W9-CPO-906

Dictionary OF Pastoral Care AND Counseling

Dictionary OF Pastoral Care AND Counseling

RODNEY J. HUNTER

General Editor

H. NEWTON MALONY
LISTON O. MILLS
JOHN PATTON

Associate Editors

ABINGDON PRESS • *Nashville*

DICTIONARY OF PASTORAL CARE AND COUNSELING

Library of Congress Cataloging-in-Publication Data

Dictionary of pastoral care and counseling / Rodney J. Hunter, general editor . . . [et al.].
   p.   cm.
  Includes bibliographical references.
  ISBN 0-687-10761-X (alk. paper)
  1. Pastoral theology—United States—Dictionaries. 2. Pastoral counseling—United States—Dictionaries. I. Hunter, Rodney J.
  BV4011.D43   1990
  253'.03—dc20   89-29781
                               CIP

Publication Staff

   Editors: Carey Gifford, Davis Perkins, and Joseph Crockett (all formerly of Abingdon Press), Ulrike Guthrie.

  Copyeditors: Angelika Fisher, Joyce King.

  Proofreaders: Eleanor Brownfield, O. C. Dean Jr., Rebecca Dean, Faye Federman, Ulrike Guthrie, Marian Lord, Susan Nease, Marella Synovec, Terri Thornton, Johnny Wrye.

  Coordinators: Helen Pouliot, Johnny Wrye.

  Formatting: Glenn Hinton

  Styling: Tommy Mullins

  Proofs: George Clark

  Typesetters: Joyce Adams, Reba Blackwell, Frances Dennis, Belinda Felker, Kathy Harding, Sylvia Marlow, Shirley Mitchell, Deborah Ogleton, Chris Street, Charlene Tolbert.

  Makeup: Gayl Carter, Mary Lynne Galbreath

  Design: Leonardo M. Ferguson

In Appreciation

T he associate editors and I wish to express our gratitude and appreciation for the superb contributions, cooperation, and encouragement we have received from our hundreds of authors, advisors, and consultants through the long process of creating this volume. We wish especially to thank the management and editors of Abingdon Press for their vision in sponsoring this book, their generous investment in it, and their support of our editorial goals and concerns: Ronald P. Patterson, and editors Carey Gifford, who conceived the project, Joseph Crockett, Davis Perkins, and Ulrike Guthrie. To Ulrike we owe a special word of thanks for her extraordinary ability and dedication in seeing the book through its final stages.

Dean Jim L. Waits of the Candler School of Theology, Emory University, provided ongoing encouragement and institutional support enabling the *Dictionary* to come to completion, and we are deeply grateful to him for his significant participation. We are grateful also to the Visiting Scholar Program of the Lilly Endowment for its assistance in enabling the participation of our Principal Editorial Consultant, Glenn H. Asquith, Jr., and to the Board of Governors of the Georgia Association of Pastoral Care for their interest, understanding, and indirect financial support in connection with the work of Associate Editor John Patton.

We wish to express our special thanks to editorial consultants Glenn H. Asquith, Jr., James E. Dittes, and Orlo Strunk, Jr., for their invaluable assistance at many points. In particular we are indebted to Glenn Asquith, Jr., for his extensive involvement in the project's final two years, and to President Roger H. Martin of Moravian Theological Seminary for making his participation possible. We are grateful too for the valuable contributions of our Board of Editorial Advisors in suggesting author prospects and providing other helpful assistance.

We wish to acknowledge with personal appreciation also the many others who gave extraordinary, dedicated assistance, among whom are: Dorcas Ford-Doward, Matthew Hartsfield, Kenneth Kroemer, Patricia Lewis, Walter Lowe, Donna Meyers, Marion Moss, Anita Ostrom, Helen Patton, Kristan Pope, Theresa Prestwood, Damaris Ramirez, Nancy Savage, Virginia Schinkel, Lory Skwerer, JoAnn Stone, Donna Viselli, and Diane Wright.

On a personal note, I wish to give special thanks to my family, Ann and David, for their loving forbearance and support; to my student assistant, Matthew Hartsfield; to Carey Gifford and Ulrike Guthrie of Abingdon Press; to Glenn Asquith for his invaluable participation and colleagueship; and especially to my associate editors, Liston Mills, H. Newton Malony, and John Patton, for their immense creative labors and devotion to this task over many years—and for their personal support, colleagueship, and good humor at every stage.

RODNEY J. HUNTER
General Editor

Board of Editorial Advisors

Abbreviations

BIBLICAL REFERENCES

Old Testament

Genesis	Gen.	Proverbs	Prov.
Exodus	Exod.	Ecclesiastes	Eccles.
Leviticus	Lev.	Song of Solomon	Song of Sol.
Numbers	Num.	Isaiah	Isa.
Deuteronomy	Deut.	Jeremiah	Jer.
Joshua	Josh.	Lamentations	Lam.
Judges	Judg.	Ezekiel	Ezek.
Ruth	Ruth	Daniel	Dan.
1 Samuel	I Sam.	Hosea	Hos.
2 Samuel	II Sam.	Obadiah	Obad.
1 Kings	I Kings	Jonah	Jon.
2 Kings	II Kings	Micah	Mic.
1 Chronicles	I Chron.	Nahum	Nah.
2 Chronicles	II Chron.	Habakkuk	Hab.
Ezra	Ezra	Zephaniah	Zeph.
Nehemiah	Neh.	Haggai	Hag.
Esther	Esther	Zechariah	Zech.
Job	Job	Malachi	Mal.
Psalms	Ps.		

Apocrypha

1 Esdras	I Esd.	The Song of the Three Holy Children	Song of Three Children
2 Esdras	II Esd.	Susanna	Sus.
Tobit	Tob.	Bel and the Dragon	Bel and Dragon
Judith	Jth.	Prayer of Manasses	Pr. of Man.
The Rest of Esther	Rest of Esther	1 Maccabbes	I Macc.
The Wisdom of Solomon	Wisd. of Sol.	2 Maccabees	II Macc.
Ecclesiasticus	Ecclus.		
Baruch	Bar.		

New Testament

Matthew	Mt.	Luke	Lk.
Mark	Mk.	John	Jn.

New Testament (Continued)

CPE   Clinical Pastoral Education
KJV   King James' Version (Bible)
LXX   Septuagint
NAB   New American Bible
NAS   New American Standard (Bible)
NEB   New English Bible
NT   New Testament
OT   Old Testament
TET   Today's English Translation

Note: Biblical passages are quoted from the Revised Standard Version (RSV) unless otherwise indicated.

Preface

This *Dictionary* provides useful information, guidance and insight for a wide range of religious caregivers. These include: parish pastors, priests, and rabbis; specialized pastoral counselors, pastoral psychotherapists, and religious workers; theologians, theological students, and other scholars. Many lay caregivers and therapists will also find it helpful and stimulating. More than twelve hundred articles provide concise, authoritative information on virtually every topic related to pastoral care and counseling, practical and theoretical, and its authors represent a wide ecumenical cross section of the field and related disciplines.

The book is also, we believe, easy to use. Its bibliographies and cross referencing enable the reader to find information quickly, see the interrelation of topics, and identify additional sources of information and insight. To facilitate ease of use, we have adhered to the fundamental concept of a dictionary: an alphabetical arrangement of brief, concise articles, which we have knit together through an extensive cross-referencing system.

However, the *Dictionary* also includes articles and essays of all lengths that go well beyond providing basic information. By offering critical perspectives and creative insights, these articles contain abundant resources for the assessment and future development of contemporary practice. Thus the book is also an "encyclopedic dictionary," and is a potential resource and stimulus for research and teaching and for the future development of pastoral care and counseling.

Basic Aims

The *Dictionary* has the following fundamental objectives:

(1) To provide practical information and guidance for pastoral care and counseling practitioners. The *Dictionary* aims to be practical, and many of its articles are written by practicing pastors and counselors or scholars who are closely related to the practice of the field. Often it articulates insights hitherto available only through oral tradition.

At the same time it challenges and seeks to broaden the popular meaning of practice and practicality. It is our conviction that a right understanding of practice, especially in religious ministry, must include questions of truth, conviction, meaning, and value. Pastoral care and counseling are fundamentally religious endeavors. However concrete, mundane, and "human" its tasks and problems, it is essential that these religious and moral meanings be kept in view.

Thus, in designing and editing this volume, we have sought to avoid a "cookbook" approach that would reduce care and counseling to a mass of techniques aimed at ameliorating human ills narrowly conceived. The *Dictionary* includes, of course, numerous practical topics. But these articles seek to define human need and pastoral response more broadly, richly, and deeply. They offer perspectives, insights, questions, and suggestions—not pigeon-holed problems and quick-fix techniques. The *Dictionary's* underlying concept of practicality therefore contrasts, in some measure, with prevailing notions of what is "practical," and argues for a larger, deeper, and more religiously authentic meaning of practicality in contemporary ministry.

(2) To integrate practice with theological and social scientific theory. Theory and practice need to and can speak to each other. Thus we have tried to show, first, that deeper questions of meaning, truth, and faith are present in the immediate problems of care and counseling, and second, that theoretical and theological ideas often have empirical and practical dimensions. Naturally, some articles focus more on practice and others more on theory, but many combine both, and cross references supply further connections, often revealing unexpected insights.

Over its long history, pastoral care and counseling has provided an impetus for deepened theological understanding, just as theological developments have shaped and reshaped pastoral practice. This is because practice is not simply applied theory. As the "wisdom of experience," practice is also itself a source of theory, just as theoretical thinking is a kind of practice. Thus we have aimed to promote a thoughtful, critically minded practice, and a practical, humanly rich and caring mode of theorizing.

In terms of disciplines, the *Dictionary* aims to promote dialogue (a) between the social sciences and the theological disciplines, and (b) between pastoral care and counseling and other expressions of ministry such as preaching, teaching, worship, church leadership, and social witness. The need for more serious work at all of these intersections is widely recognized today, and we believe the *Dictionary* can make a helpful contribution to this task.

(3) *To provide focus and identity for contemporary pastoral care and counseling.* Without imposing more focus or order than seemed possible or justified, it was our aim to organize the *Dictionary's* diverse topics around a basic perspective on pastoral care and counseling, as much as seemed possible and appropriate at this time in the discipline's history. The importance of focus is evident when one considers the enormous variety of topics and disciplines represented in this volume, reflecting the complexity of the field today—everything from theology, psychology, and mythology to family theory and therapy, crisis ministry, psychoanalysis, spiritual direction, feminist therapy, the special needs of the dying, the value of ritual, and the pastoral use of the telephone.

Central to the articulation of focus and identity is the definition of terms. The *Dictionary* regards pastoral care and counseling as the theologically informed ministry of religiously faithful persons to individuals and families. More specifically, *pastoral care* is considered to be any form of personal ministry to individuals and to family and community relationships by representative religious persons (ordained or lay) and by their communities of faith, who understand and guide their caring efforts out of a theological perspective rooted in a tradition of faith. *Pastoral counseling* is a more specialized and structured form of religiously based care, distinguished by its degree of contractual formality (a helping contract or covenant between the parties) and by the special expertise of the helping person.

Because the term "pastoral" often carries a Christian connotation, we have sometimes employed cognate terms like "Jewish care" and "Native American care," though we have not sought to limit the meaning of "pastoral" exclusively to the Christian tradition. While some may regard "pastoral" as overly restrictive, implying a narrow clericalism or professionalism, we trust that the rich historic connotations of the term will not be overlooked, especially its long association with tender personal care, healing, and compassion, and that its continuing value be recognized and appreciated.

To express the *Dictionary's* pastoral identity and focus we have also attempted to fashion an appropriate, even at points distinctive, vocabulary for its entries. This sometimes meant departing from prevailing psychological or professional terminology (e.g. "counselee" instead of "client" in explicitly pastoral contexts). In a few instances it has also meant drawing

in, as article titles, terms that have become established in the American pastoral care and counseling movement through oral tradition (e.g. PERSONAL STORY, SYMBOL, AND MYTH; STRUCTURING; HUMAN CONDITION/PREDICAMENT; PILGRIMAGE).

(4) *To promote ecumenical consciousness and understanding.* The American pastoral care and counseling movement, from which this volume basically derives, had its origins in North American Protestantism, and the book largely reflects the concerns and perspectives of that tradition. Nonetheless it seemed of vital importance that a serious attempt be made to include other pastoral traditions as a first step (in many instances) at ecumenical consciousness raising and comparative understanding.

The *Dictionary* therefore includes articles on Roman Catholic, Orthodox, and Jewish topics in pastoral care and counseling, and on common topics written from diverse ecumenical and interfaith perspectives—e.g. MINISTRY (Roman Catholic Tradition); PERSON (Jewish Perspective). There are also brief treatments of Mormon, Asian and Islamic care and counseling, as well as Native American, West Indian, and African traditional religion and methods of care. It also includes a wide range of perspectives within Protestantism, relating the clinical pastoral care and counseling movement to current critical thinking as well as to the emerging counseling movement in the evangelical churches.

(5) *To promote practical and scholarly research within the pastoral care and counseling movement.* The pastoral care movement began around the turn of the century with an awakening of interest in the relationship between religion and health and with the insights of the new psychology of religion. From these origins it progressed through a significant rapprochement with dynamic psychiatry and psychology to produce a profound reorientation in the theories and methods of pastoral care. The result was a deepened sensitivity to the needs and dynamics of persons, the development of a psychologically sophisticated therapeutic orientation in ministry, the "psychologizing" of many other aspects of ministry and religious practice, and the creation of a major field of specialized practice with its own paraecclesial institutions and professional standards. The movement also deeply impacted theological education. Today its influence extends far beyond Protestantism, and far beyond North America.

At the same time important critical concerns have arisen about these developments and their influence. Questions of sexism, racism, psychologism, subjective individualism, clericalism, ahistoricism, and a lack of moral and religious criticism have been among the more serious concerns raised by critics, while in recent years representatives of the movement itself have begun to advance new understandings. It is therefore a time of stock taking, of ferment, and of promise for the future.

One of our aims was to respond to this historical moment as a unique opportunity. Articles like BLACK AMERICAN PASTORAL CARE; FEMINIST ISSUES IN PASTORAL CARE; LAY PASTORAL CARE AND COUNSELING; MIGRANT WORKERS; PERSONALISM AND PASTORAL CARE; TRADITION AS MODE OF CARE, and many others offer possibilities for broadening the field's horizons and generating new methods and understandings of care.

On the theoretical side we have given special attention to social perspectives, history, philosophy, theology, and ethics, as titles like SOCIAL JUSTICE ISSUES, PRUDENCE, and MORAL DILEMMAS IN PASTORAL PERSPECTIVE, PHILOSOPHY AND PSYCHOLOGY indicate. To stimulate historical interest, the *Dictionary* also includes over two hundred short biographies of individuals who have contributed significantly to the development of pastoral care and counseling, emphasizing more recent figures but including major representatives of the long ecumenical tradition of pastoral care and spiritual guidance.

Articles like BIBLE, USE AND INTERPRETATION OF; TEACHING; EVALUATION AND DIAGNOSIS, RELIGIOUS, and many others suggest new methods or open new doors of practice. Others bring psychological theories current in care and counseling under theological scrutiny or explore the psychological and pastoral implications of particular theologies—e.g. ANALYTICAL (JUNGIAN) PSYCHOLOGY AND THEOLOGY, PROCESS THEOLOGY AND PASTORAL CARE. All facets of specialized pastoral counseling are critically reviewed as well in articles like ECONOMIC DIMENSIONS OF PASTORAL COUNSELING, PASTORAL COUNSELING CENTER, SPECIAL-IZATION IN PASTORAL CARE, and PASTORAL PSYCHOTHERAPY, the latter with cross references to SPIRITUAL DIRECTION and PASTORAL CARE (History, Traditions, and Definitions).

In many respects this *Dictionary* represents an important chapter in the history of the pastoral care movement, the culmination of a remarkable period of renaissance in the long history of pastoral care. But it also represents an attempt to assess the current field critically and to stimulate new developments. Undoubtedly much remains to be done on all of these topics, whose treatment was necessarily limited by constraints of space. But if it makes a satisfactory start simply at *naming* important issues and *suggesting* future directions, then this in itself, we believe, will be a valuable contribution to research and development in the field.

More importantly, however, we hope it will make a useful contribution directly to practitioners and those whom they serve. To them, in their suffering and in their patient efforts at faithful care, we are pleased to dedicate this volume, in the name of the One in whose care we all live and move and have our being.

RODNEY J. HUNTER

General Editor

Contributors

Joe Boone Abbott, D. Min.
Pastoral Care and Counseling
Baptist Medical Center
Birmingham, Alabama

William Seth Adams, Ph.D.
The Episcopal Theological
    Seminary of the Southwest
Austin, Texas

LeRoy Aden, Ph.D.
Lutheran Theological Seminary
Philadelphia, Pennsylvania

Clark S. Aist, Ph.D.
St. Elizabeth's Hospital
Washington, D.C.

Daniel Aleshire, Ph.D.
Southern Baptist Theological Seminary
Louisville, Kentucky

Frank S. Alexander, J.D.
School of Law, Emory University
Atlanta, Georgia

Joseph L. Allen, Th.D.
St. Vladimir's Orthodox Seminary
Crestwood, New York

Leslie C. Allen, Ph.D.
Fuller Theological Seminary
Pasadena, California

Stephen Allison, Ph.D.
Abilene Christian University
Abilene, Texas

Herbert Anderson, Ph.D.
Catholic Theological Union
Pasadena, California

Ray S. Anderson, Ph.D.
Fuller Theological Seminary
Pasadena, California

S. M. Anderson, S.T.D.
Samaritan Counseling Center of Hawaii
Honolulu, Hawaii

Richard Anthony
Private Practice
Berkeley, California

M. Kathryn Armistead, M.A.
Bellshire United Methodist Church
Nashville, Tennessee

William V. Arnold, Ph.D.
Union Theological Seminary in
    Virginia
Richmond, Virginia

Robert J. Arnott, Ph.D.
School of Theology at Claremont
Claremont, California

James B. Ashbrook, Ph.D.
Garrett-Evangelical Theological
    Seminary
Evanston, Illinois

Homer U. Ashby, Jr., Ph.D.
McCormick Theological Seminary
Chicago, Illinois

Glenn H. Asquith, Jr., Ph.D.
Moravian Theological Seminary
Bethlehem, Pennsylvania

Bruce E. Atkinson, Ph.D.
Private Practice
Memphis, Tennessee

Dean Aufderheidi, Ph.D.
U.S. Army
Savannah, Georgia

David W. Augsburger, Ph.D.
Mennonite Biblical Seminary
Elkhart, Indiana

Joyce A. Babb, L.C.S.W.
Counseling Associates
Pasadena, California

Daniel G. Bagby, Ph.D.
Seventh and James Baptist Church
Waco, Texas

Jack Balswick, Ph.D.
Graduate School of Psychology
Fuller Theological Seminary
Pasadena, California

David Barash, Ph.D.
Department of Psychology
University of Washington
Seattle, Washington

Henlee H. Barnette

David R. Barstow, D.Rel.
Pilgrimage Press, Inc.
Atlanta, Georgia

Les Beach, Ph.D.
Hope College
Holland, Michigan

Walter Becker, Ph.D.
La Vie Counseling Center
Pasadena, California

Marine G. Behrens, Ph.D.
Department of Psychology
Whittier College
Whittier, California

Benjamin Beit-Hallahmi, Ph.D.
University of Haifa
Haifa, Israel

David G. Benner, Ph.D.
Redeemer College
Fresno, California

Colleen Zabriskie Benson, Ph.D.
Covina Psychological Services
Covina, California

Richard D. Berrett, Ph.D.
Central Valley Counseling
and Therapy Center
Ancaster, Ontario, Canada

Stephen Bevans, Ph.D.
Divine Word Theologate
Chicago, Illinois

William G. Bixler, Ph.D.
Clinical Psychology
Manassas, Virginia

Jerome H. Blass, Ph.D.
Bergenfield-Dumont Jewish Center
Bergenfield, New Jersey

Paul M. Blowers, Ph.D.
Emmanuel School of Religion
Johnson City, Tennessee

Benjamin Preston Bogia, M.Div.
University of Kentucky
Lexington, Kentucky

Mark Bohner
Ph.D. Candidate
Fuller Theological Seminary
Pasadena, California

William Bolling
Atlanta Food Bank
Atlanta, Georgia

Martin Bolt, Ph.D.
Calvin College
Grand Rapids, Michigan

Richard Bondi, Ph.D.
Candler School of Theology
Emory University
Atlanta, Georgia

Roberta C. Bondi, D.Phil.
Candler School of Theology
Emory University
Atlanta, Georgia

Donald S. Bosch, Ph.D.
Private Practice
Pasadena, California

William P. Boyle, Th.M.
Georgia Association for Pastoral Care
Atlanta, Georgia

Carol Brainerd, R.N.
Hospice
Pasadena, California

Gary Brainerd, Ph.D.
Private Practice
Pasadena, California

Luisa S. Brakensiek, Ph.D.
Pacific Psychological Resources
Simi Valley, California

Menachem M. Brayer, D.H.L., Ph.D.
Yeshiva University
New York, New York

Lucy Bregman, Ph.D.
Department of Religion
Temple University
Philadelphia, Pennsylvania

Milo L. Brekke, Ph.D.
Brekke Associates
Minneapolis, Minnesota

D. G. Brenner

Peter Bridge, D.Min.
Pennsylvania Foundation
of Pastoral Counseling
Wyncote, Pennsylvania

C. W. Brister, Ph.D.
Southwestern Baptist
Theological Seminary
Fort Worth, Texas

Gary Brock, D.Min.
Vanderbilt University Medical Center
Nashville, Tennessee

David Brokaw, Ph.D.
Azusa Pacific University
Azusa, California

Nathan C. Brown, Ph.D.
Pacific Psychological Resources
Simi Valley, California

Robert C. Brown, Ph.D.
Hope College, Retired
Holland, Michigan

Rodney C. Brown, Th.M.
RJR Nabisco, Inc.
Winston-Salem, North Carolina

Sammi B. Brown, M.D.
Atlanta, Georgia

Sandra R. Brown, Ph.D.
Abbott-Northwestern Counseling Center
Minneapolis, Minnesota

Thomas E. Brown, M.Div.
S.T.D. Candidate, Emory University
Butler Street CME Church
Atlanta, Georgia

Victor B. Brown
Aquinas Junior College
Nashville, Tennessee

Victor L. Brown, Jr., D.S.W.
Brigham Young University
Provo, Utah

Warren S. Brown, Ph.D.
Graduate School of Psychology
Fuller Theological Seminary
Pasadena, California

Don S. Browning, Ph.D.
The Divinity School
University of Chicago
Chicago, Illinois

Richard G. Bruehl, Ph.D.
Private Practice
Nashville, Tennessee

Gerald Bubis, M.S.W.
Hebrew Union College
Los Angeles, California

Rodger K. Bufford, Ph.D.
Psychology Division
Western Conservative Baptist
Seminary
Portland, Oregon

Reuven P. Bulka, Ph.D.
Congregation Machzikei Hadas
Ottawa, Ontario, Canada

J. Russell Burck, Ph.D.
Rush Presbyterian-St. Luke's
Medical Center
Chicago, Illinois

John E. Burkhart, Ph.D.
McCormick Theological Seminary
Chicago, Illinois

Richard E. Butman, Ph.D.
Department of Psychology
Wheaton College
Wheaton, Illinois

Nancy Evans Bush, M.S.
International Association for
Near-Death Studies
Storrs, Connecticut

Julian L. Byrd, S.T.M.
The Methodist Hospital
Houston, Texas

Lisa Sowle Cahill, Ph.D.
Department of Theology
Boston College
Chestnut Hill, Massachusetts

Alastair V. Campbell, Th.D.
Faculty of Divinity
University of Edinburgh
Edinburgh, Scotland

Isaac Canales, Ph.D.
Fuller Theological Seminary
Pasadena, California

Donald Capps, Ph.D.
Princeton Theological Seminary
Princeton, New Jersey

Francine Cardman, Ph.D.
Weston School of Theology
Cambridge, Massachusetts

Sue Webb Cardwell, Ph.D.
Christian Theological Seminary
Indianapolis, Indiana

John Carmody, Ph.D.
University of Tulsa
Tulsa, Oklahoma

Jackson Carroll, Ph.D.
Hartford Seminary
Hartford, Connecticut

John D. Carter, Ph.D.
Rosemead School of Psychology
Biola University
La Mirada, California

Ronna Case, D.Min.
Bethany United Methodist Church
Bakersfield, California

J. L. Cedarleaf, B.D.
Association for Clinical Pastoral
    Education
Sacramento, California

Joseph Champlin
Diocese of Syracuse
Syracuse, New York

Brian H. Childs, Ph.D.
Columbia Theological Seminary
Decatur, Georgia

Judith Z. Clark, M.A.
Applied Psychological Services
Laguna Niguel, California

Walter H. Clark, Ph.D.
Andover Newton Theological
    Seminary, Emeritus
Cape Elizabeth, Maine

Bowman L. Clarke, Ph.D.
Department of Philosophy
University of Georgia
Athens, Georgia

Paul W. Clement, Ph.D.
Psychology Resource Consultants
Pasadena, California

William M. Clements, Ph.D.
The Medical Center
Columbus, Georgia

Howard Clinebell, Ph.D.
Pastoral Psychology and Counseling
School of Theology at Claremont,
    Emeritus
Claremont, California

Nancy J. Cobb, Ph.D.
California State University, Los Angeles
Los Angeles, California

Gary R. Collins, Ph.D.
Liberty University
Lynchburg, Virginia

Timothy Collister, Ph.D. Candidate
Fuller Theological Seminary
Pasadena, California

David G. Congo, Ph.D.
Free to Soar Ministries
Mission Viejo, California

Quinn R. Conners, O.Carm., Ph.D.
Washington Theological Union
Silver Springs, Maryland

Jim Conway, Ph.D.
Mid-Life Dimensions
Fullerton, California

Sally Conway, M.S.
Mid-Life Dimensions
Fullerton, California

Gail Paterson Corrington, Ph.D.
Department of Religion
College of William and Mary
Williamsburg, Virginia

John H. Court, Ph.D.
Graduate School of Psychology
Fuller Theological Seminary
Pasadena, California

Pamela Couture
Candler School of Theology
Emory University
Atlanta, Georgia

Harold Coward, Ph.D.
University of Calgary
Calgary, Alberta, Canada

Fred B. Craddock, Ph.D.
Candler School of Theology
Emory University
Atlanta, Georgia

Robert W. Crapps, Ph.D.
Department of Religion
Furman University, Emeritus
Greenville, South Carolina

Grover E. Criswell, M.Div.
Ohio Pastoral Counseling
    Services, Inc.
Dayton, Ohio

Lawrence S. Cunningham
Department of Theology
Notre Dame University
Notre Dame, Indiana

Glen W. Davidson, M.Div., Ph.D.
School of Medicine
Southern Illinois University
Springfield, Illinois

Daniel C. DeArment, Th.M.
Presbyterian-University of
    Pennsylvania Medical Center
Philadelphia, Pennsylvania

O. L. DeLozier, Jr., M.Div.
Georgia Association for Pastoral Care
Atlanta, Georgia

Vincent deGregoris
Eastern Baptist Theological Seminary
Philadelphia, Pennsylvania

Lori M. Dick, D.O.
College of Osteopathic Medicine
    of the Pacific
Pomona, California

James E. Dittes, Ph.D.
The Divinity School
Yale University
New Haven, Connecticut

William C. Dixon, D.Min.
Samaritan Counseling Center
Portland, Oregon

Thelma F. Dixon-Murphy, Ed.D.
The Institutes of Religion and Health
New York, New York

Carl B. Dodrill, Ph.D.
School of Medicine
University of Washington
Seattle, Washington

Marlin Dolinsky, M.S.
San Bernadino, California

Doris Donnelly, Ph.D.
John Carroll University
University Heights, Ohio

John P. Donnelly, S.J.

Mary Ann Donovan, S.C., Ph.D.
Jesuit School of Theology
Berkeley, California

Constance Doran, Ph.D.
Patton State Hospital
San Bernadino, California

Robert M. Doran, S.J., Ph.D.
Regis College
Toronto, Ontario, Canada

Ted Dougherty, Ph.D.
Department of Religion
Wake Forest University
Winston-Salem, North Carolina

Marjorie Doyle, Ph.D.
United Church of Christ
New York, New York

John W. Drakeford, Ph.D.
Southwestern Theological Seminary
Fort Worth, Texas

Edgar Draper, M.D.
University of Mississippi Medical
   School
Jackson, Mississippi

Alvin C. Dueck, Ph.D.
Mennonite Brethren Biblical Seminary
Fresno, California

Regis Duffy, O.F.M., S.T.D.
Department of Theology
Notre Dame University
Notre Dame, Indiana

David C. Duncombe, Ph.D.
The Landberg Center for Health
   and Ministry at U.C.S.F.
San Francisco, California

Deryck Durston, S.T.M.
Eger Lutheran Homes
Staten Island, New York

Myron Ebersole, M.A.
University Hospital
Pennsylvania State University
Hershey, Pennsylvania

Bruce Ecker

David N. Elkind
Department of Psychology
Tufts University
Medford, Massachusetts

Charlotte Ellen, M.S.W., Ph.D.
Private Practice
Santa Barbara, California

J. Harold Ellens, Ph.D.
Private Practice
Farmington Hills, Michigan

Gary S. Eller, Ph.D.
White Haven Presbyterian Church
Memphis, Tennessee

Craig Ellison, Ph.D.
Alliance Theological Seminary
Nyack, New York

Robert S. Ellwood, Ph.D.
School of Religion
University of Southern California
Los Angeles, California

James G. Emerson, Ph.D.
Calvary Presbyterian Church
San Francisco, California

Richard C. Erickson, Ph.D.
Veterans Administration Hospital
Portland, Oregon

Barry K. Estadt, Ph.D., P.A.
Centennial Counseling Center
Columbus, Maryland

John Estelle
Ph.D. Candidate
Fuller Theological Seminary
Pasadena, California

Michelle Estelle
Ph.D. Candidate
Fuller Theological Seminary
Pasadena, California

C. Stephen Evans, Ph.D.
St. Olaf College
Northfield, Minnesota

Richard O. Evans, M.Div.
Littleton United Methodist Church
Littleton, Colorado

Eric Evenhuis, D.Min.
Bethesda Counseling Service
Upland, California

William Johnson Everett, Ph.D.
Emory University
Atlanta, Georgia

James W. Ewing, Ph.D.
San Diego, California

Jacob Ezhanikatt
Montfort College
Bangalore, India

Heije Faber, Th.D., D.Psych.
University of Leiden,
   and Tilburg University, Emeritus
Maarn, The Netherlands

Gabriel Fackre, Ph.D.
Andover Newton Theological School
Newton Centre, Massachusetts

Roy W. Fairchild, Ph.D.
San Francisco Theological Seminary
San Francisco, California

Randall M. Falk
Congregation Ohabai Shalom
Nashville, Tennessee

Donald Falkenberg
Western Career Development
   Center, Retired
Pasadena, California

John W. Fantuzzo, Ph.D.
University of Pennsylvania
Philadelphia, Pennsylvania

Edward Farley, Ph.D.
Vanderbilt University
Nashville, Tennessee

Fran Yeager Fehlman, Ph.D.
Miramar College
San Diego, California

James Fenhagen, D.D.
The General Theological Seminary
New York, New York

Peter E. Fink, S.J., Ph.D.
Weston School of Theology
Cambridge, Massachusetts

James Finley, Ph.D.
Private Practice
Pasadena, California

Irwin H. Fishbein, D.Min.
Rabbinic Center for Research
   and Counseling
Westfield, New Jersey

Robert G. Fishman

O. Ray Fitzgerald, Ph.D.
Methodist Hospital
Memphis, Tennessee

John L. Florell, Ph.D.
BroMenn Counseling Services
Bloomington, Illinois

Jennifer J. Fog, Ph.D.
Private Practice
Pasadena, California

Rhea H. Forman, Ph.D.
Blauchard Valley Psychological
   Services
Findlay, Ohio

Leila M. Foster, J.D., Ph.D.
Private Practice
Evanston, Illinois

James W. Fowler, Ph.D.
Candler School of Theology
Emory University
Atlanta, Georgia

David W. Foy, Ph.D.
Graduate School of Psychology
Fuller Theological Seminary
Pasadena, California

James G. Friesen, Ph.D.
Shepherd's House Counseling Center
Van Nuys, California

James Gaffney, S.T.D.
Loyola University
New Orleans, Louisiana

Patrick Daniel Gaffney, C.S.C.,
   Ph.D.
Department of Anthropology
Notre Dame University
Notre Dame, Indiana

E. Clinton Gardner, Ph.D.
Candler School of Theology
Emory University
Atlanta, Georgia

Sol L. Garfield, Ph.D.
Washington University
St. Louis, Missouri

Peggy L. T. Garrison
Bethany Theological Seminary
Oak Brook, Illinois

Volney P. Gay, Ph.D.
Department of Religion
Vanderbilt University
Nashville, Tennessee

Randy Georgemiller, Ph.D.
Associated Clinical Psychologists, Ltd.
Des Plaines, Illinois

Charles V. Gerkin, B.D.
Candler School of Theology
Emory University
Atlanta, Georgia

S. H. Getsinger

P. R. Giblin

Dean Gilliland, Ph.D.

Allen R. Gilmore, Ph.D.
The Pastoral Counseling and
   Consultation Centers of Greater
   Washington
Washington, D.C.

Joseph V. Gilmore, Ph.D.
Private Practice
Hamilton, Massachusetts

Hany M. Girgis, Ph.D.
Fuller Theological Seminary
Pasadena, California

Dean R. Given, Ph.D.
South Coast Psychological Services
Santa Barbara, California

Anne Glasser, Ph.D.
Private Practice
Santa Monica, California

Donald J. Goergen, O.P., Ph.D.
Dominican Province of St. Albert
   the Great
Chicago, Illinois

Joseph Goering, Ph.D.
Department of History
University of Toronto
Toronto, Ontario, Canada

Herb Goldberg, Ph.D.
California State University,
   Los Angeles
Los Angeles, California

F. Gonzalez

Winston E. Gooden, Ph.D.
Graduate School of Psychology
Fuller Theological Seminary
Pasadena, California

Richard L. Gorsuch, Ph.D.
Graduate School of Psychology
Fuller Theological Seminary
Pasadena, California

Larry Kent Graham, Ph.D.
The Iliff School of Theology
Denver, Colorado

W. Ralph Graham, M.S.
American Protestant Correctional
   Chaplains Association
Stone Mountain, Georgia

Brian W. Grant, Ph.D.
Christian Theological Seminary
Indianapolis, Indiana

Thomas J. Green, J.C.D.
Department of Canon Law
Catholic University of America
Washington, D.C.

Graeme M. Griffin, Ph.D.
United Faculty of Theology
Melbourne, Australia

Lucille Sider Groh, Ph.D.
The Samaritan Pastoral Counseling
   Center of Evanston/Wilmette
Evanston, Illinois

Earl A. Grollman, D.D.
Beth El Temple Center
Belmont, Massachusetts

Dennis Guernsey, Ph.D.
Graduate School of Psychology
Fuller Theological Seminary
Pasadena, California

Shirley C. Guthrie, Th.D.
Columbia Theological Seminary
Decatur, Georgia

James D. Guy, Ph.D.
Rosemead School of Psychology
Biola University
La Mirada, California

Peter J. Haas, Ph.D.
Vanderbilt University
Nashville, Tennessee

Vernita R. Haddy, M.A., M.F.C.C.
Edgemont Hospital
Los Angeles, California

Mark Hadlock, Ph.D.
Philhaven Hospital
Lebanon, Pennsylvania

B. John Hagedorn, Ph.D.
Pastoral Counseling and
   Consultation Center of Greater
   Washington
Washington, D.C.

Beverly S. Hagner, Ph.D.
Private Practice
Glendale, California

Emily S. Demme Haight, Ph.D.
Center for Religion and
   Psychotherapy of Chicago
Chicago, Illinois

Norbert F. Hahn Ph.D.
Candidate, Emory University
St. John's Lutheran Church
Atlanta, Georgia

Charles E. Hall, B.D.
Private Practice
Prairie Village, Kansas

Quentin L. Hand, Ph.D.
The KEY Pastoral Counseling Center
Huntsville, Alabama

Kenneth Hansen, M.Div.
Laird Counseling Center
Glendora, California

G. Simon Harak, S.J., Ph.D.
Religious Studies
Fairfield University
Fairfield, Connecticut

Gary L. Harbaugh, Ph.D.
Trinity Lutheran Seminary
Columbus, Ohio

Walter Harrelson, Th.D.
The Divinity School
Vanderbilt University
Nashville, Tennessee

Howard L. Harrod, Ph.D.
The Divinity School
Vanderbilt University
Nashville, Tennessee

Archibald D. Hart, Ph.D.
Graduate School of Psychology
Fuller Theological Seminary
Pasadena, California

Phyllis P. Hart

Bruce M. Hartung, Ph.D.
Onondaga Pastoral Counseling
   Center
Syracuse, New York

Harold Hatt, Ph.D.
Phillips Graduate Seminary
Enid, Oklahoma

John C. Haughey, S.J.
St. Peter's Catholic Church
Charlotte, North Carolina

John R. Haule, Ph.D.
C. G. Jung Institute - Boston
Boston, Massachusetts

Charles G. Helms, S.T.D.
Presbyterian Family Life Center
Charlotte, North Carolina

Kenneth W. Henke, Ph.D.
Haverford College
Haverford, Pennsylvania

Roberta Hestenes, D.Min.
Eastern College
St. Davids, Pennsylvania

J. Michael Hester, Ph.D.
The Southern Baptist Theological
    Seminary
Louisville, Kentucky

Richard L. Hester, Ph.D.
Southeastern Baptist Theological
    Seminary
Wake Forest, North Carolina

John H. Hewett, Ph.D.
First Baptist Church
Asheville, North Carolina

David Hickel
Ph.D. Candidate
Fuller Theological Seminary
Pasadena, California

Paul Hiebert, Ph.D.
Fuller Theological Seminary
Pasadena, California

Ross T. Hightower, D.Min.
Georgia Association for Pastoral Care
Atlanta, Georgia

Gordon Hilsman, D.Min.
Memorial Medical Center
Ashland, Wisconsin

E. Glenn Hinson, D. Phil.
The Southern Baptist Theological
    Seminary
Louisville, Kentucky

Sol Hofstein, D.S.W.
Federation of Jewish
    Philanthropists of New York
New York, New York

E. Brooks Holifield, Ph.D.
Emory University
Atlanta, Georgia

Lawrence E. Holst, S.T.M.
Lutheran General Health Care
    System
Park Ridge, Illinois

Kenneth A. Holstein, Ph.D.
Department of Psychology
Wheaton College
Wheaton, Illinois

Robert E. Honour, M.Voc.Reh.
McDivitt and Street
Charlotte, North Carolina

Ralph W. Hood, Jr., Ph.D.
University of Tennessee
Chattanooga, Tennessee

Thomas C. Hood, Ph.D.
Department of Sociology
University of Tennessee
Knoxville, Tennessee

Edwin A. Hoover, Ph.D.
Christ Hospital
Oak Lawn, Illinois

James F. Hopewell, Ph.D.
    (Deceased)
Candler School of Theology
Emory University
Atlanta, Georgia

Denise Dombkowski Hopkins, Ph.D.
Wesley Theological Seminary
Washington, D.C.

Thomas Hopko, Ph.D.
St. Vladimir's Orthodox
    Theological Seminary
Crestwood, New York

John F. Hotchkin, S.T.D.
National Conference of Catholic
    Bishops
Washington, D.C.

Mark D. Houglum, M.Div.
St. Paul Lutheran Church
Kodiak, Alaska

Beth Houskamp, Ph.D. Candidate
Fuller Theological Seminary
Pasadena, California

Donald C. Houts, Ph.D.
Illinois Area Pastoral Care and
    Counseling, United Methodist
    Church
Champaign, Illinois

William E. Hulme, Ph.D.
Luther Northwestern Seminary
St. Paul, Minnesota

Richard A. Hunt, Ph.D.
Graduate School of Psychology
Fuller Theological Seminary
Pasadena, California

Ann Covington Hunter, M.S.W.
Hemophilia of Georgia, Inc.
Atlanta, Georgia

Rodney J. Hunter, Ph.D.
Candler School of Theology
Emory University
Atlanta, Georgia

J. Imbach

Paul E. Irion, M.A.
Lancaster Theological Seminary
Lancaster, Pennsylvania

Steven S. Ivy, Ph.D.
V. A. Medical Center
Nashville, Tennessee

Carroll E. Izard, Ph.D.
Department of Psychology
Vanderbilt University
Nashville, Tennessee

Edgar N. Jackson, Ph.D.
Corinth, Vermont

Gordon E. Jackson, Ph.D.
Pittsburgh Theological Seminary,
    Emeritus
Pittsburgh, Pennsylvania

Walter Jacob, D.H.L.
Rodef Shalom Congregation
Pittsburgh, Pennsylvania

Murray Janson, D.D.
University of South Africa
Pretoria, South Africa

Gerald P. Jenkins, D.Min.
Counseling Center
Georgia Baptist Medical Center
Atlanta, Georgia

Theodore W. Jennings, Jr., Ph.D.
Bakersfield, California

J. H. Jennison, Ph.D.
University of California Medical
    School
Irvine, California

Homer L. Jernigan, Ph.D.
School of Theology
Boston University
Boston, Massachusetts

Paul Jersild

Paul Jewett, Ph.D.
Fuller Theological Seminary
Pasadena, California

Ben Campbell Johnson, Ph.D.
Columbia Theological Seminary
Decatur, Georgia

Cedric B. Johnson, Ph.D.
Bethesda Counseling Center
Santa Monica, California

Dale A. Johnson, Th.D.
The Divinity School
Vanderbilt University
Nashville, Tennessee

Paul J. Johnson, III
    Ph.D. Candidate
Emory University
Atlanta, Georgia

Theodore M. Johnson, Ph.D.
Philhaven Hospital
Lebanon, Pennsylvania

Robert E. Johnston, S.T.D.
ADVCACARE Inc.
Charlotte, North Carolina

Pamela M. Jolicoeur, Ph.D.
Department of Sociology
California Lutheran College
Thousand Oaks, California

Alan Jones, Ph.D.
Grace Cathedral
San Francisco, California

Merle R. Jordan, Th.D.
School of Theology
Boston University
Boston, Massachusetts

Emma J. Justes, Ph.D.
Northern Baptist Theological
  Seminary
Lombard, Illinois

Samuel E. Karff, D.H.L.
Congregation Beth Israel
Houston, Texas

Robert L. Katz, D.H.L.
Hebrew Union College
Jewish Institute of Religion
Cincinnati, Ohio

Elizabeth Kearney, M.S.
Pasadena Unified School District
Pasadena, California

Jasper N. Keith, Jr., S.T.D.
Columbia Theological Seminary
Decatur, Georgia

Paul Kelly, Ph.D.
Counseling Ministries
La Mesa, California

David H. Kelsey, Ph.D.
The Divinity School
Yale University
New Haven, Connecticut

Howard E. Kennedy, M.Div.
United Methodist Church, Retired
Port St. Lucie, Florida

Kevin R. Kennedy
Ph.D. Candidate
Fuller Theological Seminary
Pasadena, California

Kirk A. Kennedy, Ph.D.
Department of Psychology
Malcolm Grow Medical Center
Andrews Air Force Base
Camp Springs, Maryland

Elizabeth Kilbourn, M.A., M.Div.
Anglican Diocese of Toronto
Toronto, Ontario, Canada

John P. Kildahl, Ph.D.
Clinical Psychologist
Postgraduate Center for Mental
  Health
New York, New York

Robert L. Kinast, Ph.D.
Center for Theological Reflection
Madeira Beach, Florida

Robert R. King, Jr., Ph.D.
Counseling Ministries
Blue Jay, California

Stephen D. King, M.Div.
Ph.D. Candidate
Vanderbilt University
Nashville, Tennessee

C. Benton Kline, Ph.D.
Columbia Theological Seminary
Decatur, Georgia

James A. Knight, M.D.
School of Medicine
Louisiana State University
New Orleans, Louisiana

Ward A. Knights, D.D.
The Universalist Church
Tarpon Springs, Florida

John Koenig, Th.D.
The General Theological Seminary
New York, New York

Ronald L. Koteskey, Ph.D.
Department of Psychology
Asbury College
Wilmore, Kentucky

Catherine Koverola, Ph.D.
University of Manitoba
Winnipeg, Manitoba, Canada

Charles H. Kraft, Ph.D.
School of World Missions
Fuller Theological Seminary
Pasadena, California

Douglas A. Kramer, M.D.
Department of Psychiatry
University of Wisconsin
Madison, Wisconsin

Pesach Krauss
Sloan-Kettering Cancer Center
New York, New York

Calvin Kropp, S.T.D.
Georgia Association for Pastoral
  Care
Atlanta, Georgia

Joseph C. Landrud, Ph.D.
Hill Avenue Grace Lutheran
  Church
Pasadena, California

James N. Lapsley, Ph.D.
Princeton Theological Seminary
Princeton, New Jersey

Cameron Lee, Ph.D.
Graduate School of Pscyhology
Fuller Theological Seminary
Pasadena, California

Perry LeFevre, Ph.D.
Chicago Theological Seminary
Chicago, Illinois

Robert C. Leslie, Ph.D.
Pacific School of Religion
Berkeley, California

Douglass Lewis, Ph.D.
Wesley Theological Seminary
Washington, D.C.

H. D. Lewis, B.Litt., D.D.
King's College, University of
  London, Retired
London, England

Elizabeth Liebert, S.N.J.M., Ph.D.
San Francisco Theological Seminary
San Anselmo, California

Alvin J. Lindgren, D.D.
Garrett-Evangelical Theological
  Seminary, Emeritus
Evanston, Illinois

James Loder, Ph.D.
Princeton Theological Seminary
Princeton, New Jersey

James C. Logan, Jr.

A. Adams Lovekin, Ph.D.
Samaritan Counseling Center
Albuquerque, New Mexico

Walter J. Lowe, Ph.D.
Candler School of Theology
Emory University
Atlanta, Georgia

Lyman Lundeen, Ph.D.
Lutheran Theological Seminary
Philadelphia, Pennsylvania

B. Lynn Lusk, Psy.D.
Private Practice
Claremont, California

David Lyall, Ph.D.
St. Mary's College
University of St. Andrew
Seattle, Washington

Masamba ma Mpolo, Ph.D.
African Association for Pastoral
  Studies and Counseling
Kinshasa, Republic of Zaire

Archie J. MacLachlan

Steven A. Moss, M.H.L.
B'nai Israel Reform Temple
Oakdale, Long Island

Akbar Muhommad, Ph.D.
State University of New York
Binghamton, New York

Richard A. Muller, Ph.D.
School of Theology
Fuller Theological Seminary
Pasadena, California

James M. Murphy, M.D.
Blanton-Peale Graduate Institute
New York, New York

Gary E. Myers, Ph.D.
Candler School of Theology
Emory University
Atlanta, Georgia

S. Bruce Narramore, Ph.D.
Rosemead School of Psychology
Biola University
La Mirada, California

Allen Nauss, Ph.D.
Christ College, Irvine
Irvine, California

Theron S. Nease, Ph.D. (Deceased)
Columbia Theological Seminary
Decatur, Georgia

Holly S. Nelson, D.Min.
Vanderbilt University Medical
   Center
Nashville, Tennessee

James B. Nelson, Ph.D.
United Theological Seminary of the
   Twin Cities
New Brighton, Minnesota

M. S. Nelson

R. Arne Newman, Ph.D.
Graduate School of Psychology
Fuller Theological Seminary
Pasadena, California

Carol A. Newsom, Ph.D.
Candler School of Theology
Emory University
Atlanta, Georgia

George Niederauer, Ph.D.
St. John's Seminary
Camarillo, California

Tsyugikazu Nishigaki, D.Min.
Seiwa College
Nishinomiya, Japan

William M. Nolan, D.Min.

Henri J. M. Nouwen, Ph.D.
Daybreak-L'Arche
Toronto, Ontario, Canada

Ronald L. Numbers, Ph.D.
University of Wisconsin
Madison, Wisconsin

Leo J. O'Donovan, S.J.
Georgetown University
Washington, D.C.

Wayne E. Oates, Th.D.
Southern Baptist Theological Seminary
Louisville, Kentucky

Leon Oettinger, M.D. (Deceased)
Private Practice
Pasadena, California

William B. Oglesby, Jr., Ph.D.
Union Theological Seminary in
   Virginia
Richmond, Virginia

Richard R. Osmer, Ph.D.
Union Theological Seminary in Virginia
Richmond, Virginia

Anita R. Ostrom, M.Div.
Ph.D. Candidate
Emory University
Atlanta, Georgia

David S. Pacini, Ph.D.
Candler School of Theology
Emory University
Atlanta, Georgia

C. Eddie Palmer, Ph.D.
Department of Sociology and
   Anthropology
University of Southwestern
   Louisiana
LaFayette, Louisiana

William Pannell, D.D.
Fuller Theological Seminary
Pasadena, California

Peter J. Paris, Ph.D.
Princeton Theological Seminary
Princeton, New Jersey

Duane Parker
Interfaith Health Care Ministries, Inc.
Rhode Island Hospitals
Providence, Rhode Island

Duane F. Parker, Ph.D.
Association for Clinical Pastoral
   Education
Decatur, Georgia

Colin Murray Parkes, M.D., F.R.C.
   Psych.
Department of Psychiatry
The London Hospital Medical
   College
London, England

Sharon Daloz Parks, Th.D.
Weston School of Theology
Cambridge, Massachusetts

Les Parrott, Ph.D.
Seattle Pacific University
Seattle, Washington

George W. Paterson, Ph.D.
University of Iowa Hospitals and
   Clinics
Iowa City, Iowa

E. Mansell Pattison, M.D.
   (Deceased)
Medical College of Georgia,
   Emeritus
Augusta, Georgia

John Patton, Ph.D.
Columbia Theological Seminary
Decatur, Georgia

William O. Paulsell, Ph.D.
Lexington Theological Seminary
Lexington, Kentucky

Robert L. Pavelsky, Ph.D.
Private Practice
Corona, California

Jordan Pearlson, J.D., D.D., M.H.L.
Temple Sinai Congregation
Toronto, Ontario, Canada

Robert Peel, L.H.D.
The First Church of Christ,
   Scientist
Boston, Massachusetts

Cliff Penner, Ph.D.
Private Practice
Pasadena, California

Joyce Penner, M.S.
Private Practice
Pasadena, California

Paul J. Peterson, Ph.D.
Associated Psychological Services
St. Cloud, Minnesota

James L. Philpott, S.T.D.
Private Practice
Chattanooga, Tennessee

William E. Phipps, Ph.D.
Davis and Elkins College
Elkins, West Virginia

Dayanand David Pitamber, Th.D.
Satyaniketan Dharmvigyan
   Mahavidyalaya
Allahabad, U.P., India

Stuart A. Plummer, M.Div.
Private Practice
Denver, Colorado

James N. Poling, Ph.D.
Colgate Rochester Divinity School
Rochester, New York

Pablo Polischuck, Ph.D.
Massachusetts General Hospital
Boston, Massachusetts

Kenneth Polite, Ph.D.
Rosemead School of Psychology
Biola University
La Mirada, California

George Polk, S.T.M.
Bethany Hospital
Chicago, Illinois

Ronald Ponsford, Ph.D.
Northwest Nazarene College
Nampa, Idaho

Jack Nusan Porter, Ph.D.
The Spencer Group
Newton, Massachusetts

Jean Porter, Ph.D.
The Divinity School
Vanderbilt University
Nashville, Tennessee

Mark Poster, Ph.D.
Department of History
University of California, Irvine
Irvine, California

Paul W. Pretzel, Th.D.
Private Practice
Arcadia, California

Max Price, Ph.D.

L. Rebecca Propst, Ph.D.
Lewis and Clark College
Portland, Oregon

Paul W. Pruyser, Ph.D. (Deceased)
The Menninger Clinic
Topeka, Kansas

Robert E. Puff
Ph.D. Candidate
Fuller Theological Seminary
Pasadena, California

Claude P. Ragan, Ph.D.
Private Practice (Psychology)
Greensboro, North Carolina

Lewis Rambo, Ph.D.
San Francisco Theological Seminary
San Francisco, California

Carole A. Rayburn, M.Div., Ph.D.
Private Practice
Silver Spring, Maryland

Calvin Redekop
Department of Sociology
Conrad Grebel College
Waterloo, Ontario, Canada

G. Lloyd Rediger

James Reed, Ph.D.
The Toronto School of Theology
Toronto, Ontario, Canada

Daniel Rhoades, Ph.D.
School of Theology at Claremont
Claremont, California

James T. Richardson, J.D., Ph.D.
Department of Sociology
University of Nevada
Reno, Nevada

Charles R. Ridley, Ph.D.
Graduate School of Psychology
Fuller Theological Seminary
Pasadena, California

Leo Rippy, Ph.D.
Board of Higher Education,
   United Methodist Church (Retired)
Nashville, Tennessee

Thomas Robbins, Ph.D.
Rochester, Minnesota

Cecil M. Robeck, Jr., Ph.D.
Fuller Theological Seminary
Pasadena, California

Georgiana G. Rodiger, Ph.D.
Private Practice
Pasadena, California

Jack R. Rogers, Th.D.
Presbyterian Church (U.S.A.)
Louisville, Kentucky

Joel Jay Rogge, J.D., D.Min., Ed.D.
Ipswich, Massachusetts

Wayne G. Rollins, Ph.D.
Assumption College
Worcester, Massachusetts

Andrew J. Rooks, M.D.
CPC Horizon Hospital
Pomona, California

R. S. Rosa

Marcia S. Rosenberg, Ph.D.
Clinical Psychologist
Fresno, California

Stanley Rosenman, Ph.D.
Private Practice
New York, New York

Kenneth P. Ross, Ph.D.
Private Practice
Hollywood, California

R. J. Ross

G. Wade Rowatt, Ph.D.
The Southern Baptist Theological
   Seminary
Louisville, Kentucky

Gloviell Rowland, Ph.D.
Department of Early Childhood
   Education
California State University,
   Los Angeles
Los Angeles, California

Michael Rulon, Ph.D.
Covenant College
Chattanooga, Tennessee

Theodore Runyon, Th.D.
Candler School of Theology
Emory University
Atlanta, Georgia

Horace O. Russell, D.Phil.
Eastern Baptist Theological
   Seminary
Philadelphia, Pennsylvania

Walter Saft, Dr. Theol.
Friedrich Schiller University
Jena, East Germany

Don E. Saliers, Ph.D.
Candler School of Theology
Emory University
Atlanta, Georgia

Terence J. Sandbek, Ph.D.
Charter Hospital of Sacramento
Sacramento, California

Randolph K. Sanders, Ph.D.
Walker and Associates
New Braunfels, Texas

John A. Sanford, M.Div.
Private Practice
San Diego, California

Gary R. Sattler, Th.D.
Fuller Theological Seminary
Pasadena, California

Joachim Scharfenberg, Dr. Theol.
Institute for Practical Theology
University of Kiel
Kiel, West Germany

Chris R. Schlauch, Ph.D.
Boston University
Boston, Massachusetts

Carl D. Schneider, Ph.D.
Grady Memorial Hospital
Atlanta, Georgia

Clarence H. Schnelling, Ph.D.
Iliff School of Theology
Denver, Colorado

Carla Egly Schuler, Ph.D.
Kaiser Mental Health Center
Los Angeles, California

Paul G. Schurman, Th.D.
School of Theology at Claremont
Claremont, California

Charles E. Scott, Ph.D.
Department of Philosophy
Vanderbilt University
Nashville, Tennessee

Harvey Seifert, Ph.D.
School of Theology at Claremont
Claremont, California

Sanford Seltzer, D.D.
Union of American Hebrew
    Congregations
Brookline, Massachusetts

Henry A. Selvey, M.D.
Georgia Association for Pastoral Care
Atlanta, Georgia

Virginia Staudt Sexton, Ph.D.
Department of Psychology
St. John's University
Jamaica, New York

James H. Shackelford, Ph.D.
Parkside Pastoral Counseling Center
Park Ridge, Illinois

Martin E. Shoemaker, Ph.D.
Personnel Institute of Canada
Vancouver, British Columbia, Canada

Steven F. Shoemaker, Ph.D.
Children's Bureau of Los Angeles
Van Nuys, California

William J. Short, O.F.M., S.T.D.
Franciscan School of Theology
Berkeley, California

Patricia P. Shropshire, Ph.D.
Georgia Association for Pastoral
    Care
Atlanta, Georgia

Lou H. Silberman, D.H.L.
Vanderbilt University, Emeritus,
University of Arizona
Tucson, Arizona

Debra L. Silver, M.Div.
S.T.D. Candidate
Emory University
Atlanta, Georgia

C. Dene Simpson, Ph.D.
Northwest Nazarene College
Nampa, Idaho

Chaplain John N. Sims, D.S.M.
Baptist Medical Centers
Birmingham, Alabama

A. W. R. Sipe, M.S.
Timonium, Maryland

Lory Skwerer, M.Div.
Atlanta, Georgia

Catherine S. Smith, Ph.D.
Associated Psychological Services
Pasadena, California

Douglas K. Smith, Ph.D.
Counseling Associates
Los Olivos, California

Kermit W. Smith

Luther E. Smith, Jr., Ph.D.
Candler School of Theology
Emory University
Atlanta, Georgia

Marcia R. Smith, Ph.D.

Thomas A. Smith, M.C.S., Ph.D.
Religious Studies
Loyola University
New Orleans, Louisiana

John Snarey, Ed.D.
Candler School of Theology
Emory University
Atlanta, Georgia

Samuel Southard, Ph.D.
Fuller Theological Seminary
Pasadena, California

Richard M. Spielmann, Th.D.
Colgate Rochester Divinity School
    Bexley Hall/Crozer Theological
    Seminary
Rochester, New York

Bernard Spilka, Ph.D.
University of Denver
Denver, Colorado

Russell P. Spittler, Ph.D.
Fuller Theological Seminary
Pasadena, California

Edward Springman, M.Div.

Ira C. Starling, Jr., M.Div.
United States Navy
Washington, D.C.

Clyde J. Steckel, Ph.D.
United Theological Seminary
    of the Twin Cities
New Brighton, Minnesota

Edward V. Stein, Ph.D.
San Francisco Theological Seminary
San Anselmo, California

Robert G. Stephanopoulos, Ph.D.
Holy Trinity Archdiocesan Cathedral
New York, New York

Irwin R. Sternlicht, Ph.D.
C. G. Jung Institute of Los Angeles
Los Angeles, California

Howard C. Stevenson
Division of Child Mental Health
State of Delaware
Wilmington, Delaware

Charles W. Stewart, Ph.D.
Pastoral Psychotherapy Associates
Bethesda, Maryland

Allison Stokes, Ph.D.
Hartford Seminary
Hartford, Connecticut

D. Lee Stoltzfus, Ph.D.
L.I.F.E. Management Systems
Monrovia, California

Alvin J. Straatmeyer, Ph.D.
Private Practice
Glendale, California

Aunë J. Strom, Ph.D.
Private Practice
Pasadena, California

George W. Stroup, Ph.D.
Columbia Theological Seminary
Decatur, Georgia

Orlo Strunk, Jr., Ph.D.
Grand Strand Pastoral Counseling
    Service
Myrtle Beach, South Carolina

R. Scott Sullender, Ph.D.
Walnut Valley Counseling Center
Diamond Bar, California

Ronald H. Sunderland, Ed.D.
Equipping Lay People for Ministry,
    Inc.
Houston, Texas

David K. Switzer, Th.D.
Perkins School of Theology
Southern Methodist University
Dallas, Texas

Charles Edward Taylor
Laguna, California

Charles W. Taylor, D.Min.
The Church Divinity School of the
    Pacific
Berkeley, California

Palmer C. Temple, M.Div.
St. Luke's Training and Counseling
    Center
Atlanta, Georgia

Anthony C. Thiselton, Ph.D.
St. John's College
University of Durham
Durham, England

J. Donald Thomas, M.D.
Huntington Hospital
Pasadena, California

Robert V. Thompson, M.Div.
First Baptist Church
Evanston, Illinois

Edward E. Thornton, Ph.D.
The Southern Baptist Theological
  Seminary
Louisville, Kentucky

Martin Thornton, S.T.D.
  (Deceased)
Truro Cathedral
Cornwall, England

Steven M. Tipton, Ph.D.
Candler School of Theology
Emory University
Atlanta, Georgia

John R. Tisdale, Ph.D.
Cedar Crest College
Allentown, Pennsylvania

Mary Ann Tolbert, Ph.D.
The Divinity School
Vanderbilt University
Nashville, Tennessee

Lee E. Travis, Ph.D. (Deceased)
Graduate School of Psychology
Fuller Theological Seminary
Pasadena, California

Mark Trotter, M.Div.
First United Methodist Church
San Diego, California

Gene M. Tucker, Ph.D.
Candler School of Theology
Emory University
Atlanta, Georgia

Judith E. Turian, Ph.D.
U.S. Naval Regional Medical Center
Long Beach, California

Ralph L. Underwood, Ph.D.
Austin Presbyterian Theological
  Seminary
Austin, Texas

Julia Upton, R.S.M., Ph.D.
St. John's University
Jamaica, New York

Edward Collins Vacek, S.J., Ph.D.
Weston School of Theology
Cambridge, Massachusetts

A. J. van den Blink, Ph.D.
Colgate Rochester Divinity School
Rochester, New York

Bryan Van Dragt, Ph.D.
Private Practice
Gig Harbor, Washington

Adrian van Kaam, Ph.D.
Institute of Formative Spirituality
Duquesne University
Pittsburgh, Pennsylvania

Charles A. Van Wagner, S.T.D.
Life Enrichment Center
Raleigh, North Carolina

Hendrika Vande Kemp, Ph.D.
Graduate School of Theology
Fuller Theological Seminary
Pasadena, California

Vernon Vande Reit, Ph.D.
Private Practice
Pasadena, California

Mary Vander Goot, Ph.D.
Psychology Associates
Grand Rapids, Michigan

John Vannorsdall, Ph.D.
Lutheran Theological Seminary
  at Philadelphia
Philadelphia, Pennsylvania

Bruce Vaughn, M.Div.
Ph.D. Candidate
Vanderbilt University
Nashville, Tennessee

John Monroe Vayhinger, Ph.D.
Clinical Psychologist
Colorado Springs, Colorado

G. Daniel Venable, Ph.D.
Valley Psychological Center
Sacramento, California

Adrian M. Visscher, D.Psy.
St. Paul University
Ottawa, Ontario, Canada

Paul C. Vitz, Ph.D.
Department of Psychology
New York University
New York, New York

Garry A. Vogelpohl, D.Min.
St. John's Lutheran Church
Nashville, Tennessee

David W. Waanders
New Brunswick Theological Seminary
New Brunswick, New Jersey

Edwin R. Wallace, IV, M.D.
Department of Psychiatry
  and Health Behavior
Medical College of Georgia
Augusta, Georgia

Ernest Wallwork, Ph.D.
Department of Religion
Syracuse University
Syracuse, New York

Roger N. Walsh, M.D., Ph.D.
Department of Psychiatry
  and Human Behavior,
  University of California, Irvine
Irvine, California

Michael Ward, Ph.D.
University of Southern California
  Medical School
Los Angeles, California

David Lowes Watson, Ph.D.
General Board of Discipleship
The United Methodist Church
Nashville, Tennessee

Peggy Way, Ph.D.
Eden Theological Seminary
St. Louis, Missouri

Robert Weathers, Ph.D.
Graduate School of Education
  and Psychology
Pepperdine University
Culver City, California

Timothy T. Weber, Ph.D.
Private Practice
Colorado Springs, Colorado

Eugene S. Wehrli, Ph.D.
Eden Theological Seminary
St. Louis, Missouri

Christine Wenderoth, Ph.D.
Columbia Theological Seminary
Decatur, Georgia

Ernest White, Ph.D.
The Southern Baptist Theological
  Seminary
Louisville, Kentucky

James F. White, Ph.D.
University of Notre Dame
Notre Dame, Indiana

Susan J. White, Ph.D.
Westcott House
Cambridge, England

Scott Cabot Willis, Ph.D.
Veterans Administration Medical
  Center
Portland, Oregon

R. Ward Wilson, Ph.D.
King College
Bristol, Tennessee

Edward P. Wimberly, Ph.D.
Garrett-Evangelical Theological
  Seminary
Evanston, Illinois

Charles Winquist, Ph.D.
Department of Religion
Syracuse University
Syracuse, New York

While every effort has been made to contact contributors and include accurate, up-to-date information regarding titles and affiliations, the reference book editor at Abingdon Press would welcome any corrections to the above list.

ABANDONMENT. *See* CRUELTY AND SADISTIC BEHAVIOR; GRIEF AND LOSS; RAGE AND HOSTILITY.

ABORTION (Ethical Issues). The central considerations in the dilemma of abortion are: (1) physiological and social relation of sexual activity to procreation; (2) the status and rights of the unborn life or fetus; (3) the welfare and rights of the pregnant woman; and (4) the interests of others, such as the father, family, and the religious and civic communities. Abortion is a moral problem precisely because the situations out of which it arises present conflicts of values and rights. The weighing of these values is not a specifically or exclusively "religious" issue. However, the Christian doctrines of creation and redemption bring to the problem of abortion a respect for the lives of all persons, especially the innocent, as well as a commitment to enhance their quality. The Christian images of sin, cross, forgiveness, and reconciliation allow recognition of the brokenness of the human condition, the reality of moral conflict, and the frequent necessity of sacrificing some values for the sake of others. Christian groups disagree about whether and when abortion is morally valid, but few disagree that it is tragic, even when morally warranted.

1. Bible and Tradition. Different evaluations of abortion in Christian history and in the present arise from different interpretations of the values at stake. Scriptural references to abortion are few. The Hebrew Bible stipulates merely that if men quarreling cause a woman to miscarry, the guilty one shall pay a fine to the woman's husband. Only if the woman herself is killed must the attacker give "life for life" (Exod. 21:22–23). The NT makes no specific reference to abortion, but does reject drugs and potions *(pharmakeia)* — which may include abortifacients (Gal. 5:20; cf. Rev. 9:21; 18:23; 21:8; and 22:15). In biblical, patristic, medieval, and Reformation Christianity, avoiding reproduction was seen as sinful, the life of the unborn was accorded high value, women were thought to have few rights of independent self-determination in family or society, and abortion was associated with sexual immorality. Some patristic and medieval authors argued that the fetus does not receive a soul until its body has developed a substantially human form. Abortion of the unformed, unensouled fetus was considered seriously sinful but not homicide. In the eighteenth century, the Roman Catholic Church shifted decisively toward the position that life deserves the utmost care from conception, and by the late nineteenth century had limited abortion to only a very few life-against-life cases in which the fetus dies as an indirect result of an operation designed to save the mother. Protestant denominations vary in justifications for abortion but generally place more weight on the responsibility of the individuals concerned to decide, especially the pregnant woman.

2. Contemporary Discussion. An important element in the current debate is the feminist critique of patriarchy in church, family, and society. Some argue that access to abortion is essential to guarantee control over reproductive capacity, and to permit women to join equally with men in the political, economic, and domestic spheres. Others respond that more effective social support of women with difficult pregnancies would enhance women's freedom while permitting recognition of the fetus as an entity with at least some independent value and rights.

Another aspect of the modern discussion is advanced understanding of and control over gestation and birth. Knowledge of fetal development has fueled controversy over fetal status. Biological "lines" or phases such as conception, implantation, the appearance of brain activity recordable by electroencephalogram, and viability outside the womb have been suggested variously as the points at which the fetus acquires some essential characteristic necessary for human life to have protectable status. Further, the possibility of predicting congenital defects makes it possible to perform abortions in response to so-called "fetal indications." Abortion of abnormal fetuses raises questions of whose interests should be determinative of such decisions, and whether the arguments justifying them also justify infanticide.

In summary, Christians continue to debate the status of the fetus and of its rights in comparison to the right of those whom its continued development affects, especially its mother. While some Christians condemn abortion in all but the most extreme cases, others view it as the right of any woman who chooses it. A broader consensus exists in favor of abortion as an option when the mother has been victimized by rape or incest, when her physical health is seriously endangered, or when the child will be severely abnormal. Precise criteria for such abortion decisions continue to be refined.

Bibliography. E. Batchelor, ed., *Abortion: The Moral Issues* (1982). D. Callahan, *Abortion: Law, Choice, and Morality* (1970). J. Connery, *Abortion: The Development of the Roman Catholic Perspective* (1977). C. Gilligan, *In a Different Voice* (1982). B. W. Harrison, *Our Right to Choose: Toward a New Ethic of Abortion* (1983). M Kutkin, "Tay-Sachs and the Abortion Controversy," *J. of Religion and Health,* 20 (1981), 224–42. J. T. Noonan, ed., *The Morality of Abortion: Legal and Historical Perspectives* (1970). T. J. Silber, "Abortion: A Jewish View," *J. of Religion and Health,* 19 (1980), 231–39.

L. S. CAHILL

ETHICS AND PASTORAL CARE; MORAL DILEMMAS IN PASTORAL PERSPECTIVE; MORAL THEOLOGY AND PASTORAL CARE. *See also* CONSCIENCE; FAMILY, CHRISTIAN *or* JEWISH THEOLOGY AND ETHICS OF; MORAL DEVELOPMENT. *Compare* DISAGREEMENT, DIFFERENCE, AND CONFLICT IN PASTOR-PARISHIONER RELATIONSHIPS.

ABORTION (Pastoral Care). The care and counseling of women and couples (and sometimes men individually) who are considering the termination of an unwanted or otherwise problematic pregnancy, or of persons who have previously undergone an abortion. While most abortion counseling involves women only, men may also be included. Pastors may wish to consider and encourage their participation since the men too are involved and often feel they have no one with whom they can express their feelings and concerns.

Abortion counseling today is done against the background of a society that is deeply conflicted over the moral and legal issues in abortion, and which is undergoing pervasive cultural ferment concerning all questions related to sexuality, marriage, and childraising. In this atmosphere, the pastoral care of persons contemplating or recovering from abortion is, needless to say, a sensitive and complex matter. But while abortion presents a moral dilemma in pastoral care, a look at the broader picture reveals that there need be no incompatibility between holding a particular moral position oneself, as pastor or counselor, while assisting an individual to reach a free decision of conscience. It is in any case extremely important that the counselor be in touch with his or her own feelings and values concerning abortion, without feeling compelled to limit the counselee's freedom of conscience.

1. Preabortion Counseling. The fact that someone seeks or is willing to be involved in counseling before terminating a pregnancy indicates that the individual's mind is not entirely settled on the matter. The circumstances and motivations may be very different from situation to situation, however, and it is important for the pastor not to prejudge what the decision means for the persons involved. Some, like many middle-class adoles-

cents, may be in a state of crisis and feel the need to reach a decision quickly. Under pressure, normal problem-solving mechanisms may be inadequate for the situation. The counselor's task is then to help the person expand her level of awareness so she can reach a decision with more internal freedom and a greater range of choice. Others, for example, women with limited economic means and large families to support, while not panicky, may for practical reasons feel that they have little choice. Still others, including older women with established families, may or may not be resolved about having the abortion, but in either case may find value in talking through the considerations and moral ambiguities with an understanding person. Such people may have a deep sense of reverence for life, but struggle with equally deep concern about the future welfare of the child, the family, and themselves if the pregnancy is continued.

Pastoral conversation and questioning should try to elicit the counselee's motives for seeking an abortion. Pregnancy and abortion can have various meanings even for persons in similar circumstances, so it is important to ask and to listen. It is often helpful to the counselees themselves to express and talk through their feelings and motives, and pastors should encourage them to do so insofar as that seems wanted and useful. The pastor can assist by asking simple, direct questions and listening well, and at times by providing appropriate information and moral perspective.

Since pregnancy can have many meanings, it is important for pastors to be alert to the range of possibilities. Sometimes a pregnancy is only a surface issue, an expression perhaps of family or developmental problems. In such situations abortion would be a temporary or partial solution to the underlying problem. When this is the case, the pastor can help the counselee understand the abortion decision in the context of its deeper meanings. This may expand the individual's perspective and enable a more free and responsible decision. If the woman's chief concern is with society's reaction to her pregnancy, as is sometimes the case with adolescents or unmarried women who come from conservative religious communities, the counselor's loving, nonjudgmental interaction can be an important indicator that the world will not automatically reject her if she chooses to continue this pregnancy or if she decides to have an abortion. Sometimes pregnancy is a source of fear in itself and can spark anxiety attacks and nightmares. Such reactions can be explored as a way of acknowledging the normal impact of pregnancy as well as its specific meanings for this woman. Still others, often young and frightened, may perceive the developing fetus in their wombs as little more than a problem to be gotten rid of. Such persons can be helped toward a broader understanding and more responsible decision for or against abortion if the helping person acknowledges with them their fear and sense of pressure and helps them to imagine the possibility of alternatives. For all abortion counselees, considering both short-term and long-term consequences is important. These include psychological as well as social consequences that may be entailed in either alternative, including the possibility of unexpected emotional side effects if one has an abortion, and the realistic considerations of social support and economic resources if one does not.

2. Postabortion Counseling. An individual's immediate reaction to abortion is generally relief. Long-term reactions are less clearly predictable, however; the data concerning long-term emotional effects of abortion are ambiguous, and questions can be raised about the depth, authority, and slant of particular studies. Some studies show little negative effect; others suggest that an emotional price is sometimes paid for abortion which does not appear until long after the event. When the latter is the case, it appears to vary in intensity with the subjective meaning and the real or imagined severity of one's own action (e.g., sense of guilt).

In any case abortion involves grieving. As in mourning other losses, grief reactions in abortion vary widely in kind and intensity depending on many factors. They are usually intensified, however, to the extent that conflicting desires and feelings about the fetus are present. A complicating factor in abortion grief is the psychologically ambiguous status of the fetus. This may make the mourning process both easier in some ways and more difficult in others. It is often the case also that abortion is an isolating experience socially and emotionally, making pastoral care and presence all the more important.

In terms of grief and recovery, the crucial questions are the general circumstances of the pregnancy and what the fetus represents subjectively to the persons involved. A woman who has undergone an abortion might have lost a fetus whose importance was peripheral or negligible to her, or the result of rape or incest, or she might have lost a severely depressing problem; the abortion may therefore leave her with a profound sense of relief. But, psychologically, she might also have lost a symbol of motherhood and womanliness, of love, of hope, of self-esteem, or sense of future. The fetus may have been the dreamchild of youth or the fullness of womanhood — or punishment for trying to be grown-up. Determining what exactly has been lost, therefore, is a key factor in appreciating the individual's reaction and the most helpful pastoral responses. To determine the possibility of psychological complications, and to anticipate the intensity of the grief reaction, it is therefore necessary to determine the centrality of that which has been lost, as well as the circumstances under which that loss occurred.

As in other grief reactions, it is entirely possible that, while one's immediate reaction may be that of profound relief, repressed feelings can come to consciousness later and cause a more severe reaction. Because of the immediacy of the reaction, a woman might be focusing exclusively on dealing with this surface problem while repressing any other emotional feelings. Bugen's study on grief is very helpful in understanding the severity of these reactions.

Although some people quickly conclude that abortion is always preventable, the events which led to the pregnancy itself might not have been preventable, which could lessen the severity of the reaction. Again, the woman's immediate impulse might be to overlook the preventability in the face of her desire to eliminate the immediate problem. One should also take into consideration the circumstances which led to the decision to abort. These circumstances might include interpersonal conflicts, family planning, threat to fulfillment of life goals, emotional instability, financial difficulties, age, illegitimacy, adultery, rape, or fear of genetic defect.

Specific social, legal, religious, and cultural norms must also be taken into consideration, for they possess at least the potential for compounding the concepts of centrality and/or preventability. Reverence for life is a universal concept, not restricted to any religious group. Thus even a woman who is not actively affiliated with a church group could have a profound religious response to an abortion.

Some of the more typical pathological preoccupations among women who have had unresolved long-term grief reactions to abortion, for which professional help may be appropriate, include fantasies of the fetus as an identifiable baby and as a growing child (particularly at the anniversaries of the abortion), neurotic guilt for murder, fear of bodily injury as a result of the abortion, fear of future defective or deformed babies as punishment, and concern for secrecy.

It is quite possible, therefore, that the needs of a woman who has undergone an abortion will be identical with those of any individual who has suffered a severe loss, and in some respects might even be more intense because of an underlying feeling of guilt.

Bibliography. L. Bugan, "Human Grief: A Model for Prediction and Intervention," *American J. of Orthopsychiatry*, 47 (1977), 196–206. D. Mace, *Abortion: The Agonizing Decision* (1972). C. Parkes, *Bereavement: Studies of Grief in Adult Life* (1972). P. J. Riga, "Counseling, and the Abortion Issue," *J. of Pastoral Counseling*, 17:2 (1982), 44–5. L. Scott, "Possible Guidelines for Problem Pregnancy Counseling," *Pastoral Psychology*, 23–4 (1972), 41–9. D. Switzer, *The Dynamics of Grief: Its Sources, Pain, and Healing* (1970). J. Upton, "The Hidden Grief of Abortion," *Pastoral Psychology*, 31 (1982), 19–25. J. Wallerstein *et al.*, "Psychological Sequelae of Therapeutic Abortion in Young Unmarried Women," *Archives of General Psychiatry*, 27 (1972), 828–32.

J. UPTON

MORAL DILEMMAS IN PASTORAL PERSPECTIVE. *See also* DECISION/ INDECISION, PSYCHOLOGY OF; FAMILY, JEWISH *or* PASTORAL CARE AND COUNSELING OF; GRIEF AND LOSS; GUIDANCE, PASTORAL; RESPONSIBILITY/IRRESPONSIBILITY, PSYCHOLOGY OF; VALUES IN COUNSELING AND PSYCHOTHERAPY; WOMEN. *Compare* MISCARRIAGE; MOTHER-INFANT BONDING; PREGNANCY.

ABSOLUTION. *See* BLESSING AND BENEDICTION; PENANCE, SACRAMENT OF.

ABSTINENCE. *See* ALCOHOL ABUSE, ADDICTION, AND THERAPY; ASCETICAL PRACTICES; SELF-DENIAL.

ACADEMY OF RELIGION AND MENTAL HEALTH. *See* RELIGION AND HEALTH MOVEMENT.

ACCEPTANCE. The therapeutic posture of receiving or taking in another person; an attitude of caring for and of holding in valued esteem another person as a person of distinct particularity.

Genuine acceptance is a primary characteristic of the therapeutic relationship in most forms of insight therapy. Carl R. Rogers considered it one of the six necessary and sufficient conditions for therapeutic change. Historically, Rogers developed acceptance in relation to, and as a correction of, the tendency of the counselor "to pass some type of evaluative judgment upon the client." Acceptance is not agreement or approval; rather, it is a warm and positive evaluation of the individual whether or not the person lives up to or conforms with the therapist's values or expectations. Acceptance is also not synonymous with appraisal. It does not evaluate the individual's experience in terms of what is important or worthy; instead it respects and cherishes the individual's experience for its own sake. In this sense, acceptance is permissiveness. It is a suspension of all judgment, but unlike permissiveness it does not come out of a *laissez-faire* attitude. Instead it is a deep and genuine affirmation of the individual in the totality of her or his experience.

Rogers emphasizes the unconditional nature of acceptance. He maintains that the therapist should prize every facet of the client's experience, no matter how negative or positive. In his later writings, Rogers prefers the phrase "unconditional positive regard" to the less radical term "acceptance."

Genuine acceptance serves several purposes in the therapeutic process. It is the *conditio sine qua non* of a positive and enduring relationship between client and counselor. Furthermore, it provides a safe atmosphere in which clients can explore and experience their inner world of feelings and meanings. Rogers believes that it also enables clients to achieve self-acceptance. As clients experience the acceptance of the therapist, they gradually begin to take the same attiude toward themselves, feeling a "dawning respect for, acceptance of, and, finally, even a fondness for" themselves. The achievement of increased self-acceptance is crucial to Rogerian healing, for it represents a re-union with the depths of one's experiencing and an ability to live spontaneously out of the fullness of one's being.

Pastoral counselors recognize the importance of genuine acceptance for the same reasons that psychotherapists do. In addition, they emphasize the symbolic role of the pastor's acceptance as not only personal acceptance but as signifying an infinitely transcendent acceptance. Ultimately, the pastor witnesses to and makes concrete God's unconditional acceptance of the human being who is basically unacceptable. This paradoxical truth is crucial to Christian healing, for it frees individuals from the compulsive need to make themselves acceptable and assures them of God's unqualified love.

Bibliography. C. R. Rogers, *Client-Centered Therapy* (1951). For a theological discussion: T. Oden, *Kerygma and Counseling* (1966).

L. ADEN

GRACE AND PASTORAL CARE; GRATITUDE; FORGIVENESS; LOVE; THERAPEUTIC CONDITIONS.

ACCEPTANCE OF GOD'S WILL. *See* GOD'S WILL, ACCEPTANCE OF.

ACCIDENT PRONENESS. *See* SELF-DESTRUCTIVE BEHAVIOR.

ACCIDENTS, PASTORAL CARE IN. *See* CRISIS MINISTRY; EMERGENCY, PSYCHOLOGY OF PASTOR IN; TRAUMA.

ACCIDIE. *See* APATHY AND BOREDOM.

ACCOUNTABILITY. *See* LEGAL DIMENSIONS OF PASTORAL CARE AND COUNSELING; RESPONSIBILITY/ IRRESPONSIBILITY.

ACCREDITATION. Basically an American phenomenon that emerged around the turn of the twentieth century to ensure quality education and to establish some standards for general collegiate and professional education.

Accreditation is to be distinguished from certification. Persons are certified to practice a profession. Educational programs and institutions are accredited. Both certification and accreditation serve the general welfare by ensuring a certain quality of performance, a certain standard of excellence.

Accreditation is an ordered process by which educational programs and institutions are periodically reviewed by recognized accrediting agencies. Each accrediting organization publishes standards for educational programs. For instance, the Association for Clinical Pastoral Education has standards for programs of basic, advanced, and supervisory CPE, and the American Association of Pastoral Counselors has standards for training programs in pastoral counseling. Although there are differences in procedures, the accreditation process in the pastoral care and counseling organizations involves the following steps in the initial and subsequent periodic accreditation reviews.

The accreditation review usually involves conducting a program of self-study and a written documentation of that study by the applicants; an on-site review of the institution, staff, curriculum, and program resources and governance by a team selected by the accrediting agency; a written report with recommendations by the site review team; and the publication of the accredited status granted by the agency. Periodic reviews of the educational program are regularly made within five to seven years to determine continuous compliance with established standards.

Accreditation is a status granted to an educational program and institution that are found to be in compliance with stated criteria of educational quality. An accredited status ensures a certain quality of excellence in an educational program that may qualify graduates for admission to higher or more specialized programs or for professional practice. Additionally, an accredited status may determine eligibility for membership in an association of similar institutions. Beyond this official understanding, accreditation also provides a periodic review of peers, and thereby promotes continuing education with corrections and blessings from colleagues. It fosters exchange of ideas and methods of practice, and it provides some structure for the enhancing of the profession and the promoting of community, which, in the long run, may be the most valuable benefits of the accreditation process.

By enactment of federal legislation, the U.S. Office of Education provides criteria for, determines eligibility of, and publishes a listing of accrediting agencies. Organizations desiring recognition as accrediting agencies must be approved by standards and procedures published by the U.S. Office of Education. For example, the Association for Clinical Pastoral Education (ACPE), at its inception as an organization in 1968, requested recognition by the U.S. Office of Education as an accrediting agency for programs of CPE and since then has been listed continuously in the *Federal Register*.

J. N. KEITH, JR.

STANDARDS FOR PASTORAL COUNSELING. *See also* AMERICAN ASSOCIATION OF PASTORAL COUNSELORS; ASSOCIATION FOR CLINICAL PASTORAL EDUCATION; PASTORAL COUNSELING CENTER. *Compare* CERTIFICATION; LICENSURE.

ACEDIA. *See* APATHY AND BOREDOM.

ACHIEVEMENT MOTIVE. *See* COMPETITIVENESS; MOTIVATION.

ACT PSYCHOLOGY. *See* DYNAMIC PSYCHOLOGY.

ACTING OUT. The replication of forgotten memories, attitudes, or conflicts by action rather than words and without awareness on the part of the person. Although particularly relevant in the psychoanalytic process where it is referred to as "acting out in the transference," it may occur outside of the analytic situation; for example, in undersocialized children who have failed to establish a normal degree of affection with others. It is also seen in adults as an inappropriate way of expressing feelings, although in its original psychoanalytic meaning a key requirement is its *unconscious* genesis and its relation to the analytic process.

O. STRUNK, JR.

PSYCHOANALYSIS (Therapeutic Method and Research); *Compare* PATIENCE/PATIENTHOOD; RESPONSIBILITY/IRRESPONSIBILITY, PSYCHOLOGY OF; RESISTANCE; WORKING THROUGH.

ACTION. *See* BEHAVIOR; FEELING, THOUGHT AND ACTION IN PASTORAL COUNSELING; THEORY AND PRAXIS.

ACTION/BEING RELATIONSHIP. The focus of pastoral supervision upon the relationship between what the supervisee is and what he or she does. The use of the philosophical categories action and being is not necessary to the supervisory process, but it calls attention to the fundamental issue of how what one is relates to what one does.

Recent pastoral care education has held that it is not enough to learn how to perform certain actions and to theorize about them. The central issue in learning to be a minister is integrating theory and practice through one's person. The relation between action and being, therefore, is explored through the question, "How does this action or thought of yours relate to who you are and the kind of minister you are becoming?"

This kind of supervisory intervention is more than a practical strategy. It presupposes that the acquisition of the practical knowledge of ministry involves at least some change in the whole person. Normatively, something should happen that integrates action and being.

Related to the Christian theological tradition, that presupposition might be stated in this way: (1) Jesus Christ exemplifies ministry in both his person and his action, a perfect integration of action and being; (2) in contrast, those who follow him in ministry do not possess the integration of what they are and what they do; (3) pastoral supervision of ministry, therefore, involves confronting this discrepancy as a challenge to facilitate integration. The action/being relationship is, thus, a "condition report" on where the student is in developing a ministry integral to his or her person.

Even though there has been a general consensus within the pastoral care movement that "pastoral" supervision involves the supervision of whole persons rather than of particular behaviors, maintaining that focus is difficult. The concern for integration represents a tension for both supervisor and supervisee and even the best students and supervisors tend to resolve the tension by narrowing the supervisory focus to behavior. Rather than asking, "How does what you did relate to what you are?" the supervisor is tempted to ask the narrower question, "How can you do it better?"

The action/being relationship describes a point of view that resists behavioral reductionism. It represents the conviction that the best in pastoral caring involves the offering of oneself to others in relationship. What one does should be a natural expression of what one is. Christians base this norm upon an interpretation of the person of Jesus Christ as a unity of his action and being.

J. PATTON

SUPERVISION. *See also* CHRISTOLOGY AND PASTORAL CARE; FEELING, THOUGHT, AND ACTION IN PASTORAL COUNSELING; PHILOSOPHY AND PSYCHOLOGY. *Compare* BEING/BECOMING RELATIONSHIP; EXISTENTIALISM AND PASTORAL CARE; HUMAN CONDITION/PREDICAMENT (Clinical Pastoral Perspective).

ACTION-REFLECTION. *See* CASE STUDY METHOD; SUPERVISION; THEORY AND PRAXIS.

ADAMS, JAY E. *See* NOUTHETIC COUNSELING; FUNDAMENTALIST PASTORAL CARE.

ADAPTION. *See* ADJUSTMENT, CONCEPT OF; EGO STRENGTH; PSYCHOSOCIAL DEVELOPMENT.

ADDICTION. *See* ALCOHOL *or* DRUG ABUSE, ADDICTION AND THERAPY.

ADJUNCTIVE THERAPIES. A term used to describe those therapy modalities which supplement private psychotherapy within clinical, educational, and industrial environments. Adjunctive therapies may serve as an auxiliary to private psychotherapy, or they may be utilized as the principle treatment modality. Adjunctive therapies are essentially wholistic and humanitarian; they are thus a rich resource for pastoral care and counseling as a mode of preventative therapy in association with community mental health programs. Humanistically oriented adjunctive art therapists believe the whole person can be treated through creative expression (art, dance, drama, music, poetry, etc.) because creative work is compatible with integrating body, mind, spirit, and emotion.

All of the adjunctive therapy modalities are specialized fields of training, requiring specific education and supervised training. They are used mainly with physically, emotionally, and mentally handicapped adults and children, both in private and group therapy, and are conducted by a licensed professional or a qualified paraprofessional who is under professional supervision. Many of these therapy modalities overlap.

1. **Art Therapy** is characterized by the use of art media (paintings, drawings, sculptures, collages, clay modelings, sandplay, etc.) to help clients express themselves nonverbally through symbolic communication. Clients learn to interpret the meanings of their creative productions, thereby contacting the unconscious basis of emotional problems. Although art therapy, like art education, may teach technique and media skills, it is less product-oriented because it is more concerned with the individual's inner experience.

2. **Dance Therapy** is the psychotherapeutic use of rhythmic movement to assist the client to express spontaneous activity, relieve tensions and feelings, and release potential for interactions with others. Dancing as a healing ritual has its roots in antiquity. For centuries peoples of all cultures have expressed their joys and their sorrows through the ritual of dance, communicating with their gods, and exorcising their demons, conquering pain and gaining inner strength. A basic premise underlying dance therapy is that there is an integral relationship between mind and body; all movement reflects both intrapsychic dynamics and interpersonal functioning.

3. **Drama Therapy** uses theories and techniques from theater and psychotherapy. The basic premise for drama as therapy is that theatrics provide a natural vehicle for internal dramas within the psyche to be externalized onto the theater of life, expediting the resolution of emotional conflicts and facilitating individual and social change.

   a. Psychodrama is a group therapy method developed by J. L. Moreno in 1925. The therapist is the director, the patient is the protagonist (actor), and the group, composed of trained workers or former patients as "auxiliary egos," play various roles that reflect thoughts and feelings the protagonist may not yet be able to verbalize. The therapist determines which life situations from the patient's history are to be reenacted and also serves as a catalyst to evoke conflicts of psychological importance. As a therapeutic approach for children, psychodrama helps children listen to and cooperate with one another, as well as express feelings, fantasies, and reality-oriented concerns. Puppetry, dramatic games (pantomime and interviews), dramatic plays (writing and producing them), and encounter techniques are commonly used methods for children.

   b. Sociodrama, an outgrowth of psychodrama, is mostly used in clinical, educational, and industrial settings. Role playing is employed mostly for practical purposes (sales problems, applying for a job, staff relationships, etc.). The process of acting out new social roles helps the individual gain insight into the motivation and expectations of self and others with more objectivity. Sociodrama facilitates alternative modes of action, new adaptive methods, and tests capacities for change.

4. **Industrial Therapy** is based on the premise that paid work is essential to the integrity of chronic patients in mental hospitals who suffer from emotional disorders, if they are to be rehabilitated and reintegrated into the community as self-respecting human beings. Industrial therapy programs provide paid work in sheltered workshops within the hospital environment, or in jobs outside of the mental hospital. Opportunities to develop good work habits, new trades, and skills bring self-esteem and meaning to the mental patient through paid work and its character-developing qualities, such as responsibility, punctuality, dedication, loyalty, obedience, honesty, and the feeling of being of service to others. Although the use of unpaid work as treatment for the mentally ill has a long history, it is only recently that industrial psychologists have recognized the necessity for an emphasis on paid work as a means to restore the mental patient through social and cultural rewards.

5. **Music Therapy** is based on the premise that sound, in the form of music, has the power to heal the whole person, involving body, mind, spirit, and emotion. The emphasis in music therapy is on *sound* and its effect on the psyche and physiology, as opposed to the *kind* of music used or *standards* of music achievement. Although the music therapist is a modern phenomenon, music as a curative agent for affliction of soul and spirit is not. Throughout antiquity physicians, philosophers, priests, and musicians have observed and used music as a healing agent, as David soothed King Saul with his harp (1 Sam. 16:23). The belief that disease may be cured through divine intervention has always been a part of pagan religious faith. Later, the early Christian church and Christian Fathers tried to eliminate from music all traces of its evil pagan influence through the planned use of music to provide a spiritual, elevating experience. Art and music were commissioned to adorn cathedrals and enhance the effect of the ritual, the liturgy, and the processions of the faithful. This symphony of aesthetics was meant to bring the faithful nearer to God, putting them in a receptive and spiritual mood, moving the heart, alleviating sadness, and calming the angry spirit.

6. **Occupational Therapy** (OT) provides an opportunity to maximize the patient's potential for health and growth by using activities involving skill (arts and crafts, work projects, and activities of daily living skills) to work toward a specific goal that is evaluated by the therapist. The process whereby the therapist matches the patient to the therapeutic activity is guided by available information and observation of the patient regarding social, psychological, vocational, cultural, and ethnic factors. OT is among the best organized and most universally employed activities in mental institutions.

7. **Physical Therapy** practitioners work in hospitals, nursing homes, schools for handicapped children, rehabilitation centers, community health centers, industries, and also as educators. The physical therapist is skilled in planning, organizing, and directing programs for the rehabilitation of patients of all ages who are disabled by

an illness or an accident, or were born with a handicap, and/or are suffering from physical and emotional trauma. The therapist relieves pain, using physical means (e.g., exercise, massage, heat, water) and equipment such as diathermy and ultrasonic machines. Patients are directed in the care and use of wheelchairs, braces, canes, crutches, and so forth.

8. **Play Therapy** is characterized by the use of play activities in psychotherapy with children and is the most widely used technique of child therapists. Play materials (puppets, dolls, dollhouses, cars, guns, crayons, cards, games, etc.) are used as media for children to express their emotional life. The therapist accepts their inner feelings and encourages further exploration of feelings through the play media, which can symbolize many things to the child. The therapist accepts the child's symbolism exactly as it is, responding in constant sensitivity to the child's attitudes, and conveying a consistent and sincere belief in the child. Play therapy uses many psychiatric and psychological techniques for diagnosis and is used in a wide variety of childhood disorders.

9. **Poetry Therapy** uses poetics (lyrics, poetry, prayer, etc.) as a scaffolding to express and share the common human experience evoked through the universal and timeless symbolism inherent in poetics. The metaphor, simile, rhyme, and rhythm in poetics serve as a catalyst that activates fantasies and brings to catharsis archetypal images buried deep within the psyche; emotions are purged through the directed use of reason implicit in the poetic expression. Poetry as therapy is a gentle tool: poetic symbols embody the perspective or worldview of the person perceiving the symbol, allowing clients to identify with the poem in their own understanding, resolving conflicts at their own pace. Poetry therapy has also been found to evoke an aesthetic and spiritual dimension of awareness similar to religious devotional expression.

10. **Recreational Therapy** provides recreational activities to teach resocialization: to facilitate social contacts, diminish isolation, stop inertia, and promote self-confidence. Community groups and other volunteers (singers, musicians, etc.) contribute special services to the milieu program.

Bibliography. J. Alvin, *Music Therapy* (1975). J. Diamond, *BK: Behavioral Kinesiology* (1979). M. P. Hall, *The Therapeutic Value of Music Including the Philosophy of Music* (1982). S. Halpern, ed., Tuning the Human Instrument: An Owner's Manual (1978). D. C. Houts, "The Structured Use of Music in Pastoral Psychotherapy," *J. of Pastoral Care*, 35 (1981), 194–203. E. Kramer, *Art as Therapy with Children* (1971). A. Lerner, "Poetry Therapy," in R. J. Corsini, ed., *Handbook of Innovative Psychotherapies* (1981). K. J. O'Connor and C. E. Schaefer, *Handbook of Play Therapy* (1983). M. Samuels and N. Samuels, *Seeing with the Mind's Eye: The History, Techniques, and Uses of Visualization* (1975). A. Stark, "Dance-Movement Therapy," in L. E. Abt and I. R. Stuart, eds., *The Newer Therapies: A Sourcebook* (1982). H. Wadeson, "Art Therapy," in L. E. Abt and I. R. Stuart, eds., *The Newer Therapies: A Sourcebook* (1982). W. Winick, *Industry in the Hospital: Mental Rehabilitation Work* (1967). L. R. Wolberg, *The Technique of Psychotherapy* 2d ed. (1967); see ch. 8 for information on the Adjunctive Therapies.

M. Yablonsky, *Psychodrama: Resolving Emotional Problems Through Role-Playing* (1976).

V. R. HADDY

PSYCHOTHERAPY. *See also* DRAMA *or* MUSIC AS MODE OF CARE. *Compare* MILIEU THERAPY.

ADJUSTMENT, CONCEPT OF. An ideal of mental health in which one's drives for satisfaction are so balanced with social, legal, and ethical limits and expectations that dynamic tensions can be periodically and satisfactorily reduced. The individual can live in acceptable relationships with others and with personal gratification.

Q. L. HAND

PSYCHOSOCIAL DEVELOPMENT; RESPONSIBILITY/IRRESPONSIBILITY. *See also* PSYCHOLOGY IN AMERICAN RELIGION. *Compare* ALIENATION/ESTRANGEMENT; INTERPERSONAL THEORY.

ADJUSTMENT DISORDERS. A group of mental disorders whose common feature is their development in reaction to a psychosocial stress as described in the third edition of the American Psychiatric Association's *Diagnostic and Statistical Manual of Mental Disorders (DSM-III)*. The *DSM* classification includes eight types of adjustment disorders, categorized according to the primary reaction occurring in the person in response to the psychosocial stressor. These disorders are of interest because their etiology is psychosocial by definition as opposed to other causes such as developmental, organic, drug-induced, or genetic.

1. **General Features.** The main elements of an adjustment disorder are (a) that it begins within three months of the onset of a psychosocial stressor, (b) that the psychosocial stressor be identifiable, and (c) that the disorder be either one of social or occupational functioning, or that the reaction to the stressor be considered excessive. Stressors can be single or multiple, can be isolated events or chronic situations, and can include the transition from one developmental stage to the next. Stressors vary in severity, especially when the duration, timing, and developmental stage of the person are taken into account. An adjustment disorder ceases to exist when a level of psychological maturity is achieved allowing the person to adapt to the psychosocial stressor, or following the termination of the stressor. An adjustment disorder diagnosis is not used when the symptoms meet the criteria for other *DSM-III* diagnoses, when the symptoms are attributable to the exacerbation of a previously existing disorder, or when there is no identifiable psychosocial stressor. Normal grieving is not considered an adjustment disorder.

2. **Types.** The *DSM-III* types and their primary stress responses are: *a. Adjustment disorder with depressed mood* (dysphoria, tearfulness, self-criticism, hopelessness, etc.); *b. Adjustment disorder with anxious mood* (anxiety, e.g., nervousness, inability to concentrate, hyperventilation, palpitations, etc.); *c. Adjustment disorder with mixed emotional features* (combines anxiety, depression, or other emotional symptoms); *d. Adjustment disorder with disturbance of conduct* (rules or laws are broken, rights violated, or major societal norms transgressed); *e. Adjustment disorder with*

mixed disturbance of emotions and conduct (mixed emotional and behavioral symptoms); *f. Adjustment disorder with work (or academic) inhibition* (occurs in an individual whose previous functioning in these areas has been satisfactory; mild anxiety or depression usually present); *g. Adjustment disorder with withdrawal* (social withdrawal without significant anxiety or depression); *h. Adjustment disorder with atypical features* (occurs when responses cannot be classified as above).

3. **Clinical Example.** A previously happy ten-year-old boy who functioned well among peers and at school gets involved in fights and shows deteriorating grades in school one month after the onset of his parents' marital difficulties. The diagnoses are adjustment disorder with disturbance of conduct and adjustment disorder with academic inhibition. It could be argued that in a child the academic dysfunction represents a variant of depression, and that the correct diagnosis is therefore adjustment disorder with mixed disturbance of emotions and conduct. The problems resolve following the parents' successful marital therapy.

4. **Brief Note Concerning Treatment.** Since the one constant in the adjustment disorders is knowledge of the precipitating stress, treatment logically has two elements. One is to assist the person in the development of a higher level of adaptation to the psychosocial stress involved. This might be through individual psychotherapy, family therapy, behavioral therapy, educational efforts, etc. Consideration in the choice of approach must be given to the psychological and chronological maturity of the client at the time of the occurrence of the stressor, and the nature, duration, and severity of the stressor. The second element appropriate in most situations is emotional supportiveness on the part of the therapist. This may be especially true in cases where the psychosocial stressor involved is presumed to be time-limited. He or she might also work toward augmenting the natural supportive function of the family to achieve the same effort or even as the sole form of treatment. Sometimes this is the most efficient and least complicated approach.

Bibliography. American Psychiatric Association, Adjustment Disorder, *Diagnostic and Statistical Manual of Mental Disorders* 3d. ed. (1980), pp. 299–302. J. H. Greist, "Adjustment Disorders," in J. H. Greist, J. W. Jefferson, and R. L. Spitzer, eds., *Treatment of Mental Disorders* (1982), pp. 419–28.

D. A. KRAMER

ADJUSTMENT, CONCEPT OF; DIAGNOSTIC AND STATISTICAL MANUAL III; STRESS AND STRESS MANAGEMENT. *See also* MENTAL HEALTH AND ILLNESS; EVALUATION AND DIAGNOSIS, PSYCHOLOGICAL; PSYCHOPATHOLOGY, THEORIES OF. *Compare* BEHAVIORAL DISORDERS OF CHILDHOOD.

ADLER, ALFRED (1870–1937). One of the original members of the Vienna Psychoanalytic Society, who became its first defector in 1911. Founding the school of Individual Psychology, Adler shifted the theoretical emphasis from the Freudian focus on libido to the ego's striving for power. Critical aspects of Adler's theory include an individually unique (and fictional) goal, which is teleological and directs the ego's striving; the unconscious as "the unknown part of the goal"; "style of life" as the organizing structure for personality, which is a unified relational system; the significance of the individual's "apperceptive schema" and the social situation; as well as *social feeling* or *social interest* as the primary defense (Ansbacher).

Adler's "psychology of religion" emerged in dialogue with Ernst Jahn, a Lutheran pastor. In 1933 they coauthored *Religion und Individualpsychologie,* criticizing the integrative efforts of Pfister, Allers, Kunkel, and Runestam. Adler regarded Individual Psychology as a form of religion, linking it with theological anthropology and regarding it as a worldview that subordinates all other efforts to the ultimate goal of ideal community and the strengthening of social interest.

Bibliography. H. L. and R. R. Ansbacher, *The Individual Psychology of Alfred Adler* (1956). P. Roazen, *Freud and His Followers* (1971). H. Ellenberger, *The Discovery of the Unconscious* (1970).

H. VANDE KEMP

INDIVIDUAL PSYCHOLOGY. *See also* EGO PSYCHOLOGY AND PSYCHOTHERAPY; NEOFREUDIAN PERSONALITY THEORIES AND PASTORAL CARE.

ADLERIAN PSYCHOLOGY. *See* INDIVIDUAL PSYCHOLOGY.

ADMINISTRATION. *See* LEADERSHIP AND ADMINISTRATION.

ADOLESCENTS. Adolescents are persons in the developmental stage first marked by the onset of puberty and concluding with the ill-defined time of entering adulthood. Adolescence is unknown in primitive societies that cannot afford the luxury of biologically mature members remaining comparatively unproductive and dependent upon their parents. Hence, Western psychological adolescence is a cultural phenomenon resulting from a delay in the assumption of adult roles.

During adolescence a number of highly significant physical, intellectual, and social changes occur that are perplexing and bewildering to adolescent and adult alike. Successfully undergoing these many changes and consolidating them into a unity is the main task of adolescence. This process of coming to know who one is, what one believes and values, and what one wants to achieve is called forming an identity. The task is made more difficult in today's Western society because of its emphasis upon the autonomy of the individual, the marked decline of any consensus regarding values and beliefs, and the limited and fragmented character of rite-of-passage rituals.

Adolescents have two basic psychosocial needs while they are engaged in their odyssey toward identity. First, they need something to believe in. They search for people and ideas in whose service it would seem worthwhile to prove themselves trustworthy. When they have hope in the future and confidence in themselves they may form high ideals and engage in extremely worthwhile service. Second, they need a sense of belonging—of being in community. This provides a temporary sense of identity and is a buttress of external support while they build an internal foundation for their identity. The church is in a unique place to sustain both of these needs, provided that it understands the developmental changes and needs of the adolescent.

1. **Physical Development.** Changes marking the onset of puberty begin at about twelve for girls and fourteen for boys. For males, the sexual urge is urgent and aims toward a rapid discharge of tension in orgasm. Sexual urges are closely tied to physical urges, and adolescent males often respond to a wide variety of environmental cues. In females sexual feelings are much more diffuse and intertwined with other feelings. Female sexual arousal is generally less climax-oriented and is more of a state to be enjoyed indefinitely than as a mere prelude to orgasm. Adolescent girls often report that the tenderness and warmth of being held is more enjoyable than the sexual act itself. Adolescents, especially boys, are often conscious of, and troubled by, an awareness of the conflict between their physical urges and their conscience or moral awareness.

Adolescents fall in love primarily with themselves, projecting their own romantic idealism onto almost anyone who offers the slightest encouragement. For the male, love is idealized; he feels his sexuality as almost antagonistic to love. For the female, her still diffuse sexuality is decidedly secondary to love. Falling in love may increase the chance of girls becoming sexually active, but will likely, at first, reduce the intensity of the boy's advances.

2. **Intellectual Development.** Around the age of twelve adolescents begin to develop the ability to think abstractly, to consider various solutions to a problem without actually trying each of them, and to compare the real against the possible. They can now analyze a situation to its conclusion and reach a decision on the basis of mental processes. Their conceptual world expands, and they become interested in understanding God, their faith, and how it relates to the world. This new thinking capacity allows for a heightened self-awareness and more critical thinking about the world around them. They may become quite egocentric. This arises out of a need to master and become more comfortable with a new way of thinking and the need to work toward their own identity, the latter of which benefits enormously from their new analytical skills. They no longer uncritically accept the teachings of authority figures and benefit more from adults who will patiently assist them in working out their own beliefs and values. Often they will go through a period of naive idealism. This process is necessary for adolescents to gain extensive practice in using their new intellectual powers and in developing their own identity. There are unique opportunities for spiritual growth as adolescents are actively seeking people and ideas in which to put their faith. At the same time they are often fearful of making a commitment, which may be too similar to their childish dependency on adults, from which they are trying to escape. Some may, paradoxically, express their need for faith in statements filled with cynicism and mistrust.

3. **Social Development.** Changes occur as adolescents begin making the transition from being dependent children to adults. Part of developing an identity involves moving away from both emotional and financial dependency upon parents. Adolescents feel very ambivalent over leaving the dependency of childhood versus meeting the demands of peers and society for more independent living. They will demand the privileges associated with adulthood while failing to accept the responsibilities that accompany them. Adults recognize that these go together, but adolescents may see the responsibilities as being imposed by adults and merely serving as degrading reminders of their dependent status. When this happens adults need to remember that adolescents are acting out their own ambivalence.

Few adolescents really feel in control. Many feel trapped between alien physical and emotional impulses and unreasonable adult demands. Many are unsure as to whether they even want responsibility for controlling all the new sensations welling up within themselves. Underneath the grumbling and protestations, the adolescent may feel a sense of relief and being cared for when parents or other adults step in and impose their authority. This also frees them to regain their dependent status with a minimum loss of face from peers since the restrictions are imposed from outside.

4. **Caring for the Adolescent.** Adults can help adolescents develop new intellectual skills and gain confidence in their ability to move toward a more independent existence. Adults need to change their approach to decision making, especially in family relationships, to allow more opportunity for the adolescent to participate. They should sit down and help the adolescent make good choices by examining various potential solutions and looking at their possible consequences. When working with young adolescents (12–14) they will need to provide much of the structure and advice, while for middle adolescents (15–16) adults may be partners in the solution. Older adolescents (17–19), who have benefited from years of previous work, can usually handle the process by themselves, and adults can limit their activity to giving input when asked. This democratic style is critical for the adolescent's development. A *laissez-faire* approach fails to provide adequate structure and training while an authoritarian style fails to provide the adolescent with an opportunity to struggle with and grow from the process of decision making.

Adults may be overly restrictive because of their awareness of the adolescent's current limitations and the perils of the outside world. But, out of a well-founded desire to protect, they fail to recognize the need for struggle if the adolescent is to mature into adulthood. Often the adult's need for control conflicts with the developmental needs of the adolescent. Yet changing to a more flexible way of relating is necessary if the adolescent is to be prepared to meet the challenges and responsibilities of adulthood.

In working with adolescents, the pastor or pastoral counselor will be most effective if he or she assumes the role of "adult guarantor" (Irwin) in the young person's life. This posture provides the adolescent with assurance that he or she can indeed master the turbulent struggles of this stage and develop an identity that has meaning and purpose.

When more serious difficulties arise, such as academic difficulties, family and interpersonal conflicts, delinquency, involvement with alcohol or drugs, or emotional disorders, it is important not to lose sight of the continuing role of family dynamics, especially with younger adolescents. Young people often appear more independent than they in fact are (or feel), and their problems are often more significantly related to family dynamics than may at first appear. The troubled adolescent may, for example, be unconsciously expressing family conflicts through the role of family scapegoat. Thus many pastoral counselors are reluctant to involve adolescents individually in counseling or psychotherapy, preferring to work with the whole family. For the parish pastor in such situations, it is important to bear in mind family contexts and relationships and to relate to family systems as well as to the individuals when extending pastoral care as an "adult guarantor" to troubled adolescents.

Bibliography. J. Stone and J. Church, *Childhood and Adolescence* 3d. ed. (1975). E. Erikson, *Identity, Youth and Crisis* (1968). J. Oraker, *Almost Grown* (1980). C. M. Shelton, *Adolescent Spirituality* (1983). C. Stewart, *Adolescent Religion* (1967). P. W. Irwin, *The Care and Counseling of Youth in the Church* (1975). T. Lidz, *The Person* (1968). L. Sherrill, *The Struggle of The Soul* (1968).

S. F. SHOEMAKER

LIFE CYCLE THEORY AND PASTORAL CARE. *See also* BAPTISM AND CONFIRMATION; BAR MITZVAH/BAT MITZVAH; DIVORCE, CHILDREN AND ADOLESCENTS IN; FAMILY; GRIEF AND LOSS IN CHILDHOOD AND ADOLESCENCE; SOCIOLOGY OF RELIGIOUS AND PASTORAL CARE. *Compare* CHILDREN; PARENTS/PARENTHOOD; YOUNG ADULTS.

ADOPTION. Adoption is the process whereby one or more adults, not the biological parents of a minor child or children, become recognized by a court of law as the parent or parents of such a child or children. In any given year in the U.S., it is estimated that 3.5 percent of those under eighteen are adopted (Schwam and Tuskan, 1979, p. 342).

Questions surrounding adoption include places for adopting parents to go for help, who is involved in the adopting process, and the church's role in establishing a supportive climate for both adopting parents and children.

Parents seeking to adopt a child have three major places in the community to go for help: (1) Public support agencies; (2) voluntary support agencies; (3) independent placement through a physician or lawyer. Adoption laws prohibit the buying and selling of babies and outline procedures for biological parents, the intermediary, and adopting parents to follow. In agency adoptions social workers make the home visit, prepare adopting parents to receive the child, and follow through with the placement itself.

With more universal acceptance of birth control and later marriages of white middle-class couples, the number of white babies has diminished, leaving mainly minority, handicapped, and older children available for adoption. Babies from Third World countries and from immigrant families are also available. The church and other community agencies can help change community attitudes toward accepting such racially mixed families.

Pastoral care of couples considering adoption may involve a variety of concerns. The couple may need further help in accepting their inability to produce children together. If one spouse is physically more responsible for this fact, his or her feelings about this may need explora

tion in the light of the decision to take action on adoption. Pastoral support may be needed for the actual decision to adopt or for the means chosen to pursue adoption. Should the couple have decided to adopt a child who is difficult to place, their feelings about this may need further exploration. Particularly in non-agency adoptions, they may need to talk about their feelings toward the biological parents of the child. Should adequate social work preparation not have taken place, discussing with the prospective parents the importance of telling the child about the adoption is important, noting that the child may desire to visit the biological parent(s) in some cases. The pastor may find appropriate ways to emphasize the couple's religious faith in entering into this parental vocation together.

Bibliography. J. S. Schwam and M. K. Tuskan, "The Adopted Child" in *Basic Handbook of Child Psychiatry* (1979).

C. W. STEWART

FAMILY, JEWISH *or* PASTORAL CARE AND COUNSELING OF PARENTS/PARENTHOOD; SOCIAL SERVICES AND PASTORAL CARE. *See also* CHILDREN; FOSTER CHILDREN AND FOSTER PARENTS; INFERTILITY; MOTHER-INFANT BONDING; STEPFAMILIES.

ADULTERY. *See* INFIDELITY, MARITAL.

ADULTS. *See* LIFE CYCLE THEORY; YOUNG ADULTS; MIDLIFE PERSONS; OLDER PERSONS.

ADVICE-GIVING. The procedure whereby a caregiver introduces an *a priori* set of values or belief criteria and uniquely applies these to the specific life situation of the other person(s) in a pastoral relationship. It has a long history in pastoral care, especially in the form of applying codified religious truths and norms to specific personal and interpersonal situations. This can be seen in classical spiritual direction, religious discipline, and exhortation. Advice-giving has traditionally been called inductive guidance since it seeks to lead a distressed person toward established guidelines, whereby he or she can reach a life decision.

When the pastoral care movement began to adopt the methods and principles of modern psychology in the 1920s, advice-giving was all but abandoned since it tended to thwart the process of uncovering the complex conscious and unconscious dynamics which motivate human activity. Instead, the movement was shaped by an eductive guidance which emphasized the drawing of values and criteria out of an individual's own experience in order to integrate his or her intrapsychic dynamics and assist decision making in specific life situations. Advice-giving, or the sharing of *a priori* convictions, if done at all, was bracketed and introduced as a pastoral caring function outside the counseling process.

In recent years, with the rise of interest in spiritual direction, moral inquiry, and issues of pastoral identity, assertiveness, initiative, and authority in the pastoral counseling movement, advice-giving has gained some renewed acceptance. There is also a growing awareness that many persons seeking the acceptance and caring of pastoral counseling are searching beyond the relief of needs and distress for counsel on the right ordering of life. In the more evangelical conservative approach to pastoral counseling (e.g. Jay Adams), advice-giving is viewed as a key counseling tool. In the mainstream of the movement, advice-giving is used more in service to eductive guidance or as the context in which this eductive guidance takes place.

In general, advice-giving is appropriate in the pastoral relationship when: (1) the aim is to provide resources that might not have been seen otherwise; (2) it is ascertained that a person primarily seeks new information rather than delving into the dynamics motivating his or her questioning; (3) it appears advice-giving would be an effective therapeutic intervention when one is urgently needed to block a destructive pattern or vicious circle in order for a more healthy pattern to emerge.

In all instances, advice-giving should be introduced in a spirit of dialogue with the other so that the carer can assist the other in exploring his or her response to the advice-giving.

C. M. MENDENHALL, III

CLINICAL PASTORAL PERSPECTIVE; GUIDANCE, PASTORAL; SUGGESTION, PERSUASION, AND INFLUENCE. *See also* PRUDENCE (Moral Theology); WISDOM. *Compare* LISTENING.

ADVOCACY. Religious functionaries have, for millennia, advocated the causes of those who appealed to them for counsel. They have intervened with friends and families, community gatherings and government. They have represented those for whom they advocated as individuals and members of a class. In part, Anglo-American legal advocacy and the system it gave rise to originally developed out of procedures for ascertaining God's will in a case.

As rational procedures gradually came to supplant direct appeals to deity, the rule of law began to evolve. Under it, first ethical principles, then economics, political, psychological, and sociological ones, came to supersede divine will as standards of justice. Lawyers came to supersede clergy as advocates. Justice became increasingly a secular concern.

Over the past two centuries, pastors have begun to reclaim their earlier role as advocates for those who seek their care and counsel. More and more are coming to realize that only in an ideal world can each individual become enabled, with proper guidance alone, to act effectively on their own behalf to secure justice. In the world in which we actually live, familial and social inculcation all too often give rise to disabling attitudes and personality patterns which can be highly resistant to modification. Systemic obstacles within the family, community, and society often render individual action in one's own behalf futile.

The pastor who counsels, like many other helping professionals, will sometimes need to intervene as advocate for the counselee if the requisite systemic change is to be brought about which will enable the counselee to secure a living situation in which counseling can be effective. The pastor who advocates, unlike most other helping professionals, will often need to learn to live in the dynamic tension created by any conflict which may appear between societal norms for justice and the

counselee's own way of religious or spiritual development.

To the extent that pastoral practice overlaps secular activity, a dilemma is unavoidable. The problem stems from the fact that God's will for any particular individual cannot always be rationally determined, while people need rational norms within which to be able to function consciously. Social orders embody these rational norms, and are evaluated by how well they adhere to them. The question for the pastor who advocates thus becomes how to adequately represent and accommodate the unfolding, seemingly irrational will of God without undermining the developing but necessarily rational social order.

No less important is the unavoidable conflict between the counselee's advocacy needs and the power needs of the pastor who advocates. In the political realm, one must be especially vigilant to discriminate between these needs.

J. J. ROGGE

CONSCIOUSNESS RAISING; PROPHETIC/PASTORAL TENSION IN MINISTRY; SOCIAL JUSTICE ISSUES IN PASTORAL CARE. *See also* ASSERTIVENESS IN MINISTRY; AUTHORITY, PASTORAL; BLACK *or* FEMINIST THEOLOGY AND PASTORAL CARE; ETHICS, PROFESSIONAL; LIBERATION THEOLOGY AND PASTORAL CARE; VALUES IN COUNSELING AND PSYCHOTHERAPY. *Compare* EXPLOITATION/OPPRESSION; VICTIMIZATION.

AELRED OF RIEVAULX. *See* CLASSIC LITERATURE IN CARE AND COUNSELING (Roman Catholicism).

AFFAIRS. *See* INFIDELITY, MARITAL.

AFFECT. *See* EMOTION; FEELING, THOUGHT, AND ACTION IN PASTORAL COUNSELING.

AFFECTIONS, RELIGIOUS. *See* PSYCHOLOGY IN AMERICAN RELIGION; RELIGIOUS EXPERIENCE.

AFFECTIVE DISORDER/AFFECTIVE PSYCHOSIS. *See* MANIC-DEPRESSIVE (BIPOLAR) DISORDER; ORGANIC MENTAL DISORDER AND ORGANIC BRAIN SYNDROME; PERSONALITY, BIOLOGICAL DIMENSIONS OF; PSYCHOSIS.

AFFIRMATION. *See* ACCEPTANCE; COMMUNITY, FELLOWSHIP AND CARE; GRACE AND PASTORAL CARE; THERAPEUTIC CONDITIONS.

AFFLUENCE/THE AFFLUENT. *See* LIFESTYLE ISSUES; SOCIAL STATUS AND CLASS FACTORS; RICH PERSONS; VIPs.

AFRICAN PASTORAL CARE MOVEMENT. In the Western sense, pastoral care and psychiatry are relatively new disciplines in Africa. While both were part of the colonial and missionary medical and theological heritage, they have aroused the interest of researchers, governments, and church institutions only within the last twenty years. Recently, both disciplines have become subjects of university and seminary study, though both were, in essence, aspects of the indigenous African religious and medical systems. Specialized healers and priests provided assistance, guidance, diagnosis, and care to both groups and individuals.

1. History. The 1958 Bukavu and 1959 Tananarive pan-African conferences on mental disorders and psychiatry were the first on the continent to address issues concerning psychological problems and personality traits of the peoples in Africa and Madagascar. Dr. Lambo of Nigeria was the only black African psychiatrist at the Tananarive Conference. Since then, three conferences on African psychiatry have been held, in 1961, 1968, and 1977, with heavy participation of African psychiatrists. The *Review of African Psychopathology (Revue de Psychopathologie Africaine)* and *The African Journal of Psychiatry* have become important instruments for research and publication of studies.

The 1955 Accra Conference on Christianity and African Culture emphasized the importance of the Africanization of theology and church ministry. This conference stimulated African churches and scholars to reflect on the nature and challenges of ministry (Busia, 1955; Nketia, 1963). The search for a contextual theology and ministerial praxis became the leitmotiv of African churches and theologians. Two major concerns of pastoral care and psychology, family life and mental health, may serve to focus the pastoral dimensions of this search.

a. Family life. The 1963 All-Africa Conference on the Christian Home and Family Life analyzed such issues as customary marriage, bride price, polygamy, the essence of Christian marriage, population education and family planning, trial marriage, divorce and remarriage, prostitution and single parenthood, and called for appropriate family life education and counseling services within the churches. The relationship between marriage and family life in traditional Africa (Mbiti, 1973), sensitivity to problems arising out of African marriage customs, and the understanding of the psychocultural, economic, and political dynamics of divorce and polygamy, have become areas of pastoral focus. The establishment of groups for the management of adolescent fertility, for personal growth using psychodrama, as well as for families' action-reflection intended to effect social change and personal maturation, are some of the educational experiments being tried in the pastoral care of family life.

In helping persons and families understand the impact of change on both individual and group identities, the church takes into account the dynamisms of African extended family systems. The extended family system reinvents itself by using its inherent capacity to be the center *par excellence* of support and confrontation among and for its members, thus enabling the individual as well as the entire family, through dialogue and rituals of reconciliation, to deal constructively with conflicting and inhibiting personal drives and cultural and religious values. This family arrangement seems to create a psychosocial atmosphere conducive to personal growth and family cohesion. Furthermore, the family is enabled to become an agent of social change (Pobee, 1979).

b. Mental health. The 1967 Consultation on Practical Theology in Yaoundé and the Ibadan first Ecumenical Consultation on Biblical Revelation and African Beliefs not only stimulated work in specifically African theology (Dickson and Ellingworth, 1969; Appiah-Kubi and Torres, 1979; Nyamiti, 1971; Mbiti, 1974), but challenged

African theologians to deal with issues of disease, health, and healing from an African perspective.

2. Emerging Orientations and Issues. The African pastoral care movement has been developing three major orientations: the first is rooted in Western theories, seeking to describe pastoral care in European patterns of pastoral theology (Tjega, 1971; Nomenyo, 1971). The second is a purely descriptive and academic interpretation of health and healing using African patterns of thought and traditional therapies (Mwene-Batende, 1981). The third approach attempts to integrate both systems and uses African cultures, biblical theology, and Western psychodynamically oriented psychotherapy and proposes pastoral implications for the churches (Lutahoire, 1979).

The following three dynamics need further theoretical and practical research for contextual development of pastoral care in Africa: (1) the importance of understanding the parishioner's or client's worldview, (2) the importance of incorporating cultural concepts of illness and health into the therapeutic process, (3) the necessity of inserting insight-oriented approaches into the pastoral care and therapeutic process in order to promote emotional release or catharsis, personality growth, and an awareness of one's identity in relation to that of the group.

Bibliography. K. Appiah-Kubi and S. Torres, *African Theology en Route* (1979). K. A. Busia, "Ancestor Worship, Libation, Funerals," in S. G. Williamson, ed., *Christianity and African Culture* (1955). K. A. Dickson and R. Ellingworth, *Biblical Revelation and African Beliefs* (1969). S. Lutahoire, *The Human Life Cycle Among the Bantu* (1979). Masamba ma Mpolo, *J'ai été trompée* (1978); "La cure d'âme et la souffrance," in *Manuel de Théologie Pratique* (1971); *Sorcellerie et pastorale* (1977). J. S. Mbiti, "La théologie africaine," in *Spiritus*, 56 (1974), 307–21; *Love and Marriage in Africa* (1973). Mwene-Batende, "La sorcellerie, la divination, la thérapie et leurs fonctions sociales dans la société lignagère kumu," in *Combats pour un christianisme africain* (1981). S. Nomenyo, "La cure d'âme auprès de familles," *Manuel de Théologie Pratique* (1971). C. Nyamiti, *African Theology* (1971). J. S. Pobee, *Toward an African Theology* (1979). J. Tjega, "La cure d'âme," *Manuel de Théologie Pratique* (1971).

M. MA MPOLO

INTERNATIONAL PASTORAL CARE MOVEMENT; PASTORAL CARE MOVEMENT. *Compare* SOUTH AFRICAN PASTORAL CARE MOVEMENT.

AFRICAN TRADITIONAL RELIGION, PERSONAL CARE IN. Research done in recent years has brought to light complex patterns of psychosocial and medical systems existing in African traditional societies. Diviners, herbalists, therapeutic groups, and a variety of healers specialized in the diagnosis and treatment of illnesses, including mental disorders and deviant behaviors.

1. Cosmology. African cosmology is perceived and lived as one composed of seen and unseen spirit-beings. They constitute life-forces which constantly interact with, and thus influence, the course of human life for good or for bad (Mbiti, 1970). The departed ancestors are part of this constellation of living spirits. By virtue of being part of the extended family and living in the proximity of God, the Creator, the ancestors are endowed with special powers. Therefore, they enable the birth of children and protect the living family members from attack by malevolent spirits. As those who sanction the moral life of both individuals and community, the ancestors punish, exonerate, or reward. Thus, the health of the living depends to a great extent on their relationships within the extended family and with their ancestors who mostly communicate their wishes through dreams (Pobee, 1978). Evil divinities coexist with other spirits. The Vusugu of Kenya believe that an evil divinity uses witches and sorcerers to bring about misfortune and illness and to cause the death of human beings (Mbiti, 1970).

Thus, traditional African cosmology is dynamic. It recognizes and integrates the duality of mind and body, magic and rationality, order and disorder, negative and positive powers, and individual and communal consciousness. The maintenance of personal and social equilibrium in the midst of this apparent dualism becomes the major role of traditional diagnosis, psychotherapy, and medical systems.

Beliefs in witchcraft and sorcery form the most important cosmological and medical etiological category of the traditional African systems studied thus far. Evans-Pritchard (1937) demonstrated that the Azande used witchcraft and sorcery as symbolic interpretations of misfortune, illness, and death. Kluckhohn (1944) views these beliefs as functional in that they are used as a channel through which people deal with feelings of hatred, hostility, frustration, jealousy, guilt, and sexual fantasies, the expression of which is culturally discouraged. These beliefs therefore engender abreactions which prevent the formation of severe neurosis. They perform the psychological function of dealing constructively with ambivalent feelings aroused by the ambiguity of both the cosmological and social orders.

2. **Health and Illness.** A large quantity of literature exists describing the traditional etiological and diagnostic system. Organic factors such as bad diet, heredity, stress, anger, hostility, rivalry, anxiety, fear, fatigue, ambivalence, and identity crisis, can bring on illness. Such psychological factors, however, are almost always perceived as having a precipitating function in individuals whose vulnerability has been exploited by the possessive power of malevolent forces (P'Bitek, 1971; Dawson, 1974).

Etiology and diagnosis in the context of traditional African thought pose the following basic question: "*Who* is the cause of my illness? Is it I, or is it someone else?" In this context, organically manifested symptoms are always the result of some aggression and are thus not just physically induced. What is essentially sought in every illness, either somatic or emotional, is the *significance* of such disease.

3. **Diagnosis.** Diagnosis is always synthetic: it searches for and announces the cause of illness by providing its sociopsychological and spiritual significance. The consequences of such an illness for the individual and the community are also indicated. This approach obviously differs from the classification method characteristic of Western psychiatry. In African thinking, mental disorder is perceived to be persecution of, or more precisely, aggression against the individual self by other socio-cultural and spiritual selves. Thus, the ancestral spirits participate in the therapeutic process primarily by solving relationships arising from the violation of traditional norms. The healer, on the other hand, orchestrates significant events capable of reconciling broken relationships. Thus, diagnosis aims at clarifying the type, the nature, and the significance of each conflict which is supposed to be the basic cause of illness. There are as many types of mental disorder as there are possible conflicting relationships.

4. **Healing and Care.** The restoration of broken relationships, the reestablishment of social equilibrium, and the revitalization of individual identity within the context of the renewed community are the major means and dynamic ends underlying traditional therapies and healing processes in traditional African societies. Care for the troubled person is a process involving many steps, usually beginning with a tentative consensus reached by the family members. The kin diagnostic group, that is, a therapeutic palaver, led by the extended family's elders, brings together the clan in order to fathom the meaning of the patient's illness (Janzen, 1978). In certain places, for example, in the Congo of central Africa, the elders perform therapeutic rites in which members of the matriclan and the patriclan of the patient discuss the case and then terminate the session with a rite of reconciliation.

A second consensus is sometimes sought by the healer through meeting with the wider community. Here, the symptoms yield their symbolic significance. The patient becomes the visible sign of the underlying dynamics within the group and of its value. The socialization of guilt and of the individual as well as the communal confessions, provide a catharsis. Public acknowledgment of the fault brings about reconciliation of the patient with others. Symbolic psychodrama, exorcism, and rites to effect reconciliation with the ancestors and good spirits are traditional therapeutic devices which help the community and the individual to bring into consciousness and reenact symptoms and myths which are part of traditional African systems of illness and of health.

Bibliography. G. Bibeau *et al.*, *Traditional Medicine in Zaire* (1980). J. Dawson, "Urbanization and Mental Health in a West African Community," in A. Kiev, ed., *Magic, Health and Healing* (1974). E. E. Evans-Pritchard, *Witchcraft, Oracles and Magic Among the Azanda* (1937). J. M. Janzen, *The Quest for Therapy in Lower Zaire* (1978). C. Kluckhohn, *Navaho Witchcraft* (1944). J. S. Mbiti, *Concepts of God in Africa* (1970). Masamba ma Mpolo, "Kindoki as Diagnosis and Therapy," *Social Science and Medicine*, 15-B (1981), 405–13. O. P'Bitek, *Religion of the Central Luo* (1971). J. S. Pobee, *Toward an African Theology* (1979).

M. MA MPOLO

CARE OF SOULS *(Cura Animarum)*; CULTURAL ANTHROPOLOGY OF RELIGION, DISCIPLINE OF; SHAMAN; SOCIOLOGY OF RELIGIOUS AND PASTORAL CARE; SOCIOLOGY OF RELIGION. *Compare* BLACK AMERICAN PASTORAL CARE; NATIVE AMERICAN *or* WEST INDIAN TRADITIONAL RELIGION, PERSONAL CARE IN; RELIGION; SOUL (Black Church); WITCHCRAFT.

AFRO AMERICAN PASTORAL CARE. *See* BLACK AMERICAN PASTORAL CARE.

AFTERLIFE. *See* ESCHATOLOGY; HEAVEN AND HELL, BELIEF IN; SURVIVAL (Occult).

AGAPE. *See* LOVE.

AGED PARENTS/AGED PERSONS. *See* AGING; PARENTS/PARENTHOOD; OLDER PERSONS.

AGENCIES, SOCIAL. *See* SOCIAL SERVICES.

AGGADAH. *See* JEWISH LITERATURE IN CARE AND COUNSELING.

AGGIORNAMENTO. *See* VATICAN COUNCIL II.

AGGRESSION AND ASSERTION. Aggression is a form of behavior in which persons express their rights, thoughts, and feelings without regard for the rights, thoughts, and feelings of other persons. Aggression may lead to psychological or physical injury of others or to property destruction. Assertion, by contrast, is a form of behavior in which persons express their honest thoughts, rights, and feelings (both positive and negative) in a way that respects these factors in other persons.

These definitions, based on those in the *Principles for Ethical Practice of Assertive Behavior Training* (Alberti and Emmons), suggest a clear difference between the two constructs and contradict some lay definitions which tend to see the two terms as nearly synonymous. Assertion includes respect for the rights and feelings of others and may include both positive expressions — joy, love, and so forth — and negative ones — anger, refusal, and the like. Aggression ignores the rights and feelings of others and most often focuses on negative expression.

In reality, however, distinguishing between the two is much more complex and difficult than these definitions suggest. For one thing, the two terms grow out of different fields of psychology that have not been integrated with each other. For this reason it is important to understand these backgrounds before attempting to discriminate between these terms.

1. **Background.** *a. Aggression.* Freud believed in an innate, internal aggressive drive. The aggressive drive can be triggered by external stimuli but is invariably associated with internal conflicts and represents the expression of a primary self-destructive drive — the "death instinct" turned outward.

Similar to Freud's theory in its emphasis on internal factors is the ethological theory of Konrad Lorenz. Lorenz felt that both humans and animals have an aggressive instinct, which functions via a "hydraulic system." That is, if the aggression is not expressed, it builds up until it finally explodes into the environment. Lorenz believed that the human instinct to aggress must be given expression but can be handled non-lethally through aggressive rituals and sublimation. This theory has been criticized because there is little physiological evidence to support the hydraulic system notion.

The frustration-aggression theory (Dollard, Doob, Miller, Mowrer, and Sears) disagrees with the notion of an innate aggressive instinct but does suggest an aggressive drive as a natural response to the experience of frustration. Frustration here is taken to mean interference with any goal-directed activity. The drive can be reduced through aggressive activity. Berkowitz and others have substantially modified the theory by pointing out that other factors besides frustration can lead to aggression and that frustration may not lead to aggression invariably.

While differing in other aspects, each of these theories implies an aggressive force that is inherent to humans and animals. However, physiological evidence indicates that the concept of an internal aggressive force may not be nearly so important or warranted by the evidence as these theories maintain. Research by Schachter and Singer and others indicates that the body's physiological condition during anger and aggression is often little different than its condition during fear or other arousal states. In fact, experiencing anger or behaving aggressively seems to involve a subtle interaction between physiological, cognitive, and environmental factors.

This latter view represents the essence of the more recent theory of aggression known as social learning theory. Its proponent, Albert Bandura, argues that aversive experiences lead to emotional arousal, which can lead to any one of a number of learned responses of which aggression is only one. Bandura's theory does not rule out the possibility of aggressive drives or instincts but it indicates the powerful force of learning and environmental stimuli in the process of aggression.

b. Assertion. Unlike aggression, assertion is a term whose roots lie in clinical and counseling psychology and more specifically in behavior therapy. For this reason, much more work has been done to help people become assertive than to develop a theoretical foundation for defining assertion.

Initially assertion was seen in a very general sense as a behavior closely akin to expressiveness. Wolpe (1973) defined assertion as "the proper expression of any emotion other than anxiety toward another person." He also argued that assertion includes the expression of positive as well as negative emotions and stressed that assertion was different from aggression.

As time progressed, a few practitioners began to use the terms aggression and assertion almost interchangeably but most adopted the definition of assertion stated at the beginning of this article. In addition, the realization developed that assertion is not a static personality trait but instead represents a large variety of learned behaviors. These commonly include making and refusing requests, expressing positive and negative emotions, giving and receiving compliments, expressing personal rights, making conversation, and so forth. Instead of being seen as generally assertive or nonassertive, most individuals are more adept at certain types of assertive behaviors than others and in certain types of situations.

2. **Differentiating Between Aggression and Assertion.** Robert Alberti suggests that a more adequate way of differentiating between assertion and aggression is by contrasting the terms on several dimensions. With some modifications, these dimensions include intent, behavior, interpersonal effects, physiological effects, and the social-cultural context.

a. Intent. The intent of an aggressor is to express and gain personal goals through manipulating, dominating, or hurting the other person. The foundational intent is an adversarial one in which the aggressor competes with the other person for control. In assertion the intent is to express oneself and gain personal and common goals through negotiation, expression of intimacy, or firmness. The approach is honest and noncompetitive.

b. Behavior. Aggressive behavior is typified by threatening or intimidating body language and verbal expressions, and in some cases by punishment. By contrast, assertive behavior is firm but expressions are non-threatening and encourage further discussion. Verbalizations over conflict issues tend to focus on the feelings of the assertor rather than blaming or berating the other person. For example, one form of assertive communication is called the "I message." In this form an assertor might say, "When the yard doesn't get cut, I get upset and I'd like to see the yard done soon" rather than, "You've never cut that yard and you probably never will."

c. Physiological effects. For some years a notion popularized by Konrad Lorenz and others suggested that the expression of aggression leads to a decrease in physiological tension levels and thus to subsequent decrease in aggression. This catharsis hypothesis is usually illustrated as being something like a pressure valve. Noxious stimuli build up aggressive impulses within the individual, so it is important to release this pressure from time to time either actively in reality through aggressive acts or passively, vicariously, or symbolically or, for example, through observing ritualized aggressive activities such as football.

More recent research suggests that this hypothesis is of limited validity. Releasing aggressive impulses does seem to lead to an immediate reduction in physiological tension. However, subsequent aggressive acts tend to increase rather than decrease. In addition, since aggressive acts rarely lead to a final resolution of the interpersonal problems that were the focus of aggression, physiological tension generally returns quickly.

Successful conflict resolution is one of the chief factors determining long-term decreases in physiological tension and aggressive behavior. Assertive behavior, as well as certain other behavioral styles, leads to a decrease in physiological tension levels and often results in conflict resolution as well. Several clinicians have noted a tendency on the part of clients to be less aroused by minor slights and provocations after assertiveness training than before.

d. Interpersonal effects. This dimension requires differentiating aggression from assertion by the responses of the other person instead of by the acts themselves. Presumably assertion leads to openness, conflict resolution, negotiation, and assertion from the other person, while aggression leads others to respond either with appeasement and withdrawal or with counter-aggression and hostility. The difficulty with contrasting aggression and assertion on this dimension is that no two persons respond to an assertive or aggressive message in the same way. Respondents bring a host of personal variables to the situation which may in part determine how they respond. For example, if the respondent is an extremely sensitive person, any serious communication whether assertive or aggressive may be perceived and dealt with

as a threat. Still, the research evidence suggests that the probability of a positive interpersonal response is greater with assertion than with aggression (Hollandsworth and Cooley, Hull and Schroeder).

e. Social-cultural context. The proliferation of interest in assertiveness training on a national and worldwide basis has made professionals increasingly aware of culture as a factor determining whether a communication is viewed as assertive or aggressive. If, say, a non-Western culture values interpersonal silence and submission highly, a behavior which might be seen as assertive in Western culture would likely be viewed as aggressive there. At the same time a culture in which there is great emphasis on confrontation and violence might view an "I-message" assertion as meek and spineless.

3. **Therapeutic Implications.** Several popular approaches to therapy and counseling have stressed the importance of emotional ventilation and confrontation as a means of self-growth and positive mental health. Counselees are advised to scream, beat pillows, or use encounter bats, and to confront parents, spouses, and significant others. Some within the church have, with good intentions, supported this movement. However, as previously argued, there is in fact very little evidence to support the long-term efficacy of these ventilative approaches. At best such techniques lead to short-term reduction in physiological tension. Unfortunately, they also tend to miss the most crucial factor needed not only for tension reduction but also for long-term satisfaction, namely conflict resolution. When persons have the assertive skills needed to resolve conflicts with relatives and others, ventilation and aggression become of secondary importance.

Bibliography. Alberti's dimensions for differentiating between aggression and assertion are found in "Was that assertive or aggressive?" by R. E. Alberti, *Assert: The Newsletter of Assertive Behavior* vol. 7, (1976) p. 2. Adapted for reproduction for *Dictionary of Pastoral Care and Counseling* by permission of Impact Publishers, Inc., Box 1094, San Luis Obispo, CA 93406. Further reproduction prohibited. Additional bibliography: R. Alberti and M. Emmons, *Your Perfect Right* 4th ed. (1982). A. Bandura, *Aggression: A Social Learning Analysis* (1973). L. Berkowitz, "Experimental Investigations of Hostility Catharsis," *J. of Consulting and Clinical Psychology*, (1970), 34:1–7. J. Dollard, L. Doob, N. Miller, O. Mowrer, and R. Sears, *Frustration and Aggression* (1939). S. Freud, *Beyond the Pleasure Principle,* (1920) SE vol. 18. J. Hollandsworth and M. Cooley, "Provoking Anger and Gaining Compliance with Assertive Versus Aggressive Responses," *Behavior Therapy*, (1978), 640–46. D. Hull and H. Schroeder, "Some Interpersonal Effects of Non-assertion, Assertion and Aggression," *Behavior Therapy*, 10 (1979), 20–28. K. Lorenz, *On Aggression* (1966). S. Schachter and J. Singer, "Cognitive, Social, and Physiological Determinates of Emotional States," *Psychological Review*, 69 (1962), 379–99. J. Wolpe, *The Practice of Behavior Therapy* 2d ed. (1973).

R. K. SANDERS

ASSERTIVENESS IN MINISTRY; ASSERTIVENESS TRAINING AND THERAPY; CONFLICT AND CONFLICT MANAGEMENT; POWER; RAGE AND HOSTILITY; VIOLENCE. *See also* ANTISOCIAL PERSONS; DOMINEERING PERSONALITY; JUVENILE CRIME AND DELINQUENCY; PASSIVE-AGGRESSIVE PERSONALITY. *Compare* ANGER; RESPONSIBILITY/IRRESPONSIBILITY, PSYCHOLOGY OF; SOCIOBIOLOGY.

AGGRESSIVE BEHAVIOR, CHILD'S. *See* Behavioral Disorders of Childhood.

AGING. The process of change which occurs after physical maturity has been reached. Generally, aging is defined as occurring at three levels: biological aging, psychological aging, and sociological aging (Birren and Schaie). Biological aging includes those changes in structure and function of the body organs and systems which occur across time. It may also refer to the progressive loss of functional capacity which eventually results in death. Psychological aging refers to changes in adaptive capacities and behavior due to greater experience. Sociological aging encompasses changes in roles, social behavior, and social expectations across a lifetime.

Needless to say, these three areas interact considerably across the life span, but do not progress at the same rate. Functional age is a concept which encompasses all three. How an individual performs on a variety of ability tests is indicative of functional age, and thus reflects physical, cognitive, and social functioning in the environment. It should be apparent that the human life cycle is a continuum from conception to death, with growth, development, and aging used to refer to what transpires between the two ends of the continuum.

1. Demographics and Research. The population of the U.S. is becoming increasingly elderly. In 1981 over twenty-five million persons were 65 years or older, which was approximately eleven percent of the population. This is up from four percent at the turn of the century. This change is due to a declining birth rate accompanied by an increase in life expectancy, from forty-eight years in 1900 to seventy-three years in 1978 (76.5 for women and 68.7 for men). This has resulted in more and more adults being outside the work force through retirement, and in increased social and governmental programs for older people.

Many of the findings of aging research are inconclusive and even contradictory, depending on the research design utilized and the aging model used as rationale. Longitudinal studies experience subject dropout which distorts any findings, while cross-sectional studies may reflect only generational differences or cohort effects rather than true aging effects. Thus there is much controversy about the nature and degree of decline of various abilities. Future aging research will undoubtedly employ complex designs that will more likely isolate true aging factors.

2. Theory. Why do people (as well as all other creatures) age? Three theoretical approaches have been developed to explain the aging process (cf. "Shock," in Birren and Schaie). The genetic theory suggests that cells are programmed to die after they have divided a certain number of times — perhaps from damage to the cellular DNA or other causes. The "wear and tear" theory, a nongenetic explanation, proposes that time itself produces changes in the cells that reduce their capacity to function properly. The physiological theory of aging points to deterioration of organ systems, such as the cardiovascular system, or impairment of physiological control mechanisms. It is likely that aging is so complex a process that it is best explained by a combination of these theoretical approaches. There is general consensus

that aging is not a disease and that we probably inherit a maximum life span at birth; but there is no consensus about the length of that life span. However, stress is generally seen as the most important environmental factor affecting the rate of aging.

Schaie's (Birren and Schaie) three models of aging are most commonly referred to in current aging literature. The "irreversible decrement" model refers to progressive, inevitable decline in abilities after a maximal level of functioning is reached sometime during adulthood. The "decrement with compensation" model suggests that some of the increasing decrements can be overcome or remedied with intervention. The model subscribed to by most personality researchers is the "stability" model, which proposes that once maturity is reached, behavior remains stable.

3. Aging as Decline. One of the most prominent themes of aging is decline or loss. This is unfortunate in that it has led to much ageist thinking, which associates certain negative expectations with all persons over a certain age. While losses do occur in the sensory and psychomotor domains during much of adulthood, the rate of decline varies from one function to another. In addition the variability of personal attributes increases across the life span, so age-based expectations alone are often invalid. Sensory and psychomotor losses may be balanced by increased verbal facility through the fifth and sixth decades. Hearing impairments are the most common and most debilitating of sensory losses, but only occur in twenty-six percent of persons over age seventy-five. Reaction time increases with age, as does cautiousness, but generalized creative endeavors increase through the sixth and seventh decades. Cognitive losses are thought to be the result of disease processes rather than genetically caused primary aging processes. Certainly the fear of loss of memory is far greater than any actual loss as it occurs in most people. Women in particular are likely to experience the loss of a spouse (half of all women over sixty-five are widows — U.S. Department of Health, Education, and Welfare, 1976). And while reduced income is a concern for many older people, women alone account for three-fourths of the elderly who are officially under the poverty index (Butler and Lewis, 1982). Eighty-six percent of persons over sixty-five have some chronic health problem (1972, U.S. DHEW). These are examples of the changes associated with aging that are viewed negatively. However, aging is one of life's ever-present processes which inevitably produces changes. These changes are natural but are unique, as each aging individual is unique.

Bibliography. J. E. Birren and K. W. Schaie, *Handbook of the Psychology of Aging* (1977). R. N. Butler and M. I. Lewis, *Aging and Mental Health* 3d ed. (1982).

C. Z. BENSON

LIFE CYCLE THEORY AND PASTORAL CARE; OLDER PERSONS, JEWISH *or* PASTORAL CARE AND COUNSELING OF; OLDER PERSONS, MENTAL DISORDERS OF; PERSONALITY DEVELOPMENT; REMINISCENCE THERAPY; RETIREMENT.

AIDS (Pastoral Issues). Acquired Immune Deficiency Syndrome (AIDS) is a disease that cripples the body's defenses against infection. The Human Immunodeficiency Virus (HIV) immobilizes the key blood cells which in healthy people activate the immune system, leaving the body defenseless against certain cancers and opportunistic infections. HIV may also enter the central nervous system, leading to dementia and paralysis. Many individuals live for years without symptoms of HIV infection. However, by the mid-1980s the mortality rate for persons experiencing full manifestation of AIDS was 80 percent at twenty-four months and approaching 100 percent at four years. More recent advances in medical treatment and the development of new drugs have increased the life expectancy of persons with AIDS (PWAs), particularly when treatment is begun before the onset of symptoms.

When people become seriously sick or disabled they experience social isolation and a number of deep-seated fears: fear of infection and impairment, of uncertainty, of stigmatism and ostracism, and of death. Regardless of its nature, a serious health crisis results in emotional stress associated with significant changes in outlook over a short period. In turn, this may involve adaptive changes in personality of a brief or long-term nature.

These factors are all present in the lives of PWAs. However, these features are exacerbated by deeper fears related to stigmatization and ostracism arising from the disease's association with its two main patient populations, homosexual males and intravenous drug users. Because AIDS is primarily a sexually transmitted disease, and because of societal taboos related to gay lifestyles, prostitution, and drug abuse, patients in these population groups must confront such issues at a time when the diagnosis thrusts each into a confrontation with death from which there is no relief. Those who have contracted the disease in other ways, e.g. through heterosexual contact, blood transfusions (primarily until 1985 when blood began to be stringently screened), or as an unborn child in the infected mother's womb, suffer similar stigmatization and ostracism. In any event, PWAs have "fallen into death's realm of power." Just at the point when they are most in need of support and compassion, they are most vulnerable to the deepest pain and threat.

It is important for pastors and counselors to remember that the threats faced by PWAs are also confronted by parents and other family members, lovers, and friends. Like the patient, the family and friends struggle to come to terms with the disease and its inevitable end in the context of societal attitudes toward AIDS and PWAs. This anguish is deepened for parents who learn that their son is gay at the time when they learn he has AIDS. Parents may learn that their son-in-law is bisexual or has been infected by a prostitute when they learn their daughter has AIDS. In many cases, denial and bewilderment will often be replaced by a sense of helpless rage.

Pastoral care of PWAs is a response to grief. Experience suggests that the most basic need is a climate in which grieving people may tell their stories of loss or threatened loss. This in turn must be shaped by an openness to the specific needs of the patient or family members. To the extent that PWAs have usually experienced rejection and derogation, they are searching for acceptance and affirmation. In particular, gay men seek understanding and acceptance of their being and lifestyle. The degree of hostility to both gay men and drug users indicates a need for advocacy of both their personal needs and their patient rights. In end-stage disease, advocacy may include representing the patient's wish to discontinue invasive therapies and to maintain comfort without life-prolonging intervention. Since many patients with AIDS face loss of mental faculties, the caring person may raise with the patient the matter of arranging power of attorney, should mental deterioration make it impossible for the patient to act on his or her behalf.

People facing threat of imminent death look for some way to find meaning, both in their lives and in their deaths. It is inappropriate to "preach at" the patient or at family members in such a setting. It goes without saying that this ministry is one that excludes the kind of empty moralizing that treats the other as an "it." One of the most creative attempts to analyze the caring role of the helping person is suggested by Alan Keith-Lucas (1972). He contends that effective help and support are offered only when composed of three elements: reality, empathy, and support. This concept is presented in summary form via three caring responses: Reality — "This is it"; Empathy — "I know it must hurt"; and Support — "I am here to help you if you want me and can use me," or, more succinctly, "You don't have to face this alone." Reality by itself is harsh, and can be destructive. It is only reality approached with empathy and support that is truly a caring ministry.

In addition to compassionate pastoral ministry to PWAs and to the circle of people immediately affected, it must also be remembered that neither the carer nor the patient and family functions in a vacuum; each is a member of a wider community. The pastor bears a unique opportunity and responsibility to minister not only to the people immediately affected, but to the "worried well" in the wider societal groupings of which they are members. This may mean interceding at the patient's request with an employer, or assisting the patient to obtain legal assistance and other benefits. This issue raises a further matter, namely, the prophetic aspect of pastoral care, or the pastoral care of the "system" (Shelp and Sunderland, 1985). The pastoral function relates to the church's role as a mediating and reconciling agency in the community. This function is furthered by the provision of appropriate educational opportunities for the general public — a task for which the local congregation is well suited. The exploding effects of AIDS and the emotions of hurt and bewilderment it has stirred will only be alleviated through the efforts of people who meet the challenge with compassion, and, to the extent it is possible, that proper level of dispassionate response that encourages people to work and talk with one another to heal the wounds created by fear and grief.

Bibliography. J. Ablon, "Stigmatized Health Conditions," *J. of Social Science and Medicine*, 15B (1981), 31. A. Keith-Lucas, *Giving and Taking Help* (1972). K. Seybold and U. B. Mueller, *Sickness and Healing* (1981). R. H. Sunderland and E. E. Shelp, *AIDS: A Manual for Pastoral Care* (1987); also *AIDS and the Church* (1987); *The Pastor as Prophet* (1985); *AIDS: Personal Stories in Pastoral Perspective* (1986).

R. H. SUNDERLAND

DYING, PASTORAL CARE OF; SICK, PASTORAL CARE OF. *See also* CHRONIC ILLNESS; GRIEF AND LOSS; LIFESTYLE ISSUES IN PASTORAL CARE; LONELINESS AND ISOLATION; PROPHETIC/PASTORAL TENSION IN MINISTRY.

AL-ANON FAMILY GROUPS. Al-Anon is a worldwide fellowship of men and women whose lives are or have been deeply affected by someone else's drinking. Related to Alcoholics Anonymous, it is a spiritual program in which persons discover that no situation is hopeless and that their serenity does not depend upon another person. Faith in a Higher Power helps them learn to live peacefully one day at a time.

Al-Ateen is a similar organization for adolescents. ACOA is an AA-related group for Adult Children of Alcoholics.

ANONYMOUS

ALCOHOLICS ANONYMOUS. *See also* SUPPORT GROUPS.

ALCOHOL ABUSE, ADDICTION, AND THERAPY. A progressive compulsive-addictive illness, the primary characteristic of which is the continuing excessive use of alcoholic beverages in ways that damage one or more areas of a person's life — mental and/or physical health, family life and social relationships, job and economic viability, creativity, and spiritual wholeness. To say that an alcoholic's drinking is *compulsive* means that psychologically the desire is driven to some degree from an unconscious level and to that degree is beyond volitional control. *Addictive* refers to a physiological adaptation of the organism to the presence of alcohol so that acute distress (withdrawal symptoms) and craving are experienced when the person stops drinking. The term *progressive* refers to the fact that the illness usually develops through predictable stages and if not treated eventually will result in irreversible dysfunction and death. The illness conception of alcoholism, recognized today by the American Medical Association and World Health Organization, does not eliminate the ethical aspects of the problem. It simply shifts the focus from holding alcoholics responsible (and blaming them) for their compulsive drinking (over which they have relatively little control), to emphasizing their responsibility to get help and learn how to live without alcohol.

Terms in this field often are used with varying meanings. *Problem drinking, compulsive drinking,* and *chemical dependency on alcohol* are approximate symptoms of *alcoholism.* However, *problem drinking* sometimes is used more broadly to include non-addictive alcohol abuse such as driving an automobile after drinking. The term *chronic alcoholism* refers to the advanced stages of the illness during which severe medical and sometimes psychiatric complications occur.

Alcoholism is America's third largest health problem (following heart disease and cancer). More people are addicted to alcohol than to all other chemicals combined (with the exception of nicotine and caffeine). It is estimated that nearly ten million persons are at some stage of this illness, and each person with alcoholism is surrounded by a circle of pain in the lives of others, resulting from the alcoholic's excessive drinking. In our society,

many people develop multiple addictions — to alcohol plus a variety of prescribed and/or street drugs.

1. General Features of Alcoholism. Understanding the nature of the problem is essential preparation for counseling alcoholics effectively. Alcoholism is an incurable, potentially fatal, but highly treatable disease. For reasons not fully understood a certain percentage of those who use beverage alcohol develop the illness (approximately seven percent in America). The essence of the problem is increasing dependence on alcohol and loss of control of the amount or the occasion of one's drinking. Increased dependence and loss of control usually occur gradually (often five to fifteen years). In a small minority of alcoholics, the addictive process occurs much more rapidly, often after a traumatic crisis or loss.

There are at least three major types of alcoholism. The most common type in America is the *steady-drinker-with-binges,* whose heavy daily drinking is punctuated by occasional binges of several days or longer. The second type is the *periodic alcoholic,* who usually is abstinent between binges. This type may suffer from pronounced manic-depressive mood swings. Third and most difficult to identify is the *plateau alcoholic,* who drinks more-or-less continually but seldom seeks maximum intoxication or goes on binges. Instead such persons keep their blood alcohol level at a fairly constant level much of the time, a level that permits them to continue functioning but in seriously impaired ways.

Most alcoholism (other than the plateau type) involves frequent drunkenness, but not all drunkenness is symptomatic of alcoholism. *Recreational drunkenness* is a common form of behavior in which groups of people use alcohol to release their "child" sides to play. *Social desperation drunkenness* refers to intoxication to anesthetize suffering from social discrimination and injustice (e.g., among Native Americans). Frequent intoxication, whatever its motivation, tends to produce increased addictive drinking on the part of some.

The terms *high bottom* and *low bottom* alcoholics refer to the degree of personal and social disintegration alcoholics must experience before they become open to outside help. *Low bottom* or skid row alcoholics are what most people picture when they hear *alcoholic.* Actually such alcoholics probably constitute five percent or less of all alcoholics in America.

2. Causes and Predisposing Factors. *a. Physiological and psychological factors.* Alcoholism is a complex illness of the whole person. Extensive research over four decades has failed to discover a simple or single cause to explain why some "social drinkers" become addicted and others with similar drinking patterns over many years do not. Psychological, sociocultural, physiological, pharmacological, and spiritual causative factors are involved in producing alcoholism, in varying degrees from one person to another. The cliché "Alcoholism comes in people not in bottles" is accurate in the sense that over ninety percent of Americans who drink do not become addicted. But as a report by the World Health Organization's Committee on Drugs Liable to Produce Addiction shows, the pharmacological properties of alcohol do play an appreciable role in the etiology of alcoholism, though other factors also must be present. It would be accurate to say that alcohol lends itself to persons who tend to form compulsive-addictive behavior patterns relatively easily.

The "soil of addiction," which makes some people receptive to the seeds of addiction, usually includes psychological problems present before the person began drinking. Alcohol is widely used in most cultures because of its anesthetic or pain-diminishing effects. It is particularly attractive to prealcoholics because it can temporarily deaden awareness of painful anxiety, guilt, inner conflict, loneliness, and low self-esteem. Personality disturbance underlying the addictive process may be severe (psychoneuroses, psychoses, or character disorders) or relatively mild. Some severely disturbed persons do become addicted, but one does not have to be a psychological cripple to become an alcoholic, particularly if one is in a heavy-drinking culture or group.

Alcoholics drink so much because they hurt so much, but their excessive drinking increases the painful feelings that made alcohol so attractive in the first place. Thus a vicious, self-feeding cycle of increased drinking to overcome the painful effects of previous excessive drinking is established.

Why do only certain persons become alcoholics among all those who have elevated levels of inner pain? A few researchers hold to the hypothesis that there is a metabolic peculiarity that predisposes certain persons to this addiction. Atypical metabolic patterns have been identified in the advanced stages of some alcoholics. But whether these are predisposing causes or consequences of damage to the organism from prolonged excessive drinking is not yet known. Biochemical changes may be involved in the irreversibility of loss of control in most alcoholics —that is, the fact that once persons cross from controlled to uncontrolled drinking they ordinarily cannot recover the ability to drink in controlled fashion.

b. Sociocultural factors. Learned social and cultural factors probably are primary determinants of why only certain psychologically vulnerable people become addicted. These factors are reflected in the high rates of alcoholism in some cultures (e.g., Ireland and France) and among some heavy-drinking groups in America, and the contrasting low rates in other cultures (e.g., Italy) and groups (e.g., Orthodox Jews). A World Health Organization study comparing attitudes toward drinking and drunkenness and rates of addiction in some twenty-five cultures discovered this principle: the more easily accessible alcohol is, and the more heavy drinking is regarded as "normal" behavior in particular cultures or subcultures, the less psychological pain is required in individuals to produce alcoholics. In all cultures, social disapproval of drunkenness is much stronger for women than men. This probably accounts for the considerably lower rates of addiction among women.

Thus, alcoholism can be prevented on two interrelated levels — by rearing psychologically healthy children (with less anxiety) and by fostering more constructive attitudes toward, and thereby stronger social controls on, drunkenness in a society. The gradual increase, since the founding of Alcoholics Anonymous (AA), of the percentage of Americans who regard alcoholism as a disease that can be treated (seventy-nine percent in 1982) means that social attitudes are making it easier to seek help.

c. Spiritual causes. An understanding of the spiritual causes of alcoholism illuminates the unique role of ministers. There is a dynamic relationship between alcohol and alcoholism, on the one hand, and religious strivings, fear of death, and meaninglessness, on the other. Bill W., the co-founder of AA, said on one occasion, "Before AA we were trying to find God in a bottle." William James suggested in his Gifford Lectures that the sway of alcohol is due to its power to stimulate the mystical faculties in human beings, and that drunken consciousness is one form of mystical consciousness. The widespread use of alcohol in religious rites related to the mysteries of human existence (e.g., birth, marriage, death) is based on its power to symbolize the transcendent and the ecstatic. Clinical evidence suggests that for many alcoholics, alcohol is not a *symbol* of the transcendent dimension of life: it *is* their transcendent dimension. The abortive attempt to satisfy spiritual needs by nonreligious, chemical means is probably a significant cause of many addictions, including alcoholism. Addiction can be understood as a form of idolatry — that is, making a false absolute out of a substance that is not ultimate. Persons attempting to satisfy spiritual needs by alcohol eventually discover that their god betrays them, turning out to be a demon, which makes their spiritual alienation, emptiness, and longing all the worse. Full recovery must include developing healthy ways to satisfy the universal spiritual needs for trust, values, meaning, experiences of transcendence, forgiveness, and development of one's higher self or soul.

3. Treatment Goals and Resources. a. Goals. Therapy with alcoholics has four goals: (1) motivating them to accept their need for help; (2) detoxification and medical treatment of problems resulting from withdrawal (e.g., agonizing hangover or *delirium tremens*) and prolonged malnutrition from "drinking their meals" (e.g., cirrhosis of the liver); (3) enabling them to interrupt the addictive cycle by learning to avoid taking the first drink; (4) helping them rebuild their lives and relationships without alcohol; learning to satisfy in interpersonal and spiritual ways the needs that they had attempted to satisfy by means of alcohol. The mainstream view of most alcoholism counselors and treatment approaches (including AA) is that permanent abstinence is the only realistic and viable objective for alcoholics. (This view has been challenged by a small minority of scientists and therapists in the field; cf. Pattison, 1977.) Counseling, psychotherapy, and marriage and family counseling frequently are helpful in achieving this goal. Full recovery — the achievement of stable sobriety (abstinence) within a constructive lifestyle — often takes several years, with temporary "slips" occurring, particularly during early stages of the process. Because alcoholism is an illness involving whole family systems, it is important to involve the family in treatment.

b. Resources. Most alcoholics resist facing their need for help long after the need is obvious to those around them. Openness to help comes when they "hit bottom" or "surrender." This occurs when the fear and grief of terminating drinking is outweighed for a time by the fear of the painful consequences of continuing to drink and by the faint hope of finding something better. Alcoholics ordinarily do not hit bottom as long as persons close to them (e.g., spouse, parent, employer) protect them from the painful consequences of their excessive drinking. Vernon Johnson (1980) has developed an innovative way of motivating alcoholics to accept help using a planned and unified confrontation by their family and other significant persons.

Getting alcoholics to a physician or to a detoxification center may increase the possibility of their achieving permanent sobriety. But if treatment stops with medical help, it seldom results in full recovery because the person has not learned how to avoid reactivating the compulsive-addictive cycle. Regular, ongoing participation in AA is the most widely available and effective means by which alcoholics can interrupt this cycle and achieve stable sobriety. In a deeply caring group of persons who are living proof that it *is* possible to recover, the newcomer acquires hope again and learns how to avoid taking that first drink which, for alcoholics, usually leads to intoxication.

Rebuilding one's whole life and lifestyle without alcohol is a demanding and essential part of recovery. AA's twelve-step program is an invaluable resource in this process for many alcoholics. In fact more alcoholics recover in AA than in all other treatment approaches combined. But residential treatment centers using medical help, group therapy, intensive education about the nature of alcoholism and recovery, individual counseling (often by recovered alcoholics trained in counseling), *and* frequent AA meetings often are effective with those for whom AA alone is not enough. Whatever the treatment, alcoholics must learn that their uncontrolled drinking is their first and most urgent problem and must be given top priority.

Antabuse (a drug which provides a period of enforced sobriety by its biochemical incompatibility with alcohol) is a therapeutic adjunct that is helpful to some people who cannot break the addictive cycle by AA methods alone. In some cases a dynamic religious experience may also break the drinking cycle, as illustrated by the recovery of Bill W. (AA's co-founder) and by the alcoholism programs of the Salvation Army and the rescue mission.

4. **The Role of the Church.** Ministers and their congregations can fulfill five valuable roles in the treatment and prevention of alcoholism:

a. *Encouraging help-seeking.* The first step is to help bring hidden alcoholics and their families out of hiding and to accept help. In spite of the availability of treatment resources, the majority of alcoholics still die untreated because their problem is hidden or they deny their need for help. In sermons and other public statements clergy can communicate enlightened understanding of alcoholism and the hope for recovery. A congregation's alcohol education program should acquaint people with the warning signs of early-stage addiction (e.g., increased dependence, memory loss after drinking) and give them opportunity to hear AA and Al-Anon speakers tell their inspiring recovery stories. Thus hidden and resisting alcoholics and their families can be encouraged to seek help sooner. In pastoral care and counseling, ministers should be alert to the signs that may indicate drinking problems — for example, evidence of drinking excessively or at inappropriate

times, escalating marital conflict, or emotional disturbance in children.

b. *Pastoral counseling with alcoholics.* The counseling of alcoholics involves using the basic principles of educative counseling, which integrates relevant information (about alcoholism, the recovery process, AA, and other treatment resources) with counseling aimed first at helping alcoholics accept AA and/or other treatment. If pastors are able to combine caring and confrontation with communicating information, they can help alcoholics and their families get to potentially life-saving help. AA can provide crucial help that a non-AA pastor cannot, and vice versa; therefore, it is essential to encourage alcoholic counselees to attend AA meetings regularly while receiving counseling. By using counseling skills, ministers can help AA members who request this help to deepen their moral inventory. As facilitators of spiritual healing and growth, clergy can be of unique help to alcoholics and their families in working through spiritual conflicts and enriching the essential spiritual dimension of their recovery.

c. *Pastoral counseling with families of alcoholics.* Counseling for spouses, children, and parents of alcoholics is a major opportunity for clergy, occurring more frequently than opportunities to help alcoholics directly. Alcoholism is a family illness both in the sense that interaction in the family system often helps to perpetuate the drinking, and in the sense that most members of the family are themselves deeply disturbed by the alcoholic's drinking behavior.

The key to counseling with spouses and parents of alcoholics is the Al-Anon principle of *release.* This means letting go of their inappropriate sense of responsibility for getting or keeping the alcoholic sober, and of their obsessive, counterproductive attempts to control the alcoholic's drinking by alternating overprotective and punishing behavior. Release by family members also involves severing the alcoholic's control over them by deciding to do all they can to have more constructive, fulfilled lives, regardless of what the alcoholic does or does not do about his or her drinking. To the degree that release is accomplished by a spouse, the neurotic marital interaction that keeps the alcoholic from hitting bottom will tend to be interrupted. Referral of adult family members to Al-Anon and adolescents to Alateen groups will give them massive emotional support from persons who understand from the inside the agony of living with an alcoholic. These two groups encourage participants to use the Twelve Steps to heal and renew their own lives. Ministers trained in marriage counseling can provide important additional help to couples in rebuilding their marital and sexual relationship as a part of recovery.

d. *Church initiatives in the community.* A valuable outreach dimension of the ministry of congregations and clergy is support of community alcoholism resources. This may involve inviting AA and Al-Anon groups to use church facilities, supporting the local National Council on Alcoholism group, helping to establish outpatient or inpatient treatment facilities, writing state legislators to support enlightened alcoholism bills, encouraging general hospitals to establish alcoholism programs, helping to set up an alcoholism program in one's business (many companies have these), or simply attending open meetings of AA and Al-Anon to get acquainted with members, learn from them, and express one's affirmation of their programs. This last form of outreach can help deepen a minister's emotional understanding of alcoholism and build relationships with persons who can be significant assets in making referrals. A church's lay pastoral care teams should include stable AA and Al-Anon members of each sex.

e. Prevention. Programs aimed at prevention constitute a key contribution of clergy and congregation and should occur on three levels: First, parent education and mutual support can help the pastor and congregation nurture the self-esteem and responsibility of children and youth, which are the best defenses against the misuse of alcohol and other consciousness-altering drugs. Second, alcohol education and counseling can help develop constructive social attitudes and controls on drinking and drunkenness. Third, by helping alcoholic parents recover, the probabilities of future addiction and other personality problems among their children will be lessened. (The incidence of alcoholism among adult children of alcoholics is approximately five times that of the general population, probably not because the illness is hereditary, but because of the emotional trauma of living with an alcoholic parent.)

5. **The Special Needs of Alcoholic Women, Youth, and the Aged.** These special populations of alcoholics have recently begun to receive needed attention and should be of concern to churches and ministers. The gap between rates of male and female alcoholism is narrowing in America. Alcoholism among *women,* often hidden and of the plateau type, is tremendously complicated by the institutional sexism that damages women's self-esteem in our society. Problems around sex role identity, marriage, children, and sexual adjustment seem to be more prominent causative factors in female than in male alcoholics. Fortunately, treatment programs designed to meet the special needs of alcoholic women, using women as counselors, are becoming available.

The major alcohol problem of *adolescents* is not addiction *per se* but drinking and driving. However, the excessive drinking that sets the stage for alcoholism (prealcoholism) is common among teenagers, and the number of youth and young adults in AA has increased dramatically in recent years. The identity-establishing task of youth often is complicated and delayed by using alcohol and drugs to cope rather than struggling to use and thereby develop personality potentialities. Clergy and lay persons who work with teens need to be knowledgeable regarding alcohol and alcoholism to help them make constructive decisions in this hazardous area of their lives.

There is a sizable and increasing alcohol and drug problem among the *elderly.* Some life-long moderate drinkers become alcoholics after retirement. (Older people sometimes use alcohol and prescription drugs to self-medicate depression caused by forced retirement.) Long-time excessive drinkers often develop alcohol-related mental and physiological complications during their older years. Many elderly persons are members of congregations. Enabling them to develop satisfying lives and find mutual support can help them avoid the destructive misuse of alcohol and prescription drugs.

Bibliography. *Alcoholics Anonymous* 3d ed. (1976). Anon., *Living with an Alcoholic with the Help of Al-Anon* rev. ed. (1980). H. Clinebell, Jr., *Understanding and Counseling the Alcoholic, Through Religion and Psychology* rev. ed. (1968) "Philosophical-Religious Factors in the Etiology and Treatment of Alcoholism," *Quarterly J. of Studies on Alcohol,* 24 (Sept., 1968). V. E. Johnson, *I'll Quit Tomorrow* rev. ed. (1980). E. M. Pattison *et al., Emerging Concepts of Alcohol Dependence* (1977). J. E. Royce, *Alcohol Problems and Alcoholism: A Comprehensive Survey* (1981). M. Sandmaier, *The Invisible Alcoholics: Women and Alcohol Abuse in America* (1980). G. E. Vallant, *The Natural History of Alcoholism* (1983).

H. CLINEBELL

ALCOHOLICS ANONYMOUS; AL-ANON FAMILY GROUPS; DRUG ABUSE, DEPENDENCE, AND TREATMENT; MENTAL HEALTH AND ILLNESS. *See also* PSYCHOPATHOLOGY, THEORIES OF; PERSONALITY, BIOLOGICAL DIMENSIONS OF. *Compare* EATING AND DRINKING.

ALCOHOLICS ANONYMOUS. "A fellowship of men and women who share their experience, strength, and hope with one another that they may solve their common problem and help others to recover from alcoholism" (AA Preamble).

1. **Philosophy.** AA views alcoholism as an allergy of the body coupled with an obsession of the mind, causing progressive physical, emotional, and spiritual deterioration. The alcoholic feels compelled to drink despite overwhelming evidence of destructive effects and despite firm resolve to drink moderately or not at all. Release from the compulsion to drink is viewed as a gift that is given one day at a time and is dependent on maintenance of a fit spiritual condition. This spiritual way of life is achieved through working the twelve-step program of recovery outlined in the fellowship's textbook, *Alcoholics Anonymous* (3d ed., 1976). The first step addresses powerlessness over alcohol and the unmanageability of life. It is the only step that deals with physical abstinence from alcohol. Steps two through nine help the alcoholic develop a trusting relationship with a personal Higher Power, or God, and achieve humility through writing and sharing an honest moral inventory, making amends, and allowing God to remove hobbling character defects. The final three maintenance steps call for continuing daily inventory and amends, conscious contact with God through prayer and meditation, and service to others. Since emphasis is placed on the concepts of Higher Power or personal understanding of God, this program has become acceptable to individuals of every religious persuasion as well as to agnostics and atheists.

AA meetings are held for the purpose of sharing the process of recovery. Twelve traditions provide spiritual principles for the AA group with anonymity as the cornerstone. The single requirement for membership is a desire to stop drinking. AA is nondenominational, autonomous, and self-supporting (*Twelve Steps and Twelve Traditions,* 1953).

2. **Background: Growth and Effectiveness.** AA was serendipitously started in Akron, Ohio, in 1935 when Bill Wilson, a sober alcoholic stockbroker, shared his experience and hope with Bob Smith, a despairing alcoholic surgeon. The fellowship took its name from the title of the book *Alcoholics Anonymous* written by Bill

Wilson and the first one hundred sober members. They were deeply influenced by the Oxford Group movement. AA became known publicly after an article by Jack Alexander appeared in the *Saturday Evening Post* in 1941. AA's membership is now over 1,000,000 with 48,000 groups in 110 countries. Its membership includes 30 percent women, 15 percent under thirty, and 25 percent dually addicted. Fifty percent of those who remain three months in AA, sober or not, subsequently stay sober and active for the next year. Eighty percent of members sober in AA for one to five years remain sober and active for the next year. Thirty-three percent are currently referred through counseling and treatment facilities (*AA Grapevine*, March, 1982).

Al-Anon is a similar program for family members of alcoholics. Gamblers Anonymous and Narcotics Anonymous are mutual-help organizations based on AA principles.

Bibliography. Bill W., *Alcoholics Anonymous* (1976). Anon., *12 Steps and 12 Traditions* (1953) and *A. A. Grapevine,* March 1982. E. Kurtz, *Not-God: A History of Alcoholics Anonymous* (1979).

J. E. TURIAN

ALCOHOL ABUSE, ADDICTION, AND THERAPY. *See also* AL-ANON FAMILY GROUPS. *Compare* GROUP COUNSELING AND PSYCHOTHERAPY; RELATIONSHIP NETWORK; SELF-HELP PSYCHOLOGIES; SUPPORT GROUPS.

ALIENATION/ESTRANGEMENT. A type of human relation in which familiarity transforms into strangeness. Such relations may characterize human existence without hope for removal, or they may be limited to changeable, individual situations.

The two words elaborate each other. The basic sense of *alienate* is transfer of title, and alienation means to cause to be withdrawn or transferred. Alienation occurs, for example, when attachment is changed into separateness or when identity changes into otherness. The opposite of alienation is reconciliation. To estrange means to remove or to make strange. Estrangement happens when something is taken away or kept at a distance. It has the sense of disuniting, and joining or endearing are its opposites.

Human beings have to deal with alienation and estrangement all the time. We experience the transformation of familiarity and identity into strangeness and otherness in the ordinary passage of time in which our present transforms into our past and the possibilities that we bear become no longer possible. Change and alienation seem to be companions. We are also distanced from what has been close to us or from an undifferentiated part of us in all experiences of birth and creation: something comes forth and leaves us. We carry in our lives the possibility for our death: we are our own capacities for final loss of life, a strange difference that makes part of our being seem strange to us. As parts of a larger whole we find ourselves at a distance from ourselves to the extent that we are apart from the whole and are a part of the whole. Any relation to deity or to nature or to the universe that is a part of our being would constitute a continuous differencing in our lives in which we would be at a distance from ourselves as mundane, particular, or finite. We are thus characterized by differences in our

being that are lived in experiences of alienation and estrangement.

We may also experience transformations of familiarity and unity into strangeness and fragmentation in ways that are limited to our own characters or to the character of the time and society in which we live. Whenever one lives as though one were essentially different from the way one is, one experiences alienation and estrangement in some form. One might, for example, not be able easily to perceive things as unities or to have a sense of oneself as unified. Or one might experience phobia or anxiety regarding anything that reminds one of the denied aspect. Further, if we live in a society that punishes or opposes something essential to our character, we will be estranged from our society as we participate in it and depend on it. If our moral principles oppress something vital for our lives, we will live by an alienating moral code. And if our existence is constituted by numinous presence or by the sustaining presence of God, a life without religious sensibility in some form would be one characterized by alienation. We would make something close to us strange by the way we lived.

In determining whether an experience of alienation is to be accepted or eliminated, one needs to discover in the alienation what is familiar and strange, close and distant, intimate and foreign. Are these constituents aspects of human beings generally or are they subject to alteration and elimination? The clinical task might be for one to learn how to live in acceptance of experiences of estrangement. Or the task might be to replace experiences of estrangement with those of close and open relation.

Bibliography. H. Arendt, *The Human Condition* (1958). M. Boss, "Anxiety, Guilt, and Human Liberation," *Review for Existential Psychology and Philosophy* (1963). A. Camus, *The Myth of Sisyphus* (1955). H. Hendin, *The Age of Sensation: A Psychoanalytic Exploration* (1975). S. Kierkegaard, *Sickness Unto Death* (1980). H. Marcuse, *Reason and Revolution* (1941). R. May, *Existence* (1958). J. P. Sartre, *Existentialism and Human Emotions* (1957). P. Tillich, *Systematic Theology,* vol. 1 (1951).

C. E. SCOTT

ANOMIE/NORMLESSNESS. *See also* ANXIETY; APATHY AND BOREDOM; EVALUATION AND DIAGNOSIS; LONELINESS AND ISOLATION; SIN/SINS; SOCIAL CHANGE AND DISLOCATION; SOCIAL ISOLATION. *Compare* DOUBT AND UNBELIEF; EXISTENTIALISM AND PASTORAL CARE.

ALIENS. *See* CULTURAL AND ETHNIC FACTORS IN PASTORAL CARE; MIGRANT WORKERS AND FAMILIES; SOCIAL CHANGE AND DISLOCATION; SOCIAL STATUS AND CLASS FACTORS.

ALLPORT, GORDON (1897–1967). An American psychologist who was a pioneer in the study of personality and the psychology of religion. The younger brother of Floyd Allport, an eminent social psychologist, Gordon Allport's focus was on the development of a theory of personality that was neither psychoanalytic nor behavioristic. He stressed the individual nature of personality and the uniqueness of the individual. His concept of the "functional autonomy of motives" deemphasized the instinctual drives behind motivation and placed emphasis on the mature and independent person. Besides his studies on personality, Allport studied the difference between mature and immature religion, and out of this he developed the concepts of intrinsic and extrinsic religion. *The Nature of Prejudice* (1954) has become his most influential work, and *The Individual and His Religion* (1950) has contributed significantly to understanding the psychology of religion.

Bibliography. G. Allport, *Personality: A Psychological Interpretation* (1937); *Becoming* (1955). H. N. Malony, "The Contribution of Gordon Allport to the Psychology of Religion," *J. of American Sociological Association* (1971).

S. C. WILLIS

HUMANISTIC PSYCHOLOGY.

ALPHONSUS DE LIGOURI. *See* LIGOURI, ALPHONSUS DE.

ALTERED STATES OF CONSCIOUSNESS. *See* CONSCIOUSNESS; PSYCHEDELIC DRUGS AND EXPERIENCE; RELIGIOUS EXPERIENCE. *See also* FAITH HEALING.

ALTRUISM. *See* COMPASSION; LOVE; SACRIFICIAL BEHAVIOR. *See also* SELF-TRANSCENDENCE; VIRTUE, CONCEPT OF.

ALZHEIMER'S DISEASE. *See* NEUROLOGIC ILLNESSES.

AMBIVALENCE. (1) Contradictory emotions or attitudes toward a person or object. (2) Uncertainty as to which approach or attitude to take. The psychological term "ambivalence" is taken from dynamic psychology, where it refers specifically to the simultaneous presence of love and hate, or of desire to approach and desire to retreat from another.

Though Freud believed that ambivalence is innate, rooted in the dualism of the instincts of life and death, today it is more commonly theorized that ambivalence is rooted in childhood experiences. The child needs its parents for survival, emotionally as well as physically. As the parent provides food, shelter, attention, and love the child responds positively, with love and with imitation of and identification with the parents. Love for these providers, who are also powerful in the child's perspective, grows. But the parent may act in ways which hurt or jeopardize the safety of the child or which thwart the child's expression or attainment of its wishes. Reactions of anger, even rage, can build. If both emotions are intense and enduring they become a part of the child's ongoing emotional pattern in relation to the parents. Held at an unconscious level, these emotions remain active in motivating behavior.

As the child grows, appreciation for parental support may be the positive dimension. Hatred for parental use of support to control the growing child and resentment of expectations that the child fulfill the parent's dreams may be the negative side. Actions toward the parent will vary, depending upon which emotion is dominant, and may be impeded and decisions made difficult (as in obsessive-compulsive neurosis) because of the dual and contradictory response patterns that have been developed.

As a result of the common phenomenon of transferring past experiences into the present ("transference"), a person's ambivalence toward a parent may focus on other persons in later years. Pastors, for instance, as God's representatives and hence authorities, may be substituted unconsciously for one's childhood authorities. A minister may be the target of a parishioner's ambivalence without the parishioner's awareness that this has happened. Pastors may be similarly ambivalent toward their parishioners.

The positive dimension of the ambivalence may cause both the parishioner and the pastor to set unrealistic or contradictory expectations of each other. For example, the parishioner may be lavish in complimenting the pastor, but when the pastor does not call as often as wanted or seek the parishioner's advice enough, the parishioner's anger may seem unreasonable. The negative side may get expressed in unfair criticism or active opposition to the minister, or the parishioner may leave the congregation as a way of rejecting the hated parental-substitute, the pastor.

When a parishioner's actions toward the pastor express conflicting responses at inappropriately intense levels, ambivalence should be considered as one explanation. Recognition of ambivalence and its resolution usually require a counseling relationship.

Accurate recognition and assessment of parishioner ambivalence will assist the minister to accept and respond constructively to these irrational reactions, and may aid in assisting the parishioner in securing appropriate counseling or to obtain similar help for oneself. It is helpful to remember that intense ambivalence often indicates the presence of unresolved emotional issues from earlier significant relationships impacting on present experience rather than a simple realistic reaction to present relationships or circumstances. Pastorally, it is often helpful simply to encourage ambivalent persons to articulate both sides of their ambivalence and invite them to explore its meaning via associations and memories.

Q. L. HAND

EMOTION; MOTIVATION; RESISTANCE. *See also* DISAGREEMENT, DIFFERENCE, AND CONFLICT IN PASTOR-PARISHIONER RELATIONSHIPS; PSYCHOANALYSIS; RAGE AND HOSTILITY. *Compare* DECISION/INDECISION.

AMBROSE OF MILAN, ST. (ca. 339–397). Roman Catholic bishop of Milan, Italy; one of the great church fathers.

Pastoral care permeated the life, works, and ministry of Ambrose in many ways, perhaps best summarized with five modern regions of pastoral care: (1) *counseling and soulcare* for the bereaved and mourning, the misguided, those seeking perfection, the virgins dedicated to God; (2) *worship and homiletics:* lively and inspiring, singing-oriented services, well-crafted, bible-based preaching; (3) *outreach/social ministry:* giving funds (including his personal wealth) to the poor, special care for the helpless, patron of the orphans; (4) *pastoral care and ethics:* criticizing the excesses of the upper classes, holding the state morally accountable; insisting on separation between church and state, submission of state to church in matters of faith; practical application of morality; stress of four virtues; (5) *congregational ministry:* a strong emphasis on a sense of community among believers, care of the common good against troublemakers, assistance to the needy, affirmation of good members.

N. F. HAHN

EARLY CHURCH, PASTORAL CARE AND COUNSELING IN.

AMERICAN ASSOCIATION OF PASTORAL COUNSELORS (AAPC).

A membership organization that promotes pastoral counseling. Such promotion is carried out by standards and processes for certification of individuals and accreditation of institutions for the practice and teaching of pastoral counseling. AAPC promotes research, monitors legal concerns, supports publications, provides continuing education, approves supervision, serves as a liaison to religious bodies, and encourages collegial relationships in pastoral counseling.

AAPC, organized in 1963, is the major organization for pastoral counselors in the U.S. Membership includes persons in Canada and other countries throughout the world. It is governed by a Board of Governors, which consists of members elected as chairpersons of the ten regions, the nine Association standing committees, and three officers. The administration of the AAPC is through the employed Executive Director and staff located in the Washington, D.C. area.

Membership includes individuals and institutions. Individual membership is granted through three levels of certification: Member, Fellow, Diplomate. Fellow is considered the master clinician and Diplomate the teacher. Institutional membership is granted through accreditation as a pastoral counseling delivery center and approval as a training program.

Affiliation includes both individuals and institutions in several categories. Pastoral Counselor-in-training is for persons engaged in education to become a certified member; Pastoral Affiliate is for pastors of local congregations who choose not to be certified; Professional Affiliate is for persons of other mental health professions; and International Affiliate is for pastoral counselors in countries outside the U.S. who choose to be related to the AAPC. Institutional Affiliate is for centers and schools who are in the process of accreditation or whose purpose is not suitable for accreditation but whose institution desires a relationship with the AAPC.

The Code of Ethics regulates the standards of practice and behavior of pastoral counselors. The professional quality of pastoral counselors is maintained by adherence to this Code, active involvement in a religious body, participation in continuing education, and consultation through peer review.

Annual meetings are held in the spring and regional meetings in the fall. AAPC maintains collegial relationships with other pastoral care organizations and is a participant in the International Committee of Pastoral Care and Counseling.

J. W. EWING

ACCREDITATION; CERTIFICATION; PASTORAL COUNSELING MOVEMENT; STANDARDS FOR PASTORAL COUNSELING. *See*
also ASSOCIATION FOR CLINICAL PASTORAL EDUCATION; ECUMENICAL RELATIONSHIPS IN THE PASTORAL CARE AND COUNSELING MOVEMENTS; HISTORY OF PROTESTANT PASTORAL CARE (UNITED STATES); THEOLOGICAL EDUCATION AND THE PASTORAL CARE MOVEMENT.

AMERICAN CATHOLIC PSYCHOLOGICAL ASSOCIATION. *See* COUNSELING, ROMAN CATHOLIC.

AMERICAN FOUNDATION OF RELIGION AND PSYCHIATRY. *See* PASTORAL COUNSELING MOVEMENT; RELIGION AND HEALTH MOVEMENT.

AMERICAN INDIANS. *See* NATIVE AMERICANS.

AMERICAN PASTORAL CARE AND COUNSELING. *See* HISTORY OF PROTESTANT *or* ROMAN CATHOLIC PASTORAL CARE (United States); PASTORAL CARE *or* PASTORAL COUNSELING MOVEMENT.

AMES, EDWARD SCRIBNER (1870–1958).

American psychologist of religion. Graduated from Yale Divinity School in 1892 and was granted the first Ph.D. in philosophy from the University of Chicago in 1895. For two years a *private docent* at Chicago, he then taught for three years at Butler College, before becoming pastor of Hyde Park Church of the Disciples of Christ from 1900 to 1940 and teacher, board member, and dean of the Disciples Divinity House from 1896 to 1945. He resumed teaching philosophy at Chicago in 1900, retiring in 1935. Ames taught the first course in the psychology of religion at Chicago in 1905. In *The Psychology of Religious Experience* (1910), the first attempt at a "handbook" in this field, he concentrated on anthropological studies and the early stages of religion, emphasizing that religion is an affirmation of society's highest values. In *Religion* (1929) Ames articulated the Instrumentalist position, which regards sacredness as the product of social interest, and God as reality idealized, contrasting his position of "extreme personalistic theism" with the orthodox positions of transcendent and absolute theism.

Bibliography. *Beyond Theology: The Autobiography of Edward Scribner Ames* (1959). Garrison, *Faith of the Free* (1940).

H. VANDE KEMP

PSYCHOLOGY OF RELIGION (Theories, Traditions, and Issues). *See also* PSYCHOLOGY IN AMERICAN RELIGION.

AMES, WILLIAM (1576–1633).

English Puritan divine and casuist. After studying with William Perkins at Cambridge, Ames became the preeminent Puritan authority on "cases of conscience."

Both a pastor to the English church in Rotterdam and a professor at the University of Franeker in Holland, he defined theology as "the doctrine of living to God" and hence as a "practical" rather than a "speculative" discipline (The Marrow of Sacred Divinity, 1642, pp. 1, 4). His understanding of theology led him to include in his systematic treatises long discussions of ethical and pastoral issues.

Though he treated casuistic divinity as a part of dogmatic theology, Ames also wrote texts devoted solely to pastoral questions, the most celebrated being his *Conscience with the Power and Cases Thereof* (1643), which was still being used at Yale College and other American schools in the eighteenth century. As a disciple of Perkins, he depended heavily on the dialectical methods of the French logician Petrus Ramus, and hence described both pastoral conversation and preaching as being marked by rigorous logical analysis and syllogistic reasoning, as well as by close attention to biblical passages. As much as any other theologian, he established the standard patterns of Puritan pastoral care in England and the American colonies.

E. B. HOLIFIELD

CASUISTRY, PROTESTANT.

AMIDAH. *See* JEWISH PRAYERS.

AMISH PASTORAL CARE. *See* SECTARIAN PASTORAL CARE.

AMNESIA. *See* NEUROLOGIC ILLNESSES; MEMORY; LOSS OF FUNCTION.

AMNIOCENTESIS. The needle extraction of the amniotic fluid which bathes the developing embryo inside the uterus. The amniotic fluid can be used diagnostically to determine the fetus' sex, maturity, and the presence or absence of certain congenital defects or chromosomal abnormalities, such as Down's Syndrome.

D. THOMAS

ABORTION; DOWN'S SYNDROME; MORAL DILEMMAS; PREGNANCY.

AMPUTATION. *See* CRISIS MINISTRY; GRIEF AND LOSS; LOSS OF FUNCTION.

ANABAPTISTS. *See* SECTARIAN PASTORAL CARE; SIMONS, MENNO. *See also* MINISTRY(Protestant Tradition).

ANALYSIS. *See* ANALYTIC (JUNGIAN) PSYCHOLOGY; PSYCHOANALYSIS; SELF-ANALYSIS. *See also* THEORY IN PASTORAL CARE AND COUNSELING, FUNCTIONS OF.

ANALYST. A psychotherapist who separates and identifies the motivational components (biological and learned) or parts of a seeker's behavior to the end that the client's insight will result in attitudinal and/or behavioral changes. *Analysts* may use psychoanalytical, Jungian, Adlerian, or other similar psychotherapeutic systems which involve a long-term therapeutic alliance.

Q. L. HAND

ANALYTIC (JUNGIAN) PSYCHOLOGY *or* PSYCHOANALYSIS (Therapeutic Method and Research); PSYCHOANALYST. *Compare* CLINICAL PSYCHOLOGIST; PSYCHIATRIST/PSYCHIATRY.

ANALYTICAL (JUNGIAN) PSYCHOLOGY (Personality Theory and Research). 1. Introduction and Overview. The life of the psyche, as experienced by Carl G. Jung, Swiss psychiatrist, 1875–1961, does not conduct itself in logical, codifiable, predictable ways that permit systematic theory and research in the sense understood by contemporary science. Regarding himself as a radical empiricist who simply reported psychological realities, Jung, on principle, abjured writing systematic theory, and the only research he found appropriate was the careful observation of psychological experience in himself, in his patients, and in the myths, art, and rituals of the human race. The best introductory overview to psychological reality, as perceived by Jung, is to understand the incongruity between that reality and systematized theorizing or "scientific" research, an incongruity which was reflected, for example, in his disagreement with Freud, whom he saw captive, in the name of "science," to a mechanistic philosophy emphasizing outer, predictable, physical phenomena at the expense of the inner, intangible, and whimsical events which constitute the more urgently real and fundamental psychic realities.

Psychological reality as experienced, for all of its irrationality, surprise, and particularity, has its own reality, autonomy, authority, and it needs to be heeded as it presents itself. It is only constricted and distorted by being codified into "lawful" generalities and "explained" by reduction to categories other than itself, as though the individual's psychological experience is real only when accounted for by what is more physical and more reproducible.

"My empirical temperament is more eager for new facts than for what one may speculate about them, although this is an enjoyable pastime" (*Collected Works,* 18, p. 6). "Under the influence of scientific assumptions not only the psyche, but the individual man, and indeed all individual events suffer a leveling down . . . that distorts the picture of reality to a conceptual average. . . . It displaces the individual in favor of anonymous units that pile up into mass formations" (*Collected Works,* 10, p. 252).

In heeding the transcending irrationality of the psyche, which he did not hesitate to call "soul," Jung honored not only its depth and its autonomy, but also its wholeness, in at least three senses: its intrinsic healthiness; its compositeness, especially its embrace of competing and opposite elements; and its collective nature, transcending the experience of any individual. Jung saw psychology as far more than the study of pathology. Pursuing the broadest and deepest arenas of human experience, he was concerned with the *meaning* of spirit, of the numinous, of creativity, as well as the relationship between psyche and soma. Jung objected, as in his disputes with Freud, to the one-sided attention to the dark, disruptive, shadow aspects of the psyche without adequate recognition of the light, creative playfulness and self-healing capability of the psyche, just as he equally objected to the suppression and neglect of the alien and evil as an important element of human experience.

Philosophically, in dealing with a world of opposites, Jung may be described, in one respect, as a psychological Hegelian not unmindful of the push of instinctual "matter" but equally conscious of the pull of the spirit at the same time. The human spirit, for Jung, is the essential protagonist in the struggle for personal integration and self-fulfillment. Another way of stating his position would be that the concern of the psyche is not simply the release of imprisoned sexuality, nor even the omnipotence of scientific certainty, but the discovery of "soul," that is, the discovery of its authentic being.

What Jung had in mind for the "spirit" did not necessarily imply either a divine existence or a supernatural faith, but the well accepted concept of the human spirit, the aspirations expressed historically in works of the graphic arts, literature, science, politics, and even sports, in fact in every sphere of human endeavor.

This new appreciation of the reality and wholeness of the psyche, which in turn makes possible a new worldview of unity, can, however, only be achieved by one individual at a time. This process, was referred to by Jung as *individuation*. This is the development of the individual to maturity and fulfillment, and is marked by the progress of the ego in becoming increasingly aware of its origin out of the larger, archetypal psyche (the Self) and the nature of its relationship to that phenomenon.

2. **The Personal Unconscious and Complexes.** Jung's work grew out of his early experimental research into the nature of psychological complexes, "focal or nodal points of psychic life," as inferred from such common experiences as slips of the tongue and lapses of memory. This recognition that unconscious elements interfere with conscious intentions was first established through the word association test. What may seem to be a simple stimulus can constellate a set of reactions in the unconscious that will determine the attitudes, the emotions, the level of blood pressure (in fact, a whole range of psychosomatic responses), and thus ultimately, gross behavior. The polygraph is based on those early researches by Jung.

The complex is autonomous, it has a life of its own and is not under the control of the conscious part of the psyche, namely, the ego. "Certain complexes arise on account of painful or distressing experiences in a person's life . . . these produce unconscious complexes of a personal nature. . . . But there are others that come from quite a different source. . . . At bottom they are irrational contents of which the individual has never been conscious before" (*Collected Works*, 8, "The Structure and Dynamics of the Psyche").

Experience has shown that complexes are not infinitely variable, but rather belong to definite categories. Some of them have acquired popular, if not hackneyed, designations, for example, the inferiority complex, the anxiety complex, the power complex, the mother or father complex. Jolande Jacobi makes the distinction between "morbid" and "healthy" complexes which seem to be related to Jung's distinction between personal complexes and complexes of the collective unconscious (the objective psyche).

Complexes are rendered less painful and harmful by making them as conscious as possible so that they may interact cooperatively with the conscious ego, and become subject to choice, rather than function autonomously.

3. **The Collective Unconscious (Objective Psyche), Archetypes, and Myths.** Jung readily admitted to the extraordinary difficulty he encountered when he introduced the concept of the collective unconscious to the scholarly world. "The collective unconscious . . . is part of the psyche which can be negatively distinguished from a personal unconscious by the fact that it does not, like the latter, owe its existence to personal experience, and consequently is not a personal acquisition . . . the contents of the collective unconscious have never been in consciousness . . . but owe their existence exclusively to heredity. Whereas the personal unconscious consists for the most part of *complexes*, the content of the collective unconscious is made up essentially of *archetypes*" (*Collected Works*, 9, p. 42).

The understanding of the archetype is central to the concept of myth, symbol, the structure of the psyche, and its operation. One way of describing an archetype is a pattern of psychic energy, a system of readiness for action. It is at the same time an image, an emotion that is found universally in each human being, a pattern of energy shared by each individual, in every generation. How this pattern of energy expresses itself, that is, the form or shape it assumes, varies from place to place and from era to era. The core of the archetypal pattern, however, remains inviolate. Most frequently, people experience the archetypes as images in dreams, fantasies, fairytales, myths, and certain collective rituals.

For example, particular mythological images represent collectively meaningful values for a culture as long as they are in agreement with the psychological needs arising out of the unconscious (objective psyche) of the majority of persons in a particular historical period. Whenever a traditional mythic image loses its adequacy as a living symbol, it appears to be "dead." The Sumerian-Akkadian Tiamat, the Egyptian Isis, the Babylonian Ishtar, and the Greek Aphrodite no longer evoke awe even in those areas of the world where they once did.

In contrast however, today the image of Mary in Christian theology or the image of Devi in Hindu theology evokes awe and a religious attitude. From this view of events, it would not be unreasonable to conclude that contrary to what we have frequently heard since the time of Goethe, if not before, it is not that "God" has "died," but rather that a particular mythic image of the archetype has lost its potency. The myth-forming energy does not die, but continues to generate new images that represent valid meaning for the majority once again.

4. **The Masculine and the Feminine and the Principle of Opposites.** The terms *masculine* and *feminine* refer not to biological distinctions, or to persons of different gender, but to psychological characteristics, images, functions, and concepts. For example, the image of a sword with its capacity to cut, penetrate, separate, and divide has been considered masculine in its symbolic nature. The image of a stewing pot with its capacity to receive, contain, sit passively on the stove, and allow for the transformation of its contents has been considered feminine in its nature.

The presence of the *syzygy*, the conflict between the opposites, is universal. One of the more basic forms in which we experience this conflict, consciously as well as unconsciously, is in terms of the opposites of the masculine and the feminine. It stands as principal among the psychological problems facing us.

Initially, Jung drew a parallel to the concepts of Logos and Eros. "The concept of Eros could be expressed in modern terms as psychic relatedness and that of the Logos as objective interest" (*Collected Works*, 10, p. 123). But he came to prefer the parallel with the ancient Chinese concepts of the yin and yang as introduced to him by the Chinese classicist, Richard Wilhelm.

The yang principle, or the archetypal masculine, encompasses the generating or creative element; it is the initiating energy; it symbolizes driving energy, the moving aspects of strength, essentially from the center outward; it is aggressiveness and arousal. It represents the qualities of heat, light, and dryness as characterized by the sun. The yang represents heaven and spirit; it is manifest in discipline and separation, yet the positive and orderly, hence the individuation process.

On the other hand, the yin principle encompasses the receptive, the containing and enclosing; it represents yielding, withdrawing, the centripetal, ingoing direction of energy; it is form-giving and gestalting; it is the dark womb that gives birth to drives, instincts, and sexuality; it represents the cool and wet; it symbolizes the earth and moon, space and darkness; it is negative, undifferentiated, chaotic, and collective.

According to Wilhelm, the relationship between yin and yang is complementary. The receptive power of the yin is the perfect complement of the creative yang element. They do not meet in combat; they are not opposites, but serve to complete each other.

Individual men or women are not expected to be exclusively "masculine" or "feminine." Rather each person possesses both traits. The psychology of a man is determined by varying degrees of masculine factors and a recessive or background functioning of the feminine elements. Conversely, the psychology of a woman is formed by varying degrees of feminine qualities against the background expression of masculine elements.

The *anima* represents the archetype of the feminine principle or yin element in a man; the *animus* represents the archetype of the masculine principle or yang quality in a woman. The anima and the animus tend to function as separate and independent personalities. Just as each man and woman is different from other men and women, so each anima and animus is composed of a different prominent set of elements. In our struggle for individuation, we must discover and make conscious that "other" within; how it thinks, feels, tends to act, what it likes or dislikes. The contrasexual personality is much like a problematic partner and must be treated with attention, consideration, and also with discipline.

The effect of the anima or the animus on the ego is profound. It immediately fills almost the entire ego with its needs. When a man is seized by the anima, he exhibits compulsive moodiness, sentimentality, self-pity, withdrawal, depression, morbid sensitivity; in other words, he behaves as an inferior example of a woman. However, with a relatively conscious relationship to this inner feminine, the anima becomes an invaluable helpmate. It can provide a feeling capacity and allow for the expression of compassion and patience, make spontaneity possible, with a less routinized, rigidly determined exis-

tence. Perhaps most important, the anima assists in the process of judgment — valuation in the form of the feeling function is a critical aspect of decision making.

An animus-possessed woman is dominated by preconceived notions; opinions become more important than facts. She is argumentative, dogmatic, and continually overgeneralizes. She argues not to discover truth, but simply to be "right" she seeks to dominate, control, and to win. The unaware woman behaves as a partially, and therefore poorly, functioning example of a man. The animus in a woman corresponds to the paternal Logos in the same way that the anima in a man corresponds to the maternal Eros. As such, it may serve the woman well only if she develops the requisite consciousness of that inner masculine. Through the figure of the father, the animus expresses not only conventional wisdom and opinion, but also what we have referred to as the "spirit," that capacity for philosophical and religious thought, as well as those attitudes dependent upon it. When integrated, the animus functions as a mediator between the conscious and the unconscious, thus making available to her the ability to reflect, to deliberate, and the very basis for organized self-knowledge.

5. **The Persona** is the image one presents to society, the impression one makes upon others, while attempting to conceal one's 'true' nature. The persona is a complex of relationships between ego consciousness and society, along with its expectations. The more one identifies with this outer, idealized image, the more one falls under the influence of the contrasexual side of the psyche in the form of anima or animus.

The term *persona* derives its meaning from the mask worn by the actors of Greek antiquity to indicate the roles they played. Metaphorically and symbolically it turns out to be an excellent term. For in the course of analysis the mask is dissolved. The persona image is recognized as the mask for the elements operating in the collective unconscious.

6. **The Shadow** is the part of the personal unconscious concerned with traits, qualities, attitude contained in an image of the same sex, that cannot be accepted or even tolerated by the individual. The nature of the shadow is distinguished, therefore, from the functions of the anima or the animus, which represent collective aspects of the unconscious. Since everything in the unconscious is at one time or other projected, the shadow expresses itself in more or less intense emotional reaction to those same traits and behaviors in others, while denying its existence in itself. This mechanism makes working with the shadow the commonly and frequently used path to the transpersonal and collective side of the psyche.

7. **The Ego and the Self.** Jung distinguished between the ego and the Self, "inasmuch as the ego is only the centrum of my field of consciousness, it is not identical with the totality of my psyche, but merely a complex among other complexes. Hence, I discriminate between the ego and the Self, since the ego is only the subject of my consciousness, while the Self is the subject of my totality: hence it also includes the unconscious psyche. In this sense the Self would be an (ideal) factor which embraces and includes the ego," (*Collected Works* 6, p. 425).

8. **Dreams.** A special form of expression and communication by the unconscious psyche, dreams are regarded with special respect by Jung. He did not distinguish

between latent and manifest dream content as did Freud. The dream speaks clearly, though in its own language. Dreams neither censor nor distort content material. The dream reveals rather than hides meaning; that is, it points to something not yet known. Dreams speak in symbols and mythic motifs, the image-language of the objective psyche. The contents of dreams do not refer solely to pathology and destructive drives, but also to that which is healthy, normal, and creative, a reminder of how Jung respectfully regards psyche as a whole.

Bibliography. J. Jacobi, *Complex/Archetype/Symbol in the Psychology of C. G. Jung* (1959). C. G. Jung, *Collected Works,* trans. by R. F. C. Hull. *Memories, Dreams, Reflections* Bollingen Series 20 (1963). C. G. Jung, *Man and His Symbols* (1964). E. C. Whitmont, *The Symbolic Quest* (1969). R. Wilhelm and C. F. Baynes, *I Ching or Book of Changes* (1967).

I. R. STERNLICHT

PERSON; PERSONALITY THEORY. *See also* DREAMS (Theory and Research); MYTHOLOGY AND PSYCHOLOGY; PSYCHOLOGY OF RELIGION (Theories, Traditions, and Issues); SYMBOLISM/SYMBOLIZING; The UNCONSCIOUS. *Compare* BEHAVIORISM (Theories and Research); HUMANISTIC PSYCHOLOGY (Theories and Research); PHILOSOPHY AND PSYCHOLOGY; PSYCHOANALYSIS AND THEOLOGY; PSYCHOANALYSIS (Personality Theory and Research); PSYCHOLOGY, WESTERN; PSYCHOSYNTHESIS. *Biography:* JUNG.

ANALYTICAL (JUNGIAN) PSYCHOLOGY (Therapeutic Method and Research). Analytical Psychology does not prescribe any particular method of psychotherapy, unlike Freudian psychoanalysis which includes both a theory of personality and a prescribed method of treatment. This is because analytical psychology believes that the psyche is too complex and unknown to be restricted to any one method of treatment. This lack of a fixed methodology makes Jungian analysis flexible. Jungian therapists can and do work as marriage counselors, family therapists, and with groups, and Jungian principles can be adapted for work with children as well as with adults of all ages. Nevertheless, there is what might be called "classical" Jungian analysis and this article will concentrate on describing this process.

1. **The Classical Method.** The classical analytical situation occurs in one-to-one (individual) therapy, and has two somewhat differing approaches. At one end of the spectrum is an approach that is clinical and reductive, and more closely resembles the Freudian model. At the other end of the spectrum analysts work with their clients in a dialectic manner in which both therapist and patient are personally involved. In the first approach the medical model is more dominant, in the second approach the interaction may be conversational, although always relevant to the client's needs and situation. Within the two ends of this spectrum there are as many variations of method as there are individual analysts. But all would agree that Jungian analysis involves the analysis of unconscious contents, such as dreams and fantasies, where such material is available. A distinction is often made between therapy and analysis, the former consisting of work with the ego and the events of daily life, and the latter involving working through material from the unconscious. In actual practice, therapeutic intervention and analytical work may both be involved in a single psychotherapeutic session.

In spite of individual variations, analysts working in a classical style tend toward certain psychotherapeutic modalities. Many of these originated with Jung himself, for although Jung did not prescribe any definite way to do therapy he did work with people in his own distinctive way. Since most of the originators of Jungian psychology were analyzed by Jung it was natural that Jung's particular way of doing therapy should have influenced later analysts.

While Freud, for instance, had the patient reclining on a couch with the therapist behind him, Jung preferred to sit with his patients face-to-face. Jung felt this was important in order to emphasize the active role the client plays in the therapeutic process. He also wanted to confront, rather than avoid, the relationship that develops between therapist and client.

Originally, Freudian psychoanalysts were almost exclusively medical people, but Jungian analysts came from varied professional backgrounds. In medical parlance the person being treated is called the patient. Many Jungian therapists, however, prefer to call the people whom they see clients, counselees, or analysands.

2. **Particular Emphases: Dreams, Transference, and Creative Expression.** Jungian analysis attempts to make unconscious psychological processes accessible to consciousness, so that they can be understood and related to the events of conscious life wherever possible. The analysis of dreams is frequently utilized by Jungians for this purpose, and clients are usually encouraged to remember, record, and work with their dreams in a variety of ways. It is believed that as a person gains insight into and relates positively to the unconscious, natural healing tendencies are released; Jung, along with Carl Rogers and others, believed that healing lies within the individual (though Rogers did not take into account the unconscious).

In addition to the achievement of insight, Jungian therapy focuses on the process of "transference" which takes place in analysis between analyst and analysand. The transference includes all those factors that the client brings into the relationship with the therapist. These will include the client's hopes, expectations, and fears, and the feelings of warmth or antipathy that may arise between the two. There may also be unconscious factors involved. For instance, a client may repeat with the therapist a pattern of reaction that stems from an early relationship with a parent. Or there may be archetypal images projected onto the therapist, such as that of the Saviour. The analyst will also bring his or her psychological factors into the relationship, and a discussion of these factors, called the counter-transference, also may be involved in the therapy.

Jung regarded the relationship between therapist and client as extremely important and wrote about the transference extensively. He went so far as to indicate that the bottom line of success in therapy was the effect of the personality of the therapist on that of the client. It is hoped, of course, that the psychological consciousness and integration of the personality of the therapist will have a positive and beneficial effect on the personality of the client. Thus, there must be the right rapport between the two, and it is not unusual, when this does not exist, for a therapist to recommend that a client see another analyst.

Jungian therapy also frequently encourages the expression of the psyche and its creativity as an important part of therapy. Methods that lead to the creative expression of the psyche include dancing, painting, sculpting, music, creative writing, physical exercise, keeping a journal, and a special method for coming to terms with unconscious contents which Jung called "active imagination."

In the process of active imagination, the ego, fully awake and alert, discourses with, contemplates, or develops a story relating to images or symbols that have arisen spontaneously from the unconscious in dreams or fantasies. The intent of active imagination is to differentiate and reconcile the standpoints of consciousness and the unconscious. Gestalt psychology uses a somewhat similar method but is more extraverted and involves a group of people. Techniques such as "guided imagination" also have Jung's active imagination as their antecedent.

3. Goals and Process of Therapy. All methods of treatment have certain goals. In Jungian therapy there are, of course, the goals that the client brings into the therapy, for example, the alleviation of distressing symptoms, or the improvement of a relationship. The analyst naturally must take these goals into consideration, but in a general way the analyst has a broader goal in mind which is the individuation of the client. Individuation refers to the lifelong process that seeks to bring about a whole, integrated personality. The essence of this process is the establishment of a living relationship between the ego, as the center of the conscious personality, and the "Self," the center of the whole personality. Analysts believe that the analysis of dreams, the nature of the transference, and, in certain cases, the use of active imagination, greatly facilitate this process. Jungian therapy understands that as a person individuates a healing process is set in motion, and that the ultimate goal of analysis is to aid this process because this alone can lead to well-being. It is this emphasis that makes Jungian analysis synthetic and teleological in its emphasis, as distinguished from Freudian therapy which is more causal and reductive.

People often ask how long Jungian analysis takes. Analysts report that clients may see them for a few weeks or for several years. Because Jungian analysis may lead a person into his or her process of individuation, analytical work often educates and equips people to continue to pay close attention to unconscious material even though formal analytical work has come to an end.

4. Training in Jungian Therapy. Jungian analysts are trained at various training institutes in major cities throughout the world. Requirements for admission to a training program vary from one institute to another but always include: (1) Considerable prior personal analysis with a Jungian analyst; (2) Prior professional qualification in the field of psychotherapy. Training programs vary in their content but generally include instruction in the concepts of Jungian psychology through seminars and lectures, supervision of counseling by experienced analysts, continuing personal analysis, and a control case. The programs may take four to six years of part-time work and culminate in an examination by a certifying board composed of analysts from more than one training institute.

5. Relevance to Pastoral Counseling. Jungian methods should be readily adaptable by pastoral counselors. While certain Jungian concepts may prove problematic

from the standpoint of Christian theology, such as Jung's treatment of the problem of evil, many Jungian methods of therapy should prove useful. Examples of active imagination occur in the Bible (the Temptations in the wilderness, and Elijah's talk with God on Mt. Sinai). Dreams, so valued in Jungian analysis, are often cited by Scripture as ways in which God speaks to us. The idea that there is a process of individuation aiming at wholeness should fit naturally into the conceptual framework that underlies the pastor's approach to counseling.

Jung's typology has been particularly useful to therapists of many different persuasions, and has also been used extensively in research by people employing the Myers-Briggs Type Indicator, or some similar test for determining personality typology along Jungian lines. Research by Jungian analysts and scholars also goes on extensively wherever the archetypal structure of the psyche is revealed in fairy tales, anthropological findings, religious lore, alchemy, and any other area in which the human psyche spontaneously represents itself.

Bibliography. M. Fordham, *Jungian Psychotherapy* (1978). J. Hall, *Jungian Dream Interpretation: A Handbook of Theory and Practice* (1983). B. Hannah, *Jung: His Life and Work.* C. G. Jung, *The Collected Works of C. G. Jung,* 20 vols. (1953–79), esp. vol. 16, *The Practice of Psychotherapy; Memories, Dreams, Reflections* (1961). J. A. Sanford, *The Invisible Partners* (1980). M. Stein, ed., *Jungian Analysis* (1982). M. L. von Franz, *The Interpretation of Fairy Tales* (1973). E. C. Whitmont, *The Symbolic Quest* (1969).

J. A. SANFORD

PSYCHOTHERAPY: PSYCHOTHERAPY AND COUNSELING (Research Studies and Methods). *See also* DREAM INTERPRETATION; GUIDED IMAGERY TECHNIQUE; RELIGION AND PSYCHOTHERAPY; TRANSFERENCE; The UNCONSCIOUS. *Compare* PSYCHOANALYSIS (Therapeutic Method and Research); *also* HUMANISTIC PSYCHOTHERAPIES; BEHAVIOR THERAPIES. *Biography:* JUNG.

ANALYTICAL (JUNGIAN) PSYCHOLOGY AND PASTORAL CARE.

"Healing may be called a religious problem," Jung wrote (*Collected Works,* 11, par. 523). His views of the nature of human experience and of the goals and methods of psychotherapy readily convey a tacit religious quality and resemble many aspects of pastoral care. His most fundamental and passionately held affirmations resonate with affirmations generally held by practitioners of pastoral care.

These include (1) his abiding belief that life is deeply rooted in transpersonal power and is given benign and energetic direction by that power; (2) his persistent commitment to the transformation of the alien; (3) his honoring of the mysterious; (4) his robust pursuit of wholeness (i.e., health and holiness); and, above all, (5) his sense that such wholeness is not achieved by manipulating behavior or circumstances — not by "doing" anything — but rather is received as a gift, a consequence of an enlarged and appreciative attitude — a "faith" perhaps — toward the richness of life, a deliberate orientation of self, an active, intentional, and hearty relationship with life, a delight in all of life as a gracious gift.

Healing (according to Jung) is by aligning oneself, in zestful consciousness, with what is, not by changing reality or by selectively designating some of reality as good and some as bad, to be shunned. Saving is by a kind of conversion, a reorientation of one's outlook, to a trust in the grounding of life (though mysterious), and a trust that behavior that follows from this reorientation of self (though unpredictable), will be fitting. Jung reportedly suggested that religion is the courage to look inside and be faithful.

Jung's understanding of healthy human experience and of healing processes, then, seems to engage a pastoral care perspective that emphasizes, not behavioral adjustment and control, not "works," but postures of faith in response to grace. He believed that his views reflected and developed the fundamental perspectives of Christian (and other) traditions, and he passionately wanted to purge existing theological and ecclesiastical formulations from literalisms and accretions which he regarded as spiritually debilitating distortions.

Jung practiced without explicit theological doctrine, remained metaphysically agnostic—the transcending power is transpersonal, not necessarily transpsychic— and persistently criticized the many confining structures and strictures he found in prevailing religious practices and formulations, especially as he experienced these in his minister-father and in the Swiss Protestant church.

So, too ready an identification of his views with those of pastors is inappropriate. Although he did express the often quoted opinion that the problem of his patients, without exception among those over thirty-five, was "that of finding a religious outlook on life . . . none of them has been really healed who did not regain this religious outlook," he immediately followed this remark with the warning: "This of course has nothing to do with a particular. . . . church" (*Collected Works,* vol. 11, par. 509).

This article will attempt to identify several of the fundamental perspectives with which Jung would want to illuminate and clarify pastoral care.

1. Fundamental Principles. Jung's wisdom for the pastor and the pastor's people may be best summarized in two principles: *a. Fullness of life.* The surprises, annoyances, mysteries, stresses, conflicts, paradoxes, and irrationalities of life, which are often regarded as evil or alien and which are shunned or subdued in a shortsighted attempt to make life more "perfect," are in fact authentic, valid, meaningful, and constructive parts of the endowment of life, to be consciously welcomed and deliberately befriended. Wholeness is the goal, not perfection, which constricts and limits. Dreams, puzzling coincidences, competing tendencies within the same person, fits of rage, "neurotic" fears—these are some of the intrusive irrationalities which Jung learned to be curious about, not fearful of. There is a largeness to life, an "always more"-ness, reminiscent of William James's zestfully embraced "pluralistic universe." The contours of any particular experience or episode of life should not close off and define as alien other experiences or perspectives, but, rather, require and invite complementarity and completion from just those dimensions of life which are mysterious and "alien" to the present experience.

This celebration of the richness of life appears to be Jung's equivalent to a doctrine of grace. It resembles Augustine's emphasis on the redemptive power resident in creation and his subordination of the question of "evil" to the question of "being."

b. Autonomous reality of "soul." Inner life and experience—especially the life of imagination and symbol, and especially unconscious patterns and energies—for which Jung was not unwilling to use the name of "soul," commonly regarded as "subjective," unreliable, and derived, are, in fact, highly "objective," trustworthy, reliably discerned and reliably heeded, autonomous, and authoritative. Unconscious processes are a self-generating resource, not a repository of trauma, as Freud would have it. Imagery, "symptoms," dreams, intuitions, irrationality, baffling surprises—these things are transcendent and autonomous, not somehow a product of the person having the experience, not derived from and reducible to other events. This is the principal significance of the concept known popularly as the "collective unconscious" (perhaps better called an "objective, transpersonal unconscious"), the insistence on the priority and autonomy of fundamental archetypal patterns of psychological life, shapers of, not products of, the historical events of individual and cultural experience.

According to this view of Jung, we do not enter life empty of personality or psychological patterns and resources, just as we do not enter it with unformed bodies waiting to be shaped by experience. Instead, each member of the human species is the inheritor of an inventory of behavior patterns, archetypal "personalities" as rich and as beneficial as the chemical and anatomical marvels that are part of the evolved human biological heritage or the instinctual patterns with which birds, insects, and other species are endowed, forged by eons of evolution into powerful and useful strategies of life. These behavioral patterns take shape in our experience in the imagery of dream and legend, and also as our own behavior comes to act out or as we project onto others patterns, like the little boy, the queen of heaven, the trickster, the ice queen, the shadow, *et al.*

Adaptive and benign as these patterns are in principle, the result of evolutionary gain, they can, like generally benign biological processes, run amok when left unattended and unbalanced by other processes. A person who becomes, for the moment, possessed by the archetype, is not himself or herself. The remedy is in the conscious recognition, much aided by personifying, that it is the archetype who is in control ("That is just the kind of thing the trickster does"), and having objectified this agent, choosing whether this is a role the Self wishes to play at this time, and if so, to bring it under the conscious control of the Self.

c. Therapeutic implications. It is especially in the kind of events that occasion pastoral care—in the passions and addictions that people pursue; in the stress they create and sustain in relations with family, employers, pastors, fellow church members; in anxieties and forebodings; in intense ambivalence and internal conflict—that we can see forces that are to be regarded not as pathological or peculiar, but as ancient scripts—habits of the soul, as it were—universal and valuable, parts of the human experience, though perhaps temporarily misplaced or unbalanced.

The pastoral response is to enable persons to see *through* the events and crises, to be aware of the particular psychological energies at play, to be aware of them as distinctly separate from the Self, yet to welcome them as fundamental and appropriate parts of the human heritage (not peculiarly personal afflictions), to be aware of them as only part, though perhaps a temporarily dominant part, of human experience, not as consuming masters or monsters.

The Jungian strategy of therapy and pastoral care can perhaps be summarized as a twin rhythm of *relativizing* and *relating*. The patterns of behavior, moods, roles, "symptoms," "personalities," "neuroses" that one finds oneself pursuing are not absolute requirements, are not to be identified with the Self. They are objectively distinguishable from the Self, can be held at arm's length, are only a small portion of one's potential experience. Objectifying these, relativizing these — in Jung's tactic of choice, by personifying them — encountering them consciously as distinct and autonomous phenomena, one can avoid becoming unconsciously and passively possessed by these psychological energies. Instead one can consciously choose whether and how to integrate them deliberately. With the freedom of this choice, one embraces, befriends zestfully what one wills. One relativizes them so as to be able to relate to them. One relates to them consciously so as to be able to relativize them.

These principles can be summarized in Jung's own words. He wrote of his mid-crisis discovery: "The essential thing is to differentiate oneself from these unconscious contents by personifying them, and at the same time to bring them into relationship with consciousness. That is the technique for stripping them of their [disruptive, fragmenting] power. It is not too difficult to personify them as they always possess a certain degree of autonomy, a separate identity of their own" (Jung, 1961, p. 187). Conscious life, the sense of Self, is not to be shrunk (as, e.g., seems to be Freud's strategy) to avoid or defend against irrational and disconcerting eruptions, but to be expanded to encounter them. But the encounter presupposes them as distinct and finite entities. The conscious Self, enhanced and strong, declines to accord them the idolatrous power and priority they can be accorded unconsciously.

These strategies find expression in the principles of "consciousness-raising" and "choice as empowerment" advocated among contemporary minority or feminist or other groups experiencing oppression. They regard it as essential to their "liberation"—in a way that Jung would endorse — to identify the external agencies dominating their experience and to exercise deliberate choice about their relationship with those agencies.

d. *Contrast with Freudian outlook.* Both Freudian and Jungian therapies proceed by *analysis,* that is, the discovery "within" or behind pathologies and other intense or distressing emotional experiences and roots in phenomena which are not obviously connected with the conscious problematic experience. But there are at least three fundamentally important differences:

(1) Freud's analysis finds the sources in (traumatic and, in principle, avoidable) events in the individual's personal history — consequences of a "fall." Jung's analysis finds them in the structures of human nature, held in common with other humans in quite different historical and cultural contexts — part of creation.

(2) Freud identifies the sources as distortions to be neutralized; making them conscious is for the purpose of controlling and countering them. Unconscious forces are to be guarded against. Jung identifies the sources as creative resources to be welcomed and used; making them conscious is for the purpose of integrating them into one's psychic domain. Unconscious forces are to be freely and deliberately befriended.

(3) Freud generally dismisses the face value of the conscious experience, the apparent fears, angers, etc. They are not reliable guides to the true meaning of the event, but are misleading. The root experience and *its* emotional consequences are the psychological reality; the immediate experience is distorted by, as well as derived from root experience. Jung credits the face value of the immediate experience as having its own validity. The archetypal energies may be autonomous and driving, but the forms they take in conscious experience are valid in their own disclosures.

In consequence of these differences, the Jungian pastoral caregiver has good grounds for regarding a distressed counselee with esteem, acceptance, and hope. The distress that occasions the pastoral care may be regarded not primarily as pathology or defect — enhancing the despair and low self-regard the client already feels as well as enhancing a status difference between the client and a caregiver perceived as the steward of health whose knowledgeable expertise is required to rescue the distressed. Instead, the presenting distress is regarded, like any other life experience, as a gift to be carefully received; whatever mystery surrounds it and whatever meaning it contains, as in any life experience, will be best explored by resources available to the counselee in the experience itself, not by resources in the possession of the caregiver.

2. **An Example of Jung as a Pastoral Caregiver.** Olga Fröbe-Kapteyn was a lay student of Jung's who, as a volunteer, assisted in organizing an annual Jungian conference, Eranos. When Jung became aware of the distress she felt as a conflict between her responsibilities as a mother and the appeal of her semi-professional responsibilities, he wrote to her, by hand, the following letter on August 20, 1945 (C. G. Jung *Letters,* vol. 1, p. 375):

Dear Frau Fröbe . . . . . Your present situation is the result of pressure of circumstances which are unavoidable. It is *conflicts of duty* that make endurance and action so difficult. Your life's work for Eranos was unavoidable and right. Nevertheless it conflicts with maternal duties which are equally unavoidable and right. The one must exist, and so must the other. There can be no resolution, only patient endurance of the opposites which ultimately spring from your own nature. You yourself are a conflict that rages in itself and against itself, in order to melt its incompatible substances, the male and the female, in the fire of suffering, and thus create that fixed and unalterable form which is the goal of life. Everyone goes through this mill, consciously or unconsciously, voluntarily or forcibly. We are crucified between the opposites and delivered up to the torture until the "reconciling third" takes shape. Do not doubt the rightness of the two sides within you, and let whatever may happen, happen. Admit that your daughter is right in saying you are a bad mother, and defend your duty as a mother towards Eranos. But never forget that Eranos is also the right thing and was latent within you from the beginning. The apparently unendurable conflict is proof of the rightness of your life. A life without inner contradiction is either only half a life or else a life in the Beyond, which is destined only for angels. But God loves human beings more than the angels. With kindest regards, Yours sincerely, C. G. Jung. [Reprinted by permission of Princeton University Press.]

In Jung's view, Frau Fröbe's internal conflict is not abnormal, avoidable, or resolvable, not the result of fault or flaw to be remedied, but is itself confirming and constitutive of the "rightness" of her life. There is not an "evil" in this situation to be subdued, but the energies of life in its wholeness to be embraced. Further, the energies at play in her experience are not distinctively or privately hers but are part of the endowment she shares with the human race. Especially, the balance of opposites is, for Jung, a fundamental structure of human nature. The pastoral care consists in helping Frau Fröbe to admit these processes to consciousness and to choose to make them her own, part of her Self (or else consciously to reject them) rather than to let herself be disturbed and possessed by them.

3. A Jungian Vision of Ministry: Hermeneutic of the Alien. From earliest cultures it has been the office of the priest, the holy person, the minister of religion to guide transactions with the alien and mysterious, with all that invades from precincts beyond everyday "normalcy," with that which is alienated and alienating, erupting and disrupting, with the powers—whether regarded as spiritual or demonic, sickness or sin—which leave ordinary contours of life broken and distorted. The minister is expected to lead in dealing with what is deemed "troublesome" or "awesome"—especially as these two blend with the disconcerting intrusions from beyond one's ken and control, from what is experienced as the "other world." The common inventory of personal distress—alcoholism, death, divorce, *et al.*—which typically comes to the minister's attention in calls for pastoral care, is appropriate and central to this priestly office of the minister, intransigent remnants of a once larger domain of the alien and mysterious, much of which has now been ceded to the secular authorities in law, medicine, politics, nuclear physics, etc. So, too, are the oppressions, injustices, and inequities that clamor for the minister's attention as calls to "prophetic" ministry, and which are similarly a proper function of the traditional priesthood.

The response to the alien and mysterious which Jung recommends resembles perhaps more that of a high priesthood, that of a mystic or a shaman, than that of a magician or a medicine man. Jung recommends a response which is not fearful but is open, trusting, expectant, curious, naive, and childlike. Not a response to manage or subdue or conquer the alien, but a response that is a hermeneutic of the alien, a strategy to discern its meaning and message, a message expected, in some fundamental sense, to be "good news." The "priestly" response to "pastoral" (and "prophetic") problems is a strategy of making—or perhaps better, *acknowledging*—contact with the alien and transcendent, an immediate,

intimate contact and mutual embrace. The priest enlarges our ken to include the alien, to discover our oneness with the oneness of life.

The common response to pastoral problems today, however, is governed by medical and management models: remedy, repair, correct; subdue the mystery, rebuff the alien, restore life to "normalcy." (Freud is part of this medical tradition.) The pastor is problem-solver, trouble-shooter, and coach. The pastor exercises power and authority to exorcise and subdue the alien. The time reference is largely toward the past: restore a previous equilibrium; find the problem-making defect in the past; undo the past sin.

In contrast to such a managing of distress—making matters well again—is the attitude illustrated by the personal episode recounted about Jung by his secretary Aniela Jaffé (Jaffé, p. 197). When he could not find a file folder of material he wanted to show a visitor, instead of calling the secretary for help, Jung intentionally got along without it, precisely because he was actively curious, and expectant, about what life had in store in providing the absence of the folder. He joyfully trusted life's promise to expand experience beyond his own initial agenda. Jung's time reference is toward the future, which he expects to be more whole, completing and compensating for the present, embracing what now appears to be alien or mysterious or a "problem." Events take their meaning and shape from this future, not from norms or determinants of the past. Becoming consciously aware of what *is* is more important than trying to make matters as they "should be," a judgment always based on too partial and past-oriented norms. One aspires to wholeness, not perfection, which always excludes something crucially valid.

4. Suggestions for Pastoral Care. Just as the healthy and mature life, in Jungian perspective, consists not so much in methods and tactics, like a Freudian ego, as in certain settled perspectives about life (which this article has attempted to convey), so neither does Jungian therapy consist so much in techniques and methods as in outlook. The pastoral caregiver cannot and need not aspire to any expert techniques of an experienced Jungian clinician, nor to the Jungian's intimacy with the wide range of symbols and archetypal figures that abound in human legend and dreams. But some illustrations can be given here of how Jungian perspectives might influence a pastoral caregiver.

For situations of remorse and regret, the attitude may be: You did what you seemed to need to do at that time. Own it. But now the question is, what happens next, coming out of that episode? Perhaps this is not unlike Jesus' attitude towards the woman taken in adultery (Jn. 7:53–8:11).

For other situations of stress or "pathology" in which persons seem to be "not themselves," the attitude may be something like this: This experience *is* your life at this moment; it needs to be lived into and through. There is more to life than this moment; compensation, corrective balance, completion will come, peace in place of guilt, direction and self-control in place of aimlessness, concern for other in place of selfishness, generosity of spirit in place of narrowness, love in place of scorn. But this newness will come most likely in unscheduled, unexpected, unscripted ways and times. The new will come and be received more clearly the more clearly and earnestly, the more self-consciously one lives into (and hence through) the present experiences. The way to welcome what is to come is to welcome what is. A Christian pastor may find this attitude an expression of the Lent/Easter and Advent/Christmas themes of patient, trusting expectancy.

The pastor may be especially receptive to reports of "unusual" experiences, especially those that seem irrational and irrelevant, all the distracting interruptions to routines and efficiencies, in conversations, in church life, in anyone's life. This may include "coincidences" and surprises, dreams and other moments of imagination, distracting trivia or stories in a committee meeting, scenes or figures from TV shows or films that a parishioner or counselee finds engaging. Such experiences need not be analyzed or made relevant, but simply attended to, admitted into presence, harbingers of messages and resolutions that will appear clear in their own time. This is perhaps something like Jesus' preference for letting parables speak for themselves. The pastor may also be content, in counseling or in preaching, to tell stories which seem to be inherently compelling—wanting to be told—without feeling the need to explain them, draw morals, or even necessarily understanding the story or knowing why it seems to demand a telling.

Sensing that current intense struggles, in a troubled marriage, for example, are, in part, acting out internal and unconscious struggles, the pastor will avoid becoming also captured by this complex and may encourage backing off from preoccupation with the details of the marital troubles in favor of reflection about unconscious relationships each partner has with their own psychic figures. A man may need to be more alert to encounters with female figures in dreams and fantasy than to be examining endlessly the disputes with his wife, or he may need to be encountering his own shadow rather than finding fault with his boss.

The pastor need not suffer unfair criticism personally or defensively, but can be ready, gently, not aggressively, to hear overtones of parishioners' unconscious struggles with parts of themselves.

As a special kind of expectancy, the pastor may be alert to corrective balance which is available to a one-sidedness and narrowness of life. It is just when a person seems a most entrenched fundamentalist or most achievement-oriented and controlling, that compensating religious or romantic sentiments may become insistent. Shunned, they may take possession in radical and destructive ways — in religious cultism or in shabby affairs. The pastor, encountering such one-sided people in conversation, in sermons, for example, may help them to be aware, e.g., in dreams or daydreams, of these budding, novel, perhaps awesome energies, and in the awareness better to assimilate them.

Bibliography. A. Jaffé, *The Life and Work of C. G. Jung* (1971). C. G. Jung, *Collected Works*, vol. 11 (1969); *Memories, Dreams, Reflections* (1961). G. Adler, ed., *C. G. Jung: Letters* (1973).

J. E. DITTES

PASTORAL CARE (History, Traditions, and Definitions); PASTORAL COUNSELING; PASTORAL PSYCHOTHERAPY. *See also* ACTION/BEING RELATIONSHIP; DREAM INTERPRETATION IN PASTORAL COUNSELING; INTERPRETATION AND HERMENEUTICS, PASTORAL; MODELS IN PSYCHOLOGICAL AND PASTORAL THEORY; RELIGION AND PSYCHOTHERAPY; SYMBOLIC DIMENSIONS OF PASTORAL CARE RELATIONSHIPS. *Compare* BEHAVIOR MODIFICATION AND PASTORAL COUNSELING; HUMANISTIC PSYCHOLOGY *or* PSYCHOANALYSIS AND PASTORAL CARE; *also* FEELING, THOUGHT, AND ACTION IN PASTORAL COUNSELING.

ANALYTICAL (JUNGIAN) PSYCHOLOGY AND RELIGION.

C. G. Jung's views on religion, which dominated his writing during the last twenty years of his life, were natural and inevitable extensions of his psychological observations and formulations. Though he insisted that he limited himself to psychology and eschewed theology with a sometimes professed agnosticism, his extended sense of psychic realities and his passionate concern for life to be fundamentally rooted and well directed propelled him into addressing concerns that are generally thought of as religious. His views, then, tended to be more normative than analytical or descriptive and suggest a passionate ambivalence here characterized as that of a prophet or reformer wanting to rescue the best of his tradition from the worst of his tradition. Although he touched, with much appreciation and curiosity, on other religions, he concentrated his attention on Christianity, about which he apparently felt a fervent ambivalence, beginning with his childhood in the manse of a highly conventional Swiss Reformed pastor.

This article will first characterize this "prophetic" posture, then summarize Jung's more constructive affirmations of the inherently religious nature of human experience, then review his critical appraisal of some prevailing religious practices and concepts.

1. **Jung as Reformer of Religion.** *a. Prophet.* Jung's views of religion are perhaps best understood as those of a prophet or reformer, intent on identifying and salvaging what he regarded as authentic and essential (though often only implicitly present) in the Christian tradition, and equally intense in his call for that tradition to grow beyond a one-sidedness in which it is stuck (especially in its insistence on a highly transcendent God) and beyond paralyzing literalisms, rationalisms, and perfectionisms that dangerously remove religion from its origins and mission in experience. Jung saw himself calling his culture back from the brink of a self-destruction induced by religious impulses gone awry and into a new age of a vital and mature religion that would evolve from a transformed Christianity.

This "prophetic" outlook—finding tremendous religious power implicit but abandoned and unrecognized in extant Christianity — emerged, Jung was to report at the end of his life (*Memories, Dreams, Reflections*), in his earliest days, when powerful religious experiences in visions and dreams, sometimes "gracious," often dark and foreboding, seemed to him vital, valid, self-authenticating, and starkly contrasted with the pallid, routinized, intellectualized, unprobing, formulaic "faith" espoused by his Swiss pastor father, who retreated from the intense experiences and doubts the boy found so energizing and "gracious." Jung's experience with his mother was similarly teasing; she seemed to him to possess a mystical and spiritually vital "personality #2" for which he yearned to have access but which he found locked away, inaccessible, inside a conventional *hausfrau* "personality #1."

This "prophetic" posture is a characteristic which Jung shares with many of the well-known psychologists and sociologists of religion of this century, who have consistently organized their analyses around the difference between what they regarded as a more authentic, psychologically intense, fundamental or primary expression of religion and those forms which are more derived, secondary, institutionalized and rationalized. One thinks, for example, of Allport's "intrinsic" and "extrinsic," James's sick soul and twice-born versus healthy minded and once-born, the church-sect typology of Troeltsch, Weber, and most other sociologists, and of course the more explicitly self-defined reformist message of popular contemporary sociologists Bellah and Berger. Even Freud's persistent fascination with religion seems to be provoked by what he perceived as the mixture of more mature and healthy high religious elements, in which he found Judaism and Christianity sourced, with the more neurotic and infantile elements he found dominant. (This contrast was symbolized for him in the story of the two Moseses, which he portrayed in his final book, *Moses and Monotheism*.)

b. Therapist. The same understanding of Jung's transformist approach to religion is made by Murray Stein (1985) who persuasively characterizes Jung's relationship to Christianity as that of a therapist, determined to heal this sick patient, indeed, to save its life, by recalling it to its proper identity. ·

c. Knight. One might also cast Jung's religious concerns as those of a knight, symbolized by a dream he had in 1938, on the eve of World War II. This dream seems to have precipitated his concentration on religion for the rest of his life. It was a dream in which he felt singularly commissioned to retrieve the Holy Grail, a search he begins in the dream by plunging into icy water (Jung, 1961, pp. 280–83).

Whether as prophet, therapist, knight, or in some other way, it is important to understand Jung's approach to religion as reflecting a profound and intense ambivalence and as expressing a fervent commitment to amelioration. He *wants* Christianity, as he must have wanted his father and mother, to become transformed, liberated, renewing its vitality in restored connection with the roots from which it arose. But to do this, it is necessary for Jung to call attention to the deadly distortions and alienations he finds extant. He finds powerful potentials in the Christian tradition for what James Hillman has called "soul-making" but also finds impossibly deadly distortions of that spiritual vitality.

2. Human Experience Inherently Religious. Jung apparently conceived of the human mind, especially the unconscious, as inherently and actively religious in at least five senses.

a. "Gifts of grace." Psychological energies are available which, if recognized and permitted, inevitably move a person, and a culture, toward wholeness. At any stage of development a person can be thought of as having reached an approximation that is partial and one-sided and for which the unconscious generates a balancing compensation. In identifying wholeness as the goal,

in contrast to "perfection,"—a goal that represents a foreshortening, an illusion, and a limitation, analogous with idolatry—and in virtually guaranteeing movement toward wholeness, if the individual "accepts" it, Jung appears to be taking a stand on an issue often debated in terms of "gospel/law" or "justification/sanctification." The phrase "gifts of grace" is his own (e.g., *Collected Works*, vol. 11, par. 501).

b. Experience of God. Psychological energies, especially those of the archetypes, generate, inevitably and actively, the human experience of God or gods (including figures such as Christs, saints, and Devil) and also generate the human capacity to relate to these figures in faith. In the often quoted interview remark "I do not need to believe in God; I *know*," (Bennet, 1966, p. 167), Jung is emphasizing this intimate psychological connection (though not necessarily endorsing the "God" of his interviewer or of many who quote the remark). It is misleading, even dangerous to ignore or deny God(s), for they will insist on their sway, often in darker fashion (as in Nazism) than if allowed consciousness. (Jung carved in stone over his doorway: "Called or not, the god will be present.") It is equally misleading and dangerous to absolutize or literalize God, as by projecting into a transcendent existence, removed from the psychic sources, or by regarding a God as final or complete, or by regarding the God, which actually is the product of psychic revelation, as the source of revelation.

c. Transcendence. These resources (which generate wholeness and gods) are transcendent to the individual (though not trans-psychological) and represent a kind of ultimate reality in which the individual is grounded. Psychological energies do have their own underived, irreducible reality and power, transcending any particular historical or symbolic representation. It is perilous to lose touch with these resources, which are simultaneously "inner" and "beyond," and to claim an autonomy, which easily becomes demonic—for example, by taking science or Marxism or theology at face value as rationalities without recognizing the powers they possess out of their origins in the unconscious.

d. Reality of symbols. These psychological energies are best encountered and acknowledged in symbols, rituals, myths—the "stuff" of religion—and also profoundly obstacled by pat doctrines, and other literalisms, with which religion is replete.

e. Appropriating revelation. As fundamental as are the unconscious sources of religious experience and the symbolic language with which they are best expressed, and as perilous as is conceptual elaboration, such as theologizing—so fraught with the abuse of taking its words too seriously and literally and losing touch with its psychic roots—it is still appropriate and necessary for the conscious mind to assimilate in its own language the disclosures of the unconscious. In "theologizing" as in any other encounter with unconscious psychological energies, it is necessary both to *relativize* them, as by personifying them and recognizing them as only part of the energies available, and, with the energies thus de-tyrannized, to *relate* to them, to own them, to make them conscious, integrated by and into the understanding of the Self.

Jung's appraisal of any aspect of religion, then, expresses his judgment as to how well it has expressed these five psychological/religious principles. In general, he finds existing religions, especially the Christianity to which he devotes his attention, to have the potential to express supremely well these religious qualities of human experience, but also to suppress them. It is especially the third and fourth principles, the need to remain in close touch with psychological sources, and to do so through imagery, that are violated.

3. **Critical Analyses.** *a. Ritual.* Jung wrote at length on his understanding of "Transformation Symbolism in the Mass" (*Collected Works,* vol. 11), the title emphasizing his insistence that the importance of ritual is in the immediate symbolic experience of the participant; preoccupation with a remote historical event is a distorting literalism. The Mass enables the participant to be in touch with and to play out significant transforming archetypal events; the ego and the unconscious (symbolized by Christ and the Father) surrender their separate autonomies (by crucifixion and by incarnation, respectively) and become integrated, or "individuated" into a new resurrected whole. Participating Catholics benefit, Jung believed, from this process and other symbolisms retained by the church, even when they do not share Jung's understanding of its importance — analogous to the therapeutic benefits of rehearsing dreams, even when they are left uninterpreted. But they are handicapped in this benefit by the church's emphasis on the historicity of the events and by doctrines of merits acquired remotely and vicariously — analogous with literal reductions of dream symbols. Such interpretations distract from the real contemporary power in the event by assuaging the pain necessary to each participant.

Similarly, Jung believed, the confessional could provide therapeutic/religious benefit — an effective alternative to formal analysis — because it provides occasion for self-reflection in mythical and symbolic language. However, as always, in practice there is the serious risk of reciting formulas, without awareness of their connection with deeper psychological energies, and also the risk that easy absolution will deprive persons of the pain necessary to seek and experience the healing realities to be discerned in one's own story. Thus, while generally deploring Protestantism's surrender to "rationalistic historicism," Jung was capable of writing that "the Protestant has a unique chance to make himself conscious of sin . . ." (*Collected Works,* vol. 11. par. 86), probably wanting to underline "chance."

b. Evil. Evil is a decided reality that must either be consciously integrated into experience and the sense of Self—illustrated by the excruciatingly painful several days it took the young Jung to acknowledge his vision of God defecating on the cathedral (1961, pp. 36–40) — or, denied such conscious integration, suffered to hold destructive sway. It is a dangerous defect in Christianity that it ignores evil (as in Augustine's *privatio bono* doctrine) or claims to triumph over it (as in the symbol of the Crucifixion), and a defect in Christian symbols of God and Christ (see below) that they remain adversaries of evil rather than provide symbols, necessary to human healing, that integrate evil.

c. God, Trinity. Important as is the integrative power of God, the Christian symbol remains incomplete, in ways that Jung discussed in various ways. Because Jung found four-someness a more completing symbol than three — a square holds two pairs of opposites together—it seemed necessary for the Christian idea of a trinitarian God to evolve further into a quaternity. His two principal candidates for the fourth member of Godhead were (1) evil, and (2) femininity. He also thought God needed to include humanity, and his *Answer to Job* recounts how God's encounter with a moral integrity in Job superior to his own provoked God's recognition of this need and hence the Incarnation. Jung also identified the mandala, because of what he found to be its powerfully whole-ing images of center and completeness, with God. Jungian thinking also allows for the partialness of any god symbol to be compensated for in a pluralism of gods.

d. Christ. Along with the Buddha, Jung found Christ a supremely powerful symbol of human Selfhood, a symbol into which Jesus fit well, but one still incomplete, like God, for the lack of femininity, for a triumph over evil rather than integration with it, and for a spiritualizing emphasis that precluded full embodiment and sexuality.

Bibliography. E. A. Bennet, *What Jung Really Said* (1966). J. P. Dourley, *The Illness That We Are: A Jungian Critique of Christianity* (1984). C. G. Jung, *Collected Works* (vol. 11, 1958) arrays most of Jung's writings on religion, including two short books, *Answer to Job,* and *Psychology and Religion.* "Introduction to the Religious and Psychological Problems of Alchemy," in *Collected Works* (vol. 12, 1968), pp. 1–37. *Memories, Dreams, Reflections* (1961) contains posthumously published autobiographical reflections. "Aion: Researches into the Phenomenology of the Self," in *Collected Works* (vol. 11, 1958). "Mysterium coniuncitionis," in *Collected Works* (vol. 14, 1970). M. Stein, *Jung's Treatment of Christianity; The Psychology of a Religious Tradition* (1985).

J. E. DITTES

PSYCHOLOGY OF RELIGION. *See also* MYTHOLOGY AND PSYCHOLOGY; PHILOSOPHY AND PSYCHOLOGY; PSYCHOLOGY IN AMERICAN RELIGION; PSYCHIATRY AND PASTORAL CARE; RELIGION AND PSYCHOTHERAPY; SYMBOLISM/ SYMBOLIZING. *Compare* ANALYTICAL (JUNGIAN) PSYCHOLOGY AND THEOLOGY; HUMANISTIC PSYCHOLOGY *or* PSYCHOANALYSIS AND RELIGION; THEOLOGY AND PSYCHOLOGY.

ANALYTICAL (JUNGIAN) PSYCHOLOGY AND THEOLOGY. This essay focuses on critical theological issues raised by analytical or Jungian psychology. It is no secret that Jung's attention to the transformative function of religious symbols in the integration of the psyche was one of the factors which led to his break with Freud and the psychoanalytic school in 1913. As far as Freud was concerned, religion and the occult constituted a "black tide of mud" which threatened to undermine the scientific validity of psychoanalytic theory. Jung, on the other hand, believed that the reality of God and the reality of the psyche were inextricably linked. How this relationship is manifest in specific religious symbols, beliefs, and behavior is explored in another essay on "Analytical (Jungian) Psychology and Religion" in this volume. Our concern here is to elucidate some of the theological assumptions and implications of analytical psychology.

1. **Foundational Assumptions.** *a. Wholeness as a paradoxical complementarity of opposites.* For over a half century until his death in 1961 Jung sought empirical evidence from the sciences and humanities to support his foundational anthropological premise regarding the wholeness of the person. In physics, particularly in collaboration with Nobel laureate Wolfgang Pauli, Jung found support for the complementarity of the physical and psychical aspects of reality. In the comparative study of religion, in alchemical literature, history, ethnology, and mythology, he discovered prototypical representations of an intrinsic paradox in the human psyche — a *complexio oppositorum* that was mediated symbolically through the archetypes of the collective unconscious. Here symbolic representations of good and evil, light and darkness, *persona* and *shadow,* and the contrasexual opposites *animus* and *anima* reflect an underlying flow of libidinal energy which is not restricted to sexual impulses but extends over the polarities of drive and spirit.

Influenced by Plato's concepts of soul *(psyche)* and participation *(methexis),* Jung referred to the psyche as a reservoir of energy created by the tension of opposites, and participating in a wider ontological domain, namely, the collective unconscious. Without opposites, there could be no balance or self-regulation. Moreover, the polarization of opposites is such that they tend to turn one into the other. This Jung called the principle of *enantiodromia* — a principle derived from Heraclitus's law of countermovement. These two principles, polarization and self-regulation or equilibrium, reflect a strong Hegelian dialectic in Jung's thought. This tension between opposites is a necessary condition for the emergence of any symbols of wholeness, most importantly, symbolic representations of God.

This paradox is evident in Jung's portrayal of the wholeness of the person as the *alpha* and *omega* of human becoming. Wholeness personified by the Self is not a state to be attained merely by conscious effort but is a process that involves the assimilation of the contents of the personal and collective unconscious. Paradox is anchored in a both/and equilibrium — e.g., both *animus* and *anima,* both good and evil — opposites which, though contradictory, are equally necessary for transformative insight into the quest for meaning. This is not to minimize the importance of struggle and conflict between opposites but to underscore the significance of resolution or synthesis in the paradox. This idealist (Hegelian) view of paradox, in contrast to Kierkegaard's existential dialectic of either/or, assumes that there is affinity between opposites. In analytical psychology, the *coincidentia oppositorum* is inherent in the collective unconscious.

b. The transcendental character of archetype, symbol, and Self. Jung used the phrase "canalization of libido" (1956, p. 142) to describe the transformation or conversion of the energy of psychological phenomena into other forms, for example, the transformation of libido into archetypal symbols. One such archetype, the Self, is an *a priori* state of wholeness rooted in the psychoid realm of the collective unconscious from which the individual ego emerges. In positing the Self as the metapsychological construct for the integration of personality Jung relies heavily on religious symbolism, thereby blurring any distinction between psychological interpretation of the wholeness of the psyche and theological interpretation of the salvation of the soul. Whereas Freud interpreted symbols semiotically and causally, Jung was captivated by the numinosity and paradoxical character of symbols and their role in the integration of the personality. He was particularly interested in the transcendence of archetypes insofar as they were beyond the total grasp of consciousness. The archetype-as-such presents itself as a symbol that is never fully knowable; hence Jung usually refers to the God-image rather than to God. As long as the archetype remains pregnant with meaning it has a numinous and transformative effect on the integration of the personality, energizing the transition to new goals. Individuation therefore should be seen not only as a psychological process but also as a quest for meaning. The latter is always more than what is consciously known. Its nucleus is a complex of mythological and religious images, ideas, and experiences.

c. Individuation as a quest for meaning and knowledge of God. Analytical psychology seeks to locate the experience of a unifying center in the personality within transcultural representations of the *imago Dei* as the highest and optimal expression of wholeness. Jung sought to accomplish this by connecting individual experience to the limitless reservoir of meaning present in the collective unconscious that is transmitted through the classics of various traditions. At the same time he refused to surrender individual experience to theological dogma. He insisted that the religious thrust of individuation is not to *believe* in God but to *know* God. The problem is that we can grasp only the image of God. Hence Jung could not make any precise distinction between the Self and the *imago Dei.*

d. Individuation as a dynamic synthesis of opposites. In reflecting on the psychotherapeutic process, Jung noted that the psychotherapist is "threatened with a conflict of duties between the two diametrically opposed and mutually exclusive attitudes of knowledge, on the one hand and understanding, on the other. This conflict cannot be solved by an either/or but only by a kind of two-way thinking: doing one thing while not losing sight of the other. In view of the fact that in principle, the positive advantages of *knowledge* work specifically to the disadvantage of *understanding,* the judgment resulting therefrom is likely to be something of a paradox" (1957, p. 19).

Maintaining a dynamic tension between opposites is a corrective to one-sidedness that masquerades as integration but which in reality is a defense against inferior, negative, or repressed aspects of the personality. This one-sidedness is exploited by dogmatic theology and positivistic science, both of which are preoccupied with the search for absolutes.

2. **Theological Themes and Issues.** *a. Theology as hermeneutics of symbol.* For Jung and his followers, the primary theological task is not to formulate a dogmatic concept of the archetypal structure of the God-image (which inevitably is distorted by our own projections) but to undertake a hermeneutical inquiry into the sym-

bolic expressions of the Self in the lives of persons. Here the analyst functions not only as clinician but also as hermeneuticist.

"The essence of hermeneutic . . . consists in adding further analogies to the one already supplied by the symbol: in the first place subjective analogies produced at random by the patient, then objective analogies provided by the analyst out of [his] general knowledge. This procedure widens and enriches the original symbol, and the final outcome is an infinitely complex and variegated picture. . . . Certain lines of psychological development then stand out that are at once individual and collective. There is no science on earth by which these lines could be proved 'right'. . . . Their validity is proved by their intense value for life" (1916, p. 291).

The hermeneutical task of widening the horizons of self-understanding beyond the context of personal life history to that of the collective experience of humanity leads to a further consideration of the epistemological assumptions in analytical psychology.

b. Evil as archetypal power. Individuation necessitates confrontation with evil. The latter is not to be understood metaphysically as the *privatio boni* (in contrast to God as the *summum bonum*) but as a primal archetype which like all the other archetypal powers of the unconscious cannot be readily integrated by the ego. Evil as such is inseparable from the archetype of the God-image. As far as Jung was concerned, the profundity of evil exceeds the demonic elements of the personal shadow. The human soul is ill-equipped to deal with evil as an autonomous power which could be mastered by the ego. Evil, like an iceberg, protrudes only its tip into the realm of the personal conscious.

The nature of the Self is such that it is both the center of our greatest creative insights and our worst destructive impulses. Thus, it is not unusual that those who attempt to master the transpersonal power of evil are also creative geniuses. Unfortunately, they succumb to ego-inflation of such magnitude that the result is the catastrophic victimization of humanity. Perhaps it is this awesome realization that led Jung to reject arguments for the non-substantiality of evil and to incorporate evil into the redemptive and creative archetype of the God-image. The Self, experienced religiously as the God-image, is the psyche's transcendent center of meaning and power and also the depth of despair and meaninglessness. In short, the Self is an ever-present possibility of a "harmony of differences that is wholeness" (van der Post, 1975, p. 219).

c. Salvation as Self-realization. In the first half of the life cycle individuation is primarily dominated by the differentiation of the ego from the Self, whereas the *telos* of the second half of the life cycle is Self-realization. The latter involves a decisive effort to integrate the conflictual aspects of the personality. But the realization of the Self is not merely a matter of our willingness to confront the unintegrated, rejected and repressed aspects of the personality. The Self is paradoxically always already and not yet. In other words, Self-realization has a definite eschatological character which may be obscured by the teleological thrust of individuation. At the core of Self-realization is the religious paradox of struggle and surrender. In the struggle for wholeness the soul inevitably surrenders to the darkness and ambiguity of the God-image. This "dark night of the soul" described by John of the Cross, Meister Eckhart, and other mystics, forms the substance of theological discourse on the encounter with non-being.

d. Jesus the Christ as archetypal symbol. Thus far we have characterized the God-image in somewhat abstract terms and have not addressed its incarnation in Jesus the Christ. Jung maintained that psychological wholeness was represented by the archetype of the Christ. In this respect the historical Jesus exemplified a universal psychological reality. But the historical Jesus is not the only manifestation of wholeness. According to Jung, "anything that a man postulates as being a greater totality than himself can become a symbol of the self" (vol. 11, 1940/1941, p. 156). However, given the human propensity for idolatry and self-deception, what appears as the "totality" can often assume demonic and destructive forms. Moreover, "totality" is not necessarily embraced as a *complexio oppositorum* but as a partiality that is absolutized.

e. Divine immanence and transcendence. Basically, the relationship of the Self to the *imago Dei* is an unresolved problem for Jung. On the one hand, the wholeness of the personality that is exemplified by Jesus Christ is consistent with Jung's understanding of the immanence of God. On the other hand, Jung was dissatisfied with a purely immanent God. But neither was he content with traditional Western metaphysical attributes of a transcendent God, namely, omniscience, omnipresence, and omnipotence. Evidently, Jung was convinced that the transcendence of God was indicated by the numinosity and ineffability of the archetype. Accordingly, he attempted to retrieve Gnostic interpretations of God that were compatible with his metapsychology, the most important of which was the idea that evil is an integral aspect of the *imago Dei*. In emphasizing the negative dialectic that is posed by evil, Jung underscores the paradoxical nature of the psyche and the metaphorical structure of theological language.

f. Evil as a necessary component of Self and God. Jung maintained that the psyche has a natural propensity "to invent analogies" (1956, p. 141). He therefore proposed that "the soul must contain in itself the faculty of relation to God, i.e. a correspondence, otherwise a connection could never come about. This correspondence is, in psychological terms, the archetype of the God-image" (p. 11). In Gnostic and alchemical texts, he discovered a powerful symbol of wholeness, namely, the marriage *quaternio*. The four constitutive elements in this union of opposites represented a primal holistic structure of light and darkness, *animus* and *anima*. Following his correspondence theory, Jung considered the *quaternio* analogous to the religious experience of the God-image and the Christian Trinity an imbalanced representation of the wholistic structure of the God-image. The missing element, the shadow side of the God-image, remains undisclosed. The apprehension of the numinosity of the shadow, though always partial is, nevertheless, a necessary element in the cultivation of the divine-human relationship, as we see in the story of Job.

If the dark side of God is indeed a constitutive feature of the *imago Dei*, then analytical psychology challenges

Christian theology to retrieve this historical tradition even if this means retrieving dangerous Gnostic elements in the history of Christianity. To acknowledge evil as a central component of the numinosity of God would revolutionize conventional notions of the perfection of God. But pastorally much is to be gained from the healing power of the shadow. Wholeness takes precedence over perfection which satisfies the demands of consciousness only. The goal of wholeness depends on conscious as well as unconscious seeking. Its realization extends beyond the particular individual, linking him or her to the wider history of humanity. Hence the projection of the shadow may take on a collective form that threatens the very existence of the universe, for example, the threat of nuclear holocaust.

3. Practical Implications and Values. In *Modern Man in Search of a Soul,* Jung anticipated much of our contemporary struggle to discover and recover transcultural and androgynous forms of spirituality and to come to terms with the problem of evil in a nuclear age. In typical Hegelian fashion, Jung views history optimistically. He construes conflict dialectically, sublating it into the integration of the Self. But this is not simply an individual project. The integration of opposites is an occasion for reconciling and healing fragmented relationships and for discovering the historical and collective symbols and stories that are definitive of the human species. In the modern era, this is especially critical in the arenas of sexism and racism. Voices of women are being heard around the world as they question the viability of contrasexual integration and seek new ways of interpreting the relevance or irrelevance of the *imago Dei* to their struggle for dignity and justice. Similarly, racism and economic oppression continue to undermine transcultural harmony.

In light of these and other threats to human wholeness, Jung's emphasis on dialectical paradox and the *coniunctio oppositorum* appears idealistic and individualistic. However, Jung was genuinely concerned about the need to preserve a vital spirituality in this fragmented universe. He refused to settle for easy "metaphysical" solutions to the conflict between good and evil, such as those given by contemporary proselytizers of privatized triumphal Christianity. On the contrary, Jung challenges theologians to treat the problem of good and evil as *"extra ecclesiam"* and to explore its psychological meaning, for example the paradoxical integration of the sacrifice of the ego and the realization of the Self in the sacrament of the Eucharist. For Jung, the Christ complex had more significance for the human journey of Self-realization than personal or ecclesiastical attempts to imitate the historical Jesus.

This is not to imply that Jung assumed that depth explorations of the collective unconscious through analytical psychotherapy could provide all that is necessary for wholeness. Analytical psychology discloses the dialectic of necessity and possibility in the transformation of the psyche. Theology places this dialectic within the context of the divine-human relationship. In the final analysis, analytical psychology and theology are engaged in a mutually critical hermeneutical enterprise that revolves around common paradoxes that punctuate our propensity for ego-inflation and self-deception while at the same time illumining aspects of the psyche that demand inclusion and moral action if we are to claim authentic membership in the human community, indeed in the body of Christ.

Bibliography. C. G. Jung, "The Structure of the Unconscious," *Collected Works,* vol. 7 (1916); "Alchemical Studies," *Collected Works,* vol. 13 (1967); "Symbols of Transformation," *Collected Works,* vol. 5 (1956); "Transformation Symbolism in the Mass," *Collected Works,* vol. 11 (1958); *The Undiscovered Self* (1957). D. Cox, *Jung and St. Paul* (1959). J. E. Loder, *The Transforming Moment* (1981), ch. 5. L. van der Post, *Jung and the Story of Our Time* (1975).

R. M. MOSELEY

PERSON; PASTORAL THEOLOGICAL METHODOLOGY; THEOLOGY AND PSYCHOLOGY. *See also* PASTORAL THEOLOGY, PROTESTANT; PHILOSOPHY AND PSYCHOLOGY; RELIGION AND PSYCHOTHERAPY. *Compare* ANALYTICAL (JUNGIAN) PSYCHOLOGY AND RELIGION; PSYCHOANALYSIS AND THEOLOGY.

ANDERSON, GEORGE CHRISTIAN. *See* RELIGION AND HEALTH MOVEMENT.

ANDROGYNY. The combined presence within an individual of socially valued, stereotypic feminine and masculine personality traits. In the most widely used definitions of androgyny, masculinity has been associated with an instrumental orientation—traits of rationality, assertion, and independence. Femininity has been associated with an expressive orientation—traits of gentleness, intuitiveness, and sensitivity. The androgynous individual combines both an expressive and an instrumental orientation.

C. S. SMITH

FEMINIST ISSUES IN PSYCHOLOGY; PERSON; SEXUALITY. *Compare* BISEXUALITY.

ANGELA OF BRESCIA (ANGELA DE MERICI), ST. *See* WOMEN IN PASTORAL MINISTRIES, HISTORY OF.

ANGELA OF FOLIGNO. *See* WOMEN IN PASTORAL MINISTRIES, HISTORY OF.

ANGER. A passion or emotion directed toward one who inflicts a real or supposed wrong. Ire, wrath, displeasure, resentment, indignation, and fury are its common synonyms. Although generally considered undesirable, anger is morally neither positive nor negative in and of itself; its effect and manifestation determine its constructive or destructive impact and hence its ethical value.

Hostility, from which anger is to be distinguished, is a state of antagonism, or animosity toward someone or something. A hostile state usually means opposition to, ill will toward, or destructive intentions with regard to its object. Hostility is synonymous with unfriendliness, animosity, and warfare. Unlike anger, hostility implies a negative orientation toward another.

The capacity for anger is a basic human endowment. Anger is aroused by a sensory perception plus an interpretation of the perception (thoughts which explain or "translate" the perception to the individual). Anger, like all emotions not based on physical stimuli, is thus "born" by an individual's thoughts; it is in part a product of interpretation and thus is always meaningful in some way. Contrary to popular belief, anger (or any other emotion) is not automatically "caused" by someone or some event, but is the result of an individual's perception and interpretation of a given situation.

Not all anger is destructive (unlike hostility which intends to be destructive). The purpose in anger may be a redemptive *or* a destructive end. Its effect depends on the particular manner employed to convey the emotion. Anger and hostility exhibit many forms and manifestations which are deeply conditioned by culture. Some cultures model constructive and therapeutic ways to channel anger; others evidence destructive forms. For most individuals, it is their families that have the greatest impact on the learnings of anger. Anger is generally interpreted as a dangerous emotion in Western culture; thus, most persons learn early to evade, ignore, or camouflage it, or to express the feeling with an accompanying moral justification (e.g., "I have good reason to be angry, a right to be angry").

Students of human behavior confirm that all individuals experience anger, and that the proper managing of this emotion entails an awareness of its presence and the learning of constructive channels for its expression. Failure to live responsibly with anger can result in costly forms of psychopathology, as seen, for example, in the common unhealthy manifestations of "disguised" anger in the American culture — depression, explosive physical behavior, intimidation, numbness, and alienation.

1. **Anger in the Bible.** The destructive and redemptive aspects of anger are evident in both Old and New Testaments. In the OT one recalls the hostility of Cain toward his brother (Gen. 4:6–8), the anger of Joseph's brothers toward him in Genesis 37–50, and God's own anger with Moses (Exod. 4:14), the whole people of Israel (Num. 25:3), the land (Deut. 29:27), Gideon (Judg. 6:39), David (II Sam. 12), and others. The Bible treats anger as a natural emotion and does not automatically condemn or approve of it. Each situation is described in its setting; anger is judged on the basis of who experienced it, for what cause, and how it was manifested. People in the Bible are described in human candor, and every emotion is reflected. On the whole, the writers of the OT do not moralize about the virtues and vices of anger. The Book of Proverbs is an exception, yet even in that compendium the main trait extolled is "slowness to anger," which is regarded as a characteristic of God (16:32; 19:11). The early view of God's anger as apparently temperamental (e.g., Gen. 18:25) seems gradually to have been modified toward a more mature understanding of a Lord of love whose "anger is but for a moment" and whose "favor is for a lifetime" (Ps. 30:5).

The NT reflects an understanding of the redemptive possibilities of anger. Incarnation is a manifestation of how God deals with anger in human relationships. Jesus expressed anger in various circumstances, on each occasion serving as a model of redemptive anger by demonstrating *concern* for individuals, as in his sorrowful anger over "hardness of heart" (Mk. 3:5) and his rebuke of the Pharisees for using religious rules as a weapon against human beings (Mt. 23:13–39). He also employed anger as an expression of *care* when confronting individuals with truth so that they would take redemptive steps for themselves (Mt. 16:23; cf. Jn. 8:31–59).

The apostolic church may not have fared as well in making anger redemptive. Paul's letters show that early Christians struggled with deeply felt differences which sometimes caused serious divisions and became destructive of young fellowships. We may conjecture that these struggles included their share of anger. Presumably, apostolic warnings to put away anger were not given without reason (Eph. 4:31; Col. 3:8), even though the writer of Ephesians, citing Jesus (4:26), clearly believed that anger is not sinful in itself ("Be angry but do not sin"), even if it can become so if not dealt with in a timely fashion ("Do not let the sun go down on your anger"). Given the amount of dissension in the Corinthian church and perhaps elsewhere, it is easy to suppose that the first Christian congregations, like so many since who have experienced tension and conflict, failed to understand and implement the positive possibilities for a deeper, more trusting common life when anger is dealt with honestly and directly. For it is certain that if real conflict and anger are ignored, major problems — mistrust, misperception, suspicion, and alienation—will develop.

2. **Assumptions About Anger.** Three misconceptions govern an inadequate management of anger by religious people: (1) the erroneous belief that all anger is sinful (and that this is the Bible's teaching); (2) the belief that angry feelings are best managed by being camouflaged or ignored; and (3) the belief—really the illusion—that the unpleasant or painful feelings such as anger, if ignored, will vanish and not continue to influence relationships.

Three corresponding points with regard to anger and its consequences therefore need to be emphasized. (1) The Scriptures agree with modern psychological studies in affirming that anger, though having destructive potential, also has positive and redemptive contributions to offer human relationships. (2) The right acknowledgment and expression of anger assists in deepening and developing social relationships; proper attention to anger can facilitate clarity of relationships and intensify commitments of care and love. (3) Unresolved or unexamined anger interferes with the effective exercise of relationships and produces confusion, misunderstanding, and alienation. Studies performed in four different churches with more than two hundred individuals, for instance, disclosed the fact that harbored anger was a primary reason for unresolved feelings, isolation between persons, and ineffective subsequent action in healing or reconciling efforts (Bagby, 1979).

3. **Pastoral Response to Anger: General Principles.** Stewards of anger should first examine their own characteristic manner of handling hostility and anger. Clergy and other counselors dealing with anger tend to handle the emotion according to their learned background. Consequently, if a minister has grown up believing that all anger is sin, he or she will usually have no inclination to explore the emotion with angry persons. Pastors and pastoral therapists will only facilitate its exploration if they themselves have examined and understood the anger in their own lives. This requires at least two operations:

First, one must discover learned attitudes about anger and its place in one's own life. Counselors need to examine and understand the anger in their own life history and their established patterns of handling animosity, especially including any destructive patterns (see below). CPE is a particularly important pastoral resource for this. It is designed partly to assist participants in discovering, accepting, and responsibly handling their feelings in ministry, and anger is often a central emotion in such training experiences. The CPE approach typically combines a concern for the outward manifestation and control of anger in relation to professional role and pastoral need, with a depth-oriented examination of one's emotional history and character and the dynamic structure of one's interpersonal relationships. Thus the issue of the management and control of this powerful emotion is related to fundamental questions about the self and relationships. There are, however, also programs for clergy that concentrate mainly on methods of cognitively and behaviorally understanding, controlling, and effectively managing anger. Conflict management experts, for example, are available to lead seminars at which church leadership can learn more effective means of channeling anger, and there are many centers and learning institutions available which assist individuals in self-understanding through psychological testing and helpful self-clarification sessions.

Second, counselors must develop redemptive avenues to channel anger. Persons responsible for anger management, such as persons in positions of leadership, should work at modeling healthy and constructive ways of displaying anger. Pastoral counselors can further enrich this modeling function through their distinctively therapeutic insights and responses to anger. These tend to bring out its potential for deepened self-understanding, more emotionally rich and rewarding relationships, and personal growth. Such counselors can also become trusted examples to parishioners who often struggle with therapeutically inadequate role models in the management of anger. Responsible use of anger includes an understanding and expression of the emotion in ways that allow for continuing communication which preserves the respect and integrity of the person to whom anger is being directed and maintains or enhances relationships.

4. **Inadequate and Pathological Forms of Anger.**
a. Depression. Much of what people call depression is believed to be anger turned upon oneself. Persons who grow up in an atmosphere that discourages open expression of anger often end up internalizing their feelings. The expression "swallow one's feelings" is descriptive. Unfortunately, such learned behavior, rather than alleviating the situation, can cause a variety of physical symptoms (ulcers, diarrhea, tension headaches, and melancholic distress) and emotional pain because such persons are punishing themselves on an ongoing basis. They are surprised if someone suggests that any negative or strong feelings may be at work within them, and usually resist suggestions that anger may be a factor in their physical or emotional distress.

Counselors can assist the angry or depressed person by gently providing an atmosphere in which anger can be voiced and received. The first step in making such anger redemptive is to acknowledge its presence, and the therapist or caring person must stimulate insight to help the person discover the negative emotions stacked up inside.

Avenues for responsible venting of feeling must also be provided. A supportive counseling atmosphere, a trusted group (in or out of the congregation), and selective friends who will listen with sensitivity may all provide safe and helpful outlets for expressions of pent-up anger and aggression. Physical exercise and active participation in sports are also effective tools to ventilate and sublimate suppressed anger in the angry-depressed.

b. Physical/verbal outbursts. Some individuals have learned to handle their anger impulsively and outwardly by "expelling" it. Such persons have usually grown up in an atmosphere where disputes were settled by "letting it all hang out" rather than by practicing impulse control through good communication and mutual problem solving. Persons who have emotional outbursts often frighten others, abuse them emotionally or physically, and are seldom aware of the manipulative intent of their actions or the impact or severity of their behavior.

Such persons usually expect people to reject them. They have learned over a long period of time that rejection is likely, and they set themselves up to cause it. Some individuals who practice this inadequate means of expressing anger do so as a cover for their own feelings of inadequacy or anxiety in certain circumstances.

A counselor who is aware of these dynamics can assist the angry/outspoken persons, at one level, by making them aware of the effect of their explosive manner on others. At a deeper level, however, the counselor offers such persons a qualitatively new kind of relationship, one in which the angry/outbursting individual is unable to alienate and manipulate the counselor and gain the hidden neurotic gratification that she or he has learned to expect from angry outbursts. Resisting all such ploys, the healing individual surprises the angry/outspoken person with acceptance and care, and steadily teaches him or her how to moderate expressions of anger and how to communicate it more effectively.

c. Fear of anger. Some people have been taught to cower under the pressure of anger. Persons who become afraid of anger most often are frightened by their own feelings and those of others. They flinch under verbal abuse, often cry, and withdraw into themselves for protection. Such inadequate responses to anger are multiplied by their fear of their own feelings, especially of anger.

The presenting signals for such unhealthy reactions to anger in others are usually a generalized anxiety (without apparent cause), a forced "meek" disposition, a perception of fear of people and gatherings of people, and a general sense of intimidation. Such persons rarely offer their opinion, certainly not in a public setting, and the whole community loses.

The most effective reversal of fear of anger is a gentle and long-term supportive relationship with someone who will "bring out" the intimidated and assist them to find courage in expressing their fears. One immediate fear is that their feelings, so far suppressed, if released, will overwhelm them and others. The patient reassurance, along with the steady reality that a counselor is not being "overcome" with their anger (at first intense, but soon quite mild if regularly expressed) can encourage this person, who has learned to ask the world for forgiveness for existing, and for the privilege of being "stepped on."

d. The angry-numb. Some individuals have learned to submerge and anesthesize their feelings by not allowing any outward expression. They have learned "not to feel." Every pastor knows individuals who are physically present in the life of the church but otherwise immobilized and apathetic. They neither contribute nor participate emotionally, for anger has "coated" their lives with a deadening anesthetic. Their healing can only take place with people who will assist them to understand the role that anger has assumed in their deadlock of feelings. Together with caring and trusted friends, they can begin the process of uncovering the layers of buried hostility which paralyze and debilitate their performance and freedom.

e. The angry-alienated. These individuals actually withdraw in the face of anger, remain unattached, removing themselves from community and from many relationships. Such persons have found withdrawal a safer way to deal with their animosities, but the ensuing alienation and isolation are a high price to pay to avoid anger. Church rolls abound with the names of individuals who have "withdrawn fellowship" under circumstances of disaffection. The main result of this mismanagement of feelings is that the anger involved is rarely dealt with; it remains as a constant source of isolation and distance in relationships, sometimes for years.

A constructive ministry with the angry-withdrawn involves a tender approach and a steadfast initiative. Unable to take initiative themselves, such victims of isolation will usually not respond at first to care or to interest expressed toward them. Patience and determination to assist them in dealing with their unresolved emotions is a first step toward their full participation in relationships. Direction and support as they explore the nature of their angry wound will also encourage them to evaluate and reconsider their approach to anger.

Constructive exploration of anger will usually include some clarity and evaluation of the motives and reasons for anger. An open, nonjudgmental attitude on a counselor's part always enhances the atmosphere required for honest exploration of strong feelings. A continued communication of respect and appreciation for the person with whom one is dealing is also an essential ingredient in redemptive work with anger and hostility. And perhaps the most important factor in a ministry with angry persons is the declared intention that anger will not be used as a means to sever a relationship, but as a shared emotion given in trust which has the potential of deepening the relationship at stake.

Bibliography. D. W. Augsburger, *Anger and Assertiveness in Pastoral Care* (1979). D. G. Bagby, *Understanding Anger in the Church* (1979). A. V. Campbell, *The Gospel of Anger* (1986). M. P. Nichols and M. Zax, *Catharsis in Psychotherapy* (1979), pp. 207ff. C. Tavris, *Anger, the Misunderstood Emotion* (1982).

D. G. BAGBY

AGGRESSION AND ASSERTION; CONFLICT AND CONFLICT MANAGEMENT; EMOTION; FEELING, THOUGHT, AND ACTION IN PASTORAL COUNSELING; RAGE AND HOSTILITY; VIOLENCE. *See also* ALIENATION; CATHARSIS; PROFANE LANGUAGE; SADNESS AND DEPRESSION; SELF EXPRESSION/SELF CONTROL; SIN/SINS. *Compare* CHRISTIAN LIFE; FORGIVENESS; MEDIATION/CONCILIATION.

ANGER AND MEEKNESS (Moral Theology). *Anger* is (a) an emotional agitation aroused by dissatisfaction and leading to an impulse to seek redress; (b) the inordinate inclination to vengeance. *Meekness* is (a) a habit of patient endurance under provocation; (b) in a pejorative sense, a spineless submissiveness.

1. Anger. Three phases of anger can be noted. Anger arises as a normal response to any of a vast array of untoward events, including physical evils like a kick or spiritual evils like unjust treatment. This discontent then quickly evokes a psychosomatic agitation which fills the body and, frequently, focuses the whole attention on the offender. Third, anger develops an impulse against the causes of the harm. Usually, if not always, some sort of responsibility is imputed to the immediate or remote causes of the offense.

Scripture indicates instances of good anger. Anger is legitimate when the perception of the evil is accurate, when the excitation is proportionate to the evil, and when the impulse is directed toward correcting the ill. Scripture also warns against anger, and—influenced by Stoicism—much of the Christian tradition has judged that morally good anger seldom occurs. The way anger so quickly absorbs a person, distorts perspective, rages out of control, and leads to violent actions has made all anger suspect. Reason, the imagination, and the heart turn away from their proper functions and become subservient to anger's fury.

The moral issue is not merely how one acts out an emotion, but also the justifiability of the emotion itself. Anger often is misdirected, for example, when it strikes out against one person because of harms received from another, say, from a parent. Like other emotions, anger can expand beyond its original cause. It can turn into a simmering rancor or into a thirst for vengeance. Anger has been included among the seven capital or deadly sins because it often inspires a host of other sins.

2. Meekness. Since anger can be legitimate, meekness is not exactly its moral opposite. Rather meekness, after the example of Jesus, is a patient endurance of both justifiable and unjustifiable harms. According to Paul, meekness is a gift of the Holy Spirit. Toward God, meekness represents a docility which does not revolt against God's sometimes burdensome will. In human interactions, meekness means a self-possession which modulates excessive reactions. The meek restrain, if not altogether suppress, anger's impulse to seek redress. Further, both rancor and a continued desire for revenge are absent in the meek. Meekness can be a deficiency if it means mere indolence, paralysis through fear, or absence of normal reactions to evil.

Meekness is, in fact, a virtue of strength. The just war tradition is based on the strength of legitimate anger. The pacifist tradition, however, is based on the strength of meekness. Patient endurance is necessary for a peaceable society, but it is also—according to the Beatitudes and Jesus' example—part of the life of one who adheres to God. Jesus is the model of one who can react with anger but also with meekness.

Bibliography. H. Fairlie, *Seven Deadly Sins Today* (1978). S. Lyman, *Seven Deadly Sins* (1978).

E. C. VACEK

CHRISTIAN LIFE; SEVEN DEADLY SINS. *See also* CHARACTER ETHICS; MORAL THEOLOGY AND PASTORAL CARE; SIN/SINS; TEMPTATION.

ANGLICAN PASTORAL CARE. A ministry of compassion with people in "the true wilderness" of life (Williams, 1965), shaped by three basic perspectives (Sykes, 1978; Wolf, 1979). (1) Anglican pastoral care is grounded in a particular way of doing theology that features "comprehensiveness" (The Lambeth Conference, 1968). (2) It is rooted in a historical, universal, and unifying view of the church and its ministry (Carey, 1954). (3) It presupposes an incarnational understanding of nature and society (Temple, 1942). Each of these perspectives, in turn, helps to articulate pastoral care for Anglicans as an art form of a community rather than a profession of an elite.

1. Anglican Theology and Pastoral Care. As Augustine and Anselm remind us, theology is faith seeking understanding. Anglicans attempt to make sense of their faith that "Jesus is Lord" by interrelating biblical revelation, teaching from doctrinal tradition, and reason, which grows out of "the best of contemporary knowledge." The Scriptures as a whole are essential for understanding because they record the historical encounter between God and people. Tradition includes the accumulated wisdom of the Judeo-Christian heritage and enables us to draw upon the insights and experiences of our religious predecessors. Reason enables us to be honest, to be open to all sorts of truths, and to engage all of our intellectual capacities and ways of knowing (Baycroft, 1980).

The implications of such a theological method for pastoral care are clear. First, one basic task of Anglican pastoral care is educational. In a variety of ways, it endeavors to develop and deepen people's comprehension of faith in Christ. In doing this, it draws on all that is available not only within the Bible and doctrinal tradition but also from reason, which grows out of the whole of life's experience informed by such intellectual disciplines as psychology, sociology, economics, political science, and philosophy. Such reliance on extra-biblical and extra-traditional authority echoes Carl Jung's acknowledgment of the "religious dimension" in psychotherapy.

A second task for pastoral care that follows from this way of "doing theology" is an ethical or moral one (Elmen, 1983). As people gain a greater understanding of Christian faith, they also search for ways to express the relation of faith to practice. In seeking to inform their conscience about responsible and faithful witness, they look for concrete ways to engage with integrity about matters of personal and social transformation. They also seek the "gift of courage" to live with the ambiguity of the moral life (Wilkes, 1981). In doing all this, they can draw upon a rich heritage of spiritual direction and casuistry.

2. Anglican Ecclesiology and Pastoral Care. While there are many different models of the church, Anglicans stress a historical, universal, and unifying expression of the church. They draw upon the ancient creedal formulation of the "one, holy, catholic and apostolic" church. In doing so, they organize their community life around the worship of God, the proclamation of the gospel, the care of persons in special need, and the pursuit of social justice (Ramsey, 1956). Central to all of these activities is a commitment to a sacramental way of life. "The sacraments are focal points for a life lived in relationship to all that conveys the humanizing grace of God in Christ. . . . The Passion of Christ becomes, in this process, the prevailing icon of all life for each of us" (Holmes, 1982).

Although the fundamental sacraments are those of baptism and the eucharist, traditionally, there are five others. Each of these touches us at different stages of our lives from birth to death. While every sacrament has specific implications in Anglican pastoral care, two in particular have a prominent place in the growth and development of persons. These are "confession" (i.e., reconciliation) and "unction" (i.e., healing) (Ross, 1975). The former enables us to deal in concrete ways with issues of guilt (legitimate or neurotic) and challenges us to live with God's unconditional and unending love. The challenge of God's unlimited forgiveness can liberate us to become whole. Unction, on the other hand, is prayer for healing. It helps us to focus on God's continuing presence in our lives and the constant divine desire that we become whole, whatever that might mean in detail. Confession and unction, of course, also assume the usual considerations and sensitivities of pastoral care and counseling.

3. Incarnation and Pastoral Care. The prologue to St. John's Gospel tells of God's creation and redemption. Central to this powerful portrayal is the proposition that "the Word became flesh and dwelt among us . . . full of grace and truth." Anglican theology presupposes an incarnational understanding of nature and society. Consequently, Anglican pastoral care does not restrict itself to the care of individuals. It also is deeply committed to a tradition of social justice, the appropriate conservation of nature, and the just transformation of society (Owen, 1980).

Anglican pastoral care, then, is much more than a profession of a select few. It is an art form lived out in a historical and contemporary community with a lay and ordained ministry. The latter is specific and highly focused; the former is general and all-pervasive. Ordained ministry includes the deacon, who serves the powerless and reminds us all, in concrete and symbolic ways, to do so also (Barnett, 1979); the priest, who is committed to a ministry of Word and sacrament, central to which is reconciliation in its many real and sacramental forms (Terwilliger and Holmes, 1975); and the bishop, an overseer who reminds the community of its unity and universality, fosters sound teaching about the faith, and speaks at times as a prophet. While the laity participate in all of this, they also remind the community of an art form of Christian caring that includes education in the faith, spiritual direction, moral and ethical discernment, the care of persons in special need, the participation in the sacraments, and the pursuit of justice and social transformation.

Bibliography. J. Barnett, *The Diaconate* (1979). J. Baycroft, *The Anglican Way* (1980). K. Carey, ed., *The Historic Episcopate in the Fullness of the Church* (1954). P. Elmen, ed., *The Anglican Moral Choice* (1983). J. E. Griffiss, ed., *Anglican Theology and Pastoral Care* (1985). U. T. Holmes III, *What Is Anglicanism?*

(1982). *The Lambeth Conference 1968* (1968). J. T. McNeill, *A History of the Cure of Souls* (1951), ch. 10. D. R. G. Owen, *Social Thought and Anglican Theology* (1980). M. Ramsey, *The Gospel and the Catholic Church* (1956). K. Ross, *Hearing Confessions* (1975). S. W. Sykes, *The Integrity of Anglicanism* (1978). W. Temple, *Christianity and Social Order* (1942). R. E. Terwilliger and U. T. Holmes III, eds., *To Be A Priest* (1975). W. Wilkes, *The Gift of Courage* (1981). H. A. Williams, *The True Wilderness* (1965). W. J. Wolf, ed., *The Spirit of Anglicanism* (1979).

J. REED

PASTORAL CARE (History, Traditions, and Definitions). *See also* HISTORY OF PROTESTANT PASTORAL CARE (United States). *Compare* ECCLESIOLOGY AND PASTORAL CARE; EDUCATION, NURTURE, AND CARE; INCARNATIONAL PASTORAL CARE; SACRAMENTAL THEOLOGY AND PASTORAL CARE; TRADITION AS MODE OF CARE.

ANIMA/ANIMUS. In analytical (Jungian) psychology, the archetypal contrasexual aspect of each sex. For a man, the *anima* is the unconscious feminine characterized by the symbol of the *Yin* (qualities of darkness, earth and moon, receptivity, instinct and flesh, synthesis, matter and the concrete). For a woman, the *animus* represents the unconscious masculine as characterized by the symbol of the *Yang* (qualities of light, heat, aggressiveness, fertility, sun, sky, spirit, word, antithesis, and separation).

I. R. STERNLICHT

ANALYTICAL (JUNGIAN) PSYCHOLOGY (Personality Theory and Research). *See also* SEXUALITY, BIOLOGICAL AND PSYCHOSOCIAL THEORY OF.

ANIMISM. *See* AFRICAN TRADITIONAL RELIGION, PERSONAL CARE IN; SOCIOLOGY OF RELIGIOUS AND PASTORAL CARE.

ANNIVERSARY DEPRESSION. A psychological disturbance generated by recollections of an exceptionally painful experience, usually close to the season of that particular trauma. The anniversary of a significant personal loss or assault to the self will frequently initiate other associations of suppressed grief and fear, thus compounding and confusing an identification of the problem's source. Events like the death of a spouse, a severe injury or illness, a divorce or bankruptcy will often provoke this type of depression and its melancholy affect.

Anniversary depressions are not necessarily linked to a *specific* age, time or season. This condition is triggered by thoughts and feelings which are blocked with varying degrees of intensity. It is characterized by an increasing succession of intrusive memories and denial signs of similar magnitude. There is a subtle, continuous preoccupation with the traumatic event. Concurrently there is a rejection of its historical impact and a disassociation of the depression from its original source. Other traumatic recollections and disappointing incidents are then absorbed into the effect of the precipitating crisis. A person suffering from this malady will also experience sleep disturbances frequently accompanied by painful and violent dream symbolism. They may also act out or reenact the crisis and ruminate about such behavior in a paranoid manner.

Another symptom of anniversary depression is the denial of pain by overactivity that seems to be productive. Pain and anger are masked by compensatory behavior. For instance, a person who has suffered from a near-fatal experience will often attempt "to make up for lost time," a defensive strategy subconsciously designed to dismiss the fear of dying. Such activities give the appearance that the effects of the precipitating crisis and/or its anniversary are no longer a cause for concern. However, it may well be that these activities or accomplishments represent a flight from anxiety linked to the trauma and other repressed associations.

Pastors can provide valuable crisis intervention in many instances of anniversary depression. One avenue or "tool" for the minister is some type of account or "calendar" of major crises revealed by the depressed person. This record may be a log of significant dates such as funerals, hospitalizations, marriages or legal divorces. Pastoral contacts a few weeks prior to such anniversaries can provide an opportunity for the counselor to discuss and even work through some unresolved grief, as well as other sources of depression that the pastor perceives as subjects for short term counseling.

In psychotherapy the anniversary of a crisis may serve as an entrée for resolution of deep psychic injuries. These wounds are typically characterized by a vague, free-floating anxiety or depressive moods which are exacerbated by confused clusters of painful memories blocked from conscious recollection.

Bibliography. D. M. Moss, "Near Fatal Experience, Crisis Intervention and the Anniversary Reaction," *Pastoral Psychology,* 28 (1979), 75–96; "New Divorce Stress Disorder: Judicial Trauma," *Marriage and Divorce Today,* 7 (1982), 1; "Using a Trauma Calendar to Help Clients/Parishioners," *Marriage and Divorce Today,* 5 (1980), 1. G. Pollock, "Anniversary Reactions, Trauma, and Mourning," *Psychoanalytic Quarterly,* 39 (1970) 347–71; "Temporal Anniversary Manifestations: Hour, Day, Holiday," *Psychoanalytic Quarterly,* 40 (1971), 123–31.

D. M. MOSS

GRIEF AND LOSS; SADNESS AND DEPRESSION. *Compare* HOLIDAY DEPRESSION; MEMORY.

ANNULMENT. *See* DECREE OF NULLITY.

ANOINTING. *See* ANOINTING OF THE SICK, SACRAMENT OF; BLESSING AND BENEDICTION; RITUAL AND PASTORAL CARE; SICK, PASTORAL CARE OF. *See also* MINISTRY AND PASTORAL CARE (Orthodox Tradition).

ANOINTING OF THE SICK, SACRAMENT OF. The Roman Catholic sacrament by which spiritual healing and often physical healing is conferred on the sick.

Although from earliest Christian times anointing with blessed oil was associated with physical healing, the first extant rite for such an anointing dates only from the ninth century. The high mortality rate in the Middle Ages caused anointing to become linked with deathbed situations. As a result, physical healing was de-emphasized and the forgiveness of sins was stressed. It was only in the 1950s that research rediscovered the physical healing aspect of the sacrament and the fact that the reception of the sacrament was not originally intended only for the dying. The Second Vatican Council (1962–65) mandated the revision of the rite for the sacrament and suggested that "anointing of the sick" was a more appropriate name than "extreme unction." The council also mandated that any Catholic who was seriously ill could receive the sacrament of the anointing of the sick. Furthermore, in deathbed situations the final sacrament should be Holy Communion (Viaticum). An interim rite for anointing (1974) stressed both physical and spiritual healing.

The sacrament of the anointing of the sick can give the sick person an inner spiritual strength that complements the body's natural powers of healing. The pastoral skills of the priest and the atmosphere in which the rite is celebrated have an impact on the effectiveness of the sacrament. While it is Christ who acts in the sacrament (*ex opere operato*), the incarnational emphasis of Catholicism has always stressed the importance of pastoral attitudes and interior dispositions (*ex opere operantis*).

Unfortunately, in many people's minds the sacrament is still associated with the deathbed. As a result, they or their families do not request it. Also, the length of the 1974 rite was somewhat impractical in a busy hospital setting. The 1983 rite of anointing emphasizes that Holy Communion (Viaticum) is the final sacrament for the dying. Ideally, anointing should take place early on in the illness. The 1983 rite also specifically envisions anointing taking place in a hospital or institutional setting.

However, since only a priest can ordinarily administer the sacrament, it would be quite time-consuming to attempt to anoint all the sick, aged, and infirm in a large parish. This may well explain why except for emergency anointings and occasional communal anointings there is ordinarily not a lot of catechesis about this sacrament on the parish level. Allowing deacons to administer this sacrament would certainly help to make the sacrament of the anointing of the sick more available to the Catholic faithful.

Bibliography. C. Davis, "Sacrament of the Sick or of the Dying," *Theology for Today*, (1962), 284–68. J. L. Empereur, *Prophetic Anointing* (1983). J. Martos, "Anointing," in *Doors to the Sacred* (1981). P. Palmer, "The Purpose of Anointing the Sick: A Reappraisal," *Theological Studies*, 19 (1958), 309–44.

G. MCCARRON

ROMAN CATHOLIC PASTORAL CARE; SACRAMENTAL THEOLOGY AND PASTORAL CARE, ROMAN CATHOLIC; VATICAN COUNCIL II AND PASTORAL CARE. *See also* BLESSING AND BENEDICTION; RITUAL AND PASTORAL CARE; SICK, PASTORAL CARE OF; SIGN OF THE CROSS.

ANOMIE/NORMLESSNESS. To be without standards for behavior.

Anomie or normlessness can be considered a type of alienation in which one finds oneself opposed to the norms of one's society as one seeks self-fulfillment. Or one might feel impelled to accomplish something important without standards for determining what is to be accomplished or how it might be done, although this sense dominates all other values and priorities. In such

situations one is at a distance from both oneself and from the norms for social acceptance, because who one is and who one ought to be do not seem to be normatively related. Obligations seem to originate at a distance from the person and appear to oppose what the person senses to be most important. The person is consequently alienated from his or her social environment and from his or her social self or personality. If, however, the norms available to one are themselves destructive for a person, a sense of normlessness may be taken as possibility for important change.

Anomie also characterizes situations in which one experiences reality without normative determination such as in some encounters with divinity, in absorbing states of serenity, or in certain intense passions. If divinity, for example, is experienced as overwhelming light, awesome enormity, or some other incomprehensible presence, one's state of mind may be elevated beyond the norms of human judgment. The occurrence will seem to be normless. In other states of unusual intensity one may also find no norms for action or judgment. One finds, rather, that *anomie* names a certain dimension of human being or human experience that appears to transcend social relations and moral agency. Further, in those fundamental experiences in which norms originate such as community, familial bonding, or participation in a culture, anomie probably occurs in the sense that one experiences the origin without norms for judging it. Such an experience could be one of mission or of nothingness and void.

Bibliography. S. Kierkegaard, *Fear and Trembling* (1983). A. Maslow, *Toward a Psychology of Being* (1968). M. Seeman, "On the Meaning of Alienation," *American Sociological Review*, 24 (1959), 783–91.

C. E. SCOTT

ALIENATION/ESTRANGEMENT; CONSCIENCE; EVALUATION AND DIAGNOSIS; MENTAL HEALTH AND ILLNESS. *Compare* ANXIETY; APATHY AND BOREDOM; SIN/SINS; SOCIAL ISOLATION.

ANOREXIA NERVOSA. A condition that is characterized by an intense fear of becoming obese, self-imposed severe dietary limitations, significant weight loss, disturbance of body image, and, in women, amenorrhea. It has no known physical cause and occurs mostly in females, with the onset between the ages of ten and thirty. Psychodynamic formulations regarding the causes are numerous. Personal traits often seen are model behavior and high achievement.

Bibliography. K. D. Brownell and J. P. Foreyt, eds., *Handbook of Eating Disorders* (1986).

J. A. KNIGHT

MENTAL HEALTH AND ILLNESS; SELF-DESTRUCTIVE BEHAVIOR. *See also* EATING AND DRINKING; PSYCHOPATHOLOGY, THEORIES OF; PSYCHOTHERAPY. *Compare* BULIMIA; OBSESSIVE-COMPULSIVE DISORDER.

ANTHONY OF EGYPT, ST. *See* EARLY CHURCH, PASTORAL CARE AND COUNSELING IN.

ANTHROPOLOGY. *See* BIBLICAL, PHILOSOPHICAL, *or* THEOLOGICAL ANTHROPOLOGY, DISCIPLINE OF; PERSON.

ANTHROPOLOGY OF RELIGION. *See* CULTURAL ANTHROPOLOGY OF RELIGION.

ANTI-SEMITISM. Discrimination and hatred against Jews, manifested for two millennia in persecution, execration, confinement, banishment, and massacre. To gain such historic pervasiveness and power, anti-Semitism evidently serves society and its members in some way. Presumably, pressures from disequilibrating internal forces are relieved; the disintegrator of Jews experiences a corresponding cohesiveness; destructiveness is safely discharged by blighting helpless Jews; casting the often envied Jew into the role of pariah refurbishes self-esteem.

Beginning the anti-Semitic drama are delusive charges that Jews defile, disease, weaken, tempt, demoralize and induce chaos in the non-Jew. Allegedly, Jews undermine society because of their intrinsically base nature. The Jew's inherent evilness finds expression in envy, greed, treachery, corruption, and lust; the Jew craves destruction of Christian values and defamation of Christian Gods. Jewish malignancy allegedly derives from uncanny qualities: rootlessness, immortality, and mysteriousness. According to this belief, Jews, as conspirators, inflict their enervating impact on the host nation in order to enslave the debilitated population. The world's boundaries alone limit the Jew's voracity for cruel dominance.

This group fantasy renders the Jew into a receptacle for unacceptable primitive feelings. Malediction of the Jew also stems from negative primal images of significant others. The child was insufficiently loved to enable the integration and taming of fragmented, horrendous imagery of key persons. Unable to employ the archaic imagery, psychic structures remain truncated.

Especially stymied is the unfolding of a mature conscience. The precursory conscience may be appeased by the sacrificial offering of Jews. Fearing unmasking of a barbaric inner world, the perpetrator is compelled incessantly to "expose" the Jew. Ongoing anti-Semitism is difficult to halt since idealizations of forebears are threatened, questions are raised about one's legacy and state of morality, and accustomed satisfactions are thwarted.

Counseling entails listening with empathy to the voicing of prejudice. Otherwise the counselor will commit the same offense as did unsympathetic parents. Probably the rage and sense of entitlement underlying intolerance were stimulated by parental thwarting of the child's need to be heard and prized. Ideally, counselor responses should be correctly timed, tactful, and tailored to the client's associations. Interpretations of prejudice will usually center on (1) the Jew being equated with a non-preferred part of the self or with an ambivalently regarded significant person, and on (2) victimizing acts toward Jews originating from the compulsive repetition of catastrophic moments suffered in early childhood.

Bibliography. R. M. Loewenstein, *Christians and Jews* (1951). E. A. Rappaport, *Anti-Judaism* (1975). J. P. Sartre, *Anti-Semite and Jew* (1948).

S. ROSENMAN

HOLOCAUST; PREJUDICE; RACISM. *See also* AUTHORITARIANISM; SOCIAL PERCEPTION, JUDGMENT AND BELIEF. *Compare* SOCIAL CONSCIOUSNESS AND RESPONSIBILITY.

ANTINOMIANISM. *See* LEGALISM AND ANTINOMIANISM.

ANTISOCIAL PERSONS. Persons who characteristically exhibit an aggressive or hostile orientation toward other people, either actively or passively. The more active expressions of the antisocial orientation include: (1) tackling problems fearlessly, in a headstrong or warlike manner, heedless of dangerous or punishing consequences; (2) inappropriate self-assertiveness, toughness, and self-reliance, with a tendency to employ intimidation as a means of social influence; (3) combativeness, a belligerent attitude, and a tendency to pick fights either physically or in more refined social, political, or economic ways; (4) vindictiveness ("I don't get angry, I get even"), or a manipulative tendency to feel hurt, to cry, to have low frustration tolerance; (5) a cynical, distrusting attitude toward others; (6) ruthless ambition and striving for power; (7) overconcern with status and prestige. Passive expressions involve, essentially, resistance to authority, though the authority dimension is often hidden from obvious view: procrastination, dawdling, stubbornness, intentional inefficiency, forgetfulness, refusal to take appropriate responsibility for past mistakes or future obligations, and refusal to accept instruction, discipline, and sacrifice in striving for achievement.

1. History of Concept in Psychology and Psychiatry. Historically, the antisocial person has been named and described with varied terms, and widely differing explanations of the origins of his or her behavior have been advanced. Cesare Lombroso (1836–1909), an Italian psychiatrist, described physical and mental stigmata of the "criminal" personality. Lombroso hypothesized that these stigmata were atavisms, or anthropological "throwbacks," from more primitive eras of humankind's development as a species. In the second half of the nineteenth century, R. L. Dudales and H. H. Goddard separately studied two families—the Jukes and Kallikaks—and sought to document the hereditary nature of crime, immorality, and pauperism in the U.S. The attempt to link antisocial behavior to constitutional or hereditary origins persists until today in the recent efforts to relate the XYY chromosome to criminal behavior. Yet the XYY chromosomal configuration can also be found in exceptional numbers among athletes and military personnel who do not have any criminal records (Friedman *et al.*, 1975, pp. 102–3, 314).

A less crude, more psychological understanding seems to begin in the scientific period with Phillipe Pinel who described these persons as having *manie sans delire* (insanity without delirium). Their main deficit was an absence of feeling. This is reminiscent of the "hardness of heart" referred to by Jesus (Mt. 19:8) and "being past feeling" referred to by Paul (Eph. 3:18–19). In 1835 the British psychiatrist J. C. Prichard described this inability to learn from experience, to have empathy for others, as "moral insanity." Through the work of Adolph Meyer in this country at the turn of the twentieth century, the terms *constitutional psychopathic state* and *psychopathic personality* became a part of psychological and psychiatric language to describe the antisocial personality. Ernst Kraepelin defined this term to mean a "morbid form of personality development" which was degenerative. By degenerative he meant a lasting morbid reaction to the stresses of life.

The first thorough clinical description of the psychopathic person was published by Hervey Cleckley in 1941 and has remained largely unchanged over the years. Cleckley refused to overidentify the antisocial personality with criminality. He noted that there are those who go to jail or psychiatric hospitals and those who do not, and those who keep up "a far better and outward appearance of being normal." "The chief difference . . . perhaps lies in whether the mask or facade of psychobiologic health is extended into material success" (Cleckley, 1964, pp. 198–99).

The Diagnostic and Statistical Manual of Disorders, Revised Edition (DSM-III-R), reiterates the hallmarks of the antisocial person: guiltlessness, inability to sustain a love relationship for as much as a year, impulsivity, emotional shallowness, superficial social charm, and inability to learn from experience. However, as Theodore Millon says, "DSM has returned to an accusatory judgment rather than dispassionate clinical formulation; what we have is but a minor variation of earlier, ill considered, and deplorable notions such as moral 'insanity' and 'constitutional inferiority.' . . . Only a minor subset of the aggressive personality [as Millon names the antisocial person] comes into conflict with the law. Many find themselves commended and reenforced in our society where tough, hard-headed 'realism' is admired as an attribute necessary for survival." Millon notes that "the arrogant patriot, the manipulative politician, the harshly punitive father, the puritanical and fear-inducing minister, the vengeful dean, the irritable and sadistic mother are a few examples of how antisocial persons appear in everyday life" (Millon, 1981, pp. 181–82.)

Millon denotes the characteristics of the aggressive or antisocial person as follows: (1) Hostile affectivity expressed in an irascible temper and verbally abusive and physically cruel behaviors; (2) social rebelliousness and a contempt for authority, tender feelings, and compassionate concerns; (3) social vindictiveness and a satisfaction in derogating and humiliating others; (4) a fearless attitude that courts and provokes danger; and (5) a shallow, superficial charm and a clever manner.

The blunt, impulsive blurting out of feelings and opinions, of aggressive or antisocial persons shocks and intimidates other people. They say what they think long before they have thought it out. The objective of this behavior is to intimidate and control others. *Rationalized* as frankness and honesty, this behavior in the long run is *sublimated* into the choice of occupation: competitive business enterprises, military careers, trial lawyers, evangelist tycoon preachers. These persons thrive by having an "enemy" upon which they *project* their vindictiveness

in the name of a specious "cause." They are power-centered personalities with an uncompromising covetousness of whatever control centers of money, prestige, and position lie within their realm of activity.

2. Pastoral Response. The intuitive pastoral response to antisocial personalities is one of disdain. A more appropriate and helpful response becomes possible, however, when the psychodynamic factors and forces in their behavior are understood. Parental rejection, abandonment, or brutality rank foremost. Another form of rejection is the symbiotic preoccupation of one or both parents with another child, making the antisocial person the "black sheep" of the family who is left to fend for himself or herself and learns that he or she cannot depend on others. In not being loved, he or she settles for being envied or feared. Pastoral approaches of gentle humor and accurate empathy for her or his history yield the best results. Yet it is important not to be afraid of such persons or allow them to intimidate one.

The identification and understanding of antisocial persons is of particular importance in the selection, preparation, and ordination of ministers. The personality makeup of candidates for the ministry has only recently begun to be considered in the qualifications for ministerial leadership. The Apostle Paul sharply discerned the "peddlers of God's word" (II Cor. 2:17), as did Peter in his first letter in the injunction to "tend the flock of God that is your charge . . . not for shameful gain" ["for the love of filthy lucre" (KJV)] not as "domineering over ["lording it over" KJV] those in your charge" (I Peter 5:2). They focus on the concern of the aggressive, antisocial personality's hungers: money and power. As the Pardoner says in Chaucer's *Canterbury Tales*:

> All my preaching is about avarice and such cursed sins, in order to make them give freely of their pennies namely to me; for my intention is to win money not at all to cast out sins. I don't care, when they are buried, if their souls go a-blackberrying.

More recent American literature, such as Sinclair Lewis's *Elmer Gantry* and Somerset Maugham's *Rain,* have epitomized the antisocial religious person. Yet it is not until a stark, gruesome tragedy such as Jim Jones and the Peoples' Church in Guyana that the populace as a whole becomes aware of the gullibility of people for being swindled by antisocial persons functioning as religious leaders.

Another point of relevance for pastoral care in relation to antisocial personalities is the need for a renewed appraisal of the transformation of personality—not just its sublimation of already existing character disorders—in Christian experience. The disciples James and John wanted power—to sit one on the right hand and one on the left hand of Jesus in his triumph over the earth. They were "sons of thunder" who angrily wanted to call down fire from heaven on the inhospitable Samaritan village. If this had simply been glossed over in sublimation, another rage-filled and sadistic pair of religious operators would have been the result. But the gentle rebuke of Jesus, the teaching of a better, more disciplined way, their death to power and control, and their being raised to walk in the newness of loving other people as Christ had loved them transformed them into a new being in Christ. Rationalization, sublimation, and projection make of a person one who, as Bunyan says, "would rather lose your company than to change his ways." Transformation through radical redemption results in a person who is teachable, empathic, and full of integrity.

Bibliography. American Psychiatric Association, *Diagnostic and Statistical Manual of Mental Disorders III-R* (1987). H. Cleckley, *The Mask of Sanity,* 4th and 5th eds. (1964, 1976). A. Friedman, H. Kaplan, and B. Sadock, *Comprehensive Textbook of Psychiatry II* (1975), vol. 1. T. Millon, *Disorders of Personality: DSM-III, Axis II* (1981). W. E. Oates, *Behind the Masks* (1987). P. Pinel, "Treatise on Insanity," in D. N. Robinson, ed., *Significant Contributions to the History of Psychology* (1977).

W. E. OATES

CRUELTY/SADISTIC BEHAVIOR; DEVIANT BEHAVIOR, THEORY OF; RAGE AND HOSTILITY; VIOLENCE. *See also* CONFRONTATION (Pastoral and Therapeutic); DISAGREEMENT, DIFFERENCE, AND CONFLICT IN PASTOR-PARISHIONER RELATIONSHIPS; LIMIT SETTING; PSYCHOPATHOLOGY, THEORIES OF; RESPONSIBILITY/IRRESPONSIBILITY, PSYCHOLOGY OF; LYING; MORAL DEVELOPMENT. *Compare* AGGRESSION AND ASSERTION; DOMINEERING PERSONALITY; MANIPULATION; PSYCHOPATHIC PERSONALITY.

ANXIETY. A psychic response of dread or fear to a vague, unspecified threat. Anxiety as a psychic condition is experienced by all human beings, although it may be triggered by different sources for different persons. There are different types of anxiety and various theories about it, but, as this article will maintain, at its core anxiety signals the threat of a fundamental loss or separation. While anxiety is considered primarily a psychological construct, it also has physiological, philosophical, and theological dimensions. Anxiety can function both as an inhibitor and a contributor to human growth and development. The constructive use of anxiety principally depends upon the individual's capacity to confront it — that is, upon courage.

1. Definitional Distinctions. *a. Anxiety and fear.* Fear is a reaction to a specific identifiable danger while anxiety is a diffuse apprehension that is unspecific, vague, and objectless. In anxiety the very existence of the individual seems threatened. Physiologically and behavioristically there may be little distinction between anxiety and fear. Both involve physiological mobilization (e.g., increased heart rate and blood pressure) and avoidant behavior (such as in phobia, procrastination, or indecisiveness).

b. Anxiety and stress. Stress suggests a more general psychological and physical fatigue and tension, which may be induced by worry, exertion, traumatic circumstances, or other distress, as well as by anxiety.

c. Normal and abnormal anxiety. Normal anxiety, sometimes referred to as primary anxiety or existential anxiety, is a natural, expected and potentially constructive dimension of life. Normal anxiety accompanies freedom and possibility, spurs us on to grow and mature, and guides us in creative means for coping with the challenges of everyday life. Another form of normal anxiety is that found in our sense of vulnerability to the powers of nature, to sickness, and to eventual death. A third form of normal anxiety is associated with isolation and alienation from others, in response to which we move toward communion with others. Abnormal or neurotic anxiety is a reaction to a threat that is (1) disproportionate to the objective danger, (2) involves repression, and (3) is managed by decreased awareness, isolation, psychosomatic reactions, and other destructive defense mechanisms.

2. Philosophical Perspectives on Anxiety. Many philosophers of the seventeenth century stressed the autonomous and prevailing power of reason. The rational faculties of the individual were to counter and control irrational fears and anxiety, such as those associated with devils, sorcerers and forms of magic that were prevalent during the Middle Ages and the Renaissance. Rationalists of the seventeenth century expressed confidence in the individual person's capacity to achieve autonomy and rationality in his or her intellectual, social, religious, and emotional life. The seventeenth century belief in the rational control of the emotions was extended in the nineteenth century by the repression of emotions.

This movement toward the separation of emotions and reason with voluntaristic effort was challenged by the existentialists. Their rejection of traditional rationalism insisted that reality can only be experienced by the whole person using feelings, thoughts, and actions. Kierkegaard believed that this full expression of the human personality reflected the freedom inherent in each individual. For Kierkegaard, freedom is possibility. However, this capacity for self-awareness of possibility brings with it anxiety. While all persons have the opportunity to move ahead in their development, the fact that the path to be taken is unknown creates anxiety. The conflicts involved in the actualization of one's personhood include "destroying the status quo, destroying old patterns within oneself, progressively destroying who one has clung to from childhood on, and creating new and original forms of living" (May, 1950, p. 39). Kierkegaard encourages the individual to confront the anxiety and guilt associated with freedom. In the individual's confrontation of anxiety-creating experiences there develops a self-strength, a capacity to "continually develop one's self out of the death throe of anxiety" (Kierkegaard, 1944, p. 104).

3. Freud. Anxiety is an essential concept in Freud's thinking: "Anxiety is the fundamental phenomenon and the central problem of neurosis" (Freud, 1926). Freud's first theory of anxiety viewed it as the result of repressed libido. Freud's second theory of anxiety (1926) viewed it not as the result but as the cause of repression. This later theory of anxiety identifies it as part of the defensive mechanisms of the ego. The ego perceives danger from the demands of the instincts and generates anxiety as a sort of alarm. The threatened danger the ego perceives is the ego's becoming overwhelmed by excitation and concomitant loss of identity, a fear contributed to by the threats of the loss of or the separation from the mother and of severe punishment from the father. These life endangering events are often disguised and/or transformed in our adult life into different symbols, objects, and rituals to which we respond with anxiety. Anxiety is always a derivative phenomenon, made up, in part, of memory traces of infantile fear and pain, which is why it shows up in expressions of the unconscious, as in nightmares.

4. Sources of Anxiety. Many life experiences foster anxiety. The feeling state is the same, but the conditions and therefore the processes that elicit the feeling are different. Rank points to the individuation/separation process as a source of anxiety. Adler identifies inferiority feelings as the source. Jung views the threat of the irrational in the collective unconscious as a primary contributor to anxiety. Horney refers to the conflicting personality trends which result from our efforts to change life patterns as sources of anxiety. For Sullivan anxiety results from our apprehension of disapproval in interpersonal relationships. May sees the threat to life values as a major source of anxiety. From some sociological perspectives, the source of anxiety is attributed to the role conflicts inherent in cultural change and social mobility. The common feature in each of these perspectives on the source of anxiety is, one may argue, the threatened loss of or separation from that which is perceived as necessary for existence.

5. Theological Perspectives on Anxiety. Paul Tillich believed that anxiety is the individual's response to the threat of nonbeing. Nonbeing not only means the threat of death, but also the threats of guilt and meaninglessness. Like Kierkegaard, Tillich suggests that the only true response to the anxiety of nonbeing is to confront it courageously by taking it into one's being. The incorporation of nonbeing into being robs nonbeing of its overwhelming threat.

For Reinhold Niebuhr anxiety is the central concept in his theological understanding of the human condition. Anxiety is our response to the paradox of our freedom and finiteness: even as we are able to transcend ourselves in order to anticipate perils, we understand ourselves all the more keenly as finite.

Anxiety has been defined as the dread and fear of possible separation from God (e.g., Stinnette) or, as in the form of "anxious striving" and "anxious longing" (Curran), as part of the process of the individual's movement toward maturity and lasting security, fulfillment, and ultimate meaning.

6. Methods of Healing Anxiety. An essential element in healing anxiety is strengthening the ego capacity of the anxious person. As the seat of anxiety the ego must be strong enough to confront anxiety without retreating through repression or other destructive defense mechanisms. The caregiver should support the ego's capacity to expand its awareness of threat and danger, thereby decreasing the possibility of denial and repression.

But the caregiver must also help the anxious person develop constructive responses to the anxiety. Confronted with the threat of separation and loss, the threat of meaninglessness, the threat of overwhelming guilt, or some other threat to one's existence, the anxious person must be helped to face the courageous task of restructuring the self. This may mean moving into another developmental stage, rearranging one's value system, or exercising one's freedom to more fully be one's self.

Faith can be an important factor in the process of confronting one's anxiety and moving through it; according to some theologies it is the indispensable factor. In this view God offers courage and strength. If the anxiety is related to the threat of separation from God, the faithful assurance of God's love, grace, and presence can help reduce the anxiety of separation. All caregivers, lay or clergy, can assist in this process. As the caregiver courageously faces with the anxious person the dreaded source of anxiety, both are enabled to experience the presence of God, which gives confidence and overcomes alienation.

Bibliography. A. Adler, *Problems of Neurosis* (1930). C. A. Curran, "Positive Anxiety in Judeo-Christian Thought," in S. Hiltner and K. Menninger, eds., *Constructive Aspects of Anxiety* (1963), pp. 105–18. S. Freud, "The Justification for Detaching from Neuroasthemia a Particular Syndrome: The Anxiety-Neurosis," *Collected Papers* vol. 1 (1963), pp. 76–106; "Inhibitions, Symptoms and Anxiety," *SE*, 20. S. Hiltner and K. Menninger, *Constructive Aspects of Anxiety* (1963). K. Horney, *New Ways in Psychoanalysis* (1939). C. G. Jung, *Psychology and Religion* (1938). S. Kierkegaard, *The Concept of Dread* (1944). I. Kutash, L. B. Schlesinger, *et al.*, eds., *Handbook on Stress and Anxiety* (1980). R. May, *The Meaning of Anxiety* (1950). R. Niebuhr, *The Nature and Destiny of Man* (1941), vol. 1. W. E. Oates, *Anxiety in Christian Experience* (1955). O. Rank, *Will Therapy* (1936). B. Spinoza, *The Ethics of Spinoza and Treatise on the Correction of the Intellect* 4th ed. (1910). M. Stein, A. J. Vidich, and D. M. White, eds., *Identity and Anxiety* (1960). C. R. Stinette, *Anxiety and Faith* (1955). H. S. Sullivan, "The Meaning of Anxiety in Psychiatry and Life," *Psychiatry*, 2:1 (1948), 1–15. P. Tillich, *The Courage to Be* (1952).

H. U. ASHBY, JR.

DEFENSE AND COPING THEORY; FEAR; FEELING, THOUGHT, AND ACTION IN PASTORAL COUNSELING; PSYCHOPATHOLOGY, THEORIES OF. *See also* ANXIETY DISORDERS; EXISTENTIALISM AND PASTORAL CARE; HUMAN CONDITION/PREDICAMENT; PERSON; PERSONALITY THEORY; PHILOSOPHY AND PSYCHOLOGY; SEPARATION ANXIETY. *Compare* GUILT; SHAME; SHYNESS.

ANXIETY, CHILDHOOD. *See* BEHAVIORAL DISORDERS OF CHILDHOOD.

ANXIETY DISORDERS. A group of psychological disorders in which anxiety and avoidance behavior are the prominent characteristics. Anxiety is a general feeling of fear and apprehension in which the specific nature of the danger is often not clearly perceived. In neurotic anxiety the emotional arousal is just as strong as in ordinary fear (where the threat is more or less clearly perceived and acknowledged by others), but the danger is internal, neither identifiable nor shared as a common threat by others in the situation (Zimbardo and Ruch, 1975).

It is not anxiety *per se* but the type and degree of stress eliciting it that determines if fear is normal or abnormal. In our modern, stressful world, many feel uneasy a good deal of the time and may even experience occasional mild anxiety attacks. Major financial reverses, loss of employment, and other unusual stresses may activate severe but perfectly normal feelings of anxiety. In neurotic reactions the anxiety is considered pathological because it tends to be chronic and is elicited by stress situations that the average individual handles without too much difficulty. Anxiety disorders are fairly common, and it is estimated that about two to four percent of the general population have at some time been diagnosed as having either a phobic disorder or some other anxiety disturbance (Coleman, *et al.*, 1980).

1. **Types of Anxiety Disorders.** *a. Generalized anxiety disorder.* This type is characterized by chronic diffuse anxiety and apprehension which may be punctuated by recurring episodes of more acute, disabling anxiety. Since neither chronic anxiety nor acute anxiety attacks appear to stem from any particular threat, the pervasive anxiety is said to be "free-floating." Individuals with neurotic anxiety are chronically apprehensive and anxious. Their vague fears and fantasies keep them continually upset, uneasy, and discouraged. Not only do they have difficulty making decisions but after decisions have been made they may worry excessively over possible errors and unforeseen circumstances that may lead to disaster. In addition to free-floating anxiety, the predominant symptoms in anxiety neurosis typically include an inability to concentrate, difficulty in making decisions, extreme sensitivity, discouragement, sleep disturbances, excessive sweating, and muscle tension.

b. Obsessive compulsive disorder. Individuals with obsessive compulsive disorders feel compelled to think about something that they do not want to think about or to carry out some action against their will. These individuals usually realize that their behavior is irrational but cannot seem to control it. Particularly common are obsessive thoughts of committing an immoral act. In compulsive reactions, people feel compelled to perform some act which seems strange and absurd to them. Some "addicted" individuals feel mounting anxiety if they cannot perform unhealthy acts such as smoking, consuming alcohol or other drugs, overeating, gambling, sexual exhibition, overspending, etc. The performance of the compulsive act usually brings a feeling of reduced anxiety and tension.

c. Phobic disorder. A phobia is a persistent fear of some object or situation that presents no actual danger to the person or in which the danger is magnified out of proportion to its actual seriousness. Some phobias involve an exaggerated fear of things that most people fear such as darkness, fires, and snakes. Others, such as phobias of open places and crowds, involve situations that do not elicit fear in most people. People who suffer from phobias usually admit that they have no real cause to be afraid, but say they cannot help themselves. Regardless of how it begins, phobic behavior tends to be reinforced by the reduction in anxiety that occurs each time the individual avoids the feared situation or stressor. In addition, phobias may be maintained in part by secondary gains, such as increased attention, sympathy, and control over the behavior of others.

2. **Diagnostic Indicators.** In understanding fear and anxiety reactions, it is helpful to assess intensity, duration, and stimulus. *Intensity* may range from mild to panicky fear. The *duration* may range from acute to chronic. An acute reaction has a sudden onset and relatively short duration but usually with intense symptoms. Acute anxiety attacks are recurring periods of panic that last anywhere from a few seconds to an hour or more. In generalized anxiety disorder the anxiety is chronic, i.e. of at least six months duration.

The *stimuli* that evoke fear may be specific and easily identified as a dog in an animal phobia or presenting a speech in speech phobia. They may also be numerous, diffuse, or unknown as in generalized anxiety disorder that is characterized by general apprehensiveness and frequent worries.

Spielberger *et al.*, (1970) have developed measures of *state* versus *trait* anxiety. *State* anxiety is viewed as focused anxiety that is associated with specific stimuli. Elevations in state anxiety are normally evoked in persons exposed to stressful situations. Examples include fear of medical procedures or test taking fear. *Trait* anxiety refers to anxiety proneness, which is a generalized personality characteristic. High trait persons experience more anxiety states because they perceive a wider range of circumstances as dangerous or threatening.

3. **Physiological Responses.** Fear, anger, and depression are the three basic negative emotions. Each of these emotions is innate and to some extent necessary for survival of the human organism. All three emotions are controlled by the subcortex or old brain, which automatically controls not only our negative emotions but also all the bodily functions and involuntary reactions that keep us alive. The physiological component of emotions is greatly influenced by the activity of various endocrine glands. These glands pump secretions directly into the bloodstream, which are carried to and influence every part of the body. In sudden fear, a hormone is circulated through the blood that brings about such widely diverse processes as dilation of the pupils of the eyes, constriction of blood vessels in the wall of the stomach, and an increase in the rapidity with which blood clots in the presence of air. Part of the sensation of fear is due to great changes in blood flow through the body. The subcortex diverts large amounts of blood away from the interior digestive organs and from the areas of the head, neck, face and even the brain to the skeletal muscles of arms, legs, back, chest, and abdomen where it is most needed for flight or fight responses. Studies have indicated that the hormone epinephrine, which is secreted by the adrenal glands, is generally associated with fear.

4. **Theoretical Explanations.** *a. Psychoanalytic theory.* According to psychoanalytic theory, an anxiety disorder is a symptom of an underlying, hidden psychic conflict. Anxiety-neurotic individuals are seen as likely to experience intense anxiety in situations that elicit "dangerous" feelings — feelings they think they should not have. In analytic theory, repression is the main technique of defense used by neurotic-anxiety individuals, who repress unacceptable hostile impulses and sexual desires. Their conflicts often began during early childhood, and the repression is not complete, as evidenced by continued diffuse anxiety.

A phobia is seen as a displacement of anxiety from a threat that originally elicited it to some other object or situation. For example, a basically insecure person who thinks she or he may be discharged from a job for poor performance may develop an elevator phobia. Fear of an elevator makes it impossible to get to the office located on the twentieth floor of an office building, which in turn protects the person from the possible humiliation of being fired. Psychoanalytic theory explains neurotic anxiety as resulting primarily from either a defense against threatening impulses or, as in phobias, a displacement of anxiety.

b. Learning theories. In learning theory fear and anxiety are understood as conditioned emotional responses. A person learns fears through classical conditioning. As Pavlov's dogs were conditioned to salivate automatically to the sound of their keeper's footsteps at meal time, a person is conditioned to produce an automatic, involuntary emotional response of fear and uneasiness. For example, a fear-eliciting stimulus of an experience with a vicious dog may produce a fear response which generalizes to other dogs and results in a dog phobia. Anxiety can also be learned through modeling or imitation learning. For example, a child may learn anxiety reactions similar to those of a parent. Studies of behavior disorders of children found that overanxious children tend to have overanxious mothers (Jenkins, 1969).

c. Cognitive behavioral theories. These theories emphasize that the quality of emotional states, such as fear, is determined by cognitive factors. They suggest that fear is determined not only by physiological responses to fear-producing stimuli but requires a cognitive appraisal and evaluation of the stimulus situation. Studies have supported the theory (Schacter, 1962, 1971; and Lazarus, 1968). In a situation perceived as threatening the cognitive appraisal results in either direct action of fight or flight or benign reappraisal in which a person reassesses the situation as less threatening, thereby reducing the anxiety state.

5. Methods of Treatment. *a. Pharmacological therapy.* The chemical agents used in such therapy include two most commonly accepted antianxiety compounds (minor tranquilizers). The most commonly used minor tranquilizers are the benzodiazepine derivatives including chlordinzepoxide (Librium), diazepam (Valium), oxazepam (Serax), clorazepate (Tranxene), and flurazepam (Dalmane). Benzodiazepine derivatives have the important property of selectively diminishing generalized fear or anxiety and leaving adaptive behaviors largely intact. They are thus far superior to many other types of anxiety-reducing chemicals, which tend to have widespread negative effects on adaptive functioning.

The other widely accepted class of prescription antianxiety compounds are the meprobamate drugs marketed under the trade names of Miltown and Equanil. Meprobamates seem to operate mainly through the reduction of muscular tension, which in turn is experienced as calming and emotionally soothing. Nevertheless, all antianxiety drugs have a basically sedative effect on the organism, and many patients treated with them complain of drowsiness and lethargy.

b. Psychoanalytic therapy. Here the focus is on treating underlying causes of anxiety. Treatment is designed to relieve repressed impulses, resolve underlying psychic conflict, and help the patient gain insight into the causes of his or her anxiety. Such psychotherapy is highly verbal and introspective and is often best adapted to individuals who are above average in intelligence.

c. Behavior therapy. The behavior therapist assumes that irrational fears are learned fears and that what can be learned can be unlearned. Thus, in treating anxiety or phobias, behavior therapists and cognitive-behavior therapists use one or more of these techniques: systematic desensitization using relaxation training; extinction (non-reinforcing of behavior); implosive therapy in which the client experiences anxiety reaction without suffering any harm; real life ("in vivo") desensitization in which the client progressively faces anxiety stimuli until the fear is extinguished; modeling, in which the client observes a model responding to a situation in an appropriate manner; positive reinforcement of less anxious responses; and learning to control irrational, obsessive thoughts that are associated with emotional responses of neurotic anxiety and fear. Behavior therapy has proven to be highly effective, particularly in treatment of specific phobias such as animal, speech, and school phobias in children. Research shows a clear-cut superiority in treating phobias using behavioral methods.

Bibliography. J. Coleman, J. N. Butcher, and R. C. Carson, *Abnormal Psychology and Modern Life* (1980). D. Cronin, *Anxiety, Depression and Phobias* (1982). I. L. Janis, *Psychological Stress* (1958). R. L. Jenkins, "Classification of Behavior Problems of Children," *American J. of Psychiatry,* 125 (1969), 1032–39. I. Marks, *Handbook of Psychotherapy and Behavior Change: An Empirical Analysis* (1978). D. Meichenbaum, *Stress and Anxiety* (1977), vol. 2. M. J. Smith, *Kicking the Fear Habit* (1979). C. D. Spielberger, R. L. Gorsuch, and R. E. Lushere, *Manual for the State-Trait Anxiety Inventory (Self-Evaluation Questionnaire)* (1973). C. E. Walker, *Learn to Relax* (1975). P. Zimbardo and F. Ruch, *Psychology and Life* (1975).

L. WRIGHT
M. PRICE

ANXIETY; FEAR; MENTAL HEALTH AND ILLNESS; PSYCHOPATHOLOGY, THEORIES OF. *See also* DEFENSE AND COPING THEORY; DIAGNOSTIC AND STATISTICAL MANUAL III; EMOTION; SEPARATION ANXIETY. *Compare* GUILT; SHAME; SHYNESS; STRESS AND STRESS MANAGEMENT.

APATHY AND BOREDOM. Both terms connote absence or lack of feeling, interest, or concern; indifference; listlessness; weariness or emptiness of spirit. *Apathy* implies the withdrawal of affect from an object, such as work, spouse, politics, or church, for which strong affect would ordinarily be expected. *Boredom* may imply some annoyance with such an object and its perceived emotional dullness. Apathy may be associated with a sense of helplessness; boredom with hopelessness, depression, self-blame, perhaps with loneliness, aging, or other occasions of loss. The apathetic person seems to be saying, "I just don't care any more," or "Why bother with X?" The bored may be saying, "I'm just too much trouble; I'm the bother." Earlier and traditionally, apathy and boredom were understood in terms of "sloth" (*acedia*), one of the "seven deadly sins."

1. Psychological Dynamics. The "erasing" of emotions and motivation where they have existed or are appropriately expected implies anxiety, painful emotions, and conflicted emotions, which are being dealt with by repression and withdrawal. The person has come to feel that there are forces at work beyond his or her powers (helplessness) and that he or she lacks internal resources for dealing with the situation (hopelessness). The mild, indirect anger that remains present—in the withdrawal the apathetic directs at another, and in the annoyance the bored feels with others or with self— suggests that more intense anger may be present unconsciously, contributing to the anxiety. In any case, it is important to recognize the condition as a symptom that is not readily changed without some attention to the underlying anxiety and conflict.

The pastor or counselor may become involved in the dynamics as one of the persons at whom the apathy or boredom is directed. The person may have experienced conflict in the church or with the pastor, or may be generalizing to the pastor or to God from other situations and relationships. In either case, the pastor will experience the lack of emotion and motivation directed at himself or herself, at church activities, and especially at the process of counseling itself or at any message of hope or encouragement the pastor may attempt to offer. The pastor may be tempted to feel it necessary to overcome the apathy toward counseling before counseling can address the apathy.

2. **Pastoral Care.** The apathetic or bored person is one of the most difficult types of persons with whom the pastor works. Because the emotional withdrawal and self-disparagement are so clearly inappropriate and "unreasonable" and perhaps personally frustrating to the pastor, it is tempting to try directly and directively to overcome the apathy or boredom and to instruct or persuade the person to revive zest and positive affect. This tactic can lead to fruitless, cyclical arguments with the pastor, for example, insisting "You're OK" and the parishioner insisting, "No, I'm not." It can enhance the person's experience of guilt and despair and drive the person further from the fellowship and ministry of the church. It fails to address the underlying dynamics. There is nothing that can be said that will directly change the mindset of the apathetic or bored person.

The most successful pastoral work with such people takes much time and energy because a considerable amount of confirmation and affirmation is needed to bolster self-worth and a sense of personal resources for dealing with underlying anxieties and conflicts. The most important tool is listening. A willingness to hear rehearsals of injustices and complaints of helplessness and hopelessness may convey a message of respect, helping to restore the person's own sense of value and dignity. The listening may also help to air and to confront some of the underlying emotional conflicts.

3. **The Apathetic or Bored Pastor.** Apathy and boredom are common afflictions of ministers. Pastors may feel overwhelmed by a sense of helplessness in the face of "the church board" or "people who won't listen" or "too much for one person to do." Anxiety grows to such painful proportions that the pastor may begin to lose interest in what happens. Long before the members of the congregation begin to be dissatisfied, the pastor may have arrived at the conclusion that "nothing really matters." When there are repeated conflicts within the church, some pastors begin to believe that they are solely responsible for the disagreements. As their anxiety grows, they may become "bored" and withdraw, expressing self-pity and disparagement about themselves and their ministries.

Sometimes a vacation is helpful, or another change of pace. However, relief will not be long-lasting if the pastor can find no outlet for the buildup of anxiety and emotional conflict. Most helpful in many instances is a support group of other pastors who can listen to stories of frustration and helplessness with understanding and empathy. This help also may be found in a counseling or therapy relationship. While the situation seldom changes, the pastor experiences a sense of relief and discovers a renewed feeling of being in control, being able to identify areas of competence and to reestablish self-esteem. Perspective is altered and the pastor's perception of self as an effective minister is revived.

Bibliography. C. S. Calian, *For All Your Seasons* (1979). S. D. Healy, *Boredom, Self, and Culture* (1984). M. Huguet, *L'ennui et ses discours* (1984). D. S. Savage, *The Apathetic and Bored Church Member* (1976). E. J. Weitzel, *Contemporary Pastoral Counseling* (1969).

B. P. BOGIA

MENTAL HEALTH AND ILLNESS; MENTAL HEALTH, PASTOR'S; SLOTH AND ZEAL (Moral Theology). *See also* ANXIETY; CONFLICT AND CONFLICT MANAGEMENT; FEELING, THOUGHT, AND ACTION IN PASTORAL COUNSELING; EMOTION; REPRESSION; SELF-ESTEEM. *Compare* ALIENATION/ESTRANGEMENT; ANOMIE/NORMLESSNESS; LIFE/ALIVENESS; LONELINESS; SADNESS AND DEPRESSION.

APHASIA. *See* LOSS OF FUNCTION; NEUROLOGIC ILLNESSES.

APOCALYPTIC THINKING AND BELIEF. *See* ESCHATOLOGY; HOPE AND DESPAIR.

APOCRYPHA. *See* OLD TESTAMENT AND APOCRYPHA.

APOSTASY. Total and willful abandonment of the Christian faith both outwardly and inwardly (by mouth and by heart) and, therefore, rebellion against the authority of God's Word (from the Greek *apostasis*, "revolt"). Traditionally, apostasy has constituted a more serious grade of both heresy (violation of Christian belief) and schism (violation of Christian unity).

The term originated in the early church under Roman persecution and gained prominence because of the social and political pressure on Christian people to abandon their faith. Apostasy, murder, and adultery were the three grave sins that the early church initially considered unpardonable. Later, forgiveness and reinstatement were permitted but only after a long and humbling public penance. The most noted transition in this matter occurred under the episcopacy of St. Cyprian in Carthage, following the first systematic, empire-wide persecution of Christians (Emperor Decius, 250 C.E.). Cyprian succeeded in reserving to the bishop (in this case, himself) the act of reinstatement, but moderated the old severity: apostasy was seen in only the most blatant instances of denial, and even here reinstatement could occur after suitable penance and exclusion from communion.

The contemporary significance of the term for pastoral care rests in whether or not the history of modern Western culture constitutes a vast, unfocused apostasy. The modern West has pursued secularity and autonomy for sustaining its life, laying aside many of its former supernatural sanctions. Have these moves constituted a revolt against the governance of God, in favor of life within the limits of reason alone? Is the modern world apostate, in regard to its own heritage? To the extent that it is, the pastoral counselor faces a complex situation.

One issue, for example, is the integrity of pastoral care itself, since the field is partially formed by the discipline of modern psychology, which may itself be implicitly apostate. In that case, this apostasy, negative in character, must be probed to see if affirmative traces of classical theological imagery remain in translated form. Psychological concepts of limit, empathy, crisis, integration and reintegration, acceptance, and goal, are examples of such affirmative traces. In that case, the counselor appropriately enters the situation of the counselee through the key of psychological language and concept. Yet even with this entry, the implicit apostasy effects an ironic reversion into the arena of faith it had proposed to replace, as psychological language yields to the appropriate, reminiscent objects of biblical narrative: covenant, incarnation, cross, resurrection, new creation, justification, and end time.

Bibliography. *The Maryknoll Catholic Dictionary* (1965). *The Oxford Dictionary of the Christian Church* 2d ed., (1974). H. von Campenhausen, *Men Who Shaped the Western Church* (1964), ch. 2. *The New Catholic Encyclopedia* vol. 1, (1967). *The Schaff-Herzog Religious Encyclopedia* vol. 1, (1892).

W. MALLARD

APOSTOLIC PASTORAL CARE. See NEW TESTAMENT AND APOCRYPHA. *See also* PASTORAL CARE (History, Traditions, and Definitions).

ARCHETYPE. In analytical (Jungian) psychology, a primordial image representing psychic contents of the collective unconscious (as opposed to the personal unconscious) frequently manifest in dreams, myths, fairy tales, and symbols. As patterns of energy not directly experienced, archetypes yield an endless variety of distinct images shared by all people universally, e.g. the mother or father imago, the hero, the tribe, or the deity.

I. R. STERNLICHT

ANALYTICAL (JUNGIAN) PSYCHOLOGY (Personality Theory and Research); COLLECTIVE UNCONSCIOUS. *See also* MYTHOLOGY AND PSYCHOLOGY; SYMBOLISM/SYMBOLIZING.

ARGUING/ARGUMENTATION. See CONFLICT AND CONFLICT MANAGEMENT; DISAGREEMENT, DIFFERENCE, AND CONFLICT IN PASTOR-PARISHIONER RELATIONSHIPS; REASONING AND RATIONALITY IN PASTORAL CARE.

ARGULA von GRUMBACH. See WOMEN IN PASTORAL MINISTRIES, HISTORY OF.

ARISTOTELIAN PSYCHOLOGY. See PHILOSOPHY AND PSYCHOLOGY; CAUSALITY IN PSYCHOLOGY, FORMS OF.

ART OF DYING (Ars Moriendi). Refers to any of a great many late medieval devotional books concerned with death and dying. Rich in pastoral and ascetical insight, this body of literature was widely used in the fourteenth and fifteenth centuries. Initially the texts were probably manuals to aid clerics in ministry to the dying. After being published as illustrated block-books and translated into vernacular languages, they came into the possession of lay people, and thus became influential for popular piety as well as for pastoral work. Texts attributed to Jean Gerson, Nicholas of Dinkelsbuehl, Thomas Peutner, and Geiler von Kaiserberg are most well-known.

T. A. SMITH

MEDIEVAL CHURCH, PASTORAL CARE IN. *See also* DYING, PASTORAL CARE OF; ESCHATOLOGY AND PASTORAL CARE.

ART THERAPY. See ADJUNCTIVE THERAPIES.

ARTERIOSCLEROTIC DISORDERS. See HEART PATIENT; NEUROLOGIC ILLNESSES.

ARTIFICIAL INSEMINATION. See FAMILY PLANNING; INFERTILITY; INFERTILITY THERAPIES, MORAL ISSUES IN.

ARTIFICIAL INTELLIGENCE. See CYBERNETIC THEORY IN PSYCHOLOGY AND COUNSELING; INTELLIGENCE AND INTELLIGENCE TESTING.

The ARTS AND CARE. See ADJUNCTIVE THERAPIES; DRAMA *or* MUSIC AS MODE OF CARE.

ASCETICAL PRACTICES. Voluntary activities, or the renunciation of certain pleasurable objects or activities, for the purpose of spiritual growth and loving service. Christian asceticism does not seek to identify particular objects as damaging or evil but begins by recognition and acknowledgement of the goodness of the body and the material world. Nevertheless, persons can become compulsive in pursuit of objects or activities so that the development of a disciplined life is necessary in order to augment personal freedom leading to emotional and spiritual growth.

Ascetic practices have been featured consistently in historic Christianity and in the Orthodox churches as a necessary part of the spiritual life. Because cultural and religious perspectives that reject asceticism are dominant in contemporary North American culture, historic and contemporary practices and attitudes will be treated sequentially.

1. **Historical.** A range of ascetic practices can be found in western Christianity, from gentle disciplines like regular prayer, watchfulness, reading, and short fasts, to harsh practices—damaging to the body and life-shortening—such as self-scourging, long fasts, dry fasts, and self-cultivated bodily discomfort or pain. In many historic descriptions of sanctity, extreme voluntary abuse of the body seems to be taken for granted.

It is difficult to understand self-imposed physical suffering as consonant with the goodness, integrity, and permanence of the body in human personhood. Frequently, historic authors were aware of abuses and cautioned care for the body and the avoidance of harsh ascetic practices.

Nevertheless, historic Christians were convinced of the usefulness of voluntary ascetic practices. They understood that altering habitual activities or one's physical condition was the most direct way to render the soul open, vulnerable, and sensitive — a prerequisite to any significant change in behavior, attitudes, or personality. Ascetic practices were seen as an irreplaceable tool for access to the soul. Disciplines of celibacy, poverty, and obedience to a spiritual leader were useful for overcoming socially conditioned styles of the pursuit of sex, power, and possessions. They were also often described as important for the clarification, concentration, and intensification of consciousness and for addressing the subtly deadening habits and addictions of daily life. Toward the realization of these goals, Evagrius Ponticus, a theologian of fourth century Egyptian desert asceticism, mentions asceticisms of prayer, vigils, reading, fasting, solitude, continence, and limiting one's intake of water. John Cassian adds to this list nakedness and poverty.

In Protestantism, and beginning with Luther, there has been criticism of asceticism as practiced in the medieval church. Luther considered ascetic practices necessary for the spiritual life, but he described them as the *result* of penitence rather than as the *means* of making the soul sensitive to its usually well-defended operation. Calvin, like the Old Testament prophets, spoke of ascetic practices in the context of public life, as a means of altering the comfortable habits that prevent communities and nations from recognizing internal injustice and /or external peril.

2. **Contemporary.** The value of ascetic practices is being rediscovered as a means of overcoming habits and addictions and of gathering and focusing energy in a culture increasingly oriented to distraction and entertainment. In order to be fully consonant with Christian faith, ascetic practices must not be directed to punishing the body or to rejecting certain objects as evil. Rather, ascetic practices must be individually designed — either by a person with self-knowledge, or by a wise and sensitive spiritual director — to address a compulsive pattern. Undertaken for a length of time, chosen in advance, these practices must also be as good for body as for soul. Short fasts which allow the body to rest from its constant labor of metabolism, fasts from media, disciplines of prayer and meditation often involving techniques of breathing and posture, temporary periods of celibacy, solitude, silence — any of these ascetic practices can be highly effective in identifying and treating deadness in soul and habituation in body. Christian ascetic practices are not in themselves ends, but can be effective as preparation for loving service. The effective creative use of ascetic practices demonstrates the unity of body and soul in spiritual growth.

Bibliography. "Ascèse, Ascéticisme," *Dictionnaire de spiritualité ascétique et mystique,* I, col. 936–1017, esp. III. "L'ascèse chrétienne," col. 960–1017; see also "Mortification," X, col. 1791–99. "Ascétisme," *DTC* I, col. 2055–77. T. à Kempis, *The Imitation of Christ.* I. Loyola, *The Spiritual Exercises.* The Collected "Sayings of the Fathers" in O. Chadwick, ed., *Western Asceticism* (1958). For contemporary treatments, see M. Miles, *Fullness of Life: Historical Foundations for a New Asceticism* (1981).

D. Nichols, *Holiness* (1981). H. J. M. Nouwen, *With Open Hands* (1972).

M. R. MILES

SELF-DENIAL; SELF-EXPRESSION/SELF-CONTROL; SPIRITUAL DISCIPLINE AND GROWTH. *See also* CELIBACY; CHRISTIAN *or* JEWISH LIFE; RELIGIOUS BEHAVIOR; RELIGIOUS LIFE (VOWED LIFE); SPIRITUAL THEOLOGY AND PASTORAL CARE; SPIRITUALITY; VOWS/VOWING. *Compare* LIFESTYLE ISSUES; MORAL BEHAVIOR AND RELIGION; PENANCE, SACRAMENT OF; PHYSICAL FITNESS DISCIPLINES; PSYCHOPATHOLOGY AND RELIGION; SACRIFICIAL BEHAVIOR.

ASCETICAL THEOLOGY. *See* SPIRITUAL THEOLOGY.

ASIAN PASTORAL CARE MOVEMENT. *See* SOUTH ASIAN *or* EAST ASIAN PASTORAL CARE MOVEMENT.

ASIAN RELIGION, SOUL CARE AND PSYCHOLOGY IN. *See* PSYCHOLOGY, EASTERN; PSYCHOLOGY AND PSYCHOTHERAPY (East-West Comparison).

ASIAN AMERICAN PASTORAL CARE. Pastoral care with Asian Americans is concerned with all the problems present in any cross-cultural work, but several distinctive issues are also involved.

1. **Identity.** Virtually every Asian American struggles with the question of identity. Set apart by Asian facial characteristics, members of this group cannot merge into white American circles even if they wanted to. Though they may be thoroughly Americanized in attitudes and behavior patterns, they tend to remain outside the mainstream of American life. They may feel like Americans, but they look like Asians and hence are torn between two cultures. Since a clear, personal identity is so crucial for developing positive self-esteem, Asian Americans are more susceptible than most Americans to the problem of a low sense of personal worth.

The identity issue is made more acute by the failure of many Americans to distinguish between the different parts of Asia where Asian Americans have their roots. Few Americans know enough about Asian history to recognize how deep-seated some antagonism is between Asian ethnic groups. For example, how many Americans are aware that the Japanese occupied Taiwan from 1895 to 1945 so that at least two whole generations of Taiwanese lived entirely under Japanese domination? For Chinese to be mistaken for Vietnamese, or for Koreans to be confused with Japanese, or for Filipinos to be misnamed Malaysians is to compound the identity problem.

An additional identity issue revolves around the generation being dealt with in terms of when migration from the home country took place. Among Japanese Americans, special Japanese names are given to the different generations; effective pastoral care must pay attention to the distinctive features of each group. The generation born in Japan which migrated to the United States are known as Issei. The first generation born in America are known as Nisei. The second and third generations born in the U.S. are known respectively as Sansei and Yonsei.

The identity issue is further compounded for recent immigrants by economic and social factors. Unlike many of the earlier streams of migration encouraged by the need for cheap labor, the more recent migrations, especially from Vietnam, have consisted largely of well-educated professional people who have fled from their own country to seek freedom in America. Confronted both by language problems and by stringent licensing procedures, these professionals are often forced to work at menial tasks far below their capacity.

2. **Exploitation.** Perhaps even more important than the identity issue is the fact that most Asian Americans have experienced exploitation and humiliation at the hands of Americans in general. Oriented to a melting pot ideal, most Americans are unaware of how little interest most Asian Americans have today in being assimilated into the mainstream culture. A good part of the resistance to being acculturated grows out of the persecution and discrimination to which many Asian Americans are still subjected.

Each wave of Asian immigration started with exploitation for economic gain. Chinese were recruited to construct the railroads, and Japanese and Filipinos were recruited to work in the sugar cane fields. When Asians began to gain an economic foothold, the fear of the "yellow peril" led to restrictive immigration policies, and the war hysteria on the West Coast in World War II led to the creation of relocation camps for all those of Japanese ancestry, commonly called "concentration camps" by Japanese Americans. Most Asians have deep-seated anger, but the special personality characteristics of typical Asians keep this anger repressed and seldom visible. Every Asian American is conscious of the fact that Hiroshima and Nagasaki were Asian cities, and that only in Asia has an atomic bomb been used against a civilian population. Pastoral care with Asian Americans begins with the recognition that Asian Americans are a part of the "other" America which has known more of discrimination and humiliation than it has known of equality and justice.

3. **Culture.** A third issue of importance where Asian Americans are concerned is the recognition of the deep roots of Asian culture. Whereas Americans in the United States are inclined to believe that the Western, American way is superior and the Eastern, Asian way is inferior, Asian Americans may well have the opposite point of view. When Chinese speak of China as the "central kingdom" around which the rest of the world revolves, they are stating their conviction of the essential "rightness" of the Chinese way. When marriage across ethnic lines is proposed, with one of the partners Asian American and the other of non-Asian ancestry, it is usually the Asian American family that is most distressed. To marry a non-Asian, in the eyes of the Asian American community, is to be degraded.

4. **Family.** A fourth issue is the highly significant place of the family in any Asian American home. Probably the sharpest difference between Asian and American ways comes in the distinction between a community versus an individual orientation to life. Most Asians think in terms of community whereas most Americans (at least in the United States) think in terms of the individual. Most Asian Americans are torn between accenting the family-oriented ways of their former culture and the individual-oriented ways of their new homeland.

Pastoral care of an Asian American inevitably involves the family. Seen from Western eyes, the relationship of parents to children, and especially of mother-in-law to daughter-in-law seems rigid and arbitrary, but seen from the perspective of Asian culture it is normal and expected. If the newly married son seems to pay more attention to his mother than to his bride, this is simply the Asian way and does not mean that he doesn't care for his new wife.

5. **Relationships.** Still another issue is found in the indirect way in which Asians go about handling personal relationships. Asian Americans are constantly pulled between the direct ways of North Americans and the indirect ways of Asians. One of the commonest areas for breakdown in communication is seen when a westerner seeks a direct "yes" or "no" to a specific question. The Asian American may give the impression of being in full agreement, when, instead, he or she is in sharp disagreement. The open expression of feeling, and especially of anger, is contrary to cultural norms. It is commonplace to find that the Nisei man who suffered through the relocation camp experience seldom raises his voice in angry protest but eats his heart out in silence. Any teacher knows how hard it is to get direct feedback that may be negative from Asian Americans steeped in the tradition of revering the older teacher.

The indirect approach so common to anyone steeped in Eastern culture finds expression in practices in pastoral care. In a way which seems foreign to most North Americans, the older brother may be called upon to play a reconciling role when tensions flare up among family members, rather than seeking a professional counselor who might be inclined to use direct confrontation in attacking problems.

6. **Ethnic Roots.** Pastoral care with Asian Americans is complicated by the fact that the Christianity known to most readers has been so bound up with Western ways that to become a Christian almost means to give up Asian heritage. Students in Asia studying in missionary schools have commonly been given Biblical names (Joseph, Peter, Jacob) so that becoming Christian has meant changing given names. The identification of Christianity with the Western world is an increasing problem in a day when sensitivity about ethnic roots has been sharpened and when an indigenous theology is being developed. The degree to which Christianity is able to foster an appreciation for ethnic roots and a recognition of a wisdom from the East often superior to the wisdom of the West may spell the difference between a pastoral care which enhances and one which denigrates.

Bibliography. D. W. Augsburger, *Pastoral Counseling Across Cultures* (1986). E. Gee *et al.,* eds., *Counterpoint: Perspectives on Asian America,* Asian American Studies Center, University of California at Los Angeles (1976). R. C. Leslie, "Counseling Across Cultures," *United Ministries in Higher Education, Monograph Number 5,* June, 1979. A. Tachiki *et al.,* eds., *Roots: An Asian American Reader,* Asian American Studies Center, University of California at Los Angeles (1971). R. Sano, compiler, *The Theologies of Asian Americans and Pacific Peoples: A Reader,* Asian Center for Theology and Strategies, Pacific School of Religion (1976).

R. C. LESLIE

CROSS-CULTURAL PASTORAL CARE. *See also* CROSS-CULTURAL MARRIAGE AND FAMILY; CULTURAL AND ETHNIC FACTORS; RACISM; SOCIAL STATUS AND CLASS FACTORS.

ASPIRATION. *See* HOPE AND DESPAIR; MORAL BEHAVIOR AND RELIGION.

ASSERTIVENESS IN MINISTRY. A behavioral methodology for training in ministry offering a theory of balanced power that is nonaggressive yet effective in interaction and negotiation.

Pastoral initiative, administration, negotiation, problem solving, and conflict management, when viewed from the perspectives of behavioral psychology, may be said to fall into three main groupings: nonassertive, assertive, and aggressive behavior. To react too strongly (aggressive behavior) or too weakly (nonassertive behavior) is seldom useful. Between these extremes lies a balanced option (assertive behavior) that is generally more effective.

1. **Theory.** In its development, assertiveness training has become a set of procedures for intentional behavioral change utilized in education and in all the helping professions. It views behavior along a continuum from passive, nonassertive behavior through active assertive behavior to explosive aggressive behavior. Individuals may act habitually from one of the three, or more commonly swing from the one extreme to the other as the nonassertive person internalizes and accumulates stress, then explodes and overreacts to persons and problems, which is followed by a contrite return to passivity.

Nonassertion entails ignoring one's own rights, thoughts, and feelings. By failing to express one's desires and allowing others to violate oneself or by expressing one's thoughts and feelings in a self-effacing, apologetic style, which permits others to ignore them, the nonassertive person invites use or abuse. The message communicated is: I'm not important — you ignore me. My needs don't matter — you can take me for granted. My goals are secondary — you may take advantage of me.

Aggression involves ignoring the other person's rights, thoughts, and feelings. By standing up for personal rights and expressing goals in a way that overpowers, intimidates, or manipulates the other, aggression violates the other person. Since the goal is domination, winning, or exploiting the other's loss, the message communicated is: I am all important — you must yield. My needs are crucial — yours are insignificant. My goals are everything — yours are nothing.

Assertion involves a balanced concern for the rights, wants, thoughts, and feelings of both self and others. The goal of assertiveness is communication, cooperation, and mutually satisfactory solutions to problem situations. Some trainers view assertiveness as claiming one's rights and getting what one wants, regardless of the other's preferences. Assertiveness in ministry follows the perspective that authentic assertiveness takes mutuality as the starting point of balanced power and responsibility.

2. **Evaluation.** *a. Theology.* The goal of interpersonal relationships is to act justly, mercifully, and responsibly. Justice is achieved by the balancing of love and power as each corrects and completes the other. Aggression values power to the exclusion of love. Loveless power seizes control at the expense of caring, violating others even in the name of truth, righteousness, or perfection. The nonassertive response, on the other hand, prizes love and eschews power. "Love and power are often contrasted in such a way that love is identified with a resignation of power and power with a denial of love" (Tillich, 1954). Assertiveness seeks to unite power and love in loving power that creates powerful love.

b. Ethics. Assertiveness in ministry recognizes that those models of assertive training that focus more on rights than responsibility, more on goals than relationship, and more on content than process are ethically invalid. Grace and truth, love and power, concern for persons and concern for ends must be kept in dynamic and creative balance. Thus the pastoral theologian thinks of relationships on two *continua* — assertiveness and affirmativeness. To be assertive (act powerfully) does not require any loss of affirmativeness (acting positively). To act in assertive and affirmative balance offers ministry that gives presence — someone to stand with — and prophetic clarity — something to stand for.

3. **Application.** Assertiveness training is a process with these two equally crucial foci. *Assertiveness* has the goals of (1) modeling the difference between assertion and aggression, and between nonassertion and polite concern; (2) helping people identify and claim their personal rights and the full rights of others; (3) reducing thinking and feeling blocks to creative change and growth; (4) skill development through role playing and life-practice methods. *Affirmativeness* has the goals of (1) modeling love as equal regard for self and other; (2) helping people differentiate between passive yielding love and active concern for the highest good for self and others; (3) integrating relational affirmativeness as positive caring with interpersonal power in effective assertiveness.

Bibliography. D. W. Augsburger, *Anger and Assertiveness in Pastoral Care* (1979). M. Emmons and D. Richardson, *The Assertive Christian* (1981). J. Faul and D. W. Augsburger, *Beyond Assertiveness* (1980). J. Wolpe and A. Lazarus, *Behavior Therapy Techniques* (1966). R. Alberti and M. Emmons, *The Professional Edition of Your Perfect Right* (1986). P. Tillich, *Love, Power and Justice* (1980 [1954]).

D. W. AUGSBURGER

AGGRESSION AND ASSERTION; AUTHORITY, PASTORAL; INITIATIVE AND INTERVENTION, PASTORAL; LEADERSHIP AND ADMINISTRATION. *See also* ADVOCACY; CONFLICT AND CONFLICT MANAGEMENT; CONFRONTATION (Pastoral and Therapeutic); POWER; STRUCTURING. *Compare* AUTHORITARIANISM; COMPETITIVENESS; PATIENCE/PATIENTHOOD.

ASSERTIVENESS TRAINING AND THERAPY. A form of behavior therapy that seeks to improve clients' skills in expressing their personal rights, thoughts, feelings, and concerns to others. Its emphasis is to train communication skills that are direct, honest, appropriate, and take into account the rights and feelings of others. The training is most often suggested for people who exhibit various self-effacing behaviors, but it has also been successfully used to help aggressive individuals develop less-abrasive communication skills. Assertiveness training has been offered to the general public as a tool for improving overall personal effectiveness.

1. Therapeutic Methods. Training is provided in either individual, group, or workshop settings. Initially, an assessment is made of the client's areas of deficiency. For example, a particular client may have difficulty making requests or effectively expressing anger. Other possible deficit areas include refusal behaviors — saying no — expressing positive or negative emotions, giving/receiving compliments, and assertiveness in special situations such as job interviewing.

Training then focuses on improving these skill deficits. The therapist usually provides clients with educative materials on what assertiveness is and how it differs from aggressiveness and self-effacement. Treatment often focuses on cognitive blocks that may inhibit assertive behavior. For example, the active church worker who wants more time with her family but finds herself saying yes to every church project, may do so because of a nagging and perhaps irrational cognition that to say no is to be seen as "a poor example of a Christian." The therapist will work with the client to identify these cognitions and substitute more rational ones. The church worker might alternatively think to herself that as a Christian she also has a responsibility to her family and that it is doubtful that people will think badly of her if she refuses another opportunity.

One key aspect of assertiveness training is the rehearsal phase. Its major assumption is that assertiveness is a learned skill best mastered by practice in a safe, instructive environment. The role of the therapist during rehearsal is to help a client focus on areas of greatest difficulty, model or demonstrate appropriate assertive behaviors, observe or participate in the client's rehearsal, and give feedback and coaching to the client about the effectiveness of the rehearsals. For example, a client may report difficulty returning a defective shirt to the store. The therapist or another group member would play the salesperson and encourage the client to enact the scene of returning the shirt. This would be practiced several times until there was evidence that the client had achieved some mastery.

One special advantage of rehearsal is that clients can receive feedback both on the more obvious aspects of their assertive behavior and on the more covert ones such as body language, voice inflection, inappropriate smiling, and poor eye contact which may negate an otherwise assertive message. The therapist coaches the client to eliminate such self-defeating behavior and encourages the client to practice his or her new assertive skills in everyday life.

The ultimate purpose of assertiveness training is not to teach clients to "get their way," but to aid them to communicate more effectively their honest thoughts, needs, and feelings. Such behavior leads to negotiation and intimacy rather than manipulation. The therapist is not interested in historical causes. It is assumed that nonassertive behaviors have been learned and that if they have been learned, they can be unlearned.

2. Assertiveness Training and the Church. Sometimes Christians resist assertiveness training, believing that it contradicts religious teachings that stress "turning the other cheek." Such an attitude is not limited, as some suppose, to the more Fundamentalist denominations. Typically such people view Christ as one who was mild and self-effacing and overlook evidence that he could also express negative emotion and be confrontive. When Jesus healed a man in the synagogue on the Sabbath (Mk. 3:1-5) it was an assertive risk for the betterment of another's life. Present-day, nonassertive people sometimes have difficulty even imagining themselves speaking up in similar conflict situations.

When one considers that most assertiveness training eschews aggression, strives for greater intimacy between people, and teaches honest communication skills, then the training seems even more consonant with a Christian ethic.

Bibliography. R. Alberti and M. Emmons, *Your Perfect Right* 4th ed. (1982). A. Lange and P. Jakubowski, *Responsible Assertive Behavior* (1976). R. Sanders and H. Malony, "A Theological and Psychological Rationale for Assertiveness Training," *J. of Pastoral Theology*, 10 (1982) 251-55.

R. K. SANDERS

AGGRESSION AND ASSERTION; BEHAVIOR THERAPIES; POPULAR THERAPEUTIC MOVEMENTS AND PSYCHOLOGIES. *Compare* HUMAN RELATIONS TRAINING; PSYCHOTHERAPY; VALUES IN COUNSELING AND PSYCHOTHERAPY; WILL THERAPY.

ASSESSMENT. *See* EVALUATION AND DIAGNOSIS; INTERPRETATION AND HERMENEUTICS.

ASSOCIATION FOR CLINICAL PASTORAL EDUCATION (ACPE). An interfaith association composed of clinical pastoral educators, theological school representatives, church agency representatives, and interested individuals. Its purposes are: (1) to promote clinical pastoral education (CPE) as an essential part of theological education and of continuing education for ministry; (2) to define standards for CPE; (3) to certify supervisors of CPE; (4) to accredit institutions, agencies, and parishes to offer programs of CPE; and (5) to provide conferences, publications, and research opportunities.

The ACPE has over 375 institutions accredited to offer programs of CPE, has over 800 certified supervisors, 2,500 individual members, and 110 theological school members. Each year over 7,000 theological students and clergypersons enroll in CPE.

CPE is professional education for ministry. It brings theological students and ministers into supervised encounter with persons in crises. Out of an intense involvement with persons in need and the feedback from peers and teachers, students develop new awareness of themselves as persons and of the needs of those to whom they minister. From theological reflection on specific human situations, they gain new understanding of the human situation. Within the interdisciplinary team process of helping persons, they develop skills in interpersonal and interprofessional relationships.

CPE is offered by accredited centers at three levels: (1) Basic CPE which focuses on ministry formation and ministry development; (2) Advanced CPE which provides continuing education in ministry development and pastoral care specialization; and (3) Supervisory CPE to develop clinical competence and learning in supervision.

The legally responsible body of the ACPE is a General Assembly, a body with representatives from each of the nine ACPE regions, representatives of the Association of Theological Schools, denominational/faith group representatives, the ACPE officers, and chairpersons of standing committees.

The work of the Association is carried out through committees such as: accreditation, certification, development, finance, historical, judiciary, research, and standards.

The ACPE is divided into nine geographic regions. Regions provide workshops and conferences in which CPE supervisors, CPE students, theological professors, and others share insights and explore issues of concern in ministry. Each year the ACPE provides a national conference as continuing education for its members.

Bibliography. E. E. Thornton, *Professional Education for Ministry* (1970).

C. E. HALL

CLINICAL PASTORAL EDUCATION; PASTORAL CARE MOVEMENT. *See also* ACCREDITATION; CANADIAN PASTORAL CARE MOVEMENT; CERTIFICATION; CERTIFIED SUPERVISOR; HISTORY OF PROTESTANT PASTORAL CARE. *Compare* AMERICAN ASSOCIATION OF PASTORAL COUNSELORS; COUNCIL FOR CLINICAL TRAINING; INSTITUTE OF PASTORAL CARE; LUTHERAN ADVISORY COUNCIL; SOUTHERN BAPTIST ASSOCIATION FOR CLINICAL PASTORAL EDUCATION.

ATHANASIUS, ST. *See* LITERATURE, DEVOTIONAL.

ATHEISM. *See* DOUBT AND UNBELIEF; GOD, DOCTRINE OF, AND PASTORAL CARE; SECULARIZATION/SECULARISM.

ATONEMENT. *See* CHRISTOLOGY AND PASTORAL CARE; FORGIVENESS; GUILT; PENANCE, SACRAMENT OF; UNDOING.

ATTITUDE. The classical approach within psychology has defined attitude as a predisposition to respond positively or negatively to a psychological object. "Psychological object" includes not only physical objects but also ideas, symbols, other people, and concepts. This definition of attitude has been at the heart of most of the research done within this area. Many psychologists use the terms attitude, interest, value, and opinion almost interchangeably.

The procedures commonly used to evaluate an attitude include Thurstone's (1928) equal-appearing intervals scale technique, summative scaling (Likert, 1932), Guttman (1944) scaling, self-ratings, and Osgood's semantic differential technique (Osgood, Suci, and Tannenbaum, 1957). All of these procedures have good reliability and validity. The results from these different scaling procedures are highly correlated and thus are interchangeable.

Attitudes have been found to relate strongly to behavior when certain conditions are met. Those conditions include situations in which the individual is engaged in decision making about the behavior, and when the situation is more strongly determined by personal preference than by values (in the sense of moral obligation). Schwartz (1968) has shown that attitudes correlate with

behavior when people are aware of the long-term consequences (and so can compare those consequences to their attitudes) and when they accept their responsibility in that situation (and so see their attitudes as relevant to their behavior). If these two conditions are not met, attitudes are unrelated to behavior.

Conscious processes other than attitudes may also influence behavior. These other processes include social norms (i.e., how we feel those people important to us will react) (Ajzen and Fishbein, 1980) and values (Gorsuch and Ortberg, 1983). In the latter case, the term "values" is used in the sense of moral obligation. Values as moral obligations can be measured through a rating on a scale of moral obligation *per se* or through methods developed by Scott (1965). Not only are values semantically different from attitudes *per se*, but they also correlate only three-tenths with attitudes as measured by the traditional instruments. Further, in situations that could be defined as morally relevant by moral philosophers, values add to the prediction of behavior over and above the classical definition of attitudes (Gorsuch and Ortberg, 1983). Hence attitudes consist of one's *personal* predisposition to respond positively or negatively and are relatively independent of moral evaluations of whether one *ought* to respond positively or negatively.

Bibliography. I. Ajzen and M. Fishbein, *Understanding Attitudes and Predicting Behavior* (1980). R. L. Gorsuch, "Attitudes, interests, sentiments, and values," in R. C. Johnson and R. B. Cattell, eds., *Functional Psychological Testing* (1985). R. L. Gorsuch and J. Ortberg, "Moral obligation and attitudes: Their relation to behavioral intensions," *J. of Personality and Social Psychology*, 44 (1983), 1025–28. L. Guttman, "A basis for scaling qualitative data," *American Sociological Review*, 44 (1944), 139–50. R. A. Likert, "A technique for the measurement of attitudes," *Archives of General Psychology*, 140 (1932), 44–53. C. E. Osgood, G. J. Suci, and P. H. Tannenbaum, *The Measurement of Meaning* (1957). S. Schwartz, "Words, deeds, and the perception of consequences and responsibility in action situations," *J. of Personality and Social Psychology*, 10 (1963), 232–42. W. A. Scott, *Values and Organizations* (1965). L. L. Thurstone, "Attitudes can be measured," *American J. of Sociology* (1928), 529–54.

R. L. GORSUCH

SOCIAL PERCEPTION, JUDGMENT, AND BELIEF. *See also* SOCIAL PSYCHOLOGY, DISCIPLINE OF; VALUES RESEARCH. *Compare* PERSONALITY TYPES AND PASTORAL CARE; MIND-CURE MOVEMENT; TEMPERAMENT.

ATTRIBUTION THEORY. *See* SOCIAL PERCEPTION, JUDGMENT, AND BELIEF.

AUGUSTINE OF HIPPO, ST. (354–430). Bishop of Hippo Regius. At age eighteen he began a search for truth which caused him to embrace successively Manichaeism, skepticism, Neoplatonism, and ultimately Christianity. From his native North Africa Augustine went to Rome and then to Milan where he fell under the influence of Ambrose, bishop of Milan. Months of struggle culminated in his baptism in 387. When he returned to Africa, Augustine organized a monastery in his hometown. The group later moved to Hippo where he was ordained priest in 391 and made bishop in 396. He spent the remainder of his life working out his interpretation of Christianity in such monumental works as *The City of God*.

As philosopher and theologian Augustine's importance in Christian history has been rarely matched. Among his many contributions is his understanding of selfhood. His view grew out of his personal struggles as reflected in his *Confessions*, a spiritual autobiography. Futile attempts to correct his profligate ways convinced Augustine that it was impossible to escape sin by mere acts of will. His moral disease was deep, inherited from fallen Adam. Deliverance from this spiritual bondage was possible only through divine grace, irresistibly and compellingly breaking upon him. Augustine's view dominated Christian pastoral psychology for over a millennium and traces remain today.

R. W. CRAPPS

EARLY CHURCH, PASTORAL CARE AND COUNSELING IN.

AUGUSTINIAN SPIRITUALITY. *See* SPIRITUALITY (Roman Catholic Tradition).

AURA. *See* PARAPSYCHOLOGY.

AUSTRALIAN AND NEW ZEALAND PASTORAL CARE MOVEMENTS. Pastoral care in both Australia and New Zealand has learned much from the modern pastoral care movement in the U.S., yet there are also notable variations between the three countries. Private practice in pastoral counseling is almost unknown in Australia but is growing steadily in New Zealand. Pastoral counseling centers on the U.S. model are uncommon in both countries but, in New Zealand especially, there is an increasing number of small, specialized centers for pastoral concerns. Most of the formal caring, however, is done within parish structures, within church institutions, or through chaplaincy roles in government institutions.

Within parishes pastoral care is often seen as the exclusive responsibility of the formally designated priest, minister, or pastor. In recent years, however, pastoral care teams and other forms of lay participation have developed in some congregations, particularly in Australia. Some of the most effective caring is done informally or incidentally to other activities. Caring for the pastors has been haphazard in most churches.

Institutionalized forms of caring by the churches in both countries have traditionally focused on caring for children and the aged. The churches also provide counseling and other forms of help for the poor, the socially disadvantaged, people in crisis (including crises of marriage and family life), and people with specific difficulties, e.g. alcohol or drug dependent people or sufferers from Huntingdon's disease. Most of these services draw their primary funding from the state but continue to call on Christian motivation and concern. It is often the availability or otherwise of government funding which shapes the caring response of the churches. There are indications in both countries that the pattern of state involvement in social welfare may change to provide for greater participation by voluntary organizations, including the churches. Many church members offer their caring through non-church organizations and programs.

Many church programs of caring have pioneered in meeting community needs. An historical example is the Presbyterian Church (now Uniting Church's) formation of the Australian Inland Mission in 1912 to serve people in the most remote areas of Australia. Bush patrol padres journeyed to these areas by camel (later by car, truck, and four-wheel drive) and hospitals were established. In 1928 the founder, Rev. John Flynn, sought to cast a "mantle of safety over the Inland" by placing pedal-operated radios in each of the scattered homesteads and by developing a medical service using radio and airplanes — now the Royal Flying Doctor Service.

Chaplaincies in general, and mental and psychiatric hospitals have provided pastoral care within their institutions as well as a context for supervised (or clinical) pastoral education. CPE programs exist in major cities in most states of Australia and many provinces of New Zealand. They have transformed chaplaincy ministries and are an important element in theological education generally. New Zealanders still tend to look to the U.S. for advanced training in supervision and for accreditation where Australia can provide these from its own resources. The Association for Supervised Pastoral Education in Australia, which sets standards for three levels of supervisor (Pastoral Supervisor, Training Supervisor and Clinical Pastoral Educator), has a history going back to 1965. It has maintained a creative link between pastoral action and theological reflection. Chaplaincies — often part-time — in the armed forces and in industry (through the Inter-church Trade and Industrial Mission) give clergy an opportunity to offer pastoral care to many people they would otherwise be unlikely to meet.

The church's care for aboriginals in Australia has changed over the years from a mission-based caring for individuals to an advocacy on behalf of aboriginal communities in issues of land rights and race relations. In New Zealand the Maori and Pacific Islander communities have established churches of their own and movements like Ratana contribute to both the religious and the political identity of the Maori people. Ratana has always had a strong healing emphasis. The Pacific Islander communities have established networks of support for people adjusting to Western society.

The pastoral literature from Australia and New Zealand is limited but growing in significance. Recent titles have included works on lay pastoral ministry, death and bereavement, marriage and divorce, care of families, crisis telephone counseling, and the role of conscience in caring.

G. M. GRIFFIN

INTERNATIONAL PASTORAL CARE MOVEMENT; PASTORAL CARE MOVEMENT.

AUTHORITARIANISM. (1) A controlling and hierarchical style of leadership or of personal relationships, sometimes called "dogmatic" in more popular usage, to be contrasted with a more democratic or egalitarian style. (2) A personality trait distinguished by rigidity, dogmatism, intolerance of ambiguity and of change, high regard for structure and hierarchy, often associated with prejudice and with conservative social and religious attitudes. The two usages seem to have arisen independently in mid-century American social psychology. There is no strong evidence or theory arguing that authoritarian personalities are especially likely to adopt an authoritarian style of leadership or of personal relationships. Indeed, the "authoritarian personality" may be more useful to characterize the compliant followers of an authoritarian leader (whether a militaristic dictator, a spouse, a therapist, or a minister) than to describe the leader (Milgram).

1. **Authoritarian Leadership.** Identification of authoritarian leadership style emerged out of studies of group dynamics (e.g., Lewin) and, to a lesser extent, out of the closely related exploration in non-authoritarian styles of personal psychotherapy (e.g., Rogers). Leaders and therapists who encouraged responsibility and initiative by their groups or clients were regarded as more effective than authoritarians who maintained their own control over the agenda, process, and outcome. This relates to debate between "high" and "low" understandings of the nature and authority of ministry (and of styles of preaching, counseling, and community leadership), whether God's call is to individual ministers who assemble community or to a community who call their ministry from among themselves.

2. **"The Authoritarian Personality."** This term found its way into the vocabulary of social psychology — in a book title by that name (Adorno, *et al.*) — out of an elaborate study of anti-Semitism, prompted by the phenomenon of Nazism; thus, the name for the popular questionnaire for identifying authoritarianism, "F-scale" (for fascism). These researchers and many others found that anti-Semitism was correlated with irrational prejudice towards other ethnic groups and that this ethnocentrism was further correlated with styles and habits of mind that could be characterized as rigidity, intolerance of ambiguity and of change, undue concreteness and stimulus-boundedness, preference for clear-cut structure and hierarchy, absolutism, aggressiveness toward perceived inferiors and obedience to superiors. Authoritarian personalities tend to maintain highly idealized views of themselves, their parents, and others close to them, corresponding to the exaggerated negative views of "out" groups.

Many studies have established that authoritarians are more likely to be found among church members and orthodox believers than among nonmembers; also more among males, the less well educated, and the politically conservative — although authoritarianism among political liberals can also be identified (Rokeach).

Can authoritarianism be modified, especially can it be modified by any resources available to the minister? To the extent that it is structured into personality, established early in life or genetically, it is relatively fixed and intractable. To the extent that it is the product of socialization, in which the individual simply acquires the outlooks and habits of mind of the subculture in which he or she was raised, a changed social context, which a church community may provide, should make a difference. To the extent — and it may be a large extent — that authoritarianism is a defensive posture, reacting to a perceived precariousness of life, status, and esteem, pastoral strategies of support, of reinterpreting perceived fears, and of identifying religious and other resources should be effective.

Bibliography. T. W. Adorno, E. Frenkel-Brunswik, D. J. Levinson, and R. N. Sanford, *The Authoritarian Personality* (1950). J. E. Dittes, "Religion, Prejudice, and Personality," in M. P. Strommen, ed., *Research on Religious Development* (1971) 356–87. K. Lewin, *Field Theory in Social Science* (1952). S. Milgram, *Obedience to Authority* (1974). C. Rogers, *On Becoming a Person* (1961). M. Rokeach, *The Open and Closed Mind* (1960).

J. E. DITTES

AUTHORITY; SOCIAL PERCEPTION, JUDGMENT, AND BELIEF. *See also* AGGRESSION AND ASSERTION; LOCUS OF CONTROL RESEARCH; POWER; RACISM; SOCIAL PSYCHOLOGY, DISCIPLINE OF. *Compare* ASSERTIVENESS IN MINISTRY; DOMINEERING PERSONALITY; INDOCTRINATION; RACISM; SEXISM; SOCIAL CONSCIOUSNESS AND RESPONSIBILITY.

AUTHORITY, CONCEPT AND THEORY OF.

Authority refers to a fundamental relationship between persons, behaviors, organizations, and ideas in which one component has, or is deemed to have, important or legitimate power over the other. The English term is rooted in the Latin "auctor," meaning "producer of a work, artist, founder of a family, writer, originator of a proposal, author of a piece of information or warrant for its truth." Authority thus refers to a person who is the source, originator, or warranty for something. The derivative, "auctoritas," from which our word descends, means "validity, origination of a proposal, expression of approval or assent, authorization, full power, command," and thus also "influence, authority, whether of a person or of things" (*Cassell's Latin Dictionary*, 25th ed.).

In English "authority" carries many meanings: the power or right to enforce obedience, a doctrine of moral or legal supremacy, the right to command or to give the ultimate decision. It can also refer to delegated or derived power given to the bearer from above. Here the word takes on the meaning of "those in authority," that is, those vested with the legitimate or traditional power to command or to influence the actions of others. Authority, however, is not limited to behavior or action, but extends to the inward, subjective dimensions of human life, as in "power over the opinions of others" or the inwardly felt power of conscience in relation to social authority. Here, subtle but far-reaching forms of intellectual, legal, and moral authority are exercised through authoritative opinion or quotation from authoritative sources.

1. **Sociological Dimensions.** Max Weber (1957, 1961) described three basic forms of authority: traditional, rational-legal, and charismatic. (1) Traditional authority is that in which the legitimacy claimed for it is believed "on the basis of the sanctity of the order" handed down from the past. (2) Charismatic authority refers to inspirational or magical qualities in a leader. (3) Rational-legal authority calls for obedience to a set of laws or policies viewed as an impersonal order within a limited area of legitimate power; this is the kind of authority most commonly associated with bureaucracy.

In the theory of organization and government, the word has two meanings: (1) authorization or empowerment and (2) ordering and control. Any one who is "without authority" is not empowered to say or do certain things and can expect to be challenged if attempting them. On the other hand, one who "has authority" not only can but is expected to say or do those things, and in many cases can empower others also to do them.

In social theory the notion of empowering or authorization usually includes the notion of legitimacy, which is often used to distinguish between authority and power. Power itself may or may not be legitimate, but authority is frequently defined as "legitimate power," that is to say, as power framed by laws, bylaws, or regulations, and therefore constitutional.

What is at stake in organizations and in whole societies is balancing the reliability of persons' behavior in their offices or roles with the organization's or society's need to be adaptive. People need to be empowered in order to be able to do what is expected, and to be controlled in order to keep the expected cooperation functioning. However, social organizations also need to engage in a perpetual process of adaptation, which usually entails dislocations in authority relationships, institutions, and regulative principles. Managing this difficult but necessary process of change may become the responsibility of all but, if breakdown is to be averted, it must be coordinated and ordered by the managerial subsystem, that is, by the existing structure of authority. Thus, administrative or governmental authority entails certain permissions and rights but not unlimited power.

2. Decline in Hierarchical Authority and Concern for Autonomy. The last eight hundred years of Western history, perhaps especially among Anglo-Saxon peoples, reflect a slow but steady decline in the acceptance of hierarchical authority. The rise of democracy, participatory management, plural executives, and the protest movements of the late twentieth century represent contemporary expressions of this trend, which dates from the beginning of modernity. The fundamental issue has to do with self-government — whether and how a people can carry it out effectively and for the benefit of society and human life as a whole.

What is being challenged is the worth of hierarchical systems of authority. Certain organization seems to indicate that participatory management and patterns of authority that enhance the empowering of human beings seem very often to be more effective than those which emphasize control. The evidence so far is ambiguous and may reflect cultural expectations. What is clear is that the call for such participatory patterns of authority is becoming worldwide. The emerging global culture seems to be generating a similarly global desire on the part of all people for a larger share in the making of decisions that shape their lives, that is, for greater authority.

3. Psychological Dimensions. This worldwide phenomenon shows up in individual psychology and development. In the life cycle of many persons in the contemporary West, for example, one's relationship to authority shifts frequently. In early childhood, the narcissism of the child provides a field in which autonomy takes its first emerging steps. With the onset of puberty, autonomy becomes powerful and pushes the individual rapidly toward self-determining adulthood in tension with a community that can be experienced as predominantly oppressive or liberating, though more commonly as a mixture of both. The socialization of girls differs from that of boys regarding the question of authority, however. The community expects boys to rebel and move sharply toward autonomy, whereas dependency patterns have been approved and encouraged for girls, with corresponding dangers: young women may fail to develop a mature autonomy; young men may fail to develop mature patterns of interdependence.

Success or failure in later life will depend heavily on the degree to which one develops adequate understandings of authority and of coping with it. Mature adulthood represents to some degree an arrival at this understanding and is often accompanied by the right to exercise it.

The basic need is to develop a dynamic sense of integrity by which one can relate to authority and values in mutually supporting ways. Throughout the life cycle there appears one fundamental question: Will authority threaten autonomy or enhance it by paving the way toward mature interdependence? The threat is always that authority should be so overbearing as to become heteronomous and thus to threaten freedom or else be so weak as to permit the threat of social and psychic chaos. A healthy balance is difficult to achieve and seems to presuppose a faith that within the self and society there is a "depth dimension" in which both autonomy and heteronomy can be rooted and united, however imperfectly and impermanently (cf. Tillich, 1963).

4. Implications for Pastoral Ministry. Modern challenges to all forms of traditional and bureaucratic authority have not spared the minister. One prominent force has been generated by recognition of the ministry of the laity, which has left many pastors unsure whether the office of the ordained ministry is different in any fundamental sense from that of the laity. Another challenge has come from increasing secularization of the culture.

In reaction, many pastors have sought to ground their authority on competence and interpersonal skill or charisma. Unfortunately these are insufficient because they tend to transform the church into a community of primary relationships (a *Gemeinschaft*) devoid of the objective secondary relationships (a *Gesellschaft*) essential to its mission. It also permits the minister's office to be transformed into a series of roles (ministries) without inherent limit, leaving a minister vulnerable to maceration and burnout.

Other ministers seek more theological grounding of their authority. Christians understand ministerial authority as rooted in Jesus Christ and conferred by the Holy Spirit in the public act of ordination. It rests on a combination of the inner call by God and the outer call by the church to the ordained ministry. It is, in this sense, related to a call different from that of the laity, a call *within* the myriad vocations of the church, and the ordination ceremony highlights that. Since it is an authority given in this manner, however, it is not an authority *over* the church but *with* the church. It is not the authority of the impersonal bureaucrat, or the autocrat, or the charismatic. It is, rather, the authority of a representative, of one who serves at the focus (Word and Sacrament) of the worshiping church. In this view, whatever authority the minister may have as ordained minister in the various ministries and missions of the church derives from that authority alone.

Bibliography. R. B. Harris, ed., *Authority: A Philosophical Analysis* (1976); also contains a large bibliography by R. T. De George. P. Tillich, *Systematic Theology* vol. 3, (1963). M. Weber, *The Theory of Social and Economic Organizations* (ET, 1957) and "The Types of Authority," in *Theories of Society*, T. Parsons, *et al.*, eds. vol. 7, (1961), 626–32.

R. J. ARNOTT

POWER; RESPONSIBILITY/IRRESPONSIBILITY. *See also* CONSCIENCE; LOCUS OF CONTROL RESEARCH; MORAL BEHAVIOR AND RELIGION; OBEDIENCE; ORGANIZATION DEVELOPMENT; SOCIAL PERCEPTION, JUDGMENT AND BELIEF; SOCIOLOGY OF RELIGIOUS AND PASTORAL CARE; SOCIOLOGY OF RELIGION; SUGGESTION, PERSUASION, AND INFLUENCE.

AUTHORITY, PASTORAL. Spiritual power, mediated through the church to influence opinion, induce belief, and lead individuals and groups to moral and evangelical action. In pastoral counseling, the skill of the pastor in personal encounters authenticates this authority. D. D. Williams speaks of real authority as arising out of the concrete incarnation of loving service, which by God's help becomes present in the care of souls.

1. **Authority Versus Authoritarianism.** *a. Influential studies of psychology of authority.* Since the founding of the journal *Pastoral Psychology* in 1950, methods of training clergy in counseling have eschewed authoritarianism. The publication of T. W. Adorno's *The Authoritarian Personality* coincided with the first issues of *Pastoral Psychology*. Adorno and other psychologists noted the ways in which authoritarian thinking corresponds to a closed, threatened personality. Nothing in the present world can erode the authoritarian personality's doctrinaire creeds rooted in a submissive, childish past. M. Rokeach later postulated that the closed-minded person holds a threatening view of the world and the open-minded person an accepting view of the world.

Where religion influences personality, Adorno and Rokeach differ, since the former finds evidence to associate religiosity with prejudice. But Rokeach finds that persons with reactionary beliefs as well as those with liberal beliefs might with equal probability be closed-minded.

G. Allport developed psychological scales to distinguish intrinsic *versus* extrinsic religion. Status-conscious individuals, generally identified as closed-minded, accept extrinsic religion for security in the world. In contrast, a minority of church members sometimes are led by an intrinsic belief system to sacrifice personal convenience and security for the sake of their devotion to God and care for those rejected by society.

b. Issues related to pastoral care. The studies of Adorno, Rokeach, and Allport pointed up an early problem in the development of pastoral counseling. How can a pastor lead an individual or group to accept the supreme authority of God over their lives without also becoming an authoritarian person or developing dependency relationships with parishioners? First attempts to answer this question appealed to client-centered counseling as the preferred mode for pastoral conversations. This type of counseling centered completely upon the inner belief system of an individual and avoided any references to the beliefs of the counselor, unless the counselee had persistently distorted the beliefs of the counselor. But J. Frank noted that he and fellow psychiatrists would be practicing brainwashing if they were consistent in the use of client-centered techniques; for clients learned that their therapists approved of them when they talked of themselves. The anxiety of clients diminished when they finally learned the hidden value system of the counselor, even as prisoners learn to confess to imaginary crimes in the minds of their interrogators and are rewarded by privileges in the prison.

Frank and other therapists began to urge an open awareness of the authority of the therapist as a healer, without falling into the authoritarianism of a heavily directive interview. This emphasis was consistent with the writings of some pastoral counselors, such as W. Oates, who insisted that a minister clearly represents the authority of God to a parishioner. The emphasis echoes theologically in D. D. Williams and in sociological analyses of the pastoral office.

H. Oliver presents four sociological designations of authority in the pastoral office: (1) the derived authority inherent in church tradition; (2) the legal responsibility allowing the pastor to serve as the representative of an established institution and to uphold the norms of that institution; (3) the charismatic impact of a saintly or heroic preacher upon those who hear; and (4) the technical knowledge offered by a pastor without coercion to those who ask for help.

In pastoral counseling the place of authority gradually gained acceptance under various nomenclatures such as "shared appraisal" (S. Hiltner), to describe the way a pastor and a parishioner can look together at an issue of behavior or belief posing a problem to either of them. Instead of a judgment handed down to the parishioner from the pastor above, a shared appraisal means a mutual view of issues by which God judges both parties. The parishioner becomes less defensive after perceiving the pastor's empathetic understanding. In biblical terms, pastoral authority combines admonition (*noutheteo*) with encouragement and comfort (*parakalao* and *oikodome*) (Rom. 15:14; I Cor. 4:14, 10:11; Eph. 6:4; Col. 3:16; II Thess. 3:15).

2. **Authority in the Pastorate.** *a. Scriptural sources.* In addition to problems about the manner of the pastor as an authority or as authoritarian, issues arise because the church is a powerful and established institution. The teachings of the church help mold pastoral authority and the expectations that others have of the pastor.

The authoritative text of the church, the Bible, presents many commands for obedience, which J. Kennedy classifies under four headings: (1) the command for Christian obedience to the discernible will of God (Acts 5:29; I Thess. 4:1; I John 5:2); (2) Christ's claim to obedience to his lordship (Mt. 7:28, 29; Mt. 23:10; Jn. 13:13; II Cor. 10:5); (3) claims of the church and its leaders to be sources of authority (Rom. 16:17-19; Heb. 13:17; II Thess. 3:14); and (4) the admonition of Christians to obey those who exercise lawful authority in the world (I Tim. 2:1-2).

Authority derived from the Scriptures can be a source of freedom rather than compliance. J. L. McKenzie vigorously protests that obedience and submission are not ends in themselves; rather, authority is one function of the Spirit and has no specific place in the church or its offices. B. Cooke and H. Küng agree with McKenzie that authority derives from the work of the Spirit of God in a humble servant rather than in a hierarchy developed from a Roman court scene. These writers contrast the authority of the world with spiritual authority (Mt. 20:25-28; Jn. 13:1-20).

b. Views of congregations and pastors. In general, congregations expect to find the authority of the pastor reflected in the pattern of worship and belief of the church and in the integration of interpersonal relationships of members. Conventional church members do not expect the pastor to be an agent of change in the life of people in the world or even to change the organization of the church to focus upon some specific social action (W. W. Schroeder, T. Evans, S. Klausner, J. Hadden).

Pastors, on the other hand, generally find their source of authority in "special leading"—God's direct planning or "natural leading"—a realization that the pastor has talents to meet needs.

3. Summary. The development of pastoral psychology since the 1950s has made several contributions to the understanding of pastoral authority. First, psychological studies have shown the deep roots of assumptions about authority in the life of both parishioners and pastors. Persons who develop an authoritarian conscience (described in Col. 2:20-23) will need counsel on the *way* they practice their faith and prejudge other people. Persons who rebel against authority may find in counseling that they are fighting parental figures from the past rather than the representative of legitimate social responsibility in adult life. The pastor can also be aware of the way parishioners project upon the pastor attitudes toward authority learned since childhood.

Second, pastoral psychology has contributed to reshaping pastoral authority by fostering new means of communication between pastor and parishioner. A pastor can share judgmental appraisals about issues with a parishioner, and still do so lovingly and realistically.

On the other hand, biblical concepts of church authority contribute to pastoral counseling a sense of the need to rely upon a power beyond self, "faith's object" (P. T. Forsyth), rather than upon professional office or personal talent.

Bibliography. T. Adorno, *The Authoritarian Personality* (1982). T. Campbell, *The Fragmented Layman* (1970). B. Cooke, *Ministry to Word and Sacraments* (1980). D. Day, *The Minister and the Care of Souls* (1977). T. Evans, "The Brethren Pastor," *J. of the Scientific Study of Religion,* 3 (1963), 43–51. P. Forsyth, *The Principle of Authority* (1952). J. Hadden, *The Gathering Storm in the Churches* (1970). J. Kennedy, *Presbyterian Authority and Discipline* (1965). S. Klausnes, "Role Adaptations of Pastors and Psychiatrists," *J. of the Scientific Study of Religion,* 4 (1964), 14– 39. H. Küng, *The Church* (1976). J. McKenzie, *Authority in the Church* (1971). W. Oates, *The Christian Pastor* (1982). H. P. Oliver, *Professional Authority and the Protestant Ministry* (1967). M. Rokeach, *The Open and Closed Mind* (1960). W. W. Schroeder "Lay Expectations of Ministerial Role," *J. of Scientific Study of Religion,* 2 (1963): 217-27. M. Stein, *Contemporary Psychotherapies* (1961).

S. SOUTHARD

ECCLESIOLOGY AND PASTORAL CARE; MINISTRY; PASTOR (Normative and Traditional Images of). *See also* DISCIPLINE, PASTORAL CARE AS; KEYS, POWER OF; PASTORAL OFFICE; PSYCHOLOGY OF RELIGION; SOCIOLOGY OF RELIGIOUS AND PASTORAL CARE; SUGGESTION, PERSUASION, AND INFLUENCE. *Compare* FAITH AND INTEGRITY, PASTOR'S; IDENTITY, PASTORAL; PERSONHOOD OF THE PASTOR, SIGNIFICANCE OF.

AUTHORITY ISSUES IN PASTORAL CARE. Authority issues in pastoral care involve: (1) being under authority; (2) being an authority; and (3) conveying authority. They also involve the relationship between pastoral identity and pastoral role and function.

1. Under Authority. In pastoral care as well as in other dimensions of ministry, the minister is *under* authority. This means that he or she cannot offer care apart from the religious body which endorses that ministry or the structure, such as a parish, hospital or counseling center, which authorizes ministry in that particular setting. There is no such thing as the private practice of pastoral care and counseling. There are, indeed, clergypersons who do counseling and psychotherapy as private practitioners, but not as pastors. The noun, "pastor," and the adjective, "pastoral," *mean* having ecclesiastical authority because one is subject to it. Ministers, lay or ordained, do what they do and are what they are as representatives. They cannot just be themselves. They represent the strengths and weaknesses of the church which ordains them, the hospital or other agency which employs them, and the professional association which certifies their competency. As persons under authority ministers are required to interpret what they do in ministry to their ecclesiastical and/or secular endorser or employer. The person or group to which they are accountable must be able to understand what they are doing as ministry; therefore, the minister has the obligation to relate his or her function to the purposes of the institutions and associations which he or she represents.

2. An Authority. In addition to being accountable to structures beyond themselves for what they are and do, ministers are themselves authorities. Persons who have been educated in the theory and practice of the faith— usually, but not exclusively, the ordained—possess an authority themselves. Mark's statement about Jesus in the synagogue at Capernaum, "as one who had authority, and not as the scribes" (Mk. 1:22) is the kind of thing that is perceived about pastors. They have something within themselves which can inspire and support. In terms of their own self-understanding and experience, this is what is usually referred to as "pastoral identity." In terms of the way others respond to them, this is the ability to function in a pastoral role. The fact that in the NT even Jesus' authority is sometimes defined negatively— "not as the scribes"—suggests some of the intangible quality of being an authority.

The way this authority is expressed varies considerably from person to person. Much of Richard Sennett's analysis of the concept of authority (1980) can be applied to authority issues in pastoral care. Pastors, for example, often fear being authoritative, that is, being called to account for what they say or being set apart from those over whom they have authority. They may express their authority paternalistically, alleging that what they do is for the good of the person over whom they exercise it. (This is what Sennett calls the "authority of false love.") They may also express it autonomously, as Sennett puts it, "without love" or without adequate concern for the persons most affected by it.

3. **Conveying Authority.** Other authority issues in pastoral care involve difficulties in conveying authority to others. Historically, the term "pastor" has sometimes designated only the person in charge of a parish or other administrative unit. Pastoral duties, therefore, seldom involve only providing ministry oneself; they also involve supervising the ministry of others. The pastor is a person in between, one who receives authority, exercises it, and conveys it to others under the pastor's oversight. This supervisory dimension of pastoral work is not an easy one to carry out. Pastors may have difficulty in letting go of any of their authority, preferring to do the job themselves. They may allegedly convey authority to others but covertly retain it by insisting that the supervisee "do it their way." They may become overconcerned about the problems of those to whom they have attempted to give authority and not provided adequate attention to the task that needs to be accomplished. Each of these examples reflects difficulties in genuinely conveying authority to others.

The authority issues related to being under authority, being an authority, and conveying authority are all related to the pastor's role and function and his or her inner sense of pastoral identity. The acceptance of the role for oneself is essential to adequate functioning in that role and in interpreting it to others. Moreover, role acceptance and satisfactory practice in functioning in it are dependent upon an evolving inner sense of identity with the role as integral to who one is. Without this developing sense of pastoral identity, the authority issues in pastoral care become extremely difficult to deal with.

Bibliography. R. Ekstein and R. S. Wallerstein, *The Teaching and Learning of Psychotherapy* (1958). J. Patton, *Pastoral Counseling: A Ministry of the Church* (1983). R. Sennett, *Authority* (1980). D. D. Williams, *The Minister and the Care of Souls* (1961). P. Young-Eisendrath and F. L. Wiedemann, *Female Authority* (1987).

J. PATTON

CONSCIENCE; DISCIPLINE, PASTORAL CARE AS; MORAL DEVELOPMENT; RESPONSIBILITY/IRRESPONSIBILITY PSYCHOLOGY OF. *See also* ANTISOCIAL PERSONS; CONFRONTATION (Pastoral and Therapeutic); GUILT; LEGALISM AND ANTINOMIANISM; OBEDIENCE (Roman Catholicism); STRUCTURING. *Compare* ANOMIE/NORMLESSNESS; DEPENDENCE/INDEPENDENCE; MORAL DILEMMAS IN PASTORAL PERSPECTIVE.

AUTISM. A serious form of childhood psychopathology characterized by a lack of social responsiveness, impairment in communication ability, and bizarre behaviors. Speech may be absent or confined to repetition of a few phrases. A lack of attachment to others, frequent self-stimulatory behaviors, resistance to change, or a fascination with objects may be observed. Professional intervention is required.

Bibliography. M. Ruter and E. Schopler, *Autism* (1978).

L. MANS-WAGONER

DEVELOPMENTAL DISORDERS; EXCEPTIONAL CHILDREN AND THEIR FAMILIES; MENTAL HEALTH AND ILLNESS; ORGANIC MENTAL DISORDER; PSYCHOSOCIAL DEVELOPMENT.

AUTISTIC CHILD AND FAMILY. *See* AUTISM; EXCEPTIONAL CHILDREN AND THEIR FAMILIES.

AUTOMATIC WRITING. *See* PARAPSYCHOLOGY.

AUTONOMY. *See* DEPENDENCE/INDEPENDENCE. *See also* DOUBT AND UNBELIEF, EGO STRENGTH.

AUTOPSY. Usually involves dissection of the body after death to determine cause of death or to gain information that could be used in the treatment of living persons. More recently the use of the term has been broadened to include a social or psychological autopsy, through which the psychologist or sociologist seeks to learn and understand the factors that have contributed to suicide and other forms of self-destructive behavior.

In the pastoral context, counselees often have questions concerning the necessity or validity of medical procedures after death. Examples of such queries include, "Why this added indignity? Hasn't she suffered enough already?" or "Will this interfere with the possibility of immortality?" or "What good will this mutilation accomplish?" Such questions reflect the mental and emotional state of the questioner and usually will best be answered from that point of view.

Often the question about an autopsy will be initiated by a member of the medical staff. Because it is apt to be an unpleasant subject it may be assigned to an intern or resident who may approach the family with a lack of sensitivity or tact. It may then be that the injured relative approaches the pastor or chaplain with a question that is more concerned with personal injury than with objective matters that have to be considered. Then it becomes the role of the counselor to confront both the injured feelings and the more practical issues.

The nature of the grief may be seen in the identification of the bereaved with the deceased. It may be that questions about the autopsy are the first step toward confronting the reality of death and the changes that are implicit in that recognition. Here the counselor may want to use questions to gently move the mourner away from identifications limited by a preoccupation with the dead body toward a more objective judgment concerning the changes death invariably produces. After some explanation and interpretation sensitive to the feelings of the bereaved, the counselor may raise questions about the meaning and function of the autopsy and the role of autopsies in the history of medicine like "Do you think the dead body has feelings?" or "Do you think the deceased would have wanted to aid medical exploration?" or "Do you understand the feelings you have about this procedure?"

It is wise to keep in mind that the chief consideration is the welfare of the bereaved person. Newer techniques of medical research may be more productive than the autopsy, so it is not as vital medically as it once was. Hospitals are not so apt to be judged now by the percentage of autopsies they report. A growing awareness of the importance of the feelings of survivors tends to modify the perception of the autopsy in the total health care perspective. Training medical personnel in communicative skills and human sensitivity would be helpful. Training pastoral persons to help people confront their own feelings and use that confrontation to produce psychological movement is a desired goal. A wise approach to the matter of the autopsy may serve both a psychotherapeutic and a spiritual purpose as the physical and the spiritual realities are brought into their proper relation.

E. N. JACKSON

DEATH, MEANING OF; GRIEF AND LOSS; MORAL DILEMMAS IN PASTORAL PERSPECTIVE. *See also* BODY.

AVARICE AND GENEROSITY. 1. Avarice. Also called covetousness or greed, avarice is an aberration of the normal desire to have things. The desire for goods is inordinate when one seeks to have more than is reasonable for the fulfillment of one's responsibilities such as the preservation and development of one's family. Avarice is also inordinate either when one becomes overly concerned about acquiring and keeping or when one is stingy in sharing. Avarice overvalues possessions, and its disorder usually appears in the sacrifices one is willing to make for them. As a major source of other sins, avarice is listed among the seven capital or deadly sins.

Money has become the chief means of exchange for goods and services. Curiously, the desire to accumulate wealth has been transvalued in contemporary Western society into something of a virtue. The amassing of wealth is said to fuel modern economies, thereby helping all, including the poor. Further, accumulating money is said to free persons from dependencies, encourage discipline, and expand human freedom and creativity. Thus avarice is said to be absolved from guilt.

There is no limit to the amount of possessions, particularly money, that a person can seek to amass. Possessions can become a goal sought for themselves, for the power and status they bring, or as a sign, for example, of God's favor or predestination unto salvation. Though economic theory claims that money has only a secular, rational function, this thesis fails to explain the irrational and even salvific importance that money often has for persons.

Miserliness is the desire to possess, without the desire to enjoy what this wealth makes possible. Profligacy is the wasteful or excessive use, dispersion, or consumption of possessions. Conspicuous consumption — often based not on actual wealth but on debt — is a form of seeking or displaying self-importance by expending resources. The Christian tradition, holding that the worth of persons is not based on how much they own or use, rejects all these abuses.

2. Generosity. This virtue is a disposition to give freely beyond what is required by justice. Because persons can legitimately find provisional security and relative identity through some of their possessions, the sharing of those possessions can be a means of self-giving. The widow's mite is a greater self-giving than the superfluities of the rich. Generosity without this self-giving is defective; giving possessions can flow from other motives, not all of which are good, for example, vanity or even contempt for creation. Giving is also defective

when it is indiscriminate, that is, when it is merely a form of self-expression or when it does not discern the helpfulness of the gift.

Christian generosity flows from three closely interrelated themes: the love of God as the giver of all gifts, the common humanity of everyone, and the humility of Christ who did not cling to his riches. Complementing these themes are the human experiences of the insufficiency of wealth for happiness, the freedom that comes from detachment, and the joy that comes from a magnanimity of the soul.

Bibliography. S. Lyman, *Seven Deadly Sins* (1978). K. Menninger, *Whatever Became of Sin?* (1973). M. Novak, *Spirit of Democratic Capitalism* (1982). L. Smedes, *Mere Morality* (1983).

E. C. VACEK

CHRISTIAN LIFE; SEVEN DEADLY SINS. *See also* CHARACTER ETHICS; GIVING AND RECEIVING; MORAL THEOLOGY AND PASTORAL CARE; SIN/SINS; TEMPTATION.

AVERSION THERAPY. A behavioral technique that is used to diminish the frequency of undesirable behavior. It generally involves the application of a painful stimulus immediately following the appearance of an undesired behavior. Although often abused as a therapeutic technique, it can be successfully used as a last resort and should *always* be used in conjunction with a plan for increasing desirable behavior.

T. J. SANDBEK

BEHAVIOR THERAPIES (Methods and Research); CONDITIONING. *Compare* IMPLOSIVE THERAPY.

AVOCATION. *See* LIFESTYLE ISSUES; PLAY.

AWARENESS. *See* CONSCIOUSNESS; PERCEPTIVENESS AND SENSITIVITY, PASTORAL.

AWE. *See* RELIGIOUS EXPERIENCE; THE HOLY.

AXIOTHERAPY. A form of counseling which focuses on clarifying the specific values at stake in any troublesome situation, asking how these values are functioning or dysfunctioning in relation to long-range fulfillment of the self, and how they might be open for review and behavioral change. The approach draws attention to the value-laden character of the psychotherapeutic process. It is a special form of value clarification except that it tends to rest within a mental health framework rather than a strictly educational one. Basic principles of axiotherapy include the following: (1) a value is a legitimate focus in the psychotherapeutic project; (2) values have motivational power in their own right; and (3) the consistency between values and behavior may be viewed as an index to psychological adjustment.

Bibliography. T. Oden, *The Structure of Awareness* (1969). O. Strunk, Jr., "Principles of Axiotherapy," *J. of Religion and Health,* 15 (1976), 241–46.

O. STRUNK, JR.

PSYCHOTHERAPY; VALUES CLARIFICATION; VALUES IN COUNSELING AND PSYCHOTHERAPY.

B

BAAL SHEM-TOV (ISRAEL BEN ELIEZER). (Master of the good name, ca. 1700–ca. 1760). Popularly referred to as Besht, which are the initials of Baal Shem-Tov. It was only in his fourth decade that Israel revealed himself and established an ever expanding circle of disciples known as Hasidim. A charismatic leader, he exalted and ennobled each human being and emphasized that future messianic redemption must be preceded by the personal salvation of each individual soul. He stressed the importance of serving God in joy and opposed unnecessary fasting and self-deprivation.

Often accused of glorifying ignorance, the Besht emphasized the concept of "devekut," or clinging to God, which could be achieved through prayer and study. He was greatly revered in his time, and after his passing his reputation continued to grow, with legends attributed to him forming a basic part of Hasidic literature.

The Baal Shem-Tov is acknowledged as the spiritual ancestral parent of many branches of modern Hasidism, which has greatly influenced Judaic expression since his death. The Besht's approach to life offers a powerful antidote to the feelings of anomie and meaninglessness.

R. P. BULKA

HASIDIC CARE AND COUNSELING; SPIRITUAL MASTERS AND GUIDES.

BAPTISM AND CONFIRMATION. The principal rite of Christian initiation. Originally a unitary ritual for adult believers involving baptism as a private rite followed by a public affirmation (later called confirmation) together with the initiate's first celebration of the Eucharist. By medieval times baptism and confirmation had become separated in the Western church into distinct rituals defined as sacraments, associated mainly with the initiation of infants and of children at puberty. (The Eastern churches have no rite of confirmation.) While theological debate has raged over the nature and purpose of these rites, much contemporary liturgical theology, Catholic and Protestant, has found renewed appreciation of their unity as an organic process of initiation into Christian faith.

This appreciation is consonant with the anthropological observation that every religious tradition includes rituals marking important life transitions such as birth and puberty. Circumcision, baptism, infant dedication, bar and bat mitzvah ceremonies, and the like all give public definition and meaning to these milestone developmental events. They also define or redefine social roles and identities, deepen social and historical solidarity, and provide occasion for the religious community, and for particular individuals within it, to affirm or renew their most cherished beliefs. Thus, for both theological and psychosocial reasons, baptism and confirmation have major significance for pastoral care.

1. **Theological Understandings.** *a. Historical.* The Christian practices of baptism and confirmation have complicated histories and have been occasions for conflict in the church since NT times. The emphasis on repentance and moral reformation more than ritual purity moves the baptism of John the Baptist beyond the proselyte baptism of Palestinian Judaism (cf. Mk. 1:1–8; Mt. 3:1–12; Lk. 3:1–17). The great missionary commission (Mt. 28:18–20) locates the authority to baptize with Jesus. In the book of Acts, baptism is connected to the giving of the Holy Spirit and entrance into the Christian community. In Pauline thought, baptism is linked to themes of repentance and forgiveness, entrance into a new context of relationships, eschatological awareness, and the reception of the Holy Spirit, commissioning for ministry, and the assurance of being God's child.

The practice of the early church in which baptism, the Chrismation, and the Eucharist were a unitary rite, presupposed that the majority of people were initiated into the Christian community as adults. The period of preparation or catechumenate that preceded the unitary baptismal initiation normally occurred during Lent. The separation of confirmation from baptism was a consequence of the increased practice of infant baptism, church growth, and the insistence that only the bishop could confirm. The unity of the initiatory rite was broken, and the rite of confirmation diminished in significance.

By the Council of Orange in 441 C.E., when "confirmation" was used for the second rite of initiation, it was clearly understood that the laying on of hands added a grace to that which was given in the "washing" of baptism. This distinction noted at the Council of Orange was refuted by the Reformers who regarded baptism as a complete sacrament to which nothing needed to be added. Luther and Calvin viewed confirmation as a human contrivance but nonetheless a useful churchly ceremony as long as it did not infringe on the proper and primary significance of infant baptism. The emphasis on consenting faith in the Anabaptist tradition created a new form of unity in the initiatory rite. In the centuries since the Reformation, the rite of confirmation has often functioned as an ecclesiastically sanctioned rite of passage into adulthood in the church and in society. Recent decisions by most major Protestant denominations to admit children to the Lord's Supper before confirmation have further modified the initiatory significance of confirmation.

b. Contemporary. With the publication (1983) of the World Council of Churches' document, *Baptism, Eucharist and Ministry,* the Christian churches have moved closer to a consensus regarding the meaning of baptism. Both infants' and believers' baptisms embody God's initiation in Christ and express a response of faith made within the believing community. Whenever or however it occurs, baptism embodies God's initiation in Christ and expresses a response of faith made within the believing community. It always includes the juxtaposition of God's gracious activity and individual responsibility. Whenever baptism occurs, it is also assumed that the baptized person will continue to grow in the understanding of faith. This developing consensus regarding Christian initiation will make it possible to work toward a common understanding of the implications of baptism for the Christian life and for pastoral care.

The introduction in the Roman Catholic tradition of the Rite of Christian Initiation of Adults (RCIA) in 1972 as a framework for adult conversion into the Christian faith has revived the importance of the community and the process of the catechumenate in Roman Catholic practice. The emergence of RCIA has shifted the focus of baptism to the formation of faith through the catechumenate and the unitary nature of the initiation. Baptism in mature adulthood emphasizes the importance of spiritual formation before as well as after the unitary rite and moves toward a vision of a church composed of well-informed, deeply committed adult persons.

Despite the conflicts and controversies that continue to surround baptism, it remains a significant symbol for the Christian's life. Baptism is God's act *and* our response. It is also both an event and a process. Nothing needs to be added to what is accomplished in the ritual act of baptizing, and yet baptism cannot be isolated from the events that precede it and succeed from it. As the momentary and complete action of God, baptism needs no supplement; the baptized one is fully initiated into the covenant of forgiveness. We are never more Christian than at our baptism. And yet the entire life of a Christian is the living out of baptism. What is appropriated at various crisis moments in the human life cycle is already given in the baptism. For that reason, it can be said that the Christian life is a daily baptism, once begun, and ever continued throughout the life cycle.

2. Pastoral Perspectives on Infant Baptism.
a. Preparation of parents. The Church's preparation of parents for the baptism of their children is concerned with the faithfulness of parents in responding to the needs of the newly born as well as with the faith of the believing family and community into which the child is baptized. Preparation for parenthood and preparation for infant baptism or child dedication are interdependent. Both require a reorientation of focus. Parenthood is an act of altruism. Although there are parenting skills to be learned, the task of the church is to help people learn that altruism is an essential dimension of parenthood. Fathers and mothers parent best when they are able to be primarily attentive to the needs of the infant. Moreover, baptism or dedication is a sign that not even children are excluded from God's love. It obligates parents to regard their children from the beginning of life as fully human, unique, and surprising creations of God, who are subjects as well as objects of love.

b. Significance for human development. Baptism or the dedication of infants also contributes to the development of human autonomy because it reminds parents that they are caretakers and not possessors of their children. We are to love, honor, protect, and respect our children from the beginning of life so that they might become autonomous enough to serve the world for the sake of Christ. Baptism is a symbolic reminder to parents that they are to hold their children in such a way that it is easy for them to leave. Our children are not "our" children, even when we love and protect and honor them as our own, because by baptism they have been initiated into a community of love and obligation that transcends each particular family. The family and the church are both "cradles" of protection and nurture that hold us for service in the world.

The sacrament of initiation in infancy both incorporates and individuates. Baptism makes an individual a particular child of God *and* locates him or her in the midst of an assembly of Christians. Baptism is the sacrament that particularizes each individual as a unique gift of God at the same time that it incorporates each one into the mystical Body of Christ. Baptism supports the process of individuation by which we come to be distinct and autonomous selves while recognizing the necessity for community for such growth in human life.

The connection between name-giving and baptism illustrates yet another meaning of baptism that has significance for human development. In whose name one is baptized is central to understanding baptism as a saving event. How one is named in the baptism is significant for the process of individuation within the family. It is important that parents are aware of the ways in which expectations carried by the name might restrict as well as enhance the development of the child's own unique way of being in the world. The name given at baptism not only identifies a child within a particular human family but also locates that child within the family of God. It reminds us to whom we belong and who we are bound to serve from the beginning of life. The name given at baptism connotes the incorporation into the family of God and remains forever as a testimony of that identity.

The purpose of the church's ministry is to help the family create the kind of welcoming environment for the newly born that will foster individual growth in the midst of community. The ritual of baptism is shaped by the same paradox of individual autonomy and community participation that determines the formation of the self in a family. Baptism, as a second birth into a second holding environment, initiates a process in which both family and church mediate a life of faith and a life of grace for individual growth. The individual's affirmation of faith in confirmation or through adult baptism focuses on identity and fidelity in the Christian life. It is a response to God's prior claim.

3. Pastoral Perspectives on Confirmation and Adult Baptism. The rite of confirmation is an action that reaffirms one's identity within the company of the baptized. It is also a pledge of faithfulness. Our willingness to become committing persons is a way of keeping faith with the God who keeps promises. The capacity to make and keep commitments, which is so central for the ethical life of the Christian, is an appropriation of our baptismal call to discipleship. For the Christian, the beginning of this call to care for the neighbor is in God's gift and promise of forgiveness. Baptism has meaning in adulthood in part because it is the lifelong reminder of the promise of forgiveness and the call to care that is given in baptism. Baptism is always an experience of privilege *and* responsibility.

If baptism, whenever it occurs, is understood as call to the ministry of discipleship, then it becomes an important link between pastoral care and vocation. The beginning of our ministry is in our baptism in the sense that we have been initiated into a "royal priesthood" through our baptism either as children or as adults. We are free to care in and for the world because we are confident that our daily tasks are a calling from God. This conviction has led some in the Roman Catholic tradition to regard the Rite of Christian Initiation of Adults as the paradigm for pastoral care. The end of care is discipleship and vocation. The Christian is encouraged to live out his or her vocation with the assurance that the God who has called each one to discipleship will also sustain each one by fulfilling the gift of forgiveness promised in baptism.

Baptism, understood as God's claim and promise as well as our response, has special significance for those who struggle with loneliness and despair. For them it is a sign of hope that we are acceptable to God even when we feel rejected by others or unacceptable to ourselves and terrified by the dread of abandonment. When we are overwhelmed by guilt, baptism is a personal sign of the promise of forgiveness that is logically and psychologically prior to our experience of that forgiveness. Helping people claim the gifts of their baptism—its enduring significance through life—is a way for providing support and healing in pastoral care.

Bibliography. R. L. Browning and R. A. Reed, *The Sacraments in Religious Education and Liturgy* (1985). A. Davanagh, *The Shape of Baptism: The Rite of Christian Initiation* (1978). R. Duffy, *A Roman Catholic Theology for Pastoral Care* (1983). T. Oden, *Pastoral Theology* (1983), ch. 8. M. Thurian, ed., *Ecumenical Perspectives on Baptism, Eucharist and Ministry* (Commission on Faith and Order, No. 166, World Council of Churches, 1983). *Baptism, Eucharist and Ministry*, (Commission on Faith and Order, No. 111, pp. 4, 348–84, World Council of Churches, 1982).

H. ANDERSON

EMERGENCY BAPTISM; RITUAL AND PASTORAL CARE; SACRAMENTAL THEOLOGY AND PASTORAL CARE; REBAPTISM; VOWS/VOWING. *See also* CHRISTIAN LIFE; CONVERSION; EARLY CHURCH, PASTORAL CARE AND COUNSELING IN; ECCLESIOLOGY AND PASTORAL CARE; LITURGICAL CHANGE AND REFORM (Pastoral Issues); SACRAMENTS, ORDINANCES, AND RITES, TERMINOLOGY AND CONCEPTS OF; SYMBOLISM/SYMBOLIZING; WORSHIP AND CELEBRATION. *Compare* BAR MITZVAH/BAT MITZVAH; CIRCUMCISION.

BAPTIST PASTORAL CARE. Baptists belong to a religious tradition which stresses the authenticating power of religious experience and therefore have understood their clergy as custodians of the inner world of their parishioners. During the last half century, Baptists, as other denominations, have been increasingly willing to apply scientific data to traditional ministerial roles, but the "care and cure of souls" cuts across their history.

1. Early English Baptists. Early English Baptists saw pastoral care and counseling primarily as discipline. They were dissenters and, until the Act of Toleration in 1689, suffered persecution under the established church. In that context rigorous discipline was necessary to preserve faithfulness. Even minor infractions were faced with candor, often culminating in expulsion of an unrepentant sinner.

The emphasis on discipline enhanced the role of preaching among early English Baptists. Long sermons were intended to make doctrine clear and instruct in requirements of the good life. During the seventeenth, eighteenth, and nineteenth centuries, preaching dominated the pastoral office. Pastors from Thomas Helwys (ca. 1550 to ca. 1616) to C. H. Spurgeon (1834–92) achieved their reputation in the pulpit. Yet those whose primary work was proclamation attended suffering people. Andrew Fuller (1754–1815), for example, came to the ministry through a rending encounter with an alcoholic and later confessed his inescapable obligation to such persons. Spurgeon, who regularly preached to congregations of over five thousand, counseled many, and his visitation of the sick during a cholera epidemic so impressed people that the rumor spread that his bedside prayers had healed hundreds. Although preaching was the primary vehicle of these early Baptists, the intentions were pastoral—the salvation, guidance, and consolation of persons.

2. Early American Baptists. The English tradition continued among early American Baptists, but in the environment of frontier revivalism. Itinerant clergy aimed to spread the gospel as rapidly as the frontier expanded. Sermons were long, intense, and instructive, intended to evangelize and enforce proper behavior. Corrective discipline of an offending person followed the English pattern. Thus pastoral care on the American frontier enhanced social control in an environment often lacking social order. After the frontier disappeared, large measures of frontier revivalism survived in American Baptist life. Corrective discipline has softened, but correct doctrine and behavior are often required for full participation in church life.

3. Black American Baptists. Among black Baptists in America pastoral care is best understood in the context of pre–Civil War slavery and continual social injustice extending beyond emancipation. If the functions of pastoral care are healing, sustaining, guiding, and reconciling (Clebsch and Jaekle, pp. 8–10), pastoral care among blacks has stressed sustaining. White religion was rejected, and blacks found in their distinctive commitments "shelter from the slavery system, an institutional framework to confound their social condition, an ideology of self-esteem and an earnest of deliverance and ultimate victory" (Matthews, p. 208).

The congregation, as much as the minister, has provided the sustaining function in black pastoral care. For the slave, church became extended family when relatives were sold away. Spirituals provided a worldview, lifting vision beyond daily toil. During the eighteenth century, mutual-aid and burial societies provided both financial resources and congregational care during bereavement. After the great migration to northern urban centers, the black church was a community in which blacks who were powerless in the depersonalized city could participate.

The black minister traditionally symbolized the sustaining function of the congregation. Aside from political and cultural features, the enthusiasm with which the black community rallied around Martin Luther King, Jr., in the civil rights movement was undoubtedly aided by a willingness to ascribe to the black minister high levels of authority for preserving the sustaining function of pastoral care. His sermons of careful rhetoric and emotional poetry, stirring visions of triumph, rest upon the symbolic role of the black minister as sustainer.

4. Chaplaincy. Both black and white Baptist clergy have served as chaplains in hospitals, prisons, industry, and primarily in the military. As military chaplains, their duties include visiting and counseling, character education, and support in crises. Military chaplaincy itself is quite old, dating to the Revolutionary War, but not until after World War I did planning become more systematic. The National Defense Act of 1920 created the office of chief of chaplains for the army, a post occupied on several occasions by Baptists. Similar developments occurred with the navy and air force with 254 Baptist naval chaplains serving during World War II.

5. Clinical Pastoral Training Among Southern Baptists. Chaplaincy during World Wars I and II was crucial in the development of pastoral care concerns among Baptists. Earlier Baptist clergy had faithfully devoted themselves to visitation and care, but their work was largely uninformed by personality sciences emerging since the late nineteenth century. War trauma made pastors more aware of their limitations and their need for specialized preparation. By the 1940s Christian ministers had moved beyond antagonism toward the personality sciences, especially psychoanalysis, and begun to utilize the new sciences in ministerial preparation. Southern Baptists played a major role in this development, sharing with other denominations a concern to educate its ministry to include clinical pastoral education.

Among Baptist pioneers in clinical pastoral education were G. S. Dobbins of Southern Baptist Theological

Seminary (SBTS) and A. E. Tibbs of New Orleans Baptist Theological Seminary (NOBTS). Tibbs introduced clinical experience requirements for his Th.D. candidates in religious psychology and counseling at NOBTS, and in 1937 Dobbins and his colleague W. O. Carver invited Seward Hiltner to SBTS to generate interest in clinical pastoral education. The SBTS plan lay dormant until World War II when the superintendent of the Louisville General Hospital appealed to the seminary for volunteers to relieve the shortage of orderlies and attendants. Supplying volunteers initiated clinical programs at SBTS.

The 1940s and 1950s witnessed the rapid and formal development of clinical pastoral education among Southern Baptists. By the late 1950s every seminary sponsored by the Southern Baptist Convention offered courses in pastoral care and counseling. Major programs existed at SBTS and NOBTS and a program later called the School of Pastoral Care had been created at the North Carolina Baptist Hospital in Winston-Salem. These three centers pioneered pastoral care education among Southern Baptists.

The Louisville program developed largely around Wayne E. Oates. His interests were quickened by his experience as a volunteer at Louisville General Hospital and encouraged by his tutor Dobbins. He sought training wherever he could find it, including a summer with Anton T. Boisen in 1945. Oates and Ralph Bonacker taught the first course in CPE at SBTS, and in 1945 he was appointed instructor in psychology and clinical training, rising through the ranks until he was made professor of psychology of religion in 1955. Although his title underscored psychology of religion, Oates's primary interest throughout his academic career has been pastoral care and counseling, that is, the development of pastors in the classical sense.

During the 1940s Oates was instrumental in establishing clinical training centers at mental and general hospitals in Kentucky and was involved in opening the clinical program at North Carolina Baptist Hospital. The North Carolina center opened in 1947 under the direction of R. K. Young, offering three types of services: six- or eight-week courses under a chaplain supervisor, a one-year chaplain's internship, and outpatient counseling. The program was connected with Southeastern Baptist Theological Seminary from 1953 to 1967, but with the establishment of the Association of Clinical Pastoral Education in 1967, it severed organic connection with the seminary. The center receives financial support from the North Carolina Baptist Convention and operates satellite training for clergy at three locations in the state.

At NOBTS the Tibbs legacy fell to his successor, John Price. In 1951 Price structured a program at the Southern Baptist Hospital, which flourished under the direction of Myron Madden, who became chaplain supervisor at the hospital in 1959.

Two other centers, although not official Baptist agencies, have had Baptist leadership and influence. The Institute of Religion in the Texas Medical Center in Houston, established in the mid-1950s, cooperated with five Texas seminaries in developing graduate programs in pastoral care and counseling. The institute has been ecumenical in its faculty and sponsorship, including

Baptist directors such as Samuel Southard and Joseph Knowles. The Georgia Association for Pastoral Care, incorporated in 1962, utilizes the personnel of seven affiliated groups to offer chaplaincy service to the public and to train seminarians. Atlanta Baptist pastors Monroe Swilley and Louie Newton participated in its establishment, Georgia Baptist Hospital was one of its affiliated institutions, and E. A. Verdery was one of its early leaders.

In 1957 the Southern Baptist Association for Clinical Pastoral Education (SBACPE) was formed. Louisville, New Orleans, and Winston-Salem leaders played major roles in the formation of SBACPE. It was distinctly concerned with accreditation guidelines for supervisors preparing ministers for pastoral care and counseling in local churches. The purpose is clearly stated in the association's standards: "To afford opportunities for persons in church-related vocations to relate theological studies to interpersonal relationships through personal supervision by a pastoral supervisor within the framework of a theological education and in relation to the ministries of the church." This orientation, different from other accrediting agencies since it is more oriented toward psychiatric preparation, has marked Southern Baptist concerns throughout its history.

The SBACPE began modestly with eighteen professors and chaplains at the organizational meeting but grew rapidly. In a decade its membership had expanded to over seventy-five, regional organizations had been structured, and non-Baptists (about twenty-five percent of its membership) had been included. In 1965 the name was changed to "The Association of Clinical Pastoral Educators" to reflect its national scope and ecumenical constituency. A year later the association was dissolved in the interest of unification with the Association of Clinical Pastoral Education.

6. The American Baptists. The American Baptist Convention has focused attention on career planning and placement. Studies in 1961 and 1962 demonstrated that Baptist pastors were generally confused about their role, felt pressed upon by their problems, and sensed a need for pastoral care themselves. A further study in 1965 isolated placement as a crucial factor in this general ministerial unhappiness.

Acting on these findings, the Commission on Ministry adopted a plan to develop regional centers to offer career guidance and placement services to ministers. In 1967 a center was opened in Wellesley Hills, Massachusetts, followed by a second center in Oakland, California. J. H. Burns developed career counseling for American Baptist clergy at the Oakland center, and a detailed description of his procedure appears in Orlo Strunk's *Dynamic Interpersonalism for Ministry* (1973).

7. Summary. The shifting organizational structures of CPE and the growth of career counseling reflect a struggle typical of pastoral care and counseling among Baptists in the 1940s, 1950s, and 1960s. Hectic activity marked the attempt to help clergy catch up with the rapidly advancing knowledge in the dynamics of personality and to understand themselves as participants in interpersonal development. Growth in seminary courses and clinical programs was so rapid that their integration with other aspects of seminary education and the life of the church was seriously threatened. Here Baptists made a significant contribution. Especially Southern Baptists, as illustrated in the purpose of SBACPE, have insisted that the final concern is to properly prepare parish clergy. Oates's writings from the 1950s, especially *The Christian Pastor* (1953), *The Bible in Pastoral Care* (1953), *Religious Factors in Mental Illness* (1955), and *Anxiety In Christian Experience* (1955), are replete with biblical references and assume the Christian community as a context for healing. Persons such as E. E. Thornton, a student of Oates, have continued this emphasis. They assume that ministers draw upon a rich pastoral heritage as shepherd of the flock and enrich that heritage by alliance with psychology and medicine. That they work in the context of a religious tradition of piety, individualism, and authenticating personal experience enhances their sense that pastoral care and counseling must be refined by contemporary science.

Bibliography. W. A. Clebsch and C. R. Jaekle, *Pastoral Care in Historical Perspectives* (1964). E. B. Holifield, *A History of Pastoral Care in America* (1983). J. T. McNeill, *A History of the Cure of Souls* (1951). E. E. Thornton, *Professional Education for Ministry* (1970) is a detailed treatment of CPE. E. P. Wimberly, *Pastoral Care in the Black Church* (1979), argues for parallel existence of sustaining and guiding functions of pastoral care in the black church. D. C. Matthews, *Religion in the Old South* (1977), may be supplemented by S. S. Hill, Jr., *Southern Churches in Crisis* (1966) and *Religion and The Solid South* (1972).

R. W. CRAPPS

HISTORY OF PROTESTANT PASTORAL CARE (United States); PASTORAL CARE (History, Traditions, and Definitions); PASTORAL CARE MOVEMENT. *See also* FUNDAMENTALIST *or* EVANGELICAL PASTORAL CARE. *Biography:* OATES.

BAR MITZVAH/BAT MITZVAH. The Jewish rite of passage which marks the transition from childhood to religious maturity. Generally observed near one's thirteenth birthday, the ceremony includes a reading of the sacred scroll (Torah) by the celebrant in the presence of family and congregation. The child usually expounds on the meaning of the passage read and conducts a portion of the worship service. A structured period of instruction prepares the child to master these tasks. The rabbi usually addresses some personal words to the celebrant about the meaning of the occasion and blesses him or her. In some synagogues the ceremony includes the physical passing of the sacred scroll from grandparent to parent to child. The service at the synagogue is typically followed by some social festivities including family and friends.

Bar mitzvah (Aramaic and Hebrew) means 'son of the commandments'. The rite is without ancient authority and has been observed only since the middle ages. In the Talmud the term simply applies to any male who has reached the age of thirteen and a day. Such a person becomes responsible for the quality of his ritual and ethical life. He is now obligated to fast on the Day of Atonement, may serve as a legal witness in a rabbinic court, and may be counted as one of the quorum (ten adult males) required for public worship.

Until the twentieth century the rite was confined to males. In the 1920s bat mitzvah, a comparable rite for girls, was introduced in some non-Orthodox synagogues. Only with the rise of the women's movement has the bat mitzvah become widespread. Orthodox congregations try to provide some equivalent but do not hold it within the context of the regular worship service.

Within the Jewish community bar and bat mitzvah have become the primary rites confirming parental responsibility to transmit the heritage and the younger generation's readiness to receive it. The congregation is thus symbolically reassured of continuity. To the family the rite heralds a new stage in the relationship between parent and child. Rabbi Elazar taught that when a child reaches this age, the father should proclaim: "Blessed is He, who freed me from the responsibility for this child" (Genesis Rabba 63:14). The child is regarded as having entered into a new period of personal accountability. He or she is given an opportunity to demonstrate skills acquired over a period of years to make a more serious appropriation of covenant commitments.

As a rite of puberty, bar/bat mitzvah coincides with a child's normal quest for greater independence. Children of this age spend increasing periods of time away from parents, are more zealous for peer approval and often adopt a more critical posture toward parental norms.

These dynamics make the period of bar/bat mitzvah potentially stressful for all members of the family. There is first the inherent ambiguity of adolescence. In western culture the thirteen-year-old is neither totally a child nor fully an adult. Parents celebrate the child's budding maturity even as they may feel disquieted by the prospect of diminishing parental control.

Tensions exhibited by parents and children which are manifestly focused on issues of adequate preparation or the assignment of specific parental roles in the ceremony may reflect deeper, often unconscious parental ambivalence on the issue of freedom and authority. In turn, the child is torn between yearning for greater autonomy and acknowledging a lingering need for dependence.

These dynamics require pastoral sensitivity. Parents function best when rabbis involve them in the preparation of the child and in the ceremony itself. The child needs reassurance that the tasks have been adequately fulfilled. A post–bar/bat mitzvah letdown is best countered by a sustained change in status. In traditional Judaism there are more structured ritual occasions to signify such change. The bar mitzvah will wear phylacteries during the daily worship service, etc. In liberal Judaism, where ritual observance is freer and less pervasive, it is more challenging to provide such tangible symbols of religious maturity. Many congregations encourage the child to continue formal religious training by entering a high school program through confirmation.

When the stresses are sensitively accommodated the bar/bat mitzvah experience is a peak moment of joy for the celebrant and the family.

Bibliography. E. Friedman, "Systems and Ceremonies: A Family View of Rites of Passage," in *The Family Life Cycle,* E. Carter and M. McGoldrick, eds. (1980), pp. 429–60. B. Sherwin, "Bar Mitzvah," *Judaism,* 22: 1 (1973), 52–65. L. Trepp, *The Complete Book of Jewish Observance* (1980), 241–46.

S. E. KARFF

JEWISH HOLY DAYS AND FESTIVALS. *See also* ADOLESCENTS; BLESSING AND BENEDICTION; FAMILY, JEWISH; RITUAL AND PASTORAL CARE; TRADITION AS MODE OF CARE; VOWS/VOWING; WORSHIP AND CELEBRATION.

BARTH, KARL (1886–1968). A major Protestant theologian and author of *The Epistle to the Romans,* which was published shortly after the First World War in German and then in English. This famous commentary on Romans stemmed the tide of modern Protestant theology, which was, in Barth's opinion, concentrating more upon humanity than upon God and God's revelation. He reasserted the authority of Scripture and the significance of theology in the life of the church.

Although Barth rejected natural theology as a basis for the revelation of God, his final work, *The Christian Life* (1981), was a perceptive exegesis of the Lord's Prayer as a basis for the identity of a human before God and of the importance of "friend" and "brother" in human relations. In this he showed the importance of Christian relationships in a community as superior to any of the other relationships existing between members of a human family.

In rejecting the importance of "orders" of creation (described by Brunner as family, society, etc.), Barth laid particular emphasis upon the Holy Spirit as instructor in personal sensitivity and upon Jesus Christ as the only model for living in this world. Because of the emphasis upon Jesus as "God's man," Barth said little about anthropology, psychology, or social psychology. Yet he was strongly influenced by Eduard Thurneysen and Johann Blumhardt, pastors who were active in the care of souls and social service. Barth may have known of the widely published experience of Blumhardt in the healing of a deranged girl through the power of prayer, but this does not appear in his brief reference to the devil and demons in his *Church Dogmatics.*

Barth was teaching systematic theology at Bonn when Hitler came to power. Barth played a leading part in the founding of the Confessing Church and the framing of the Barmen Declaration of 1934. Dismissed by the Nazis, he returned to his native Switzerland and became a professor of theology at Basel, until his retirement in 1962.

Bibliography. C. Brown, *Karl Barth and the Christian Message* (1967). T. C. Oden, *The Promise of Barth* (1969).

S. SOUTHARD

NEO-ORTHODOX THEOLOGY AND PASTORAL CARE; PASTORAL THEOLOGY, PROTESTANT. *See also* THEOLOGY AND PSYCHOLOGY; THEOLOGY AND PSYCHOTHERAPY.

BASIC ECCLESIAL COMMUNITIES. *See* LATIN AMERICAN PASTORAL CARE MOVEMENT.

BASIC TRUST. *See* LIFE CYCLE THEORY.

BATTERED WIVES/HUSBANDS. *See* FAMILY VIOLENCE; VICTIMIZATION.

BAXTER, RICHARD (1615–91). English Presbyterian divine, famed for his innovative pastoral work in the parish of Kidderminster, Worcestershire.

Baxter's fame as a pastoral writer rests largely on his *Gilvas Salvianus; or the Reformed Pastor* (1656). The book described in detail the public duties of pastors — preaching, discipline, and the administering of the sacraments — and exhorted the clergy to lead exemplary lives of faithfulness and humility. But Baxter's primary interest was in persuading English pastors to devote more of their time to "private conference," the instruction of families, and the teaching of the catechism. It was through such methods that he transformed his Kidderminster parish during his ministry of fourteen years there.

He wrote voluminously, producing treatises on such varied pastoral topics as meditation, patience, preparation for the sacrament, sickness, melancholy, assurance, joy, and death. He once said that his own bodily weakness and pain prompted him to study how to die — and hence how to live. His classic devotional treatise, *The Saints' Everlasting Rest* (1650), provides a distinctive insight into seventeenth-century Puritan attitudes toward death and dying.

His contention that the main part of pastoral care consists of teaching and guidance within a local church — and that pastors must "take heed to themselves" before they attempt such a task — has deeply influenced Protestant conceptions of ministry.

E. B. HOLIFIELD

HISTORY OF PROTESTANT PASTORAL CARE (United States).

BECOMING. *See* BEING/BECOMING RELATIONSHIP; DEVELOPMENTAL THEORY AND PASTORAL CARE.

BEERS, CLIFFORD WHITTINGHAM. *See* MENTAL HEALTH MOVEMENT.

BEHAVIOR. (1) In pastoral care and counseling, either overt actions as distinct from subjective experiences and intentions, or both together—thus any psychological action of the person. (2) In psychology, the primary dependent variable. This article describes the technical meaning.

The major types of behavior are defined in terms of activities of three systems of the body and the independent variables that control, influence, or modify them: (1) the striated muscles, (2) the smooth muscles, glands, and heart, and (3) the central nervous system (particularly the cerebral cortex). Independent variables that can impact activities within these three systems are broadly: (1) antecedent stimuli and (2) reinforcers, consequences, or feedback.

1. Reflexive Behavior. Some behaviors seem to be influenced primarily by antecedent stimuli. Known as "elicited," "respondent," "Type S," "Pavlovian," "reflexive," "classically conditioned," or "involuntary" responses, they are relatively simple, can be produced in all physiologically normal persons, and do not require prior learning. They fall into three major subcategories: (1) Somatic reflexes: movements of the striated muscles, which are elicited by an unconditioned stimulus. For example, a loud, unexpected noise will produce a startled jump. The jump is just as easily produced in a young infant as in a mature adult. (2) Reflexes of the smooth muscles, glands, or heart: movements that are controlled by the autonomic nervous system and which are elicited by an unconditioned stimulus. For example, applying an electric shock to a person's hand will cause the blood vessels of all extremities to contract. To the extent that one consciously experiences them, covert reflexes are experienced as emotional reactions. (3) Sensations: activity in a sensory reception area in the cerebral cortex triggered by the stimulation of a sensory receptor. For example, ringing a particular bell produces a distinctive auditory sensation.

Although each type of reflexive behavior can be elicited by the appropriate unconditioned stimulus, classical conditioning can give previously neutral stimuli the power to elicit them.

2. Consequence-Controlled Behavior. Other behaviors seem to be influenced primarily by events that *follow* the behaviors. Such behaviors are known as "emitted," "operant," "Type R," "Skinnerian," "instrumental," and "voluntary" responses. They are relatively complex, vary greatly among individuals, and are dependent on past learning. They too fall into three major subcategories: (1) Actions: movements of the striated muscles having the potential to modify the person's environment. The most common kinds of environmental impact are known as "reinforcers," "consequences," and "feedback." Examples include walking, talking, dancing, writing, etc. (2) Instrumental responses: voluntarily controlled activity of the smooth muscles, glands, and heart through the use of biofeedback procedures. (3) Cognitions: activity in the cerebral cortex in which symbols, signs, and images are manipulated. This final category of behavior can be self-observed only.

P. W. CLEMENT

PSYCHOLOGY, WESTERN. *See also* ACTION/BEING RELATIONSHIP; BEHAVIORISM; PERSONALITY, BIOLOGICAL DIMENSIONS OF; FEELING, THOUGHT, AND ACTION IN PASTORAL COUNSELING; LEARNING THEORIES.

BEHAVIOR, RELIGIOUS. *See* RELIGIOUS BEHAVIOR.

BEHAVIOR, SACRIFICIAL. *See* SACRIFICIAL BEHAVIOR.

BEHAVIOR MODIFICATION AND PASTORAL COUNSELING. The use of techniques of behavior modification by pastoral counselors. How widely behavior modification will extend, in comparison with psychodynamic therapies, remains to be seen. Many writers have opposed behavioral theory and application on the grounds that they are inherently manipulative and dehumanizing, while others justify their use because they are believed to be more efficient and effective than other methods.

1. Behavior Modification Techniques. Early research on conditioned responses in animal and human subjects (I. Pavlov, J. B. Watson) was followed by research in which the active and purposeful behavior of the subject was studied, not just responses to stimuli, to see whether prediction and control could be obtained (B. F. Skinner). Behavior modification methods for use on human subjects have been developed which claim to be directly based on this research, though there is controversy over whether these methods are as truly grounded in research as alleged.

a. Systematic desensitization. This technique, pioneered by J. Wolpe (1969), involves the pairing of a learned relaxation response with imagined anxiety-provoking situations, especially in the treatment of phobias.

b. Aversive and counterconditioning methods. These techniques are derived from conditioning research like that of Pavlov and Watson, and involve the use of painful external stimuli (e.g., a mild electrical impulse) paired with behavior, thoughts, or feelings which are undesirable. Counterconditioning involves the positive reinforcement of behavior which is incompatible with the undesirable behavior. These methods have been widely used with inappropriate sexual behavior, violent behavior, and with other compulsive and phobic behavior. Often these methods work quickly and dramatically, but the positive effects may not always last.

c. Operant methods. Operant conditioning involves the assessment of rewards which are predictably successful in building new desirable behaviors and which will sustain and enhance such positive behavior. Token economy operant methods (T. Ayllon and N. H. Azrin, 1968) employ actual tokens which earn points toward a rewarding event (visit to the commissary), which may be earned by an increase in positive behavior (sweeping one's room). Token economies have been widely used in schools and other institutional settings. Other operant methods include behavior assessment and contracting, self-reinforcement, and the use of biofeedback.

d. Modeling. In this technique pioneered by A. Bandura (1971), behavior change is encouraged by presenting positive examples of the behavior desired, either by actual people, on film, or in imagination. Modeling has been widely applied in school settings and in the treatment of aggressive behavior by modeling assertive but not aggressive responses to threatening situations.

e. Cognitive methods. L. P. Ullmann (1970) has argued that cognitions are covert behaviors which follow the principles of operant conditioning. Cognitive behavioral methods thus involve procedures for helping people to condition their thoughts in ways which are similar to other types of behavioral conditioning. Clients are trained in creating new images of experienced events, and thus can learn new and more appropriate responses.

2. Appropriation of Behavior Modification Techniques in Pastoral Counseling. Of the techniques summarized above, it would seem unlikely that desensitization or aversive and counterconditioning methods could ever be recommended for pastoral counseling. Those methods presuppose a degree of technical competence and of control over the lives of clients which should not ordinarily characterize a pastoral relationship.

However, it would seem entirely appropriate to recommend operant, modeling, and cognitive methods in pastoral counseling, not only because of their potential effectiveness, but also because it can be demonstrated that pastoral counseling relationships have always included random and unsystematic applications of such techniques.

In the growing but still modest literature of pastoral counseling employing behavior modification methods, such distinctions between methods are frequently made.

R. Alexander (1976) argues that operant conditioning methods are consistent with a humane and Christian ethical viewpoint, because operant conditioning stresses positive rewards in a social system of positive reinforcement rather than punishment, and thus more adequately approximates the good society which is the aim of Christian effort.

R. L. George and E. L. Dustin (1970) advocate an increased use of behavioral methods in pastoral counseling. Such usage would make the minister a more disciplined professional, a more equal partner in the counseling relationship, a better scientist, and more aware of the way in which the minister functions as a source of reinforcement in all functions of ministry. In another article, R. L. George (1972–73) argues for the efficiency and effectiveness of behavioral methods in pastoral counseling especially in eliminating nonselective reinforcement.

C. Steckel (1979) argues for a selective use of behavior modification in pastoral counseling by means of enhanced understanding and training and heightened awareness on the part of the pastoral counselor regarding informal and unacknowledged behavioral methods already found in other therapeutic approaches, and especially in forming explicit behavioral contracts with clients in counseling relationships.

H. Stone (1980) argues that behavioral methods comprise an important new set of techniques which complement other therapeutic methods. Using pastoral care experiences, Stone explains the use of relaxation and biofeedback methods to reduce stress, cognitive methods to deal with irrational ideas, operant methods to help parents deal effectively with children, and the use of systematic desensitization and other techniques such as behavioral rehearsal, thought stopping, and problem solving. Stone acknowledges and responds to criticism of behavioral methods, and urges pastors to reexamine their biases against behavioral methods.

N. L. Marvin (1980) proposes a wider use of modeling in the church and tries to show how Christ as the perfect model can be applied to less than perfect human modeling.

R. K. Bufford (1971) believes that biblical and behavioral principles are essentially in harmony on many points, and so encourages the use of behavior modification methods in child rearing, Christian education, and in pastoral and evangelistic work. He emphasizes the role of the pastor as model and the use of positive reinforcement in pastoral relationships.

While use of behavior modification techniques is advocated in the literature, there are no comprehensive studies giving evidence of the extent to which these techniques have been adopted in the teaching and practice of pastoral counseling.

3. Objections to Behavioral Methods in Pastoral Counseling. *a. Philosophical or theological objections.* Because B. F. Skinner (1953, 1971, 1974) has argued so passionately for philosophical determinism and the social benefits of increased behavioral control, many of the philosophical or theological objections (S. Koch, P. Scribner, M. Novak) have been addressed directly to Skinner, assuming that any form of behavior modification must represent Skinner's philosophy. Skinner does seem to hold that all behavior is intrinsically predictable and thus controllable. And he does allow for "counterconditioning", understood however, as the influence exerted by the subject on the experimenter, so his determinism is partially qualified.

Other behaviorists (e.g., W. Craighead, A. Kazdin, and M. Mahoney) have argued for both scientific determinism and responsible choice. Some theological writers (C. Steckel, R. Bufford) have argued for a theological appropriation of a qualified form of determinism based on the doctrine of divine providence.

b. Moral objections. Behaviorism has been vigorously opposed by those who argue that there is no moral justification for extending behavioral control over others, even for the most laudable purposes, since the inevitable result is either coercion or manipulation, in which the controlled person is not treated as a responsible moral agent. J. Kurtch (1953), A. Koestler (1967), and W. Gaylin (1973) see the threat of antidemocratic and elitist social control in applied behavior modification.

B. Häring (1975) acknowledges a limited contribution of behavior modification in demonstrating that freedom is always limited and calls for a discerning use of behavioral methods. But he affirms the reality of conscience and freedom against any behaviorist determinism.

Some behaviorists (L. Krasner, P. London) have recognized that ethical issues of new scope and magnitude are inherent in the use of behavior modification, and have proposed guidelines for their use. London sees in behavior modification an old moral question — how to use power justly. But behavioral technology places this old question in a new context, since power can be exercised in far more subtle and effective ways by using behavioral methods. What is required, according to London, is a new ethic of human awareness, so that people retain a strong measure of freedom and self-control.

C. Steckel (1979) has argued that behavior modification is ethically permissible as long as principles are observed which maximize the informed consent of the clients involved, and which require the participation of all parties involved in the determination of both moral means and moral ends. He has attempted to ground these principles in a Christian theological understanding of justice and love.

C. Ellison (1977) articulates seven specific Christian concerns from an evangelical perspective which should govern research and therapy. Among these concerns are the projection of individual dignity, the observance of the created orders, and the development of specifically biblical guidelines. In a similar vein, R. Bufford (1981) develops a biblical case for applied behavior modification, largely derived from the covenant of God's commandments and human responsibility to obey God. While theology cannot accept Skinnerian determinism, Bufford believes that much of the practical wisdom of behavior modification is compatible with biblical teachings.

c. Pastoral objections. While there is no body of literature stating uniquely pastoral objections to behavior modification on principles other than the theological or moral arguments cited above, there are nevertheless certain identifiable pastoral counseling concerns which are frequently raised in discussions among professionals. One of these is the concern that behavioral assessment, planning, and reinforcing do not allow for the free and spontaneous movement of experience so important in the

good life. A grim regimentation might be the result. It is also feared that focusing on behavior rather than thoughts or feelings may not facilitate the deeper change which many people need when they enter into pastoral counseling, but may only result in the problems reappearing in the form of some other symptoms. Some of the behavior modification applications to marriage and family counseling situations (e.g., A. Azrin, B. J. Naster, and R. Jones,) appear to view marriage and the family exclusively as mutual need, as a reinforcement system rather than as a sacrament or covenant.

4. Overcoming Objections to Behavior Modification in Pastoral Counseling. *a. Theology and ethics.* Systematic theologians and theological ethicists will need to explore behavioral theory and methods more fully than they have in the past. While freedom and determinism are familiar themes in theology, contemporary theologians (aside from the few examples cited above) have shown little interest in pursuing these themes in relation to modern behavioral psychology.

While theological ethicists have not avoided moral questions of power and control in society, they have not (with the exception of Häring, Ellison, and others cited above) sufficiently attended to the particular ethical dilemmas inherent in behavior modification. A more detailed, reflective, and selective assessment of behavior modification, including its constructive possibilities, will be needed from theological ethics if pastoral counselors are to find the kind of encouragement and guidance they require.

b. Pastoral theology and counseling. Teachers and supervisors in pastoral theology and counseling will need to reexamine their own commitments to particular therapeutic orientations and to consider the use of a behavioral perspective in analyzing the exchanges which occur in pastoral counseling. Pastoral counseling has already moved beyond advocating a particular therapeutic orientation (S. Hiltner, C. Wise) to a more eclectic approach to therapy (H. Clinebell). Nevertheless, particular therapeutic orientations still exercise a strong influence on many seminary teachers, chaplains, and pastoral counselors. Until pastoral theologians and counselors become less committed to a single therapeutic approach, behavior modification will probably not gain significant approval or use.

One fruitful approach would be the analysis of pastoral counseling processes, as presently conducted, on behavioral principles, much as J. Haley does in *The Strategies of Psychotherapy*, where the same counseling session is discussed in detail from several therapeutic orientations. Such imaginative excursions into behavioral analysis would not require a fundamental change in orientation, but might demonstrate the truly eclectic character of every counseling process.

c. General pastoral studies. A greater openness to behavior modification might emerge in pastoral studies generally if more attention were given to what D. Browning calls "method in Christian living"—those specific ways by which the faithful person seeks to express discipleship in daily life. Modern pastoral studies have tended, in reaction to Victorian moralism, to emphasize the unconditional love of God rather than specific expectations for Christian living. Browning and others are calling for a more balanced perspective on God's love and God's commandments. The fact that much of the recent positive assessment of behavior modification comes from theologically evangelical circles suggests that the liberal or mainline church bodies may be less open to the use of behavior modification.

5. The Future of Behavior Modification in Pastoral Counseling. If the objections to behavior modification discussed above are substantively addressed from theological, ethical, and pastoral perspectives, it is likely that behavior modification will gradually take its place among the various methods already used in pastoral counseling. If this work does not proceed, and if behavior modification itself should eventually lose the position of dominance it holds in many therapeutic settings, then its use in pastoral counseling will surely be modest at best.

It is almost certain that pastoral counseling will recover, in some manner, the emphasis on helping people to live as persons of religious faith, as well as maintaining its present emphasis on unconditional love and a therapeutic dissolution of harmful repressions. The centuries of tradition regarding the proper work of the rabbi, priest, or pastor will surely aid in this recovery.

Behavior modification might well become one avenue of that recovery, because it offers concepts and methods for removing undesirable behavior and for strengthening desirable behavior. The skillful pastoral counselor will need to engage the new client in a process of assessment to discover the nature of the presenting problem and the dynamics underlying it.

In the very nature of such an assessment, the pastoral counselor will be looking at behavioral dynamics while using other therapeutic orientations, and will need to enter into explicit negotiations with the counselee regarding the degree to which specific behavior is a problem to be addressed. If there is behavior to be removed or enhanced, the next phase of assessment will entail exploration of the various positive and negative reinforcing events which sustain unwanted behavior or interfere with desired behavior. If, however, this initial assessment does not yield tangible behavioral results, the versatile pastoral counselor will shift to other therapeutic orientations and methods to help the counselee discover whether something in belief, thinking, or emotions seems to be at the heart of the presenting problem.

However, if the initial assessment yields a behavioral analysis, the pastoral counselor who knows how to use behavior modification methods will then enter upon the most challenging and difficult part of the therapeutic contract — discovering the actual pattern of positive and negative reinforcements in the experience of a client(s). Some will be obvious — "I eat when I'm depressed." But others will be hidden in complex patterns — "I try to take time for prayer each day, but all I can think about are the many things I should be doing." An extended period of trial and error may ensue, in which the counselor suggests new reinforcement patterns which the counselee tries out before the next session. Out of such trial and error the counselor and client(s) eventually develop a clearer picture of the actual reinforcements which are at work.

The next phase of behavioral pastoral counseling is the development of a plan for modifying old reinforcing patterns and developing new ones. Such a plan must be the result of close collaboration between the counselee and counselor, or else an excessive dependence upon the counselor will block the kind of self-control and self-direction which the counselee needs. Such a plan may include daily activities, review periods, adjustments in patterns of life activities, all the way to changes in occupation, place of residence or marital relationships, though such major changes are usually not explored until other efforts have proven fruitless. Whatever form the specific plan takes, it needs to include both "internal events"—those thoughts or feelings which function as behavioral reinforcers — and all those "external events"— people and objects in the human environment which predispose one to certain behavior — in order to be a successful plan of treatment.

Continuing therapeutic sessions become opportunities for reviewing the plan and making any adjustments which may be required. These sessions are also used to prepare for the ongoing management of the plan which will be the responsibility of the client when the counseling sessions are concluded. Here the emphasis is on strengthening the client's ownership of the plan and the responsibility for its successful operation, in the eventual absence of the positive reinforcement of the pastoral counseling sessions.

During such behavioral pastoral counseling, the versatile counselor will not be oriented exclusively to behavioral concepts but will always be employing basic counseling skills — active listening, focusing, etc.—to be attentive to issues of belief, attitudes, feelings, and the like, which may not just be dependent upon behavior, but which may also serve as behavioral reinforcers, or which may need some attention in their own right.

If pastoral counseling in the future incorporates behavior modification in the manner suggested above, it can be expected that counseling will become more efficient and effective with those clients who have needed help with specific behavior but instead have been treated with depth exploration. It can also be expected that some issues of transference or dependence upon the counselor will be resolved more effectively, since the elements of mutual responsibility for the therapeutic contract are more consciously articulated in behavior counseling than in other therapeutic orientations. And it can also be expected that a greater balance of power (and of justice) will emerge in the counseling relationship, since counselor and counselee must be engaged in a mutual exploration and learning process rather than a treatment process in which someone presumed to be "sick" is helped by someone presumed to be "well."

Nevertheless, behavioral pastoral counseling in the future will also need to be on guard against abuses of behavior modification methods. In the churches and in pastoral counseling it will be especially important to guard against employing unquestioning obedience as a goal of behavior modification. In religious groups where believing specific doctrines and following prescribed patterns of behavior are required, it will take special sensitivity and skill on the part of clergy and pastoral counselors to keep behavior modification from becoming simply a more sophisticated procedure for enforcement of these beliefs. In religious groups which affirm a greater plurality of beliefs and actions, it will be especially important for clergy and pastoral counselors to employ behavior modification in ways which give specific shape to faith and religious life without at the same time violating the conscience of individual believers.

Bibliography. R. G. Alexander, "Can a Christian Ethic Condone Behavior Modification?" *Religion in Life* (1976), 191. T. Ayllon and N. H. Azrin, *The Token Economy: A Motivational System for Therapy and Rehabilitation* (1968). N. H. Azrin, B. J. Naster, and R. Jones, "Reciprocity Counseling: A Rapid Learning-Based Procedure for Marital Counseling," *Behaviour Research and Therapy*, 11 (1973), 366. A. Bandura, *Psychological Modeling: Conflicting Theories* (1971). D. Browning, *The Moral Context of Pastoral Care* (1976). R. K. Bufford, *The Human Reflex* (1981). H. Clinebell, *Basic Types of Pastoral Care and Counseling* (1984). W. E. Craighead, A. E. Kazdin, and M. J. Mahoney, *Behavior Modification* (1976). C. W. Ellison, *Modifying Man: Implications and Ethics* (1977). W. Gaylin, "Skinner Redux," *Harper's Magazine*, October (1973), 55. R. L. George, "Behavioral Counseling for the Minister," *J. of Pastoral Care*, 7: 2 (1972–3), 42–7, R. L. George and E. R. Dustin, "The Minister as a Behavioral Counselor," *Pastoral Psychology*, 21 (1970), 16. J. Haley, *Strategies of Psychotherapy* (1963). B. Häring, *Ethics of Manipulation* (1975). S. Hiltner, *Pastoral Counseling* (1949). S. Koch, "Psychology and Emerging Conceptions of Knowledge as Unitary," in *Behaviorism and Phenomenology*, T. W. Wann, ed., (1964). A. Koestler, *The Ghost in the Machine* (1967). L. Krasner, "Behavior Modification—Values and Training: The Perspective of a Psychologist," in *Behavior Therapy, Appraisal and Status*, in C. M. Franks, ed., (1969), p. 541. J. W. Krutch, *The Measure of Man* (1953). P. London, *Behavior Control* (1972). M. L. Marvin, "Social Modeling: A Psychological-Theological Perspective," *J. of Psychology and Theology*, Fall (1980), 211–21. W. L. Mikulas, *Behavior Modification* 2d ed. (1978). M. Novak, "Is He Really a Grand Inquisitor?" in *Beyond the Punitive Society*, J. H. Wheeler, ed., (1973). I. P. Pavlov, *Lectures on Conditioned Reflexes* (1928). P. H. Scribner, "Escape from Freedom and Dignity," *Ethics*, 83: 1 (1972), 13–15. B. F. Skinner, *Science and Human Behavior* (1953); *Beyond Freedom and Dignity* (1971); *About Behaviorism* (1974). C. J. Steckel, *Theology and Ethics of Behavior Modification* (1979). H. W. Stone, *Using Behavioral Methods in Pastoral Counseling* (1980). L. P. Ullmann, "On Cognitions and Behavior Therapy," in *Behavior Therapy*, C. M. Franks, ed., 1 (1970), 201–4. J. B. Watson, *Behaviorism* (1925). C. Wise, *Pastoral Counseling: Its Theory and Practice* (1951). J. Wolpe, *The Practice of Behavior Therapy* (1969).

C. J. STECKEL

BEHAVIOR THERAPIES (Methods and Research); PASTORAL COUNSELING; PASTORAL THEOLOGY. *See also* ACTION/BEING RELATIONSHIP; BEHAVIORISM (Theories and Research); FEELING, THOUGHT, AND ACTION IN PASTORAL COUNSELING; LEARNING THEORIES; PHILOSOPHY AND PSYCHOLOGY.

BEHAVIOR REHEARSAL. *See* BEHAVIOR THERAPIES.

BEHAVIOR THERAPIES (Methods and Research). A systematic attempt to apply empirically determined behavioral "rules" to remediate the behavior of both individuals and groups in situations of crisis. Specifically, behavior therapists seek (1) to use clinical procedures which were initially developed in the laboratory — this entails defining the relationship of the client's envi-

ronment to the presenting behavioral difficulty in a precise fashion — and (2) to apply clearly defined procedures, such as reinforcement and punishment (among others) in a manner that permits determining empirically whether or not treatment was successful. Behavioral therapists assume that even complex behavioral problems and sequences can be defined in terms of their component parts and that these components can be systematically treated.

1. **Basic Types and Procedures.** Behavior therapists define and classify behavior in several ways. *Respondent* behaviors are reflexive, that is, controlled by antecedents (the events that precede them). These include such behaviors as emotional reactions, smooth muscle responses, sensations, and somatic reflexes. Ivan Pavlov's pioneering work on classical or respondent conditioning laid the theoretical foundation for how an event could become conditioned to elicit a behavioral response. *Operant* behaviors are controlled by the events which follow them (consequences) and include cognitions, actions, and the instrumental behaviors of smooth muscles. Operant procedures became popularized following B. F. Skinner's application of laboratory based principles to clinical situations in the 1940s and 1950s. Behaviors may also be classified as excesses, deficits, or anomalies. Behavioral excesses are those behaviors in which the client engages too frequently and must be reduced, while behavioral deficits are those behaviors which the client either does not perform at all or performs at such a low rate that the behavior must be increased. Anomalies are those behaviors which, while neither an excess nor a deficit, are inappropriate or unusual for the setting in which the client currently exhibits them.

Historically, behavior therapy is a relatively new discipline and treatment approach. Isolated behavioral treatment interventions can be found dating back to the early twentieth century, but it was not until 1953, when B. F. Skinner published *Science and Human Behavior*, that operant behavioral techniques became firmly established as valid therapeutic interventions. In 1958 Joseph Wolpe published *Psychotherapy by Reciprocal Inhibition*, which elaborated the respondent (classical conditioning) origins and treatment of phobias.

Walker, Hedberg, Clement, and Wright (1981, pp. 24ff.) elaborate several tasks that are essential prerequisites to both operant and respondent behavioral treatment procedures. First, a precise definition (called a *response definition*) of the problematic or *target behavior* is necessary to insure that both client and therapist are describing the same behavior. Second, there must be an *identification* of the antecedents of respondent behaviors, and the consequences of operant behaviors which maintain the behaviors and which could be altered or rearranged in a treatment plan. Third, a *classification* of the behavior as an excess, deficit, or anomaly must be made. Fourth is a *specification* of the goals of treatment, which treatment interventions are to be used, and any behavioral assets which might effectively be used in the treatment interventions. And, fifth, there must be an *evaluation* of the treatment intervention to document that the desired changes are occurring at the desired level. Typically, a behavior therapist takes a pretreatment measure of the behavior in question and reevaluates at various points during the therapy process.

2. Techniques Based on Classical Conditioning.

a. Relaxation training. Current research indicates that muscle relaxation is an effective means of reducing anxiety (Bernstein and Borkovec, 1973). It is assumed that one cannot be both relaxed and anxious at the same time. This technique is relatively straightforward, easily learned, and the instructions can be put onto a cassette tape that clients can take home to practice. Relaxation training has been used as an intervention to reduce anxiety or as an adjunct to other therapeutic techniques which might prove anxiety provoking. Demands for each session should be kept low, and the preparation of the client and physical setting is essential to the relaxation process. Low noise levels, dimmed lights, a reclining chair, the therapist positioned so as to minimize embarrassment to the client, and low voice tones all facilitate a relaxed state for the client. Prior to beginning the treatment clients should be informed why relaxation training was chosen, briefly what to expect, and any resistances ought to be discussed. Many clients feel awkward during the first sessions and should be told that this is a normal reaction.

During each relaxation session the clients are instructed to tense various muscle groups to three quarters of their potential, then to relax them. The therapist simultaneously instructs the client to feel and examine the tension, and after five to ten seconds to relax and feel the tension "flow out" of the muscle group. The order of muscle groups, while not critical, generally begins with the extremities and proceeds to the shoulders, neck, and facial muscles. Sessions end with the client staying in a relaxed state for a brief interval and then discussing any reactions with the therapist.

b. Systematic desensitization. This technique builds on the skills acquired through relaxation training and applies them to a wide range of "phobic" or feared situations such as public speaking, dating, and test taking. Desensitization involves isolating the anxiety provoking event, constructing a hierarchy of situations from least to most anxiety producing, and imagining oneself in those situations while in a relaxed state. There are many variations on this basic technique (Wolfe, 1958; Meichenbaum, 1974). While empirical research supports its efficacy, there is no consensus as to *how* the technique actually achieves its results. An assumption of this procedure is that an imagined event can stand in place of the real one. It is therefore necessary for imagined events to produce anxiety. If the client can imagine the event and not experience anxiety, then subsequent systematic desensitization will most likely not be successful.

The selection of themes is the first critical step in the process as the therapist and client must decide *what* to desensitize. Frequently clients are unable to verbalize clearly what it is that they fear. The more specifically the situation to be desensitized can be defined, the greater the prognosis for successful outcome. The second step is the construction of a hierarchy of aversive imaginal situations from which the client and therapist should select from one to two dozen incremental situations leading up to the feared event, beginning with those which produce the least anxiety. A hierarchy should be established for each of the individual's feared situations. The client is then asked to relax, and the therapist states that he or she is about to introduce a scene which he or she wants the client to visualize as vividly as possible. The first scene from the hierarchy is then described to the client. The goal for the client is gradually to experience more anxiety provoking situations *without* becoming anxious. When the client reports that he or she is experiencing anxiety, the therapist terminates that scene and returns to one that is less threatening.

c. Implosion and flooding. These techniques are used to reduce anxiety by presenting, either imaginally or *in vivo*, the feared situation and prohibiting the client from making an escape response. The client is instructed to maximize and experience the anxiety for an extended period of time. It is believed that the client will learn that the feared event need not be feared and anxiety will be reduced. Although both interventions are in practice fairly similar, implosion techniques originated from a psychodynamic perspective while flooding is more behavioral.

3. Techniques Based on Operant Procedures.

The operant procedures mentioned below are those frequently referred to as behavior modification. These few basic principles, in various combinations, have been used to successfully treat a number of commonly seen clinical syndromes, including depression, marital discord, substance abuse and dependence, and psychotic behaviors. These techniques have also been used with children to reduce fighting, tantrums, enuresis, arguing, lying, and to increase academic and cooperative behaviors. In the present survey only the basic principles can be presented.

Operant techniques are based on the assumption that the environmental consequences of a behavior serve to maintain its presence or absence. These treatment procedures are systematic and involve various combinations of reinforcement, punishment, and extinction (i.e., neither reinforcing nor punishing) to weaken or strengthen the links between a behavior and the environment. A *reinforcer* is any stimulus which follows a behavior and increases the likelihood that that behavior will recur and increase in frequency. *Reinforcement* is the process of systematically rewarding a behavior in order for it to increase in frequency. Reinforcement occurs either when a behavior is directly reinforced through administering a rewarding consequence (food, money, tokens), or through the removal of an unpleasant stimulus (loud noise, pain, anxiety).

A *punisher* is any stimulus which follows a behavior and decreases the likelihood that that behavior will recur or at least decreases the frequency. A punisher may also be administered directly (spanking, aversive smell, shock), or indirectly by removing a pleasant stimulus (loss of privileges, money, tokens). Use of punishment is frequently associated with negative side effects. Punishment produces emotional behavior and the punishing agent may become anxiety-provoking or feared. Intermittently using punishment generally teaches at what times the behavior can be engaged in, rather than reducing the behavior, excessive punishment can be inhumane and abusive. Both reinforcers and punishers are defined in terms of their effect on behavior and not in terms of whether they are subjectively pleasant or unpleasant.

Extinction is the process of withholding the usual consequences of a behavior (usually reinforcing) in order to decrease its frequency. Problems with extinction arise when the behavior is too serious to ignore (fighting, self-injurious behavior) or is intermittently ignored. As with intermittent punishment, intermittent extinction teaches only when and when not to engage in a behavior. Additionally, when extinction is first instituted, the behavior will increase in frequency before it decreases, leading many people, especially parents, to conclude erroneously that "it isn't working." This teaches the client that if the usual consequences of a behavior are not forthcoming, increasing the frequency or magnitude of the behavior will produce the desired results.

Both reinforcement and punishment have been found to be most efficacious under the following conditions. First, the consequence is delivered as soon as possible after the occurrence of the target behavior. Second, the consequence is of sufficient magnitude to affect the behavior. Third, the person is not satiated with the consequence to the point that it is no longer reinforcing or punishing.

Various combinations of reinforcement, punishment, and extinction have been clinically used and empirically verified by behavior therapists as successful treatment interventions. *Shaping* is a method of teaching previously unlearned behaviors by systematically reinforcing gradual and successive approximations to the desired behavior. For example, teaching a child to ride a bike might include the child sitting on the bike while it is steadied by a parent, riding with training wheels, riding while steadied by a parent, and riding alone. Each step in the sequence gradually approximates the desired behavior.

Differential reinforcement is the process of reinforcing a desired behavior that is incompatible with an undesired behavior and putting the undesired behavior on extinction (ignoring it). In some instances punishing the unwanted behavior can be substituted for putting it on extinction. For example, a child in school can be reinforced for sitting at his desk, a behavior which is incompatible with wandering around the classroom, and ignored when he is out of his seat.

Response cost is the procedure of "fining" a person following a predetermined undesired behavior. Monetary fines, loss of privileges, and loss of points are contingent upon the occurrence of the undesired behavior. A unique procedure which has proven effective with children is *time out* from reinforcement. Following the target behavior the child is removed from the arena and returned after a brief interval of appropriate behavior.

Walker *et al.* (1981) delineate nine important steps in implementing an operant behavioral intervention: (1) selecting the behavior to be modified and defining it in a clear and concrete manner such that everyone involved agrees upon the target behavior; (2) deciding whether the behavior is an excess, deficit, or anomaly along with what behaviors would be desirous to develop in its place; (3) analyzing the sequence of events which are either reinforcing or punishing the target behavior and maintaining its presence (how could this sequence be interrupted? could a more desirable behavior be reinforced in place of the present target behavior?); (4) determining what type of intervention program will be used (will only reinforcement, punishment, or a combination of both procedures be needed?); (5) obtaining a fre-

quency count of the behavior prior to the introduction of treatment (known as a *baseline*); (6) implementing the treatment program; (7) after a short time period, reassessing the treatment program and making changes as needed; (8) at various intervals recording the frequency of the behavior to determine if the desired treatment changes are occurring; (9) deciding how long the treatment should continue and in what manner the treatment program might be phased out.

4. Other Behavioral Treatment Interventions.
a. Token economies. Token economies can be employed when a group of people in the same arena have common treatment needs. Typically, settings such as prisons, residential treatment facilities, or mental hospitals will predetermine which behaviors when performed will be reinforced with tokens. These tokens can be exchanged at a later point in time for a wide range of backup reinforcers. The essential components of the token economy are that the environment be controlled, target behaviors predetermined, measured objectively, and taught or reinforced with tokens that are contingent on performance of the target behavior and can be spent on backup reinforcers. Token economies are conceptually easy to understand but can be problematic to implement, requiring a great deal of foresight and planning.

b. Behavioral contracting. This has proven quite useful in negotiating, in concrete and measurable terms, agreements between two parties. These two parties can consist of spouses, parents and children, or even client and therapist. Whereas contracts are usually verbal, a written record which states what was agreed to by each party is useful should a disagreement arise later. The process of negotiating the behavioral contract is very valuable in teaching problem solving and conflict management skills. Typically, a contract will specify concretely what behavior(s) are to be changed, how much they are to be changed within a specific time period, as well as the specific reinforcer that is to be earned.

c. Assertion training. Assertion training has been frequently misinterpreted and maligned by casual observers of this technique. A more accurate label for this intervention might be social skills training. Most clinicians who work with this technique stress that the inability to make socially appropriate responses will lead to anxiety, stress, and other maladaptive behaviors. In the course of social interactions it is necessary to be able to begin, maintain, and conclude conversations, say no, make requests, and express positive and negative feelings. Assertion training attempts to teach these skills to people who cannot perform them without feelings of embarrassment, guilt, or anxiety.

Bibliography. A. Bandura, *Principles of Behavior Modification* (1969). A. S. Bellack, M. Hersen, and A. E. Kazdin, eds., *International Handbook of Behavior Modification and Therapy* (1982). D. A. Bernstein and T. D. Burkovec, *Progressive Relaxation Training* (1973). D. M. Gelfand and D. P. Hartman, *Child Behavior Analysis and Therapy*, 2d ed. (1984). M. R. Goldfried and G. C. Davison, *Clinical Behavior Therapy* (1976). D. H. Meichenbaum, *Cognitive Behavior Modification* (1977). K. L. Miller, *Principles of Everyday Behavior Analysis*, 2d ed. (1980). B. F. Skinner, *Science and Human Behavior* (1953). J. Wolpe, *Psychotherapy of Reciprocal Inhibition* (1958). C. E. Walker,

A. Hedberg, P. W. Clement, and L. Wright *Clinical Procedures in Behavior Therapy* (1981).

J. A. WOLFE

BEHAVIORISM (Theories and Research); BEHAVIOR MODIFICATION AND PASTORAL COUNSELING; PSYCHOTHERAPY AND COUNSELING (Research Studies and Methods). *See also* ACTION/BEING RELATIONSHIP; CONDITIONING; FEELING, THOUGHT, AND ACTION IN PASTORAL COUNSELING; LEARNING THEORIES; PHILOSOPHY AND PSYCHOLOGY; PSYCHOTHERAPY; THEOLOGY AND PSYCHOLOGY. *Compare* ANALYTICAL (JUNGIAN) PSYCHOLOGY (Therapeutic Method and Research); HUMANISTIC PSYCHOTHERAPIES (Methods and Research).

BEHAVIORAL DISORDERS OF CHILDHOOD. A classification of mental disorders usually first evident in childhood or adolescence. The *Diagnostic and Statistical Manual of Mental Disorders* (3d ed.) divides children's problems into five categories: (1) intellectual, (2) behavioral, (3) emotional, (4) physical, and (5) developmental. Behavioral disorders appear as problems corresponding to the first three of these, i.e., as problems in deportment or conduct (overactivity, noncompliance, aggressiveness, delinquency), as predominant manifestations of anxiety (separation and avoidance problems), and as disruptions in basic areas of physical functioning (elimination, eating, sleep, speech, and movement). They are to be distinguished from similar symptoms secondary to organic impairment, mental retardation, psychosis, major disturbances of affect, or specific learning disabilities.

1. Problems in Deportment or Conduct. Moore (1982) divides the deportment-conduct problems of children into three major areas: control problems, aggressive behavior, and delinquent behavior. These areas fall on a severity and age-related continuum from control problems to delinquent behavior. *Control problems* are often brought to the attention of a helping professional by distraught parents who express an inability to set limits effectively for their children. Children with these problems may manifest any or all of these difficulties: oppositional or other forms of disruptive behavior, temper tantrums, overactivity, or excessive whining. *Aggressive behavior problems,* which are more antisocial, consist of excessive physical and verbal aggression by the child and include such behaviors as defiance of authorities, frequent arguing, and fighting. *Delinquent behavior problems* represent the most serious social adjustment difficulties. They include such provocative behaviors as persistent truancy, substance abuse, running away, theft, sexual misconduct, and physical violence.

2. Problems Manifesting Anxiety. Anxiety disorders of childhood or adolescence can take the form of either generalized anxiety across numerous situations or anxiety specifically related to certain environmental conditions. *Generalized anxiety disorders* are characterized by over-anxiety about the future and a preoccupation with the child's own vulnerability and self-perceived incompetency. *Focalized anxiety problems* are associated with inordinate anxiety related to separation from significant others or to excessive recoiling from contact with strangers beyond that deemed developmentally appropriate.

3. Problems in Physical Functioning. Behavioral disorders of childhood that occur as disruptions in normal physical functioning are less common than conduct or anxiety disorders but are nontheless as problematic and in rare instances can be life threatening. The disorders in this category are subdivided according to the affected physical function (eliminating, eating, sleeping, speaking, and moving). The two functional elimination problems are bed-wetting (enuresis) and inappropriate passage or retention of fecal material (encopresis). Eating disorders include a refusal to eat sufficiently (anorexia nervosa) and episodes of binge eating (bulimia). Childhood sleep disorders (termed papasomias or disturbances during sleep) include somnabulis (sleep-walking) and night terrors. The latter are to be distinguished from typical nightmares because they involve a sudden onset of thrashing and crying with open eyes and rapid breathing which lasts from five to thirty minutes despite parental intervention. Stuttering is the most common speech disorder. Stereotyped movement disorders, commonly called tics, involve involuntary abnormal muscle movement. They vary in severity according to how many muscle groups are involved.

In attempting to diagnose childhood behavior disorders two major distinctions must be kept in view: (1) children are in a process of development; their behavior is therefore much more variable and responsive to environmental influences and manipulations than that of adults. (2) Usually children are brought involuntarily to the attention of the counselor because their behavior has been socially disruptive. This may unduly focus attention on the behavior itself when in fact these problems may be secondary to serious parental, marital, or family dysfunction.

Bibliography. American Psychiatric Association, *Diagnostic and Statistical Manual of Mental Disorders* 3d ed. rev. (1987). Group for the Advancement of Psychiatry, Committee on Child Psychiatry, *Psychopathological Disorders in Childhood* (1966). M. Rutter, D. Shaffer, and M. Shepherd, *A Multi-Axial Classification of Child Psychiatric Disorders* (1975).

J. W. FANTUZZO

CHILDREN; DIAGNOSTIC AND STATISTICAL MANUAL III; EVALUATION AND DIAGNOSIS, PSYCHOLOGICAL; PSYCHOPATHOLOGY, THEORIES OF. *See also* ANXIETY; FAMILY THEORY AND THERAPY; MENTAL HEALTH AND ILLNESS; PERSONALITY DEVELOPMENT; PSYCHOSOCIAL DEVELOPMENT. *Compare* ADJUSTMENT DISORDERS; JUVENILE CRIME AND DELINQUENCY; PSYCHOSOMATIC ILLNESS.

BEHAVIORAL SCIENCE. Behavioral science studies the behavior of humans and animals in the physical and social environment. Techniques include observation and experimental methods similar to those of the natural sciences. Behavioral science includes psychology, psychiatry, sociology, cultural anthropology, and related disciplines.

R. K. BUFFORD

SOCIAL SCIENCES. *See also* BEHAVIORISM; CULTURAL ANTHROPOLOGY; PHILOSOPHY AND PSYCHOLOGY; PSYCHIATRY; PSYCHOLOGY; SOCIOLOGY OF RELIGIOUS AND PASTORAL CARE; SOCIOLOGY OF RELIGION; THEOLOGY AND PSYCHOLOGY.

BEHAVIORISM (Theories and Research).

Behaviorism purports that the science of psychology should be restricted to the study of directly observable behavior and events.

Modern behaviorism began at the turn of the century. Major proponents include Pavlov, Watson, and Skinner. Originally a reaction to the mentalism of introspectionism and functionalism and characterized by intense loyalty among its adherents and strong opposition by others, behaviorism has emerged as a major force in contemporary psychology because of its influence on psychological research and its widespread practical application. Criticisms focus on behaviorism's naturalistic reductionism and determinism.

1. History. The roots of modern behaviorism can be traced to the work of Ivan Pavlov, a Russian physiologist, around the turn of the century. Almost by accident, Pavlov discovered the phenomenon that has come to be known as classical or respondent conditioning. While he was studying salivation in dogs, Pavlov discovered that, after a time, the dogs salivated even when the keeper entered the room rather than just when given food. His curiosity aroused, Pavlov began to study this process. He found that events such as the ringing of a bell, which reliably preceded giving the dogs food on a number of occasions, gradually developed the power to elicit salivation, much like the actual presence of food. Pavlov's work established the basic principles of respondent conditioning.

The American psychologist John B. Watson, dissatisfied with the mentalistic introspection and functionalism so widespread in the psychology of his day, adopted Pavlov's classical conditioning method and extended it. Watson was a strong environmentalist who discounted heredity; he argued that any type of adult could be developed from any given child with the proper training. Watson and his students extended behavioral psychology into the study of psychopathology through the study of fear responses.

E. L. Thorndike, a contemporary of Watson, developed the "law of effect," which noted that behaviors that were followed by desired outcomes tended to recur, while behavior not followed by desired outcomes did not.

With the work of B. F. Skinner begun in the 1930s, a dramatic change occurred in behaviorism. Watson had conceptualized virtually all behavior in terms of the classical conditioning model. Skinner introduced the concept of operant behavior. Also known as instrumental behavior, operant behavior follows the model of Thorndike's law of effect. Operant behavior operates on the environment to produce an effect; it involves the voluntary musculature; it is controlled by events that follow it rather than by eliciting stimuli preceding it as in respondent behavior.

Skinner concluded that operant behavior was much more varied, more flexible, more common, and of greater practical and social significance than respondent behavior. Thus operant behavior became the primary focus of behavioral research for thirty to forty years. Only recently has Skinner's view in this area been challenged with the the discovery of operant conditioning of autonomic functioning such as blood pressure and heart rate, and with the discovery that operant and respondent processes occur simultaneously in complex and inextricably interwoven patterns.

Although many others also contributed to the developing science of behaviorism, Skinner's influence still overshadows them. Despite considerable resistance from the psychological establishment, Skinner, together with his students, developed the fledgling behavioral approach into a major force in modern psychology along with the psychodynamic, humanistic, and more recently the transpersonal theories. A basic principle that Skinner articulated at the beginning of his work was that systematic study of an arbitrarily chosen behavior in a controlled environment would lead to general principles of behavior that had universal application. Although time and subsequent developments have seriously challenged this view, it has nonetheless been demonstrated that principles developed in such a contrived set of conditions have widespread applicability.

By 1948, with the publication of *Walden Two,* Skinner's behavioral utopianism had become public. Skinner's interest in social, political, and philosophical/religious issues was perhaps culminated in the publication of *Beyond Freedom and Dignity* (1971). A signer of the Humanist Manifesto II, Skinner reveals in this volume a naturalistic and humanistic utopianism that is militantly anti-Christian.

2. Concepts of Behaviorism. Ferster, Culbertson, and Boren report that behaviorism may refer to many different but related concepts. Behaviorism may be thought of as a scientific method, a body of data, a technology, a philosophy of science, or a worldview. As a scientific method, behaviorism proposes that psychology limit itself to the natural science methods of observation and experimentation in investigating the behavior of organisms. Behaviorists reject hypothetical constructs and intervening variables, concepts involving events within the organism that are not observable. However, behaviorists acknowledge that internal events such as secretion of gastric juices, contractions of the intestinal muscles, changes in blood pressure, and so on may become the subject matter of psychology provided they are in principle observable. As a body of data, behaviorism refers to the findings and discoveries that result from applying these methods.

Behaviorism's technology includes the application of behavioral discoveries to practical problems in the world about us; one example is the use of behavioral techniques to evaluate the effects of drugs on animals before commencing human tests.

Some behaviorists contend that the scientific method is the only legitimate approach to knowledge; such a view extends behaviorism to a philosophy of science. Finally, for some, most notably Skinner and his closest adherents, behaviorism is a worldview, "religion," or metaphysic—a comprehensive explanation for all that exists, not only a useful approach to the science of psychology.

3. Major Behavioral Movements. According to some theorists, the development of behavioral psychology has three overlapping but distinct movements. The first is *radical behaviorism,* represented by Watson and later led by Skinner and his followers, such as Keller, Ferster, Sherman, Bijou, and Goldiamond.

Albert Bandura is the most prominent figure in the second major movement, *symbolic behaviorism*. Bandura and his colleagues and students focus largely on the processes of modeling and imitation. They argue that much of human behavior is acquired through observational learning rather than by means of reinforced practice as suggested by the Skinnerian model. According to Bandura, the child who observes a particular behavior-consequence sequence in another person can symbolically engage in the same interaction, remember it until another occasion, and then perform the same act later, although it is novel to the child. Although clearly more cognitive, Bandura's conceptualizations continue to use the concepts of stimulus, response, and reinforcement, and thus are generally considered to fall within the behavioral traditions.

Bandura's work paved the way for the third major wave, *cognitive behaviorism*. The cognitive behaviorists contend that cognitions precede behaviors and are the key causal link in behavioral sequences rather than external stimulus events serving as discriminative stimuli. Adherents of cognitive behaviorism include Meichenbaum, Mahoney, Thoresen, and Beck.

At present, adherents of all three forms of behavioral psychology are active at the same time. It remains to be seen whether there will be a gradual disappearance of radical Skinnerian behaviorism and ascendance of cognitive behaviorism. Cognitive behaviorism might also merge with other forms of cognitive theory to form a cognitive psychology outside the mainstream of behaviorism.

4. Contemporary Research and Application. The earliest work in behavioral psychology was largely conducted in the animal laboratory. Pavlov is known for his work with dogs; Thorndike worked with cats; Watson's work was more diverse, but also emphasized the animal lab. Skinner laid much of the groundwork for modern laboratory experimentation in animal behavior. He developed the Skinner box, an automated and highly controlled experimental environment. He also developed the cumulative recorder for automated recording of behavior and contributed to the development of automated laboratory equipment.

While Skinner's original aims have not been fully realized, the value of his technological developments and automated research procedures can hardly be overestimated. Contemporary animal research continues in many areas. Among these are complex learning, including the simulation of language behavior in lower animals, such as chimpanzees and pigeons. Other research focuses on complex stimulus control, the effects of interacting schedules of reinforcement, and species-specific behavior. Much of this research is reported in *The Journal for the Experimental Analysis of Behavior*.

Another area of animal research is in behavioral pharmacology. Virtually all psychotropic medications and many others as well are first tested on animals using operant procedures. Another area of animal experimentation on the forefront of medical research is in the area of behavioral toxicology. Recent work has shown that toxic chemicals administered in doses far below lethal levels produce adverse cognitive and behavioral effects. Much of the research into the effects of potentially hazardous chemicals is conducted with animals using behavioral procedures because they are able to produce behavior that is highly predictable and yet sensitive to the small physical changes produced by subacute doses.

Contemporary behavioral research with humans is diverse and multifaceted. Early work with humans was largely focused on developing techniques for treatment of severely handicapped individuals, including the profoundly retarded, autistic children, and institutionalized psychotic persons. A second area of early behavioral research was in the area of education. Both of these lines of research continue, but have been joined by many new fields. These include behavioral studies of business and industry, including such areas as developing behavioral techniques to increase the use of containerized packaging as a cost-saving technique in shipping. Other studies have focused on conservation of gas and electricity and control of littering. In the last few years a number of journals have emerged that publish this work, including *The Journal of Applied Behavior Analysis, Behavior Therapy, The Journal of Behavior Therapy and Experimental Psychiatry*, and many others.

5. Psychological Criticism. A number of criticisms have been directed toward behaviorism by adherents of other psychological systems. Although behaviorism seeks complete objectivity, subjective factors inevitably enter into any theoretical system; even the topics chosen for investigation and the methods of investigation have subjective elements. Another criticism is that behaviorism denies thought and conscious experience, yet they are an intimate part of our natural experience. A third criticism, at least with early behaviorism, was its denial or minimization of the role of heredity. Fourth, early behaviorism was faulted for dealing with "trivial" animal behaviors rather than complex human behaviors. This criticism no longer applies. Fifth, the basic unit of behavior is largely arbitrary; this is highlighted by the contrast between Watson's molar "muscle twitch" behaviorism and Tolman's molecular behaviorism, in which the basic unit was a complex act. Finally, behaviorism is criticized for its emphasis on naturalism, mechanism, and determinism.

6. Appraisal from a Christian Perspective. Many objections to behaviorism have been raised from a Christian perspective. Most focus on behaviorism's worldview and its reductionistic emphasis on naturalism, materialism, and determinism; other criticisms focus on the overt use of reinforcement and discouragement of punishment.

The behavioristic worldview is surely the largest issue from a Christian perspective. Many critics argue that it is impossible to separate behaviorism as a scientific method, as a body of data, or as a technological application from the worldview of prominent behavioral adherents such as Skinner. While the proponents of such criticisms are often eloquent and vociferous in their objections, they confuse data and application with the theory used to explain them, and behavior theory with the worldview of its most prominent adherents. One could as plausibly argue that anyone who cites Scripture is, *ipso facto*, Christian, as argue that all proponents of behaviorism accept Skinner's behavioristic worldview.

While Scripture affirms the reality of the natural order, it also speaks of a spiritual realm which is immaterial; thus behaviorism is, at best, incomplete in this respect. What is needed is a psychology, whether behavioral or some other system, which encompasses both natural and supernatural or mental/spiritual realities.

In an extended appraisal of behavior theory, Bufford notes that determinism and its philosophical opposite, free will, are not biblical concepts. Freedom is used in Scripture in terms of freedom from the power and penalty of sin and freedom to serve God and receive God's blessings. Because the issues are more properly choice and responsibility, much of the criticism in this area is misguided.

Many objections have been expressed to the overt use of reinforcement in behaviorism. However, God is described as "a rewarder of those who seek him" (Heb. 11:6, NASB). Ironically, Skinner and his followers are also criticized because of their objections to punishment. However, Skinner's objections to the use of punishment are not only inconsistent with Scripture, they also are now inconsistent with the results of behavioral research.

Finally, behaviorism contains an implicit scientism. Scientism is the view that the scientific method is the only legitimate source of knowledge. The scientific method is of great value, but is not comprehensive; reason and revelation must be accorded their legitimate places as well.

Behaviorism has made a major contribution to the science of psychology. It is also of value to the Christian. However, the fact that it is often contaminated with humanistic, naturalistic, materialistic philosophy suggests that caution must be exercised in adopting behavioral approaches. The basic criteria that must be used are the means/ends tests. Are the methods which behaviorism advocates consistent with biblical teachings? Are the goals toward which they are used similarly consistent? If so, they are legitimate and can therefore also be used by God's people.

Bibliography. W. S. Agras, *Behavior Modification* 2d ed. (1978). A. Bandura, *Principles of Behavior Modification* (1969). J. H. Brink, "Free Will, Determinism, and Behavioristic Psychology," *Christian Association for Psychological Studies Bulletin,* 6 (1970), 11. R. K. Bufford, *The Human Reflex* (1981); "Behavioral Views of Punishment: A Critique," *J. of the American Scientific Affiliation* (1982). G. R. Collins, *The Rebuilding of Psychology* (1977). M. Cosgrove, *B. F. Skinners' Behaviorism: An Analysis* (1982). L. J. Crabb, *Basic Principles of Biblical Counseling* (1975). S. W. Ellison, ed., *Modifying Man: Implications and Ethics* (1977). C. B. Ferster, S. Culbertson, and M. C. P. Boren, *Behavior Principles* 2d ed. (1975). E. Gambrill, *Behavior Modification* (1977). D. Glenwick and L. Jason, *Behavioral Community Psychology* (1980). C. S. Hall and G. Lindzey, *Theories of Personality* 3d ed. (1978). B. Häring, *Ethics of Manipulation* (1975). M. Hersen, R. M. Eisler, and P. M Miller, *Progress in Behavior Modification* (vols. 1–16, 1975–84). H. I. Kalish, *From Behavioral Science to Behavior Modification* (1981). M. J. Mahoney, *Cognition and Behavior Modification* (1974). D. Meichenbaum, *Cognitive-Behavior Modification* (1977). S. Pinkerton, *Behavioral Medicine* (1982). H. Rachlin, *Introduction to Modern Behaviorism* (1970). G. S. Reynolds, *A Primer of Operant Conditioning* (1975). C. Rogers and B. F. Skinner, "Some Issues Concerning the Control of Human behavior: A Symposium," in R. Ulrich, T. Stachnik, and J. Mabry, eds., *Control of Human Behavior* (1966). F. A. Schaeffer, *Back to Freedom and Dignity* (1972). B. F. Skinner, *The Behavior of Organisms* (1938); *Walden Two* (1948); *Science and Human Behavior* (1953); *Beyond Freedom and Dignity* (1971); *Cumulative Record* rev. ed. (1972); *Particulars of My Life* (1976); *The Shaping of a Behaviorist: Part Two of an Autobiography* (1979). C. J. Steckel, *Theology and Ethics of Behavior Modification* (1979). C. E. Thoresen, *Behavioral Self-Control* (1974). E. Thornton, "A Transpersonal Critique of Behaviorism," *J. of Religion and Health,* 21 (1982), 8–20. L. P. Ullman and L. Krasner, *A Psychological Approach to Abnormal Behavior* 2d ed. (1975). M. S. VanLeeuwen, "The Behaviorist Bandwagon and the Body of Christ," *J. of the American Scientific Affiliation,* 31(1979), 88–91; *The Sorcerer's Apprentice* (1982). H. Wheeler, ed., *Beyond the Punitive Society* (1973). G. Wilson and C. M. Franks, eds., *Contemporary Behavior Therapy* (1982).

R. K. BUFFORD

BEING/BECOMING RELATIONSHIP. *Being* is related to *becoming* as actuality to potentiality. In pastoral care and counseling, these terms are employed to point to a fundamental polarity whose balance or tension needs to be sensitively understood, honored, and maintained. In practice this often involves a back-and-forth attention from one to the other.

1. **Change and Stability.** In the process of healing, growth, and change there is need for a certain amount of stability (homeostasis), resulting in a tension between the need for persistence or continuity and the need for change. Often this means that pastoral counseling and psychotherapy move through phases of one then the other. As new gains are made they must be consolidated and integrated as actualities; and after stability has been achieved for a time, new growth tendencies emerge, disrupting the established stability.

2. **Trust and Intentionality.** There is a sense in which personal growth is natural, a gift of God rooted in the order of creation. In the Bible it is clear, for instance, that the potential for becoming is a gift of creation: "The whole creation is on tiptoe to see the wonderful sight of the sons of God coming into their own" (Rom. 8:19, Phillips). Yet actualizing this potential involves not only trust in growth as a natural, creaturely tendency, but intentional effort and a willingness to risk. The dimension of being and the dimension of becoming must be distinguished and responded to in appropriate ways, often in some reciprocal, rhythmic fashion.

3. **Process and Accountability.** The process of personal becoming is nurtured (in the language of Carl Rogers) by unconditional positive regard, congruence ("being real"), acceptance of others, and empathic understanding. Yet the community of faith is also necessary to provide a context of meaning and values for guiding and disciplining the unfolding of human potential. (The secular growth movements often lack this perspective of accountability to the community, which is a necessary check and balance for individual development.) While the pastoral counselor lets the process (the becoming) unfold by establishing "therapeutic conditions," the community serves as a moral and religious reality reference (the being aspect), providing a structure which guides and holds the process accountable in some larger sense.

4. **Attention to Present Reality and Emergent Process.** Counseling experience reveals that there is often a deep, dynamic interconnection between paying close attention to the reality of one's present and past experience — getting "close" to it experientially — and moving forward into

new modes of personal existence. This often happens paradoxically: when counselees let go of the deliberate attempt to change or "fix" themselves and simply experience who they are in emotional depth, change may begin to happen in unexpected and creative ways; attention to one's being releases a process of becoming. And when counselees let go of some fixed perception of themselves from the past and begin to envision significant new possibilities, a deeper, more authentic affirmation of their own existence and sense of living fully in their present experience—their being—comes forth; attention to one's becoming yields a renewed and empowered sense of one's being.

Bibliography. H. J. Clinebell, *Growth Counseling* (1979), esp. ch. 5. W. E. Oates, *The Religious Dimensions of Personality* (1957), esp. ch. 11. C. R. Rogers, *On Becoming a Person* (1961), esp. ch. 6.

P. G. SCHURMAN

PHILOSOPHY AND PSYCHOLOGY. *See also* EXISTENTIALISM AND PASTORAL CARE; HUMAN CONDITION/PREDICAMENT; PROCESS, CONCEPT OF. *Compare* ACTION/BEING RELATIONSHIP.

BELIEF. *See* FAITH/BELIEF.

BELIEVER BAPTISM. *See* BAPTISM AND CONFIRMATION; BAPTIST PASTORAL CARE.

BELLIGERENCE. *See* ANTISOCIAL PERSONS.

BELONGING, SENSE OF. *See* COMMUNITY, FELLOWSHIP, AND CARE.

BENEDICT, RUTH. *See* NEW YORK PSYCHOLOGY GROUP.

BENEDICT OF NURSIA, ST. (480 – ca. 547). Roman Catholic saint and patriarch of occidental monasticism. After three early adult years of solitary penance and prayer in a cavern and a short stint as leader of a hermit community, he founded his own order of Benedictine monks in Monte Cassino.

Benedict came into prominence in two ways: first, the spiritual and pastoral-paternal nature of his personality, the holy quality of his lifestyle, and the wisdom of his teachings drew many disciples to Monte Cassino so that, in time, the monastery emerged as the center of European monasticism. Second, his personal influence was bolstered by the status of his rules for monasteries, the so-called *Rules of St. Benedict* which during the Middle Ages became the standard for all occidental monasticism. With this work, in particular its accent on the guidance of souls, discipline, order, and happiness in the faith community, Benedict reinforced the monastic emphasis upon the attainment of salvation by approved religious practices in a lasting way.

N. F. HAHN

EARLY CHURCH, PASTORAL CARE AND COUNSELING IN.

BENEDICTINE SPIRITUALITY. *See* SPIRITUALITY (Roman Catholic Tradition).

BENEDICTION. *See* BLESSING AND BENEDICTION; RITUAL AND PASTORAL CARE.

BEREAVEMENT. *See* GRIEF AND LOSS; MOURNING.

BERNARD OF CLAIRVAUX, ST. (1090 – 1153). Monastic reformer, theologian, and mystic. Born into a noble Burgundian family near Dijon in France, he entered the reformed monastery of Citeaux at the age of twenty-two. After several years he was sent to found a new monastic foundation at Clairvaux, where he served as abbot for the remainder of his life. From the monastery of Clairvaux sixty-eight other Cistercian monasteries were founded during Bernard's lifetime.

Despite his monastic seclusion, Bernard was intimately involved with public church life. He was a vigorous exponent of monastic theology, engaging in fierce polemics with the exponents of the new dialectical theology like Abelard. He was deputed by the pope to be the prime preacher of the Second Crusade (1147 – 49), and its failure was a most bitter disappointment for him. He frequently intervened in ecclesiastical affairs as his extant letters clearly indicate. His most lasting achievement was his decisive influence on the incredible growth of the Cistercian Order in the twelfth century.

Bernard's considerable body of writings reflects his view that an intense spiritual life was a prerequisite for an effective apostolate in the church. (See his classic treatises on loving God (*De Diligendo Deo*), his treatise on prayer (*De Consideratione*), and his eighty-six sermons on *The Song of Songs* (*Sermones in Cantica Canticorum*).)

Canonized a saint in 1174 and declared a Doctor of the Church in 1830, he lived on the eve of the great medieval movement of scholastic theology and is often called the "last of the Fathers."

Bibliography. G. R. Evans, *The Mind of Saint Bernard of Clairvaux* (1983). B. S. James, *St. Bernard of Clairvaux* (1957). T. Merton, *The Last of the Fathers* (1954).

L. S. CUNNINGHAM

MEDIEVAL CHURCH, PASTORAL CARE IN; SPIRITUALITY (Roman Catholic Tradition).

BERNE, ERIC. *See* TRANSACTIONAL ANALYSIS.

BETRAYAL. *See* INFIDELITY, MARITAL; RAGE AND HOSTILITY.

BEXLEY HALL PLAN. *See* PASTORAL CARE MOVEMENT.

BIBLE, PASTORAL USE AND INTERPRETATION OF. From the very beginning of the pastoral care movement in the early 1930s, the pastoral use of the Bible has been a matter of central concern (and considerable controversy). Typical of this concern is *The Art of Ministering to the Sick* (1936) by R. C. Cabot and R. L. Dicks. A chapter in this influential publication is devoted to the use of the Bible in pastoral work with hospital patients. It establishes two fundamental principles that have survived to the present day: (1) Whatever use is made of the Bible in pastoral care, it should be guided by the particular needs and circumstances of the patient, and (2) Its use should reflect pastoral sensitivity to the patient's physical and psychological limitations, acute or chronic.

When the pastoral counseling movement emerged in the late 1940s, it adopted these principles and introduced a third: (3) Whatever use is made of the Bible in pastoral care or counseling, it should be consistent with the counseling principles and methods that inform the pastoral intervention as a whole. In his chapter on religious resources in pastoral counseling in *Pastoral Counseling* (1949) S. Hiltner cites the case of a pastor who used the Bible in a counseling session in a manner that was consistent with his overall counseling approach, which was to understand, accept, clarify, and consolidate. Because this use of the Bible was consistent with sound counseling theory and method, Hiltner judged it a legitimate introduction of the Bible into the counseling process.

In what follows, this article attempts to clarify the enduring value and importance of these fundamental principles, but also critically augment them with a renewed understanding of the power of biblical texts as sources of normative understanding and illumination in pastoral care.

1. Dynamic vs. Moral Instructional Use.

From our vantage point in the 1990s, these three principles now seem axiomatic. We are therefore surprised to learn that they had to be fought for; they did not gain ready acceptance from pastors or from the majority of seminary professors responsible for training pastors. Resistance to these principles may have been due, in part, to the fact that biblical passages are chosen on the basis of the patient's needs. Thus, the need is first determined and then the text is chosen to address this need. But, some critics would say, should not the Bible be used to determine the need? If the Bible is God's Word, then it defines the need, and its understanding of the need may differ radically from any extra-biblical assessment of a patient's needs. (This critique is perhaps best articulated in E. Thurneysen's *A Theology of Pastoral Care*.)

But resistance to these principles was primarily due to the fact that those advocating them were also proponents of the new "dynamic psychology." This meant selecting biblical passages that related to the "deeper" dynamics involved, using the Bible to address the individual's intrapsychic conflicts. As W. E. Oates pointed out in *The Bible in Pastoral Care* (1953), "The Bible is the pastor's 'royal road' to the deeper levels of the personalities of his people." Those who have opposed the pastoral care movement's approach to the Bible have often done so from mistrust of its use in exploring these deeper dynamics.

This mistrust has been reasserted in recent years by J. E. Adams (1972, 1977). Adams vigorously attacks the dynamic approach to the use of the Bible and argues instead for a moral instructional use. He shares the conviction of his predecessors that biblical passages need to be chosen for the specific needs of the counselee, but he selects a passage for its moral, not dynamic, value. In his judgment, use of the Bible should be directed toward convicting the counselee of sin and encouraging a change in moral behavior. For him, this does not require probing the deeper intrapsychic conflicts of the counselee, but simply identifying how the counselee's behavior is at odds with a Christian orientation to life and using the Bible to restore or reinforce this orientation.

2. Case Illustrations.

In actual practice, there are significant differences between the dynamic and moral instructional uses of the Bible. One major difference is that, in the dynamic approach, biblical passages are chosen not for their topical relevance to the patient's problem but for their dynamic relevance. It is not assumed, for example, that biblical passages on homosexuality or divorce are necessarily the most relevant biblical resources for counseling the homosexual or couples experiencing marital discord. A parable of Jesus or a passage from Paul on an entirely unrelated topic may be more immediately relevant to the dynamics involved. This distinction between topical and dynamic relevance can be illustrated by comparing a case reported by C. A. Wise (1956) with a case from J. E. Adams (1977).

a. Dynamic relevance — Carroll Wise. Wise cites the case of a parishioner who came to his pastor because he was worried about his job, finances, the children, and especially about his wife. During counseling, it came to light that there was a time when he had felt very resentful toward his wife, and had wondered whether his resentment might get out of hand, to the point where he would harm her physically.

As time went on his resentment lessened but was replaced by worry that something might happen to her. Wise says that this counselee was experiencing anxiety, "a panic reaction to something that does not constitute an actual danger to our life, but does constitute a danger to our inner being, to our self. In John's case, anxiety was a symptom of the deeper problem of resentment." He then suggests turning to the Bible for insights into the nature and effects of anxiety, e.g. "Do not be anxious about your life" (Mt. 6:25). He does not recommend topical use of the Bible to address the man's situation, e.g. "Husbands, love your wives, as Christ loved the church and gave himself up for her" (Eph. 5:25). Nor does he cite biblical injunctions against resentment, possibly because such injunctions mainly concern resentment toward the wicked who are prospering (Prov. 23:17), but more likely because he believes the pastor should focus on the current problem, the parishioner's anxiety.

While we might challenge this decision to focus on his anxiety rather than the underlying cause (resentment), and may actually do so on dynamic grounds, this case nonetheless shows that the biblical passage is chosen for its relevance to the deeper dynamics involved in the parishioner's difficulties.

b. Topical relevance — Jay Adams. Adams' use of the Bible is virtually the antithesis of Wise's approach. He cites the example of a young couple who came to their pastor for help in disciplining their seven-year-old son. The pastor accepts the couple's claim that the problem is a disciplinary one, and brings to bear the following passages from the book of Proverbs: "Folly is bound up in the heart of a child, but the rod of discipline drives it far from him" (22:15) and "The rod and reproof give wisdom" (29:15). On the basis of these passages, the pastor encourages the couple to spank the child, but also to augment physical punishment with verbal reproof, which means confronting the boy with his sin and need for redemptive change.

This approach is not concerned with the possibility that the disciplinary problem may mask a more fundamental dynamic conflict, possibly involving the boy's attitudes toward his parents or his parents' relationship to each other. Instead, the pastor cites biblical passages that are topically related to the parents' assessment of the problem. Proponents of the dynamic use of the Bible would undoubtedly complain that the pastor never got to the heart of the problem (its underlying dynamics) but instead accepted the couple's testimony that the problem was disciplinary. Adams might well counter that the dynamic approach is often content to unearth the emotional conflict (e.g. anxiety caused by resentment) but ignores the fact that the cause of this conflict is usually sin (e.g. the sin of resentment). He might also complain that the Bible was introduced after the problem has been explored in depth, and one wonders therefore just how indispensable it was to the clarification of the counselee's problem?

3. Recovering the Disclosive Power of the Text. Such criticisms of the dynamic approach do not prompt many pastors to adopt the moral instructional approach, with its topical use of the Bible. But they do suggest the need for refinements of the dynamic approach. Today we appear to be moving toward the formulation of a fourth principle. This principle would be based on the judgment that while our predecessors emphasized the internal dynamics of the counselee, they did not pay sufficient attention to the dynamic power of the biblical text itself. This dynamic power of the text has been described in various ways, but one of the most suggestive for pastoral care is Paul Ricoeur's view that biblical texts are "world disclosive" (1971, 1978). For him, the meaning of a biblical text is not limited to what it is ostensibly about—its topical references. Instead, the text discloses a "world" that transcends its immediate situation. When we say that the listener or reader appropriates the text, we mean that they orient themselves to the world it discloses.

a. Jesus' parables. Excellent illustrations of how the biblical text discloses a world that transcends its immediate situation may be seen in Jesus' parables. Take, for example, the parable of the hidden treasure (Mt. 13:44). This parable compares the kingdom of heaven to treasure hidden in a field, which a man finds, and in his joy sells all his possessions to buy the field. Through the image of the hidden treasure, this parable discloses the world that Jesus refers to as "the kingdom of heaven." He gives insight into this other world by comparing it to a phenomenon well known to us in our everyday world ("hidden treasures"). It should be noted, however, that once the similarity between these two worlds is established, it is typically their *dissimilarity* that enables the parable to be genuinely disclosive. The kingdom of heaven is like an earthly treasure, but it is also profoundly unlike it: "Do not lay up for yourselves treasures on earth, where moth and rust consume and where thieves break in and steal, but lay up for yourselves treasure in heaven, where neither moth nor rust consumes and where thieves do not break in and steal" (Mt. 6:19-20). If we can imagine treasures that are imperishable and eternally ours, we

have entered into the world the parable discloses to us. In a very real sense it is an alien world, *unlike* anything we have yet experienced.

b. The disclosive role of the text. Once we recognize that the dynamic power of a biblical text is its capacity to disclose a world, we can also see how the Bible may play a more decisive role in pastoral care than either the pastoral care movement or its critics have envisioned. Biblical texts are not introduced into the care or counseling situation merely to augment approved counseling procedures and initiatives. Neither is it introduced to merely reinforce preconceived understandings of what constitutes Christian behavior. Rather, the Bible is introduced because it offers a new disclosure and challenges the counselee to appropriate this disclosure.

The intrapsychic dynamics of the counselee continue to inform the selection of biblical texts, but now there is much greater clarity as to why the Bible is introduced, and there is much greater expectation behind its use. Thus, a fourth principle would be: Whatever use is made of the Bible in pastoral care and counseling, it should be informed by the pastor's awareness of the disclosive power of specific biblical texts. Also, pastors will need to develop better means of identifying and evaluating the disclosive effects of biblical texts in actual care and counseling situations. What changes do they effect in the counselee who appropriates them? What criteria should we use in evaluating these changes?

c. Relation to the dynamic approach. Restoring a sense of the dynamic power of the Bible to pastoral care and counseling does not mean breaking with the dynamic approach of our predecessors. We continue to affirm their view that biblical texts are not chosen for their topical similarity to the patient's situation, but for their dynamic relevance. But we extend the rationale for this view by emphasizing that a text is chosen not only because it relates to the personal dynamics of the patient, but also because it has world disclosive possibilities owing to the dynamic power of the text itself. Furthermore, we can anticipate that as the world disclosive potential of biblical texts becomes better understood, our counseling methods will be informed more directly by these texts and less captive to current psychotherapeutic theories and techniques. This may lead in time to balancing, if not actually replacing, the third principle with its corollary: Whatever use is made of psychotherapeutic theories and techniques, it should be consistent with the disclosive power of the biblical texts employed in any given case.

d. Illustration—a new direction for Wise's case. This view that the Bible has its own dynamic power through the world disclosive potential of its various texts may seem rather abstract. How does it work in practice? We may illustrate its use by referring once again to Wise's case of the man who resented his wife, and dealt with this resentment through anxiety. Biblical texts that are expressly about anxiety, however, are unlikely to have much disclosive power. The young man is likely to say that he is aware of the biblical injunction, "Be not anxious about your life," but that this awareness has not changed anything. Moreover, if he reads this verse in context, he might contend that the anxiety to which this passage refers concerns the basic necessities of life (food and clothing), whereas his anxiety has roots in his resentment toward his wife. Ironically, the "be not anxious" passages would serve the moral instructional approach better than the dynamic approach.

A text more relevant to the dynamics involved and much more likely to have disclosive power might be Jesus' parable of the prodigal son (Lk. 15:11-32). An important dynamic of this story is the elder brother's resentment toward his younger brother for the undeserved attention he is receiving from their father. This story reveals the destructive effects of resentment on the person who harbors it. His resentment alienates him, not just from the object of his resentment (his brother), but also from others whose company he prizes (his father, and the servants and friends who have come to celebrate his brother's return). Thus, resentment has an isolating effect. We also sense from this story that resentment immobilizes the elder brother, rendering him powerless and impotent. He is able to appeal only to his past exemplary behavior and is unable to meet this new challenge with resilience and self-confidence. Thus, resentment inhibits self-growth.

The common theme of resentment in the counseling case and the parable indicates that they may have a similar dynamic, justifying the introduction of this biblical text into the counseling process. We may also assume that the man's anxiety reaction to his resentment manifests a similar alienation (perhaps not only from his wife but also his children and friends at work) and immobilization (reflected in lack of self-growth). The next step, after determining the text's dynamic relevance and diagnostic value, is to ascertain how it may also disclose to the counselee a new "world" to which he may orient himself. Does this text have dynamic power? The key to the parable's world disclosive potential is the father's response to his son's expression of resentment, "Son, you are always with me, and all that I have is yours." This statement opens a world that the counselee has not yet experienced. It is a world in which his alienation is transcended ("you are always with me") and his grounds for resentment are eliminated ("all that I have is yours"). The question is whether the counselee can envision himself in this new world, or whether he will choose instead to cling to the world his resentment has fashioned for him.

The parable cannot, of course, answer this question. It depends on whether the counselee appropriates the text and the world it discloses. But the parable does intimate what course he might take if he wishes to enter this world because this is the same course the elder brother is being challenged to take. The elder brother is challenged to come to himself (as his younger brother came to *himself*) and perceive that he has been viewing the situation incorrectly: his brother's gain is not *his* loss. The parable discloses a world in which the economics of "your gain is my loss" are replaced by "your gain enriches me." His father's assurance, "all that I have is yours," begins to open a new, alien, and dangerous world to the elder brother and anyone else who shares his psycho-economic assumptions. Thus, the question is whether the counselee can enter a new world where his wife's gain is not perceived to be his loss, but his personal enrichment. To begin seeing things this way would be the first step toward overcoming the alienating and immobilizing effects of resentment.

This perceptual change can be seen as self-growth, reflecting an expanded capacity to love another person and having the ultimate effect of Eph. 5:25 ("Husbands, love your wives, as Christ loved the church and gave himself up for her"), an effect that would not have been realized had this verse been introduced for purposes of moral instruction. Furthermore, this effect confirms the therapeutic wisdom of Proverbs 12:25: "Anxiety in a man's heart weighs him down, but a good word makes him glad." The father followed this advice when he told his son, "You are always with me, and all that I have is yours." The pastor would also have followed this advice at least implicitly, had he brought this parable to the attention of his anxious parishioner.

Bibliography. J. E. Adams, *Competent to Counsel* (1972); *The Use of the Scriptures in Counseling* (1976). R. C. Cabot and R. L. Dicks, *The Art of Ministering to the Sick* (1936), ch. 17. D. Capps, *Biblical Approaches to Pastoral Counseling* (1981). S. Hiltner, *Pastoral Counseling* (1949). H. N. Malony, "The Use of the Jewish/Christian Scriptures in Counseling," *J. of Pastoral Care*, 20 1985, 116–24. W. E. Oates, *The Bible in Pastoral Care* (1953). W. B. Oglesby, Jr., *Biblical Themes for Pastoral Care* (1980). E. H. Peterson, *Five Smooth Stones of Pastoral Work* (1980). D. A. Phillipy, "Hearing and Doing the Word: An Integrated Approach to Bible Study in a Maximum Security Prison," *J. of Pastoral Care*, 37 (1983), 13–21. P. Ricoeur, "Listening to the Parables of Jesus," in C. E. Reagan and D. Stewart, eds., *The Philosophy of Paul Ricoeur* (1978), pp. 239 –45; "The Model of the Text: Meaningful Action Considered as a Text," *Social Research*, 38 (1971), 529–62. E. Thurneysen, *A Theology of Pastoral Care*, (1962), chs. 5–8. C. A. Wise, *Psychiatry and the Bible* (1956).

D. CAPPS

PSALMS, PASTORAL USE OF; TEN COMMANDMENTS. *See also* INTERPRETATION AND HERMENEUTICS, PASTORAL; RELIGIOUS LANGUAGE IN PASTORAL CARE; REVELATION AND PASTORAL CARE. *Compare* BIBLICAL LITERALISM; OLD *or* NEW TESTAMENT, TRADITIONS AND THEOLOGY OF CARE IN; PASTORAL THEOLOGY.

BIBLE, PRINCIPLES OF CARE AND MINISTRY IN. *See* MINISTRY (Biblical Origins and Principles); OLD TESTAMENT AND APOCRYPHA, *or* NEW TESTAMENT.

BIBLICAL ANTHROPOLOGY, DISCIPLINE OF.
The study of what the Bible has to say about the origin, nature, and destiny of human beings. Contrary to traditional biblical anthropologies, the Bible neither yields a systematic or developmental picture of the human being nor supports the imposition of overarching anthropological, historical-critical, socio-psychological, philosophical, or metaphysical assumptions about human beings upon the biblical texts. Contrary also to secular psychologies, which emphasize personal autonomy and self-actualization, biblical anthropology begins with God, the One who gives human life meaning. Understanding human beings both as they are and as they are called to be by God, biblical anthropology can shape the goals of pastoral care and counseling and the attitude of the pastor, and provide both support for and critique of the psychological tools used in pastoral ministries.

1. **Traditional OT Anthropologies.** OT anthropologies have focused upon the various Hebrew terms dealing

with the makeup of the human being, namely, *nephesh* (soul/person), *bāśār* (flesh/body), *rûah* (spirit/breath), *lēb* (heart/feelings), and so forth. These terms have been forced into a systematic or developmental picture based upon older, now outmoded assumptions drawn from many disciplines.

a. Assumptions about primitive mentality. Chief among such assumptions are theories of primitive mentality offered by mid-nineteenth to early twentieth-century anthropologists who thought in evolutionary terms. They argued that modern interpreters are separated from the "primitive," ancient Israelites and Christians by a vast gap of time and culture, a gap which necessitates our thinking and viewing the world differently than they.

b. Pedersen's socio-psychological approach. J. Pedersen and H. W. Robinson developed pioneering biblical anthropologies based upon these now-rejected assumptions about primitive mentality. Describing the characteristics of Hebrew mentality systematically, Pedersen spoke of the *nephesh* (soul) and of other psychic terms such as blessing, righteousness, and honor, associated with the soul: "such as he, man, in his total essence, is a soul," which is a "totality with a peculiar stamp." This way of thinking was different from ours, as the Hebrew language itself shows with its emphasis upon totalities and connections.

c. Robinson's "corporate personality." H. W. Robinson claimed that Israel's psychology was undergirded by the concept of "corporate personality," that is, an oscillation or fluidity between the individual and the group. Though our modern individualistic morality makes corporate personality untenable to us, according to Robinson this conception shaped Israel's thinking until individualism emerged with the prophets, for example, Jeremiah and Ezekiel. This developmental view drew support from anthropologists who argued that individualism in society marked the transition from primitive (group) to modern (individualistic) thinking. Robinson pointed to the prophets as the "pioneers" of progress in morality and creative developers of "the old nomadic clan spirit." The prophets were exceptional, he asserted, for it was only with Jesus that a direct individual relationship to God was reached.

d. Historical-critical developmentalism. Such developmentalism was reinforced by nineteenth century OT scholars who embraced the historical-critical method, as classically formulated by J. Wellhausen. Wellhausen's reconstruction of Israelite religion shifted the traditional focus on the Mosaic period to the prophets as the "real climax" of Israelite religion. This shift was accomplished by Wellhausen's radical reinterpretation of postexilic Judaism as "a dead work," thinking which reinforced anti-Judaic tendencies in twentieth-century Christian theology.

e. Critique of traditional approaches. Most of the framework supporting such developmental, systematic views of the human being in the Bible is crumbling. J. Barr's semantic critique of Pedersen's circular arguments is reinforced by the criticisms of contemporary anthropologists like E. Evans-Pritchard, R. Horton, and R. Finnegan. They question whether a basic difference in modes of thought between scientific and prescientific (modern and primitive) societies actually exists and

whether one can, in the absence of historical evidence, make broad generalizations.

Robinson's reconstruction is based in part on what contemporary anthropologists reject as "a romantic stereotype" of the early nomads as brave, independent individualists whose clan spirit was reintroduced into the collectivism of Israelite life and purified by the prophets. Contemporary Bible scholars like G. Mendenhall and N. Gottwald, who view Israel's life in socioeconomic terms, have challenged older sociological studies of Israel's supposed nomadic beginnings and later shift to agriculture and city. Despite such criticism, scholars continue to use traditional anthropological approaches uncritically, as documented by J. Rogerson. Pedersen's work and Robinson's theory, for example, still provide the foundation for many contemporary OT and NT anthropologists, such as E. Rust, R. Shedd, J. Chamberlayne, N. Porteus, D. Owen, A. Johnson, K. Koch, D. Russell, G. Wright, W. Stacey, and J. Robinson.

2. Traditional NT Anthropologies. Like their OT counterparts, NT anthropologies have focused upon the various Greek terms dealing with the makeup of the human being, namely, *sōma* (body/person), *sarx* (flesh), *pneuma* (spirit/mind), *psykhē* (soul/life), and so forth, forcing them into an unsupportable systematic picture. Yet unlike OT anthropology, NT anthropology has not undergone the same comprehensive critique of presuppositions. This is due in part to the fact that views of the human being in the NT have been intricately woven into various systematic theologies, whose apologetic and dogmatic concerns have determined the shape and result of anthropological research. This has resulted in a critique of theology rather than of anthropology, or at the most, of Christian rather than NT understandings of the human being.

a. Augustine and original sin. The classic Christian understanding of the human being, with its two themes of *imago Dei* and human sin, was forged in Augustine's controversy with the Pelagians in the fifth century. Augustine argued that humans were created with certain supernatural gifts that were lost because of the Fall of Adam. Thus, humans suffer from hereditary moral disease (original sin) and legal liability (death) from which only God's grace (for some) can save the sinner. Influenced by the Neoplatonists, Augustine also argued that humans are created in the image of God and as such are capable of self-transcendence in terms of "mind" or "rational faculties of the soul." Augustine's views were modified and passed on by Thomas Aquinas in the Middle Ages, John Calvin and the Reformers, and contemporary theologians like Karl Barth, and serve as the implicit starting point for many traditional NT anthropologies, which focus on the human being as creature, sinner, and believer, for example, W. Gutbrod. Augustine illustrates the dependence of Christian anthropology upon the OT, especially Genesis 1–3, for much of its raw material; the NT presumes the creation faith of the OT.

b. Sōma in Pauline anthropology. Paul's direct statements about the nature of the human being have generally determined the anthropological picture of the whole NT. Traditionally, scholars have viewed Paul, in his preoccupation with the human tendency to sin, as the first great introspective psychologist.

Many view Paul's use of *sōma* as the centerpiece of his psychology and anthropology. *Sōma* functions as either a wholistic term for the whole person (J. Robinson, M. Dahl, W. Stacey), or as an inherently evil physical body in a dualism of body and soul which must be overcome. The latter view uses *sōma* interchangeably with "flesh" and "sin," and is characteristic of nineteenth-century arguments for strong Hellenistic influence on Paul, which are still used today. The former view draws heavily upon Pedersen and H. W. Robinson, seeing *sōma* as the person made for God, and *sarx* (flesh) as the person distanced from God.

For the existentialist Rudolf Bultmann, Pauline anthropology allows one to tackle the problems of theology. Specifically, if *sōma* does not necessarily denote physical substance but rather the wholistic sense of self-understanding and self-relationship, then resurrection (I Corinthians 15) is dematerialized into a transformation of the personality. In this way, both the "problem of history" and the problem of continuity with Judaism and traditional Christianity are overcome; what matters is only one's response to God's radical call to obedience in each concrete moment.

c. Critique of traditional approaches. Augustine's doctrine of the Fall and Original Sin has been challenged by the rationalism of the Enlightenment and the natural sciences. W. Pannenberg represents the current movement away from Augustine's dogmatic NT anthropology toward an apologetic theological anthropology which can hold its own with competing ideas in the modern world by intersecting with and thematizing aspects of modern anthropological phenomena.

Other scholars are reclaiming Genesis 2–3 in a different way for NT anthropology. C. Westermann, for example, argues that Augustine's interpretation does not accord with the intention of the story, that there was no "original state" of innocence because the tightly connected course of events in the garden is meant to be a primeval happening, a myth. The view of Adam as a historical individual who passes his Fall to his descendants is not found anywhere in the OT but only in late Jewish tradition of the second century A.D. (II Esdras 7). The Genesis narrative deals not with the origin of human beings but rather with the human experience of limits, that is, suffering, death, sin; its nuances cannot be compressed into a doctrine. P. Trible argues similarly in her rhetorical-critical study of Genesis 2–3. The divine speeches in Genesis 3 are descriptions of the consequences of disobedience, not prescriptions for punishment and behavior; they protest against the contamination of creation.

Contemporary NT anthropology also rightly avoids any dichotomization of OT and NT, and especially of OT and Pauline views of the human being. R. Jewett, K. Stendahl, R. Gundry, and P. Henry argue for a contextual approach to Paul's anthropology and against homogenizing or spiritualizing Paul by abstracting different terms from their historical situation and forcing them into an overarching framework of consistency provided by the researcher. This challenges those like W. Stacey and J. Robinson who fit all of Paul's anthro-pological terms into H. W. Robinson's "corporate personality" schema.

Stendahl criticizes those who interpret Paul's justification by faith and second use of the Law in Romans from a later, Western frame of reference (via Augustine and Luther) as a guide for the introspective conscience, a romantic model of our own frustration, and as the center of Pauline anthropology. Rather, Paul's basic concern as the Apostle to the Gentiles was with the relation between Jews and Gentiles in light of Jesus as the Messiah. This was not a real problem after the end of the first century, when Christianity's constituency was not Jewish.

The confusion over the relationship between body and soul/spirit in Paul has led scholars to distinguish between duality and dualism in Pauline anthropology. Those who see *sōma* as inherently evil in a body/soul dualism are criticized, in line with new directions in NT study, for overestimating Hellenistic influence on Paul and underestimating his Jewish background. Rather than a dualism that places body and soul in an opposition which works against the unity of differentiation, most follow Gundry in speaking of a "duality" of being that does not imply a metaphysical, ethical dualism but which recognizes two substances that belong together and are capable of separation and various operations. This anthropological duality is not expressed through Paul's formally consistent use of any two terms. The focus upon duality also helps to place Paul and NT anthropology in continuity with Jewish beliefs of Paul's own time (with the exception of Greek dualism in the Wisd. Sol. 9:15) as well as with OT anthropology.

Contra the existentialism of Bultmann, which devalues the physical body *(sōma)*, Gundry argues that Christ's incarnation and bodily resurrection reaffirm the duality of human beings first seen in creation. The *sōma* dies but will also be resurrected, proof of its worth and of its need for sanctification now. The physicalness of *sōma* affirms life in a material world and our responsibility for it, moving us away from an individualistic, spiritualized Gospel toward community and praxis. This critique intersects with that of socio-historical interpreters like W. Schottroff and D. Soelle who argue against the abstractions of idealist interpretations of the human being, and for a materialist exegesis that sees the real life of biblical people in a concrete way. Materialist thinking attempts to overcome the Western separation of spirit and matter which has contributed to a destructive economic materialism, and to recognize our dependence upon God and our need for revolutionary praxis.

Advocates of a psychological analysis of NT, and particularly Pauline texts, for example, R. Scroggs, G. Theissen, and W. Wink, agree with the materialists that the Bible speaks about the transformation of selves by God's acts. They argue that psychological models and terminology can illumine these changes, with a stress upon the reality of the transformation rather than the person's awareness of it.

3. **Contemporary Biblical Anthropologies.** *a. Basic elements.* Most contemporary biblical anthropologies agree on a few basic points. Human beings are created by God as part of the natural world but with a special relationship to that world, to each other, and to God.

Humans have a visible and an invisible side, which are interrelated. God gives human life meaning.

b. Focus on the texts. No single biblical anthropology today commands a consensus. Though the focus of biblical anthropologies may vary, most agree that one must begin with the biblical texts themselves. Beginning with the varied witness of the texts disallows any systematic biblical anthropology; rather the texts provide certain focal points for discussion. The main focus of H. Wolff's anthropology, for example, is the "surprising" agreement emerging from the texts about human beings being in dialogue with and called by God rather than objectified in themselves.

c. Anthropology and pastoral care. From a pastoral perspective, biblical anthropology can liberate human beings rather than simply lecture them as sinners. W. Brueggemann, for example, insists that the biblical metaphor of covenant, that is, our grounding in Another who initiates our personhood and who stays bound to us in loyal ways for our well-being, provides a focus for pastoral counseling. In response to this covenanting God of the Bible, the appropriate human response is to hope, listen, and answer obediently. Pastoral counseling that encourages such action rejects our self-grounding and reclaims the idea of calling, that is, a purpose for being in the world that is related to the purposes of God.

For W. Oglesby the anthropological focal points which inform the process of counseling rest in the answers to the questions in Psalm 8:4 and Genesis 3:9. Human beings are creatures in God's image with creativity, yet sinners in isolation whose life-giving relationships are broken. The search for "Adam" marks all that follows in biblical narrative, including Jesus who defines his mission as seeking "to save that which was lost" (Luke 19:10). Thus even in sin one can still respond to grace through forgiveness and restore broken relationships. S. Guthrie similarly argues that the Triune God's grace for the sinner means that pastoral counseling can (1) enable people not to *be* but to *become*; (2) give up all neutrality about the goal of becoming; and (3) "infect" people with hope.

Critics of traditional anthropology as sexist and racist also focus upon this eschatological question of becoming. J. González, for example, insists that traditionally maleness has been considered normative while femaleness has been seen as "a defective way of being human." Biblical anthropology, by not distinguishing between the descriptive and prescriptive goal of psychology, uses psychology as a tool to support such sexual stereotyping and the status quo. Based upon this anthropology, counselors simply advocate "coping." J. Nelson and D. Soelle also fault the duality of body and spirit/mind in Christian anthropology as a source of an anti-sex, anti-body and thus anti-woman bias which must be overcome.

Bibliography. R. Anderson, *On Being Human* (1982). J. Barr, *The Semantics of Biblical Language* (1961). W. Brueggemann, "Covenanting as Human Vocation," *Interpretation*, 33 (1979), 115–30. E. Evans-Pritchard, *Theories of Primitive Religion* (1965). C. González, "On the Way to Wholeness," *Theology Today*, 34 (1978), 378–85. J. González, "Searching for a Liberating Anthropology," *Theology Today*, 34 (1978), 386–94. N. Gottwald, *The Tribes of Yahweh* (1979). R. Gundry, *Sma in Biblical Theology* (1976). S. Guthrie, "Pastoral, Trinitarian Theology, and Christian Anthropology," *Interpretation*, 33

(1979), 130–44. P. Henry, *New Directions in NT Study* (1979). R. Horton and R. Finnegan, eds., *Modes of Thought* (1973). R. Jewett, *Paul's Anthropological Terms* (1971). G. Mendenhall, "The Hebrew Conquest of Palestine," *Biblical Archaelogical Review*, 3 (1970), 100–120. J. Nelson, *Embodiment* (1979). W. Oglesby, "Implications of Anthropology for Pastoral Care and Counseling," *Interpretation*, 33 (1979), 157–71. W. Pannenberg, *Anthropology in Theological Perspective* (1985). J. Pedersen, *Israel* (1926). H. W. Robinson, *Corporate Personality in Ancient Israel* (1980, [1935]). J. Rogerson, *Anthropology and the Old Testament* (1979); "The Hebrew Conception of Corporate Personality," *J. of Theological Studies*, 21 (1970), 1–16. L. H. Silberman, "Julius Wellhausen and his *Prolegomena*," *Semeia*, 25 (1982), 75–82. W. Schottroff and W. Stegemann, eds., *God of the Lowly* (1984). R. Scroggs, "Psychology as a Tool to Interpret the Text," *Christian Century*, (March 24, 1982), 335–38. K. Stendahl, *Paul Among Jews and Gentiles* (1976). G. Theissen, *Psychological Aspects of Pauline Theology* (1987). P. Trible, *God and the Rhetoric of Sexuality* (1978). C. Westermann, *Creation* (1974). H. W. Wolff, *Anthropology of the Old Testament* (1974).

D. D. HOPKINS

PERSON (Christian *or* Jewish Perspective); THEOLOGICAL ANTHROPOLOGY.

BIBLICAL LITERALISM. A hermeneutical approach to biblical interpretation which understands the Bible to "say what it means and mean what it says." Undergirding this approach is the belief that Scripture, though written through human vessels, is Scripture only because of its divine origin. Scripture, understood to be word-for-word God-given, has an authority which transcends time, culture, human reasoning, or any other ways in which attempts are made to "add to" or "take away from" its meaning. Scripture is God's truth for all times and cultures; it is not to be modified to conform to each passing (and sinful) culture. Indeed, it is sinful human nature which desires to use human ingenuity to mold God's law to our desires, rather than to conform our lives to God's way.

Literalists contend that Scripture is objective truth. No one, however, comes to a text unbiased. A complex set of assumptions, beliefs, and questions are always present in the interpreter which inevitably provide the context in which interpretation is done. This context determines such things as the particular biblical perspective which is appropriate in a given situation, how Scriptures are to be harmonized when they might appear to be contradictory, or how to find in Scripture the answers to questions which the biblical writers do not (directly) address. Literalists, although proclaiming to have only Scripture as their authority, in actuality bring to biblical interpretation a particular perspective through which Scripture is read (see Fackre). In order for literalists to claim an objective authority in Scripture, however, these subjective components of interpretation must remain implicit. It is this unacknowledged source of authority which guides the literalist and frustrates the nonliteralist.

The biblical literalist expects the pastor to have the authoritative word in matters pertaining to faith and practice. The Word of God is both necessary and sufficient as a guide to life; thus, knowledge of the Bible provides all the answers needed for living faithfully. The pastor is expected to be proficient in this knowledge and directive in counseling, providing clear answers to the problems brought by the parishioner.

Pastoral care and counseling provided to a literalist by a nonliteralist pastor is often characterized by suspicion (does this pastor carry truthful authority?) and frustration (is there any common ground from which to begin?). Diagnosis, process, and goals will be different from a nonliteralist perspective. Pastoral care and counseling in this situation is best understood as cross-cultural in nature. Crucial here is the recognition that literalism is more than an "objective" reading of the Bible; it is also a sociological phenomenon, a way of life with an order and structure which binds people into community. To attempt to change a person's theology is to risk altering preexisting relationships with both family and faith community. Literalists fear the disintegration of their entire world of meaning if even one part of it is destroyed. Acceptance of the literalists' perspective as one way of living a meaningful life is a crucial beginning point for the pastor. The challenge for the nonliteralist pastor is that of moving *within* the literalist system of convictions, allowing its own truth to surface and provide movement toward growth and resolution of the dilemma. Because of radically different foundational convictions, competing narratives, and structural issues, the difficulty of this pastoral counseling should not be underestimated.

Bibliography. J. Barr, *Fundamentalism* (1977). G. Fackre, *The Religious Right and Christian Faith* (1982). G. Marsden, *Fundamentalism and American Culture* (1980). J. I. Packer, *"Fundamentalism" and the Word of God* (1983). E. Sandeen, "The Problem of Authority in American Fundamentalism," *Review and Expositor*, 75:2 (1978). D. W. Sue, *Counseling the Culturally Different, Theory and Practice* (1981). B. Warfield, *The Inspiration and the Authority of the Bible*, S. Craig, ed. (1949).

H. S. NELSON

BIBLE, PASTORAL USE AND INTERPRETATION OF; FUNDAMENTALIST PASTORAL CARE; INTERPRETATION AND HERMENEUTICS, PASTORAL. *Compare* CHARISMATIC PASTORAL CARE.

BIBLICAL THEOLOGY. *See* OLD TESTAMENT AND APOCRYPHA, *or* NEW TESTAMENT.

BIBLIOTHERAPY. *See* LITERATURE, PASTORAL USE OF.

BILLINSKI, JOHN M. *See* PASTORAL CARE MOVEMENT.

BINSWANGER, LUDWIG (1881–1966). A Swissborn psychiatrist who broke away from psychoanalysis and developed Dasein analysis or "existential analysis." Binswanger, following his father and grandfather, became the director of the Sanatorium Bellevue in Kreuzlingen, Switzerland, and held that position for over forty years. Initially he studied psychoanalysis and became a close friend of Freud. However, he eventually came to reject the positivism, determinism, and reductionism of psychoanalytic thought and incorporated some of Heidegger's philosophy into his work. Binswanger attempted to understand the whole person by focusing upon one's "existence" or "being-in-the-world." He described three modes of existence: "Umwelt" or biological existence; "Mitwelt," existence in relationship to other persons; and "Eigenwelt" or one's relationship to oneself. Through Daseinanalysis (literally the analysis of one's being-in-the-world), Binswanger sought to reconstruct the disturbed individual's inner world of experience and move the person toward freedom, responsibility, and authentic existence.

Bibliography. J. Needleman, *Being-in-the-world* (1963).

S. C. WILLIS

EXISTENTIAL PSYCHOLOGY AND PSYCHOTHERAPY.

BIOENERGETICS. *See* POPULAR THERAPEUTIC MOVEMENTS AND PSYCHOLOGIES.

BIOFEEDBACK. The use of monitoring instruments to detect, amplify, and translate biological changes into meaningful information, which is then "fed back" to the patient so that the process or outcome can be modified voluntarily. Biofeedback has become an important method of treatment for physicians and psychologists for a wide variety of problems related to anxiety and stress. For example, in essential hypertension (high blood pressure of no known organic etiology) the level of pressure can be measured and continuously fed back to patients in such a way that they learn how to reduce the pressure. This is done by utilizing the feedback to control the state of tension, content of thought, and degree of tension that is contributing to the high blood pressure.

1. **The Concept of Feedback.** The general term "feedback" was coined by the mathematician Norbert Weiner and concisely defined by him as "a method of controlling the system by reinserting into it the results of its past performance." Every living organism is a self-regulating system owing its existence and stability to feedback mechanisms of all sorts. Infants learn hand-eye coordination by means of "visual proprioceptive feedback." By trial and error, muscles become coordinated and finally perform their complex tasks. The body also has many *endogenous* feedback systems that control functions such as blood temperature, heart rate, and muscle tension. Many are considered to be "autonomic" (i.e., they happen automatically) because there are no sensors to alert the subject to the process. Heart rate, blood pressure, residual muscle tension, digestion, and brain activity are examples of these "autonomic" functions.

Biofeedback, then, is a special application of this principle. When a sensor is inserted and information is obtained about these functions, they become "voluntary" activities to a certain degree in that they close the information loop and make a degree of control possible.

2. **History of Biofeedback.** Through the years there have been unusual reports in the scientific literature of people being able to control involuntary physiological activities, such as brief periods of cardiac arrest, voluntary acceleration of pulse rate, and remarkable control of skin temperature. In 1938, B. F. Skinner, the father of behaviorism, tried to condition the constriction of blood vessels through positive reinforcement. It was not until the late 1950s and early 1960s, however, that any real progress was made in experimentally demonstrating that voluntary control could be exercised over important body functions. This was followed during the late 1960s with

a flood of reports on the clinical effectiveness of such control. Today, biofeedback is being used (with varying degrees of success) to treat a wide variety of problems, including muscle contraction, headache, migraine headache, high blood pressure, sweat-gland activity, anxiety reactions, teeth-grinding, hyperactivity, drug addiction, chronic pain, sexual disorders, and stress symptoms. It is used by a variety of health professionals including psychologists, psychiatrists, physiological therapists, internists, cardiologists, dentists, speech pathologists, and educationalists.

3. **Future Trends.** With increased sophistication in the design of instruments to measure physiological functioning and in the understanding of body chemistry, new areas of application are constantly being developed. Space-age technology is making available extremely small and easily portable physiological instruments. Anxiety and stress are becoming better understood. Computer technology provides a high degree of accuracy in the gathering and analysis of data. Taken together, these developments may be expected to provide the decades ahead with exciting challenges as more and more physiological systems are transformed from being purely autonomic to being under voluntary control.

Bibliography. K. R. Gaarder, and P. S. Montgomery, *Clinical Biofeedback: A Procedural Manual* (1977). R. J. Gatchel and K. P. Price, *Clinical Applications of Biofeedback* (1979). I. Martin, and P. H. Venables, *Techniques in Psychophysiology* (1980).

A. D. HART

ANXIETY; BRAIN RESEARCH; PAIN MANAGEMENT/PAIN CLINIC; STRESS AND STRESS MANAGEMENT. *Compare* CYBERNETIC THEORY IN PSYCHOLOGY; HOMOEOSTASIS; MIND-BODY RELATIONSHIP.

BIOLOGICAL DIMENSIONS OF PERSONALITY AND BEHAVIOR. *See* PERSONALITY, BIOLOGICAL DIMENSIONS OF; SOCIOBIOLOGY.

BIOMEDICAL DILEMMAS. *See* MORAL DILEMMAS IN PASTORAL PERSPECTIVE; DYING, MORAL DILEMMAS IN; SICK, PASTORAL CARE OF.

BIORHYTHM RESEARCH. Biorhythm, also known as biological periodicity and biochronicity, refers to patterns of life that follow a predictable, cyclical course. While it is true that plant and animal life responds to a variety of variables such as a lunar calendar, temperature, amount of sunlight, and environmental resources, (Saunders, 1977), biorhythm theory, which generalizes from these and other variables to human thought, feelings, and behavior, has been more difficult to support.

Historically, much of the investigation of biorhythms has been based on patterns of accidents, such as industrial occurrences, and on people involved in special events, such as space flight and the difficulties encountered there. Using these data, Thommen (1973) has reviewed attempts to define periodic cycles for a 33-day intellectual rhythm, a 23-day physical rhythm, and a 28-day sensitivity rhythm. But research using random samples has yet to substantiate his position, though this may be due mainly to its complexity.

On a simpler level, research is being pursued on women's 28-day menstrual cycle and emotional reponses to it. Strughold (1971) used jetlag to illustrate what happens when our personal biological clocks are influenced by environmental variables. However, in psychiatric problems, there is insufficient data to indicate any broad type of biorhythmic process related to emotional dysfunction. Bipolar (or manic-depressive) illness has been described as being cyclic, but research has not clarified what determines the onset or reduction of these cycles. For the present, much further research is needed to support biorhythms as a major factor in human behavior.

Bibliography. D. S. Saunders, *An Introduction to Biological Rhythms* (1977). H. Strughold, *Your Body Clock* (1971). G. S. Thommen, *Is This Your Day?* (1973).

T. M. JOHNSON

PERSONALITY, BIOLOGICAL DIMENSIONS OF. *See also* MANIC-DEPRESSIVE (BIPOLAR) DISORDER. *Compare* HOMOEOSTASIS; HYPNOSIS; TEMPERAMENT.

BIPOLAR DISORDER. *See* MANIC-DEPRESSIVE (BIPOLAR) DISORDER.

BIRACIAL MARRIAGE AND FAMILY. *See* CROSS CULTURAL MARRIAGE AND FAMILY.

BIRTH. *See* CHILDBIRTH.

BIRTH CONTROL. *See* FAMILY PLANNING; MORAL DILEMMAS IN PASTORAL PERSPECTIVE; SEXUALITY, CHRISTIAN *or* JEWISH THEOLOGY AND ETHICS OF.

BIRTH ORDER. In a family, the sequence in which children are born. Francis Galton, the eminent British psychologist, was one of the first to study the role of birth order, in *English Men of Science: Their Nature and Nurture* (1874). However, the first major theoretical impetus was provided by Alfred Adler, who considered birth order one of five major variables to be explored in the description and diagnosis of personality. He described in detail the personality characteristics of oldest, youngest, second, and only children. Adler emphasized the importance of "dethronement," being ousted from the position of central attention and power with the parents, which is at the root of sibling rivalry and feelings of inferiority.

Since Adler's early writings, literally hundreds of studies have been conducted on birth order, inspired by six major groups of theories, of which dethronement was the first (Adams, 1972). Intrauterine and physiological theories emphasized the differences in the mother's health in each of her pregnancies and their impact on the child. Theories of only-child uniqueness focused on the only child as being more adult-oriented or more self-centered. Theories involving the anxiety or relaxation of the parents generally regarded the first child as the recipient of greater parental anxiety. Theories of sibling influence focus on the effect of sibling power and sex and the importance of role assignments among siblings. Finally, theories of economics have focused on the impact of birth order concerning achievement, generally emphasizing the advantage of the firstborn over later-born children. This variable is confounded by family size. Adams (1972) concluded that only two findings emerged consistently from this research: firstborns tend to attain greater educational levels, and firstborns are more dependent and affiliative. Schooler (1972) concluded that birth order research might result in clearer findings if it took into account such structural variables as family size and sex of siblings.

More recent theories have taken more of these structural variables into account, emphasizing that birth order effects are considerably modified by sex and number of siblings. As the number of children increases, parental interaction with individual children is reduced, lending some credibility to the dethronement/dispossession theory. In these situations older siblings also become the role models for the younger. Walter Toman (1969) asserts that both marriage and friendship are more successful if persons recreate the complementary relationships learned in the family. Adding sex to birth order results in multiple sibling positions one might assume, especially in larger families, and creates a unique family constellation for each of the children in a single family. Based on Toman's research, the family therapist Murray Bowen asserts that "no single piece of data is more important than knowing the sibling position of people in the present and past generations" (1978, p. 385). This more complex approach to sibling constellation, and a focus on the psychological aspects of sibling relationships, is beginning to replace the traditional birth order research.

Bibliography. Alfred Adler's various writings on birth order are summarized in H. L. and R. R. Ansbacher, eds., *The Individual Psychology of Alfred Adler* (1956). Literature reviews on birth order are found in B. Adams, "Birth Order: A Critical Review," *Sociometry*, 35 (1972), 411–439. C. Miley, "Birth Order Research 1963–1967: Bibliography and Index," *J. of Individual Psychology*, 25 (1969), 64–70. E. L. Vockell, D. W. Felker and C. H. Miley, "Birth Order Literature 1967–1971: Bibliography and Index," *J. of Individual Psychology*, 29 (1973), 39–53. B. Sutton-Smith and B. G. Rosenberg, *The Sibling* (1970). More recent theories may be found in W. Toman, *Family Constellation* (1969). M. Bowen, *Family Therapy in Clinical Practice* (1978). S. P. Bank and M. D. Kahn, *The Sibling Bond* (1982).

C. E. TAYLOR
H. VANDE KEMP

PERSONALITY THEORY. *See also* CHILDREN; FAMILY THEORY AND THERAPY; ONLY CHILDREN.

BIRTH TRAUMA. The psychological experience of being born. The prolonged, stressful birthing process represents a psychological as well as physical separation from the mother, with increased dependence on oneself. According to Otto Rank, a symbolic extension of this experience applies to conflict in interpersonal relationships, where the stress of identification and fear of loss is psychologically similar to the traumatic birthing process.

T. M. JOHNSON

ANXIETY; WILL THERAPY. *Compare* CHILDBIRTH; SEPARATION ANXIETY; TRAUMA. *Biography:* RANK.

BISEXUALITY. A term that can refer to differentiation of biological sex, a phase in sexual development, or a type of sexual orientation. Bisexuality is sometimes used to refer to persons born with male and female sexual genitalia; the more common term is hermaphrodite. It is misleading when bisexuality is used this way, for in most cases there is a clear chromosomal sex. (Nonetheless, decisions as to which sex in which to rear a hermaphrodite child require consideration of a complex set of medical and social factors.) Most develop with a single adult sexual identity and orientation.

Freud's theory of personality development held that all children are born "bisexual," that human beings have equal sexual attraction for both sexes before social factors intervene, though the social factors make critical use of anatomical differences. This concept also is critical in Freud's explanation of the etiology of homosexuality as an immature resolution of the Oedipal complex. Much of psychology has moved away from Freud's view of innate bisexuality and etiology of homosexuality, however.

In its most common and accurate usage, bisexuality refers to a person who is emotionally, socially, and sexually attracted to individuals of both biological sexes, as distinguished from heterosexual and homosexual orientations. However, there has been a great deal of controversy over whether this type of sexual attraction actually exists. It has been treated as a myth, as a developmental phase, and as pathology, that is, sexual confusion. Kinsey identified 18 percent of men as bisexual, less for women. More recent reports indicate 8–20 percent for men, 15 percent for women. Some recent literature (DeCecco and Shively; Bode) contends specifically that there is a true bisexual person, for whom sexual attraction and behavior are equal toward men and women, either happening contemporaneously or sequentially over long periods of time. But by and large this category has been ignored in research on orientation; so little is known about it. Its etiology is uncertain, as in heterosexuality and homosexuality. Biological causes and social learning theories are the two most common explanations.

Assessment is the first responsibility of the pastoral counselor, and this must include indications of emotional and social attraction as well as physical. The person must be distinguished from those who have true sexual identity confusion. The bisexual person, like the homosexual person, receives negative judgment from the traditional religious community. In counseling with such a person one should clarify orientation, then work to clarify decisions about lifestyle within the individual's moral and spiritual framework. As sexual orientation is very difficult to change in the adult, treatment considerations include assessment of motivation to change, environmental support, and consequences of chosen lifestyle.

Bibliography. J. Bode, *View from Another Closet* (1976). J. DeCecco and M. Shively, "Bisexual and Homosexual Identities," *J. of Homosexuality*, 9 (1983/84). A. Kinsey, W. Pomeroy, and C. Martin, *Sexual Behavior in the Human Male* (1948).

P. P. HART

SEXUALITY, BIOLOGICAL AND PSYCHOSOCIAL THEORY OF; SEXUAL VARIETY, DEVIANCE, AND DISORDER. *Compare* ANDROGYNY; HOMOSEXUALITY; IDENTITY.

BISHOP. From the Greek *episcopos,* a term used in some churches to designate the highest order of ordained ministry. In some churches the term is used to describe an office or pastoral and administrative function to which elected elders are consecrated. Protestant polities of the episcopal type will vary depending upon whether bishop is understood as order (hence, ordination) or office (hence, consecration.)

In the Greek language the term originally meant a civil office or overseer of those who labor. The early Christians carried the term into their church life. In the NT it is difficult to make clear distinctions between presbyters (elders) and bishops, for example, Titus 1:5; Acts 20:17 and 20:28. By the second century, however, the definition of functions and responsibilities became more precise as seen in Ignatius of Antioch. A bishop is one who exercises pastoral oversight, who is the chief liturgical figure presiding at the Eucharist, ordaining and absolving. Likewise, the bishop acquires greater fiscal control and general administrative authority in the church.

Episcopal patterns varied, mostly according to geographical location. In some locations (notably North Africa) the monarchical plan prevailed, where a bishop governed a single church. In other areas bishops of a major city supervised the bishops of smaller cities and towns. In still other instances, notably in Western Europe, the pattern developed whereby the bishop of a major metropolitan area supervised the work of the presbyters in the surrounding area. This pattern is reflected in contemporary practice in the Roman Catholic and Anglican churches. In the process of developing episcopal patterns a clearer distinction was being drawn between presbyters and bishops. This development entailed a narrowing of the specific functions of a bishop to those to which only a bishop had exclusive rights, that is, confirmation and ordination.

The Western church was organized according to episcopal polity until the Reformation. The title was retained in some Reformation churches, particularly among certain Lutheran bodies. The title is also used by Moravians, though their polity is presbyterial. Among most American Methodists the title is used for those elected and consecrated to the work of "superintendency." Twentieth-century developments in the ecumenical movement toward greater unity, as seen for example in the Church of South India, the Church of North India, and the Consultation on Church Union (COCU) in the U.S., reveal a growing awareness of the importance of the threefold order of ministry (deacon, elder, and bishop) as a means of making the church's unity manifest in the world.

Bibliography. B. Cooke, *Ministry to Word and Sacraments* (1976). E. G. Jay, *The Church: Its Changing Image Through Twenty Centuries* (1980). World Council of Churches, *Baptism, Eucharist and Ministry* (Faith and Order Paper No. 111, 1982).

J. C. LOGAN, JR.

ECCLESIOLOGY AND PASTORAL CARE; MINISTRY. *Compare* AUTHORITY, PASTORAL; ELDER; SUPERVISION.

BLACK AMERICAN PASTORAL CARE. A contextual response pattern of *agape*, empathic care to persons and families in periods of emotional and spiritual crisis. It has been developed by black Christians who understood and understand themselves to be related significantly to God. Its power is rooted in a worldview that envisages God as intimately involved in black people's lives, caring for them and sustaining them in the midst of oppression and racism.

Black American pastoral care is a form of ministry that seeks to elicit a response to God's immanent activity in black people's lives through caring patterns provided by the social context-relational values, symbols, and methods and patterns of care. The goal of its caring response has been to assist God in liberating persons from the shackles that prevent growth toward relational wholeness in time, body, mind, and in relationship to others, institutions, the environment, and to God. The functions of its caring response patterns can be understood through the traditional tasks of pastoral care, namely, healing, sustaining, guiding, and reconciling.

The caring patterns and their functions can be envisioned from an historical and developmental perspective in the black church from slavery to the present time. Moreover, these patterns are similar to the biblical models of caring in worldview and form, and as such they have had a history different from American pastoral care in general.

Contemporary black pastoral care seeks to draw on the contextual model of the past and to correlate this past model with recent behavioral science models. The efforts of contemporary black pastoral care theorists have some affinity with the recent trend in pastoral care known as growth counseling.

1. **Forms and Functions of Empathic Caring.** Historically, five key structures within the black church have carried out its caring functions. They include the symbolic worldview, the role of the black preacher, the family, the extended family, and the church as a support system. They have functioned biblically in the sense that they have contributed to the building up of community much in the same way that the early church attempted to build up the body of Christ (V. P. Furnish).

The symbolic worldview of black Christians has been cosmological. The cosmological world has been composed of the transcendent-spiritual realm and the mundane-material realm. These two aspects of reality form an interpenetrating relational unity rather than a hostile cleavage. When the mundane-material world is impacted by the spiritual realm, personal and social wholeness is the result.

In this worldview God has been and is very much involved in the everyday world assuring the availability of the resources for personal and social wholeness. The resources of the transcendent-spiritual world and God's activity are intimately related in the mind of black Christians. Thus, when they encounter God's saving activity in the world, the resources of the transcendent-spiritual world are made available, and conversion takes place. That is, their entire being becomes a relational whole; they are related to the source of human wholeness and growth; their lives are transformed, and the power to grow relationally is released (C. Johnson).

One result of the conversion has been that black Christians have sought to respond to this encounter with God through *agape* love to others. Therefore, the black preacher, the black family, the extended family, and the black church have sought to create the kinds of relational patterns that reflect the quality of God's care for them.

The relational structures have performed the traditional functions of pastoral care — reconciling, healing, sustaining, and guiding. These functions need to be defined from the perspective of human wholeness in the light of black Christian experience. *(1) Reconciling* has been the central function of black American pastoral care; its aim has been to enable persons to encounter the Source of human wholeness. *(2) Healing* has been one result of the encounter, and the power to grow toward relational wholeness is released. *(3) Sustaining* has supported the wholeness already existing when circumstances temporarily blocked growth. *(4) Guiding* has functioned to help persons make the kinds of decisions that have led to the fulfillment of their full possibilities as relational persons.

2. **Historical Periods.** *a. 1750–1910.* The traditional functions of pastoral care are evident in the brush arbor, the mourning bench tradition, and the mutual aid societies prominent during slavery and the reconstruction period. The brush arbor was a secret supportive religious meeting held by slaves in bondage where they sought to worship God freely, to express their hopes and desires without fear, and to form supportive relationships with each other while under bondage and prohibited from holding secret meetings (G. Rawick). The mourning bench tradition, which has existed since slavery and is operative in some churches today, was a place or location in the church, usually in the front, where persons under conviction of sin sat and received communal support until the spirit of the Lord touched them (C. Johnson and A. R. Raboteau). Under conviction meant that persons were aware of God working in their lives convicting them of sin and drawing them toward salvation. The mutual aid societies were support systems that were formed during slavery and the reconstruction period to assist persons to maintain physical, emotional, social, economic, and spiritual well-being through caring relationships in the face of life and circumstantial crises such as death, dying, bereavement, and loss.

All three of these supportive structures were primarily vehicles of reconciliation in that caring relationships assisted persons to encounter the Source of growth, wholeness, forgiveness, hope, and love. Moreover, these structures carried out the healing function. The worldview undergirded them, and when persons were in harmony with the Source of wholeness and when there was harmony between the spiritual realm and the material realm, healing resulted. Evidence of such healing and wholeness was the fact that the slaves and ex-slaves believed that there was a personal identity change. They believed they were no longer slaves but children of God, which meant they experienced self and social transcendence; they transcended the slave label and identity. They were not reduced to self-definitions dictated by social prescriptions of inferiority.

Sustaining persons in the midst of slavery and in the midst of life transitions was also a function of the three structures of caring. Persons were supported in their efforts to find wholeness as well as continued integrity in wholeness in those periods when growth was blocked temporarily. During those periods the three structures prevented persons from losing the growth that had already been achieved.

Persons also needed guidance in the growth process. These three caring patterns helped to guide persons to the source of wholeness as well as in the growth process after encountering God. Following conversion, for example, persons were guided and nurtured into their roles in the caring community.

In addition to these three structures of caring the black family and extended family also acted as vehicles of healing, sustaining, guiding, and reconciling. Recent evidence indicates that the black family and extended family have been very supportive of the growth toward wholeness during slavery (H. D. Gutman).

The role of the black preacher was central in these supportive structures because the pastor held up the black Christian worldview before the community as a guide, and embodied the symbolic worldview to bring it to bear on the lives of persons and families in crises (E. Wimberly).

b. 1910–1950. The caring functions of the earliest period of black American pastoral care were performed by corporate patterns of care. In this new period the same caring structures of the earlier period carried out the same functions of healing, sustaining, guiding, and reconciling with one modification. The brush arbor as a secret meeting place was no longer needed, but its function was maintained after slavery. The mourning bench tradition, mutual aid societies — especially in the South—the black family and extended family, and the role of the black pastor as symbol still existed and performed similar functions to those of the earlier period of history although there were new social conditions. The major social change after the emancipation of black people from slavery was the urban migration of black people from the South to the North. Support structures were needed to meet the needs for the new urban residents.

Storefront churches became the major supportive communities for assisting persons in making the transition from the South to the urban North, and they functioned as small extended families that provided many of the caring functions. Similar to the mutual aid society and the mourning bench tradition of the South, the storefront church carried out corporate care that assisted persons in finding wholeness in time, mind, body, and in relationships to others, institutions, environment, and to God.

c. 1950 to the present. The civil rights and the black power and consciousness movements made black people aware that they must do something about the social structures that blocked their growth as full persons participating totally in American society at all levels. Therefore social transformation and personal transformation were linked, and the preventive role of caring in the black church became prominent. In addition to the traditional supportive structures that were part of the two earlier periods, caring not only meant building up the life of persons and the caring community; it also meant addressing those social structures and conditions that hindered the healing, sustaining, guiding, and reconciling ministries of the church. Building on the eschatological worldview that God was intimately involved in the lives of people, the vehicles of nonviolent protest, black economic development and strengthening black institutions — the family and extended family, the school and the church — became complementary to the caring ministry of the church. In other words, the model of caring became intentionally wholistic although one can see major evidence of this wholistic orientation in the other two periods. However, what changed in this period was a new consciousness by the entire black church that caring also involved addressing growth blocking social systems.

3. Contemporary Theory in Black Pastoral Care. Black pastoral care as a discipline emerged in this period. As a discipline it has sought to identify, formulate, conceptualize, and transmit to others those caring principles and methods that have grown out of God's encounter and involvement with black people. In building a theory of pastoral care black theorists today build on the legacies of the past to fashion contemporary models useful in ministry in the black church. This care reflects the wholism of the corporate emphasis of the past as well as the concern for the needs of the whole person. Concern for ethical and social issues is central.

4. The Relationship of Black American Pastoral Care to Pastoral Care in General. The development of black American pastoral care can be distinguished from the pastoral care and counseling traditions emerging in the 1920s and later associated with contemporary accrediting agencies known as the American Association of Pastoral Counseling and the American Association of Clinical Pastoral Education. These organizations may not represent the total history of pastoral care and counseling in the U.S., but they do portray a significant portion of what has happened theoretically and practically in the field of pastoral care.

Until recently a significant part of the training and practice of pastoral counselors in these organizations took place outside of the parish setting and has been only marginally related to the Judeo-Christian heritage of care. The theoretical model which characterizes the early development of these groups are: (1) similarity to the medical model in training and practice, (2) the one-to-one interview, (3) the client-centered method as normative, (4) and a psychodynamic understanding of human behavior — unconscious past as determining pathological derivatives of behavior.

In contrast, black American pastoral care has been (1) related to the local church and to the historic heritage of care in the Judeo-Christian tradition, (2) corporate, (3) biblical and theological in understanding the nature of their identity as children of God, (4) supportive of normal coping skills that prevent emotional illness, and (5) focused on the resources of the total community for the care of a person's wholistic needs.

Black American pastoral care has many affinities with growth counseling, which is a recent model emerging in pastoral counseling. This model emphasizes the use of supportive methods, improving relationships, utilizing positive personality resources, supporting coping skills and constructive behavior, and dealing with present realities (Clinebell). This model has visualized the goal of caring as the growth of persons toward relational wholeness in mind, body, and toward others, institutions, environment, and God. Systems, crisis, body, and spiritual therapies are significant. It emphasizes the corporate nature of personality and corporate resources for responding to the wholistic needs of persons. Theology, ethics, and changing social systems are also crucial in this the-

ory. Black pastoral care has operated implicitly on these ideas in the past and explicitly more recently.

5. The Significance of Black American Pastoral Care. It has significance for the ongoing conceptualization of the theory and practice of pastoral care, contributes to the trend in theorizing that seeks to link caring models with the Judeo-Christian heritage of caring, and also provides one paradigm for correlating the discoveries of modern behavioral sciences with aspects of a selected community of faith. It offers a critical model for examining the assumptions undergirding modern pastoral care and contributes to building wholistic, systemic, and ethical models of caring.

Bibliography. C. Felton, *The Care of Souls in the Black Church* (1980). V. P. Furnish, "Theology and Ministry in Pauline Letters," in *A Biblical Basis for Ministry*, E. Shelp and R. Sunderland, eds., (1981), 11–30. H. G. Gutman, *The Black Family in Slavery and Freedom 1750 – 1925* (1976). D. Hurst, "The Shepherding of Black Christians," (Th.D. Dissertation, School of Theology at Claremont, California, 1981). C. H. Johnson, *God Struck Me Dead: Religious Conversion Experiences of Ex-Slaves* (1969). V. L. Lattimore, "The Positive Contribution of Black Cultural Values to Pastoral Counseling," *J. of Pastoral Care*, 34 (June 1982), 105 – 117. A. J. Raboteau, *Slave Religion: The Invisible Institution in the Antebellum South* (1978), p. 255. G. P. Rawick, ed., *The American Slave: A Composite Autobiography* (1972), 9 vols. A. Smith, Jr., "Religion and Mental Health Among Blacks," *J. of Religion and Health*, 20 (1981), 264 – 87. E. P. Wimberly, "A Conceptual Model for Pastoral Care in the Black Church Utilizing Systems and Crisis Theories," (Ph.D. Dissertation, Boston University, 1976); *Pastoral Care in the Black Church* (1979); *Pastoral Counseling and Spiritual Values: A Black Point of View* (1982).

E. P. WIMBERLY

BLACK THEOLOGY AND PASTORAL CARE; CULTURAL AND ETHNIC FACTORS IN PASTORAL CARE; HISTORY OF PROTESTANT PASTORAL CARE (United States); PASTORAL CARE (History, Traditions, and Definitions); SOCIAL STATUS AND CLASS FACTORS IN PASTORAL CARE; SOUL (Black Church). *See also* BLACK IDENTITY AND CONSCIOUSNESS; CROSS-CULTURAL MARRIAGE AND FAMILY; CROSS-CULTURAL PASTORAL CARE; EXPLOITATION/OPPRESSION; GROWTH COUNSELING; WORLD VIEW. *Compare* AFRICAN *or* WEST INDIAN TRADITIONAL RELIGION; BLACK MUSLIM CARE AND COUNSELING.

BLACK IDENTITY AND CONSCIOUSNESS. Refers to the effort by black people in the U.S. to affirm their self-worth as whole human beings in the face of negative ascriptions, behavior, and feelings toward them resulting from white racism. This affirmation has begun with an effort to reinterpret their personal and corporate identity and history in the light of a new consciousness that owns biological (black) pigmentation, that affirms their ancestral roots in Africa, that accepts the historical importance of black families and extended families, that rejects assimilation into white middle-class values at the expense of black folkways, that challenges the research that portrays black people as pathological and living in disrupted families and communities, and that affirms the traditions that make up the black community.

The motivation for this self-affirmation emerged out of an awareness that black people could take their destiny into their own hands. Starting with the success of the civil rights movement, black people learned that their lives could be internally controlled rather than externally manipulated. Acting on this new awareness, they began to experience themselves as worthwhile human beings, capable of controlling their own destiny. This new consciousness has helped black people to visualize new strengths and resources inherent in their community.

The major implication of this new racial identity and consciousness for pastoral counseling is the need to develop conceptual and therapeutic growth models of wholeness (1) that affirm the strengths of black clients rather than pathologies, (2) that visualize the strengths of black families and extended families and social network systems as sources and resources of healing, and (3) that recognize that some interactional lifestyle patterns and values governing black behavior may be different from the white middle-class orientation.

1. Review of Research. *a. Challenges to pathological theories of self-hatred.* Part of the effort to affirm wholeness in the identity and consciousness movement has been to challenge research completed on black people that has painted negative pictures of them. Significant in this research have been ideological biases that portray black people and their culture as pathological and deviant. Pathological theories have largely focused on the disorganized aspects of a selected population in the black community and have neglected and ignored the overall strength of the total black community. To counteract the pathological orientation, black researchers with a new consciousness have been exploring black life and have found a social and cultural context supportive of black personhood (Banks, 1980).

According to David Hurst (1981), a black pastoral counselor, a review of the literature on the black personality will reveal that the concept of black self-hatred has dominated the literature. In his mind the major explanation for this domination has been the prevalence of psychoanalytic interpretative frameworks which have focused on pathology and have ignored the social contexts of black people. His review also reveals that black persons are envisaged as victim, patient, parolee, and petitioner for aid. They are rarely portrayed as whole human beings with healthy coping skills who love themselves.

Hurst's critique is reflective of the growing consciousness of black scholars with regard to research carried out on black people (Banks, 1980). The following list is a compilation of the deficiencies black researchers have found in the literature done by researchers without black consciousness: (1) placing emphasis on pathology rather than on strengths, (2) moving uncritically from groups to individuals, (3) assuming uniformity of black experience, (4) placing emphasis on the lowest income groups of black subjects, (5) tending to focus on captive subjects/prisoners, mental patients, school children, (6) using poor research designs and sampling, (7) tending to deemphasize cultural factors and their influence on behavioral patterns, (8) exhibiting reluctance to treat racism as an important factor, and (9) having unexamined class biases and racial biases.

b. Emergence of the cultural variant model of the black family. In an effort to develop models that are grounded in a more realistic view of black people than the pathological and deviant models, black psychological and sociological researchers have turned to the social context that produces the black person. They have chosen anthropological research models that seek to explain individual and corporate black behavior and life from within the black community context. Rather than studying the convenient problem populations that need special therapeutic and social program attention—the mental patient, prisoner, welfare client—they have tried to visualize the black community as a whole. This approach has been called an ecological indigenous cultural approach (Peters, 1981).

Much of the research that has been done in the pathological school of thought has assumed that black culture was either culturally deviant or culturally equivalent (Allen, 1978). The culturally deviant model accepts that there are distinct cultural differences between black and white people, but this theory holds that the distinction is deviant and thus pathological. On the other extreme is the culturally equivalent model which postulates that there is no real cultural difference between black people and white people. In this theory differences are attributed to class differences rather than to distinctiveness in cultural styles inherited from Africa (Sudarkasa, 1981).

The alternative to these two theories has emerged as the culturally variant model which recognizes that there are some culturally distinctive features about black life that have been inherited from Africa. These differences should not be ignored or labeled as pathological, deviant, or merely class differences. The major difference pointed out is the communal or corporate orientation to black life when compared to the white middle-class value of individualism.

The following list of conclusions reflects research findings on the black family by black scholars employing the culturally variant model: (1) rejection of matriarchal explanations of black family organization, (2) flexibility in the allocation of roles, (3) discovery that the majority of black families are structurally complete, (4) emphasis on constructive coping skills in the face of adversity, (5) involvement of kinsfolk in child-rearing, (6) egalitarian norm functional in household, (7) rejection of the view of the ineffectual black father and husband, (8) great family and peer self-esteem reflecting communal orientation, (9) family support of strong self-images, and (10) strong emphasis on achievement in the black social context.

c. Counseling issues with the culturally different. The culturally variant orientation also has influenced the manner in which counselors perceive black clients. There are research findings which point to the fact that black counseling clients often differ culturally from many white middle-class counselees (Smith, 1981; Banks, 1980). The following conclusions are found in the research concerning black clients: they (1) are very nonverbal, (2) emphasize story telling, (3) are action-oriented more than talk-oriented, (4) have a variance in eye contact from the majority group, (5) are people-oriented more than thing-oriented, (6) prefer jobs and professions that are people-oriented, (7) view responsibility and locus of control externally, (8) view counseling as alien since families and churches deal with their inner and personal concerns, (9) seek concrete advice, (10) often reject childhood interpretations of problems, and (11) test white counselors for negative racial attitudes.

2. Implications for Pastoral Counseling. The rejection of pathological and deviant explanatory models of behavior makes the growth counseling orientation a natural alternative. This model focuses on the strengths of persons, the importance of the natural social context and systems for healing, the constructive aspects of behavior, and the preventive role of community, educational and action methodologies as well as therapeutic models. This model also rejects the hierarchical and power models of the counselor-client relationship, and in turn makes it possible for the counselor to learn from a culturally different client. Growth counseling also recognizes the impact of injustice and negative social forces on personality development and takes seriously the person's struggles with injustice. This model has the potential to affirm the role of the black social context in shaping black identity, worth, and wholeness.

Bibliography. For a review of psychological research, see D. Hurst, "Shepherding Black Christians," University Microfilms (1981), 86–95. For reviews of research on the black family, see W. R. Allen, "The Search for Applicable Theories of Black Family Life," *J. of Marriage and the Family* (February 1978), 117–29. J. Dodson, "Conceptualization of Black Families," in *Black Families,* H. P. McAdoo, ed. (1981), pp. 23–36; L. B. Johnson, "Perspectives on Black Family Empirical Research: 1965–1978," in H. P. McAdoo, (1981), pp. 87–102; M. Peters, "Parenting in Black Families with Young Children: A Historical Perspective," in H. P. McAdoo, (1981), pp. 211–24; N. Sudarkasa, "Interpreting the African Heritage in Afro-American Family Organization," in H. P. McAdoo (1981), pp. 37–53. For black identity formation, see S. T. Hauser, *Black and White Identity Formation* (1971). For reviews on research in counseling, see W. Banks, "The Social Context and Empirical Foundation of Research on Black Clients," in *Black Psychology,* R. L. Jones, ed. (1980), 447–55; E. J. Smith, "Cultural and Historical Perspectives in Counseling Blacks," in *Counseling the Culturally Different: Theory and Practice,* D. W. Sue, ed. (1981), pp. 141–85.

E. P. WIMBERLY

CONSCIOUSNESS RAISING; CULTURAL AND ETHNIC FACTORS IN PASTORAL CARE; IDENTITY; SOCIAL CONSCIOUSNESS AND RESPONSIBILITY; SOCIAL PERCEPTION, JUDGMENT, AND BELIEF. *See also* CROSS-CULTURAL MARRIAGE AND FAMILY; RACISM; SOCIAL STATUS AND CLASS FACTORS. *Compare* ASIAN AMERICAN, BLACK AMERICAN, BLACK MUSLIM, HISPANIC AMERICAN, *or* NATIVE AMERICAN PASTORAL CARE.

BLACK ISSUES IN PSYCHOLOGY. The identification, examination, and exploration of key points and matters within the broad discipline of psychology that have direct bearing on the lives of black people in America. These issues, when identified, raise critical questions of psychology from the perspective of black experience and black culture in America. While there is no homogeneous black experience or culture, selected issues related to the uniqueness of being black in America can be identified. These black issues often get ignored by what black behavioral scientists call "Euro-American psychology."

1. The Psychological Study of Black People. The major issue in relationship to black experiences and psychology is whether the traditional categories of Euro-American psychology can be applied to black subject matter. Black psychologists would point out that this type of theoretical application takes concepts and theories developed from Euro-American subjects and applies them to black subjects. For black psychologists, this approach is inadequate primarily because it ignores the unique social and cultural context in which many black people find themselves, and in many ways it has erected barriers and biases against black people as a result.

To counter the Euro-American psychological approach to the study of black people, black psychology as a discipline emerged in the late 1960s and early 1970s, and sought to study individual black behavior and mental processes from within the black social ethos of lived experiences. It focuses on the struggles, pleasures, interests, desires, habits, aims, drives, motivations, feelings, actions, and wants of individuals within a social context. It adopts systems models of understanding black individuals which envisage individual behavior and mental processes from within a particular social environment. For many black psychologists the social situation not only includes the exploration of the American social scene and black culture; it also includes the exploration of black African assumptions related to the nature of reality.

2. Cultural Variance Versus Cultural Deviance. Closely related to the first issue is the perspective through which black culture and life are viewed. Many psychologists from the Euro-American school have ignored the social context of black individuals and have compared black individuals to white individuals. When this is done, the differences between them are labeled. The white Euro-American values are normative, and black differences are labeled as pathological or deviant.

Black psychologists and behavioral scientists began to recognize the pejorative influences that this type of labeling and biased constructs were having on black people, and they proposed an alternative theoretical model for explaining the differences. The alternative explanation is called the cultural variant model. This model recognizes that the differences between white individuals and black individuals are culturally determined and represent unique cultural adaptations rather than individual adjustments. Many black psychologists point out that black behavior makes real sense when envisaged in its social context and in its African heritage.

3. Science Versus Ideology. This issue focuses on what is measurable and observable and how the measured and observed data are interpreted. Science is generally understood as objective observation, and ideology as subjective observation where investigator biases are not systematically controlled in the observation. In ideology, personal values influence the questions asked and the answers received. Black psychologists recognize how difficult it is to control ideological biases which influence objective observation and have therefore called for the recognition and acknowledgment of ideological biases in all research and theory building (W. Allen).

One major ideological bias emerging out of Euro-American psychology is the deficit theory which has its roots in the philosophy of social Darwinism (Guthrie). This theory compares whites to blacks and interprets the differences in terms of the theory of instinctual endowment and heredity. Such an orientation leads easily to deviant-oriented models of psychology and interpretations that relate to pathology. Black psychologists and behavioral scientists recognize the biases that are at work in the deficit model and have called for theories of interpretation that include the social and cultural uniqueness of black people. This critique of the deficit theory has helped to sharpen thinking on the culturally variant model.

4. The Sociology of Knowledge and the Uniqueness of the Black Experience. This issue focuses on the meaning that things have for people and how socially shared knowledge determines this meaning. The significance of the shared knowledge and meaning orientation is that it helps to provide a rationale for understanding the different ways of viewing the same reality from group to group.

A key observation here is the differences in worldview of many black people when compared to the dominant worldview existing in wider society. For example, research reveals the following about black culture: (1) a wholistic emphasis on the relationship of mind and body when compared to the mind-body dualism in Euro-American culture; (2) priority given to relational thinking as opposed to analytical thinking required in the educational system (J. Hale); (3) emphasis on oral-auditory aspects of perception which is distinct from the visual and written emphasis of wider culture; (4) a present time orientation compared to a future time orientation of dominant culture; (5) a collective group orientation rather than an individual orientation; and (6) an effort to cooperate with nature rather than to manipulate it (J. White, D. Parham and A. Parham).

5. Wholistic Synthetic Models of Personality Versus Analytical Macular Models. Black psychologists and behavioral scientists have focused on the social context of personality development in an effort to avoid the deviant and deficit models of Euro-American psychology. This has led to more attention being paid to systems theory, preventive mental health models, and growth-health-wholeness models by black psychologists and behavioral scientists. The pathological and medically oriented models that dominated psychology for a long time are pushed aside in favor of health- and strength-oriented models. Moreover, existential models of psychology and philosophy are drawn on because they emphasize the importance of experience. Black experience is central for black psychology, and existential models form a good conceptual compatibility with black psychology.

6. Indigenous Counseling Approaches Versus White Middle Class Approaches. There are certain white middle-class assumptions undergirding contemporary counseling models which may have negative influences upon those persons whose cultural experiences are different. These class-oriented models are related to the "YAVIS Syndrome"(D. Sue); each letter in this acronym stands for one descriptive characteristic of class-bound counseling orientations. White middle-class models of counseling are successful with the Young, Attractive, Verbal, Intelligent, and the professionally Successful. This is not to say that the YAVIS model is normative in describing who is attractive or intelligent. Rather, this syndrome refers to the kinds of clients who are preferred by mental health practitioners. This model places a premium on openness, psychological minded-

ness, verbal-emotional-behavioral expressiveness, insight, one-to-one action through talking, intimacy, passivity by the counselor, monolingual conversation (standard English), analytical verbal mode, self-direction, and self-exploration.

The value biases in the YAVIS model are being challenged by ethnic behavioral scientists who realize how culture and social experiences shape values and styles of counseling. Among the issues they raise are the significance of nonverbal behavior, language differences, locus of control of authority (inner or outer), locus of responsibility (personal or social), action styles and group styles of problem solving, and dialogical and responsive ways of communicating evident in Third World populations.

Black and white counselors alike are being challenged to pay particular attention to the different cultural styles individual clients and families bring into the counseling relationship. Emphasis is being placed on the utilization of the cultural styles as well as the social networks as part of the therapeutic process.

7. Talent Assessment Versus Talent Development. Black psychologists have called to the attention of educational and psychological testers the emphasis on talent assessment in intelligence, aptitude and potential with very little regard for the need to help students to develop the skills necessary to do well on these tests. Many black youth are screened out of mainstream societal opportunities because of the talent assessment orientation. Black psychologists are urging other professionals in their ranks to understand the testing process and the test making process so that they can help black students and others to develop the skills necessary to do well on these tests. There is also emphasis on research into the skills employed by black youth on an everyday basis so that these skills can be integrated into the tests. It is felt that integration of indigenous skills into the tests will make them less culturally bound and more relevant to divergent cultures. Moreover, black psychologists are urging educators to become more concerned with helping black youths to learn and to develop the kinds of skills needed to do well on the tests as they are currently constructed.

8. Methods of Relating Black Issues and Euro-American Psychology. There are generally three paradigms for relating black cultural uniqueness and Euro-American psychology: the indigenous cultural model, the correlational model, and the applicatory model. The *indigenous model* ignores the categories and theories of Euro-American psychology and draws its theories concerning individual behavior and thought processes from the uniqueness of black people, from their experiences and from their cultural inheritance from Africa. The *correlational model* recognizes the value of Euro-American psychology and seeks to correlate it with black indigenous equivalents (J. White, D. Parham, A. Parham); it seeks to enrich itself as well as Euro-American psychology through cross-fertilization. The *applicatory method* uncritically applies Euro-American psychological categories to black experiences; it ignores the uniqueness of black experiences and behavior.

9. Political Involvement Versus Scientific Objectivity. Black psychology does not take the position that psychology or the behavioral sciences should be politically neutral and value free (J. White, D. Parham, A. Parham).

Black psychologists see their theories and activities as efforts to change the sociopolitical process and to make American society more responsive programmatically to the needs of black persons.

10. Implications for Black Pastoral Care and Counseling. The theme of cultural and social uniqueness of the black experience has been common in the nine issues raised above. Not only are these issues crucial for black psychology, they are also central to black pastoral care and counseling.

Pastoral care has implicit or explicit psychological understandings of persons. Often these understandings come from Euro-American behavioral science assumptions and research. However, black pastoral care, in contrast to pastoral care in general, has sought its models for understanding persons from the cultural richness of black life. It has assumed the culturally variant orientation, and it has always operated out of ideological presuppositions which were related to the Christian faith. It has employed wholistic synthetic models of personality and has recognized the need for indigenous counseling approaches. Methodologically, it has given the priority to indigenous approaches to caring while some of the black pastoral care and counseling theorists have attempted to correlate indigenous approaches with analogous behavioral science concepts. Moreover, political involvement is assumed in black pastoral care and counseling.

The discipline of black pastoral care and counseling is a recent phenomenon with the first written works appearing in 1975 in several doctoral dissertations. However, indigenous pastoral care and counseling models have existed since the first black community was formed in America. In a real sense, the black church has been the experiential base for the kinds of issues that black psychology is now raising. There is, indeed, a great deal of cross-fertilization between black psychology and black pastoral care and counseling.

Bibliography. W. R. Allen, "The Search for Applicable Theories of Black Family Life," *J. of Marriage and the Family,* 40 (1978), 117–29. J. Hale, *Black Children: The Roots, Culture, and Learning Styles* (1982). R. L. Jones, ed., *Black Psychology* (1980). See especially articles by R. Guthrie; J. White, D. Parham, and A. Parham. D. W. Sue, *Counseling the Culturally Different: Theory and Practice,* (1981). E. P. Wimberly, *Pastoral Care in The Black Church* (1979); *Pastoral Counseling and Spiritual Values: A Black Point of View* (1982).

E. P. WIMBERLY

PSYCHOLOGY; RACISM. *Compare* CONSCIOUSNESS RAISING; MODELS IN PSYCHOLOGICAL AND PASTORAL THEORY; PHILOSOPHY AND PSYCHOLOGY.

BLACK MUSLIM CARE AND COUNSELING. "Black Muslims" is a pseudonym for the Nation of Islam organization, headed by the Honorable Elijah Muhammad ("the Messenger of Allah to the Black Man in America") until his death in 1975. Under the leadership of his son Imam Warith Deen Muhammad, the doctrinally new organization was most recently known as the American Muslim Mission. Dissolved in 1985, the former *masajid* (Arabic plural of *masjid,* mosque) became administratively independent; the former Chicago headquarters is known as Masjid Elijah Muhammad. Despite some similarities, this article does not concern the present Nation of Islam, also called the Black Muslims, led by Minister Louis Farrakhan.

Counseling in the Nation and its successor organizations was based on the premise that African Americans ("Bilalians," "Afro Americans" or "black Americans") are in need of religious and social rehabilitation. During the time of Elijah Muhammad the rehabilitation program began with the formal "acceptance of Islam," i.e., conversion to his heterodoxy. His weekly sermon, radio broadcast, and his column in the Nation's organ *Muhammad Speaks* were concerned with solutions to the psychological and social conditions of African Americans.

Adult males became members of the Fruit of Islam (FOI). They were taught the dietary laws of Islam, physical fitness and defense, personal hygiene, proper dress and behavior. They were encouraged to be self-respecting, industrious, supportive of their families, and law-abiding citizens. Indulgence in drugs, smoking, gambling, fornication, adultery, and criminal activities was proscribed. A member who was known to have such proclivities was given special attention in a private or group session. He was encouraged to sever unnecessary associations with females and nonmembers of the Nation. If he violated the behavior code, he was subject to a "trial" before the membership; if found guilty, he was reprimanded severely, suspended for a period, or both.

Adult females became members of the Muslim Girls Training and General Civilization Class (MGT and GCC) and received guidance similar to that of the males. They learned home economics, and were taught to be respectful and obedient to their fathers and husbands, within the framework of the Islamic code of conduct. They were required to cover their heads, bosoms, arms and legs in public, including the workplace.

Young students received care and counseling in the Universities of Islam, the Nation's primary and secondary schools, now called Sister Clara Muhammad Schools.

Under Warith Muhammad Muslims are urged to seek guidance from the Qur'an (Koran), Hadith (sayings of the Prophet Muhammad), *khutbas* ("sermons") of Imam Muhammad himself and other imams. Members may receive guidance from the group's weekly newspaper *Muslim Journal,* which contains the following regular columns: "Imam W. Deen Muhammad of Masjid Elijah Muhammad," "A Message of Concern to the American People," "Observations," "Science and Health," "Family Life," "The Holy Qur'an," "Hadith," "Mind Matters," "Your Health from a Dental Point of View" and "Small Business." Also, a growing number of books, records and cassette tapes on religious, theological, psychological, marital, and social matters are available for purchase. Muslim prisoners have access to Muslim chaplains, as well as printed materials. All members may address queries to the editor of the *Muslim Journal* and to Imam Muhammad.

A. MUHAMMAD

BLACK AMERICAN PASTORAL CARE; ISLAMIC CARE AND COUNSELING. *See also* BLACK IDENTITY AND CONSCIOUSNESS; PRISONERS AND PRISON CHAPLAINCY.

BLACK THEOLOGY AND PASTORAL CARE.

Black theology represents the religious dimension of a significant cultural revolution that was forged by black Americans in the mid-sixties as a new development in their struggle for racial justice. Black theology boldly asserts that a racist cultural bias in the Euro-American theological tradition has distorted the true meaning of Christianity. Assuming a prophetic stance, black theology wages an unrelenting battle against the ideological assumptions of ecclesiastical authorities and academic scholars by advocating the identification of the mission of Jesus with the liberation struggles of oppressed peoples in general, and black Americans in particular. In fact, black theology argues that solidarity with the black American struggle is a fundamental requirement of all American Christians desirous of being faithful to Jesus Christ.

1. **Historical Development.** In the midst of the activities of Christian activists in the black church-related Civil Rights Movement of Martin Luther King, Jr., and the events stimulated by the Black Power Movement, the National Committee of Negro Churchmen (N.C.N.C., later called the National Conference of Black Churchmen) published a Christian theological justification for the symbol "black power." During that period blacks found themselves alienated not only from white conservatives but also from their former allies, white liberals. Accordingly, the N.C.N.C. statement launched the first attempt since the Marcus Garvey Movement of the 1920s to separate black Christianity from the theology of the white churches. It strongly affirmed black consciousness and black power as necessary elements in the quest for liberation.

The publication of James H. Cone's book, *Black Power and Black Theology* in 1969 marked the first major explication of a black theology. As the progenitor of this new movement, Cone describes his own work as an attempt to develop a systematic explanation of the contents of a gospel of liberation that will be a motivational force and a Christian justification for the liberation struggle against racism. In other words, black theology contends that the Bible must be read in light of the struggles of oppressed black Americans whose social condition establishes for them a place of hermeneutical privilege in grasping the will of God.

Black theology is integrally related to black liberation politics. Its subject matter is the God of the black American experience; i.e., the One in whom black Americans have trusted throughout the period of slavery up to the present time. This identification of the "Jesus of the black experience" with the "Jesus of Scripture" is the principal way whereby Cone establishes common ground between the social realities of the black American experience and the claims of the NT record. But, (according to many) herein lies black theology's chief vulnerability, namely, a tendency to' identify political ideology with Christian theology. Not surprisingly, some of its strongest critics have been sympathetic theologians trying to persuade Cone to avoid the idolatry implicit in every cultural theology.

In his book, *God of the Oppressed*, Cone responds to his critics by drawing upon the resources of the sociology of knowledge in order to show the necessary relationship between the theologian's social situation and his or her theological enterprise. Further, he argues that the identification of God with the particularity of oppressed black Americans implies no exclusive election of blacks by God but, rather, represents a specific instance expressive of God's solidarity with all oppressed peoples. In fact, Cone and other black theologians appeal to the biblical claim of God's identification with the Israelite struggle for liberation as a primary ground for demonstrating the relationship between the social condition of oppressed peoples and the activity of God.

Cone argues further that God's solidarity with the black struggle for racial justice in the twentieth century is similar to his solidarity with the Israelites in effecting their deliverance from slavery. In short, black theology contends that it is consonant with the biblical understanding that God's activity in history is always seen in the liberation struggles of oppressed peoples. In this respect, black theology has made a creative contribution to theological inquiry by tracing the bias within the Bible (*viz.*, God's identification with the oppressed) thereby clarifying a theological symbol that has been obscured by the Euro-American theological tradition.

Clearly, black theology represents a revisionist method in theological scholarship that is typified by a move away from the universal realm of absolute ideation as the starting point for the theological task to the historical context of concrete reality. Hence, like all liberation theologies, black theology does not seek theological solutions for theoretical problems but, rather, theological understandings that are relative to the liberating desires and activities of oppressed peoples. Nevertheless, black theology is dogmatic and like every form of dogmatism it claims possession of absolute truth, aims at its systematization and assumes for itself an authoritative posture on all normative matters of thought and practice. The general ambivalence of the black churches to the Black Theology Movement is caused in large part by the latter's dogmatic orientation.

Black theology may be described best as radical social criticism for three reasons: (a) its wholesale condemnation of Euro-American theology's uncritical appropriation of the prevailing racist values implicit in its cultural milieu; (b) its methodological focus on praxis (i.e., the liberation struggle) as both a descriptive and normative principle: descriptive in its portrayal of the nature of human experience with which the inquiry begins, and normative in both its theological identification with Jesus the Liberator as well as its moral imperative for political action; (c) its revolutionary aim to provide theological grounds for a liberating praxis that aims at effecting radical change in all societal structures of racial oppression.

2. **The Implications of Black Theology for Pastoral Care.** The novelty of black theology's inductive approach to theological inquiry lies in its explicit affirmation of the experiences of oppressed peoples as the starting point for an understanding of God's activity in the world. This distinctive approach has constituted a radical challenge to an older style of scholarship that was interested primarily in measuring the impact of oppression on the oppressed, implying thereby that the latter were merely victims of external forces acting on them. Consequently, that older form of scholarship failed to discern those self-initiating and constructive activities of oppressed peoples.

In fact, it assumed that the oppressed were incapable of exercising any agency whatsoever. Hence, the results of such scholarship were predictable: i.e., pervasive levels of pathological disorder permeating the social, psychological, political and cultural dimensions of life among the oppressed. In fact, for a long while, it was not uncommon for scholars in all fields (black and white alike) to view the thought and practices of black religion as aberrations of their white counterparts.

The emergence of black theology has afforded blacks a perspective with which they might make a distinctive methodological contribution to all areas of religious scholarship including that of pastoral care. Since black theology represents the religious dimension of a cultural revolution among black Americans, all areas of the humanities and the social sciences have felt its impact to some degree. Hence, most recent research in the area of black American studies assumes a high measure of cognitive, moral, religious, social and political agency on the part of oppressed blacks throughout their history: agency that has enabled them (then and now) to gain significant levels of transcendence over the crippling conditions of their lives.

Black theology's efforts in identifying the liberating activity of blacks with the acts of God have hastened the demise of all feelings of racial inferiority that had plagued blacks for so many generations. Black theology has given renewed impetus to such principles as racial self-respect, self-reliance, self-initiative, self-determination and self-fulfillment; principles that formerly relied on various pragmatic arguments for their justification are now grounded theologically.

For its continuing enlightenment, however, black theology must rely on the findings of all the areas of study including the resources provided by the field of pastoral care. Further research on the psychology of oppressed peoples both as victims and as agents of liberation can help black theology in its reflections. Further, the psychology implied by black theology needs clarification and critical evaluation.

Finally, black theology's focus on the self-initiating activities of the black oppressed must be brought into relationship with the immense suffering that results from the conditions of oppression. Both the capacity to transcend those conditions and the capacity to undergo them represent two poles of the black experience that must not be separated from each other. Black theology's tendency to focus on the former and pastoral care's tendency to concentrate on the latter must be challenged by the insights of each such that both might strive for a more wholistic approach to the black American experience.

Bibliography. J. H. Cone, *Black Power and Black Theology* (1969); *God of the Oppressed* (1975). V. L. Lattimore, "The Positive Contribution of Black Cultural Values to Pastoral Counseling," *J. of Pastoral Care,* 36 (1982), 105–117. G. S. Wilmore and J. H. Cone, eds., *Black Theology: A Documentary History, 1966–1979* (1979).

P.J. PARIS

BLACK AMERICAN PASTORAL CARE. *See also* CONSCIOUSNESS RAISING; CULTURAL AND ETHNIC FACTORS; EXPLOITATION/OPPRESSION; PASTORAL THEOLOGY, PROTESTANT; PROPHETIC/PASTORAL TENSION IN MINISTRY; RACISM; SOCIAL JUSTICE ISSUES. *Compare* FEMINIST *or* LIBERATION THEOLOGY AND PASTORAL CARE; SOCIOLOGY OF RELIGIOUS AND PASTORAL CARE.

BLAME/BLAMING. *See* ANGER; GUILT; MORAL BEHAVIOR AND RELIGION; RIGHTEOUSNESS/BEING RIGHT.

BLANTON, SMILEY (1882–1966). American psychiatrist. Blanton's chief contribution to pastoral care and counseling was his service as director of the American Foundation of Religion and Psychiatry, which was affiliated with the Marble Collegiate Church in New York City. Having long wished to create a training center for clergy, he joined with Norman Vincent Peale in 1937 to establish a psychiatric clinic as a free service of the church, and with the aid of Frederick Kuether, a minister of the Evangelical and Reformed Church, he and Peale expanded the clinic in 1953 into a foundation that offered psychiatric services and Clinical Pastoral Education (CPE).

Though he was associated by the public with Peale's ideas about positive thinking, Blanton was a Freudian therapist who had studied with Freud and been psychoanalyzed by him in Vienna. A graduate of Vanderbilt University and Cornell Medical School, he studied at the Royal College of Physicians and Surgeons in London and completed a residency in psychiatry under Adolph Meyer at Johns Hopkins before serving as a psychiatrist for the U.S. Army during World War I. After teaching speech and mental hygiene for ten years at the University of Wisconsin, he organized the Minneapolis Child Guidance Clinic and taught psychiatry at the University of Minnesota Medical School. He was forty-seven when he went to Vienna to study with Freud, in search of therapeutic aids for stutterers. He was on the faculty at Cornell when Peale sought his guidance about counseling. They subsequently published *Faith Is the Answer* (1940), the book that helped to launch Peale's public career. Blanton's *Love or Perish* reflected his distinctive merging of suggestive therapy and Freudian analytic ideas.

E. B. HOLIFIELD

PASTORAL CARE MOVEMENT; RELIGION AND HEALTH MOVEMENT.

BLENDED FAMILIES. *See* STEPFAMILIES.

BLESSING AND BENEDICTION. Forms or acts which, usually through the spoken word, convey power to persons in the name of God or as an expression of confidence in one person by another. The term *benediction* refers to a prayer for or an affirmation of the reality of a blessing.

For pastoral care the roots of both words are to be found in the OT and the NT. In the OT community there were frequent pronouncements of blessing and requests for blessing upon the community as well as specific individuals and events that would affect the Israelites. Specific blessing could only be pronounced by persons holding appropriate authority, such as kings, priests, and prophets. But other forms existed as well, such as a father's blessing given to a son. In the NT church the power to bless continued to reside with appropriate authorities. For example, the Aaronic blessing was reserved for the priesthood.

Magical thinking has surrounded blessing and benediction in the tradition as well as in the present day. The most helpful way to distinguish the magical from the more strictly religious is to look for the perceived source of the power. If the power is viewed as originating with the person speaking and claimed to work specifically and /or exclusively at the bidding of said person, then the thinking is magical. In religious blessing the person is seen as servant, has no control and can make no promises other than as an expression of faith. The power rests in the Deity and shows itself at the will of the Deity through any means.

In pastoral situations there are frequent occasions in which blessing is requested explicitly or implicitly. The spoken word, the laying on of hands, and special prayers can be requested out of a complex variety of motivation and needs. The sensitive pastor would do well to listen and explore carefully before complying with such requests. A blessing "granted" where magical thinking is dominant can foster already deep feelings of low self-worth and, indeed, engender anger and hostility when the "promise" is not kept. No doubt, all of us harbor a secret wish for magic, but a request for blessing out of a felt sense of need for assurance of God's power and presence can be deeply moving and of genuine help. In this "religious" observance of blessing, the one requesting and the one pronouncing blessing become co-participants in the acknowledgment of God's presence in the past and the assurance to one another that the promise of that presence can still be trusted. At that point, the two can "bless God" in the tradition of Gen. 14:19–20 as a form of thanksgiving.

The forms of blessing and benediction are many, including: the traditional benediction at the close of worship, pronouncement of blessing at a marriage, the Roman Catholic sacrament blessing the sick, the laying on of hands, a hand on the forehead during prayer. Forms can be both formal and informal. Their intention is to convey the promise of strength to be found, not in the one who speaks, but in the God for whom that word is being spoken.

Bibliography. M. Madden, *The Power to Bless* (1970). P. W. Pruyser, "The Master Hand: Psychological Notes on Pastoral Blessing" in W. B. Oglesby, Jr., *The New Shape of Pastoral Theology* (1969).

W. V. ARNOLD

RELIGIOUS LANGUAGE AND SYMBOLISM; RITUAL AND PASTORAL CARE; SIGN OF THE CROSS. *See also* AUTHORITY, PASTORAL; SYMBOLISM/SYMBOLIZING; WORSHIP AND CELEBRATION. *Compare* ANOINTING OF THE SICK; BAPTISM AND CONFIRMATION; MAGICAL THINKING; MATRIMONY, SACRAMENT OF.

BLINDNESS. *See* HANDICAP AND DISABILITY; LOSS OF FUNCTION.

BLOOD PRESSURE. *See* BIOFEEDBACK; HEALTH AND ILLNESS; HEART PATIENT; STRESS.

BLUMHARDT, JOHANN CHRISTOPH (1805–1880). A German pastor in the Black Forest. In 1841 he was called to the sickbed of a young girl, Gottliebin Dittus, who had been diagnosed by her doctor as being possessed by a demon. (A little later similar symptoms, such as convulsions, bleedings, and serious self-injuries, were described as "hysteria" in medical literature.) Blumhardt took care of Gottliebin for two years during the course of which he enabled the patient to describe her strong inner conflict symbolically and verbally as a fight between light and darkness. This ended with the cry "Jesus is victor" and led to her complete liberation from all demonic offenses. Later almost all the parishioners of Möttlingen presented themselves for the pastor's personal counseling to confess their sins and receive absolution. In the course of Blumhardt's pastoral encouragement, many also experienced the healing of physical diseases, which led to an enormous rush of people to him from the villages around. With the help of Gottliebin and other parishioners he organized a biblically oriented parish life based on group conversations. In 1852 he built a house-church in Bad Boll from which he launched unique pastoral activities in spoken and written word. In the center of his preaching was the hope of a new effusion of the Holy Ghost and a renewal of Christianity.

His lifework consisted mainly of "living human documents," of people who through his pastoral care experienced the resolution of inner conflicts, which also had the effect of healing physical diseases. A wide variety of religious schools of thought ranging from religious socialism to Pietism and from dialectical theology as far as psychosomatic medicine claimed Blumhardt as one of their number. The latter school appreciated his "wholistic view" by which he applied his pastoral care to the very center of the personality. Others regarded him as a forerunner of modern psychotherapy because of his preoccupation with the structure of dialogue.

J. SCHARFENBERG

FAITH HEALING.

BODY. The material, visible aspect of the individual self as person. Although the body is sometimes disparaged in dualistic strains in Western and Eastern traditions, the preponderance of both traditions is for a wholistic view of human nature in which the body is regarded as an essential and valued part of personality.

1. **Cultural Background.** Biblical thought was fundamentally wholistic. The ancient Hebrews did not have a particular word for body; *nephesh* was used to refer to the self as a whole, implying a unity between the material and the immaterial, i.e. between "body" and "soul." This wholism can also be seen in the NT use of *sōma* to refer to the comprehensive unity of the self-as-person.

Greek thought ranged from glorification of the body for its strength and beauty to depreciation of the body as the prison house of the soul. The dualism reflected in this latter (Platonic) view is also found in the Christian scriptures, e.g., Mt. 10:28 and in Paul's use of *sarx* (flesh) and *sōma* (body) to contrast with *psyche* (soul) and *pneuma* (breath, spirit). Nevertheless it is clear that even for Paul human life was inconceivable apart from the body (II Cor. 5:1f; cf. I Cor. 15:35-39). And the NT as a whole clearly emphasizes the concreteness of God's care and salvation of humankind through the healing ministry of Jesus and the early church, and through the proclamation of Christian hope as resurrection of the body, as distinguished from a doctrine of the soul's inherent immortality.

Greek dualism became more pronounced, however, in the early centuries of Christian history as devout Christians sought to escape the sinfulness and corruption of the world through ascetic subjugation of bodily needs and appetites. The ascetics (from *askeo*, "to exercise," used of athletic, and subsequently moral, self-discipline) of the early church became the religious of the Middle Ages.

2. Theological Understanding. The biblical theological basis for affirmation of the body as essential to our humanity may be seen in four doctrines.

a. Creation. The Creator not only endowed the creature from the beginning with the "breath of life" but intimately "formed man of the dust of the ground" (Gen. 2:7).

b. Incarnation. He who is "in the form of God" (Phil. 2:6) is "born of a woman" (Gal. 4:4) and so partakes of our fleshly nature.

c. Salvation. As sinners it is true that human beings experience their bodily existence as drawing them away from God. The "lust of the flesh and the lust of the eyes and the pride of life, is not of the Father" (I Jn. 2:16). Witness also Paul's cry, "Who will deliver me from this body of death?" (Rom. 7:24). This is not to say, however, that the body is intrinsically evil; rather it is the instrument of sinfulness. It is from this perspective that Paul refers to the body as the "body of sin," equivalent to the "old self" which has been crucified with Christ (Rom. 6:6).

Final deliverance from "this body of sin and death" is not escape from the body, as evil *per se*, into some spiritual realm; it is rather resurrection in a new body. Having been united to Christ in baptism which is a washing of the body (Gal. 3:27), and having received Christ's Spirit who dwells in our body as in a temple (I Cor. 6:19), Christians are enjoined "to present [their] bodies as a living sacrifice, holy and acceptable to God" (Rom. 12:1) in the assurance that "he who raised Christ Jesus from the dead will give life to your mortal bodies also through his Spirit who dwells in you" (Rom. 8:11). The Christian looks forward not to redemption *from* the body but redemption *of* the body (Rom. 8:23).

Meanwhile, transformed by this hope of the resurrection, the Christian seeks to live a responsible life in the body from day to day. Paul, who had suffered much as a Christian, refers to the Christian life as "carrying in the body the death of Jesus so that the life of Jesus also may be manifested in our bodies" (II Cor. 4:10). Thus the Christian seeks to honor Christ in his or her body whether by life or by death (Phil. 1:20), knowing that all shall give account in the day of final reckoning for the deeds done in the body (II Cor. 5:10).

d. The church. In the NT there is a rich figurative use made of the concept of "the body" to interpret the corporate life of the Christian. Surely one of the most suggestive of all the images of the church is that of the body of Christ. "For as in one body we have many members, and all members do not have the same function, so we, though many, are one body in Christ, and individually members one of another" (Rom. 12:4-5). In I Cor. 12:14f. Paul uses the figure of the church as Christ's body to admonish his readers to a life of unity and mutual service in the Spirit. This metaphor assumes a literal understanding of body as the sphere of life and service to God and neighbor.

The head of the body, the church, is Jesus Christ (Col. 1:18). To speak of Christ as the head of the body is to speak of the preeminence which is his. This preeminence is due not only to his bodily resurrection as the first fruits of those who sleep, but also to his bodily suffering and death for the salvation of humankind. Christ's atoning death, the supreme revelation of the divine love, consists in a bodily act of sacrifice. While burnt offerings and sin offerings can give God no final satisfaction, yet God has prepared for Christ a body and "we have been sanctified through the offering of the body of Jesus Christ once for all" (Heb. 10:10). This atoning event of the death which Christ suffered for our redemption was and is memorialized in the eucharistic meal, the central act of worship in the ancient church. When Christians approach this table they must remember, according to Paul, that to eat and drink in an unworthy manner profanes the body and blood of the Lord. Indeed, any who eats and drinks "without discerning the body eats and drinks judgment upon himself" (I Cor. 11:29).

3. Pastoral Implications. Perhaps the most far-reaching implication of the Christian view of the body for pastoral care is in the realization that, fundamentally, the Bible and contemporary theology look upon the person wholistically. Hence pastoral care is not a "cure of souls" in a disembodied, falsely "spiritualized" sense. It is concrete care of the whole person—the feeding of the hungry, clothing of the naked, and ministry to the sick, which tie pastoral care closely to medical and other social service ministries. At the same time a wholistic approach to pastoral care will be sensitive to the relationship between emotional life and the biological aspects of the person. It will understand the impact of one's bodily condition upon psychological identity and self-esteem (e.g. in the aging process, disfigurement, or loss of function). And it will understand the body and its uses as a form of communication with the self, with others, and with God, e.g. through "body language" and somatically expressed symptoms of psychological or spiritual disorder. Similarly it will be alert to the subtle ways in which moral, emotional, and spiritual qualities of the person and of personal relationships impact bodily life and functioning.

In particular, wholistic pastoral care will affirm human sexuality and its responsible expression. According to the Christian vision, the sexual polarity of male and female is the way in which our humanity is given us by the Creator. Hence, we are always related to one another bodily and sexually. Sexuality is in fact to be enjoyed and affirmed as a central part of one's identity. Such affirmation is distinguished from the performance of sexual acts as such, which comprise only one aspect or expression of sexuality (Nelson). Paul, for example, sees in the sexual union of the wife and husband as "one flesh" (*sarka mian*) an analogy to the oneness of Christ and the Church (Eph. 5:31-32). Therefore, sexual acts are not to be engaged in casually, as promoted by the modern "sexual revolution." Sexual acts unite two bodies, i.e. whole persons, in a unique and spiritual way. In I Cor. 6:12-20 Paul condemns immorality as improper because the body is a temple of the Holy Spirit, intended to glorify God.

Bibliography. M. R. Miles, *Augustine on the Body* (1979). J. Nelson, *Embodiment: An Approach to Sexuality and Christian Theology* (1978). J. A. T. Robinson, *The Body: A Study in Pauline Theology* (1952). T. F. Tracy, *God, Action, and Embodiment* (1984).

P. JEWETT

PERSON; PERSONALITY, BIOLOGICAL DIMENSIONS OF. *See also* ASCETICAL PRACTICES; CREATION; ESCHATOLOGY; SALVATION, HEALING, AND HEALTH; INCARNATIONAL PASTORAL CARE; MIND-BODY RELATIONSHIP; PHYSICAL FITNESS DISCIPLINES; PSYCHOSOMATIC ILLNESS; SEXUAL ISSUES IN PASTORAL CARE; SEXUALITY; WHOLISTIC HEALTH CARE.

BODY IMAGE. Refers to the body as a psychological experience and centers primarily on a person's feelings and attitudes toward his or her body. It results from the way a person (1) apprehends sensations from the body itself and through the body from the outside world, (2) valuates, organizes, and integrates these sensory prehensions in the self, and (3) projects these organized prehensions back onto the body.

Body image is a basic building block in the experience of selfhood. The emerging sense of self is first a sense of a "bodily me" — an awareness of hunger, discomfort, pleasure, and visceral sensations arising within the infant. As the self develops, the infant begins to distinguish between what is inside the skin and what is outside. The child thus delineates his or her own body and sets it off from the rest of the world. A person's self image grows to include much more than a simple bodily concept; yet there remains a close causal relationship between the feeling about one's body and one's sense of self.

Fisher suggests the body is so closely related to self that the manner in which it is experienced is mirrored in the self to an unusual degree. In persons who perceive their bodies with a definite form and firmness, there appears to be a strong sense of self. These persons are effective in dealing and communicating with people. Their behavior appears independent and self-directed. For persons who perceive their body boundary as indefinite and vague, there appears to be a weak sense of self — a feeling of being open, unprotected, and vulnerable to the outside world. There is a need to create artificial structures in the outside world to compensate for lost or unreliable body boundaries. Attractive clothing, uniforms, heavy use of cosmetics and perfume may be ways of trying to construct defensible body boundaries.

The way persons in the church feel about and perceive their bodies has suffered to the extent to which the Christian theological tradition has uncritically relied on Platonic and Neoplatonic metaphysics. This metaphysic has tended towards a dualism which elevates spirit and soul above the body. Body is depreciated to the level of *sarx* — evil, corruptible, finite flesh — which is in opposition to spirit. In the wake of this dualism, a person may try to deny bodily sensations or may project on the body an image of disgust or unacceptability. In either case, the self will suffer from the label and/or will try to disassociate itself from the body. This leads to a sense of depersonaliza-tion — a sense that the person's body is strange, alien, not a part of one's self identity. In extreme cases, the person becomes cut off from the body and the contact with reality which the body mediates and psychosis results.

To the extent to which the Hebrew understanding of *basar* or the Greek understanding of *sōma* have prevailed in the theological understanding of the body, there has been a more wholistic concept of personality involving both self and body as a unity. Thus, how a person feels about body image cannot be separated from feelings about oneself.

The doctrines of the incarnation of Christ, the resurrection of the body, and the Christian community as the "Body of Christ" attest to the indivisibility of the personality and the importance of the body and one's experience of it in fostering a healthy sense of self. These doctrines provide helpful pastoral tools by pointing to the significance of body consciousness in dealing with personality problems and suggesting a corporate form of definiteness, constancy, and firmness in body boundaries which transcends one's physical, fleshly existence.

Bibliography. S. Fisher and S. Cleveland, *Body Image and Personality* 2d rev. ed. (1968). S. Fisher, *Body Consciousness: You Are What You Feel* (1973). J. A. T. Robinson, *The Body: A Study in Pauline Theology* (1952).

C. M. MENDENHALL, III

PERSONAL, CONCEPT OF; SELF CONCEPT. *See also* HANDICAP AND DISABILITY; LOSS OF FUNCTION; OBESITY; SICK, PASTORAL CARE OF. *Compare* PHYSICAL FITNESS DISCIPLINES; SOMATIZING; SOMATOTYPE.

BODY LANGUAGE. Physical movements, postures or gestures that express human feelings, attitudes, or relationship states. While the human face is capable of an immense range of expressions and communications, the entire human body also participates in the communicative process through gestures, postures, and movements that range from obvious, stereotyped patterns to extremely subtle expressions of thought and feeling.

Body language is the primary form of nonverbal communication and is employed by human beings nearly all of the time, consciously and unconsciously. However, since most body language is unconsciously generated, it is often regarded as significantly (if unintentionally) revealing of the person. In fact it is commonly regarded as a direct communication of the unconscious mind and thus a *more* candid and truthful form of communication than verbal language, which is generally calculated to express what we believe our hearers want or ought to hear.

Body language appears to have its own unique vocabulary within a particular culture, just as verbal language has. A typical example in Western culture is the man who sits stiffly in his chair, arms folded tightly, jaws set, refusing to speak freely, thus communicating defensiveness, fear, and hostility (or anger). While such instances are easily recognized, more subtle and precise "vocabularies" of body language also develop, as recent research in the body-language science of "kinesics" has shown (Lowen, 1967, 1971).

Learning to read body language well is crucially important for pastoral care and counseling because it broadens and deepens communication, opening more significant forms of relationship, especially when body language contradicts verbal language. A parishioner, for example, may protest verbally that she feels no ill will toward another parishioner, but a shifting of the eyes, a nervous adjusting of the feet, and a drawn face, together with the impression of tension and inappropriate force and pitch in the voice combine to communicate deeper feelings of anger, hostility, envy, or alienation. However, body language vocabularies vary by culture and subculture and to some extent from person to person, and always require a degree of subjective interpretation. Therefore it is important not to draw simplistic or stereotyped conclusions from body language alone, apart from a sensitive reading of the entire picture of verbal and nonverbal expression (including patterns of other nonverbal behavior) interpreted in cultural context.

Pastors also need to be attentive to their own body language in both public and private acts of ministry. While counselees or parishioners may not be consciously focused on the pastor's body language, one can be sure that a subliminal awareness of it enters significantly into the total experience of communication and ministry.

Bibliography. J. A. DeVito, *Communication* (1976). A. Lowen, *The Betrayal of the Body* (1967) and *The Language of the Body* (1971). R. S. Ross, *Persuasion: Communication and Interpersonal Relations* (1974).

J. H. ELLENS

COMMUNICATION. *Compare* BODY IMAGE; SYMBOLIC DIMENSIONS OF PASTORAL CARE RELATIONSHIPS; SYMBOLISM/SYMBOLIZING.

BODY OF CHRIST. *See* ECCLESIOLOGY.

BODY THERAPIES. Psychotherapeutic approaches which emphasize personality change and development by focusing attention and work on the physical body. Body-oriented psychotherapies attempt to integrate a person's mind, body, and emotions through various breathing techniques and, in many cases, physical movement, exercise, and stress.

The main foundation for body psychotherapies in Western culture comes from the work of Wilhelm Reich, a psychoanalytically oriented psychiatrist who studied with Sigmund Freud in the early 1920s as a member of Freud's "Viennese inner circle." Reich held that character is a more basic problem than neurosis. He felt that the way persons posture their bodies and carry tension in their bodies is indicative of their intra- and interpsychic conflicts. He believed that people literally develop "character armor" or chronic muscular tension to protect themselves from feeling, remembering, and seeing crucial and painful emotional memories and realizations. This armor consequently blocks one from being fully alive, aware, and happy in the present moment. Therapeutically, Reich believed that if character armor is first attended to, neurotic traits are easier to analyze and work through.

Reich believed that his therapy enabled individuals, like infants, to become "organismically self-regulating" and freed from unnecessary inhibition. This is also the fundamental principle of Gestalt therapy as developed by Frederick (Fritz) Perls, a student and patient of Reich's. The most direct descendants of Reich are called "medical

organamists," the principle disciple being Ellsworth-Baker. Another prominent offshoot of Reichian theory is Alexander Lowen's "bioenergetics."

Other forms of body work are occasionally combined with Reichian and neo-Reichian techniques. "Rolfing" involves a systematic stretching of the fascia to correct the alignment of the body. Structural patterning is an offshoot of this approach. It involves learning correct ways to stand, sit, and move. The Alexander technique and Feldenkrais method are two other body systems; both entail rather painless and subtle adjustments of the body that occasionally result in rapid personality changes.

All of these systems are Western forms of body psychotherapy. Eastern methods of body work were developed a thousand or more years ago, including Tai Chi and Yoga. These approaches have an added dimension in that they are potential paths for attaining higher and/or altered states of consciousness, while Western body therapies only concern themselves with personality development and the modification of character neuroses.

Bibliography. A. Lowen, *Bioenergetics* (1975); *The Language of the Body* (1958). F. S. Perls, *Gestalt Therapy* (1951). W. Reich, *Character Analysis* (1949). I. P. Rolf, *Rolfing: The Integration of Human Structures* (1977).

D. L. STOLTZFUS

POPULAR THERAPEUTIC MOVEMENTS AND PSYCHOLOGIES; PSYCHOTHERAPY. *Compare* PHYSICAL FITNESS DISCIPLINES. *Biography:* PERLS; REICH.

BOISEN, ANTON (1876–1965). Founder of clinical pastoral training for ministers and theological students. After graduating from Union Theological Seminary, Boisen served as a Presbyterian minister in rural parishes, a member of the YMCA Expeditionary Force, and supervisor of the rural survey of the Interchurch World Movement, before becoming the chaplain at Worcester State Hospital in Massachusetts and Elgin State Hospital in Illinois. During those years, he also earned a master's degree at Harvard and studied under Macfie Campbell at the Boston Psychopathic Hospital. He lectured for two years at the Boston University School of Theology and for fifteen years at Chicago Theological Seminary.

Boisen is revered as the chief founder of Clinical Pastoral Education (CPE) — a program of professional training through the long-term supervised encounter of ministers and theological students with men and women in crises in hospitals, prisons, and social agencies. After conversations with Richard Cabot, with whom he had studied social ethics at Harvard and from whom he learned the value of the first-hand study of "cases," he established the first clinical group in 1925 at Worcester State Hospital. In 1930, he and Cabot joined with others in the formation of the Council for the Clinical Training of Theological Students.

In his clinical teaching, Boisen hoped to lead students toward deeper theological insight by teaching them to view the patients in the mental hospital as "living human documents" whose pain and healing could illuminate the nature of religious experience. In his book *The Exploration of the Inner World* (1936), he argued that emotional collapse is a chaotic encounter with God that could lead either to a new integration of the personality or to a fall into total inner disarray. He thought that certain forms of mental illness manifested the existence of a "power that makes for health" immanent within the purposive movement of the natural order. His autobiography, *Out of the Depths* (1960), revealed with scrupulous honesty his attempt to interpret and learn from his own episodes of mental illness.

A student of George Albert Coe, Boisen was concerned with what he called "the basic psychology of religion," and he thought that the mental hospital offered a setting in which to study, at firsthand, "the problem of sin and salvation." His interest in turbulence and chaos within the personality deeply informed the methods and presuppositions of the Council for Clinical Training. Coe's teaching also directed Boisen's attention to the social nature of religion, and he eventually adopted Josiah Royce's notion of loyalty, which he interpreted with the aid of George Herbert Mead's descriptions of the way we form our conscience by internalizing social standards. Boisen believed that mental illness exposed the failure to grow into higher social loyalties, as well as the effort to transcend that failure. He found the insights of Freud to be useful but excessively narrow; he distrusted the effort to locate the source of mental illness primarily in childhood experiences, and he disliked any use of psychological theory that minimized the importance of ethical ideals. He also felt uneasy when the clinical traditions seemed to turn their attention to the psychological dynamics and therapeutic needs of the students themselves, insofar as that detracted from the primary task of achieving greater theological understanding.

Boisen knew Elwood Worcester at the Emmanuel Church in Boston, and his work represented in part a point of continuity with the older Emmanuel Movement. But it was the depth and intensity of his own personality, as well as the force of his ideas, that ensured his profound influence on the Clinical Pastoral Education Movement. His emphasis on the "living human document" has periodically reappeared as a guiding theme for clinical supervisors and Protestant pastoral theologians.

E. B. HOLIFIELD

HISTORY OF PROTESTANT PASTORAL CARE (United States); PASTORAL CARE MOVEMENT. *See also* CASE STUDY METHOD. *Compare* PSYCHOLOGY OF RELIGION.

BONDAGE OF THE WILL. *See* FREEDOM AND BONDAGE; WILL/WILLING.

BONDING. *See* COMMUNITY, FELLOWSHIP, AND CARE; MOTHER-INFANT BONDING.

BONE, HARRY. *See* NEW YORK PSYCHOLOGY GROUP.

BONHOEFFER, DIETRICH (1906–45). German Lutheran clergyman. As pastor and seminary lecturer in Berlin, he opposed the Nazi regime from its beginning and signed the Barmen Declaration of 1934. Continual opposition to Hitler led to his arrest in April 1943 and his execution by hanging in April 1945.

In prison Bonhoeffer developed ideas of religionless Christianity, advocating escape from dead forms of the church to inexpressible meaning that is ultimate. All churchly ritual and word, including the behavior and talk of the pastoral counselor, are at best penultimate, through which hopefully the divine Word may be manifest.

R. W. CRAPPS

SECULARIZATION/SECULARISM; SPIRITUALITY (Protestant Tradition).

BONNELL, JOHN SUTHERLAND (1893–   ). Presbyterian pastor and pastoral theologian. As the pastor of the Fifth Avenue Presbyterian Church in New York City, Bonnell proposed that pastors become adept in "pastoral psychiatry," which he defined as a ministry directed to the "healing of the soul." He believed that the goal of pastoral counseling was to bring the parishioner in touch with God and the spiritual resources that flowed from God. Impressed by his father's vocation as a staff member of the Falconwood Hospital on Prince Edward Island, Bonnell familiarized himself with the work of the European therapists, especially Alfred Adler and Karen Horney, and in 1935 began a counseling program at his Fifth Avenue Church. In his *Pastoral Psychiatry* (1938) and other similar works, he drew on the theme of "adjustment" in order to develop a method of counseling that reflected both psychological theory and a Christian theology.

E. B. HOLIFIELD

HISTORY OF PROTESTANT PASTORAL CARE (United States); PASTORAL CARE MOVEMENT.

BOOK OF COMMON PRAYER. *See* ANGLICAN PASTORAL CARE.

BOOK OF MORMON. *See* MORMON CARE AND COUNSELING.

BOOKS. *See* CLASSIC LITERATURE IN CARE AND COUNSELING; LITERATURE, PASTORAL USE OF.

BOOTH, GOTTHARD. *See* NEW YORK PSYCHOLOGY GROUP.

BORDERLINE DISORDER. A much debated diagnostic category that calls attention to the fine line between neurosis and psychosis. Various levels of the disorder respond to stress by regressing to an apparent brink of psychosis without fully entering the psychotic realm. Expressions such as "just before" or "almost" psychotic are apt descriptions for the symptoms manifested in this psychological condition. Consequently, both neurotic and psychotic symptoms are evident without a consistent behavioral pattern. The range of these symptoms may be inconsistent and frequently contradictory.

Early interactions with paternal figures are usually of a "push-pull" nature in which the infant is rewarded for regressive behavior and affection is withdrawn during periods of appropriate behavior. The basic confusion that emerges from such a process is an emotionally vulnerable, lonely, depressed, and angry state of self. While these individuals may have natural talents, they rarely experience pleasure in work or sexual activities. They are frequently self-destructive, often cross addicted, and, at times, suicidal. The capacity for impulse control is low, while manipulative disregard for others is quite high. The ability to empathize or authentically give is stunted.

Anger is a serious problem for the person with this disorder. Unpredictable outbursts of anger are often directed toward people who try to assist these individuals. This type of anger is most obvious when it is directed toward no one in particular and seemingly at the entire world. It is most subtle in messages about chronic boredom and a fundamental sense of longing for something or someone not only missing but non-existent. There is a helpless or faithless expectation that their self-void will be filled. Concurrently there is a persecutory fear.

As a result, persons who suffer from this disorder are marginally equipped for social relationships. Outwardly they may appear to be sociable, even charming, but beneath that surface there is basic mistrust. They tend to have brief, intense superficial contacts wherein there is a pressing or urgent desire for something felt as missing. This condition frequently develops into habitual patterns of clinging helplessness. Consequently, these people tolerate being alone quite poorly. They feel a need to associate with many people and consider themselves as having "close friends." Nevertheless, they cannot appreciate reciprocal care, so such relationships are brief. The conflict over giving and receiving is marred at a primary psychological level. In counseling or psychotherapy sessions these people will describe their social patterns in ways similar to a relationship with a particular parent, usually the mother. These descriptions often reveal a cycle: idealization followed by waves of manipulation, devaluation, and rejection. It is common that this cycle is active during therapy. It is also possible for the client to experience occasional psychotic transferences.

An understanding of the Borderline Disorder is important because of the label's widespread use. Though difficult to treat, people suffering from this malady can make favorable psychological progress. During psychotherapy, however, the counselor must consistently remember that this is an illness of the whole person and the individual's worldview, as well as a deep hunger for faith and a reason for being.

Bibliography. American Psychiatric Association, *Diagnostic and Statistical Manual III* (1980). R. R. Grinker, Sr., B. Werble, R. C. Drye, *The Borderline Syndrome* (1968), pp. 141–62. P. Hartocollis, ed., "Affects in Borderline Disorders," in *Borderline Personality Disorders* (1977), pp. 495–506. H. I. Kaplan and B. J. Sadock, *Modern Synopsis of Comprehensive Textbook of Psychiatry/III* 3d ed., (1981), pp. 487–90. O. F. Kernberg, *Borderline Conditions and Pathological Narcissism* (1975), pp. 24–26, 35–36, 38; also "Contrasting Approaches to the Psychotherapy of Borderline Conditions", J. F. Masterson, ed., in *New Perspectives on Psychotherapy of the Borderline Adult* (1978), pp. 84–89. D. M. Moss, "Narcissism, Empathy and the Fragmentation of Self: An Interview with Heinz Kohut," *Pilgrimage*, 4:1 (1976), 26–43.

D. M. MOSS

NARCISSISM/NARCISSISTIC PERSONALITY; PERSONALITY DISORDERS. *See also* DIAGNOSTIC AND STATISTICAL MANUAL III; EVALUATION AND DIAGNOSIS, PSYCHOLOGICAL; PSYCHOPATHOLOGY, THEORIES OF. *Compare* PSYCHOSIS.

BOREDOM. *See* APATHY AND BOREDOM.

BORN-AGAIN EXPERIENCE. A phrase designating a sudden and intense type of conversion. Among most Protestants the usage has traditionally meant an experience which is highly individualistic, underscoring a personal relationship with God. Since World War II, the phrase has become more particularized, designating a conversion which is crisis in character and to which are attached high levels of emotionality, sometimes including tongue-speaking (glossolalia). The experience often occurs after extreme internal conflict and dissatisfaction with one's lifestyle and appears as immediate surrender to new values and a dramatic change in personal behavior. For the believer the alteration is so dramatic that intellectual explanations are inadequate in light of the sense of being grasped by an outside power.

The usage is drawn from the biblical account of a conversation between Jesus and a Pharisee named Nicodemus (Jn. 3:1–21). In the interview Jesus advises Nicodemus that "unless one is born anew, he cannot see the kingdom of God" and subsequently elaborated that this birth of the Spirit is contrasted with birth of the flesh. Hence some believers have rejected gradual patterns of conversion in favor of a nonrational invasion from above. Some even insist that no conversion occurs unless it conforms to this type.

Emotional aspects of conversion which mark the born-again experience have been discussed by many researchers. In the pioneering book *Varieties of Religious Experience* (1902) William James voiced considerable admiration for religious experiences which were literally bathed in emotion. Those whose experience was "acute fever" could clarify the nature of genuine religion, whereas those whose religion was "dull habit" could tell us little. Although the dogmatic and exclusivistic attitudes of many contemporary born-again Christians would have been abhorrent to James, he insisted that intense emotionality should mark serious commitment. James and other pioneering researchers around the turn of the century observed experience which still bore marks of several great awakenings and frontier revivalism. The conversion they observed was typically dramatic, identified with revival, mourners' bench, and emotional crisis. Reacting against intellectual theorizing which marked the academic community during the late 1800s, James underscored popular forms, insisting that vital religion must incorporate "a passionate affirmation of desire" (1984).

A half century after James, Gordon Allport described a typology of conversion which he discovered among college students of the late 1940s (Allport, pp. 33–4). Conversion might occur as a definite crisis of upheaval and dramatic reorganization (the born-again experience), but more often it was a gradual awakening with no specific or traumatic event being decisive (seventy-one percent of Allport's sample). Allport concluded that our grandparents attended revival meetings and returned home with adolescents "formally converted," whereas his students usually experienced conversion less dramatically. The contemporary emphasis upon being born again may represent an attempt to recover earlier conversion patterns.

Resurgent discussions of born-again experience illustrate the attitudes which religious groups have traditionally expressed toward emotion in religion. Some believers reject emotion as an unpredictable and eccentric guide for religious commitment, while others closely identify emotion and religion. In fact, the elusive character of feeling may encourage the devotee to assume that emotion is the domain of God's work. "I feel that God is leading me to . . ." typically appears in popular religious language often with the tacit assumption that thinking may interfere with the work of the Spirit. This emphasis "is likely to spill over into intense religious practices marked by informal ritual designed to break down inhibition and encourage uncontrolled emotionality" (Crapps, p. 229).

Those who insist on the necessity of being born again sense the importance of emotion in religion. In *The Future of Religion* Freud recognized the emotional tenacity with which people hold to their religion and warned that intellectual erosion of religious emotion is risky. Further, affective commitment gives religious experience warmth and flavor, liveliness and spontaneity. Yet unencumbered emotionality risks depending on a fickle moral guide and indulging desire as the highest good. Without intellectual control, intense commitment easily becomes religious fanaticism.

The born-again experience is a strategic opportunity for pastoral ministry. The task is to conserve a vital balance between the traditional emphasis upon the importance of emotion in religion (as in Friedrich Schleiermacher, Rudolf Otto, and Jonathan Edwards) and upon formal dogma and ritual which protects against rank individualism. The former assures respect for private dimensions of religious experience and the latter maintains contact with historical structures through which God's purposes are known.

Bibliography. G. Allport, *The Individual and His Religion* (1950). R. W. Crapps, *An Introduction to Psychology of Religion* (1986). S. Freud, *The Future of an Illusion* (1928); *The Future of Religion* (1928). W. James, *The Varieties of Religious Experience* (1902); *Essays in Pragmatism* (1984). C. Johnson and H. N. Malony, *Christian Conversion: Biblical and Psychological Perspectives* (1982). G. Silverman and W. B. Oglesby, Jr., "The New Birth Phenomenon," in *Pastoral Psychology*, 31 (1983), 179 – 83.

R. W. CRAPPS

CONVERSION; FAITH/BELIEF; RELIGIOUS EXPERIENCE. *See also* EVANGELICAL PASTORAL CARE; PRAYER; PSYCHOLOGY OF RELIGION (Empirical Studies, Methods, and Problems); REBAPTISM; REPENTANCE AND CONFESSION; SPIRITUALITY (Protestant Tradition); VOWS/VOWING. *Compare* CHARISMATIC EXPERIENCE; ILLUMINATION; MYSTICISM; VISIONS AND VOICES.

BORROMEO, ST. CHARLES (1538–84). Roman Catholic cardinal and archbishop of Milan, Italy. In 1563 Borromeo became a priest and embarked on a strict ascetic lifestyle.

Borromeo's significance is tied in large measure to the Council of Trent (1562–63) where he was instrumental in supporting his superiors' impulse for reform. He is considered a great exemplar of a Tridentine bishop, an embodiment of the council's intents. His personal example and convictions — such as the lofty ideal of a bishop's responsibility, a high degree of pastoral awareness, an intense level of pastoral care, a deep interest in social problems (e.g., the plague of 1576), a zealous promotion of sacramental penance, a particular concern for the moral life of the people of Rome, the founding of educational institutions, solid administration of and effective contributions to the work of the church — are said to have had a greater effect than all council resolutions. His pastoral activities had worldwide effects.

N. F. HAHN

SPIRITUALITY (Roman Catholic Tradition); SACRAMENTAL THEOLOGY AND PASTORAL CARE.

BOSS, MEDARD (1903–). A Swiss born existential psychiatrist and psychotherapist. Boss, initially trained in psychoanalysis, turned away from Freud and Jung and became influenced by the philosophy of Heidegger and the therapy of Binswanger. Boss stressed human freedom and responsibility and argued that psychological problems resulted from abandoning one's freedom. Existence is the process of becoming, and "being in the world" is the process of relating encounters to existence. His understanding of existential therapy and dream analysis are demonstrated in his two most important works, *Psychoanalysis and Daseinanalysis* and *The Analysis of Dreams*. Boss, along with Bingswanger, was instrumental in the early integration of existential and phenomenological philosophy with the techniques of psychoanalysis.

Bibliography. M. Boss, *The Analysis of Dreams*, (1958); *Psychoanalysis and Daseinanalysis*, (1963).

S. C. WILLIS

EXISTENTIAL PSYCHOLOGY AND PSYCHOTHERAPY.

BOSTON PERSONALISM. *See* PERSONALISM AND PASTORAL CARE.

BOUNDARY THEORY. *See* FAMILY THEORY AND THERAPY.

BRAIN DAMAGE. *See* ORGANIC MENTAL DISORDER AND ORGANIC BRAIN SYNDROME; PERSONALITY, BIOLOGICAL DIMENSIONS OF. *See also* BRAIN RESEARCH.

BRAIN DEATH. *See* DEATH, BIOMEDICAL DEFINITIONS.

BRAIN DISORDERS. *See* EPILEPSY; NEUROLOGIC ILLNESSES; ORGANIC MENTAL DISORDER AND ORGANIC BRAIN SYNDROME. *See also* BRAIN RESEARCH; PERSONALITY, BIOLOGICAL DIMENSIONS OF.

BRAIN RESEARCH. The scientific study of the structure (anatomy), function (physiology), and diseases (pathology) of the central nervous systems of humans and animals. Participating in this study are individuals in the disciplines of neurophysiology, neuroanatomy, microbiology, histology, biochemistry, pharmacology, endocrinology, physiological psychology, neuropsychology, and the clinical fields of neurology and psychiatry.

The brain is studied at many levels, from the most microscopic study of the membrane of the neuron, to the most macroscopic study of the effects of particular brain damage on behavior. The following areas of current brain research are chosen to represent these various levels of investigation.

1. **Neurotransmitters.** Neurotransmitters are the chemical messages "squirted" across the microscopic junction between neurons called the synapse. Particular brain systems can, to some degree, be separated on the basis of their characteristic neurotransmitter. Different psychoactive drugs have their particular effects due to their ability to affect specific neurotransmitter systems. Recent research into the mechanism of the action of morphine led to the discovery of endorphines (endogeneous morphines), which have the property of affecting certain neural systems (e.g., those involved in pain) like a transmitter substance, but which may be released into the blood stream and thus have effects at a distance from the cells that produce the endorphine. Further research has led to the discovery of numerous other neuroactive substances (neuropeptides), some of which were previously known to be hormones. These hormone-neurotransmitters act as transmitters for local neural information flow as well as hormones with effects at some distance. Thus, there has been a blurring of the distinction between hormones and neurotransmitters. Major advances in neuropharmacology are made by identifying and learning to synthesize new neurotransmitter substances.

2. **Brain Transplantation.** Although the concept of transplanting an entire brain is still a subject for science fiction, there has been recent success in transplanting small amounts of neural tissue from one brain to another. Under certain circumstances these transplants survive and begin to form normal neural connections with the host tissue. A promising application of this research is the treatment of diseases of the nervous system which result in deficiencies in various hormones or neurotransmitters, such as dopamine deficiency in Parkinson's disease. Transplanted cells may be capable of providing a constant and normal source of deficient neurochemicals.

3. **Development of the Nervous System.** In the embryonic development of an organism most structures grow by local cell differentiation. However, neurons often must send their axons accurately to very distant parts of the body where they must synapse in the correct way on specific other cells. One of the challenging tasks of brain research is determining how the nervous system becomes correctly wired. How do the axons of neurons reach their destination and form the appropriate synaptic connections? What is the role of genetic and biological factors, and what roles do environmental influences (i.e., experience and learning) play in this process?

There is considerably more involved in nervous system development than random growth and cell contact, with *post hoc* functional differentiation. Central nervous system neurons have very specific pathways of growth and target cells. They grow as if they "know" exactly where they are going and what sort of a "person" (but not exactly who) they will meet when they arrive. The best guess is that the beacon for directional growth and synaptic connection is chemical ("nerve growth factor"). Attempts to confuse cells by changing their point of origin of growth or altering their experiential relationship to the outside world have no effect on their direction of growth and location of synapse. They still manage to find their specific targets. Experience and learning, however, play some part in determining the functional characteristics of sensory neurons, but only if the experience occurs within certain critical periods of development. However, cortical neurons, in areas of higher mental function, can apparently be induced to grow and form new synapses by learning and enriched experience at nearly any age.

4. **Information Processing in Sensory Systems.** The use of electrical recording of the activity of single neurons has been particularly productive in learning how sensory information is coded, recoded, and recognized at various levels of the sensory systems. Persisting in this research is the concept of cells whose input and output characteristics qualify them as "detectors" of particular sensory properties. In the case of vision, information processing begins with brain cells sensitive to specific small spots of light or dark in the field of vision. At higher levels of the brain's visual processing system, cells respond maximally to increasingly complex properties of visual information, such as edges or corners at specific angles, still in a small part of the visual field. At the highest levels of processing, cells respond to ("detect") meaningful aspects of visual information, such as facial features, specific body parts, and particular classes of objects, regardless of where in the field of view the object occurs. Thus, sensory information processing in the brain progresses in a manner that supports the psychological concept of a progression from sensation to perception. This "progression," however, may not be serial in time, but occur to some degree in parallel, higher and lower areas working simultaneously on the same information.

5. **Learning and Memory.** The search for the "engram," that is, the site of permanent structural or functional change that occurs with learning, is pursued at both the micro and macro levels. Research with snail-like organisms like aplysia, whose nervous systems are simple enough to be drawn as a circuit diagram, has demonstrated changes in the efficiency of information transmission across the synapse caused by experience. These changes last long enough to be a possible mechanism for short-term memory. Longer-term memory may involve permanent structural change in the synapse, or increases in the number of junctions (synapses) between active cells. On the more macro level, it appears that all cortical areas of the brains of higher animals have the capacity for memory storage and store memories specific to the type of information processing the cortical area subserves. However, at least in humans, a particular area deep within the temporal lobe (the hippocampus) seems to be necessary for forming new memories. The amnestic aspects of Korsakoff's syndrome are thought to be due to specific hippocampal damage.

6. **Neuropsychology.** This field of study attempts to describe the specific cognitive and personality changes associated with damage to different areas of the human brain. Much is being learned of the specific functions of the different areas of the cerebral cortex. This research area has been accelerated by new developments in radiography, specifically CAT (Computerized Axial Tomography), MRI (Mag-

netic Resonance Imaging) and PET (Photo Emission Tomography) scanning techniques. These methods allow one to have a three-dimensional view of the anatomy (CAT and MRI) or relative activity (PET scans) of the living and functioning human brain and to relate these findings to the behavior of the individual.

7. **Hemispheric Specialization.** One area of neuropsychology deserves particular description, that is, the investigation of the specialization of the right and left cerebral hemispheres through study of individuals who have had the large neural pathway between the hemispheres surgically severed as a treatment for epilepsy (commissurotomy or "split-brain" patients). Without this pathway, information cannot be shared between the hemispheres and, thus, each hemisphere is forced to process information on its own. Research in this area has dramatically confirmed the verbal versus visuo-spatial specialization of the left and right hemispheres, respectively, which has long been a well-accepted idea in neurology. More importantly, this research has demonstrated that the hemispheres are two potentially independent organs of thought and consciousness, each with its unique processing style. The left hemisphere processes information in a linear and logical way; while the right is more adept at recognizing patterns of simultaneously occurring information. The impact of this area of brain research has been felt in such distant disciplines as education, artificial intelligence, and philosophy.

Bibliography. D. G. Jones, *Our Fragile Brains: A Christian Perspective on Brain Research* (1981). E. Kandel and J. Schwartz, *Principles of Neural Science* (1981). D. M. MacKay, *Brains, Machines and Persons* (1980). B. Pansky and J. A. Delmas, *Review of Neuroscience* (1980).

W. S. BROWN

BIOFEEDBACK; PERSONALITY, BIOLOGICAL DIMENSIONS OF; MIND-BODY RELATIONSHIP. *See also* LEARNING THEORIES; MEMORY; ORGANIC MENTAL DISORDER; PSYCHOSURGERY. *Compare* SENSORY DEPRIVATION RESEARCH; SLEEP AND SLEEP DISORDERS.

BRAIN WAVES/BRAIN SCAN/BRAIN TUMOR. *See* BRAIN RESEARCH. *See also* NEUROLOGIC ILLNESSES; ORGANIC MENTAL DISORDER AND ORGANIC BRAIN SYNDROME.

BRAINWASHING. *See* INDOCTRINATION. *See also* DEPROGRAMMING.

BREAKDOWN. *See* PSYCHOPATHOLOGY, THEORIES OF; PSYCHOSIS.

BRIDGET OF ULSTER, ST. *See* WOMEN IN PASTORAL MINISTRIES, HISTORY OF.

BRINKMAN, ROBERT E. (1909–72). American Methodist chaplain, clinical pastoral educator, and psychologist. Brinkman served from 1938 to 1947 as director of the Council for Clinical Training. Influenced by Freudian psychoanalytic theory and by Wilhelm Reich's depictions of character and its expression in bodily structure, Brinkman conceived of clinical training as an exposure to therapeutic

wisdom that would enable students to "experience" other persons. Trained as a supervisor under Carroll Wise at Worcester State Hospital, Brinkman became an administrative assistant for Helen Flanders Dunbar when she was director of the Council for Clinical Training. Her studies of psychosomatic medicine confirmed his convictions about the interrelation of psychic and somatic structures. His work as director of the council evoked considerable criticism from supervisors who feared that he was substituting psychological concerns for pastoral ones. Uncomfortable in the pastoral role, he became a practicing psychotherapist in New York in 1947.

E. B. HOLIFIELD

PASTORAL CARE MOVEMENT.

BRITISH PASTORAL CARE MOVEMENT. The modern pastoral care movement in Britain advances a long tradition of pastoral care in Britain, which has been characterized by a rich diversity of approach, reflecting various traditions of church and theology. The writings of Richard Baxter and John Keble are significant expressions of Reformed and Anglo-Catholic understandings of spiritual direction. Earlier in this century J. G. McKenzie (1929) and H. Guntrip (1956, 1971) laid the foundations of a fresh approach, like Boisen in North America, responding to inadequacies which they perceived in education for pastoral ministry. Both found in the work of Sigmund Freud insights relevant for pastoral care and exercised an important influence through their psychotherapy, teaching, and writing. Later, L. D. Weatherhead (1951) made a critical analysis of the contributions of Freud, Jung, and Adler to pastoral work.

1. **Recent Developments.** The modern British pastoral care movement finds a self-conscious expression in the Association for Pastoral Care and Counseling (APCC) established in 1972 to promote communication between a number of groups concerned with pastoral care and education. Among the most important of these were the Clinical Theology Association, the Richmond Fellowship for Mental Welfare and Rehabilitation, the Westminster Pastoral Foundation, the Dympna Centre, certain Anglican dioceses, and some universities involved in pastoral education.

The Clinical Theology Association was founded by Frank Lake, a former medical missionary, who in 1958 began seminars for ministers and lay people. While Lake's early theories drew heavily upon the work of Guntrip and Melanie Klein, with their emphasis upon the earliest experiences of childhood, his later writings stressed the significance for pastoral care of the intrauterine experience, especially in the first trimester of gestation. The Richmond Fellowship was formed in 1959 to carry out a program of education in the field of human relationships based upon the fellowship's therapeutic communities. The Westminster Pastoral Foundation was set up in 1970 by William Kyle, a Methodist minister with experience in the American Clinical Training movement. The Dympna Centre, a Roman Catholic organization for counseling and training, was established in 1971 by the Reverend Louis Marteau.

Contemporaneously, certain dioceses of the Church of England appointed advisers in pastoral care and counseling. The unique arrangement whereby certain secular universities have been able to inaugurate courses leading to a diploma in pastoral studies has also been highly significant. An influential voice was that of R. A. Lambourne of Birmingham University. He opposed a too rapid move toward institutional structures with an over-professionalized understanding of ministry based on a problem-solving, counseling-orientated approach. His vision encompassed a pastoral care that was "lay, corporate, adventurous, variegated and diffuse." Whether Lambourne's views shaped, or merely reflected, a peculiarly British perspective, only history will judge.

2. **Contemporary Features.** Although a division of the British Association for Counseling, the national organization identifies itself as an Association for Pastoral Care and Counseling. Pastoral counseling is not normally regarded as an autonomous profession, but rather an activity that is part of a wider ministry of pastoral care. There has consequently been little pressure for the accreditation of either individuals or organizations. While APCC offers an accreditation procedure, this is primarily seen in terms of a tool for assessment, education, and growth rather than a professional qualification. The clinical setting has been less important than in other countries, though supervised hospital placements have been integral to some courses (e.g., in Edinburgh University and in two London teaching hospitals). There is, however, in Britain as a whole, an increased awareness of the need to develop an approach to education for pastoral care based upon a thorough understanding of supervisory processes.

Bibliography. R. Baxter, *The Reformed Pastor* (1956 [1656]). A. V. Campbell, *Rediscovering Pastoral Care* (1981). H. Guntrip, *Mental Pain and the Cure of Souls* (1956); *Psychology for Ministers and Social Workers* 3d ed. (1971). M. Jacobs, *Still Small Voice: An Introduction to Pastoral Counseling* (1982). J. Keble, *Letters of Spiritual Counsel and Guidance* (1870). F. Lake, *Clinical Theology* (1966); *Tight Corners in Pastoral Counseling* (1981). R. A. Lambourne, "Objections to a National Pastoral Organization," *Contact,* (no. 35, 1971). L. Marteau, *Words of Counsel* (1978). J. G. McKenzie, *Souls in the Making: An Introduction to Pastoral Psychology* (1929); *Guilt: Its Meaning and Significance* (1962). L. D. Weatherhead, *Psychology, Religion and Healing* (1951). F. Wright, *The Pastoral Nature of the Ministry* (1980).

D. LYALL

INTERNATIONAL PASTORAL CARE MOVEMENT; PASTORAL CARE MOVEMENT. *See also* CLINICAL THEOLOGY. *Compare* WESTERN EUROPEAN PASTORAL CARE MOVEMENT. *Biography:* BAXTER; KEBLE; LAKE; LAMBOURNE; WEATHERHEAD.

BROTHER, PASTOR AS. *See* PASTOR (Normative and Traditional Images).

BROTHER LAWRENCE OF THE RESURRECTION—(NICOLAS HERMAN) (1611–91). Carmelite friar and mystic. Born Nicolas Herman, he was a soldier for nearly twenty years before joining the Discalced Carmelite monastery in Paris where he lived as a humble lay brother and community cook until his death. After his death Joseph de Beaufort published his scattered writings and letters in 1691 together with a report of four conversations the two had in the 1660s. In English translation this collection is entitled *The Practice of the Presence of God.*

Brother Lawrence's spiritual teaching centers on his conviction that a person can sanctify his or her ordinary life by the conscious cultivation of the presence of God in and around the circumstances of daily living. To develop this continuing sense of God while going about the business of life was both a method that Brother Lawrence proposed in order to "pray without ceasing," and a strategy for overcoming any false dichotomy between the life of action and the life of contemplation.

L. S. CUNNINGHAM

SPIRITUAL MASTERS AND GUIDES; SPIRITUALITY (Roman Catholic Tradition).

BROTHERS/BROTHERHOOD. *See* CHILDREN; COMMUNITY, FELLOWSHIP, AND CARE; FAMILY; MEN.

BROWNING, DON S. *See* PASTORAL THEOLOGY, PROTESTANT; THEOLOGY AND PSYCHOLOGY.

BROWNING, W. P. *See* EAST ASIAN PASTORAL CARE MOVEMENT.

BRUDER, EARNEST. *See* PASTORAL CARE MOVEMENT.

BRUDERHOF. *See* SECTARIAN PASTORAL CARE.

BRUNNER, EMIL (1889–1966). The pastoral emphasis of Brunner is best seen in *Eternal Hope* (1954), an extensive study of the Christian view of last things. In this and other works he speaks of revelation as the truth that is indirectly communicated and therefore can be grasped only by faith as an active decision. Like Kierkegaard, Brunner sees faith as a risking of oneself upon God's word.

Brunner was the first major theologian to work out the "I-Thou" definition of a concrete fellowship in which truth is an encounter (*The Divine-Human Encounter,* 1943). He argued that the leap of faith is necessary because reason has gone wrong in humanity. Ideas have become imperialistic. He saw the answer for this deviation in the shape of a personal encounter with God who is disclosed in Jesus Christ. This is revelation.

Brunner always maintained that some light of reason is available through the image of God and through God's Creation. The upholding of this doctrine was important as a foundation for moral theology in a time when Karl Barth was severely restricting the point of contact for God's grace to special revelation. Brunner also developed a theological basis for social psychology in his doctrine of the orders of life which progressed from interpersonal relationships and family relationships to the social structures of our political and cultural life. Christ serves as the mediator to bridge the gulf between God and humanity and between persons.

In *The Misunderstanding of the Church* (1953) Brunner sought a pastoral relationship in which *ecclesia* would be understood as a spiritual community rather than as an institution.

From 1924 to 1955, Brunner occupied the chair of systematic and practical theology at the University of Zurich.

S. SOUTHARD

NEO-ORTHODOX THEOLOGY AND PASTORAL CARE.

BUBER, MARTIN (1878–1965). Born in Vienna, from his early days he was very active in efforts to reestablish the Jewish State in Israel. In his mid-twenties he began to study Hasidism, and wrote prolifically. Buber is most famous for his philosophy of dialogue, formulated in his book *I and Thou,* originally published in 1923. In this work, and as further developed and amplified in his later writings, Buber distinguishes between the I-Thou and I-It relationships. The I-Thou relationship is one of mutuality and openness, the I-It relationship is not authentic dialogue but one in which the other is used to satisfy one's own needs. In Buber's formulation, the I-Thou and the I-It relationships interact. Buber's concept of dialogue is further developed in his *The Knowledge of Man* (1965).

Buber lectured at the University of Frankfurt, where in 1930 he was appointed professor of religion. In 1938 he settled in what was then called Palestine and served as professor of social philosophy at the Hebrew University until 1951.

R. P. BULKA

EXISTENTIALISM AND PASTORAL CARE; I AND THOU.

BUCER, MARTIN (1491–1551). German Protestant Reformer and pastor. His book, *Von der wahren Seelsorge,* contains the first biblically and theologically grounded theory of the care of souls. No longer is the care of souls determined by sacramental penance or aimed at comforting tempted consciences. Bucer's new key word is "improvement" (*Besserung*), his central theological image is the church as the body of Christ, and his intent is the establishment of Christ's reign in the church. This means the serious realization and earnest practice of Christianity in daily life, particularly in the care and concern of Christians for one another. Thus, each individual Christian is entitled, indeed obligated, to engage in the care of souls in a wholistic fashion. To that end, Bucer combines the spiritual and the material, the ecclesial and the internal form of faith, addresses individuals as well as the faith community as a whole, upholds the law in its strictness while superseding it with the Gospel. He combines toughness with consideration, a biblical basis with practical pastoral experience. He extends his pastoral concern to include soul care for "healthy" members of the community as well as for the poor and for the "heathens, Jews, and Turks."

N. F. HAHN

REFORMED PASTORAL CARE.

BUDDHIST SOUL CARE. *See* COMPASSION; PSYCHOLOGY, EASTERN; PSYCHOLOGY AND PSYCHOTHERAPY (East-West Comparison).

BULIMIA. An episodic, rapid ingestion of quantities of food, accompanied by awareness that the eating is abnormal, terminated by abdominal pain or nausea, and fol-

lowed by self-disgust and depression. Bulimics exhibit concern about their weight and attempt to control it by dieting, vomiting, or use of cathartics and diuretics. The disorder, occurring mostly in females, usually begins in adolescence or early adult life.

Bibliography. K. D. Brownell and J. P. Foreyt, eds., *Handbook of Eating Disorders* (1986).

J. A. KNIGHT

MENTAL HEALTH AND ILLNESS; SELF-DESTRUCTIVE BEHAVIOR. *See also* EATING AND DRINKING; OBSESSIVE-COMPULSIVE DISORDER; PSYCHOPATHOLOGY, THEORIES OF; PSYCHOTHERAPY; SADNESS AND DEPRESSION. *Compare* ANOREXIA NERVOSA; OBESITY.

BULLINGER, HENRY. *See* REFORMED PASTORAL CARE.

BULTMANN, RUDOLF (1884–1976). New Testament scholar and theologian. Bultmann, whose career was spent in both Germany and the U.S., is best known for his concentration on demythologizing biblical texts in favor of *kerygma*, the essential and timeless truth behind the texts.

Bultmann contributes to pastoral care and counseling through his analysis of acceptance. Acceptance comes not from measuring up to norms, social or personal, but from radical obedience: hearing and responding to divine unconditional love, which enables one to respond to life with openness and thereby discover one's best self (see his *Theology,* 1, pp. 316–7.).

R. W. CRAPPS

EXISTENTIALISM AND PASTORAL CARE.

BUNYAN, JOHN (1628–88). English Nonconformist clergyman and writer. He became a believer after his marriage in 1648, largely through reading books supplied by his devout young wife. After a decade of religious struggle, Bunyan was formally recognized as a minister in 1657 and remained associated with a Bedford congregation until his death. Most of 1660–72 was spent in Bedford jail because of his nonconformist views. During imprisonment he both wrote extensively and ministered to fellow prisoners.

For Bunyan life was essentially warfare with Satan as the opponent. This plight informs his autobiographical *Grace Abounding to the Chief of Sinners* (1666) and his own experience is generalized in the story of every Christian as told in the classic *The Pilgrim's Progress* (1678). Both works recount continuous onslaughts by Satan against which the basic defense is Scripture. For Bunyan pastoral care was essentially assistance to fellow pilgrims in this inescapable struggle.

R. W. CRAPPS

CLASSIC LITERATURE IN CARE AND COUNSELING (Protestantism); SPIRITUALITY (Protestant Tradition).

BURIAL. The traditional Judeo-Christian means of disposing of the dead body. Originally, burials took place in the church building, later church yards and cemeteries were consecrated, continuing the symbolism of the communion of saints. These were later joined in secular form by municipal or proprietary cemeteries.

1. **Psychological Significance.** Burial is an intentional separation of the dead body from the community of the living. In addition to its practical consequences of avoiding pollution and enabling decomposition of the body in the earth, there is the psychological function of acting out the transition from a relationship of interactive presence to a relationship of memory. Mourners are helped by coming to terms with the finality of death. Relationships as they have been experienced with the deceased are ended by separation from the body, and living relationships must provide the support necessary for mourners to reorganize their lives without the effective presence of the deceased.

2. **Theological Significance.** The act of burial is usually accompanied by a service of committal, which is both liturgically and emotionally the climax of the funeral. The committal service most often used, based on the *Book of Common Prayer*, has dualistic overtones more in keeping with Hellenistic ideas of immortality than the NT concept of resurrection, committing the soul to God and the body to the earth. Promises of heavenly bliss or immediate entry into larger life may preclude the force of the Gospel message that new life is hoped for out of death. Burial represents the reality of death.

Burial is also a way of reflecting care for the body rather than simply discarding it as refuse. Eusebius describes how in a plague in Alexandria pagans merely threw their dead into the streets, while Christians prepared the bodies of their dead and buried them.

3. **Existential Ambivalence.** Both the psychological and theological implications of burial reflect an ambivalence very commonly felt by mourners. While there is a necessary apprehension of the finality of death, there is also a sense in which in burial something of the presence of the deceased is maintained at the site. This is why we visit the tombs and graves of famous personages. In our culture this is partially supported by assumptions of preservation of the body by embalming, caskets, and vaults. It is further supported by our customs of memorialization: tombstones, flowers, and visits to the grave. As persons occupied space in life there is the feeling that they are related to a particular space in death.

This ambivalence is unavoidable, representing the incapability of the human psyche to admit totally the finality of death. Our pastoral concern is to help mourners turn from their investment in relationship to the deceased to reinvesting their psychic energy in living relationships.

Bibliography. O. Cullmann, *The Immortality of the Soul or Resurrection of the Dead?* (1958). P. E. Irion, *The Funeral and the Mourners* (1979 [1954]); *The Funeral: Vestige or Value?* (1977 [1966]). C. M. Parkes, Bereavement (1972). B. Throckmorton, Jr., "Do Christians Believe in Death?" *Christian Century* (1969), 708-10.

P. E. IRION

FUNERAL; MOURNING CUSTOMS AND RITUALS. *See also* WORSHIP AND CELEBRATION; RITUAL. *Compare* CREMATION; MEMORIAL SERVICE; MEMORIAL SOCIETY.

BURIAL, JEWISH. *See* FUNERAL AND BURIAL, JEWISH.

BURKHART, ROY (1895–1961). Clergyman. After receiving his Ph.D. at the University of Chicago, Burkhart was a high school principal for four years before becoming a minister. He is best known for a long pastor-ate at First Community Church, Columbus, Ohio, where he led the church in a person-oriented ministry with special attention to marriage and family counseling.

Burkhart believed that people's lives are basically changed in small groups and counseling situations. Sermons are important, but their significance depends upon growth that occurs through face-to-face encounters afforded in vital church groups.

In four articles in *Pastoral Psychology* Burkhart describes features of the program at First Community Church. "The Service of Memory" (1 [June 1950], 22–7) discusses design of the funeral to help persons utilize their Christian faith to manage bereavement. "A Program of Pre-Marital Counseling" (1 [October 1950], 25–33) describes a program of guidance to assist young people in understanding the nature of love and to prepare them for marriage. Families with children up to twelve are the concern of "The Church Program of Education in Marriage and the Family" (2 [November 1951], 10–14). "Full Guidance Counseling" (2 [April 1952], 23–31) advocates use of a variety of methods, especially nondirective techniques, in these programs.

Because of such programs First Community Church and its pastor have been recognized as pioneers in applying pastoral psychology to parish life. Burkhart has served as national director of youth work for the United Brethren Church, as trustee of the International Council of Religious Education, and as chairman of the Commission of Christian Education of the National Council of Churches. His writings include *The Secret of Happy Marriage* (1949), *Understanding Youth* (1938), and *From Friendship to Marriage* (1938).

R. W. CRAPPS

PASTORAL CARE MOVEMENT. *See also* CONGREGATION, PASTORAL CARE OF; COMMUNITY, FELLOWSHIP, AND CARE.

BURNOUT. A syndrome, often occurring among individuals in helping professions, involving emotional and physical exhaustion, depersonalization, and a feeling of reduced personal accomplishment. Other symptoms include: headaches, gastrointestinal disorders, lingering colds, loss of weight, sleeplessness, shortness of breath, feelings of tension and anxiety, overuse of food, coffee, or chocolate, memory loss, irritability, daydreaming, tendency to blame, withdrawal, cynicism, marital dissatisfaction, impatience, feelings of inferiority, emotional flatness, loss of interest in hobbies, preoccupation with one area of one's life, and spiritual dryness.

1. **Causes.** There are several theories about the causes of burnout. Maslach (1982) and other social psychologists believe that burnout can be understood best by focusing on situational, environmental, and demographic factors, such as long working hours, little feedback regarding one's work, lack of family time, low salary, understaffing, life changes, unrealistic expectations, lack of time off, and inability to control one's schedule. This view supports the pastoral observation that people — whether church school teachers or pastors — do not burn out from overwork so much as from lack of support.

Internal factors may also be involved, however. Freudenberger (1980) represents a psychoanalytic position which believes that intrapsychic or personality tendencies are a more reliable explanation of burnout. These include need for approval, workaholic qualities, authoritarianism, unassertive acts, overly sensitive reactions, "type A" personality, poor self-worth, and the "messiah" complex — the belief that only "I" can do everything best. Clinical pastoral experience along this line points also to identity issues, especially in pastors who attempt to fill diverse or conflicting roles and become confused about their pastoral identity in the attempt.

Instead of the linear causality of external or internal factors, a third model, proposed by Heifetz and Bersani (1983), understands burnout as a cybernetic interplay of situational, intrapsychic, interpersonal, physical, and spiritual factors. The combination of these five factors leads to burnout when the homeostatic balance among them is heavily weighted on one and not compensated by another. To illustrate, individuals feeling the pressure of unrealistic expectations imposed by others (an external factor) find it necessary to maintain homeostasis by drawing on internal self-confidence (internal factor) or spiritual resources. They may further enhance homeostasis by directly confronting the persons having the expectations (interpersonal variable). If these complementary efforts do not compensate for the external stress, the individuals are likely to experience burnout. This view assumes a wholistic understanding of persons; each area affects the other, and it is the combination that leads to burnout.

2. **Prevention.** The following suggestions can enable pastors and other helping professionals to prevent burnout. (1) Gain a clear understanding of personal strengths and weaknesses; this helps one distinguish between external and internal sources of stress and to seek help when appropriate. (2) In order to gain a sense of purpose and priorities, carefully plan one's directions, focus on essentials, and learn to say no without feeling guilt or giving offense. (3) Structure changes in the environment that will relieve the stress, and adjust to factors that cannot be changed; such steps might include spreading unpleasant tasks between enjoyable ones, guarding productive time for creative pursuits, eliminating repetitive annoyances, learning to separate leisure activities from work, and attending workshops to gain new practical ideas. (4) Develop interpersonal relationships in which one can experience support and affirmation. (5) Take action to resolve interpersonal conflicts and differences. (6) Learn constructive ways of dealing with anger. (7) Achieve a balance between empathy for people and overinvolved sympathy, which diverts one from central issues. (8) Develop relaxation and recreational outlets by learning at least one relaxation technique, exercising, getting proper rest, having a balanced diet (with restricted sugars), making occasional retreats to nature, avoiding states of helplessness by taking control, and implementing a coping strategy in tough situations. (9) Seek professional help when that seems warranted.

The symptoms of burnout can be thought of as a built-in alarm system in the body signifying that life is out of balance. With proper attention to these symptoms, balance can be restored and burnout can be prevented.

Bibliography. K. Albrecht and H. Selye, *Stress and the Manager* (1979). E. Brachter, *The Walk-on-Water Syndrome* (1984). S. Daniel and M. L. Rogers, "Burnout and the Pastorate: A Critical Review with Implications for Pastors," *J. of Psychology and Theology,* 9 (1981), 232–49. H. J. Freudenberger, *Burnout* (1980). L. Heifetz and H. Bersani, "Disrupting the Cybernetics of Personal Growth: Toward a Unified Theory of Burnout in the Human Services," in B. Farber, ed., *Stress and Burnout in the Human Service Professions* (1983). C. Maslach, *Burnout: The Cost of Caring* (1982). J. Warner and J. D. Carter, "Loneliness, Marital Adjustment, and Burnout in Pastoral and Lay Persons," *J. of Psychology and Theology,* 12 (1984), 125–31.

D. G. CONGO

MENTAL HEALTH, PASTOR'S; PASTOR, PASTORAL CARE OF; STRESS AND STRESS MANAGEMENT. *See also* ASSERTIVENESS; PRAYER AND WORSHIP LIFE, PASTOR'S; RELAXATION, PSYCHOLOGY AND TECHNIQUES OF; REST AND RENEWAL, RELIGIOUS TRADITIONS OF. *Compare* ANXIETY; COUNTERTRANSFERENCE; FAITH AND INTEGRITY, PASTOR'S; SADNESS AND DEPRESSION.

BUSHNELL, HORACE (1802–76). American Congregationalist pastor and theologian. His chief influence on pastoral care came through his theological reflection, especially through his revisioning of the character of spiritual growth. In his *Christian Nurture* (1847, 1861) Bushnell insisted that the children of Christian parents should grow up as Christians without ever knowing themselves as being otherwise. The book was a criticism of an excited revivalist piety, and it helped alter American Protestant conceptions of both the family and the church. Bushnell urged that pastors recover a sense of the organic relations that influenced spiritual growth through the unconscious and unintended exertion of power over character. The book became a classic of the Religious Education Movement in the twentieth century, when Bushnell's ideas seemed particularly compatible with innovations in developmental psychology.

Bushnell had an indirect influence on pastoral care through his reflections on theology and theological language, which helped prepare the way for the liberal New Theology of the later nineteenth century. He insisted that theological language is far more akin to poetry than to science, and that therefore the rationalistic orthodoxy of his era was doomed to failure. Bushnell believed that theological doctrines appeal not so much to the logical understanding as to the imagination and the aesthetic apprehension of faith. He therefore attempted to define the Christian doctrines of the Trinity, the Atonement, and the nature of Christ in a form that recognized the symbolic status of religious language.

Bushnell was an active pastor of the North Church (Congregational) in Hartford, Connecticut. There he experimented with various pastoral techniques, such as reserving his study one evening each week for conversations with young men. His main influence, though, was that of a theologian who recognized the power of social groups to nurture spiritual growth.

E. B. HOLIFIELD

HISTORY OF PROTESTANT PASTORAL CARE (United States).

BUSINESS PERSONS AND BUSINESS CHAPLAINCY. *See* INDUSTRIAL AND BUSINESS CHAPLAINCIES.

C

CABOT, RICHARD C. (1868–1939). American physician and ethicist. A hematologist and cardiologist at the Harvard Medical School, Cabot pioneered in the use of the case method and established the first clinical pathological conferences in medical education, founded Harvard's Department of Medical Social Work, and assisted in the early development of Clinical Pastoral Education (CPE). After resigning his post at Massachusetts General Hospital in 1920, he taught social ethics at Harvard University and later at Andover Newton Theological Seminary.

Cabot's 1925 article, "A Plea for a Clinical Year in the Course of Theological Study," helped stimulate interest in CPE, and he assisted Anton Boisen in the organization of the first clinical program, implemented at Worcester State Hospital. In 1930 he became a founder and first president of the Council for the Clinical Training of Theological Students; he also helped establish the Theological Schools' Committee on Clinical Training in 1938.

In 1936 Cabot and Russell Dicks published a book that helped to change the understanding of pastoral care in American Protestantism. *The Art of Ministering to the Sick* popularized Cabot's notion that creative listening by the minister could help patients discover the direction in which God—defined as "the power in ourselves that makes for health"—was leading them. By helping men and women discover their "growing edge," the minister could foster healing and health.

His ethical vision and clinical methods remained important in the Clinical Pastoral Education movement, especially at the Institute for Pastoral Care organized in Boston in 1944.

E. B. HOLIFIELD

HISTORY OF PROTESTANT PASTORAL CARE (United States); PASTORAL CARE MOVEMENT.

CABRINI, FRANCES XAVIER, ST. *See* WOMEN IN PASTORAL MINISTRIES, HISTORY OF.

CALENDAR, LITURGICAL. *See* LITURGICAL CALENDAR; RITUAL AND PASTORAL CARE.

CALIFORNIA PSYCHOLOGICAL INVENTORY (CPI). *See* EVALUATION AND DIAGNOSIS, PSYCHOLOGICAL.

CALL TO MINISTRY. The self-understanding held by ordained clergy or clergy candidates in relation to their sense of vocation. The notion of a call accents the idea that such persons feel chosen or selected for this particular role rather than viewing it primarily as a personal career choice. This self-understanding needs to be viewed in terms of its theological grounding, its social scientific meanings, its guidance aspects, and contemporary trends.

1. Theology. The clergy's claim to special vocation (calling) is based in the NT understanding of the vocation or calling of all believers into discipleship. This general calling is marked by baptism. The believer is then commissioned to witness to the gospel through love of God and neighbor and participation in the priesthood of all believers. Within this body some are then selected for a representative ministry with particular responsibility for Word and sacrament, a calling marked by ordination. The biblical basis for this special calling is found in the calling of the Twelve, the selection of the deacons in the book of Acts, and in the commissioning of the apostles. The traditional description of call has been colored by Paul's account of his own call on the road to Damascus. However, ministers have claimed a variety of understandings of their personal call to ministry.

A helpful fourfold typology of the call to ministry has been provided by H. Richard Niebuhr (1956): (1) The call to be a Christian which comes to all believers; (2) The secret call which directs one into a special form of ministry; (3) The providential call which describes the gifts and graces of an individual, marking him or her as an obvious candidate for carrying out certain types of ministry; (4) The ecclesiastical call by means of which a congregation or other ecclesial institution certifies a person for ministry in a particular setting. Some persons claim all four of these as normative for the call to ministry, while others would claim only one or two as normative.

2. Psychology. It is important to respect the mystery and possible spiritual significance of a sense of calling while, at the same time, attempting to be attentive to its range of psychological meanings. These can vary from the extreme of being a healthy, realistic expression of an emerging clarity about one's ultimate identity and vocation in relation to God, with other persons in human society and history, to pathologically confused and conflicted attempts to solve psychological and interpersonal problems through religion, to many mixtures of psychological strength and weakness in between. In sorting out these factors it is a sensitive and complex question to decide how psychological and theological factors and criteria of assessment should be related.

Yet while psychology may not be able to exhaust the meaning of a sense of calling, it can illuminate it in important ways. When reflecting psychologically, it is helpful to consider the sense of call from at least two perspectives. *Developmentally*, one may ask how the sense of calling expresses the normal developmental issues and processes at this time in this person's life. In an adolescent, for instance, it may be deeply related (positively or negatively) to normal developmental issues of identity ("finding oneself"), while in a person of middle years it may be much more oriented toward the struggle to develop a sense of responsibility and care for others and to find a sense of meaning and purpose beyond oneself.

In relation to mental health and illness, the question is whether the experience of feeling called is dynamically related to an unconscious attempt to resolve conflict or meet other needs within oneself or in one's interpersonal relationships. For example, it may represent an attempt to create a sense of self in the face of radical self-doubt and emptiness, to confirm personal worth against feelings of low self-esteem, to atone for guilt with parents or other internalized authorities, or to gain love and respect from peers, or power over them. In serious psychopathology the sense of divine call can form a prominent part of a delusional system of grandiosity, suspicion, and persecution.

3. Guidance. Simple conversation exploring the subjective meanings of a sense of call can be helpful to persons uncertain — or overly certain — of its validity, either to add psychological insight and confirmation to its sense of authenticity and "rightness" or to raise significant questions for further reflection before major decisions are made.

A useful adjunctive counseling resource, the Theological School Inventory (TSI), is a widely used instrument for research or guidance of candidates for ministry in relation to descriptions of call or self-understanding of those entering ministry. The major emphasis is descriptive of motivational factors and how these are perceived by the candidate. Such self-reporting instruments can be of help to pastoral counselors or others offering guidance to candidates. When the counselor finds that there is evidence of delusional thought processes that have been interpreted in terms of traditional theological language, the counselor must rely on standard reality testing questions and devices for judgment as to treatment or referral.

Counselors might be prepared for an increase in the use of traditional theological terms in the descriptions of religious experiences such as a call to ministry in the light of a number of second career students, the strength of the charismatic movement within many churches, and the general interest in spirituality within the contemporary culture.

Bibliography. A. T. Boisen, *The Exploration of the Inner World* ([1936], 1972). P. M. Helfaer, *The Psychology of Religious Doubt* (1972). R. A. Hunt, S. W. Cardwell, and J. A. Dittes, *Guide to Interpreting the TSI* (1976). L. Marteau, "Assessment for the Priesthood and Religious Life," *Clergy Review* 67 (1982), 31-35. H. R. Niebuhr, *The Purpose of the Church and Its Ministry* (1956). T. C. Oden, *Pastoral Theology* (1983), ch. 1. C. W. Stewart, *Person and Profession* (1974). J. N. M. Wijngaards, "Assessing Spiritual Experiences," *Clergy Review* 67 (1982), 253-60. World Council of Churches, *Baptism, Eucharist, and Ministry* (1982).

C. H. SCHNELLING

MINISTRY; RABBINATE; VOCATION. *See also* CAREER DEVELOPMENT AND GUIDANCE (For Pastors); CLERGY, EMPIRICAL STUDIES OF; GOD'S WILL, ACCEPTANCE OF; PERSONHOOD OF THE PASTOR, SIGNIFICANCE OF; THEOLOGICAL STUDENTS, PASTORAL CARE OF. *Compare* RELIGIOUS LIFE (VOWED LIFE).

CALLING AND VISITATION, PASTORAL. The pastoral call refers to the traditional prerogative of ministers to take initiative toward persons in response to need. Traditionally, it encompasses home and hospital visits for purposes of education, nurture and care, evangelism, organization, and discipline.

Of all professionals, the pastor has the unique privilege and responsibility of relating to persons in their home environment, which is the best place for observing human interaction. For example, a home with two parents, one grandparent and four children creates forty-nine possible relationships. To take a person out of the home and counsel them in a carefully insulated one-to-one encounter merely adds another interaction. It does little to give insight into the other forty-nine relationships.

The importance of this fact in its more practical form has been recognized in recent years by those in the fields of family therapy and social work. These other professionals increasingly feel that they must be at the center of life's complex interactions if they are to have a clear picture of what is really happening to the people involved. However, nearly all other professionals may come into the home only under special circumstances and then usually on invitation and by appointment. It is usually only the pastor who is considered to be so close to the family that a visit may be made on the basis of an initiative that is part of a pastoral function.

However, problems with the pastoral call do exist in contemporary ministry. In families where both parents work or where television and other leisure activities make excessive demands on people's time and attention, the traditional approach to the pastoral call needs to be reassessed. Not only a priority of calls may be necessary, but also a more carefully planned call may well take the place of a once casual approach. Nevertheless, this does not make invalid the pastor's privilege and responsibility of taking initiative toward persons in his or her care.

Four types of call can be classified: crisis, promotional, organizational, and pastoral interest. Crisis calls would involve accidents, deaths, critical illness, arrests, or catastrophes like fire and flood. These take priority over other activities. Promotional calls relate to new people in the community, new or prospective members, and the growth potential of the parish. Organizational calls are more specifically focused on educational, financial, and other institutional aspects of parish life. Pastoral interest would have to do with the aged, the shut-in, and the inactive.

Traditionally, pastoral calling has had a strong social and spiritual quality. In the past, the pastor simply appraised the family's welfare and invited all present to share in Bible reading and prayer. Contemporary training in pastoral care and counseling makes it possible to enrich the pastoral call by observing stressful conditions and insecurities. Emerging problems may be dealt with before they become critical. Wisely directed queries may be used to open up the subject, and while the persons may not enter into what is considered a formal counseling session some of the benefits may be achieved. This may range from talking with a youth about vocational choice, to educational planning, or dealing with dilemmas of religion and ethics. The call may provide a chance to discuss in depth the spiritual, personal and familial concerns of persons as well as church activity.

As long as ministry is built on human relationships, the pastoral call, formal or informal, in home or hospital, with an individual or a family group will have a primary claim on pastoral energy and skill. However, the care of persons has always been the responsibility of the entire community of faith. Therefore, the training and involvement of lay persons in pastoral calling will significantly enhance the effectiveness of this aspect of congregational care.

Bibliography. S. M. Coyle, "A Covenanting Process in Pastoral Home Visits," *J. of Pastoral Care* 39:2 (1985), 96 – 109. T. C. Oden, *Pastoral Theology: Essentials of Ministry* (1983), ch. 12.

E. N. JACKSON

CONGREGATION, PASTORAL CARE OF; CONVERSATION, PASTORAL; FAMILY, PASTORAL CARE AND COUNSELING OF; PERCEPTIVENESS AND SENSITIVITY, PASTORAL. *Compare* CORRESPONDENCE; INITIATIVE AND INTERVENTION; TELEPHONE, PASTORAL USE OF.

CALVIN, JOHN (1509 – 64). Protestant theologian and reformer. Born and educated in France, Calvin came almost incidentally to Geneva in 1536 and accepted H. Farel's invitation to organize the Reformation there. After squelching opposition to their leadership, Calvin's rule was uncontested, and he took steps to make Geneva an ideal community under God. The experiment represents the most extensive attempt in Protestant Christendom to give pastoral guidance to an entire city.

Calvin organized ministers and elders in Geneva to supervise the daily life of all citizens. Affairs were to be judged by God's law so that Geneva could be a model of Reform ideals. Elders were to make "fraternal correction," but severe punishment, including expulsion or even execution (as with Servetus), could be meted to the gross sinner or unrepentant heretic.

The stern discipline which Calvin enforced in Geneva was counterbalanced by a more gentle Calvin as pastor. His letters recount numerous instances of an empathetic pastor caring for troubled parishioners. He writes to bereaved persons with sincere warmth and personal feeling, but his advice is not maudlin. He leans heavily upon Scripture and speaks with comforting certitude. Death seems to have been a crisis which brought out the pastor in Calvin.

R. W. CRAPPS

REFORMED PASTORAL CARE.

CALVINISM. *See* PASTORAL CARE (History, Traditions, and Definitions); REFORMED PASTORAL CARE. *See also* HISTORY OF PROTESTANT PASTORAL CARE (United States); SOCIOLOGY OF RELIGIOUS AND PASTORAL CARE.

CAMPUS MINISTRY. *See* COLLEGE STUDENTS AND COLLEGE CHAPLAINCY.

CANADA, HISTORY OF PASTORAL CARE AND COUNSELING IN. *See* CANADIAN PASTORAL CARE MOVEMENT; HISTORY OF ROMAN CATHOLIC PASTORAL CARE IN CANADA.

CANADIAN ASSOCIATION FOR PASTORAL EDUCATION. The Canadian Pastoral Care movement may best be discussed by examining the national pastoral care organization. The Canadian Association for Pastoral Education (CAPE) is the only national organization in Canada having responsibility for the training, accreditation, and certification in supervised pastoral education (SPE). The movement for SPE had its beginnings in 1951 when two Canadian Baptist clergy, Earle McKnight and Archie MacLachlan, who had trained in the Boston area of the U.S., returned home and ran summer units simultaneously, one in Nova Scotia and one in Ontario. In 1957, with the support and encouragement of Dr. Charles Feilding, an Anglican, the Reverend Elliott McGuigan, S. J., and the Reverend Jack Breckenridge, of the United Church, the Toronto Institute for Pastoral Training was set up as an integral part of the Toronto School of Theology. In 1962, the first pastoral training center in the west of Canada was begun in Calgary by W. E. Mullen. During the next two years interested people from across the country were brought together to discuss the possibility of forming a national association for clinical pastoral education (CPE). Finally on December 16, 1965, a constitution was accepted that gave the new association its title, the Canadian Council for Supervised Pastoral Education (CCSPE). Eight years later, in January, 1974, the name was changed to CAPE.

Structurally, CAPE differs from its American parents. Since all of the first CAPE supervisors had trained in the U.S., they perceived at firsthand the struggles to bring together various groups under the umbrella of the Association for Clinical Pastoral Education (ACPE). They were also aware of the splitting of function between the pastoral counseling wing (the American Association of Pastoral Counselors (AAPC)) and the supervised pastoral educational wing (ACPE) and their separate institutions.

So when CCSPE was founded, it brought together the functions of both ACPE and AAPC under one organization. This polity has required constant dialogue, which has created a healthy tension within the association. In the 1980s total reciprocity in certification was established between CAPE and ACPE.

Similarly, in 1974, a pilot project was established under the guidance of Claude Guldner for the training and certification of specialists or practitioners, and since then there has been a steadily increasing number of specialists in the three streams of institutional ministry, pastoral counseling, and pastoral care or parish-oriented practitioners. Currently there is increasing expectation that those entering supervisory training should have achieved specialization as practicing ministers first.

There are several major issues with which CAPE is struggling. The first is the tension that exists between the understanding of SPE as a movement, a counterculture within denominational structures, as against the increasing formalization and standardization of SPE into something of a "church" itself, with its own quasi "bishops" and territories and canons. Whether what was once a prophetic anti-institutional movement might become a regularized component of denominational institutions is an issue that the Association must address.

Secondly, has the need to redress the balance of ecclesiastical Docetism caused the Association to emphasize the insights of social science till the most neglected element in the verbatim is "theological reflection"? There is a movement for stronger theological and liturgical development as well as new insights in spirituality. CAPE has also been called to reassess its high investment in individual care and counseling and to consider its responsibility to minister to institutions, systems, and society in general.

Canada is a country founded on the recognition of minority rights. Ironically, there are very few minorities represented in the supervisory ranks of CAPE. In the specialist category, the minority groups have a much higher representation, especially women, as well as an increasing number of women supervisors. In 1980–81, CAPE had its first woman president, and the first as well in the clinical pastoral movement.

Canadians have not been much involved in research and scholarly publication. To encourage this aspect of CAPE's life, a research prize was instituted in 1979 and is awarded annually. Beyond its borders, CAPE shares jointly with ACPE and AACP as a partner in publishing *The Journal of Pastoral Care* and is a fully participating member of the International Committee on Pastoral Care and Counseling.

E. KILBOURN

CANADIAN PASTORAL CARE MOVEMENT. *Compare* ASSOCIATION FOR CLINICAL PASTORAL EDUCATION; THEOLOGICAL EDUCATION AND THE PASTORAL CARE MOVEMENT.

CANADIAN COUNCIL FOR SUPERVISED PASTORAL EDUCATION (CCSPE). *See* CANADIAN PASTORAL CARE MOVEMENT.

CANADIAN PASTORAL CARE MOVEMENT.

The modern history of pastoral care in Canada is most clearly revealed in the development of the Supervised Pastoral Education movement (hereafter SPE). This movement evolved from unconnected and varied origins. Persons who had trained in the U.S. began training programs in Canada reflecting the orientations of the programs in which they had participated. The Canadian Council for Supervised Pastoral Education (CCSPE) was formed in Toronto in 1965 and changed its name to the Canadian Association for Pastoral Education (CAPE) in 1974. In 1989, there were training programs in all Canadian provinces, sixty-seven training centers, and a total membership of 1200, of which 353 are Roman Catholics. There are four regional organizations in Ontario and one additional organization serving the Atlantic provinces (Nova Scotia, New Brunswick, Prince Edward Island, and Newfoundland).

1. **Beginnings.** Charles Feilding was an Anglican from Nova Scotia studying at General Seminary in New York in the late twenties when New England was in intellectual ferment over psychoanalysis. When he took his first and only course in Supervised Pastoral Education (SPE) at Worcester State Hospital under the supervision of Anton Boisen, Feilding was a classmate of Seward Hiltner. This experience had a profound effect on Feilding, for although he took no more courses he became dedicated to promoting SPE as a part of every clergyman's experience. When, a few years later, he became professor of Moral Theology in Trinity College at the University of Toronto, Feilding worked intensively at persuading church and medical authorities in Toronto to inaugurate a program of Supervised Pastoral Care in their hospitals. It was not until 1958, however, that the first SPE course was offered at Toronto General Hospital. That course was under the direction of Jack Breckenridge, who had trained at Massachusetts General Hospital.

Meanwhile Boisen became chaplain at Elgin State Hospital near Chicago, and in 1936 sent a promotional agent to Queen's University at Kingston, Ontario, and to the University of Toronto. A. V. Bentum, a student at Knox College in Toronto, enrolled in a course at Elgin State Hospital under the leadership of Boisen and Donald Beatty. Bentum then went to the University of British Columbia for social work training before going to Vancouver Island as a supervisor of social work. Feeling the need for further training, he enrolled at the Menninger Clinic, and following that spent many years as a social worker in California.

In 1937 an evangelist for SPE, Robert Brinkman, came to the Toronto area. His first students did not continue in pastoral ministry but Brinkman's efforts were not fruitless. On a visit to McMaster University he planted seeds that led Ernest Bruder to take extensive training between 1941 and 1944 at Ann Arbor, Rochester, and Greystone Park. Following that he became the chaplain of St. Elizabeth's Hospital in Washington, D.C. and the editor of the *Journal of Pastoral Care* (*JPC*). From there he exercised a profound influence over developments in Canada.

Archie MacLachlan was another in whom the seed took root. Enrolling at Andover Newton in the fall of 1947 after taking his S.T.M. under the supervision of Philip Guiles, he took six weeks of training at Worcester State Hospital and another six weeks at the Boston City

Hospital under John Billinsky. MacLachlan went on to Harvard on the recommendation of Guiles to complete his master's degree in clinical psychology. During the summer vacation of 1949 he acted as an assistant supervisor with Lester Potter at what was then called the Massachusetts Memorial Hospital.

2. **History of Program Development.** *a. Ontario.* In order to reestablish himself in Canada, MacLachlan accepted a position as a director of Christian education at Yorkminster Baptist Church in Toronto. It took him some time to discover that Dean Stewart, of the McMaster Divinity College, had been favorably impressed by Anton Boisen while serving as a pastor in Oak Park, near Chicago. Stewart welcomed MacLachlan because he had hoped, during his tenure as dean, that he would be able to incorporate SPE into the curriculum of McMaster Divinity College. The big questions confronting them were: What institution would be willing to launch a Supervised Pastoral Education Program, and how could such a venture be financed? MacLachlan received a cool response from the church communities.

In a meeting with an old friend, Jack Breckenridge, he discovered that Breckenridge had taken two courses of SPE in Boston and had recently accepted appointment by his conference to be the United Church of Canada Chaplain at the Mountain Sanatorium (TB) in Hamilton. Breckenridge was sure that the superintendent of the sanatorium would be interested, and offered to introduce MacLachlan to Dr. Hugo Ewart. Ewart was enthusiastic about the idea. He had been the prime mover in getting the Hamilton Conference of the United Church of Canada to appoint Breckenridge as the first full-time, trained chaplain to a public institution in Canada.

The first official course in Ontario and Western Canada was offered by an interdenominational Board of Directors through the Department of Extension of McMaster University in 1952. It was a six-week course financed by a $40 tuition fee and a $750 grant from the Atkinson Foundation. Only three students could be persuaded to enroll — a Baptist and two United Church of Canada ministers — but the following year enrollment increased to ten and was more ecumenical in composition. The enrollment continued to grow until it was necessary to use the facilities of two general hospitals and a mental hospital to accommodate the program. After initiating the program in Hamilton, McLachlan moved to Winnipeg and, while pastor of a church there, conducted a one-and-a-half-day-a-week program of SPE. The project was so successful that it was carried on for the next two years that MacLachlan remained in the city. Its appeal was such that two Portage la Prairie ministers drove fifty miles through winter weather to attend. Among those who participated were Murray Thompson (later the pioneer of SPE in British Columbia) and Greer Boyce, (who eventually became the professor of pastoral care at Emmanuel College in Toronto).

In 1959 MacLachlan became the first chaplain of the Ontario Hospital in Hamilton. He and Jack Friesen were appointed chaplains to Ontario Mental Hospitals that summer, the first trained chaplains employed by the Ontario Government. As chaplain, MacLachlan accepted invitations from clergy in many communities to speak about the work of the chaplain and the relation of religion to mental health. He promoted seminars and conferences in such widely separated places as Sudbury, Montreal, London, St. Thomas, Kingston, Owen Sound, and Whitby. This led to an increase in chaplaincy appointments in mental hospitals, correctional institutions, and institutions for the mentally retarded.

In 1972 MacLachlan accepted the invitation to become the first director of the Kingston Institute for Pastoral Care, located at Queen's University, and he attained the status of full professor at Queen's Theological College. This program increased the emerging focus on the parish. The original students were clergy (of several denominations). They were involved in the program four days a week. The program included lectures, verbatim seminars, interpersonal group seminars, book reports, and weekly critical incident reports for group discussion.

In 1983 Robert Thompson, minister of Northlea United Church in Toronto, invited MacLachlan to supervise him while together they offered a parish-based program with Roman Catholic as well as Protestant students. Most of the students, regardless of denomination, were expected to do some of their pastoral visitation in the parish of the church where the program was being offered. Having obtained acting supervisor status after this program, Thompson has conducted three subsequent courses which have been more completely parish based and fully ecumenical. The results have been most satisfactory both for the students and for the parish. Similar programs have been offered by Father James Hannah in Holy Name Parish (also in Toronto) and by Professor Kenneth Jackson of McMaster Divinity College in a Baptist parish in Dundas, Ontario. Probably the most significant development of the first decade was the organization of the Toronto Institute of Pastoral Training (TIPT). Feilding had labored hard and long to cultivate the interest of the Toronto medical community. He organized discussion groups, which included such men as the dean of medicine of the University of Toronto, and some of the most important department heads. He involved the superintendent of the Toronto General Hospital and the Toronto Hospital for Sick Children, and he brought together members of the medical and the church community for discussion. Notable among the church leaders were Elliott McGuigan, of the Jesuits, who was to be a senior advisor at Vatican II, and Harold Vaughan who was the director of the Board of Colleges and Schools for the United Church of Canada, a man with outstanding fund-raising skills.

In spite of all of his efforts Feilding did not seem to be able to allay the anxieties of most of the key people he had assembled. Finally in May of 1957 he called a meeting at Trinity College in Toronto composed of the key doctors of the medical faculty, the dean, the head of medicine, the head of psychiatry, the superintendent of the Toronto General Hospital, and a distinguished guest from the Boston medical community. To support him in making his presentation Feilding had invited his college associate, Gordon Watson, along with guests from the Hamilton project, Dr. J. N. Senn, superintendent of the Hamilton Psychiatric Hospital and Dr. Hugo Ewart, the superintendent of the Mountain Sanatorium, along with MacLachlan. Ewart was unable to attend but sent a strong letter in support because of the work that was being done by the chaplain and the training program in the sanatorium.

The result of that meeting — after long and strenuous discussion—was Feilding's proposal for the formation of a Toronto Institute for Pastoral Training which would be responsible for training programs in the Toronto area. This was approved and a Continuing Committee was set up to be responsible for selecting a supervisor and making the necessary arrangements for launching a training program in the spring of 1958. Although there were no Roman Catholics on the initial Board of TIPT and no Roman Catholic candidates in the first program, the fact that they had been consulted and were kept apprised of developments meant that when the national organization came into being the Roman Catholics were ready to be involved.

It should be noted at this point that the organization which later became known as the Toronto Institute of Human Relations (TIHR) had its beginnings when Mervyn Dickenson returned from training at Boston University in 1961. He was not interested in becoming an institutional chaplain; rather, he was interested in pastoral counseling, but there were no churches looking for staff members with his training and skills. Finally he persuaded Royal York Road United Church in Toronto to allow him the use of their facilities. While establishing himself in this new pastoral role, he found fellowship and an opportunity to work out some of his ideas with men who had been at graduate school with him who were now in the Toronto area serving as chaplains. It was only natural that when it came time to think about organizing what later became known as CAPE, he and others interested in counseling were included in the scope of the new organization.

b. The Atlantic provinces. The roots of SPE development in the Atlantic provinces go back to Earle McKnight who went from Nova Scotia to Andover Newton Theological School in 1939, where he had become interested in SPE as a student of Philip Guiles. During the summer of 1940 he went to Chicago to take a course under the direction of Beatty and Boisen. Upon graduation McKnight returned to Nova Scotia as a parish minister. While serving in Fredericton he was asked by Andover Newton to supervise a student, Charles Taylor, who would serve as a chaplain, under the classification of "psychological intern," in the Victoria General Hospital during the summer of 1951, for academic credit. Halifax is at least 200 miles away from Fredericton, and the supervision had to be conducted by correspondence; and the curriculum of the course was specified by Andover Newton. (Taylor had taken a three-month course at Boston City Hospital under the direction of Guiles and the supervision of Billinsky in 1950.) In 1952 Andover Newton assumed responsibility for the course at the Victoria General Hospital, and Taylor was given the status of supervisor for the project. He persuaded four of his fellow students to participate in the program under the classification of "psychological interns". In 1953 Acadia University assumed responsibility for the program and its site was moved to Kentville Sanatorium where the participants were recognized as "chaplains in training."

Acadia thus became the first Canadian university and divinity college to incorporate SPE into its curriculum.

c. Manitoba. After fifteen years in "successful parish ministry" Gordon Toombs, having completed his Ph.D. from Edinburgh University, went to study at the Menninger Foundation in 1961. He felt the need to improve his ability in personal relationships. At the end of his second year he returned to Winnipeg to start a counseling service in a downtown United Church. In 1963, in response to local requests, he started a half-day-per-week seminar for clergy to develop counseling skills. This non-credit seminar continued for several years. Toombs also lectured to ministerial students at the United Church College in alternate years until the college closed in 1970. He and Jim McKay, chaplain at Winnipeg General Hospital, recognized a need for SPE in Winnipeg; so they organized a program and invited the Reverend Donald Houts of St. Paul's Seminary in Kansas City to provide direction for a three-month program during the summer of 1967 and again in 1968. Following this experience with Houts, Toombs received supervisory status. Subsequent courses were offered by the Department of Extension of the University of Manitoba at the Winnipeg General Hospital. Thus, in 1969 Toombs became the first Canadian to direct an accredited course in Western Canada.

While these developments were taking place in Winnipeg, Kenneth Beale, who was American trained, was getting things started through Brandon University in Brandon, Manitoba. In 1969 and 1970 he offered a course for local clergy. However, in 1971 he accepted a position in Ontario so there were no further courses offered in Brandon until Orton Anderson became chaplain at the Brandon Mental Hospital and Rudi Katerburg became chaplain at the Brandon General Hospital. Jointly they started a program in 1972. Both of these men were full supervisors. Anderson had received his training in Hamilton while Katerburg, having commenced his training in Hamilton, had completed most of it in Toronto under the supervision of Bert Massiah.

d. Alberta. The beginnings of SPE in the province of Alberta did not have the traditional SPE origin. In 1962 the Pastoral Institute of Calgary, located in the center of the business district of the city at Central United Church, offered its first pastoral counseling and matrimonial services under the guidance of the Reverend W. E. Mullen. In response to what he felt was an urgent need in Calgary, Mullen took training in counseling at the American Institute of Family Relations in Los Angeles. On his return to Canada in 1961 he obtained the support of the Marriage Guidance Council, the Calgary Presbytery of the United Church of Canada, the Board of Central United Church, and formed a board of directors recruited from several professional groups in the area. Although it had financial difficulties which taxed the budget of the Marriage Guidance Council of the United Church for some time, from the outset it was so overwhelmed with clients that it had to begin training personnel immediately.

By 1968 it became obvious that a hospital chaplaincy program was needed in Calgary. Two groups became aware of this need almost simultaneously. The United Church appointed the Reverend James Taylor, who had taken his training with Murray Thompson in Vancouver and at Menninger Clinic, to the position of United Church Chaplain at the Foothills General Hospital in that year. In the same year an ecumenical organization, known as the Hospital Pastoral Care Association of Alberta, came into being largely in response to the efforts of a number of Roman Catholic priests and sisters.

Taylor moved cautiously and was able to gain the confidence and support of the Hospital Pastoral Care Association to the extent that he was able to offer a program of training in Pastoral Care in January of 1970. The format of the program indicates something of Taylor's response to the local needs and the cautiousness of the clergy in the area. He applied to the Accrediting and Certification Committee of the Canadian Council for Supervised Pastoral Education for approval to offer a full quarter of training for the program. The time structure was designed to offset resistance that might have been expressed by clergy saying: "I would like to take the course but my church could never think of me taking three months off." Clergy attended full-time for the first week in January. Then they attended Monday and Tuesday until the approach of Easter. There was a break until after Easter when the two-day-per-week schedule was resumed for six weeks. This was followed by a break until early June, when the students were required to return for three final intensive weeks of training. The program worked well, but through the experience Taylor discovered that such caution was not necessary. The next year he adopted the format of the three month full-time quarter of training. With this format the program has continued to expand in size and broaden in ecumenical scope.

e. British Columbia. After a two-year residency at the Houston (Texas) Institute of Religion, Murray Thompson became the United Church chaplain at Vancouver General Hospital in 1963. He had hoped that it would be an ecumenical appointment but it did not materialize as such. Thompson served seven years and was able to organize courses for parish clergy without the official recognition of the hospital. His students were recruited exclusively from the United Church ministry, for the United Church had a policy of requiring placements on mission fields during the summer months. In 1967 Thompson succeeded in breaking through this policy; of his seven students, four were seminarians.

During the same year (1967) Thompson first became aware of Bert Bentum, who had become involved with the Westminster Foundation. After several years of operation the foundation was incorporated in 1967 to train clergy in skills of applied ministry. Its founder, the Reverend Fred Metzger, a Presbyterian of Hungarian origin, invited Bentum to give lectures from time to time to his students at Riverview Hospital where the foundation program was being offered. This appealed to Bentum so much that he gave up his job with the Government of British Columbia and returned to parish ministry. This made it convenient for him to participate in the program at the Riverview Hospital at Port Coquitlam.

Bentum, having heard of the newly founded Canadian Council for SPE, received full supervisory status in 1968 and was one of the first to receive that status from the

Accrediting and Certification Committee of the Canadian Council for SPE. This made it possible for him to move into Riverview Hospital and offer accredited courses, until he and Metzger decided to go their separate ways in 1970.

In the meantime Thompson had succeeded in organizing and incorporating the Pastoral Institute of British Columbia. Its aim was to promote interdenominational cooperation, which would make it possible to have an ecumenical chaplain in the Vancouver General Hospital who could offer accredited courses in SPE, and who could have the support of the religious training institutions in Vancouver. In 1969 he was able to get sufficient cooperation from the Anglicans, Presbyterians, and the three Lutheran bodies besides the United Church to organize and incorporate the Pastoral Institute of British Columbia.

Thompson served as president of the Canadian Council for SPE from 1968 to 1969. When Bentum obtained full supervisory status in 1970 he became more involved with Thompson and the Pastoral Institute, but this relationship was not very satisfactory and it ended with Bentum's retirement in 1972.

f. Saskatchewan. Several factors contributed to the slow development of SPE in Saskatchewan. The first factor is that of geography and the lack of large urban centers. The second is that during the fifties "sensitivity groups" had had a great appeal and met a real need in that area. In the sixties and seventies church leaders were not prepared to respond to the time demands and concentration involved in SPE programs. Women in religious orders were feeling the need of training in hospital ministries, but SPE programs were not yet ready to accept non-clergy in their programs. Orton Anderson had become chaplain of the mental hospital in Weyburn in 1963 and had to overcome many prejudices about the role of clergy in hospitals from a very conservative religious community, and ignorance of need on the part of the government. At neither level did they seem ready to accept the role of hospital chaplain, which Anderson was trying to offer. In 1972 he moved to Brandon where there was a more accepting attitude on the part of the public and the government authorities.

A. J. MACLACHLAN

AMERICAN ASSOCIATION OF PASTORAL COUNSELORS; ASSOCIATION FOR CLINICAL PASTORAL EDUCATION; HISTORY OF PROTESTANT PASTORAL CARE (Canada); INTERNATIONAL PASTORAL CARE MOVEMENT; PASTORAL CARE MOVEMENT.

CANCER PATIENT. "Cancer" is a lay term, derived from the Latin word for "crab," (creeping ulcer). The term applies to a broad spectrum of malignant neoplasms (new and abnormal formations of tissue, e.g., a tumor, or "growth"), which are divided into two categories, carcinoma and sarcoma. Carcinoma refers to a new growth or malignant tumor which occurs on the skin and in mucous membrane tissue, for example, lungs, stomach lining, and intestines. Sarcomas arise in connective tissue such as muscle or bones, and may affect organs such as bladder, kidneys, liver, lungs, and spleen. Cancer is invasive and, if not benign, tends to metastasize, that is, travel from one point of the body to another.

Metastasis usually refers to the manifestation of a malignancy as a secondary growth arising from the primary growth in a new location. Spread is by the lymphatics or blood stream.

Prior to the outburst of AIDS, cancer was described as a demoralizing disease which had replaced tuberculosis as the most feared illness. Sontag noted that cancer patients are lied to, not just because the disease is perceived to be a death sentence, "but because it is felt to be obscene — in the original meaning of that word: ill-omened, abominable, repugnant to the senses." As recently as 1985, Slaby and Glicksman stated that cancer is probably feared more than any other disease. "There is horror of being given the diagnosis, of treatment of the disease, and of the death associated with it." Patterson stated that cancer has evoked popular fears which transcend its deadliness.

All illness carries with it a sense of isolation from family and community, and hence is perceived as a stigmatized state by the patient (Patterson; Ablon; Parsons; Goffman). In this context, it is important for the pastoral care provider to address these issues, assuring cancer patients that they are worthy of compassion and acceptance. This ministry is to be directed to patients and their immediate circle of family and friends. One of the strongest and surely most lasting of perceptions on the part of cancer patients is that even family members and close friends may pull away from them. A spouse may desert or divorce the patient, and friends may cease their visits. Ministry to cancer patients is thus characterized as a grief ministry to a person facing catastrophic losses or anticipated losses. These include the loss of well-being and security, self-esteem, and self image, identity as an active, productive member of a family and community, and dreams, aspirations and goals around which life has been organized (Sunderland).

Among the choices faced by patients and loved ones is the question whether to embark on a new drug therapy which is experimental in nature and perhaps accompanied by serious side effects. Some patients choose to accept the risks to grasp at any hope of averting death or in order that their sufferings may help others. Patients on experimental or other protocols may need to be reassured that it remains in their power to withdraw from the treatment when they choose to do so. The practice of medicine and law now provides for patients who wish to cease all intervention, and patients may even decline to be fed and hydrated. Such patients may be transferred to a hospice setting, either institutional or in the patient's home. The latter eventuality calls for a team of helpers, for example, from the patient's congregation, who will complement nursing care by hospice personnel, and assist the family when the patient wishes to die at home. Pastoral care providers may be called upon to assist patients to make these decisions, and/or to help family members understand the patient's wishes.

Patients and family members may also be confronted with the realization that hospital, medical, and nursing care costs may reach such a level that the family's economic security is threatened. Such a realization may be accompanied by feelings of helplessness, anger, and guilt, and the care provider should be alert to respond to these feelings with acceptance and compassion. Cancer care in the larger, tertiary-level medical centers is often provided to patients who have traveled across the country in search of a new drug or other therapy. In this event, both the patient and accompanying family member may experience isolation from customary support systems. Local congregations can assist such families by assigning members to visit out-of-town or out-of-state patients and families. Assigned lay ministers should receive training for this function, and continue their work under supervision.

Bibliography. J. Ablon, "Stigmatized Health Conditions," *J. of Social Science and Medicine,* 15 B (1981) 5 – 9. E. Goffman, *Stigma: Notes on the Management of Spoiled Identity* (1963). T. Parsons, *The Social System* (1951). J. T. Patterson, *The Dread Disease* (1987). A. E. Slaby and A. S. Glicksman, *Adapting to Life-threatening Illness* (1985). S. Sontag, *Illness as Metaphor* (1979). R. H. Sunderland, "Grief Recognition and Response," in *AIDS: A Manual for Pastoral Care* (1987), pp. 30ff.

R. H. SUNDERLAND

SICK, PASTORAL CARE OF; SICK AND DYING, JEWISH CARE OF; SUFFERING. *See also* CRISIS MINISTRY; HEALING; HOSPITALIZATION, EXPERIENCE OF; PAIN; PATIENCE/PATIENTHOOD. *Compare* DYING, PASTORAL CARE OF; HEART PATIENT; SURGICAL PATIENT.

CANDIDATES, MINISTERIAL. *See* THEOLOGICAL STUDENTS.

CANON LAW. *See* CODE OF CANON LAW; ECCLESIOLOGY.

CANON LAW SOCIETY OF AMERICA. A professional association of over 1,600 members largely in the United States which fosters the understanding and proper use of canon law in the Catholic Church. Formed in November 1939 in Washington, D.C., the Society has promoted canonical-pastoral approaches to key ecclesial issues and taken a leading role within the United States in revitalizing canon law in such areas as matrimonial tribunal procedures and due process structures. The Society has recently been involved in continuing education in and the preparation of an extensive commentary on the 1983 Code of Canon Law for the Latin Catholic Church. The Society's activities are expedited through a board of governors composed of a president, vice president, secretary, treasurer, and consultors. An executive coordinator facilitates various services provided for the members, e.g. professional publications, and expedites various undertakings such as conventions and symposia. Standing and *ad hoc* committees promote the Society's interests in various areas of canonical theory and practice.

T. J. GREEN

CODE OF CANON LAW; HISTORY OF ROMAN CATHOLIC PASTORAL CARE (Canada *or* United States); PASTORAL THEOLOGY, ROMAN CATHOLIC. *See also* CASUISTRY, ROMAN CATHOLIC; DIVORCE AND REMARRIAGE (Roman Catholicism); ECCLESIOLOGY, MORAL THEOLOGY, *or* VATICAN COUNCIL II, AND PASTORAL CARE.

C.A.P.E. *See* CANADIAN ASSOCIATION FOR PASTORAL EDUCATION.

CARDIAC PATIENT. *See* HEART PATIENT.

CARDINAL VIRTUES. *See* CHARACTER ETHICS; MORAL THEOLOGY; VIRTUE, CONCEPT OF.

CARE AND COUNSELING (Comparative Terminology). *See* PASTORAL CARE AND COUNSELING (Comparative Terminology).

CARE GROUPS. *See* GROWTH GROUPS.

CARE OF SOULS (Cura Animarum). The traditional term for pastoral care. The primary meaning of the Latin word *cura* is "care," although it also includes the notion of "healing." The word *anima* was the most common Latin translation of the Hebrew *nephesh* ("breath") and the Greek *psyche* ("soul"). "Soul" has many shades of meaning in Scripture. In Gen. 2:7, when God breathed into his nostrils, the man became "a living soul," yet the same word, *nephesh,* is used in Gen. 2:19 to describe animals (though translated "living creature"). In the NT "soul" stands for the essential human being, with emphasis on its transcendent destiny. The care or cure of souls, then, is distinguished from other helping enterprises by its consistent reference to ultimate meaning.

The term "care of souls" is used in three ways. (1) Its broadest use sums up the work of the office of priest, including leading worship, preaching, visiting, and organizing parish life. In this sense, "care of souls" acknowledges that all acts of ministry have as their ultimate aim the salvation and perfection of persons under God. In the Roman Catholic and Episcopal traditions a "curate" was one who had received the cure of souls by legitimate appointment to the office of parish pastor or assistant pastor. The bishop, likewise, exercised this care toward the diocese, and the pope toward the whole church.

(2) In a narrower sense, "care of souls" describes a particular strand of pastoral care tradition, *Seelsorge,* stemming from the Reformation and especially prominent in Lutheran pastoral theology. According to McNeill (1951), Lutheran practice rejected the compulsory nature of the confessional, but maintained it as a searching personal conversation on religious problems. Pastors gave priority to visiting the sick, the dying, and prisoners. Most important, they implemented Luther's recovery of the NT idea of mutual correction and encouragement, the "care of all for the souls of all," states McNeill.

(3) The "care of souls" is sometimes used as a synonym for pastoral care. Clebsch and Jaekle (1975) define the care of souls as "helping acts done by representative Christian persons directed toward the healing, sustaining, guiding, and reconciling of troubled persons whose troubles arise in the context of ultimate meanings and concerns."

The goals and methods of pastoral care have varied according to the age and culture. In a review of three hundred years of Protestant pastoral care in America, Holifield (1983) concluded that Pietism's preoccupation with the welfare of the individual soul became the seedbed for the growth of popular psychology. In turn, the new psychology reshaped the Protestant vision of the self,

so that the goal of pastoral care moved "from salvation to self-realization" under God.

The ancient term "cure of souls" reminds contemporary pastors of their apostolic forebears who, in the spirit of Jesus, met human pain with compassion and human guilt with grace and forgiveness.

Bibliography. W. A. Clebsch and C. R. Jaekle, *Pastoral Care in Historical Perspective* (1975), pp. 1, 4. F. Greeves, *Theology and the Cure of Souls* (1962). S. Hiltner, *Preface to Pastoral Theology* (1958), pp. 82–172. E. B. Holifield, *A History of Pastoral Care in America* (1983), p. 356. J. T. McNeill, *A History of the Cure of Souls* (1951), pp. 189–90. See also J. R. Haule, "The Care of Souls: Psychology and Religion in Anthropological Perspective," *J. of Psychology and Theology* 11 (1983), 108–16.

A. L. MEIBURG

PASTORAL CARE (History, Traditions, and Definitions). *Compare* JEWISH CARE AND COUNSELING; PASTORAL COUNSELING; PASTORAL PSYCHOTHERAPY; PSYCHOTHERAPY; SEELSORGE; SPIRITUAL DIRECTION (History and Traditions).

CAREER. *See* WORK AND CAREER.

CAREER DEVELOPMENT AND GUIDANCE (For Pastors). A process for mid-career stock-taking based on the premise that what religious professionals do for a living should, as much as possible, provide them with a reasonable degree of occupational satisfaction. Clergy, clergy candidates, and other religious professionals are given professional assistance in (1) assembling a relevant mass of psychological and vocational self-information; (2) engaging in in-depth reflection upon this information; and (3) in the context of this counselor-guided self-study planning for the actualization of their vocational potential.

Robert D. Rasmussen (1970) has described the process as "roughly comparable to putting a camera into your hands and teaching you how to take motion pictures of yourself in the conduct of your daily work," and as a process "by which persons are assisted in (a) assessing their abilities, interests, values, work experience, and career goals; (b) restating or altering their future occupational plans; and (c) integrating and implementing their clarified self-concept with the reality of their occupational situations" (Rasmussen, 1970).

Church career counseling has its roots in the general field of vocational counseling, but it has been modified to take account of the special characteristics of church-related occupations. It is not seen as a form of pastoral counseling or of psychological counseling. Usually brief and sharply focused, it does not intend therapeutic goals realized over an extended period of time. Rather, it attempts to assist the person in his or her own self-actualizing as a decision-maker.

The project is not to be viewed as the church's "hired hand," pressuring persons to remain in the ministry, anymore than it exists to encourage persons to leave a troubled occupation. In fact, "most of those who use such services intend to remain within the church occupations" (Rasmussen).

The movement has not been without its critics and its detractors. The main criticism from the psychological community is that such career counseling does not have a theoretical base which appreciates the deep nature of vocation, thus restricting its treatment to surface factors (Rulla, 1971). On the ecclesiastical side, criticisms have been based mostly on the fact that the methodological armamentarium comes from behavioral and social sciences, not from within the theological and ecclesiastical communities.

At the same time, the church has long needed a "humane method for an honorable exit from ministry" (Rasmussen), a fact made blatantly manifest following Vatican II when thousands of Roman Catholic priests and nuns left the church without their decision of exodus being examined and worked through.

Career development counseling centers function out of several different models, but most centers have a minimal staff consisting of a career counselor, a part-time clinical psychologist, a medical consultant, and an administrative assistant. Although there are some philosophical and methodological differences evident in the movement, most participants would agree with the assertion that such career work is a process, not a single event. Procedures, too, differ, although most centers follow a procedure similar to the following:

Prior to a person's arrival at a career development center, a guided autobiographical questionnaire is placed in his or her hands, along with an inventory of those activities and achievements which have been meaningful to the participant. This latter inventory becomes the basis for a rather painstaking analysis of the individual's effectively demonstrated abilities, thus producing a skill-bank capable of replication in future development.

Also prior to the person's actual experience with the career development, he or she is asked to complete, under the direction of a test proctor, a battery of standardized vocational and psychological tests as well as specialized instruments designed by career development counselors in their attempt to tailor-make their counseling to the needs of each individual client.

During the career development planning process the client will spend one-and-a-half to two hours with a staff clinical psychologist. This personality assessment attempts to provide the client with a fair and accurate picture of personality makeup. The client's time with the psychologist is followed by a case conference between the psychologist and the career counselor. The resulting full report becomes a part of the client's total data bank.

Where appropriate, spouse participation is invited and encouraged. Spouse perspective often adds an invaluable dimension to the religious professional's work.

Strict professional confidentiality is practiced by all centers in the Church Career Development Council network. No information is released to the client's denominational officials, or to any person or agency, except upon the client's own authorization.

Costs for these services vary according to the client's relationship with one of the center's participating regional denominational bodies. Most mainline Protestant groups and some Roman Catholic orders provide subsidy for their ordained clergy, applicants for ministerial candidacy, brothers in religious orders, religious sisters, etc.

Approximately twenty regionally located career development centers are accredited by the Church Career Development Council, Inc. and by an accreditation arm of the American Association for Counseling and Development. Locations of centers and brochures describing their services are available from the Church Career Development Council office.

Bibliography. R. Bolles, *What Color Is Your Parachute?* (1982). T. Brown, "Career Planning," in *Creating an Intentional Ministry,* J. Biersdorf, ed., (1976). W. Coville, *et al., Assessment of Candidates for the Religious Life* (1968). J. Kinnane, *Career Development for Priests and Religious* (1970). H. Malony and D. Falkenberg, "Ministerial Burnout," in *Leadership* (Fall, 1980). E. Mills, "Career Development in Middle Life," in *Evolving Religious Careers,* E. Willis, ed., (1970). G. Jud, E. Mills, and G. Burch, "Summary of Findings," in *Ex-Pastors — Why Men Leave the Parish Ministry* (1970). R. Ragsdale, *The Mid-Life Crises of a Minister* (1978). R. Rasmussen, "Resources for Career Development," in *The Continuing Quest,* J. Hofrenning, ed., (1970). L. Rulla, *Depth Psychology and Vocation* (1971).

D. FALKENBERG

PASTOR, PASTORAL CARE OF; VOCATION. *See also* CALL TO MINISTRY; MINISTRY; RABBINATE; WORK AND CAREER. *Compare* CLERGY, EMPIRICAL STUDIES OF.

CARICATURES OF THE PASTOR. *See* PASTOR, STEREOTYPES AND CARICATURES OF.

CARING COMMUNITY. *See* COMMUNITY, FELLOWSHIP, AND CARE. *See also* CONGREGATION; RELATIONSHIP NETWORK; RELIGIOUS AND UTOPIAN COMMUNITIES; THERAPEUTIC COMMUNITY; SUPPORT GROUPS.

CARMELITE SPIRITUALITY. *See* SPIRITUALITY (Roman Catholic Tradition).

CASE STUDY METHOD. An organized and systematic way of studying and reporting various aspects of a person, family, group, or situation using a predetermined outline of questions or subjects. In clinical supervision the case study method is frequently used as a method of reporting, analyzing, and evaluating a pastoral encounter or counseling session. It is also used as a teaching method in many disciplines, including theological education, where a particular pastoral situation is reported and discussed in a classroom setting.

1. **Development and Use.** The use of stories or parables for purposes of instruction is an ancient precursor of the modern case study method. The prophet Nathan, for instance, used a story of a rich man and a poor man to confront King David with the meaning of his behavior (II Sam. 12:1–6), and Jesus used stories like those of the Good Samaritan (Lk. 10:29–37), the householder (Mt. 21:33–41), and the man with two sons (Lk. 15:11–32) to teach the Kingdom of God.

a. Education. In modern times, the case study method as an educational device was introduced by Christopher Langdell, the first dean of Harvard Law School, in 1870. Langdell believed that students should learn principles of law by studying and mastering actual court cases dealing with particular situations. From these, students learned the process of making legal decisions by understanding the relevance of particular cases to general situations, rather than attempting to apply general rules to a specific instance. By the early twentieth century, the more progressive medical schools and schools of social work used the case study method to teach diagnostic skills and to supervise students' work (see Anton T. Boisen below).

The Harvard Business School has had a major impact on education in many fields through extensive use of the case study method in its curriculum (see McNair). The Association of Theological Schools, in cooperation with the Harvard Business School, has formed a Case Study Institute, which provides many cases on numerous subjects for use in theological schools and churches, available through published bibliographies. Written in the action/decision model of the Harvard Business School, these cases give detailed accounts of situations illustrating the concerns of pastoral care, pastoral counseling, church administration, ethics, church history, theology, and other related subjects.

The case study method has been used pedagogically in the field of history to provide descriptions of persons, places, or events that give the student a deeper understanding of a particular historical period (see Rosell), and has been developed into a form of historical research, psychohistory, by Erik Erikson and others. Erikson has published extensive case studies exploring the psychosocial development of Martin Luther, Gandhi, and Thomas Jefferson.

b. Psychology. The case study has been especially important in the field of psychology as a means of describing, analyzing, and interpreting clinical issues in the lives of individuals. Freud wrote extensive case histories to illustrate and describe his clinical findings. These were typically a chronological account of Freud's sessions with a patient, giving data concerning presenting problems, behavior, symptoms, and therapeutic interventions, and concluding with a clinical discussion and analysis of the case. Other case studies in psychology have utilized categories such as present illness, personal history, family history, psychiatric findings, hospitalizations, psychometric findings, and clinical summary. In psychology, a distinction is made between the *case study,* which usually deals with a problem of adjustment during a relatively short period of time, and the *life history,* a more comprehensive, long-term analysis of a person's life issues (see Bromley).

c. Pastoral theology. The case study method has been important in the conceptualization and teaching of pastoral theology. Hiltner (1958) used the detailed pastoral notes of Ichabod Spencer, a Presbyterian minister in the mid-nineteenth century, to define and illustrate the functions of shepherding. Hiltner believed that one-to-one relationships could provide the starting point for the study of basic principles in pastoral theology. Thornton (1964) used an extensive case study of "Mr. Mills" to approach subjects such as repentance, salvation, and faith. Oates (1970) provided vivid case examples to describe the relationship between religion and mental illness.

d. Clinical Pastoral Education (CPE). i. Anton T. Boisen. The use of the case study method in CPE originated with Anton T. Boisen, the founder of CPE. His belief that the study of theology in the classroom must be supplemented with a reading of the "living human documents" led him to recruit four theological students for the first unit of CPE at Worcester (Massachusetts) State Hospital in 1925. His case studies of mentally ill people were motivated partly by his desire to understand and validate his own experience of mental illness. (See Boisen 1936, 1946, 1955, and 1960 for examples and applications of his case study method with individuals and social groups.)

Boisen first became acquainted with the case study method while studying with George Albert Coe at Union Theological Seminary in New York (1909–10). In Coe's seminar on mysticism, Boisen read Delacroix's careful case analyses of Saint Teresa, Madame Guyon, and Heinrich Suso. Another major influence on Boisen's method was Richard C. Cabot, with whom Boisen studied at Harvard Divinity School. Cabot's book *Differential Diagnosis* was based on his clinical pathological conferences at Harvard Medical School. This educational procedure pointed to diagnosis on the basis of known facts as the most important part of learning from the "human documents." Boisen attended Cabot's social ethics seminar on preparation of case records for teaching purposes (1922–23). Boisen also learned the case study method in social work from Miss Susie Lyons of the Social Service Department at Boston Psychopathic Hospital (1923–24). By applying case study principles as a social worker, Boisen found that he could study the whole person in his or her social setting and deal with significant factors such as motives, values, and religious experience.

In CPE, Boisen's basic goal was to help theological students form their own theology from an empirical base. In the introduction to an unpublished collection of his case studies, which he distributed to CPE centers, Boisen noted that their use was not primarily for students to learn skills but rather to enable students to build a theology through a careful study of religious experiences and beliefs. He believed that a detailed survey of a patient's family, religious, and developmental history, as well as the present illness, was the most important activity for CPE students because it would enable them to understand the patient and provide a basis for discussion of the meaning of the patient's illness and treatment. In this way, students were able to read the "living human documents." (For a more detailed description of Boisen's case method, see Asquith, 1976 and 1980.)

ii. Russell L. Dicks. Beginning his work as chaplain at Massachusetts General Hospital, Dicks developed another approach to the case study method—the "verbatim." Adapted from social work, though with precursors in earlier centuries of pastoral care, the verbatim was more suited to short-term pastoral care in a general hospital, where Boisen's life history method would have been difficult and, in many cases, less relevant to crisis intervention during physical illness.

In the verbatim, Dicks sought to reproduce, as closely as possible, the actual conversation between chaplain and patient (see Cabot and Dicks). Such a focus became the cornerstone for supervision and evaluation of pastoral work in CPE. It enabled reflection upon the effectiveness, appropriateness, and congruence of the pastor's response to a person in crisis. While Dicks was indeed concerned about the ways in which a person's religious beliefs functioned during illness, his verbatim dealt more with method and practice than with the theological reflection inherent in Boisen's life histories. Boisen, while affirming the importance of good pastoral care, became increasingly concerned, as the CPE movement progressed, that it was focusing more on psychological method than on theological understanding of human experience. Nevertheless, the testing and formation of a student's theology continues to be a basic purpose of CPE, and the case study method remains as one of the primary tools by which this objective is achieved.

e. Other uses. In supervision of pastoral psychotherapy, which is usually conducted in a formal office setting, the case study method is centered upon a taped segment of a particular session. Its presentation is usually preceded by an oral or written report of basic data about the counselee, family and marital history, diagnosis, therapeutic issues and goals, and summary of the relationship to the point of the current session. The use of audio or video tape enables the supervisor to focus more completely upon the dynamics between client and therapist.

The case study method has been employed to study and understand one particular aspect of a person's life. Satir's "Family Life Chronology" gives the individual and collective history of family members in therapy. Draper's "Religious History Inventory" surveys the origins, current functions, and future orientation of a person's religious faith in order to assess its impact upon other aspects of his or her life. In such uses, case information is not gathered in a routine, mechanical way; these are rather guidelines for the investigation of particular subjects.

The case method is also used in training lay persons for all aspects of work within the local church. In Christian education, it can be a tool for developing skills of teachers and youth advisors (Fallaw). In the verbatim or process report form, it is used for supervision of laity in visitation, outreach, and crisis intervention.

In courses such as business, law, and theology, cases usually take the form of a description of a previous event outside of the student's experience. In supervision of pastoral work, the case usually reports and evaluates the student's own experience in a particular situation or encounter.

2. Methodology. *a. Current applications.* The most frequently used type of case study in pastoral care and counseling is that of the student's own experience. This may be recorded according to the following outline.

I. Background Information
  A. Basic facts about the person or situation
  B. Conditions leading to the pastor's involvement
  C. Summary of pastor's relationship to person or situation up to the point of the report, including other persons or professionals involved
  D. Nature of pastor's preparation for the visit, session, or situation, including intended goals
  E. Physical description of the person(s), environment, and first impressions at beginning of event
II. Description of Event

This may take one of several forms:
  A. Verbatim account of entire session, including pauses, non-verbal communications, exterior events, etc., with each statement labeled and numbered according to persons involved
  B. Process report of event, written in prose form summarizing the content of all verbal and non-verbal interchanges
  C. Combination of verbatim and process reporting, which gives verbatim account only of short, critical segments of event
  D. Audio or video tape of event, or segment of it
III. Evaluation
  A. Identification of theological and psychological issues inherent in the session
  B. Evaluation of pastor's role in the event in light of stated goals and in terms of strengths and weaknesses of method, including a statement of what was learned or resolved in the event
  C. Citing of relevant literature which may assist the pastor in dealing with this and future events
  D. Questions for discussion of the case

Comprehensive case reports of this type can become lengthy, so supervisors, pastors, and educators continually experiment with alternatives that achieve the same goals. One alternative is the incident report, a one-page description of a critical event in a student's training process (Perske) or a problem situation that calls for group consensus on a possible solution (Pigors and Pigors).

Another method, adopted by the Academy of Parish Clergy for continuing education seminars, requires each participant to write a one-page case with four parts: background, description, analysis of issues and relationships, and evaluation of the pastor's effectiveness (Glasse). Confining this information to one page forces the writer to identify critical information and focuses upon the alternatives for action in the given situation.

b. Guidelines for use. Standards for the effective use of the case study have been suggested by those who have had extensive experience with this method. Glasse notes that a case study should include a clear statement of the pastor's goals in the situation, a point of choice between alternate courses of action, and attention to significant details that affect the case. Bromley offers basic rules for the preparation of psychological case studies, including the need for accuracy and truthfulness in reporting and a comprehensive statement of the full "ecological context" in which the person lives.

A study of historic and contemporary uses of the case study method suggests several guidelines for its use in pastoral care.

1. Discussion and analysis of case studies should make use of, but also *transcend,* behavioral science perspectives. In the pastoral care movement it has been the temptation to rely heavily upon the behavioral sciences for understanding of a person's life issues and to give only secondary attention to theological themes that might be

inherent in the case. This can be addressed by examining the goals for use of a case study; is it being studied to make one a better therapist or a better theologian? The former is not pastoral care without equal attention to the latter.

2. A case used in pastoral care should be *theologically provocative,* having inherent issues that stimulate theological thinking among those using the case. Initially, it often requires skill and effort on the part of the teacher or supervisor to make such theological issues apparent to students in pastoral care; ultimately, a case study should enable students to make this identification on their own and thus gain skill as pastoral theologians. If this cannot be done without a great deal of effort and speculation then the case may not be suitable for use.

3. Some principles should emerge out of a case study with *universal* application to the pastor's work. The case should not be too narrow in focus but should have wider application to an understanding of theology and basic life issues.

4. The case should be interpreted from an *informed* perspective. While Boisen asserted the importance of studying the nature of human experience, he also disapproved of students who did not read to supplement their clinical learning. Theological and psychological dynamics can only be accurately identified from the foundation of a basic body of knowledge. To be fully effective, a case study should stimulate and make use of clinical reading on the issues raised in the case.

5. A final concern in case studies is *confidentiality.* Deep and sensitive material about a person's life is usually presented. The presentor often feels a sense of betrayal of confidence, which can cause resistance in reporting the full story. In situations where the identity of the counselee, parishioner, or patient must be disclosed, tapes or materials should be erased or destroyed after use. When the identity of the person is not necessary, it should be disguised. In supervision, the person is frequently not the central focus; the main emphasis is rather upon the presentor of the case. The case study is a tool for facilitating growth and skill in identifying and dealing with the various dynamics present in the case.

3. **Evaluation.** Bromley and Runyan have noted the shortcoming of subjectivity in the presentation and discussion of case studies, and the fact that a study is frequently presented by one person to a group of like-minded persons. Thus there is value in having the analysis and conclusions of a case study subject to the critical examination of others — especially those with differing theoretical points of view. A balanced discussion and critique adds to the wider application of principles inherent in the case.

The case study has proven to be an effective method for giving students a working knowledge of the principles of any given discipline. A well-prepared case study does not point to one easy and quick solution; it forces those discussing the case to return to the basic tools and knowledge of their discipline and apply them to life situations. Thus the case study method is effective in enabling students to master the complex material of disciplines such as theology, psychology, and ethics (see Veatch). A good case presentation can broaden one's awareness of the magnitude and depth of critical life issues; it can sharpen analytical, philosophical, or theological skills; and it can develop a person's tolerance of disagreement and ambiguity. Such a case can help to make students and teachers colleagues, rather than adversaries, by engaging them in a mutual search for the truth in the practice of their profession.

The regular use of the case study method can also add depth to the practice of pastoral care. In the face of many responsibilities, the pastor is often tempted to make superficial judgments based on inadequate information. The investment of time spent in learning the history and details of a person's situation will enable the pastor to be more prescriptive, and therefore more effective, in his or her pastoral care and counseling.

Bibliography. G. H. Asquith, Jr., "The Case Study Method of Anton T. Boisen," *J. of Pastoral Care,* 34 (1980), 84–94; "The Clinical Method of Theological Inquiry of A. T. Boisen," unpublished dissertation, Southern Baptist Theological Seminary (1976). A. T. Boisen, *The Exploration of the Inner World* (1936); *Out of the Depths* (1960); *Problems in Religion and Life* (1946); *Religion in Crisis and Custom* (1955). J. Breuer and S. Freud, "Studies on Hysteria," (*SE,* vol. 2). K. Bridston, et al., *Casebook on Church and Society* (1974). D. Bromley, *Personality Description in Ordinary Language* (1977), ch. 8. R. C. Cabot and R. L. Dicks, *The Art of Ministering to the Sick* (1936), ch. 18; *Cases in Theological Education* (1981). N. Cryer and J. Vayhinger, *Casebook in Pastoral Counseling* (1962). E. Draper, *et al.,* "On the Diagnostic Value of Religious Ideation," *Archives of General Psychiatry,* 13 (1965), 202–7. E. Erikson, *Life History and the Historical Moment* (1975). W. Fallaw, *The Case Method in Pastoral and Lay Education* (1963). S. Freud, *Three Case Histories,* P. Rieff, ed., (1963). J. Glasse, *Putting It Together in the Parish* (1972), chs. 7–8. S. Hiltner, *Preface to Pastoral Theology* (1958). M. McNair, *The Case Method at the Harvard Business School* (1954). W. E. Oates, *When Religion Gets Sick* (1970). R. Perske, "The Use of a Critical Incident Report," *J. of Pastoral Care,* 20 (1966), 156–61. P. Pigors and F. Pigors, *Case Method in Human Relations* (1961). G. Rosell, "Clio in the Classroom: The Use of Case Studies in the Teaching of History," *Theological Education,* 13 (1977), 168–74. W. Runyan, *Life Histories and Psychobiography* (1982). V. Satir, *Conjoint Family Therapy,* rev. ed., (1967), 112–35. C. S. Calian, "Case Study Materials and Seminary Teaching," *Theological Education,* 10 (1974), 136–217. E. E. Thornton, *Theology and Pastoral Counseling* (1964). R. Veatch, *Case Studies in Medical Ethics* (1977).

G. H. ASQUITH, JR.

CLINICAL PASTORAL EDUCATION; THEOLOGICAL EDUCATION AND THE PASTORAL CARE MOVEMENT; VERBATIM. *Compare* EMPIRICAL THEOLOGY AND PASTORAL CARE; ROLE PLAY; TEACHING. *Biography:* BOISEN; CABOT; COE; DICKS.

CASEWORK. *See* SOCIAL CASEWORK.

CASSIAN, JOHN. *See* CLASSIC LITERATURE IN CARE AND COUNSELING (Roman Catholicism); EARLY CHURCH, PASTORAL CARE AND COUNSELING IN.

CASUISTRY, JEWISH. *See* JEWISH CARE AND COUNSELING.

CASUISTRY, PROTESTANT. The art of applying general moral and pastoral principles to particular questions of conduct and conscience. Casuistic textbooks began appearing among Protestants—especially in England and Holland—in the late-sixteenth century, and they soon became the standard manuals for pastoral care and counsel. They combined ethical prescriptions with methods of pastoral inquiry and standards of clerical judgment. In scope they embraced issues ranging from politics and economics to clothing and recreation, but their primary purpose was to help the pastor discern and treat the spiritual ailments that tormented "all poore distressed consciences" (H. Holland, Introduction, *The Works . . . of Richard Greenham,* 1599). Therefore, they encouraged the spread of an introspective piety and became especially popular among the American Puritan ministers, who used them to analyze the stages in the order of salvation.

1. **Emergence.** The explanation for the sudden appearance and proliferation of writings on casuistry is complicated. Roman Catholics had long taunted Protestants for lacking a casuistic tradition. The success of Elizabeth I in thwarting institutional reform in the Church of England impelled religious reformers to concentrate their attention on individual piety and reformation. The Reformed and Anglican doctrinal emphasis on sanctification created a demand for moral guidebooks. And the preoccupation with the doctrine of election in the late-sixteenth century engendered widespread anxiety about salvation. The resulting "problem of assurance" required that ministers become cartographers of the inner life, able to chart the normal stages of a pilgrim's progress. For whatever reasons, the English theologian William Perkins published his famous *Discourse of Conscience* in 1596, and other theologians followed his example. William Ames, an English refugee to Holland, extolled Perkins's formative influence when he wrote his own text, *Conscience with the Power and Cases Thereof* (1630), which remained a standard authority in England, Holland, and America well into the eighteenth century.

2. **Introspective Methods.** The treatises ensured that Protestant pastoral care would be a wide-ranging enterprise that embraced not only spiritual growth but also civic responsibility, familial duties, economic morality, and political attitudes. But especially in the American colonies where Puritan influences shaped the religious ethos, the casuistic texts encouraged an introspective piety by offering detailed descriptions of the order of salvation. Perkins, for instance, outlined ten stages of religious growth: (1) an inward or outward "cross" exposing the self's insufficiency, (2) an awareness of "law," (3) a recognition of the power of sin, (4) legal fear, (5) a consideration of the promise of salvation, (6) initial faith, (7) doubt and despair, (8) assurance, (9) evangelical sorrow, and (10) joyful obedience. The informed pastor, using such a series of descriptions, could distinguish the legal fear of stage four from the doubt and despair of level seven and thereby know how to comfort—or admonish—an anxious parishioner. The treatises also informed pastors how to apply general ethical principles to specific ambiguous cases. And they presented examples of proper casuistic inquiry: Perkins, for instance, provided lists of questions that could unearth the "causes" of spiritual distress, followed by other lists of questions that could clarify the "effects" of inner dispositions.

3. **The Role of Logic.** The casuistic writers usually had considerable training in logic, and that training deeply informed their conception of pastoral counsel. A number of them, for instance, developed patterns of pastoral inquiry and diagnosis using the logic of Petrus Ramus, a sixteenth-century French logician. Ramus and his followers had tried to identify and classify the concrete terms implicit within more general conceptions. Each abstract word, they thought, could be subdivided into at least two other more concrete terms, each of which could then be further subdivided, until every logical notion was clearly understandable. The logician could then confidently combine the words into propositions.

Perkins, following the Ramist procedure, instructed pastors that a spiritual malady like "distress of mind" could be subdivided into two modes: fear of condemnation and despair of salvation. Each form of distress arose from temptations, which could also be subdivided into two modes: temptations of trial, which tested faith, and temptations of seducement, which were demonic seducements into evil. Temptations of trial could then be further divided into two types: they could be struggles with a wrathful God or afflictions designed by God to test faith. Temptations of seducement were subject to similar divisions. By adroit questioning, pastors could use such a method of analysis to discern the religious state of distressed parishioners. They could assure a worried saint, for instance, that his or her spiritual pain was an outward affliction of trial producing a fear of condemnation, not a blasphemous temptation of seducement producing despair. Logical analysis was thus at the heart of pastoral counsel among Perkins's followers. Not every casuistic text used a Ramist logic, but they all reflected some pattern of logical analysis and inquiry.

The casuists proposed, then, that pastors employ a method of inquiry, logical classification, syllogistic reasoning, and persuasive argumentation. They taught the minister to begin each session of counsel by asking questions. Upon receiving a sufficient number of answers, the pastors used the prescribed pastoral logic to diagnose the ailment. Then the task was to convince the parishioner that the diagnosis was correct. Most casuists believed that pastors could be most convincing when they combined their diagnostic conclusions with biblical truths in such a way as to form syllogistic arguments. Their procedures, they thought, were therefore both rational and biblical. They constituted what the clergy called an "answering method," permitting them to carry on a "methodical" pastoral conversation. (The word "method," derived from the field of logic, became a technical term referring to the rational procedures advocated by the casuists.)

4. **Decline.** The casuistic "method" prevailed in America until the mid-eighteenth century when, for several reasons, it declined. First, more descriptive treatments of pastoral issues, like Jonathan Edwards's *Treatise Concerning Religious Affections,* became popular among the clergy. Second, the emergence in England and Scotland of "moral philosophy" as a new kind of specialized ethical inquiry superseded the interest in the older style of casuistic ethics. Third, the popularity of "moral sense" theories in ethics seemed to make irrelevant the painstaking moral reasoning that had marked the casuistic tradi-

tion. And finally, the growing disinclination, after the eighteenth-century revivals, to insist on a highly educated clergy meant that a smaller proportion of pastors had to read the casuistry texts in college. By the early nineteenth-century, the educated clergy read not casuistic treatises but the new textbooks in "pastoral theology," along with separate texts in "moral science." The casuistic tradition gave way to more specialized modes of inquiry. But most of the pastoral theology texts, which were focused initially on homiletics and evangelism, failed to retain the expansive scope of the earlier books on casuistry.

The Protestant casuists, like their Catholic predecessors and contemporaries, had promulgated a highly rationalistic view of pastoral counsel, but they had succeeded in directing the pastor's attention to both private spiritual issues and matters of broad social concern. They also had recognized the ambiguity of particular moral judgments without thereby surrendering a confidence in ethical principles. And they had located pastoral concerns squarely within a broad theological context. The tradition never disappeared entirely, but the residues that remain in the twentieth century are found mainly among Christian ethicists, who still debate abut the relationships between general moral principles and the concrete situations that call for ethical decisions.

Bibliography. For further analysis, see E. B. Holifield, *A History of Pastoral Care in America: From Salvation to Self-Realization* (1983). Two illuminating primary sources are W. Perkins, *The Whole Treatise of the Cases of Conscience* 2d ed., (1617) and W. Ames, *Conscience with the Power and Cases Thereof* (Latin, 1630; English, 1643). See also T. Wood, *English Casuistical Divinity During the Seventeenth Century* (1952).

E. B. HOLIFIELD

HISTORY OF PROTESTANT PASTORAL CARE (United States); MORAL THEOLOGY AND PASTORAL CARE; PASTORAL CARE (History, Traditions, and Definitions); SIN/SINS. *See also* CONSCIENCE (Protestantism); ETHICS AND PASTORAL CARE; REASONING AND RATIONALITY IN PASTORAL CARE. *Compare* CASE STUDY METHOD; EVALUATION AND DIAGNOSIS, RELIGIOUS; GUIDANCE, PASTORAL; JEWISH CARE AND COUNSELING; MORAL DILEMMAS IN PASTORAL PERSPECTIVE; PASTORAL THEOLOGY, PROTESTANT. *Biography:* AMES, Edward Scribner; EDWARDS; PERKINS.

CASUISTRY, ROMAN CATHOLIC. Casuistry may be defined as the method of applying general principles of any discipline to particular cases. However, casuistry usually refers specifically to the methodology by which general moral or legal rules are applied to concrete situations; so understood, casuistry today is generally associated with Roman Catholic moral theology. Within that formal discipline, it is employed both to illustrate general principles, and to guide confessors and others in the application of those principles to specific cases.

While casuistry has been in bad repute since the eighteenth century, it is a necessary part of any practically oriented system of morality. Nonetheless, it is fair to say that Catholic moral theology places a distinctive emphasis on casuistry. And this fact provides an important key to understanding the relationship between Catholicism's moral thought and its pastoral practice; the development of Catholic casuistry reflects the tensions inherent in a moral theology that is at once a juridical and a pastoral discipline.

On the one hand, the development of Catholic moral theology has been closely tied to the development of the sacrament of penance and canon law. Hence, it has tended to focus on determining permissible and forbidden kinds of actions, rather than concentrating on, for example, general principles or inner dispositions. While this focus has sometimes become legalistic, it is rooted in the church's sense of what is required for its own integrity. But at the same time, moral theology has been shaped by a pastoral tradition of special concern for the spiritually weak. Pastors and theologians have usually brought this concern together with the church's juridical claims by focusing on determining minimal standards of behavior and extenuating circumstances. Naturally, casuistry has played a crucial role in these determinations. And while moral theology has sometimes fallen into casuistical laxism, at its best it reflects a realistic and nuanced sense of the integral relation between the individual's actions and his or her intentions and attitudes.

1. Historical Developments. Casuistry has always played a role in the church's moral reflections. The patristic era saw a number of lively casuistical discussions, often centered around the embarrassing behavior of scriptural heroes and some saints. (Should Jacob have lied to Isaac? Should certain virgins have submitted to rape, rather than jumping off a cliff?) Esoteric as they might now sound, these discussions had important practical implications. At the same time, pastors were called on to provide casuistical guidance for everyday problems related to truth-telling, self-defense, wealth and commerce, and marriage and family life. This tradition of pastorally oriented casuistry continued through the Middle Ages, contributing substantially to the development of Catholic moral theories of the just war, commercial practices, and marriage and sexuality.

As Kirk observes, casuistry flourished in both Catholic and Protestant circles from the time of the Reformation until the end of the seventeenth century. At that point, "Reformed casuistry died as sudden a death as any in history" (Kirk, p. 203). In Catholicism, on the other hand, the seventeenth and eighteenth centuries are considered the golden age of casuistry; they also saw bitter disputes over casuistical laxism.

In response to the requirement of the Council of Trent that sins be confessed by species (kind) and number, moral theology in the sixteenth century focused increasingly on casuistry. By the end of this century, the manuals for the training of confessors (the *Institutiones morales*) had assumed a standard form, which emphasized the study of cases of conscience. As a part of this study, these manuals offered guidance for the confessor who is not certain how to guide the perplexed or erring penitent through the theory of *probabilism*. Probabilism simply holds that in doubtful cases, a confessor may give absolution if he has reason to do so, even if he also has what seems to be a stronger reason to refuse absolution. Hence, this theory represents an attempt to reconcile the demands of God, and ecclesial integrity, with the needs of penitents struggling with the ambiguities of life and their own weaknesses.

The difficulty was that probabilism was perceived as leading to an unacceptably lax interpretation of Christian morality. No doubt, it was abused by some confessors, although as Kirk argues, a sympathetic reading of the probabilists suggests that they were more sensible, and more compassionately wise about human life, than they are usually thought to have been (Kirk, pp. 207–12). In any event, the probabilists, most of whom were Jesuits, were bitterly opposed both by the more rigorist Dominicans and by the Jansenists. Public opinion tended to favor the rigorist view, and as a result both casuistry and the Jesuits got a bad name that is with them still. Finally, this controversy was effectively settled by Alphonsus Liguori (1696–1787), "the Prince of Moral Theologians," whose own theory (equiprobabilism) was ultimately less important than the judicious opinions he offered on a variety of cases. It should be noted that while Liguori avoided the extremes of laxism, he was not nearly rigorist enough for many of his contemporaries. Nonetheless, the Holy See has declared that his opinions on all subjects could safely be followed; that is, Liguori's casuistry was not declared to provide the one right view on every case, but to be always within the verge of acceptable options for a Catholic confessor. Practically, his influence has been immense.

Casuistry has continued to play an important role in Catholic moral theology through the present time. Since Vatican II, however, the context for casuistry has changed significantly, at least in this country, due to changing attitudes toward the sacrament of penance. For many, this sacrament is no longer seen primarily as the kind of private court that it became in the Counter-Reformation; in any case, its use seems to be declining. At the same time, many priests and laity in the U.S. are more willing to allow persons of uncertain ecclesial status (for example, divorced and remarried Catholics) open access to the sacraments. In this context, casuistry can no longer focus on the juridical judgements of confessors. Casuistry continues to play a significant role in contemporary moral theology, but now it is more often used to illuminate the ways in which a person's actions reflect his or her fundamental dispositions, than it would have been in the Counter-Reformation church.

2. **Contemporary Issues.** Certain casuistical principles have received considerable attention recently.

a. The principle of double effect. This principle is receiving considerable scrutiny, especially in connection with medical cases. It attempts to provide guidance in situations in which both good and bad effects will accrue from a contemplated action. As traditionally formulated, it holds that the action is permissible if (1) it is not intrinsically morally evil in itself (unlike, for example, murder or adultery), (2) the evil effect is not the casual means by which the good effect is produced, (3) the evil effect is not intended for its own sake, and (4) there is a proportionate reason for permitting the evil action.

The difficulty with these criteria is that they seem to produce counterintuitive results, especially in some medical cases. Hence, a number of moral theologians have recently advocated either modifying this principle drastically, or else abolishing it. Others insist that in spite of the difficult cases, this principle acknowledges the necessary linkage between certain kinds of actions and certain intentions and attitudes better than any proposed alternative. The issues at stake are complex; further reading is suggested in the bibliography.

b. Cooperation. In what circumstances may a person assist in performing a morally wrong act? The complex traditional answer to this question continues to be significant, again especially with reference to medical cases (for example, the situation of nurses required to assist at abortions). Simply put, the doctrine of cooperation holds that no one may ever cooperate with a morally wrong act if he or she approves of what is being done (formal cooperation); however, a person may cooperate in an act of which he or she disapproves morally, if he or she has a proportionate reason for doing so, proportionate reason being determined in relation to the degree of cooperation involved, as well as to the agent's purpose in cooperating (material cooperation). To switch examples, a confirmed pacifist could therefore work in a munitions plant, if she had no other means whereby to support her family.

c. Epikeia. In the wake of the most recent revision of the Code of Canon Law (1983), the principle of epikeia is receiving renewed attention. In Catholic tradition, this principle simply holds that (human) laws should be applied in accordance with the presumed good intention of the lawmaker, who cannot have foreseen all circumstances, and who (presumably) would not have wanted a law to bind in circumstances in which its application would be harmful. So, for example, a diabetic can assume that the church precept to fast on Good Friday does not apply to him, if fasting would seriously injure his health. He would not have to ask for a dispensation in order to exempt himself from the observance of this law. It has been observed that this principle is more at home in a Roman than in an Anglo-American legal system; if it were more widely recognized in this country, Catholic canon law would be seen to be far more flexible than many assume it to be.

Bibliography. J. Coriden *et al.*, eds., *The Code of Canon Law: A Text and Commentary* (1985). G. Cragg, *The Church and the Age of Reason 1648–1789* rev. ed., (1970). C. Curran and R. McCormick, eds., *Readings in Moral Theology No. 1: Moral Norms and Catholic Tradition* (1979). J. Dedek, *Titius and Bertha Ride Again* (1974). E. Hamel, "Casuistry," *New Catholic Encyclopedia*, vol. 3, (1967), 195–7. B. Häring, *The Law of Christ*, vol. 1 (1965). E. Healy, *Medical Ethics* (1963). G. Kelly, *Medico-Moral Problems* (1960). K. Kirk, *Conscience and Its Problems* rev. ed. (1936). R. McCormick and P. Ramsey, eds., *Doing Evil to Achieve Good* (1978). "Moral Theology," *New Catholic Encyclopedia*, vol. 9, (1967) 1109–25.

J. PORTER

MORAL DILEMMAS IN PASTORAL PERSPECTIVE; MORAL THEOLOGY AND PASTORAL CARE; PASTORAL CARE (History, Traditions, and Definitions); ROMAN CATHOLIC PASTORAL CARE; SIN/SINS. *See also* CANON LAW SOCIETY OF AMERICA; CONSCIENCE (Roman Catholicism); ETHICS AND PASTORAL CARE; HISTORY OF ROMAN CATHOLIC PASTORAL CARE (Canada *or* United States); LEGALISM AND ANTINOMIANISM; PENANCE, SACRAMENT OF. *Compare* CASE STUDY METHOD; EVALUATION AND DIAGNOSIS, RELIGIOUS; JEWISH CARE AND COUNSELING; MORAL DILEMMAS IN PASTORAL PERSPECTIVE; PASTORAL THEOLOGY, ROMAN CATHOLIC; SPIRITUAL THEOLOGY AND PASTORAL CARE. *Biography:* LIGUORI.

CAT SCAN. *See* BRAIN RESEARCH.

CATASTROPHE, PUBLIC. *See* Disaster, Public.

CATECHUMENATE/CATECHETICS. *See* Baptism and Confirmation; Education, Nurture and Care; Roman Catholic Pastoral Care; Teaching.

CATHARSIS. Derived from a Greek word meaning "to cleanse or purify," and commonly referred to as the "ventilation of feelings," catharsis generally refers to the process in which there is a sudden, overwhelming expression of emotion (e.g., crying), which results in release of tension. Though usually a normal and naturally therapeutic response to situations of grief, guilt, anger, or overwhelming stress, catharsis has special significance in counseling and psychotherapy. There it occurs most significantly through the recall and expression of repressed traumatic experiences and attendant feelings. Some contemporary therapies, such as Gestalt and Primal Therapy, emphasize catharsis, while others, like Behavior Modification, criticize it for its tendency to reinforce negative behavior. In any case a distinction must be made between encouraging, for example, aggressive *behavior* as cathartic versus the usually beneficial psychotherapeutic process of expressing aggressive *feelings,* and between the mere *expression* of feelings and some attempt to *understand* them and to *integrate* their significance into subsequent self-understanding and behavior.

The concept of catharsis was first introduced in 1893 by Breuer and Freud as a result of their work with patients suffering from hysteria. Essentially such patients experienced a great deal of anxiety and often manifested physical symptomatology for which no physiological etiology could be established. Using hypnosis as the vehicle for recalling the repressed memories and their affect, Breuer discovered that the particular symptoms disappeared. However, they discovered that their method did not remove the basic hysterical disposition of the patient, nor did it prevent similar symptoms from emerging. As a result, Freud developed psychoanalysis, in which catharsis was expanded into a more complex process known as "working through." Hypnosis was replaced by the technique of free association, which requires the patient to say whatever comes to mind. The analysis of resistance to free association gives important clues as to the content of the repressed memories which underlie the symptoms and behavior of the patient.

Emotional and spiritual catharsis has been an important part of healing rituals and religious experience (especially in Pentecostal and revivalist traditions), where the emphasis is on cleansing and rebirth. In conversion and confession there is often an emotional release. The intensity of these experiences may be related to the degree to which unconscious material emerges. However, even a powerful cathartic experience can produce only transitory results. As psychoanalysis has moved from catharsis to working through, so a deeper and more lengthy process is involved in turning oneself around following conversion and confession.

In pastoral care and counseling, catharsis is an important factor in enabling a person to move through the grief process or to assimilate other traumatic experiences or losses. The confession and release of a flood of emotions such as fear, anger, and guilt prepare the way for the longer-term process of responsibility.

Bibliography. J. Breuer and S. Freud, "Studies on Hysteria" (*SE* 2). M. P. Nichols and M. Zax, *Catharsis in Psychotherapy* (1977). T. J. Scheff, *Catharsis in Healing, Ritual, and Drama* (1979).

D. S. BOSCH

CRYING; FEELING, THOUGHT, AND ACTION IN PASTORAL COUNSELING; PSYCHOTHERAPY; SELF-EXPRESSION/SELF-CONTROL. *See also* EMOTION; PSYCHOANALYSIS. *Compare* STRESS AND STRESS MANAGEMENT.

CATHOLIC CHARITIES. *See* Counseling, Roman Catholic.

CATHOLIC PASTORAL CARE. *See* Roman Catholic Pastoral Care.

CATHOLIC-ORTHODOX MARRIAGE. *See* Orthodox-Catholic Marriage.

CATHOLIC-PROTESTANT MARRIAGE. A marriage involving a Catholic and a baptized Protestant is commonly called an "interfaith marriage," or in ecumenical usage a "Christian intermarriage" or "ecumenical marriage." An earlier term, still in use, is "mixed marriage."

Each Christian communion or denomination generally has its distinctive culture, which shapes the attitudes of its members concerning such matters as conception, sexual relations, children, divorce, and family ritual. In an interfaith marriage these differences can become a source of disharmony, with the further possibility that one partner may compromise values with ensuing resentment or guilt. In Catholic tradition, as a means of protecting the Catholic party, the church discouraged these marriages. In recent years, however, especially since the Second Vatican Council, a more open attitude toward interfaith marriage has been evident, as reflected in the 1983 *Code of Canon Law.* Important changes have been instituted relating to the raising of children, the wedding service, and the ecumenical family's religious life and worship. The church has also encouraged premarital counseling and continuing pastoral support for interfaith couples, not simply to alleviate difficulties but, more positively, to enhance the ecumenical possibilities for moral and spiritual growth.

1. **Changes in Catholic Law and Attitudes.** Because "mixed" marriages were seen to constitute a danger to the faith of the Catholic spouse and the family's children, an impediment to such marriages was established in church law; no Catholic could validly enter such a marriage unless first dispensed from the impediment by the Catholic bishop for certain specific "canonical reasons."

In 1967 Pope Paul VI removed this impediment from the law in his apostolic letter *Matrimonia Mixta.* Thereafter, with the permission of their bishop, Catholics could enter such mixed marriages for any just and reasonable cause. At the same time the pope waived the prior requirement of canon law that other Christians sign promises that children be baptized and brought up as

Catholics. Now only the Catholic party entering a mixed marriage is asked to promise to do what can be done to share the Catholic faith with future children. The other Christian party is to be informed of the Catholic partner's promise.

At the same time Pope Paul VI modified what had previously been the Catholic Church's nearly universal insistence that all mixed marriages involving a Catholic partner be entered into according to "the canonical form," that is, in the presence of a Catholic priest and two witnesses. Thus the 1983 *Code of Canon Law* specifies that Catholic bishops may dispense from the required canonical form "if serious difficulties pose an obstacle to its observance" and as long as there is "some public form of celebration of the marriage" (Canon 1127).

As the provisions of Catholic law changed, one can also perceive a gradual shift in Catholic attitudes toward ecumenical marriages as revealed in successive statements of the popes. While inter-Christian marriages involving Catholics could be more readily provided for, the emphasis at first remained on the undoubted difficulties couples in such marriages must face rather than on the positive ecumenical contribution they might make. This was not unexpected given the higher incidence of marital breakup in exogamous marriages. Thus, while Pope Paul VI's *Matrimonia Mixta* of 1967 observed that "mixed marriages . . . do not, except in some cases, help in re-establishing unity among Christians," by 1980 John Paul II was speaking more positively of the ecumenical role of mixed marriages, noting that such marriages "contain numerous elements that could well be made good use of and developed, both for their intrinsic value and for the contribution that they can make to the ecumenical movement . . . [especially] when both parties are faithful to their religious duties." Thus an effort should be made "to establish cordial cooperation between the Catholic and the non-Catholic ministers from the time that preparations begin for the marriage and the wedding ceremony even though this does not always prove easy." While in fact it has not always proven easy, pastoral practice in recent years has evidenced great strides forward in this area and has gained important experience in implementing these new laws and attitudes.

2. Premarital Counseling. One of the most important components of the church's total ministry to ecumenical couples is premarital counseling, preferably by both pastors conjointly or collaboratively, concerning the religious issues involved in their marriage. These issues focus especially on the upbringing of future children and the family's religious life together. In discussing these and related matters Catholic deacons and priests are of course expected to show respect for the conscience and religious liberty of the partner who is not a Catholic, just as they hope such respect will be shown for the religious rights and duties of the Catholic partner by the Protestant minister.

Regarding the upbringing of children, pastoral experience has led to certain practical conclusions. If it is at all possible to do so, it is better for the couple, acting jointly prior to their marriage, to come to a clear determination concerning the religious formation of children and then to hold to it unless serious new factors in the future demand a reconsideration. As a married couple they will have to make many serious decisions jointly. Their capacity to reach this decision together is one clear indication of their readiness as persons to enter married life. When the couple's decision is known beforehand, they also may be somewhat protected from ensuing tensions between their families who may seek to exert claims on the religious upbringing of children once they are born and eliciting strong bonds of affection. If, on the other hand, the couple find themselves truly unable, even with the help of counselors, to come to an agreement about the religious upbringing of future children, they have *prima facie* reason to pause and reconsider their situation. They may be facing incompatibilities of a serious nature, which they shall no more be able to resolve in married life than before it.

Pastoral experience has also convinced many counselors that it is not a solution to defer this question with the proposal that when the children are old enough they may choose their church allegiances for themselves. By prompting children to defer and avoid a childhood identification with one church community, such an approach does not readily provide a secure religious orientation for young children or a sense of true belonging to the church. As they grow older and are asked to come to a decision, having to choose for the father's or mother's side can be psychologically very stressful, especially for a child approaching adolescence.

Thus there is a real advantage in taking such matters up prior to the marriage and dealing with them in a sensitive, respectful, and realistic manner. There is clearly an additional advantage when it is possible for the ministers of both churches of the couple to offer such counseling jointly or collaboratively. In such a setting further confidence is gained that both parties' religious rights and obligations in conscience are being respected and that neither is being subjected to one-sided pressure.

In addition to child-raising concerns, the couple also should be encouraged to explore the ways in which they will develop a life of shared prayer, devotion, and service in their household while still being members of distinct religious communities. A family that cannot discover a common life of prayer in which all members can share equally is missing an important life-sustaining element. Concrete possibilities will vary, depending on how divergent their religious backgrounds and communities are. Again, an approach that matches respect with realism is called for and here, too, expert pastoral counseling can serve to point out possibilities the couple themselves may not have been aware of.

Since personal religious discussion may not have been a prominent feature of their conversations while dating, ecumenical couples need to be alerted to the fact that many people sense their religious interests, commitment, and fervor rising in the early years of marriage. Otherwise when this phenomenon occurs, it may be misinterpreted as a distancing factor in the marriage — the attempt of each partner to assert a distinct identity over against the other in a competitive way.

3. The Wedding Service. The actual celebration of the marriage offers possibilities for Catholic ministers to join with or be joined by other ministers in ways that were not open before Vatican II. There can be little doubt that when the churches and religious communities through their representative ministers show themselves united in prayer and give support for a couple entering a mixed marriage that a strong and hope-filled message is conveyed to all, especially to the couple, their family, and friends. It is an important teaching moment.

The Catholic Church in the U.S. stresses that there should be only one celebration of the marriage following an established public form, not double or successive wedding ceremonies. When the marriage is celebrated according to the canonical form of the Catholic Church, the Catholic minister (deacon or priest) is the one who will witness the exchange of marital consent by the couple. If the marriage is celebrated according to another religious rite — with the requisite dispensation from the canonical form — the Catholic minister may take an active part, but not the leading ministerial role or one on a par with the minister of the church whose marriage service is being followed. The ministers themselves arrange in advance for the proper distribution of their roles in keeping with these guidelines set down by the National Conference of Catholic Bishops in 1968.

4. **Ongoing Pastoral Support and Worship Life.** Since Vatican II the Catholic Church in collaboration with other churches has made genuine progress in developing new and more supportive ways to assist couples in their preparation for and celebration of mixed marriages. A need remains to be met in offering support for ongoing married life. In spite of all that is done in preparation for their marriage, mixed couples can still feel marginalized by their religious communities after marriage. Mixed-marriage families often tend to fall in the gaps between the churches. When attending each other's churches, the nonmember can subtly (and sometimes not so subtly) be made to feel an outsider. The difficulties for the couple to remain active and in regular attendance at two different churches are undeniable. Obviously much more must be done to extend more effective pastoral care to the special needs of these couples. (The matter is not entirely free of controversy among Catholics. The Catholic Marriage Encounter movement, for example, is divided into two wings, one that welcomes non-Catholic Christians, the other restricting itself exclusively to Catholics.)

Since Vatican II the Catholic Church has made no special provisions for mixed-marriage couples in terms of joint worship or sacramental sharing. However, the church has adopted new policies in this field that have significance for ecumenical couples and families. Perhaps the most important of these is the encouragement now given to all Christians to participate to the extent possible in one another's worship. At the same time, because Catholic theology continues to regard sacramental sharing as a sign of full communion (or of a very high degree of communion) with the church, the new policies also place clear restrictions on sacramental participation. They provide for exceptions, but these are in response to individual need and are not granted as a matter of regular practice.

In general, these provisions (summarized in Canon 844 of the 1983 *Code of Canon Law*) permit a non-Catholic Christian in need to be admitted to a sacrament if he or she (1) spontaneously requests it, (2) is unable under the circumstances to receive it from his or her own minister, and (3) is properly disposed, approaching the sacraments as a Christian should, in faith and with repentance for personal sins. Catholics in need may similarly request the sacraments from ministers of other churches whose sacraments the Catholic Church regards as valid.

Bibliography. "Gaudium et Spes" ["Pastoral Constitution on the Church in the Modern World"], in *Documents of Vatican II* (1966). "The Christian Family," in *Vatican Council II, More Postconciliar Documents* (1982). G. A. Kelly, "Marriage, Mixed." in *New Catholic Encyclopedia* (1967).

J. F. HOTCHKIN
J. MILLER

CROSS-CULTURAL MARRIAGE AND FAMILY; MARRIAGE AND MARITAL CARE; MATRIMONY, SACRAMENT OF. *See also* CODE OF CANON LAW; VATICAN COUNCIL II AND PASTORAL CARE. *Compare* DIVORCE AND REMARRIAGE.

CAUSALITY IN PSYCHOLOGY, FORMS OF.

In psychology, causality refers to whatever principles are employed to account for the occurrence of psychological events in relation to other psychological (and nonpsychological) factors and events.

In common speech, terms like *reason, motive,* and *condition* are often used to express the notion of psychological causality, with a particular emphasis or perspective in each case. A *reason,* for instance, explains or justifies a result ("The reason for his suicide attempt was his arrested adolescence.") A *motive* refers to an intentional, productive state of mind that causes results: "Her motive for stealing was hunger." In the case of *reason,* the emphasis falls on explanation; with *motive* it falls on need or desire. *Conditions,* however, can also be regarded as causes. In that case it is the interplay of events in part/whole relations rather than explanation or desire that comes especially into focus, though conditions can also refer to factors that are judged to be necessary (though not sufficient) for a particular event to occur.

1. **Aristotle's Classic Theory.** The most complete framework for considering forms of causality in Western psychology is provided by Aristotle. Aristotle's account of the four causes in his *Metaphysics,* although frequently modified and argued, underlies all later Western conceptions of causality, including those operative in contemporary psychological theory and practice.

In his classic account Aristotle distinguishes between formal, material, efficient, and final causes. *Formal cause* is the essential or charactistic form of a thing — that which makes it what it is — including its capacity to act or respond (including, for example, a person's capacity to act and respond in therapy). A person's character may be regarded as a formal cause of his or her actions, as when we say that a certain person was rude "because he is a hostile person." A broad conception of mental health can function as a formal cause when that conception gives shape to a therapeutic process. Formal cause might also be considered to be God's conception of what an individual essentially is and is capable of becoming, or it might be a forming essence existing in itself which gives shape and definition to the existence of things.

Material cause is the matter out of which something is to be wrought, for example, the stone for the statue or the psyche at a certain stage as the material for further psychological development.

Efficient cause is the immediate agency of change, for example, heat causing the water to boil or abuse causing hatred. A person's trust of a therapist can be the efficient cause of the development of a trusting relationship with a family member.

The *final cause* is the end or goal *(telos)* of a process, that toward which one aims; for example, to be a fully functioning individual or a loving and supportive family. The final cause of an experiment could be explanatory knowledge or academic honor.

2. Contemporary Psychology. Experimental psychology, with its research model found primarily in physics, employs efficient causality as virtually the sole form of causality underlying its conceptual schemes and research. This emphasis makes the bridge between experimental psychology and most clinical approaches difficult, since a wide variety of conditions and influences appear to cause human behavior and states of mind. In most clinical situations no one kind of causation plays an exclusive or clearly dominant role. Most of these situations appear instead to justify a concept of causation as a totality or whole of contingencies that issues in certain consequences. Whereas in experimental psychology causes and influences must be tightly controlled and variables limited with an eye to explanation, in clinical work conditions and consequences are given in a maze of variabilities that make simple linear conceptions of cause and effect inadequate. Similarly, when psychology is limited to a study of traits or types, such an emphasis on formal causation would appear to be overly limiting in a way analogous to the overemphasis on efficient causation in experimental psychology. If a psychological method, clinical or experimental, is unable to designate Aristotle's formal, material, efficient, and final causes in that approach and in the events that it studies, one may assume a narrowness of view that is probably distorting.

Forms of psychological causality are decisively influenced by what one considers to be fundamental human needs, interests, and situations. If one interprets human beings as moved primarily by appetitive drives, satisfaction of those drives would define the most essential therapeutic goals. Or if the drive for a meaningful life is found to be fundamental, discovery of energy-giving meanings would be the basic goal of therapy.

Abraham Maslow's theory of a hierarchy of needs, hypothesized to account for human growth and satisfaction, provides an example of a theory that employs each of Aristotle's four causes and illustrates the close relationship between a theory's causal and motivational concepts.

A therapist following Maslow's theory would determine which needs must be met first in order to free the person for satisfaction of "higher" needs; for example, before the need for loving intimacy can be met, one must meet the need for security. Each accomplished stage would be the material cause for the next step. Need fulfillment constitutes the final cause, being the goal toward which one aims, and is expressed through particular final causes like security, intimacy, and peak experiences. The formal cause is the structure of needs in human beings. The efficient cause is what meets the need in a given situation.

An alternative approach similarly involving all four of Aristotle's types of causality theories, like some family systems theories, that conceptualize an organic interplay of social, cultural, historical, and individual factors. Therapy based on such theories attempts to cause changes in the whole by modification of certain of the parts. In such a systemic approach one first defines some inclusive whole, whether family, the family's society, a language structure, or some other environment, then sees how the whole and the parts condition (i.e., cause) each other, mutually define their goals, jointly shape their immediate agencies, and together provide the material from which changes will occur and the forms of what is to be and can be.

3. Conclusion. Aristotle did not see adequately the interplay of history and causation, and one might reject or justifiably ignore his metaphysics. But the types of causes that he designated appear to name fundamental constituents in the life process and still provide a useful and insightful framework for assessing psychological theories.

Some notion of causality is implicit if not explicit in most psychologies, and theories often differ significantly from one another according to the kinds of causal principles they employ. Being aware of these differences can be important in making critical evaluations of particular psychologies as well as for considering their appropriateness for theology and for pastoral care and counseling.

Bibliography. Aristotle's *Metaphysics,* I.3. R. G. Collingwood, *An Essay on Metaphysics* (1940). A. Maslow, *Toward A Psychology of Being* (1962). M. Bunge, *Causality* (1959). D. Hume, *An Enquiry Concerning Human Understanding* (1982 [1748]). C. G. Jung, *Synchronicity* (1973). V. Frankl, *The Doctor and the Soul* (1955). For Aristotle and contemporary psychology see also J. R. Averill, *Patterns of Psychological Thought* (1976), 131–82.

C. E. SCOTT

PERSON (Philosophical Issues); PHILOSOPHY AND PSYCHOLOGY. *See also* FREEDOM AND DETERMINISM; MODELS IN PSYCHOLOGICAL AND PASTORAL THEORY; MOTIVATION; WILL/WILLING.

CELEBRATION. *See* WORSHIP AND CELEBRATION; RITUAL AND PASTORAL CARE.

CELEBRITIES. *See* VIPs.

CELIBACY. A way of life in which one chooses not to marry for religious reasons. In effect, this is also a choice of sexual abstinence.

Celibacy is a part of both the Hindu and the Buddhist ideals of religious perfection. It existed but was never prominent in Judaism. In the West it has been a Christian institution, primarily Orthodox and Roman Catholic. Celibacy is not absent from Anglican and Protestant Christianity but it has not played a prominent role there. Within Roman Catholicism one must distinguish two kinds of celibacy: clerical celibacy and the celibacy associated with religious life. The former is required of Roman Catholic priests by church law; the latter is a chosen way of life, ordinarily lived in common, with its origins in monasticism, and associated with religious vows.

1. History. Catholic practice has traditionally seen celibacy as based on Scripture. Mt. 19:10-12 is no longer interpreted by exegetes as necessarily referring to celibacy; thus the only clear biblical basis is I Cor. 7:25-40, in which Paul presents celibacy as his own opinion rather than as a teaching from Jesus.

The celibacy associated with religious life is linked to the history of monasticism. Monastic life in its origins was a lay movement and its celibacy was not related to priesthood or diaconate. Clerical celibacy is a later development than monasticism. During the first centuries of the Christian church, bishops, priests, and deacons were not forbidden to marry.

In Eastern Orthodoxy, monasticism was the milieu for celibate life. It was generally permissible for priests and deacons to be married; bishops, however, were expected to be celibate. In the West, the first legislation requiring clerical celibacy dates from the Spanish Council of Elvira, 306 C.E. Early legislation did not apply to the universal church but followed the pattern of regional councils and customs. It was not until the twelfth century that a general council (the First Lateran Council, 1123) legislated the obligation of celibacy for the whole of the Latin Church and also declared (in the Second Lateran Council, 1139) that marriages contracted by clerics were invalid. The Reformation did not accept clerical celibacy and chose a married clergy. Calvin was open to celibacy as a personal option but not as general practice. The Council of Trent continued to require celibacy of the Roman Catholic clergy.

2. Theology. In Christian history there has never been only one theology of celibacy. Varied motives were operative for different people.

Celibacy involves an individual's attentiveness to his or her experience of God. The God of Abraham, Isaac, and Jacob is a God who calls people forth to play a role in history or fulfill a vocation. Celibacy involves a discernment of how God is present and active in the life of an individual and rests upon this sense of vocation in a person's religious experience.

Some persons experience their relationship with God in such a way that they want to give themselves more fully to God; they want to "give their lives completely to God." They feel called to an intimacy with God such that they choose not to have a human partner. Traditionally this has been expressed in language of mystical or spiritual marriage. Its basis is the felt love of an individual for God or the desire for a more contemplative life.

Others experience their relationship to God as a call to service—self-sacrifice for the sake of ministry. An unmarried person may be able to be more available to the poor or the sick, or for teaching or evangelization. Celibacy in this case involves an apostolic consciousness or pastoral sense.

For some, celibacy implies witness, a radical giving of testimony to the faith. The martyr in Christian history exemplified the ideal of witness. With the closing of the age of martyrdom, the monk or nun or ascetic became a new form of radical witness. Witness is often seen as eschatological (as for Paul), i.e., bearing witness to a life that transcends present existence. Today, witness is also associated with a view of celibacy as a counter-cultural statement, or as the desire to live more radically the Christian value system.

Some experience celibacy as freeing—not simply as freedom *from* the responsibilities of marriage and family but freedom *for* God, for service to others, for missionary work, or for taking radical social stands.

Thus celibacy includes many realities such as vocation, mysticism, contemplative life, pastoral availability, service, freedom, witness, radical discipleship, self-sacrifice, and asceticism. Rarely are all of these operative in one individual. They express centuries of Christian experience in which Jesus was a prime example.

3. Psychology. *a. Sexuality.* The Christian ascetical tradition associated human sexual pleasure with concupiscence and sin. Sexual abstinence was therefore viewed as a more complete victory over the flesh than Christian marriage. Thus celibate people can readily deny sexual feelings or needs. With changing attitudes, celibate people are increasingly aware that being celibate does not mean being nonsexual, though normal sexual feelings in a celibate person can create fear, destructive guilt, and social withdrawal. The person needs to learn ways of expressing felt responses that do not lead to genital sexual intimacy. Both feelings and behavior can be sources of conflict. Increased sexual awareness can lead to acting out what is inconsistent with celibacy. Celibacy can also raise sexual identity questions.

b. Intimacy. While celibate people maintain that genital expression of sexual affect is not a basic human need, they perceive the need for tactual expression and intimacy differently. Some maintain that it is better for a celibate person to refrain from close interpersonal relationships or particular friendships. Others desire close affective relationships and struggle with how to integrate them into a celibate life.

c. Motivation. Factors such as sexual denial, homosexuality, or a fear of intimacy do influence a person's choices regarding celibacy. There are thus three levels of motivation that a person needs to distinguish: (1) the level of the ideal, discussed in the theology of celibacy above; (2) the level of psychosexual development, which involves unconscious factors; and (3) the level of specific decision. The first level is not valid if it is used to avoid the second, psychological level. It then functions as rationalization. If a person is attentive to the second level, then the theological ideal can function constructively at the third level where a person chooses how to live the Christian life. Celibate motivation, however, can never dismiss the supra-psychological level of faith which plays a decisive role and does not fear psychology. Greater understanding of the second level of personal motivation does not determine a choice but enhances the freedom to make a choice.

4. Pastoral Considerations. Guidance for a celibate person demands both religious and psychological sensitivity. Spiritual counseling alone can reinforce denial, avoid unconscious motivation, risk failing at the task of intrapsychic integration, or diminish the freedom that comes from greater self-awareness. Psychological counseling alone can ignore the reality of the spiritual life, of a celibate individual's experience of God and faith, of the personal meaning that comes from committed Christian discipleship, and can place greater value on psychological needs at the expense of broader social concerns. Counseling must deal with the reality that celibacy remains an ideal of Christian life (although not the only ideal) and also the reality that celibates are human beings facing the tasks of adult development. A freely chosen adult celibacy is experienced as a gift from God given for the sake of others. However, it is not a gift that comes without struggle. Nor does it deny the equally valid gift of Christian marriage.

Pastoral counseling of celibate people frequently involves one or several of the following: (a) vocational issues, such as whether an individual wants to be celibate, or how to deal with the obligatory character of a clerical celibacy; (b) the areas of sexual or relational counseling; (c) faith and prayer.

Bibliography. G. A. Aschenbrenner, "Celibacy in Community and Ministry," *Human Development* 6/1 (1985), 27–33. P. Delhaye, "History of Celibacy," *The New Catholic Encyclopedia*, III (1967), 369–74. D. J. Goergen, *The Sexual Celibate* (1975). "Separation Anxiety and Celibate Friendship," *Review for Religious*, 35 (1976), 256–64. A. Greeley, *The Catholic Priest in the United States — Sociological Investigations* (1972). R. Gryson, *Les origines du célibat ecclésiastique* (1970). P. Keane, "The Meaning and Functioning of Sexuality in the Lives of Celibates and Virgins," *Review for Religious*, 34 (1975), 277–314. E. Kennedy and V. Heckler, *The Catholic Priest in the United States — Psychological Investigations* (1972). C. Kiesling, *Celibacy, Prayer and Friendship* (1978). A. Plé, "The Place of Relationships in the Life of the Priest," *Clergy Review*, 67 (1982), 209–19. E. Schillebeeckx, *Celibacy*, (1968). S. Schneiders, "Non-Marriage for the Sake of the Kingdom," in Pope Paul VI, ed., *Widening the Dialogue* (1974). M. Thurian, *Marriage and Celibacy* (1959).

D. J. GOERGEN

RELIGIOUS LIFE; SEXUALITY, CHRISTIAN THEOLOGY AND ETHICS OF; VOWS/VOWING; *See also* ASCETICAL PRACTICES; CHRISTIAN LIFE; MINISTRY, ROMAN CATHOLIC; FAITH AND INTEGRITY, PASTOR'S; SELF-DENIAL. *Compare* LIFESTYLE ISSUES; LUST AND CHASTITY (Moral Theology).

CENTERING/CENTEREDNESS. *See* MEDITATION.

CERTIFICATION. Etymologically, a term meaning "to make certain"; from two Latin words, *certus* (certain), *facere* (to make). The National Commission for Health Certifying Agencies defines certification as "a process by which a professional organization or association grants recognition of competence to an individual who has met the standards or predetermined qualifications specified by that organization or association" (1979, p. 4).

The Association for Clinical Pastoral Education (ACPE), the American Association of Pastoral Counselors (AAPC), and other professional organizations of clergypersons have certification commissions or committees.

ACPE has become the standard-setting, accrediting, certifying, resource agency in the field of clinical pastoral education (CPE). It accredits CPE programs in institutions, agencies, and parishes, and certifies supervisors to conduct these programs. Requirements for certification are formal and specific. The process emphasizes a candidate's ability to demonstrate the pastoral, supervi-

sory, and conceptual competence essential for conducting CPE. Certification is granted in three stages: Supervisory Candidate (training level, two or three years); Associate Supervisor (supervisor of two units of CPE, status subject to annual review); and Supervisor. Prerequisites include formal requirements, such as academic degrees, pastoral experience, and CPE that includes supervisory training (ACPE, 1989).

AAPC provides certification for ministers trained in pastoral counseling. The organization also accredits pastoral counseling centers and approves training programs. There are three levels of certification: Member, Fellow, and Diplomate. These levels cover a range of functioning from supportive counseling to extended pastoral psychotherapy and the supervision of pastoral counselors in training. Certification is granted to those who have met formal and technical requirements and can demonstrate their professional competence as pastoral counselors (AAPC, 1981).

Certification is the leverage used by public and private agencies, as well as professional peers, to assure effectiveness. Theological seminaries are assured through the standards for becoming a certified supervisor that theological students will receive competent supervision. The public is assured that pastoral counselors are competent to function as pastoral psychotherapists. Because the public does not presume to be able to assess the competence of a pastoral service provider, certification, as in all professional service fields, is shaped largely by professional peers. Certification also has a gatekeeping function for those already certified, assuring them that those who enter their field are competent to function as professional peers (Aist, 1980).

Bibliography. "Perspectives on Health Occupational Credentialing," Report of the National Commission for Health Certifying Agencies (September 30, 1979). Association for Clinical Pastoral Education, Inc., "The Standards of the Association for Clinical Pastoral Education, Inc.," (1989). The American Association of Pastoral Counselors, *Handbook* (December, 1981). C. S. Aist, "Professional Certification in the Clinical Pastoral Field," *J. of Supervision and Training* 3 (1980), 101–05.

L. L. McGEE

CERTIFIED SUPERVISOR; STANDARDS FOR PASTORAL COUNSELING. *See also* AMERICAN ASSOCIATION OF PASTORAL COUNSELORS; ASSOCIATION FOR CLINICAL PASTORAL EDUCATION. *Compare* ACCREDITATION; LICENSURE; SPECIALIZATION IN PASTORAL CARE.

CERTIFIED SUPERVISOR. Formerly called "chaplain supervisor," a pastoral or clinical theological educator who supervises the learning practice of pastoral care and counseling in institutions, agencies, and parishes. Competency in supervision is assured through a certification process offered by professional organizations such as the Association for Clinical Pastoral Education (ACPE) and the American Association of Pastoral Counselors (AAPC). Training and standards for becoming a certified supervisor are provided by these organizations.

L. L. McGEE

CERTIFICATION; CLINICAL PASTORAL EDUCATION; SUPERVISION, PASTORAL. *See also* AMERICAN ASSOCIATION OF PAS-

TORAL COUNSELORS; ASSOCIATION FOR CLINICAL PASTORAL EDUCATION.

CHANGE, PERSONAL. *See* PSYCHOTHERAPY. *See also* CRISIS, DEVELOPMENTAL.

CHANGE, SOCIAL. *See* SOCIAL CHANGE AND DISLOCATION.

CHAPLAIN/CHAPLAINCY. *Chaplain* refers to a clergyperson or layperson who has been commissioned by a faith group or an organization to provide pastoral services in an institution, organization, or governmental entity. *Chaplaincy* refers to the general activity performed by a chaplain, which may include crisis ministry, counseling, sacraments, worship, education, help in ethical decision-making, staff support, clergy contact and community or church coordination.

Chaplaincy may be provided by an institution such as a general or mental hospital, prison, school or college, by a business organization, or the armed forces. Although many faith groups and institutions use "pastoral care" synonymously with "chaplaincy services," some prefer to use "pastoral care" to refer to any services performed by either ordained or non-ordained persons, but reserve "chaplaincy services" for activities performed by ordained ministers, priests, or rabbis. In the U.S. Armed Forces only the terms "chaplaincy" and "chaplaincy services" are used.

The term chaplain originated with the appointment for personal ministry of a non-parochial cleric to a monarch, ecclesiastical authority or nobleman who owned a chapel. Chaplains then began serving in military units, and later in institutions such as hospitals, prisons, schools, and diplomatic facilities.

Chaplaincy has developed a variety of specialized forms in its various settings. Military, prison, hospital, and business chaplaincies, for instance, are generally viewed as distinct forms of specialized ministry with corresponding career tracks, and within some of these forms, such as hospital chaplaincy, chaplains often specialize further, for example in pediatric, geriatric, oncology, hospice, mental health, or chemical dependency ministries. In these settings the chaplain is generally recognized as a member of the institutional team functioning with specialized skills. Many chaplains, however, also consider it important to keep non-specialized care and concern for all persons related to the organization as the principal feature of their identity and work even when they also provide more specialized counseling. Their ministries emphasize caring relationships with staff, institutional authorities, and family members as well as the organization's primary or majority population.

Chaplains may be employed on a full-or part-time basis. They may be compensated by the institution, by a denomination, church or synagogue, by a separate funding organization, or may contract their services individually or through a contracting organization. Many clergy also volunteer their services as chaplains, as many parish ministers do for local hospitals. Since the 1920s, many chaplains have been clinically trained to function in their particular type of facility. Chaplaincy organizations have been certifying chaplains for competency to function in specialized ministries since the 1940s.

Basic requirements for functioning as a chaplain usually include an ecclesiastical endorsement from the chaplain's denomination or faith group, ordination or commission to function in a pastoral care ministry, and the theological training expected by the chaplain's denomination. Exact requirements vary by denomination and by institution and have been changing in recent years. The Roman Catholic church, for instance, has not required hospital chaplains to be ordained since 1980, which opened this ministry to women. Since the 1920s, many chaplains have been clinically trained to function in their particular type of facility or ministry.

K. W. SMITH

SPECIALIZATION IN PASTORAL CARE; COLLEGE STUDENTS AND COLLEGE CHAPLAINCY; GENERAL HOSPITAL CHAPLAINCY; INDUSTRIAL AND BUSINESS CHAPLAINCIES; MENTAL HOSPITAL CHAPLAINCY; MILITARY SERVICE AND MILITARY CHAPLAINCY; POLICE OFFICERS AND POLICE CHAPLAINCY; PRISONERS AND PRISON CHAPLAINCY. *See also* CLINICAL PASTORAL EDUCATION.

CHAPLAIN SUPERVISOR. *See* CERTIFIED SUPERVISOR.

CHAPLAINCY. *See* CHAPLAIN/CHAPLAINCY.

CHARACTER, MORAL. *See* CHARACTER ETHICS; MORAL DEVELOPMENT. *See also* FAITH AND INTEGRITY, PASTOR'S.

CHARACTER, PASTOR'S. *See* FAITH AND INTEGRITY, PASTOR'S.

CHARACTER AND PERSONALITY (Comparative Concepts). Like many psychological terms, "character" and "personality" have been used in multiple ways. Sometimes the two words are used synonymously. For example, we might say "Sam is an interesting character," but we might just as readily say "Sam has an interesting personality." Even psychoanalysts have used the two words interchangeably. Thus, a patient might be described as having an "oral character structure" or an "oral personality organization."

Etymologically, the word character — a Greek root meaning "engraving" — thus suggests deeply ingrained structures. Personality comes from the Latin word for mask and often connotes something more superficial than character. Current usage may reflect these origins. Psychologists tend to employ character in reference to the static or unchanging aspects of the person, but to use personality to mean something more active, dynamic, and perhaps potentially changeable.

Taking a more detailed look at the variety of meanings attached to "personality," Allport (1937) compiled fifty discrete definitions from the psychological literature, which he organized into five broad categories: (1) *omnibus* — summing up the individual by enumerating various important characteristics, (2) *interactive* — describing personality as the organization of discrete behaviors into an integrated whole, (3) *hierarchical* — stressing the various layers or developmental stages of personality, (4) *adjustment* — suggesting that personality emerges from one's attempts to cope with environmental demands, and (5) *distinctiveness* — emphasizing those qualities which set individuals apart from one another. Allport's own definition incorporates elements from the latter four categories:

Personality is the dynamic organization within the individual of those psychophysical systems that determine his unique adjustments to his environment (1937, p. 48).

Returning to character, several additional meanings are noteworthy: (1) In contrast to the wholistic nature of personality, character is sometimes considered to be just one of the elements or subsystems making up personality. For example, an omnibus definition may describe personality as consisting of character, habits, and attitudes. (2) Character is also used to connote an organization of qualities that are judged relative to ethical standards: "She is of honorable character." The word personality rarely implies goodness or badness.

Allport proposed an interesting solution to the semantic problems raised by these terms. He distinguished between the two by defining character as "personality evaluated," and personality as "character devaluated." Using Allport's simple distinction, the science of psychology is concerned primarily with the study of personality, while discussions of character more properly belong to the disciplines of theology, philosophy, and ethics.

Bibliography. G. W. Allport, *Personality: A Psychological Interpretation* (1937). C. Hall and G. Lindzey, *Theories of Personality* 3d ed. (1978).

D. BROKAW

PERSON; PERSONALITY THEORY. *See also* MORAL DEVELOPMENT; MORAL THEOLOGY AND PASTORAL CARE; PHILOSOPHY AND PSYCHOLOGY.

CHARACTER ARMOR. *See* BODY THERAPIES.

CHARACTER DISORDERS. *See* PERSONALITY DISORDERS.

CHARACTER ETHICS AND PASTORAL CARE. *Character* refers to that relatively enduring combination of natural capacities and historical accidents which distinguish one individual from another and which together describe the element of consistency in the self's relation to the world. *Character ethics* refers to that analysis of character which seeks to provide a normative language for guiding individuals and communities in their character forming functions. A *theological ethics of character* does this with particular attention to the role played by religious beliefs and practices in this formation. Character ethics and pastoral care intersect when an ethics of character is employed as a norm, goal, or critical perspective, in the pastoral care of members of a particular believing community, whether in the theoretical understanding of that care or in the practical activities of care within the community.

1. **Character in the Philosophic Tradition.** Ethics in general has always had to do with the relationship between the vision of the good one holds and the problems of embodying that good within the constraints of finite historical existence; thus character ethics is concerned with the relationship between ideal visions of the good human being and the task of living out those visions in real life circumstances. Both the content of the visions and the ways of implementing them are subjects of ethical reflection, and traditions differ in their analysis of each. They also differ in the significance they give to the concept of character itself in the larger task of ethics. Some see ethics primarily as a matter of delineating the principles and rules of moral action (what should we *do?*); others emphasize the forming and testing of images of the good person or society (what should we *be?*). The former tends toward universalizing abstraction, the latter toward concreteness and particularity; the former tends to formulate principles, the latter to tell and reflect upon stories. Traditions differ in their analysis of the nature of the ultimate human good and of the elements of character and their role in its formation.

a. Classical ethics. The issues surrounding character were important for Aristotle and Aquinas, because they were concerned about connecting the flow of time and change in historical existence with enduring structures of human nature. They saw an inherent connection between an individual's concrete life in the world and her or his pursuit of human goodness. Goodness found concrete expression in the form of specific moral habits or skills — called virtues. The self was formed out of these habits or skills of the good life and tempted by vices away from it. Character was conceived as the structure of selfhood which would best express the normative relation between goodness and transient human existence.

A very different attitude was taken by thinkers of the Enlightenment. For them, the moral problem was not how to embody the good within the flux of history (e.g., how to define and achieve character) but how to establish human autonomy over against the contingent institutions and traditions of history. This they attempted by appealing to reason for the grounding of human autonomy, with reason conceived as a capacity transcending the vagaries of history.

Thus the Enlightenment did not find much use for the language of character. It viewed character either as an accidental feature of no moral significance, or significant only when reducible to the rule of universal rationality in everyday life. A person of good character was one who was able to abstract herself or himself from historical, affective, or other nonrational influences on moral choice.

Nineteenth and early twentieth century philosophy inherited this rationalist influence, and "good character" became closely tied to a description of the traits necessary to become a more completely rational person. Ironically, but perhaps inevitably, this narrowing of the moral to the purely rational discouraged critical thinking about the nonrational features of character. Thus a particular culture's notion of what qualities constituted a good woman or man was allowed to take the place of more sustained reflection on the formation and exercise of real human capacities in relation to ideals of human goodness.

From about the middle of the present century, however, philosophical attention has turned to issues well expressed in the language of character. These include the cultural and narrative context of all human capacities, reason included; the complex relationships between belief and behavior, desire and action; and the historical and temporal development both of moral language and of people themselves. (See Aristotle, Hauerwas, MacIntyre, and Meilander.)

b. Contemporary theological ethics. Christian theological ethics emphasizes the transforming effect of grace on nature, holds transformation to be discernible in the life of specific individuals, and thus is concerned to speak of a language of transformation and change in concrete human communities. It is also concerned to hold together characteristic features of the self in relation to the world, that is, to conceive of the self only in its relation to the world, not as a separable or distinct entity (as in the Platonic idea of soul). It also seeks to avoid the Enlightenment divorce of the rational and universal from the affective and particular.

To that end four elements in the contemporary understanding of character may be described. These elements include (1) our capacity for intentional action, (2) our involvement with feelings, (3) our subjection to the accidents of history, and (4) what might be called our heart, or our capacity for exercising imagination, memory, and the desire for union, here understood as a pursuit of the good both in personal integrity and in union with others. Here an ethics of character draws on the categories of image, metaphor and narrative to speak of the ways in which stories make available to the heart the direction and characteristics of a life well lived. Here also appears the importance of the concrete images, metaphors, and stories which offer possibilities for shaping character, and of the historical communities in which that formation takes place, as they form the irreducible vocabulary with which the language of the heart is spoken. (See Bondi, Hauerwas, Meilander, and Niebuhr.)

2. Contribution of Character Ethics to Pastoral Care. Little direct attention has been paid to character ethics in the modern pastoral care movement. This was perhaps due to the heavily psychological interests of the field and to the notion of value neutrality borrowed from psychotherapy. However, pastoral care and counseling became involved in character ethics indirectly insofar as it followed psychoanalytic or other psychological schools in discussing character under the heading of personality theory. Personality theory generally defines motivational and other qualities of the "normal" and ideal person and distinguishes healthy from psychological types. Moreover, all care of persons including pastoral care assumes some notion of the healthy or ideal person (however secular, latent, or general) as a goal toward which the care is directed. It also operates with some sort of norm for discriminating desirable from undesirable character. Hence it is always possible to reflect on pastoral care from the standpoint of character ethics.

How character ethics might contribute to pastoral care in large part depends on how pastoral care understands itself and the enterprise of ethics. When pastoral care sees the task of ethics as primarily the rational analysis of obligations, rights, and principles, it also has a limited use for the language of character. An ethics of character is inevitably concerned with the formation of particular individuals within communities expressing a vision of the good in concrete images and stories. Those who hold to the primacy of reason and principles in ethics as well as pastoral care often feel that the concreteness of an ethics of character disqualifies it from a universalizable public discourse, and thus its usefulness lies chiefly in its ability to exemplify or illustrate moral principles and convictions (see Browning).

Where pastoral care emphasizes the ongoing network of dynamic relations in which individuals and communities are enmeshed, and where its understanding of rationality is tempered by the limitations imposed by historicity, it finds the language of character more congenial. Here it focuses on the relation between stories and self-understanding on the one hand, and the experience of life in the world on the other. An individual may better understand her or his life as itself a story, come to some awareness of the larger narratives which lend structure and meaning to personal life stories, and in this way come to participate more fully in the formation of her or his character. Because an ethics of character provides a language of history, transformation, and direction, it offers a vocabulary for self-reflection that may enable critical appropriation of the ways one has been shaped up to the present, and some sense of participation in the shaping one will undergo in the future; that could well contribute to the tasks of pastoral care both in crisis intervention and in long-term nurture and growth (see Gerkin and Patton).

By treating human capacities and the specific historical narratives grounding them, the language of character offers to pastoral care a means of imaginatively recreating the past and participating in alternative futures. It provides an avenue for exploring explicitly Christian images that contribute to the universe of meaning in which a given individual or society exists and in which pastoral care occurs. The elements of character and their formation will remain particularly important to a religion like Christianity, which at its heart calls not for correct doctrine but for the new creation of a people disposed to love.

Bibliography. Aristotle, *Nicomachean Ethics* (1975). R. Bondi, "The Elements of Character," *J. of Religious Ethics* 12:2 (1984), 201–18. D. Browning, *Religious Ethics and Pastoral Care* (1983). C. Gerkin, *Living Human Documents* (1984). S. Hauerwas, *Character and the Christian Life* (1975; 2d ed. 1985). *The Peaceable Kingdom* (1983). A. MacIntyre, *After Virtue* (1981). G. Mailander, *The Theory and Practice of Virtue* (1984). H. R. Niebuhr, *The Responsible Self* (1963). J. Patton, *Pastoral Counseling* (1983).

RICHARD BONDI

CHARACTER AND PERSONALITY (Comparative Concepts); ETHICS *or* MORAL THEOLOGY, AND PASTORAL CARE. *See also* ACTION/BEING RELATIONSHIP; MORAL DEVELOPMENT; PERSONAL STORY, SYMBOL, AND MYTH; REASON AND PASSION; REASONING AND RATIONALITY IN PASTORAL CARE. *Compare* EVALUATION AND DIAGNOSIS, RELIGIOUS; SEVEN DEADLY SINS.

CHARACTER FORMATION. *See* CHARACTER ETHICS; MORAL DEVELOPMENT.

CHARCOT, JEAN-MARTIN (1835 – 93). The greatest neurologist of his time, Charcot founded the Salpetrière School of hypnosis and became known as the "Napoleon of Neuroses" for his contributions to the theoretical understanding of hysteria, somnambulism, catalepsy, and dual personality. He founded two of the earliest journals relating art and medicine, and offered a "scientific explanation" of demoniacal possession, which he regarded as a special form of hysteria. While Charcot's ideas have remained controversial, his status as a major contributor to dynamic psychology is unchallenged. Part of his influence on dynamic psychology was through Freud.

H. VANDE KEMP

HYPNOSIS; HYSTERIA.

CHARISMA. See SUGGESTION, PERSUASION, AND INFLUENCE; SOCIOLOGY OF RELIGIOUS AND PASTORAL CARE.

CHARISMATIC EXPERIENCE. In theology a charismatic experience is a subjective mystical experience of an objective grace or gift of the Spirit given to an individual. A charismatic leader, as in politics or the military, is one who has a personal quality, a magic of personality, or some personal gift which elicits popular loyalty or enthusiasm from followers. This sociological phenomenon was first described by Max Weber ([1922] 1957) who borrowed the term from Christian theology.

Paul lists nine gifts of the Spirit in I Corinthians 12:8 – 11. Although these gifts were prominent in the beginning of the Christian church, they almost disappeared until they were revived in the twentieth century by the Pentecostal churches, the neo-Pentecostal movement and the Catholic charismatic renewal. Various psychological and sociological models have been offered to explain these manifestations, though probably the best way to understand them is to interpret them theologically as mystical experiences with psychological and sociological aspects.

1. Scriptural Basis. In I Cor. 12:8–11, Paul lists nine gifts of the Spirit which are not intended to be complete but rather illustrative. "One may have the gift of *preaching with wisdom* given him by the Spirit; another may have the gift of *preaching instruction* given him by the same Spirit; and another the *gift of faith* given by the same Spirit; another again the *gift of healing,* through this one Spirit; one, the power of *miracles*; another, *prophecy*; another the gift of *recognizing spirits*; another the *gift of tongues* and another the *ability to interpret them*" (Jerusalem Bible).

The designation "pentecostal" is used today by those who emphasize the gift of tongues as it was manifested on the day of Pentecost (Acts 2:1–11). The designation "charismatic" is used by those who see the gift of tongues as one of a number of spiritual gifts given to Christians (as emphasized by Paul).

2. Historical Sketch. In the Acts of the Apostles, there are many references to charismatic experiences (e.g., Acts 2:1–11, Acts 4:29–31; 10:44–48; 20:22–23; 21:4). These experiences are also mentioned in the Ante-Nicene Fathers (e.g., Ignatius, Irenaeus, and Tertullian). By the end of the third century, however, these charismatic phenomena died out of the normal life of the church because of their abuse in the heresy of Montanism. A few individuals may have experienced them down through the centuries (i.e., Vincent Ferrer, Louis Bertrand, Francis Xavier), but it is hard to verify such occurrences historically. In the seventeenth century charismatic experiences were encouraged by the French Huguenot prophets of the Cevennes and the convulsionaries of Saint-Medard. In the nineteenth century charismatic experiences were highly structured in the Catholic Apostolic church, and they also were manifested in the Holiness movement which came out of Methodism.

At the beginning of the twentieth century, the classical Pentecostal movement revived the use of these gifts of the Spirit. Gradually, sectarian churches were formed. In the 1950s, a neo-Pentecostal movement began in the mainline Protestant denominations. Beginning in 1967, a charismatic renewal erupted within the Roman Catholic church in the U.S. Cross-cultural manifestations of charismatic experiences have been cited in Judaism and in Islam (Dermeghen, 1953).

3. Psychological Issues. Two issues are prominent in attempting to understand these unusual charismatic experiences. The first is whether these experiences are pathological; the second is whether there is any psychological model which is best for understanding them.

Classical Pentecostals were originally often called "Holy Rollers" because of many ecstatic manifestations which were prominent in their meetings, i.e., jerking, swooning, and rolling. William James ([1902] 1958) considered these phenomena as manifestations of nervous instability. The most common psychiatric interpretation of them has been hysteria (Janet, [1907] 1924). Schizophrenia with catalepsy has also been suggested (Cutten, [1927]).

More recent research, however, has not substantiated these earlier claims of pathology (Alland, 1962; Kiev, 1963, 1964). Well-designed research studies with control groups have not found Pentecostals to exhibit pathology in the clinical sense (Kildahl, 1972; Wood, 1965). Even such a deviant population as the snake-handling Pentecostals in Appalachia have not been found to be mentally disturbed. (Gerrard, *et al*, 1966; Schwarz, 1960). Linguistically, glossolalia has been demonstrated not to be similar to schizophrenese, i.e., psychotic speech, though modern linguistic analyses of glossolalia have not substantiated the claim that glossolalia is indeed a language in the usual sense of having a vocabulary, syntax and grammar (Samarin, 1972).

A number of psychological models have been used to explain charismatic experiences. These models have reflected the development of the field of psychology itself. Freud ([1910] 1963) encouraged his friend and associate Oskar Pfister, a Swiss pastor, to conceptualize dynamically a case of glossolalia. Pfister (1912) concluded that his patient had regressed to an infantile state (cf. Flournoy, [1900] 1963). Repression of unconscious conflicts was the interpretation which Laffal (1965) made of the glossolalia of neo-Pentecostals at Yale University. Following Jungian psychology, Kelsey (1964) interpreted glossolalia as a breakthrough from the collective unconscious. Ego-psychology investigators originally conceptualized the ego as being able to be autonomous in some functions and to be free from unconscious conflicts at times (i.e., Hartman, [1939] 1958, 1964). Therefore, one could experience "regression in the service of the ego" which would be creative, as for example in wit, poetry, and art (Kris, [1934] 1953). Numerous investigators have applied this explanatory concept to glossolalia (Alland, 1962; Kildahl, 1972; Lapsley and Simpson, 1964a, 1964b; Pattison, 1968). Goodman (1972) insisted that charismatic experiences were manifestations of an altered state of consciousness (ASC), i.e., of trance. Samarin (1972) countered that an ASC was not necessary and that glossolalia, for example, could be learned behavior without trance (cf. Alland, 1962). In conclusion, these various psychological models have heuristic value, but there is no consensus among psychologists concerning how to understand charismatic experiences.

4. **Sociological Issues.** The one major sociological paradigm for understanding the early classical Pentecostals has been the deprivation model. Classical Pentecostals in the first half of the twentieth century came from a deprived or disinherited segment of North American society, i.e., from the lower socioeconomic classes (Anderson, 1979). According to the deprivation model, charismatic experiences would compensate for poverty and low social status. These deprived groups formed sects since they did not feel welcome in the more established churches. Glock (1973) has delineated five types of deprivation: economic, social, organismic, ethical, and psychic. He maintains that economic deprivation produces the sects, including classical Pentecostals.

However, Bradfield (1979) demonstrated that neo-Pentecostals did not meet the criteria of economic or social deprivation. Organismic, ethical, and psychic deprivation seemed more evident. The deprivation model seems deficient in explaining the more recent sociological manifestations of charismatic experience, i.e., for the neo-Pentecostals and the Catholic Charismatics. Also, this model would no longer apply to classical Pentecostals in the second half of the twentieth century as it did in the first half.

Sociological analysis has revealed certain variables of internal set or attitudes that people bring to their charismatic experiences. These include a felt need for physical or emotional healing because of a personal crisis (Bradfield, 1979), and the need for renewed spiritual vitality (Greeley, 1974). Theorists have used the models of a rite of passage (Hutch, 1980), a token of group acceptance (Lapsley and Simpson, 1964a), a rite of initiation (Ranaghan, 1974), a structured role enactment (Holm, 1978), and a bridge-burning act of commitment (Gerlach and Hine, 1968) to explain the internal set of individuals who seek the charismatic experiences.

A number of environmental factors have been identified which make the occurrence of charismatic experiences more likely for an individual. Gerlach and Hine (1970) discovered that recruitment along lines of preexisting social relationships, i.e., family and friends, is an important factor. Some modeling by way of demonstration facilitates the learning process (Samarin, 1972). Paradoxically, even some opposition seems to keep the Pentecostal movement alive and more vital (Gerlach and Hine, 1968). Although no single factor or combination

of factors of internal set or environmental factors characterizes any single charismatic person, these factors are thought to be operative in some manner in every case.

5. **Theological Interpretation.** Although charismatic experiences have been interpreted to be sectarian in nature as opposed to being aspects of institutional church life, probably the best way to understand these experiences is to accept them as mystical experiences which can occur either in sects or in churches (Troeltsch, 1931 [1911]). Sociological analysis has demonstrated that the most powerful factor predisposing Catholic charismatics to seek charismatic experiences is a religious quest rather than compensating for deficits either sociologically or psychologically (Heirich, 1977). This religious quest may well be the most powerful factor for classical Pentecostals today and for neo-Pentecostals as well. In other words, the best way to understand charismatic experiences may be to view them as a form of mysticism which has its own validity (Malony and Lovekin, 1985).

Bibliography. A. Alland, "Possession in a Revivalist Negro Church," *J. for the Scientific Study of Religion,* 1-2: (1962), 204–13. R. M. Anderson, *Vision of the Disinherited: The Making of American Pentecostalism* (1979). C. D. Bradfield, *Neo-Pentecostalism: A Sociological Assessment* (1979). G. B. Cutten, *Speaking with Tongues: Historically and Psychologically Considered* (1927). E. Dermeghen, *Muhammad and the Islamic Tradition* (1953). T. Flournoy, *From India to the Planet Mars: A Study of a Case of Somnambulism with Glossolalia* ([1900] 1963). S. Freud, *Psychoanalysis and Faith* ([1910] 1963). L. P. Gerlach and V. H. Hine, "Five Factors Crucial to the Growth and Spread of a Modern Religious Movement," *J. for the Scientific Study of Religion,* 7 (1968), 23–40; *People, Power, and Change: Movements of Social Transformation* (1970). N. L. Gerrard, L. B. Gerrard, and A. Tellegen, *Scrabble Creek Folks: Part II, Mental Health* (1966). C. Y. Glock, "On the Origin and Evolution of Religious Groups," in C. Y. Glock, ed., *Religion in Sociological Perspective* (1973). F. D. Goodman, *Speaking In Tongues: A Cross-Cultural Study of Glossolalia* (1972). M. E. Greeley, "Charismatics and Non-Charismatics, A Comparison," *Review for Religious,* 33 (1974), 315–35. H. Hartman, *Ego Psychology and the Problem of Adaptation* ([1939] 1958); *Essays in Ego Psychology* (1964). M. Heirich, "Change of Heart: A Test of Some Widely Held Theories About Religious Conversion," *American J. of Sociology,* 83 (1977), 653–80. N. G. Holm, "Functions of Glossolalia in the Pentecostal Movement," in T. Källstad, ed., *Psychological Studies of Religious Man* (1978), pp. 141–58. R. A. Hutch, "The Personal Ritual of Glossolalia," *J. for the Social Scientific Study of Religion,* 19 (1980), 255–66. W. James, *The Varieties of Religious Experience* ([1902] 1958). P. Janet, *L'état mental des hystériques* ([1907] 1924). M. T. Kelsey, *Tongue Speaking: An Experiment in Spiritual Experience* (1964). A. Kiev, "Beliefs and Delusions of West Indian Immigrants to London," *British J. of Psychiatry,* 109 (1963), 356–63. A. Kiev, *Magic, Faith, and Healing* (1964). J. P. Kildahl, *The Psychology of Speaking in Tongues* (1972). E. Kris, ed., *Psychoanalytic Explorations in Art* ([1934] 1953). J. Laffal, *Pathological and Normal Language* (1965). J. N. Lapsley and J. H. Simpson, "Speaking in Tongues: Token of Group Acceptance and Divine Approval," *Pastoral Psychology,* 15 (1964), 48–53; "Speaking in Tongues: Infantile Babble or Song of the Self? Part II," *Pastoral Psychology,* 15 (1964), 16–24. H. N. Malony and A. A. Lovekin, *Glossolalia: Behavioral Science Perspectives on Speaking in Tongues* (1985). E. M. Pattison, "Behavioral Science Research on the Nature of Glossolalia," *J. of American Scientific Affiliation,* 20 (1968), 73–86. O. Pfister, "Die psychologische Enträtselung der religiösen

Glossolalie unter der automatischen Kryptographic," *Jahrbuch für Psychoanalytische und Psychopathologischen Forschungen*, 3 (1912), 427–68. K. M. Ranaghan, "Rites of Initiation in Representative Pentecostal Churches in the United States, 1901–1972," Ph.D. dissertation, University of Notre Dame (1974). W. J. Samarin, *Tongues of Men and Angels: The Religious Language of Pentecostalism* (1972). B. Schwarz, "Ordeal by Serpents, Fire and Strychnine" *Psychiatric Quarterly*, 34 (1960), 405–29. E. Troeltsch, *The Social Teachings of the Christian Churches* ([1911] 1931). M. Weber, *The Theory of Social and Economic Organizations* ([1922] 1957). W. W. Wood, *Culture and Personality Aspects of the Pentecostal Holiness Religion* (1965).

A. A. LOVEKIN

ECSTACY; PRAYER; RELIGIOUS EXPERIENCE; SANCTIFICATION/ HOLINESS. *See also* SPIRITUALITY. *Compare* BORN-AGAIN EXPERIENCE; CONVERSION; HAPPINESS; HOLY, The; MYSTICISM; TRANCE; VISIONS AND VOICES.

CHARISMATIC HEALING. *See* FAITH HEALING.

CHARISMATIC PASTORAL CARE. The delivery of pastoral services within, or from out of, a religious environment marked by beliefs and practices characteristic of the Pentecostal churches. Having emerged in the opening decades of the twentieth century, this family of Christians teaches a post-conversional baptism in the Holy Spirit — a personal religious crisis experience issuing in enhanced joy, holiness, and fervor. This experience is accompanied, initially or eventually, by a replication of the extraordinary NT spiritual gifts — most usually speaking in tongues (glossolalia). Other gifts include prayer for physical and emotional healing, vernacular and often highly specific prophecy.

The charismatic movement spans virtually the whole range of Christendom, including the Roman Catholic and Eastern Orthodox sectors as well as the major strands of the Reformation (Reformed, Lutheran, Anglican, and Anabaptist). According to global church statistician David Barrett's *World Christian Encyclopedia*, there were in 1980 over 51 million Pentecostal Christians worldwide in more than 1,200 of their own denominations — making the Pentecostal tradition the largest sector in Protestantism. Adding Christians who remain within the mainline churches, including Roman Catholics, and who profess to have adopted Pentecostal beliefs and practices (these all form the diffuse "charismatic movement"), the figure swells to above 100 million Pentecostal charismatics worldwide in the mid-1980s.

1. **Features of Charismatic Religious Practice.** Pastoral nurture in a charismatic context will yield encounter with one or more of the following:

a. Healing. "Prayer for the sick," as a regular part of church services, marked Pentecostal churches even before they organized into denominations. Charismatics extended the therapeutic quest to "inner healing" as well — spiritually wrought rectification of psychological disorder. This often involves prayers that follow the development of the subject's own biography from birth through childhood to adolescent conflicts and adult disruptive episodes (divorces, job loss, family crises, etc.).

But pastors will frequently meet with the unfinished theological agenda of the Pentecostal worldview: what are the principles by which some persons for whom prayer is offered do recover, or at least improve — while others do not?

b. Failed healings. Some in the Pentecostal and charismatic movements teach a distorted definition of faith — which is viewed as the bold right to demand healing of God, accompanied by the need to demonstrate faith by actions that imitate the sought outcomes rather than attend to the present realities. Numerous media evangelists reflect this view. Even among the Pentecostal and charismatic churches, pastors have to provide care in cases of failed healings.

c. Exorcism. Pentecostal charismatics believe in both angels and demons. What health care professionals may diagnose as mental disorders readily described in the DSM III, enthused laity (often encouraged by clergy who share the pandemonic construct of cosmic realities) will attribute to demonic powers. Habits or weaknesses may be attributed to demons of lust, laziness, alcohol, or suicide.

Hence, exorcisms occur. Formats vary from refined use of liturgical paragraphs from the Roman Catholic missal to the faddish and even bizarre — such as coughing up various demons, at a moment specified by the evangelist, and spitting them into brown bags (quickly sealed) brought to the church service for the purpose.

d. Glossolalic prayer. Charismatic believers take freedom to use their own glossolalia gifts within limited prayer groups where the practice is understood and valued. The pre-war research of Anton Boisen, for whom religious glossolalia indicated personality disorder and social deprivation, has been displaced by that of later scholars, such as Newton Malony. Glossolalic subjects are no less "normal," nor any less needy, than non-Charismatic devotees even in the same congregation. It is the elitism implicit in the use of glossolalia which calls for pastoral reminders of the content and context of I Corinthians 13.

e. Laying on of hands. Contrary to the touch-deprivation that marks current Western societies, Pentecostal charismatics favor handholding in congregational prayer and singing. Greater religious significance accompanies the laying on of hands. It was a natural extension of the practice when media evangelists called for "laying your hand on" either the radio or TV or else on the affected part of the listener's own body as "point of contact" for prayer.

f. Resting in the Spirit. Also called "slain in the Spirit" among classical Pentecostals, this term describes a faint in which the individual falls backwards, prostrate and motionless. In earlier decades it was a frequent consequence of group prayer. More recently the action follows (some would say, is caused by) the prayers of evangelists — often with hands placed on the heads of the persons for whom prayer is offered. It is not uncommon to position aides behind the persons prayed for to catch them and ease the descent.

The phenomenon was a frequent accompaniment of the ministry of Kathryn Kuhlman. A Roman Catholic priest who directs an orphanage reports that children who "rest in the Spirit" gain visions of Jesus and conversations with him. Persons who undergo this experience usually rise quietly in a brief time to rejoin the proceedings.

g. Word of knowledge. This gift of the Spirit appears in the list of charismata at I Cor. 12:8 ("utterance of knowledge"; *"word* of knowledge" comes from the KJV, widely preferred by classical Pentecostals and means the public disclosure (usually by a leader, at times by a congregant) of some alleged fact about a person that is not a matter of common knowledge. Typically, a healing evangelist will announce, perhaps pointing in a general direction within an assembled congregation, that someone present suffers a certain malady. A person so affected will rise and attest the accuracy of the disclosed secret. Prayer for healing follows. The practice has suffered abuse when alleged "words" are given for highly specific life-direction guidance—business options or marital choices, for example.

2. Approaches to a Positive Pastoral Response. Most major denominations have charismatic service committees which strive to balance charismatic piety with denominational loyalty. These agencies cultivate networks of charismatic practitioners whom inquirers may consult. Publications, conferences, and seminars address general and specific problems from pastoral standpoints anchored firmly within the denominational traditions.

The International Order of St. Luke the Physician has roots that go back to 1932, when Episcopal clergyman John Gaynor Banks established an agency aimed at recognizing healing as a normal mode of ministry. Some 7,000 members (20 percent clergy) make use of its journal *Sharing* and attend locally sponsored conferences.

The Association of Christian Therapists counts over 2,000 members. It is Roman Catholic but ecumenical and charismatic, an organization of lay and professional persons who link medical care and prayer for healing.

Among periodicals of practical help are: *Wholeness: A World Digest of Christian Healing* (New Zealand), *New Covenant, Pastoral Leadership,* and *Ministries.*

Bibliography. Statistics: D. B. Barrett, *World Christian Encyclopedia* (1982). Selective global historical survey: W. J. Hollenweger, *The Pentecostals* (1972) and R. Quebedeaux on *The New Charismatics II* (1983). American Pentecostalism: V. Synan, *The Holiness-Pentecostal Movement* (1971). Insightful critical exposition: G. A. Wacker, Jr., "The Function of Faith in Primitive Pentecostalism," *Harvard Theological Review* 77 (1984), 353–75; *also* D. L. Clark, "An Implicit Theory of Personality, Illness, and Cure Found in the Writings of Neo-Pentecostal Faith Teachers," *J. of Pastoral Theology* 12 (1984), 279–85. Internal and external critiques: R. Spittler, ed., *Perspectives on the New Pentecostalism* (1976). On healing, a Roman Catholic charismatic viewpoint: F. MacNutt, *Healing* (1974). Problems, from a Pentecostal viewpoint: D. Gee, *Trophimus I Left Sick* (1952) and D. E. Harrell, Jr., *All Things Are Possible: The Healing and Charismatic Revivals in Modern America* (1975). On glossolalia: the older view, A. Boisen, "Religion and Hard Times: A Study of the Holy Rollers," *Social Action* 5 (Mar. 15, 1938), 8–35; the newer assessment: H. N. Malony and A. A. Lovekin, *Glossolalia: Perspectives from the Social-behavorial Studies* (1985). L. Parker, *We Watched Our Son Die* (1980). R. Quebedeaux, *By What Authority: The Rise of Personality Cults in American Christianity* (1982).

R. P. SPITTLER

PASTORAL CARE (History, Traditions, and Definitions); HOLY SPIRIT, DOCTRINE OF, AND PASTORAL CARE. *See also* BLESSING AND BENEDICTION; ECCLESIOLOGY AND PASTORAL CARE; EXORCISM; FAITH HEALING; PRAYER IN PASTORAL CARE. *Compare* EVANGELICAL *or* FUNDAMENTALIST PASTORAL CARE; PIETISM AND PASTORAL CARE; SECTARIAN PASTORAL CARE.

CHARITY. *See* GIVING AND RECEIVING; LOVE; *also* VINCENT DE PAUL, ST.

CHASTITY. *See* LUST AND CHASTITY. *See also* EVANGELICAL COUNSELS; RELIGIOUS LIFE.

CHEKHOV, ANTON. *See* CLASSIC LITERATURE IN CARE AND COUNSELING (Orthodoxy).

CHEMICAL ECSTASY. *See* PSYCHEDELIC DRUGS AND EXPERIENCE.

CHEMOTHERAPY. *See* CANCER PATIENT.

CHILD ABUSE AND NEGLECT. *See* FAMILY LAW; FAMILY VIOLENCE.

CHILD CARE/CHILD RAISING. *See* PARENT EFFECTIVENESS TRAINING; PARENTS/PARENTHOOD.

CHILD-PARENT CONFLICT. *See* FAMILY; FAMILY THEORY AND THERAPY; PARENTS/PARENTHOOD.

CHILDBIRTH. Historically, researchers have focused on the physical aspects of childbirth. Recently, this has shifted to two other factors that influence a woman's experience of childbirth: social/cultural mores and personality characteristics of the mother.

Differences in the philosophy of obstetrics in the Netherlands and the U.S. illustrate the first of these. In the U.S. childbirth is considered a medical procedure performed by a physician in a sterile isolated environment. In the Netherlands childbirth is viewed as a natural phenomenon which usually needs no intervention but only close observation and moral support. High risk cases are delivered in hospitals in the Netherlands and low risks are often delivered at home with a midwife and family members present. Surprisingly, the death rate of infants is lower in the Netherlands than in the U.S. Less surprising is the finding that women who deliver babies at home find childbirth to be a more satisfying experience and are less depressed than woman who deliver in hospitals.

Another custom that influences the experience of childbirth is the presence of the father. Fathers present at the birth of their children tend to form earlier attachments and spend more time with their infants than fathers who are not present. More interesting is the finding that women who experience childbirth as "mystical" or "rapturous" are women whose husbands are present at the childbirth.

Also influential in the childbirth experience is the mother's personality. The personality trait most studied is that of anxiety. Women high in anxiety tend to have longer labors, have more uterine dysfunctioning, and have more highly active babies than women low in anxiety.

Newton's research suggests a relationship between childbirth and other female functioning. For example, women who dislike childbirth tend to dislike menstruation, breastfeeding, and closeness to their infants. Newton calls women "trebly sensuous" and she discusses the psychological and physiological similarities between undrugged childbirth, orgasm, and lactation. She encourages women to experience and enjoy all their sexuality rather than focusing only on orgasm.

Breen finds that women who adjust well to childbearing are generally more individuated than women who do not adjust well. They also tend to be active rather than passive which is contrary to the cultural stereotype of femininity.

None of these studies is conclusive and more research is needed to adequately understand the social/cultural and personality factors that influence childbirth. Enough is known, however, to suggest that the experience of childbirth can be enhanced to the extent to which a woman feels good about herself as an individual and as a woman, and to the extent to which she feels supported by those around her.

Bibliography. D. Breen, *The Birth of a First Child* (1975). A. Macfarlane, *The Psychology of Childbirth* (1977). M. Mead and N. Newton, "Cultural Patterning of Perinatal Behavior," in S. A. Richardson and A. F. Guttmacher, eds., *Childbearing, Its Social and Psychological Aspects* (1967). N. Newton, *Maternal Emotions* (1955); "Trebly Sensuous Woman," *Psychology Today,* (July, 1971), 68–72.

L. S. GROH

PARENTS/PARENTHOOD; PREMATURE BIRTH; PREGNANCY. *See also* BODY; FAMILY, PASTORAL *or* JEWISH CARE AND COUNSELING OF; MOTHER-INFANT BONDING; WOMEN. *Compare* FAMILY PLANNING; MISCARRIAGE.

CHILDHOOD, BEHAVIORAL DISORDERS OF.
See BEHAVIOR DISORDERS OF CHILDHOOD.

CHILDISHNESS. *See* REGRESSION; RESPONSIBILITY/ IRRESPONSIBILITY. *See also* NARCISSISM.

CHILDLESSNESS. *See* INFERTILITY.

CHILDREN. While persons between the ages of zero and twelve usually represent a sizable proportion of those to whom a pastor or religious worker may minister, the pastoral care and counseling of children has only recently received specialized attention. The particular needs, developmental issues, and problems of persons in this stage require focused attention in order for ministry to be effective.

1. Understanding the Child. For the pastor, the most important dimension of working with normal children is to be concrete. The younger the child, the less capable he or she is of having abstract thought. Jean Piaget, Swiss biologist and psychologist, has shown that children generally learn, reason, and relate in concrete terms until about the age of twelve, when more abstract thinking begins to develop. Thus, to be able to communicate and help children, the pastor must leave the world of the intellect and get into the concrete world of things and experiences. For children, words are secondary to experience.

To work with children, pastors need to be genuinely interested in what they are doing. Children read feelings

very well and can quickly recognize insincerity. A pastor must also be able to play, have a sense of humor, and use symbols, such as toys. Finally, a pastor who offers pastoral care or counseling to children must be open-minded and able to adjust to the quick shifts of the child's mind.

Most children show their feelings or express their problems in actions, rather than by telling about them. In relating to children, pastors use stories, play with toys, use music, or role-play situations, whether they are involved in education, pastoral care, or counseling. With children who have developed fine motor skills (over the age of six years), pencil and paper exercises like drawing pictures of their families, themselves, or their fantasies are often used.

Whether the child is in a normal situation such as learning about prayer, a Bible story, learning values in role play, or is a child who is trying to adjust to divorce by playing with family figures, action is the vehicle of change and learning. In pastoral care with normal children, concrete actions, words, and symbols are important in communicating concern. Physical touch or contact along with parallel play provide an entrée to children and lets them know they are cared about. In older children, noncompetitive games that allow the game players to share their feelings and experiences help children learn it is all right to share with the pastor and peers. Normal children also respond well to group activity where they gain a sense of belonging and learn the support of fellowship and positive peer pressure. Here the pastor needs to have some experience working with group dynamics to be of maximum effectiveness. Similar to group activity is family interaction led by the pastor. This is more than the family night supper; it is planned family activities that promote togetherness and teach communication, negotiation, and conflict resolution. Major denominations and workshop groups have produced guidebooks for numerous planned activities to help groups of families learn these skills (see Dill, 1986; Sawin, 1979, 1984). These activities teach younger children and particularly adolescents to talk and negotiate about problems rather than act them out.

Good pastoral care with children provides a natural bridge for the pastor to help when problems develop, whether those problems are of a crisis nature or more long-term.

2. Methods of Pastoral Care. A number of different ways to treat problems are available to pastors. Since most younger children are oriented around actions rather than speech, they often play out their feelings and problems or act out solutions. A method of working with children has evolved this century known as *play therapy,* in which children alone or in groups play in a room designed to let them express themselves most fully. The therapist's task is to interpret the play or reflect the feelings he or she sees in the child's play. Sometimes the whole family is involved with a problem that initially is presented as the child's. The counselor often interprets the young child's play or helps the family see and experience the problem as belonging to the entire family as a system rather than just to one member. The pastoral counselor can also deal with the child in the parent's presence, thus teaching the parent how to handle a specific problem by demonstrating practical ways to change behavior. The pastor helps the parent to understand the child's concrete thought processes and how to relate to them. This approach changes depending on the age and development of each child. Children under six years of age are very reactive to the world around them and form their impressions of their world through interactions. They react to what they see modeled and to what works for them. For example, a child may resist developing speech if she or he can get what is wanted by pointing. In this case, the parent must learn to present alternatives that take speech rather than gesturing. No amount of talking will change the child's behavior: only action will work. Touch, parallel play, rhythm, music, and doing activities are the best ways of communicating with children at this age.

Though children have developed considerable intellectual abilities by their sixth birthday, they are still heavily dependent on concrete activities to form their understanding of things around them. As they enter school, relationships become important, and they spend more time outside the home. At this age, children still show their problems rather than articulate them. Speech, however, can parallel action, and as a child plays, he or she starts to translate what was meant by the same words.

For instance, an eight-year-old experienced situational school phobia. He would read the newspaper, listen to the radio and T.V. to hear the weather predictions for the next day. He would closely check the sky upon awakening and keep records of weather predictions and how the weather actually turned out. On rainy or predicted rainy days, he would refuse to go to school, or if an unexpected rain shower happened at school, he would become ill and have to return home. He had experienced a tornado not more than a mile from his home and reported he was fearful a tornado would destroy his home. In play therapy, it quickly became apparent that *home* really meant mother. She was an over-protective, frightened person who had helped foster her son's fear. By helping the mother and son deal with their fear, the problem was alleviated. After a close relationship has developed, touch is still appropriate at this age, but in a more limited way. Play is more structured, as in games, and big muscle activities such as running, jumping, and pounding help to release emotions. Interpretations and instruction are the best ways to communicate at this level.

3. **Behavior Problems.** The pastor who works with children needs to develop a repertoire of treatments which will relate to the developmental stage and the particular problems children have. Some of the most common complaints about preschool children a pastor sees, whether in making parish calls or in a counseling situation, revolve around behavior problems that typically parents or other caregivers cannot tolerate.

Hyperactivity is one of the more common complaints about younger children. This term describes not only nonstop activity but often destructive, irritating, and demanding behavior as well as a short attention span. Modern pediatricians do not diagnose hyperactivity until a child is over five years old. Often behavior labeled as hyperactive by parents, day-care workers, nursery school personnel, or church workers is actually a sign of depression, anxiety, or parenting or family problems. Because children develop at different rates, no matter what their chronological age, children who have developmental delay are sometimes labeled hyperactive. Most children mature beyond the behavior that is characterized as hyperactivity. For others, structure, childproofing the child's environment, employing multiple care givers, individual attention, and supportive relationships for parents often help both children and parents through this stage. Ritalin, a stimulant that has a paradoxical effect on children, is often given when a child has been diagnosed as hyperactive, but needs to be used very cautiously. Teaching parents patience and explaining that most children outgrow overactive behavior may be the most important contribution a pastor can make in dealing with this problem.

A second area of complaint involves elimination, that is, enuresis, lack of bladder control, and encopresis, lack of bowel control. First complaints about enuresis can come from a lack of understanding of bladder control. Usually children can achieve daytime bladder control from one to three years of age. Nighttime control problems often persist for some time. Bed-wetting is a common complaint. Again, maturation is an important element in any physical mastery. Often parents expect children to gain total control before it is physiologically possible. Unless there has not been a significant dry period of from three to six months at night, then enuresis is usually not a problem. About five percent of children still bed-wet beyond their thirteenth year.

If there has been a significant dry period, and bed-wetting reappears, it could be because of emotional problems. One of the most common of these is the birth of a new sibling. The problem will usually disappear if the child is reassured of his or her place in the family and finds that the new arrival is here to stay.

Other types of elimination problems can be physical and should be checked out medically. There are few consistently proven ways to handle enuresis. Many methods have shown limited success: restricting fluids, expanding the bladder by waiting until the last minute to urinate, using alarm devices that wake the child when they begin to wet their bed, vitamin therapies, using magnesium and calcium, and medication, primarily Tofranil or tricyclic medications over a two-week period. Most of these approaches have little side effect and can be helpful; however, the medication can be very dangerous if not carefully controlled by parents. Accidental ingestion of tricyclics is the second highest cause of poisoning death in young children.

The problem of encopresis has many more emotional ramifications than enuresis. Usually, after bowel control is established, bowel problems not caused by disease or diet are the result of control issues between the parent and child. Fecal accidents in the pants, hiding feces in drawers, the furnace, and other annoying places often represents an expression of anger and frustration on the part of the child. Family therapy or counseling between the parents and child usually is the most helpful.

A third area of major complaint is nightmares, fear, anxiety, and depression. Children who are too young to articulate their problem very well often experience their feelings, dreams, or environment as intolerable and try to withdraw. Sleep disturbance and withdrawal are common symptoms with these children. Simple behavioral methods, such as telling the children to go back and finish the nightmare positively, the way they want it to end, can help eliminate some fears. Counseling with family members is also helpful, along with helping the child act out fears and fantasies through play therapy, and enlisting the help of friends or a weapon to ward off danger in the dream. When children are of school age, chief complaints surround learning difficulties, minimal brain dysfunction, problem behavior, childhood depression, separation anxiety, and even asocial behavior. Most of these problems involve classroom activity, but often reflect home problems. Methods involving understanding and the establishment of structure or special education classes can help children to cope with these problems.

4. **Spiritual Development.** The combined research of psychology and religious studies has provided important insights for understanding a child's spiritual development.

Psychologically, Erik Erikson has noted that the primary developmental tasks of children from birth to adolescence include trust versus mistrust, autonomy versus shame, initiative versus guilt, and industry versus inferiority. Pastoral theologians, however, have noted that these tasks also have a religious dimension. Lewis Sherrill (1963) asserts that a child's first (and ongoing) encounters with the love of a parent have strong relevance for how the child will also perceive the love of God. Therefore, a stable and trustworthy relationship with parents lays the foundation for the child's capacity to trust God. An unpredictable, abusive, or harshly judging parent will likewise affect the qualities which the child attributes to God as authority.

Donald Capps (1983) also notes that the accomplishment of these developmental tasks of childhood have strong implications for the child's moral and religious development, including the child's personal sense of hope, will, purpose, and competence. These stages also can affect the planning and use of ritual in church life (cf. Holmes, 1982). Fowler (1987) points out that the stages of faith development usually associated with childhood (such as intuitive-projective and mythic-literal) should be considered in understanding the various ways in which a congregation is "present" to a child through worship, Christian education, and pastoral care.

Attention to these kinds of insights will enable the pastor to minister to children with sensitivity and skill.

Bibliography. V. Axline, *Play Therapy: The Inner Dynamics of Childhood* (1947). D. Capps, *Life Cycle Theory and Pastoral Care* (1987). R. Clapp, "Vanishing Childhood," *Christianity Today*, 28:8 (1983), 12–19, and 28:9 (1984), 18–24. R. Coles, *Children of Crisis*, 5 vols. (1967–77). E. R. Dill, "Planning for all Ages: Intergenerational Events can Build Bridges in a Church," *Christian Ministry*, 17:2 (1986), 16–18. D. Elkind, *The Child's Reality: Three Developmental Themes* (1978). J. W. Fowler, *Faith Development and Pastoral Care* (1987); *Stages of Faith* (1981); "Gifting the Imagination: Awakening and Informing Children's Faith," *Review and Expositor*, 80 (1983), 189–200. U. Holmes, *Young Children and the Eucharist* (1982). A. Lester, *When Children Suffer* (1987); *Children in Crisis* (1985). J. Piaget, *The Development of Thought* (1977); *Moral Judgment of the Child* (1948); *Play, Dreams, and Imitation in Childhood* (1962). M. M. Sawin, *Family Enrichment with Family Clusters* (1979); "How the Family Shapes Religious Believing and How Religious Education Can Shape the Family," *American Baptist Quarterly*, 3 (1984), 53–62. L. Sherrill, *The Struggle of the Soul* (1963), ch. 2; *Understanding Children* (1939).

J. L. FLORELL

CHILDREN, PASTOR'S; DIVORCE, CHILDREN AND ADOLESCENTS IN; DYING CHILD AND FAMILY; EXCEPTIONAL CHILDREN AND THEIR FAMILIES; FAMILY, PASTORAL *or* JEWISH CARE AND COUNSELING OF; FOSTER CHILDREN AND FOSTER PARENTS; GRIEF AND LOSS IN CHILDHOOD AND ADOLESCENCE; ONLY CHILDREN; STEPFAMILIES. *See also* ADOPTION; BIRTH ORDER; MATERNAL DEPRIVATION; MOTHER-INFANT BONDING. *Compare* LIFE CYCLE THEORY AND PASTORAL CARE; PARENTS/PARENTHOOD.

CHILDREN, CONVERSION OF. *See* CONVERSION; EVANGELIZING.

CHILDREN, DEATH OF. *See* DYING CHILD AND FAMILY; FUNERAL, CHILD'S.

CHILDREN, DISCIPLINE OF. *See* PARENTS/PARENTHOOD; PARENT EFFECTIVENESS TRAINING.

CHILDREN, DIVORCE AND. *See* DIVORCE, CHILDREN AND ADOLESCENTS IN.

CHILDREN, PASTOR'S. Those children who are reared, at least in part, during the time their father or mother serves as pastor of a local congregation. This distinction of identity is required because ministers' children reared in other settings do not experience the same domestic dynamics as do those for whom the parish is their family context. Insufficient data is presently available to contrast both the different effects on children when the father is pastor and when the mother is pastor, and the impact of the parent's position on the child according to the time in the child's life when a parent becomes a pastor.

Pentecost (1964) has noted that pastors' children ". . . are seldom allowed to live completely normal lives." This "glass bowl" effect does permeate the pastor's family existence.

Because the boundary between the role of father or mother and role of the pastor is usually blurred, the boundary between family and profession is also blurred to varying degrees. A prominent consequence of this for pastor's children is the question of personhood integrity versus becoming an extension of the pastor's role. Some pastors' children flourish in the added attention afforded by the parent's role, while others experience it as an odious burden. Pastors' children routinely experience unrealistically high family role expectations and significant social pressure. Other negative factors include the requirement to suppress or make inaccessible certain feelings and reactions to life situations. While in some pastors' families the inaccessibility of parents because of pastoral responsibilities results in experiences of emotional deprivation, in others the profession seems to make parents more available. A large negative impact results from children hearing criticisms of the pastor parent without any framework for processing such attacks. Similarly, some pastors' children experience exclusion or negative treatment both in the church and in society because they are pastors' children. Some pastors' children are overwhelmed by the pressures and, in rebellion, reject all connections with qualities or patterns that exhibit the lifestyle associated with the ministry.

The advantages for pastors' children are generally overlooked. The large number of persons in highly successful occupations who grew up as pastors' children suggests that for many children it is a positive experience. Pastors' children have the advantage of seeing a strong sense of life purpose modeled by their parents. This clear sense of values and moral decision-making contributes to the development of internal life controls, positive character, spiritual growth, and spiritual concern for both family and church.

The development of pastors' children has received scant attention in the literature except as isolated chapters in books on pastors' wives or families. An exception to this paucity of materials is *Parenting in the Minister's Home* by Terry Peck. His list of development issues for pastors' children suggests areas for parental attention: love, uniqueness, self-worth, anger, stress, sexual development, discipline, spiritual growth, parental mistakes, burnout effects, and launching concerns.

The ultimate question, beyond all the circumstances of life in a pastor's home, concerns the quality of the relationship between the parent and the child. Yet no parent, even the pastor, can legitimately take full responsibility for the outcome of a child's life, except in rare and flagrant circumstances.

Bibliography. T. Peck, *Parenting in the Minister's Home* (1988). D. H. Pentecost, *The Pastor's Wife and the Church* (1964). R. M. Stevenson, "Children of the Parsonage," *Pastoral Psychology* 3:3 (1982), 179–86.

E. WHITE

MARRIAGE AND FAMILY LIFE, PASTOR'S. *See also* CHILDREN; PARENTS/PARENTHOOD.

CHILDREN OF GOD/FAMILY OF LOVE. *See* NEW RELIGIOUS MOVEMENTS.

CHILDREN'S HOME. *See* CHAPLAIN/CHAPLAINCY; GRIEF AND LOSS IN CHILDHOOD AND ADOLESCENCE. *See also* FOSTER CHILDREN.

CHIROPRACTIC HEALING. That process of healing which results when a chiropractor makes adjustments to the spine, primarily using his or her hands. These adjustments have two main aims: one, to relieve pain caused by pressure on nerves resulting from spinal misalignment; and two, to release the body's own healing powers so that healing may occur throughout the body. In what follows, chiropractic healing will be considered in three parts: 1. History of Chiropractic, 2. Chiropractic Theory, and 3. Importance for Pastoral Care.

1. History of Chiropractic. Chiropractic health care in North America began with Dr. Daniel David Palmer who, in 1895, restored to hearing by spinal manipulation a man who had been deaf for seventeen years. Three years later he opened a school of chiropractic in Daven-

port, Iowa, a school now known as The Palmer School of Chiropractic (Kelner). Since then, the profession of chiropractic has developed to what is now generally recognized as a legitimate healing profession. Most insurance companies reimburse for chiropractic services and over twelve million people annually seek chiropractic care (Green).

2. Chiropractic Theory. Chiropractic is built upon three related scientific theories and clinical principles. The first is that disease may be caused by nervous system disturbances. The nervous system coordinates the activity of cells throughout the body. Any condition which irritates the nervous system will disturb that activity and in turn lead to disease. Second, disturbances in the nervous system can be caused by derangements in the musculoskeletal structure. Off-centerings or subluxations of vertebral and pelvic segments, which are common in most persons, can lead to nervous system irritation and disturbances. Third, nervous system disturbance can cause and/or aggravate disease in various organs and parts of the body. Subluxations may trigger or exacerbate headaches, asthmatic syndromes, spastic colons, and many other conditions (Schafer). Chiropractors are concerned, therefore, not only with the functioning of the spine and pelvis but with the whole person. They believe that their healing methods bring relief to pain resulting from subluxations, and also that chiropractic adjustments will promote healing throughout the entire organism, including the body and the mind.

Traditional chiropractic treatment seeks to correct or reduce a subluxated, hypermobile, or fixated vertebral or pelvic segment by using a specific, predetermined adjustment. The purpose of this adjustment is to normalize the relationships within and between the segments and relieve the neurological, muscular, and vascular disturbances caused by the subluxation (Schafer). The spine consists of thirty-three bones, called vertebrae, and has more than fifteen hundred supporting muscles and ligaments. Through the spine passes the spinal cord, which has thirty-one pairs of nerves that originate in the brain and leave the spine through openings between the vertebrae. Special cushions, called discs, which lie between the vertebrae, act as shock absorbers and allow for motion and flexibility. Subluxations, or derangements in the spine, can lead to disc and nerve disturbances and other problems throughout the organism (Schafer).

As has been indicated, the major form of therapy used by chiropractors is spinal manipulation or adjustment using the hands. The ability to make that adjustment requires a great deal of skill, not unlike that required by a surgeon. The chiropractor relies upon X-rays as well as the many years of training in the chiropractic art to arrive at the precise adjustment needed at a given time. When allowed by state laws, many chiropractors also use adjunct methods of healing, such as acupuncture, massage, and electrical stimulation of muscle groups. They may also advocate diet and vitamin therapy in their effort to treat the whole person. But the primary technique is the skillful use of the hands.

3. Importance for Pastoral Care. It is important that pastoral care practitioners, whether they be parish pastors, pastoral counselors, or educators, be familiar with chiropractic medicine. Many of their parishioners or clients will have back problems and may suffer from back-related problems. Medical doctors are seldom trained to deal with spinal disturbances and those who are may too quickly resort to surgical techniques when chiropractic healing may be the treatment of choice.

Perhaps the most important implication for pastoral care from chiropractic is its emphasis on wholistic healing and that if not impeded the body and mind will tend to heal themselves. A study of the theory of chiropractic healing should help anyone practicing pastoral care to appreciate anew the innate resources of the human person.

Bibliography. L. Green, "Are You Deranged?," *Outsider* (August, 1987). M. Kelner, *et al., Chiropractors: Do They Help?* (1980). R. A. Leach, *The Chiropractic Theories* (1986). B. J. Palmer, *The Science of Chiropractic* (1911). R. C. Schafer, *Chiropractic Health Care* (1977).

C. KROPP

HEALING. *Compare* OSTEOPATHIC HEALING.

CHOOSING, CHOICE. See DECISION/INDECISION, PSYCHOLOGY OF; FREEDOM AND DETERMINISM. *See also* COMMITMENT.

CHRIST, IMITATION OF. See CHRISTIAN LIFE; CHRISTOLOGY AND PASTORAL CARE; SPIRITUAL DISCIPLINE AND GROWTH.

CHRISTADELPHIANS. *See* SECTARIAN PASTORAL CARE.

CHRISTENING. *See* BAPTISM AND CONFIRMATION.

CHRISTIAN CONCILIATION MOVEMENT. An association of conservative Protestant peacemaking ministries committed to applying biblical principles and procedures in the resolution and reconciliation of disputes among Christians within the framework of the local church.

1. **History and National Scope.** The Christian Conciliation movement was begun in 1980 by a group of attorneys in Albuquerque, New Mexico, led by Laurence Eck, and was subsequently promoted nationally by the Christian Legal Society, a national association of conservative Protestant lawyers. Currently, Christian Conciliation Service programs are in operation across the U.S. and in several foreign countries. Most of these local programs are members of the national Association of Christian Conciliation Services, which is affiliated with the Christian Legal Society.

2. **Scriptural Foundation.** The ministry is based on the scriptures, which direct Christians to resolve their disputes within the framework of the church rather than in the secular courts (e.g., Mt. 18:15–20; I Cor. 6:1–7) and scriptures that emphasize the importance of reconciliation and unity in the Body of Christ (e.g., Mt. 5:22–23; I Cor. 12:12–27; Eph. 4:1–16).

3. **Goals and Services.** The goals of this ministry are threefold: (1) to assist individuals to resolve disputes and reconcile broken relationships using biblical principles and procedures; (2) to educate, train, and equip pastors, church leaders, lawyers, counselors and therapists, and

individual Christians to be peacemakers in their professional practices and personal lives; and (3) to exhort and equip the church to return to its scripturally mandated ministry of resolving disputes among Christians.

Christian Conciliation services include: (1) biblical counsel to individuals involved in disputes; (2) mediation and arbitration of disputes; and (3) educational seminars and books, tapes, and other educational materials on biblical conflict resolution, peacemaking, and church discipline.

Mediations are conducted by panels of three trained volunteers — typically, a lawyer, a pastor, and a layperson with expertise in the area of dispute. During each mediation, the mediators attempt to: (1) understand the facts; (2) identify the issues in dispute and the applicable biblical principles for each issue; (3) discern and eliminate the underlying, root causes of the dispute; (4) help each party reconcile with God; (5) help the parties reconcile with one another; and (6) bring the parties to an agreement on what God's will is for how the dispute should be resolved. Disputes typically include: broken marriages, family conflicts, contractual and business disagreements, disputes over debts, personal injury cases, professional malpractice, inter- and intra-church conflicts, and disputes involving Christian organizations.

Bibliography. L. Buzzard and L. Eck, *Tell It to the Church: Reconciling Out of Court* (1982).

D. A. MONTGOMERY

MEDIATION/CONCILIATION; RECONCILING. *Compare* CONFLICT AND CONFLICT MANAGEMENT; CONFRONTATION (Pastoral and Therapeutic); EVANGELICAL PASTORAL CARE; FORGIVENESS; PEACE-MAKING AND PASTORAL CARE; PROBLEM SOLVING.

CHRISTIAN COUNSELING. See EVANGELICAL PASTORAL CARE.

CHRISTIAN EDUCATION/FORMATION. See EDUCATION, NURTURE, AND CARE; SPIRITUAL DISCIPLINE AND GROWTH; TEACHING.

CHRISTIAN-JEWISH MARRIAGE. See JEWISH-CHRISTIAN MARRIAGE.

CHRISTIAN LIFE. The life of Christ as lived by those for whom Christ is supremely important; a way of life known by its inner spirit and not merely its outward forms.

Among Christian traditions, the "Christian life" has no one particular form. Limited clarification of meaning can come from "defining" the term in the usual dictionary sense. Depending on the tradition, descriptive definition weights either the mystical or moral, the individual or corporate, the sacred or secular, the belief or faith, the virtue or ability, the perfection or wholeness aspects of Christian life. Such variability demands that we go beyond objectively describing forms of the Christian life to ways of illumining its inner dynamics. "Discernment" commends itself as one such way. The pastoral art of discernment serves to identify those whose personal relationship with Christ has supreme importance to them. Yet a further step toward clarifying the meaning of the

Christian life is possible as we undertake the "fostering" task of nurture and sustenance in ministry. These two processes enable internalization of Christ's own life and allow his Spirit to conform the spirit of one's inner life to his image. The person so nurtured and sustained knows his or her life as a "Christian life," whatever its outward form. Conversely, those not living the Christian life can have no direct knowledge of it.

1. Introduction *a. The variety and relativity of meanings.* The term "Christian life" lacks a single universally accepted meaning. Even within Christendom, it is often used interchangeably with "religious life" and "spiritual life," and occasionally with "the life of faith," "discipleship," the Christian "way," "pilgrimage," or "journey," and others. Each of these terms has acquired a particular set of meanings by virtue of its use within the religious and cultural traditions which give it currency. For the term "Christian life" there are secular meanings, Protestant meanings, Jewish meanings, Catholic and Unitarian meanings—and multiple meanings within single traditions and denominational groups. Descriptively then, the term "Christian life" is relative to the use and understanding of the defining group; there is no one accepted meaning.

Theologically, there are acceptable meanings and there are unacceptable meanings. Doctrinal claims are little affected by the variety and relativity of such meanings. Even non-Christian traditions may assert doctrinal certainty concerning the term "Christian life." Our present task, however, is best limited to a range of meanings given this term by traditions claiming to be "Christian" and to foster the Christian life.

b. Three modes for clarifying meanings. There are three general ways of clarifying the term "Christian life" in the context of pastoral care and counseling. The first is by *descriptive definition*—a largely conceptual task—that relies primarily on the disciplines of historical and systematic theology. The second way is by *discernment.* Here the defined meanings of the Christian life are used to identify particular persons or groups who do and who do not evidence the Christian life. This is a diagnostic task that belongs mainly to the disciplines of ascetical and pastoral theology. The final way of clarifying the term "Christian life" is through *fostering* the Christian life. This involves the pastoral tasks of nurturing and sustaining, and belongs most properly to the disciplines of pastoral care and counseling.

The process of clarifying the meaning of Christian life moves between these three modes, from the most conceptual (descriptive definition) to the most empirical (fostering), through the mode that combines them both (discernment). We are concerned with a life process which is inherently dynamic and whose shape may best be clarified by a process reflecting these dynamics.

c. The dynamics of the Christian life. The dynamics underlying a Christian life reflect at least four major forces moving through that life at any one time. There is first of all the unique set of personality traits of the individual Christian. Just as unique are the life events and circumstances that interface with his or her personality. To this comes the particular will, desire, or call of Christ for this person, as best as he or she can distinguish it. And finally there is the Christian's own denomina-

tional expectations of how a Christian should live. The day-by-day interaction of these forces influences significantly the form a person's life will take. Although there are Christian traditions that minimize the importance of some of these factors, there can be little doubt that the last quarter century has brought to Western Christianity an increasing awareness of and sophistication about the psychological and sociological forces shaping the way we live as Christians. Even theologically it is now widely accepted that no one Christian life will be like another. If anything, the hallmark of the Christian life has become its diversity of forms.

2. The Descriptive Mode. *a. Six dimensions of Christian life.* These forms may be seen as constituting at least six "dimensions" of religious life in the Christian tradition and are presented below in the mode of descriptive definition.

i. mystical/moral. The Desert Fathers and those in cloistered orders have been regarded by the Christian church as exemplifying a "high," difficult, and privileged form of the Christian life; a life which is ordered around long periods of prayer and worship, where God and Christ are to be approached in a direct and contemplative way. Christians of quite a different disposition have seen the Christian life principally in terms of faithful adherence to the moral teachings of Christ, with little regard for mystical theology or contemplative practice. This latter tradition has taken both an individual and a social form in this country, with late seventeenth-century Puritanism typifying the individual form and the early twentieth-century "social gospel" the social form. Salvation and mystical union with God are the goals which cluster at the mystical pole of this dimension, while obedience, social obligation, and divine approval are the goals that constitute the moral end.

ii. sacred/secular. Ritual and sacrament have provided many Christians with a focus and guide for living. This liturgical life appoints for one's encounter with God special times, places, objects, persons, and acts, with the grace thus imparted believed to infuse all other activities of life. At the other end of the spectrum are those who see the Christian life as celebrating the goodness and vitality of divine presence in all times, places, beings, activities, and things.

iii. individual/corporate. The disciple, follower, or pilgrim model of Christian life historically has emphasized the lonely journey of the Christian wending his or her way through life. Temptations, trials, consolations, and important decisions constitute the landmarks, with other persons seen either as incidental to or the occasions for individual growth in the Christian life. In marked contrast stands corporate or group-centered Christian life. Whether in the traditional gathered community or in the more modern "cell" or "T" groups, the Christian life is seen essentially as the property of this constituted "body of Christ" and only derivatively as the property of the individual member.

iv. belief/faith. Some Christian traditions regard unwaivering belief as the *sine qua non* of the Christian life, while others regard it with suspicion, emphasizing instead the redemptive activity of Christ with the Christian regardless of belief or confession. The former stress the conscious work of the Spirit and the latter a less conscious or intentional state where faith is essentially a deeply integrated disposition of the Christian personality toward God or Christ.

v. virtue/ability. Known by its "fruits," the Christian life has been seen as manifesting and/or consisting of certain behaviors and attitudes. The classical form of this model is comprised in the nine Christian virtues of Gal. 5:22—love, joy, peace, patience, kindness, goodness, faithfulness, gentleness, and self-control—the living of which is considered indicative of and often synonymous with the Christian life. Another view holds that any behavior or attitude can express the Christian life if it springs from a God-given sense of rootedness which *enables* one to see oneself and the world clearly and to respond appropriately.

vi. perfection/wholeness. Saintliness is popularly regarded as the epitome of the Christian life, yet Christians have a divided view on what makes for a saintly life. On the one side is the life of perfection commended by Christ in Mt. 5:48, and on the other side are Paul's beloved backsliding "saints" of I Corinthians 1. In the latter, saintliness may consist more in "wholeness" (as Jungians propose) than in perfection, an awareness and acceptance of both the good and bad within. Jesus' startling response to the rich young man in Mk. 10:18, "Why do you call me good? No one is good but God alone," gives us pause to wonder whether even goodness is a property of an exemplary life.

b. The limits of descriptive definition. Such diversity would seem to make difficult the task of descriptively defining the term "Christian life." No doubt it is simpler for those standing within a particular tradition or historical period where the Christian life implies homogeneity in personality, life experiences, discernment of call, and denominational background; and which assumes that most, if not all, true Christians are cast from the same mold and follow the same path. Such a view is finding far fewer adherents than in former times, which may be yet another sign that pluralism and diversity in religious things have come of age.

This diversification of forms in the Christian life has brought a new perspective to both theology and pastoral care. The most influential herald of this perspective is probably Søren Kierkegaard, who was rediscovered in the 1940s. Kierkegaard's entire literature may be seen as a polemic against the tendency of his time to "define" the Christian life. As a shrewd pastoral theologian, he saw the Christian life as much too important a thing to be defined: other things might be defined with impunity but not the Christian life. That was to be lived; and out of the experience of living would come clarity. The experience could be represented by words, hence definitions, but these words could neither be propounded nor understood by one not living the Christian life. They were simply passwords among family members.

It is Kierkegaard's story about the "knight of faith" that perhaps best epitomizes this polemic for pastoral theology today. It is rumored that in all Denmark there is no greater Christian than this knight; so spies are sent out that it might be discovered how he lives. Yet all they find is a "complacent burgher" who cannot be distinguished from his neighbors by the way he looks, talks, or conducts his life. Yet Kierkegaard, the "psycholo-

gist," can. He instructs his reader not to look to the outward forms, whether saintly or common, but to the inward "movements of infinity" that have no outward expression. What distinguishes the knight from others is something so deep and personal that it cannot be seen, known, or communicated directly—and that is the Christian life, discerned and fostered by its substance and not its form.

In the understanding and doctrine of most Christian traditions, this "substance" (if we may call it that) has very much to do with the life of Christ. It is the spirit or inner principle of Christ's life that becomes in us the Christian life. Borrowing from biology we may say that the Christian life has a unique and distinguishable genotype, but as many phenotypes as there are Christians. Since the phenotypes of form do not readily distinguish the Christian life from the non-Christian one, neither do they define the Christian life in a helpful or accurate way.

3. The Mode of Discernment. *a. Identification and recognition.* The pastoral art of discernment provides a helpful perspective here. Definition and description function best when elucidating qualities of things. It is primarily a rational and logical activity. Discernment, on the other hand, has more to do with dynamic processes, generally life processes. It is mostly an intuitive activity. It is similar to the experience of recognizing a childhood friend years later, in a way that seems uncanny. Everything about him or her has changed; not even the most complete F.B.I. description would have enabled us to recognize this person, yet we do. What we recognize is the *person,* and not a conglomerate of definable qualities about the person. Jesus was no stranger to this art. What he sought in someone, he recognized immediately, identifying a Christian life (technically, a pre-Christian life) from the midst of the unlikely group of people from which he chose his disciples and those whom he called and healed.

Discernment is not only a pastoral art practiced by Christ and by ministering Christians, it is the threshold to the Christian life. It is the process that allows us to identify, recognize, and then focus our attention on another person. As Christ discerns each of us in this deeply personal way, we are known by him. It is Christ's nature to do this, the essence of his Christ-ness. In a word, it *is* his life. So, also, is our life a Christian life as we identify, recognize, focus on, and draw close to this Life, this Person who discerns us so. It is the inward riveting of our two lives that allows him to be Christ and us to be Christians, him to live his Christ-life and us to live our Christian lives. And although the outer form of our Christian lives may differ radically (and at times confusingly), our inner lives converge on his to become one, one substance and one genotype.

b. Valuing. It is then the high value one places on the Person of Christ—matching the high value he places on us—that sets us apart as Christians and enables us to live a Christian life. No matter how exemplary a life we may live, it is not a Christian life if our personal relationship to Christ is of little importance. Christian traditions, despite their diversity on questions of form, seem fully agreed here. This sense of personal importance is to be understood commonly. For each of us there are persons of great importance and persons of less importance.

A Christian life is the life in which Christ becomes for us the most important person. He asked those who would follow him to regard even their families of less value than himself (Mt. 10:34–39; 12:46–50; 19:28–29). To be committed wholly to the Christian Church, Christian doctrine, or even the *idea* of a personal Christ is not enough. It is the degree of investment in this other Person that enables a Christian life.

4. The Fostering Mode. *a. Internalization.* As discernment nudges us from the conceptual to the personal realm in understanding Christian life, the process of fostering takes us a step further. In this step we go from recognizing and valuing a person to allowing our relationship with this person to shape our lives. A common understanding of interpersonal dynamics illumines how the power of an important relationship can influence and change the way someone lives. A parent with an infant, a special teacher with a child, a mentor with a young adult, and a man and a woman in marriage are relationships in which internalizing change is always happening. In a Christian life this happens with Christ, a step in which Christ begins to be transformed from the most important person in relation to me to an equally personal presence and power within. The Freudian understanding of parental "incorporation" by the child may provide a picture of this dynamic. Through the parent-child relationship, and to the degree the parent is valued by the child, the child begins to assimilate the parent's values —which in turn begin to change the way the child behaves and sees the world. Where this happens in a normal manner, the parent still exists for the child as an autonomous person; but now the parent (teacher, mentor, spouse, or Christ) is also internalized.

b. Nurturing and sustaining. The most basic notion of the Christian life requires this step of internalization. First of all it is the deepest and most powerful way that one person can affect another. It is also the way to personal knowledge, a knowledge from within that results from being changed by another. The Christian life is by its nature experienced and known only to those whose lives are being shaped continually by Christ from within. This is basically a "fostering" process, in the sense of both nurturing and sustaining. Change occurs only in growth, and growth occurs only with nurture. In the Christian life one grows from the "old" to the "new" as one is fed from without and within by Christ.

Equally important is how we are sustained by this inside/outside Christ. Without sustenance all change and all life would vanish instantaneously. Yet only those who come near to perishing, who know the extreme fragility of life, seem to have the experience of being sustained in life. Christian life requires this awareness through its intimate involvement with suffering and death, where the Person of Christ is seen to sustain the slender thread by which both our earthly and our eternal lives are suspended; and this by virtue only of his deep and mysterious concern for us.

All life is then nurtured and sustained by Christ; but a Christian life is one that is lived in radical awareness of this and is being continually shaped by this awareness. Of all ways we have of discovering the meaning of Christian life, none may be so powerful. It is the task of pastoral care to "foster" Christian life through nurture

and sustenance, but in such a way that focuses on Christ and not the minister, and allows Christ to do the ministering. Kierkegaard has described the task of the pastoral ministry as the art of putting people "in the way of the Truth," and getting out of the way yourself. In order for this to happen, we must allow a personal relationship with Christ to develop, a relationship so deep that it internalizes, and in internalizing, shapes one's very substance to his own image. At that point the clearest meaning of the Christian life is perceived, because one already is living it.

5. Conclusion. We have then not so much a "definition" of the Christian life as a way of living it and a related method for clarification. This method moves the inquirer from the most abstract level (descriptive definition) to the most empirical level (fostering) as it also moves him or her from objective detachment to involvement in the Christian life itself. By way of analogy we may picture the mode of descriptive definition as providing a window to the Christian life; the mode of discernment as leading one to the threshold of Christian life; and the fostering mode as enabling one to experience the Christian life from within—by living it. Each of these modes implies and requires the others, whether simply to clarify the meaning of the "Christian life" or to live it.

Bibliography. D. Capps and W. Capps, *The Religious Personality* (1970). F. Cardman, *The Shape of Christian Life* (1980). D. Duncombe, *The Shape of the Christian Life* (1969). H. Hurnard, *Hinds' Feet in High Places* (1977). St. Ignatius, *The Spiritual Exercises* (1964[1535]). St. John of the Cross, *Dark Night of the Soul* (1959[1584]). S. Kierkegaard, *Concluding Unscientific Postscript* (1941); *Fear and Trembling* (1938); *For Self-Examination* (1940); *The Sickness Unto Death* (1941). Br. Lawrence, *The Practice of the Presence of God* (1963[1666]). W. Pannenberg, *Christian Spirituality* (1983). P. Pruyser, *The Minister as Diagnostician* (1976). J. Sanford, *Evil: The Shadow Side of Reality* (1981). F. Vanderwall, *Spiritual Direction: An Invitation to an Abundant Life* (1981).

D. C. DUNCOMBE

FAITH/BELIEF; HOPE AND DESPAIR; LOVE; SPIRITUALITY; SANCTIFICATION; VOCATION. *See also* COMMITMENT; GRACE; GRATITUDE; HAPPINESS; LIFESTYLE ISSUES IN PASTORAL CARE; MORAL BEHAVIOR AND RELIGION; SOCIAL CONSCIOUSNESS AND RESPONSIBILITY. *Compare* APOSTASY; JEWISH LIFE; RELIGIOUS LIFE; SEVEN DEADLY SINS.

CHRISTIAN-NONCHRISTIAN MARRIAGE. *See* CROSS CULTURAL MARRIAGE AND FAMILY.

CHRISTIAN PSYCHOLOGIST. A person who is both a psychologist and a Christian. Although the term seems self-explanatory, the variety of types of Christian psychologist, as well as the emphases they give to either Christianity, psychology, or an integration of the two, makes the term more complex.

1. Emphasis on Psychology. For some Christian psychologists, their faith has little effect on their practice of psychology, which thus does not differ from that of non-Christians. Academic psychologists of this type do research on the same topics as secular psychologists, and their theoretical explanations are no different. They see the spiritual aspects of people as irrelevant to psychology.

Clinical-counseling psychologists of this type use the same counseling techniques as do secular psychologists. As psychologists, they make little effort to deal with sin or spiritual problems, but treat people as secular therapists would. One major difference from some secular psychologists is that this type will not attack general Christian beliefs in their counselees, although they may challenge what they perceive as neurotic forms of Christianity. These Christian psychologists are not widely known because they do not advertise themselves as Christians.

2. Emphasis on Christianity. Other Christian psychologists place the greater emphasis on Christianity. Their psychological training, if any, has little effect on their practice of psychology. Academic psychologists of this type call for a complete restructuring of psychology, beginning with a new set of assumptions. Although several psychologists have called for such a rebuilding of psychology, none has succeeded in building radically new Christian systems of psychology.

Applied psychologists of this type tend to see all psychological problems in terms of spiritual problems. They usually reject psychological treatments for such problems and use direct confrontation of sin, Bible reading, and prayer as therapy. In terms of treatment, they differ little from a common-sense, lay-Christian approach. Adams's "nouthetic counseling" and Solomon's "spirituotherapy" are examples of this. Christian psychologists of this type are widely known through their books, seminars, and lectures.

3. Integration of Both. Assuming that all truth is God's truth, still other Christian psychologists attempt a balanced integration of Christianity and psychology, rather than making one discipline dominant. During the 1970s the movement to integrate psychology and Christianity flourished. Some theoretical Christian psychologists show how psychological concepts and practices parallel theological concepts and practices (Carter and Narramore, ch. 3). Others claim that psychology and theology are working at different levels (Myers). Still others attempt to reinterpret psychology from a Christian perspective (Koteskey).

Applied psychologists of this type use both psychological and Christian practices (Collins). They have some Christian conception of personality and may use client-centered therapy along with prayer, behavior modification along with repentance, or some variation of psychoanalytic therapy along with confession and forgiveness. A pastor referring a parishioner to a Christian psychologist should know the psychologist's theological and psychological frame of reference. His or her theological position should be compatible with the counselee's, and the therapy should be appropriate for the problem.

Christian psychologists of this type have formed associations since the mid-twentieth century. Roman Catholics formed the American Catholic Psychological Association, which became Psychologists Interested in Religious Issues, and is now a division of the American Psychological Association. Protestants formed the Christian Association for Psychological Studies. Both of these organizations are open to Christians of all denominations. Many research psychologists interested in Christianity are members of the Society for the Scientific Study of Religion.

Two journals which publish articles by Christian psychologists are the *Journal of Psychology and Theology*, begun in 1972, and the *Journal of Psychology and Christianity*, begun in 1982.

Bibliography. J. Adams, *Competent to Counsel* (1970). J. Carter and B. Narramore, *The Integration of Psychology and Theology* (1979). G. Collins, *Psychology and Theology* (1981). R. Koteskey, *Psychology from a Christian Perspective* (1980). D. Myers, *The Human Puzzle* (1978). C. Solomon, *Handbook of Happiness* (1971).

R. L. KOTESKEY

CHRISTIAN PSYCHOTHERAPIST. *Compare* CLINICAL PSYCHOLOGIST; EVANGELICAL PASTORAL CARE; PASTORAL COUNSELOR; PASTORAL PSYCHOTHERAPY; PSYCHOLOGIST; PSYCHOLOGY IN AMERICAN RELIGION; VALUES IN COUNSELING AND PSYCHOTHERAPY.

CHRISTIAN PSYCHOLOGY. *See* INTEGRATION OF PSYCHOLOGY AND THEOLOGY; PASTORAL THEOLOGY, PROTESTANT.

CHRISTIAN PSYCHOTHERAPIST. Used to describe a wide variety of individuals engaged in counseling, the term suffers from a great deal of ambiguity since both "Christian" and "psychotherapist" have such a broad range of meanings. Although "psychotherapist" is sometimes loosely used to refer to individuals engaged in the entire range of interpersonal interventions from short-term advice-giving through classical psychoanalysis, it is more appropriately limited to those professionals who thoughtfully apply psychological principles and techniques in order to resolve emotional problems or disorders. Psychotherapists typically work from a relatively well-defined theoretical foundation which includes conceptualizations regarding human nature, personality development, motivation, psychopathology, and the processes of change or personality growth.

As applied to psychotherapists, "Christian" has been used to refer to (1) any therapist who is a Christian, (2) any therapist who conceptualizes the counseling process in terms of Christian concepts and values, or (3) a therapist who actively incorporates biblical principles and concepts into the therapeutic process. In the first usage, the therapy is not necessarily different from "non-Christian" therapy except for the person of the therapist. Christian therapists operating from this perspective, while they may see their therapy as an expression of their Christian commitment, do not attempt to offer uniquely Christian counseling. Their Christian faith is reflected largely in their caring and in their sensitivity to counselees' spiritual interests and needs.

The second group of therapists conceptualizes therapeutic process in terms of a Christian understanding even though they may not verbalize these conceptualizations in distinctly biblical language. They consider the relationship between the scriptural teachings on sin and psychological views of psychopathology, for example, and they let their understanding enlighten and shape their therapeutic activities. They may also attempt to understand their patients' struggles as a conflict within individuals who are both bearers of the image of God and suffering from the results of sin. Because their understanding of the counselees' problems is informed and guided by scriptures, these Christian psychotherapists may diverge from secular theorists on issues such as personal responsibility and the handling of emotions such as guilt and anger. They do not, however, bring scriptural passages directly into the counseling process.

Therapists in these first two categories may distinguish between spiritual and emotional problems and choose not to bring biblical principles and values directly into therapy because they see spiritual and emotional growth as somewhat distinct processes or because they believe this would interfere with the patient's autonomy and freedom of choice.

The third group of therapists goes beyond conceptualizing the therapeutic process in Christian terms to actively verbalizing the patients' struggles in Christian (or biblical) terms. These therapists may draw on specific biblical passages and principles in helping patients come to grips with the origin, nature, and resolution of their adjustment problems. They may bring relevant scriptures to bear on problems such as guilt and forgiveness, marriage and divorce, self-esteem or interpersonal conflicts. This group of therapists includes a diverse collection of individuals ranging from very directive and didactic therapists to those who utilize an insight-oriented depth therapy. Their commonality is found not in their therapeutic orientation or style but in their incorporation of biblical principles and concepts in their therapeutic endeavors. Therapists in this third category also tend to view patients wholistically and do not believe a clear cut separation of spiritual and emotional issues is either possible or desirable.

Bibliography. J. O. Jeske, "Varieties of Approaches to Psychotherapy: Options for the Christian Therapist" in *J. of Psychology and Theology* (1984) 12:260–69.

S. B. NARRAMORE

CHRISTIAN PSYCHOLOGIST. *Compare* EVANGELICAL PASTORAL CARE; PASTORAL COUNSELOR; PSYCHOLOGY IN AMERICAN RELIGION; PSYCHOTHERAPIST; SPIRITUAL DIRECTOR; SPIRITUAL MASTERS AND GUIDES; VALUES IN COUNSELING AND PSYCHOTHERAPY.

CHRISTIAN SCIENCE. A religious organization and teaching, best known for its emphasis on spiritual healing.

Highly controversial, Christian Science has been subject to widely varying interpretations, but two objective facts are central to its history. The Church of Christ, Scientist, was founded in 1879 with the avowed purpose of reinstating "primitive Christianity and its lost element of healing." Its founder, Mary Baker Eddy (1821–1910), a New England woman of Calvinist background, was the author of the denominational textbook *Science and Health with Key to the Scriptures* which contains the definitive statement of Christian Science theology, metaphysics, and practice.

1. **Theology.** Few churches have a membership so thoroughly grounded in doctrine and theology. Emphasis in the denomination is on spiritual education. Small yearly classes instructed by a teacher of Christian Science are formed into continuing "associations." Although entirely a church of lay members, this educational struc-

ture as well as the role of the Christian Science practitioner helps to provide an effective form of pastoral relationship. In Eddy's own classes, the first three days were always devoted exclusively to a consideration of the nature of God. This has set the pattern for all subsequent Christian Science classes; it is also the starting point for all Christian Science treatment (i.e., prayer). The first sentence on page one of *Science and Health* reads: "The prayer that reforms the sinner and heals the sick is an absolute faith that all things are possible to God,—a spiritual understanding of Him, an unselfed love."

Elsewhere Eddy wrote, "As Christian Scientists you seek to define God to your own consciousness by feeling and applying the nature and practical possibilities of divine Love" (*Message for 1901.*) In common with other Christians she saw this "divine Love" as having been uniquely incarnated and exemplified in Jesus Christ, who is regarded by Christian Scientists as the Son of God though not as "very God of very God." The Supreme Being was to be understood both from the supreme example of Jesus and from the practical experience of discovering one's own authentic being as a loved child of the infinitely caring and shepherding power which he addressed so intimately as Father.

Christian Scientists frequently couple that term with the concept of divine motherhood in the compound metaphor of Father-Mother. They find biblical authority for further defining deity as all-embracing Life, Truth, Spirit, Mind, Soul, Principle. These terms, capitalized to differentiate them from their ordinary mundane meanings, are regarded as enriching in concrete ways the recognition of God as the infinite Person from whom all health or spiritual wholeness is derived. Ideal "manhood" (i.e., personhood) is held to have been revealed to the world through the life of Jesus, from his virgin birth to his resurrection and final "ascension" above all material limitation. But it is also to be experienced progressively by his followers as, in true spiritual fellowship, they study to "let this mind be in you which was also in Christ Jesus" (Phil. 2:5 KJV).

2. **Metaphysics.** A 1948 academic study (Steiger) concluded that Eddy had done something new by evolving a metaphysic that *healed.* She herself claimed that physical healing was the "least part" of Christian Science, subordinate to the whole process of spiritual regeneration. But she also saw it as an essential element of the kerygma "scientifically" understood. As *Science and Health* puts it: "'The Word was made flesh.' Divine Truth must be known by its effects on the body as well as on the mind, before the Science of Being can be demonstrated. Hence its embodiment in the incarnate Jesus,—that life-link forming the connection through which the real reaches the unreal, Soul rebukes sense, and Truth destroys error."

Eddy was of course not the first to think of Christianity as science and of God as principle. Not only the early church fathers, but also such later giants as Aquinas and Calvin used these terms. But that was before the immense sophistication of modern scientific method, rooted in controlled experiment and empirical verification, changed their meaning. Eddy realized that without the pragmatic component no religious system could claim to be scientific. Hence her emphasis on spiritual healing as the crucial evidence of the substantiality of Spirit in a world increasingly looking for causality in matter.

Christian Scientists insist that their view of reality as entirely spiritual does not make meaningless the whole of human life or discount it as mere illusion. While matter is regarded as a false, limited mode of thinking from which the manifold ills and errors of the flesh proceed, human history is held to be a record of spiritual evolution when rightly viewed — a history of progressive breakthroughs of spiritual reality into material appearances, restructuring thought, reshaping experience, revealing new possibilities of being. The magnitude of the task and the urgent needs of the human condition, they believe, demand great humility of the would-be healer. Eddy herself had a good deal to say about the need for patience, compassion, and realism in human affairs.

3. **Practice.** To the Christian Scientist there is no such thing as a miracle — if this word is taken to mean an infraction of law. Love, being Principle, must operate as law. "The miracle of grace is no miracle to Love," Eddy wrote (*Science and Health*), and an official publication of the church (*Century of Healing*) explains: "Christianity does not usually put repentance and rebirth into the category of miracle. In the same way, physical changes following a changed relationship to God do not seem mysterious to the Christian Scientist for whom matter is an expression of thought."

This is where Christian Science metaphysics makes a notable difference. The traditional Christian who accepts that God creates both germs to cause disease and drugs to cure it finds no inconsistency in combining prayer for healing with reliance on medicine. The logic of Christian Science excludes such a position and makes it necessary for the Christian Scientist to decide which one he or she will rely upon in a given situation — a choice, however, that is left to individual decision.

Though many people turn to Christian Science in the first place for healing of mind, body, or human situation, those who accept it as a permanent way of life are apt to regard such healing as a confirmatory sign rather than an end in itself. This at least is the ideal. From its earliest days there have been adherents who have wanted to turn it into a faith healing cult, a smart success philosophy, or a revival of second-century gnosticism. So far none have succeeded. Eventually they all run up against the tenacious Christianity of the movement's founder who, through her writings, still shapes Christian Science thinking. Her concern extended far beyond the healing of physical ailments, as illustrated by her founding of *The Christian Science Monitor* in 1908 to help bring Christian values to bear in a healing way on the larger ills of the world.

The Christian Science movement today is composed of The Mother Church—The First Church of Christ, Scientist, in Boston — and some 3,400 branch churches, societies, and college organizations in 50-plus countries. Like many other denominations it has had some decline in numbers during the past two decades but has made some gains in third-world countries. A number of families have now followed Christian Science as a way of life for four or five generations. Its indirect influence on the current Christian healing movement in the traditional churches has undoubtedly been considerable, and it shares with them what Eddy gave as the purpose of all genuine spiritual healing: "to attest the reality of the higher mission of the Christ-power to take away the sins of the world" (*Science and Healing*).

Bibliography. M. B. Eddy, *Science and Health with Key to the Scriptures* (1934); *Message to The Mother Church for 1901* (1898). S. Gottschalk, *Emergence of Christian Science in American Religious Life* (1973). R. Peel, *Mary Baker Eddy: Years of Discovery* (1966); *Years of Trial* (1971); *Years of Authority* (1977). H. W. Steiger, *Christian Science and Philosophy* (1948).

R. PEEL

HISTORY OF PROTESTANT PASTORAL CARE (United States); MIND-CURE MOVEMENT. *Compare* SECTARIAN PASTORAL CARE. *Biography:* EDDY.

CHRISTIAN SCIENCE PRACTITIONER.

A person engaged in the public practice of Christian Science healing.

1. **Qualifications.** In one sense every Christian Scientist is expected to be a practitioner of his or her religion. But for practical purposes the term is reserved for those who give full time to the healing ministry and whose names have been accepted for listing in the directory of practitioners in the monthly *Christian Science Journal.* Apart from the short course of intensive instruction which most serious students of Christian Science take with an authorized teacher, the practitioner's training is a lifelong discipline of prayer, study, application, and spiritual growth. At the time of listing in the *Journal*, evidence of Christian character and successful healing work must be submitted.

2. **Status.** A practitioner is not as such an officer of the church. The practitioner's ministrations are for anyone who seeks them; they are not restricted to a single congregation or to Christian Scientists only. The healing sought is not merely of physical difficulties but of grief, stress, obsessions, addictions, marital crises, business problems, depressive states — the whole range of contemporary ills. A person seeking help is referred to as a patient rather than a client, and the relations between practitioner and patient are regarded as strictly confidential. The practitioner is self-supported in the same way as a general practitioner of medicine, through the patients' payments.

3. **Role.** As a religious vocation, the practitioner's role is closer to that of the pastoral counselor than of the professional therapist. It involves no physical diagnosis or even psychological analysis in the usual sense. It starts with prayer and ends with prayer. Counseling is not directed toward specific actions or decisions but toward turning the patient more wholeheartedly to "divine Love" for the sought-after answer to a problem. Prayer may uncover obstructive or destructive tendencies in the patient's thinking, but the practitioner's work is to see that these are no part of the patient's God-given spiritual identity. A key passage in Eddy's *Science and Health* reads: "Jesus beheld in Science the perfect man, who appeared to him where sinning mortal man appears to mortals. In this perfect man the Saviour saw God's own likeness, and this correct view of man healed the sick."

Bibliography. M. B. Eddy, *Science and Health with Key to the Scriptures* (1934). R. Peel, "The Christian Science Practitioner," *J. of Pastoral Counseling,* 4 (1969), 39–42; "Christian Science and Value Clarification," *Voices: J. of the American Academy of Psychotherapists,* 13 (1977), 62–66.

R. PEEL

SPIRITUAL MASTERS AND GUIDES. *Compare* PASTOR.

CHRISTIAN THERAPY UNIT. Christian programs in psychiatric hospitals have been around since the 1960s but have become increasingly popular in urban areas where Christian subcultures are strong. Christians who seek professional counseling want to know that their Christian values are respected. In the past, Sigmund Freud and Albert Ellis have spoken out against combining religion and therapy, stating that religion is neurotic. Times have changed and a growing number of Christians in the field of psychology are writing books, speaking on the radio, and advancing concepts about inner healing, rebuilding the family, and Christian therapy in psychiatric hospitals.

Christian hospital programs are variously called Christian Psychiatric Programs, Christian Behavioral Medicine Programs, and Christian Therapy Programs. Most of the programs are similar in their design, purpose, and delivery of services. They offer a variety of activity therapies, psychotherapies, chemotherapies, and theological input. In all such programs, three sources of information are used together: psychology, theology, and medicine. For the psychological and theological input, the programs usually offer various forms of traditional therapy groups along with integration of pertinent scriptures on basic principles of mental health. There may be special emphasis on topics such as forgiveness, guilt, anger, grief, substance abuse, sinning, and being sinned against. For the medical input, patients are evaluated to rule out non-psychological causes for their breakdowns such as diseases and tumors. Psychiatrists also evaluate whether medicine might be of benefit to the patient. In addition to a psychiatrist, a private therapist spends the time to help the patient pull together all that is being learned while in the hospital and apply it to life.

During the course of the hospitalization, the patient goes through three basic phases. First, there is an adjustment to accepting the crisis and to the new surroundings, and an orientation to the hospital rules and opportunities. Usually after one to three days the patient begins to move into the working phase, participating in various activities and talking about problems. This opens the door for expression of suppressed feelings and dealing with problems in a more effective and healthy way, gaining a new perspective on what was previously overwhelming and avoided. The final phase involves new plans to cope, solidify gains, and to prepare to leave the hospital and return home. This may involve the family and pastor in supportive planning sessions.

Pastors, employers, and family members are often first to notice a person may be in the process of emotional collapse. Being aware of sources of Christian professional help and when to refer can be invaluable.

B. L. LUSK
E. EVENHUIS

MENTAL HOSPITAL/MENTAL HOSPITALIZATION. *Compare* CHRISTIAN PSYCHOTHERAPIST; GROUP COUNSELING AND PSYCHOTHERAPY; HAVURAH; MILIEU THERAPY; THERAPEUTIC COMMUNITY.

CHRISTMAS. *See* HOLIDAY DEPRESSION; LITURGICAL CALENDAR.

CHRISTOLOGY AND PASTORAL CARE. Christology is reflection upon the one whom the Christian community confesses as Lord and Savior. In Christ we know God as a human person, and pastoral care is a ministry to persons. Thus pastoral care, like all of Christian ministry, is engaged at the point of "linkage" between Christ and particular human persons.

The question of the linkage between Christ and particular persons is treated in both the classical and the modern Christologies. But the linkage may be approached from either of the two *sides,* so to speak: beginning with Christ or beginning with particular persons. And in this regard there is a marked difference of tendency between the modern and the classical Christologies.

On the one hand, the particularly *modern* question of relevance urges one to approach the linkage from the side of human experience, asking, "How does the figure of Jesus relate to me, or to human experience as I know it?" One begins with human subjectivity, which thus becomes the interpretive touchstone. Accordingly, Christ is understood as exemplifying, deepening, and correcting an understanding of personhood which has already been given, to a significant extent, within common human experience. Indeed there is a distinct tendency in this approach to regard the significance of Christ as residing primarily in this very process: the process whereby human self-understanding, often assisted by appropriate pastoral care, is deepened and corrected in the light of Christ.

The modern approach may be said to begin with experience, move to Christ, and then return to (an altered) experience. In equally schematic terms, *classical* Christology tends to proceed in the opposite sense: beginning with Christ, seeing human destiny as included in the person and work of Christ, and then returning to the reality of Christ with renewed appreciation. If the modern approach so insists upon beginning with experience, it may be because of a distinctively modern concern that apart from experience there might *be* no linkage, no effective connection, between Christ and ourselves. At the heart of classical Christology, in contrast, is the conviction that, quite apart from the vagaries of our experience, *a linkage is already given.* Indeed, this is so on two counts: first, because in Christ God took on human nature, in which we all participate; and second, because in Christ God has willed the redemption of all of humankind, ourselves included, and indeed the redemption of all of creation. For the classical tradition this givenness is not merely speculative or incidental. It is the foundation for our hope and deeply related to the very meaning of grace.

From the perspective of the modern approach, the crucial task for pastoral care becomes one of helping the individual make the connection between Christ and his or her own experience; and the redemptive work of Christ consists in large part, perhaps exclusively, in the achievement of that new self-understanding. For the classical approach, the emphasis falls instead upon making available to the individual, through word and sacrament, the reality of that which has already been accomplished (whatever the eschatological reservations) in the life, death, and resurrection of Jesus Christ.

As we seek to trace these issues more fully, we shall begin with what is perhaps more familiar, the modern approach. Then, having seen something of the strengths and limitations of the modern procedure, we shall be in a better position to understand and appreciate what is for many the less familiar, classical alternative.

1. **The Modern Period.** Friedrich Schleiermacher may be regarded as the fountainhead of the distinctively modern approach to Christology. His reworking of theology was inspired by a clear awareness that it was necessary — and possible — for the Christian faith to engage modern science on its own terms. Was science grounded in experience? Very well, theology could be grounded there, too — provided only that experience be understood with sufficient depth. For faith is not mere superstition, it is rooted in a sense of our "absolute dependence" upon the divine reality. Jesus of Nazareth, in this perspective, is the one in whom the religious awareness was most fully realized, least clouded by denial and sin. To show this, Schleiermacher supplemented his more directly theological works with a *Life of Jesus* which sought to fulfill a twofold purpose: to meet the standards of modern historical criticism while simultaneously displaying the peculiar power of Jesus' personality.

To find in the personality of Jesus the key to Christian faith, and the contemporary relevance thereof, was the common goal of the many subsequent "lives of Jesus." These efforts, quite various as they were, succeeded in showing that science and history were not inimical to religious belief, and they pointed beyond the Enlightenment notion that faith could be reduced to a few spare ethical concepts. They found in the historical person of Jesus something which transcended abstract ideas, establishing the necessary linkage between his time and our own; and for that something a fitting term is "personality."

In 1906, however, Albert Schweitzer's study of *The Quest for the Historical Jesus* called this entire enterprise into question. Schweitzer argued that the biographers had, on scant historical grounds, projected their own particular preconceptions upon the figure of Jesus. Specifically, he noted that all resisted the cardinal characteristic which clearly *was* true of the historical Jesus, namely, his fervent belief in an immanent end of history. The suspicion began to spread (abetted by the writings of Feuerbach) that the lives of Jesus were indeed a projection, a misguided effort to dilute and domesticate the disturbing strangeness of the figure of Jesus.

Thus there appeared in the twentieth century a challenge to nineteenth-century liberalism in the form of the dialectical theologies of Barth, Bultmann, Tillich, and others. These new Christologies sought not to deny the eschatological strangeness, but to make of it the very basis of Christian proclamation. They saw in the crisis which the gospel precipitates the very meaning of Christ for our lives. Undoubtedly, the biographers too had

understood Christ as challenging us, as summoning us to decision, but for them the challenge was generally one of living up to certain ideals which we already more or less endorse. Now, in the theologies of crisis, Christ was understood as challenging all of our all-too-human plans and ideals, calling us to a life of radical openness and faith.

But the new movement itself contained a fundamental ambiguity. At issue was the modern insistence, which we have already noted, upon the importance of experience. For one side of the movement, Christ was understood as the paradigm of *the experiences* of crucifixion and resurrection — experiences which were taken as common to all of human life, and as providing the connection between Christ and one's own life situation. In this direction lay religious existentialism, as exemplified by Tillich. For the other side of the movement, however, Christ was increasingly understood as the one who in his radical otherness stands apart from *all* of our experience — including the deepest religious experience, and including the predictable processes of difficulty and growth — and who, though judging our experience, redeems and fulfills it as well. This was the perspective which led Barth to disavow religious existentialism as simply a further, more dramatic extension of religious liberalism, and to undertake a distinctively Christocentric retrieval of the classical tradition.

2. **Assessment of the Modern Approach.** There can be little question that the pastoral care movement has invested heavily in a combination of theological liberalism and existentialism. With occasional exceptions, the movement has been characterized by a quest for experiential relevance and a high regard for the findings of modern science. It has been chary of any doctrine which seemed badly grounded in experience. Accordingly, Christology tended to become, in a manner not unlike that of the earlier "lives of Jesus," a search for those teachings and experiences in Jesus' life and ministry which found resonance in the life experience of the contemporary individual. The result was a Christology which was more positively "incarnational," both in the sense that it portrayed Jesus as a truly human person who had known the extremes of struggle, joy, and suffering; and in the sense that it brought religious belief into contact with aspects of the individual's experience that had hitherto seemed to be unreligious, and possibly unacceptable (e.g. Wise, 1966). It has been, in this regard, a healing and wholistic Christology.

Nevertheless, there are problems which arise when this becomes the predominant or even the exclusive way of dealing with the reality of Christ. For one thing, there is the suspicion, voiced by Schweitzer's earlier critique, that we tend to make our own preoccupations the exclusive lens through which we filter our understanding of Christ. In the past Jesus has been portrayed as everything from the great Crusader to the world's greatest salesman; in our own therapeutically oriented culture, it is all too predictable that he would be presented as history's greatest therapist. A second, related issue is that posed by the church's ongoing struggle with the tension between relevance and identity (see Moltmann, 1974, p. 7.) By coming down so emphatically on the side of relevance to the culture at large, the pastoral care movement runs the risk, as some have noted, of losing sight of that which makes it specifically Christian. If this is so, then surely the issue must be engaged at the point of Christology.

Finally, as we have seen, the modern approach does tend to rearrange the very shape of christological thinking (cf. McIntyre, 1966). In the classical tradition there is a sequence which, within that context, would appear quite obvious. First there are certain things which Christ has accomplished—paying for our sins, defeating the devil, or whatever—and then, subsequently and as a result, there is the believer's experiencing of these benefits in his or her particular life. Nothing could seem more logical. But the modern mind, with its prizing of experience, regards as magical or mythological the notion of receiving benefits that have already been accomplished, independently of our experience. Thus it has fashioned an alternative approach that begins with experience, perhaps as question, then proceeds to Christ, perhaps as answer, and finally returns to the individual's experience, which may now be transformed in light of the individual's recognition of the significance of Christ. The procedure is well adapted to the modern situation; but it does tend to define the saving effect of Christ as being the effect of a certain experience, or the result of the recognition of a certain experience; and as thus dependent upon it.

Without minimizing the very real difficulties of the classical approach, it is possible to appreciate within it what one might call a certain liberating confidence. While life undoubtedly remains a struggle, there is the assurance that everything does not depend on us. Christ has won the victory, paid the price; salvation has been secured. If these things are not true, there is no gospel. If they are true, then the task of pastoral care is to free people from the effort to save themselves, and to make the saving reality accessible to them, by sacrament and word.

For its part, the modern pastoral care movement, instructed by existentialism, has insisted that human experience is always in process and always ambiguous, and that theology is always eschatological, always a theology of hope. All this is true enough. But does it follow from this that the good news of the gospel is *only* a hope based on an ambiguity? Are we simply whistling in the dark? Or is there in fact a reality that exists in gracious independence of us, to which we can witness and hold? Is there in fact a reality which, by virtue of its very independence, can ground our hope, calling our experience into question—and producing a positive transformation?

3. The Classical Period. Approaching the classical tradition in this light, one may find in it not a series of metaphysical exercises, but a remarkably rigorous effort to safeguard the reality of which we have just spoken: the reality of Christ's saving work. A key example is the Council of Nicaea's affirmation that Christ is *homoousios*, "of the same nature," with God. Athanasius makes clear the reasoning behind this term when he argues that if Christ were but a creature, he could not save us—"for how could a creature, by a creature, partake of God?" (*Against the Arians*, 2:67). Salvation, as Athanasius well understood, is not simply a relative improvement in human affairs; for any merely relative improvement might just as readily be reversed. Salvation is rather the

definitive overcoming of death, a virtual reenactment of Creation. Clearly, then, the one who has accomplished such a thing must be "of the same nature" with the Creator.

St. Augustine was especially clear as to why Christology needs to begin with a given reality. For he was keenly aware that our natural tendency is to love ourselves rather than God, and this misdirected love was not just a sentiment but a wrong orientation of our entire being. The first requirement, therefore, was that our very being, as fallen human nature, be freed and transformed by God's grace. Then, gradually and always imperfectly, we might become experientially aware of the wonder of what God has done. This theological conviction is apparent even, and perhaps especially, in Augustine's most intensely personal work, his *Confessions*, which is indeed an example of what St. Anselm later termed "faith seeking understanding." Augustine's reflection upon his own life takes the form of a prayer addressed to God; and specifically a prayer suffused with gratitude, a thanksgiving for what God has done. It is thus, in light of God's gracious activity, that Augustine seeks to understand his own experience, to understand himself.

Augustine's procedure in the *Confessions* is paradigmatic of the classical approach to pastoral care. The individual's particular story is placed within the context of the larger, encompassing story of God's redeeming activity. We come to see that all of Creation is good, that there is a created order which we had denied, and that the God to whom we are restored is, in God's own reality, a community of love: the Trinity. The means by which one is restored to one's rightful place within the created order and within the divine community is, appropriately enough, a concrete order and community, namely, the church. The classical tradition thus raises questions about the viability of a "private" pastoral counseling that proceeded without any concrete connection to the sacraments or to the community of faith (cf. Thornton, 1956).

Insistence upon a prior reality does not, however, preclude significant insight into human subjectivity. Here again Augustine is the classic case; for to an extraordinary degree his thought is the premodern turning point for the distinctively modern, Western understanding of human inwardness, and particularly for the modern association of personhood with freedom. In his thinking, the role of the will comes to the fore, and the shape of one's will and affections—in short, the direction of one's loving—became constitutive of the self. For Augustine the human is not a simple entity, but a coming together of memory, understanding and will; and in this interpenetrating threeness he thought to glimpse a vestige of the Trinity.

And here again motifs evident in Augustine reappear variously in other classical figures and movements. Because sin is rooted in self-absorption, a certain self-forgetfulness becomes the goal of Christian devotion. The aim of faith, in the classical understanding, is, in a very real sense, to allow Christ to become the true subject of one's life. But accomplishing such self-forgetfulness requires that the individual (or often the individual's spiritual advisor) have a shrewd comprehension of the workings of human subjectivity. It is no accident that distorted teachings regarding Christology should have as their correlate distorted practices regarding the human person (see Sabom, "Heresy and Pastoral Care"), and that some of the cardinal insights of modern personality theory should be indebted to the experiential sensitivity of such pastor-theologians as Saints Benedict and Ignatius of Loyola.

4. Theories of Christ's Work. Under the broad heading of Christology we have been discussing both the understanding of Christ's *person* and the general significance of his *work*. It may be useful now to attend briefly to a secondary matter, namely, the various theories that have sought to explain more specifically the nature of the work of Christ. Three of these theories fall within what we have called, quite generally, the classical tradition and thus provide a way of making some initial distinctions within that tradition. And all of the theories are useful as ways of indicating how differences in Christology go hand in hand with differences in pastoral care. But one must always remember what the theologians have too often forgotten, that the theories are always to remain subservient to the reality they wish to illumine.

One of the earliest formulations is St. Paul's affirmation that Christ "died for our sins" (I Cor. 15:3). In these few words there is already an implicit interpretation, one which depicts Christ as *suffering a punishment* and doing so in our place. In speaking the language of requirement and punishment, this approach draws upon a certain theological understanding of law at the same time as it proclaims the good news of the overcoming of the law. Pastoral care in this context will seek to help persons become aware of their sinfulness or will address those points where they are already so aware; but it will wish to do so in such a way that the "No" of God's judgment is always enclosed within the redemptive "Yes" of salvation.

Distinct from this first approach is that in which Christ is seen as *offering a work of penance*. Whereas punishment assumes the imagery of public law, penance suggests private devotional practice. More importantly, a punishment comes as a requirement, whereas a work of penance may be a gift freely offered, which thus results in a certain "merit." The medieval church in particular understood itself as entrusted with the grace or merit accruing from Christ's death, which the church then made available through the sacraments. This is one way, though not the only way, in which the administration of the sacraments may be understood as central to pastoral care.

In contrast to these relatively objective accounts, it is customary to distinguish the theory according to which Christ's work is one of *exercising a moral influence*. While this interpretation originated with Anselm, it has flowered in the modern period, which has been attracted by the theory's more subjective orientation. On this account, Christ shows forth the love of God. Beholding him, I myself become more loving; and that effect, that inward transformation, is in itself the reality of redemption. Pastoral care thus becomes primarily an effort to encourage and inspire, to model and persuade.

In the first two approaches, there is a fundamental level at which the pastor's actions will be efficacious regardless of his or her individual worth. In classical Roman Catholicism the sacraments are effective *ex opere operato*. On the alternative, i.e., moral influence theory, greater emphasis falls upon the pastor's calling to "be Christ" to others — here once again is the characteristic modern turn whereby personality and experience provide the link — and accordingly a greater stress may be placed upon the minister's moral character.

Finally, Gustaf Aulen in *Christus Victor* has pointed out the importance of those accounts which depict Christ as *winning the victory* over the powers of darkness and death. This theory — or better, this complex of images — has roots running deep in early Christian proclamation and worship. It reappears powerfully in the thought of Martin Luther, for whom it serves as an antidote to the tendency, apparent in both of the first two theories, to postulate an unchanging moral order within which one interprets — and all too often confines — the saving work of Christ. Implicit in such theologies is a two-step process according to which we must first be rendered acceptable before we can be accepted. One may wonder whether such contingent acceptance is indeed what is meant by forgiveness (see Hendry, 1959). In Luther salvation is rather the triumphant gesture, at once loving and all-powerful, whereby God strides across the great divide and embraces us, just as we are, in Christ. The imagery of spiritual triumph would seem to imply that pastoral care, whatever else it may be, must always retain a certain dimension of exorcism: which is to say that it must at one and the same time take seriously the powers of evil and refuse to bargain with them.

5. Contemporary Issues. An abiding issue in pastoral care has been the tension, mentioned earlier, between relevance and identity. In his influential *Basic Types of Pastoral Care and Counseling*, Howard Clinebell argues persuasively that there is a spiritual dimension to the many forms of counseling and care, and indeed to human life generally (p. 107). To help make this point, the author defines the "spiritual" quite broadly. It is that which concerns one's relation to time in the largest sense, i.e. to eternity (p. 115), and that which concerns one's capacity for a fundamental wholeness and growth. But such breadth of definition, while it serves well the cause of relevance, contributes little to the clarification of a specifically Christian identity. One hears a great deal about the spiritual, but remarkably little about Christ — or even about the Holy Spirit.

Daniel Day Williams's *The Minister and the Care of Souls*, while close to Clinebell's work in many respects, offers a more developed Christology. The book is especially valuable for its insistence that the work of Christ as portrayed in the New Testament be understood in personal (or better yet, interpersonal) terms (p. 87). In his own portrait of Christ, Williams places emphasis upon Christ's humanity and upon Christ as the one who reveals to us our own "essential humanity" (p. 17). The result is a Christology exhibiting many of the strengths and many of the limitations of the earlier liberal theology. Christ is depicted as fully human, meeting us at the point of our own need, and of the needs of other persons. But one is left with the impression that Christ's work of salvation is more or less identical with this act of revelation, and that Williams remains perhaps deliberately vague as to the character of Christ's divinity.

In contrast, Eduard Thurneysen's *A Theology of Pastoral Care*, which appeared in German in 1946, self-consciously seeks to ground pastoral care in a more classical Christology. Instructed by the theology of Karl Barth, Thurneysen understands pastoral counseling as "the conversation which is based on preaching and leads back to it" (p. 107). Whereas preaching is public, counseling is private; nevertheless it continues the task of preaching, which is to witness to the Word—the Word who is not simply a general concept or a common attribute of humanity, but the Word who is the person Jesus Christ.

Williams and Thurneysen are thus representative of the two distinct approaches to the task of effecting the necessary linkage between Christ and particular individuals. In Williams the linkage is made by an "essential humanity" which one already knows, to some degree, on the basis of common experience. The task of counseling, then, is to help us to recognize the ways in which our understanding is deepened, corrected, and transformed in the light of Christ. Thurneysen, approaching the issue from a classical viewpoint, and particularly from the Reformed tradition, would argue that such a process of recognition disguises a subtle form of law, in that it still stakes its hope on certain human capacities (cf. Thurneysen, p. 76). Thurneysen requires, or rather he believes that the gospel requires, that there occur in the course of the pastoral conversation a certain crucial "breach" (p. 131). This reflects his conviction that we must hear as proclamation, because we cannot believe on our own, that the truly important encounter between God and the human is not our encounter with God, but is the encounter that has already taken place in the life, death, and resurrection—and thus in the person—of Jesus Christ.

This line of argument is vigorous in affirming Christian identity. But many observers have been concerned that any introduction of a "breach" within the counseling process would necessarily entail a neglect of the counselee's concrete, subjective experience—or even a rejection thereof—and thus a loss of relevance. To some extent these objections may be the result of Thurneysen's particular style, which is indeed somewhat confrontational. That style, however, is not the only way in which the classical tradition may be appropriated, as is apparent from Thomas C. Oden's more nuanced treatment of the matter in *Kerygma and Counseling*. "Empathy," Oden writes, "is the process of placing oneself in the frame of reference of another . . . . Incarnation means that God assumes our frame of reference, entering into our human situation of finitude and estrangement, sharing our human condition even unto death" (p. 50). Another valuable appropriation of the classical tradition, somewhat more oriented to sacrament than to proclamation, is the relatively neglected work of Martin Thornton, e.g., his *Pastoral Theology: A Reorientation*.

6. **Conclusion.** The strength of the classical Christologies may be said to lie in a certain liberating objectivity, which is founded upon the conviction that salvation has indeed been accomplished in Christ; and that by baptism into the body of Christ, one participates in that salvation. This bold affirmation need not imply that those outside the church are not saved; but it does mean that the

troubled believer within the church is given something quite specific—something quite incarnational and sacramental—that she or he can hold on to. For this approach the whole welter of human emotions, the hopes and fears and conflicts which are so central to pastoral care, do continue to be important. But anxieties about the future are always secondary, in this perspective, to the reality of what has already been accomplished in Jesus Christ. This relativization of experience is not a disregard for pastoral care, but a different approach to it. It is an approach which can say at an appropriate moment that if you are on the bus (so to speak), you are indeed on the bus, regardless of how you happen to feel about it. And this surely is one legitimate form which the gospel of grace may take.

There is always the danger, however, that a healthy objectivity may devolve into an abusive objectivism; and that faith in what has been accomplished in Christ may become the excuse for triumphalism, complacency, and a fixation upon the past. The truth of the classical tradition must be rescued again and again from the embrace of a shallow traditionalism. And in this struggle, one must claim as an indispensable resource the modern insistence upon freedom, experience, and the openness of the future.

What is required, in briefest terms, is a sense of objectivity without objectivism, a sense of subjectivity without subjectivism, and a proper recognition of that which the faith may claim as accomplished as well as of that which remains open-ended. But how is this to be effected? In *The Trinity and the Kingdom* (pp. 3–4), Moltmann affirms that experience is indeed important—but that what matters in the end is not our own experience, but rather *God's* experience. Given that crucial turn, Moltmann can interpret life, death, and resurrection of Jesus as the decisive revelation and enactment of God's own personhood. There emerges an understanding of God as the passionate God who engages the suffering of the world to the point of death, and who takes that suffering into the very Godhead.

In such a vision all time is redeemed. Past and future are drawn together. It then becomes clear that for Christology and for pastoral care, for orthodoxy and for "orthopraxis," it is of crucial importance that one avoid the trap of pitting past against future: as if one had to choose between saying "salvation has been accomplished in Jesus Christ" and saying "the future is genuinely open." Rather the good news of the gospel is that precisely *because* of what has been accomplished in Christ, and precisely because it *has* been accomplished for certain—therefore the future which was closed is opened, and life has indeed become possible.

Bibliography. G. Aulen, *Christus Victor* (1931). R. W. Battenhouse, ed., *A Companion to the Study of St. Augustine* (1955). D. S. Browning, *Atonement and Psychotherapy* (1966). R. Bultmann, *Jesus and the Word* (1934). W. A. Clebsch and C. R. Jaekle, *Pastoral Care in Historical Perspective* (1964). H. Clinebell, *Basic Types of Pastoral Care and Counseling* rev. ed. (1984). F. W. Dillistone, *The Christian Understanding of Atonement* (1968). R. S. Franks, *The Work of Christ* (1962). A. Grillmeier, *Christ in Christian Tradition* 2d ed. (1975). G. S. Hendry, *The Gospel of the Incarnation* (1959). R. J. Hunter, "Moltmann's Theology of the Cross and the Dilemma of Contemporary Pastoral Care," in T. Runyon, ed., *Hope for the Church* (1979), pp. 75–92. G. E. Jackson, *Pastoral Care and Process Theology* (1981). K. E. Kirk, *The Vision of God* (1966). E. Käsemann, *Jesus Means Freedom* (1969). G. A. Lindbeck, *The Nature of Doctrine* (1984). W. Lowe, "Christ and Salvation," in P. C. Hodgson and R. H. King, *Christian Theology* rev. ed. (1985), pp. 222–48. J. McIntyre, *The Shape of Christology* (1966). J. T. McNeill, *A History of the Cure of Souls* (1951). J. Moltmann, *The Crucified God* (1974); *The Trinity and the Kingdom* (1981). H. R. Niebuhr, *Christ and Culture* (1951). T. C. Oden, *Kerygma and Counseling* (1966); *Pastoral Theology* (1983). J. Pelikan, *The Christian Tradition* (1971–   ). J. M. Robinson, *A New Quest of the Historical Jesus* (1961). W. S. Sabom, "Heresy and Pastoral Care," in *J. of Pastoral Care*, 36:2, 76–86. F. Schleiermacher, *The Life of Jesus* (1975). A. Schweitzer, *The Quest for the Historical Jesus* (1961). J. Sobrino, S. J., *Christology at the Crossroads* (1978). M. Thornton, *Pastoral Theology: A Reorientation* (1956); *The Rock and the River* (1965); *The Function of Theology* (1968). E. Thurneysen, *A Theology of Pastoral Care* (1962). D. D. Williams, *The Minister and the Care of Souls* (1961). C. A. Wise, *The Meaning of Pastoral Care* (1966).

W. J. LOWE

GRACE, REVELATION, *or* SALVATION, AND PASTORAL CARE. *See also* CHRISTOTHERAPY; CROSS AND RESURRECTION; INCARNATIONAL PASTORAL CARE. *Compare* GOD, DOCTRINE OF, AND PASTORAL CARE; TRINITY AND PERSONHOOD.

CHRISTOTHERAPY. The term refers to a form of psychotherapy based on the assumption that Christ is the healer of the wounded psyche and spirit of persons through the power of the meaning and value he incarnates. Although developed in its most systematic form by Bernard J. Tyrrell (1975; 1981), the notion has its roots in the theology of Bernard Lonergan and in the psychiatric theory of Thomas Hora. Tyrrell himself sees Christotherapy as a contemporary expression of the perennial stress in the Christian tradition on Christ as healer of the whole person. In this sense, Christotherapy is one of a growing number of attempts to relate the *content* of the Christian message to the modern expression of psychotherapy.

Bibliography. B. L. Lonergan, *Method in Theology* (1972). B. J. Tyrrell, *Christotherapy: Healing Through Enlightenment* (1975; 1981). H. Wolff, *Jesus the Therapist* (1987).

O. STRUNK, JR.

PSYCHOTHERAPY; PSYCHOTHERAPY AND THEOLOGY. *See also* CHRISTOLOGY AND PASTORAL CARE; COUNSELING, ROMAN CATHOLIC; PASTORAL THEOLOGY, ROMAN CATHOLIC.

CHRONIC ILLNESS. "Impairments or deviations from normal which have one or more of the following characteristics: are permanent, leave residual disability, are caused by non-reversible pathological alteration, may be expected to require a long period of supervision, observation or care" (L. Mayo, quoted in Strauss and Glaser, 1975).

Chronic illness represents a major proportion of total illnesses. Approximately one half of the population of the United States is affected by one or more chronic illnesses. The rate is higher in lower income and advancing age groups although many young people also are affected.

The increasing rate is related to improved control of infection and advances of medical technology, which save many who would otherwise be terminally ill.

Though hospital patients are treated for acute conditions, many patients in fact suffer from the acute phase of chronic diseases: arthritis, cancer, heart, kidney, respiratory diseases, and others. The chronically ill face recurring crises, frequently a downward trajectory leading to social isolation, disruption of family life, extensive expense, and death.

1. General Strategies for Care. Basic steps for treatment of the chronically ill include the following. (1) Recruitment and coordination of multidisciplinary persons and agencies capable of providing help. (2) Prevention of crises or prompt care when they occur. (3) Minimalization of debilitation. (4) Prevention of withdrawal and isolation. (5) Patient and family acceptance of disease. (6) Dealing with economics of treatment and loss of income.

The achievement of an optimum quality of life for patient and family is the major strategy and goal of all care. Normalization includes attention to family needs, physical requirements, optimal rehabilitation, attention to accessibility of buildings and streets, provision for mobility and assistance in accepting a new state of normality. Full normalization includes affirmation of personal worth and life meaning with the chronic illness.

2. Pastoral Care. Pastoral care should seek to help the chronically ill deal with the problems of theodicy, personal worth, and spiritual meaning, as well as to support the psychosocial aspects of adjustment. Adjustment to chronicity requires working through the conflict phases of grief over loss of a more ideal self, including shock, denial, anger, depression, defensive compensation, acceptance, and adjustment.

In view of the unlikelihood of cure, pastoral care for the chronically ill is usually directed toward support, comfort, care, and relief. The function of pastoral care is to assist the chronically ill to grow toward a wholeness that transcends the limitation of their illness. Although chronicity would appear to limit the goal of healing, normalization that leads to functional wholeness entails a realistic view of healing as contrasted to a more idealized view.

Sustaining includes the provision of comfort, support, and standing by when it appears that little can actually be changed in the person's illness or impairment. However, it is precisely in relation to chronicity that hope and the exercise of autonomy, though limited, are essential. When pastoral care encourages the person to optimize remaining personal capacities, it can help to avoid encouraging inordinate dependency.

Guiding in pastoral care calls for patient education of resources of the spirit from within more than the externals of persuasion, interpretation, direction, and the like. Guiding the person with chronic impairment means shared exploration of the meaning of the experience and the resources that might enable growth toward optimal function.

Normalization in pastoral perspective recognizes persons as spiritual beings whose lives are given value through realization and actualization of God's enabling grace. Pastoral care seeks to enable the chronically ill to accept the limits of all human experience, including "the suffering of this present time," and to respond to the resources of faith and hope that enable them to move toward the "glory that is to be revealed" (Romans 8).

Bibliography. V. Frankl, *The Doctor and the Soul* (1955); also *Man's Search for Meaning* (1963). S. Hiltner, *Preface to Pastoral Theology* (1958). S. Hunt-Meeks, "Pastoral Care and the Psychomaintenance of Chronic Illness," *Pastoral Psychology,* 29 (1981), 231–43. H. Kushner, *When Bad Things Happen to Good People* (1981). W. Oates, ed., *Pastoral Care in Crucial Human Situations* (1969). A. Strauss and B. Glaser, *Chronic Illness and the Quality of Life* (1975).

M. EBERSOLE

SICK, PASTORAL CARE OF. *See also* EVIL; HEALTH AND ILLNESS; PAIN; PATIENCE/PATIENTHOOD; SUFFERING. *Compare* HANDICAP AND DISABILITY; LOSS OF FUNCTION.

CHRYSOSTOM, ST. JOHN (349–407). Patriarch of Constantinople, prolific writer, outstanding preacher, advocate of prophetic as well as priestly ministry, exemplar of ascetic, caring, and holy living.

In Chrysostom's time the existential human dilemma was seen as the struggle with sinfulness for which the traditional remedies of rebuke, formal penance and counsel, preaching, and the sacraments no longer provided sufficient care of the soul. Chrysostom, among others, favored adding personalized soul care by humble and conscientious pastors, something he performed with great diligence in his own ministry, as well as the abolition of private confession.

Yet Chrysostom combines individual soul care with care about the material and social dimensions of life such as politics, class differences between the excesses of the rich and the needs of the poor, and moral and administrative reform for the church and its clergy. This combination features a strong preference for the guiding function of pastoral care.

N. F. HAHN

CLASSIC LITERATURE IN CARE AND COUNSELING (Orthodoxy); EARLY CHURCH, PASTORAL CARE AND COUNSELING IN; PASTORAL CARE (History, Traditions, and Definitions).

CHURCH. *See* COMMUNITY, FELLOWSHIP AND CARE; CONGREGATION; ECCLESIOLOGY AND PASTORAL CARE.

CHURCH OF GOD. *See* SECTARIAN PASTORAL CARE.

CHURCH WORKERS. *See* VOLUNTEERS, PASTORAL CARE OF.

CHURCH YEAR. *See* LITURGICAL CALENDAR; RITUAL AND PASTORAL CARE.

CHURCH-SECT DIFFERENCES IN PASTORAL CARE. The church-sect distinction refers to a typology developed by Ernst Troeltsch (1931) as a means of facilitating the analysis of the social forms of religion. The typology presents contrasting ideal types of religious communities (never found in pure form) representing two fundamentally different orientations to the existence of the church in the world. In the "church type," by which Troeltsch had in mind the established state churches of Europe, the Christian community functions and views itself in continuity with the values and institutions of the larger social order; one is born into the church and (ideally) everyone belongs to it. The sect-type, by contrast, emphasizes discontinuity, difference, and separateness from society, and voluntary membership on the basis of personal commitment. A "church" is characterized by universalism and inclusiveness in its values; a "sect" bids one to strict adherence to narrowly defined, distinctive, and exclusivist group norms. Sects stress inward personal religious purity and piety, often in antagonism to the world; churches insist on equality of all people and are oriented positively to the world. A sect values informality and egalitarianism; a church is organized more formally (often hierarchically) and becomes protective of its institutional forms. As H. R. Niebuhr also showed, the church-sect typology can provide a powerful analytic tool for understanding the social form of religious life, though it needs to be modified to apply to American mainline denominations which represent something of a mixed type though with significant churchly emphases.

1. **Implications for Pastoral Care.** Though the distinction is only partly applicable to most American churches, real differences of this general sort can be identified in the style of pastoral care they offer. Central to church-sect differences is the degree of trust and rejection by the group of its immediate social and cultural milieu. Whereas a mainline denomination trusts the larger secular society to provide resources for pastoral care, a sect rejects them. The church is more community, group, and socially oriented in its pastoral care and less dependent on the authority and personal charisma of the pastor. The sect is more exclusive in its claim of the authority of the Scriptures, formal teachings, and manuals of the group used by the pastor. It generally does not trust the power of social agencies and health care professionals unless these are sectarian adherents.

As regards authority, sect adherents are encouraged to submit to the authority of the pastor and the Bible. The aims of pastoral care are defined in largely moralistic terms. In contrast, mainline denominations look less to the personal, charismatic authority of the pastor to provide the group's authoritative interpretation of the Word of God, and instead draw from their institutional authority, sacraments, and acceptance of human and health care resources available in the larger community. A church pastor claims less strict personal authority and trusts non-church forms of care to assist in pastoral care responsibilities, while nonparish ministers of the church type identify closely with nonreligious helping professions.

2. **Examples.** While the general differences in pastoral care implied in the classic church-sect typology are useful in understanding different clergy and church styles, distinctions are not always clear-cut and transitions are frequently evident. The following vignettes illustrate both the types and the ambiguities and transitions:

A Presbyterian pastor—a church-type—ranks illness, death, family conflict, and job-related tensions as principal pastoral care needs. She reads widely from psychological literature and terms her 'common sense' approach as an appeal to the presence or Providence of God in all of life: "Do your best, trust in God, and you have no need to fear." As a mainline pastor she encourages parishioners to "try to use all the knowledge we have at hand."

An Episcopal rector reports that his pastoral care role is to help parishioners clarify personal problems. Once the "real" problem is identified the person is referred for any extensive care. He monitors closely the professional care community, including fees, peer reputation, and relationship with social agencies. All care except that for crises such as bereavement is referred. He is a classic church-type pastor.

A Roman Catholic priest vigorously claims that pastoral care belongs to the whole church community. He notes that Roman church pastoral care was traditionally located in the sacraments, with little time for acts of overtly nonreligious personal caring. His laity gradually are coming to understand, however, that pastoral care is not solely a priestly task, and they can contribute to and receive in this area. In evaluating his own pastoral care, he claims that above all he is a spiritual guide. If he perceives that any efforts to reconcile family and interpersonal conflicts begin to alienate him from any of the individuals involved, immediately he refers to psychological counselors. In moral situations he focuses on spiritual matters as an expression of his own personal gifts and interests. His pastoral care is a mixture of the church (sacramental) type and the sect (personal authority) type.

A Mennonite pastor has recently undertaken clinical pastoral education (CPE). Earlier, he would press "to get them to see how they messed up spiritually." He would try to help the laity to "process sin before the Lord" because the community would not press publicly for confession but would uphold a strict view of church rules. This placed a heavy burden of guilt on the laity. Now more patient in working with parishioners, he explores with them the developmental aspects of their problems and refers them much more often to social agencies. This is sectarian in transition due to the "universalism" of CPE.

A Nazarene minister defines her task to "be there," to be available to listen. Not eager to involve herself directly, she reminds individuals of their need to face problems and use spiritual means available to them: repent, straighten out your lives, let the Lord lead. The church board has to act against unrepentant members occasionally, but the decisions are based on the manual. This is a sectarian approach; the pastor and lay leaders quietly but powerfully enforce adherence to the manual.

A Pentecostal pastor says most of his pastoral care concerns marital problems. He strictly follows a manual that "deals with any area or problem in the family." Procedures are clearly and fully described and interpretations are given on specific biblical passages aimed to respond to specific problems. The pastor gauges his care by the question, "What would the Lord want?", although receiving Christ is not a prerequisite for receiving his pastoral care. He is direct in stating what he wants parishioners to do between counseling sessions. The pastor and parishioner(s) join hands to pray to conclude each session. He may visit in the home to discuss

and promote progress. He may use a worship service to offer pastoral care through healing and confession. Or he may tell a person that he will talk to them later "in a more special, spiritual way." The personal charisma of the Pentecostal pastor meets the group expectations that he is the expert; he takes initiative and directs but does not publicly coerce. Pastoral care is explicitly based on teachings derived from biblical passages about a particular problem. This is a classic sectarian approach to pastoral care.

3. **Parallels of The Pastoral Care Movement to Sect Groups.** If one considers the history of the pastoral care movement in the U.S. from the 1930s to the present, one detects a sectarian beginning that gradually began to move toward a "church" orientation with a restrictive, less ideologically "pure" self-understanding of its power. Psychological insights were once the *sine qua non* of an uncompromising faith commitment to the modern pastoral care movement, giving the movement a sectarian character despite its positive orientation to secular psychology and social science. As the sectarian use of psychoanalysis and Rogerian counseling and anthropology loosened, there emerged a new openness to theology, to spiritual formation and direction, and to the use of prayer and the Bible in pastoral care and in Clinical Pastoral Education. Purely psychological approaches gave way to the larger theological environment of pastoral theology. The sectarian, closed, doctrinaire aspect of the movement subsided.

Bibliography. J. L. Adams and S. Hiltner, eds., *Pastoral Care in Liberal Churches* (1970). J. E. Dittes, "Typing and Typologies: Some Parallels in the Career of Church-Sect and Extrinsic-Intrinsic," *J. for the Scientific Study of Religion* (1971) 375–83. H. R. Niebuhr, *The Social Sources of Denominationalism* (1929). R. Richey, ed., *Denominationalism* (1977). E. Troeltsch, *The Social Teaching of the Christian Churches* (ET 1931). M. Weber, *The Protestant Ethic and the Spirit of Capitalism* (ET 1930).

P. A. MICKEY

PASTORAL CARE (Varieties, Traditions, and Issues); SOCIAL STATUS AND CLASS FACTORS IN PASTORAL CARE; SOCIOLOGY OF RELIGIOUS AND PASTORAL CARE; SOCIOLOGY OF RELIGION. *See also* AUTHORITY ISSUES IN PASTORAL CARE; MINISTRY; PASTORAL CARE MOVEMENT.

CIRCUMCISION. The ritual of circumcision, which is known in Hebrew as *B'rit Milah,* the Covenant of Circumcision, according to Jewish tradition occurs on the eighth day after the birth of a boy unless there is a medical reason why it should be postponed. The circumcision finds its scriptural basis in God's commandment to Abraham to remove his and his sons' foreskins as a symbol of the covenantal relationship between God and God's people (Gen. 17:9-14; 23–27). The ritual procedure welcomes the male child into this Covenant of Abraham, but it does not make the child Jewish as he is already Jewish if, according to traditional Judaism, his mother is Jewish.

The circumcision is usually performed by a Mohel, a ritual circumciser, who since he is also a rabbi, recites the prayers in addition to removing the foreskin. A rabbi may be present in addition to the Mohel to recite certain prayers and to instruct the parents as to their role at the ceremony.

The circumcision begins with the godparents bringing the infant into the room in which the circumcision will be performed. They are greeted by those gathered with the words, "Blessed be he who comes in the name of the Lord."

As Abraham circumcised his son, the religious requirement to perform the *B'rit Milah* is engendered upon the father. If he is not a Mohel, then he must give over his obligation to do so to the Mohel. This is done in a public statement by the father.

The Mohel begins the removal of the foreskin. As he does this he recites various prayers which express the obligation of bringing the child into the Covenant of Abraham. After the foreskin is removed, the parents give thanks to God for this special and joyous moment by drinking sweet sacramental wine.

The child is then given his Hebrew name as he has been welcomed into the Covenant of Abraham. This name not only identifies him within the household of Israel, but it identifies his soul to God as well. The boy will be known by this name for the rest of his life (except in cases of severe illness when the name can be changed). A person's name always includes his father's name except when the person is sick and the mother's name is used. The child would be known as so-and-so the son of so-and-so.

A *MiShabayrach*, a prayer for recovery from the circumcision, is then recited. This prayer, in addition to asking for healing, asks that the parents be blessed with wisdom in raising their child properly, and in turn that he be a source of blessing to them as he lives a life worthy of good deeds.

The ritual is concluded by the Mohel or rabbi blessing the child with the priestly benediction from Num. 6:24–26, "May the Lord bless thee and keep thee. May the Lord shine His face upon thee and be gracious unto thee. May the Lord lift up His face to thee and grant thee peace." This is then followed by a festive meal for those in attendance.

S. A. MOSS

FAMILY, JEWISH THEOLOGY AND ETHICS OF; JEWISH HOLY DAYS AND FESTIVALS. *Compare* BAPTISM AND CONFIRMATION; COVENANT AND CONTRACT; RITUAL AND PASTORAL CARE.

CIVIL LAW. *See* LEGAL DIMENSIONS OF PASTORAL CARE AND COUNSELING.

CIVIL RIGHTS MOVEMENT. *See* BLACK-AMERICAN PASTORAL CARE.

CLAIRVOYANCE. *See* PARAPSYCHOLOGY.

CLARE OF ASSISI, ST. *See* WOMEN IN PASTORAL MINISTRIES, HISTORY OF.

CLARK, ELMER TALMAGE (1886–1966). An active churchman in the Methodist Episcopal denomination, Clark was a prolific writer on the topics of church history, home missions, stewardship, and the Wesleyan

revival, and edited *The World Parish Series*. Clark earned his place in the historical annals of the psychology of religion through the publication of *The Psychology of Religious Awakening* in 1929. Interested in possible changes in conversion phenomena since Starbuck's (1899) study, Clark employed a questionnaire to study 2,174 subjects. He found three types of religious awakening: (1) the classical or *definite crisis* type (6.7 percent); (2) the *emotional stimulus* type (27.2 percent); and (3) *gradual awakening* (66.1 percent). Clark's subjects thus differed substantially from Starbuck's, for whom the *definite crisis* was most common, and whose average age at conversion was 16.4 years. The *gradual awakenings* of Clark's subjects occurred at an average age of 12.7 years. He regarded the *gradual awakening* as more normal, and believed that the sense of sin, depression, moral failure, fear, and dread associated with sudden conversions reflected impediments and blockages due to emotional disturbance. Clark's study remains one of the most widely cited in conversion literature.

Bibliography. E. T. Clark, *One Hundred Years of New Madrid Methodism: A History of the Methodist Episcopal Church* (1912); *The Rebirth of Protestantism in Europe* (1925); *The Rural Church in the South* (1924); *The Negro and His Religion* (1924); *Social Studies of the War* (1919); *What Happened at Aldersgate?* (1938); *The Psychology of Religious Awakening* (1920). Starbuck, *The Psychology of Religion* (1899).

H. VANDE KEMP

PSYCHOLOGY OF RELIGION (Empirical Studies, Methods, and Problems).

CLASS, SOCIAL. *See* SOCIAL CLASS FACTORS.

CLASSIC LITERATURE IN CARE AND COUNSELING (Judaism). *See* JEWISH LITERATURE IN CARE AND COUNSELING.

CLASSIC LITERATURE IN CARE AND COUNSELING (Orthodoxy). For present purposes, "classic literature" will be taken to include not only the works of the fathers of the church, e.g. Basil the Great, John Chrysostom, Gregory the Theologian, Gregory Nyssa, Simeon the New Theologian, Romanos Melodist, etc., but also the great modern writers of fiction from Eastern European countries where Orthodoxy has had its deep, pervasive, and formative influence—such figures as Dostoevsky, Kazantzakis, Chekhov, Tolstoy, even Solzhenitsyn. These modern literary figures do not describe or theorize about pastoral care in the modern Western manner, but their literature reflects the natural integration of church and society, of pastoral caring and generic human caring, which marks Orthodox culture. Thus it reflects much of the spirit and style of Orthodoxy's tradition of care, and also richly expresses Orthodoxy's deep theological and psychological interest in the understanding of persons.

As a means of illustrating some of the major themes and emphases of this tradition the present article focuses on three representative figures: St. John Chrysostom, Leo Tolstoy, and Anton Chekhov. The most fundamental and pervasive of these themes is *theodicy* (from *Theós* and *dike,* literally "the justification of God"). All the literature that truly represents the ethos of the Eastern Orthodox church — and by extension those lands in which Orthodoxy has its roots — is infused with the question of theodicy. This concern is woven into the lives of both those who write and, in the case of the modern authors, the characters about whom they write. In that literature one finds the application of theology to circumstance. This "application" is known in the Orthodox church as *periptosis,* the true task for *pastoral care.* What God has done in creating life, in manifesting God by his "two arms" (St. Gregory Nazianzen), i.e., God's Word (Christ) and God's Spirit, is constantly used to interpret and measure the persons and their predicaments, as the authors deal with them. This is done, even though the human capacity to fully know God, i.e., "in His Essence," remains human and limited, precisely subject to its own nature. This is the teaching known as *akatályptos,* or the "incomprehensibility of God." Thus, one always finds such literature enveloped in a certain "mystery," beyond which the human being cannot cognitively pass, although in his soul he intuits the message of such mystery. This intuitive knowing, of course, is the deepest kind of knowing, one which touches the mind, heart, and soul of human persons.

1. St. John Chrysostom. Among all his theological works, Chrysostom wrote two classics from which any contemporary pastor could easily profit: *Letter to a Young Widow* and *Letters to Olympias.*

In his *Letter to a Young Widow* Chrysostom writes as though he were a pastor in our own age who knows the turmoil that is occurring in this young woman's life. The counsel he offers is personal and tender: "Since they who are stricken with sorrow ought not to spend their whole time in mourning and tears, but to make good provision also for the healing of their wounds . . . it is a good thing to listen to words of consolation." With a great sense of timing and as one engaged in the therapy of grief, Chrysostom writes that he could not do this earlier, "while the storm was still severe" lest that "would add fuel to the flame." His letter, now written "after the thunderbolt [of shock] has fallen," enters the various dimensions of her present state, e.g., her youth and suffering, security and wealth (her husband was obviously wealthy), affection and sexuality ("keep thy bed in his honour sacred from the touch of any other man"). In all such words, Chrysostom is both practically and profoundly aware of the unhappiness and calamities of human life. These have come about because of the moral corruption of the pervading society, and in her case, particularly because of the war in which the Emperor Theodosius was engaged (and at that time seemed to be losing to the Goths). In that war many young women were widowed, each suffering under her own special circumstances. Rather than falling into self-pity, gloom, despondency or reckless indifference which the Pagans might do, Chrysostom reminds her that the Christian is to "see through" the predicament, making it work *for* the person in acquiring the eternal hope of the gospel. In this way, the young widow is not to be *taken* by the situation, but is rather to *take hold of it,* to *own* it, and to *use* it to grow spiritually.

In his *Letters to Olympias* Chrysostom addresses a deaconess who was an heiress of a great fortune, married at

sixteen, and widowed at eighteen. Her wealth and its disposition brought her into conflict with the Emperor Theodosios who wanted her to marry a young Spaniard. In his letters — there are six — Chrysostom offers the same advice of hope in the gospel as he did to the young widow, but now applies it to both her wealth and the various ecclesiastical problems with which she was disturbed.

Giving her wealth lavishly in support of the work of the church to the sick and poor, Olympias had to be warned by Chrysostom about such indiscriminate liberality. Her wealth, after all, is a trust given by God which must be used discreetly. Such advice, of course, made enemies for Chrysostom among many bishops and clergy who hoped to profit themselves from her gifts and generosity.

Regarding the church, he asks Olympias why she is "sorrowful and dejected." "Is it because of the fierce black storm which has overtaken the Church?" But he adds, "I do not abandon the hope of better things, considering who is the pilot in all this". All that concerns her is "transitory and perishable," the only thing which is truly terrible being *sin.* Chrysostom brings questions of evil and injustice analogically to the Christ of the gospel who also thus suffered "railings, insults, reproaches and gibes inflicted by the enemy." Further, all this is the manner of God's dealing: "He does not put down evils at the outset." Despite what humans think, it is "God Himself who orders all things according to His inscrutable wisdom." Olympias' only true and Christian task is to "reckon-up" the misfortunes of this world, the form of which is passing away, with the eternal world which is yet to come in glory, and of which we now have a foretaste. "Divert your mind from despondency and derive much consolation" from this task of "reckoning-up," he challenges her.

In both these examples, then, St. John Chrysostom calls upon the tradition and Scripture of Christianity as transmitted in the "mind of the Church," and as it speaks to the human dilemma.

2. Tolstoy's *Anna Karenina.* One of the many themes of Leo Tolstoy's *Anna Karenina* focuses upon the saying of Jesus "that he who finds his life will lose it, and he who loses his life for my sake will find it" (Mt. 10:39; cf. Lk. 9:24). In the Eastern world the virtue of losing one's life to find it pervades the Christian ethos, giving basis to the church and the culture, to family and society; but it is important to understand its distinctively Eastern interpretation. In traditional Orthodox cultures it is not one's uniqueness, self-realization, or autonomous individualism which is valued, as in the West. What is valued is *life in community* in which alone one can truly know one's identity and truly "find" oneself. In this light, "loss of self" is best understood as a proper interpretation of "self-denial," a virtue little respected—if even recognized— in the Western world today. The difficulty is obvious, since self-denial strikes painfully at one's basic identity as a human being. One discovers that one *is* selfish, that one spends one's time in a demanding body and soul and as a particular person who makes demands on others.

The message of losing and finding oneself is dramatized and clarified in *Anna Karenina* by two prominent characters: Anna and Konstantine Levin. Anna quickly moves to center stage because of her unique beauty and charm. A woman who can sweep into a room in a beautiful ball gown, with all eyes turned upon her, Anna has an intensely enchanting power as she spins a web of self-deception around her adulterous love-affair with the Count Vronsky.

But always the camera angle shifts to Levin, who lives out an entirely different life story, most of which takes place on his own country estate. Levin presents an almost comic contrast to the passionate Anna. He deals with hay and piglets, with farming and peasants. But while other "gentlemen farmers" are enjoying the fruit of their ownership, Levin is never quite content. He observes the simple faith of the peasants and of his wife, Kitty and, identifying with them, he asks: "Why can't I believe?"

Anna, meanwhile, is off touring Europe with her Count, has a child by him, does a little "patio gardening," and utterly charms everyone she meets. She has everything — social standing, attention, adventure — *uniqueness*. In contrast, if Levin gets what he wants, he seems not quite sure he deserves it. Two more different characters could scarcely have been devised: Anna, who seems to be "finding" herself, and Levin who seems to be "losing" himself.

Having attained everything she wanted, having "found herself" through self-assertion and the enjoyment of her unique personality, Anna finds herself tormented by greed, doubt, and jealousy. What if Vronsky loved another woman the way he loved her? What if Vronsky only wanted her for her body, and what if her body lost its beauty to him? How could she cling to those things she had "found" by her self-assertion? Ultimately, she decides that death, in Tolstoy's words, is "the only way of restoring his love for her in *his* heart, of punishing him, and of gaining the victory in the fight which an evil spirit was waging in her heart against him." Thus, in a famous scene, Anna's life of self-affirmation and fulfillment ends as she throws herself under a train.

But unlike TV dramatizations of the novel, Tolstoy does *not* end the story there. He takes us back to the country, where we find Levin wrestling with his love for his wife and son, Mitya. Why, he is wondering, do I not feel the intense caring for my son? Was something wrong with him? Levin has invested himself, lost himself, and denied himself for his family and his servants — and still he questions himself.

Suddenly, a terrible thunderstorm comes up. Kitty and Mitya are not in the house. Lightning strikes and their favorite oak tree comes crashing down. Suddenly he feels himself breathing a desperate prayer: "Dear Lord, dear Lord, not on them!" Tolstoy's words: "And though he thought at once how senseless was his prayer that they should not be killed by that *already* fallen oak tree, he repeated it, for he knew that he could do nothing better than to utter that senseless prayer." They *are* safe. But Levin remains deeply moved, for in that moment he came to understand both his love for them, and his ultimate dependency on God.

3. Chekhov's Short Stories.
If Tolstoy broods upon issues of theodicy via the epic novel, Anton Chekhov realizes the same goal through the short story. His stories are "shot-through" with images of church-life and human predicaments. One of the most famous of his stories is entitled *The Bishop*. There one is taken into the personal thoughts and concerns of "Bishop Pyotr" (Peter), as he struggles with the psychological effects of "feeling distant" from his mother, who comes to visit him. While such distance might be a "respect" which she gives him due to his position, he perceives it rather in terms of "loneliness." She is comfortable with the other people, but not with him. Such themes are clearly psychological, but they also show an author working out Christian thematics through such problems of interpersonal relations.

Chekhov realizes his message by using incidents, time and places which are *sui generis* Orthodox. In *The Letter*, for instance, the aged Father Anastasy, on the Eve of Easter, overstays his visit with the younger Father Fyodor (the "dean" of the parishes in that district); this is a most inappropriate time for such a visit. However, along with Deacon Liubimov, Father Anastasy struggles to work out a "family problem" with his son and seeks help from the more refined Father Fyodor. With his help, the widowed Deacon writes a stern letter to his son; but later, convinced by the elder priest to "forgive," the Deacon, in a comic and paradoxical postscript to his harsh letter, shows Christian compassion for his wayward son, thus undermining the sternness which he wished to project at the outset of his letter!

Chekhov's stories are not about church-life in the narrow sense of the word; they are about people in crisis and cultural predicament. However, the context in which these crises and predicaments are worked out, and the themes that pervade such stories as *Easter Eve, A Nightmare, The Murder, Uprooted* and *The Steppe*, are clearly Eastern Orthodox. As such, they portray a deep sensitivity to human need and suffering and generate a vision of what it means to care "pastorally" in the widest sense of the term, and certainly in the truest sense of the Orthodox tradition in which church and society are integrally related.

4. Conclusion.
One must of course read such works oneself to grasp the full import of even what little has been presented here. But if we return to Tolstoy, it can be said that like those who wrote before and after him — all of whom can represent the Eastern Orthodox literature — he hardly writes a "novel"; rather he portrays a "piece of life" that gives an expansive vision of God and humanity. The closing words of *Anna Karenina* may suffice to make this point:

> . . . there will still be the same wall between the holy of holies of my soul and other people, even my wife. I shall still go on scolding her for my own terror, and being remorseful for it. I shall still be as unable to understand with my reason why I pray, and I shall still go on praying. But my life now, my whole life apart from anything that can happen to me, every minute of it, is no more meaningless as it was before, but it has the positive meaning of goodness which I have the power to put into it.

Bibliography. J. L. Allen, *The Ministry of the Church: Image of Pastoral Care* (1986). W. A. Clebsch and C. R. Jaekle, *Pastoral Care in Historical Perspective* (1964). R. J. Deferrari, ed., *The Fathers of the Church: A New Translation*, 69 vols. (1948–   ). J. T. McNeill, *A History of the Cure of Souls* (1951). T. C. Oden, *Pastoral Theology: Essentials of Ministry* (1983); *Crisis Ministries*

(1986). J. Quasten, *et al.*, *The Works of the Fathers in Translation*, 40 vols. (1946–). A. Roberts and J. Donaldson, eds., *The Ante-Nicene Fathers*, 10 vols. (1885–1896; 1979). H. Wace and P. Schaff, eds., *A Select Library of the Nicene and Post-Nicene Fathers of the Christian Church*, 14 vols. (1887–1892), vol. 9.

J. L. ALLEN

MINISTRY AND PASTORAL CARE (Orthodox Tradition). *See also* EARLY CHURCH, PASTORAL CARE AND COUNSELING IN; PASTORAL CARE (History, Traditions, and Definitions). *Compare* EASTERN EUROPEAN PASTORAL CARE MOVEMENT. *Biography:* CHRYSOSTOM.

CLASSIC LITERATURE IN CARE AND COUNSELING (Protestantism).

Writings that have significantly influenced the understanding and practice of pastoral care in the Protestant traditions since the Reformation. The literature noted here is organized by chronological periods.

1. The Sixteenth Century. Pastoral concern over abuses of the sacrament of penance (confession), particularly the sale of indulgences, gave rise to the Protestant Reformation in the sixteenth century, though these concerns had been present for several preceding centuries. Significantly, on All Saints' Eve, 1517, Luther posted his Ninety-five Theses, in part because of his concern for the effect on simple people of the sale of indulgences. While affirming the value of confession, Luther claimed that the authority to hear confessions and absolve from sin rested upon all believers, not just upon the clergy. He interpreted the binding and loosing passage of Mt. 18:18 as authorizing all Christians to exercise a priestly office toward one another.

Luther was a skilled spiritual director and confessor who did not allow his other responsibilities to deter him from this pastoral task. On April 16, 1521, he appeared before the Diet of Worms. The hearing was continued on the following day. Yet at dawn, before his second appearance, he went to the bedside of Hans von Minckwitz, a dying knight, to hear his confession and administer the sacrament. Many such examples of Luther's care for the sick are found in his *Table Talk*.

Luther's letters, the earliest classical literature of Protestant pastoral care, provide a vivid glimpse into how Luther responded to persons facing a variety of personal crises. One such letter was addressed to Frederick the Wise, Elector of Saxony, who became seriously ill in the summer of 1519. His court chaplain, Georg Spalatin, asked Luther to write a word of spiritual consolation. "I cannot," wrote Luther, "pretend to be deaf to the voice of Christ crying to me out of your Lordship's flesh and blood, 'Behold here am I sick.'" His letter (*The Fourteen of Consolation*, 1520) then proceeds to a scripturally based meditation on fourteen themes of spiritual cure: seven aspects of evil and seven blessings of God.

While many of Luther's works have significance for Protestant pastoral care, neither he nor Calvin wrote a specific treatise on the cure of souls. Calvin followed Luther in his view that confession to God should be followed by confession to fellow humans. Citing Jas. 5:16, he urged Christians to confess their faults "one to another." Confession could rightly be made to any church member, but, in addition, Calvin suggested that people in spiritual distress also seek consultation with the pastor, though this was optional, not required.

Calvin was a gentle, persuasive, and concerned pastor. This facet of his life is less well known than his career as the stern reformer who organized Geneva under a system of rigorous ecclesiastical supervision. He conducted an extensive correspondence with a variety of persons facing illness, poverty, oppression, and family conflict. So important was pastoral work to Calvin that Jean Daniel Benoit, who studied his care of souls in detail, concluded that Calvin's theology was in fact derived from his effort to be a better pastor (Benoit, 1947). Calvin's pastoral letters reflect his unwavering confidence in the biblical revelation for spiritual guidance and support. Repeatedly he urged his readers to reflect on the truth of the Holy Scriptures in the midst of their distress.

The earliest Protestant writing on the pastoral office as such was a sermon by Huldreich Zwingli, chief preacher in Zurich. Originally delivered at the Zurich Disputation in January, 1523, it was published as *Der Hirt (The Pastor)* in 1524, the title borrowed from the early patristic document, the *Shepherd* of Hermas. Concerned about the abuses of the pastoral office, Zwingli appeals to pastors to follow his leadership in the path toward reform. The first section of the book is a biblical description of the character of the true shepherd. The second part condemns "false prophets."

Since *Der Hirt* was intended to persuade Swiss pastors to support the Protestant cause, it is not primarily a text on the care of souls. Nevertheless, its warmth and piety helped to create a positive sense of the significance of pastoral care.

The most significant Protestant work on pastoral care of the Reformation period was written by Martin Bucer, whose *On the True Cure of Souls* appeared in both Latin and German editions in 1538. Bucer, the leader of the Reformation at Strasbourg, held an interesting mediating position between Lutheranism and the Reformed movement. He claimed to be Lutheran, and by the Wittenberg Concord of 1536 he and his followers from southern Germany were included in the Lutheran movement. Yet John T. McNeill (1951, p. 177) suggests that his influence was probably greater among Calvinists. In any case, like other reformers Bucer based his assertions on the authority of Scripture, but he emphasized mutual care in the Christian community. In Ezekiel's portrait of God as the Good Shepherd (Ezek. 34:16), Bucer found a model for the Christian pastor: "I will seek the lost, and I will bring back the strayed, and I will bind up the crippled, and I will strengthen the weak, and the fat and the strong I will watch over; I will feed them in justice."

2. The Seventeenth Century. The Reformation in England was rooted in the efforts of evangelicals such as Latimer and Tyndale to make the Bible available to laity —efforts that cost them their lives. Within the context of the political reforms of Henry VIII, English churchmen developed their own ecclesiastical system, which made penance and absolution mandatory.

Mid-seventeenth-century England was torn by civil war and religious strife. During this period classic pastoral literature is best illustrated by the works of Anglican and Puritan clergy who wrote to offer guidance when priestly counsel was not available. Confession and the cure of souls concerned a number of Anglican writers, of whom the best known is Jeremy Taylor (1613–67). Chaplain to Charles I, Taylor served briefly with the royalist army. After the king was murdered, he moved to Wales, where he remained during Cromwell's rule. There in 1650 he wrote *The Rule and Exercise of Holy Living,* and the following year a companion volume, *The Rule and Exercise of Holy Dying.* In these well-known works, Taylor offers guidance for Christians facing the crises of life. *Holy Dying,* however, was intended not so much as counsel for the sick and dying as for the well. It was a manual to help people prepare themselves for the trials and tribulations that are the inevitable reminders of mortality. Taylor understood illness as sent by God for spiritual growth. He wanted to help individuals learn from their pain and gave examples of appropriate prayers to be offered by the sick person.

Richard Baxter (1615–91) represents the best of the Puritan tradition of pastoral care during this century. At twenty-six he went to Kidderminster in Worcester County, an unpromising community of about four thousand, where he became an earnest and effective preacher, attributing his success to his pastoral work. In his classic work, *Gildas Salvianus, the Reformed Pastor* (1656), Baxter stressed the importance of the care of the individual. While still a bachelor, he developed a program of family pastoral care, spending at least an hour with each of the eight hundred families of his church each year. (His clerk scheduled fifteen or sixteen families for interviews in Baxter's house each Monday and Tuesday.) Baxter tried to give each person time for private conversation. When some of his peers in the clergy complained that they did not have time to know all their church members individually, Baxter urged them to hire an assistant out of their own salary, since it was preferable to live on a partial salary than to neglect a single soul.

In support of his ministry with the sick, Baxter developed a consultative relationship with a "godly and diligent" physician. His effectiveness in cases of depression widened his reputation as a counselor. Popular in its own time, *The Reformed Pastor* influenced many later pastoral theologians. McNeill claims that "for Protestant ministers," because of its urgency, originality, and appeal, "no other book quite ranks with it."

Whereas Jeremy Taylor had served with loyalist forces in the civil war, his contemporary, John Bunyan (1628–88), had fought for Parliament. A tinker's son, rowdy and profane, Bunyan came under the religious influence of a devout young woman whom he married in 1648. He joined a nonconformist church and soon began preaching. After the restoration of Charles II, Bunyan was arrested for preaching without a license and confined in the Bedford jail for twelve years. Here he ministered to his fellow prisoners, studied the Bible, and wrote extensively. Among his works from prison was *Grace Abounding to the Chief of Sinners* (1666), in which he recounts his own inward struggle against the devil, and, during a second imprisonment, *The Pilgrim's Progress* (1678), a work which describes the spiritual warfare of everyman— "Christian." *Pilgrim's Progress* has been called "the most influential modern Protestant manual of personal piety" (Clebsch and Jaekle 1975, p. 272). Bunyan drew his authority not from university training in theology but

from the King James Bible and his own immediate religious experience, and his writings reinforced these two sources as normative for pastoral care in the free-church tradition.

3. The Eighteenth Century. Pastoral literature of the eighteenth century gave special attention to accounts of conversion experiences that marked Pietism in Europe, evangelicalism in Britain, and the Great Awakening in America. These mystical experiences, sometimes accompanied by strange behavior, were regarded as significant opportunities for pastoral care. The literature of this period is represented by Jonathan Edwards and John Wesley.

The preaching of Jonathan Edwards (1703–58) launched the first of the great revivals in America about 1734. Minister at Stockbridge, Massachusetts, Edwards preached a rigorous Calvinism, including unconditional election, with a fervor and power that sometimes led his hearers to respond by weeping, shrieking, or fainting. Surprised by such phenomena, Edwards at first was not sure whether to credit these responses to the devil or the Holy Spirit.

Edwards's *Treatise on the Religious Affections* (1746) was the first American work on the psychology of religion. His purpose for the work was to set forth an understanding of the dynamics of religious feelings in order to communicate the gospel more effectively. The *Treatise* reflects his understanding that in God's design of human nature "affections are very much the spring of men's actions." Therefore true religion must appreciate the role of the affections in motivating behavior, including conversion.

Edwards described and classified various mental dispositions, recognized the significance of individual differences, and opposed the concept of a uniform pattern for conversion. As an aid to self-examination and reflection, he not only kept a journal but also reviewed his dreams every morning, seeking to discover his "prevailing inclinations." The *Treatise,* which drew on this remarkable pioneering research and reflection, shaped the psychological understanding of religion for the next hundred years and beyond.

John Wesley (1703–91), whose father, Samuel, was a minister of the Church of England, was trained at Oxford and for two years served as curate to his father at Epworth. His *Journal* (1735–90), which is a record of his lifelong ministry as a leading preacher of the Evangelical Revival in Britain and one of the classic documents of Protestant evangelical ministry, is filled with pastoral insights and observations. Wesley felt a keen pastoral concern for his converts, many of whom were experiencing the hardship and deprivation that accompanied the Industrial Revolution. To the masses of the crowded cities and the farms Wesley brought a message of hope. He invited his hearers to respond to the leading of the Spirit of God and held forth the possibility of a new life as a gift of God's grace.

Because Wesley knew that new converts needed continued support, he organized "bands" for mutual confession and discipline, rules for which appear in his *Journal* under the date of December 25, 1738. The following year, "societies" began to be formed and consisted of "classes" of twelve men and women meeting once a week under a class leader. Class members shared their troubles, confessed their shortcomings, and encouraged one another in a fellowship of concern. In addition, the societies developed rules of acceptable conduct, which not only forbade profanity, drunkenness, and quarreling, but also encouraged members to feed the hungry, clothe the naked, and visit the sick. This mutual care of souls powerfully transformed poor folk from anonymous victims of society into named and known members of the family of God.

Less well-known than the *Journal* is Wesley's *Primitive Physick* (1747), a religiously oriented home medical guide of which twenty-three editions were published during Wesley's lifetime. The love of God, he noted, is the "sovereign remedy of all miseries." By keeping the passions under control, the love of God offsets the illnesses resulting from passion. Likewise, the inner peace produced by the gospel is a powerful means of health and long life.

The work of Edwards and Wesley laid the foundation for a pastoral psychology that appreciated both the dynamics of religious experience and the spiritual power of the small group.

4. The Nineteenth Century. Again, during the nineteenth century, pastoral care was reshaped by changes in the culture. As classic examples of a burgeoning literature, Ichabod Spencer's *A Pastor's Sketches* (1850) represents an antebellum perspective, and Washington Gladden's *The Christian Pastor and the Working Church* (1898) typifies the changes in pastoral awareness that had occurred by the latter part of the century.

Ichabod Spencer (1798–1854) was a Presbyterian minister who held a long pastorate in Brooklyn, New York. His "sketches" are in fact detailed reports of his pastoral conversations. The book's subtitle, *Conversations with Anxious Inquirers, Respecting the Way of Salvation,* illustrates the revivalistic image of Protestant pastoral care during the antebellum period.

The Second Great Awakening not only touched the frontier, but also took the form of an urban revivalism. Educated ministers applied the current faculty psychology to their pastoral work in order to lead "anxious inquirers" to wholehearted repentance and faith. Spencer blended gentle tact with spiritual urgency in his appeal to the will. Even by 1840 theological seminaries had begun to develop chairs of pastoral theology, often linked to homiletics, and a number of faculty were beginning to write handbooks of pastoral theology. But few were as widely circulated or as warmly appreciated throughout the century as Spencer's *Sketches*.

During the nearly fifty years between Spencer's sketches and the appearance of Gladden's *Christian Pastor,* America had been torn by the Civil War, had become an urban and industrial power, and had put its faith in technology and progress.

The optimism of the times was symbolized in the other half of Gladden's title *"and the Working Church."* He spoke of numerous groups within the church whose diverse needs called for special organizations: children, young people, and the poor. The pastor equips lay leaders to share with him in the "work" of saving, teaching, and shepherding men, women, and children. Group work was the method. In fact, according to Seward

Hiltner (1958, p. 48) "group work in the church in the contemporary sense virtually begins with Gladden."

In a chapter entitled "The Pastor as Friend," Gladden portrays the minister as the kind of person "to whom the heart of anyone in need of a friend would instinctively turn." To accept the outpouring of hearts filled with doubt, sorrow, anxiety, and despair requires tenderness, warmth, and strength. Gladden favored collaboration with physicians in the care of the sick. At the same time he was convinced of the health-giving potential of effective pastoral care.

By 1900, the church had acquired the organizational profile familiar to twentieth-century Christians. Pastoral theology was firmly established in the theological curriculum. Theologians were exploring the significance of pastoral care of the "new psychology" of William James and the psychoanalytic theories of Sigmund Freud.

5. The Twentieth Century. During the 1920s two physicians, William S. Keller of Cincinnati and Richard C. Cabot of Boston, helped to launch a new form of education for pastors. Keller began a summer school designed to teach social ethics through placement of seminarians in social agencies. Cabot called for a "clinical year," which would help the young minister discover the "growing edge" of the soul. From their separate efforts emerged the program of professional training known as Clinical Pastoral Education (CPE). The purpose of its founders was to improve the functional skills of pastors in dealing with persons in crisis situations. Their chief methods were placement of trainees in situations of acute need, close supervision, and disciplined theological and ethical reflection.

In 1925, with Cabot's help, Anton T. Boisen began clinical training at Worcester State Hospital, where he served as chaplain. Boisen had earlier experienced a schizophrenic breakdown with religious manifestations. *The Exploration of the Inner World* (1936) is the story of his experience and of his hope for a more therapeutic use of religion in caring for the mentally ill.

In the same year that Boisen's book appeared, Cabot and a young Methodist minister, Russell L. Dicks, published *The Art of Ministering to the Sick.* Dicks demonstrated the healing power of listening through verbatim reports of conversations with patients. He also wrote lyrical prayers to remind them of their ultimate hope. The book was widely read and used for decades.

During the economic boom that followed World War II, the popularization of psychology gave impetus to the rapid growth of CPE. Almost all theological seminaries added courses in pastoral care and counseling. Four pastoral theologians, some of whom had studied with Boisen and all of whom were well acquainted with his work, provided intellectual leadership during the fifties and sixties.

In *Pastoral Counseling* (1949) Seward Hiltner of the University of Chicago described a method of "eductive counseling." Carroll Wise of Garrett Biblical Institute combined personalist theology and dynamic psychology in *Pastoral Counseling: Its Theory and Practice* (1951). Paul Johnson of Boston University treated *The Psychology of Pastoral Care* (1953) from the perspective of interpersonal psychiatry. The strong influence of Carl Rogers is evident in all three of these works. Wayne Oates of the

Southern Baptist Theological Seminary interpreted the role of *The Christian Pastor* (1951) from the dual perspective of scripture and the social sciences. The work by Oates, revised twice, has served as a text for more than thirty years. The others were superceded by later works by both their authors and others.

In the last quarter of the century, the literature of pastoral care and counseling has been voluminous and increasingly varied and creative in responding to human pain under rapidly changing social conditions. Yet certain themes in pastoral work appear to be timeless, and the classics still have much to teach the modern pastor.

Bibliography. For source selections and overview essays see W. A. Clebsch and C. R. Jaekle, *Pastoral Care in Historical Perspective* (1975). For historical discussions see S. Hiltner, *Preface to Pastoral Theology* (1958). E. B. Holifield, *A History of Pastoral Care in America* (1983). C. F. Kemp, *Physicians of the Soul* (1947). J. T. McNeill, *A History of the Cure of Souls* (1951). E. E. Thornton, *Professional Education for Ministry* (1970). For excellent bibliography see T. C. Oden, *Pastoral Theology* (1983). For representative Luther selections see A. Nebe, *Luther as Spiritual Advisor* (1894). T. G. Tappert, ed., *Luther: Letters of Spiritual Counsel* (1955). For Calvin see J. D. Benoit, *Calvin, directeur d'ames* (1947).

A. L. MEIBURG

PASTORAL THEOLOGY, PROTESTANT; PASTORALIA. *See also* PASTORAL CARE (History, Traditions, and Definitions). *Compare* JEWISH LITERATURE IN CARE AND COUNSELING. *Biography:* BAXTER; BOISEN; BUCER; BUNYAN; CABOT; CALVIN; DICKS; EDWARDS; GLADDEN; JOHNSON; LUTHER; OATES; SPENCER; TAYLOR; WESLEY; WISE; ZWINGLI.

CLASSIC LITERATURE IN CARE AND COUNSELING (Roman Catholicism).

Literature, primarily of the West, that has exercised formative influence on the ministry of pastoral care and counseling and that offers resources for the development and renewal of that ministry today. Works from the Greek patristic tradition are also significant for Roman Catholic pastoral theology and practice and should be consulted as well.

Classically, this ministry and its literature have been treated under the rubric of "cure of souls," although such a description does not do justice either to the scope of the tradition or to the range of concerns encompassed by pastoral care and counseling, a terminology only recently appropriated by Roman Catholics. Traditionally, the ministry of pastoral care in the Roman Catholic context has been as much communal as individual, sacramental (liturgical) as devotional, concerned with practice (sanctification and the disciplines of Christian life) as with faith (Justification). Roman Catholic literature of pastoral care, then, includes works addressed both to individuals and communities, as well as those addressed to pastors — bishops, priests, abbots, abbesses, and others exercising pastoral supervision. Works in this tradition can be broadly comprehended under six headings: initiation; exhortation (Christian life); reconciliation (sin and forgiveness); spiritual direction and discernment; consolation (death and dying); and pastoral office.

Representative or illustrative works in each category will be discussed. The extensive literature of monastic life, expositions of monastic rules, treatises on prayer, contemplation and mystical experience, as well as hand-books on preaching and instruction or exhortation in social ministries (e.g., health care, care of the poor) will not be considered here.

1. **Initiation.** In the early church, the model of pastoral care was the catechumenate and the context of care was mission (evangelization), as R. Duffy has observed. The process by which new members were welcomed, instructed, and initiated into the community was a lengthy one of pre- and post-baptismal catechesis and liturgical formation, primarily under the direction of the bishop. The earliest work of this genre is Cyril of Jerusalem's *Catechetical Lectures* and *Mystagogical Catecheses* (mid-fourth century, Greek), though the outlines of the baptismal rite and its meaning are already sketched out by Tertullian ca. 200 CE (*On Baptism*). The western counterpart to Greek catechetical instructions is found in Ambrose of Milan's *On the Sacraments* (ca. 390), six catecheses preached by the bishop in the week after Easter, recapitulating for the newly baptized the meaning of the baptismal rite in which they have just participated, reinforcing their belief in the reality of the body and blood of Christ which they have received in the Eucharist, and reviewing the content of the Lord's Prayer as a guide to the Christian life on which they have embarked. *On the Mysteries* by the same author offers a briefer treatment of similar material from about the same time.

Augustine's *First Catechetical Instruction* (*De catechizandis rudibus*, sometimes translated "on catechizing the simple") is another work from the literature of initiation that sheds light on the pastoral nature of this ministry. The treatise (ca. 405) is addressed to pastors, advising them on the theory of catechesis and instructing them in its practice, both in terms of what material must be presented, the manner of its presentation, and the way in which this must be appropriately adapted to the particular persons being instructed. In addition to offering long and short versions of a sample catechetical discourse, Augustine encourages the catechist to maintain a willing disposition even when the work of instruction may seem wearisome.

In addressing different aspects of the process of Christian initiation, both Ambrose and Augustine offer insights into the personal and pastoral dimensions of conversations about the faith, whether these are with individuals or groups, prospective converts or long-standing parishioners.

2. **Exhortation.** Instruction in Christian living and in the formation of Christian character is the aim of works of exhortation and encouragement. Ethical treatises and theories of virtue have an obvious bearing on this literature but belong more to the history of theological ethics than to pastoral care and counseling. The two treatises singled out here suggest the range of available material.

Tertullian's treatise *On Patience* (ca. 200) is in many ways a model work of this sort. It presents an astute analysis of the virtue of patience, grounded, one cannot help but think, in the author's knowledge of his own limitations in this regard, as well as in a theological understanding of the patience of God with humankind, and particularly the patience of Jesus Christ in the incarnation, which was a patience even to death. The analysis of impatience is equally astute, from its demonic origins to its mundane causes and manifestations. Tertullian concludes by demonstrating that patience is the foundation of the goods promised in the beatitudes and the necessary condition of charity; when practiced in body and spirit, it is patience that brings persons to God.

In a quite different vein, Aelred of Rievaulx's *On Spiritual Friendship* (ca. 1165) responds to a request for instruction on the subject from one of the monks in the community over which he presided as abbot. Beginning from classical definitions of friendship, Aelred examines the nature of friendship and its basis in the divinely willed society of all creatures, the benefits of friendship and its contribution to virtue, and the ways in which and with whom friendship may be cultivated and preserved throughout life. His reflections on friendship are instructive for all those seeking to live a Christian life, not simply for those in cloistered community.

Helping persons to embody the values of patience and friendship in their lives is an aspect of Christian formation that can speak to contemporary issues such as burnout and commitment that arise frequently in the ministry of pastoral care and counseling today.

3. Reconciliation. Much of the history of the cure of souls in Roman Catholicism has been treated in terms of the development of a system of penitential discipline, as in J. McNeill's classic work. Numerous early controversies witness to the centrality of the issue of sin and forgiveness in the Christian community.

Tertullian is again a prime example. His treatise *On Penitence* (ca. 204) reflects the common practice of the time. The purpose of Christian repentance is to further the work of God's mercy; as an occasion of both repentance and conversion, baptism effects the forgiveness of the new Christian's previous sins. After baptism, there may be one — but only one — further opportunity for the forgiveness of serious sin, involving public penance and a period of exclusion from communion. Tertullian's stern treatment of the practice of penance took an uncompromising turn after he had associated himself with the heretical but disciplinarily rigorist Montanist sect. In his essay *On Purity* (213 ff.), Tertullian insists that there is no possibility of forgiveness for serious post-baptismal sin. Though the community may pray for the sinner, forgiveness must be left entirely to God's future disposition.

Controversy about forgiveness of sin continued in the disputes about whether the sin of apostasy could be forgiven, and by whom, that arose in the period after the Decian persecution (250 ff.). The issue of episcopal authority and the ecclesiastical regulation of penance played as important a role in these conflicts as did concern for the welfare of the would-be penitent. In time, however, agreement was reached on even this difficult question, and the practice of a penitential discipline that could be undertaken many times during a Christian's life gained acceptance throughout the western church, particularly after the time of Pope Gregory the Great (died 604). As the medieval penitential system continued to develop, handbooks of penance came into being for the use of those hearing confessions. J. McNeill and H. Gamer have collected and translated many of these so-called penitentials (sixth to twelfth centuries), which distinguish and catalog the various kinds and occasions of sins and prescribe the appropriate penances to be assigned. While both sins and penalties may strike the contemporary reader as obsessively scrupulous or excessively harsh, the handbooks offer an insight into the seriousness with which Christian life and discipline were regarded.

Reflection on appropriate standards of Christian behavior, the need for both communal and private forums for confession and forgiveness, and the efficacy of human repentance and divine mercy might serve to deepen compassion for the sinner at a time in which judgmental moralism is on the increase. It might, as well, strengthen the foundations of the ministry of pastoral care and counseling when confronted with the prevalent extremes of guilt and anxiety on the one hand and narcissism on the other.

4. Spiritual Direction and Discernment. The literature of spiritual direction and discernment is vast, extending from the early ascetic movement through centuries of monastic culture and into the era of the Reformation and beyond. In the initial development of asceticism the teacher-disciple relationship was the primary means for instructing those new to this way of life. A good deal of later monastic literature could in turn be characterized as directed toward spiritual formation and, at least in passing, discernment. As the social context of the church changed radically with the division of western Christendom during the Reformation, matters of formation and discernment shifted locale from the monastery to the active apostolate of both clergy and laity.

It is in the deserts of Egypt, Palestine, and Syria in the fourth century that western Christianity discovered the foundations of the ascetic practice which it later developed into its own distinctive forms, primarily through the institution of monasticism. John Cassian's *Conferences* (ca. 425) record the teachings he absorbed during approximately ten years among the hermits and communal ascetics of Egypt. Although written for the monks in the community he eventually founded in Marseilles in ca. 425, the *Conferences* represent a major current of influence on western asceticism and its concomitant practices of spiritual direction and discernment. In presenting the discourses of various monastic teachers (the "Abba" or "father" to whom the neophyte went for guidance), Cassian offers psychologically astute advice on spiritual growth and discipline. Conferences on such topics as "The Monk's Goal" (the perfection of charity and the contemplation of God) or "On Perfection" (an examination of the reasons for which persons undertake the life of perfection) are occasions for teaching not only about ascetic practices but about the discernment (or "discretion") that undergirds them. Seemingly distracting thoughts in prayer or contemplation, for example, may come from God as well as from ourselves or from the devil. Similarly, a person may undertake the ascetic life out of fear of hell or hope of reward, in which case stability of character will never be attained; but if love of God is the source of motivation, the person will increase in charity and grow into God's image and likeness.

In the radically different context of the Counter-Reformation, Ignatius Loyola continued the tradition of direction and discernment begun in the desert more than a thousand years earlier. During a period of convalescence from wounds received in battle, Ignatius embarked on a reform of life that would lead him to an extended period of prayer and conversion at Manresa, where he began to evolve a method of prayer and discernment. The *Spiritual Exercises* (published in 1548) quickly became the basis of formation and spiritual direction in the Society of Jesus (founded by Ignatius in 1540), and they remain the distinctive feature of Jesuit spirituality to this day.

The meditations of the *Exercises* are divided into four "weeks," each organized around a central theme. Sorrow for sin and thankfulness for the grace and forgiveness of Christ the Savior characterize the first week; meditation on the kingdom of Christ and on the Two Standards (Christ's and Lucifer's) sets the tone for the second week's contemplation of the life and ministry of Jesus, leading to consideration of the call of Christ in one's own life; contemplation of the passion directs the third week toward a compassionate entering into Christ's suffering love; and the fourth week focuses on generous and loving presence to the risen Christ and the presence of God in all things. The "Rules for the Discernment of Spirits" that follow after the outline of the Exercises are consonant with much of the ascetic-monastic tradition but bear a distinctively Ignatian stamp, keyed as they are to the weeks of the *Exercises*. It is not so much in the reading as in the experiencing of the *Exercises* that it is possible to appreciate their versatility and power in leading persons to discover within themselves the love of Christ and to respond freely and generously to its promptings.

While Cassian wrote for monks and Ignatius for an order of priests, Francis de Sales wrote for lay people, and particularly for women. His pastoral concern as a bishop was in the guidance of souls seeking to practice devotion in the ordinary circumstances of their lives. To this end he wrote the *Introduction to the Devout Life* (1609) for one of his penitents, to assist her in striving for the true love of God to which anyone, in any walk of life, might aspire. The *Introduction* is a sensible, humane, and gentle guide to finding and loving God in all things through the purification of the soul from sin and the affection for sin, in the cultivation of prayer and the simple (rather than the extraordinary) virtues, and in overcoming the temptations that will always beset humankind in this life. It is Francis de Sales's great gift to have understood that devotion is a universal Christian vocation, and to have evolved a practical and rather ordinary way for lay people to pursue this call. In this the *Introduction* speaks not only to the Counter-Reformation context in which it was written, but also to the need for a truly lay spirituality that is so strongly felt today.

Experience in the disciplines of the spiritual life, understanding of its pitfalls, and insight into the workings of the human heart are only a portion of the heritage of spiritual direction and discernment that pastoral ministers might draw on in response to the growing interest in spirituality and the practice of prayer among contemporary Christians.

5. **Consolation.** Letters of consolation, sermons on death and resurrection, reflections on the death of a friend or family member, and treatises on the art of dying from nearly every century witness to that unavoidable pastoral situation, the end of life. Among the extensive correspondence of St. Jerome are a number of letters of consolation, the most famous of which is Letter 108, a memorial of the life of his companion and colleague, Paula, written to her daughter Eustochium in 404. More typical of consolatory literature than this almost hagiographical memorial of Paula, however, is Jerome's Letter 39 to that same Paula on the death of her daughter Blaesilla in 385, evidently of ascetic excesses. Writing to console her mother, Jerome praises Blaesilla's faith, holiness, and learning, gives voice to his own grief even as he tries to ease Paula's, and struggles to make sense of the ageless problem of the untimely death of the young and innocent. After contrasting OT accounts of mourning and grief with the joy that is proper to those who believe in the resurrection of Jesus, Jerome concludes by having Blaesilla address her mother from beyond the grave with a recapitulation of his argument and an admonition not to grieve the Lord with her mourning.

Jerome's difficulties in dealing with grief reflect the strong and persistent influence of Stoic ethics on western Christianity. A similar conflict between human emotion and the Stoic ideal that characterized the appropriate Christian response to death is graphically represented by Augustine in his descriptions in the *Confessions* (397–400) of the death of a close friend (Book 4) and of his mother, Monica (Book 9).

By the fifteenth century, attention had shifted from the problem of bereavement to that of preparation for one's own death. Works on the *ars moriendi* or art of dying well circulated in popular block-books (woodcuts accompanied by a spare text) and in learned tracts; Latin, French, and English originals, as well as translations and abridgments abounded. A good example of the genre is *The Book of the Craft of Dying,* a Latin treatise of unknown authorship popular in England in the mid-fifteenth century. In commending the practice of dying well, the author advises on how to avoid the principal temptations that arise when one is facing death (temptations regarding faith, desperation, impatience, complacency, and love of temporal things), and offers instructions on how to minister to the spiritual needs of the dying person. These include assisting them in reviewing their life and faith through a series of questions, counseling and encouraging them to repentance, and praying with them; sample prayers illustrate this final point.

As Christian theology has integrated the insights of modern psychology, pastoral approaches toward death and dying have advanced beyond the limitations of Stoic ethical theory or medieval understandings of human nature. But in an age poised almost equally between the massive denial of death and the pervasive fear of annihilation, where dying can be prolonged indefinitely and life manufactured, these classic works of consolation can perhaps serve as reminders of the way in which death still marks human living and challenges human meaning.

6. **Pastoral Office.** Reflections on the nature of pastoral office do not appear until the latter part of the fourth century, though vigorous advocacy of the bishop's authority can be found before this in the writings of Ignatius of Antioch, Irenaeus, and Cyprian. In the West it is Ambrose who first elaborates the responsibilities of pastoral office in a treatise *On the Duties of the Clergy* (ca. 391). Patterned after Cicero's *De Officiis,* Ambrose's work exemplifies the appropriation of classical culture that so marked Christianity in this period, and is as much a

presentation of a Christian theory of virtue and practical ethics as it is a treatment of pastoral office. The duties of the clergy are simply those of the Christian raised to a higher degree, to which are added the counsels of perfection.

Although Gregory the Great composed his *Pastoral Care* or *Pastoral Rule (Liber Regulae Pastoralis)* as an apology for his own reluctance to assume the office of bishop of Rome, the treatise (591) came to shape the understanding of pastoral office throughout the Middle Ages. In the first of its four parts Gregory begins to paint a portrait of the pastor as a governor (i.e., guide or director) of souls who is to teach by the example of his own life; the picture of the pastor's character and life and the manner in which he is to conduct his office is further elaborated in the second part. The remainder of part one is given over to discussion of the ambiguities and difficulties of discerning who is fit for pastoral rule. Both those who seek and those who avoid office can be selfishly motivated, and in either case the desire for personal advantage ultimately works to personal as well as ecclesial detriment. The third and longest section of the work is an explanation of how the pastor should teach those in his care by taking into account the crucial differences in their circumstances, personalities, vices, and virtues. In thirty-six contrasting pairs (or pastoral case studies, as T. Oden views them), Gregory demonstrates how personal context determines the appropriate method of exhortation. The treatise concludes with a brief warning against pride on account of either the pastor's virtuous life or his effective teaching.

The papal office itself is the subject of Bernard of Clairvaux's *Five Books of Consideration* (completed in 1152–53) addressed to Pope Eugene III, who had briefly been a monk in Bernard's monastery. The first four books treat various aspects of papal office and power; the fifth reflects on knowledge of God and the nature of the celestial hierarchy. The centerpiece of Bernard's pastoral advice on the exercise of the highest office in the church is the virtue of consideration, that faculty of thought by which truth is sought in practical affairs. In order to allow time for consideration, Bernard urges Eugene to clear his schedule of unnecessary clutter, to delegate responsibilities, and to take care of his own needs. Properly schooled in self-knowledge, Eugene will better be able to address himself to the needs of the church and the papal household, which require urgent attention. Finally, it is in the consideration of God and the things which are above that Eugene will find his homeland.

Although the context of ministry has changed considerably from the time of either Gregory or Bernard, many of the demands and the dangers of pastoral office have remained the same: self-aggrandizement and the temptation to indispensability still threaten to subvert ministry; lack of time for prayer and reflection causes activity to replace care; and disregard for the complexities of human nature and the diversity of pastoral contexts makes for impersonal, ineffective pastoral relationships. Reflection on the classic literature of pastoral care and counseling may assist the minister in the self-knowledge, care of self, and compassionate understanding of others that is the necessary foundation of any ministry that hopes to be humane, helpful, and genuinely Christian.

Bibliography. History and Literature: W. Clebsch and C. Jaekle, *Pastoral Care in Historical Perspective* (1964). R. Duffy, *A Roman Catholic Theology of Pastoral Care* (1983). K. Leech, *Soul Friend* (1977), 34–89. J. T. McNeill, *A History of the Cure of Souls* (1951). T. Oden, *Care of Souls in the Classic Tradition* (1984). Primary Sources: Aelred de Rievaulx, *Spiritual Friendship*, Cistercian Fathers Series 5 (1974). St. Ambrose, *On the Duties of the Clergy*, in *Saint Ambrose, Select Works*, Nicene and Post-Nicene Fathers 10 (2d ed., 1969); *The Mysteries, On the Sacraments*, in *Saint Ambrose, Theological and Dogmatic Works*, Fathers of the Church 44 (1963). St. Augustine, *Confessions*, (ET 1961); *First Catechetical Instruction*, Ancient Christian Writers 2 (1962). Bernard of Clairvaux, *Five Books on Consideration*, Cistercian Fathers Series 37 (1976). J. Cassian, "Conferences," in *Western Asceticism*, Library of Christian Classics 12 (1958). Pope Gregory the Great, *Pastoral Care*, Ancient Christian Writers 11 (1950). Francis de Sales, *Introduction to the Devout Life* (ET 1950). D. Fleming, S.J., *The Spiritual Exercises of St. Ignatius: A Literal Translation and a Contemporary Reading* (1978). Jerome, *Letters*, in *St. Jerome, Select Works*, Nicene and Post-Nicene Fathers 6, 2d series (2d ed. 1954). *Medieval Handbooks of Penance*, Records of Civilization 29 (1938). Tertullian, *On Penitence* and *On Purity* in *Tertullian, Treatises on Penance*, Ancient Christian Writers 28 (1959); *On Patience*, in *The Writings of Tertullian*, The Ante-Nicene Fathers 3 (rep. 1980).

F. CARDMAN

PASTORAL THEOLOGY, ROMAN CATHOLIC; PASTORALIA; ROMAN CATHOLIC PASTORAL CARE. *See also* PASTORAL CARE (History, Traditions, and Definitions). *Compare* JEWISH LITERATURE IN CARE AND COUNSELING. *Biography:* AMBROSE OF MILAN; AUGUSTINE OF HIPPO; BERNARD OF CLAIRVAUX; FRANCIS DE SALES; GREGORY THE GREAT; IGNATIUS OF LOYOLA; TERTULLIAN OF CARTHAGE.

CLASSICAL CONDITIONING. *See* CONDITIONING.

CLASSICAL PSYCHOLOGY. *See* EARLY CHURCH, PASTORAL CARE AND COUNSELING IN; PHILOSOPHY AND PSYCHOLOGY, WESTERN.

CLEMENT OF ALEXANDRIA, ST. *See* EARLY CHURCH, PASTORAL CARE AND COUNSELING IN; LITERATURE, DEVOTIONAL.

CLERGY, EMPIRICAL STUDIES OF. Research studies which employ measures of observable or recorded data provided by or about clergy whose primary focus of occupational responsibility is an organized parish or congregation meeting regularly for worship in a specific geographical locality. Not included are studies of seminarians or of clergy serving specialized ministries such as campus ministers, foreign missionaries, pastoral counselors, teachers, or ecclesiastical administrators.

The most complete bibliography of studies of all kinds of clergy, published in 1965 (Menges and Dittes) with a supplement in 1967 (Menges), summarized close to a thousand studies. This article is based upon an initial review of more than four hundred reports and abstracts but refers to only a limited number of the studies. Included are those which appear representative of the categories employed or which seem especially significant.

1. Three Approaches to Defining Ministry. Three paths have been taken to define ministry through the use of empirical research. Each path has led to a different definition.

a. Functional definition. In 1934 May assembled about a thousand statements of activities of clergy and through content analysis identified a limited number of categories. Twenty years later Blizzard followed a similar approach and suggested a set of six practitioner roles: preacher, pastor, teacher, priest, administrator, and organizer. In 1973 Nelson *et al.* used factor analysis to define five integrative roles which were judged to comprise the whole of the pastor's work: traditional (including evangelism, preaching, and shepherding), counseling, administration, community problem-solving, and Christian education. Similar sets of factors, roles, or functions have been prepared for separate denominations, specifically Roman Catholic and Lutheran. An additional manner of categorizing the pastoral task was employed by Webb and Hultgren who used ratings by clergy of all specialties to validate the factor analysis of seminarians' interests. Ten roles were identified: counselor, administrator, teacher, scholar, evangelist, spiritual guide, preacher, reformer, priest, and musician.

b. Personal definition. The major example of the second path began with both personal and task-oriented competencies which were expected to lead to effective or ineffective ministry. The study, carried out under the sponsorship of the Association of Theological Schools (ATS), which represented Protestant, Roman Catholic, and Jewish denominational groups, elicited eleven second-order factors or themes of ministry (Schuller *et al.*, 1975). Six involved an orientation to content areas of ministry for functioning as a pastor: (1) community and world, (2) spiritual concerns and personal faith commitment, (3) congregation development through worship and liturgy, (4) persons experiencing stress, (5) a priestly-sacramental ministry, and (6) denominational awareness and loyalty. Four referred to styles of ministry: (1) an open, affirming style, (2) a legalistic, docetic privatism, (3) congregational leadership, and (4) theologian in life and thought. The last referred to characteristics which would disqualify a person as a pastor. As with the functional definition similar studies have been conducted for United Methodists, Lutherans, and a group of Roman Catholic and Protestant clergy.

c. Theological definition. The third approach is illustrated first by the work of Longino and Hadden who examined the religious beliefs of 7,443 parish clergy from six major Protestant denominations. They identified a unidimensional structure of belief among the clergy portrayed by a continuum from a literal to a demythological interpretation of the faith. A similar continuum seems to exist among Jewish rabbis.

J. Carroll's study in 1971 found that clergy could be separated into three groups arranged along a theological continuum according to distinct types of seminaries attended. Blanchard later (1981) showed that Carroll's graduate school seminaries produced change-oriented pastors, the religious community type produced an orientation toward the local parish, and the vocational school seminaries produced a style of ministry between the other two. Further substantiation for the thesis that ministerial practice is associated with type of seminary training or denominational and theological emphasis is

offered by the results of the ATS Readiness for Ministry study (Schuller *et al.*, 1980) which revealed distinctive profiles of ministerial competencies and characteristics for fourteen individual denominational groups.

2. Behavior Associated with Separate Functions. Only four functions have been studied with more than a slight degree of interest. Counseling has received the greatest share of attention. The other three roles are community and social involvement, administration-leadership, and preaching.

a. Community and social involvement. The social action function of the clergy ranges from participation in civic and community groups and activities to oral and behavioral protest about major social problems.

An analysis of data obtained in 1952 from Episcopalian clergy and laity led Glock *et al.* to assert the importance of challenging the church toward social action rather than restricting it only to providing comfort in the stresses of life and to the assurance of an everlasting existence. After reviewing results of a study of a random sample of ten thousand clergy among six major Protestant denominations, Hadden (1969) predicted a forthcoming crisis because of lay opposition to the clergy's involvement in civil rights and other issues. Strommen *et al.* (1972), however, found no such wide diversity among Lutherans in beliefs, practices or social values.

In a nationwide survey of Presbyterian clergy and laity Hoge *et al.* (1978) located support for Hadden's crisis statement when they found disagreement between the two groups on the use of evangelism or social involvement as the form of mission and outreach beyond the local congregation. Further study revealed, however, that the divisions lay not between the minister and laity, but along theological lines in both groups. Quinley (1969) had also found that activist clergy in the Vietnam War debate were more liberal theologically and politically than their counterparts. Nelsen *et al.* (1973) affirmed the use of political viewpoint as a good predictor of protest, and both Nelsen *et al.* and Hoge *et al.* referred in addition to an ideological commitment to a humanistic Christianity as a prime characteristic of the pastor involved in social action.

Stark *et al.* (1971) tried to identify more basic reasons why a sample of Protestant ministers from nine major denominations in California spoke out from pulpits on social issues or refrained from doing so. Religious convictions again stood out as the major factor, especially for conservative clergy who emphasized the importance of individual salvation as the solution for social ills.

In addition to the theological, political and ideological variables, another factor has been associated with the lack of protest involvement. Campbell and Pettigrew's study of Little Rock pastors at the time of the integration crisis in that city showed that the expectations of parishioners opposed to integration kept some pastors from following their own inclinations.

b. Preaching. Difficulty in objective assessment has probably hampered the initiation of empirical research studies on preaching. Sermon topical content was a focus of the research by Stark *et al.* referred to above in the social action area. Dobbins found that pastors who included material related to counseling in their sermons also tended to spend more time in counseling each week than did other clergy. Other studies have focused on the pastor's self-concept and nonverbal communication.

c. Administration-leadership. Among the few research studies in this area Ashbrook's work is probably the most distinctive. He found that behavior of leaders who were sensitive to people and also skillful in facilitating their work was positively associated with criteria of effectiveness for the organization.

d. Other functions. Limited empirical investigation has been completed in other areas including evangelism, personal-spiritual development, teaching, and work with the mentally retarded.

3. Characteristics of Pastors. Many empirical studies of pastors deal with personal and demographic characteristics including beliefs and attitudes.

a. Demographic and background data. Most studies provide in connection with their investigations some demographic data, such as age, education, length of experience, parish location, and size. Statistical compilations are provided by many denominations in separate publications and by individuals for select groups such as rural clergy, black pastors, and diocesan priests. The National Council of Churches has also sponsored more ambitious studies crossing denominational lines.

b. Personality and interest patterns. Use of the *Myers-Briggs Type Indicator* among clergy has revealed a ministerial personality common to a plurality of pastors. It is an extroverted, feeling type that evidences warmth, is best at jobs that deal with people, likes to have matters settled and decided, and exhibits loyalty to respected institutions and causes. The pattern has appeared in several studies including those of Protestant clergy, Jewish rabbis, United Church of Christ ministers and Lutherans.

Lenski (1963) found that Roman Catholic clergy were more inclined than Protestants to stress the importance of obedience to authority in contrast with emphasizing intellectual autonomy.

In the area of interests special scales have been developed for Roman Catholics and Lutherans. Webb's *Inventory of Religious Activities and Interests* has proved to be a significant contribution to pastoral research.

c. Satisfaction, stress, and career change. No common picture of satisfaction and dissatisfaction among clergy appears across the studies dealing with this factor. However, there does appear to be some agreement in the significance of low pay, inadequate promotion opportunities, and lack of support and adequate supervision as characteristics of dissatisfaction. Mills and Hesser suggest that such factors become more serious stress items as clergy subjectively perceive them as being unjust.

Hoge *et al.* (1981) related the concept of clergy satisfaction to a vocational commitment to one's present pastorate and to ministry in general. They found that the clarity with which pastors discern expectations from their parishioners and others in terms of roles rather than a myriad of tasks is significantly correlated with present vocational commitment. Both clarity and lack of conflict (among expectations from self, congregation and denomination) are important for general vocational commitment. The findings of M. Johnson *et al.* and of Gleason, both of whom refer to the proliferation of activities as a

determinant of stress, would appear to support the need for clarity of roles.

Satisfaction, dissatisfaction, and stress serve also as overarching concepts which affect a decision for career change. Factors used in deciding about projected changes include materialistic reasons of finding an attractive church of a larger size (Nelsen and Everett) and a higher offered salary (Mitchell), as well as evidence of a previous or projected fruitful ministry (Mills).

Personal role conflicts, clergy-lay disagreements on social action, and the cost of celibacy among Roman Catholics have been additional factors. Other studies of career change have concentrated upon individual denominations and attempted to identify characteristics of persisters and of those who left the ministry (United Church of Christ, Southern Baptist, Roman Catholic, Episcopalian, United Methodist, Church of God, Lutheran, Unitarian, and United Presbyterian).

The most comprehensive study of career development among clergy was completed by Hall and Schneider (1973) with Roman Catholic priests of the Hartford, Connecticut, diocese. They found that current satisfaction and performance, along with one's future career development, are significantly affected by organizational factors which include work challenge, autonomy, and supervisory behavior.

d. Beliefs, attitudes and values. In several major surveys of the clergy, attitudes toward various ecclesiastical and social issues have been identified, such as priests' freedom to marry (Fichter) and economic and political values (Lenski). Other attitudes have also been investigated, including euthanasia, death education, preschool children, ageism, family functioning, sex stereotyping, and the use of the courts.

Of greater significance to researchers seems to have been the relationship between theology and certain attitudes or values. Stark *et al.* revealed a clear line between orthodoxy and anti-Semitism. Driedger showed that doctrinal conservatives with other-worldly emphases favored control of personal and public morality while doctrinal liberals who portrayed a this-worldly view were concerned chiefly with civil liberty.

In his survey of Methodist and Baptist pastors in Oregon, B. Johnson (1966, 1967) noted a distinct relationship between liberal theology and a liberal stance on various public issues. However, conservatives held varying positions on the same issues. To explain his findings he suggested that liberals may be more inclined than conservatives to invest social issues with religious significance and thus he maintained distinct liberal social views.

Tygart's study supported Johnson's conclusions but suggested further that though theological beliefs may stimulate initial socio-political attitudes and actions, one's political ideology tends to strengthen and direct the type and degree of involvement. Hammond *et al.* introduced the concept of clergy authority as another influencing factor. They found that the type of authority assumed by the clergy (legal, pragmatic, or charismatic) significantly affected formality in the church, liberal social attitudes, social involvement, and professional involvement. Legal authority is derived from the pastor's training and is recognized by ordination. According to the pragmatic type the pastor feels that authority must be demonstrated regularly, while a charismatic authority is linked with a divine calling.

e. Unique groups of clergy. Demographic data about women clergy have been prepared by the National Council of Churches. The few studies available suggest an increasing acceptance but little evidence for their increased professionalization (Royle; Bock). According to Bradshaw, clergy who have suffered psychological breakdown and have obtained treatment have used the ministerial role to satisfy immature needs and did not employ adequate means to cope with various stresses without great psychic cost. Other clergy groups studied include those in a multiple staff ministry, clergy couples, divorced clergy, and retired clergy.

4. Characteristics of Effective Pastors. At least twenty studies have been completed which have obtained ratings of pastoral performance. Most have used global or overall measures while a few have concentrated on specific functions in the ministry.

a. Global effectiveness. Although a number of situational variables and background or experiential characteristics have been investigated, only higher academic achievement in college and seminary (Nauss, 1974a) and a comparatively low degree of mobility, especially with only a few pastorates of brief tenure (Jackson; Nauss, 1974b), seem characteristic of the more effective clergy.

Included among the personality and skill variables with a higher degree characteristic of effectiveness than for satisfactory performance are: productive energy (Jackson), concern for people (Douglas, Jackson), desire for and expression of autonomy (Dyble), leadership skills (Douglas; Jackson; Ashbrook; Harris; Nauss, 1973), skills of communication (Dyble; Benson and Tatara), a theoretical orientation; (Dyble), satisfaction with work in a local parish (Ashbrook), emotional stability (Harrower; D. Carroll) and an extroverted trait (Jackson; Nauss, 1973).

b. Effectiveness according to function. The decision to investigate pastoral effectiveness according to separate functions was based in part upon the recognition that more clergy would likely display high levels of performance in one or several functions than in all the tasks of ministry. Rader and Benton have both found distinct characteristics among pastors effective in their counseling or pastoral care function. Unique profiles in each of the functions assessed have been found among effective United Methodist, United Presbyterian, and Lutheran clergy (Cochran; Dyble; Nauss, 1983). Characteristics that appear in each of the different function groups are a positive viewpoint or attitude, use of feedback, high motivation related to job dimensions, and high satisfaction (Nauss, 1983).

5. Means Used To Effect Change in Pastors. Many clergy along with their sponsoring church bodies are usually very inclined to develop ways in which they can improve or develop their knowledge and skill. Surveys of clergy needs which would serve as topics for continuing education have been conducted in a number of different denominations and local groups.

Some studies have also been conducted which use pre- and post-test measures to assess particular methods of effecting change. Higgins and Dittes were able to reduce differences of role expectation between clergy and laity in two churches through open discussions. Methods used in other studies include training programs in alcoholism, use of a booklet on management procedures, a consultation program in bereavement ministry, a mass media course, a workshop on the elderly, special learning activity projects, and a seminar for psychological and theological growth.

The most frequently employed means of effecting change has been Clinical Pastoral Education. Measured changes have occurred in helping clergy become more positive and less defensive (Thomas *et al.*), developing and maintaining a desire for self-actualization (Geary), and developing an open, free, and accepting style of authority (Beech).

6. Conclusion. Pastoral styles seem to vary a great deal. How may this variety be described and explained? Five significant variables have arisen through the empirical research of the past half century: denominational affiliation, theological beliefs, source and type of pastoral authority, personality, and certain organizational conditions. It is possible that these factors, together with other situational variables, may lead to specific styles, though the research designs that have been employed in the past and their results have not offered a causal connection.

Characteristics of the various levels of performance, except for the effective level, have not been clearly identified. Past empirical studies suggest that perceiving one's ministry in terms of random activities or generalized functions may be one such characteristic. In addition to clarifying the performance levels, future research will likely focus on different areas and styles of ministerial service as well as many of those which have to date received inadequate attention.

Bibliography. J. Ashbrook, "Ministerial Leadership in Church Organization," *Ministry Studies*, 1 (1967), 5–32. L. Beech, "Supervision in Pastoral Care and Counseling," *J. of Pastoral Care*, 24 (1970), 233–9. J. Benton, "Perceptual Characteristics of Episcopal Pastors," Ph.D. Diss. (1964), University Microfilms, vol. 25, 7, 3963. D. Blanchard, "Seminary Effects on Professional Role Orientations," *Review of Religious Research*, 22 (1981), 346–61. S. Blizzard, "The Minister's Dilemma," *Christian Century* 25, (1956), 508–09. E. Bock, "The Female Clergy: A Case of Professional Marginality," *American J. of Sociology*, 72 (1967), 531–9. S. Bradshaw, "Ministers in Trouble," *J. of Pastoral Care*, 31 (1977), 230–42. E. Campbell and T. Pettigrew, "Racial and Moral Crisis," *American J. of Sociology*, 64 (1959), 509–16. D. Carroll, "A Follow-up Study of Psychological Assessment," in W. Bier, ed., *Psychological Testing for Ministerial Selection* (1970), pp. 159–80; "Structural Effects of Professional Schools on Professional Socialization," *Social Forces* (1971), 61–74. J. Cochran, "A Study to Identify Critical Elements Associated with Effective and Ineffective Behaviors of United Methodist Ministers," *Dissertation Abstracts* 43 (1982), 398–9. A. R. Dobbins, "The Function of the Sermon in the Pastor's Role as Counselor," *Dissertation Abstracts,* 31 (1971), 6341–2. A. W. Douglas, "Predicting Ministerial Effectiveness," Ph.D. Dissertation, Harvard University (1957). L. Driedger, "Doctrinal Belief: A Major Factor in the Differential Perception of Social Issues," *Sociology Quarterly*, 15 (1974), 66–80. J. Dyble, "Report to Ad Hoc Ministry, Study Committee," unpubl. MS., Office of Research, Board of Education, United Presbyterian Church, U.S.A. (1972). J. Fichter, *America's Forgotten Priests* (1968). T. Geary, "Personal Growth in CPE," *J. of Pastoral*

Care, 31 (1977), 12–17. J. Gleason, "Perception of Stress Among Clergy and Their Spouses," *J. of Pastoral Care,* 31 (1977), 248 – 51. C. Glock, B. Ringer, and E. Babbie, *To Comfort and To Challenge* (1967). J. Hadden, *The Gathering Storm* (1969). D. Hall and B. Schneider, *Organizational Climates and Careers* (1973). P. Hammond, L. Salinas, and D. Sloane, "Types of Clergy Authority," *J. for the Scientific Study of Religion* (1978), 241–53. W. Harris, "The Use of Selected Leadership, Personality, Motivational, and Demographic Variables in the Identification of Successful Ministers," *Dissertation Abstracts,* 33 (1973), 9, 4833. A. M. Harrover, "Mental Health Potential and Success in the Ministry," *J. of Religion and Health,* 4 (1963), 30 – 58. P. Higgins and J. Dittes, "Change in Laymen's Expectations of the Minister's Roles," *Ministry Studies* 2 (1968), 5–23. D. Hoge, E. Perry, and G. Klever, "Theology As a Source of Disagreement about Protestant Church Goals and Priorities," *Review of Religious Research,* 19 (1978), 116 – 38. D. Hoge, J. Dyble, and D. Polk, "Influence of Role Preference and Role Clarity on Vocational Commitment of Protestant Ministers," *Sociological Analysis* 1:42 (1981), 1–16. D. Jackson, "Factors Differentiating between Effective and Ineffective Methodist Ministers," Ph.D. Diss. (1955), University Microfilms, vol. 15 (2), 2320. B. Johnson, "Theology and Party Preference among Protestant Clergymen," *American Sociological Review,* 31 (1966), 200 – 8. B. Johnson, "Theology and the Position of Pastors on Public Issues," *American Sociological Review* 23, (1967), 433 – 42. M. Johnson, H. Lohr, J. Wagner, and W. Barge, *The Relationship Between Pastors' Effectiveness and Satisfaction* (1975). G. Lenski, *The Religious Factor* (1963). C. Longino and J. Hadden, "Dimensionality of Belief Among Mainstream Protestant Clergy," *Social Forces,* 55 (1976), 30 – 42. M. May, "The Profession of the Ministry," in *The Education of American Ministers* vol. 2, (1934). R. Menges, "Studies of Clergymen: Abstracts of Research, Supplement I," *Ministry Studies,* 1 (1967), 5–79. R. Menges and J. Dittes, *Psychological Studies of Clergymen* (1965). E. Mills, "Career Change in the Protestant Ministry," *Ministry Studies,* 3 (1969), 5–21. E. Mills and G. Hesser, "A Contemporary Portrait of Clergymen," in G. Bucher and P. Hill, eds., *Confusion and Hope* (1974), pp. 17–31. H. N. Malony, *Current Perspectives in the Psychology of Religion* (1977); "Ministerial Effectiveness: A Review of Recent Research," *Pastoral Psychology,* 33 (1984), 96 – 104. R. Mitchell, "Polity, Church Attractiveness, and Ministers' Careers," *J. for the Scientific Study of Religion,* 5 (1966), 241–58. A. Nauss, "Ministerial Effectiveness Research: Past and Future." *Concordia Seminary Studies* (1974a); "The Relation of Pastoral Mobility to Effectiveness," *Review of Religious Research,* 15 (1974b), 80 – 6; "Seven Profiles of Effective Ministers," *Review of Religious Research,* 24 (1983), 334 – 46. H. Nelsen, R. Yokley, and T. Madron, "Ministerial Roles and Social Action Stance," *American Sociological Review,* 38 (1973), 375–86. H. Nelsen and R. Everett, "Impact of Church Size on Clergy Role and Career," *Review of Religious Research,* 18 (1976), 62–73. H. Quinley, "Hawks and Doves among the Clergy," *Ministry Studies,* 3 (1969), 5–20. B. Rader, "Pastoral Care Functioning," *Ministry Studies,* 3 (1969), 18 – 27. M. Royle, "Women Pastors: What Happens After Placement?" *Review of Religious Research,* 24 (1982), 116 – 26. D. Schuller, M. Brekke, and M. Strommen, "Criteria," in *Readiness for Ministry* (1975). I. D. Schuller, M. Brekke, and M. Strommen, eds., *Ministry in America* (1980). R. Stark, *et al., Wayward Shepherds* (1971). M. Strommen, et al., *A Study of Generations* (1972). J. Thomas, L. Stein, and M. Klein, "A Comparative Evaluation of Changes in Basic Clinical Pastoral Education Students," *J. of Pastoral Care,* 36 (1982), 181–93. C. Tygart, "The Role of Theology Among Other 'Belief' Variables for Clergy Civil Rights Activism," *Review of Religious Research,* 18 (1977), 271–78. S. Webb, *An Inventory of Religious Activities and Interests* (1968) Education Testing Services in Atlanta, *Ministry Inventories:* Tests in Print. S. Webb and D. Hultgren, "Differentiation of Clergy Subgroups on the Basis of Vocational Interests," *J. for the Scientific Study of Religion,* 12 (1973), 311–24.

A. NAUSS

RABBIS, *or* RELIGIOUS, EMPIRICAL STUDIES OF; THEOLOGICAL STUDENTS, EVALUATION AND EMPIRICAL STUDIES OF. *Compare* PERSONHOOD OF THE PASTOR, SIGNIFICANCE OF; PSYCHOLOGY OF RELIGION (Empirical Studies, Methods, and Problems).

CLERGY, MARRIAGE, FAMILY, AND DIVORCE OF. *See* DIVORCE, *or* MARRIAGE AND FAMILY, PASTOR'S.

CLERGY COUPLES.

A married couple in which both the wife and husband are ordained clergy. The term has become an umbrella term for many life experiences and styles of ministry. Some clergy couples are serving as co-pastors of a church or parish. Some are serving as senior pastor and associate pastor. Others are serving separate parishes. Some situations find one spouse serving a church and the other serving in a specialized ministry such as chaplaincy or pastoral counseling. Some clergy couples are even ordained in different denominations. Some reside in one parsonage or manse; others in two. Some live in the same proximity of each other; others have positions which require them to live great distances apart.

1. **Concerns.** Any marriage requires adjustment, give and take, and interpersonal sensitivity in order to deal with the many stress situations which arise. There are particular stresses when one person is clergy, but when two clergy persons are married, the stress and adjustments are multiplied; add to this the possibility of children or other family members and it can become an almost explosive situation.

Arranging schedules of two busy persons, with inevitable disruptions, can be difficult. If the two are in a co-pastorate this might be lessened, but in the case of a couple serving different churches or in two different positions or locations, scheduling becomes very complex. The problems include finding time for communication, for meals, for time together, for leisure, for family responsibilities, and simply to be alone.

Clergy couples, above all, must learn to be trusting and flexible and to respect each other's calling and responsibilities. It is imperative to make time to check out each other's commitments, reserve personal and family space, preserve personal time for each individual's needs, and make a real effort to abide by decisions and plans jointly agreed upon. Clergy couples need to be flexible to crises, unexpected problems, interruptions, and unscheduled events such as crisis counseling and funerals. Respecting one another's commitments, even if not fully comprehended, is necessary for mutual support and sensitivity.

Personal time together is very important but it often must be scheduled. Couples should find it helpful and meaningful to schedule dinner dates, lunches, concerts, theatres, or just time to "get away from it all" by getting into the car, parking in the shade, talking, laughing, and listening—no phone, no interruptions, and no one around. Also, short trips can be planned, with or without the children.

Family and children add another dimension of concern to the role and work of clergy couples. There is always the tension in ministers' families of how much their children should be involved in the "work" of the church; it adds yet another dimension when both mother and father are clergy. Time must be set aside for the children. However, if clergy couples can take time to relate to each other, and relate their needs and concerns to church authorities, the authorities will generally be sensitive to their needs. There are, nonetheless, exceptions to this statement. Many church authorities continue to have difficulty accepting women who are ordained, and even more difficulty with ordination of a woman spouse of an ordained clergy person. Some church persons simply cannot accept the "preacher's wife" as clergy. They just do not "fit the role"—the role that has often been stereotyped: the preacher's wife who always plays the piano, prays, or serves tea. In the author's experience, women who offer the most resistance to women clergy and the women of clergy couples, are usually the non-ordained wives of clergy.

Another concern of clergy couples is location or appointment. There are few churches that have full-time co-pastorates or associates where the couple can serve together, especially with both receiving a respectable, full-time salary. Equally difficult is to find two churches that are near enough to each other. If one of the pastors is more skilled than the other, or (in the appointment process of some denominations) if one pastor should be moved and the other not moved, there is the question of where the two may live. If there are school-age children, where they attend school is also an issue. In some denominations clergy couples who choose to serve one church together may incur some loss in salary, pensions, and medical benefits because one or the other of the spouses is not considered "full time."

2. **Rewards.** Although the concerns and problems associated with clergy couples are many, and will become increasingly so as the number of clergy couples increases, there are many rewards and advantages in being a clergy couple. Even some of the "concerns" may also be benefits. Housing, for example, may be such that a couple might be able to invest in some equity if one or both are receiving a housing allowance. Also, both spouses can work together and have their own time, with more flexibility of scheduling than might be possible if one spouse was in another profession. This can also at times be helpful in the raising of children. Schedules may be more easily adjusted when one spouse can be at home while the other is engaged in pastoral duties. Also, there is some time for each person to be creative in his or her own way, each supporting the other, ultimately being more effective in the local church.

The new phenomenon of clergy couples is a blessing as well as a challenge to the church. Clergy couples bring a new expression of incarnational, covenantal theology in their separate or related ministries. New possibilities in ministry are emerging from clergy couples, and fulfilling marriages are evolving from this partnership. When couples pursue visions of servanthood and love with a colleague and partner, new possibilities of service and fulfillment come into view, even though there are still many personal, practical, and institutional issues to be worked through.

Bibliography. R. L. and M. C. Detrick, "Marriages of Two Clergy-Persons," *Pastoral Psychology,* 30 (1982), 170–8. D. C. Houts, "Marriage Counseling with Clergy Couples," *Pastoral Psychology,* 30 (1982), 141–50. D. R. and V. C. Mace, "Marriage enrichment for clergy couples" *Pastoral Psychology,* 30 (1982), 151–9. E. M. Rallings and D. J. Pratto, *Two-Clergy Marriages: A Special Case of Dual Careers* (1984). J. P. and N. J. von Lackum, *A Report on Clergy Couples,* National Council of Churches (1979).

M. J. ZIMMERLI
R. ZIMMERLI

DUAL CAREER MARRIAGE. *Compare* MARRIAGE AND FAMILY LIFE, PASTOR'S.

CLERGY/LAITY DISTINCTION. *See* ECCLESIOLOGY; MINISTRY.

CLIENT (Terminology). *See* COUNSELEE/CLIENT/PARISHIONER TERMINOLOGY.

CLIENT-CENTERED THERAPY. A theory and method of constructive personality change developed by Carl R. Rogers. Originally named nondirective counseling, it first came into professional view during the early 1940s. In 1951 Rogers changed the name to client-centered therapy (CCT) to emphasize a positive focus on human capacities (Rogers, 1951). In 1974 the name was changed to person-centered therapy (Meador and Rogers, 1984) but the client-centered or Rogerian designation has retained its popular usage.

1. **Basic Focus and Assumptions.** Rogers has identified CCT with the so-called "third force" in psychology, or "humanistic psychology." Unlike psychoanalysis, CCT holds an optimistic view of human personality and focuses on present rather than past experience; unlike behaviorism, it investigates the inner experience of persons rather than observable behavior, and holds that behavioral change evolves from within the individual rather than through the manipulation of external contingencies.

Rogers's theory of personality assumes that (1) human beings are experiencing beings; (2) behavior can be understood only from a person's internal frame of reference; (3) the value of life resides in the present; (4) humans are innately good and trustworthy; (5) humans tend toward self-actualization; (6) deep relationships are a basic human need; (7) growth occurs through self-discovery; (8) people do the best thing possible when given the right conditions; and (9) the theory applies to all people. Rogers was aware that human beings are capable of great evil, hostility, and self-alienation, but believed that these propensities were the result of negative "conditions of worth" imposed on children by family and society, not essential or inevitable attributes of personality.

2. **Theory of Therapeutic Change.** The central thesis of CCT states that if the therapist has certain interdependent attitudes—namely, congruence, unconditional positive regard, and empathic understanding—then

growth will occur in the client. Rogers calls these attitudes "necessary and sufficient" conditions of therapeutic personality change (Rogers, 1957) and holds that if these conditions are present, therapeutic change will invariably occur.

Congruence, or genuineness, denotes the ability of therapists to be fully self-aware and open to their own inner experiencing. *Empathic understanding* denotes the ability of therapists to immerse themselves in the feeling world of their clients and effectively communicate their understanding back to the client. *Unconditional positive regard,* a nonpossessive caring or acceptance of the client's individuality, reflects the therapist's trust in the actualizing process and belief in the client's self-discovery of personal resources. Thus, eschewing rigid methodology or techniques, CCT finds in the personal qualities of the therapist the impetus for client growth.

3. Key Concepts. Several concepts in CCT theory are central for understanding the nature of therapeutic process and the gains that can be achieved in therapy. *Self-concept* refers to one's perception of oneself. *Self-experience* refers to one's actual psychological experiences, regardless of self-concept. *Ideal self* refers to the self-concept one would most like to possess. Psychological problems derive from incongruence between the perceived (or "symbolized") self and actual self-experience, accompanied by tension and internal confusion, and imposed on the individual by family and society: children learn to falsify the symbolizing of their own experience in order to maintain parental love and protection.

Therapy seeks to allow the self-concept to represent more accurately the individual's self-experience through an experience of unconditional positive regard which allows greater freedom for self-actualization, more full and accurate awareness of one's experiencing, and thus fuller psychological functioning (Rogers, 1961). The goal of therapy is therefore the fully functioning person—the person who symbolizes his or her own experiencing accurately and therefore lives in a way that most fully expresses and develops his or her potential as a human being while mutually supporting such growth in others.

A number of reflective critiques are available ranging from agreement to rejection of Rogers's views, and from critical scholarship to pejorative confrontation and polemic. Rogers himself, however, has insisted on the verifiability of his approach via scientific research (C. R. Rogers, E. T. Gendlin, D. J. Kiesler, and C. B. Truax, 1967), and many of his contemporary followers continue to emphasize the need for empirical research to demonstrate the effectiveness of the person-centered approach to counseling, to psychotherapy, and to family, social, and cultural change (R. Levant and J. M. Shilien, 1984). Theological critiques have become a part of the pastoral care and counseling literature (e.g., T. Oden, 1956; D. Browning, 1987).

Bibliography. D. Browning, *Religious Thought in the Modern Psychologies* (1987). R. Fuller, "Carl Rogers, Religion and the Role of Psychology in American Culture," *Humanistic Psychology* 22 (1982), 21–32. F. Greve, "Client-Centered Therapy," in M. Gilbert and R. Brock, eds., *The Holy Spirit and Counseling* (1985). R. F. Levant and J. M. Shlien, eds., *Client-Centered Therapy and the Person-Centered Approach: New Directions in Theory, Research, and Practice* (1984). B. Meador and C. Rogers,

"Person-Centered Therapy," in R. Corsini, ed., *Current Psychotherapies* (3d ed., 1984). T. C. Oden, *Kerygma and Counseling* (1966). C. R. Rogers, "A Theory of Therapy, Personality, and Interpersonal Relationships as Developed in the Client-Centered Framework," in S. Kock, ed., *Psychology, A Study of a Science,* vol. 3 (1959); *Counseling and Psychotherapy* (1942); *Client-Centered Therapy* (1951); "The Necessary and Sufficient Conditions of Therapeutic Personality Change," *J. of Consulting Psychology,* 21 (1957), 95–103. C. R. Rogers, *et al., The Therapeutic Relationship and Its Impact: A Study of Psychotherapy with Schizophrenics* (1967).

C. R. RIDLEY

HUMANISTIC PSYCHOTHERAPIES; PHENOMENOLOGICAL PSYCHOLOGY AND PSYCHOTHERAPY; PSYCHOTHERAPY; SELF PSYCHOLOGIES. *See also* INTERNAL FRAME OF REFERENCE. *Biography:* ROGERS.

CLINEBELL, HOWARD (1922–). An internationally recognized author, teacher, leader, pastor, counselor, supervisor, and consultant in the field of pastoral psychology. Since 1959 he has been professor (now emeritus) of pastoral psychology and counseling at the School of Theology at Claremont, California. His major clinical and academic training was received at DePauw University (B.A.), Garrett Theological Seminary (B.D.), William A. White Institute (Certificate of Applied Psychiatry for Ministry), and Columbia University (Ph.D., Psychology of Religion). He has written and/or edited over thirty books and fifty articles, several of these with his wife, Charlotte Ellen.

Clinebell has profoundly shaped the growth of contemporary pastoral psychology. He was the first president of the American Association of Pastoral Counselors. His book *Basic Types of Pastoral Counseling* (1966, revised 1984), perhaps the most widely used seminary textbook for pastoral counseling, helped expand the scope of pastoral approaches from individual/intrapsychic dynamics and nondirective methods to a more inclusive focus on interpersonal dynamics and more directive human potentials approaches.

Clinebell's emphasis on human potential—the aspirations, possibilities, and strengths of the human soul and psyche—has led him to develop a "Growth Counseling" approach to actualizing and liberating human life. In the field of pastoral psychotherapy, this "Growth Counseling" orientation has been one of the few to address human development in relation to feminist, social, political, and global consciousness raising. Clinebell's lifestyle as well as his pastoral theory, has embodied a creative zest for embracing human thoughts, emotions, actions, spirituality, and relationships in a wholistic way.

C. M. MENDENHALL, III

PASTORAL CARE MOVEMENT; PASTORAL COUNSELING MOVEMENT.

CLINICAL PASTORAL EDUCATION (CPE). CPE is professional education for ministry which brings theological students, ordained clergy, members of religious orders, and qualified laypersons into supervised encounter with living human documents in order to develop their pastoral identity, interpersonal competence, and spirituality; the skills of pastoral assessment, inter-professional collaboration, group leadership, pastoral care and counseling; and pastoral theological reflection.

Emerging in the 1920s, CPE began in a search for the laws of the spiritual life adequate for times of personal crisis. Drawn to the methods of medical education, psychology, and social work, and reacting against the limitations of classical theological education, the founders launched an educational innovation that has significantly influenced pastoral ministry both in parishes and in mental and general hospitals, prisons, social agencies, and campuses. It has also helped to move theological schools toward a professional model of education and stimulated the emergence of associations of pastoral supervisors in many countries of the world.

1. History *a. Beginnings 1923–1944.* CPE began in a search for religious meaning in personal crises requiring hospitalization and for principles of social engineering relevant to urban problems of poverty and family disintegration. CPE began in a mental hospital in Worcester, Mass., (1925), and almost simultaneously in a cluster of social service agencies in Cincinnati, Ohio, (1927). The Massachusetts General Hospital in Boston hosted the first CPE program in a general hospital (1930).

The founders, the Rev. Anton T. Boisen of Worcester, Mass., William S. Keller, M.D. of Cincinnati, and Richard C. Cabot, M.D. of Boston adapted the methods of professional education in psychiatry, social work, and medicine respectively. Organizations fostering CPE as an educational innovation for theological students and ministers were formed in Boston on January 21, 1930, and in Cincinnati in 1927.

During the 1930s the Council for Clinical Training developed standards for training and for the pastoral supervision of trainees in CPE. Helen Flanders Dunbar, M.D., and the Rev. Seward Hiltner established a primary identity with theological education and ecumenical Christianity. Chaplain supervisors, such as the Rev. Russell L. Dicks, developed new methods, particularly the "verbatim." Others such as the Rev. Carroll Wise refined the case study methods of medicine and social work as a tool of pastoral assessment and theological reflection. A personal difference between Dunbar and A. Philip Guiles, later a professor at Andover Newton Theological Seminary, triggered The Council for Clinical Training to move to New York City. A new organization, The New England Theological Schools Committee on Clinical Training, was formed to promote programs in the Boston area. In 1944 the group incorporated as The Institute of Pastoral Care (IPC).

Meanwhile, in Cincinnati, Keller's innovation became formalized as the Graduate School of Applied Religion (1936)—a year-round operation with the Rev. Joseph Fletcher as director. Students sought "to correlate the social with the spiritual approach," and "to 'tie-up' the practical social approach with the pastoral office."

In 1944 supervisors of the three groups, seminary deans and presidents, and representatives of the Federal Council of Churches met in Pittsburgh for the first National Conference of clinical pastoral training. This event marks the end of the beginning phase of CPE. It generated a vision of a common identity and eventual unification of sponsoring organizations. Most impor-

tantly, it defined the goals and methods of CPE with enough consensus to set the parameters within which CPE developed during the next four decades. Then, as now, the heart of CPE was supervised encounter with living human documents. Robert Brinkman, Director of the Council, defined clinical training as "the performance of pastoral work under competent supervision, such work being recorded and submitted for evaluation and criticism." "The supervisor must demonstrate not only 'some teaching ability, but primarily the ability to enable others to observe for themselves, to evolve their own conclusions and applications, and above all to grow' " (R. Powell, 1975).

b. Developments 1944–1984. Agreement on standards for CPE in 1953 sustained a thrust toward organizational unity. A final merger of the Council for Clinical Training, The Institute of Pastoral Care and two denominationally identified groups—the Lutherans and the Southern Baptists—did not occur until November 17, 1967. The story of struggle, maturation, creativity, and growth in CPE up to 1967 is told in Edward E. Thornton's *Professional Education for Ministry: A History of Clinical Pastoral Education* (1970).

c. Affinities and assumptions. CPE links theological education and ministry with the world of health, welfare, and penal organizations primarily. Tension between the needs and values of seminaries and the clinical settings in which CPE occurs has shaped the enterprise throughout its history. At every juncture, however, CPE has identified itself finally as a part of theological education. Its ministry is a function of the sponsoring church or synagogue and is grounded in the different soteriologies and ecclesiologies thereof. CPE offers a method of interpreting human experience, not a theological construction. The method begins within a given theological framework, examines specific ministry events or cases descriptively, enters into dialogue with the appropriate behavioral science information and the minister's own intuitive wisdom, engages in theological reflection, and then forms a pastoral assessment and plan for ministry.

At the core of CPE is the process of supervision. Program standards, accreditation of training centers, and the certification of practitioners all revolve around the supervisory process. CPE supervision takes place in a bipolar field—fostering competence in ministries to deeply troubled persons and psychosocial and spiritual growth in supervisees.

Two views of the self have shaped supervisory assumptions and goals from the beginning of CPE. Holifield (in *A History of Pastoral Care in America*, 1983) sees supervisors torn between two ideals. Both were expressions of progressivism in education and moral reform in religion, but were based on different ethical presuppositions. The Boston group (IPC) drew from Scottish common sense a reliance on rationality and self-control. Ethical formation meant stability and growth: facing the facts, overcoming self-deceptions, conforming to the real. Supervisors focused on finding the "growing edge" and trusting the immanent divinity to carry one to health and meaning in life. Theirs was the optimistic, "once born" religious experience (as described by William James in *The Varieties of Religious Experience*, 1902). The New York group (CCT) exalted freedom and autonomy. Drawing on depth psychology, they defined the self with images of conflict, non-rational feelings and inner chaos. They pursued the goal of freedom—freeing persons from rigid, destructive patterns and self-expectations. Liberation required understanding one's inner conflicts. Theirs was the pessimistic, "twice born" religious experience of James's *Varieties*. In 1936 two classics of the CPE literature appeared reflecting these two orientations: Cabot and Dicks, *The Art of Ministering to the Sick,* and Boisen, *The Exploration of the Inner World*.

Subsequent developments have blended these ethical ideals into every region and resolved many of the arguments derived from them. Underlying tensions remain, but a sense of divine providence in the emergence and unfolding of CPE transcends the differences. From Boisen's sense of "The Guiding Hand" to Gerkin's "The Power of the Future" (1984), CPE leaders have confessed their faith in and obedience to a transcendent reality manifest at least for the moment in CPE.

2. Goals. *a. Pastoral identity.* The foundation and center of CPE goals is the formation of pastoral identity in seminarians and clergy. Assumption of responsibility for providing ministry and positive identification with colleagues in ministry contribute to the sense of one's self as a representative of God and of a specific community of faith, the bearer of a religious tradition, and the affirmation of one's authority as a minister. Other elements integral to pastoral identity in CPE include the following.

b. Interpersonal competence. Shaped by Russell Dicks' use of the verbatim in the 1930s, Carl Rogers' client-centered therapy in the 1940s, as well as sensitivity training and the encounter group movement of the 1950s, CPE continues to place high value upon interpersonal competence. The skills of active listening, interpretation, and confrontation serve the goals of congruent communication and authentic personhood in relation to others. The context of learning communication skills is three-fold: one-to-one caring relationships, small groups for support and growth (often called the Interpersonal Relationship [IPR] Group), and interprofessional interactions related to the maintenance or change of the institutional system in which CPE is provided.

c. Professional competence. CPE balances personal and professional formation at all levels of education. Basic CPE units develop competence in pastoral care appropriate to all ministry settings. In advanced levels, however, the goal of professional competence is shaped by the requirements of specialized pastoral care inherent in the setting in which CPE is offered. Pastoral care specialists are expected to achieve competence levels equal to or beyond that of other professional persons in their setting.

d. Integration of theology and ministry. Integrating theology and ministry has been an especially difficult goal to achieve in CPE. Classical, rationalistic models of theological reflection do not connect readily with empirical methods and intuitive modes of knowing. Tillich's method of correlation received a great deal of attention in early CPE literature and process theology in the 1960s and 1970s. Phenomenology prevailed in CPE programs, however. With the 1980s came narrative theology and Charles Gerkin's case for pastoral care in "a hermeneuti-cal mode." A hermeneutical mode assumes that a person is a myth maker and that every person's story may be told both in an authentically theological language and in a scientifically psychological language. Both paradigms are needed. Each must remain discrete. Integration does not blur the two language systems; it links them in amplifying both the forces (dynamics) and meanings (images and symbols) of the stories with which pastoral ministry is concerned.

e. Spiritual guidance. Concern for the life of the spirit surfaced as a major goal in the ACPE Conference of 1976 as Henri Nouwen presented lectures published later as *The Living Reminder* (1977). Subsequently several supervisors developed original methods for involving CPE students in reflection on their relationship with God. Some empirical studies of spiritual growth in CPE have been published as well. Efforts at reshaping pastoral care and counseling to deal explicitly with both the problems of living and matters of the spirit are under way. As a result, an early overemphasis on psychodynamic and psychotherapeutic understandings is giving way to a more balanced inclusion of theological wisdom about spiritual formation and spiritual guidance. A link is being forged with Boisen's assertion that "the purpose and goal of CPE is to bring students into a more meaningful relationship with God."

f. Ethical awareness. The decade after the incorporation of the ACPE (1967–77) saw a rapidly expanding awareness of the needs of minorities in CPE. Blacks began to raise consciousness about their needs in CPE during the 1960s and women in the 1970s. The 1977 ACPE Conference highlighted issues as diverse as medical ethics, the physically handicapped, sexism, the celibate student, blacks, hospice patients, and emotionally blocked students. Subsequently, gay and lesbian supervisors have claimed a place for themselves in CPE and a start has been made toward a literature on supervising gay and lesbian students in CPE. More limited attention has been paid to international students, the poor, and couples in CPE. Ecumenical awareness has been an integral aspect of the structure and content of CPE from its beginnings.

3. Methods. *a. Responsibility and reflection within a graded, competency-based curriculum.* Responsibility for ministry as a clergyperson and disciplined reflection on the ministry given constitute the bipolar force field within which CPE methods are formed. Parishioners, patients, clients, inmates— these are the primary instructors in CPE. The organizational context in which ministry occurs impacts educational outcomes in profound ways as well (see Rader, 1980). Educational methods are the many ways by which students learn to pay attention to the recipients and contextual determinants of their ministry, to become open to their own and others' experience in providing ministry, to integrate their theory and practice, and so to improve effectiveness in achieving their goals in ministry.

CPE programs function at three levels: basic, advanced, and supervisor-in-training. (See "Standards for the Accreditation of CPE Centers to offer Designated Programs of CPE and for the Certification of CPE Supervisors, 1983," for description of competencies prerequisite to completion of each level of CPE). Within this graded, competency-based curriculum, students provide ministry under supervision. Supervision is the heart of the learning process, functioning through multiple structures of responsibility and reflection.

b. Verbatims and case conferences. The verbatim, developed by Russell Dicks for hospital ministry in the early 1930s, expands pastoral record keeping by recording conversation sequences as they are remembered by the minister. While used in nearly every CPE program for many years, the verbatim is now being replaced by audio and video recording.

The case study method was advocated by Boisen and Richard Cabot in the 1920s. Paul Johnson and others in Boston's "Cabot Club," during the late 1930s, modeled case conferences on the clinical pathological conference in medical education. The case conference examines ministry events and long-term processes with an eye to multiple variants. Pastoral assessment and ministry plans are formulated in the languages of both science and theology. The case conference, likewise, is still used in nearly all CPE programs.

Verbatims and case conferences characterize "the quiet, intense spirituality of the pastoral care movement." They assume that human experience has value for theological understanding and that a relationship with God is "dialogical, not monological." They have spearheaded the emergence of a new paradigm for pastoral ministry in which pastoral conversations are open to systematic reflection, and participation gains equal standing with proclamation as a method of communicating the faith. Verbatims in particular are the royal road into a student's personal learning issues. Selective memory characterizes verbatims and gives them a "dreamlike" quality, affording clues to personal meanings. Like impressionistic paintings, verbatims reveal a student's self-experience. Miscolorations and gaps are as revealing as accurate descriptions. Grist for the supervisory mill is provided, therefore, both in what is recorded and in what is omitted (see Burck, 1980).

c. Seminars and personal growth groups. CPE seminars are as varied as the specializations associated with CPE settings. Similarities among CPE seminars cluster around didactic agendas, reflection and analysis of sermons and worship leadership appropriate to a given setting, and sharing and reflection on personal and historical expressions of spirituality. Most CPE programs provide intensive small group experience as well, designed to provide peer support in coping with the novelty and risks involved in doing CPE and to develop self-understanding, interpersonal competence, and personal growth in psychosocial and spiritual dimensions of the student's life. CPE's goal of balancing professional and personal formation unfolds in the repertoire of seminars and personal growth groups typical of CPE programs.

d. Supervision. The Association for Clinical Pastoral Education, Inc. (ACPE), confers its highest level of certification on supervisors. The structures and processes of accountability are complex, vigorous, and carefully monitored by the ACPE. Peer review of would-be supervisors occurs prior to their entering supervisory training, in mid-process (by certifying supervisors to offer CPE on

their own), and at the completion of a period of autonomous functioning.

A profile of fully certified supervisors, based on mean scores in a study by Seaton-Johnson and Everett (1980) shows the "typical" supervisor of the 1970s to be a forty-seven-year-old Caucasian male. He would hold a Master of Divinity degree, be employed as a chaplain earning between $20,000 and $35,000 per year, and have had fifteen years experience as a pastoral care specialist. He would have invested in two to three years of psychotherapy and would identify himself as a psychodynamically oriented minister. If asked, he would say that he would not choose to leave his chaplain supervisor rule under "any conditions."

Normally a supervisor screens CPE applicants, makes admission decisions, and inducts them at once into contract learning. Once a student's learning goals are synchronized with program and institutional goals, the supervisor facilitates the student's goal achievement, conducting mid-course and final evaluations for guidance and assessment purposes.

Most supervisors assume that care plus confrontation equals growth. Supervisors pay attention both to the student-patient (or parishioner) relationship and to the student-supervisor relationship. Personal identity and professional competence issues, relationship and technique issues, authority and parallel process issues, individual and systemic issues appear frequently in supervisory conversations. Supervisors discriminate learning issues such as the above from problems about learning. Problems about learning may require interventions ranging from verbal confrontation to referral for psychotherapy or marital therapy to termination from the program. Basic to the supervisory relationship is involvement, acceptance, and unconditional positive regard.

Supervisors pay serious attention to educational theories relevant to their function as clinical pastoral educators. Representative of these concerns is the publication of the *Journal of Pastoral Care*, dating from 1947, and the *Journal of Supervision and Training in Ministry*, launched in 1978. Innovations in supervision and studies of supervisory concerns appear regularly in these journals as well as in the annual ACPE Conference Proceedings. *Pastoral Psychology* and the *Journal of Religion and Health* publish studies relevant to CPE supervision less frequently.

e. Innovation in CPE methods. A survey of CPE literature from the formation of the ACPE (1967) to 1983 shows variety and vitality among clinical pastoral educators. The marathon sensitivity group (Dorn and Evans, 1969) and gestalt approaches were tested experimentally (Knights, 1970 and 1978) along with education for interdisciplinary teamwork (Van de Creek and Rower, 1970; Meiburg, 1971). Original uses of "play" in CPE (Close, 1975), of Milton Erickson style hypnosis (Close, 1981), and of "story day" (Frazier, 1978; Summers, 1981) followed.

The research of Carkhuff on communication skills (Markham, 1977), systems perspectives on marital and family therapy (Anderson and Fitzgerald, 1977), marriage enrichment innovations (Hackett and Hackett, 1977), and neuro-linguistic programming (Schmucker, 1982), added depth to the interpersonal competence methods of CPE. "Open Agenda Conferences" (Mason,

1979), "Research as a Curriculum Component" (Gibbons and Myler, 1978), spirituality seminars (Buckell, 1979; Kenny, 1980), and the use of the arts in CPE (Kenny and Hammond, 1983) demonstrate balanced attention to personal and professional aspects of CPE. Even the standard methods of verbatims and case conferences were examined and enriched during this period (Barry, 1983; Mason, 1979).

4. Varieties of Settings. From the beginnings in mental hospitals, general hospitals, and social agencies, CPE moved into prisons, university campuses, and medical schools, into military establishments and parishes.

The dream of offering CPE in the minister's own clinic, i.e., the parish, has stimulated numerous pilot programs. One of the first and most durable was established in 1965 by Robert K. Nace in Zion's Reformed-United Church of Christ in Greenville, Pennsylvania. Nace maintains that CPE in a parish setting is qualitatively different from CPE in an "institutional setting." The "living human document" in parish CPE "is no longer the person in 'crisis and/or pathology' but rather the person in normal, ordinary, routine pilgrimage of life" (Nace, 1981).

CPE is also now international in scope. Although begun in North America—in the United States in the 1920s and soon thereafter in Canada—CPE took root during the post-World War II years in Northern Europe, Southeast Asia, New Zealand and Australia, Africa and South America.

5. Outcomes. New educational and therapeutic activities usually justify themselves with testimonials initially. When carefully researched studies of effectiveness appear, the enterprise has come of age; youth has given way to maturity. Effectiveness studies of CPE programs appeared as early as 1947 (Brick), and continued to appear regularly thereafter (Thomas, *et al.*, 1982).

Early studies demonstrated positive changes in students' self-perceptions and role-perceptions, supporting claims of effectiveness in the primary goal of basic CPE to develop clear pastoral identity. Subsequent studies have confirmed the findings of positive changes in an initial quarter of CPE, but demonstrated a wash-out process during the months immediately following CPE. Only one factor appears not to diminish in the absence of subsequent reinforcement, i.e., the desire to be self-actualized (Grant, 1975; Geary, 1977).

Several comprehensive studies of the membership of the ACPE have been published during the past decade. A study sponsored by the *Journal of Pastoral Care*, based on the return of 1,357 questionnaires, found that high educational standards were operative as well as high continuity in basic values during the first fifty years of CPE (Florell, 1975). An independent analysis of CPE supervisors—their identity, roles and resources—(based on 665 responses) compiled data that confirmed the findings of the Florell study (Seaton-Johnson and Everett, 1980). In 1982 the ACPE Research Committee completed a research project on the criteria that clinical pastoral educators use as they evaluate students. The study was done cooperatively with the Association of Theological Schools' Director of *Readiness for Ministry* research as phase one of a search for accurate measurements of the educational outcomes of a basic unit or an internship of CPE. Next steps will be pilot studies to discover how to measure these desired outcomes, and finally, a before and after study of a wide sample of CPE students (Rowatt, 1982).

6. Issues. Two concerns constitute the nuclei around which the issues cluster in CPE. As professional education for ministry, CPE is centered (a) on being "for ministry" and (b) on "professional education" as its way of doing education for ministry.

a. Being "for ministry." Whatever the faith assumptions of CPE supervisors and their sponsors, CPE seeks to translate those assumptions into ministry. Psychological assumptions about the nature of the self and ethical commitments to the goals of change may be divergent, but CPE maintains the tension between ideals and the givens of a specific situation. Theories must always come to terms with the practice of ministry. Praxis must always be examined in the light of theory.

Theory itself contains constant tensions as well. In CPE, theory is always a plural reality: theology and psychology and sociology and systems theory, and so on. The ultimate point of reference can never be found in any one theoretical perspective. Every perspective becomes partial in the process of being employed "for ministry."

Ministry may occur in any context—worshiping congregation, hospital, agency, prison, school, inner city streets or back roads of the rural poor—yet the primary thrust of CPE is to offer religious ministry. Tension always exists, therefore, between the needs and values of the setting in which CPE occurs and the faith and ministry commitments of CPE itself. To provide religious ministry in nonreligious settings is to minister from a marginal position. Marginalization, then, becomes a constant reality shaping the CPE experience. Marginalized persons are low-power persons in terms of institutional decision making but may become even more highly developed in their interpersonal and spiritual awareness. Living on this boundary generates an anxiety level that manifests itself in a constant display of issues for CPE. One of the ironies with which CPE lives is the relative absence of CPE programs in the minister's own clinic, i.e., local congregations. The differences between nonreligious settings and worshiping congregations may prove to be far reaching in both assumptions and outcomes for CPE in the future.

b. Doing "professional education." Other issues cluster around the role of professional education as the method of choice in equipping persons for ministry. Professions thrive on research. Outcome studies continue with more and more sophistication. Studies of pastoral assessment based on research in faith development, for example, are promising. The historic alliance of CPE and the psychology of religion gain strength as a result of awakenings to spirituality and spiritual formation. Research on the history of pastoral care, on ministry in cross-cultural perspectives, and recognition of the centrality of story in theological reflection all enrich CPE and strengthen its alliance with theological education.

Intensive supervision of both the doing and the being aspects of education for ministry perpetuates tension within the CPE process. How to make the most of the creative possibilities of the tension and how to do so for growing numbers of women and minorities in CPE are questions that occupy supervisors continually. Certification, accreditation, and judicial issues are perennial as clinical pastoral educators strive to maintain quality control of CPE and to win recognition thereof from related accrediting bodies.

Commitment to "professional" standards in an enterprise centered in "being for ministry" generates tension also between professionalization and authentic spirituality. Confidence in the divine providence manifest in the emergence of CPE is maintained by fidelity to both professionalism and spirituality in ministry. By tolerating the tension and by attitudes of openness to change, inclusiveness toward related groups, freedom and encouragement for innovation, and face-to-face accountability among peers, the treasures of CPE are safeguarded. They are held in open hands—open to need and open to the future.

Bibliography. H. Anderson and C. G. Fitzgerald, "The Use of Family Therapy as Preparation for Ministry Within CPE and Seminary Context," *1977 ACPE Conference Proceedings*, The Association for Clinical Pastoral Education, 53–5. A. M. Barry, "Creating For Learning: Verbatim Alternatives," *J. of Supervision and Training in Ministry*, 6 (1983), 56–61. A. O. Bickell, "Theology/Spirituality Seminars," *J. of Supervision and Training in Ministry*, 2 (1979), 30–9. A. Boisen, *The Exploration of the Inner World* (1936). M. Brick, "Some Clinically Trained Ministers and the Program of Their Churches," unpublished doctoral dissertation, Teachers College, Columbia University, 1947. R. Burck, "Pastoral Expressionism: Verbatims in the Pastoral Paradigm," *J. of Supervision and Training in Ministry*, 3 (1980), 39–56. R. Cabot and R. Dicks, *The Art of Ministering to the Sick* (1936). H. T. Close, "A Visit with Milton H. Erickson: The Grandfather of CPE," *J. of Pastoral Care*, 35 (1981), 52–7. H. T. Close "Play in CPE," *J. of Pastoral Care*, 24 (1975), 241–7. R. V. Dorn and W. R. Evans, "CPE—Marathon Sensitivity Group," *J. of Pastoral Care*, 23:3 (1969), 175–7. J. L. Florell, "After Fifty Years: Analysis of the National ACPE Questionnaire 1975," *J. of Pastoral Care*, 29 (1975), 221–32. R. T. Frazier, "The Use of One's Story in CPE," *J. of Supervision and Training in Ministry*, (1978), 17–25. T. F. Geary, "Personal Growth in CPE," *J. of Pastoral Care* (1977), 12–17. C. Gerkin, *The Living Human Document: Re-Visioning Pastoral Counseling in a Hermeneutical Mode* (1984). J. L. Gibbons and D. C. Myler, Jr., "Research As a Curricular Component in CPE," *J. of Supervision and Training in Ministry*, 1 (1978), 36–45. G. Grant, "An Objective Evaluation of an Eleven-Week Supervised Pastoral Education Program," *J. of Pastoral Care*, 29 (1975), 254–61. E. Hackett and M. Hackett, "Implications of Marriage Enrichment for CPE," *1977 ACPE Conference Proceedings*, The Association for Clinical Pastoral Education, 130–1. S. Hiltner, *Preface to Pastoral Theology* (1958). E. B. Holifield, *A History of Pastoral Care in America* (1983). W. James, *Varieties of Religious Experience* (1902). D. E. Kenny, "CPE—Exploring Covenants with God," *J. of Pastoral Care*, 34:2 (1980), 109–13. D. E. Kenny and S. Hammond, RSCJ, "Readiness for Ministry, CPE and Arts," *J. of Supervision and Training in Ministry*, 6 (1983), 33–55. W. A. Knights, Jr., "A Gestalt Approach in a Clinical Training Group," *J. of Pastoral Care*, 24:3 (1970), 193–8. W. A. Knights, Jr., "On Being a (Gestalt) CPE Supervisor," *J. of Supervision*, 1 (1978), 26–35. G. W. Markham, "Using Carkhuff Helping Skills Training in CPE," *1977 ACPE Conference Proceedings*, The Association for Clinical Pastoral Education, 127–9. R. C. Mason, Jr., "Open Agenda Conferences: Purpose and Method," *J. of Supervision and Training in Ministry*, 2 (1979), 22–9. A. L. Meiburg, "Conjoint Clinical Education: An Interdisciplinary Experiment," *J. of Pastoral Care*, 25:2 (1971), 116–21. R. Nace, "Parish Clinical Pastoral Education: Redefining the Living Human Document," *J. of Pastoral Care*, 35:1 (1981), 58–68. H. Nouwen, *The Living Reminder* (1977). R. Powell, *CPE: Fifty Years of Learning* (ACPE, 1975). B. Rader, "The Organizational Context of Supervision and Training," *J. of Supervision and Training in Ministry*, 3 (1980), 87–99. G. W. Rowatt, "What Does ACPE Expect of Ministry?" *J. of Pastoral Care*, 3 (1982), 147–159. F. Schmucker, "The Interpretation of Tongues," *J. of Supervision and Training in Ministry*, 5 (1982), 61–76. A. Seaton-Johnson and C. Everett, "An Analysis of Clinical, Pastoral Supervisors: Their Identities, Roles and Resources," *J. of Pastoral Care*, 3 (1980), 148–58. T. Summers, "Story Day in CPE," *J. of Supervision and Training in Ministry*, 4 (1981), 37–48. J. Thomas, *et al.*, "A Comparative Evaluation of Changes in Basic Clinical Pastoral Education Students in Different Types of Clinical Settings as Measured by the Adjective Check List and the Experience Scale," *J. of Pastoral Care*, 3 (1982), 181–93. E. Thornton, *Professional Education for Ministry* (1970). L. Vandecreek and J. Rower, "Education for Interdisciplinary Teamwork," *J. of Pastoral Care*, 24:3 (1970), 176–84.

E. E. THORNTON

ASSOCIATION FOR CLINICAL PASTORAL EDUCATION; EDUCATION IN PASTORAL CARE AND COUNSELING; PASTORAL CARE MOVEMENT; SPECIALIZATION IN PASTORAL CARE. *See also* CASE STUDY METHOD; SUPERVISION, PASTORAL; THEOLOGICAL EDUCATION AND THE PASTORAL CARE MOVEMENT; VERBATIM.

CLINICAL PASTORAL PERSPECTIVE.

Rooted in the psychology of persons and in the supervised practicums of law, medicine, and social work that emerged at the turn of the century. Earlier pastoral perspectives and practice served primarily to encourage and enable persons to adapt or adjust to the prevailing faithful religious community, and those unable to adapt or adjust were marked as lost souls. Most clergy were unaware that developmental deviations, conflicts, and intense emotion might lie at the root of a person's inability to conform or adapt to the community. With the dawning of a psychology of persons, the use of case study practicums, and the publication of Freud's lectures on psychoanalysis, pastoral education and care began to revise and enlarge its focus.

In 1908, Elwood Worcester, rector of the Emmanuel Episcopal Church in Boston, established a church clinic for the healing of troubled souls. In 1923, in Cincinnati, Dr. William Keller invited theological students to participate in a social case work practicum. In 1925, in Boston, Dr. Richard Cabot urged theological schools to include a clinical year in the curriculum. These developments set the stage for the introduction of the clinical pastoral perspective in theological study. The perspective presumes that personal needs and concerns of people are most adequately met in ministries informed by functional education. Because the clinical pastoral perspective has more to do with people than concepts, it is illuminated most clearly by stories of the people who forged its shape.

Anton Boisen is acknowledged as the founding father of CPE. On being hospitalized, he recognized that his experience was analogous to the religious conversion phenomenon. As chaplain at Worcester (Mass.) State Hospital, Boisen was convinced that theology students and clergy in ministries to, and studies of, hospitalized "living human documents" could deepen their understanding of pastoral ministry and amplify their pastoral practice. In 1926 at Worcester, with the cooperation of Dr. William Bryan, superintendent, the first CPE group assembled. In supportive ministries with patients, the students observed behaviors and listened to life stories, delusions, fantasies, and hallucinations. Using Boisen's case studies as a model, the students developed case reports. Representative case studies were then discussed in supervisor-student case seminars, designed to educe pastoral diagnostic impressions and pastoral care implications. The case study process produced usable pastoral insights and led to the accumulation of a body of pastoral knowledge available for subsequent clinical and academic study. Boisen's ministry-based study of "living human documents" continues to endure as a facet of the clinical pastoral perspective.

Even though Boisen was critically aware of his "living human document," he did not elect to include student "human documents" in his educational agenda. Fred Kuether, a contemporary of Boisen, while not neglecting patient documents, was convinced that pastoral study of student documents was as important to clinical learning as patient documents. At the same time Kuether acknowledged that the complexity of serious student self-study could tax the limits of clinical programs. (Boisen, for instance, took years to explore his inner world.) Kuether formalized the study of the student's "living human document" as a curriculum component. He encouraged students to express their feelings, reactions, attitudes, values, and assumptions in order to provide content for self-study. He accurately assumed that in-depth understanding of one's own humanity could result in a more effective ministry. New dimensions of the self-study facet appear in sharing of, and reflection on, longitudinal life stories. It is noteworthy that ACPE standards for basic CPE state as program objectives: "To become more aware of oneself as minister," and "To become aware of how one's attitudes, values, and assumptions affect one's ministry."

Carroll Wise, who succeeded Boisen at Worcester, asserts that pastoral relationships are an intrinsic facet of the clinical pastoral perspective. Pastoral relationships are elusive, following random rather than regular orbits. The many variables occasioned by emotion, attitude, action, level of maturity, and differing life stories preclude definitive generalizations about relationships. Nevertheless, Wise holds that the incarnational quality of a relationship is revealed when a pastor and a parishioner become personally and deeply involved in a pastoral relationship—a quality that leads to salvation and resurrection. Flexible functional study of relationships can yield clues about the powerful forces that both clash and blend in these encounters. By perceiving these clues pastors make pastoral rather than academic use of their insights.

Russell Dicks, as a general hospital chaplain, saw little value in using the case study or pastoral relationship facets in his educational ministry, and introduced the verbatim report as his prime educational method. By verbatim reports students noted the process and content

of their pastoral conversations with patients. In evaluation seminars and supervisor-student conferences the verbatim description of the process and content of the pastoral interview was analyzed. There the students discovered that a pastoral response can determine the direction and depth of pastoral communication. These insights enabled the students to listen to fragile concealed human concerns, and to respond sensitively to patient needs. Dicks's contribution enriched the clinical pastoral perspective by adding process evaluation to case study and relationship reflection.

Other methodological modifications such as video- and audiotaping, role play, and chaplaincy rounds continue to add new facets to the clinical pastoral perspective. The unique and particular missions of agencies which sponsor functional educational programs usually tend to expand the perspective.

Is the clinical pastoral perspective applicable beyond its traditional field education, CPE, and pastoral care and counseling usage? Is it applicable to studies of social documents, moral and ethical issues, administrative structures, etc.? Some experimental, functional, educational programs have focused on public, social, and ethical matters, yet the question remains unanswered. Broadening the application of the clinical pastoral perspective may require radical revision of existing CPE supervisory training, different styles of ministry, and unique new centers of learning. If that takes place the perspective may no longer be *pastoral.*

To summarize, the clinical pastoral perspective emerges out of, and is actualized in, functional education. It aims at improving pastoral practice rather than providing cognitive content. The clinical pastoral perspective stands alongside the academic perspective and asks its educational programs to provide the theological and psychological wisdom necessary for creative reflection. Applied to practice, the clinical pastoral perspective requires informed, mature, motivated learners and competent supervisors working together in a setting congenial to functional learning.

Bibliography. Association for Clinical Pastoral Education, *Standards* (1985). A. Boisen, *Exploration of the Inner World* (1936); *Out of the Depths* (1960). R. Cabot and R. Dicks, *The Art of Ministering to the Sick* (1943). S. Freud, *A General Introduction to Psychoanalysis* (1943). B. Holifield, *A History of Pastoral Care* (1983). W. James, *Varieties of Religious Experience* (1902). E. Thornton, *Professional Education for Ministry* (1970). C. Wise, *The Meaning of Pastoral Care* (1966).

J. L. CEDARLEAF

COMPASSION; INTERPRETATION AND HERMENEUTICS; PASTORAL CARE (Contemporary Methods, Perspectives, and Issues); PERCEPTIVENESS AND SENSITIVITY, PASTORAL; PHENOMENOLOGICAL METHOD OF PASTORAL CARE. *Compare* EDUCATION, NURTURE, AND CARE; EVALUATION AND DIAGNOSIS; LEADERSHIP AND ADMINISTRATION; TEACHING.

CLINICAL PSYCHOLOGIST. Clinical psychologists apply principles and methods from psychological science to the assessment and alleviation of behavioral, intellectual, and emotional disorders and discomforts. (A *counseling psychologist,* by contrast, generally works with people who have milder emotional or personal problems.)

Most clinical psychologists receive training patterned after the "scientist-professional" model, which involves study of research techniques, as well as the accepted findings of psychological science. Clinical psychologists also receive doctoral and post-doctoral clinical training, that is, supervised experience in working with the recipients of their services. Most states require licensure for the independent practice of clinical psychology. A listing of those qualified to function at the level of independent practice is found in the *National Register of Health Service Providers in Psychology,* which is published biannually.

A clinical psychologist may work in a variety of settings, such as a mental health clinic, a hospital, or in private practice. Many specialize in working with certain populations, such as children or the elderly.

Clinical psychologists use psychological tests and other assessment techniques to evaluate the nature and causes of an individual's psychological distress or dysfunction. Interventions practiced by the clinical psychologist are directed at alleviating behavioral dysfunctions, emotional conflicts, and personality disorders. Individual psychotherapy that relies heavily on verbal communication between the psychologist and the client continues to be a mainstay of clinical psychology, though many practice interventions that involve behavioral reeducation, environmental manipulation, group psychotherapy, or family therapy.

In addition, many clinical psychologists work in the areas of consultation to other professionals, of designing programs for delivering services, and of supervision and evaluation of the delivery of services. Moreover, expertise in designing and conducting research continues to be one of the most important contributions of clinical psychologists, since other mental health professionals tend to have less training in this area. The psychological profession tends to value research training as a skill to be applied in daily clinical activities as well.

C. P. RAGAN

INTERPROFESSIONAL TEAMS AND RELATIONSHIPS. *Compare* MARRIAGE AND FAMILY THERAPIST; PSYCHIATRIST/ PSYCHIATRY; PSYCHOLOGIST; PSYCHOTHERAPIST; SOCIAL WORKER.

CLINICAL PSYCHOLOGY. The application of findings and techniques from the various branches of psychology to the study of abnormal behavior, the measurement and evaluation of mental and behavioral disorders, and interventions in them. The field of clinical psychology has its historic roots in early forms of mental measurement and began to flourish with increased demand for services at the end of World War II.

C. P. RAGAN

PSYCHOTHERAPY. *Compare* PSYCHIATRIST/PSYCHIATRY; PSYCHOLOGY; SOCIOLOGY OF RELIGIOUS AND PASTORAL CARE.

CLINICAL THEOLOGY. This term is understood in two primary ways within the pastoral care movement. In a generic sense it refers to the theological reflection that grows out of clinical experience, such as in Clinical Pastoral Education (CPE), where one encounters the depth experiences of Anton Boisen's "living human doc-

uments." Understood more specifically, clinical theology refers to the organization and school of pastoral studies in Great Britain, which was founded by Frank Lake, who authored the large and influential volume *Clinical Theology* (1966; abridged version, 1987).

J. PATTON

BRITISH PASTORAL CARE MOVEMENT; PASTORAL THEOLOGY, PROTESTANT. *Compare* EMPIRICAL THEOLOGY; EXPERIENTIAL THEOLOGY. *Biography:* LAKE.

CLOWN, PASTOR AS. *See* PASTOR (Normative and Traditional Images).

CODE OF CANON LAW (Roman Catholicism). The primary legal document governing the Latin Catholic Church. Issued by Pope John Paul II on January 25, 1983, after a nearly eighteen year drafting process, it took effect on November 27, 1983. It largely replaced the 1917 code, which was revised in light of Vatican Council II and the needs of contemporary pastoral practice. Composed of 1752 canons, it is divided into seven books treating the following issues: general legal principles, the status of various church members (laity, clergy, religious), church organization at the universal, national, regional, and diocesan levels, the church's teaching and sanctifying missions, ecclesiastical temporal goods, ecclesiastical sanctions, and judicial and administrative procedures.

T. J. GREEN

CANON LAW SOCIETY OF AMERICA; CASUISTRY, ROMAN CATHOLIC; ROMAN CATHOLIC PASTORAL CARE. *See also* ECCLESIOLOGY AND PASTORAL CARE; MINISTRY, ROMAN CATHOLIC; MORAL THEOLOGY AND PASTORAL CARE.

COE, GEORGE ALBERT (1862–1951). American religious educator and psychologist of religion. A professor of religious education at Union Theological Seminary (New York) and Teachers' College, Columbia, Coe helped organize and direct the Religious Education Society of America.

Coe's efforts to appropriate the New Psychology for the churches contributed not only to a revised appraisal of the traditional Protestant Sunday School but also to a renewed appreciation for methods of pastoral care and counseling that were grounded in psychological research. His own research into the psychology of religion convinced him that the functionalists were right when they turned their attention from isolated states of consciousness to the interests and preferences of concrete persons. He believed, too, that such functional psychologists as John Dewey were correct when they argued that growth, occurring within a network of social relationships, was the highest ethical end. Hence he concluded that the aim of religious education was "the growth of the young toward and into mature and efficient devotion to the democracy of God, and happy self-realization therein" (*A Social Theory of Religious Education,* 1917, p. 55).

He believed that religious education was ideally a form of "social interaction" that would alter the individual's outlook toward the social good. He thought also that such a progressive conception of education had clear therapeutic implications. "Cooperative thinking" could release the personality from its self-imposed limitations by forming the "habit of being free and freely cooperative" (*The Motives of Men,* 1928, p. 209).

Such insights confirmed Coe's belief that the care of souls, like education itself, could become "a system of organized and proportioned methods based upon definite knowledge of the material to be wrought upon, the ends to be attained, and the means and instruments for attaining them" (*The Spiritual Life,* 1900, p. 21). It was no surprise that religious educators offered the first modern classes in pastoral counseling in the American Protestant seminaries.

Coe worked for a "scientific" understanding of pastoral care, a Sunday School informed by functional and developmental psychologies, and a recognition of the therapeutic capacities of free interchange within small and intimate groups. Many of his views failed to survive the neoorthodox revolt against liberalism in the early 1930s, but the Protestant pastoral care traditions in the U.S. remain indebted to some of his central insights.

E. B. HOLIFIELD

HISTORY OF PROTESTANT PASTORAL CARE (United States); PASTORAL CARE MOVEMENT. *See also* EDUCATION, NURTURE, AND CARE.

COERCION. *See* INDOCTRINATION; POWER; VIOLENCE.

COGNITIVE BEHAVIORISM. *See* BEHAVIORISM.

COGNITIVE/CONATIVE PROBLEM IN PSYCHOLOGY AND COUNSELING. The cognitive/conative problem may be characterized as the basic question in the psychology of motivation: whether human behavior is governed primarily by the emotions, impulses, and desires, or by cognition.

1. **Two Types of Theory.** Two opposing types of psychological theories deal with the relationship of cognition to the active part of the mental life. According to the first, an emotion, desire, physiological need, or passion always serves as the inducement to behavior. Reason is here viewed as "the slave of the passions" (David Hume) and as not capable of generating ends of action on its own, apart from those provided by antecedent needs or desires. Classical psychoanalytic theory is commonly interpreted as the leading example of this first approach (see Allport, 1961, pp. 202, 207–8). For Freud, reason has a bureaucratic function: it manages the various forces impinging upon the ego from within and without as efficiently as possible, without making substantive claims of its own.

In the second type of theory, reason provides the motive for action, motivating the person toward what is objectively *desirable,* as opposed to what is subjectively *desired.* The passions play a predominantly negative role in this theory by disturbing reason's pursuit of its own goals. The cognitive developmental psychology of Lawrence Kohlberg, which builds upon the work of Jean Piaget, is the leading contemporary representative of this second approach. The central hypothesis of Kohlberg's theory is that each stage in a person's cognitive moral development possesses a unity of organization that deci-

sively affects all conduct at that stage. Kohlberg also contends that cognitive beliefs and judgments determine emotional states rather than vice versa (see Beck, 1971, p. 392).

2. **Mediating Positions.** In recent years, there have been movements toward mediating positions within both the psychoanalytic and the cognitive developmental traditions. Criticism of Freud's drive discharge theory (Holt, 1967) as well as the theoretical revisions proposed by psychoanalytic ego psychologists like Heinz Hartmann and Erik Erikson have encouraged recognition among psychoanalysts of the crucial role played by cognition in human conduct. In Erikson's influential revision of Freudian theory (Erikson, 1950; Wallwork, 1973) some of Piaget's discoveries are incorporated into a broader ego-social model of personality growth that presupposes Freud's work on biologically triggered stages. At the same time, neo-Piagetians have attempted to expand the Piagetian model of development beyond cognition in such a way as to encompass emotional aspects of personality development (cf. J. Fowler, 1981, and R. Kegan, 1982).

Emotions are constituted in part by certain beliefs and judgments about the context in which they are experienced (Bedford, 1957). Fear, for example, is always associated with the *idea* that something bad is going to happen; otherwise, it is not properly described as fear. Cognitivists are thus correct to insist that different affects cannot be qualitatively distinguished without reference to cognitive structuring. But this does not necessarily deny the well-established clinical evidence that we are often unaware of the emotions that are moving us. While unconscious emotions are no longer defined as instinctual discharges that occur independently of cognitive processes, vague feelings like sadness and anxiety may still be felt and responded to in behavior without any conscious ideational awareness, because the necessary beliefs that more precisely identify these emotions are unconscious.

3. **Implications for Counseling.** Many types of counseling work in large part by helping the client discover and cognitively understand (by redescribing) the context to which he or she has been responding emotionally without conscious awareness. For example, the woman who is moody and experiences difficulties in her work and marriage may find in therapy that her inexplicable reactions are not caused by current events or circumstances but by something else — say, the death of a parent shortly before the onset of her symptoms. Her moodiness and depression turn out to be unacknowledged grief, a response to an earlier relationship. In order to identify cognitively the context to which a person is responding unconsciously, it is not sufficient to know the person's conscious beliefs, though this information certainly may be helpful. It *is* essential to follow the subtle clues that the individual provides regarding the possible hidden meanings of one's ego-alien behavior. For counseling to be effective, both the cognitive and affective sides of the personality need to be engaged, as Freud first realized. In fact, where anxiety is the prevailing presenting emotion, intellectual insights often will be resisted defensively until the therapist — through

empathy—finds some way of reaching the person behind the mask.

Bibliography. G. Allport, *Pattern and Growth in Personality* (1961), pp. 196–274. C. M. Beck, *et al.*, *Moral Education* (1971). E. Bedford, "Emotions," *Proceedings of the Aristotelian Society*, n.s. 57 (1957), 281–304. E. Erikson, *Childhood and Society* (1950). J. Fowler, *Stages of Faith* (1981). For a critique, E. Wallwork, "Morality, Religion, and Kohlberg's Theory," in B. Munsey, ed., *Moral Development, Moral Education, and Kohlberg* (1980) 269–97; and "Religious Development," in J. Broughton and D. J. Freeman-Moir, eds., *The Cognitive Developmental Psychology of James Mark Baldwin* (1982), pp. 335–8. M. Hoffman, "Moral Development," in P. Mussen, ed., *Carmichael's Manual of Child Psychology* 3d ed., vol. 2, (1970), pp. 261–359. R. R. Holt, ed., "Motives and Thought," *Psychological Issues* (1967). R. Kegan, *The Evolving Self* (1982). A. Kenny, *Action, Emotion and Will* (1963). L. Kohlberg, "Stage and Sequence," in D. Goslin, ed., *Handbook of Socialization Theory and Research* (1969), pp. 347–480; "Continuities in Childhood and Adult Moral Development Revisited," in P. B. Baltes and K. W. Schaie, eds., *Life-Span Developmental Psychology* (1973); *The Philosophy of Moral Development*, (1981) vol 1. For a critique, W. P. Alston, "Comments on Kohlberg's 'From Is to Ought'," in T. Mischel, ed., *Cognitive Development and Epistemology* (1971), pp. 269–84. R. S. Peters, *The Concept of Motivation* (1974). E. Wallwork, "Erik Erikson: Psychological Resources for Faith," in R. Johnson and E. Wallwork, *Critical Issues in Modern Religion* (1973), pp. 322–61.

E. WALLWORK

FEELING, THOUGHT, AND ACTION IN PASTORAL COUNSELING; PHILOSOPHY AND PSYCHOLOGY; REASON AND PASSION. *See also* EMOTION; MOTIVATION; PERSONALITY THEORY; PSYCHOTHERAPY; RATIONAL-EMOTIVE PSYCHOTHERAPY; REASONING AND RATIONALITY IN PASTORAL CARE. *Compare* PSYCHOLINGUISTIC THEORY; STRUCTURALISM.

COGNITIVE DEVELOPMENT. Cognition as used in modern psychology deals with that which becomes known by an individual, that is, the ideas a person forms about the self and the world. Cognition as a concept was addressed by both Plato and Aristotle. In their writings, the notion of mind was divided into three principal areas: cognition (knowing), feeling, and the will. In the general sense, cognition deals with how an individual's representation of reality comes about from personal experiences of it. To speak of a "cognitive event" is to speak of one's own awareness of reality based on either subjective or objective interests. Cognition requires a distinction between its contents, that is, personal ideas about the real world and processes, i.e. meaning, mechanisms by which ideas arise and are transformed in one's brain.

1. **Stage Theory.** Cognitive development concerns the acquisition and retention of knowledge. The skills involved in these functions are primarily cognitively mediated and have to do principally with intelligence and stages of the brain's development. The newborn infant holds particular interest for those who study the interrelationships of genetic and environmental factors as they affect memory, thought, behaviors, and, most importantly, formation of personality and intellect. Over the past several years, Jean Piaget has examined the development of the child's cognitive growth in more depth than anyone else, and his theories have gained worldwide recognition.

The main thrust of Piaget's theory is that there are discreet stages of mental development, each of which is characterized by a different form of reasoning. Piaget was not primarily concerned with establishing normative data for children; rather, most of his studies revealed an emerging, cognitive complexity determined by the child's own biological growth. He distinguished four stages of intellectual development: sensory motor, pre-operational, concrete operations, and formal operations. Sensory motor functions of the human infant are the predominant focus for the first twenty-four months. From the ages of approximately two to seven, the pre-operational stage is characterized by symbolic functioning where the infant begins using words or objects to represent some thought. An egocentric view of the world is held by the child during this stage. From ages seven to twelve years, approximately, children demonstrate an ability to conduct mental operations on concrete objects. They also start to group objects into classes and order them on the basis of their relations according to size, shape, volume, etc. When these features give way to a child performing mental operations on objects in such a way that they learn that these objects will appear differently to others standing in a different position from theirs, egocentric thinking gradually gives way to a different point of view via a differentiation process, that is, logical operations for abstract concept formation (reasoning) ability.

Piaget's work is replete with hundreds of examples of cognitive changes from perceptual ignorance to logical abstraction, as well as from simple to complex mental events paralleling the development of higher cortical activities in the human brain. The development of higher mental functions in the human brain, its neurobiological bases through various regulated processes, its relation to memory, learning, attention, and other brain-behavioral functions are as yet inadequately comprehended.

The investigations of Alexander Luria as to higher cortical functions in humankind have explored in detail neuropsychological aspects of brain-behavior relationships and cerebral dysfunctions. As Piaget viewed the mind as a dynamic system which passes through qualitatively different levels of differentiations and integrations, Luria held to the notion that the human brain, as a whole, was involved in the most complex brain-behavior functions and is dynamic in its mediation of psychological processes as well as flexible in terms of environmental stimuli.

It was principally through the seminal ideas of L. S. Vygotsky that Luria's views on language and cognitive development took shape. Vygotsky's influence created the basic framework within which linguistic and neuropsychological ideas were interpreted. He was concerned with the issue of how linguistic and neuropsychological phenomena fit into an account of human cognition. The method of genetic explanation, also called "comparative evolutionary method" by Luria provided the foundations for Vygotsky and Luria's approach to the study of inner speech development—a significant part of the child's mental development.

Many experimental techniques have been used to generate a vast body of knowledge which has shaped our views of infancy and infant capabilities. The impact of the first three to five years of life has received intensive investigation by such researchers as the following: Burton White, Sheldon White, T. Berry Brazelton, Jerome Kagan, Richard Kearsley, Philip Zelazo, T. G. R. Bower, John and Elizabeth Newson, J. McVicker Hunt, Paul Mussen, John Conger, Robert McCall, Jean Piaget, Lewis Lipsitt, John Flavell, to name a few. Research by these authors can be found in the developmental psychology literature as well as cognitive development literature.

2. Relationship to Brain Maturation. Maturation of cognitive abilities in relation to the brain's growth is highly influential for emotional/personality development. A generalized sequence of cognitive abilities which then leads to cognitive competencies occurring over time is as follows. At two months of age it has been shown that an infant can demonstrate a difference in "knowing" versus "experiencing." It is the degree of experience which varies from what one knows. It is the ability of memory, which is the essential function to emerge during the first year of life, if not the first six months of life, that is crucial in a child's mental development. By at least two years of age, in normally developing infants, memory for past experience develops. Next, active memory emerges, that is, incoming information is related to knowledge for the first time. Then, symbolization competency as to how experiences are represented in a child's mind occurs. Next, the ability to infer the cause of an event transpires, including appreciation of "right" versus "wrong". Finally, children become aware of their reflecting capacity, that is, the ability to act and become self-aware.

These are some of the more fundamental aspects of developments that take place, mediated by the brain, which afford the infant with new capacities to emerge in the infant's cognitive development. At approximately eighteen to twenty-four months after birth, the notion of anxiety emerges. Somewhat later, between twenty-four and thirty-six months of life, "shame" and "guilt" emerge in the repertoire, as well as "failure" and "pride" on the part of a child. A "prepared" set is present at about this time of life for evaluation of the young child's actions as to "right" versus "wrong." What is probably occurring, experts believe, is the further development of inhibitory systems in the brain's activities. It is the maturation of the brain's varied information-processing abilities, contingent upon maturing brain systems, that permits self-awareness, that is, conscious thinking ability, to come about, emerging anywhere from twelve to thirty-six months in the infant. At this point, it is believed that an infant is capable of distinguishing between knowing about his or her self and experiencing events in the real world that have some kind of an exterior, causal basis.

3. Developmental Disabilities. It is important to acknowledge that inadequate encoding of early experiences, stimulation (sensory), brain insult, nutritional deficiency, anoxic conditions, hereditary defects, can impose differing degrees of restrictions on the brain's cognitive capacities. Practically speaking, it is important to describe as clearly as possible the events and patterns in the child's developmental abilities before raising questions as to a child's disability, level of retardedness, or

impaired maturation trend. All of these observations can be referred to a physician, developmental psychologist, or developmental resource specialist to determine whether the cognitive development of a particular child is in fact "abnormal".

Some of the major factors influencing cognitive development that can lead to aberrant patterns, regressions, and disabilities are as follows: the relationship between biological maturation and psychological experience; emergence of new cognitive competencies in any field, especially social competency development; personality formation and temperamental style; effects of poor environments on mental development; central nervous system maturation; sexual differentiation factors; effects of malnutrition on the growing fetal/infant brain; the role of culture in the course of one's cognitive development; development of perceptual and linguistic competencies; memory development at an early age; verbal cueing capabilities applied to verbal symbolic information-processing competencies; mother-infant relationships over the first thirty-six months of life; object relationship development; and styles of information processing of different types of subject matter. Any interruption due to deficiencies in one or more of the above areas can affect a child's cognitive development.

As newer results continue to flood the journals and new theories emerge in producing models of cognitive developmental processes that affect competency development, a better understanding will no doubt emerge illuminating the breadth and scope of the key changes that are possible during this early period of life. How the brain effects control over higher mental processes, and how behavior of others affect these processes, are matters for further research.

Bibliography. A. W. H. Buffery, "Sex differences in the neuropsychological development of verbal and spatial skills," in R. M. Knights and D. J. Bakker, eds., *The Neuropsychology of Learning Disorders* (1976). L. B. Cohen, J. S. De Loache, and M. S. Strauss, "Infant perceptual development," in J. D. Osofosky, ed., *Handbook of Infant Development* (1979). H. T. Epstein, "Growth spurts during brain development," in J. S. Chall and A. F. Mirsky, eds., *Education and the Brain: The 77th Yearbook of the National Society for the Study of Education, II* (1978). S. Grossberg, "How does a brain build a cognitive code?" *Psychological Review* (1980) 1–51. J. Kagan, R. B. Kearsley, and P. R. Zelazo, *Infancy: Its Place in Human Development,* (1978). J. Kagan and H. A. Moss, *Birth to Maturity* (1983). A. R. Luria and F. I. Yudovich, *Speech in the Development of Mental Processes in the Child* (1959). L. V. Majovski, "Higher Cortical Functions in Children: A Developmental Perspective," in *Handbook of Clinical Child Neuropsychology* (1988). J. Oates, ed., *Early Cognitive Development* (1979). L. S. Vygotsky, "The Problem of Age-Periodization of Child Development," *Human Development* (1974), 24–40; L. S. Vygotsky, *Mind in Society: The Development of Higher Psychological Processes* (1980).

L. V. MAJOVSKI

COGNITIVE PSYCHOLOGY AND PSYCHOTHERAPY; PERSONALITY DEVELOPMENT. *See also* COGNITIVE/CONATIVE PROBLEM; DEVELOPMENT, CONCEPT OF; IMAGINATION. *Compare* CYBERNETIC THEORY; EVALUATION AND DIAGNOSIS, PSYCHOLOGICAL; FAITH DEVELOPMENT RESEARCH; LANGUAGE DEVELOPMENT; MORAL DEVELOPMENT; STRUCTURALISM.

COGNITIVE DISORDERS. *See* ORGANIC MENTAL DISORDER AND ORGANIC BRAIN SYNDROME.

COGNITIVE DISSONANCE THEORY. A cognitive consistency theory proposing that individuals need consistency (consonance) among their cognitions (thoughts). Leon Festinger (1957) first published the theory that if two cognitions do not "go together" (e.g., "I hate exercise" and "I just jogged two miles") cognitive dissonance will occur. Dissonance is an uncomfortable state, and a person experiencing dissonance will seek to resolve it by either changing one of the dissonant cognitions ("I really like exercise after all") or adding cognitions ("I exercise because the Surgeon General says exercise lowers the chances of having a heart attack").

Research on cognitive dissonance has often produced surprising results. Aronson and Mills (1959), for example, found that college women who underwent a severe initiation for what turned out to be a dull group, indicated that they liked the group *more* than women who underwent a mild initiation. In other words, as predicted by dissonance theory, when women held two inconsistent cognitions ("I went through a lot to get into this group" and "This group is so dull that the initiation was not worth it"), they altered one of their cognitions to reduce dissonance ("This group is actually quite interesting").

Dissonance theory has been applied to two kinds of situations that involve a discrepancy between attitude and behavior. In the first, dissonance results when an individual must select one of two equally attractive alternatives. According to dissonance theory, an individual reduces post-decisional dissonance by changing his or her evaluations of the two alternatives. For example, an individual who must choose between Hawaii and Alaska for a vacation trip and settles on Hawaii might later think, "Hawaii is much more exciting; I love the sand and the sun; Alaska will probably be too cold; I would have had a terrible time in Alaska." In other words, the individual increases the value of the chosen alternative and decreases the value of the other.

In the second situation, dissonance arises when persons are forced to behave counter to their private attitudes. As a result, either the behavior or the attitude must change to bring cognitions into harmony again. Festinger and Carlsmith (1959) illustrated this phenomenon in their classic study of forced compliance, with subjects paid either one dollar or twenty dollars to complete a boring task. Those paid only one dollar tended to say that the task was enjoyable, not boring.

One can reduce dissonance by either changing behavior, adding new cognitions, adjusting to the dissonant state, or, most commonly, changing attitudes.

Bibliography. E. Aronson and J. Mills, "The Effect of Severity of Initiation on Liking for a Group," *J. of Abnormal and Social Psychology*, 59 (1959) 177–81. L. Festinger, *A Theory of Cognitive Dissonance* (1957). L. Festinger and J. Carlsmith, "Cognitive Consequences of Forced Compliance," *J. of Abnormal and Social Psychology*, 58 (1959); 203–10. L. Festinger, H. W. Riecken, and S. Schachter, *When Prophecy Fails: A Social and Psychological Study of a Modern Group that Predicted the Destruction of the World* (1956).

L. S. BRAKENSIEK

SOCIAL PERCEPTION, JUDGMENT, AND BELIEF; SOCIAL PSYCHOLOGY, DISCIPLINE OF.

COGNITIVE PSYCHOLOGY AND PSYCHOTHERAPY. Cognitive psychology attempts to understand how people think. Cognitive psychotherapy applies this knowledge to the problem of how the individual can be helped to cope with emotional problems such as depression or stress.

1. Cognitive Psychology. At present, cognitive psychology is dominated by the information processing approach, which organizes cognitive processes into a sequence of ordered stages. Each stage reflects an important step in the processing of cognitive information. Contrary to earlier theorizing in this area, however, this sequence of information processing is not a cold deterministic process initiated at one point in the environment, then automatically carried through to completion by the organism. Rather, information processing is now seen as at least partially under the control of the perceiver: the individual imposes a conceptual schema upon incoming information. This conceptual schema, a product of the individual's knowledge and conceptual structure, then directs and organizes the processing of the information from the environment. This organizational process has been termed intentionality (cf. Anderson, 1980).

Cognitive psychology's theory of the emotions generally posits two factors as necessary for emotional arousal and evaluation: bodily arousal, which can be a product of genetics or chemical input, and evaluation, which is an interpretative process based upon past experiences and accrued conceptual categories.

2. Cognitive Psychology's View of Psychotherapy. Cognitive therapy strives to change not only individual cognitions (first step) but the global manner in which an individual construes reality. Neither is the emphasis on urging individuals to give up a particular perspective (e.g., "I am incompetent") but to aid them in strengthening an incompatible belief (e.g., "I am competent at that specific task"). The therapist thus attempts to change the individual's focus of attention. The person is taught to focus on incompatible beliefs until a crisis ensues in which original assumptions are questioned and the individual's core concepts change. Cognitive therapy sees the negative, superficial cognitions as a manifestation of core assumptions. Thus, cognitive psychotherapy aims at changing the individual's deep structures or underlying meaning patterns. According to certain theorists, some of these structures can be changed even if the individual is not fully aware of them.

Most cognitive psychotherapies consist of three phases: (1) The presentation of the cognitive rationale for the therapy to the patient, in which patients are told that they can learn to control their emotions by first learning to become aware of their underlying thoughts, then learning to substitute alternative thoughts. Such a rationale lets patients in on the process or therapy, and also instills a belief in the possibility of self-control or self-efficacy, the crucial ingredient of mental health according to cognitive theorists. (2) A process in which the individual is made aware of his or her thoughts, generally involving the client in some type of record- or log-keeping. Patients may be asked to write down their thoughts either at specific times of the day, or when they become anxious or depressed. Some therapists also encourage their patients to use retrospective imagery during sessions to become aware of thoughts they had in a previous anxiety- or depression-provoking situation. (3) Training the client to verbalize alternative cognitions or cognitions incompatible with the pathogenic cognitions of which they have become aware. This verbalization can take several forms, for example, having the patient write down the alternative thoughts or verbalize the thoughts to one's self, covertly or overtly.

3. Current Techniques in the Cognitive Psychotherapies.
There are four principal approaches to cognitive psychotherapy (see Mahoney and Arnkoff, 1978). *(1) Behavioral self-control.* These techniques include cognitive techniques in which individuals are taught to control the impact of the environment upon them by choosing which environment they will expose themselves to (stimulus control procedure). They also are taught to control their reactions to the environment by learning to monitor their behavior in particular situations and to decide when to reward or punish themselves. This entire process is labeled cognitive because research suggests that self-reinforcement involves the individual's beliefs and expectancies concerning what is rewardable behavior. Such a process could also be termed behavioral, however, inasmuch as individuals are encouraged to change their rewarding behavior. Research suggests that both self-monitoring and self-rewarding have therapeutic efficacy. There is still insufficient evidence to evaluate the efficacy of the stimulus control process, however.

(2) Covert conditioning. This is a class of techniques which attempt to produce a physical conditioning process by focusing on internal thoughts and images. In covert *counterconditioning,* for instance, the individual attempts to imagine aversive scenes and cope with them; in *thought-stopping* clients are taught to say "stop" to themselves when they begin to engage in negative ruminations. There is no substantial evidence so far supporting the efficacy of these techniques.

(3) Cognitive restructuring. This category of cognitive techniques includes rational-emotive therapy (RET), the self-instructional techniques of Meichenbaum and the cognitive therapy of Aaron Beck. Meichenbaum's approach focuses on the idiosyncratic thought patterns of the individual and attempts to give the patient self-instructional training for use in certain situations. Meichenbaum's emphasis is on the construction of a positive set of self-talk skills, not on destroying negative beliefs as in RET. Beck's cognitive therapy combines the above: individuals learn both to recognize maladaptive cognitions and to develop more adaptive cognitions. Beck goes further and gives the patient behavioral assignments to test the incorrectness of the old maladaptive thoughts or the correctness of the new thoughts. An increasing number of therapy outcome studies have documented the efficacy of both Beck's and Meichenbaum's models.

(4) Coping skills and problem solving. This approach comprises a heterogeneous collection of procedures which seek to give individuals a repertoire of skills to aid in adjustment. Typically, these include training in self-instructional procedures, how to talk to one's self in a difficult situation, relaxation training, and performance rehearsal. Imagery may be used here, not as a conditioning process but as an opportunity for rehearsal. The teaching of problem solving skills is seen as an aspect of coping skills, and individuals are taught the basic steps of problem solving: specifying the problem, collecting information, identifying causes, examining options, narrowing options, comparing data, and revising plans. Generally, the coping skills and problem-solving techniques are considered to be effective procedures for teaching individuals to deal with stressful situations and offer much promise for the future.

4. Theological Evaluation.
Because cognitive therapy lays stress on the functioning of the individual's rational and cognitive capabilities as a source of mental health, there is a danger of elevating reason and cognitive organizational capacity until it becomes the source or criterion of all information and knowledge, including religious knowledge. This leads to an excessive rationalism with no room for transcendent sources of knowledge (revelation) — the problem first posed by Immanuel Kant. It also suggests an idolatrous overestimation of the mind and a disparagement of the role of the physical and biological factors in mental life — the position of idealistic philosophies. Perhaps this elevation of mind attests to an inherent idealism in cognitive psychology, as well as a ready affinity to Eastern religions, as suggested by some work on the nature of consciousness (Shapiro and Zifferblatt, 1976).

On the positive side, however, cognitive therapy's emphasis on argumentation with oneself is reminiscent of the *imago dei* as defined by Reinhold Niebuhr (1941). Niebuhr (borrowing from Augustine) pictures the image of God in the individual as that aspect of the individual which is capable of dialogue with oneself and is thus self-conscious. The human is also capable of stepping back from one's "self" and evaluating it in a moment of self-transcendence. According to Niebuhr, self in dialogue with self is the essence of humanness. Thus, similarly, this seems to receive direct expression in cognitive psychology's control models, which postulate that self-control and self-efficacy, the essence of mental health, are achieved when the individual becomes aware of self-statements and becomes able to stand back from them and argue with them.

Moreover, argumentation with self-statements can be done from the standpoint of any norm. Just as Ellis earlier applied the norm of stoicism to the healthiness of self-statements, so a transcendent norm can be applied to one's internal dialogue — for example, the thoughts and words of Christ as the ultimate, transcendent Word of God. Dialogue with self alone, apart from such a norm, limits transcendence, whereas a transcendent norm more fully allows the self to step out of its own process and be interpreted. Indeed, Niebuhr suggests that individuals only know themselves when confronted in this way by God. Jesus as God Incarnate and also as perfect humanness is thus a mirror for self-knowledge and understanding.

Finally, the unique way in which the cognitive and behavioral techniques have been combined in the cognitive therapy paradigm allows for a more wholistic concept of the individual than is possible in either the psychoanalytic model (with its emphasis on mind only) or on behavioral therapy (with its emphasis on nature and the impact of the environment only). Because of this inclusiveness, and because cognitive therapy emphasizes self-dialogue and the possibility of self-transcendence, this model may be said to express fundamental features of the biblical — especially the Hebraic — view of the person as both physical, subject to the vicissitudes of the environment and the natural world, and self-transcendent, made in the image and likeness of God.

5. Applications in Pastoral Counseling. *a. Use of scriptural and theological concepts.* The ample use of scriptural and/or theological categories in all three phases of the cognitive therapy process is one use of this model in pastoral care and counseling. For example, in the first phase of therapy, it is possible to reinforce the rationale that one's thoughts have an impact upon emotional adjustment through the use of scriptural or theological concepts (for example, Rom. 8:5). The presentation of internal dialoguing with self as a unique manifestation of the image of God can also provide a theological rationale.

In the second phase, insight into cognitions, the Psalms laud the value of self-examination (e.g., Psalm 139), and both scripture and tradition are rich in models of self-examination.

The third phase of cognitive therapy, replacing maladaptive thoughts with healthier thoughts, allows a generous use of concepts from all aspects of Christian literature or tradition. For example, one characteristic of the depressed individual is the tendency to think in "all or nothing" categories; one must be perfect or one is worthless. Romans 3:23–24, for example, can provide a useful replacement thought for themes of such perfectionism. Likewise, the tendency toward emotional reasoning among depressives — "because I feel bad, I must be bad" — can be countered with statements from Christian mystical tradition. St. John of the Cross, for example, contends that emotional darkness or desolation is not necessarily a sign of God's disfavor, and can indeed be evidence of increased spirituality, a phase in one's spiritual journey. That is, depression is not necessarily a sin.

b. Use in meditative disciplines. Meditation has been defined as the focusing of one's attention in a non-evaluative manner. Research in cognitive therapy (Shapiro and Zifferblatt, 1976) suggests, however, that even when concentrating in a "non-evaluative manner" — presumably without evaluative cognitions — the individual is actually making a cognitive construction: "Whatever I think is OK." Likewise, Christian traditions of meditation, especially Ignatian spirituality, seek to transcend ordinary cognition by making copious use of mental images of spiritual subjects. According to the cognitive perspective, however, these images are actually thoughts within a visual mode, which contain much more information than would normally be available in an abstract mode. Even meditation in the tradition of St. John of the Cross, commonly called contemplation because of its attempt to arrive at imageless or contentless

prayer (as in the Eastern tradition), could be construed as cognitive. Essentially, the individual within this framework learns to tell himself or herself that it is acceptable not to have an image, that whatever darkness is experienced is acceptable and, indeed, is part of the contemplative path.

The act of telling oneself that whatever one experiences is acceptable can have important positive effects, however. Construing negative emotions like anxiety or depression as acceptable and, indeed, as stages on a path of contemplation can be freeing for overanxious or depressed individuals, who often become anxious simply about the possibility of experiencing negative emotions.

Ignatian meditative techniques can also be useful in dealing with depression or anxiety. Individuals in these states often experience a great deal of negative imagery; Modifying that imagery or neutralizing that imaging can often lessen depression (Propst, 1982). It is thus only a simple step to encourage such individuals to substitute religious imagery for their negative images.

Bibliography. J. Anderson, *Cognitive Psychology and Its Implications* (1980). M. Mahoney and D. Arnkoff, "Cognitive and Self-control Therapies," in S. Garfield and A. Bergin, eds., *Handbook of Psychotherapy and Behavior Change,* 2d ed. (1978). R. Niebuhr, *Nature and Destiny of Man,* vol. 1 (1941). L. R. Propst, "Cognitive Therapy via Personal Belief Systems," in L. Abt and I. Stuart, eds., *The Newer Therapies* (1982). D. Shapiro and S. Zifferblatt, "Zen Meditation and Behavior Self-control," *American Psychologist,* 31 (1976), 519–32.

L. R. PROPST

COGNITIVE DEVELOPMENT; PHILOSOPHY AND PSYCHOLOGY; PSYCHOLOGY, WESTERN; PSYCHOTHERAPY. *See also* COGNITIVE/CONATIVE PROBLEM; CYBERNETIC THEORY; DREAM THEORY AND RESEARCH; FEELING, THOUGHT AND ACTION IN PASTORAL COUNSELING; IGNATIAN SPIRITUALITY; IMAGINATION; MEDITATION; MIND; PROBLEM SOLVING; PERSON (Philosophic Issues); RATIONAL EMOTIVE PSYCHOTHERAPY; REASONING AND RATIONALITY IN PASTORAL CARE; SPIRITUAL DIRECTION. *Compare* BEHAVIOR THERAPIES; GESTALT PSYCHOLOGY AND PSYCHOTHERAPY; ILLUMINATION; INTELLECTUALIZATION; INTUITION; REASON AND PASSION; THEOLOGY AND PSYCHOLOGY.

COHABITATION. Usually a man and woman sharing the same household without marriage for at least six months. "There have been few developments relating to marriage and family life which have been as dramatic as the rapid increase of unmarried cohabitation (Glick and Spanier, 1980, p. 20). The number of cohabiting couples has more than tripled since 1970. According to the 1985 census, there were 1,988,000 such households in the U.S. Glick and Spanier report that blacks contribute disproportionately higher numbers, and that among total populations, cohabiting couples are characterized by lower income levels and higher unemployment.

1. Sociological Studies. The first sociological studies of cohabitation in the U.S. were of college populations (Henze and Hudson; Peterman, Ridley and Anderson; Bower and Christopherson). Later studies surveyed were of males in the Selective Service (Clayton and Vass, 1977). However, Glick's and Spanier's studies utilized Census Bureau statistics on marital status and living arrangements and gave readers a better idea of the nature of the phenomenon. Studies have also been carried out in

Sweden, and attempts are being made currently to study cohabitation in other parts of the world. The practice apparently increased in Western Europe during the 1970s as it did in the U.S.

The increase in cohabitation reflects a complex of social factors: increased sexual freedom, postponement of marriage, a trend toward smaller families, a relaxation of parental pressure toward early marriage, a decrease of social stigma related to divorce, liberalization of norms relating to lifestyles, and a decrease in the authority of the church. Society, however, still has a high stake in marriage and a stable family structure. Though attitudes toward cohabitation are changing, the unmarried couple will still encounter social barriers and psychological problems that need to be faced realistically.

2. Issues Involved in Cohabitation. Marriage involves three parties: the man, the woman, and the state. In cohabitation, the couple chooses to have the benefits of living together without the intrusion or the protection of the state; most issues surrounding cohabitation eventuate from this choice. Psychologically, the couple probably is motivated by a desire for companionship, sexual privilege, and sharing of quarters without the legal constraints of marriage. Partners can leave the relationship upon notice with responsibility only to themselves. Couples enter such relationships desirous of freedom from the social expectations represented by traditional marriage.

Legal issues are the biggest ones for the unmarried couple to work through. Common law marriage, once universally recognized, has legal status today in only a dozen states and the District of Columbia. A couple without a registered marriage license faces problems, particularly concerning taxation, inheritance, and the legitimacy of children born to the union. If one partner has been previously married and brings a child into the new home, the custody of the child may be questioned. Laws vary from state to state regarding cohabitation; in some states such activity is still considered immoral and illegal so that the couple find themselves with few legal rights. New state legislation is currently being written to take account of this relationship.

Separation between unmarried couples when one or both want to break up the relationship poses the greatest problem. Since the celebrated Marvin versus Marvin "palimony" case in California in 1979, courts have had to deal increasingly with the rights of such partners at the time of separation. Most states now recognize that (1) the unmarried spouse has a right at time of separation to bring claims against the partner; and (2) among contracts, implied and express, implied contracts (unwritten but expressed) represent valid claims.

The interpersonal issues that unmarried couples face depend on the commitment each has made to the relationship, which varies from person to person and from one period of social history to another. Fidelity to each other may or may not be assumed. How each enters into the conjugal roles — in particular, economic support, pooling of resources, assumption of responsibility for house and property — depends upon each partner's desires, and these may change. What may be entered into as a convenience during college years is difficult to break up because of emotional ties. Even though most of these liaisons exist in urban areas or areas surrounding colleges and universities, the couples must face up to how the larger community views their relationships. For these reasons, cohabitation is often a situation couples enter into before marriage or after divorce. There is an unstable and tenuous quality to such relationships, particularly because of the lack of a contract.

3. Pastoral Counseling. The Christian church stands behind marriage either as a sacrament or a covenanted relationship and, for that reason, cohabiting couples often expect pastors and priests to disagree with their desire to live together outside marriage. However, pastoral counselors can most effectively help cohabiting couples work toward a responsible relationship in keeping with Christian values by helping them reflect on the quality of their relationship in a noncondemning way. Pastoral counseling typically involves (1) couples who are facing interpersonal conflicts and who want to resolve them in their current state; (2) cohabiting couples who come to the pastor seeking marriage; (3) cohabiting couples seeking separation, with the problems of children of the union included in their set of issues.

Cohabiting couples facing interpersonal conflicts may reveal dynamics similar to those present in married couples, and to that extent may be counseled in somewhat the same way so far as resolving immediate problems is concerned. Especially in short-term counseling the most useful approach involves the pastor's serving as mediator, attempting to help the couple work toward a contract that represents a common understanding of their individual rights and duties. Such a contract can be oral or written; some lawyers are now providing an outline of such a contract, which a couple may write out and change as needed. A cohabitation agreement is intended to prevent either party from taking unfair advantage of the other within the arrangement or at the time of separation (see Englehardt, 1981).

In counseling unmarried couples who are experiencing interpersonal conflict, the pastor should nonetheless be alert to the fact that the lack of a marital commitment often introduces subtle but important differences into the counseling situation, especially if deeper personal needs are involved or longer-term therapeutic counseling seems indicated. Many pastoral counselors therefore feel that extended counseling with unmarried couples is dynamically unwise and to be avoided. They believe that such counseling implicitly presupposes a commitment between the partners that has not in fact been made, thus blurring individual identity and responsibility in the developing commitment. Others believe that these risks can be effectively managed and that constructive outcomes can sometimes be achieved, at least by well-trained and experienced counselors. In either case there are obvious questions of moral responsibility related to the pastor's representation of the church and perhaps his or her own moral views as well. These issues must be carefully thought through in relation to the pastor's desire to offer care that is fundamentally accepting, noncondemning, and constructively helpful.

Cohabiting couples who come to the pastor to be married — and these represent the majority of those whom he or she will see — will need premarital counseling that stresses the nature of the commitment they seek to make to each other before God and in the eyes of the state. Emotional blocks that each has experienced to marriage before this time and their current motivation to marry should also be explored. Family backgrounds particularly need to be discussed, as the reasons for the couple's prior cohabitation are probably related to their view of their parents' marriage, a sibling's divorce, or some other negative experience. Ideas regarding fidelity, family financial planning, and having children are important to discuss, as such couples may have been inhibited in their communication with each other because of the tentativeness of their union. The religious service itself should include all the elements of the ritual and should enable the couple to found their union on mutual commitment within a religious community.

Unmarried couples seeking separation may approach the pastor or may be referred by other members of the family desirous of helping the couple. With state laws varying so widely on the legal status of cohabitation, however, the pastor would do well to have the couple see a lawyer. Responsibilities to one's ex-partner, deciding who gets custody of the children, distribution of property, etc., are complicated issues that need arbitration by legal counsel. Laws are changing so rapidly that unless a pastor wants to do a lot of legal research it is impossible to be up to date on these matters. If only one party, say the woman, seeks out the pastor and feels as though she has been treated unfairly at the time of separation, the pastor may need to support her psychologically while she seeks legal redress. Care and custody of children of the union may need particular attention. There is a trend toward eradicating legal provisions that have previously discriminated against children born out of wedlock. Whether cohabitation will be recognized by law and in the eyes of society as an emerging social institution is yet to be seen.

Bibliography. D. W. Brown and V. A. Christopherson, "University Student Cohabitation: a Regional Comparison of Selected Attitudes and Behavior," *J. of Marriage and the Family*, 39 (1977), 477–54. R. R. Clayton and H. L. Vass, "Shacking Up: Cohabitation in the 1970s," *J. of Marriage and the Family*, 39 (1977), 273–84. G. Douthwaite, *Unmarried Couples and the Law* (1979). L. S. Englehardt, II, *Living Together: What's the Law?* (1981). J. M. Eskelaar and N. Katz, eds., *Marriage and Cohabitation in Contemporary Societies* (1980). P. C. Glick and G. B. Spanier, "Married and Unmarried Cohabitation in the United States," *J. of Marriage and the Family*, 42 (1980), 19–30. L. F. Henze and J. W. Hudson, "Personal and Family Characteristics of Cohabiting and Non-cohabiting College Students," *J. of Marriage and the Family*, 36 (1974), 722–27. E. D. Macklin, "Non-marital Heterosexual Cohabitation: a Review of the Recent Literature" *Marriage and Family Review*, 1 (1978), 1–12. D. J. Peterman, C. A. Ridley, and S. M. Anderson, "A Comparison of Cohabiting and Non-cohabiting College Students," *J. of Marriage and the Family*, 36 (1974), 344–54. J. S. Bureau of the Census, "Marital Status and Living Arrangements," (Oct., 1985) Current Population Report SP 20, No. 402.20.

C. W. STEWART

FAMILY; MARRIAGE. *See also* COMMON LAW MARRIAGE.

COLLECTIVE UNCONSCIOUS. In Jung's psychology, the source of primordial human memories which are inherited in the brain structure at birth as a result of repeated, cumulative racial experiences. Within the collective unconscious reside the archetypes, the evolved latent ancestral knowledge of the human race. When structured by individual growth, these represent universal reactions to typical human situations, e.g., birth, death, and relationships with the divine and between the sexes.

H. COWARD

ANALYTICAL (JUNGIAN) PSYCHOLOGY (Personality Theory and Research); ANALYTICAL (JUNGIAN) PSYCHOLOGY AND PASTORAL CARE *or* RELIGION *or* THEOLOGY; ARCHETYPE; MYTHOLOGY AND PSYCHOLOGY; UNCONSCIOUS.

COLLEGE STUDENTS AND COLLEGE CHAPLAINCY. Students, for the purpose of this entry, are persons engaged in a program of study in an institution of higher learning, whether they are undergraduates, graduates, or in a professional school. College chaplaincy is a religious ministry, usually headed by an ordained person, which provides the members of an academic community with opportunities for worship, the non-credit study of religious texts and issues, and for pastoral counseling and the experience of religious community. The disestablishment of religion in Western culture is now complete in most academic institutions, including those still supported by the churches. Most students, therefore, work in a secular setting and most chaplaincies are now at varying distances from the center of the institutions' central purposes. The secularity of most academic institutions conditions both the needs of the students and the form of the ministry provided by the chaplain.

1. **Students.** The life of a student is still seen as a deviation from the norms of society which assume that at this chronological age a person will enter the work force, establish independence from the family, marry, and contribute to the joint income. Although most families and all academic institutions affirm the work of scholarship, many students are uneasy about their privileged position, the financial strain upon the family, the postponement of sexual commitment, and uncertainty about their future employment. Though most students were exposed to heterogeneous values in secondary school, the values of their homes were normative. These values are challenged in the classroom and dormitory, and many students are pressed to begin the task of affirming or denying the values which shaped their adolescence. Increasingly, academic institutions make no integral provision for assisting students with this process, and chaplains and counselors fill a role once performed by professors and administrators. The impact of experimentation with alcohol, drugs, and sexual practice, often delayed by the academically oriented until the college years, is accentuated by the relative freedom and diversity of values within the college community. While it is true that many students with strong religious training become less involved in the college years, it is equally true that some students who have had no previous religious experience choose to explore what it is that motivates and shapes the lives of their religiously committed peers. There is no single response to the academic work itself. The majority

of students are unthreatened by it and are unexcited by either content or process. A few students experience the euphoria of insight and manifest a concentration of energy, neither of which is easily comprehended by peers or the general population.

2. Chaplaincy. There are three major types of chaplaincies. The college chaplain (Dean of the Chapel) is employed by the institution and charged with serving all of its members. Major religious traditions also send chaplains, primarily to serve those of their denomination. It is increasingly common for conservative Christian groups such as Inter-varsity and Campus Crusade to send trained workers to evangelize and nurture students. The college chaplain is charged with the oversight of the various ministries.

College and denominational chaplains most often center their ministries in corporate worship. Around this center, students, and sometimes faculty members, are gathered for Bible study, discussion of ethical issues, fellowship, and social action. Non-denominational groups center their work in Bible study, instruction, outreach, and the development of a supportive community. From time to time, various chaplaincies cooperate to accomplish a campus-wide conference, mission, or program of social action.

College and denominational chaplains are theologically trained, ordained by their traditions, have CPE experience, and have usually had at least one prior professional position. One-third to one-half of their time is spent in counseling. The college chaplain spends additional time in crisis counseling.

3. Campus and Parish Resources. College chaplains usually form alliances with the deans charged with student affairs in common concern for the quality of life within the institution. The referral of students by professors to chaplains is common, as is referral from chaplains to the school's counseling center. It is not uncommon for the counseling center and the chaplains to work together to provide group work in such areas as the use of alcohol and sexual relationships.

The congregations and synagogues surrounding a college often serve students by providing continuity with their previous religious experience and a non-threatening community.

Chaplains are accountable to their respective denominations but find major support among their peers. Professional conferences, denominational and ecumenical, provide both standards and continuing education.

Bibliography. R. Rankin, ed., *The Rediscovery of Spirit in Higher Education* (1980). G. W. Jones, ed., "Campus Ministry," *Counseling and Values* 20:2 (1976). K. Underwood, *The Church, the University, and Social Policy*, 2 vols. (1969).

J. VANNORSDALL

CHAPLAINCY; YOUNG ADULTS.

COLOSTOMY. The creation of a surgical opening (an ostomy) between the skin and any portion of the large bowel, performed as a permanent or temporary diversion of the fecal stream. Pathologic conditions necessitating a colostomy are congenital defects, neurogenic disease, trauma, inflammatory disease (including radiation injury), and cancer. Patients' attitudes affect their accep-

tance of the procedure and willingness to live with its limitations. Because "potty training" plays an important role in childhood development, the threat of losing control of elimination functions has emotional as well as physical significance. The presence of a stoma affects self-esteem and body image; very personal and private parts of one's life become exposed. Patients leave the hospital carrying a surgical scar and an altered process of elimination that will demand attention every day.

A counselor needs to understand the world of colostomy patients. No question posed by patients or family members is insignificant if counselors want them to feel that the ostomy is acceptable and not repulsive. Patients cannot accept an ostomy unless they can care for themselves. Therefore patients need to be taught how to perform their own care. They need time for demonstration, for participation, for practice with supervision until they become proficient in handling the entire procedure. As patients learn to care for themselves, they become comfortable with touching the stoma and washing the skin, and realize that the stoma is now just another bodily part. It is important that partners also be supported through a similar phase of adjustment.

Initially colostomy patients are threatened by loss of life. Gradually, however, as they recover, their attention shifts to their role in the family and in society, work life, and sexuality. An ostomy can interfere with patients' attitudes about all these areas, particularly the latter. A man with an ostomy is still very much a man, and a woman with an ostomy is very much a woman. Spouses need to be encouraged to touch each other and to confirm their feelings for each other, their own sense of self-worth, and their sexuality. A couple needs to view the ostomy as an integral part of their relationship, to consider how their sexual activity will be affected, and to learn how to manage the appliances. Both partners need to feel that they have permission to discuss their sexual concerns, to develop communication with an accepting person. Patients need to be reassured, need time to tell their stories and to explore ways of dealing with problems related to employment, financial resources, and socialization, as well as sexuality.

The pastor can provide an accepting atmosphere in which permission is given to explore all avenues. The pastor must remain alert to any clue patients offer, opening areas for exploration and helpful integration. If the couple should need intensive therapy for any of their concerns, including sexuality, the pastor should know how to make appropriate referrals.

E. J. MAHNKE

BODY IMAGE; CRISIS MINISTRY; HANDICAP AND DISABILITY; LOSS OF FUNCTION; SURGICAL PATIENT.

COLUMBARIUM. *See* BURIAL; CREMATION.

COMFORT/SUSTAINING. To console and strengthen; to stand alongside to lend support and encouragement when the situation cannot be changed, at least not immediately; to carry on a ministry of sustenance as long as circumstances preclude healing.

In contemporary pastoral care and counseling, sustaining is seen as one of three or four pastoral functions within pastoral ministry. This understanding is spelled out most explicitly in Seward Hiltner's *Preface to Pastoral Theology* and in *Pastoral Care in Historical Perspective* by William A. Clebsch and Charles R. Jaekle. According to these authors, the basic function of pastoral care and counseling is to heal, to restore the individual to a state of functional wholeness. When that is not possible, as for instance in times of loss through death, pastoral care takes the form of sustaining, of comforting and strengthening in order to help the individual cope with the situation. Thus sustaining is a distinct ministry, important in its own right, though it also presses toward healing when that is possible.

A ministry of sustaining is also to be distinguished from guiding. Guiding means helping an individual to decide upon an appropriate course of action, either by educing the answer from his or her own inner resources or by confronting him or her with other, outside considerations and resources. To these three functions Clebsch and Jaekle add a fourth—the function of reconciling. Reconciliation becomes the primary concern of pastoral care and counseling when it centers on broken relationships. The relationships may be person-to-person or person-to-God, but in any case reconciliation is seen as a distinct function when it is not considered an integral dimension of the other three functions.

1. **Historical Roots of Sustaining.** Sustaining is a modern cognate for the word "comfort." Comfort is a biblical term, used more frequently and in a wider sense in the KJV than in the RSV. Its basic meaning is to speak to someone in a friendly way, to draw close to the person in need. This drawing close encompasses two dimensions: consolation and admonition or, in other words, undergirding and urging on. Hiltner believed that in modern usage comfort has lost the connotation of urging on and has come to mean simply soothing or even making comfortable. He proposed the use of "sustaining" as a way to recapture the original meaning of comfort. His proposal is faithful not only to the concrete implications of the biblical term but also to its theological ramifications. Consolation and admonition parallel the larger biblical structure of indicative and imperative. This parallel means that comfort — especially God's comfort—involves both gift and task, both a receiving and a doing. It also acknowledges the fact that comfort can become "a doing what is possible" only because it is first "a receiving of solicitous care and concern." In a word, comfort as task proceeds from comfort as gift, and not vice versa.

According to Clebsch and Jaekle, the ministry of sustaining has been a fourfold process in the church, especially when enacted with individuals who have suffered a devastating loss. The first endeavor is to help these individuals hold the line against further loss or excessive retreat. Once accomplished, preservation gives away to consolation, to relieving their sense of misery by surrounding them with a sense of support and hope. The third phase is consolidation, that is, encouraging these persons to use the resources they have available to begin a process of rebuilding. This sets the stage for the final task: redemption. The individual is helped to face the future and to build "an ongoing life that once more pursues its fulfillment and destiny on a new basis."

2. **Sustaining as Crisis Counseling.** A special form of sustaining is called crisis counseling. Crisis counseling deals with traumatic situations that cannot be changed immediately, and therefore calls for a ministry of consolation and admonition. Its three-step methodology (often called the ABC method of intervention) is similar to Clebsch and Jaekle's fourfold process, except that it is stated in more psychological terms. The first step is called *achieving* contact with the person in crisis, not just physical contact but more so the establishment of a genuine relationship of empathy and trust that conveys care and support. The second step is *boiling* the problem down to its essentials. In this phase, the pastor concentrates on getting a deep and accurate understanding of the person's situation and tries to help him or her clarify the exact source and nature of the crisis. The final step, called *coping* with the problem, is a conflation of Clebsch's and Jaekle's consolidation and redemption. It involves the establishment of a realistic plan of action, based on an inventory of the individual's internal and external resources, and represents a definite attempt to put that plan into effect as a move beyond the crisis into a new way of life.

3. **Theological Dimensions of Sustaining.** For pastoral care and counseling, a ministry of sustaining is grounded in the theological belief that all comfort comes ultimately from God. In the OT, God's sustaining presence is mediated through Scripture, through the prophets, and especially through "God's Servant" who brings the promise of final deliverance. In the NT, comfort comes from Jesus Christ or, more specifically, it is the gift of good news granted in Jesus Christ. Christ as comfort addresses two basic types of human affliction: death and suffering. In terms of death, Christ is comfort because he has broken the power of death by his resurrection and has become the promise of eternal life. In terms of suffering, Christ comforts either by consoling and strengthening in the midst of affliction or by delivering the person from it. In either case, Christians accept suffering for Christ's sake and thus become members of a fellowship in which they receive the comfort of God. In turn, they are able to comfort others who are in any affliction with the comfort with which they themselves have been comforted by God (II Cor. 1:3–7). In this way, the Christian fellowship of suffering becomes a fellowship of mutual care and comfort.

Pastoral care and counseling lives in this hope and works toward this end. At the same time, it recognizes that comfort in any ultimate sense is an eschatological promise, not a present achievement. A certain measure of comfort can be and is gained in the immediate situation, but final deliverance from death and suffering will be accomplished only at the end of time. Pastoral care and counseling, then, should seek to make real God's sustaining presence in our interactions with each other, knowing that we are sharing in Christ's sufferings and that he is participating in ours, but it must also labor under the realization that ultimate comfort is not possible in the present age.

4. **Sustaining and Black Pastoral Care.** Black pastoral care in America has been a notable instance of a ministry of sustaining. As Clebsch and Jaekle point out, sustaining becomes dominant in historical epochs when

immediate solutions cannot be found for personal or social conflicts. Because black people have lived under slavery and oppression, a ministry of sustaining, which combines both consolation and admonition, both present and eschatological hopes, has been a dominant form of black pastoral care and counseling on both a congregational and a clerical level. Through a variety of means — prayer meetings, church fellowship, Negro spirituals, the rite of baptism, and an optimistic theological worldview—the black church has sustained and given courage to its people. By its depth and its breadth black pastoral care is an epitome of the ministry of sustaining in situations of prolonged suffering.

Bibliography. G. A. Buttrick, *Interpreter's Dictionary of the Bible,* vol. 1, (1962), p. 662. W. A. Clebsch and C. R. Jaekle, *Pastoral Care in Historical Perspective* (1964). S. Hiltner, *Preface to Pastoral Theology* (1958). H. T. Weyhofen, *Trost: Modelle des Religiösen und Philosophischen Trösters und ihre Beurteilung durch die Religionskritik* (1983). E. P. Wimberly, *Pastoral Care in the Black Church* (1979).

L. ADEN

CONSOLATION; GRIEF AND LOSS; MOURNING CUSTOMS AND RITUALS; PRESENCE, MINISTRY OF; TOUCHING/PHYSICAL SUPPORT. *See also* CRYING; PROVIDENCE; SHEPHERD/ SHEPHERDING; SUPPORT GROUPS; SUPPORTIVE THERAPY; WORSHIP AND CELEBRATION.

COMMANDMENTS. *See* TEN COMMANDMENTS.

COMMITMENT. Any binding social relationship created by an act of promising, choosing, and self-giving, maintained by trust, dedication, and hope together with the force of moral obligation, circumstance, cost, or sacrifice. Alternatively, especially in social psychological literature, commitment is often defined as persistence in a course of action that is meaningful and important despite obstacles, costs, or alternative possibilities (Brickman). The two meanings are complementary, pointing in the first instance to commitment's social character (binding relationship), and in the second to its most prominent behavioral feature (persistence).

1. General Features. Whether in love, friendship, marriage, work, career, moral life, or religion, commitment is a complex and profoundly important human activity involving certain distinctive features: (1) A *juxtaposition of freedom and constraint:* commitment combines free choosing and intentionality with the creation and acceptance of obligation. It is freedom limiting itself, and obligation freely performed. (2) *Cost and sacrifice:* one is not genuinely committed until a price is paid, a sacrifice made, or a promissory act performed ("I do"); this makes the relationship socially binding or the action costly to undo or reverse. (3) *Future orientation:* undertaken by sacrifice or promissory act in the present, commitment aims to structure the future; thus it requires faith and hope. (4) *Social complexity:* commitments are never really simple or singular but always involve multiple social and cultural "objects." Commitment to one's spouse or profession, for instance, also entails commitment to the abstract values, social obligations, and institutions which those relationships involve; likewise, *abstract* commitments (e.g. to ideals, values, or symbols)

entail *concrete* social actions, institutional relationships, costs, and consequences. (5) *Variable with respect to social change:* commitment can be conservative and conformist, or individualistic, innovative, and divergent from established norms and practices (e.g. prophets, social reformers, cultural innovators).

2. Sociology of Commitment. Though commitment is popularly viewed as an individual act, it must also be understood as a group function, even when its social dimensions are not obvious. This is because all commitments are inherently social; they respond to social circumstances and create social consequences.

Every society and every institution must generate and sustain commitment, and commitments in one form or another are no doubt essential for individual welfare. In the modern world, however, commitment has become especially important — and problematic. Today individuals must make many choices for themselves that once were prescribed by community and tradition; cultural meanings and values that support commitment have weakened in authority and influence; and secularism, pluralism, individualism, and rapid social change undermine commitment in countless ways (Bellah; Mead; Rieff; Wheelis). Thus commitment has emerged as a major personal, social, and pastoral problem.

Kanter's (1972) theory, developed for analyzing divergent communities (communes), is nonetheless helpful for understanding any group commitment sociologically. Defining commitment as "the willingness of people to do what will help maintain the group because it provides what they need" (p. 66), Kanter distinguishes three kinds of social processes or "mechanisms" involved in creating and maintaining commitment, each of which *detaches* individuals from existing or competing involvements and *attaches* them to the group: (1) *continuance* — economic "sacrifice" for and "investment" in the group; (2) *cohesion*—"renunciation" of outside emotional ties and emotional "communion" within the group; and (3) *control*—"mortification" of one's former identity and rediscovery or "transcendence" of self through the group's meaning system. Kelley's popular work on conservative churches (1977) utilizes similar ideas, but emphasizes control mechanisms almost exclusively. Other studies (e.g. Gerlach and Hine; Brickman) have defined stage-like sequences for commitment.

3. Social Psychology of Commitment. Defining commitment solely in terms of persistent action, Brickman and associates (1987) offer a powerful theory based on cognitive dissonance and social perception theories in social psychology. Brickman distinguishes control motivation, "extrinsically" oriented in terms of seeking rewards or avoiding harm, from commitment motivation which occurs in the absence of reward and in the presence of obstacles or other negative factors and is thus pursued for "instrinsic" reasons of meaning and value. In committed friendship, for example, one values one's friend for his or her own sake, not solely for sex, social status, or the like; in committed activities like a religious calling or even a hobby, one persists because of their felt meaning and value. Such committed or intrinsically motivated action gradually comes about, says Brickman, as persons seek to justify or find reasons for actions previously taken that "commit" them little by little to their consequences (technically, "reducing dissonance"). In order for commitment to develop, such actions must occur in ambiguous situations where there is a "negative element," be freely chosen, and entail a willingness to accept consequences. Then one gradually develops intrinsic motivation for one's actions; one becomes inwardly "committed" to them. Thus, contrary to popular intuition, the subjective attitude of commitment, which sustains one through adversity and distraction, *follows* rather than precedes behavioral acts of commitment. Brickman's theory makes use of numerous research studies and offers powerful insights into many forms of commitment, from weight reduction and romantic love to religion. He also maintains that persons who develop significant commitments are less prone to mental distress and illness and more able to live deeply satisfying and meaningful lives, especially if they develop commitment to life itself in the face of suffering and death.

4. Psychology of Commitment. From a humanistic or "self-actualizing" perspective commitment can be motivated by distorted self-awareness (Rogers) or unmet needs and deficiencies (Maslow.) In either case it functions as a device for self-maintenance, *or* it can be an expression of one's deepest organismic valuing process (Rogers) or the development of one's inherent powers (Maslow). Commitment's subordination of self to society or transcendent "other" stands in some tension with the self-actualization principle of these psychologies.

Jung's and Erikson's theories would also seem to emphasize developmental aspects of commitment, especially unconscious ones. For Jung, ordinary social commitments as well as profound spiritual ones emerge out of archetypal depths as well as conscious ego functions, and always involve unconscious attempts to develop and unify the psyche, whatever their outward social aims and dynamics. For instance, a commitment may at one level be the psyche's attempt to express a dominant function (e.g. introversion) or develop a latent one (e.g. extroversion), or (especially in later life) to integrate projected archetypes in quest of the Self. Erikson's (1964) "life cycle" theory implies that each psychosocial life stage task is a kind of commitment process and suggests that commitment means different things at different stages of the life cycle. For instance, commitments of middle adulthood inwardly draw upon the accrued strengths ("virtues") and limitations of previous developmental stages (e.g. hope, will) in achieving "generativity," the capacity to work and care for future generations.

Psychoanalytically, commitment may be viewed as an ego operation in which specific object relations are secured, modelled after developmentally primitive relations (e.g. parents), and subjected to rigidifying reinforcement through intrapunitive superego pressures (evident, in extreme form, in authoritarianism). Thus the dynamics of guilt and shame play a significant role in psychoanalytic understandings of commitment, as well as "regressive" processes—attempts to recover childhood securities and partially to suspend or compromise the reality-oriented functions of adulthood (e.g. by believing that one can control the future and secure relationships against loss). However, this need not be pathological; commitment may also serve the person's realistic long-term interests, though commitment is a psychologically complex and risky process at best (Schlesinger). There is some question whether or in what way any of these theories can envision genuinely sacrificial, self-transcending commitment free of conflict or pathology, however.

Feminist perspectives have added yet another dimension. Jung (1953), Gilligan (1983), Chodorow (1974) and others contend that women in Western patriarchal culture give higher priority to maintaining relationships than to asserting autonomy. By inference, commitment would seem less problematic for women than for men, or problematic in different ways, and may typically manifest a more intuitive, "emergent," less rational and decisional style. Commitment threatens the masculine emphasis on autonomy, will, and control; the woman's challenge is to achieve greater individuality and self-affirmation (less "self-sacrifice") in committed relationships.

5. Theology and Ethics of Commitment. Though "commitment" in the contemporary sense of self-giving, self-binding promissory action is relatively recent (late nineteenth century), virtually the entire Jewish and Christian heritage is about commitment in one form or another. The basic biblical concept here is *covenant*, with its themes of calling and vocation, binding relationship, mutual fidelity, moral obligation, promise, faith, hope, and love—as well as sin, judgment, forgiveness, and redemption—themes developed with respect both to divine-human and human-social relationships. The emergence of commitment as a social and personal concern in late modern individualistic societies gives occasion for reappropriating this tradition, especially the question of the value and meaning of commitment itself.

Of the many perspectives offered by the Christian tradition on commitment, three may be noted: (1) All commitments involve an act of trust and hope; they reach out beyond the self, beyond what can be directly predicted or controlled, to a hoped-for future in relationship to another; thus, at least implicitly, they reach out for God—for the primordial and ultimate Ground of trust and hope, however distorted or contrary to divine will they may be in particular instances (Tillich, Pannenberg). (2) Commitment thus gives finite, concrete historical expression to human destiny, requiring a willingness to live creatively and concretely in history, under the conditions of limitation and death. (3) The history of commitment (biblical and postbiblical) manifests repeated human failure at committed living, and leads to the disclosure that only commitment rooted in unconditional divine grace, forgiveness, and empowerment can ever "succeed." Such "success," however, occurs dialectically through motifs of failure, forgiveness, and restoration, not through perfectionistic effort.

6. Pastoral Implications. (1) The church must courageously speak and live a "call to commitment" sufficiently faith-filled, sacrificial, and hopeful to call individuals out from private interests into the community of faith in service to the world. Commitment occurs only to the extent that one is not afraid to embrace significant challenge, cost, and sacrifice; only what is worth paying, sacrificing, and dying for is worth living for. (2) At the same time, the church, in issuing calls to commitment, must recognize its tendency for such calls to become moralistically demanding, oppressive, aggressive, and hostile if issued apart from a genuinely felt and lived sense of need, failure, and grace. Divorced from its deepest religious insights, commitment easily becomes a code word legitimating new forms of exploitation, legalism, sadistic demand, and masochistic obedience. (3) Pastoral care and leadership must, on one hand, challenge persons to live beyond themselves in committed relationships and moral pursuits, while on the other hand compassionately support and understand the difficulties and failures inevitably involved in doing so. This combination has never been easy, and has its peculiar difficulties in the modern situation. But it is well to remember that in its depth its difficulties are not social or psychological only, but spiritual, involving the whole drama of covenantal life with one another and with God.

Bibliography. R. N. Bellah *et al., Habits of the Heart* (1985). N. Chodorow, "Family Structure and Feminine Personality," in M. Z. Rosaldo and L. Lamphere, *Women, Culture, and Society* (1974). E. Erikson, *Insight and Responsibility* (1964). S. Freud, *Group Psychology (SE,* 18/67); *Civilization and Its Discontents (SE,* 21/59). L. P. Gerlach and V. H. Hine, *People, Power, and Change* (1970). C. Gilligan, *In Another Voice* (1983). J. C. Haughey, *Should Anyone Say Forever? On Making, Keeping, and Breaking Commitments,* (1975). R. J. Hunter, "Commitment as Psychological Process: Theory and Pastoral Implications," *Pastoral Psychology,* 24 (1976), 190–205; "The Act of Personal Commitment," unpublished Ph.D. dissertation, Princeton Theological Seminary (1974). C. G. Jung, *Two Essays in Analytical Psychology* (1953). R. M. Kanter, *Community and Commitment: Communes and Utopias in Sociological Perspective* (1972). D. M. Kelley, *Why Conservative Churches Are Growing* rev. ed. (1977). M. Mead, *Culture and Commitment* (1970). E. O'Connor, *Call to Commitment* (1963). W. Pannenberg, *Theology and the Kingdom of God* (1969); *What Is Man?* (1970). P. Rieff, *The Triumph of the Therapeutic* (1966). C. R. Rogers, "Freedom and Commitment," in *Freedom to Learn* (1969). K. D. Sakenfeld, *Faithfulness in Action: Loyalty in Biblical Perspective* (1985). H. J. Schlesinger, "Developmental and Regressive Aspects of the Making and Breaking of Promises," in *The Human Mind Revisited,* S. Smith, ed. (1978); "Mature and Regression Determinants of the Keeping of Promises," in *Adulthood and the Aging Process* (1980). E. E. Thornton, *Theology and Pastoral Counseling* (1964). P. Tillich, *The Courage To Be* (1952). A. Wheelis, *The Quest for Identity* (1958).

R. J. HUNTER

FAITH/BELIEF; PROMISING; VOCATION. *See also* DECISION/ INDECISION; FORGIVENESS; FREEDOM; FRIENDSHIP; GRACE; HOPE AND DESPAIR; LIFE CYCLE THEORY; LOVE; MARRIAGE; MORAL BEHAVIOR AND RELIGION; RELIGIOUS AND UTOPIAN COMMUNITIES; RELIGIOUS LIFE; RESPONSIBILITY/ IRRESPONSIBILITY; SACRIFICIAL BEHAVIOR; SANCTIFICATION/ HOLINESS; SOCIAL CONSCIOUSNESS AND RESPONSIBILITY; TIME/TIME SENSE; VOWS/VOWING. *Compare* ALIENATION/ ESTRANGEMENT; ANOMIE/NORMLESSNESS; APOSTASY; DOUBT AND UNBELIEF; INFIDELITY, MARITAL; NARCISSISM.

COMMITMENT (Psychiatric Hospitalization). *See* MENTAL HOSPITAL/MENTAL HOSPITALIZATION.

COMMITTEE OF TWELVE. *See* PASTORAL CARE MOVEMENT.

COMMON LAW MARRIAGE. In some jurisdictions, a legal union between a man and woman established

when they present themselves as married. Their intention to be known as married is signified by use of a common name, a joint bank account, etc. Known cohabitation alone does not constitute a common law marriage, though continual cohabitation for a period of years is usually a factor in determining that such a marriage exists.

Q. L. HAND

COHABITATION; MARRIAGE.

COMMUNES. *See* RELIGIOUS AND UTOPIAN COMMUNITIES.

COMMUNICATION. Behavior designed to exchange meaning between organisms. The loveliest quality of humanness is the potential for efficient use of language. Through language humans can hurt but also heal, manipulate but also exchange meaning, express sickness and sin but also praise God and share the consolation of the gospel. The ability to share the meaning of life with one another is, undoubtedly, the supreme expression of God's image reflected in our humanness.

1. Elements of Communication Theory. In either case words work as tools for exchange of meaning only because a given culture has a general agreement about what their meanings are. This is also true for nonverbal communication, which can express meaning, attitude, feeling, or intent. Nonverbal language, often referred to as body language, may include posture, facial expression, limb movements, proximity to others, orientation toward another person, dress, and nonverbal sounds. It may or may not be accompanied by verbal language.

A lively debate continues among communication theorists whether the communicating person transfers to the receiving person a "package of meaning" through the channel of language, or whether the communication process is stimulated into actualized experience, meaning percepts already latent in the receiving person. Kant thought that communication, as all experiences of knowing, was of the latter type, language effecting a specific impact upon the cognitive and emotive functions of persons which activates or stimulates notions, insights, percepts, and feelings already present but dormant.

The process of communication is depicted graphically in Figure 1 (on the following page). This diagram clarifies the structure of communication as the process of who says what to whom, in what channel, with what effect. Numerous dynamically interacting elements constitute the process. The sender experiences an emotive level need and the psyche raises this largely subconscious need to a semiconscious or conscious level so that it may be translated into a notion. The notion is then refined and given precision through a cognitive process that evaluates the need sensation, the notion it has generated, and the idea in which it is now realized, and begins the conceptualization of a formal thought or percept. Depending upon whether a person is right- or left-brain dominant, the thought may be conceptualized linguistically or pictorially.

The formalized thought is then encoded in body or verbal language — that is, it is given symbolic form. Nonverbal language or body language seems to be a more

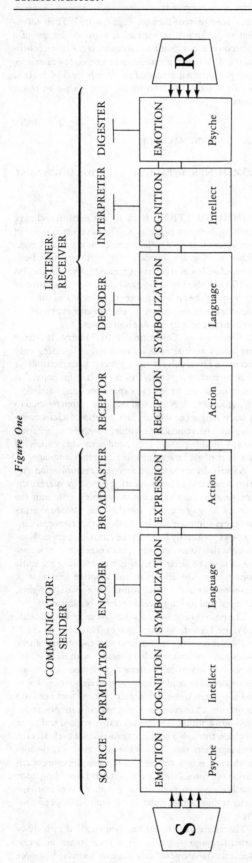

Figure One

direct expression of the needs and notions of the unconscious mind than is verbal language, forging a more direct link between psyche and symbolic encoding. However, body language is culturally conditioned, therefore learned, so there must also be a cognitive element in the process linking sensation to the symbolic encoding.

The thought or percept, now encoded in language, is ready for broadcast to the receiver through the verbal or nonverbal language channel. The receiver grasps the linguistic signal, decodes the symbology, interprets the cognitive material, and registers it in the psyche, deciding at the same time what to store in the memory and what to discard or repress.

This process contains many subprocesses. As the sender is sensing, encoding, and broadcasting the message, both extrinsic and intrinsic feedback are also in process. Intrinsic feedback is that experience in the sender by which each stage of his or her communication is being internally evaluated in terms of previously stored memory, rational reflection, learned defenses, and moral critique. Extrinsic feedback is the communicator's experience evaluating the setting and responses of the receiver and the conditions of the communications environment, and modifying the message appropriately. Simultaneously the receiver also engages in both of these feedback processes.

2. **Problems in Communication.** Moreover, there is always significant distraction, called static, functioning in any communication process. Static may be generated by the difference between the verbal and nonverbal language of the sender, physical noise or distracting activity in the environment, offensive language on the part of the sender, or inappropriate behavior by the receiver. Static is usually activity or circumstance that overloads some aspect of the communication process with extraneous emotional content, distracting the communication process from the main message. If a preacher should employ profanity in a sermon, for instance, the congregation would remember the inappropriate language, not the sermon. The inappropriate language would raise emotional static of such intensity that it would absorb all the energy and attention which should be concentrated upon the sermon. In such a case, the system is overloaded with extraneous emotion, and communication is obstructed.

Thus there are many points in any communication process at which a breakdown can occur: in the sender or receiver, at each of the points of transition to increasingly sophisticated development of the thought or percept, between the psyche and intellect, between the intellect and the symbolic encoding, between the encoding and the expression, or between the expression and the perception by the receiver. Moreover, sender and receiver may not "speak the same language." Modern culture is vocationally and linguistically tribalized and, therefore, filled with jargon. So a sender and receiver may have different functional communication channels, preventing them from tuning themselves well to one another.

At its best, communication is a two-way process, with senders and receivers constantly alternating roles, employing the principle of feedback in order to confirm or revise the accuracy of their hearing of each other. This entails both "active listening," the careful concentration

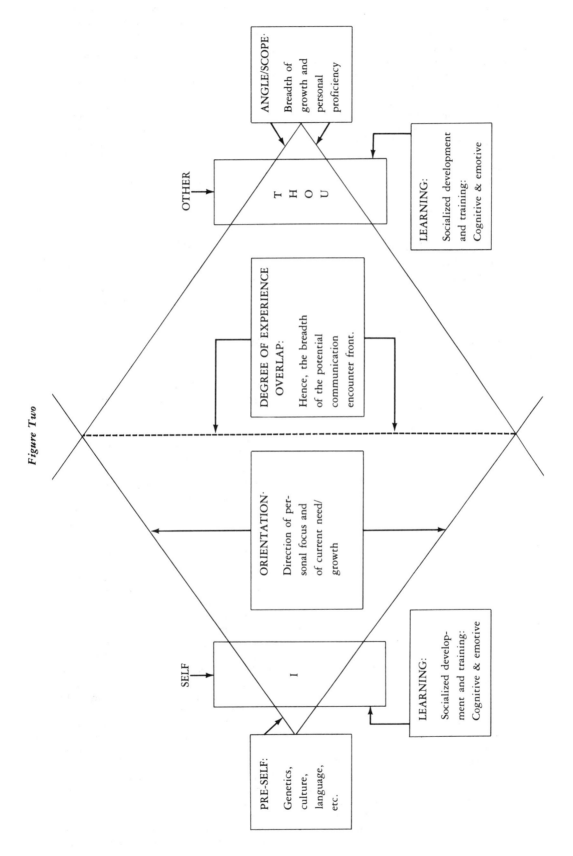

Figure Two

on what the partner is saying rather than a preoccupation with what one wishes to say next, and "efficient expression," the accurate and coherent symbolizing of one's intended message with a minimum of jargon and static. These principles are depicted in Figure 2, on previous page, which makes clear how important two-way communication is, how crucial is the orientation of the communicators toward each other, the significant role played by breadth of personality and training or development, the benefit of commonality in their symbolic vocabularies, and the significant extent to which their experience-overlap enhances their interaction.

3. **Pastoral Communication.** Communication may be said to comprise the "central nervous system" of all ministry; hence the insights of communication theory are vitally important for the practice of ministry. Two principles in particular may be emphasized: *(1) Dialogue.* Communication in which there is a frequent alternation of sender and receiver roles, and the use of feedback to increase accuracy and reduce static, is dialogical. It is the most efficient form of communication and is generally thought to be essential to therapeutic communication in particular. Though not always identified by name as such, dialogic communication has nevertheless been heavily emphasized in modern pastoral care and counseling (e.g., Hiltner, 1949; Clinebell, 1986). At a simple level dialogical communication means that direct interaction — a visit, a conversation, an opportunity to touch, to see, to hear, and to respond interactively with one's "receiver'—is more effective as a means of relating the Gospel to specific need than, say, a lecture or a prophetic proclamation. At a deeper level, it means that pastoral communication involves a real art, a studied, disciplined attempt to enter into dialogical relation with other persons, and to overcome the temptation to seize control over situations by speaking without first having carefully listened and sought correction of one's understanding (Howe, 1963).

(2) Wholism. The principle of wholistic communication combines verbal and nonverbal aspects of communication into a coherent message in which the one does not distract from or subvert the other. Such coherence is regarded as important in all caring and therapeutic ministries and, like dialogue, has been stressed as a key principle in the modern pastoral care movement. Clinical pastoral training, for example, emphasizes an awareness of the emotional dimensions of one's communications as well as the cognitive, and stresses the importance of coherence between what one says verbally and what one feels and communicates nonverbally. Such coherence is not a matter of communicational technique alone, however, but a function of a deep coherence within the pastor and in the pastor's interpersonal relations — a coherence in the entire communicational style or structure of one's life, intrapsychically and socially, verbally and nonverbally, cognitively and emotionally.

The model here may in many ways be Jesus' own ministry of communication, in which the spoken word and the healing or compassionate deed constituted a single, unified expression of the divine Word. In its deepest meanings, therefore, communication theory may be said to point toward him in whom there was perfect, full, wholistic communication of divine grace, in whom

person and message were one, and who entered fully into the human condition to hear as well as to speak, with accuracy and effectiveness, to the human predicament.

Bibliography. J. E. Baird, Jr., and S. B. Weinberg, *Communication, The Essence of Group Synergy* (1977). H. A. Bosmajian, *The Rhetoric of Nonverbal Communication* (1971). J. B. Carr, *Communicating and Relating* (1979). H. J. Clinebell, *Basic Types of Pastoral Care and Counseling* (1984). J. A. DeVito, *Communication, Concepts and Processes* (1976). J. H. Ellens, "A Theology of Communication: Putting the Question," *J. of Psychology and Theology,* 2 (1974), 132–39; "Psychodynamics of Mass Media Society," *J. of Psychology and Theology,* 7 (1979), 192–201. S. Hiltner, *Pastoral Counseling* (1949). R. L. Howe, *The Miracle of Dialogue* (1963). B. E. Myers and M. T. Myers, *Communicating When We Speak* (1975). R. S. Ross, *Persuasion: Communicating and Interpersonal Relations* (1974).

J. H. ELLENS

BODY LANGUAGE; CONVERSATION, PASTORAL; INTERPRETATION AND HERMENEUTICS, PASTORAL; MARRIAGE COMMUNICATION; PREACHING; PSYCHOLINGUISTIC THEORY IN PSYCHOLOGY AND COUNSELING. *See also* DOUBLE BIND; LANGUAGE DEVELOPMENT; PRESENTING PROBLEM; SPEECH DISORDERS AND THERAPY; SYMBOLISM/SYMBOLIZING. *Compare* SILENCE.

COMMUNICATION, MARRIAGE. *See* MARRIAGE COMMUNICATION.

COMMUNICATION, PRIVILEGED. *See* CONFIDENTIALITY; LEGAL DIMENSIONS OF PASTORAL CARE AND COUNSELING.

COMMUNION (EUCHARIST). The term "communion" is used in at least three primary senses. (1) It may refer to the partaking of the bread and the cup at the Eucharist, or Lord's Supper. Thus a "communion rite" is the act of the whole assembly's receiving Eucharist, whether standing, kneeling or sitting. (2) "Communion" designates the living relationship between human beings, and between the divine and the human as a characteristic of the church, as expressed in the hymn, *For All the Saints:* "O blest communion, fellowship divine." (3) When Protestants speak of *the* Communion, they generally refer to the whole liturgical complex of words, symbols, and actions which constitutes the Eucharist — derived from the Greek word meaning "thanksgiving." Roman Catholics, Anglicans and Episcopalians tend to use the term in the first sense, to refer to the communion rite itself. Throughout Christian history different traditions have used various terms to designate the whole liturgy: Mass, Eucharist, Lord's Supper, the Divine Liturgy, the Breaking of Bread, or the Holy Communion.

In all Christian traditions, however, communion (or Eucharist) is the central act of Christian worship, and one of the primary "means of grace" by which spiritual care is made visible, immediate, and effective for individuals and for the church as a community. Thus its importance for pastoral care, understood in the most comprehensive sense, can scarcely be exaggerated. This continues to be true even though, since the advent of the pastoral care movement, conversational forms of care, including formal pastoral counseling and pastoral psychotherapy, have emerged as major expressions of the church's pastoral ministry, especially in Protestantism. The relationship of these forms of care to communion and other ritual expressions has not been adequately worked out, theologically or practically, in the pastoral care and counseling movement or in the church as a whole. It may be be assumed, however, in view of the diversity of gifts and ministries in the church (I Cor. 12:4-11), that their proper relationship should not be competitive but complementary.

1. **Fourfold action.** The Christian eucharistic liturgy combines the ancient pattern of the ministry of the word derived from Jewish synagogue services, with the "fourfold" action of the table: Bread and wine are taken (offertory), blessed (prayer of thanksgiving), the bread is broken (fraction), and cup and bread are given (communion rite). This fourfold action, derived from the words and acts of Jesus with the disciples at the Last Supper, consists of one verbal and three nonverbal acts. Only the great prayer of thanksgiving, sometimes called the prayer of consecration, is fully verbal, praising and thanking God for God's glory and mighty acts in history, focusing upon salvation accomplished in Jesus Christ. This singular prayer invokes God's Holy Spirit upon the people and the bread and the cup, praying also for unity in Christ that the church may fulfill its mission in the world.

For the other three actions — taking the gifts, breaking the bread, and the giving and receiving — few, if any, words are needed. Thus, while various "words of administration" are employed at the distribution such as "The Body of Christ, the Bread of Heaven," or "the blood of Christ, the cup of salvation" (often accompanied by "broken for you" and "shed for you"), the communion rite itself is the most corporately interactive point of the whole eucharistic liturgy. The fourth of the actions is the most obviously communal focus in the whole service of worship, for this involves physical communion of the people of God.

2. **Theological Images.** Several foundational images of the Lord's Supper, or Holy Communion, emerge from the NT and earliest Christian eucharistic practices. These images bear directly upon pastoral and theological understandings of eucharistic reform and renewal in the church today. First is the image of the Eucharist as a meal of *joyful thanksgiving*. This is clear from the account in Acts: "And breaking bread from house to house, they were taking their meals together with gladness and sincerity of heart, praising God and having favor with all the whole people" (2:46–47, NAS). For the first generation of Christians, this was a feast of the resurrection. The subsequent loss of the meal context diminished the connection between home and church. Recent reforms have emphasized both the symbolism of a shared meal and a less penitential, more joyful style of celebration.

The second image is of *remembering*. The whole life and ministry, suffering, death, and resurrection of Jesus Christ is to be remembered in and through this meal. The words of institution, *eis ten emev anamnesin* (I Cor. 11:24; Lk. 22:19), carry the force of command to the community: "Do my *anamnesis*." This corporate action of remembering involves genuine encounter with the reality and power of what is recalled—the whole person and work of Christ.

A third image is that of *fellowship or communion*, a participation in the life of Christ. To eat and drink at this meal is to hold communion with and in the presence of the Lord. This is made especially clear in Paul's question: "Is not the bread which we break a sharing (*koinonia*) in the body of Christ? Since there is one loaf, we who are many, are one body, for we all partake of the one bread" (I Cor. 10:16–17, NAS).

The actual giving and receiving of the bread and cup is linked to another basic image: Christ's own sacrificial self-giving for the sins of the world. The image of "Christ our Passover who was sacrificed for us" (I Cor. 5:7) is the very basis of meaning and power in the communing. To celebrate Eucharist together is to remember and to experience as actual all of Christ's work—his sacrificial self-giving. On this basis alone can we understand the sense in which, by our participation, we are "offering our bodies" back to God as "living sacrifices" (Rom. 12:1, NAS). This is possible because the meal is also an action of the Holy Spirit; it is undertaken by virtue of the animating work of the Spirit in the midst of the people.

A final image which illuminates the significance of Communion is eschatological. The meal itself is a *foretaste of the heavenly banquet*. Thus, like the Jewish Passover, participation in this meal looks forward to when it "finds its fulfillment in the kingdom of God" (cf. Lk. 22:16; Mt. 26:29; Mk. 14:25). Here we may speak of eucharistic participation of the whole assembly as a kind of rehearsal and anticipation of what God is bringing about: reconciled relationships, restoration of peace and justice, true mutuality on earth, and the reign of God in all things.

3. **Forms of Practice.** The theological dimensions of these governing images are intrinsic to the matter of the human experience of communing. The style of distributing and receiving communion must show pastoral sensitivity and integrity if these images are to be understood and lived at the affective and volitional levels of worship. The early church stood for communion while the dominant practice in the Anglican, Lutheran and Roman traditions until recently has been to kneel at an altar rail. English Puritans and certain "free-church" traditions (Congregationalists, Presbyterians, English Methodists) receive while seated. Each practice forms the communicants in certain fundamental attitudes and dispositions toward the meaning of the sacrament.

The same is true of the manner in which the bread and cup are presented and consumed. For the first thousand years and in recent reforms, the people have received both the bread and the cup in the hand. The use of individual cups is a late nineteenth century development which has been the primary mode, until recently, for most free-church Protestants.

4. **Pastoral Dimensions.** Despite the range of specific variants in practices, certain basic pastoral concerns are common to all Christian traditions wishing to deepen eucharistic faith and life. (1) Is the meal celebrated with care, human insight, and genuine hospitality? (2) Is the relationship between those who serve and those who receive in the spirit of Christ? (3) Are the healing and reconciling powers of the Eucharist made manifest? (4) Is

the sacrament understood as a fully communal action, with ethical implications for how the church is to serve the world and live together "in Christ?" (5) Is there adequate pastoral and catechetical preparation of the whole assembly, ministers of communion and the people, for "full, conscious and active participation" (*Constitution on the Sacred Liturgy*) which will deepen over time? The quality of experience and interaction at the communion rite and the integrity of the whole eucharistic celebration expresses as well as forms the perception of pastoral care in the common life and mission of the congregation.

These fundamental principles pertain not only to the celebration of communion in public worship but also to those occasions when communion is celebrated with individuals in special need or distress, as with the sick and dying. Here communion may serve to renew and strengthen faith, overcome isolation by uniting individuals symbolically with the whole church, and communicate the love of God in simple, sensory forms that seem especially appropriate in times of crisis. It is also true that communion continues to be associated primarily with themes of guilt and forgiveness in Western Christianity, despite the broadening theological emphases of recent reforms. Because these and other themes of need and failure often emerge significantly in life crises, it may be especially important to celebrate communion at such times. This is particularly true if done in conjunction with simple conversation articulating the crisis experience and offering suggestions of ways in which its themes may find expression and gracious response in the Eucharist. In the midst of human frailty and failure, such a Eucharist celebration affirms that indeed nothing in all creation will be able to separate us from the love of God in Jesus Christ our Lord (Rom. 8:39).

Bibliography. G. Fourez, SJ, *Sacraments and Passages* (1981). R. W. Hovda, *Strong, Loving and Wise* (1977). J. F. White, *Sacraments As God's Self-Giving* (1983), chs. 3, 6. World Council of Churches, *Baptism, Eucharist and Ministry* (1982).

D. E. SALIERS

CHRISTOLOGY, GRACE, *or* SACRAMENTAL THEOLOGY, AND PASTORAL CARE; LITURGICAL CHANGE AND REFORM (Pastoral Issues); WORSHIP AND CELEBRATION. *See also* CHRISTIAN LIFE; LITURGICAL AND DEVOTIONAL LIFE, ROMAN CATHOLIC TRADITION OF; RITUAL AND PASTORAL CARE; VATICAN COUNCIL II. *Compare* COMMUNITY, FELLOWSHIP, AND CARE; CONGREGATION, PASTORAL CARE OF; ECCLESIOLOGY AND PASTORAL CARE; SACRAMENTS, ORDINANCES, AND RITES, TERMINOLOGY AND CONCEPTS OF; SYMBOLISM/SYMBOLIZING.

COMMUNITIES, RELIGIOUS. *See* RELIGIOUS AND UTOPIAN COMMUNITIES; RELIGIOUS LIFE (VOWED LIFE).

COMMUNITY. *See* COMMUNITY, FELLOWSHIP AND CARE.

COMMUNITY, FELLOWSHIP, AND CARE (Christian). Etymologically, the term *community* refers to the obligations, gifts, or services that persons bring to one another; thus, what they have, they have partly "in common." A contrasting term is *immunity*, "not under obligation, exempt." Bodies of faith should not experience themselves as immunities from, but as resources for,

persons. *Community* is similar to *covenant*, which suggests an overcoming of barriers between strangers and an identifying of ways in which they can be resources for each other (to love one another). *Fellowship* means a *laying together of money or property*, hence a partnership or a society, a mutuality of care and a sharing of material resources in support of care. Thus community, fellowship, and care points to the caring functions inherent in all communal experiences which can be brought forward in explicit ways in the life and work of religious communities.

All pastoral care occurs against a communal background, and communities of faith have an interest in the well-being of their members. Often unnoticed, much natural caring occurs among members of a body of faith. Persons in similar situations find their way to one another. In a sewing circle women talk about the needs and concerns of many persons in the congregation, consider how to meet them, and refer some to clergy. Even gossip can perform constructive caring functions. In some church fellowship groups, members telephone needy members daily, bring in meals, drive them to appointments, even shop—concrete acts of kindness whose symbolic significance as gestures of care goes beyond their practical value, important as that may be.

All aspects of a church's life reveal pastoral needs and afford opportunities for care, whether by clergy or by other members. In addition to illnesses, bereavement, family problems, and other such needs, congregations also generate pastoral needs as a result of living and working together as a community of faith. In situations where opinions differ, for example, some persons experience undue anxiety, doubting themselves or fighting others. Moreover, bodies of faith always fall short of their ideals. Called to be saints, members can become dismayed or cynical when they see sin in others or in themselves. Such experiences call for an atmosphere, a tradition, of understanding and care in the fellowship as a whole, as well as specific acts of caring.

In some religious traditions, care of members is from the beginning a task of the entire congregation; in others, it is delegated to professional staff who are expected to have care-giving skills, allocate time to individual pastoral care, provide confidentiality, and—especially in situations of acute crisis—bring the symbolic richness of the ordained pastoral role as a resource to those in need. Even where caring is institutionally specialized through ordained clergy, however, members generally exercise a kind of "stewardship of suffering" among themselves through their relationships, often providing as much or more care in that way as through the "official" care by clergy. Not only by reaching out, but also by making their struggles available to one another, members deepen communal ties and strengthen one another through identification. Moreover, many persons actually need to help others as part of wrestling with their own difficulties, a truth dramatically demonstrated by Alcoholics Anonymous, one of the most powerful exemplifications in our time of the healing power of communal care.

It is also important to remember that there are inevitable limitations in the care that professional clergy can provide. The minister, for instance, may not have been divorced, fired, or pregnant before wedlock, but some members have been, and they frequently bring an immediate and useful understanding of the painful experience lacking in even the most empathic minister who has not shared the particular experience. While this does not mean that helpful care can only be given by those who have suffered the same problem, it does point to the special bond that can exist between fellow sufferers, forming a community of care, a "stewardship of suffering," that makes available the healing and sustaining power of shared affliction.

Bibliography. R. Burck, "Pastoral Care and the People of God," *Pastoral Psychology*, 30 (1982), 139–52 (includes other references). B. W. Grant, "Fitness for Community: A Response to Laings and Kohut," *J. of Pastoral Care*, 38 (1984), 324–37. L. Malarskey and D. J. Marron, "Evaluating Community Interaction," *Human Development*, 3, 3 (1982), 17–24.

J. R. BURCK

CONGREGATION, PASTORAL CARE OF; FRIENDSHIP; LAY PASTORAL CARE AND COUNSELING; RELATIONSHIP NETWORK. *See also* EATING AND DRINKING; ECCLESIOLOGY AND PASTORAL CARE; GROUP COUNSELING AND PSYCHOTHERAPY; HAVURAH; JEWISH CARE AND COUNSELING; RELIGIOUS AND UTOPIAN COMMUNITIES; RITUAL CARE; SOCIOLOGY OF RELIGIOUS AND PASTORAL CARE; THERAPEUTIC COMMUNITY. *Compare* ALIENATION/ESTRANGEMENT; LONELINESS AND ISOLATION; PRIVACY AND SOLITUDE.

COMMUNITY, FELLOWSHIP, AND CARE (Jewish).

Counseling has been considered the duty of everyone in the Jewish community rather than being delegated to a leadership group. Until the eighteenth century, there was no professional rabbinate, and even after that time rabbis rarely considered pastoral duties primary.

1. **Associations** (200 C.E.–Present Time). Special groups dedicated a portion of their life to help people during life cycle crises. Most larger Jewish communities had a *havurah* (fellowship) which visited the sick (*biqur holim*) and another which buried the dead and comforted the bereaved (*havurah qadishah*) (*Bible, Talmud,* Moed Katan 27b; Abraham, 1896; Neuman, 1948). The responsibility for such groups was shared by the entire community.

Sick-care societies on a communal basis did not appear until the Spanish-Jewish period. They may have begun as early as the thirteenth century in Spain (Neuman, II, 161ff). Such societies were responsible for the physical and spiritual welfare of all who were ill, burial of the dead, and counseling of the bereaved.

Similar societies were founded in Germany in the seventeenth century, probably under the influence of Spanish-Jewish immigrants (Marcus, 1947, p. 64). At the same time we find such societies beginning in Italy. Throughout Central Europe they patterned themselves somewhat after Christian groups which also cared for the sick, but two major differences continued to exist between the Jewish organizations and their Christian counterparts. The Christian organizations were also social clubs and tended to look only after their own sick members. The Jewish Brotherhood had few social overtones and worked for the benefit of the entire community. These societies, often called "Holy Brotherhood" or "Brotherhood of Loving Kindness," were motivated by strong religious forces. Their constitutions often quote Psalm forty-one or the *Ethics of the Fathers*—"By three things is the world upheld; by Torah, service, and by deeds of loving kindness" (*Pirqê 'Avot* 1.2) or "thou shalt love they neighbor as thyself" (Lev. 19.18).

The brotherhoods were tightly organized and funded through the community. All the members of the brotherhood were duty-bound to serve in whatever capacity they could. There were rigid schedules of visiting the sick and caring for the bereaved. As much attention was given to religious and emotional needs as to the physical needs of the sick. The basic feeling of these groups was best stated by Dr. Abraham Wallich, a seventeenth century university-trained physician, who in his *Sefer Harefuot* felt that sickness must be cured not only by physical, but also by spiritual means. Whole manuals were written for the guidance of those who counseled the sick and the bereaved. Many of them like *Maabar Yabak, Yosef Ometz, Sefer Haredim, Refuat Neshamah,* and *Sefer Hahayim* were very popular and went through many editions.

Special associations for the care of women were established, and literature in the vernacular Judeo-German appeared for them by the eighteenth century.

2. **Hassidism.** A somewhat different response to the needs of the pastoral care was evolved by the Hassidim of the eighteenth and nineteenth centuries. This group, which rebelled against the elitist intellectualism of Polish rabbinic Judaism, was led by charismatic leaders who established hereditary positions. The leader (*rebbe*) helped his followers through every stage of life, and they turned to him at each crisis, whether it was of a religious, economic, or psychological nature. This highly personal and directive counseling continues among Hassidim to this day. The scope of this counseling and its nature depended on each Hassidic leader. The numerous Hassidic tales collected by disciples enhanced the reputation of each Hasid, made a moral point, and provide us with an insight into counseling techniques. No single method, however, evolved (Dubnow, 1931; Dresner, 1960; Buber, 1947; Schachter and Hoffman, 1983).

3. **Modern Times.** Since the Emancipation of the Jewish community (1800), a professional rabbinate as well as a variety of social agencies have evolved to provide leadership. Counseling services for the Jewish community did not develop until the 1930s. Some education in pastoral counseling is currently demanded by all rabbinic seminaries. This combines modern insights with the classical Jewish tradition.

Bibliography. I. Abraham, *Jewish Life in the Middle Ages* (1896), ch. 18. M. Buber, *Hasidism and Modern Man* (1966); *Tales of the Hassidim* (1947). S. Dresner, *The Zaddic* (1960). S. Dubnow, *Geschichte des Chassidismus* (1953). R. L. Katz, *Pastoral Care and the Jewish Tradition* (1985). J. Marcus, *Communal Sick-Care In The German Ghetto* (1947). A. A. Neuman, *The Jews in Spain* (1948), vol. 2, ch. 18. Z. Schachter and E. Hoffman, *Sparks of Light, Counseling in the Hassidic Tradition* (1983).

W. JACOB

HAVURAH; JEWISH CARE AND COUNSELING; JEWISH HOLY DAYS AND FESTIVALS, PASTORAL DIMENSIONS OF. *Compare* CONGREGATION, PASTORAL CARE OF; OLD TESTAMENT AND APOCRYPHA, TRADITIONS AND THEOLOGY OF CARE IN; RELATIONSHIP NETWORK; RELIGIOUS AND UTOPIAN

COMMUNITIES; RITUAL AND PASTORAL CARE; SOCIOLOGY OF RELIGIOUS AND PASTORAL CARE.

COMMUNITY MENTAL HEALTH MOVEMENT.

A mental health movement originating in the 1960s, developed to prevent serious mental illness through an emphasis on mental health education, early intervention and referral, and psychiatric treatment available near home. The movement created new opportunities for clergy and mental health professionals to work together in local communities; it also contributed to the developing pastoral counseling field in significant ways.

1. **History.** Prior to World War II, mentally ill people were removed from local communities to live in state supported "insane asylums." These institutions tended to be large, poorly decorated and maintained facilities. Able-bodied patients were assigned jobs within the institution, such as working on the asylum farm to produce food for patients. Progressive state programs provided recreational activities while most institutions offered only room and board. The asylums were located away from populated areas since the patients were considered dangerous. Attempts were made to help patients through various medical treatments using insulin, cold packs, electroshock, and surgery.

After World War II, public thinking changed about mental illness. American psychiatrists, such as William and Karl Menninger, began to persuade the public that the insane are mentally ill people needing psychiatric treatment. People who worked in state insane asylums during the war as alternative service, such as Mennonites, started working to create more humane and effective facilities to care for the mentally ill. Newly discovered medications reduced anxiety, relieved depression, and controlled aggressive behavior. These factors led to a mental health reform movement in some states during the 1950s. The movement emphasized psychiatric treatment, not just custodial care.

Building upon the mental health reform movement, the U.S. Congress passed the Mental Health Act in 1955, which established a Joint Commission to determine mental health needs and to review existing mental health programs. In 1961 the Commission issued its findings, which President John Kennedy and Congress implemented, launching the Community Mental Health movement.

The movement encouraged citizens to study local mental health needs and to create new programs designed to meet those needs. Federal funding was made available on a matching basis to develop community mental health centers, designed to serve specified geographical catchment areas, which were smaller than the areas covered by the large state hospitals. The goal of these mental health centers was to provide mental health services near home, thus reducing the need to remove emotionally troubled persons from their homes, families, and jobs.

Mental health associations and community mental health centers grew rapidly and became the backbone of the Community Mental Health movement. Already established mental health associations, which were lay groups providing mental health education for citizens, also grew in influence. Clergy were involved in many of these mental health associations.

Most importantly a new institution, the community mental health center, was established. Federal guidelines specified that each center was to provide a range of mental health services including: (a) inpatient treatment; (b) outpatient treatment; (c) part-time hospitalization; (d) 24-hour emergency service; (e) consultation; (f) diagnostic and evaluation services; (g) after-care placement and follow-up; and (h) mental health education.

The Community Mental Health movement had several significant consequences for the American public. The movement encouraged the view that mental health is as important as physical health, with the underlying assumption that any person or family in the community might develop emotional problems that could be helped by therapy or counseling. Perhaps more important, the movement developed a philosophy that mentally or emotionally troubled people could be helped while living at home and continuing employment in the community; they did not have to be removed from the community to a state hospital in another town. This philosophy of treatment eventually reduced the number of patients in state psychiatric hospitals and led to some hospitals being closed.

2. **The Religious Community and the Community Mental Health Movement.** In 1957 a major mental health study discovered that forty-two percent of those individuals seeking help for life problems would first contact clergy; further, the study found that sixty-four percent of those persons receiving help from clergy reported satisfaction with the help they received (see Veroff, Kulka, and Dorran, 1981). These findings were significant in identifying the important role clergy play in helping individuals and families cope with life crises.

There are many reasons why clergy are contacted so often by people seeking help. Clergy are available in most local communities and can be called upon in crisis situations; they have flexible hours and can respond immediately to a crisis situation; usually they do not charge fees for services, making them available to all citizens regardless of income; they can initiate home visits; and they often are motivated for and educated in helping distressed people. Moreover, religious rituals provide important, socially shared personal care in life transitions, such as marriage, birth, illness, and death.

Some clergy, recognizing the need for clinically trained mental health professionals in their communities, have served on mental health center boards and helped to create new mental health programs. Others have viewed mental health professionals with suspicion and distrust, concerned that mental health professionals may be "secular humanists" critical of religious beliefs and practices.

Mental health professionals moving into the community have, in turn, viewed clergy in differing ways. Some professionals see clergy as established caregivers and work with clergy to improve the quality of pastoral and other care available in the community. Others either ignore clergy or are suspicious of their helping efforts, while envying the established position of clergy in the community as caregivers with easy access to troubled people in their home environment.

3. **Clergy and Mental Health Staff.** As community mental health centers grew, three basic models of clergy-

staff cooperation emerged: education, pastoral consultation, and staff chaplain/pastoral counselor.

a. Education. The educational model brings clergy and center staff together to improve mutual understanding of each others' helping role, theoretical assumptions, and counseling techniques. This model has been implemented in several ways.

One mental health center, for instance, has sponsored a monthly reading-discussion group for clergy and center staff in which participants select readings from theology and the behavioral sciences. In these discussions participants developed relationships while broadening their understanding of the others' contributions to troubled people. Out of one of these reading groups a staff social worker and clergy person developed a support group for elderly citizens in the community experiencing emotional problems. The group met at the clergyman's church, which was centrally located in the community and was open to all elderly persons in the community.

At another mental health center the staff decided that while clergy were important primary mental health caregivers, they needed help in strengthening their therapeutic interventions. The staff invited interested clergy to a series of seminars designed to assist them in recognizing serious mental illness and in learning therapeutic techniques that could be used to prevent further illness or to refer persons to the center staff. This educational effort was part of the center's goal to strengthen the helping role of frontline caregivers in the community, such as teachers, physicians, police, and judges. Clergy in the program were encouraged to maintain their pastoral identity and role while providing better therapeutic intervention for parishioners experiencing life crises. The center staff served as educators and consultants to the clergy while being ready to receive referrals from them.

b. Pastoral consultation. A pastoral consultation model has been developed in other centers. In this model the center employs a part-time, clinically trained pastoral consultant who meets with clergy, individually or in groups, to discuss case material from the clergy's involvement with people seeking help—often problems of marital conflict, parent-teenager communication, employment difficulties, death, and aging. The consultant may invite the center staff to share perspectives on the situation, which provides mutual learning for the staff and clergy. The consultant also meets with center staff to help them better understand the patient's religious beliefs and practices.

c. Staff chaplain—pastoral counselor. In the staff chaplain/pastoral counselor model, the center employs a clinically trained pastor as a member of the staff. This chaplain shares staff responsibilities for carrying out the goals and programs of the center and is a member of the center's committees. He or she also provides pastoral visitation and pastoral counseling for patients and families of the center, and in some centers develops an accredited Clinical Pastoral Education (CPE) program for area clergy and theological students.

Clergy working in mental health centers are required to have certification in CPE and/or pastoral counseling, and are encouraged to pursue advanced degrees.

4. Community Mental Health and the Pastoral Counseling Movement. As the public began to accept the need for counseling to cope effectively with life crises, many looked to community mental health centers for help, though many others preferred to seek help from clergy specially trained in pastoral counseling. Religious groups therefore formed pastoral counseling centers to which area clergy could refer parishioners needing long-term counseling.

In some communities cooperation has developed between pastoral counseling centers and community mental health centers, with mutual referral and consultation increasing the effectiveness of both programs. In other communities, however, pastoral counseling centers and community mental health centers exist independently and competitively, lacking direct or formal contact.

Bibliography. E. Bruder, "A Time of Challenge," *Pastoral Psychology*, 16 (1965), 5–7. R. K. Bufford and T. B. Johnston, "The Church and Community Mental Health: Unrealized Potential." *J. of Psychology and Theology*, G. Caplain. *Principles of Preventive Psychiatry* (1964). A. Duval, "The Expanding Role of the Minister As Community Health Services Develop," *Pastoral Psychology*, 16 (1965), 8–12. E. Ediger, "A Community Mental Health Center and the Churches," *Pastoral Psychology*, 17 (1966), 34–41. G. Gurin, *Americans View Their Mental Health* (1960). C. Hall, "New Frontiers in Mental Health," *Pastoral Psychology*, 17 (1966), 6–8. H. N. Maloney, "The Demise and Rebirth of the Chaplaincy," *J. of Pastoral Care*, 29 (1975), 129–34. D. Parker, "Pastoral Consultation Through A Community Mental Health Center," *Pastoral Psychology*, 17 (1966), 42–46. E. M. Pattison, "Functions of the Clergy in Community Mental Health Centers," *Pastoral Psychology*, 16 (1965), 21–26. I. Rosen, "Some Contributions of Religion to Mental and Physical Health," *J. of Religion and Health*, 13 (1974), 289–94. J. Slaughter, W. Nisi, R. Bennick, R. Carlson, "Roles of Chaplains in Community Mental Health," *Hospital and Community Psychiatry*, 29 (1978), 797–800. J. Veroff, R. A. Kulka, and E. Dorran, *Mental Health in America* (1981).

D. PARKER

INTERPROFESSIONAL TEAMS AND RELATIONSHIPS; MENTAL HEALTH MOVEMENT; MENTAL HOSPITAL/MENTAL HOSPITALIZATION. *See also* HALFWAY HOUSE; PSYCHOLOGY IN AMERICAN RELIGION. *Biography:* MENNINGER.

COMMUNITY PSYCHIATRY/PSYCHOLOGY. A form of psychiatry and psychology resulting from the Mental Health Studies Act of 1955 which has evolved to include six defining features: (1) a service area of 75,000–200,000 people; (2) comprehensive services including inpatient, outpatient and emergency care, partial hospitalization, community consultation and education programs; (3) continuity of care allowing patients and staff to move from one service to another with relative ease; (4) emphasis on prevention of mental illness; (5) researching of available services with the goal of preventing mental illness, shortening hospital stays, and eliminating residual disabilities after an illness; and (6) evaluation of program effectiveness through empirical research.

R. L. PAVELSKY

COMMUNITY MENTAL HEALTH MOVEMENT; MENTAL HEALTH AND ILLNESS. *Compare* MENTAL HOSPITAL/MENTAL HOSPITALIZATION.

COMMUNITY RESOURCES FOR PASTORAL CARE. *See* SOCIAL SERVICES AND PASTORAL CARE.

COMPARATIVE PSYCHOLOGY. Comparing the behaviors of different species of animals, especially infrahuman species. Comparisons between human beings and other animals are appropriate, but more helpful are comparisons of two or more infrahuman species. In practice, the field of comparative psychology should simply be labeled "animal behavior" because relatively few studies of a truly comparative nature have been done.

The goals of comparative psychology can be summarized as: (1) the identification and classification of behavior; (2) determining the relations between behaviors, both within and across species; (3) studying the origin and development of behavior; (4) selection of specific animals and behavioral situations that merit specialized study; and (5) the development of theory that subsumes and predicts the observed behaviors.

The reasons for studying infrahuman behavior are generally considered to be: (1) knowledge of the specific animal for its own sake; (2) practical application of animal behavior for human welfare; (3) ethical restrictions on some types of research with humans sometimes do not apply to animal studies; and (4) the animal can be used as a model for fundamental processes that occur in higher level species.

Historically, the foundation of comparative psychology was laid by Charles Darwin and his student George J. Romanes in such classic works as Darwin's *Expression of Emotion in Animals and Man* (1873) and Romanes's *Animal Intelligence* (1883), *Mental Evolution in Animals* (1884), and *Mental Evolution in Man* (1889). The interest and controversy sparked by these writings led many others to become concerned with the internal control of behavior and related phenomena. By the turn of the century three specific approaches — ethology, comparative psychology, and neurobiology — were developing independently of each other. The ethological approach developed mainly in Europe and is characterized by the work of Karl von Frisch, Konrad Lorenz, and Niko Tinbergen. They sought to study animal behavior in natural settings and dealt primarily with species-specific differences, evolution, and phylogenetic relationships. The comparative psychology position developed in North America through the work of Karl Lashley, Edward C. Tolman, Clark L. Hull, B. F. Skinner, D. O. Hebb, and Frank A. Beach. These researchers used rigorous, statistically analyzed, laboratory studies of the albino rat to explore animal models of learning and memory. The neurobiological approach focuses on the specific nerve cell mechanisms mediating small components of behavior. Representative of neurobiology is the work of Ramon y Cajal, Charles Sherrington, Hodgkin, Huxley, Sir John Eccles, and Eric Kandel.

Humorously, yet seriously, the 1949 address to the American Psychological Association by Frank Beach offered a classic perspective and historical indictment of comparative psychology, ultimately leading one to conclude that psychology knows more about albino rats, clipped-wing pigeons, and college sophomores than any other living organisms, none of which are representative of their species! Little has changed since, except that comparative psychology is gradually disappearing as a distinctive field.

Bibliography. F. A. Beach, "The Snark Was a Boojum," *The American Psychologist*, 5 (1950), 115–24. M. R. Denny, ed., *Comparative Psychology: An Evolutionary Anaylsis of Animal Behavior* (1980). D. A. Dewsbury, ed., *Comparative Psychology in the Twentieth Century* (1984). J. L. Gould, *Ethology: The Mechanisms and Evolution of Behavior* (1982). J. W. Grier, *Biology of Animal Behavior* (1984).

C. D. SIMPSON

PSYCHOLOGY. *Compare* BEHAVIOR; PERSONALITY, BIOLOGICAL DIMENSIONS OF.

COMPASSION. From a Latin word meaning to bear, to suffer. In common use it suggests sympathy or pity for the plight of another, to be moved emotionally by the other's tragic situation or distress. In current pastoral care usage the desire to relieve suffering, implicit in pity, is present, but without the condescension that pity may connote. Compassion is more like empathy (feeling with) than sympathy (feeling for).

1. Psychological Dimensions. Psychologically, compassion appears to be rooted in the capacity to reconstruct the situation of another imaginatively and to respond to it emotionally in ways shaped by the meanings and values of the culture. From the combination of these capacities emerge two features that distinguish true compassion from a merely sentimental or impulsive response: the inclination toward informed, intelligent actions and the willingness to risk and give of oneself to alleviate suffering.

The ability to reconstruct another's situation imaginatively entails the capacity to maintain sufficient cognitive distance to avoid mistaking one's own reactions for the other's while remaining emotionally close to one's own vulnerability to suffering and participation in the common experience of being human. In addition, detailed knowledge or insight into the life story, personality, and character of the other person can aid this imaginative reconstruction and emotional intimacy, and can sometimes make a crucial difference in evoking a compassionate attitude instead of one that is indifferent or judgmental. For example, the frequently overwhelming themes of childhood neglect and abuse in the life stories of violent criminals may reverse one's initial perception and evoke compassion in place of condemnation. In other situations, however, the opposite may be true: deeper knowledge and insight into the apparent suffering of another, such as one with chronic somatic distress, may undermine compassion by disclosing levels of intentionality, deception, and manipulation not previously evident. For compassion to emerge in these situations an even deeper level of knowledge and insight into the deceptive and manipulative behavior itself is required, together with more developed capacities for emotional identification and acceptance. The love of one's enemy may therefore constitute the deepest test of compassion.

What psychological factors enable such imaginative, emotional, and self-transcending moral action to occur? The process is elusive and little understood, though it may be supposed that a compassionate attitude is more likely to develop in persons who have grown up in compassionate families. Compassion provides an emotional atmosphere in which all aspects of the human condition are dignified and in which acceptance of human limitations and the encouragement of human abilities may prevail. Such families nurture love for self and others rather than chronic fear of impending judgment and castigation, in which persons turn against their own humanity and develop self-hate. This makes it easier for children to feel the distress of others and to develop a sense of kinship with and support for a wide variety of persons, grounded in a sense of fundamental human likeness that transcends social, cultural, and situational differences.

2. **Cultural Dimensions.** Cultural meanings and values, as well as individual experiences that may have confirmed them, appear to be important in either developing or narrowing such emotional and imaginative capacities. Various social norms can either widen the ability to allow oneself to see and feel another's anguish or can encourage one to ignore, deny, or rationalize it. Norms that encourage compassion tend to teach the belief that to participate in another's suffering can somehow be redemptive. They may teach a variation of the Golden Rule, encouraging persons to develop self-awareness of their prejudices and a desire to transcend social boundaries that limit imagination. Moral and religious traditions may foster the development of compassion by providing explicit teachings on the virtue of compassion or by offering idealized stories and images of it (cf., the classic medieval image of St. Martin sharing his cloak with a beggar, or Christ's words of forgiveness on the cross). In addition, teachings concerning the solidarity of human beings with one another and perhaps with creation itself, the precariousness of human life and our shared vulnerability to tragedy, suffering and sin, and the supremacy of mercy, forgiveness, and caring concern over judgment and condemnation serve to evoke and support compassion by generating a moral and spiritual universe in which compassion is felt to be grounded in the ultimate character of reality.

3. **Compassion in the Major Religious Traditions.** As a virtue, compassion is valued in both Eastern and Western religious traditions, though they differ in subtle but significant ways. In Mahayana Buddhism, compassion is the motive for taking the Boddhisattva vow: the renunciation of the wish to escape from existence until all sentient life is freed from suffering. In Judaism, compassion or *rachamin* is the first of the thirteen attributes of God listed in Exod. 34:6, in a passage that has become part of the High Holy Days liturgy. Because compassion is an attribute of God, humans are enjoined to imitate it. In Christianity, desire to identify with and be present for the sufferer in his or her situation is intrinsic to faith in Christ. Compassion as a motive begins with the pathos of God, is manifest in the divine compassion revealed in Jesus (see, for example, Mt. 9:36), and shapes Paul's experience and teaching of the centrality of the Paschal mystery in Christian life.

The religious rationales underlying compassion as a virtue also differ in important but subtle ways among these traditions. In Buddhism, compassion for living beings is expressed in helping them to achieve Enlightenment (complete understanding of ultimate truth) and thereby escape the karmic necessity of rebirth. Because the Buddha believed that desire and worldly attachment lead only to suffering, the many sacrifices and charitable acts of the Boddhisattva do not imply a valuing of earthly life but are done in the service of helping the creature escape the phenomenal world.

The Hebrew *rachamin* links compassion to the idea that all human beings are related. In Judaism, however, the intertwining of compassion with obligation and justice emphasizes actions rather than feelings. The obligations to all people prescribed in the Torah reveal an awareness of human interdependence: welcoming the stranger, judging righteously, and caring for widows, orphans, and the poor. In Jewish tradition compassion, as a moderating force, is necessary for justice; it is not in opposition to the law. Without compassion righteous judgment (the interpretation of the law appropriate to a particular situation) could not occur.

Christianity inherits the Jewish emphasis on the value of human life, but the centrality of the cross introduces the motif of "suffering with" into the Christian concept of compassion. The NT views disease and death as humankind's enemy, against which Jesus as the Christ manifested God's redemptive love and power by teaching, healing, and exorcizing. Compassion is linked to an acceptance of God's love for humanity and the intrinsic or created worth of every individual as a child of God, while the cross is the sign of God's compassionate participation in the suffering of creatures and the forgiveness of their sin. The Christian who accepts divine compassion is liberated to share with others and thereby extend and participate in the compassionate, reconciling work of God in history.

Compassion is the cardinal virtue of the pastoral tradition, the indispensable quality that motivates and deepens all charitable, healing, and caring acts into events of moral and spiritual significance. The compassionate pastor is therefore one who exemplifies a deeply felt sense of solidarity with suffering persons transcending class and culture, yet one who maintains the distance necessary for sustaining suffering persons in their search for an authentic understanding of the meaning of their afflictions.

Bibliography. L. Blum, "Compassion," in A. Rorty, ed., *Explaining Emotions* (1980), pp. 507–17. J. J. Gill, "Empathy Is at the Heart of Love," *Human Development*, 3:3, 29–41. R. L. Katz, *Empathy* (1963). J. McNamara, *The Power of Compassion* (1984). D. P. McNeill, D. A. Morrison, and H. J. M. Nouwen, *Compassion* (1982). M. L. Matics, *Entering the Path of Enlightenment* (1970). J. Moltmann, *The Crucified God*, 2d ed. (1974); *The Trinity and the Kingdom* (1981). H. J. M. Nouwen, *The Wounded Healer* (1972); *Reaching Out* (1975). T. I. Rubin, *Compassion and Self-Hate* (1975).

J. EZHANIKATT
Q. L. HAND
L. SKWERER

EMPATHY; FORGIVENESS; LOVE; SUFFERING. *See also* CHRISTIAN *or* JEWISH LIFE; COMFORT/SUSTAINING; COURAGE; MORAL DEVELOPMENT; MORAL THEOLOGY AND PASTORAL CARE. *Compare* PERCEPTIVENESS AND SENSITIVITY, PASTORAL; PERSONAL STORY, SYMBOL, AND MYTH IN PASTORAL CARE; PHENOMENOLOGICAL METHOD IN PASTORAL CARE; SACRIFICIAL BEHAVIOR; SELF-TRANSCENDENCE.

COMPETENCY, PASTORAL. *See* Technique and Skill; Wisdom and Practical Knowledge. *See also* Education in Pastoral Care and Counseling; Licensure; Standards for Pastoral Counseling.

COMPETITIVENESS. The act of contending against another person or other persons or against normative standards to gain exclusive goals, goods, trophies, status, or recognition.

Competitiveness is an inescapable trait which Western culture generally believes is essential for the development of personality. Like other traits, competitiveness in its extremes becomes pathological and counter to sound growth. Pastoral care is concerned with the healing of pathological competition and the fostering of healthy competitiveness in the service of growth.

Competitiveness is a characteristic of every person's life process and is necessary for personality development and survival. The processes of differentiation and individuation are competitive in that the developing child defines his or her own identity in opposition to other persons. Initially, parents are the objects of competition, then siblings, and finally peers. Competition is also operative in sustaining life, as one enters the work place as a competitor for the productive position commensurate with one's abilities. Competition has been an accepted motivation in education as well as courtship and marriage. Competition determines one's position in the social structure. Competitiveness is inescapable and the question to be addressed by the pastor is how one competes.

Like most character traits, competitiveness is detrimental in both of its extremes. Adults who have failed to learn how to compete adequately have severe emotional handicaps in carrying out normal functions of living. Social interaction and earning a living become major obstacles. On the other hand, excessively competitive persons are subject to life-crippling stress as well as difficulty with interpersonal relations. Specialists in pastoral counseling will see both in their practice, and the parish ministers will encounter them as members of their congregation who need help.

The church has often found itself opposed to the secular world in its attitude toward competitiveness. While religious teachers and publications often proclaim that competitiveness is contrary to the cooperative nature of the NT community, secular publications laud competitiveness as the way that ambitious, upwardly mobile persons can strive for success in their chosen field. A more pastoral view must honor the inescapability of competitiveness, while recognizing the Christian warning of the dangers of competitiveness as destructive to the community. The pastor's concern is to ameliorate the extremes of competitiveness and to help those with such a need to restore a balance to their competitiveness.

Difficulties with competitiveness involve a distorted estimate of one's own abilities or an unrealistic establishment of goals. As is the case with many emotional disorders, health lies in the correction of distortions. This goal may be addressed through preaching, brief pastoral counseling, or long-term, intensive psychotherapy, depending on how deeply embedded in the character one finds the distortions.

Bibliography. G. Hardin, *Promethean Ethics* (1980). H. Ruben, *Competing* (1980).

R. T. HIGHTOWER

AGGRESSION/ASSERTION; CONFLICT AND CONFLICT MANAGEMENT; POWER. *See also* FAMILY THEORY; GROUP DYNAMICS; INTERPERSONAL THEORY. *Compare* ANTISOCIAL PERSONS; DOMINEERING PERSONALITY; MANIPULATION.

COMPLEX. A constellation of experiences and feelings around a single concept which mediate between one's conscious and unconscious world, according to Carl Jung. Complexes shape the manifestation of unconscious thoughts when they press against the ego, such as those in dreams and psychosomatic symptoms. Psychoanalysts have identified several complexes, such as the Oedipal and Electra complexes, which often relate directly to family dynamics.

T. M. JOHNSON

ANALYTICAL (JUNGIAN) PERSONALITY THEORY; PSYCHO-ANALYTIC PERSONALITY THEORY.

COMPULSION. *See* Obsessive-Compulsive Disorder.

COMPUTER (as Psychological Model). *See* Congregation, Pastoral Care of; Cybernetic Theory in Psychology and Counseling.

CONATIVE/COGNITIVE PROBLEM. *See* Cognitive/Conative Problem in Psychology and Counseling.

CONCENTRATION. *See* Hypnosis; Meditation.

CONCILIATION. *See* Christian Conciliation Movement; Mediation/Conciliation.

CONCUPISCENCE. *See* Lust and Chastity.

CONDITIONING. A means by which an organism's behavior is modified as a direct function of environmental influences. The two basic forms of environmental influences affecting behavior change are the classical and the instrumental conditioning paradigms. In the classical paradigm, behavior change is a result of the temporal association or pairing of a neutral event with a naturally stimulating event until the neutral event acquires the eliciting properties of the stimulating event. Behavior change in the instrumental or operant conditioning paradigm is a function of the effect of stimulating consequences on spontaneously emitted responses. These two conditioning paradigms represent the simplest forms of learning.

1. Classical Paradigm. Classical conditioning (also known as respondent conditioning) was first described by Pavlov, who discovered that the dogs in his physiological laboratory would salivate at the sight or sound of the attendant who usually brought them food. These dogs were "classically" conditioned. There are three basic steps in this form of conditioning. Before it occurred, the sight or sound of the attendant (neutral event) produced no salvation response, and food (stimulating event) naturally elicited or produced salivation (unlearned response). During conditioning, the sight and sound of the attendant were temporarily associated with the salivation-producing food. After conditioning, the sight and sound of the attendant alone were sufficient to produce salivation (learned response).

2. **Operant Paradigm.** Instrumental or operant conditioning is most closely associated with the animal experiments of B. F. Skinner. In the puzzle-box experiments of his predecessor, Thorndike, a hungry cat was placed in a confining cage in which some sort of unlocking device (e.g., handle or knob) was mounted inside the box. When this device was manipulated, the door would fall open and the animal could then get a bite of food outside the door. It was discovered that initially the animal would exhibit a wide range of randomly occurring behaviors from its repertoire in attempting to gain access to the food. The particular behavior that proved instrumental in producing access to the food (pushing the handle) gradually became the one most emitted. Random responding gave way to efficient performance, which reliably produced the rewarding event. In this paradigm, the conditioned response is the one that contingently produced the stimulating event.

3. **Distinctions.** Both instrumental and classical conditioning involve the modifying effects of stimulating environmental events on an organism's behavior, but in all other respects they are functionally distinct from one another. In classical conditioning the critical element involves the pairing of two events (e.g., attendant and food), which *elicit* an involuntary response from the organism (salivation). In instrumental or operant conditioning, the crucial relationship is between the voluntarily *emitted* response and the stimulating event (i.e., reward or punishment) that it produces. In the classical paradigm the environment (i.e., the pairing of neutral and stimulating events) acts on the organism to produce a response, whereas in the operant paradigm, the organism's response acts on the environment to produce stimulating events.

Bibliography. E. Hilgard, *Conditioning and Learning* (1975).

J. W. FANTUZZO

BEHAVIORISM; BEHAVIOR MODIFICATION AND PASTORAL COUNSELING; BEHAVIOR THERAPIES; LEARNING THEORIES. *See also* CAUSALITY IN PSYCHOLOGY, FORMS OF; SCRIPT; SHAPING; TOKEN ECONOMY.

CONDITIONS, THERAPEUTIC. *See* THERAPEUTIC CONDITIONS.

CONDUCT PROBLEMS, CHILDREN'S. *See* BEHAVIORAL DISORDERS OF CHILDHOOD.

CONFESSION/CONFESSIONAL. *See* PENANCE; REPENTANCE AND CONFESSION.

CONFESSION, SEAL OF. *See* SEAL OF CONFESSION.

CONFESSOR. (1) In early Christian usage, an honorific title for those who suffered persecution in service to the Orthodox faith but did not die as martyrs. (2) In the Roman Catholic sacrament of penance, the priest who receives the private confessions of the individual penitent, usually on a regular basis. The confessor functions as sacramental judge, correcting and consoling the penitent's conscience, and, according to privileges established by canon law, designating specific means for absolution of sins and restoration to grace. This judicial role is further complemented by the confessor's duty as spiritual counselor, instructing and inspiring the penitent in the devout life. In other traditions, the minister or rabbi may have a similar symbolic role as confessor, especially in the context of pastoral care and counseling.

P. M. BLOWERS

PASTOR; PRIEST; SPIRITUAL DIRECTOR. *See also* CASUISTRY; PENANCE. *Compare* PASTORAL COUNSELOR; SPIRITUAL MASTERS AND GUIDES.

CONFIDENTIALITY. The socially and legally accepted right of any person to the privacy of their thoughts, feelings, writings, and other personal effects. Privileged communication is an even stronger principle, codified in law, that confidential communications, both verbal and non-verbal, are, in certain relationships, protected from enforced public disclosure even in the courts. Such relationships have historically included those of husband and wife, and attorney and client. This protection in more recent years, and with much less clarity, has been extended to such other relationships as clergy-penitent, physician-patient, psychologist-client, psychotherapist-client and, in some states, family members. The most restrictive privilege law was enacted by the Federal Government in 1975 protecting disclosure of confidential information regarding treatment of drug and alcohol abuse patients (Title 42 of the Code of Federal Regulations).

Simply put, confidentiality refers to privacy while privilege refers to the legal protection of that privacy. It is illuminating to consider the criteria which are deemed necessary in order to extend the protection of the privilege to confidential communications. The criteria were formulated by the legal scholar of Northwestern University, John H. Wigmore. (1) The origination of the communication must occur within the confidence that it will not be later disclosed. (2) The necessity of confidentiality must be essential to the realization of the purpose and maintenance of the relationship. (3) The community must give sanction to the relationship as one which should be protected and fostered in the service of public well-being. (4) The destructive effects which would occur to the relationship if the confidential communication(s) is (are) disclosed must be greater than would be the benefit toward the carrying out of justice in the litigation involved. In most cases, confidential pastoral communications are considered to meet these criteria.

Few issues have resulted in more anxiety and concern over the relationship between civil and religious interests than has that of confidential and privileged communications made to professional clergy. This was certainly not in the minds of those New York legislators who enacted the first privilege statute governing communications to clergy in 1928. As clergy and their related church organizations have increasingly become involved in providing mental health services in parish work and in pastoral counseling or chaplaincy, the matter has become significantly more complex. The central reason for this is that communications to clergy which are made to them in their professional capacity are protected (privileged) from disclosure in ways which communications made to many other social service professionals are not. Thus arises not only interprofessional antagonisms but legitimate concern that public well-being is not, in fact, protected by such laws which limit the public's need to know. The restriction placed on disclosure of information which otherwise might be of benefit in the judicial process seems, to many, less appropriate when it is not strictly considered confessional or penitential.

Enumerated in Article IV of the Bill of Rights, and considered essential to the development of trust and confidence in professional pastoral relationships, confidentiality can be defined as the commitment by both parties not to disclose communications between the parishioner/client and the clergyperson to a third party without the expressed consent of the parishioner/client. From the confessional booth to the clergy counseling office, it is recognized that a parishioner/client must be totally free to communicate the most private of thoughts and feelings if healing and reconciliation are to occur. This places a great responsibility on the parish pastor who interacts with the same person in counseling, church meetings, social gatherings, and worship.

The information given in confidence to the pastor is the property of the parishioner, so any protection from disclosure belongs to the parishioner *not* to the pastor. Many have mistakenly understood that the pastor is privileged (protected) when, in fact, it is the parishioner's communications which receive this protection.

Confidentiality points clearly to the fact that clergy, as recipients of certain information, whether as parish pastor, pastoral counselor or chaplain, stand at the interface of civic and religious responsibility. Only in certain situations, e.g., the requirement by state laws to report child abuse, is the matter clear. In addition, it should be noted that in most states information shared in marital, family or group counseling sessions is not privileged since it is shared in the presence of other persons. Thus, though the commitment to confidentiality remains applicable regardless of the number of persons in a counseling session, the courts may likely not consider such information privileged.

The best approach to follow for clergy in parish ministry would be to inform church members of their professional commitment to confidentiality in all their counseling and related activities. There is only one professionally accepted exception to this principle. In a situation where professional consultation is sought with another professional, it is considered that such a breach in confidentiality is acceptable as long as it is solely for the benefit of the parishioner/client. The person(s) should be informed that their confidences will be shared with a third party for this purpose and their permission secured in writing. Parish clergy can generally expect that communication made to them in their capacity as clergy will be protected, by law, from disclosure with the above noted exceptions in group

settings. Chaplains, in their comparable role as spiritual advisors must also maintain the confidentiality commitment and would be subject to the same clergy-privilege statutes. Clergy in full-time pastoral counseling ministry should adhere to the confidentiality provisions found in the Code of Ethics of the American Association of Pastoral Counselors. Communications made to clergy functioning full-time as psychotherapists are less clearly privileged since the confessional or penitential intent of the clergy-penitent privilege is not well demonstrated. However, the privilege is often, in fact, not questioned, which then raises an important ethical question for the pastoral counselor as to whether or not the privilege should be invoked in order to avoid testimony or release of records when the relationship in question is much more psychotherapeutic than confessional.

With the widespread use of computerized information storage, distribution and retrieval, record auditing, insurance reimbursement, etc., it is questionable as to whether confidentiality is really possible. However, the values surrounding personal privacy and their importance in building pastoral relationships of trust and security must be guarded in the ministry of the church.

Bibliography. American Association of Pastoral Counselors, *Handbook* 2d ed. (1975), p. 28. E. Augspurger, "Legal Concerns of the Pastoral Counselor" in *The Organization and Administration of Pastoral Counseling Centers* (1981), pp. 131–48. L. Foster, "Privileged Communications: When Psychiatrists Envy the Clergy," *J. of Pastoral Care*, 33, (1976) 116–21. T. Klink, ed., "Pastoral Confidentiality and Privileged Communication," *Pastoral Psychology*, 17:162 (March, 1966), 3–46. W. H. Tieman and J. C. Bush. *The Right to Silence: Privileged Clergy Communication and the Law* (1983). J. H. Wigmore, *Evidence in Trials at Common Law*, vol. 8 (1961), p. 527.

E. A. HOOVER

ETHICS, PROFESSIONAL; LEGAL DIMENSIONS OF PASTORAL CARE AND COUNSELING; RECORD KEEPING. *See also* COVENANT AND CONTRACT IN PASTORAL COUNSELING; PROFESSIONALISM.

CONFIRMATION. *See* BAPTISM AND CONFIRMATION.

CONFLICT, CONGREGATIONAL. *See* CONFLICT AND CONFLICT MANAGEMENT; CONGREGATION; DISAGREEMENT, DIFFERENCE, AND CONFLICT IN PASTOR-PARISHIONER RELATIONSHIPS; JEWISH CARE AND COUNSELING.

CONFLICT, FAMILY. *See* FAMILY, PASTORAL *or* JEWISH CARE OF; FAMILY THEORY AND THERAPY; FAMILY VIOLENCE. *See also* CRISIS MINISTRY.

CONFLICT, MARRIAGE. *See also* MARRIAGE; MARRIAGE COUNSELING AND MARITAL THERAPY. *See also* CRISIS MINISTRY.

CONFLICT, PASTOR-PARISHIONER. *See* DISAGREEMENT, DIFFERENCE, AND CONFLICT IN PASTOR-PARISHIONER RELATIONSHIPS. *See also* CONFLICT AND CONFLICT MANAGEMENT; CONGREGATION, PASTORAL CARE OF.

CONFLICT, PSYCHOLOGICAL. *See* MENTAL HEALTH AND ILLNESS; PSYCHOPATHOLOGY, THEORIES OF.

CONFLICT, UNCONSCIOUS. *See* PSYCHOANALYSIS (Personality Theory and Research).

CONFLICT AND CONFLICT MANAGEMENT.

Webster's Dictionary defines "conflict" as: "to fight, clash, struggle." As a result, the word is usually thought of negatively, as is the experience of conflict. This article acknowledges the negative quality of human conflict but also maintains that conflict is a natural, inevitable, and central part of human existence, that conflict can be loving and creative, and finally, that persons can learn to manage conflict in ways that are constructive, healthy, and loving rather than destructive, unhealthy and alienating.

1. Roots of Human Conflict. Recognizing three unique characteristics of personhood can provide a helpful perspective on human conflict. First, each individual sees and experiences the world through his or her own perceptual framework, which structures the world. This framework provides categories through which we order and relate our experiences and out of which we make choices about actions to take. Thus it gives meaning to both our experience and action.

Second, humans are intentional, willful beings. Each has goals which he or she wants to accomplish, and these goals are targets toward which we direct our actions. Even when we are not fully clear about our goals our actions are intentional, directed toward that which would be meaningful and fulfilling from our perspective.

Third, humans are social beings. We live and work out our identity within the context of other persons. From our earliest awareness of others through the maturing process, we discover that other persons are like us. They perceive the world from their perspective. They have goals which they are pursuing. These sets of intentions and goals inevitably claim some of the same space and the same resources of others.

In short, to be human means to have conflict. Despite our wish to avoid conflict, we continue to seek our own fulfillment and wholeness. This goal-directed action inevitably encounters and conflicts with other humans' pursuits of their own goals. The only option we have is not *whether*, but *how* to deal with the inevitable human conflict.

2. Styles of Managing Conflict. We all have our own styles of dealing with conflict. These styles become ingrained patterns of responses and initiatives in the face of conflict. They largely determine how effective or ineffective, creative or destructive we are in managing conflicts. It is possible, but not easy, to change styles.

Altering attitudinal and behavioral patterns such as conflict styles requires at least three phases. The first is awareness of our styles and under what conditions we tend to use them. There are many ways to understand our styles. One excellent instrument which provides a clear theoretical framework as well as a rating of how we use each style is Teleometric's *Conflict Management Survey*.

A second step in the change process is intentionality and practice. Changing the way we deal with conflict requires identifying specifically which behavioral expression of a style we want to change and then practicing that new behavior over and over again. For example, if our primary style is to withdraw from conflict immediately, a first behavioral change might be to commit ourselves to remain on the conflict scene at least five minutes. Gradually we experience that we will not be destroyed by conflict. Then we can practice next steps such as communication skills or identifying our goals that are being blocked in the conflict situation.

A final step toward change requires the reinforcing of the new behavioral pattern. It must be rewarded and socially supported. Otherwise our tendency is to revert to the more comfortable and familiar pattern. Alcoholics Anonymous, as one example, has long recognized, and effectively used, the support and reinforcement principle to change entrenched destructive patterns of behavior.

Most of us feel a great deal of inadequacy, anxiety, and guilt about the ways we manage conflict. Recognizing different styles should also include understanding that there is no one perfect style of managing conflict. The various styles are appropriate under different circumstances. Creative conflict management includes recognizing that we all manage conflict, affirming our abilities, recognizing our styles, and learning to use them appropriately in different circumstances.

3. Role of Pastoral Leaders. Conflict is not only a personal phenomenon; it is also communal. A community's effectiveness in dealing with its conflicts will depend largely on its leaders. In the church, the pastor has a primary role in conflict management. Many pastors want to deny, conflict, or suppress it in the church, or avoid their role as manager. Too often in churches conflicts are not dealt with openly and publicly. Apathy, alienation, and hostility among the members result.

To be an effective leader, a pastor must encourage creative conflict in the congregation; that is, develop an atmosphere and communal processes in which members can express their hopes and dreams, share their differences, search together for goals and alternatives that will allow each person to accomplish what is important to him or her while together investing in the mission of the church.

By engaging clergy and laity together in the exploration of the church's mission, and by managing the conflict that inevitably arises from the different interpretations of that mission, the church can experience a new creativity and vitality. Growth is only possible, however, when management processes within the church function to encourage expression of diverse hopes, make the differences visible, and explore alternatives for attaining divergent goals. The pastor, effective or not, is the primary manager in the system. For the health and vitality of the church and its members, conflict management must be a pastoral priority.

4. Conflict and Love. Love is the norm for a Christian life. If conflict is inevitable, even necessary in human existence, can we love others and be in conflict with them at the same time? Too often the church has interpreted conflict to be the opposite of love. Not only is that a mistaken notion, but it has been one of the fundamental causes of the inadequate dealing with conflict in the church. Rather, loving, caring for others, investing deeply in them, and risking part of ourselves makes our conflicts intense.

Remember our uniqueness as persons. We are intentional, goal-directed, making choices always from our own perspectives. With our model being the all-inclusive love of God, to love others is to affirm their right and necessity to have their own goals and unique perspectives. We are to love and affirm all, not just those who agree with us or whose goals we support and regard as right.

On the other side of the coin we need those who differ with us. Growth toward wholeness as persons is no natural unfolding. It is an arduous, often painful struggle. We frequently discover our blind spots, our biases, our areas of needed growth through those who conflict, disagree, and stand over against us. Resistance from others enables us not only to perceive our own limitations and weaknesses but to gain insight into our identity and intentions. Seen thus, conflict, if acknowledged and faced, can be a gift of God's grace set before us.

Finally, to love others means we must also share our hopes and intentions with them and see that the goals of others in the community are held up. Not to lift up this reality for others is not to love them or ourselves. A loving and caring community is one that not only provides for this sharing and its resulting conflict but also encourages it.

5. Guidelines for Managing Conflict. The following principles are recommended as helpful guidelines for creative conflict management. While they may seem simple or obvious, the key is being able to internalize and use them in those moments when rationality deserts us, when reflection and planning time are nonexistent, when the stakes are high, and when our anxiety is intense. It requires persistence and practice for individuals and organizations to increase their capacity and skill in managing conflict.

Two suggestions may help in learning and internalizing the principles. First, practice one principle at a time, instead of trying to change everything at once. Second, use the principles as a checklist to assist in remembering them.

a. Help others feel better about themselves. Persons and organizations manage conflict best when they are feeling secure and good about themselves. They are more open to the goals of others, clearer about their own intentions and can see and agree to a wider range of alternatives. When they are feeling bad about themselves the opposite reactions set in. Though aware of these differences, in conflict persons' intentions and actions are often to attack, to put others on the defensive and to make them feel worse about themselves.

b. Strive for effective communication. Effective communication consists of attentive and reflective listening and sending messages with the knowledge that one's perspectives and messages are uniquely one's own. Effective communication is central to creative conflict management. In sending messages, persons should remember that they are perceptions and perspectives, not absolute facts. The more important part of communication, however, is receiving the message. More distortion and misunderstanding occurs with the receiver than the sender. Two things should be practiced for effective receiving. First, listening at all levels — verbal and nonverbal. Second, checking with the sender to see if one is understanding the message correctly. These skills can be practiced and learned.

c. Examine and filter assumptions. Beware that all persons inevitably make assumptions about other persons and situations that have no basis in reality and, in turn, act on them without ever checking their validity. People even have the tendency to nurse these assumptions and hide them from the light of examination. These unexamined assumptions very often contribute to destructive conflict. Creative conflict management should include a reminder to see whether or not the assumptions one is acting upon are true.

d. Identify goals. Identifying what a person, group, or organization is trying to accomplish—what is wanted—is usually the most important element in conflict management. The existence of a conflict means that there are two or more persons' intentions and actions trying to occupy the same space at the same time. Until persons identify what each party wants or is trying to accomplish, in short, what their goals are, they can never manage the conflict.

e. Identify the primary issue. Many persons want to offer a quick solution to the conflict often before they are even clear about the central issue. Persisting until the issue is clear is complicated by the fact that most conflicts have multiple issues. Rarely, however, can all of the issues be effectively worked on at once. It is more helpful to focus on at least one main issue until an alternative is found. A good conflict manager continues to ask, "Is this the primary issue?" Once an alternative is found for that issue, it will help manage the other related issues as well.

f. Develop alternatives for goal achievement. Search for alternatives that will allow all parties to achieve that which is important and fulfilling to them. Everyone knows that this goal is not always attainable. But, if persons do not begin with that as their goal, they will often settle the issue too quickly and inadequately. Belief that such alternatives can be discovered is crucial to creative conflict management.

6. Conclusion. Creative conflict management intends to point to a style that is constructive rather than destructive to persons and groups. Creative means having the ability or power to create; to create is to bring into being something that does not now exist. Creative conflict management, then, means building new relational possibilities, new alternatives for action that presently do not exist and that are satisfying for both parties. The goal of creative conflict management from a ministry perspective is to enable all parties to achieve that which is vital and important to them. The principles are intended as guidelines to that end.

There are numerous planning methods that can spur the creativity of individuals and groups, but none work unless the people have a sense of hope, unless they believe new possibilities can be discovered. The church needs first to remember and proclaim its good news, that in God all things are possible. Hope can also come from the affirmation that conflict can be a source of redemption, as, through it, the church examines its mission more closely. That sense of hope can empower the church and its members for a more creative future.

Bibliography. J. L. Allen, *Love and Conflict: A Covenantal Model of Christian Ethics* (1984). D. W. Augsburger, *Anger and Assertiveness in Pastoral Care,* (1979). A. C. Filley, *Interpersonal Conflict Resolution* (1975). L. Hart, *Learning From Conflict: A Handbook for Trainers and Group Leaders* (1981). S. B. Leas, *Leadership and Conflict* (1983). S. B. Leas and P. Kittlaus, *Church Fights: Managing Conflict in the Local Church* (1973). D. Lewis, *Resolving Church Conflicts* (1981).

D. LEWIS

AGGRESSION AND ASSERTION; DISCIPLINE, PASTORAL CARE AS; MEDIATION/CONCILIATION; POWER; RECONCILING. *See also* ANGER; CONFRONTATION (Pastoral and Therapeutic); FAMILY VIOLENCE; FORGIVENESS; PROBLEM SOLVING; RAGE AND HOSTILITY; RESISTANCE. *Compare* ALIENATION/ESTRANGEMENT; COMPETITIVENESS; PEACE-MAKING AND PASTORAL CARE.

CONFRONTATION (Pastoral and Therapeutic). In a therapeutic context, to bring a counselee face-to-face with avoided aspects of his or her feelings and behavior. The usual objectives are self-understanding, clarification of reality, and inner-directedness.

This view of confrontation focuses primarily upon the inner world of the counselee and interaction with others. The pastoral counselor attends carefully to the counselee's facility and readiness to engage avoided aspects of the self and utilizes clarification, interpretation, and other interventions as procedures of confrontation.

Confrontation also means face-to-face encounter of counselor and counselee. This perspective focuses upon the therapeutic relationship, the otherness of the counselor, and views the interaction of counselor and counselee as the matrix for growth. The counselor attends carefully to the counselee's response to him or her as the other. The counselee experiences the counselor's otherness through empathic presence, authentic response, and active participation in the search to understand his or her life history and present experience.

An authentic pastoral and therapeutic response often requires introduction of a different view and an examination of the present experience; this is necessary for forgiveness and reconciliation. Without the response of the other a person is limited to the purview of self and others shaped often by uncorrected childhood narcissism and grandiosity.

The counselor's active participation is often a difficult posture to achieve. The counselor must attend carefully to the counselee's readiness and self-direction in the search to understand. The timing of confrontation, therefore, should rest on the counselor's assessment of the counselee's psychological inclination, observing ego function, and guardedness. It serves no therapeutic purpose to confront a defensively protected person who sustains a deficit of observing ego function.

In addition to the encounter with self and other, confrontation means that a counselee will encounter the moral context for his or her life even when there may be no specific conversation about "what is right." The pastoral counselor as a representative of a specific community, tradition, and moral/ethical view enlarges the con-

text of the therapeutic encounter. Thus, the counselee's process toward inner-directedness is amended in counseling through confrontation of the moral/ethical context for decision making. Avoiding a moralistic and judgmental posture, the counselor participates in the counselee's identification and subscription of values for living.

Pastoral confrontation rests upon the counselor's hermeneutical task: to participate through the relationship in a person's coming to new interpretations and views. The task may move to whatever level the counselee shows personal readiness and facility for attaining. Where there is sufficient personal adequacy and motivation, the counselee may confront a new interpretation of self, others, and God that offers greater potential for personal liberation, interpersonal reconciliation, and responsible participation in life.

Bibliography. D. S. Browning, *The Moral Context for Pastoral Care* (1976). L. G. Colston, *Judgment in Pastoral Counseling* (1969). J. C. Hoffman, *Ethical Confrontation in Counseling* (1979).

G. P. JENKINS

AUTHORITY, PASTORAL; DISCIPLINE, PASTORAL CARE AS; WORKING THROUGH. *See also* ASSERTIVENESS IN MINISTRY; CHRISTIAN CONCILIATION MOVEMENT. *Compare* CONFLICT AND CONFLICT MANAGEMENT; DEPROGRAMMING; INTERPRETATION AND HERMENEUTICS, PASTORAL; LIMIT-SETTING; POWER; REALITY PRINCIPLE; STRUCTURING.

CONFUCIAN SOUL CARE. *See* PSYCHOLOGY, EASTERN.

CONFUSION. *See* MENTAL HEALTH AND ILLNESS; ORGANIC MENTAL DISORDER AND ORGANIC BRAIN SYNDROME.

CONGREGATION, JEWISH CARE AND COUNSELING IN. *See* JEWISH CARE AND COUNSELING.

CONGREGATION, PASTORAL CARE OF. The ministry of oversight and nurture offered by a religious community to its members, including acts of discipline, support, comfort, and celebration.

1. Biblical Basis. *a. Heritage of the Old Testament.* Throughout the Jewish scriptures, the injunction to care for members of the community receives the strongest emphasis. It is couched in terms of conforming to the Lord's ways and serving him with all one's heart (Deut. 10:12ff.). Israel must know that the Lord their God is "God of gods and Lord of lords, the great, the mighty, and the terrible God," who secures justice for widows and orphans and loves the alien (v. 17).

This theme, repeated endlessly in the Bible, stresses that taking care of the community is central to the identity of the people of God. The prophets protested that one of the reasons for God's great and terrible acts against Israel was its failure to shepherd and nurture those members of the community whose claim upon it lay in their very helplessness and need for support.

The term "pastoral," familiar in the Christian community, denotes the community's care of its members. It derives from the figurative language of Jewish scriptures and, supremely, from the Lord's care of Israel (Palms 23; 80). Jeremiah and Ezekiel extended the image of "caregiver" to the leaders of Israel, the King and his prophets, who frequently were castigated for their failure to fulfill their duties as shepherds of the flock (e.g., Ezek. 34:8).

Judaism has always stressed the obligation to show kindness to those in need; the Hebrew *zedakah* equals righteousness (Deut. 24:13; Isa. 32:17; Ps. 106:3); *gemilut hesed*, the bestowing of kindness, is the rabbinical term for such care. Charity (in the sense of I Corinthians 13) may be regarded as a free tribute of love; but in Judaism, charity is an act of duty incumbent upon those in a position to meet the needs of others. Such charity is righteousness insofar as God, the giver of all blessings, claims from divine blessings a share for the disadvantaged, and, as the Creator, claims a part of the earth's benefits on behalf of the orphan, the widow, and the stranger (Deut. 15:10, 11).

b. *Witness of the New Testament and Early Church.* To the early Christian community, only Jesus could fulfill the role of *the* shepherd. The disciples' role in caring for the "flock" derived from Jesus' charge to them. Thus, they participated in his pastoral function. This responsibility to care for (love) one another is emphasized in the Fourth Gospel and in the Johannine Epistles, where the members' love for one another, by which the world will know that they are truly the Lord's disciples, is the highest expression of the evangel. Through their ministry to each other, they are to exemplify Jesus' ministry to his disciples. The washing of the disciples' feet (Jn. 13:1–17) symbolizes the caring ministry that is to be the core of the community's life. The community is to live in and for such mutual service, apart from which there is, effectually, no revelation, no faith, and, particularly, no ministry and no church (Moody-Smith, 1981, p. 226).

In the Ante-Nicene Church, pastoral care became a clerical function that, by the third century, was centralized in the episcopate. Pastoral ministry was delegated by the bishop to deacons, and, subsequently, to presbyters, whose task became that of gathering the flock, keeping it unified, and protecting its members from threat (Cooke, 1980, pp. 60–66; 350ff.).

The expectation that the clergy would provide pastoral care to the congregation has remained as strong in mainline Protestant churches as in the Roman Catholic church. For example, although the past three decades have witnessed a growing awareness that the task devolves on laypeople as much as upon the clergy, the pastoral care literature from Hiltner (1949) to Oglesby (1980) addresses a clergy audience. The implicit assumption has been that the task, for all practical purposes, rests upon the ordained pastor. Nevertheless, the recognition by the Reformers and their successors that pastoral care is a ministry of *the congregation,* and that laypeople, like clergy, share in the NT *charismata* that equip them for that ministry, is given increasing credence. Equipping laypeople for pastoral ministry has emerged as one of the most urgent tasks facing congregations.

2. **Scope of Pastoral Care of the Congregation.** Pastoral care has evolved in two directions: general pastoral *care* directed to the membership, and a more intensive and individual pastoral *counseling* to members facing personal or family crisis and stress.

a. Changing role of the pastor. Until recently, clergy and laity alike have expected that the ordained pastor would make regular pastoral visits to members' homes as the primary expression of pastoral ministry. While many clergy undoubtedly still maintain a rigorous schedule of home visits, the practice has been inhibited by the growth in size of congregations and the geographic scattering of members throughout large metropolitan areas.

One of the consequences of urbanization for the shape of the congregation's ministry to its members has been the restriction of clergy pastoral visitation to periods of crisis in the lives of families. Both pastor and parishioner still believe that visitation by the clergy is incumbent in such crises as hospitalization and bereavement. Other, less crisis-oriented care, such as that to the elderly and homebound, falls in the same category. Yet the physical capacity to fulfill this ministry, if left exclusively to the clergy, has been greatly reduced; as a result, clerical pastoral care of the congregation is greatly limited in scope.

As the function of pastoral care has grown to incorporate the ministry of both clergy and laity, its scope also has been extended. The training of selected laypeople to participate in pastoral care enables the congregation to undertake a more comprehensive ministry. Paul apparently was aware of the need and opportunity for a broad-based ministry: "Let love for our brotherhood breed warmth of mutual affection. . . . Contribute to the needs of God's people. . . . With the joyful be joyful, and mourn with the mourners. . . . Care as much about each other as about yourselves" (Rom. 12:9–16, NEB).

b. Intentional nature of pastoral care. Paul's admonitions to those called to help others implies a further characteristic of pastoral care: it should be intentional in nature. Much conversation between members is an expression of love and concern for one another, and thus is to be commended; but it may fall outside the definition of ministry, which, by its very nature, should be self-conscious and purposeful. What constitutes ministry as pastoral care is not the extent to which care lacks any special representation of Christian faith, but that that ministry is offered self-consciously in the Lord's name.

Some writers have been so emphatic on this issue that they have maintained that unless there is specific identification of the name in whom the ministry is offered, the conversation cannot be regarded as pastoral at all. Thus, Clebsch and Jaekle (1964) maintain that on many occasions works of charity, welfare, or education closely associated with the Christian ideal of love for the neighbor are hardly "pastoral" if they lack any specific representation of faith. To some extent Oden (1983) expresses the same concern, although not with the same force. He urges that the pastor be ready always to speak in overtly religious words. If pastoral visitation fails that purpose, it may succeed in being pleasant conversation but it is hardly pastoral dialogue.

As an alternative to this restrictive perception of pastoral care stands a second perspective. Pastoral care may be defined not in terms of the *content* of the dialogue but in terms of the *intentionality* of the pastor—whether

ordained or lay. From a Christian perspective, the criterion then becomes the fact that the lay or ordained pastor ministers self-consciously in the name of Christ, determining in the course of the conversation itself the extent to which any overt witness is made to that faith that is the ever-present reality in which the visit is grounded. Even the familiar images of Mt. 25:31ff. do not eliminate this notion of intentionality. Those whom the Lord welcomed had chosen a lifestyle of self-giving service. Further, the gospels present the very ministry of Jesus as insistently self-conscious and intentional (e.g., Mt. 7:4; Jn. 9:4).

c. Presence of the Word as evangelism. The foregoing suggests another nuance of pastoral care — the act of ministry may be offered not only through the medium of the caring words of the pastoral visitor, but in the pastor's "presence" itself. "Presence" is a word very much in common use, and to affix "Christian" to it only begs many questions. The term is used in one context to describe the experience of being there, in the name of Christ, often anonymously, listening before one speaks. In such a situation, "presence" may precede witness; in another sense, the very presence *is* witness.

If this premise is granted, two further statements may be advanced: First, pastoral care of the congregation is far more intimately related to what has been called "evangelism" than has been recognized previously, and can be presented as the primary and fundamental form the gospel may take in a particular situation. Thus, a visit to a family newly arrived in the parish may be perceived as a *pastoral* visit that may or may not be characterized as an *evangelistic* visit, in the traditional sense of that term. The same may be true of other pastoral situations. For, second, pastoral care of the congregation must now incorporate any act of care or nurture extended from the congregation to its members. This ministry would include visits unrelated to specific events, visits that manifest the congregation's continuing pastoral concern for each family — regular phone contacts with homebound members; the use of birthday and other greeting cards; the reading of the names of deceased members on the anniversaries of their deaths or on All Saints Day; the celebration of attainments or achievements.

The recognition is growing that significant anniversaries should occasion pastoral care visits. This applies particularly to the initial period of bereavement. There appears to be a broad consensus among widowed members, for example, that congregations quickly forget their need for a ministry of continuing support in the post-funeral period. Occasions for pastoral ministry include the twelve-month period following a death; wedding anniversaries and family birthdays; and the major public holidays.

The congregation's need to record information, such as important anniversaries, that should issue in pastoral visits has given increasing urgency to the trend toward using computers to facilitate pastoral care of the congregation. This development further emphasizes the importance of the careful structuring and organization of the congregation's pastoral care of its members, which should be undertaken with the highest degree of responsibility and commitment. The thoroughness of the

congregation's ministry — for example, ensuring that visits are not overlooked — may be as important as the sensitivity and spiritual direction of the visits themselves.

3. **Pastoral Care and the Eucharist.** One of the emphases brought to the ministry of pastoral care of the congregation in recent years has been a renewed attention to the relationship between pastoral ministry and the Eucharist. It is the loving commitment of each Christian, and of the church as the corporate community, to express compassion and care for a hurt and suffering humanity. The ministries of God's people grow out of and find highest expression in the worship of the people of God. The community offers that work as a unique sacrifice that embraces all acts of ministry and finds its supreme symbolic moment in the Eucharist (Cooke, 1980, p. 203 ff.; Newbigin, 1983, p. 10.5).

One of the contemporary forms this relationship has taken has been the development of a "lay Eucharistic ministry" within the Roman Catholic and Episcopal churches. Recognizing that the pastoral needs of the church demanded changes, in order not to deny parishioners the Eucharist in extraordinary situations, the Holy See provided for the appointment, upon request from the parish pastor, of laymen and laywomen as special, auxiliary, or "extraordinary" ministers of the Eucharist (N.C.C.B., 1973). This practice has extended the congregation's pastoral care of its members within the context of the Eucharistic celebration.

On the theological premise that pastoral care of the congregation is a response to the liturgical life and practices of the church, and, in particular, draws its inspiration from the Eucharist, it is noteworthy that in some denominations (e.g., Roman Catholic, Presbyterian) the full participation of children in the Eucharist has been authorized. This, with other initiatives, has raised the question of the extent to which children receive pastoral care with the same intentionality as that provided for adult members. Pastoral care education has tended to focus more on ministry to adult members than to children. A strong case can be made that special provision should be made for pastoral care of children in the congregation, where that ministry has been overlooked.

Bibliography. R. Burck, "Pastoral Care and the People of God," *Pastoral Psychology*, 30, 4 (1982), 139–52. W. A. Clebsch and C. R. Jaekle, *Pastoral Care in Historical Perspective* (1964). B. Cooke, *Ministry to Word and Sacrament* (1980). S. M. Coyle, "A Covenanting Process in Pastoral Home Visits," *J. of Pastoral Care*, 39 (1985), 96–109. E. H. Friedman, *Generation to Generation: Family Process in Church and Synagogue* (1985). S. Hiltner, *Pastoral Counseling* (1949). K. Kohler in I. Singer, ed., *The Jewish Encyclopedia* (1901). D. Moody-Smith, in E. E. Shelp and R. H. Sunderland, eds., *A Biblical Basis for Ministry* (1981). National Conference of Catholic Bishops, *Bishops' Committee on the Liturgy, Study Text 1* (1973). L. Newbigin, "Studies in 1st Peter" in R. H. Sunderland, ed., *Equipping Laypeople for Ministry* (1983). T. Oden, *Pastoral Theology* (1983). W. Oglesby, Jr., *Biblical Themes for Pastoral Care* (1980).

R. H. SUNDERLAND

CALLING AND VISITATION, PASTORAL; COMMUNITY, FELLOWSHIP, AND CARE; ECCLESIOLOGY AND PASTORAL CARE; LAY PASTORAL CARE AND COUNSELING; PASTORAL CARE (Contemporary Methods, Perspectives, and Issues). *See also* COMMU-

NION/EUCHARIST; LEADERSHIP AND ADMINISTRATION; LITURGICAL CHANGE AND REFORM (Pastoral Issues); PREACHING; TEACHING; VOLUNTEERS; WORSHIP AND CELEBRATION; *also* JEWISH CARE AND COUNSELING (History, Traditions, and Contemporary Issues); OLD TESTAMENT AND APOCRYPHA, *or* NEW TESTAMENT, TRADITIONS AND THEOLOGY OF CARE IN; ROMAN CATHOLIC PASTORAL CARE. *Compare* DISAGREEMENT, DIFFERENCE, AND CONFLICT IN PASTOR-PARISHIONER RELATIONSHIPS; FRIENDSHIP, PASTOR-PARISHIONER; GROWTH GROUPS; RELATIONSHIP NETWORK; SUPPORT GROUPS.

CONJOINT MARRIAGE AND FAMILY THERAPY. Refers to the psychotherapy of a married couple or family meeting together. The marital dyad may be treated as a subsystem of a larger family system. Conjoint family therapy includes all members of the family system which as a whole may be seen as the focus of therapeutic attention.

R. E. JOHNSTON

MARRIAGE COUNSELING AND MARITAL THERAPY.

CONSCIENCE. A deeply felt, active, inclusive sense of moral approval or disapproval, rooted in the emotionally directive experiences that occur in the early years of childhood. At the same time it is an active, inclusive, moral perspective, subsuming all other evaluative perspectives. Conscience therefore develops in a tension between an accusing structure of repression and a guiding sense of moral discernment. The Christian tradition has stressed both the ontological guilt and the moral guidance of conscience. Pastoral care requires not only awareness of emotional abnormalities and forgiveness of ontological guilt, but also recognition of the importance of moral dialogue within a wider community of faith.

1. **The Dynamics of Conscience.** Freud described conscience as a repression of deeply felt impulses caused by standards that are internalized from persons (parents) who are both loved and feared during the early years of life. Such repressions result in a sense of shame and guilt. Ego psychologist Erik Erikson has theorized that shame and guilt are also accompanied by more positive qualities of ego strength such as autonomy and initiative. The sense of ego strength leads to a guiding "ethical sense" rather than moral repression. Conscience may therefore develop from proto-moral qualities of autonomy and initiative to a more mature guiding sense of identity and creativity.

Freud discovered that the infant takes in restrictions put upon it by parents or other caretakers as a kind of primitive conscience. Because of fear of loss of love, these restrictive standards are taken into the personality largely at an unconscious level. If the repression is too severe, or the trauma too great, the child may develop an enduring compulsive personality in which she or he feels the strongest obligation to standards such as cleanliness, order, and restraint. In the extreme, such a conscience can become paranoid. The earliest experiences of violating such norms are felt as shame in the presence of the parents.

Between the ages of three and six, the child takes in a more developed set of standards by a process of identification with the loved and feared parents. These standards include guilt about sexual and aggressive impulses. The resulting conscience is deeply felt, largely unconscious, and very enduring. Guilt regarding many imaginary ideas and many impulses is now added to the shame about more simple prohibitions that characterize the primitive conscience. Excessive repression can result in depression, paranoia, and/or compulsive disorders.

Erikson describes a more positive ethical sense that develops alongside of the accusing conscience described by Freud. In the first year of infancy trust and hope develop alongside of mistrust. During the second and third years of life a sense of autonomy modifies the sense of shame. During the third to sixth year a sense of initiative transforms the sense of guilt described by Freud. The psychosocial attitudes of trust, autonomy and initiative are foundational to ego strength throughout life. While they do not lead directly to moral evaluation, their absence leads to a conscience characterized by shame and guilt. They may therefore be called proto-moral virtues.

Another powerful description of the guiding conscience has been stimulated by Jean Piaget. According to Piaget, the moral judgment of young children is characterized by unilateral respect wherein they attribute a kind of magical divine authority to all adults. As children interact and mature, they come to understand that moral judgments gain their authority from mutual agreement. Lawrence Kohlberg has refined this process to six stages of development: naive egoism, punishment-obedience, concrete reciprocity, interpersonal mutuality, social order, social contract, and universal principle.

From what has been said it is evident that conscience moves through certain developmental stages. During infancy and early childhood, proto-moral attitudes of trust or mistrust, autonomy or shame, initiative or guilt are established. The preschool child has a mystical, magical attitude to authority, an attitude that may be carried into later life. The school-age child develops a sense of competence or incompetence along with a very legalistic way of thinking about what is fair, again a perspective that may be carried into later life. Youth and young adults gain a sense of identity and a capacity to look at behavior from various perspectives. Commitment to a guiding perspective is basic to the mature adult process of moral discernment.

2. **An Inclusive Moral Perspective.** A widely accepted moral psychology has looked upon conscience as a faculty alongside of other faculties of the personality. Conscience is rather to be considered the total self in the process of moral evaluation. Maturity of conscience then depends upon the degree to which all the impulses and understandings of a person are consciously brought to bear in the activity of moral discernment. While the strongly accusing conscience lacks integration within the total self, discerning moral evaluation is integrative for the total self, and is furthermore an interactive process within the wider community.

Faculty psychology has looked upon conscience as a voice within, an isolated capacity for moral evaluation within personality. H. Richard Niebuhr has argued persuasively that conscience rather ought to be considered as an evaluative process of the total person. All the processes of personality, including impulses, perceptions, ideals, and loyalties are brought to bear in evaluating a particular behavior, either intended or completed. Conscience is thus the inclusive moral perspective of the self, that which subsumes all other perspectives. It is in touch with the deepest loyalties and commitments of the self, with the central tendency to ego integration. While the accusing conscience has the character of a separate faculty, conscience as the inclusive evaluative process of the total person is not so separated.

James Gustafson has suggested that moral discernment is more than awareness of circumstances, attention to rules of conduct, consideration of principles, and commitment to ideals. Discernment is an act of the total self that brings all of these elements to bear in a process of moral evaluation. It seems close to what Erikson means by the ethical sense. Information, intentions, rules, moral reasoning, discussion, and ideals are all important to moral discernment. The concept of discernment therefore seems most appropriate as a characteristic of the mature conscience.

Conscience is closely related to community. Freud observed that a community is made up of those who have internalized the same accusing conscience. Similarly Erikson observed that the ethical sense is shaped by common social ideals. Conscience reflects the various social, religious, and ethnic groupings of people. Dialogue and discussion are the processes by which the moral discernment of the members of a community is shaped.

3. **Conscience and Faith.** The Apostle Paul taught that conscience is always to be respected. In Christian tradition conscience was thought to guide all persons according to universal moral principles. The tradition also has considered ontological guilt and dread to be the roots of the unredeemed conscience.

In the NT Paul distinguishes between a strong and a weak conscience, but he intends generally the opposite of contemporary usage. For Paul a weak conscience is one that insists upon refraining from meat dedicated to idols, even though idols are known to have no divine reality (I Corinthians 8). The strong conscience is not bound by the falsity of idolatry, but can adjust to various circumstances and to the various convictions of others. Nevertheless, Paul always respects the integrity of conscience. He will never violate another person's conscience, no matter how weak or strong, lest the person be deprived of the capacity to change and grow. He constantly affirms that in his mission he has been true to Christ and to his conscience. He also sees conscience as a bond between the individual and the community. The juxtaposition of conscience and Christ by Paul suggests that conscience is incomplete unless transformed by Christ.

In Christian tradition conscience has often referred to the immediate awareness by every person of the universal moral law. This law was considered to be expressed in the Ten Commandments. While the restrictions of the accusing conscience serve to preserve communities and cultures, the content does not seem to contemporary social scientists to be so universally similar as it was thought to be in previous centuries. The community ideals by which moral discernment is shaped are subject to cultural and historical variation, yet discernment is analogous to the traditional idea of guidance by the moral law.

The Augustinian-Lutheran tradition points out that a genuinely inclusive and benevolent moral evaluation is impossible for existing human beings. Therefore the concern for an inclusive and genuinely valid moral evaluation evokes a deep sense of human fallenness. Not only the accusing conscience, but also the guiding conscience brings on a sense of God's condemnation. However, Christ atones not only for ontological shame and guilt, but also for the inadequacy of human discernment. In Christ persons are freed of the dread of death, and are renewed or regenerated in their discernment. Christ becomes the center of the most inclusive moral evaluation, and he becomes the center of a re-established relationship with other persons. As persons are sanctified in Christ, they are enabled to grow in the process of discernment.

4. **Conscience and Pastoral Care.** The pastor and the community of faith may offer a variety of resources to those with difficulties of conscience. Pastoral care can include a transforming relationship, assurance of the grace of God in Christ, discernment of ambiguity, moral education, ethical dialogue and decision, and referral when necessary.

The most immediate care a pastor can offer a person with a disturbance of conscience is a transforming relationship. This includes a Pauline respect for the integrity of the weakest conscience. It involves a relationship in which various impulses and perceptions hidden beneath the accusing conscience can be brought before the light of discernment. It involves hearing and responding to the pain and anger of hidden impulses with a kind of acceptance and understanding that becomes a prototype for the new way that a person can begin to view himself or herself. The attitude of the pastor toward other persons can become the vantage point from which their own self-evaluation can begin to change.

Pastoral care has all of the resources of faith to offer. There is the grace of God in Christ to relieve ontological shame, guilt, and the fear of death. There are the sacraments within the healing community. There is confession within a set of caring and trustworthy relationships, which can be the beginning of release from accusation. Individual and corporate prayer and worship can become a transforming reality. Bible study can encourage discernment, and Christian service can offer an opportunity to act upon the guiding moral vision in Christ.

Pastoral care can also be keenly aware of the ambiguity of religious expression. All of the religious resources just mentioned can be used in the service of the accusing conscience. Often condemnation is voiced in the form of the highest ideals and the most idealistic relationships. Discerning pastoral care will sense the difference between religion in the service of a weak conscience and religion as an expression of mature vision. Perhaps all religious expression is a mixture of both, and therein pastoral care is always to be carried out in the awareness of God's forgiving, renewing, empowering grace.

Pastoral care can also be aware of the importance of ethical clarification and dialogue in the process of moral discernment. Pastoral care that is utterly accepting of all feelings and behaviors may be helpful in eliciting the deeper impulses in the accusing conscience, but dialogue and moral evaluation are necessary to moral discernment.

Pastoral care will therefore be willing to explore the ethical vision of people in relation to the communities to which they are loyal. Pastors may not only listen, but also enter into moral discussion, sharing their own convictions when appropriate. Moral education and dialogue belong to pastoral care and moral discussion within the community of faith is a healing resource when not dominated by the mood of the accusing conscience.

When severe disturbances of conscience require therapeutic skills that pastors do not possess, they must be willing to make referrals to properly qualified persons. Pastors can continually pray for the maturity of conscience that comes from seeking God's will, and from being instructed by others at points where they would otherwise be unable to see. Pastors can live out of and share their own moral discernment that is rooted in a deep awareness of God's grace in Jesus Christ.

Bibliography. D. Bonhoeffer, *Ethics* (1971). W. Conn, *Conscience: Development and Self-Transcendence* (1981). E. Erikson, *Childhood and Society* (1950); *Insight and Responsibility* (1964). S. Freud, *New Introductory Lectures* (1933); *Totem and Taboo* (1938). *Group Psychology*, CWP, 18 (1966). J. Gustafson, *Ethics, A Theocentric Perspective* (1981). P. Lehmann, *Ethics in a Christian Context* (1979). D. Miller, *The Wingfooted Wanderer* (1977). J. Piaget, *Moral Judgment of the Child* (1948). C. Pierce, *Conscience in the New Testament* (1955).

D. E. MILLER

MORAL DEVELOPMENT; MORAL THEOLOGY AND PASTORAL CARE; PERSON; RESPONSIBILITY/IRRESPONSIBILITY, PSYCHOLOGY OF; RIGHTEOUSNESS/BEING RIGHT. *See also* AUTHORITY; CASUISTRY; COMMITMENT; ETHICS AND PASTORAL CARE; GRACE; FREEDOM AND BONDAGE; GUILT; LEGALISM AND ANTINOMIANISM; MORAL DILEMMAS; OBEDIENCE; REPENTANCE AND CONFESSION; SELF-EXPRESSION/SELF-CONTROL; TEMPTATION. *Compare* ANOMIE / NORMLESSNESS; SOCIOPATHIC PERSONALITY.

CONSCIENCE (Orthodoxy). *See* MINISTRY AND PASTORAL CARE (Orthodox Tradition).

CONSCIENCE (Judaism). In Judaism, the closest equivalent to conscience would be the concept, the good instinct, or the *yetzer ha-tov.* The ideal in Judaism is for persons to integrate the instinctual energy — represented by the so-called evil instinct *(yetzer ha-ra)* — with the *yetzer ha-tov* which would make possible a moral life following the principle of *imitatio dei.* Judaism has a consistently strong emphasis on personal ethics and moral behavior. The task of the counselor would be to help individuals liberate powers of creative conscience and to sublimate the instinctual drive towards immature gratification and impulsive defiance of moral codes.

An early reference to the process of conscience can be found in I Sam. 24:5 which reports that the heart of David smote him after he had torn the garment of King Saul. The phenomenon of guilt is reflected in the experience of Cain who protested that his punishment for the killing of his brother was too great for him to bear. Another term used in the Bible (I Kings 19:12) is "the still small voice"—this designated the call of God which is felt within individuals and which leads them to identify with God and to follow in God's ways. The basic theme of justice in Judaism is conveyed in Jer. 9:23–24;

God practices loving kindness, justice, and righteousness. The philosopher Maimondies was later to suggest that righteousness signifies the inner state of a good conscience.

In rabbinic literature, the concept of *yetzer* is associated with the heart and with the kidneys. These organs were felt to be the seats of reason and judgment and also of feeling and of morality. The theme of conscience is also conveyed by the term *harata,* indicating remorse over immoral or objectionable behavior. *Harata* is a step leading to repentance and to the processes of personal confrontation emphasized in Rosh Hashanah and Yom Kippur. In the Jewish view, our conscience calls upon us to follow the ways of God and to engage in *hesed* or loving kindness.

Conscience in Judaism can also be seen as referring to matters which are left to the discretion of the heart and which are beyond specific laws. These are *debarim ha-mesurim la-leb.* Another Hebrew term is *hayyav,* designating moral obligation. Medieval Jewish philosophers used the term *sechel* to designate the intellect as well as the feeling of inner obligation. Later medieval literature included works of *musar* — dealing with the duties of the heart and issues in ethical behavior.

In Judaism the conscience cannot be equated with the superego. It is a sense of personal responsibility for doing good which is implanted within the individual and which reflects the spark of the divine and which distinguishes persons from animals.

Counselors can help the individual distinguish between objective and neurotic guilt. Real guilt indicates a consciousness of having done some injury to oneself or to another person. The task of the counselor is to help the individual sublimate destructive impulses, to dissolve irrational guilt, and to help discover and implement life affirming values congruent with the will of God.

In counseling, we distinguish between a peace of mind orientation which could tranquilize moral demands and the more confrontational orientation which at its best promotes the moral growth of individuals. The conscience in Judaism is related to principles of *imitatio dei* and *kedusha* — the sanctification of human life.

R. L. KATZ

ETHICS AND PASTORAL CARE; PATIENTS, JEWISH CARE AND COUNSELING OF; PERSON (Jewish Perspective).

CONSCIENCE (Protestantism). A fundamental human awareness of the demand for integrity and wholeness of the self before a transcendent Other.

In its origins, "conscience" *(syneidesis)* is a Hellenistic rather than a Hebraic term. It referred to a faculty implanted in human nature. Its proper function was to protect persons from evil by causing pangs of guilt for the transgression of moral limits. It was experienced primarily as bad conscience in relation to past actions. The corresponding Hebrew term meant "the heart." The two ideas rest upon fundamentally different forms of anthropology. Although the Greek term does not appear in the Gospels, it occurs thirty times in the NT. In adopting the concept to answer his opponents at Corinth, Paul pointed out its relativity and the need to limit it by consideration for the weaker brother (I Cor. 8:9–13). In Rom. 2:14–15 and 13:5 Paul interpreted 'the pains of conscience as the inner manifestation of God's wrath. The accusing conscience—whether of the Gentile or of the Jew—discloses a fundamental contradiction in life under the law. The inability to live by the law, whether the latter is known by nature or by revelation, points to the universal need for grace.

Following Paul, the Reformers also spoke primarily of the accusing conscience. For Luther conscience is an expression of God's wrath; it includes the divine judgment not only upon disobedience of the law but, more fundamentally, upon pride. Even for believers conscience remains primarily the accusing conscience which is related dialectically to grace. For Calvin conscience is experienced not only as guilt before the law but more deeply as "indolence and ingratitude" (*Institutes* I, 5:15). To the accusing conscience God appears as enemy. Revelation of God's grace transforms the conscience and frees the latter for "joyous obedience." In comparison with Luther, Calvin has a larger place for a "good conscience" in his doctrine of sanctification. Whereas conscience remains an accuser for Luther, for Calvin its primary role in the believer is that of moral guidance and direction.

The Reformers' view of conscience differs sharply from the noetic conception of Aquinas. For Aquinas, conscience is an innate rational capacity for moral self-assessment; its function is to guide human behavior in accordance with right reason. Despite such differences, however, there is general agreement among all Christians that conscience is inviolable and also that it is not infallible. While the voice of conscience ought always to be obeyed, it ought not to be equated with the voice of God.

The Christian conscience is not only instructed by Christ; it is also formed by the nurture of the affections and the Christian virtues. Greater attention to God's creative work through the socio-psychological processes of moral experience would enable Protestants to bridge the gap between law and grace in their understandings of conscience. To the extent that God's creative work is acknowledged in the natural conscience, conversion means a radical transformation of the latter in the context of sanctification.

Bibliography. E. Mount, *Conscience and Responsibility* (1969). C. A. Pierce, *Conscience in the New Testament* (1955). M. R. Weed, "Conscience in Protestant Ethics," Ph.D. dissertation, Emory University (1978).

E. C. GARDNER

CASUISTRY; ETHICS AND PASTORAL CARE; MORAL THEOLOGY; PERFECTIONISM. *See also* PERSON (Christian Perspective).

CONSCIENCE (Roman Catholicism). Historically, problems of conscience have been a central concern in Roman Catholic spirituality, pastoral care, and moral theology. The Catholic emphasis on penitential practice naturally highlighted the importance of conscience and emphasized the role of the confessor as an expert in questions of conscience, while the practical problem of instructing confessors led to the development of moral theology as a distinct theological discipline. Under the impetus of the Council of Trent, moral theology emerged in the sixteenth century as that branch of Catholic theology which assists the conscience in coming to decisions about the moral goodness or sinfulness of particular acts.

Thus Catholic pastoral practice and theory in the period from Trent to Vatican Council II (1962–1965) were highly legalistic, occupied with problems of applying authoritative norms and principles to complex human situations. Though the individual Catholic had an obligation to come to responsible individual decisions of conscience and was in theory free to follow those decisions even if opposed by the church, in practice it was assumed that decisions of conscience would conform to official church teachings.

After Vatican Council II the worldview of historical consciousness began to temper the classical worldview that had predominated in Roman Catholicism. A more scripturally based ethic began to complement the natural law emphasis of Catholic pastoral care and moral theology, and personalism mitigated the excessive reliance on authoritative teachings. These developments accorded a new autonomy to individual decisions of conscience.

Current Roman Catholic pastoral practice and moral theology and their relationship to conscience may best be viewed within the context of spirituality. Spirituality deals with the individual's relationship with God. Current moral theology is essentially discursive reasoning that assists the individual conscience in determining what is sinful and what is not. As a result, the individual can with God's grace begin to deal with the obstacles that hinder his or her relationship with God (the purgative stage of spirituality). As that relationship deepens, the conscience is less preoccupied with avoiding sin and more concerned about simply pleasing God. Moral theology gives way to ascetical theology. Intuitive and affective decisions of conscience coexist with discursive reasoning (the illuminative stage of spirituality). As the individual's relationship with God deepens further, the conscience is primarily concerned with loving God and the neighbor. Ascetical theology gives way to mystical theology. Discursive reasoning is almost submerged in decisions of conscience that are primarily intuitive and affective (the unitive stage of spirituality).

Bibliography. C. Curran, *Themes in Fundamental Moral Theology* (1977); "Discipleship: The Pastoral Minister and the Conscience of the Individual," *Clergy Review,* 68 (1983), 271–81. B. Haring, *The Law of Christ* (1961–1966) 3 vols. T. O'Connell, *Principles for a Catholic Morality* (1978).

G. McCARRON

CASUISTRY; ETHICS AND PASTORAL CARE; PENANCE, SACRAMENT OF; MORAL THEOLOGY; SCRUPULOSITY. *See also* PERSON (Christian Perspective).

CONSCIENTIOUS OBJECTORS. *See* MORAL DILEMMAS IN PASTORAL PERSPECTIVE; PROPHETIC/PASTORAL TENSION IN MINISTRY; SOCIAL CONSCIOUSNESS AND RESPONSIBILITY.

CONSCIENTIOUSNESS. *See* PERFECTIONISM; SCRUPULOSITY. *See also* RESPONSIBILITY/IRRESPONSIBILITY, PSYCHOLOGY OF.

CONSCIOUSNESS. In philosophy, psychology, and ordinary speech consciousness has a variety of different meanings that relate to the perception of what passes or occurs in a person's mind.

Consciousness has been technically defined in phenomenology as intentionality. Consciousness as awareness of an object is an unreflective act and an irreducible given in human experience. The meaning of consciousness is derived from this primary given. Theories that elaborate introspection or retrospection, subjectivity, states of consciousness and systems of consciousness are grounded in intentionality. Whatever else consciousness might be, the immediate awareness of an object is its first meaning in the phenomenological orientation, and on this level of consciousness is unreflected. Consciousness is here simply the perception of an object or succession of objects.

This first definition of consciousness is primary but incomplete because the existence of consciousness in human experience includes consciousness of itself. In perception, consciousness is not only the seeing of an object but the *awareness* of seeing the object. This awareness is a reflective act. It regards the primary act of seeing the object as an object itself. Consciousness thus takes itself as an object. Such reflective consciousness establishes an inwardness that accompanies all our conscious thought. This is the "I" which, though not discernible as a separate entity of the mind, nevertheless presents itself in the consciousness of the world of objects. Therefore, consciousness can be considered the conjunction of the reflective "I" with the primary perception of the object.

The consciousness of the apprehension and constitution of the "I" or ego by reflective consciousness often extends the empirical mapping of consciousness into acts of introspection and retrospection. Consciousness then means self-consciousness or ego-consciousness. The reason for this extension is explained by William James when he notes that the universal fact is not the existence of feelings and thoughts but the experience of "I think" and "I feel." James rejects the ordinary understanding of consciousness as an object to be examined and simply identifies consciousness with experience. It is the "I" in the experience of consciousness that complicates the meaning of consciousness as a simple state of awareness. We are not simply aware of the world but we are aware of our being aware.

It would be easy then to understand consciousness as a state, system, or thing subject to introspective investigation. Psychoanalysis has especially sought to elaborate the concept of consciousness, topographically and systematically (P. Ricoeur, 1974, p. 99).

One of the fundamental hypotheses of psychoanalysis is that "consciousness is an exceptional rather than a regular attribute of psychic processes" (C. Brenner, p. 2). It was at the extremities of ordinary experience (dreams, parapraxes, hypnosis, neurosis, psychosis) that Freud discovered gaps or absences that challenged the primacy of a natural attitude toward consciousness as the sole determinant of meaning. He argued that the skewed nature of conscious experience of these points of extremity engendered processes such as repression, displacement, substitution, and symbolization which further conditioned the manifest content of conscious experience. These processes suggested the existence of an unconscious mind existing with and complementing the conscious mind. Freud wrote of the concept of the unconscious that "It is necessary because the data of consciousness have a very large number of gaps in them; both in healthy and in sick people psychical acts often occur which can be explained only by presupposing other acts, of which, nevertheless, consciousness affords no evidence" (*SE* 14, p. 166). Consciousness entails a meaning that goes beyond its primary definition.

Consciousness as a primary concept is never fully explicit. It always contains an implicit reference to the conditions that make consciousness possible (Ricoeur, p. 101). Theories of consciousness presented in transcendental philosophers as psychoanalytic psychologies significantly alter our understanding of experience by their investigations and descriptions of the conditions which make consciousness possible. Consciousness becomes a highly overdetermined concept so that experience is mediated through pure concepts of the undertaking (Kant), a psychological work of repression and its derivations (Freud), or through the realization of archetypal patterns and motifs (Jung and Hillman). The contributions of transcendental philosophy, phenomenology and depth psychologies is that consciousness never discloses itself without a remainder. In each of these disciplines this remainder is thought to be a witness of consciousness to consciousness that alters both the meaning and ground of experience. In these disciplines our conscious perceptions are viewed not as primary experiences of objects, but as experiences mediated by preconscious conditions of the mind. The concept of the "I" that accompanied the primary given when consciousness reflected upon itself raises doubts about the simplicity and immediacy of objective experience, implies the existence of transcendental conditions and psychodynamic forces within the ordinary register of conscious thought.

An implication of these theories of consciousness for counseling and ministerial practice is the discrediting of literalism in the interpretation of experience on any level. Metaphorical and symbolic meanings must be assumed in the reporting of material in textual traditions, community awareness and self-knowledge. Counseling and ministry must therefore be interpretive disciplines if they are to attend to the full range of conscious experience situated against a complex background or reservoir of unsaid meanings. Thus the act of consciousness reflecting on itself raises the need for interpretation. And, for communities or individuals to be conscious of themselves, the first representations of primary conscious experience must be allowed to unfold in the patterns of meaning that constitute their possibility for their situation. Consciousness itself is the first witness to metaphorical meaning when it becomes its own object and the interpretation of conscious experience is an ongoing elaboration of metaphorical meaning.

Bibliography. C. Brenner, *An Elementary Textbook of Psychoanalysis* (1957). S. Freud, *SE* 14 (1964). J. J. McDermott, ed., *The Writings of William James* (1968). P. Ricoeur, *The Conflict of*

Interpretations (1974). J. P. Sartre, *The Transcendence of the Ego* (1957).

C. WINQUIST

MIND; UNCONSCIOUS. *See also* MEMORY; PERSON (Philosophical Issues); PHILOSOPHY AND PSYCHOLOGY; SELF-UNDER-STANDING; SELF-TRANSCENDENCE.

CONSCIOUSNESS, RACIAL. *See* BLACK IDENTITY AND CONSCIOUSNESS.

CONSCIOUSNESS, SOCIAL. *See* SOCIAL CONSCIOUS-NESS AND RESPONSIBILITY.

CONSCIOUSNESS RAISING. According to one authority, consciousness raising means "becoming aware of social issues in a deeply involved and responsibly personal way in which an understanding of self is related to an understanding of others, both individually and collectively" (Crook, p. 398). This generally involves the discovery that one's private and personal existence is shaped in fundamental respects by specific social patterns and processes of which one had not been previously aware, such as economic and class interests or patterns of racial and sexual power. One gains an expanded perspec-tive on who one is, coming to see one's "private" self as in fact also a social or public self, shaped, limited, and oppressed by public value systems and by large configu-rations of social, economic, and political power.

In particular, "consciousness raising" usually refers to a revision in the understanding of one's personal needs and problems. Difficulties one had previously believed to be of individual origin (e.g. marriage unhappiness as the result of personality limitations) are now seen in a new light, as caused in some crucial respect by oppressive social forces (e.g. sexism). Moreover, the former, indi-vidualistic consciousness (e.g. that I as a woman have a psychological problem relating to men) is now interpre-ted as a deception perpetrated by the oppressing forces (my former individualistic, psychological self-understanding was sociologically created by a sexist meaning and value system).

1. Political Origins and Context. In its widest and most favorable sense, consciousness raising may be viewed as one dimension of growth toward full potential as members of the human family; it has to do with leaving behind limited perspectives of reality and embracing more inclusive images, concepts, and modes of actions. The term is more often employed, however, in the context of liberationist politics, principally Third World and black liberation movements and the women's movement. Paulo Freire (1970), for instance, uses the term *conscientizacao* to refer to his revolutionary method of Third World teaching. Ignorance and lethargy are the products of economic and political domination, leading to a "culture of silence." Freire's method of literacy education expands the awareness of selfhood in oppressed persons to the point where they awaken from their leth-argy, begin to look critically at their social situation, and take initiative to transform it. In feminist consciousness raising, "From the personal to the political" has become the key phrase.

2. Consciousness Raising and the Church. In many respects, the church tends to function as a conservative social instrument, promoting the adjustment of individ-uals to the existing social order despite its rhetoric and programs of social change. One way it does this is by maintaining a sharp distinction between public and pri-vate life, and by directing its caring ministry toward problems defined and addressed entirely as private or personal. Consciousness raising, however, attempts to *unite* public and private in new conceptions of self and society. It may therefore offer the church a method for moving beyond the public-private split and its tendency to promote adjustment to the status quo. By integrating consciousness raising methods into its educational and counseling ministries, the church could become more effective in promoting critical social awareness and cre-ative involvement in efforts aimed at social transforma-tion, while simultaneously engaging persons in deeply personal ways at points of felt need.

In recent years, for example, some churches have applied consciousness raising methods to the problem of sexism. By putting persons "in touch" with their oppres-sion, consciousness raising groups help both men and women question the sex roles imposed on them and increase their awareness of other social pressures. Group participants generally begin by discussing their experi-ences in an individualistic, personal mode, but eventu-ally come to see the social, cultural, and political com-mon denominators of their experience. The focus of discussion is not on psychological analysis or coping strategies but on social awareness and action, since there are "no personal solutions to social problems."

3. Consciousness Raising, Therapy, and Encoun-ter. Consciousness raising is to be distinguished from psychotherapy and encounter, although good therapy and encounter should have a consciousness raising effect. Therapy generally assumes the "medical model": the client is sick or in any case the problem lies within the client, client's family, or client's personal relationships. From the point of view of consciousness raising, how-ever, it is important to avoid the idea that persons or personal relationships are sick and need to be cured; it is society that is sick. Consciousness raising groups there-fore seek to help persons become aware of the sick social structures and value systems that oppress them, and rid themselves of the "false consciousness" through which they would blame themselves for society's oppression.

Consciousness raising groups also differ from encoun-ter groups and rap (or discussion) groups. The idea in consciousness raising is not to be confronted or to "unload" so much as to revise one's understanding of oneself and society and to see more clearly its personal effects in one's own life. This does not mean that con-sciousness raising groups are primarily didactic, how-ever; the education involved is highly experiential and personal.

4. Critique. Consciousness raising presents pastoral care and counseling with a new tool for expanded influ-ence and offers the church a new way of bringing its pastoral and prophetic ministries together. It is impor-tant, however, that its strengths and limitations be care-fully appraised. One issue is how consciousness raising can be constructively related to therapeutic care and counseling (if it can), assuming that both are important. What modifications would be necessary in each? And how is consciousness raising to be distinguished, theoretically or in practice, from conversion and indoctrination? Are new perceptions and understandings actually "perceptions" and "understandings," or are they more accurately understood as altered belief structures and values systems? A further question is whether the methods of consciousness raising oversimplify the issue of responsibility. Critics charge that, while consciousness raising methods can liberate and empower people to take initiative to change oppressive social forces, they can also function for some persons as an unhelpful, even antitherapeutic rationalizing of personal problems if they shift responsibility indiscriminately or inappropriately from psychological to social and political terms. Consciousness raising asks the counter question: Is not pastoral care and counseling in danger of an "indiscriminate" and "inappropriate" shifting of responsibility from social and political terms to those of private personhood and psychology in matters pertaining (for example) to sex, race, and economics?

Underlying these questions are more basic ones that will need to be thought through in coming years as pastoral care and counseling seeks to appropriate the methods of consciousness raising. What is the relation between individual and social process? How can psychological perspectives be related to sociological ones in pastoral assessment, care, and counseling? And, most generally, how can ministry best facilitate the healing and redemptive transformation of self and society together?

Bibliography. C. H. Clinebell's *Counseling for Liberation* (1976), ch. 6. H. J. Clinebell, *Basic Types of Pastoral Care and Counseling* rev. and enlarged ed. (1984), pp. 340–48. C. H. Crook, *The Evolution of Human Consciousness* (1980). P. Freire, *Pedagogy of the Oppressed* (1970). S. Julty, *Men's Bodies, Men's Selves* (1979), pp. 13–30. National Task Force on Consciousness Raising, *Guidelines to Feminist Consciousness Raising* (1976).

P. G. SCHURMAN

CRITICAL THEORY; PROPHETIC/PASTORAL TENSION; SOCIAL CONSCIOUSNESS AND RESPONSIBILITY; SOCIAL JUSTICE ISSUES IN PASTORAL CARE. *See also* BLACK THEOLOGY *or* FEMINIST THEOLOGY *or* LIBERATION THEOLOGY, AND PASTORAL CARE; LIFESTYLE ISSUES IN PASTORAL CARE. *Compare* ADVOCACY; ENCOUNTER GROUPS; PEACE-MAKING; ROLE PLAY; SOCIOLOGY OF RELIGIOUS AND PASTORAL CARE.

CONSENT. *See* CONFIDENTIALITY; COVENANT AND CONTRACT; LEGAL DIMENSIONS OF PASTORAL CARE AND COUNSELING.

CONSERVATIVE JUDAISM. A branch of Judaism which emerged in the middle of the nineteenth century. It holds that God's will, first revealed at Sinai, is progressively disclosed through the historical experiences of the community of believers. Jewish law and custom reflect the collective wisdom and faith of the community, and so undergo continual evolution. Although Conservative Jews generally maintain a traditional lifestyle, they remain open to change (the ordination of women as rabbis, for example). Approximately thirty-five percent of affiliated Jews in the U.S. identify themselves as Conservative Jews.

P. J. HAAS

JEWISH CARE AND COUNSELING.

CONSOLATION. Consolation is an ancient ministry of pastoral care, often referred to as "the consolation of the brethren." It is based on the reality that life can be hard to endure, and that God's people are not spared the sufferings of the human family. We are afflicted with pain, disappointment, discouragement, and bereavement. But God's people have been given resources to cope with these trials — one of which is the ministry of consolation.

The ministry of consolation is a ministry of empathy, of compassion. "The beginning of healing is in the solidarity with the pain" (H. Nouwen). Jesus' ministry is described in similar terms: "He had compassion on them and healed their sick" (Mt. 14:14).

The ministry of consolation is frequently a parental ministry, in which the consoler, figuratively or even literally, holds the sufferer as one would comfort a hurt and frightened child. Such consolation is an anodyne for pain. Job's consolers came together "to console with and comfort him" (Job 2:11). They did this in their cultural ways of showing compassion. But when Job finally expressed his deep feelings of despair, they were offended. They ceased consoling and began reproving him. They went from "nurturing parents" to "critical parents." Job did not appreciate the change. "Miserable comforters, all of you" (Job 16:2).

The ministry of consolation is an incarnation of God's consolation. "Comfort, comfort my people, says your God," (Isa. 40:1). God is the great consoler. "I will never fail you or forsake you" (Heb. 13:5). But in our afflictions we can *feel* forsaken. In ministering to a woman who felt guilty over her "lack of faith" in that she struggled with the anguish that God had forsaken her, a pastor consoled her with the reminder that Jesus struggled with this same anguish. His cry of dereliction, "My God, my God, why hast thou forsaken me?" (Mt. 27:46) speaks for all Jobian sufferers. His identification with his people included this agony of despair. He was "in every respect tempted as we are" (Heb. 4:15). Although Jesus' crucifixion identifies with our pains, it is his resurrection that provides the consolation of hope in the midst of empathy.

The consoler needs to listen and to accept the despairer's cry. Since God can accept the protest of Job and the despair of Jesus, those who incarnate God's consolation have this acceptance as their model. Listening is the bridge for the reception of compassion. Besides listening to the lament of the afflicted, the consoling minister usually offers the comfort of scriptural assurances and the intercession of prayer.

Through this ministry of consolation the afflicted may catch a glimpse of the God who often seems hidden as they struggle with the dread of abandonment. It is then that God's human representatives are helpful in reinforcing the sufferer's faith through their consoling care.

Bibliography. H. J. Nouwen, *Reaching Out* (1975).

W. E. HULME

COMFORT/SUSTAINING. *See also* CLASSIC LITERATURE IN CARE AND COUNSELING; GRIEF AND LOSS; MOURNING CUSTOMS AND RITUALS.

CONSTITUTIONAL PSYCHOLOGY. *See* SOMA-TYPE.

CONSULTATION. Pastoral consultation is a process in which another person is utilized in matters of personal and professional concern in a mutually dependent manner which stimulates intellectual and emotional development and expands personal awareness. It differs from pastoral supervision in that the consultant has responsibility only to the consultee(s), not for the matters brought up in the consultation.

Contrasting significantly with this definition are the assumptions behind a more familiar view of consultation: "Let's call in a consultant and see where we are going wrong." Long an integral part of the business and industrial community, this style of consultation implies that some corrective action is needed or some knowledge is missing which the consultant may provide.

After being called in, the consultant suggests a corrective procedure or supplies the needed knowledge. The consultee utilizes the newly acquired information to effect the desired goal. The value of this style of consultation is well known and generally accepted. The consultant relies heavily on an acquired body of knowledge, good business principles and an ability to stay abreast of current techniques and procedures. This style of consultation is most effective where a product or highly technical engineering is involved. The success of this style of consultation is not dependent upon the consultant's awareness and understanding of his or her own person even though these may be desirable qualities.

Pastoral ministry is built upon the view that all persons are unique as created beings and unique in development; therefore, the most effective approach is personal and relational. Being knowledgeable and articulate are desirable qualities, but an open, honest relationship is primary.

1. The Relational Aspects of Pastoral Consultation. The pastoral minister, by virtue of the desire to minister to persons, needs a different understanding and style of consultation, not only as a consultant to parishioners but in seeking consultation in personal and professional matters. This understanding and style is essentially personal and relational and proceeds on the belief that the task of the minister is performed within the context of his or her relationship with the person being served. It further holds that every person is a created, spiritual being, free to develop in his or her own unique way. Understanding and respecting these precepts is basic to all pastoral work. When these fundamental relational principles support the consultation process, it allows the consultant and consultee to participate freely in mutual trust and respect. Mutual dependency can be acknowledged without embarrassment and a sense of celebration pervades the encounter.

When these principles are not a part of the consultation, competitiveness develops. Mutuality is not experienced and usually simplistic advice and simplistic solutions dominate. The folly of disregarding relational principles is dramatized in the fable of the monkey and the fish. In this fable, the monkey sees the fish in the water and exclaims, "You poor fellow, you are going to drown. Here, let me help you!" Then the monkey lifts the fish out of the water and hangs him out to dry.

Effective pastoral consultation, like all pastoral work, requires an understanding and commitment to fundamental relational principles in which persons exchange honest emotional responses, stimulate personal awareness and expand consciousness. To take the time and risk to speak to another person openly and honestly and resist the temptation to effect a quick cure or take a patronizing stance promotes personal satisfaction and fulfillment. It also guards against the painful sense of isolation and the failure to live up to unrealistic expectations, both of which frequently plague the ablest of ministers.

2. Freedom of Choice in Pastoral Consultation. Once again the discussion of consultation in a pastoral framework needs to be contrasted with the usual understanding of that term. In the business and industrial communities, the consultant usually makes an assessment of the situation and then suggests a course of action that will remedy the problem. There is ample freedom in this process to utilize a consultant in the first place and to reject whatever is offered in the final analysis. Once again, however, a tangible product or technology is involved. The consultant brings into the situation any new knowledge or advanced technology in the particular field with the confidence that what he offers is best.

In pastoral consultation there is no corresponding product or technology. The consultant and consultee are unique individuals, each developing in their own way. This means that, in the strictest sense, no one knows what is best for another person. With this understanding and a commitment to this kind of freedom, the consultant and consultee are free to participate in a relationship in which all the human factors can be viewed. This process may be unpleasant and uncomfortable, but where it is understood that the consultant does not know best, compassion and trust support the relationship. Freed from the burdensome task of knowing what is best for another, the consultant is able to open his or her own person and offer a variety of responses and impressions with the confidence that the consultee can pick and choose what is useful. Similarly, the consultee, when freed from the illusion that someone else knows what is best, is able to accept numerous responses from a variety of people with the confidence that his or her own person will utilize the feedback advantageously and select a course of action out of an inner wisdom. With this understanding, one can easily see why pastoral consultation comes with an admonishment that the consultation process should not be used quickly but, like leaven in bread, should be allowed to work slowly.

3. Authority in Pastoral Consultation. Pastoral consultation, in contrast with the usual understanding of that term, places authority in the consultee rather than the consultant. When the pastoral consultant offers consultation, trusting the authority of the consultee, and when the consultee accepts consultation, trusting his or her own inner wisdom, then the personhood of both parties is not only affirmed but enhanced. Confidence is built in the inner authority and mutual respect is experienced. Where each person is seen as having his or her own competent inner authority, intradependency takes on an enjoyable quality where give and take flow freely. Vulnerability is non-threatening and the richness of one's emotions is experienced. Where this view is not accepted, dependency is experienced as inferiority, self-disclosure is fraught with anxiety, and the authority of the inner person is mistrusted. Reliance on an outward authority usually results.

4. **Theological Perspectives in Pastoral Consultation.** The utilization of the consultation process within the pastoral framework described above affords an awareness of the intrinsic worth of every individual, and an awareness of the developmental posture of all creation. Nothing is static; all things are being created.

Finally, the pastoral approach to the consultation process is creative by virtue of being unlimiting and unpredictable. This process stimulates the development of an independent/relatedness gestalt which opens avenues whereby the self can find fulfillment by knowing itself and its relatedness. This, in turn, forms a new self, more aware of its independence and more aware of its relatedness. The new self can then form a gestalt whereby fulfillment can again occur by knowing itself and its relatedness. This process provides the possibility of awareness that we are indeed created in the image of God—perpetually creative.

O. L. DELOZIER, JR.

INTERPROFESSIONAL TEAMS AND RELATIONSHIPS; PASTORAL COUNSELING; PROFESSIONALISM. *Compare* REFERRAL; SUPERVISION, PASTORAL.

CONTEMPLATION. See MEDITATION; MYSTICISM; RELIGIOUS LIFE; SPIRITUAL DISCIPLINE AND GROWTH. *See also* IGNATIAN SPIRITUALITY.

CONTEMPLATIVE PSYCHOLOGIES. See SPIRITUAL PSYCHOLOGIES.

CONTEXTUAL LEARNING. See CASE STUDY METHOD; SUPERVISION; TEACHING.

CONTEXTUAL THEOLOGY. Theology which is constructed with maximal concern for its relevance to the cultural context in which it occurs. Contemporary attempts at theological contextualization frequently carry such labels as "Black Theology," "Liberation Theology," "African Theology," "Melanesian Theology," and the like.

All theologizing is done from a particular point of view, in terms of the perspectives (including the biases) of the producers of the theology. Those who are doing the theologizing have particular questions in their minds arising from their life experience within the culture in which they participate. As they study and reflect on the Scriptures (and/or other sources to which they look for assistance) they seek to discover and formulate answers to those questions. In this way, theology comes into being.

The term "contextualization" was defined by Shoki Coe (1973) as preferable to the term "indigenization" which has been widely used as a label for the ideal toward which cross-cultural witnesses to Christianity strive in non-Western contexts. To many missiologists, the latter term has come to connote too static an understanding of what should happen when Christianity is introduced into a given culture. A term like contextualization is felt to have a more dynamic meaning (see Taber, 1979).

Since its introduction, the term has gained fairly wide currency among missiologists in both liberal and conservative camps. Anthropologically oriented conservatives have largely embraced the concept and sought to point out its relevance both in missiological contexts and in describing the process by means of which Western theologizing is done (see Taber, 1978; Buswell, 1978; Kraft, 1979). Conservative theologians tend to be suspicious of both the term and the process, perhaps due to the fact that the term originated within the liberal camp (see Nicholls, 1979; Henry, 1980). Conn (1978), a conservative theologian-missiologist with cross-cultural experience, is a notable exception.

1. **Historical Use.** Advocates of contextualization see this process as part and parcel both of the NT record and of the theologizing activity of all subsequent interpreters of Christianity. This is the process that the Apostles were involved in as they sought to take the Christian message that had come to them in Aramaic language and culture and to conceptualize it for those who spoke Greek. In order to contextualize Christianity for Greeks, the Apostles gave themselves to the expression of Christian truth in the thought patterns of those to whom they spoke. Indigenous words and concepts were used to deal with such topics as God, church, sin, conversion, repentance, initiation, and most other areas of Christian life and practice.

The early Greek churches were in danger of being dominated by Hebrew theology, just as many non-Western churches today are in danger of being dominated by Western theologies. The Apostle Paul and others, however, struggled against the Hebrew Christians to develop a contextualized Christian theology for those who thought according to Greek conceptual patterns. In doing this they had constant conflict with many of the Hebrew church leaders who felt it proper to simply impose Hebrew theological concepts on new converts (see Acts 15). These conservative Hebrews were, as von Allmen (1975) points out, the heretics against whom Paul fights for the right for Greek-speaking Christians to have the gospel contextualized in their language and culture.

It was a similar battle that Martin Luther and the other reformers fought in the sixteenth century for the rights of Christians to think theologically in German rather than in Latin. Later, the Anabaptists and others struggled against the Lutherans for the right to contextualize Christianity in their own cultural forms. The history of denominationalism in Europe and America is full of such struggles. A like situation exists in many missionized countries today where peoples of non-Western cultures are finding that the theological formulations of generations of Western theologians are often irrelevant to the pressing problems that they need to deal with. Contextualization becomes, therefore, the way to escape the conceptual domination of the West (Boyd, 1974) just as political independence has become the way to escape political domination.

2. Method. Some might feel that the intensive investigations of generations of Western theologians must surely have produced a once-for-all set of theological understandings that can simply be passed on from culture to culture. Those who have been involved in attempts to contextualize Christian theology in non-Western cultures have not, however, found this to be true. The questions, addressed by Western theologians (particularly academic theologians) are very often quite different from those being asked by village Africans, Asians, Latin Americans and even non-academic North Americans. It is discovered, rather, that

> Any authentic theology must start ever anew from the focal point of the faith, which is the confession of the Lord Jesus Christ who died and was raised for us; and it must be built or re-built (whether in Africa or in Europe) in a way which is both faithful to the inner thrust of the Christian revelation and also in harmony with the mentality of the person who formulates it. There is no short cut to be found by simply adapting an existing theology to contemporary or local taste (von Allmen, 1975, p. 50).

The contextualization of Christian theology is, therefore, not simply the passing of a "product" that has been developed once for all in Europe or America. It is, rather, the imitating of the process that the early Apostles went through. Since the materials from which the theologizing is done are the same biblical materials, the essential message will be the same. The formulation of that message, the relative prominence of many of the issues addressed, and, indeed, the presence or absence of certain issues will, however, differ from culture to culture. NT teaching concerning the superiority of the power of Christ to that of evil spirits is, for example, a much more prominent part of contextualized African or New Guinean theology than of American theology. Advocates of theological contextualization frequently draw a parallel between contextualization and the Incarnation of Jesus Christ (Coe, 1973). They suggest that just as in Christ God participated fully in a given human culture, though his origin lay outside of that culture, so in contextualization the theologizing process participates fully in the cultural realities in which the formulations take place, even though the stimuli (e.g., the Bible and other revelatory activity on the part of God) have their origins outside of the receiving culture. Incarnation, of course, involves more of life than thinking, articulating, and writing.

Incarnational/contextualized theologizing is seen, therefore, as an activity that embraces all of living rather than something relegated to small portions of living (such as thinking behavior). Non-Western and non-academic theologizing even in Western contexts is seen more as something that is lived than as something that is merely written. It is also seen as something that everyone does rather than simply the activity of a few academically trained specialists. Theologizing is, therefore, seen as expressed through ceremony, ritual, singing, informal conversation, and all other aspects of life. Indeed, persons may formally articulate theological beliefs which are different from those beliefs which they practice or express in ceremony, ritual, etc.

Contextualization of theology is, therefore, something that is always happening whenever people ponder or otherwise express their faith. It takes many forms, only some of which are recordable in writing. It may be done formally (as by those with academic training in theology) or informally (as by everyone, including academics, in the living, ritualizing, etc. of the faith). Even academic theologizing may be done in terms of perspectives other than those traditionally recognized as Theology. (See Kraft, 1979 for an appeal for and exemplification of this contention.)

Bibliography. R. H. Boyd, *India and the Latin Captivity of the Church* (1974). R. M. Brown, "The Rootedness of All Theology," *Christianity and Crisis* (1977), 170–74. S. Coe, "Authentic Contextuality Leads to Contextualization," *Theological Education,* 9 (1973), 24–25. H. M. Conn, "Contextualization: Where Do We Begin?" in C. E. Armerding, *Evangelicals and Liberation* (1977), pp. 90–119. C. F. H. Henry, "The Cultural Relativizing of Revelation," *Trinity Journal* (1980), 153–64. C. H. Kraft, "The Contextualization of Theology," *Evangelical Missions Quarterly* (1978), 31–36; *Christianity in Culture* (1979). B. Nicholls, *Contextualization: A Theology of Gospel and Culture* (1979). C. R. Taber, "Contextualization: Indigenization and/or Transformation" in D. M. McCurry, ed., *The Gospel and Islam* (1979), pp. 143–54; "Is There More Than One Way to Do Theology?" *Gospel in Context* (1978), 4–10; "The Limits of Indigenization in Theology," *Missiology* (1978), 53–79. D. von Allmen, "The Birth of Theology," *International Review of Mission* (1975), 37–55.

C. H. KRAFT

THEOLOGY. *Compare* EXPERIENTIAL THEOLOGY; LIBERATION THEOLOGY AND PASTORAL CARE.

CONTINUING EDUCATION. *See* EDUCATION IN PASTORAL CARE AND COUNSELING; SPECIALIZATION IN PASTORAL CARE.

CONTRACEPTION. Pastoral responsibility does not usually include the giving of contraceptive information, but it does involve having it or knowing where to find it. Pastors should be able to raise pertinent questions about the adequacy of a parishioner's contraceptive knowledge and practice. Issues about contraception are often a part of the family tension shared with pastors or they may be part of the underlying concern of a teenager in the parish who has become sexually active. In order to function adequately in pastoral work, the clergy need to know and be able to consult with a family physician and/or gynecologist who can provide up-to-date information about contraception.

1. Methods. Until 1960 there were few contraceptive options available to sexually active adults, and the so-called "natural methods"—the calendar and rhythm method—were often unreliable. In 1960, the birth control pill offered women a reliable means of contraception that could be decided upon more or less rationally and taken at a time separate from the emotionally laden immediacies of the sexual relationship.

The original birth control pill (BCP) worked by giving the woman a balance of the two major female hormones, estrogen and progesterone. Early BCPs contained approximately twenty times more progesterone and three times more estrogen than present-day BCPs, and thus had an increased incidence of side effects such as nausea, bloating, and even vascular problems such as phlebitis (inflammation of the veins), strokes, and embolism (blood clots).

Today there are over thirty types of birth control pills, ranging from normal strength (considerably lower dose than earlier pills) to low estrogen pills (with fewer side effects), and to the newer mini-pills (with significantly lower levels of hormones, but more potential problems with unwanted bleeding). Side effects from the current pills range from bloating, weight gain, and breast engorgement to nausea and depression. Weighing the fear of pregnancy against these significant physical problems is often very difficult for both the patient and the physician.

Women over thirty-five who smoke or have a family history of heart problems experience a significant increase in the incidence of heart disease due to taking oral contraceptives. These women are faced with the dilemma of risking heart disease, stopping smoking (with all of its concomitant anxiety), or opting for a scary change in birth control.

Misconceptions regarding the dangers of birth control pills add to the anxiety of women. Birth control pills probably do not cause an increased incidence of breast or cervical cancer. BCPs actually reduce the risks of premenstrual tension, painful periods (dysmenorrhea), ovarian and uterine cancer, and pelvic inflammatory disease (PID). For most women, BCPs are a safe method of contraception.

Another method of contraception is the intrauterine device (IUD). IUDs render the uterus lining hostile to sperm and eggs through the production of cells which destroy both. IUDs can also cause painful cramping and heavy bleeding. Once an acceptable alternative to the pill, IUDs have recently received negative publicity and, because of side effects resulting in litigation, all but a few have been taken off the market. Because of this, many women who have used IUDs successfully are now having to make other contraceptive choices.

Another contraception form, the barrier method, offers excellent protection. Diaphragms are soft, dome-shaped devices that fit over the cervix and, when used with a spermicide, act as both a physical and chemical barrier. Their major drawback is that sex must be planned, thus often interfering with the spontaneity of the sexual encounter.

A recently developed sponge offers convenience and simplicity. Loaded with a spermicide, it offers twenty-four hours of protection. Although a good choice, many men and women complain of irritation from this and other spermicides.

Condoms are still used by many men and are the contraceptive choice that places the responsibility sometimes on the male. Condom use has virtually no side effects, yet some men refuse to use them because they "interfere with normal feeling." Their use has greatly increased, however, with the AIDS epidemic.

Today, there are two alternative methods of so-called "natural" planning, which can be effective if practiced properly. The basal body temperature method charts days that are safe for intercourse by checking a woman's temperature. Normally, it will drop slightly prior to ovulation, then rise about 1/2 degree immediately after. The mucus method monitors the changes in the quantity and quality of cervical mucus. The mucus changes to cloudy and sticky as ovulation nears, and clears as ovulation begins. These methods are unreliable if not properly understood because of the potential for mistiming.

2. **Sterilization.** Perhaps the most difficult contraceptive decision is permanent sterilization. Available to the female (tubal ligation) and the male (vasectomy), the decision to have either of these procedures is difficult and emotional. The tubal ligation, in which the fallopian tubes are cut to prevent the passage of the egg, is safe and effective, yet requires surgically entering the abdomen and either an out-patient visit or a short hospital stay. Vasectomies, in which the vas deferens (the male tube carrying sperm) is cut, is an out-patient procedure and carries minimal risk. Physiologically, there is little difference between the two procedures; psychologically, the difference widens. If a woman's self-image is centered around her ability to bear children, a permanent sterilization may be perceived as "taking away" her identity, thus creating both physical and psychological post-operative problems.

Many men fear a vasectomy, not because of the surgical procedure, but because of the myths surrounding "cutting the tubes." Men are often afraid that they will lose their desire for sex, their ability to have an erection, and even their masculine voice. A vasectomy does not interfere with the flow of the male hormone, testosterone, and therefore does not interfere with male sex characteristics. The only difference consistently reported by men who have had vasectomies is a slight change in orgasmic feeling due to changes in the consistency of the fluid ejaculated.

3. **Special Concerns.** Teenage women pose a special contraceptive problem. The increased incidence of early sexual experiences and the resulting increase in teenage pregnancies makes the proper handling of this contraceptive decision important and difficult. Teenagers often will confide in their physician or pastors that they are sexually active, yet are naive or afraid to seek information about preventing pregnancy. They may not be aware of their options or may harbor their parents' misconceptions or outdated information regarding these choices. Most fear their parents will find out that they are sexually active. The confidentiality and patience shown by the pastor and the physician are paramount to the teenager's understanding of the responsibility to prevent pregnancy.

Even though an understanding of all sexually transmitted diseases (STDs) is important, the stigma of herpes warrants special attention. The emergence of the "herpes scare" has created a new attitude toward both casual and long-standing sexual relationships. Genital herpes is caused by two viruses, both referred to as herpes simplex. Herpes simplex Type 1 (HSV-1) infects the mouth and lips, producing the common cold sore or fever blister. Herpes Type 2 (HSV-2) is the predominant cause of genital herpes and is almost always transmitted sexually. The chances of contracting herpes from toilet seats or hot tubs is so negligible that its occurrence is considered very rare.

No antibiotic will kill herpes, but the recent discovery of Acyclovir provides some hope. All herpes viruses have the same characteristics: after the initial sexual transmission, the virus lies dormant in certain nerve cells, periodically resurfacing to cause new outbreaks and symptoms. Recurrent outbreaks may be precipitated by stress, menstrual periods, other infections, fatigue or, more commonly, for no known reason. The frequency of these outbreaks varies from weekly to every year or so. They cause intense pain, itching and irritation, along with a fever, and flu-like symptoms.

The fear of contracting herpes and other STDs has had the effect of curtailing casual sexual encounters. Likewise, once a person has contracted herpes, the fear of spreading it has strained many new relationships. Even though theoretically herpes can only be spread when there is an active sore, one must realize that herpes victims, especially women, are often never quite sure when they have an active lesion. A thorough understanding of both the physical and emotional realities of contracting herpes can help people with the disease adjust and, in most cases, lead normal sex lives.

4. **Conclusion.** Positive sexual relationships contribute significantly to a person's emotional well-being. Thus, anyone wishing to understand the "total" person must gain an appreciation of the complexity of contraceptive decisions made in these sexual relationships.

There are many contraceptive options open to a couple, and each carries potential physical and psychological consequences. Because contraceptive decisions are an integral part of any new relationship, professionals dealing with interpersonal relationships should be well-grounded in a basic understanding of these contraceptive choices.

A. P. MORLEY, JR.

FAMILY PLANNING; SEX EDUCATION. *Compare* PREMARITAL COUNSELING.

CONTRACTS IN PASTORAL COUNSELING. *See* COVENANT AND CONTRACT; LEGAL DIMENSIONS OF PASTORAL CARE AND COUNSELING.

CONTRITION. *See* PENANCE; REPENTANCE AND CONFESSION.

CONTROL. *See* SELF-EXPRESSION AND SELF-CONTROL. *See also* CYBERNETIC THEORY IN PSYCHOLOGY AND COUNSELING; LIMIT SETTING.

CONVALESCENT HOME. *See* CHAPLAIN/CHAPLAINCY. *See also* CHRONIC ILLNESS; HANDICAP AND DISABILITY; NEUROLOGIC ILLNESSES.

CONVERSATION, PASTORAL. Conversation is an event of communication between two or more persons, occurring in a specific place and in a specific frame of time. Generally speaking, therefore, pastoral conversation is communication in which one of the persons has a pastoral identity which gives shape and substance to the conversation. It is the unique shape and substance which makes it pastoral, however, and not the mere fact that

one participant is ordained. Although religious language and practice may be used in the conversation, this does not necessarily make it pastoral, either. Rather, it is the fact that the identity and role of the pastoral person are significant and are the basic reason the conversation is taking place which provides the context of pastoral conversation.

In this context, any specific agenda takes on pastoral and spiritual concern, regardless of the use or non-use of religious language or resources such as Scripture and prayer. The symbolic role of the pastoral person is a significant dynamic in pastoral conversations. This may be illustrated by the person who calls a pastoral counselor and says, "My husband and I are having conflict in our marriage and need counseling, but we want to have it with someone who is a minister as well as a counselor." In this kind of transaction, the conflict in the marriage, whatever it may be, takes on spiritual significance due to the symbolic role of the pastoral person. It follows, therefore, that whatever counseling approach is used, as long as the context of the relationship maintains this symbolic dynamic and preserves pastoral identity, it is pastoral counseling.

The nature of pastoral conversation has been influenced by a number of persons from the field of psychotherapy. No one has had more of an impact, however, than the noted author and psychotherapist, Carl Rogers. In their classic volume entitled, *The Art of Pastoral Conversation,* Heije Faber and Ebel van der Schoot draw heavily from the work of Rogers to characterize the process of pastoral conversation. The following points from Rogers' client-centered approach are relevant for and congruent with pastoral conversation. They are the three fundamental conditions for a therapeutic relationship.

1. **Empathic Regard.** Basic to Rogers's understanding of therapeutic communication is the principle of empathy. The counselor must be able to hear the client from the perspective of the client, responding to feeling on the experiential track of the client. This is congruent with an incarnational theology in which Jesus Christ is viewed as the empathic reality of God, coming where we are, experiencing life from our perspective, and enabling us to move beyond our caughtness and limited vision.

2. **Establishing Acceptance.** In order for rapport to develop and a therapeutic relationship to emerge, the counselor must accept the client for who he or she is, without imposing prejudice and judgmental bias. This does not mean that a pastor must give up his or her own value system. Neither does it mean everything the counselee does is appropriate. It simply means that there is a basic positive regard, caring, and valuing of the other person without just seeing the other person as a collection of behaviors. Theologically, it is the doctrine of grace in human relationships.

3. **Being a Real Person.** Rogers insists that the counselor be a genuine, open, honest, and disclosive person. He rejects hiding behind professional expertise as phoniness which blocks personal growth and meaningful communication. Pastors who hide behind a clerical mask fail to make creative use of pastoral conversation. If the pastor *plays* the role of pastor, he or she will not be very

effective with perceptive parishioners. He or she has to *be* a pastor.

These three conditions underlie any meaningful pastoral communication. While many other dimensions could be employed, these are fundamental for pastoral conversation in any context. Although there is no total unanimity about the approach of Rogers among pastoral communicators, there would be a higher incidence of agreement here than with any other basic approach. With these conditions operative, one can then expand the variety of responses beyond Rogers's system and still remain faithful to the integrity of pastoral conversation. Other approaches which are more direct, cognitive, interpretive, or behavioral can be used creatively as long as the traditional pastoral functions of healing, sustaining, and guiding are actualized in a manner which preserves pastoral integrity and caring for the individual, couple, family, or group involved.

Bibliography. D. E. Bratton, "Teaching the Art of Caring Conversation: An Enabling Ministry for Hospital Chaplains," *American Protestant Hospital Association Bulletin*, 44:2 (1980), 48–50. H. Faber and E. van der Schoot, *The Art of Pastoral Conversation* (1965). G. B. Noyce, *The Art of Pastoral Conversation* (1981). E. E. Peterson, "The Ministry of Small Talk," *Leadership*, 5:3 (1984), 88–89. C. R. Rogers, *Client-Centered Therapy* (1951). C. B. Truax and R. R. Carkhuff, *Toward Effective Counseling and Psychotherapy* (1967).

C. R. WOODRUFF

COMMUNICATION; INTERPRETATION AND HERMENEUTICS, PASTORAL; LISTENING; PERCEPTIVENESS AND SENSITIVITY, PASTORAL. *See also* PASTORAL CARE (Contemporary Methods, Perspectives, and Issues); TECHNIQUE AND SKILL. *Compare* CORRESPONDENCE, PASTORAL.

CONVERSION. In Hebrew and Greek the words translated as "conversion"—*shub, strephein, epistrephein,* and *metanoia*—mean to turn, turn again, and return. Though these words do not always carry specifically religious meanings in the Bible, in certain contexts within the Hebrew Bible they connote the alterations in people's thoughts, feelings, and actions as they turn from idols to the true God or when they repent, that is, return to the covenant relationship with God. In the NT "conversion" refers specifically to people's response to the call of God in Christ.

1. Types of Conversion. Present-day meanings of conversion refer to a variety of changes or turnings. To take into account the importance of the cultural, social, and religious settings, we may delineate four types of conversion. First, *tradition transition* is the decision of an individual or a group to change affiliation from one major religious tradition to another, for example, from Buddhism to Christianity or from animism to Islam. Such conversion is typical in a context of cross-cultural contact. Second, *institutional transition* involves the movement of an individual from one subgroup (such as a denomination) to another *within* a major tradition, for example, from the Southern Baptist Church to the Episcopal Church. Third, *affiliation* is the change from noninvolvement to involvement with a religious group, behavior, and/or ideology. Because many people are being reared within secular families, affiliation is becoming increasingly prominent. Joining new religious movements is a common form of affiliative conversion. Fourth, *intensification* is the deepening of commitment and involvement people experience when they move from being a nominal or apathetic member of a religious group to being people for whom religion is the central focus of life.

Lofland and Skonovd (1981) have proposed a psychoreligious typology they call "conversion motifs." Different religious movements deploy various images and strategies of conversion that elicit and shape the experience of people converting in diverse settings. The motifs provide the metaphors, ideas, or defining contours of the converting process. They believe that there are six major "conversion motifs" operative today: intellectual, mystical, experimental, affectional, revivalistic, and coercive.

In the past, conversion referred only to the initial turning to faith and/or a religious organization. Recently, however, some theologians have emphasized the importance of conversion as a continuing process of the whole person throughout an entire lifetime. They inquire into the effects of the process in the domains of the intellect, morality, and emotions, as well as the realm of religious experience. Thus, the converting person is seen to be continually transformed through a combination of profound intellectual change, emotional maturation, increasing ethical sensitivity and behavior, and an intensifying love of God and humanity.

The varieties of conversion experiences reported in the literature are vast. Some tend to focus on dramatic "born again" experiences and others describe conversion as a slow and subtle but profound process.

2. Stages of Conversion. Whatever the precise nature of a particular conversion, it can be described as a process with seven discernible stages. The model outlined below is an adaptation of the work of Tippett (1977) and Lofland and Stark (1965). It is not intended to be normative for every conversion but it is a heuristic device designed to organize the findings of researchers and to provide a framework for the interpretation of the phenomenon; indeed, stage models should be adapted for specific forms and settings of conversion.

a. Context. Understanding conversion wholistically requires that the overall matrix in which conversion takes place must be accounted for. The cultural, social, and religious settings can facilitate and obstruct the conversion process and influence both the form and content of the myths, rituals, and symbols that are options for people in different settings. The context includes the larger environment, or the macrocontext, and the smaller setting, or the microcontext, of the individual, family, and community. The context provides the ethos, options, and models that are available to people. Individualistically oriented studies of conversion tend to ignore or trivialize the crucial importance of the context. An adequate understanding of conversion requires that the relevance of cultural, social, and religious vicissitudes be taken into account. Not only are these factors relevant to the external world of the potential convert, but they influence individuals in terms of their identity and consciousness.

b. Crisis. Ordinarily people live their lives within the bounds of conventional and normal routines. Stress is dealt with adequately and equilibrium maintained.

However, events within the macrocontext and/or within the personal life of individuals creates a disruption that opens people to new options. Most scholars of conversion agree that crisis is a necessary, but not sufficient, cause for conversion. People in the crisis stage experience a painful awareness that goes beyond mere dissatisfaction or restlessness: they see their lives as banal, destructive, meaningless, alienated, selfish, or indifferent to spiritual matters. The habitual ways of living are experienced now as ineffective and inauthentic, and change becomes existentially imperative.

c. Quest. In this stage people seek new ways of thinking, feeling, and behaving. They may experiment with options like astrology, encounter groups, political activities, new religious movements, or psychotherapy. Seekers are alert to new ways of thinking or acting that will relieve dissatisfactions with old modes of living. Most scholars agree that potential converts are active participants in their own transformation. Exceptions to this point of view are those who see some groups as manipulating the vulnerabilities of people in crisis and merely taking advantage of their attempts to improve their lives.

d. Encounter. At this stage seekers may find a person (an advocate) or a group whose message strikes a responsive chord, offering a new or rediscovered way of achieving salvation. Seekers establish a relationship with the advocate and the group and begin to perceive new possibilities for meaning in life. Most social scientists note that the encounter generally takes place via kinship and friendship networks. When these do not exist, often a friendship style of relationship is cultivated in order to facilitate the persuasion process. Needless to say, such situations can easily been misused.

e. Interaction. Through interaction with the advocate and group, potential converts begin to find specific needs addressed. Typically, four categories of needs are addressed during this period: the need for an intellectual system of meaning; the need for an emotional sense of belonging; the need for new modes of action or "techniques for living"—that is, specific guidelines and methods for living in accordance with the values of the new orientation; and, in many cases, the need for a leader who embodies the ideals and mobilizes the vision of the group.

f. Commitment. In this stage, the converts decide the new way of life is superior to the old and actively break with the past. Often a ritual is necessary to mark the break and the new commitment—baptism, for example, or the "testimony" that allows converts to articulate the new perspective from which they now view their lives. A Christian convert may perceive the preceding stages as reflecting the grace of God in leading the person to accept the gift of salvation in Jesus Christ.

g. Consequences. Consequences vary from convert to convert, but the experience of a new way of life and a sense of power consolidates the new beliefs and behaviors. In Christian conversion there should be a continuing process of growth and renewal in relationship with God. A common metaphor for this process is pilgrimage. If a convert fails to begin this pilgrimage following the initial commitment event, the convert may well leave the new faith. After the initial enthusiasm peaks, new converts sometimes experience a post-conversion depression,

during which the high hopes fade and the intense joy of finding the new faith diminishes. Without proper pastoral care, the convert may begin to question the validity of the new life and faith. The transition to a sense of pilgrimage and growth is often facilitated by guides who model a religious life of discipline and growth. As people mature in faith, they gain a sense that all of one's life is a pilgrimage toward a life of deepening relationship with God.

3. Understanding and Interpreting Conversion. The best way to understand conversion is to see it as a process that takes place in a dynamic force field of people, events, experiences, ideas, and groups. Cultural, social, personal, religious, spiritual, and other dimensions all infuse and shape the process in numerous ways in different settings. Motivations for converting are multiple and cumulative. Motivations vary from mere compliance to others' wishes to profound experiences of God, the discovery of life's meaning, and the resolution of emotional conflict. Social scientific studies and theological analyses of conversion point to the conclusion that conversion is a multifaceted, complex process that must be understood by using a number of different scholarly approaches combined with profound respect for the mystery of human transformation.

Theologically, conversion is the encounter of a person with God. The experience occurs in many different ways for different people. The stage model suggests one way of organizing data gathered from many sources. Although the model has been presented in terms of an individual's search for meaning, the authentic conversion experience is not merely to assuage personal dissatisfaction. Rather, conversion is a process in which God makes us all vulnerable to the transcendent. Conversion is the radical alteration of a person's life as it changes focus from self to God and from self to the service of others. Thus conversion is a lifelong process of breaking away from any obstacle or idol and turning to the living God and to the needs of other human beings. Such a transformation is made possible through the gift of God's transcendent grace.

Bibliography. A survey of the extensive literature about conversion may be found in L. R. Rambo, "Current Research on Religious Conversion," *Religious Studies Review*, 8 (1982), 146–59. *The Varieties of Religious Experience* (1902), by William James remains a classic study of religious conversion. The stage model proposed in this article is an adaptation of J. Lofland and R. Stark, "Becoming a World-Saver: A Theory of Conversion to a Deviant Perspective," *American Sociological Review*, 27 (1965), 862–75 and A. R. Tippett, "Conversion as a Dynamic Process in Christian Mission," *Missiology*, 5 (1977), 203–21. J. Lofland and N. Skonovd, "Conversion Motifs," *J. for the Scientific Study of Religion*, 20 (1981), 373–85. Although not mentioned in this article, pathological distortions of conversion are possible. See L. Salzman, "The Psychology of Religious and Ideological Conversion," *Psychiatry*, 16 (1953), 177–87. A recent survey can be found in C. Johnson and H. N. Malony, *Christian Conversion: Biblical and Psychological Perspectives* (1982). For a fine integration of theology and developmental psychology see W. Conn, *Christian Conversion: A Developmental Interpretation of Autonomy and Surrender* (1986). See also J. E. Loder, *The Transforming Moment* (1981). For a collection of historic and contemporary accounts of conversion experience see H. T. Kerr and J. M. Mulder, eds., *Conversions: The Christian Experience* (1983).

L. RAMBO

PSYCHOLOGY OF RELIGION (Empirical Studies, Methods, and Problems); RELIGIOUS DEVELOPMENT; RELIGIOUS EXPERIENCE; SALVATION AND PASTORAL CARE. *See also* CHRISTIAN LIFE; COMMITMENT; EVANGELICAL PASTORAL CARE; EVANGELIZING; FAITH DEVELOPMENT RESEARCH; NEW RELIGIOUS MOVEMENTS. *Compare* BAPTISM AND CONFIRMATION; BORN-AGAIN EXPERIENCE; FAITH DEVELOPMENT RESEARCH; ILLUMINATION; REPENTENCE AND CONFESSION.

CONVERSION (JEWISH CARE AND COUNSELING).

Judaism welcomes men and women who embrace the Jewish faith of their own free will. The Hebrew term for a convert to Judaism is *Ger Tzedek*, meaning, literally, a righteous sojourner. The phrase is often abbreviated to *Ger* in the masculine and *Gioret* in the feminine. In English, the word *convert* and phrase *Jew by Choice* are used interchangeably. Judaism is emphatic in stressing that no distinctions are to be made between born Jews and those who become Jewish through the process of conversion lest the latter be considered anything other than legitimate members of the Jewish community. Descriptive terminology is used only for purposes of record keeping and sociological research.

1. **History and Requirements.** The most famous convert in Jewish history is Ruth, a Moabite woman whose plea to her Jewish mother-in-law, Naomi, is recorded in the biblical Book of Ruth, (1:16) "Entreat me not to leave you or to return from following you, for where you go, I will go, and where you lodge, I will lodge, your people shall be my people and your God, my God." According to Jewish tradition, Ruth is the great-great-grandmother of King David from whose descendants the Messiah will come. This tribute is testimony to Judaism's high regard for men and women who wish to become Jews.

History records that Jews actively missionized in the Graeco-Roman world. It is clear from accounts in both the NT and Rabbinic literature that pagans frequented the synagogue and that Judaism was a well-known faith in antiquity. However, during the reign of Constantine the Great, Jews were forbidden to proselytize on pain of death. The practice was never revived. From then on, potential converts to Judaism were also discouraged. Such individuals were reminded of the consequences attendant to linking their lot with a persecuted people subject to upheaval and even death. It became customary to turn individuals away as many as three times in order that they might thoroughly probe their own motivations for considering conversion.

Judaism respects the integrity of other approaches to God. Jews do not believe that any faith has a monopoly on religious truth. Today, a growing number of individuals are choosing to become Jewish. A number of factors have contributed to interest in Judaism. These include: the impact of living in an open society, the decline of anti-Semitism, prohibition of discrimination in the work place, and greater interaction between Jews and non-Jews socially and professionally. But the need to fully examine one's reasons for becoming Jewish is as crucial now as it was in years past.

Candidates for conversion should weigh the impact of that decision upon other members of their family, in particular parents and siblings. Sometimes the announcement that one is becoming Jewish will evoke bitter reactions from loved ones. On occasion, parents may even become estranged from a son or daughter. Often one's initial exposure to Jews and Judaism comes about as a result of a romantic involvement with a born Jew. Love for a Jewish mate and the desire to placate potential Jewish in-laws, however commendable, are not sufficient reasons for converting. Becoming a Jew necessitates a commitment to the ideals and principles espoused by Judaism. Converting for the purpose of pleasing others often results in dissatisfaction and unhappiness later on. That is why, historically, rabbis did not sanction conversions performed solely for the sake of marriage and are still disinclined to officiate under those circumstances.

2. **Process.** *a. Instruction.* The process of conversion is lengthy and intense. Persons are required to undergo a period of formal instruction which may vary from six months to a year or more in length depending upon the rabbi responsible for the course of study. The curriculum usually includes theology, history, the festival and life cycle of Judaism, Zionism, the nature and structure of the Jewish community and comparative religions with emphasis upon the differences and similarities between Judaism and Christianity.

If a candidate for conversion is contemplating marriage to a Jewish partner, the latter is also encouraged to participate in the academic program. This is done in order to emphasize the family aspects of Jewish practice and observance. It serves to underscore the responsibility of the born Jewish partner in fashioning the Jewish home. Upon the completion of the course of study, the prospective convert is again reminded by the rabbi that converting to Judaism is a serious decision and its ramifications should be carefully evaluated. If the candidate still has any doubts, she or he is strongly advised against converting. Since there are no time restrictions governing when a conversion can take place, the candidate is assured that at some future date when doubts have been resolved the opportunity will be available.

Prospective converts should understand that conversion to Judaism is not achieved instantaneously. It involves a growing process of change and adaptation. Jews by Choice confront a number of dilemmas. Authenticity is of major concern. Converts often wonder whether they will be able to become full-fledged members of a group with a unique cultural heritage including special foods and even certain verbal expressions. Ethnicity needs to be put into proper perspective. Yet however significant this may be, the essence of Judaism is its religious core. Others have difficulty giving up the celebration of Christmas. The matter is often less one of theological belief in the birth of the Christian Messiah than in dealing with lingering memories of pleasant aromas and family conviviality. Even though some Jews observe Christmas as a secular occasion, Judaism emphasizes its religious implications. Those persons who believe in the divinity of Jesus should not consider conversion to Judaism. It is a conviction incompatible with the teachings of Judaism.

b. Ritual. Should the candidate wish to proceed, a ceremony of conversion is then initiated. Orthodox and Conservative Judaism require that both male and female converts undergo *Tvilo,* meaning ritual immersion. Ritual immersion generally takes place in a facility designed for that purpose, called a *Mikveh.* By virtue of this act, one is symbolically reborn as a son or daughter of the household of Israel. Appropriate benedictions are recited by the convert during the immersion.

According to Jewish law, men are also obligated to undergo ritual circumcision in keeping with the injunction in the Book of Genesis, to circumcize one's son as Abraham circumcized Isaac. Circumcision represents a permanent sign of the covenant between God and the Jewish people. The ritual is called *Brit Miloh,* the Covenant of Circumcision. In those instances where a male convert has already been circumcised, a symbolic drop of blood is drawn in fulfillment of the obligation. Reform Judaism considers both ritual circumcision and ritual immersion optional, requiring only that a requisite period of formal instruction precedes the conversion. As there are differences between the various branches of Judaism regarding the precise rituals and criteria necessary for converting, Orthodoxy does not recognize the validity of conversions performed under Reform auspices. Candidates for Reform conversion are made aware of this situation when they initially speak with a Reform rabbi in order that they can made decisions which will affect not only themselves but the Jewish status of any children they may bear in the future.

The ceremony is witnessed by three persons, generally rabbis or other learned Jews. The prospective convert is expected to confirm that she or he has made this choice voluntarily and that all previous religious affiliations have been relinquished. The convert promises to be active in the life of the Jewish community and to raise any future children as Jews. The convert recites the words, "Hear O Israel, the Lord is our God, the Lord is One," and is then given a Hebrew name, usually one of her or his choosing, as well as a certificate attesting to the act of conversion. The ceremony concludes with a blessing rendered by the presiding rabbi. The conversion ceremony can either be conducted privately or during a public service of worship in the synagogue. The matter is dependent upon the preference of the person becoming Jewish.

S. SELTZER

JEWISH CARE AND COUNSELING (History, Traditions, and Contemporary Issues). *See also* JEWISH-CHRISTIAN MARRIAGE; PENITENTS, JEWISH CARE AND COUNSELING OF.

CONVERSION DISORDER. *See* HYSTERIA.

CONVERTS. *See* EVANGELIZING; CONVERSION.

CONVICTION OF SIN. *See* GUILT; REPENTANCE AND CONFESSION.

COPING THEORY. *See* DEFENSE AND COPING THEORY.

CORRESPONDENCE, PASTORAL. The use of letters or other forms of communication to express pastoral concern or as a concrete act of pastoral care. Such correspondence may be supplementary to directly personal acts of care or, especially in case of great distance, may take the place of direct care.

1. History. The letter as a vehicle for the expression of pastoral concern has a long history. The OT includes letters from Jeremiah (29:1–32) to the exiles in Babylon and from Elijah to Jehoram King of Judah (II Chr. 21:12–15). The pastoral concern in the OT is often a prophetic call to repent. The NT has numerous examples of letters as expressions of pastoral care. Concerned that "the brethren who are of the Gentiles in Antioch" have had their minds unsettled by unauthorized ministers, the elders send them a letter to reinforce the verbal reassurance they will get from emissaries Judas and Silas (Acts 15:22–29). Paul's letters to Timothy and Titus include expressions of loving care as well as pastoral instruction.

The diversity of form (personal, group, instructional, authoritative) of the letters found in Scripture has given rise to a rich tradition of pastoral correspondence in subsequent centuries. Most prominent have been the official letters issued by ecclesiastical authorities such as bishops and denominational executives. Though many of these are authoritative pronouncements to which a reply is not expected, it is important to be aware of this very strong tradition in the exercise of pastoral responsibility. An example would be the pastoral letters sent out periodically by the U.S. Catholic Bishops (Nolan).

The use of the pastoral letter by those in authority has not, however, been restricted to official matters. Augustine (354–430), bishop of Hippo, writes to the consecrated virgin Sapida expressing care and offering guidance in a time of mourning. He writes also to his fellow priest, Nobilius, expressing regret that he cannot be present at the dedication of a sacred building. Augustine's words illustrate the usefulness of the pastoral letter when the pastor cannot be present in person. He writes that his "heart's desire would carry my poor body to you, were it not that infirmity renders this impossible" (Cunningham). The mystic, Catherine of Siena (1347–80) authored numerous letters of spiritual guidance. In her correspondence with Pope Gregory XI she tried to influence his decisions out of her pastoral concern for the church and its leadership (Scudder). Martin Luther (1483–1546) wrote many letters of spiritual guidance with the particular goal of encouraging people to have faith (Tappert). Teresa of Avila (1515–82) proved in her letters that her own great dedication to the interior life did not keep her from a deep pastoral concern for others (Allison Peers). Francis de Sales, (1567–1622), bishop of Geneva, was a prolific letter writer. The predominant theme was care for the spiritual growth of his correspondents (Stopp). John Keble (1792–1866), a Victorian clergyman of the Church of England, gave practical advice in his letters about how to live a moral life (Clebsch). His letters often urged the recipients to write to him regularly. Apparently he saw correspondence as an integral part of his pastoral ministry. Lutheran pastor Oskar Pfister's correspondence with Sigmund Freud is an excellent example of a pastoral correspondence in which the pastor's deep caring is utterly consistent and faithful although the two people corresponding come from very different viewpoints (Meng). Dietrich Bohoeffer's letters from prison are another example of the use of pastoral correspondence to overcome physical limits (Bonhoeffer).

2. **Pastoral Use.** The *official pastoral letter* continues to be widely used across denominational lines. Recent popes have continued to make liberal use of the official encyclical letter and the executives of most Protestant denominations continue to make use of the letter to announce official policy. There does not seem to be much question about the usefulness of such letters for official purposes. Certainly the written form of the communication protects it from the distortions to which it is vulnerable in the oral form. In addition the letter can be easily duplicated or printed. It not only reaches a wide readership but places a copy in their hands for future reference. Ecclesiastical authorities do not, however, restrict their use of the pastoral letter to official pronouncements. In many instances a pastoral letter is simply *exhortatory* in nature. For instance a bishop or church authority may send a letter to all congregations at the beginning of a particular liturgical season encouraging a spirit of generous giving in a denomination-wide campaign to help the needy. A step removed from the official pastoral letter is the letter written by a local parish pastor to all members of a congregation. Though this too may outline some official pronouncement or directive, it more usually expresses pastoral caring for the membership and encourages them toward attitudes or behaviors which contribute to their spiritual growth. Such pastoral letters continue to enjoy wide use in current pastoral practice. At the very least this basic level of group pastoral communication seems necessary. Advanced communications technology has conditioned the average person to expect accurate and speedy communication from those who occupy positions of responsibility.

In spite of its long history, the value of *personal pastoral correspondence* is not as easy to assess. This is partly due to its very personal nature. The most accurate evaluation of its pastoral usefulness is probably the personal judgment of the two persons involved in the correspondence. Pastoral practice is to some extent a matter of style. For some pastoral persons, engaging in pastoral correspondence is experienced as a natural and integral part of their pastoral work. For others it is not experienced this way at all. A key issue here seems to be the amount of value placed on *frequent* pastoral contact whether personal or not, as opposed to *in-person* contact whether frequent or not. Clearly when great distance or physical limitation is involved personal contact is impossible. In this case the letter or telephone call becomes the best pastoral option. When distance is not a factor, however, the value to be placed on pastoral correspondence is less clear. Those who place very little value on anything less than in-person contact will probably not generate a great deal of correspondence. On the other hand those who believe letters and telephone calls are important reinforcers of the connection already made by in-person contact may find letter-writing to be an important aspect of their work. In current pastoral practice letters are commonly used to announce upcoming or ongoing events and invite partic-

ipation. Letters of condolence or congratulation, too, are common as are letters of thanks for gifts or services rendered to pastor or parish. Baptist pastor C. W. Brister (1964) describes pastoral correspondence as "a specific ministry of friendship and encouragement." He recommends its use in the following instances: A personal letter of introduction from a new minister, personal letters of thanks for gifts or courtesies, personal congratulatory letters on such occasions as birthdays, anniversaries, and graduations. Brister emphasizes the need for correspondence to be personal and warns against form cards or printed letters which tend to be considered promotional by the recipients. Whether or not a pastoral relationship develops in such a way as to lead to an *ongoing correspondence* seems to be dependent on the style of the individual pastor and the availability of the pastor to such a development. It is also, of course, dependent on the degree to which such form of pastoral contact is deemed valuable by the particular parishioner involved.

3. **Recent Developments.** Sophisticated photo copiers, touchtone telephones and videophones, menu-driven computer programs, word processors with a mail-merge capacity, computer modems, fax machines, advanced cable-TV applications are all propelling us into an age of instant communication. The availability of this technology to the person doing pastoral ministry can greatly increase his or her power to reach people with various expressions of pastoral care. The power of the computer to organize and retrieve data can free up time for more in-person contact or for more personal forms of pastoral correspondence. The capacity of a word processor quickly to merge personal data profiles with numerous form letters can contribute to the efficient writing of more meaningful and personally relevant letters. Distance becomes less of a factor with sophisticated telephone and video links. However, as long as people are accessible to in-person pastoral contact, the technologies should be used to supplement that contact rather than replace it. For all their value it is important to remember these technologies have not yet made "Beam me up, Scottie!" a reality. Unlike the fictional characters in the television series "Star Trek" (1966–69), we have not yet found a technique which can produce an immediate state of personal presence out of a previous state of personal absence. The capacity to personalize "Dear Member" into "Dear Sue" is a useful technique of communication but in itself it hardly represents a great advance in the true caring availability of one human being to another.

Bibliography. E. Allison Peers, ed., *The Letters of Saint Teresa of Jesus,* vol. I (1951). D. Bonhoeffer, *Prisoner for God, Letters and Papers from Prison* E. Bethge, ed., (1958 [1953]). C. W. Brister, *Pastoral Care in the Church* (1964), pp. 153–54. W. A. Clebsch and C. R. Jaekle, *Pastoral Care in Historical Perspective* (1983), pp. 309–20. M. Dods, ed., (J. G. Cunningham, trans.), *Letters of St. Augustine, Bishop of Hippo* (1872–75) on microfiche, pp. 460–65. S. Freud and O. R. Pfister, *Psychoanalysis and Faith: the Letters of Sigmund Freud and Oskar Pfister* (1963). H. J. Nolan, ed., *Pastoral Letters of the United States Catholic Bishops* (1983). P. Rossman, *Computers, Bridges to the Future* (1985). V. Scudder, ed., *Saint Catherine of Siena as Seen in Her Letters* (1905), pp. 115–29. E. Stopp, trans., *St. Francis de Sales,*

Selected Letters (1960). T. G. Tappert, ed., *Luther: Letters of Spiritual Counsel* (1955).

P. BRIDGE

PASTORAL CARE (History, Traditions, and Definitions); CLASSIC LITERATURE IN CARE AND COUNSELING; COMMUNICATION.

COSMETIC SURGERY. *See* SURGICAL PATIENT.

COSMOLOGY AND PASTORAL CARE. *See* ESCHATOLOGY.

COUNCIL FOR CLINICAL TRAINING. An organization existing from 1930 to 1967 which established clinical education programs in mental hospitals, general hospitals, and correctional institutions for the training of theological students and clergypersons.

The Council was an organizational expression of a revolution which was taking place in professional education for ministry from the impact of theological liberalism, dynamic psychology, interest in the relationship of medicine and religion, and the discovery of the importance of experiential methods of learning for professional persons.

At its inception the Council provided a forum for discussing the relationship of medicine and religion and an organizational structure for developing clinical training programs, recruiting students for the programs, and enlisting the cooperation of theological schools. By 1940 the Council had fourteen clinical training centers, nineteen supervisors, fifty-five students, and an official relationship with the Association of Theological Schools in the U.S. and Canada. By 1967, its last year of existence, the Council had eighty-four centers, ninety-one supervisors, and thirty-seven seminary members.

According to the 1952 Council standards, clinical training was "a firsthand learning experience under accredited supervision which provides theological students and clergymen with opportunities for intensive study of problems in the field of interpersonal relationships and which seeks to make clear to the student, in understanding and practice, the resources, methods, and meanings of religion as they are expressed through pastoral care."

The legally responsible body of the Council was a self-perpetuating board of governors initially composed of persons from the fields of medicine and religion, and later composed of a majority of chaplains who had been approved or accredited by the Council to supervise students. After the first decade of its existence, the policies and procedures of the Council were largely shaped by what was at first called the conference of supervisors (later the assembly of supervisors and its committees) which handled such matters as standards, curriculum, certification, and accreditation.

The Council participated in numerous cooperative ventures with other groups involved in the clinical training of clergypersons. These included participation in national conferences on clinical training, the Committee of Twelve, the formation of joint standards, and joint accreditation experiments. These cooperative ventures provided opportunity for serious discussion of the possibility of creating a single CPE organization.

In 1967 the Council for Clinical Training joined with the Institute of Pastoral Care, the Association of Clinical Pastoral Educators, and the Department of Institutional Chaplaincy and Clinical Pastoral Education of the Lutheran Council in the U.S. to form the Association for Clinical Pastoral Education, Inc. The Council for Clinical Training, Inc. was legally dissolved.

Bibliography. E. E. Thornton, *Professional Education for Ministry* (1970).

C. E. HALL

ASSOCIATION FOR CLINICAL PASTORAL EDUCATION; HISTORY OF PROTESTANT PASTORAL CARE (United States); PASTORAL CARE MOVEMENT. *See also* CLINICAL PASTORAL EDUCATION.

COUNSEL, SPIRITUAL. *See* SPIRITUAL DIRECTION; SPIRITUAL MASTERS AND GUIDES. *See also* EVALUATION AND DIAGNOSIS, RELIGIOUS; PASTORAL COUNSELING.

COUNSELEE/CLIENT/PARISHIONER (Terminology). The choice of a designation for recipients of pastoral care or counseling implies a structure for the relationship.

A *counselee* is one who receives advice. As used in psychology this term connotes a person seeking help from a professional counselor, implying a recognition of need and often the payment of a fee.

A *client* is one employing the services of a professional person, such as those employing lawyers, investment counselors, or psychologically trained counselors.

A *parishioner* is either (1) a person living within the area assigned to one priest or one local church or (2) a member of a congregation. Originally a parish was a geographic area assigned to one priest for religious oversight; all persons living within the parish were his responsibility. In later use the term was applied to members or constituents of a congregation regardless of geographic location.

Terms used to describe other persons in social relationships imply the speaker's orientation. A store owner who has "customers" suggests their purchase of a product or service. A gambler referring to others as "suckers" sees them as objects to cheat in a quest for money. The physician treating "patients" has established their suffering from illness or injury and the application of medical knowledge and skill as the structure of the relationship.

The minister who calls the recipient of pastoral care or counseling a counselee or client relies on secular disciplines for name and structure. Both terms imply the helper's superior knowledge; limited, contractual relationships with the person; and monetary payment for counseling. As pastoral counselors have practiced their ministry in nonchurch settings, it has been difficult to call those seeking help "parishioners." Since those seeking help often come from many congregations (or none) and since pastoral counseling centers are dependent upon payments from those aided, both "counselee" and "client" have seemed appropriate terms.

Both terms, however, lack ecclesiastical referents, and their secular rootage makes the spiritual dimension of pastoral counseling appear superfluous. The placement of pastoral counseling centers in public buildings and hospitals has contributed to this secular appearance, and a pastoral counselor using these terms can in fact begin to see himself or herself primarily as "therapist" instead of "pastor" or "minister."

Names that aid the pastoral counselor to see the person seeking help in a religious context will enhance the *pastoral* aspect of pastoral counseling and help individuals to see themselves as searching for wholeness rather than as "sick," "maladjusted," or dependent upon professionals. One such possibility is the term "seeker." By indicating a search or pilgrimage, "seeker" connotes initiative, intentionality, and movement by the one asking aid. "Seeker" is also reminiscent of "pilgrim," one traveling toward a place of healing and blessing not always clearly known in advance. A "seeker" joins others traveling the same way and welcomes the assistance of a guide. Those who serve as guides know more about exploring new territory, but seekers do their own walking as they travel together. Thus "seeker" implies a context compatible with Judeo-Christian meanings and values and, though not commonly used at this time, may offer an appropriate term for the pastor's relation to those searching for wholeness.

Q. L. HAND

PASTORAL CARE (Contemporary Methods, Perspectives, and Issues); PASTORAL COUNSELING; PASTORAL PSYCHOTHERAPY. *See also* COUNSELING AND PSYCHOTHERAPY (Comparative Concepts); PILGRIMAGE METAPHOR.

COUNSELING. See Pastoral Counseling. *See also* Counseling, Roman Catholic; Counseling and Psychotherapy (Comparative Concepts); Family Theory and Therapy; Jewish Care and Counseling; Marriage Counseling and Marital Therapy.

COUNSELING, JEWISH. See Jewish Care and Counseling. *See also* Hasidic Care and Counseling; Jewish Literature in Care and Counseling.

COUNSELING, JOURNALS IN. See Journals.

COUNSELING, MARRIAGE AND FAMILY. See Family Theory and Therapy; Marriage Counseling and Marital Therapy.

COUNSELING, PASTORAL. See Pastoral Counseling.

COUNSELING, ROMAN CATHOLIC. Contemporary counseling within the Roman Catholic tradition has its roots in two major sources: (1) the emergence of scientific and clinical psychology, along with attempts to integrate contemporary psychological theory and technique within the church's ministry of pastoral care; and (2) the implementation of the church's social ministry through the counseling services of Catholic Charities. The future of pastoral care and counseling is likely to be profoundly affected by two current trends: (1) the development of academically based professional training programs in pastoral care and counseling; and (2) the expansion of lay ministry in both parishes and institutions.

1. The Emergence of Contemporary Psychology. The origins of activity in the field of psychology in the U.S. can be traced to Monsignor Edward A. Pace, charter member of the American Psychological Association (1892). Fr. Pace, after studying psychology under Wundt and physiology under Carl Ludwig at Leipzig, established the first psychology laboratory at the Catholic University of America in 1891. It was in this setting that Fr. Thomas Verner Moore completed doctoral studies and subsequently conducted prolific studies leading to a major work, *Cognitive Psychology* (1939), which attempted to throw light on the intellectual life of the human person. Parallel to the influential work of Thomas Verner Moore in the U.S., Roman Catholic acceptance of the new science of psychology was greatly enhanced by the work of Cardinal Désiré Mercier, who introduced scientific psychology into the Catholic University of Louvain in 1891, firmly believing in the reconciliation of philosophy with modern science and especially with psychology. Albert Edouard Michotte continued this tradition, teaching at Louvain from 1905 to 1946 and directing its psychological laboratory for twenty-five years. Another European, Agostino Gemelli, Franciscan priest, physician, psychologist, a graduate of Louvain in 1911, gained wide acceptance for psychology in Italian society and in the scientific community.

The 1950s were years of unprecedented activity on the part of psychologists at Roman Catholic institutions. Fr. Moore published a second major work, *The Driving Forces of Human Nature* (1950), attempting to integrate the philosophical and theological disciplines with psychology and psychiatry. In 1952, Fr. Charles Curran at Loyola University in Chicago published *Counseling in Catholic Life and Education* with a preface by Eugene Cardinal Tisserant commending the book for its integration of theology and philosophy with modern psychological science. Magda B. Arnold and John A. Gasson, with other prominent Roman Catholic psychologists, published another attempt to deal with the whole person (*The Human Person*, 1954), including a section on self-integration through religion. During this period Fordham University established the Institute for Pastoral Psychology (1955) to assist clergy in understanding emotional problems encountered in pastoral ministry and in formulating a better understanding of the relationship between clergy and the professional psychotherapist. At the same time the Institute for Mental Health was established at St. John's University (1954) in Collegeville, Minnesota, to bring psychiatrists, psychologists, and clergy together in an ongoing dialogue.

During the 1950s and into the early 1960s large numbers of Roman Catholic clergy entered doctoral programs in psychology at the Catholic University, Fordham University, Loyola University and other degree programs throughout the country with a view to bringing the insights of the contemporary helping professions to the work of ministry in their respective dioceses and religious communities. The American Catholic Psychological Association (ACPA), founded in 1948 out of a collective interest in dealing with the study of the human person from a thoroughly wholistic point of view, continued to gain in membership and in professional and scientific influence.

A significant highlight of the 1950s for Roman Catholic psychologists was an invited address by Pope Pius XII to the thirteenth Congress of the International Association of Applied Psychology on April 10, 1958. The pope affirmed psychology in its scientific and clinical aspects and offered personal reflections on essential elements to be embraced by Roman Catholic psychologists. Defining personality as "the psychosomatic unity of man insofar as it is determined and governed by the soul," the pope stressed that: (1) the unity of the person is psychosomatic: the mind influences the body and the body influences the mind; (2) the self is a unique and universal center of being that is endowed with self-mastery and self-disposition and is ordinarily responsible for its decisions; (3) every person must be treated with profound respect as a child of God; and (4) the human person has the ability and obligation to complete the image of God in his or her personality by following objective norms dictated by conscience and revelation. The pope closed with a series of moral guidelines stressing repeatedly the need for free and informed consent of the subject studied. This address represented the highest level of affirmation for Roman Catholic psychologists who had only recently emerged from decades of controversy regarding the integration of the theological and philosophical disciplines with scientific psychology.

During the 1960s a number of books appeared attempting to integrate psychological insights with vocational and spiritual development and with the practice of ministry (e.g., Godin, 1965). The first degree program in pastoral counseling at a Catholic educational institution was established at Iona College in 1963 in response to a demand from Roman Catholic clergy for training in counseling. In 1965 the National Association of Catholic Chaplains was founded in order to further the training and professionalism of ministers within health care and institutional ministry. Courses in counseling were introduced into Roman Catholic seminaries along with the development of professional field education drawing upon the insights of the behavioral sciences. A revitalization of the ministry of spiritual direction began as practitioners and theoreticians attempted to incorporate many of the insights of developmental psychology and group dynamics into the ministry of spiritual direction. A large number of clergy and vowed religious utilized their scientific and clinical training in programs of seminary and religious formation.

The 1970s were marked by significant progress in incorporating the religious dimension into the field of psychology. Members of the American Catholic Psychological Association, working toward an acceptance within the American Psychological Association of the validity of religion and religious behavior as an object of research, and imbued with post-conciliar ecumenism, reorganized into an ecumenical organization under the title Psychologists Interested in Religious Issues (PIRI) in 1971. Under the leadership of Fr. William Bier, SJ and Virginia Sexton, PIRI won acceptance as Division 36 of the American Psychological Association in 1975, establishing a place within mainstream psychology for the study of religious behavior and religious experience.

Illustrative of the emerging integration of the psychological and theological disciplines, master's degree and advanced certificate programs in pastoral counseling for clergy, vowed religious and lay ministers emerged from the psychology department of Loyola College of Maryland in 1976. Ecumenical in philosophy, faculty, and student body, the Loyola program is wholistic and ministerial in nature, attempting to integrate contemporary counseling theory and technique within the context of the church's ministry of pastoral care and counseling. It was accredited for chaplaincy training by the National Association of Catholic Chaplains in 1982 and is the first Roman Catholic academically based program to be awarded full accreditation by the American Association of Pastoral Counselors (1985).

2. **Counseling Services of Catholic Charities.** Much of the counseling ministry of the Roman Catholic Church has been under the auspices of Catholic Charities, which was founded as the National Conference of Catholic Charities (NCCC) in 1910, with the following statement of purpose:

> "The national Conference has been created to meet a definite situation. It aims to preserve the organic spiritual character of Catholic Charity. It aims to seek out and understand causes of dependency. It aims to take advantage of the ripest wisdom in relief and preventive work to which men have anywhere attained, and to serve as a bond of union for the unnumbered organizations in the United States, which are doing the work of Charity. It aims to become, finally, the attorney for the Poor in Modern Society, to present their point of view and defend them unto the days when social justice may secure to them their rights."

Historically, the early development of Catholic Charities in the U.S. had two main thrusts, one institutional and the other parochial. Many religious communities were founded to meet health and social needs, establishing institutions to further their work among the new immigrants who found it difficult to become acclimated to American society. At the same time virtually every parish became a cultural as well as religious center, providing for a variety of educational and social needs. In the 1920s and 1930s a number of factors converged to give impetus to a new direction for the church's charitable effort: new governmental social programs, the professionalization of social work, and the entry of large numbers of Catholics into the economic mainstream of society. Catholic Charities became increasingly "professionalized" and focused on child welfare and casework services to families. Today most Catholic Charities agencies and institutions see themselves as part of the total community serving anyone who is in need.

In the theology of Catholic Charities, counseling and other human services are viewed as ministries of compassion flowing from the good news of the gospel:

> "As an integral expression of the Church of Christ we are charged not simply with attempts to meet human need, but with the further challenge of a reflective penetration of every expression of need as a revelation of the human condition that all men share. . . . All men bear within them the riches and dignity of human

nature so that as one man discovers and gives expression to his need all men find in him a mirror of themselves. Thus, instead of fostering a division between those who help and those who are helped, Catholic Charities must foster the compassion reflected in the gospel wherein men experience themselves in each other. . . . Services provided by the Catholic Charities Movement should be evidently sacramental, that is, transparencies of the mercy and love of Christ" (NCCC, 1972, p. 17).

The longstanding identification of the Catholic Charities movement with social casework has been extended to many areas to encompass broad responsibility for leadership in the total field of human services. This includes, in addition to casework and counseling services, activity in the areas of health, housing, credit unions, social action, family life, and recreation and youth activities. There is a growing recognition that human problems should be met in a variety of ways through the utilization of various disciplines working together as a team for preventive as well as restorative activity. Currently the NCCC, representing over one thousand diocesan agencies and several affiliated organizations, has commissions addressing families and children, unmarried parents, the elderly, and housing.

While the focus of diocesan charities differs, there is an increasing movement toward the parish as a service community as well as a place of worship. This includes an understanding of social services as enabling the parish not only to meet the needs of its own parishioners but also to be a responsible leadership group within a neighborhood, utilizing and contributing to the community's various institutional systems. Pilot projects involving the provision of counseling services for a group of area parishes, coordinated by the diocesan office, have emerged with increasing frequency in the 1980s with a view to meeting the increasing need for counseling services at a time when the number of ordained clergy in the parishes continues to decline.

3. The Future in Light of Current Trends. In 1965 the Decree on the Apostolate of the Laity of Vatican II highlighted lay participation in the priesthood of Christ. One Vatican commentator observed: "For centuries this concept has been on the back burner, set on simmer. The Vatican Council put the ministry of the laity on front burner and turned the setting up to high."

Theological schools that have made programs available to religious and laity seeking to prepare for ministry but without ordination have experienced lay and religious enrollments of from one-third to one-half of their student bodies. At the same time specialized institutes of pastoral studies specifically designed for non-ordained ministers continue to emerge and prosper. Further evidence of the expansion of the ministry of the non-ordained is found in the membership statistics of the National Association of Catholic Chaplains. From a clerical organization of seven hundred priests in 1972, the NACC has grown to include 3,201 members in 1984, 1,116 of whom are priests, with 2,085 non-ordained members, a growth of over two thousand percent in thirteen years. In response to the growth in lay ministry in general and to the emergence of the career, full-time, professionally trained lay minister, the bishops of the

U.S. issued a joint pastoral letter in 1980 entitled *Gifted and Called*. The revised Code of Canon Law, promulgated on January 1, 1983, made significant changes in expanding the role of the laity in ministry.

Whatever specific forms of ministry may develop in the future, current trends suggest an increasing role of non-ordained ministers, including laity and vowed religious in the pastoral care and counseling ministry. The movement of Catholic Charities toward decentralization of counseling services in favor of parish-based support systems suggests an increasing role at the parish level for the lay minister of pastoral care and counseling. At the same time, given the decline of ordained priests and the current staffing of health care institutions by non-ordained ministers of pastoral care and counseling, it is projected that the majority of health care chaplaincies will be staffed by vowed religious and lay ministers.

In the past the professional affiliation of Roman Catholic clergy and religious with psychology (and to some extent with psychiatry) and the major commitment to human services through the profession of social work under the aegis of Catholic charities have constituted the primary foci of Roman Catholics interested in the counseling ministry. More recently, individual clergy, religious and lay ministers have affiliated with the American Association of Pastoral Counselors, constituting approximately five percent of the membership as reported in the 1984 AAPC directory. Given the increasingly prominent role of laity in the counseling ministry within the Roman Catholic Church, the future of Roman Catholic participation in AAPC is likely to be profoundly affected by the status of lay ministry within AAPC.

Bibliography. C. Curran, *Counseling in Catholic Life and Education* (1952). A. Godin, *The Pastor as Counselor* (ET, 1965). National Conference of Catholic Charities, "Toward a Renewed Catholic Charities Movement" (1972). T. F. O'Meara, *Theology of Ministry* (1983). Pius XII, "Address to the Thirteenth Congress of the International Association of Applied Psychology" (April 10, 1958).

B. K. ESTADT

HISTORY OF ROMAN CATHOLIC PASTORAL CARE (United States); VATICAN COUNCIL II. *See also* CHRISTOTHERAPY; FORMATIVE SPIRITUALITY; PASTORAL CARE MOVEMENT; PASTORAL COUNSELING MOVEMENT; ROMAN CATHOLIC PASTORAL CARE. *Compare* CASUISTRY; JUDAISM AND PSYCHOLOGY; RELIGION AND PSYCHOTHERAPY; SPIRITUAL DIRECTION. *Biography:* GODIN.

COUNSELING, VALUES IN. *See* VALUES IN COUNSELING AND PSYCHOTHERAPY.

COUNSELING, VOCATIONAL. *See* VOCATION (Protestantism).

COUNSELING AND PSYCHOTHERAPY (Comparative Concepts). For many years definition of and distinction between these two terms have been unresolved issues, rooted in the social and institutional origins of the various helping professions. When in 1942 Carl Rogers published his now-classic *Counseling and Psychotherapy,* he both recognized and took a stand on an issue that already had become controversial and, more than forty years later, remains so. At the time, many psychiatrists had determined that psychologists should not be allowed to practice psychotherapy. Although that issue remains alive in some quarters even today, generally it has been settled by educational and training institutions, the courts, state licensing boards, insurance companies, professional organizations, and praxis. In fact, both clinical and counseling psychologists do practice psychotherapy. Further, it is relatively safe to say that more non-medically trained professionals practice psychotherapy than do medically trained persons.

1. **Assumptions About Practice.** Distinctions between the two terms have depended on assumptions about the nature of psychotherapy and the nature of counseling: either counseling and psychotherapy are two terms for the same process or project; or counseling and psychotherapy are distinctively different processes and projects; or counseling and psychotherapy are not identical but similar, and the overlap is both significant and critical. To date no one of these assumptions or claims has become clearly dominant. The issue continues to generate discussion, argument, research, professional conflict, theoretical nuances, practical techniques — even wearisome unconcern.

At what might be called the folk level of the profession, the issue appears settled, as illustrated by a sentence from a brochure sent out by a local mental health facility: "We offer counseling for short-term, ordinary kinds of problems and psychotherapy for problems that have a longer, deeper history." Implicitly the foci are *length* and *depth*, two aspects commonly used to compare counseling and psychotherapy. Both notions offer problems, especially in light of "newer therapies," which do not necessarily correlate length and depth, and which challenge older meanings of these terms.

Perhaps more differentiating and to the point is the argument that counseling primarily focuses on decisions and plans persons must make to play productive roles, irrespective of whether they are sick or well, normal or abnormal. In the framework of counseling, then, consumers are clients, not patients; and the essential concern is with enhancement and realization of possibilities and potentialities, rather than with limitations and illnesses of the individual. Still, as the literature clearly indicates, psychotherapy — at least some forms of it—has similar, even identical, concerns and foci.

2. **Conceptual Redefinition.** One of the most conscientious, imaginative, and risky attempts to untangle the conceptual underbrush of this issue has been suggested by James F. T. Bugental, an existential-humanistic psychotherapist. He suggests that the notion of "being levels of therapeutic growth goals" provides the organizing principle for making heuristic differentiations and comparisons between such terms as counseling and psychotherapy. His continuum runs from counseling through psychotherapy to evocation. Essentially, counseling has to do with adjustment and coping, therapy with renewal and growth, and evocation with emancipation and transcendence. Each mode uniquely configures a variety of factors: the primary mental realm to be dealt with, focus of attention, reality assumptions, goals, presence or absence of crisis, nature of the therapeutic alliance, length and commitment, life significance, and symptoms (see Figure 1, on following page).

Although the presence of a relatively new term, "evocation," makes Bugental's scheme more complex, it does appear closer to reality than a simple length/depth notion. Certainly it offers a sense of the complexity involved in making meaningful and honest comparisons when dealing with the counseling/psychotherapy issue.

3. **Pastoral Implications.** The problem and controversy have touched the pastoral care and counseling movement as well. Although the term counseling has held a rather firm place in the movement, in recent years the phrase "pastoral psychotherapy" has emerged. Carroll Wise, for instance, has claimed that psychotherapy is a more accurate designation for what the religious professional does when engaged in depth encounters with others. Arguing biblically and etymologically, he claims that pastoral psychotherapy treats the living person as *a total reality*, an organic unity broken and in need of healing. Of course, Wise's perspective rests heavily on his understanding of what general psychotherapy itself is —and that remains an open question in need of far greater clarification than has been achieved thus far.

Bibliography. S. A. Appelbaum, "Challenges to Traditional Psychotherapy from the 'New Therapies'," *American Psychologist*, 37 (1982), 1002–08. A. H. Brayfield, "Counseling Psychology," *Annual Review of Psychology*, 14 (1963), 319–50. J. F. T. Bugental, *Psychotherapy and Process: The Fundamentals of an Existential-Humanistic Approach* (1978). C. R. Rogers, *Counseling and Psychotherapy* (1942). D. Smith "Trends in Counseling and Psychotherapy," *American Psychologist*, 37 (1982), 802–09. C. A. Wise, *Pastoral Psychotherapy: Theory and Practice* (1980).

O. STRUNK, JR.

PASTORAL COUNSELING; PASTORAL PSYCHOTHERAPY; PSYCHOTHERAPY. *See also* COUNSELEE /CLIENT/PARISHIONER TERMINOLOGY.

COUNSELING AND PSYCHOTHERAPY (Research Studies and Methods). *See* PSYCHOTHERAPY AND COUNSELING (Research Studies and Methods).

COUNSELING CENTER. *See* PASTORAL COUNSELING CENTER.

COUNSELING PSYCHOLOGY. A branch of psychology which focuses upon a person's learning and relationship difficulties, uses tests and interviews to diagnose the problem, and interviews to resolve it. Counseling psychologists in private practice do evaluations, as well as marriage, vocational, and adjustment counseling. The differences from clinical psychology are not sharply defined.

Q. L. HAND

COUNSELING AND PSYCHOTHERAPY (Comparative Concepts). *Compare* CLINICAL PSYCHOLOGY.

COUNSELOR. The term "counselor" is used in two commonly understood ways: (1) one who advises, such as a lawyer, a supervisor of children or youth in a camp setting, a faculty member who advises students, one whose profession is counseling, and advisers in many

Figure 1. Comparisons among six levels of psychotherapy goals.

	Deficiency Motivation				Growth Motivation	
Category	Counseling		Therapy		Evocation	
	Adjustment	Coping	Renewal	Growth	Emancipation	Transcendence
Mental realm	Conscious	Conscious and preconscious	Preconscious	Preconscious and unconscious	Unconscious	Inner vision
Focus of attention	Content	Content	Content more than process	Process more than content	Process	Inner search
Reality assumption	Consensus self-and-world concept	Consensus self-and-world concept	Same but some self change	Reconstructed self-and-world concept	Fluid self-and-world concept	Nonattachment
Goals	Change behavior to fit world demands	Develop skills to interact with world	Replacing nonfunctional self-percepts	Life reorganization and revitaling	Freeing from "self"-domination, flowing being	Openness to ultimate awareness
Crisis?	No	No	Traumatic catharsis	Incomplete	Nearly always	Death and rebirth
Nature of alliance	"Professional" detached	"Professional" friendly	Some transference	Transference	Transference neurosis	Companions in the unknown
Length and commitment	Short-term, minimal investment	Moderate investment, medium term; group methods often especially helpful	Moderate investment, medium term; group methods often especially helpful	Long-term, important life investment	Major life commitment; expectation of true life change even after therapy	Major life commitment; expectation of true life change even after therapy
Life significance	Incidental	Helpful to better life	Important life changes	Life change, enrichment	Basic revision of life perspective	Basic revision of life perspective
Symptoms	Symptom relief	Symptom relief	Symptoms worked through	Symptoms worked through	Symptoms unimportant	Symptoms unimportant
Typical therapy	Behavior modification	Group therapy	General psychotherapy	Ego analysis, depth therapy	Existential psychotherapy	Transpersonal therapy

other areas of life; (2) one who is trained to use interviewing and other psychological methods to reduce behavioral and emotional or other adaptive problems.

Counseling interviews may be structured for the mutually agreed-upon goal of receiving advice from one who is considered expert in a particular field of knowledge or in order to explore various behavioral alternatives in the light of one's history and personality. Although counselors who are adequately trained clinically may be flexible enough to move from an advice-giving mode to a more therapeutically oriented one, the majority of counseling is structured toward the achievement of one goal to the exclusion of another.

Although the authority of clergy to advise has long been accepted, the use of "counselor" to describe clergy is fairly recent. Interest in pastoral interviewing skills was expressed in the 1930s. C. T. Holman's, *The Cure of Souls* (1932) had chapters on "The Case Work Method in the Cure of Souls" and "Spiritual Therapeutics." Books were written on topics like *Pastoral Psychology* by K. R. Stolz (1932), J. R. Oliver's *Pastoral Psychiatry and Mental Health* (1932), and *Pastoral Psychiatry* by J. S. Bonnell (1938). R. Cabot and R. Dicks, in *The Art of Ministering to the Sick* (1936) discussed listening methods and reported interview verbatims. An early use of "pastoral counseling" occurs as a chapter heading in Stolz's book. Other titles included C. J. Schindler, *The Pastor as Personal Counselor* (1942), R. L. Dicks, *Pastoral Work and Personal Counseling* (1947), and S. Hiltner, *Pastoral Counseling* (1949).

C. R. Rogers' *Counseling and Psychotherapy* (1942) was especially influential during these years. Its "non-directive method" offered a conversation technique that appeared easy to learn, and its theory of "unconditional positive regard" seemed congruent with theological concepts of divine action. Clergy could see themselves as "therapists" without lengthy training. Pastoral care teachers made extensive use of this book.

The image of counselor, developed in psychology and adapted by clergy, is of a person trained in psychotherapeutic and theological methods of assisting others to cope with their personal and interpersonal difficulties. The pastoral counselor has the authority of both ordination and psychotherapeutic training without the additional responsibilities usual with the parish pastor or the medically based psychiatrist.

Bibliography. E. B. Holifield, *A History of Pastoral Care in America* (1983).

Q. L. HAND

COUNSELING AND PSYCHOTHERAPY (Comparative Concepts); COUNSELING, ROMAN CATHOLIC; PASTORAL COUNSELOR. *Compare* CONFESSOR; PSYCHOTHERAPY; SPIRITUAL DIRECTOR.

COUNSELS (Moral Theology).

Medieval and modern Roman Catholic theology acknowledge the occurrence of divine invitations which do not strictly entail obligations, and whose acceptance is regarded rather as supererogation than as duty. Main examples derived from the NT are voluntary poverty and celibacy. Adoption of these counsels by groups of perfectionist Christians was fundamental to the development of monasticism. Since monasticism's success was found to depend on submission to appropriate regulations and superiors, obedience, in that sense, was judged practically indispensable to a community life of poverty and celibacy. As a result, poverty, celibacy, and obedience came to be referred to as the three evangelical counsels, regarded as the defining attributes of consecrated religious life.

J. GAFFNEY

PRUDENCE (Moral Theology); MORAL THEOLOGY AND PASTORAL CARE.

COUNTERTRANSFERENCE.

Exaggerated positive and negative feelings, fantasies, and behavior in the counselor or therapist that are "transferred" from some other, earlier relationship onto the client, and are thus inappropriate to the reality of the current therapeutic relationship (in contrast to the client's "transference" reactions to the therapist). Some contemporary writers use the term to refer to all of the counselor's feelings and reactions to clients. As these definitions suggest, the term has undergone a great deal of change since Freud first introduced it in 1910 (in his paper "The Future Prospects of Psychoanalytic Therapy"). Some writers contend that "countertransference" has been so widely misapplied that its usefulness is now in question.

1. The Countertransference Debate. While Freud introduced the term, he did not pursue it systematically in his writings. Strangely, the topic lay essentially untouched for forty years when a major theoretical debate ensued, a debate that continues as one of the most controversial topics in the theory and practice of all relationship-centered therapies.

a. Countertransference as problem. Freud's limited writing on countertransference gave rise to a twofold usage. One approach, the "classical," received most attention in the early years of the development of psychotherapy, as represented by the following statement: "We have become aware of the countertransference which arises in [the physician] as the result of the patient's influence upon his [unconscious] feelings" (Freud, 1910, pp. 144–45). Freud urged all analysts to begin their work with a self-analysis and to continue this process to deeper levels so that blockages to the relatively objective observation of patients could be guarded against and removed. Thus, countertransference feelings were viewed essentially as a hindrance to be excised from the therapeutic field.

In his paper "On Transference Love" (1915) Freud drew out the antitherapeutic consequences of unanalyzed (i.e., unresolved) countertransference. There he pointed out that when strong "in love" feelings emerge in male therapists toward their female patients, the gratification and reciprocation of these feelings will foreclose on the possibility of getting to the neurotic roots of the patient's problem. Thus the frustration of such wishes and the refusal to join in with such mutually gratifying fantasies or behavior is necessary for the development of self-knowledge and the maturation of the patient's personality. If falling in love over and over again would solve deeper emotional conflicts, there would be no need for psychotherapy.

This "classical" position of non-gratification, abstinence, and non-interference was the standard ideal for many years. Countertransference was viewed essentially as a problem to be solved.

b. Countertransference as therapeutic tool. Later, in a different vein that anticipated subsequent developments, Freud proposed a second usage of the term. The analyst "must turn his own [unconscious] like a receptive organ toward the transmitting [unconscious] of the patient. . . . So the doctor's [unconscious] is able . . . to reconstruct [the patient's] [unconscious]" (1912, pp. 115–16). In this passage Freud points toward a constructive use of the therapist's reactions to the patient, perceiving that an understanding of these reactions is a necessary condition of the therapeutic process.

2. **Contemporary Views.** *a. Use of the therapist's personality.* Beginning about 1950 with the writings of Fromm-Reichmann in the U.S., Winnicott, Racker, and a number of other writers, a new emphasis upon the nature of the therapeutic relationship as a special interpersonal setting began to shed new light particularly upon the positive dimensions of countertransference reactions. Fromm-Reichmann (1950), for example, was among the first to elaborate on the importance of the use of the therapist's personality in both its real (that is, generically human) and unconscious aspects. She taught that the stance of the therapist ought to be that of a participant-observer; without engaging the patient at every level there could be no progress or maturation. However, she also cautioned against the indiscriminate use of therapists' reactions to patients and strongly advised all who choose to undertake therapeutic work to have their own therapy.

b. Present status of the concept. Since 1950 many writers representing numerous therapeutic orientations have developed and debated the concept (Epstein and Feiner, 1979; Menninger, 1958; Rogers, 1951; Snyder, 1961; Wise, 1980). The results have been both enlightening and confusing. At one extreme are those who claim that they do not experience or identify transference and countertransference phenomena at all. They claim to deal only with the conscious and objective aspects of the therapeutic relationship. At the other extreme are those who see all reactions of the therapist as caused by the client. Thus, if a therapist feels sexually aroused or angry with a client, these feelings are viewed as being caused by the client's behavior toward the therapist and are thus utilized as valid observational data. Widely diverse positions have been taken as the sole truth in the confusion and controversy on this subject.

3. **Countertransference in Pastoral Counseling.** Despite these widely varying points of view, countertransference is still a cornerstone of any relationship-centered pastoral counseling process. In both its problematic and constructive aspects, countertransference needs to be well understood by the clinical pastor. Giving in to any extreme view is fraught with danger to the therapeutic process.

a. Countertransference problems. Careful clinical research (e.g., Langs, 1976) has shown the destructive, anti-therapeutic effect of a therapist's projective identifications toward clients. When this occurs, the therapist's view of and response toward clients is based largely upon the unconscious projection of the therapist's own unresolved conflicts onto the client. Such unconsciously determined behavior as conspiring with a client to avoid certain material, blocking of feelings by intellectual interpretations, responding in anger or over-solicitousness to a client on a consistent basis—all forms of acting out (e.g., forgetting appointments, not establishing firm boundaries, sexual involvement, going to sleep, keeping the relationship on a social basis, etc.) are anti-therapeutic and clearly the responsibility of the therapist. They need to be dealt with, not in direct communication with the counselee, but in the pastor's own supervision, consultation, or personal therapy. Consistent and chronic problems of this nature with a variety of counselees indicate a serious therapeutic need in the pastoral counselor. (See DeWald, 1964; Chessick, 1974; and Wise, 1980 for reliable and detailed discussions of these issues.)

b. Constructive aspects. Unquestionably, despite potential distortions and difficulties, one's unconscious reactions, feelings, and fantasies are invaluable sources of information and insight about the person with whom one is working. For example, the kinds of memories elicited in the pastoral counselor by the relationship with a particular counselee often provide a reliable guide to the developmental level at which the client is operating. Likewise, fantasy images engendered by the material a counselee presents may be the best clue one can obtain for understanding what a person is trying to communicate about himself or herself. Finally, empathic responses to the feelings of the counselee, as well as realistic feelings of anger toward provocative behavior, often enable the pastoral counselor to make contact with persons in deep ways that add immeasurably to the maturational process in both counselee and pastoral therapist.

4. **Dealing with Countertransference Problems.** *a. Internal process.* In the last analysis, the ability to thread the needle between total narcissistic indulgence and the failure to attend to and utilize one's responses to counselees will be determined primarily by the maturity and personal honesty of the pastoral therapist. When compulsive feelings or fantasies occur in the clinical pastor they should be dealt with internally, with or without consultation. This requires an honest (and sometimes painful) exploration of the meanings of the countertransference for oneself—its relation to one's own unresolved maturational issues, emotional needs, significant relationships, and one's moral and religious values. The aim of such self-assessment is thus to direct the pastor back to the true sources of the contertransference for appropriate responses at those points and away from spurious and destructive efforts to resolve one's own personal issues through the counselee. The ongoing therapeutic discipline of dealing with countertransference thus opens up profound issues of personal integrity and growth for all therapists and counselors, and for this reason has been regarded as a key issue in the clinical education of pastors and pastoral counselors.

b. Consultation, supervision, and therapy. While the internal process lies at the heart of dealing with countertransference, it is frequently helpful and at times necessary to enlist the aid of a clinically capable consultant or supervisor in facing and exploring countertransference issues. The discipline of learning to identify the need for such help, and seeking it, is fundamental to pastoral counseling and expresses the commitment of the field to therapeutic effectiveness and moral integrity. It is therefore a common practice for clinical supervisors to focus on countertransference issues and for experienced pastoral counselors occasionally to seek consultation on an *ad hoc* basis.

If persistent countertransference patterns arise in response to many counselees, however, serious attention should be given to further intensive psychotherapy for the pastor. In some cases, the suitability of the pastoral counselor's personality to therapeutic work may need to be questioned.

c. Special problems with religious counselees. A small but significant literature exists on the special problems of religious therapists with religious clients (Spero, 1981; cf. Stern, 1985). While a shared value system and point of view may be helpful in establishing a therapeutic alliance, such thoughts, feelings, and symbolic content may open the door to collusion between the pastoral counselor and his or her counselee. A pastoral counselor of the same faith may be better able to understand and respond to a counselee's constructive and destructive uses of religion, but on the other hand may be reluctant to interpret or challenge shared beliefs or practices when they are being utilized defensively against self-understanding.

It is particularly incumbent upon pastoral counselors to be alert to their role-related countertransference reactions when working with persons of very similar or very dissimilar religious backgrounds. As with most other countertransference issues, the key to effective usage of these feelings is the self-understanding, maturity, and moral integrity of the pastor.

Bibliography. R. Chessick, *The Technique and Practice of Intensive Psychotherapy* (1974). W. J. Collins, "The Pastoral Counselor's Countertransference as a Therapeutic Tool," *J. of Pastoral Care,* 36 (1982), pp. 125–35. P. DeWald, *Psychotherapy, a Dynamic Approach* (1964). Epstein and Feiner, eds., *Countertransference* (1979). S. Freud, "Observations On Transference Love", *SE* 12 (1915), pp. 158–74; "Recommendations for Physicians Practicing Psychoanalysis," *SE* 12 (1912), pp. 109–20; "The Future Prospects of Psychoanalytic Therapy," *SE* 11 (1910), pp. 139–52. F. Fromm-Reichmann, *Principles of Intensive Psychotherapy* (1950). R. Langs, *The Bi-Personal Field* (1976). K. Menninger, *Theory of Psychoanalytic Technique* (1958). E. Racker, *Transference and Countertransference* (1968). C. Rogers, *Client Centered Therapy* (1951). W. U. Snyder, *The Psychotherapy Relationship* (1961). M. H. Spero, "Countertransference in Religious Therapists with Religious Patients," *American J. of Psychotherapy,* 35:4 (1981), 565–75. E. M. Stern, ed., *Psychotherapy and the Religiously Committed Patient* (1985). D. W. Winnicott, *Through Pediatrics to Psychoanalysis* (1975). C. A. Wise, *Pastoral Psychotherapy* (1980).

R. G. BRUEHL

PSYCHOANALYSIS (Therapeutic Method and Research). *See also* CONSULTATION; PASTOR, FAITH AND INTEGRITY *or* MENTAL HEALTH; SELF-UNDERSTANDING; SUPERVISION.

COUPLES, UNMARRIED. *See* COHABITATION.

COUPLES THERAPY. Referred initially to the psychotherapy of an identified patient done with the spouse present as a consultant. In contemporary usage, it refers generally to the psychotherapy of any couple seen conjointly with each partner and their relationship identified as foci of therapeutic attention.

R. E. JOHNSTON

MARRIAGE COUNSELING AND MARITAL THERAPY.

COURAGE. The ability to face threats to one's security or well-being, manifested either as courage "for the sake of," or courage "in spite of."

An act of courage "for the sake of" occurs within a structured and rational world when one faces threats to the order of that world. In the Middle Ages, courage "for the sake of" was refined into a patrician style of life called knighthood. The vocation of the knight was to defend king and church, the sources of order and meaning.

The knight remains the model of courage for those whose world is structured and meaningful. The soldier who gives his life to defend his nation from danger is answering the call to preserve society's values from destruction. The faithful who die for the sake of the gospel are exemplifying faithfulness to Christ. The person of high principle who makes sacrifices for the sake of integrity, is witnessing to the reality of what is eternal. In these instances courage is demonstrated as the ability to face that which threatens the established order or the source of meaning. It is action "for the sake of."

In the nineteenth century, the existentialist paradigm replaced a stable, meaningful world "out there" with a self-created world threatened by forces that would overwhelm the individual. The courageous person in an existentialist vision of the world is not one who sacrifices for the sake of an objective ideal, but who acts in spite of the absurd.

The existentialist paradigm was formulated by Søren Kierkegaard who used the Genesis story of Adam as the diagnosis of the human condition. Kierkegaard saw life as a paradox of the infinite and the finite. We are created in the image of God and yet made of dust of the earth. The infinite dimension of the self enables us to see ourselves as isolated individuals with a beginning and an end. I not only know that "all must die," I know that someday I must die. This knowledge is the source of anxiety. Most people hide from anxiety by conforming to the world (e.g., bourgeois morality, capitalist ethic, worship of the state). The courageous individual risks either despair or faith by facing the truth of existence and defying the world. Faith, as "courage-in-spite-of," is defined after the example of Abraham, whose courage to risk his future in spite of the absurd resulted in his possessing it.

The most systematic development of courage "in spite of" was outlined by Paul Tillich in *The Courage To Be* (1952). Tillich defined courage as the act of facing up to the ontological contradictions of existence. Based on a Kierkegaardian definition of human life as paradox, Tillich said that to be human is to be threatened with non-being. Awareness of non-being, anxiety, takes three forms: ontic anxiety (fate), moral anxiety (guilt), and spiritual anxiety (meaninglessness). When a civilization's structure of order and meaning disintegrates, anxiety becomes endemic. Ontic anxiety was dominant at the end of the ancient world, moral anxiety at the end of the Middle Ages, and in our time, the end of the modern era, the dominant anxiety is spiritual. Courage, for Tillich, is the "courage to be" in spite of the threat of non-being manifested as death, guilt, or meaninglessness.

Psychologists, such as Ernest Becker, who stand in the existentialist tradition, see the primary fact about human existence as anxiety about death as non-being (annihilation anxiety). Becker interprets the Narcissus myth to mean that the motivating power in human behavior is the need to know oneself as counting for something, having "cosmic specialness." He sees Freud's great contribution as revealing that human beings live lives of deception in order to hide their true condition as finite and conditioned beings. We are not in control of our lives. Given this understanding of existence, courage is the honesty to accept the fear of death, and the fact that we must rely on "vital lies," systems of ideas, or powers beyond our own, for cosmic significance.

Bibliography. E. Becker, *The Denial of Death* (1973). P. Tillich, *The Courage To Be* (1952).

M. TROTTER

EXISTENTIALISM AND PASTORAL CARE; FAITH/BELIEF; SPIRIT, HUMAN. *Compare* ANXIETY; FEAR.

COVENANT AND CONTRACT.

The terms "covenant" and "contract" represent two basic dimensions of all pastoral care and counseling. Covenant refers to the element of trust and pledged faithfulness to one another which establishes and undergirds the caring or counseling relationship. Contract, on the other hand, denotes the mutual expectations of the relationship and its specific terms, such as time, place, frequency and duration of meetings, and any fee arrangements. Covenant and contract are subtly interrelated in a way which constitutes an important dynamic of all caring relationships.

Covenant is the commitment mutually shared by the caregiver and the care-receiver or receivers to engage in a relationship which is intended to promote greater health and wholeness. In actual practice the covenant ordinarily emerges slowly as trust and mutual participation in the relationship development. Even so, the covenant exists in some form when the caregiver and the care-receiver begin the relationship.

In essence, the caregiver promises to bring to bear all his or her knowledge and skill and to be faithful in dealing with the care-receiver. At times the promise is assumed and may or may not be discussed in any overt form. In like fashion, the care-receiver promises to enter the relationship with conviction and with a commitment to engage in the partnership of resolution. Here also there is usually a tentative aspect which is present and which marks the relative uncertainty found in entering on an uncharted course. Ordinarily the receiver looks to the giver to demonstrate the validity of the relationship as it unfolds. Ideally, the covenant does not change as the relationship develops; rather it becomes more overt and visible than at the beginning. Nevertheless, its essence is the mutual commitment of both persons to engage in the process of healing.

Contract is a term utilized to describe the actual procedure being followed in the healing relationship as a means for carrying out the intent of the covenant. It includes the particular expectations of the care-receiver as well as the expectations of the caregiver. The caregiver draws on knowledge, skill, and experience for dealing with destructive ploys manifested by the care-receiver and attempts to relate in the fashion which seems most appropriate at any given time in the process. In carrying out this purpose the caregiver is conscious that the relationship is atypical in that it avoids the customary "small talk" of social relationships, has definite limits regarding times and duration of meeting, and deals with issues often denied or obscured by the care-receiver. The commitment of the caregiver enables him or her to respond to the various emotional and behavioral aspects of the care-receiver so as to provide an experience of release from crippling attitude and behavior toward a more open style of life.

The care-receiver moves toward greater openness as the process goes forward while being aware of the reality that growth is uneven and progress may, at times, seem slow in coming. In the atypical relationship the care-receiver (or receivers) find opportunity for experimenting with different fashions of relating in the context of the stability of the caregiver. Whereas the covenant is the basic "given" of the relationship, the contract changes from time to time as progress occurs. A continual renegotiation of the contract is made as the care-receiver moves toward taking more and more responsibility for personal growth and wholeness.

The covenant is fulfilled when the caregiver and the care-receiver mutually affirm the completion of the process. Ideally, this represents the growing ability of the care-receiver to function in a constructive and creative fashion without recourse to the atypical kinds of relationships essential to stabilize personal life. The conclusion of the covenantal relationship includes an openness for the care-receiver to return, as needed, from time to time in the ongoing pilgrimage of life. In a less than ideal situation, the caregiver and the care-receiver(s) conclude that the relationship is not helpful for whatever reason. Such a conclusion results in termination with the possibility of referral.

Bibliography. R. C. Erickson, "Covenant Making and Pastoral Counseling," *Pastoral Psychology*, 30 (1981), 113–21. K. J. Kaplan and M. Kaplan, "Covenant Versus Contract as Two Modes of Relationship Orientation," *J. of Psychology and Judaism*, 4/2 (1979), 100–16. K. Menninger, *Theory of Psychoanalytic Technique* (1958), ch. 2. W. B. Oglesby, Jr., *Biblical Themes for Pastoral Care* (1980), ch. 2.

W. B. OGLESBY, JR.

COMMITMENT; LEGAL DIMENSIONS OF PASTORAL CARE AND COUNSELING; PROMISING; RESPONSIBILITY/ IRRESPONSIBILITY, PSYCHOLOGY OF; TRUST. *See also* CONFIDENTIALITY; FEES IN PASTORAL COUNSELING; LIMIT-SETTING IN PASTORAL CARE AND COUNSELING; STRUCTURING.

COVENANT GROUPS. *See* GROWTH GROUPS.

COVETOUSNESS. *See* AVARICE AND GENEROSITY.

CPE. *See* CLINICAL PASTORAL EDUCATION.

CPI (California Psychological Inventory). *See* EVALUATION DIAGNOSIS, PSYCHOLOGICAL.

CRAZINESS. *See* PSYCHOSIS.

CREATION, DOCTRINE OF AND PASTORAL CARE.

This topic may be defined as the relationship between theology and methods of practical ministry arising from the doctrine that God has made all that is, and that all that God has made is good in some fundamental sense (despite the mysterious presence of evil in the natural order), especially as God uses the good creation in our salvation.

We may be grateful heirs of the Reformation for this reason: that through the centuries we have continued to proclaim the heart of the gospel message, namely, that in Jesus Christ all people can, without merit, find salvation. But we frequently fail to realize that this salvation encompasses the whole of humanity, indeed, the whole of creation. In other words, we have not always connected the doctrine of salvation with the doctrine of creation.

1. The Broken Link Between Creation and Care.
The Dutch professor of practical theology Heitink (1977, p. 111) declares that the human being as sinner has completely eclipsed the human being as creature. As a result, everything uttered about the human way of being is governed by and confined between the poles of sin and grace. Between these two poles "spiritual life," as distinct from "daily life," runs its course. This is where pastoral care comes in, in the guise of "spiritual care," operating between the poles of confession and absolution. Such an approach in fact reduces the gospel and restricts both our concept of humanity and our ministry.

We realize how far-reaching the matter is when we consider our picture of Jesus. The Dutch systematic theologian Hendrikus Berkhof vividly makes the point: how strange it is that "while innumerable people through the centuries have first of all been fascinated and gripped by the picture which the evangelists draw of the earthly Jesus, the study of the faith has for centuries hardly shown any interest in the life of Jesus" (1979, p. 293). Just so, in the Creed we simply skip from "born" to "suffered," as if in the interval there had been no noteworthy events involving Jesus. And yet, without the life of Jesus both cross and exaltation would hang suspended in midair.

Elsewhere Berkhof (p. 322) has indicated how the relationship between the Holy Spirit and creation has been similarly overlooked. The Spirit's work is in effect limited to the personal (spiritual!) life of the Christian, whereas truly scriptural thought would trace his steps throughout the created world.

2. Reforging the Link Through the Sciences. To begin anew to view the doctrine of salvation in conjunction with the doctrine of creation would have major implications for pastoral care. It would certainly mean, first, that pastoral theologians would not object in principle to finding out what the human and social sciences have to teach us about human beings. Unfortunately some Christians and Christian counselors still have grave objections to such cross-influencing, because they fear that these other sciences might usurp (practical) theology. Both Catholic and, to a lesser extent, Protestant tradition have clung to the idea denoted by the term "general revelation," a revelation implicit in God's relation to creation, that all people can experience everywhere at all times. Traditionally this level of revelation has remained secondary to the revelation of God in Jesus Christ, and, especially in conservative Protestant theology, care has been taken lest a door be opened to "natural theology" or a naturalizing of grace.

It is very interesting, however, that Karl Barth (who flatly rejected the doctrine of *analogia entis* in this connection) nevertheless tries to assign a proper place to "profane humanity" in the last part of his discussion of reconciliation, when he guardedly describes the "other words" from *extra muros ecclesiae* as "true words" and "parables of the kingdom" (1935, IV/3, pp. 122, 128).

Pastoral theology naturally concerns itself with special revelation (salvation), but must also take account of God's general revelation (creation). Pastoral theology would be foolhardy not to learn what it can from the other sciences. Of course it would be even more foolish to forfeit its theological character in the process.

3. Placing Fellow Creatures in Pastoral Relationship Under God. Giving full recognition to both creation *and* salvation might also help us to resolve the dilemma of what Riess calls kerygmatic counseling as opposed to partner-centered pastoral counseling (1973, pp. 153, 186). Kerygmatic counseling has the commendable purpose of proclaiming the message of salvation to the individual in the counseling situation. The danger is that it may lose sight of the fact that the counselor is a creature, a human being. Besides the fact that in the NT the word "proclaim" encompasses so much more than just a person who knows informing another who desires to know, the unique circumstances and background of the other person must be borne in mind: the gospel is communicated only through dialogue, a dialogue that entails an encounter and an experience. Only when the counselee experiences the counselor as a fellow pilgrim can the counselee find help. Pastoral care must have due regard for both the gospel and the human recipient of its message. On the other hand, emphasis on creation discourages the counselee in partner-centered counseling from dominating to such an extent that only the human remains, and God is pushed out altogether. This would imply that creation has no need of redemption.

4. Creation That Groans in Travail. *a. Redemption of all creation.* Redemption means that *creation* must be redeemed. It is tragic that Christians should have believed for so long that redemption means not the salvation *of* the world, but salvation *from* the world. In the NT (especially in the synoptic Gospels) salvation is very closely associated with the Kingdom of God and brings deliverance in the broadest sense of the word. Verkuyl describes the Kingdom of God as the new dispensation that began with Christ, that will be consummated by him, and in which all relationships will be renewed: the relationship between God and humanity, but also the relations between individuals, nations, sexes, generations, and races (1976, p. 270). God's "kingdom" is "the restored creation." The glorified Lord is not only head of his church but also, and above all, Lord of all creation. Fortunately the reign of God has become increasingly focal in pastoral theology. Seitz writes that pastoral care continues and concentrates God's incarnation in human individuals and society; the vehicle is the church, Christ's body, and thus pastoral care is God's concern for men and women to achieve wholeness within the ambit of God's kingdom (1968, p. 292). Heitink maintains that the kingdom of God encompasses the whole of reality (p. 161). Pastoral care must reach the individual in his or her unique circumstances, in oppression by relentless structures, in personal weariness and strain; if not, it legitimizes the status quo, implies that creation has no need of salvation, and promotes individualization of religion.

b. Pastoral comfort and tragic reality. Although salvation includes the whole of creation, it will not be realized finally until the dawn of the *new* creation. For this reason, the pastoral counselor continually has to deal with "those situations that as total situations cannot be changed, or at least cannot be changed at this time" (Hiltner, 1958, p. 116). In such situations pastoral care will have to proffer something accorded great emphasis in Scripture — comfort.

What does that mean? One thing it does not mean is the solution of all problems. In the past the church has been far too ready with answers. Berkhof puts this very aptly: the doctrine of faith has always explained the presence of suffering and death in God's good creation and the struggle for life in nature as the wages of sin (p. 170). It was taken for granted that the good creation was the equivalent of the static Greek ideal of perfection, which did not allow for such dissonances; and that these latter were brought about by the great cataclysm of sin. It followed that these things were a punishment in which humanity had to acquiesce. We now know, however, (in view of the chronology of fossils) that strife, suffering, death, and natural catastrophes existed millions of years *before* the appearance of *homo sapiens.* Thus we have to admit to a tragic element in creation, to much sorrow for which no one can be blamed, to much affliction that no one can efface. What we cannot do is to explain it. It would seem that God never intended to call into existence a ready-made and complete world, but that creation must pass through a history of resistance and struggle, suffering and dying.

Therefore comfort in this context does not mean escape from reality. It aims rather to help men and women to accept the brokenness of creation as part of existence, at the same time that they resist and radically modify the human lot. In the end, however, there must always be the realization that God will one day inaugurate a new creation. The Christian faith propounds eschatology.

5. At Once Both Sinful and Justified. Rather than denying human sinfulness, the previous point actually emphasizes it. Sin is no deplorable error of distant forebears, not a lot imposed from without, but a deeply rooted flaw in the creaturely structure of human beings, rendering them guilty. Consequently, anyone who works with a person in this created order is working with (and is) a sinner.

When one deals with fallen human nature, however, one is dealing not only with a sinner but also with someone innately oriented to God, created in God's image and likeness, and called to become so more and more (Col. 3:10). Apparently Genesis 1 would have us know that whereas the gods cannot be compared with Yahweh, people can (König, 1982, pp. 102–10). Pastoral care aims to realize this likeness — to mention but one example — to teach us to forgive one another *as God* in Christ forgave us (Eph. 4:32). It also quite definitely means that true human nature is to be found in relationship to God, and that we achieve self-actualization only in realizing this relationship. Anyone who fails to recognize this works against the interests of humanity.

One can never speak of creation and the creature without mentioning Christ. He stands at the beginning and end of history. He is the first-born of creation (Col. 1:15), the true person in the image of God, human as God intended us all to be. Berkhof remarks that we find Jesus' humanity difficult to grasp: it is a solitary presence in our human world, an example that we do not follow and consequently an indictment of our brand of humanity; but also an invitation to something far better that God has in mind for us. Jesus is the foretaste and promise of the new humanity (p. 298).

Pastoral care functions on the assumption that this creation belongs to God; that God's kingdom already is dawning among us; that the humanity exemplified by Jesus can break through in the lives of people and triumph on our planet; that in Jesus the fulfilment of it all is firm and secure. He, the first-born of creation, who has given us the first fruits of the Spirit (Rom. 8:23), is the guarantee that in the fulness of time the ripened fields will be harvested in the new creation.

Bibliography. K. Barth, *Die Kirchliche Dogmatik,* IV/3 (1935). H. Berkhof, *Christian Faith* (1979). G. Heitink, *Pastoraat als Hulpverlening* (1977). S. Hiltner, *Preface to Pastoral Theology* (1958). A. König, *Here Am I!* (1982). R. Riess, *Seelsorge* (1973). M. Seitz, "Exemplarische Seelsorge," in R. Bohren, ed., *Wort und Gemeinde (Festschrift für E. Thurneysen)* (1968). J. Verkuyl, *Inleiding in de nieuwere Zendingwetenschap* (1976).

M. JANSON

CHRISTOLOGY; ESCHATOLOGY; GOD; NATURE AND GRACE; PERSON; PROVIDENCE; SALVATION; SIN/SINS. *See also* NEO-ORTHODOX THEOLOGY AND PASTORAL CARE. *Compare* EVIL.

CREATIVITY. *See* IMAGINATION.

CREMATION. Disposition of a dead body by incineration. Frequently the term cremation is used to describe a more general pattern of post-death activities which includes immediate disposition of the body without embalming or other preparation, without ritualization or public participation.

1. Counseling Families. Cremation involves several pastoral opportunities. One is counseling with families who are considering cremation, assisting them in exploring and evaluating their motivation. Religious questions may be involved. Except for very conservative Protestants and orthodox or conservative Jews, there are no theological objections to cremation. Most churches are permissive. Recent revisions of Roman Catholic canon law have removed the church's objections to cremation.

a. Positive motives. These motives for planning cremation are aesthetic, social, or economic. Some persons prefer the swift, clean process of incineration to the slower natural process of decomposition. Some individuals prefer cremation as a means of land conservation. Still others see cremation as a way of reducing costs associated with the preparation of the body.

b. Counterproductive motives. Other motives, particularly those associated with the speedy disposition of the body, may in some instances be questionable because they do not contribute to effective mourning. Where there is effective emotional realization of the fact of death and the finality of its consequences for relationships, immediate cremation poses no problem. But where primary intention is to avoid contact with the body of the deceased, to escape personal involvement in formal post-death activities, to truncate the pattern of mourning customs and rituals, or to avoid public sharing of feelings of loss, there is an unwillingness to undertake the grief work associated with death.

2. **Pastoral Rituals.** The second pastoral opportunity is the conducting of a funeral or memorial service. Where immediate cremation is carried out, a public service of worship may be arranged later. In other instances a funeral may be conducted in the customary fashion with the committal service modified. If possible the pastor and family should accompany the body to the crematory. Families have commented that a committal service at the crematory provides a sense of fitting separation from the deceased rather than having the feeling that they did not carry through the entire mortuary process.

3. **Committal of Ashes.** A further pastoral opportunity involves the final disposition of the ashes following cremation. Some families will elect not to reclaim the ashes but to leave their disposition to the crematory or funeral home. Others will purchase an urn for placement in a columbarium. Alternatively, the ashes may be interred in a family burial plot, or the family may prefer to strew the ashes at some location of special meaning for them. In some areas commercial services will strew the ashes at sea. Whenever possible, the pastor should offer to participate in the final disposition of the ashes, providing closure in a worship setting of commendation and committal.

Bibliography. P. E. Irion, *Cremation* (1968). C. J. Polson, R. P. Brittain, and T. K. Marshall, *The Disposal of the Dead* 3d ed. (1975).

P. E. IRION

FUNERAL; MEMORIAL SERVICE. *See also* DEATH, MEANING OF; MEMORIAL SOCIETY; PERSON. *Compare* BURIAL; FUNERAL AND BURIAL, JEWISH.

CRIMINAL AND ANTISOCIAL BEHAVIOR. *See* ANTISOCIAL PERSONS; DEVIANT BEHAVIOR.

CRIPPLED PERSONS. *See* HANDICAP AND DISABILITY. *See also* LOSS OF FUNCTION; NEUROLOGIC ILLNESSES.

CRISIS, DEVELOPMENTAL. The disruption of life by expected, as contrasted with unexpected, happenings. The birth of a child and retirement are examples of developmental crises while automobile accidents or cancer are examples of accidental crises. Persons can prepare for developmental crises by looking ahead and planning ways of dealing with anticipated changes; such preparation can be facilitated by growth groups and educational opportunities.

H. N. MALONY

DEVELOPMENT, CONCEPT OF; LIFE CYCLE THEORY; PERSONALITY DEVELOPMENT. *See also* GROWTH GROUPS; SUPPORT GROUPS.

CRISIS INTERVENTION THEORY. A practical theory that can be implemented by sensitized laypersons or by professional clergy and mental health workers of any theoretical persuasion. Crisis intervention theory (CIT) involves five sequential steps.

1. **Understanding Crisis as Homeostatic Upset.** A crisis is an upset in homeostasis. CIT has as its basic proposition that each person develops a certain homeostasis in his or her life. This basic stance toward life may reflect a relatively high level of functioning or a low level of functioning. In CIT the level of functioning is less important than the homeostatic nature of the basic stance toward life. As long as the homeostasis is not disturbed, there will be no crisis (although there may be lifestyle dissatisfaction). Consequently a person functioning at a high level of adaptive behaviors may have a crisis in his or her life; a person functioning at a low level of adaptive behaviors, for example, a chronic neurotic, may also have a crisis in his or her life.

2. **Recognizing the Kind of Imbalance.** In order to accomplish long-term stabilization it is necessary to identify both the kind of and the deeper source of the homeostatic imbalance. That there is a homeostatic imbalance will be evidenced by the onset or intensification of emotional distress (anxiety, depression, guilt or anger) or disorientation. The crisis intervention counselor will find that the various kinds of emotional distress or disorientation have their source in one of four dimensions. (1) In the *intrapersonal* dimension the source is within the individual and arises from the individual's inability to cope with his or her own cognitive, emotional, or behavioral impulses. (2) In the *interpersonal* dimension the source is the individual's relationship(s) with others and arises from the individual's inability to enter into constructive problem solving with others or from communicative dysfunction within the relationship. (3) In the *physical* dimension the source is the individual's health and arises from the individual's inability to cope with life-threatening or chronic illness, or physical malfunction. (4) In the *spiritual* dimension the source is the individual's response to God or the religious community and arises from the individual's inability to respond to the redemptive message. It is important to note that while elements of all four dimensions generally are present, one dimension typically predominates, and that one would be identified as the principal source of the homeostatic imbalance and thus its basic kind or character.

3. Recognizing the Cause of the Crisis. In order to bring relief to the immediate crisis it is necessary to identify the immediate or precipitating cause of the homeostatic imbalance, which usually comes from one of three situations. (1) A *loss of support,* when the person experiences a real or imagined loss of someone or something with whom he or she has established very close emotional ties. While this would generally be a family member, it could be a pet or a national or religious leader. (2) A *loss of control,* when the person experiences a sense of helplessness and powerlessnesss in the face of what is perceived as an overwhelming threat or a set of impossible demands. (3) A *new or unique situation,* when the person is confronted with a situation that calls for adaptive behaviors that he or she has not yet had opportunity to develop. This category includes new situations, such as an occupational change, or previously experienced situations in a new environment, such as moving into a new home.

4. Achieving Short-Term Stabilization. According to CIT, by the time the crisis counselor has identified the kind and cause of the crisis, short-term stabilization has begun. This is accomplished through the development of a model to help the person understand the cause and cure of the current crisis. The model of understanding develops as the crisis counselor coaches or facilitates the person's understanding of his or her current situation and, through understanding and support, begins to develop a sense of regained control over his or her life. The model of understanding is then used as the beginning point to help the person generate a program for long-term stabilization that will seek to remedy the problems identified as the source and cause of the homeostatic imbalance.

5. Achieving Long-Term Stabilization. Long-term stabilization results as the crisis counselor supports the person through the program for long-term stabilization. This program may include legal, medical, psychological, or pastoral counseling and intervention.

Bibliography. R. Edwards, *The ABC Method of Crisis Intervention Counseling* (1973). A. Freedman, H. Kaplan, and B. Sadock, *Comprehensive Textbook of Psychiatry* 2d ed. (1975). H. Parad, *Crisis Intervention: Selected Readings* (1965). R. Pavelsky, *Proposal for the Development of a Crisis Service at Circle City Hospital* (1979).

R. L. PAVELSKY

CRISIS MINISTRY. *See also* EMERGENCY, PSYCHOLOGY OF PASTOR IN; GUIDANCE, PASTORAL; PASTORAL INITIATIVE AND INTERVENTION; THEORY IN PASTORAL CARE AND COUNSELING, FUNCTIONS OF. *Compare* CYBERNETIC THEORY IN PSYCHOLOGY AND COUNSELING; HOT LINE CRISIS MINISTRIES; RAPE COUNSELING.

CRISIS MINISTRY. Within the Judeo-Christian tradition crisis ministry has been generally understood as the caring response of the people of God to persons experiencing distress because of disruptive events and relationships. Disruptive events may be situational in that they involve the intrusion of circumstances by accident or unexpected changes in the life situation of the persons involved, or they may be developmental in that they are related to transitions in the life cycle of individuals or families. Ministry here refers both to the ministry of the laity as well as of ordained persons in the exercise of their representative and symbolic roles.

The role of religious ministry in crisis situations has a long history in the Judeo-Christian tradition. The Book of Psalms has a preponderance of psalms of either individual or communal lament prompted by times of crisis. Likewise, as J. T. McNeill states, "The prophets were the crisis theologians of their era" (1951, p. 11).

William Clebsch and Charles Jaekle identify four functions which pastoral care in the Christian churches has served: healing, sustaining, guiding, and reconciling.

In the American Protestant religious experience of the seventeenth and eighteenth centuries, the religious and therefore ministry dimensions of crisis experience tended to take on the more narrowly spiritual focus of the life of the troubled soul. The minister as recognized expert in matters related to the activity of God and of satanic powers in the struggles of the soul, was called upon to exercise an active ministry of persuasion designed to convince troubled persons of the truth and applicability of the gospel for their situation. In this period "crisis" could include both unusual stress in the life of the soul and crucial or critical spiritual issues in relation to salvation.

With the coming of the modern period in pastoral care and counseling, crisis ministry began to deal with the more psychologically understood meaning of developmental crises and adaptational crises, and situations of personal and family crisis precipitated by some event that disrupts the normal flow of life. Specializations in crisis ministry began to develop in the 1930s and 1940s, with some pastors developing crisis ministries in medical and surgical hospitals focused on the care of persons undergoing physical illness and death, or with critical mental and emotional illness. *The Art of Ministering to the Sick* (1936) by Russell L. Dicks and Richard Cabot, was an important landmark in establishing the role of pastoral ministry in the care of the physically ill. Anton Boisen's work as a mental hospital chaplain, culminating in his *Exploration of the Inner World* (1936), opened the way to a specialized crisis ministry with the mentally ill. Parish pastors likewise focused on their one-to-one ministry with parishioners suffering from these crucial life experiences.

In this changing cultural context, which was strongly shaped by the impact of psychological and psychotherapeutic ways of considering personal and family crises, the focus for crisis ministry likewise took a psychological turn. The more specifically spiritual or religious dimensions and concerns inherently present in human crisis continued to provide an underlying structure of symbolic meaning and ultimate significance for critical events and even developmental transitions. But the more immediate occasion for ministry began to be seen in more psychological and relational terms. In brief, pastoral crisis ministry became adapted to the society and its culture. The new forms of crisis ministry and the theory that undergirded them were shaped to fulfill psychologically structured goals of support, assurance of care for others and attention to personal meanings and feelings concerning events and relationships. Theologically grounded goals for crisis ministry began to be correlated with psychologically informed purposes.

Recent developments in crisis ministry theory in situations of death and dying provide a significant example of the predominance of psychologically conceived purpose in much of the practice of crisis ministry in the modern situation. The influential work of Elisabeth Kübler-Ross and others represented a primarily psychological interest in the care of persons undergoing terminal illnesses. An often rudimentary correlation is made between this psychological purpose and a more theological intention to communicate and represent the supportive presence of God with the sufferer, i.e., God does not abandon the dying person in his or her death.

In the modern period, the pastoral care of persons whose crisis involves death and bereavement has often become paradigmatic for all crisis ministry. Death is in many ways the ultimate form of crisis in human finite life. The crisis of living toward death or recovery from loss by bereavement has generally been found by researchers such as Kübler-Ross to involve a series of stages or intertwining themes. Thus death and grief ministry can be conceived in terms of shepherding a time-bound process through identifiable stages moving either toward acceptance of death or recovery from grief.

Kübler-Ross identified five stages in the process of coming to acceptance of one's own death, namely, denial and isolation, anger, bargaining, depression and acceptance. By contrast, other theorists, such as Gerkin (1979) and E. S. Shneidman (1976) propose a set of interlocking themes or alternating states of consciousness that vacillate between denial and acceptance accompanied by varying degrees of exploration of the meaning of one's own death. Y. Spiegel (1977) posits four stages in the bereavement process: shock, control, regression, and adaptation. D. K. Switzer (1970) suggests a six-stage process in grief: shock, numbing, struggle between fantasy and reality, breakthrough of grief, selective memory and pain, and finally, acceptance of loss and affirmation of life.

For all these theorists, the caring response in crises related to the death of a loved one consists in sensitive location of the person at some point in the process of dying or grief, accompanied by a supportive and accepting relationship that encourages the working through of grief and anxiety.

This ministry has provided paradigms for other common human experiences involving loss, such as divorce, vocational transition such as job loss or failure, retirement, and dislocation related to job changes, as well as crises which may also result in similar grief manifestations. As with bereavement, these crises tend to be more or less time-bound. Even developmental crises such as the transition from adolescence to adulthood or the mid-life crisis are understood by some theorists in ways akin to the crisis of bereavement. Crises such as acute marital conflict or intergenerational conflict in families are also often presented to the helping professional as temporary, acute, and perhaps amenable to short-term intervention.

The notion of crisis ministry as involving a time-bound intensive effort to assist persons in working through a temporary period of particular stress received a further impetus from another development in the secular helping professions. In the 1960s the presence of large numbers of persons seeking help from secular agencies and practitioners of the helping professions in an increasingly urbanized society prompted a search for time-limited approaches to human problem solving. From these efforts came a cluster of methodologies that has come to be known as crisis intervention theory.

The concept of crisis intervention was first proposed as a short-term therapeutic response to personal and family crises by psychiatrists Gerald Caplan and Erich Lindemann. A crisis, according to Lindemann's theory, refers to any event or situation occurring in the life of an individual or family that interrupts the homeostatic balance and thus creates a situation in which "the habitual problem-solving activities are not adequate and do not lead rapidly to the previously achieved balanced state" (Parad, p. 21).

Consequently, the purpose of crisis intervention becomes that of relating to the person(s) in a crisis to restore the previous balance and habitual patterns of coping with life problems as expeditiously as possible. Using that frame of reference, some pastoral care theoreticians have proposed that pastoral crisis ministry should embrace similar goals and their concomitant methodologies. Both D. W. Switzer (1974) and H. K. Stone (1976) incorporate this form of crisis intervention theory into their proposals for a relatively simple "ABC method" of crisis pastoral counseling. The method employs three basic steps: (1) Achieving contact and a relationship of trust with the person(s) involved in the crisis. (2) Boiling down the problem to its essentials by focusing on the present situation, the source of the stress, and attempting to identify the nature of the threat to the individual(s). (3) Assisting the person(s) under stress to cope actively with the problem (Switzer, pp. 88–101; Stone, pp. 32–48). When the person is again able to utilize customary coping mechanisms to cope with the crisis situation, the pastoral counselor withdraws from the situation which has then become stabilized.

Other pastoral care theorists, most notably C. V. Gerkin (1979) have, however, questioned on both psychological and, more forcefully, on theological grounds, the adequacy of crisis intervention theory as a theoretical base for pastoral crisis ministry. Pastoral response to crisis situations in individuals and families must be informed not only by a psychological theory of crisis experience that relates what is experienced in crisis to the ongoing growth and maturation of the person, but also by a theology of ministry in crisis situations that incorporates a theological understanding of human crises. As the theologian Carl Michaelson proposed, crises are crucial situations that plumb three levels of human concern that involve faith and doubt. A crucial situation is "an inescapable situation requiring decision," a situation in which "it is being determined whether one will live or die," and a "momentous" situation in that "there is in it a dimension of ultimate significance." Pastoral concern needs therefore to move beneath and beyond the level of resolution of practical crisis problems and the restoration of persons to their state of life prior to the crisis-precipitating event. Crisis events, whether developmental or situational in origin, contain implications concerning the most profound questions of meaning and religious faith. Human finitude and vulnerability before the contingencies of disease, accident, and death, as well as human frailty and failure in relationships and purposes are made most apparent and experientially visible in times of crisis. Ultimate questions become immediate and existential in times of such crises as life-threatening illness or bereavement, acute marital crisis, or family disorganization. Pastoral response to crisis needs therefore to attend to these ultimate dimensions of crisis experience in order that ministry may both respond to spoken and unarticulated questions of meaning and open the way for exploration of the connections between experienced crisis and the experiences of faith and doubt.

Crisis experience from this perspective evokes in critical ways questions concerning the presence or absence of God in the concreteness of human finite life. Likewise, crisis experience evokes questions concerning the meaning of suffering, the ultimate grounding for human hope even in apparently hopeless situations, and the reality of forgiveness for human participation in the causation of crisis events. Thus crisis experience evokes fundamental questions of faith, and crisis ministry has as its central focus and purpose the intention of responding to these questions in whatever form they may be explicitly or more indirectly presented by persons in the crisis situation.

Theologically, a crisis situation may be defined as any human experience in which one encounters the fundamental questions of the meaning of life, its finite boundaries and limits, and its basic vulnerability. Crisis ministry, seen theologically, concerns itself with the response of the people of God to those experiences. The theologically defined purpose of crisis ministry has to do not only with the restoration of persons to the ordinary flow of crisis experience, but with the transformation of life in harmony with God's purposes. Hope and expectation thus become key ingredients in the stance of ministry in crisis, as does openness to the reality of suffering which crisis experience entails.

To embrace a theologically defined purpose for crisis ministry underscores yet another important element in crisis ministry with significant psychological as well as broader hermeneutical implications. It suggests the pastoral responsibility to attend carefully to the particularities of the crisis experience both in terms of their psychological and life process dynamics and in terms of their meaning. A given crisis event may be expected both to have widely varying and highly nuanced meanings to different persons, and involve highly particular psychological dynamic implications and reverberations. Crisis ministry at its best thus demands a highly sensitive and nuanced response on the part of the pastor that emerges from a careful interpretation of both the meaning issues that the event symbolizes for the person and the psychological impact of the event, given the particular personality, socio-economic situation, and family dynamics of persons involved. Here the techniques suggested by crisis intervention theory need to be enriched by the skills and practical theological knowledge of the pastor as hermeneutical guide and interpreter.

Pastoral crisis ministry likewise entails the pastor's full use of the sacramental and other ritually symbolic resources of the Christian community and tradition. In certain situations the appropriate and sensitive sharing of Scripture and prayer, along with use of other symbolic religious language can have powerful supportive meaning and help the crisis victim place the crisis experience in a context of faith seeking understanding. Ritual and sacramental practices need, of course, to be carried out in ways that comport with the desires and affirmed meanings understood by the persons in the crisis.

Beyond his or her own pastoral work, the pastor's crisis ministry also includes exercising facilitating leadership in equipping and enabling the ministry of the laity in community expressions of support and concern for those undergoing crisis. Pastoral leadership here has several important dimensions: (1) The pastor, through preaching, teaching, and his or her own example, can sensitize and stimulate a congregation to the value and opportunities for a caring ministry of lay persons for fellow parishioners and others undergoing the ordinary crises of life. (2) Educational programs may be developed that inform congregants as to what sorts of acts, gestures of concern, and ways of relating are truly helpful to persons in various kinds of crisis. (3) Organizational leadership that facilitates the caring ministry of lay people, e.g., by organizing existing lay groups such as church school classes, adult women's, men's, and youth groups for intentional crisis support ministries or, on occasion, the development of informally structured groups of persons within the congregation who share particular forms of crisis (widowhood, divorce, common illnesses such as cancer or heart disease, or early retirement, etc.).

Crisis ministry is in many respects the most crucial aspect of a pastor's care and counseling work. Its function is deeply rooted in the Judeo-Christian tradition concerning the care of persons in times of distress. Its practice calls upon the pastor to exercise a broad range of skills, from careful socio-cultural, psychological, and hermeneutical analysis to sensitive theological and ethical reflection. It engages the pastor both in close personal encounter with persons at crucial times in their lives and in exercising the skills of leadership and sensitization of the laity as they fulfill their ministry as members of the body of Christ. Crisis ministry tests the capacity of the Christian community and its ordained representatives to fulfill their calling to "bear one another's burdens and so fulfill the law of Christ" (Gal. 6:2).

Bibliography. A. Boisen, *Exploration of the Inner World* (1936). W. A. Clebsch and C. R. Jaekle, *Pastoral Care in Historical Perspective* (1964). R. L. Dicks, *The Art of Ministering to the Sick* (1936). C. V. Gerkin, *Crisis Experience in Modern Life: Theory and Theology for Modern Life* (1979). E. Kübler-Ross, *On Death and Dying* (1969). E. Lindemann, "Symptomology and Management of Acute Grief," *The American J. of Psychiatry*, Sept. (1944). J. T. McNeill, *A History of the Cure of Souls* (1951). C. Michaelson, *Faith for Personal Crises* (1958). D. M. Moss III, "Near-Fatal Experience, Crisis Intervention and the Anniversary Reaction," *Pastoral Psychology*, 28 (1979), 75–96. H. J. Parad, ed., *Crisis Intervention: Selected Readings* (1965). E. S. Shneidman, *Death: Current Perspectives* (1976). Y. Spiegel, *The Grief Process* (1977). H. K. Stone, *Crisis Counseling* (1976). D. K. Switzer, *The Minister as Crisis Counselor* (1974).

C. V. GERKIN

JEWISH CARE AND COUNSELING; PASTORAL CARE (Contemporary Methods, Perspectives, and Issues). *See also* COMFORT/SUSTAINING;

DISASTER, PUBLIC; EMERGENCY, PSYCHOLOGY OF PASTOR IN; EVALUATION AND DIAGNOSIS, PSYCHOLOGICAL; GUIDANCE, PASTORAL; HOT-LINE CRISIS MINISTRIES; REFERRAL; TRAUMA. *Compare* DIVORCE (Care and Counseling); DYING; FAMILY VIOLENCE; GRIEF AND LOSS; MARRIAGE COUNSELING; MENTAL HEALTH AND ILLNESS; RAPE AND RAPE COUNSELING; SICK, PASTORAL CARE OF; VICTIMIZATION.

CRISIS, PUBLIC. *See* DISASTER, PUBLIC.

CRITICAL THEORY. The thought of the Frankfurt School, a movement of social and philosophical reflection originating in Germany in the 1920s. In opposition to the predominant positivist theories of science which would have reduced all knowledge to the ordering of "objective" data, the Frankfurt School sought to reinstate the role of praxis and the imagination.

The critical theorists held that to make room for such creative activity, one must dispel the popular myths, the oppressive common sense, of the dominant social order. For assistance in this effort, the Frankfurt School turned to the works of Marx and Freud. This decision may seem paradoxical, since these two "masters of suspicion" are commonly dismissed as being reductionistic themselves; but members of the School were at pains to show that the seemingly more attractive theories which sought to replace Marx and Freud generally boiled down to adaptationist positions, that is, arguments for fitting in, which subtly reinforced the status quo. As an alternative, the School urged that the (apparent) materialism of the earlier thinkers be appropriated as a penetrating critique of the ideologies or idealizations which served to cover over the *actual, functional* reductionism of the dominant social order. Thus critical theory sought to bring together the classical theories of Marx and Freud, just as in its concrete research it undertook to reintegrate the often isolated disciplines of psychology and sociology.

Historically, the School was deeply affected by the experience of fleeing Nazi Germany in 1933 and settling for a period in the U.S., where Erich Fromm and Herbert Marcuse became widely known. Fromm gradually distanced himself from the group, yet he retained the characteristic project of reconciling Freud and Marx. Marcuse was adopted in the 1960s as a symbol of social protest. His thought, often oversimplified by opponents and advocates alike, is represented by *Eros and Civilization* (1955) and *One-Dimensional Man* (1964). However, the core of the School's ongoing work must be sought in the writings of Max Horkheimer and Theodor Adorno: examples are their *Dialectic of Enlightenment* (1972) and Adorno's difficult, but magisterial *Negative Dialectics* (1973).

While Horkheimer and Adorno are sometimes faulted for being relentlessly negative, some recent critical theorists have argued that human praxis has an inherently positive orientation toward hope and liberation. Jürgen Habermas has powerfully renewed critical thought by reformulating it in terms of a comprehensive theory of human self-reflection and communication (*Knowledge and Human Interests,* 1971). In theology, Horkheimer's stress upon the disruptive significance of the memory of past suffering has influenced Jürgen Moltmann (*Crucified God,* 1974) and Johann Baptist Metz (*Faith in History and*

Society, 1980). Aspects of critical theory may be seen in much of current liberation theology.

Bibliography. T. W. Adorno, *Negative Dialectics* (1973). T. W. Adorno and M. Horkheimer, *Dialectics of Enlightenment* (1972). A. Arato, ed., *Essential Frankfurt School Reader* (1978). J. Habermas, *Knowledge and Human Interests* (1971). D. Held, *Introduction to Critical Theory* (1980). R. Jacoby, *Social Amnesia* (1975). M. Jay, *Dialectical Imagination* (1973). M. Lamb, *Solidarity With Victims* (1982). W. Lowe, *Evil and the Unconscious* (1983). H. Marcuse, *Eros and Civilization* (1955); *One-Dimensional Man* (1964). J. B. Metz, *Faith in History and Society* (1980). J. Moltmann, *Crucified God* (ET 1974). T. Schroyer, *Critique of Domination* (1973).

W. J. LOWE

THEORY AND PRAXIS. *See also* PHILOSOPHY AND PSYCHOLOGY; SOCIOLOGY OF RELIGIOUS AND PASTORAL CARE.

CROSS, SIGN OF. *See* SIGN OF THE CROSS.

CROSS, STATIONS OF. *See* SPIRITUALITY (Roman Catholic Tradition).

CROSS AND RESURRECTION. The juxtaposition of these central symbols of the Christian faith has special meaning in pastoral care and counseling, pointing both to its foundations in the person and work of Christ and to the ongoing dynamics of Christian life and suffering and care in his name.

1. As Signifying the Christological Foundations of Pastoral Care. There is only one difference between pastoral counseling and other forms of counseling, but it is a uniquely distinctive one. The difference is that pastoral counseling operates within the compass of the cross and resurrection of Jesus Christ. This means that it fulfills its function in the ambience of God, who in Christ lowered himself to the level of the cross, as Moltmann puts it, to the point where he became the crucified God. The implications are tremendous.

If he who is Lord could become obedient unto death (the cross), if human beings could be worthy of such an infinitely great ransom (I Cor. 6:20), then no counselor can merely hear out his or her counselee with clinical sensitivity, insight, and empathy. No: each person, and each person's special situation, must move him or her to action. After all, the cross has shown us the ghastly injustice that people (and their structures) can perpetrate in the lives of others, and can do so, moreover, with a semblance of law and righteousness, in the name of God, using religion and piety as instruments.

But, further, the cross reveals that humanity's most dire need does not lie in external circumstance but in itself, and offers a place where counselor and counselee alike can be radically and finally redeemed from guilt and sin (I Jn. 2:2) and may become truly free (Jn. 8:36).

But the cross was not the end. Through the resurrection God legitimized the life and passion of Jesus. The endless struggle to preserve life ends merely in losing it; but the resurrection tells us unequivocally that because Christ lives, we can venture to believe, knowing that what was begun in and through Jesus can never be stopped. God in Christ will triumph, even if we see nothing of that triumph as yet; even if we must still suffer and eventually die. For the believer this means being able to accept all that cannot be changed as yet, through the bounteous comfort of his passion and resurrection (II Cor. 1:3–11); at the same time it means that there is no need to acquiesce in anything at all anymore. We can rebel against things, radically change them, on the strength of Christ's resurrection; and if for the time being we still have to die, we know that death is a vanquished death which has been swallowed up in victory (I Cor. 15:54).

2. As Signifying Ongoing Themes in Pastoral Practice. The cross-resurrection symbol points also to a vital relationship that must be maintained in Christian life and in pastoral care and counseling, between several pairs of polar or dialectical opposites: fact and possibility, powerlessness and power, despair and hope, suffering and fulfillment, sin and forgiveness, failure and new beginnings. The symbol is rich with such meanings, and more could perhaps be elaborated. In each instance it seems important to maintain a balance or interaction between the opposing terms. Thus it is important not to lose sensitivity to the reality of evil and suffering in times of joy or fulfillment, and not to live as if one were beyond sin, suffering and limitation by virtue of, say, becoming Christian or experiencing deep therapeutic change. The juxtaposed symbols of cross and resurrection serve as a reminder of the ongoing complexity and unfinished quality of even the most worthy or successful lives, while at the same time pointing in faith to the unfathomable possibilities that lie beyond human power in the love and strength of God.

The cross-resurrection symbol is also frequently employed in contemporary pastoral care and counseling as a way of expressing the opposing tensions experienced in therapeutic change or transformation. The therapeutic client or counselee is said to undergo a kind of cross-resurrection struggle as old styles of personal subjectivity and behavior patterns die and new ones seek to come into being; dreams, for instance, may include cross and resurrection imagery in persons wrestling profoundly with themselves.

While cross and resurrection function as expressive metaphors in care and counseling, pointing to the ultimate significance of things experienced there, the symbolism can be used to sanctify tensions or dynamics that may not merit such interpretation and legitimation. All experiences of suffering are not necessarily cross-like — for example, sufferings one brings upon oneself in spite or self-pity as a means of manipulating others, etc. Similarly, some experiences of fulfillment and joy may be falsely based, for example on unjust social privilege, self-deception, or the superficial resolution of personal problems. The pastoral theological task is therefore to seek appropriate theological understanding of these symbols and to develop criteria for distinguishing their appropriate from their inappropriate uses in pastoral situations.

Bibliography. R. J. Hunter, "Moltmann's Theology of the Cross and the Dilemma of Contemporary Pastoral Care," in T. Runyon, ed., *Hope For the Church* (1979). J. Moltmann, *The Crucified God* (1974). W. E. Oates, *Pastoral Counseling* (1974).

R. J. HUNTER
M. JANSON

CHRISTOLOGY *or* ESCHATOLOGY AND PASTORAL CARE. *See also* HEAVEN AND HELL, BELIEF IN; HOPE AND DESPAIR; LIFE/ALIVENESS; SUFFERING. *Compare* HUMAN CONDITION/ PREDICAMENT.

CROSS-CULTURAL MARRIAGE AND FAMILY.

Marriage is a communally recognized and normatively prescribed relationship between at least two persons that designates economic and sexual rights and duties owed each to the other or others and provides the primary means in a society by which offspring are recognized as legitimate and accorded birth status rights.

Marriage, the contractual or covenantal relationship between a wife and a husband, is a cultural rather than an authentically universal human experience. Family, the collective body of persons who live in one household or descend from one common progenitor, is a widely varied human institution, occurring in such a diversity of forms that it is difficult to claim "family" as a universal. Yet all people live in relational networks. Family, as a concept, has little meaning in some cultures. There is not even a word for "family" in some parts of Latin America and Africa. In Botswana, the nearest equivalent word means "compound," the place where people live.

The family as a social ideal and basic unit of society in the West emerged with the creation of the middle class and the mobile nuclear family with a division of labor between husband, wife, and children. In other cultures and traditions there is the clan, the tribe, the dwelling unit, the community as more recognized units of human relationships.

1. Marriage and Family Across Cultures. Viewed cross-culturally, marriage is frequently a relationship between groups rather than just between individuals. Such an inter-family union exists beyond the life span of either partner. Marriage is not only a sexual, parental, social relationship, it is also an exchange which transfers rights and obligations between the contracting parties which are often political as well as economic. All societies have restrictions, taboos and boundaries which prohibit or permit certain unions. No society allows indiscriminate mating.

Marriage has highly varied definitions and forms. It may be predominantly an economic, political, tribal, civil, legal, romantic, religious, impulsive, reverent, heterosexual, homosexual, monogamous, polygamous, polyandrous, endogamous, exogamous, trial, serial, or experimental relationship. In all times and places people have explored the possibilities of marriage and its potential variations.

The three characteristics of marriage which are almost universal traditions are permanence, fidelity, and need-fulfillment, although these elements are expressed in such different ways in various cultures that variety is as noteworthy as commonality. In some cultures, permanence is stressed much more than need-fulfillment, in others fidelity is prized of one sex and optional of the other. The most striking contrasts are in the areas of expectations. In traditional cultures, expectations focus on the functional and are more easily fulfilled. In the West, expectations are inflated by social values of intentional and expressive rather than traditional marriage.

2. The Bicultural Marriage. The marriage of persons from different cultures demands that either person join the partner's culture in one-way adaptation or that both seek to be bicultural. Inevitably a third culture—a metaculture—is formed which both partners share. It is composed of elements from both cultures combined into a new construct. The pastoral therapist must be culturally capable of entering all three cultures with respect for and authentic contact with each of these worlds of experience. The therapeutic support of both persons and of the marriage—of all three cultures—requires that both persons be encouraged to sustain a clear cultural identity in their families of origin while achieving an intentional marriage with strong identifications.

In traditional marriage, central issues are familial loyalty, intergenerational obligations, and the duty of reproduction. Personal fulfillment and affectional needs are optional. In contemporary Western intentional marriage, personal fulfillment and affectional needs are central, and family loyalty, intergenerational obligations and the duty of reproduction are optional. The traditional marriage is a contract between families maintained by communal cohesion; the intentional marriage is a covenant between persons maintained by internal cohesion. In the first, tasks and roles are clearly defined, in the second they are negotiated and shared without socially fixed roles. Divorce in traditional communities is seen as a more communal event, but in intentional marriages divorce is seen more as an issue of mutual consent of the participants. Bicultural marriages inevitably must choose between mutually exclusive traditions or seek to incorporate elements of each in the creation of an intentional marriage without a dangerous discontinuity with either past.

The family as a system functions in recognizable patterns in any culture. The dynamics of union and separation in human relationship, of immature attachments and mature associations in the life cycle, and of absorption in another or abandonment of the other are present in all human networks. However, the assumptions about what is appropriate closeness and distance, dependence and interdependence, individuation or affiliation must be defined in contextually congruent ways. Marital or family therapy in a second culture requires keen awareness of the cultural context of the family system and of its dynamics within the larger system.

3. **A Theology of Paradox and Balance.** The theologically grounded pastoral counselor recognizes the paradoxical dimensions of all marriage and family relationships. These paradoxical elements include the worth of both person and group; the needs for independence and interdependence; the goals of conformity and diversity; the responsibility to both the previous generation and the present one; the concern for family security and safety for outer directed service; the private and personal and the public and communal nature of marriage; the biological as well as the spiritual family. A pastoral theology which recognizes the values in both elements of these poles of human wholeness will seek a balance appropriate to the culture's central values which refuses to sacrifice either the person or the group, the family security or the service to others, the vertical or the horizontal loyalties. Every culture contains skewed elements which oppress its members. The pastoral caregiver seeks not to change the culture from without, but to elicit change and evoke

transformation from within. The goal of pastoral therapy is not only immediate tension release in healing but long-term transformation toward greater wholeness, justice and humanness.

Bibliography. D. W. Augsburger, *Pastoral Counseling Across Cultures* (1986). D. Mace and V. Mace, *Marriage: East and West* (1960). M. McGoldrick, *et al.*, *Ethnicity and Family Therapy* (1982).

D. W. AUGSBURGER

CULTURAL AND ETHNIC FACTORS IN PASTORAL CARE; FAMILY; MARRIAGE. *See also* CATHOLIC-PROTESTANT MARRIAGE; JEWISH-CHRISTIAN MARRIAGE; ORTHODOX-CATHOLIC MARRIAGE; ORTHODOX-PROTESTANT MARRIAGE. *Compare* SOCIAL PERCEPTION, JUDGMENT, AND BELIEF; SOCIAL STATUS AND CLASS FACTORS IN PASTORAL CARE.

CROSS-CULTURAL PASTORAL CARE. Any pastoral ministry in which two or more of the participants, including the minister as helper, represent more than one culture. The key to working across cultures lies in recognizing personal bias. Cultural patterns that deviate from our own are neither better nor worse but are simply different. To appreciate differences instead of being disturbed by them lies at the heart of effective cross-cultural pastoral care. Moreover, the appreciation of distinctive differences opens the way to understanding rather than judgment, and so makes communication more possible.

Another essential is to avoid simplistic explanations. Note, for example, how inappropriate it is to speak simply of Japanese Americans without singling out Issei (Japan-born), Nisei (first-generation Americans, most of whom grew up in relocation camps), Sansei (second generation), and Yonsei (third generation). Even more inappropriate is to refer simply to Asians without distinguishing the many ethnic groupings that fall under this one classification.

Pastoral care across cultural lines calls for several distinctive approaches. In the first place, pastoral care as counseling is largely a Western, American experience. In most places in the world, other than the U.S., counseling is thought of as a family concern and is generally handled within the family. Often the best approach is to work indirectly through a family member, such as the older brother.

A second approach accents the place of community. Many cultures are community-centered rather than individual-centered. In Chinese culture, for example, it is the impact on the family rather than on the individual that is the major consideration.

A third approach calls for some kind of specific activity on the part of the helping person. It is not enough to listen sympathetically or even to be "present" in a genuine way. This is no place for a remote, uninvolved, "professional" stance. This is the place for warm, concerned caring demonstrated in specific acts. Seeking out the person or the family involved in a home is often more appropriate than waiting for the person in distress to ask for help.

A fourth approach involves the use of specifically religious resources. It is often in cross-cultural problems that the crucial significance of a religious orientation to life emerges. Many cultures give a more prominent place to religious faith than they do to psychological insight.

An unexpected dividend from working with persons of another culture is the light that is thrown on the differences found among people of the same culture. Differences in gender, or in age, or in social class, or in economic condition, all play important roles in pastoral work and need to be acknowledged.

Bibliography. D. W. Augsburger, *Pastoral Counseling Across Cultures* (1986). A. Dueck, "American Psychology in Cross-Cultural Context," *J. of Psychology and Theology*, 11 (1983), 172– 80. R. C. Leslie, "Counseling Across Cultures," Monograph #5, United Ministries in Higher Education (June, 1979). A. J. Marsella and P. B. Pedersen, eds., *Cross-Cultural Counseling and Psychotherapy* (1981). D. E. Wingeier, "The Ministry as Cross-Cultural Communication," *The Circuit Rider*, 3 (1979), 3–5.

R. C. LESLIE

CULTURAL AND ETHNIC FACTORS IN PASTORAL CARE. *See also* MISSIONARIES, PASTORAL CARE OF; SOCIAL PERCEPTION, JUDGMENT, AND BELIEF; SOCIOLOGY OF RELIGIOUS AND PASTORAL CARE. *Compare* ASIAN AMERICAN *or* BLACK AMERICAN *or* HISPANIC AMERICAN PASTORAL CARE; JEWISH CARE AND COUNSELING; NATIVE AMERICANS, PASTORAL CARE OF.

CRUELTY/SADISTIC BEHAVIOR. Actions which inflict pain and suffering; delight in another's suffering; getting sexual pleasure as the result of another's suffering; intent to gain power or favor from Satan or a satanic group by inflicting pain and suffering.

1. The Kinds Of Behaviors That Bring Suffering. These are varied and have many causes. For example: (1) Life's expectations are "mapped out" early in a child's life; these expectations are followed and further developed in subsequent years, until a major intervention alters the early mapping. When a child is told he or she is bad and is treated violently, for instance, violent behaviors will show up later in life. Violent or perverse sexual experiences in early life produce mapping which results in repeating these experiences when older. (2) There is a cycle that perpetuates victimization from generation to generation. When a teenage boy hurts or sodomizes a younger boy, the latter is likely to act out the same behavior a few years later with a younger child. The victim thus becomes the victimizer in order to decrease pent-up feelings left from the trauma experienced when he was the victim. (3) Child abusers have usually been abused themselves as children. The causes include modeling after the abusive parent, release of pent-up victimized feelings, and enactment of early mapping. (4) Some believe they will receive power or favor from Satan or a satanic group if they behave in the most malicious and horrible ways possible (see Pratney; Warnke). Killing animals and infants as sacrifices to Satan, and forcing preschool children to drink the blood and urine and eat the flesh and feces of these sacrifices, are examples of Satanic/ritualistic abuse. (See Passport Magazine, and J. Hossingsworth.)

2. Identifying Victims. This is where the pastoral counselor can be of immediate help if informed what to look for. (1) For adult victims of childhood cruelty or sadistic behavior, the memories of the events are often deeply repressed, and the client will begin to uncover the memories well after counseling has begun. Care must be taken when the repressed memories do emerge, because the client will usually go through a period of disorganization— from a few days to a few months—and may become suicidal. Support, encouragement, and a supportive social network are important during this time. (2) For many child victims the memories are also repressed. In addition, there are often threats to the life of the child, the family, or pets if the secret (the abusive behavior) is divulged. Some indicators pointing toward child abuse include: the child's relationships are extremely superficial; the child appears out of touch with reality; the child is self-destructive; the child may be intense or agitated; the child may fall behind in classwork because of sleepiness. If these indicators are present, it may be possible to inquire with an adult about physical symptoms, including vaginal discharge or bleeding, bedwetting (enuresis), "soiling" pants (encopresis), or excessive masturbation. Signs of Satanic/ritualistic abuse include the following: a preoccupation with blood, urine, and feces; candles and costumes appearing in the child's stories; dismemberment of animals and infants mentioned by the child; questions from the child about taking drugs; the child expresses fear of going to jail; the fear emerges that "bad people" (as Satanists often call themselves) will break into the house and kill the child or burn the house if the secrets are disclosed.

3. Counseling the Victims. Victimizers almost never seek treatment (see M. S. Peck).

Counseling with adult victims of childhood cruelty or sadistic behavior usually requires a substantial commitment of the counselor. It takes a lot of energy and the willingness to go at a slow pace to work with these people. If that commitment seems difficult, it would probably be better for the client to be referred to another counselor. The most important element in therapy is to establish trust, as these clients did not have trust built into their "maps" during formative years. Trust develops in the presence of a safe therapeutic relationship.

Treating child victims requires a counselor who specializes in child treatment. Here the counselor should tell the child to disregard threats and tell all secrets. It is important to get the child to disclose as much as possible, in order to get the agitated feelings healed.

Bibliography. "America's Best Kept Secret," *Passport Magazine*, *Special Report* (1986). J. Hollingsworth, *Unspeakable Acts* (1986). M. S. Peck, *People of the Lie* (1983). W. Pratney, *Devil Take the Youngest* (1985). M. Warnke, *The Satan Seller* (1972).

J. G. FRIESEN

AGGRESSION AND ASSERTION; ANTISOCIAL PERSONS; PERSONALITY DISORDERS; VIOLENCE. *See also* ANGER; DEVIANT BEHAVIOR, THEORY OF; PSYCHOPATHOLOGY, THEORIES OF; RAGE AND HOSTILITY; SOCIOPATHIC PERSONALITY.

CRYING. The expression of pain, grief, or distress by weeping and sobbing; shedding tears with or without making a sound.

Humans are the only creatures who weep, and the universality of tears would indicate a deep biological base. The cathartic effect of crying has long been known. Stress alters the chemical balance of the body and crying helps to restore balance by the excretion of these substances, e.g., catecholamines. Thus suppression of tears may lead to a variety of physical and psychological complaints and problems. The taboo against tears for males may contribute to their higher incidence of stress-related disorders.

Comments on the physical significance of tears, however, do not exhaust their meaning. Infants respond both to internal and external stimuli with tears, i.e., to pain, discomfort, fear. Later, children utilize "operant crying" to manipulate the environment if the consequences are beneficial in their eyes, e.g., adult attention. Adults cry in pain, grief, anger, sympathy, and identification, and also in times of pleasure or joy when deeply touched.

Crying has, then, a variety of manifestations and meanings. With the infant and grief-stricken, it is a means of soliciting support and calling attention to need. With the happy and satisfied, tears may portend a sense of ecstasy and of the ephemeral quality of life. Too few tears may foster stress and illness while too many may suggest depression and the need for pastoral intervention. Even so, culture dictates to a great degree the appropriateness of one's tears. Thus women are permitted tears whereas in some circles men are not. Certainly it is improper to cry on the job, or in public places, or before a frightened child both because it connotes weakness and is a source of embarrassment to onlookers. Finally, religion is often utilized to reinforce these social sanctions. A moral imperative comes to undergird certain cultural attitudes about the relation of strength and weakness and faith and unbelief to crying.

The above would suggest that crying involves both intrapsychic and interpersonal/social dimensions and dynamics. Gregory the Great observed that some cry to cleanse themselves from sins in earnest while others bathe themselves in tears like the sow, who was washed only to return to the mire. Gregory comments that behavior (in this instance tears) may reflect one's circumstances (the interpersonal) or one's temperament (the intrapsychic).

Intrapsychically, crying may reflect the need for emotional release and the attempt to resolve an intrapsychic conflict. Such would certainly seem to be true in the case of infants or of persons suffering loss. The acknowledgment of pain through tears confesses vulnerability and invites support and attention. But tears may also simply be a signal of the conflict itself and not an effort at resolution. Thus the person who habitually cries when dependency needs are touched, finding them frightening and humiliating, confesses that shame and anger are the stuff of his or her tears.

In the same manner, tears may have varying interpersonal meanings. In Horney's terms, they may reveal efforts to move towards, away from, or against others. In such instances they are intended to have an environmental effect, i.e., to elicit sympathy, or create a smokescreen so that one may escape, or in a hostile fashion to manipulate and control others through guilt and intimidation.

The pastoral response to crying involves an assessment of a number of factors. How crying fits a person's individual history; how crying is related to a given culture and social class; how it is related to a given stage of development; and how various religious traditions regard crying — all these are ingredients to understanding the meaning of tears in a given instance. Perhaps the basic question pastors must ask is whether tears reveal genuine pain, joy, need, or anger and indignation and thereby enhance and enrich the quality of life and relationships or whether they serve to obscure and hinder dealing with the genuine issues of our common life.

S. W. CARDWELL

CATHARSIS; COMFORT/SUSTAINING; GRIEF AND LOSS. *See also* CONSOLATION; TOUCHING/PHYSICAL SUPPORT.

CULTS. *See* NEW RELIGIOUS MOVEMENTS.

CULTURAL AND ETHNIC FACTORS IN PASTORAL CARE. An emerging area of research and practice that by definition concerns issues which arise when counseling persons with dissimilar cultural and ethnic backgrounds. Consideration of ethnic factors typically focuses upon situations where the counselor is identified with mainstream culture and unilingual, and the client a member of an ethnic minority. Scant literature exists concerning the counselor as member of an ethnic minority and the counselee non-ethnic. Ethnicity may be viewed as a primary bonding, an identification and context of belonging, shared by groups with common language, behaviors, histories, lifestyles, values, and norms. Ethnic considerations are usually related to factors of race, social class, religion, and gender within a sociocultural context of pluralism and minority or subordinate status with the dominant culture. The great diversity of ethnicities, as well as variations within each ethnic group and varying status within the dominant culture, complicates the development of theory and skills.

Counseling is viewed as a communication process which intends to be of assistance to a client, but is impeded when both parties send and receive messages with different meanings which come out of differing worldviews. Some literature views the basic principles of counseling as valid when placed within an awareness of the importance of differing ethnic and cultural meanings. Others view traditional counseling principles as invalid, having been developed without awareness of differences which can substantively affect goal, process, and outcome of counseling. The literature urges being alert to renewed ethnocentricity and ethnic stereotyping as well as to psychological and political considerations concerning client participation in the dominant culture.

1. **Underlying Assumptions in Counseling.** In Western societies, counseling is normatively reflective of: (a) the philosophical assumptions of a white, majority, dominant, middle class mainstream culture which emphasizes the universal nature of the human, and (b) norms of mental health which may not be congruent with alternate orientations, allow for the persistent power of ethnic shapings of identity, or consider how closely self-image is related to ethnic and cultural background and status.

Alternate worldviews or symbol systems may not be given credence within counseling orientations that assume that its perspectives and processes fit any individual in any culture, ethnic community, age, sex, or social class. A counselor may work toward goals of self-actualization, autonomy, self-control, or insight in processes that emphasize intimacy and self-disclosure in non-structured settings over long periods of time, where neither goal nor process intersects the client's worldview, expectations or life experiences. The counseling orientation may assume that the locus of control lies within the self, whereas an alternate culture may value or experience control as outside or other-located. It may value self-responsibility as central in assimilation or participation within a sociopolitical system of the dominant culture, whereas a member of an ethnic minority may have experienced being left out, unwanted, oppressed, or discriminated against. A counselor may value change through intrapsychic insight, while the client expects direct help in specific and immediate situations.

Thus consideration of ethnic factors implicitly and explicitly critiques the philosophical assumptions of counseling systems which are not inclusive of cultural and ethnic diversity, and which have an unacknowledged stance of ethnic, economic, or color blindness that can lead to impairment within the counseling processes, mis-diagnosis and treatment, and a loss of the differing subtleties of meaning within both verbal and non-verbal communication. Counseling may fail to assist clients both within their own worlds and with relationships with the dominant culture. Thus the literature calls Western counseling to task for failing to view the meanings of the persistence of ethnicity, as well as for missing such dynamics as learned helplessness among the ethnic poor and the positive valuations to be accorded ethnic identity within mental health perspectives. It may also be critiqued for operating with self-evident assumptions of a "melting pot" valuation without regard for profound issues of acculturation, assimilation, and experiences of marginality and/or oppression.

2. Specific Ethnic Considerations Within the Counseling Process. There may be different forms of greeting behaviors, meanings in non-verbal communications such as eye contact, expressive gesture, body movements, and perspectives on distance, space, and intimacy. Differing understandings of the locus and possibility of control and responsibility in social discourse and expectations of obligation in relation to biological and ethnic family may be present. Valuations concerning self-disclosure, the desired outcome of counseling and the nature of time and style of client investment in the process may vary radically. Ethnic factors may also affect the authority with which the counselor is invested, including counselor credibility, and there may be overt or covert power dynamics, especially when the counselor is viewed as representative of the dominant or oppressive culture. Such factors lead toward the sending and receiving of messages which are misinterpreted, substantively affecting matters of goal, process and outcome.

The literature is unclear as to whether it is necessary or preferable for counselor and client to share a common ethnic and cultural identification with strong arguments on either side. Emerging literature suggests that knowledge of the client's ethnic identifications and cultural symbolic systems and context is crucial, and that there is no guarantee that shared ethnicity or culture will in itself assure efficacious counseling.

3. Preparation of the Counselor. The literature reports the lack of training programs paying specific attention to ethnic and cultural differences. A consensus is emerging that preparation for cultural fluency, or cross-cultural expertise should be normative in preparation for counseling in a multicultural society, and there is growing insistence that this should become a dimension of the ethics of the various counseling professions. The counselor should be expected to recognize his or her own ethnic and cultural biases and assumptions to the same depth that one considers intrapsychic awareness and motivations. The culturally fluent counselor will be aware of personal cultural biases, the cultural inclusiveness of operative theoretical framework, and the need for a repertoire of resources and skills to invite and sustain a working counseling relationship and communication process that is congruent with the client's world.

Preparation for counseling that includes attention to cross-cultural and ethnic factors will have as its goal finding ways of bridging cultural differences in order to work effectively, on the client's behalf, with culturally and ethnically different clients. The counselor needs preparation and supervision to recognize and respond to tests of one's credibility; to have specific knowledge of ethnic and cultural variations; to avoid new stereotyping; and to consider social and political forces affecting both a particular ethnic group and individual variations within that group. Attention to the attitudes, behaviors, goals, and skills of the counselor within ethnic context becomes a prerequisite for effective counseling.

4. Future Research and Directions. Four directions are particularly crucial: (a) The adequacy of theoretical frameworks which allow for wide variation in ethnic and cultural and individual worldviews and dynamics; (b) the sparse offerings presently available in theories and proven practices in inter-cultural communication; (c) concern for the paucity of research that has come out of real counseling interactions between counselors and clients of differing orientations; and (d) issues of "matching" or referral. While it may be clear that communication is enhanced when there is a similar worldview, this similarity in itself is not sufficient, due to intracultural and intraethnic diversity and other factors such as race, social class, sex, gender, and religion.

Bibliography. D. W. Augsburger, *Pastoral Counseling Across Cultures* (1986). P. Bogia, "Where Are You Coming From: An Examination of Cultural Factors in Groups," *Pastoral Psychology*, 28 (1979), 21–26, R. Brislin, *Cross-Cultural Encounters* (1981). J. Dillard, *Multi-Cultural Counseling* (1983). D. J. Hesselgrave, *Counseling Cross-Culturally* (1984). V. L. Lattimore, III, "The Positive Contribution of Black Cultural Values to Pastoral Counseling," *J. of Pastoral Care*, 36:2 (1982), 105–17. R. C. Leslie, "Counseling Across Cultures," *United Ministries in Higher Education* (1979). K. Parker, "Problems and Possibilities of Cross-Cultural Supervision," *Pastoral Psychology*, 26 (1978), 263–73. P. B. Pedersen, *et al.*, *Counseling Across Cultures* (1981). D. W. Sue, *Counseling the Culturally Different* (1981). A. Wolfgang, ed., *Nonverbal Behavior* (1984).

P. WAY

CROSS-CULTURAL PASTORAL CARE; SOCIAL STATUS AND CLASS FACTORS IN PASTORAL CARE; SOCIOLOGY OF RELIGIOUS AND PASTORAL CARE. *See also* ASIAN AMERICAN *or* BLACK AMERICAN *or* HISPANIC AMERICAN PASTORAL CARE;

BLACK IDENTITY AND CONSCIOUSNESS; JEWISH CARE AND COUNSELING; LIFESTYLE ISSUES IN PASTORAL CARE; NATIVE AMERICANS; SOCIAL PERCEPTION, JUDGMENT AND BELIEF; POOR PERSONS; RICH PERSONS. *Compare* CHURCH-SECT DIFFERENCES IN PASTORAL CARE; CONSCIOUSNESS RAISING.

CULTURAL ANTHROPOLOGY OF RELIGION, DISCIPLINE OF.

The anthropological study of religion is allied with sociology, psychology, and comparative religions. Its unique contributions lie in its data — mainly the study of non-Western tribal and folk religions — and in its method of cross-cultural comparison.

Three major sets of questions have occupied the anthropological study of religion: (1) questions about the origins of religion and its place in the broad expanse of human history; (2) questions about the nature and functions of religions within societies; and (3) questions about the meaning of religious ideas and symbols.

1. The Origins of Religion. Like medieval Christian theology, nineteenth and early twentieth-century science sought to explain human affairs in terms of a single comprehensive history; but unlike theology it did so in naturalistic terms. Following the lead of Conte, the early anthropologists postulated an evolution of religious beliefs and practices from a simpler, more uniform past to the complex heterogeneous present. Like Conte, who divided history into three stages of intellectual development—theological, metaphysical or philosophical, and scientific—they attributed this evolution to the growth of human rationality.

E. B. Tylor traced the origins of religion to an earlier belief in spirit beings that arose when primitive humans, reflecting on the nature of dreams and death, came to the conclusion that humans have invisible souls that leave the body and wander to distant places. Later, he said, they extended this notion of a spirit or soul to animals, plants, and even inanimate objects. True religion began when humans began to worship ancestors by offering them food and drink. From a belief in spirits, Tylor argued, it is only a small step to belief in the "continuance" of these spirits beyond death in an afterworld, in their "embodiment" in objects, in "possession" in which they enter living persons, in powerful spirits or "gods," and in "fetishes" or special objects inhabited by these gods. R. R. Marett argued that belief in spirits was preceded by a stage in which humans experienced a sense of awe at the great forces of nature and came to believe in a mysterious impersonal power or *mana*.

Sir James Frazer traced the origin of religion to magic and postulated the mental progress of humans from magic to religion to science. Early humans, he argued, were prelogical, and they developed magic on mistaken notions of causality based on similarity (pouring water produces rain), and contagion (acts performed on some part of a person's body, such as hair clippings, affect that person).

Opposition to evolutionary theories of religion came from two quarters. Andrew Lang and others argued that many simple societies have a belief in an all-powerful creator, God, a belief evolutionists attributed only to advanced universalistic religions, while in the U.S., Franz Boas and his students A. L. Kroeber and Leslie Spier called for empirically based history to replace the "armchair speculation" that had characterized evolutionary theories. Their chief contribution was a series of historical accounts of religious change among the tribes of North America.

2. Functional Approaches. During the period between the world wars, anthropological theories of religion were heavily influenced by positivist theories formulated in psychology and sociology that held that social phenomena, like natural phenomena, obey laws discoverable by empirical observation and human reason. These theories were materialistic and sought to explain religions in terms of the functions they serve in maintaining the organization of societies.

Sigmund Freud saw religion as an essentially neurotic expression of unconscious psychological conflicts and redirected psychic forces centering around the Oedipus complex and infantile helplessness. In *Totem and Taboo* (1913) he traced the origins of religion to an early case of patricide and primal incest by a band of sons, and to the resulting ambivalence toward the father who, at first, became the totem and then, by projection, the god of the band. In later studies Freud elaborated on the nature of religion as a projection of authority figures. For the most part anthropologists rejected as fanciful Freud's story of religion beginning in a case of primal incest. However, a few, such as Geza Roheim and George Devereux, accepted Freud's thesis and sought to show from tribal data that in religion the neurotic mind transfers its suppressed wishes onto external objects, which it makes sacred.

Far more influential was Emile Durkheim's functionalist theory, which held that religion plays a vital role in maintaining order in a society. For Durkheim religion was a set of symbols that refer not to supernatural beings but to the society itself. Gods, spirits, and other religious symbols represent the society as a whole or some of its parts. By ordering these symbols in rituals, the nature of the social order is affirmed; by declaring these symbols sacred, the egocentric impulses of individuals that threaten to destroy that order are suppressed. As individuals participate in religious rituals, they affirm their place in and subordination to the society. Religions therefore serve vital positive functions in maintaining societies. Their explicit beliefs, however, cannot be taken as valid statements about how the people view reality.

The leading anthropologists to adopt functionalist approaches to the study of religion were A. R. Radcliffe-Brown, who believed that the objects venerated by a people were those directly or indirectly essential for their survival; E. E. Evans-Pritchard, who analyzed the function of witchcraft among the Zande; R. F. Fortune, who studied sorcery among the Dobu; and Raymond Firth, who investigated the ritual cycle of the Tikopia.

Bronislaw Malinowski, although a functionalist, recognized the importance of religious beliefs *qua* beliefs. He refused to treat people as anonymous individuals trapped in social webs and their ideas as merely social projections. All people, he said, have folk sciences by which they seek to meet their human needs. Religion and magic are rational responses to the universally experienced emotions of stress that arise when these sciences fail. The difference between the two is one of purpose. Magic is utilitarian and instrumental. It is used to influence events such as unforeseen calamities that are beyond normal human control. Religion, on the other hand, is an end unto itself. It provides people with an explanation for suffering, crisis, and death, and thereby assures them that the world is indeed orderly and meaningful.

3. **Meaning-oriented Approaches.** Before World War II, anthropologists began to look at religions as systems of meaning — as folk theologies about the ultimate nature of reality. One of the first to take this approach was L. Levy-Bruhl, who saw primitive religions as products of prelogical mentalities governed by emotions and mystical analogies. His thesis, however, was largely rejected by anthropologists such as Paul Radin who pointed out that intellectuals in tribal societies do reach high levels of philosophical sophistication.

Daryll Forde, Marcel Griaule, and others have shown that religious myths and rituals give expression to the fundamental beliefs people have about reality — in other words, their worldviews. Taking a problem-solving approach, Clifford Geertz holds that religion provides answers to the three fundamental human experiences that threaten to make life meaningless: the problem of bafflement when human explanation systems fail, the problem of suffering and death, and the problem of injustice or feeling of moral disorder and chaos. It answers these by appealing to higher realities outside of daily experience.

Claude Levi-Strauss and the cognitive structuralists contend that religions are essentially mental systems for organizing and storing abstract information. This is not, as Forde and Geertz would argue, information people have about the real world. Rather it is information about the conceptual categories people create in their minds. In other words, rituals and myths shape the thought worlds of the people. While this approach has produced some elegant interpretations of particular religions, many anthropologists question whether the abstract interpretations do not reflect more the cognitive structures of the anthropologists than those of the people.

Edmund Leach, Mary Douglas, and Victor Turner have taken a broader approach to the study of human classification systems. Douglas argues that religion helps maintain fundamental classifications by treating things that fall between the categories as either sacred or polluted. Rituals and taboos therefore serve as conceptual boundary markers, setting off various types of social reality. For example, the human life cycle rites — birth, initiation, marriage, and death — mark important transitions in the life of an individual, and thereby create a sense of order in life. Turner has applied the same approach to the study of community rituals and to pilgrimages.

After a long period in which religion was seen only as a stage (often pathological) in the development of human thought, or as a means for organizing and integrating a society, it has now become an object of anthropological research in its own right as a system of human beliefs defining the ultimate character of reality and humankind's role within it.

Bibliography. M. Douglas, *Natural Symbols* (1970). E. Durkheim, *The Elementary Forms of Religious Life* (1915). J. G. Frazer, *The Golden Bough: A Study in Magic and Religion* (1955 [1911]). W. A. Lessa and E. Z. Vogt, eds., *Reader in Comparative Religion* 4th ed. (1979). C. Levi-Strauss, *The Raw and the Cooked* (1969). B. Malinowski, *Magic, Science and Religion* (1984 [1925]). V. W. Turner, *The Drums of Affliction* (1968); *The Ritual Process* (1969). See also J. R. Haule, "The Care of Souls: Psychology and Religion in Anthropological Perspective," *J. of Psychology and Theology,* 11 (1983), 108 – 18.

P. HIEBERT

RELIGION. *See also* AFRICAN, NATIVE AMERICAN, *or* WEST INDIAN TRADITIONAL RELIGION; JOURNALS IN RELIGION, THEOLOGY, AND THE SOCIAL SCIENCES, INTERDISCIPLINARY; MYTHOLOGY AND PSYCHOLOGY; NEW RELIGIOUS MOVEMENTS; RITUAL AND PASTORAL CARE; SACRIFICE; SHAMAN; SYMBOLISM/SYMBOLIZING. *Compare* PSYCHOLOGY OF RELIGION; SOCIOLOGY OF RELIGIOUS AND PASTORAL CARE; SOCIOLOGY OF RELIGION.

CULTURE AND PERSONALITY. *See* PERSONALITY, SOCIETY, AND CULTURE.

CURE OF SOULS *(Cura Animarum).* *See* CARE OF SOULS.

CURIOSITY. *See* MOTIVATION.

CURRAN, CHARLES. *See* COUNSELING, ROMAN CATHOLIC.

CURSING. *See* PROFANE LANGUAGE; VOWS/VOWING; WITCHCRAFT.

CYBERNETIC THEORY IN PSYCHOLOGY AND COUNSELING. "Cybernetics" comes from the Greek word *kybernetes* meaning "helmsman" or "steersman." The word "governor," referring to a control mechanism on a machine or to a leader of the state, comes from the equivalent Latin word. In the 1940s, N. Wiener coined this term to refer to the science of control and communication in animal and machine. During World War II the development of cybernetics was accelerated because of its military applications, such as aiming guns at moving targets.

As the science of control and communication in humans and machines, cybernetics is a bridge or umbrella science, combining the biologist's concern with adaptive organism, especially the central nervous system, and the engineer's concern with systems analysis. This bridging draws in other areas, such as physics, psychology, and information theory. Cybernetics offers a dynamic and functional perspective, which is significant for the psychologist at the levels of understanding, preventing, and treating problems.

1. **Homeostasis and Feedback.** Homeostasis is the maintenance of organization despite the tendency toward disorder. A common example is the thermostat, which maintains a constant temperature within a range of minor variations. Another example is an automatic pilot which keeps a ship or plane on course within minor deviations. Homeostasis is more complicated in an organism, but a similar system of control maintains various levels, such as body temperature or blood sugar.

In a psychological system homeostasis is even more complex. The homeostatic defiance of entropy implies that determinism is not complete. This has been likened to Freud's recognition of a deep irrational component in humans. We exercise a system of control to integrate the personality and to keep mood swings within a reasonable range. Schizophrenia is a consequence of insufficient control to integrate the personality, and manic-depressive psychosis is a consequence of extreme mood shifts.

Feedback makes self-correction possible by basing behavior on past performance. It is the process of feedback that makes it possible for a machine or organism to act purposefully, thereby overcoming the natural tendency toward disorder. Feedback makes possible behavior that is not merely automatic but adaptive, responding to actual rather than anticipated performance. A counselor employing feedback must not merely receive, but adapt on the basis of the information. The principle of feedback can be employed to discover both where the counselor is failing to understand or being misunderstood, and to guide the counselor in adjusting his or her course accordingly.

2. **Computer Models and Programming.** One of the most prominent areas of human-machine interaction involves computers. However, there are different types of computers. Digital and analogue computers differ in that the former's operations are discrete (states of all or none, yes or no only) and the latter are continuous. Digital computers are more common because they have more universal or general application. There is debate as to whether the psychological organism is fundamentally digital, since neurons are either firing or not firing.

Another distinction is between algorithmic and heuristic computers. Algorithmic computers work with a precisely specified pattern of decision procedure and work through all the possibilities, regardless of how remote and unlikely they may be. This becomes unwieldy in complex problems. Heuristic computers employ a selective decision procedure. They decide on the most likely possibilities and explore only these. Psychological organisms are clearly heuristic.

3. **Applications and Relation to General Systems Theory.** Cybernetics has had various applications. By patterning action on the model of the computer, the individual can become more efficient. Through biofeedback, rehabilitation can be enhanced and accelerated.

However, the more significant applications of cybernetics have been social rather than individual. The application to technology is sometimes called "cybernation," a combination of cybernetics and automation. Psychological issues raised by this development include the occasional feeling of threatened self-image by a person taking orders from a computer (and perhaps displaced by one) and, in general, the highly rationalized approach to human and organizational relations implicit in computerized management. At another level, clearly evident in popular culture, computers may be changing the way people think of themselves and one another. Terms like feedback, programming, and information processing have become part of our psychological vocabulary, especially among counseling professionals. Whether this development in language betokens a shift in our understanding of persons toward greater depersonalization and mechanization, or simply a useful addition to psychological thinking, is an important, if so far unanswered, question.

The most constructive and significant impact of cybernetics on pastoral care and counseling, however, has come by way of general systems theory. Developed by L. von Bertalanffy, general systems theory has roots in psychobiology but is concerned to study systems as such rather than specific systems. Some identify cybernetics and general systems theory as opposite sides of the same coin, while others see them as distinct but related.

Wholism, synergism, and isomorphism are basic principles of cybernetics and general systems theory. One does not deal with individual components but with a system. It is not possible to change one item without changing the systems of which it is a part. The whole is greater than the sum of its parts. The individual does not behave in isolation but in the context of a series of interrelationships. One should be concerned not only with the units in a system but with the links that relate them. The pastor, for instance, is a shepherd of systems, guiding church influence on behavior (Pattison, 1977). Or again, it is not the husband or wife that is the client, but the marriage; not the parent or child, but the family (Switzer, 1974; Sandholm, 1982).

A computer program is a full set of instructions. The computer must not only be informed of the data to be read, but also when to read the data. The computer must be informed of all the steps to be followed and of the sequence to follow, taking into account all possible alternatives. A flow chart is a graphic presentation of the program. One question for psychological methodology is whether a computer program and/or flow chart gives us a precise way of expressing mental processes or whether they give us a way for computers to reach the same goals that humans or animals reach by mental processes.

4. **Artificial Intelligence and Theological Issues.** Artificial intelligence (AI) is the performance by machines of tasks requiring perceptual and reasoning abilities, for example, playing games, processing languages, solving problems, proving theorems, and recognizing patterns. AI is closely related to cognitive psychology.

Philosophers, such as K. M. Sayre and J. M. Crosson of the Philosophic Institute for Artificial Intelligence at the University of Notre Dame, have explored philosophical issues raised by AI, such as: Can machines learn? Can machines have feeling or consciousness?

Although philosophers had been debating issues of AI for some time, H. E. Hatt (1968) was one of the first to identify significant theological issues raised by AI (see also Studdiford, 1967). Is a human being nothing more than a highly complex cybernetic system? Can we continue to affirm the reality of human freedom and responsibility if machines can make judgments and decisions? If so, are freedom and responsibility exclusively human qualities or can machines at a high level of complexity also achieve some measure of freedom and responsibility? How can we maximize the humanizing potential and minimize the dehumanizing potential of cybernetics? Taking E. Brunner's concept of the *imago dei* as responsibility, Hatt argues that freedom and determinism, in both humans and machines, are not opposites, but concomitants, and that the relation of freedom and determinism is the ground of responsibility.

Bibliography. N. Wiener, *Cybernetics* 2d ed., (1961 [1948]) is seminal. Wiener explores the impact of cybernetics on society in *The Human Use of Human Beings* 2d ed.,(1954 [1950]) and on religion in *God and Golem, Inc.* (1964). K. Menninger, *The Vital Balance* (1963) provides a theory of psychopathology based on homeostasis.

Systems theory is developed by L. von Bertalanffy, *General Systems Theory* (1968), esp. chs. 8–9 on psychology, on which also see Bertalanffy, *Robots, Men and Minds* (1967). The systems approach has been applied to pastoral care by E. M. Pattison, *Pastor and Parish* (1977). Narrower applications can be found in W. R. Beavers, "The Application of Family Systems Theory to Crisis Intervention," in D. K. Switzer, *The Minister as Crisis Counselor* (1974), and in G. L. Sandholm, "A Systems Perspective to Marriage Counseling," *Pastoral Psychology,* 31 (1982), 118–28.

Artificial Intelligence concepts, techniques, and programs are discussed in A. Barr, *et al., The Handbook of Artificial Intelligence* 3 vols. (1981–1982). Artificial intelligence's relation to cognitive psychology is developed in H. A. Simon, *The Sciences of the Artificial* (1969), ch. 2. The theological significance of cybernetics is explored by H. E. Hatt, *Cybernetics and the Image of Man* (1968) and K. Vaux, *Subduing the Cosmos* (1970). See also W. E. Baumzweiger-Bauer, "Ethical Monotheism and Mental Structure," *J. of Psychology and Judaism* (1980), 5–15. W. B. Studdiford, "Willing in Androids," in J. N. Lapsley, ed., *The Concept of Willing* (1967).

H. HATT

HOMEOSTATIS; PSYCHOLOGY; SYSTEMS THEORY. *See also* COGNITIVE PSYCHOLOGY AND PSYCHOTHERAPY; COMMUNICATION; FAMILY THEORY AND THERAPY; HEALTH AND ILLNESS; MODELS IN PSYCHOLOGICAL AND PASTORAL THEORY; PHILOSOPHY AND PSYCHOLOGY. *Compare* COMPARATIVE PSYCHOLOGY; ECOLOGICAL PSYCHOLOGY; PSYCHO-LINGUISTIC THEORY IN PSYCHOLOGY AND COUNSELING; THEORY AND PRAXIS.

CYNICISM. *See* ANTISOCIAL PERSONS.

CYPRIAN OF CARTHAGE, ST. (ca. 200/210–258). Bishop of Carthage, prolific writer, spiritual and moral leader, martyr.

Cyprian's adult conversion produced a transformed man who distributed his wealth to the poor, committed himself to discipline (e.g., chastity), and who valued the unity of the church above all else. His personal steadfastness, consistency, and care authenticate his writings and his episcopacy.

The cruel reality of Christians suffering from persecution and plague provides the backdrop for Cyprian's pastoral care. He writes supportive and inspirational letters to those suffering—writings which establish him as the earliest author of consolation literature in the classical vein. At the same time, he is an advocate of strict though compassionate discipline for lapsed believers by resisting pandering and cheap grace, by rejecting exomologesis prior to readmission to the fellowship, by positioning the office of bishop as the guardian of norms, and by seeking to reconcile various factions for the sake of the unity of Christ's church.

N. F. HAHN

CLASSIC LITERATURE IN CARE AND COUNSELING (Roman Catholicism); EARLY CHURCH, PASTORAL CARE AND COUNSELING IN.

CYRIL OF JERUSALEM. *See* CLASSIC LITERATURE IN CARE AND COUNSELING (Roman Catholicism).

D

DAIMONIC. Any natural function which has the power to take over the whole person. The concept is best explicated in existential psychology but appears as somewhat parallel to that of idolatry in religious psychology. Examples of the daimonic are sex and eros, anger and rage, and the craving after power. The daimonic may be either creative or destructive and is normally both.

Bibliography. R. May, *Love and Will* (1969).

O. STRUNK, JR.

EXISTENTIAL PSYCHOLOGY AND PSYCHOTHERAPY. *Compare* THE DEMONIC.

DANCE THERAPY. *See* ADJUNCTIVE THERAPIES.

DASEINANALYSIS. *See* EXISTENTIAL PSYCHOLOGY AND PSYCHOTHERAPY.

DAY, DOROTHY (1897–1980). Devoutly practicing, yet nonconformist, Roman Catholic writer, journalist, columnist, and social activist in the U.S. Co-founder of the newspaper, *The Catholic Worker*, and initiator of the hospitality houses for the poor.

The embodiment of two themes in the life of Dorothy Day make her an important figure for the field of pastoral care: (a) a profound spirituality and deep commitment to the church; and (b) a rare, active, and personal commitment in published word and personal deed to the plight of the poor, homeless, and disenfranchised.

Dorothy Day's unifying center was a strong religious conviction about God's love for all of creation, the unity of all creation, and the need for an urgent reformation of the social order which would make God's universal love believable again to those upon whom social arrangements had thrust feelings of alienation from that love.

With one foot in the daily operations of actual ministries and the other in the reflective domain of intellectual thought and writing, ministering in the actual context of pastoral care as well as critically addressing its moral context, Dorothy Day was a *praxis* theologian *par excellence*.

N. F. HAHN

SOCIAL JUSTICE ISSUES IN PASTORAL CARE; SPIRITUALITY (Roman Catholic Tradition).

DEACON (Gk. *diakonos,* "servant".) One of the orders of ordained ministry in the polity of certain churches, while a lay function in the polity of other churches. The NT origins of deacons as a distinct ministry are difficult to trace with clarity. Most NT scholars no longer consider Acts 5:1–6 as the origin of an order as such. In fact, the word *deacon* never appears in Acts. Irenaeus (ca. 130–ca. 200) was the first to claim that the passage in Acts refers to an order of ministry. In Phillippians 1:1 the clearest technical sense of the term appears, where the greeting contains the words "all the saints . . . with the bishops and deacons." Even here it is questionable if these special functions of ministry were initiated through the imposition of hands. Throughout the NT there is not sufficient evidence that the various functions of ministry carried with them special status conferred through the imposition of hands. Certainly the various ministries had the community's blessing, but in the earliest period the church seems to have had a more organismic rather than hierarchical form.

In the post-NT church the deacon was attached to the bishop. The deacon performed liturgical functions such as reading the Epistle and Gospel lessons at the Eucharist, receiving the alms offerings, and performing pastoral functions such as visiting the poor, needy, and ill. The servant role was threefold: service to the bishop (administrative), service to the congregation (liturgical), and service to the world (pastoral-social).

During the patristic and medieval periods the functions of the deacon were reduced as increasing emphasis was placed upon the subordinate role which the deacon played in the church hierarchy. The designation of the deacon as an order inferior to the priesthood provided in the Western Church a transition from a subordinate but permanent diaconate to a transitional diaconate as preliminary to elder's (presbyter's) ordination. The transitional diaconate as a probationary period for priesthood or elder's ordination is a practice in the Anglican Church and the United Methodist Church. In Calvinist and the Reformed tradition the deacon has no liturgical responsibilities. Diaconal responsibilities are administrative (supervising the alms offering) and pastoral (caring for the ill). In churches with more pronounced congregational polity, such as Baptist, the deacon assists the pastor in "serving" the elements of the Lord's Supper as well as rendering pastoral care. In the Lutheran Church the deacon is an assistant pastor, though fully ordained.

The Second Vatican Council foresaw the possibility of a permanent diaconate. The deacon, where authorized, could perform baptisms, celebrate the Eucharist, officiate at weddings, and administer last rites. In 1982 the Faith and Order Commission of the World Council of Churches released the results of a five-year study and consultation which represents a major ecumenical consensus regarding baptism, eucharist and ministry. The participating churches included Eastern Orthodox, Lutheran, Anglican, Reformed, Methodist, Disciples, Baptist, Adventist and Pentecostal churches. The document advocated a permanent diaconate which would represent to the church its calling as a servant in the world. Several Protestant denominations are studying the possibilities for a permanent diaconate functionally distinct from but not hierarchically subordinate to other orders — a full and equal order.

Bibliography. J. M. Barnett, *The Diaconate: A Full and Equal Order* (1981). B. Cooke, *Ministry to Word and Sacraments* (1976). J. G. Davies, "Deacons, Deaconesses and the Minor Orders in the Patristic Period," in *J. of Ecclesiastical History,* 22 (1963), 1–15. E. Schweizer, *Church Order in the New Testament* (1961), translated by F. Clarke. World Council of Churches, *Baptism, Eucharist and Ministry* (1982).

J. C. LOGAN, JR.

ECCLESIOLOGY AND PASTORAL CARE; MINISTRY. *See also* ELDER; LAY PASTORAL CARE AND COUNSELING.

DEAFNESS. *See* HANDICAP AND DISABILITY; LOSS OF FUNCTION.

DEATH (Meaning and Theory). *See* DEATH, BIOMEDICAL DEFINITION OF; DEATH, MEANING OF (Christian); DEATH AND DYING, PSYCHOSOCIAL THEORIES OF; DEATH RESEARCH AND EDUCATION; DYING, MORAL DILEMMAS IN; NEAR-DEATH EXPERIENCE; PERSON (Jewish Perspective).

DEATH (Pastoral Care). *See* DYING, PASTORAL CARE OF; DYING CHILD AND FAMILY; DYING, MORAL DILEMMAS IN; SICK AND DYING, JEWISH CARE OF.

DEATH, BIOMEDICAL DEFINITION OF. The need for precise medico-legal definitions of death is the product of post-1950 advances in medical technology. The ancients defined death as "the departure of the breath of life," technically determined by holding a mirror to the nostrils of the person. Today we can maintain heart and lung function, assess brain function, and evaluate the causes, consequences, and reversibility of the whole body as an organism.

Death is defined as the permanent cessation of functioning of the organism as a whole, even though individual organs may continue to function for a time. The organism as a whole refers to spontaneous and innate activities which require integrated action of most organ systems and produce at least limited response to the environment. Thus death is a biological definition of irreversible loss of organismic function.

The death of a "person" is not a biological term but is a psychological, social, philosophical, and theological concept, referring to the essential elements of existence significant to the nature of a "person." Thus a human organism may be "alive," but not be a "person." Examples include an infant born with severe brain damage, a person who is comatose without consciousness, and organic or senile brain deterioration with "loss of the personality." Permanent absence of consciousness and cognition are the criteria of a "non-person," but not a definition of biological death of the organism. Pre-literate societies often used death of the person as a defining criterion to allow malformed infants and sick or senile persons to die or be killed. Today similar issues of voluntary and involuntary euthanasia revolve around the ambiguous situations of death of the person versus biological death of the organism.

In 1978 a U.S. Presidential Commission developed a model statute to define biological death, "The Uniform Determination of Death Act," which states: "An individual who has sustained either (1) irreversible cessation of circulatory and respiratory functions, or (2) irreversible cessation of the entire brain, including the brain stem, is dead. A determination of death must be made in accordance with accepted medical standards." The intent of this statute is to remove the determination of death from legal disputation and restore judgment to the "private sphere" of joint physician and family discernment. It presupposes the existence of accepted medical standards and procedures to determine irreversibility of organ function and integrated organism operation even in the presence of artificial life-support systems.

Complicating conditions in making such a biologic determination of irreversible death include: (1) drug and metabolic intoxication which may give a false picture of brain and cardiopulmonary suppression, (2) hypothermia which may mimic brain death, (3) young children in whom irreversible brain damage is difficult to assess, and (4) biological shock in which reduction in circulation may produce temporary non-response.

Bibliography. J. A. Fruehling, ed., *Sourcebook on Death and Dying* (1982). D. J. Horan and D. Mall, eds., *Death, Dying, and Euthanasia* (1980).

E. M. PATTISON

DEATH AND DYING, MORAL DILEMMAS IN; DEATH, MEANING OF; DEATH RESEARCH AND EDUCATION. *See also* PERSON.

DEATH, CHILD'S. *See* DYING CHILD AND FAMILY; FUNERAL, CHILD'S.

DEATH, JEWISH CARE AT. *See* SICK AND DYING, JEWISH CARE OF.

DEATH, MEANING OF (Christian). Death is the temporal limit of all finite existence. Its meaning depends on the perspective from which it is viewed, that is, biological, psychological, sociological, or theological. In Christian theology death is interpreted in relation to God the Creator, Judge and Redeemer of life. The death and resurrection of Christ are central in this interpretation. The hopeful realism of a biblically rooted theology of death stands in contrast to both death-denial and death-acceptance in modern culture.

1. Biblical Views of Death. *a. Old Testament.* Death is understood in different ways in the OT: (1) As a given limit that God has set for all creatures (Isa. 40:6 ff.; Ps. 90:10). Hence while premature or violent death is feared, finitude and mortality are not seen as intrinsically evil: the patriarchs died "old and full of years" (Gen. 25:8). (2) As a continual threat to full human life experienced in boundary situations like sickness, loneliness, and exile. Since life consists in relationship with God within the covenant community, experiences of alienation from this source are death-like and are feared and lamented. (3) As the result of a primordial divine curse caused by human sin (Genesis 2–3). All suffering and death is construed as divine punishment for violations of the covenant or the moral order of creation (but cf. the book of Job). (4) As God's enemy, which will be defeated at the end of history (Isaiah 26; Daniel 12). In late Jewish apocalypticism the persistence of unjust suffering prompts the hope that God will raise the dead and establish justice universally.

b. New Testament. Diverse understandings of death are also apparent in the NT. Although the early church unanimously affirms that God has acted through Christ to assure final victory over death, tension is evident between seeing death strictly as enemy and seeing death and resurrection as the pattern of God's way of salvation. God's coming kingdom is signaled by Jesus' forgiveness of sins, healing of the sick, and raising of the dead. Yet Jesus also calls his disciples to give up their old way of life in order to find new life (Mk. 8:34 ff.).

Different dimensions of death are implicit in the NT portrayals of Jesus' own death. While Matthew and Mark stress Jesus' experience of abandonment, Luke describes Jesus as serenely trusting in God and praying for his persecutors as he dies. For Paul death is the wages of sin (Rom. 6:23) and the last enemy (I Cor. 15:26). As Adam brought death, so Christ brings new life (Rom. 5:12 ff.). Christians die with Christ in baptism and in everyday discipleship in hope of participating in his resurrection. Whereas Paul interprets the cross kenotically (Phil. 2:5 ff.), John views it triumphantly (Jn. 19:30). Christ is the resurrection and the life (Jn. 11:25), and he gloriously finishes the work of salvation on the cross. Correspondingly, Paul emphasizes more the commencement, John more the present actuality of new life in believers by the power of the Spirit of Christ.

2. Traditional Theology of Death. *a. Death as separation of body and soul.* Two doctrines have been especially prominent in traditional Western philosophical and theological interpretations of death. The first is the doctrine of death as the separation of body and soul and the related belief in the soul's immortality. Whereas the biblical view of human life is wholistic and rejects all dualisms, the doctrine of the soul's immortality encourages death-denial, individualism, deprecation of bodily existence (the body as prison and death as emancipation), often including an attitude of detachment or apathy toward physical and emotional needs. These views, inherited by the church from Platonic metaphysics, have been widely criticized in both modern anthropology and biblical studies (cf. O. Cullmann, 1958).

b. Death as consequence of sin. The doctrine of original human immortality lost as a result of the Fall and the related belief that all death is a divine punishment comprise the other major theme of traditional theologies of death. Both Augustine's interpretation of Original Sin and some theories of the Atonement presuppose a causal connection between sin and death. Due in part to modern knowledge that death belonged to the created order before the appearance of humanity, the traditional teaching that all death is caused by sin has lost credence.

3. Modern Theology of Death. In addition to rejecting the inherent immortality of the soul as a trivialization of death, modern theology emphasizes the multidimensionality of death, including the possibility of it being the "natural" conclusion of life. The result of sin is not that we must die but that we die in fear and estrangement. Karl Barth argues that death belongs to the limitation of human life as created by God, that under the conditions of sin death confronts us *de facto* as guilty creatures unable to justify our lives, but that through faith in Christ we are "liberated for natural death," that is, set free to live and die in the confidence that God, who is gracious and faithful, is Lord not only of life but also of death. Karl Rahner's theology of death stresses its double-sidedness: death is something that happens to us and that we are called in faith to accomplish. As seen preeminently in the faithful dying of Jesus, death is both an event passively endured and an act of self-entrustment to the mysterious and gracious reality of God. As an act of self-surrender to God, death is a recapitulation and completion of the whole of Christian life as directed toward free, unconditional love of God and self-giving service of others. Modern theologians sensitized by social criticism distinguish between mortality as a condition of finite existence and socially manufactured death, that is, the violent ending of life caused by poverty, exploitation, and war. While a doctrine of natural death has its place, it becomes misleading if it ignores either the darkness of death in actual human experience or the evil of socially inflicted death.

4. Death-Denial in Modern Culture. The widespread denial of death in modern culture has been a recurrent theme of modern literature (e.g., L. Tolstoy, *The Death of Ivan Ilych*) as well as the subject of many scientific studies. Aggravating factors have been the breakdown of traditional symbol systems expressing confidence in the continuity of life, the erosion of the extended family, the increased sense of individual isolation, and the threat of nuclear holocaust, which endangers not only the lives of individuals and societies but all life on earth (see Lifton, 1979). Both denial and acceptance of death in modern culture are rooted in the conviction that death is the ultimate reality. Modern fear of death focuses as much on the process of dying as on death itself. Having learned to value independence and activity and to abhor dependence and passivity, many persons fear above all the helplessness of dying (see Bermann, 1973). This fear of complete dependence is intensified by the possibility of being kept alive artificially by modern medical technology when all valued life capacities are irretrievably lost.

5. Theology of Death and Pastoral Ministry. A theology of death for pastoral ministry will include the following emphases: (1) The value of the diversity of biblical understandings of death in addressing the many different aspects of death experienced by people. No single formula or image (e.g., friend, enemy) encompasses the multidimensionality of death. (2) The profound relationality of human existence. As we love we become vulnerable because our lives are intertwined with the lives of others. Grief is the appropriate response to the loss and separation experienced in death. The Bible contains a rich literature of mourning (e.g., Psalms 22, 88, cf. Mk. 15:34), which honors the outpouring of protest in grief. (3) The ultimate Christian confidence in face of death is neither one's accomplishments, progeny, nor supposed immortality, but the grace of God decisively revealed in Jesus Christ. Nothing can separate us from the love of God in Christ (Rom. 8:38 ff.). (4) The awareness of the incompleteness of the work of redemption, of the continuing "groaning of creation." Faith in God refuses to justify the horrors of history or the tragedies of personal experience. The resurrection of Christ from the dead is the basis and paradigm of hope in God's final victory over all evil. Such hope sustains believers in their struggles and prayers for a world hospitable to full life for all.

Bibliography. L. R. Bailey, Sr., *Biblical Perspectives on Death* (1979). J. D. Bane, *et al.*, eds., *Death and Ministry* (1975). K. Barth, *Church Dogmatics* III/2, par. 47 (1956). E. Becker, *The Denial of Death* (1973). E. Bermann, *Scapegoat: The Impact of Death-Fear on an American Family* (1973). O. Cullmann, *Immortality of the Soul or Resurrection of the Dead?* (1958). H. Feifel, ed., *New Meanings of Death* (1977). E. Jüngel, *Death: The Riddle and the Mystery* (1975). E. Kübler-Ross, *On Death and Dying* (1969). R. J. Lifton, *The Broken Connection: On Death and the Continuity of Life* (1979). L. Mills, ed., *Perspectives on Death* (1969). K. Rahner, *On the Theology of Death* (1961). E. S. Shneidman, ed., *Death: Current Perspectives* 2d ed. (1980). P. Steinfels and R. Veatch, eds., *Death Inside Out* (1975).

D. L. MIGLIORE

ESCHATOLOGY AND PASTORAL CARE. *See also* CROSS AND RESURRECTION; DEATH, BIOMEDICAL DEFINITION OF; DEATH AND DYING, PSYCHOSOCIAL THEORIES OF; GRIEF AND LOSS; NEAR-DEATH EXPERIENCE. *Compare* DEATH AND DYING, MORAL DILEMMAS IN; LIFE/ALIVENESS; SACRIFICE; SICK AND DYING, JEWISH CARE OF; SUICIDE.

DEATH, MEANING OF (Jewish). *See* PERSON (Jewish Perspective).

DEATH, PASTORAL CARE AT. *See* DYING.

DEATH, PSYCHOLOGY AND SOCIOLOGY OF. *See* DEATH AND DYING, PSYCHOSOCIAL THEORIES OF.

DEATH AND DYING. *See* DEATH; DYING. *See also* ESCHATOLOGY AND PASTORAL CARE.

DEATH AND DYING, PSYCHOSOCIAL THEORIES OF. Systematic analyses of the role of death in human life, and of the process of dying as a human situation. This subject divides rather sharply between theories developed within the context of care for the dying and bereaved, and theories aimed at integrating wider philosophical and cultural concerns into depth psychology. As a result psychologies of dying make their own philosophical and cultural assumptions, while some of the most provocative psychosocial theories of death are skimpy in citing clinical data and are uninterested in the unique situation of the dying person.

1. **The Ambiguous Legacy of Freud.** Both the above situation and the uneasy role of death in contemporary psychology stem in part from the influence of Freud in this area. Freud postulated a "death instinct," *Thanatos,* a force locked in perpetual conflict with Eros or the pleasure-principle. Supporting evidence included the compulsion to repeat unpleasant experiences, resistance in therapy, and other symptoms not directly associated with death. Yet his idea was that a pervasive force works in us which is aimed toward the cessation of tension, motion, and life. According to Bakan, although the "death instinct" may not focus upon the conscious experience of dying, it is no coincidence that Freud developed this idea during his long painful struggle with cancer. Perhaps his encounter with death gave the "death instinct" its existential plausibility for Freud.

However, even were that the case, the great majority of American theorists and clinicians influenced by Freud have not found this idea either plausible or necessary. A far more acceptable thesis of psychoanalysis has been that symbolism — of death, or immortality — is primarily defensive in function. In the unconscious there is neither time, nor negation, nor death. All attempts to cope with or encounter death founder upon this supposed fact. This view legitimates a cultural denial of death, for any hope to integrate death with the deeper levels of human experience is ruled out by the theory itself. Moreover, explicit fears of death or fantasies of dying were often interpreted as defensive symbolic expressions of other anxieties such as castration. Certainly, due to this theoretical bias, all explicit references to immortality and/or transcendence of death were seen as instances of denial.

Finally and ironically, Freud's legacy includes his own personal heroic stoicism in facing his own death. His eighteen-year struggle with cancer became a model for how impending death and constant pain can be faced with realism.

2. **Dying as a Process.** Given the above, it is not surprising why dying as a psychological situation was neglected as a source for theorizing. If the unconscious is truly oblivious to death, then whether one is clinically dying or healthy makes no difference. Yet then, seemingly suddenly, the work of Elisabeth Kübler-Ross (1969) with the dying received massive attention, especially her claim that at the deepest emotional level, "acceptance" of death is possible.

Kübler-Ross, although not the only one to theorize on the psychology of dying, has been by far the most influential. Her work probably derives from that of Lindemann in the 1940s on bereavement. Lindemann describes a process of "grief work" in which the bereaved gradually come to accept a death. In Kübler-Ross's psychology of dying, this "work" becomes a five-stage process, an endopsychic, spontaneous progression from "denial" through other states such as anger and depression, accompanied but not determined by physical deterioration. The goal of this process is "acceptance," requiring the de-cathexis (withdrawal) of emotional bonds with the living, and an overall nondefensive posture of "letting go." Although the image of "stages" imply straightforward linear progression, this is a naive reading of the basic theory.

Whatever its clinical validity, this model has at least two distinct merits. First, this "stages" approach allows for grouping a large range of clinical phenomena. Second, it assimilates dying as a human situation into a larger framework of coping with loss. Death, even one's own, becomes a loss—and the hope is that one can accept loss and reach a state beyond even the stoic resignation which Freud, for one, exemplified. Avery Weisman (1972), who also theorized on the psychology of dying, never claimed Kübler-Ross's style of "acceptance" as a realistic goal. Weisman held out only the modest hope that denial could be overcome, and that rueful realism in the face of death's pain might be achieved. Weisman's theory perhaps because of its relatively somber tone has never "caught on" the way Kübler-Ross's has with the general public. By the early 1970s, there was a very large number of popular self-help books on the subject, all influenced by Kübler-Ross, and almost all tacitly substituting a Rogerian-Maslowian psychological framework for the original Freudian foundation. At the level of theorizing, these popular works, like Kübler-Ross's, assume a harmony or congruence between the human organism and its psyche, so that death as a "natural" process need not be intrinsically threatening.

3. **Death in Psychological Theorizing.** *a. Existentialist influences.* While in the psychologies of dying, death is grasped primarily as one type of loss, in existential psychologies death is the unique conditioner of all human experience. Our awareness of death characterizes our entire existence as a "being-toward-death," and no experience or area of life can be interpreted adequately apart from this. In existentialist literature, protagonists confront their own deaths and in so doing can achieve an authentic relation to their lives. Psychological appropriations of existentialism usually include this theme, and thus set "existential psychologies" in sharp contrast to "mainstream" American theories. Two prominent examples illustrate this. Ludwig Binswanger's "The Case of Ellen West" (1944) reconstructs the life-world of an anorexic suicide in terms of Heideggerian categories. For Binswanger's subject, her suicide was her most authentic act, in an existence relentlessly engaged in "being-toward-death." It is significant that Binswanger used this particular case history as a vehicle to present his own Heideggerian revision of psychoanalysis.

The second example is Ernest Becker's *The Denial of Death,* another attempt to integrate existential and Freudian thought. Becker considers the fear of death and the need to deny mortality and vulnerability as more basic motivations than sexuality. Hence, childhood experience is reconstructed as the battleground upon which an unsuccessful defensive struggle against the possibility of one's own nonbeing is waged. In adults, culture provides symbolic "hero-systems" to continue this impossible denial of death. Becker insists that the perpetual conflict between death's reality and our pervasive denial cannot be avoided, mitigated, or truly resolved.

b. The influence of mass death. A very different factor has played a role for another important psychosocial theorist, Robert Lifton. Lifton's *The Broken Connection* (1979) revises Freudian theory along the lines of Eriksonian ego-psychology, postulating nondefensive ego capacities, and reciprocity between culture and the individual. Lifton's two most important contributions to a theory of death are, first, his view on modes of symbolic immortality, and second, his incorporation of twentieth-century history. Lifton holds that symbolism expressive of continuity with the future, or of transcendence of death, is appropriate to human beings. Such symbolism is more than a defensive denial of death. Lifton's careful and sensitive discussion makes it possible for him to appreciate the subtlety with which death and immortality symbolism have functioned in an enormous range of cultural and developmental contexts. Yet Lifton's most distinctive contribution is his research on the drastic influence of twentieth-century experiences of mass death. Hiroshima, the Holocaust, and above all, the prospect of total annihilation through nuclear war, make expressions of symbolic immortality even at the individual level precarious. These historical possibilities alter our personal relation to death. Because all continuity is threatened, we can no longer presuppose the tie to the future that, for all other generations, made individual mortality bearable. Thus Lifton locates the cause of today's denial of death not in the unconscious or human nature itself, but in equally devastating and inescapable forces within history.

Bibliography. D. Bakan, *The Duality of Human Existence* (1966). E. Becker, *The Denial of Death* (1973). L. Binswanger, "The Case of Ellen West" in R. May, S. Angel, and H. Ellenberger, eds., *Existence* (1967 [1944]). S. Freud, *Beyond the Pleasure Principle* in SE 18. E. Kübler-Ross, *On Death and Dying* (1969). R. Lifton, *The Broken Connection* (1979). E. Lindemann, "Symptomatology and Management of Acute Grief " *American J. of Psychiatry* 101 (1944). A. Weisman, *On Dying and Denying* (1972).

L. BREGMAN

DEATH, MEANING OF; DEATH RESEARCH AND EDUCATION; NEAR-DEATH EXPERIENCE. *Compare* DEATH, BIOMEDICAL DEFINITION OF; ESCHATOLOGY; GRIEF AND LOSS; LIFE/ALIVENESS; SURVIVAL (Occult); WILL TO LIVE.

DEATH EXPERIENCE. *See* NEAR-DEATH EXPERIENCE.

DEATH INSTINCT/DEATH WISH. *See* DEATH AND DYING, PSYCHOSOCIAL THEORIES OF; PSYCHOANALYSIS (Personality Theory and Research); SELF-DESTRUCTIVE BEHAVIOR.

DEATH RESEARCH AND EDUCATION. Refers to the systematic investigation of problems and issues about human mortality and the application of investigative findings to learning activities particularly of the professions.

1. The Distinguishing Characteristic of Modern Research. Examination of the written artifacts of any era reveals a universal concern with death. A juxtaposition of fear and fascination about mortality lies at the center of speculation about life and its reasons and death and its causes. Neither concerns about dying and death nor extensive literature expressing those concerns distinguishes the modern era from past generations, however. What does distinguish our times is the use of scientific method to explore the age-old and universal concerns.

The scientific investigation of dying and death refers to the systematic study of a hypothesis in which a common method allows empirically verifiable results to be repeatedly duplicated by other investigators. The findings of scientific investigation, which are changing constantly, should not be confused with its method. As methods become refined, conclusions about the hypothesis of study must be revised.

2. Varieties of Investigative Methods. Aristotle used the syllogistic method assuming that deductive logic would prevent the kinds of fallacies common to assumed knowledge based on tradition, the authority of a person in political power, or common sense. Tradition provides a transfer of wisdom from one generation to the next but it can also be repetition of a predecessor's mistakes. By definition, an authority is correct and conflicting ideas are erroneous. Common sense, at best, reflects opinion of the times. Syllogistic method challenged the earlier knowledge base about dying and death and, more importantly, eventually led to the quest for empirical proof.

Empirical methods include (1) analysis of individual case histories, (2) participant observation in which the investigator joins a group being analyzed and records the behavior of the members, (3) retrospective analysis of historical data, and (4) projective techniques which attempt to identify private meanings that subjects under investigation give to death and dying. An assumption of empirical methodology is that findings from the sampled population can be generalized to a wider population, an assumption not always valid.

More objective than empirical methods are scientific methods which are well-tested, carefully controlled for variables, empirically verifiable observations which lead to a quantifiable data base. Examples of scientific methods include (1) observations of a statistically significant sample population which contains controls and checks to establish reliability and validity, (2) survey research, (3) analysis of archival data (epidemiology) and (4) laboratory experimentation. Knowledge about dying and death may come by way of opinion, faith, or argument but that knowledge is "privileged" data based on the experience of one or a few persons. Scientific knowledge results from research publicly ascertainable and demonstrably evident to all persons using the same method.

3. Principal Topics of Modern Investigation. Most scientific investigation has focused on the physiology of dying which has led to improved control of pain, better techniques of palliation, and corrected methods of forensic investigation. Such research has led to a more inclusive definition of death, adding cessation of brain function to the cause of arrested cardiac and pulmonary function as criteria for establishing the time of death.

By extension of the hypothesis, "death is . . . ," dying, too, has been redefined to focus on what leads to cessation of bodily functions. Much research between World War II and the Vietnam War focused on dying from cancer. In part, this concentration reflects the shift from a majority of deaths in North America occurring from acute infectious disease or trauma, to chronic disease processes. Investigation of nonfatal losses has led to a wholly new set of rehabilitative specialities.

Investigations by the behavioral sciences have tended to focus on the psychological notion of situational "adaptation," e.g., how do the critically and terminally ill cope with their health crises? As a consequence, new definitions and distinctions have entered both the therapeutic and pastoral literature, e.g., denial, despair, hope, self-esteem. New techniques of professional intervention are also foci of extensive investigation such as analysis of the emotional needs of children, adolescents, and the elderly, the efficacy of individual psychotherapy, family or group therapy, and survivors' group interactions.

Investigations by the social sciences have tended to focus on relational and comparative questions: How members of families interact, how Protestants contrast in coping skills with Roman Catholics, what rituals in faith traditions best meet criteria of therapeutic interaction. Also extensive in the literature are analyses of how situations of living in the twentieth century are contrasted with those of previous generations, and the reasons for the differences.

Investigations of the behavioral and social sciences have made a noticeable impact on pastoral care and have moved the historian E. B. Holifield to describe the history of pastoral care in America as a shift in focus from salvation to self-realization.

4. Impact on Education. *a. General learning.* One of the most applied findings of research in thanatology has led to death and dying courses at all levels of learning. Usually, these courses are designed to overcome the pervasive distancing of death-related experiences in our culture. In contrast to the common event, prior to the twentieth century, of witnessing death in the home, many children have grown into adulthood in the past half century without ever seeing a dead body. Many modern values and metaphors of communication are designed to avoid such experiences. As a consequence, large numbers of North American society have been ill-prepared to cope with loss in general and death in particular. Primary and secondary school curriculum directors have been challenged to provide representative experiences of loss through various media. Public television, radio, and print media have changed noticeably since the 1970s to make realistic references to death in contrast to older euphemisms of avoidance.

b. Training for the professions. In 1969, Dr. Elisabeth Kübler-Ross published her book, *On Death and Dying*. Despite being unscientifically collected and erroneously analyzed, her data did demonstrate that, contrary to the assumptions of the times, physicians and other health-care providers seldom had the same perceptions of dying and death as did patients. Her findings caught the attention of a wide audience. A variety of courses were developed for nurses, social workers, chaplains, and other members of the helping professions throughout the continent.

The impact of these courses was at least threefold: Members of the helping professions were challenged to become better aware of their own fears and fascinations with death and dying; the needs of terminally ill patients and their families became acceptable concerns of the professional; and each of the major professions began major research efforts to expand data bases, to improve therapies of intervention, and to promote better communication with patients. Numerous surveys of educational offerings for the social worker, in nursing, funeral service, ministerial and medical education reveal that significant changes have occurred in professional education since 1970 in which the protocols of professional competence have come to include definable behaviors of assistance (rather than avoidance) to the terminally ill.

Bibliography. E. Kübler-Ross, *On Death and Dying* (1969). T. Rodabough, "How We Know About Death: Research Strategies," *Death Education,* 4 (1981), 315–36.

G. W. DAVIDSON

NEAR-DEATH EXPERIENCE; SURVIVAL (Occult). *Compare* SUICIDE RESEARCH.

DECALOGUE. *See* TEN COMMANDMENTS.

DECEPTION. *See* LYING. *See also* RESPONSIBILITY/IRRESPONSIBILITY, PSYCHOLOGY OF.

DECISION/INDECISION, PSYCHOLOGY OF. The action of deciding, from the Latin *to cut.* Reaching a determination; settling an issue; resolving a course of action; ruling on an issue; concluding with a final judgment about some matters in dispute. Indecision is inability to decide; vacillation; irresolution; hesitancy.

The psychology of decision is linked closely with personality strength and maturity. Several psychological theories help explain the common fear of deciding (i.e., fear of cutting). Difficulties in separation and individuation, castration fears, Oedipal conflicts and self-actualization are all related to the action of deciding. Aristotle wrote, "It is hard at times to decide what sort of thing one should choose — and still harder to abide by one's decisions." Biblical references include Josh. 24:15 ". . . choose this day whom you will serve . . ." and Mt. 16:15 "But who do you say that I am?" Decisions are a part of personal and spiritual growth.

1. Free Will and Determinism. Determinism is the philosophical theory that all events, including decisions, are completely determined by previously existing causes. A person cannot be held responsible for a decision, given everything, including one's personality, that preceded the choice. The theory of free will, (indeterminism) on the other hand, holds that one's actions are not completely determined by preexisting causes. The issue is unsettled in philosophy and psychology. The counselor can best proceed pragmatically with the hope that counselees can increase their freedom with the insights and new behavior developed through counseling.

2. Psychodynamics and Ego Psychology. Psychodynamics, defined as the inner psychic forces which move the personality, provide a picture of the multiple factors which empower a decision. In addition to physical, constitutional factors (e.g., retardation), a decision is produced in the face of (a) biological drives, (b) intrapsychic conflicts, (c) unresolved childhood needs, (d) typical character patterns, and (e) environmental pressures. For example, an author may or may not decide to work on a manuscript based on (a) a need for sleep, plus (b) a desire to and fear of surpassing one's father, plus (c) a desire to vindicate one's memory of feeling inferior to one's high school classmates, plus (d) chronic, personal workaholic character patterns, plus (e) an imminent vacation trip long planned with one's spouse. The resolution of those competing and/or synergistic psychodynamic forces, some conscious, some out of awareness, will lead to a decision to write, or not to write, or not to decide at all, which of course is also to decide. All these factors may usefully become part of counseling a person with problems in making decisions.

Ego psychology focuses on adaptation (deciding), specifically the deciding between the forces of the id, the superego and the environment. Ego strength may be defined as the ability to choose and reach productive goals. The healthy ego weighs alternatives, and in the face of conflict and anxiety, decides. Pathological decisions are regarded as the product of a weak ego. The strong ego is likened to the successful captain of a ship (i.e., one's personality). Analogously, the leadership tasks of the ego include managing the ship's engine below decks, directing the ship's crew which may want to mutiny or cooperate, estimating the powers of wind and waves, and ultimately keeping a hand on the rudder so the ship moves where the captain decides. Effective counseling develops ego strength, the ability to choose, and carry through one's decision.

3. Pathology of Decision Making. Pathology in decision making is at two opposite ends of the compulsive-impulsive continuum, namely, over-control to under-control. The compulsive delayers fear losing their boundaries if they cannot keep perfect control, and forestall decisions. Impulsive persons act out their impulses in haste to avoid anxiety which arises if they experience conscious awareness of their personal involvement in a decision. Decision making is a potential problem for several diagnostic categories of neuroses, personality disorders, and psychoses. The obsessive-compulsive counselee feels inner pressure to control everyone and everything in his or her environment in the hope of avoiding risks in living. Such needs for complete certainty often make decisions and subsequent action nearly impossible. The insecure doubter devises a living style and a myriad of habits that limit freedom and can lead either to constricting compulsions or phobic attempts to avoid danger.

The passive-aggressive person procrastinates decision and action, and thereby expresses aggression; the sociopath acts on immediate self-serving impulse; the psychotic decides without adequate reference to reality factors. Counseling strategies must vary according to the pathology of the counselee.

4. Counseling Theory, Strategy and Technique.
Counseling the person with a conflict about decisions calls for developing insight about the roots of the problem, and changing behavior. Counselees profit from observing, understanding, confronting, and working out their unsuccessful patterns. The following approach to counseling is based on a combined psychodynamic, ego psychology and cognitive behavior therapy approach.

A major cause of decision problems is low self-esteem. Decision-making is most difficult when one's self-worth is publicly connected to the decision, for example, an architect designing his own home. Fearing evaluation by important other persons, and possible negative exposure, a desire for perfection grows. Counseling requires that the client understands that his or her ultimate-reason-for-being is not being tested in a decision.

A second cause of decision problems is that a decision is a commitment, it cuts off other options, and is seen as a loss of freedom. Counseling offers the insight that few decisions are irreversible, and that passive-aggressive indecisiveness is even more costly.

A third cause of decision problems is the fear of success, rooted (according to psychoanalytic theory) in the fear of killing one's parent, being attacked by others for being "king-of-the-hill," or losing the friendship of one's peers. Counseling provides opportunity to explore the erroneous thinking behind the fear of success, and offers the more accurate thought that success, not failure, brings rewards.

A fourth reason is that some decisions are problematic simply because they mean getting involved in some burdensome act. Counseling weighs the pros and cons of fight or flight, and reasons that the gains of a completed term paper outweigh the discomfort of an incomplete one.

The counselor is advised to be active, because the impulsive counselee can easily control the counseling by aggressive "acting-in" during the sessions, and conversely the compulsive client is apt to delay effective work by endless ruminating. The active counselor will promote efficiency by intervening sooner rather than later, supporting while pushing for new behavior. Dealing in the present, including the client's behavior during the session, is crucial for counseling success. Impulsives want to avoid present anxiety by deciding something, deciding anything. Compulsives usually live in the future, preoccupied with trying to control how things will turn out. Compulsives therefore need to recognize that they avoid current feelings and behavior, and deny responsibility for their present moment. The counselee needs to internalize the responsibility for the problem—it is not circumstance but oneself, that makes a decision difficult.

Counseling proceeds effectively in a relaxed milieu where safety and security predominate, the fear of error is minimized, and decisions assume less awesome proportions. Counselees profit from being encouraged to set deadlines, and to make decisions, both within the counseling session, and between sessions. They strengthen their skill, develop insight about their behavior processes, and learn that they do not need to make perfect decisions, nor are decisions necessarily permanent.

The psychological need to be all-knowing and all-powerful can be analyzed as a defense against feeling human and finite. The arrogance of this view, and its ultimately self-defeating consequences, can be worked through by careful exploration of the client's neurotic desire for perfection and control.

Finally, counselors themselves are well-advised not to be perfectionists in their attitudes toward their counselees; this will help to provide the environment of acceptance which is necessary for healthy decision-making. As Winston Churchill observed, perfectionism is spelled p-a-r-a-l-y-s-i-s.

Bibliography. American Psychiatric Association, *DSM III*, rev. ed. (1986). Aristotle, *Ethics III* i. 43. A. Beck, *Cognitive Therapy and the Emotional Disorders* (1976). G. and R. Blanck, *Ego Psychology* 2 vols. (1974, 1979). E. Erikson, *Insight and Responsibility* (1964). J. Martorano and J. Kildahl, *Beyond Negative Thinking* (1989). L. Wolberg, *The Technique of Psychotherapy* (1967).

J. P. KILDAHL

COMMITMENT; DEPENDENCE/INDEPENDENCE; FREEDOM AND BONDAGE; WILL/WILLING. *See also* DOUBT AND UNBELIEF; GRACE; OBSESSIVE-COMPULSIVE DISORDER; RESISTANCE. *Compare* ASSERTIVENESS TRAINING AND THERAPY; RESPONSIBILITY/IRRESPONSIBILITY, PSYCHOLOGY OF.

DECOMPENSATION. A term referring to a breakdown in the optimal psychic functioning of an individual. This results from failure of the defense mechanisms, which normally serve as psychological protection from overwhelming vulnerability. An example of this process is seen when a person who has experienced a previous schizophrenic episode begins again to display symptoms characteristic of schizophrenia.

M. ESTELLE

DEFENSE AND COPING THEORY; PSYCHOSIS. *Compare* HALLUCINATION; PANIC.

DECREE OF NULLITY. In Roman Catholic canon law the declaration that an act is not legally recognized, applicable especially with reference to the sacrament of matrimony. A judgment of nullity rendered by the initial tribunal must be confirmed by an appeal tribunal in order for the marriage to be declared invalid. The grounds for annulment are of three types: (a) invalidating impediments—insufficient age; impotence; prior relationship of blood, religion or law; holy orders; solemn religious vows; (b) inadequate external manifestation of consent and (c) insufficiency of consent—intention not to cohabit; simulation of consent; conditional consent; lack of sufficient maturity of judgment. This decree has no effect on the legitimacy of children born of the union, and frees the Catholic party to enter a subsequent sacramental marriage.

Bibliography. *The Code of Canon Law* (1983). R. Lawler, D. Wuerl, and T. Lawler, *The Teaching of Christ* (1983).

E. A. MALLOY

DIVORCE AND REMARRIAGE (Roman Catholicism). *See also* CODE OF CANON LAW (Roman Catholicism).

DEDICATION. *See* COMMITMENT; VOWS/VOWING.

DEFENSE AND COPING THEORY. The concept of human self-defense is as old as human reflection on our behavior. Human defenses are biological, psychological, and social. Our bodies shiver in the cold to defend against freezing, we cringe in protective posture during an argument, we rush to rescue our children from an accident. The concept of defenses was given a central place in psychological theory by Freud in 1920 with his structural theory of psychic operation. The ego was posited to protect the organism from undue anxiety by mediating intrapsychic conflict between id, superego, and reality demands. The ego constructed defenses against each and produced compromise solutions to assuage the demands of all three. The operations of the ego were thus called "ego defenses."

1. **An "Open Living Systems" Model.** Freud's model is a reductionistic, mechanistic, "closed system" concept akin to a refrigerator, in which the ego defenses protect the inside of the refrigerator from getting hot. It is a static model, in that the human (refrigerator) goes nowhere. Its function and purpose is to keep cool. Defenses were thought to be the source of psychopathology.

In contrast, current ego psychology is based on an "open living systems" model. Here each element of the human organism contributes to the overall coping or adaptive function of the organism. There are no "defenses" as such, since each function contributes to the operation of the organism as a whole. The human acts to *preserve functions,* not a steady state. In turn, the preservation and maintenance of functions generates *purposive action.*

Purposive action is the consequence of responses to instinctual drive stimuli which represent *human preservation principles.* In lower animals the instinctual drives determine action. However, as we ascend the phylogenetic ladder (amoeba, worms, fish, birds, apes, human beings) we observe a decrease in direct determination of action by instinct and increasing psychological and social determination of action. In human beings we can no longer speak of instinctual behavior, but rather of instinctual principles. For example, with a few moments of oxygen deprivation the human will not only breathe harder, but loosen a collar and cry for help. On the other hand, a sexual drive stimulus may not be evoked except in special social circumstances and may not result in any sexual action by the person. Thus the person *processes* instinctual drive stimuli in accord with human preservation principles, rather than merely defending against instincts or satisfying instinctual demands.

2. **Human Preservation Principles.** There are three preservation principles that are reflected in human system actions. *a. Life preserving actions.* These are human actions to obtain food, water, air, temperature regulation (shelter), and body protection against pain or attack. These actions are mediated by brain monitors. In the young infant we see immediate stimulus-response reflexes, then simple conditioning responses, and later in adulthood there is complex social behavior required to produce life-preserving action (saving money to buy food). In the mentally retarded, in brain-damaged persons, and in psychotic persons, the life-preserving

actions are mostly retained. In severe pathology, these actions (or defenses) are compromised and death will eventuate (profound retardation, coma, catatonia, withdrawn depression). Life-preserving actions are in constant operation and highly automated.

b. Self-preserving actions. These include primary bonding to the nurturant parent and ego operational skills such as thinking, feeling, skilled body action. These actions emerge as the infant matures into a capacity to interact with external objects. This biological-social interaction creates intrapsychic structure: a stable memory of nurturant mother, the ego ideal memory of idealized others, the superego memory of good/bad behavior, and the ability to refine thinking, feeling, and the manipulation of objects. It also results in the construction of a self-construct or memory of identity. To function and survive as a person one must first achieve effective functions and then learn to use each function selectively when appropriate. When these actions are not learned well or used well, self-preservation is compromised. For example, poor bonding results in a borderline character disorder which cannot tolerate loneliness. Poor skill acquisition results in learning disabilities. Poor choice of actions such as trying to be an opera singer even though tone-deaf may result in self-deprecation. Much of self-preserving action becomes automated social behavior.

c. Species-preserving actions. This includes reproductive sexual action and social bonding action between parent and child and with a community. One cannot engage in effective species preserving action until and unless one is successful in life-preserving and self-preserving action. These actions are the least automated, most selective, and discontinuous in life.

3. **Integrative Systems.** Life-, self-, and species-preserving actions all require biological, psychological, and social *functions* combined in order to achieve a successful preservative action. This requires synthesis and integration of biopsychosocial operations of the organism. Thus there is no one set of "defensive functions" apart from the total human system. Rather, the human acts in effective or ineffective preservation as a whole act. The human has two systems to achieve integrative action.

a. Amygdala-visceral forebrain. This is the so-called "primitive brain" because it is well developed in mammals, and lies underneath the uniquely large frontal cortex or "new brain." The amygdala receives information from the body (pain, hunger, thirst), from the ego (thoughts, feelings), and the world (objects). Experimental studies indicate that the amygdala mediates: (1) general arousal, orienting reactions, sleep, (2) antagonistic behavior (fight, defense, predatory attack), (3) feeding activities, (4) sexual behavior, (5) reward and punishment in self-stimulation, (6) bonding behavior. The amygdala makes a primitive integration of events and produces a primitive preservation action. In addition, the amygdala makes a primitive *interpretation* of events as either threatening or preservative. In either case, the amygdala sends a signal to the front cortex, experienced as a basic tonic affect, which we label as the experience of "me." If the amygdala interprets a threat, the me experience is one of organismic dysequilibrium, while if the interpretation is one of preservation, the me experience is one of organismic equilibrium. Obviously the amygdala, a primitive brain process, may misinterpret body, ego, and object events. Thus we may experience me as threatened when we are not, or vice-versa. However, the frontal cortex also can recode amygdala interpretations. This occurs in human maturation when we learn to reinterpret events as a non-threat to our existence and recode our amygdala. Then we can tolerate challenge, stress, and even disasters without the amygdala generating a dysequilibrium signal. These data explain why some people are thrown into panic by slight events, while others tolerate and survive events like the Holocaust. This set of processes may be termed the "neurobiological basis for existential angst or peace."

b. Frontal cortex. The second integrative and interpretive system resides in the frontal cortex. Certain functions are subsystems, such as the cognition system, the emotional system, and the body skills system. But in addition there is a unique set of integrating, synthesizing, and choosing ego operations, often termed the "executive" operations. These are experienced as the "I" experience. This "I" can observe and change the thought system, the emotional system, the self-construct system, the memory system, and the amygdala system. The classical formulation of ego defenses dealt with the vicissitudes of the programmed and automated ego subsystems, which operate akin to a mechanistic computer operation. But this ignored the executive operations and the "I" experience thereof, which is the basis for personal freedom, for personal responsibility for one's actions, and for the capacity for moral choice.

4. System Psychopathology. In contrast to the classical view of pathological defenses which produce psychopathology, the open systems model views psychopathology as the result of (1) malfunction of a specific operation, or (2) the continued use of functions at an immature level of integration (fixation of functions), or (3) the loss of integrative capacity resulting in return to immature function (regression), or (4) inept and ineffective executive integration.

a. Malfunction operations. The immune system of the body normally produces immunity to infection, but if it malfunctions it produces asthma and allergic reactions. The normal "defense" has malfunctioned and created a pathology. Similarly, the amygdala may normally interpret threat or preservation, but if the coding is not modified with maturation, the amygdala will malfunction and signal threat when there is none. The person then may experience repetitive anxiety attacks, panic states, or become chronically defensive.

b. Fixation of immature operations. This is the hallmark of "personality disorders." They employ self-preserving actions typical of the preschool child, which were normal and adaptive at that age. But the same automated ego operations are inflexible, stereotyped, and maladaptive to adult life situations. These persons are life- and self-preserving, but have poor species-preserving capacity. They defend life and self well at the expense of others.

c. Regression in operations. This is typical of acute crises and stress reactions. The person is unable to synthesize current events and respond in a preservative fashion. They "defend" by retreating from the reality context. For example, a couple is arguing over the discipline of the children. The husband cannot simultaneously cope with the misbehavior of the children, his wife's demands, and his own uncertainty about himself as a father. He retreats to a simpler level of responding as a child, resulting in pouting and rage.

d. Inept and ineffective integration. This occurs when a person has not acquired the capacity for specific self-observation and self-evaluation. Thus the person depends upon automated behavior that might have been effective in prior contexts, but is now ineffective. New synthesis and integration is required. For example, an executive has lost his job and searches futilely for an identical job instead of reviewing his skills and abilities for different job opportunities. Or consider a couple whose children have left home, who continue life as before, yet wonder why they feel useless and depressed.

5. Arousal Management. *a. Response to stimuli.* The human organism is always processing stimuli. In a steady state the organism is at rest or at work without change in the arousal level. However, new or intensified stimuli produce organismic arousal. This is signalled by physiological signs of increased heart rate, more peripheral blood flow, increased muscle tension, and increased attention to stimuli. If this activation leads to effective action, the body and mind arousal are experienced as normal concomitants of the action (for example, getting worked up for a game). But if there is arousal and activation *without* effective action, we experience the body and mind arousal as the *experience of anxiety.* By analogy, if we start a car, press the accelerator, but leave the gears in neutral, the car will shake and roar in arousal without action. We may consider normal action as starting the car and driving when stimulated to do so. Conversely, starting the car when stimulated and then trying to decelerate the engine without driving is "neurotic defensive behavior." That is, the main purpose of action is to reduce the experienced anxiety, rather than generate effective purposive action.

b. Normal response sequence. In the normal sequence the human responds thus: (1) I am coping in a steady state. (2) New arousal occurs. (3) I cannot continue in my current coping style. (4) I create a new coping style by (a) changing my values or goals, (b) changing my responses or (c) changing my environment.

Effective coping may break down due to a number of factors such as: (1) overwhelming stress or disaster, (2) competing reality demands that overwhelm the synthesizing capacity, (3) lowered capacity to respond due to physical fatigue, illness, or psychological depletion of energy.

c. Abnormal response sequence. Whatever the cause, when effective coping does break down, the human organism responds in a preservative action to *reduce anxiety rather than take effective action.* Thus internal function improves, but external action deteriorates. This is the paradox of neurotic and psychotic defenses.

In this abnormal sequence the following pattern occurs: (1) I am coping in a steady state. (2) New arousal occurs. (3) My current coping style begins to break down. (4) I cannot synthesize and integrate a new coping style. (5) I regress to earlier immature levels of coping to reduce anxiety. (6) I feel like I am coping better, even though I am not — which I ignore. (7) The new situation is not resolved, because I have not created a new solution. (8) I am now operating in an internally adaptive style, and externally maladaptive style.

The above process can result in various levels of "defensive adaptation," ranging from temporary to chronic, simple to severe: (1) simple temporary anxiety; (2) simple chronic anxiety; (3) temporary neurotic reconstitution (depression, somatization, conversion reaction); (4) temporary severe disorganization (depersonalization, fuge, panic); (5) chronic severe disorganization (immobilization, catatonia, psychosis).

Since all defensive adaptations are "pseudo-solutions," the original stimuli, conflicts, or competing demands recur. Since the person has retreated from a new synthesis, they immediately respond with the same "pseudo-solution." That is, they repeat the same neurotic or psychotic sequence with the generation of the same symptoms over and over. This is called the *neurotic repetition compulsion*.

6. A Hierarchy of Coping Styles. All normal synthesizing operations require some degree of *repression*, which is the unconscious process of preventing stimuli from reaching consciousness. In neurotic coping styles, there is such a high degree of repression that the person is unaware of the nature of the stimuli, and therefore responds only to the anxiety generated, rather than to the stimuli. In psychotic defenses, by contrast, there is too little repression, hence the reality of the stimuli is ignored and the pseudo-solution offers a delusional reinterpretation of the stimuli.

With the above in mind we can examine four levels of coping styles in relation to reality stimuli.

Level I. Psychotic Coping Styles, common in psychosis, dreams, childhood. Examples are: denial of external reality, fixed distortion of external reality (hallucinations), and delusional projection (paranoia).

Level II. Immature Coping Styles, common in personality disorders and adolescence. Examples are: fantasy (schizoid withdrawal, denial through fantasy), projection, hypochondriasis, passive-aggressive behavior (masochism, self-harm), acting-out (compulsive delinquency, perversions).

Level III. Neurotic Coping Styles, common in everyone. Examples are: intellectualization (isolation, undoing, obsessionalism, rationalization), reaction formation, idealization, displacement (phobias, wit, conversion reactions), dissociation (neurotic denial).

Level IV. Mature Coping Styles, common in healthy adults. Examples are: sublimation, altruism, suppression, anticipation, humor.

All of these examples have been labelled "ego defenses," but that misrepresents the differences of "pathology" at each level. At Level I, there is a pseudo-solution, great distortion of reality, and associated malfunction of many ego operations; while at Level IV, none of this is true.

All normal and healthy people use all of these "ego defenses" (except at Level I) at least some of the time. The difference between healthy and pathological uses are: (1) Healthy people use higher level defenses more consistently. (2) Healthy people shift in their use of defenses for synthetic adaptation. (3) Healthy people use lower levels less frequently for shorter periods. (4) Healthy people are more aware of their use of lower level defenses, tend to avoid or eliminate such use, and seek to use higher levels.

7. Conclusions. All humans need to employ effective defenses. More accurately, we must achieve and utilize effective life-, self-, and species-preserving actions. The pejorative connotation of ego defenses is a misinterpretation of the requirements for survival. Perhaps the only truly defenseless persons are infants, fools, and psychotics.

All of the biopsychosocial operations of the human being provide important functions. Even delusions and hallucinations are important developmental operations in the young child. The hallmark of defenses is not a set of pathological operations, but rather the style of utilization of different mechanisms. A specific mechanism can be seen as operating in a normal or pathological fashion only within the context of the whole human action at the moment. For example, denial of illness is a normal life-preserving mechanism in the dying.

Finally, all humans are simply human. None of us copes effectively all the time. None of us always synthesizes and integrates life effectively all the time. All of us demonstrate ineffective, inept, inefficient, and neurotic responses some of the time. None of us has the capacity to transcend the intransigent flaws of our fallen human nature. We all fail to preserve our own existence.

Bibliography. Y. Ben-Ari, *The Amygdaloid Complex* (1981). F. K. Berrien, *General and Social Systems* (1968). A. Freud, *The Ego and the Mechanisms of Defense* (1937). J. Loevinger, *Ego Development* (1976). K. Menninger, M. Mayman, and P. Pruyser, *The Vital Balance* (1963). E. M Pattison, "Ego Morality," *Psychoanalytic Review*, 52 (1968), 187. G. E. Vaillant, *Adaptation to Life* (1977).

E. M. PATTISON

HEALTH AND ILLNESS; MENTAL HEALTH AND ILLNESS; PSYCHOPATHOLOGY, THEORIES OF. *See also* ANXIETY; BRAIN RESEARCH; EGO; EGO PSYCHOLOGY AND PSYCHOTHERAPY; OBJECT RELATIONS THEORY; PSYCHOANALYSIS; REPRESSION; *also* CYBERNETIC THEORY; SYSTEMS THEORY. *Compare* MODELS IN PSYCHOLOGICAL AND PASTORAL THEORY; STRESS AND STRESS MANAGEMENT; WILL TO LIVE.

DEFENSE MECHANISMS. In his second theory of psychic apparatus in 1920, Freud postulated an ego structure which mediates or "defends" the human organism from overwhelming demands of instincts, superego, and reality forces. In 1936 Anna Freud coined the term "ego-defense mechanisms" to describe a variety of neurotic coping strategies employed to "defend the ego." In psychoanalytic theory today, defense mechanisms are distinguished from mature ego "coping mechanisms."

E. M. PATTISON

DEFENSE AND COPING THEORY. *For specific defense mechanisms see* DENIAL; DISPLACEMENT; DISSOCIATION; IDENTIFICATION; INTELLECTUALIZATION; INTROJECTION; MORALIZING; PROJECTION; RATIONALIZATION; REACTION FORMATION; REGRESSION; REPETITION COMPULSION; REPRESSION; SUBLIMATION; SUPPRESSION; UNDOING.

DEFENSIVENESS, PASTORAL. In psychoanalytic theory, defense mechanisms are employed by the ego to relieve the pressure of excessive anxiety. Operating at the unconscious level, they serve to deny, falsify, or distort reality as a way of coping with a threatening situation. As human beings, clergypersons are susceptible to the very same defense mechanisms so exhaustively identified in the traditional psychoanalytic literature (A. Freud, 1957). There is no hard evidence that ministers or priests, for example, are immune from, or more vulnerable to, rationalization tendencies or to displacement than are non-clergy. Seen intrapsychically (as defenses were originally conceived) the same defense mechanisms which frequently produce a wide spectrum of psychiatric symptoms function just as devastatingly in clergy as in non-clergy. The human psyche is non-vocational — *not* a respecter of persons.

Once this is said and appreciated, it must be acknowledged that our modern and more systemic ways of thinking complicate the issue considerably. The psyche is an abstraction and defense procedures are formed contextually, which means that some varieties of conditions of life do nurture certain kinds of defenses and pathological conditions more than do others. The religious professional's context may then be inclined to produce some psychic conflict more so than other professions (McGinnis, 1969). Unfortunately, the empirical research on this issue is lacking; but there is sufficient clinical evidence to suggest that there may be certain factors in the clegyperson's context which would encourage a sort of "pastoral defensiveness"—a defensiveness which, though observable in all persons, finds in the religious environment an especially fertile soil.

1. **Moral masochism.** Perhaps the most comprehensive defense — or adaptive syndrome (the issue is not settled) — is moral masochism. Sigmund Freud (1956) first drew attention to the existence of masochistic trends in the instinctual life of human beings. He noted three forms of masochism: erotogenic masochism, feminine masochism, and moral masochism. He placed special importance on moral masochism, which he saw essentially as a sense of guilt which is mostly unconscious. Later clinicians expanded the term to include nearly any psychic process or behavior in which self-induced suffering is evident. Its pervasiveness is exemplified in the following view of a contemporary psychoanalytic clinician:

"Whether sanctified in religious practices as embodied in aspects of the Christian ethic, in mortification and its most extreme variant, asceticism; or institutionalized in the passively endured personal and mass desolation of warfare; or evidenced in the tenets of medieval court chivalry wherein 'courtesy' demanded complete acceptance of the unattainability of the female, in elaborate rituals or unrequited love . . . ; or exalted in the lyrical, though morbid, often necrophilian torrents of the Romantic movement; or inhering in the very texture of Western civilization wherein, in its beginnings, society was so structured that some groups of men were submissively obeisant to other groups in power, which had its full flowering in the facist ideology — masochistic phenomena remain a disturbing accompaniment of the human condition" (Panken, 1967).

Whether such pervasive phenomena have a special and clear presence in the religious sphere is problematic, although the psychoanalyst Theodor Reik (1941) certainly thought so and demonstrated the associations in detail in his classic study, *Masochism in Modern Man*. But whether moral masochism is itself pathogenic or salugenic remains a moot and perplexing issue, although many of its characteristics appear to fit well certain religious and theological perspectives (Strunk, 1982).

2. **Moralism.** At a more personal and specific level, moral masochism as a state or general condition often finds expression in moralism — that is, the tendency to see all things evaluatively or in a right/wrong format. Given the essentially normative nature of ministry, it is easy to see how moralism might be utilized by the religious professional with great frequency. He or she — through education, training, and perhaps even through temperament—learns well a moral set, thus drawing on the moralistic propensity with a natural flair. Such a tendency avoids a purely descriptive account of life's various situations and pumps into them ethical and moral meanings. Often, too, moralism leads to closure— albeit at times premature — thus reducing the need to deal with complex issues where nuances and shades of meanings are involved. In this sense, moralism serves more a defensive function — protecting the pastoral person from psychic discomfort and anxiety, at the same time providing a rationale for such a tendency in terms of theological "truths" or religious generalizations.

3. **Generalization.** Indeed, the religious project itself often breeds generalizations in a variety of ways. Religion, after all, makes exceedingly broad truth claims — claims which gain much of their appeal and power from their overly comprehensive nature. When this sort of theological way of thinking is personified, it can easily lead to generalization-type behavior. As a psychic process, generalization is when a person reaches a judgment applicable to a whole class, often on the basis of experience with a limited number of that class. The result of such a propensity may vary but certainly one outcome is the oversimplification of phenomena. Generalization, on the other hand, protects one from ambiguity — but often at the expense of seeing reality as a whole. Again, whether such a tendency is more apt to appear in the pastor than in other persons is a moot point. But the opportunity to utilize such a defense is amply available given the broad and lengthy agenda of the typical religious project.

4. **Intellectualization.** Another equally subtle defense which may have special availability to the pastor is intellectualization. In this process the individual uses elaborate ideas and reasons to deny the existence of unconscious feelings and to avoid recognition of them. Thus, a pastor may harbor pathological anger but may deny the condition by claiming that she or he is merely expressing "righteous indignation" over some social injustice, finding at the same time many biblical and theological reasons for taking a hard stand on that issue. Social psychologists have observed with some consistency, for instance, that peace demonstrators at times manifest strong aggressiveness, especially against the police or others who would question their actions. Still, such demonstrators have available to them a massive reservoir of ideas which can be woven into a form of rationalization quite difficult to penetrate. In the case of the religious person, such a reservoir of ideas and intricate notions may tran-

scend the empirical and contain powerful numinous qualities.

5. Religion and pathology. A key factor in such defensiveness is the unconscious nature of the processes, not the actual behavior itself. Whether moralism, generalization, intellectualization, or any other defense is pathological depends primarily on their unconscious quality.

Perhaps more important for pastoral persons to realize is the broader issue of whether religion itself, by its very nature, contains an unusually large possibility for the development of pathological thought and behavior. For instance, ecclesiogenic neurosis, a term utilized by some European psychiatrists, claims that there are indeed psychic illnesses which are caused by the widespread "tabooizing" education of churches where sexual and erotic areas of life are banned from open discussion but at the same time considered to be immoral, forbidden, or even threatened with punishment (Cumbee, 1980). A similar postulate is expressed strongly and clearly by Solignac in his *The Christian Neurosis* (1982) where a great deal of religion, especially of a conservative and dogmatic bent, is targeted as a producer of pathological behavior.

That such a perspective — the intimate tie between pathology and religion — may provide a large contextual horizon for "pastoral defensiveness" seems reasonable but the specifics of the association remain both problematic and complex.

Bibliography. D. W. Cumbee, "Depression as an Ecclesiogenic Neurosis," *J. of Pastoral Care*, 34:4 (1980), 254 – 67. A. Freud, *The Ego and the Mechanisms of Defense* (1957). S. Freud, "The Economic Problem of Masochism," in *Collected Papers*, 2 (1956), 255 – 68. T. C. McGinnis, "Clergymen in Conflict," *Pastoral Psychology*, (Oct. 1969), 13–20. S. Panken, "On Masochism: A Revaluation," *Psychoanalytic Review*, 54 (1967), 135 – 47. T. Reik, *Masochism in Modern Man* (1941). P. Solignac, *The Christian Neurosis* (1982). O. Strunk, Jr., "Moral Masochism and the Religious Project," *The Bulletin of the National Guild of Catholic Psychiatrists*, 28 (1982), 25–33.

O. STRUNK, JR.

DEFENSE AND COPING THEORY; MENTAL HEALTH PASTOR'S. *Compare* EMPATHY; PERCEPTIVENESS AND SENSITIVITY.

DÉJÀ VU. *See* PARAPSYCHOLOGY.

DE LASZLO, VIOLET. *See* NEW YORK PSYCHOLOGY GROUP.

DELAYED STRESS DISORDER (DSD) *See* POST-TRAUMATIC STRESS DISORDER.

DELINQUENCY. *See* ANTISOCIAL PERSONS; BEHAVIORAL DISORDERS OF CHILDHOOD; DEVIANT BEHAVIOR.

DELIRIUM. *See* ORGANIC MENTAL DISORDER AND ORGANIC BRAIN SYNDROME.

DELUSION. A personal belief which is maintained despite irrefutable evidence to the contrary. Delusions serve the purpose of dealing with such feelings as inferiority, anger, and frustrations of hopes. Thus, for example, an individual can overcome gross feelings of inferiority by entertaining the delusion of being the person of Christ (a delusion of grandiosity). Delusions are to be distinguished from *illusions* in that the latter are misinterpretations of stimuli.

A. J. STRAATMEYER

HALLUCINATION; PSYCHOSIS. *Compare* VISIONS AND VOICES.

DEMENTIA. *See* ORGANIC MENTAL DISORDER AND ORGANIC BRAIN SYNDROME; PSYCHOSIS.

DEMON POSSESSION. *See* EXORCISM; The DEMONIC.

DEMONIC, The. That realm of experience in which power, usually evil, is felt to be exercised by agents not under direct human control. Often these agents are thought of as superhuman, and sometimes as personal. In the latter case they may be called spirits, demons, angels, Satan, the devil, etc. Originally the Greek word *daimon* denoted a lesser, animistic deity, which could be either protective or threatening. In Stoic philosophy the word was internalized and came to mean the divine element residing in humans. Nevertheless, popular belief in demons as external forces always existed alongside the derived meaning and usually prevailed over it. Often demons were identified with spirits of the dead who might be conjured into appearing but who also had wills of their own and could choose to vex or possess humans.

The Greek conception of demons plays only a small role in the OT, although the phenomenon is certainly known (I Sam. 28:13; Deut. 18:10 ff.). On the other hand, stories like those of the tempting serpent (Gen. 3:1 ff.) and the "sons of God" who cohabit with human females (Gen. 6:1 ff.) both reflect and encourage speculation about superhuman agents of evil. So do the many OT references to angels, who can be thought of as good or evil, though ultimately under God's control. Satan, for example, was originally a deceiving or accusing spirit from God's heavenly court (I Chr. 21:1; Job 1–2). In Judaism and Christianity almost every meaning for the demonic set forth above comes into some prominence. This historical fact must be evaluated with care by those framing contemporary strategies of pastoral care and counseling.

1. Preoccupation with the Demonic in Ancient Judaism. Particularly in intertestamental Jewish literature thoughts about the demonic become conspicuous. Fallen angels especially take on clearer identities. According to one tradition, evil spirits, the offspring of the rebel angels in Gen. 6:1: ff., oppose God's rule on earth by introducing illness, weaponry, temptations to fornication, and oppressive governments into human life (Tobit; I Enoch 6 – 16; Jubilees 15:31). Sometimes demons are associated with idolatry (Joseph and Aseneth 12–13) or are seen to be the source of uncleanliness (I Enoch 99). Occasionally Satan is named as leader of the evil spirits (Jubilees 10), but other names for this superior power occur as well (e.g., Azazel, Belial, Beliar). In the Community Rule from Qumran (I QS 4) the dualistic view appears that the "spirit of falsehood" resides equally with the Holy Spirit in every human being, both having been emplanted by God.

All of this intertestamental literature presupposes to some degree an apocalyptic or two-age view of reality. God retains control over the present evil age, but only in a way that requires great human suffering and effort. From the historical point of view it is legitimate to link increased speculation about demons with Israel's experience of subjection to hostile foreign governments. In rabbinic Judaism, especially after the second Jewish war against Rome in 135 C.E., apocalyptic thought tends to recede and evil spirits usually descend to the status of lesser capricious forces. More and more they lose their lofty angelic character; one may combat them effectively by the practice of Torah.

2. New Testament Interpretations of the Demonic. The NT writers share many presuppositions about angels, demons, and the present evil age with those who produced the non-canonical Jewish literature of their day. Unlike their contemporaries, however, they believed that with the coming of Jesus, God had begun to destroy the domain of the evil powers in a final and irreversible way. Jesus performed many exorcisms and was reported to have withstood the devil's temptations to personal power (Mt. 4:1–11; Lk. 4:1–13). He also interpreted his actions as the central thrust of God's eschatological war against Satan: "If I by the Spirit of God cast out demons, then the kingdom of God has come upon you" (Mt. 12:28; cf. Lk. 11:20; Jn. 12:27–32). Especially in the epistles, Jesus' death and resurrection are pictured as God's triumph over angelic powers (Col. 2:13–15; I Pet. 3:22; Heb. 2:5–9), or at least as the decisive blow in this process (I Cor. 15:20–28).

Paul and the author of Revelation emphasize the ongoing dimension of the struggle against the "god of this world" (II Cor. 4:4). According to the apostle, believers live in an interim period at the juncture of the ages. Through the Holy Spirit it is a time filled with infinite promise; but it is also a time of danger, for the demonic powers are now mounting their final counterattack. This means that even the everyday structures of life (e.g., marriage, business, rejoicing, mourning), quite normal in themselves, may be co-opted by the powers to tempt believers into bondage (I Cor. 7:29–31). Paul sees the enslaving powers at work in such entities as death, sin, and the law (I Corinthians 15; Galatians 4); he believes that they can use for their dark purposes "things present . . . things to come . . . height, depth . . . [and] anything else in . . . creation" (Rom. 8:38 ff.). To the extent that they oppose God's new order, human governments become agents of the demonic (I Cor. 2:6 ff.; Revelation). God and Christ help the believer to endure these endtime trials, but one must exercise the gift of discernment to detect the powers of this age (Rom. 12:1 ff.), for they tend to hook proud people where they feel secure in knowledge (I Corinthians 8; 10:11–22). Some modern interpreters have stressed the connection between oppressive political or religious authorities and the frequent language about the demonic in the NT (see esp. P. Hollenbach, 1981). Bultmann has correctly seen that Paul modifies the mythology of Jewish apocalyptic by showing how the demonic powers are characteristically experienced in existential categories.

3. Modern Encounters with the Demonic. Recent wrestlings with the demonic in Judeo-Christian thought are more widespread than current pastoral literature would suggest. Kierkegaard may have been the first to relate Paul's existentialist impressions of the demonic to personality structures. He wrote of narcissistic people so shut up in themselves that they had come to love their bondage above all else and shunned contacts with any liberation from the outside, or else raged against it. These personalities Kierkegaard termed "demoniacal." As therapy he recommended the patient, silent presence of another with indirect communication. Paul Tillich took up similar biblical insights in his frequent references to the demonic, among which one finds a discussion of how ordinary time and space become diabolical when emptied of being. Tillich's student Rollo May explores some implications of his teacher's thought about the demonic for the practice of psychotherapy, although he also shows himself influenced by the old Stoic view.

On a more cosmic plane, literature growing out of the Nazi period, and especially the Holocaust, raises anew the spectre of a corporate evil, which is more than the sum total of human choices (see, e.g., Elie Wiesel's *Night*). Similarly, William Stringfellow has examined American political and spiritual life through images of the demonic provided by the book of Revelation. Surprisingly realistic portraits of men, women, and institutions possessed by demons appear in the novels of C. S. Lewis and Charles Williams. Although Freud did not reckon with the demonic as such, he laid great stress on society's need to restrict the boundless forces of the instincts, both of "life" and of "death." Moreover, his work stands as a necessary warning against the demonizing of other people (an unbiblical notion) by the projection upon them of one's own unresolved conflicts. Jung (1954) wrote explicitly about the demonic, associating it with the destructive tendencies of the archetypes and locating it finally in the Godhead. In a work on the discernment of spirits Morton Kelsey (1978) provides an adaptation of the Jungian position for pastoral care and counseling shaped by charismatic Christian views.

In summary, one may say that the demonic, along with the two-age conceptions linked to it in the NT, requires considerable attention today as a category for understanding and guiding pastoral care and counseling. At the very least, the psychic forces exerted by social-political-economic systems, from the international to the local, need to be taken more seriously in ministering to individuals. It is significant that some recent secular thinking about family systems (R. D. Laing, L. Pincus, and C. Dare) describes problems which, from a classical Judeo-Christian standpoint, resemble nothing so much as the demonic at work.

Bibliography. R. Bultmann, *Theology of the New Testament* (1951–1955). W. Foerster, *"Daimon," Theological Dictionary of the New Testament*, vol. II, (1964). S. Freud, *Civilization and Its Discontents* vol. 21, in *SE* (1930). P. Hollenbach, "Jesus, Demoniacs, and Public Authorities," *J. of the American Academy of Religion* (1981), 567–88. C. G. Jung, *Answer to Job* (1954). M. Kelsey, *Discernment* (1978). S. Kierkegaard, *The Concept of Dread* (1944 [1844]) and *Sickness Unto Death* (1954 [1849]). R. D. Laing and A. Esterson, *Sanity, Madness and the Family* (1970). C. S. Lewis, *That Hideous Strength* (1945). R. May, *Love and Will* (1969). L. Pincus and C. Dare, *Secrets in the Family* (1980). W. Stringfellow, *An Ethic for Christians* (1973). P. Tillich, *Systematic Theology* (1951–1963). C. Williams, *All Hallows Eve* (1948). E. Wiesel, *Night* (1972).

J. KOENIG

EVIL; EXORCISM; WORLD VIEW. *See also* EXISTENTIALISM AND PASTORAL CARE; JESUS; NEW TESTAMENT, TRADITIONS AND THEOLOGY OF CARE IN. *Compare* DAIMONIC; PARAPSYCHOLOGY; PSYCHOPATHOLOGY AND RELIGION; WITCHCRAFT.

DENIAL. A defensive process whereby painful thoughts and feelings associated with reality are unconsciously rejected or evaded. While in some instances of denial the facts of reality might be consciously accepted, their personal and emotional significance is unconsciously disavowed; one seems oblivious of their significance. Usually these painful thoughts and feelings are reflective of unpleasant or unwanted aspects of the self.

D. HICKEL

DEFENSE AND COPING THEORY; DEFENSE MECHANISMS; NEUROSIS. *Compare* REPRESSION; SUPPRESSION.

DENIAL OF DEATH. *See* DEATH AND DYING, PSYCHOSOCIAL THEORIES OF.

DENIAL OF SELF. *See* SELF-DENIAL. *See also* SACRIFICIAL BEHAVIOR.

DEPENDENCE/INDEPENDENCE. Dependence/independence represents one continuum used to describe the human psyche and interpersonal functioning. Personality types can be classified according to a person's relative degree of psychological dependence/independence. At one pole is the overly dependent person who needs the support, approval, and presence of others in order to feel secure, adequate, and lovable. At the other extreme is the overly independent person who needs no one and who prides him- or herself on being self-sufficient. Both extremes are never as simple as they first appear and facades often disguise a hidden opposite dynamic. Theological perspectives offer a critique of both extremes and argue for the essential interdependence of all of life.

1. The Dependence/Independence Continuum. The dependence/independence continuum is a relative scale of two opposite qualities: independence and dependence. At each pole are the extremes and at each point along the continuum there is a relative blending of dependence and independence. Most people, representing the middle portions of the "bell curve," are a mixture of dependent and independent features. In other words, most humans have needs in both areas: the need for the affection, love and approval of others (dependency needs) and the need to be competent, to be self-sufficient and to have a sense of personal power (independency needs). Generally, a person is functioning in a healthy manner, when he or she is getting both types of needs satisfied.

While people have a certain preferred style in regard to dependence/independence, it is also true that circumstances may cause some flexibility in functioning. For instance, a person may act/feel more independent in a work situation than he or she does in a home environment. In addition there will be periods of "situational dependency" such as bereavement, unemployment, illness or hospitalization. Such situations momentarily force people to be or feel more dependent than they might normally be or feel. A person who is able to adapt his or her interpersonal functioning to meet the demands of a new situation or life-stage is generally considered to be more healthy than the person who cannot. People who are highly rigid, especially at either extreme of the continuum, usually have the most psychological difficulties.

2. The Overly Dependent Person. At one extreme is the overly dependent person. This kind of person has strong, sometimes over-powering, needs to be dependent on other people. She or he needs the presence, approval and support of others in order to feel secure, adequate and competent. Such people may have other related problems, like depression, jealousy, hypersensitivity, suicide impulses and passivity, and tend to lean on others and find it difficult to make independent decisions. It is easy to imagine that such people are very vulnerable in crises, like a marital dissolution or a death of a loved one, that knocks out their usual support system. On such occasions dependent people feel abandoned, overwhelmed and helpless.

Dependent people are attracted to the church. They find the presence of a nurturing community, the virtue of humility and the promise of comfort all very appealing. Authoritarian religion, which provides simple clear answers and reduces the need to make independent decisions, is even more alluring. Dependent people tend to be very active in church affairs. They tend to be very loyal, dependable workers. Typically, they are not strong leaders. The church can easily institutionalize dependency for such people by providing a safe structure, a set of comfortable beliefs and a built-in support system. Yet, a wise and sensitive pastor can also gradually and persistently help dependent people to become more independent by giving them more responsibilities in the congregation, by assisting them to think independently, by encouraging them to develop further vocational skills and by teaching them that assertiveness is not a sin.

3. The Overly Independent Person. At the other extreme is the overly independent person. Compared to the "dependent personality," modern psychology has devoted relatively little attention to the problems of the excessively independent person. This is due, in part, to a strong cultural bias in America that defines independence and even excessive independence as desirable. Western culture admires the "rugged individualist." Pastoral traditions, however, particularly those that deal with the dangers of pride, offer some resources.

Pastors are less likely to see the overly independent person in church. Such people usually do not attend church regularly because, after all, they do not need others, the church or God. More often, a pastor only hears complaints about the excessively independent person from his or her church-going spouse. Often overly independent people have a difficult time in emotional situations, like bereavement. Showing emotion, especially weeping, is perceived as a sign of weakness. Therefore they resist crying and repress pain. For these same reasons they may make poor marriage partners. They resist sharing tender emotions, and thereby block marital intimacy. They act as if they need no one but themselves.

Overly independent people tend to avoid consulting their physicians, even when sick. They often deny that they have any weakness—physical or otherwise. Such extensive denial patterns can, of course, lead to more serious health or interpersonal problems. If they have to enter a hospital, even for a brief period, they find the forced dependency difficult to cope with. Typically, they make poor patients; sometimes angry or depressed. Death, the ultimate robber of independence, is particularly difficult for them to deal with. Yet, such crises often give pastors their only opportunity to minister to these people.

C. G. Jung posited that whenever there is a personality characteristic in the extreme, such people have a hidden opposite characteristic that is repressed in order to maintain the onesidedness. According to this principle of compensation, the psyche fights to balance itself by giving expression to this opposite feature. The male alcoholic, for example, argues that he can stop drinking anytime he wants. He does not need any doctor, AA group or hospital program. Yet, anyone who has worked with alcoholics knows that their over-independence only masks a deep dependency. Similarly, overly dependent people have a hidden strong side. There is great power in many of the manipulative "games" that dependent people play to get their needs met. The key to working with these people is to help them "own" their power and to use it in more direct and open ways, thereby reintegrating their independent side into their consciousness.

4. **Dependence, Independence, and Interdependence in Theological Perspectives.** Theologian Friedrich Schleiermacher made a distinction between absolute dependence and relative dependence. The feeling of absolute dependence, which is the essence of religion, has a divine object. Relative dependence refers to all other human dependencies. If humans recognize their absolute dependence upon God, then all other human dependencies become relative. From this perspective, the overly dependent person is understood as someone who has absolutized human dependencies. They have idolized them. Such people actually need to become more dependent upon God, thereby freeing themselves to view their human dependencies for what they are: of relative importance.

St. Paul offers another perspective on this issue when he uses the image of a body to describe the church (I Corinthians 12). Each member of the church, like each body part, is different and has a unique contribution to make if the whole organism is to live and flourish. His vision of the community of faith is one characterized by interdependence. For Paul, interdependence is both a descriptive and a normative statement. Humans are essentially interdependent. Humans need God, God needs humans. We need others, others need us. People need the natural order, the natural order needs human stewardship. People who are overly independent or overly dependent deny this essential interdependence of life. Only when they allow the tension between dependence and independence to be transcended by the dynamic of interdependence do they find their health and salvation (cf. Gilligan).

Bibliography. D. W. Augsburger, *Anger and Assertiveness in Pastoral Care* (1979). H. T. Blane, *The Personality of the Alcoholic: Guises of Dependency* (1968). C. Gilligan, *In a Different Voice* (1982). C. G. Jung, "The Psychology of the Unconscious," *Collected Works*, vol. 7 (1953), pp. 1–117. H. Parens and L. J. Saul, *Dependence in Man: A Psychoanalytic Study* (1971). F. Schleiermacher, *The Christian Faith* (1928). S. Southard, *People Need People* (1970). P. Tournier, *The Strong and Weak* (1963).

R. S. SULLENDER

DECISION/INDECISION, PSYCHOLOGY OF; FREEDOM AND BONDAGE; RESPONSIBILITY/IRRESPONSIBILITY, PSYCHOLOGY OF. *See also* EGO STRENGTH; IDENTITY; SELF/SELFHOOD. *Compare* AGGRESSION AND ASSERTION.

DEPERSONALIZATION NEUROSIS. *See* NEUROSIS.

DEPRAVITY/ORIGINAL SIN. *See* SIN/SINS.

DEPRESSION. *See* SADNESS AND DEPRESSION. *See also* HOLIDAY DEPRESSION; MANIC-DEPRESSIVE (BIPOLAR) DISORDER.

DEPROGRAMMING. Any process of counter-indoctrination that persuades a convert to a "cult" to relinquish involvement with the group, its views and practices. The term "cult" refers to a variety of stigmatized groups, usually religious and/or therapeutic in their primary aims, which deviate significantly from the social mainstream. Deprogramming is frequently coercive: the convert is abducted from the group, physically confined and subjected to psychologically assaultive techniques for breaking up "programmed" beliefs and attitudes. Coercive deprogramming is most commonly carried out by professional deprogrammers hired by parents of adult children involved in cults.

In this article we briefly describe coercive deprogramming and the ongoing, complex controversy regarding it, which involves interrelated issues of mental health, civil liberty and religion.

1. **Process of Coercive Deprogramming.** Involuntary deprogramming begins with forcible abduction and physical confinement, often in a specially prepared motel room guarded by hired deprogrammers and their assistants. Concerned relatives of the cult member sometimes participate in the abduction, as do police when custody is legally authorized (see section 2).

Deprogramming typically consists of up to four days of sustained and forceful verbal assault, sleep deprivation and, in some cases, physical violence. The fatigued and highly stressed deprogrammee is deliberately enraged and humiliated by blasphemous and scatological abuse of the cult's charismatic leader and beliefs, and is mocked, insulted and degraded with accusations of sexual crimes, prostitution, etc. The deprogrammer harangues the captive convert with evidence of the cult's use of mind control, compelling testimonies of deprogrammed ex-members, and fallacies in cult doctrine. These arguments provoke the deprogrammee into emotionally charged debate, deemed essential for successful deprogramming. Deprogrammers sometimes resort to physical violence to provoke emotional turmoil and angry argumentation in cases of silent or ritualistic responses from converts, such as chanting.

In these ways deprogrammers forcibly impress upon the deprogrammee's mind the view that he or she is a victim of cultist mind control or brainwashing, and is incapable of objective, independent thinking, and that the cult's belief system is false. Successful deprogramming is sometimes followed by several weeks at a special rehabilitation facility where systematic instruction in Bible interpretation and in the psychology of mind control lead the deprogrammee to reevaluate the cult experience and to reidentify with the social and religious mainstream.

2. Legal Status of Deprogramming. From the legal standpoint there are three kinds of deprogramming: voluntary, legal and extra-legal. Deprogramming is *voluntary* when the individual willingly meets with deprogrammers either before joining, during membership or after leaving the cult. Coercive deprogramming is *legal* when carried out after a judge has granted temporary custody under existing guardianship or conservatorship laws, on the basis that the convert is mentally incapacitated by cultist indoctrination. Custody is usually granted in *ex parte* hearings in which the judge confers with the parents' lawyers; the cult member is not represented. Legal deprogramming has become rare since 1977 when a California appellate court barred the use of existing conservatorship statutes to imprison cultists (*Katz vs. Superior Court*). Legislation has since been introduced in several state legislatures to give judges broad discretionary authority to remove persons from "coercive" and deceptive groups and to allow forced treatment under private auspices.

In the great majority of cases, the abduction and coercive deprogramming of an adult convert is an *extra-legal* vigilante action without a court custody order. However, the courts have been extremely tolerant of extra-legal abductions, and usually acquit or refuse to prosecute hired abductors out of sympathy for parents. Unsuccessfully deprogrammed individuals have obtained criminal convictions or civil decisions against their abductors in a small fraction of cases. As of mid-1983, the U.S. Supreme Court has refused to review all deprogramming cases appealed to it and has let stand both pro- and anti-deprogramming appellate court decisions.

3. Arguments for Coercive Deprogramming: the Anti-Cult Perspective. The "anti-cult" movement is composed primarily of relatives of converts and disaffected ex-converts, and is led by medical and legal professionals. The anti-cult analysis maintains that converts to intense, unconventional religious groups have no pre-existing motives for conversion, but rather are "captured" by cultist techniques that are so efficacious as to constitute "mind control" or "brainwashing." Cult members are psychologically enslaved, incapable of critical reason, and therefore not responsible for what they think, feel and do. Since the conversion is due to induced mental pathology, it is actually a pseudo-conversion, with zombie-like obedience to malevolent cult masters. The forcible undoing of this condition by coercive deprogramming is, then, a necessary therapeutic intervention desperately needed by the convert. Constitutional protection of religious freedom does not apply to cult members because freedom of religion implies freedom of thought as a prior condition.

Intense, nontraditional religious commitment and practices are viewed as having "coercive" and even "hypnotic" effects that benumb free will and enslave the devotee. Sudden changes of values, stereotyped discourse with restricted vocabulary, humorlessness, disinterest in public events, and absolutistic thinking are all considered to be symptoms of cult-induced mental impairment syndromes. The effectiveness of coercive deprogramming in "liberating" converts from cultist bonds is interpreted as proving the psychopathological nature of cultist involvement.

Coercive deprogramming is assigned a moral as well as medical legitimacy and urgency, in the anti-cult view. Groups stigmatized as "cults" tend to be authoritarian and manipulative in their leadership, communal and totalistic in their social organization, aggressive in their proselytizing, and systematic in their programs of indoctrination — all offensive to fundamental American values of individuality, freedom and rationality. Thus the rescue of American sons and daughters from cultist entrapment becomes both morally and medically imperative.

4. Arguments Against Coercive Deprogramming. Critics of deprogramming emphasize that their arguments — unlike the anti-cult rationale — are grounded in a substantial body of social scientific research, including over 250 reports in scholarly journals.

According to survey results (see R. Anthony) authoritarian cults that isolate members from mainstream society contain less than one percent of all Americans involved in unconventional religious groups. The research literature shows the mental health effects of the "new religions" to be exceedingly complex and varying greatly from group to group. Numerous beneficial mental health effects have been identified (Robbins and Anthony, 1982). The anti-cult characterization of these groups as monolithic in deception and harmfulness thus seems a drastic over-generalization.

The mind-control model has been found seriously inaccurate even for authoritarian, isolationist cults. The "capture" of converts is refuted by research revealing preexisting individual motivation for, and seeking of, involvement. Other studies document a large voluntary turnover in supposedly mind-controlled groups, contradicting the notion that members are helpless without outside intervention. The exercise of individual choice makes cultist involvement an issue of religious freedom, and First Amendment protection remains fully applicable.

Retrospective accounts by deprogrammed ex-members are often cited as confirming mind-control allegations, but deprogrammers, anti-cult therapists and parents usually have a major hand in shaping the ex-convert's reconstructions and interpretations. In a study of 100 deprogrammed and voluntary ex-members of a large authoritarian group, mainly the deprogrammed ex-members believed they had been brainwashed (Solomon, 1981).

It is noteworthy that the current wave of sectarian religiosity follows two earlier periods of evangelical fervor in American history, from 1720 to 1740 and from 1820 to 1850, and that the authors of the Constitution established the separation of church and state expressly to accommodate intense religious sensibilities among citizens.

Modern psychiatry champions secular rationality and traditionally is hostile towards religious perspectives. The allegation of "brainwashing" and the reframing of the "new religions" as predominantly a mental health issue can be seen as an arbitrary but effective rhetoric for waging a covert ideological war. The "medicalization" of the cult issue extends the jurisdiction of the medical profession into religious and social realms. The mind-control model puts anti-cultists in a humanitarian role while it medically legitimizes religious persecution and the enforcement of worldviews and lifestyles acceptable to families and mainstream society. Yet, coercive deprogramming itself closely resembles the "mind control" that deprogrammers supposedly despise.

The authors agree that while the harmful extremes demonstrated by some groups show that public scrutiny is warranted, coercive deprogramming is unsuitable from psychological and civil libertarian standpoints.

Bibliography. T. W. Adorno, E. Frenkel-Brunswick, D. J. Levinson and R. N. Sanford, *The Authoritarian Personality* (1950). R. Anthony, "The Fact Pattern Behind the Deprogramming Controversy: An Analysis and an Alternative," *Review of Law and Social Change* 9, (1980), 73 – 90. R. Anthony and T. Robbins, "Deprogramming, Brainwashing and the Medicalization of Deviant Religious Groups," *Social Problems* 29, (1982), 283–97. For a classic text on mind control: R. Lifton, *Thought Reform and the Psychology of Totalism* (1963). Cited in Section 4 is T. Solomon, "Integrating the Moonie Experience," in *In Gods We Trust: New Patterns of Religious Pluralism* (1981), 275–94.

B. ECKER
T. ROBBINS
R. ANTHONY

NEW RELIGIOUS MOVEMENTS. *See also* ETHICS, PROFESSIONAL; LEGAL DIMENSIONS OF PASTORAL CARE AND COUNSELING. *Compare* CYBERNETIC THEORY IN PSYCHOLOGY AND COUNSELING; INDOCTRINATION; MANIPULATION.

DEPTH PSYCHOLOGY. The psychology of the unconscious and the nonrational. Its task is the exploration of dreams, fantasies, complexes, defenses, and related processes which access the daimonic. Its major goal is the integration of the conscious and unconscious selves. In the U.S. the term most commonly refers to analytical (Jungian) psychology but also to psychoanalysis and other psychologies emphasizing the unconscious.

H. VANDE KEMP

ANALYTICAL (JUNGIAN) PSYCHOLOGY; PSYCHOANALYSIS; UNCONSCIOUS. *Compare* DEMONIC; DYNAMIC PSYCHOLOGY; EXISTENTIAL PSYCHOLOGY; INDIVIDUAL PSYCHOLOGY.

DESENSITIZATION. *See* SYSTEMATIC DESENSITIZATION.

DESIRE. *See* LOVE; LUST AND CHASTITY; MOTIVATION; REASON AND PASSION.

DÉSIRÉ MERCIER, CARDINAL. *See* COUNSELING, ROMAN CATHOLIC.

DESPAIR. *See* HOPE AND DESPAIR; SADNESS AND DEPRESSION.

DESTINY, HUMAN. *See* ESCHATOLOGY; PERSON (Christian *or* Jewish Perspective).

DESTRUCTIVE BEHAVIOR. *See* AGGRESSION AND ASSERTION; ANTISOCIAL PERSONS; RAGE AND HOSTILITY; SELF-DESTRUCTIVE BEHAVIOR.

DETACHMENT, PROFESSIONAL. *See* OBJECTIVITY, PROFESSIONAL; PHENOMENOLOGICAL METHOD IN PASTORAL CARE.

DETERMINISM. *See* FREEDOM AND DETERMINISM. *See also* CAUSALITY IN PSYCHOLOGY, FORMS OF.

DETOXIFICATION. *See* ALCOHOL ABUSE, ADDICTION AND THERAPY.

DEVELOPMENT, HUMAN. *See* HUMAN DEVELOPMENT.

DEVELOPMENT, PERSONALITY. *See* LIFE CYCLE THEORY; PERSONALITY DEVELOPMENT, BIOLOGICAL AND SOCIALIZING FACTORS IN; PERSONALITY THEORY. *See also* ANALYTICAL (JUNGIAN) PSYCHOLOGY, PSYCHOANALYSIS, *or* HUMANISTIC PSYCHOLOGY (Personality Theory and Research); COGNITIVE, EMOTIONAL, LANGUAGE, MORAL, *or* PSYCHOSOCIAL DEVELOPMENT.

DEVELOPMENTAL CRISIS. *See* CRISIS, DEVELOPMENTAL.

DEVELOPMENTAL DISABILITY. *See* HANDICAP AND DISABILITY; MENTAL RETARDATION.

DEVELOPMENTAL DISORDERS. One of five major groups of mental disorders usually beginning or first evident during infancy, childhood, or adolescence as described in the American Psychiatric Association's *Diagnostic and Statistical Manual of Mental Disorders (Third Edition)*, also known as the "*DSM*-III." This grouping includes thirteen diagnoses divided into six which relate to distortions in development (Pervasive Developmental Disorders) and seven which relate to delays in specific areas of development (Specific Developmental Disorders). The developmental disorders are of interest because they affect the aspect of childhood which most differentiates it from adulthood, that being the multiple lines of rapidly and relatively predictably occurring change which characterize normal development. Mental retardation is not considered a developmental disorder in the DSM-III classification. It is categorized separately as a generalized intellectual disorder. It can occur simultaneously with any of the developmental disorders.

1. Pervasive Developmental Disorders. The six specific diagnoses represented in this category all describe disorders involving abnormalities in the development of multiple psychological functions. These include, for instance, attention, perception, reality testing, motor movement, attachment behavior, affective expression, and quality of play. It must be emphasized that it is the abnormal development, as opposed to across-the-board delays, of these psychological functions which is important. Some areas may be delayed. Others will have evolved in a direction and to an endpoint that would be abnormal for any stage. Others may even appear advanced. These multiple and marked discrepancies in development result in a significant impairment in social skills, language, and response to the environment.

a. Infantile autism. The main characteristics are a profound avoidance of interaction with others, including such traits as failure to establish eye contact or exhibit a social smile, bizarre mannerisms, delayed or absent language development, including most frequently echolalia and pronoun reversals (usually substituting "you" for "I" or not using the pronoun form), affective aloofness, and a fascination with lights and twirling objects. Its main features must be present prior to thirty months of age. Some parents report signs from the beginning while others indicate they arose after a period of relatively normal development, even after beginning language development. The attachment system is heavily affected, and it is probable that many of the final features of this disorder are secondary to this involvement. A moderate percentage of children with infantile autism are put at increased risk for this disorder by the presence of some other disorder, usually a neurological one. There appears to be a genetic risk factor as well, as identical twins have a high concordance for the development of autism.

b. Childhood onset of pervasive development disorder. The characteristics of this disorder are essentially those of infantile autism. However, this diagnosis applies when their onset is between thirty months and twelve years of age. It is usually a milder condition than infantile autism.

2. Specific Developmental Disorders. The seven diagnoses in this category represent disorders in which there is significant impairment in specific developmental areas in a child whose development is otherwise normal.

a. Developmental reading disorder. This is the most common of the specific developmental disorders. It is often called "dyslexia." It can only be diagnosed on IQ tests which have verbal and performance subtests.

b. Developmental arithmetic disorder. IQ tests are required to establish this diagnosis. It is not a common disorder.

c. Developmental language disorder. This refers to the delayed acquisition of language. There are two types.

i. Expressive type. Children with this disorder have severe lags in vocal expression even though they understand words and concepts normally.

ii. Receptive type. Both the expression and the understanding of language fail to develop. These children often attempt to communicate nonverbally through gestures.

d. Developmental articulation disorder. One or several of the later-acquired speech sounds are mispronounced consistently.

3. Treatment. The Pervasive Developmental Disorders require a comprehensive and long-term approach to treatment. Early identification and intervention are important. Individual psychotherapy aimed at augmenting the child's minimal relationship capabilities is combined with family psychotherapy whose purpose is to facilitate membership in a family of a child who is "different." Anti-psychotic medication is sometimes used in low dosage. Educational programs must be tailored to the child's specific developmental levels.

The treatment for the Specific Developmental Disorders is primarily educational. Learning disability classrooms, tutoring, and speech therapy are used as appropriate. Psychotherapy is employed when an emotional difficulty is contributing to or results from one of these disorders.

Bibliography. American Psychiatric Association, *Diagnostic and Statistical Manual of Mental Disorders,* 3d. ed., (1980) M. S. Mahler, *On Human Symbiosis and the Vicissitudes of Individuation,* vol. 1: *Infantile Psychosis* (1968).

D. A. KRAMER

EXCEPTIONAL CHILDREN AND THEIR FAMILIES; HANDICAP AND DISABILITY; PERSONALITY DEVELOPMENT. *See also* DIAGNOSTIC AND STATISTICAL MANUAL III; EVALUATION AND DIAGNOSIS, PSYCHOLOGICAL. *Compare* MENTALLY RETARDED PERSONS, JEWISH CARE AND COUNSELING OF; LANGUAGE DEVELOPMENT; MENTAL RETARDATION; SPEECH DISORDERS AND THERAPY.

DEVELOPMENTAL PSYCHOLOGY. Developmental psychology is the branch of general psychology concerned with the characteristics and processes of human and animal behavior which change from conception to death. Human developmental periods include prenatal, infancy, toddlerhood, childhood, adolescence, and young adulthood, middle age, and senior adulthood. A variety of categories of behavior are studied including personality, language acquisition, moral and faith development, social behavior, psychosexual, cognitive, and motoric development. Both normal and atypical patterns are investigated.

The field of developmental psychology is concerned with (1) delineating the cause of behavioral change, (2) determining whether the changes are universal or unique to particular groups and cultures, and (3) discovering when particular changes occur.

There is considerable debate among theorists regarding the etiology (cause) of developmental change, the debate couched usually in terms of environment/heredity or nature/nurture. The current trend focuses on the interaction between environment and heredity.

G. ROWLAND

PERSONALITY DEVELOPMENT; PERSONALITY THEORY AND RESEARCH; PSYCHOLOGY, WESTERN. *See also* COGNITIVE, EMOTIONAL, MORAL, PSYCHOSOCIAL DEVELOPMENT; FAITH DEVELOPMENT RESEARCH.

DEVELOPMENTAL THEORY AND PASTORAL CARE. The root meaning of development is to unwrap or unfold something, such as a wrapped package or a rolled up banner; hence the contemporary understanding of development as an unfolding of a living organism's latent possibilities. In this sense development is roughly comparable to growth. The development of a plant or animal, for example, refers to the changes through which it passes in the course of its maturation.

Various philosophers, psychologists, and theologians, however, have given the concept of development a more specific meaning. R. S. Peters (1975) provides a particularly helpful definition. Peters argues that the concept of development involves three elements: (1) a pre-existing structure, (2) an invariant sequence, and (3) an end state. Viewed along these lines, development refers to the gradual unfolding of the pre-existent structure of a living organism through specifiable stages toward a predetermined *telos* or end. This definition articulates the essential features of the concept as it has been employed in the two major schools of developmental psychology that have impacted contemporary religious thought and ministry, life cycle theory and structural-developmental theory.

1. **Life Cycle Theory.** This type of developmental theory focuses on the entire course of human life, setting forth stages which persons pass through as a result of biological maturation, intellectual development, and alterations in social roles and statuses which correspond to these changes. The interplay of psychological and sociological factors in this approach has led many persons to refer to it as a "psychosocial" theory (Erikson, 1964).

Consistent with the three components of development identified above, life cycle developmentalists include an understanding of the pre-existing structure or ground plan of human development, an identification of an invariant sequence of stages through which it passes, and an understanding of the end point of this process. In general, this school describes the ground plan of development in terms of the epigenetic principle. Closely associated with the study of the embryo, this principle views persons as following a genetically inherited schedule of maturation in which new capacities emerge or diminish at given points throughout the life cycle.

This schedule serves as the foundation for the sequence of stages, which are described in a wide variety of ways: developmental tasks, seasons, predictable crises, life passages, and eras. Broadly speaking, these refer to a set of predictable issues which confront the individual as a result of inner growth and corresponding outer changes. While there is great variation in the way that societies respond to the developing person's ability to take on new social roles, life cycle developmentalists argue that there is an underlying, common pattern of human development that can be identified across cultural lines. Erik Erikson, for example, argues that every person faces the crisis of basic trust versus mistrust during infancy, regardless of the very different ways that parenting takes place from one culture to another or the variety of parenting styles within a given culture (Erikson, 1963).

The third element of the concept of development, the end point of the process, serves not as a philosophical *telos* luring the developmental process forward, but as the culmination of the way that the earlier stages have been negotiated. For example, Erikson's final developmental crisis, integrity vs. despair, focuses on "the acceptance of one's one and only life cycle and of the people who have become significant to it . . ." (Erikson, 1968, p. 139). How persons handle this crisis is deeply influenced by the strengths or deficiencies accruing from prior development. Thus long-standing feelings of inferiority may first emerge during the fourth stage, subsequently influence the whole course of one's life, and come to the fore in the final stage ("integrity versus despair and disgust") with an intensity that makes a despairing evaluation of the past almost inevitable. Hence, while continuing to be conceptualized in accordance with the epigenetic principle (the emergence of predictable developmental tasks during the final stage), the end point of the developmental process in life cycle theories also is portrayed as the result of a historical process culminating in the negotiation of the earlier stages.

2. **Structural-Developmental Theory.** The structural-development school portrays the three elements of development quite differently. This school builds on an insight dominant in philosophy since Kant: knowledge of the world is not a simple copy of external reality, but, in part, is a function of the mental categories which persons use to organize their experience. Structural developmentalists argue that the Kantian categories of knowing have a developmental history. Hence, "structural-developmental" refers to the fact that persons are viewed as passing through various stages of development in the way that they structure their experience.

The pre-existing structure or ground plan of the developmental process is viewed primarily as the inheritance of genetically given potentials which may or may not be activated by the environment with which persons interact. Thus, unlike the epigenetic principle, this school views the ground plan as a combination of internal and external factors: of basic human possibilities which are elicited by and interact with the social world.

In Jean Piaget's theory, for example, the ability to reason in a hypothetico-deductive fashion, achieved during the stage of "formal operations," is not simply inborn (Piaget, 1958). It results from a combination of factors including the gradual maturation of the brain, increased motility, the kind and quality of one's schooling, and the complexity of the social world with which the developing person interacts.

The second and third elements of the concept of development, as portrayed by the structural developmentalists, also differ from the perspective offered by life cycle theorists. Structural developmentalists identify clearly demarcated stages of development which refer not to a predictable set of life issues but to an underlying pattern of knowing. Each stage employs a qualitatively distinct style of organizing or operating on experience. These stages follow an invariant sequence; each builds on those that came before it and assumes the developmental advances which they achieved. Development, thus, is seen as a cumulative process.

At the same time the whole developmental process is conceptualized in terms of the *telos* or end state toward which it is moving. Cognitive or ego competencies which emerge at any given stage are viewed as steps toward the more adequate structuring of experience represented by the final stage. Developmental theories in this school, as such, are inherently normative; a value judgment in favor of the final stage or end state is built in. Piaget, for example, presents formal operations, the final stage of his theory, as a *more adequate* mode of reasoning than those of earlier stages, affording greater flexibility in the way persons can investigate and think about the world (Piaget, 1969).

This complex picture of development, as both building on achieved competencies and moving toward the normative end point represented by the final stage, is ultimately based on a concept of development conceived as the increasingly complex differentiation and reintegration of cognitive or ego functions. This concept of development does not, like life cycle theories, conceptualize development as a passage through predictable life crises, but rather as a series of qualitative shifts in a person's way of structuring knowledge and experience of the external world.

3. Pastoral Implications. Developmental psychology has played a far more important role in theories of education than in pastoral care and counseling. In part, this is due to the fact that educators are concerned with normal developmental process across the life span as they attempt to set forth an integrated curriculum. Pastoral care and counseling, in contrast, has more frequently been drawn to theories of psychotherapy and depth psychology in its attempt to offer assistance to persons in specific crisis or need.

Clearly, however, there is a place for developmental theory in pastoral care and counseling. First, it can serve as a helpful diagnostic tool for discerning the nature of the crisis confronting a minister. Is it a normal developmental crisis? Is it a long-term characterological disorder? Is it a result of situational stress?

Second, developmental theory can offer a helpful perspective for relating ethical and theological concerns to pastoral situations. As Don Browning, Charles Gerkin, and others have pointed out, it is not adequate for ministers to bracket out moral and theological concerns in their pastoral appropriation of psychology (Browning, 1983; Gerkin, 1984). The perspectives afforded by faith and moral development enable the minister to grasp these issues in terms of the strengths and limitations of a particular stage characterizing the person in crisis (Fowler, 1981, 1987; Kohlberg, 1976). It also provides the caregiver with insight into how he or she can offer moral or theological guidance in ways that the person in crisis can meaningfully understand.

Developmental theory, however, should not be appropriated uncritically. Cultural anthropologists have raised questions about the cross-cultural validity of the supposedly invariant stages which these theories offer (Snarey, 1985; Munroe, Munroe, and Whiting, 1981). Those who have done research on the experience of women and minorities have also argued that developmental theories reflect a male and/or white bias, not only in the sequencing of stages, but more importantly in the very categories by which the stages are described (Gilligan, 1982). Of great importance in this regard is the claim that many of these theories place an overemphasis on rational autonomy and individuation. A third criticism is primarily theological. There may be some danger, when appropriating developmental theories in pastoral work, that these theories unwittingly advance an understanding of the religious life that centers on human achievement and moral advancement. The priority of God's self-disclosure and forgiving love can easily be shuffled to one side in an attempt to assist persons up the ladder of faith or morality.

Bibliography. D. S. Browning, *Religious Ethics and Pastoral Care* (1983). E. Erikson, *Childhood and Society* (1963); *Identity: Youth and Crisis* (1968); *Insight and Responsibility* (1964). J. W. Fowler, *Stages of Faith* (1981); *Faith Development and Pastoral Care* (1987). C. V. Gerkin, *The Living Human Document* (1984). C. Gilligan, *In a Different Voice* (1982). R. Kegan, *The Evolving Self* (1982). L. Kohlberg, *Collected Papers on Moral Development* (1976). D. Levinson, *The Seasons of a Man's Life* (1978). R. Munroe, R. H. Munroe, and B. Whiting, eds., *Handbook of Cross-Cultural Human Development* (1981). R. S. Peters, "Education and Human Development," R. F. Dearden, *et al.* eds., *Education and Reason* (1975). J. Piaget, *The Growth of Logical Thinking from Childhood to Adolescence* (1958); *The Psychology of the Child* (1969). J. Snarey, "Cross Cultural Universality of Social-Moral Development: A Critical Review," *Psychological Bulletin,* 97 (1985), 202–32.

R. R. OSMER

LIFE CYCLE THEORY AND PASTORAL CARE. *See also* AGING; PERSONALITY DEVELOPMENT; PERSONALITY THEORY; *also* CHILDREN; ADOLESCENTS; YOUNG ADULTS; MIDLIFE PERSONS; OLDER PERSONS; *also* COGNITIVE, EMOTIONAL, FAITH, HUMAN, LANGUAGE, *or* MORAL DEVELOPMENT. *Compare* PILGRIMAGE METAPHOR; PROCESS, CONCEPT OF. *Biography:* ERIKSON.

DEVIANT BEHAVIOR, THEORY OF. A major aspect of social disorganization, often expressed in acts of crime and in antisocial behavior. The major thrust of this article will deal with selected ways in which the study of crime and antisocial behavior has recently been approached.

1. Definitional Complexity. The nomenclature of deviance is complicated, conflicting, and overlapping; the attendant issues of free will and responsibility are ripe with controversy and confusion; and the nature of societal response to deviance is arguably one of the central themes of history. Human rights, civil rights, tolerance and intolerance, love, charity, forgiveness, and good will all reflect in some measure the degree of importance attributable to the phenomena of rule making and rule breaking. Sociology, in particular, claims as its subject matter the topics of norms and social order. Correspondingly it must deal with norm violations and social disorder. These topics form the cornerstones of sociological inquiry and are relevant points of departure for the current undertaking.

Social order depends upon normative behavior in order to avoid chaos. Norms are standards of behavior made up of folkways, mores, regulations, and laws. The violation of norms constitutes rule breaking, immorality, illegality, and criminal behavior. Questions routinely arise about the role of the powerful in defining and reacting to the behavior of those less powerful and about the lack of standardized treatment for those apprehended for deviant acts (McCaghy, '1980, pp. 21–26). Questions abound from students of deviant behavior as to the situational, contextual, and relative nature of norm violation. Legal scholars, legislators, enforcement officials, and court personnel work constantly to provide sane and solid societal responses to deviant behavior but use a judicial system noted for its hair-splitting and adversative techniques. Individuals, when confronted with their own deviant behavior, use a variety of techniques to justify, rationalize, excuse, deny, and redefine their actions. Pastoral counseling often attempts to bring about a common definitional assessment of an act or set of actions whereby a common response or solution can be derived. However, one of the variables so important in the basic equation that makes us truly human is our ability to be confused, uncertain, flexible, adaptable, and deceitful to ourselves and others. Counselors will never become obsolete as long as the human condition remains one involving definitional complexity, symbolic constructionism and the "interpretation" of events and actions. Let us explore these conditions in relation to the impact they have upon our concept of social order.

The Stimulus-Interpretation-Response Model. The stimulus-response (S-R) model holds that a particular stimulus will evoke a predictable response from an organism. Some species behave in ways over which they have no control. Some animals spawn, build nests, migrate, and obtain food in predictable, genetically predetermined, ways. They are programmed to act and do so without thought or consideration of the consequences of their actions.

Humans have the advanced capacity of thought and reflection. The essential component of civilized behavior is one of considering the impact of one's actions upon another and of choosing one course of action over another. Prior to the civilized act, however, a component of interpretation is involved, one in which symbols are perceived, evaluated, and stored in memory and thus used in the interpretive process. We are not mandated to act in a direct-drive, stimulus-response, fashion. Between the stimulus and response in humans occurs an interpretation, a denotative and connotative function that sets us apart from other species.

The stimulus-interpretation-response (S-I-R) model, therefore, allows our ascendancy over other species, and liberates us from the confining patterns of predetermined action. This liberation, however, in allowing flexibility of response contains the seeds of social conditioning, learning, and necessitates the process of socialization whereby one absorbs the symbols of one's culture. The process is imperfect, imprecise, and never-ending. This liberation contains basic elements of growth and freedom but simultaneously awards us the capacity for destructive antisocial conduct. This two-edged sword allows variability in social organization but ensures elements of social disorganization; it allow us to establish customs of conformity and sets the stage for nonconformity, deviance, and crime.

Because of the flexibility of social organization allowed by the S-I-R model, some have written of the normality of deviance (E. Durkheim).

Due to the components of the S-I-R model of behavior, it is impossible for people to exhibit the exact sameness of perception, sentiment, and individual consciousness necessary for homogenous and totally predictable action. This diversity in the human condition constantly propels a heterogeneity of action. Yet there are limits to the degree of heterogeneity allowable if a semblance of social order is to prevail. Anarchy and chaos would defeat the species. A balance between freedom and constraint is at best a precarious balance and one in which we find not only an abstract intellectual challenge but also a real field of concern in everyday counseling situations. Let us briefly review some of the classic concepts that seek to sensitize us to the multiple ways in which we respond to a mutable world.

2. **Positions of Relativity.** Deterministic positions, those that posit direct and specific causal links between exact, concrete, and operationalized phenomena are seldom found in the social sciences. If theoretical formulations between variables are demonstrated, these formulations are more likely to be correlational than causal and are more likely to be cast in sets wherein a host of independent variables are examined in relation to one dependent variable. The "cause" of juvenile delinquency, for example, has not been found within the social sciences. This is true not because of the lack of sophistication and conceptual ability of the researchers but because of the complexity and "relative" nature of so much human behavior. Even our most important correlational variable, that of socioeconomic status, fails the test of causation when examining the dependent variables of delinquency, crime, deviance, and antisocial behavior. Some poor neighborhoods are known for their law-abiding nature while some ghettos are continually besieged by criminal activity.

Even with the technological advancements in data collection, storage, retrieval, and manipulation we are still reminded of the complex character of human behavior each time we review the basic tenets of the relativist positions within the discipline. More specifically, what are some of these tenets and what do they tell us about crime and antisocial behavior?

a. Symbolic Interactionism. Sheldon Stryker (1980, p. 11) acknowledged the complexity and relativity of human behavior when he advised that the world did not have to be viewed as "deterministic" and that behavior need not be seen as caused to the point that ". . . it must be possible to explicate a complete set of causes sufficient to account for every case without exception of some behavior." Stryker's position takes into account the indeterminate nature of behavior but falls short of stating that behavior is random, in which case, as noted above, anarchy and chaos would prevail. "The symbolic interactionist sees . . . choice, self-direction, and self-control as socially derived, that is, as rooted in social interaction," (Stryker, 1980, p. 11). This basic tenet of symbolic interactionism allows us to explore several related concepts, each sensitizing us to special caveats if we seek deterministic and casual explanations of crime and deviant behavior.

The term "cultural relativism" means that the "function and meaning of a trait are relative to its cultural setting" (Horton and Hunt, 1984, p. 69). Likewise, and by extension, subcultural relativism refers to the fact that members of smaller groups are capable of defining the function and meaning of a trait in ways unique to their subculture. Therefore, to attempt to force a definition of proper, good, legal, or beneficial upon a group of people with different views of the world is to run the risk of creating conflictual situations.

The term "definition of the situation" is a popular and useful concept when studying human responses to life situations. Lodged within symbolic interactionism, the concept is often associated with W. I. Thomas and his famous theorem ". . . if men define situations as real, they are real in their consequences," (quoted in Stryker, 1980, p. 31). This concept emphasizes the importance of the subjective processes through which lives are experienced on a day-to-day basis. When one considers the idea that "trivial" acts may lead to violent outbursts in bars on Saturday nights one recognizes the viability of the theorem.

What is trivial depends upon the definition of the situation. Therefore, when someone defines something as nontrivial or "real" it is often real in its consequences. Lethal outcomes frequently result from self-fulfilling prophecies set into motion by an unknown mixture of variables. Each situation is different because it is constantly in the process of being defined, of being constructed.

The "social construction of reality" (Berger and Luckmann, 1966) is the process whereby persons create meaning through interaction. Physical properties may remain real regardless of our definition of them but symbolic meanings are much more subjective than are physical objects. Society is an abstraction apart from the people who populate a region. As Horton and Hunt (1984, p. 16) note: "But society is also a *subjective reality*, in that for each person, the other persons, groups, and institutions are whatever that person perceives them as being." The recognition of the constructed nature of reality prompted a number of scholars, particularly in the 1960s and '70s in the United States, to focus on the processes involved in constructing crime and deviance. The resulting ideas are contained in the societal reaction or "labeling" perspective. This perspective uses symbolic interactionism as a springboard from which to understand how an act becomes labeled criminal, non-criminal, or something else entirely.

b. Societal Reaction. The study of defining is the study of power. Given that behavior is relative to time, place, circumstance, context, subculture, etc., it seems inevitable that some will attempt to force their definition of the situation on others and that conflictual situations will automatically arise. Some would argue that civilized group members enter into social contracts with one another in a consensual manner in order to ward off the savage and brutish attacks of rogues, bullies, criminals, insane persons, and misfits. This is often the layperson's concept of social organization and social justice — the greatest good for the greatest number — wherein law-abiding citizens protect civilization against a forceful and dangerous minority of miscreants.

H. S. Becker (1963, p. 9), however, turns our attention to the definitional process by writing:

> Social groups create deviance by making the rules whose infraction constitutes deviance, and by applying those rules to particular people and labeling them as outsiders. From this point of view, deviance is not a quality of the act the person commits, but rather a consequence of the application by others of rules and sanctions to an "offender." The deviant is one to whom that label has successfully been applied; deviant behavior is behavior that people so label.

Extending and refining this argument, E. Sagarin (1976, p. 25), adroitly points out that "The English language is constructed in such a way that we speak of people *being* certain things when all we know is that they *do* certain things" (italics in original). "The behavior is real, but the identity is an invention," (Sagarin, 1976, p. 31).

Thus, the relativist position asks us to consider whether or not we want to accept definitions and labels that others attempt to saddle us with, even labels not necessarily bad, deviant or criminal. The challenges faced by those working for women's rights, rights of welfare recipients, prisoner rights, gay rights, etc., point out the relative and conflictual nature of the definitional process.

3. **Conclusion.** For many, the relativist position lacks precision, is void of meaningful theory, and falls short as a causal explanation of antisocial behavior. Recently many have begun returning to more "sober" explanations of deviant behavior, seeking once again the security of deterministic theory. The labeling theorists have been accused of "ontological gerrymandering" (Woolgar and Pawluch, 1985) and conflict theorists appear weakened by attractive, simplistic, and often incorrect theoretical formulations about human behavior. But the relativists, the subjectivists, constructionists, and perceptionists have made their presence known and have sensitized scholars and politicians to the basic tenets of their positions. Even if researchers, practitioners, and counselors within the human services arena turn to biology, nutrition, chemistry, theology, or demonology in their search for the causes of deviant behavior, the relativists have been heard and will hopefully serve as a constant reminder of the marvelous and mysterious nature of human action whether it be labeled conformist or deviant.

Bibliography. H. S. Becker, *Outsiders: Studies in the Sociology of Deviance* (1963). P. L. Berger and T. Luckmann, *The Social Construction of Reality: A Treatise on the Sociology of Knowledge* (1966). P. B. Horton and C. L. Hunt, *Sociology,* 6th ed. (1984). S. Lukes, *Durkheim: The Rules of Sociological Method and Selected Texts on Sociology and its Method,* translated by W. D. Halls (1982). C. H. McCaghy, *Crime in American Society* (1980). E. Sagarin, "The High Personal Cost of Wearing a Label," *Psychology Today* (1976), 25–31. S. Stryker, *Symbolic Interactionism: A Social Structural Version* (1980). S. Woolgar and D. Pawluch, "Ontological Gerrymandering: The Anatomy of Social Problems Explanations," *Social Problems,* 32 (1985), 214–25.

C. E. PALMER

ANTISOCIAL PERSONS; JUVENILE CRIME AND DELINQUENCY; SEXUAL VARIETY, DEVIANCE, AND DISORDER. *See also* LIFESTYLE ISSUES IN PASTORAL CARE; RESPONSIBILITY/IRRESPONSIBILITY, PSYCHOLOGY OF. *Compare* MORAL BEHAVIOR AND RELIGION.

DEVOTIONAL LIFE AND PRACTICES. *See* PRAYER; PRAYER AND WORSHIP LIFE, PASTOR'S; SPIRITUAL DISCIPLINE AND GROWTH; SPIRITUALITY. *See also* JEWISH HOLY DAYS AND FESTIVALS; JEWISH PRAYERS; LITURGICAL AND DEVOTIONAL LIFE, ROMAN CATHOLIC TRADITION OF.

DEVOTIONAL LITERATURE. *See* LITERATURE, DEVOTIONAL.

DEWEY, JOHN (1859–1952). American philosopher and educator. As a professor of philosophy and education at the University of Michigan, the University of Minnesota, the University of Chicago, and Columbia University, Dewey developed a functional psychology, an "instrumentalist" conception of meaning and truth, and a vision of education as a "reorganization" of experience that had as its end the sustaining of "growth."

Dewey's *Democracy and Education* (1916) was especially important for the later pastoral theology traditions. In that book he defined education as a "reconstruction or reorganization of experience," which enhanced the meaning of that experience and increased the ability to direct the course of subsequent experience. Such a view of education presupposed an assumption that the achievement of selfhood was a "process," and that the self's greatest good was "growth." No fixed end defined the goal of the process; growth itself was the end, and the purpose of formal education was to organize the powers that would ensure further growth. Dewey's view of education also presupposed that "true" ideas were not embodiments of a static and absolute "truth" but instruments with which the organism adjusted itself actively and constructively to a natural and social environment.

The earliest proponents of Dewey's ideas within the churches were the religious educators who tried to reorganize the Protestant Sunday School in accord with the ideals of progressive education. Insisting that teachers remain sensitive to the interests of their pupils, they formulated the aim of religious education as growth toward a Christian maturity that enabled the young to devote themselves to other persons within "the democracy of God." Religious growth was an adjustment to a divine environment.

The religious education movement sensed the therapeutic potential of Dewey's ideas. George Albert Coe at Columbia Teachers' College argued that the ideal of cooperative thinking envisioned by Dewey could release the personality from its self-imposed limitations. Hence the religious educators became teachers of pastoral counseling within the seminaries, and they drew on Dewey for their conception of counseling as "problem solving" that promoted "personality adjustment."

The pastoral theologians who published texts on the cure of souls during the 1930s depended heavily on the metaphor of "adjustment," which, largely through Dewey's influence, had begun to permeate liberal theology. Charles Holman's *The Cure of Souls* (1932) and Karl Stolz's *Pastoral Psychology* (1932) both taught that the task of the religious counselor was to help persons achieve adequate moral and religious adjustment.

Dewey also exercised some subtle influence on the tradition of Clinical Pastoral Education (CPE). The patriarch of that tradition, Anton Boisen, who had studied under Coe, hoped that clinical training would help students understand the "function" of religion. And the sensitivity to "process" and "growth" that marks clinical supervision reflects, in part, a continuing debt to Dewey's ideas about education.

Pastoral theologians now rarely cite Dewey's works, but they remain indebted to both his vision and his vocabulary.

E. B. HOLIFIELD

HISTORY OF PROTESTANT PASTORAL CARE (United States); PRAGMATISM AND PASTORAL CARE.

DIACONATE. *See* HISTORY OF ROMAN CATHOLIC PASTORAL CARE (United States); ROMAN CATHOLIC PASTORAL CARE.

DIAGNOSIS. *See* EVALUATION AND DIAGNOSIS; INTERPRETATION AND HERMENEUTICS, PASTORAL.

DIAGNOSTIC AND STATISTICAL MANUAL III

(DSM-III). The latest description and classification of "mental disorders" published by the American Psychiatric Association in 1980; a slightly revised volume (DSM-III-R) was published in 1987.

1. Background. Earlier attempts at nosological classification resulted in the American Psychiatric Association's *Diagnostic and Statistical Manual of Mental Disorders* (DSM) published in 1952 and the *Diagnostic and Statistical Manual of Mental Disorders, Second Edition* (DSM-II) appearing in 1968. The original DSM sought to bring some degree of systematization into the field of classifying mental disorders and to align it with International Classification of Diseases (ICD). One of the unique features of the original DSM was the use of the term "reaction" which seemed to imply that mental disorders were the result of a combination of psychological, social, and biological factors. This particular term was dropped from both the DSM-II and the DSM-III to the dismay of those who saw it as yielding to the "medical model" which emphasizes primarily the organic component.

The DSM-III had its initial impetus in 1974 when the American Psychiatric Association appointed a task force which was to begin work on a new diagnostic manual. In the process of its development, the DSM-III went through a number of drafts which were prepared by a total of fourteen advisory committees. The task force maintained a close liaison relationship with numerous other professional organizations which, it was hoped, would result in a broader acceptance of the final product.

Extensive field trials were conducted for two years during which reportedly a total of 12,667 patients were evaluated by approximately 550 professional clinicians. The writers of the DSM-III concluded that when the results of the field trials were assessed, the majority of those involved had responded favorably and that the possibility of greater reliability and diagnosis seemed evident, as compared with the DSM-II.

2. Purposes. The DSM-III task force had a number of specific purposes in mind as it drafted the volume. For one thing, the DSM-III was intended to provide an avenue of communication among professionals by providing a common language. Further, it was hoped that the end product would be useful in understanding the nature of the disorders, in treatment planning, and in predicting outcome (prognosis). Also, among the intentions of the authors of the DSM-III was that of making it useful in research because of the increased precision with which disorders were described and diagnoses could be made.

The aim of the task force was to avoid introducing new terminology when possible. At the same time diagnostic terms and classifications which "had outlived their usefulness" were to be excluded.

3. Special Features. Because of the distinctive features of the DSM-III, it is approximately ten times longer than its immediate predecessor. Among the descriptors of the disorders in the manual are: (1) the *essential features* which describe the particular characteristics of the disorder and provide the criteria for diagnosing it as such; (2) the *associated features* which, in some cases, are also present but which are not required for the diagnosis; (3) the *age at onset* or the time at which the particular disorder normally first becomes manifest; (4) the *course* or usual progression of the disorder; (5) the degree of *impairment* in everyday functioning with specific focus on social and occupational aspects; (6) the *complications* in which the disorder may eventuate, e.g., a major depression resulting from substance abuse; (7) the *predisposing factors* which place individuals in a category of higher risk or greater likelihood of developing the disorder; (8) the *prevalence* of the disorder or percentage of people who develop the disorder if they live to the usual age of onset; (9) the *sex ratio* referring to the relative frequency with which the disorder is found in females and males; (10) the *familial pattern* which addresses the extent to which the disorder appears to be more common among biologically related family members than in those not so; and (11) the *differential diagnosis* referring to those disorders which need to be considered and seen as distinct from the one under consideration (i.e., those disorders which are to be ruled out).

A significant change from its predecessors was the fact that the DSM-III no longer has the nosological category of neurosis although some neuroses are listed in parenthesis, e.g., Obsessive Compulsive Disorder (Obsessive Compulsive Neurosis). This resulted from the fact that no agreement could be reached among theoreticians regarding the definition of a neurotic disorder. The disorders which in the DSM-II were categorized as neurotic are incorporated into the affective, anxiety, somataform, dissociative, and psychosexual disorders in the DSM-III.

Of special significance is the emphasis which the DSM-III gives to diagnostic criteria. Although clinical judgment is still required regarding the extent to which the criteria are met, the fact that the DSM-III does specify them makes the manual much more precise than its predecessors. The likelihood of agreement in the assessing of mental disorders is considered to be greatly increased because of this and thus greater reliability is established. This implies that the DSM-III is more usable as a clinical instrument in treatment planning because a more precise diagnosis has been reached. The DSM-III has also made possible greater precision in the area of research because the diagnostic criteria enhance the likelihood that specific disorders are indeed being studied.

Another of the truly distinctive features of the DSM-III is the multiaxial approach to evaluation. The person being evaluated is viewed along five axes. These are: (1) All of the clinical problems or syndromes which are the focus of evaluation and treatment are listed on this axis (Axis 1) except for those on Axis 2. (2) Personality disorders (long-standing, deeply-entrenched behavioral, cognitive, affective, and interpersonal patterns which establish a contextual setting for and affect the nature of the disorder in Axis 1 and the treatability of the individual) and Specific Developmental Disorders. (3) Physical disorders or conditions which are ordinarily considered to have a bearing on the *causation* or *treatment* of the disorders listed on Axis 1 or 2. (4) Severity of the psychosocial stressors which are considered to be implicated in the etiology or progression of the primary disorder. These stressors are rated on the scale of one to seven (representing the summed effect of all stressors) and are generally seen as occurring within one year of the current disorder. This axis thus considers the psychosocial environment in which the disorders on Axis 1 are imbedded. (5) Highest level of adaptive functioning in the past year which is deemed to have prognostic importance because of a tendency to return to an earlier level of adaptive functioning. The areas of functioning which are under consideration on this axis are: social, occupational, and leisure time.

A feature of the DSM-III not found in earlier editions is the assessing of personal stresses and strengths as specified on Axes 4 and 5. It is generally agreed that these factors bear heavily on understanding the primary disorder, planning of treatment, and prognosis.

Another fundamental concept which deserves underscoring is the fact that the DSM-III emphasizes that it is *disorders* which are being classified rather than individuals. For this reason, words such as "hypochondriac" and "paranoid" are avoided; instead reference is made to "individuals who experience a hypochondriacal disorder," or "persons suffering from a paranoid disorder."

4. **DSM-III-R.** A revision and update of the DSM-III was published by the American Psychiatric Association in 1987. Compiled in the same way as the DSM-III, this revision reflects further research on and use of the diagnostic categories found in the DSM-III. While major categories are basically unchanged, DSM-III-R gives further clarification and delineation of some disorders. One notable change is that "Ego-dystonic Homosexuality" has been removed as a category because of its rare use in diagnosis and treatment. The DSM-III-R has also added three disorders in an appendix as "Proposed Diagnostic Categories Needing Further Study." These include "Late Luteal Phase Dysphoric Disorder" (related to menstrual cycle), "Sadistic Personality Disorder," and "Self-Defeating Personality Disorder."

5. **Criticisms.** One of the criticisms leveled against the DSM-III is that it is too heavily oriented in the direction of the "medical model." At the same time, many consider it to be much less so than other classification systems. The fact that liaison was maintained with numerous other professional groups who were allowed to be heard seems to have had the effect of tempering a medical emphasis. The inclusion of Axes 4 and 5 highlights the fact that the persons suffering from disorders are seen as living in a psychosocial environment and are therefore not viewed or treated from the standpoint of a "medical model" alone.

Another criticism which many have deemed to have considerable weight is the fact that too many behaviors or syndromes are called mental disorders when really they should not be (e.g., developmental reading disorder).

Other criticisms of the DSM-III include the assertion that the prognostic statements have not been sufficiently tested to the point of reliability. Some have criticized the DSM-III for yielding excessively to "special interest groups" which exerted pressure for either the inclusion or exclusion of certain disorders. The DSM-III has also been criticized for its lack of precision in judging the severity of the psychosocial stressors and the highest level of functioning. Finally, some charge that it does not sufficiently incorporate the knowledge gleaned from recent research.

Bibliography. American Psychiatric Association, *DSM-III Case Book: A Learning Companion to the Diagnostic and Statistical Manual of Mental Disorders* 3d ed., (1981).

A. J. STRAATMEYER

EVALUATION AND DIAGNOSIS, PSYCHOLOGICAL; PSYCHIATRIST/PSYCHIATRY; PSYCHOPATHOLOGY, THEORIES OF. *See also* MENTAL HEALTH AND ILLNESS.

DIALYSIS PATIENT. *See* CHRONIC ILLNESS; HANDICAP AND DISABILITY; LOSS OF FUNCTION.

DICKS, RUSSELL (1906–65). American pastoral theologian. A Methodist minister, Dicks served as a hospital chaplain at Massachusetts General Hospital and other hospitals, as well as a professor of pastoral care at Duke University Divinity School.

As one of the first chaplain supervisors of Clinical Pastoral Education (CPE) in a general hospital, Dicks pioneered in the supervisory use of written "verbatims"—word-for-word transcriptions — of pastoral conversations. He believed that study of the direct encounter between a student and a patient could reveal whether or not the student understood what was happening in the interchange. His method represented a departure from Anton Boisen's technique of having students in clinical settings write detailed case histories of the patient's physical and emotional development.

Dicks was a prolific writer, and in 1936 he and Richard Cabot published *The Art of Ministering to the Sick,* an influential study of the "directed listening" through which the minister could elicit in patients an awareness of the power within themselves that made for good health. In subsequent years, he wrote devotional material for the sick, along with numerous books on pastoral counseling. The analysis of pastoral conversations in his 1939 publication *And Ye Visited Me* popularized the use of verbatim material in textbooks on pastoral care. Dicks was active in the early development of the Institute of Pastoral Care, which was founded in Boston in 1944, and he also served for several years as the editor of the journal *Religion and Health.*

Dicks was important primarily because of his pioneering use of the verbatim transcript as an instrument of clinical supervision and as an illustrative device in textbooks on pastoral care and counseling.

E. B. HOLIFIELD

PASTORAL CARE MOVEMENT.

DIETING. *See* OBESITY AND WEIGHT CONTROL.

DIRECTOR, SPIRITUAL. *See* SPIRITUAL DIRECTOR.

DISABILITY. *See* HANDICAP AND DISABILITY; LOSS OF FUNCTION.

DISAGREEMENT, DIFFERENCE, AND CONFLICT IN PASTOR-PARISHIONER RELATIONSHIPS. Problems in pastoral relationships frequently consist of thoughts and feelings leading to clashes or contention between pastors and those for whom they provide care. Differences and disagreements in attitude, conviction, and affection may lead to relational conflict. Sometimes such conflict may be ignored. But when persons seek or need pastoral attention, ignoring differences is often impossible. Significant religious, theological, political, and lifestyle distinctions are present in every congregation. This article outlines five conflictual situations and suggests a framework for analysis and action. It asks how the pastor should relate and how differences might be faced.

Conflict with pastors sometimes occurs when persons are engaged in intense religious pilgrimage. The conflict may represent competing motives and attitudes within the individual. Usually the more vigorous the conflict between pastor and parishioner, the more foundational the inner conflict of the person. A pastoral response which accepts the conflict and attempts to relocate it within the individual is often helpful. To argue or take sides is more likely to diminish the person and his or her vitality. Helping persons to become curious about their loyalties, convictions, and directions calls for the pastor to reflect their dilemmas and to raise their awareness of their ambivalence. In such instances the timing of challenge and interpretation are crucial to pastoral action.

Second, conflict may occur when parishioners assume that pastors share their life perspective and anticipate confirmation of their chosen direction. In this situation the pastor must be careful to use convictions neither to close off the other's conflict nor to take a rigid take-it-or-leave-it stance. Many problems brought to the pastor are genuine dilemmas in which hurt, courage, and concern are core needs. Pastors may be clear and explicit about their own values and convictions, but the goal is to establish genuine dialogue in which ambiguity is minimized and in which the parishioner is supported in reaching a clear sense of "yes" or "no" and assuming responsibility for his or her particular situation.

A third occasion which gives rise to overt differences arises in cross-cultural settings. Differences are inevitable when nationality, lifestyle, race, or socio-economic gaps exist between pastor and parishioner. The danger of such situations is that an attitude of supremacy will be expressed or that dehumanizing actions will occur. Pastors are challenged to recognize that there are cultural variants as to what is meaningful, healthy, and religiously correct. They will need to be particularly sensitive to avoid premature judgments, to be clear about their own values while avoiding imposing those values on the other, and to value the subjective world of the parishioner. This assumes that a key to ministry is that pastors receive others into their world without imposing their viewpoint, ideology, or way of doing things on them as a condition for offering love, friendship, and care.

A fourth perspective is that conflict is one step in the transformational process. This perspective assumes that change is an unavoidable human experience and that change produces internal and external conflict. Frequently the content of this conflict will be negative feelings and/or thoughts. The pastoral role in such situations is to help the person "bear conflict in expectancy." He or she attempts to accept that there is no absolute human authority, emphasize complexity rather than superficiality, accept subjective perceptions and personal differences, positively value stress, and develop multidimensional relationships.

A final source of conflict involves the limits of human vision. This limit is clearly related to developmental differences in the ways persons construct their faith perspectives. People develop in a variety of ways as to how they attend authorities, how they use religious symbols, and how they judge "what counts" in making moral judgments. These differences suggest that pastors be patient with self and others when they construe experiences in fundamentally different ways. If pastors take seriously the internal world of others, then the roots of conflict may at least be appreciated and pastors can choose whether forgiveness or discipline is an appropriate reconciling response for the pastor or parishioner.

The pastor's responses depend upon the level of conflict, the personal characteristics of those involved, and the circumstances of that particular situation. The five categories outlined provide some guidance in conflictual situations when ministry must go on either because of or in spite of the differences. Central to every perspective, however, is appreciation for the subjective worlds of pastor and parishioner. Courage and persistence are required in order to bear conflict and nurture differences in these situations.

Bibliography. J. Dittes, *The Church in the Way* (1967). S. Hiltner, *The Counselor in Counseling* (1952). J. Loder, *The Transforming Moment* (1981). H. Nouwen, *Reaching Out* (1975). W. Oates, *Pastoral Counseling in Social Problems* (1966).

S. S. IVY

CONFLICT AND CONFLICT MANAGEMENT; CONGREGATION, PASTORAL CARE OF. *See also* AUTHORITY, PASTORAL; CULTURAL AND ETHNIC FACTORS; POWER; SOCIAL STATUS AND CLASS FACTORS; PROPHETIC/PASTORAL TENSION; SOCIAL PERCEPTION, JUDGMENT, AND BELIEF; SYMBOLIC DIMENSIONS OF PASTORAL CARE RELATIONSHIPS. *Compare* FRIENDSHIP, PASTOR-PARISHIONER.

DISASTER, PUBLIC. Any circumstance in which, over a short space of time, a large number of people suffer major loss or damage to person or possessions. It includes natural catastrophes or "Acts of God" as well as personmade disasters, be they deliberate or accidental. It does not include individual or familial griefs and losses which affect only a few people. Nor does it include the widespread losses of non-material objects (self-respect, dignity, hope for the future, etc.) which may result from major social changes (e.g. unemployment).

Disasters, by their nature, disrupt the fabric of society, destroy and hurt people, and evoke psychological and social reactions which may themselves cause further misery and sow the seeds of more disasters. But, like personal losses, disaster can be transcended; the experience of communal grief can set in train the rebirth of "communitas" and of spiritual and moral values which may previously have declined.

Pastors are often in key positions to influence the course of the events which lead up to and follow disasters.

In their roles as community leaders, parent-figures, ritual specialists, caregivers and witnesses to ultimate meaning, they are greatly needed at such times and they will find that many doors are open which previously were closed.

1. **The Reaction to Disaster.** Researchers have recognized a general pattern of orientation and response to disasters:

a. Anticipation. Many disasters (tornadoes, bush fires, floods) can be generally and even locally predicted; so, too, may civil disturbances, mining and other industrial disasters. Sadly, these predictions are all too often ignored or misunderstood. Precautions taken are inadequate, and many individuals react as if they were immune. Those who act upon warnings are likely to be seen as alarmist, and no one is more unpopular than the bringer of bad tidings.

b. Impact. Consequently, the immediate impact of disaster is often one of numbness and disbelief. People may be dazed and immobile or they may rush into action without proper thought for the consequences. Rescue attempts are often hindered by the hectic activities of would-be helpers, communications become blocked, leaders ignored and people attempting to leave the center of disaster may find their escape blocked by people gravitating toward it. Despite this, widespread panic is rare and tends to occur only if a group of people perceive that their escape route is blocked. More often disasters give rise to striking examples of self-sacrifice and dogged refusal to give up hope.

c. Recoil. As the awful irreversible reality of what has happened begins to sink in, emotional reactions of anxiety and fear occur, often with feelings of helplessness, bewilderment and fatigue. Victims now become aware of their need for help and may actively seek it. Demands for immediate succor may outstrip the resources available and angry reactions are common. Individuals and families tend to see themselves as at the center of the disaster and, while mutually supporting each other, are inclined to expect protection from a social system that may no longer exist. Others may be buoyed up by a sense of elation and relief at having survived.

d. Grief. As time passes both relief and anxiety begin to diminish and a fuller appreciation of the scale and implications of the disaster is established. Anger and disillusionment with protective powers — be they community leaders, parents, God or God's representatives, the clergy and ministers — may be expressed in irrational and hurtful ways. Victims find themselves compulsively repeating in their minds and in their conversation the events leading up to the disaster as if, even now, they could find out what went wrong and put it right. The urge to find someone to blame may lead to scapegoating; rumors abound, and everybody, including community leaders and journalists, is in danger of getting caught up in a wave of vengeful bitterness.

At the same time much of the anger is directed inwards. Just as a physically sick person can feel ashamed of being sick, so a disaster-stricken community feels ashamed of itself. Apathy and dejection are widespread and people give up hope in any worthwhile future. These emotions are, of course, the normal reactions of grief.

They occur after any major loss but their scale and pervasiveness create special problems in a disaster area.

When a disaster has struck, the sense of invulnerability which causes people to ignore warnings is lost and they may become excessively anxious, overprotective toward their children and over-concerned about other possible disasters. It is not surprising that the physical accompaniments of anxiety and tension may be misinterpreted as signs of physical or mental "breakdown" and that people often seek help from doctors and other caregivers. Unfortunately, the drugs which are often prescribed liberally to people in a disaster tend to confirm a sick self-image and sometimes lead to habit formation. They may even delay and distort the healthy expression of grief. So, too, do self-prescriptions of alcohol whose disinhibiting effect adds further to the risks of irrational expression of anger.

e. Recovery. Anger in itself is neither good nor bad, although it can lead to good or bad behavior. As time passes, irrational and harmful outbursts become less common and, if circumstances are right, people become able to channel their distress in creative and constructive directions. The wish to bring something good out of the bad thing that has happened—to find a worthwhile use for discontent — can lead to an increase in the birth rate, increased community involvement in charitable activities, or quite conscious efforts to ensure that similar disasters can never occur again. Yet while reparative activities help to reestablish the victims' sense of personal and communal worth, they do not undo what has happened. A dead child can never be replaced nor a lost home rebuilt. Hence grief is necessary despite whatever money or other resources can provide in compensation, and grief tends to go on for far longer than people expect. In fact, it is probably true to say that a community does not "recover" from a major disaster; it is permanently changed. Anniversaries become times of renewed grief and the survivors remain bound to the dead by their duty to remember and idealize them and to make manifest the evidence that their influence continues in the world and that this influence is good. Hence memorial scholarships, libraries, parks and other benefits "keep alive" the memories of the dead by enhancing the lives of the living.

2. **Sociopathology.** Individual losses can give rise to pathological grief and mental illness and, in like manner, communal grief can give rise to lasting problems which may permeate the society in which they arise. Comparative studies of disasters are few but it is already possible to identify factors that may determine why it is that some communities go into decline while others emerge unscathed or even strengthened by the tempering effect of a calamity:

a. Lack of forewarning is associated with prolonged disorganization and a much greater sense of outrage than is the case when disasters are expectable and where plans for relief already exist.

b. The scale and distribution of casualties are important variables. Thus a plane crash may kill a large number of people but, if they come from a large number of communities, the grief which results will be spread out within each community without severely disrupting that community. Obviously, however, a disaster which affects a large proportion of the population of one community will be locally more devastating in its effects.

c. Disasters which take out or damage key persons within a community or which leave them so afflicted with grief that they are unable to provide calm and rational leadership, undermine the social supports which are important sources of reassurance and security.

d. Disasters which split up communities so that people are relocated in haphazard manner without regard to the structure of their social unit have the same effect. Events of these kinds provide no buttress against the chaos-producing effects of anger and bitterness with consequent loss of trust in authority and in a secure foundation for society.

e. Isolated communities may have learned to be self-reliant but this very self-reliance may prove a problem if the scale of the disaster outstrips the resources locally available to cope with it. Suspicion of outsiders may hamper and discourage those who make the effort to offer support and it is likely that they will withdraw to leave the community to solve its own problems.

f. Communities at the bottom of the social status ladder whose morale is never high. Disasters easily destroy what little communal pride and self-confidence already exists and the provision of too much outside aid may encourage unhealthy dependence. Sadly it is these very communities that are least able to foresee or prevent the occurrence of disaster.

g. When *feelings of bitterness* precede the disaster and a community perceives itself as underprivileged and / or threatened, the communal reaction may add fuel to this discontent and lead to an escalation of civil disturbance.

3. **Pastoral Care and Counseling.** Wherever possible, pastoral care should be attempted *before a disaster occurs.* This is a thankless task since nobody likes to be a "Prophet of Doom," and we should expect resistance to any suggestion that we should look forward to the things we do not look forward to. Such resistance is itself a sign of fear, and it may be necessary to allay the fear by emphasizing the value of preparation. Those whose faith enables them to accept the transitory nature of human life and the impermanence of territory and possessions will be less perturbed by disaster than others, such as those whose religious observance is expected to persuade God to protect them from misfortune.

During the *impact and recoil phase* the ability of pastors to remain calm in the face of chaos will be tested. Fortunately, their ritual functions provide them with clearly defined and understood roles to perform. The ministry to the dying may well take priority over other activities, but support to the injured and the bereaved must be a close second priority. Even if injuries and loss of life are minimal, the pastor's symbolic role is such that his very presence in the midst of ruin may help to reassure people that God's representatives continue to care.

At such times it is essential to establish a clear line of communication and command. Clergy and religious people may find themselves having to take a lead simply because other community leaders are absent or ineffective. Or they may use their own authority to set up and support an improvised leadership structure to meet the emergency. This is no time for democratic government; those who are able and calm must act decisively to care for those who are disabled and distraught, and they may need at first to repress their own feelings of distress in order to do so.

But repression is a dangerous defense if it is continued for too long. Carers can act in many ways to *support and encourage the expression of grief* and to provide opportunities for people to talk, cry, and rage. They should not attempt to block such expressions of grief, although it may sometimes be necessary to attempt to persuade people to turn their anger in directions where it will do good rather than harm or reassure others who are being unjustly accused.

If it is all right for the disaster-stricken population to grieve, then the same must surely be the case for the carers. In fact, it would be hard to believe that carers really care unless they show some appropriate emotional response. The problem for the carer is to continue to give emotional support to others while not denying his or her own need for emotional support. For this reason it is most important for those who take on caregiving roles to make time to meet together and to support each other.

Carers from outside the disaster area, who are themselves less personally traumatized, may find their own most important function in supporting the indigenous caregivers. There is a great need for organizations, such as the Red Cross, who provide rescue services, to recognize the need for continuing psychological support to community leaders into the aftermath of a disaster. Meetings between caregivers also improve liaison and act as a model for the creation of similar *mutual support groups* throughout the afflicted community.

One should not be surprised if some of these groups become vehicles for the expression of irrational emotions or the execution of inappropriate or harmful plans. Community leaders may be placed in the agonizing position of having to decide whether to join such groups in the hope of bringing some rationality into their activities or to disown them in the hope of reducing popular support. There are no simple answers, and it is inevitable that friends will be offended, pride hurt and carers rejected by those for whom they care. If caregivers expect such things they will be less hurt by them when the time comes.

Disasters naturally tend to evoke the sympathy of people from outside the disaster area. Helpers flood in and offers of financial and other aid will be received from all directions. Although much of this help will be welcome, it is essential to organize a proper response if further chaos is to be avoided.

Newspaper and television reporters will help to bring the disaster into public awareness and, if wisely advised, will often draw in further help. But their intrusive search for news may cause them to focus their attention on the most disturbed members of the community and they easily get caught up in the search for scapegoats. Community leaders will do well to set up a press office in order to ensure that responsible and accurate information is given, rumors corrected and a mutually helpful working relationship developed with the media. Pastors and other counselors may find themselves in a position to reach out to large sections of the community, and the intelligent use of press releases and similar means can allay fear and generate support systems.

During the recovery phase the need for continued emotional support will diminish and exciting and creative developments become possible. People want to believe that good can come out of evil, and sensitive counsel can encourage the development of many worthwhile changes.

A disaster demolishes the complex structure of meanings and assumptions which all of us take for granted. We need time to grieve, to grasp desperately at straws from the past, to strive to undo what cannot be undone. Only then can we begin to take stock of what remains and to look again at our basic assumptions about life and death.

Bibliography. F. Ahearn and R. Cohen, eds., *Disasters and Mental Health: An Annotated Bibliography* (1984). A. H. Barton, *Communities in Disaster* (1970). E. Bromet, *Three Mile Island: Mental Health Findings* (1980). R. Chinnici, "Pastoral Care Following a Natural Disaster," *Pastoral Psychology*, 33 (1985), 245–54. H. Dieck, *The Johnstown Flood* (1889). T. E. Drabek and W. H. Key, *Conquering Disaster: Family Recovery and Long-Term Consequences* (1983). J. P. Reed, Jr., "The Pastoral Care of Victims of Major Disaster," *J. of Pastoral Care*, 31 (1977), 97–108. P. Sorokin, *Man and Society in Calamity* (1942).

C. M. PARKES

CRISIS MINISTRY; EMERGENCY, PSYCHOLOGY OF PASTOR IN. *See also* POST-TRAUMATIC STRESS DISORDER; SOCIAL SERVICES AND PASTORAL CARE; SURVIVOR PSYCHOLOGY; TRAUMA; VICTIMIZATION. *Compare* HOLOCAUST; SOCIAL CHANGE AND DISLOCATION; WARTIME PASTORAL CARE.

DISCERNMENT OF SPIRITS. In Christian tradition an important distinction is made between "spiritual discernment" and "the discernment of spirits." The first is a general ability to understand and interpret a person's spiritual state and religious experience. According to ancient and orthodox authority this may be a charismatic gift (I Cor. 12:10) or a skill acquired by experience, or some combination of both. Wise pastors are generally able to discern those under their care who are endowed with particular gifts and graces, and whose spiritual health and integrity is such as to make them key members of a Christian community. Conversely, they should be able to guide good and faithful people whose immaturity may be leading them along false paths of prayer.

"Discernment of spirits," on the other hand, is a much more complex and technical process, based upon a profound ascetical theology of which there is an enormous literature spanning Christian history. This has its biblical basis in such texts as I Cor. 2:6–16; 12:1–11; I Jn. 4:1–6, which were expounded and expanded throughout the ages by the Desert Fathers, especially Cassian, St. Anthony, St. Bernard, Denis the Carthusian, and Scaramelli, and reached something of a final sophistication in St. Ignatius Loyola and St. John of the Cross. This traditional wisdom, dealing with a most delicate matter, remains of much pastoral value, but here possibly more than anywhere its underlying sense has to be translated from ancient and medieval concepts into contemporary terms, aided by modern psychological sciences.

1. **Recovering the Spiritual Tradition.** The bulk of these ancient writings speak of good and bad spirits, personified into angels and demons directly influencing prayer and spiritual experience. It needs to be recog-

nized, however, that belief in an unseen spiritual world, expounded in detail by the doctrine of a hierarchy of being by St. Thomas Aquinas; an invisible but real world populated by the heavenly host of cherubim and seraphim, angel and archangel together with the spiritual influence of the saints in the church triumphant; all of this is perfectly logical orthodox doctrine. Playing fast and loose with symbolic imagery, the ancient writers sound naive to modern ears, but they express a firm orthodoxy and point to depths of religious experience that the modern psychologist is unable to explain away. Rather than demons and angels, the contemporary pastor might prefer to deal with spiritual experience in terms of misinterpretation and self-deception, and to interpret the Spirit's leading by sanctified rational thought. But ultimately the underlying truths remain the same: it is a matter of terminology.

A further difficulty in the ancient tradition is that, as with prayer in general, it is inclined to concentrate on the mystical rather than on the ascetical; that is, on the rare rather than the common levels of religious experience. In ordinary pastoral practice, the concern is with a correct interpretation of these common levels; is this or that experience a genuine disclosure of the will of God? And what does it mean? We speak somewhat glibly of the "leading of the Spirit"; we frequently pray for the "guidance of the Spirit." But how does God the Spirit directly guide? Can God's influence really lead us into correct decisions? Or can we be misled into mistaking the Spirit for something else, perhaps our personal hopes and aspirations? What are the criteria?

2. Sources and Kinds of Discernment. Modern pastors should struggle with the ancient wisdom; such studies can be fruitful and rewarding. But greatly to simplify by way of introduction, the traditional sources of spiritual perception may be classified under three main headings: there are good angels, demons, and those movements of the soul that arise from natural intelligence. Translated, there are healthy spiritual insights issuing from healthy prayer, correctly and conscientiously interpreted; there is erroneous interpretation arising out of sinful distortion or self-seeking; and human decision growing on right belief.

Again greatly to simplify for normal pastoral practice, the orthodox authorities provide the following concensus:

(1) The will of God, disclosed in prayer, may be mysterious but *it cannot be irrational, futile, or useless.* There are many amusing and doubtless apocryphal stories to illustrate the point, like the nun who jumped into the icy river in reparation for drinking too much wine! She was sure that this was God's command; her superiors were wisely doubtful! Contemporary examples are not far to seek, such as the unhappily married family man who claims a sudden call to the solitary life as pious excuse for evading his proper responsibilities.

(2) A genuine leading of the Spirit always *embraces a moral content.* Consoling experiences of the presence of God are frequently offered to the immature beginner for sustenance, renewal, and strengthening, while the validity of such experience depends upon action on behalf of others. God does not offer self-disclosure to men and women purely for their own self-satisfaction.

(3) Genuine experience leading to action involves *humility and abandonment.* It frequently implies an interior peace because all is seen as under the dictates of divine providence. God would appear to have little sympathy for spiritual panic!

(4) Genuine spiritual leading implies *flexibility of purpose.* God has disclosed special purposes throughout history — from St. Paul to Albert Schweitzer — but God is unlikely to provide a detailed career blueprint. A continuous waiting upon God, acceptance of contingency and disappointment, is the outcome of true humility.

(5) Essential background to the discernment of spirits is consideration of a person's *total spiritual state.* God is bound to nothing, and God may call the most unlikely to heroic service, but sin is still the root cause of distortion.

3. Call to Ministry as Example. As but one practical example for a final illustration, we might look at the most common case of discernment in the modern Western world: the call to Christian ministry. Someone feels such vocation, claiming to be moved by the Spirit, directly invited by God to serve as priest, minister, or pastor. Within any reputable Christian community such claims have to be tested, and the five points above may be called into play:

(1) Ministry requires certain qualities: intellectual ability, leadership, compassion, a thirst for prayer. God can still overrule any deficiency, but the plain lack of all such qualities makes the vocation suspect. (2) Is there any motive of self-satisfaction, social status, arrogance? Where is the moral content? (3) Is there any foreseen, or hoped for, career structure? or genuine abandonment? utter self-oblation? (4) Is there flexibility of purpose, true humility, or are there personal reservations within the heart of the candidate? (5) And what of the candidate's overall spiritual state?

Bibliography. For the historical tradition *see* St. Athanasius, *The Life of Antony,* R. C. Gregg, trans. (1980), ch. 26. Cassian, *Conferences,* Part 1, chs. 16–23; also Parts 2, 7. St. Bernard, *Sermon 33.* St. Ignatius Loyola, *Spiritual Exercises,* D. L. Fleming, trans. (1978). St. Teresa, *Way of Perfection,* chs. 37–39. St. John of the Cross, *Ascent of Mount Carmel,* Part 2, ch. 26, pp. 3–8. St. François de Sales, *On the Love of God,* bk. 8, chs. 9–14; bk. 9, chs. 1–10. Augustine Baker, *Sancta Sophia,* (1972) sec. 4, paras. 9–21. G. B. Scaramelli, *Directorium Ascenticum,* (ET 1924, vol. I, pp. 104 ff. *passim.*) For modern studies and commentary see M. Thornton, *Prayer: A New Encounter,* 2d. ed., (1974, pp. 93–95). *See also* J. de Guibert, *The Theology of the Spiritual Life* (1954). A. Poulain, *The Graces of Interior Prayer,* ET 2d. ed., (1950). R. Garrigou-Lagrange, *The Three Ages of the Interior Life* (1947).

M. THORNTON

INTERPRETATION AND HERMENEUTICS, PASTORAL. *See also* CALL TO MINISTRY; GUIDANCE, DIVINE, ILLUMINATION; SPIRITUAL DISCIPLINE AND GROWTH; SPIRITUAL THEOLOGY; SPIRITUALITY. *Compare* EVALUATION AND DIAGNOSIS, RELIGIOUS; SOCIAL PERCEPTION, JUDGMENT AND BELIEF; VISIONS AND VOICES.

DISCIPLESHIP. *See* CHRISTIAN LIFE; SPIRITUAL DISCIPLINE AND GROWTH. *See also* COMMITMENT.

DISCIPLINE, CHILD. *See* PARENTS/PARENTHOOD. *See also* BEHAVIORAL DISORDERS OF CHILDHOOD; PARENT EFFECTIVENESS TRAINING.

DISCIPLINE, PASTORAL CARE AS (History). The problem of discipline in the pastoral care of the Christian church must be seen against the background of the accomplishments of Judaism. The emphasis in ancient Israel on the central role of the law for the organization of everyday life led to a gradual decline in the widespread use of magic, sorcery, and divination. The early sages and later scribes of Israel replaced guidance through magic with guidance and counsel based on the rational interpretation of the covenant law. But the problem of discipline in Christian pastoral care has centered on how to maintain ethical seriousness in its guidance of everyday behavior without becoming entrapped in the destructive grip of a legal and moral rigorism. Striking the proper balance between moral seriousness and the regenerative gestures of acceptance and forgiveness has become all the more challenging in the face of the moral pluralism and relativity that characterize modern societies.

1. **Discipline in Ancient Israel.** Christians are inclined to think about their religion against the background of the alleged excessive moral rigorism of Pharasaic Judaism. They often overlook the fact that Pharisaic Judaism is the culmination of a long process of a unique kind of spirituality and a unique strategy for the organization and guidance of everyday individual and communal life. The Israel of the Exodus was a loose assortment of pariah people — a "guest" people living at the margins of the more established culture — who were finally unified around faithfulness to God's covenant *(berith)* and law *(Torah)*. The breakthrough in religio-cultural evolution that this represented was the replacement of guidance through the magical ministrations of shamans or oracles by guidance through appeals to the authority of a divinely legitimated law which itself had to be validly interpreted. This shift led to the emergence of new classes of holy personages; ecstatic war magicians, such as Samuel, gradually were replaced by Levitical priests, prophets, wise men, wise women, and later scribes and rabbis.

Priests and sages were especially important for the guidance and discipline of everyday life. The Levitical priests were closely associated with the cultic activity of the Israelite confederacy. They gained their prestige from their knowledge of Yahweh's commandments and from their expertise in complementing the law and expiating guilt, especially for kings, princes, and other prominent private persons who were trying to avoid disaster by learning the law and being reconciled to it when they faltered.

Although wise men and women, or sages, on the other hand, knew and interpreted the Jewish law, they also had access to other strands of ancient practical wisdom from Egypt, Mesopotamia, and Greece. Possibly even less esoteric than the priests, these ancient sages directed and disciplined lives on the basis of argument and reasoned admonition. But they were far from elitists and aristocrats; they identified their reasoned, practical, moral teachings with the alluring feminine figure of Wisdom,

who invited all ages and classes to "fill yourselves with my fruits" (Eccl. 24:12).

Gradually, a third class of holy personages emerged in ancient Israel. These were scribes who at one time may have been secretaries to priests but who gradually became an independent group of scholars. The people who gathered to hear them interpret the law constituted the core of the earliest synagogues. The scribes were the authors of the Midrash—the oral exposition and interpretation of the Torah. These scribes became the rabbis of the first century C.E. with whom Jesus may have been identified.

Reflection on the role of law in ancient Judaism and its rational and scholarly interpretation in the care of souls can remind contemporary pastors of an easily forgotten truth. Although Christians often contrast this legal rationality of ancient Israel with the NT emphasis upon love, forgiveness, and grace, it should also be contrasted with magic. In contrast to the guidance of life through resort to divination, magic, and sorcery, Judaism more and more emphasized a practical, this-worldly rationalization of life around interpretation of the moral and ritual aspects of the written and oral law.

2. **Discipline in the New Testament.** This background of Jewish practical religious laws constitutes the major religio-cultural context for care and discipline in the NT. Of course, even this highly visible and deeply felt tradition had also been profoundly influenced by various popular Greek philosophies, which emigrated to Israel after the victories of Alexander the Great and the later occupations of Rome. Yet there is no particularly strong emphasis on the role of discipline in Jesus' ministry as it is portrayed in the Synoptic Gospels. Jesus is represented as having profound respect for the law. He was addressed frequently as Rabbi, indicating, as John McNeill suggests, that he may have had the formal training of a rabbi. Yet his approach to the law was closer to that of the liberal Pharisees and was humanely oriented toward seeing a line of continuity between the will of God and the needs of human beings. Jesus was interested in the needs of individuals, performed acts of healing, and used a fresh, warm, yet provocative manner of addressing people.

Whatever Jesus thought or did in the area of discipline must be set within the context of this total picture. Jesus' commission to Peter in Mt. 16:19 probably gives us more insight into patterns of discipline in the early church than it conveys knowledge about Jesus' actual practices. The words addressed to Peter, that "whatever you bind on earth shall be bound in heaven, and whatever you loose on earth shall be loosed in heaven," clearly convey a high image of disciplinary authority. In addition, Matthew represents Jesus as giving specific instructions for handling occasions when one member of the church has sinned against another (Mt. 18:15–17). The injured person should ask privately for redress. If the offender refuses, the injured person should return to the offender with witnesses and state the case again. If this does no good, the injured person is to take the complaint to the church, and if the offending brother "refuses to listen even to the church, let him be to you as a Gentile and a tax collector." This, too, is linked with the power of the keys to "remit or retain sin" and probably represents a rather advanced stage of the church's development. This passage became central to the medieval Catholic church's understanding of the power of the papacy to "bind" and "loose" the movement of souls into heaven. A similar passage granting this authority to the apostles can be found in Jn. 20:22–23. Although in these passages the basis of authority seems to shift from Peter to the whole church, or to the apostles, one is still struck by how they all seem to testify to the importance of discipline in the early church.

In the letters of Paul, we find the apostle concerned about the immorality of a particular individual in the Corinthian church (I Cor. 5:1–7). He urges that the person be removed from the fellowship of the church. Even here, however, Paul holds out the possibility of acceptance, comfort, and forgiveness for those who repent and are open to these blessings (II Cor. 2:5–11).

These different references to the disciplinary practices of the early church witness to the truth that in spite of the centrality of grace and forgiveness in the early church, there was indeed great concern for the maintenance of certain orderly codes of everyday behavior. Responsibility and cooperation among those who are members of the "one body" of Christ, genuine love for one another, contributions to the saints, and not offending the conscience of the weaker members — these are just a few of the more central behavioral expectations that early Christians placed on one another. It has sometimes been observed that Paul's call to early Christians to live holy, sober, upright, and godly lives has parallels with some of the moral values of the widely popular Stoic philosophies of the day. But in contrast to Stoic catalogues of virtues, the early Christian views of moral virtue were imbued with a lively sense of spiritual existence not known to the Stoic tradition. An example of this can be found in Tit. 2:11–13, where the author writes: "For the grace of God has appeared . . . training us . . . to live sober, upright, and godly lives . . . awaiting our blessed hope."

One cannot fully understand the nature of pastoral care and its dimensions of discipline until one comprehends the time perspective of the early church, which was dominated by the consciousness of the imminent return of Christ and his inauguration of the kingdom of God. Christian existence was seen as primarily a matter of mutual sustaining of the faithful until the Second Coming. Individuals were exhorted to be steadfast in this expectation, to continue to provide for themselves in their worldly vocations, to remain unmarried if single, and to continue married even if one's spouse were not a Christian. Mutual edification (*aedificatio mutua*) and fraternal correction (*correptio fraterna*) in small groups and among friends were the primary modes of mutual support, and criticism was generally given in the context of warm, forgiving, and loving relations.

3. **Discipline in the History of the Church.** The nature of pastoral discipline shifts considerably throughout the history of the church, depending upon a variety of historical circumstances. The waning expectations about the early return of Christ, the persecution of the church, the later establishment of the church, the effort to sustain the imperial church, the Protestant Reformation, and finally the move toward privatization and secularism in the modern nations of the West all had their implications for the nature of pastoral care and pastoral discipline.

a. Pastoral discipline and the persecutions. The early church quickly became an object of both Jewish and Roman persecution. Throughout the second century, tension grew between the church and the empire, generally centering around the refusal on the part of Christians to participate in state cults and to pledge absolute obedience to the emperor. However, some Christians did compromise and renounce their Christian faith. This raised the difficult question about which types of sins and lapses from the faith could be forgiven. The task of reconciling lapsed Christians gradually became standardized in the newly emerging office of the bishop. Tertullian (160–220) took a rigorist stand in the controversy. He developed the practice of exomologesis, which required sinners to publicly confess their sins before the entire congregation while also doing penance of a kind commensurate with their misdeeds. But Tertullian felt that the sins of idolatry, unchastity, and homicide could not be forgiven by the church (although perhaps by God) even through exomologesis — a position that Cyprian later took steps to liberalize.

b. Pastoral discipline and the imperial church. With the Constantinian establishment of the church in the fourth century, the mentality of Christians suddenly shifted from that of an outgroup to that of an ingroup with access to and support by the highest powers of civil authority. The church, its bishops, and pastoral care were now cast into a new role, which entailed socializing and assimilating diverse groups, cultures, and nations of southern and northern Europe into the new religio-cultural synthesis created by the marriage between the church and the Holy Roman Empire. This new task was supported by various forms of Platonic and Neoplatonic philosophy, which saw the universe as a great hierarchically organized chain of being. With the help of these philosophies and its developing sacramental system, the church gradually developed a model that saw its bishops and priests as the controllers of the traffic or flow of souls up and down this great chain. The church, invoking the authority of Mt. 16:19, saw itself as the keeper of the keys. Pastoral care and pastoral discipline were seen as forms of guidance by which individuals were inducted into progressively higher degrees of perfection along this chain of being.

The teachings of the Benedictine monks of the sixth century constitute a good illustration of how the process functioned. The Benedictine discipline consisted of a twelve-step ladder of humility; this pattern provided a hierarchical model of pastoral discipline that was influential far beyond the confines of the Benedictine monasteries themselves. The first three rungs of the ladder—to fear God, to despise one's own desires, and to obey the church—were prescribed for laymen as well as priests and monks.

This process of religio-cultural synthesis was even further supported by Pope Gregory the Great (590–604). Gregory's *Book of Pastoral Rule (Liber regulae pastoralis)* was full of shrewd yet sensitive insights into human nature, but it took the stance that pastoral care entailed the firm yet humble exercise of authority over souls needful of competent guidance into the moral and spiritual truths of the church.

Throughout the Middle Ages pastoral care took the form of what William Clebsch and Charles Jaekle have called inductive guidance (1964). This involved inducting novice Christians into deeper and sounder understandings of the faith and disciplining them when they faltered. In addition to the Benedictine rule and Gregory's *Pastoral Rule*, the Celtic penitential books played a pivotal role in this guidance. These were practical manuals, written by Irish and Welsh monks as early as the sixth century, that were distinguished for their methods of cataloging sins and stipulating appropriate penances. Though at first resisted by many bishops who feared the independence that such manuals gave to local clergy, by the ninth century the penitentials had become the chief resource for the parish priest's effort to rule over and instruct his flock.

c. Pastoral discipline and the Reformation. It is partly against the background of the moralistic excesses of the penitential system, however, that the Protestant Reformation came about. The Reformation constituted a serious blow to the Catholic synthesis of theology and practical guidance. Luther dispensed with the penitentials and their rules for establishing sins and penances. Lutheranism also abolished regular private confession, the form of confession that had gradually replaced the public confession of the exomologesis. More informal and occasional private confession was emphasized instead. In the place of these traditional Catholic forms of guidance and discipline was Luther's doctrine of the priesthood of all believers and the individual's immediate recourse to God's direction through prayer and meditation.

Luther simultaneously reduced the role of church and priest in the guidance of souls and heightened guidance through an unmediated relation to God. But the practical consequences of these moves in both Lutheranism and Calvinism may have functioned to increase the role of secular guidance as well. As Weber pointed out in his famous Protestant ethic hypothesis, the Lutheran doctrine of vocation *(Beruf)* sanctioned the Christian's secular occupation as an appropriate arena for expressing gratitude for one's salvation. It may be, as Weber suggests, that the reduction of guidance by church, penitential, and priest unwittingly increased the role of guidance by secular social structures empowered by the emerging dynamics of modern systematic capitalism.

But the idea of a lonely individual conscience standing before God would not be entirely accurate to describe everything that happened in pastoral care and discipline during the Reformation. Mutual edification and fraternal correction of small groups characterized a good deal of the life of later Protestant groups. This is especially true of Martin Bucer and his following and the Pietists associated with Philipp Jakob Spener. But it was also characteristic of the Methodist class meetings and love feasts and to some extent of various Presbyterian and Congregational groups on the American frontier.

4. Problems with Discipline in the Modern Church.

Pastoral care during the twentieth century seems to have gradually lost interest in the question of discipline, especially in the mainline Protestant churches (less so in the Catholic churches and the more conservative Protestant denominations). There are probably several reasons for this decline. First, the secularization of modern societies has left institutional religion with far less influence over the lives of individuals. The church and its ministry have had much less authority to exercise and have been far less potent in shaping lives, especially at the level of concrete attitudes and behaviors. The church, therefore, has been in a defensive stance and has related to its people primarily through warmth and acceptance, for fear that a more directing posture would actually alienate people and cause them to leave.

Second, along with secularization has come heightened pluralism in ethics and lifestyle. People everywhere seem far less certain than they once were about the acceptable limits of everyday behavior. The churches themselves seem more reluctant to invoke their authority in sanctioning clearly discernible approaches to work ethics, sexual ethics, child rearing ethics, and related normative issues pertaining to adulthood, manhood, and womanhood.

And finally, there has been the impact of modern psychotherapeutic psychology on the care and counseling of the church. Most of contemporary secular counseling and psychotherapy has understood itself as working out an ethically neutral value framework. Because of the dialogue that has gone on between secular psychotherapy and pastoral counseling, some of the value-neutral understandings of the secular theories have influenced the self-understanding of the church's pastoral care. Many contemporary theories of pastoral care and counseling emphasize primarily the values of acceptance, insight, clarification, and support. This is especially true of those pastoral counseling theories influenced by the writings of Carl Rogers.

But there is some evidence of a new interest in the role of moral guidance in pastoral care. The earlier works of O. Hobart Mowrer, *The Crisis in Psychiatry and Religion* (1961) and *The New Group Therapy* (1964), raised the ethical and disciplinary issue for the churches but received only a modest hearing. In a considerably different vein, Don Browning's *The Moral Context of Pastoral Care* (1976) and John Hoffman's *Ethical Confrontation in Counseling* (1979) may have gone further in establishing once again the question of moral guidance and discipline as a proper concern for the full reality of the church's pastoral care and counseling.

Bibliography. D. S. Browning, *The Moral Context of Pastoral Care* (1976). J. C. Hoffman, *Ethical Confrontations in Counseling* (1979). C. Jaekle and W. Clebsch, *Pastoral Care in Historical Perspective* (1964). J. T. McNeill, *A History of the Cure of Souls* (1951). O. H. Mowrer, *The Crisis in Psychiatry and Religion* (1961) and *The New Group Therapy* (1964). M. Weber, *Ancient Judaism* (1952) and *The Sociology of Religion* (1964).

D. S. BROWNING

PASTORAL CARE. *See also* ECCLESIOLOGY AND PASTORAL CARE; JEWISH CARE AND COUNSELING; MORAL THEOLOGY AND PASTORAL CARE; OLD *or* NEW TESTAMENT, TRADITIONS AND THEOLOGY OF CARE IN; SOCIOLOGY OF RELIGIOUS AND PASTORAL CARE; SPIRITUAL DIRECTION, HISTORY AND TRADITIONS OF. *Compare* MORAL BEHAVIOR AND RELIGION.

DISCIPLINE, PASTORAL CARE AS (Principles and Methods). *See* PASTORAL CARE (History, Traditions, and Definitions).

DISCIPLINE, SELF. *See* ASCETICAL PRACTICES; SELF-EXPRESSION/SELF-CONTROL.

DISCOURAGEMENT. *See* HOPE AND DESPAIR; SADNESS AND DEPRESSION; SELF-ESTEEM.

DISCRIMINATION, RACIAL. *See* RACISM.

DISEASE. *See* HEALTH AND ILLNESS.

DISFIGUREMENT. *See* BODY IMAGE; SELF-ESTEEM.

DISGRACE. *See* SHAME.

DISLOCATION, SOCIAL. *See* SOCIAL CHANGE AND DISLOCATION.

DISOBEDIENCE. *See* ADJUSTMENT DISORDERS; BEHAVIOR DISORDERS OF CHILDHOOD; OBEDIENCE (Roman Catholicism); PARENTS/PARENTHOOD.

DISORDERS, PSYCHOLOGICAL. *See* MENTAL HEALTH AND ILLNESS; PSYCHOPATHOLOGY, THEORIES OF. *See also* ADJUSTMENT DISORDERS; ANXIETY DISORDERS; BEHAVIORAL DISORDERS OF CHILDHOOD; BORDERLINE DISORDER; DEVELOPMENTAL DISORDERS; FUNCTIONAL DISORDER; MANIC-DEPRESSIVE (BIPOLAR) DISORDER; OBSESSIVE COMPULSIVE DISORDER; OLDER PERSONS, MENTAL DISORDERS OF; ORGANIC MENTAL DISORDER AND ORGANIC BRAIN SYNDROME; PERSONALITY DISORDERS; POST-TRAUMATIC STRESS DISORDER; SLEEP AND SLEEP DISORDERS; SPEECH DISORDERS AND THERAPY.

DISORIENTATION. *See* PSYCHOSIS.

DISPENSATION. The relaxing in a particular case of obligations or impediments arising from ecclesiastical laws or vows made in institutions governed by the Roman Catholic Church. There must be serious and justifiable reason for a dispensation. Since the church institutes and sanctions ecclesiastical laws and vows, it can also dispense from them. However, the church cannot dispense from obligations arising from divine law, from natural law, or from civil law; the distinctions between these are clearly spelled out in Catholic moral theology.

W. M. NOLAN

ROMAN CATHOLIC PASTORAL CARE. *Compare* ECCLESIOLOGY AND PASTORAL CARE; KEYS, POWER OF.

DISPLACEMENT. A defense mechanism in which impulses are unconsciously redirected to a substitute object because the person who elicited the feelings is too threatening. When the expression seems inappropriate they are redirected toward safer or more socially accept-able targets. An example is an employee who becomes angry at his or her boss and later, at home, without conscious awareness of the connection, kicks his or her dog.

J. ESTELLE

DEFENSE AND COPING THEORY; DEFENSE MECHANISMS.

DISPOSITION. *See* TEMPERAMENT.

DISSOCIATION. A term used to designate a sudden, involuntary, but often temporary alteration in consciousness. Psychoanalytically, dissociation is viewed as an unconscious defense mechanism where threatening attitudes, ideas, and feelings become distinctly separated from the rest of the psyche. This "splitting" of mental processes may result in the display of wandering behavior, multiple personalities, and memory loss.

S. MEHARG

DEFENSE MECHANISMS; MULTIPLE AND DISSOCIATIVE PERSONALITY. *See also* DEFENSE AND COPING THEORY; NEUROSIS.

DISSOCIATIVE PERSONALITY. *See* MULTIPLE AND DISSOCIATIVE PERSONALITY. *See also* DEFENSE AND COPING THEORY.

DISTANCE. *See* INTIMACY AND DISTANCE; OBJECTIVITY, PROFESSIONAL; PHENOMENOLOGICAL METHOD IN PASTORAL CARE.

DISTRUST. *See* SUSPICIOUSNESS AND PARANOIA. *See also* TRUST IN PASTORAL RELATIONSHIPS.

DIVINE GUIDANCE. *See* GUIDANCE, DIVINE; PROVIDENCE, DOCTRINE OF, AND PASTORAL CARE.

DIVINE LAW. *See* ETHICS AND PASTORAL CARE; MORAL THEOLOGY AND PASTORAL CARE. *See also* GOD'S WILL, ACCEPTANCE OF; TEN COMMANDMENTS.

DIVINE LIGHT MISSION. *See* NEW RELIGIOUS MOVEMENTS.

DIVINE WILL, ACCEPTANCE OF. *See* GOD'S WILL, ACCEPTANCE OF.

DIVISION 36, AMERICAN PSYCHOLOGICAL ASSOCIATION. *See* COUNSELING, ROMAN CATHOLIC.

DIVORCE (Care and Counseling). The process of dissolving a marriage by severing the spiritual, emotional, physical, and legal covenant between marriage partners. **1. The Process.** In spite of its pain, divorce has the potential to stimulate growth and to become a creative opportunity for personal reassessment and redirection. Pastoral care and counseling for divorce involves understanding the complexities and stages of the process and the impact divorce has, not only on couples but also on their families and communities.

a. Marital adjustment. To view divorce as a single action taken on a day in court is to misunderstand a highly complex process that may begin years before any open discussion of parting has occurred or any legal action contemplated. Couples may prepare for divorce, quietly separating bank accounts and other finances, returning to school to retool for earning a living, developing independent social lives. Within the marriage, the processes of disenchantment and disillusionment and the erosion of love may begin. Covert and overt conflicts emerge as couples struggle to make their relationship work, fighting for what they value. When the struggle fails to produce a common vision and to renew the relationship and reconcile the differences, physical separation and legal divorce can follow. However, there are couples who choose to remain legally married in spite of emotional divorce. Such couples fall short of the vision of covenant relationships that our religious heritages depict for marriage and may complicate the counselor's understanding of divorce. (Lederer and Jackson discuss these marriages under their category of stable-unsatisfactory.)

For couples who do part, physical separation is one of the most painful points in the divorce process, the point where an undeniable tear in the relationship has occurred. While some couples do mend this tear, it is only possible with mutual effort and hard work. Too often it is not possible for both partners, at the same time, to recommit to working on their marriage. Weiss's research indicates that even when reconciliations do occur, subsequent separations are likely.

b. Divorce adjustment. Once physical separation and legal divorce occur, partners are thrown into the world of the formerly married and into the realities of starting over. Often taking a number of years to work through, this period can be an opportunity for the individual to grow and achieve a greater degree of maturity and personal integration. Fisher's research indicates that divorced persons have the potential for achieving even higher levels of functioning than their married counterparts. For those who do not adjust to divorce successfully, it is possible to remain stuck for a lifetime, bemoaning the loss and clinging to the past. Sequentially, the following challenges are most likely to be encountered in the divorce process.

2. Expectable Challenges in the Adjustment Period. Denial is one of our basic defenses when we feel threatened, and it is, understandably, commonly used when people face the ending of their marriage. We have been taught that divorce is wrong, sinful, a social illness, something that happens to losers. Coming to accept reality requires courage and faith, and acceptance of divorce is necessary before further movement in the process can occur. Then other social, emotional, and spiritual challenges emerge.

Loneliness is something we face whether married or single. However, divorce brings home vividly the awareness of one's existence as an individual. The challenge is to learn to bear the sense of alienation and loss, while discovering a sense of comfort and peace in solitude. Though there may be an initial flight into frenzied activities and social involvements, ultimately the process calls one to face oneself.

Guilt and rejection are closely tied to acceptance and loneliness. Often the one who initiates the legal action struggles with the guilt of hurting someone he or she has cared for, of going against deeply felt values and beliefs about marriage. And the one who is left struggles with a strong sense of rejection, self-doubt, and pain. The challenge for both persons and for counselors is to place the experience of ending the relationship into realistic perspective. Guilt can motivate the divorced person to learn from the experience so as not to repeat it. Unrealistic, neurotic, or self-destructive guilt serves no valid purpose, however. Similarly, the feeling of rejection can motivate self-examination and growth, rather than leading to a total self-indictment that is unrealistic and neurotic, again serving no healthful purpose. Divorce may have been the healthiest choice for all concerned; or it may have been the best the couple could do.

Grief, the process of mourning the losses in a divorce, is painful yet necessary. Many attempt to avoid the pain, but the complex and multiple losses must be faced and mourned. Persons divorcing lose a close, intimate friend and companion, a lover, someone to share the responsibilities of parenting. They lose financially, with everyone taking a cut in standard of living. They lose possessions, pets, neighbors, homes, and in-laws and extended family networks. They lose the same kind of contact with their children, whether they are the custodial or noncustodial parent. They may lose status, their place in the community. No facet of life remains untouched. Each of these losses calls for courage to grieve and move on. Hesitancy to experience the pain of grief is normal yet may paralyze some people. Successful handling of these losses strengthens a person's capacity to face whatever life may bring.

Self-concept and self-esteem are intricately involved in the divorce process. There is no life crisis that calls for more confidence and integration of self than divorce. At the same time, there is no crisis that is more destructive to self-concept and esteem. Rebuilding a realistic and positive picture of self is one of the major challenges for the divorcing person and the counselor. The wounds and injuries and challenges and problems involved in the process are met more easily when the sense of self is secure, esteem is high, and there are reminders that we are children of God, accepted and loved.

Friendships do not avoid the impact and stress of divorce. Maintaining solid friendships and a support network is critical for making it through the process; however, many old friendships get lost. Some friends cannot understand, others take sides, and yet others feel threatened and withdraw. Still others are part of the in-law relationships, making their status ambiguous. Most persons going through the process are challenged to build a new friendship network, to take initiative and assertively create a new support base just when their social resources are at an all-time low. At this time persons often, though usually temporarily, drop out of the couples-world and seek friends among other singles. The person usually develops a much broader and more tolerant attitude towards singles and later may include both singles and couples in his or her friendship network.

Disentanglement from a former love relationship is a complex task. For parents, the task is even more com-

MARRIAGE/REMARRIAGE

PERIOD OF POST-
DIVORCE ADJUSTMENT

ISSUES: Lifestyle decisions
                 Growing/Repetition

INTERVENTIONS: Individual Therapy
                 Marriage Tribunal
                 Support groups

PERIOD OF MARITAL
ADJUSTMENT

ISSUES: Lifestyle
                 Values
                 Goals
                 Friends
                 Family Relationships
                 Sexual Intimacy

INTERVENTIONS: Marriage counseling
                 Couples communication
                    and enrichment groups
                 Supportive individual
                    counseling

PERIOD OF DIVORCE ADJUSTMENT

ISSUES: Acceptance
                 Loneliness
                 Rejection/Guilt
                 Grief
                 Self-Concept
                 Self-Esteem
                 Friendships/Support
                 Disentanglement
                 Anger
                 Sex
                 Trust/Intimacy
                 Freedom to be
                    Single or
                    Committed in a
                    relationship

INTERVENTIONS: Divorce adjustment
                    seminars
                 Support groups
                 Individual supportive
                    therapy
                 Divorce Mediation

PERIOD OF DISENCHANTMENT

ISSUES: Disillusionment
                 Erosion of Love
                 Conflict
                 Giving Up/Giving In

INTERVENTIONS: Intensive marriage and
                    family therapy

PHYSICAL SEPARATION

plex. The often subtle and intricate ways couples intertwine their lives makes letting go difficult. Dividing possessions and sharing responsibilities for parenting call for a willingness and ability to disengage emotionally from one's former spouse and to deal with problems fairly and justly. Particularly for parents, the challenge is to separate out the marital and parental relationships and to work together in the best interest of the children. Often this is so difficult that both relationships get severed, to everyone's detriment.

Anger, a necessary aid in the process of emotionally disengaging, is one of the strongest feelings that divorcing persons experience. Rooted in feelings of hurt, abandonment, and helplessness, the rage some experience is frightening and unlike any anger they have felt before. Learning to channel and use this anger and energy constructively is a major challenge. Divorce provides an opportunity to learn new ways to express and handle anger productively in problem solving.

Sexual identity and relating sexually as a single person are issues raised by the divorce process. There is often an initial period of disinterest in sexual relations and, if attempted, they may lead to experiences of impotency or little enjoyment. Sometimes, hypersexual activity occurs as a way of re-establishing a sense of worth as a man or as a woman, or as a way of assuaging loneliness or seeking revenge. Eventually, the sexual pattern that was normal for that person will re-establish itself. The challenge is how to reconcile one's beliefs and values with the single lifestyle. Those going through divorce often search for a morality they can live with. They are likely to move from law and order and class values to more universal principles as guides for their moral reasoning and decision making (Kohlberg).

Trust and intimacy in social relationships come late in the divorce adjustment process. Persons going through the process are generally cautious and tentative, avoiding new wounds. As they begin to feel more confident and in charge of their lives, they experience a freedom to choose, to choose to be single or to be in a committed relationship. Significantly, many divorced persons remarry within the first year. This fact does not contradict the statement that trust and intimacy come late. Rather, it indicates that for many individuals a double task is involved. Not only does the divorce process need to be faced and worked through, but also comes the building of a new relationship. It is not surprising that second marriages have a higher casualty rate than the first. Without allowing time to heal and to learn from the ending of a love relationship, the possibility of repeating the earlier, unsuccessful pattern is very high.

3. **Interventions.** Pastoral care and counseling for divorce must begin with an understanding of the process described above. Interventions need to be guided by the stage of the process and the needs present. The diagram (on the following page) summarizes the process and possible interventions. Regrettably, couples often come to therapy as a last-ditch effort. Encouragement to seek help early is critical. Helping couples in the formative period of their marriage with marriage counseling, couples communication or enrichment groups, and supportive counseling may prevent the process of erosion and provide the context for understanding marriage as a mutual project, demanding love, commitment, and work.

During the period of disenchantment, more intensive marriage and family therapy may be helpful. At the point of physical separation, supportive individual counseling may be useful, though this tends to provide a forum for rumination. Time-limited, didactic-experiential divorce adjustment seminars appear to have the greatest potency for this acute crisis time and are also useful during the period of divorce adjustment (Fisher, Weiss, Kessler). Ongoing groups, offered through churches and synagogues, where the membership is highly fluid, are also helpful. Divorce mediation, an emerging option to adversarial divorce, offers a process of working through some of the disentanglement and parenting issues in a creative and humane way.

It is not until the period of divorce adjustment and post-divorce adjustment that individual therapy can produce real fruits. It is during these periods that the individual can deeply search his or her own contribution to the divorce and learn from it. For Roman Catholics, this process of self-examination may involve the marriage tribunal and the annulment process.

The general stance the pastor or pastoral counselor needs to take toward divorce is that of support, suspending judgment while calling those involved to learn and grow from the experience.

Bibliography. P. Bohannon, *Divorce and After* (1970). S. Campbell, *The Couple's Journey* (1980). B. Fisher, *Rebuilding* (1981). R. Gardner, *Parents' Book About Divorce* (1977). J. Haynes, *Divorce Mediation* (1981). M. Hunt and B. Hunt, *The Divorce Experience* (1977). F. Kaslow, "Divorce and Divorce Therapy," in A. Gurman and D. Kniskern, eds., *Handbook of Family Therapy* (1981). S. Kessler, *The American Way of Divorce* (1975). M. Krantzler, *Creative Divorce* (1974). W. Lederer and D. Jackson, *The Mirages of Marriage* (1968). I. Ricci, *Mom's House, Dad's House* (1980). C. Sager and B. Hunt, *Intimate Partners* (1979). R. Weiss, *Marital Separation* (1975). M. Wilcox, *The Developmental Journey: A Guide to the Development of Logical and Moral Reasoning and Social Perspective* (1979). J. Young, ed., *Divorce Ministry and the Marriage Tribunal* (1982).

J. H. SHACKELFORD

DIVORCE, CHILDREN AND ADOLESCENTS IN; MARRIAGE; MORAL DILEMMAS IN PASTORAL PERSPECTIVE. *See also* CHILDREN; DECISION/INDECISION, PSYCHOLOGY OF; FAMILY LAW; FORGIVENESS; GUIDANCE, PASTORAL; LEGAL DIMENSIONS OF PASTORAL CARE AND COUNSELING; MEDIATION/CONCILIATION; MORAL THEOLOGY AND PASTORAL CARE; RECONCILING; RESPONSIBILITY/IRRESPONSIBILITY, PSYCHOLOGY OF; VOWS/VOWING. *Compare* DIVORCED PERSONS; INFIDELITY (Marital); JOURNALS IN MARRIAGE AND FAMILY COUNSELING.

DIVORCE, CHILDREN AND ADOLESCENTS IN.

The offspring, adopted or natural, of two adults whose marriage is coming to or has come to an end. This article will focus primarily on those offspring whose ages are less than twenty years, although there are certainly aftereffects that must be faced by adult children of divorced or divorcing parents. The term "children" refers ordinarily to offspring under the age of thirteen. "Adolescent" refers to a person between the ages of thirteen and twenty. Increasingly, stepchildren are included in this description. Multiple divorces result in stepchildren going through these effects when a second or third marriage of the natural or adoptive parent ends in divorce. All too often the needs of children and adolescents are neglected during and after a divorce. Attention tends to center on the adults. While care for the divorcing parties is going on, the offspring are suffering a variety of emotional upheavals, including grief, anger, rejection, assaulted self-esteem, and anxiety about the future. Pastoral care and, frequently, counseling during divorce, should include both preadolescent and adolescent children in some way and thus attempt to prevent later, more exaggerated, difficulties.

1. **The Response of Children to Divorce.** Children in the latent and prepuberty years are very conscious of relational issues that go on among significant adults. They derive much of their internal sense of security and well-being from the relative health of their family system. While parents may attempt to conceal intense conflict, children are usually quite conscious of it. When the tension is not discussed or even acknowledged by the parents, the children tend to become more anxious or fearful. They may even feel caught between their intuitive "knowledge" that something is wrong and the fear of being called silly or wrong if they say something about it.

Along with the acute sensitivity to and dependency on those significant relationships, children typically possess a great sense of power about their ability to influence the state of relationships. Much of this, of course, comes from a not-yet-well-developed sense of differentiation from the parents. For example, if the child wishes bad things for a parent and that parent later suffers in some way, the child feels responsible.

This tension between dependency and power comes into bold relief with children when divorce occurs. On the one hand, there is a strong sense that their world (and thus they themselves) has been shattered. On the other hand, the child often feels responsible for what has happened. ("What did I do wrong, Mommy?" or "If you won't divorce, I promise to. . . .")

Some children, depending on age, maturity, and circumstance, may articulate these fears very openly. Others retreat into silence, appearing unresponsive and unwilling to talk. Regardless of the external appearances, however, the major issues calling for attention include the sense of helplessness and despair, and the sense of responsibility for what has happened, often seen in a "special burden" to "fix it."

2. **The Response of Adolescents to Divorce.** Teenage children are developmentally wrestling with issues of significance, competence, and power. Experiencing the dissolution of the marriage of parents is a major threat to those developmental issues. Suddenly the significance of the adolescent seems to be undermined. Parents are making decisions that will affect the teenager deeply, and some of these decisions don't *seem* to take the well-being of the son or daughter seriously. The parents, and those seeking to help, often fail to give much attention to the feelings of the adolescent. Autonomy and independence suddenly become all too real! Further, a sense of competence is undermined. Witnessing the breakup heightens a consciousness of the inability to "do anything" about it. The feeling is one of helplessness and a sense of powerlessness.

Erik Erikson notes that the crucial value of adolescence is faithfulness. What the teenager witnesses in divorce is an ending of faithfulness, accompanied by the fear and / or outrage that his or her own significance, competence, and power could be (and are being) damaged by this divorce or ending.

Manifestation of this grief will vary widely from anger, to acting out, to apparent lack of caring, to depression. Nonetheless, it is important to have some sensitivity to these developmental issues that are likely to be meaningful to the adolescent.

3. **The Pastoral Care of Children and Adolescents in Divorce.** Children and adolescents, as noted earlier, enter into a grief process long before formal steps of divorce take place. There is a loss of security and sense of certainty about their own status and worth. Often the grief is unspoken out of the fear that saying something will result in more radical separation than is already being experienced.

Consequently, the pastoral care of marital conflict should be broadened to include the children and adolescents in the family. Since these offspring will not ordinarily take the initiative to ask for help in direct ways, it becomes the pastor's responsibility to take initiative toward them. There is a variety of ways in which this may be done, and more of them are informal than formal.

One form of pastoral care is that of *assurance*. Children like to know that they have been noticed. If visiting in the home, the pastor should take some time to speak with the child, giving assurance that the child may count on being visited (and seen!) as well. The aim is to provide interest and concern about what is going on *with the child* in the midst of this experience. If the process has moved to formal steps toward divorce, giving the child an illustrative book can be the entry to conversation about what is happening.

Adolescents may not be as readily available as children. They may need to be sought out and told that the pastor wants to care for them as well as the parents. Assurance consists of letting these sons and daughters know that they are noticed, remembered, and invited to receive pastoral care as well. If the pastor uses a family systems approach, these children and adolescents will be included in significant ways in the counseling process itself.

Another form of pastoral care is continued and planned *conversation*. As the pastor shows a willingness to listen to "how it is" with children and adolescents, some of the security and significance issues begin to be met in new ways. With children it may literally be necessary to have a "bag of tricks" for these conversations. Paper, pencils, crayons, puppets, storybooks — all become vehicles for the child to tell his or her own story about what is happening. Adolescents will often respond more openly on neutral turf. The formality of an office may be too threatening if they fear being seen as the "poor kid" whose parents are breaking up. Long walks, driving somewhere in the car, talking while "on errands" may be contexts within which more can be said because of the comforting presence of distractions for the moments in which *much* is being said.

Third, the pastor can serve as an *interpreter* of sons and daughters to divorcing or divorced parents. Often the pain in the process does result in a tunnel vision on the part of the parents. They forget or miss or need not to see the pain of their children. The pastor can be a gentle but firm reminder that, though perhaps no longer married, they are still parents. And, as parents, they need to be attentive to the needs and pain of their children, whatever their ages.

Bibliography. W. V. Arnold, *When Your Parents Divorce* (1980). E. H. Erikson, *Toys and Reasons* (1977). S. Fraiberg, *The Magic Years* (1959). R. A. Gardner, *The Boys' and Girls' Book About Divorce* (1970). *Psychotherapy With Children of Divorce* (1976). C. L. Jewett, *Helping Children Cope with Separation and Loss* (1982). A. D. Lester, *Pastoral Care With Children in Crisis* (1985).

W. V. ARNOLD

DIVORCE (Care and Counseling). *See also* ADOLESCENTS; CHILDREN. *Compare* GRIEF AND LOSS IN CHILDHOOD AND ADOLESCENCE.

DIVORCE, PASTOR'S. Divorce among pastors is less frequent than in the general population but has been increasing in recent years. While many of the same factors are involved in clergy divorce as in other kinds, certain stresses specific to ministry are also involved. And while attitudes, especially in the "mainline" denominations, are becoming more accepting of clergy divorce, traditional values also remain strong. In any event, a pastor's divorce always impacts a congregation powerfully, calling for a deepened understanding of ethical norms in relation to human realities, and for a renewed understanding and experience of community.

1. **Rate.** It is estimated that in 1980 there were approximately 280,000 male clergy serving as pastors of parishes, of whom approximately eighty percent were married. Assuming a divorce rate of nearly one percent, each year over 2,000 clergy marriages end in divorce. This estimate does not include clergy women, clergy serving in positions other than as pastors of parishes, and clergy who were divorced prior to entering the ordained ministry.

In recent decades the divorce rate for clergy has increased. However, it is difficult to determine how much the rate has increased. In 1960 the divorce rate for clergy was 0.2 percent, increasing to 0.4 percent in 1970. A crude estimate for the early 1980s is that less than one percent of all married clergy divorced in a given year. By comparison with the general population of the U.S. in the early 1980s, approximately two to three percent of all marriages end in divorce in a given year.

By comparison with the recent past, however, divorce among pastors has increased greatly. By comparison with the general population, divorce among clergy is still much lower. Most divorced persons, including clergy, marry again. It may be estimated on the basis of an accumulated divorce rate, for example, that over a ten-year period approximately ten to fifteen percent of clergy marriages will end in divorce, a rate that is about one-fourth of that of the general population.

Divorce rates are most appropriately calculated on the basis of the number of divorces in the population at risk of divorce. To compare the number of marriages in a given year with the number of divorces in the same period is not an appropriate measure of rate of divorce, since the base groups are not the same. The most appropriate statistic is the number of divorces that eventually occur in a given number of marriages. In the U.S., for example, approximately thirty to forty-five percent of first marriages in a given year will have ended in divorce fifteen years later, with about half of these divorces occurring within the first two years of marriage. Divorce rates are highest in the U.S., followed by the U.S.S.R., Denmark, Sweden, Egypt, and England. Changes in the rates, however, are affected by changes in divorce laws, increased accuracy of reporting divorce, and other factors, in addition to the quality of the marriages themselves.

2. **General Factors That Increase Clergy Divorce.** Societal and personal factors that increase divorce in the general population also operate on marriages in which one spouse is a pastor. *a. Social factors.* In most industrialized, technological countries, there are higher expectations for happiness in marriage, conception can be controlled, divorce is more widely accepted, mobility of persons is greater, and women as well as men have access to education and job opportunities. In this context, congregations and church leaders tend to become more tolerant and accepting of divorce. Increasingly in many churches and denominations, a pastor may divorce and still be able to serve as a pastor in the denomination, sometimes even in the same congregation. This increased tolerance of divorce permits clergy in an unhappy marriage to divorce when in years past they would either have tolerated the miserable marriage or left the ministry because of divorce.

b. Personal and interpersonal factors. Often cited as causes of divorce are difficulties in areas such as money, sexual relations, parenting pressures, relatives, career concerns, and alcoholism. These are usually expressions of more basic underlying factors that destroy the marriage relationship. Among these interpersonal factors are disagreement about goals and expectations as individuals and as a couple, inability to solve conflicts constructively, lack of commitment to each other and the marriage, poor skills for communicating love and affirmation, and inappropriate time management. These interpersonal factors and skill deficits often result from inadequacies in the spouses' own family systems and personal development.

3. **Factors Specific to Clergy Divorce.** Many marriage therapists suggest that the pressures and stresses on clergy marriages are similar to those on marriages involving other careers, and the fundamental dynamics that produce divorce among clergy would also produce divorce if the marriage involved some other career. Several studies, however, indicate that there are some factors that are unique for marriages involving pastors. Among these are time pressures from being pastor, the pastor's evening and weekend work schedule, expectations (real or assumed) of the congregation that the minister's marriage and family approach perfection, lack of family privacy, frequent moves required by the denomination, and commitment of pastor to church or career in preference to marriage and family. In addition, the vows of commitment to the ordained ministry ask the individual to put allegiance to God above all other human commitments, which includes marriage. These disadvantages,

of course, are common to most clergy marriages, so one may infer that divorce occurs when the couple does not have the commitment or the abilities to resolve these issues satisfactorily.

4. **Women Clergy and Divorce.** Most research to date has involved male clergy and their non-clergy wives. Although the number of ordained women is increasing in some denominations, less is known about the marriage dynamics and divorce rates for married female pastors. The Hale, King, and Jones study (1980) of 878 United Methodist clergywomen showed slightly over fifty percent married, about thirty percent single, ten percent separated or divorced, and ten percent widowed. Since this included many women still completing their preparation for ordination, these percentages will likely change as more women achieve experience equivalent to male clergy.

Marriages in which both spouses are ordained clergy typically face all of the usual issues that can produce divorce plus the added dimensions of coping with a two-career marriage that has many possibilities for career cooperation or competition.

5. **Factors That Produce Success in Clergy Marriages.** It is also instructive to consider the reasons that the divorce rate for clergy is lower, and likely to stay lower, than the divorce rate for the general population. Compared to other career groups, pastors and their spouses are more likely to have good communication skills, to share common goals, to come from family backgrounds that support good marriage skills, and to have the interpersonal resources necessary to continue in a successful marriage. In addition, clergy marriages have shared religious commitments and spiritual resources, a unity of purpose in ministering to others, the nurturing support of the congregation, respect in the community, many friendship networks, opportunities for the spouse to be involved in the pastor's work, and interesting challenges and opportunities. In some ways these advantages reflect the couples' underlying positive perspectives that may come from their own family systems and their involvements in the religious community. It is possible that the influences that attract persons to careers in the ordained ministry may also tend to facilitate more satisfying marriages. More research on these hypotheses is needed.

6. **Congregational and Pastoral Aspects of Clergy Divorce.** Clergy couples, whether the man, woman, or both are clergypersons, continue to face an assumption by church leaders and by parishioners that if their faith were strong enough they would not have to divorce. It is still difficult for many religious persons to understand that one can accept the failure of a particular marriage as a fact of life without negating a belief in the indissolubility of marriage as a norm for living. The divorce of clergypersons is theoretically no different ethically from the divorce of any member of a congregation. Practically, however, because of the symbolic and administrative leadership role of the pastor, it is a different problem because of the wider ranging effect of the divorce on the total community. As a leader of that particular congregation a pastor has a greater responsibility for the effect of his or her actions upon that community. In reality this is not fair to pastors or to their families, but it is a fact to be dealt with.

Both clergy and the church have needs in the face of clergy divorce. Parishioners may feel that if the clergy cannot stay married then surely their own marriages are at risk. Clergy who divorce may feel blamed by threatened parishioners and ecclesiastical officials, stripped of self-worth and self-esteem, and cast out of the community of faith. Furthermore, they may be perceived as unacceptable leaders in other ministry situations because of their marital failure. The needs of divorced clergy include helping both in accepting their responsibility for the failure of their broken marriage and the sin that contributed to that failure and in discovering the possibility of grace and reconciliation with congregations and church officials from whom they feel estranged. Pastors' spouses whose identity was strongly related to their place in the congregation perhaps need the most assistance in finding who and where they are without dependence on the role of their former spouse. Congregations need an ongoing interpretation of the relation of sin and grace with respect to this particular issue. Sin does not permanently destroy a community but may provide opportunity for a deeper experience of the meaning of community.

Bibliography. S. R. Brown, "Clergy Divorce and Remarriage" *Pastoral Psychology,* Spring (1982). W. Douglas, *Ministers' Wives* (1965). H. Hale, Jr., M. King, and D. M. Jones, *New Witnesses: United Methodist Clergywomen* (1980). R. A. Hunt, *Ministry and Marriage* (1976). D. Mace and V. Mace, *What's Happening to Clergy Marriages?* (1980).

R. A. HUNT

DIVORCE; MARRIAGE AND FAMILY LIFE, PASTOR'S; PASTOR, PASTORAL CARE OF. *Compare* CLERGY *or* RABBIS, EMPIRICAL STUDIES OF; CLERGY COUPLES; MARRIAGE.

DIVORCE AND REMARRIAGE (Judaism). Because of the complex patterns of adaptation of the Jewish community, attitudes toward Jewish religious law (*halacha*) range from binding to persuasive to irrelevant. Nowhere is this more apparent than in practices relating to religious divorce and the implications of remarriage. At stake are a series of disabilities, primary among them the status of children and their descendants.

Illegitimacy in Judaism is not based upon a child's birth before marriage but is a function of the right of a husband to exclusive sexual access to a woman consecrated to him. The children of a woman who had been a partner in a properly consecrated marriage but whose divorce and remarriage did not include the religious dissolution of her previous marriage are regarded by strongly committed Jewish traditionalists as illegitimate (*mamzerim*). For those who regard Jewish religious law as binding, this taint would restrict the children of such liaisons as limited in marriage opportunities to those of similar lineage.

Because of the severity of this rule and because of the shattering effect of sudden discovery by less traditionally oriented Jews of unanticipated impediments to marriage with a more traditionally oriented co-religionist, Reform and Conservative Judaism therefore have sought doctrinal and legal methods to protect the modern Jewish divorcee.

Conservative Judaism has attempted to remain within the traditional legal framework. By incorporating into the religious marriage contract (*ketuba*) a clause giving their rabbinic court the right to annul a marriage, the Conservative Movement gives to the wife the ability to initiate religious divorce proceedings and to protect her offspring by a future husband in ways not available to her in normative Orthodox practice.

Reform Judaism in its early stages attempted to eliminate Jewish religious divorce. The status of a marriage was to be determined by civil, not religious, law. Two major influences have prompted reconsideration of this position: the granting of the right to determine matters of personal status to ultra-orthodox elements in the State of Israel, and a growing religious sentiment to evolve liturgical devices to mark the conclusion of a marriage. Many reform rabbis attempt to protect divorcees and their future offspring by counseling them to obtain a more traditional religious divorce (*get*) even though the absence of this procedure is not regarded as an impediment to remarriage.

The classic Orthodox procedures for religious divorce call for the highest level of legal and scribal competence. With rare exceptions, the wife must depend upon the husband to initiate the process. His refusal would leave her divorced in civil law but unable to remarry a traditionally oriented partner. Most Orthodox rabbis will cooperate fully in attempting to resolve such a conflict.

Divorce severely upsets the normative life patterns of observant Jews. Home ceremonies are structured in ways which presume both parents. The absence of the other often encourages the remaining spouse to utilize a child of the opposite sex as a religious surrogate partner. A young son is encouraged to "be the man of the house" and bless the wine on the eve of Sabbath or Festivals, a young daughter to bless the candles. Counseling patterns which focus on the reconstruction of the family system should be sensitive to the child's ambivalence and vulnerability as well as the parent's unconscious compulsions to lean upon the child.

Life cycle ceremonies in the synagogue are never easy for the divorced and remarried. It is at these events that counseling is most often sought. The presence of the "replacement spouse and pseudo parent" and the old agenda of hurt and counter-hurt add to an already considerable burden of anxieties for the parent. At a Bar/Bat Mitzvah, the child usually longs for the day about which he or she has dreamed: the day when his or her real parents and his or her real family are once again a unit. At a wedding, the interplay of divorced parents is a brutal reminder of the fragility of modern marriage at precisely the moment when the bride and groom would prefer not to be reminded. Because three generations are often involved and because of the pressures built into Jewish family life, these moments often call for pastoral skills even more than liturgical competence.

Bibliography. R. P. Bulka, "Some Implications of Jewish Marriage Philosophy for Marital Breakdown," *Pastoral Psychology* 30 (1981), 103–12.

J. PEARLSON

DIVORCE (Care and Counseling); JEWISH CARE AND COUNSELING; REMARRIAGE (Pastoral Care). *See also* MARRIAGE AND MARITAL CARE (JEWISH PERSPECTIVE); MORAL DILEMMAS IN PASTORAL PERSPECTIVE. *Compare* JEWISH-CHRISTIAN MARRIAGE; MORAL THEOLOGY AND PASTORAL CARE.

DIVORCE AND REMARRIAGE (Orthodoxy). In the Orthodox Christian teaching and practice, marriage is accepted as a Sacrament (*Mysterion*), a gift of grace which involves both God and human society. Marriage is "given" to a male and a female, based upon love, respect and mutuality as a freely received physical, moral, and spiritual covenantal relationship. Man and woman consecrate their covenant of mutuality into a communion with each other "in Christ," revealed in the union of Christ and the church (Eph. 5:21–33). As the church is the foretaste of the eternal Kingdom and an actual participation in the new age inaugurated by Christ, so the special vocation of marriage reveals eternal joy, communion, and new creation.

In faithfulness to both the Scriptures and the tradition, Orthodoxy sees Christian marriage ideally as indissoluble. Yet, this is not understood in a strict legalistic sense, but rather in dynamic terms, as an ideal cooperation of divine grace and human freedom. Sin and human failure can and do lead to the dissolution of a marriage. The church, sorrowfully and with a sense of pastoral solicitude, is forced to recognize the reality of moral ambiguity, human weakness and temptation, scandal and misunderstanding, which may lead to the betrayal of the ideal of Christian marriage, if the grace of marriage has not truly been received or is not bearing fruit. A ministry of guidance, healing and reconciliation through penance is exercised in such cases. A fresh opportunity is tolerated only by condescension to human weakness, as the entire liturgical and canonical tradition indicates. In practice, however, there is a tendency to be more lenient and accommodating than the stated position would have.

It would be proper to say, then, that the Orthodox church tolerates divorce and admits the possibility of remarriage. It does not "grant" divorces, nor does it "recognize" them, except as legal actions of the state which are a necessary precondition to considering a pastoral accommodation to the issue. Divorce is considered a grave sin; but in practice there is forgiveness through penance, and remarriage is possible. Yet, although second and third marriages are permitted under certain circumstances, this practice is discouraged. A fourth marriage is forbidden.

Remarriage is permitted after the death of a spouse, when the surviving partner may enter into a second marriage. Strictly speaking, the "order of second marriage" is to be used in all cases of successive marriage. It is a penitential service, very different from the normal rite of crowning; full of admonitions and reminders of human weaknesses; somber and humbling. The reasoning is consistent with the vision of marriage as an anticipation of the eternal Kingdom and that the first marriage is unique and ideal. The norm is maintained of marriage as indissoluble and eternal, a gift of grace and faith which reveals the joy of perfect communion. Usually, however, the rite of "second marriage" is observed only when both parties are entering into a successive marriage.

In the instance when a marriage has broken down, steps may be taken by church authorities to minister to the situation and to the persons involved. If, upon petition of a separated person, a case is to be adjudicated by the bishop or by a spiritual tribunal appointed by him, certain procedures are followed. These procedures may vary from diocese to diocese or within various jurisdictions of Eastern Orthodoxy. In general, however, a formal action must precede any rite of "second marriage," which is granted only by the permission of the bishop as the normal minister of the principle of "economy."

Adultery and fornication are primary causes for the formal dissolution of a marriage. In such cases it is decided that the ideal of Christian marriage is entirely defeated and the scope of marital fidelity is destroyed. It is seen as a type of moral death. Other causes for dissolution of marriage which have been considered as valid for the church are: plotting against one's life by the spouse; sexual impotence; procuring or inducing abortion; insanity; abandonment for more than three years; imprisonment lawfully for more than seven years; fraudulent or forcible marriage; incurable alcoholism, addiction, or gambling; compromising the honor or dignity of the spouse through illicit affairs; and the voluntary acceptance of the monastic life.

In all cases, a civil court action must precede any consideration by the church tribunal in reviewing the circumstances for issuing an ecclesiastical divorce and the granting of permission to remarry according to the rite of "second marriage" (*digamia*). Usually, the parish priest is required to investigate this matter thoroughly, to exhaust all avenues of possible reconciliation and to submit a report for the consideration of the tribunal. The petitioner must be present at a hearing and after due process a decision may be handed down allowing a successive marriage in the church. Spiritual direction, penances, and pastoral solicitude are offered to both parties.

Orthodox canon law forbids the administration of sacraments to other than members of the Orthodox church. In no case may a divorced person who is not an Orthodox communicant receive marriage by an Orthodox priest. For obvious reasons, conversions to Orthodoxy solely for the purpose of sacramental remarriage are not permitted.

R. G. STEPHANOPOULOS

DIVORCE (Care and Counseling); MINISTRY AND PASTORAL CARE (Orthodox Tradition); REMARRIAGE (Pastoral Care). *See also* MARRIAGE; MORAL DILEMMAS IN PASTORAL PERSPECTIVE; MORAL THEOLOGY AND PASTORAL CARE. *Compare* JEWISH-CHRISTIAN MARRIAGE; ORTHODOX-CATHOLIC MARRIAGE; ORTHODOX-PROTESTANT MARRIAGE.

DIVORCE AND REMARRIAGE (Protestantism).

Protestant churches have differed greatly in their approach to divorce and remarriage in the past 450 years. Luther and Calvin led the reformers in rejecting the Roman view that marriage is a sacrament. Their rejection meant that divorce was not an attack on the mystery of grace working in the true sacraments like baptism and Eucharist. It did not undermine the sanctity of the church. Because Roman sacramentality had been tied to the validity of the marriage contract, the reformers also

had to reject the use of annulment to end marriages. That is, people could not appeal to original impediments to the marriage contract in order to separate from each other and remarry. It also meant that matters of divorce came under the control of government rather than the church.

Three basic thrusts emerged among reformers in the wake of this rejection of sacramentality: the Lutheran "Two Kingdoms" emphasis on the protection of faith, the Calvinist theocratic emphasis on obedience to the New Covenant, and the radical independents' emphasis on personal dignity. All of them argued from biblical texts rather than from the nature of sacrament.

While Luther rejected marriage's sacramentality he held it to be a sacred order of creation, to be dissolved only because of adultery. However, at the same time he assigned matters to the magistrate, who would develop laws and policies designed to preserve order and peace rather than advance faith ideals. Christians were enjoined to uphold their faith in God no matter what the condition of their marriage and to endure its rigors patiently. However, the church could not use the civil arm to force fractious people to dwell together. The church could only refuse to remarry them, though it could remarry the innocent party to a civil divorce.

Calvin was equally rigorous in his attack on divorce and remarriage as a divine ordinance, appealing to Christ's injunctions against divorce as essential to creation itself. Although these matters were to be controlled by the state, Calvin saw the state as the instrument of the church for the perfection of the world. Christians, indeed everyone, would have to pray for the grace to sustain their marital situation or to live without remarriage, though separated from their original spouse. His compatriot, Ulrich Zwingli, though agreeing in the main with Calvin's approach, turned to OT norms for divorce and remarriage, thus allowing for a more liberal approach, even in a theocratic state.

In the next century, John Milton, relying on earlier, more liberal interpretations by Martin Bucer and Heinrich Bullinger, argued that divorce should be allowed on the basis of fundamental incompatibility. He turned to Genesis to maintain that the chief purpose of marriage was companionship rather than procreation, constraint of lust, or sacramentality. Though this position was subsequently rejected by the Puritan reformers and successive Protestant theologians, it slowly began to permeate Protestant culture. Today it represents the majority position.

In these three strains we see three different ethical emphases, which produce in turn typical challenges to pastoral care and counseling. The Lutheran position still reflected concern for the preservation of one's given status in life. One's primary duty is to live faithfully in that position. Therefore, the primary pastoral concern is how to preserve a trust in God in the midst of the pain as well as the enjoyment of one's marital state. In the event of divorce, pastors must seek first of all to preserve this faith.

Because Calvinists tend to see marriage as a vocation to perfect the world, pastoral care must seek to strengthen the will and capacity for dependence on God's grace in order to bend one's marital and familial situation to produce some common good for society. Divorce entails a failure of will and a breaking of covenant. Pastoral care must then deal with the resolution of guilt and the restructuring of will, inclination and behavior.

Among the independents and their heirs, for whom marriage is neither primarily ecclesial nor civil but personal, pastoral care seeks to help people identify what they need in order to preserve their dignity and well-being. Divorce is an occasion for discovering one's personal center and growing further in faith, which links it back to some elements in Lutheran positions.

Over these four centuries, Protestant churches have moved from the defense of the order of a largely kin-based society to the nurture of the personal interiors of relatively autonomous participants in a society of markets and publics. The contemporary ascendancy of the independents' position would not be possible without economic and civil equality between men and women. Today, churches might reclaim some of their earlier societal concerns by focusing on the preservation of parental ties and provision for economic fairness as crucial expressions of faith, hope and love in the upheavals of divorce and remarriage.

Bibliography. H. Dombois, "Unscheidbarkeit und Ehescheidung in den Traditionen der Kirche," *Theologische Existenz Heute,* 190 (1976). W. J. Everett, *Blessed Be the Bond: Christian Perspectives on Marriage and Family* (1985). V. N. Olsen, *The New Testament Logia on Divorce: A Study of Their Interpretation from Erasmus to Milton* (1971).

W. J. EVERETT

DIVORCE (Care and Counseling); REMARRIAGE. *See also* MARRIAGE AND MARITAL CARE; MORAL DILEMMAS IN PASTORAL PERSPECTIVE; MORAL THEOLOGY AND PASTORAL CARE. *Compare* CATHOLIC-PROTESTANT MARRIAGE; JEWISH-CHRISTIAN MARRIAGE; ORTHODOX-PROTESTANT MARRIAGE.

DIVORCE AND REMARRIAGE (Roman Catholicism).

The enormous upsurge in the divorce rate in the U.S. from 1962–75 created grave pastoral problems for all the American churches, especially the Roman Catholic. As Catholics began to divorce and remarry in record numbers, a serious reevaluation of the Catholic church's teaching, discipline, and pastoral care ensued. American Catholicism historically had taken strong stands for the permanence of marriage and against divorce and remarriage; negative attitudes toward those who divorced and remarried were deeply internalized in the Catholic people.

In the late nineteenth and early twentieth centuries many Catholic immigrants came to the U.S. from nations which did not permit civil divorce; as a response to the new, liberalized divorce laws passed in many of the states in the post Civil War period, the American Catholic bishops, meeting together in Baltimore in 1884, attached an excommunication to a second marriage "outside the Church" after civil divorce.

When the U.S. divorce rate began to rise dramatically and unexpectedly in the 1960s, Catholic response was initially characterized by shock and denial, but soon pastors, canon lawyers, and theologians began to respond. Church lawyers through their professional organization, the Canon Law Society of America, persuaded the American bishops to request from Rome special experimental procedural reforms to expedite the granting of annulments in the U.S.

1. **Marriage and Canon Law.** Catholic theology sees the celebration of Christian marriage as a faith experience expressing the church's teaching on the permanence of marriage to the world and offering men and women access to deeper union with the Lord. The sacrament of matrimony involves an interaction between the Lord and the believer within the church community. Church law governing sacramental practice attempts to ensure the authenticity and integrity of the couple's encounter with Christ. Canon law tries to safeguard the integrity of the marital relationship not only for the benefit of the parties themselves but also for the well-being of society as a whole. An annulment means that, contrary to appearance, a given marriage duly celebrated in a church ceremony does not meet the legal requisites for community recognition. The contract the couple entered into on their wedding day is, in fact, invalid. This may result from a deficiency extrinsic to the couple, for example, not marrying before a priest and two witnesses in an approved ceremony, or from deficiencies intrinsic to the couple, like an incapacity to sustain a lasting marriage relationship or perhaps a defective attitude regarding the traditional values of permanence, fidelity, and procreation.

The New Code of Canon Law (1982) sees Christian marriage as a commitment to a total life relationship in faith that ideally reflects God's unfailing love for his people. The traditional qualities of permanence and exclusivity create the milieu in which a community of life and love flourishes and in which a genuinely human procreation and education of children takes place. This heightened understanding, drawn from Vatican II's teaching on marriage (*Gaudium et Spes,* nos. 47–52) has made the conditions requisite for a valid marriage more demanding, and has led to a considerable broadening of the grounds for annulments.

The 1970s witnessed an expansion of tribunal personnel and services throughout the U.S. in an attempt to bring relief to those whose first marriages were invalid, and thus enable them to have their second marriages approved by the church. Whereas approximately seven hundred annulments were granted in the U.S. in 1967, seven thousand were granted in 1973, a year after the new norms were implemented. (About 40,000 annulments were granted in 1982.) Of some eight million living Catholics who have ever been divorced, about seven to ten percent have received annulments of their first marriages. (At least half of those ever divorced are estimated to be remarried.) The experimental American norms were modified in the revised universal Code of Canon Law (1982) restoring in the U.S. some of the time-consuming features of the previous law, while maintaining the expanded grounds for annulment.

As a gesture of pastoral concern and reconciliation, the 1884 law of excommunication was removed in 1977 by Pope Paul IV at the request of the American bishops, and in 1980 during the "Year of the Family," the bishops called for local churches to develop ministry to the separated and divorced as part of a national pastoral plan to help "hurting families." A 1981 survey of the Bishops National Family Life office found that 67 percent of the American dioceses had developed some form of ministry to the divorced.

2. Pastoral Care. The backbone of Roman Catholic pastoral care to the divorced has become the locally based support group, in which the divorced themselves help others through the difficult adjustment process following broken marriages. Commenting on useful interventions for crises and other stressful situations, sociologist Robert S. Weiss has stated that although no systematic information is available, unsystematic observation suggests that the most useful form of help is support. Support is furnished by a helper (who may or may not be professional) who is accepted as an ally by the distressed individual. Divorced Catholics groups draw upon peer-counseling and self-help models, and reinforce them with an understanding of the church as God's people, caring for and ministering to each other. The groups build upon sound principles of grief processes and recovery drawn from the behavioral sciences and complement them with pertinent themes of death and resurrection from Christian spirituality. The groups insist upon personal recovery and establishing an autonomous single life after divorce as their main goal, warning against hasty remarriage as a solution. Some of the diocesan ministries and local groups have begun to develop second marriage preparation programs since 75 percent of the divorced eventually choose to remarry. Special groups for children are developing in many places.

In 1975 in Boston a network organization was founded, the North American Conference of Separated and Divorced Catholics (NACSDC) to connect the grassroots divorce ministry in the U.S. and Canada. Through its national and regional conferences, clergy workshops, and publications, the NACSDC has facilitated the development of an array of support groups, retreats, seminars and conferences which give shape to divorce ministry. The "Beginning Experience" (BE) was begun in 1974, providing an intensive forty-eight hour group grieving process facilitated by the divorced and widowed themselves; by 1982 over a hundred BE teams were offering about three hundred weekends a year in the U.S. and Canada.

Calls for reevaluation of Catholic teaching and discipline surfaced at the 1980 Synod of Bishops in Rome. Pope John Paul II reaffirmed traditional teaching on the permanence of marriage, yet insisted that the divorced and invalidly married remain part of the church community and that the Church as a "merciful mother" must offer them pastoral care. On his pastoral visit to England in June 1981 the Pope prayed for the divorced and those who minister to them.

The reception of the Eucharist by those in invalid second marriages remains a much-discussed theological and pastoral issue. Although the Pope reaffirmed the traditional norm of excluding them from Communion, many theologians and canonists argue that this norm admits of many exceptions and that those who are living in solid, Christian marriages should be offered the Eucharist as a support to them in their new commitments. Many Catholic pastors encourage such persons in second marriages to receive Communion, working out with them a conscientious decision about the appropriateness of receiving Communion in a confidential discussion, referred to as the "internal forum solution."

The bishops at the 1980 Synod called on the Pope to study the Orthodox practice which provides church approval for some second marriages. The relationship of the two divergent disciplines on divorce and remarriage remains a significant continuing issue in ecumenical discussions.

Bibliography. T. Mackin, *What Is Marriage?* (1982). K. T. Kelly, *Divorce and Second Marriage* (1982). A. Cherlin, *Marriage, Divorce, Remarriage* (1981). E. Schillebeeckx, *Marriage: Human Reality and Saving Mystery* (1965). R. Weiss, *Marital Separation* (1975). E. and J. Whitehead, *Marrying Well* (1981). J. Young, *Ministering to the Divorced Catholic* (1979); *Divorcing, Believing, Belonging* (1984).

J. J. YOUNG

DIVORCE (Care and Counseling); REMARRIAGE; ROMAN CATHOLIC PASTORAL CARE. *See also* CANON LAW SOCIETY OF AMERICA; DECREE OF NULLITY; MARRIAGE; MARRIAGE TRIBUNAL; MORAL DILEMMAS IN PASTORAL PERSPECTIVE; MORAL THEOLOGY AND PASTORAL CARE. *Compare* CATHOLIC-PROTESTANT MARRIAGE; JEWISH-CHRISTIAN MARRIAGE; MATRIMONY, SACRAMENT; ORTHODOX-CATHOLIC MARRIAGE; SEPARATION, MARITAL (Roman Catholicism); VATICAN COUNCIL II AND PASTORAL CARE.

DIVORCED PERSONS. *See* DIVORCE (Care and Counseling).

DIX, DOROTHEA LYNDE (1802–87). A prominent humanitarian who led the crusade for improvement in the care of the mentally ill in the U.S. during the mid-1800s. Dix highlighted the need for states to take responsibility for providing the mentally ill with humane, medically grounded institutional care. She used her connections with influential wealthy people to initiate pressure upon state legislatures.

Dix directed her original efforts toward her native Massachusetts. After visiting a mental hospital, she left the field of teaching and embarked fulltime upon a career as a reformer. In Massachusetts alone, her work in the 1840s resulted in an enlarged hospital and a growing consciousness of the needs of the mentally ill that became the model for thirty-two hospitals in other states. Dix embraced the cause of the mentally ill and traveled widely throughout the U.S. and Europe on their behalf until her death.

B. HOUSKAMP

MENTAL HEALTH MOVEMENT.

DOBBINS, GAINES S. *See* BAPTIST PASTORAL CARE; PASTORAL CARE MOVEMENT.

DOCTOR, PASTOR AS. *See* PASTOR (Normative and Traditional Images). *See also* HEALING.

DODDRIDGE, PHILIP (1702–51). English minister, author. Doddridge was a non-conformist who valued religious liberty and inquiry. Yet his keen pastoral eye also realized the dangers of too much freedom. Therefore, in his many popular writings on topics of devotional and practical import as well as in his pastoral ministry, he offered specific exercises as well as general guidance for the spiritual life. His *Rise and Progress of Religion in the Soul* (? 1804) is a classic. Also, he enabled the laity for the ministries of visitation and soul care.

N. F. HAHN

SPIRITUAL DIRECTION, HISTORY AND TRADITIONS OF.

DOGMATIZING/DOGMATIC PERSONALITY.
See AUTHORITARIANISM; PREJUDICE.

DOMESTIC LAW. *See* FAMILY LAW.

DOMESTIC VIOLENCE. *See* FAMILY VIOLENCE.

DOMINEERING PERSONALITY. One who tries to exert excessive control and influence over persons, places, or things. The need to influence or control others (dominance need) is a fundamental dimension of human personality. Edwards (1959), for example, considers dominance to be one of fifteen basic personality variables. Leary (Carson, 1969) sees "dominance/submission," along with "affection/hostility," as the two basic dimensions of interpersonal interaction. The recent literature on assertiveness training (e.g., Wolpe, 1973) gives much attention to the proper expression of any emotion (other than anxiety) toward another person, using terms similar to the appropriate need for dominance or control.

Dominance, in and of itself, is not maladaptive, and in appropriate measures, is characteristic of desirable degrees of "ego-strength" or "responsible assertiveness." However, when someone becomes fixed in a particular mode of interaction and develops a rigidity of interpersonal relatedness, dominance leads to conflict.

What the layperson would describe as a domineering personality is, at times, part of the symptom complex of more traditional diagnostic categories, like the personality disorders in which excessive dominance can be part of a longstanding style, not easily altered. An excessive need for dominance also can be a feature of more severe disorders like the schizophrenias, paranoias, and affective conditions. Most theorists (e.g., Johnson, *et al.*, 1981) would argue that these patterns are the result of learning and/or experiential factors. Obviously, dominance can facilitate vocational success, but when it becomes exaggerated or overused, interpersonal difficulties inevitably arise. Untreated, such patterns continue throughout adult life, although they dissipate to a degree in middle or old age.

Extremely domineering people are very difficult to deal with. Such persons are often poor candidates for change because they themselves are not distressed, nor are they motivated to change. Although there can be disastrous effects on the quality of relationships at home, work, or church, such persons often have minimal insight into how their interpersonal style might account for such tensions.

Assuming that a person has a tendency to become domineering as a way to gain social approval or bolster a sense of mastery or control, one goal of pastoral care might be to assist the individual in developing a more intrinsic basis for self-worth and more effective interpersonal strategies. Dominance may reflect a basic emotional need that can be explored in a counseling relationship. More carefully monitoring interactions with such persons and being more candid and congruent in group settings are other ways to help such individuals obtain needed feedback (see Augsburger, 1981, for helpful suggestions). The counselor would need to develop sufficient trust and rapport in order to evidence by commitment that he or she "cares enough to confront."

Bibliography. D. Augsburger, *Caring Enough to Confront* (1981). R. Carson, *Interaction Concepts of Personality* (1969). A. Edwards, *Edwards' Personal Preference Schedule* (1959). C. Johnson, *et al.*, *Basic Psychopathology* (1981). J. Wolpe, *Psychotherapy by Reciprocal Inhibition* (1958). P. F. Schmidt, *Coping With Difficult People* (1980).

R. E. BUTMAN

AGGRESSION AND ASSERTION; ANTISOCIAL PERSONS; MANIPULATION. *Compare* AUTHORITARIANISM; COMPETITIVENESS.

DOMINICAN SPIRITUALITY. *See* SPIRITUALITY (Roman Catholic Tradition).

DONATISM. *See* EARLY CHURCH; ECCLESIOLOGY AND PASTORAL CARE.

DONIGER, SIMON (1895–1978). Founder and editor of *Pastoral Psychology*. After establishing this influential journal in February 1950, Doniger edited it for nineteen years. His brother Lester acted as business manager, Seward Hiltner as pastoral consultant. Doniger selected *Pastoral Psychology* articles to be reprinted in the numerous books he edited, including *Religion and Human Behavior* (1954) and *The Nature of Man: in Theological and Psychological Perspective* (1962). As a social worker specializing in behavior problems of children, he directed a child guidance agency in Newark, New Jersey, for twenty years prior to his journal tenure.

Born in Poland, Doniger emigrated to the United States at age sixteen. In the U.S. Army during World War I, he was stationed in St. Elizabeth's Hospital in Washington, D.C., where he observed "shell-shocked" soldiers. He earned degrees from New York University only after he had achieved professional stature: B.S. (1935), M.A. (1936), and Ph.D. (1938).

Bibliography. S. Hiltner, "Simon Doniger," *Pastoral Psychology*, 20:190 (1969).

A. STOKES

PASTORAL CARE MOVEMENT; RELIGION AND HEALTH MOVEMENT.

DOUBLE BIND. In communications theory, a situation in which two messages conflict because they are at different levels, a bind which is "doubled" by the fact that the listener cannot escape the situation or comment on the discrepancy.

Inspired by Russell's theory of logical types, the double bind was first described in 1956 as an etiological factor in the development of schizophrenia by G. Bateson, D. D. Jackson, J. Haley, and J. H. Weakland. The necessary ingredients for a double bind include: (1) two or more persons, one of whom has physical and/or psychological survival value for the other; (2) repeated experience, so that the double binding pattern is a recurrent theme; (3) a primary negative injunction involving the threat of punishment; (4) a secondary injunction conflicting with the first at a more abstract, or metacommunicational, level and also involving the threat of punishment; (5) a tertiary negative injunction that prohibits the listener from leaving the field or stepping outside the frame of reference; (6) functional autonomy of the process so that the listener learns to perceive the world in double-bind patterns. In addition, the paradoxical behavior demanded by double-binding is in itself of a double-binding nature, so that a vicious circle of pathological behavior and communication is established.

The most critical aspect of this theory is the *doubling*, which occurs when the person is unable to comment on the conflicting messages either because of the power hierarchy in the situation or the lack of insight into the logical structure of the communication. Faced with the necessity for action or choice, and unaware of the fact that true choice is impossible, the listener will follow some predictable patterns associated with classic symptoms of schizophrenia. He or she may conclude that a vital clue is being overlooked, and develop a paranoid pattern of searching for such clues. Or the person may try to comply with all injunctions literally, exhibiting the foolishness of the hebephrenic. Emotional withdrawal from the situation is also possible, resulting in autistic and catatonic symptoms.

The logical structure of the double bind is not inherently pathological, and it is possible to construct therapeutic double binds. Early examples of this include Dunlap's "negative suggestion," Frankl's "paradoxical intention," and Rosen's "*reductio ad absurdum.*" Mirroring the structure of its pathogenic counterpart, the therapeutic double bind presupposes an intense relationship that has survival value for the client. In this context an injunction is given that reinforces the behavior the client wants to change, implies that this reinforcement is the agent of change, and thereby creates a paradox by implying that the client is changed by remaining unchanged. Compliance with the injunction demonstrates that the client is in control of the behavior, thus changing its meaning and context, while resistance to the injunction involves giving up the problematic behavior. The therapeutic contract prevents the client from withdrawing or otherwise dissolving the paradox, and the client "wins" in either case.

Bibliography. A sophisticated analysis of the double bind may be found in P. Watzlawick, J. H. Beavin, and D. D. Jackson, *Pragmatics of Human Communication* (1967). A simpler explication is given in V. Satir's *Conjoint Family Therapy* (1967). The original description, critiques, historical refinements, and further extensions of double bind theory are included in C. E. Sluzki and D. C. Ransom, eds., *Double Bind* (1976).

H. VANDE KEMP

FAMILY THEORY AND THERAPY; PARADOXICAL INTENTION. *See also* COMMUNICATION; MARRIAGE COMMUNICATION. *Compare* WILL/WILLING.

DOUBT AND UNBELIEF. Doubting implies uncertainty and difficulty with decision making. Unbelief is a more definite and resolute state of mind, implying a fixed position that is considered normative. Many doubters conceal their uncertainty and indecision; many unbelievers proclaim their chosen stance. The opposite of doubt is certainty or confidence; the opposite of belief is unbelief or disbelief. Some theologians (e.g., Tillich) see doubting not as the opposite but as a dynamic ancillary to belief, leading to the synthesis of faith as an existential "affirmation in spite of. . . . "

1. Unbelief, Disbelief, and Secularization. *Unbelief* is often used derogatorily; some of its historical cognates such as *infidel, heathen, scoffer* bespeak a fierce and narrow partisanship to a particular religion. It is difficult for believers to be fair to unbelievers; there is pressure on people to believe in *something,* often leading to the insinuation that unbelievers must be, after all, "religious" in some hidden or perverted way. Such judgments are forms of religious totalitarianism.

Disbelief is a better term for the selective rejection of a specific religious tenet or practice, for example, the Protestant rejection of Catholic Mariology and praying to saints. (This example shows that certain disbeliefs can be salient ingredients of religious, and even ecclesiastic, innovation.) *Unbelief* is better used for the global rejection of religious ideas and practices and overlaps with *irreligion* and *atheism.* Neither of these terms should be confused with *agnosticism,* which is based on a delicate epistemological consideration that pleads for not committing oneself to unknowable entities or unverifiable propositions.

Disbelief should be distinguished from the phenomenon known as *secularization.* In advanced pluralistic societies the power and scope of religion have decreased in proportion to those of other institutions such as the state, the arts, science, and the law; membership and attendance in the historic churches have diminished. There are at least two very different forms of secularization: (1) Secularization by drift, antagonistic to religion, was enhanced by the Enlightenment and subsequently changing views of the human condition, including critiques of religion by philosophers and other scholars. Marxist criticism has unmasked religion as an ideology to hold the underclasses in socioeconomic enslavement. Rational criticism in the Feuerbach-Freud tradition takes up the idea of God as a projection of human grandiosity and as fantasy fulfillment of infantile dependency cravings. Both critiques state that religion contributes to human alienation, socially or psychologically. (2) Secularization by religious and theological purpose leaves to the public domain or seeks to realize in the world much of what was formerly done by and in churches, such as social welfare, nursing the sick, education, advocacy for the oppressed. This kind of religious secularization takes a high view of the public sector (as in H. Cox's early work) and is appreciated by sociologists (e.g., Weber, Parsons) who hold that the secular order sometimes approximates the normative values of religion, such as in compassion, charitableness, or justice.

2. Forms of Unbelief. What are the major forms of selective disbelief, global unbelief, and irreligiosity? Some clues come from landmark formulations in the psychology and sociology of religion, and from certain theological works. (1) When Schleiermacher accentuated a feeling of utter dependency and an attitude of reverence as crucial to religion, self-reliant enlightened people who believed in humankind's increasing competence (e.g., in medicine, science, food production) could dismiss his plea and hold themselves unsuited to the humility he required. (2) When Otto defined the *numen* as *mysterium tremendum et fascinosum* and speculated that responsiveness to the *numen* might be a matter of talent, some unbelievers could claim to lack such a talent or to have missed out on opportunities for its stimulation. (3) James stressed the "reality of the unseen" in religion, which could be used to define some forms of unbelief as lack of imagination. And in seeing belief as decision making, James suggested that one can passionately decide not to decide, that is, leave some questions open and arrive at an agnostic position. (4) For Freud, the idea of God as Providence is linked to infantile human feelings of omnipotence alternating with helplessness; in religion one compromises by ceding a portion of one's omnipotence to God while retaining some of it for influencing God to act in one's favor. And since Freud unmasked much pious humility as having a narcissistic core, particularly in fantasies about life after death, unbelief can be seen as emancipation from infantile concerns or as a stance of radical intellectual honesty. Moreover, when religious indoctrination is a form of thought control, curious and rational minds can wrestle themselves free from the taboos to which they have been subjected. (5) Leaning on Otto and Freud, Erwin Goodenough has located a part of the *tremendum* within the person, in the Id, where it elicits both awe and terror and is felt as dangerously potent. One can shield oneself from this internal terror by means of a protective blanket (of repression); on that blanket appear all kinds of ideograms (symbols) that hint at the hidden content by culturally transmitted notions. These symbols, indicating tentative meanings, are to the modern mind closer to hypotheses than to doctrinal verities; the modern mind approaches religion more as search than as find. In this scenario some unbelief can be understood as disbelief in the validity or relevance of certain ideograms on the blanket, or as skepticism about the good fit of any ideogram to the ineffable reality behind the blanket.

3. **Disbelief and Social Realities.** Belief, unbelief, disbelief, faith, and doubt are ways of dealing with objective ambiguities as well as subjective ambivalences. Since religion is in most cases culturally transmitted rather than personally invented, the problems are multiplied by the ambiguities and ambivalences, the hypocrisies, disloyalties, spurious rationalizations, or inane simplisms the learner encounters in the instructors. And because in pluralistic societies religious instruction tends to pit one belief against another, any particular belief entails a particular disbelief. Religious affiliation entails both a positive and a negative identity ("I am a Methodist, not a Baptist") in which beliefs of any sort become objects of love or hate, each held or rejected with tenacious strength.

4. **Rationales for Disbelief.** Life is governed by inescapable themes with which everyone has to come to terms. What major life themes organize beliefs and are occasions for unbelief or disbelief?

a. Dependency and autonomy. Many people are highly aware of their creaturely contingency and make their utter dependency the cornerstone of their belief system; some may even have a morbid need to act dependently. Others stress their own initiative and feel that human beings can exert some mastery over their lives and their natural and social ambience; they detest passivity, assume much responsibility for themselves and society, and their boundless curiosity respects no taboos. They do their free thinking zestfully. From here to the position of dispensing with the idea of God as a limit-setting factor and of refusing to tinker with the fact of mortality is a step toward autonomy; the latter may have its own admirable humility if it renounces the wish for instant or total gratification of passive-dependent, responsibility-surrendering needs. Dependency and autonomy also involve the question of *obedience:* to whom, for what? Once seen as a virtue, obedience has lost its mandatory status; one may instead emphasize the right to selective disobedience, for example, in civil disobedience.

b. Mystery. In a technological culture the emphasis is on mastery, not mystery; and what cannot be mastered may come to be seen as absurd or irritating. Nihilism dwells on senselessness. Positivism limits itself to what is tractable and graspable. Yet some major modern thinkers (Buber, Marcel, Kafka, Kierkegaard) hold that mystery is inherent in all deep human experiences and that it points to some transcendent power or quality. Unlike solvable puzzles or tractable problems, encounters with mystery reverse the normal subject-object relation: mystery grasps us rather than our grasping it.

The problem (mystery) of evil has proven to be a stumbling block for religious belief; while it leads some to embrace a rescuing, benevolent, or meaning-giving God, it has led others to reject the very idea of God, let alone a benevolent one. Since some belief in benevolence is Pollyannaish and involves a denial of obvious malevolence, critics of this position have a rational point. Moreover, since numinosity may be experienced in wonders of nature, artistic beauty, scientific discovery, or intense human affection, not everyone is disposed to conjecturing from such experiences to a divine transcendent being. Disbelief in the supernatural and aversion to religious speculation may sometimes derive from distrust in the imagination, which is indeed often dangerously (pathologically) overworked in the religious. The idea of mystery and the positing of transcendent powers need careful cognitive and emotional sifting; as modes of symbolic thought they are vulnerable to intrusions from the autistic as well as the realistic spheres, and subject to gross distortion. Spotting such distortions may turn some people off from the very idea of mystery, which to them equals mystification.

c. The will to believe, and choosing between the options. James felt that, barring indifference, to know the truth and avoid error one must take a position, with the attending risks. But some people pursue truth without heed to error, whereas others who fear to be duped specialize in avoiding error while losing interest in truth; some beliefs are passionately positive (and possibly sloppy), while other beliefs are overly cautious (and rather contentless). Choosing seriously requires that the available options are live (personally relevant), forced (unavoidable), and momentous (not trivial).

Many religious propositions meet these criteria and require choosing precisely because they lie beyond purely logical argument and scientific proof. Religion as a whole is one large option: does one accept its usefulness, accuracy, or pertinence to oneself, or does one choose to be an unbeliever — in either case with consequences for the integrity of thought, for the modulation of feelings, for the prompting of one's actions, and for the quality of interpersonal relations? But conversely, the developmentally acquired thought patterns, moods and affects, action patterns, and relational styles will have much bearing on the way anyone chooses between the options, and even on the kind or scope of options perceived. The choices made or avoided are deeply embedded in personality factors, including the self-concept. James described what certain types of religion do to and for certain personality types, and vice versa. Like many others, he saw mystical experience as the acme of religion — erroneously, to some. Sober minds who attach greater value to observed behavior than to private musings may avoid all religion if defined as mystical experience; they may prefer an ethical to a religious stance, and be content with normal states of consciousness.

d. Providence. Most people who think of Providence at all are interested in the divine intention *toward themselves,* and often think of it in quasi-parental imagery. Moreover, theological parlance about Providence is saturated with images derived from three social system models: family, church, and state, each portraying a kind of caring and demanding a kind of loyalty. Although the idea of Providence has been discredited by various abuses (e.g., the *deus ex machina* involved in miracle belief, and "explaining" natural events by a "God-of-the-gaps"), people in adversity are still prone to ask: "Why?" or "Why me?" It takes a stoical mind to forego such questions, but some people are trained to be Stoics. Coming to terms with Providence entails coping with malevolence and avoiding meritoriousness about benevolence. It takes sufficient experience of benevolence, with its attending buildup of trust, to see the point in the idea of Providence; it is an empty, if not offensive, idea to those who do not have the experience. A crucial aspect of belief or disbelief in Providence is whether or not one has any ground for hoping in tragic situations — for true hoping as differentiated from blithe wishing.

e. Reality and fantasy. Much unbelief and disbelief appear to hinge on definitions of reality (how large it is, what it encompasses, whether or not it goes beyond the sensory world, whether it is only outside or also inside persons, etc.), and on being comfortable with or leery of the imagination. Religious ideas and practices are, like the arts, music, literature, and science, of a symbolic order and have an illusionistic status. They are unlike sensory reality and different from highly personal autistic musings (as in dreams). It takes training and aptitude to think and act symbolically, and certain acquired brain lesions can undo an established aptitude. While some people love ritual, others are out of touch with it. Dedicated realists feel ill at ease with speculative ideas, which they consider flighty and fantastic. Such cautionary posi-

tions are quite understandable in the face of religion's large heritage of wild, gruesome, wishful, revengeful, and morbid fantasy materials.

5. Disbelief and Personal Maturing. Pastors as well as clinicians are impressed by the tenacity of childhood beliefs in many adults; this observation supports another one, namely, that religious beliefs, ideas, and practices often remain undeveloped in otherwise well-endowed, educated, and intelligent people. This selective backwardness of religion in people with a developed artistic taste, business shrewdness, or professional knowledge strongly suggests that in such cases religion is more a matter of the superego (early conscience) than of the ego. Functioning as a set of prescriptions and proscriptions, its adhortations and strictures are deemed incontestable and nothing is done to make the childish belief (locked into an obedience morality) a reasoned and reasonable faith that has dealt with life's ambiguities and human ambivalences. Since this species of religious beliefs is sometimes very vocal or pressureful in the political and legislative sphere, it begs for a critical or militant response and is not a negligible factor in producing unbelievers of various sorts.

Unfortunately, the terms *believers* and *unbelievers* are all too often handled as categorical descriptions of a presumably lifelong stance. Far too little attention has been paid to changes in belief, disbelief, and unbelief occurring during any person's lifetime, and to the possibility that some oscillations may be age-specific. There is insufficient systematic knowledge about religiosity and beliefs in old age and in terminal phases of illness; all we have are anecdotal narratives that show great variation. It is known that adolescence is for many a time of religious search and experimentation, and that it yields a high incidence of reported conversions. It is also known, but only anecdotally, that certain impactful life events (e.g., emotional or physical trauma, near-death experiences, unexpected exposure to exquisite goodness, exposure to charismatic persons) can prompt people to revise their beliefs and disbeliefs, sometimes drastically. But what in general prompts revision of beliefs? And should not all beliefs and disbeliefs be constantly revised during the journey of life? If the development and maturing of religious beliefs and its alternatives involve periodic revisions, this process entails a deep belief in tolerance (toward self and others) as a supreme virtue.

Beliefs and disbeliefs are deeply embedded in interpersonal relations, whether the latter are dominated by love or hate. James recognized that often "our faith is faith in someone else's faith." Similarly, our disbeliefs may be the afterglow of other people's disbeliefs. Some people need a moratorium on their beliefs; others may need to break away from parental beliefs, and most religious founders or innovators have been controversial revisionists.

Bibliography. H. Cox, *The Secular City* (1968). L. Feuerbach, *The Essence of Christianity* (1841). S. Freud, "The Future of an Illusion," *SE,* vol. 21, pp. 3–56 and "Civilization and Its Discontents," *SE,* vol. 21, pp. 59–145. E. Goodenough, *The Psychology of Religious Experiences* (1965). W. James, *The Will to Believe, and Other Essays in Popular Philosophy* (1897). *The Varieties of Religious Experience* (1902). K. Marx and F. Engels, *On Religion* (1884). R. Otto, *The Idea of the Holy* (1917). T. Parsons, Introduction to M. Weber's *The Sociology of Religion* ([1922]

1963). P. Pruyser, *Between Belief and Unbelief* (1974). F. Schleiermacher, *On Religion* ([1799] 1955). P. Tillich, *Dynamics of Faith* (1957). M. Weber, *The Sociology of Religion* ([1922] 1963).

P. W. PRUYSER

FAITH/BELIEF; PSYCHOLOGY OF RELIGION (Empirical Studies, Methods, and Problems). *See also* DECISION/INDECISION; DEPENDENCE/INDEPENDENCE; FANTASIZING; MYSTICISM; PROVIDENCE; RELIGIOUS EXPERIENCE; SECULARIZATION/ SECULARISM; SOCIOLOGY OF RELIGION; WILL/WILLING. *Compare* ALIENATION/ESTRANGEMENT; ANOMIE/NORMLESSNESS; EVALUATION AND DIAGNOSIS, RELIGIOUS.

DOUKHOBOR. *See* SECTARIAN PASTORAL CARE.

DOWN'S SYNDROME. Once called Mongolism, Down's Syndrome is a common form of mental retardation caused by a chromosomal abnormality. Small physical features, poor muscle tone and coordination, slanting eyes, and an increased occurrence of heart and other congenital defects may be observed. Although physical and mental development are delayed and limited, the wide range in intellectual, social, and occupational abilities precludes stereotyping.

Bibliography. J. L. Philpott, "By the Waters of Babylon: The Experience of Having a Down's Syndrome Child," *Pastoral Psychology* 27, 155–63.

J. L. PHILPOTT

EXCEPTIONAL CHILDREN AND THEIR FAMILIES; HANDICAP AND DISABILITY; MENTAL RETARDATION. *Compare* AMNIO-CENTESIS.

DRAFT COUNSELING. *See* MORAL DILEMMAS IN PASTORAL PERSPECTIVE. *See also* LEGAL DIMENSIONS OF PASTORAL CARE AND COUNSELING; PROPHETIC/PASTORAL TENSION IN MINISTRY; SOCIAL CONSCIOUSNESS AND RESPONSIBILITY.

DRAMA AS MODE OF CARE. Drama may be seen as a method of doing pastoral care when it communicates the gospel and takes place within a supportive, nurturing, healing community of faith. Drama in the church is usually understood to be a ministry rather than purely an artistic pursuit, a form of entertainment, or a profit-making effort. Therefore, the purpose and context of church drama fundamentally shape its meaning and method.

1. **Religious Drama.** Religion and drama have been intimately interrelated from earliest times. Drama has its roots in the gestures, myths, symbols, and rituals common to the natural rhythms of life and the movements of the universe, and functions as a vehicle of religious expression for primitive peoples. Drama continues to have an important place in the church and synagogue today because of its ability to touch people at the depths of their imaginations, to open them to the presence of mystery, and to mediate the symbols of their faith.

   a. *What makes drama religious.* For many people, religious drama brings to mind images of pageants portraying the great stories of the Bible: a reenactment of the Nativity or the events of Passion week. In its broadest definition, however, drama is religious not because of its use of biblical characters, theological language, or material drawn from our Judeo-Christian heritage. Drama is religious because of its ability to express ultimate concern about human existence, to examine and challenge the values of contemporary society, to explore the continuing mystery of the divine-human encounter, and to explain the nature, purpose, and meaning of human life. In this sense, religious drama need not be overtly religious, nor must it exclude "secular" drama that occurs outside the church.

   b. *Symbolic nature.* Religious drama is both an expression of faith and an event that gives birth to faith. It is difficult to express religious experience in words alone. The language of religious expression is symbol, and drama is a generous medium for symbol. Drama employs sight and sound, motion and distance, time and space: "real" objects symbolically employed to create an atmosphere or event wherein one might be open to the new life our Creator inspires.

   Drama leans heavily on the metaphoric quality of the symbols it employs. The audience experiences the play (which is not "real") as though it were reality. The stage becomes a frame, setting apart the drama from the audience. Stylized, fantastic, or symbolic staging, scenery, costumes, language, and movement all join to remind us that this is "play," with the implicit suggestion that it is harmless. We are free to identify with the characters and join in the plot with impunity or without fear of reprisal. What occurs is paradoxical: what is acted out on stage is more real than reality; fiction is truer than truth. This allows us to see who we are from a different and revealing perspective. Like David on hearing Nathan's story of the little lamb, we recognize ourselves and realize, "you are the one."

   c. *Context.* When a dramatic event occurs as a part of church program, it takes on religious meaning. Even when a church group produces a traditionally secular piece primarily for entertainment purposes, its context shapes the meaning of the play. The imagery and symbolism suggest a new understanding and significance to the dramatic event. A senior high group, for instance, may perform a play to raise money for a mission project. Because it is done in the church it takes on theological significance.

2. **Forms and Uses.** Religious drama takes many forms, including plays, dramatic poetry, prose, liturgy, or choral readings. These are written or designed to be used in a variety of ways: *formal theater,* the conventional production of plays; *liturgical drama,* dramatized sermons, children's stories, portions of the liturgy, or other events that take place in the sanctuary as a part of the service of worship; *readers' theater,* the dramatic reading of scripts, with little or no attempt to portray characterization or plot development through the use of movement, scenery, costuming, lighting, or other dramatic devices; *impromptu dramatization,* spontaneous or informal dramatic play with children, and role-playing as an educational tool for teaching and training adults; *dramatic play,* stunts or skits with young people or adults at camps, retreats, or other informal settings; *nonverbal expressions,* such as clowns, mime, and dance; *liturgy,* the pomp and pageantry of many religious festival celebra-

tions, including formal and informal liturgies, may be appropriately labeled drama.

3. Drama as Ministry. *a. Theological perspective.* Because a religious drama program is a ministry, its values will not be the same as those of the secular theater, and the results of its efforts will be measured by different standards. The worth of any caring ministry of the church should be judged by the effect it has on those who serve as well as its contribution to those who are served. Such a program should be recognized as a ministry not only in its witness to those who attend performances, but to those involved in its production as well. Ideally, this approach will incarnate the word and will of God throughout each step of the process.

b. Planning and approach. Plays are selected not for their popular appeal or profit potential but because of their witness to God's love and justice in confronting important and timely issues. Those chosen for cast and crew are recruited not solely for their skills and talents but also because of their need for the support and nurture such an experience might offer. From auditions to rehearsal to performance, this process fosters growth and enrichment. Participants are able to try out new behavior or look at themselves in a different light and find affirmation, support, and encouragement. Forgiveness becomes more important than precision, and acceptance takes precedence over polish.

4. Drama as Ministry Through Community. *a. Caring medium.* The community that is formed through a church drama program can become a medium for healing, forgiveness, liberation, and love. Working together in such a group creates a sense of belonging and gives people a feeling of purpose that comes from working for a cause larger than themselves. Self-esteem is generated as participants experience affirmation of their talents and abilities. For some, this may be the only way they feel able to contribute to the church.

b. Growth experience. Being part of a play production can be a learning and growth-enhancing experience. It is often an intergenerational effort in which individuals are exposed to lifestyles and attitudes different from their own. People may feel supported by discovering that others are struggling with the same issues they are. They may be affirmed by those who share their views, or challenged by those who differ. The symbolic nature of drama provides fertile ground for exploring questions of life and faith in greater depth than is possible in other settings. Moral and spiritual issues may be addressed on stage through characterization and interpretation or in informal discussions backstage or after rehearsals.

c. Pastoral function. A church drama program can serve a pastoral function by providing easy access to a caring community. Its variety of tasks — from set construction, costuming, and publicity design, to handling properties and taking tickets — call out a multitude of gifts that require varying levels of skill and commitment. It is a ready-made, task-oriented group to which people with a wide range of pastoral needs may be referred. The unemployed, recently retired, or parents whose children have "left the nest" will discover numerous ways to devote their time to a meaningful endeavor. Those who are divorced, widowed, or new to the community will find a place where they feel comfortable and quickly

begin to establish new relationships. Struggling adolescents are exposed to different role models and find new mentors. Marginal or alienated people who might feel excluded from other church programs may be incorporated into a drama group with little risk because many of the tasks are minimal and require little skill or commitment.

From the challenge of its prophetic witness on opening night, to the laughter and celebration of the final cast party, drama can be a vital mode of pastoral care in any church.

Bibliography. B. Way, *Development Through Drama* (1973). J. Hodgson, ed., *The Uses of Drama* (1979).

W. C. DIXON

COMMUNITY, FELLOWSHIP, AND CARE; PLAY. *See also* RITUAL AND PASTORAL CARE; SELF-EXPRESSION/SELF-CONTROL. *Compare* ADJUNCTIVE THERAPIES; MUSIC AS MODE OF CARE; TRADITION AS MODE OF CARE.

DREAM INTERPRETATION IN PASTORAL COUNSELING. Because of the value of dreams for revealing the depths of personality, their interpretation is of exceptional importance in all depth psychotherapy. However, because certain dreams may be of special spiritual significance or represent genuine religious experiences, dream interpretation should occupy a place of even greater significance in pastoral counseling. Because of the knowledge and experience required, dream interpretation will be of interest especially to the pastoral counseling specialist. However, there are some pastors with special interest in and knowledge of dreams who meaningfully employ dream interpretation in their pastoral care. This article will summarize basic principles and techniques from the perspective of depth psychology.

1. Principles. Dreams reported in pastoral counseling should be considered to be about what is going on in the depths of the dreamer's personality rather than about external persons and events. For instance, if one reports a dream about a great battle — even if it were a real historical battle with real military leaders — it should be understood that this refers symbolically to a conflict in the unconscious depths. There are, indeed, some dreams that contain literal information about the external world, and there are others that reveal feelings and attitudes about real people in the external world. However, in contrast to these two kinds, virtually all of the dreams presented in pastoral counseling may be assumed to refer more or less entirely to the dreamer's own personality. Therefore, the pastoral counselor should understand that the figure of the dreamer in his or her own dream (i.e., the figure who is "I" in my dream) stands for the dreamer's conscious ego; everything else in the dream may be taken as symbolic of some aspect of the dreamer's personality (including internalized object representations). An exception to this rule is the occasional dream symbol that refers to the pastoral counselor.

Dreams should be seen as compensatory. They reveal to us what we are ignoring, or they show the repressed aspects of our personalities. A corollary of this principle is that an interpretation is not correct if it only articulates something we already consciously know.

Dreams should be seen as presenting a visual metaphor of the deeper *psychological* significance of what is currently going on in the dreamer's life. An interpreter understands that a dream says in effect, "In your life it is as though . . ." and then presents a pictorial metaphor. For instance, a dreamer reported a dream in which he was playing casually on the beach when suddenly a huge tidal wave began approaching; the dream concluded with the person realizing that he could not escape it. The pastoral counselor came to understand that the dream was saying to the dreamer, "In your life it is as though you had been playing undisturbed but now are overwhelmed in a terrifying way — as though by a tidal wave." Further, the pastoral counselor and the dreamer came to see that the tidal wave represented the upwelling of the unconscious which the dreamer could no longer avoid.

Complementary to the principle above and building upon it, some dreams should be recognized as presenting a visual metaphor of the deeper *spiritual* significance of what is going on in the dreamer's life. Some dreams present archetypal symbols, i.e., symbols of a universal significance with antecedents in myth and religious literature. Moreover, these dreams may have a numinous feeling tone, i.e., feelings that range from the eerie, uncanny, unearthly, weird, ghostly, or mildly ecstatic to experiences of *mysterium tremendum et fascinosum*. The archetypal symbols place the dreamer's particular predicament in the context of the universal human predicament, and the numinous tone lets the dreamer and interpreter know that they are approaching holy ground. Archetypal dreams, which may be extremely powerful, may reveal an astonishing wisdom and artistry at work in the depths — much greater than that possessed by the dreamer's conscious ego. Morton Kelsey and John Sanford have both made excellent theological arguments that one may still meaningfully speak of certain dreams as media of divine revelation.

The dreamer him or herself is the final authority as to whether a certain interpretation is accurate. In some cases the dreamer will experience a "tingle of recognition" when an accurate interpretation has been formulated. Other times the dreamer will provide indirect confirmation by the recall of more dreams which show progress in the growth process or by the realization of more insight.

Ideally, in the course of interpretation, the dreamer will experience the feelings, conflicts, and processes revealed in the dream. That is, dream interpretation that is therapeutically or spiritually effective is not merely an intellectual exercise but an experiential process.

Dream interpretation in pastoral counseling is a collaboration between two authoritative partners. While the dreamer is the source of final confirmation about an interpretation, the pastoral counselor brings something essential also. The more adequate the counselor's theory (of personality development, psychopathology, psychotherapeutic process, etc.), the better equipped he or she is for partnership in understanding the meaning of a dream.

Since dreams arise from the area of the personality that is naturally childlike, playful, and imaginative, the pastoral counselor should take a childlike and playful approach to dreams. Similarly, some dreams arise from an area of the personality that is capable of awe, wonder, and spiritual ecstasy. In these cases, the pastoral counselor should assume the same attitude and not attempt to explain away or ignore the numinous tone.

2. Technique. The principles above imply a great deal about technique; some suggestions follow, roughly in order of importance.

The pastoral counselor should pay attention first to the feelings in the dream, especially those feelings in which the dream culminates. If a dreamer presents a dream which culminates in feelings of violent anger, the pastoral counselor may be certain that whatever else the dream means, the feelings of violent anger need to be taken seriously. An interpretation that is not congruent with the dream's feeling tone is inevitably off the mark.

The second thing to which the pastoral counselor must give attention is the dream's basic theme. This should be done before concentrating on particular symbols. While each dream is unique and there are no fixed meanings to particular symbols, there is some commonality of meaning to particular dream themes. If the dreamer and pastoral counselor come up with nothing else, attention to the affect and the theme of the dream will give some idea of what is going on in the dreamer.

The pastoral counselor should seek the associations (i.e., whatever thoughts, feelings, memories, ideas spontaneously come to mind) of the dreamer first to the basic theme and then to particular symbols. If a dreamer produces no associations, it should be understood that he or she is blocking. The pastoral counselor will then turn from the content of the dream to an exploration of this resistance; understanding the resistance to association to the dream will itself throw light on the dream. Furthermore, whatever else the dreamer communicates during the session should be taken as association to the dream. The associations give an indication of what the theme and particular symbols subjectively mean to the dreamer.

Among the associations of the dreamer, it is helpful to get the triggering event or sequence of events which stimulated the dream. One can be sure that any dream has been stimulated by some event or sequence in the life of the dreamer. The dream shows pictorially the unconscious meaning of these events to the dreamer.

After the dreamer has provided associations, the pastoral counselor may share and use his or her associations to the dream.

The pastoral counselor should bear in mind that dreams frequently contain much irony and humor and often employ puns as a way of communicating. Being alert to figures of speech in dreams will help in understanding. For instance, a dream may picture the dreamer sitting on top of a fence in order to show that the dreamer is, in a figure of speech, "straddling the fence" on a certain issue.

Bibliography. J. Campbell, *The Hero With a Thousand Faces* (1949). M. Elidae, *Myths, Dreams and Mysteries* (1975). A. Faraday, *The Dream Game* (1974). J. Fosshage and C. Loew, eds., *Dream Interpretation: A Comparative Study* (1978). R. Greenson, *Explorations in Psychoanalysis* (1978), chs. 20, 23. C. G. Jung, *Dreams* (1974); *Man and His Symbols* (1964); *The Archetypes and the Collective Unconscious, Collected Works*, 9:1 (1969). M. Kelsey, *God, Dreams, and Revelation* (1974). R. Langs, *Technique in*

Transition (1978), ch. 18. R. Otto, *The Idea of the Holy* (1923). J. Sanford, *Dreams: God's Forgotten Language* (1968).

C. G. HELMS

INTERPRETATION AND HERMENEUTICS, PASTORAL; PASTORAL COUNSELING; PASTORAL PSYCHOTHERAPY. *See also* PERSONAL STORY, SYMBOL AND MYTH IN PASTORAL CARE; SELF-UNDERSTANDING. *Compare* ANALYTICAL (JUNGIAN) *or* HUMANISTIC PSYCHOLOGY, AND PASTORAL CARE; FANTASIZING; GUIDED IMAGERY TECHNIQUE; ILLUMINATION; JEWISH CARE AND COUNSELING; PSYCHOANALYSIS AND PASTORAL CARE; SYMBOLISM/SYMBOLIZING.

DREAM THEORY AND RESEARCH. 1. Dream Theory. *a. Judeo-Christian precedents.* Our Jewish forebears understood the function of dreams primarily as messages from God. To the ancient Jewish people with their deeply rooted monotheistic faith dreams were of great consequence. Yahweh communicated his wishes and warnings directly to his people via the medium of dreams. Dream imagery symbolically pointed to an alternative, waking-life context to which God was directing the dreamer.

Biblical dream interpretation consistently applied this theocentric approach. For example, Daniel offered King Nebuchadnezzar a clear moral and spiritual admonition in Daniel's interpretation of the King's dream of a great tree and its eventual demise (Dan. 4:1–37).

Christianity brought with it various minor amplifications of the traditional Jewish approach to dream interpretation. Books such as the Gospel of Matthew are replete with divine advice given through the vehicle of dreams. Church fathers such as St. Clement, St. John Chrysostom, and St. Augustine viewed dreams as pathways to a more intimate grasp of God. These church leaders pointed out that the origin of dreams is in the depths of the human psyche, placed there by God for purposes of instruction and edification for the dreamer.

b. Freud. In *The Interpretation of Dreams* (1900), Sigmund Freud opened the way to a new approach to understanding dreams. For Freud, dreams functioned primarily to release and express repressed instinctual urges. The motive for dreaming was no longer God; rather, instinctually oriented wishes in search of fulfillment served as the catalyst for dream fantasy and imagery. Dreams focused on the preverbal, prelogical, "primary process" language of the dreamer. Dream symbols provided "the royal road to the Unconscious."

Freud's emphasis was not on the manifest, more obvious, content of a dream so much as on the latent, more subtle, content. Within his retrospective, psychopathology-oriented assumptive framework, Freud viewed the latent content of dreams more often than not as expressions of sexual and/or aggressive instinctual urges. Certain dream symbols were labeled as pointing directly to instinctual analogues, for example, long, slender objects were phallic images, and hollow containers were the vaginal counterparts.

Dream interpretation, for Freud, focused on the technique of free association, where the dreamer was asked to spontaneously verbalize whatever came to awareness in regards to specific elements of a given dream. Freud's technique of free association aimed at exploring the latent, symbolic nature of dreams.

c. Jung. The next major contribution to dream theory came from Carl G. Jung, originally a student of Freud's. Dreams, for Jung as for Freud, opened the dreamer to heretofore unconscious elements of his or her psyche. However, for Jung, the stress was on the healing function and psychospiritual content, rather than the cathartic function and instinctual content (as in Freud), of dreams. Within Jung's framework, the developmentally more advanced aspects of dreams (i.e., psychospiritual content) found expression in universal, archetypal imagery. Because Jung operated, much more than Freud, within a teleological, health-oriented perspective, he had a greater tolerance for spiritually inclined amplifications of dreams.

d. Contemporary approaches. Contemporary schools of dream theory, such as transpersonal psychology, have moved toward providing a comprehensive means to incorporating Freudian, Jungian, and biblical (or other overtly spiritual) perspectives on dream theory. The transpersonalist views dreams as carrying interpretable messages from any, or all, of several different levels of individual functioning. The motive of dreams is a many-faceted one, meeting or expressing the multiform biological, psychological, and spiritual needs of the dreamer.

Within this perspective, dream symbols carry both pathology-oriented and growth-oriented material from all levels of personality. For example, a dream of a long, slender object may suggest: a penis and related sexual instincts (a possible Freudian explanation), a heavy club for breaking through interpersonal or intrapsychic barriers to healthy individuation (a possible Jungian explanation), a vine which invites one to climb the ladder to heaven and spiritual growth (a possible biblical, or overtly spiritual, explanation), and other possibilities.

One helpful contribution from transpersonal psychology is in its emphasis on the simultaneous manifestation, in the dream, of several distinct levels of the person. Pre-egoic, instinctual concerns coexist with egoic, psychosocial concerns, which coexist with trans-egoic, spiritual concerns, all within the complexities of a given sequence of dream images and symbolism.

Dream interpretation, from the transpersonal perspective, begins at the level of physical-bodily-instinctual symbolism (for example, the long, slender object as a penis), searching here for any emotional resonance between the dreamer and the dream imagery. Once insight has been gained at this level, the next step is to analyze the dream symbolism at the level of intellectual-psychosocial-relational experiences (for example, the long, slender object as a heavy club for breaking through personal limitations), again with the goal of working through emotionally charged dream associations. Finally, the dream is examined for spiritual-transcendental-numinous symbolism (for example, the long, slender object as a vine reaching to the heavens) which may have been evoked in the dreamer.

2. Dream Research. As we relax toward the sleeping state, there occurs a definite reduction in the frequency and intensity of external stimuli being actively processed in the brain. Laboratory research with sensory deprivation suggests the emergence of a predominantly nonverbal, image-oriented awareness as we move into sleep. For example, at the nebulous dividing line between wakefulness and sleep, we may experience hypnagogic images, which metaphorically relate to our most recent pre-sleep thoughts.

Electroencephalographic (EEG) technology has allowed for research with brain waves, opening up our understanding of the various stages of sleep. These stages correlate with the activity of dreaming. Our sleep begins at an initial, relatively light stage, and subsequently grows deeper through three distinct stages. This biological process of the brain at rest then reverses itself, as we emerge back up through the sleep cycle to a lighter, more alert stage. Characterized by rapid eye movement (REM), this latter stage is where most dreams take place.

We cycle through REM sleep and correlated dream phases half a dozen times per night, with initial periods of dreaming of five minutes, and later periods of dreaming of thirty minutes. EEG research indicates that the average adult spends about twenty percent of total sleep time in dreaming each night.

3. Applications for Pastoral Care and Counseling.

a. Active imagination. Within the tradition of Jung, dream amplification by means of active imagination permits the conscious ego opportunity to discourse, via dream images and symbols, with the shadow side (that is, less conscious and perhaps less acceptable aspects) of one's personality. The dreamer records the significant symbols and characters across an entire series of dreams. The symbols or characters are encouraged to dialogue with one another in this process of active imagination.

One easy method for active imagination involves typewriting an imaginary dialogue between dream characters or symbols. Character #1 is represented in upper-case letters; character #2 in lower-case. This discipline opens the dreamer up to the healing, integrative powers of effective dream self-interpretation.

b. Dream journaling. Another approach to dream interpretation involves working in a systematic, analytical way with one's own dream images. Pragmatically, the dreamer first records on a bedside tablet the content of the dream, in as much detail as possible, immediately upon awakening. Next, any feelings evoked by the various dream images are recorded. Metaphors which can be linked to the dream images are brainstormed and recorded. Finally, the waking context of one's life previous to the dream, with associated thoughts, feelings, and events, is noted as it refers to the dream content. Collecting a series of such dream worksheets over time often proves to be illuminating for the dedicated self-interpreter of dreams.

Bibliography. C. Brenner, *An Elementary Textbook of Psychoanalysis* (1973). N. R. Carlson, *Physiology of Behavior* (1977). S. Freud, *The Interpretation of Dreams* (1950 [1900]). R. R. Greenson, *The Technique and Practice of Psychoanalysis* (1967). C. S. Hall and V. J. Nordby, *A Primer of Jungian Psychology* (1973). B. Hannah, *Encounters with the Soul: Active Imagination as Developed by C. G. Jung* (1981). C. G. Jung, *The Structure and Dynamics of the Psyche* (1960); *Man and His Symbols* (1964). L. C. Kolb, *Modern Clinical Psychiatry* (1977). M. Ullman and N. Zimmerman, *Working with Dreams* (1979). K. Wilber, "The Developmental Spectrum and Psychopathology: Part II, Treatment Modalities," *J. of Transpersonal Psychology*, 16 (1984), 137–66.

R. WEATHERS

BRAIN RESEARCH; PSYCHOTHERAPY AND COUNSELING (Research Studies and Methods). *See also* ANALYTICAL (JUNGIAN) PSYCHOLOGY; COGNITIVE PSYCHOLOGY AND PSYCHOTHERAPY; EVALUATION AND DIAGNOSIS, PSYCHOLOGICAL; HUMANISTIC PSYCHOLOGY; HUMANISTIC PSYCHOTHERAPIES; PSYCHOANALYSIS (Personality Theory and Research); SLEEP AND SLEEP DISORDERS. *Compare* FANTASIZING; IMAGINATION; RELIGIOUS EXPERIENCE; SYMBOLISM/SYMBOLIZING.

DRINKING. *See* ALCOHOL ABUSE, ADDICTION AND THERAPY; EATING AND DRINKING.

DRIVE/DRIVES. *See* MOTIVATION.

DRUG ABUSE, DEPENDENCE, AND TREATMENT. *Drug abuse* refers to the use of any chemical substance, licit or illicit, which endangers or harms the physical, mental, emotional, social, or spiritual health or well-being of the user or other people.

Drug dependence refers to the most serious form of drug abuse and is characterized by a compelling need or craving to use a drug, regardless of the consequences, due to (a) psychological dependence, where the drug's effects are considered essential for well-being; and/or (b) physical dependence, where the body has adjusted to and requires the presence of the drug in order to maintain homeostasis and to avoid withdrawal symptoms. However, because it is not always possible to make a clear distinction between the psychological and physiological aspects of dependence, drug dependence should be viewed as on a continuum ranging from mild to severe.

Treatment refers to the help given to drug-dependent individuals, and others close to them, which interrupts the dependency process and initiates the process of recovery in which each person learns constructive ways to live more fully without abusing drugs.

Throughout history, men and women have used and abused various drugs. In biblical times, alcohol and other drugs were used for health and ritual purposes, but the immoderate use of alcohol and the use of drugs in connection with sorcery and magic were clearly condemned (Barnette). Today the problems of drug abuse and dependence have become a global concern, reaching epidemic proportions in many countries. In the U.S., drug abuse has spread throughout society and includes many kinds of mind- and mood-altering substances (Blum). Although alcohol is the most widely abused drug, Americans increasingly have become "polydrug" users who abuse and become dependent upon more than one drug.

Abuse of drugs may initially be a matter of choice, but for some people voluntary abuse can lead to dependence. The complex process by which a person progressively loses control over, and becomes compelled to continue, drug use despite adverse consequences is similar to the manner in which people become trapped in other compulsive, harmful patterns of behavior such as overeating, gambling, and sexual obsessions.

Without intervention, drug dependency is a progressive, destructive, and potentially fatal condition for which everyone in society pays a price. Fortunately, increasing numbers of people are overcoming the social stigma attached to drug problems and seeking help to break out of the trap of dependency. The pastor is likely to encounter many drug-dependent persons as well as family members in need of help and can play a unique and important role in their recovery and growth as whole persons and families.

1. **Drug Dependence.** *a. Causes and perpetuating influences.* Drug dependence is a complex problem that has no single or simple cause, but instead arises from and develops according to the interaction of many factors — pharmacological, biological, psychological, sociocultural, and spiritual. An understanding of these factors is important for those who wish to offer effective therapeutic or preventive help.

Regardless of their differences, all drugs of abuse have in common the ability to alter the user's physical, mental, or emotional state. The more immediate, potent, and desirable these changes, the greater their reinforcement value and the higher the probability of drug abuse and dependence. With many drugs the development of tolerance, where increasingly larger doses are needed to achieve the desired effect, and physical dependence also contribute to and perpetuate drug abuse and dependence. Drug abuse can be viewed as essentially a conditioned response resulting from continued drug use that has been reinforced by the pharmacological effects of the drug.

Pharmacological research and learning theories offer only a partial explanation for drug dependence; they do not explain initial drug use nor why some drug abusers, but not others, become dependent. Research points to the influence of social and cultural conditions, such as the widespread availability and acceptability of drugs, affluence, media exposure, peer group influence, and socioeconomic pressures that foster and perpetuate individual drug abuse and dependence.

Parental role models and family environment also exert a strong influence. Children whose parents abuse alcohol or other drugs are at high risk; "without intervention, forty to sixty percent of children of alcoholic parents become alcoholics themselves" (Ackerman). Many substance abusers come from backgrounds characterized by familial dysfunction such as broken homes, parental neglect or rejection, enmeshed relationships, and unresolved dependency/autonomy conflicts (Clinebell; Kaufman and Kaufmann; Platt and Labate).

Sociocultural factors do not account for individual differences within the same environment; not all persons from high risk backgrounds become substance abusers nor do all substance abusers come from high risk backgrounds. Biological and psychological factors may account for some of these differences. Scientists continue to search for a specific hereditary factor or preexisting biological condition that would account for vulnerability to drug dependency (Gottheil, *et al.*; Lettieri, *et al.*).

Personality traits have also been cited as predisposing factors. Although certain psychological characteristics (e.g., low frustration tolerance; impulsiveness; low self-esteem; ambivalence toward authority; heightened levels of stress, anxiety, guilt, and anger) frequently appear in substance abusers, there is no single "addictive personality type" that characterizes all substance abusers or predicts who will become one. In addition, some of these characteristics may actually be an effect, rather than a cause, of drug abuse and dependence.

Often overlooked in secular research, but of crucial significance, especially for the pastor, are the spiritual causes of drug dependency. In a world characterized by rapid social change and the erosion of traditional beliefs, practices, and institutions, drugs hold out the promise of instant pleasure or relief — at least temporary — from feelings of emptiness, powerlessness, meaninglessness, and alienation from self, others, and God.

Etiological theories raise significant pastoral issues and challenges. If drug abuse represents, at least to a large degree, a tragic response to the problems and unmet emotional and spiritual needs within individuals and society, the fact that so many people "turn to drugs and not the church for a sense of meaning, love, community, and transcendence is a clear, valid judgment on what the modern church has become" (Cassens). It is a judgment, certainly, but also a challenge for the church today to reach out in love. For pastors this often raises the ethical question of whether drug dependence is a sickness or a sin, the answer to which influences one's relationships and effectiveness with such individuals.

At one extreme, the "all-sin" view, which sees drug dependents as weak or immoral people who bear full responsibility for their problems, generally results in a moralistic, judgmental attitude that reinforces their feelings of inadequacy, rejection, and guilt and makes them less open to help. An "all-sickness" view, which sees dependents as helpless victims who bear little, if any, responsibility for their problems, often leads to a condescending or unconstructive approach, which does not help them to honestly confront, admit, and take responsibility for changing their destructive patterns of behavior. A more constructive view would take into account both the many complex causal factors and the drug dependency process which limit a person's ability to be completely self-determining as well as the basic tendencies of human nature such as the abuse of personal freedom, egocentricity, and self-deification, which alienate us from God and keep us from a life of genuine fulfillment without drugs. Thus, a reinterpretation of this moral question from a combined understanding of the complex etiology of drug dependence and a Christian theology which accepts drug dependents as individuals who share humanity's basic problems, needs, and weaknesses is more likely to lead to a compassionate and constructive approach. Such a view is compatible with the position of the American Medical Association and many helping professionals: that alcoholics and other drug dependents suffer from a diagnosable, primary, progressive, chronic "disease" from which, with help and an acceptance of responsibility for change, they can and do successfully recover.

b. Development and consequences. Etiological theories suggest causative and perpetuating influences in dependence but do not predict who will become drug dependent. Stages of development and their consequences, however, are essentially predictable once the dependency process has been initiated. Regardless of the drug used, most drug dependent individuals and others close to them go through a similar series of emotional and behavioral changes that make them increasingly dysfunctional (Johnson; Johnson Institute; McCabe; Wegscheider).

Briefly, the early stages of dependency are characterized by a growing preoccupation with and reliance upon the drug's effects, especially during times of stress. Usual activities and relationships are neglected as the person adapts his or her lifestyle to accommodate increasing drug use. As dependence increases, the individual develops ingenious ways to obtain, use, and conceal drugs.

Blackouts, or chemically induced periods of amnesia, may begin to occur. These are associated with increasing "loss of control," where the user progressively loses the ability to stop drug use once started or to predict how he or she will act. This leads to out-of-control behavior, growing problems in different areas of life, and increasing feelings of shame, guilt, anxiety, and self-hatred. A return to the chemical for relief only initiates a vicious cycle of compulsive use, uncontrollable behavior, and adverse consequences and negative feelings. Increasing blackouts and memory distortions as well as the development of psychological defenses such as denial, rationalization, projection, and repression may bring temporary relief but put the user further out of touch with reality, and unable to see drug use as a problem.

Whatever the original problems for which drug use may have been a symptom, drug use has now become the primary problem that requires direct treatment. Unfortunately treatment is often delayed or prevented by family members and others who, in trying to adjust to the dependent, progress through similar stages in which they learn unhealthy, defensive roles and patterns of behavior that support or contribute to the dependency. The odds of relapse are high for dependents whose families do not receive treatment but retain their own dysfunctional behavior patterns.

In the advanced stages, chemical use is continuous and leads to further deterioration in all areas of life. Abrupt reduction or cessation of drug use may result in unpleasant or life-threatening withdrawal symptoms, evidence that physical dependence is complete. Without intervention to arrest the process, the dependent loses everything—friends, family, job, health, even his or her defense system — and is left with nothing but chronic pain and despair. In the end, dependency can lead to premature death or, positively, to surrender and recovery.

The costs to society of drug abuse and dependence are high. Drug abuse plays a significant role in serious crime, family violence, traffic accidents and fatalities, lowered employee productivity, poor academic achievement, delinquency, and places a great strain upon medical, educational, and other human services. Perhaps most tragic is the amount of human suffering and untold loss to society of human potential.

2. **Treatment and Recovery.** *a. Intervention.* It is no longer accepted as true that the dependent must "hit bottom" before he or she can be treated and recover. Several effective techniques have been developed to intervene to bring the dependent to treatment sooner (McCabe; Johnson; Keller).

Generally, the persons who first seek help are family members or "significant others" close to the dependent. Because of their own defenses and negative feelings, however, they may be unable to see or to admit that a drug problem exists and instead present the counselor with a variety of other difficulties such as marital con-

flicts, financial concerns, delinquency, illness. The perceptive pastor recognizes the symptoms of drug dependency, provides information about the disease and its effects on the entire family, encourages family members to seek help for themselves, and offers additional supportive counseling as needed. As family members learn to change their own unhealthy behavior patterns and allow the dependent to experience the negative consequences of drug use, the dependent's recognition of a drug problem and the need for outside help may be hastened.

On occasions where the pastor has an opportunity to meet with the dependent, it is essential to try to establish a therapeutic relationship that can help to motivate the dependent for treatment. Knowledge of and skill in applying general counseling principles and methods as well as specific techniques for working with drug dependents are important and include building trust and rapport, accepting and accurately reflecting feelings, exploring and dealing directly with the immediate problem of drug use and its consequences rather than underlying causes, sharing information about the progressive symptoms of dependency in such a way that the dependent begins to question his or her own pattern of drug use, avoiding overprotective or other "enabling" behaviors, and—when necessary — using constructive, nonjudgmental confrontation to help the dependent see the reality of his or her condition (Clinebell; Johnson; Keller).

b. Treatment alternatives. Since drug dependency is a complex, multidimensional problem that affects whole persons and families, effective treatment must also be wholistic and multidisciplinary. The wise pastor will not try to assess or to treat drug dependency alone, but will develop firsthand knowledge of community resources specializing in drug problems, know his or her own skills as well as limitations and refer to appropriate additional resources, and be willing to share responsibility for providing help and support throughout the treatment and recovery process.

Most treatment efforts today fall into one of the following categories, plus variants or combinations: detoxification; residential, drug-free; outpatient, drug-free; or chemical approaches (Glasscote, *et al.*; Mothner and Weitz; Platt and Labate). Detoxification involves the gradual reduction of drug dosages, and sometimes the administration of other drugs, in order to minimize the discomfort, pain, or potential danger associated with termination of drug use. Withdrawal from drugs is necessary before meaningful treatment can begin but does not constitute rehabilitation.

Treatment can be residential or outpatient, long- or short-term, voluntary or compulsory, chemically assisted or drug-free. Some programs treat only the dependent, but an increasing number include concerned others as well. The goal of most treatment is to break the cycle of dependency and to initiate a process of individual and family recovery in which each person learns to live a more satisfying, productive life without drugs. This generally involves helping dependents and family members recognize and relinquish their denial and other delusional defenses, accept the illness and one's own part in it, recognize and share feelings, change unhealthy behaviors and rebuild the family system, and make a commitment to an ongoing recovery program (Wegscheider).

Many dependents and families will benefit from an intensive, concentrated period of residential treatment followed by treatment in an outpatient setting. Continued involvement in a Twelve Step recovery program such as Alcoholics Anonymous, Narcotics Anonymous, or an Al-Anon Family Group is also highly recommended. Specific treatment methods vary; however, many programs utilize self-help concepts developed by groups like Alcoholics Anonymous (AA) and residential therapeutic communities that emphasize individual motivation and participation, group therapy, peer support and confrontation, and the positive role of former abusers as counselors.

Two major chemical approaches that exist in the difficult treatment of heroin addiction are methadone maintenance, a narcotic substitution method, and narcotic antagonist therapy, which uses chemical compounds to block the euphoriant effects of opiates. Numerous concerns and problems are associated with these methods; however, they may be helpful to some heroin addicts, particularly when used with other supportive services (Platt and Labate).

Accurate evaluation and comparison of various treatment approaches and their effectiveness is complicated by numerous research and methodological problems. It is apparent, however, that no single approach provides all the solutions, and that the most effective treatment is one that utilizes a variety of methods according to individual and family needs.

c. Recovery. Treatment of the acute phase of drug dependency is only the beginning of a lifelong recovery and growth process. During the early stages of individual and family recovery and involvement in treatment and/or a program like AA's Twelve Steps, the pastor's role is primarily a supportive one. In later stages, skilled pastoral counseling can play a vital part in helping dependents and families reorganize their lives without drugs and develop their full potentials as human beings. This includes individual, marital, and family counseling to help dependents and families resolve personal and interpersonal difficulties; assistance to those who request it in working on the "moral inventory" steps of Twelve Step recovery programs; and guidance and support that foster spiritual awareness and growth. Pastors are cautioned to be sensitive and to take care not to offer religious solutions too quickly to dependents lest this lead to a superficial emotional response and avoidance of personal responsibility rather than a genuine acknowledgement of the need for and acceptance of God's grace and redemptive love.

The pastor, through example and teaching, can also prepare, challenge, and encourage the church to become a place where dependents and their families can experience the acceptance, fellowship, and support that will facilitate their recovery and restore them to full relationship with themselves, with others, and with God.

3. **Conclusion.** The question and the challenge facing the pastor and the church today is not whether but rather how it will confront the tragic problems of drug abuse and dependence. Effective treatment requires the cooperation and help of everyone, including the pastor and the church. If drug abuse and dependence represent an attempt to satisfy spiritual and other human needs, it would appear that within the corporate body and fellowship of the church lies our best hope for both its prevention and treatment.

Bibliography. R. Ackerman, *Children of Alcoholics* (1978). H. Barnette, *The Drug Crisis and the Church* (1971). K. Blum, *Handbook of Abusable Drugs* (1984). J. Cassens, *Drugs and Drug Abuse* (1970). H. Clinebell, Jr., *Understanding and Counseling the Alcoholic* rev. ed. (1968). R. Glasscote, *et al.*, *The Treatment of Drug Abuse* (1972). E. Gottheil, *et al.*, eds., *Etiologic Aspects of Alcohol and Drug Abuse* (1983). V. Johnson, *I'll Quit Tomorrow* rev. ed. (1980). Johnson Institute, *Chemical Dependency and Recovery Are a Family Affair* (1979). E. Kaufman and P. Kaufmann, eds., *Family Therapy of Drug and Alcohol Abuse* (1979). J. Keller, *Ministering to Alcoholics* (1966). D. Lettieri, *et al.*, eds., *Theories on Drug Abuse* (1980). T. McCabe, *Victims No More* (1978). I. Mothner and A. Weitz, *How to Get Off Drugs* (1984). J. Platt and C. Labate, *Heroin Addiction* (1976). S. Wegscheider, *Another Chance* (1981).

J. A. BABB

ALCOHOL ABUSE, ADDICTION, AND THERAPY; ALCOHOLICS ANONYMOUS; MEDICATION; MENTAL HEALTH AND ILLNESS. *See also* GROUP COUNSELING AND PSYCHOTHERAPY; PSYCHEDELIC DRUGS AND EXPERIENCE; PSYCHOPATHOLOGY, THEORIES OF; SUPPORT GROUPS. *Compare* BIOLOGICAL DIMENSIONS OF PERSONALITY AND BEHAVIOR; EVALUATION AND DIAGNOSIS, PSYCHOLOGICAL.

DRUGS. Any substance used as a medicine or in the preparation of a medicine; a narcotic, especially one that is habit-forming. In present society, the term "narcotic" is usually used pejoratively of a drug, except when the drug is used in connection with many of the medications used in psychiatry. The term *medicine* is used when referring to substances which are seldom or never abused. Drugs and medicines can be useful and life-saving, and can enhance the quality of life. Abused or misused they can injure or destroy.

1. **Historical Development.** Drugs and medicines have been in use since before recorded history. The lore of the medicine man, the shaman, and the healer has been passed down to the contemporary practitioner. For example, alcohol is almost as old as humanity; the uses of castor oil and opium were mentioned in the Eber Egyptian Papyrus written more than one millennium before Christ; aspirin was developed from the folk medicine of Canadian Indians, while cocaine came from indigenous Peruvians. But despite this historical heritage humans still only had fewer than twenty therapeutic drugs by the end of the nineteenth century. In 1907, after 606 attempts, Ehrlich's "Magic Bullet" (an arsenic compound) was discovered and used in the treatment of syphilis—an event of major significance since syphilis was an endemic disease which maimed and destroyed the mind, and killed untold numbers of persons. However, the success of this systematic research did not immediately influence drug development.

2. **Synthetic Drug Development.** In the 1930s researchers began to replace the herb, root, tree, and plant derived medicines with synthetics. One of the first of these "tailored" drugs was Dilantin (phenytoin). Wishing to develop a better anticonvulsant than phenobarbital, two physicians systematically made numerous

compounds based on the barbituric acid nucleus until they eventually discovered Dilantin, still now a major medicine for controlling seizures. The lessons learned from this discovery are now used to explore the potentials of many old and new medications. Since sulfonamides changed the treatment of bacterial diseases in the 1930s, more effective medicines have been discovered than in the preceding thousands of years. Medical development of drugs is now developing rapidly in two directions: whereas many drugs have been formulated for effective use in a broad spectrum of diseases, others have been discovered which are increasingly specific in their treatment of particular diseases.

Penicillin, originally derived from a mold, opened new vistas in antibacterial therapy. Along with synthetic derivatives and other mold-derived antibiotics, penicillin is effective against many bacterial diseases and syphilis. Beta-blockers such as propranolol (Inderal) have vastly altered the treatment of heart disease. Thyroid, insulin, growth stimulators, and other hormones are effective in many areas of endocrinology, including those relating to post-menopausal problems. Asthma and other allergic symptoms are also responsive to medication.

3. **Psychoactive Drugs.** Among the most widely used and misused drugs are the psychoactive agents. There are anti-anxiety, anti-depressant, and other psycholytic drugs. Major and minor tranquilizers, sedatives and stimulants, drugs to relieve tics, all have useful places. Although it is frequently said that psychiatric patients are often over-medicated, this ignores the thousands of mental patients who filled the hospitals before the discovery of Thorazine. Mental institution rosters constantly increased, relative to population increases, from the time records were kept until 1954 when chlorpromazine (Thorazine) was first used for the treatment of schizophrenia. Many who had been hospitalized returned to their homes and now work and live in the community.

Psychiatric drugs are often referred to as psychotropic (*psycho*, mind; *trepien*, turn) or psychoactive and are substances which act directly on the brain to affect various functions including perception, cognition, emotions, attention, and learning.

The evolution of word usage has caused confusion about some psychoactive drugs. "Tranquilizer" and "sedative" are now often considered equivalent terms by nonmedical individuals. In medical usage, however, *sedated* has come to mean drowsy, slow to respond, impaired cognition, obtunded; while *tranquilized* is taken to mean well-ordered, calm, contemplative, with improved function. It is true that side effects such as drowsiness occur but these can usually be relieved by modification of dosage.

Some therapists have called psychoactive drugs chemical strait jackets which prevent effective therapeutic counseling and psychotherapy. Other experts, however, believe that psychoactive drugs stabilize the patient/client, improving insight and making the patient more accessible for psychotherapy.

4. **Stimulant and Psychotropic Drugs.** The use of "stimulant" drugs in the treatment of children with Attention Deficit Disorder (ADD), Minimal Brain Dysfunction (MBD), hyperactive children, and hyperkinetic behavior syndrome is a major therapeutic issue of the day. In this field, as in many concerned with psychotropics, proponents point out the stabilizing effect on behavior, the improvement in learning and coordination, and the improved social adjustment which results from drug use. Others argue that drugs do not cure psychiatric illnesses, but only control or alleviate them. The dangers of side effects are pointed out, and the possibility that drugs may be required for the rest of the patient's life is emphasized. The same is true of diabetics and insulin.

Much of this dichotomy of thought arises from a disagreement on the causes of "emotional" illnesses. Much literature suggests that schizophrenia, hyperactivity, depression, and other illness are primarily physiological in origin rather than environmental-psychological. Environmental stress is considered as only a part of the cause, by many, although there are some who still firmly believe that organicity plays only a minor role in emotional/psychiatric illnesses. This confusion is not new or unusual. Adolph Meyer was concerned about the relative importance of organic versus environmental causes in *dementia praecox* (schizophrenia) in 1895.

Alcoholism looks like an acquired condition yet there is strong data to support a hereditary factor or at least a predisposition to the disease. An increased incidence of alcoholism in the fathers of hyperactive children is well documented. It is also common to have a family history of alcoholism even though some of the family members have never seen each other.

Antibiotics have almost eliminated some of the contagious diseases. Mastoiditis, osteomyelitis, meningitis, are seldom seen by the physician or the general public. Scarlet fever and pneumonia are easily treatable in most instances, yet in the 1930s a child with staphlycoccic pneumonia had little chance for survival. Side effects and allergic reactions do occur and can result in rashes, discomfort or even death.

5. **Safety of Drugs, and Drug Abuse.** There is no such thing as a "safe" drug. Any medicine that is potent enough to produce controls or cures can do harm. The same is true of counseling. Treatment by the physician, the psychologist, the psychiatrist, or the pastor without searching for the cause, treatment by method not by individual, treatment by bias not from knowledge is dangerous and may well do more harm than good. It is important for the medical or psychological therapist to explain the possible side effects of the treatment modality and also to put it in perspective.

Drug abuse as the result of therapeutic use or misuse can occur; yet use and abuse differ greatly. In the treatment of ADD a daily dose of 50–75 milligrams would be considered high, yet "speed freaks" (amphetamine abusers) use 500–1,000 mg of "speed" a day "mainlining" (injecting) it. There have been several studies on the addicting/habituating effect of amphetamines in hyperactive children. All of the studies and reviews have concluded that there was no evidence to support the concept that stimulant drug therapy led to abuse. The same is probably true of most psychoactive drugs if they are monitored and wisely used.

This does not mean that some drug-treated ADD children do not end up abusing alcohol and other "recreational drugs" but it seems that the incidence is no greater than in control populations. How much abuse is due to the drug and how much is due to the temperament of the person is still unresolved. Treatment programs for abuse are still unsatisfactory. If we better understood the cause we would be much closer to a competent, successful, treatment routine.

Many new *"therapeutic" treatment programs* are now being used for conditions which have commonly been treated by counseling or drugs. One that has received much publicity is the Finegold dietary approach to hyperactivity. It excludes food dyes, additives, and to some degree simple sugars. The media has devoted reams of copy to this alternative therapy although all controlled studies have shown it to be of little or no value. The same can be said for the treatment of schizophrenia and other illnesses by megavitamins and large mineral supplements.

Vitamins are seldom considered drugs yet the medical profession in general feels that they are among the most abused substances. Although there are a number of diseases that can be brought on by overuse of vitamins the public is constantly encouraged to buy and use them. There is probably little need for regular use of these vitamins and their use should be as judiciously explored as is the use of psychotherapeutic, anticonvulsant, or antibiotic drugs.

6. **The Placebo Effect.** Drugs and medications may also work by the placebo effect. This effect occurs when a medication that is chemically inert effects curative or symptomatic changes. When the patient and/or curer has confidence that the prescribed medication has curative power, a process that is not totally understood is set in motion that will lead to a cure of the illness or a decrease in the symptomatology. The belief system elicits subtle changes in the neuro-endocrine and immunological systems of the body, stimulating active biochemical changes in the patient's body. Current research would indicate that endorphins, a natural morphine-like pain-reducing substance in the human body, may play a part in this curative effect. Even when a medication is not chemically inert, the placebo effect may play a part in the patient's improvement.

L. OETTINGER
D. THOMAS

BIOLOGICAL DIMENSIONS OF PERSONALITY AND BEHAVIOR; MEDICATION; PSYCHEDELIC DRUGS AND EXPERIENCE. *See also* ALCOHOL ABUSE, ADDICTION, AND THERAPY; DRUG ABUSE, DEPENDENCE, AND TREATMENT.

DRUGS, PSYCHEDELIC. *See* PSYCHEDELIC DRUGS AND EXPERIENCE.

DRUGS IN COMMON USE AND ABUSE. (*See* Charts on the following pages).

DRUNKENNESS. *See* ALCOHOL ABUSE, ADDICTION AND THERAPY. *See also* EATING AND DRINKING; GLUTTONY AND TEMPERANCE; RESPONSIBILITY/IRRESPONSIBILITY, PSYCHOLOGY OF.

DSM-III/DSM-III-R. *See* DIAGNOSTIC AND STATISTICAL MANUAL III; EVALUATION AND DIAGNOSIS, PSYCHOLOGICAL.

DUAL CAREER MARRIAGE. A husband-wife relationship in which both spouses are gainfully employed (or serve in a formal volunteer position) whether full- or part-time. More than fifty percent of couples in the U.S. are dual career couples. Unique stresses result, but definite assets lure couples into continued dual employment.

1. **Stresses.** Dual career couples experience stress peculiar to their situation. Competition between jobs often heads the list as persons argue over whose job comes first. Job related relocation for one partner places further major strain on the relationship. Male and female role expectations generate adjustment problems until homemaking chores are shared, in mutually satisfactory ways. Two spouses face three jobs: his, hers, and homemaking. Creative coping responses to the demands of homemaking lead two-career spouses to eat out more often, seek convenience devices, lower their expectations for house care, as well as employing others to tend to routine maintenance (maids, condominium contracts, etc.).

The care of children surfaces as a further area of difficulty. Child care centers, live-in sitters, and relatives are the three primary resources of two-career parents. Alternating shift work seems to be a less than desirable choice for working parents. Generally, time pressures on both-working couples result in isolation from peers and the extended family, because they are too busy to maintain durable friendships. These couples often stretch their working time at the expense of recreation and worship.

Contrary to popular opinion, however, dual career marriages are as stable and as effective as one-career marriages. Two-job spouses divorce at about the same rate as others. Their offspring do not have a higher rate of delinquency or school drop-out. Daughters of working couples achieve higher scores in school and complete more years of education. Sons are not adversely affected unless the father is dysfunctional as a family member.

2. **Assets.** One obvious asset, more money, misleads some couples. A second job (or a volunteer position) means extra expense. Money is the reason most couples take up two careers but personal satisfaction is the big asset that keeps them in dual careers.

Personal satisfaction comes from secondary gains such as increased social contact, gratification from contributing to society, and a greater sense of personal freedom. Employment and volunteer activities mean interaction with other persons; this increases opportunities for gratifying experiences as well as increased feelings of personal worth. When a husband and a wife pursue closely related vocations they usually challenge each other to increase productivity on the job.

Two factors emerge as key variables in the satisfaction of two-career couples: flexibility and mutual commitment. When both mates involve themselves outside of the home, changes in routines, role expectations, and relationships of power result. The capacity to accept these changes leads to increased satisfaction. Each partner's commitment to the other's goals correlates positively to overall adjustment to dual careers. Couples who support each other's out-of-the-home work report higher levels of marital bliss. The degree of overall commitment to a spouse supports this latter variable.

Pastoral care of two-career couples has developed around pastoral responses to the stress areas, support of

CONTROLLED SUBSTANCES: USES AND EFFECTS

	Drugs	Trade or Other Names	Medical Uses
NARCOTICS	Opium	Dover's Powder, Paregoric, Parepectolin	Analgesic, antidiarrheal
	Morphine	Morphine, Pectoral Syrup	Analgesic, antitussive
	Codeine	Codeine, Empirin Compound with Codeine, Robitussin A,C	Analgesic, antitussive
	Heroin	Diacetylmorphine, Horse, Smack	Under investigation
	Hydromorphone	Dilaudid	Analgesic
	Meperidine (Pethidine)	Demerol, Pethadol	Analgesic
	Methadone	Dolophine, Methadone, Methadose	Analgesic, heroin substitute
	Other Narcotics	LAAM, Leritine, Levo-Dromoran, Percodan, Tussionex, Fentanyl,* Darvon, Talwin, Lomotil	Analgesic, anti-diarrheal, antitussive, *surgical anesthetic.
DEPRESSANTS	Alcohol	Beer, spirits, whiskey, wine.	Anti-anxiety, sedative, hypnotic
	Chloral Hydrate	Noctec, Somnos	Hypnotic
	Barbiturates	Amobarbital, Phenobarbital, Butisol, Phenoxbarbital, Secobarbital, Tuinal	Anesthetic, anti-convulsant, sedative, hypnotic
	Glutethimide	Doriden	
	Methaqualone	Optimil, Parest, Quaalude, Somnafac, Sopor	Sedative, hypnotic Almost never used because of abuse potential
	Benzodiazepines	Atarax, Ativan, Azene, Clonopin, Dalmane, Diazepam, Librax, Librium, Serax, Tranxene, Valium, Verstran	Anti-anxiety, anti-convulsant, sedative, hypnotic, surgical anesthetic All benzodiazepines are basically anxiolytic (anti-anxiety) drugs, but are often used for sedative effects and for muscle relaxant effects. Combined with alcohol or other sedative drugs the effect is synergistic, i.e., each intensifies or multiplies the effect of the other when used in combination.
	Other Depressants	Equanil, Miltown, Noludar, Placidyl, Valmid	Anti-anxiety, sedative, hypnotic
STIMULANTS	Cocaine	Coke, Crack, Flake, Snow	Anti-hemorrhagic, Local anesthetic
	Amphetamines	Biphetamine, Delcobese, Desoxyn, Dexedrine, Mediatric	Hyperkinesis,
	Phenmetrazine	Preludin	narcolepsy
	Methylphenidate	Ritalin	Anti-hyperactivity in pre-pubertal children
	Other Stimulants	Adipex, Bacarate, Cylert, Didrex, Ionamin, Plegine, Pre-Sate, Sanorex, Tenuate, Tepanil, Voranil	
HALLUCINOGENS	LSD	Acid, Microdot	None
	Mescaline and Peyote	Mesc, Buttons, Cactus	None
	Amphetamine Variants	2.5 DMA, PMA, STP, MDA, MMDA, TMA, DOM, DOB	
	Phencyclidine	PCP, Angel Dust, Hog	Veterinary anesthetic, psychogenic in humans
	Phencyclidine Analogs	PCE, PCP, TCP	
	Other Hallucinogens	Bufotenine, Ibogaine, DMT, DET, Psilocybin, Psilocyn	None
CANNABIS	Marijuana	Pot, Acapulco Gold, Grass, Reefer Sinsemilla, Thai Sticks	Investigational treatment of glaucoma, anti-nausea with chemotherapy patients.
	Tetrahydrocannabinol	THC	As above; active ingredient in marijuana
	Hashish	Hash	None
	Hashish Oil	Hash Oil	None

CONTROLLED SUBSTANCES: USES AND EFFECTS

	Drugs	Physical Dependence	Psychological Dependence	Tolerance	Duration of effect in hrs.
NARCOTICS	Opium	High	High	Yes	3-6
	Morphine	High	High	Yes	3-6
	Codeine	Moderate	Moderate	Yes	3-6
	Heroin	High	High	Yes	3-6
	Hydromorphone	High	High	Yes	3-6
	Meperidine (Pethidine)	High	High	Yes	3-6
	Methadone	High	High	Yes	12-24
	Other Narcotics	High-Low	High-Low	Yes	Variable
DEPRESSANTS	Chloral Hydrate	Moderate	Moderate	Possible	5-8
	Barbiturates	High-Moderate	High-Moderate	Yes	1-16
	Glutethimide	High	High	Yes	4-8
	Methaqualone	High	High	Yes	4-104
	Benzodiazepines	Mod-High	Mod-High	Yes	4-8
	Other Depressants	Moderate	Moderate	Yes	4-8
STIMULANTS	Alcohol	Low-High	Low-High	Yes	1 hr./oz. alcohol
	Cocaine	High	High	Yes	0-3
	Amphetamines	High	High	Yes	2-4
	Phenmetrazine	Possible	High	Yes	2-4
	Methylphenidate	Possible	High	Yes	2-4
	Other Stimulants	Possible	High	Yes	2-4
HALLUCIN-OGENS	LSD	None	Degree unknown	Yes	8-12
	Mescaline and Peyote	Unknown	Degree unknown	Yes	8-12
	Amphetamine Variants	High	Degree unknown	Yes	acute effect days, long-term withdrawal months
	Phencyclidine	Degree unknown	High	Yes	Sometimes precipitates schizophreniform psychosis, esp. in borderline patients.
	Phencyclidine Analogs	Degree unknown	Degree unknown	Possible	Variable
	Other Hallucinogens	None	Degree unknown	Possible	Variable
CANNABIS	Marijuana	Moderate	Moderate-high	Yes	2-4 hours acute; some effects last weeks
	Tetrahydrocannabinol	Moderate	Moderate-high	Yes	2-4 hours acute; Some effects last weeks
	Hashish	Degree unknown	Moderate	Yes	2-4
	Hashish Oil	Degree unknown			2-4

CONTROLLED SUBSTANCES: USES AND EFFECTS

	Drugs	Ususal Methods of Administration	Possible Effects	Effects of Overdose	Withdrawal Syndrome
NARCOTICS	Opium	Oral, smoked	Euphoria drowsiness, respiratory depression, constricted pupils, nausea	Slow and shallow breathing, clammy skin, convulsions, coma, possible death	Watery eyes, runny nose, yawning, loss of appetite, irritability, tremors, panic, chills and sweating, cramps, nausea
	Morphine	Oral injected smoked			
	Codeine	Oral, injected			
	Heroin	Injected, sniffed, smoked			
	Hydromorphone	Oral, injected			
	Meperidine (Pethidine)	Oral, injected			
	Methadone	Oral, injected			
	Other Narcotics	Oral, injected			
DEPRESSANTS	Chloral Hydrate	Oral	Slurred speech, disorientation, drunken behavior without odor of alcohol, increased anxiety	Shallow respiration, cold and clammy skin, dilated pupils, weak and rapid pulse, coma, possible death	Anxiety, insomnia, tremors, delirium, convulsions, possible death
	Barbiturates	Oral, injected			
	Glutethimide	Oral, injected			
	Methaqualone	Oral, injected			
	Benzodiazepines	Oral, injected			
	Other Depressants	Oral, injected			
	Alcohol	Oral, inhaled	As above, and impaired, hypertension, hemorrhaging, brain atrophy		
STIMULANTS	Cocaine	Sniffed, injected, smoked	Increased alertness, excitation, euphoria, increased pulse rate and blood pressure, insomnia, loss of appetite	Agitation, increase in body temperature, hallucinations, convulsions, possible death. Atypically, most severe reactions, eg. death, can occur with first usage	Apathy, long periods of sleep, irritability, depression, disorientation, hyper verbality
	Amphetamines	Oral, injected			
	Phenmetrazine	Oral, injected			
	Methylphenidate	Oral, injected			
	Other Stimulants	Oral			
HALLUCIN-OGENS	LSD	Oral	Illusions and hallucinations, poor perception of time and distance	Longer, more intense "trip" episodes, psychosis, possible death, depression (severe in some) including suicidal preoccupation	Hallucinatory "Flashbacks" long after detectable levels of drug are gone, periods of severe anxiety
	Mescaline and Peyote	Oral, injected			
	Amphetamine Variants	Oral, injected			
	Phencyclidine	Smoked, oral, injected			
	Phencyclidine Analogs				
	Other Hallucinogens	Oral, injected, smoked, sniffed			
CANNABIS	Marijuana	Smoked, oral	Euphoria, relaxed inhibitions, increased appetite, disoriented behavior, decreased judgment, memory impairment, decreased motivation, fatigue paranoia, possible psychosis	Fatigue, paranoia, possible psychosis	Insomnia, hyperactivity, decreased appetite occasionally reported, irritability, continued symptoms of possible effects
	Tetrhydrocannabinol				
	Hashish				
	Hashish Oil				

Source: Drug Enforcement Administration, *Drug Enforcement Fall 1979*, (Washington, D.C.: U.S. Department of Justice); revised by D. McRight

equal rights, and programming alternatives in the local church. Two-career marriages need further specific research from pastoral care specialists.

G. W. ROWATT

FAMILY, HISTORY AND SOCIOLOGY OF; MARRIAGE; VOCATION; WORK AND CAREER. *Compare* CLERGY COUPLES; PARENTS/ PARENTHOOD.

DUNBAR, HELEN FLANDERS (1902–59). Pioneer in psychosomatic medicine and a founder of clinical pastoral education (CPE). A woman who dazzled many by her keen intelligence, academic degrees, driving ambition, formidable style, and beauty, Dunbar dropped her first name early in her career to mislead readers into thinking that she was male.

After her graduation from Bryn Mawr (1923), Dunbar earned an A.M. and Ph.D. from Columbia (1924, 1929), a B.D. from Union Theological Seminary (1927), and an M.D. from Yale (1930). She managed simultaneous studies in philosophy, theology, and medicine by employing two secretaries. During her final year of medical school she assisted in clinics in Vienna and Zurich, and visited the shrine at Lourdes to observe the relation of faith to healing.

In 1925, the year that Anton Boisen began introducing clinical training for divinity students, Dunbar worked with him at the Worcester State Hospital. In 1930 she became director of the newly formed Council for the Clinical Training of Theological Students, and later hired Seward Hiltner as executive secretary. Under their leadership clinical training (CPE) became established in theological seminaries.

Dunbar is remembered chiefly for her work in psychosomatic medicine. She compiled a massive bibliography, *Emotions and Bodily Changes,* a standard reference work updated several times. She popularized her research in *Mind and Body* (1947) and other publications. Dunbar also founded the journal *Psychosomatic Medicine* (she served as editor-in-chief from 1938 to 1947), and the American Psychosomatic Society (1942).

Dunbar's first husband, Dr. Theodore Wolfe, brought orgone therapist Wilhelm Reich to America and was his English translator. Her second husband, George Henry Soule, Jr., an editor of *The New Republic,* fathered her only child, born in 1941. In Dunbar's later years the quality of her work deteriorated as she relied on alcohol to deal with stress and emotional pain. Some interpreted her death by drowning as a suicide.

Bibliography. A. Stokes, *Ministry After Freud* (1985). R. C. Powell, *Healing and Wholeness,* unpublished doctoral dissertation, Duke University (1974).

A. STOKES

PASTORAL CARE MOVEMENT; RELIGION AND HEALTH MOVEMENT.

DUTY, SENSE OF. *See* CONSCIENCE; RESPONSIBILITY/ IRRESPONSIBILITY, PSYCHOLOGY OF. *See also* OBEDIENCE; VIRTUE, CONCEPT OF.

DYING, JEWISH CARE OF. *See* SICK AND DYING, JEWISH CARE OF.

DYING, MORAL DILEMMAS IN. Refers to concepts of right behavior which, because of changes in sites where dying occurs, roles of persons making decisions about care of the dying, and definition of death, place both terminally ill patients and their caregivers in conflict and competition. These changes have shifted priorities of care from traditional behaviors incorporated in faith traditions and social mores to contemporary behaviors defined by technological capabilities and protocols of professional competency.

1. **Traditional Ethics.** Earliest evidence of moral consideration for the dying is found in India. The Buddhist Emperor Asoka, who died in 238 B.C., was concerned about the safety and health of Hindu pilgrims seeking to reach the holy waters of the Ganges at Varanasi (Benares). He ordered shelters, or hospices, to be built and guideposts to be erected giving directions as well as advice. Ethical imperatives called for care of the vulnerable pilgrim. Piracy, overcharging, neglect, and other behaviors which took advantage of the vulnerable were defined as immoral.

Building of shelters (hospitals or hospices) and articulating values of care found later in the Middle East and Europe suggest Asokan influence and cultural exchange along the trade routes of Asia Minor. The metaphors of life used in many faith traditions are those of pilgrim, wanderer, or traveler, and the paradigm for ethical behavior is care of the vulnerable pilgrim. Jesus' parable of "The Good Samaritan" is part of that tradition.

For many eighteenth century Christians in North America, the road of life was to be traveled giving highest priority to faithfulness or obedience to God. Death of the body, no matter how painful, was an insignificant threat when compared to the possibility of death of the spirit. Depending on the faith tradition one would examine, priority or emphasis was given to obligations for encouraging the dying patient's acts of belief, for giving sustenance, or for providing shelter.

As best as scholars can determine, most people preferred a slow dying process to a quick death so as to have time to put one's affairs in order; and the role of caregivers was to support the vulnerable in such endeavors. Whatever befell an individual, life and death were defined as part of God's purpose and an individual's life had an end (*telos*), as part of that purpose. While Bunyan's *Pilgrim's Progress* is Calvinist in theology, in metaphor and value it was as universal an expression of ethical principles for death and dying as one can find in the literature of the time. These principles were dominant in North America until the twentieth century.

In the nineteenth century West, there have been at least two strong imperatives for a pilgrim's actions: the right of self-determination in making decisions about how one travels the road of life versus the obligation to follow a map ordained by the Giver of Life. The secularization of mores has tended to emphasize the former imperative; faith traditions have tended to emphasize the latter.

2. **Changes Which Pose Moral Dilemmas.**
a. Change in sites of dying. In 1980, about five percent of reported deaths were children or adolescents and most died in hospitals. In 1900, by contrast, over half of reported deaths were children fifteen years of age or

younger and most died in their homes. In 1980, in most metropolitan areas of North America, between seventy and eighty percent of reported deaths occurred in an institution of care, whereas in 1900, that percentage of reported deaths occurred in the home.

b. Change in roles of care. As the major site of death shifted from the home to the health care institution, the roles of caring shifted from family and friends to members of health care professions. Given the pluralism of the population treated in health care institutions, directions for moral behavior shifted from the imperatives of faith traditions and the mores of communities to protocols defined by each association of health care professionals. These protocols, for a variety of historical and economical reasons, not only shifted the roles of caring but the power of decision-making into the hands of professional caregivers, particularly physicians. The questions of self-determination or faith obedience that had been reflective of the pilgrim's progress were displaced by the questions of who shall decide and what options will be provided for terminally ill patients and their families within the limits of professional competency — a shift in the ethics of caring for the dying from *all* adherents of a tradition to only the professionally certified.

c. Change in definition of death. Changes in sites and roles of care led to a redefinition of death. A significant implication of the shift of decision-making to health care professions (a shift some critics call "a will to play God") was the need to determine which patients "at risk of dying" should receive care when the protocols for caring required scarce expertise and resources. Triage logic — the rough determination whether expertise and resources will make a difference in maintaining a patient's cardiac and respiratory signs, and, since 1970, brain functions — was developed in World War I to help physicians decide who among the injured should receive treatment. That logic has been incorporated into the protocols of acute care hospitals for determining not only what treatments will be provided but at what moment death will occur. Triage logic presumes precise expertise and leads to precise determinations measured by machines. The advent of sophisticated life-prolonging techniques like artificial respirators and heart-lung machines has shifted the definition of death from being a part and process of the pilgrim's journey of meaning in life to a programmed moment as the end of the pilgrim's vital signs. With the change in definition has come redefinition of concepts of right behavior.

3. Contemporary Ethical Dilemmas. In 1980, a group of physicians identified the following dilemmas as the most perplexing in their care of dying patients: whether to tell patients the truth about the severity of their diagnoses; how rigorous the caregiver should be with the principle of confidentiality between physician and patient as opposed to sharing data of diagnosis and care with members of the patient's family; whether applying therapy requires the patient's *informed* consent; what priority should be given to therapies designed to cure as opposed to those designed primarily for comfort; and how to behave ethically on behalf of the patient while maintaining professional relationships with other caregivers.

In addition, many bioethicists also include the dilemmas of whether it is morally permissible to withhold or to withdraw treatment from a dying adult patient in order to shorten or reduce suffering; whether in cases of intractable pain health care professionals should cause death either by direct or indirect means; whether knowledge or resources for hastening one's own death should be made available to dying patients; and how much costs of care should enter into decisions about how to care for the terminally ill.

These dilemmas, and others, represent changes in ideas and behaviors of care which either challenge traditional values or so alter the mores by which decisions are made as to turn the pilgrim's possibility of living and dying for a *telos* (purpose) into a *finis* (finality). Like the pilgrim in Bunyan's epic, a terminally ill patient in the twentieth century runs high risk of falling through the trap door to hell at the very threshold of fulfilled life, tripped by treatment received while vulnerable.

4. Implications for Pastoral Care. In contrast to earlier centuries, definition and practice of pastoral care for the terminally ill today is largely institutionally based. Mores of home and parish are subordinated to protocols of health care institutions. The tests of effective pastoral care include whether patients understand as a part of their faith structures how to face and resolve moral dilemmas likely to be confronted when terminally ill; whether terminally ill patients are supported in being a primary decision-maker about their care; whether such patients are permitted to change their decisions with regard to therapy options; and whether the terminally ill and their families are provided orienting rituals for making their final pilgrimage together.

Bibliography. Information Planning Associations, *A Bioethical Perspective on Death and Dying: Summaries of The Literature* (1977). The President's Commission for the Study of Ethical Problems in Medicine and Biomedical and Behavioral Research, *Deciding to Forego Life-Sustaining Treatment: A Report on the Ethical, Medical, and Legal Issues in Treatment Decisions* (1983). W. T. Reiche, ed., *Encyclopedia of Bioethics* (1978). P. Steinfels and R. M. Veatch, *Death Inside Out: The Hastings Center Report* (1975). R. M. Veatch, *Death, Dying and the Biological Revolution: Our Last Quest for Responsibility* (1976).

G. W. DAVIDSON

GUIDANCE, PASTORAL; MORAL DILEMMAS IN PASTORAL PERSPECTIVE. *See also* DEATH; DEATH RESEARCH AND EDUCATION; DYING, PASTORAL CARE OF; MORAL THEOLOGY AND PASTORAL CARE; SICK AND DYING, JEWISH CARE OF; SUICIDE (Ethical Issues); WILL TO LIVE. *Compare* DECISION/INDECISION, PSYCHOLOGY OF; ESCHATOLOGY AND PASTORAL CARE; ETHICS AND PASTORAL CARE; EVALUATION AND DIAGNOSIS, RELIGIOUS.

DYING, PASTORAL CARE OF. That special, personalized ministry to dying persons, and their families, wherein the pastor symbolically represents the community of faith and at the same time provides the warmth of individual human caring.

There is a tendency to consider dying persons from an abstract point of view, which may enable a necessary objectivity. However, this necessary process should not isolate the dying from the living. A principal task in pastoral care is to include the dying, not separate them as if they were different in some basic sense. By providing care the pastor binds more closely together the living with the dying. The pastor's care is a tangible and concrete presence which makes available the powerful symbolic message that the community of the faithful, the hopeful, and the loving is present amidst this last crisis.

1. Demographic Factors. In the United States approximately 7.5 percent of the population are under five years of age and almost twelve percent are over sixty-five. These figures become particularly significant when compared to earlier decades. Since 1900 there has been a thirty-six percent decrease in the percentage of children under ten years of age, and a 257 percent increase in the percentage of the population over sixty-five. Once they reach old age, persons now have more years of life expectancy than ever before. Thus, it is easy to see that the U. S. is becoming an older society; the population is living longer and longer.

One consequence of this fundamental population shift is that death is becoming more closely associated with advanced age. In less than eighty years, there has been a 300 percent increase in the percentage of deaths among persons over sixty-five. The family relationships of this age group are also noteworthy. Seventy-seven percent of men over sixty-five live with their spouse; only fifteen percent live alone. In contrast, over fifty percent of women over sixty-five are widowed, and forty-one percent live alone. Women outlive men and are therefore more likely to experience widowhood in old age.

There are some remarkable differences across the life span in the causes of death. What kills the young adult does not necessarily kill the octogenarian. The three leading causes of death for males aged fifteen to twenty-four are accidents, homicides, and suicides. For females the same age they are accidents, homicides, and malignancies. For all persons over sixty-five, however, the leading causes of death are heart diseases, malignancies, and strokes. Generally speaking, then, the young tend not to approach the point of death gradually, with conscious opportunities for preparation. On the other hand, the elderly are not only much more likely to die, but are also much more likely to be aware of their dying condition prior to the moment of death.

2. Basic Principles. Everyone is unique; dying persons are no exception. Several overarching themes appear relevant to the general process of dying, yet each person who is dying is involved in an unusual set of circumstances that will never be repeated. While general themes, stages and theological doctrines have been taught and believed to be relevant to dying, it is best to enter each relationship with a dying person with an open mind. One must suspend temporarily the rational, cognitive certainties so carefully constructed for personal understanding and pay attention first and foremost to the unique dying person within one's pastoral care. One must be prepared to facilitate the death of another human being on that person's own terms, not merely within the framework of meaning that the pastor brings into the relationship.

Sensitive and creative pastoral care does not present a formula for meaning, but encourages the emergence of those themes from personal life that are best lifted up within the realm of faith, hope and love, for mutual experience and eventual transformation into new meaning within the context of awareness of God's loving presence. Sensitive and creative pastoral care of the dying does not provide an answer from the faith tradition before the individual's question is ever spoken, much less heard or understood. The role of pastoral care is to help bridge the gap between the individual's question and the experienced answer of the faith tradition. Ideally, this answer should be from the faith tradition already appropriated by the dying person.

Unfortunately, the context for pastoral care of the dying elderly is likely to be a hospital. Hospitals are best suited for the treatment of acute diseases, yet they are often poorly prepared for the treatment of a person with a terminal illness; hence, the development of the hospice concept. Fortunately, the pastor can still be the one who is willing and able, along with family members and close friends, to facilitate expression of the dying person's experience of illness.

a. Barriers. Because the pastor must enter the dying person's realm of meaning in order to render sensitive pastoral care, it is important that this ministry's paradoxical nature be recognized. No one, pastor included, is completely comfortable with the immediate, piercing realization of one's own personal death. This sort of awareness has been described as an *ego chill* that causes a shivering up and down the emotional spine. Because this chill is uncomfortable, there is an instinctive attempt to minimize or banish from awareness any partial identity with the dying person. One frequently observed mechanism of this kind is a "flight into faith" that has the characteristics of denial. Another is the reflexive and mechanistic "flight into ritual," be that ritual extemporaneous prayer, Bible reading, a rite of healing, or exhortation, or even the Eucharist. Faith, ritual and religious symbol each may have a vital role in pastoral care of the dying, of course. However, they need to be part of a conscious plan of care, not a means of soothing the pastor's ego chill.

Still another protective mechanism is simply avoidance. It is all too easy to avoid the dying person by focusing attention on the living, grieving family so that opportunities to enter the dying person's realm of meaning are minimized. Avoidance and flights into faith and ritual result from a natural inclination to avoid discomfort. The paradox comes from awareness of the dying person's need to be honest and open and therefore of the pastor's need to be honest and open yet at the same time not too vulnerable, since this often results in protective reactions that do not serve the cause of pastoral care.

Dying requires hard work. The dying person must cope with the disease process itself—pain, discomfort, loss of strength—and with a variety of other issues as well. Very little in the dying process is entirely new, however. How the person has coped with life's adversities on previous occasions will probably be replicated in greater or lesser fashion as the person copes with death.

b. The unknown. Since by definition a person dies only once, the process of dying is itself an unknown. Since death has become a phenomenon of old age, the dying person may have had few models of "how to die." Death is no longer experienced within the family in familiar surroundings across the life span. Now, death tends to happen in the hospital, beyond day-to-day experience. Therefore, not only is death itself the unknown, but the process of dying and the process of giving and receiving care during the latter phases of the illness are also likely to be unknowns. Characteristic attitudes toward the unknown are aroused, particularly in the early phases of dying. Where the unknown has been experienced in the past as threat, then the unknowns of dying will probably arouse fear until enough experience has been gained to lend predictability to the situation.

c. Loneliness. The dying person is often not in a position to mix with other people in a normal social fashion. Weakened, even bedridden, the dying person cannot engage in many social activities. Attending church may be impossible, for example, although listening to the service on the radio or on tape may contribute to a sense of participation in the community. There also comes a time when the dying person has less need for interaction with other people. Usually, however, this occurs nearer to the actual point of death, when the dying person has disengaged from much of life. Learning how to cope with loneliness when one's usual mechanisms for coping are blocked can be a significant aspect of the dying process. The mere presence of the pastor helps to ameliorate the loneliness and boredom that result from social isolation.

d. Grief. Loved ones may be grief stricken over the impending death of a significant family member, yet the dying person is giving up everybody and everything. Routine activities, cherished roles, and long-held dreams are being gradually lost. The loneliness of dying, as others necessarily go about living, implies partial loss of support from friends rarely seen. The grief of dying is therefore not all anticipatory grief. Much of it is present and ongoing, as one more activity, role, dream or person is stripped away.

Like the living who grieve, dying persons experience the entire range of human emotions — anger, fear, resignation, hope, denial, depression, humor, pain — as they cope with their losses. Yet, the process of dying is the backdrop that remains a part of each day. Pastoral care facilitates the experience and expression of self-grief, knowing that any emotion or longing is acceptable in the presence of God. The pastor's acceptance of the unacceptable, without soothing platitudes or flights into faith or ritual, can enable dying persons to accept the unacceptable in themselves, even celebrate the lowering of pretensions in their relationships to self and God.

e. Letting go. This may well be one of the more difficult aspects of dying. In previous decades the ideals and skills of mastery and self-control have been practiced, perhaps even overlearned, in a society that aggrandizes self-determination and the illusion of independence. Letting go is different from *giving up*, which implies a passive resignation to fate and a withdrawal of the inner self from others and even from reflective self-awareness. *Letting go* is an active process of trust, an opening up of the self to one's inability to control the future, an active giving over of the self to the care of One beyond human finitude. It is a blessing of personal dependence on others for a while, and on God forever. If life's delicate balance between control and dependence, trust and mistrust, should ever so gently tilt toward letting go at any point during the dying process, then surely the grace of God has been present. Pastoral care may enable this to happen, but faith is a gift from God.

Bibliography. G. W. Davidson, *Living With Dying* (1975). C. A. Garfield, ed., *Psychosocial Care of the Dying Patient* (1978). E. A. Grollman, ed., *Concerning Death: A Practical Guide for the Living* (1974). E. Kübler-Ross, *On Death and Dying* (1969). G. Kuykendall, "Care for the Dying: A Kübler-Ross Critique," *Theology Today*, 38 (1981), 37 – 48. W. W. Morris and I. M. Bader, eds., *Hoffman's Daily Needs and Interests of Older People*, 2d ed. (1983). T. C. Oden, *Pastoral Theology* (1983), ch. 18. G. Patterson, "Death, Dying, and the Elderly," in W. M. Clements, ed., *Ministry with the Aging* (1981), pp. 220 – 34. B. Spilka, J. D. Spangler, C. B. Nelson, "Spiritual Support in Life-Threatening Illness," *J. of Religion and Health*, 22 (1983), 98 – 104. B. Spilka, J. D. Spangler, and M.P. Rea, "The Role of Theology in Pastoral Care for the Dying," *Theology Today*, 38 (1981), 16 – 29. B. Spilka, J. D. Spangler, M. P. Rea, and C. B. Nelson, "Religion and Death: The Clerical Perspective," *J. of Religion and Health*, 20 (1981), 299 – 306. *Statistical Abstract of the United States,* 104th ed. (1984).

W. M. CLEMENTS

COMFORT/SUSTAINING; CRISIS MINISTRY; DEATH; ESCHATOLOGY AND PASTORAL CARE; GRIEF AND LOSS; HOPE AND DESPAIR; SICK AND DYING, JEWISH CARE OF. *See also* ANOINTING OF THE SICK, SACRAMENT OF; ART OF DYING (Ars Moriendi); GOD'S WILL, ACCEPTANCE OF; HOSPICE; LOSS OF FUNCTION; MORAL DILEMMAS IN PASTORAL PERSPECTIVE; PRAYER IN PASTORAL CARE; RITUAL AND PASTORAL CARE; SICK, PASTORAL CARE OF; SUFFERING; WILL TO LIVE. *Compare* NEAR-DEATH EXPERIENCE.

DYING CHILD AND FAMILY. A dying child confronts the family, the pastor, and the faith community not only with an anguishing crisis of meaning and faith, but also, dynamically, with a profound threat to the entire family system, its structure, functioning, roles, alliances, and emotional health. As individuals and as a unit, the family experiences extreme stress. Withdrawing from all external activities to manage the internal stress, isolation becomes an unanticipated result. Pastoral care requires, in addition to providing basic sustaining care, an understanding of these dynamics and methods of appropriate intervention when particular difficulties appear. It also often requires, at appropriate times, helping the child and family interpret their painful experience realistically and honestly through the resources of religious faith and community.

1. **Family Dynamics. *a. Child.*** The child facing death experiences many of the same emotions which any dying person faces: fear, anger, guilt. Communication of these emotions may be more difficult, however. The family's desire to protect the child (so thwarted in other areas) may establish patterns of communication which deny the child opportunities to express fears and concerns openly. Further, the child's verbal and cognitive skills are at a different level than those of adult family members.

The ability to conceptualize death is age-related. The very young child (two to three years) has little comprehension of the meaning of death. Children from three to five begin to understand it, but cannot comprehend its finality. From approximately ages six to nine, children tend to personify death, which may give them a sense of control through bargaining with this personified power.

The child who is frequently hospitalized senses the loss of authority which parents undergo during this time, and often becomes highly manipulative. As authority becomes vested in medical personnel, the child may experience strong fears of possible parental abandonment. Reassurance of parents' love and support, firm setting of limits to curb manipulation, and as much normal parenting as possible will do much to allay the child's natural fears.

b. Parents. Studies show that divorce rates following the death of a child can range from fifty to ninety percent. The stress on the marital relationship brought on by prolonged serious illness, frequent separation of the spouses due to the child's hospitalizations, feelings of guilt when leaving the child to find time together, all lead to gradual distancing in the marital relationship. The mother-child bonding tends to grow stronger as the mother withdraws from external concerns to care for her ill child; fathers generally assume greater responsibility over management of the household and other children. Patterns of isolation develop as each spouse seeks to protect the other from a portion of the burden, and as other potential resource people withdraw out of respect for their privacy and grief. Mothers lose their ordinary means of self-fulfillment: work identity, spouse relationship, normal parenting role. Fathers suffer many of the same losses. Career decisions must be made in light of health insurance, financial concerns, and medical care availability. In addition to added family responsibilities, a parent may need an additional job to pay high medical expenses. When significant medical decisions must be made, a frequent source of conflict between spouses arises over quantity versus quality of life decisions.

c. Siblings. Brothers and sisters are often protected from knowledge of what is happening. Nevertheless, they perceive the rearrangement of the family structure and functions, and sense highly charged emotions. Provocative behavior, accident proneness, and feelings that nothing ought to be enjoyed are usually engendered by feelings of guilt. Siblings need opportunities to resolve old quarrels, to be told that they are not responsible for the child's illness, and that they are loved and will be cared for despite the tragedy. Siblings can become the innocent recipients of parental anger over the injustice of the illness. Children may even invoke this anger to gain parental attention, or to bring parents out of depression and grief. Siblings may feel angry themselves over the death, and may fear and fantasize about their own death. They may also feel anger at the dying child for usurping so much time, attention, and affection.

d. Grandparents. Grandparents exhibit a threefold grief: for themselves, for their children, and for their grandchild. They may express difficulty in accepting the diagnosis, placing parents in the awkward position of defending it. Open communication between parents and grandparents may provide important emotional resources.

2. **Communication Patterns.** It is important to realize that family communication patterns during a child's terminal illness were developed as part of the family system prior to the illness. Patterns which were previously effective may become dysfunctional when challenged by this stress, while former communication problems are magnified by it. A pattern of flexible openness seems to best serve both the dying child and the restructuring family system, even though it sometimes brings the threat of difficult questions and possible chaos. Mutual pretense (both child and parent know the truth, but pretend they do not) is a pattern which allows family roles to be maintained. Denial (closed awareness) may be an appropriate response at certain times, e.g. when gathering emotional strength to face a crisis or during times of remission when life can proceed normally. Overly used, however, closed communication patterns lead to isolation of individuals and preclude intimacy.

Christian faith is often employed as a denial mechanism. Pastoral intervention which enables families to move toward more open sharing of painful emotions can broaden and deepen the family's faith system, as members struggle openly with their pain in the context of faith.

3. **Restructured Family.** Loss of any family member results in the temporary collapse of the family structure because its integrity is severely disrupted. The family must adapt to the loss by shifting roles, affections, and alliances. If this is not done intentionally, someone may suffer in the process. This new balance is obtained at great cost, and against a background of pervasive loss. A family whose former structure was rigid will have greater difficulty than the family with a flexible structure.

Children may be emancipated before they are ready. This is particularly likely to happen to children not physically present in the home. Sometimes a child will be "parentified" (cast into the role of a parent) when the parents find themselves needing support in their grief. This child may bypass his or her grief in order to fulfill the family need, but it will eventually surface in other ways. The child who appears to accept the death without a struggle is the one statistically most likely to have problems later. Open communication and flexibility allow the family to experiment until a satisfactory new system emerges.

4. **Pastoral Care.** Often the simple presence of the pastor is enough to begin opening channels of communication. The most important focus for pastoral support and counseling is the marital couple; the dying child and siblings are best supported by the parents themselves. Restoring the couple's ability to address each other's needs is vital. Recreation should be encouraged. Discovering which tasks are currently overwhelming the spouses that others might perform, and mobilizing support networks among family, church members, and friends, can lighten the burden. Persons are usually available and willing, but reluctant to intrude without invitation. Breaking down the isolation of individuals and of the family unit is essential. Helping the family to see its structural patterns which emerged during the illness and afterwards may be helpful in identifying who may be getting left out, who is being relied on too heavily, or who may be assuming an inappropriate role. As the pastor perceives areas of potential dysfunction, preventive parent counseling may resolve problems before they become more serious. Supporting, promoting, and enabling covenantal relationships between spouses, family members, and family and faith community is an important goal of pastoral care.

It is unusual today for a child to be considered dying until shortly before death occurs. Medical terminology has shifted from "terminal" to "life threatening illness," embodying an important shift in the religious interpretation process as well. The nature of God's role in the world, particularly in relation to this crisis event, becomes critically important. How do human actions and responses effect God's actions? Parental anguish in the face of overwhelming helplessness usually results in regression to early childhood beliefs about God, miracles, prayer, and illness as punishment for sins (real or imagined). Thus, the particular religious questions which arise must always be addressed in the context of the particular family and its history. To assume that all persons bring the same questions to their experiences, or that the same question means the same thing to different families, is to miss the particularity in which ministry will be most meaningful. For example, "Why is my sister (daughter) dying?" may be responded to by the pastor as if it were a theological question, yet it may be a request for better medical information; it may be a cry of anguish which needs to be heard rather than answered; it may be the beginnings of a confession of sin (by patient, parent, or sibling) which must be taken seriously before forgiveness can be experienced. Initial religious questions are usually reflective of only secondary, and thus safer, concerns. An atmosphere in which questions (and even rage at God) are considered faithful responses to tragedy will allow the deeper questions and pain to surface. Only then can pastor and person bring these particular, ultimate questions before God, and together discover ways to live faithfully toward some glimpse of meaning.

A relationship of trust, built by quiet listening and honest answering, is imperative in speaking with children about religious issues. Allow the child to lead the conversation; keep answers as simple as possible; proceed no further than the child indicates a readiness to hear. Children whose previous experiences have given them a sense of basic trust in others will be better able to trust that God will continue to care for them during this difficult time, and after death. The pastor's presence implicitly embodies this presence and love of God in their lives.

Bibliography. M. Bluebond-Langner, *The Private Worlds of Dying Children* (1978). R. W. Buckingham, *A Special Kind of Love: Care of the Dying Child* (1983). J. Claypool, *Tracks of a Fellow Struggler: How to Handle Grief* (1982 [1974]). K. Doka, "Pastoral Counseling to the Dying Child", *J. of Pastoral Counseling*, 15 (1980), 34–40. W. M. Easson, *The Dying Child*, 2d. ed. (1981). E. Grollman, *Talking About Death: A Dialogue Between Parent and Child* (1970). R. Hare-Mustin, "Family Therapy Following the Death of a Child", *J. of Marital and Family Therapy*, 5 (1979), 51–8. F. Herz, "The Impact of Death and Serious Illness on the Family Life Cycle," in *The Family Life Cycle: A Framework for Therapy*, E. Carter and M. McGoldrick, eds. (1980), pp. 223–40. J. Kisner, "A Family Systems Approach to Grief," *Pastoral Psychology*, 28 (1980), 265–76. T. Krulik, B. Holaday, and I. Martinson, *The Child and Family Facing Life-Threatening Illness* (1987). E. Kübler-Ross, *On Children and Death* (1983). I. Moriarty, "Mourning the Death of an Infant: The Siblings Story," *J. of Pastoral Care*, 32 (1978), 22–33. E. M. Pattison, *The Experience of Dying* (1977). T. A. Rando, *Parental Loss of a Child* (1986). O. J. Sahler, ed., *The Child and Death* (1978), esp. Section I: "The Family and the Fatally Ill Child." H. S. Schiff, *The Bereaved Parent* (1977).

R. W. Willis, "Some Concerns of Bereaved Parents," *J. of Religion and Health*, 20 (1981), 33–40.

H. S. NELSON

COMFORT/SUSTAINING; DYING, PASTORAL CARE OF; GRIEF AND LOSS; SICK AND DYING, JEWISH CARE OF. *See also* CHILDREN; DEATH; GRIEF AND LOSS IN CHILDHOOD AND ADOLESCENCE; HOPE AND DESPAIR.

DYNAMIC INTERPERSONALISM. A comprehensive theory of ministerial practice developed by Paul E. Johnson, a pioneer in the pastoral psychology and counseling movement. Essentially a synthesis of the personalism of Edgar Sheffield Brightman, Harry Stack Sullivan's interpersonal psychiatry, the individual psychology of Gordon W. Allport, and the liberal theology of Paul Tillich, dynamic interpersonalism represents an attempt to form a comprehensive theory of personality capable of undergirding a variety of expressions of ministry, particularly pastoral care and counseling. Much of Johnson's emphasis was on the necessity of holding to an *open* system in which communal aspects are fully appreciated, holding that no person is truly a person in himself or herself alone, but only as she or he enters into mutual relationship with other persons. Johnson's conviction that a Christian praxis ought to be based on many systems of inquiry (theology, psychology, sociology, anthropology, etc.) may be contrasted to those which hold that the base of pastoral counseling must be theological or biblical alone.

Bibliography. P. E. Johnson, *Person and Counselor* (1967); "The Trend Toward Dynamic Interpersonalism," *Religion in Life,* 35 (1966), 750–52. O. Strunk, Jr., ed., *Dynamic Interpersonalism for Ministry* (1973).

O. STRUNK, JR.

PERSONALISM AND PASTORAL CARE. *Compare* INTERPERSONAL THEORY; PERSON; PERSONALITY THEORY (Varieties, Traditions, and Issues). *Biography:* JOHNSON.

DYNAMIC PSYCHOLOGY. A psychology concerned with mental forces or mental energy, most generally emphasizing motivation, will, affects, and the unconscious. The phrase "dynamic psychology" was apparently coined by Robert Woodworth around 1910. The single term "dynamic" was probably first used by Leibnitz, who contrasted it with "static" and "cinematic" in physics. Herbart applied the term to psychology, distinguishing static from dynamic states of consciousness. The French physiologists used the term to contrast functional paralyses with organic ones. By the time Hughlings Jackson adopted the term in 1874, "it designated the physiological aspect in contrast to the anatomic, the functional in contrast to the organic, the regressive in contrast to the status quo, and it expressed at the same time the energetic aspect, even including at times the connotation of conflict and resistance" (Ellenberger, 1970, pp. 290–91).

1. **Historical Origins.** The principal source of dynamic psychotherapies and dynamic psychiatry lies in the work of the early mesmerists and hypnotists. Van Helmont's "animal magnetism" was used as a healing force by Gassner, Mesmer, the brothers de Puysegur, and many

others in France, Germany, and England during the seventeenth and eighteenth centuries. During the nineteenth century, mesmerism was transformed into hypnotism and applied as an anesthetic (by Elliotson, Esdaile, and Braid) as well as a therapeutic method (by Liebault and Charcot). Applications of hypnotism culminated in Janet's theory of hysteria, Freud's development of free association, and Morton Prince's research on dissociation.

A second source of dynamic psychology was the act psychology begun by Leibnitz, who stressed the activity and unity of the mind, and hinted at an unconscious in a doctrine of degrees of consciousness. Herbart developed this notion of a "limen of consciousness" (a threshold into consciousness), which was later tested experimentally by Fechner. Later act psychologists stressed the notion of active ideas and motives as basic to conceptions of conflict and theories of motivation.

A third source lies in the motivational doctrine of hedonism begun by Hobbes, who regarded motives as being based on expectations of pleasure and pain. This doctrine was continued in the works of Locke, Hartley, Bentham, and the Mills, culminating in the twentieth century in Thorndike's Law of Effect (responses that have satisfying consequences are strengthened while those followed by discomfort are weakened) and Freud's pleasure principle.

2. Major Dynamic Psychologists. Sigmund Freud was probably the greatest of the dynamic psychologists. He regarded the unconscious as active, striving, and powerful, and regression as a sign of conflict between the ego and unconscious desires. Another great dynamist was William McDougall, who challenged the mechanical nature of behaviorism and pleaded for a "purposive behaviorism," developing his hormic psychology as a prime example. McDougall regarded instincts as goal-directed, liberating their energy to guide the organism toward a goal. This purposive notion reappeared in E. C. Tolman's learning theory, the cognitive psychology of E. B. Holt, and the various psychologies of attitude and set.

Other dynamic psychologies of major importance are those of Robert Woodworth, Kurt Lewin, and Henry Murray. Woodworth stressed the organism's role as an intervening variable between stimulus and response. Lewin, in his field theory, regarded persons as mobile organisms, attracted by positive valences or goals and repelled by negative ones. He emphasized the concept of tension in describing motivations and needs. Murray formulated a list of needs very similar to McDougall's listing of instincts. Influenced by all these theorists, Gordon Allport epitomized the dynamic personality theorist.

Bibliography. The history of clinical dynamic psychologies and psychiatries may be found in: H. Ellenberger, *The Discovery of the Unconscious* (1970). G. Zilboorg and G. W. Henry, *A History of Medical Psychology* (1969). L. Weatherhead, *Psychology, Religion and Healing* (1951). A review of developments in academic dynamic psychology may be found in: E. G. Boring, *A History of Experimental Psychology* (1950) ch. 26. E. Heidbreder, *Seven Psychologies* (1933) ch. 8. A. A. Roback, *History of American Psychology* (1952) chs. 20–22. For an application to theology, see S. Hiltner, *Theological Dynamics* (1972).

H. VANDE KEMP

PSYCHOANALYSIS, ANALYTICAL, *or* HUMANISTIC PSYCHOLOGY; PSYCHOLOGY. *See also* EMOTION; HYPNOSIS; MOTIVATION; PSYCHIC ENERGY; UNCONSCIOUS; WILL/WILLING. *Compare* CAUSALITY IN PSYCHOLOGY; COGNITIVE/CONATIVE PROBLEM IN PSYCHOLOGY AND COUNSELING; FACULTY PSYCHOLOGY; MODELS IN PSYCHOLOGICAL AND PASTORAL THEORY.

D'YOUVILLE, MARIE-MARGUERITE. *See* WOMEN IN PASTORAL MINISTRIES, HISTORY OF.

DYSFUNCTION, SEXUAL. *See* DYSFUNCTION AND SEX THERAPY.

DYSLEXIA. *See* DEVELOPMENTAL DISORDERS; LEARNING DISABILITY.

E

EARLY CHURCH, PASTORAL CARE AND COUNSELING IN. Study of pastoral care in the early church covers two periods: the period in which it was illegal to be a Christian in the Roman Empire, and the period in which Christianity was not only legalized but also was the favored religion of the empire. For the purposes of this article the first begins after the writing of the last book of the NT and ends with the last persecution of Christians at the beginning of the fourth century. The second is inaugurated by the emperor Constantine and the rise of monasticism. Where the early church ends and the church of the Middle Ages begins is harder to determine, but again for the purposes of this article, we will arbitrarily cut off with Gregory the Great's *Pastoral Care.*

The content of pastoral care in the early church was shaped by two assumptions that both pre- and post-Constantinians made about the care of Christians. First, that while each person was responsible for the living out of her or his own Christian faith, to be a Christian meant to function as a member of the Christian community. Pastoral care was therefore strongly oriented toward the needs of the whole community, rather than those simply of the individual apart from the community. Second, that human beings were made in the image of God, and only as they functioned as the image of God could they be whole and healthy people. This image included rationality, with its two major components: the ability to choose the good and the ability to love. Pastoral care, then, also was directed to helping the individual live in accordance with that image, in spite of conflicts that person might have with the larger culture. In pre-Constantinian Christianity we see these assumptions especially in their dealing with martyrdom and the question of post-baptismal sin; in post-Constantinian Christianity they are particularly visible in the rise of monasticism and the way it affected the larger church.

1. Pre-Constantinian Pastoral Care: The Integrity of the Community. Pre-Constantinian Christianity can be characterized by its relationship to the world of its time: it was in the world but not of it. On the one hand,

in the Roman Empire of the period, it was illegal to be a Christian; Christians were identified as atheists who were undermining the state. On the other hand, Christians lived in communities which did, indeed, reject a good number of ordinary careers as threatening Christian integrity by the way in which they were entwined with state religion. A large proportion of pastoral care during the period, therefore, had to be directed to three interrelated areas: (a) preservation of a tradition handed faithfully from one generation of Christians to the next, (b) preservation of the purity of the church and its faithful members, and (c) support and help for those who needed to lay down their lives for the sake of their witness to the Christian truth.

a. Preservation of tradition. Though there was such a thing as infant baptism, most people entered the Christian community during this period through adult baptism. It was a basic conviction of the early church that to be a Christian one must have both a knowledge of and faith in Christian realities as they were handed down through the apostles, and a lifestyle in which one lived out these realities. Baptism, therefore, was preceded by a three-year catechumenate for the thorough training of the new Christian in doctrine, worship, and lifestyle. Training of the catechumens, therefore, would have been one major task of pastoral care.

A good deal of time, apparently, was also spent in the further development of Christian character after baptism as we see, for example, by the writings of Clement of Alexandria (ca. 200) and Origen of Alexandria (d. 253). In this enterprise the early church drew upon and thoroughly Christianized some of the traditions and literature of the pagan philosophical schools of their day, especially in their understanding of psychology and the virtues.

b. Preservation of the purity of the church. Baptism, during this period, was held to bring about the forgiveness of any sins committed before baptism. Christian communities at this time strongly emphasized love and care for one another, both emotionally and physically. Individual sin after baptism, therefore, was understood to threaten both the community and the individual. The three major sins of adultery, murder, and apostasy committed after baptism were particularly serious. Another major area of pastoral care, therefore, was dealing with post-baptismal sin.

Tertullian, a North African churchman of the second century, believed that the ethical requirements on Christians were stricter than they had been for the ancient Israelites. Putting great emphasis on the need for purity within Christian communities, he believed that while there could be one repentance for minor sin after baptism, there could be no further sinning and repenting of that sort. Furthermore, after baptism there could be no repentance for the three most serious sins of apostasy, adultery, and murder. Dispute over these rigorous standards caused a serious breach in the North African church that continued into the time of Augustine's battle with the Donatists.

On the more tolerant side, however, the *Shepherd of Hermas*, a widely used early second-century document, taught that God accepts repentance for one sin committed after baptism, apparently even for apostasy or adultery. Hermas at this point is representative of the main thrust of the church that persisted well into the Constantinian period in the West (as late as the sixth century), where repentance was permitted for only one sin after baptism.

It is important to note that the repentance of which we are speaking in this early period was not a private matter between God and the individual, or the individual and the priest: it required public humiliation and confession to the congregation, begging its forgiveness, followed by a long public penance. The stages of this penance, and the length of time each stage took, were gradually institutionalized over the centuries that followed. By the end of the fourth century in the East, Gregory of Nyssa, for example, was recommending a twenty-seven-year period of penance for murder.

c. Martyrdom and apostasy. Because Christianity was illegal during this period, the possibility of persecution was part of the expectation of what it meant to be a Christian. Persecution was sporadic, sometimes consisting of mob harassment, sometimes of neighbor denouncing neighbor to the government, sometimes of organized and systematic persecution by the government. In every place, however, it was understood that the Christian might be called upon at some time to lay down her or his life in martyrdom in order finally to fulfill the calling of the Christian.

A major pastoral concern during times of persecution was the encouraging of those who were to be martyred, to firm them up and remind them of the witness they were about to make to the world, of their ability to set tender family ties aside for the sake of Christ, and of their lack of fear of death because of their trust in its defeat by the Resurrection. We see the kind of pastoral situation martyrdom created in a very early account, the *Martyrdom of Perpetua*.

The martyrdom of the leadership of a community presented a special problem in the pastoral care of the community. We see a pastoral response to such a threat in the letters Bishop Ignatius of Antioch sent to the Christian communities to which he wrote on the way to his own martyrdom in Rome. These letters were intended to strengthen the commitment and resolve of the communities over against this threat, teaching them to understand martyrdom as the highest form of Christian witness both to the community itself and to those outside the community.

The worst pastoral problem created by martyrdom, however, was how to deal with those who had either run away from it or who had given in under it, betraying both God and the community. Congregations all over the empire were torn by the conflict between those who believed apostasy of this sort was unforgiveable, and those who believed that this, too, could be forgiven after repentance and a proper period of penance. Many of those who advocated forgiveness had themselves been tortured or imprisoned and survived. In North Africa, the Donatists, rigorists who rejected forgiveness for apostasy, believed that only by such rigorism could the faithful transmission of apostolic tradition be maintained and baptisms thus be valid. The split in the church over this issue was serious enough to last into the Arab conquests of the seventh and eighth centuries.

2. **Post-Constantinian Pastoral Care.** The last serious persecution of Christians began under the emperor Diocletian in 303. In 312, Constantine recognized Christianity as the favored religion of the empire, and with the exception of the situation under Julian the Apostate, from that time on Christianity was entwined with the life of the state. Martyrdom had come to an end, and pastors were faced with a new problem: how to keep Christianity from simply merging with and absorbing the non-Christian culture around it.

a. The monastic ideal. The rise of monasticism offered both a direct and an indirect solution. At the end of the third century, Anthony, the orphan of Egyptian peasant parents, responded to the biblical story of the rich young ruler by divesting himself of all he owned in order eventually to move into the Egyptian desert as the first monk. Soon, others took up the life in loose groups, or solitarily, and a few years later, another Egyptian, Pachomius, founded the first organized communities. By the end of Anthony's life in 356, the Egyptian desert held thousands of men and women, and monasticism was thriving in Palestine and Syria as well. At the beginning of the sixth century Benedict of Nursia became the founder of monasticism in the West.

Though there were some monastics who held themselves apart from the world, for most of them the goal of monastic life was the perfect love of God and neighbor. The route to this love was a long training that was based in a psychology of the day originally drawn from Plato, but also containing Stoic elements. In its monastic version, human beings were created in the image of God; this meant the were made able to know God, choose the good, and love. As a result of the Fall, however, their vision was distorted by the presence of the passions — obsessive or otherwise destructive states of mind or habitual behavior that make love impossible. One of the main concerns of those who took up this life was the defeat of the passions and the restoration of the image of God.

b. Monastic care and counseling. In early monasticism, the person (rarely a priest) who exercised pastoral care over these men and women was the *abba* (male) or the *amma* (female). The first job of the *abba* or *amma* was the formation of the monastic Christian character. Working from the principle that each person has different spiritual needs, dependent upon that person's disposition, strong points, and passions, the disciple would reveal all his or her thoughts to the teacher who would work with the disciple to determine that person's individual needs. Because their passions very often made them blind to their true condition, the disciples trusted the *abba* or *amma* to understand the disciple's thoughts, words, and body language, sometimes better than the disciple. Once the diagnosis was made, the *amma* or *abba* recommended a course of behavior to the disciple for the control of the passions based on the needs and strengths of that individual. The enormous variety in types of pastoral care, depending on the different personalities of teachers and students, is remarkable.

Evagrius Ponticus (d. 399) was one of the most influential of these teachers. With great psychological insight, he not only understood the passions in great depth but also gave advice about analyzing dreams with respect to the passions, and advised keeping a journal record of the occasions of passions in order to control them. Through John Cassian and, later, Gregory the Great, his influence was as great in the West as in the East.

What they all had in common, however, was the goal of love in the Christian life, and in order to achieve it, they advocated a very strong policy of being non-judgmental and forgiving toward those who sinned. In the light of the importance of the question of post-baptismal sin in the pre-Constantinian era, as well as in the church in the West during this period, their position was truly radical. One *abba*, for example, was asked about the appropriate length of penance for serious sin; he replied that, if a person were truly repentant, a few days would be enough.

Increasingly as time went on in this period, the leadership of the church was drawn from monastic circles, and it would appear that in certain circles there was some conflict over whether celibacy was an ideal for non-monastics as well as monastics. Very early, Syrian Christianity had not thought it possible for Christians to be both baptized and married. Though the church firmly rejected such a position, tensions remained, intensified by the ambiguity with which sexuality was regarded in society as a whole at that time.

c. Congregational care and counseling. Within the larger society, individual holy men served an important function by exercising a pastoral leadership that overlapped with priestly pastoral care to a considerable extent. Holy men are seen from the fourth century onward, especially in the East, offering counseling help on an individual basis to lay people in matters ranging from marital problems and land disputes to taxation and other difficulties with the government.

Apart from this, clergy dealt with their congregations as they had in the past, but with the interesting addition of extensive pastoral correspondence, as we see in numerous collections of letters from the period. The letters of Theodoret of Cyhrrus (ca. 393–ca. 466), for example, illustrate a pastor's ability to offer his parishioners condolences, exhort them to generosity toward refugees

from North Africa fleeing barbarian invasions, and give out various advice on public and private matters, drawing both on scriptural language and classical pagan literary motifs.

Around 591 in the West, Gregory the Great (pope from 590) wrote a handbook of pastoral care for bishops called *Pastoral Care*. In this classic document Gregory incorporates and systematizes most of the theological insights and methods of ancient monastic pastoral care, drawing particularly on the influence of Evagrius Ponticus from whom he took the notion of the seven deadly sins. This work, though lacking in subtlety compared to the writings of the desert fathers, provided a useful system of pastoral practice and remained the most influential piece of writing on pastoral care well into the Middle Ages.

Bibliography. R. C. Bondi, *To Love As God Loves* (1987). W. Clebsch and C. Jaekle, *Pastoral Care in Historical Perspective* (1964). J. McNeill, *A History of the Cure of Souls* (1951). T. Oden, *Care of Souls in the Classic Tradition* and *Pastoral Theology* (1983). Oden's books provide helpful bibliographies. Useful collections of ancient pastoral writings include "The Sayings of the Fathers" in O. Chadwick, trans. and ed., *Western Asceticism* (1958); B. Ward, trans. and ed., *The Sayings of the Desert Fathers* (1975). Gregory's *Pastoral Care* is in Henry Davis, trans., *Ancient Christian Writers*, Vol. 2 (1950).

R. C. BONDI

PASTORAL CARE (History, Traditions, and Definitions). *See also* MINISTRY AND PASTORAL CARE (Orthodox Tradition); ETHICS AND PASTORAL CARE; PHILOSOPHY AND PSYCHOLOGY; ROMAN CATHOLIC PASTORAL CARE. *Compare* JEWISH CARE AND COUNSELING (History, Traditions, and Contemporary Issues); MEDIEVAL CHURCH, PASTORAL CARE IN. *Biography:* GREGORY THE GREAT; HERMAS; TERTULLIAN OF CARTHAGE.

EAST ASIAN PASTORAL CARE MOVEMENT.

The Pastoral Counseling movement in East Asia has not developed as rapidly as in Southeast Asia mainly for two reasons: English is not commonly used in daily life in Japan, Korea and Taiwan, and cultural tradition. In these countries family ties are so close that it has not been the custom to bring personal or family troubles to someone outside the family circle. It was considered a disgrace to do so. However, rapid industrial development followed by urbanization has undermined the traditional function of the family, and the need for assistance from individuals and/or agencies outside the family has been increasing. It is in this situation that pastoral counseling has been accepted and need for it has been growing.

Japan. In 1951 American educators led by W. P. Lloyd visited Japan and suggested promotion of student counseling, which resulted in a visit by Carl Rogers in 1952. Rogers made a lecture tour all over Japan and made an enormous impact on schoolteachers. Thus school counseling and vocational guidance permeated the schools rather quickly. In the church setting, however, it came very slowly. In 1953, W. P. Browning, an American missionary, started to teach pastoral counseling at Tokyo Union Theological Seminary. In the late 1950s and early 1960s a few Japanese pastors who studied in the U.S. came back and started to teach at other seminaries. But it was not until 1964 that the term "pastoral counseling" began to be heard more widely in the church. In this year, the first Japanese version of CPE was held at Kyoto Baptist Hospital, featuring Paul E. Johnson as guest speaker. About sixty pastors participated in a week-long program. After this, for several years, a week or ten days of CPE was held each year at different Christian hospitals; this continued until the students' riots in the 1970s.

Meanwhile, the Japan Institute of Pastoral Counseling (JIPC) was organized in 1963 and began publishing a journal. Basic books by Wayne Oates, Seward Hiltner, and Howard Clinebell were translated into Japanese. Kwansai Pastoral Counseling Center in Kobe and Growth Counseling Center in Tokyo began functioning in the early 1980s followed by Christian Counseling Center in Tokyo in the mid-1980s. In 1984 the Second Asian Conference on Pastoral Care and Counseling was held in Tokyo. Nearly one hundred people attended this conference, including Clinebell and other American leaders in the field. As a result of this conference the Pastoral Care and Counseling Association of Japan (PCCAJ) was organized to be a more inclusive body, which may enable it to have a more powerful impact upon the Japanese Christian church in the future.

Korea. Pastoral counseling began to be taught in 1956 at the Methodist Seminary in Seoul. As the Christian church grew, the need for pastoral counseling became more urgent in theological education. Pastors who studied in the U.S. came back to teach at different seminaries. Many basic books were translated into Korean, and CPE began to be offered at the Department of Theology and Graduate School of Yonsei University in cooperation with Severence Hospital.

Taiwan. The contribution of Mackay Christian Hospital is notable. In 1962 a counseling room was started in that hospital. The chief psychiatrist of Taiwan University Medical School backed up the program, and it was officially approved in 1967. In 1970 a masters program in pastoral counseling led by Theodore Cole was opened at Taiwan Theological School in cooperation with the Graduate Theological School of Southeast Asia. With financial help of the American church a family counseling center was opened in Taipei in 1971, which was later incorporated into the counseling center of Mackay Hospital.

Another influential center is Changhua Christian Hospital, under the leadership of Peter Hsian Chih Shih. When he came back to Taiwan after a year's study in the U.S., he started CPE at this hospital in 1967. The next year he extended the program to a six-weeks course and held it five times a year. In 1977 he started a supervision course, which became a three-year program beginning in 1986. In 1975 the Taiwan CPE Association was organized with three Christian hospitals, Mackay, Changhua, and Catholic Hospital.

T. NISHIGAKI

PASTORAL CARE MOVEMENT. *Compare* PSYCHOLOGY AND PSYCHOTHERAPY (East-West Comparison); SOUTH ASIAN PASTORAL CARE MOVEMENT.

EASTER. *See* LITURGICAL CALENDAR. *See also* CHRISTOLOGY AND PASTORAL CARE; CROSS AND RESURRECTION; HOLIDAY DEPRESSION.

EASTERN EUROPEAN PASTORAL CARE MOVEMENT. Professor Otto Haendler, one of the pioneers of the pastoral care movement in Eastern Europe, commented that after World War II "the era of the sermon changed to the era of pastoral care." Because he believed that the work of Freud, Adler, and Jung could promote and deepen the work of pastoral care, Haendler began to make use of their theories in his teaching. Particularly influenced by Jung, Haendler realized and taught that one can only accept another person to the degree that one has accepted oneself. His work was influential with a number of subsequent leaders in the movement in both Eastern and Western Europe, such as Joachim Scharfenberg, Klaus Winkler, Hans-Joachim Thilo, and Heinrich Fink.

In the early 1970s pastors of the socialist countries came in contact with the pastoral care movement in the U.S. The work of Heije Faber, a Dutch pastoral theologian who had studied in the U.S., was particularly influential. The major psychological influence, however, was the work of Carl Rogers, whose methods were seen to be consistent with Christian teaching. Rogers's understanding of human beings, however, presented theoretical problems because its humanistic optimism contrasted radically with the theological view that the human being can be healed and saved only by God. The acceptance of Rogers' methods and the questioning of his theories was a major point of discussion within the Eastern European pastoral care movement.

In 1975 the conversation with the West, which had taken place primarily through psychological and pastoral care literature, became more direct and personal. In that year, for the first time, ministers from East Germany had the opportunity to participate in an international pastoral care conference at the Baptist Seminary at Ruschlikon, near Zurich, Switzerland. In 1977 the first pastoral care conference held in a socialist country, which involved persons from both Eastern and Western Europe, took place in Eisenach, (German Democratic Republic). There were also observers from other parts of the world, including the U.S. This conference was the impetus for the formation of a national pastoral care organization in East Germany, which has provided for the extensive interchange of experience and thus stimulated improvement in the quality of pastoral care in the churches. This positive development was continued by two conferences following in the subsequent four years, one in Western Europe, in Edinburgh, Scotland, and one in the East, at the Catholic University in Lublin, Poland.

Clinical Pastoral Education in Eastern Europe takes place in a number of clinical centers, for example, Halle, Berlin, and Halberstadt. One of the first East German supervisors, Günther Steinacker, at the Deaconess Hospital in Halle, conducts a training program that involves essentially the same elements as American CPE: daily visits in the hospital; the writing of verbatims; individual supervisory sessions; group sessions designed to aid self-awareness and self-expression; daily meditation on biblical texts; relaxation training, etc. The clinical course is approximately six weeks in duration. CPE-type training also takes place in the theological faculties of universities, especially at Rostock, Leipzig, Halle, and Jena.

In addition to hospital training, in a number of places East German pastors meet together under the leadership of a supervisor to examine their pastoral experiences and to increase their self-awareness. A book, *Seelsorgepraxis: Erfahrungen, Klärungen, Erkenntnisse* (1981), describes what is actually happening in these counseling groups. The bishops of the churches of the German Democratic Republic are interested in and supportive of both types of clinical training.

The present situation in Eastern European pastoral care is characterized by two contrasting tendencies: a strong interest in modern psychological methods, and a recovery of the pastoral tradition. Pastors are thoroughly convinced that the contributions of modern secular psychotherapy should be integrated into pastoral practice. The work of Freud, Adler, Jung, Fromm, and Rogers has been particularly influential. Rogers's greatest influence has been to encourage pastors toward a greater awareness of feeling and self-expression. On the other hand, there has been a conviction that pastoral interaction should not be limited to a focus on feelings alone, which has led to an emphasis upon wisdom from the classical pastoral tradition. Augustine, Gregory the Great, Luther, Taylor, and Schleiermacher, representing the consensual mainstream of the ecumenical pastoral care tradition, have been the chief contributors and demonstrated their enduring practical usefulness. The pastoral care movement in Eastern Europe has been in touch with both the worldwide pastoral care movement and the pastoral tradition of the Christian church.

W. SAFT

PASTORAL CARE MOVEMENT; INTERNATIONAL PASTORAL CARE MOVEMENT. *Compare* WESTERN EUROPEAN PASTORAL CARE MOVEMENT. *Biography:* FABER.

EASTERN ORTHODOX TRADITION. *See* MINISTRY AND PASTORAL CARE (Orthodox Tradition). *See also* DIVORCE AND REMARRIAGE (Orthodoxy); LITERATURE IN CARE AND COUNSELING (Orthodoxy); ORTHODOX-PROTESTANT *or* ORTHODOX-CATHOLIC MARRIAGE; SACRAMENTAL THEOLOGY AND PASTORAL CARE, ORTHODOX; SPIRITUALITY (Orthodox Tradition).

EASTERN RELIGION, SOUL CARE, AND PSYCHOLOGY. *See* PSYCHOLOGY, EASTERN. *See also* NEW RELIGIOUS MOVEMENTS; PSYCHOLOGY AND PSYCHOTHERAPY (East-West Comparison).

EATING AND DRINKING. While these behaviors are normally related to the body's acquisition of nutrients, they are also intimately associated with the way a person relates to himself or herself, other people, the world, and even God. To know the manner, quantity, and context in which a person eats and drinks is to know something about his or her psychosocial makeup. Food and drink have such intense emotional significance that they are often linked with events in the spiritual, personal, and interpersonal dimensions of life that have nothing directly to do with nutrition.

Sigmund Freud underscored the basic developmental significance of eating and drinking patterns in his theory of the earliest ("oral") phase of psychosexual development. During this phase the child's life centers around the mouth and its functions. Psychoanalytic theory traces a number of human character traits to the experiences and drives of this oral phase. If, in the initial oral sucking period, the child has an emotionally and physically satisfying experience, this theory holds that he or she may identify with the nurturing mother and begin to develop as generous, altruistic, and self-assured. Frustrations or conflicts encountered in this phase may lead to pessimism and overdependence on others for personal needs. In the later oral biting period the child becomes more aggressive and independent. Ambivalence experienced at this time may lead to unresolved anger and insecurity. Insatiable appetite and alcoholism are human conditions which are purported to originate in difficulties experienced during the oral phase.

Fritz Perls carried oral aggression and human development a step further. For Perls, aggression is necessary to individual growth as a person assimilates the world. To be assimilated as a healthy, integral part of one's self, nourishment — whether mental, physical, emotional, or spiritual — must be digested. This requires aggressive destruction of the structure of the nourishment. Thus, the use of the mouth becomes a paradigm for the way a person relates to and integrates his or her world. If natural oral aggression is blocked, the person is reluctant to chew or even bite, and he or she may relate to the world by swallowing it whole (introjection) or putting the reluctance to chew or bite on someone else (projection) or on an introjected part of him or herself (retroflection). In Perls's view, the blockage must be confronted and the natural chewing and digesting allowed to proceed in order to avoid or remedy personality disorder.

Not only are eating and drinking patterns related to personal development, but also to human social systems. In his work with anorexics and bulimics in the family context, Salvadore Minuchin notes that these patterns of eating are functional in maintaining family stability where enmeshed and disengaged relationships between family members exist. Kintner, *et al.* (1981) and Moos, *et al.* (1977) empirically substantiate that family members exhibit the values of the family environment through their own eating and drinking behaviors. In general, families with poor eating and drinking habits tend to be dysfunctional, exhibiting a high level of conflict, control, and organization while those with good eating and drinking patterns appear functional, cohesive, expressive, independent, and exhibit an active relational orientation.

Patterns of eating and drinking are also related to religious experience. Offering food or drink or abstaining from them (fasting) are symbolic ways in many societies of showing devotion to deities. Significant religious events are celebrated with festivals centered on eating and drinking. In the Christian tradition, eating and drinking reach their culmination in the communion or Eucharist, with its emphasis on digesting the brokenness of Christ's body before wholeness is obtained and the reconciliation of human and divine relationships through an act of atoning death orally received and consumed. The symbol of the Eucharist can become an important pastoral resource in helping persons confront the intrapersonal and interpersonal dynamics that may contribute to maladaptive patterns in eating, drinking and living.

Bibliography. H. Bruch, *Eating Disorders* (1973). D. Cappon, *Eating, Loving and Dying* (1973). E. H. Erikson, *Childhood and Society* (1963). P. Farb and G. Armelagos, *Consuming Passions* (1980). S. Freud, *New Introductory Lectures on Psychoanalysis* (1933). M. Kintner, *et al.*, "Relationship Between Dysfunctional Family Environment and Family Member Food Intake," *J. of Marriage and Family*, 43 (1981), 633–41. S. Minuchin, *Psychosomatic Families* (1978). R. Moos, *et al.*, "Family Characteristics and the Outcome of Treatment for Alcoholism," *J. of Studies on Alcohol* (1977), 77–88. F. Perls, *Ego, Hunger, and Aggression* (1969 [1947]).

C. M. MENDENHALL III

GLUTTONY AND TEMPERANCE (Moral Theology); LIFESTYLE ISSUES IN PASTORAL CARE. *See also* AGGRESSION AND ASSERTION; ANOREXIA NERVOSA; BODY; BULIMIA; OBESITY AND WEIGHT CONTROL. *Compare* ALCOHOL ABUSE, ADDICTION AND THERAPY; ASCETICAL PRACTICES; COMMUNITY, FELLOWSHIP, AND CARE; NEED/NEEDS; RITUAL AND PASTORAL CARE; SYMBOLISM/SYMBOLIZING.

ECCLESIOLOGY AND PASTORAL CARE. The way Christians are "gathered" in the name of Christ and as a consequence exercise pastoral ministries as a shared responsibility. The term "ecclesiology" has been a polemical term since the sixteenth-century debates. In the eighteenth and nineteenth centuries, the connection between ecclesiology and pastoral care reflected institutional and historical concerns more than a theological point of view. In the twentieth century, the relationship of ecclesiology and pastoral care has been reexamined within the larger question of praxis and theory. Praxis is understood here as a sphere of action that generates its own implicit theoretical system. Ecclesial praxis refers to the actions of a Christian community and their implicit meanings.

An important element in any definition of church must be the purpose of its gathering: to do the work of the gospel or to be "in mission." In any historical epoch, when the Christian community loses sight of its mission, institutional goals may become primary concerns. The profile of the Christian community is, in fact, shaped by its prevailing sense of evangelization and mission in view of the inbreaking of the Kingdom of God. The mission of the church is both a response to and a proclamation of the Kingdom of God. Pastoral care cannot be defined outside the context of the mission of the church to proclaim God's reign.

A second crucial element in defining church is the foundational and perduring role of the Holy Spirit. The NT church gradually clarified its awareness that the Holy Spirit empowers the community to do the work of the gospel. Long before any systematic development of pneumatology or Trinitarian theology, the Spirit was seen as the operative force that enabled flawed Christians to be the "body of Christ." A traditional witness to this belief is the Eucharistic *epiclesis* or "calling down" of the Holy Spirit for both the sanctification of the bread and wine and the community that it might be the body of Christ.

Ecclesiology, then, is the systematic study of the Christian church as a "disciple group," gathered by the power of the Spirit in the name of Christ to proclaim his "good news"—the actualization of the Kingdom of God. In the contemporary study of ecclesiology, the scriptural, historical, systematic, and psychosocial dimensions of church are examined. These theoretical elements are compared with ecclesial praxis. By its very nature a productive and realistic study of ecclesiology cannot be divorced from the ways in which the church pastorally cares for the people of its time. Pastoral care may, in fact, be regarded as a praxis ecclesiology in that it delineates the operational definitions of mission, Kingdom, and salvation within a Christian community.

1. New Testament Foundations. Although there are ongoing exegetical discussions about the underlying concepts of church in the NT, one uncontested characteristic of NT writers is that their experience of and theories about the Christian community are not as dichotomized as subsequent systematic ecclesiologies sometimes tend to be. Paul, for example, does not construct a theory of church and then attempt to apply it to the Corinthian situation. Failures of local churches to proclaim credibly the gospel and to minister with sensitivity to one another are occasions for Paul to develop the theological and pastoral implications of "being gathered" (*sunerkhesthai en ekklésia*) in the name of the Lord. In line with our specific concerns about pastoral care, there are several descriptions, rooted in the NT discussion of church, that are particularly helpful. These descriptions are not meant to be exhaustive but rather to retrieve the careful balance between theory and praxis in the early Christian communities.

a. The cross of Christ. First, the church is seen as a community shaped by the Cross. One of the most important factors in the ecclesial formation of early communities is the deepening awareness of the salvific meaning of the death of Jesus. Biblical scholars continue to study the various stages of this awareness in the pre-Pauline and Pauline churches. From a systematic perspective the importance of these developments might be stated in this way: as the Christology, so the ecclesiology of the community. As we shall see, this connection in turn shapes the pastoral care of each community.

A well-known example is the Corinthian community. These Christians seem to have emphasized the importance of an exalted Lord to the detriment of the meaning of his death for them. Paul's pastoral corrective is the "word of the Cross" (I Cor. 1:18). Paul clearly teaches that the community takes its form and focus from its ongoing appropriation of the meaning of the Cross. The apostle reminds the community that his gospel proclamation centered on a crucified Christ (II Cor. 2:2).

The community's misunderstanding of his proclamation has betrayed itself in its praxis: quarreling and divisions (I Cor. 1:10–15), moral disorders (I Cor. 5, 6), and a shocking insensitivity to the poorer Christians (I Cor. 10:19–22). In effect, Paul describes a self-serving ecclesiology premised on a similar Christology. Paul's antidote is to clarify a central implication of the Eucharist, which he understands as the proclamation of the death of the Lord until he comes (I Cor. 11:26).

Paul has prefaced this teaching with his discussion in I Cor. 10 of the meaning of "participation" (*koinōnia/metexein*) as a dynamic and unifying experience. From the very nature of this "sharing" in the Body and Blood of

Christ, he deduces the oneness of the community (I Cor. 10:16–17) and offers the ideal of apostolic imitation and its practical corollary: to seek the advantage of others for the sake of their salvation (I Cor. 10:33). This Pauline development agrees with the consensus of exegetes that the growing awareness of the meaning of Christ's death in the early communities was linked to their celebration of the Lord's Supper. In brief, Paul deduces the nature, mission, and ministries of the Christian community from his conviction that Christ was someone "on account of others" (*huper pollōn*). The pastoral care of the community is both measured and enabled by the unique self-gift of Christ.

b. The body of Christ. The church is also seen as the unified and ministering body of Christ. Paul employs several complementary images to describe his pastoral ideal of a Christian community. In his early response to the divisions within the Corinthian community the apostle insists on a redemptive unity that is rooted in one Spirit and one Lord (I Cor. 12:11; in the later Pauline corpus, see Eph. 2:13–14, 19).

The test of each ministry is whether it "builds up" (*oikodomein*) the church (I Cor. 14:4–5, 12). This Pauline edification is a gradual process of appropriating the gospel message and proclaiming it credibly to others. This process of "building up" cannot be understood apart from the mission of the whole community. In other words, the liturgical and theological activity of the community is measured and clarified by its praxis of "building up" the church.

In his letter to the church at Rome, Paul again proposes unity as a practical result of Christian identification with Christ. The apostle's teaching about the crucified and risen Christ's gift of justice, presented within the corporate image of his new reign (Rom. 5:10–21), is linked to his discussion of initiation as dying and rising with Christ (Rom. 6:3–10). This latter idea resonates with Paul's earlier teaching about being baptized into one body (I Cor. 12:13). In other words, Paul does not conceive of the church as a group of individually saved members. Rather he begins with the corporate nature of salvation, which enables the church to be the body of Christ and draws out its corollaries for the community—"so that we might bear fruit for God" (Rom. 7:4, NAB). In view of Paul's cosmic view of redemption, this service includes those outside as well as those within the community.

c. The Kingdom of God. The church is the community of God's future. Although there are a number of ecclesiologies and eschatologies in the NT, there is an overriding conviction that salvation will only be fully realized when we are gathered into the Kingdom of God. The church, gathered in the Lord's name, already proclaims and symbolizes the ultimate unity of that Kingdom (Eph. 3:10). The writer of the letter to the Ephesians, for example, in using the Pauline leitmotif of "building up the body of Christ" (Eph. 4:12–16), keeps in view its ultimate purpose—the Kingdom: "The 'body is built up' so that the church can be an effective sign and expression of the cosmic mission of Christ" (Senior and Stuhlmueller, 1983, p. 205).

The later patristic image of Christ as "medicus" (doctor) also develops some of these eschatological themes. In commenting on Jesus' saying that it is the sick who need a doctor (Mk. 2:17), Origen, for example, speaks of Jesus as the heavenly physician and the church as his room of healing (Homily 8 on Levit.). Leaders of Christian communities are urged to be like compassionate physicians to the spiritually sick in their midst (Apostolic Constitutions, 2). The healing Christ, as a sign of the coming of the Kingdom, is the model for the church as a healing community.

The vision of God's gathered people at the end of time in the book of Revelation provides the continuing goal and criterion for the mission and ministries of the church. Ultimately, there is no authentic pastoral care in the Christian church that does not take its definition and direction from the Kingdom of God. Conversely, when eschatology no longer challenges the ecclesial awareness of Christians, their sense of pastoral care inevitably becomes privatized.

2. The Catechumenate as Contemporary Model. By the end of the second century, a process of Christian formation for initiation into the church known as the catechumenate seems to have been widespread. This process of conversion, usually extending over several years, involved the baptized and candidates in a comprehensive reevaluation of experiences, lifestyles, and values in light of the gospel message. Implicit in this catechumenal process is an integrated model of church, ministry, and mission that can provide a contemporary frame of reference for the discussion of ecclesiology and pastoral care.

The catechumenate is ecclesiology in praxis. The most striking feature of the catechumenal process is that it models elements of an authentic Christian community and calls both candidates and baptized to commitment to that ideal. When implemented correctly, the catechumenate is designed to clarify the operational (as opposed to purely theoretical) definitions of salvation, church, sin, mission, and ministry within the whole community. In other words, the goal of effective pastoral care is the same as that of the catechumenate—to enable people to welcome the gospel implications of incorporation into Christ in initiation. Both the catechumenal process and pastoral care uncover the redemptive needs as well as the potential service of each member of the community. The deepening ecclesial self-awareness of the community, in turn, gives direction and scope to this pastoral care in at least two ways.

First the catechumenal model provides pastoral care with an evangelical challenge to call the whole community to continuing conversion and renewal. In the face of the residual temptation to compromise gospel witness and living, catechumenal evangelization becomes a hallmark of effective pastoral care. This ongoing proclamation of the gospel reminds the community of its prophetic and eschatological role of symbolizing the power of Christ's death by its unity as the body of Christ. Consequently, effective pastoral care is measured not only by its impact on the individual but also on the ways it enables the community as a whole to fulfill its mission.

Second, pastoral care in the ecclesial model of the catechumenate is concerned with maintaining the intentionality of the community and its members, that is, its intention to be shaped by the transcending values of the

Kingdom of God rather than by subtle forces of institutional routinization. Effective pastoral care helps the community to be honest by fostering ecclesial self-awareness in how it prays and what it does. Personal intentionality revolves around the individual's reappropriation of gospel values in each life stage with its specific challenges and tasks within the context of his or her church community. Effective pastoral care assists the individual in uncovering operational motivations and recovering the vision of the Kingdom and its practical corollaries for his or her participation in the mission of the church. Pastoral care, then, deals with the intentions of the church and its members in their actual praxis.

Finally, the various dimensions of healing that derive from pastoral care within an ecclesial context are brought to common focus in the mission of the church. The catechumenate leads to a sacramental healing that enables the individual to "build up" the community, which is the body of Christ. Psychological and physical dimensions of pastoral care also enable its recipients to care for others as part of their ecclesial commitment.

Bibliography. R. Banks, *Paul's Idea of Community* (1980). R. Duffy, *A Roman Catholic Theology of Pastoral Care* (1983). R. Duggan, ed., *Conversion and the Catechumenate* (1984). J. Hainz, *Ekklesia. Strukturen Paulinisches Gemeinde-Theologie und Gemeinde-Ordnung* (1972); *Koinōnia: Kirche als Gemeinschaft bei Paulus* (1982). M. Kehl, *Kirche als Institution* (1976). W. Klaiber, *Rechtfertigung und Gemeinde: Eine Untersuchung zum paulinischen Kirchenverständnis* (1982). F. Klostermann, *Gemeinde-Kirche der Zukunft. Thesen, Dienste, Modelle* (1974). H. Ludwig, *Die Kirche im Prozess der Gesellschaftlichen Differenzierung* (1976). W. Meeks, *The First Urban Christians* (1983). N. Mette, *Theorie der Praxis* (1978). P. Minear, *Images of the Church in the New Testament* (1960). J. Murphy-O'Connor, "Eucharist and Community in I Corinthians," *Worship*, 50 (1976), 370–85 and 51 (1977), 56–69. H. Rikhof, *The Concept of Church: A Methodological Inquiry into the Use of Metaphors in Ecclesiology* (1981). E. Schillebeeckx and B. Van Iersel, eds., "Revelation and Experience," *Concilium*, 113 (1979). D. Senior and C. Stuhlmueller, *The Biblical Foundations for Mission* (1983). K. Rahner, "Grundlegung der Pastoraltheologie als praktischer Theologie," *Handbuch der Pastoraltheologie*, F. X. Arnold, *et al.*, eds., Vol. 1 (1972), 117–229.

R. DUFFY

CONGREGATION, PASTORAL CARE OF; MINISTRY; PASTORAL CARE (History, Traditions, and Definitions); PASTORAL THEOLOGY. *See also* AUTHORITY, PASTORAL; PASTORAL OFFICE; VATICAN COUNCIL II; WOMEN IN PASTORAL MINISTRIES, HISTORY OF. *Compare* COMMUNITY, FELLOWSHIP, AND CARE; ECUMENICAL RELATIONSHIPS IN THE PASTORAL CARE AND COUNSELING MOVEMENTS; JEWISH CARE AND COUNSELING; LAY PASTORAL CARE AND COUNSELING.

ECKHART, MEISTER

ECKHART, MEISTER (ca. 1260–1327). Dominican preacher, theologian, and mystic. Born in Thuringia, Eckhart entered the Dominican Order in Erfurt while still in his teens. He studied at Paris and Cologne, held two lectureships at Paris, served in administrative positions in the Dominican Order in Germany, and was professor of theology at Strasbourg from 1312 to 1323. He died while en route to Avignon to defend himself against charges of heterodox teaching. Some of his theological propositions were posthumously condemned in 1329.

Eckhart's writings, both in Latin and in the vernacular, reveal a negative mysticism that emphasizes the dynamic of all things coming out from God and flowing back to God; an idea found in St. Augustine of Hippo and other Christian Neoplatonists. Eckhart's emphasis on the transcendent purity of God's nature and the human need for detachment are fundamental poles of his mystic thought. Eckhart was influential in his own day (the mystics John Tauler and Henry Suso were his disciples) and our own. His contemporary influence can be detected in theologians like Paul Tillich and philosophers like Martin Heidegger. His rather paradoxical emphasis on God's transcendence and a "this worldly" mysticism has ensured him a following among modern spiritual writers who regard him, along with John of the Cross, as the "mystic's mystic."

Bibliography. E. College and B. McGinn, eds., *Meister Eckhart* (1981). V. Lossky, *Theologie négative et conaissance de Dieu chez Maître Eckhart* (1960). R. Schürmann, *Meister Eckhart: Mystic and Philosopher* (1978).

L. S. CUNNINGHAM

MYSTICISM; SPIRITUALITY (Roman Catholic Tradition).

ECOLOGICAL PSYCHOLOGY

ECOLOGICAL PSYCHOLOGY. A wide variety of subspecialties within the broader discipline of psychology, devoted to understanding the role of the environment in the scientific explanation of psychological phenomena (Mace, 1983). It attempts to study the interrelationship between the animal and the real environment within which it exists, viewing the proper unit of analysis as the organism in its natural surroundings, rather than the isolated organism (Cutting, 1982). While strictly controlled laboratory experiments can provide useful data, ecological psychology focuses on naturalistic field studies that include the interactive relationship between the living being and its environment.

To appreciate the contribution of ecological psychology, it is necessary to see it more as a philosophical revolution within the field of science than as a distinct discipline. In fact, it has been regarded by some as the most controversial reform in scientific method to occur in experimental psychology (Gibbs, 1979). In all areas of psychological research, such as the study of perception, memory, learning, development, social influence, and attitude change, there has been a radical call for studies that are sensitive to the contextual continuities and potentialities of human and animal behavior. Ecologically informed researchers maintain that it is no longer acceptable to design experiments that confirm what is already obvious to the logical mind. Hypothesis-forming is now to be valued over hypothesis-confirming research. Even more importantly, studies must be designed to obtain results that are generalizable to the real world, requiring that research be conducted in the natural environment rather than in the laboratory.

This reform represents a reaction to the traditional approach used in psychological research, which has typically valued certainty over authenticity, external over internal validity, method over meaning, manipulation over understanding, rigor over sensitivity to human subtlety, and narrow quantification over broad qualitative inquiry (Gibbs, 1979). Ecological inquiry seeks to balance these polarities both by incorporating a naturalistic spirit into laboratory experiments and by utilizing experimental methods in field work. While traditionally the scientific method was thought to require the insulation of laboratory manipulations and measures from the natural environment in order to control unidentified intervening variables, ecological psychology maintains that including these possible environmental variables is necessary for the authenticity, generalizability, and applicability of the findings.

The International Society of Ecological Psychology was formed in 1982 in an effort to unite those of various specialties within experimental psychology who are interested in studying the relationship between the person's or animal's capacities and the resources of the environment (Mace, 1983). In addition to psychologists, the Society also includes artists, architects, computer scientists, biologists, ethologists, physicians, physicists, linguists, mathematicians, physiologists, and philosophers.

The impact of ecological psychology on experimental research has been profoundly important. Its revolutionary implications continue to be evaluated and debated among both scientists and social philosophers.

Bibliography. J. E. Cutting, "Two ecological perspectives: Gibson vs. Shaw and Turvey," *American J. of Psychology,* 95:2, (1982), 199–222. J. C. Gibbs, "The meaning of ecologically oriented inquiry in contemporary psychology," *American Psychologist,* 34:2 (1979), 127–40. W. M. Mace, "Proceedings of a meeting of the International Society of Ecological Psychology," *J. of Experimental Psychology: Human Perception and Performance,* 9:1 (1983), 151–57.

J. GUY

PSYCHOLOGY. *Compare* COMMUNITY PSYCHIATRY/PSYCHOLOGY; CYBERNETIC THEORY IN PSYCHOLOGY; FIELD THEORY; PHILOSOPHY AND PSYCHOLOGY; SOCIAL SCIENCES.

ECONOMIC DIMENSIONS OF PASTORAL COUNSELING. *See* FEES IN PASTORAL COUNSELING; PASTORAL COUNSELING CENTER. *See also* MONEY.

ECSTASY. A state in which persons feel themselves to be in direct contact with what they perceive to be divine. The state is usually associated with extremes of consciousness, ranging from excessive agitation to total passivity, sometimes occurring in sequence. Typically total or partial suspension of awareness occurs, accompanied by the feeling that one's body is controlled by spiritual forces. This state is often defined as a trance, but independent confirmation of this is difficult to obtain. The state can occur spontaneously or be induced deliberately by a wide variety of techniques such as music and dancing, solitary meditation, physical discipline, or drugs. It may be associated with visions, speaking in tongues (glossolalia) or self-mutilation directed toward spiritual ends. Ecstasy is particularly common in cultures in which belief systems legitimate either soul loss or possession. Often ecstasy is explained in terms of soul loss followed by spirit possession but either explanation can exist independently. When ecstatic states are interpreted as union with, rather than mere contact with, the Divine, they become identical with mystical states.

Ecstasy has been reported throughout history and in virtually every culture. Numerous examples occur in the OT (e.g., Num. 25, I Kings 17, 26–28) and in the NT (e.g., Acts 2, 4; II Cor. 12, 1–4). The experience was normative for the Hebrew prophets and the Mohammedan dervishes. In the Middle Ages it occurred in outbreaks of tarantism and St. Vitus's dance. In modern times it is frequent in less advanced cultures, particularly as an initiation rite for shamans or inspired priests. Its occurrence in advanced cultures is also frequent and well documented. In the modern Western world it is often associated with the rise of new religious movements and the revitalization of older religions. The extreme emotional intensity of ecstasy, whether active or passive, has probably accounted for its ambivalent interpretation in modern times as throughout history. However, efforts to dismiss ecstasy as mere emotionalism are unwarranted. Likewise, while ecstasy often is associated with what might otherwise be indicators of diseases or deficiencies, the integration of even seizures and trance states into meaningful systems of culturally supported beliefs make facile claims to psychopathology insufficient.

Ecstasy is best viewed as a universal human potential that can and often does have both positive social and psychological functions. For instance, ecstatic states function to provide a radical equality of persons in terms of access to the Divine, to permit expression of otherwise unacceptable emotions, and to provide theological belief systems with experiential confirmation. Ecstasy is particularly functional when embedded within theological belief systems that can both legitimate its expression and contain its excesses.

Bibliography. M. Eliade, *Shamanism* (1964). A. M. Greeley, *Ecstasy* (1974). J. R. Haule, "'Soul-Making' in a Schizophrenic Saint," *J. of Religion and Health,* 23 (1984), 70–80. M. Laski, *Ecstasy* (1968). I. M. Lewis, *Ecstatic Religion* (1975). T. K. Osterreich, *Possession* (1974 [1921]).

R. W. HOOD, JR.

CHARISMATIC EXPERIENCE; MYSTICISM; RELIGIOUS EXPERIENCE. *Compare* HAPPINESS; PEAK EXPERIENCE; SPIRITUALITY; TRANCE; VISIONS AND VOICES.

ECSTASY, CHEMICAL. *See* PSYCHEDELIC DRUGS AND EXPERIENCE.

ECUMENICAL MARRIAGE. *See* CATHOLIC-PROTESTANT MARRIAGE. *See also* CROSS-CULTURAL PASTORAL CARE.

ECUMENICAL RELATIONSHIPS IN THE PASTORAL CARE AND COUNSELING MOVEMENT.

The pastoral care and counseling movement has contributed significantly to ecumenical relationships from its beginnings in the 1920s and 1930s. Its early leadership included a Congregational minister, Anton Boisen, a Unitarian physician, Richard Cabot, and an Episcopalian layman, Robert Keller, all of whom were concerned with ministry outside the parochial and denominational boundaries.

In the 1940s and 1950s, many Protestant clergypersons moved outside their denominational traditions to minister with people in clinical settings. Often these clergy were rebelling against traditional religious beliefs and values which they considered too limiting and moralistic for effective ministry with people in crisis. These clergy experimented with new learnings from the behavioral sciences which they felt deepened and stretched their narrow theological views. In the process a common bond formed in this new movement as professional pastoral care associations were formed offering support and encouragement for clergy engaged in this new method of theological study and pastoral practice. These associations were formed with a strong ecumenical spirit. Often clergy found involvement in these new associations as important as in their denominational affiliations.

During the 1960s and 1970s Roman Catholic clergy and religious sisters entered the pastoral care movement to resolve faith issues and to prepare for ministry in hospitals and other clinical settings. They participated in CPE programs and enrolled in secular degree programs in increasing numbers. This development brought Protestant and Roman Catholic clergy together for learning and service in a way that challenged each other's assumptions, stereotypes, and religious beliefs. Some Catholic clergy and religious became significantly involved in the established pastoral care organizations, while others formed a new national association to certify priests and sisters for ministry with people in crisis.

Pastoral care associations developed certification standards and procedures for clergy ministering in clinical settings. This process is conducted on an ecumenical basis; it involves the presentation of pastoral work to an ecumenical committee which decides whether the person is competent to practice in a ministry specialty such as supervision, counseling, or chaplaincy.

As ecumenical relationships have developed in the pastoral care and counseling movement, persons in training have struggled to develop a pastoral identity consistent with their religious traditions yet meaningful to their new ministry with people of different faiths. As clergy minister with people in crisis and meet in seminars with students from different religious traditions, their theological assumptions and religious practices are challenged. This has led to the development of a pastoral theology that is uniquely ecumenical in nature. Ritual practices, however, have remained essentially denominational, and Roman Catholic liturgy and Protestant worship practices have continued to be separated in the clinical settings.

In general, the common practice of pastoral care and counseling in the clinical setting has contributed significantly to relationships among many religious traditions. The further involvement of persons from Judaism and other traditions will no doubt continue to enrich this process.

D. F. PARKER

CLINICAL PASTORAL EDUCATION; PASTORAL CARE MOVEMENT; PASTORAL COUNSELING MOVEMENT; THEOLOGICAL EDUCATION AND THE PASTORAL CARE MOVEMENT. *See also* AMERICAN ASSOCIATION OF PASTORAL COUNSELORS; ASSOCIATION FOR CLINICAL PASTORAL EDUCATORS; ECCLESIOLOGY AND PASTORAL CARE; INTERNATIONAL PASTORAL CARE MOVEMENT; JOURNALS IN PASTORAL CARE AND COUNSELING; JUDAISM AND PSYCHOLOGY; VATICAN COUNCIL II AND PASTORAL CARE.

EDDY, MARY BAKER (1821–1910).

EDDY, MARY BAKER (1821–1910). Founder and initial leader of the religious movement of Christian Science. Reared in the church, Eddy was religious since childhood, sensitive to God's presence, and curious about mental and spiritual causation.

Her cure from a severe injury under the hypnotic treatment by one P. Quimby impressed Eddy with the healing power of the mind. In *Science and Health with Key to the Scriptures* (1875) she forged the Christian Science faith stance from Quimby's thoughts on hypnotism and Christian teachings. Through the lens of pastoral care we see, first, that Eddy represents that unique class of magnetic, believing individuals who manage to translate a high-level spiritual motivation into productive material achievements. Second, her life and work are reflections of pastoral care in the century of Schleiermacher: a highly emotional and highly individualistic form of religiousness providing a cushion against the bumps of life by sustaining the last religious bastion unconquered by Enlightenment reason: the human soul.

N. F. HAHN

CHRISTIAN SCIENCE; HISTORY OF PROTESTANT PASTORAL CARE (United States); HEALING.

EDUCATION, GRADUATE. *See* PASTORAL THEOLOGY, GRADUATE EDUCATION IN. *See also* EDUCATION FOR PASTORAL CARE AND COUNSELING; THEOLOGICAL EDUCATION AND THE PASTORAL CARE MOVEMENT.

EDUCATION, NURTURE, AND CARE. *Education* is the systematic and intentional effort to transmit, evoke, or acquire knowledge, attitudes, values, or skills (Cremin). It should not be viewed exclusively in terms of schooling or the promotion of cognitive competencies but focused upon a wide range of items which are intentionally taught and learned. *Nurture* refers to a certain type of education, one that is based on a biological model of growth. It can be defined as the provision of nourishment to a living organism in order to help it to develop and flourish. *Care* refers to concern for the well-being of another. It is frequently used to designate an attitude of "tender and solicitous concern" toward those in need (Hiltner).

This article discusses the theoretical nature, significance, and relationship of these fundamental terms. The article on TEACHING deals with their practical implementation—how the educational work of the church can be done from a pastoral perspective.

1. **Care as a Constitutive Dimension of Human Existence.** In recent philosophy, Martin Heidegger (1962) has most forcefully explicated care as a constitutive dimension of the being of humans. In his philosophy, care (*Sorge*) refers to the dimension of human existence by which humans are open to Being. Humans alone stand out (*ecstasis*) from the dumb rhythms of nature and relate to objects, persons, and events as part of a meaningful world. They are "possibilities" for human existence. Care is that openness to Being which allows possibilities for meaning to emerge. The opposite of care is apathy or numbness.

Care is more than a generalized openness to Being, however. Two more specialized uses add significantly to the understanding of this concept. One focuses upon care as the sort of relationship in which the well-being of another is recognized as having a claim upon the self. A parent's care for his or her child, for example, involves a relationship in which the well-being of the child is determinative of the parent's attitudes and actions. Here, questions of moral responsibility come to the fore.

A second, closely related understanding of care harks back to its more common meaning which was pointed to in the initial section. Here, care refers to an attitude of tender and solicitous concern for those in need. This linkage of care with the needy is crucial. Human openness to Being and the recognition of the moral claims of others on the self meet their severest challenge in the face of suffering. There is a universal human tendency to shrink back when confronted by the suffering of others and to repress the memory of suffering, our own as well as others, (Metz; Freud). To exercise concern for others in need thus constitutes a limit experience in which the entire enterprise of human caring is brought into focus (Tracy). Why should one endure the pain of caring for others who are suffering? What sustains care in the face of the obliteration and severe distortion of others?

2. Education as a Constitutive Dimension of Human Existence.
While care points to the openness to Being which constitutes humans as human, education points to the finitude and temporality of such caring. The etymology of education is helpful in this regard. It is significant that the Latin *educere* means both "to bring up" and "to lead out" (cf. Dewey). The former sense will be referred to primarily in terms of "formation" and the latter, "transformation." Education is a generic dimension of human existence; to be human is to engage in a process of education involving the formation of perduring elements of self and their ongoing transformation in response to unique contexts of experience.

Education as formation involves the "bringing up" of a person. While this concept seemingly implies something done *to* persons *by* others (parents, teachers, or educational institutions, for example), what is in mind here is something different: the "taking form" of a human being with indefinite potentialities into something that is concrete and limited. Education as formation is the acquisition of such qualities as concrete values, transactional styles, and an identity which perdure and give form through time. Philosophers of education have resorted to terms like character (Aristotle), habits (Dewey), and excellences (Frankena) to designate that which is formed in the educational process.

Transformation, by contrast, focuses upon the "leading out" dimension of education. It refers to the reconstruction of the self or some dimension of experience, and takes account of the developmental dimensions of human existence. More fundamentally, it calls attention to the temporality of human existence: the fact that the past is not strictly determinative of human life, but unfolds in a unique and open-ended present, affording the possibility of a genuinely new future. Education can never be satisfied merely with the formation of persons but must focus on the ongoing transformation of the self and community in ways that are consistent with the possibilities of a given historical context.

Formation and transformation alone do not constitute education. Any living being in nature takes concrete form and undergoes a series of transformations, for better or worse. What makes an experience or setting educational is its systematic and intentional pursuit of formation and transformation in light of a self-conscious moral ideal. Only certain attitudes, information, values, and skills are transmitted and evoked. Only certain processes of growth and change are encouraged. Education, as such, is inevitably normative. It is based on a vision of the Good giving shape and direction to formation and transformation. Human existence which is devoid of education in this sense is less than fully human. This leads us to consider the relationship between education, nurture, and care.

3. The Nurture of Care in Education.
Care and education cannot exist without one another. Care is the substance of education, for it is human openness to Being which is formed and transformed. Moreover, care in its deeper senses — the recognition of the moral claims of others and concern for their well-being in the face of suffering—is present in some form in every moral vision which informs education. It may be helpful to think of the relationship between these two realities in terms of a reformulated understanding of nurture.

Nurture implies the provision of nourishment to a living being in order to allow it to grow and flourish. While this concept has historically been associated with a liberal vision of religious and secular education (and its organicist understandings of growth and development), it can be appropriated in a radically different concept of education. To care, in its deepest sense, is to show concern for the well-being of others, especially the suffering other. The nurture of care in education, thus, involves the task of confronting humans with the reality of human suffering and questions of moral responsibility in the face of the claims of others, items which can hardly be said to emerge naturally out of human experience. It points toward the nurture of an ever-widening arc of inclusiveness in which the community of those who matter takes on universal proportions, embracing the living and the dead, the victims of history, as well as the successful.

4. Education, Nurture, and Care as Forms of Christian Ministry.
To this point, this article has described education, nurture, and care as generic features of human existence. To exist as a human in any real sense is to engage in the activities of care and education. The conceptual distinctions which have been developed may throw light on those forms of Christian ministry which are typically referred to as pastoral care and Christian education.

From one perspective, pastoral care and Christian education are specialized forms of care and education as they have been described in the previous sections. Pastoral care is the activity of offering, in the name of Jesus Christ, tender and solicitous concern to persons in need. Christian education is concerned with the systematic and intentional formation and transformation of the members of the Christian community. From another perspective, however, care and education are transformed when brought into a theological perspective which is grounded in the Christian faith. In ways that are consonant with the Christian story, they are understood as normatively ordered under and toward God.

Human care, as openness to Being, is viewed more fundamentally as the created capacity for openness to God, a readiness for covenant fellowship with the Author of all being. It is no accident that Paul Tillich has taken a concept that is closely related to care, "concern," and used it to describe faith as a generic feature of human existence (Tillich). Human caring always takes place in relation to an "ultimate concern," that which is cared about most deeply, exerting an ordering impact on life. Likewise, education, as the systematic and intentional formation and transformation of finite, temporal humans in conjunction with a moral ideal, is construed by Christian theology as an activity which is properly carried out only when the good is determined in relation to God.

Theology, thus, views care and education as theonomous, as finding their proper grounding and fulfillment in the sovereign God. Moreover, it recognizes the fact that care and education as constitutive dimensions of human existence are deeply distorted in the normal course of human affairs. It speaks of a fall and the reality of sin by which care becomes, not the ground for an openness to God or other beings, but a curving in upon the self and its own concerns. It acknowledges the ways in which the dialectic of formation and transformation in education is destroyed by idolatry, which issues, not in the nurture of a widening circle of care for the commonwealth of being, but a defensive protection of the finite causes of closed communities.

It is on the basis of a clear recognition of the radical distortion of human care and education that the Christian story witnesses to redemption in Jesus Christ. In Christ, human care—that openness to Being which reaches its fullest expression in the acknowledgment of the moral claim of another and the willingness to endure the pain of identification with the suffering other—finds its true expression and fulfillment. In Christ, the educational processes of intentional formation and transformation issue in a life which shares the universalism of care for all of being which characterizes the sovereign, gracious God.

In both cases, what is found is not a denial of that which is given in creation but its redemption, its proper ordering and restoration under God. Pastoral care and Christian education, thus, as ministries of the church, seek to carry on the work of Christ in which the true meaning of care and education, as constitutive dimensions of human existence, are redeemed. The church, under the tutelage of Christ, is to care in ways that witness to the human community its vocation of caring which was given in creation. It points, first of all, to Christ's care, of which its own is a pale approximation. In its educational ministry it is concerned with the nurture of the fullness of care in all spheres of life, the formation and transformation of persons toward a universalism of care under the sovereign God.

As constitutive dimensions of human existence and as ministries of the church, care and education stand in the closest relations. In an age of specialization and technical expertise, it is important to remember the ways that both pastoral care and Christian education find their proper unity disclosed in Jesus Christ.

Bibliography. L. Cremin, Traditions of American Education (1977). J. Dewey, Democracy and Education (1916). W. Frankena, Three Historical Philosophies of Education (1965). S. Freud, "The Interpretation of Dreams," SE 4. S. Hiltner, Preface to Pastoral Theology (1958). M. Heidegger, Being and Time (1962 [1926] pp. 225–8. J. B. Metz, Faith in History and Society (1980). P. Tillich, Systematic Theology vol. 1, (1951) pp. 12–14, 211–15. D. Tracy, Blessed Rage for Order (1975), pp. 93–108.

R. R. OSMER

TEACHING. See also BAPTISM AND CONFIRMATION; CONGREGATION, PASTORAL CARE OF; COMMUNITY, FELLOWSHIP, AND CARE. Compare JEWISH CARE AND COUNSELING; JEWISH LITERATURE IN CARE AND COUNSELING.

EDUCATION, THEOLOGICAL. See THEOLOGICAL EDUCATION AND THE PASTORAL CARE MOVEMENT.

EDUCATION FOR PASTORAL CARE AND COUNSELING. The process of professional training required to prepare persons for the effective practice of ministry. There are two essential dimensions of this educational process—academic and clinical. The goal of the academic dimension is to learn the psychological, psychotherapeutic, and theological theories that constitute the conceptual foundation of pastoral care and counseling. The goal of the clinical dimension is to learn, through supervisory and therapeutic experiences, to use one's conceptual and personality resources effectively in the practice of these healing, wholeness-nurturing arts. This statement will describe both the educational experiences required to prepare one to do competent care and counseling in generalist ministries (including parish ministry), and the additional educational preparation needed for effectiveness in specialized ministries of pastoral counseling and psychotherapy.

1. **Clinical Education for Care and Counseling.**
a. Essential personal qualities. The key to being a healer and growth enabler in one's ministry is the mental wholeness and spiritual vitality of one's own personality. Six characteristics seem to be crucial in the personalities of effective counselors. Enhancing these wholeness-enabling personality strengths is the fundamental objective of clinical education: (1) congruence—authenticity and genuineness; personal integration and self-awareness; (2) non-possessive warmth, caring, and respect; (3) empathetic understanding—the ability to enter, to an appreciable degree, into another's inner world of meanings and feelings; (4) a sturdy sense of one's own identity and self-worth; (5) personal aliveness, continuing growth, and openness to oneself and others; and (6) an awareness of one's own areas of continuing need for healing and growth—accepting oneself as a "wounded healer," to use Henri Nouwen's apt phrase.

b. Types of learning experiences. The following types of learning experiences have proved most productive in enhancing a theological student's or minister's personality resources for relating in healing, growth-nurturing ways.

i. One's own psychotherapy. Personal therapy is an invaluable part of the education of all persons seeking to enhance their caring and counseling skills. Extensive psychotherapy is an essential foundation for the graduate education designed to prepare one to become a competent specialist in pastoral counseling and psychotherapy. Effective psychotherapy increases self-awareness and self-esteem, and thereby enhances empathetic awareness and esteem of others; it strengthens one's ability to relate constructively and communicate clearly; it reduces a counselor's unconscious conflicts which otherwise are projected unwittingly onto the recipients of ministry including counseling. Individual and group therapy tend to have a complementary effect; therefore both are desirable in pastoral counseling training.

Psychotherapists who do psychotherapy with those preparing for specialization in pastoral counseling should have a high level of competence, which is validated by appropriate credentials in their professional associations (as pastoral counseling specialists, clinical psychologists, clinical social workers, or psychiatrists), state licensing, and a positive reputation among professional colleagues who are familiar with their therapeutic skills. A substantial part of the training therapy of counseling pastors and pastoral counseling specialists should be with a *pastoral* psychotherapist whose training and competence are demonstrated by membership in the American Association of Pastoral Counselors (AAPC), at either a Fellow or a Diplomate level. (A list of such persons and information about membership requirements and training programs may be obtained from AAPC.)

ii. Clinical Pastoral Education (CPE). This consists of doing ministry for eleven weeks or more with people in crises. This ministry is done under the intensive supervision of a rigorously trained chaplain who has been accredited by the Association for Clinical Pastoral Education (ACPE). Like psychotherapy, CPE provides a depth encounter with oneself and one's pattern of relating. Furthermore, doing ministry under supervision with those in crises confronts seminarians and ministers in ways that challenge their intellectual assumptions, working hypotheses, and styles of relating. This often produces the kind of theological, cognitive, and emotional dissonance required to trigger both personal and professional growth. Thus, CPE offers unique learning opportunities that strengthen one's relational resources for all dimensions of ministry. The caring and counseling skills of persons preparing for or involved in generalist ministries can be increased significantly by a quarter or two of CPE. Persons preparing for specialized counseling ministries should have several quarters of CPE including at least one in a mental hospital or mental health facility. (A list of accredited CPE supervisors and centers may be obtained from ACPE.)

iii. In-service supervision. One of the most valuable and readily accessible ways of strengthening one's personality resources and interpersonal skills is to arrange for regular supervision of one's pastoral care and counseling by a well-trained pastoral counseling specialist or a mental health professional. Providing such in-service training is one of the most important ways by which pastoral counseling specialists can help increase the care-giving effectiveness of those in general ministries. A pastor can arrange to meet weekly or bi-weekly with a qualified supervisor. Or a small group of ministers can contract for such supervision, thus reducing the cost and adding the peer sharing, confrontation, and support that can significantly enrich the learning opportunities of those being supervised. Adequate preparation for specialized counseling ministries must include extensive, interprofessional supervision. (See AAPC standards below.) Many pastoral counseling centers offer supervision and consultation for those in general ministries.

iv. Professional growth experiences. Participating in professional courses, workshops, and seminars utilizing clinical/experiential learning methods can stimulate one's personal and professional growth simultaneously. Such educational opportunities are offered by many theological seminaries, pastoral counseling centers, hospital chaplaincy services, and some community mental health programs. The action-reflection teaching methods employed in these learning experiences often include: (1) learning from in-depth case studies, verbatim reports of pastoral contacts, and audio-or-video-recorded sessions presented by the participants from their caring and counseling ministries; (2) audio-and/or video-recorded and "live" demonstrations of caring and counseling methods by the instructor-supervisor and by the students; (3) skill practice sessions in which the instructor and students rotate in the roles of "counseling pastor," "troubled parishioner" and "observer coach"; and (4) small growth group sessions to increase the interpersonal and pastoral effectiveness of the trainees.

As in the case of clinical supervision, small clusters of pastors can arrange to meet weekly or bi-weekly for mutual support, peer supervision, and role playing of counseling problems from their ministries. Leadership of such professional growth-support groups can be rotated among the participants. But to increase the learning, arrangement should be made by the group for a trained supervisor-teacher to lead the group. Attending such a group or participating in an intensive workshop, seminar, or retreat, periodically, can provide the professional updating and renewal that are needed at regular intervals to avoid pastoral care burnout. Most graduate programs designed to train pastoral counseling specialists include a variety of such in-depth professional growth experiences.

v. Spiritual disciplines and other forms of self-care. Taking time to open oneself to the artesian spring of God's ever-present love and forgiveness through regular meditation, prayer, and reading that is both feeding and energizing, can reduce stress, rejuvenate one's wilting inner aliveness, and thus enable one to have something healing to offer others in caring ministries.

2. **Learning Foundational Theory.** *a. Need for theory.* Personal-professional growth through therapeutic and clinical learning has been discussed first to emphasize the foundational importance of this in all pastoral care and counseling education. But it is also essential to learn basic theological, psychological, and psychotherapeutic theory. This knowledge provides cognitive maps to guide one in understanding both of the enigmas of human behavior and the methodologies needed for effective care and counseling. Learning workable theory is an essential and complementary part of one's total educational preparation for developing competence in pastoral counseling. As seminarians and ministers grow in the healing personality attributes described above, their understanding of psychodynamic and counseling theories, and of spiritual resources from their theological

heritage, becomes increasingly functional in ministering to people confronting life crises, losses, conflicts, and burdens.

b. Areas of theoretical learning. At some point in one's professional education — during college or seminary, in advanced degree programs in pastoral care, or in continuing education courses, workshops, or seminars — it is necessary to acquire (and update on a continuing basis) a *working* understanding of these areas:

i. Normal personality growth and development, including the psychology of the various stages of childhood, adolescence, and adult, and the differences between the development of women and men (see Gilligan).

ii. The social and cultural context within which one ministers, including a sociological understanding of the institutions, mores and norms, the positive resources as well as oppressive forces in one's culture, as these influence and mold the health and sickness of individuals, families, and communities.

iii. Psychology and sociology of religion, including an understanding of religious experience, beliefs, and institutions, as these impact and reinforce sickness or health in the lives of individuals, family systems, and congregations. This understanding is the bridge which enables one to use religious resources such as prayer, scripture, sacraments, and congregational practices in healing, growth-nurturing ways, in one's practice of teaching, caring, and counseling.

iv. Pastoral history and identity, including an understanding of the history and heritage of pastoral care and spiritual direction as resources in forming one's professional and pastoral identity, and in implementing the theological-religious uniqueness of that identity and orientation in one's pastoral care and counseling.

v. Theories of illness and health, emphasizing the dynamics and interdependency of psychological, psychosomatic, interpersonal, and spiritual factors from the perspective of both abnormal psychology and wholistic health; and an understanding of the implications of spiritual, value, and meaning-of-life issues for sickness and health.

vi. Marriage and family dynamics, including an understanding of the profound and unsettling changes in women's and men's identities and relationships, the family systems perspective, and the basic theory and methods of marriage and family enrichment and counseling.

vii. Group dynamics and counseling theory, including the forces operating in any group and the methods by which leaders of groups and social systems can enable the interaction within them to become more nurturing of mutual wholeness. Because clergypersons work with large and small groups in many aspects of their ministries, including caring and counseling, acquiring an understanding of group dynamics and creative group leadership is a vital part of preparation for ministry.

viii. Methods of care and counseling that are normative in the practice of either a generalist or a specialist in this ministry.

To prepare for a *generalist ministry* of care and counseling, clergy need to know the basic theory and methodologies of short-term crisis intervention, longer-term supportive care and counseling, bereavement care and counseling, marriage and family crisis counseling, refer-

ral counseling, educative counseling (e.g., preparation for marriage, parenthood, retirement, etc.), growth groups leadership, training of lay carers, and counseling on spiritual, ethical, and meaning issues.

To prepare for a *specialized ministry* of pastoral counseling and psychotherapy, clergy must know the basic theory and methodologies of these types of counseling, psychotherapy, supervision, and teaching, in addition to those needed in generalist ministries: differential diagnostic and treatment planning skills, longer-term pastoral psychotherapy for more dysfunctional persons, utilizing resources from a variety of contemporary psychotherapies, reconstructive marriage and family therapy, therapy for pathological grief responses, group psychotherapy, therapy for persons suffering from pathogenic beliefs and value systems, clinical teaching and supervisory theory and skills (for use in training seminarians, providing continuing education and consultation for persons in generalist ministries, and consultation to professionals in the other therapeutic disciplines on ethical and theological issues), administrative and organizational development skills (for use in directing a pastoral counseling center, etc.).

3. Resources for Advanced Training in Pastoral Counseling. Unfortunately, the required courses, field education, and internships in most seminary M. Div. curricula are not fully adequate to prepare clergy for the counseling demands of the typical parish ministry. Furthermore, new approaches and resources in pastoral counseling are emerging constantly. Clergy in either generalist or specialized counseling ministries, who wish to keep their skills updated and sharp, must, throughout their professional careers, engage in continuing education experiences, including disciplined reading in the blossoming literature of this field.

Here are some major resources for both post-seminary continuing education and training for specialized ministries:

a. Advanced clinical programs. The nearly four hundred ACPE-accredited training programs in this country offer a wealth of opportunities for clergy to receive intensive supervision of their ministry to persons. Year-long, stipendiary internships are offered by some CPE centers. Such an experience provides a strong foundation of clinical learnings for those preparing for a specialized pastoral counseling ministry or chaplaincy. Becoming a "chaplain supervisor," accredited by ACPE to direct CPE programs, involves a rigorous process of advanced clinical education, including extensive supervision of one's clinical teaching skills. Many pastoral counseling centers offer advanced clinical education programs including year-long internships.

b. Advanced degree programs. A considerable number of seminaries now have post-M.Div. programs (e.g., D.Min.), in which advanced education in pastoral psychology and counseling is a popular focus. As noted below, a post-seminary degree in pastoral counseling is required to move beyond the AAPC "Member" level to "Fellow." This is the minimum level of training and competency to qualify as a pastoral counseling specialist. A Ph.D. in pastoral psychology and counseling (or its equivalent in professional achievement) is required to become a "Diplomate." This degree increasingly is being regarded as normative for those in advanced specialized ministries of teaching, research, and psychotherapy.

A variety of Ph.D. programs in this field exist in seminaries and in university graduate departments of religion. To complete such a program usually requires three-and-a-half to five years, during which there is rigorous academic and clinical learning which aims at enabling the student to integrate theological and psychological resources for healing and wholeness, and to achieve a high level of competence as both a theoretician and practitioner.

An alternate route to competency as a minister who specializes in counseling (common among Roman Catholic clergy) is to take a post-seminary degree in one of the mental health disciplines — e.g., clinical psychology. The disadvantage of this educational path is that the essential integration of psychological and theological resources is not built into such graduate programs. If the integration occurs, it must be done on one's own. The advantages of such an approach are certification in a mental health profession, which may open secular as well as church-related professional opportunities, and increased likelihood of receiving payment for one's therapeutic work from health insurance.

4. **AAPC Membership Requirements.** The membership requirements of AAPC, the major standard-setting guild of those with advanced training in pastoral counseling, provide a striking example of the multifaceted nature of pastoral counseling education. Examining these may illuminate the relationship between training standards and levels of competency, and between the clinical, academic, and churchly requirements for the different levels of membership. (The following three paragraphs are quoted or slightly paraphrased from the 1978 AAPC *Handbook*.)

a. Member level. (Ministers who have demonstrated competence to do limited, brief, or supportive pastoral counseling independently, or to do in-depth pastoral counseling under direct supervision, and to integrate counseling insights into the total pastoral function.) *Requirements:* A baccalaureate and an M.Div. degree; membership in good standing as a minister in a recognized faith group; three years' experience in ministry, and a continuing responsible relationship with one's local religious community; satisfactory completion of one unit of CPE and of at least 375 hours of pastoral counseling for which one has received at least 125 hours of interdisciplinary supervision dealing with both theological and psychological issues; a continuing consultative or supervisory relationship, preferably with a Fellow or Diplomate of AAPC.

b. Fellow. (Ministers who have demonstrated the ability to work as pastoral counselors at an advanced level of competency, provide leadership in interpreting the theological dimension of human wholeness, and do supervision of trainees under supervision.) *Requirements:* Satisfy the requirements for Member; plus an advanced degree (M.A., S.T.M., D.Min., etc.) in pastoral counseling or its equivalent, requiring one year of academic work beyond the seminary degree; at least 125 hours of interdisciplinary supervision of at least 1,000 hours of pastoral counseling (beyond the Member requirement); sufficient theological and psychotherapeutic investiga-

tion of one's own intrapsychic and interpersonal processes so that one is able to protect counselees from one's problems and deploy oneself to the maximum benefit of the counselee; give evidence of (a) an understanding of the counseling and psychotherapeutic process, (b) an ability to develop a counseling or psychotherapeutic relationship, (c) an ability to perform a leadership role in the context of the religious community, and (d) an ability to integrate one's professional role and personal identity.

c. Diplomate. (A minister who demonstrates the ability to work as a pastoral counselor and as a supervisor of ministers and pastoral counselors in training at an advanced level of competency; teach and supervise persons in pastoral ministry and/or pastoral counseling in congregations, or in pastoral counseling centers, or in schools; demonstrate ability to conceptualize the relationship of the psychotherapeutic disciplines to the theological interpretations and guidance of life). *Requirements:* Satisfy the requirements of Fellow, plus demonstrate competence in the practice of supervision of ministers in training in pastoral counseling, having supervised at least five supervisees for a minimum of thirty hours each, while receiving at least fifty hours of supervision of that supervision; demonstrate significant performance in at least three of the following—Ph.D. or equivalent, research, publication, leadership in AAPC, teaching and/or supervising pastoral care and counseling, contributing to church and community.

5. **Education for the Future.** To equip counseling pastors and pastoral counselors for ministry in our world of rapid social change, both the academic and clinical dimensions of education must be continually rethought in the light of these prominent needs and trends in our society:

a. Integrating heritage. To respond to the acute, escalating spiritual and ethical crises in our culture, pastoral counseling education must be more imaginative in equipping clergy to draw on the rich healing resources of their religious heritage. In this way they can maximize their unique counseling role as healers of spiritual and ethical pathology and enablers of that spiritual-ethical wholeness which is the integrating center of whole-person health.

b. New technology. To respond to the multiple problems and new possibilities generated by the hi-tech revolution, the education of pastoral counselors must equip them to utilize the new technology (e.g. computers, video-recording, etc.) in all aspects of their therapeutic and preventive work, *and* to help this amazing technology become more humanizing and less depersonalizing in its impact on human consciousness and relationships.

c. Wholistic orientation. To respond to the dominant hyper-specialization, compartmentalization, and pathology-orientation within the healing arts, *and* to the widespread longing for wholeness in our society, the education of pastoral counselors needs to equip them to function in more wholistic and health-oriented ways that move far beyond the limitation of the old medical model.

d. Systemic orientation. To respond to the growing need for more systemic and ecological ways of understanding human problems *and* liberating human possibilities, the education of pastoral counselors must equip them to transcend the hyper-individualistic orientation of the mainstream of traditional psychotherapy by reclaiming and utilizing in their practice of counseling, the relational, systemic biblical understanding of persons in relationships in community.

e. Social empowerment. To respond to the growing awareness of the radical interdependence of individual healing and growth, on the one hand, and societal healing and transformation, on the other, the education of pastoral counselors must help them integrate the pastoral and the prophetic dimensions of their tradition, making the central goal of all care and counseling the *empowerment* of people to work with others to heal each other *and* the social malignancies (e.g., racism, sexism, ageism, poverty and economic exploitation, domestic, intergroup, and international violence, and nuclearism) that are among the root causes of individual, family, and community pathology.

f. Cross-cultural perspectives. To respond to the challenges of the planetary communication network and the increasing interaction of cultures in our "global village," the education of pastoral counselors must enable them to transcend the middle-class, caucasian, North American-European, mainly male origins of the pastoral counseling movement, to become skilled in cross-cultural counseling and open to learning from persons with radically different backgrounds.

g. Consciousness-raising. To respond and contribute to the liberating changes in the basic identity of women (and therefore of men) in our world, the education of pastoral counselors must raise their consciousness by increased awareness of the crippling effects of systemic sexism in our culture, the church, and (most important) in themselves. It must teach them to integrate consciousness raising as an indispensable part of all their healing and growth work; define wholeness in androgynous ways; and identify the hidden male biases in most "objective" studies of human development and psychotherapeutic theory.

h. Non-traditional families. To respond to the unprecedented changes occurring in marriage and family life and the proliferation of varied lifestyles in our society, the education of pastoral counselors must better equip them to bring healing and growth to persons in divorce, remarriage, and blended families, and in non-traditional committed relationships (e.g., co-habitating couples, gay couples, intentionally generated "family" support systems, etc.).

i. Right-brain capacities. To respond to the growing need for balancing our rational, analytical, intentional left-brain dominated lives (in a left-brain, technological society), with the fuller development of our metaphoric, artistic, intuitive, wholistic, right-brain capacities, education of pastoral counselors must become more right brain in both its methodologies and content. In this way it can equip trainees to let a playful dance between the functions of the two brain hemispheres enrich their counseling, teaching, supervision, writing, *and* their personal lives.

j. Uses of leisure time. To respond to the needs and opportunities created by longer life expectancy, and the dramatic increase in the amount of leisure available in technological societies, education of pastoral counselors must challenge and equip them to generate innovative programs and healing approaches to the wholeness needs of persons in the mid-years and beyond, and more creative uses of leisure by people at all ages. In short, the challenges and opportunities confronting future-oriented educators of pastoral counselors are unprecedented, enormous, and very exciting!

Bibliography. Association for Clinical Pastoral Education, *Handbook* (1978). H. Clinebell, *Basic Types of Pastoral Care and Counseling* (1984), especially ch. 17. "Revisioning the Future of Spirit-Centered Pastoral Care and Counseling," in G. L. Borchert and A. D. Lester, eds. *Spiritual Dimensions of Pastoral Care* (1985). E. E. Thornton, *Professional Education for Ministry, A History of Clinical Pastoral Education* (1970).

H. CLINEBELL

CLINICAL PASTORAL EDUCATION: SPECIALIZATION IN PASTORAL CARE. *See also* CERTIFICATION; PASTORAL THEOLOGY, GRADUATE EDUCATION IN; PROFESSIONALISM; SUPERVISION; THEOLOGICAL EDUCATION AND THE PASTORAL CARE MOVEMENT; THEORY IN PASTORAL CARE AND COUNSELING, FUNCTIONS OF.

EDUCTIVE GUIDANCE. *See* GUIDANCE, PASTORAL.

EDWARD THE CONFESSOR, KING (ca. 1003–66). Charismatic healer and the last Anglo-Saxon king of England. He ascended the throne in 1042 stepping into political instability. Although he lacked what seemed to be much needed political toughness and personal power, he is remembered for virtues like piety, generosity, gentility, unworldliness, asceticism, and chastity. A great sponsor of monastic and church institutions, his major accomplishment was the construction of Westminster Abbey. After his canonization in 1161, because of his working of miracles and of his visions, he became one of England's most popular saints. He is remembered especially for healing a form of tuberculosis by the laying on of hands.

N. F. HAHN

FAITH HEALING; MEDIEVAL CHURCH, PASTORAL CARE IN.

EDWARDS, JONATHAN (1703–58). American Puritan pastor and theologian in Northampton and Stockbridge, Massachusetts. Edwards wrote widely on pastoral topics, but his most significant publication was his *Treatise Concerning Religious Affections* (1746), which he wrote intending to prove that the Great Awakening was a true work of God, but which turned out to be a rich and complex description of the religious inclinations and of the "signs" that ministers and others could use in discerning whether the affections truly had been transformed. By arguing that true religion consists mainly in holy affections, Edwards accented his idea that deep human affections are the springs of human activity, and that the pastor could therefore not afford to deal with people simply at the superficial level of intellectual assent. He also suggested that most of the popular signs of spirituality—ranging from zealous enthusiasm to feelings of assurance—are untrustworthy, and that true religious affection consists in a sense of the beauty and excellency of divine things that transcends all self-preoccupation.

He became deeply engaged in the eighteenth-century debate over pastoral methods, arguing that pastors should avoid premature or careless consolation of distraught souls, lest they block the way to the genuine humbling of the heart that a religious crisis should produce.

His treatise on the religious affections represented a departure from older methods of pastoral casuistry and a forerunner of the efforts to ground pastoral insights on the careful observation of the varieties of religious experience.

E. B. HOLIFIELD

HISTORY OF PROTESTANT PASTORAL CARE (United States). *See also* CASUISTRY, PROTESTANT.

EFFECTIVENESS STUDIES, PASTORAL. *See* CLERGY, EMPIRICAL STUDIES OF; PSYCHOTHERAPY AND COUNSELING (Research Studies and Methods); EMPIRICAL RESEARCH IN PASTORAL CARE AND COUNSELING.

EFFICIENT CAUSE. *See* CAUSALITY IN PSYCHOLOGY, FORMS OF.

EGO, PHILOSOPHICAL CONCEPT AND PROBLEM OF. *See* PERSON (Philosophical Issues); PHILOSOPHY AND PSYCHOLOGY; SELF, PHILOSOPHY OF.

EGO, PSYCHOLOGICAL MEANINGS AND THEORY OF. Mental agency responsible for carrying out executive functions, like planning and problem solving. The term "ego" is the Latin first-person pronoun, "I"; the concept ego is not equivalent to what one calls oneself. Psychology claims scientific status precisely to the degree it distinguishes between the ego, an experience-distant agency, and the self, an experience-near aspect of ordinary consciousness. Folklore, religion, and literature are rich in insights about the self. To this wealth of insight people may add their own observations; but they cannot enrich so easily the natural sciences. Hence psychologists have struggled to claim a special territory for investigation. They did so by either avoiding questions of the self and studying observable behavior, or they described the workings of a hypothetical agency which they alone observed systematically: the ego.

This struggle has shaped the development of psychological theories of the ego. Since "ego" refers neither to a natural object, nor simply to the "self," theory alone determines what the term designates. There are as many definitions of ego as there are distinct ego psychologies.

1. Ego and Consciousness. In prescientific societies and within religious traditions the ego is identified with the self. The self is identified almost completely with one's conscious experience, that is the "I" of ordinary life. Consciousness stamps us as humans and marks us as unique individuals; my hopes and fears are *mine* alone. Both the history of religions and studies of infants reveal that human beings perceive themselves at the center of their worlds. Phenomenologically they are correct. The self is precisely that portion of our world which is the terminus of our sensations and the source of our conscious will (see James; Gibson). Aristotle, like Plato, esteemed vision above all the other senses because it alone permit-

ted one to perceive how one's environment is arrayed around the self (H. Jonas). Western psychologists have ineluctably diminished Aristotle's claim.

Traditional peoples ascribe to the gods their most cherished attribute: consciousness. This reaches a sublime form in the OT when the Divine says of itself, "I am who I am" (Ex. 3:14). Jesus' claims to special wisdom are marked by the extraordinary way he employs the first-person pronoun when he proclaims, "You have heard that it was said . . . . But *I* say unto you" (Mt. 5:21ff.) (see E. Stauffer).

Descartes countermanded this religious identification of self with ego. His famous argument, "I think, therefore I am," bespeaks a deep anxiety: without constant ego processing—thinking—my self, "I", might cease to be (Guntrip). This obsessive doubt permeates Descartes's attempts to delimit the self and assign it a relationship to God. God is that Being who guarantees my continuity. Subsequent English and German philosophers pursued Descartes's problem; even the atheists believed knowledge of self paralleled if not equaled the knowledge of God. David Hume argued one could know neither: we know directly only that we are a bundle of temporary sensations; of our essential self we know nothing. Kant and his followers argued the opposite.

2. Typology of Ego Psychologies. Scientific psychology was born in nineteenth-century German laboratories. William James was an early student. Would traditional conundrums of the mental and moral sciences yield to strictly objective methods? Could their practitioners tell us what human beings were? Indeed, what is the "I" or "I-ego" and what are its boundaries? Based upon how they answer James's questions we can place ego psychologists along a spectrum. Jamesians are at one extreme, Jungians at another.

According to Jamesians, the ego varies by context. Numerous American psychologists who follow James, often unknowingly, define the ego according to the set of sentiments and beliefs one may ascribe to a particular individual.

According to Freudians, the ego is a psychological organ, phylogenetically evolved, which promotes adaptation by developing, out of an undifferentiated matrix, inherited capacities, like memory, impulse control, and self-observation. Hence the ego is defined neither by consciousness, nor personal experience. On the contrary, Freud says in *The Ego and the Id* (1923), it is unknown how much of the ego is unconscious. Post-Freudian psychoanalysts have revised Freud's concepts, expanded the set of ego functions, and described the ego's intrinsic energies (H. Hartmann; R. W. White). Object relations theorists, particularly in Britain, and self psychologists in the U.S. have scrutinized the ego's ability to retain and amplify feelings of a coherent self or "ego-identity" (see P. Federn; H. Kohut; D. W. Winnicott; H. Guntrip; K. Guettler).

According to Jungians, the ego is neither the center nor the master of the personality. In his late texts Jung limits the ego to that portion of the psyche available to consciousness. Hence its size and importance vary; it is not the regulator of psychological life but one of its regulated portions. In cultures like ours where consciousness is overvalued, the psyche automatically redresses the resulting imbalance. Hence in successful treatment, ego-consciousness diminishes and non-ego functions, represented by archetypical entities, emerge automatically (see Jung; M. Fordham; J. Hillman).

3. **Implications for Psychotherapy.** These distinct theories of the ego entail distinct theories of therapy. Jamesians emphasize the need to examine and alter the pathogenic context. Freudians focus upon the need to reorder and repair cognitive deficits, hence they champion the goals of insight and self-regulation. Jungians attempt to evoke the appearance of non-ego attributes, like hidden artistic talent, with which their patients can balance off the burden of excessive self-consciousness.

Because they disagree about the nature of the ego and the goals of treatment, members of these three groups disagree about the definition of ego-boundaries. Consequently, Jamesians seek to decrease their patients' sense that their symptoms are ego alien while Freudians seek to deepen that feeling by demonstrating how defensive behaviors which are initially ego-syntonic become ego-dystonic with insight. Jamesians link one's problems to one's context. Freudians link them to one's internal attempts to adapt to that context. Jungians seek to expose the ego's presumptions of supremacy; the truly healthy personality is centered on the unconscious self (or Self) not the conscious ego.

Bibliography. E. Erikson, *Childhood and Society* (1978). P. Federn, *Ego Psychology and the Psychoses* (1952). S. Freud, *The Ego and the Id* (1962 [1923]) in *SE* 19. M. Fordham, *Jungian Psychotherapy* (1978). J. Gibson, *The Ecological Approach to Visual Perception* (1979). K. Guettler, *Concepts Covered by the Terms "Ego," "Id," and "Superego" as Applied Today in Psychoanalytic Theory* (1971). H. Guntrip, *Schizoid Phenomena, Object Relations and the Self* (1969). H. Hartmann, *Ego Psychology and the Problem of Adaptation* (1964 [1939]). J. Hillman, *Revisioning Psychology* (1975). W. James, *Textbook of Psychology* (1892). H. Jonas, *The Phenomenon of Life* (1966). C. G. Jung, *Two Essays on Analytical Psychology* (1977). H. Kohut, *The Analysis of the Self* (1971). D. Phillips, "Ego" in *Encyclopedia of Religion and Ethics*, J. Hastings ed., vol. 5, (1928) pp. 227–31. E. Stauffer, "Ego" in *Theological Dictionary of the New Testament*, 2, pp. 343–62. R. W. White, *Ego and Reality in Psychoanalytic Theory* (1963). D. W. Winnicott, *Playing and Reality* (1971).

V. P. GAY

ANALYTICAL (JUNGIAN) PSYCHOLOGY *or* PSYCHOANALYSIS (Personality Theory and Research); PERSONALITY THEORY (Varieties, Traditions, and Issues). *See also* PHILOSOPHY AND PSYCHOLOGY. *Compare* IDENTITY; PSYCHE; SELF, PHILOSOPHY OF; SELF PSYCHOLOGIES; SOUL.

EGO-ALIEN. *See* EGO, PSYCHOLOGICAL MEANINGS AND THEORY OF.

EGO BOUNDARY. *See* EGO, PSYCHOLOGICAL MEANINGS AND THEORY OF.

EGO DEFENSE. *See* DEFENSE AND COPING THEORY.

EGO-DYSTONIC/EGO-SYSTONIC. *See* EGO, PSYCHOLOGICAL MEANINGS AND THEORY OF.

EGO IDEAL. The set of positive images and roles toward which the ego strives, similar to Erik Erikson's notion of "ideal identity." A conscious aspect of the superego according to classic psychoanalysis. The superego is a precipitate of the resolved Oedipus complex; the ego ideal a precipitate of the superego.

V. P. GAY

PSYCHOANALYSIS (Personality Theory and Research).

EGO-IDENTITY. *See* EGO, PSYCHOLOGICAL MEANINGS AND THEORY OF; IDENTITY.

EGO INVOLVEMENT. A measure of how individuals perceive that their environment responds to their understanding of their needs. Social psychologists, especially Muzafer Sherif, measure it by assessing how persons attend selectively to information that enhances their self-esteem. High ego-involvement is analogous to secondary narcissistic investment.

V. P. GAY

SELF-ESTEEM. *Compare* DEFENSIVENESS, PASTORAL; EGOTISM; EMPATHY; PRIDE AND HUMILITY; SYMPATHY.

EGO PSYCHOLOGY AND PSYCHOTHERAPY. That chapter or field of psychoanalytic psychology which focuses on and explicates the meanings and functions of the ego. Although commonly referring to a diverse literature which amplifies, extends, and revises Sigmund Freud's ideas in a variety of directions, it is properly inclusive of Freud's writings, beginning in his earliest work and undergoing constant development and modification.

This essay examines the evolving field of ego psychology through an analysis of the developing concept ego in the context of the developing psychoanalytic theory and therapy. It expressly attends to technical and not colloquial meanings. Ego is not identical to the awareness or feeling of one's own self, nor to individual, nor to personality. Ego does not name the "subject" as opposed to the "object" of experience; it is not one's own person as opposed to other persons. The concept ego is complex, multireferential, and inherently ambiguous for a number of reasons. Ego refers to qualities and phenomena of human subjectivity which are at the limit if not beyond the capacities of language. The concept itself is situated in and derives its meanings from three contexts: psychoanalysis as an investigative procedure, as a treatment method, and as a scientific discipline. The terms ego, ego psychology in particular, and psychoanalysis in general, have undergone and continue to undergo revision.

1. **Theory.** *a. 1880s–1900.* From its inception in Freud's earliest writings, the concept ego has had many meanings in a diversity of contexts. It designates the "person's self as a whole," including the body, as distinguished from other selves; and it refers to a certain area of the psyche having a privileged position at the center of the person, involving particular attributes and functions.

In a psychological context, Freud uses "ego" to name three different dimensions of the personality: the subject who directs and oversees activities; certain mental functions having to do with both external and internal reality;

and the "dominant mass of ideas," a more or less organized unity of thoughts and values which are acceptable to and expressive of the person.

With regard to the external world, the ego implements perceptual-cognitive functions having to do with "reality-testing": thought, perception, judgment, reflection. With respect to the internal world, the ego exercises functions of "defense," protecting itself from the re-experience of painful memories, thoughts, and affects. Pathology represents the failure of defense, especially of repression, in "the return of the repressed." Neurotics "suffer mainly from reminiscences," that is, past real-fantasy events.

In a "metapsychological" and "biological" context of the person *qua* organism, the ego is regarded as an organization of neurones. It presupposes the capacities of testing reality, of distinguishing external from internal reality, such that "psychical primary processes" are inhibited and moderated in the activity of "psychical secondary processes."

b. 1900–1915. Throughout this period there is little direct examination and elaboration of the concept ego, though several of its qualities and attributes can be discerned in the new "topographical" (unconscious-preconscious-conscious) model of the mind. Aside from the proposal that the ego is the carrier of the wish for sleep, Freud focuses on the activity of "censorship" rather than on the broader activity of defense. Conflict — a central motif in Freud's thought — is spoken of less in terms of a painful idea *vs.* the dominant ideational mass, or of a wish *vs.* the system preconscious-conscious, but more in terms of ego *vs.* desire, and later, of "ego-instincts" *vs.* sexual instincts.

In the highly productive years 1914–15, the ego becomes a psychic system, differentiated into ego, ego-ideal, ideal ego, and superego. It is a psychic location from which energy is sent to "objects" (persons) and toward which energy is sent from objects, including one's self. The ego presents itself as an object to be loved. Through the process of "identification," the ego "internalizes" an aspect of an external object, making that aspect a part of itself, internally.

c. 1915–1937. What had been up to this point a gradual and constant revision of the concept of ego during this period becomes a dramatic reorientation, wherein the foundation of modern "ego psychology" is laid. In Freud's *The Ego and the Id* (1927), the ego is an agency of the mind, a coherent organization of psychic processes, developed via identification, exercising a diversity of functions: consciousness, sense perception, perception and expression of affect, thought, control of motor action, memory, language, defense mechanisms and defensive activity in general, control, regulation, reality testing. In mediating among the demands of the "id" (instinctual desire and aggression), of the "superego" (ideals, prohibitions, and inhibitions), and of external reality, the ego "serves three masters." It differentiates out of the id, which essentially guides its course.

The ego assumes a more potent and active role in Freud's *Inhibitions, Symptoms, and Anxiety* (1927). Rather than simply naming a system of functions, it names that which constructs and integrates these functions. In addition to reacting to demands, it actively anticipates them

and organizes processes: the ego can exert control over, as well as be dependent upon, the id and the superego. In introducing a developmental view of anxiety, Freud intimates but does not propose a picture of the development of ego functions and of the ego in general.

Anna Freud's *The Ego and the Mechanisms of Defense* (1936) marks the completion of a theoretical and therapeutic shift from "id psychology" to "ego psychology," where the ego and not the id (or the unconscious) is the focus of observation and interpretation. In this study, she identifies a broader range of defenses, links their origin to particular developmental phases, and explains how they serve adaptive (progressive) as well as protective purposes.

d. 1937-present. Ego psychology in this extended phase expands in several directions through the writings of many contributors. The revisions and reorientation of this period involve several features. Psychoanalytic psychology becomes a general developmental psychology, inclusive of pathology and health, id and ego, conflict and adaptation, intrapsychic and interpersonal relations. We examine some of these shifts through the varied ideas of Heinz Hartmann, René Spitz, Margaret Mahler, Erik Erikson, and briefly through a number of other thinkers.

As the "father" of modern ego psychology, Hartmann amplified as well as qualified Freud's thinking in several key areas. Psychoanalysis had arisen as a study and theory of psychopathology but had gradually moved in the direction of becoming a "general developmental psychology," a theory of normality and health as well as of illness, an understanding of consciousness and of the ego as well as of the unconscious and of the id. Hartmann introduced the theme of adaptation and set it alongside the motif of conflict. Human existence and development could not, according to Hartmann, be understood solely nor primarily in terms of conflict: a reciprocal, mutually enhancing relationship exists between the organism and its environment.

The direct corollary to this juxtaposition of conflict and adaptation is the proposal that there are two "spheres" of psychic functioning. Drawing upon Freud's comment that the "id and ego are originally one" (1937), Hartmann asserts that ego and id developed out of an "undifferentiated matrix." On one hand is the sphere of intrapsychic conflict; on the other, a "conflict-free" sphere, wherein the ego, having its own energy source, develops somewhat independently and autonomously. In an "average expectable environment," the ego has the capacities of changing itself to comply with the demands of reality ("autoplastic adaptation"), changing reality to suit itself ("alloplastic adaptation"), and, by implication, finding an adaptive environment. Conflict arises in contexts in which the "fitting together" of organism and environment is absent or impeded.

Spitz and Mahler, though working independently of one another, extended ego psychology in parallel ways. Each pursued Freud's idea that in the case of children, direct external observation could not only complement but also validate findings made through the classical psychoanalytic approach, namely, via introspection and empathy. Through their studies of the pre-oedipal period, of the mother-child dyad, and of the child's psychological processes, each constructed a theory of early psychological development.

Erikson's writings expand Freud's and Hartmann's thoughts. As in Hartmann, the motifs of conflict and adaptation are taken together: instincts and culture, the individual and the collective, are both counterposed as well as potentially complementary. Development must, according to Erikson, take into account not only intrapsychic processes, and the mother-child dyad, but interpersonal, environmental, and cultural factors: development is not only "psychosexual"—it is "psychosocial." The personality develops not only during the first five years of life but throughout the life cycle. It does so according to an innate "epigenetic plan," involving the progressive mastery and solution of phase-specific tasks throughout eight stages.

A few of the number of figures who have contributed to the evolution of ego psychology deserve mention. David Rapaport sought to integrate the new ego psychology with Freud's id psychology and with social psychology, in constructing a general psychoanalytic psychology. Robert White, seeking to transform psychoanalysis from a theory of pathology to a general psychology, concentrated on the concept of independent ego energies and its consequences for the theory as a whole. Edith Jacobson, focusing on the child's dual acquisitions of his or her sense of self and of other selves, formulated a developmental model which integrates the theories and insights of Freud, Hartmann, Rapaport, Mahler, and others. The British school of object relations and the self psychology of Heinz Kohut represent two theoretical lines which presuppose and extend modern ego psychology in contemporary psychoanalytic theory.

2. Therapeutic Method and Technique. Freud's approach arose as a cathartic method: conflicts were regarded as repetitions of traumatic memories which were to be resolved by re-experiencing them in the therapy, such that their original affects were discharged. If neurotics suffered mainly from reminiscences, the goal of therapy was to "fill in the gaps in memory," to make what was unconscious conscious. Toward this end, the client was asked to report whatever comes into his or her mind with as little censorship as possible. The therapist follows this report with "evenly hovering attention," attempting to understand and help the client understand more fully what was and is happening.

Gradually this approach was modified and refined into a method of interpretation and reconstruction. The therapist assists the client in understanding how current conflicts, particularly as they are re-enacted in the therapeutic setting and relationship, are the repetition of past conflicts and attempted maladaptive solutions. It is through this experiential, lived, cognitive-affective process that the capacities of the adult ego are enlisted, and new adaptive solutions are considered and constructed. In this way, the goal of therapy is the "expansion of the ego": "where there was id there shall ego be."

The revisions of psychoanalytic theory in ego psychology have not modified its fundamental therapeutic principles; but, these revisions have had considerable impact on therapeutic method and technique, especially in regard to diagnosis (assessment) and treatment (intervention). In light of the revised understanding of the ego as processing external reality, the internal world, and organizing the fit between the two, "ego assessment" focuses on how a therapeutic problem or conflict may be a matter of inner capacities, environmental conditions, and/or the interrelation between them. Based on an understanding of the ego as functioning in defensive and adaptive ways, ego assessment focuses on discerning and evaluating a person's characteristic defense mechanisms as well as his or her particular areas of conflict-free functioning. Arising out of an appreciation for a general developmental psychological approach, ego assessment concentrates on such developmental issues as: the level of ego development (the highest level of psychosexual development a person has attained); the level of ego strength (the autonomous ego resources available for modification and change at the particular time); the level of object relations (the quality of interpersonal relations, as understood developmentally); and the level of anxiety (the nature, quality, and intensity of anxiety).

In conjunction with expanding and specifying diagnostic tools, ego psychology has contributed to broadening and particularizing treatment skills and modes of intervention. Ego-oriented clinical approaches may be differentiated into ego-supportive and ego-modifying. Though of course this distinction is more shaded than clear-cut, the former refers to those interventions aimed at restoring, sustaining, or deepening adaptive capacities as well as strengthening autonomous ego functions, whereas the latter points to transmuting personality structures and patterns.

In summary, ego psychology has extended the therapeutic diagnostic and treatment armamentarium; it has provided a developmental paradigm for more precise assessment and intervention; and, finally, it has established psychoanalytic psychotherapy as a viable approach to pathology across the clinical spectrum from psychosis to borderline personality disorder to neurosis.

3. Problems in Ego Psychology. There are a number of problems in ego psychology which warrant discussion but which, due to limitations of space, can only be mentioned. The most fundamental problem rests with the concept itself. It may be argued that the term "ego" has become inclusive of so many meanings as to be unacceptably ambiguous if not empty. Is the ego finally to be understood as an "entity" which acts, directs, and organizes, and/or is it a "taxonomy" of psychic functions which somehow loosely fit together? Should this ambiguity be resolved by renaming certain of these referents, as Hartmann, Jacobson, and Kohut have done with the term "self," or are such conceptual distinctions false solutions which avoid the ambiguity Freud intentionally exploited from the beginning?

It has been asserted that ego psychology fails to blend with its psychoanalytic foundation in a consistent and coherent way, that it tries unsuccessfully to unite a revised vision of the ego with an outdated picture of the id. Furthermore, some have argued that in the focus on and explication of the ego system, the nature of the systems of id and superego and the intersystemic relations between the agencies have been sorely neglected. Last, from a clinical point of view, while proponents have claimed that ego psychology enhances diagnostic and treatment skills, there are those who assert that this perspective tends to encourage a mechanical, depersonalized, "experience-distant" approach to therapy, wherein the therapist treats the ego, the id, the superego, and not the "person."

4. Pastoral and Theological Implications. Psychoanalytic ego psychology explicitly as well as implicitly portrays images of human nature, action, and fulfillment and thereby is a perspective which not only informs and enhances but also competes and conflicts with Judeo-Christian religious traditions.

Christian theology and pastoral care and counseling benefit from the findings and insights of ego psychology in theoretical as well as practical ways. Ego psychology suggests the possibility as well as the plausibility of thinking of faith, and of thinking theologically, in developmental terms. This is not to propose that theology be developmental in form; rather, it is to assert that a theology which takes into account the differentiation between successive phases of human development may be more reflective of the problems and potential solutions of human life. Ego psychology enhances the broadly clinical activities of pastoral care and counseling in providing a framework for assessing, referring, and/or treating a broad range of disturbances to which the clergy are exposed. It is a perspective particularly helpful to the pastor because it takes into account the parishioner's (or client's) inner psychological capacities, his or her environmental situation, and the fit between the two as areas to be understood and potentially modified.

At the same time, ego psychology is a perspective which both competes as well as conflicts with Judeo-Christian theologies and faiths. This competition and conflict revolves around the fact that in contemporary Western culture, psychological theories and faith systems serve a common function: the organization of inner life. In so doing, they each provide a "map" through which the self experiences itself and its world. This map implicitly as well as explicitly examines and explains how and why human beings think and act as they do, how they might and should think and act more "appropriately," and how change toward such ends may and should be effected.

The map provided by ego psychology, or, the maps provided by ego psychologists, not only compete but conflict with the maps of theological perspectives. As a psychology, by definition ego psychology reduces problems, issues, dynamics, actions to a secular, "scientific" level, one having an express focus on the individual. Ego psychology inherently implies if not asserts that the questions and problems themselves are not religious-theological nor normative-ethical; that they are not basically communal or "transcendent"; that "ought" can be derived from "is."

In summary, ego psychology has been and can continue to be an invaluable resource for the practices of pastoral care and counseling, and for ministry and theology in general. At the same time, as in the use of any theoretical and practical resource, how it properly fits with the needs, goals, and values of ministry must be subject to careful and critical examination and evaluation.

Bibliography. G. Blanck, "Crossroads in the Technique of Psychotherapy," *Psychoanalytic Review,* 56 (1970), 498–510. G. Blanck and R. Blanck, *Ego Psychology: Theory and Practice* (1974–79). D. S. Browning, *Generative Man: Psychoanalytic Perspectives* (1973). E. Erikson, *Childhood and Society* (1964); *Insight and Responsibility* (1964); *Identity: Youth and Crisis* (1968). A. Freud, *The Ego and the Mechanisms of Defense* (1968). S. Freud, *The Ego and the Id* (1927); *Inhibitions, Symptoms, and Anxiety* (1927); *Standard Edition of the Complete Psychological Works of Sigmund Freud* (1981). E. G. Goldstein, *Ego Psychology and Social Work Practice* (1984). H. Guntrip, *Psychoanalytic Theory, Therapy, and the Self* (1971). H. Hartmann, *Ego Psychology and the Problem of Adaptation* (1958); *Essays on Ego Psychology: Selected Problems in Psychoanalytic Theory* (1964). H. Hartmann, E. Kris, and R. M. Loewenstein, "Comments on the Formation of Psychic Structure," *Psychoanalytic Study of the Child,* 2 (1946), 11–38. R. R. Holt, "The Past and Future of Ego Psychology," *Psychoanalytic Quarterly,* 44 (1975), 550–76. E. Jacobson, *The Self and the Object World* (1964). G. S. Klein, "The Ego in Psychoanalysis — A Concept in Search of an Identity," *Psychoanalytic Review* 56, (1970), 511–25; *Psychoanalytic Theory: An Exploration of Essentials* (1976). H. Kohut, *The Analysis of the Self* (1971). E. Kris, "The Development of Ego Psychology," *Samiksa,* 5 (1951), 153–68; "Ego Psychology and Interpretation in Psychoanalytic Therapy," *Psychoanalytic Quarterly,* 20 (1951), 15–30. J. Laplanche and J. B. Pontalis, *The Language of Psychoanalysis* (1973). M. S. Mahler, *The Selected Papers of Margaret S. Mahler* (1979). W. W. Meissner, "Psychoanalysis as a Theory of Therapy," *International J. of Psychoanalytic Psychotherapy,* 4 (1975), 181–218. D. Rapaport, *The Collected Papers of David Rapaport* (1967). R. W. White, *Ego and Reality in Psychoanalytic Theory* (1963). B. Wolman, ed., *Psychoanalytic Techniques* (1967).

C. R. SCHLAUCH

OBJECT RELATIONS THEORY; PSYCHOANALYSIS (Therapeutic Method and Research *or* Personality Theory and Research). *See also* PERSONALITY THEORY; PSYCHOTHERAPY. *Compare* INDIVIDUAL PSYCHOLOGY; NEOFREUDIAN PERSONALITY THEORIES AND PASTORAL CARE; SELF PSYCHOLOGIES; WILL THERAPY.

EGO STRENGTH. Assessment of a person's ability to maintain appropriate ego functioning, especially under duress. Psychotherapy aims to increase ego strength by repairing deficits in reality-testing, control of drives, object relations, thought processes, and defenses. Similar concepts are ego autonomy (S. Freud, Heinz Hartmann), ego identity (Erik Erikson), and adaptive regression in the service of the ego (Ernst Kris).

V. P. GAY

EGO PSYCHOLOGY AND PSYCHOTHERAPY; PSYCHOANALYSIS (Personality Theory and Research). *See also* DEFENSE AND COPING THEORY; IDENTITY; SELF-ESTEEM. *Compare* EVALUATION AND DIAGNOSIS, PSYCHOLOGICAL.

EGOISM. *See* LOVE.

EGOTISM. A sense of supreme importance of oneself. A character flaw, not a psychiatric disorder, it designates an excess of self-love at the expense of object love. Egotists are primary narcissists; they suffer no conflict, no guilt, and have no urge to alter themselves.

V. P. GAY

NARCISSISM/NARCISSISTIC PERSONALITY; PRIDE AND HUMILITY (Moral Theology). *See also* DEFENSE AND COPING THE-

ORY; EGO (Psychological Meanings and Theory). *Compare* EGO STRENGTH; SELF-ESTEEM; SPECIALNESS, SENSE OF.

ELCHANINOV, FATHER ALEXANDER. *See* YELCHANINOV, FATHER ALEXANDER.

ELDERLY PERSONS. *See* AGING; OLDER PERSONS, PASTORAL *or* JEWISH CARE OF.

ELDERS. In the NT the word *presbyteros* is translated "elders." The earliest Palestinian church was administered collegially by a board of such elders (see Acts 11:30; 15:22). An early responsibility of the elders was to supply presbyters for the churches established through Paul's missionary endeavors. Several NT passages indicate that in the earliest period of the church the presbyter or elder was an "overseer" or *episkopos* (see Acts 20:17f.; Phil. 1:1; and Tit. 1:5, 7). In the earliest period the elder was the presiding bishop of a local congregation. While elders are not mentioned in the Pauline Epistles, in the Pastoral Epistles they govern by teaching, preaching, and pastoral ministry. They are anointed and empowered through the laying on of hands (I Tim. 4:14). These functions of the elder closely parallel the functions of the priesthood in Israel. By the second century a distinction developed between the bishop who presided over a council of elders and the elder whose authority was derived from the bishop. Not until the second and third centuries, however, did the church distinguish clearly a threefold pattern of ministry—bishop, elder, and deacon.

In contemporary church polity the term elder plays a significant role in the Reformed tradition and other traditions influenced by it. Even within the Calvinistic tradition a distinction is made between presbyter and elder. The presbyter is an ordained elder whose responsibility is primarily to word and sacrament, while a layperson may be ordained an elder to share responsibility with the pastor for the administration and ordering of the church's life. The distinction Calvin maintained was between teaching elders (ordained pastors) and ruling elders (ordained laypersons).

The Anglican tradition ordains deacons as a transitional order toward priesthood, which is a permanent order. Somewhat the same practice has continued in American Methodism as seen in the policy of the United Methodist Church. In the United Methodist Church, however, the elder is ordained to a threefold responsibility of word, sacrament, and order. Other Christian bodies, such as Disciples of Christ, also ordain elders for the purpose of pastoral oversight of the church. In the Moravian Church, deacons are consecrated (not ordained) as presbyters, as the second order of ministry.

Bibliography. B. Cooke, *Ministry to Word and Sacraments* (1976). W. Niesel, *The Theology of Calvin* (1956). E. Schweizer, *Church Order in the New Testament* (1961).

J. C. LOGAN

MINISTRY; ECCLESIOLOGY AND PASTORAL CARE. *See also* BISHOP; DEACON; LAY PASTORAL CARE AND COUNSELING.

ELECTROCONVULSIVE THERAPY (ECT). A treatment in which seizures are elicited in order to alleviate severe mental disorders, most commonly major depressions. The treatment involves first inducing general anesthesia, and then applying controlled amounts of electrical stimuli to the patient's skull which traverses portions of the brain. This causes a seizure which in turn produces the therapeutic effect. Seizures are typically elicited once every two to three days for a total of eight to twelve administrations, with the exact number being dependent upon symptom amelioration. The precise mechanisms through which seizures produce therapeutic effects are not known with certainty. However, research suggests that seizures increase the permeability of the blood-brain barrier and increase levels of neurotransmitters which may decrease psychological difficulty in a manner similar to antidepressant medication.

ECT was not judiciously used early in its development (1940s–1950s). This undoubtedly contributed to the very negative impression most persons retain regarding ECT. The differences between past and present usage of ECT are striking. Patients were commonly treated with high numbers of ECT over many years. Similarly ECT was thought to be a panacea and used to treat widely varying mental disorders. Currently, it is used in a much more limited fashion. It is not normally utilized until other treatment interventions have been attempted without success (such as psychotherapy and antidepressant medication). Further, large numbers of treatments do not typically occur. Moreover, it is used more specifically with mood disorders when the symptoms delineated below are present.

These symptoms are usually associated with very severe mood disorders, such as profound and unremitting sadness or dysphoria with these symptoms being worse in the morning, terminal insomnia (early awakening), anorexia, weight loss, paucity of speech, slowed thinking, motor inertia, suicidal thoughts and impulses, and feelings of guilt, hopelessness and worthlessness. Further, delusional and psychotic processes, when the content of such processes relates to guilt, self-blame, persecution, bodily disease and nihilism, suggest that ECT may be an effective treatment. The above symptoms are thought to reflect an "endogenous depression," one which is predominately physiologically based as opposed to "reactive depressions" which are the reaction to situationally based stressors. ECT is thought to ameliorate endogenous depressions but not reactive depressions.

Most studies comparing the therapeutic effectiveness of ECT with other treatment interventions in treating mood disorders suggest that ECT is of greater therapeutic efficacy than antidepressant medication.

The greatest liability of ECT is the confusion immediately experienced after treatment and memory difficulties that persist for longer periods of time. However, research clearly shows that these sequelae are time-limited. The patient will probably be somewhat confused for the first thirty minutes after treatment. One to two hours after the treatment, though, impairment may not be noticeable to the casual observer. After six ECT treatments the patient may retain a mild to moderate memory deficit. He or she may not be able to recall certain things that occurred prior to ECT. Additionally, the patient may experience difficulty consolidating new memories. However, usually by three months, and more clearly by six months subsequent to treatment, all memory deficits have usually been resolved.

ECT is a treatment which has been beset by much negative publicity. However, as research now demonstrates, the therapeutic benefits of its usage in specific cases, even in light of the side effects noted above, suggest it to be the treatment of choice for many patients.

Bibliography. R. Abrams and W. B. Essman, *Electroconvulsive Therapy: Biological Foundations and Clinical Applications* (1982). M. Fink, "Myths of 'Shock' Therapy," *American J. of Psychiatry*, 134 (1977), 991–96. R. G. Harper and A. Weins, "Electroconvulsive Therapy and Memory," *J. of Nervous and Mental Disease*, 161 (1975), 245–54. L. R. Squire, "Electroconvulsive Therapy and Memory Loss," *American J. of Psychiatry*, 145 (1977), 997–1001. I. S. Turek and T. E. Hanlon, "The Effectiveness and Safety of Electroconvulsive Therapy," *J. of Nervous and Mental Disease*, 164 (1977), 419–31.

T. COLLISTER

MENTAL HEALTH AND ILLNESS; MENTAL HOSPITAL CHAPLAINCY; PSYCHOPATHOLOGY, THEORIES OF; PSYCHOSIS. *Compare* PERSONALITY, BIOLOGICAL DIMENSIONS OF; BRAIN RESEARCH; MEDICATION; MIND-BODY RELATIONSHIP; PSYCHOSURGERY.

ELLIOTT, HARRISON (1882–1951). Educator. After succeeding George Albert Coe at Union Theological Seminary, Elliott served for twenty-five years as professor of practical theology and head of the department of religious education and psychology. He pointed out the enormous import of the development of psychology in *The Bearing of Psychology upon Religion* (1927) and helped introduce courses in mental hygiene into the seminary curriculum. His skill in group process and discussion greatly influenced his student Carl Rogers. With his wife, Grace Loucks Elliott, he co-authored *Solving Personal Problems* (1936) and from 1941–1945 regularly hosted meetings of the New York Psychology Group.

Elliott earned a B.A. from Ohio Wesleyan University (1905), a B.D. from Drew Theological Seminary (1911), an M.A. from Columbia (1922), and a Ph.D. from Yale (1940). Early in his career he worked for the Methodist Church in China and was secretary of the International Committee of the YMCA.

A. STOKES

HISTORY OF PROTESTANT PASTORAL CARE (United States); NEW YORK PSYCHOLOGY GROUP; PSYCHOLOGY IN AMERICAN RELIGION.

ELLIS, ALBERT. *See* RATIONAL EMOTIVE PSYCHOTHERAPY.

EMBARRASSMENT. *See* SHAME; SELF-ESTEEM.

EMBODIMENT. *See* BODY; INCARNATIONAL PASTORAL CARE (Protestantism).

EMERGENCY. *See* CRISIS INTERVENTION THEORY; CRISIS MINISTRY; DISASTER, PUBLIC.

EMERGENCY, PSYCHOLOGY OF PASTOR IN. An emergency is generally understood as an unexpected occurrence or set of circumstances that demand immediate action. With respect to pastoral care, an emergency demands that whatever care is given be given immediately and without reflection beforehand. Emergency and a crisis are often identified, but their meanings are quite different. A crisis is a turning point, a decisive or crucial time, a time of great danger or trouble that affects the long-term outcome of the situation. Its major psychological feature is that it demands reflection and thoughtful decision. In contrast, the major psychological feature of an emergency is that it demands that there be no reflection, only immediate action. The circumstances of the emergency appear to be saying that what is done is less important than that something be done now. In a crisis there is time; in an emergency there is no time.

The psychological effect of an emergency upon a pastor is similar to its effect upon anyone — a felt need to take immediate action. Because a pastor's social role and personal identity is one in which he or she is a learned person committed to helping people, an apparent emergency may make a greater demand on the pastor than upon one who can avoid any expectation of expertise. Although the demand of any emergency seems to be "Do something!" the actual need is for the pastor to decide quickly whether, in fact, something really must be done now.

If one rules out certain physical emergencies, such as apparent heart attacks, choking, life-threatening accidents, suicidal or homicidal behavior, all of which require quick behavioral and not distinctively pastoral response, most pastoral emergencies are crises, not emergencies. This means that there is time after all, and an appropriate pastoral response is to discover the meaning of the apparent emergency and how to respond to it as a crisis.

The person who presents an emergency to a pastor is saying, "You've got to do something to save me; the situation is intolerable." (A frequent variation on the request for emergency help is when the seeker anxiously demands that the pastor do something about somebody else.) The pastor, who is supposed to be a person who cares and who is quite vulnerable to guilt for not caring, has a comparable need on his or her part to do something immediately to take away the requesting person's pain or panic. The pastor's feelings of importance are accentuated because this person has come to him or her in this apparently dire situation, saying, "Be my rescuer. I am inadequate and dependent on you alone for help. Take over my life and responsibilities." If there is exaggeration here, it is only slight, and it underscores the major features of the situation: the seeker's helplessness, the opportunity for heroic behavior on the part of the pastor, and an assumption on the part of both that reality is external and circumstantial, unrelated to personality structure and longer-term needs. The apparent emergency has recreated the early life situation of the parent and child.

The word "apparent" has been used repeatedly in this article in order to emphasize the fact that there are very few real psychological or pastoral emergencies; therefore an appropriate response to an emergency is doing just what it seems cannot be done: examining the situation and the persons involved in it to see what is going on. In what way does either the seeker or the pastor need the emergency to relieve anxiety or to avoid what is happening in life or in the pastoral relationship? Emergency behavior actually rules out pastoral care and substitutes, instead, immediate relief. Pastoral care always involves looking at the persons involved (including the pastor) as well as the situation and dealing with the whole person, not just the problem presented.

J. PATTON

CRISIS MINISTRY; INTERPRETATION AND HERMENEUTICS, PASTORAL. *See also* MENTAL HEALTH, PASTOR'S; PANIC. *Compare* CRISIS INTERVENTION THEORY.

EMERGENCY BAPTISM. Emergency baptism refers to any baptism performed under life-threatening conditions, most often with critically ill, deformed, or injured newborns and infants. The request for emergency baptism is rarely casual. In every instance a few unhurried moments of reflection will make clear that significant meaning is attached to this pastoral act by either parents, relatives, physicians, or nurses.

The pastoral imperative is to respond—with dispatch, but not panic. If the request comes from unreasonable fear, the pastor does not need to contribute to the hysteria. One usually can assume that the sacramental claim comes from a life-threatening setback to a newborn child. This "sacramental emergency" usually means inconvenience. Subjectively the pastor may want to attend to the matter quickly, but to "sprinkle and run" is not a faithful response. Assessment time before the baptism and moments of debriefing afterwards may prove immensely rewarding.

An emergency baptism is a communal event. If we are called to minister in an unknown situation, we need to make some initial inquiries: Can you tell me about the child? Are parents or relatives here? What is their religious background? Do they have a parish priest or minister? Who among the staff has been caring for the child?

Launching into the actual baptismal act without first taking some measure of these variables is a mistake. We do well to avoid playing into a magical view of the sacrament. Inviting the nurses, doctors, and family to stand with the child during baptism makes a positive statement about the larger Christian family. Time taken to build this momentary community will be meaningful.

Roman Catholic tradition emphasizes the sacrament of baptism as a precondition to church membership. Among some Catholic hospital personnel there may be a tendency to baptize all infants, especially those with potential illness. While from the Protestant perspective this practice may seem unnecessary, wisdom dictates that the pastor examine his or her own bias. The commitment to the sacrament is clearly a symbol of concern and respect. Persons who go to the trouble of calling a pastor or chaplain are reflecting their commitment to the welfare of the child; such quality of concern is worthy of support.

On occasion families decide after a pastoral conversation *not* to baptize a child. When a family requests emergency baptism prior to their infant's surgery, it may

become clear that their own tradition practices "believers baptism" and that they are responding to magical pressure from outside individuals. When pastoral conversation uncovers this subtle coercion, faithfulness may mean waiting and trusting that their child is in the care of God and in time will be able to take a place in the congregational fellowship of his or her parents.

P. C. TEMPLE

BAPTISM AND CONFIRMATION. *See also* CRISIS MINISTRY; DYING, PASTORAL CARE OF. *Compare* BLESSING AND BENEDICTION; CHILDBIRTH; LIMBO.

EMMANUEL MOVEMENT. An organization formed in 1904 with the general aim of bringing together the forces of medicine and religion to promote healing both mind and body under the conviction that Jesus Christ heals in the contemporary world as he did in NT times.

In 1904 Elwood Worcester, rector of the Emmanuel Episcopal Church in Boston, Massachusetts, in cooperation with several prominent New England physicians, established a clinic for spiritual healing. The clinic's activities, housed in Worcester's church, were dubbed the "Emmanuel movement" by the press. Spectacular reports of healings drew national attention. In 1908 Worcester, in collaboration with his ministerial associate, The Rev. S. McComb, and Dr. I. Cariat, a prominent physician on the faculty of Tufts Medical School, published *Religion and Medicine,* a volume that set down clearly the philosophy undergirding the movement. The book drew mixed reviews; but its influence was enhanced when it was included in the Surgeon General's *Progress of Medicine During the Nineteenth Century.*

Unlike other healing cults of the time, the Emmanuel movement built on enlightened and sophisticated notions in both medicine and religion. Its approach to healing was based on four principles: (1) the person is a composite of mind and body; (2) religion should clearly and emphatically value the therapeutic efficacy of medical treatment of organic disorders; (3) the relation between organic and functional disorders should be a legitimate domain for spiritual healing; and (4) the contributions of the medical profession to health and welfare are in no sense to be minimized. As Worcester was later to summarize it: "What distinguishes this work from all healing cults . . . is its frank recognition of Religion and Science as the great controlling forces of human life and the attempt to bring these two highest creations of man into relations of helpful cooperation."

Despite these serious intentions to relate high scholarship in both medicine and religion to the area of praxis, the movement was sputtering by the early 1930s and dead by 1940. Thornton (1970) suggests three reasons for the movement's demise: (1) it failed to train ministers; (2) Worcester did not himself grow and change with the rapid developments in psychiatry; and (3) the relationships between physicians and clergy, integral to the movement, broke down.

As an item in the history of the medicine-religion dialogue, the Emmanuel movement holds a minor but nevertheless important place, particularly in the development of wholistic tendencies in medicine and health care. Perhaps of equal significance, from the perspectives of the pastoral care and counseling movements, were its spinoffs in regard to later developments in the mental hygiene movement, the hospital care offered by chaplains, and the establishment of clinical pastoral education (CPE) as a part of theological education.

Bibliography. C. J. Scherzer, "The Emmanuel Movement," *Pastoral Psychology* (1951), 27–33. E. E. Thornton, *Professional Education for Ministry* (1970). E. Worcester, S. McComb, and I. Coriat, *Religion and Medicine* (1908). E. Worcester and S. McComb, *Body, Mind and Spirit* (1931).

O. STRUNK, JR.

HISTORY OF PROTESTANT PASTORAL CARE (United States); PASTORAL CARE MOVEMENT; RELIGION AND HEALTH MOVEMENT. *Biography:* WORCESTER.

EMOTION. At the level of conscious experience, a state of feeling that has motivational and cue-producing properties that organize and guide cognition and action; at the motor-expressive level, a characteristic configuration of movements, primarily facial, secondarily vocal-postural-gestural; at the neurochemical level, a particular set of brain mechanisms, neural pathways, and neurotransmitters, whose activation is responsible for the motor-expressive and experiential components and for increased activity in the cardiovascular, respiratory, and other life-support systems, the latter bodily changes being noticeable only in more intense emotional situations.

1. **Components.** Although differences on particulars remain, most major emotion theorists agree that emotion is complex and must be defined at different levels or in terms of different components. An emotion, it is generally agreed, has neurophysiological, expressive, and experiential components. Key differences among theorists are largely in regard to the first and last of these components. Some think the key neurophysiological processes occur primarily in the autonomic ("involuntary") nervous system, which controls cardiovascular functions, respiration, and other visceral activities. Others think that the generation of emotion comes from the somatic nervous system, which innervates the muscles of facial expression and all the muscles over which we have voluntary control. According to this view, autonomic-visceral changes are consequences of emotion. The weight of the evidence seems to be coming down in favor of the latter theorists but the issue is not settled.

At the experiential level, opinions divide on whether emotion necessarily includes *cognition* that is based on some transformation of sense data or is simply a state of *feeling* that is based on patterned (untransformed) sensory input. The latter position holds that "feeling is first," the primal mental process, and that emotion at the level of conscious feeling is coordinated with thought and action through biological and experiential development. A related issue concerns the role of cognition in the generation of emotion experience. Some investigators hold that cognitive evaluation or appraisal of an incentive event is a *sine qua non* of emotion (Lazarus, 1980; Plutchik, 1980), whereas others maintain that cognition is only one of several vehicles for activating emotion.

There is some evidence for the latter position, but the issue is still being debated.

There is greatest consensus among behavioral scientists on the nature of the expressive component of emotion because it is this component on which there is the most robust and widely accepted empirical data. It is generally agreed that in human beings the expression of the emotions is most highly differentiated in the face and voice. There is incontrovertible evidence for the correspondence between certain patterns of facial and vocal activity and certain emotions and there is rapidly increasing evidence that these expressive behaviors are of signal importance in human development and human relationships.

2. **Research.** *a. Neurophysiological.* There have been numerous advances in the knowledge of particular brain mechanisms involved in emotion. The brain areas closely linked to emotions, particularly the structures of the limbic system, are among the phylogenetically oldest parts of the mammalian brain. This suggests a critical role for the emotions in human evolution. Direct stimulation of limbic structures elicits emotion and emotion-specific behavior. For example, stimulation of the medial areas of the hypothalamus elicits rage behavior in the cat (Flynn, 1967). In contrast, lesions of the amygdala block aggressive behavior and produce docility in the normally fierce lynx and agonti (Schreiner and Kling, 1956).

Clinical observations of brain-injured human patients have also shown correspondence between certain structures and specific emotional responses. Although this evidence does not indicate that there is an "anger center" or "fear center" it does show that some emotions are more related to certain brain structures than to others. The same principle holds for hormones and other neurotransmitters. These data help define emotion by specifying their biological nature.

b. Expressive. The first widely acclaimed work on the expressive component of emotions was authored by Charles Darwin (1872). His hypothesis that certain emotional expressions are innate and universal has been convincingly confirmed by contemporary scientists (Eibl-Eibesfeldt, 1972; Ekman, Firesen, and Ellsworth, 1972; Izard, 1971). Fundamental emotions that are recognized and labeled similarly across cultures include interest, joy, surprise, sadness, anger, disgust, contempt, fear, and shame. Genuine, spontaneous facial and vocal patterns of the emotions serve three social functions. They (a) signal the inner experience or state of feeling (b) influence the thought and actions of observers, and (c) may provide information about when the activator of emotion is external.

In some relationships and under certain circumstances emotional expressions prescribe precisely the behavior of the perceiver. For example, most one-year-old infants will cross the normally fear-eliciting deep side of a visual cliff if their mothers exhibit a joyful, smiling face, but none will cross if confronted with mother's fearful expression (Klinnert *et al.*, 1983). Such dramatic examples of expression-motivated behavior may not be so common in adult behavior, but emotional expressions continue to add critical information and emphasis to linguistic communication. We tend to be unaware of our virtually automatic search for expressive cues to the "real" significance of the spoken word.

c. Experience. The third component of emotion is variously labeled subjective experience, phenomenological aspect, or feeling. It is most typically the referent when people use the word emotion. Theorists, like Zajonc (1980) and Izard (1977) who hold that the third component of emotion is essentially a state of feeling, believe that there are separate systems for emotion and cognition. Zajonc (1980) has presented evidence indicating that people can make affective responses (preferences) among briefly exposed objects even though they cannot reliably say whether they have ever seen the objects. That is, they can sort the objects on the basis of preference but not in terms of "objective" features which enable cognitive discrimination.

The influence of emotional experience on perception, cognition, and action has been demonstrated in a number of investigations. Experience of emotion is integral to empathy, and sadness and grief are critical in maintaining family and community cohesiveness (Averill, 1962; Izard, 1977). Emotional experiences as well as emotional expressions are key forces in the establishment of the first social bond (infant-mother attachment) and all subsequent interpersonal ties. Experimentally induced joy has been shown to increase altruistic behavior (Salovey and Rosenhan, 1982) and resistance to temptation (Fry, 1975).

3. **Functions.** There is substantial empirical support for the assumption that each of the emotions of human experience has adaptive, motivational functions. For example, interest motivates learning, exploration, and creative endeavors. Joy facilitates social interaction and alleviates stress. Anger mobilizes energy for action against frustrating barriers which may include insults to personal integrity and oppression. Shame motivates development of skills and competencies that strengthen the self and make it less vulnerable to humiliation. Guilt, believed by some to be a fundamental emotion despite its lack of a characteristic expression, fosters reparation and the development of a sense of personal responsibility.

One can reason that emotions maintain their adaptive functions even in psychopathology. There is firm evidence that the so-called affective symptomatology of depression is not a unitary affective state but rather a pattern of discrete emotions including sadness, anger, and shame (Izard, 1972). Sadness can serve an adaptive function in depression by slowing down mental and motor functioning, giving the individual time to focus on and attend to the problem. Anger's power to energize and activate can prevent the sadness from becoming totally immobilizing and overwhelming. Finally, shame can help ameliorate depression by motivating self-protective and self-strengthening behaviors, counteracting the loss of self-esteem that often figures in the etiology of the disorder.

Bibliography. J. R. Averill, "A Constructivist View of Emotion," in R. Plutchik and H. Kellerman, eds., *Emotion, Theory, Research and Experience* (1983). C. R. Darwin, *The Expression of Emotions in Man and Animals* (1872). I. Eibl-Eibesfeldt, "Similarities and Differences between Cultures in Expressive Movements," in R. A. Hinde, ed., *Nonverbal Communication* (1972). P. Ekman, W. V. Friesen, and P. C. Ellsworth, *Emotion in the Human Face: Guidelines for Research and an Integration of Findings* (1972). J. P. Flynn, "The neural basis of aggression in cats," in D. C. Glass, ed., *Neurophysiology and Emotion* (1967). P. S. Fry, "Affect and Resistance to Temptation," *Developmental Psychology* (1975), 466–72. C. E. Izard, *The Face of Emotion* (1971); *Human Emotions* (1977); *Patterns of Emotions: A New Analysis of Anxiety and Depression* (1972). M. Klinnert, J. Campos, J. Sorce, R. Emde, and M. Svejda, "Emotions as behavior regulators," in R. Plutchik and H. Kellerman eds., *Emotions in early development*, vol. 2, *Emotion: Theory, research and experience* (1983). R. S. Lazarus, "Thoughts on the relations between emotion and cognition," *American Psychologist*, 37 (1982), 1019–24. R. Plutchik, *Emotion, a Psychoevolutionary Synthesis* (1980). R. C. Roberts, *Spirituality and Human Emotion* (1982). P. Salovey and D. L. Rosenhan, "Effects of Joy, Attention and Recipient's Status on Helpfulness," (1982), unpublished manuscript. L. Schreiner and A. Kling, "Rhinencephalon and Behavior," *American J. of Physiology*, 184 (1956) 486–90. R. B. Zajonc, "Feeling and Thinking: Preferences need no inferences," *American Psychologist*, 35 (1980), 151–75.

C. E. IZARD

AMBIVALENCE; CATHARSIS; FEELING, THOUGHT AND ACTION IN PASTORAL COUNSELING. *See also* COGNITIVE/CONATIVE PROBLEM IN PSYCHOLOGY AND COUNSELING; MIND-BODY RELATIONSHIP; PERSON (Philosophical Issues); PHILOSOPHY AND PSYCHOLOGY; REASON AND PASSION. *Compare* ANGER; ANXIETY; APATHY; BOREDOM; ECSTASY; FEAR; HAPPINESS; LOVE; MANIC-DEPRESSION (BIPOLAR) DISORDER; PAIN; RAGE AND HOSTILITY; SADNESS AND DEPRESSION.

EMOTIONAL DEVELOPMENT. 1. Historical Perspective. The research and discussion of emotional development in the past century has included a mixture of very well and very poorly conceived studies. Emotions are not easily defined operationally, and many behavioral scientists believe emotions are objectively unknowable. These researchers frequently turn to animal studies which can be well controlled and are methodologically reliable, unlike many studies done with humans. The difficulty with the findings taken from animal studies is that they are often irrelevant and give little information about the study of emotional development in humans.

Historically, Bridges (1932) was one of the first researchers to study emotional development. Though her data were based on observation rather than experimentation, her work is still referred to today and her basic assumptions of emotional development have had a great impetus into further research in this area. She believed that children are born with the capacity for showing only undifferentiated excitement. By about the age of three months, children are able to differentiate excitement into positive and negative aspects, namely delight and distress. Following this early period, children show an increasing differentiation until about two years of age. At this age, the emotions of fear, disgust, joy, and affection are expressed and these new emotions are similar to the most complex adult emotions.

Since Bridges, the two emotions most studied have been smiling and crying, which represent pleasure and displeasure. Researchers have found that smiling occurs early in infants, supporting the belief that pleasure is an innate emotion. However, infants quickly begin smiling when human faces are presented, suggesting that emotional responses are learned. Today, researchers generally believe that emotions are a result of an interaction between innate and environmental influences. Research on infant crying has produced similar results, finding that crying is also both the product of inheritance and given situations.

Another area of research interest in emotional development involves the effects of deprivation on children. In the past, researchers investigated how children raised in institutions compared to children raised under usual family conditions. These early researchers believed that children raised in institutions were intellectually impaired and emotionally flat compared to the other group. Today these early conclusions about deprivation are viewed with skepticism, because the results are often not justified by the research findings. Yet modern researchers still believe there is some effect from early deprivation, though this emotional disturbance may result from the breaking, even temporarily, of ties with familiar individuals and places.

2. Infancy. Emotional development in human beings is a continuous and gradual process which occurs throughout life. The basic types of emotional expressions are present at an early age. Emotional patterns which are established may change throughout life, but when change occurs, it is normally slow.

Compared to adults, infants have slower fluctuations of affective responses to varied stimulations. Infants are unable to keep their internal environments stable, and they are easily upset. For example, when infants are pleased, they are pleased all over. Their whole body, not just a smile, indicates how they feel. But these expressions may fade quickly, and seconds later infants may be angry all over; they kick, cry enthusiastically, and get red in the face. Infants' moods change so quickly that it is almost frightening for the caretakers. This instability of emotional response is, however, normal. If infants are raised in an emotional atmosphere which is loving and consistent, their emotions will stabilize and develop normally.

3. Early Childhood. There is a steady differentiation of emotional responses during early childhood. Some general trends during this period include a response to a wider range of emotion-evoking situations, an increasing control of emotional manifestations, and a greater awareness of the role and feelings of others.

Researchers have probed the emotions of anxiety, aggression, fear, and creativity, with some interest also in socialization, affection, humor and interests. Fear, for example, is typically believed to be learned, though there is a predisposition to fear certain things (animals, the unknown). Most aggression is also believed to be evident or learned by the end of early childhood years. From the research on these various emotions, four generalizations have been made: (1) There is a growth from the diffuse to the specific; (2) there are responses to a wider variety of stimuli as one grows older; (3) the role of maturation and readiness increases; (4) there is increasingly wide variation of emotional response dependent upon environmental stimulation, especially upon parental models and parent-child interaction.

4. Middle Childhood. Researchers frequently report the important role of infancy and early childhood in shaping emotional responses. However, though most researchers believe that little can be done about the basic potentiality of human being by age six, growth is always an interaction of the individual with the environment. The environment may be changed and manipulated and the patterns of personal reaction to the environment may be modified.

During this period, there is a sharp reduction in temper outburst; children learn to satisfy their needs in more positive ways. Fears are also reduced, though old fears of the unknown and animals usually change to fears of school, social relationships, and other situations related to their experience. Emotional responses, as well as being a function of age and maturity, are outcomes of cultural conditioning mediated through key adults.

5. Late Childhood. Preadolescents have the same emotional needs as individuals of other ages, although the specific ways they fill these needs involve somewhat different approaches. They need to feel that significant others love them, that they are needed, and others respect their privacy. With a growing sense of emotional maturity, preadolescents become more capable of handling emotional stress.

Although these older children often pull away from any outward physical affection, such as a kiss or a hug, they really want to be loved. Parental affection is best shown by evidencing an interest in their activity, by conversing with them on an adult level, and by regarding their sporadic aloofness from adults as being normal.

The emotional expression of preadolescents often confuses adults because these manifestations are inconsistent and equivocal. However, these emotional behaviors are normal for this age group and may even be considered as desirable signs of maturing. Such manifestations include their noncommunicativeness with adults, their teasing of young siblings, their apparent carelessness in matters of dress, their tendency to wander afield without permission, and their antagonism to or aloofness from the other sex.

6. Adolescence. During adolescence, emotional patterns become more stabilized. Achieving emotional independence for adolescents has its roots in the past, namely when they began school as children. From this point on, their contact with peers expanded and their sphere of autonomous activities widened. Now emotional patterns are more stabilized and are approaching the consistency seen in adulthood.

Some researchers disagree with this statement that adolescence is a time of emotional stability. They argue that adolescence is a time of emotional and psychological discontinuity because achieving emotional independence in modern Western society is particularly difficult for adolescents. Prolonged education forces young people to be financially dependent on their parents for many years. Urbanization decreases the opportunity for adolescents to execute adult responsibilities. Child labor laws and automation have reduced the opportunity for this age group to work if they desire. Rapid changes in technology and the complexity of the world produce indecision in adolescents and threaten their sense of security. Despite these cultural forces which threaten the emotional stability of adolescents, these young adults can achieve emotional independence, especially when adults help support their autonomy and identity.

7. **Adulthood.** As adolescents move into adulthood, emotional independence and maturity become more stable. Throughout life, however, emotions continue to slowly develop and change as the external and internal forces in people's lives change. These changes are continuous, active, and have an adaptive function. One major difference during this period of life is that emotional growth involves an increased concern for the welfare of others, expressing both identity and compassion for others.

Certain factors can alter the course of emotional development in adulthood. The situations which elicit various emotions may change. Emotional development also takes place through changes in the coping reactions of people. Changes in the social conventions as to what is proper to experience, express, or both may affect emotional development. And, finally, emotional expressions may change with development.

Bibliography. K. Bridges, *The Social and Emotional Development of the Pre-school Child* (1931). C. Malatesta and C. Izard, *Emotion in Adult Development* (1984). K. Scherer and P. Ekman, *Approaches to Emotion* (1984).

R. E. PUFF

EMOTION. *Compare* EVALUATION AND DIAGNOSIS, PSYCHOLOGICAL; MATERNAL DEPRIVATION; PERSONALITY DEVELOPMENT, BIOLOGICAL AND SOCIALIZING INFLUENCES IN.

EMPATHY. The ability to identify with and experience another person's experiences. This is accomplished by (as much as possible) suspending one's own frame of refrence in order to enter the perceptual and emotional world of the other. Empathy is vital in the counseling situation. If a counselee feels that the counselor empathically and truly understands him or her, the counselee is more likely to trust the counselor with deeper feelings and enter the therapeutic process more deeply and productively.

Bibliography. J. J. Gill, "Empathy is at the Heart of Love," *Human Development,* 3 (1982), 3:29 – 41.

D. E. MASSEY

LISTENING; PERCEPTIVENESS AND SENSITIVITY, PASTORAL; PRESENCE, MINISTRY OF; THERAPEUTIC CONDITIONS. *See also* PHENOMENOLOGICAL METHOD IN PASTORAL CARE; TECHNIQUE AND SKILL IN PASTORAL CARE. *Compare* IDENTIFICATION.

EMPIRICAL RESEARCH IN PASTORAL CARE AND COUNSELING. Empirical research is a systematic investigation aimed at finding new or substantiating facts and relationships between facts (or factors) that help further the understanding of a problem or problems and the rules or interactions that govern them.

Broadly speaking, research in pastoral care and counseling, like research in other professional fields, is of two kinds: (1) *empirical studies,* which examine actual events of care and counseling (and the human problems to which they are addressed); and (2) *theoretical studies,* which analyze or construct the concepts and images (e.g. asssumptions, metaphors, meanings, values, and causal hypotheses) which define the problems and guide the

practice of pastoral care and counseling. It is important to recognize the close connection in principle between these two even though many research studies give a dominant or even exclusive attention to one over the other.

1. **Three Methods of Empirical Research.** In pastoral care and counseling there are three predominant methods of gathering information: the case study, correlational, and experimental. All three involve observations of behavior. These methods differ in terms of the research questions they ask, the types of observations that are made, the circumstances surrounding the observations, and how the data from the observations are handled.

a. Case studies. In the case study method, an in-depth analysis of a single individual using qualitative terms and concepts is frequently used. The research question may highlight an unusual problem, or demonstrate how to work with a particular individual. Most pastors learn this method in seminary and are heavily exposed to it in basic Clinical Pastoral Education. A sample question might be: "How are theological issues addressed in dealing with a heart attack victim?" Observations such as verbatim reports are based on work with a particular individual or problem in depth, within the context of pastoral care or counseling, drawing on themes as they relate to other individuals, and contributing to theory or raising research questions to be examined using other research methods. One problem with this approach is its lack of generalizability to other populations or individuals.

b. Correlation studies. The correlational method examines the relationship between two or more variables, quantitatively looking at the extent one variable changes with another variable. The research question is usually stated in the form: "Do variable A and variable B go in the same or opposite direction?" For example, ministers' personality traits might be measured on a personality profile like "16 personality factors (16PF)," or the "Minnesota Multiphasic Personality Inventory (MMPI)," (A), and those measures might be correlated with their choice in ministry—parish ministry or pastoral counseling (B). This relationship is expressed through a correlation coefficient, which expresses the relationship in a range of values from + 1 indicating positive relationship, 0 representing no relationship, and -1 indicating negative relationship. Usually the closer the correlation coefficient is to + 1 or -1 the more statistically significant the findings. This approach is useful for gathering information about how variables relate to each other, but does not lend itself to making cause and effect statements.

Another popular form of correlational research used in pastoral care and counseling is opinion survey. The question asked here is to what extent certain options correlate, or go together with sex, social class, church affiliation, or political affiliation?

c. Experimental studies. The experimental method looks at the quantitative relationship between one or more conditions which are systematically varied and are expected to cause change in a person's behavior. This approach represents the greatest degree of control, which in research refers to systematically varying, randomizing, or holding constant the conditions under which observations are made. The purpose of having control within research is to reduce the number of alternative explanations for why and how behavior is influenced. In experimental research, the condition which is directly varied is called the independent variable. The dependent variable is thought to depend on the conditions varied by the experimenter. An experimental hypothesis is a statement about the effect of the independent variable upon the dependent variable (if A, the independent variable, then B, the dependent variable). For example, if Doctor of Ministry students in pastoral counseling complete a course in diagnosis, then they will be able to diagnose different kinds of emotional problems. The Doctor of Ministry course work is the independent variable and ability to diagnose is the dependent variable. Control could be achieved through randomly assigning some D. Min. students to the pastoral counseling course, while others did not take the course, then testing both groups' diagnostic ability. True experiments are very difficult to achieve in pastoral care and counseling because the tight controls required do not fit well in real life. The advantage of a true experiment is that it sharply reduces rival explanations of the results.

Most experiments in pastoral care and counseling are really what is called quasi-experimental designs. The quasi quality comes from the inability of the researcher to control fully the scheduling of treatment or exactly who gets treated. The researcher attempts to control other possible influences on the experiment as well as possible and to interpret results in the same manner a true experiment is interpreted.

Relevant to each of these methods is literature research. This involves an extensive library search on a specific subject. The gathering together of material from many different sources provides a foundation of information not available in one source.

Good research is usually characterized by clear conceptualization that is specific, good operationalization of these concepts and an extensive review of what has been done previously.

2. **Research Design.** In doing research, the researcher constructs a research design. Important issues are: who will be the subject(s), how will the subject(s) be selected, what will be tested, how will change be evaluated or observed, and what instruments will be used to evaluate change?

The subject pool in pastoral care and counseling usually comes from staff, counselees, students, parishioners and workshop participants. Selection is usually done subjectively or scientifically. Scientific methods involve matching preselected criteria or randomization, subjects are chosen randomly, using a random table of numbers. Classification variables may be conducted by any relevant method, such as age, religious affiliation, or training.

Research looks at change in behavior, attitude or skill. Types of data include self report, observation, and indices measurement. Self report is the simplest method of gathering data, but it is also the least accurate, in that subjects may act differently than they report. Observers can be watching the subjects, or measuring their behavior on a certain variable by testing. This provides a more accurate measure than self report, but may still be influenced by the subjects' awareness of being tested or observed. Indices measurement uses records or accounts intended for other uses to observe subjects so they do not know they are being observed. This usually guarantees that subjects' natural behavior is being observed, but since the records are meant for another purpose they may not accurately reflect the variable being studied. Studies that use several measures are more powerful than single measures.

3. **Significance, Reliability, and Validity.** In pastoral care and counseling, methods of establishing significant results range from those bearing clinical significance to those bearing statistical significance. Research may report observations on a single subject or involve complicated statistical designs using computerized multifactoral designs. There are two inferential techniques. The first is called parametric, where assumptions are made about the values of population parameters such as a normal bell-shaped distribution of scores, in multiple groups internal difference between groups is the same, and observations are drawn at random from the group being studied. The second is called nonparametric or distribution free statistics. The only assumption nonparametric statistics makes is that observations are drawn at random. Parametric techniques are usually more powerful than nonparametric statistics. About seventy percent of the statistics reported in the *Pastoral Care and Counseling Abstracts* from 1972–1982 used simple statistical procedures like T-tests (the ratio of a statistic to its standard error stated in terms of probability, or p value, that the results could happen by chance. P values of 0.01 or 0.05 are accepted as highly significant) or X^2 (compares an obtained distribution to an expected distribution to see if differences are higher than would occur by chance) and were presented as parametric statistics.

Closely related to significance in studies measuring variables are the problems of establishing reliability and validity. Reliability means how accurate or consistent the instrument is in measuring what it is supposed to measure. Validity is the extent to which the instrument used to measure the dependent variable is useful, that is, measures what it is supposed to measure. An intelligence test may be highly accurate and consistent (reliable) in measuring something, but not valid (useful) in measuring intelligence.

4. **Recent Research and Emerging Issues.** The general research topics reported in *Pastoral Care and Counseling Abstracts* include the nature of ministry, the education of the religious professional, the delivery of care and counseling services, and attitudes or opinions about pastoral care and counseling issues. These are important topics, though by no means exhaustive of the range of possibilities.

It is clearly crucial to the development of pastoral practice to have sound, well conceived and well executed studies of many kinds pertinent to the wide range of pastoral problems and practices. Such studies can not only open new vistas but correct existing misunderstandings and ineffective methods. Even more important than expanding the topical range of pastoral research may be improvement in pastoral research methodology itself. Several points may be worth noting in this connection.

One of the first areas that should be addressed is the task of developing explicit definitions and operationally precise concepts for the functions of pastoral care and counseling. Precise definitions and conceptual formulations, though often difficult to write, have the important function of clarifying the contents of key concepts and the relations among concepts, showing their underlying order when it exists or revealing confusions and gaps in our knowledge when they may exist. In studies of marriage counseling, for instance, it may be useful to define "marriage" as (let us say) voluntary, heterosexual, exclusive and goal oriented—four terms which give boundary to the concept, clarifying, simplifying, and systematizing its meaning. By defining a concept in this way we analyze a complex subject into its components, each of which may then be studied in relation to each other and to other variables in marriage and pastoral marriage counseling.

Another issue today is the need for pastoral researchers to grapple more explicitly with how individual differences in skill, style, interest, temperament, and theological orientation affect the doing and the outcomes of pastoral care and counseling, and how such individual differences must qualify generalized research conclusions about pastoral method. An extremely talented hospital chaplain, for instance, may handle crisis situations in a fashion that another chaplain, even highly trained, could not begin to emulate and which could not and should not be generalized as a prescription for everyone. Idiosyncratic matters of personal style, temperament and personality no doubt always play a significant role in creative ministry; but how such factors can be acknowledged and properly evaluated in empirical research methodologies is a major unresolved (and largely unexamined) question. It is perhaps fair to say that this is one of a number of research issues related to the larger question of whether pastoral care and counseling is more "art" or "science."

Another major issue emerging clearly in recent years is the need for pastoral research to come to grips more directly with its "social location" or perspective. Research is always conducted from within a particular social and historical context which inevitably shapes and limits the design of the research and the generalizability of its findings. In particular, the social class, sex, race, age, and culture, institutional location, and historical epoch of the researchers may be expected to influence the way problems are conceptualized, the methods employed to study them, and the way findings are identified and interpreted. Empirical research in pastoral care and counseling will need to develop methods of taking such factors into account critically and systematically. This does not—and cannot—mean eliminating such factors in the interest of pure "objectivity"; but it does mean attempting to be critically aware of the particular limitations and opportunities they impose on our attempts to gain reliable knowledge.

A particular and much neglected need is to develop better understandings of how to relate the ethical and theological commitments of the religious community to persons in a variety of circumstances. Pastoral care and counseling has tended to focus heavily on emotional and social dynamics of individuals and families but has so far not become as skilled in the art of relating those processes to the pastoral functions of moral and spiritual interpretation and guidance.

Finally, a closely related issue is the question of whether research in this field should attempt to become genuinely theological, or "practical theological," in its methodology, as well as social scientific, and if so, how. "Empirical research" has tended to mean "social scientific" research almost exclusively. While much is to be gained from careful appropriation of social scientific methods, it may be asked whether even the best social science can ever be entirely adequate to the unique needs of pastoral research. Pastoral work of all kinds intends to relate to people at the deepest levels of their existence in the context of relationships to the whole human community, the cosmos, and ultimately to God. What may be the implications for empirical research in pastoral care and counseling if this profound, wide-ranging intentionality is taken seriously as fundamental to pastoral care and counseling, and hence the one aspect of it that most requires diligent study? Can it be studied empirically? If so, how?

Bibliography. For research method: A. J. Bachrach, *Psychological Research: An Introduction,* 3d ed., (1972). J. Barzun and H. F. Graff, *The Modern Researcher,* rev. ed., (1970). For recent examples or discussion of empirical research in the field: *Abstracts of Research in Pastoral Care and Counseling* (1972). D. W. Augsburger, *Pastoral Counseling Across Cultures* (1986). S. W. Cardwell, "Why Women Fail/Succeed in Ministry: Psychological Factors," *Pastoral Psychology,* 30 (1982), 153–62. J. W. Fowler, *Faith Development and Pastoral Care* (1987). C. V. Gerkin, *The Living Human Document* (1984). E. B. Holifield, *A History of Pastoral Care in America* (1983). *J. of Pastoral Care* (Pastoral Assessment Issue) 34 (1980), 73–130; *J. of Pastoral Care* (Research Issue) 35 (1981) 73–124. H. N. Maloney, "Ministerial Effectiveness: A Review of Recent Research," *Pastoral Psychology,* 33:2 (1984), 96–104. T. C. Oden, *Pastoral Theology* (1983). A. Stokes, *Ministry After Freud* (1985). E. E. Thornton, *Professional Education for Ministry* (1970). R. J. Wicks, R. D. Parsons, and D. E. Capps, *Clinical Handbook of Pastoral Counseling* (1985).

J. L. FLORELL

JOURNALS IN PASTORAL CARE AND COUNSELING; PASTORAL CARE (Contemporary Methods, Perspectives, and Issues); PASTORAL COUNSELING. *See also* CAUSALITY IN PSYCHOLOGY, FORMS OF; CLERGY, EMPIRICAL STUDIES OF; JOURNALS IN RELIGION, THEOLOGY, AND THE SOCIAL SCIENCES, INTERDISCIPLINARY; MODELS IN PSYCHOLOGY AND PASTORAL THEORY; PASTORAL THEOLOGY; VALUES IN COUNSELING AND PSYCHOTHERAPY. *Compare* EVALUATION AND DIAGNOSIS; PASTORAL THEOLOGICAL METHODOLOGY; PSYCHOLOGY OF RELIGION (Empirical Studies, Methods, and Problems); PSYCHOTHERAPY AND COUNSELING (Research Studies and Methods); PSYCHIATRY AND PASTORAL CARE; THEOLOGY AND PSYCHOLOGY.

EMPIRICAL THEOLOGY AND PASTORAL CARE. "Empirical Theology" refers to the distinctive theology that emerged in the Divinity School of the University of Chicago during the first half of the twentieth century (Meland, 1969). "Pastoral care" refers here to the movement within the American Christian churches during the same time period which focused on the appropriation of the emerging social sciences. After defining "empirical theology," this article will refer to Seward Hiltner's role in bringing the interests of empirical theology and pastoral care movement together, and then will suggest areas in which empirical theology can make an increasing contribution to pastoral care in the future.

1. **Definition.** The development of empirical theology is a complex phenomenon with many variations. On the most general level, empirical theology refers to "a method of inquiry that presumes to find knowledge and its verification by appealing to experience" (Meland, p. 8). This definition distinguishes empirical theology from other forms of theology which find their authority in revelation or the realm of ideas. Persons committed to an empirical method start with human experience as the source of the knowledge of truth and return to experience as the verification of generalizations about the structures of experience. It is empirical theology's specialized views and methods concerning the empirical method which distinguish it from other contemporary views and methods such as historicism, liberalism, and phenomenology. Daniel Day Williams lists four criteria for empirical theology as it developed at the Chicago School (Meland, 1969, pp. 176–77):

First, by "experience," empirical theology means "the felt, bodily, psycho-social organic action of human beings in history. Other writers use phrases such as "lived experience," "vital immediacy," (Meland) "give-ness of relations and the primacy of bodily feelings or causal efficacy," (Loomer) to indicate experience in its breadth and depth. Empirical theologians are opposed to efforts which reduce experience to sense perception, to intuition and feeling, or to religious experience understood psychologically. Rather, they include all experience, including its full historical context—even the immanence of God—in their definition. Experience is "a complex of events subtly and ambiguously envisaged . . . data that can be envisaged only in a context, that is, within relationships, where relationships are deemed experienceable" (Meland, 1969, p. 12). This radical form of empiricism distinguishes empirical theology from other forms of theology which also focus on experience.

Second, without denying that God may also have a transcendent nature beyond experience, empirical theologians insist that God's presence is immanent in experience and is at least partially knowable. Henry Nelson Wieman, following William James, spoke of the "more" within experience which cannot be reduced to human action or thought; for Meland, "immediacy and ultimacy traffic together." Others like Daniel Day Williams (1968) use traditional language to speak about God within the fullness of experience, and are concerned specifically with the presence and action of God in the Judeo-Christian tradition. Some of this school have focused their work on the philosophical and metaphysical issues of such a view of God (Hartshorne), while others have focused on the historical record of God's activity (Meland, Williams).

Third, empirical theology as a method moves from the richness of concrete experience to generalizations about the structure of experience. This distinguishes the method of empirical theologians from deductive, rational methods, though there is disagreement within empirical theology on the value of metaphysical thought.

Fourth, empirical theology holds that generalizations about experience are always less than experience itself, and therefore have "the status of tentative and correctable assertions, subject to criticisms and never exhaustible of the concreteness of reality" (Williams, 1968, p. 177). Concrete experience is prior, both logically and perceptually, and all conceptions of the structures of experience are abstractions which facilitate understanding of some aspects of experience, but inevitably distort and diminish experience in its richness and complexity.

2. **Contributions to Pastoral Care.** The historical connections between empirical theology and pastoral care await detailed study. There are notable similarities between the two movements, especially in the shared interest in concrete human experience and a distrust of abstract rational theology. However, this shared interest points to parallel development in the same historical period rather than deep historical connection. Thornton (1970, pp. 26–28) notes that the formative influences on the early leaders were progressive education, theological liberalism, and the professions of medicine and social work. Of the early leaders, Anton Boisen ([1936] 1971, p. 151f, 183) was strongly influenced by empirical theology as seen in his interest in the social context of experience and the function of religion as an integrating philosophy of life.

The principal representative of empirical theology within the field of pastoral care, however, was Seward Hiltner. "Hiltner's approach represents a fusing of the Boisen legacy of a clinical approach to theology with the more philosophically based empiricism of the later Chicago school" (Lapsley, 1969, p. 40). However, there is evidence that, as an empirical theologian, Hiltner was a minority voice in a pastoral care movement which became increasingly preoccupied with clinical competence and organization and more interested in the methods of phenomenology and the existentialist theologies than in empirical theology.

3. **Implications for Pastoral Care.** There seems to be increasing interest in empirical theology by pastoral care specialists, and several fruitful areas for dialogue. (1) Empirical theology and pastoral care share a commitment to concrete experience as a source of knowledge about human life and God. Empirical theology can contribute to more breadth and depth in understanding concrete experience and its sociohistorical context.

(2) Empirical theology and pastoral care share an interest in the immanence of God within concrete experience. Pastoral care has had difficulty finding literal and metaphorical ways of speaking about God within the clinical context. Empirical theology can contribute a philosophical basis for God's immanence and theological guidance for speaking about God in concrete terms. This may help overcome some of the paradoxes that have blocked pastoral care in the development of its theology.

(3) Empirical theology and pastoral care share an urgency about the dialogue of the Christian tradition with the human sciences. Through its perspectival method, empirical theology sees all symbol-systems as abstractions which elucidate certain aspects of experience, but which must be held tentatively. More profound truth emerges as one engages in a correlation of perspectives, and methods of "critical correlation" are

being developed in empirical theology which would be helpful to pastoral care and lead to the clarification of a theology of pastoral care (see Browning, 1983).

In summary, there is obviously a strong compatibility between empirical theology and pastoral care based on certain shared assumptions. To this point, the two movements have developed relatively independently, with the exception of Seward Hiltner and his students. However, there is evidence of a convergence of interests which could be productive for the future.

Bibliography. A. Boisen, *The Exploration of the Inner World,* ([1936] 1971). D. Browning, ed., *Practical Theology,* (1983), see especially chapters by Browning and Tracy. C. Hartshorne, *The Divine Relativity* (1948). S. Hiltner, *Preface to Pastoral Theology* (1958). J. Lapsley, "Pastoral Theology Past and Present," in *The New Shape of Pastoral Theology,* W. B. Oglesby, ed. (1969). B. E. Meland, ed., *The Future of Empirical Theology* (1969); see especially articles by Meland, Loomer, Ogden, and Williams. E. E. Thornton, *Professional Education for Ministry* (1970). D. D. Williams, *The Spirit and the Forms of Love* (1968).

J. N. POLING

PASTORAL THEOLOGICAL METHODOLOGY; PROCESS THEOLOGY. *See also* EXPERIENCE; PASTORAL THEOLOGY. *Compare* EXISTENTIALISM AND PASTORAL CARE; EXPERIENTIAL, LIBERATION, *or* NEO-ORTHODOX THEOLOGY; THEOLOGY AND PSYCHOLOGY *or* PSYCHOTHERAPY. *Biography:* BOISEN; HILTNER; WIEMAN; WILLIAMS..

EMPOWERMENT. *See* GRACE. *See also* ADVOCACY; ASSERTIVENESS TRAINING AND THERAPY; HUMAN DEVELOPMENT; POWER.

EMPTINESS, SENSE OF. *See* NARCISSISM/NARCISSISTIC PERSONALITY; SADNESS AND DEPRESSION.

ENCOUNTER. *See* CONFRONTATION (Pastoral and Therapeutic); ENGAGED ENCOUNTER; MARRIAGE ENCOUNTER.

ENCOUNTER GROUPS. A somewhat controversial use of the techniques of group dynamics in the establishment of short-term, highly intensive, often emotional, personal growth experiences. Critics claimed the events were psychologically destructive and designed to meet the leaders' needs. Supporters pointed to changes in attitudes and efficiency in interaction with others. Some participants achieved a sense of freedom with these groups and adopted participation in them as a way of life.

L. MORGAN

GROUP COUNSELING AND PSYCHOTHERAPY. *Compare* CONSCIOUSNESS RAISING; GROWTH GROUPS; HUMAN RELATIONS TRAINING.

ENCOURAGEMENT. *See* COMFORT/SUSTAINING; COMMUNITY, FELLOWSHIP, AND CARE; HOPE AND DESPAIR.

ENERGY/ENERGY LEVEL. *See* MOTIVATION; TEMPERAMENT.

ENGAGED ENCOUNTER. A weekend live-in program for engaged couples. The original Roman Catholic program and both Protestant and Jewish adaptations include presentations by several married couples and a member of the clergy on topics such as self-knowledge, communication, the wedding ceremony, decision making, and morality and sexuality. After making written personal reflections, the participants discuss the issues with their partners.

S. BEVANS

MARRIAGE ENCOUNTER. *See also* RETREATS (Roman Catholicism); COUNSELING, ROMAN CATHOLIC.

ENGAGEMENT, MARITAL. *See* MARRIAGE AND MARITAL CARE; PREMARITAL COUNSELING. *See also* COMMITMENT.

ENLIGHTENMENT. *See* ILLUMINATION; PSYCHOLOGY, EASTERN.

ENRICHMENT, MARITAL. *See* MARRIAGE ENRICHMENT.

ENTHUSIASM, RELIGIOUS. *See* CHARISMATIC EXPERIENCE; HOLY SPIRIT; RELIGIOUS EXPERIENCE.

ENVIRONMENTAL PSYCHOLOGY. *See* ECOLOGICAL PSYCHOLOGY.

ENVY AND GRACIOUSNESS (Moral Theology). Envy is a dissatisfaction at some good or quality belonging to another which is experienced as devaluing one's self-worth. Graciousness is a delight in the good or quality possessed by another.

1. **Envy.** It is normal for persons to grasp their identity by comparing themselves with others. When another's spiritual or material goods are experienced as challenging their adequacy, persons may feel a loss of self-esteem. In an effort to overcome dissatisfaction and reestablish self-esteem, the envious are ready to devalue the other as the cause of their loss of self-worth.

Envy is distinct from emulation which is a desire for the kind of good possessed by another, experienced as a new possibility for oneself. Envy is also different from a healthy competitive spirit which perceives another's activities or attainments as a stimulus for effort rather than as a sign of personal defeat. Envy is distinct from indignation which is anger at the unworthiness of another to possess a good. It is also different from hatred which is directly oriented against the whole (and not merely some possession or quality) of the other person. Though common usage often conflates envy and jealousy, jealousy focuses on the loss of something that is one's own, while envy is directed to what belongs to another. The envious may not want to actually possess another's good; they want only that the other's "superiority" be despoiled.

Paul says that envy excludes from the kingdom of God. Augustine called it the supremely diabolical sin; Chrysostom ranked it head of the vices; and Basil called it the incurable evil. Envy is singular among the "seven deadly sins" because the other six vices, for example, lust or pride, at least initially offer some pleasure or triumph for the self. Envy, by contrast, begins with a perceived loss of self-worth; rather than leading to actions that enhance the self, it seeks to devalue the other. Hence, particularly in spiritual matters, the tradition considered envy one of the worst sins.

Willful envy is morally blameworthy insofar as it erodes proper self-love, devalues what is good in another, and weakens or destroys human community. Thus it is a failure to accept one's God-given self, to hope for the actualization of one's own gifts and graces, and to love one's neighbor. Envy, further, is morally suspect insofar as it easily leads to other evils such as detraction or even destructive deeds.

2. **Graciousness.** Graciousness flows from a sense of a God-affirmed self-esteem. It takes pleasure in another's gifts as enhancements of God's creation. The gracious person is unhappy at another's good qualities, successes, or attainments only if these goods might in fact lead to some greater harm, like pride or avarice. Graciousness is formally distinguishable from love because love is directed first of all to the whole person and only derivatively to the goods that person possesses. Still, love wills the good of another and thus is gracious.

Bibliography. A. van Kaam, *Envy and Originality* (1972). M. Klein, *Envy and Gratitude* (1975). H. Schoeck, *Envy* (1969). A. and B. Ulanov, *Cinderella and Her Sisters: the Envied and the Envying* (1983).

E. C. VACEK

CHRISTIAN LIFE; SEVEN DEADLY SINS. *See also* CHARACTER ETHICS; MORAL THEOLOGY AND PASTORAL CARE; SIN/SINS; TEMPTATIONS. *Compare* GRACE; GRATITUDE.

EPIGENESIS. Originally, a biological theory holding that development of an organism proceeds, partly by genetic design and partly by interreaction with the environment, from a simple, undifferentiated state to states of increasing differentiation and complexity operating as a functional whole. (It replaced preformation in which the organism was believed to be fully formed in the germ cell and to develop simply by becoming larger.) The "epigenetic principle" has been applied to psychological development, especially in cognitive psychology (Jean Piaget), psychosocial developmental theory (Erik Erikson), and moral and faith development theories (Lawrence Kohlberg and James Fowler). In psychology its significance lies in its notions that (1) early developmental stages persist in some form in later stages and that (2) within a basic (i.e. genetic) "groundplan" new features can emerge as a result of environmental interaction.

G. ROWLAND

DEVELOPMENTAL THEORY AND PASTORAL CARE; LIFE CYCLE THEORY AND PASTORAL CARE.

EPILEPSY. A disorder of the central nervous system that manifests itself in recurrent seizures. There are two basic classifications of seizures. Those which involve only one part of the brain at the outset are called partial or *focal seizures.* In their simplest form, the person may experience sensations or motor twitches in one part of the body (often an arm or a leg) with no other signs. The attack may last only a few seconds and the person may be quite able to talk and to continue activities. The more complex focal seizures are often called temporal lobe or *psychomotor seizures;* more than half of all adults have attacks of this type. The person may say or do strange things that are uncharacteristic, including picking at clothes, trying to talk but not making sense, and doing other activities that are not purposeful.

In contrast, *generalized seizures* involve the entire brain at the outset. Absence ("petit mal") seizures typically involve momentary loss of responsiveness and are seen most commonly in childhood. They are sometimes accompanied with fluttering of the eyelids and are usually only a few seconds in duration. The other very common type of generalized seizure is the tonic-clonic ("grand mal") seizure, which is a convulsion and which typically manifests itself with rigidity followed by convulsive movements of the arms and legs. Such an attack is considered a medical emergency if it lasts more than a few minutes or there is more than one consecutive attack.

Epilepsy is a clear indication that, at least at times, the brain is not functioning well. Even between seizures, abnormal brain waves are usually detected by an electroencephalograph (EEG). Difficulties in certain aspects of thinking, remembering, and problem solving are detectable even between seizures in many people with epilepsy. Most commonly there are problems in memory, but persons with seizures may also have difficulty in focusing on tasks and in functioning efficiently.

The social and psychological effects of epilepsy are often of considerable significance. Since seizures appear only intermittently and frequently without warning, they tend to put the person constantly on edge. And because the condition may limit normal activities (such as driving) and stigmatize one socially, persons with epilepsy may develop a negative self-image. Moreover, some religious groups equate epilepsy with demon possession and thus cause more anxiety and guilt feelings in the already overburdened individual.

Individuals with epilepsy need understanding concerning the neurological basis for their difficulties, and they need acceptance rather than rejection. If a person is experiencing frequent seizures, a medical reevaluation should definitely be considered. If social and/or emotional problems are displayed, referral to a qualified counselor familiar with seizure disorders is suggested. Neuropsychological testing may be required to evaluate the extent of emotional difficulties and losses in abilities, if any.

Bibliography. H. Gastaut, "Clinical and electroencephalographical classification of epileptic seizures," *Epilepsia,* vol. 2 (1970), pp. 102–13. H. Sands, *Epilepsy: A Handbook for the Mental Health Professional* (1982).

C. B. DODRILL

HANDICAP AND DISABILITY; ORGANIC MENTAL DISORDER. *See also* BODY IMAGE; BRAIN RESEARCH; EXCEPTIONAL CHILDREN AND THEIR FAMILIES; PSYCHOSURGERY; SELF ESTEEM.

EPISCOPAL PASTORAL CARE. *See* ANGLICAN PASTORAL CARE; BISHOPS.

EPISTEMOLOGY. *See* PHILOSOPHY AND PSYCHOLOGY; WISDOM AND PRACTICAL KNOWLEDGE; REVELATION.

ERHARD SEMINAR TRAINING (est). *See* POPULAR THERAPEUTIC MOVEMENTS AND PSYCHOLOGIES.

ERIKSON, ERIK H. (1902–). Psychoanalyst and psychosocial theorist. Erikson is a figure of gigantic proportions for pastoral care and the study of religion. Standing in the psychoanalytic tradition of Freud, he has extended Freud's theory of psychosexual development into an eight-stage, wholistic view of the life cycle. In a tradition that has focused its diagnostic power on pathology, he has characterized human health and strength. In a tradition that focused on unconscious processes and defenses, he has attended to patterns of consciousness and meaning. In a tradition that has reached against moralism and the misuse of religion in cultures, he has offered new approaches to ethics and virtue, and to the role of faith and religion in personal and societal life. In a tradition that has been criticized for confining its interpretative power to individuals and the nuclear family, Erikson has sought to study the interaction of body, psyche, society, and culture in the development of persons. Erikson is the principal founder of psychohistorical method. He introduced the concept of identity and clarified the function of the ego in its work of synthesis, adaptation, and integration of experience and selfhood.

Erikson's first book *Childhood and Society* (1950, 1963) brought him widespread recognition and established his perspective upon child development as the interplay of a biological and epigenetic "ground plan" with a family's and culture's meanings and images and a society's institutions.

Young Man Luther (1958) brought recognition to Erikson beyond academic circles. In his study of this "young great man" Erikson explored how a gifted person, willing to undertake the "dirty work" of his era, could, by struggling to break through with his own young adult issues, mint a solutional pattern for an unfolding new era.

In *Insight and Responsibility* (1964) Erikson writes about Freud and psychoanalytic method, characterizing the "disciplined subjectivity" which lies at the heart of psychoanalytic method. Here Erikson makes explicit his concern with the ethical and with virtue.

In *Youth: Identity and Crisis* (1968) Erikson explores the dynamics of identity formation and of the alienation of youth expressed in *negative* identity formation. This book explores "pseudo-speciation" in which insecure majorities can project upon minorities (Jews, Blacks, women, in these studies) the repressed and denied qualities in their own personal and collective psyches. *Gandhi's Truth* (1969) is the biggest and most ambitious of Erikson's books. In studying the personal, cultural, and religious roots of Gandhi's development and use of *Satyagraha* — non-violent pursuit of the social truth that is justice — Erikson discloses his own passionate calling to take on the "dirty work" of his epoch: the struggle for global peace with justice. Here he also illumines in greater depth his conception of the calling and character of *homo religiosus*.

Erikson has been blessed with unusual freedom to pursue his research, his therapeutic practice, and his vocation as writer and mentor to an era. In the thirties he practiced child psychoanalysis in Boston and enjoyed appointments at Harvard and Yale Universities. In the forties he conducted a private practice in San Francisco and was associated with the Institute of Child Welfare at the University of California, Berkeley. In 1950 he taught for a short time at Berkeley, but ended his relation to that university by resigning rather than sign a "loyalty oath" in the early phases of the McCarthy era. In the fifties he worked at the Austin Riggs Center and commuted regularly to Pittsburgh to work at the Western Psychiatric Institute. In the sixties Erikson was Professor of Human Development at Harvard. In the seventies and eighties he and his wife, Joan Serson Erikson, have continued an active life of research, writing, and occasional lecturing and seminar leadership.

J. W. FOWLER

EGO PSYCHOLOGY; LIFE CYCLE THEORY; IDENTITY; PSYCHOLOGY OF RELIGION (Theories, Traditions, and Issues).

EROS. *See* LOVE.

EROTIC FEELINGS AND FANTASIES. *See* FANTASIZING; SEXUAL ISSUES.

ESCHATOLOGY AND PASTORAL CARE. The doctrine of "the last things," that is, of the end of this world-epoch and of the beginning of God's new world order, the doctrine of the end and goal of humankind and of the cosmos. It is a theological doctrine of the future because it looks for the end and consummation of the world from God who is the Creator and also the creation's Redeemer. It is the Christian doctrine of the future insofar as it derives from God's faithfulness revealed in the history of Christ, in his death, and in his resurrection from the dead, and insofar as it hopes for the future as Christ's Parousia. Since this hope for the coming of Christ is grounded in the remembrance of Christ's history and in its re-presentation in the gospel and in the Eucharist, it is neither a speculation nor a dream but a grounded promise. Personal and social hopes for the future, as well as personal and social fears of catastrophes, must be oriented to the grounded promise of Christ, if they are properly to be called Christian.

Christian eschatology, which at its core speaks of "Christ and his parousia," stands in a historical and logical relationship to Jewish eschatology, which derives from the Torah and the kingdom of God, and to Islamic eschatology, which hopes for a universal reign of God. If Abraham is the father of the Jewish, Christian, and Islamic faiths, then these three religions are aligned eschatologically through Abraham's promise.

By virtue of the re-presentation of Israel's history and the history of Christ, Christian eschatology opens up three horizons of expectation for the future: (1) individual eschatology—life until death and eternal life (2) collective eschatology—history and the kingdom of Christ, judgment, and the kingdom of God; and (3) cosmic eschatology—creation and nature, the destruction of this world-order and the creation of the new heaven and the new earth.

1. **History.** In the development of the church and of theology in the West, cosmic eschatology was reduced to the eschatology of history, and collective eschatology was reduced to individual eschatology. Consequently pastoral care was reduced to the "care of souls" (*cura animarum*) and became centered on the preparation of individuals for a "good death" and on the eternal life "after death." For a long time, the salvation of the soul in "the beyond" functioned as the eschatology of the pastoral care of the souls. Only in certain messianic groups was a collective eschatology preserved. They expected the bodily resurrection of the dead on the Last Day and therefore assumed that the soul either dies along with the body or falls into a state of "soul-sleep."

Only in the twentieth century, with the rediscovery of biblical eschatology, did hope as preparation for the coming kingdom of God come to the fore: pastoral care was understood as the "call to the kingdom of God" (Christoph Blumhardt, Eduard Thurneysen) encompassing body and soul, individual and community, community and society, society and nature. The "salvation of the soul" was tied to the *diakonia* of the body; the awakening of faith was bound up with working together in God's kingdom in the world. Thus, pastoral care can no longer be only the individual care of souls but must be extended to a corporate care of souls, that is, the establishment of a brotherly and sisterly community. The care of souls by the pastor must be embedded in group care of souls and in the therapeutic ethos of the community. Then, pastoral care occurs as Luther explains it in the "Schmalkald Articles" III/4 (1537): *"per mutuum colloquium et consolationem fratrum,"* the care of souls is a task of the entire community and happens in "mutual conversation and consolation among brethren." It addresses the personal problems of individuals, the common problems of families, the social problems of society, the problems of the natural environment and of one's own embodiment. The more theology rediscovers today the necessity and the meaning of collective, historical, and cosmic eschatology, the more pastoral care will liberate itself from its traditional, individualistic narrowness and become a comprehensive care for the kingdom of God. For we always care only as far as we are capable of hoping.

2. **The Spirit of God in Life and in Death.** From very early times Christian individual eschatology adopted the Platonic doctrine of the immortality of the soul. Thereby, however, it let its Christian character slip away. According to Plato, death is "the separation of the soul from the body." Whether this separation is mourned as a loss or is celebrated as a liberating, festive occasion, this concept presupposes an ontological dualism: the soul is immortal, everlasting, incapable of suffering; the body is mortal, transitory, and subject to suffering. In death, only the mortal part of the human being passes away while the immortal soul returns to the realm of ideas. Through an imaginative [*geistige*] anticipation of death (*meditatio mortis*), the individual becomes conscious of his or her immortal soul. "Know thyself," that is, "remember that you will die." One's entire life, therefore, serves to prepare one for death. The Christian *ars moriendi* literature has its origin in this Platonic teaching about the soul and about death.

When the early Christian expectation of the immediate Parousia of Christ disappeared, the hope for the bodily resurrection of the dead was replaced by this individual hope for the deliverance of the soul through death in a "life after death." Even in the NT there is the individual hope for being wholly with Christ immediately after death (II. Cor. 5:6; Phil. 1:23). Yet this individual hope does not exclude universal hope; it rather includes it. Hope for the redemption of the soul and hope for the redemption of the body supplement one another (Rom. 8:23).

But where, then, does the soul remain after the individual death and before the general resurrection of the dead? Medieval theology resolved this problem with the assumption of an "intermediate state," the *purgatorium:* after death, souls enter into a fire of purification in order to be united with the resurrected body on the Last Day. This conception does, indeed, provide persons with hope for redemption beyond individual death, but it also empties universal hope, because everything depends on the purification of the soul.

However, only that which does not live bodily can be immortal. Only bodiless (i.e., unlived, empty) life cannot die. The doctrine of the immortality of the soul is, in reality, a teaching about unlived life. In contrast to this, the NT uses the image of the grain of seed, which falls into the ground and dies — otherwise it remains solitary. And when it dies it bears a rich harvest (Jn. 12:23; Mt. 10:39; Lk. 17:33; I Cor. 15:42 – 44). In other words, life that is not being lived and does not die remains solitary and barren. That is death before life. Lived and therefore mortal life, however, is hopeful and productive. It is life before death.

Human life is alive insofar as it is being loved and affirmed. The more passionately we live, the more we experience the joy and rich abundance of life. But along with this we also experience the pain of dying. Only life truly lived can die. Unlived life cannot die. The modern "denial of death" is the price paid for the apathy of modern life. The true *ars moriendi* is not the preparation of the soul for the hereafter but the devotion of body and soul in love, that is, the *ars amandi*. In hope for the God who resurrects the dead, humans can wholly live their lives in love and can also wholly die.

Is there, then, *no "intermediate state" for the soul?* That old conception transfers the time of the living to the dead. That is misleading. For the dead themselves, the time between their individual deaths and the day of the resurrection is only "a moment" (M. Luther). *Where, then, are the dead now?* According to Paul, they are under the ruling power of Christ, which now extends over the "living and the dead" (Rom. 14:8–9). Christ will lead the dead to the resurrection and, eventually, destroy death (I Cor. 15:55–57). *Does something immortal exist already in this life prior to death?* The soul is not immortal but the *spirit of God* is immortal, which already here, in this life, fills believers with the power of the Resurrection (Rom. 8:11). Wherever the life-giving Spirit is experienced, there eternal life is experienced before death. Wherever persons get close to the creative ground of lived life, death disappears and they experience continuance without perishing. "Whoever believes, will live, even though he die" (Jn. 11:25 NEB). The same is also valid for love.

What, then, is death? Death, then, is neither the separation of the soul from the body nor the end of body and soul but the transformation of the spirit of life, which fills body and soul, into the new, transfigured world-order of God. Death is no end and no separation, but a transformation into the life eternal. Dying persons experience "the way through the gate" (E. Kübler-Ross), and those who mourn for the dead participate, in their grief, in this transformation. Christian care of "souls" is in reality care for the spirit of life which, here and now, makes body and soul alive in love and which, penetrating through and beyond death, will transform the entire lived life into the life everlasting.

3. The Redemption of the Body and the New Creation. The experience of the presence of *God's spirit* grounds the hope for the kingdom of God in which soul and body, heaven and earth will be redeemed. Paul has developed this universal *cosmic eschatology:* "The anxious expectation of the Creation awaits the revelation of the children of God" (Rom. 8:19). The Revelation of John promises "a new heaven and a new earth" (21:1). That includes hope for "the redemption of our bodies" (Rom. 8:23). If we disregard the time-bound apocalyptic conceptions, this means: there is no personal hope in God's spirit without the bodily, the social, and the cosmic hope for the kingdom of God.

In the experience of God's Spirit persons are not being separated *from* their bodies in a Platonic manner but they wait for the redemption *of* the body, that is, they wait for the new body entirely permeated by God's Spirit—the "spiritual body." "All works of God end in a bodily state" (Oetinger). This bodily hope can only be fulfilled when not only believers but the entire Creation becomes free. Therefore, hope for the "redemption of the body" is always bound up with hope for "the new earth," in which "death shall be no more . . . nor crying . . . nor pain" (Rev. 21:4 [KJV]). There is no realistic individual eschatology without this cosmic eschatology. The destiny of the individual person is inseparably tied to the destiny of God's entire creation. Therefore, Christians look not for the destruction but for the transformation of creation into the kingdom of God. God's judgment over all godless being is the beginning of this eschatological transformation.

Christian hope brings persons into a deep solidarity with the whole suffering Creation. That hope binds humanity to a "faithfulness to the earth" (Nietzsche). From this there follows a care for peace over against the nuclear destruction of the world; for justice over against the progressive oppression of peoples of the Third World; for the life of creation over against the proliferating destruction of the natural environment.

Pastoral care in this wide horizon is the engagement of the entire community of Christ on behalf of the life of the Creation against universal death and against the powers of death in the midst of life. Whoever surrenders and renounces the hope for the kingdom of God collaborates with the powers of death. Such is the temptation of the religious and political apocalyptic of the impending global catastrophe: "Armageddon in our generation."

Christian hope is no blind optimism but a knowing resistance: Whoever knows the danger hopes for deliverance, and whoever hopes for deliverance resists the paralyzing fear. "If the world perished tomorrow, I still would plant an apple tree today," Luther is said to have remarked.

The apocalyptic system of fear, then, only has a Christian meaning if it serves the establishment of a messianic system of hope. Over against apprehensions of a nuclear, economic, and ecological holocaust, which are widespread these days, the Christian community will assert its hope for the kingdom of Christ crucified for the world, in order that humanity may in time turn back from death to life. Turning back in personal and in public life is the praxis of Christian hope.

Bibliography. P. Althaus, *Die letzten Dinge: Lehrbuch der Eschatologie* (1957). O. Cullmann, *Immortality of the Soul or Resurrection of the Dead? The Witness of the New Testament* (1958). C. Gerkin, *Crisis Experience in Modern Life* (1979). J. Hick, *Death and Eternal Life* (1976). E. Kübler-Ross, *Interviews mit Sterbenden* (1981) and *Was können wir noch tun?* (1982). [ET, *Questions and Answers on Death and Dying* (1974)]. J. Moltmann, *Theology of Hope* (1967). J. Robinson, *In the End, God* (1950). E. Thurneysen, *A Theology of Pastoral Care* (ET 1962). F. Wright, *Pastoral Care for Lay People* (1982).

J. MOLTMANN

DEATH; DYING, PASTORAL CARE OF; HOPE AND DESPAIR; PERSON (Christian Perspective *or* Jewish Perspective); SALVATION AND PASTORAL CARE; SICK AND DYING, JEWISH CARE OF. *See also* CARE OF SOULS (Cura Animarum); CROSS AND RESURRECTION; HEAVEN AND HELL, BELIEF IN; LIMBO; SOUL. *Compare* CREATION *or* PROVIDENCE, DOCTRINE OF, AND PASTORAL CARE; GRIEF AND LOSS; NEAR-DEATH EXPERIENCE; SURVIVAL (Occult).

EST (ERHARD SEMINAR TRAINING). *See* POPULAR THERAPEUTIC MOVEMENTS AND PSYCHOLOGIES.

ESTRANGEMENT. *See* ALIENATION/ESTRANGEMENT; DIVORCE (Care and Counseling). *See also* CONFLICT; DISAGREEMENT, DIFFERENCE, AND CONFLICT IN PASTOR-PARISHIONER RELATIONSHIPS.

ETERNAL LIFE. *See* ESCHATOLOGY AND PASTORAL CARE; HEAVEN AND HELL, BELIEF IN. *See also* LIFE/ALIVENESS.

ETHICAL DILEMMAS. *See* MORAL DILEMMAS IN PASTORAL PERSPECTIVE.

ETHICS, PROFESSIONAL. The system of moral principles which guides the practice of a profession. A profession is generally understood to be an occupation which involves standards of competence and responsibility, oriented to meet the needs of client groups and ultimately the common good of society. A professional is entrusted with "dangerous knowledge," making decisions for or with less knowledgeable and therefore vulnerable clients, who will be affected for better or worse. Therefore, the necessary reflection on the moral meaning of professional behavior needs to be informed by a process of ethical reasoning and by a system of belief and values that allows normative judgment. Norms provide a context of accountability. Thus, the profession normally maintains an autonomous, self-regulating association with an exacting ethical code to which members are personally committed, and with structures for control based on this code, in order to maintain the integrity of the profession, mutual trust, and collaboration. In the case of pastoral care and counseling, accountability beyond the profession is to the client or parishioner, to the wider circle of persons who might be affected, to trainees/supervisees and colleagues, to the faith group, to the public, and ultimately, to God.

The following discussion, based largely on the codes of ethics of various pastoral care and counseling associations, will be organized around issues of (1) being, (2) knowing and doing, and (3) helping as related to faith group, clients, parishioners, trainees, supervisees, colleagues and other professionals. These include lifestyle, competence, accuracy of representation, continuing education, limits of practice, avoidance of exploitation, and confidentiality.

1. **Being.** The being pervades the knowing, doing, and helping. The pastoral role, seen as symbolic of the church and of God, is very powerful, invested with deep emotional significance and crucial to the "doing" and the "helping." It is subject to distortions (transference), both positive and negative, and can be easily exploited. Therefore the ethical issues are even greater than for other helping professions. There are also the specific issues of relation to faith group and of lifestyle — including "sensible regard for moral, social and religious standards," realizing the damaging effect of violations on counselees and parishioners, faith group, colleagues, and the profession. Relation to church or faith group is integral to role identity, and includes ordination or equivalent, endorsement, and active participation in whatever ways are appropriate to the particular ministry and to the individual situation.

2. **Knowing and Doing.** Knowledge and skills comprise competence. Ethical issues include: (1) *accurate representation of level of competence,* including degrees earned, meeting generally recognized standards, certifications and levels of membership in professional organizations as well as in announcements and advertising, which should be dignified and objective. It is the responsibility of the pastor to correct any misrepresentations thereof by others; (2) unrealistic *promises* regarding the process or outcome of pastoral care and counseling should be avoided; (3) in *publications and speeches,* due regard for the limitations of present knowledge, modesty and scientific caution should prevail, without exaggeration, sensationalism, superficiality, or any form of misrepresentation; (4) *private opinions* should be differentiated from those of faith group, profession or organization; (5) *continuing professional development* through educational experiences is essential to avoid obsolescence as well as to increase competence; (6) *practice should be limited* to the level of competence achieved and referrals made when appropriate.

3. **Helping.** The use of knowledge and skills for the helping and healing of persons involves issues of relationships with all concerned.

a. Clients/parishioners. The helping relationship, called on, as it is, in times of crisis, always evokes powerful emotions — of need, of anxiety, of some degree of helplessness and dependence on the part of the counselees and parishioners, activating the basic feelings of childhood and the projection on pastors of hopes and expectations once experienced toward parents. This powerful bond, even more powerful due to the symbolic role of the pastor, makes the relationship especially vulnerable to exploitation. Pastors need to be particularly aware of this, and of their own responses, in order to avoid exploitation to meet their own needs in various ways: (1) *proselytizing:* Respect for the religious convictions of clients/parishioners requires that the pastors' influence not be used for the imposition of their own theology or values; (2) *personal needs:* The best interests of the counselees and parishioners preclude using these relationships to meet pastors' needs for affirmation, for power, for affection, for having others dependent on them. Sexual involvement or misconduct is exploitive and destructive, even after official termination, since the counselee's feelings and transference continue. Therefore, the relationship must be maintained on a professional basis; (3) any *financial* arrangements are always to be discussed at the start and handled in a businesslike manner. However, pastors should be ready to render service to persons in crisis when needed, without remuneration; (4) concern for the total health needs of the person means that *referrals* to other professionals/agencies are made when indicated; (5) *confidentiality* is absolutely essential to the pastoral care and counseling relationship, whether with individuals, couples, families or groups, so that counselees and parishioners will be able to discuss their concerns openly and with the utter honesty needed. Records must be stored so as to assure security and confidentiality. Information is to be released only by written permission; for use in publications, the identity of the person is thoroughly disguised with this so stated. In situations where there might be limits on confidentiality, these limits should be spelled out explicitly beforehand.

It is in matters of confidentiality that some of the more difficult ethical decisions arise, for example, when there is danger to the person or threat to another. The court decision in *Tarasoff vs. Regents of the University of California* stated that "privilege ends where public peril begins."

b. Supervisees. These principles also apply to supervisory and training relationships. The limits of confidentiality within the supervisory staff should be spelled out. In pastoral counseling formal therapy should not be provided by one's current supervisor or administrator.

c. Colleagues and other professionals. The receiving or paying of a commission for referrals of counselees, the soliciting of others' counselees, and disparagement of colleagues or other professionals to counselees and parishioners are considered unethical. The offering of specialized counseling services to persons currently receiving counseling or therapy from another professional is done only with prior knowledge by that professional. It is important to develop and maintain interprofessional relationships for the sake of consultation and referral, for collegial association, and for cooperation for mutual growth.

Professional ethics, then, not only contributes to mutual trust and collaboration and maintains integrity and public image, but also protects the professional against pressure, both internal and external, for the kinds of harmful behavior suggested above.

Bibliography. D. M. Campbell, *Doctors, Lawyers, Ministers* (1982). G. Corey, *et al.*, *Professional and Ethical Issues in Counseling and Psychotherapy* (1979). J. Hendrix, *Invitation to Dialogue: The Professional World* (1970). K. Lebacqz, *Professional Ethics: Power and Paradox* (1985). J. Macquarrie, ed., *Dictionary of Christian Ethics* (1967). R. K. Merton, "Some Thoughts on the Professions in American Society," *Brown University Papers* 37:9 (1960). D. Reeck, *Ethics for the Professions* (1982). W. H. Tiemann and J. C. Bush, *The Right to Silence: Privileged Clergy Communication and the Law* (1983).

S. W. CARDWELL

LEGAL DIMENSIONS OF PASTORAL CARE AND COUNSELING. *See also* CONFIDENTIALITY; ETHICS AND PASTORAL CARE; FAITH AND INTEGRITY, PASTOR'S; PROFESSIONALISM. *Compare* ADVOCACY; OBJECTIVITY, PROFESSIONAL.

ETHICS AND PASTORAL CARE. Until the modern era, all care and counseling of the troubled, the sick, the dying, the sinful, and the depressed went on within the context of some discernible religious and ethical structure of meaning. In the modern period, various new secular psychologies arose that claimed to address human problems within a framework that was neutral to any religious or ethical values. But there are good reasons for believing that the modern psychologies, rather than being neutral, have simply introduced alternative religio-ethical visions, some of which are compatible and some incompatible with various expressions of the Western religious tradition.

1. Brief Historical Review. A glance at Western methods of care and counseling reveals that care and guidance of the troubled, sinful, and ailing were always shaped by broader religious and ethical commitments. In ancient Judaism, care was frequently administered by a class of holy men called wise men. They often counseled individuals out of the resources of both the Deuteronomic codes as well as various Wisdom traditions common to the ancient world. Later a class of legal secretaries or scribes arose who both systematized and recorded the Mishnah (the oral law) and also counseled groups in congregations (the early synagogues) about the meaning of the law for their daily lives. Such instruction and guidance was never just ethical. It was placed within larger religious narratives about God's creation of a good world, the recalcitrance of humans in following God's righteous will, and God's readiness to forgive Israel if the people would only turn to the way of righteousness once again.

John McNeill (1951) points out that Jesus' own care and counsel took place within moral teachings which had considerable continuity with some Wisdom traditions. But Jesus' vision of the in-breaking of the Kingdom of God, the immediacy of his own personal contact with the suffering person, and his preference for working with people in small groups, clearly conveyed the idea that the effective agency of change and renewal was the Spirit of God witnessed to by Jesus' own person. Although the law was not the effective agent of change for Jesus, rather than lowering the demands of the law, some commentators (e.g., Erwin Goodenough) believe Jesus actually upgraded the demands for moral seriousness by placing the emphasis on adherence to the inner meaning of the law rather than on its external, objective requirements.

For the large part, the early church followed the delicate balance that Jesus achieved. Although Paul did de-emphasize the ritual law of Judaism and saw grace as the agent of change in the life of any troubled person, he still used much of the Jewish moral law to measure the righteousness of the Christian life. In the post-Pauline church, expectations about the immediate return of Christ continued to grow and tended to organize care and counsel around the question of how to sustain the faithful until that time arrived. Moral guidelines for the Christian life took on the qualities of an "interim ethic." Traditional Jewish moral codes, now mixed to some degree with Greek and Stoic codes, were amended in both fact and spirit to fit this interim situation.

The early persecutions of Christians by various civil authorities led the church to defend its identity by narrowing and dogmatizing its ethics, its understanding about when individuals had lapsed, its procedure for excommunication, and the grounds for possible reconciliation. This trend deepened when the Constantinian establishment of Christianity as the official religion of the Roman Empire forced the church to absorb and educate vast numbers of southern and northern European pagans. This led to the establishment and widespread growth among the laity of the Benedictine monastic ladder of humility and spiritual growth. In addition, at the end of the sixth century, Gregory the Great codified the church's ethical rules and instructed pastors to induct new or recalcitrant members into conformity with these codes. At the same time elaborate methods for penance, forgiveness, and reconciliation were being developed, partially influenced by Gregory the Great, in the highly influential Welsh and Celtic penitentials, or books of instructions for confessors, which constituted the backbone of pastoral care in western Europe until the time of Luther.

Martin Luther's decisive break with the Catholic Church also meant a break with the penitential system that had brought ethics and pastoral care together since the time of Gregory the Great. Pastoral care and counsel in the Protestant church during and after Luther's time proceeded without reference to a systematized set of ethical rules or "forum of conscience." The ethical life was more of a "sign" of salvation than a condition of it. Decisions of right and wrong were more a matter to be worked out in prayer between the individual and God. Or, as was the case in some pietist Lutheran or Reformed groups and among the Methodists, the rule of the penitentials was replaced by the moral discernment of the praying and mutually examining group of Christian friends.

Although the move toward Protestant individualism had much to do with the trend in western societies toward understanding care and counseling as either ethically relative or value neutral, this trend cannot fully be explained without reference to the growing pluralism and secularity that accompanied the modernizing process that characterized these societies. Nor can it be explained without reference to the rise of the secular psychologies.

2. Modern Attempts at Neutrality. The move toward images of moral neutrality in care and counseling, even in the church, is further illuminated by observing the intimate interaction between modern psychology and the modernizing process. As society in the West became more industrialized and as the process of division of labor and the split between the realms of home and work increased, traditional ethical perspectives became increasingly stripped of their customary religious and social legitimations. It is within this situation of increasing moral pluralism, moral confusion, and moral relativism that the modern psychologies and psychotherapies play a special role. They seem to offer troubled, broken, and anguished people ways of getting the help they need by using psychological technologies that present themselves as neutral.

a. In psychology. Sigmund Freud, clearly the dominant figure in psychology in the modern period, aspired to liberate psychoanalytic practice from any other form of ethics except a professional ethic. His follower Heinz Hartmann addressed the issue more directly in his *Psychoanalysis and Moral Values* (1960) by claiming that psychoanalytic theory is essentially a practical science or "kind of technology" that is neutral to all questions of moral value. Such attitudes toward the moral neutrality of psychotherapy and counseling continued in the highly influential work of Carl Rogers. Rogers was widely read by ministers and was influential on several early leaders of the pastoral psychology movement, especially Seward Hiltner. Rogers believed that all counseling should proceed in a value neutral atmosphere in which the counselor would help the client to free himself or herself from the imposed moral standards "conditions of worth" of others, especially one's parents or parental surrogates.

In addition, the therapist should help the client to listen to his or her own experience, especially his or her bodily wisdom, as a source for an autonomous and self-directed value system, one that the therapist would have no direct influence in forming. Rogers tried to facilitate this nonjudgmental and nonmoralistic attitude with his famous nondirective or client-centered reflection of the client's communication.

b. In pastoral care and counseling. The contributions of two outstanding pastoral theologians, Seward Hiltner and Howard Clinebell, can be understood in light of Roger's attempt to maintain an attitude of moral neutrality in care and counseling. It must be said at the beginning, however, that neither Hiltner nor Clinebell go as far as Rogers. Yet the influence that Rogers had on these figures — and most pastoral theologians from the 1950s through the 70s—may have led them in his direction and caused them not to see the full complexity of the issues about the relation of pastoral care and ethics.

Hiltner believed most care and counseling should be basically eductive in nature. By this he meant that the pastor should bring a nonjudgmental, client-centered attitude to the relation. The pastor should use the method of empathic reflection to "educe" or bring forth from troubled persons their own inner initiatives. In addition, the pastor's empathic reflections were also designed to help persons bring forth their own value resources as the framework within which their problems could be solved. Hiltner made a distinction, however, between two perspectives on the relation of ethics and care. He acknowledged a community ethic as well as an individual ethic and maintained that either one could be dominant. He was situational in believing that the total context dictated whether the pastor should work principally for the good of the group or the good of the individual in particular situations.

Clinebell affirmed much of the usefulness of Hiltner's client-centered model but amended it considerably with what he called his "revised model" of pastoral care and counseling. He acknowledged the importance, on certain occasions, of using the eductive, relatively value-free and insight-oriented approach of Hiltner. But he also believed there was a wide range of human problems where more supportive, reality-confronting, future-oriented, information-giving, directive, and actional approaches to care and counseling are more appropriate.

This new stance, partially influenced by the work of Hobart Mowrer and William Glasser, led Clinebell much further toward confronting the question of ethics in pastoral care. For if the minister needed at times to give suggestions, information, accentuate the positive strengths of individuals, and yet also confront them with their limitations, this more properly forces the question as to where the minister gets the moral authority necessary to make these judgments. The answer for Clinebell appears to be that the minister simply must assume the authoritative status of the moral tradition of the Christian faith. This, of course, opens many serious questions because it is precisely this tradition at several points, especially in the area of sexual, family, and gender role issues, that seems to be more open for question. Clinebell's revised model seems to be calling for a closer relation between pastoral care and ethics, but he leaves open the question as to whether this ethic should be either confessionally or critically derived.

3. Recent Models for Relating Ethics to Care. Three models are now exercising some influence on those interested in developing a closer relation between ethics and pastoral care and counseling. First, there is the model developed by William Glasser, influenced to some extent by Hobart Mowrer, and used by Clinebell in his revised model of pastoral counseling. Glasser believes that the term "mental illness" should be replaced by the word "irresponsibility." There is no mental illness according to Glasser, just people who do not know how to satisfy their basic needs for relatedness and responsibility. Helping people, whether a teenage delinquent or a schizophrenic in a hospital, entails developing a relationship of involvement and acceptance within which the counselor teaches the troubled person new ways to fulfill his or her needs responsibly, without depriving "others of the ability to fulfill their needs."

Glasser, however, seems not to be fully aware that this move toward ethics brings up the highly complex question as to how the counselor or therapeutic institution actually goes about critically justifying the various ethical concepts and theories of responsibility that they may raise as normative for those they help, be they parishioners, clients, or patients. Glasser and his Christian followers may be right in believing that ethics is good for mental and spiritual wholeness, but they run into difficulty over their uncritical view of ethics — their own and those of others.

John Hoffman offers a second model in his *Ethical Confrontation in Counseling* (1979). Hoffman builds an excellent case for the actual role of ethical confrontation within the context of care and counseling relationships. He makes a fourfold distinction with regard to various states of conscience. There are some *unconscious* functions of conscience that are (a) negative and (b) some that are positive. Furthermore, there are (c) positive and (d) negative *conscious* functions of the conscience. Hoffman is appreciative of Freud and Rogers for pointing out the unique difficulties involved in counseling with individuals with problems in the negative conscience, by which he means the guilt-ridden aspects of the unconscious superego. But much good can come from ethical confrontation (both affirmation and critique) of the other aspects of conscience, especially the conscious dimensions of conscience. Hoffman learns from Luther and Calvin about the role of acceptance, and its analogue in justification by faith, in granting us that "right to be" necessary to confront both our neurotic guilt as well as the genuine ethical claims that we must acknowledge.

Don Browning in *The Moral Context of Pastoral Care* (1976) and *Religious Ethics and Pastoral Care* (1983) acknowledges the need, upon occasion, for actual moral confrontation in care and counseling relationships. But he is more concerned about the moral *context* of care and counseling and believes that the pastor has special obligations to establish this context. Browning acknowledges that in some types of counseling relations the moral context should be temporarily "bracketed" or heuristically suspended so that the counselor and client can be free to look at underlying psychodynamics and concentrate on restoring primitive initiatives that are prerequisite for health and moral responsibility. But this momentary suspension of the moral point of view should not be overgeneralized in such a way as to undermine the wider moral outlook that should inform and guide care and counseling relationships. Browning believes that it is now time for the church to give more attention to a critical grounding of its ethical horizon, especially with regard to life cycle ethics that are so crucial to its care and counseling. In an effort to do this, he has developed a five-level understanding of practical moral reason, which can be used to solve moral problems relevant to establishing firm moral contexts. In addition, this five-level understanding of moral reason can be converted into levels for religious, ethical, and psychological diagnosis of personality or character (Browning, 1983).

Finally, it may be noted that an underlying issue in the contemporary situation has to do with what *sort* of ethics to relate to pastoral care, an ethics of *action* (principles, rules, and goals of right conduct) or an ethics of *disposition* or *character* (images and narratives of the good person). Much recent pastoral care and counseling has in effect emphasized the latter; the field's therapeutic concerns and values are primarily guided by images or concepts of, for example, the healthy, authentic, or appropriately developing person—the kind of person one should *be*. Less attention has been given to the role of pastoral care in guiding or discovering what one should *do*. The inter-

play of "being" and "doing" is undoubtedly a perennial issue in pastoral work, but it remains for contemporary pastoral theory to clarify the proper relationship from an ethical as well as practical point of view.

Bibliography. D. S. Browning, *The Moral Context of Pastoral Care* (1976); *Religious Ethics and Pastoral Care* (1983). W. Glasser, *Reality Therapy* (1965). H. Clinebell, *Basic Types of Pastoral Counseling* (1966). S. Hiltner, *Preface to Pastoral Theology* (1958). J. Hoffman, *Ethical Confrontation in Counseling* (1979). H. Hartmann, *Psychoanalysis and Moral Values* (1960). O. H. Mowrer, *The Crisis in Psychiatry and Religion* (1961). J. N. Poling, "Ethical Reflections and Pastoral Care," Parts I and II, *Pastoral Psychology*, 32 (1984), 106–14; 160–70. C. R. Rogers, *Client-Centered Therapy* (1951). *For history see* J. T. McNeill, *A History of the Cure of Souls* (1951); also W. Clebsch and P. Jaekle, *Pastoral Care In Historical Perspective* (1967); E.B. Holifield, *A History of Pastoral Care in America* (1983).

D. S. BROWNING

MORAL DILEMMAS IN PASTORAL PERSPECTIVE; MORAL THEOLOGY AND PASTORAL CARE; PASTORAL CARE (History, Traditions, and Definitions); VALUES IN COUNSELING AND PSYCHOTHERAPY. *See also* CHARACTER ETHICS; GRACE; GRATITUDE; GUIDANCE, PASTORAL; LIFESTYLE ISSUES IN PASTORAL CARE; SIN/SINS; SOCIAL JUSTICE ISSUES IN PASTORAL CARE; SOCIOLOGY OF RELIGIOUS AND PASTORAL CARE. *Compare* CHRISTIAN LIFE; JEWISH CARE AND COUNSELING (History, Traditions, and Definitions). *Biography:* CLINEBELL; GREGORY THE GREAT; HILTNER; LUTHER.

ETHICS COMMITTEE. *See* HOSPITAL ETHICS COMMITTEE.

ETHNICITY. *See* CULTURAL AND ETHNIC FACTORS IN PASTORAL CARE.

ETHNOPSYCHIATRY. *See* RELIGION AND PSYCHOTHERAPY.

EUCHARIST. *See* COMMUNION/EUCHARIST.

EULOGY. *See* FUNERAL.

EUROPEAN PASTORAL CARE MOVEMENT. *See* EASTERN *or* WESTERN EUROPEAN PASTORAL CARE MOVEMENT.

EUTHANASIA. *See* MEDICAL-ETHICAL DILEMMAS, JEWISH CARE AND COUNSELING IN; MORAL DILEMMAS IN PASTORAL PERSPECTIVE.

EVALUATION AND DIAGNOSIS, PSYCHOLOGICAL. This combined term involves two separate but integrally related subjects. *Psychological evaluation* refers, in general, to an assessment procedure in which a combination of psychological test, clinical interview, and case history data are used in an attempt to describe a certain psychological characteristic or characteristics of an individual or group. Examples are intelligence, academic/vocational achievement, or personality. Psychological evaluations can also be used to assess interpersonal processes such as communication patterns in marital relationships. Group interaction processes in military, church, industrial, and other social settings can also be ascertained. As currently practiced, psychological evaluation is a result of several decades of evolution and development.

Psychological diagnosis is a process in which an attempt is made to determine whether an individual has an abnormal condition and, if so, to distinguish this condition from other maladies or abnormalities.

Psychological evaluation and diagnosis is a process in which psychological assessment procedures are used in an attempt to formulate a psychological diagnosis.

1. Psychological Evaluation. *a. The Psychological Assessment Process.* This is a complex process for answering clinical questions in which different kinds of data about persons are utilized. These include personal and social histories, interviews, standardized psychological tests, and behavioral observations. The process involves four steps.

i. Defining the problem to be answered. Before collecting data the psychologist must know what the referral question is. In the past, psychological evaluations were often undertaken with the far too general request to "evaluate the person for me." Such a request was usually understood to be a request for a case study of the person's intellectual ability and personality characteristics. Today, psychological evaluations are much more focused and are usually called psychological "assessments" to depict this more specific objective. The first step in the assessment process, therefore, is determining a referral question or clinical problem to be addressed.

The clinical problem or referral question can be a concern psychologists have about persons they are treating or it can be a concern identified for them by another professional with whom they are consulting. Such questions as the following are typical of the problems to which psychological assessment is directed: Is this person psychotic? How much intellectual ability does this individual have? What is the suicidal potential of this person? Is this individual a suitable candidate for a certain vocation? What is the personality pattern underlying certain behavior? Has treatment changed the sociopathic tendencies in this person? What was the mental condition of this person at the time of the crime? Does this person have enough inner controls to risk being a parent?

Related to the need to be very clear about the referral problem or question is the responsibility of psychologists to agree to answer only those problems which are specifically focused and for which they feel they have the knowledge and skill. The determination of the question to be addressed involves a consultative process between the psychologist and the teacher, doctor, agency, or psychiatrist. No professional psychologist bypasses this essential step of clarifying the problem to be addressed and stating what they can and cannot answer.

ii. Collecting the pertinent data. This involves determining what kind of data to collect and how to collect it. In the past, standardized batteries of certain procedures were routinely used to answer almost every referral question. The thought behind such standardized batteries was that every question had connections with every aspect of the individual. Thus, even specific questions pertaining, for example, to intellectual ability, behavioral inclinations, somatic complaints, communication

disorders, etc., had their relationships with other aspects of the individual and in answering them without noting these relationships the counselor would run the risk of misinterpreting the data.

More recently, however, this approach has been judged to be uneconomical in that it forced individuals to go through extensive evaluation procedures most of which were often only tangentially related to the question of interest. Reports based on these procedures often included interpretations which were not used and/or were so generally presented that they were confusing.

Current psychological assessments are focused and involve a selection of procedures from the types and options that are available. These will be discussed in more detail in the next section. Briefly, however, they include clinical interviews, social and personal history, standardized tests, and behavior observations.

iii. Interpreting the data. The third step in the assessment process involves making inferences based on interpretations and comparisons of the data gleaned from the above procedures. These inferences are then confirmed, rejected, and combined into certain hypotheses that pertain to answering the problem for which the assessment was conducted. Hypotheses rather than firm conclusions are the results of the assessment process. Since human behavior is complex and involves multiple causation, any presumption that the assessment process can do more than make informed hypotheses is illusory.

iv. Communicating the answer. The final step in the assessment process involves the communication of these hypotheses to the referral source. If the referral source is the psychologist himself or herself, the results of the assessment should be summarized in a written form for the case record, and specific ways in which the procedure will impact the ongoing treatment process should be detailed. Furthermore, if the person is an adult a method for communicating the hypotheses to them should be clearly planned and executed. Adults should not undergo psychological evaluations for which they do not receive feedback.

If the referral source is another professional or an agency such as a school, court, or denominational body, then the report of the hypotheses should be tailored for the best use of the assessment by the individual who will implement the hypotheses. Thus, the format and the content of the report will vary. There is a pervasive professional opinion that far too many reports in the past emphasized psychological test scores which were overinterpreted by persons untrained in their use. Where the referring source is another professional, however, these data are often needed to make the best use of the report. Yet another common problem with past reports has been that they were too long and not useful because they did not address directly ' enough the questions which prompted the assessment in the first place.

2. Psychological Diagnosis. Sometimes referred to as the process of "psychodiagnosis," psychological diagnosis has been defined as the procedure of ascertaining whether an individual has an abnormal condition and, if so, in what ways this condition differs from other maladies or abnormalities.

a. Use of the Diagnostic and Statistical Manual of Mental Disorders (DSM III-R). No single issue in the realm of psychological assessment is more controversial and subject to more criticism than that of psychodiagnosis. There have been many reports in the past of lack of agreement among psychologists and the overuse of serious psychiatric diagnoses among persons from the lower social classes. However, the newest editions of the *DSM* have attempted to provide a basis for more valid and reliable agreement on various diagnostic issues. The *DSM* is a set of guidelines similar to those proposed by the World Health Organization for physical illnesses.

Now in a revision of its third edition, the *DSM III-R* provides clear-cut criteria for ascribing a given diagnosis to persons coupled with a set of other diagnoses to rule out before making a definite decision. It is generally accepted that most psychiatric diagnoses are less clear-cut than, for example, diagnoses of physical illness in general medicine. To illustrate this, the *DSM III-R* provides guidelines for distinguishing among suspicious feelings, paranoid ideas, paranoia, and paranoid schizophrenia—diagnoses which have often been confused in the past.

b. Symptom and syndrome description. In developing a diagnosis, the psychologist first attempts to describe or delineate symptoms. A symptom is defined as any observable sign or behavior that is atypical and suggestive of an underlying mental condition. For example, illogical thought is most frequently considered to be a sign of psychosis. Usually, symptoms do not appear in isolation, but group themselves together in related manners. These are called syndromes.

The term "syndrome" refers to a set of symptoms which occur together to form a pattern. Usually, a syndrome does not indicate a specific diagnosis but may suggest several conditions. Other factors must be considered before a final determination is made. This process of determining how patterns fit together is called differential diagnosis.

c. Differential diagnosis. This is the process of determining which specific diagnostic conditions a syndrome, or syndromes, suggest. A psychologist, for example, might observe that an individual had illogical or confused thoughts, an attention deficiency, a decrease in abstract thinking ability, peculiar thought content, and a marked disturbance in their emotional expressions. This set of behaviors, or syndrome, suggests a psychotic condition. At this juncture, the psychologist has the task of determining whether the psychosis is more likely to be a functional disorder, such as schizophrenia, or an organic disorder, such as a toxic psychosis. "Functional" refers to those mental disturbances which do not have their origin in biological pathology. "Organic" refers to those mental conditions which have their cause in some disturbance of the physical body.

The process of differential diagnosis is enhanced by supplementing the observed behavior syndromes with case history, clinical interview, and standardized test data. Through bringing all of this information to bear on the symptom picture, the psychologist is often able to prove one or more inferences, to rule out certain pathologies and causes, and to make a definitive decision. However, this decision is in the form of inferences rather than of clear causal connections. Differential diagnosis in the mental health field is most often a logical reasoning process leading to an inference rather than a certain assertion of causation or determination.

d. Difficulties and ambiguities in diagnosis. The determining of a differential diagnosis is an idea borrowed from the medical model. In medicine, physical ailments typically have a single cause which must be determined before appropriate treatment commences. This is very often difficult to determine in mental disorders, however. Psychologists, for example, are frequently asked to determine whether a given disturbance is organic or not. Since research has rarely shown that the brains of mental patients differ radically from those of nonmental patients in autopsies, such a distinction is difficult to make. Consequently, the either/or implications of differential diagnosis for mental disorders is often erroneous. In many cases, individuals are found to manifest criteria of several conditions simultaneously or they may fail to manifest any clear symptom picture despite the fact that their behavior is clearly maladaptive.

Many psychiatric patients will not fit any discrete (i.e., single) diagnostic category. As the rigor of operational criteria develops and increases through such publications as the *DSM III-R,* the number of such persons is apt to increase too. Conversely, as the diagnosis of mental disorders becomes more meaningful, the number of persons discretely diagnosed will probably decrease. If psychologists are asked for a diagnosis, such as might be requested by law or bureaucratic policy (court, state hospital), it would be appropriate to use a classification such as "Non-Specific Condition." This diagnosis could be accompanied by a description of the salient features of the condition. Where this would be allowable, the use of multiple diagnostic impressions should be employed, accompanied by an additional statement clarifying whether these are considered equally or arranged in some order of priority (e.g., primary diagnosis and then a secondary diagnosis).

In the case of primary and secondary diagnosis, the use of Axis 1 and Axis 2, as recommended by the *DSM III-R,* could also be applied. Axis 1 refers to the overall symptom pattern seen at the present moment, while Axis 2 refers to the inferred personality structure which underlies the pathology. In the *DSM III-R* this is termed the "multiaxial model."

3. **Standardized Procedures for Psychological Evaluation and Diagnosis.** There are several procedures used in psychological evaluations. These include clinical interviews, behavioral observations, standardized psychological tests, social histories, and case studies, and will be reviewed separately.

a. Clinical interviews. The interview is the most basic and most important assessment tool available to the psychologist. Through this process, the examiner not only obtains specific information from the client but also makes observations regarding appearance, behavior, mannerisms, speech, articulation, reasoning processes, emotional tone, and self presentation. These observations are often summarized in a composite statement about the client's mental status. These conclusions become the foundation against which to compare most of the other data.

Different interview approaches may be used for different reasons. Generally, it is recommended that the examiner begin with open-ended questions which allow clients to express themselves in their own style, words, and method of organization. This allows the psychologist to make unencumbered observations about the client's spontaneous behavior. Also, this procedure minimizes problems related to clients possibly reacting to the examiner, looking for cues as to which answers are right or wrong, and, therefore, not presenting information from their own point of view.

Open-ended questions are followed by clinical procedures intended to facilitate voluntary information by keeping the client talking, to clarify information or styles which have been observed, and to confront inconsistencies in content or feelings. A final phase of interviewing often incorporates direct questions intended to obtain specific information which has not been shared.

The clinical interview, discussed above, provides opportunity for observing self-presentation, reactive, and defensive behavior in clients. It does not provide opportunity to observe persons in their natural environment. Other options for behavioral observation upon which to make hypotheses must be found.

Every person referred to the psychologist for evaluation will have behaved or acted inappropriately in his or her natural environment. These behaviors will be reported to the examiner in print or by word of mouth prior to the examination. Depending upon the reliability of the source, the psychologist will put more or less trust in these reports. Where the source is trusted, these reports will be taken as if they were direct observations. Determining client reaction to these reports will become a significant part of the evaluation process. Quizzing clients regarding the accuracy of the reports, their awareness of the inappropriateness of their behavior, their experience at the moment, and their response to being queried about it are important aspects of the evaluation.

Self-monitoring is a powerful way to include self-observations in the psychological evaluation. In the course of assessment, the ability of clients to exercise self-control and introspect becomes an important behavior to include. In the course of treatment, it is equally important to assess improvement through these same procedures of self-observation.

b. *Standardizing psychological testing.* Psychological testing has become a mainstay of the procedures used in psychological evaluation since attempts were made to select fit soldiers for World War I. Since then, great progress has been made in the "standardization" of these procedures. Several issues have been of prime concern in the increasing sophistication of psychometric theory.

The first issue has to do with the idea of a "test" itself. Tests, whether given in a classroom or a clinic, are shorthand ways of predicting general behavior on the basis of limited behavior. For example, a final test in a calculus course assumes that the selected problems that are posed are a legitimate sample of all the problems that could be faced by persons with a knowledge of calculus. Furthermore, the hour-long format of the test assumes that an hour is a long enough period to assess this general knowledge of calculus.

The same assumptions underlie the concept of "test" used in psychological evaluation. It is assumed that the questions on a given test of personality, ability, intelli-

gence, vocational preference, behavioral style are a legitimate sample of all questions that could be asked in these areas. It is further assumed that the time allowed for taking these tests is sufficient to get a sample that can be generalized to the way that persons behave in the other twenty-three hours when they are not being tested.

In addition to the question of "what is a test?" there is the question of whether the test actually measures what it says it measures and whether the scores on the test would be the same from day to day. The first issue is the question of validity, while the second issue is the question of reliability. Since most tests are paper and pencil, multiple choice, or verbal response tests, there is always the question of whether these types of behavior really measure what a person could, for example, do with calculus out on an engineering construction site or whether their personality, for example, tends to be as hypermanic in daily life as the test results would seem to suggest.

Psychological tests should address these concerns of validity, reliability, and content. Increasingly, "standardized" means that a given test has passed minimal standards in these respects.

The Eighth Mental Measurements Yearbook is the most authoritative source for assessing the degree to which a given test used in pscyhological evaluation has met minimal standards of definition, validity, and reliability. It reviews over fourteen hundred tests. A quarter of them deal with personality, a fifth with vocational preference, fewer than ten percent with intelligence and aptitude, and the rest with a variety of concerns such as speech, hearing, neuropsychology, and achievement. A selection of the ones that are most widely used in psychological assessment will be noted in the section to follow.

"Psychological testing" refers to a process of administering, scoring, and interpreting these standardized psychological tests. As defined here, psychological testing has been used in a wide variety of institutions in our society. Schools, business enterprises, governmental agencies, and churches have all used psychological tests to select persons for a variety of positions and activities. Underlying the process of psychological testing has been the premise that these are effective, reliable tools for their purposes. Yet a great deal of research data indicates that psychological tests have very questionable validity and reliability.

The problem of validity arises because the nature of psychological measurement is indirect. Intelligence, personality, and anxiety, for example, are traits that cannot be assessed directly because they are hypothetical constructs with no unambiguous, tangible expression.

In regard to the reliability of psychological tests, we need to pay special attention to the difference between "states" and "traits." States are characteristics that vary from day to day, as for example, emotional moods. Traits are those characteristics that remain stable across time, as for example, intelligence. However, it should be obvious that the earlier in life a characteristic is measured the less confidence we can have that it will remain stable. The measurement of intelligence at four years of age is less reliable than intelligence measured at fourteen years of age. This is even more true of personality characteristics.

Generally speaking, psychological tests have relatively poor reliability and validity except for those that measure intelligence and school achievement. Thus, they should never be relied upon in assessment by themselves but should always be combined with the other sources of data noted in this article. Moreover, great care should be taken to assure that those who use the tests are trained in their administration and interpretation, otherwise the results will be compromised because of inept administration, or falsely interpreted because of overgeneralization.

The usage of standardized tests usually follows a three-level classification. "A" level tests are those for which no specialized training is needed and which are computer scored and need no individual interpretation. Tests such as the Mooney Problems Check List, the Life History Questionnaire, the Inventory of Religious Activities and Interests, and the Wide Range Achievement Test are examples of A-level tests. "B" level tests are those that require some basic knowledge of psychometric, ability, and personality theory as well as practicum training in administration. Such tests as the Wechsler scales for measuring intelligence, the Taylor-Johnson Temperament Assessment, the Sixteen Personality Factors Test, the California Psychological Inventory, the Strong Vocational Interest Blank, and the Myers-Briggs Type Inventory are examples of B-level tests. "C" level tests are those reserved only for persons with advanced training in personality theory and projective test interpretation. Tests such as the Thematic Apperception Test, the Rorschach Ink Blot Test, the Minnesota Multiphasic Personality Test, and the Incomplete Sentences Blank belong to this category of tests. It may be somewhat helpful to think that A-level tests can be given by those with Bachelors degrees, B-level tests can be given by those with Masters degrees, and C-level tests can be given by those with Doctors degrees. Test publishers will usually require attestations of education and training before they will sell tests at any of these levels.

c. Social and personal histories. After the initial statement of the problem a person is having, the taking of a personal and social history usually follows. This is a structured interview process in which the following general issues and particular emphases are addressed:

(1) developmental history: pregnancy, birth, infancy, the mastery of basic skills, and preschool experiences;

(2) physical history: the physical health of the individual, childhood diseases, accidents, traumas, attempts at compensation or strengthening;

(3) family history: birth order, sibling interactions, family stability, inherited physical conditions, family values, communication patterns, special needs;

(4) educational history: school experiences in pre-elementary, junior and senior high school, and post high school experiences and training;

(5) interpersonal history: friendships, romantic involvements, intimate relationships, work associations;

(6) work history: vocational preferences, work habits, positions held, financial security;

(7) religious history: quests for meaning, spiritual pilgrimages, working beliefs, associations with organized religion.

Although most referral questions should be focused, as we have noted, there is frequently a need to contextualize the problem within a personal history. While a complete history would involve all of the above themes, a more specialized history might focus on one or more of them.

d. Case studies. Although somewhat rare in contemporary psychological evaluations, case studies are still used for didactic purposes. Case studies bring together data from all of the above sources in a complete presentation of the personhood of an individual. In efforts to understand other human beings fully, students are often asked to assimilate personal data from interviews, tests, history, observations, etc. into a report that reflects such understanding. While this very general focus characterizes most case studies, it is useful for more limited purposes in that it illustrates the consistency of personality when a total picture is provided.

e. Standardized psychological tests. Below is a list of the most commonly used tests in psychological evaluation. Care should be taken to remember their uncertain standardization and the difficulty in inferring characteristics which exist in the minds of human beings. Furthermore, it should not be forgotten that the distinction between states of mind and traits of behavior is an important one.

i. Tests requiring no special training. (1) *Mooney Problems Check List:* This is a list of problems experienced by persons at different ages ranging from grade seven through adulthood. Persons are requested to check problems they have and to circle those which are most pertinent. Problem areas such as vocation, family, sex, religion, personality, friendships, morals, school, courtship, etc. are surveyed.

(2) *Inventory of Religious Activities and Interests:* This is a 120 item list of activities associated with parish ministry. Responses are used to evaluate ministerial candidates and practicing clergymen on the following dimensions: counseling, administration, teaching, spiritual guidance, evangelism, scholarship, preaching, worship leadership, social action, and music leadership. It is useful for vocational counseling and is computer scored.

ii. Tests requiring some advanced training. (1) *Wide Range Achievement Test:* This is the most widely used individual test of school achievement on spelling, reading, and arithmetic. The test is timed and includes problems in calculation, comprehension, and spelling.

(2) *The Sixteen Personality Factors Test:* A factor analytic based test of personality based on the theories of Raymond Cattell, this instrument is used for persons of sixteen and over although tests based on these theories are available for both children and young adolescents. It can be computer scored. The test measures bipolar characteristics: reserved/outgoing, less intelligent/more intelligent, affected by feelings/emotionally stable, humble/assertive, sober/happy-go-lucky, expedient/conscientious, shy/venturesome, tough-minded/tender-minded, trusting/suspicious, practical/imaginative, forthright/astute, self-assured/apprehensive, conservative/experimenting, group-dependent/self-dependent, undisciplined/self-controlled, relaxed/tense. Four second-order factors can also be scored: introversion/extroversion, low anxiety/high anxiety, sensitivity-emotionalism/tough poise, dependence/independence.

(3) *Myers-Briggs Type Indicator:* A personality test based on the theories of Carl Jung, the MBTI provides four scores along bi-polar dimensions: extroversion ver-

sus introversion, thinking versus feeling, judgment versus perception, and sensation versus intuition. This list can be computer scored. It is widely used in ministerial selection, personal development, and staff training.

(4) *Strong Campbell Interest Inventory:* This is the most widely used general tool for assessing vocational preferences. It assesses interest in six general vocational themes (realistic, investigative, social, artistic, enterprising, and conventional), twenty-six basic interest areas, and over a hundred specific occupations. Computer scored, it is useful for persons aged sixteen and older.

(5) *California Psychological Inventory:* Next to the MMPI, to be discussed in (iii) below, the CPI is the most widely used objective personality test. It measures personality from an interpersonal or social standpoint along eighteen dimensions: sociability, social presence, self-acceptance, sense of well-being, responsibility, socialization, self-control, tolerance, good impression, communality, achievement via conformance, achievement via independence, intellectual efficiency, psychological-mindedness, flexibility, and femininity. Six additional scores can be gleaned from the results: empathy, independence, managerial interests, work orientation, leadership, and social maturity. The CPI can be computer scored.

iii. Tests requiring very advanced training. These tests require sensitive intuition and are often based on free response rather than objective answers.

(1) *Thematic Apperception Test (TAT):* A projective test of personality based on interpretation of stories given in response to a sample from among twenty cards of pictures ranging from farm scenes to surrealistic graveyard scenes to blank cards. Interpretations are based on Henry Murry's theory of the construction of fantasy, the choice of heroes, the dynamics of problem solving, and the nature of motivation. The TAT has been used for many years in psychodynamic evaluations of personality dynamics.

(2) *Rorschach Ink Blot Test:* This is a projective test of personality based on interpretations of perceptions seen in free response to ten cards presented to the person one at a time. There are standard norms for an average number of responses for given age groups, popular responses, poor and good form perceptions, and the process of analysis whereby the blots are handled. It is useful to the intuitive clinician for making intuitions about preoccupations, perceptual distortions, abnormal thought processes, and anxieties.

(3) *Minnesota Multiphasic Personality Inventory (MMPI):* An objective personality test of 566 questions designed to assess psychopathology along ten clinical scales: hypochondriasis, depression, hysteria, psychopathic deviate, masculinity/femininity, paranoia, psychasthenia, schizophrenia, hypomania, and social introversion. There are also four validity scales to check for the tendency to leave out questions, to lie, to fake badly, and to fake well. This is the most widely used single instrument for assessing abnormal personality. It has forty years of research behind it and is relatively unchanged. It can be computer scored and intuitively interpreted. Profile interpretation has been the most common type of analyses.

Bibliography. American Psychiatric Association, *The Diagnostic and Statistical Manual of Mental Disorders,* 3d ed. rev., (1987). A. Anaetasi, *Psychological Testing,* 5th ed., (1982). O. K. Buros, ed., *The Eighth Mental Measurements Yearbook* (1978). M. P. Maloney and M. P. Word, *Psychological Assessment: A Conceptual Approach* (1976).

M. P. MALONEY

DIAGNOSTIC AND STATISTICAL MANUAL III; PSYCHOPATHOLOGY, THEORIES OF. *See also* MENTAL HEALTH AND ILLNESS; PSYCHIATRY AND PASTORAL CARE; PSYCHOPATHOLOGY AND RELIGION. *Compare* INTELLIGENCE AND INTELLIGENCE TESTING; INTERPRETATION AND HERMENEUTICS, PASTORAL; SOCIAL PERCEPTION, JUDGMENT AND BELIEF.

EVALUATION AND DIAGNOSIS, RELIGIOUS.

Rather than imitate medical and psychological methods and categories, the pastor can guide distressed counselees and parishioners into making assessments of themselves in terms relevant to the religious perspectives they share and the implied contract between pastor and counselee.

1. **Distinctiveness of Pastoral-Theological Diagnosis.** Clinical Pastoral Education (CPE) has familiarized practicing pastors with medical, psychiatric, and psychological diagnosis, and with the nomenclature used in these disciplines to describe untoward conditions, illnesses, character patterns, symptoms, or syndromes. However, these disciplines are not basic, but *ancillary* sciences to the caring and counseling work of pastors, who have a unique contract with the persons they seek to help. An autonomous, specifically pastoral-theological kind of diagnosing must be envisaged in order to do justice to the counselee's expectations and to preserve the integrity of the pastoral role.

Each discipline has its specificity and rests on a particular combination of one or more basic sciences, ancillary sciences, applied sciences, unique skills or techniques, and a preferred language system. While the helping professions have learned much from each other and often overlap in their intentions (if not interventions), each of these professions represents a unique perspective on the human troubles they address — both diagnostically and therapeutically. The helping professions stand apart from purely academic disciplines by their use of "transformational knowledge" that is, an often insufficient or impure knowledge base that is heavily influenced by wisdom emerging from praxis, and is affected by the ethical mandate to "do something" (knowledgeably or venturesomely) to urgently alleviate the patient's or client's acute suffering.

Accordingly, pastoral care and counseling is an autonomous professional enterprise and function within a unique theoretical and operational perspective by which to address human suffering and foibles. The profession must be responsive to the spoken or unspoken expectations of the people who seek pastoral help, including the opportunity to evaluate themselves and their troubles in the light of their faith or their religious tradition, with the aid of an expert. Such responsiveness is all the more important in view of the fact that a high percentage of troubled persons seeking help turn *first* to their pastors; whether because of the latter's assumed easy accessibility, the trust bestowed on them, the knowledge the pastor may already have of their personalities, or the like-mindedness or shared religious outlook they assume to exist between their pastors and themselves. In any case, persons seeking help from pastors expect a specific professional approach, attuned to their religious convictions and tradition. Moreover, since religions typically admonish their adherents to self-evaluation and self-scrutiny, counselees often expect to do some introspection and to get expert guidance in that task.

2. The Pastoral-Diagnostic Interview. *a. General approach.* When pastoral help is sought, the person's unspoken if not spoken agenda includes coming to know oneself, getting a hold on one's plight, prudently casting about for remedial action, or acceptance of an unchangeable situation — all within a pastoral-theological or religious perspective. The apprehensive curiosity of counselees about themselves and their problems should, however, be matched by a technical and professional curiosity about them by their pastors, who have the obligation to come to know their parishioners or counselees before attempting meliorative interventions. How might such pastorally led self-diagnosing proceed and what is needed to conduct a pastoral-diagnostic interview?

The pastor should restrain the impulse to help promptly by words or actions, many of which are bound to misfire when the counselee's problem is ill-defined or poorly understood. The pastor can instead be justifiably curious about the counselee and find legitimate professional satisfaction in thoroughly exploring the person's subjective views of self and world, ethical stances, motives, relations to other people, values, and relations to the Divine. Technically, the pastor should make use of his or her own basic and applied sciences, professional skills, and language system (and additional derivatives from ancillary disciplines if mastered) in conducting the assessment process.

While psychologists have devised questionnaires to get at a person's religious ideas and conduct, and while psychiatrists may investigate their patients' religious orientation as part of clinical case studies, their assessments are couched in psychological terms guided by psychological concepts and theories appropriate to these disciplines. We may therefore ask what concepts and techniques would be germane to a pastoral-theological assessment. What religious or theological variables can be used that have the power to pinpoint individual differences, and thus do justice to the uniqueness of the person being pastorally evaluated?

Since purposefully conversing with their people is a unique and inestimable pastoral asset, pastors should use conversational rather than mechanical diagnostic techniques. Most tests are not good enough to obtain the really interesting subtleties that make a difference.

b. Conceptual guidelines. As in other helping professions, the diagnostic conversation is to be aided by conceptual guidelines that the diagnostician believes to be phenomenologically rich and sensitive to individual differences. Highly abstract and all-encompassing conceptions (e.g., human depravity, mortality) have little discriminating power. What counts are medium-level concepts about which theoretical and practical knowledge has been acquired that make a good fit with both lay religiosity and professional theology and that can bring out anyone's unique response to life and to the religious propositions that have come one's way. There are several possibilities:

(1) One could pursue the counselee's *awareness of the holy* and how this affects a sense of creatureliness. For what kinds of beings, powers, ideas, or values does the person have a feeling of reverence; on what does he or she utterly depend? Is there an experience of awe, bliss, humility — and in what situations; any sense of mystery, self-abnegation, or acceptance of one's contingency? What are the person's idols for which sacrifices are willingly made, in time, money, or devotion? Exactly what and where is the Divine, if any, in the person's life and worldview?

(2) One can pursue the person's *sense of providence*, especially since many pastoral encounters are initiated by tragic happenings that lead persons to ask "What is God's intention *for me?*" or "Why?" and "Why me?" Everyone wants to know the divine intention toward himself or herself, which makes this theme fertile for exploration. How and where and in what proportion does the person see benevolence and malevolence? Belief in providence can be smothered by feelings of great personal competence and self-sufficiency, in which case the whole notion of providence is only a spurious abstraction. The idea of providence is existentially relevant to the difference between *wishing* and *hoping*: the wisher is at best only an apocalyptist who seeks reversals of an unfortunate fate and fulfillment of revengeful fantasies; the hoper is an eschatologist who lets God be God, asks for no more (and no less!) than God's presence in his or her affliction, and does not insist on God delivering special fantasized favors. All such personal variations on the theme of providence throw light on what people believe their God has promised them, and these notions of God's alleged promises are often very primitive, literalistic, and self-serving.

(3) Another diagnostic guidepost is *grace*: how does it function, if at all, in the person's life, toward self or others? Its close ties with guilt feelings, self-regard, atonement attempts, forgiving and forgiveness make it a discriminating diagnostic variable, as is the closely allied one of *repentance*. Does the person assume any responsibility for his or her troubled situation—too much, or too little? Or is there a perverse pride in being the "greatest of all sinners" and therefore beyond repentance and refractory to grace?

(4) A person's *sense of communion* is worth exploring: with whom or what, if any? Feelings of alienation, separation, and isolation frequently come to the fore in pastoral contacts — what is their ground and how are they played out, perhaps in congregational life? Conversely, some people define their "community" much too narrowly, solely with like-minded, like-situated, and like-believing "safe" people.

(5) Finally, pastors may wish to explore their counselees' *sense of vocation*, taken in the broad sense of their active participation in the scheme of creation and providence and living with a sense of purpose. This variable speaks to one's fundamental attitude toward life and the world: is it energetic, enthusiastic, and involved, or lukewarm, detached, cynical, and full of "bad faith?" Does the person seek a wide range of experiences and not

mind shouldering some risks, or does everything have to be maximally controlled and safe?

Variables such as these can lead to fertile diagnostic explorations in an otherwise quite conversational interview. They will not only help the pastor in obtaining data about the counselee and in organizing these observations, but they may be used as topical promptings for the counselee to pursue in the latter's attempt at self-assessment. The result of such diagnostic explorations is of course not a label (which would be almost useless anyway) but ideally a coherent, more or less narrative capsule statement that sums up the counselee's problems in experiential terms, and therefore may give clues to well-chosen meliorative moves.

Bibliography. P. W. Pruyser, *The Minister as Diagnostician* (1976). *See also*, C. Ludwick and T. H. Peake, "Adapting a Clinical Religious History Format for Pastoral Intervention with Adolescents in Psychiatric Treatment," *J. of Psychology and Christianity*, 1:2 (1982), 9–15. J. Wijngaards, "Assessing Spiritual Experiences," *Circuit Rider*, 67 (1982), 253–60. *Compare*, G. H. Asquith, Jr., "The Case Study Method of Anton T. Boisen," *J. of Pastoral Care*, 34 (1980), 84–94.

P. W. PRUYSER

INTERPRETATION AND HERMENEUTICS, PASTORAL; DISCERNMENT OF SPIRITS. *See also* FAITH DEVELOPMENT RESEARCH; RELIGIOUS BEHAVIOR; RELIGIOUS EXPERIENCE; RELIGIOUS LANGUAGE AND SYMBOLISM. *Compare* EVALUATION AND DIAGNOSIS, PSYCHOLOGICAL; PSYCHOPATHOLOGY AND RELIGION; SOCIAL PERCEPTION, JUDGMENT AND BELIEF.

EVALUATION AND DIAGNOSIS, SOCIAL. *See* SOCIAL SERVICES AND PASTORAL CARE.

EVANGELICAL COUNSELS. The three invitations of Christ which traditional Christianity has seen as useful in following him more perfectly. They are poverty, celibacy (or chastity), and obedience. These counsels are the basis for the corresponding vows of poverty, chastity, and obedience, fundamental to most monastic and religious orders and congregations. The celibate and virginal Christ invites his followers to a life of celibacy (Mt. 19:10–12). He invites the rich young man to divest himself of his possessions (Mk. 10:17–22). Obedience is implied in Christ's conferring authority upon Peter (Mt. 16:18–19), and his commissioning the apostles to go and make disciples of all nations.

Bibliography. T. Aquinas, *Summa Theologiae*, II-II, Q. 186, Arts. 3–8.

V. B. BROWN

RELIGIOUS LIFE; SPIRITUALITY, ROMAN CATHOLIC; VOWS/VOWING.

EVANGELICAL PASTORAL CARE. Derived from a Greek term meaning "gospel" or "good news," the evangelical label usually refers to a theologically conservative segment of Protestantism that includes Lutherans, Presbyterians, Baptists, Charismatics, Fundamentalists, and others who accept three basic doctrines. These are the supreme authority of the Bible (as opposed to that of the church) in all matters of faith and conduct, emphasis on

justification by the free grace of God through faith in Christ as Lord and Savior (instead of a doctrine of justification through faith and works), and belief in the universal priesthood of all believers (Wells and Woodbridge, 1975).

1. **Historical Perspective.** Like other believers, evangelical caregivers have long been involved in the "four pastoral functions" of healing, sustaining, guiding, and reconciling (Clebsch and Jaekle). Until recently, however, evangelical pastors and seminaries have tended to remain apart from the mainstream pastoral counseling movement.

Several reasons could account for this separation. Most of the early leaders in pastoral care and counseling—Boisen, Dicks, and Hiltner, for example—were theologically liberal and their conclusions appeared to be inconsistent with evangelical theology. The works of Freud and Jung were cited freely in early pastoral counseling publications and Rogerian client-centered counseling was the preferred methodology. Sin, forgiveness, or the Scriptures were rarely mentioned; greater emphasis was placed on insight, unconscious motivation, the childhood roots of behavior, and building better relationships. All of this left evangelicals feeling uncomfortable and theologically at odds with the pastoral counseling mainstream.

More conservative Christians first avoided the pastoral counseling movement and then began to develop counseling approaches of their own. Over a quarter of a century ago, for example, a Californian psychologist named Clyde Narramore quietly began to train pastors and missionaries in a biblically based type of counseling. Jay Adams, despite his lack of formal training in any of the mental health professions, argued persuasively that liberal theology and secular psychology have no place in Christian counseling. He developed his own directive-confrontational system of *nouthetic counseling* and spurred on other evangelicals to develop approaches that clearly were consistent with the teachings of Scripture.

Within the past two decades, evangelicals have produced an abundance of Christian counseling books, have launched their own graduate schools of counseling and psychology, have developed both journals and respected professional societies, have established pastoral counseling courses in most of their colleges and seminaries and, in many respects, and have taken a lead in the field of pastoral care and Christian counseling.

2. **Present Status.** In November of 1988, almost 1,300 evangelical counselors gathered in Atlanta, Georgia, for an International Congress on Christian Counseling which focused on the present status and future prospects of evangelical pastoral care and counseling. The participants included psychologists, psychiatrists, social workers, and pastors, who came from around the world and represented a variety of theoretical persuasions and theological perspectives.

3. **Professional Counseling.** Over twenty-five years ago, Fuller Seminary launched a professional doctoral program in psychology. Rosemead Graduate School of Professional Psychology followed shortly thereafter, and later a doctoral program was begun at Western Baptist Seminary in Portland, Oregon. Other programs at the doctoral level are currently being developed and several

master's degree programs are now well established at evangelical seminaries (such as Trinity and Denver Conservative Baptist), Christian colleges (such as the Wheaton College Graduate School) and several denominational institutions.

Evangelical graduates from these and more secular schools have established a network of Christian counseling centers throughout North America. Best known, perhaps, are the Minirth-Meier Clinic in Dallas, Texas, and various Christian therapy units being developed in hospitals nationwide by an evangelical organization known as Rapha based in Houston, Texas.

Several professional organizations have been founded by evangelicals and many publish journals or newsletters. Best known is the Christian Association for Psychological Studies (CAPS) with its *Journal of Psychology and Christianity*. Now well-established is Rosemead's *Journal of Psychology and Theology,* founded in 1973 as "an evangelical forum for the integration of psychology and theology."

4. Pastoral Care. As evangelicals have worked to develop master's and doctoral programs in professional psychology and counseling, pastoral care has been given less attention. Most evangelical seminaries require only one or two courses in pastoral care and counseling; few require CPE training. This may reflect both a distrust of the liberal theological perspective in much CPE training, and a difficulty in finding CPE placement for students in evangelical seminaries — many of which tend to be large.

Graduates of evangelical seminaries, like their non-evangelical colleagues, are involved daily in providing pastoral care, but apart from some emerging or developing D. Min. programs, there are few good quality training opportunities or publications for evangelical pastoral caregivers.

5. Paraprofessional Involvement. Evangelicals have given serious attention to Gal. 6:2 where Christians are instructed to "bear one another's burdens." Despite some mistrust of small groups and belief in strong pulpit ministries, many churches have emphasized the support and guidance that come when groups of believers meet regularly to study the Bible, pray together, and carry each other's burdens.

The training and use of Christian lay counselors has become increasingly popular within recent years. Although many churches develop their own training programs, others rely on pre-packaged workshops. The most influential of these is the Stephen Series, based in St. Louis, Missouri, that is advertised as "a complete system of lay caring ministry." Following an intensive two-week training period, church members return to their own congregations to train others in people-helping skills.

Initially, churches selected certain members to be lay counselors. More recent emphasis has been on training church leaders (such as deacons and elders) in caring skills, and there appears to be a movement to train and involve entire congregations in active caregiving.

6. Progressive Influences. Within the diverse and growing evangelical movement, a variety of activities are contributing indirectly to pastoral care. These activities include media presentations, political involvement,

studies in the psychology of religion, and publication of evangelical counseling books.

a. Media presentations. Despite the fall of some prominent television evangelists, evangelicals tend to dominate religious programming in the U.S. media. It could be argued that broadcasting church services is not the best approach to pastoral care, but many people — including shut-ins or those with no local church connections — apparently find comfort and hope in listening to Christian radio and watching television services.

b. Political involvement. During the early years of the fundamentalist movement many theologically conservative Christians appeared to have little interest or involvement in social issues. The social gospel of liberal Christianity was widely noted and evangelical efforts to alleviate suffering often went unnoticed.

As a group, however, evangelicals have always been involved in social action. With the emergence of the Moral Majority early in the 1980s, many fundamentalists and charismatics got involved in political activity, and many joined fellow believers in organizations such as the National Association of Evangelicals, World Vision, Compassion, Food for the Hungry, World Relief, and other evangelical organizations involved in practical social outreach. Evangelical books and magazines (such as *World Christian* and *Sojourners*) often emphasize the importance of understanding and getting involved with relief activities and political activism.

These organizations and publications are not involved in traditional pastoral care, but they focus attention on needs and provide for the physical and spiritual needs of many who suffer. In the political field, the Family Research Council (an organization that merged recently with Focus on the Family) and the Evangelical Fellowship of Canada are actively involved in helping people through political change.

In spite of evangelical church members who are isolationist and suspicious of psychology, there is new interest and significant progress in evangelical counseling and pastoral care. This is healthy growth that is likely to continue well into the next century.

Bibliography. G. Benner, ed., *Baker Encyclopedia of Psychology* (1985). M. Bobgan and D. Bobgan, *Psychoheresy: The Psychological Seduction of Christianity* (1987). A. Clebsch and C. R. Jaekle, *Pastoral Care in Historical Perspective* (1983). G. R. Collins, *Innovative Approaches to Counseling* (1986); *Christian Counseling: A Comprehensive Guide,* rev. ed. (1980). R. F. Hurding, *The Tree of Healing* (1987). D. Korem, *Powers: Testing the Psychic and Supernatural* (1988). J. Randi, *The Faith Healers* (1987). D. F. Wells and J. D. Woodbridge, eds., *The Evangelicals* (1975).

G. R. COLLINS

PASTORAL CARE (History, Traditions, and Definitions). *See also* CHRISTIAN CONCILIATION MOVEMENT; COMMUNITY, FELLOWSHIP, AND CARE; CONGREGATION, PASTORAL CARE OF; INTEGRATION OF PSYCHOLOGY AND THEOLOGY; LAY PASTORAL CARE AND COUNSELING; PASTORAL THEOLOGY, GRADUATE EDUCATION IN; SOCIAL JUSTICE ISSUES IN PASTORAL CARE; SPECIALIZATION IN PASTORAL CARE. *Compare* PASTORAL CARE MOVEMENT; *also* CHARISMATIC, FUNDAMENTALIST, *or* SECTARIAN PASTORAL CARE; PIETISM AND PASTORAL CARE.

EVANGELIZING. Evangelizing is the witness of the whole church to the lordship of Jesus Christ over the world. This good news is made explicit in the proclamation of the saving activity of God in Jesus which is expressed both in preaching and in a life of loving action. It both points to God's love and calls for a commitment to discipleship.

Normatively speaking, pastoral care and evangelism are two complementary functions of the church. As such they cannot be separated. Evangelism implies care for persons; pastoral care presupposes Christian commitment on the part of the caregiver and an implicit call to commitment for the one receiving care. While the pastoral care and counseling movement recognizes that the receiver of care need not be a professing Christian, practically speaking, Christian care will implicitly or explicitly entail formation in and by the language of the faith simply because the ministering person has been so formed.

1. **Historical Perspectives of Evangelism.** Two general perspectives appear to lie behind the varying forms of evangelism: the ecclesial and the pietistic. The ecclesial perspective assumes that the church itself functions as mediator of the Word through preaching, worship, and sacrament, and in the fellowship of believers. In this perspective, evangelism emphasizes calling persons into the whole life of the church as the medium through which Christ is known and discipleship to him is formed. It views the event of evangelism and conversion as a gradual and social process. The pietistic perspective, with its emphasis on subjective, experiential knowledge and commitment, assumes that evangelism leads one toward a direct, unmediated and personal encounter with Jesus Christ that leads to a surrendering of the self to him in an act of explicit, conscious decision and commitment.

With the impact of eighteenth and nineteenth century pietism in Europe and the Great Awakening in North America, the term evangelism has come to be associated almost exclusively with its pietistic form. On the other hand, the christian education movement, as seen in Horace Bushnell, and the pastoral care and counseling movement, have developed pastoral theologies that emphasize a positive assessment of natural processes and show preference for gradualism and mediation of the holy. Such emphases are more compatible with the ecclesial form of evangelism, while the more theologically conservative pietistic approach to evangelizing retains its emphasis on an unmediated encounter with Christ, often (though not necessarily) accompanied by a generally critical evaluation of the human sciences and a distrust of natural processes in matters of faith. This has led to a tension between evangelism and the pastoral care and counseling movement. This tension lies more in the differing approaches to evangelizing than between two functions of the church as such. The question therefore to be asked is how these two functions can be critically revised and developed in a way that expresses their theological unity and enables them to be functionally complementary. This involves considering what tensions exist between evangelism in its pietistic form and the pastoral care and counseling movement. It also requires an exploration of what these two perspectives of pastoral action may share

and how an enlarged understanding of each may contribute to a more nuanced understanding of both.

2. **Tensions and Theoretical Differences Between Evangelism and the Pastoral Care and Counseling Movement.** What has been characterized by some as mutual hostility between the movement and evangelism is in fact conflict between very close relatives. That is to say that both are deeply concerned with the individual and his or her feelings (at times to the point of anti-intellectualism); both value inner experience and consider external authority to be verified in personal subjectivity. However, in recent history the pastoral care and counseling movement, which has drawn heavily from secular schools of psychology, has often been critical of evangelism.

One quite practical element behind this criticism may be found in the adaptation of pastoral counseling programs to the rules of the private, state, and federal institutions in which much of the training of chaplains and pastoral counselors takes place. In these medical and psychiatric hospitals proselytizing is avoided if not forbidden for legal as well as therapeutic reasons. Other pastoral counseling centers, often designed on the medical model, consider it an ethical matter to inquire into psychological and religious issues with a scrupulous regard and respect for the existing (or nonexisting) religious affiliation of the counselee. Since there has been little training of counselors in the pastorate, where evangelizing might be more accepted, the assumptions of state institutions and the medical model of counseling centers have remained dominant.

A large part of the mutual hostility between the pastoral care and counseling movement and evangelism is also rooted in their differing aims and theoretical foundations. The care movement, allied with psychology and psychotherapy, both seeks to respect the integrity of other persons and value the development of insight on the part of those receiving care. Some forms of pastoral counseling, modeled after Rogerian counseling, use a phenomenological method in which the counselor seeks to enter into the client's frame of reference without attempting to convey any of his or her own. Hence what is sought is not the conversion of another person to the counselor's faith perspective but rather the cultivation of insight or "congruence" on the part of other persons. Authority is thought to be situated in the subjective experience of the individual, as expressed in the ideals of the mental health field and psychotherapy, rather than in an objective body of material such as Scripture and theology. This philosophical alliance of pastoral care and counseling with psychotherapy suggests that pastoral counseling may also have adopted the materialism and positivism of psychology which rejects any metaphysical explanation of phenomena. Thus, the field of pastoral care, to the extent that it adopts this bias, limits both its own capacity to describe, understand, and evaluate the experience of persons and its vision of what the care of persons may include.

In the early part of the twentieth century there was also the bias among psychologists that religion is in some way pathological. At this time evangelism was closely associated with revivalism. Out of this context Frederick Davenport and others gave eyewitness reports of revivals as "fervent appeals to the feelings and imagination rather than to intelligence." A revival was considered to be a form of impulsive social action that began with unstable persons in the community and often led to uncontrolled mental and nervous traits (Davenport, 1910). This perception of psychological exploitation and hysteria at revivals, coupled with the later psychoanalytic assessment of religion as neurotic, resulted in a negative evaluation of evangelism, though in the last half of the twentieth century some balance has been restored between the perspectives of psychology of religion and evangelism.

In the early days of the pastoral care and counseling movement evangelism was not considered unhealthy in itself. Anton Boisen, for example, cited only the methods known in his day as unhealthy: treatment without diagnosis, morbid emotionalism, questionable techniques. Contrary to eschewing evangelism, he called pastors to a new form of evangelizing—albeit a thoroughly liberal model—which would summon individuals to come to terms with their ultimate loyalties, that is, loyalties to the collective values of religion which serve the interests of humanity as a race (1936, pp. 181–2). It was with the rise of the CPE movement that pastoral care and counseling became so heavily influenced by psychoanalysis, thus parting ways with its earlier rooting in Boisen's empirical study of religious experience. Some literature in the movement, however, retains a constructive approach, seeing pastoral care and counseling as an enabling ministry that liberates persons for a faithful life (Thornton, Oden, Lapsley). Other pastoral theologians point to the evangelistic intent inherent in pastoral care and counseling (Oden, Gerkin). These, however, are closer in style to the ecclesial form of evangelism than to the pietistic.

3. **Some Caveats for Evangelists.** *a. Evangelism and the conflicted self.* In the early days of the psychology of religion school, William James combined the study of conversion with the study of mysticism, differentiating "healthy minded" religion from the religion of the "sick soul" which was characteristic of American models of conversion in that era. While healthy minded religion, and by extension evangelism, is little questioned by pastoral counselors, doubts are usually expressed about conversion which is characteristic of the "sick soul." By this phrase James referred to those who lived in "morbid fear" (1958, pp. 133–8), a fear which he thought not necessarily related to mental illness but which has been broadened by later psychologists to include pathological elements. This fear he thought could be found most readily in the sudden conversion of adults who are repenting from real or imaginary sins, those who are "twice born." Such persons, sensitive to the tragic elements in life, find salvation within religions that address evil directly (e.g., Christianity, Buddhism). The concern of the psychologist from these early days has been that the emotionally manipulative forms of evangelism prey on such "sick souls." It is, of course, recognized that, while the language of repentance may be used by such persons, revivalistic religion seldom appears as a precipitating factor in psychoses (Oates, 1950; Southard, 1982). This suggests that a troubled person may take a flight into religion or religiosity in an attempt to avoid, repress or mask deep anxiety and guilt while never truly experiencing the grace and forgiveness that evangelism ought to express.

b. Manipulation versus sensitive interpersonal relationships. A high degree of manipulation has been observed in the exhortations of evangelists for immediate decision. This was confirmed by the observation of nineteenth century "inquiry meetings" where anxious and confused people were told how they felt and what they were to believe. Persons intoxicated with their own experiences are blind to the needs of others and insist that every person find Christ in the manner they did. Such an evangelistic style represents a power syndrome directly related to narcissism in that it exhibits grandiosity: an exaggerated sense of self-importance, manipulation of others and emotional isolation. The condemnatory preaching, legalistic presentation of Scripture and impulsive manipulation of dependent and anxious persons which characterize the "instant evangelism" of the twentieth century is antithetical to the client-centered, reflective, nonauthoritarian, and gradual approach to change that has characterized the emerging field of pastoral care and counseling since the 1950s.

c. Impulse versus insight. The high-pressured techniques for mass evangelism which had become standard by the 1920s were based on impulsive decisions made by "anxious inquirers." These techniques were a complete reversal from the careful, patient, and personal inquiry of pastors concerning those who were "awakened" in the great revivals in the 1700s and early 1800s. Such an aggressive and authoritarian style was also in contrast to the emerging emphasis on a gradual, insight-oriented approach in pastoral care and counseling. Criticism of the aggressive techniques of mass evangelism has been leveled at the short-lived and often contradictory results of impulsive decisions. Such unsatisfactory results can often be attributed to an unsuccessful attempt at resolving psychological conflicts (as suggested above) by taking refuge in a conversion which is finally pseudoreligious and escapist. Such a neurotic maneuver can find high-pressured techniques of evangelism attractive in that it allows one to avoid personal responsibility and insight into one's own behavior and personality.

d. Group psychology. Contemporaries of the revival movement of the early part of this century also cite the "psychology of the group" as a problem, suggesting that persons in a group tend to revert to "primitive" emotions and an undifferentiated group mind which is easily swayed by a passionate and gifted speaker. Individual reason in such a group is either lost or overcome (Davenport, 1910). In his *Group Psychology and the Analysis of the Ego* (1921) Sigmund Freud reiterates these concerns and takes them further. The throwing off of customary repressions and surrendering of personal responsibility in such a group context is accompanied by an increase in suggestibility as persons begin to collectively adopt the group's leader (or symbolic "head," e.g., Christ in the church) as a shared ego ideal. Freud goes further to suggest that the condition of the individual in a group is actually hypnotic in that one uncritically surrenders to another person's authority and control.

e. The evangelizing of children. Philip Helfaer (1972) suggests that early aggressive or manipulative evangelism of children may provide the occasion for "precocious identity formation," since a childhood faith commitment typically occurs at the height of inner conflict in a child's development. The danger in such early repression is found in its subsequent limitation on the capacity to love, an impoverishment and rigidity of mental life due to the repression of fantasy and feeling, an inability to tolerate ambiguity which results in psychological splitting (i.e., perceiving self and others as either totally good or totally evil), primitive ego defenses such as denial, projection, distortion, and the narrowing of consciousness, as well as a conflictual wish for and fear of fusion. Such early repression is costly for the individual in that it requires considerable energy to defend oneself from both a punitive superego and the threat of inundation by primitive instinctual drives.

4. Pastoral Care Contributions to Understanding Evangelism. *a. The interpersonal process of evangelizing.* Some theorists (D. D. Williams, E. Thornton) hold that pastoral care and counseling are based on the assumption that a person's relationship to God is directly related to the quality of her or his human relationships. Thus it is the pastor's task to help persons to focus on human relationships that are significant to them, as well as on their relationship to God. Others (Oates, 1956 symposium on *Evangelism and Pastoral Psychology*) suggest that the primary contribution of pastoral psychologists to evangelism lies in bringing one's skills as a counselor to bear upon the motives of both the evangelist and the convert. These skills cover a broad range of theory and technique in pastoral counseling. As Paul Tillich wrote in the 1956 symposium, the evangelist cannot ask how we communicate the gospel so that others will accept it, for there is no method. To communicate the gospel means putting it before the people so that they are able to decide for or against it. Our purpose is to enable others to make a genuine decision, to witness to the way in which we have made this decision and why it is necessary for a decision to be made.

In contrast to pastoral evangelism, Gerkin (1984) discusses the evangelistic nature of "pastoral counseling in the hermeneutical mode." Within the interactive play of the counseling relationship, he suggests, there occurs a fusion of the horizons of meaning between the counselor and the help-seeker such that, while the individual's personal authority to hermeneutically structure her or his own life is respected, persons who have already had significant involvement in the Christian community are likely to experience alterations in their appropriation of Christian symbols and meanings. For others, however, the outcome is less certain. While the pastoral counselor will on occasion necessarily be explicit about his or her own Christian commitment, it is not the task of the counseling relationship to be evangelistic in a confrontational way. Rather, the personal narrative structure of the counselee may in a gradual and implicit way become intertwined with the Christian narrative structure that undergirds the counseling process and the person of the counselor. This new fusion and any open acknowledgment of it varies in degree from person to person.

b. Stress and crisis. Periods of stress or change in adult life may be opportunities for evangelism, as much as they are moments that call for pastoral care. While research may suggest that life transitions become the occasion for joining a church on the part of persons who have been Christians by name, it also often suggests that persons facing crisis, experiencing their own finitude and vulnerability, may be more open and willing to hear the gospel message.

A crisis or life transition is certainly not an occasion to exploit a vulnerable person. However, it is quite likely a time when pastoral responsibility calls for evangelism as well as care. From an ecclesial perspective, the crucial issue is one of style and timing, since a premature or overly aggressive expression of evangelistic intent can often alienate and break off communication. However, a more subtle and low-key style of evangelizing may be more appropriate for and more likely to be heard by persons who are either already somewhat active in the church or are nominally Christian.

While some of the more ecclesial types of theories of pastoral care suggest that evangelism makes explicit what is already implicit in care others state that pastoral care is a relationship which "seeks to open both pastor and parishioner to glimpses, signals, and signs of God's presence, to engender the quality of expectancy of God's disclosure" (Gerkin, 1979).

A more proclamatory and pietistic style of pastoral care, on the other hand, views a pastoral situation as an occasion that calls for preparing the way for a divine-human encounter (E. Thornton, 1964). Such a perspective seeks to interpret human experience from a theological perspective, attentive more to the ultimate concerns in a particular situation (repentance, salvation) rather than to the penultimate concerns (emotional, psychological). What is sought then is a decision for and commitment to Christ and the community of faith.

c. Pastoral assessment. All pastors, clinically trained or not, find it necessary in their work to make assessments. The body of theory that has developed out of the pastoral care and counseling movement informs and broadens the range of assessments that can be made with respect to the psychological maturity and health of persons in the Christian community.

The importance of developmental theory for understanding individual needs at particular stages in life has long been recognized by the movement. This theory can also inform evangelism about the various life needs and concerns of persons at differing times in their life journeys. While Jungian psychology points out that there is a point in adult life when one's attention and energies shift from the outer arena of life to the inner journey of developing consciousness and individual personality, stage theorists are more detailed in their descriptions of the various successive phases of cognitive and psychosocial growth. From such a perspective evangelists may recognize that a variety of approaches are needed for addressing persons at differing stages. A few examples can illustrate the usefulness of developmental and stage theory (Erikson, Piaget, Kohlberg, Fowler).

Some point to the "age of discretion or accountability" (late childhood and adolescence) as the optimal age for receptivity to the commitment called for by evangelists. At this age a youth arrives at the capacity for formal operations, that is, she or he is now able to work with symbols and abstract principles. As the formation of a personal identity is the major psychosocial task of this age, it is at this time that the formative quality of the tradition's abstract theological principles and moral values is most influential in a young person's emerging identity. Authority, however, remains external to the self at this stage. The danger is that one might become dependent on and permanently subject to the authority of others. It is at this stage that coercive and manipulative forms of evangelism take their highest toll. While more recent traditions of evangelism may target this age as the "age of discretion" because it is capable of commitment, it would be well for such evangelism to be tempered by an awareness of the sensitivity of this age.

By contrast, persons at a later stage of life may have moved beyond a reductionistic and critical phase to be able to see the many sides of an issue at one time, attending rather to the interrelatedness of things. Persons at this stage tend to recognize all religious traditions as relative, not merely to each other but also to the truth they seek to convey. The danger at this stage is that one may fall into a paralyzing passivity, complacency, or cynical withdrawal due to this paradoxical understanding of truth. A creative evangelism will be sensitive to this possibility and seek to point toward that divine reality which has certainly already grasped these persons, and to the possibility of an inclusive community of being. Also, evangelism to persons at this stage may well be less a matter of preaching the Word and more one of inviting people to work actively for transformation of the world.

Childhood remains a time when meaning is conserved and expressed in stories. The problem at this stage is that meaning is also trapped within a narrative structure. Children are not capable of drawing general concepts or principles from stories. We see here that, while it remains unreasonable to demand a commitment from such young persons, exposure to the stories and larger narrative of the faith can have a profound impact on forming their capacities to perceive and interpret (or understand) the nature of the world around them. The evangelistic dimension of Christian education takes this into account.

Religious maturity has been described in a general way by Gordon Allport (1962) who offers criteria by which mature religious sentiment may be recognized. While they cannot apply directly to a new convert who is by definition young in the faith, these criteria may be regarded as elaborating a life goal and aim for both the experienced person of faith and for one who is new to religion or to a particular expression of it, suggesting the form but not the content for a mature religious character. For those whose conversion process is gradual, these criteria for developing maturity may seem to follow along as if of one single movement. Evangelism that addresses these persons will recognize that conversion is an ever-deepening life process which yearns to listen to a steady and graceful prophetic voice. It is the nature of sudden converts, however, to seem to have fallen in love. The initial intensity and clarity of their religious vision is destined to be enshrouded in mystery again, only to be worked out eventually in the arduous process of seeking to live a faithful life. Allport suggests that "the significance of the definite crisis or emotional stimulus lies in

the hunger it arouses, and in the charting of a direction of search for appeasing this hunger" (1962, p. 34). This would suggest that the pastoral, if not the evangelistic, response to such persons would consist of enabling a person to remember the source of grace, reinterpret his or her life in terms of the new vision and grow toward a mature form of faith.

d. The success of revivals. The greatest resistance to the relationship between evangelism and pastoral counseling has been in the area of revivalism, yet Southard found (1982) that four aspects of counseling contributed to the enduring success of revivals: (1) an open concern for people; (2) diligent pastoral care; (3) responsible fellowship; (4) fervent personal and practical preaching. These include authenticity and commitment, the expression of concern for people, humanity and life relatedness, and a call to realistic commitment. Finally, a revival makes an enduring impact upon individuals when campaigns are closely associated with the work of pastors and Christian fellowships.

5. **Emerging Issues.** While some underlying assumptions of the pastoral care and counseling movement have an affinity with those of pietistic forms of evangelism, e.g., valuing personal experience and feeling, considering subjective experience to be equally or more authoritative than the objective formulations of church tradition, other assumptions basic to the movement are more congruent with an ecclesial kind of evangelism, i.e., gradual change and a relationship with Christ that is mediated through both persons and structures. This suggests that a rapprochement between the pastoral care and counseling movement and evangelism of the pietistic sort will have to come to a deeper understanding and valuing of both human development as a process of discovery (held to be important in care and counseling) and divine encounter that requires a decision and life commitment (considered central to modern evangelism).

A question that has hitherto received little attention is the different nature of women's experience. While some theorists in the field of pastoral care and counseling and church education have made inroads on this issue, the repercussions this might have for evangelism have not yet been explored.

Similarly, the nature of evangelism as it relates to racial and ethnic minorities remains relatively unexplored. What personality dynamics are involved, and what is the nature and function of authority in such contexts?

Such approaches anticipate questions concerning the ways evangelism seeks to socialize persons into specific forms of culture, and what the normative principles and rites of passage of this culture might be. The pastoral care and counseling movement, by contrast, remains more ambiguous about its socializing function, seeking to enable persons to live in voluntary association with others and with groups in a pluralistic liberal culture which has a relativizing impact on values.

An enduring question posed to the field of pastoral care and counseling is what need there may be for an explicit and personal decision for Christ and a commitment in faith to a particular church community. This concern has heretofore remained largely implicit in pastoral care and counseling, practitioners assuming that a decision of some sort is or will be made and enacted. This has been the secularizing impact of the movement's early alliance with psychology. Evangelism, meanwhile, focuses explicitly on the question of responsibility in faith. Further integration of these two fields of concern will challenge the pastoral care and counseling movement to come to terms with the need for decision and commitment. Evangelism, with its frankly acknowledged external authority, also challenges the pastoral care and counseling movement to acknowledge its own implicit external authorities and value commitments.

A final and perhaps more pervasive issue that needs exploration is the nature of authority in modernity. Sociologists point out that with the rise in secularization and pluralism in modern Western culture there is an undermining of external authority structures and an increase of voluntarism in church membership. Indeed, it is possible that forms of evangelism that are based on a sales model may have arisen in response to this cultural ethos. While a theological judgment needs to be made about this in itself, the larger question facing evangelists concerns the meaning and method of evangelism in the twentieth century. What is the place of faith, the role of decision and the nature of commitment in this era of increased communication and mobility, rapid change, and cultural pluralism with its attendant diffusion of the lines of authority?

Bibliography. G. Allport, *The Individual and His Religion* (1950). A. Boisen, *Exploration of the Inner World* (1936). F. Davenport, *Primitive Traits in Religious Revivals* (1905). J. W. Fowler, *Stages of Faith* (1981). S. Freud, *Group Psychology and Analysis of the Ego* (1921), p. 18. C. V. Gerkin, *Crisis Experience in Modern Life* (1979); *The Living Human Document* (1984). P. Helfaer, *The Psychology of Religious Doubt* (1972). S. Hiltner, *Preface to Pastoral Theology* (1958). W. James, *Varieties of Religious Experience* (1978). L. Kohlberg, *The Psychology of Moral Development* (1984). J. N. Lapsley, *Salvation and Health* (1972). P. Lynch, "Adult Christian Formation: Pastoral Responsibility," *Clergy Review,* 67 (1982), 100–3. W. Oates, "The Role of Religion in Psychosis," *Pastoral Psychology,* May (1950); Behind the Masks (1987). T. Oden, *Contemporary Theology and Psychotherapy* (1967); *Kerygma and Counseling* (1966). J. Piaget, *The Moral Judgment of the Child* (1965). S. Southard, *Pastoral Evangelism* (1982). E. Thornton, *Theology and Pastoral Counseling* (1964). D. D. Williams, *The Minister and the Care of Souls* (1961).

S. SOUTHARD
A. R. OSTROM

CONVERSION (Jewish Care and Counseling); SALVATION AND PASTORAL CARE. *See also* BORN-AGAIN EXPERIENCE; COMMITMENT; COMMUNICATION; CONVERSION; REPENTANCE AND CONFESSION; SUGGESTION, PERSUASION, AND INFLUENCE. *Compare* EDUCATION, NURTURE, AND CARE; PREACHING; RENEWAL MOVEMENTS AND PROGRAMS; TEACHING.

EVIL. That which causes harm, depriving a being of some good which is proper to that being. *Moral* evil (in religious terms, sin) is the result of a deliberate choice. In contrast, *natural* evil (e.g., an unpredictable earthquake) stems from circumstances beyond human control.

The theological "problem of evil" arises when one affirms (1) that God is good, (2) that God is omnipotent, and (3) that evil exists. Many treatments of the problem would deny or qualify one or another of these premises. Classical Christianity, however, has insisted upon all three—even at the price of acknowledging that the matter may at least partially surpass human understanding.

1. The Classical Formulation. The great exponent of the classical Christian viewpoint regarding evil is St. Augustine, whose pilgrimage from Manichaeanism through Neoplatonism to Christian faith provides a key to the logic of the classical position. The Manichaean view of evil was dualistic. To explain the fact that there is both good and evil in the world, the Manichaeans postulated that the conflict of good and evil dates back to the very origin of things: there had been a good and a bad creator. The straightforward common sense of this position makes it appealing even today, but a harsh price is paid for such dualism; for entire realms of the natural world come to be seen as inherently evil and the reality of salvation is cast in doubt. Against this position the mature Augustine argued that no created being is inherently evil. Evil lies not in the thing itself but in an inordinate love of the thing, that is, in bestowing upon the finite a love whose proper goal is the Infinite.

In formulating this argument Augustine was greatly assisted by Neoplatonic philosophy. So far from positing a radical split at the origin of things, Neoplatonism sought a primal unity in which Being and the Good would converge. This source of all reality they conceived as a primal fullness, a *plenitude* transcending all defect and bearing all goodness within it. Native to that goodness was a certain expansiveness or generosity. Like sunlight which refracts into many colors or an inexhaustible fountain cascading over many levels, the Good sought to bestow itself as widely as possible.

This vision of the Good seemed to Augustine a philosophical anticipation of Christian truth. Evil, he argued, is not a reality in and of itself; it is not a rival power on equal footing with God. Rather, evil is a dependent reality, the result of an absence or *privation*. This is not to dismiss evil as mere illusion; the hungry person finds the absence of food all too real. But it is to say that the reality of evil is precisely the reality of an absence or deprivation: not a rival reality but a violence done to the one true reality, which is the fullness of creation.

The threads of Augustine's thought converge in his anthropology. God deemed it good, an expression of the divine beneficence, to create beings endowed with freedom. Those beings, human and angel, rebelled: they turned from reality toward illusion, namely, the illusion that evil might, after all, be a reality to be acquired and worshiped. All suffering, Augustine believed, is in some fashion a consequence of that original perversion.

2. Modern Experience. The modern period has experienced a pendular swing from an initial optimism to increasing pessimism about the human prospect. For the eighteenth-century Enlightenment the advances of the natural sciences were evidence that suffering was not in fact inevitable. Human confidence expanded to such an extent that natural evil was no longer regarded as a profound contradiction in the nature of things; it seemed rather a series of discrete and manageable problems. Similarly, moral evil seemed merely a function of ignorance, requiring only a more enlightened education.

The idealist philosophers of the nineteenth century retained something of this hopefulness. But the failure of the French revolution had given them a sense of the tragic; Hegel spoke of "the butcherblock of history." To comprehend such violence, they gave greater place to the dark, passionate side of human experience. Yet they believed that by acknowledging and claiming this dark side, humankind could find its way toward a greater enrichment of life, a fuller integration. Goodness for the idealists lay not in some distant past nor in an ethereal heaven, but in the pain and struggle of human life, a struggle in which God's own selfhood was at stake.

Modern optimism expired in the trenches of World War I. The mark of modern consciousness became ironic disillusionment, an awareness of senselessness and loss. There followed the Holocaust, an effort to wipe out an entire people, to erase an entire past. And now humankind faces the threat of a nuclear cataclysm, which would cancel not only the accomplishments of the past but the very possibility of a future.

To confront such horror is to experience the absence of meaning — and indeed the absence of God. Existentialism is the philosophic expression of this searing experience. In *Being and Nothingness* Sartre portrays the isolated individual "condemned to freedom," a stranger cast upon an indifferent cosmos where the only certainty is death. Yet even in this extreme case the human mind continues to seek to make sense of things by drawing upon inherited traditions. One discerns in Sartre echoes of the Enlightenment defense of human freedom and the nineteenth-century desire to assimilate to oneself the very thing that is most threatening.

3. **Theological Response.** Theology too has struggled, in the face of modern experience, to wrest a blessing from its tradition. Remarkably, the greatest help often came from the very notions which Enlightenment rationalism had disdained: concepts of eschatology, apocalyptic, human rebellion, and radical evil. Amidst the wreckage of Enlightenment confidence, Barth, Tillich, Niebuhr (and subsequently Ricoeur) argued that the high drama of scripture was in fact a profounder sort of realism. The venerable notions of idolatry and pride became keys for understanding the contemporary ironies of history whereby humankind's greatest achievements had turned into instruments of destruction. Yet at the same time that the biblical tradition was being renewed, the predominant, Augustinian formulation of that tradition came under critical scrutiny.

a. *Regarding creation.* Traditional theology seemed oriented toward the past, toward the lost perfection from which the creature had fallen; redemption itself seemed primarily a restoration of that lost condition. In contrast, John Hick in particular has argued for an "Irenaean" theology inspired by Greek patristic sources, for which creation, even before the Fall, was oriented toward a final consummation. Might it not be in light of that final realization, rather than some restored past, that we can best interpret evil?

In recent theology there is general agreement on such a future orientation, but debate over how that future is to be understood. To what degree is the movement toward final consummation an extension of history as we presently know it — and to what degree is it radically different? Process theologians place considerable confidence in a generalized notion of process; thus their vision of history, while insisting upon genuine novelty, is relatively continuous. In contrast, Jürgen Moltmann and J. B. Metz contend that the effect of the reality of evil is precisely to overthrow every effort to view the world or history as a coherent whole. Their views of the final consummation tend to emphasize its discontinuity from all that we presently know.

b. *Regarding the Creator.* There is widespread agreement that Augustine's Neoplatonism led him into an unfortunate interpretation of God as *apatheia*, without feeling or passion. The notion fits well with Augustine's still influential dictum that "our hearts are restless until they rest in Thee," but it suggests the image of a complacent deity fastidiously aloof from the passion and pain of this world. It is this concept that accounts for much of the "protest atheism" of our time: atheism born not of skepticism but of moral indignation.

But here too agreement on the problem leads to vigorous debate over the solution. Granted God is deeply engaged in the struggles of this world, how are we to conceive of this engagement? Is it best understood in terms of certain limitations and structures which are so much a part of reality that they are binding even upon God, as in process thought? Or should the emphasis be on God's free decision to identify with suffering, as in Moltmann's account of the Father's passionate giving up of the Son on the cross?

4. **Pastoral Response.** The historic viewpoints on evil reassert themselves in contemporary psychotherapy. Humanistic psychology carries forward a certain Enlightenment confidence in human freedom and insight. Jungian psychology reaffirms the idealist effort to incorporate the dark side of experience. Existential psychology seems to alternate between Enlightenment hopefulness and the bleaker, Sartrean vision. Freudian psychoanalysis is even more complex. While Freud's view of the unconscious undercuts the Enlightenment confidence in reason, there is in Freud's theory and method a certain tenacious rationalism. And yet the insight at which Freud's rationalism arrived is often a chastened recognition of human tragedy and limitation.

Confrontation with the problem of evil, largely tacit in secular schools of psychotherapy, becomes explicit in pastoral care and counseling. For if the unconscious is at least in part the result of past trauma, therapy must entail a sort of "archeology of suffering." When this painful exploration is attempted in a pastoral context, it is bound to raise religious questions. Much of the therapeutic process is a struggle to admit the pain of one's past. Yet in and through such recognition the aim is also to achieve healing, a healing which is strong and compassionate enough to bear the recognition of pain. To attempt such a process within a religious or quasi-religious context calls for a certain balance which, in its own way, is analogous to that sought by earlier theological approaches to the problem of evil.

Therapeutic healing requires *some* sort of vision of wholeness, a wholeness not only of the self but of the world the self inhabits. The world cannot remain divided simplistically between "good" parts and "bad" parts, which are then related in some magical fashion. In overcoming Manichaeanism, Augustine forged for all time an alternative to such divided thinking. The notion of evil as privation, recognizing that evil is real and yet not a subsistent reality in its own right, provides the conceptual framework for a process that is central to pastoral counseling and care: namely the process of *integration*, the accepting and embracing of all within the created order. This process is further supported by Augustine's other key concept, that of plenitude, which expresses a sacramental awareness that simply to *be*, as such, is itself a good that is worthy of celebration.

At the same time, those with pastoral experience may well be wary of the classical formulation in two regards. First, the tradition has tended to explain all evil and suffering in terms of the Fall. In one astonishing passage Augustine holds that "all suffering is either sin or the consequence of sin." In theological terms, this seems to represent a neglect of the distinctive problem posed by natural evil; it is difficult to imagine that before the Fall wolves were committed vegetarians. In therapeutic terms, this viewpoint tends to encourage the common human tendency to lay upon some person, whether oneself or another, responsibility for difficulties that are an inherent part of living in the world.

Second, one may regret the historic tendency for Augustine's vision to be transformed into a neat system, an "explanation" of evil. Many may look to some form of existentialist protest or a more dynamic position oriented toward the future. But existentialism can lead to a renewed form of Manichaeanism with all the attendant problems, and as Hegel's example shows, a dynamic element does not of itself free one from having a system. When one addresses the problem of evil in the appealing terms of growth, development, and the future, it becomes dismayingly difficult to avoid the implication that the end will justify the means.

Two insights gleaned from pastoral experience are especially valuable at this juncture. On the one hand, we must acknowledge that real suffering has the effect of placing us before the cross, where all explanations fail. One can only cry out or fall silent. As Paul Ricoeur and the Frankfort school of critical theory have both argued, the experience of evil contradicts every human system. It shatters "the moral vision of the world."

At the same time one repeatedly encounters testimonies to the deep and almost inexplicable comfort which individuals have found in the simple fact that another person was present, sharing in some minuscule way in the pain of the experience. For a number of theologians such testimony has opened the way to a renewed theology of the cross, proclaiming the cross as God's response not only to the specific problem of human sin but to *all* the pain and conflict of this world.

5. Conclusion. Despite its great difficulties, or rather because of them, the problem of evil is certain to continue as an important area in the dialogue between pastoral care and constructive theology. The ongoing discussion must seek to do justice to modern experience, but it is also likely to give further evidence of the enduring value of the classical formulation. It may be found that the limitations of the tradition arose less from its fundamental vision than from the effort to present that vision as a metaphysic, rather than as a proclamation and a promise.

Bibliography. For the classic position: A. Farrer, *Love Almighty and Ills Unlimited* (1962). For a comprehensive survey and alternative proposal: J. Hick, *Evil and the God of Love* (1966). See also J. P. Sartre, *Being and Nothingness* (1956). P. Ricoeur, *The Symbolism of Evil* (1967). J. Moltmann, *The Crucified God* (1974). S. P. Schilling, *God and Human Anguish* (1977). In a more popular vein: H. S. Kushner, *When Bad Things Happen To Good People* (1981). C. S. Lewis, *The Problem of Pain* (1944); *A Grief Observed* (1961). A. McGill, *Suffering: A Test of Theological Method* (1968). R. Capon, *The Third Peacock* (1971). Regarding theology and psychotherapy specifically: W. Lowe, *Evil and the Unconscious* (1983). Of special pastoral interest: D. G. Meyers, *The Inflated Self: Human Illusions and the Biblical Call to Hope* (1980). T. Oden, *Pastoral Theology* (1983), ch. 15.

W. J. LOWE

CREATION *or* PROVIDENCE, DOCTRINE OF, AND PASTORAL CARE; SIN/SINS; SUFFERING. *See also* DEATH, MEANING OF; DEMONIC; JUDAISM AND PSYCHOLOGY; PAIN; SIN AND SICKNESS; THEOLOGY AND PSYCHOTHERAPY.

EVOLUTION. *See* CREATION, DOCTRINE OF, AND PASTORAL CARE; CULTURAL ANTHROPOLOGY OF RELIGION; SOCIOLOGY OF RELIGIOUS AND PASTORAL CARE.

EXCEPTIONAL CHILDREN AND THEIR FAMILIES. Children who have social and educational needs requiring individualized attention due to cognitive, emotional, or physical impairment or to superior intellectual skills. These include those who are mentally retarded, blind, deaf, crippled, or emotionally disturbed, as well as those who are gifted. Members of this diverse group share the common problem of being unable to benefit sufficiently from those social institutions which have been established to promote the growth and welfare of children. As a result of being "different," exceptional children and their families are faced with problems and experiences that are foreign to most families, such as the special challenges in adjusting to the fact that the child is exceptional and the need to find community support resources.

The impact of an exceptional child on the family varies depending upon the nature of the child's abilities and disabilities, the stability and resources of the family, and the social support systems that are available. As a rule, the family is placed under additional stress emotionally, socially, financially, and spiritually. A central theme that runs through each of these areas is the question of the value of the child who is not "normal." When the child is perceived by the family or the society as less than adequate or deficient, a different course of adjustment will be seen than when the child is perceived as a unique individual with abilities and characteristics that are also valued, perhaps for their differences. Commonly, a confusing array of sadness, anger, and guilt is experienced when the child is viewed as damaged or defective. Parents are often prone to feel responsible for their child's difficulties and the accompanying guilt can lead to inappropriate parenting. Some may try to overcompensate through indulgence; others may withdraw. Successful coping depends upon the recognition and acceptance of each of these emotional reactions.

With gifted children, problems may stem instead from a tendency to expect more from them than their level of emotional maturity allows, or from valuing the child solely for his or her intellectual abilities while neglecting other aspects of the child's personality. In both situations, adjustment depends upon integrating the child's exceptional characteristics with the rest of his or her personhood. Maladjustment follows an overemphasis of the exceptional trait to the neglect of the whole person.

For many families, coping with an exceptional child can lead to a "crisis of faith," which can be resolved positively by an increased respect for the diversity of God's creations or negatively by the perception that the child is a punishment from God. Similarly, the experience can lead either to a turning to or a turning away from God and the church. In this instance, sensitive, assertive pastoral counseling may impact not only the family's continued relationship to the church but also the ability of the family to cope with the problems it faces.

Socially, the family must help to pave the way for the acceptance of their child into a wider social radius. By communicating acceptance and valuing of the child and a willingness to face the problems that arise, the family not only encourages the child to adopt a similar attitude but also demonstrates a model for others in the community.

The financial stress that accompanies the birth of an exceptional child is a direct result of the child's need for individualized attention. A large proportion of the burden may come from the many medical costs associated with physical impairments. Additional costs may come from complex equipment needed to compensate for a lack of skills. For example, specially designed prosthetics, wheelchairs, computers, typewriters, and reading aids are often available but costly. For families with limited financial resources these may offer only an additional means of frustration. On top of these costs, for many exceptional children individual tutoring and/or nursing may be required. Very few families are able to address these needs adequately by themselves.

Exceptional children are the responsibility not only of the families to which they are born but also of the wider community. Recently this responsibility has been recognized in the "right to education" movement, which resulted in legislation requiring individualized educational instruction for exceptional children. The impact of this movement is widespread, yet comes into conflict with increasing economic crises. As a result the families of children who have the right to specialized services often are required to take an advocacy role to secure their rights. Local parents' groups exist which offer support and information, often from those who have faced similar problems. In addition, private and public social services agencies must be approached for spiritual, emotional, and financial support.

Bibliography. B. S. Dohrenwend and B. Dohrenwend, eds., *Stressful Life Events: Their Nature and Effects* (1974). *Exceptional Child Education Resources*, a quarterly publication of The Council for Exceptional Children, Information Services Unit. P. M. Ferguson and L. J. Heifetz, "An Absence of Offering: Parents of Retarded Children and Their Experiences With the Clergy," *Pastoral Psychology*, 32 (1983), 49 – 57. G. W. Paterson, *Helping Your Handicapped Child* (1975). J. R. Lachenmeyer and M. S. Gibbs, *Psychopathology in Childhood* (1982).

L. MANS-WAGONER

FAMILY, PASTORAL CARE AND COUNSELING OF; SOCIAL SERVICES AND PASTORAL CARE. *See also* AUTISM; CHILDREN; DEVELOPMENTAL DISORDERS; EVALUATION AND DIAGNOSIS, PSYCHOLOGICAL; GIFTED CHILD; HANDICAP AND DISABILITY; MENTALLY RETARDED PERSONS.

EXCLUSIVE BRETHREN. *See* SECTARIAN PASTORAL CARE.

EXCOMMUNICATION. A person is said to be in a state of excommunication when he or she is formally denied communion or fellowship with the church. Since the Christian community is regarded as most visibly present in its eucharistic celebration, excommunication generally takes the form of an ecclesiastical sanction which renders one ineligible to receive the sacrament of the Lord's Supper. Excommunication may result when a person sets himself or herself against some aspect of the faith, morality or discipline of the Christian community. Continued pastoral concern aims at the ultimate restoration of the individual to full communion with the church.

S. J. WHITE

DISCIPLINE, PASTORAL CARE AS; ECCLESIOLOGY AND PASTORAL CARE; SACRAMENTAL THEOLOGY AND PASTORAL CARE. *See also* APOSTASY; DIVORCE AND REMARRIAGE (Roman Catholicism).

EX-CONVICTS. *See* PAROLEES AND EX-CONVICTS.

EXERCISING. *See* OBESITY AND WEIGHT CONTROL; PHYSICAL FITNESS DISCIPLINES; PLAY.

EXHIBITIONISM. *See* SEXUAL VARIETY, DEVIANCE, AND DISORDER.

EXHORTATION. *See* PREACHING; REASONING AND RATIONALITY IN PASTORAL CARE. *See also* ADVICE-GIVING; DEFENSIVENESS, PASTORAL; SUGGESTION, PERSUASION, AND INFLUENCE.

EXISTENTIAL PSYCHOLOGY AND PSYCHOTHERAPY. Derived from European philosophical existentialism, existential psychology is more concerned with fundamental affirmations about the nature of human beings and human being, than with the close analysis of personality structures and processes more familiar in American psychology. More a point of view and a protest against the perceived captivity of human experience by systems of thought than it is a system of thought itself, existential psychology affirms the fundamental reality of individual human being as experienced, not to be generalized, reduced, or abstracted into categories, elements, essences, or theories which are somehow presumed more "real" or fundamental than the raw experience itself. Also, in defying fixed categories, it affirms a radical potential for change. These themes, of course, pervade many other humanistic psychologies (e.g., Allport, Jung, Rogers) which do not take the name "existential."

Existential psychologists especially attend to such questions as how human beings come about and develop, how interpersonal and social worlds are constructed, the nature of human feelings and emotions, processes of personal and social change, the nature of human pain and suffering, joy and ecstasy, and the nature of optimal human existence.

Some of the major contributors to existential psychology are: Paul Tillich, Søren Kierkegaard, Karl Jaspers, William James, Paul Ricoeur, Ronald D. Laing, J. F. T. Bugental, Edmund Husserl, Amadeo Giorgi, Martin Buber, Ludwig Binswanger, Friedrich Nietzsche, Viktor Frankl, Erwin W. Straus, Rollo May, Adrian van Kaam, Aaron Gurwitsch, Jean-Paul Sartre, Henri P. Ellenberger, Albert Camus, Eugene T. Gendlin, Earnest Keen, J. H. Van Den Berg, Martin Heidegger, Peter Koestenbaum, Alfred Schutz, Maurice Merleau-Ponty, Gabriel Marcel, and Max Scheler.

Most of these persons are European, for the roots of existential psychology lie in European philosophy and theology rather than traditional or mainstream psychology or psychiatry. Indeed, existential psychology grows out of a philosophical foundation which differs substantially from that of contemporary science.

1. **Basic Approach.** Existential psychology relativizes all perspectives or systems including its own. Any perspective is a partial abstraction and is useful and true in its own way. The essential nature of human beings *can* be understood and described from the perspective of physics or chemistry, biology or theology, psychology or anatomy, or any other.

According to this philosophy of science, there is no real, basic, irreducible stuff of which human beings are composed. Human beings are no more basically nerves and cells than they are carbon and nitrogen, no less neutrons than spiritual essences, no more animal instincts than living matter. So there is no hierarchy of sciences. Theology is not reducible to psychology, nor is sociology to biology. The assumed "basic nature" of human beings simply shifts as one moves from one way of understanding and describing human beings to another.

Existential psychology is merely one of several psychologies, and it has merely one of several ways of understanding and describing the basic nature of human beings. It is recognized that other psychologies hold that humans are comprised of agencies such as cortical excitations, incentives, hormones, aggressive instincts, egos and unconscious wishes, viscerogenic needs, biological drives, conditioned and unconditioned stimuli, social interest, primary drives, and stimulus-response bonds.

2. **Being-Existing-Experiencing.** If existential psychology has any fundamental concept, it is that persons are understood and described in terms of "ways of being" or "ways of existing" or "modes of experiencing," the shorthand for which is "potentials for being-existing-experiencing." These *potentials* are the presumed constituents of human nature, the stuff of which human beings

are comprised—but only from the perspective of existential psychology.

This means that even the most basic foundation of human beings is understood and described in terms of potentials for being-existing-experiencing. But such understanding must stay close to the individual's raw experience and is not to be generalized or abstracted. Early in the development of existential psychology, it was posited that there were a few shared dimensions or fundamental ways of being-existing-experiencing. But this notion has been largely replaced by the conviction that there are no such shared universal potentials. Instead, most existentialists hold that each person may well have a singularly unique set of basic potentials for being-existing-experiencing.

Indeed, the more carefully any given person's own set of potentials is described, the more exactly and concretely each potential is specified, the easier it is to understand that each person's set of potentials may be singular and unique. Accordingly, it is essentially inaccurate to presume that there are common or universal modes of being-existing-experiencing (unless the level of description is so general as to be virtually meaningless).

Each person's potentials are to be described concretely and specifically as they are for this person at this time. For example, one potential for being-existing-experiencing may be described as letting the other go, setting the other free, letting the other person be. Another may be described as being exposed and vulnerable, raw and open, defenseless and assailable. Still another may be described as joining with, blending into, fusing with. Yet another may be described as ejecting, blasting out, exploding.

3. **Rejection of Dichotomies.** *a. Mind vs. body.* Because there is no fundamental division into psychology and biology, theology and chemistry, physics and sociology, the human body is just as important in existential psychology as feelings and behavior. Accordingly, the human body is understood and described with the same concepts and constructs used to understand and describe feelings, behavior, and potentialities for being, for existing, and for experiencing.

b. Person vs. objective world. Existential psychology rejects any fundamental dichotomy between person and objective world, an assumption held by most other approaches, and replaces this familiar notion with Heidegger's assumption of "phenomenological world construction." This means that human beings construct their own meaningful worlds, and that each person's ways of being-existing-experiencing are at the same time ways of being in their worlds, ways of responding and reacting to their worlds, and ways of constructing their own worlds. Each person's worlds are assumed to represent various kinds and levels and shapes of each person's personal realities. As the person substantially changes, so too can and will the personally constructed worlds undergo change. In earlier existential thinking, these worlds were divided into the world of physical and biological reality (*Umwelt*), the world of social and interpersonal human relationships (*Mitwelt*), and the world of relationships with one's self (*Eigenwelt*). Today, however, this threefold division is replaced by a more flexible concept of multiple worlds of phenomenological realities.

4. Processes of Change. What are the provisions for change, for growth and development, for optimal ways of being and existing? Change occurs on the twin axes of actualization and integration. Actualization refers to the capacity of each potential for being-existing-experiencing to be realized or brought forward or fully experienced. Integration refers to the nature of the relationships between and among each person's potentials for being-existing-experiencing, their capacity to become integrated (harmonious, peaceful, welcoming, positive) with one another. The word "capacity" is critical, for existential psychology declines the package of inborn pushes and pulls (e. g. "drives" or instincts) which characterize most other psychologies. There are no biological or biopsychological sequences of growth or development, no force toward becoming mature, no constitutional wellsprings pushing or pulling the person toward authenticity, spirituality, social consciousness, normality, health or whatever else. This is the element of existentialism that has engendered a fatalistic pessimism in some European thinkers (e. g., Sartre).

However, most American existential psychology holds out the possibility for each person to move in the direction of ever-increasing actualization and integration of his or her own array of potentials for being-existing-experiencing. For the person, or for collective persons, this posits the capacity for being-existing-experiencing everything which is there, for maximally integrative relationships occurring within and between these possibilities, and, even more dramatically and radically, for personally or socially constructed external worlds to change in a direction which mirrors and provides for the integrative actualization of these potentials for being-existing-experiencing.

Some see theological implications in the vision of a single human being or human beings collectively reaching higher plateaus of existence, transcending ordinary modes and ordinary worlds.

5. Schools of Psychotherapy. Adapting these processes of change, existential psychotherapy owes its beginnings to the work of a handful of existential psychiatrists, notably Ludwig Binswanger and Eugene Minkowsky. There are two distinguishable approaches.

a. Existential analysis. In this approach change is believed to occur through two means: (1) existential insight and understanding, and (2) a special patient-therapist relationship involving a genuinely human meeting of two persons. Unlike the insight and understanding of unconscious forces, wishes, and instincts of psychoanalysis, existential psychology's emphasis is upon insight and understanding of one's own existential potentials for being and existing. The existential analytic family of psychotherapies includes those who label their work as Daseinsanalysis, existential therapy, phenomenological therapy and logotherapy.

b. Experiential therapies. Instead of relying on existential insight and understanding, or some kind of patient-therapist relationship as the means of change, the experiential therapies focus directly on the event of experiencing itself, seeking for the most full and complete (i.e., unblocked or undistorted) experience possible.

Among the experiential psychotherapies are Gestalt therapy, feeling-expressive therapy, provocative therapy, focusing therapy, emotional flooding therapy, and cathartic therapy.

6. Principles of Therapy. In accord with existential psychology's value system, its way of conceptualizing human beings and their ability to change, there are some distinctive features in actual psychotherapeutic practice. For example, bestowing upon the patient a characteristic of choice, responsibility, and letting-be means there is no imposing of therapy upon the person. Starting therapy, ending therapy, taking each step in the therapeutic process are all determined in large measure by the patient rather than the therapist. As another feature, the declining of subject-object relationships means that the person is not placed into the role of an object that is evaluated, assessed, reported about, intervened into, programmed for change, or modified.

There are six processes of therapeutic change in existential psychotherapy: (1) the person undergoes change by means of insight and understanding of one's own personal modes of existing-being-experiencing in concert with a developing sense of choice, freedom, and responsibility for these modes. It is a process of seeing and grasping one's own potentials for existing-being-experiencing, and exercising choice for or declining these ways of being-in-the-world; (2) change occurs through a process of therapeutic encountering between therapist and patient. This is a fully genuine meeting of the two persons, an open confrontation and full "being-with-one-another," a risking of existential clashing which culminates in transformation and existential growth; (3) change occurs by means of the carrying forward of one's own potentials for existing-being-experiencing. This is a process of opening up, of actualization, of fuller being and existing and experiencing one's own potentials; (4) change occurs by means of an internal process of therapeutic encountering between the person and one's own deeper potentials for existing-being-experiencing. It is the internal encounter which risks existential clashes and which culminates in an integrative meeting, welcoming, touching intimacy between patient and inner potentials; (5) change occurs by means of the wholesale disengagement from one's own substantive continuing personality structure, identity, or self, and the wholesale entering into the deeper existences, deeper modes of being, deeper experiencings. This is the process of existential death and rebirth in which the innermost core of the person undergoes radical transformation into a new and authentic being; (6) change occurs by means of the opening up of new worlds, the construction of new and changing life situations, and the risking of actual new and changing ways of being-existing-experiencing in worlds of one's own construction.

Bibliography. J. F. T. Bugental, *The Search For Existential Identity* (1976). R. May, H. F. Ellenberger, and E. Angel, eds., *Existence* (1958).

A. R. MAHRER

EXISTENTIALISM AND PASTORAL CARE; PERSONALITY THEORY (Varieties, Traditions, and Issues); PHENOMENOLOGICAL PSYCHOLOGY AND PSYCHOTHERAPY; PHILOSOPHY AND PSYCHOLOGY; PSYCHOLOGY; PSYCHOTHERAPY (Varieties,

Traditions, and Issues). *See also* ACTION/BEING RELATIONSHIP; ALIENATION AND ESTRANGEMENT; FREEDOM AND DETERMINISM; HUMAN NATURE, PROBLEM OF; I AND THOU; WILL/WILLING. *Compare* EXPERIENTIAL PSYCHOTHERAPY; HUMAN CONDITION/PREDICAMENT; HUMANISTIC PSYCHOLOGY (Theories and Research); HUMANISTIC PSYCHOTHERAPIES (Methods and Research); SELF-ACTUALIZATION/SELF-REALIZATION; SPIRITUAL PSYCHOLOGIES; TRANSPERSONAL PSYCHOLOGIES; WILL THERAPY. *Biography:* BINSWANGER; BUBER; FRANKL; JAMES; KIERKEGAARD; MAY; TILLICH.

EXISTENTIALISM AND PASTORAL CARE.

The terms "existentialist" and "existentialism" are used in a broad, popular sense and in a stricter, philosophic sense. In the broader sense, an existentialist is any person who is seriously concerned, involved rather than detached; and whose thinking is engaged, committed — embodied in actual living or derived from lived experience. In the stricter sense, the terms apply to a specific philosophic movement arising out of the nineteenth century (Kierkegaard, Nietzsche) and coming to fruition in the present century (Heidegger, Sartre, Buber, *et al.*), and to those persons directly influenced by it. It is by examining this movement that we can best understand the relationship of existentialism to pastoral care and counseling.

1. **The Philosophic Movement.** While the thinkers gathered under this heading are quite diverse, they have in common a repudiation of the rationalistic reduction of human existence found in both idealism and positivism. In addition, they share a somewhat similar view of the human situation, though they may pose radically different responses to that situation.

Specifically, they find the clue to human existence in the depth of human subjectivity, in the individual's finite freedom as that freedom is shaped and distorted by the anxiety it arouses. Anxiety, in turn, leads to inner conflict, to action which is defensive, cutting off the self 's growth and development, or to hostile, aggressive action which injures the fabric of human relationships. Such anxiety is fundamentally an anxiety before death or other loss, or before the possibilities of freedom. Guilt, despair, and meaninglessness are terms that characterize the inner conflict, the loss of unity and wholeness in the person. Objectification, dehumanization, and depersonalization are terms used to characterize the consequent style of relating to others. Defensiveness, alienation, self-centeredness, and hostility reflect the loss of openness and mutuality.

As a part of their emphasis on human freedom these writers call for responsibility, for decision and intensity of living, and for a kind of self-transcendence which some call authentic existence. In their view of the human problem the atheistic and religious existentialists agree. Where they disagree is on the question of whether there is any extra-human resource that can help resolve the human predicament, whether there is anything that transcends the human situation, offering healing to the community or to the person. Thus existentialism is not so much a shared philosophical system as a shared protest against the depersonalization and alienation of human existence, and a shared perspective on the human condition.

While philosophic existentialism has antecedents in earlier thought, its roots in the modern world are to be found in such figures as Pascal, Kierkegaard, and Nietzsche. In the twentieth century it might be said to include such diverse writers as Heidegger, Sartre, Jaspers, Berdyaev, Buber, Bultmann, and Tillich. Though the existentialist philosophers have shaped psychological thought quite directly in existential psychiatry and psychology (Binswanger, May, Bugental, Yalom, *et al.*), the influence of existentialism on pastoral care has come largely through the religious existentialists, particularly through such figures as Tillich, Buber, and Bultmann. Through them its contribution has been substantial, in both direct and indirect ways.

2. **Relationship to Pastoral Care.** The most substantial influence of existentialist thought on Christian theology and pastoral care has been its contribution toward the rediscovery of the depth of the Christian view of the human situation. The existentialist exploration of the darker side of human experience (anxiety, guilt, despair, meaninglessness) has helped Christian thought and practice to recognize once again that there is something radically wrong at the heart of human existence. There is a disorder within the self that lies below the level of behavior and consciousness, though it is reflected in behavior and may be present at the level of feeling and conscious awareness. This disorder is not simply accidental, growing out of the peculiar circumstances of a given individual's life. It is rather characteristic of human existence as such, though it inevitably finds expression in the response of the individual to the particular events and experiences of his or her life history. Such an assessment of the human condition leads to a fresh understanding of the seriousness of the need which the church and its ministry of caring must address. The classical distinction between *sin* and *sins* expresses this more profound and realistic grasp of the human problem. What is wrong with human being and becoming is wrong not simply at the level of behavior and conscious will.

The implication of this renewed realism about the human predicament for pastoral care is that pastoral care must go beyond simple instruction, moralistic judgment, and exhortation, beyond appeals to human will power or to social good will. It is not enough to give good advice, not enough to attend to the level of conscious awareness. The failure to be fully human is a "sickness" that eludes self-healing. The lost unity of the self, the freedom which has become bondage, and the inability to love others or the self are beyond human healing. Therefore, the ministry of care must be a ministry of grace, a grace which is mediated through embodied action and not simply verbalized. The word of acceptance, if it is to reach the depth dimension of human need, must be mediated by concrete relationships that reach below the level of consciousness. The healing word is not an abstract word, it is an incarnate, embodied word.

Those who take this view seriously can see at once what it is that distinguishes pastoral care from other caring functions. Pastoral care addresses the ultimate and universal dimension of the human problem. This distinctive concern continues to be present when pastoral care addresses the penultimate dimensions of behavioral, organic, or emotional disorder, or when it works at the level of education, ethical counseling, or other forms of caregiving. The universal human problem finds expression within the contingent disorder and within the other human needs addressed by all caregivers. Pastoral care is not limited to those called pastors. Doctors, psychotherapists, teachers, as well as all other laypersons, may become and often are channels of the grace that transforms human disorder and conflict, whether that grace be inlaid in the folds of life, present in a clearly defined helping relationship, or embodied in the silent word of acceptance and confirmation expressed by the one who stands beside the bed of a helpless, dying person.

The preceding paragraphs illustrate concretely what may be said to be a second important contribution of existentialism to pastoral care. The views of existentialist thinkers have made possible what might be called a recovery of Christian language. They have made it possible to formulate in a new and important way what has been expressed symbolically and mythically in traditional Christian thought and experience. Through demythologization (R. Bultmann) or by means of the interpretation of symbols in existentialist categories (P. Tillich) the older language has become once again filled with meaning. Through the existential interpretation of Christian symbols, a language has been found that can reach beyond the Christian community itself into the world of medicine, psychotherapy, education, and the arts to express the substance of what religious faith and practice are about.

3. **Relationship to Pastoral Counseling.** The contribution of existentialism to pastoral care in the narrower and more specialized sense of pastoral counseling and pastoral psychotherapy is also substantial. On the one hand existential analyses of the human situation have not only made the counselor aware of what distinguishes such care from ordinary secular counseling and psychotherapy; they have also provided the ground for distinguishing and relating a religious understanding of the human problem to that developed by the various depth psychologies. The depth psychologists, like the existentialists, have seen that the human problem lies deeper than behavior and conscious awareness. Psychoanalysis and other forms of depth psychology may be said to be psychologies of the human existential situation. They disclose the sickness of the self under the conditions of existence. Their phenomenological descriptions of inwardness and their analyses of the dynamic elements in the individual's self-defeating actions parallel those of existential analysis. Such similarity makes possible the utilization of insights from both perspectives in the care and treatment of troubled persons.

But existentialism may also help the one engaged in pastoral care preserve a critical stance in relation to the psychological theories of depth psychology. For example, the distinction between universal, existential anxiety and neurotic anxiety makes it possible to understand the limits of psychological treatment. It is not possible to eliminate the universal existential structures that mark every life, though it may be possible to alleviate or annul the destructive effects of the contingent factors which produce neurosis or psychosis. Further, there is a distinction between real guilt and neurotic guilt, pointing to the necessity of making the important differentiation between genuine acceptance and forgiveness, and the elimination of guilt feelings. What these observations

mean is that no simple optimism about the human condition and its healing is possible.

On the other hand, some forms of depth psychology miss the full vision of what is possible even under the conditions of existence. Paul Tillich would point to the fact that implicit in the existential understanding of human existence is an essentialist vision. There is a depth of human love and a kind of human relatedness that transcends eros or libido and the self-defending strategies of the human condition. A movement toward openness and communion is possible in response to grace. New life and new being are possible, for there are transcendent grounds for a healing which transcends the actions of the human caregiver.

Much of existentialism's strength and power has come from its attention to the single concrete individual, to the personal dimension of human experience. Its use of phenomenological description is one of the modes of that attention. So too, one of the strengths of depth psychology has been its focus on the individual case, on the history of the single individual disclosed in therapeutic encounter.

These have been enduring resources for the pastoral counselor and pastoral psychotherapist, giving insight to the counselor's own work and modeling a method of working with individuals. But this resource is also something of a handicap. Many existentialists and perhaps most depth psychologists have neglected the societal and communal contexts which frame the individual life. In consequence they may also neglect the structures of disordered social existence which impinge upon the individual. There are of course existentialists who have emphasized the social dimension of human being and becoming (Buber and Marcel) or who have explicitly sought to correct the individualistic perspective of a given existential interpretation (D. Soelle in relation to Bultmann). To be aware of this one-sidedness of many of the existentialists is to call attention to a real or potential gap in pastoral psychotherapy. Liberation theology in particular should make those involved in pastoral care aware of the need for resources that lie beyond both existentialism and depth psychology.

Bibliography. M. Buber, *The Knowledge of Man* (1965). R. Bultmann, *Theology of the New Testament*, 2 vols. (1952, 1955). G. Izenberg, *The Existentialist Critique of Freud* (1976). C. Hanly, *Existentialism and Psychoanalysis* (1979). P. LeFevre, "The Snare of Truth," in P. Homans, ed., *The Dialogue Between Theology and Psychology* (1968). R. May, *Existence* (1958). P. Tillich, *The Courage to Be* (1952); *The Meaning of Health: Essays in Existentialism, Psychoanalysis, and Religion* (1984). J. Wahl, *Philosophies of Existence* (1969). J. Wild, *The Challenge of Existentialism* (1955). I. Yalom, *Existential Psychotherapy* (1980).

P. LEFEVRE

EXISTENTIAL PSYCHOLOGY AND PSYCHOTHERAPY; HUMAN CONDITION/PREDICAMENT; PASTORAL THEOLOGICAL METHODOLOGY; PASTORAL THEOLOGY. *See also* ACTION/BEING RELATIONSHIP; ALIENATION/ESTRANGEMENT; BEING/BECOMING RELATIONSHIP; I AND THOU; PHENOMENOLOGICAL METHOD IN PASTORAL CARE; PHILOSOPHY AND PSYCHOLOGY; THEORY IN PASTORAL CARE AND COUNSELING, FUNCTIONS OF. *Compare* EMPIRICAL, EXPERIENTIAL, LIBERATION, NEO-ORTHODOX, *or* PROCESS THEOLOGY, AND PASTORAL CARE; INTERPRETATION AND HERMENEUTICS, PAS-

TORAL; THEOLOGY AND PSYCHOTHERAPY; WILL TO LIVE. *Biography:* BINSWANGER; BUBER; 'BULTMANN; KIERKEGAARD, MAY; TILLICH.

EXOMOLOGESIS. As a *general term* in patristic literature, confession of sins to God or to human beings; confession of benefits; acknowledgment of truth. As a *technical term,* applied in second through fourth centuries to procedure for reconciliation of penitents, involving a penitential way of life: "sack-cloth and ashes," fasting, and prayer (Tertullian). These acts constitute public confession of guilt to God but also, by the very nature of the acts, to the church. Also known as second penitence, baptism culminating first penitence, it was available only once in a lifetime.

Bibliography. B. Poschmann, *Penance and the Anointing of the Sick* (1964). Tertullian, *On Penance,* Ancient Christian Writers 28 (1950). K. Rahner, *Penance in the Early Church* (1982).

M. A. DONOVAN

EARLY CHURCH, PASTORAL CARE AND COUNSELING IN. *See also* PASTORAL CARE (History, Traditions, and Definitions); REPENTANCE AND CONFESSION. *Compare* GROUP COUNSELING AND PSYCHOTHERAPY; PENANCE, SACRAMENT OF; RECONCILING.

EXORCISM. Invoking the name of God to expel an evil spirit believed to inhabit or possess a person or, by extension, a place or object. As a form of spiritual healing, exorcism presupposes belief in and putative evidence of *possession,* the condition of being under the influence or domination, whether internal or external, of a supernatural being such as a god, demon, ghost, spirit, witch, or even an artifact or natural entity such as an animal which is able to control the behavior of the possessed person whether partially or fully, constantly or intermittently.

1. Spirit Possession and Exorcism in History. Both spirit possession and exorcism have figured prominently in world religions from antiquity to the present. In the Christian West, however, possession has been generally attributed to Satan or demons. Over the past two centuries, belief in demons and other spirits, along with their ability to assume control of human behavior, has largely disappeared from Western civilization in the wake of the development of empirical science and especially the widespread acceptance of medical psychotherapy.

That such beliefs and practices should nevertheless persist is not startling, considering the long centuries of human history when fear of demons and possession was virtually universal. In Europe alone, from the late Middle Ages to the Enlightenment, hundreds of thousands of men, women, and children were ritually executed on the merest suspicion of witchcraft, one of the chief acts and evidence of which was causing possession, as in the cases of those burned and hanged in seventeenth-century France and New England, including both Protestant and Roman Catholic clergy.

But at least since the sixteenth century in Europe, and perhaps for much longer elsewhere, the likelihood that a supposedly possessed person could deceive or be deceived led to the useful distinction between true possession and false or pseudo-possession. This may be defined as the delusion that oneself or another person is possessed by an evil spirit, often accompanied with behavioral phenomena traditionally associated with possession but in fact induced by natural factors such as physiological, psychological, or sociological stresses and structured according to culturally available patterns of belief.

2. Possession and Pseudo-Possession. With certain possible historical exceptions now little susceptible of proof or disproof, true possession cases, in which the onset and course of the behavioral symptoms cannot be explained or treated by ordinary medical or psychiatric means, are so extremely rare, if they exist at all, as to be considered clinically negligible. But several kinds of "pseudo-possession" can be distinguished in addition to psychotic reactions. One of these is induced trance behavior, which includes "cinematic neurosis", that is, imitative behavior induced by exposure on the part of impressionable or suggestible persons to presentations of possession behavior in motion pictures, television, print media, including religious broadcasting. Similar mimetic behavior can result from the impact of live religious services, demonstrations, and theatrical presentations. Such behavior ordinarily lacks the severe derangement of personality characteristic of psychosis. It may, on the other hand, signal the onset of a psychotic episode.

Another sort of pseudo-possession is religious enthusiasm, the result of high expectation based on a strong shared belief system and sometimes deliberate social manipulation. Its forms include theriomorphism (the belief that one acquires animal powers), as in medieval berzerkers, Mau Mau terrorists, etc.; voodoo and macumba; and pentecostalism.

Hypnosis is also a kind of pseudo-possession. Finally, it must also be noted that certain events and experiences of monstrous evil, threat, or danger are sometimes interpreted as demonic possession—such as the crimes against humanity perpetrated by the Third Reich or the mass murders of Charles Manson—as well as more ordinary obsessions, compulsions, addictions, and chronic conditions such as fear of animals, acrophobia, alcoholism, allergies, and some classes of compelling moral fault, especially sexual sins.

3. Normative Considerations. a. Scriptural basis. Exorcism was practiced in Judaism before the Christian Era, and there is scriptural and post-scriptural evidence for its continuation in the early church. The term *exhorkizo,* "to adjure," was not used of Jesus or of his disciples, however (Acts 19:13). "Casting out" unclean spirits was signified by the word *ekballein* (Mt. 8:16; Lk. 11:14), which was often coupled with *therapeúō,* "to heal or cure" (Mk. 1:34; Lk. 6:18; 8:29). In Acts 10:38 the word *iáomai,* which also means "to heal," is similarly employed. Casting out spirits was part of the healing ministry; significantly, the primary meaning of *therapeúō* in Greek is "to serve God."

b. Early Christian practice. Ritual exorcism was included in the sacramental observance of baptism from a very early period. However, the "possession" implied was essentially external, forensic, and collective. In early Christian services, *energumenoi,* demented and spiritually troubled members of the community, were segregated among penitents and catechumens under the care of minor clerics, who were eventually called "exorcists."

Such disturbed persons were routinely prayed for by the whole community, but they seem not to have been subjected to extended rituals of exorcism such as those developed in the Middle Ages and Post-Reformation Era.

c. Present belief and practice. Christian denominations vary widely with regard to such beliefs and the practice of exorcism. Modern liberal Protestantism has tended to reject both belief and practice (at least outside of instances recorded in the Bible), while many evangelical and especially Pentecostal traditions maintain literal belief in possession and foster the practice of public exorcism. The Roman Catholic and Orthodox traditions have historically affirmed the possibility of possession and admitted the practice of exorcism under usually strict ecclesiastical control, though current trends in theology and pastoral care incline toward the liberal Protestant position rather than that of evangelical fundamentalism. In the Catholic Church, the minor order of exorcist and the ritual of exorcism were suppressed after 1971. Some Orthodox and Hasidic Jews accept the possibility of possession by the spirit of a deceased human being (*dybbuk*) and the practice of exorcism, but liberal Judaism rejects both.

d. Scientific studies. The incidence and characteristics of possession and exorcism have been documented and subjected to analysis for over seventy years by anthropologists, psychologists, and sociologists. In terms of economic function, that is, its value in reestablishing social harmony, the dialectical drama of possession and exorcism has been interpreted by social scientists as a means of surfacing and discharging psychic tension within a family group or on a much larger scale, as was evident in the witchcraft mania in Nigeria during that nation's struggle to attain and preserve its independence. (*See* M. Marwick, 1970.)

Such a theory, which has been advanced independently by many researchers and substantiated by cross-cultural investigation throughout the world, bears an obvious similarity to the psychological account of the possession and exorcism of particular individuals — of surfacing, identifying, and alleviating stress.

Interpreted as arising from outside, whether of the individual or the group, possession (and, subsequently, exorcism) may be more "successful" than if envisioned as arising from within, because such interpretation exonerates the person or the group from guilt or complicity. Because such rituals *can* successfully alleviate stress, however, they are likely to be repeated in the event of further stress. Thus, a recurrent dialectic is set up, the net effect being to trap individuals and societies in a behavioral habit that provides immediate relief but fails to address the real sources of distress.

4. **Pastoral Practice.** Persons seeking pastoral care and counseling with regard to fears and beliefs about possession are often deeply disturbed, and may require extensive counseling, often in the mode of crisis intervention. Persons apparently exhibiting moderate to severe psychopathology should be firmly but compassionately guided to competent psychiatric agencies for evaluation and treatment. Such persons will most likely also have deep spiritual needs, which should not be overlooked in the referral process. In any case their concerns must not be dismissed or belittled because they conflict with ideas or beliefs held by those they approach. While the imagery of possession, through which radical threat and evil are experienced, may seem unrealistic, the felt danger and the need for emergency help are clearly, if only subjectively, real, and worthy of serious pastoral respect and response.

Bibliography. D. Bakan, *The Duality of Human Existence* (1966), pp. 38–101. J. Cortes and F. Gatti, *The Case Against Possessions and Exorcisms* (1975). F. Goodman, *et al.*, *Trance, Healing, and Hallucination* (1974). J. Lhermitte, *True and False Possession* (1963); "Pseudo-Possession," *Soundings in Satanism*, F. Sheed, ed., (1972), pp. 12–35. M. Marwick, ed., *Witchcraft and Sorcery* (1970). R. May, *Love and Will* (1969). J. Mischo, "Possessions Diaboliques: Diagnostics interdisciplinaires et perspectives psychohygeniques," *Concilium*, 103 (1975) 81–98. T. Oesterreich, *Possession, Demoniacal and Other*, (1966). R. Prince, ed., *Trance and Possession States*, (1968). W. Sargant, *The Mind Possessed* (1975). R. Woods, "The Possession Problem," *Chicago Studies*, 12 (1973), 91–107; "The Devil, Evil and Christian Experience," *Listening*, 12:2 (1977), 21–42.

R. J. WOODS

EVIL; The DEMONIC; PASTORAL CARE (History, Traditions, and Definitions). *See also* MEDIEVAL CHURCH, PASTORAL CARE IN; PSYCHOPATHOLOGY AND RELIGION; SALVATION, HEALING, AND HEALTH. *Compare* FAITH HEALING; SIN AND SICKNESS.

EXPECTATION. *See* HOPE AND DESPAIR. *See also* ESCHATOLOGY; TIME/TIME SENSE.

EXPERIENCE. Participation in or encounter with reality. The term "experience" is also used of the practical knowledge gained through such participation or encounter.

Experience is sometimes contrasted with reflection. In such cases, emphasis is placed upon the immediacy of the occurrence, which excludes detached reflection. However, when used in the second sense, as denoting knowledge gained, "experience" actually *includes* reflection (or the result of reflection) as well as the original immediacy.

Clarification of the term is important to pastoral counseling and pastoral care in a general sense because these activities draw upon experience. But more specifically it is important because a primary goal of pastoral work is precisely the fostering of personal openness to, and understanding of, experience.

1. **Interpretations of Experience.** Broadly speaking, one may distinguish two ways of understanding the nature of experience. One may think of experience as being built up out of primary elements or "sense data," or alternatively one may regard experience as emerging from the wholeness of an original relationship.

a. Sense data. From the time of early Greek philosophy, experience has been understood as the perception of ourselves in the world of objects by means of the senses, particularly sight. Scientific methodology has codified this notion of sense perception into principles of precise observation intended to yield verifiable knowledge. An experience is considered true and universal if it can be repeated and experienced anew under similar circumstances. Laws are formulated as patterns of repeatable experience, in the hope that, when such laws are sufficiently ordered and systematized, the course of future experience may be confidently predicted.

b. "Being-in-the-world." Another understanding of experience does not regard sense data as the primary mode of experiencing. The more elemental level of awareness which this understanding claims, is of ourselves and others as being mutually interactive, with the capability of memory and anticipation. According to the "radical empiricism" of William James, experience begins with an original whole, a "blooming, buzzing confusion," within which the person then seeks to make distinctions. Martin Heidegger's notion of "being-in-the-world" asserts that experience does finally not rest upon the objectification of reality, but rather upon an original concern, an implicit understanding of Being which places the person in relationship with all other elements of the world. Thus one's sense of the whole is not the cumulative result of observation and generalization; rather it is the original concerned relatedness upon which the very capacity for detached observation depends. From this it follows that laws for the prediction of experience are not as important as the underlying capacity for freedom and responsibility.

2. Uses of Experience. *a. Prediction and control.* In the realm of science and technology the ability to predict and control reactions is essential. This ability is in part built upon the collected experiences of enough practitioners, from which concepts are constructed in order to guide further practice. Prediction and control are essential abilities in such fields as medicine and the natural sciences.

The ability to predict and control in the behavioral sciences, such as psychology, is less sure. Yet even in such practices as pastoral care and counseling the ability to "build on experience" is important. While only the most radical of behaviorists would argue that all human behavior is subject to discernible laws, it is true that human memory of prior experiences allows for reasonable navigation through various tasks. Much pastoral care and counseling is possible because of the collective wisdom of generations of pastoral caregivers.

Practical wisdom is most difficult to define. It most likely is the result of being open to new experiences, with critical reflection upon the experience and pastoral action in response to the event. Such critical reflection does not rest upon merely subjective evaluation. The teachings of the faith tradition and the critical evaluations of other pastoral workers are also an essential part of the reflective process. While rote and a purely technical approach to pastoral care is to be avoided, it is difficult to deny the usefulness of prior experience in guiding practice in the present. Works such as Kübler-Ross's study *On Death and Dying,* while open to abuse, are very helpful in offering the pastoral care minister the fruit of the collected experiences of others.

b. Enlightenment. H. G. Gadamer has argued that in its pure sense, experience is always new. Only through being surprised can we really acquire new experiences. For an experience truly to be an experience, according to Gadamer, it must run counter to our expectations. Thus insight is more than just knowledge of a given situation; it also involves liberation from something that deceives us and holds us captive. Such experience is essential to

enlightenment; it challenges defensive preconceptions which keep one closed to change. Pastoral care is limited as long as it is delivered by a person who has become closed to experience through an over-reliance on psychological or scriptural prescription. The deeper dimensions of reality become accessible through what Thomas Klink has called "cross-grained" experience: the often difficult confrontation between categorical and specific knowledge.

c. The religious dimension. If experience in the most fundamental sense is always new experience, then it has religious implications. New experience challenges our expectations and illusions of being in full control of our lives. In this fashion experience confronts us with our human finitude. No human is master of the future. Anton Boisen, in particular, pointed this out when he described acute psychotic experience as a religious crisis. In psychosis the apparatus for predicting the future, explaining everyday life, and describing self-identity fails. The struggle to regain balance in this eruptive situation is a religious one. William James, like Boisen though with less extreme experiences in mind, also described the role of the new in religious experience. Experience, James argued, always begins negatively as it confronts human limitation and the absoluteness of the barricade between the human and the divine. Both Boisen and James believed that eruptive experience and its resolution have religious as well as therapeutic significance. Pastoral care and counseling is in a unique position to address both of these facets.

3. **The Experienced Pastor.** While the experienced pastor may well be one with much practical experience and wisdom, he or she is also one who is open to new experience, in the awareness of his or her limitations and the limitations of others. In this sense the true value of experience is in engendering a capacity to be open to surprise. This is particularly important in pastoral care and counseling, where attentiveness to the specific is crucial. To be closed to the particular and the unique in a pastoral experience is not only to miss the essential ministerial act of shepherding, but also to succumb to human pride and sin—the mistaken notion that one has the power to predict and control the future. This is by no means to deny the accumulative aspect of experience, for at the same time there are organizing principles one must incorporate if one is to act at all.

The experienced pastor, then, is one who is open to experience and willing to reflect upon it, and also one who is able to abstract and conceptualize.

Bibliography. I. G. Barbour, *Issues in Science and Religion* (1966). A. T. Boisen, *The Exploration of the Inner World* (1971). H. G. Gadamer, *Truth and Method,* (1975). M. Heidegger, *Being and Time* (1962). W. James, *The Principles of Psychology* (1890); *The Varieties of Religious Experience* (1958). T. W. Klink, "How Is Supervision Carried Out?" in *Clinical Education for the Pastoral Ministry* (1958). B. E. Meland, ed., *The Future of Empirical Theology* (1969).

B. H. CHILDS

EXPERIENTIAL PSYCHOTHERAPY; EXPERIENTIAL THEOLOGY; PHENOMENOLOGICAL METHOD IN PASTORAL CARE; PHILOSOPHY AND PSYCHOLOGY; WISDOM AND PRACTICAL KNOWLEDGE. *See also* EMPIRICAL THEOLOGY, EXISTENTIAL-

ISM, *or* PROCESS THEOLOGY, AND PASTORAL CARE. *Compare* RELIGIOUS EXPERIENCE.

EXPERIENCE, PRACTICAL. *See* WISDOM AND PRACTICAL KNOWLEDGE.

EXPERIENCE, RELIGIOUS. *See* RELIGIOUS EXPERIENCE.

EXPERIENTIAL PSYCHOTHERAPY. A type of psychotherapy which assumes that experience is the fundamental category for describing life and health and which uses the therapeutic relationship to facilitate the human capacity for experiencing. In contrast, psychopathology is understood as "non-experience." What people return to again and again is hunger for meaning in their ordinary experience. "They seek the assurance that they can move into the flow of life, experiencing fully both their person and the other" (Malone, 1981). Experiential theory, according to Gendlin, "holds that change depends upon whether the ongoing living and experiencing process moves fuller and further, in just those respects in which previously it has held back. Experience is basically process, it is living, and not just this or that content" (1974, p. 238).

The term "experiential psychotherapy," first appeared in the title of an article by Felder, Malone, Warkentin, and Whitaker (1962). According to Mahrer, "there is no single experiential psychotherapy. There is a family of experiential psychotherapies, more or less sharing a common humanistic-existential theory of human beings" (1983). Experiential psychotherapists are generally understood to be those who find techniques and theoretical systems that are most congruent with who they are and which allow for the fullest and most sensitive expression of their personality and character in relating to patients.

Experiential psychotherapy theory and practice is relevant for pastoral care and counseling because of the experiential nature of learning from supervised pastoral experience. Students are expected to learn from their experience, and to learn to enhance their experience as well. The "being with" the patient or parishioner emphasized by good CPE supervision is inescapably experiential. So also is one of the guiding images for pastoral care and counseling—the theological symbol of the incarnation.

Bibliography. R. E. Felder, T. P. Malone, J. Warkentin, and C. Whitaker, "First Stage Techniques in the Experiential Psychotherapy of Chronic Schizophrenic Patients," in *Current Psychiatric Therapies*, vol. 2 (1962). E. T. Gendlin, "Client-Centered and Experiential Psychotherapy" in D. A. Wexler and L. N. Rice, eds., *Innovations in Client-Centered Therapy* (1974). T. P. Malone, "Psychopathology as Non-experience," *Voices* (1981). T. P. Malone and P. T. Malone, *The Art of Intimacy* (1987). A. R. Mahrer, *Experiential Psychotherapy: Basic Principles* (1983).

J. PATTON

EXISTENTIAL PSYCHOLOGY AND PSYCHOTHERAPY; EXPERIENCE; PHENOMENOLOGICAL PSYCHOLOGY AND PSYCHOTHERAPY; PSYCHOTHERAPY. *See also* ACTION/BEING RELATIONSHIP; BEING/BECOMING RELATIONSHIP; PHILOSOPHY AND PSYCHOLOGY. *Compare* COGNITIVE PSYCHOLOGY AND PSYCHOTHERAPY; HUMANISTIC PSYCHOTHERAPIES (Methods and Research).

EXPERIENTIAL THEOLOGY. Theology that makes use of experience or depends upon it. The term is widely if somewhat loosely used by pastoral counselors or other practitioners in contrast to academic theology of the classroom or to a theology based upon Scripture or tradition. What must be asked of those who speak of "experiential theology" in this way is (1) what do you mean by experience? and (2) how do you relate theology to experience?

Some call theology experiential (or "empirical") in order to make it parallel to science with its empirical basis, using experience in the sense of what is observable or verifiable. But God and God's ways with the world are neither directly observable nor empirically verifiable. Others see experiential theology as that based upon a special kind of experience—a mystical vision or an awareness of the holy. Such a theology often discounts traditional understandings and may even exclude from doing theology those who have not had the appropriate kind of experience.

More appropriate for the pastoral counselor is the relating of theology to the spiritual or religious quality of some (or perhaps all) human experiences. One can discern the dimension of transcendence or the holy in certain experiences, often called "limit experiences," and one can appeal to that dimension for doing theology. How one appeals to experience in doing theology is a more subtle issue. A helpful way to understand what is involved is provided by Tillich's (1951) distinction of source, norm, and medium for theology.

Experiential theology may mean that the content of theology is found in experience. To speak about human nature, for example, or the Holy Spirit, is to rely upon what can be experienced of human beings or of the Spirit. This may mean that only what has been personally experienced is admitted to theology, but more often it is also the experience of the community, and tradition as historical experience or the Bible as record of experience. Only what has been experienced can be the source for theology.

Some would not deny that there may be other sources for theology, beyond or parallel to experience, such as revelation given in Scripture or the dogmatic formulations of the church or rational insight. The question for them, however, is what is to be the norm for selecting from these various sources. Some, including some pastoral counselors, would say that experience is the norm. What the Bible says about the human being is to be used for theology as it corresponds to the findings of experience, or what the church says about the Spirit is how we experience the Spirit. The truth or usefulness of sources other than experience is determined by their agreement with experience.

Some would not make experience the norm or even an appropriate source for theology. Yet they speak of theology as experiential, meaning that experience is the way in which we receive and interpret the revelation of God, which alone is the source of theology. The reality of what it is to be human or the reality of the Spirit is to be found only in revelation which transcends experience. Only through our experience, however, do we receive or understand that reality. Theology is experiential in having experience as the medium for doing theology. Experiential theology then may mean theology done on the basis of experience, or in conformity to experience, or simply in the context of experience.

Bibliography. P. Tillich, *Systematic Theology,* vol. 1, 1951).

C. B. KLINE

EXPERIENCE; PASTORAL THEOLOGICAL METHODOLOGY; THEOLOGY AND PSYCHOLOGICAL STUDIES. *Compare* CONTEXTUAL THEOLOGY; EMPIRICAL THEOLOGY; EXISTENTIALISM; PROCESS THEOLOGY; SPIRITUAL THEOLOGY.

EXPERIMENTAL PSYCHOLOGY. A method of investigation in which certain factors are directly manipulated ("experimented with") in order to see their effects on behavior, while other factors are controlled, or held constant.

The areas within psychology that rely on the experimental method of investigation to advance in understanding typically include learning, motivation, emotion, human performance, sensation, perception, language, comparative and physiological psychology.

M. RULON

PSYCHOLOGY. *See also* BEHAVIORISM (Theories and Research); COGNITIVE PSYCHOLOGY AND PSYCHOTHERAPY. *Compare* CLINICAL PSYCHOLOGY; DEVELOPMENTAL PSYCHOLOGY.

EXPLOITATION/OPPRESSION. Oppression/exploitation are twin evils which plague humankind and the environment. The former is derived from the Latin *oppressus,* "to be pressed against," and has come to mean generally the unjust exercise of authority or power; the latter comes from the Old French *esploit,* achievement, utilization, profitable management; hence, to use for one's own advantage or selfishly. Obviously both of these vices can be utilized together against the individual, society, and the environment.

1. Biblical and Theological Perspectives. Biblical injunctions against oppression and exploitation abound in the Judeo-Christian tradition. As any good concordance will show, more than a dozen different words are used for oppress, oppressed, oppressor, and oppression in the Bible. Among these are "to bruise," "to put down," "to distress," "to crush." Socially the problem must come under the judgment of justice. Oppressive rulers, corrupt judges, and unscrupulous business persons are called upon to repent and to practice justice (Ps. 10:17–18; Jer. 7:5; Amos 5:10–24; Js. 2:6).

In the light of God's justice, oppression is a gross evil. As Cone contends, God appears to take the side of the oppressed, especially those who are bruised and powerless. And the character of an individual or an institution can be measured by the way they treat the defenseless.

At the interpersonal level, agape-love is the primary norm of action against oppression and exploitation. It is the basic motivation of conduct and means to will the well-being of the other as well as oneself (Lk. 10:25–37; Rom. 13:8–10; I Cor. 13). Agape-love and justice are inseparable. Justice is love's instrument to provide direction and to give it concreteness. Justice desentimentalizes love and love makes justice just. Love

and justice are the criteria of pastoral care and counseling. It is the counselor's calling, like that of the ancient Hebrew prophets to "establish justice" in the community (Amos 5:15), and like that of Jesus "to set at liberty those who are oppressed" (Lk. 4:18).

Philosophical theologian Martin Buber (1937) reminds us that we exist in two fundamental relationships: I-Thou and I-It. The I-Thou is basically the realm of persons and the I-It the realm of things. The I-Thou, the primary word of relation and togetherness, is characterized by mutuality, care, and concern. I-It is the primary term for experiencing and using, and is lacking in mutuality. But the Thou can become an It and be treated as such.

Examples of how the I-It can become a destructive relationship between one person and another are numerous. An employer may treat his employees as machines; wives may treat their husbands as things, and vice versa; and a doctor may treat a patient as merely a "case," an object to be manipulated and exploited. To thus "thingify" a person is to dehumanize and denigrate him or her. It is to fall victim to the "Medusa complex" in which persons are reduced to objects or things.

A conviction that every person is of inherent worth is essential to effective pastoral care. Clients soon become aware of whether or not the therapist really cares or is subtly using them. Immanuel Kant, for example, insists that everything in creation can be used by humans as a means to an end — except an individual. We are, therefore, to "treat humanity, whether in thine own person or in that of any other, in every case as an end withal, never as a means only." Why? Because the individual is a rational creature, an end in him- or herself, subject to moral law and sacred by virtue of undivided freedom. One's freedom, not virtue, is the source of one's dignity. To be deprived of one's freedom is to experience exploitation in depth.

2. Exploitation in Counseling. At the personal level, oppression and exploitation have significance for the pastoral counselor. Failure of the pastoral counselor to make referrals when persons need to see a psychologist or psychiatrist is oppression. Pastors have been sued for malpractice for not referring deeply psychotic and suicidal patients to health professionals. It should be kept in mind that pastoral counselors may deal effectively with neurotic disorders, but they have little expertise in dealing with psychotics and schizophrenics. Clinical pastoral education should be helpful in developing skills in knowing when and how to refer persons for more specialized therapy.

Using a counselee for one's own therapy needs is both oppression and exploitation. Every counselor needs a counselor, but the client is not that person. Using clients for one's own therapeutic needs is treating them as objects or things. This sort of behavior should be avoided because a sense of being dehumanized may be a major factor in a client's illness.

Closely related to this issue is that of failure to set a goal for termination of the counseling. It is possible that the counselor seeks to prolong the therapy sessions over a long period of time for monetary gain or to meet personal emotional needs. On the other hand, the client may seek to prolong the sessions due to loneliness and the need for at least one person who will listen. To avoid creating perpetual patients an end-time can be set.

Confidentiality is a basic right of every client or patient. It is absolutely essential to the maintenance of trust and to the client's peace of mind, health, and happiness. "Protective privilege," of course, is no absolute. However, there are certain limitations to confidentiality for the protection of the individual and society. As the Tarasoff (1974) decision puts it: "Protective privilege ends where public peril begins." But it may be that the pastoral counselor would prefer, in some cases, to practice civil disobedience by remaining silent.

Sexual exploitation of the client is all too frequent. No one is immune to this temptation. Strong sexual feelings may arise during the counseling session. Freud was adamant in his stand against the therapist becoming sexually involved with patients. This he saw as a violation of the analytical process and exploitation of the individual.

Therapy that is effective is always emotionally demanding for both therapist and client. Hence, the therapist has the opportunity to exploit the patient by adopting a paternalistic posture toward the client. This can be an unhealthy attitude because it may denigrate one's autonomy. Ethically, it may destroy one's liberty without one's consent.

Failure to keep commitments with a client, whose time and schedule is just as important as that of the therapist, is exploitation. A sensitive and empathetic pastoral counselor will be troubled if commitments are not kept. An old saying puts it this way: "It's the promises we keep that let us sleep; it's the promises we break that keep us awake."

Finally, the pastoral counselor may exploit the counselee by prematurely pronouncing guilt forgiven. Simply to quote the Bible, that if we confess our sins, God will forgive us, is not enough. The patient may agree that God forgives sin, but still feels guilty because the dynamics of the guilt feelings have not been dealt with.

3. **Oppression/Exploitation in Society.** At the larger social level oppression and exploitation can be seen worldwide. Oppressive dictatorships exist in many countries. Racial discrimination exists in almost all societies. Sexism is global. In the U.S. women are still paid approximately one-third less than men for the same work. Ageism, prejudice toward the elderly, is a growing phenomenon in America. Elderly people, due to a loss of health and power, are often exploited by both individuals and institutions.

Economic exploitation is widespread, especially in Third World nations; but the U.S. also is plagued with the problem. Migrant workers are locked into economic bondage along with illegal aliens who fear to make any demands for more decent wages.

Long periods of unemployment can be hazardous to both physical and mental health. A definite correlation exists between unemployment and the rise of such health problems as alcoholism, hypertension, depression, apathy, family tensions, child abuse, stomach ailments, and other stress related diseases.

Pastors and pastoral counselors can help clients become more aware of the facets of oppression and exploitation: oppressive family dynamics which hinder self-actualization, work relationships in which the client may be the victim of exploitation, and the dehumanizing impact of societal oppression, racial, political, and religious.

Bibliography. M. Buber, *I and Thou* (1970 [1937]). J. Cone, *God of The Oppressed* (1975). P. E. Hopkins, "On Being a Compassionate Oppressor," *Pastoral Psychology,* 34 (1986), 204 – 13. I. Kant, *Fundamental Principles of the Metaphysics of Morals* (1949), pp. 47–57. *Tarasoff vs. Regents, Univ. California,* 118 Calif. Rep. 129, 519, P 2d 553, 1974.

H. H. BARNETTE

ADVOCACY; SOCIAL CONSCIOUSNESS AND RESPONSIBILITY; SOCIAL JUSTICE ISSUES IN PASTORAL CARE; VICTIMIZATION. *See also* CONSCIOUSNESS RAISING; HOLOCAUST; PREJUDICE; PROPHETIC/PASTORAL TENSION IN MINISTRY; RACISM; SEXISM. *Compare* LIBERATION THEOLOGY AND PASTORAL CARE; POWER.

EX-PRIESTS. *See* LAICIZATION.

EXTENDED FAMILY. *See* FAMILY, HISTORY AND SOCIOLOGY OF; FAMILY THEORY AND THERAPY.

EXTRAMARITAL SEX. *See* INFIDELITY.

EXTRASENSORY PERCEPTION (ESP). *See* PARAPSYCHOLOGY.

EXTRAVERSION. *See* ANALYTICAL (JUNGIAN) PSYCHOLOGY (Personality Theory and Research); PERSONALITY TYPES AND PASTORAL CARE.

EXTREME UNCTION. *See* ANOINTING OF THE SICK, SACRAMENT OF.

EXTREMISM. *See* AUTHORITARIANISM; SOCIAL PERCEPTION, JUDGMENT, AND BELIEF. *Compare* ANTISOCIAL PERSONS; COMMITMENT; FAITH/BELIEF; NEW RELIGIOUS MOVEMENTS.

F

FABER, HEIJE (1907–   ). Dutch writer, scholar, psychologist of religion, and theological educator. He earned a doctorate in the philosophy of religion at Leiden and became a pastor in the Dutch Reformed Church. Because he preached opposition and took part in resistance activities, he was forced to go into hiding when the Nazis invaded the Netherlands. While "under cover," he studied psychology, later earning a second doctorate with a dissertation entitled "On Being Sick." Beginning in 1958, Faber held academic posts, first in Leiden, later in the theological faculty at Tilburg. He became well known outside the Netherlands and taught in many countries. He served as a guest professor at Perkins School of Theology and at Princeton Theological Seminary, and received an honorary doctorate from Meadville Theological School. In 1978 he retired to Maarn, where he continued to write and publish.

Shortly after receiving his appointment in Leiden, Faber spent three months studying with Seward Hiltner in Chicago, becoming deeply interested in clinical pastoral education. That the Netherlands has one of the strongest clinical pastoral education programs in the world is largely owing to his influence.

Faber's interests range widely; his writings comprise more than one hundred books and articles. He has a particular interest in psychoanalytic approaches to religious experience. His book-length works include studies of life in the parsonage, aging, illness, the nature of ministry, the relationship of church and society, and, most recently, spirituality. Those available in English include *The Art of Pastoral Conversation* (1965, with Ebel van der Schoot), *Striking Sails* (1984), and *Above the Treeline* (1989).

Faber was deeply influenced by the client-centered counseling of Carl R. Rogers. His colleague Wybe Zijlstra defined Faber's approach to ministry: "The pastor walks with another person along the road in order to discover *together* what the liberating truth for the other may be." Faber's personal style, a combination of old-fashioned elegance of manners with a deep warmth, friendliness, and concern, makes Zijlstra's comment a description not only of Faber's approach to ministry but of his approach to human relationships.

K. R. MITCHELL

INTERNATIONAL PASTORAL CARE MOVEMENT; WESTERN EUROPEAN PASTORAL CARE MOVEMENT.

FACULTY PSYCHOLOGY. A philosophical theory that accounts for various mental activities by distinguishing powers or faculties of the mind that control specific mental functions. A system of faculty psychology was developed by eighteenth-century Scottish philosophers Thomas Reid (1710–96) and Dugald Stewart (1753–1818). Faculties including memory, abstraction, external perception, conception, judgment, and imagination "explained" mental phenomena such as remembering, loyalty, musing, etc.

Bibliography. T. Reid, *Essays on the Intellectual Powers of Man*, A. Woozley, ed. (1941).

M. BOHNER

PSYCHOLOGY. *Compare* DYNAMIC PSYCHOLOGY; MIND.

FAILURE, SENSE or EXPERIENCE OF. *See* GUILT; SHAME. *See also* LOCUS OF CONTROL RESEARCH; SADNESS AND DEPRESSION; SELF-ESTEEM.

FAIRBANKS, ROLLIN J. (1908–83). Pastor, civilian chaplain of a wartime naval air base, hospital chaplain, and professor of pastoral theology at Episcopal Theological School in Cambridge, Massachusetts.

After holding pastorates in Michigan, where he also worked as a labor mediator, Fairbanks became the Protestant chaplain at Massachusetts General Hospital. Working closely with Paul Johnson, in 1944 he founded the Institute of Pastoral Care, an educational foundation in Boston for clinical pastoral training. He served until 1950 as its first executive director. He also served as the founding editor of the *Journal of Pastoral Care* (1947) and as the director of the Pastoral Counseling Center in Boston.

Influential primarily because of his administrative achievements, Fairbanks also consistently represented the position that clinical supervisors and pastoral counselors should attend explicitly to the ethical dimension of their tasks.

E. B. HOLIFIELD

PASTORAL CARE MOVEMENT.

FAITH/BELIEF. Like a multifaceted jewel, *faith* exhibits a complex combination of interrelated dimensions. Though it defies easy or simplistic definition, the principal dimensions of faith can be characterized as: (1) the foundational dynamic of trust and loyalty underlying selfhood and relationships. In this sense faith is a human universal, a generic quality of human beings; (2) a wholistic way of knowing and valuing, in which persons shape their relations with self, others and world in light of an apprehension of and by transcendence. Faith, in this sense is "meaning-making." Here, also, faith is a generic and universal feature among humans; (3) the unifying and life-directing response of persons, mired helplessly in alienation or self-groundedness, to the gift of divine grace. This radical understanding of "justification by grace through faith" is central in subgroups of several major religious traditions; and (4) obedient assent to revealed truth. Here, too, major subgroups in several traditions, in different ways, stress this dimension of faith. It is a peculiarity of the English language that there is no verb form of the word faith. In the course of this discussion we shall have to remember that faith is an active way of being, committing, seeing, and interacting. It has some of the connotations of a verb, not just those of a noun.

In many ways faith is central in the context, the dynamics, and the substance of pastoral care. The healing or regrounding of trust, the recovery or transformation of sustaining meaning, the mediation of grace and forgiveness and the consequent reintegration of life, and the discernment of fundamental norms for belief and action — each of these dimensions of faith stands close to the heart of pastoral care.

1. **Religion, Belief, and Faith.** *a. Faith and religion.* Faith is often used synonymously with religion, as when someone asks, "Of what faith are you?" Historian of religion W. C. Smith suggests that what we often call a "religion" we should refer to instead as a "cumulative tradition." A cumulative tradition comprises the expressions of the faith of people in the past. It can include scriptures, symbols, moral teachings, rites, music, dances, prayers, art, and architecture. It can include myths, narratives, catechetical materials, theologies, creeds, doctrines, sacraments, and a host of other elements. A given cumulative tradition is constituted by all the media that have evolved to conserve, celebrate, and communicate a people's experiences with the sacred, and to form people in appropriate relationship to it and to each other. Like a dynamic gallery of art, a living cumulative tradition addresses contemporary people and becomes what Smith calls "the mundane cause" that awakens present faith. Religious faith, on the other hand, is the person's or group's way of *responding* to the sacred as mediated through the forms of the cumulative tradition. In this sense, faith is the personal appropriation of relatedness to the transcendent. It is the quality of relationship of persons to the sacred as awakened and formed in the interplay of the cumulative tradition and their experiences of the holy (Smith, 1962, chs. 6–7).

b. Faith and belief. Believing or beliefs can be important constituent parts of faith as well as central aspects of cumulative traditions. It is a mistake, however, to equate faith with belief or believing. The Hebrew term most frequently identified as faith, *emunah,* connotes "firmness" and "trust, dependence and loyalty to God," even in face of apparent contradictions. The Greek *pistuo,* and the Latin *credo,* are often translated as "I believe." These terms, according to Smith, are more accurately rendered as "I rest my heart," "I pledge my total allegiance," or "I commit myself, body and soul." In Hindu the term denoting faith, *sraddha,* means literally a "resting of the heart" and connotes the attitude of engagement or involvement with the deeper meaning of things. In Islam, *iman* (faith) means a commitment of the self; the *mu'min,* the man of faith, is the one who accepts religious truth and says to it with his life and devotion a whole-souled "yes" (Smith 1977, pp. 71 ff.; 1979, pp. 69 ff.).

Although the force of such terms was at one time captured in the English "I believe," these rich meanings can no longer adequately be rendered with the modern usage of that phrase. Until the early modern period (sixteenth century on) "believe" carried much the same range of meaning as that associated with "to set the heart upon." Smith says, "Literally and originally, 'to believe' means 'to hold dear': virtually, to love." Modern German usage of the verbform *beliebt* still means "cherished," or "held dear." But in modernity the connotation of "I believe" has changed significantly.

Smith sees three broad movements in this transition in the cultural meaning of *believe* and *belief.* First, the *object* referred to with the word almost always was understood as personal when *believe* was first used to translate *credo* and *pistuo,* but in the nineteenth and twentieth centuries it far more frequently has a proposition as its object: "I believe *that.* . . ." Second, in the early usage, the subject of the verb "to believe" was almost always in the first person singular or plural: "I believe, we believe." In the present era statistically it is far more likely to be found with third person subjects: "He or she believes, they believe." Third, there has been a shift in reporting from what is believed as true, to what is believed as of neutral or noncommittal import, to what is believed as likely to be erroneous or false (Smith, 1979, pp. 117–20).

c. Summary comparison. In sum, faith needs to be distinguished from religion and from belief or believing. Particular religions, understood as cumulative traditions, are the collective expressions of the faith of people of the past. The components of a cumulative tradition conserve and communicate the experiences of the sacred and their meanings which have been given to a people. Religious faith is the personal orientation of lives toward the sacred that is awakened and formed by socialization into a religious cumulative tradition. Belief or believing may be an essential aspect of a cumulative tradition, but it cannot be equated with faith. Belief tries to bring faith to expression. But faith is more than intellectual assent to propositions of dubious verifiability. Statements of belief can be based on self-deception, on partial self-awareness, or on outright hypocrisy. Faith, on the other hand, constitutes practical commitment that involves both conscious and unconscious aspects. It is a moral and existential orientation of the total self to that which has the value of the sacred for a person or group.

Having distinguished faith from religion and belief, while trying to maintain their relatedness, we turn now to the effort to characterize in more depth the four central dimensions and dynamics of faith identified in our opening definition.

2. Faith as a Foundation of Selfhood and Relational Life.

Prior to its religious formation and self-consciousness, faith constitutes a generic foundation of human selfhood and community. Erik H. Erikson (1963) establishes as the first challenge of the newborn and her or his nurturing environment the development of "basic trust." Such pervasive trust — and trustworthiness — is foundational for all other human strengths and virtues. It underlies a person's capacity to "be there" for others, for causes of import, and for one's own becoming. Erikson sees that the struggle for basic trust, in the midst of ongoing tendencies toward basic mistrust, extends to one's sense of the character of the larger world and, indeed, to the character of the "ultimate environment."

Josiah Royce (1912) helps us see that perhaps the most distinctive feature of human beings lies in the fact that we are creatures who live by promises and by shared loyalty to "causes" that transcend us. Royce invites us to see that we literally live by faith, and that faith has a *triadic* or *covenantal* structure. When we use language in oral or written communication, for example, there is a bond between writer-speaker and hearer created not just by the sharing of information, but also by the implicit promise to use language truthfully and faithfully. The triadic pattern of faith is represented here by the "cause" of truth-telling, or fidelity to truth. When children in the dyadic relation with their parents struggle with learning to obey their parents' directives, they are not only learning how to relate to their folks, but are also constructing an understanding of the "causes"—the values, the beliefs, and worldview—to which their parents are loyal, and which inform the shaping of specific rules and standards.

In science, business, medicine, or economy, as well as in political and international life, we live by many such tacit "covenants" as well as by a number of explicit ones. The triadic structure of faith in our lives is made visible as much by our disloyalties, our breaches of promise, as it is by our experience of relying upon the fidelity, the "good faith," of personal and collective others.

Faith, therefore, is a generic dimension of human being and social life. It is a dynamic pattern of trust and loyalty that links one in mutuality with others, and to "causes" of mutual loyalty. It is a deep-going confidence that one can depend upon the fidelity of others, upon the self, and upon a coherence and reliable source of worth and meaning close to the heart of things.

The absence of faith, in this sense, is phenomenologically an experience of emptiness, abandonment, or non-belonging. It is the sense of being un-grounded, separated, and not established in worth. It leads on to feelings of shame, doubt (in the self, others, and the ultimate environment) and to a sense of invalidity. When pressed far enough these feelings can issue in nonspecific rage and destructive pathology.

3. Faith as a Wholistic Way of Knowing and Valuing.

Ernest Becker calls us *homo poeta*, the human being who lives by *meaning*. Faith is the generative power by which we compose wholistic images of the ultimate conditions of existence and their meaning. Images, in this sense, are internal representations of states of affairs which incorporate both what we "know" and how we feel about what we "know." Such imaging provides the contexts within which we construe our relatedness to others, to the world, to ourselves, and to God. A principal German term for imagination is *Einbildungskraft,* literally, the "power (*Kraft*) of forming (*Bildung*) into one (*Ein*)." Faith involves the power of imaging a coherent and meaningful "universe" which gives purpose, joy, and hope to our lives in the midst of everyday relations, experiences, sufferings, losses, and gains.

In this imaging, faith is neither irrational nor nonrational. Rather, it is grounded in a comprehensive rationality that combines intuition, judgment, and combinatorial originality, as well as analytic and critical reasoning. Symbol, narrative, gesture and form arise from the imaging of persons in response to experiences that have revelatory quality and power. They (the symbols, narrative, gesture, and form), in turn, evoke and activate the imaging of others in what may be called "convictional knowing."

It is the character of faith as a knowing that it draws its imaging in response to the apprehension of and by *value* — by that which instantiates supreme worth. We form the imaginal orderings of our most inclusive realm of experience in relation to that center or those centers of value which ground and confer value and worth upon us and upon our strivings. "Worth" and "worship" are etymologically related. We worship that which has supreme worth for us, and in relation to which our lives and strivings are confirmed in transcendent worth. This is Paul Tillich's characterization of faith as the "state of being ultimately concerned" (Tillich, 1957).

Faith as the valuing-knowing relation of trust in and loyalty to transcendent truth and love could be illustrated from many religious traditions. An apt instance comes from Hindu traditions where Sankara characterized *sraddha* by joining *astikya-buddhi* ("an awakeness to transcendence") with *bhakti*. "It would be attractive," says Wilfred Cantwell Smith, "to translate this [combination] somewhat as follows: Faith is awakeness to transcendence accompanied by an adoring devotion to it and a permeating participation in it" (Smith, 1979, pp. 64–65).

The opposite of *sraddha,* "unfaith," is best rendered, says Smith, with "one's heart is not in it." In biblical traditions, including Islam, unfaith is either *disobedience* — a "not-knowing" that is at least partially willful, or *idolatry* — the attribution of "God-value" to a finite center or centers of value.

4. Faith as Response to the Gift of Divine Grace.

In these first two dimensions faith is seen in terms of continuity between human experiences of fidelity and care, and trust in the ultimate conditions of existence. Stress is laid upon the created gifts of humankind to respond to "signals of transcendence" and personally and corporately to compose and respond to symbolic, mythic, and ideological representations of an ultimate coherence and meaning in life and the world process, despite tragedy, suffering, and the presence of contradictions in self and social relations. Now we must bring into focus that dimension of faith which stresses the sense of radical *discontinuity* between the "natural," and even the "religious," and faith. This will mean giving explicit attention to the role of the equally radical gift of transforming, releasing, reconciling, and restoring grace.

The need for radical re-grounding of one's life from alienation, defensiveness, and meaninglessness is heightened in Christian teaching about the justification of one's life by God's grace, received through the openness and courage of faith. In its doctrines of "the fall" and "original sin" Christian faith, especially in its Augustinian and Protestant formulations, understands humankind to be helplessly mired, like persons caught in quicksand, in efforts to find a grounding for our lives. The remnants of the *imago dei* in us — the evidences of our having been created in the image of God — are hopelessly diffused and distorted. Prior to the offering and receipt of God's radical gift of justifying, restoring grace in faith, humans live in the tragic condition of being divided selves, unsound, potentially and actually destructive, and turned in upon the self. In the Christ, God's love and grace become enfleshed, and the great "Yes" of God creates the possibility for the liberation, restoration, healing, and re-grounding of our lives in relation to God and the neighbor.

From this vantage point of radical transformation some Christian theologians have seen that there is a continuum of God's grace that helps to account for the first two dimensions of faith we described. God's "prevenient grace" is effectively working even when persons seem to be in a "state of nature" or under the curse of the Fall, enabling us to use reason in the conduct of human affairs, to respond to the imperatives of justice, and to hunger for salvation.

Without the radical gift of God's transforming love in grace, we are lost, helpless, rebellious, and defensively self-grounded, and we constitute the most lethal element in the universe. Faith is the response to grace in and by which we are transformed and restored.

5. Faith as Assent and Commitment to Truth. In Judaism and Islam, in somewhat different ways, and in those branches of Christianity where doctrinal formulations are understood to conserve and express directly the contents of divine revelation, faith is understood to be obedient assent to the explicitly revealed content of God's will.

Smith, writing about Islam, says: "Without any question, the fundamental concept in the Qur'an, overwhelmingly vivid, is that of God presented as Creator, Sovereign, and Judge; powerful, demanding, succoring, majestic; laying upon mankind inescapable imperatives and offering us inexhaustible rewards. The fundamental category on the manward side is that of faith: the positive recognition and acceptance of the divine summons, the

committing of oneself to the demands, and thus being led to the ultimate succor" (Smith, 1979, p. 39).

In Judaism, *Torah* or Way is the gift of God by which the people of Israel are called and formed for covenant partnership with God. Assent to the promises of God, and to the covenant, becomes the determining part of the lives of Jews through their daily observance of the commandments, the *Mitzvoth,* graciously required by the Law. Observance was never intended for legalistic self-justification. Rather it leads to a deep internalization of covenant faithfulness and relatedness. It is meant to form persons for — and keep them responsively in — covenant faith.

Both Islam and Judaism give rise to forms of assent and commitment to truth that can be described as "orthopraxy"—right observance, faithful adherence, and obedience to the revealed commands and laws of God.

For Christian groups best characterized in relation to this dimension of faith the issue has been, rather, "Orthodoxy"—right belief. Christians can and do understand the role of doctrine in different ways. George Lindbeck (1984) has distinguished two Christian understandings of doctrine which, in relation to the dimension of faith we consider here, offer contrasting patterns of faith as assent to revealed truth. The first of these approaches to doctrine he speaks of is the "propositional" understanding. Here doctrine is taken to be the Scripture-inspired, Spirit-shaped formulations — in the only appropriate language — of God's revealed truth and will. Doctrines — and the creedal statements that "contain" them—therefore, must be "believed" if one is to be rightly related to God in faith and practice. Lindbeck's other approach to doctrine that concerns us here is the one he calls "cultural linguistic." The point of this second understanding is related to what we said about Torah observance above: it is through participation in Christian community, hearing the Scriptures read and preached, receiving the sacraments, attending to personal and corporate prayer, and striving to be faithful in the love of God and neighbor, that the deep structure of orthodox faith is formed within us. Doctrine serves a function analogous to the rules of grammar in language: it helps to test the validity and truth of Christian language and living.

6. Conclusion. This brief account of four dimensions of faith suggests that, indeed, faith is a universal aspect of human corporate and personal living. Since the Enlightenment and the secularizing tendencies it accelerated many persons in the West and elsewhere have found themselves going about the business of forming faith, explicitly or implicitly, from ideological and personal options not mediated by historic "cumulative traditions." Marxism, psychoanalysis, humanistic psychology, scientism, materialism, and so-called "secular humanism" are but a few such orientations. Underneath the search for meaning and personal significance for one's life, there is also the hunger for community, and for grounding in that which is ultimately worthy, real or true.

Bibliography. E. Becker, *The Birth and Death of Meaning,* 2d ed., (1971). G. Ebeling, *The Nature of Faith* (1961). E. H. Erikson, *Childhood and Society,* 2d ed., (1963). J. W. Fowler, *Stages of Faith* (1981). A. J. Heschel, *God in Search of Man: A*

Philosophy of Judaism (1985). G. Lindbeck, *The Nature of Doctrine* (1984). H. R. Niebuhr, *Radical Monotheism and Western Culture* (1960). J. Royce, *The Sources of Religious Insight* (1912). W. C. Smith, *The Meaning and End of Religion* (1962); *Belief and History* (1977); *Faith and Belief* (1979). P. Tillich, *Dynamics of Faith* (1957).

J. W. FOWLER

FAITH AND WORKS; FAITH DEVELOPMENT RESEARCH; RELIGION; SPIRITUALITY. *See also* COMMITMENT; COURAGE; GRACE; RELIGIOUS DEVELOPMENT; REVELATION AND PASTORAL CARE; SANCTIFICATION; THEOLOGY AND PSYCHOLOGY. *Compare* DOUBT AND UNBELIEF; HOPE AND DESPAIR; LOVE; SOCIAL PERCEPTION, JUDGMENT AND BELIEF.

FAITH, PASTOR'S. *See* FAITH AND INTEGRITY, PASTOR'S.

FAITH AND INTEGRITY, PASTOR'S. Although one can show nuances in the meaning of the terms, pastoral faith and pastoral integrity are inseparable. The life of faith is the process whereby integrity of being, simplicity of character, and wholeness of the expression of life is developed. Faith is the assurance of things hoped for and the conviction of things not seen (Heb. 11:1). Integrity is the inner sense of freedom from crippling ambivalence about that assurance and those convictions. Integrity is that wholeness and completeness which the process of the life of faith is always striving to bring into being. Pastoral faithfulness is the persistent movement of the pastor toward the completeness and simplicity of life for which we use the word integrity as a name.

Faith is defined in NT Greek as that which causes trust, reliability, the keeping of a solemn promise or oath, i.e., the keeping of one's commitments, and acting in good faith (Mt. 23:23). Further, faith means trust or confidence, especially trust or confidence in God. In relation to Christ it means belief or trust in the Lord's help in physical and spiritual distress. More profoundly, faith in Jesus Christ means investing oneself with an undivided mind and heart in Jesus Christ and his way of life. This is why early Christians spoke of themselves as being *in* the way of Jesus Christ. In the teachings of the Apostle Paul faith is spoken of as a gift of God (I Cor. 12:9), and as a body of treasured convictions or teachings (Rom. 1:5; Gal. 1:23). In the book of Hebrews faith is portrayed throughout as the courage to be a follower of Jesus Christ with no empirical knowledge of the exact outcome of this investment of life. This is congruent with faith as portrayed in Jas. 2:14a as indivisible from action or *erga*, work. *Erga* is the inside of the hand of which faith is the back side.

From this brief overview of NT meanings, pastoral faith refers to the pastor's dependability to convey accurately the relationship he or she has with God. The distinctiveness of the pastor as a caring person is that he or she verbally and nonverbally is aware of his or her relationship to God, faithful to it, and unashamed of it.

Also, pastoral faith means that the pastor is cautious in making promises, carefully inspecting the balance of responsibility with others and the Otherness of God. Once having made promises, he or she measures his or her effectiveness in terms of faithfully keeping those promises he or she has made.

In the third place, pastoral faithfulness implies that the pastor has wholeheartedly sought out the way of life, the schema of existence set forth in the way of Jesus Christ, and conveys that spirit without pretense, ostentation, or hesitation. This especially applies to his or her "close-in" relationships to colleagues, parishioners, and counselees. This is not necessarily a "sweet" relationship at all times. It calls for standing and, having stood all, to stand (Eph. 6:12–13) in the battle with principalities and powers in social action as well as being considerate and kind to people.

In the fourth place, pastoral faithfulness is another way of describing pastoral courage to take the leaps of faith into the unknown in responses to the demands of maturity. In the book of Hebrews, we are encouraged to go on from the first principles of God's Word to maturity in partaking of the solid food appropriate for the mature. Paul Tillich (1952; 1957) called this "the courage to be." Faith is seen as a dynamic, flowing, growing process, not as a static entity falling in upon itself. All that is workable in developmental psychology is relevant to this dynamic approach to pastoral faith. In a sense, the pastor has a primary responsibility to continue to grow as long as he or she lives and not to "plateau out" or consider himself or herself as "over the hill" in the intention to use all his or her faculties "by practice to distinguish good from evil" (Heb. 5:14).

Integrity also has several shades of meaning in the biblical story. In the first place, it means simplicity as opposed to duplicity in one's intentions. In Gen. 20:5–6, Abraham gave Sarah to King Abimelech of Gerar for sexual purposes and told him she was his sister. But God spoke to Abimelech in a dream and, at the threat of death to him, advised him she was "a man's wife." Abimelech did not approach her sexually, even though Sarah herself said: "He is my brother." Abimelech contended with God saying: "Lord, wilt thou slay innocent people? . . . In the integrity of my heart and innocence I have done this." Then God said: "Yes, I know that you have done this in the integrity of your heart and it was I who kept you from sinning against me; therefore, I did not let you touch her" (Gen. 20:6).

In this sense of simplicity and unadulterated motive, integrity points to the internal forum of dialogue with God. This is a constant use of the word in Job, where the Lord says of Job to Satan: "He still holds fast his integrity although you moved me against him, to destroy him without cause" (Job 2:3). Even Job's wife knew this of him after Job was afflicted with sores. She said: "Do you still hold fast to your integrity? Curse God, and die" (Job 2:9). In response to Bildad the Shuhite's chauvinistic diatribe on the original nature of man's sinfulness: "How can he who is born of woman be clean?" (Job 25:4), and the inability of man to understand God's power (Job 26:14), Job said: "Far be it from me to say that you are right; till I die I will not put away my integrity" (Job 27:5). Pastoral integrity, then, is consistent candor in a pastor's personal prayers. He or she is not guileful, in the tradition of Nathanael, who even expressed his most negative feelings to Jesus (Jn. 1:47). Pastoral integrity is the antithesis of the person who supposes that a "double-minded man, unstable in all his ways, will receive anything from the Lord" (Jas. 1:7–8).

Søren Kierkegaard (1971) spoke of the unity of being or existing as a self before God. He called it purity of heart, to will one thing. The vision of God is the blessing that attends being who we are in our prayers before God and being no one else — neither the "good me," the "bad me," nor the "not me," to use Harry Stack Sullivan's (1953) terms — but simply me. As Aristotle said of the rational person, he is just what he or she is and nothing else.

Thus far the definition of pastoral integrity has focused upon its vertical dimension of the pastor's relation to God. Pastoral integrity has a horizontal, or interpersonal and social, dimension. Duplicity, double-mindedness, and unreliability contaminate human relationships as well as our relationship to God. A serene integrity before God provides fortitude for maintaining integrity with one's fellow human beings. The prophet Micah says that God's requirement of us is that we do justly, love mercy, and walk humbly with God. The humble walk is with God, and the pastor's integrity is sabotaged if he or she interprets humility before God as an obsequious, hand-wringing anxiety about the opinions others have of him or her. Maintaining pastoral integrity consists of doing justly and showing mercy toward one's neighbor. His or her "yes" is "yes" and "no" is "no." He or she can stand, and having stood all, stand in the convictions of his or her faith in God. Hardness of heart is not part of this, because the pastor with integrity is open, teachable, and empathic. Yet he or she has his or her *own* integrity to assert. This polarity points up the relationship between a pastor's faith and his or her integrity.

A final meaning of pastoral integrity may be found in Tit. 2:7: "Show yourself in all respects a model of good deed, and in your teaching show integrity . . ." The Greek word used here is *aphthorian*. This refers to the soundness, sensibleness, and purity of a pastor's teaching. The context implies an integrity between the way one lives and what one teaches. More broadly, one can interpret this to mean that he or she teaches only that which he or she genuinely believes and does not play "word games" with those whom he or she teaches. Paul summarizes it well: "We have renounced disgraceful, underhanded ways; we refuse to practice cunning or to tamper with God's word, but by open statement of the truth we would commend ourselves to every man's conscience in the sight of God" (II Cor. 4:1–2). *That* is pastoral integrity.

This passage reaches back to Rom. 1:5 and Gal. 1:23 where "the faith" is seen as a body of treasured convictions. Each pastor in his or her preaching, teaching, counseling, and personal struggle of the soul forges on the anvil of these functions the convictions that cause him or her to say, "Here I stand," as did Martin Luther. He or she may be ever so flexible but these convictions for him or her are the "unbendables" that give stature and stability as well as flexibility to the very backbone of his or her spiritual life. In this sense pastoral integrity is that which holds a pastor up, enables a pastor to hold out for what he or she believes, and gives him or her comfort to hold on to when things get rough.

Pastoral faith and integrity are not static realities. They are like a riverbed and its stream. The life of faith a pastor lives flows in process. As has already been indicated, the

faith, as viewed from Hebrews, is a movement unceasing toward maturity. The movement calls for courage, as Paul Tournier puts it in *A Place for You* (1968), to quit or leave one place or time of security and to seek out and to find another place and time of security. We always know that we "look for a city whose builder and maker is God" and that we have "no sure dwelling place." The person of faith with courage seeks for the city of God; in doing so he or she maintains integrity of being. The person without faith and courage shrinks back and loses integrity. The riverbed of integrity is eroded by the lack of a maturing faith. The erosion takes place because life moves on anyhow. If we do not move with the flow of life's maturing demands, then life itself becomes the force that sets us aside, pushes us aside, and has its own way. Time flies; places do not remain the same; neither do persons fail both to age and to succeed at keeping things. Relationships change, and people are never in a static condition. Aristotle said that life is motion; the faith and integrity of the pastor are his or her movement toward simplicity, wholeness, and integration of his or her personhood before God.

The faith of the pastor is also demonstrated in relationship to counselee, parishioner, and friends in his or her integrity. He or she is steadfast, "amidst good report and evil report," as one confessional covenant puts it. His or her integrity manifests itself in the life of faith as a "self-sameness" or continuity of being that "weathers" the climatic conditions of years of service.

Furthermore, the pastor's faith and integrity are expressions of each other in the professional life of a minister. The Christian minister is ordained by a body of Christian believers. He or she took that ordination as a profession of solemn covenant to proclaim the good news of Jesus Christ, bring good news to the poor, to set at liberty those in bondage, to bring sight to those that cannot see, and to be a liberator of the oppressed. His or her faith is embodied in this profession; and his or her integrity is that faith in action as he or she professionally carries out that profession with clean hands and a pure heart, with a spirit that has not lifted itself up to vanity nor sworn deceitfully.

Bibliography. U. T. Holmes, *Spirituality for Ministry* (1982). S. Kierkegaard, *Either/Or* (1971). T. C. Oden, *Becoming a Minister* (1987). H. S. Sullivan, *The Interpersonal Theory of Psychiatry* (1953). P. Tillich, *The Courage to Be* (1952); *The Dynamics of Faith* (1957). P. Tournier, *A Place for You* (1968).

W. E. OATES

PRAYER AND WORSHIP LIFE, PASTOR'S. *Compare* AUTHORITY *or* IDENTITY, PASTORAL; MENTAL HEALTH, PASTOR'S; PASTOR, PASTORAL CARE OF; PERSONHOOD OF THE PASTOR, SIGNIFICANCE OF.

FAITH AND MORALS. *See* MORAL BEHAVIOR AND RELIGION; MORAL THEOLOGY.

FAITH AND WORKS. In Christian theology, faith and works refer to two contrasting ways of relating to God — specifically, antithetical ways to be right with God and to receive God's approval. The one — faith — is centered in God and relies on God's graciousness; the other—works—is centered in the person and relies on human effort.

1. Theology. The antithesis of faith and works first came to clear expression in St. Paul and later through "Paul's most impassioned interpreter," Martin Luther. Though differing in certain respects, Paul and Luther are essentially united in their fundamental convictions on this matter. Both of them see faith and works as diametrically opposed ways of relating to God. Faith and works are not single responses but complete ways of life, each with its own special prescription of how sinful persons can be reunited with God: faith decries human effort and relies on God's unmerited and unmeritable love; works elevate human effort and represents an attempt to win God's love by obeying the divine law and doing God's will. According to Paul and Luther, each approach results in a completely different mode of existence. Living by faith leads to freedom from the compulsive demands of the law, forgiveness of sins, and the manifestation of such fruits of the Spirit as love, peace, joy, patience, and kindness (Gal. 5:22). Living by works, whether moral or ritual, engulfs the person in a feverish attempt to live up to the endless demands of the law in order to achieve perfection and to be worthy of God's love and respect. For Paul the former is salvation; the latter is self-righteousness and spiritual death.

The relation between faith and works, though antithetical in the sense noted, is complex and requires at least two further distinctions. First, faith can lose its essential character by being converted subtly into a form of merit-seeking "work." It then becomes an achievement, a claim upon God, a human reason for being accepted by God. Over against this understanding, Christian theology has maintained that authentic faith is an act of trust, free from manipulative motivations. It is fundamentally a gift and not a work, a grateful response to God's initiative and not an achievement that the person can claim or possess. Second, faith is not an endpoint in the Christian life but a beginning. It should lead to works. As a reception of God's forgiveness and a release from guilt, faith frees the person to do works of love and service, not as a way to earn merit before God but as an expression of joy and appreciation for what God has given. Works done in this spirit are the only God-pleasing ones, for all others are done out of selfish concern. Or as Paul puts the point: "Whatever does not proceed from faith is sin" (Rom. 14:23).

2. Pastoral Relevance. Contemporary pastoral care and counseling have not used faith and works as dominant categories. Pastoral theologians have recognized the importance of faith and works implicitly, but given the heavy influence of dynamic and developmental psychologies they have often used psychological categories to illuminate this fundamental dynamic in human life (e.g., basic trust and acceptance vs. mistrust, anxiety, and guilt). Nevertheless, the doctrine of faith and works is useful, and in some sense essential, to pastoral care and counseling. It describes styles of life that are fundamental to the human situation and thus basic to pastoral situations. Individual psychological development, for instance, as Erik Erikson has shown, may be viewed as a series of psychosocial struggles originating in questions of "basic trust" and culminating in questions of accep-

tance, which express issues closely related to traditional faith-works concerns (Erikson, 1959). Clinically, people who seek counseling are often locked into a feverish attempt to make themselves acceptable to themselves and even to God by their own efforts. They may even try to use the process of counseling itself for this purpose. In any case, they operate in counseling on the assumption that to be healed they must discover and do the right thing, that healing is a matter of performing the right action or series of actions. The concept of faith adds a basic and necessary correction. It indicates that being healed is finally not a matter of *doing* something but a matter of *receiving* something. It shows that wholeness cannot be willed, that the restoration of broken relationships cannot be achieved by efforts that are designed to placate or please. Healing may not come without effort—sometimes without prolonged and costly efforts—but in a deeper sense it is given and not earned or brought into existence by ourselves. In fact, it often comes at the point of defeat when we give up all attempts to effect it.

Bibliography. L. Aden, "Faith and the Developmental Cycle," *Pastoral Psychology*, 24 (1976), 3: 215–30. G. A. Buttrick, *Interpreter's Dictionary of the Bible* (1962), vol. 2, pp. 222–34. E. H. Erikson, *Identity and the Life Cycle* (1959). J. W. Fowler, *Stages of Faith* (1981). R. J. Hunter, "Law and Gospel in Pastoral Care," *J. of Pastoral Care*, 30 (1976), 146–58. P. Tillich, *Dynamics of Faith* (1957).

L. ADEN

FAITH/BELIEF. *See also* CONSCIENCE; FREEDOM AND BONDAGE; GRACE; GRATITUDE; LEGALISM AND ANTINOMIANISM. *Compare* FORGIVENESS; MORAL BEHAVIOR AND RELIGION; RESPONSIBILITY/IRRESPONSIBILITY, PSYCHOLOGY OF.

FAITH DEVELOPMENT RESEARCH. An organized research endeavor, associated principally with James W. Fowler and his colleagues, which inquires into the ways persons compose their guiding representations of the ultimate conditions of existence and shape their lives in correlation with those representations. In this research faith is conceptualized as the active, patterned process by which persons construe their relations to self, others, and world in light of their awareness of relatedness to the ultimate conditions of existence. Theological sources for this conception of faith include notably H. Richard Niebuhr, Paul Tillich, and Wilfred Cantwell Smith.

Faith development research began in 1972. Fowler's research and resulting theoretical constructions, expanded by the work of others, have begun to be appropriated in those fields of practical theology most closely related to human formation and transformation, principally religious education and spiritual formation. Their relevance to pastoral care and counseling and to pastoral theology seems equally promising, though these fields have not thus far made extensive use of them.

1. The Concept of Faith. In its broadly cognitive focus faith development theory draws its psychological resources in large measure from the constructive developmental traditions growing out of the work of Jean Piaget, though it also relies on the life cycle perspectives of Erik Erikson, Daniel Levinson, and others. To do justice to its subject matter, however, faith development theory insists that faith, as a "knowing," is more wholistic than the conceptions of knowing developed from the philosophies of Hume, Descartes, and Kant, which tend to separate cognition and the affections. Faith, as knowing, holds together the rational and the passional. "Faith is a knowing born of religious love." As this quotation from Bernard Lonergan suggests, faith involves *axiology*—valuing—as well as *epistemology*—knowing. In faith persons relate themselves to another and to others in *trust* and *loyalty*. Faith involves a "resting of the heart" (W. C. Smith, 1979).

Faith development research does not presume, however, that all faith is religious faith. It also seeks to interpret the patterns and contents of meaning-making in the lives of persons who have no significant connections with religious communities or traditions.

2. **Research Method.** Research is primarily based on a life history, a semi-clinical interview which is detailed in the *Manual for Faith Development Research,* (Fowler, Mosley, and Jarvis, 1985). Faith development theory in the Fowler version is based on a U.S. sample of interviews with more than five hundred persons from ages four to ninety. The sample includes an approximately equal number of males and females. Protestants and Catholics are well represented. Jews are present in the sample, as are Blacks, though both groups are under-represented. The sample includes a substantial number of nonreligious respondents.

3. **Principal Findings.** Faith development research has identified seven structural-developmental stages of faith which may be briefly summarized as follows:

a. Primal faith. The pre-linguistic, largely pre-conceptual forming of the infant's disposition toward an environment that is gradually coming to be recognized as distinct from the self. The child begins to form pre-images of faith that draw their feeling and content from the quality of the child's interaction with the primary caregivers in the environment, and from her or his organismic funding of hope. The seeds of basic trust and mistrust, of self-worth and its opposite, take root in the soil of this rudimentary stage.

b. Intuitive-projective faith. Typically forming between ages two and six, this stage builds upon the acquisition of language and the awakening of imagination. In the absence of cognitive operations which would allow for reversibility of thought and the testing of perceptions, children grasp experience in powerful images. Attentive to the gestures, rituals, and words adults use in their languages of faith, children's capacities for attention to mystery and the numinous can be focused and formed by their perceptions of adults' faith and convictions.

c. Mythic-literal faith. Taking form usually between ages seven and twelve, this stage marks children's abilities to question their images of faith, testing them in accordance with the teachings of valued adults and with their own more developed capacities for reversing their thought sequences and testing their perceptions. New capacities for perspective-taking allow them to overcome the previous stage's embeddedness in their own perceptions and imaginations. With a firm grasp of cause and effect relationships children in this stage form and conserve their meanings by way of narrative and story. Their interpretations of stories and beliefs, however, tend to be literal and one-dimensional. Though this stage has its rise typically in middle childhood, researchers find many adolescents and a fair number of adults best described by this stage.

d. Synthetic-conventional faith. Beginning around age twelve another revolution in meaning-making occurs for many youth. New cognitive abilities (Piaget's "early formal operations") make it possible for youth to begin to construct the images of self they believe significant others hold: "I see you seeing me; I see the me I think you see." Soon the reciprocal of this insight becomes apparent: "You see you according to me; you see the you you think I see." Mutual perspective-taking brings a qualitatively new degree of self-consciousness; it also evokes an awareness of the interiority—the "personality"—of the self and of others. In the emerging challenge of achieving a unity of the images of self reflected by others (identity) the young person also works at unifying a set of attitudes, beliefs, and values (faith) that will support an identity and link him or her to the interpersonal circle of valued persons upon whom identity and faith depend. Stories and symbols conveying meaning are seen by persons in this stage as multi-dimensional and affectively charged. But they are not critically reflected upon as symbols, nor are their meanings systematically related to each other. Many adults of all ages seem to have equilibrated their growth in identity and faith at this stage, and continue to be particularly dependent upon interpersonal relations and the external authority of groups or institutional roles for maintaining the shape of their identity and faith.

e. Individuative-reflective faith. Between seventeen and twenty some young persons begin a transition from the previous stage to one in which self-reflection is no longer so dependent upon others, but upon the emergence of a capacity for dialogue between the selves others see and a self "accessible only to me." This capacity depends upon the development of a "third-person perspective," upon self-other relations. Identity and faith now become matters of self-reflective awareness and choice. No longer so dependent upon the interpersonal support of others to maintain identity and faith, one locates authority within the self. Symbols, stories, and rituals are questioned by persons moving into this stage; their meanings come to be seen as separable and restateable in conceptual terms. Authenticity, autonomy, and clarity about the boundaries of the self tend to be valued by persons described by this stage.

f. Conjunctive faith. In some adults, usually after age thirty-five, the clear boundaries formed in the previous stage demand to be revised. New attention to polarities and ambiguities in the self and in life call for recognition (i.e., being both young and old; being both male and female; being both constructive and destructive persons; having both conscious and unconscious determinants of behavior). Truths adequate for the grounding of life come to be seen as multidimensional and as containing paradoxes. The tensions involved in maintaining several perspectives on truth simultaneously come to be seen as dimensions integral to truth. A post-critical rejoining of symbols and meanings in a "second naiveté" is related to the emergence of a more porous and receptive stance toward the reality of others. In this stage persons manifest a kind of "epistemological humility." They tend to avoid ideological over-confidence because of a heightened awareness of the degree to which the reality of Being exceeds the adequacy of all human efforts to grasp or represent it.

g. Universalizing faith. This rare stage involves the culmination of a process of de-centration from self and of re-centration beyond self which has been underway throughout the sequence of earlier stages. The knowing and valuing that are faith, in this stage, no longer center in the self or its extensions as the axis from which meaning is made and maintained. The self now finds its true depth through a grounding in Being. Those in whom this stage is manifest show evidence of loving other persons and classes of persons from a standpoint that participates in God's loving. This gives their ways of relating and leading a radical thrust. They create zones of liberation and transformation by virtue of a faith that gives rise to a transvaluation of valuing. They call all persons to relations of love and justice in a commonwealth of Being.

Studies completed or in progress have related faith development research to a wide range of topics including pastoral care and counseling (Fowler, 1987). Alternative approaches to the Fowler model to the study and interpretation of faith development include the work of A. M. Rizzuto (1979), J. Loder (1981), W. W. Meissner (1984), F. Oser (1980), and A. Vergote (1969).

Bibliography. C. Dykstra, S. Parks, and B. Wheeler, eds., *Faith and Development: Critical Reflections on James Fowler's Theory of Faith Development* (see especially articles by Browning and Lyons, and by Schneider) (1986). J. W. Fowler, *Stages of Faith* (1981); *Becoming Adult, Becoming Christian* (1984); *Faith Development and Pastoral Care* (1987). J. W. Fowler, S. Keen, and J. Berryman, *Life-Maps* (1985 [1978]). J. W. Fowler, A. Vergote, and C. Brusselmans, *Toward Moral and Religious Maturity* (1980). J. W. Fowler, R. S. Moseley, and D. Jarvis, *Manual for Faith Development Research* (1985). D. Heller, *The Children's God* (1986). J. Loder, *The Transforming Moment* (1981). B. Lonergan, *Method in Theology* (1972). W. W. Meissner, *Psychoanalysis and Religious Experience* (1984). H. R. Niebuhr, *Radical Monotheism and Western Culture* (1960). F. Oser, "Stages of Religious Reasoning," in Fowler and Vergote (1980). A.-M. Rizzuto, *Birth of the Living God* (1979). W. C. Smith, *The Meaning and End of Religion* (1963); *Faith and Belief* (1979). P. Tillich, *Dynamics of Faith* (1957). A. Vergote, *The Religious Man* (1969).

J. W. FOWLER

FAITH/BELIEF; RELIGIOUS DEVELOPMENT; THEOLOGY AND PSYCHOLOGY. *See also* COGNITIVE DEVELOPMENT; DEVELOPMENTAL THEORY AND PASTORAL CARE; PSYCHOLOGY OF RELIGION (Empirical Studies, Methods, and Problems); STRUCTURALISM; THEOLOGICAL METHODOLOGY. *Compare* EVALUATION AND DIAGNOSIS, RELIGIOUS; MORAL DEVELOPMENT.

FAITH HEALING. Improving health in body, mind, or spirit by means of prayer or other extranormal states of consciousness, usually occurring apart from orthodox medicine and considered miraculous.

Faith healing is an ambiguous term used chiefly in the U.S. to refer to diverse phenomena under the auspices of Christian Scientists, psychotherapists, spiritualists, and parapsychologists, theosophists and physicians, ordained clergy and free-lance evangelists, meditators and psychics, and cultists of many varieties.

Phenomena associated with faith healing have a history as ancient as the human race. They are documented in every region and culture of the globe and occupy a prominent place in the Hebrew-Christian Scriptures, particularly in the ministry of Jesus. Research in psychic phenomena began in the eighteenth century collecting and classifying documented case studies, and since the 1960s a burst of research activity has been taking place in transpersonal psychology laboratories. Interpretations of the data fall into two main categories: religious and parapsychological. Applications focus on a paradigm shift in philosophic and theological assumptions about reality, lifestyle issues, and the practice of healing arts in medicine, psychotherapy and religious ministries.

1. Types of Healing. *a. The problem of typology.* Since all effective healing may in some sense be faith healing, classification becomes most difficult. Mutually exclusive categories such as physical, mental, and faith healings cannot be supported scientifically because of findings of the "placebo effect" in all types of healing. Interventions into a patient's body by physical-chemical agents, X-rays, and operations are known to vary in their effectiveness according to the faith of the patient in the physicians and the treatments used. Similarly psychotherapy outcomes show a marked placebo effect. Ordinarily, however, the terms used for faith healing assume either supernatural intervention resulting in miracles or paranormal states of consciousness. The following categories offer some clarification of pathways in a jungle of luxuriant events and interchangeable terms.

b. Types based on the perceived agent of healing. *i. Faith healing.* The agent of healing is perceived to be the faith of the healer or of the person in need of healing or both. Faith healing usually presupposes a religious belief system operative in the healer and shared to some degree by the person needing healing. The power to heal is believed to be a gift from God, given to some but not available to most people.

ii. Spiritual healing. The agent of healing is perceived to be the Spirit of God or the spirits of the dead. Mind-body interactions are understood to involve entities of an unseen world and usually to take the form of a religious experience. Access to the spiritual realm is potentially open to everyone.

iii. Psychic healing. Alternate states of consciousness are believed to be the effective agent of psychic healing. Sometimes called "mind cures," psychic healing presupposes the power of mind over matter. The capacity to function in an alternate state of consciousness is a universal human potential. Nonsensory states of consciousness effective for healing are those that open one to clairvoyant and transpsychic realities.

In clairvoyant reality there are no boundaries. All things flow together. A person is to the whole as a single note to a symphony or a brush stroke to a watercolor painting. In transpsychic reality a person is a separate entity but also a part of the whole so fully that no line of separation is possible, like a wave in the ocean. Fervent intercessory prayer illustrates the transpsychic state, whereas accurate visualization of events in a distant time and place illustrate the clairvoyant state of consciousness.

iv. Charismatic healing. The agent of healing is perceived to be the person who is endowed with charisma. The gift may be a divine endowment or the mysterious power associated with high rank as with chieftains and monarchs. Charismatic healing in a religious context is often indistinguishable from faith healing. Charismatic and faith healing differ from spiritual and psychic healing in that the ability to heal is considered a special and exclusive gift in the former types but a universal human possibility in the latter.

v. Prayer healing. Prayer is perceived to be the effective agent of healing and prayer is a resource available to everyone. Prayer healing may be synonymous with any of the above types so long as prayer is employed. No distinctions apply with regard to the person who prays or the state of consciousness involved.

vi. Hypnotism. A hypnotist is perceived to be the effective agent of healing, using a technique of induction with a suggestible client. Suggestibility appears to be determined by the factor of trust in the hypnotist. Methods of hypnotic induction may be learned and employed successfully by anyone.

c. Types based on the healer's state of consciousness and intentionality. LeShan (1975) differentiates two types as follows:

i. Type I. The healer employs psychic healing in a clairvoyant state of consciousness. The healer is not intentionally seeking a specific healing; *being with* the healer prevails over *doing to*. A unitive experience involving healer and the person seeking healing occurs at an intense and profound level carried by the force of love. The healing that results may appear random, but is believed to be directed by the healed person's organism to the site most in need of healing. The healer characteristically feels energized rather than drained by the experience.

ii. Type II. The healer employs a method typically described as faith healing, involving focused concentration and touch or the laying on of hands. The healer intentionally seeks a specific cure and usually follows a prescribed ritual or set of guidelines. In Type II the healer experiences energy flowing through the body, often as vibrations or heat in the hands. Healers may perform Type II in either a sensory, clairvoyant, or transpsychic state of consciousness. Because effort and concentration are employed, healers are typically drained by their healing work. Preliminary research suggests that the results of Type II healings are not as lasting as Type I and occasionally cause problems to become worse before they improve.

2. **Varieties of Rituals and Guidelines.** *a. Three modes of ministry.* Among Christian communions healing ministries take one or more of three forms: (1) a pastoral ministry of compassion and outreach; (2) a ministry of prayer healing, specifically seeking the recovery of health; and (3) a sacramental ministry, celebrating the paschal mystery of Christ crucified and risen, working in the life of the person who is ill. A variety of rituals and guidelines reflect differing priorities among these three modes of ministry.

b. Catholic communions. All three modes of healing ministry mark the Catholic communions, but with changing emphases throughout the centuries. Prior to the ninth century the Latin Church, for example, emphasized the ministry of prayer healing in the context of a compassionate pastoral outreach to the sick. In the Middle Ages the sacrament of anointing the sick became associated chiefly with the dying. Extreme Unction as a sacramental preparation for death reflected the spiritualizing tendencies of the period. The Second Vatican Council restored the original rite to its primary place as a healing ministry so that, today, all three modes receive balanced attention. In performing the rite a priest functions in an ordinary or sensory state of consciousness and offers a Type II healing with prayers, anointing with oil and the laying on of hands.

c. The Church of England and the Episcopal Church in the U.S. Drawing upon the history of the Latin Church and with an eye on "modern pastoral experience and therapeutic psychology," the Church of England revised its healing rites in the 1930s. The Episcopal Prayerbook (1979) is in substantial agreement. Unction (anointing with oil) with the laying on of hands is a sacramental rite for the sick, prescribed in the context of an attentive and therapeutic pastoral care ministry. As in the Catholic rites, the Anglican and Episcopal services of healing are performed in a sensory state of consciousness and according to the Type II pattern.

d. Other Protestant (non-Pentecostal) communions. Moving away from sacramental understandings of healing ministries, many mainline Protestant denominations provide guidelines for prayer healing of the Type II variety but emphasize primarily the ministries of pastoral care and counseling for the sick. This trend has been reinforced strongly by clinical pastoral education (CPE) since the 1930s. CPE programs occur primarily in hospital settings, take on a medical-psychological coloring, and tend to avoid any appearance of support for extranormal states of consciousness in healing.

In the 1970s the literature of pastoral psychology began to reflect concern to recover the ancient rites of anointing and the laying on of hands and also to explore alternate states of consciousness for their potential in stimulating both religious experience and optimal organismic functioning.

The neo-pentecostal or charismatic movement is the main force in stimulating the recovery of prayer healing in mainline denominations, however. To a limited extent spiritual healing and psychic healing are being explored as well, using both the Type I and the Type II patterns.

e. Pentecostal communions. Pentecostalism, dating from 1906, emphasizes faith healing and charismatic healing as primary modes of ministry to the sick. Although charismatic healing was prominent from the beginning, a wave of healing revivalism burst on the American scene from 1947–52. William Branham, Kathryn Kuhlman, and Oral Roberts were among the best known healers of the period. Organizational skills and teaching methods became more important than faith healing to the success of Pentecostal evangelists from the 1950s on, but Type II healings continue to be the primary method in both the original Pentecostal and neo-pentecostal groups. Themes of demonology, speaking in tongues, prosperity, and prophecy accompany the witness of healing in neo-pentecostalism.

Faith healing continues to be the prototype for Pentecostal healing ministries. Guidelines call for a religious setting, a sense of pilgrimage on the part of the person seeking healing, a setting that provides a host of friends and a charismatic healer who truly loves the unwell person. The person needing healing is asked to declare a genuine desire to get well. Public confession of sins and declaring one's reasons for getting well may follow. Typically a ritual formula ensues with a positive prognosis, then either touching, holding, stroking, or anointing with oil, and finally a prayer and a command to be healed.

f. New Age healing. New Age modalities of healing range from therapeutic massage, acupuncture, aerobic running, swimming, dance, and tennis, to gardening, nutritional pharmacology, planet medicine, wilderness encounter, and the vision quest. They include Creation Spirituality, Eriksonian Hypnosis, Psychosynthesis, Jungian journey inward, Neurolinguistic Programing, and Leonard Energy Training; Tai Chi, Yoga, Ohoshiatsu, Karate; the Hakomi Method, Feldenkrais Awareness, Rubenfeld Synergy, and Intensive Journaling. One can gain the power of Shamanism, learn reflexology, hear the inner voice, study astrology, therapeutic touch, clinical herbology, or creative visualization. Explorations in sacred geometry, sacred architecture, transformational theatre and a host of meditative arts await the New Age devotee of self-realization. Healing may be sought in music, painting, dance, clowning, and wholistic health retreats.

In spite of their diversity New Age techniques are alike in assuming a spiritual as opposed to a materialistic view of reality. They pursue one goal, self-realization, along many paths, and they share the main assumptions and methods of psychic healing. Alternate states of consciousness inform their cosmology and their programs for health and healing. When specific healings are undertaken, they tend to fit the patterns previously described as spiritual healing and psychic healing. Both Type I and Type II healings are found in the New Age repertoire. The use of touch and movement is far more intensive than in the touch and anointing rituals found in faith healing and prayer healing. Radical differences mark the interpretations of healing events between classical Christian and New Age practitioners of the healing arts.

3. The Biblical Basis. *a. The Old Testament.* Fundamental to Hebrew beliefs about healing is the monotheistic concept that disease and healing belong to God alone. To see disease as punishment from God and to seek God's favor for the healing of disease was to inhibit the magical practices of the surrounding cultures. Priestly rituals and incantations were everywhere in the Semitic world. Hebrew priests, in contrast, developed and enforced sanitary legislation (preventive medicine) and warned their people that to rely on the healing powers of nature deities would invite the wrath of the one true God. Healing for the Hebrew people, then, required faith in the supernatural intervention of God and obedience to his laws which protect the social hygiene of the community.

b. The New Testament. Jesus, like no other religious healer, made healing a central theme in his ministry. Out of thirty-five specific miracles reported in the

NT, twenty-six relate to healing in one way or another. Nineteen works of healing are reported in the Acts of the Apostles and references to prayer healing occur in the epistles. It is no wonder that Christianity is preeminent among the world's religions in its concern for healing.

i. New Testament principles. The NT sets Jesus' healing ministry in the context of three principles: (1) the importance of the human body. God is Creator of the flesh; God is incarnate in the flesh; and God promises the resurrection of the flesh. The body is never seen as evil in the NT but rather as "the temple of the Holy Spirit." So the believer is exhorted to "glorify God in your body" (I Cor. 6:19–20); (2) the supremacy of the eternal. Although the body is important, its care is never to become an end in itself. Jesus warns, "it is better for you to enter life maimed or lame than with two hands or two feet to be thrown into the eternal fire" (Mt. 18:8). The body is a means for glorifying God, not the end in itself; (3) the unity of personhood. Consistently Jesus links healings with the forgiveness of sin. In healing the sick Jesus proclaims salvation. Sickness and sin are twin heads of the evil whose overthrow is signaled in the ministry of Jesus.

ii. The meaning of Jesus' healing ministry. Jesus' acts of healing reveal his compassion on the sick and the handicapped, his perception of sickness as a symptom of evil in the world, and supremely, his own messiahship and the coming of the new age. In the healing work of Jesus, he himself becomes a sign of God's presence in the midst of disease and death. In his healing miracles he calls people to repent and believe the Good News that the Kingdom of God is at hand.

iii. Christ's commission to the Church. Christ's commission to continue his own healing ministry was clear in the church's apostolic tradition. He directs his disciples on missions to preach and to heal (Mk. 6:13). The apostles continued to heal in Jesus' name after his death and resurrection, as recorded in Acts, and the gift of healing is included among the charismas of the Holy Spirit in I Cor. 12:9, 28–30.

Central to the understanding of early church practice is the passage in Jas. 5:13–16. Prayer healing is combined with the anointing with oil, a standard treatment of the day, and healing is a wholistic experience: "The Lord will raise him up; and if he has committed sins, he will be forgiven. Therefore confess your sins to one another, and pray for one another, that you may be healed" (Jas. 5:15–16). While disagreement surrounds the question of sacramental healing, no doubt remains that prayer healing is urged upon leaders of the community of faith, that confession of sins and mutual intercession is an integral part of the healing ministry, and that its aim is to improve health in body, mind and soul in radical dependence upon God for the results.

4. Contemporary Research. *a. A paradigm clash.* Faith healing of all types triggers a paradigm clash for everyone schooled in the faith assumptions of modern scientific materialism. In an ordinary sensory state of consciousness only the "see-touch" domain seems real. Cause and effect appears to work in only one direction, from lower mineral and bio-chemical forms upward, acting upon psychic, social, and spiritual functions. Deciding to gain control over nature, including human nature, requires the classical methods of science: observation, objectification and quantification. The consequence of conformity to the old paradigm is to gain more and more control over nature while becoming more and more alienated from nature, including one's own human or spiritual nature.

Phenomena such as faith healing require a psychospiritual rather than a physical paradigm through which to see what is happening. The new paradigm appears as a person accepts an alternate state of consciousness (clairvoyant or mystical consciousness) and discovers that psychic phenomena are also real. Cause and effect then is known to work from the higher psycho-spiritual functions downward, acting upon social, interpersonal, and psychic functions and also upon biochemical processes and mineral formations. Desiring continues to shape knowing. So in desiring connectedness with nature, a person learns meditative ways of participating in nature. The result of trusting the new paradigm is to gain more understanding and freedom to move in the psychospiritual domain and a profound oneness with all that is. Once a person makes this paradigm shift the so-called psi phenomena, including spiritual healing and psychic healing, are seen as "natural," alongside primarily physical and psychological modes of healing.

The basic issue for research into extranormal phenomena is not, therefore, a problem of method but of the paradigm or window through which to examine reality. Since the eighteenth century, however, research has choked on questions of method—attempting to understand psycho-spiritual realities within the limited field of vision of the old paradigm.

b. Established conclusions. Given the dominance of scientific materialism as *the* faith of Western civilization, psychical researchers have labored to make the case for psychic reality within the old paradigm. Using the technologies of biofeedback, electroencephalography, the monitoring devices of dream laboratories, the chemistry of psychedelic drugs, and the techniques of relaxation and meditation, parapsychologists have established an impressive array of conclusions about the reality of the extra-normal, its forms and functions. (See J. Rossner, 1979, and A. Sheikh, 1984, for complete and documented summaries.)

However, apart from assumptions about the underlying process, some studies have attended to the validity of the results claimed by faith healers.

Francis Galton conducted a survey of the life expectancies of ministers, religious professionals, bankers and lawyers in the late 1800s. He concluded that prayer did not extend life and, thus, was not efficacious.

In an early study of members of the Church of Christ, Scientist, Strunk (1955) concluded that most of their claims for healing could be attributed to misdiagnosis in that while many of these persons had been judged to be incurable, they nevertheless were cured psychosomatically.

Pattison, *et al.* (1973) studied forty-three fundamentalist Pentecostal persons who claimed a total of seventy-one healings. They concluded that these persons evidenced a strong need for social acceptance and affiliation and that they tended to use repression and denial as psychic defenses. Although they reported no lasting

changes in their symptoms, physical healing was not the dominant result they sought. They looked on their illnesses as providential and the initial faith-healing experience as strengthening of their faith.

In a study of the relationship between healing and the will to live, Simonton (1973) studied 152 cancer patients who had followed a visualization regime for a period of up to two years. In almost every case improvement, or lack of it, was correlated with the patients' positive or negative attitudes and their involvement in the visualization procedures.

Anderson (1977) initiated a study in England substituting spiritual healing for radiation therapy and found that over half the patients survived beyond their physician's expectations and, furthermore, many were told no trace of the cancer could be found.

In an investigation of the importance of expectations of persons seeking healing, Westerebeke *et al.* (1977) questioned persons who went to the Philippines to be healed by psychic healers. Receiving healing correlated highly with confidence in psychic healing in general and with past experience with the paranormal.

In a later investigation of these Filipino psychic healers, Allison and Malony (1980) reported cases of legitimate and validated healings coupled with just as objective cases of fraud in both healing methods and claimed results.

A Soviet study of the effects of faith healing examined thirty patients who were treated by Alexi and Victor Krivorotov, a father and son healing team. The patients were diagnosed as suffering from real physical ailments. Then they were treated by the Krivorotovs for one week. All showed improvement and some were completely cured (cf. Meeks, 1977).

Less optimistic than these reports was the Strauch (1959) study of 650 patients who were observed up to fourteen months after treatment by spiritual healers. Although sixty-one percent reported they were improved, only a few showed objective healing.

These studies are but a few of the investigations that have been conducted. As can be seen, they vary widely in terms of methodology and conclusions. The reported results are mixed, at best, in regard to the efficacy of faith healing.

One of the more balanced approaches to this issue has been that of the Harvard physician, Herbert Benson, who wrote *Beyond the Relaxation Response*. This volume explored the power of faith and meditation in healing. Benson described studies which demonstrated the efficacy of the "faith factor" which he suggested combined relaxation with belief in the tenets of the world's great religions. "Belief," Benson contended, was the essential factor in faith healing.

5. **Interpretations.** Before interpretation of a faith healing is possible three conditions must apply: (1) a healing has taken place (improvement in the health of body, mind, and/or soul is alleged by the healed person, and if possible confirmed by independent observers); (2) the healing has depended on a nonmedical intervention; and (3) the healing is extraordinary and medically unaccountable. At this point interpretations diverge into two camps.

a. Religious. The religious explanation is simply that the healing is supernatural, a miracle. The miracle may be further interpreted as work of the Holy Spirit, an answer to the prayers of compassionate friends, the work of a holy person or a holy place (such as a healing shrine) or a result of the faith of the person requiring healing.

Most prayer healing is understood by its practitioners as an aid to religious experience, having as its ultimate goal the spiritual growth and well-being of the healed person. Many consider such healings to be "telescoped time therapy," that is, "a radically speeded-up version of the potential normal healing process." At this point religious and parapsychological interpretations converge.

b. Parapsychological. Parapsychologists believe that extranormal events, including psychic healings, conform to laws of psychic life that are beginning to be understood. So-called gifts of healing are the manifestations of a universal human potential that is more fully developed in some persons than in others. "Para"-psychology is the science of psychic phenomena that exist "alongside of" the sensory awareness of the "see-touch" world. To speak of the "extra"-normal is to use an intentional double-entendre, not only larger than normal in the sense of awesome but also more truly human, implying that psychic phenomena are primary and more basic to human survival than cognitive abilities.

When it comes to hypothesizing about the actual process activated in psychic healing, most parapsychologists and religionists agree that self-healing mechanisms of the unwell person are activated. Optimal organismic functioning is stimulated and time is shrunk in the healing event.

6. **Applications.** Philosophical, theological and life-style issues have become apparent in discussing the paradigm clash triggered by faith healing and other extranormal happenings. At an applied level, faith healing holds promise for medicine, psychotherapy, and religious ministries as well. Selected cases illustrate possible applications in these fields.

a. In medicine. A controlled study on the practical application of psi ability as an adjunct to medical diagnosis demonstrated the value of psychics in the diagnosis of cases that are misdiagnosed by physicians in preliminary medical examinations (approximately twenty percent of all cases). A group of eight psychics were ninety-eight percent accurate in locating pain sites and determining personality traits and eighty percent accurate in diagnosing illnesses.

b. In psychotherapy. Multiple studies demonstrate the possibility of inducing telepathy in subjects, thereby enabling a therapist to know the thoughts and intentions of others or to project one's own thoughts to them. Similarly the capacity for precognition may be self-induced, enabling therapists and clients alike to anticipate the consequences of patterned behaviors and take corrective measures.

c. In religious ministries. All of the above capacities may be employed in the care of others. More importantly the ministry of intercessory prayer may be enhanced through improved understanding of how to enter the state of consciousness in which extranormal phenomena ordinarily occur.

By firm ethical commitment to use extra-normal interventions under the mandate of the commandments to love God wholeheartedly and neighbor as self, religious communities may set a standard and develop a social conscience that will redeem the parapsychological arts from self-serving and destructive uses and so enhance the healing powers of the entire human community.

d. In pastoral applications. Pastors often encounter claims of faith healing. It is not uncommon for parishioners to seek faith healing when traditional medical treatment fails or when a malady is declared incurable. Church members in both settings where faith healing is overtly practiced and where it is not look to faith healers for help in times of crisis. The ways in which pastors respond to these situations are a function of their tradition, their polity, their beliefs, and their culture.

As had been noted, healing by faith has a long history in the life of the Christian church dating from the healing miracles of Jesus himself. Faith healing was an expectation in the life of the early church. Although kept alive in some traditions, healing by faith went into a decline and has been revived only in the twentieth century among mainline churches as well as pentecostal communions. However, it is still not the norm in conventional Protestantism. Nevertheless, healing services are typical in such widely different settings as Episcopal and Assembly of God churches.

However, most pastors offer prayers for healing at the bedsides of sick persons. They expect their prayers to be efficacious, if only in the mental attitudes of the sick. Here is where beliefs play an important role. The differences are great, but as has been said, pastors usually have a medium, if not a deep, belief in the importance of healing by faith. While these convictions may be expressed in far less flamboyant ways than those of faith healers who hold mass services, the underlying beliefs are often similar.

How pastors react to the claims of their members that cancers have been removed, functioning restored, or limbs repaired by faith healing is a question that can only be answered by reflection and forethought. As has been noted, tradition, culture, and personal convictions play an important role in pastoral attitudes toward these claims. Where faith healing is an expectation, a welcome, positive attitude toward such claims might be predicted. In fact, pastors may engage in such endeavors. Where faith healing is not expected, pastors would do well to anticipate such encounters and be proactive in how they will react to parishioners who inquire of them or who claim such healings. That faith healing will be an important part of Western culture for some time to come is a foregone conclusion.

Bibliography. S. H. Allison and H. N. Malony, "Filipino Psychic Surgery: Myth, Magic or Miracle," *J. of Religion and Health,* 20:1 (1981), 48–62. G. Anderson, "Paranormal Healing in Great Britain," G. Meek, ed., *Healers and the Healing Process* (1977). H. Benson, *Beyond the Relaxation Response* (1984). A. Castiglione, *History of Medicine* (1969). J. Fosshage and P. Olsen, eds., *Healing Implications for Psychotherapy* (1978), see chapters by J. Frank, S. Krippner, and J. Goodrich in particular. C. Gusmer, *And You Visited Me* (1984); *The Ministry of Healing in the Church of England* (1974). D. Harrell *All Things Are Possible* (1975). C. R. B. Joyce and R. M. C. Welldon, "The

Objective Efficacy of Prayer: A Double Bind Clinical Trial," *Reader in Psychopharmacology* (1964). L. Le Shan and H. Margenau. *Einstein's Space and Van Gogh's Sky* (1982). *Pastoral Psychology* Special Issue on "Religion and Parapsychology," 21:206 (Sept., 1970). E. M. Pattison, N. A. Lapine, and H. A. Doerr, "Faith Healing: A Study of Personality and Function," *J. of Nervous and Mental Disease*, 157 (1973), 397–409. J. Rossner, *From Ancient Magic to Future Technology* (1979). A. Sheikh, ed., *Imagination and Healing* (1984). A. Shilkh, *Faith Healing* (1981). O. C. Simonton quoted in J. S. Bolen, *Meditation and Psychotherapy in the Treatment of Cancer* (1973). I. Strauch, "Zur Frage der geistigen Heiling," *Psychoenergetic Systems*, 23:1 (1959), 73. O. Strunk, Jr., "Motivational Factors and Psychotherapeutic Aspects of a Healing Cult," *J. of Pastoral Care*, 9 (1955), 213–20.

E. E. THORNTON
H. N. MALONY

FAITH/BELIEF; HEALING; RELIGION AND HEALTH; SALVATION, HEALING, AND HEALTH; SICK AND DYING, JEWISH CARE OF; SICK, PASTORAL CARE OF. *Compare* EXORCISM; SUGGESTION, PERSUASION, AND INFLUENCE.

FALL/FALLENNESS. *See* ALIENATION/ESTRANGEMENT; HUMAN CONDITION/PREDICAMENT; SIN/SINS.

FAMILY, CHRISTIAN THEOLOGY AND ETHICS OF. The attempt to understand the family in light of Christian belief and experience, and to offer a normative vision of family life and relations aimed at embodying Christian convictions in everyday life.

The family in some form is a feature of human society that predates Christian theological and ethical reflection on it. That reflection proceeds first by seeking to understand the family as a social and cultural phenomenon; second, by recollecting sources of insight and interpretation from Scripture, tradition, and experience; third, by articulating theological frameworks for understanding the family; and fourth, by offering practical ethical reflection and pastoral care in daily living and in times of particular need. The family bears important theological and ethical significance as an arena where Christian beliefs seek daily expression and where future generations are raised and nurtured.

1. The Family as Institution and Relationship. The family is a social institution and a special relationship. As an institution it locates individuals in a network of responsibility and gives them a role in the transmission of culture. As a special relationship it is part of an individual's identity and character, which it both forms and expresses for good or for ill.

The family as a social institution regulates sexual intercourse, offspring, lines of descent, property, and inheritance. It helps in the division of labor for daily living and supports the external economic roles of its members. It is heavily involved with the socialization of the next generation, a task it shares in an uneasy balance with other social institutions (see Lasch). Many structures of family life have arisen over the centuries to fulfill these functions (see Elshtain; Blustein). Christian theology and ethics try to do this in ways appropriate to Christian belief and experience.

Family membership constitutes a special relationship unlike others formed in the public sphere, though it shares certain characteristics with friendship and commitment to a profession, belief, or cause. These relationships are special because they both form and express an individual's identity and character. Persons in one special relationship are not interchangeable with those in another, as each person has become part of the character of the others in the relation. This intensely personal feature of the family is often in tension with the more impersonal demands arising from its function as a social institution. How this tension is to be regarded is an important feature of any Christian vision of the family (see Bondi).

2. Sources of Christian Theology of the Family. Christian theology of the family exhibits a wide range of sources. Each represents a synthesis of belief, tradition, and experience, which any given theology of family life interprets in its generation. The sources are often contradictory or conflicting in general outlook and in particular ethical and pastoral emphasis, making contemporary interpretation both necessary and difficult. Six important sources may be briefly described.

a. Jewish tradition. Jewish tradition influenced Christian thought through the Hebrew scriptures and through first century C.E. Jewish culture. The books of Genesis, Proverbs, and Hosea form the core of much Christian thought on the family (see Augustine, Barth, Luther, Bromiley), and the patterns of Jewish family life and law form the background for NT writings on these topics. Three themes emerge from the Jewish tradition: Sex is a good of creation ordained by God for procreation and pleasure; marriage and the family are human institutions ordained by God that can be understood as a covenant similar to that between YHWH and Israel; women and men have definite yet dignified roles in marriage and family life (see Feldman).

b. Greco-Roman tradition. The family is always lived and interpreted in a definite cultural context. While many cultures have shaped Christian thought on the family, four themes from the Greco-Roman culture of Christianity's youth still have significant influence: Marriage is a secular contract entered by consent of the individuals and dissolvable by legal action; the state can and should regulate marriage and divorce but be reluctant to interfere in daily family life; sex by nature is primarily for procreation and secondarily for pleasure; any felt religious dimension to marriage and family life is a private matter.

c. Christian scripture. In addition to the themes from Hebrew scripture just mentioned, the writings of the NT offer a rich diversity of thought on marriage and the family, of which the safest thing that can be said is that no one vision emerges. Two sorts of sources can be seen: Scriptural passages that explicitly discuss marriage, family life, and related issues, and broader NT themes that have been or might be used to interpret family life and relations. Since the former tend to be highly specific and embedded in Jewish and Greco-Roman traditions, and the latter tend to be more all-encompassing and their application to the family more arguable than clear, there is often considerable friction between these two kinds of sources. For example, one could cite Eph. 5:22–33 to emphasize the headship of the husband over the wife (as Christ over the church), while on the other hand one could develop the themes of radical freedom and equality from Gal. 3:23–29; these two starting points would yield conflicting views of the proper relationship between husband and wife (see Bromiley; Bondi). As a result, the use of scripture varies widely from one interpretation to the next and often depends on views of the authority and function of scripture developed quite independently from reflection on marriage and family life.

d. Augustine of Hippo. The need to synthesize this diversity of sources with human reason and experience arose early in the history of the church. The most notable and lasting such attempt was made by Augustine of Hippo. For Augustine the family was a social institution ordained by God for the propagation of the race and the containment of sexual lust. There were three goods of marriage and family: offspring, marital fidelity, and sacrament, by which he meant an enduring sign of commitment and faith analogous to the union between YHWH and Israel, Christ and the church. Augustine's position greatly influenced later thought, most explicitly in the Catholic tradition where the importance of sacrament was considerably expanded in the development of canon law on marriage (see Makin). But it was also widely influential in Protestant thought where Augustine's definition of the goods of marriage and family set the terms if not the outcome of theological debate.

e. The Reformation. By the time of the Reformation four criteria for a valid Christian marriage had emerged: consent, contract, church ceremony, and consummation. These were based chiefly on Augustine's synthesis and the laws and customs of medieval Europe. The chief impact of the Reformation was to eliminate the requirement of a church ceremony and with it the sacramental (but not the symbolic) character of marriage. Family life was upheld by the Reformers as a secular reality especially blessed by God. Family relations were often interpreted on models drawn from Hebrew scripture (see Luther and Barth).

f. Romantic love and individualism. From the sixteenth century onward elements of Romantic love—personal fulfillment, idealistic sex roles, physical pleasure, disdain of time and change—became incorporated into a popular understanding which sought that love in an institution basically experienced as toil and child-rearing. The evident tensions in this union have been exacerbated in the twentieth century by the rise of individualistic tendencies which see the family as a means of self-expression. The resulting conflict between the institutional demands of marriage and family and the desire for a qualitatively "good" experience of family life poses many challenges to Christian theology and ethics (see Hauerwas).

3. Theological Frameworks for Understanding the Family. The family received four normative foundations in the sources just noted. The *physical* emphasizes the family as the ordained framework for primarily procreative sexual intercourse. The *social* emphasizes the propagation and rearing of children and the mutual relations of the family members. The *spiritual* emphasizes the covenantal, sacramental, or providential character of the family. The *personal* emphasizes individual experience within institutional forms and the qualitative enrichment of that experience over time. Theological understandings of marriage and family life are distinguishable by the relative primacy given one or more of these foundations and by the way they draw on the sources mentioned above to support and articulate that interpretation. Such understandings cut across denominational and confessional lines. Five understandings may be noted briefly (see Bondi).

a. Contract and natural union. These understandings depend chiefly on the physical and social foundations for the family. They see the family as a social institution entered into by a private contract which may be blessed by the church. They focus on the establishment and dissolution of marriage bonds rather than on daily family life, and they tend to use economic, legal, or socio-psychological language to articulate their perspectives. Where explicitly religious dimensions are present they are thought of as added by private consent (contract) or diffused through creation in general and this institution in particular (natural union). Theologies tending toward these understandings often fall back on their cultural context to provide the ethical and pastoral assistance to be discussed in section four below.

b. Covenant and command of God. These depend more on a spiritual foundation for the family and order the physical, social, and personal foundations in terms of how the covenant or command of God is understood. The ambiguity of the covenant analogy and the difficulty in discerning God's commands are the chief difficulties with these understandings. It makes a great difference whether the key interpretative feature of the covenant analogy is taken to be obedience, steadfastness, or faithful love, or whether God's commands are found in Scripture (and where), church or community authority, or personal revelation. Theologies tending toward these understandings often have a difficult time incorporating the family as a personal relationship that must be lived in a non-Christian society where culture does not straightforwardly reinforce (let alone embody) covenant or command.

c. Vocation of fidelity. Seeing marriage and family life as a vocation allows for the incorporation of the institutional and personal features noted previously without collapsing their distinction. A vocation in the everyday sense is a socially structured personal choice, and Christian fidelity is a theological and ethical shaping of that enterprise. This understanding emphasizes the spiritual and personal foundations for the family and orders the physical and social within them. This is especially important in an age where sexual relations, child-rearing, and family life are often pursued in separate or overlapping social settings. Single-parent families, families with multiple sets of parents and children through remarriages, and the desire of couples who do not practice procreative sex (whether through homosexuality, continence, contraception, or disability) require an understanding of family life capable of including but not ordered around the traditional physical and social foundations. Theologies tending toward this understanding often turn to a covenantal or sacramental interpretation of the spiritual foundation for marriage in order to prevent the personal foundation from privatizing the relationship.

4. Ethical Reflection and Pastoral Care. Theological frameworks set the context for seeing priorities and possibilities in ethical reflection and pastoral care. A large part of such reflection and care must be devoted to critical investigation of what frameworks, theological and otherwise, are actually shaping practice. Yet ethics and pastoral care must move from critique to practice; indeed, these are but two parts of the same movement of appropriating and embodying Christian faith. This practice focuses on the Christian family in daily life and in times of tragedy and despair, seeking to bring the solidarity of the larger Christian family to bear on the families of its members.

a. The Christian family in daily life. Ethical reflection and pastoral care must begin by focusing on the long-term needs of the Christian family. Preparation for marriage, sustaining the family within church and community, and nurturing family life are tasks that are both ethical and pastoral. The connection between ethics and pastoral care is more visible in some theologies than in others but is never wholly lacking. At best, the theological ethicist offers a normative vision of family life and the reflective categories and skills of interpretation that will enable individuals to perform their own synthesis of Scripture, tradition, and experience. The pastoral care specialist assists this process by making accessible the social skills and psychological insights helpful to it, and by offering assistance in articulating the theological and cultural context within which a given Christian family seeks to live. Such coordination of effort is vital in an arena like the family, which forms the intersection of so many aspects of life and faith and where future generations are raised and nurtured (see Hauerwas; Mace; E. Whitehead and J. Whitehead).

b. Tragedy and vision in the Christian family. Ethics has too often been confined to supplying injunctions for family living, and pastoral care to picking up the pieces of lives shattered at least in part on those injunctions. The need for the combined efforts of ethics and pastoral care in preparing for, sustaining, and nurturing the family in a normative vision is nowhere more apparent than in moments of tragedy in family life. Indeed, we would not know what would morally constitute a tragedy, or what would be the appropriate pastoral response, in the absence of such long-term theological reflection. Divorce, abortion, death, adultery, suicide, murder, depression, spouse and child abuse, and a host of other devastating moments in family life are not understandable as tragedies *for Christians* apart from a sense of how the odd vision of the Christian faith would have us see and respond to them. In the absence of that vision Christians lose sight of what the family is about, and thus it and its tragedies are governed by other beliefs and experiences. The theology and ethics of family life are necessary precisely because without them there would be married Christians but no Christian families. That would be a serious blow to the ability of Christians to embody their faith in this world, and to understand themselves as somehow part of one family in Christ.

There is an immense literature on the topic.

Bibliography. Augustine, *The Goodness of Marriage; Commentary on the Literal Meaning of Genesis.* K. Barth, *Church Dogmatics* 3:4 (1961), pp. 116–285. Neo-orthodox perspective: J. Blustein, *Parents and Children* (1982). Western philosophical perspective: R. Bondi, *Fidelity and the Good Life,* unpublished dissertation, University of Notre Dame (1981). G. Bromiley, *God and Marriage* (1980), theological perspective centered on Scripture. J. B. Elshtain, *The Family in Political Thought* (1982), historical essays in Western tradition. D. Feldman, *Marital Relations, Birth Control and Abortion in Jewish Law* (1974). S. Hauerwas, *A Community of Character* (1981), pp. 155–229. W. Kasper, *Theology of Christian Marriage* (1980), continental Catholic perspective. C. Lasch, *Haven in a Heartless World* (1979), criticism of social scientific treatment of family. M. Luther, "The Estate of Marriage," *Luther's Works,* vol. 45; *The Christian in Society* 2; *Lectures on Genesis, ad. ser.* D. Mace, *Close Companions* (1982), Marriage Enrichment handbook. Detailed historical treatment by American Catholic: T. Mackin, *What is Marriage?* (1982). E. and J. Whitehead, *Marrying Well* (1981), detailed theological and psychological treatment. J. C. Wynn, *Family Therapy in Pastoral Ministry* (1982), pastoral counseling perspective.

RICHARD BONDI

FAMILY, PASTORAL CARE AND COUNSELING OF. *See also* COMMITMENT; ETHICS AND PASTORAL CARE; FAMILY PLANNING; MATRIMONY, SACRAMENT OF; LOVE; MORAL THEOLOGY AND PASTORAL CARE; SEXUALITY; VOCATION. *Compare* FAMILY, JEWISH THEOLOGY AND ETHICS OF; MARRIAGE; PERSON.

FALSE CONSCIOUSNESS. *See* CONSCIOUSNESS RAISING.

FAMILY, DYING CHILD'S. *See* DYING CHILD AND FAMILY.

FAMILY, ETHICS OF. *See* FAMILY, CHRISTIAN, *or* JEWISH, THEOLOGY AND ETHICS OF.

FAMILY, HISTORY AND SOCIOLOGY OF. The historical and sociological study of the family in the U.S. focuses on changes in its structure and function in the context of industrialization and more recent economic and social changes.

1. Industrialization and the Nuclear Family. *a. Parsonian theory.* When historians began to take seriously changes in the institution of the family they were brought face to face with the dominant sociological paradigm, the Parsonian theory of the rise of the nuclear family. Parsons (1955) had theorized about the family in terms of the modernization thesis. As society moved toward an industrial, urban, democratic pattern, a new family pattern was needed which would maximize the mobility of workers. Faced with the requirements of the market economy, families that were embedded in hierarchical, stable village communities where tradition prevailed in all matters of daily life were no longer functional. A process of change began in which functions that had been part of family life began to be stripped away and separate institutions were created to perform them, the prime example being education. The family pattern that remained at the end of this process was, according to Parsons, a nuclear one in the sense that it was left with only the most essential, universal attributes. These were embodied in the parental figures: families reproduced and raised children; in the nuclear family the father performed the instrumental function and the mother the emotional or nurturant function. Parsons's theory of the nuclear family worked to legitimize the middle-class nuclear family by claiming that it expressed the universal functions of the family and also that it fit perfectly the needs of modern society. No other family type could provide free, autonomous workers who could change location or skill at the whim of the market, while at the same time provide a new generation of workers who could be trained by the state.

b. Actual peasant family life. When historians examined closely the transformation of the family at the beginning of the industrial revolution Parsons's theory of family modernization came under attack. Aries (1965) showed that the pre-industrial family was more than simply a nuclear family with excess functional baggage. In Europe before the industrial revolution a form of village sociability characterized daily life in which the family barely existed as a distinct social unit. Privacy in marital relations was unheard of as the village regulated sexual pattern and child-rearing practices. Children were regarded as miniature adults with no separate needs or distinct emotional stages. The entire community participated in all spheres of life from work and religion to love and leisure activities. For Aries the change to the nuclear family was at best a mixed blessing: the isolation of the middle-class family from wider networks of sociability was a serious disadvantage of modern conditions.

c. Noble family life. Historians also found that the family life of the European aristocracy did not fit easily into the Parsonian scheme. Flandrin (1976), among others, discovered a distinct family pattern among the nobility that could not be seen in Parsonian terms. Aristocratic families were organized into lineages in which the existing couple was only a point on a continuum that stretched back into the distant past and forward into the future. The current noble couple were regarded as trustees of the line, in no sense free to do as they pleased but obligated to care for the condition of the house. Noble families lived entirely public lives, with retainers, clients, and servants constituting a social unit of some forty to two hundred people. The noble household was a political center dominating the surrounding countryside. Marital relations were formal and entirely public; even the design of the chateau revealed little concern for privacy. Children were raised by servants and left the home for another chateau to be reared outside the parental setting. Sexual fidelity was not the norm among nobles, who lived what Stone (1977), a historian of the British nobility, called "serial polygamy." Marriages were arranged by parents whose concern was not for the domestic compatibility of the couple but for the political advantage of the line.

d. Working-class families. If the peasant and noble families did not resemble the Parsonian model for pre-industrial families, so the early industrial working-class family raises further questions for the modernization thesis. Tilly and Scott (1978) studied the transformation of peasants into workers and the impact this change had on family life. They found that workers did not readily adopt the nuclear family pattern. In fact, workers resisted the threat of industrial society to their communities, protesting against those forces which worked against the solidarity of their collective life. Instead of eagerly accepting the freedom and autonomy promised by market conditions they attempted to preserve the feature of mutual assistance that characterized their communities. They rejected the privacy and isolation of the nuclear family in favor of women's networks and men's fraternal institutions, such as the tavern. Early union organizing in the Midwest, for example, attempted to build on these features of working-class family life rather than encourage the nuclear family pattern. A study by Young and Wilmott on the London working class indicated that it was not until after World War II that large numbers of working-class families abandoned the urban neighborhood for the suburbs and began to resemble the middle-class pattern of the nuclear family.

Other studies of the nineteenth century working-class family, such as that by Donzelot (1979) on France, showed that the nuclear family was not freely adopted by the early industrial working class as the Parsonian model would suggest, but was imposed. In France two forms of coercion can be identified. On the one hand middle-class women attempted to instill virtues associated with the nuclear family (thrift, cleanliness, scrupulous supervision of children) into working-class mothers through philanthropic and quasi-social welfare institutional activities. On the other hand, the state began to formulate policies that would coerce the working class into nuclear family patterns. From the regulation of orphanages in the early part of the nineteenth century to the formation of social welfare institutions, the state worked to compel the adoption of a family pattern, the nuclear one, that Parsons regarded as the paragon of freedom.

2. Twentieth Century Families. In recent decades the nuclear family has been rejected by the vast majority in the U. S. and other industrial or post-industrial nations. It is estimated that at most fifteen percent of families in the U.S. in 1980 conformed to the classical nuclear family pattern: only the husband works outside the home, there are small numbers of children, and there has been no divorce. This also challenges the Parsonian model of the fit between the nuclear family and industrial society.

However, at the same time that behavior patterns deviate from the nuclear family norm, aspirations for the nuclear family remain strong. The apparent travail of the nuclear family in recent decades has been a cause for serious concern by social scientists, the government and the public at large. The deviations are treated as symptoms or disorders.

a. Family as victim of attack. One common explanation for the situation is stated by Lasch (1977). Until the 1920s the family, in Lasch's view, was a haven from the cold, threatening world of the marketplace. The father's authority and the mother's nurturance provided a humane, warm bastion against the vagaries of capitalist society. Then the outside world started to intrude upon the privacy of the home, disrupting the authority of the father, encouraging the mother to find interests outside the home and enticing the children to find their social reference in the peer group. The state, the social sciences and the helping professions descended upon the family with the intention of assisting it but with the result of destroying it, Lasch laments.

The theory has a psychological component, relying loosely on psychoanalytic theory: In the traditional nuclear family the father's authority and the mother's devotion and sacrifice were the keys to the healthy development of the child. The mother's love and attention began the Oedipal process in the child; the father's stern paternalism served as a testing ground for the child's rebellious feelings. Thus the child learned independence, developed a strong superego, in psychoanalytic language, by doing battle with the father's authority. Free citizens, capable of resisting the state's injustice, were formed in the bosom of the nuclear family.

After the 1920s this delicate equilibrium began to be shaken: The authority of the father was substituted by that of teachers, doctors, psychologists, clergy, social workers, and so forth. For her part the mother began to find interests outside the home in careers and leisure activities, rejecting a life of sacrifice for one of excitement and fun. As a consequence relations in the home became distant and confusing for the child. The Oedipal process did not proceed smoothly: the child's loving feelings lost their natural object and reverted to the self; the child's hostile feelings found no limiting authority and were not repressed. The superego was not formed in the same way and as a result the narcissistic personality was born. In the culture of narcissism the individual is incapable of self-control and genuine love for another. Impulsively the narcissist attempts to gratify his or her slightest desires, without being able to criticize or resist outside forces such as the state. In Lasch's depressing view the culture of narcissism is a breeding ground for the totalitarian state. While current psychoanalytic orthodoxy tends to support Lasch's position and while it does ring a chord of verisimilitude among those who bemoan current mores, in the end his argument conceals more than it reveals about the history and condition of the family in advanced industrial society.

b. Fragility of nuclear family. i. Economic stress. Other theories would stress the fragility of the isolated nuclear family in the face of twentieth century economic changes. The birth and spread of the corporation destroyed small-scale manufacturing, agriculture, and retail establishments in favor of large, bureaucratic institutions. In this process millions of middle-class fathers lost entrepreneurial control of property and became salaried employees. The *petit bourgeois* class, the backbone of the nuclear family, was shorn of the basis of its authority, a loss which was no doubt felt in the home. At the same time women did begin to seek careers outside the home. In the context of a dual career family, childrearing practices would certainly have to change. The new situation was not necessarily a disaster and creative solutions have been developed in thousands of homes. Nevertheless, what these circumstances did underline was the inherent limitations of the isolated nuclear family to cope with social transformations. Without deep ties to the community, neighborhood, church or kin groups, even grandparents, the nuclear family compels the couple to rely on their own limited resources, not always with the best results for the couple or their children.

It was the condition of isolation and vulnerability that led the family to seek the support of outsiders (teachers, therapists, clergy, social welfare workers), not intrusion from outside, as Lasch has it.

ii. Value changes. Another source of change in family was the change in priority of values. Perhaps beginning in the 1920s, people began to reject the restrictions of the Victorian compromise, that is, respectability of the home in exchange for an absence of warmth, emotional growth and sexual fulfillment. The Victorian husband found life's rewards in work and in the huge industry of prostitution. The wife was limited in her interests to the maintenance of the home and the upbringing of the children, a restriction many see as unnecessary and harsh. After the 1950s individuals began demanding more of life and the limitations of the nuclear family once again appeared too restrictive. Economic affluence coupled with high levels of education was a mixture that did not bode well for the Victorian compromise.

Prominent developments — divorce, abortion, rejection of parenthood, rejection of marriage, experimental arrangements such as group marriage — were all giving up the Victorian priority on stability of the home for more personal satisfactions and flexibility in adult development. The spread of consumerism is also part of this conjuncture.

These later views disagree with Lasch and place the blame for the culture of narcissism on the unfortunate restrictions of a family form which, in the name of privacy, forbids authentic commitments to the community and places an inordinate burden on two isolated people to fulfill all the needs that complex, modern life affords.

3. A Summary Interpretation. The dispute over the fate of the nuclear family in advanced technological society will no doubt continue to excite the work of social scientists. Surely no simple answer exists or it would already have been discovered. A theory needs to be developed which avoids the (Parsonian) glorification of the fit of the nuclear family with industrial capitalism and the (Laschian) condemnation of modern social developments.

a. Pluralism of family patterns. First the family needs to be studied historically with an appreciation of the real differences in family patterns that have existed. Social scientists need to avoid the tendency to seek universals of the family because this exercise most often ends in justifying the prejudices the investigator began with. Only by studying family types that are seriously at variance with our own and that we perhaps find at first glance repugnant can we appreciate the specificity of our own family form as well as its limitations.

For example, peasants, in pre-industrial society, beat their children routinely and systematically. While that is perhaps repugnant to modern observers, it can be understood. The beatings were part of a family system which gave priority to the child's place in the wider village community, thus allowing the child a flexibility and multiplicity in adult role models and objects for identification. In the modern nuclear family, by contrast, where affection, not beatings, are the primary sanction of parents, unwanted behavior of the child is greeted with the loss of parental love. In a situation where the child has no other resort than to the parents the withdrawal of love can be more devasting and damaging than the beatings experienced by the peasant children, who, after all, were not maimed by the whip physically nor usually emotionally shaken.

b. Autonomy of family. Once an appreciation for historical differences of family types is assured the investigator comes up against another common danger: finding too close a fit between the family and society. Liberals find the nuclear family to fit perfectly with capitalist democracy; Marxists find the family to be a reflection of the mode of production. Neither position will do. It is best to presume nothing of the sort and to study the family as a relatively autonomous sphere of social life, with its own dynamics and its own modes of domination.

Families do not oblige social theorists with a neat fit. We have seen that the working class did not adopt the nuclear family in the early stages of industrialization. Another disjuncture between the family and society occurred more recently. It was the middle class, those who allegedly fit best into society, who raised children that protested the Vietnam War, created a youth counter-culture, began the movements for women's liberation, ecological balance with nature, reform of the churches and expanded social choices such as divorce and freer sexual preferences. All of this contradicts the conventional wisdom of both liberalism and Marxism.

c. A pattern of love and authority. Given an appreciation for the historical nature of the family and for its significance as a locus of social life, the following paradigm may be proposed for further study. The family is centered on a particular pattern of love and authority, based on hierarchies of sex and age, which is best revealed in the interaction of the parents and children through the first three stages of the latter's life. Other indices are important for a complete account of the family but this one reveals extraordinary differences between family types and indicates the limitations of each without loading the categorical deck in favor of any (Poster).

In the classical middle-class nuclear family of the nineteenth century, both love and authority are concentrated in the parents. The mother has the duty of total moral supervision of the child. Extremely intense emotions characterize relations within the family. Through the first three stages of the child's life a pattern exists in which the child must sacrifice bodily pleasure to win and keep parental affection. In the oral stage there is a rigid feeding schedule. During the anal stage parents insist on early and complete bowel control. During the genital stage childhood masturbation is absolutely forbidden. In the little dramas that concern the events of early childhood, the child is faced with a heightened ambivalence toward the parents.

The process, which Freud terms the Oedipus complex, is unique to the nuclear family and is its hallmark. Only where parental figures are personalized through deep love feelings and intensified through complete authority over the child does such ambivalence exist that identification is internalized. The child will become capable of enormous self-repression and hence will appear as the autonomous individual in democratic and market institutions. The child will also have a deep need to reproduce the nuclear family by finding a substitute for the parent of the opposite sex toward which to reproduce in adult form (romantic love) the early exclusive attachment.

d. Advantages and costs of nuclear family. The pattern of the nuclear family has been with us for some time. It has certain strong advantages over other family types: it provides a setting of warmth, love and domesticity, but it has done so in the past at the expense of strict gender typing and the isolation of the child from the community. It affords virtually the only emotional arena in industrial society and in that capacity elicits strong support. Yet by limiting emotional life to itself it reinforces the cold, arms-length relations with the outside world. As individuals demand more from life than can reasonably be satisfied by a single mate it is a question whether the nuclear family in some form will continue or whether other institutions will begin to take on the character of a true community, establishing relations of deep commitment, caring, and affection instead of the endless repetition of the mercantile contract.

Bibliography. P. Aries, *Centuries of Childhood* (1965). J. Donzelot, *The Policing of Families* (1979). J. L. Flandrin, *Families* (1976). S. Freud, *New Introductory Lectures on Psychoanalysis* (1965). K. Keniston, *Young Radicals: Notes on Committed Youth* (1968). C. Lasch, *Haven in a Heartless World: The Family Besieged* (1977); *The Culture of Narcissism: American Life in An Age of Diminishing Expectations* (1979). T. Parsons, *et al.*, *Family, Socialization and Interaction Process* (1955). M. Poster, *Critical Theory of the Family* (1978). L. Stone, *The Family, Sex and Marriage in England, 1500–1800* (1977). L. Tilly and J. Scott, *Women, Work and Family* (1978). M. Young and P. Willmott, *Family and Kinship in East London* (1957).

M. POSTER

FAMILY THEORY AND THERAPY. *Compare* FAMILY VIOLENCE; MARRIAGE; PARENTS/PARENTHOOD; RELATIONSHIP NETWORK; SOCIAL STATUS AND CLASS FACTORS IN PASTORAL CARE; SOCIOLOGY OF RELIGIOUS AND PASTORAL CARE.

FAMILY, JEWISH CARE AND COUNSELING OF.

With the destruction of the great Temple in Jerusalem in 70 C.E. Judaism moved from a shrine-centered religion to a religion focused upon observance, congregational gathering and the sanctified home. The home was regarded as a "small sanctuary" with roles clearly defined and each member of the family given tasks designed to raise the sense of holiness of even the most simple and routine of acts. So great was the focus upon the home and the interrelation of generations, that until recently when Hebrew borrowed a word from the Greek, the Hebrew language had no word for the abstraction of continuing national experience. Until it borrowed the Greek word for "history," the Hebrew language had regarded history simply as "generations," the linkages of emerging Jewish families.

Against the coldness and hostility so often encountered in the outside world, a God-centered home environment and a sanctified family structure became the core experience in Jewish life. In order to understand the relationship of the Jews to their faith and to their life sequence, one must begin not with the synagogue but with the Jewish home and with life cycle milestones which often involve the synagogue but find their dynamics in the family environment.

The birth of a Jewish child immediately places sacred obligations upon the parents. A son is named at his circumcision, which becomes the moment of his being brought into the Covenant of Abraham. The ceremony takes place on the eighth day even if that day is the Day of Atonement or the Sabbath. Only when the health of the child prevents it is the circumcision delayed. A daughter is named in the presence of a congregation, usually at the synagogue. In the Ashkenazic tradition (which is the source tradition for most of North American Jewry) the child will carry both English name(s) and Hebrew name(s). A beloved ancestor is posthumously honored by giving the name continuity through the newborn. A current tendency to have smaller families increases the tensions surrounding the baby naming as both the mother's and father's families vie for the honor of having a beloved name attached to the newborn. The rabbi's role will include counseling the families in achieving some compromise or combination in the choice of name, guiding the parents to choose the appropriate Hebrew name (especially when there is a change of gender involved which would change the Hebrew). The naming ceremony suggests life routine for the child, praying that parents may share the joy of being with the child as the child becomes immersed in Torah, guided into a good and lasting marriage and trained in the obligations of religiously motivated deeds of loving kindness.

The religious education of a Jewish child begins quite early. Jewish minority status has historically required a formal religious education to shape the child's awareness, values, and liturgical competence. There is a beautiful old European tradition that the child on the first day of his schooling will simultaneously be given a Hebrew book and a drop of honey on his tongue so that the process of learning will be sweet and tasteful for him or her. The parental options will vary from Sunday school systems to mid-week Hebrew systems to full-time separate Jewish day-schools. The choice of an educational system forces parents to encounter their own priorities and their own value systems. This is not always accomplished without significant intergenerational tensions. Strangely enough it is often the grandparents who themselves were shaped by a greater element of old country ethnic momentum who are most committed to the open society and the public school. Many times it is the younger generation whose ethnic momentum has diminished who want their children to have the specifics which can only be given by a separate Jewish school system. Again the rabbi plays the role of a counselor trying to develop with the family a pattern which resolves tensions in a manner best leading to the well-being and the religious character formation of the child.

Coming of age ceremonially in Judaism was once primarily focused upon sons. The Talmud suggests that at the age of thirteen a son becomes responsible for obeying God's Commandments (*Bar Mitzvah*). A tradition developed requiring the lad to stand in the presence of a congregation, to read from the Torah scroll with competence and skill, and often to display further indications of his readiness as an educated Jew to assume his emerging role as an adult in the community. At thirteen, a son is regarded as an adult and may be counted in the required quorum of ten for congregational prayer. This ceremony has special validity in Western culture. At precisely the time when most boys are threatened by the

rapid maturation of girls their own age, and by their own glandular transitions, Judaism signals the youngster that coming of age is not to be found in smoking cigarettes or other anti-social assertions of independence but manhood may be found in accepting a demanding, sanctified challenge and mastering it. The lad then must stand up at a service and indicate to everyone important to him and his family that he is capable of assuming adult skills and responsibilities.

Since the turn of the century, in response to egalitarian treatment of women, there has been a growing custom among Conservative, Reform and Reconstructionist Jewish communities for a daughter to have Bat Mitzvah. In many congregations, this would entail a parallel pattern for girls to do liturgically precisely what boys do at that age, thus signaling the growing responsibility of women in the continuity of Jewish tradition and in the survival of Jewish religious institutions.

Once again the joy of the ceremonial moment interweaves with the tensions of preparation. Sensitive tasks include the choosing of some relatives for ceremonial honors while excluding others. Resistance by the child to the training program and family tensions arising out of the forthcoming festive occasion often bring the rabbi into counseling situations which demand sensitivity and skill. It is to the rabbi that the task will frequently fall of recognizing the intense need of grandparents for some form of specific recognition as the busyness of parents often ignores them and their needs. A rabbi sensing their dilemma will often arrange for specific moments of recognition and reassurance.

In the process of raising children few milestones offer quite as many complex challenges and difficulties as does the time of marriage. The interacting complexities increase geometrically as future in-laws meet to approve or disapprove and to try to negotiate harmoniously. Personality conflicts, different anticipations of religious observance, the allocation of the financial responsibilities of what is often a very costly and lavish occasion are among the most frequent precipitates of a visit to the rabbi. Some very observant families will refuse to participate in or even attend a wedding if held in a more liberal Reform and Conservative synagogue, thereby attempting to coerce the other in-laws into a setting acceptable to themselves. Many liberal parents will give ground at this point in the belief that the well-being of the couple may require giving in to the demands of the more observant set of parents. Greater numbers of liberal Jews who are equally convinced of the rightness and the quality of their own religious commitment will refuse to go along with the coercion. Again the rabbi becomes the negotiator and the conciliator. Of extreme importance to many will be the issues brought about where there has been a prior divorce by the wife. A religious divorce is essential before a woman may be allowed to participate in a traditional marriage. Even where the couple is not orthodox in observance, there are very severe implications for the children of a marriage where an acceptable religious divorce has not been obtained prior to the marriage ceremony. Illegitimacy in Judaism is not a function of birth prior to marriage; rather, illegitimacy involves the birth of a child by a father other than the husband to whom a woman is consecrated. In the absence of a form of deconsecration through a religious divorce (*get*) the entire line of descendants may be barred from marriage with traditionally oriented untainted family lines. Since many North American Jews are simply unaware of the implications of a woman's remarriage after civil divorce it is the obligation of the rabbi to point out some of the implications to her and where possible to guide her in making critical decisions affecting the future of children who may be born to her new marriage.

The openness of North American society and the secularization of values has led to a level of exogamous marriages previously unknown in Jewish life. In many of these cases, the non-Jewish spouse will choose to convert to Judaism through some form of study program. This process is often intricate and demanding. There are many traditionalists who look upon marriage as an inadequate rationale in the accepting of converts. On the other hand, the great survival instinct of the Jewish people often creates pressures which are contrary to this traditional opinion. The rabbi involved in a conversion process has to develop sensitivities which may lead him to refuse to convert the person planning marriage to a Jew. Conversion involves a careful assessment of motivation and the identity-change difficulties involved in an honest and sincere reshaping of religious orientation. Even where the parents of the potential convert are enthusiastically in favor of the conversion and the marriage, their very existence and the pattern of their religious observance as well as their continued involvement with their grandchildren fight against the process. Rabbinic counseling in intermarriage situations and in the conversion involved therein calls for the highest level of empathy with the converting partner and in many cases insight into the Jewish partner and why it is that this partner deliberately sought to marry someone whose roots and family background did not parallel his or her own. Premarital counseling is highly desirable and careful guidance indicating the additional problems faced by those who cross religious boundaries are all essential.

Greater longevity coupled with greater mobility has created special problems for the Jewish family. When family members remain within reasonable proximity traditional values tend to stay intact. A continuing personal involvement with aging parents and grandparents, continuing supportive relationships of the community even to those aged who do not have responsible descendants, remains one of the glories of Jewish community values. But families separate and parents move away. Divorce is not only a function of the young. Divorce and remarriage offer special problems to descendants who may feel some diminished responsibility for the linear ancestor but little or no responsibility for the spouse of that ancestor. From their early teens children and grandchildren begin looking forward to "going away to college." Many never return. Their children know their grandparents not as intimates but as somehow special people visited on rare symbolic occasions. The fact that many parents and grandparents leave what had been the familial community and move to other regions of the country contributes to a breakdown in not only family support but the supportive role of community agencies. The rabbi therefore finds himself with a wonderful set of values but

geographical and emotional impediments which make their application extremely difficult.

Counseling encounters will frequently deal with after-death guilt as well as death-bed expressions, hostility, and feelings of desertion. In spite of extensive charitable contributions (which may be the highest of any ethnic group in the world) the Jewish community finds itself hard pressed to deal with not only the physical needs of an aging population (many of whom survive below the poverty line) but with special emotional needs as the Jewish community strives to fulfill long-standing religious obligations designed to retain the dignity and well-being of the aged.

Many couples faced with aging parents find themselves simultaneously faced with children in their twenties and thirties whose life pattern has yet to come into focus. Early presumptions that parents had adequately provided for their own financial retirement and expectations that children by their mid-twenties would be self-sufficient are often not realized. The "middle generation" finds itself harassed and troubled, wondering when there will be a time without draining obligations — a time when they can simply enjoy years together. Judaism is very clear in setting responsibilities both to parents and to children. These intergenerational tensions, especially where the "middle generation" is educated in an ideal which they have somehow failed to fulfill, lead to intricate problems involving guilt, anger, and lack of self-worth.

Self-worth as a mirror of conflicting values occupies a very important part in rabbinic counseling. The secular society and current Jewish attitudes place upon Jewish children a heavy responsibility to "succeed." Because of the tendency of the community to honor those who make significant economic gifts to the community and its institutions or those who have made extraordinary contributions to humanity, there is growing anxiety among young Jews who have difficulty finding their own path through the forest. Young people confuse "being a success" with the right to be Jewish. Many counseling situations, such as those dealing with the retreat into cults, bring to the surface this particular self-image of being "unsuccessful," of being the less-than-achieving sibling. These individuals tend to carry the distorted conception that Judaism is available only to those who have achieved notably. Not only is the "success" syndrome a profound challenge to the rabbi's therapeutic capacities but the attempt to balance the consumerism, the narcissism, the self-centered dimensions of our culture against the self-acceptance inherent in Jewish values tax his capacities to the utmost. The refuge of the young into internal frontiers aided and abetted by fashionable mysticism and consciousness distorting drugs offers to the rabbi a challenge that he shares with many of his colleagues in the Christian ministry.

Judaic counseling therefore is a full life cycle challenge beginning with prenatal counseling with the young parents and continuing on to after-death counseling with the descendants. Judaic counseling draws from the very rich sources of Jewish tradition but must somehow translate these effectively within a general culture which frequently signals values and objectives directly contrary to everything which Jewish tradition attempts to teach and to sanctify.

Bibliography. G. B. Bubis, *Saving the Jewish Family* (1987). M. McGoldrick, *Ethnicity in Family Therapy* (1982).

J. PEARLSON

FAMILY THEORY AND THERAPY; JEWISH CARE AND COUNSELING. *See also* BAR MITZVAH/BAT MITZVAH; CIRCUMCISION; JEWISH HOLY DAYS AND FESTIVALS; SEXUALITY AND SEX COUNSELING (Jewish Perspective). *Compare* JOURNALS IN MARRIAGE AND FAMILY COUNSELING; MARRIAGE AND MARITAL CARE (Jewish Perspective); SINGLE PERSONS, JEWISH CARE AND COUNSELING OF.

FAMILY, JEWISH THEOLOGY AND ETHICS OF.

Nothing is more important to the Jewish religion or the Jewish ethos than the family. Judaism is the religion of the Jewish people, which is likened to a family from its inception. Indeed, in patriarchal times, the Jewish community was precisely a family and God's promise of fruitful increase was a promise to the clan of Abraham, Isaac, and Jacob and his children. The fate of the community in Genesis hangs upon the fidelity and security of the primal family. Throughout its history the Jewish family has been the matrix of Jewish civilization.

1. Biblical. In biblical Judaism, the family (*mishpahah,* and other terms) is polygynous and endogamous as well as patriarchal. While several wives are clearly permitted, many are not common, and when a man marries several women, he often suffers for his choice. Abraham has only one wife at a time, and Isaac only one; Jacob means to marry only Rachel, but Leah is also forced upon him by their father. A royal person, like Solomon, with many wives is considered objectionable, partly for that reason, by most Biblical writers.

There is a continuous tendency to marry close to the group, typically to marry cousins, and this leads to the position that only marriage among Jews is proper. The strength and the unity of the community has always been closely tied to endogamous marriage. In the Bible, it is only renegades like Esau who tend to marry out, and after the restoration, Ezra insists on expelling the foreign women whom the Jews, left in the Land of Israel, have married.

The Bible does not describe a ceremony of marriage. In all probability the basic act was one of intercourse, which the Talmud still regards as a minimally satisfactory legal marriage. Deut. 24.1 prescribes a basis for divorce which is both simple and equivocal. The rabbis debated whether only a grave offense sufficed for divorce, or whether almost anything that displeased the husband could be cause to divorce his wife. Clearly, divorce was an option for biblical men, but we do not usually hear of its employment even in very difficult marriages. Only sterility, ascribed inevitably to the woman, seems to have been sufficient reason for separation. Biblical marriage and divorce appear to us as civil acts, though for biblical Jews the distinction between religion and civil law is almost invisible.

The purpose of marriage is the procreation of children. The characteristic Jewish tendency to perhaps overvalue children begins in biblical times. Nothing is thought of as more catastrophic than to die childless, and nothing is more rewarding than a large and loyal family. One's "name" is carried on by one's offspring, particularly male offspring, and the Levirate obligation (Deuteronomy 25) is meant to fulfill the need of a deceased brother for a son to carry on his lineage and his self. While the Bible normally forbids marriage to sisters, if one's brother dies, a man is obligated to offer his widow the opportunity to bear children in honor of her first husband. Adultery, forbidden by the Ten Commandments and elsewhere, is particularly heinous because it confounds the clear line of parents and children, rendering the perpetuation of one's "name" doubtful.

The biblical family is surrounded by obligations like circumcision of newborn males and, insofar as death rites are described, they are understood as being gathered to one's ancestry. The family is the basic unit of biblical life and even of the community of the dead. Judaism is one great family and, in the messianic future, the whole world will become one still greater family of families, as Amos envisions. A Jew is born into a family, lives in a family, dies to return to the clan, and ultimately is included in the great human family itself.

2. Rabbinic. Rabbinic Judaism may be conceived as a theology of family. The primary commandment is to marry and raise children. The number of children required as a minimum is usually held to be two, perhaps one of each sex. Both husband and wife must consent to any marriage, and must be old enough to understand their commitment fully. Marriage between strangers is not allowed, though families can arrange matches or have matches arranged, subject to the couple's later approval.

The purpose of marriage is companionship in its fullest sense. This includes the sexual rights of both parties (the wife's rights are especially clearly delineated) and the need to be together in a more than formal sense. Marriage is effected by a legal document, a gift, or even by intercourse itself, provided that the intercourse is meant to bind the couple in wedlock and that they are otherwise permitted to one another. A man may divorce his wife by mere repetition of a formula, at least in principle, but the wife's financial and personal rights are increasingly protected by the stipulations of her *ketubah,* the document signed before the wedding which prescribes her husband's obligation in case of their divorce or his death. Divorce, though not stigmatized, was rare in Jewish circles, though even some outstanding sages were divorced, and divorced persons usually remarried. Couples who could not have children or who could not give each other true companionship were not required to remain permanently together in an unhappy marriage.

Much of rabbinic law describes the obligation of children to their parents, the reverse being understood as far less in need of detailed commandment. The obligation to honor one's parents included both father and mother, grandparents, in-laws, and even older siblings. The law embodied a far-reaching web of obligation, beginning with pious gratitude expected toward those who gave us life. Children were expected to live near their parents normally, so that they could continue to offer them personal service. They were expected to support their aging parents financially, and to reverence them by not invading their personal space nor demanding their private time. "Honor" meant obedience to lawful parental authority, and both generations were subject to a divine law which cuts across all merely human lines.

It was well understood by the rabbis that there would be inevitable conflict between parents and children, especially married children. One's duty to one's spouse clearly superseded any putative obligation to one's parents, and a wicked parent was not to be obeyed, though even he or she was, somehow, still to be honored. Problems of senile and disturbed parents are not unknown to the rabbis, and their solutions are pragmatic and realistic, though never abandoning the sacred principle of parental honor.

Resolution of conflict between the generations is a strong desideratum of rabbinic thinking. Time and effort, counseling and meditation help to ameliorate intergenerational animosity, which is neither to be ignored nor sentimentalized, but also not ratified. The Jewish family is conceived of as a real, human family with real and lasting hostility as well as real and lasting bonds of affection, both of which are inextricably connected. It is not perfect parents whom we are to honor, nor are children thought to be capable of honoring their parents without the precise and continuous direction of rabbinic law. Parents must continually restrain their desires to control the next generation, and children must continually refine selfish desires to abandon their own obligations. But partial resolution is possible in the short run for many conflicts, and, in the messianic future, children and parents will at last be fully reconciled (Mal. 4:6). Perhaps intergenerational harmony is at the essence of messianic expectation and hope. The messianic age signifies an all-embracing, all-fulfilling eschatological clan, one partly foreshadowed already by our own little family itself.

3. Medieval. S. D. Goitein has described the medieval Sephardic Jewish family of the Mediterranean world from materials found in the Genizah of Cairo, where official documents were placed. He notes the extraordinary attention to family throughout the Jewish world. Though families were not very large, children were welcomed and usually named for their beloved ancestors. They provided not merely economic safety nets for parents, but, far more important, they were sources of pleasure and opportunities to teach Jewish values to a new generation. Endogamy, practiced even more closely than in rabbinic times, meant that families were usually cross-related and normally very, very close. An extended family raised the children of each as quasi-siblings and indoctrinated them all in the religious culture of their community. Families undertook joint economic projects and often lived off the patrimony that they jointly inherited.

Medieval Jewish marriage was sanctified by law and belief, by courts and conscience, though divorce was always possible, even easy, for couples who both desired it. Parents had an important voice in choosing their children's spouses, sometimes a decisive one, though since marriages often took place between cousins or other close relatives, the couple knew one another very well long before the wedding. The ceremony itself was both a legal contracting and a religious celebration, often both elaborate and protracted. The documents of marriage and the courts which authorized them tried consistently to shore up the wife's protection, even in the setting of a fully patriarchal system, and usually with success. For example, despite the prevalence of polygamy, no man could take a second wife, or even a female slave, without his wife's permission. Occasionally, she would actually urge him to add another spouse to relieve her of household or sexual responsibility.

Women represented a "world within a world," separated in so many ways, yet bound to the male world by ties of affection and economic need. The names of these Sephardic women were rarely biblical; they more often spoke of mastery and power in their Arabic forms, ("Lioness," "Mistress of Cities"). Women took responsible economic roles and often traveled widely. They knew less Torah but had more worldly wisdom than some of their men. Some were affluent, many independent, in a world where slaves did the hard work and men made the money. If their husbands mistreated them (and some did), they had easy recourse to a judge who would inevitably protect battered wives, even where the evidence for brutality was slender. A husband was not allowed even to curse, much less to strike his wife in anger. If he did, he would learn to be sorry.

Widows and orphans were gathered, more informally than legally, into a family by tacit adoption. Widowers almost always remarried soon, and widows almost as often. But if a woman was left alone, or if children were orphaned, the larger family of families was quick to provide for their needs and to give them shelter and surcease.

4. Modern. The contemporary Jewish family is more disparate, assimilated and difficult to describe than its predecessors. Children are clearly still cherished and protected, but the Jewish birth rate is one of the lowest in the world, and actually threatens the future demographic possibilities of the group. Intermarriage is on the rise, perhaps reaching forty percent in some areas, but there is a good deal of conversion to Judaism, among women in particular. Divorce is also much more common than in the past, but remarriage remains the usual pattern. The Jewish community has not yet created institutional forms for its single components. It seems that, while familial ties and familial conflict remain important, the modern nuclear Jewish family is becoming not only smaller but also cooler and more remote. We can look forward to families that look rather less like a traditional Jewish family, with working mothers, protean fathers and only children who must quickly learn to act like adults.

A number of models suggest themselves for the Jewish family in our time. It has been likened to a corporation with the father as the chairman of the board, the mother as manager and the children as stockholders. Each has a commodity to sell and needs that only the others can fulfill.

Some Jewish families play, instead, at paradise. They are, indeed, "havens in a heartless world," hermetically shut out from the ills and threats of the greater political world around them. Regression is not only permitted to each member of the family, but expected. A recurring nursery scene is obsessively repeated, leaving no member strong enough or mature enough to face the real and impersonal world beyond the walls of home.

Other Jewish families are more like a cult. They practice child-worship, living for the successes and perfections of the offspring, sacrificing for their future in an orgy of mutual gratification. The ceremonies of Judaism are, in this model, inevitably childish: Bar Mitzvah becomes the most crucial day in the family's life, and Passover is reduced to eating the bread of a pre-historic paganism. The young can be systematically seduced, persuaded, adored, manipulated and used as machines for the gratification of parental needs that are otherwise unfulfilled.

In the U.S. the most common family model seems to be the congressional. Each member has a vote, perhaps the father has a veto. Competition and compromise mandate small successes and the limits of power on each member of the group. Indignation and loss of dignity, as Erikson has pointed out, may be the price we pay for a stasis in which families meet one another's most pressing needs without ever pressing the other to transcend those very needs. Checks and balances can reduce conflict to manageable proportions, but they do not inspire a religious faith or moral achievement.

The most authentic Jewish model is perhaps still the school. From rabbinic times on, the Jewish family has considered as its primary obligation the care and training of its young, mutual self-criticism and life-long instruction of its old. Such a family is neither a retreat nor a political alternative. It is a necessary role for a family of families. It results in a millennial tradition of clan and clan-responsibility. It is a place where human dialogue is possible and a place where human community is foreshadowed. Martin Buber's "I and Thou" is most likely an idealized description of Jewish marriage, or of the relationship of parents and children.

A wise counselor of the Jewish family would search out those elements of their togetherness that promise therapeutic education. He or she would look for mutuality, responsible rebellion, achievement without invidiousness. He or she would encourage the separation of functions between the generations and a mature acceptance of parental authority, paralleled by traditional Jewish honoring of parents, but in a context more open to change and to self-consciousness than in the past. Such a family would be a school for primary process: touching, fondling, kissing—but also letting go. It is a setting for Torah: instruction in skills and acceptance of norms. It is necessarily both repressive and remissive, uniquely close and yet carefully non-suffocating. This is, of course, an ideal, but it is also a metaphor for the great messianic family of the future, when all the families of the earth will live in peace and love. For our own Jewish family to be such a metaphor is already to bring it into the scope of eternity itself.

Bibliography. G. Blidstein, *Honor Thy Father and Mother* (1975). E. B. Borowitz, *Choosing a Sex Ethic: A Jewish Inquiry* (1969). R. de Vaux, *Ancient Israel: Its Life and Institutions* (1961), pp. 19–55. S. D. Goitein, *A Mediterranean Society III: The Family* (1978). K. J. Kaplan, M. W. Schwartz, M. Markus-Kaplan, "The Family: Biblical and Psychological Foundations," *J. of Psychology and Judaism* 8 (1984), 77–196. M. Lamm, *The Jewish Way In Love And Marriage* (1980). C. G. Montefiore and H. Loewe, *A Rabbinic Anthology* (1974 [1938]), XXII–XXIV. R. Patai, *Sex And Family In The Bible And The Middle East* (1959). A. J. Wolf, *"Toward A Theology Of Family,"J. of Religion and Health*, 6:4 (1967) 280–89. M. Zborowski and E. Herzog, *Life Is With People* (1962 [1952]).

A. J. WOLF

DIVORCE AND REMARRIAGE (Judaism); FAMILY PLANNING; JEWISH LIFE; MARRIAGE (Jewish Perspective); SEXUALITY, JEWISH THEOLOGY AND ETHICS OF. *Compare* FAMILY, CHRISTIAN THEOLOGY AND ETHICS OF; PERSON (Jewish Perspective).

FAMILY, PASTORAL CARE AND COUNSELING OF.

The church has always regarded the family as its special concern. In Western societies it was the church that validated marriages and legitimated the birth of children. For most of its history, the church's care for families has been subsumed under the sacramental and ritual life of faith. Religious rites associated with birth, puberty, marriage, and death continue to be modes of care that enable individuals and families to live through the stress that usually accompanies change and loss. The recent development of the family systems perspective has introduced new approaches to the care of individuals and families.

1. The Church as an Advocate for the Family. So far as we know, there has always been something like what we call the family to protect and nurture those who are young. Only recently, however, we have begun to explore the ways in which the whole human story might be told in terms of household events. The history of Israel is often carried by family stories. Although the continuity of the church as the New Israel is not dependent on family lineage, the early Christian community is often described in family metaphors. The Bible everywhere assumes the significance of the family as a context for criticism and care even though its importance is modified by the claims of discipleship.

The church has sought throughout its history to establish and maintain the sanctity of the home. It has taught that the family is the vehicle for God's continual creation and rule. In ways that have ignored the diversity across cultures, the church has sometimes declared that there is only one family structure that fulfills the plan of God. Within some branches of Christianity, it is still claimed that questions about sexual expression and procreation are the province of the church and not the family. Nonetheless, the church continues to be an advocate for family life and a context in which questions about the purpose of the family can be examined and debated.

2. Pastoral Care and the Family Life Cycle. The family is an organism of change. Some of that change is unexpected. Some of it is inevitable as individuals within the family grow up and grow older. Because the family is always changing, adaptability is one of its essential characteristics. To believe in a God who is always making something new means that change is an unavoidable dimension of each family structure.

We have assumed that individuals change throughout the entire life cycle according to relatively predictable phases. So do families. Every individual life cycle crisis is also a family crisis. Individual transitions into and out of different family roles—such as leaving home, getting married, becoming parents, coping with widowhood—are interrelated with changes in the family as a system. These life cycle ceremonies provide a framework for families to change as well. They are "hinges of time" on which doors can open or close for several generations. The church's access to families at these nodal events is a privilege and an opportunity for a ministry with individuals and with entire families for the sake of growth and stability.

3. Attending to Individual and Communal Needs. Pastoral ministry with families in the midst of a life cycle transition often requires attending to individual needs *and* attending to the needs of the family as a whole in a balanced way. The dialectic between individual and community, being separate and being together is embodied in the ritual life of the church. On the one hand, the rituals of the church focus on incorporation into community: we are baptized into the whole company of the faithful; the Eucharist is a community meal; marriage makes "one flesh" of two separate individuals. On the other hand, rituals of the church are also moments which foster individuation. At every significant moment in the life of a Christian, each one is identified as a distinct and unique child of God. The ministry of care with individuals experiencing a life cycle crisis is also a ministry to family which itself is in a crisis requiring adaptation and change. Our ministry with families is at the same time a focus on the individuals in the midst of community.

The pastor's access to families at significant life cycle events provides unparalleled opportunities for ministry to the organism as a whole as well as to individuals. The pastoral task at each life cycle event is to reframe the transition in terms of the family as a whole so that the family might be a healing resource rather than a source of tension. Religious rites and family rituals provide necessary structures of transition that balance individual development and family change by honoring autonomy and celebrating community simultaneously.

4. Leaving and Joining for the Sake of Getting Married. The wedding is a family ritual set in the midst of the process of getting married. It is, at one level, the merger of two systems that are competing for dominance. Those tensions are frequently evident at the wedding rehearsal. At other times marital conflicts over incidental matters between the newly married may be unacknowledged expressions of loyalty to one's family of origin that evokes a battle to determine which family's tradition will shape the emerging patterns of this newly forming unit.

The paradox of leaving and joining (cleaving) forms the emotional framework for this process of getting married. Premarital work is most effective when it can help the bride and groom continue to disengage from their families of origin in order to begin engaging with one another in the task of forming a new family. If both families of origin understand the process of getting married as an event of the whole family system, there is also the possibility of affecting more than one couple and more than one generation (H. Anderson 1984).

5. The Addition of Children as Both Gift and Challenge. The arrival of a child into the worlds of family and church is both a gift and a challenge. It is a gift of new life because the unpredictable but creative energies of the newly born invigorate human community and reaffirm our belief in the future that God continues to make new. The addition of children is also a challenge to change because it requires that a family modify previously determined and sometimes fixed patterns of interaction in order to create a hospitable space for the new child.

The arrival of a child may signal a significant set of losses — loss of privacy, loss of energy, loss of time, loss of role, loss of emotional availability—which a young family may choose to ignore. Pastoral visitation and the rites of passage at birth both provide opportunities to attend to the loss and grief that are a part of an otherwise happy event.

Religious rituals of initiation and naming that surround the birth of children provide a framework for the family as a whole to engage in the care of its generations (Patton and Childs, 1988). The way in which a family understands the needs for individuation from the beginning of life will enhance the later process of leaving home. Families that are reluctant to adapt to change and slow to respect difference and unwilling to admit that their children are growing up and growing older are likely to establish rules that will exaggerate the ordinary turbulence of adolescence. It is particularly important that the rituals of the church around adolescence encourage diversity while affirming continuity.

Ministering with families of adolescents is difficult because it is a time of turmoil during which parents and children alike are expanding their horizons and developing their gifts for the world. Without a solid interactional frame of reference during this period in the family's history, it is easy for a pastor to take sides and thereby increase rather than decrease the family's tension. Being close without being co-opted by the family is always the pastor's delicate task.

6. Thinking Interactionally About People and Families. The development of an approach to the pastoral care of families that goes beyond ritual has been influenced by the emergence of the family therapy movement in the second half of the twentieth century. This therapeutic change is first of all an epistemological shift toward an interactional perspective on human nature. Thinking interactionally begins with the whole, with the interconnectedness of all life and the interdependence of the parts within the whole family in particular. From this perspective, it makes little sense to focus on individual emotional trouble apart from the distress of the system as a whole. Reframing or redefining family or congregational difficulties in terms of the whole system is the beginning of change (Friedman, 1985).

This interactional or systemic perspective about people has wide-ranging implications for the helping process in general and the pastoral care of families in particular. The helping person is looking for patterns of interaction and sequences of behavior within the organism as a whole more than the dynamics of individuals within the family system. Thinking interactionally about people in families means that intrapsychic conflicts are understood in the light of the interpersonal context and symptoms point in the direction of the whole rather than individual parts. The goal of a therapeutic intervention is to effect a change in the whole family system that will in turn benefit each individual within the family.

7. Characteristics of the Family as a Human System. Most versions of family systems theory hold several assertions in common: (1) the family is a system with a life of its own that transcends the sum of the individuals within it; (2) the dynamic forces operating within a family are as complex as the forces operating within an individual personality; (3) many of the most important processes going on in families remain hidden; (4) one extremely powerful process visible in all families is the family's tendency to keep itself (a) in existence, and (b) as unchanged in form and structure as possible; (5) one means that the family commonly uses to maintain itself is to assign significant roles to family members who collude in the process by accepting the assigned roles; (6) families, like individuals, come to exist, develop, flourish, and end in a life cycle that has certain predictable elements.

The family functions best when it maintains a delicate balance between the needs of the individual and the needs of the community or system as a whole. It is sustained by a careful synchrony between being intimate and caring *and* being separate and divergent. Boundaries are clear but permeable. In a sense, the family is always living in paradox. Rules are unambiguous but flexible. Loyalties are moveable but dependable. Roles are necessary but individuals are never defined by them. Children leave home so they can return. Parents let their children go so that they are free to belong to the family. The family is a context for individual growth when its individual members are committed to the family as a whole. The family that changes together is more likely to stay together.

8. Implications of the Interactional Perspective for Pastoral Care. *a. Taking initiative.* The introduction of family therapy interventions into the practice of pastoral ministry has emphasized anew the importance of pastoral initiative in general. In contrast to the nondirective or Rogerian approach that has dominated pastoral care for some time, the family systems perspective encourages greater activity on the part of the helping person. As a result there is less emphasis on the presumed neutrality of the helper and more deliberate and open use of the subjective reactions of the helper. This greater activity on the part of the helper in the therapeutic process presupposes clarity about one's authority and a willingness to use one's power in appropriate ways.

b. Home visitation. Because the contexts in which we live are important, family therapists have used home visits as a regular part of assessment and treatment. Visiting a family's home provides an unparalleled opportunity to learn about interactional patterns, values, how conflicts are dealt with, individual styles of living and ways of being together as a family that can best be learned by observing families in their natural habitat. A pastor who approaches his or her ministry from an interactional or systemic perspective will be committed to and comfortable with the traditional privilege of calling on parishioners in order to understand them more clearly and help them more effectively.

c. Circular rather than linear causality. Thinking in terms of family systems introduces a different and more circular way of understanding causality. When fault-finding and blaming are a part of the weaponry used in family, forgiveness and healing are more difficult. Parents will point to a child as the family's scapegoat if there is trouble in the marriage; husbands and wives may unwittingly sacrifice a child in order to keep the focus away from their relationship. The pain of divorce is exacerbated by the intent of one or both spouses to locate the blame for the divorce on the other spouse. If, however, causality is more circular than linear, purity is more difficult to maintain because responsibility is shared by the whole system. Pastoral insistence on the mutuality of fault in troubled marriages and families must be done carefully when people are in pain but it can enhance the possibility of mutual forgiveness and reconciliation.

d. Small change makes large change. It is often said from a family systems perspective that a small change will make for a large change. Although families (like individuals) seek help, thinking that a major overhaul of their family is the only solution, a seemingly small change in the family's structure, rules, allocation of role responsibility, distribution of power, or pattern of communication may be enough to unstick the system. The first, and most difficult task, is to reframe the family's problem in terms of the whole. The pastor's ability to think interactionally may be the small change that will make for large change in the family system. Expertise in family therapy techniques is less important for effective pastoral work with families than this capacity to think systemically and to be close to families without being caught up in their emotional swirl.

e. Differentiated pastoral leadership. The emphasis on the whole in family systems thinking does not diminish the importance of the differentiation of its parts. A family functions best when the boundaries that separate the parts are clear but permeable. Leaving home is a process of differentiating the self in the interest of autonomy and for the sake of the possibility of intimacy and forming a new family. The differentiation of the self is equally important in pastoral leadership in general and the care of families in particular. An organism tends to function best when its "head" is well differentiated. The effectiveness of one's pastoral ministry with congregations and with families finally depends more on the leader's capacity for self-definition than on the ability to motivate or change others (Friedman, 1985).

9. Pastoral Marriage Counseling from a Systemic Perspective. A systems perspective on pastoral counseling with troubled marriages begins with the assumption that the problem is with the whole rather than one individual part of the whole. The behavior one spouse complains about is often created and maintained by the whole system including one's family of origin. The circular causality that is characteristic of a systemic perspective keeps the focus on mutual accountability. Thinking interactionally about troubled marriages points to the importance of clarifying relationships with families of origin, uncovering buried grief that may be generations old as well as rectifying functional or affectional imbalance within the marital dyad.

Once couples have determined to divorce, the church has a special opportunity it has not always fulfilled to help people live through the grief of divorce. The capacity to begin a new relationship that will endure depends very much on how previous bonds have been "terminated" and grieved for. Very often, pastoral work with individuals who are marrying for the second time must begin by doing unfinished grief work from the previous loss. It is important to note that children may sometimes be the private bearers of that grief.

Preparing people for a second marriage is enhanced by looking at the whole system. Families of remarried persons are likely to be structurally top-heavy because of the proliferation of grandparents as well as stepparents. They are also commonly confused about boundaries and conflicted about loyalties. When a second marriage occurs there are hidden losses for the child who has been a surrogate spouse. The myth that the second marriage will be perfect creates its own terror. Because marrying a second time is so complex, pastors need to be prepared to help people sift through a number of emotional minefields that could undo a relationship before it has a chance to begin.

10. Chronic Illness in the Family and Pastoral Care. More and more attention is being given to the impact of chronic illness on the family and the impact of the family on the development of chronic illness. If one begins with the conviction that a family's emotional system mirrors the same kind of delicate balance that each individual organism must achieve, then it is possible that whether and how a family member gets sick may have much to do with the kind of stress being experienced by the family organism as well as that person's position in the system. Sickness in the family, especially if it is chronic, may be an expression of the organism's dis-ease. Individual pastoral care of the chronically ill, necessary as it is, should not preclude attending as well to the whole organism that may in fact be the occasion for the chronic illness. Recognizing the interdependence of family life will have wide-ranging consequences for pastoral ministry of which care for the chronically ill is one illustration.

There is hardly anything more complex and yet more critical than the church's response to the increase of violence in the family. Religious communities need to be critical of the ways in which the Bible, for instance, has been misused in support of violence toward women and children in the family. Despite the fact that religious beliefs have been used to support family violence, the church may be the only healing context in society. Because the church is a community that understands and does not ignore the presence of sin and evil in human life, it should be able to respond to perpetrators as well as victims of family violence with firm limits and genuine compassion. The church is a community of the forgiven and a forgiving community, and as such it is a place that should welcome both the abusers and the abused.

11. Family Pastoral Care and Larger Social Systems. Although the church regards itself as a guarantor of family well-being, it has not always functioned effectively as an advocate for public policy favorable to the family. As a result, family structures in our society have been significantly influenced by the implicit values of industrialization. The concern for the larger social, economic, and political context of the family is an extension of systems thinking. The church needs to add its voice to the debate about a public policy for the family particularly on behalf of poor families, minority families, and other families that have been disenfranchised by society.

Religious congregations continue to have significant opportunities to strengthen family life through programs in parent education or marriage enrichment, through support groups for families with special needs, through day-care centers and other forms of assistance for marginal groups, and through the creation of communities that provide a surrogate extended family for people who have been cut off from their roots. In all of these efforts, the church needs to be careful lest its efforts of support reinforce an already diminishing sense of competence in families today. Alongside its programs that are intended to promote family well-being, the church needs to provide a hospitable atmosphere for families who are discouraged or fearful or who fail to be all they would like to be or who have experienced more stress than they were able to endure.

12. The Family and Christian Discipleship. The family is a necessary component of creation. Despite wide diversity of form and function throughout human history, the family has fulfilled God's intent to provide a context for creation and care in order to ensure the continuity of humankind. From the perspective of Christian discipleship, however, the family can never be an end in itself. In order to be a vital human organism, the family is always moving outside itself for the sake of justice, peace, and freedom in ever-widening human communities.

The fundamental paradox is: the family is necessary for human life to continue *and* its significance is always limited. The systems perspective on family life enables us to acknowledge that growth toward autonomy is most likely to occur in families where the rules are flexible, the roles interchangeable, and the rituals dependable. It is the call to discipleship, however, that vitalizes family life by pushing us out of nurturing contexts into those ever-enlarging circles of human interaction in which God continues to make all things new.

Bibliography. D. A. Anderson, *New Approaches to Family Pastoral Care* (1980). H. Anderson, *The Family and Pastoral Care* (1984). E. H. Friedman, *Generation to Generation: Family Process in Church and Synagogue* (1985). J. Patton and B. H. Childs, *Christian Marriage and Family: Caring for our Generations* (1988). C. W. Stewart, *The Minister as Family Counselor* (1979). J. C. Wynn, *Family Therapy in Pastoral Ministry* (1982).

H. ANDERSON

FAMILY THEORY AND THERAPY; CONJOINT MARRIAGE AND FAMILY THERAPY; CROSS-CULTURAL MARRIAGE AND FAMILY. *See also* ADOPTION; STEPFAMILIES; COHABITATION; DIVORCE; EXCEPTIONAL CHILDREN AND THEIR FAMILIES; FOSTER CHILDREN AND FOSTER PARENTS; JOURNALS IN MARRIAGE AND FAMILY COUNSELING; MARRIAGE; PARENTS/ PARENTHOOD; REMARRIAGE; MARRIAGE AND FAMILY THERAPIST; RUNAWAYS; SINGLE PARENTS. *Compare* LIFE CYCLE THEORY AND PASTORAL CARE; MARRIAGE AND FAMILY LIFE, PASTOR'S; SINGLE PERSONS.

FAMILY, SOCIOLOGY OF. See FAMILY, HISTORY AND SOCIOLOGY OF.

FAMILY, SUICIDE'S. See SUICIDE (Pastoral Care).

FAMILY, THEOLOGY OF. See FAMILY, CHRISTIAN *or* JEWISH THEOLOGY AND ETHICS OF.

FAMILY CONFLICT. *See* FAMILY, PASTORAL *or* JEW-ISH CARE AND COUNSELING OF; FAMILY THEORY AND THERAPY; FAMILY VIOLENCE.

FAMILY COUNSELING/FAMILY COUNSELOR. *See* FAMILY, PASTORAL *or* JEWISH CARE AND COUNSELING OF; FAMILY THEORY AND THERAPY; MARRIAGE AND FAMILY THERAPIST.

FAMILY DYNAMICS. *See* FAMILY THEORY AND THERAPY.

FAMILY LAW. The law, both criminal and civil, that involves family relationships. Churches and synagogues treat birth, marriage, and death as events to be marked with special ritual observance and with understanding of spiritual significance. Therefore, pastors and pastoral therapists are often in a strategic position to serve families at these points of change in family structure. A knowledge of the law affecting the families in the jurisdiction in which the professional is working is essential.

1. **Law Affecting Children.** With medical advances and new social attitudes toward children and family, the law has had to develop to cover new situations. Not too long ago, adoption was an innovation. Now with genetic engineering, the law is again growing in order to evaluate and define the interests and rights of persons who bring their conflicts to the courts and legislatures.

The possibilities of *in vitro* fertilization and implantation in the same woman or in a second woman have resulted in legally complex relationships. *In vitro* gestation will provide even more questions regarding legal responsibility and liability. When the law is uncertain, the parties involved may attempt to bring clarity to the situation by entering into contracts spelling out the consequences of foreseeable events.

Adoption is a concept with which we are now familiar. Through adoption legal responsibility for an individual (minor or an adult) is transferred by a court from natural parents to other persons. However, adoption is a fairly recent innovation in the U.S. It was not permitted at common law and in the U.S. was first authorized by statute in the 1840s. Adoption without parental consent is even more recent and is authorized in special situations such as proof of parental unfitness. Often statutes provide for three stages in the adoption process: (1) termination of the legal rights of the natural parents toward the child; (2) an interim decree giving the adoptive parents custody and providing for a placement evaluation; and (3) a final decree of adoption based on what is in the best interest of the child. Once the adoption is court-approved, it is usually permanent unless there is evidence of a fraudulent concealment or ignorance of a disability. Under most statutes the original birth certificate and the court record of the adoption are placed beyond the reach of the child and outsiders without a court's authorizing access. The adoptee, the natural parents, and the adopting parents may have different interests and feelings regarding the access by the adoptee to information about the natural parents.

Artificial insemination by a donor raises a host of legal questions that go well beyond those that are inherent in a legal adoption. With sperm banks and the freezing of sperm, a child can be conceived years after the father's death. This new development has required rethinking of legal concepts regarding illegitimacy, support demands, and inheritance of property.

Genetic counseling and screening—both voluntary and compulsory—raise questions about the rights to reproduce if there will be substantial injury to the offspring. Knowledge of genetic defects can be both beneficial and harmful to the carrier. Knowledge known but withheld from a patient can result in lawsuits. Rights to abortion and actions for wrongful life illustrate the complexity of newly developing law. Deformed newborns, the duty to prolong a child's life, and the child's right to die are other problem areas complicated by the inability of the child to give an informed consent to a choice.

What are the legal consequences when a child and parents disagree about psychiatric treatment or pastoral therapy? Does the minor have the right to treatment against the wishes of the parents? Does the minor have the right to refuse treatment if the parents are trying to force it on the child or adolescent? What are the parental rights to commit a minor to an institution? What happens to confidentiality of communication if a minor is in treatment and the parents pay for the treatment? Should the age of the minor make any difference in the rights granted? It would be helpful to be able to point to clear-cut legal decisions on these issues. However, often the law is not easy to ascertain because of the lack of statutes or cases on the subject. The best protection for the practitioner is to consult a lawyer and to be aware of law that does exist in the jurisdiction. For example, there are statutes in many states that cover specific situations such as child abuse, gunshot wounds, and some infectious diseases that require certain persons to report to governmental agencies even though general rules regarding confidentiality must be broken to do so.

Children who disobey the law are treated in a different manner than adults. Juvenile courts in the U.S. are considered civil courts rather than criminal. Until the 1967 Supreme Court case of *In v. Gault*, it was not clear that the child had some of the constitutional rights and other legal safeguards that protect the adult offender. Juvenile court judges often complain of the frustration of having to send children who have never been taught to obey the law to institutions in which they are not likely to reform. The cost of institutional care for these minors is great. The protection of the children and the protection of society from the acts of these youths are continuing concerns.

The pastoral therapist also may need an awareness of the laws regarding treatment of children in schools and institutions. Token economies and behavior modification provide special legal problems because of the element of coercion. Rights of retarded children and their families may be of interest to pastors. The minor who is a research subject or a transplant donor is accorded special legal protections by the law. Because children often do not have the capacity to protect themselves when their interests conflict with those of adults, the law has found it necessary to give them special treatment not accorded competent adults.

2. **Marriage and Cohabitation.** Changes in family structures have forced changes in the law. Lawyers today

have to deal with high divorce rates, serial marriages, cohabitation of unmarried couples, employment of both partners, homosexual "marriages," and various forms of multiple sexual relationships. However, marriage is not just a private relationship but has a contractual nature in which the state has an interest. In the U.S., state law governs marriage and divorce and may vary from jurisdiction to jurisdiction.

Because clergy are involved in the solemnization of marriages, it is important that they know the provisions of the governing statutes. There are conditions a couple must meet before the marriage will be considered valid. Often, the statutes indicate the responsibilities of officiating clergy for filing marriage certificates with the responsible state official. Penalties may be specified for failure to comply.

While statutes governing marriage and divorce have tended to become less restrictive, leaving more freedom to the couple, the rights of one partner against another can be enforced. Property and child custody rights may be accorded even cohabiting but unmarried couples. It is not unusual for formal contracts to be signed before the marriage that specify the rights and duties of the parties. Care must be taken with such contracts because there are some provisions that will make the agreement unenforceable because they are against public policy. Annulments of marriages may take place if consent to the marriage is based on a delusional belief or if there is intentional concealment of a serious mental disability. Some knowledge of the applicable state laws regarding marriage will be helpful to the pastoral therapist.

The laws governing divorce also are changing. State statutes specifying the grounds of divorce or of no-fault divorce are of consequence in marriage counseling. Leaving home by one of the partners of a marriage may be a therapeutic maneuver, but it may have legal consequences of being considered desertion that will be harmful to the person involved. Confidentiality becomes a special problem for the therapist who may be called to testify about admissions made in family therapy. The law governing confidentiality of therapy sessions involving more than one patient is not clear in many jurisdictions. The currently popular divorce mediations also may present the practitioner with legal and ethical questions regarding the representation of more than one person and unauthorized practice of law if the proper scope of mediation is not carefully observed.

Child custody is another problem that may involve parents, relatives, or others in legal maneuvers. Although the "best interest of the child" is the guiding principle in custody decisions, it does not give the answer to what to do with the child. Parental rights often become the battlefield. Visitation rights, child support payments, joint custody issues — all present situations in which the balancing of interests is difficult. Moreover, as conditions affecting the best interest of the child change with the growth of the child, so may the custody provisions.

Children have long been recognized as potential victims for abuse, although only recently has the prevalance of incest been acknowledged. Now, with the rights of women being given increasing attention, the problems of rape and battery are being reinterpreted from the time in which the husband and wife were considered legally one — that one being in all too many situations the husband. Violence toward the elderly also is being uncovered. Increasing occurrences of suicide and murder by young persons have dispelled the picture of youthful innocence.

Family violence constitutes a significant element in police work. The family therapist needs some acquaintance with what to do when the criminal law is violated and what duties and responsibilities may exist to break confidence to report clear and present danger in the family circle. Pastors and pastoral therapists do well to become acquainted with their law enforcement procedures and officials.

3. **Competence and Capacity of a Family Member.** Although competence and capacity issues are not limited to the family, it is in the family setting that the issues may be especially acute, and it is the family member who may need to take charge when a relative cannot function. Normally, a person will be released from a contract only if so incapacitated as to believe that the contract is a completely different type of agreement. The senile or manic-depressive family member can wreak havoc with the financial security of other family members and can be a danger to him- or herself. Responsibility for the debts of a spouse may place a marital partner in financial difficulties. State statutes exist that provide for a conservator of the estate or a guardian of the person.

Wills, by which a person can dispose of an estate after death, require less capacity than contracts or the appointment of conservators because the chance of fraud is less. In order to make a valid will, the person should know what property exists to be given away, have a plan for its disposition, and be aware of the natural objects of concern. These requirements do not mean that property must be given to the family — only that recognition must be present that the person making the will is aware that there are family members who might expect to receive something from the estate. Persons are presumed to be sane until the contrary state of affairs is proved. Often, a family can avoid expensive court supervision of property by consulting a lawyer about the possibility of the establishment of trusts or the use of a power of attorney while the relative is alive, and about the possibility of a will and other estate planning to expedite the disposition of property upon death.

Perhaps the most difficult role for many family members is the care and protection of a dying relative. Questions may arise as to when the family has to take over the decision-making process because of the incapacity of the dying person to make a rational choice about life-sustaining measures. Physicians often consult family members even where there is capacity in the patient in order to protect themselves against the threat of malpractice suits by the relatives. Death also is a concern of the law that treats subjects such as the definition of death, autopsies, and burials.

4. **The Roles of Pastor and Pastoral Therapist.** The pastor or pastoral therapist may be involved in different roles in situations calling for the application of family law. When filing a marriage certificate with the proper state authorities, the pastor may be charged by statute to act on behalf of the state. Sometimes the pastor or pasto-

ral therapist will be treating the family or a member of the family in therapy and may be asked to testify by one person against a relative to whom the professional also owes a fiduciary duty. The administrator of a counseling center may be charged with responsibility for having family client interests protected and for seeing that staff members have continuing education opportunities to keep them abreast of legal developments that impinge on their work. The pastor or pastoral therapist may serve as an employee of a church school or a state institution with a primary loyalty to the employer but with various obligations to different family members. Theological training may equip a person to serve as an ethicist at a hospital. Pastors may be asked to serve on institutional review boards charged with the protection of research subjects. It is important for the professional in these various roles to be aware of the legal implications and liabilities of actions taken in dealing with a family.

Access to good legal advice is important and probably best secured through a continuing relationship with a lawyer who can become familiar with the professional responsibilities of the client. Because family law is changing with shifts in social and economic conditions affecting human relationships, it is not safe to assume that knowledge of the law acquired at the present time will suffice in the future. However, it will be helpful for the pastor to explore the public information pamphlets, professional seminars, and lawyer referral services provided by local and state bar associations. The review of subjects in this article is designed to alert the professional as to when to seek advice or to recommend to family members the need for legal counsel because of potential liability.

Bibliography. D. Bazelon, "Courts and the Rights of Human Beings, Including Children," in I. Berlin, *Advocacy for Child Mental Health* (1975). I. Berlin, "The Rights of the Retarded Child and His or Her Family," in I. Berlin, *Advocacy for Child Mental Health* (1975). L. Foster, "Group and Family Records," in H. Schuchman, L. Foster, and S. Nye, *Confidentiality of Health Records* (1982). A. Holder, *Legal Issues in Pediatrics and Adolescent Medicine* (1977). N. Lavori, *Living Together, Married or Single: Your Legal Rights* (1976). S. Ross and A. Barcher, *The Rights of Women* rev. ed., (1983). H. Schuchman, "Children's Records," in H. Schuchman, L. Foster, and S. Nye, *Confidentiality of Health Records* (1982). R. Schwitzgebel and R. Schwitzgebel, *Law and Psychological Practice* (1980). R. Slovenko, *Psychiatry and Law* (1973).

L. M. FOSTER

FAMILY VIOLENCE. *Compare* CHILDREN; FAMILY, HISTORY AND SOCIOLOGY OF; LEGAL DIMENSIONS OF PASTORAL CARE AND COUNSELING.

FAMILY LIFE, PASTOR'S. *See* MARRIAGE AND FAMILY LIFE, PASTOR'S.

FAMILY PLANNING. Frequently understood as a synonym for contraception, family planning can more accurately and usefully be thought of as the act of considering and, finally, deciding if and when and in what way to become parents. The process of family planning can contribute significantly to a couple's development of personal as well as sexual intimacy with each other. It most often becomes a pastoral issue at two points: (1) during pre-marital interviews, when the pastor raises the question of the couple's views on having children; and (2) when tension arises in a couple's relationship because of differing positions on the issue.

1. **If We Are To Have Children.** Because of the effectiveness of contraception, the choice about becoming parents may be a more difficult one now than at any time in history. Choosing to make a significant change in one's lifestyle is generally more difficult to do than to adapt to a change for which one is not fully responsible. In earlier generations, couples often dealt with the question by just letting pregnancy occur without seeing it as a choice that one or both of them had made. Now, the responsibility for having children is much more difficult to avoid. It is easier for partners to blame each other for the decision and, in the process, to add that tension to the change in lifestyle that parenting brings. Pastors can assume that the issue of being or not being parents is an issue or has been an issue with virtually every couple they see in pastoral care or counseling.

Moreover, family planning is not just a relational or psychological issue. It is an ethical and theological one as well. This is the primary reason it needs to be raised in a pre-marital interview. How one contributes to the future generation is important for the way one understands oneself as a human being. One does not literally have to have children to contribute to the next generation. In fact, part of one's contribution may be deciding not to, but choosing instead to find ways of nurturing or guiding the children of others. Whatever the decision, taking some responsibility for the future generation is an important way in which persons express their care for the world beyond themselves.

2. **When We Are to Have Children.** There is a burden of choice in the timing of parenting as well as in the decision about being parents at all. The issue here is physical, psychological and ethical/theological. There are biological factors which, though changing because of changing factors in health care, are inescapable. If a couple is to become parents, it must be done during a particular time relatively early in their life together. The decision to become parents affects the career goals of both, usually the woman's more than the man's, but inevitably both careers will be affected. The husband, for example, who is committed to the concept of a two-career marriage may find himself modifying his views in the light of what he may have to do in parenting to allow his wife to continue her career path. This, again, is an ethical and theological issue as well as a relational and psychological one. It affects and is affected by one's view of what human beings are and should be.

3. **In What Way We Are to Have Children.** This dimension of family planning may involve the number of children a couple chooses to have, the lengths they will go to become biological parents or to find satisfactory means of adoption, how they will express and develop their personalities as actual parents or how they will contribute to the future generation in a parental way without literally becoming parents. Again, these issues have obvious biological, psychological and theological/ethical dimensions. They become pastoral issues when a couple is open to or seeks pastoral care in dealing with

them. What the pastor needs in order to assist a couple with their issues of family planning is: (1) information about and understanding of at least some of what a couple is facing; (2) a point of view of his or her own about the biological, psychological and ethical/theological issues involved; and (3) enough personal sensitivity to assist a couple in making responsible decisions about family planning rather than surrendering their decisions to an external authority.

J. PATTON

CONTRACEPTION; FAMILY, CHRISTIAN *or* JEWISH THEOLOGY AND ETHICS OF; PARENTS/PARENTHOOD. *See also* ADOPTION; GENETIC COUNSELING; GUIDANCE, PASTORAL; LIFESTYLE ISSUES IN PASTORAL CARE. *Compare* ABORTION (Pastoral Care); MORAL BEHAVIOR AND RELIGION; MORAL DILEMMAS IN PASTORAL PERSPECTIVE; SEX EDUCATION.

FAMILY THEORY AND THERAPY. Family theory is a way to conceptualize the life of the family unit. It involves understanding the individual within the context of a dynamic family system with its own unique developmental stages, history, and cultural relatedness. Family therapy is a way of joining and restructuring a dysfunctional family system.

1. **Principles of Family Theory.** *a. The individual in family context.* Family system theory is based on the concept that the context in which a person lives affects the inner processes of that person. Each individual lives within the context of a family. Family system theory hypothesizes that changes in the context will produce changes in the individual.

Studies in many fields (sociology, psychology, animal behavior, and medicine) help support the connection between context and individual. Within the field of family theory, Toman explores the effect of birth position (first born, youngest, etc.) on identity and personality characteristics. Framo's studies of married couples explore the connection between husband and wife roles and expectations in each spouse's family of origin. Parental and spousal behavior is often copied from the context in which the individual is reared. Medical studies supervised by Minuchin indicate the relatedness of such diseases as anorexia nervosa and brittle diabetes to an individual's position within the family as well as to the dysfunction of the family system.

b. A dynamic system. In family system theory, the family is seen as a dynamic, open system, affected by the greater socio-cultural system in which it exists. The family has a structure, yet that structure is always in transformation, varying between the tension of change and the calm of stability. As time passes and members join and leave the family, the system restructures itself. The family system is seen as having to adapt to changing circumstances, yet having to maintain a sense of continuity to enhance the psycho-social growth of each of its members. Both flexibility and consistency are required attributes of a dynamic family system.

c. Developmental stages. During the normal restructuring of a family system over time, the family will pass through the following developmental stages:

i. Intimacy versus idealization and disillusionment. The work of this stage is to achieve intimacy as a couple with realistic perceptions of each partner as a whole person.

Partners must assume responsibility for themselves and negotiate differences to achieve mutual support and nurture in an unidealized, realistic way.

ii. Replenishment versus turning inward. At this time children are born and parenting begins. A major problem of this stage is that some mothers and fathers forget that good parenting begins with and must be maintained by a good marriage relationship.

iii. Individualization versus pseudo-mutual organization. During this stage, elementary-aged children begin to differentiate and become increasingly self-sufficient. If the movement from family interests to individual interests is inhibited, a fusion of family members occurs, producing an enmeshed, pseudo-mutual organization.

iv. Companionship versus isolation. As teenaged children move into their own social peer networks, parents must re-evaluate their own roles as spouses. Adolescents need parents who are fulfilled in their own adult spousal relationships.

v. Regrouping versus binding or expulsion. The young adult child moves out of the family during this stage. If the family can regroup and restructure itself, this movement away can be accomplished. If not, the young adult either is bound to the family and cannot leave or is expelled from the family and cannot return.

vi. Rediscovery versus despair. In this postparental stage, the couple must rediscover themselves and their spousal commitment. All children have now grown and left home, and the pre-retirement parents must form new experiences and new community connectedness.

vii. Mutual aid versus uselessness. In this final stage of family development, the retired couple mutually aid and support each other. A new sense of connectedness must be established with children and grandchildren.

d. Generational histories. As one family passes through its developmental stages another family begins. Children grow and marry, transforming parents into grandparents and initiating new sequences of family development. Parenting styles, spousing styles, coping styles, personality characteristics, and relational styles are often rooted in a three-generational history of an individual's family system. It is often helpful, therefore, to explore with an individual the history of the preceding generations to get a more complete understanding of the total family context (Bowen, 1978).

e. Socio-cultural interconnectedness. Not only is the family context influenced by the individuals forming its history, it is also affected by the greater context in which it exists. Family theory is beginning to look at this greater context, that is, cultural conditions, socio-economic status, ethnic values, religious belief systems, and governmental structures to see its effects on the development of the family and its members.

2. **Principles of Family Therapy.** *a. Health and wholeness within the individual and the family.* Family therapy begins with a positive premise. Within each individual there resides an energy which moves that individual forward in progressive stages of growth. If this energy is not restricted, the individual will have the ability to perceive, comprehend, and choose actions to continue the life process toward wholeness and health. Families also will move forward in progressive stages if their members are free to interact with each other in ways

that do not block the flow of creative energy. The family, therefore, is a living organism with a tendency toward both maintenance and evolution.

b. Individual problems as the result of dysfunctional family transactional patterns. Family therapy looks at the individual as part of the family. Individual problems, therefore, are conceptualized as a result of dysfunctional interactions within the family, which alter the context and thus the inner processes of the individual living within that context. If individual problems are seen as the result of maladaptive behavior within that social unit of the family, new ways of solving individual problems can be conceived.

c. Altering dysfunctional family patterns by changing sequences and structures. The structural school of family therapy conceptualizes the family as an organism and sees the symptoms as a reaction of the organism under stress. The goal of this school is alteration of the structure of the organism to reduce the stress. This is done by challenging the structure, the symptom, and the family view of reality.

The strategic school of family therapy conceptualizes the problem more in terms of specific repeated interactional sequences between members of the family. The symptom is seen as a protective, sacrificial act by one family member to preserve the family homeostasis. The goal of the strategic therapist is to identify the dysfunctional aspect of the interactional sequences and to alter the sequences surrounding the symptom, thus rearranging the organization and producing change.

d. The role of the family therapist as enabler. The family therapist is the person called upon by the family to help alter its own internal structure and functioning. The therapist must join the family system as a new member and from within assist the family in its own restructuring. Thus, the family therapist is seen as an enabler, helping the family to change itself.

3. Methods in Family Therapy. *a. Working with the whole family unit.* Since individual problems are conceptualized as a result of dysfunctions within the living human organism of the family, therapy must begin with the presence of the whole family unit, including residential grandparents or other extended-family members. In separated, divorced, or second-family systems, absent family members such as a former spouse can be represented by empty chairs.

Initial sessions are especially critical since family members will attempt to align with the therapist and convince him or her of their family worldview. If important family members are not present at the initial sessions, alliances could be made between members and therapist which could prove non-therapeutic when the absent family member is introduced into the therapy.

b. Seeing the identified patient as a family symptom-bearer. It is often an individual's behavior that prompts the movement toward therapy. The identified patient is seen by the family as the problem. The family therapist must see the patient not simply as the possessor of some form of individual pathology but as a family symptom-bearer. According to the structural school, the patient is reacting to the family organism stress in a way that makes it more contained and obvious. For example, a child's bedwetting might be seen as a reaction to a more subtle, yet more powerful family stress arising from an unresolved intimacy problem between the parents. The strategic school would more readily interpret the child's behavior as a way of drawing the family's concern to himself rather than to the parental dyad, thus preserving the status quo between the parents.

c. Seeing the symptom as a family metaphor. The symptom itself can be conceptualized as a metaphor for other actions causing greater stress within the family. For example, a daughter's run away behavior could be related to her father's withdrawal from his spousal relationship. A symptom may also be a dysfunctional expression of a healthy need. A boy's fear of animals may be a mechanism for creating contact with his father since the fear prevents his leaving the house without his father. The description of the behavior of the identified patient may also be a metaphor for the behavior of another family member. A mother who describes her son, the identified patient, as disrespectful, cold, and unloving may more accurately be describing her perception of her husband's behavior.

d. Joining the family system. Since a family system is a living organism, it will attempt to incorporate the therapist as a new member of the system in a way that will continue the family homeostasis. The therapist will need to join the family system in order to earn his or her right to lead and enable the family restructuring. The therapist must join, but he or she must not be dissolved by the ego mass of the family system.

Joining can be accomplished in a number of ways. Structural theorists suggest that the therapist begin by maintaining the structure already present in the family system. In this way the therapist is accepted within the current expectations and behavioral rules of the family and, once accepted, can begin to alter the structure from a position within it. Maintenance is accomplished by upholding the structure and hierarchy of the family system. Deferring to the father as the head of the household, asking permission from a husband to speak to his wife or from a mother to speak to her child continues interactional patterns already established in the family. Once joining has reached an acceptable level, restructuring can begin. When restructuring raises stress and anxiety to non-therapeutic levels, the therapist can return to joining functions, thus reducing stress and gaining new acceptance.

In addition to maintaining, the therapist can join the family system by tracking. Tracking is a method of adopting the content of the family communication and following it and then using it to produce the desired restructuring. By tracking the content of the communication presented by the family, by asking clarifying questions, and by exploring and expanding the meaning of the content the therapist gains entry into the mind-set of the individual members of the family. Using the content symbolically, the therapist can make restructuring suggestions that will be accepted by the family without their feeling challenged or confronted. A third method of joining is twinning, in which the therapist couples with the family's style, affect, and behavior. The therapist can duplicate the family's style of communication, or by duplicating body posture and movements, can affiliate with a certain family member.

Minuchin has suggested that joining can be done from different positions of proximity. In the close position the therapist joins by specific affiliation with individual members of the family system. In the medium position, the therapist becomes the active neutral listener, gently following and tracking the content and exploring actions that can be taken to change the behavior talked about in the content. The third or disengaged position sounds like a contradiction, yet it allows the therapist to join the family from the distanced position of an expert who makes observations or gives assurance.

e. Restructuring the family system. Having successfully joined the family system, the therapist experiences and observes the dysfunctional aspects of the family and begins the process of restructuring. The aim of restructuring is to free the family symptom bearer, to reduce conflict and stress in the family, and to help the family learn and experience new ways of coping. There are three major ways to accomplish restructuring:

i. Challenging the symptom. Since the symptom is a result of dysfunctional family patterns of interaction, one way to challenge the symptom is to challenge the interactions of the family. Rather than settling for verbal remembrances of actions and feelings, it is far better to have interactions happen within the therapy room so that the therapist can observe the patterns, see where the sequences of behavior break down, and suggest alternatives.

Another way of challenging the symptom is to help the family focus on some dysfunctional interactional pattern other than the presenting symptom. By shifting the focus, the symptom loses some of its intensity, and the family begins to think in terms larger than the presenting symptom.

ii. Challenging the family structure. The therapist can restructure a family system by observing current family boundaries and then altering them. By observing the way the family and its subsystems interact with each other—including where family members sit, who talks, who is silent—the therapist can challenge boundaries by having family members move or by asking quiet members to talk and more verbal members to listen and observe. Homework, tasks, and directives for action outside the therapy hour continue and strengthen the new boundaries.

Another way to challenge family structure is to change the hierarchial relationships already established within the family system and its subsystems. By joining with and supporting family members who do not currently enjoy much power, the therapist can unbalance the accepted hierarchy and create new stress within the family structure.

A third method is to emphasize the complementarity of all its members. The presenting problem of the identified patient can then be relabeled as a problem of the whole family.

iii. Challenging the family reality. In restructuring a family system the subtle, yet powerful family worldview will have to be challenged and altered. The therapist must understand this worldview and be able to see how and where it encourages and supports the dysfunctional behavior of the system. One way to challenge the worldview is by using universal symbols. This allows the

therapist to call on a transcendent power and allows the family to accept alternative ways of seeing things that are not directly confronting. Another way is to challenge family myths and perceptions of history where appropriate. A third way uses the power of the therapist as expert, allowing a different explanation of reality and experience to be entered into the family thinking.

4. **Implications for Pastoral Care.** *a. The family as the vehicle of faith.* The Judeo-Christian faith is a faith communicated through people and through families. The OT centers around the stories of families beginning with Adam and Eve. The faith was developed and transmitted by and through patriarchal families. The NT continues to enhance the family as the vehicle of faith through the stories of Mary, Joseph, and Jesus. Faith is proclaimed by individuals rooted in their own family structures.

In our contemporary religious community the family is still a vital part of the telling and retelling of the story of faith. Of all current institutions, the church is one of the few that serves and gathers whole families into its life. The rites of church burials, baptisms, and marriages are family events. Ministry is accomplished within the framework of the family. It is, therefore, important that the deliverer of pastoral care see beyond the individual and perceive the context and structure of the individual's family system.

b. The pastor as family consultant and educator. The pastor, because of love and concern for the persons and families touched by his or her ministry, has the opportunity and the challenge of becoming a family consultant and educator. The pastor can develop programs, sermons, and lessons to discuss family roles. Workshops can give expertise in handling family stress through negotiation and compromise. Experts in the field of family life can be invited to discuss family issues. Church policies can be altered to allow more family interaction in services and activities. Theology can be taught through family gatherings.

c. The pastor as family counselor. Persons who are hurting often go to a pastor as the first person with whom they will discuss their problems. A well-trained pastor will know how to assess the presented problem and either take on the counseling or make an appropriate referral. A knowledge of family system theory allows the pastor to see the person in context and, therefore, to conceptualize the problem in a way which gives greater alternatives for support and help.

d. The congregation as a family. Knowledge of family system theory and family therapy can also encourage the pastor to see the congregation as a family and to interact with it accordingly. The pastor can be aware of the developmental life stages of the congregation related to such factors as the ages of its members. Congregational events and services can be seen as extensions of family life and can be designed to involve all levels of membership. A system of congregational pastoral care can be developed in which laity are organized to support each other during developmental and situational crises. Conflicts and stress within the congregation can be explored from a systems point of view so that negotiation and compromise can be achieved between congregational subsystems. The entire life of the congregation can be experienced through the theories of family systems and can be altered beneficially through the theories of family therapy.

Bibliography. H. Anderson, *The Family and Pastoral Care* (1984). M. Bowen, *Family Therapy in Clinical Practice* (1978). H. Fishman and S. Minuchin, *Family Therapy Techniques* (1981). J. L. Framo and I. Boszormenyi-Nagy, eds., *Intensive Family Therapy: Theoretical and Practical Aspects* (1965). E. H. Friedman, *Generation to Generation: Family Process in Church and Synagogue* (1985). A. S. Gurman and D. P. Kniskern, *Handbook of Family Therapy* (1981). J. Haley, *Problem Solving Therapy* (1976). K. J. Kaplan, M. W. Schwartz, and M. Markus-Kaplan, "The Family: Biblical and Psychological Foundations," *J. of Psychology and Judaism,* 8 (1984), 77–196. S. Minuchin, *Families and Family Theory* (1974). S. Rhodes, "A Developmental Approach to the Life Cycle of the Family," *J. of Social Casework,* 58 (1977), 301–11. C. Stewart, *The Minister as Family Counselor* (1979). W. Toman, *Family Constellation: Its Effects on Personality and Social Behavior,* 2d ed. (1969).

B. J. HAGEDORN

FAMILY, PASTORAL CARE AND COUNSELING OF. *See also* DOUBLE BIND; FAMILY, HISTORY AND SOCIOLOGY OF; JOURNALS IN MARRIAGE AND FAMILY COUNSELING; MARRIAGE AND FAMILY THERAPIST; STEPFAMILIES; SYSTEMS THEORY. *Compare* MARRIAGE COUNSELING AND MARITAL THERAPY.

FAMILY THERAPIST. *See* MARRIAGE AND FAMILY THERAPIST.

FAMILY THERAPY. *See* FAMILY THEORY AND THERAPY.

FAMILY VIOLENCE. Behavior between family members that is, in fact, criminal assault, including punching, choking, knifing, shooting, and sexual assault. This violence may take various forms, such as wife-beating, child abuse, and incest. Emotional abuse and child neglect are frequently involved as well.

Recent evidence indicates that domestic violence may well be the most common crime in America. It is now being recognized as a major social problem, after being dismissed for centuries as unimportant.

1. Social Attitudes. The most ancient legal documents, going back as far as the Code of Hammurabi, explicitly permitted domestic violence. It was viewed as the right of the husband to discipline his wife and children in any way he saw fit, including the right of capital punishment. The government was not permitted to interfere in this exercise of patriarchal privilege (Dobash and Dobash, 1979).

In time, gradual restrictions were placed on the ways in which men could exercise this right. In English common law, this eventually resulted in the famous "rule of thumb," which stated that a man had the right to beat his wife with any stick that was no bigger around than his thumb (Dobash and Dobash, 1979).

In the nineteenth century, various social reform movements made child and wife abuse less palatable. In 1871 an Alabama court ruled that men no longer had the right to beat their wives, and in 1874 the first legal action was taken to protect an abused child — under laws designed to prevent cruelty to animals. However, as late as 1910, the U.S. Supreme Court ruled that a man could not be prosecuted for assault and battery against his wife, because the court might damage domestic tranquility if it interfered in what happened behind closed doors at home (Langley and Levy, 1977).

Today, the laws of every state are viewed as prohibiting assaults on family members just as they prohibit assaults on strangers. However, these laws are poorly enforced in domestic situations. In many communities, when battered women call the police for help, they find that the officers are reluctant to get involved. The batterer is rarely arrested, and the victim is often discouraged from pressing charges. Criminal prosecution of these cases is rare. If the case does go to court, the proceedings usually take many months before the trial occurs. Even if convicted, the batterer is unlikely to be sent to jail and in most cases is merely placed on probation. These difficulties explain why many victims decide to drop the charges against the assailant in these cases.

Not only the legal system but society in general is remarkably tolerant of violence in the family. In a survey taken in 1976, 31.3 percent of the husbands and 24.6 percent of the wives saw "couples slapping each other" as normal, necessary, or good (Straus, Gelles and Steinmetz, 1980).

2. Frequency. Family violence was once thought to be rare. However, in the past decade, many studies have provided evidence that domestic violence is remarkably common in America today. Although surveys show that only ten percent of domestic violence incidents are reported to the police, police departments report that domestic violence calls occupy much of their time. In a study conducted in Chicago in 1974, the police received more requests to respond to family violence than to all other serious crimes combined (Langley and Levy, 1977).

These cases are not trivial. Domestic violence situations may well lead to death or serious injury. In 1971, one third of all female homicide victims in California were murdered by their husbands. It has been estimated that about one thousand children are killed by their parents each year as a result of abuse or neglect, and many more are seriously injured. Domestic violence calls are regarded as the most dangerous for police, accounting for about one-quarter of all police injuries and fatalities received in the line of duty (Langley and Levy, 1977).

To give an estimate of how common family violence may be in the population as a whole, two major sociological surveys have been conducted using random sampling techniques. The first, carried out in 1976, used a representative sample of 2,143 households through the U.S. Interviewers asked the husband (or wife in fifty percent of the households) what methods of conflict resolution they used, ranging from rational discussion to use of knife or gun. Twenty-eight percent of the families reported at least one spousal assault incident at some time in their marriage, sixteen percent reported a violent incident in the past twelve months, and four percent reported violence in the past year that was life-threatening in nature (Straus, *et al.,* 1980). A similar study conducted in 1979 with 1,793 housewives in Kentucky produced very similar figures. With nearly fifty million couples living together in America, these studies give an estimate of two million households in which life-threatening spousal assaults occur each year.

In one controversial finding, the 1976 survey found that wives were reported to engage in as many violent behaviors as husbands, although the husbands' violence was somewhat more severe and frequent. This surprising data has generated much debate over the prevalence of battered husbands, since it does not support the findings of most police, hospital and counseling programs, which report that only about one to two percent of spousal assault victims are husbands (Dobash and Dobash, 1979). Critics have pointed out that the survey did not ask if any of the wives' behavior was in self-defense, nor did it ask about the level of injury that resulted from violent behavior.

In the 1976 study, 3.6 percent of the parents reported using abusive violence toward their children in the preceding twelve months. This category excluded spanking, but did include kicks, bites, punching, beating, threats, or actual use of a gun or knife (Straus, et al., 1980). The sexual assault of children was not investigated in this study, but another survey indicated that almost one-fifth of girls and one-eleventh of boys have been sexually molested at some time in their lives. At least half of the assailants were family members of the child victims (Finkelhor, 1979).

Abuse of parents, particularly the elderly, by their grown children is also being reported increasingly to hot-lines and other social agencies. However, there are no reliable estimates of the prevalence of this form of abuse at the present time.

Christian families are not exempt from domestic violence. A survey of Methodist churchwomen in 1981 revealed that sixty-eight percent had some personal experience with family violence — including wife-beating, child abuse, and incest (Fortune, 1982).

3. **Causes.** The causes of domestic violence are poorly understood at the present time. However, research in this area has identified certain "risk factors" that are associated with a high rate of domestic violence. While family violence is found in every socioeconomic and ethnic group, it is more frequent in young, poor, minority, and urban families. It is also increased markedly by unemployment of the husband. These are all factors that produce increased social stress on the family (Schulman, 1980; Straus et al., 1980). Physically handicapped persons and pregnant women are at greater risk of being abused by family members. This may be because their special needs also place more stress on the family's resources (Straus, et al., 1980).

Many studies indicate that family violence is a learned behavior; it is the way batterers have been taught to cope with stress. A high percentage (most studies indicate fifty percent or more) of abusive adults were abused as children themselves or witnessed violence between their parents (Rosenbaum and O'Leary, 1981; Straus, et al., 1980; Sweeney and Key, 1982). Even if they did not witness violence in their own home as children, batterers have had many opportunities to witness culturally approved violence elsewhere in society.

Violent behavior in the family is not only modeled, it is also reinforced. When violent acts occur, they are often followed by positive consequences. First, there is the immediate internal release of tension that accompanies any vigorous physical activity. Batterers feel better when they have "gotten things off their chests." For batterers, violence may well be their only form of emotional release, the only way they know how to relieve tension. Secondly, violence often produces compliance by others — it gets the batterer what he or she wants. Thirdly, the negative consequences that one might expect to follow violence — arrest, conviction, divorce — often do not occur for a long time, or are prevented from occurring at all by the "forgiving" family.

Violence in the family, especially wife-beating, is often associated with alcoholism or drug abuse. However, even after successful treatment of the alcohol or drug problem, domestic violence frequently persists. For this reason, alcohol or drug abuse cannot be viewed as a "cause" of domestic violence.

Only a small percentage of batterers seen in counseling programs appear to be psychotic. The others are frequently described as dependent, possessive people with problems of impulse control. They tend to deny and minimize their violence, and try to blame their problems on others — often their families. Male batterers often have a "macho" facade, but underneath they are frequently passive people with low self-esteem, who have difficulty asserting themselves without resorting to aggression (Sweeney and Key, 1982; Walker, 1979, 1981).

4. **Victims' Persistence in Abusive Relationships.** Abused children or frail elderly people who are battered frequently are completely dependent on their abusers, have no financial resources to leave, and no place to go.

There are many similar external or social reasons that may keep battered women from leaving abusive relationships. First, the woman may receive intense pressure from family and church to stay in her marriage at all costs. Second, she may be economically dependent on her husband. Even when she has a job, a woman on average earns only sixty percent as much as a man, and supporting herself and her children may be difficult or impossible for many women. If she does want to leave, the woman may have no place to go. Until the past decade there were virtually no places that offered emergency housing for women and children, although there were many shelters for homeless males. Finally, the woman may be ignorant of her legal rights and unaware of available shelters or other services (Martin, 1976).

There also may be internal or psychological factors that make it difficult for battered women to leave abusive relationships. One early theory was that women must stay because they were masochists and enjoyed being beaten. However, people who have worked extensively with battered women report that this is rarely—if ever—the case, and that virtually no woman reports enjoying being beaten. The feelings evoked by being assaulted are not pleasurable, but rather terrifying.

Many battered women, in fact, appear to stay with the batterer because they are virtually paralyzed by fear. This syndrome, described as "learned helplessness" by psychologist Lenore Walker, is also seen frequently in other victims of uncontrollable violence, such as prisoners of war, rape victims, and terrorist hostages. In order to survive, they become passive and numb and try to disturb their assailants as little as possible. They may come to view their assailants as omnipotent and may even try to defend them to others (Walker, 1979).

Another psychological pattern seen in some battered women has been called the "missionary syndrome." These women stay with their men out of a desire to reform them and help them overcome their violence or other problems. Warm, maternal, and frequently devout Christians, "missionaries" endure battering with martyr-like stoicism, hoping that their patient forgiveness will eventually lead the batterer to reform. Far from eliminating domestic violence, this strategy simply provides further reinforcement for it.

Attempts to find a distinctive psychological profile of battered women has been fruitless. However, many therapists describe battered women as commonly suffering from low self-esteem, tending to minimize the violence, and often unaware of their own needs and physical reactions (Walker, 1979, 1981).

5. Characteristics of Violent Families. Violent families tend to deny the violence, especially to outsiders, and concentrate on maintaining a successful, even happy, facade. Frequently, they are isolated socially, with few friends and outside contacts. They try to meet all of their emotional needs within the family, and become enraged when other family members fail to meet their excessive, unrealistic demands.

In wife-beating, Walker (1979) has pointed out that the violence is rarely continuous, but often shows a cyclic pattern with three phases: tension-building, which may last months or years; an aggressive outburst that may be triggered by a minor event; and a final period of loving contrition after the abuse is over. This honeymoon period often provides the only reward that the victim experiences in the relationship.

Once violence begins in a marriage, it rarely stops without outside intervention. It typically increases over time in both frequency and intensity. The pattern of escalating violence often continues until it terminates in divorce, serious injury, or death.

6. Sources of Help. The majority of victims of family violence suffer in silence, not seeking help anywhere. Frequently, when victims of violence *do* turn to others for aid, they are blamed themselves for the assault. They are often asked, "What did you do to provoke this?" This phenomenon of "blaming the victim" is a common response naive observers make to any disaster, including rape, fire, flood, and auto accidents. Social psychologists theorize that this is the way people may seek to maintain their view that the world is just and predictable, and that those who suffer some disaster must, therefore, have done something to deserve it. The victims themselves also engage in this process and, therefore, may share in blaming themselves for the assault they have suffered.

a. Police. Despite the reluctance of many police departments to get involved, it is still important to report domestic violence incidents. In fact, it is *mandatory* now in every state for most professionals, including pastors, to report child abuse to the police or other child protective agencies. Police action and criminal prosecution are important steps in giving the message that domestic violence is not acceptable behavior and that it is, in fact, a crime. Furthermore, a court order for counseling is the only way many abusers will ever enter

treatment. However, the court process is a lengthy ordeal for victims, and they often need support and encouragement to continue in it.

b. Restraining orders. Most states now enable victims of domestic violence to obtain temporary orders from the court that require the batterer to leave the home and stay away from the victim for a specified period of time. Evidence collected by several legal advocacy clinics indicates that these orders are effective in stopping violence while they are in force in about seventy-five to eighty percent of cases.

c. Shelters. For battered children, thousands of foster homes and treatment facilities are now available. In most cases, court orders are necessary to place children in them. In addition, there are now over 400 shelters for battered women in the U.S. They provide emergency housing at low or no cost for women and their children for a brief period of time — usually up to one or two months. During this time the woman is offered a safe place to stay (the shelter locations are usually confidential) and various counseling and advocacy services that enable her to explore her options and decide what she wants to do. Shelters frequently offer support groups for women once they leave, and also may offer counseling to the batterer.

d. Counseling. Battered women and other victims of family violence frequently report that when they have sought counseling it was not helpful or even seemed to make the violence worse. They often say that the therapist did not seem well-informed about domestic violence and appeared to share the popular attitudes about it: treating it as trivial or blaming the victim. Unfortunately, many therapists have received no training at all in handling domestic violence situations and may not see enough of these cases to develop expertise on their own.

It is important to recognize that counseling is a stressful experience in itself, and that for persons who have learned to be violent in times of stress, counseling of any kind may initially increase the risk of violence. Many untrained counselors may seem to be exonerating the abuser, and this, too, may free him or her to be even more violent.

For these reasons, it is important to refer violent families to experienced therapists with special training in domestic violence. Most shelters and child protective agencies have referral lists of such specialists in their communities. In certain situations, however, it may be necessary for pastors to engage in counseling these families. Therefore, pastors need to be aware of the current developments in the field of domestic violence counseling.

Most experts agree that conjoint marriage counseling and family therapy are *undesirable* techniques to use at the beginning of treatment. In these settings the victims may be afraid to reveal the depth of the problem and the abuser may use the sessions to further abuse the victim verbally (Walker, 1979, 1981). Therefore, most domestic violence treatment programs first see the abuser and the victim separately. If alcoholism or drug abuse is also involved, this should be treated before anything else is attempted. The next priority is to stop the violence rather than to enhance the relationship or improve communication. Many therapists prefer to place the abuser and victim in separate groups, but individual therapy is effective and may be all that is possible. During this phase physical separation may be helpful to ensure the safety of all family members.

During the initial phase of treatment for the batterer the focus is on accepting responsibility for the violence and learning anger control. This involves helping the batterer to develop awareness of the physiological signs of mounting tension, learning to prevent tension from escalating by relaxation, "time-outs," and taking positive assertive action to achieve one's goals. Batterers are taught to look at their pattern of negative "self-talk" (e.g., "She has no right to push me around like this") and replace it with more positive alternatives (e.g., "I don't have to lose control over this. I can talk about it calmly").

Meanwhile, the emphasis for the victim is on providing support, ensuring safety, and enhancing self-esteem. After their initial numbness wears off many victims feel intense anger about being abused and need a safe place to ventilate their feelings. With child victims, play therapy and art therapy are valuable techniques to aid in this expression of feeling.

Once the counselor is confident that the abuser has acquired reliable anger control, and if the victim is willing, then couple or family counseling may be employed to improve communication, learn nonviolent methods of resolving conflict, and clarify unrealistic expectations (Sweeney and Key, 1982; Walker, 1979, 1981).

Two national organizations provide particularly valuable services in child abuse situations. Parents Anonymous provides self-help groups, patterned after Alcoholics Anonymous, for parents who have abused their children. Parents United offers similar groups for incest victims and for their parents.

As with alcohol and drug abuse, family violence abusers rarely enter treatment without external pressure — either separation, the threat of divorce, or a court order. Family violence is a deep-seated problem, and altering this pattern is a difficult and painful process. A few counseling sessions, a religious experience, or a few promises to change are rarely enough. However, the prognosis for change is quite good for those who complete domestic violence programs. While no comprehensive outcome research has been published to date, some programs are estimating that violence stops in about eighty percent of the families they treat.

7. **The Church's Response.** *a. Serving the victim.* As part of its traditional ministry to people in crisis, the church can provide emergency help for victims of domestic violence. It can provide information about existing services and help victims obtain the legal, medical, and other aid they need through persistent advocacy on the behalf of the victim. In areas without shelters, the church might develop a network of host homes to provide temporary housing for victims. In areas with shelters, the church can support their work with donations of money and materials, and by supplying volunteers.

b. Healing the family. The church can also help victims and their families recover from the long-term effects of violence through counseling services and sponsoring support groups such as Parents Anonymous. Furthermore, the church can offer violent families a chance to build positive bridges to other people and break out of their isolated way of life.

c. Challenging society. There is a critical need for the church to offer society a nonviolent image of family life. Family-life education programs can provide instruction in nonabusive ways of parenting and resolving family conflict. Pastoral premarital and postmarital counseling can address issues of domestic violence prevention. The church and its leaders can model nonviolent modes of treating their own families as well as the family of God.

Second, the church can be a powerful force in reducing the social stresses that enhance the risk of domestic violence. Sexism, racism, and poverty are the soil in which family violence grows.

Finally, the church has a moral responsibility to speak out against domestic violence, labeling it clearly as evil. The church is in a strategic place to address the tacit social approval that has permitted family violence to flourish in our society.

Bibliography. S. Bentley, "The Pastoral Challenge of an Abusive Situation," *J. of Religion and Health,* 23 (1984), 283–89. R. Clarke, *Pastoral Care of Battered Women* (1986). R. W. Dobash and R. Dobash, *Violence Against Wives* (1979). D. Finkelhor, *Sexually Victimized Children* (1979). M. Fortune, "The Church and Domestic Violence," *Theology News and Notes,* June (1982), 17–21. J. Garbarino and J. K. Hershberger, "The Perspective of Evil in Understanding and Treating Child Abuse," *J. of Religion and Health,* 20 (1981), 208–17. C. H. Kemp and R. E. Helrfer, *The Battered Child* 3d ed., (1980). J. E. Korbin, ed., *Child Abuse and Neglect: Cross-Cultural Perspectives* (1981). R. Langley and R. C. Levy, *Wife Beating: The Silent Crisis* (1977). D. Martin, *Battered Wives* (1976). A. Rosenbaum and K. D. O'Leary, "Marital Violence: Characteristics of Abusive Couples," *J. of Consulting and Clinical Psychology,* 49:1 (1981), 63–71. M. Roy, ed., *The Abusive Partner: An Analysis of Domestic Battering* (1982). M. A. Schulman, *A Survey of Spousal Abuse Against Women in Kentucky* (1980). M. A. Straus, R. J. Gelles, and S. K. Steinmetz, *Behind Closed Doors: Violence in the American Family* (1980). S. Sweeney and L. J. Key, "Psychological Issues in Counseling Batterers," *Theology News and Notes,* June (1982), 12–16. L. E. Walker, *The Battered Woman* (1979); "Battered Women: Sex Roles and Clinical Issues," *Professional Psychology,* 12:1 (1981), 81–91.

C. DORAN

CRISIS MINISTRY; FAMILY, JEWISH *or* PASTORAL CARE AND COUNSELING OF; FAMILY LAW; VICTIMIZATION; VIOLENCE. *See also* AGGRESSION/ASSERTION; INCEST; LEGAL DIMENSIONS OF PASTORAL CARE AND COUNSELING; MARRIAGE COUNSELING AND MARITAL THERAPY; RAGE AND HOSTILITY; RAPE; SOCIAL JUSTICE ISSUES AND PASTORAL CARE.

FANATICISM. *See* AUTHORITARIANISM; SOCIAL PERCEPTION, JUDGMENT, AND BELIEF. *Compare* ANTISOCIAL PERSONS; COMMITMENT; FAITH/BELIEF; NEW RELIGIOUS MOVEMENTS.

FANTASIZING. The creative process of mental imagery. Flowing as a visual stream of images, metaphors, symbols, and dramatic sequences, fantasy forms a major part of the internal world of experiencing. Most feelings are generated by a person's fantasy life. Visualization is thus at the center of the human bio-computer. Generated primarily from the right hemisphere of the brain, fantasy exerts a powerful affect bodily, intellectually, emotionally, and perceptually. Fantasy can block, influence, or shape the experience of external reality. This symbol-forming activity gives birth to artistry, creativity, and intuition. While often uniquely personal, fantasizing, according to Jungian theory, can also embody universal or archetypal symbols that emerge from the subconscious.

An important dimension of the pastoral counseling relationship often revolves around the sharing and exploration of the counselee's fantasizing process. Through this activity counselees invite participation in their inner worlds of experiencing. The very act of sharing, especially if this material has been surrounded with feelings of shame or guilt, can facilitate emotional release and a greater self-acceptance. The unfinished business of the past, especially images of childhood tied to traumatic events, can significantly influence current fantasy life and can directly affect a person's self-image, mood, feelings, thoughts, and interactions. Bringing these emotionally charged images into awareness enables one to live more fully in the present.

Fantasizing can play a valuable integrative role by bridging the conscious and the unconscious, rational and affective, mental and physical aspects of personality as well as bringing together the inner and outer worlds of reality. Working with the fantasy life of the counselee, the counselor invites him or her to see the patterns and themes, symbols and metaphors that are the "stuff" of their internal drama.

The engagement of the imagination facilitates working through impasses, resolving conflicts, integrating disowned parts of the personality, exploring polarities, and expanding the boundaries of awareness. In the counseling session, counselees are often asked not only to share their fantasizing processes but to use imagery to experiment with seeing things differently.

In one fantasy technique, called identification, clients act out various parts of themselves as an avenue of integration. They may put this or that aspect into dialogue with a conflicting one to achieve a new harmony. This technique is also used to explore new patterns of interaction by dramatizing troublesome situations. In this way, fantasizing becomes a rehearsal of modified ways of being in the world.

A major involvement with the fantasizing process can be the discerning of projections—psychological processes in which disowned traits of the self are experienced as belonging to others. Another meaningful focus is often the realizing of "fear fantasies" anticipated with future events. Sometimes these are only remotely conscious.

Guided fantasy can also evoke the exploration of personal meanings. In this technique, the counselor may have the counselee visualize going on a journey, climbing a mountain, encountering someone like a wise old man and engaging in a conversation. While many variations can be used, the intent is to foster a process in which new directions are discovered and symbols emerge for the journey of self-actualization.

In the counseling relationship the counselor often shares his or her own fantasies as a means of responding to the material the counselee offers. These spontaneous associations that emerge as metaphor, symbol, or story facilitate the counselees' exploration and invites them to tune to their own visualization processes.

Bibliography. R. Assagioli, *Psychosynthesis* (1965). G. M. Cordner, "The Spiritual Vision Within," *J. of Pastoral Care,* 35, 42–51. M. James and D. Jongeward, *Born to Win* (1971). J. Jaynes, *The Origin of Consciousness in the Breakdown of the Bicameral Mind* (1976). C. Jung, *Symbols of Transformation* (1956). F. Perls, *Gestalt Therapy Verbatim* (1969). M. Samuels and N. Samuels, *Seeing with the Mind's Eye* (1975). J. Stevens, *Awareness* (1971). J. Zinker, *Creative Process in Gestalt Therapy* (1977).

G. E. CRISWELL

GUIDED IMAGERY TECHNIQUE; IMAGINATION; PERSONAL STORY, SYMBOL, AND MYTH IN PASTORAL CARE; PLAY. *Compare* DREAM INTERPRETATION; PASTORAL COUNSELING.

FASTING. *See* ASCETICAL PRACTICES; EATING AND DRINKING. *See also* SPIRITUAL DISCIPLINE AND GROWTH; SELF-DENIAL.

FASTS, JEWISH. *See* JEWISH HOLY DAYS AND FESTIVALS.

FATALISM, BELIEF IN. *See* HOPE AND DESPAIR; LOCUS OF CONTROL RESEARCH; PROVIDENCE.

FATHER/FATHERING. *See* PARENTS/PARENTHOOD.

FATHER, GOD AS. *See* GOD, IDEAS AND IMAGES OF.

FATHER, PASTOR AS. *See* PASTOR (Normative and Traditional Images).

FEAR. A rational reaction to an objective identifiable external danger, which may involve flight or attack in self-defense. In neurotic anxiety, by contrast, the emotional arousal is just as strong but the danger is internal, neither identifiable nor shared as a common threat by others in the situation (Zimbardo and Ruch, 1975).

1. The Psychology of Fear. Fear is an innate, involuntary response to danger or threat. The perception of danger impels the individual toward either a "fight" or "flight" response. In face of extreme danger an individual may panic or freeze, suffer somatic symptoms like nausea or incontinence, or become unable to function in an organized manner. Such behavior is commonly observed in disasters like fires, in military combat, and in the sudden death of a relative or friend.

Realistic fear appears to be healthy for a person. Too little fear may have as bad an effect on health as too much fear. Moderate levels of fear, for example, have been associated with better adjustment to surgery than low or high fear levels (Janis, 1958). Moderate fear appears to help patients plan future reactions and modulate stress and induces a kind of "emotional inoculation."

2. Pastoral Care. Because, in simple fear, the threat is real, a therapeutic response (concerned with psychopathology) by the pastor or caregiver is not generally appropriate. Neurotic conflict or emotional or cognitive disorder may be triggered or intensified by realistic environmental threats, however, so there is always a need to assess the reality of the threat together with the health and appropriateness of the fear and other responses. Insofar as the threat is external and real and the fear seemingly appropriate and uncomplicated by serious pathology, the best pastoral response may be little different from the best "human" response, namely simple human presence, a supportive "standing by" without attempts to provide unrealistic reassurances or to rationalize away strong feelings, combined with whatever realistic help can be given for countering the danger. (It is generally not necessary or helpful to offer condescending pastoral assurances that one's fear is "natural" or "healthy.") If the fear seems seriously exaggerated — either too great or too little for the actual threat—it may also be helpful and wise, in addition to remaining alert for pathological features, to provide some gentle reality orientation by reviewing the circumstances, distinguishing fact from fearful fantasy or speculation, and helping the person or persons become appropriately aware of the strengths and resources available to them.

Prayer or other acts of liturgical care may also be appropriate, depending on the faith and theological understanding of both the pastor and the persons involved. Such specifically religious care-giving should not be offered as a means of denying reality or substituting for such realistic action as may be possible and appropriate, but as a way of helping the fearful be reminded of the strengthening presence and grace of God in every circumstance of life, from whose care "neither death, nor life . . . nor anything else in all creation can separate us" (Rom. 8:38–39).

Bibliography. I. L. Janis, *Psychological Stress* (1958). O. Pfister, *Christianity and Fear* (1948). D. K. Switzer, *The Minister as Crisis Counselor* (1974). P. Zimbardo and F. Ruch, *Psychology and Life* (1975).

L. WRIGHT
M. PRICE
R. J. HUNTER

ANXIETY; CRISIS MINISTRY. *See also* EMOTION; FEELING, THOUGHT, AND ACTION IN PASTORAL COUNSELING. *Compare* CATHARSIS; COURAGE; FAITH/BELIEF; SHYNESS; TRUST.

FEAR OF GOD. See The HOLY; EVALUATION AND DIAGNOSIS, RELIGIOUS; RELIGIOUS BEHAVIOR; RELIGIOUS EXPERIENCE.

FEEDBACK PRINCIPLE. *See* COMMUNICATION; CYBERNETIC THEORY IN PSYCHOLOGY AND COUNSELING.

FEELING, THOUGHT, AND ACTION IN PASTORAL COUNSELING. Feeling, thought, and action are sequentially linked in the human personality, representing the chain of events by which emotions are expressed as concrete action. Biblical anthropology affirms the integrity of humans and honors each of these aspects of human functioning and their essential unity. Most of the psychotherapies that have emerged over the years have focused on either feelings, thoughts, or actions while neglecting the other two. Sound pastoral counseling practice recognizes the importance of all three linked

integrally if it is to be true to its biblical heritage of the essential wholeness of the human being.

Feelings are the subjective experience of one's current emotional state which may be a response to inner and outer stimuli. In primitive organisms or in newborn infants, feelings result in immediate responsive action without cognitive selection. In the more developed human personality, with intelligence and freedom, thought permits the assessment of the feeling state and selection among many possibilities of responsive action. The more developed the personality, the greater is the awareness of possibilities for action and the more likely that the response will further the growth and nurturance of the person. Feelings, thoughts, and actions are equally important in this sequential chain and none of them can be ignored when considering human development and functioning.

The Bible, both OT and NT, considers the human being as a whole. In the OT, the "heart" is seen as the seat of feelings and thoughts and as the source of actions (Gen. 6:5; Ps. 14:1; Jer. 29:13). No distinction is made nor superiority assigned to any of these functions. All three are addressed as responding to God and equally in need of discipline (I Sam. 2:1; Ps. 5:9; Ps. 51:10; Prov. 12:25; Jer. 24:7). The NT continues the theme of wholeness and the equality of feeling, thought, and action. Both Jesus and Paul were concerned with feelings (Mt. 5:28), thought (Phil. 2:5), and action (Mt. 7:21). Each is seen as part of the human whole and in need of redemption. Biblical anthropology that is true to its source in Scripture will honor the integrity of the human personality. The human being has its source in the Creator God who is the source of feelings, thoughts, and actions severally and in totality.

Because they are not linked by a common anthropology, secular psychotherapies have not manifested this essential unity of feeling, thought, and action. Each of the founders and developers of psychotherapeutic theories has reflected his or her own view of human personality which usually contains a bias toward one of the three aspects at the expense of the others. Transactional analysis and rational emotive therapy emphasize cognitive thought. Behavior modification and reality therapy stress action. Client-centered therapy and Gestalt therapy focus on feeling. The assumption is that a change in one focus eventuates in a consequent change in the other two without further attention. The danger inherent in this approach is that a problem in one area becomes an object of concern, and that objectification is detrimental to the empathy which is essential to the relationship that promotes personality change and growth.

Effective pastoral counseling includes a relationship in which empathy is the salient feature. The counselor needs a sense of the client's total experiencing regardless of what is presented as the presenting problem. The presenting problem may be presented as depression or inner deadness (feeling), obsession (thought), or compulsions (action). The presented focus cannot be ignored, but the pastoral counselor must have a sense of what the presenting problem means to the client in terms of the whole sequential chain of feeling, thought, and action, both currently and historically. The pastoral counselor also should be able to hear and respond to a shifting focus as the client's process leads him or her through changing emphases. A limited psychotherapeutic theory makes this empathic response difficult and might inhibit the therapeutic process.

The change and growth that occurs in psychotherapy is virtually always accompanied by a strong feeling experience. The change is manifest in altered behavior which is a cognitive response to the feeling. Through empathy, the pastoral counselor affords support, understanding, and acceptance, and through projective identification, provides a model for the growth. He or she is more useful to the client in this process, if he or she responds to the client as a unity of feeling, thought, and action.

Bibliography. W. Gaylin, *Feelings* (1979). E. J. Gendlin, "A Theory of Personality Change," in P. Worschel and D. Byrne, eds., *Personality Change* (1964). W. B. Oglesby, Jr., "Pastoral Care and Counseling in Biblical Perspective," *Interpretation*, 27 (1973), 307–26. P. Olsen, *Pastoral Care and Psychotherapy* (1961).

R. T. HIGHTOWER

COGNITIVE/CONATIVE PROBLEM IN PSYCHOLOGY AND COUNSELING; PASTORAL COUNSELING; TECHNIQUE AND SKILL IN PASTORAL CARE. *See also* CATHARSIS; PERSONAL STORY, SYMBOL, AND MYTH IN PASTORAL CARE; PSYCHODRAMA; REASONING AND RATIONALITY IN PASTORAL CARE. *Compare* BEHAVIOR THERAPIES; COGNITIVE PSYCHOLOGY AND PSYCHOTHERAPY; EMOTION; PHILOSOPHY AND PSYCHOLOGY; PRAGMATISM AND PASTORAL CARE; PSYCHOTHERAPY; REASON AND PASSION.

FEELINGS, OWNERSHIP OF. *See* EXISTENTIALISM AND PASTORAL CARE; FEELING, THOUGHT, AND ACTION IN PASTORAL COUNSELING.

FEES IN PASTORAL COUNSELING. Charges for counseling that are normally, but not necessarily, monetary amounts.

1. **The Need for Fees.** According to Karl Menninger, counseling "must involve a sacrifice, otherwise it becomes a matter of indifference in the patient's life. It is deeply rooted in the human mind that what is cheap is of little value and what is dear is valuable" (Menninger, p. 35). Without sacrifice, the counselees may fail to become partners in the counseling process. They may end counseling too soon, feeling guilty about taking so much of the counselor's time, or never become deeply involved in counseling since it has not required a significant commitment. The setting of an appropriate fee can contribute to both the counselor's and to the counselee's responsibility and well-being.

Parish pastors receive their income through contributions given to the church, and generally provide counseling for little or no remuneration. But fees are the major source of income for pastoral counselors and pastoral counseling centers, and must be charged. Ethical and theological questions about the appropriateness of fees for a service understood as religious ministry are inseparable from the larger questions of the proper uses of money and how professional services which involve the sharing of one's person are to be compensated for, whether those services involve teaching, consultation, preaching, etc.

2. **Types of Monetary Fees.** Counselors charging monetary fees tend to use one of two methods, a standard fee or a sliding fee scale.

a. Standard fee. With the standard fee policy, everyone is charged the same amount. That amount is determined by a combination of factors: other counselors' fees, the cost of providing the service (the break-even fee), the amount of income a counselor feels he or she must earn, the counselor's perceived value of service provided, and the counselor's other available sources of income.

The advantages of using a set fee are very attractive. There is no need for funding, provided the fee is high enough to cover expenses. Other advantages include low administrative cost, ease in budgeting, and a clear understanding of the counseling fee prior to the counselee's first session. In addition, some counselees will have a lower fee under this system. Yet, unlike the sliding scale policy it does not require those who can afford more to pay a higher fee.

The standard fee policy, however, is not designed for people who cannot pay the full amount. Pastoral counselors, therefore, often use a variation of the traditional policy which enables them to serve lower-paying counselees. Counselors on programs using this alternative system establish a financial aid fund, usually with money from contributed sources. Money from the fund is then used to pay the difference between what the counselee can actually pay and the cost of providing his or her counseling.

John Hinkle describes the primary advantage of this approach: "It helps fulfill the commitment to service-regardless-of-ability-to-pay through (1) the financial aid fund and (2) increasing third-party contributions through a more attractive context for giving." Many contributors are more interested in giving when they know their money will be used directly to help people who otherwise would be unable to receive counseling.

b. Sliding fee. The most common method of determining a counselee's fee has been the sliding scale. With this approach, the amount a counselee is charged is based upon his or her ability to pay. Typically, a counselor uses a graph which indicates what people at various levels of income should be able to afford for counseling. This amount is usually in the area of eight to ten percent of their gross family weekly income. Once the suggested amount is determined using the graph, the counselor makes allowances for the counselee's particular situation, considering such things as family size, outstanding financial obligations, and other potential sources of payment (e.g., a parent or an insurance company). An adjusted fee is then established, and the counselee is responsible for that amount.

For the sliding scale to be effective, the average fee received must equal the cost of providing the service: otherwise, additional funding must make up the difference. In order to maintain the necessary average payment, some people need to pay more than their counseling actually costs. They make up the deficit resulting from others paying less than the cost of counseling.

The sliding scale is easy to use, requires little administrative time, and enables counselors to see low-income counselees. On the other hand, the sliding scale has three major disadvantages. It can be difficult to maintain a sufficient number of high-income payers and/or contributors to balance out those who cannot afford to pay the cost of providing the service. Secondly, this approach is dependent upon "involuntary contributions." The more affluent people subsidize the therapy of others even though they may not want to. This sense of coercion or unfairness can be detrimental to the therapeutic process. Finally, persons at the bottom end of the sliding scale may feel they are getting "cheap" counseling, knowing their cost is well below the standard rate. This also can hinder the counseling.

The most common variation of the sliding fee scale involves using a limited slide, which requires that a minimum fee be paid unless special arrangements can be made.

3. Alternative Means of Payment. *a. Third-party reimbursement.* Pastoral counselors sometimes qualify for third-party reimbursement — e.g., payments from insurance companies, corporate employee-assistance programs, or church-assistance funds. The conditions for receiving money from these sources vary considerably and are influenced by such factors as state law, the credentials of the pastoral counselor, and corporate contracts.

b. In-kind payment. To make in-kind payment, counselees give volunteer work to a charitable or service organization in return for counseling sessions. Using this concept, the pastor directs the counselees to the kind of work that will increase their self-esteem by enabling them to help others. From the onset, the pastor and counselees work together in a contract of exchanged hours of service.

There are several advantages in using in-kind payment. Counselees do not feel they are accepting charity. They invest in the counseling process and take it seriously. The community benefits from the volunteer work. And, in-kind payment can be excellent therapy for the persons involved. By working with other people, lonely or mildly depressed individuals fill a void in their own lives and gain perspective.

The main disadvantage of in-kind payment is that it takes time to help people find appropriate volunteer placements and to follow up on how they are doing their assigned tasks. In-kind payment can also be used in conjunction with monetary payment programs. For example, some counselees who make a monetary payment are assigned volunteer work for therapeutic purposes.

4. Setting and Collecting Fees. Most pastoral counselors initially find it difficult to set and collect fees. There are good reasons, however, for the counselor to assume this responsibility. The fee helps define the counseling relationship. The counselor has more information about the counselee, and therefore knows what constitutes a fair fee. Finally, payment often provides a situation in which therapeutic issues (related to resistance, anger, etc.) may surface and then be resolved in the treatment process.

Whoever sets and collects the fees must be acquainted with fee guidelines and with the program's financial needs, and must know how to work with counselees in a sensitive but firm manner. If not the counselor, this person should keep the counselor informed of any unusual behavior or accumulated debt on the side of the counselee. People seeking counseling are frequently suffering from uncertainty and the inability to follow through with intentions. The person setting and collecting the fees should not contribute to these problems. The fee should be clear and the payment policy firm.

Bibliography. J. C. Danco, "The Ethics of Fee Practices: An Analysis of Presuppositions and Accountability," *J. of Psychology and Theology*, 10 (1982), 13–21. J. E. Hinkle, Jr., "The 'Robin Hood' Policy: Ethical and Practical Issues Growing Out of the Use of Fee Scales in Pastoral Counseling Centers," *J. of Pastoral Care*, 31:2 (1977), 119–24. K. Menninger, *Theory of Psychoanalytic Technique* (1958). J. C. Carr, J. E. Hinkle, Jr., and D. M. Moss III, eds., *The Organization and Administration of Pastoral Counseling Centers* (1981).

R. J. ROSS

COVENANT AND CONTRACT IN PASTORAL COUNSELING; JEWISH CARE AND COUNSELING; PASTORAL COUNSELING; PASTORAL COUNSELING, ECONOMICS OF. *See also* ETHICS, PROFESSIONAL; LEGAL DIMENSIONS OF PASTORAL CARE AND COUNSELING; MONEY; PROFESSIONALISM; VALUES IN COUNSELING AND PSYCHOTHERAPY.

FELLOWSHIP/FELLOWSHIP GROUPS. *See* COMMUNITY, FELLOWSHIP AND CARE; GROWTH GROUPS; PIETIST PASTORAL CARE; SUPPORT GROUPS. *See also* FEMINIST ISSUES IN PSYCHOLOGY; FEMINIST THERAPY.

FEMINIST THEOLOGY AND PASTORAL CARE. Theology that seeks to empower women to personal creativity and self-confidence by enabling them to remember that they too are created in the image of God. Feminist theology is done by women who take women's experience into account when interpreting Scripture, ritual, and dogma. Frequently it criticizes aspects of "patriarchal religion" such as the "maleness" of God in imagery, language, and function, the origin of sin, the history of human origins, hierarchical structures, and the dualities of good/evil, mind/body, transcendent/immanent, inner/outer, heaven/earth, sacred/secular, and male/female. Conventional thought frequently associates men with the first term in each of the dualities and women with the second. From this follows the popular belief that "men are to women as God is to human-kind" (Schaef). Historically, these unquestioned assumptions have been used to justify the political, economic, and social inequalities of the sexes. In addition to unveiling such hidden "patriarchal" assumptions, feminist theology pays particular attention to how the male orientation of Scripture, theology, and religious practice manifests itself in language, imagery, doctrine, and ritual, and what effect these have on women's identities and roles in the church. It advocates female images of God, reinterpretation of Scripture, and inclusive language.

1. Directions and Contributions to Theological Discussion. Feminist theology has developed in both exodus and reformist/liberationist formulations. Many women find the traditional religious structures too confining and too slow to change, so they are leaving the churches to embrace Goddess worship, nature religions, and humanistic personal spirituality (Daly, Christ, Spretnak, Goldenberg, Stone). The revisionist/

liberationist movements, on the other hand, call for the full participation of women in ministry and church government, a retranslation of the Scriptures that incorporates inclusive language and images, and the reinterpretation of problematic Scripture passages (Ruether, Fiorenza, Lardner-Carmody, Wilson-Kastner, Mollenkott, Scanzoni, and Hardesty). While these two approaches vary in their radicalness, both have provided women with permission to seek and use female-formulated images of womanhood and power. Both have provided a process of identifying strong female models in Scripture, mythology, history, and personal lives by asking, "What were women doing when. . . ?"

Another major feminist contribution to theological reflection lies in the focus on the process and context of theological reflection rather than on the content. This enables men and women to move from the law-and-rule-abiding approach of childhood religion to a more self-reflective spirituality, one that considers the broader spiritual significance of events and beliefs in terms of personal connection to and participation in the world. All feminist theologians promote women's quest for identity, equality, personal improvement, and empowerment in the world. Some also consider the impact of these changes on men.

2. Contributions to Larger Society. One important political implication of the feminist challenge to dualisms, especially the us/other dualism, is that women can no longer be seen as "other." If women are no longer seen as "other," the logic and threat of the "other" declines and with it the justification for war, racism, sexism, and exploitation of the environment.

It is not possible to correct the past imbalances of a male-dominated society without theological reformation, since religion has provided legitimacy to male power. Feminist theology strives to reduce the dichotomization of gender roles and the deification of the "masculine" type. A primary approach to these concerns has been an insistence on inclusive (nonsexist) language in Scripture, theology, and ritual—a crucial insistence because language determines thought and sets behavioral limits. Critics of feminist theology have argued that the words "man" and "mankind" are generic terms that include both women and men. Recent studies in linguistics, dreams, and imagery, however, have shown that the unconscious is extremely literal in its interpretation of language, despite conscious rationalizations otherwise.

3. Religion and Women's Identity. Feminist theologians have recognized the formative role of religion in creating and complicating the problems of identity for women in a society modeled after a patriarchal religious worldview. They seek total transformation of society and not merely the assimilation of a few "token" women. Yet it is in this call for transformation that feminists meet some of their most challenging critics. Many agree that the predominant male language and imagery of traditional religion has hurt and stifled women, and yet they question the relevance of consciously self-generated alternative religious images and symbols. Some critics suggest that feminist theologians only want to replace male images with female ones and thereby change the balance of power. Perhaps balance does demand a swing from one extreme to the other. Some women are developing alter-

native images through re-exploration of goddess myths and remnants of cave paintings. Others are searching history for women's contributions that have been overlooked. But the issue is not really one of determining the authenticity of the images—distinguishing "natural" religious images from the "arbitrary" images of culture, for instance. All images are products of culture to some degree; the role of culture cannot be eliminated. Rather, the issue is how women can determine their loyalties to particular images when all images, as "arbitrary" expressions of culture, are in question.

3. Implications for Pastoral Care. Feminist theologians raise issues that are emotionally charged for both men and women. They challenge tradition and thus threaten change. The lines of support are not drawn between men and women but across the gender line. The discussion of concerns is heated and often angry because of women's experience of inequality on one hand and men's fears and insecurities on the other. Women and men both fear abandonment and abuse.

Individual and collective struggles with these issues follow a grief process of denial, anger, bargaining, depression, acceptance, and hope. The loss grieved for is the loss of naiveté and the security of knowing what to expect, even though the expected has not been working. This process of challenge and change has profound implications for pastoral care. Each stage needs to be accepted and facilitated without judgment. Women may deny that a problem exists, or that their depression comes from repression of urges to be who they are, rather than from their personal failing to be what someone expects. They may feel angry at having sold themselves short or at having been denied equality. As women begin to ask for what they want bargaining results in little increments because they do not feel worthy of more. Depression sets in with the realization that things will never be as they once were and with women's fear that they may be inadequate to the quest for self-acceptance. The acceptance in the process comes with accepting God's love, and realizing the internal and external beauty of women's will and contribution to the world. The process ends with hope for a world of equality and full valuation of both sexes.

4. Suggestions for Pastoral Caregivers. To incorporate practically the insights of feminist theology in pastoral care the caregiver should: (1) consider that women undergoing identity re-formation best profit by seeing a woman caregiver who has worked through these issues; (2) use inclusive language unless referring to a gender-specific situation; (3) set the goal of facilitating women's sense of self and empowerment rather than a sense of coping and adjustment; (4) encourage women to identify models of strong women through suggested reading, wise-woman imagery, and women's support or consciousness-raising groups; (5) validate the exploration of alternative images of divinity, including the wise woman or goddess; (6) facilitate the development of a new and stronger self-concept based on trust of personal and community experience; (7) explore and use reinterpretations of problematic scriptural passages; (8) reread and reinterpret Bible myths in such a way as to give women their rightful place in history; (9) be careful not to project male experience onto female experience without checking out its appropriateness; (10) encourage experimentation with new behaviors; (11) work through any discomfort raised by these issues with a peer or supervisor; and (12) see women as beautiful daughters of God regardless of the forms of their struggle.

The pastoral caregiver should encourage men to: (1) work on their own fears and angers that arise as a loved one explores her concerns; (2) understand the grief process for both men and women; (3) experiment with new behaviors; and (4) incorporate the feminine within themselves. Together men and women should learn to tell the truth without fear or judgment and to contract for new behaviors in a way that encourages frequent re-evaluations.

Bibliography. C. Christ, *Diving Deep and Surfacing* (1980). C. Christ and J. Plaskow, eds., *Womanspirit Rising* (1979). S. Collins, *A Different Heaven and Earth* (1974). M. Daly, *The Church and the Second Sex* (1968); *Beyond God the Father* rev. ed. (1985); *Gyn/Ecology* (1978). E. Fiorenza, *In Memory of Her* (1983); N. Goldenberg, *Changing of the Gods* (1980). D. Lardner-Carmody, *Feminism and Christianity* (1982). V. Mollenkott, *Women, Men and the Bible* (1977). E. Pagels, "Christianity's Masculine Orientation," *New Oxford Review* (March, 1979). R. Ruether, *New Woman, New Earth* (1975). L. Scanzoni and N. Hardesty, *All We're Meant to Be* (1974). A. Schaef, *Women's Reality* (1981). M. Stone, *When God Was a Woman* (1976). C. Spretnak, *Politics of Women's Spirituality* (1982). P. Trible, *God and the Rhetoric of Sexuality* (1978). P. Wilson-Kastner, *Faith, Feminism and The Christian* (1983). P. Zulkosky, *The Wise Woman in Guided Imagery*, Ph.D. Dissertation, School of Theology at Claremont (1984).

P. ZULKOSKY

ADVOCACY; CONSCIOUSNESS RAISING; PROPHETIC/PASTORAL TENSION IN MINISTRY; SEXISM; SOCIAL JUSTICE ISSUES IN PASTORAL CARE; WOMEN. *See also* CULTURAL AND ETHNIC FACTORS IN PASTORAL CARE; EXPLOITATION/OPPRESSION; PASTORAL THEOLOGICAL METHODOLOGY; PASTORAL THEOLOGY; SOCIAL STATUS AND CLASS FACTORS IN PASTORAL CARE. *Compare* BLACK THEOLOGY *or* LIBERATION THEOLOGY, AND PASTORAL CARE; SOCIOLOGY OF RELIGIOUS AND PASTORAL CARE.

FEMINIST THERAPY. Emerges from the philosophy and process of consciousness raising, and from the developing theory of a new psychology of women.

A new psychology of women views the mythology of feminine evil as an expression of the misogyny and gynephobia of historical and contemporary society. It affirms the physiological and psychological development of the female from birth to adulthood as independent and life-affirming rather than as derivative from or inferior to male development.

A new psychology of women assumes that most gender characteristics and role assignments traditionally described as innate are in fact culturally evolved and proscribed; that those qualities traditionally assigned to women (passivity, dependence, weakness) are maladaptive both psychically and functionally, and that others (nurturance, cooperativeness, emotionality) though viewed as positive, are culturally devalued; that many characteristics assigned traditionally to men, though not devalued (aggressiveness, dominance, power) have become increasingly maladaptive for men individually and for global human survival.

A new psychology of women assumes that traditional psychological "knowledge" about the behavior, abilities, and psychological characteristics of both women and men supports stereotypical beliefs about the sexes, and that these beliefs in turn support existing legal, political, economic, and social inequalities between the sexes. Thus women are prevented from developing those qualities of strength and independence which lead to successful functioning in the public world; men are cut off from the human qualities of nurturance, affiliation, and cooperativeness so crucial to survival on the planet.

A new psychology of women, like feminism itself, supports an integrative approach to the subjective and the objective, the rational and the intuitive, the expressive and the instrumental, the scientific and the metaphysical, the carnate and the incarnate.

Early studies by Weisstein, Chesler and Broverman, *et al.*, document the double standard of mental health for women and men, and describe the sexist, racist, and elitist nature of most "therapy." These studies pinpoint the beginnings of feminist therapy in the early 1970s. Feminist therapy challenges the ways in which sex, race, and class affect the kind of help people get. It sees powerlessness often at the root of "psychological disorder." It rejects the equation of money and power with human value.

Feminist therapy rejects preconceived notions or goals for mental health in either sex. It refuses to equate marriage and motherhood with success as a woman, or money and prestige with success as a man. It values a variety of lifestyles among women and men, women and women, men and men, adults and children. Feminist therapy does not view divorce as failure nor the single-parent family as less than whole. It challenges the oppressive character of marriage and the nuclear family for women and has no stake in the preservation of a marriage for its own sake. Feminist therapy focuses on the valuing of women's experience both historically and immediately and asks the question, "What would the world be like if women's experience were taken into account and valued?" While nonsexist or humanistic therapy encourages individual development free of stereotyped gender restrictions, feminist therapy goes further. It examines and seeks to change society politically, economically, socially.

There is no one body of knowledge and theory, or set of practices to which all feminist psychologists or therapists would subscribe. Some elements, however, are implemented or expressed in therapy by most feminist therapists. Most feminist therapists: (1) encourage clients to interview more than one therapist before settling on one who is most likely to be helpful; (2) freely communicate information about their own training, experience and style of counseling; (3) use a sliding scale in fee setting, recognizing particularly that a woman's ability to pay does not necessarily reflect her father's or husband's income; (4) work with women in groups where their experience can be validated by other women; refer them to feminist consciousness raising groups; (5) avoid jargon, psychological testing and diagnostic labels where possible as essentially sexually, racially and economically biased and dehumanizing; (6) encourage equality between client and therapist by their nondefensiveness and self-disclosure; articulate their own biases, acknowledge their mistakes, open themselves to learning from those with whom they are working; (7) encourage female clients to discover competent female role models in every area of society; (8) suggest feminist reading resources appropriately and encourage their clients to participate in political action according to their interests; (9) encourage women to claim their own personal space and time; help them to challenge their own appeasing behaviors and low aspirations, especially in marriage and motherhood; validate their independence and self-reliance; (10) place major emphasis on body work: (a) in the form of self-healing, physically and spiritually, through breathing, movement, meditation and other body therapies and (b) by encouraging women to take control of their own bodies through understanding their physiological processes and claiming the right to choose how they will function sexually and reproductively — whether or not to engage in sexual activity at all, and with whom, whether or not to initiate or terminate pregnancy; (11) encourage women to examine their own sexuality from the standpoint of compulsory heterosexuality and the lesbian experience; (12) encourage women to uncover the rage which all women have internalized as a result of centuries of misogyny and their own individual experience, and to find healing ways of expressing it; and (13) encourage women to observe and evaluate images of women prevalent in the media, in the male language structure, in representations of deity; encourage women to explore the days when deity was female and to claim their own Wise Woman within.

In marriage and family counseling, a feminist therapist is conscious of the effects of socially enforced sex roles as major components of a couple's or family's concerns. She recognizes that most systems theories are based on a patriarchal family model and require modification from a feminist point of view. She is alert to dominance and submission issues like who does the talking and touching, how role assignments are understood and implemented, who is valued and for what, how money and power issues are intermixed, who is identified as the "problem." She questions the ethics of preserving marriages or family solidarity at the expense of the wife/mother's independence and full range of choices about her life. She encourages a woman to use her power directly by stating her feelings and needs rather than indirectly through manipulation, depression, illness or nagging. She helps a couple to assess the interrelation of sex and power between them. Cognizant of the statistics about rape, battering, and incest, she is on the alert for hidden or overt clues to the presence of such behavior. She takes into account differing cultural norms but she does not allow these to interfere with facilitating female independence.

A feminist therapist working with men is conscious of the ways in which the oppressor is also the oppressed. She encourages men to assess the ways in which cultural stereotypes have limited them: in their valuing of achievement versus affiliation, in their capacity to feel and express emotion, in their choices about sexuality, in their physical health. She encourages men to inform themselves about women's concerns and issues and to acknowledge their biases and the ways in which these are played out in their relationships with women. She encourages men to explore feelings and practices about fatherhood and to be aware of their subtle internalized as well as manifest violence against women. She encourages men to become aware of how sexism has limited men as well as women.

Feminist therapists may be grounded and function in one or more traditional psychological schools. Whatever theories and methods they espouse are always assessed and moderated according to the feminist guidelines articulated above.

1. Can a Man Be a Feminist Therapist? In the combined mental health disciplines, two-thirds of clients are women while seven-eighths of therapists are men. Because of the sexism in society and because of the ways in which women and men are taught to view themselves and each other, there are always elements of power and powerlessness between women and men. Both sexes behave differently with each other than they do with members of their own sex. There are some things women will not talk about with a male counselor. The power and emotional significance of men as men cannot be overestimated. Girls learn early that men have greater political, social, and physical power. They learn early that they are expected to develop even their own identity in relation to males — as daughter, mother, wife. Women are likely to view themselves as weak in relation to men. Even the most benevolent male therapist, then, reinforces traditional stereotypes about the power differential—that women are dependent on the good father for validation as women. It is difficult for a woman to validate her own strength and independence while working with a man. Even if he encourages these qualities in her, she is likely to feel she is being given her freedom, rather than claiming it for herself. The man is likely to agree.

A number of studies have explored attitudes among therapists to the double standard of mental health. Among the findings are the following: (1) male therapists find it harder than female therapists to acknowledge sex biases in themselves; (2) male therapists are more apt than are female therapists to assume that women are envious or seductive, and to have a negative view of women's mental health; (3) male therapists are more apt to be threatened by and to discourage a woman's anger; (4) the male therapist in marriage or family therapy is likely to be allied, consciously or unconsciously, with the husband/father; and (5) some studies suggest that sex-role biases are more significant than sex of therapist in determining attitudes toward women's mental health.

Since the sex ratio of clients to therapists is unlikely to change dramatically within the foreseeable future, what is crucial is feminist consciousness raising among women in general, so that they can recognize sexist biases in therapists. Women do not need a male therapist because they have problems with men. What they need to know is not that some men are "different," but that they themselves can become strong and independent. Women have problems relating to men because men have abused their power. Men can help by changing themselves and the power structures they participate in, including the institutions of therapy and of pastoral care. When they are working with women, they can do everything in their power to inform themselves, to uncover their own biases, to encourage women to be with other women in consciousness raising groups and with female mentors, and to refer them to feminist therapists.

2. Relevance for Pastoral Care. Since they represent both institutionalized religion and institutionalized psychology, both of which continue to be tenaciously patriarchal, ministers and pastoral counselors are as subject to sexist biases as anyone else. In both religious and psychological settings, men are likely to be predominantly the dispensers of care and women the receivers. While all ministers and pastoral counselors need to examine their own inevitable biases and the ways in which they help to perpetuate male power and dominance, male pastoral counselors particularly need to examine their competence for working with women. Ministers, even more than other male therapists, are vulnerable to the tendency of many women to project supernatural powers onto them. For many women, and often for themselves, male ministers seem to speak with the voice of the male God. It is crucial that male pastoral counselors make a serious commitment to implementing the thirteen standards and practices listed above, particularly those related to encouraging women to participate in consciousness raising and to look toward other women rather than to men for validation. Whereas a female counselor can identify herself as similarly oppressed when working with women, especially of her own color and economic group and as being on a similar journey, male counselors must see themselves as oppressors and therefore with limited effectiveness in working with members of an oppressed group. At the same time, they must struggle to unearth the ways in which they themselves are oppressed, not by women, but by the cultural demand for their own dominance. Ruether suggests that men must avoid *trivialization and ridicule* in response to women's liberation. They must avoid *co-optation*, that is, assuming that they are equally oppressed, or know more about feminism than women do. "Deeper male conversion from sexism involves a willingness to enter into risks himself. He has to recognize his own profound fear of loss of affirmation by the male group ego if he departs from his male roles" (Ruether, *Sexism and God Talk*, 1983, p. 191.) Individual practitioners of pastoral care, as well as the institution of pastoral care, can do this only with a continued questioning and evaluating of their attitudes about women.

Bibliography. I. Broverman, "Sex-Role Stereotypes and Clinical Judgments of Mental Health," *J. of Consulting and Clinical Psychology,* 34 (1970), 1–7. P. Chesler, *Women and Madness* (1972). Cleveland Women's Counseling, "Guidelines for Women Seeking Psychotherapy," 3d ed. (1977), pp. 133–46. R. Hare-Mustin, "A Feminist Approach to Family Therapy," *Family Process,* 17 (1978), 181–94. E. Maccoby and C. Jacklin, *Psychology of Sex Differences* (1974). J. Miller, *Toward a New Psychology of Women* (1976). E. Rawlings and D. Carter, *Psychotherapy for Women* (1977). J. Robbin and R. Siegel, eds., *Women Changing Therapy* (1983). N. Weisstein, "Psychology Constructs the Female" in V. Gornick and B. Moran, eds., *Woman in Sexist Society* (1971).

C. ELLEN

CONSCIOUSNESS RAISING; WOMEN. *See also* PHILOSOPHY AND PSYCHOLOGY; PSYCHOTHERAPY; VALUES IN COUNSELING AND PSYCHOTHERAPY.

FÉNELON, FRANÇOIS DE LA MOTHE (1651–1715). French theologian, writer, spiritual director, and bishop. Fénelon served in Parisian parishes and as a tutor and spiritual director to nobility. Elected to the French Academy in 1693, he was consecrated bishop of Cambrai in 1695. His involvement with Madame Guyon and her Quietist circle, however, led to the condemnation of certain of his ideas by the Vatican in 1699. Fénelon also earned a reputation as a social and educational theorist and his influence on future thinkers of the French Revolution was not inconsiderable.

Disgraced at the royal court, Fénelon remained a zealous pastor of his diocese until his death. His primary pastoral legacy was his extensive spiritual correspondence with high-ranking ladies and military officers whom he served as spiritual director. Fénelon's letters of spiritual counsel are part of the classic literature of this genre. Though his brush with Quietism lessened his appeal to Roman Catholics, his works have been widely read in Anglican circles. Fénelon wrote perceptively and boldly, searching out self-deception and self-love and encouraging simple obedience, faith, and love of God in those whom he directed.

L. S. CUNNINGHAM

SPIRITUAL DIRECTION, HISTORY AND TRADITIONS OF.

FESTIVALS, JEWISH. *See* JEWISH HOLY DAYS AND FESTIVALS.

FETISHISM. *See* SEXUAL VARIETY, DEVIANCE, AND DISORDER.

FIDELITY. *See* COMMITMENT; FAITH/BELIEF; RESPONSIBILITY/IRRESPONSIBILITY, PSYCHOLOGY OF. *See also* APOSTASY; INFIDELITY, MARITAL; VIRTUE, CONCEPT OF.

FIELD THEORY. The attempt to describe personality development and behavior as a function of one's total psychological reality or life space. Originated by Kurt Lewin in *A Dynamic Theory of Personality* (1935), it has been applied extensively to group dynamics and broad issues of social concern and is the basis of environmental psychology. Field theory is well described in C. S. Hall and G. Lindzey, *Theories of Personality* 3d ed. (1978) pp. 383–435.

M. G. BEHRENS

PERSONALITY THEORY (Varieties, Traditions, and Issues); SOCIAL PSYCHOLOGY. *See also* ECOLOGICAL PSYCHOLOGY; GROUP DYNAMICS; SYSTEMS THEORY.

FIELDING, CHARLES. *See* CANADIAN PASTORAL CARE MOVEMENT.

FINANCES. *See* FEES IN PASTORAL COUNSELING; MONEY.

FINANCIAL PLANNING. *See* MONEY.

FINITUDE. *See* CREATION, DOCTRINE OF; HUMAN CONDITION/PREDICAMENT; LIMIT SETTING; REALITY PRINCIPLE; REALITY TESTING; REALITY THERAPY.

FITNESS. *See* PHYSICAL FITNESS DISCIPLINES. *See also* BODY IMAGE; HEALTH AND ILLNESS; OBESITY AND WEIGHT CONTROL.

FLETCHER, JOSEPH F. (1905–   ). American ethicist and clinical pastoral educator. Fletcher emphasized the social and prophetic dimensions of pastoral psychology, and between 1935 and 1944 he expanded the Graduate School of Applied Religion in Cincinnati, Ohio into a clinical center supplementing the work of theological seminaries. In 1944 he moved to the Episcopal Theological School in Cambridge, Massachusetts, where he served as professor of pastoral theology and Christian ethics, associate editor of the *Journal of Pastoral Care,* and a trustee of the Institute for Pastoral Care. He criticized the separation of the prophetic and the therapeutic in Clinical Pastoral Education (CPE).

Educated at Yale Divinity School, Berkeley Divinity School, and the University of London, Feltcher served as the curate of an inner-city church in London, a chaplain in a private school, and a research director for the Protestant Episcopal Church before moving to Cincinnati. Through his experiences there in CPE and counseling, Fletcher began to develop the moral perspective that came to be known as "situation ethics," the view that moral judgments must emerge not from absolute general principles but from an informed and loving response to the complex variables in each situation. He sometimes described situational ethics as simply "case" or "clinical" ethics. The publication of his *Situation Ethics* in 1966 evoked considerable interest and debate.

He influenced pastoral care, as well, through his explorations of medical ethics, and near the end of his career he became a professor of medical ethics at the School of Medicine of the University of Virginia. Throughout his involvement with CPE Fletcher emphasized the social and ethical dimensions of pastoral care.

E. B. HOLIFIELD

CLINICAL PASTORAL EDUCATION; PASTORAL CARE MOVEMENT.

FLOODING. A technique of behavioral therapy in which a person is guided in realistic images of feared situations, with the goal of extinguishing abnormal avoidance responses. In implosion, a variation of flooding, the therapist also introduces images of the person's worst fantasies about the object. While this method has proved effective, it has more recently been replaced by actual exposure to the feared situation or object.

G. H. ASQUITH, JR.

BEHAVIOR THERAPIES (Methods and Research); IMPLOSIVE THERAPY.

FOOD. *See* EATING AND DRINKING. *See also* GLUTTONY AND TEMPERANCE; OBESITY AND WEIGHT CONTROL.

FOOL, PASTOR AS. *See* PASTOR (Normative and Traditional Images).

FOOLISHNESS. *See* WISDOM AND PRACTICAL KNOWLEDGE.

FORGETTING/FORGETFULNESS. *See* MEMORY; REPRESSION. *See also* ANTISOCIAL PERSONS.

FORGIVENESS. The act of rendering null and void the penalty owed by a wrongdoer to an offended party; hence a term having legal or quasi-legal qualities denoting a release from a debt. An essential element of forgiveness is the wrongdoer's awareness of having offended and owing a penalty. At the same time, the offended party grants forgiveness unconditionally. In this sense the act transcends the retributive nature of punishment for a crime.

Forgiveness always has a social context. It is a transaction between God and humanity, between two or more persons, or even between two or more "selves" in the developmental history of one person. Forgiveness is not the equivalent of reconciliation, however; it is the means by which barriers to reconciliation (which may or may not follow) are removed.

1. **Fundamental Characteristics of Forgiveness.** *a. Legal/obligational presuppositions.* In both the OT and the NT, forgiveness is understood in legal terms. The most common OT term for it is *shalach,* which means a lifting up or a removal of a past event that may inhibit a present one. In the NT (and LXX), *aphiemi* is most often used to denote forgiveness, and like the Hebrew word it represents the idea of sending away or remitting. J. N. Lapsley (1966) has argued that these biblical words deal with questions of obligations, and obligations can exist only in a legal framework.

The legal dimensions of forgiveness are evident even in the psychic processes described by Lapsley. Using the work of Freud and others, he describes a young child's making of "contracts" with parents or other caretakers. Often these contracts, or expectations, are made without the knowledge of the adults, yet when the child perceives a violation of the contract he or she expects restitution. Such expectations become part of one's personal history and must be dealt with in later relationships, especially if they become controlling in the new relationships.

This legal understanding of forgiveness has important implications for pastoral work with adults. Often the pastor will be asked to help someone who seems to live under a "contract" that was made years before, but which is no longer appropriate. While the original emotional contract may have been made with a parent, it does not necessarily apply to a spouse, a colleague, or a child, and it can create serious difficulties.

b. Divine-human relationship as context of all human forgiveness. It can be claimed that the essence of Christianity is summed up in one sentence: "God forgives sin through Jesus Christ." Usually the understanding of God's forgiveness of sin has been articulated in the doctrine of the atonement, which essentially says that

God has graciously pardoned human sin through the ministry and death of Jesus, thereby allowing the divine-human relationship that God intended. While God's forgiveness is a gracious act, not dependent upon human action, the person aware of guilt and shame and aware of God's forgiveness is called to respond in devotion and gratitude. James Emerson (1964) calls this larger dimension of grace and gratitude the "context of forgiveness," which he distinguishes from specific acts of forgiveness. Without reference to this context, all acts of forgiveness between humans are merely "good deeds" and can be rendered trivial.

Forgiveness cannot be considered merely within the potentially abstract context of the divine-human relationship, however. The doctrine of atonement, for instance, can become merely rationalistic, making it difficult for individuals to discern what concrete role they can play in the communication of forgiveness. Forgiveness must have some communal and transactional dimension: there must be two or more persons involved in order to speak of it. While doctrine can offer the context of forgiveness, forgiveness cannot be understood apart from community. The church is the community that responds to God's forgiveness through confession, worship, discipline, and witness.

2. Forgiveness and the Processes of Human Life.
a. Relation to guilt and shame. In the Christian tradition forgiveness has generally been associated with guilt. Guilt follows acts of transgression for which forgiveness is sought. According to J. Patton (1985), however, shame may be more important for understanding forgiveness than guilt, since shame has to do with one's whole self rather than with particular acts of transgression. Moreover, it is a condition that all share. Shame is the realization that others see us as we really are, and not our pretensions. Like shame, forgiveness is a realization that we are more *like* those who have offended us than we are *different* from them. Forgiveness from this perspective is a realization of this fact rather than an act of condescension by a righteous person toward a sinful one. Forgiveness of guilt tends to separate the righteous from the unrighteous, while forgiveness in the face of shame acknowledges our commonality.

b. Relation to reconciliation. It is a mistake to equate forgiveness with reconciliation (Lapsley), for while forgiveness is an indispensable prelude to reconciliation, reconciliation does not necessarily follow forgiveness. Frequently one may forgive violations of a contract or covenant but not desire to continue in relationship with the offender. This is the case in many divorces. Although forgiveness does suggest something negative — the violation of a trust—it also allows for a positive starting over; for the process of forgiveness to be complete, the forgiving party must remove all bind or hindrance from the forgiven party. Forgiveness allows at least potentially for the renegotiation of further relationships.

3. Pastoral Implications and Issues. *a. Interpersonal.* Quite often a pastor's investigation of how a parishioner understands the function of forgiveness can be used diagnostically. Does the person understand himself or herself as capable of feeling the forgiveness of God? Is forgiveness so foreign to the interpersonal life that the forgiveness of God makes no sense? Can the person recognize personal guilt and shame? Can the person release himself or herself from resentment in order to forgive? Are lasting relationships important enough to require forgiveness? Just as important, does the person forgive in order to please, without the offender's feeling any remorse? If this is the case, then the forgiving person is vulnerable to continued disappointment and resentment.

The notion of acceptance is central to both the theological and the therapeutic understandings of forgiveness (D. D. Williams, 1961). One must feel accepted for what one is and is struggling to become in order for forgiveness to have any impact. The pastor, then, must enter into the struggles of the other with the faith that grace is a reality, so that he or she can be a witness for divine forgiveness. The pastor's self-knowledge is important. Can the pastor accept those aspects of the other that he or she does not accept in himself or herself? Can the pastor forgive the violation of his or her own feelings by the ones being ministered to?

b. Marriage and family. Marriage entails contractual and covenantal arrangements. While recently there has been some interest in formal and legal marriage contracts, most marriages begin with unacknowledged expectations. According to C. Sager (1967) these expectations entail: (1) an understanding of marital styles; (2) expectations of satisfaction of biological and psychological needs; and (3) external foci such as career and lifestyle. Much difficulty arises because, more often than not, these expectations are held without one's spouse or children being aware of them. Often a spouse can feel that the other has not fulfilled an implicit expectation. Once expectations are made explicit, forgiveness can be explored as a way of moving beyond the difficulty.

With explicit expectations a married couple can either accept the elements of the contract or covenant as reasonable, or they can reject them as unacceptable and try to renegotiate them. It is at this point that reconciliation might follow forgiveness. Many a divorce results when one forgives unreasonable expectations but leaves little or no room for renegotiation. In this case forgiveness can literally be understood as a letting go without hindrance or bind; in a family with children, forgiveness allows for the continued relationship between parent and child.

c. The local church. The local church has often been compared to a family, and insofar as that comparison is justified, forgiveness has a vital place in the church. Indeed it has been suggested that where there is a church, there too, should be a forgiving community. This is true not only in the church's obligation to preach ultimate divine forgiveness but also in its obligation to follow the teaching of Eph. 4:32 and the Lord's Prayer. Clearly, then, the pastor has a responsibility to educate the congregation in forgiveness by word and example. It is clear too that the pastor must, at some level, understand the pastoral role as having some inherent authority by virtue of the calling to ministry and the responsibilities of professional education and practice. The pastor mediates and participates in the process of forgiveness. It is here that the pastor may find it useful to be informed about conflict management (Raush, 1974).

d. The church and the world. The 1967 Confession of the United Presbyterian Church makes it clear that "to be reconciled to God is to be sent into the world as his reconciling community" (Part II, section A. 1). The confession further states that since the forgiving Christ is the model for ministry, forgiving others is a response to that model. While there are many complicated issues involved in world problems, it seems incumbent upon the pastor to encourage the church to study the issues with forgiveness in mind, especially if that study includes the prayerful wish for forgiveness of our own violations of trust. Issues of world hunger, the distribution of wealth, and proliferation of nuclear arms are clear issues that entail some measure of forgiveness.

Bibliography. G. Aulen, *Christus Victor*, (1960). J. G. Emerson, *The Dynamics of Forgiveness* (1964). W. Klassen, *The Forgiving Community* (1967). J. N. Lapsley, "Reconciliation, Forgiveness, Lost Contracts," *Theology Today*, 25 (1966), 44–59. H. R. Mackintosh, *The Christian Experience of Forgiveness* (1934). J. Patton, *Is Human Forgiveness Possible?* (1985). W. A. Quanbeck, "Forgiveness," *The Interpreter's Dictionary of the Bible*, vol. 2, pp. 314–19. H. L. Raush, *et al.*, *Communication, Conflict, and Marriage* (1974). C. Sager, *Marriage Contracts and Couple Therapy* (1967). L. Smedes, *Forgive and Forget* (1985). V. Taylor, *Forgiveness and Reconciliation* (1948). D. D. Williams, *The Minister and the Cure of Souls* (1961).

B. H. CHILDS

GRACE AND PASTORAL CARE; GUILT; PENANCE, SACRAMENT OF; REPENTANCE AND CONFESSION. *See also* CHRISTOLOGY AND PASTORAL CARE; FREEDOM AND BONDAGE; GRATITUDE. *Compare* ACCEPTANCE; CONFLICT AND CONFLICT MANAGEMENT; COVENANT AND CONTRACT; HEALING OF MEMORIES; MEDIATION/CONCILIATION; UNPARDONABLE SIN; UNDOING.

FORMATION, MINISTERIAL *and* PASTORAL.
See CALL TO MINISTRY; THEOLOGICAL STUDENTS; VOCATION. *See also* CLINICAL PASTORAL EDUCATION; EDUCATION IN PASTORAL CARE AND COUNSELING; THEOLOGICAL EDUCATION.

FORMATION, MORAL AND SPIRITUAL.
See MORAL DEVELOPMENT; SPIRITUAL DISCIPLINE AND GROWTH. *See also* EDUCATION, NURTURE, AND CARE; FAITH DEVELOPMENT RESEARCH.

FORMATIVE SPIRITUALITY.
A science, art, and discipline serving the ministry of spiritual counseling, teaching, and direction developed by the Roman Catholic spiritual writer and psychologist Adrian van Kaam. Formative spirituality is rooted in "formation science," a newly emerging human science with its own methods and meta-language. Formation science examines critically and systematically the life directives implied in empirical formation traditions, customs, dynamics, conditions, and problems, together with their possible solutions.

The formation of a distinctively human or spiritual life is potentially central to the experience of every person. Formation science addresses the transcendent quality of this experience by means of its own methodology. Its research designs aim at the understanding of spiritual formation as observable within the life worlds or "formation fields" of individuals and communities. This exploration critically and creatively takes into account whatever may have been disclosed about distinctively human formation by other sciences, arts, ideologies, and traditions. The ultimate criterion of the effectiveness of the findings of formation science is the confirmation by persons applying these findings within their own traditions.

The methodology of formation science involves eight categories: (1) selection of scientifically generalizable topics rooted in concrete formation events; (2) prescientific and scientific articulation in the language of formation science of the structures of these events; (3) elucidation of the dynamics embedded in these structures and their fields of meaning; (4) critical consultation of relevant auxiliary arts, sciences, and formation traditions; (5) translation of the results of consultation into the meta-language of formation science; (6) transposition of the translated findings into the scientific framework of the topic under consideration; (7) integration of the topic thus researched within the overall evolving theory of spiritual formation; and (8) empirical application and critical reality testing in formation counseling, spiritual direction, and a variety of related ministries in pastoral care and education. It is possible to articulate these findings critically within one's own faith tradition or that of others. As such the science of formation is not identified with any specific ideological or religious tradition.

Examples of topics thus investigated include the role of memory in the unfolding of foundational identity and commitment; the process of moving from an idealizing stance toward a consonant formation of ideals; spiritual appropriation of the past as a movement from resentment to gratitude; the formative experience of waiting as a passage from living in illusion to living in reality; creative response to limitedness; the movement from anger to compassion; moving from envious comparisons toward respectful community living; the lived experience of personal conflict, its implications for spirituality; and the emotional response to separation from loved persons.

Bibliography. A. van Kaam, *The Art of Existential Counseling* (1966); *Formative Spirituality*, 4 vols. (1983–1987); *Foundations for Personality Study: An Adrian van Kaam Reader* (1983); *Studies in Formative Spirituality* vol. 1 (1980). See also T. J. Kreuch, "Adrian van Kaam's Psychology and Religious Personality Model." *J. of Psychology and Christianity*, 2 (1983), 39–50.

A. VAN KAAM

SPIRITUAL DIRECTION, HISTORY AND TRADITIONS OF; SPIRITUAL DISCIPLINE AND GROWTH; SPIRITUALITY, ROMAN CATHOLIC. *See also* COUNSELING, ROMAN CATHOLIC; RELIGION AND PSYCHOTHERAPY; RETREATS (Roman Catholicism); SPIRITUAL THEOLOGY AND PASTORAL CARE. *Compare* LOGOTHERAPY; POPULAR THERAPEUTIC MOVEMENTS AND PSYCHOLOGIES; PSYCHOTHERAPY; PSYCHOSYNTHESIS.

FORNICATION.
See SEXUALITY, CHRISTIAN *or* JEWISH THEOLOGY AND ETHICS OF.

FORTITUDE.
See COURAGE; EGO STRENGTH; PATIENCE/PATIENTHOOD. *See also* MORAL THEOLOGY; VIRTUE, CONCEPT OF.

FOSDICK, HARRY EMERSON (1878–1969). Liberal Baptist preacher at Riverside Church in New York City and professor of practical theology at Union Theological Seminary in New York.

Remembered primarily as a preacher and a proponent of theological and social liberalism, Fosdick insisted that "personal counseling" was the center of his ministry, and he urged ministers not only to learn counseling skills but also to treat the sermon as an occasion for "counseling on a group scale." In the 1920s he created controversy when he called on Protestant ministers to develop their own version of the Catholic confessional. To discover how that might be done, he turned for help to Thomas Salmon, the medical director of the National Committee for Mental Hygiene. Thereafter Fosdick spent much of his time each week in consultations with the distressed.

His primary goal as a counselor was the formation of character. He hoped to encourage people to accept themselves, assume responsibility for their own lives, and devote themselves to the service of others. Though Fosdick, out of his own experience, had an intense sensitivity to inner turmoil, he also held the optimistic view that religious faith could help persons release the power within themselves and achieve inner harmony. His accent on the "practical use of faith" bore some resemblance to the American tradition of New Thought. Fosdick's favorite psychologist was William James, who convinced him that a positive and affirmative mental disposition could engender healing in the divided personality. His autobiography, *The Living of These Days* (1956), provides useful information on attitudes toward pastoral counseling in the 1920s. His popular treatise *On Being a Real Person* (1943) represents his distinctive style of combining religious and psychological insights.

Fosdick was one of the best-known radio preachers in America (1926–46), and he helped convince a considerable segment of the liberal Protestant clergy to deliver topical sermons on such topics as the mastery of depression, the conquest of fear, and the overcoming of anxiety. He pioneered in the effort to exploit the insights of modern psychology for the work of the minister.

E. B. HOLIFIELD

PASTORAL CARE MOVEMENT; PREACHING.

FOSTER CHILDREN AND FOSTER PARENTS. A foster parent is someone who assumes the authority and responsibility of parenting for an unknown, but generally limited period of time, in order to provide emotional, mental, and physical support for a child or children. A foster child is a minor who, due to circumstances in his or her natural family, has been placed by a parent, relative, or the state in a foster program.

1. Placement Issues and Concerns. A child may be placed in a foster program for any number of reasons: because of the death of a parent (or both); at the request of parents who can no longer manage delinquent behavior; for parental neglect or abuse; because of the instability of parents; in response to a temporary family emergency; and others. The removal of a child from the natural home/parents is likely to be as traumatic as the circumstances that necessitated the move. Some children have been able to cope and even thrive in an unsatisfactory home environment while others have not. It is therefore difficult to anticipate the emotional state of a child entering a foster home. A child may anticipate that the new situation will be even worse than home.

Foster parents are advised at the time of placement of the rights of natural parents, such as visitation arrangements and telephone privileges. Though contact with the natural parents might appear to do more harm than good, it is generally essential for a good placement. It may calm the child's dread of abandonment; it may help the child to keep the parent(s) in a realistic perspective. The interaction between the natural parent(s) and child is enhanced if foster parents are able to maintain a family atmosphere in which emotional boundaries are clear but permeable.

2. Continuing Care and Termination. The ability of foster parents to maintain a continuing relationship with the natural parents of the child is crucial but seldom easy. Natural parents may be faithful in visitation or they may have little or inconsistent contact with their child or children. Natural parents may be grateful for help or they may regard foster parents with hostility as adversaries rather than helpers of the natural family. Despite these complications, foster parents should not judge or label the natural family; the child does not have to hate one to love the other.

Although the requirements vary, individuals desiring to become foster parents must meet standards in parenting ability, housing, sanitation, home safety, family health, etc. Foster parents are expected to nurture and support the child's physical, emotional, and social development. It is particularly necessary that a foster parent be able to discipline in a fair and nonviolent manner.

Because of a foster child's need to be loved and the temporary nature of the relationship, a foster parent needs to love without possessing and without expecting remarkable change. An effective foster parent is a generative person who is able to invest in a child for the child's sake. The foster child also brings a unique gift to the family. In that sense, being a foster parent is an experience of mutuality as well as an act of altruism. Because it is difficult not to become attached, foster parents learn the necessity of grieving a loss in order to love again.

3. Role of the Church. Foster parent programs are based on the conviction that parents have limits as well as responsibilities. It is self-evident that parents cannot do with their children whatever they wish. It is not so clear who should intervene for the sake of the children or by what criteria social workers and other authorities decide that a child shall be removed from her or his natural parents. The church has a stake in those programs (such as foster parents) that seek the common good of both children and parents. In the process of developing public policies about the family, it is essential that the church be a clear and knowledgeable participant lest the state, by default, become the guarantor of the family in the public sector. Therefore, foster programs initiated by the state should not be isolated from the church or the family in the exercise of responsible care of troubled children and families.

Bibliography. Children's Bureau, Office of Child Development, U. S. Government Printing Office, *Children Today.* E. Felker, *Foster Parenting Young Children: Guidelines from a*

Foster Parent (1974). A. Kadushin, *Child Welfare Service* (1974). M. Reistroffer, *What You Always Wanted to Discuss About Foster Care But Didn't Have the Time or Chance to Bring Up* (1971).

H. E. ANDERSON

CHILDREN; PARENTS/PARENTHOOD. *See also* FAMILY, CHRISTIAN *or* JEWISH CARE AND COUNSELING OF. *Compare* ADOPTION; STEPFAMILIES.

FOX, GEORGE (1624–91). Founder of Quakers (Society of Friends). The beginnings of Quakerism are traced directly to the religious enthusiasm of George Fox, an Englishman whose personal experience convinced him that religious truth comes by way of God's voice speaking to the soul. In 1652 Fox joined a group of seekers meeting regularly for fellowship. His moral earnestness and organizing abilities enabled him to emerge as leader. Over the years 1652–84 the message of this Society of Friends spread rapidly over England and into Ireland, the Netherlands, and North America.

Fox's conception of pastoral care is based directly upon his emphasis upon inwardness and direct experience. Since inward spirituality in which the Spirit moves directly upon the human soul is the possession of all, no believer has exclusive rights to divine truth. Therefore, Fox opposed a professional, paid ministry and thereby promoted the concept of pastoral care rooted in mutual responsibility.

R. W. CRAPPS

QUAKER PASTORAL CARE.

FRAME OF REFERENCE. *See* INTERNAL FRAME OF REFERENCE.

FRANCIS DE SALES, ST. (1567–1622). Catholic bishop, spiritual writer, and religious founder. Educated at the University of Paris and later, in the law, at the University of Padua, he was ordained a priest in 1593, consecrated a bishop in 1599, and named by the pope as bishop of Geneva (Switzerland) in 1602. He founded, with Jane Frances de Chantal, the women's order of the Visitation of Our Lady in 1610. The episcopacy of Francis de Sales was characterized by an emphasis on preaching, catechetical work with the young, close pastoral care of parishes, and his own skill as a spiritual director.

His writings fill twenty-six volumes in the collected edition but two works have attained the status of classics. Between 1608 and 1609 he wrote *The Introduction to the Devout Life,* a manual of piety which stressed sanctification in this world. Praised for its limpid prose, *The Introduction* was best loved (especially by lay readers) for its world-affirming spirituality. The *Treatise on the Love of God* (1616) was written with the Visitation nuns in mind, a profound and original meditation on the birth and nurture of the virtue of supernatural charity in the soul.

Francis de Sales was canonized a saint by Pope Alexander VII in 1665 and declared a Doctor of the Church in 1877 by Pope Pius IX.

Bibliography. M. Henry-Couannier, *Francis de Sales and his Friends* (1964).

L. S. CUNNINGHAM

SPIRITUAL DIRECTION, HISTORY AND TRADITIONS OF SPIRITUAL MASTERS AND GUIDES; SPIRITUALITY (Roman Catholic Tradition).

FRANCIS OF ASSISI, ST. (1182–1226). Roman Catholic deacon, founder of three Franciscan orders, spiritual leader, miracle worker, author of the famous peace prayer.

Coming from a wealthy family and enjoying the pursuant privileges, Francis experienced a radical conversion in 1205 to a life of poverty and service modeled after Christ.

St. Francis is remembered not only for his exemplary ascetic lifestyle, but also for his spirituality, the many miracles he performed in response to all sorts of human requests, his advocacy of fraternal charity, his loyalty to the mission and work of the church, a ministry to both the privileged rich and the needy masses. Particularly significant are the social or public implications of his work: through personal example and through word and deed, Francis and his associates converted numerous persons of wealth and stature and encouraged others to make charitable gifts, thereby providing a spiritual force against the emerging social trends of secularism and acquisitiveness.

N. F. HAHN

SPIRITUALITY (Roman Catholic Tradition).

FRANCISCAN SPIRITUALITY. *See* SPIRITUALITY (Roman Catholic Tradition).

FRANKL, VIKTOR (1905–). The father of the third Viennese school of psychotherapy, known as logotherapy. Logotherapy, aptly described as "healing through meaning," is the formulation of Frankl's concept of the human being in the cosmos. This concept was formulated in Frankl's early years, and through his concentration camp experiences during World War II those conceptions were reaffirmed and energized. Frankl received Doctor of Medicine and Doctor of Philosophy degrees from the University of Vienna. After the war he was the head of the neurology department at the Polyklinik Hospital in Vienna, even performing lobotomies, yet at the same time was a champion of the human spirit, as is evidenced throughout his writings.

Frankl was professor of neurology and psychiatry at the University of Vienna Medical School, as well as distinguished professor of logotherapy at the United States International University. Ever since his book *Man's Search for Meaning* appeared on the North American scene in 1959, his influence on Western thought has grown exponentially. His twenty-six books have been translated into nineteen languages. Among his major works are *The Doctor and the Soul, Psychotherapy and Existentialism, The Will to Meaning, The Unconscious God,* and *The Unheard Cry for Meaning.* Many German language books have not been translated into English, nor has his play, titled *Synchronization in Buchenwald.* Aside from this, Frankl has authored countless articles on logotherapy and has made over fifty lecture tours in the U.S.

Frank's emphasis on the search for meaning as the primary motivational force in each human being remains a powerful antidote to the feeling of anomie and meaninglessness that is felt by many individuals in our modern, technologized society. Judging by the pattern of the past decades, Frankl's thought is likely to become an even more powerful presence on the global scene.

R. P. BULKA

LOGOTHERAPY.

FREE ASSOCIATION. The "fundamental rule" of psychoanalysis, developed by Sigmund Freud. The patient is asked to verbalize whatever comes to awareness, that is, thoughts, fantasies, wishes, feelings, setting aside his or her usual censoring. Patient and analyst work to understand the patient's inner life and conflicts by examining the data which this procedure produces, including the patient's blockages and seemingly irrelevant thoughts. The goal is self-knowledge, freedom, and an enhanced ability to choose.

S. A. PLUMMER

PSYCHOANALYSIS (Therapeutic Method and Research). *Compare* FANTASIZING.

FREEDOM AND BONDAGE. These terms point to the theological problem of the nature and limits of human volition with respect to salvation and our relation to God, especially as that problem was first propounded by Paul and pursued by Augustine, Luther, and Calvin, all of whom denied that the will has the power to be efficacious in and of itself with regard to ultimate matters. In contemporary pastoral care and counseling, the theme was reasserted by some early leaders of the pastoral care movement who found a convergence between this classic theme in Protestant theology and the insights of modern dynamic and "depth" psychologies, particularly psychoanalysis, which illuminate the complex inner bondages of human motivation and behavior.

Taken together, the terms "freedom" and "bondage" suggest a paradoxical if not contradictory view of human willing: freedom asserts that humans have the ability to determine the direction and shape of their lives; bondage asserts that they are unable to extricate themselves from evil. In contemporary pastoral care and counseling, both assertions most often come to focus in the question, "In what sense, if any, do persons have the ability to heal themselves and restore their broken relationships, when healing and restoration are understood profoundly as a basic, total choosing of life and well-being centered in God over against self-centered, life-destroying options?"

1. A Dynamic Psychological Perspective. Dynamic psychology in general depicts personality as a system of forces in mutual tension and ongoing change. In the history of the modern pastoral care movement it was Freud's dynamic psychology in particular—psychoanalysis— that most stimulated and shaped thinking about the psychological possibilities and limits of human freedom.

In Freud's theory, personality has a threefold organization: "id" refers to the person as impulsive desire ("instinct"); "ego" to the person as reason, reality orientation, and executive function (organization and control); and "superego" to the person as inwardly compelled and constrained by moral demands and prohibitions. It is the concept of ego that embodies Freud's idea of freedom. The ego's primary function is to seek out objects in the external world that give real satisfaction to the desires of the internal world (id). To accomplish this task the ego "interpolates between desire and action the procrastinating factor of thought." This means that persons are not driven blindly to fulfill the wishes of the id but have the capacity to deliberate and to decide—that is, to choose.

At the same time, Freud was a professed determinist, and in his theory the capacity to deliberate and choose is profoundly (if not paradoxically) limited by unconscious forces and processes. At the deepest level, choosing involves the response one makes to anxiety, the ego's signal of impending internal danger from the impulsive demands of the id. Here the ego must choose between the emotionally dangerous gratification of instinct and a lapse into unconscious forgetfulness of the id's desires— what he called "repression." Repression, which in some sense is universal for Freud, thus modifies freedom radically. Individuals are pushed toward repression by forces that impinge on them before they develop the capacity to intrude "the procrastinating factor of thought," forces which include a phylogenetic inheritance from primeval history and the individual's experience of ontogenetic helplessness as a newborn. Repression means that humans unconsciously deny and renounce certain libidinal and aggressive desires—the deepest truth about themselves—realities that constitute fundamental, ineradicable motive forces in their existence.

The immediate results of repression may be positive, even life saving, because repression controls impulses felt to be dangerous. But its long-term consequences are deleterious. Repression creates a state of inner estrangement in which libidinal desires are not stripped of their driving power, nor do they diminish with time. Instead they continue to press for satisfaction, manifesting themselves in devious and subtle ways, e.g., as symptoms, as dreams, as psychopathology, as slips of the tongue. The end result is a distortion in development in which individuals are tied to their past, in which they live, and respond to the present in terms of some previously unassimilated desire or experience. In a word, they are captive to a pernicious bondage of repressed desire from which they cannot unfetter themselves by their own efforts.

To be free of infantile determinisms persons must be helped to unearth and to live through the denied desires. Freud's whole therapeutic endeavor revolves around this goal—to make conscious the unconscious. This goal presupposes a kind of freedom, yet it rests on a simple yet profound observation: that freedom begins with the recognition, the awareness, of how profoundly we are in fact determined.

2. A Pauline-Augustinian Theological Perspective. Within the Pauline-Augustinian tradition, as developed by the sixteenth century reformers, the question of human freedom and its limits is also a major concern and the subject of profound reflection. One contemporary representative of this tradition on the question of freedom and bondage is Reinhold Niebuhr, whose thought converges in certain respects with Freud's while yet, as Christian theology, differing radically from Freud's atheistic materialism.

For Niebuhr, freedom is the power of the self to determine the direction and action of the total self. Persons can transcend themselves and the natural world, and therefore they are free in a twofold sense: They can choose between various alternatives and they can choose their own "total end." Niebuhr focuses on the second ability. He believes that persons always retain the capacity for self-determination, but he also believes that the exercise of that freedom is ambiguous on every level of human existence. Stated in terms of bondage, Niebuhr maintains that the self can *envision* being unselfish but it cannot *be* unselfish.

Freedom is always ambiguous, because universally human beings fall into sin. They turn from God as the source of life and attempt to be the source of their own fulfillment. This egoistic turning puts everything out of order, but it does not destroy a person's essential being. Niebuhr is asserting the paradoxical stance that the person is free yet not free. The self can function in different ways: "Sometimes the self acts and sometimes it contemplates its action" (Niebuhr, p. 259.) The self in contemplation is the self transcending itself. It stands above its acts of thought and deed and becomes aware of its sin, of its egoistic self-assertion. It is not a universal self that has escaped finitude and limitation, but it is a reflective self that is conscious of its concrete attempts to resolve the insecurities of finitude by the pretensions of absolutism.

In Niebuhr's thought, the self in contemplation is the epitome of human freedom. It means that persons are free to discover that they are not free. They can transcend themselves and realize that their previous actions are distorted by egoism. This is a moment of radical freedom.

Yet it is in this moment—the moment of greatest freedom—that the individual's final and irrevocable bondage to sin is exposed. It shows that persons are free in a limited and always ambiguous way. They fall prey to the "Pharisaic fallacy," assuming that their "present ability to judge and criticize the undue and unjust claims of the self in a previous action is a guarantee of . . . virtue in a subsequent action" (Niebuhr, vol. 1, p. 277). This pretension, which is itself an egoistic assertion, is not true; for, according to Niebuhr, when the self acts it always manifests egoism and even uses its previous transcendent perspective as a rationalization for its self-centered activity. In a word, every "act" of the self is colored inescapably by the taint of sin.

This inescapable corruption of freedom highlights the degree to which Niebuhrian theology emphasizes human enslavement. Human beings can neither escape nor suspend the pernicious law of self-centeredness, not even if they gain knowledge of its operation in previous actions. They cannot stand outside of self-love long enough to be or to do anything which is not denigrated by selfishness. Even an increase in the power and the scope of freedom does not annul the operation of self-love; for "as freedom develops, both good and evil develop with it" (Niebuhr, vol. 2, p. 95). Thus persons are captive to the law of egoism. They have the capacity to contemplate an unselfish act, but they are powerless to do it. This is the depth of their bondage, the intense ambiguity of their moral and spiritual paralysis.

3. Implications for Pastoral Ministry. Niebuhr and Freud appear to converge at least at two points: both assert a deep level of bondage to self as intrinsic to the human condition (though for very different reasons), and both hold a paradoxical view of freedom as involving a right knowledge of one's bondage. Such ideas are admittedly not popular in American culture. Humanistic and behaviorist psychologies, in particular, and their current pastoral derivatives reject this psychology and theology as too pessimistic regarding the natural human potential for healing, growth, and fulfillment. In response, Freud and Niebuhr (again, for very different reasons) would surely find such humanism self-deceived with regard to the alienation, pathology and sin, and shallow in its vision of human fulfillment.

In any case, if ministry is concerned with healing the deepest levels of human impotence and conflict, pastoral care and counseling would be well advised to take these views of the human situation seriously. For whatever else pastoral care and counseling do, they must ultimately address the impotence of persons and help to empower them to do what is fulfilling. From the Pauline-Augustinian perspective this is no counsel of despair, despite its paradoxical view of human freedom. For this tradition also holds that the depth of the human bondage is matched at every point by an even greater depth of divine grace. Thus pastoral care and counseling are called to mediate a transcendent, transforming power that enables the person to live out the unique bondages of his or her life from a new center, a revitalized will, liberated, open and authentically responsive to God, the true source of human good. Only then are persons free to determine their "total end" in a genuinely authentic and fulfilling way.

Bibliography. S. Freud, *The Ego and the Id, SE* 19; *Inhibitions, Symptoms, and Anxiety, SE* 20; *New Introductory Lectures on Psychoanalysis SE* 22. R. Niebuhr, *The Nature and Destiny of Man* vols. 1 and 2 (1953). In pastoral theological literature see: S. Hiltner, *Theological Dynamics* (1972), ch. 1. R. J. Hunter, "Law and Gospel in Pastoral Care," *J. of Pastoral Care,* 30 (1976), 146–58. D. Roberts, *Psychotherapy and a Christian View of Man* (1953), pp. 94–117. E. E. Thornton, *Theology and Pastoral Counseling* (1964).

L. ADEN

FAITH AND WORKS; FORGIVENESS; GRACE; GRATITUDE; GUILT; LEGALISM AND ANTINOMIANISM; WILL/WILLING. *See also* CONSCIENCE; SIN/SINS; RESISTANCE. *Compare* COMMITMENT; DECISION/INDECISION, PSYCHOLOGY OF; HUMAN CONDITION/PREDICAMENT.

FREEDOM AND DETERMINISM. Freedom is often taken minimally to mean absence of constraint or coercion. In this context the emphasis falls on freedom of choice. One is free when one can choose without obstacles or restraints on his or her capacity to choose and can take initiative according to his or her interests. Freedom also can mean the spontaneity of human being: one is free in spontaneous self-enactment. Or human freedom may be interpreted as the bare capacity to be, which transcends all states of identity.

Determinism is the claim that human actions are caused by an agency or situation external to human being, such as fate, God, natural law or environment, or by a nonvoluntary force within human being such as blind urge, personal history, or genetic inheritance. Within a pastoral context the issue of freedom and determinism is whether the state of mind that brings a person to seek help is inevitable, or whether it can be significantly changed by pastoral-therapeutic experiences.

1. **Freedom of Choice.** Freedom of choice is not so much an issue of whether a person's actions are caused as it is a question of whether a person can determine his or her actions within a causal sequence. Can a person genuinely choose among possibilities and be responsible for actions which he or she initiates? Or is the task of pastoral care or therapy to discover what is inevitable for a person and to provide an occasion for increased intelligence and acceptance regarding inevitabilities? Most therapists, pastoral or secular, probably are convinced that therapeutic experiences make a difference in people's lives and that one of the differences can be a higher degree of self-determination by the person. Such experiences of growth in self-determination may make the question of whether there is freedom of choice seem abstract. At the same time there appear to be many psychological situations that are beyond help other than through superficial medication or some form of chemical alteration. In those situations one may well wonder if the Greek's view of unbending Fate was right, that there is a fundamental dimension of reality which yields to nothing and in which choice does not exist.

2. **Freedom as Appropriation.** The power of self-awareness is often noted in clinical literature. One form of self-awareness, intellectualization, consists in mere observation without psychological change. But other types of self-awareness develop through experiential encounter in which a person comes to know aspects of his or her psychological world and is changed through this knowledge. The counselee's clinical problem or concern, say fears of being homosexual or a fear of insanity, may or may not be changed by this self-knowledge, but as the person appropriates this self-understanding, he or she makes room for it in his or her relationships and day-to-day experiences, and finds that the kind of controlling power that had been exerted by the problem changes. The person can remember it, anticipate it, make adjustments in light of it, or, at deeper levels, experience qualitative change in his or her attitude or emotional relationship to the difficulty, "appropriating" it more profoundly into the sense of self. The person is more self-aware, whole, and some would say freer.

3. **Freedom and Possibility.** People who experience the world as hopeless or totally determined have no sense of possibility. When the present time is lived as qualified by possibility, on the other hand, nothing seems totally finished. The future conditions even out the events of the past. The past happens in the novelty of a continually emerging future which may recast the meaning of the past and which in most cases makes finality in the present impossible. This kind of freedom, the freedom of possibility or of being possible, can be said to characterize self-enactment of human being, to constitute its spontaneity. Freedom in this case originates in the possibility of human being, not in deliberate acts of choice.

4. **Freedom and Anxiety.** Within the phenomenological / existential orientation particularly, one finds discussions of freedom as an indeterminate capacity to be, which transcends identity states. The potentiality for being is experienced as a depth state of unease called existential anxiety (distinct from psychological anxiety, which characterizes specific individuals only and can be eliminated, at least in principle). This potent indeterminacy of human being is a capacity for change and means that no specific identity state or subjective constitution is necessary for human being. When freedom is interpreted in this way, nonfreedom is usually considered to be one's denial of the transcending state of one's being. Such denial occurs when a person is ensnared by the concerns of everyday living and is oblivious to the questions and the depth issues related to human being, such as the inevitability of ignorance and death and the possibility of profound courage and joy.

Bibliography. M. Boss, *Anxiety, Guilt, and Psychotherapeutic Liberations* (1970). F. Copleston, *History of Philosophy*, vols. 2, 3 (1960). S. Kierkegaard, *Sickness Unto Death* (1980). J. N. Lapsley, ed., *The Concept of Willing* (1967). Lucretius, *On the Nature of Things* (1969). J. S. Mill, *On Liberty* (1978).

C. E. SCOTT

CAUSALITY IN PSYCHOLOGY, FORMS OF; PERSON (Philosophical Issues); PHILOSOPHY AND PSYCHOLOGY. *See also* PROVIDENCE; PSYCHIC DETERMINISM; WILL/WILLING. *Compare* DECISION/INDECISION, PSYCHOLOGY OF; FREEDOM AND BONDAGE; HOPE AND DESPAIR; NATURE AND GRACE; SELF-TRANSCENDENCE.

FREEDOM AND PROMISCUITY, SEXUAL. *See* SEXUALITY, CHRISTIAN *or* JEWISH THEOLOGY AND ETHICS OF; SEXUAL ISSUES IN PASTORAL CARE; SEXUAL VARIETY, DEVIANCE, AND DISORDER.

FREUD, SIGMUND (1856–1939). The founder of psychoanalysis was born to Jewish parents in Freiberg, Moravia. Following a liberal humanistic and scientific education at the University of Vienna and its medical school, Freud pursued residency training in psychiatry, internal medicine, and neurology. Although he soon abandoned the anatomic and physiologic research he had pursued under Ernst Brücke, the mechanistic philosophy he imbibed there stayed with him, to some degree, throughout his career. Nevertheless, Freud's clinical work was to take him increasingly away from his mechanistic scientific origins to a purposeful approach to human psychology.

Through his work with Charcot and his conversations with Breuer, Freud had become convinced that hysterical symptoms, whatever their etiology, could be approached psychotherapeutically. This, coupled with the poor results from somatic therapies, led Freud to hypnotic suggestion in 1887. In 1889 he returned to France to improve his hypnotic technique under the tutelage of Liébault and Bernheim.

Gradually, from 1889 to 1895, Freud's psychotherapeutic technique evolved from hypnotic suggestion through hypnotic catharsis to free association in waking consciousness. From his clinical work and collaborations with Breuer, Freud concluded that the etiology of hysteria was a psychical one — the repression or strangulation of painful, disagreeable memories and affects associated with traumatic experiences. The treatment consisted of undoing the repression of the unconscious memories and affects through the free association method.

In *Studies on Hysteria* (1895) Freud clearly recognized the role of repressed sexuality in the etiology of neurosis. From 1895 to 1900, through his clinical work and self-analysis, he would become more and more convinced of the importance of sexual factors. The turning point occurred in 1897, when Freud discovered that his hysterics' accounts of seduction, which he had hitherto believed to be literally true, were often fantasies. This awoke him to the importance of psychical reality. He also uncovered, in his patients and himself, the Oedipus complex — an unconscious constellation of sexual longing for the parent of the opposite sex and rivalrous hatred toward the one of the same sex.

The year 1899, when *The Interpretation of Dreams* was published, is generally considered the birthdate of psychoanalysis. Here Freud introduced the topographic theory of the mind (the conscious, preconscious, and unconscious), the concept of primary and secondary process mentation, of dreams as the disguised fulfillment of unconscious wishes, and of dreams and neurotic symptoms as compromise formations. Soon afterward Freud advocated the significance of transference — the patient's repetition of historically determined patterns of behavior in the present. The interpretation of the historical roots of the patient's transferential behaviors came to be viewed as the cornerstone of psychoanalytic treatment.

From 1900 to 1926 Freud's ideas underwent considerable development and modification. However, he seldom totally discarded his earlier conceptions but usually incorporated them into — or allowed them to lie alongside — his later ones. Freud's growing appreciation of the defensive operations of the psyche, as they manifest themselves to the therapist in the form of resistance, led him to lay the foundations of ego psychology from 1920 to 1926. *Group Psychology and the Analysis of the Ego* (1921) and *The Ego and the Id* (1923) flesh out the structural theory of the psychic apparatus — id, ego, and superego. Along with this came the understanding that defensive maneuvers and moral ideals and prohibitions can be quite as unconscious as the impulses they oppose.

Inhibitions, Symptoms, and Anxiety (1926) presented the seminal theory of the relationship between unconscious intrapsychic conflict, anxiety, and symptom formation. In conflict an unconscious affect-laden fantasy (id impulsion), disagreeable to the demands of the superego or society, threatens to rise into consciousness, raising the possibility that it might then be translated into action. The unconscious ego experiences this as an imminent danger situation. In order to prevent the feared response from superego or society, the ego generates anxiety. This "signal anxiety," as it is termed, is unpleasurable. Since the psyche moves toward pleasure and away from pain (in accordance with the pleasure principle), the ego blocks the offending impulse from awareness and removes the need for signal anxiety. When the defense mechanism fails, a symptom results. A symptom is therefore a compromise between the unconscious fantasy striving for expression and the defense against it.

In tandem with these conceptual innovations Freud's therapeutic writings take increasing cognizance of the importance of analyzing the resistance. In other words, it becomes just as important to know why a patient is withholding a fantasy or feeling (i.e., to discern the fear that motivates the resistance) as it is to uncover the unconscious feeling or fantasy itself.

After 1926, though Freud continued to write on psychoanalytic psychology, the bulk of his original thinking shifted to culture. Among his most important contributions are his ideas on social cohesion (Freud, 1921, 1930). He came to view the bonds that unite the members of society as aim-inhibited (or sublimated) libido and the mutual identification of individuals with one another through the incorporation of a similar set of ideals. Repression of aspects of both sexuality and aggression were considered vital to the maintenance of group cohesion.

Through his impact on psychoanalysis, dynamic psychiatry, social psychology, and psychotherapeutic approaches in general, Freud remains the most influential psychologist of modern time.

Bibliography. C. Brenner, *An Elementary Textbook of Psychoanalysis*, rev. ed., (1973). S. Freud, *Introductory Lectures on Psycho-Analysis, SE*, 15, 16(1915–1916); *Civilization and Its Discontents SE*, 21 (1930) pp. 64–145.

E. R. WALLACE

PSYCHOANALYSIS. *See also* HISTORY OF PROTESTANT PASTORAL CARE; JEWISH CARE AND COUNSELING; PSYCHOLOGY IN AMERICAN RELIGION.

FREUDIAN PSYCHOLOGY. *See* PSYCHOANALYSIS.

FRIEND, PASTOR AS. *See* FRIENDSHIP, PASTOR-PARISHIONER; PASTOR (Normative and Traditional Images).

FRIENDS, SOCIETY OF. *See* QUAKER TRADITION OF CARE.

FRIENDSHIP. An enduring primary interpersonal relationship between two or more persons who share common interests and activities. Friendship is characterized by a mutual and reciprocal desire to be together for these common purposes and by varying levels of self-disclosure and intersubjective bonding.

Friendship is similar to primary kinship relationships by the character of the bonding which may occur, but differs with respect to its voluntary nature. Its outcomes or benefits include various combinations of personal support and affirmation, intellectual stimulation, professional enrichment, utilitarian assistance, and awareness of limitations. Friendship helps overcome loneliness, promotes capacities for cooperation, develops personal confidence, substitutes for family relationships, and assists with other crucial individuation and socialization tasks. Friendships may also contribute to antisocial behavior and personal dissolution.

1. **History.** Plato, Aristotle, Cicero, Augustine, Bacon, Montaigne, Emerson, and Schleiermacher have written classical essays on friendship. The moral character of friendship has played a central part in these and other interpretations. In the Graeco-Roman world friendship

was viewed as a form of love, called *philos*, and regarded as the instinctual natural basis for all positive social relationships. It was basically a male prerogative. The most pure form of *philos* was expressed in the student-teacher relationship of the philosopher and pupil. It sometimes included homosexual relationships and the practice of pederasty. The chief moral questions centered on whether good men needed friendship, thereby implying incompleteness and lack of perfection, whether evil men were capable of friendship, and whether particular friendships worked against more impersonal, disinterested, and universal forms of love. Generally, friendship was seen as possible only between virtuous men, and its proper object was the well-being of the friend. It both compensated for public evil and neglect, and contributed to the public good.

More recent writings about friendship have emphasized the psychological, sociological, and ethnological dimensions of friendship. Psychological studies, for example, have focused on such matters as intimacy, loneliness, self-disclosure, caring, bonding, and life cycle factors in friendship formation and maintenance. These perspectives shift the focus of moral concern away from the nature of virtue required by persons for friendship to exist and tend not to define friendship itself in primarily moral terms.

2. **Moral and Religious Dimensions.** The moral issues related to friendship have tended to turn on the idea that friendship is one type of love, characterized by mutuality, or *philos*, which stands in moral tension with other types of love, such as altruism, agape, sacrificial love, eros, epithemis, and libido. Many of these moral questions are largely avoided, however, when friendship is instead regarded as a particular type of interpersonal relationship in which all the dimensions of love are required, and in which one becomes normally, but not exclusively, focal. Under these circumstances, friendship is viewed as a mutual relationship which is not necessarily exclusive (as in the case of marriage), and which involves relative degrees of self-sacrifice, altruism, erotic feelings, and the commitment to achieve something beautiful in the world which transcends the friendship relationship itself. Closer inspection reveals that reciprocity is not all that occurs; friendship challenges, relativizes, and transcends egocentricity. It is a context for care for the other quite apart from a calculated response. And while friendships may stand in tension with other loyalties, they may just as well enrich and develop them. Further, it is no longer clear that impartial, disinterested, and universal forms of love are more virtuous than those which are based upon particular contextual knowledge of the needs of the receiver.

Friendship is experienced as both an achievement and as a gift. It is based upon a dialectical interplay of integrity and responsiveness. Integrity defines a person's interests, style, and commitments; it locates the individual socially and leads to potential contact with others. Responsiveness defines a person's capacity to be influenced, shaped, and changed. It is the ability to enter into novel experiences and to greater levels of self-discovery. Religiously, the onset of friendship is often experienced as providential. The acceptance and understanding within friendship are experienced as a means of divine grace, the bonding as a dimension of covenantal community, and the growth and outcomes as evidence of God's power for bringing into being new personal and social creations.

Bibliography. L. A. Blum, *Friendship, Altruism and Morality* (1980). L. K. Graham, "Ministers and Friendship," Ph.D. dissertation, Princeton Theological Seminary, University Microfilms (1978). M. E. Hunt, *Fierce Tenderness: Toward a Feminist Theology of Friendship* (1986); "Personal Growth Through the Friendship Encounter," *Humanitas*, 6 (1970), 137–252. L. B. Rubin, *Just Friends: The Role of Friendship in Our Lives* (1985).

L. K. GRAHAM

COMMUNITY, FELLOWSHIP, AND CARE; LOVE; RELATIONSHIP NETWORK. *Compare* LIFESTYLE ISSUES IN PASTORAL CARE; LONELINESS AND ISOLATION.

FRIENDSHIP, PASTOR-PARISHIONER. A relational bond of mutual respect and support between clergy and congregants in ecclesiastical contexts. Such a bond anticipates durable relationships among members of the Body of Christ who share common interests, participate in Christian ministries, bless each other's lives, bear one another's burdens, and relate from altruistic motives.

1. **Biblical Foundations.** Transforming friendship is anticipated in God's invitation to persons shut up in life's loneliness: "Call to me and I will answer you" (Jer. 33:3). To enjoy friends one must offer friendship to others (Prov. 18:24), ideally loving the neighbor as oneself (Mk. 12:33). Just as Jesus Christ claimed his followers as friends (Jn. 15:15), so the Christian pastor identifies with parishioners.

2. **Ethical Considerations.** Some authorities warn pastors against familiarity and advise an essential detachment from parishioners. Though a minister must be professionally effective as a spiritual leader, motivator, and change agent to an entire congregation, at the same time, the pastor can relate as a friend to individual members and families. A Christian pastor's availability to and goodwill for the flock are indispensable requisites for ministry. In turn, special church friends provide a supportive network, nurturing the pastoral family. As God's messenger among diverse personalities, the pastor discovers varied levels of friendship—from informal contacts to profound touches of grace and mutual care.

3. **Pastoral Approaches.** The gift of friendship is a socializing and redeeming gesture, creating spiritual family ties within a congregation. Marked by freedom and mutuality such comradeship cannot be forced, but may be offered, exchanged, or even refused. True friendship endures physical separation and the passing of time and engenders respect and trust that permit difference, even disagreement. For friendship to remain a vital force, the individuals involved must nourish relationships and heal impaired bonds. Friendship assures that one is accepted, understood, and loved. In friendship's power, one faces enemies, endures hardships, flourishes in ordinary times, and endures to the end. Just as all true neighbors do, the pastor and parishioner who are friends will sustain each other's lives and provide fiber for ethical decisions and strength for daily living.

Bibliography. D. Allen, *Love* (1987). C. W. Brister, *Take Care* (1978). C. S. Lewis, *The Four Loves* (1960). M. E. Marty, *Friendship* (1980). W. E. Oates, *The Christian Pastor* 3d ed., (1982). A. Plé, "The Place of Relationships in the Life of the Priest," *Clergy Review,* 7 (1982) 209 – 19.

C. W. BRISTER

COMMUNITY, FELLOWSHIP, AND CARE; CONGREGATION, PASTORAL CARE OF; FRIENDSHIP; RELATIONSHIP NETWORK. *Compare* AUTHORITY, PASTORAL.

FRIGIDITY. *See* SEXUAL DYSFUNCTION AND SEX THERAPY.

FROMM, ERICH (1900 – 80). Psychoanalyst and social critic whose work synthesized Freudian psychology and Marxian social theory. Born in Germany, the only child of an orthodox Jewish family, Fromm's early study of the OT and Talmud began a lifelong interest in societal ethics and religion, though he renounced his Jewish faith in 1927. After study at the universities of Heidelberg (Ph.D, 1922) and Munich, Fromm completed psychoanalytic training and began the Frankfurt Psychoanalytic Institute. He later was an early leader in "The Frankfurt School," a group of social scientists who developed social critical theory from Freudian and Marxian sources. In 1934 Fromm emigrated to the U.S. and became associated with Harry Stack Sullivan and Karen Horney. Fromm taught at a number of leading American universities and later at the National Autonomous University of Mexico, Mexico City.

From the time of the publication of Fromm's first book, *Escape from Freedom* (1941), until his death, his voluminous writings were widely read in both popular and academic circles. Influenced by both Freud and Marx, Fromm became widely known as both a psychologist and a critic of capitalist culture. His influence in relation to pastoral care and counseling is thus by virtue not only of having received attention by many of the leaders of the pastoral care and counseling movement over three decades of its rapid expansion, but also because many persons seeking the help of pastors had avidly read his exceedingly popular writings.

Bibliography. J. S. Glen, *Erich Fromm: A Protestant Critique* (1966). Don Hausdorff, *Erich Fromm* (1972).

C. V. GERKIN

CRITICAL THEORY; NEOFREUDIAN PERSONALITY THEORIES AND PASTORAL CARE. *See also* PSYCHOANALYSIS.

FRUITS OF THE SPIRIT. *See* CHRISTIAN LIFE; HOLY SPIRIT; SPIRITUALITY. *See also* CHARISMATIC PASTORAL CARE.

FULFILLMENT. *See* ESCHATOLOGY; HAPPINESS; SELF-ACTUALIZATION. *See also* PERSON.

FUN. *See* HUMOR; PLAY; WIT AND HUMOR IN PASTORAL CARE.

FUNCTION, LOSS OF. *See* LOSS OF FUNCTION.

FUNCTIONAL DISORDER. A physical or psychological disorder whose cause, continuation, or exacerbation cannot be attributed to organic factors but appears to be psychological in nature. An example is severe back pain for which no physiological explanation exists to account for either its etiology or intensity; the pain is thus assumed to be "functional," representing the somatization of psychological conflicts.

A. J. STRAATMEYER

EVALUATION AND DIAGNOSIS, PSYCHOLOGICAL; PSYCHOPATHOLOGY, THEORIES OF. *Compare* PSYCHOSOMATIC ILLNESS; SOMATIZING.

FUNCTIONALISM. *See* CULTURAL ANTHROPOLOGY OF RELIGION.

FUNCTIONS OF MINISTRY. *See* MINISTRY.

FUNDAMENTALIST PASTORAL CARE. Fundamentalism is characterized by an inerrant biblical hermeneutic, a separatist attitude, and loyalty to an authority-centered group; thus, fundamentalist pastoral care is primarily distinguished by its pervasive literalistic and legalistic use of the Bible as an authoritative pastoral resource for interpreting, diagnosing, and responding to human problems and crises. Typically, the fundamentalist pastor or lay caregiver represents the Bible with considerable pastoral authority, and often adopts a confrontational stance in relation to parishioner or counselee, a stance believed to be an expression of care in the best interest of the person or persons involved.

1. **Origins and Defining Characteristics of Fundamentalism.** According to Sandeen (1967) the roots of fundamentalism extend into the unofficial alliance between two newly formed nineteenth century theologies — dispensationalism and the Princeton theology — at the Niagara and Northfield Conferences. Representatives from both theologies repeatedly appeared on speaking platforms together as they fought against modernism and suggested several fundamentals of the faith. Over a period of time various organizations adopted different lists of the fundamentals (e.g., *The Fundamentals,* 1910) which today have developed into a five-point statement of fundamentalism: the inerrancy of Scripture, the Virgin Birth, substitutionary atonement, bodily resurrection of Jesus, and either the miracle-working power of Jesus or the Second Coming of Jesus. Thus, fundamentalism was a faith perspective offered in response to the problems of nineteenth century modernism. Through its history it has been a changing movement with diverse constituents who have opposed forms of modernism perceived to be leading to the demise of Christianity (cf. Marsden, 1980).

Fundamentalism's central tenet is a doctrine of biblical authority that affirms the absolute and inerrant authority of Scripture for life, faith, and theology. Other characteristics of fundamentalism derived from this tenet. In the late 1940s, the neo-evangelicals, those who had been called fundamentalists but who had become more tolerant of other Christian perspectives, sought dialogue and cooperation in mission. Thus, another distinguishing characteristic of fundamentalism is the doctrine of holiness or separation that influences fundamentalists to avoid dialogue and cooperation with those perceived to be willful disobeyers or deniers of Scripture. Such persons are often described as militant antimodernists. Although these two characteristics best distinguish fundamentalism, Barr (1977) suggests a third: loyalty to an authority-centered group. Fundamentalists are loyal to a local, regional, or national group of fundamentalists that is centered around an authoritative leader whom they respect and to whom they look for guidance.

2. Jay Adams as Representative. Among fundamentalist pastoral writers today Jay Adams is the most widely known and influential, and may be taken as a fair representative of contemporary fundamentalist pastoral care and counseling.

Adams emerged after a long period during which the social sciences had decisively influenced mainline pastoral care. He expressed several criticisms of this development: that pastoral care was losing its identity in relationship to the church, ministry, the Bible, and theology; that private practice counseling had little accountability to the church; and that the social sciences had more authority than the Bible as a guide for pastoral care. In response to these criticisms, Adams offered his own alternative, "nouthetic counseling," or more inclusively, a nouthetic pastoral method that makes explicit in an innovative way the traditional fundamentalist pastoral method.

a. Noutheticcounseling. "Nouthetic" is a transliteration of a Greek verb found eight times in the NT and for which Adams could find no adequate English translation, but which points to the basically spiritual character of Bible-centered counseling. Adams insists that nouthetic counseling is the counseling theory and practice taught in the Bible. In brief, nouthetic counseling aims at personal change from sin to faith and righteousness, "brought about by confrontation out of concern" for the counselee's benefit. At its core, nouthetic counseling perceives itself as biblical counseling, counseling that is to be taught by the inerrant, infallible, and authoritative Word of God and empowered by God's Spirit. It evolves from a literalistic and legalistic biblical hermeneutic and is a rational, problem-entered, behavior-oriented approach. Its major emphases include: (1) Change. Adams presupposes that persons are sinners who are responsible for their sinful behavior. Although problems do arise because of biological or accidental causes, more often than is acknowledged, problems arise from sinful living patterns (or even sinful responses to biologically or accidentally caused problems) that must be changed "in God's way." Two types of needs for change arise: change that leads to salvation and change that is part of the sanctification process. In both cases Adams uses the inerrantly biblical hermeneutic for diagnosis.

(2) Confrontation. One cannot be healed or saved by means of one's own resources. But there is hope. The Bible provides the basic text for living, providing both the way to salvation and solutions to every human problem. The nouthetic counselor is involved face-to-face with the counselee and refuses to avoid unpleasant issues. The counselor verbally confronts the counselee with biblical principles in order to convict the counselee of the sinful basis of the problem and to correct the problem by training the counselee in the new way of life. Some fundamentalists write out a list of scriptural passages to be read and obeyed, though Adams insists on the importance of explaining the prescribed principles and relating them to the problem at hand. One might also note that a pastor with a nouthetic approach must feel certain of his pastoral identity and authority, since his principles not only allow but also call upon him to confront at appropriate times.

(3) Concern. The motivation for the confrontation is love for this person who was created in the image of God. The change sought is for the benefit of the counselee.

b. Pastoral counseling in general. Adams understands pastoral counseling to be one aspect of the pastoral ministry. Indeed, he understands it to be akin to shepherding in its efforts to put "new life into one by convicting and changing, encouraging and strengthening after trial, defeat, failure, and/or discouragement" (1975, p. 14). Pastoral counseling is a ministry of the church, done by representative persons of the church, preeminently by the ordained pastor, but also by trained laity. As a ministry of the church, it takes place within the context of a body of believers who practice mutual edification and correction. In fact, the counseling session itself often includes other persons significantly related to the counselee in respect to the presenting problem.

c. Separatism. Adams strictly adheres to the doctrine of separation. First, Adams asserts that the best training for pastoral counseling is not to be found in a school of psychology or of medicine but in a seminary that provides a proper biblical and theological foundation. Second, Adams insists that one avoid all sources that do not hold biblical presuppositions. The Bible is the textbook for counseling. Admittedly, Adams does say that science may illustrate, fill in generalizations, and challenge human interpretations of the Bible. However, except for occasional references to sleep studies, one finds little evidence that Adams acknowledges that he has been informed by other disciplines, disciplines that he calls non-Christian. Further, Adams designates the evangelical view that all truth is from God as a ruse of Satan. Third, he perceives psychology and psychiatry as having incorrectly informed pastoral care and as having crossed into the turf of pastors who are the only true doctors of the soul (or psyche). Fourth, Adams is very concerned that the pastor protect his flock from those holding false doctrine. This, in effect, separates him from other Christians. Here one observes the loyalty to a group that is authority-centered and which, in fact, gains its identity from its allegiance to an inerrantly biblical hermeneutic and its separation from all groups representing other perspectives.

d. Critique. Adams accurately sees pastoral care and counseling as having to some extent forgotten its theological and ecclesial roots. In this way he holds mainline caregivers accountable. Yet his Scripture-centered response to this problem is extreme. (1) Adams's approach tends to reduce Scripture to legalistic prescriptions for solving the problems of life. (2) It offers a static and deceptively simple view of reality in which truth and right can be known and obeyed unambiguously. (3) In addition to attacking the social sciences, Adams often misrepresents them due to a simplistic misunderstanding of their theories. (4) Although his reclaiming of pastoral authority has merit, his extreme emphasis on authority may hinder psychological, intellectual, and spiritual maturity. Furthermore, nouthetic counseling's rational and certain approach can come across as impersonal, emotionally distant, and insensitive.

Bibliography. J. E. Adams, *The Big Umbrella* (1972); *The Christian Counselor's Manual* (1973); *Competent to Counsel* (1972); *Pastoral Counseling* (1975). J. Barr, *Fundamentalism* (1977). D. O. Beale, *S.B.C.: House on the Sand?* (see "Appendixes", 1985). D. E. Capps, *Biblical Approaches to Pastoral Counseling* (1981). J. A. Carpenter, "Fundamentalism," in S. S. Hill, ed., *Encyclopedia of Religion in the South* (1984). S. G. Coles, *The History of Fundamentalism* (1931). N. F. Furniss, *The Fundamentalist Controversy, 1918–1931* (1954). G. M. Marsden, *Fundamentalism and American Culture* (1980). E. R. Sandeen, "Toward a Historical Interpretation of the Origins of Fundamentalism," *Church History,* 36 (1967), 66–83.

S. D. KING

PASTORAL CARE (History, Traditions, and Definitions). *See also* BIBLICAL LITERALISM; ECCLESIOLOGY AND PASTORAL CARE; INTEGRITY THERAPY. *Compare* CHARISMATIC, EVANGELICAL, *or* SECTARIAN PASTORAL CARE; PIETISM AND PASTORAL CARE.

FUNERAL. A worship service or public ritual marking the death of an individual, including the disposition of the dead body by burial or cremation. Usually a funeral involves a clergyperson, so it can be seen as one element in the pastoral care of the bereaved. Funerals are an integral part of the mourning process, assisting individuals in coping with their grief and social groups in reintegrating without one of their members.

1. Relation of the Funeral to the Mourning Process. It is very important to see the funeral integrated into the whole mourning process, which can be conceptualized in three steps. The early stage, acute grief, centers on the disruption caused by the death of a significant other. It struggles to come to terms with the reality of that loss and its consequences. Mourners tend to be confused, seeking to grasp ways in which they can learn to cope with their loss. During the time of acute grief the mourners most closely related to the deceased are surrounded by family and friends.

A later stage, extended grief, is a more private experience in which mourners, with less structured social support, have to reorient their lives without the presence of the deceased. For most persons this period lasts at least a year.

The funeral is part of a transitional stage that comes between the shock and numbness of early grief and the slow working through of the varied feelings tied to the loss and the gradual reorganization of daily life. Thus, the funeral relates to the goals and tasks of both acute and extended grief. It participates in the ongoing grief work and should be consistent with the best understanding of grief and mourning.

2. Dimensions of the Funeral. *a. Religious.* Virtually all of the great religions give meanings to death and its aftermath. Malinowski and other anthropologists see religion growing out of human dread of death, and van Gennep describes death ritual as a rite of passage for the deceased and the mourners. In the Christian faith community the funeral is intended to convey several central meanings: the hope for new life in the face of death, the unshakable love of God, and the comforting concern of the fellowship.

b. Social. A social group, a family or community, has a life of its own. It regards the death of one of its members with a sense of loss. But at the same time the life of the group goes on. The funeral is an adaptive social structure in which a group both reaffirms the strength of its identity and acknowledges the necessary restructuring of the relationships within it.

c. Psychological. The funeral can also meet the psychological needs of the individual mourners. It undergirds the process by which the bereaved cope with their loss and points them to vital resources as they reshape their lives without the deceased.

These three dimensions blend together, each making particular contribution which complements the positive functions of the others. Although it is possible to define and design the funeral according to a single dimension, the effectiveness of the funeral in meeting the needs of the bereaved is proportionate with the number of dimensions involved.

3. Purposes of the Funeral. *a. Reenforcing awareness of loss.* Grief work invariably involves pain. Mourners must be sufficiently motivated to give psychic energy to that process. An important prerequisite for such motivation is an awareness that a significant loss has been sustained. Cognitively, bereaved persons usually acknowledge within a short period the fact of the death. Emotionally, awareness of the loss penetrates more slowly. Deeply ingrained feeling patterns take time to shift into new modes.

The funeral can help to reenforce awareness of the loss in several ways. The funeral is drama, providing an occasion for acting out the ending of visual contact and separation from the body of the deceased. The committal of the body is a demonstration of the finality of death in terms of the conclusion of the relationships of life. The funeral offers additional reenforcement of consensual validation because a number of people are feeling and responding to a sense of loss, making it more real.

b. Sanctioning the remembering process. Lindemann pointed to the essential role of memory in grief work with his "learning to live with memories of the deceased." Mourning involves making a transition from relating to a personal presence to relating to a memory. Such memory, particularly in acute grief, is painful, and the natural inclination is to avoid those things which cause discomfort; hence the value of supporting the memory process.

Some form of personalization of the funeral is possible even in the most formal liturgical patterns. The homily offers one such opportunity; use of a factual obituary another. Here mourners can be reminded of the relationships they have had with the deceased and can review the meaning of that person for their lives.

Recognizing that recollections early in the grief process are almost always positive, even idealized, pastors have sometimes been fearful of personal references in the funeral, lest they exaggerate or become overly sentimental. However, the purpose is factual description of details of the life of the deceased to support and sanction the remembering process.

c. Enabling expression of feelings. In the funeral there is a ritualized permission to mourn. Society regards expression of feelings of loss appropriate in the ritual setting. It is ironic that some funerals have a prescriptive dimension, telling mourners what they should or should not be feeling.

A permissive attitude is important to open the way for dealing with profound feelings after the funeral. Although feelings toward the deceased expressed during acute grief are usually positive, most relationships also involve negative feelings. The resulting ambivalence, if not brought to awareness, can produce considerable inner conflict. The openness of the funeral to the expression of feelings can enhance and enable persons to allow feelings of grief and ambivalence to surface and be dealt with later in the mourning process.

d. Providing support. Grief, like any pain, is intensely personal, but its impact is somewhat mitigated by the support of others who share in the loss. The funeral affords several channels for such support. Families tend to gather when a member dies. The funeral indicates the place of the deceased and the mourners in the family and the larger community. The reaffirmation of kinship patterns is seen in the ways in which people are notified of the death of a relative, the seating pattern at the funeral, and various participatory roles.

Attendance of relatives and friends at the funeral, as well as caring gifts of flowers and memorials, demonstrates support. The funeral assists the supportive process through congregational participation: unison or responsive readings, hymns, corporate prayers, and in some instances the Eucharist.

e. Guiding reorganization of life. Gradually mourners resume a relative normalcy without the deceased, but the reorientation process takes a year or more. The funeral takes only a few hours of this extended process, but it is a pivotal moment in the shift from the past to the future. The ritual enacts a turning of attention from the body of the deceased (which emotionally for many mourners still constitutes a presence) to the support of the community of the living. Mourners experience two crucial realities in the funeral. First, they separate themselves from the body of the deceased in the committal service. Secondly, they find that comfort and strength are felt in the supportive care of others, indicating that living relationships are a vital resource for their reorganization during the entire mourning process.

Gorer and others have pointed out that deritualization has exacted a heavy toll because bereaved persons are given no effective guidance through the extended mourning process, yet the limited guidance of the funeral can help point the way.

f. Affirming meaning. From the earliest times of human intelligence, people have sought to explore the meaning of death. Both philosophy and theology have participated in this quest. Recurrent questions have been: Why do all living things die? What causes death? What happens when one dies? Is there any justice in death? Many different belief systems offer poetic or metaphorical answers to such queries. These answers are often articulated in the funeral.

In the Christian church the central belief inspiring such answers is the resurrection hope. It forms the basis for the selection of Scripture readings, the offering of prayers, and the teaching of the homily. From its earliest times the church has confidently hoped that new life will emerge from death as a gift of grace. This new life, as described in the NT, is neither an exact reproduction of the present life nor the complete abrogation of that life. There is both continuity and discontinuity. The hope for new life is the foundation for the coping process of the Christian funeral. The destructive force of death is not denied, but there is the confident hope that new life is given.

4. Forms of the Funeral. There is a tremendous variety of local customs, ethnic traditions, family patterns, and liturgical practices which affect any given funeral. In times of crisis persons tend to look to the familiar and the customary for stability. To know that one does not totally have to invent ways for coping with the crisis is highly supportive.

Customs are not accidents but have their beginnings in efforts to meet particular needs. Through repetition over a period of time the self-conscious intention may become obscured and the customary practice may seem to have degenerated to an empty form. However, customs may still have some value so long as the original needs are present. Custom becomes needlessly confining only when those needs no longer exist or if superior ways for meeting the needs are available.

Especially in ministries not closely circumscribed by ecclesiastical regulation, pastors often find themselves less than satisfied with the context of customs — parish, family, ethnic — which prevail in a given community. Because of regional variations some customs followed in a community may not be identical to those with which the pastor is familiar. A common temptation for pastors is to attempt a restructuring to their familiar patterns. It is a far more helpful ministry to try to understand existing customs and their functions before attempting drastic reshaping.

Custom also involves the variety of religious forms of the funeral. If the deceased or the bereaved family is affiliated with a Christian church, there will be some guidance from the liturgical tradition of the denomination or congregation. Although there is a broad spectrum of such traditions, they fall into two major categories: churches with formal liturgical practices and those with informal worship patterns.

In churches with a strong liturgical heritage there will be a highly structured funeral service that is related to an acknowledged historical tradition and is prescribed by ecclesiastical regulation, rather than being arbitrarily shaped by the minister of the congregation. The strength of such a practice is that the same funeral service is followed for all baptized Christians, regardless of their circumstances. Usually there is provision in the homily for recognition of the unique dimensions of the life that has been lived. Because of its conserving quality, highly liturgical language avoids sentimentalism, while preserving awareness of human mortality and its tragic consequences.

In other churches, worship services, including funerals, are more informal. However, even though they might not follow historical liturgical forms, they are often, nonetheless, patterned informality. By repetition a structure is set. In funerals the informal patterns are often strongly influenced by local custom, as well as by the point of view and experience of the minister. Within these variables the informal funeral offers a high degree of flexibility and opportunity for personalization. For those reasons it sometimes risks exaggerated sentimentality. The most effective way of assuring the helpfulness of the informally structured funeral is to understand clearly and comprehensively the purposes of the funeral.

Because in most communities a religious officiant is a *de facto* requirement, families from the half of the population who do not belong to any church or synagogue are confronted with a problem when death occurs. If they wish to mark the death with a funeral, they have little option but to turn to a pastor whose church regulations do not prevent participation. The pastor is then confronted with the choice of conducting the service in accordance with regular Christian content or modifying it to emphasize the social and psychological dimensions of death and bereavement without strong emphasis on theological meanings. Such a conventional funeral can be a service to grieving families because it makes available some resources for coping with their loss, even though they do not participate in the meanings of the faith community.

5. Critiques of the Funeral. Like any institutionalized ritual, the funeral is frequently critically evaluated, both positively and negatively. As circumstances change, it is quite possible that portions of rituals will become dysfunctional. Well-founded, objective, reasoned criticism can be a valid means for making necessary and appropriate changes in social customs and ritual responses. Such critiques can be offered on psychological, sociological, economic, or theological bases (See Bowman, Farrell, Morgan). The goal of such critiques must be the more effective achievement of the objectives sought in the funeral: the separation from the deceased and the strengthening of mourners in the process of coping with their loss.

At the same time it must be recognized that the impulse to criticize the funeral can be the result of a dislike for anything that is associated with death. Negative reaction to the funeral may be for some a displacement of negative reaction against death, an acting out of the frustration and anger that is felt when confronted with mortality.

A common criticism of the funeral is that in its contemporary forms it is a "pagan" ritual. Very often this critique is directed at the involvement of the body of the deceased in the funeral. Based on a dualistic valuation of the spiritual and the derogation of the physical, any attention to the dead body is regarded as "pagan" ostentation. This criticism misses the point that such dualistic assumptions are much more attuned to Hellenistic Platonic philosophy than to the more unitary understanding of the human person contained in Scripture.

Another major criticism of the contemporary funeral is based on economics. There are those who seriously contend that funerals are needlessly expensive, causing many bereaved families to overspend, diverting money from meeting more legitimate needs. Extravagance is never justifiable, nor could one condone economic exploitation of families distraught with grief. Where such abuses occur, the economic criticism of the funeral is valid. But it can also be argued that the functional values of the funeral justify a reasonable expenditure for accomplishing the dignified disposition of the body and the provision of the psychological, social, and religious resources of the ritual.

A third criticism of the funeral is that it is an obsolete ritual. It is undoubtedly true that rituals can lose their meaning when they are cut off from their roots. But mortality remains a present reality and the benefits of ritualizing the death of a person are widely supported by the behavioral sciences (see Feifel, Fulton, Gorer, Irion). Custom and tradition can be very confining if thought of as externally imposed. But one need not be slavishly obedient or compelled to conformity. Custom should be understood as a resource to be drawn upon voluntarily and selectively. It provides a pattern based on the accumulated experience of others for meeting a crisis, a map by which mourners can chart their course.

One final criticism might be directed to the clergy. Too often pastoral care of the bereaved is heavily focused on acute grief and the funeral. This rite should be seen as an important component in *ongoing* pastoral care through the extended period of grief, rather than as a substitute for such care.

6. Current Developments in Funeral Practice. One trend increasingly seen is greater flexibility in funeral planning. While there is a stable central core containing the historical liturgical tradition or the more common practices of the informal standard, one also sees efforts at innovation. Flexibility is a response to pluralism, recognition that the spectrum of personal viewpoints and needs is so wide that a single funeral pattern cannot be helpful to everyone. Flexibility will be constructive if it focuses on new and better ways to achieve the purposes of the funeral for specific mourners. Some ways in which this flexibility is demonstrated are: inclusion of memorial comments by friends or relatives, devising services with secular rather than religious language, and greater family participation in the processes of caring for the body of the deceased or in the interment process.

Funeral practices during the past century appear to have undergone a process of simplification which continues to the present. In many communities the custom of public viewing or visitation is no longer followed. Increasingly the committal service is conducted at the church or funeral home rather than at the graveside or crematory, truncating the family participation in separating it from the deceased. In some areas, following many deaths no funeral is held. The body of the deceased is disposed of immediately following death with no ceremonial accompaniment. Sometimes a memorial service is held at a later time. In other instances there is no formal memorialization.

Perhaps more common than this is the increasing privatization of the funeral, which is attended only by family or a few close friends. Sometimes this is intentional, where a family prefers to mark the death only in the family circle, rather than as a congregation or larger community. Sometimes socio-economic factors make it very difficult for persons other than the immediate family to attend the funeral. In many instances the value of a supportive community is diminished, reflecting the general loss in our time of the sense of belonging to a larger community.

There are also some trends related to the economics of funerals which have bearing on the form and function of the funeral. A number of groups, seeking to resist funeral costs, have developed plans which accomplish only the economical disposition of the corpse with little or no ritualized resource for coping with grief. Also, prearranging is increasingly practiced. An individual or family will plan, and sometimes prepay, for a funeral which may not take place for some years. While there may be some economic advantage in doing the funeral planning apart from bereavement, it has the by-product of possible dissociation of the funeral from the specific needs which may be strongly felt at the time of the death. Prearrangement should be regarded as advisory rather than absolutely fixed, and families should have the opportunity to make such modifications as they might find specifically helpful in coping with their grief.

An increased interest in death in recent history has had a positive effect on funeral practices. As understanding of the dynamics of confronting mortality has developed, the rationale for many funeral practices has been clarified, and people have been sensitized to the resources available for coping with death and grief through ritual.

Bibliography. E. Bendann, *Death Customs* (1930). L. Bowman, *The American Funeral* (1959). N. Cassem, "The First Three Steps Beyond the Grave," in V. Pine, *Acute Grief and the Funeral* (1976). J. Farrell, *Inventing the American Way of Death* (1980). H. Feifel, *New Meanings of Death* (1977). R. Fulton, *Death and Identity*, rev. ed., (1976). I. Glick, R. Weiss, and C. Parkes, *The First Year of Bereavement* (1974). G. Gorer, *Death, Grief, and Mourning* (1965). P. E. Irion, *The Funeral and the Mourners* (1979 [1954]). *The Funeral: Vestige or Value?* (1977 [1966]). E. Jackson, *The Christian Funeral* (1966); E. Lindemann, "Symptomatology and Management of Acute Grief," in *Pastoral Psychology*, 14 (Sept. 1963) 136. B. Malinowski, *Magic, Science and Religion* (1954). L. Mills, "Pastoral Care of the Dying and the Bereaved," in L. Mills, ed., *Perspectives on Death* (1967). E. Morgan, *A Manual for Death Education and Simple Burial*, 8th ed., (1977). P. Rosenblatt, R. Walsh, and D. Jackson, *Grief and Mourning in Cross-cultural Perspective* (1976); "A Service of Death and Resurrection," *Supplemental Worship Resources*, 7 (1979). A. van Gennep, *The Rites of Passage* (1960 [1908]). Y. Spiegel, *The Grief Process* (1977). G. Vernon, *Sociology of Death* (1970).

P. E. IRION

DEATH, MEANING OF; FUNERAL DIRECTOR; GRIEF AND LOSS; MEMORIAL SERVICE. *See also* BURIAL; COMFORT/SUSTAINING; COMMUNITY, FELLOWSHIP, AND CARE; CREMATION; HOPE AND DESPAIR; MOURNING CUSTOMS AND RITUALS; RITUAL AND PASTORAL CARE; WORSHIP AND CELEBRATION.

FUNERAL, CHILD'S. The death of a child, whether suddenly or after prolonged illness, is an unanticipated and devastating loss. Inevitably, questions of theodicy arise, such as, "Why would a loving and powerful God allow this to happen?" or "What is the relationship between God's will and this tragedy?" It is out of a profound sense of helplessness — parental and pastoral— that the issues of God's love and power emerge.

When death approaches, parents often cry out in desperation for an intervention by God. The child's death becomes a major test of faith. It may be interpreted as punishment for some real or imagined sin, or as evidence of an uncaring or even nonexistent God. Anger, bitterness, and despair are normal reactions. The child's death brings a loss of innocence, an overwhelming sense of vulnerability in a world we cannot control. Basic trust is shaken. Continuity with future generations is partially or fully severed.

These are some of the issues that must be confronted in planning the child's funeral. The funeral functions as the centering point for pastoral care. Growing out of a relationship with the family, the pastor designs the service to incorporate the particularity of their loss within the context of God's promises of resurrection and hope, and to help them to articulate their faith questions. Pain must be shared before healing can occur. Easy or pious answers, however, minister more to the pastor's anxiety than to the family's pain. Labeling the event as "God's will" may temporarily relieve the guilt which parents inevitably bear, but it may also circumvent the search for meaning and growth in faith, or even cause a turning away from God. The pastor brings greater comfort through the promise that the family need not suffer alone.

It is important that the service celebrate the life of the child in relationship, affirming that the meaning of life lies not in its length but in the love which surrounds it. This love survives death and is both the source of the pain and the resource for healing. Those gathered incarnate God's presence with the family. Here is found a visible sign of hope in the midst of unbearable sadness.

Bibliography. B. C. Birch, "Biblical Faith and the Loss of Children," *The Christian Century*, 100 (1983), 965 – 67. C. M. Chakour, *Brief Funeral Meditations* (1971). J. Claypool, *Tracks of a Fellow Struggler* (1974). R. W. Willis, "Some Concerns of Bereaved Parents," *J. of Religion and Health*, 20 (1981), 133–30.

H. S. NELSON

COMFORT/SUSTAINING; FUNERAL; GRIEF AND LOSS; HOPE AND DESPAIR. *See also* CHILDREN; COMMUNITY, FELLOWSHIP, AND CARE; DEATH, MEANING OF; FAMILY, JEWISH *or* PASTORAL CARE AND COUNSELING OF; PROVIDENCE, DOCTRINE OF, AND PASTORAL CARE. *Compare* DYING CHILD AND FAMILY.

FUNERAL AND BURIAL, JEWISH. According to Jewish tradition, the funeral is a unique event for both the family and the community. The funeral, a rite of separation, acknowledges that someone has died, while offering support to the loved ones left behind.

Unlike in many religions, the Jewish funeral usually takes place within a day or two after the death has occurred. One must remember that Judaism evolved in the hot climate of the Middle East, where bodies would quickly decompose. Unless people are unusually close friends of the mourners, they usually do not disturb the family during the brief period between death and burial. This allows the bereaved the necessary time to work through the many details of the funeral as well as affording them the opportunity to experience their own personal grief. In the *Pirke O'vot* (*Ethics of the Fathers*), it is written: "Do not appease thy fellow in the hour of his anger, and comfort him not in the hour when his dead lies before him."

The Jewish funeral helps the survivors to bear the painful loss. The rabbi recites those prayers which are expressive of both the spirit of Judaism and the memory of the deceased. The most commonly used scripture is Psalm 23, which expresses the faith of the members of the flock in the justice of the Divine Shepherd. Various Psalms — "O Lord, what is man?" — epitomize the thought that although "our days are a passing shadow," there is immortality for those who have "treasured their days with a heart of wisdom." During the recitation of the prayer *El Molay Rachamim* ("God, full of mercy"), the name of the deceased is mentioned. The eulogy of the dead (*Hesped*) is included in the service to recognize not only that a death has occurred, but that a life has been lived.

Tradition deems it a most worthy deed for the friends not only to attend the funeral service but to follow the procession to the Jewish cemetery. This, the *Halvawyat Hamat*, is the ultimate demonstration of honor and respect. At the graveside, after the recitation of the *Kaddish*, the prayer of condolence is offered: "*Ha-maw-Kom Y'na-chem Es'chem B'soch Sh'aw A-vay-lay Tzee-yon Vee'roo-shaw-lay-yim*—May the Eternal comfort you among the other mourners for Zion and Jerusalem."

Following the funeral, the *Shiva* (literally, "seven"), the seven days of intense mourning, begins. Acquaintances visit the bereaved and offer their condolences during this specified mourning period. Jewish tradition dramatizes the reality that even though individuals may die, caring friends still remain.

Some friends bring food to the home for "the meal of condolence," with the thought that life must continue for the survivors. Flowers generally are not sent either to the funeral home or the house of the bereaved; it is felt that the monies may best be spent to help others less fortunate through charitable donations, and newspaper obituaries often make such a request. This is the family's recommendation for remembrance, but it does not necessarily exclude other forms of expression.

It is always appropriate to express condolences with a sympathy card or, preferably, an individual letter. A sharing of personal memories is the most meaningful record that the bereaved will read and reread in the future. Love and memory will never die.

Bibliography. N. Linzer, *Understanding Bereavement and Grief* (1976).

E. A. GROLLMAN

GRIEF AND MOURNING, JEWISH CARE IN; JEWISH HOLY DAYS AND HOLIDAYS FESTIVALS. *See also* JEWISH PRAYERS; MOURNING CUSTOMS AND RITUALS. *Compare* BURIAL; FUNERAL.

FUNERAL DIRECTOR. Funeral Director emerged as a vocation in the twentieth century as a response to urbanization and specialized sanitation techniques in the preparation of bodies for burial. More recently funeral directors have come to function as the primary source and organizer of services at the time of death. Thus the relationship between them and the minister is a crucial one.

The funeral director tends to be an anomolous member of the professional community. Working with people in times of emotional crisis calls for professional insight, yet the role also calls for the providing of merchandise and services such as transportation and public facilities for private services. While most professionals have facilities provided and financed by the community, such as hospitals, schools, courthouses, and churches, funeral directors provide their own facilities. This deviation from the norm causes problems and misunderstandings.

Pastors and funeral directors share the responsibility for ministering to bereaved persons; at times this produces an adversary relationship from which the bereft suffer. It is therefore important to have a clear understanding of lines of responsibility and cooperation. The funeral director is, in a real sense, a director or conductor who orchestrates a large variety of activities, personal and social, that go into the rites, rituals, and ceremonies that provide a proper atmosphere for expressing valid feelings and for providing group support.

The earliest evidences of civilized behavior appear in the physical remains of ancient funeral practices. Cro-Magnon humans, the diggings in Persia 70,000 years ago, and the Pyramids give evidence that reveals how early people confronted death and grief. As Nazi activity showed, it is only the sick civilization that tries to deny the value of life and the ceremonial practices that verify that value. The function of the cathedral as a burying place and the cemetery adjacent to the church indicates a long-standing relationship of religion and the rites and rituals surrounding death and grief. In this relationship a funeral director may be either a good ally or an unfortunate adversary.

From the pastoral care perspective, the encounter at the time of death is rich in opportunity for psychological movement, because very deep feelings are prevalent. People can be easily offended or unusually responsive. Thus it becomes important that the funeral process serve effectively to meet the needs of people. To this end, the funeral includes a series of psychological and spiritual steps that may best be performed in a logical manner, as outlined in the nine parts of the funeral process indicated in the Service of Death and Resurrection prepared by The United Methodist Church for the ministry of the church at death, (found in Supplemental Worship Resources #7). It is thus important that both funeral director and pastor be acquainted with the concept of the funeral as a process rather than as an event.

Until recent years the funeral director, like former generations of clergypersons, had little education but considerable motivation to serve. Now, in most parts of the country, educational standards are set and licensing after proper examination is required. In most training schools for funeral directors, courses in crisis psychology and crisis management are taught. This may make the funeral director a well informed colleague on the team of professionals who serve the community and its needs in time of death. Thus cooperation between pastor and funeral director can become a benefit to the bereft.

E. N. JACKSON

BURIAL; CREMATION; FUNERAL; FUNERAL AND BURIAL, JEWISH; MEMORIAL SERVICE.

FUTURE/FUTURE ORIENTATION. *See* ESCHATOLOGY; HOPE AND DESPAIR; TIME/TIME SENSE.

G

GAMBLER'S ANONYMOUS. *See* ALCOHOLICS ANONYMOUS; GROUP COUNSELING AND PSYCHOTHERAPY; SUPPORT GROUPS.

GAMBLING. To gamble is to take a calculated risk for monetary or personal gain. Two-thirds of all Americans engage in some form of legal gambling such as casinos, bingo, office pools, lotteries, dog and horse racing, and jai alai. Illegal gambling, such as numbers and bookmaking, draws additional millions each day. Even speculation on the stockmarket is a form of gambling. For a subset of people, gambling becomes a pathological behavior pattern with extensive social and economic complications. Compulsive gamblers are unable to resist the urge to gamble regardless of the consequences. For such individuals, the result is almost invariably financial loss because, in almost all games of chance, the odds are greatly against the bettor.

There are at least fifteen million compulsive gamblers in the United States. In the present psychiatric nomenclature, compulsive gambling is classified as a disorder of impulse control. It is characterized by inability to resist gambling combined with compromise of family, personal, and/or vocational pursuits. In severe cases this may be further complicated by involvement in criminal activity or by borrowing money from illegal sources to finance gambling. Gamblers who commit crimes usually do so as a result of financial desperation, rather than because of more severe character pathologies. Substance abuse, depression, and anxiety may also be present in some cases. Compulsive gambling is generally considered an acquired behavior which is the result of environmental influence rather than an innate biological predisposition. While the term compulsive is used to describe these behaviors, the disorder is distinct from obsessive-compulsive disorders which consist of repetitive stereotyped acts such as cleaning and checking.

Given the number of pathological gamblers, surprisingly little empirical research has been conducted. In the domain of treatment, the literature describes primarily behavioral techniques. Extensive work has been done on risk-taking and decision-making in laboratory experiments, but it is not known how these findings generalize to compulsive gamblers. Most studies are confounded by other factors, for example, the trivial nature of the tasks, use of college students rather than clinical populations as subjects, lack of possible financial gain, and the absence of ego-involvement. The majority of the literature on compulsive gambling consists of the opinions of clinicians who have worked with such individuals. This results in a number of theoretical positions on the etiology as well as the treatment of the disorder.

In behavioral terms, gambling provides a variable schedule of reinforcement. This type of schedule creates behavior patterns that are highly resistant to extinction. It is the occasional win that promotes the behavior.

Some authors believe that the thought of gambling creates a state of arousal that leads to the behavior. Gambling may produce positive emotional arousal by eliciting cognitive states such as pride, courage, or release from reality. Therefore, it may be that gamblers experience an unpleasant tension if they refrain from gambling.

Gambling may also be conceptualized as adult play. According to Freud, play has four functions: wish fulfillment, conflict reduction, temporary leave of absence from reality, and the shift from a passive to an active state.

Other psychodynamically oriented experts focus on the role of conflict reduction in gambling. The conflict may be over unconscious aggression and/or early oedipal issues. Gambling may be a form of self-punishment for such forbidden urges and thereby reduces conflict.

Still others suggest that gamblers may need to take risks which are satisfied by wagering. Such individuals may be described as sensation-seekers who take monetary and perhaps social risks in gambling that provide needed stimulation. Also, gambling has been conceptualized as an addiction, with similar dynamics and treatment requirements.

There are several treatments possible for compulsive gamblers. Behavioral treatments focus on the teaching of self-control techniques and may employ methods such as aversion therapy and imaginable desensitization. The treatment of choice for various intrapsychic orientations is individual therapy aimed at resolving conflicts. Gamblers Anonymous is a self-help group similar to Alcoholics Anonymous. Participation includes public admission of the problem and group support for members. While not a religious organization, participants are encouraged to utilize belief in a higher power to aid in overcoming their difficulties.

Treatment and referral of such individuals requires recognizing that gambling may only be a portion of the total problem. Gamblers commonly do not seek assistance until the situation has become quite extreme. Thus, assessing not only the gambling problem but also emotional, financial, legal, and interpersonal circumstances is important.

Bibliography. E. Bergler, *The Psychology of Gambling* (1974). H. R. Lesiour, "The Compulsive Gambler's Spiral of Options and Involvement," *Psychiatry,* 42 (1979), 790–87. H. Milt, *Compulsive Gambling,* Public Affairs Pamphlet No. 598 (1981). S. Winston and H. Harris, *Nation of Gamblers* (1984).

M. R. SMITH

MORAL THEOLOGY AND PASTORAL CARE; RESPONSIBILITY/ IRRESPONSIBILITY, PSYCHOLOGY OF. *See also* BORDERLINE PERSONALITY; LIFESTYLE ISSUES IN PASTORAL CARE; MONEY; OBSESSIVE-COMPULSIVE DISORDER. *Compare* CHRISTIAN LIFE; JEWISH LIFE.

GAMES. *See* MANIPULATION; PLAY; TRANSACTIONAL ANALYSIS.

GAUME, ABBÉ JEAN JOSEPH (1802–79). French Catholic priest, theologian, author of 45 works.

Known for a life of piety, zeal, and friendliness, Gaume is identified chiefly with two causes: the recovery of early Christian authors for Catholic spiritual direction and catechetics, and the practice of auricular confession. Both of these subjects are treated extensively in his popular work, *Le Manuel des Confesseurs* (1837), and they are combined insofar as Gaume advocates a form of pastoral care that relies on the methods of spiritual directions of great Catholic masters. Termed "auricular confession," this method is a most directive form of counseling. As a prescriptive type of guidance it assumes the superiority of the spiritual director over the troubled person who receives information, exhortation, admonishment— even threats— from the helper.

This method was the dominant mode in eighteenth and nineteenth century France, and its diligent exposition in *Le Manuel* makes Gaume an important figure for the field of pastoral care.

N. F. HAHN

ROMAN CATHOLIC PASTORAL CARE; SPIRITUAL DIRECTION; SPIRITUALITY (Roman Catholic Tradition).

GAY LIFESTYLE AND RIGHTS. *See* HOMOSEXUALITY; LIFESTYLE ISSUES IN PASTORAL CARE.

GEMARA. *See* JEWISH LITERATURE IN CARE AND COUNSELING.

GENDER. *See* SEXUALITY.

GENERAL HOSPITAL CHAPLAINCY. Religious ministry rendered in the context of a primarily medically oriented health care institution.

A general hospital is a health care institution that accepts persons with a wide variety of illnesses and injuries and covers the complete range of ages. Distinctions between general hospitals and specialty hospitals such as psychiatric or rehabilitation facilities are diminishing as general hospitals expand their areas of care to include potentially any health related activity oriented to diagnosis, treatment, or prevention. The modern general hospital is a product of the late nineteenth and early twentieth centuries as the number of hospitals increased from under 200 to over 4,000 in 1920. This increase followed the developments of the germ theory of disease, aseptic surgery, diagnostic modalities such as radiology, and improvements in physician training. Pastoral care by trained chaplains in general hospitals began in the 1930s.

1. History. The pattern for general hospital chaplaincy in the early 1900s was for a hospital to secure the services of a retired minister without any special training to visit patients. The first instance of a general hospital appointing a clinically trained chaplain was the employment of Austin P. Guiles in 1930 at Massachusetts General Hospital. His successor in 1933, Russell Dicks, powerfully influenced the expansion of the minister's place in the general hospital with the 1936 publication (with Richard C. Cabot) of *The Art of Visiting the Sick.* The American Protestant Hospital Association adopted standards for general hospital chaplains in 1940.

The use of trained hospital chaplains expanded dramatically after World War II as a result of increased familiarity with military chaplaincy and the growing Clinical Pastoral Education (CPE) movement. Founding members of the College of Chaplains (1946) were primarily general hospital chaplains. The Veterans Administration established a Chaplaincy Service in 1945, although chaplains had been serving in a predecessor institution since 1866. By the early 1970s, 43 percent of hospitals had a chaplaincy service; in 1985, 65 percent of hospitals (4,100) reported having chaplaincy services.

A milestone in the recognition of general hospital chaplaincy was the 1967 statement on chaplaincy by the American Hospital Association (AHA):

> The American Hospital Association recognizes that chaplaincy programs are a necessary part of the hospital's provision for total patient care, and that qualified chaplains and adequate facilities, as well as the support of administration and medical staff, are essential in carrying out an effective ministry for patients.

This was followed by publication of the AHA *Manual on Hospital Chaplaincy* in 1970. The concept of the general hospital chaplain is in agreement with the modern health care philosophy which recognizes the need for total patient care, including the physical, mental, spiritual, and social dimensions of life. The chaplain is a symbol that the institution recognizes the impact of values, morals, ethics, rituals, and religious beliefs on the health/illness continuum.

2. Structure. Hospital chaplaincy programs have several different patterns, depending on such factors as size of hospital, financial resources, hospital ownership, and administrative philosophy. The major patterns are: (1) full-time chaplain(s) offering direct service and education for ministers such as CPE; (2) full-time chaplain(s) offering direct service; (3) part-time chaplain(s) offering direct service or organizing the services of local ministers; and (4) a volunteer program utilizing local ministers. Financial support patterns also vary, including: (1) full funding by the hospital; (2) partial funding by the hospital and by an outside source; and (3) full funding by an outside source such as a denomination or group of churches.

3. Tasks. Although many of the tasks are similar to other chaplaincy ministries, the context of general hospital chaplaincy is unique. Circumstances of birth and death, chronic disease and disability, high technology, short stays, and high costs influence the chaplain's goals and methods. The experience of a patient in a general hospital is affected by the loss of control over one's own life; by fear of pain, discomfort, the unknown, and death; and by hope for cure, for improvement, or for survival. The anxiety of human finitude is the theological context in which diminished health, loss of functioning, and loss of life is threatened. This anxiety raises issues of faith—how one views the world, how one views God, how one finds meaning, and whether one can trust. In the midst of a host of professionals who focus on particular aspects of disease, the chaplain focuses on the whole person. The chaplain is not concerned with the disease alone, but with how significant dimensions of the patient's life are affected by the disease or injury. The chaplain's perspective is wholistic and centered on meaning, value, and relationships. The chaplain brings to the bedside the pastor's role as a representative of God and the religious community; affirmation that one may enjoy fulfillment and meaning in spite of pain and disability; and the hope that, whatever the outcome of the course of the illness, one may feel secure in God's hands. Hope is transformed from wishing for concrete results into confidence in One transcending human limitations.

In these circumstances the general hospital chaplain offers support, comfort and consolation for patients; counseling with patients about a variety of problems and decisions; sacramental ministry; pastoral care and counseling of staff; worship leadership; liaison relations with community, clergy, and churches; education of clergy; development of community relations; and administration.

The general hospital chaplain has been compared to the clown in a circus (see Faber). Trapeze artists and high wire walkers are impressive and awesome with their feats of skill and daring, but the audience cannot personally identify with them. The clowns come between acts and bring the show back in perspective as the audience identifies with their human follies. In the general hospital environment of high technology, esoteric languages, and superbly skilled staff, the chaplain brings a human dimension and introduces the transcendent by presence, prayer and rituals.

4. Training. The usual requirements for becoming a general hospital chaplain include a college degree, the basic seminary degree, the equivalent of a full year of CPE, and endorsement by one's denomination.

5. Issues. Some issues in most chaplaincy ministries are highlighted in the general hospital setting. The chaplain constantly reaches out to strangers who will be institutionalized for only a brief time. The frequent turnover of "congregation" requires that the chaplain look to the institution's staff as a more steady constituency. The staff have their own particular needs aggravated by a high-intensity, life and death setting which provides frequent opportunities for pastoral care and counseling. Teamwork is a challenge as the chaplain may have opportunities to write in charts and serve on interdisciplinary teams, and to seek consultation and exchange of information with other team members in brief encounters.

Church relationships for the general hospital chaplain are similar to other chaplaincies. The chaplain must maintain dual institutional loyalty (both to the church and to the hospital), maintain credentials in a particular denomination, and receive emotional and ecclesiastical support from the denomination. While there is less of an inherent conflict between church and institution in the case of a health care chaplaincy (objectives are similar: health, healing, wholeness), there may still be some struggle over control of the chaplain's ministry regarding particular goals and evaluation.

The dominant issues in modern general hospital chaplaincy relate to changes in the institution. An explosion in technology has given medicine the ability to push the limits of life from birth to death. New procedures raise ethical questions such as the prolongation of life by machines, test tube conception, surrogate mothering, genetic counseling, informed consent, euthanasia, etc. Additional ethical questions are raised by changed reimbursement schedules, government regulations, rising medical costs, and allocation of health care resources. General hospital chaplains may have opportunities to address these issues on hospital ethics committees, in administrative offices, and in church forums.

New challenges for general hospital chaplains are briefer hospital stays and sicker patients; the proliferation of outpatient facilities and home health care; an aging population which constantly increases the percentage of the elderly in hospitals; and staff members experiencing additional stress due to shortage of available personnel.

Bibliography. American Hospital Association, *Manual on Hospital Chaplaincy* (1970). R. C. Cabot and R. L. Dicks, *The Art of Ministering to the Sick* (1936). H. Faber, *Pastoral Care in the Modern Hospital* (1971). A. M. Kuby and C. M. Beloge. "AHA Surveys Chaplaincy Programs," *Hospitals, J. of the American Hospital Association,* 48 (1974), 98–102. L. E. Holst, ed., *Hospital Ministry: The Role of the Chaplain Today* (1985). L. D. Reimer and J. T. Wagner, *The Hospital Handbook,* 2d ed., (1988).

W. R. MONFALCONE

CHAPLAINCY; INTERPROFESSIONAL TEAMS AND RELATIONSHIPS; MINISTRY. *See also* PASTORAL CARE MOVEMENT; SALVATION, HEALING, AND HEALTH.

GENERAL SYSTEMS THEORY. *See* SYSTEMS THEORY.

GENERALIZING. *See* DEFENSIVENESS, PASTORAL.

GENERATIONAL CONFLICT. *See* FAMILY THEORY AND THERAPY.

GENEROSITY. *See* AVARICE AND GENEROSITY (Moral Theology); GRACE; GRATITUDE. *See also* LOVE; SACRIFICIAL BEHAVIOR; VIRTUE, CONCEPT OF.

GENETIC COUNSELING. Interpreting genetically related birth defects and health problems to at-risk individuals and families. Genetic counselors help counselees to comprehend medical facts, including diagnosis, prognosis, and available treatment; understand available options for subsequent pregnancies; and make informed decisions in an emotionally supportive climate.

Bibliography. M. W. Clark, "The Pastor as Genetic Counselor," *J. of Religion and Health,* 20 (1981) 317–32. National Center for Education in Maternal and Child Health, "Resources for Clergy in Human Genetic Problems: A Selected Bibliography" (1985).

M. K. ARMISTEAD

AMNIOCENTESIS; FAMILY PLANNING; MORAL DILEMMAS IN PASTORAL PERSPECTIVE. *See also* DECISION/INDECISION, PSYCHOLOGY OF.

GENETICS/GENETIC DISORDERS. *See* BIOLOGICAL DIMENSIONS OF PERSONALITY AND BEHAVIOR; GENETIC COUNSELING. *See also* SOCIOBIOLOGY.

GENOCIDE. *See* HOLOCAUST.

GENTILES. *See* CONVERSION (Jewish Care and Counseling); JEWISH-CHRISTIAN MARRIAGE.

GERKIN, CHARLES V. *See* PASTORAL THEOLOGY, PROTESTANT.

GERONTOLOGY/GERIATRIC CARE. *See* AGING; OLDER PERSONS, PASTORAL *or* JEWISH CARE AND COUNSELING OF.

GESTALT PSYCHOLOGY AND PSYCHOTHERAPY. Gestalt is a German word meaning whole or pattern. A Gestalt is a pattern of elements that forms a meaningful whole. A song, for example, is a group of notes which when put together in a certain pattern form something more than the sum of the parts. If these parts are analyzed or taken apart, the whole is lost. The emphasis of the early Gestalt psychologists — M. Wertheimer (1925), W. Köhler (1929), K. Koffka (1935), and K. Goldstein (1939) — was not on analysis as in traditional psychology but rather on looking after meaningful, perceptual patterns. In this movement terms such as proximity, Prägnanz, similarity, organizational set, direction, absorption, resistance, and stability entered psychological experimentation, later to be utilized in applied fields. Learning and growth were seen primarily as reorganizing assimilated material into new ways of seeing things — the "aha" experience.

1. Gestalt Psychotherapy. Gestalt psychotherapy was developed by Frederick and Laura Perls (1951, 1973). Frederick was a psychiatrist who was not satisfied with the Freudian psychology in which he was trained. Laura was a psychologist who had studied with the early Gestaltists. In the late 1930s and 1940s they developed Gestalt therapy.

Gestalt therapy incorporates the major concepts of Gestalt psychology as well as incorporating concepts from Sigmund Freud, Carl Jung, Wilhelm Reich, humanistic psychology, existentialism, and phenomenology.

Gestalt psychology, especially as it has found expression in counseling and psychotherapy, has influenced pastoral care and counseling in a variety of ways. At the onset of the modern pastoral care movement, much pastoral care and practically all pastoral counseling was based on a talk model of doing counseling, usually patterned after either psychoanalysis or client-centered therapy. In the early 1950s, however, at a time when pastoral counseling specialists were searching for newer and different modalities, Frederick Perls published *Gestalt Therapy* (1951), which summoned the psychotherapeutic community to focus more on emotional spontaneity and sensitivity to the body, which could lead to insight, greater awareness, a healthy expressiveness, and more acute identification of feelings.

Although many pastoral care persons remained opposed to such seemingly radical notions, a significant number were attracted to the innovations, particularly to the variety of techniques being developed e.g., guided fantasy, daydreaming, role-playing, the use of imagery, double-chair encounters, relaxation instruction. Frequently such techniques took form in what came to be called the human potential therapies and the growth counseling settings, and they found their way into pastoral care activities, especially pastoral counseling, CPE group counseling, and marriage and family enrichment work (H. Clinebell, 1972; T. C. Oden, 1972).

The emphasis in Gestalt therapy is working with the whole person. The focus of therapy is "in the now" and on the "how." There is very little analyzing. Analyzing is seen as usually being rationalization, a "head trip," rather than an activity leading to change. In the Gestalt approach the therapist sets up experiments or exercises to help clients see and accept what they are doing and how they are doing it. With this *awareness* the client has a choice of continuing to behave that way or doing something new to see if the new behavior is more satisfying.

2. Central Concepts. *a. Organism-environment field.* The Gestalt approach holds that an individual perceives his or her environment as a total unit of meaning; he or she responds to all experiences. The whole is perceived in one of two ways, as "figure," those stimuli to which he or she attends, and "background," the stimuli to which he or she does not attend. The "figure" or foreground has meaning only in the context of the background.

The person's foreground is continually changing with one foreground flowing into another. This flow of Gestalts or patterns is the basis of our experience. This experience is a constantly changing process. In any given situation what is "foreground" for one person may not be for another, making each of us unique.

b. Organismic self-regulation. The flow of individual experience is far from random, however. What becomes foreground for an individual is based upon his or her own need system at the moment. When a person is functioning freely, he or she will make contact with the environment in ways that meet the needs of the organism. This is conceptualized as the wisdom of the organism, and the process is called organismic self-regulation (Goldstein, 1939).

Organismic self-regulation comes out of direct organismic experiencing. It is based on our awareness of our whole being and thus is intuitive rather than intellectual.

c. Psychological homeostasis. Organismic self-regulation functions to keep the person centered or balanced. Following this inner knowing allows one to meet one's needs as best one can, given the organism-environment field one is in at the time. The organism is regulated by its own psychological homeostasis, so that when one is thirsty, getting a drink becomes foreground; when one is lonely, finding some personally satisfying contact becomes foreground. The most pressing need will come to the foreground and orient the person to maintain a balance or homeostasis.

d. Awareness. Awareness is the central method by which we can contact our environment and meet our needs and thus experience balance and satisfaction. Awareness is a kind of organismic self-knowing and is always in process. It is through awareness that we can know what is "right for us." Awareness of our organism gives us a sense of direction and motivation to become more fully who we are. Awareness clarifies for us what our most pressing need is and what options we have to meet that need. With awareness of our organism and our environment we have choice and freedom. With that choice and freedom we can contact, act on, or interact with, our environment to meet our needs. Without awareness, contact is incomplete and a weak or poor Gestalt is formed. This results in unfulfilled needs and dissatisfaction.

3. The Therapy Process. *a. The paradoxical theory of change.* Gestalt theory holds that change and growth take place when one becomes what one is, rather than when one tries to be what one is not. Change at a personality level does not happen by trying to be better, saying, "I should change," by coercion or persuasion or by interpretation or "guidance." Growth takes place by first fully owning what we do and how we do it. Gestaltists believe we need to know where we are before we can move to a new place. Paradoxically, it is by standing still and becoming aware of ourselves just as we are that we become able to grow and expand our boundaries. This philosophy also holds for the therapist who needs to be authentic. Therapy is a risk-taking relationship where both client and therapist share their experience of the moment. It is an exercise in being fully truthful and expanding our awareness of ourselves.

b. Acceptance. Based on the paradoxical theory of change it becomes clear that acceptance is a central task in the therapy process. First there is clarifying and finding out just who and what one is, how one behaves, thinks, and feels; the second step is to accept oneself. Self-acceptance is difficult for many clients. The therapist functions as a model, for when clients own where they are and are truthful about themselves, the natural organismic response of the therapist is acceptance. This helps the clients to accept themselves as well.

c. Responsibility. When one owns who one is and what one does and accepts oneself as one is, then one has taken responsibility for oneself in Gestalt terms. Responsibility means a person does not blame friends, God, culture, or parents for one's actions, but claims them as one's own. It is by taking responsibility for ourselves that we gain freedom and choice. With freedom and choice we become the "master of our ship" and can choose to change.

d. Support. Before a client can change, support is necessary. Since we exist in an organism-environment field in order to change and grow we must have support from our environment. This includes such basic support as air, water, and food, and, equally important, the support of friends, family, community, and our own selves. In therapy, when a client is growing, risking, pushing out his or her boundaries, or trying new behaviors, it is important that the therapist authentically support this movement.

In summary, by being aware of who, what, and how we are, by accepting and owning this, by being clear about what we want, and by having a support system we have the freedom to grow, be satisfied, and be free to be a service to the organism-environment field of which we are a part.

4. Importance for Ministry and Religious Values. The Gestalt approach lends itself to being incorporated in part or as a whole in pastoral care (e.g., W. A. Knights, 1970). A number of clergy have been fully trained as Gestalt therapists. Much more common, however, are pastors who incorporate parts of Gestalt therapy into their counseling and work with individuals, families, groups, and congregations (Clinebell, 1972).

In terms of values, the concepts of acceptance, owning, and acknowledging openly who and what we are, being clear about our needs, freedom, responsibility, and support all fit into basic Christian values. The emphasis on present experiences or the now in Gestalt is not a hedonistic emphasis. Gestaltists focus on living *in* the now, not *for* the now. This promotes awareness rather than hedonism. There are, however, some aspects of the Gestalt philosophy and its "ultimate metaphor" which appear to run counter to much of traditional Christianity's "metaphysical horizon" (T. C. Oden, 1972).

Depending upon a particular pastor's orientation, the concept of organismic self-regulation may go beyond trust of self or parishioners; however, it is important to know that in Gestalt that process goes beyond or behind our defenses, our games, and our avoidances to the essence of what we are. In Gestalt, self-knowing may be interpreted as the deepest kind of God-given self-knowing. It is being true to our innermost wisdom, our conscience.

This inner wisdom is also applied to our relationship to our neighbor and to the world around us. Psychological development in Gestalt terms goes from dependency to independency to interdependency. It is in the last stage, interdependency, when we are able to "love our neighbor as our self," and it is in the earlier two stages where we learn to love ourselves.

Bibliography. D. S. Browning, *Religious Thought and the Modern Psychologies* (1987). H. Clinebell, *Growth Groups* (1972). K. Goldstein, *The Organism* (1939). W. A. Knights, "A Gestalt

Approach in a Clinical Training Group," *J. of Pastoral Care*, 24 (1970), 193–98. K. Koffka, *Principles of Gestalt Psychology* (1935). W. Köhler, *Gestalt Psychology* (1929). T. C. Oden, *The Intensive Group Experience: The New Pietism* (1972). F. Perls *et al.*, *Gestalt Therapy* (1951); *The Gestalt Approach* (1973). W. Wertheimer, *Gestalt Theory* (1925). V. Vande Reit, M. Korb, and J. Gorrell, *Gestalt Therapy: An Introduction* (1980).

V. VANDE REIT

PERSONALITY THEORY *or* PSYCHOTHERAPY (Varieties, Traditions, and Issues); PSYCHOLOGY. *See also* PHENOMENOLOGICAL PSYCHOLOGY AND PSYCHOTHERAPY; PHILOSOPHY AND PSYCHOLOGY; POPULAR THERAPEUTIC MOVEMENTS AND PSYCHOLOGIES. *Compare* HUMANISTIC PSYCHOLOGY *or* PSYCHOTHERAPIES; SELF PSYCHOLOGIES. *Biography:* PERLS.

GESTURES. *See* BODY LANGUAGE; COMMUNICATION; DRAMA AS MODE OF CARE; RITUAL AND PASTORAL CARE; SYMBOLIC DIMENSIONS OF PASTORAL CARE RELATIONSHIPS.

GET. A Jewish divorce contract. Although the GET is based on Deut. 24:1, "He writes her a writ of divorce . . . ," its wording was established only in Roman times. The GET contains the name of the husband, the name of the wife, the husband's declaration that the wife is free to remarry, and the signature of witnesses. A GET is always given to the wife by the husband. A woman who is not given a GET may not remarry, according to traditional Jewish Law, and is termed an "agunah" (lit. 'anchored woman').

P. J. HAAS

DIVORCE AND REMARRIAGE (Judaism).

GHOST. *See* PARAPSYCHOLOGY; SURVIVAL (Occult).

GIBBONS, JAMES CARDINAL (1834–1921). Roman Catholic archbishop of Baltimore and influential leader of the American Catholic Church. Gibbons's great apologetic work, *The Faith of Our Fathers* (1876), exhibited the contemporary pastoral theological style of "naturalness, cheer, and informality" regarding pastoral topics (e.g., penitential confession), as did his later *Ambassadors of Christ* (1896), which stressed the family as context for religious education.

N. F. HAHN

PASTORAL THEOLOGY, ROMAN CATHOLIC.

GIFTED CHILD. A child whose academic, intellectual, or artistic abilities make it possible for him or her to function at a level of achievement far above that of his or her chronological peers. The positive characteristics most often observed in these children are: verbal precocity, a highly developed sense of humor, an attention span beyond that of their peers, an ability to synthesize, analyze, see relationships, and make high levels of cognitive transitions. Gifted children may also have a high level of sensitivity and difficulty with socialization and self-image.

E. KEARNEY

EXCEPTIONAL CHILDREN AND THEIR FAMILIES. *See also* CHILDREN; FAMILY, JEWISH *or* PASTORAL CARE AND COUNSELING OF; INTELLIGENCE AND INTELLIGENCE TESTING.

GIFTS OF THE SPIRIT. *See* CHARISMATIC EXPERIENCE; CHRISTIAN LIFE; HOLY SPIRIT; SPIRITUALITY.

GIVING AND RECEIVING. Human interaction usually involves giving and receiving on the part of both parties. A satisfactory human exchange is one in which the giver and the receiver come away with feelings of positive regard for each other. In a pastoral care relationship, giving and receiving need to be kept in balance. If this is not done, the giver becomes depleted and may need to look for artificial props to avoid the burnout that follows a sustained imbalance between giving and receiving.

1. **Postures of Giving and Receiving.** "Give, and it will be given to you" (Lk. 6:38) are words addressed to givers that are also a reminder that givers must be receivers if they are going to be sustained. There are postures of giving that prevent a mature relationship from developing between pastor and parishioner and there are also ways of giving that sustain growth and relationship between them.

a. Signs of immature exchanges. Giving can usually be measured by its results along with the feelings it leaves in its wake. Negative results come when giving increases the dependency of the one receiving. Such giving may have the aim of expanding a pastor's worth or power. Other examples of giving that bring negative results are: giving that draws attention to the giver, giving that leaves guilt or obligation in the one receiving, giving that leaves resentment in the one receiving, giving that produces shame in the receiver, giving that makes the receiver less potent, giving that is self-serving, giving that is seductive in nature.

b. Signs of mature exchanges. Mature giving will include some of the following: giving that seeks to meet needs of both parties, giving that includes at least some of the self, giving that provides the one receiving with a chance to give or share the self.

2. **The Nature of Exchanges in Pastoral Care.** Only a beggar would expect to get silver or gold from a pastor. This was the case of the man lame from his birth who was placed before the Temple in Jerusalem to beg. The Apostle Peter let the beggar know that he had no material gifts to offer, but brought him the healing of his infirmity (Acts 3:1–10).

Pastors are not usually looked to as owners or dispensers of material wealth. On the other hand parishioners traditionally look upon themselves as the material support of the clergy. Hence in these relationships custom dictates that pastoring persons give in the area of nonmaterial gifts. For example, pastors give counsel, advice, support, care. In other words they give "spiritual gifts," or service that may be difficult to measure in terms of material worth. In contrast, the parishioner, as receiver of the nonmaterial offerings of the clergy, is usually expected to give something material and measurable.

3. **The Factor of Obligation.** *a. In pastoral care.* Parishioners traditionally expect pastoral care in times of crisis such as sickness, accident, misfortune, and death. However, there are occasions when their needs extend

beyond normal expectations. This may leave a person with a sense of obligation or unpaid debt if a pastor goes beyond the call of duty in support and care.

When the parishioner feels obligated for pastoral care, such feelings can be better handled through open discussion. The pastor who ignores these feelings and keeps on giving may force too much indebtedness. This can then lead to such results as a parishioner withdrawing to get away from the feelings or, on the opposite side, one may give the pastor a lavish gift that is inappropriate in order to assuage feelings of debt.

Where obligation is discussed freely, the parishioner will need the honest input from the minister in order to assess a proper method of discharging it. This could be anything from an extra amount of giving to the church budget to a gift of one's services to the church. Once a commitment is made, the pastor will expect fulfillment.

b. In pastoral counseling. In pastoral counseling where pastors give large amounts of time to one person or family, there needs to be an agreement ahead of time about the parishioner dealing with the obligation that may build.

In more formal pastoral counseling the client and counselor can manage a balance between giving and receiving by agreeing on a fee that is mutually acceptable. If there are reservations on either side, these need to be expressed at the start. For example, a client with a unique hardship faces the counselor, asking for a very low fee. The counselor will do well to voice reservations about doing such for an unlimited time. The counselor may grant a certain number of sessions at a reduced rate. At the end of the period the matter of obligation can be more fully evaluated from both sides.

4. The Matter of Initiative. *a. In pastoral care.* The pastoral role is one of the few social roles — if not the only one — that allows initiative in offering services and help. When a crisis is known, a pastor is expected to go to the one in need. The pastor offers to give, yet the one in crisis still makes the decision about whether the help offered will be accepted.

Timing in the pastoral initiative is crucial. Critical situations need immediate response. One call at the peak of a crisis can be of more avail than a dozen calls made too long after the fact. Pastoral support given in an attempt to make up for tardiness has greatly reduced value. For example, five minutes with a parishioner facing surgery can be more valuable than five hours in post-surgical visits. Perhaps this is all symbolized in the timing of a cup of cold water to the thirsty person.

b. In pastoral counseling. Initiative is reversed where formal counseling is concerned. Here the client or parishioner is left with making a claim for specialized help from a pastor or professional counselor. When a parishioner takes the initiative to seek help from a pastor or a pastoral counselor, the response needs to be professionally dependable. A request for help puts an ethical burden on the pastoral helper to refer the one in need to a more qualified professional helper if the pastor is unable to meet the need. The fact that a client gives the pastor authority to help does not mean the pastor is thereby qualified. Pastors should work within the limits of their special abilities. For example, a client with pathological depression will not usually come within the province of

pastoral counseling: Such a person will need additional medical and psychiatric attention.

5. Theological Aspects of Giving and Receiving. The NT admonition is, "You received without pay, give without pay" (Mt. 10:8).

Forgiveness and grace announced in the gospel are the core material of the Christian witness. If one has received this, there is an obligation to give it to others who have not received it.

The flow of the "debt," theologically understood, is forward. One does not owe another for communicating the word of forgiveness and grace; the only indebtedness is to the one who has not heard or received it.

This model of giving is parallel to that seen in family life when the father gives to his son or daughter without a demand that they pay back. Such a father expects that the son or daughter keep the giving flowing down to the grandchildren and so on through the generations. This actually becomes that father's reward.

"You received without pay, give without pay" has nothing to do with a fee for services or pay for honest work. It is important for a pastor or pastoral counselor to remember that light and water as symbols of the divine gift are free in themselves. Pastoral care and counseling, in dealing with and handling priceless commodities, needs the material support of parishioners in this process. There is also support in the words, "the laborer deserves his wages —" (Lk. 10:7), which Jesus spoke to those he sent forth as witnesses.

The blessing and affirmation of another person in pastoral care is an act of passing along a gift rather than originating one. It becomes an act of giving what one has received. Perhaps the primary model of giving and receiving goes all the way back to Abraham. God is seen as blessing Abraham with an expectation that Abraham give to others what he has received (Gen. 12:2).

Bibliography. R. Lee, "The Practice of Ministry," *J. of Pastoral Care,* 26 (1972), 33–9. M. Neisser, "The Sense of Self Expressed Through Giving and Receiving," *Social Casework* (May 1973), 294–301. K. A. Olsson, *Meet Me on the Patio* (1977), pp. 39–53.

M. C. MADDEN

MONEY; SELF-EXPRESSION/SELF-CONTROL. *See also* GRACE; GRATITUDE; INTIMACY AND DISTANCE; LOVE; SELF-TRANSCENDENCE. *Compare* POWER; SACRIFICIAL BEHAVIOR.

GLADDEN, WASHINGTON (1836–1918). Congregationalist pastor, pastoral theologian, and advocate of the social gospel.

His book *The Christian Pastor* (1898) attempted to define the pastoral task in an era when urban Protestant churches in America tended to multiply internal organizations and promote social fellowship. His vision of pastoral care corresponded to the activist temper of Protestant progressivism. Hence he emphasized the administrative work of the pastor, though he also reflected the prevailing Protestant admiration for the princes of the pulpit—the gifted preachers in the influential urban pulpit. As an active pastor in Columbus, Ohio, Gladden embodied both ideals: he was a celebrated preacher and an advocate of progressive social causes. In his brief comments on pastoral counseling, Gladden proposed that pastors make a vigorous appeal to the will, but that they do so with sympathy, cheerful informality, and unpretentious naturalness.

E. B. HOLIFIELD

HISTORY OF PROTESTANT PASTORAL CARE (United States).

GLASSER, WILLIAM. *See* ETHICS AND PASTORAL CARE; REALITY THERAPY.

GLOSSOLALIA. *See* CHARISMATIC EXPERIENCE.

GLUTTONY AND TEMPERANCE (Moral Theology). 1. *Gluttony,* an inordinate desire for the pleasures connected with the sense of taste, a preoccupation with consumption that overrides both natural self-regulation and love of the object and its creator; one of the seven deadly or capital sins. 2. *Temperance,* the virtue opposite to gluttony, an attitude of rational self-control that seeks enjoyment in moderation, eliminating excesses of either consumption or abstinence.

Christian tradition has primarily associated gluttony with eating, and secondarily with drinking, though more recent interpretation has broadened the concept to include other preoccupations with consumption. From the early Christian centuries to Chaucer's time, writers focus primarily on the physical ugliness and social impropriety of being too interested in food. The classic image is of a man riding a swine. Many of the writings echo Clement of Alexandria in descriptions of the unsightliness of persons "in such a hurry to feed themselves that both jaws are stuffed out at once. . . ." Chaucer also focuses on external behavior, wanting to eat too early, too much, with too much enthusiasm, or with overmuch attention to the food's aesthetic quality.

Early and late there has been awareness that the external self-stuffing is the symptom of an internal poverty that is the root of the sin. Dante's gluttons try to feed the soul with food for the body, and most contemporary writers (Olsson; Grant) observe that the food and drink are an escape from self, an attempt to quell unmeetable ego needs. A formative dynamic in gluttony is the turning to the things one can consume as a substitute for the peace and fulfillment that come from fellowship with God and the Creation.

There is an idolatrous and an addictive element to all gluttony, as food, drink, and experience replace God as the dominant factor in the state of the self. A major factor in gluttony is always the self's failure to heed its body's signals that it has had enough, whether the commodity consumed is food, drink, aesthetic experience, or anything else.

Contemporary writers increasingly are pointing out that this preoccupation is sinful in its negative pole as well: a pickiness that refuses mundane food, an abstemiousness which places aesthetic values of the experience of consuming above the physical benefits.

Christianity has been somewhat unsettled in naming and describing the state opposite to gluttony. Spiritually there has been no confusion, the emphasis always being on "hunger and thirst after righteousness," seeing the mouth as an organ for praise first and ingestion second, and seeking first the Kingdom of God. But how that is to be lived out has remained a puzzle.

There has been an uneasy tension between temperance and abstinence as possible alternatives, with neither gaining a clear decision. Temperance is most often found in the lists of virtues, but it is clearly a Greek and Roman ideal, depending more on rational ability to identify excess than fits easily into a more Hebraic faith. It is oddly dispassionate. By Tertullian's time Christian morality moved in the direction of absolute separation from those elements of physical pleasure deemed suspect by the church, and for various branches of Christendom total avoidance of specific acts or substances continue to be seen as the antidote to gluttony. Some critics object that abstinence requires a negative preoccupation as dangerous as the glutton's positive one, and counsel a more Hebraic reverence for a rhythmic life, characterized by an alternation between eating and abstaining, with the social and religious context and the body's own cues governing the shifts from one emphasis to the other.

Bibliography. Clement of Alexandria, "On Spiritual Perfection," in J. B. Oulten, *Alexandrian Christianity* (1954). B. W. Grant, *From Sin to Wholeness* (1982). W. F. May, *A Catalogue of Sins* (1967). K. A. Olsson, *Seven Sins and Seven Virtues* (1962).

B. W. GRANT

CHRISTIAN LIFE; EATING AND DRINKING; LIFESTYLE ISSUES; SEVEN DEADLY SINS. *See also* CHARACTER ETHICS; MORAL THEOLOGY AND PASTORAL CARE; SELF EXPRESSION/SELF CONTROL; TEMPTATION; SIN/SINS. *Compare* ASCETICAL PRACTICES; OBESITY AND WEIGHT CONTROL.

GNOINSKIEJ, JADWIGE. *See* WOMEN IN PASTORAL MINISTRIES, HISTORY OF.

GNOSTICISM. *See* PHILOSOPHY AND PSYCHOLOGY, WESTERN; REVELATION AND PASTORAL CARE. *See also* ANALYTICAL (JUNGIAN) PSYCHOLOGY AND THEOLOGY.

GOAL ORIENTATION. *See* CAUSALITY IN PSYCHOLOGY, FORMS OF; COMPETITIVENESS; MOTIVATION.

GOD, DOCTRINE OF, AND PASTORAL CARE. The exposition of beliefs held by a living religious tradition concerning the nature of God and God's relation to the world, including discussion of the limits of what can be known and said about God, especially in regard to God's presence in those moments in human experience that occasion pastoral care.

A doctrine of God is "normative" when it functions in the common life of a religious tradition to provide the rules governing *what* is deemed appropriate to say about God and *how* to say it. In biblically shaped traditions, the normative doctrine of God holds that only analogies can be used to characterize God. Furthermore, adequate talk of God must balance contrasting types of analogy: first, because God is "mystery," analogies for how God is "for us" must be balanced against analogies for how God is "in Godself"; then, talk of how God is "in Godself" must balance analogies for God's "goodness" against analogies for God's "greatness"; and talk of how God is "for us" must balance analogies for God as Creator with analogies for God as Redeemer, and both with analogies for God as Fulfiller. "Pastoral caring," one of many activities comprising the common life of religious traditions, addresses persons' troubles which "arise in the context of ultimate meanings and concerns" (W. Clebsch and C. Jaekle). Since it is done in the context of *ultimate* concerns, it inevitably involves expression of beliefs about God, which need to maintain the balances outlined in normative doctrine of God. If it fails to hold those balances, it risks deepening rather than easing people's troubles.

1. **Normative Doctrine of God.** This discussion is confined to doctrine of God held by biblical religious traditions, traditions in whose common life biblical writings function to call the community into being, to sustain and correct it. These traditions hold that, although God is present to us, our capacities for experience and knowledge are wholly inadequate to God. Consequently, God can only be described in analogies generally drawn from the Bible. Although there are several such communities, Jewish and Christian, with significantly different doctrines, it is possible to outline common themes in normative doctrine of God.

The most basic theme is that an adequate doctrine of God must hold two poles in tension. Together they signify that God is "mystery." Thus God is present to us as One "for us" (*pro nobis*), the ultimate ground of our being and worth, faithfully engaged in our common life for our well-being; and yet God is always prevenient ("comes before") in both action and being. God becomes present *before* any action by us either deserves or resists it. That is true because in becoming present God always remains faithful to God's own reality (*in se*), which is (in crucial respects) always *before* our reality, which means that God's being and worth are not dependent on any other reality than God's. (The question, in *which* respects God's reality is "prior" to ours, is a point on which traditions differ.) Experientially, this is expressed by saying that God is present as both gracious, that is, intimate in a freely loving way, and glorious, that is, awesome in majestic and even terrifying ways.

Doctrinally the same point is made by noting that "divine immanence" and "divine transcendence" are not antithetical concepts but are best understood adverbially as qualities of God's relationships. God is immanent in a "transcendent" way; that is, God is present, but in ways that escape our powers to understand, anticipate, or control. And God is transcendent in an "immanent" way; that is, (in crucial respects) God is free of, or not dependent on, any other reality for being and worth, and in ways that are fully capable of intimate engagement in our lives.

This doctrine provides the basic rule for talk about God: God's faithfulness to us must be characterized by "personal" analogies (i.e., like a person, God loves, helps, becomes angry, grieves, etc.) which must be kept in polar tension with nonmaterialist or "spiritual" analogies for God's faithfulness to Godself (i.e., unlike anything made of matter, God *in principle* cannot be an object of sense experience, comprehension, or control).

Further, normative doctrine of God deals with God *in se* and God *pro nobis*. In each topic contrasting poles are held in tension. God *in se* is at once good and great. The goodness of God is expressed in a variety of analogies

drawn from human relationships: God is for us as a shepherd is for the sheep, a parent for a child, a lover for the beloved, a wise teacher for a disciple. Doctrinally, it is a "goodness" that is freely and wisely *loving*, capable of caring for another's well-being without prior conditions or constraints; because it is wise, it is *unconstrainedly knowing* (omniscient), and because it is utterly free, it is capable of being *present everywhere (omnipresent)*. The greatness of God is expressed in a variety of analogies usually drawn from power relationships. It is like the power exhibited by a potter working with clay, a king ruling a nation, a judge deciding a punishment, a storm. Doctrinally, it is a "greatness" that is freely *creative*, that has the capacity to be effectively productive of the other's being, growth, and fulfillment, and that is not limited by any constraints that are ultimately rooted in realities other than God (*omnipotent*, "all powerful"). "Divine goodness" and "divine greatness" are dialectically related concepts. God's goodness is a "great" goodness: divine love is a freely *creative* love. God's greatness is a "good" greatness: divine creativity is a freely loving creativity.

Keeping the right balance between these two sets of analogies for God's reality *in se* has proven controversial since God, as transcendent, is not dependent on any other reality for being (greatness) or worth (goodness). God is in those respects not vulnerable to or changeable by any other reality (i.e., God is *immutable*). But as immanent, does God not have something analogous to human emotions, and can they not change? Most traditional theology has judged that divine immutability includes the unchangeability of God's "emotions" or "passions" (*impassibility*). Much modern theology has concluded, to the contrary, that analogies for divine goodness (e.g., parental love and suffering) are meaningless unless God can be said to be capable of something analogous to changeable emotions. Clearly normative doctrine of God will have important implications in the practice of pastoral care.

Normative doctrine about God *pro nobis* holds in balance three significantly different modes in which God is faithfully engaged in our lives: God as Creator, as Redeemer, as ultimate Fulfiller. These correlate roughly with three families of biblical narratives and the nonnarrative texts that reflect on them. Properly speaking, however, they do not correlate with the three "Persons" of the traditional Christian doctrine of the Trinity. Rather, the entire Godhead is said to be present *pro nobis* in each mode. Each is a different *way* in which God is transcendently immanent and immanently transcendent. In each, God is free, loving, and creative, but in relation to different aspects of human being and worth.

As Creator, God is present as the freely creative ground of our existence and of the continuing reliability and intelligible natural and moral order of our world. No sharp distinction may be made between God's originating and continuing creativity. Creating in love, God also *grounds our worth*. We are worthy of respect simply because our existence is itself God's loving gift, not because of our own qualities or achievements. God as Creator is also the ground of the meaningfulness of the passage of time, since a major aspect of the created realm is its temporality. Doctrinally: as Creator, God is also Providential Lord.

As Redeemer, God is present as the freely loving *re*-creator of creatures damaged and deformed by evil undergone and evil done. This is a mode of God's presence distinct from God as Creator, first, because the sheer fact of creation does not entail logically or metaphysically that beyond sustaining us in a deformed existence, God must or may set us free from the bonds of our deformities. Second, while God's freedom to be for us as Creator is not constrained by any antecedent conditions, God's freedom to be present as Redeemer is a freedom to be present in terms of our creatureliness. Election and predestination express doctrinally the temporal dimension of redemption, meaning that God's redemptive presence is prevenient to our accomplishments and decisions.

As Fulfiller, God is the ground of those developments in history that move the created realm to its divinely destined consummation at the end of time (*eschaton*). This way of God's being for us is distinct from God's presence as Creator in that nothing about the ongoing reliability and orderliness rooted in creation entails that the world will or does now "move toward" any consummation. It is distinct from God's presence as Redeemer in that beyond healing and restoration, fulfillment is creative of new and richer modes of creaturely experience of justice and peace.

The temporal dimension of each of these modes of God's presence *pro nobis* raises a question with theologically controversial answers. Given that God, as Providential Lord, Electing Lord, and Eschatological Lord, is present for us in relationship (i.e., in time) and in ways appropriate to our condition as finite, sinful, and unfinished creatures, how do we best explicate the relationship between divine grace and creaturely response? In each of these three modes of divine presence is "grace" irresistible? Or are we to be said to cooperate with it? Here there is no normative doctrine. However, what *is* required by normative doctrine is that talk of God *pro nobis* hold these three modes of divine presence together in a balance.

2. Doctrine of God in the Practice of Pastoral Care. To understand pastoral care as helping acts "directed toward the healing, sustaining, guiding and reconciling of troubled persons whose troubles arise in the context of ultimate meanings and concerns" (Clebsch and Jaekle, p. 4) is to stress that pastoral care is distinct *in principle* from the "helping professions" in that some "dynamic" (S. Hiltner) doctrine of God is inescapable and determinative in the practice of pastoral care. It is inescapable because pastoral care is addressed to troubles arising in the context of *ultimate* meanings and concerns. It is dynamic in that its personal appropriation by troubled persons is an ingredient in the very *process* of their dealing fruitfully with their problems. It is determinative because only an adequate understanding of God can help empower troubled persons. Inadequate doctrine of God may result in disempowerment. Hence, a normative doctrine of God must function to provide criteria for both guidance and critical self-correction in the very practice of pastoral care.

In sustaining and guiding, for example, pastoral care aims, among other things, to nurture in distressed persons a trust in the ultimate worth and meaningfulness of life, which is expressed normatively in doctrine of God as Creator. Such trust, however, is deformed if it is not also

informed by doctrine about God as Redeemer and Fulfiller. If Creation is treated as the dominant, or sole, mode of God's presence to troubled persons, then all the evil, whose reality threatens the troubled persons' confidence in the worth and meaningfulness of life, is understood as directly caused by God's creativity. This is evident in a pastoral caring which encourages accepting *all* that occurs as "providential."

Doctrinally, what is inadequate is that the transcendence of God's creativity is stressed at the expense of the immanence of divine love and respect for the creature's integrity. God's greatness *in se* is stressed at the expense of God's goodness, and faith is deformed into something close to resignation. Or creation may be treated one-sidedly as the dominant mode of God's presence when divine creativity is simply equated with psychological dynamics that are a part of every person's "created" nature. The doctrine of God as Creator rightly opens us to all the wisdom the several sciences can offer concerning the structure and dynamics of creatures, since they are the concrete effects of God's presence as Creator. But if God's presence is *equated* with these, then the immanence of God's creativity is stressed at the expense of the transcendent freedom of divine love, and trust in God is deformed into trust in one's native capacities.

In "reconciling," pastoral care aims to nurture in persons a love that responds to God's reconciling and forgiving love and goes beyond the demands of justice but does not negate them. Divine love is expressed normatively in doctrine of God as Redeemer. Human responding love, however, will be deformed if Redemption is treated as the sole relevant mode of God's presence. Reconciliation is needed in the face of alienation from God, others, and oneself, a circumstance in which all three are somehow wronged. When reconciliation is understood as rooted in one's learning first to forgive oneself, rather than in a preveniently forgiving love of oneself, and when forgiveness is separated from accountability and repentance for alienating actions, then God's presence as forgiving Redeemer is separated from God's presence as Creator of continuing moral order and intelligibility in the world. The immanence of God's forgiving love is sentimentalized by being stressed at the expense of the constancy of the transcendent divine creativity that holds us accountable for our own deformities ("divine judgment") and keeps us under constant pressure to change deeply ("divine wrath"). The responding love that is being nurtured is correspondingly sentimentalized into "forgiving and forgetting."

Further, in healing and sustaining, pastoral care aims at nurturing in troubled persons a hope for a world more just and peaceful, which is expressed normatively in a doctrine of God as Fulfiller. This hope is deformed if fulfillment is treated as the dominant mode of God's presence. This is reflected in pastoral caring when troubled persons are encouraged to think their broken lives would be fulfilled if they adopted practices designed to help escape a hopelessly evil world and to prepare for a new world discontinuous with this one, which God would "bring in." There hope is turned into world-denying resignation. This also happens in pastoral caring that encourages troubled persons to focus primarily on the cultivation of ecstatic experiences of the presence of the Holy Spirit. There hope tends to be turned into "magic-thinking." Each of these cases illustrates how normative doctrine of God may shape the context of pastoral care, functioning not only as a guide for *what* is to be expressed to persons troubled about ultimate meanings and concerns, but also *how* it might best be expressed.

Bibliography. K. Barth, *Church Dogmatics* II/1 (1957). D. Browning, *Atonement and Psychotherapy* (1966). W. Clebsch and C. Jaekle, *Pastoral Care in Historical Perspective* (1964). J. Cobb and D. Griffin, *Process Theology* (1976). S. Hiltner, *Theological Dynamics* (1972). H. P. Owen, *Concepts of Deity* (1971). P. Pruyser, *The Minister as Diagnostician* (1976). P. Tillich, *Systematic Theology* I (1951). H. Zahrnt, *The Question of God* (1969).

D. H. KELSEY

PROVIDENCE, DOCTRINE OF, AND PASTORAL CARE; THE HOLY; TRANSCENDENCE (Divine); TRINITY AND PERSONHOOD. *Compare* CHRISTOLOGY, HOLY SPIRIT, *or* REVELATION, AND PASTORAL CARE; THEOLOGY.

GOD, IDEAS AND IMAGES OF. For approximately forty years, polls have consistently reported that ninety-four to ninety-eight percent of Americans affirm a belief in God. Such belief, however, may be less important than the nature of the deity in which faith is expressed. God concepts become almost impossibly diverse if one goes beyond the confines of Western civilization. Reasonable circumscription is, however, attainable when the Judeo-Christian tradition is stressed.

God concepts appear to be sensitive indicators of development, psychological maturity, and psychosocial well-being. Considering the prevalence of avowed belief, and its potential psychological significance, surprisingly few empirical efforts have been directed at understanding God concepts. Discussion articles of an anecdotal or theoretical nature have been published for over a century, but objective, methodologically sophisticated psychological research in this area is relatively rare.

1. **Complexity.** A few studies and a fair amount of theory have been concerned with the multidimensionality of God images. Developmental thinkers (Pitts) have noted that anthropomorphic ideas in young children are replaced by more abstract formulations in adolescence (Elkind, 1971). Still, human-like representations are probably held to some degree by most religious people throughout life.

Utilizing advanced statistical procedures, it has been shown that adjectives descriptive of the deity combine to yield meaningful patterns (Gorsuch; Spilka, Armatas, and Nussbaum). The strongest clusters were: conceptions of (1) a loving and forgiving deity; (2) God as punitive and threatening; (3) an omni-God (omnipotent etc.); (4) a stern father; (5) a blessed and holy being; (6) a remote, impersonal deity; and (7) a divine kingly figure. The terms considered most descriptive of God were: divine, loving, just, eternal, and infinite. Least descriptive were: jealous, damning, mythical, avenging, and inaccessible.

Gorsuch further studied these images and organized them hierarchically. He found eight, often similar patterns, six of which combined to form two higher-level

inclusive images. One of the latter consists of characteristics that relate God to humanity through such concepts as wisdom, divinity, power, and righteousness. This was called a "benevolent" deity. The second composite included the more human qualities of charity, fairness, faithfulness, love, support, mercy, and warmth. This image was labeled the "companionable" deity. The higher level combination of these two patterns was seen as a traditional Christian image of God.

Data gathered from 1948 to 1974 suggest a tendency for college students to perceive God less and less as a benevolent deity. Features contributing to the companionable image have remained fairly constant. The latter also constitute the dominant view held by these respondents (Potvin, Hoge, and Nelsen).

2. **Development.** Most research on childhood images of God has been guided by the theories of Piaget and Freud. Studies inspired by Piaget's views are largely concerned with cognitive growth, while those influenced by Freud stress emotional development.

a. Piaget. The developmental theory of Jean Piaget has had a profound effect on studies of religious understanding in children. Basically, this perspective defines qualitatively different cognitive stages in childhood and early adolescence through which, it is hypothesized, all normal individuals progress. Thinking proceeds from early global, undifferentiated, and concrete expressions to a final mature stage in which ideas and images are differentiated and abstract (Elkind, 1971).

In keeping with this position, David Elkind (1970) claims that religion is a normal and natural outcome of intellectual growth. The concept of God is said to result from a human need to "represent" the world mentally. One thus attempts to tie language and thought to concrete symbols. God is apparently easily imagined to be like powerful human adults, initially one's parents. According to Williams (1971), this analogy is facilitated by the child's perception of "his parents as all-powerful, all-knowing, and divine" (p. 62).

Some researchers rephrase God-concept development in terms that suggest alternative possibilities. Harms observed a beginning "fairy tale" stage (3–6 years) followed by a "realistic" stage (7–12 years). Finally after age thirteen, growth terminated in an "individualistic" period. DeConchy stressed successive expressions of attributivity (7–10 years; emphasizing God's attributes), personalization (11–14 years; God as person), and interiorization (14–16 years; God is defined abstractly).

b. Freud. Freud's view is that the God concept is really derived from the images children have of the characteristics of human fathers. Early in development, the child is said to rely on the protection and strength of the father. Growing awareness of paternal limitations implies a need for the same security and the idea of a universal all-knowing, powerful father — God is thus created. This has stimulated much research, virtually all of which suffers from serious defects in design and analysis. In their review, Beit-Hallahmi and Argyle claim support for the broad psychoanalytic principle that religious ideas relate to family relationships.

What was originally regarded as a simple research problem has been shown to be exceedingly complex. One must control for the fact that mother, father, and God images are closely related because of the nature of language and what is learned within a culture and religious institutions (Spilka, Addison, and Rosensohn; Vergote and Tamayo). Many basic operational and measurement questions have also been raised, and these may invalidate almost all of the work undertaken on this issue to date.

3. Correlates. God images seem to reflect rather fundamental psychological characteristics of the individual. A number of studies have affiliated these ideas with indices of personal well-being. Self-esteem and views of God as loving and supportive go together. The latter are also correlated with an intrinsic-committed faith that stresses a search for truth and utilization of religion as a guide to everyday living. Perceptions of God as restrictive, controlling, and vindictive are associated with low self-esteem, general maladjustment, signs of poor personality integration, and an extrinsic-consensual religious outlook that employs faith for personal aggrandizement and security (Benson and Spilka). Distorted and negative God concepts have generally been observed among the severely emotionally disturbed (Lowe and Braaten).

Conceiving God as loving is also allied with feelings of closeness to both parents and perceptions of the self and parents as loving figures (Spilka, Addison, and Rosensohn). Connoting the deity as impersonal, distant, and uninvolved in human affairs is affiliated with ethnic prejudice (Spilka and Reynolds). In this latter instance, the image of God held does not serve as a model or guide for one's behavior and attitudes; neither is there any question of personal accountability.

Bibliography. B. Beit-Hallahmi and M. Argyle, "God as a Father-Projection: The Theory and the Evidence", *British J. of Medical Psychology*, 48 (1975), 71–5. P. Benson and B. Spilka, "God Image as a Function of Self-Esteem and Locus of Control," *J. for the Scientific Study of Religion*, 12 (1973), 297–310. J. P. DeConchy, "God and the Parental Images," in A. Godin, ed., *From Cry to Word: Contributions Towards a Psychology of Prayer* (1985), pp. 85–94. D. Elkind, "The Origins of Religion in the Child," *Review of Religious Research*, 12 (1970), 35–42; "The Development of Religious Understanding in Children and Adolescents," in M. Strommen, ed., *Research on Religious Development* (1971), pp. 655–85. R. L. Gorsuch, "Dimensions of the Conceptualization of God," in J. Matthes, ed. *International Yearbook for the Sociology of Religion*, 2, (1967), pp. 187–99. E. Harms, "The Development of Religious Experience in Children," *American J. of Sociology*, 50 (1944), 112–22. W. L. Lowe and R. O. Braaten, "Differences in Religious Attitudes in Mental Illness," *J. for the Scientific Study of Religion*, 5 (1966), 435–55. W. Pitts, *Concept Development and the God Concept in the Child: A Bibliography* (1977). R. H. Potvin, D. R. Hoge, and H. M. Nelsen, *Religion and American Youth*, U. S. Catholic Conference (1976). A. M. Rizutto, *The Birth of the Living God* (1979). B. Spilka and J. F. Reynolds, "Religion and Prejudice: A Factor-Analytic Study," *Review of Religious Research*, 6 (1965), 163–68. B. Spilka, J. Addison, and M. Rosensohn, "Parents, Self, and God: A Test of Competing Theories of Individual-Religion Relationship," *Review of Religious Research*, 16 (1975), 154–65. B. Spilka, P. Armatas, and J. Nussbaum, "The Concept of God: A Factor-Analytic Approach," *Review of Religious Research*, 6 (1964), 28–36. A. Vergote and A. Tamayo, *The Parental Figures and the Representation of God* (1980). R. Williams, "A Theory of God-Concept Readiness: From the Piagetian Theories of Child Artificialism and the Origin of Religious Feeling in Children," *Religious Education*, 66 (1971), 62–6.

B. SPILKA

IMAGO DEI; THE HOLY; TRANSCENDENCE (Divine); TRINITY AND PERSONHOOD. *Compare* EVALUATION AND DIAGNOSIS, RELIGIOUS; IMAGINATION; THEOLOGY.

GOD'S WILL, ACCEPTANCE OF. To accept God's will is to affirm the unique way in which God's love becomes manifest in our life. Accepting God's will has nothing to do with a passive submission to an external divine power which imposes itself on us. To the contrary, it is an active claiming of an intimate relationship with God, in the context of which we discover our deepest vocation and the desire to live that vocation to the fullest.

1. A Life According to God's Will. This is very concisely expressed by the Apostle Paul: we ask "that you may be filled with the knowledge of his will in all spiritual wisdom and understanding, to lead a life worthy of the Lord" (Col. 1:9). By spiritual understanding, Paul means an insight into the spiritual interconnectedness of all things. Through such an insight we can situate ourselves in time and space. God's will is the inner working of God's love that leads us to a way of life in response to creation and history in as far as they are an expression of that same divine love. By seeing more and more the interconnectedness of things (the Desert Fathers spoke of a *theoric physike:* a vision of how things hang together) we come to an experiential knowledge of our unique place in the world. This heart knowledge enables us to live a life "worthy of the Lord," that is, a life that responds to our true place in creation and history.

The Spirit which we have received through Jesus Christ gives us this knowledge of God's will. It is the Spirit of love that calls forth from us a life that is worthy of the Lord. Paul describes such a life as a life that is "worthy of the Lord and may please him in every way: bearing fruit in every good work, growing in the knowledge of God" (Col. 1:10, NIV). A life according to God's will manifests itself in three ways. It is a unified life: acceptable to God in all its aspects, physical, emotional, and intellectual. It cannot be a divided life, since love leads to harmony among all the parts of our existence. It also is a fruit-bearing life — not necessarily a successful and productive life, but a life that bears the fruits of love. Love is always fruitful. It belongs to the essence of love that something new is being born from it. Finally, it is a life that increases our knowledge of God. The more we respond to God's unique way of loving us the deeper our heart will know the God who loves us. Knowing God and loving God can never be separated. Therefore, the more integrated and the more fruitful our life becomes, the deeper our insight will become of God's love for us.

2. Pastoral Implications. This vision of God's will has its implications for pastoral ministry. The pastor can never say what God's will is for an individual person, but is always again called to help individual persons to "read" with the eyes of love the concrete situation in which they find themselves. A war, an illness, a death, an earthquake, or a successful harvest, a promotion or an award can never be simply called God's will that needs to be accepted. They are the concrete context in which a person is asked to discern how God's love is becoming manifest. The task of the pastor is to help parishioners listen to how the Spirit of God is moving them in their particular historical context. Based on Paul's words, questions can be raised such as: How can this situation lead you to a fuller integration of your life? How can it bear fruit in your life? How can it give you a deeper insight in God's love for you?

Acceptance therefore can never mean submission or resignation. When we see ourselves in a relationship of love with God, there will always be something of a lover's struggle. Jesus himself lived this intensely when he prayed in Gethsemane: "Father, if thou art willing, remove this cup from me; nevertheless, not my will, but thine, be done" (Lk. 22:42). In our relationship with God there will be feelings of rejection as well as attraction, anger as well as gratitude, fear as well as love. There will be the ups and downs of a true love relationship in which the partners have to discover and rediscover each other day by day. But we can be sure of one thing: "If we are faithless, he remains faithful, for he cannot deny himself" (II Tim. 2:13).

Often we need to struggle long and often in darkness, not able to see God's faithful love in our concrete life situation. In such a situation the pastor is called to represent God's faithfulness and stay with parishioners in their anguish, praying unceasingly that God will reveal to them the new way of loving to which they are invited. In the pastoral relationship the protesting question, "Why did this happen to me?", has to gradually and gently be converted into the searching question, "To which new way of love is God calling me because of what did happen to me?" The answer can never be given once and for all, because there is always more to live and more to love. But as we grow deeper into life and love, we will constantly be confronted with the choice between rejecting God's faithful love and affirming the always deeper way in which that love touches us. Only in this way, can "accepting God's will," be a meaningful expression.

H. J. M. NOUWEN
J. IMBACH

EVALUATION AND DIAGNOSIS, RELIGIOUS; GUIDANCE, DIVINE; OBEDIENCE (Roman Catholicism); PROVIDENCE, DOCTRINE OF, AND PASTORAL CARE. *See also* CHRISTIAN LIFE; JEWISH LIFE; VOCATION. *Compare* CALL TO MINISTRY; PATIENCE/PATIENTHOOD; PRIDE AND HUMILITY (Moral Theology); SUFFERING.

GODFORSAKENNESS. *See* SUFFERING.

GOD-TALK/RELIGIOUS LANGUAGE. *See* RELIGIOUS LANGUAGE. *See also* SALVATION AND PASTORAL CARE.

GODIN, ANDRÉ, S.J. (1915–   ). Jesuit priest, educator, psychologist, and author, born in Gembloux, Belgium. He obtained his Ph.D. in philosophical psychology at the University of Brussels (1942), a Licentiate in Theology from Louvain University (1947), and the Master of Arts degree in psychology from Fordham University (1951). He acquired the theoretical foundations and extensive practice in counseling and guidance during

his post-doctoral work at the Centre de Consultations Médico-psychologiques in Brussels. Godin's major fields of interest and research are the psychology of religion, psychotherapy and psychoanalysis, and group dynamics applied to pastoral psychology.

Father Godin is professor of psychology of religion at the International Center Lumen Vitae in Brussels. As editor of *Studies in the Psychology of Religion* he stimulated numerous sound empirical investigations on the psychology of religion, and in his capacity as a dedicated professor he trained many graduate students and directed their research. His own research and publications span a broad field encompassing religious development, religion and personality, pastoral psychology, and the psychological factors in religious education. Father Godin is the author of *The Pastor As Counselor* (1966) and coauthor of *Death and Presence* (1972).

V. S. SEXTON

PASTORAL THEOLOGY, ROMAN CATHOLIC; PSYCHOLOGY OF RELIGION.

GODLESSNESS. *See* SECULARIZATION/SECULARISM; SIN/SINS.

GODPARENTS. Persons who serve as witnesses or sponsors for a candidate for Christian baptism. Usually such sponsorship involves special responsibility for the continuing support and nourishment of the candidate's life in Christ. The origins of the practice of this sponsorship lie in the early centuries of the church, when members of the Christian community would bring forward individuals inquiring about the faith, and would vouch for their sincerity and good character. The sponsor also exercised special concern for the individual during the often lengthy catechumenate period. Through the centuries which followed, there was a proliferation of ecclesiastical regulations concerning the appropriate number and gender of godparents, and their responsibilities. Today the role of godparents (often formally referred to as "sponsors") is most significant in those denominations which practice infant baptism, for example, Roman Catholics, Episcopalians, Lutherans, United Methodists, and Presbyterians. The godparents usually take an active part in the rite of baptism, and promise to uphold the child in his or her Christian life.

S. J. WHITE

BAPTISM AND CONFIRMATION; PARENTS/PARENTHOOD. *See also* FAMILY. *Compare* CIRCUMCISION.

GONORRHEA. An infectious inflammation of the mucous membranes of the genital tract caused by the bacteria Neisseria gonorrhoeae, transmitted primarily by sexual contact. Untreated it can lead to complications such as pelvic inflammatory disease, prostatitis, endocarditis, and infectious arthritis.

J. D. THOMAS

SEX EDUCATION.

GOODNESS/GOOD WORKS. *See* CHARACTER ETHICS; FAITH AND WORKS; MORAL THEOLOGY; VIRTUE, CONCEPT OF.

GOSPELS, THE. *See* JESUS; NEW TESTAMENT.

GRACE AND NATURE. *See* NATURE AND GRACE.

GRACE AND PASTORAL CARE. Grace in Christian theology refers to the unconditional, comprehensive, empowering love of God for the world. God's grace was manifested fully in Jesus Christ (Jn. 1:14; Rom. 5:2) and is present in the world through the power of the Holy Spirit. As one of the central concepts of Christian theology, grace combines the covenantal theme of God's overflowing, undeserved forgiveness of sinful humanity with a sense of divine power to liberate, redeem, and renew human life. God's grace empowers human beings to live graciously, in faith and gratitude to God and in a spirit of forgiveness and peace with others (I Cor. 1:3ff.), and is expressed also through particular spiritual "gifts" (or "graces") that God gives to the church for its upbuilding and edification (I Cor. 12:4ff.; Eph. 4:11–16).

The relation between this fundamental set of Christian affirmations and pastoral care is multifaceted and complex. It may be immediately apparent, however, that the doctrine of grace is not only fundamental to Christian life, but has particular significance for care and counseling ministries. In the following discussion, the various ways in which this doctrine has related to pastoral care over the centuries, and some of the ways it relates today, are sketched in broad terms under several thematic headings. In each of these discussions it is suggested that certain basic tensions within the doctrine have practical as well as theoretical significance for pastoral care. It is also suggested that, to some extent, the history and structure of pastoral care itself can be understood in terms of the various ways the church has lived out the implications of these doctrinal tensions in its personal caring ministries.

1. Grace as Forgiveness and as Empowerment. The conjunction of these central covenantal themes in the concept of grace points to a profound and abiding tension in the history of pastoral care related to the theological themes of justification and sanctification. There is or ought to be no contradiction between these conceptions. But there has always been a certain tension between them, and thus implicitly between conceptions of grace in terms of forgiving love, in contrast to the demands of the Law, and grace as constructive empowerment for new life, the power of growth in Christian virtue.

One pole of this tension is the "Law-Gospel" theme. This theme focuses on *moral and spiritual failure* and conceives pastoral care as an embodiment of the grace of forgiveness in relation to the Law's necessary work of judging, confessing, forgiving, and being absolved of sin (Hunter, 1976). The traditional Catholic penitential system epitomizes the sacramental form of this meaning of grace in its distinctive way, but pastoral care as confession and the pastor as confessor, whether through formal (ritualized) or informal means, is a widespread historical tradition expressing one of the fundamental meanings of pastoral care over the centuries.

The recent pastoral emphases on "acceptance," the value of presence, gracious relationship, Rogers's "unconditional positive regard," and the like, even though they do not necessarily define and deal with human beings in explicitly moral terms of failure and forgiveness, stand in this broad tradition as well, as many have noted. When pastoral care is conceived as the embodiment of a spirit of grace — of hospitality, of warm, unjudgmental caring — it is implicitly assumed that a danger of rejection, condemnation, or guilt exists to which the ministry is responding with the grace of forgiveness or "acceptance."

The other pole of the forgiveness-empowerment tension focuses on *moral and spiritual possibilities*. When pastoral care has emphasized sanctification and the power of grace to renew and reform human life, on the other hand, disciplines of moral guidance and of spiritual direction and formation become central to the understanding of pastoral care. Even among liberal Protestant pastoral counselors this emphasis appears in "growth counseling" (Clinebell), and together with a renewed interest in spiritual formation and direction, often with the aid of humanistic or Jungian psychology, faith development theory, or other developmental frameworks. It also appears in forms of counseling concerned with raising consciousness and altering lifestyles regarding social issues (e.g., feminism).

When the accent falls on grace as forgiving love (as in classical Lutheran piety), the Christian life — the process of sanctification—tends to be construed as a deepening of the awareness of sin and forgiving grace, and an accompanying deepened sense of faith, gratitude, and freedom from the burden of sin and guilt, with less emphasis on (and more hesitancy about) any notion of accomplished or progressive growth in virtue. When grace as the power of spiritual growth (or "formation") is emphasized (as in the Catholic tradition and certain forms of Protestantism), justification tends to be viewed either as mainly appropriate to an early phase or moment or as a periodic or occasional necessity when one relapses in the life of moral and spiritual development. But it may also be integrated more profoundly into the conception of sanctification as an abiding theme of Christian life even if the accent falls primarily on constructive possibilities.

When the "justification" theme is given priority in these recent clinical traditions, it takes the form of attending especially to the givens and realities, spiritual or otherwise, of the human situation—a sense of the "caughtness" of life and its existential boundaries. Accepting life's unchangeable boundaries and realities need not amount to a counsel of futility or despair or an entrapment in conservative social attitudes, any more than an emphasis on the possibilities of change and growth need to be superficial or Pollyannaish, though both perversions are possible. It can mean a deepening of wisdom and an enhancing capacity for exercising realistic responsibility over those things which one is in fact able to change.

2. Grace as Transcendent or as Immanent in Its Operation. The difference here has to do with how much God's redeeming work is held to be internal to and cooperative with natural human powers (given the state of fallenness), and how much it transcends, addresses, or confronts human capacities with a power not their own.

It would be misleading to suggest a sharp dichotomy here as the only theological possibility, but there is a basic difference of emphasis and, at times of basic theological position. The question at the heart of the matter concerns the assessment of the nature and effects of sin on moral and spiritual capacities. In its classic form it is the debates over the "freedom" or the "bondage" of the "will." The Augustinian position that human beings in the fallen state cannot will the good (that is, God) and need grace from beyond themselves (from God) to be saved, is opposed to the Pelagian insistence on a fundamental continuing capacity for right moral choice, with grace serving a supportive or supplemental role, as in various sorts of "semi-Pelagianism."

This dispute concerning the possibilities and limits of human moral power plays out pastorally in a variety of significant ways that are directly related to different conceptions of grace, that is, of the way in which God's love becomes present and effective for salvation in human life. When the "bondage of the will" is affirmed, grace becomes necessary and is typically conceived as coming to human beings essentially from beyond themselves, through Word and Sacrament, rather than occurring more immanently within, as a cooperative or enabling power releasing or cooperating with natural human powers. It would be a mistake to overemphasize this contrast, since theologies of transcendence may also envision grace as intimately present in the experience of the individual (it need not be purely formal or mechanical even if it has often degenerated in that direction); similarly, immanentalist positions may maintain a sense of the profound "otherness" of the God within while holding to a notion that grace utilizes, frees, or otherwise supports and cooperates with "the will."

A priority on transcendence leads to conceptions of the pastoral or ecclesial task that give a central role to outside intervention in some form, since humans are believed not to have the crucial resources within. The sacramental system is one such form. Another, secular version is seen in modern pastoral counseling in the psychoanalytic theory of transference and its derivatives, which emphasize the essential role of the therapist and the therapeutic relationship in some way. While transference dynamics do not eliminate the need for therapeutic effort on the part of the patient or counselee any more than sacramental worship eliminates significant participation by the worshiper, it does presuppose that fundamental healing cannot take place by self-analysis or introspection; it requires the presence of an emotionally significant relationship managed therapeutically in certain ways designed to be effective against the deep-seated defenses and resistances of the personality — its "bondage."

3. Institutional and Charismatic Expressions of Grace. If grace is the power of God's redeeming and life-giving love active in human affairs, it becomes pastorally necessary to specify where this divine power occurs or is to be found — or how it finds us. Of course, in one sense the question is unanswerable: God cannot be confined to any human institution or book; the Spirit blows where it will. This fundamental insight of faith, rooted in reverence and awe of God, stands in tension with the Christian conviction that God is active in a unique and particular way through a history of revela-

tion, its Scriptures, and through the church with its ministries of Word and Sacrament, service and fellowship. Grace is thus "institutionalized" in a qualified but fundamentally important sense: uniquely present in but not bound to its historical, institutional forms.

This tension between "charismatic" and "institutional" expressions, like the other tensions considered in the doctrine of grace, leads to varying pastoral styles and priorities. The institutional forms in pastoral care have mainly emphasized the sacramental ministry. The needs of the sick, the dying, the troubled, the confused, and the wayward are then typically provided for through formal prayer and other ritual participation. Ritual brings God's grace near, as it were — makes it available, close, sensual, dependable, even (in Max Weber's sense) "routine." The charisma, the effervescent, uncontrollable new wine of the spirit is, sociologically speaking, "routinized."

There are of course counterparts to the traditional ways of "routinizing charisma" in contemporary care and counseling. The professionalization of pastoral ministries in recent years, including the rise of certified clinical chaplaincy and the pastoral counseling movement and the development of sophisticated counseling skills, may all be viewed as necessary or inevitable ways of institutionalizing the charisma of the healing arts, which in their origins tended to have less professional formality and more therapeutic "charisma" about them. And just as traditional forms of institutionalized caring through the sacramental and related systems bred controversy and conflict over which institutions and which credentials are qualified for the authoritative mediation of divine grace, so these tendencies appear also in recent contentions over standards of certification and accreditation and the relations between the various secular and pastoral healing professions.

The more "charismatic" conception of divine grace and ministry finds its purest or most obvious expression in the inspired, usually unofficial ministries of gifted healers, seers, spiritual masters, and extraordinary pastors. Their power to care emanates in some sense from themselves as spirit-filled persons rather than from institutional office, though it has often occurred within the formal ranks of the ministry as well, as with the great spiritual directors and pastoral confessors of all traditions.

The principal *ordinary* expression of the charismatic side of the pastoral field is simple conversational care. In conversation, more than in formal sacramental or homiletic ministries, one functions with degrees of uncertainty, contextual analysis, responsiveness, and improvisation. Pastoral authority is located more directly in the "gifts and graces" of the pastor as a person and as one trained and developed both in the life of faith and in the pastoral arts. As in all "charismatic" expressions of grace, these qualities, like the wind, cannot ultimately be called forth by simple intention or be institutionally controlled, though they can be related in varying, sometimes unstable degrees to the necessary ongoing forms and structures of ecclesial life.

4. Grace in History and in Nature. In the broad Christian tradition thinking about grace, though focused on the redemption and renewal of human life, is not limited to human beings alone or to the course of human history, but is also understood to be cosmic in scope. It is the whole world that God redeems, and the grace revealed in Christ is present in the full expanse of God's creative work in the cosmos (Col. 1:15–20). This idea has not been greatly emphasized or developed theologically, especially in the West, but it may have increasing importance for Western pastoral care and counseling. This is because it points to the integral relation between human existence and nonhuman natural processes. Such conceptions are not foreign to contemporary pastoral care. Twentieth century developments in the field have, for example, included a serious engagement with issues of health and the relation of health to religion, a topic which forces consideration of the role of the body, physiological processes, the environment, and transindividual social processes in personality and human relations. The pervasive concern for the relation of mental health to religion is also germane here, for theories of psychopathology (and health) postulate various nonpersonal psychological forces, systems, and processes that contribute integrally to mental health and to religion. These notions have been commonplace in contemporary pastoral counseling (e.g. pastoral family therapy), though a concern about their impersonality sometimes leads to existentialist or humanistic psychological themes as correctives.

Pastoral care and counseling, like secular psychiatry today, must struggle with how these seemingly impersonal, even mechanistic conceptions (and their related pharmacological and behavioral therapies) relate to human personhood. Specific therapies (religious and nonreligious) position themselves variously on a continuum of possibilities regarding this question of fundamental perspectives. Theologically, the question is not entirely new, given the cosmological implications of biblical Christology. The contemporary question is whether or how to conceive the natural order as the bearer of divine grace, and how in any case such natural processes may both limit and contribute to the vital concerns of human life. The problem for pastoral theology at this point is thus an instance of the larger topic of ecological theology, the theology of nature and of the place of human history in nature and of nature in history. Answers to those questions will obviously have direct bearing on how pastoral care and counseling are understood and practiced, and how these caring ministries of the church will relate to their secular scientific counterparts, with their heavily naturalistic and often mechanistic worldviews and related therapeutic technologies.

Bibliography. H. Clinebell, *Basic Types of Pastoral Care and Counseling* rev. ed. (1984). C. V. Gerkin, *Crisis Experience in Modern Life* (1979). J. Haroutunian, *God With Us* (1965). E. B. Holifield, *A History of Pastoral Care in America* (1983). R. J. Hunter, "Law and Gospel in Pastoral Care," *J. of Pastoral Care* 30(1976), 146–58. J. N. Lapsley, *Salvation and Health* (1972). J. T. McNeill, *A History of the Cure of Souls* (1951). T. Oden, *Kerygma and Counseling* (1966). J. Oman, *Grace and Personality* (1925). E. Thurneysen, *A Theology of Pastoral Care* ET (1966).

R. J. HUNTER

CHRISTOLOGY, ECCLESIOLOGY, ETHICS; SALVATION, *or* SACRAMENTAL THEOLOGY, AND PASTORAL CARE; FAITH; FORGIVENESS; FREEDOM AND BONDAGE; NATURE AND GRACE; SANCTIFICATION/HOLINESS; SPIRITUAL DISCIPLINE AND GROWTH; WILL/WILLING. *See also* ACCEPTANCE; ENVY AND GRACIOUSNESS; GIVING AND RECEIVING; LEGALISM AND ANTINOMIANISM; RIGHTEOUSNESS/BEING RIGHT. *Compare* AVARICE AND GENEROSITY; MORAL BEHAVIOR AND RELIGION; RESPONSIBILITY/IRRESPONSIBILITY, PSYCHOLOGY OF; SPIRITUALITY; THERAPEUTIC CONDITIONS.

GRACIOUSNESS. *See* ENVY AND GRACIOUSNESS; AVARICE AND GENEROSITY; GRACE; GRATITUDE.

GRADUATE EDUCATION IN PASTORAL COUNSELING *and* **PASTORAL THEOLOGY.** *See* EDUCATION IN PASTORAL CARE AND COUNSELING; PASTORAL THEOLOGY, GRADUATE EDUCATION IN; SPECIALIZATION IN PASTORAL CARE.

GRANDIOSITY. *See* EGOTISM; NARCISSISM; PRIDE AND HUMILITY.

GRANDPARENTS. *See* PARENTS AND PARENTHOOD. *See also* FAMILY, HISTORY AND SOCIOLOGY OF; FAMILY THEORY AND THERAPY.

GRATITUDE. The appropriate, spontaneous, joyful response to an act of forgiveness, favor, or other kindness shown to one by another, especially if unexpected or undeserved. Whether in response to God or other persons, gratitude is integrally related to gracious actions, and may be defined as the ideal or normative response to them.

1. *Motivational Complexity.* Ideally, gratitude should be spontaneous and uncomplicated, but in reality, and psychologically, this is not always so. Seward Hiltner, for example, notes the difficulty people have maintaining a sense of gratitude over time, and the ways in which honest gratitude can become mixed with other motives (Hiltner, 1972). The recipient of a major gift may in time begin to take it for granted; the ebullient gratitude of a patient to the physician may quickly fade when the danger is past. While such gratitude may be sincere at the time, often it is short-lived; the sense of thankfulness subsides; the patient recovers and gets on with normal life, and the doctor is seen as simply having done the job paid for.

Other forms of such "reactive gratitude" (as Hiltner calls it) are seen in counseling relationships where promises of sobriety, marital fidelity, or steady work patterns are offered in return for "just one more chance," yet in time the sense of gratitude for the opportunity passes and the former destructive behaviors return. It is important to underscore that the gratitude shown in these instances need not be seen as insincere; indeed, it is often ardently sincere at the time. But even deeply felt gratitude is, regrettably, often short-lived.

Why this is so is not immediately obvious, but the reason may lie somewhere in gratitude's motivational dynamics; more must be going on than meets the eye. One possibility, as Hiltner suggests, is that mixed with a genuine sense of gratitude may be an unconscious resentment at the dependency experienced by the receiver of any truly unmerited gift or gracious favor. Dependency easily leads to resentment, as any parent of teenagers can attest, and acts of giving and generosity create dependency by implying a relationship of power or superiority over the recipient, however unintended. The experience of receiving gifts, favors, or forgiveness therefore is never far removed from the anxiety of powerlessness or inferiority. To the extent that this dynamic is operative in given situations, gratitude may more understandably fade or lead into contradictory, "unappreciative" subsequent behavior.

2. True and False Gratitude. Hiltner's "reactive gratitude" should not be confused with "false gratitude." In false gratitude, the expression of thanks may *seem* genuine but, unlike the reactive kind, it really is not. Instead, it is a ploy, conscious or unconscious, to divert attention from the self's essential responsibility and to manipulate others instead. This pattern is often seen in alcoholics who claim they can handle their own problems; when it appears that they cannot, and must be bailed out of trouble by some Alcoholics Anonymous member or clergyperson, the individual will often heap praise and thanks on the helper. This may sound convincing and heartfelt but its psychological meaning may be quite unrelated to real gratitude; it may in fact be intended to divert attention from one's own responsibility and to set the stage for future manipulation of the helping person.

False gratitude can of course occur in all family and interpersonal relationships. A parent's expression of gratitude to a child for spontaneously cleaning his or her room may (though need not) be manipulative rather than genuinely thankful—treating the child's kindness (if that is what it is) as a service for which payment is due but under the guise of gratitude. Such "gratitude" is a reward, not an expression of thanks, as well as a device for getting him or her to do it again. Similar misrepresentations can occur in sexual and marital relationships, where subtle forms of payment and manipulation may be involved in what are presented as acts of self-giving and gratitude.

In all such instances a manipulative strategy poses as gratitude. But what fundamentally disqualifies the response as gratitude is its loss of connection with grace. A gift is falsely treated as though it were the fulfillment or creation of an obligation. And the individual's response to it is misrepresented as gratitude when in fact it is a payment, psychologically. Genuine gratitude and thanksgiving, however, are free, not obligated, just as the act which prompts them must be free and gracious—in some sense always undeserved and "beyond the call of duty."

3. Gratitude and the Christian Life. In Christian perspective, gratitude, as the truly appropriate and comprehensive response to God's grace in Jesus Christ, is the fundamental orientation for Christian life, the basic motive and perspective for all true worship and faithful living. It is fundamental to any act of Christian worship and basic to Christian social and ecological responsibility. A sense of gratitude is utterly incommensurate, for example, with the greed and exploitation inherent in patterns of economic, sexual, and racial injustice. Even the tacit acceptance of nuclear contamination or the possibility of nuclear holocaust expresses a profound lack of gratitude for God's Creation.

Given the psychological complexity of gratitude, its tendency to fade, and its potential for perversion, it is apparent that even this seemingly simple and primary disposition of the heart requires correction and development. Theologically, one might say that gratitude, like everything human, stands in need of God's judgment, redemption, and sanctification. If this is so, gratitude is both a primary, spontaneous outpouring of the heart in response to acts of kindness, favor, and forgiveness, and a disposition or virtue to be cultivated, corrected, and developed over time. We must, in a sense, learn gratitude, and practice it; yet in another sense, gratitude is always free and spontaneous, the joyful human response to all that comes to us beyond what we earn or deserve, freely and graciously.

Bibliography. S. Hiltner, *Theological Dynamics* (1972).

B. H. CHILDS

ENVY AND GRACIOUSNESS; GRACE AND PASTORAL CARE. *See also* AVARICE AND GENEROSITY; DEPENDENCE/INDEPENDENCE; SPIRITUAL DISCIPLINE AND GROWTH; WORSHIP AND CELEBRATION. *Compare* MORAL BEHAVIOR AND RELIGION.

GRAVESIDE SERVICE. *See* BURIAL.

GREED. *See* ENVY AND GRACIOUSNESS; AVARICE AND GENEROSITY.

GREEK ORTHODOXY. *See* MINISTRY AND PASTORAL CARE (Orthodox Tradition).

GREEK PHILOSOPHY AND PASTORAL CARE. *See* PHILOSOPHY AND PSYCHOLOGY, WESTERN.

GREGORY OF NYSSA. *See* EARLY CHURCH, PASTORAL CARE AND COUNSELING IN; LITERATURE, DEVOTIONAL.

GREGORY THE GREAT, POPE (540–604). Gregory became pope in 590, in a time of cultural transition, social instability, expansion of the Roman Church, and political turmoil.

It is for his profound calming and pace-setting Christian influence—through his writings, administration, and personal example—on the beliefs, practices, and morals of individuals and nations that Gregory earned his stature.

Gregory's seminal work, *Pastoral Care,* reflects his larger agenda and achievement in the domain of soul care. It sums up the pastoral wisdom of the church fathers for practical use, stresses the connection between inner and outer affairs in soul care, cautions against undue attention to worldly matters, and recognizes the embeddedness of most concerns in a framework of ultimate meaning. Its focus on the guiding aspect of the pastoral office intends to counter a proliferation of sacramental rites and practices and to strengthen the pastoral function of personal ministry in order to provide ongoing disciplinary and consolatory support for persons' continuous struggles with sin and temptation.

N. F. HAHN

PASTORAL CARE (History, Traditions, and Definitions); EARLY CHURCH; MEDIEVAL CHURCH.

GRIEF AND LOSS. The complex interaction of affective, cognitive, physiological, and behavioral responses to the loss by any means of a person, place, thing, activity, status, bodily organ, etc., with whom (or which) a person has identified, who (or which) has become a significant part of an individual's own self.

The power of grief to disrupt the total life of a person derives from the interaction between the physiological inheritance of an infant and growing child with the significant other people and events of her or his life. As a part of this process, attachments are formed and the individual self is developed from the perceived attitudes of significant others toward oneself. The breaking of these attachments in grief, the loss of the other, is experienced as one's *own* breaking, the death of significant aspects of one's own self.

Grief is a process with identifiable stages during which one gives up that which is lost, withdraws emotional investment in the physical reality of the other, effects gradual reinvestment of one's self in the images of the other which are a part of the self, and renews meaningful activities and relationships without the lost one. All of the stages must be gone through at the person's own pace in order for positive reorganization to take place.

Pathological grief refers to the blocking of the usual movement through the process, with the person fixating on one or a few feelings and/or behaviors of some stage prior to resolution. Intense ambivalent feelings toward the deceased have been repressed, and this repression stands in the way of the mourning which needs to take place.

Pastoral care of the bereaved attempts through frequent conversations to facilitate grieving: expressing feelings, remembering, accepting the reality of physical death, experiencing one's own value as an individual, and discovering meaning in one's life in the midst of the events. The funeral is also considered to be a part of the pastoral care of the bereaved.

1. **The Dynamics of Grief.** *a. Psychoanalytic theory.* Freud spoke of mourning as the process of withdrawing libido which had been directed toward the lost loved object and redirecting it toward another object. An internal reaction is triggered, since the lost object had in some sense become a part of our own ego. The process of freeing the libido and redirecting it takes place bit by bit over a period of time (Freud, 1914).

The pastoral psychologist Edgar Jackson (1957) built his approach on that of Freud, but made additional contributions in his discussion of the relationship between the child's early experiences of deprivation and the later loss of the person by death, of the death of an emotionally related person as a reminder of one's own finitude, and of the significant role in one's life of a system of values for providing meaning and coherence for all of life's experiences.

Spiro, a rabbi, also elaborates a psychoanalytic approach particularly relevant to the pastor. Spiro relates Jewish mourning customs to the social and the unconscious personal needs of the bereaved (Spiro, 1967). A more recent, detailed psychoanalytic exposition of the dynamics of grief that also pays attention to sociological factors, theological issues, and the minister's role, is that of Spiegel (1978).

b. Interpersonal theory. A synthesis of the ideas of several theorists with particular relevance to understanding grief has been made by Switzer (1970). Switzer sees the development of the self as arising from the interactions of a particular human being with the particular physical and social environment. The learning of attitudes toward one's self and the external world, including other human beings, derives from the perceived behavior of the primary caregiving person(s) toward the infant and small child. Among the very important early behaviors of these caregiving people are the "going away" and "being absent" behaviors. From the very beginning of extrauterine life the infant learns that the absence of the caregivers inevitably produces physical discomfort and even pain, which quickly is learned as psychological discomfort, the threat to one's well-being when the caregivers leave or prepare to go. From this base Switzer develops a theory of grief as the reactivation of the early experiences of separation anxiety by a contemporary loss. Guilt as moral and existential anxiety, as fear for our own being rising out of our awareness of our finitude, our helplessness in certain situations, and our mortality, contributes to the overwhelming disruptive power of the experience, since the loss of the other is experienced as the loss of one's own self.

Sullender (1979) criticizes Switzer's failure to note unique differences between infantile mourning and adult grief. While Switzer's work does note some striking differences between them (the various aspects of existential anxiety, for example), other differences between infantile and adult separation experiences need to receive more attention. In addition, a predominant reaction in grief, the affect of sorrow, is not accounted for, and probably is not directly related to separation anxiety as such.

c. Biological-psychological conceptions. Bowlby and Parkes are major contributors to an understanding of grief based upon a combination of ethologists' studies of the behavior of animals, using these findings to make suggestions concerning the source and meaning of human experiences of attachment and separation, and upon some of the interpersonal and psychoanalytic approaches already mentioned. The bonding of infants to adults is a need passed on to human beings from higher primates by patterns of imprinting, and there is an inherent striving toward the accomplishment of this process (Bowlby). The breaking of attachments calls forth typical searching and mourning behaviors which have resulted from imprinting, and requires the processes of detachment and reattachment.

Parkes states "that the pining or yearning which constitutes separation anxiety is the characteristic feature of the pang of grief" (1972, p. 6).

d. Summary. Any comprehensive theory which assists in understanding the reaction of grief will need to take into account both the *common* and the *unique* physiological givens of the human being as a particular personality is developed in the interaction of that human being with the primary caregivers and with other persons and events. Psychoanalytic emphases on internal psychic processes must also be integrated into such a theory.

2. **Grief as a Process: Stages and Behaviors.** Parkes stated it most clearly: "Grief is a process and not a state.

Grief is not a set of symptoms which start after a loss and then gradually fade away. It involves a succession of clinical pictures which blend into and replace one another" (1972, pp. 6–7).

In the highly selective review which follows, it will be noted that there is no reference to the popular work by Elisabeth Kübler-Ross (1969). Some writers have referred to the stages of dying she describes as stages of grief. While there are some similarities in behaviors, there are some very significant differences as processes. To attempt to force her stages of dying on post-loss grieving is distorting and misleading.

a. Stages. As early as 1955, pastoral theologian Wayne Oates proposed a very helpful theory of grief outlining a progression of stages: (1) The shocking blow of the loss in itself; (2) the numbing effect of the shock; (3) the struggle between fantasy and reality; (4) the break-through of a flood of grief; (5) selected memory and stabbing pain; (6) the acceptance of the loss and the affirmation of life itself (1955, pp. 52–5).

A more thoroughly developed picture is provided by Spiegel. (1) Spiegel notes *shock* as the first stage, including disbelief, emotional numbness, occasional outbreaks of pain and tears, a frequent lack of awareness of external events and conversations, and difficulty in thinking clearly. (2) The *control* stage follows, characterized by both the self-control of the grief-stricken and that which is demanded by other persons with whom one must deal. Spiegel describes the person as often passive, having difficulty in carrying out decisions, experiencing distance between one's self and the external world, a sense of the unreality of it all, a depersonalization, feeling empty or dead inside, and trying to act as if the loss had not occurred.

(3) The third stage he refers to as *regression*. The organization of the self which had been based upon interaction with the other can no longer be sustained under the impact of the reality of the loss. Earlier forms of feeling and reacting begin to dominate and are often independent of the realities of the present environment. There are experiences of pain, uncertainty, fragmentation, heightened emotionality of all kinds, weeping, anger, complaining, becoming exhausted and withdrawing, seeming apathy, self-centeredness, preoccupation with and often idealization of the deceased, grasping at simple explanations including religious ones, a pervasive sense of helplessness, and a variety of control and defense mechanisms directed against the pain and the fear of loss of control.

(4) The final phase is *adaptation*, the step-by-step giving up of regressive behaviors. In their place more adaptive responses arise as the loss is recognized to its full and final extent. This makes necessary the very painful giving up of expectations of interaction with the deceased, accompanied by a restoration of the person within one's own individual personality. In so doing, recontact with the present external world takes place (Spiegel, 1978, pp. 62–83).

Many of the behaviors mentioned by Spiegel and others are also described by Parkes, but Parkes's stages contribute additional understanding because they grow out of empirical research. His first stage is *numbness and denial,* although elements of denial operate in the other stages as well. Parkes's research indicates that the usual period of time for this stage is five to seven days.

The second stage is *yearning,* intense painful longing for the deceased, preoccupation with thoughts of that person, searching behavior, illusions of thinking that one has seen the person, dreams and fantasies, auditory and occasionally visual hallucinations, self-reproach, identification with behaviors, activities, or illness of the deceased (especially a terminal illness), and thoughts and feelings of suicide. This stage usually lasts for several weeks.

The third stage is *disorganization and despair,* beginning with some reduction of the intensity of yearning, the diminishing of the magnitude of the other emotional reactions. There are various degrees of apathy and aimlessness, and the inability to see a positive future. The majority of respondents in the research were still in this stage a year following the loss.

Finally there is *reorganization*. The internal task of removing one's energy from the person who had died, while not necessarily finally accomplished, and perhaps never is, is substantially accomplished, and the bereaved person begins to see a hopeful future without the physical presence of the deceased and to experience the present as meaningful. Parkes's study of widows indicates that even after thirteen months the majority of his research subjects could not be said to have completed their grieving process.

b. Comments on process, stages, and behaviors. Since grief is a process with stages, it is essential for a person to go through each one of the stages completely in order to reach a positive resolution of the whole grief reaction. This reorganization is accomplished when the person is capable of living approximately as meaningfully, happily, and effectively as prior to the loss. To continue to repress and suppress the feelings involved in grief, to go about one's usual business as if there had been no loss, to attempt to skip stages or not do what needs to be done to work out the internal psychological tasks and the external social tasks is to thwart the process of resolution and reorganization.

Grief understood as a process also communicates to us that it is usually a transient, although not smoothly and rapidly moving, period of time. This means that the feelings and thoughts and most of the behaviors of grief as they appear *during the process* are normal. Many powerful ones may be experienced at the same time, some may be in conflict with one another, and together they may be absolutely overwhelming to the individual. These reactions are in themselves not to be feared, even reactions such as hallucinations, if they do not persist, do not seriously interfere with one's daily activities or the process of grief, and if one does not base one's decisions and behavior upon them. While it is not uncommon for grieving persons to feel intense anger or to have thoughts of suicide, the actual behaviors of violence and suicide have to be resisted.

It is crucial that the minister be aware of these data in order to evaluate where a person is in the process, to facilitate the movement of the process without seeking to force it too rapidly, to be alert to a person's attempts to leap over a stage, not to be frightened in the presence of behaviors unfamiliar to the minister herself or himself, to be able to assure persons that they are not losing their minds, yet to be able to take with utmost seriousness their suicidal thoughts and feelings and potential violence toward others.

3. **Pathological Grief.** Pathological (morbid, atypical, unresolved) grief is that condition of the bereaved in which he or she does not reach the final stage of the process or is not continuing to make progress toward positive resolution within six to eight months after the loss. Given this approximate period of time, a fixation on a particular symptom or a particular segment of a specific stage of the normal grief process may be noted (usually either stage two or stage three of Parkes's scheme), with the adoption in a rigid and inflexible manner of one or a small select number of the mechanisms or behaviors of that stage. This fixation is in contrast with the usual grief process when there is the experimental testing of the various behaviors over a period of time, discarding those which are not functional in the maintenance and the restructuring of the self, and then going on to utilize in a constructive and adaptive way several of those which facilitate self-maintenance and growth.

Researchers have pointed out certain distinguishing dynamics of pathological grief. Parkes indicated that as a result of his comparison of the grief of psychiatric patients and that of widows from the general population, the only discernible differences were that the psychiatric patients had a greater intensity of guilt and that the behavior of self-reproach persisted for a longer period of time. There was also the tendency for the early grieving of this group to be delayed, that is, a lapse of two weeks or more between the loss and the beginning of the pangs of grief (1972, pp. 107–8).

Volkan (1970) specifies the universality of a love-hate ambivalence in the persons with pathological grief whom he has treated, though such ambivalence is involved at least to some degree in all grief. Obviously it is quite minimal in some; thus it is the presence of *intense, exaggerated*, or *repressed* ambivalence which seems to be involved in pathological grief.

This condition may look like any one of a number of disorders or forms of human unhappiness: depression, bitterness, anxiety attacks, general irritability and/or outbursts of anger, or even more severe symptoms of emotional disorder.

Ministers can play a very important role in identifying such persons and being effective pastors to them. Understanding the source of their unhappy and often difficult behavior can give a different perspective on the way in which they relate to others and therefore can lead to the pastor's establishing a more constructive relationship with them. More frequent visits and conversations with those persons may eventually begin to focus on the relationship of their present unsatisfactory lives to their incompleted grief. Even though there is a possibility that the person will resist the minister's efforts, the minister may discover that the person's intensity of dissatisfaction with her or his present life is sufficient to overcome the threat of feeling the pain and the person may be open to referral to the appropriate helping professional.

4. **Needs of the Bereaved.** Since many of the needs of the grief-stricken have been referred to in the foregoing discussion, it remains only to gather them together in summary form. The list is somewhat, but not precisely, chronological. The needs are: (1) to accept in one's own mind the reality and finality of the physical death; (2) to become aware of and express all of the feelings one has toward the deceased person, the loss of the person, and sometimes concerning the mode of death (lingering and painful illness, sudden accident which seems to be the clear fault of the deceased or some other person, suicide, etc.); (3) to break the emotional ties with the deceased in the sense of not attempting to invest emotionally in that person and behave toward the person as if he or she were still physically present; and by not seeking to get one's continuing needs met directly through that person; (4) to break habitual patterns of speech and other behaviors which assume the other's continued physical existence; (5) to affirm one's own self as worthwhile in and of one's self apart from interaction and connection with the deceased; (6) to reaffirm and therefore to allow to come back to life those characteristics and behaviors of the deceased with which the person had previously identified, and which can now be experienced as continuing to contribute to the ongoing and growing life of the grieving person; (7) to cultivate both old and new family relationships and friendships; and (8) to rediscover meaning in and for one's own life.

In the meeting of the first seven needs, the emotional and relational meaning foundation of the person's life is already being re-established. In addition, the human being strives naturally and constantly toward ways of thinking about human experience that bring some sense of coherence, which help the person understand her or his own experience and lead to the effective sharing of that experience and that meaning with others, and which are also stimulating and reinforcing to the entire grieving process.

5. **Pastoral Care of the Bereaved.** Effective pastoral care for bereaved persons is based upon the capacity of the pastor to relate closely to persons undergoing intense emotion, a knowledge of the dynamics and stages and behaviors of grief and the needs of the bereaved, and an awareness of findings like those of Parkes which make clear that early full grieving, allowing one's self to feel and to express those feelings both verbally and nonverbally, tends to lead to the most constructive resolution of the process, while the repression or suppression of the early reactions to the loss tend to lead to a greater severity of the grief symptoms later (Parkes, 1970, p. 450).

The process by which pastoral care is accomplished is by frequent visits with the grieving, assisting persons to express themselves by asking about what has taken place and by responding with accurate empathy. The pre-funeral visit can be a time of assisting people to talk about the deceased so that their own memories are activated, the feelings and expression of emotions are facilitated, and in the process, the minister is gaining information both about the deceased and the bereaved that will lead to the development and execution of a more pastorally effective funeral.

The funeral should be viewed as a worship service of the community, yet also as a part of the pastoral care process. Its goals are to affirm the reality and finality of the physical death of the person, to encourage remembering and the sharing of memories, to facilitate the identification and expression of feeling, to bind persons to one another in community, to provide conditions and resources which may assist growth in faith and hope, and to celebrate the life of the deceased before God in context of appropriate religious meanings and ritual expressions.

In continued pastoral visits, it is helpful to ask the bereaved about what their feelings are right at the moment, review the death and the events surrounding the death, and discuss their most vivid memories of the person and the feelings connected with those memories.

One difficult task of many grieving persons, which is especially difficult in terms of pastoral guidance, is the allowing of sufficient time for mourning, not covering it up by premature decisions to move and to get rid of all reminders, or by one's work and a flurry of activities, yet at the same time, beginning to return, as quickly as one is actually ready, to daily activities, responsibilities, and the re-establishing of old or developing new relationships.

In many situations an awareness of family systems dynamics is critical. Each individual family member must be ministered to, but the family as a whole needs also to be considered. Children of whatever age must not be overlooked by the pastor. Though their grief is not identical to that of adults, nor the way they express it, the impact of the loss upon them may be at least as great. Adults often need encouragement to give extra loving attention to children in the family at a time when the adults themselves feel as if they have less to give. Unfortunately, some families expect sameness in thinking and feeling among their members and become angry with or ostracize one another for differentness. The pastor may be able to help by pointing out differences in grief reactions of people of different ages and with different relationships to the deceased. The pastor can help family members to understand and tolerate differences and to communicate more fully and clearly with one another.

Finally, families face difficulties in the reassignment of both instrumental and affectional roles. A perceptive pastor can call to their attention the need for whole family negotiation, helping family members resist the undiscussed assignment of particular new roles to various members who do not want them or who are not developmentally mature enough for them, or the undiscussed taking over of certain roles of the deceased by one family member. (See Switzer, 1974, ch. 5).

Bibliography. J. Bowlby, *Attachment* (1969). S. Freud, "Mourning and Melancholia," *SE* 14, pp. 125–53. E. Jackson, *Understanding Grief* (1957). E. Kübler-Ross, *On Death and Dying* (1969). K. Mitchell and H. Anderson, *All Our Losses, All Our Griefs* (1983). W. Oates, *Anxiety in Christian Experience* (1955). C. Parkes, *Bereavement* (1972); "The First Year of Bereavement," *Psychiatry*, 33 (1970), 444–67; " 'Seeking' and 'Finding' a Lost Object," *Social Science and Medicine*, 4 (1970), 187–201. Y. Spiegel, *The Grief Process: Analysis and Counseling* (1978). J. Spiro, *A Time to Mourn* (1967). R. S. Sullender, "Three Theoretical Approaches to Grief," *J. of Pastoral Care*, 33 (1979), 243–51. D. K. Switzer, "Awareness of Unresolved Grief: An Opportunity for Ministry," *The Christian Ministry*, July (1980), 19–23; *The Dynamics of Grief* (1970); *The Minister as Crisis Counselor* (1974). V. Volkan, "Typical Findings in Pathological Grief," *The Psychiatric Quarterly*, 44 (1970), 1–20.

D. K. SWITZER

COMFORT/SUSTAINING; DEATH, MEANING OF; DYING, PASTORAL CARE OF; ESCHATOLOGY AND PASTORAL CARE; FUNERAL; HOPE AND DESPAIR; GRIEF AND MOURNING, JEWISH CARE IN; PROVIDENCE, DOCTRINE OF, AND PASTORAL CARE; SADNESS AND DEPRESSION; SUFFERING. *See also* AUTOPSY; CONSOLATION; CRYING; MOURNING CUSTOMS AND RITUALS; SUICIDE (Pastoral Care); WIDOWS/WIDOWERS. *Compare* HANDICAP AND DISABILITY; LOSS OF FUNCTION; SOCIAL CHANGE AND DISLOCATION; SUPPORT GROUPS.

GRIEF AND LOSS IN CHILDHOOD AND ADOLESCENCE. A child growing up today is all too aware of the reality of death, perhaps more than adults realize. Even at a very young age, the child is confronted with death: a pet is killed, a grandfather dies, a leader is assassinated. And, of course, television provides pictures of death in living color.

Yet children's feelings and perspectives are often overlooked. Too often the pastor comforts the adult mourners but pays scant attention to the "little ones." The child should be allowed to participate with the family in the commemoration of a deceased loved one. Silence only deprives him or her of the opportunity to share grief.

1. Can Children Understand Death? Psychologist Maria Nagy, studying Hungarian children in the late 1940s, discovered three phases in the child's awareness of mortality. The child from three to five may deny death as a regular and final process. Death is like sleep: you are dead, then you are alive again. This child experiences what he or she considers "death" many times each day, such as when the parents go to work.

Between five and nine, children accept the idea that a person has died, but may not understand it as something that will happen to everyone and particularly to themselves. Around the age of nine and ten, children recognize death as an inevitable experience that will occur even to them.

These are all rough approximations with many variations. Robert Kastenbaum points out that adolescents and even some adults have childlike views of death. They "know" that death is inevitable and final, but most of their daily behavior is more consistent with the conviction that personal death is an unfounded rumor.

a. Are euphemisms a helpful explanation of death? The question arises constantly about what we should tell a child when death occurs. Should we not acknowledge that a person has died? Should we say that a grandparent became ill and went to a hospital to recuperate, hoping that the child will eventually accept the absence?

Evasions indicate the clergyperson's uncertainty about children's capacity to deal with existing situations. It encourages youngsters to "forget about things" and does not prepare them to deal with life's realities. We should never cover up with a fiction which we will repudiate someday. There is no greater childhood need than trust and truth.

b. Should we share religious convictions with children? Of course! Religion is concerned with the mystery of death as well as the meaning of life. But in giving religious interpretations, be honest and translate theological concepts into the language and comprehension of the child.

Suffering and death should not be linked with sin and divine punishment. Children experience enough guilt without the added measure of God's chastisement.

c. Should youngsters attend the funeral? Again honesty is the best policy. Children should be told of a loved one's death *immediately,* in a familiar setting and by a parent or someone close to them. They should be given the opportunity to attend the funeral. To deprive them of this sense of belonging could shake their future mental health.

Explain in advance the details of the funeral; this will lessen the child's anxieties. However, a child who does not wish to attend the funeral should never be forced to go. Gently suggest that sometime later he or she might visit the cemetery.

2. Do Children Experience Grief? Mourning and sadness are appropriate emotions for people of all ages. The more meaningful the relationship, the more intense the feeling of loss.

According to John Bowlby of Tavistock Clinic, London, each child may experience three phases in the natural grieving process. The first is protest when the child cannot believe the person is dead and attempts, sometimes angrily, to regain the deceased. Next is pain, despair, and disorganization when the youngster begins to accept the fact that the loved one is really gone. Finally, there is hope, when the child begins to organize his or her life without the deceased.

a. Should the child be discouraged from crying? The child whose loved one dies should be allowed to express grief. Don't be afraid of causing tears. So often adults deliberately veer the conversation away from the deceased, not understanding that the worst thing possible is for the child to repress tears. Grief that is stoically bottled up inside may later find release in an explosion more serious to the child's inner makeup.

b. What are other responses to death? For the child, death may bring a variety of reactions.

i. Denial. The child may seem unaffected because he is trying to defend himself against the death by pretending it has not happened. This response signifies that the child has found the loss too great to accept and is pretending secretly that the deceased is still alive.

ii. Bodily distress. "I have no appetite." "I had a nightmare." Anxiety expresses itself in physical and emotional symptoms.

iii. Hostile reactions to the deceased. "How could Daddy do this to me? Didn't he care enough about me to stay alive?" The child feels deserted and angry.

iv. Hostile reactions to others. "Dad didn't take proper care of her; that's why Mom died." Resentment is projected outward in order to relieve guilt by making someone else responsible for the death.

v. Replacement. The child makes a fast play for the affection of others as a substitute for the person who has died.

vi. Assumption of mannerisms of the deceased. The child tries to take on the characteristics of the deceased by walking or talking like him or her.

vii. Anxiety. The youngster becomes preoccupied with the physical symptoms that ended the deceased's life. He transfers the symptoms to himself in a process of identification.

viii. Idealization. In the attempt to fight off unhappy thoughts, the child becomes obsessed with the deceased's good qualities, falsifying the deceased's real life and character.

ix. Panic. "Who will take care of me now? Suppose something happens to Mommy!" This state of confusion and shock needs a parent's supportive love: "My health is fine; I will take care of you."

x. Guilt. Children are likely to feel guilt, since in their experience bad things happen to them because they were naughty. The parent's desertion must be a retribution for their wrongdoing. Therefore they search their minds for the "bad deed" that caused it.

These are some of the reactions of children as well as adults. Some come at the time of death; some never appear. Others may be delayed, since children often repress their emotions and attempt to appear calm in the face of tragedy. As clergy we can give vital support for the terrible pain of separation.

c. Guidelines for concerned clergy. i. Do not avoid the subject of personal death. Mental health is not the denial of tragedy, but the frank acknowledgment of painful separation.

ii. Do not discourage the emotions of grief.

iii. Do not tell a child euphemisms, half-truths, or circumlocutions. Honesty is the only policy.

iv. Do share your religious convictions as to faith, God, immortality, prayer, and death. But have more concern for the welfare of the bereaved than for the protection or promotion of religious institutions.

v. Do make referrals to other supportive people. Seeking further help from a mental health professional is not an admission of weakness, but a demonstration of strength and love.

vi. Do remember that the process of adjustment to death is longer than the funeral. The height of depression is six to nine months after death! Make frequent visits and encourage the child to talk about his or her feelings.

vii. Do be human. Express your own emotions of grief; shed a tear — physically and spiritually — to touch the child in pain. Just remember the words of Thornton Wilder, "There is a land of the living and a land of the dead and the bridge is love — the only survival, the only meaning."

E. A. GROLLMAN

CHILDREN; DYING CHILD AND FAMILY; FUNERAL, CHILD'S; GRIEF AND LOSS; GRIEF AND MOURNING, JEWISH CARE IN. *See also* FAMILY, JEWISH *or* PASTORAL CARE AND COUNSELING OF. *Compare* DIVORCE, CHILDREN AND ADOLESCENTS IN.

GRIEF AND MOURNING, JEWISH CARE IN. Judaism is more than a creed; it is a way of life. And death is a reality of life. Since there are diverse ways in which Jews throughout the ages have viewed life, so there are different approaches by which Jews practice the rites of death. For example, traditional Judaism is opposed to cremation as a denial of belief in bodily resurrection. On the other hand, a prominent liberal rabbi in Cleveland writes, "I have no particular faith in physical resurrection. About one in ten funerals in which I officiate involves cremation." Orthodox rabbis may not permit autopsies, yet almost all Conservative and Reform rabbis do. Thus there is no unanimity of acceptance as to the rites of burial and manners of mourning.

One becomes a mourner (Hebrew, *Ovel*) upon the death of one of seven relatives: father, mother, husband, wife, son or daughter, brother or sister, including half-brother or half-sister. A child less than thirteen years old is not obliged to observe the rituals of mourning.

From the moment that Jews learn of the death of a loved one, there are specific religious rites that help to order their life. A most striking expression of grief is the rending of the mourner's clothes (*Keriah*). In the book of Genesis, when Jacob believed that his son Joseph was killed, the father "rent his garments" (37:34). Today many mourners indicate their anguish by cutting a black ribbon, usually at the funeral chapel or at the cemetery prior to interment. The ceremony is performed standing up, to teach the bereaved to "meet all sorrow standing upright." For a parent, the tear is made on the left side over the heart; for others, it is on the right. *Keriah* is visible for the week of *Shiva*.

Shiva ("seven") refers to the first seven days of intensive mourning beginning immediately after the funeral, with the day of burial counted as the first day. One hour of the seventh day is considered a full day. Mourning customs are not observed on Sabbaths and festivals. The bereaved remain at home, receiving a continuous stream of condolence calls. This helps to keep the minds of the bereaved active and their attentions engaged. Also, it is important because the companionship lends the comfort of the loving concern of family and friends.

Even though a minor is exempt from many of the mourning rites, the youngsters should not be arbitrarily dismissed from the family gathering. They should be afforded the chance to face grief and mingle with loved ones. Some enlightened adults have helped children feel they are important by allowing them to share in the family duties, such as answering doorbells and telephones, assisting with chores, and even preparing the *Seudat Havra-ah*, the meal of consolation. They are given the opportunity to help and be helped.

Immediately upon returning from the cemetery the *Shiva* candle is kindled and remains burning for the entire seven days. Before his death, the great sage Judah Hànasi instructed that a light should be kept aflame in his home, for "light is the symbol of the divine. The Lord is my light and my salvation."

Following the *Shiva* comes the *Sh-loshim,* the thirty days. The mourners resume normal activity but avoid places of entertainment. At the end of thirty days ritualistic mourning is over, except in the case where the deceased was a parent, when mourning continues for an entire year.

The adults might attend the *Minyan* (daily worship) and the Sabbath services. They read aloud the *Kaddish* prayer, originally not a liturgy for the dead, but a pledge from the living to dedicate one's life to the God of Life, "Magnified and Sanctified." This is the highest approach to commemorate the memory of a loved one. Each time during the year that the mourners recite the *Kaddish,* they reinforce both the reality of death and the affirmation of life. They openly display their own needed concern and profound feeling of being a good son, daughter, father, mother, brother, sister, or spouse. They participate with others who are also suffering the emotional trauma of bereavement. They belong to the largest company in the world—the company of those who have known anguish and death. This great, universal sense of

sorrow helps to unite human hearts and dissolve all other feelings into those of common sympathy and understanding.

The complete mourning period for those whose parents have died concludes twelve months from the day of the death. For other relatives *Sh-loshim* concludes the bereavement.

Anniversaries of the death (*Yahrzeit*) are observed annually on the date of death, commencing on the preceding day and concluding on the anniversary day at sunset. *Kaddish* is recited in the synagogue and the *Yahrzeit* candle is kindled.

The service of commemoration of the tombstone or plaque is called the "unveiling." The time of the unveiling may be any time after *Sh-loshim* and usually before the first year of mourning is over. Unveilings are not held on the Sabbath or during festivals. Any member of the family or a close friend may intone the appropriate prayers, usually a few Psalms, the *El Molay Rachamim* ("God, full of compassion") and the *Kaddish*. Visitation at the grave may be made as often as one wishes following the initial thirty-day period.

The memorial prayer of *Yizkor* ("May God *remember* the soul of my revered") is said four times a year during the synagogue worship: *Yom Kippur, Shemini Atzeret, Pesach,* and *Shavuot*. It is not usually recited during the first year of mourning.

Jewish rituals are community rituals. They are performed by those who share a religious sameness. The traditions create a sense of solidarity, of belongingness—the feeling that one is a member of the group with all the comfort and gratification that such a cohesiveness brings.

Judaism is strict in limiting mourning to the given periods and the customary observances. Excessive grief is taken as want of trust in God. The faith holds it as desirable that with time the havoc wrought by death should help to repair itself. Though no one is ever the same after a bereavement, he or she is expected, when mourning is over, to take up existence for the sake of life itself. The garment that the pious mourner rends can be sewn and worn again. The scar is there, but life must resume its course. The observance of the Jewish laws and customs of mourning helps the mourner face reality, gives honor to the deceased, and guides the bereaved in the reaffirmation of life.

There are different approaches to a concept of life after death. O. Lazarus, in *Liberal Judaism and Its Standpoint,* summarizes a Reform Jewish attitude toward death: "We cannot believe in the resurrection of the body that perishes with death. We feel, however, that there is that within us which is immortal, and is not bounded by time and space. It is this, man's soul, as it is called, which continues, so we believe, to live after the death of the body."

The Orthodox Jew is committed to a belief in recompense, immortality, and resurrection. The scales of cosmic equity will end up in balance with the body of the dead arising from the grave to be reunited with the soul. In the presence of all the multitudes of all generations, God will pronounce judgment of bliss or damnation.

The Conservative movement has retained some of the prayers in the liturgy where belief is expressed in resurrection and immortality of the soul. For many, the concepts are not regarded literally but rather figuratively and poetically. Some retain the speculative rabbinic and medieval view of the soul as a distinct entity enjoying an independent existence.

Even within each of the three Jewish movements, there is latitude for differences of opinion. While there are many thoughts, none is declared authoritative and final. The tradition teaches, but at the same time it seems to say there is much we do not know and still more we have to learn. And even then, only God can completely discern the mysteries of life and death.

Bibliography. E. A. Grollman, *Living when a Loved One Has Died* (1977); *Explaining Death to Children* (1967). M. Lamm, *The Jewish Way in Death and Mourning* (1969). J. Riemer, *Jewish Reflections on Death* (1978).

E. A. GROLLMAN

FUNERAL AND BURIAL, JEWISH; JEWISH PRAYERS; JEWISH CARE AND COUNSELING. *See also* FAMILY, JEWISH CARE AND COUNSELING OF; GRIEF AND LOSS; MOURNING CUSTOMS AND RITUALS; RITUAL.

GROUP COUNSELING AND PSYCHOTHERAPY.

The arranged use of a selected collection of people who work together to attain goals that are considered: (1) as enhancing to the psychological, spiritual, or functional well-being of the participants, (2) as involving a decrease of distress resulting from aberrations of behavior, thinking, or feeling. Generally this takes place within specified time-limited experiences, and the behavior of a designated leader as well as the members of such a group is governed by an accepted rationale designed to promote the attainment of the agreed-upon goals.

While group counseling and group therapy cannot be absolutely differentiated, both include characteristics that can be designated as lying on a continuum between theoretical extremes. Thus we may differentiate group counseling from group psychotherapy by noting that group counseling generally lies near one end of a particular continuum, while group therapy falls near the other end.

The first differentiating continuum spans the poles between groups having goals for enhancing one's well-being versus groups having goals for correcting disturbances. Group counseling is more often associated with the former and group therapy with the latter. Group therapy may be viewed as enhancing, but often this goal is seen as only secondary to the loss of symptoms. In general, group therapy deals more with problems (or at least with more serious problems), group counseling more with issues of growth and enhancement.

A second distinguishing continuum has to do with belief in the power of the therapeutic experience to create change. Group counseling is generally acknowledged to be less powerful and group therapy to be more powerful. This gives group therapy a greater sense of mystique, magic, and potential for good or ill. Terms describing group therapy as more "intense," pursuing more "depth," or being more "thorough" than group counseling suggest this sense of power and mystique.

Given these considerations (and further reinforcing them), group therapists are expected to have more expertise than group counselors. Their training is more thorough, longer, and more credentialed; accordingly, their services are often more expensive.

It is somewhat ironic, therefore, that with respect to leader *activity*, group therapists are typically understood to be *less* active than the group counselors, as Stein *et al.* (1982) note. This is due to the fact that group counseling usually is more structured than group therapy; it has more limited goals, stronger didactic intent, and requires greater management by the leader.

1. **Group Counseling.** Participants expect a group endeavor labeled "counseling" to require a less intense commitment than group therapy. The entire scope of the project is understood to be limited in depth, power, and capacity to create change. To this end, the purpose of the experience is generally specified during recruitment of participants. Within the experience of the therapy itself, subject matter for conversation is limited more or less to what has previously been specified or to what would be considered contributory to it. This is done to prevent group members from assuming unwarranted expectations and trying to bend the group behavior in therapeutic directions, only to become disappointed when this neither happens nor is allowed.

a. Group composition. The selection of group members depends to some extent upon the stated goals of the group, but fundamentally two alternatives exist: (1) homogeneous selection, (2) heterogeneous selection. In the former some characteristic of an individual is considered prerequisite to membership in a specific group. Thus, a history of alcohol abuse may determine membership in a group concerned with abstinence; an age prerequisite between fourteen and eighteen may determine membership in a group dealing with adolescent sexuality. In a heterogeneous group, on the other hand, one seeks a broad spectrum of characteristics among members. A group may be homogeneous in one dimension (e.g., married) while heterogeneous in others (e.g., age, race, social class). Homogeneous selection offers a more rapid sense of solidarity (cohesion) within a group, whereas heterogeneous selection brings more experience to bear on any particular topic.

It is generally recommended that one select group members by individual contact with prospective participants (or couples, as appropriate) before undertaking the group experience. This is not always necessary or possible. As a general rule, the more ambitious the goals and the more limited the access and egress of members during the group experience, the more important is prior individual assessment of prospective members. In general one wishes to avoid including individuals who are known to be overly argumentative, inordinately demanding, attention seeking, habitually complaining, easily injured (insulted, hurt, disappointed, etc.), highly manipulative, or excessively blaming. Individuals known to be unstable should be included only with all due caution.

b. Structural arrangements. Group counseling as well as group therapy always takes place within a contractual agreement among group members. An important item within such an agreement is the amount of time that such an experience will involve. Naturally one has considerable latitude in specifying this, and it may well be negotiated early in the group's history. The group may be convened once or many times and each session may be one to two hours in length or even longer. Intermittent sessions are conveniently limited to one to three hours each (norm: one and a half hours), while single sessions may last as long as desired. Fatigue factors introduce psychological phenomena that dictate caution after about three hours of continuous meeting. The length of each session and the number of sessions should be specified beforehand unless otherwise agreed.

The optimum size of a counseling group depends upon what method of counseling is employed. If a group is to be more structured (see below) and leader-centered (as in didactic styles of leadership), it may more comfortably include a larger number of persons. Conversely, if more interaction among members is desired, a smaller group is appropriate. The recommended limits of size for a largely interactional group are between four and twelve members.

The setting of the experience can be very important but cannot be specified in principle beyond noting that it must satisfy the requirements of members and leader. It is good to avoid wide-open spaces, interfering environmental noise, and physically uncomfortable seating.

c. Methods. There are possibly as many methods of doing group counseling as there are individuals who do it. However, two dimensions of method are fundamentally important: (1) leader-centered versus interactional, and (2) structured versus unstructured. A very active group leader may choose an essentially didactic approach to counseling, in which an agenda is taught to a group of participants. Comments, questions, and responses may be solicited, but it always remains clear that the leader is teaching and imparting information. This is basically how group therapy began. This method has three distinct advantages: it requires little knowledge of the operation of groups, it can be done with almost any size group, and it is generally well under the control of the leader.

Interactional group counseling depends relatively more upon the actual interaction of the members and leader or members with other members. Discussion, problem solving, and, in general, concerted effort characterize this method. The leader's participation may be very limited, often confined to focusing comments. Interactional counseling requires a leader more skilled in group direction, typically offers a more intense experience, and usually limits group size, as previously noted.

A *structured* group counseling experience is one that is programmed. It proceeds according to a set of directions conveyed to the participants. These may specify either leader-centered or interactional styles, but either way the behavior within the experience is specified. Examples of structured group experiences abound in what are known as "encounter groups" and may be found in books such as *Here Comes Everybody* by William Schutz. *Unstructured* group counseling lacks this programmed quality; what happens within the experience is less planned. One allows the experience of the group to unfold—and it often does so in unpredictable ways.

It should be noted that any particular style may exist anywhere on the continuums represented by these alternative methods. In group counseling, however, a certain amount of structure is always presupposed by virtue of the need to adhere to the limitations imposed by the original contract.

2. Group Therapy. *a. Structural arrangements.* Since the difference between group therapy and group counseling exists not so much in how it is done as in what the expectations are, the structural arrangements for conducting therapy groups vary much the same as in counseling groups and according to the same principles. Nevertheless, since therapy groups generally deal with more delicate situations, it is wiser to set up smaller groups. Most therapists prefer to work with four to ten individuals, thus allowing more attention to be devoted to each participant. Eight is often felt to be the ideal number (Yalom, 1975).

Two types of ongoing groups exist—closed and open. A closed group starts with a specified number of people and continues to completion without adding members, even if some of the original ones drop out. An open group loses old members and gains new ones throughout its history.

Like the counseling group, a therapy group may have a homogeneous or heterogeneous composition. The same considerations apply as with counseling groups. In a group not homogeneous for sex, it is ideal to have an even distribution of women and men, although in practice this is not always possible.

Member selection should almost always begin with individualized selection since more is at stake. Different authors advise the avoidance of different types of patients; so it appears likely that one simply needs to learn from experience what type of patient one works well with, and select on the basis of that. Most authors advise against treating schizophrenics in predominantly non-schizophrenic groups. Manipulative, antisocial, or sociopathic persons, and people who tend to act rather than feel or think cause trouble in groups of predominantly neurotic people. Yalom advises against including schizoid individuals (very withdrawn and asocial) in therapy groups, but this author has had good experience with the practice. If it is done, patience is the key—such persons may take years to gain benefit.

Therapy groups are usually conducted for an hour and a half once a week (range: once every two weeks to three or four times per week). Groups that demand considerable energy on the part of the therapist may do well to meet less often and for a shorter period of time (e.g., adolescent groups usually meet for an hour at a time).

Yalom, among others, believes that for one to obtain significant improvement, at least a year to a year and a half in group therapy is required. However, this may well refer to more long-term change than symptomatic relief, which may occur in two months or so.

Time-limited groups, where the contract specifies the length of the experience, may be useful, but this is much more typical of group counseling. Limiting the duration of a group usually cannot adequately take into account the individual requirements of all the participants.

Marathon groups (with sessions running twelve to twenty-four hours or longer) may be useful with any particular group or individual within a therapy group as an occasional powerful incentive to change. The extended time creates fatigue that enhances emotional intensity and often increases one's capacity to experience feeling in general. The marathon group may produce a "peak experience" conducive to more rapid change.

However, some caution is required regarding the use of this technique, for the more intense the experience, the more likely it is that one will see some bad results. (See Lieberman *et al.* [1973].)

The physical environment may be more important to a therapy group than to a counseling group. A smaller space, more physical comfort, and a sense of isolation and security go a long way in promoting group solidarity and individual ease.

b. Basic technique. Therapy groups consist of a specific number of individuals having the common goal of therapy with the understanding that this is to be done within the group experience. Included within the group, but in a special position, is a leader. The leadership function, however, may be divided among two or more people, giving rise to co-therapy. Each method has its advantages and disadvantages. Co-therapy usually enhances a therapist's sense of security and thus may be advisable for inexperienced therapists. Co-therapy also may be more comfortable in novel or particularly stressful group situations. Where co-therapy is undertaken, the relationship between the co-therapists becomes as important as almost everything else going on in the group — the relationship is like a small marriage regardless of the sexes of the individuals involved. Because of this, solo therapy may be easier or preferable for some.

Groups without leaders are also possible. Usually they consist of individuals who are knowledgeable of group therapy or they occur as an alternative to meeting with the leader. Generally, the group creates a leader anyway, though this person may not be best suited for the role of "therapist."

The actual conduct of a group therapist may take two forms, focusing either on individual therapy in the group or on the group as a whole. While these forms simply reflect a different focus of attention, the actual behavior of therapists practicing each alternative varies considerably. Individual-in-group psychotherapy is just what the term states — the therapist pays attention to and deals with each individual in turn just as he or she would do in individual therapy. The group acts as a "Greek chorus," reflecting, commenting, observing, and occasionally assuming the therapist role. The group-as-whole therapist, on the other hand, attends to the process of the group (hence this is also known as "process group therapy") — how each individual fits into it, and how the individual's behavior adapts him or her to the role assumed.

c. Leadership function. Following the analysis established by Lieberman *et al.* (1973), we may understand a therapy group leader as having four basic functions: (1) nurturing (2) stimulating (3) managing, and (4) interpreting. (Analyses vary, but for the most part they fit the Lieberman model.)

Nurturing includes comforting, showing sympathy, giving, understanding, and offering support, encouragement, and attentiveness. This activity encourages attachment, security, and a sense of well-being. It also encourages dependency, which makes nurturing an activity to be used in moderation.

Stimulating refers to maintaining a level of emotional arousal conducive to progress. Theoretically, an optimal level of arousal exists, but determining what is optimal is difficult. Too little arousal is safe but of limited value regarding change; too much is dangerous. Experience is needed to judge how much, when, and with which groups stimulating is necessary.

Managing refers to the administrative function of the leader: setting limits, providing time and space, and controlling the parameters of group activity. Managing is easy, but too much management frustrates learning in a group, while too little produces anarchy and confusion.

Interpreting is believed to be the most important function of a leader. It consists in providing explanations for behavior, cognition, and emotion inside and outside of the group experience. The therapist provides a rationale that explains life in integrated logical terms and is used to dissect and rearrange elements of behavior so that problems of living are solved and distress is decreased.

d. Therapeutic rationale. Having a rationale for what one does as a therapist is important, whether working with groups or individuals, and all therapists have such rationales to a greater or lesser extent. These rationales are always learned, though not entirely learned in formal training programs. In all likelihood, most practitioners simply adapt an academically learned rationale to what they already believe or have learned through experience. The efficacy of the rationale is probably determined by many factors, not least of which is the personhood of the individual practicing it (see Smith, *et al.,* 1980). How well a therapist succeeds with a particular rationale may depend more upon how well he or she understands it, and (possibly) on how much she or he believes it to be effective, than on the inherent merits of the theory itself. A group therapist is generally known, however, by the rationale he or she uses.

3. **Training.** The kind of group counseling or therapy one proposes to do will determine how much and what kind of training is required. As noted, one should seek more and longer training for group therapy than for group counseling. The rationale one desires to use also may determine the extent of training. For example, the use of an intricate, involved rationale such as psychoanalytic theory requires considerable training, while group counseling based on a spiritual or theological rationale that incorporates psychological principles may require less training (depending on the depth and complexity of the spirituality involved). In general, however, the structure inherent in the counseling framework is used to avoid deviations that require more extensive understanding and skill. Clergy doing group therapy generally do so with a well-integrated rationale, combining elements of theology with elements of extensively learned psychological theory. In addition, any group therapist does well to integrate knowledge from many other sources as well — physiology, sociology, philosophy, literature, history, and so forth.

Doing group therapy requires skill. For those who are sure of themselves and competent, it is a very powerful instrument that is rewarding and exciting to use. It is efficient, economical, and may be as effective (if not more effective) than individual therapy. It is certainly the most natural of the psychotherapies, for it treats aberrancy in the context within which aberrancy exists — the (social) group.

Bibliography. M. A. Lieberman, I. D. Yalom, and M. B. Miles, *Encounter Groups: First Facts* (1973). W. C. Schutz, *Here Comes Everybody* (1971). M. L. Smith, G. V. Glass, and T. I. Miller, *The Benefits of Psychotherapy* (1980). A. Stein, H. D. Kibel, J. W. Fidler, and H. I. Spitz, "The Group Therapies," in J. M. Lewis and G. Usdin, eds., *Treatment Planning in Psychiatry* (1982), pp. 44–85. I. D. Yalom, *The Theory and Practice of Group Psychotherapy* 2d ed. (1975).

Further sources of a general nature include R. J. Corsini, *Methods of Group Psychotherapy* (1957). H. I. Kaplan and B. J. Sadock, *Comprehensive Group Psychotherapy* (1971). I. D. Yalom, *The Theory and Practice of Group Psychotherapy* 2d ed. (1975).

For works on theory, see G. S. Gibbard, J. J. Hartman, and R. D. Mann, *Analysis of Groups* (1974). P. E. Slater, *Microcosm* (1966). D. S. Whitaker and M. A. Lieberman, *Psychotherapy Through the Group Process* (1964).

For psychoanalytic group therapy see H. E. Durkin, *The Group in Depth* (1964). S. H. Foulkes, *Therapeutic Group Analysis* (1964). S. Scheidlinger, ed., *Psychoanalytic Group Dynamics* (1980).

For Gestalt group therapy, see E. Polster and M. Polster, *Gestalt Therapy Integrated* (1973), ch. 10.

For transactional analysis in groups, see E. Berne, *Principles of Group Treatment* (1966).

H. A. SELVEY

GROUP DYNAMICS, PROCESS, AND RESEARCH; PSYCHO-THERAPY. *Compare* CHRISTIAN THERAPY UNIT; COMMUNITY, FELLOWSHIP, AND CARE; ENCOUNTER GROUPS; GROWTH GROUPS; HUMAN RELATIONS TRAINING; ROLE PLAY; SUPPORT GROUPS; THERAPEUTIC COMMUNITY.

GROUP DYNAMICS, PROCESS, AND RESEARCH.

The study of individuals interacting in small groups. The word "dynamics" in this context implies complex and interdependent forces that act within the group setting. Various disciplines, such as sociology, religion, psychology, and education, as well as industry, have engaged in research and application of the principles of group dynamics. Further, theoretical orientations that cut across discipline barriers have evolved, and the diversity of approaches to the study of group dynamics has produced a body of literature and research that is rich, diverse, and occasionally inconsistent.

1. Major Theoretical Orientations. The academic field of group dynamics, initiated by Kurt Lewin's research at the University of Iowa in the 1930s, is concerned with the nature and development of group process as well as the way in which membership, composition, structure, physical setting, and leadership affect process. In many instances, conclusions regarding these issues are still under debate among the proponents of the various theoretical orientations. The principal positions in the field today include the following:

(1) *Field theory.* Kurt Lewin, the reputed founder of modern group dynamics, developed field theory. Closely associated with Gestalt psychology, field theory holds that behavior is the result of a field of interdependent forces. Using a method of analysis similar to that of physics, Lewin analyzed individual and group behavior as parts of a system of interdependent forces. Field theory has proven to be more useful as a descriptive tool, however, than as a systematic theoretical formulation of group processes.

(2) *Interaction theory.* This approach views the group as a system of interacting individuals. The relationship of three elements — activity, interaction, and sentiment — are examined to explain all aspects of group behavior. Sociological psychologists have adopted this theory for its usefulness in describing naturally occurring groups.

(3) *Systems theory.* Similar to interaction theory, systems theory emphasizes structure (roles and positions, for example). Systems theory also focuses upon group "inputs" and "outputs" in relation to the larger social environment.

(4) *Empirical-statistical orientation.* In the 1940s Raymond Cattell utilized factor analysis and other statistical procedures in an attempt to discover basic aspects of group behavior. Cattell isolated three dimensions or "panels" in groups: population traits, meaning the characteristics of the individual members; syntality, the "personality" of the group as a whole; and internal structure, that is, the relationships and organizational characteristics of the group.

(5) *General psychology.* This view attempts to extend the principles of individual behavior, such as learning, motivation, and perception, to the group setting. It has been criticized for not taking into account the unique reality of the group as a whole.

(6) *Psychoanalysis.* Based upon Freudian theory, this approach addresses motivational and defensive processes of the individual in terms of group structure. Transference issues involve other members as well as the group leader. A theory of group process has evolved directly from the psychoanalytic orientation, and it has also influenced other process theories. This view, however, has not stimulated much empirical research.

(7) *Reinforcement theory.* Thibaut and Kelly's exchange theory is a major example of this orientation, which attempts to explain interpersonal behavior in terms of rewards and costs and behavior sequences. Group process is analyzed in relation to the adjustments individuals make in attempting to solve problems of interdependency. The greatest contribution of their theory at present lies in the organization of empirical data.

(8) *Transactional approach.* Group behavior is explained in terms of an interchange of inputs and outputs. Group members are viewed in light of valued contributions they are able to make to the other group members. For example, a leader who is helpful and meets group expectations may exchange these resources for influence, status, and esteem.

2. Methods. Three principal methods have been employed in group dynamics research. (1) *Field studies* are conducted in naturally occurring situations, and the groups (such as a family or a school class) usually have a prior history. The researcher attempts to observe naturally occurring events without changing them, though in the field *experiment* the researcher introduces variations in the natural setting in order to study their effects.

(2) *Laboratory experiments* involve arranged groups and are conducted in a laboratory setting for the purpose of investigating a specific group phenomenon. The National Training Laboratory (now known as the NTL Institute for Applied Behavioral Science), formed in Bethel, Maine, in 1947, still specializes in formal and informal laboratory experiments for teaching group

dynamics. NTL's "T-groups" are designed to be educational rather than psychotherapeutic.

(3) *Role playing.* Participants are asked to assume particular roles to study the effects of particular types of behavior on group process, as in Lewin, Lippitt, and White's classic 1939 study of social climates. Adult leaders assumed leadership roles that were either democratic, autocratic, or laissez-faire with groups of ten-year-old boys to determine the effect of leadership style on productivity and group climate.

3. **Group Process.** *a. Developmental phases.* Groups develop over a moderately long period and probably never reach a completely stable state. Much early development is oriented toward establishing a social structure including rules, norms, and roles. There appear to be stages in group development, however, that occur somewhat universally regardless of group structure.

Research generally agrees as to the progression of stages occurring in a normally developing group. The initial stage is often labeled "orientation" or "encounter." The group is initially uncertain and somewhat fearful. Group members tend to search hesitantly for meaning and for the means whereby the group's goal or primary task will be achieved. They also attend to social relationships and to concerns over safety, acceptance, inclusion, and solidarity. Group members generally desire clear leadership as well as agreement and harmony among members.

The second phase is often characterized by the terms "conflict," "dominance," and "differentiation." In this phase a social pecking order is established as members attempt to establish their preferred levels of initiative and power. Disenchantment with the leader and intermember leadership struggles occur. Rebellion against the leader may sometimes take the form of trying to "elect" a leader covertly from among the membership or of deflecting group anger through scapegoating. By the close of this phase, members generally hold a less idealized view of the leader, and individual member differences are beginning to be viewed in a positive rather than fearful light.

The third phase is characterized by cohesiveness and group productivity. Roles and norms are well established. There is generally an increase in morale, mutual trust, and self-disclosure (the group's chief concern is with intimacy and closeness) and a greater freedom to confront problems as they arise and to apply group problem-solving skills.

Stage four is often termed "separation." Members are concerned with making sense out of what has transpired throughout the history of the group. Solidarity concerns may reemerge in an effort to ward off the impending "death" of the group. Members may once again start to rely heavily upon the leader.

b. Group membership and composition. There is good evidence that the way group membership is selected has an impact on group process. While some of this experimental research has been criticized for regarding observer bias and the duration of the groups under study, general guidelines for optimal group composition have nevertheless been derived. Research suggests that groups composed of members with similar attitudes tend to be the most cohesive, while conflict over basic principles generally has a negative effect on group process. When a group agrees on principles but disagrees over their application, the conflict generally tends to enhance cohesiveness. Also, when a group is composed of individuals with diverse conflict areas and patterns of coping, but with similar degrees of vulnerability and capacity to tolerate anxiety, there is generally a positive effect upon group dynamics.

Research also indicates that certain types of individuals do not function well in groups because of their interpersonal style. Alcoholics, depressives, psychotics, and somaticizers generally tend to impede the progress of a heterogeneous group; however, homogeneous groups of these individuals (e.g., Alcoholics Anonymous) tend to have a greater success rate than mixed groupings. Unconventional group members whose behavior is unpredictable also tend to inhibit group functioning.

Group size is generally cited as a significant variable also, but there is some debate over ideal size. Psychoanalytic group theory maintains that eight is ideal; sociologically oriented research tends to favor five-member groups. There is a general consensus that more than ten members tends to diffuse individual participation and lessen member satisfaction. However, in larger groups, members are more likely to find an "attractive other" who satisfies interpersonal needs.

c. Group structure. Structure refers to the internal organization and procedures of a group. Each group member, by virtue of membership itself, contributes to and limits the possibilities of a given group's structure; each holds a specific position in any given group; each evaluates every individual, including him or herself, in terms of prestige or importance in the group. This evaluation determines status, which in turn determines an individual's place in the group hierarchy.

The set of expected behaviors associated with any given position constitutes the individual's role. Individuals can play a variety of roles, depending upon the group, but roles within groups tend to become stereotyped, especially in the second phase of group development.

Another aspect of group structure is the development of norms, that is, rules of conduct established by the members of the group in order to maintain behavioral consistency. Often, group norms are established covertly, as when a habitual manner of proceeding evolves into a norm without a formal discussion to establish it as such. For example, a group may begin its first few sessions with leader commentary, and this initial practice may become tacitly accepted as the norm or proper way of proceeding; a new member who innocently attempts to start the discussion may be surprised at the degree of disapproval this norm-violating behavior produces.

d. Physical setting. Numerous studies have been conducted on the effects of physical setting on group behavior, though many of these effects seem to depend upon individuals' expectations. In one study (Baker, 1937) productivity increased when workers were told that music being played would have a positive effect on production; but when workers were told the purpose of the music was interference, productivity declined.

Specific effects of size and attractiveness of setting as well as noise level, have also been assessed. For instance, the effects of group interaction on task performance seem to be intensified in a small room as opposed to a larger one. Surroundings perceived as ugly tend to elicit more fatigue, discontent, and hostility than attractive group settings. Lighting and sound also appear to affect group interaction: a dimly lit room seems to decrease eye contact and cuts down on verbal interaction, while unpredictable noise tends to lead to frustration and impede task performance.

e. Leadership. The group leader exercises social control and is often the focus of the group. Because of the significance of the leader role within the group, a considerable amount of research has been generated about this vital factor in group dynamics.

The leader's role is to oversee the setting and attainment of group goals, and group leaders tend to be endorsed by members in relation to the success of the group in meeting its goals. Effective leadership is believed to be characterized by task-related abilities, sociability, and motivation to be leader. Studies further suggest that democratic leadership results in greater member satisfaction than does autocratic leadership. However, in stressful situations leaders tend to behave in a more authoritarian manner. Leader techniques can also directly influence group cohesiveness; leaders who preface negative feedback with positive feedback tend to increase cohesiveness, while those who characteristically begin with negative communication tend to diminish group cohesiveness.

Bibliography. K. Baker, "Pre-Experimental Set in Distraction Experiments," *J. of Group Psychotherapy*, 16 (1937) 471–86. D. Cartwright and A. Zander, eds., *Group Dynamics: Research and Theory* 3d ed. (1968). K. Lewin, R. Lippitt, and R. White, "Patterns of Aggressive Behavior in Experimentally Created 'Social Climates,'" *J. of Social Psychology*, 10 (1939) 271–99. J. Luft, *Group Processes* (1970). M. Shaw, *Group Dynamics* 3d ed. (1981). J. Thibaut and H. Kelley, *The Social Psychology of Groups* (1959). I. Yalom, *The Theory and Practice of Group Psychotherapy* (1975).

J. Z. CLARK

GROUP COUNSELING AND PSYCHOTHERAPY; GROWTH GROUPS; SUPPORT GROUPS. *See also* DYNAMIC PSYCHOLOGY; LEADERSHIP AND ADMINISTRATION; SELF-HELP PSYCHOLOGIES; SYSTEMS THEORY. *Compare* RESEARCH IN PASTORAL CARE AND COUNSELING; RITUAL AND PASTORAL CARE.

GROUP MARRIAGE. *See* MARRIAGE (Christian).

GROUP PSYCHOTHERAPY. *See* GROUP COUNSELING AND PSYCHOTHERAPY.

GROUPS. *See* GROWTH GROUPS; SELF-HELP PSYCHOLOGIES; SUPPORT GROUPS.

GROWTH. *See* DEVELOPMENTAL THEORY; LIFE CYCLE THEORY; PERSONALITY DEVELOPMENT, BIOLOGICAL AND SOCIALIZING FACTORS IN; SPIRITUAL DISCIPLINE AND GROWTH.

GROWTH COUNSELING. A human wholeness approach to the help process developed in the theorizing and practice of pastoral counselor Howard Clinebell. Its goal is to facilitate the maximum development of a person's possibilities at each stage of the life cycle in ways that enable the growth of others and contribute as well to the development of a society in which all persons have the opportunity to develop and use their full potentials. It is the name given to growth-oriented care and counseling, therapy, and education that seek to enable persons to liberate themselves from whatever is blocking their growth toward wholeness. Pastoral growth counseling draws on the growth resources of traditional and contemporary psychotherapies and growth-oriented psychologies and integrates these with the rich growth resources from the Hebrew-Christian tradition. The pastoral counselor is perceived as a liberator whose task is to facilitate the process through which persons liberate themselves to live more freely and to actualize their maximum constructive possibilities as whole persons.

Growth counseling is also an integrating conceptual system that draws eclectically on a number of therapeutic models from behavioral science for its growth orientation, with special resources taken from the human wholeness movement, relational, systems, and radical therapies and from the spiritual growth therapies. It is a growth, health, and systems model rather than an individualistic, hierarchical, pathological, and medical model, and it seeks to focus on the person's strengths and possibilities as well as on pathologies. As a model of caring its usefulness is not limited to ordained persons; rather, it emphasizes a variety of growth-enabling relationships and is designed to be used by secular therapists as well as pastoral counselors. It can take place in a variety of settings involving many methods that facilitate growth possibilities of persons.

1. **Philosophical Foundations.** *a. Historical origins.* The foundations for contemporary views of wholeness and the nature of the growth process are related to nineteenth-century organismic biology where growth of living things was envisioned as goal-directed and organismic. This view replaced the medical model of the closed system, which was the foundation of Freud's psychic determinism. Howard Clinebell has recognized the limitations of the mechanistic and medical orientations of his earlier neo-Freudian training in counseling and psychotherapy and has integrated that training with organismic views of ego-psychology, action-oriented therapeutic methods, and relational and systems approaches to growth counseling. In this way goal-directed behavior, as well as pathological or growth-blocking behavior, could be addressed.

b. Presuppositions, humanistic foundations, the nature of personality. The fundamental principles of organismic views of growth are the law of evolution, universal interrelatedness, circular causality, and open systems. Growth is envisaged as a movement toward increasing evolutionary organization and differentiation. Reality is pictured as an interrelated collection of wholes, and causal relationships are envisaged as feedback loops rather than as linear cause and effect. Living organisms are open systems that influence and are influenced by other systems.

Humanistic assumptions also undergird contemporary theories of growth. Organisms are in the process of being and becoming; they are goal-directed, and these processes need to be supported by life systems. Within this humanistic orientation the human personality is viewed as symbol-creating and as contextual in nature. By contextual it is meant that the personality is an open system that is influenced by historical, social, cultural, and group interaction processes. However, in this orientation persons can transcend the contextual processes because of their symbol-creating ability.

2. **Theological and Ethical Foundations.** *a. Theological foundations.* The deepest universal growth need in all persons is to develop our transcendent possibilities. Spiritual strivings are most central to all human beings, and persons strive to overcome the spiritual alienation that is at the core of their being. Thus, within persons there is an inherent and relational push and pull that is transpersonal and transcendent and draws and pushes them to fulfill themselves in relationship to a larger spiritual reality.

For persons in the Judeo-Christian tradition the source of all growth and creativity is God, and biblical images undergird and empower growth-centered approaches to pastoral care and counseling, in the view of Howard Clinebell. He draws on the biblical motifs of liberation, hope, the kingdom of God, growth as a gift from God, the image of God, and Jesus as an example of what it means to be a whole person, in order to illustrate the biblical foundations of growth counseling. Clinebell is also aware of the deep resistance to growth within human nature and draws on the biblical view of sin as deeply blocked growth to bring an open-eyed realism to growth counseling.

b. Ethical foundations. Growth counseling is based on the human wholeness ethic and the ecological ethic. To actualize one's own wholeness in ways that also help others to develop their potentials is the human wholeness ethic. This ethic is crucial for Clinebell because persons often actualize their own selves at the expense of others in our sexist, racist, ageist, and individualistic society. The ecological ethic is concerned for and committed to the whole ecological system where growth takes place. The concern is not only with personal transformation, but also with empowering persons to work for social transformation. One should be concerned with changing those institutions and structures that hinder and block growth.

c. The church. The church has the capacity to be salugenic—health and growth producing—as well as pathogenic—sickness producing and growth blocking. The church's task is to be a center of wholeness which liberates growth potentials rather than blocking them. Pastoral growth counseling draws on the church's rich growth traditions in its effort to become salugenic.

3. **Six Dimensions of Growth.** Clinebell outlines six dimensions of wholeness, all of which are involved in growth counseling. These dimensions are interdependent and are an organic unity in the growth process. These include growth in a person's mind, body, in relationships with others, within the biosphere or ecosystem, in groups and institutions that sustain growth, and in the spiritual dimension. Growth in one area influences growth in the other five areas. Thus, self-fulfillment and self-actualization cannot take place in isolation from the six dimensions. Genuine and sustained self-actualization always involves transcendence and results from self-other, self-society, and self-environment fulfillment.

4. **Goals, Processes, Methods, and Vehicles of Growth Counseling.** *a. Goals of growth counseling.* Growth counseling seeks to facilitate, liberate, and accelerate potentialization and the ongoing growth of persons in all their interdependent relationships. It utilizes the growth, health, and hope perspectives to help persons discover and develop the gifts of God—the deep unused strengths and capacities for greater wholeness. It is concerned with liberation in all six dimensions of a person's existence and with enabling them to grow intentionally toward the future. There is also the concern to educate and reeducate persons so that they can take full responsibility for their own growth and to help them to learn constructive values, attitudes, and relationship skills.

b. Processes, methods, and vehicles. Growth counseling seeks to awaken hope for growth through care, confrontation, and coaching. The counselor expresses caring through genuine affirmation of a person's strengths in nonmanipulative ways. The counselor also integrates confrontation with caring through speaking openly about the way persons are limiting and blocking their growth. The counselor concentrates on the immediate context, feelings, and behaviors that lead to self-esteem, and coaches persons in order to help them awaken and nurture realistic hope for change through developing and implementing enabling plans for growth.

The counselor's attitudes and person are crucial in growth counseling. One must develop a growth-hope perspective; continue to develop one's own potential for growth so that one can see fully other's growth possibilities; become familiar with knowledge of the nature and dynamics of human growth, especially the stages and transactions of the life cycle; and become aware of how values and contemporary social problems such as racism, sexism, and ageism impact the way men and women perceive themselves and truncate wholeness. With regard to life crises the counselor envisages the period of transition as growth opportunities.

The counselor utilizes a variety of approaches to help people move toward growth goals, including individual counseling, crisis intervention, systems approaches to marriage and family counseling, enrichment groups, educational and consciousness raising and social action groups, and natural social growth networks. The counselor or growth enabler is free to choose a variety of relationships, systems, behavioral and body educational and therapeutic approaches to growth. The counselor as liberator needs to become an integrated eclectic and draw relevant insights and methods from a variety of sources for conceptual and therapeutic models.

5. **Conclusion.** Growth counseling is indeed appropriate for persons who are growing in normal ways throughout the life cycle. It is also useful for those persons suffering more severe growth blockages including emotional and characterological problems. This latter dimension needs fuller exploration in future theorizing and research in growth counseling.

Bibliography. H. J. Clinebell, *Growth Counseling for Mid-Years Couples* (1977); *Growth Groups* (1978); *Growth Counseling* (1979); *Contemporary Growth Therapies* (1981). D. M. Moss, "Growth Counseling: A Dialogue with Howard Clinebell," *J. of Religion and Health,* 23 (1984), 179–96. E. P. Wimberly, "A Conceptual Model for Pastoral Care in the Black Church Utilizing Systems and Crisis Theories," (Ph.D. Dissertation, Boston University, 1976).

E. P. WIMBERLY

HUMANISTIC PSYCHOLOGY AND PASTORAL CARE; GROWTH GROUPS; PASTORAL COUNSELING; SPIRITUAL DISCIPLINE AND GROWTH. *See also* PSYCHOLOGY IN AMERICAN RELIGION; PSYCHOTHERAPY (Varities, Traditions, and Issues). *Compare* JEWISH CARE AND COUNSELING; MODELS IN PSYCHOLOGICAL AND PASTORAL THEORY; SUPPORTIVE THERAPY.

GROWTH GROUPS. A type of small group existing under a variety of names, all of which share as their central purpose the enhancement and development of members of the group. Such groups may be called sharing groups, discipleship groups, fellowship groups, covenant groups, care groups, marriage enrichment groups, women's liberation groups, action groups, family clusters, and so forth. One type of growth group prevalent in many churches is the home Bible discussion group. A central element in all such groups is an emphasis on interpersonal relationships combined with the desire for expanded awareness, understanding, and growth.

Growth groups differ from therapy groups in their emphasis on growth-oriented discussions rather than on pathological issues. They differ from encounter groups in that they explore ideas and actions as well as feelings, and have a lower level of intensity in most interactions. Growth groups often use written materials as a resource for the group's interaction. Good communication patterns and an understanding of group dynamics are essential to healthy growth groups.

Membership usually ranges from three to twelve people. Leadership patterns vary from reliance upon a single designated leader, a team of two or three leaders, or a pattern in which leadership is passed from member to member. Leaders are often spoken of as facilitators or enablers, rather than as authoritative teachers or therapists, to emphasize their role as guides or encouragers helping group members discover and utilize their full potential.

Groups may organize around three basic means of growth: sharing, study, action, or some combination of these. Sharing groups spend much of their time exploring personal issues, needs, and concerns. Tools used may include sharing questions and relational games. Self-disclosure of feelings is seen as a means to unlocking hidden barriers and resistances to personal growth and interpersonal relationships. Study groups spend a major portion of their time discussing a story or passage from the Bible or other study material of which the content is dealt with on a personal level that includes the struggles, feelings, hopes, and intentions of the members. Action groups seek growth through preparation and involvement in meaningful member-chosen action arising from convictions or critical issues, needs, and concerns. Christian growth groups that combine sharing, study, and/or

action often include prayer as an additional element in their group life.

Bibliography. H. Clinebell, *Growth Groups* (1977). G. Cosby, *Handbook for Mission Groups* (1975). L. Evans, *Covenant to Care* rev. ed., (1982). R. Hestenes, *Using the Bible in Groups* (1983).

R. HESTENES

GROUP DYNAMICS, PROCESS, AND RESEARCH; HUMANISTIC PSYCHOLOGY AND PASTORAL CARE; SPIRITUAL DISCIPLINE AND GROWTH. *See also* COMMUNITY, FELLOWSHIP, AND CARE; CONGREGATION, PASTORAL CARE OF; PSYCHOLOGY IN AMERICAN RELIGION; SOCIOLOGY OF RELIGIOUS AND PASTORAL CARE. *Compare* ENCOUNTER GROUPS; FORMATIVE SPIRITUALITY; GROUP COUNSELING AND PSYCHOTHERAPY; GROWTH COUNSELING; HAVURAH; SUPPORT GROUPS.

GUIDANCE, CAREER. *See* CAREER DEVELOPMENT AND GUIDANCE (For Pastors).

GUIDANCE, DIVINE. A description of God's activity of preserving, concurring in, and governing the destiny of individuals, universal history, and the natural order. In the language of Christian theology, divine guidance is understood in terms of the doctrine of providence. In the practice of pastoral care, questions about divine guidance or providence occur frequently. They are often raised by the issue of theodicy — how God's goodness and omnipotence can be reconciled with the reality of evil.

Theologically, the discussion of divine guidance cannot be separated from discussions about the nature of God, God's relation to the world, what is meant by an "act of God," and the relation of divine freedom to human freedom. There have been many different theological responses to these issues. At one end of the theological spectrum are those theologians who stress convictions about the sovereignty of God and insist that every event is a part of God's plan for individuals and for creation as a whole. John Calvin, for example, argued that the concepts of chance and fortune were "depraved opinion," and that all events are governed by "God's secret plan." At the other end of the spectrum are theologians who insist on the autonomy of the human will. A variety of mediating positions can be found between these two ends of the spectrum. In contemporary theology one of the best known of these mediating positions is process theology. Charles Hartshorne and John Cobb argue that God is internally related to the world in such a manner that God can be said to "lure," if not direct, the created order to its proper end.

In the literature of pastoral care, questions about divine guidance are often discussed in terms of the nature of faith, especially faith understood as an act of trust. Seward Hiltner, for example, argues that the attribute of God that is most appropriate in discussions of divine guidance or providence is God's trustworthiness. Hiltner insists that divine guidance does not necessarily entail a doctrine of predestination which separates God's power from God's grace and good will. The deeper problem, Hiltner observes, is one of cosmology — how to interpret God and God's relation to the world. God's trustworthiness and God's guidance of individuals does not necessarily absolve individuals of their freedom and responsibility.

Bibliography. T. Aquinas, *On the Truth of the Catholic Faith*, III/2 (1956). Augustine, *The City of God* (ET 1972). K. Barth, *Church Dogmatics*, III/3 (1960). J. Calvin, *Institutes of the Christian Religion* (ET 1960). D. Evans, *Struggle and Fulfillment* (1979). L. Gilkey, *Reaping the Whirlwind* (1976). J. Hartt, "Creation and Providence," *Christian Theology* (1983), 115 – 40. J. Hick, *Evil and the God of Love* (1966). S. Hiltner, *Theological Dynamics* (1972), 55–80.

G. W. STROUP

ILLUMINATION; PROVIDENCE, DOCTRINE OF, AND PASTORAL CARE; DISCERNMENT OF SPIRITS. *See also* GOD'S WILL, ACCEPTANCE OF; RELIGIOUS EXPERIENCE; REVELATION AND PASTORAL CARE. *Compare* DREAM INTERPRETATION IN PASTORAL COUNSELING; EVALUATION AND DIAGNOSIS, RELIGIOUS; INTUITION; VISIONS AND VOICES.

GUIDANCE, PASTORAL. The act of helping a person or persons find their way through an unfamiliar, confusing, or difficult situation, often in which some kind of decision making or action is involved, as in solving family problems, making life decisions, or pursuing a spiritual discipline. In contemporary pastoral literature guidance is usually distinguished from support, care, healing (or therapy), and reconciling as fundamental expressions of the caring ministry, though elements of all may be and usually are present in each. Different styles of guiding also have been distinguished, for example, "inductive" guiding, which applies *a priori* principles to concrete situations, and "eductive" guiding, which attempts to elicit the individual's own sense of direction and resources for decision making from within (Clebsch and Jaekle, 1964).

Though guidance is one of the principal activities undertaken as a part of pastoral care, it may be the least studied of these activities. After several decades of neglect, and in some circles contempt, guidance seems to be the subject of study once again, in new forms.

1. Reclaiming Guidance. One of the most influential contributors to the pastoral-theological enterprise, Seward Hiltner, made a significant place for guidance in his pastoral theology. Hiltner divided the overall work of the minister into three major categories: communicating the gospel, shepherding the flock, and organizing the fellowship. Within the category of shepherding, Hiltner suggested three major subcategories: *healing, sustaining,* and *guiding.* The fourth category — *reconciling* — was suggested by William Clebsch and Charles Jaekle (1964). Hiltner termed his approach "eductive" because he emphasized the importance of the pastor's "educing" or drawing out the parishioner's inner sense of direction and decision-making capacities.

Hiltner's view of guidance is expressed in the metaphor of the guide in the North Woods, who has knowledge of the territory not possessed by the traveler who needs a guide. The traveler, on the other hand, knows what his or her own goal is, and the guide does not. It is mandatory for the guide to respect the traveler's sense of purpose and destination, and advisable for the traveler to accept the guide's wisdom about means of accomplishing the purpose. We may take the metaphor a little further than Hiltner takes it; if the guide has serious questions about the appropriateness of the traveler's purpose or destination, the guide may and should raise appropriate questions and, if necessary, withdraw from the contract.

Thus, although much thinking in pastoral care and counseling has made little use of it, there has been in recent pastoral theology a framework for thinking about guidance as a useful activity in pastoral work.

2. Objections to Guidance. The process of guidance has been criticized as a legitimate part of pastoral work on the grounds that it is too directive. The powerful impact, beginning in the mid-1950s, of the client-centered or nondirective philosophy of Carl Rogers made guidance an almost unacceptable concept among many ministers. Guidance implies direction, and the concept behind the word *nondirective* was taken with utter seriousness by many ministers, particularly those interested in counseling.

The word *guidance* suggests to many that there is an inequality or unevenness in the helping relationship, with the helper somehow "one-up." If there is any accuracy in that perception at all, then in what does that inequality really consist? Does it imply specific skill in one or another form of a helping process? Does it imply a greater knowledge of some kind? Does the contract for help in formal counseling imply a one-up, one-down relationship? Does the pastoral relationship imply it? To what extent is pastoral care or its more formal, contracted sibling, pastoral counseling, a guidance process? Or is guidance not to be considered a part of counseling at all?

From the 1950s until very recently, training in pastoral care and counseling has had a strongly nondirective element. Students were taught that to offer direction, to speak from any frame of reference other than that of the help-seeker, was manipulative. (This actually involved a misdefinition of the word "manipulative" by equating it with all direction and guidance instead of reserving it to denote directing another person for one's own gain.) Nor was this true only of those being trained in centers influenced by Rogers's thinking. There were — and are — centers in which the dominant mode of thinking is psychoanalytic; in such centers the active, guiding participation of the pastor or pastoral counselor also may be discouraged.

3. New Forms of Guidance. Pastoral care activities — both responsible and irresponsible — that are far more ready to use a guidance process have been more in evidence recently. They vary widely in their theoretical and practical approaches. Let us examine four processes recently or presently in use among pastors, all of which use elements of guidance.

Family therapy is quite openly a guidance process: direct suggestions may be made, help-seekers may be asked to move their chairs so as to be closer to or more distant from each other or the helper, "homework" assignments may be given. Theories and techniques in family therapy differ widely, but even the least directive thinkers in family therapy operate by making some kind of active intervention with families, and offer guidance. In family therapy, the helper is bound to respect the family's goals in seeking help, although it is possible to question those goals and to refuse the contract if, say, the family wants the process used to "fix" a scapegoated child.

Sensitivity training, popular among clergy a few years ago, was a guidance process that largely hid its manipulative qualities under a guise of openness. Participants were guided into certain forms of behavior. In sensitivity training the group often assumed the right to determine a person's identity; introducing oneself in such a group by anything except a casual nickname was often taboo.

Nouthetic counseling, articulated by Jay Adams in such works as *Competent to Counsel* (1974), is one contemporary theory of pastoral counseling that holds that the pastor should be very directive indeed. This theory takes as its starting point the conviction that people seeking help are often confused, dependent, and certainly out of touch with God's will for their lives. Adams holds that the well-trained, thoughtful, prayerful pastor knows what a parishioner should do, and that it is the pastor's obligation to announce that course of action to the help-seeker and, if need be, to insist upon it. The nouthetic approach is reminiscent of early periods of Christian history and operates by placing an unusual (for this period of history) amount of authority in the hands of pastors. Hiltner's image of the North Woods guide will clearly not do here. The guide knows not only how to get where the visitor is going; the guide also knows what the visitor's goals and purposes should be, and is derelict in duty by not insisting that the visitor accede to the guide's sense of what the goals should be.

Spiritual direction is another recent development that evokes consideration of guidance. Long a practice with its own processes and disciplines among Roman Catholics, spiritual direction has begun to be more important in Protestant circles as well. Spiritual direction may mean a variety of activities, but in general it assumes that there is a person seeking to come in touch with spiritual depths and riches not yet understood or integrated, and that there is someone — again, the North Woods metaphor — more familiar with the territory who can assist the seeker. Unlike counseling or psychotherapy, spiritual direction is not necessarily concerned with problems in living that need solutions. Rather, it is concerned with the movement back and forth between life in the spirit and life in the world, and the integration of the two. The writer currently most familiar to Protestants as an interpreter of spiritual direction is Henri Nouwen, who offers in his writings direct examples of the use of guidance. Adrian van Kaam is a more systematic writer about guidance and spiritual direction.

Recent developments in pastoral theory have also had a guiding flavor, though the term itself is not always employed, as in the works of Don S. Browning (1976), Donald Capps (1983), and Charles Gerkin (1984).

Bibliography. J. Adams, *Competent to Counsel* (1974). F. M. Bockus, "The North Woods Revisited: New Developments in Guiding," in W. B. Oglesby, ed., *The New Shape of Pastoral Theology* (1969). D. S. Browning, *The Moral Context of Pastoral Care* (1976). D. Capps, *Life Cycle Theory and Pastoral Care* (1983). C. V. Gerkin, *The Living Human Document* (1984). S. Hiltner, *Pastoral Counseling* (1949); *Preface to Pastoral Theology* (1958). H. J. M. Nouwen, *Reaching Out* (1975). A. van Kaam, *Religion and Personality* (1980).

K. R. MITCHELL

ETHICS AND PASTORAL CARE; MORAL DILEMMAS IN PASTORAL PERSPECTIVE; MORAL THEOLOGY AND PASTORAL CARE; PASTORAL CARE (History, Traditions, and Definitions); SPIRITUAL DIRECTION. *See also* ADVICE-GIVING; ETHICS, PROFESSIONAL; HUMAN RELATIONS TRAINING; INTERPRETATION AND HERMENEUTICS, PASTORAL; JEWISH CARE AND COUNSELING; MEDICAL-ETHICAL DILEMMAS, JEWISH CARE AND COUNSELING IN; PASTORAL COUNSELING; REASONING AND RATIONALITY IN PASTORAL CARE; REFERRAL; SUGGESTION, PERSUASION, AND INFLUENCE; VALUES CLARIFICATION. *Compare* ADVOCACY; EVALUATION AND DIAGNOSIS, RELIGIOUS; MORAL BEHAVIOR AND RELIGION; INITIATIVE AND INTERVENTION; VALUES IN COUNSELING AND PSYCHOTHERAPY.

GUIDE, PASTOR AS. *See* PASTOR (Normative and Traditional Images); SPIRITUAL DIRECTOR; SPIRITUAL MASTERS AND GUIDES.

GUIDED IMAGERY TECHNIQUE. A method which utilizes a person's ability to create images in one's own mind for some specific therapeutic purpose. Guided imagery has been used to facilitate relaxation, change physiological states (e.g., lower blood pressure, reduce anxiety), solve problems, overcome fears, resolve conflicts, and bring healing to past traumatic events. Basically, psychotherapists have used guided imagery as a method to simulate reality. The counselee might be asked to use his or her mind to imagine or picture a particular situation. The therapist would then use various techniques, such as questions, directives, or descriptions (Shorr, 1983), to guide the counselee through the image and toward a helpful or meaningful resolution. Currently, there are a number of different therapies or specific ways in which the technique of guided imagery is used. Systematic desensitization and implosion therapy are two very successful behavioral techniques that have utilized guided images.

In recent years, pastoral counselors and Christian therapists have used the guided imagery technique in the healing of memories (Linn and Linn, 1974) or inner healing (MacNutt, 1974). Quite often, a very traumatic event in someone's past will have long-lasting and far-reaching effects in that person's life. The goal sought after in the healing of memories is to replace the traumatic material in the memory with new material that can become a source of healing for the individual (Stapleton, 1976). Briefly, the method is for the counselor to ask the person to imagine in his or her mind a returning to that particular traumatic event. Once the person has imagined that event or situation and can describe it, then, instead of reliving the event as they remember it happening, the person is also asked to visualize Christ entering into that situation and remaining there with them (Stapleton, 1976). Christ can now become an experiential source of forgiveness, strength, compassion, love, or any other kind of healing for that person in that particular situation. This new, re-experiencing of a past event, situation, or relationship transforms the way in which that event, situation, or relationship is preserved in memory. Thus, Christ and all his healing power are now a part of what is remembered.

Bibliography. D. Linn and M. Linn, *Healing of Memories* (1974). F. MacNutt, *Healing* (1974). J. Shorr, *Psychotherapy Through Imagery,* 2d ed., (1983). R. Stapleton, *The Gift of Inner Healing* (1976).

S. C. WILLIS

COGNITIVE PSYCHOLOGY AND PSYCHOTHERAPY; FANTA-SIZING; IMAGINATION. *See also* TECHNIQUE AND SKILL IN PASTORAL CARE. *Compare* DREAM INTERPRETATION.

GUIDES, SPIRITUAL. See SPIRITUAL MASTERS AND GUIDES. *See also* SPIRITUAL DIRECTOR.

GUILES, AUSTIN PHILIP (1894–1953). American theological educator. He assumed a leading role in the formation of the Council for Clinical Training of Theological Students (1930), the New England Theological Schools Committee on Clinical Training (1938), and the Institute of Pastoral Care (1944).

Envisioning clinical training as a discipline to produce professional competence, Guiles argued that clinical experience should be a regular part of the education of ministers within the theological seminary. At a time when there was still tension between clinical educators and seminary faculties, he introduced clinical training to Andover Newton Theological Seminary, and he helped, in 1938, to form the committee that would reinforce the growing amity between clinical supervisors and theological faculties in the Boston area.

Guiles received his own clinical training under the supervision of Anton Boisen and then served as a chaplain at Massachusetts General Hospital. He lost his chaplaincy when he began to write—and to insert in the medical records—psychiatric evaluations of some patients. He then became the first field secretary and interim director of the Council for Clinical Training of Theological Students, before joining the faculty of Andover Newton in 1931 as director of Clinical Training. After a policy dispute with Helen Flanders Dunbar, he left the council and worked closely with Richard Cabot in the effort to expand clinical training to the seminaries of New England. Because of Cabot's distrust of psychiatry, Guiles tended to promote general hospitals, rather than mental hospitals, as the settings for clinical pastoral training. But the Institute of Pastoral Care, which he helped establish in 1944 to promote clinical education within theological schools, soon began to use both mental and general hospitals.

He also founded pastoral counseling centers under the auspices of Andover Newton. Guiles tried to promote interest in what he called "clinical theology," but he remained influential primarily as an organizer and administrator of clinical programs.

E. B. HOLIFIELD

PASTORAL CARE MOVEMENT.

GUILT. Objectively, guilt refers to acts or behavior which violate laws, codes, or moral values held by the community to which the individual is linked. Subjectively, guilt-feeling is the emotion accompanying self-judgment or knowledge that one has transgressed values in some way important to the self. In some instances, guilt-feeling may accompany impulses toward, or contemplation of, value transgression, thus having a prospective function as a conscience warning signal.

In the following discussion, guilt, an aspect of human life and pastoral care, is treated as a boundary phenomenon. Its theological roots and its systemic and dynamic structure and development are explored, with an attempt to clarify normal existential guilt over against clinical aberrational forms. Helpful as well as disruptive aspects of the theological/pastoral approach to guilt are elaborated (Stein, 1968).

1. Biblical and Theological Prologue. Guilt is taken seriously from beginning to end in the Scriptures as the clear sign of alienation from God, others, and self. It is a corollary of the presence of sin. It is not just perceived as an individual reality but also as a communal reality. One at odds with God because of sin would bring judgment on the whole community.

This corporate sense implied a crucial participation of the community in the recognition of guilt, the resolution of guilt, and the avoidance of guilt. Hence, it was a central issue in human life. Its seriousness entailed the shedding of blood of prized animals, the ritualized cleansing of contamination, the expulsion by scapegoating of sufficiently offensive members, and, on occasion, death for grievous offenses. The law and priestly codes clearly and minutely clarified conditions of infraction and appropriate responses to the guilt incurred.

By the time of Christ, the codes and religious rituals had become oppressive and in themselves an alienating as well as a unifying force. Classical Christian interpretation sees Jesus as the liberating Christ, as God's once-for-all self offering: a blood sacrifice overcoming divine-human alienation and confirming the faith that *no* human dereliction can separate a person from the love of God or from God's proffered forgiveness. This was the good news that liberated humankind in an ultimate sense from bondage to guilt and which the Apostle Paul perceived and preached so radically and so powerfully. This was the kairotic event celebrated in the sacrament of communion, the kerygmatic reality entered into through baptism.

The problem for theology and therapy since those early days of the faith, and even to this moment, is *pen* ultimate. Christendom did not absorb adequately or dynamically its own good news of unconditional love and forgiveness. In Pfister's (1944) terms, the church left Christ's analytic (love-oriented) resolution of guilt and reinvoked a synthetic (conditional, works-methodological) approach.

Because of confusion over the early expected results of baptism and its eschatological significance, the church began to intrude authoritarian and clerical guidance over guilt and morals, imposing classes of venial and mortal discriminants on behavior, legislating control of remorse and penitence and prescribing norms for the confessional (See Schär, 1973). All this, while settling some confusion, generated a new distortion, instituted a hierarchical effort to control inner processes, to prescribe some forms and proscribe others, an external frame for an internal reality.

By the time of the Reformation, authoritarian abuses led to fear and rebellion in the believer and, in Luther's case, to the need for a rediscovery of freedom from guilt through the grace of God and justification by faith alone, attested by Scripture alone. This break with institutional authority reinternalized many guilt issues and opened the door (largely through the Enlightenment) to liberation of the individual. This liberation from the strictures of ecclesiastical hierarchy did not mean total liberation, but only liberation to a wider reference community and the attachment of guilt to values more pluralistically and idiosyncratically construed.

The penultimate issues continued: guilt was still present, codes still stressed communal strictures (often severe in Protestant communities), and sanctions were still imposed. Yet a process had begun: the voice of independent reason had gained a foothold in the theological and ecclesiastical framework and even the lay individual's input had entered the moral equation.

Lehmann's terms, the "decline" and "fall" of conscience, refer to the fact that this mushrooming individualization of conscience has led to a growing sense of moral isolation, of guilt-in-a-vacuum, of narcissistic or solipsistic decision-making (Lehmann, 1963).

The infusion of anthropological and sociological findings from other cultures into the moral dialogue has widened moral individualism. Kantian conviction about the "moral law within" has been applied to the structure and fact of conscience, but the notion that the *contents* of conscience are universally concordant has given way to the belief that while humans seem to have a universal moral concern and potential for guilt, the codes that are connected with that concern vary widely and can only precariously judge each other.

Many would concur with Paul Tillich that while morality "as the pure form of self-affirmation is absolute, the concrete systems or moral imperatives, the 'moralisms,' are relative" (Tillich, 1955). This, Tillich goes on to say, is *not* relativism, a philosophical attitude which he holds to be self-contradictory, but rather is the acknowledgment of humankind's finitude and its dependence on the contingencies of time and space. Protestantism at its best, he believes, has the right to protest against any "moral content which claims unconditional character," and implicitly against the guilt it engenders.

Current theological thought, resonant to the above problems as well as the issues of contextual ethics, has concerned itself vitally with both the nonauthoritarian bent of humanistic ethics (e.g., Maslow, 1971, and Fromm, 1947) and the empirical efforts of such psychologists as Piaget (1977) and Kohlberg (1981) and numerous others to explore and clarify what they contend are invariable cross-cultural developmental cognitive stages and structures, which impinge on moral decision making.

2. **The Psychodynamics of Guilt.** Modern understanding of the guilt process necessarily involves an orientation of the discussion to particular theories of personality. Currently, three dominant emphases are notable as bases for explaining moral development and behavior. These are the psychoanalytic, cognitive-learning, and behavioral theories. (See Hall and Lindzey, 1978; Lickona, 1976). Clinicians and students of moral behavior are frequently indebted to insights from all three of these orientations. Sigmund Freud's (1930, 1933) initial theories of identification have been refracted by many subsequent research studies and criticized vigorously by neo-Freudians and ego-analysts as well as those outside the psychoanalytic tradition. Nevertheless, they constitute original and seminal nodal points in the discussion of guilt. For purposes of brevity, this presentation will largely be restricted to the psychoanalytic explanation of the guilt process.

Freud spoke of guilt as "a topographical variety of anxiety." He was alluding to the topography of the psyche. In his latest theory (the structural theory), he proposed a tripartite structure of the psyche: id, ego, and superego. Id (Latin for *it*) is the instinctual base of the personality, which is a psychoid locus of the biological energies of the organism. These energies are unconscious and elementally seek discharge and homeostatic balance, becoming conscious as they are symbolized in the ego. Freud considered the sexual and aggressive drives to be the most significant in personality formation. These he ultimately labelled *eros* and *thanatos* drives. The ego channels these into expression and contact with the external world through its executive, defensive, perceptual, and communicative functions.

The small child, up to the age of three or four, may experience shame and fear of punishment, rejection or loss of love, but, according to Freud, does not yet feel guilt. It is not until the third component of the psychic structure, the superego (in German, das Überich — the 'over I') is established that the child begins to feel true guilt feelings or moral anxiety. This third aspect of the psyche begins to crystallize sometime between the ages of three and six, a period Erikson (1959) designates as the crisis of "initiative vs. guilt."

Freud believed that the superego is a part of the psychic structure that is internalized in the process of development as the result of identification with a parent figure or parent surrogate, usually the father. He recognized, however, that the superego structure, which monitors ego and id processes (like an internal parent), is a combination of identification to some degree with *both* parents in the typical nuclear family (Freud, 1927, p. 44).

Freud believed that the superego was formed as a result of the anxieties produced in the child by the Oedipal conflict — a conflict which was generated by the child's desire to possess completely the opposite-sexed parent and the resultant hostility and fear that ensued in relation to the same-sexed parent, now experienced as an obstacle to this complete realization. The anxiety generated by these conflicting impulses led, he thought, to identification with the parental superego and its values as a defense against the impulses as well as their concordant repression and partial neutralization during the "latency period" of childhood.

The superego draws its energies from the id and is largely unconscious. This internalized parent (parents) acts as a focal symbolic representative of the values which the parent absorbed from the community and religio-social tradition. Actions, thoughts, and impulses are now monitored automatically and often unconsciously. Any of these that contradict the internalized values evoke what Freud labeled "topographically defined anxiety" or guilt (see Freud, 1930). This monitoring process is experienced by the individual much as the former parents were experienced (often distorted by fantasy) in terms of sanctions or approval. The superego is able to influence behavior by withholding love, rejection, or aggressive action against the ego (self-punishment). The aggression may take the form of self-hatred, low self-esteem, or actual destruction of the person in suicide or slow forms of suicide as evidenced in some crime, severe asceticisms, neurosis, psychosis, addictions, and so forth.

Freud ultimately subsumed under the term superego two functions, one positive and one negative: ego ideal ("Thou shalt") and conscience ("Thou shalt not"). Living up to the former led to positive feelings of self-esteem and self-love or healthy pride (eros turned on the ego). Violating genuinely held values led to conscience indictment, experienced as love withheld or self-punishment (aggression turned on the ego). Thus it may be seen that the superego (internalized parent) reflects or contains both a *cognitive* element (value contents) and an *emotional* or feeling element (negative guilt-anxiety or, when affirmative, the elation of self-love and esteem).

The *cognitive*, or value, aspects of the superego are learned largely through parental admonition, verbalization, and signaling. The more fundamental and primitive feeling aspects are mixtures of pre-Oedipal and Oedipal confluences of erotic and aggressive emotions in varying combinations, some of them in sadistic or masochistic intensity. These may reflect directly, or fantastically distort, parental modeling. Some current studies by Piaget and Kohlberg of socialization and value-acquisition concentrate upon the cognitive developmental sequences, with less attention to the emotional substructure of conscience.

Freud assumed that any civilized person would feel guilt. His book, *Civilization and its Discontents,* holds guilt to be a *sine qua non* of civilization. It is a braking principle through which a society internalizes and turns otherwise destructive aggression back on the self. Its *normal* form he called "remorse" (literally, "eating again"—a word which captures the uniquely persistent gnawing quality of guilt). Freud's greater interest was turned to the problem of neurotic guilt. It was not until he made the distinction between normal and neurotic guilt that the church was able to minister with full effectiveness in the arena of guilt.

3. Normal Existential Guilt. Martin Buber once wrote: "Man is the being who is capable of becoming guilty and is capable of illuminating his guilt" (Buber, 1971, p. 113). What is illumined varies as different thinkers assess it. Some, such as Freud, hold that the contents of the superego are purely relative to the taboos and sanctions of whatever environment the individual was reared in. In this view, guilt feelings are essentially oriented to local or parochial value violations, even though there is much similarity around the world (especially regarding murder and incest). Others, such as Immanuel Kant and many theological writers hold that the guilt points to a moral law within which is reliable and inviolable. St. Paul speaks of Gentiles who have "the law written on their hearts" (Rom. 2:15). Many modern psychologists contend that the *potential* for guilt is present in any normal member of a group holding shared values but that the value *contents* will vary widely around the globe. For example, World War II studies of soldiers showed that American G.I.s were prone to guilt over killing. German soldiers were more inclined to feel guilt over disobeying an order (Hulse, 1948). The question again arises whether widely varying values necessarily imply complete value relativity. So long as relativity can be shown at all, who can presume to judge another? Is all guilt circumstantial to location, an accident of fate? Or is there such a thing as guilt which reflects a universal

truth, a fundamental order of life? Secularists and religionists fall on both sides of the answer, though most theologians tend to hold for what might be called "existential guilt."

According to Buber, existential guilt "occurs when someone injures an order of the human world whose foundations he knows and recognizes as those of his own existence and of all common human existence." He qualifies this by adding, "what I call existential guilt is only an intensification of what is found in some measure wherever an authentic guilt feeling burns" (Buber, 1971, p. 92). Existential guilt is often called "real" guilt, "normal" guilt, or "authentic" guilt. It is usually the theologian who extends the structural relationship of this communal human reality to a cosmic order, reflecting a divine intent.

One of the problems of religious history involves the question of this extension of human expectations onto God. Where punishment for guilt is concerned, unconscious cruelty may be projected. Moralisms can lead to the spirit of legalistic righteousness, which confronted Jesus. Paul Ricoeur (1970, p. 299) writes that "faith goes beyond the ethics of righteousness." To use R. S. Lee's psychoanalytic way of expressing this point, Christianity reflects an "ego religion" more than a "superego religion," meaning essentially that God's ultimate moral purposes transcend our best moralisms and even the most authentic sense of guilt (Lee, 1948).

4. The Pathology of Guilt. With some exceptions, both the theological and psychological worlds have noted and dealt with the aberrations which the guilt process may take. Early Catholic confessional guides warned the priest about "The Scrupulous"—the unrelievable confesser who, in spite of all assurance, could not accept grace. This was an early delineation of what today would be commonly called the obsessive-compulsive syndrome.

Typically, guilt pathology falls into two rather polar forms: *too intense guilt*, usually seen in classical neurotic and psychotic symptoms, and conversely, an *absence* or *confusion of guilt*, characterized by terms such as "character disorder," "personality disorder (antisocial and dyssocial," or the older less definitive term "psychopathy." Variations on these are seen in narcissistic disorders and borderline personalities. These patterns, always somewhat unique to the individual, are usually marked by distinctions in the degree and type of identification with early models.

When significant survival figures are over-invested (introjected), the internal monitoring may be too aggressive, threatening, or sadistic. Ego functions and defenses may become too stylized, rigid, and symptomatic. Anxiety, especially moral anxiety or guilt, dominates the picture, and routinized ways of avoiding or trying to dissipate it develop. Hysteric repression, depressive self-castigation, obsessive-compulsive ritualization with reaction-formation, isolation of affect, or idealization may ensue. Inadequate ego function accompanied by overwhelming primary processes may eventuate in psychotic levels of maladaptation.

Situations in which guilt seems either absent or ineffective signal distortions of character usually associated with failures of identification. Inappropriate, absent, uncaring, or sadistic modeling may provoke superego lacunae sufficient to mar any effective bases for social adjustment or creative participation in communal values except at superficial, expedient levels. Such persons, notoriously dramatized in a Hitler ("Morality is meaningless") or Goering ("You can take your morality and stick it up"), commonly exact a great price from society for such a value-vacuum or distortion (see Lickona, 1976).

5. Conflicting Issues in the Treatment of Guilt. One of the most intransigent aspects of the efforts by the church to deal with guilt was rooted in the interweaving of normal existential guilt with pathological guilt. To treat all guilt uniformly is similar to treating all physical problems uniformly. (The prescription of vigorous physical exercise for obesity might well kill a person with a cardiac problem.) Similarly, heaping moralistic demands on pathologically guilty persons may only compound the pathology. Or, conversely, attempting nonconfrontational "acceptance" of a person with a character disorder may do the same. Even asserting forgiveness to a person who cannot get in touch with the roots of his or her alienation, self-hatred, grandiosity, or narcissism may not remove guilt.

Much of the early hostility of the healing professions toward the church was provoked by occasional clergy insistence on heightening the self-recrimination of already guilt-burdened persons. Penance and acceptance were too often conditioned by authoritarianism, and guilt was not infrequently used punitively and manipulatively, even when it was done unconsciously. Often enough, instinctual drives of self-assertion or sexuality were in themselves condemned as demonic, thus heightening internal conflict and guilt.

Subsequent to clarification of normal and pathological forms of guilt, it has become possible to differentiate to some degree the varying tasks of psychotherapy and religious forgiveness. The task of psychotherapy, insofar as possible, is to restore internal balances of structure, which will permit relatively normal ranges of self-esteem, self-restraint, and appropriate self-other boundaries *vis-à-vis* common values in the shared social order, with an optimal potential for moral anxiety when genuine values are transgressed.

The task of the religious carer is empathically to accept persons in the givenness of their human frailty, affirming the forgiveness and love of God in Christ and assuring the penitent, by attitude and word, that worth is based on God's gift and assertion, not on degree of excellence. *Metanoia,* or conversion to a new level of life, is a response of gratitude — not a *condition* of God's love but a *reaction* to it.

When a person cannot "accept his or her acceptance," but is under the domination of pathological structures (organic, developmental, or traumatic-situational), then referral to an appropriate psychiatrist or psychotherapist is in order, conditioned by the skills and limits of the pastoral counselor.

Problems are compounded by the fact that many of them are complex *mixtures* of pathological and normal existential guilt. A growing rapprochement is evident between pastoral counselors and the other helping professions, revealing an increased awareness of the interfabrication of issues once treated only by the priest or by the physician or therapist.

6. A Christian Stance. The outlines of the Christian attitude toward guilt encompass at least the following: (a) Both unmitigated self-condemnation and moral pride are inappropriate. (b) God in Christ has affirmed our worth and our forgiveness. (c) We are liberated from alienation and the power of sin and guilt when we accept and live in the context of God's love. This entails confession of guilt, reformation of life, and restitution of wrong, where possible. (d) Koinonia, the fellowship of believers, shapes and informs our values and conscience, enabling us to grow in responsible love toward God, others, and ourselves. (e) Responsibility of the forgiven believer entails forgiveness of others, restoration of broken relationships, and a serious participation in the sustaining of the community of faith which proclaims and lives out God's forgiving love. (f) Intellectual and moral integrity witness to the complexity of guilt and the complication of life by the structures of evil. These also entail recognition of the skills of therapists and behavioral scientists (often nontheological) in analyzing and clarifying mental dynamics and psychopathology. The Christian will refer to and utilize these skills and insights where possible and appropriate to the healing of human brokenness. (g) The aim of the pastoral counseling of guilt is to help the guilty person discern the real and/or neurotic quality of the guilt, deal therapeutically with the latter, and, where existential guilt is present, help the person appropriate, assimilate, and share God's love, forgiveness, and acceptance, moving toward personal and communal wholeness.

Bibliography. M. Buber, "Guilt and Guilt Feelings," in R. W. Smith, ed., *Guilt: Man and Society* (1971) p. 113. E. Erickson, *Identity and the Life Cycle* (1959). S. Freud, *Civilization and its Discontents* (1930); *New Introductory Lectures on Psychoanalysis* (1933); *The Ego and the Id* (1927). E. Fromm, *Man for Himself* (1947). W. Hulse, *Report on Proceedings, International Congress on Mental Health* (1958) pp. 52–53. C. Hall and G. Lindzey, eds., *Theories of Personality* 3d ed. (1978). L. Kohlberg, *The Philosophy of Moral Development* (1981). R. S. Lee, *Freud and Christianity* (1948). P. Lehmann, *Ethics in a Christian Context* (1963) pp. 327–43. T. Lickona, *Moral Development and Behavior* (1976). A. Maslow, *The Farther Reaches of Human Nature* (1971). J. Piaget, *The Moral Judgment of the Child* (1977). O. Pfister, *Christianity and Fear* (1944). P. Ricoeur, *Freud and Philosophy: An Essay on Interpretation* (1970) p. 299. H. Schär, "Protestant Problems with Conscience," in C. Nelson, ed., *Conscience* (1973) pp. 79–94. E. Stein, *Guilt: Theory and Therapy* (1968). P. Tillich, "The Nature of a Liberating Conscience," in I. Galdstone, ed., *Ministry and Medicine in Human Relations* (1955) pp. 127–40.

E. V. STEIN

CONSCIENCE; FORGIVENESS; MORAL DEVELOPMENT; REPENTANCE AND CONFESSION; RESPONSIBILITY/IRRESPONSIBILITY, PSYCHOLOGY OF; SIN/SINS; UNPARDONABLE SIN. *Compare* ANXIETY; EXISTENTIALISM; GRACE; HUMAN CONDITION/PREDICAMENT; NEUROSIS; PSYCHOPATHOLOGY, THEORIES OF; SHAME; UNDOING.

GURU. *See* SPIRITUAL MASTERS AND GUIDES.

H

HABIT. *See* MORAL DEVELOPMENT; MORAL THEOLOGY. *See also* LEARNING THEORIES; JAMES, WILLIAM.

HAENDLER, OTTO. *See* EASTERN EUROPEAN PASTORAL CARE MOVEMENT; PASTORAL THEOLOGY, PROTESTANT.

HALAKAH. Lit. "walking," a normative rule defining Jewish religions or moral behavior, and so, by extension, the entire system of Jewish law. In its classical sense, the term was used to distinguish the legal portions of Scripture and Talmud from "aggadah"—the exegetical, theological, or narrative portions. In current use, it generally refers to the particular practices, procedures, and rites accepted as normative by Orthodox Judaism.

P. J. HAAS

JEWISH CARE AND COUNSELING (History, Traditions, and Contemporary Issues); JEWISH LITERATURE IN CARE AND COUNSELING. *Compare* CASUISTRY; MORAL DILEMMAS IN PASTORAL PERSPECTIVE.

HALFWAY HOUSE. A residential program that serves as a transitional bridge between institutional care and community life. The halfway house emphasizes supervised participation of its residents (typically six to eight) in all aspects of daily living, with the goal of preparing the residents for self-management and independent living.

J. FOG

COMMUNITY MENTAL HEALTH MOVEMENT. *See also* COMMUNITY, FELLOWSHIP, AND CARE; PAROLEES AND EX-CONVICTS; THERAPEUTIC COMMUNITY.

HALL, CHARLES E. *See* PASTORAL CARE MOVEMENT.

HALL, GRANVILLE STANLEY (1844–1924). American psychologist and educator. As a professor of psychology at Johns Hopkins, where he founded one of the first psychological laboratories, and as president and

professor of psychology at Clark University in Worcester, Massachusetts, Hall not only produced studies of adolescence and senescence but also helped to initiate the study of the psychology of religion.

He was the first American academic psychologist to argue—in a lecture in 1881—that the age of religious interest and of sexual maturity coincided, so that adolescence was the normal stage of religious impressionability and conversion. He therefore interpreted conversion as a natural and universal process at the stage when life pivoted from self-centeredness to deeper care for others. Hence Hall stands as an early figure in the application of developmental psychology to an understanding of religion, both in his popular text on *Adolescence* (1904) and in his early studies of the moral and religious training of children.

He was probably more important, though, as an administrator and organizer. He made Clark University a center, however briefly, for the study of the psychology of religion. His *Journal of Religious Psychology and Education* was the most important vehicle of the psychology of religion movement. And he was responsible for bringing Freud and Jung to America in 1909 to lecture on psychoanalysis.

E. B. HOLIFIELD

PSYCHOLOGY OF RELIGION (Theories, Traditions, and Issues).

HALLUCINATION. A perception which occurs even though the related sensory organ has received no actual stimulation. Hallucinations can involve any of the senses (sight, touch, taste, hearing, smell) and usually suggest psychological conflict such as a guilt-ridden person being berated in the voices heard (auditory hallucination). Hallucinations are to be distinguished from illusions (misinterpretation of stimuli) and dreams.

A. J. STRAATMEYER

PSYCHOSIS. *Compare* DECOMPENSATION; PANIC; VISIONS AND VOICES.

HALLUCINOGENS. *See* PSYCHEDELIC DRUGS AND EXPERIENCE.

HANDICAP AND DISABILITY. A permanent condition of limitation in the ability to perform essential tasks. The cause may be congenital, or the onset may be gradual or sudden, by disease, accident, or war. Language usage varies, but it is clear that persons are not defined by a condition that limits some part or dimension of their activity. Persons with handicapping conditions include those whose disability or difference in appearance or behavior creates a problem of mobility, communication, intellectual comprehension, or personal relationships, which interferes with their social activity and/or participation.

The World Health Organization clearly delineates three widely used terms: (1) impairment, the loss or abnormality of a psychological, physiological, or anatomical structure or function, causing functional limitations to perform those activities usually carried out by the organ or systems affected; (2) disability, any restriction or lack of ability to perform an activity in the manner or within the range considered normal for a human being, that is, disturbances within areas of task, skill, behavior; (3) handicap, a disadvantage resulting from an impairment or disability that limits or prevents the fulfillment of a role that is normal for that individual. Thus an impairment is the cause; a disability is what a person cannot do; a handicap is the social barrier, attitude, or condition that restricts participation.

1. **The Community Context of Care.** Care must overcome a social/cultural and ecclesial community's negative response to disability and blemish. Through historical attitudes that have related sin to disability, and Western cultural attitudes that emphasized independence, persons with disabilities have frequently been viewed with fear, threat, or awkwardness. Because they have been named by their disability (i.e., the blind, the deaf, the lame, the dumb), rather than their personhood (i.e., persons with a disability or persons with handicapping conditions), they have been viewed as objects or recipients of care. Such attitudes can make a disability worse, as they lead to exclusion, invisibility, or being viewed solely as recipients of services provided by others.

Care begins with visibility, access, and invitation to full participation in community, recognizing that the disability is just one dimension of personhood. Thus the goal of pastoral care for persons with disabilities is their full equality and participation in community as whole persons. Agents of care must work with the attitudes of the whole community as they have led to physical and attitudinal barriers to full access and participation. As stewards of access, care providers thus invite partnership and reciprocity with persons with disabilities. Within the context of total community, recognition is also developed that disabilities cut across racial, social, sexual, ethnic, and age populations, and that no one is free from disability at some point of the life cycle.

2. **Special Care and Counseling Considerations.** As with any special population, a whole range of situations and feelings and a great diversity of responses must be expected. Consideration must be given to matters of onset and their differing meanings, namely, congenital, gradual, or sudden. Persons with disabilities must cope with personal and physical barriers and limits without surrendering their possibilities of finding alternatives, creative participation, and social usefulness. There may be feelings of grief, anger, and mourning over lost capacities or possibilities, as well as negative feelings about self-concept and body image. There may be ambivalent feelings about independence or premature dependency, as well as those of vulnerability, loneliness, and frustration.

The person with a disability is a social person, and the family context must be considered. Dynamics of overprotection or guilt within the disabled person or family member(s) may be present. The person may experience difficulties in personal relationships and with feelings and expressions of sexuality. There may be dynamics within the person or family that have developed through isolation, exclusion, or social invisibility, or from experiences of having been pitied or patronized. As in any counseling, attention must be paid to the differing meanings of individual and family narrative, including their broader social matrix:

The varying conditions of disability may call for slow, sustained efforts to find alternatives to normal social intercourse, in which care may focus on sustaining and supportive systems and standing by. The person or family may disclose needs for ethical reflection or moral guidance in matters of sexuality, marriage, having children, and issues of life and death. In broader social context, pastoral care and counseling for persons with handicapping conditions is interprofessional, and it is probable that pastoral caregivers will work with members of other helping professions, for example, doctors, physiotherapists, nurses, social workers, other mental health professionals, and technicians in facilitating the use of mechanical helps. It is important that the pastoral helper have knowledge of the particular disability, its prognosis, and related emotional effects. The caregiver should also be aware of self-help groups and advocacy organizations of persons experiencing the disability and their families as rich community resources.

3. **Related Theological Issues.** Christian community is not complete without the full participation of persons with handicapping conditions, whose past isolation must be reconciled within the wholeness of the family of God. God's love is not contingent upon physical perfection, and historical ties between faith and wholeness, sin and disability—which have led to fear, threat, and resulting isolation—must be corrected. Issues of suffering, finitude/limitation, and meaning, when there is no apparent physical healing, must be addressed. Mature understandings of the suffering servant and the finding of perfection through weakness may be helpful. Theological understandings of the nature of God's power and love, as well as of the meaning of healing, will be relevant.

The full inclusion of persons with physical limitation within Christian community invites the sharing of their gifts of ministry with full equality, and makes indispensable witness to all persons who both accept finitude/limitation while refusing unnecessary barriers to the possibilities of their full personhood with human community.

Bibliography. L. G. Colston, *Pastoral Care with Handicapped Persons* (1978). J. Cox-Gedmark, *Coping with Physical Disability*

(1980). J. van Dongren-Garrad, *Invisible Barriers: Pastoral Care with Physically Disabled People* (1983). T. Gould, "A Guide to Eliminating 'Handicappism' in Language," *New World Outlook* (May 1983). W. Kern, *Pastoral Ministry with Disabled Persons* (1985). G. Müller-Fahrenholz, ed., *Partners in Life: The Handicapped and the Church*, Faith and Order Paper No. 89, World Council of Churches (1979). H. O. Ohlsberg, *The Church and Persons with Handicaps* (1982). H. H. Wilke, *Creating the Caring Congregation: Guidelines for Ministering with the Handicapped* (1980); *Strengthened with Might* (1952); "Is Our Theology Disabled?: A Symposium on Theology and Persons with Handicapping Conditions," Health and Welfare Ministries Division, General Board of Global Ministries, The United Methodist Church (1982) or "God's Power and Our Weakness," Task Force of Persons with Disabilities of the Consultation on Church Union, G. F. Moebe, ed. (1982).

P. WAY

EPILEPSY; EXCEPTIONAL CHILDREN AND THEIR FAMILIES; LOSS OF FUNCTION; MENTALLY RETARDED PERSONS. *See also* BODY IMAGE; GRIEF AND LOSS; PATIENCE/PATIENTHOOD; PROVIDENCE, DOCTRINE OF, AND PASTORAL CARE; VICTIMIZATION.

HANDICAPPED CHILD AND FAMILY. *See* EXCEPTIONAL CHILDREN AND THEIR FAMILIES; HANDICAP AND DISABILITY; LOSS OF FUNCTION.

HANUKKAH. *See* JEWISH HOLY DAYS AND FESTIVALS.

HAPPINESS. The subjective judgment that a positive relation exists between an individual's present circumstances and her or his vision of what constitutes a good life. Happiness is not simply a feeling, nor is it the same as pleasure. All things being equal, one would prefer to be happy, but instead one usually pursues relative happiness within the constraints set by historical circumstances and one's vision of the good life. Happiness thus accrues to the life well lived. It is good relative to its existence in a constellation of goods, rather than being an end in itself. Happiness lies in relations, not in things or acts.

Happiness has been suspect in moral philosophy, because its pursuit as an end (usually as a form of pleasure) tends to weaken bonds between people and denigrate social and corporate concerns. This sets people over against each other in competition for the resources of individually pursued happiness. In pastoral care a similar concern exists that happiness not be another way of pursuing self-fulfillment without considering the relational context of the self in which that happiness is constituted. Christian theology in particular provides good grounds for holding that the happiness of others is a necessary part of the happiness of individuals. This should not, however, be connected with a false sense of self-sacrifice to demean the value of happiness rightly perceived.

Thus in pastoral care, as in theological ethics, *unhappiness* may well be a more important category. While it would be hard indeed to come up with a satisfactory substantive definition of happiness, it is possible to ascertain whether a person is subjectively unhappy, and then to investigate the discrepancy between the moral context of happiness for that person and the actual conditions of that person's life. Unhappiness of a persistent sort tells us something is wrong with the set of relations in which a person lives, and thus invites further reflection on which elements in those relations are contributing to the unhappiness. The persistent unhappiness of groups or classes of people may also be a clue to situations of abuse or injustice in a wide range of social situations.

In this light even the experience of happiness is not in itself necessarily good. One may *feel* happy for reasons that are morally questionable either for one's own long-term vision or for the well-being of others. Happiness cannot be pursued as a moral or therapeutic good if it is so narrowly defined as to require the unhappiness of others or the undercutting of wider moral vision.

Bibliography. Aristotle, *The Nichomachean Ethics* (1975), a classic discussion of connection between happiness and goodness in a well-lived life. D. Evans, *Struggle and Fulfillment* (1979), connects psychology of religion and moral philosophy on relation between virtue and happiness. T. Oden, *Pastoral Theology* (1983), connects happiness with wholistic view of pastoral care.

RICHARD BONDI

ETHICS AND PASTORAL CARE; MORAL THEOLOGY AND PASTORAL CARE. *See also* CHRISTIAN LIFE; EMOTION; GRACE. *Compare* CHARACTER ETHICS AND PASTORAL CARE; CHARISMATIC EXPERIENCE; ECSTASY; GRATITUDE; SADNESS AND DEPRESSION; SELF-ACTUALIZATION/SELF-REALIZATION; SELF-ESTEEM.

HARE KRISHNA. *See* NEW RELIGIOUS MOVEMENTS.

HARMS, CLAUS (1778–1855). German Lutheran pastoral theologian, provost at Kiel. His three-volume *Pastoraltheologie* (1830–34) is credited with founding and shaping the discipline of pastoral theology, in addition to and independent of practical theology, by using as the basis for reflections the experiences, encounters, and dilemmas of pastors. His detailed treatment of the professional demands upon pastors is one of the most progressive in the field of personal guidance. Harms favored the restoration of private confession, suggested the then novel job description of "pastor for visitation and outreach," proposed university training courses for the ministry, and expressed his desire for ministers to be qualified in "psychiatry."

N. F. HAHN

PASTORAL THEOLOGY, PROTESTANT.

HASIDIC CARE AND COUNSELING. Hasidism is a popular, charismatic Jewish movement originating in Southern Poland in 1734. A Hasid (literally, pious) is one who has accepted a *rebbe* as a guide and spiritual director and has allied himself with a Hasidic congregation. Israel ben Eliezer founded the movement. Born in about 1700 in the Ukraine, he came to be known as the Baal Shem Tov (Master of the Good Name). The movement spread rapidly among Eastern European Jews and continues to occupy an important place in the Jewish community.

1. **Origin.** During the seventeenth and eighteenth centuries, the life of the ordinary Jew in Eastern Europe was characterized by political and social oppression, persecu-

tion, and ostracism. Efforts among the poor and uneducated to gain or regain their dignity as persons and as a community and to assuage a deep yearning for greater contact with Jewish life were generally unsuccessful. Among the rabbis and the leisured, a retreat to the world of the spirit was possible through a study of Jewish literature and the Talmud. But the anguish of the masses who sought to escape the inferior position in which they were held and to participate in a religion they could understand was largely unacknowledged.

It was into this void that the Baal Shem Tov stepped. Firmly grounded in the Jewish Mystical Tradition (Kabbala) and possessed of unusual gifts of speech and imagination, he insisted that the primary duty to seek God and to find one's place in his purpose required neither great learning nor long prayers. God is to be found all about us and the path to him is not despair and gloom but the awareness of his presence in joy and lightness of heart and in acts of love and mercy.

Initially Baal Shem Tov ministered to the religious and emotional needs of his neighbors from his position as a teacher of children. However, as his reputation grew, persons traveled great distances to seek his benediction and his advice on relations with God and each other. His ideas were presented simply, usually embellished and illustrated with examples and stories from daily life. His followers, known as Hasidim, included any number of important religious leaders, many of whom became *rebbes* themselves and established congregations. Baal Shem Tov came to be regarded as having direct contact with God, serving as an intermediary and as a defender of the Jewish people before the Almighty. Stories of miracles were associated with his name and although he left no writings, his words were transmitted orally by his followers and he became a legendary figure. More scholarly successors, like Magged of Meseritch, sought to undergird his teaching with traditional Jewish learning and the writings of the mystics. They also began to train *rebbes* to carry on the movement.

During the course of these developments Hasidism experienced considerable opposition. The Hasidim's emphasis on prayer as opposed to study and on emotion rather than intellect caused their opponents (Mitnaggedim, i.e., Orthodox Jews) to accuse them of attempting to destroy learning, dignity, and the Jewish Tradition. Finally, the Hasidim were excommunicated and a period of persecution and animosity continued until a common enemy, the eighteenth-century Enlightenment, which caused the various factions within Judaism to unite. Even in the midst of this conflict, Hasidism continued to expand and to provide examples of saintliness, wisdom, and spirituality to Jewish life.

The price the Hasidim paid for their acceptance as a legitimate expression of Jewish life was to see once spontaneous practices become institutionalized. Schachter suggests that this resulted in a suppression of their more exuberant and emotional expressions and a surrender of some aspects of their work, for example, meditative techniques. Following the bloodlines of the original leaders, Hasidic dynasties emerged all over Europe, some faithful to the original intent, while others took on regal characteristics and removed themselves from the people. The ideal that a religious leader ought to be expert in the Tradition and in Jewish Law came to characterize the Hasidic *rebbe*. But the commitment that he not neglect or be aloof from the people and from his primary task of bringing all Jews closer to God receded.

2. Care and Counseling. What the Baal Shem Tov brought to a dispirited people was the hope of a life unified in all its parts, personal, interpersonal, and metaphysical. He captured their alienation and personal and social ostracism with his characterization of life as exile. By utilizing classical mystical concepts, he insisted that the separations they experienced between good and evil, rich and poor, male and female, mercy and judgment, all their inner and outer contradictions contained holy sparks separated from their true source in God. The entire cosmos possesses immense and largely unacknowledged possibilities so that all that exists is to some degree estranged from the source of its life.

The task of the Hasidic master or *rebbe,* then, was to gather up these fallen sparks everywhere. They sought to provide a path to unification and vital relatedness to God for those unable, either through want of learning or leisure or because of the pressing distractions of life, to pursue the traditional way of study and debate of the Torah. The uneducated needed a guide. They needed to be reminded by instruction and example that no situation in life should be neglected. The divine sparks are always present, and the inner exaltation of raising these sparks to their source follows from devoted attention to the vicissitudes and activities of daily life. Thus whatever one does, whether prayer, work, family life, or play, becomes an occasion for participation in the unification and fulfillment of the universe. Despair, self-pity, and sadness are marks of distance from God; ecstasy, physical liveliness in song and dance, and devotion and service reflect a life bound to God.

These *rebbes* or *zaddikim* (righteous ones) were the key to the Hasidic communities. They were known as Teachers of the Way. Their participation with the people enabled them to serve as examples, so that the task of the Hasidim was to emulate the *rebbe* in works of charity, justice, prayer, song, and ecstasy. As intermediaries their lives were understood to be a reflection of the unification of earth and heaven, body and soul, male and female, etc. By simply observing their daily activities, the Hasidim could learn about wholeness. As Woocher says, "The Hasidic communal ideal rested on a faith in the power of simplicity, joy, and the encounter with a counselor and healer, who himself embodied wholeness and intimacy with people and God, to effect a unification embracing all the dimensions of human life (p. 30).

At the heart of the *rebbe's* relation to the Hasidic community was the *yehidut*. The *yehidut* (literally, "oneing") involved a private meeting with one's *rebbe* which at its best reflected a sacred encounter among the *rebbe,* the Hasid, and God. Generally a Hasid met with his *rebbe* annually and at all the major turning points of his life, for example, at bar mitzvah, with the decision about the choice of a partner. At times of crisis the Hasid was also expected to consult with his *rebbe*. The sessions were formal and private. The Hasid prepared ritually and spiritually for the event and gave thought to the issues/dilemmas he wished to present. Moreover, simply by appearing for the *yehidut*, the hasid agreed to abide by the *rebbe's* advice and instruction and to offer a gift to help support him.

The bond between Hasid and *rebbe*, then, required a life-time commitment. Each stage and place in life offered opportunities to gather the sparks, to observe the injunctions of the Torah, to perform good deeds *(mitzvot)*, and to do *teshuvah* (repent or return and ascend to one's divine source of origin). The *rebbes* were astute in their efforts to uncover and to understand the Hasid's inner life and situation. As the movement grew, specialization occurred among the *rebbes,* and referral to another master or to a *mashpiyim* (influencer) was possible. Only after this effort to understand did they offer prescriptions for action, prescriptions which might include meditative techniques, acts of charity, healings, and miracles. They saw the depressed, the financially distressed, the barren, the abandoned, those with family conflict, and the politically oppressed, always seeking ways to encourage relatedness to God in the midst of life. And at the conclusion of the *yehidut*, they offered their blessing, frequently a whispered word cherished as a mutual pact among Hasid and *rebbe* and God.

This relation to the *rebbe*, as reflected in the *yehidut* formed the basis for communal life among the Hasidim. More often than not, the Hasid would emerge from his meeting with his master to celebrate in song and dance the blessing that was his. For the meeting was understood to transcend simple personal distress and to link persons to each other and, finally, to the purposes of God in the unification of his creation. Thus the substance of the *yehidut* became the stuff of daily interchange among the Hasidim, linking them to each other and to the Almighty.

3. Present State. A renewal of interest in the Hasidic tradition reflects both the psychological and the theological wisdom and insight it contains. Martin Buber and Elie Wiesel have each acknowledged their indebtedness to the tradition. In Buber's case, his formulation of the I-Thou relationship owes much to the encounter in the *yehidut* between *rebbe* and Hasid. In the psychological sphere, Woocher demonstrates the possible dialogue of Hasidic thought with neo-Freudian, Jungian, humanistic, and even behaviorist theories. He also notes that Hasidic attempts to "embody growth" and "wholeness" resemble the work of Rogers, Maslow, Fromm, and Frankl. Any number of scholars have also demonstrated the affinities of the *yehidut* to some contemporary work in psychotherapy. Schachter especially has delineated these affinities. But each of these writers is also careful to point out that the transcendent dimension of Hasidic thought, expressed in myth, mystery, and religious symbolism, moves beyond the personal and social aspects of contemporary psychology. Finally, Hasidic psychological insight was an expression of Torah.

Within the Hasidic community there appears to be no acknowledged relation between their thought and contemporary psychology. Indeed, within Judaism generally, there seems to be a certain tension between its Reformed and Conservative expressions and the Hasidim, and one dimension of this tension is the differing attitude among these groups towards secular knowledge. Hasidic orientation and training are more closely akin to the Orthodox tradition as this is modified by their allegiance to their particular dynasties.

Bibliography. M. Buber, *Tales of the Hasidim* (1947). S. Grayzel, *A History of the Jews* (1947). E. Hoffman, *The Way of Splendor* (1981). J. C. Safier, "Hasidim, Faith and Therapeutic Paradox," *J. of Judaism and Psychology,* 3:1 (1978), 38–47. S. Schachter and E. Hoffman, *Sparks of Light: Counseling in the Hasidic Tradition* (1983). M. H. Spero, "Discussion: On the Nature of the Therapeutic Encounter Between Hasid and Master," *J. of Judaism and Psychology,* 3:1 (1978), 48–59. J. S. Woocher, "The Kabbalah, Hasidim and the Life of Unification," *J. of Judaism and Psychology,* 3:1 (1978), 22–37.

L. O. MILLS

JEWISH CARE AND COUNSELING (History, Traditions, and Contemporary Issues); ZADDIK. *See also* JEWISH LITERATURE IN CARE AND COUNSELING; JUDAISM AND PSYCHOLOGY. *Compare* COMMUNITY, FELLOWSHIP, AND CARE; PIETISM AND PASTORAL CARE.

HATE. *See* RAGE AND HOSTILITY. *See also* AGGRESSION AND ASSERTION; ANGER AND MEEKNESS.

HAVURAH.—Fellowship. The Hebrew root is *haver* (friend), thus, a group of friends. First found among the Essenes and Pharisees as communes, havurah took the form of community service-oriented groups with specific tasks; for example, ministering to the family of the newborn, the wedding party, the family in mourning, and so forth. (Neusner, 1967, 1970, 1972; Peli, 1984; Tal, 1974).

Three forms are manifest in Judaism today: residential and/or neighborhood communes, fellowship groups outside the synagogue, and synagogue-sponsored groups. Most contemporary commentators — such as Neusner (1972), Reisman (1977), Schulweis (1975), Wasserman (1979), and Bubis (1977) — ascribe properties and functions that include goals of fellowship, study, and service. Disagreement exists as to the degree to which friendship must underlie pursuit of other goals. Neusner especially differentiates between fellowship which bonds *despite* friendship and the more widely held premise that friendship becomes an essential element. Most research confirms the essential importance of relationships, group size, and shared interests (Wasserman, 1979, 1983; Reisman, 1977).

Prior research (Fein, 1972; Reisman, *et al.,* 1977) established a great degree of anomie among Jews. Kinship theory (Pattison, 1975) explains the familial overtones to be found in most successful havurot. Psychological (non-related) kinship groups evolve, which in many instances take the place of family in moments of stress — both painful and pleasurable — such as births, bar mitzvah and bat mitzvah ceremonies, weddings, divorces, and deaths.

Theoreticians suggested that intensive personal experiences in small havurah groups should result in measurable changes in behavior. Major studies on synagogue-sponsored havurot do not confirm this (Bubis, Wasserman, and Lert, 1983; Reisman, 1977). Members' attitudes seem to be more positive toward synagogues, more caring about each other, but specific ritual behaviors show no significant change. Intangible and informal dimensions of identity were not measured by the research instruments.

Extensive personal interviews suggest that havurot have much greater potency as fellowship groups when they function as sources for serious study and acquisition of knowledge (Schulweis, 1975; Bubis and Wasserman, 1983; Reisman, 1977). Research has indicated a higher degree of learning readiness than is present among non-havurah members. Perhaps insufficient time has passed since the great and relatively recent explosion of havurot throughout the country. Non-synagogue-affiliated havurot have more ardent ideologies and focus on the religious and spiritual dimensions of membership to a greater degree than seems to be the case in synagogue-affiliated havurot (Axelrod, 1968; Gendler, 1972; Sheingold, 1982). The non-synagogue havurot are more likely to be found on the East Coast and are more comprehensive in their dimensions. Far more frequently they encompass prayer and religious observance than the friendship aspects that seem more normative in synagogue-affiliated groups.

In synagogues, the role of the rabbi varies. In some instances rabbis are the key figures in forming and nourishing havurot while just as frequently key lay people or nonrabbinic synagogue staff are key figures (Braun, 1977).

Many rabbis oppose the prospect of havurot being founded in their synagogues, wrongly concluding that small groups would be more likely to break away or disaffiliate as a result of increased satisfaction in havurot. Some research, however, suggests this is not the case, but that allegiance to the synagogue is enhanced (Bubis and Wasserman, 1983).

Havurot are not panaceas for serving the disgruntled and the peripheral. Intimacy is an outgrowth of havurot experiences, but service to the congregation is not a guaranteed outcome. It is a powerful tool for helping people deal with their own interests and needs as Jews. The degree to which their ancient roles as servers to others rather than to self will or should gain primacy remains a question in our day.

Bibliography. A. S. Axelrod, "Havurot Shalom: A Clarification," *Reconstructionist* (December 20, 1968), 30–36. B. Braun, "Havurah as a New Dimension in Congregational Life," in G. Bubis, ed., *Serving the Jewish Family* (1977). G. Bubis, "Facing New Times," *Central Conference of American Rabbis J.*, 20/4 (1973), 9–13. G. Bubis, ed., *Serving the Jewish Family* (1977). G. Bubis and H. Wasserman, with A. Lert, *Synagogue Havurot: A Comparative Study* (1983). L. Fein, R. Chin, J. Dauber, and B. Reisman, *Reform Is a Verb* (1972). E. Gendler, "Old-New Ways in Jewish Worship," *Hadassah Magazine*, 54/3 (Nov. 1972), 16–17, 45. J. Neusner, *Contemporary Judaic Fellowship in Theory and in Practice* (1972); *The Havurah Idea* (1967); *Judaism in the Secular Age: Essays on Fellowship, Community and Freedom* (1970). E. M. Pattison *et al.*, "A Psycho-social Kinship Model for Therapy," *American J. of Psychiatry*, 132 (1975), 23–30. P. Peli, "The Havurot That Were in Jerusalem," *Hebrew Union College Annual* (1984). B. Reisman, *The Chavurah: A Contemporary Jewish Experience* (1977). H. Schulweis, "The Changing Nature of the Synagogue," *Central Conference of American Rabbis Convention Proceedings* (June 1975). C. Sheingold, *New Pockets of Jewish Energy* (1982). U. Tal, "Structures of Fellowship and Community in Judaism," *Conservative Judaism*, 25/2 (Winter 1974), 3–12. H. Wasserman,

"The Havurah Experience," *J. of Psychology and Judaism*, 3 (1979), 168–83. A. J. Wolf, "Three Havurot," *Central Conference of American Rabbis J.*, 22/1 (1975), 34–36.

G. BUBIS

JEWISH CARE AND COUNSELING (History, Traditions, and Contemporary Issues). *See also* COMMUNITY, FELLOWSHIP, AND CARE; JUDAISM AND PSYCHOLOGY; RELATIONSHIP NETWORK. *Compare* CONGREGATION, PASTORAL CARE OF; GROUP COUNSELING AND PSYCHOTHERAPY; GROWTH GROUPS.

HEADACHE. *See* PAIN MANAGEMENT/PAIN CLINIC. *See also* BIOFEEDBACK; PSYCHOSOMATIC ILLNESS.

HEALER, PASTOR AS. *See* PASTOR (Normative and Traditional Images).

HEALING. The process of being restored to bodily wholeness, emotional well-being, mental functioning, and spiritual aliveness. Christian modes of healing have always distinguished themselves by achieving a spiritual advance in connection with the healing process. Healing may also refer to the process of reconciling broken human relationships and to the development of a just social and political order among races and nations. In recent times, healing and wholeness have become metaphors for religious views of salvation.

1. Old Testament View of Healing. For Christians, concern for healing has its roots in the OT. The Hebrews pictured the world as good. There was a unity of mind and body, created by God. Whereas health was viewed as a blessing from God, a reward for righteousness and faithfulness to the Mosaic covenant, illness was often regarded as divine punishment or chastisement for transgression. Health and holiness were therefore positively related and were united in the concepts of *shalom* and righteousness. Holiness refers to a sense of personal unity and integration of one's being in dynamic relationship to God, world, and community out of choice. It eventuates in the notion of a centered and covenanted life, set apart for a morally committed existence in the world. This existence is characterized by *shalom*, or bodily wholeness and being at peace with self, God, and neighbor. It is a righteous life inasmuch as it is characterized by deliverance from one's enemies, personal integrity, and living fitly in the world as a member of the covenant community with God. There is a social dimension to salvation and the health which attends it, extending to relationships among nations as well as an ecological dimension involving stewardship of the earth. Thus, healing and salvation are linked insofar as they both involve restoration to dynamic wholeness in body, mind, spirit, society and the world, and derive from being in proper relation to God. The book of Job revises the view that all illness and affliction are divine punishments upon sin and adds the perspective that illness results from an evil agency deriving its power indirectly from God and operating apart from human intention and virtue. Rather than necessarily reflecting a broken relationship with God, bodily and emotional affliction may overtake the faithful and may eventuate in a spiritual and theological advance whether or not physical healing actually occurs.

2. New Testament View of Healing: The Ministry of Jesus. The NT portrays Jesus as vitally concerned with healing the physical, moral, and mental diseases of persons, and commanding his followers to do the same. About one-third of the Gospel accounts describe various healings performed by Jesus, and the early church reported dramatic healings by its leaders and members. The NT regards healing as an indication of the presence of the Kingdom of God, in which restoration of bodily wholeness, emotional well-being and mental functioning take place in the context of a spiritual advance. Jesus and his followers believed that sickness and disease resulted from demon possession rather than from divine punishment of personal or corporate sin. Illness and disease were regarded as forms of bondage to evil forces, taking place in the depths of personal being apart from personal choice or control. Jesus' method of healing evoked latent attitudes of faith and the desire for wholeness and linked these with the healing power of God who hates evil in all its forms. Thus, Jesus provided an opportunity for human faith and divine power to coalesce in creating a new order. Restoration of bodily, emotional and mental capacities were not the only concern of this new order, but restoration of these faculties was included in it. As in the OT, salvation and health were integrally related, both were seen as blessings from God who opposes sin and evil, of which sickness and personal disorder are expressions. The mind, body, and spirit were understood to comprise a dynamic unity. The witness of Jesus, however, also advanced the idea that though personal attitudes play a part in the healing process, they may be overwhelmed by evil agents which distort the personality and cause bodily, emotional and spiritual disorder. Further, Jesus commanded his followers to heal the sick.

3. Healing in the Early Church. For the first three centuries, the ministry of healing was made central in the worship and mission of the apostolic church, and was practiced regularly by those recognized as having this capacity. Unlike the Gnostics, who viewed the body as subordinate and therefore denigrated it, the early church affirmed the goodness of the body and regarded the human being as a unity of mind, body, and spirit. During this period, healing became more sacramental and was combined with anointing and exorcisms.

Beginning in the fourth century, the emphasis in the church began to change. The body began to be seen as less important than the spirit, and illness was increasingly regarded as the result of divine chastisement and discipline. The precariousness of life increased as the Roman Empire was in decline, furthering the sense of God's wrath and reinforcing the growing tendency to regard the spirit and the material world as opposed. The practice of anointing for healing gave way by the ninth century to the practice of anointing for death.

4. Healing in the Later Middle Ages. In the later Middle Ages, under the impact of Aquinas and Aristotle, the body and reason were regarded as instruments for this world, the soul for the next. The soul, mind, and body were ordered hierarchically and increasingly had little to do with one another, though such was not Aquinas's original intention.

In spite of this divorce of healing from salvation and the view that illness results from divine chastisement, healing was practiced in the Middle Ages. There were monastic orders of healers and hospitalers. Relics and shrines provided means of healings, and these were reported at the hands of some of the great saints and leaders of the church. One example is when Bernard of Clairvaux, attending the funeral of Malachy, the primate of Ireland, healed the withered hand of a boy by placing it upon the hand of the dead saint. Numerous healings were attributed to Dominic, the founder of the Dominican order, St. Francis, John of Beverly, Bishop of York, St. Francis Xavier, and many others. However, many of the stories of healing performed by the saints were too fanciful to sustain credibility, and under the growing view that illness was a divine chastisement and that the welfare of the spirit was more important than that of the body, physical healing was no longer an integral part of the church's life and mission. By the Council of Trent in 1551 there was no longer room in the church's understanding for a rite of healing. The church came to regard the needs of the body to be in conflict with those of the spirit and attempted to control the development and practice of medicine. Priests were required to attend patients before physicians; physicians ignoring this rule were sanctioned by the church.

5. Healing during the Reformation. The Reformers continued the medieval emphasis upon the welfare of the soul, and regarded illness as a punishment, health as a blessing. Though the reformers encouraged compassion toward the ill and emphasized prayers for healing and a time for support and encouragement of the afflicted, they regarded illness as an opportunity to reaffirm God's mercy and grace by receiving the release from sin occasioned by the chastisement of illness. If the sick person should die, it was regarded as a merciful release from the sin and evils of this world, and the time to receive fully the blessings of God only partially realized on earth. Luther and Calvin did not believe in miraculous physical healings, but affirmed that the true miracle was the spiritual healing of the soul by God's grace through faith. Physical or emotional illness could thus be viewed as contributing to a spiritual advance whether or not healing occurred, so long as the healing of the soul through forgiveness took place.

6. Post-Reformation Views of Healing. Since the Reformation, Western culture has witnessed a radical reversal of the emphasis upon the spiritual healing of the soul. Beginning in the seventeenth and eighteenth centuries under the influence of Descartes and Newton, there developed an emphasis upon the health of the body and the natural physical processes of living. These have had far-reaching consequences for religious viewpoints. Descartes developed a dualistic view in which he affirmed that "there is nothing included in the concept of body that belongs to the mind, and nothing in that of mind that belongs to the body." To Descartes, the material universe, though a creation of God, was nothing but a machine. He believed that there is no purpose in organic life, no spirituality in matter. Nature worked according to mechanical laws. Everything in the universe was explained according to the movement of its parts and described in mathematical, logical fashion. And though

Descartes believed that mind and matter were unified in God, this idea dropped aside in the appropriation of his thought.

Sir Isaac Newton carried forward and synthesized Descartes' views. He developed universal mathematical laws describing the working of the solar system, and confirmed Descartes' view of the universe as a large mechanical system operating according to these laws. He came to understand that the basic structure of reality was material. He argued that the building blocks for the elements of reality in the finest form are small, solid, indestructible objects out of which matter was made, and existed in certain mathematically predictable relationships. And though God created the material particles, the forces between the particles, and the fundamental laws of motion governing the interactions of the particles, God has left the world basically to run on its own in a machine-like way. God was viewed as a transcendent and remote monarch who orders things from high above, without direct involvement. In this dualistic and deterministic worldview everything that happens is explained as causal; everything in the universe can be predicted in linear fashion, once the elements at work in a given context are identified.

7. **Modern Understanding and Medical Practice.** This worldview has been the underlying basis for modern medical practice. The body is regarded as a well-ordered machine that functions according to predetermined patterns. Illness is the breakdown of this functioning. Healing consists in establishing the natural functions or processes and then restoring them through the appropriate intervention. These functions can be isolated to particular parts of the body, with no assumption that there is a connection between all the parts, and between the body and its social and physical environment. Neither is it assumed that emotions, mental functions, values, and spiritual capacities play a part in the processes of disease and healing. The person is regarded as an isolated ego inside the body. Mental work has been given higher status then manual work.

This worldview has contributed to the development of large industries to develop and improve the body. It has spawned a massive pharmacological emphasis in medical treatment, and provided substantial impetus to surgery and the organ transplant phenomenon. Religiously, in its more severe form, it has led either to atheism or to the repudiation of any meaningful view of God as a benevolent and effective agent in the concrete events of the world. At the other extreme, many religious persons have simply denied the validity of these scientific perspectives and have maintained allegiance to earlier theologies which affirm the importance of healing the soul's relation to God. The natural and bodily worlds are thought to be of a lower order. Other religiously based persons have tried to accommodate the Cartesian-Newtonian view by revising their theological understandings to include a positive evaluation of the natural and secular, and to regard medical healing as originating in God, whether or not it is carried out by believers. The various responses to the Cartesian-Newtonian worldview, however, have led to ongoing tension between the sacred and the secular, and to the specialization of function which secularism has bred. The larger result is a situation where physicians rarely treat the emotions or the spiritual capacities and environmental contexts of persons, and psychologists and ministers have little to do with the life of the body and its processes.

8. **Issues of Brokenness and Healing in the Twentieth Century.** In the twentieth century there have been converging religious and secular forces which question the Cartesian-Newtonian worldview, and recapture some of the Jewish and early Christian views about the unity of body, emotions, spirit, society, and the cosmos in the process of disease and healing. Individuals, societies, and nations are described in some important Christian literature, notably that of the World Council of Churches, as in need of healing from their brokenness and liberation from bondage to forces of evil which have captured them. The dualistic and deterministic worldview is in itself regarded as an expression of sin's estrangement inasmuch as it divides and fragments that which God created to be related. In individuals, this brokenness is expressed in unabated identity crises, in persistent estrangement from one's roots, in ongoing difficulties with what it means to be male and female and to relate to families, in struggles over depression arising from frustrated aspirations, aging, illness, and a sense of meaninglessness and isolation. On a national and global scale it is characterized by oppression, lack of education and jobs, and the selfish, greedy use of the earth's resources eventuating in the pollution of air, water, and land.

According to recent World Council of Churches statements, the religious call in the modern world is to share, to be a healing presence where it is needed, whether between cultures, races, generations, women and men, races and religions, or oneself and one's family. Healing has once again, as in its biblical rootage, become connected with salvation, *shalom,* and holiness, and with the transformation of the personal and the social fabric of existence.

9. **Pastoral Theology and Therapy for Healing.** The theoretical and practical contributions of Hiltner, Lapsley, and others have both reflected and spawned a major concern for health and healing in modern pastoral practice. Nearly all seminaries have major curricular offerings in pastoral care and counseling, and much of the average minister's time is taken in ministries related to the restoration of bodily wholeness, mental functioning, interpersonal reconciliation, and spiritual aliveness. A number of programs training pastoral care and counseling specialists have emerged to support the growing number of persons focusing their ministries in the area of personal and interpersonal healing. The College of Chaplains of the American Protestant Hospital Association, the Association of Clinical Pastoral Education, and the American Association of Pastoral Counselors are but a few of the professional groups which support the various healing ministries in today's religious world. Though their emphases and methods may vary, persons in these groups are united in the conviction that illness and personal distress is an opportunity for the healing power of God to work in a transforming manner. The mind, body, and environment are understood to be interconnected in the processes of disease and healing,

and religious perspectives and methodologies are broadly interpreted to play a potentially important role in the healing of persons.

10. Modern Pastoral Approaches to Healing. Within current pastoral practice, there are two major approaches to the processes of healing, with variants and nuances of interpretations within them. One is the practice of spiritual-charismatic-sacramental healing. Morton Kelsey has interpreted this mode in many of his books, especially in *Healing and Christianity*. The other is the pastoral counseling or pastoral-psychotherapy approach which draws upon modern psychotherapeutic modes for much of its self-understanding and methods. Seward Hiltner, James Lapsley, Wayne Oates, Howard Clinebell, Carroll Wise and others have written about and practiced this mode of pastoral healing.

a. Spiritual-charismatic-sacramental healing. Akin to the relatively direct form of healing ascribed to Jesus and the early church, it has been carried forward by great healers throughout the history of the church. Of the numerous forms of this healing, nearly all involve a combination of bodily restoration and emotional renewal with an attendant spiritual advance. It is usually performed by a recognized healer and carried out in a communal context involving a variety of religious practices. Occasionally exorcisms are performed by those having the gift of healing. The processes involved in spiritual healing include spiritual discernment on the part of the healer, washing and anointing, laying on of hands, prayer — sometimes in tongues — confession of sins, singing praises to God, and meditation. The eucharist is sometimes celebrated at healing services. It is theorized that the latent faith and desire for wholeness on the part of the ill person are awakened by the healer in the healing context, and linked with the saving and healing power of God who works through persons with special gifts. It still constitutes a frontier for critical examination in order to assess more fully its distortions and excesses, as well as its achievements and potential for being incorporated into other models and practices of healing in the church.

b. Pastoral counseling and pastoral psychotherapy. With roots in the guidance of penitents in the Middle Ages, this approach has evolved in its modern form through dialogue primarily with the psychologies of Freud, Jung, Rogers, Erikson, Berne and, more recently, with some of the family systems perspectives delineated by Satir, Ackerman, Bowen, Minuchin, and others. This dialogue has allowed the pastoral care and counseling movement to recapture its classical understanding that the body, mind, spirit, and environment are dynamically related and that for healing to occur it must engage the depths of the personality and its situation in the world. These perspectives make it clear, once again, that healing involves a liberation from bondage to forces which work in spite of conscious, willful, or rational intentions. The pastoral counseling movement has thus rediscovered that healing involves a new relation to oneself, to one's neighbor, and to God. In relation to self, one is enabled to overcome crippling dependencies and counterproductive strategies of living, to be released from destructive negative emotions, to find a sense of purpose and direction, to experience the harmonious working of one's personal aspirations and natural instincts, to be reconciled to one's limitations, and to be aware of one's continuity with and participation in the human race and its enterprises. In relation to one's neighbor, egocentricity is abated, compassion and empathy increased, one's behaviors become less dominated by anxiety, fear, and hostility, and a growing capacity for cooperation and collaboration result. Differences of opinion and conflict are regarded as opportunities for enrichment. One is better able to balance giving and receiving, work and pleasure, the conscious and the unconscious, the personal and the social. In relation to God, one experiences acceptance rather than punishment, rejection, or indifference. An awareness of God's continual providence may emerge, as well as a sense of being called or drawn to new patterns of living and new forms of work. An inner freedom in relation to God predominates, which eventuates in a spontaneous confidence and impulse to worship joyfully. One begins to identify with God's compassion for all of the living and to see the world in inclusive rather than chauvinistic terms. Since the healing of one's relationship with God often involves a radical restructuring of one's concepts of God, one becomes more tolerant of other religious perspectives, and capable of being influenced by them without losing one's own rootedness.

11. The Role of the Caregiver in Healing. The pastoral caregiver, counselor, or therapist is not the healer, but is the one who takes the major responsibility for creating the conditions by which healing may occur in the special relationship between the pastoral healer and those seeking assistance. The relationship of openness, trust, mutual exploration and learning, acceptance and establishment of limits between the parties allows the depths of the predicament and the latent impulses toward healing in the parishioner, or the parishioner's milieu, to become apparent and to effect a healing process. Sometimes the caregiver helps families or groups restructure their relationships in such a way that the conditions for health are more optimal, and helps interpret the religious dimensions of the disease and healing processes. This interpretation generally affirms that the pastoral helper represents or reflects God's incarnational presence in the sufferings of the world and points to God's saving and renewing work in the structures of this world. Religious interpretation, in addition, involves the difficult assignment of helping parishioners discover how internalized theologies and religious practices contribute to attitudes and behaviors which maintain their illnesses. The healing process therefore often involves considerable theological reworking at the dynamic level of the personality.

12. Future Directions in Modes of Healing. One frontier confronting the church is the need to bring together both modes of healing, addressing one another at both the conceptual and practical levels. In current practice, they tend to reflect the sacred/secular split so endemic in the modern world, and operate out of worldviews which do not tend fully enough to healing in all the dimensions of human experience. The charismatic- spiritual mode tends to neglect the emotional, cognitive, and relational dimensions of experience, while emphasizing the physical and the spiritual. It emphasizes continuity with historic theological interpretations and is in tension with modern viewpoints.

The pastoral-psychotherapeutic mode minimizes the spiritual and bodily in favor of the emotional, cognitive, and relational dimensions of experience. It is more comfortable with contemporary worldviews, and sometimes appears to be in tension with historic Christian views.

Another frontier is the need to develop models of healing which bring the social, political, economic, and ecological dimensions of health and healing into dialogue with the spiritual, emotional, and physical. Neither the charismatic-sacramental nor the pastoral-psychotherapeutic approaches have transcended their foundations in individual psychology and Western bourgeois culture.

In addition, there is a need for pastoral theological interpretations of healing to incorporate perspectives and practices from Native American, Asian, African, and Spiritualistic sources. Rather than being seen as superstitious and primitive, these powerful orientations may enable us to further regain the wholism of our early Judaic and Christian heritage and to more fully witness to the saving power of God in the world.

Bibliography. F. Capra, *The Turning Point: Science, Society, and The Rising Culture* (1982). W. A. Clebsch and C. R. Jaekle, *Pastoral Care in Historical Perspectives: An Essay with Exhibits,* (1964). S. Hiltner, *Religion and Health* (1943); *Preface to Pastoral Theology* (1958). M. T. Kelsey, *Healing and Christianity in Ancient Thought and Modern Times* (1973). J. N. Lapsley, Jr., *Salvation and Health: The Interlocking Processes of Life* (1972). A. Weil, *Health and Healing: Understanding Conventional and Alternative Medicine* (1983). World Council of Churches, "Healing and Sharing Life in Community," Issue Paper, 4 (1983).

L. K. GRAHAM

FAITH HEALING; HEALTH AND ILLNESS; MENTAL HEALTH AND ILLNESS; RELIGION AND HEALTH MOVEMENT; SALVATION, HEALING, AND HEALTH; SICK AND DYING, JEWISH CARE OF; SICK, PASTORAL CARE OF. *See also* PATIENCE/PATIENTHOOD; PROVIDENCE, DOCTRINE OF, AND PASTORAL CARE; PSYCHIATRY AND PASTORAL CARE; RELIGION AND PSYCHOTHERAPY. *Compare* CHIROPRACTIC HEALING; EXORCISM; OSTEOPATHIC HEALING.

HEALING, CHIROPRACTIC AND OSTEOPATHIC. *See* CHIROPRACTIC HEALING; OSTEOPATHIC HEALING.

HEALING RITES AND RITUALS. *See* FAITH HEALING; HEALING. *See also* CHARISMATIC PASTORAL CARE; RITUAL AND PASTORAL CARE.

HEALING AND SALVATION. *See* SALVATION, HEALING, AND HEALTH, THEOLOGY OF.

HEALING OF MEMORIES. This term as used by its adherents refers to the prayerful process whereby the presence of Jesus Christ is symbolically introduced into a person's painful memory by one who functions as the intervenor. The counselee is encouraged to relive the painful memory or set of memories in as much vivid detail as is possible, in order that the particular memory may be reconstructed in a positive way.

Although many practitioners use the method, five writers have provided the primary descriptive literature. (1) Michael Scanlon (1974) focuses on the inner healing

brought about by prayer. (2) Dennis and Matthew Linn (1978) describe inner healing as the process in which they "take the hand of Jesus and lead Him back to a hurt" that the person does not want to see. The "healing of a memory drains out our old fears and feelings and pours in Christ's feelings." (3) Theodore Dobson stresses the presence of Jesus in the life of the person even at the time of the painful memory, and notes that the healing of memories rests upon the promise that time need not be a barrier for healing deep hurts of the past. (4) For Francis MacNutt (1979) inner healing involves "walking back in time with Jesus" in order to effect healing. The basic idea is that Jesus, "the same yesterday, today and forever," will "fill with his love all those places that were so empty for so long, once they have been healed and drained of the poison of past hurts and resentments." (5) Ruth Carter Stapleton (1977) focuses upon the "little child within us" who hurts, whom we have rejected, who failed to receive healthy love or was neglected. "That little child within us must harken to the healing love of Jesus Christ."

Bibliography. T. E. Dobson, *Inner Healing: God's Great Assurance* (1978). D. and M. Linn. *Healing Life's Hurts: Healing Memories Through Five Stages of Forgiveness* (1978). F. MacNutt, *Healing* (1974); *The Power to Heal* (1979). M. Scanlon, *Inner Healing* (1974). R. C. Stapleton, *The Gift of Inner Healing* (1977).

D. GUERNSEY

HEALING; MEMORY; PERSONAL STORY, SYMBOL, AND MYTH IN PASTORAL CARE. *See also* EVANGELICAL PASTORAL CARE; MEDITATION; TIME/TIME SENSE. *Compare* FORGIVENESS; PASTORAL COUNSELING; REMINISCENCE THERAPY; REPENTANCE AND CONFESSION.

HEALING OF RELATIONSHIPS. *See* COMMUNION/EUCHARIST; FORGIVENESS; PENANCE; RECONCILING.

HEALTH, MENTAL. *See* MENTAL HEALTH AND ILLNESS.

HEALTH AND ILLNESS. Health and illness are not the discrete, reciprocal, precisely, and physiologically defined categories commonly supposed, any more than is the distinction between mental and physical health (or illness). It is useful to distinguish between "unwellness" (the subjective experience of the individual), "patienthood" (a social role), and "disease" (the medically identifiable disorder). One or two of these conditions may be present without the other(s). "Disease" as a static condition is challenged by holistic, organismic, functional thinking, which understands "symptoms" as coping, conflict-solving strategies, thus blurring the distinction between health and illness. Health can be regarded as a set of positive attributes, not just the absence of illness. The distinction between illness and other categories of deviation, such as crime, immorality, or character flaw, depends on changing historical, cultural, and philosophical influences. So, too, with the understanding of the relation between health (as a medical goal) and salvation (as a pastoral goal); linguistically speaking, do the two terms refer to discrete, related, or identical processes?

1. **Unwellness, Patienthood, Disease.** If one feels unwell, one may be prompted to seek help from an expert for diagnostic study and possible remedial intervention. If this help is sought from a medical expert, one assumes temporarily and provisionally the role of patient, and depending on the diagnostic outcome, the expert may legitimize the unwell person's claim to patienthood, which may involve exemptions from certain duties and perhaps a right to certain benefits or ministrations.

In professional medical perspective the presenting subjective unwellness is studied in technical terms, such as disease, injury, defect, lesion, wound, disorder, dysfunction, ailment, malady, and is addressed by an intricate conceptual apparatus that dwells on symptoms, signs, processes, basic and proximate causes, precipitating conditions, stress points and stress reactions, predispositions, the time sequence in which symptoms and signs arise, and a host of other considerations that derive from medicine's basic and applied sciences and its lore of pragmatic knowledge. A disease or pathogenic process can be present without symptoms; the person is not a patient though diseased. Complaints may be presented without evidence of any known disease; this may lead to a physician giving the patient a "clean bill of health" and questioning his or her claim to patienthood.

2. **Physical-Mental Dualism.** Ages of dualistic thought have yielded a conventional distinction between physical and mental (often called "emotional") illness, and a parallel distinction for health. In this framework one can be physically ill and mentally healthy, and vice versa. Unfortunately, the complaints about feelings of unwellness that drive people to the medical profession are frequently so vague or so complex that the apparent neatness of this convention is not viable. Hence, old dualistic premises have given way to newer organismic, wholistic, and process philosophies of medicine, and to multiperspectival or multidisciplinary approaches to illness and health. Nosologies are no longer based on the ideal of physicalistic reduction; psychological and social causes (primary, secondary, or precipitating) are now envisaged as viable explanations of known diseases and states of unwellness.

In pastoral encounters with unwellness or disease a similar set of philosophical assumptions appears to operate. Under religious aegis the classical body-mind dualism had long ago been amplified into a tripartite division of body, mind, and soul (or spirit), each conceived as a distinct entity and often ranked in a hierarchical order of importance. This scheme is equally liable to break down in the face of the presented complaints, the desired pastoral ministrations, and the complexity of subjective experience and objective reality. Pastoral thought too has moved to wholistic, organismic, and process assumptions and has become familiar and comfortable with multi-disciplinary approaches.

3. **Pastors and Suffering.** Strictly speaking, pastors do not deal directly with disease (which is to be defined medically) or with patienthood (which is to be certified medically), but they are often forced to deal with subjective states of unwellness, and must frequently address the life situation of people medically verified as patients. The latter are then the pastor's subjects of concern and care — as persons, as people in need of special attention or support, as sufferers, as afflicted individuals, or as "children of God." In a word, pastors represent a profession that does something to suffering by placing it in a unique perspective that addresses its omnipresence, its possible meanings, its roles in life, its impact on people's integrity, its ultimate origins, and its ultimate implications.

Such a pastoral-theological focus on suffering entails some redefinition of the terms *health* and *illness* and introduces concepts of a special kind: salvation and sin, hope and despair, trust and distrust, belief in benevolence or malevolence, doom and rescue, embeddedness and alienation, faith and disgust, acceptance and rebellion, creatureliness and arrogance. In cases of medically certified severe or terminal illness the patient may have to come to terms with dying and death, with concerns for his or her loved ones or dependents, and a host of other feelings and cares that in pastoral perspective are part and parcel of the human contingency and should ideally be on everybody's agenda. In other cases the presented suffering has no medical grounds and involves no risk of life but consists in moral conundrums or compunctions, problems of loyalty or fidelity, puzzlement about one's lot, anger or disenchantment about actual or threatened losses, and confusions about the demands of faith that round off to a global idea of evil, misfortune, or unwelcome fate that elicits metaphorical allusions to sickness, pain, or anguish (e.g., Kierkegaard's "sickness unto death").

4. **Psychiatry and Suffering.** The expanded reach of psychologically oriented psychiatry since psychoanalysis (as distinguished from a dogmatically physicalist psychiatry in which all mental aberrations are declared to be brain disorders) has spawned a new terminology, for example, mental disorder, emotional illness, stress reaction, adjustment failure, internal conflict, and personality defect. In the course of several decades the key phrases used in psychiatric classification systems have moved from *disease,* via *reaction,* to *disorder* as the latest all-encompassing substantive noun, preceded by adjectival qualifications. This terminological progression is in part responsive to the increasing multiplicity of formulated complaints for which people seek psychiatric help. Many of these complaints are not of aches and pains, physiological malfunctions, or bodily changes, but come close to what pastors are compelled to respond to: deviant or maladaptive behavior; problems of attachment and loss; states of anxiety, guilt feelings, or shame; conditions of profound loneliness, sadness, or apprehension; problems of sexual identity; and immoral or illegal acts. The scope of what is covered today by the term *mental illness* is much larger than it was a century ago, and the theoretical models used to explain it and alleviate the suffering it imposes have multiplied, more so in the psychological and social than in the organic-medical direction.

5. **Disease as Coping, Life-Maximizing Process.** These historical developments of professions and their uses by the population pose an intriguing quasi-Platonic question: Is mental disorder (now used as an encompassing term) one or many? Many subsidiary questions follow. If the answer is one, is the apparent diversity of forms (subjective complaints and behavioral features) due to the diversity of individuals — each mentally ill person being a unique specimen of a unitary basic flaw? If the

answer is *many,* are there categorical units of form that can be described, conceptualized, and clearly distinguished from other units? If so, by what criteria? And what discipline or profession will offer the basic conceptions? Does reality in the naturalistic and empirical sense offer some clues, or is the grouping bound to be an artificial one, that is, the product of some purely theoretical scheme?

Though the answers given to these questions vary widely and have given rise to very different schools of thought (and practice), there are nevertheless some leading ideas that have taken root in many of the so-called helping professions and that constitute a kind of ecumenical agreement. Notably, organismic thinkers have convincingly argued that human beings are not stable entities with fixed characteristics, not substances or mechanical contraptions, but versatile, adaptive, plastic, and self-regulating organisms equipped with a multitude of coping devices by which they meet impinging external and internal changes and maintain their integrity. Their structures and functions influence each other. Process thinkers have argued that becoming overrules being, and that people (as well as the universe) are constantly engaged in processes of transformation, in which all parts influence all wholes, and vice versa. Everything is in evolution. Dynamic thought has argued that people are bundles of energy, constantly absorbing, transforming, and transmitting dynamic pulsations; and that the vital processes of life — from vegetative to ideational orders — are better seen as plays of force-and-counterforce than as linear events. Moreover, dynamic thought gives much weight to unconscious processes, to perpetual strivings for satisfaction, to the roles of love and hate in all covert and overt behavior, and to the presence of internal conflicts in many subjective complaints and behavioral aberrations. And all three orientations appear to agree with James's principle of pluralism, which holds that the important things in life are not to be reduced to simple cause-and-effect connections but beg for being considered in terms of multiple perspectives, multiple causes, and multiple attempts at melioration.

Thus, today, clinicians and researchers feel free to consider multi-generational family dynamics as a possible factor in cancer proneness; to consider many so-called accidents as being unconsciously "arranged" by the victims; to link certain known diseases to lifestyles, dietary habits, and insufficient physical exercise; and even to see many prevalent symptoms of a seemingly somatic kind themselves as ways of coping with stress or as boomerang effects of coping efforts. In psychodynamic perspective many forms of suffering can be seen as attempts made by the person to solve a conflict, to minimize its psychic duress, to salvage as much as possible of comfort and satisfaction of basic needs, and to ward off a yet worse condition that always lurks around the corner, namely, eventual death. The last motif is of great importance and should be given considerable weight, because all individual life is by definition contingent and fragile — it moves always and inevitably toward its own demise. This fact has been conceptualized by Freud in the death-drive, in which it is given an impetus of its own that is perpetually present and operative, counteracted by the forces that seek to maintain life as long and with as much well-being as possible.

6. Reclassifying Mental Disorder. Given these foundational constructs (which round off to an elementary nosology or philosophy of illness and disorder), it might be possible to reconceptualize the broad scope of mental disorder, including proneness or reactions to physical illness, and even a great deal of general human distress, as ways of coping with upsetting or disequilibrating life events and conditions. Since all helping professionals do their work under a sense of urgency, they begin by provisionally ranking or grading any disorder that comes their way: they typically judge the presented condition as "mild," "moderate," or "severe,' by whatever criteria. Such a coarse quantitative grouping makes much practical sense and could be used as zones on a larger continuum that stretches from health and normal well-being at one pole to death at the other pole. So approached, health can be soberly and realistically envisaged as covering a span that includes the ordinary portion of common human unhappiness, the little neuroticisms of everyday life, and a variety of common temporary upsets and stresses, and is characterized by the use of fairly effective, expedient, and psychologically or socially inexpensive coping devices that keep the person equilibrated under changing outer and inner conditions, and yield the person a workable amount of satisfaction. The ratio of energetic and nutrient supplies that come into the organism and the energies expended on the coping maneuvers are favorable: gratifications are obtained at a normal, moderate cost, and without serious side effects; and in cases of more glorious health the potential for further growth, productivity, and creativity is even enhanced.

Seen from this end of the continuum and keeping in mind the other end, at which life gives way to death, all disorder is a more or less drastic form of dyscontrol, in which efforts at self-regulation and organismic equilibration entail an increasingly higher cost in energy, have increasingly risky side effects, yield steadily diminishing gratifications, and entail ever more profound regressions. The ratio of life force to death force (or, less metaphysically formulated, of libidinal to aggressive engagements) becomes ever more unfavorable, until the organism gives up, as it may do in suicide or by extreme exhaustion.

Just such a nosology has been proposed by Menninger, Mayman, and Pruyser in *The Vital Balance* (1963). It describes five orders of dyscontrol beyond the healthy zone of effective self-regulation through the ordinary coping devices of everyday living, by focusing on the way in which containment and control of aggression (self- or other-directed) is attempted, but in progressively more costly, risky, regressive, haphazard, desperate, and ineffectual ways.

The first order of dyscontrol or dysfunction comprises what is commonly called "nervousness" and consists essentially in the overuse of normal coping devices, such as hypersuppression, hyperrepression, hypervigilance, hyperemotionalism, hyperkinesis, hyperintellection, hypercompensation, and somatization of worries into minor somatic and sexual dysfunctions, but all without detectable regression and without grossly diminished reality contact.

In the second order of dyscontrol the upsurge of aggressive feelings leads to rather drastic control attempts by blocking their discharge from awareness (e.g., in fainting, sleepwalking, phobias); by displacing the discharge to the body (e.g., by self-imposed asceticism, self-mutilation, intoxication, or developing intractable so-called "functional" physical illnesses); by symbolic or magical changes of the aggressive discharge (e.g., in compulsions, rituals, obsessions, sexual perversions); or by building a once-attempted emergency coping device into a character trait or habit, whether or not it fits the occasion (e.g., leading to various personality deformities of a schizoid, fraudulent, infantile, narcissistic, or addictive kind). In all these cases the condition is likely to come to public notice and entails interferences with work, productivity, and reality testing; it causes friction in social relations and causes unhappiness by yielding rather meager gratifications, typically dire enough to cause these persons to seek help, or to be referred for help by others.

In the third order of dyscontrol the aroused aggression can no longer be contained but leaks out with only minimal disguise—sometimes in episodic fashion, which suggests abrupt and rather gross ego failure followed by spontaneous recapturing of control, sometimes in chronic or habitual fashion. The first subgroup comprises sudden outbursts of violence, vandalism, seizures, or binges, which appear to stand for releases of pent-up aggressive impulses (often without rational target), often in a diminished or altered state of consciousness and followed by amnesia for the episode. In other cases the violence is somewhat more directed, as in homicidal assaultiveness, or leads to states of demoralization, delirium, or overexcited manic bouts. The second subgroup comprises chronic and repetitive aggressive behavior, overt rebelliousness, hooliganism, and habitual engagement in vice and crime, which are likely to make these persons into public enemies that even members of the helping professions tend to reject. During these aggressive outbursts reality is at least momentarily flouted, and grossly so, and foresight is very poor; yet at other moments considerable shrewdness, planning ability, realism, and even amiability are displayed.

The fourth order of dysfunction comprises extreme forms of disorganization, regression, and reality repudiation commonly encountered in so-called psychotic or dereistic states, in which destructive forces come close to demolishing these persons from within, thwarting their contact with reality; arousing uncontrollable primitive fantasies; displacing rational thought by animistic, magical, or hypersymbolic speculations; tumbling them into uncontrollable and overwhelming moods of sadness, guiltiness, wickedness, or unwarranted euphoria; disorganizing their motoric behavior; making them confused, bewildered, and disoriented; and often prompting delusional preoccupations with cosmic schemes, profound suspiciousness (as in paranoia), grandiosity, or ideas of being persecuted or sacrificed. Obviously, the libidinal gratifications in these cases are minimal and sometimes barely keep these persons alive; and the boomerang effects of their maneuvers such as social withdrawal, relinquishing reality adherence, and seeking refuge in regression, together with the intense panic to which they feel close, have many secondary disorganizing effects. Many of these states are, however, reversible and sometimes lead to a kind of rebirth that can entail great subsequent productivity, insight, sensitivity to others, and overall well-being.

The fifth order of dyscontrol comprises the greatest extremity of exhaustion and self-destructiveness, and includes suicide. Menninger sees the latter as the outcome of a strong wish to die, to kill, and be killed, that is, as being overwhelmed by all the salient forms of aggression that enlist some remaining ego function to plan and execute the terminal act. But in other cases the approach to death is a passive one, occurring by "giving up" and "shutting off" one or more of the vital processes.

This nosology combines psychodynamic and psychoeconomic considerations and takes a wholistic view of the interactions of physical, mental, social, and moral processes. It allows for mental expression of somatic events and for the somatizing of mental events. It takes subjective complaints just as seriously as objective signs and behavioral symptoms. It refers explicitly and forthrightly to the contingency of the human condition (what theologians would call creatureliness) by postulating a death-drive whose stirrings form a fundamental tone in the harmonic series of life. It allows for fluid transitions between intensities and forms of disorders, and indeed between health and illness, including the momentary or situational regressions and lapses that even the most healthy persons may undergo.

7. **Redefining Health.** There is no consensus on descriptions and definitions of health. Ideal or optimal definitions would cover a narrower span than statistical definitions based on "normalcy" in the commonsense meaning of that term (i.e., "not recognizably sick"). Moreover, historical and culturally determined changes in the span of conditions covered by the term illness affect the span of what is called health, for example, conditions formerly seen as character flaws or moral weakness may come to be seen as forms of mental illness, thus enlarging the latter rubric. It should be kept in mind, however, that designating any condition as illness does not cancel the viability of placing that condition in another perspective as well. A condition can be at once illness, crime, sinfulness, and immorality.

Convinced that mental health is more than the absence of mental illness, Jahoda has tried to formulate criteria for "positive mental health": active adjustment, a personality that is integrated, undistorted perception. A widely held view of health defines it negatively, as absence of impairment of structure and function. Others define health as effective coping with expectable stresses, and not a few theorists equate health with self-actualization. Ego psychologists envisage different levels of health by subjecting the concept of health to a developmental point of view and ranking the qualities of various ego functions.

Bibliography. M. Jahoda, *Current Concepts of Positive Mental Health* (1958). J. Loevinger, "The Meaning and Measurement of Ego Development," *American Psychologist,* 21 (1966), 195–206. K. Menninger, M. Mayman, and P. Pruyser, *The Vital Balance* (1963). K. A. Menninger, *Man Against Himself* (1938).

R. L. Numbers and D. W. Amundsen, eds., *Caring and Curing: Health and Medicine in the Western Religious Traditions* (1986).

P. W. PRUYSER

MENTAL HEALTH AND ILLNESS; RELIGION AND HEALTH; SALVATION, HEALING, AND HEALTH; SIN AND SICKNESS. *See also* EVALUATION AND DIAGNOSIS; MIND-BODY RELATIONSHIP; PAIN; PSYCHOSOMATIC ILLNESS; SUFFERING. *Compare* FAITH HEALING; HEALING; HEALTH CARE DELIVERY; SICK, PASTORAL CARE OF; SICK AND DYING, JEWISH CARE OF; WHOLISTIC HEALTH CARE.

HEALTH AND RELIGION. *See* SALVATION, HEALING, AND HEALTH. *See also* FAITH HEALING; HEALTH AND ILLNESS; RELIGION AND HEALTH MOVEMENT.

HEALTH AND SALVATION. *See* SALVATION, HEALING AND HEALTH.

HEALTH CARE DELIVERY. The delivery of a range of health services to patients in the home, medical office, hospital, extended and specialty care facilities.

1. The Patient. A patient may be described as an individual who seeks help with a medical symptom or distress. Help-seeking behavior varies according to social class, ethnic group membership, and religious persuasion. Members of the upper classes are more likely to seek medical attention than members of the lower classes; members of advanced cultures are more likely to seek help than those of cultures which are primitive and fatalistic; and there is religious diversity: there is a greater probability, for instance, that Jews and Episcopalians will seek help than Christian Scientists or Catholics (Leigh and Reiser, 1980).

Upon contact with service providers, the patient is expected to assume the role of patient, which includes a willingness to reveal intimate information, to submit to physical exam and intrusive tests, and to conform to treatment regimens. Though everyone resists this role to some degree, the non-compliant or uncooperative patient may be treated with impatience or disbelief (Leigh and Reiser, 1980).

The patient seeks relief of distress and expects health providers to assuage fears associated with the distress. Providers on the other hand, operating from a medical model, focus first on underlying causes, with the view that relief of distress may follow later (Leigh and Reiser, 1980). Since determination of cause can be a lengthy process, there is often some incongruity between the patient's emotional needs and desires and the medical provider's responses. Moreover, when diagnostic information becomes available, it may not be shared with the patient. "Many studies indicate there is a higher level of dissatisfaction on the part of patients about the amount of information physicians provide than about any other aspect of medical care" (Leigh and Reiser, 1980, p. 26).

Once cause is determined, patients may be faced with loss of function, freedom, self-image, or life itself. The counselor in the health delivery setting witnesses the expression — or denial — of these realities.

2. Onset of Illness. Some patients minimize the cues the body sends about disease and/or distress. Because symptoms can be and often are transient, their passing may suggest spontaneous cure. Patient compliance is particularly difficult to achieve with diseases which are silent killers, such as tuberculosis (TB) and hypertension. Primitive, pseudo-religious notions that illness constitutes retribution, punishment, or fate may deter others from seeking treatment.

But for most, sooner or later treatment is sought. Whether an illness is catastrophic or not, it is emotionally charged with the universally frightening realm of the *unknown*. For perhaps the first time in their lives, patients do not have the *control* they thought they had over their body and, by extension, their life; they encounter their own mortality.

Illness intrudes into the body and lifestyle of patients, bringing mental and often physical pain, expense, inconvenience, and uncertainty. When hospitalization is required, patients experience isolation and depersonalization as well. Illness means loss of health, freedom, and the familiarity of family, home, possessions, and regular work and activities.

3. Family. Similar emotions afflict families, who also experience loss and feelings of helplessness. In contrast, family members may feel (but may not attempt to hide) relief or even pleasure that pain and punishment have come to one they dislike. There may also be mixed emotions with feelings of guilt. Especially in life-threatening illness, though potentially in any illness, old, unfinished emotional business is bound to be tapped by the crisis in the patient and family alike. Since participants may not be fully aware of their feelings or may feel anxious in expressing them, counseling care should be made available to families as well as patients. Deliverers of health care should encourage the expression of feelings, both positive and negative, and provide opportunities for doing so.

4. Medical Staff. Staff in health care facilities also react emotionally to illness. In the best of circumstances, patients in pain are troubled, disoriented by new regimens, feel deprived by loss of the old, anxious to go home, frightened or angry, and can be cantankerous. Some medical and hospital units, like surgical units where most patients survive, are easier to face than others. But certain assignments are unendingly stressful and heartrending, because hope is at a premium and frequently dashed; these include cancer services, renal dialysis units, intensive care, rehabilitation, burn units, and sometimes pediatric and emergency care centers.

Clinicians need both thin and thick skins. An endless cycle of sick and often miserable people pass through the medical setting. It is draining, demoralizing, and ultimately disorienting; providers find it difficult to generate or hold a balanced view of life. However, being sensitive and understanding is an essential of good health care. Some hospitals and medical centers address staff "burnout" through rotation of assignments, discussion groups, training, bonus payments, and shorter work weeks.

This problem is compounded by rapid changes which have occurred over the past twenty years in health delivery settings. Patients, far from expressing gratitude, are increasingly litigious. Mechanization has increased the technical level of expertise required of staff and has placed machines in the way of direct patient care, reducing rewards of providing service. Regulation has increased the cost of service and accountability of providers to the degree that a correct and thorough chart note may seem as important to the staff as the medical intervention itself. Hospital and clinic administrators, saddled with increased costs in every area and reduced third party payments, are concerned with cost savings, productivity standards, and other components of the "bottom line." Clinical staff, focused on quality care, see administration as only concerned with profit.

5. **Public Sector Health Care.** Public health is provided to indigents and others lacking resources by the community for the protection of the community. Originally intended to protect the populace from contagion (e.g., hepatitis, TB), public health services have expanded in most major cities and county seats to include the full range of inpatient and outpatient departments, provided through civil service or, increasingly, by contracts to private providers. Services are delivered on an ability-to-pay basis and reach the poor, the unemployed, and the underemployed.

Controlled by tax dollars, public sector services may be inadequate or understaffed, resulting in long waiting lists for appointments, long waits at the time of appointments, loss of charts in labyrinthine service centers, cursory examinations, impaired quality of services, lack of translating services, poor follow-up, insensitivity to feelings, and a host of other problems. While these may also occur in the private sector, the singular distinction is that in private service centers the patient has a choice and a voice.

6. **The Counselor.** It behooves the counselor to be familiar with medical conditions, treatment and prognosis so as to realistically appraise his or her role. The counselor may be needed to soothe the spirit through a crisis in one case, to prepare the patient and family for a chronic lifestyle change in another, or to help the patient and family accept an inevitable death in a third. The counselor may see signs of clinician burnout and can be of help. With such information, the counselor may determine where the need is greatest and, understanding the unique human problems of patients under various medical circumstances, can provide understanding and support. The counselor may also effect humanization of patient treatment by bringing special needs to the attention of staff.

Bibliography. S. P. Kimball, *The Biopsychosocial Approach to the Patient* (1981). E. Kübler-Ross, *On Death and Dying* (1969). H. Leigh and M. F. Reiser, *The Patient: Biological, Psychological and Social Dimensions of Medical Practice* (1980). M. E. P. Seligman, *Helplessness* (1975). H. Selye, *The Stress of Life* (1956).

M. S. ROSENBERG

HEALTH AND ILLNESS; HOSPITALIZATION, EXPERIENCE OF; WHOLISTIC HEALTH CARE. *See also* ADVOCACY; POOR PERSONS; MENTAL HEALTH AND ILLNESS; PROPHETIC/PASTORAL TENSION IN MINISTRY; SOCIAL JUSTICE ISSUES IN PASTORAL CARE.

HEALTH CARE, WHOLISTIC. *See* WHOLISTIC HEALTH CARE.

HEART PATIENT. Cardiovascular disease is the number one killer in the U.S., claiming more lives than all other causes combined. The heart carries profound symbolic importance for humans as the citadel of affection and love; therefore, heart disease is a profound issue psychologically and spiritually as well as physically.

1. **Physical and Emotional Considerations.** The issue of pain control and its underlying causes is primary in patient care. Treatment in both acute and chronic patients focuses on cardiac stability and assisting the recovery process. Careful attention is given to preserving life and sustaining the physical resources of the patient. Sedation of the patient is for both physical and psychological reasons. The existential predicament and a repressed awareness of one's finitude underscore profound dependency needs within the patient; security and self-esteem are threatened. Confidence (trust) in one's body is challenged, and the needed "illusion of control" is overthrown.

2. **Pastoral Care Considerations.** *a. Acute phase.* At the acute stage a religio-suppressive approach is indicated (assurance, modest optimism, reassurance of God's presence and care); whereas a religio-expressive approach (catharsis, insight, interpretation) is appropriate as the patient's physical condition improves. The pastor must respect the patient's need of ego defenses, especially during the acute phase. As patients become more "body confident," they can more creatively deal with their experience/predicament. The psychological needs of human touch, emotional and spiritual support, and empathetic relationships are very important. The more subtly manifested spiritual needs of assurance and community are integral parts of the patient's needed support. In the acute phase of illness, relationship problems within the family may surface, giving the clergyperson an opportunity to observe and experience the dynamics of the family system. Active listening and religious ritual support is indicated rather than uncovering suppressed feelings.

b. Recovery. Following the acute phase is the second level of recovery, when the patient is moved from the intensive care unit to a general floor. Issues of lifestyle (stress, type A behavior, etc.) take on importance as recovery is linked with prevention of recurrence. Along with changes in eating, working, and other life habits, patients may be encouraged to reassess their lifestyles. Many patients experience some depression at this time.

c. Home based convalescence. This third phase provides opportunities of self-exploration for the patient when the minister takes the initiative in visiting following hospitalization. The focus of the relationship is to explore life habit changes and to be a potent ally as the patient encounters natural family resistance to any lasting significant changes in relationship patterns.

3. **Specific Goals for Pastoral Care of Heart Patients.**

(a) Initial pastoral support; use of role and religious resources; (b) Pastoral support of family; (c) Pastoral aid in the integration of the "being sick" experience, being especially sensitive to finitude issues; (d) Development of a plan of continual pastoral involvement with the patient in concert with the physician's plan: (i) Provide regular follow-up visits or introduce patient to a support group; (ii) Structure formal counseling for those who are depressed or anxiety-bound; (e) Periodic pastoral checkup for one year to determine pastoral care needs of patient.

Bibliography. G. W. Paterson, *The Cardiac Patient* (1978); "Pastoral Care of the Coronary Patient and Family," *J. of Pastoral Care*, 39, 249–61.

J. B. ABBOTT

CRISIS MINISTRY; SICK AND DYING, JEWISH CARE OF; SICK, PASTORAL CARE OF. *See also* HEALING; HOSPITALIZATION, EXPERIENCE OF; PAIN; PATIENCE/PATIENTHOOD; RITUAL AND PASTORAL CARE; SUFFERING. *Compare* CANCER PATIENT; DYING, PASTORAL CARE OF; SURGICAL PATIENT.

HEAVEN AND HELL, BELIEF IN. In the Christian tradition, the conviction that God's ultimate purposes for humankind shall be realized either in a state of beatitude that involves an eternal enjoyment of the Divine Presence or in a condition of radical separation from God in the case of the sinner who freely refuses the grace of repentance.

Both at the level of theological doctrine and of personal piety there is a wide divergence among Christians as to how the biblical images of heaven (salvation) and hell (damnation) are to be interpreted. Historically, some Christians have believed in a literal place of reward or punishment for individuals immediately upon death (the particular judgment) or after a period of purification through suffering (the Roman Catholic doctrine of purgatory), and for all persons at the culmination of time (the last or general judgment). The notion of "limbo" as a state of happiness in which the deceased is nonetheless deprived of the full vision of God was adduced in the fourth century to handle the problem of the innocent who may have died before being baptized. By contrast, many contemporary Christian thinkers have found it more faithful simply to leave open the question of the exact nature, though not the certainty, of God's final fulfillment of human life and hopes, as well as the matter of whether it must be asserted as a matter of revelation that any human being ever has or ever will evade the infinite mercy of God.

While respecting this pluralism of interpretation, a pastoral perspective on the belief in heaven and hell can be guided by several theological and psychological considerations. (1) All eschatological assertions may be heard as both statements of the believer's understanding of God and as expressions of his or her own most profound desires, fears, and expectations. (2) The understanding of God predominant in Christian revelation is that God is the creator and supreme lover of humankind whose will is to save and whose will is inevitably fulfilled (Lk. 19:10). Personal beliefs in heaven and hell that are excessively characterized by themes of judgment, condemnation, and separation might well be determined more by personal dynamic factors than by the image of God disclosed in revelation. (3) The imagery of heaven most salient for individuals and communities may be a key to a pastoral understanding of "the heart's deepest yearning," those hopes that are foundational for serious religious life. (4) The belief in God's future may easily become individualized and privatized unless its corporate and ecclesial dimension is reasserted. Human solidarity in both sin and salvation is a central biblical insight. Pastorally this means that any discussion of heaven and hell must always be located in the context of the Christian community's redemptive mission in history.

J. McDARGH

ESCHATOLOGY AND PASTORAL CARE; FAITH/BELIEF; HOPE AND DESPAIR; RELIGIOUS LANGUAGE AND SYMBOLISM, PSYCHOLOGY OF. *See also* CROSS AND RESURRECTION; DEATH, MEANING OF; LIMBO; RELIGIOUS BEHAVIOR. *Compare* EVALUATION AND DIAGNOSIS, RELIGIOUS; NEAR-DEATH EXPERIENCE; SYMBOLISM/SYMBOLIZING.

HEBREW SCRIPTURES AND SACRED WRITINGS (Traditions and Theology of Care). *See* JEWISH CARE AND COUNSELING; JEWISH LITERATURE IN CARE AND COUNSELING.

HELL, BELIEF IN. *See* HEAVEN AND HELL, BELIEF IN.

HEREDITY. *See* PERSONALITY, BIOLOGICAL DIMENSIONS OF; GENETIC COUNSELING; PERSONALITY DEVELOPMENT, BIOLOGICAL AND SOCIALIZING INFLUENCES IN; SOCIOBIOLOGY.

HERMAS (second century). Former Roman slave, author of the widely used apocalyptic work, *The Shepherd,* which features, disjointedly and repetitively, moral teachings and a penitentiary sermon. Marked by a disinterest in theology and confused thinking on Christology, and held together by a simple piety, this work is nonetheless significant in several ways: It provides insight into the development of asceticism among Jewish Christians. With the tradition, it stresses penance as a means for the forgiveness of sins. Its new emphasis is the final possibility of penance and forgiveness for the new problem of post-baptismal sins in the face of an apparent delay of the parousia. Thus, it reflects a critical stage in the development of the ecclesial system of penance.

N. F. HAHN

EARLY CHURCH, PASTORAL CARE AND COUNSELING IN.

HERMENEUTICS. *See* BIBLE, PASTORAL USE AND INTERPRETATION OF; THEOLOGY AND PSYCHOLOGY.

HERPES. The common name given to genital herpes, an ulcerative or vesicular disease of the genitals caused by the herpes simplex virus, spread primarily by sexual contact. Its clinical course is often marked by stressful and painful exacerbations after periods of remission. Genital herpes should not be confused with diseases caused by other human herpes viruses: "cold sores," chickenpox, herpes zoster or "shingles," or infectious mononucleosis.

D. THOMAS

SEX EDUCATION; SUFFERING. *Compare* HANDICAP AND DISABILITY.

HETEROSEXUALITY. *See* SEXUALITY.

HEX. *See* MAGICAL THINKING; WEST INDIAN TRADITIONAL RELIGION, SOUL CARE IN; WITCHCRAFT.

HIGH BLOOD PRESSURE. *See* PSYCHOSOMATIC ILLNESS; STRESS.

HILLEL. Hillel the Elder lived from the end of the first century B.C.E. until ca. 9 C.E. and is generally recognized as being the greatest sage of the Second Temple period. He was the acknowledged leader of the community, the title "Elder" indicating his rank as being at the very head of communal leadership. Hillel was an outstanding personality, widely respected in all spheres. He was renowned for his humility, pursuit of peace, and patience; the Talmud is replete with episodes of his kindly, understanding, and accommodating manner, even in the most taxing situations.

Hillel's concern for the common individual is reflected in such items as his establishment of the *prozbul,* a document that served the interests of the poor, who would have had difficulty gaining loans since by biblical law all loans are abrogated on the sabbatical year. Hillel rooted his *prozbul* document in biblical verse, and thus was able both to maintain the biblical regulation and to address the plight of the common people.

In addition, Hillel is famous for his disputations on legal matters with Shamai. These schools argued on religious matters, and with few exceptions, the law always followed the opinion of Hillel.

Hillel is the author of many classic statements which express fundamentals of Jewish faith. An outstanding Talmudic scholar as well as an outstanding individual, Hillel's influence on Jewish thought and Jewish life remains intact to the present. In almost every Jewish community throughout the world, there is usually at least one institution which carries his illustrious name. His empathy and sensitivity are classic models of particular importance in the counseling situation.

R. P. BULKA

JEWISH CARE AND COUNSELING (History, Traditions, and Contemporary Issues); JEWISH LITERATURE IN CARE AND COUNSELING; SPIRITUAL MASTER AND GUIDES.

HILTNER, SEWARD (1909–84). American Presbyterian minister and pastoral theologian. A prolific writer who published at least ten books and over five hundred articles on pastoral care and pastoral theology, Hiltner served as executive secretary of the Council for Clinical Training of Theological Students (1935–38), executive secretary of Pastoral Services for the Federal Council of Churches (1938–50), professor of pastoral theology at the University of Chicago Divinity School (1950–61), and professor of pastoral theology at Princeton Theological Seminary (1961–80).

No pastoral theologian has had more influence than Hiltner on the development of pastoral care traditions in modern America. He helped to establish a style of counseling that attracted widespread interest. In his *Pastoral Counseling* (1949), Hiltner advocated an "eductive method" that would help the pastor distinguish moralistic exhortation and ineffectual advice from a style of counseling that drew on "the creative potentialities of the person needing help." Hiltner's method was similar to the client-centered methods of psychotherapy proposed by Carl Rogers, and Hiltner's book helped to introduce Rogerian themes to the American clergy. But Hiltner developed his ideas independently and always retained a sensitivity to the need for ethical clarification and pastoral identity on the part of the pastoral counselor. In later years, he emphasized the ecclesial setting for pastoral counseling and the importance of the pastor's "precounseling" relationships in the parish. He also discouraged the assumption that pastoral counseling and pastoral care were synonymous.

Always seeking a basic theory of ministry and of pastoral care, Hiltner published a *Preface to Pastoral Theology* (1958), in which he argued that the task of pastoral theology was a disciplined inquiry into the healing, sustaining, and guiding activities of the minister and the church. He distinguished three overarching "perspectives" on pastoral activity — shepherding, communicating, and organizing — and insisted that the pastoral theologian was to find, within the shepherding activities of healing, sustaining, and guiding, a theological wisdom that could illumine all the church's functions and its theological doctrines. He believed that a pastoral counselor's struggle with a marriage problem or a family conflict could provide new insight into the gospel — an insight perhaps available through no other source.

Convinced of the power of social and cultural pressures to shape human perceptions, Hiltner made several cultural studies of pastoral issues. He helped stimulate interest in the problems of older people, the pastoral implications of the Kinsey Report on sexual behavior, and ministry to alcoholics. He also served on the National Committee for Mental Hygiene and urged churches to support the mental health movement.

As a clinical student of Anton Boisen and an early proponent of Clinical Pastoral Education (CPE), Hiltner worked closely with the Council for Clinical Training of Theological Students, always with the aim that CPE should be understood as a part of pastoral and theological training, not as a substitute for it or a general training in counseling methods. He also labored to define the chaplaincy, constructing, in alliance with Russell Dicks, the first statement of standards for chaplains in hospitals and other institutions.

As a teacher, he was among the first to combine the use of case histories, which he learned from Anton Boisen, with close attention to verbatim transcripts of pastoral conversations.

He served as the consultant for the journal *Pastoral Psychology,* and his many articles in that journal helped to ensure his influence among American clergy who were especially interested in pastoral care and counseling.

E. B. HOLIFIELD

HISTORY OF PROTESTANT PASTORAL CARE (United States); PASTORAL CARE MOVEMENT; PASTORAL THEOLOGY, PROTESTANT; PSYCHOLOGY IN AMERICAN RELIGION; THEOLOGICAL EDUCATION AND THE PASTORAL CARE MOVEMENT, PROTESTANT; THEOLOGY AND PSYCHOLOGY. *Compare* EMPIRICAL *or* PROCESS THEOLOGY, AND PASTORAL CARE; PRAGMATISM AND PASTORAL CARE.

HINDU SOUL CARE. *See* PSYCHOLOGY, EASTERN; PSYCHOLOGY AND PSYCHOTHERAPY (East-West Comparison).

HISPANIC AMERICAN PASTORAL CARE. The care given to Americans of Spanish descent by pastors and priests. Hispanics are a fast growing minority in the U.S., and offer a heterogeneous mosaic of multiethnic and multicultural dimensions. They are subject to a number of stressors which impinge upon their well-being and functioning, but they tend to underutilize the resources available to them in the mental health field. Unique features of Hispanic culture call for alternative strategies for pastoral care and counseling. Traditional approaches geared to middle-class Anglos may fail to address the needs arising from such contingencies. An awareness of cross-cultural factors is essential to effective ministry to Hispanics.

1. **Population Characteristics.** *a. The Hispanic mosaic.* Hispanics represent a mosaic of varied dimensions, with Mexican-Americans (both immigrants and Chicanos), Puerto Ricans, Cubans, Central and South Americans saturating various regions of the U.S. The majority of Hispanics prefer to live in urban centers. Several major cities have been associated with particular Hispanic cultures: Los Angeles has a distinct Mexican-American presence; New York receives a Puerto Rican influx; Miami has become a Cuban haven; and in general, all major cities have distinct pockets of different nationalities which cluster and revolve around dynamic interplays of a cross-cultural nature. As an example, the Greater Los Angeles area has more than 600 Hispanic Protestant churches, representing more than 20 denominations.

b. Commonalities and heterogeneity. Within this multiplicity of national groupings among Hispanics there are nonetheless a few common denominators. The Spanish language is one unifying factor. In spite of idiomatic and regional expressions and accents, Spanish serves as a common means for international communication among these persons. A second major factor, which has an impressive uniformity in the literature of social scientists who dedicate efforts to Hispanic issues, is the family. Although most writings are impressionistic, some empirical data has emerged regarding the structure and function of the Hispanic family which validates some stereotypes while discarding others. Widespread accounts of "typical" patterns include an authoritarian father and a submissive mother, with indulgent affection toward children and strict discipline for purposes of control. Sex roles appear to be more clearly delineated compared to Anglo patterns, although the rigidity of such roles has at times been exaggerated. Males appear to dominate their wives in situations in which adherence to tradition is stressed, while they also appear to overprotect their daughters and venerate their mothers, creating ambivalences in perceptions and relationships between the sexes. Respect for older members as well as for authority figures is expected.

The pastor or priest, in this context, enters the system as a respectable, dignified, reliable, and trustworthy figure from whom guidance and care is expected. In terms of values, importance is given in general to *"respeto, honor y dignidad"* (respect, honor, and dignity), and a "word of honor" appears to be as important as a written statement. Some sort of physical contact, such as an "abrazo" (hug) or handshake, is expected in a personalistic style of relating, greeting, and departing from one another. Verbal rather than written contacts are preferred, and "being there in person" takes precedence over impersonal phone contact or communication in written form. In time orientation, the "here and now" has often been cited as an adopted stance in the cultures of Hispanics, as compared to future orientations of the Anglos. Emotional expressiveness appears to be encouraged in both males and females, with suppression of negative feelings only in cases in which they could convey an idea of "weakness."

Heterogeneity also plays a major role in relationships among Hispanics. Several nationalities may have functional needs to merge when confronting oppression, and they may adopt common stances for survival purposes. Nevertheless, ethnic, racial, and national clusters are common, with pockets of given Hispanic groups practicing ethnocentrism. Factionalism, regionalism, and nationalism are part of the Hispanic scene, and discrimination and prejudice may be practiced among these peoples, expressing political, social, historical, economic, and religious barriers.

c. Stressors impinging upon Hispanics. Oppressing variables or stressors include (1) poor communication in English among older members, who are often natives from original Latin American or Hispanic cultures; (2) a poverty cycle — lower income, unemployment, depressed social status, deteriorated housing, and minimal political influence; (3) the survival of agrarian traits that are inadequate to the process of survival in technological settings; (4) seasonal migration in some cases, with the consequent uprootedness and displacement; and (5) acculturation to a society perceived as prejudiced, hostile, and rejecting those who are regarded as different.

2. **Special Needs and Caring Systems.** *a. Concrete services.* A great deal of pastoral care centers around basic needs of Hispanics related to socioeconomic conditions, lack of awareness of community resources, and poor ability to deal with several societal agencies. Such care involves aspects of social work, advocacy, translation, and even transportation of people who have to struggle with the immigration system, the welfare system, the social security system, the educational institutions, and the police.

b. Emotional problems in the family. Pastoral care involves the elucidation of problems that arise from contacts of the family with extrafamilial sources or societal agencies, cultural pressures upon its members, and contextual oppression. Intrafamilial stress due to intergenerational difficulties arising from uneven levels of acculturation and assimilation offer a challenge also. Problems include child management, adolescent acting-out, juvenile delinquency, and school related difficulties. At times, misunderstanding and misdiagnosing in school settings add to familial pressures, as parents experience a dissonance between their perceptions of their child and the school reports, especially in areas such as academic performance, intelligence level, and competitiveness. Single-parent families are not uncommon among parishioners, with burdened women who present multiple needs for support. Extended families offer unique problems of their own, with enmeshed boundaries, confused expectations, lack of differentiation, lack of personal space, and unclear roles and communication.

Pastoral care necessitates the knowledge of how such systems work and maintain unique homeostatic balance. In some cases, neglect and abuse arising from poor impulse control may engage the pastor in crisis intervention strategies. In extreme cases, suicidal gestures, surrounded with dramatic features which indicate intense styles of expression of despair, call for careful management and consultation with other professionals.

c. Wholistic perspectives. Pastoral care encounters a series of somatic complaints among Hispanics, with symptoms related to stress and anxiety (headaches, dizziness, chest pains, hyperventilation, fainting spells, etc.). Bodily preoccupations and pain syndromes appear as common complaints. "Nerves" and "dolor de cerebro" (literally "brain pain") appear to correlate with tension headaches and stress syndromes, and pastors may confront a mixture of physical, emotional and spiritual elements in such complaint systems. At times, the elucidation of depressive states from pain syndromes appears to be functionally impossible. In some extreme cases, seen in primitive responses born out of repressed anger, unacceptable feelings, or poor reality testing, the incidence of an "ataque" may occur. Such hysterical manifestation accompanied by dramatic gestures, agitation, crying, and fainting might be difficult to differentiate from temporal lobe epilepsy, as unaccustomed helpers may witness.

Operant behaviors may serve as negative attention-getting maneuvers to mobilize others around, disclaim responsibility for emotional expressiveness, or to elicit guilt feelings. Pseudo-hallucinations, auditory in nature, are reported in few cases. Being culturally syntonic in cases that stress a personal awareness of a divine call, such phenomena may prove difficult to elucidate among religious practitioners. Divine calls and special messages given in epiphanic fashion are not alien to Hispanics from Catholic backgrounds, and they are in some cases syntonic to charismatic movements among Protestant Hispanics.

In general, pastoral care involves working with uprooted people who suffer from feelings of separation from love objects, security, and who may experience a lack of belongingness in spite of being descendants of those who inhabited the land for more than three centuries. Alienation, helplessness, and despair due to stressors of socioeconomic, political, and cultural nature create a challenge that necessitates a wholistic approach in the care of people struggling for relevance, meaning, and participation in the American scene.

3. **Alternative Approaches.** *a. Underutilization of resources.* As social scientists have indicated (Padilla *et al.*, 1976), Hispanics are prone to suffer more than other ethnic groups from the stressors impinging upon them. Nevertheless, they underutilize the mental health resources available to them. Explanations for such findings are given in terms of discouraging institutional policies such as the geographical location of the providers, language barriers, culture-bound values held by helpers, and class-bound values as well. Ethnocentrism

and institutional racism may play a role in the failures reported, as well as the lack of openness and disclosure on the part of counselees. Most theoretical approaches in counseling have emphasized the verbal, cognitive, emotional, and behavioral expressiveness in therapeutic situations, with encouragement toward personal disclosure of an intimate nature. Such approaches have been geared to the young, attractive, verbal, intelligent, and successful people, and those individuals who would fail to conform to such expectations would be regarded as resistant, defensive, superficial, or as poor candidates for counseling. Remedial approaches, on the other hand, tended to oversimplify the situation and allowed for class-linked therapies, which stressed highly structured, behavioral, concrete approaches with present and problem- oriented flavor.

b. Sensitivity to idiosyncracies. Care and counseling that emphasizes middle-class orientations which stress cultural superiority in terms of achievement, arts, crafts, technology, science, and other elements of Americana, need to develop a proper cultural sensitivity to elements regarded as valuable, salient, and essential in the Hispanic cultures. Pastors need to pay attention to idiosyncracies present in terms of time orientations, assessing the degree to which short or long-term proposals are needed in processes of change in attitudes, character, and conduct of parishioners. They need to pay attention to the whole person rather than compartmentalize into physical, emotional, or spiritual complaint systems. Aristotelian cause-effect or linear relationships between events must allow room for more global perspectives, giving importance to the interplay between the individual and society, culture and religion, oppressive contexts, and survival stances among Hispanics.

Beyond the reflective approaches and the concern for intrapsychic insight, pastoral care needs to attend to the cries for liberation and integration of Hispanics into the American scene. Without engaging in simplistic approaches, pastors serving Hispanic communities may balance their stances in terms of perspectives which combine reality-based, problem-oriented, and present-oriented elements with more logotherapeutic, insightful, cognitive-affective as well as dynamic flavors. Such a stance implies the recognition of Hispanics as people whom God has called and expects to respond at all levels, whose potential needs to be actualized by means of proper care. The ability to understand, be empathic, and sensitive to linguistic, sociocultural, communicative idiosyncracies is essential. Training of pastors to serve Hispanic peoples may prove irrelevant unless such factors are taken into account. Ethnic, anthropological, sociological, and historical elements are a necessity in a curriculum which pretends to address the issue.

Finally, the care of Hispanics involves the preeminence of the role of spiritual guide, as some normative data suggests (Polischuk, 1980). A developmental style of leadership that emphasizes a personalistic, caring, warm, spontaneous style and offers guidance, counsel, empathic care, and concern for Hispanics, is the highest ranked role among ministers surveyed. Pastors may consider the advantages of their position toward Hispanics, as compared to other professionals in the helping profession: they offer free or low cost help; they are personalistic; and they act within the counselee's milieu and have access to the familial context. They are more available, even beyond therapeutically assigned hours, being accessible with more frequency and able to engage with more intensity; and they offer spiritual relevance. Such factors may prove to be functionally significant in the efficacy of pastoral care as compared to other human service providers.

Bibliography. V. Abad, J. Ramos, and E. Boyce, "A model for service delivery of mental health services to Spanish-speaking minorities," *American J. of Orthopsychiatry*, 44, (1974) 584–95. Alvarez, *et al., Latino Community Mental Health* (1974). E. S. LeVine and A. Padilla, *Crossing Cultures in Therapy* (1980). C. L. Holland, *The Religious Dimension in Hispanic Los Angeles* (1974). A. M. Padilla and R. A. Ruiz, *Latino Mental Health* (1974). P. Polischuk, "Personality characteristics and role preferences among Hispanic Protestant ministers" Ph.D. dissertation, Fuller Theological Seminary (1980).

P. POLISCHUK

CROSS-CULTURAL PASTORAL CARE; CULTURAL AND ETHNIC FACTORS, *or* SOCIAL STATUS AND CLASS FACTORS, IN PASTORAL CARE. *See also* CROSS-CULTURAL MARRIAGE AND FAMILY; MIGRANT WORKERS AND FAMILIES. *Compare* ASIAN AMERICAN *or* BLACK AMERICAN PASTORAL CARE; EXPLOITATION/ OPPRESSION; PASTORAL CARE (History, Traditions, and Definitions).

HISTORY, LIFE. *See* CASE STUDY METHOD; EVALUATION AND DIAGNOSIS; LIFE CYCLE THEORY; PERSONAL STORY, SYMBOL AND MYTH; REMINISCENCE THERAPY.

HISTORY OF JEWISH CARE AND COUNSELING. *See* JEWISH CARE AND COUNSELING.

HISTORY OF PASTORAL CARE AND COUNSELING. *See* PASTORAL CARE (History, Traditions, and Definitions).

HISTORY OF PROTESTANT PASTORAL CARE (Canada). *See* CANADIAN PASTORAL CARE MOVEMENT.

HISTORY OF PROTESTANT PASTORAL CARE (United States). The term "pastoral care" in the seventeenth and eighteenth centuries referred to the entire panoply of clerical duties: preaching, administering sacraments, governing in the congregation, studying in private, and praying in solitude, as well as "the private treating of souls in the great affair of their eternal salvation" (J. Edwards, *The Great Concern of a Watchman for Souls*, 1743, pp. 28, 42–47). Such a view persisted, but seminary courses and textbooks in "pastoral theology" began as early as 1810 to distinguish between pastoral and homiletical topics, with the assumption that pastoral activity referred to comfort, admonition, and evangelism with individuals and small groups. By the twentieth century, a few pastoral writers, especially in the Emmanuel Movement, understood pastoral care almost exclusively as the "healing" of groups and individuals, and by the 1930s some ministers virtually equated pastoral care with private conversations between a pastor and a parishioner. By the 1950s, seminary courses in pastoral care were usually understood to be mainly about counseling, often with an implicit ethic of

self-realization derived largely from psychological theorists. Such an understanding, though, led to debate. No consensus dominates the current scene, but most pastoral theologians would define pastoral care as the dimension of Christian ministry concerned distinctively with personal and interpersonal forms of human needs, and most would also agree that counseling is only one of its aspects.

1. **Early American Pastoral Care.** *a. The principle of hierarchy.* The pastors in the American colonies performed their duties with a shared agreement about the hierarchical ordering of reality. They envisioned pastoral care — the "cure of souls" — as a means to restore the relation between a transcendent God and the fallen creature. Lutheran Pietists viewed sin as dead "faithlessness" and practiced a method of "soul analysis" taught at the University of Halle in Germany, in which they probed for feelings of spiritual dryness before inquiring about a subjective sense of comfort or joy. Orthodox Lutherans accused them of being too rigid. Puritan theologians, accenting the "disobedience" in sin, followed the prescriptions of Reformed casuistry and taught their parishioners to discern introspectively the signs of their regeneration. Their opponents criticized the preoccupation with feelings of conviction and rebirth. Traditional Anglicans often tended to view sin as "disorder" and to see pastoral care as the ordering of Christian life and worship within a comprehensive parish. Their critics accused them of formalism and laxity. Whatever their views of sin and their pastoral methods, however, most Protestants agreed that the cure of souls nurtured a development through specifiable stages or levels toward salvation.

To be a pastor, then, was to interpret, in preaching, private conversation, and corporate discipline, the activity of God and the acts of supernatural beings. The clergy were specialists in supernatural mysteries and Christian piety. But they also believed in rational methods of care, whether sermons or casuistic "answering methods." In their pastoral conversations, especially, they used a method of inquiry and analysis derived from logic. Such pastoral writers as William Perkins and William Ames taught pastors to analyze pastoral concepts like "temptation" or "scruples" logically, and then to formulate conclusions about particular cases by combining their analyses with passages of Scripture in patterns of syllogistic reasoning. Reflecting the assumptions of a hierarchical society, moreover, the textbooks in casuistry argued that distressed parishioners should submit themselves obediently to clerical wisdom. And the clergy also took for granted a hierarchical psychology that depicted the soul as a gradation of higher and lower powers, the highest of which was reason. Pastoral care, therefore, whether in sermons or in conversations, consisted usually of rational argumentation.

b. Understanding versus the affections. The eighteenth-century revivals, however, revealed deep differences about psychology, theology, and pastoral method. The opponents of the revivals insisted that a transformed understanding of religious truth was far more important than "raised affections." The revivalists claimed that the affections were the deeper powers of the soul, so that to linger at the level of the understanding was to risk superficiality. Jonathan Edwards's *Treatise Concerning Religious Affections* (1746) concluded that true religion consisted "chiefly in affections." As theologians, therefore, the revivalists argued that a deep "conviction" of sinfulness and an experience of "rebirth" were necessary to change the deep-seated affections. The critics of the revival replied that God gently nurtured the soul by eliciting its assent to truth without such inward agonizing. The two groups therefore disagreed about pastoral methods. Both sides believed that pastors were to discern and interpret the spiritual status of parishioners, but the critics of the revival wanted the pastors to judge solely on the basis of public behavior, while the revivalists insisted on a judgment about the hidden religious inclinations. The revivalists, moreover, thought that the greatest danger was the temptation to offer premature comfort, thereby foreshortening the struggle with sin, while their opponents believed that the worst pastoral offense was a severity of judgment that, by withholding comfort, produced despair.

The tensions endured for decades, as did the hierarchical presuppositions, but in the early nineteenth century the writings on pastoral theology revealed a new set of preoccupations.

2. **Antebellum Pastoral Care. a. Urbanization.** The handbooks of pastoral theology in antebellum America mirrored the social changes that transformed an agricultural economy into a maturing town and industrial order. The transition from the family craft system to mercantile and factory capitalism established sharper lines of division between the town and the country, for the new commerce required urban concentration, produced urban wealth, and exalted urban values. The respectable townsfolk wanted to view themselves as enlightened and rational; at the same time, they produced a culture that glowed with sentimentality. Writers on pastoral topics sensed the implications of the change for ministerial behavior. The ministry was becoming a "career" in the modern sense, with many ministers expecting to advance upward through several pastorates, moving toward the urban pulpits. At the same time, the urbanization of revivalism ensured the triumph of an experiential evangelical piety within the smaller towns and cities. The resulting ideal of "Christian gentility" and the emergence of American "pastoral theology" were closely related.

b. Pastoral theology and the ideal of gentility. Pastoral theology flourished initially in the seminaries founded by denominations that took for granted that the urban middle classes belonged to them — such schools as Andover, Princeton, and Harvard. The subject consisted mainly of instruction in rhetoric and preaching, but the titles of the professorial chairs distinguished "sacred rhetoric" from "pastoral theology," indicating that homiletical guidance did not exhaust the topic. Pastoral training embraced such issues as ministerial judgments about religious experiences, methods of private conversation, the leadership of devotional groups, and clerical etiquette. The well-known teachers and authors on pastoral topics—such as Ezra Stiles Ely, Samuel Miller, Heman Humphrey, Enoch Pond, Archibald Alexander, William Meade, Ichabod Spencer, and James Cannon — were usually urban Presbyterian, Congregationalist, or Episcopal ministers, known for their cultivated bearing. The large popular denominations did not neglect the

topic: the Methodists published an edition of the *Pastoral Theology* of the Swiss theologian Alexander Vinet, and the Baptists read Francis Wayland's *Apostolic Ministry*, though even in the churches of the masses, "pastoral theology" was a field for urbane gentlemen, not for frontier exhorters. The standard textbooks, such as Pond's *Young Pastor's Guide: Or Lectures on Pastoral Duties* (1844) or Cannon's *Lectures on Pastoral Theology* (1859), were intended to help the preacher construct "polished and finished" sermons and to guide the pastor in decorous private intercourse with the refined classes. The manuals were also the products of a revivalist piety that defined the work of the clergy as the "conversion of souls" through preaching, exhortation, and devotional groups. Hence the primary topics were earnest preaching and pious conversation.

The handbooks advocated one overarching ideal: the physician of souls was to be a Christian gentleman. Hence they taught the clergy how both sermons and conversations could embody the ideals of rationality and refinement. They urged pastors to visit their parishioners; they taught, in popular Baconian fashion, "inductive" schemes of classifying spiritual states; they outlined the stages in the order of salvation; they illustrated modes of argumentation that could move the will; and they instructed ministers in rules of etiquette. The consensus was striking. Only among Lutherans and Episcopalians were there disagreements, focused always on the appropriateness of mandatory private auricular confession.

c. Rational orthodoxy and mental philosophy. Two intellectual traditions helped shape the consensus. The first was a "rational orthodox" theology that commanded almost universal assent among the mainline clergy. According to rational orthodoxy, Christian theology was susceptible to rational verification through the traditional "evidences of Christianity," so preaching and private conversation also often assumed the form of persuasive discourse, colored always, however, by a tincture of sentimentality designed to move the heart. The second—the new writings in "mental philosophy"—supposedly provided the clergy with an understanding of the subtleties of volition, understanding, and sensibility. Some of the era's prominent mental philosophers—Thomas Upham, Asa Burton, Frederick Rauch, S. S. Schmucker, and Gilbert Haven—were themselves clergymen who wrote from the conviction that pastors should "be at home in the philosophy of the human intellect" (Burton, *Essays on Some of the First Principles of Metaphysicks, Ethicks, and Theology*, 1824, p. 82). When the popular Brooklyn minister Ichabod Spencer published his *Pastor's Sketches* in 1851, describing in verbatim form his conversations with "anxious inquirers," his manual reflected both the assumptions of rational orthodoxy and the accepted principles of mental science, as well as the concern for gentility that marked the skillful practice of pastoral care.

3. **Late Nineteenth and Early Twentieth Century Developments. a. The natural style.** Soon after the Civil War, pastoral theologians began to write not so much of gentility and decorum as of force and vitality. The war had created a disdain for "feeble sentimentalities." The new biology and technology had spawned a fascination with metaphors of power and energy. The popular society became obsessed by the 1890s with

sports and physical culture; politicians and philosophers alike praised the "strenuous life." At the same time, Protestant parish life underwent a striking change, one symbol of which was the "church parlor." Churches became centers not only for worship but for other social activities. The first generation of postwar pastoral writers therefore argued that pastoral work must accord with "nature" and adapt itself to the new parish.

The older methods endured, but the new pastoral handbooks—such as Thomas Murphy's *Pastoral Theology* (1877), G. B. Willcox's *Pastor Amidst His Flock* (1890), James Hoppin's *Pastoral Theology* (1885), and Washington Gladden's *Christian Pastor* (1898)—assumed that strength of Christian character required a capacity for forcefulness, and they defined a "natural" style of pastoral care as the cultivation of a manly, cheerful, informal, and persuasive bearing. They urged ministers to be "masculine" and "robust," partly to overcome the objection that preachers should not engage in the "effeminate" business of gentle conversation and to show that pastoral work could itself be "natural and manly." By avoiding stiffness and formality, the pastor would invite companionship, and the best pastor was the friend, the comrade. Pastors were to be cheerful. They were to avoid morbid topics, especially in the sickroom. They were often to show their sympathy merely by pressing the sufferer's hand in silence. They were to understand rather than primly condemn. They were never to assume that persons crushed with calamities could be satisfied by homilies. "Let them weep for a while," wrote Willcox, "nature must have her way" (Willcox, *Pastor Amidst His Flock*, 1890, p. 147). The main appeal in pastoral care, though, was still directed to the will. Washington Gladden admired the physician who used a "vigorous moral treatment." He wanted pastors to do the same.

b. The new psychology. By the 1880s, however, both psychologists and liberal theologians were discovering more complex conceptions of the natural. Ideas of subconscious vitality and divine immanence complicated the simple association of naturalness with forceful informality. William James and the functional psychologists could write as much as anybody about willpower, muscular tone, and forceful character, but they also developed an increasing interest in what James and others called the "subliminal self" and hence in the ways in which surrender to the subconscious could engender self-assertion. At the same time, the American medical establishment finally relented in their scorn for European psychotherapy, and by 1906 they listed "psychotherapy" as a separate topic in their official index of medical papers. The result was spirited debate about the relative values of verbal suggestion, creative assertion, rational reflection, and psychoanalysis. And the liberal theologians, meanwhile, wrote increasingly of a God immanent in natural order and human experience.

The new psychologists of religion subsequently began to redefine what a "natural style" of pastoral care might mean. Such writers as G. Stanley Hall, William James, and James Leuba argued that religious experiences reflected natural processes that could help adolescents negotiate their crises, adults find "harmony with the universal life," and social groups maintain inner stability. They were also interested in how the new "science of

religion" could establish a wiser "soul-midwifery": they urged pastors to trust natural processes and stages of development; they emphasized the power of religious growth to induce "self-surrender" if the pastor did not press for premature decisions, and they urged pastors to plumb the depths of the subliminal consciousness.

c. Psychotherapy and the Emmanuel Movement. The first serious effort to transform pastoral care in the light of the new learning began in 1905 among some Episcopalians at the Emmanuel Church in Boston. The Emmanuel Movement attracted national attention for almost a decade, partly through its journal *Psychotherapy*. The founders — Elwood Worcester and Samuel McComb — believed that every minister practiced "psychotherapy" and that the Church therefore had to face anew the question whether it would be guided by tradition or science. Working with the Boston neurologist Richard Cabot and the medical professor James Jackson Putnam, the ministers began a counseling movement that spread from coast to coast. Its central idea was that the "law" of effort and the "gospel" of relaxation belonged together. Relaxation was the prelude to moral self-control. So the clergy were to take some ideas from Sigmund Freud and other physicians and devise a process of counseling that began with relaxation (often through rhythmic breathing, muscular relaxation, and visual imagery) and then proceeded through "tranquilizing suggestions" that would penetrate the subconscious mind. Then the pastor could educate the conscious faculties. The movement soon faded from view, but it helped to introduce the new psychology and psychotherapy into the churches at a time when both were barely understood within the hospitals.

4. Developments Between the Wars. *a. Ferment in pastoral care: the ideal of adjustment.* Journalists referred to the 1920s as a period of "psychological revival" in American culture, and the decade's pastoral writers shared the popular interest in Freudian slips and the power of suggestion. To most ministers, according to Mark A. May's report on "The Profession of the Ministry" (1934), pastoral duties still meant primarily calling from house to house, though many pastors revealed their dissatisfaction with such visits. But the report also predicted that "work with individuals is to become one of the permanent and most important aspects of the future ministry." And there was, indeed, ferment in pastoral care. Such pioneers as Harry Emerson Fosdick called for a Protestant form of the "confessional" and tried to refashion the sermon in the image of the counseling session. By 1937, the Federal Council of Churches created a Commission on Religion and Health, and its executive secretary, Seward Hiltner, announced that the Mental Hygiene Movement was reshaping clerical attitudes toward pastoral care. Hiltner began using case studies to train students in pastoral care issues.

For most of the pastoral writers, the dominant theme of the new pastoral care was "adjustment." Influenced by John Dewey, the Mental Hygiene Movement, the European psychotherapists, and the Religious Education Movement (especially the writings of George Coe), a few seminary professors — Harrison Elliott at Union Seminary in New York, Gaines Dobbins at Southern Seminary in Louisville, Charles Holman at the University of Chicago, Karl Stolz at the Hartford School of Religious

Education—began teaching courses in "pastoral psychology" that taught counseling methods to aspiring ministers. Most believed that the clergy could lead their parishioners toward ever higher levels of "adjustment" to self, the neighbor, and God. Holman's *The Cure of Souls: A Socio-Psychological Approach* (1932) described "soul-sickness" as inadequate religious or moral "adjustment," and Stolz's *Pastoral Psychology* (1932) announced that human life was a "sequence of adjustments" in which pastors helped people reorganize themselves. The *Pastoral Psychiatry* (1938) of the Presbyterian pastor John Bonnell recommended counseling techniques derived especially from the accent on "realistic adjustment" in Alfred Adler's "individual psychology."

b. The CPE Movement: dynamic psychology and insight. Within the Clinical Pastoral Education movement that had begun in the early twenties, a few writers began seeking an alternative to "adjustment." Clinical training, as it was then called, was a long-term supervised encounter with men and women in crises in hospitals, prisons, and social agencies, which gradually altered prevailing views of pastoral care. The founders of the New England Theological Schools Committee on Clinical Training hoped that clinical supervision would enhance pastoral skills and promote ethical formation in the student. The founders of the Council for the Clinical Training of Theological Students emphasized that it could also help ministers use pastoral care to free persons from rigid and destructive legalism. In 1936 the emerging clinical tradition helped to produce two early classics of the nascent pastoral care movement: the physician Richard Cabot and the chaplain Russell Dicks published *The Art of Ministering to the Sick*, in which they urged the pastor to learn the art of "good listening," which could discern the "growing edge" of the soul and nurture the purposive healing force within each person. The liberal theologian Anton Boisen published his *Exploration of the Inner World*, in which he advanced the notion that emotional collapse was a chaotic encounter with God that could lead either to a new integration of personality or a fall into total inner disarray. Boisen viewed clinical training as a study of "living human documents" whose pathological eruptions could become the key to understanding the self. He was not interested primarily in the inculcation of specific pastoral skills, but his views about the self's inner turmoil deeply influenced emerging notions of pastoral care.

Boisen felt uneasy with Freudian psychoanalytic ideas, but his heirs found themselves drawn to a Freudian and neo-Freudian analysis of the self that highlighted its inner conflicts. They advised the clergy to learn from dynamic psychologies, and thus they intensified doubts about the ideal of adjustment. Rollo May's *Art of Counseling* (1939) combined theology and dynamic psychology in a proposal that pastors, rather than encouraging "adjustment," should try to elicit understanding and insight. By the 1940s, the ideal of insight had superseded that of adjustment as a goal of Protestant pastoral care, and increasingly the heart of pastoral care was coming to be viewed as individual counseling.

5. **Post-War Developments.** *a. The renaissance of pastoral care.* The Second World War produced the greatest upsurge of interest in psychology in the nation's history, and the churches responded, both with a popular piety that presented religion as "God's psychiatry" and with a movement to improve pastoral care through increased attention to counseling. During the 1950s, the mainline seminaries invariably offered courses on counseling, the clinical education movement established 117 training centers, the churches founded at least 84 counseling centers, hundreds of hospitals created chaplaincy positions, and thousands of clergy subscribed to such journals as *Pastoral Psychology* (1950) and *The Journal of Pastoral Care* (1947). The affluence of the postwar white-collar society ensured that pastoral theologians now had the resources to popularize their convictions. Indeed, such critics as H. Richard Niebuhr worried that the teaching of pastoral care and counseling had assumed disproportionate influence in Protestant seminaries.

Four theologians of diverse views assumed intellectual leadership in the postwar renaissance. In 1949, Seward Hiltner at the University of Chicago published his *Pastoral Counseling*. Two years later, Carroll A. Wise at Garrett issued *Pastoral Counseling: Its Theory and Practice*, and Wayne Oates at Southern Baptist Theological Seminary came out with *The Christian Pastor*. In 1953, Paul Johnson at Boston University published his *Psychology of Pastoral Care*. Despite their disagreements, they shared some common emphases: they valued individual counseling; they shared in the current intellectual revolt against "mass culture," and they affirmed the new theological critique of moralism and legalism. Hence they warned ministers against "moralizing" and promoting cultural conventions in their counseling, recommending instead a pastoral attitude of acceptance and understanding. Some of the new accent on acceptance reflected the writings of the psychologist Carl Rogers, whose book on *Counseling and Psychotherapy* (1942) became a standard text among clinical groups and in theological seminaries. Rogers's methods of "client-centered" counseling were intended to bring the latent powers of the true self to full expression; the primary aims were growth and self-realization.

b. Later developments and emerging issues. During the 1960s, however, the Rogerian style came under fire from two sides. Both groups of critics believed that Rogers had overlooked the interpersonal context of human development; both found new insights in developmental and interpersonal psychologies (hence the new emphasis on group dynamics); both sought deeper theological grounding for pastoral care. But the first group, represented by Paul Johnson and Howard Clinebell, believed that the new humanistic psychologies had discovered possibilities of growth that even the earlier Rogers had overlooked, and that the presuppositions of Rogerian counseling were too individualistic. The second group, represented by Hiltner and Oates, became more amenable to ethical and religious guidance in counseling, and they also warned against the tendency of pastoral writers to seek a borrowed identity from psychotherapy. They continued to define pastoral counseling by designating the Church as its proper context, and they argued that the preoccupation with counseling had distorted the broader meaning of pastoral care.

By the end of the sixties, the pastoral care movement was divided. Should the focus remain on counseling?

Should pastoral counseling be located solely within the church? Should there be pastoral counseling specialists who work in counseling centers or established private practice? The American Association of Pastoral Counselors was formed in 1963 as an organization designed primarily for specialists. But Hiltner and Oates argued that private pastoral practice, at least, was a contradiction in terms, and when Hiltner wrote *Ferment in the Ministry* (1969) he discussed pastoral care as a broad enterprise in which counseling was only one activity among many.

The interest in pastoral counseling has by no means diminished, but increasingly during the 1970s pastoral writers turned their attention to an array of topics, especially to ethics, worship, and pastoral leadership. More pastoral writers began, like Oates and Hiltner earlier, to seek a vocabulary drawn more from theological sources and less from psychology. The distinction between care and counseling became increasingly accepted, and Protestants attended more carefully to the entire church as the locus and agent of pastoral activity. The earlier tensions, however, did not disappear.

Bibliography. For a detailed history, see E. B. Holifield, *A History of Pastoral Care in America: From Salvation to Self-Realization* (1983). The classic text is W. T. McNeill's *History of the Cure of Souls* (1951), and one should also consult the collection of documents by W. Clebsch and C. Jaekle, *Pastoral Care in Historical Perspective* (1964). There are some excellent articles in H. R. Niebuhr and D. D. Williams, eds., *The Ministry in Historical Perspectives* (1956). See also D. Hall, *The Faithful Shepherd* (1972) and D. M. Scott, *From Office to Profession* (1978), and the older work by Charles Kemp, *Physicians of the Soul* (1947).

E. B. HOLIFIELD

PASTORAL CARE (History, Traditions, and Definitions); PASTORAL CARE MOVEMENT; PASTORAL COUNSELING MOVEMENT. *See also* ANGLICAN, BAPTIST, LUTHERAN, REFORMED, *or* METHODIST PASTORAL CARE; ASIAN AMERICAN, BLACK AMERICAN, HISPANIC AMERICAN, *or* NATIVE AMERICAN PASTORAL CARE; CASUISTRY, PROTESTANT; EMMANUEL MOVEMENT; MIND-CURE MOVEMENT; PERSONALISM; PASTORAL THEOLOGY, PROTESTANT; PSYCHOLOGY IN AMERICAN RELIGION; PRAGMATISM; THEOLOGICAL EDUCATION AND THE PASTORAL CARE MOVEMENT. *Compare* CHRISTIAN SCIENCE; MORMON CARE AND COUNSELING; QUAKER TRADITION OF CARE. *Biography:* AMES, EDWARD SCRIBNER; BOISEN; BONNELL; CABOT; CLINEBELL; COE; DEWEY; DICKS; EDWARDS; ELLIOTT; GLADDEN; FOSDICK; HALL; HILTNER; HOPPIN; HOLMAN; JAMES; JOHNSON; LEUBA; MAY; OATES; PERKINS; POND; SPENCER; STOLZ; WISE; WORCESTER.

HISTORY OF ROMAN CATHOLIC PASTORAL CARE (Canada).

The praxis of ritual-sacramental types of pastoral care in Roman Catholicism has always been preserved alongside the conversational, informal forms. Socio-historical and church developments in Canada since the Second World War, concurrent with the impact of the Second Vatican Council (1962–65), had a profound effect upon both types of pastoral care. The changing institutional influence of the church, the radical transformation in the traditional source of ministers, newly emerging pastoral needs, and the consequent search for contemporary information and approaches in pastoral practice and education, changed prevailing negative attitudes toward the behavioral sciences and led to new developments in pastoral care.

1. **Early Pastoral Care.** The Roman Catholic church began its presence in Canada with the arrival of French explorers in 1534. Today it numbers nearly eleven million or forty-six percent of the Canadian population. Of these, Franco-Canadians constitute forty-nine percent, over five million in Quebec alone.

Concentrating on the conversion of the native peoples, the church, together with the pioneers, built a new society. The clergy were close to the people and gave early pastoral care a strong cultural identity, first among Francophones, and later also among the Irish, Ukranian, and Italian immigrants. In Quebec, church and state responsibilities were administratively and financially long intertwined, and a powerful presence of the church persisted well into the twentieth century. In all of Canada a church triumphant lasted until the 1950s. It provided a stable, if hierarchical, infrastructure for the many religious men and women who carried, particularly in Quebec, most of the educational, social, and health care institutions. Priests and religious had a privileged presence in pastoral care and indeed in all of Catholic life, and enjoyed a high status among the faithful.

In a church operating from clear codes of religious and moral expectations and conduct, sacramental and symbolic actions of pastoral care such as confession had a more pronounced role than personal encounter and dialogue. Conversational pastoral care consisted mainly in visiting the poor, the sick, and the dying, in home visits and occasional chats. Catholic pastoral care was largely ritual and formal.

2. **Transitions caused by World War II and Vatican II.** *a.* *Changes in society and church.* The global phenomena of industrialization, urbanization, consumerism, materialism, and the secularization of a church-oriented society were in evidence before 1939. Rapid social and political developments in Canada after World War II thoroughly changed the unique position of the church and its traditional forms of pastoral care. This was expedited by the Second Vatican Council which encouraged a positive relationship between church and world, and by a nonhierarchical understanding of the church as the community of all believers in a nonhierarchical model.

The post-war immigrant wave from diverse ethnic, racial, and religious backgrounds, enriched the Canadian cultural mosaic, diffused the existing cultural characteristics of pastoral care, and stimulated openness to religious pluralism and tolerance of differences. A growing nationalism culminated in the Canadian Constitution of 1982. Meanwhile in Quebec, a secular nationalism in the cultural domain, long supported by the church's infrastructure and further carried by the bourgeois elite of the liberal professions, gave way to a varied economic and political nationalism according to social strata and the visions of political parties.

In a gradual but accelerating evolution, educational and social institutions, as well as health care under the control of the church and religious orders, were by 1970 transferred to the state, which provided universal health care insurance, old age pensions, unemployment assistance, and family allowances. Apart from removing from the church many traditional charitable and pastoral care opportunities, it also created a large, now secular, infrastructure and bureaucracy in which people tend to become depersonalized.

In this secularization process, actively encouraged by the Church, family and church-oriented Judeo-Christian values were traded in by many for economic goals and consumer values. The liberalization of divorce and abortion laws also reflected a new situation among Roman Catholics. Furthermore, a dramatic drop in church attendance to forty-five and thirty-five percent in Canada and Quebec respectively, and in the practice of individual confession, eroded the traditional accessibility base of much of the praxis of pastoral care.

These socio-historical and ecclesiastical developments signaled the quest for a personalized sacramental care, especially in the preparation for baptism and marriage, and necessitated a rethinking of the role of conversational forms in Catholic praxis.

b. Changes in persons. The status and roles of priests and religious were further affected by the insistence of Vatican II on lay coresponsibility for the mission of the church and on the ideal of Christian marriage. A significant drop in vocations, further precipitated by a dramatic exodus of priests and religious from active ministry, reduced their now rapidly aging numbers by thirty-eight percent.

However, freed from institutional burdens, religious women in particular pioneered on the periphery of society a significant evangelical presence to the poor, the abused, the outcast, and the homeless, accentuating the need for a reorientation in contemporary pastoral care.

Concurrently, universal access to education on all levels produced a laity able and willing to do their share.

3. **Pastoral Care and the Behavioral Sciences.** In this search for pastoral adaptations, the historic call of the Second Vatican Council for a balanced use of the behavioral sciences as well as the pastoral letters of the Canadian bishops constituted timely directives. In a concerted attempt to respond to such urgent questions as marriage breakdowns, crises in the meaning of life, and various social and relationship problems, the church turned also to the human sciences.

Laity with behavioral and clinical skills were invited to minister to the confused, the lonely, the young, to those torn apart by marital and family strife, often in new types of church sponsored services complementary to civil efforts.

Large numbers of priests and religious returned to school. Some took part in the CPE programs of Protestant American origin, later organized in Canada as the Canadian Association for Pastoral Education (CAPE) on an interdenominational basis. Many enrolled in theological schools such as bilingual Saint Paul University, which had engaged human sciences professionals to assist in their interdisciplinary pastoral education curriculum. They were increasingly joined by lay persons, now constituting sixty-five percent of pastoral students. Government standards for pastoral departments of institutions under its control, also strengthened the cooperation between theology and the human sciences.

New forms of conversational pastoral care as a needed complement to traditional sacramental ministry are increasingly carried by newly trained pastoral workers, and tend to become dissociated from the services of the ordained priest.

a. Positive aspects. The recourse to the behavioral sciences helped to build a harmonizing link between the sacramental and conversational dimensions of pastoral care. It greatly enhanced a deeper understanding of how social and psychological human conditions foster or hinder Christian faith and life in the world today, and provided new directions in sacramental-ritual pastoral care and an impetus for new conversational forms. Consequently, both types have become more relational, merciful, and healing, less judgmental and authoritarian. Progressive growth in Christian faith and practice is encouraged, moral norms are offered in greater openness to a perplexed individual conscience, and sin and guilt are laid before a merciful and forgiving God as brokenness to be redeemed.

For a church no longer able to assert itself institutionally, conversational care is a relatively new phenomenon. Its dialogical nature becomes an invitation to Christian responsibility in faith and practice.

b. Negative aspects. At a time that religious experience became privatized and the church withdrew into the private domain, the recourse to *all* social sciences in the service of ecclesial action, especially in conversational pastoral care and education, has given way to psychological knowledge and methods. The functionalism of certain schools of psychology and their immanentism in the absence of an adequate pastoral theology in conversational pastoral care and education are a cause for concern.

The problematic relationship between a still largely deductive and systematic theology and the predominantly inductive and nonnormative human sciences leaves conversational pastoral education and practice vulnerable in its specific task to announce the Good News and its Christian kerygma.

In a society where God is no longer self-evident, and an immanent salvation through individual growth and mental health holds for many an ultimate meaning, it is tempting to equate uncritically pastoral conversation with psychotherapy.

A biological and deterministic functionalism, apart from a human culture or ignorant of recent developments in the behavioral sciences regarding religious experience, easily leads from a valid methodology (i.e., reductionism) to an ideological neglect of the transcendent. The widespread adoption of psychological models in pastoral training and practice without an acknowledgment of their methodological bias or a theological commitment to kerygmatic specificity, leaves the compatibility of psychological and Christian views on human existence unexplored.

In this transition period of the Church in Canada, from a predominantly sacramental-ritual care to a balanced inclusion and development of its conversational forms, the latter is often exercised without an institutional liaison to the tradition and support of the Christian community. When practiced in isolation from liturgical-sacramental pastoral care, from other ministries, and from the church's pastoral network resources, the kerygmatic specificity of pastoral conversation weakens, the indispensable role of faith tends to be down-played, and the effectiveness of the personal encounter for all types of problems and for all strata of the population over-rated.

Lastly, as pastoral conversation becomes self-contained and modeled on psychological practice, pastoral agents must negotiate between immanence and transcendence, between function and calling, between theology and the human sciences, as they struggle to preserve a sense of mission.

These concerns are not adequately addressed in pastoral education.

4. Hopes for the Future. The progress of Roman Catholic pastoral care in Canada, and of the related theological and human sciences as well, is subject to the two limitations of ignorance and zeitgeist: ignorance, for one discovery waits upon the other that opens the way for it; but discovery and its acceptance are also limited by the zeitgeist, the habits of thought particular to the culture of any region or period.

A critical understanding of the time-bound, culturally and historically determined values in both behavioral and theological wisdom, as well as a redefinition of the relationship between pastoral practice, critical analysis, and Christian mystery will be required.

In a common effort, theologians, human sciences experts, and pastoral practitioners must discern the dimensions and evolution of pastoral care issues and continually search for a new coherence between faith and culture, without closing any window on Christian faith and life.

They must simultaneously and convincingly insist upon the strength and riches of the Christian tradition, of both the *traditio*, that is, the community of believers unbrokenly passing on the faith, and of the *tradita*, that which is believed.

They are challenged to create those perspectives which allow the Christian kerygma, so characteristic of the sacramental-ritual types of pastoral care, also to be evoked and awakened in its conversational forms.

The Group of Researchers in Pastoral Studies, a learned society established by university pastoral faculties across Canada, and the journal *Pastoral Sciences* have made the dialogue between the theological and human sciences their special goal.

History shows that, when pastoral specificity is lost, pastors are thrown back upon the patterns, procedures and functions of the various other helping professions, as was the case in the medieval church. Consistent efforts are needed to develop truly interdisciplinary educational models and pastoral care approaches in firm dialogue with other ministries of the Christian community, so that the Good News may remain the inspiration and goal of pastoral practice.

Bibliography. E. G. Boring, *A History of Experimental Psychology*, 2d. ed., (1950). Canadian Conference of Catholic Bishops, *Ad Limina Report* (1983); *Communiques, Declarations, Pastoral Letters* (1942–1958); *Program of Priestly Formation* (1981). W. A. Clebsch and C. R. Jaekle, *Pastoral Care in Historical Perspective* (1964). A. Flannery, ed., "Gaudium et Spes," "Lumen Gentium," "Message to Men of Thought and Science," "Optatam Totius," *Conciliar and Post-Conciliar Documents of Vatican Council II* (1975); "La Religion au Québec," *Pro Mundi Vita Dossiers*, 3 (1977), 1–36. V. Schurr, "Théologie Pastorale," *Bilan de la Théologie de XX Siècle*, 2 (1970), 569–626. A. M. Visscher, "Theology and Psychology: Reflections on Interdisciplinarity and Method in Pastoral Studies," *Pastoral Sciences*, 2 (1983), 87–113.

A. M. VISSCHER

COUNSELING, ROMAN CATHOLIC; MINISTRY (Roman Catholic Tradition); PASTORAL CARE (History, Traditions, and Definitions); ROMAN CATHOLIC PASTORAL CARE. *See also* PASTORAL THEOLOGICAL METHOD; THEOLOGY AND PSYCHOLOGY. *Compare* CANADIAN PASTORAL CARE MOVEMENT; LITURGICAL CHANGE AND REFORM; VATICAN COUNCIL II AND PASTORAL CARE.

HISTORY OF ROMAN CATHOLIC PASTORAL CARE (United States).

The history of pastoral care in the U.S. from a Roman Catholic perspective cannot be separated from the history of pastoral care in the universal church. What the church in this country does now reflects both an ancient tradition and the current thrust of Catholicism beyond its borders. This article briefly sketches that long history of pastoral care, highlights the major influences upon pastoral care in the worldwide church over the past two centuries and shows their application to the situation here in the U.S.

1. The Church's Triple Mission. The Roman Catholic church, from the very beginning and now in every country throughout the world including the U.S., sees itself quite simply as called to carry on the mission of Jesus. The church takes as its own the task to prolong Christ's triple ministry of praying, speaking, and acting in worshipping God, of preaching the good news about a present or eventual liberating salvation to those in darkness and the shadow of death, and of healing those who hurt in any way.

This means, of course, that every Catholic, either alone or with others, must pray, spread the gospel message, and help heal the hurting. Only the Creator knows to what extent each person fulfills this duty in an informal, semiprivate and individualized way. However, the church has likewise discharged this responsibility in a formal, public, and communal manner during every century of its existence.

2. History of Formalized Pastoral Care. Clusters of Catholic Christians have thus regularly gathered together and in a church-approved manner made prayer, preaching, or healing their major and officially approved task.

We see that in the Acts of the Apostles (2:42–47) as those first Christians "devoted themselves to the apostles' instruction and the communal life, to the breaking of bread and prayers." The first deacons (Acts 6:1–7) would wait on tables and daily distribute food so that the Twelve could concentrate on prayer and ministry of the word. One of the first bishops, Peter, cured the crippled man in the name of Jesus (Acts 3:1–9).

Over the subsequent centuries, hierarchical church leaders—namely popes, bishops, priests, and deacons—naturally have walked that path of prayer themselves, preaching and healing and urging others to do so. Moreover, women and men have joined together in community life as vowed religious to concentrate on one or all three of those tasks.

If there is a pattern in this history of Roman Catholic pastoral work, it would be the emphasis that these three dimensions of care seemed to be discharged in the main by officially designated "church people," either persons with sacred orders and members of the hierarchy or consecrated religious with vows of poverty, chastity, and obedience. Lay persons obviously prayed, spread the Good News, and helped others, but they did so normally as individuals and not generally as a formalized group.

3. Early "Church People" Pastoral Care in the U.S. The Catholic church in the U.S. for the most part followed that pattern for the first two centuries or up until about the 1950s. Lay people, to quote a commonly made observation, were only supposed to "pray, pay, and obey." The actual pastoral care work would then be performed by the "professional" church people.

Thus, for example, cloistered Trappist monasteries and Carmelite convents sprang up across the U.S., where consecrated men and women spent their lives in solitude and prayer. Elizabeth Seton in 1809 established her Sisters of Charity, a religious community of women, to staff Catholic schools and teach as Jesus taught.

To be sure, lay Catholics on their own exercised all types of individual pastoral care. In addition, there were organizations like the St. Vincent de Paul Society, the Legion of Mary, Holy Name Society, Altar-Rosary Society, and Confraternity of Christian Doctrine, which formally involved lay persons in these three pastoral care ministries. But it was the common practice and understanding that "Father" or "the Sisters" took care of these matters. Lay persons paid the bills; church people did the pastoral caring.

4. Sowing Seeds for Twentieth-Century Change.
a. The liturgical movement. During the first half of the twentieth century, three developments stirred the waters and sowed seeds that eventually would alter in a radical way this clergy and religious dominated approach to pastoral care and open avenues for fuller lay participation: the liturgical movement, papal teaching on social justice matters, and lay apostolate techniques. Each of these factors, while coming from and vital throughout the universal church, were also very operative and influential in the Catholic church of the U.S.

The Roman Catholic liturgy was, practically speaking, frozen in the form produced by the Council of Trent and its implementing committees in the middle of the sixteenth century. That uniformity and stability worked well for several hundred years, but around the turn of this century visionary and concerned church leaders sensed that it no longer responded satisfactorily to the needs of a rapidly changing world. Moreover, considerable research into liturgical history had given a clearer view of what public worship could and should be.

As a result, over the next fifty to seventy-five years, pressures for reform of the liturgy emerged from below, and sporadic, piece-meal, but significant modifications were decreed from above. The movement from below, which started in monastic settings of both Europe and the U.S. (e.g., St. Meinrad and Collegeville) and gradually spread to parish situations (e.g., Holy Cross, St. Louis), urged the adaptation of practices that were considered outlandish: vernacular in the liturgy, active involvement of lay persons in worship, altars facing the people. These recommendations were not received universally with open arms by either the hierarchy or the general populace. Change is usually difficult and painful for institutions and for individuals.

Nevertheless, there were from above some Vatican approved alterations in the form of liturgical worship. Pope St. Pius X (1903–14), for example, issued a series of decrees which proved to be the first authorized steps in a long and yet remarkable process, completely transforming Roman Catholic worship. He said, in a statement to be cited often over the next fifty years, "The prime and indispensable source of the true Christian spirit is the active participation of the faithful in the sacred mysteries of the church." He urged Catholics to receive Communion earlier (at the age of reason around seven instead of twelve or so) and frequently, even daily; he stressed the value of congregational singing. Those were revolutionary concepts at that time.

There were a few officially promulgated liturgical changes after Pius X's directives, but until World War II and immediately thereafter, the major thrust of the liturgical movement was an ongoing effort from below to study, recommend, and plead for further reforms.

b. Social justice encyclicals. Several papal documents on social justice also contributed substantially to a shift from exclusively clerical and religious pastoral care to full lay participation.

In 1891, Pope Leo XIII, concerned about the harmful effects of the Industrial Revolution, growing socialism, and the loss of working people from the church, issued his encyclical *Rerum Novarum*, "On the condition of the laboring class." Received with enthusiasm and translated into several languages, the document gave a new and fresh incentive to Catholic social efforts. That spawned a variety of projects, many involving laypersons, designed to study existing structures and systems, note injustices, and work for reforms. Forty years later, Pope Pius XI published his *Quadragesimo Anno* in which he reaffirmed the principles of social and economic justice taught in *Rerum Novarum*.

The healing ministry of Christ and his church was now no longer seen exclusively as giving food, clothes, medicines, or a bed to individuals, but also as examining systems or structures which oppress the poor and struggling to correct these unjust situations. Moreover, this was to be the task primarily of laypersons, rather than mainly the work of clerics or religious.

c. Lay apostolate techniques. In 1925 Pope Pius XI gave his attention to what was termed Catholic Action and started a process which further helped reverse the process of clericalism in the church and foster the role of laypeople in pastoral work. In 1933 he formulated a principle and publicized it before the German Catholic Youth meeting in Rome, a statement which would frequently be quoted over the next decades. The visionary pontiff urged "participation and cooperation of laity in the hierarchical apostolate of the church."

A wide variety of movements or organizations abroad, but likewise in the U.S.,—for example, the Catholic Youth Organization, Young Catholic Workers, Young Catholic Student, and Christian Family Movement,—subsequently developed in response to that vision. These and many others gathered laypeople in small and large groups, sometimes following a philosophy or process of "observe, judge, and act," to determine how best as

Catholic women or men they could bring Christ to the marketplace.

Such efforts reached probably a minority of Catholic people, were more or less productive and lasted for shorter or longer periods of time, but they served as forerunners to the massive change in the role of laypersons within the church to occur at the time of the Second Vatican Council.

5. Three Vital Encyclicals in the 1940s. If the liturgical movement, papal teaching on social justice, and embryonic lay apostolate activities stirred waters and sowed seeds for future shifts in pastoral care, Pope Pius XII with three encyclical letters in the 1940s established theological bases for the monumental developments to come after him.

One of the encyclicals, on the Mystical Body of Christ (1943), taught that the church was not simply a hierarchical structure but a living organism, a community of believers linked together by ties of grace in which each person through baptism possesses both a right and responsibility to build up the kingdom. Another encyclical, on the Bible (1943), acknowledged with praise the work of contemporary scriptural scholars and urged Catholics to read, study, and pray the inspired Word. One on the liturgy (1947), the first encyclical on public worship in the church's history, provided both approbation and cautions for the directions in which liturgical promoters were moving.

6. From World War II to Vatican II. Between World War II and the Second Vatican Council (1962–65), the double top-down and bottom-up influences for change in the thrust of pastoral care continued, but with ever-increasing intensity and frequency. Both the rapid rate of external modifications and the urgency of enthusiasts reflected the fast and radical transformations in society and contemporary civilization.

a. Changed eucharistic regulations. Several seemingly minor, but actually major, official church reforms occurred, which significantly altered the way Catholics worshipped and pastoral care personnel served others.

The fast before Communion, previously from midnight, was shortened to three hours, then to one. This instantly multiplied the number of people receiving Communion at mass or confined within their homes. A related development, permission to celebrate the Eucharist at other than morning hours, opened up the possibility of masses at night in parishes, the Eucharist in homes on a host of occasions and, ultimately, anticipating Sunday worship, celebration of the Eucharist in the late afternoon or early evening on Saturday.

b. Vernacular in the liturgy. A gradual introduction of the vernacular within certain liturgical rites broke the Latin-only barrier and paved the way for the more total vernacularization of Roman Catholic worship in the U.S. after the Vatican Council. The initial translations centered on several more common blessings and frequently used rituals such as marriage or last rites for those near death.

c. Congregational participation. Even though the pope a half century earlier had called for congregational participation in word and song, serious implementation of this on a wide level did not occur until that interim period between the end of the great war and implemen-

tation of the Second Vatican Council. Again, liturgical supporters, the Liturgical Conference most notably, worked for this ideal and Roman directives reiterated the desired goals of active participation.

7. Pope John XXIII and the Second Vatican Council. *a. Major thrusts.* The election of elderly Pope John XXIII in 1958, a supposedly interim pontiff, stands, of course, as a milestone in the history both of the Catholic church in general and of pastoral care in particular. This beloved leader decentralized the Vatican administration, instituted distinctive ecumenical measures, and sought to bring the church into closer touch with the modern world. The last of these efforts, among others, led him to convene the Second Vatican Council in an attempt to open the windows of the church and allow some fresh air to enter the structure.

b. The council and its documents. When the 2,540 voting bishops assembled for the opening session in Rome on October 11, 1962, few, if any, understood just how far-reaching the impact of this ecumenical council upon the church and the world would be. The preliminary documents, which had been drawn up and distributed in general, merely restated with new terms older concepts and practices. However, the bishops, whose proceedings were being communicated worldwide by radio and television, soon indicated that these simple reformulations would not suffice. With that began a lengthy, remarkable, and complex process of studies, proposals, debates, redrafts, new discussions, and final votes on many church topics. When the work of the council concluded during an impressive celebration on December 8, 1965, in St. Peter's Square at Rome, the bishops with the new pontiff, Paul VI, had approved sixteen major documents.

The very listing of subjects covered by those decrees reflects the extensiveness of their labors: the sacred liturgy, the means of social communication, the dogmatic constitution on the church, Eastern Catholic churches, ecumenism, pastoral office of bishops, up-to-date renewal of religious life, the training of priests, Christian education, the relation of the church to non-Christian religions, divine revelation, apostolate of lay people, religious liberty, missionary activity, ministry and life of priests, and the church in the modern world.

c. Liturgy experience. Because of the nearly century-long research and renewal on the liturgy, which had preceded the council, this topic was the first one ready for debate. While in the eyes of some, reforming rules that govern the church's public worship may have seemed a relatively inconsequential matter, it proved providential that the bishops considered these proposals before moving on to others. As they returned home after completing the initial session and celebrated liturgies according to the new concepts, if not the new regulations, they experienced the church in a different way. These men saw before them possibilities of community worship, biblical preaching, vernacular rituals, diverse ministries fulfilled by laypersons, and a liturgy better connected with life. When they subsequently recommended and discussed, for example, the Dogmatic Constitution on the Church, their judgments were flowing out of lived events from back home, whether that was in the U.S., South Africa, Latin America, or western Europe.

8. Implementation of Vatican II. *a. Liturgical books.* Implementation of the conciliar decrees required time, especially with regard to the liturgy constitution. The fathers in effect voted to update all of the official worship books based on the best scholarship available in various related disciplines and built upon the reforms already introduced, which we have mentioned above. A corps of around eighty international experts undertook this task, a massive, decade-long project, which began to bear its first fruits around 1970.

b. Gap between official and unofficial church. Unfortunately, we were simultaneously undergoing a cultural explosion, a future shock of changes in the sixties throughout the U.S. While officially authorized liturgical reforms, for example, were coming, they were not coming fast enough for many Catholic religious leaders. Consequently, some took renewal into their own hands and introduced new ways of worship and pastoral care often at sharp variance with traditional laws and approved procedures. That made for a painful gap, awkward distancing, and uncomfortable relationships between those in authority, or who upheld in principle or taste the law and those in direct ministry who saw the need immediately to adjust their approach to the rapidly shifting American scene.

c. Healing in the 1970s. This chasm closed somewhat in the seventies. Antiauthority or antiinstitutional attitudes diminished a bit, consultation processes on the parish, diocesan, or national level, became more commonplace, and the revised liturgical books appeared. The latter ingeniously combined elements of unity, diversity, and richness.

9. Revised Worship Texts. *a. Order of Mass.* The *Order of Mass*, for example, introduced in 1970, preserved the unity of its 1570 predecessor, but without the uniformity of the *Roman Missal* issued four hundred years earlier. Instead, while providing a core rite to be observed everywhere in the world, it offered within this framework an openness of options to be selected and adapted by the local worshiping community. Moreover, the authorized mass books, the sacramentary and lectionary, contained an enormously rich collection of prayers and biblical texts for use at mass.

b. Other rites and ecumenical impact. The other liturgical books for such rites as baptism, marriage, care of the sick, and funerals that were published around the same time or later in the seventies followed that triple pattern. Their excellence, and the fact that several Protestant, Anglican or Episcopalian, and Orthodox scholars contributed as consultants to the committees implementing the council, led many mainstream Christian bodies to use these texts or resources for the reform of their own worship manuals. This in turn facilitated further cooperation between Catholic and other Christian clergy of the U.S. in areas like common preparation of Sunday homilies or sermons, shared nuptial services, and ecumenical prayer events.

c. Need to study all Vatican II documents. Many people today—profound theologians and persons in the pews, popular speakers and pastoral workers—cite the Second Vatican Council in support of their views or practices. However, not all have read the documents, nor does everyone refer to them correctly. Any student of pastoral care in the U.S. would do well to read the sixteen documents in their entirety and also the many Vatican decrees published afterwards, which implement or clarify them. (See Flannery, 1975, 1982.)

10. Pastoral Care's Triple Mission Today. In the first half of this century, we saw that there were three developments sowing seeds for what was to come: the liturgical movement, social justice encyclicals, and lay apostolate techniques. Those efforts are now reaching maturity and are evident on all levels in the Catholic church throughout the U.S.

a. Worship. While implementation of the liturgy reforms varies in degree and style from parish to parish and clergy to clergy, one witnesses, universally, renovated sanctuaries with altars facing the people, vernacular liturgies, congregational participation, creative developments, and multiple lay ministries like Communion distributors, readers, leaders of song, ushers, greeters, musicians, choirs, and members of liturgy committees. The description of the early Christians in Acts 2 and 6 could be applied more easily now to Roman Catholic parishes than perhaps might have been the case in past decades.

b. Preaching the liberating gospel. Both the documents of the Second Vatican Council and the Synod of Bishops in 1971 have taught that working for social justice is to be seen as an essential part of the Christian message and as an expected duty for every Christian. We see the impact of this teaching in a diversity of ways, from the U.S. National Conference of Catholic Bishops' pastoral letter on war and peace in 1983 to the fast multiplying human development groups in parishes seeking to identify and root out causes of injustice on the local scene.

c. Help for the hurting. Finally, the scattered, faltering steps of the lay apostolate in the first half of this century have become a veritable stampede in our own day. The theology of the church proposed in the council, the specific encouragement of lay ministries also taught at Vatican II, and the practical need and value for laypersons recognized on the parish level today have produced an enormous growth in the number of lay ministers and their types of activities. Permanent deacons have been reintroduced in the church who work with alcoholics, visit jails, and care for residents of nursing homes. Volunteer and employed, full- and part-time laypersons, women and men, bring Communion to those confined to their houses; they prepare parents for baptism, children for sacraments, and couples for marriage; they help the bereaved bury their dead; they visit those who mourn; and they share their experiences of pain or hurt with others suffering similar troubles.

Jesus touched those who were hurting and healed them. The Catholic church carries on this pastoral care work in our own day, but no longer just by clergy and consecrated religious women and men, but also through a vast array of laypeople.

Bibliography. J. M. Champlin, *Christ Present and Yet to Come* (1971); *The Proper Balance* (1981). A. Flannery, ed., *Vatican Council II* (vols. 1, 2; 1975, 1982). J. Gremillion, *The Gospel of Peace and Justice* (1976). R. P. McBrien, *Catholicism* (1981); *The Rites of the Church*, (vols. 1, 2; 1976, 1979). R. K. Seasoltz, *The*

New Liturgy: A Documentation (1966). Two journals of special significance for Roman Catholic pastoral care are *Worship* and *Homiletic and Pastoral Review*.

J. CHAMPLIN

COUNSELING, ROMAN CATHOLIC; PASTORAL CARE (History, Traditions, and Definitions); ROMAN CATHOLIC PASTORAL CARE. *See also* PASTORAL THEOLOGY, ROMAN CATHOLIC; PSYCHOLOGY IN AMERICAN RELIGION; THEOLOGICAL EDUCATION AND THE PASTORAL CARE MOVEMENT, ROMAN CATHOLIC; VATICAN COUNCIL II AND PASTORAL CARE. *Compare* PASTORAL CARE MOVEMENT.

HISTRIONIC PERSONALITY DISORDER. *See* HYSTERIA.

HIV INFECTION. *See* AIDS (Pastoral Issues); HANDICAP AND DISABILITY.

HOLIDAY DEPRESSION. An emotional reaction to holiday events and related cultural messages that promote celebration, characterized by various expressions or symptoms which range from mild discouragement, pessimism, and listlessness to despondency, persistent unpleasant tension, and melancholic ruminations of a limited nature. Decisions about how to behave seem to be extremely "difficult," if not "impossible." Such choices as which church service or social party to attend, what gift to purchase, or whether to mail a seasonal card sometimes provoke a sense of anguish. This behavior frequently has the appearance of *accidie*, a so-called deadly sin describing deep restlessness and inability to either work or pray. Often this level of the depression is complicated by drug and alcohol abuse.

Left unattended, some people experience an even more intense reaction, and the holiday depression can result in suicide, particularly close to a lonely Christmas Day. Those who suffer with this intensity often report preoccupations with morbid dejection, isolation, somatic disturbances, insomnia, fatigue, loss of appetite, and constipation. Their sadness, internalized anger, and expectations of being unwanted are overshadowed by exaggerations of past peccadilloes or "sins of omission." It is not uncommon that they recount their misfortunes with monotonic expressions like "If only . . . ," or "I can't seem to . . . ."

In families, holiday depression frequently follows a dynamic pattern or "calendar" of discord: by mid-fall the vacation-like nature of the summer has worn off; Halloween is the initial signal that the "holiday strip" is imminent; that strip is heralded by Thanksgiving; tension builds, but is suppressed; a hidden message, "Don't spoil Christmas for the sake of the children," is expressed by a variety of commercial agencies; Christmas brings the false exchange of "gifts"; the inauthenticity of such exchanges provokes greater tensions for those who witness or participate in the process; finally New Year's Eve, an alcohol-related party or other social situation further escalates the stress. This sequence, if repeated often enough, can result in divorce, especially if an attorney is contacted who does not appreciate the importance of referring the family for psychotherapy or pastoral counseling.

While this pattern of holiday depression is common, the "strip" is not the only period of holiday stress. Easter,

for example, occurs close to the time when most Americans calculate their income tax. For many, self-worth and financial profile become confused, if not equated, creating a period of marked anxiety and insecurity, which breed depression.

Independence Day is another occasion for potential holiday depression. The event usually extends over a long weekend when temperatures are high. Family gatherings are often noisy and involve alcohol. Since preteen children are commonly at home, parents may seek more childcare assistance from their spouses, and family quarrels can result. A special dilemma is experienced on July 4th by Vietnam veterans for whom the holiday may rekindle uniquely painful feelings. Many veterans also complain about noises, high temperatures, and humidity that remind them of the land where they risked their lives in a long-undeclared war for a country that has failed to honor them. The high incidence of divorce, crime, and suicide among Vietnam veterans points to an obvious need for crisis intervention or support groups during a time when the holiday theme involves patriotic recognition of a war America *did* win.

While holidays do not necessarily provoke depression, pastors need to recognize its possibility. A "Trauma Calendar" (*see* Anniversary Depression) can be a valuable aid. Tracts are also useful, but the pulpit is the most powerful vehicle. Advent and Christmas sermons can address the subject of depression by reflecting on the Slaughter of the Innocents; likewise, Easter is contingent on Good Friday. With the blend of such homiletical themes, ministers can offer religious perspectives, resources for prevention, and encouragement for those who experience symptoms of holiday depression, to seek personal or family counseling.

Bibliography. J. E. Baker, "Monitoring of Suicidal Behavior Among Patients in the VA Health Care System," *Psychiatric Annals,* 14 (1984), 272–75. K. Menninger, *Whatever Became of Sin?* (1973), pp. 146–48, 189. D. M. Moss, "Vietnam Veterans," *Harvard Business Review,* 5 (1986), 134–5.

D. M. MOSS

SADNESS AND DEPRESSION. *Compare* ANNIVERSARY DEPRESSION; APATHY AND BOREDOM; GRIEF AND LOSS; JEWISH HOLY DAYS AND FESTIVALS, PASTORAL DIMENSIONS OF; LITURGICAL CALENDAR; POST-TRAUMATIC STRESS DISORDER.

HOLIDAYS, JEWISH. *See* JEWISH HOLY DAYS AND FESTIVALS.

HOLINESS. *See* SANCTIFICATION/HOLINESS; SPIRITUAL DISCIPLINE AND GROWTH; SPIRITUAL THEOLOGY AND PASTORAL CARE; SPIRITUALITY.

HOLINESS PASTORAL CARE. *See* CHARISMATIC PASTORAL CARE.

HOLISM/HOLISTIC HEALTH. *See* WHOLISTIC HEALTH.

HOLMAN, CHARLES T. (1882–1968). Baptist pastor and pastoral theologian. A native of England who grew up in Canada, Holman served several Baptist churches in Canada and in 1923 became a professor of pastoral theology at the University of Chicago. He also served as dean of the Baptist Divinity House at that university.

One of the first North American ministers to take seriously the "New Psychology," Holman helped popularize the theme of "adjustment" as a guiding motif for pastoral ministry. In his study of *The Cure of Souls* (1932), he described "soul-sickness" as inadequate religious or moral adjustment. The task of the religious counselor, he thought, was to encourage adjustment to other persons and to God by promoting devotion to noble causes and values and by bringing people into the rich social environment of the Christian community.

E. B. HOLIFIELD

HISTORY OF PROTESTANT PASTORAL CARE (United States); PASTORAL CARE MOVEMENT; PSYCHOLOGY IN AMERICAN RELIGION.

HOLOCAUST. In contemporary history "the Holocaust" refers to the most tragic period in Jewish history, the years from 1933 to 1945, from the beginnings of the anti-Semitic "Nuremberg Laws" to the gas chambers of Auschwitz. Though legalized anti-Semitism in Germany began much earlier and was more methodical than most people assume, the period of the Holocaust itself began on January 30, 1933, with the Nazi seizure of power, and it ended on May 8, 1945, with the unconditional surrender of Nazi Germany. During these twelve years nearly six million Jews were murdered, including one-and-one-half million children, plus countless thousands of non-Jews.

The term "holocaust" itself refers to the complete destruction of a race or people. Derived from the Greek *holocaustos*, meaning "burnt whole," a burnt sacrifice or offering that is consumed by fire, it is an old word for a new crime. The Hebrew term *Sho'āh* and the Yiddish term *Hurban* are even more poetic: the sacrifice of the Jewish people on an altar as a burnt offering to God.

"Genocide," on the other hand, is a new word for an old crime. The term first appeared in print in 1944 in Polish legal scholar Raphael Lemkin's book, *Axis Rule in Occupied Europe.* It is a hybrid word consisting of the Greek *genos* (nation, tribe) and the Latin suffix *-cide* (killing). Lemkin felt that the destruction of the Armenians during World War I and the Jews during World War II called for a legal concept that would accurately describe the deliberate killing of entire human groups. Thus, genocide is a legal term defining crimes against humanity, while Holocaust is a sociological and theological concept denoting the "burning" or sacrifice of an entire people.

The past decade has seen a dramatic increase in both governmental and academic recognition, at high school and university level, for Holocaust and genocide studies and memorialization.

Pastoral Care: But it is not only about the deceased that significant interest is being shown; Holocaust survivors and their families continue to be a pastoral concern of the Jewish community today. The Holocaust has had a profound impact on Jewish and Christian theology as well as on interfaith relations. In the field of pastoral care, one of the primary issues raised by this event is what place the teaching and prophetic perspectives of ministry should have in the care of persons and congregations.

Pastoral issues for Christians: The issue of the Holocaust touches on the very basis of faith for Judaism. How could some of the world's most Christian countries allow such crimes of genocide to happen, some indeed with the support of their religious leaders?

In the face of daily global atrocities, a certain psychic numbing inevitably occurs. Yet deplorably little pastoral ministry occurs for Holocaust victims, and more is necessary. The National Conference of Christians and Jews and the American Jewish Committee are two examples of organizations through which the healing process can continue. Mutual respect can be cultivated through small church, synagogue, and campus groups, in which aspects of the Jewish and Christian faiths are discussed. This can pave the way for true redemption and self-enlightenment. There is a great need for all people to be better informed about the facts of the Holocaust and the history of anti-Semitism, and this understanding will facilitate healing.

The therapy group and counselor: An upsurge of interest in the Holocaust in the late 1970s led to an increased number of therapy and discussion groups. There is a very real problem of identity for such therapy groups, since in the usual sense the members are neither mentally nor physically ill, but rather are resilient and healthy, though exhibiting deep sociological syndromes of guilt and fear. Thus, the complexity of the Holocaust trauma and the effectiveness of the groups demands and depends on a highly trained, sensitive therapy leader. Ideally, the counselor must bring not only caring coupled with theology, but true Torah philosophy. Interestingly, it is chiefly the children of survivors, not the survivors themselves, who seek such therapy.

There is now a greater degree of knowledge about Holocaust survivors and their children, yet though the Jewish community cares for them in a socio-emotional sense, most people are still inadequately trained to deal with the impact of the trauma.

1. Faith and Theology in the Post-Holocaust Era. The Holocaust has had an enormous impact on religious thinking though it has taken society nearly four decades to come to grips with it. This, however, is understandable. Because of psychic numbing, it was probably impossible psychologically to contemplate the Holocaust immediately after the war. The Holocaust itself is unthinkable. However, in this era we are *all* survivors of the Holocaust in some sense, and in attempting to reflect on its meaning a new, post-Holocaust theology is needed.

Steven Katz (1976) has identified nine types of responses to the Holocaust: (1) The Holocaust is like all other tragedies. It merely raises again the question of theodicy and the problem of evil, but it does not significantly alter the problem or contribute anything new to it. (2) The classical Jewish doctrine of *mi-penei hata'einu* ("because of our sins we were punished") which evolved in the face of earlier calamities, can also be applied to the Holocaust. Thus, Israel was sinful and Auschwitz was its just retribution. (3) The Holocaust is the ultimate in vicarious atonement. As the "suffering servant" of whom the prophet Isaiah speaks, Israel suffers and atones for the sins of others. (4) It is a modern *Akedah* (sacrifice of Isaac), which is a test of our faith. (5) It is an instance of the temporary "Eclipse of God," a time when God is absent from history or inexplicably chooses to turn away. (6) It is proof that "God is dead," in that if there were a God, God surely would have prevented the Holocaust; since this did not happen, then God does not exist. (7) As the maximization of human evil, it is the price humanity has to pay for freedom. The Nazis were human beings, not gods. Auschwitz reflects badly on humanity, but it has no implications for our understanding of God's existence or perfection. (8) It is revelation; it issues a call for Jewish affirmation. Implicit is the commandment: Jews, survive! (9) The Holocaust is an inscrutable mystery. Like all of God's ways it transcends human understanding and demands faith and silence.

These views are represented by people as diverse as Abraham Joshua Heschel, Richard Rubenstein, Emil Fackenheim, Elie Wiesel, Ignaz Maybaum, and Eliezer Berkovits. Each of these theologians has unique and sometimes opposing perspectives on the Holocaust.

a. Death of God. Rubenstein holds the most radical viewpoint. Because of the Holocaust he feels that he must reject God and the meaningfulness of existence. There is no divine will, nor does the world reflect divine concern. This existential point of view is provocative though of course ultimately unfulfilling.

b. The Jews' sacred obligation. In direct opposition to Rubenstein, Rabbi Emil Fackenheim, a Holocaust survivor, has perhaps the most joyful and optimistic — one might say "Hasidic" — approach to the subject. For him, Auschwitz was an "epoch-making event" in Jewish history, since it calls into question the historical presence of God. Yet Jews must affirm the continued existence of God in Jewish history, even at Auschwitz, and the commanding voice of God, even out of the Holocaust. The message of that God is that Jews are under a sacred obligation to survive, to remember their martyrs, and to keep the Faith. To stop being Jews would in fact give Hitler a posthumous victory over them.

c. Atonement for human sin. Maybaum sought meaning from within traditional Jewish responses to suffering. For him, unlike Rubenstein and Fackenheim, Auschwitz is *not* a unique event in Jewish history but the reappearance of a classic and sanctified event. Maybaum dramatically asserts that in Auschwitz Jews suffered vicarious atonement for the sins of humanity: Auschwitz is the *Golgotha* of modern times. Moreover, Maybaum sees the *Hurban* as both destruction and, remarkably, as progress, for out of this destruction came much good— the rebirth of Israel and the building of the United Nations. Like Rubenstein and Fackenheim, Maybaum is sensitive to the commanding role of God. God was not absent during the Holocaust; God was there. Indeed, Hitler was God's agent. Yet behind this perspective lies not despair but the affirmation of faith and a redemption beyond death.

d. The hidden face of God. Berkovits offers a more traditional response to the Holocaust than the others. He emphasizes that the Holocaust was the culmination of a long history of Christian anti-Semitism. While the Holocaust was an immense injustice, it was, sadly, also countenanced by God. Yet Berkovits's concern is to make room for Auschwitz in the divine scheme despite the fact that the Holocaust was an unmitigated moral outrage. He draws attention to the biblical expression *hester panim* ("the hiding face of God") in which mysteriously and without human cause (i.e., sin) God turns away from man and woman. God's hiddenness, however, has good features. It creates the possibility of human action. It allows humans to be more human. It allows for more choice between good and evil. Like Fackenheim, Berkovits commands Jews to have faith in God and in Judaism despite God's mysterious ways.

2. The Holocaust and Israel. Of these four thinkers. Fackenheim and Berkovits are the most committed to Zionist interpretations of the Holocaust, though all of these theologians are Zionists. Maybaum would see Israel as the creation of the Holocaust; emerging out of the flames of Nazism, it is the miraculous in-gathering of the exiles to the Holy Land. Thus, the Holocaust and Israel are inexplicably and eternally intertwined. Fackenheim would agree and add that the Holocaust produced a desperate determination in the survivors as well as among those who identified with Israel to end the vacillation and bickering and produce a State! Their suffering as a people unified them as a people.

It is Berkovits who presents the most passionate theological linkage of the Holocaust to Israel. To him, the rebirth of Israel is contemporary revelation; it is the voice of God speaking to the world. The return to Zion is the ultimate vindication of God's presence in history and of God's love for humanity. Berkovits also gives what is perhaps the most poetic metaphor of all: if at Auschwitz one witnessed the "hidden face of God," then the rebirth of Israel is God smiling upon us.

Bibliography. E. Berkovits, *Faith After the Holocaust* (1973). R. P. Bulka, ed., "Holocaust Aftermath: Continuing Impact on the Generations," Special issue of *J. of Psychology and Judaism*, 6/1 (Fall/Winter 1981). E. L. Fackenheim, "The Holocaust and the State of Israel," *Encyclopedia Judaica Yearbook* (1974); *Quest for Past and Future* (1970); *God's Presence in History* (1972). V. E. Frankl, *Man's Search for Meaning* (1963). E. A. Grollman, ed., *Rabbinical Counseling* (1966). S. Katz, "Jewish Faith After the Holocaust: Four Approaches," *Encyclopedia Judaica Yearbook 1975/76.* H. S. Kushner, *When Bad Things Happen to Good People* (1981). I. Maybaum, *The Face of God After Auschwitz* (1965). J. N. Porter, *Confronting History and Holocaust: Collected Essays 1972–1982* (1983 — esp. "Is There a Survivor's Syndrome?" "On Therapy, Research, and other Dangerous Phenomena," and "The Affirmation of Life After the Holocaust: The Contributions of Bettelheim, Lifton, and Frankl"); "Social-Psychological Aspects of the Holocaust," in B. Sherwin and S. Ament, eds., *Encountering the Holocaust: An Interdisciplinary Survey* (1979); *Genocide and Human Rights* (1982). J. Robinson, "Holocaust," *Encyclopedia Judaica* 8 (1971). R. Rubenstein, *After Auschwitz* (1966). T. G. Schur, *Illness and Crisis: Coping the Jewish Way* (1987). M. Spero, *Judaism and Psychology: Halachic Perspectives* (1980). D. Szonyi, *The Holocaust: An Annotated Bibliography and Resource Guide* (1986). A. J. Twerski, *Let us Make Man: Self-Esteem Through Jewishness* (1987).

J. N. PORTER

ANTI-SEMITISM; JEWISH CARE AND COUNSELING (History, Traditions, and Contemporary Issues); RACISM; VICTIMIZATION; VIOLENCE. *See also* HEALING OF MEMORIES; POST-TRAUMATIC

STRESS DISORDER. *Compare* The DEMONIC; EVIL; FORGIVE-NESS; PROVIDENCE; SUFFERING; THEOLOGY (Judaism).

The HOLY. A term signifying the mysterious, numinous, and ineffable power of the divine, apprehended in religious experience. Twentieth-century use of the term comes from Rudolf Otto's ground-breaking book *The Idea of the Holy*, first published in 1917. This essay discusses Otto's work, subsequent development of his approach, and some criticisms of it.

1. Otto's Idea of "the Holy." The early years of the twentieth century saw the rise of several reductionistic theories of religion. Those of Frazer, Durkheim, and Freud are still well known. All of these theories held in common the idea that the core or essence of religion lay in some emotion or belief or reality not itself intrinsically religious (for example, fear of nature's powers). Religion became a by-product of essentially nonreligious factors, important as these might be. Otto's book took issue with this claim. The core or essence of religion is, he said, an experience of the holy, the sacral, of the numinous. Such an experience involves a sense of fear, wonder, and awe. Otto spoke of the *mysterium tremendum* and "the element of fascination" to express the dual nature of the holy. It inspires fear, but also attracts. An example of such a religious experience would be Isaiah's vision in the temple (Isaiah 6). Experiences such as this lie at the core of all living religion. Therefore, religion cannot be "explained" reductionistically in terms of factors having no intrinsic connection to this sense of sacrality.

Otto did not argue whether or not some object in reality corresponds to the human apprehension of the holy. He did not construct a proof for the existence of God, but was concerned with the phenomenon of religious experience. He is therefore a pioneer in the scholarly method known as the "phenomenology of religion" founded by William James.

2. Phenomenological Study of Religion. Continuing Otto's approach, other scholars examined religious experience in more detail and depth. Van Der Leeuw's *Religion in Essence and Manifestation*, Wach's *The Comparative Study of Religions*, and Eliade's *The Sacred and the Profane* all rely on Otto's work. These scholars are slightly less "psychologically" oriented than Otto, in that they focus less exclusively on individual experience of the holy and more on how symbols and communities convey the presence of the holy. Nevertheless, like Otto, they all wish to ground religion in some transrational apprehension of a reality (the sacred) beyond the ordinary (the profane), a reality that manifests itself within the phenomenal world. They describe patterns of these manifestations or "hiero-phanies" (Eliade's term) and claim such patterns are universal and can be discovered underneath the enormous variety of specific religious beliefs and practices.

3. Criticisms. The "holy" need not be identified with the Lord Yahweh of Jewish and Christian tradition. Although Otto's best examples come from the Bible, the sense of the holy can be found, he claims, among primitive peoples, Buddhists, and those with no religious beliefs. Yet Otto's description of the experience seems heavily dependent on the sense of God as transcendent, just, a Lord of nature, and on features of history peculiar to the Western, Abrahamic monotheistic traditions.

Another criticism is that Otto does not really defeat reductionism as successfully as he and others hoped. If one grants that "the idea of the holy" lies at the heart of religion, it is still possible to postulate a nonreligious origin for such an experience. For example, the holy could be explained in terms of projected Oedipal longings (Freud) or the mysterious power of society (Durkheim).

Nevertheless, the major contribution of Otto remains. He focused attention on powerful religious experience and away from more abstract elements of theological belief. He showed how behind such beliefs might lie dramatic encounters of real persons with forces mysterious and awe-inspiring.

Bibliography. E. Durkheim, *The Elementary Forms of the Religious Life* (1961 [1912]). M. Eliade, *The Sacred and the Profane* (1959). S. Freud, *Totem and Taboo, SE,* 13. W. James, *The Varieties of Religious Experience* (1902). R. Otto, *The Idea of the Holy* (1958). G. Van Der Leeuw, *Religion in Essence and Manifestation* (1963 [1933]). J. Wach, *The Comparative Study of Religions* (1958).

L. BREGMAN

GOD; RELIGIOUS EXPERIENCE; TRANSCENDENCE, DIVINE. *See also* MYSTICISM; REVELATION AND PASTORAL CARE; SYMBOLISM/SYMBOLIZING. *Biography:* OTTO.

HOLY CARD. *See* LITURGICAL AND DEVOTIONAL LIFE, ROMAN CATHOLIC; ROMAN CATHOLIC PASTORAL CARE.

HOLY COMMUNION. *See* COMMUNION/EUCHARIST.

HOLY DAYS. *See* LITURGICAL AND DEVOTIONAL LIFE, ROMAN CATHOLIC; LITURGICAL CALENDAR.

HOLY MEDAL. *See* LITURGICAL AND DEVOTIONAL LIFE, ROMAN CATHOLIC.

HOLY OIL. *See* ANOINTING OF THE SICK, SACRAMENT OF. *See also* RITUAL AND PASTORAL CARE.

HOLY ORDERS. The sacrament which confers the powers of the ministerial priesthood. All the faithful share in the priesthood of Christ, but some are called to the "sacred power of Orders, that of offering sacrifice and forgiving sins and of exercising the priestly office publicly on behalf of men in the name of Christ." (Doc. of Vatican II, "The Priesthood in the Church's Mission"). The plural "orders" is used because there are three degrees of participation in the ministerial priesthood. The order of the "episcopos" is the fullness of the priesthood by which one is made successor of the apostles and sharer in their mission of authority in the Church. By the order of "presbyteros" one shares in the work of the episcopacy, and by the diaconate, the initial stage of orders, one receives authority to baptize, preach, witness marriages, and assist the presbyteros in the serving of the people.

W. M. NOLAN

MINISTRY (Roman Catholic Tradition); WORSHIP AND CELEBRATION; VOCATION (Roman Catholicism). *See also* ECCLESIOLOGY AND PASTORAL CARE; PRIEST; RITUAL AND PASTORAL CARE; VOWS/VOWING. *Compare* LAICIZATION, ROMAN CATH-

OLIC CARE AND COUNSELING IN; RELIGIOUS LIFE; SACRA-
MENTS, ORDINANCES, AND RITES, TERMINOLOGY AND
CONCEPTS OF.

HOLY SPIRIT, DOCTRINE OF, AND PASTORAL CARE.

The doctrine of the Holy Spirit is the
teaching of the Christian community concerning the
identity, the action, and the effect of the Spirit of God.
In order to demonstrate the relation of this doctrine to
the understanding and practice of pastoral care, it will
first be necessary to describe the state of this doctrine and
the root biblical metaphor from which it has been generated. It will then be possible to indicate some of the ways
in which pastoral care may be understood as a spirited
and a spiriting praxis, that is, as an activity which is
based upon, and is a vehicle for, the work of the Holy
Spirit.

1. **Description of the Doctrine.** *a. Theological discussion.* In the first five centuries of Christianity the
doctrine of the Holy Spirit received its formal definition.
The most basic element of this definition is the determination that the Holy Spirit is to be understood as the
third person of the Trinity and thus equal in divinity
with the Father and the Son. Beyond this, the Spirit was
associated with the life of the church, the forgiveness of
sins, and the hope of the resurrection (Apostles' Creed),
and defined as "the Lord, the giver of life" and as the
source of prophetic speech (Nicene Creed). These relatively scant and formal definitions and associations did
not acquire the definiteness of form and richness of content which characterize the christological and trinitarian
doctrines of the same era. As a consequence the doctrine
of the Holy Spirit remains something of an open agenda
for theological reflection.

In the modern period considerable attention has been
given to this doctrine and to the many issues which have
come to be associated with it (baptism, regeneration,
"spiritual gifts," etc.). Indeed more treatises are devoted
to this set of issues in any given decade of the modern
period than in the first several centuries of the church's
life. The profusion of literature on the subject has not,
however, produced a consensus with respect even to the
most important features of the doctrine. Thus the work
of the Spirit may be associated primarily with the church,
with knowledge, with astonishing or mysterious power,
with special ecstatic experiences, with creation, regeneration, and sanctification. The indeterminate character of
this doctrine provides special problems as well as opportunities for linking it with the theory and practice of
pastoral care.

b. The biblical metaphor. The open and fluid state
of theological reflection upon this doctrine has the result
that any attempt to clarify it must pay particular attention to the biblical narratives, expositions, and poetry
from which it is derived, and in particular, to the meanings and associations conveyed by the terms "ruah"
(Hebrew) and "pneuma" (Greek), which are usually
translated as "spirit."

The biblical terms "ruah" and "pneuma" share a common range of meanings including wind, breath, force,
power, and vitality. In general, "spirit" is that which
overpowers or empowers with the latter meaning coming
to predominate in the NT. The central meaning of

"spirit" (whether natural, human, or divine), in a positive sense, is that which produces life, vitality, or liveliness. This is the basis for the identification of the Holy
Spirit as the Lord, the giver of Life in the Nicene Creed.
Thus, in biblical literature, "spirit" is most often associated with life or with renewal, increase, or abundance of
life. Those individuals who exemplify this liveliness to a
significant degree are singled out as special recipients of
spirit, especially when they function in such a way as to
protect or to increase the life of the people as a whole.
Thus judges, kings, prophets, songwriters, philosophers, and warriors are spoken of as spirited in that they
both exemplify and convey to others a fuller measure of
liveliness and vitality. In the NT this vitality is understood to be shared by all although enacted in different
ways according to a variety of fruits or gifts of the Spirit.

In general, then, the work of the Holy Spirit may be
understood as authorizing and empowering persons for
tasks and responsibilities within the community and as
producing an abundance of life or liveliness within the
community as a whole. We are thus led to view pastoral
care first as an activity which is authorized or empowered
by the Holy Spirit, and second as an activity which aims
at the general increase of life and liveliness among those
to whom it ministers. Accordingly we will describe
pastoral care as a spirited praxis, an activity deriving
from certain "gifts" of the spirit, and as a spiriting praxis
(aiming at the increase of "fruits of the Spirit").

2. **Pastoral Care as Spirited Praxis.** In the light of the
doctrine of the Holy Spirit and its biblical basis, pastoral
care may be understood as an activity authorized and
empowered by the divine Spirit and so as spirited praxis.
This view of pastoral care is grounded in the authorization to forgive sins (and so to release the neighbor from
the power of brokenness and bondage).

a. The forgiveness of sins. The disciples' reception of
the Holy Spirit following the resurrection of Jesus is
defined in the Gospel of John as the authorization to bind
and loose (Mt. 18:18). The principal expression of this
authority throughout the life of the church has been the
practice of confession leading to the pronouncement of
absolution. Modern pastoral care and counseling may be
viewed as the continuation and transformation of this
practice, and so as the direct descendant of the activity of
binding and loosing, which Matthew's Gospel makes
paradigmatic for spirited activity, generally among the
followers of Jesus.

Pastoral care and counseling may thus be viewed as
that activity authorized and empowered by the Holy
Spirit, which seeks to liberate (loose) persons from the
binding forces of grief, guilt, and other expressions of
intrapsychic and interpersonal brokenness, so as to
enable them to live more abundantly, generously, or
fully.

Like the practice of confession and spiritual guidance
of which it is the descendant, pastoral care operates
within the sphere of discourse and so is indebted to the
insights of modern talk-therapy crucial to psychology
and psychoanalysis. The association of the work of the
Holy Spirit with this same domain of discourse in biblical and theological reflection (prophetic speech, spirited
proclamation and hearing of the Gospel, etc.) further

strengthens the relationship between this doctrine and the practice of pastoral care.

b. The gifts of the Spirit. That pastoral care seeks healing and growth by means of language (that is, in hearing and speaking) entails that the gifts of the Spirit most closely associated with pastoral care are those of wise hearing (discernment, wisdom) and healing or liberating speech (interpretation, spirited utterance, etc.).

The practice of pastoral care requires the capacity to attend carefully to the speech of the other person so as to discern the signs of brokenness and healing. Since the publication of Freud's *Interpretation of Dreams* (1913), psychology has been associated with this task of a disciplined and discerning attention to the discourse of the other in all its manifestations. In the biblical tradition the accumulation and deployment of the wisdom necessary to this task is always understood as a gift or empowerment of the divine Spirit. Thus the Holy Spirit is the Spirit of wisdom and understanding which searches the heart and which uncovers that which is hidden. (Significantly the OT wisdom tradition influences those apocalyptic writings whose form is often that of the interpretation of dreams.) In addition the gift of discernment (which distinguishes the overpowering forces of disease from the empowering forces of healing and so tests the spirits) is of obvious importance for the practice of pastoral counseling.

In the Nicene Creed the Holy Spirit is linked to prophetic utterance. While prophetic speech is more often linked in the OT to oracles pertaining to the public or political sphere, this is generalized in the early Christian community to include all instances of address which summon the hearer into renovation and enhancement of authentic life. Thus admonition and exhortation are also spirited utterance. Pastoral care is not only a wise and discerning listening but also an appropriate, truthful, and liberating speech. The capacity to speak in ways which loosen the bonds of brokenness and invite the other into new and richer life is a further way in which pastoral care is a gift of the Holy Spirit.

3. Spiriting Praxis. Pastoral care may be understood not only as authorized and empowered by the Holy Spirit but also as the vehicle which serves and imitates that Spirit in the enhancement of appropriate or genuine vitality.

a. The pastoral relationship. While the pastoral relationship is often understood in terms of metaphors of contract and covenant, its association with the doctrine of the Holy Spirit suggests that this relationship may also be understood in terms of adoption and friendship.

The spirit of adoption (Rom. 8:15) is the spirit which attests to the unconditional acceptance of the other in spite of all overt and hidden forms of weakness and brokenness. By means of this adoption the Spirit restores the other to the authentic human dignity represented by such biblical images as sonship and image and likeness of God. This is an appropriate picture of the aim of pastoral care which establishes a relationship of unconditional acceptance and of respect and seeks to confer dignity and responsibility upon the other.

Thomas Aquinas understood the Holy Spirit in terms of friendship. In this view the Holy Spirit befriends us and conveys to us the love of God. Thus the Spirit, like

a friend, draws near to all our secrets, never betraying us but gently summoning us to richer and fuller life. This, too, suggests important dimensions of pastoral care which employs its gifts and disciplines to befriend the other, to bear the other's burdens, to establish trust and respect and to seek the genuine (rather than illusory) good of the other.

b. The aim of pastoral care. The pastoral relationship, whether understood as covenant or as adoption and friendship, aims at the healing of brokenness and the fostering of authentic and abundant life. The contrast between the effects of brokenness and the characteristics of abundant health and vitality is expressed by the Pauline contrast between flesh and Spirit. (Gal. 5:16–25). While this language has often been misunderstood and harmfully employed, it may nevertheless serve as the foundation for an understanding of pastoral counseling from the perspective of the doctrine of the Holy Spirit.

In this view 'flesh' indicates the pseudo-life which is rooted in anxiety and shadowed by death. It expresses itself in enmity and envy, which destroy the basis of human community. The compulsion to appropriate the other for the mere satisfaction of momentary or unlimited desire (lust) or to make the other subservient to one's own will to power (pride) attests to the destructive dynamics of desire rooted in fear for oneself and in an all-consuming anxiety. The modern work of psychoanalysis in uncovering the dynamics of desire thus continues and enriches the analytical insight of such pastoral theologians as Paul, Augustine, Aquinas, and the Reformers. The spirited contest against the forces of intrapsychic and interpersonal brokenness, which is pastoral care, draws appropriately from both theological and psychoanalytic insight into the dynamics of anxiety and desire.

Yet the positive notion of spirited life found in biblical literature goes considerably beyond psychological theories of acceptance and adjustment. The stoic resignation so nobly exemplified by Freud stands in contrast to biblical and theological discussion of the 'fruits of the Spirit'. A pastoral praxis which is informed by the doctrine of the Holy Spirit will aim not at resignation, accommodation, or adjustment but at the spirited vitality which expresses itself in freedom from anxiety, in generosity and loyalty, and in the exuberance of joy. Thus, despite pastoral care's indebtedness to psychotherapeutic theory and practice, it seeks to foster forms of life which do not merely conform to the norm of a broken and despirited world, but which exhibit traces of transcendent Spirit.

Bibliography. Aquinas, *Summa Theologica* (1272) I q. 36–38. Basil, *On the Holy Spirit* (374). H. Berkof, *The Doctrine of the Holy Spirit* (1964). K. Rahner, *The Spirit in the Church* (1979). J. Moltmann, *The Church in the Power of the Spirit* (1977). T. Oden, *Pastoral Theology* (1983), ch. 14.

T. W. JENNINGS

GOD, DOCTRINE OF, AND PASTORAL CARE; SPIRIT; TRINITY AND PERSONHOOD. *See also* CHARISMATIC EXPERIENCE; CHARISMATIC PASTORAL CARE; ESCHATOLOGY AND PASTORAL CARE; GUIDANCE, DIVINE; ILLUMINATION. *Compare* ECCLESIOLOGY AND PASTORAL CARE; EVALUATION AND DIAGNOSIS, RELIGIOUS; GOD, IDEAS AND IMAGES OF; LIFE/ALIVENESS.

HOLY WATER. *See* DEVOTIONAL LIFE AND PRACTICES, ROMAN CATHOLIC. *See also* RITUAL AND PASTORAL CARE.

HOME VISITATION. *See* CALLING AND VISITATION; CONGREGATION, PASTORAL CARE OF.

HOMELESS PERSONS. P. Marin captures the difficulty of reaching a clear definition: "The word 'homeless'. . . has become such an abstraction, . . . applied to so many different kinds of people, with so many different histories and problems, that it is almost meaningless." But Marin and others agree with Baxter and Hopper that the homeless are people whose "primary nighttime residence is in the publicly or privately operated shelters or in the streets, in doorways, train stations and bus terminals, public plazas and parks, abandoned buildings, loading docks and other well-hidden sites known only to their users." The homeless find themselves in this condition because for various reasons they cannot consistently house and feed themselves. The shelter "industry" has become increasingly acceptable to the system as a simple, inexpensive, and politically inoffensive solution to the complex problem of housing.

1. **How Many and Who They Are.** The sheer number of homeless people reached an all-time high in America in the 1980s. Almost everyone agrees on that point. Disagreement arises over the national figure. In 1984 the Department of Housing and Urban Development estimated the number to be 250,000. Two years earlier the Washington-based Community for Creative Non-Violence had estimated the number to be three million. Most other studies fall somewhere between these two estimates. The fact remains that the number of homeless people steadily increased during the eighties.

From a pastoral care perspective the total number has no relevance; that the tragedy exists at all demands response. Wherever a problem exists, so do causes and solutions. For example, the population described as "homeless" has changed drastically since the late seventies. In 1985 the General Accounting Office reported the average age of homeless persons to be thirty-four, younger by sixteen years than the average age of homeless people in the sixties. Other findings of the GAO reveal that single women comprise 13 percent of the overall homeless population, families 21 percent, and minorities 44 percent. Families with children make up the fastest growing segment of the homeless population in America, according to a 1986 study by the National Coalition for the Homeless.

Displacement alone cannot cause long-term homelessness. When locating alternative housing is impossible, however, there exists the ingredient for long-term homelessness. The Community Service Society of New York reports that as affordable housing becomes more scarce, economically unstable households increasingly fall prey to further financial difficulties, and already poor housing deteriorates more. Decent housing then drops from the range of procurable goods.

Homelessness also results from many contributing factors, simplified into the following categories: economic problems—job loss or other loss of income; deinstitutionalization—lack of community care residences for the displaced mentally ill; and addiction— lack of residential care facilities for treatment of substance abuse.

2. **Pastoral Responses to National Problem.** While affordable housing stock shrinks, more and more churches and synagogues respond by reaching out to shelter the population in most need. It is difficult to face the fact that in spite of the generous response to the crisis by the religious community, shelters are intolerable substitutes for homes. The religious and private communities now have the responsibility of moving the corporate and political communities to develop preventive measures and long-term solutions to the problem.

Homelessness is a national problem, but there is no national policy to address it. Instead, policies of the past have actually contributed to the problem. Cuts in entitlement programs have pushed already desperate individuals over the brink into homelessness. Society has difficulty accepting the concept that "a society owes its members whatever it takes for them to regain their places in the social order" (Marin). Many of the people who now live in shelters and on the streets have kept what they consider their part of an unspoken social contract, and that requires that one look at the motives of the system that is party to that contract. Inevitably the dilemma of choice between social justice and human charity arises. The difficulty in solving that problem for society must challenge and attract its serious members.

Bibliography. K. Hopper and J. Hamberg, *The Making of America's Homeless* (1984). Massachusetts Association of Mental Health, *Homelessness: An Integrated Approach* (1985). P. Marin, "Helping and Hating the Homeless," *Harper's Magazine*, 274 (January 1987) 37–44.

W. BOLLING

SOCIAL SERVICES AND PASTORAL CARE; SOCIAL STATUS AND CLASS FACTORS IN PASTORAL CARE; POOR PERSONS. *See also* ADVOCACY; EXPLOITATION/OPPRESSION; PROPHETIC/ PASTORAL TENSION IN MINISTRY; SOCIAL JUSTICE ISSUES IN PASTORAL CARE. *Compare* LIBERATION THEOLOGY AND PASTORAL CARE.

HOMEOSTASIS. Literally meaning "to stay the same," homeostasis has become a familiar concept in the behavioral sciences most commonly applied to interpersonal systems (viz., the family and the marital dyad). Secondary applications refer to larger social systems (i.e., organizations, communities) and to intrapsychic and physiological systems.

Physiologist Walter Cannon coined the term in 1932 to characterize the self-regulation demonstrated by organisms to maintain states of relative physiological constancy, such as body temperature and blood sugar. A parallel example from the mechanical sciences is the thermostat, a self-contained, error-activated device designed to regulate temperature. Both may be classified as operating systems involving a reciprocal relationship of self-contained and environmental elements.

According to general systems theory, a constant state of action-reaction exists between two or more associated components in relationship. This ongoing relationship is characterized by a fluid balance or equilibrium (homeostasis). The homeostatic principle dictates that patterns of relating, once established, will persist in the relatively balanced state, and variation or change will automatically be resisted as part of the system's survival.

The fundamental process involved in a system's homeostasis is the feedback loop, a reciprocal sequence in which system output is reintroduced into the system as information about the output's consequences. Feedback may be either positive or negative; both are vital to any organic system. Negative feedback typifies homeostasis and is often used synonymously with it. Negative, or constancy feedback, functions to decrease the system's deviation from a set norm or pattern, and thus maintains equilibrium, while positive, or variation feedback amplifies systemic deviation. If uncontrolled, positive feedback will lead to systemic breakdown and disorganization.

In any interpersonal system, behavior and communication may be viewed as feedback loops, insofar as the behavior and communication of each person is affected by that of the other person or persons. Interactional psychology considers interpersonal relationships (particularly marital dyads and families) as open, adaptive, information processing systems, functioning in accord with various general systems principles. Thus it is postulated that, for example, the family system's established interactional patterns represent a delicate balance, or homeostasis, which is intrinsically resistant to change.

Although less well developed, the idea of intrapsychic homeostasis also has been advanced. Psychiatrist Nathan Ackerman brought the homeostasis model to bear on the dynamics of the individual personality system as well as the group interpersonal system (i.e., family and society). He viewed homeostasis as a life-protecting principle for creative adaptation, which assures a control to prevent organisms being overwhelmed by traumatizing stimuli. Ackerman's discussion implies that personality consists of an integration of homeostatic processes, as a wholistic organism, and that the environmental systems overarch and embrace this integration. In the same vein psychiatrist Karl Menninger and associates (1963) have constructed a major theory of mental health and illness based on a hierarchy of homeostatic "levels of control."

Bibliography. N. Ackerman, *Family Process* (1970). W. B. Cannon, The Wisdom of the Body (1967 [1932]). K. Menninger, M. Mayman, and P. Pruyser, *The Vital Balance* (1963).

W. BECKER

CYBERNETIC THEORY IN PSYCHOLOGY; GESTALT PSYCHOLOGY; SYSTEMS THEORY. *Compare* PERSONALITY, BIOLOGICAL DIMENSIONS OF; BIORHYTHM RESEARCH; MODELS IN PSYCHOLOGICAL AND PASTORAL THEORY.

HOMICIDE. *See* VICTIMIZATION; VIOLENCE. *See also* ANTISOCIAL PERSONS; DEVIANT BEHAVIOR, THEORY OF.

HOMILETICS. *See* PREACHING.

HOMOPHOBIA. *See* HOMOSEXUALITY.

HOMOSEXUAL MARRIAGE. The concept of marriage, though understood somewhat differently in various ages and civilizations, has always signified the existence of a special relationship between two people. From a Christian perspective, the couple is blessed before God

with the implied approval, and under the watchful eye, of the congregation; it is a celebration of commitment before the witness of fellow believers. From a civil perspective, those married can enjoy benefits and legal sanctions. With a single voice, both the church and the state deny privileges to couples of the same sex.

The existence of homosexual or gay (used here to refer to male and female) couples, and their desire to have their relationship acknowledged in a ceremony of marriage is not new (see reference below). The reasons for a homosexual couple wanting to marry are as many and varied as those for heterosexuals, including wanting to provide a stable home for children who are either adopted or from a former marriage. The larger emphasis, though, is associated with the desire to be accepted by the "straight" (heterosexual) community. Homosexuals who consider themselves Christian, and many who do not, feel that they are no less deserving of the blessings accorded those who are united before God and the congregation. Indeed, for the majority who were raised within the church and who feel subsequently ostracised, the issue is one of reacceptance.

Society as a whole is coming to a more informed understanding of the nature of homosexuality. The vast majority of clinical evidence suggests that the homosexual orientation is not chosen and cannot be changed, even when motivation and desire are present. Additionally, the stereotypic brevity of gay relationships can be understood to be a function of a society in which isolated gays are not valued or supported in their relationships by the people that matter most to them. As noted above, coupling has been overtly discouraged.

These issues are of increasing concern to the more thoughtful in the church. The fundamental issue, though, concerns the needs of gay Christians: affiliation, fellowship, and understanding. At present only the Unitarian Church and the Metropolitan Community Church (the "gay" church with sizeable congregations in most urban centers) have ceremonies established for homosexual marriage, most often called "union." It is not uncommon (statistics are difficult to establish) for ministers of mainline churches to perform private union ceremonies under the aegis of their own consciences. Privately, these ministers agree that homosexuals should not be punished for something that is not of their own choosing. The secretiveness implied in the above, though, does not answer the needs of many Christian gays for acceptance into the larger community. The establishment of the gay church was largely a response to this. These issues will become increasingly familiar as the church finds fewer and fewer reasons to keep its back turned on its brothers and sisters who are homosexual.

Bibliography. J. Boswell, *Christianity, Social Tolerance, and Homosexuality* (1980).

K. P. ROSS

HOMOSEXUALITY; MARRIAGE; SEXUALITY.

HOMOSEXUAL PASTOR. Largely as a result of the gay movement, the subject of homosexuality has been receiving increased attention by churches. The subject remains volatile, with most Christians rejecting with emotion the suggestion that a homosexual lifestyle should be acceptable to the Christian community. However, the level of understanding in the churches generally seems to be improving. The traditional stance of a blanket condemnation of homosexuality, based on certain passages in the OT and NT, is now being challenged on the basis of empirical studies which have afforded a better understanding of this phenomenon.

A conclusion of current research which has been increasingly recognized is that a distinction must be made between homosexual *orientation* and homosexual *behavior*. This distinction has led several mainline denominations to conclude that homosexual behavior is sinful, but the orientation itself should not be so identified. This perspective has been applied to the case of homosexual pastors, with the conclusion that the church may ordain a homosexually oriented person if that person is committed to a life of celibacy.

This raises a critical dilemma for homosexual pastors. If they are not committed on religious grounds to a life of celibacy, then the church's ruling will appear to be unjust in singling out for condemnation the one form of sexual expression which is inherent to their orientation. One can argue that the church should help to create the atmosphere of acceptance which would enable homophiles to live openly with their partners, thereby helping to establish a norm of fidelity which would create a more stable and healthy situation both for homosexuals and society as a whole. But for a homosexual pastor to live openly with a partner would at the present time be a great offense to many congregations. It would clearly imply the church's condoning of homosexual behavior.

The fact that homosexual pastors have functioned for years without being challenged because of incompetence or inadequacy related to their sexual orientation would lead to the conclusion that, as a general rule, their homosexuality does not affect their performance adversely any more than does the sexuality of heterosexual pastors. Capacities for empathy and understanding in a variety of interpersonal settings are dependent upon many qualities other than one's sexual preference. It is likely that difficulties with various counseling situations, for example, vary as much among different homosexual pastors as they do among heterosexual pastors.

Gay movement advocates will often argue that homosexual males are generally more inclined to enter the helping professions. It is maintained that their rejection of machismo involves a sensitivity to human relationships and greater capacity for empathizing with others. One must be careful about idealizing, however. The need for heterosexuals is to recognize first the *personhood* of homosexuals and their capacities for ministry which should not be rejected simply on the basis of their sexual orientation. However, avowed homosexual pastors realize that their church's position usually prevents them from advocating or teaching an equal theological and moral standing to all sexual behavior. Whether covert or public, the homosexual pastor is clearly in a difficult position. Churches and pastors should profit from a continuing discussion of this issue.

Bibliography. J. F. Becker, "Formation for Priestly Celibacy: Pertinent Issues," *J. of Pastoral Counseling,* 22 (1987), 65–76. A. K. Berliner, "Sex, Sin, and the Church: The Dilemma of Homosexuality," *J. of Religion and Health,* 26 (1987), 137 – 42. M. Boyd, *Gay Priests: An Inner Journey* (1986). G. D. Comstock, "Aliens in the Promised Land?" *Union Seminary Quarterly Review,* 41 (1987), 93–104.

P. JERSILD

PASTOR. *See also* AUTHORITY, PASTORAL; CLERGY, EMPIRICAL STUDIES OF; FAITH AND INTEGRITY, PASTOR'S; IDENTITY, PASTORAL; MENTAL HEALTH, PASTOR'S.

HOMOSEXUALITY. The orientation of sexual need, desire, or responsiveness toward other persons of the same gender. Homosexual desire, if present, may be repressed or conscious. If conscious, this desire may be frustrated, sublimated, or actualized. If actualized as a pattern of sexual behavior, this may be rigorously hidden from others (closeted) or it may be disclosed. Homosexual desire or behavior may be exclusive or may coexist in varying degrees with heterosexual desire and behavior. The terms "homosexual," "gay," and "lesbian" should be applied only to persons whose conscious sexual desire and experience are exclusively or primarily directed toward other persons of the same sex. "Homosexual orientation" will designate the presence of a conscious primary sexual preference for persons of the same sex, whether or not this is actualized in overt sexual behavior.

1. **Scientific and Cultural Perspectives.** *a. Descriptive studies.* Since World War II, and especially in recent years, this subject has received growing and increasingly careful attention. While most attention has been focused upon male homosexuality, there is significant recent literature on female homosexuality as well. Homosexuality is found in almost all cultures where it may be variously permitted, institutionalized, celebrated, or prohibited. In Western industrial societies homosexuals constitute a significant minority (five to ten percent) of the population distributed randomly across social, economic, racial, and geographical (including rural-urban) groups.

For males there is no correlation between homosexuality and effeminacy in mannerism or passivity in behavior. For females there is no correlation with masculinity in appearance or aggressiveness in behavior. The desire to dress or appear as a member of the opposite sex (transvestism) is found among a small minority of homosexuals and heterosexuals, but the great majority of transvestites are heterosexual. The desire to alter external sex characteristics to conform to a strong identification of oneself with the biologically other sex (transexual) is typically a heterosexual rather than a homosexual phenomenon. There is no evidence to suggest that homosexuals are more likely than heterosexuals to seduce minors or to engage in coercive or violent sexual activity. Nor does a person become homosexual through exposure to homosexual role models or by being seduced or raped by a homosexual. The origins of heterosexual and homosexual (and bisexual) preference are not clearly understood but appear to be deeply rooted and, for the most part, unalterable. Contemporary studies emphasize the diversity of homosexual life-styles and personality types. Homosexuals appear to be no more or less likely to be happy, successful, well-adjusted, artistic, moral, conservative, or religious than heterosexuals.

b. Psychological theory and practice. Homosexuality has been the object of intense debate among psychologists, psychoanalysts, and psychiatrists. Since Freud considered homosexual libido to be present in all persons, and since neurosis was understood to be a function of repression, homosexuality was classed by Freud and his early followers not as a neurosis but rather as a perhaps unfortunate but not pathological fixation at an early stage of sexual organization. However, many psychiatrists in the middle of this century postulated that homosexuality derived from the interdiction of a biologically stronger heterosexual libido. This made possible the classification of homosexuality as a neurosis. This theory was substantiated by a series of corollary theses: that male homosexuality could be associated with an overpowering mother and/or a distant or unavailable father in early familial experience; that a homosexual orientation was therapeutically reversible; that homosexuality could be correlated with an overidentification with the opposite sex parent or desire for same sex parent; etc. Many of these theses have had to be revised as studies became available comparing homosexual and heterosexual populations.

Most theorists now reject the classification of homosexuality as a neurosis or as pathological, while still acknowledging that homosexuals may have problems, disorders, or neuroses associated, in particular cases, with homosexuality. A significant minority opinion continues to hold that homosexuality is a neurosis or personality disorder, while rejecting or modifying previous formulations of this classification.

c. Cultural perspectives. While there is no evidence of increase in the relative size of the homosexual population, a number of factors have contributed to the growing visibility of homosexuality in our culture. These may include urbanization, democratization, the effect of various civil and human rights movements, and increased attention to sexuality and to the availability of diverse sexual expressions. The result is a changing perception of the status of homosexuality in our culture. Some examples:

i. Legal changes. Under the influence of Roman and common law traditions most states have had vaguely worded statutes proscribing sexual behavior understood to include (although not restricted to) homosexual activity. A growing number of states have repealed or revised such laws with the result that sexual activity in private between consenting adults (including homosexuality) is neither prohibited nor punishable by law. In addition, gay rights statutes that prohibit discrimination against homosexuals have been enacted in a few areas.

ii. The "gay world." Homosexuality was once hidden from public view as much as possible to avoid social stigma, loss of job and friends, or prosecution. Most urban areas now have a visible gay subculture including bars, restaurants, political and legal action groups, religious, educational, and social organizations, newspapers, and medical and counseling services. Many of these organizations engage in "consciousness-raising" activities in the community at large in an attempt to overcome the still predominantly adverse response of society to homosexuality.

iii. Ecclesial debate. While most denominations maintain a strong disapproval of homosexual activity, there is significant debate within each of them concerning this stance. Most denominations favor the protection of the rights of homosexuals in society at large. Perhaps the most vigorous debate concerns the ordination of persons who openly identify themselves as (or are discovered to be) homosexuals. Most denominations are on record as opposing such ordinations in principle, although several of these have made occasional (and fervently contested) exceptions in practice.

2. The Judeo-Christian Tradition. Pastoral care and counseling draws not only upon the insights of the human sciences but is also informed by the Judeo-Christian tradition in the development of its response to homosexuality. In this connection, the work of biblical and historical scholarship and the reflections of theological ethics are pertinent.

a. Biblical scholarship. Homosexual *orientation* is not mentioned in biblical literature, although a variety of forms of homosexual *behavior* are occasionally made the subject of narrative or legal instruction. The narrative concerning the destruction of Sodom and Gomorrah includes a scene of threatened homosexual rape of God's representatives. Contemporary scholarship suggests that most and perhaps all other authentic references to homosexual behavior in the Bible refer to the practice of homosexual cultic prostitution. Apart from rape, cultic prostitution, and unbridled sexual self-aggrandizement, no specific references to homosexuality are to be found.

Despite the absence of specific reference to homosexuality as such, certain basic themes characteristic of biblical literature as a whole may be applied to homosexuality. Traditionally the themes of creation and of covenant have been understood to preclude homosexual activity and to encourage the institutions of marriage and family. Other perspectives that emphasize biblical themes of reconciling love or of eschatological transformation are somewhat more likely to be open to the development of alternative forms of sexual expression, while still insisting that sexuality (like other aspects of life) must seek to mirror or appropriately respond to the activity of God.

b. Church history. It is regularly supposed that Christianity has always been adamant in its condemnation of homosexuality. This belief must be tempered in view of the evidence that the church has typically protected persons accused of homosexual behavior from the excesses of popular outrage or legal retribution. Thus the church has consistently opposed popular calls for the excommunication of homosexuals and the imposition of capital punishment by state authority (e.g., Justinian, Henry VIII), insisting that homosexual behavior be dealt with by the pastoral office of the church. To this extent the position of many denominations supporting decriminalization and equal protection under the law for homosexuals is consistent with longstanding ecclesial practice. More recent research has indicated that historically the church has occasionally taken an even more accepting stance toward homoerotic relationships.

c. Theological ethics may be broadly characterized as traditionalist or revisionist in approach to homosexuality. The traditional view deals with homosexual behavior as a more or less serious departure from the divine will. This position does not maintain that homosexual orientation is itself sinful. Concerning salvation, sexual orientation is as irrelevant as race, gender, or even hair color. What is in question is homosexual behavior, rather than orientation. Since this view holds that the only appropriate form of sexual behavior is that which occurs within the context of a relationship of love and loyalty sanctified in the marriage of a man and a woman, it follows that homosexual sex acts have the same standing as premarital or extramarital sex (or of sex acts within marriage which violate the covenant of love between the two spouses). Such acts, although by definition sins, by no means exclude one from the covenant of grace, but rather must be made the subject of confession and repentance. Nor are all sexual acts outside the sphere of true marriage on an equal footing. Rape is not the same as sex between unmarried but mutually caring lovers. Nonmarital sexual relations that do not betray a covenant with another person are not as grievous as those which do. A traditional theological ethics that characterizes homosexuality as sinful is thus to be distinguished from the caricature of this position, which uses religious language to express an extreme hostility toward homosexuals.

Nevertheless, with the growth of the social scientific understanding of homosexuality, there is a growing body of theological opinion that rejects the a priori classification of homosexual activity as sinful (Pittenger, McNeill). Instead, sexual orientation is understood as a gift that is to be expressed in ways that embody the values of commitment and mutuality characteristic of genuine love. This means that all persons, whether homosexual or heterosexual, are called to form a style of sexual behavior exemplifying these values and to renounce styles of manipulation, depersonalization, self-aggrandizement, and destructiveness. Marriage and celibacy remain paradigms of appropriate sexual style, but are not taken to be the only possible ways of living out this commitment. Traditionalists maintain that even this qualified or provisional acceptance of homosexual lifestyle must inevitably weaken the normative value of marriage and is likely to lead to a permissive approach to sexual ethics that is blind to the dangers of trivializing human sexuality or of giving free rein to desires that become destructive. This debate, which is relatively recent, has reached no conclusion so far.

3. **Pastoral Care.** Depending on the theological and psychological perspective, the goal of pastoral care may be viewed as the sublimation of homosexual orientation or as the facilitation of a more integrated and maturely actualized homosexuality. The apparent divergence of these goals has very little effect upon the actual practice of pastoral care, since sublimation cannot be effectively achieved without integration. Moreover, the pastoral needs of persons of homosexual orientation are, in general, identical to those of other persons: the healing of the scars inflicted upon them by early and recent experience, loss, grief, and guilt, and help in the formation of styles of life that are more candid, generous, and joyful.

Homosexuals tend to have less in common than do heterosexuals. Only in one respect are they likely to share a common trait: that they regularly encounter from church and society the judgments that their sexual orientation (and especially any actualization of this orientation) is sinful, shameful, pathological, or maladjusted. This collision between a homosexual orientation and an antihomosexual ethos produces a condition of conflict, which is apt to color other conflicted or painful situations

and may generate requests for pastoral care. Four areas call for particular comment.

a. Self-esteem and personality integration. The collision between a homosexual orientation and a cultural disvaluation of homosexuality makes especially difficult the integration of sexuality with other aspects or dimensions of the self. Sexuality may then be split off from one's existence in such a way as to become completely depersonalized, or may be overvalued in compensation for cultural images leading to preoccupation and obsession. To the extent to which the negative valuation of homosexuality is internalized, it may lead to a crippling negative self-preoccupation (self-loathing) or be repressed, requiring the expenditure of inordinate psychic resources to defend against the threat to self-esteem. When these difficulties exist, the appropriate pastoral responses are those which encourage candor and reflect unwavering respect for and appreciation of the other. Within this context it may be possible to foster a more realistic appraisal of the self and of one's capacities and opportunities for more constructive attitudes and patterns of sexual involvement.

b. Relationships with family and straight friends. Because of the negative valuation of homosexuality many persons find it necessary to conceal not only their sexual behavior but their orientation as well. The burden of hiddenness may become insupportable or may lead to an attenuation of contacts with nonhomosexuals, thereby increasing preoccupation with sexual orientation at the expense of other aspects of one's personality. Thus, one of the most painful and urgent issues confronting many homosexuals is the degree to which it may be possible to be frank about homosexuality with family members and with heterosexual friends and associates.

The desire to "come out of the closet" may be closely associated with an attempt to overcome negative self-image and to integrate sexuality with other aspects of the personality. On the other hand, "coming out" may be expressive of self-destructiveness, or excessive preoccupation with sexual identity, and unrealistic with respect to anticipated responses. Pastoral care may be helpful in facilitating mature judgment with respect to this issue. The homosexual's development of a candid appraisal of the motivation for this move, a realistic assessment of likely responses, and a commitment to talk through adverse reactions are important barometers of readiness to take the irrevocable step of disclosing one's homosexuality to those whose love and respect one values most.

Pastoral care may also be requested by parents who become aware, through disclosure or discovery, of the homosexuality of one of their children. The culturally widespread (but scientifically discredited) supposition of parental responsibility for the origin of homosexuality may produce a strong sense of guilt, shame, or failure. Moreover, communication between family members may be blocked by anger, a sense of mistrust, or mutual betrayal. Pastoral care may be of help in encouraging candor with respect to such feelings and in facilitating their integration with the love and respect that characterize family ties. Many cities now have support groups to which appropriate referral may be made for family members of gay persons.

c. The development of homosexual relationships.

The opprobrium directed against homosexuality may be a major factor in the development of a style of sexual behavior, which separates sexuality from other, perhaps more important, relational values. Especially among male homosexuals, a pattern of casual anonymous sexual encounters may develop despite the person's apparent desire for a more durable relationship characterized by loyalty, respect, and love. This split between actual pattern and desired context of sexual expression may reflect or generate a sense of guilt, shame, or futility. Pastoral care may be helpful in identifying this division, exposing its roots and ramifications, and in assisting the person to move toward a more satisfying pattern of relationships. Even if the counselor is persuaded that the most desirable goal of pastoral care is the sublimation or alteration of the homosexual orientation itself, this need not be inconsistent with the encouragement of more wholistic homoerotic relationships in which obsessional and reductive modes of sexual behavior are replaced with modes more productive of spontaneity (freedom from compulsion), generosity, and commitment.

d. Relationship to church and faith.

A sense of conflict between homosexuality and strong religious faith may be exaggerated by a misunderstanding of the traditional Christian view of homosexuality which confuses that view with popular antihomosexual rhetoric. The correction of this misunderstanding, through education and consciousness raising in the churches and through interpretation and explanation of this and revisionist alternatives, may be an important part of a pastoral response to homosexuality.

Within the traditional framework it is important for pastoral care to foster the distinction between the divine intention of gracious transformation and the cultural (and internal) voice of accusation and rejection. The distinctions between orientation and behavior and between more and less destructive behavior may also have great pastoral value.

Many persons of homosexual orientation and religious commitment have found participation in denominationally related organizations for "gays and friends of gays" to be of value in overcoming the apparent contradiction in these two strongly held values. Most denominations have such organizations or caucuses, but perhaps the best known are Dignity (Roman Catholic) and Integrity (Episcopal). Other homosexuals, especially of a more pentecostal or evangelical background, have found the Metropolitan Community Church, a predominantly homosexual denomination, to be a congenial church home. While affiliation with gay ecclesial groups has the disadvantage of effecting only a partial reconciliation with the community of faith as a whole, referral to such groups may be an appropriate pastoral response for many persons.

Bibliography. A cross section of perspectives from the human sciences, including psychology, is to be found in H. M. Ruitenbeek, *The Problem of Homosexuality in Modern Society* (1963); and in J. Marmor *Homosexual Behavior* (1980). Recent scientific studies include: M. S. Weinberg and C. J. Williams, *Male Homosexuals* (1974). A. P. Bell and M. S. Weinberg, *Homosexualities* (1978). W. H. Masters and V. E. Johnson, *Homosexuality in Perspective* (1979), and A. P. Bell *et al*, *Sexual Preference* (1981). The last three deal with both male and female homosexuality. Other influential studies include: M. Hoffman, *The Gay World* (1968). C. A. Tripp, *The Homosexual Matrix* (1975). Important legal information is found in the American Civil Liberties Union handbook, *The Rights of Gay People* (1975).

A cross section of theological viewpoints is contained in H. Twiss, ed., *Homosexuality and the Christian Faith* (1978), and in E. Bachelor, ed., *Homosexuality and Ethics* (1980). Historical studies include D. S. Bailey, *Homosexuality and the Western Christian Tradition* (1975), and J. Boswell, *Christianity, Social Tolerance and Homosexuality* (1980). Influential calls for a revision in the church's position on homosexuality are to be found in N. Pittenger, *Making Sexuality Human* (1970), and J. J. McNeill, *The Church and the Homosexual* (1976). Specific attention to pastoral care is to be found in C. R. Jones, *Homosexuality and Counseling* (1974). A useful source book is T. Horner, *Homosexuality and the Judeo-Christian Tradition: An Annotated Bibliography* (1981).

T. W. JENNINGS

HOMOSEXUAL MARRIAGE; HOMOSEXUAL PASTOR; IDENTITY; PERSONALITY DEVELOPMENT; SEXUALITY. *See also* LIFESTYLE ISSUES *or* SOCIAL JUSTICE ISSUES IN PASTORAL CARE. *Compare* BISEXUALITY; SEXUAL DYSFUNCTION AND SEX THERAPY; SEXUAL VARIETY, DEVIANCE, AND DISORDER.

HONESTY. *See* TRUTH-TELLING. *See also* CONSCIENCE; RESPONSIBILITY/IRRESPONSIBILITY, PSYCHOLOGY OF; VIRTUE, CONCEPT OF.

HOPE AND DESPAIR. Hoping is a realistic and adaptive response to extreme stress or crisis in which the person acquires a patient and confident surrender to uncontrollable, transcendent forces. As a general existential condition with subdued ego feelings, hoping contrasts with wishing, which implies more urgent ego claims and controls aimed at particular objects and goals. It also differs from the self-assertiveness of optimism. Similarly, despair may be regarded as a more objectless and profound depressed state of being than, for example, grief, which attaches to specific loss. Despair and hope are better seen as in complex dialectical relation than as simple antonyms.

Through history the terms have carried a complexity of meaning. The Greeks and Romans had a skeptical or cynical attitude toward hope. The OT speaks about as often of trust as of hope; in the NT the word hope prevails. The Apostle Paul makes faith and hope distinct and coequal parts of his triad of abiding virtues. Popular opinion associates hope with almost anything upbeat. Despite dictionary definitions, expectation cannot be equated with hope; nor can the latter be defined as desire. Though despair means literally "un-hope," it cannot without qualification be equated with depression, sadness, or a melancholy mood. For Kierkegaard, despair includes a kind of spite; for Tillich it comes close to lack of courage; for many existentialists it indicates a state of inner emptiness or meaninglessness; and popular usage brings despair close to inconsolable grief.

1. Phenomenology of Hoping.

Against a long tradition in the psychological literature that sees hoping as part of one great impulse of desiring, the Christian existentialist G. Marcel, in a phenomenological study of hoping, finds it to be very different from wanting, hankering, craving, and other synonyms of wishing. By shifting from the noun *hope* to the verb *hoping,* Marcel takes the latter as a psychological process or activity that can be studied introspectively and objectively.

Under what circumstances can hoping occur? When a person feels caught or is visited by a calamity. For when everything goes well and as wished, there is no reason to hope. In modern parlance, hoping is a response to stress of a kind and intensity that does not allow escape, denial, repression, or other form of psychic refutation. Examples are incurable or terminal illness, severe losses, physical or mental captivity, dire threats to one's physical or mental integrity, or being severely curtailed in one's action radius. On the whole, good reality contact and reality testing are prerequisites for hoping.

What is the content or object of hoping; what can a person legitimately hope *for?* On this point Marcel draws a sharp line between wishing and hoping. Wishing is generally directed toward distinct and circumscribed, if not concrete, objects: a desired birthday present, money, a suitable mate, perfect health, special knowledge or skill, or, as the popular phrase goes, "the moon." The farmer wishes for rain after a drought; the breadwinner wants a salary raise. The more specific the object, the more likely it is that wishing is indulged. In contrast, the object of hoping is a global, more or less existential condition rather than a thing: one can hope to be delivered, to be set free, to become enlightened, to be understood, to be reconciled with others, to be forgiven, to die a good death, no matter how grim the present reality is. Using the nature of the object as criterion, a great deal of what popularly passes for hoping thus turns out to be wishing.

2. Dynamic Psychology of Hoping. *a. Ego dimensions.*
With these phenomenological distinctions in mind, a dynamic psychology of hoping would contrast the impulsivity, restlessness, and determined ego feeling in wishing with the relative quiescence, relaxation, and subdued ego feeling in hoping. Wishing involves determination and attempts at control; it is aided by willing. Hoping is closer to an attitude of surrender to uncontrollable, transcendent forces, whose power must first be acknowledged and whose benignity is assumed. The "I" in wishing is an action center, a claimant, and often an operator; in hoping the "I" has a degree of modesty and is open to unexpected revelations. Marcel distinguishes hoping also from optimism; the latter leads often to argumentative self-assertion as against the opinion of others. Optimists (like pessimists) see situations only from their own mood-determined angle and are prone to say: "If you could only see things the way I do, you would. . . ." Hopers lack the arrogance of optimists (and pessimists) and do not elevate themselves above others; they remain humble and respectful vis-à-vis the facts. Hence, in hoping one shuns prediction and does not claim rights or certainties.

b. Developmental dimensions. The psychoanalyst William Scott has constructed an early developmental sequence that runs from waiting, via anticipating and pining, to hoping. Hungry infants wait for the hallucinatory image of food to become an actual sensation; they learn to anticipate the satisfaction that is under way; and they may later come to pine for the mother who, they know by now, will typically satisfy her children. Hoping, according to Scott, allows the inevitable waiting to be peaceful and relies on the mother's own need to give to her child what she can. Hoping also derives from accumulated experiences that convey the lesson that it takes time for favorable change to occur. Scott's infantile paradigm moves from primitive wishful thinking in terms of hallucinated content at one pole to the beginnings of reality-oriented thought and interpersonal attitudes at the other.

c. Temporal dimensions. Scott's psychodynamic developmental sequence squares well with Marcel's idea about the role of temporal dimensions in hoping. The hoper is future-oriented in the sense of seeing reality as a process and therefore essentially open-ended. For a hoping person the future is open to novelty because reality is seen as resourceful. Lest this vision deteriorate into blind optimism or magical thinking, it is useful to reflect again on the differences between the objects of wishing and hoping. Whereas hoping is open-ended and trusting toward its object, wishing is concrete and insatiable; even the sky is not the limit when one considers the lavishness of accumulated human fantasies about mansions in heaven, inexhaustible supplies of beer in Walhalla, or pleasure maidens in paradise — all of which are extrapolated from past terrestrial experiences, with considerable embellishments.

3. Despair.
The difference in object between wishing and hoping may also be used to distinguish negative states such as sadness, grieving, and despondency from despairing. In sadness and grief some specific loss may be pinpointed, but despair is often without object. Kierkegaard held that despair *over* something is not yet properly despair. Similarly, it is held that in profound clinical depressions patients are unable to say what they are depressed about—theirs is a pervasive condition of gloom. Yet, in support of Kierkegaard's observation that despair has an ingredient of defiance or spite, clinicians can frequently find a hard core of self-righteousness behind the presenting gloominess of depressed patients. The depressed patient is somewhat like the arch pessimist who bitingly insists that: "If you could see things *my* way, you also would despair." Despair isolates the individual or, as in certain forms of depression, pits person against person. In contrast, hoping — with its global object — does not pit the hoper against others but is more often than not a shared experience, even a contagious one.

4. Pastoral Theological Implications.
These stark theoretical contrasts between hoping and wishing, global and specific objects, altruistic and egocentric attitudes, and modesty and pretentiousness may have to be softened in any individual case. Since in psychodynamic theory the mind is seen as stratified (i.e., operating concomitantly at conscious, preconscious, and unconscious levels and engaging in both primary and secondary process thinking), it makes sense to approach hoping and wishing, and hoping and despairing, as zones on a continuum, with most cases a mixture. If, by definition, hoping presupposes a rather accurate reality assessment of an untoward condition and a tragic sense of life, the process also involves a worldview or an ontology. This is one reason why hoping is theologically and pastorally an important human function to assess, both generically and in the individual case.

a. The practical importance of hope. As helping professionals know, a hopeful attitude can mitigate or stem the ravages of illness, while a despairing posture is likely to hasten a malignant process. Surviving in concentration camps has reportedly sometimes depended on hope, belief, or trust. Thus, there appears to be a margin of attitudinal influence on the physiology, mechanics, or field of forces that determine a condition and its outcome. To take such psychological effects on the outcome of any disastrous or malignant process into account, the world needs to be conceptualized as a process that is open to novelty and is creative, while otherwise orderly and lawful. Does a person who hopes have some kind of process view of reality (and of his or her own existence), even if only intuitively? And does the hoping person, again perhaps only intuitively, realize and prize the positive effect, however small, of hoping on his or her condition and its outcome? On empirical grounds, both questions merit an affirmative answer, which is reinforced by the typical desire of friends and professional helpers to "give hope" or "bring hope" to the sufferer. Hope is apparently considered an asset, sometimes a healing agent, and often is at least a palliative.

b. Ultimate issues in hoping. Biblical literature offers an interesting distinction between apocalyptic and eschatological thought that runs parallel with wishing and hoping respectively. Apocalyptic thought is full of concrete imagery derived from past and present experience and often involves a revenge motif: God will reverse the roles between oppressors and victims. The evildoers will be punished, and the downtrodden will be exalted in quite concrete ways. In contrast to such specificity of object derived from extrapolations from the past, eschatological thought is of extreme sobriety and leaves the arrangements and disclosures entirely to God. In the Pauline "Now we see through a glass darkly . . ." view, no concrete object is specified; nothing is arranged by human fantasy; no revenge is emphasized. The eschatologist lets God be God and asks for no more than God's presence in the last hour or the age to come.

Consequently, the hoping/wishing and apocalypse/eschatology distinctions can provide pastoral clues to the role that promises play in the mental or spiritual life of anyone. Some persons appear to know exactly what "their" God has promised them, and they will, if need be by extortionist prayers and threats, hold the heavenly Father to His promise! They let their fantasy supply the realization of every wish and read the fantasy as a divine promise: family reunions in heaven, freedom from care, or an angelic existence. Others are content with the promise of God's abiding presence in their life and death; still others assume no divine promise toward themselves at all. Thus, notions about providential promising can give a carte blanche for wishing, offer grounds for hoping, or restrain the fervor of desire. These different positions, in turn, suggest variations in such character traits as demandingness or feelings of entitlement versus humility.

Psychologically, as Scott's paradigm shows, hoping for the infant relies on a belief in the mother's benevolent intention; she is seen as wishing to satisfy her child. A theological paradigm for hoping similarly requires trust and confidence in a God who has benevolent intentions toward creatures, possibly augmented by incarnational demonstrations thereof. A metaphysical paradigm for hoping would have to insist on some cosmic benevolence that ultimately transcends the obvious malevolence by which existence is tainted. In all paradigms of hoping there is a belief (despite insufficient objective demonstration of its tenability) that the world, the cosmos, is a process and thus has a forward edge moving into the unknown, the not-yet-revealed, the creative—in a word, into the transcendent that can throw new light on or even alter present conditions. Despite its resistance to proof or demonstration, this belief can be subjectively very strong and abiding; its presence and intensity (barring pathological reality distortion) suggest that the person has experienced "good mothering" leading to trust. The great psychological, theological, metaphysical, and pedagogical question is how such realistic trust and soberly grounded hope can be safeguarded from distortion by wishful thinking and delusional schemes that "promise the moon."

Bibliography. S. Kierkegaard, *The Sickness unto Death* (1941). G. Marcel, *Homo Viator* (1944). K. Menninger, "Hope," *American J. of Psychiatry*, 116 (1959), 481–91. P. W. Pruyser, "Phenomenology and Dynamics of Hoping," *J. of the Scientific Study of Religion*, 3 (1963), 86–96. W. C. M. Scott, ed., *Selected Contributions to Psycho-analysis* (1957). P. Tillich, *The Courage to Be* (1952).

P. W. PRUYSER

ESCHATOLOGY AND PASTORAL CARE; SADNESS AND DEPRESSION. *See also* CROSS AND RESURRECTION; HEAVEN AND HELL, BELIEF IN; PROMISING; SELF-DESTRUCTIVE BEHAVIOR; SUICIDE; TIME/TIME SENSE; WILL TO LIVE. *Compare* DOUBT AND UNBELIEF; FAITH/BELIEF; EVALUATION AND DIAGNOSIS, RELIGIOUS; IMAGINATION.

HOPPIN, JAMES M. (1820–1906). Professor of practical theology at Yale Divinity School. Defining pastoral theology as "the art of applying truth," Hoppin believed that pastors were, above all, preachers, and that they became "pastors" mainly in order to learn how to preach more effectively. His *Office and Work of the Christian Ministry* (1870) and his *Pastoral Theology* (1884) dealt, therefore, primarily with homiletics, though he also urged his students to develop a "masculine," "virile," and "natural" style of pastoral conversation.

E. B. HOLIFIELD

PASTORAL *or* PRACTICAL THEOLOGY, PROTESTANT.

HORNEY, KAREN (1885–1952). An influential personality theorist who expanded upon traditional psychoanalytic theories by emphasizing the social dimensions of persons. Born in Germany, she left the church early in life, received psychoanalytic training in Berlin, and later emigrated to America. Horney founded her work upon the premise that classical Freudian theories laid a false foundation for further research and practice within the psychoanalytic movement. Her work, with its interpersonal emphasis, represented a schism from the common biological view of persons.

Horney greatly influenced the psychology of women by objecting to the Freudian concepts of genital inferiority and penis envy as determining factors in women's feelings and attitudes. Her interpersonal model, with its social and cultural emphases, presented an alternative construct for understanding women and their problems.

Horney outlined ten neurotic needs that develop out of a basic anxiety acquired during a stressful and unstable childhood. For many persons, Horney notes that life consists of a driven search for potential means of coping with this anxiety and the needs that arise from it. People cope using three major interpersonal styles: moving toward, against, or away from people. She hypothesized that these interpersonal styles, in extreme forms, lead to dependence, aggression, or isolation in relation to others. A neurotic person is one who conceptualizes inflexible coping strategies and therefore skews their interpersonal styles toward these extremes.

Bibliography. K. Horney, *Self Analysis* (1942); *Neurosis and Human Growth* (1950); *Our Inner Conflict* (1945).

B. HOUSKAMP

NEOFREUDIAN PERSONALITY THEORIES AND PASTORAL CARE.

HOSPICE. A program of health care delivery designed to control and relieve the emotional, physical, and spiritual suffering of the terminally ill. A hospice program may provide services primarily in the person's home, on an inpatient basis, or as a combination of inpatient and home care. An interdisciplinary team provides physical symptom management and psychological, sociological, and spiritual services as they are needed. Family members as well as the dying person receive care, and the bereaved are supported through the recovery period. The purpose of hospice care is to create an environment in which one can maintain quality of life to the fullest extent and then die peacefully without actively prolonging life or accelerating death.

1. Historical Perspective. The term "hospice" derives from a medieval word for a place of shelter for travelers on a difficult journey. The current use of the term comes from England. Dr. Cicely Saunders, a British physician who was discontented with the manner in which dying patients were treated in hospitals, is credited with developing the concept. She saw that doctors and nurses were afraid to talk about the "failure" of death and often offered extensive treatment that had no realistic hope of cure. She believed that dying patients did not need to be subjected to multiple tests, to being awakened when they wanted to sleep, or to having either inadequate medicine to manage the pain or to being given so much medicine that they were stupefied.

Out of these observations, Dr. Saunders researched methods for relieving pain and established a new kind of hospital with flexible services, where families could visit, the patients could bring some of their own belongings, and medical technology and machines were used properly. This hospital was the prototype of inpatient hospices today.

In the U.S., the hospice movement began in the 1970s; by 1984 there were more than one thousand hospices. Some were started by home health agencies; others were a cooperative effort by several community organizations. A few were developed as part of convalescent homes or skilled nursing facilities, and some were established by hospitals as palliative care units.

As the hospice movement grew, so did government and insurance regulations. Since many of the hospices were grass roots efforts, they found it difficult to meet these regulations and were forced to begin a process of reevaluation as they attempted to meet regulations, respond to the community needs, and maintain high standards of care.

It is still to be determined whether the primary role of the hospice will be one of improving standards of care for terminally ill within the traditional care system, or whether it will exist as a separate, highly visible, alternative form of health care.

2. Philosophy of Hospice. The philosophy of the hospice movement is a radical departure from the high technology and curative approach of traditional medicine. Family members and dying persons alike face moral dilemmas, often brought about by extraordinary advances in technology. As medical technology tends to postpone death rather than prolong life, the distinction between life and death becomes nebulous. This makes it difficult for the patient, the family, and the medical community to know when to withdraw treatment.

Legal issues are increasingly being clarified in right-to-die laws, in court decisions on end-of-life treatment, in the legalizing of the living will and other such documents, and in the rulings of informed consent and the right to refuse treatment. These clarifications have provided support for the views of persons not wishing to be maintained on life-support systems but wanting to have quality of life. Hospice's philosophy is intended to provide an environment in which this support can be expressed.

Components of the hospice philosophy are: (1) low technology, focusing on the appropriate use of machines or equipment, (2) respect for individual choices and personal dignity, (3) focus on quality rather than quantity of life, (4) attention to physical comfort, especially the relief of pain, (5) attention to psychosocial and spiritual needs, (6) involvement of and support of the family or significant others.

3. Organization and Delivery of Services. Hospice programs differ from one community to another but have certain characteristics in common. The hospice program is normally an autonomous, centrally administered program of coordinated outpatient and inpatient services. It is primarily concerned with home care but uses inpatient services as a backup if home care is not feasible. These services are usually available on a seven-days-a-week, twenty-four hour basis.

Care is focused on comfort rather than cure. Symptom control includes managing pain, nausea, vomiting, and other symptoms as effectively as possible. Efforts are made to assist with emotional issues by helping patient, family, and friends cope with the many feelings of anticipatory grief. Attention also is given to spiritual concerns and faith issues raised in the midst of suffering and impending death.

Health care is provided under the direction of a qualified physician who may be the medical director of the hospice or the patient's own attending physician. Because patient and family needs are varied and often extensive, the services are provided by an interdisciplinary team, which includes medicine, nursing, social work, physical, occupational, and speech therapy, as well as volunteers, pastors, homemakers, and home health aides. Services are coordinated within the team; patient and family are included in decisions of patient care.

Most hospice programs have a heavy emphasis on utilizing volunteers who are specially selected and extensively trained to augment staff services. They provide vital services other than clinical care, such as transportation, companionship, recreational opportunities, and emotional support.

The staff makes provisions for its own support and communication, where there are opportunities for members to discuss their concerns one to one or in a group as part of a plan to manage their own individual and team grief.

Hospices extend their services to the family during bereavement, frequently by utilizing bereavement groups or one-to-one support. Provision of services is usually based on need rather than ability to pay.

4. **Pastoral Role.** The spiritual concerns of some hospice patients include a desire to participate in meaningful rituals, sacraments, or resources of the church. For many, spiritual needs are expressed as a struggle with the meaning of death, the meaning of suffering, life after death, or guilt and forgiveness.

The pastoral role with the terminally ill, therefore, is often twofold. It may be one of offering comfort and consolation through the administering of sacraments, scripture reading, or prayer for those who have established these rituals as ones that bring comfort and consolation. It may also be one of enabling the patient or family to explore questions of purpose and meaning. Within this supportive atmosphere, patients and families can safely express their fears and feelings and may seek guidance and counsel. Frequently the most effective pastoral role is that of a good listener.

The pastoral role in relation to the local hospice varies from community to community. Some hospices are outgrowths of services of a particular church and therefore have a definitive provision of pastoral services to their clientele. Others with looser ties may have a spiritual needs or pastoral committee, or have a referral list of churches and ministers within the community who are willing to provide pastoral care. Other hospices may simply encourage and support the role of the individual's own religious affiliations and support systems.

Whatever the arrangement for pastoral services of a particular hospice, the pastor may add to a person's quality of life by knowing what hospice resources the local community provides for terminally ill persons and by making appropriate referrals to them.

Bibliography. C. Corr and D. Corr, *Hospice Care, Principles and Practices* (1983). V. W. Franco, "Reverence for the Humanity of the Dying: The Hospice Prescription," *J. of Pastoral Care,* 36 (1982), 46–55. E. Kübler-Ross, *On Death and Dying* (1969). P. Rossman, *Hospice: Creating New Models of Care for the Terminally Ill* (1977). C. Saunders, *The Management of Terminal Disease*

(1978). J. Zimmerman, *Hospice: Complete Care for the Terminally Ill* (1981).

C. BRAINERD

DYING, PASTORAL CARE OF. *See also* COMMUNITY, FELLOWSHIP, AND CARE; DEATH; GRIEF AND LOSS. *Compare* ESHATOLOGY AND PASTORAL CARE.

HOSPITAL. *See* HOSPITALIZATION, EXPERIENCE OF; HOSPITAL VISITATION; MENTAL HOSPITAL/MENTAL HOSPITALIZATION.

HOSPITAL CHAPLAINCY. *See* GENERAL HOSPITAL CHAPLAINCY; MENTAL HOSPITAL CHAPLAINCY; SICK, PASTORAL CARE OF.

HOSPITAL ETHICS COMMITTEE. With the rapid development of medical technology and the ability of medical science to alter and prolong human life, have come new questions and issues that demand multidisciplinary, as well as interfaith and cross-cultural, responses. Biomedical ethics committees have been formed to address concerns requiring input from medical, moral, ethical, legal, and spiritual value systems. Initiative and leadership in the development and functioning of hospital ethics committees has frequently come from hospital chaplains.

Hospital ethics committees generally serve three broad purposes: educational, establishing good decision-making practices, and insuring congruency of hospital's mission statement and actual practice.

The highest priority of these committees is usually educational, with education of the committee regarding bioethical issues and decision making occurring first, and education of the institution following. The educational task may be achieved through literature review, observation of other institutional ethics committees, review of relevant institutional policies, retrospective review of cases presented by physician members of the committee or other medical staff members.

Additional methodologies may include: conducting conferences or ethics rounds on nursing units; staff surveys to ascertain problems, needs or concerns to be addressed; providing film and print resources; inviting outside speakers. The development of guidelines or policies is the second task. As hospital policies and procedures are studied, revised, and drafted to cover new areas, the input of nursing and medical staff, as well as administration, is helpful in this process.

Another function of the committee is consultation. In most hospitals this is a voluntary process sought by physicians, nurses, or other members of the health care team in the midst of a difficult situation. Many retrospective case reviews are done before a concurrent consultation is attempted. The consultation process is open in some hospitals with patient family members, as well as many members of the care team, participating. Other committees do their deliberation in closed sessions. In most hospitals the opinion of the committee is advisory to the decision makers, usually the physician-patient-family triad.

Committees vary also as to whether special meetings are called for consultations, or done only at scheduled times, although flexibility as to meetings and a strategy for convening the committee on short notice appears to be operative with more active committees. Membership of committees ranges from under twelve to more than twenty. Central to all is representation of a variety of disciplines as well as community and faith groups.

The progress of the committee frequently hinges on the leadership. A keen interest in bioethics, desire to see the committee function well, respect by peers, ability to facilitate discussion and communication among differing disciplines, philosophies, values, etc., are important requisites for the chairperson. Secretarial support is also vital to the success of a committee. Committees are accountable to different authorities such as the medical staff, the administration, or the governing body of the hospital. There is reasonableness to the idea that a committee of the governing body is best able to address all bioethical issues of the institution.

Bibliography. G. R. Anderson and V. A. Glesnes-Anderson, eds., *Health Care Ethics: A Guide For Decision Makers* (1987). B. Hosford, *Bioethics Committees: The Health Care Providers Guide* (1986). R. Cranford and E. Dondera, *Institutional Ethics Committees and Health Care Decision Making* (1984). President's Commission for the Study of Ethical Problems in Medicine and Biomedical and Behavioral Research, *Deciding to Forego Life Sustaining Treatment* (1983).

J. L. BYRD

ETHICS AND PASTORAL CARE; GENERAL HOSPITAL CHAPLAINCY; INTERPROFESSIONAL TEAMS AND RELATIONSHIPS; MORAL DILEMMAS IN PASTORAL PERSPECTIVE. *See also* CONSULTATION; DYING, MORAL DILEMMAS IN.

HOSPITAL VISITATION. Hospital visitation, viewed as a dimension of pastoral care and counseling, is ministry to hospitalized patients and their family members. It is most often associated with the ministry of the clergy, but hospital visitation may also be effectively done by trained lay ministers who have been authorized to visit on behalf of their church or religious congregation. A newspaper reporter observing a particular pastor's ministry in a hospital setting described the pastor as "supportive, helpful, and not in the way, all at the same time." This may be as useful a description as one can state of what good hospital visitation should be.

Although "not being in the way" may simply seem to be a negative injunction, it underscores the fact that the hospital visitor comes to the hospital as an outsider. That fact needs to be recognized in a number of practical ways. Pastoral visits, for example, should ordinarily not be very long; fifteen or twenty minutes is often sufficient, and more can easily become a burden to the patient, especially when he or she is tired or in some discomfort. Though hospital visits may on occasion develop into extended pastoral conversation about life issues, they are best not viewed primarily as counseling occasions requiring extended time but as simple, symbolically rich opportunities for being present with the patient and family in a concerned and supportive way.

As an outsider, it is also appropriate and important that the visitor, lay or ordained, identify himself or herself to persons in authority on the floor where the patient is located, indicating that he or she is a pastor or lay visitor who has come to see a particular patient. Persons who will be visiting regularly on a particular hospital unit should usually become acquainted with the person in charge of that unit or the nurse regularly assigned to the care of the patient being visited. Such a procedure is respectful of the authority of the nursing staff and allows them to advise the visitor of any limitations on visitation or procedures which need to be observed. It also respects the authority of the visitor as one having an appropriate reason to be with the patient, and the hospital staff can prevent or reduce unnecessary interruptions of the visit. It is important that hospital visitors be allies in the care of the patient and family and "not in the way" of each other.

The hospital visitor, whether lay or clergy, should be helpful. He or she needs to be sensitive to the patient's physical condition, mood, and whether the visit seems to be helpful to the patient or to the patient's family. All of the skills which the visitor may have developed as a listener can be useful in hospital conversation. Perhaps most important is being responsive to the patient's present feelings and state of mind rather than trying to make him or her be some other way. If patients or families are sad, they probably have good reason for being so, and the visitor can be most helpful by responding sensitively to that mood rather than trying to change it. If the patient or family is cheered by the visit, it is most likely that this occurs because of the visitor "being with them where they are" rather than bringing in cheer from the outside. The helpfulness of the visitor may also include doing things for the patient or family that they are not prepared to do for themselves. The major caution about this is that the visitor follow the lead of the patient rather than deciding beforehand what needs to be done.

In addition to being helpful and not in the way, hospital visitation should be supportive. This means that the visitation is primarily intended to maintain continuity of relationship and prior religious meanings rather than to confront the patient with new things to be done in life or faith. There may be some exceptions to this view, but insisting upon change in the patient through aggressive religious witness or other means is generally inappropriate in a hospital setting. A supportive visit is one which enables the patient or family to maintain the faith in, and relational connections to, those things which are most important to them. The lay or ordained hospital visitor is a representative of religious meanings and community and offers support to the patient primarily through serving as a reminder of them.

It is in this context that the question of prayer with patients is best understood. While the pastor must judge each situation individually, it is important to remember that prayer by the pastor in the hospital is a strong ritual expectation of many church members who may feel hurt or deprived if the pastor does not offer to pray with or for them. On the other hand, prayer is not always wanted or appreciated and sometimes meets strong objection. A simple question will usually suffice to determine what is most appropriate and helpful. In situations where prayer is explicitly requested, it is often helpful to talk briefly about the request itself and what the person is seeking through it. In any case, when prayer is offered, it is important that it express something of the life situation as experienced by the patient and family, including their hopes, fears, and desires (without resorting to magical or unrealistic thought), while also setting these human concerns in the context of the mystery of God's reality and love. This is often especially meaningful if done, in part, in the language of the Psalms and other scripture. The prayer thus helps to remind patient and family of what they already know in faith, and so to support them with the specific resources of the tradition in their hour of special need.

Bibliography. R. C. Cabot and R. L. Dicks, *The Art of Ministering to the Sick* (1963 [1936]). L. D. Reimer and J. T. Wagner, *The Hospital Handbook* (1984).

J. PATTON

SICK, PASTORAL CARE OF; SICK AND DYING, JEWISH CARE OF. *See also* ANOINTING OF THE SICK, SACRAMENT OF; CALLING AND VISITATION, PASTORAL; COMFORT/SUSTAINING; HEALING. *Compare* CONVERSATION, PASTORAL; CRISIS MINISTRY; PRAYER IN PASTORAL CARE; RITUAL AND PASTORAL CARE.

HOSPITALIZATION, EXPERIENCE OF. Hospitalization refers to the act of being admitted to or placed in a hospital for treatment. The focus of the treatment may be physical illness or injury, emotional or psychological distress, or both. The treatment may be for a brief time or for extended periods. The experience of hospitalization refers to its effects on persons. Regardless of the illness or type of hospital, certain core dimensions of the experience are similar.

1. Being Hospitalized. Entering a hospital usually reflects a crisis in the life of the patient and his or her family. The crisis has at least two dimensions: the fact of the illness with its attendant uncertainties, pains, disruptions, and distress, and the crisis of the hospital, a strange environment to most patients, reflecting an unaccustomed social world inhabited by apparently efficient people, speaking a strange language, and determining among themselves how the patient's life is to be ordered.

What patients bring to illness and hospitalization, then, is themselves, their histories, relations, and understandings. The crisis of illness and hospitalization happens precisely at this point of self-understanding. Gradually or suddenly, a patient loses the illusion of health, adequacy, and control and is designated as "sick," a patient, a "case." Depersonalization and loss of status often accompany this designation. Whereas society values competence and independence, illness confirms the patient as weak, in need of care, and helpless. A life formerly characterized by self-sufficiency is transformed into one defined by discomfort, incapacity, and symptoms. This betrayal of the self by the body diminishes self-esteem and dislocates the patient.

In a variety of ways the hospital as institution may exacerbate this crisis of self-understanding. For example, hospital organization and procedure frequently encourage the sense of inadequacy and helplessness by fostering dependency. The implicit promise of many hospital procedures is that "if you (the patient) will place yourself in our hands, then we will make you well." This assumption legitimates the unanswered questions, the disregard for ordinary canons of modesty, and the exposure of

intensely personal information as necessary to insure recovery. It also implies that any feeling of indignity or violation expressed by the patient may be perceived as a lack of cooperation. The impact of many routines and procedures is essentially to remove responsibility from the patient in the name of care and cure.

The crisis of self-understanding may also be intensified by the patient's removal from family and friends. Networks of support are replaced by a community of strangers specially uniformed for their function and perceiving the patient as a reflection of his or her symptoms. Though this professional presence provides security, it does not provide the personal support which family, friends, and clergy, now relegated to the fringes of the patient's life, previously did. Patients themselves sometimes compound their isolation by seeking to "spare the family" and others by withholding information about their thoughts and feelings. Family and friends may isolate the patient by refusing to acknowledge the fact of illness in their wish for things to be as they were.

Obviously the fruit of this experience includes the possibility of anxiety and shock, grief and guilt, and uncertainty and apprehension both about the treatment and the future. One dimension of this anxiety results from the patient's perception of the social meaning of a particular illness, "clean" or "dirty" (for example, gall bladder surgery is clean while cancer is dirty). To some degree it may also stem from the social notion that persons are responsible for their health and illness, qualities seen as tantamount to either sin or failure. At times the apprehension is intensified by the sense that doctors and families are withholding information and making decisions behind the patient's back. This general uncertainty exacerbates pain and makes coming to terms with the illness and a general sense of hopefulness more difficult. It frequently compounds questions about finances and insurance and the resumption of one's various roles and fosters a yearning for a magical cure.

Rudolph Moos sums up this experience of crisis by describing the patient's primary task as "coping." He delineates seven "adaptive tasks" as essential. The first three of these have to do with the particular illness the patient is experiencing and include discomfort, incapacity, and symptoms; the fact of hospitalization and the various sorts of medical or surgical treatment; and the maintenance of adequate relations to the medical staff. Four additional adaptive tasks are more general and are related to any illness: maintaining a reasonable emotional balance, maintaining a satisfactory self-image, maintaining relations with family and friends, and preparing for an uncertain future.

2. Institutional Variations. I mentioned earlier that there was a core phenomenon in the experience of hospitalization and I have attempted to describe certain dimensions of that experience. However, any number of factors cause variations in the intensity and character of the patient's time in a hospital. For example, the nature and severity of the illness influences the patient's response. The different social perceptions of the illness affect the way a patient experiences and responds to a given illness. And the nature of the hospital affects both the patient's response and the attentiveness the staff may provide for the more personal dimensions of the experience. Hospice care, for example, has as a goal careful attention to the adaptive tasks mentioned above.

Beyond question hospitalization for mental illness is the most striking instance of the potentially debilitating effects of illness on the person. This is because most hospitalization for mental illness cuts the patient off from his or her community for extended periods of time and places him or her in an enclosed and regimented setting. Entrance to this institution connotes to the patient and to society that one is in some way flawed at one's core. Subsequent procedures upon admission foster what Goffman describes as a "process of mortification," wherein the freedom and privacy which serve to define selfhood are defiled.

This process of "dis-aging" and "dis-statusing" bespeaks a sequence of changes in the self. Initial shock and sense of abandonment frequently manifest themselves in bitterness and isolation. The patient may avoid contact to preserve the past and to postpone dealing with what he or she feels they have become. The staff may discredit the patient's self-understanding and encourage the patient to accept its diagnosis and view of the self. The patient's history, available to all the staff, seeks to demonstrate that the patient does not have a viable self. In effect, then, the control manifested in a general hospital becomes more or less complete in a mental hospital. The patient is placed in the hands of physicians and staff and is governed by their rules.

Pastoral Response. A pastoral presence may be invaluable to hospitalized persons. This is especially true during the entry stage of the experience as the patient comes to terms with the fact of illness. At the same time the quality of the pastoral presence is improved considerably if the pastor acquires the information, understanding, and skill which enables him or her to relate realistically to the patient. Such matters as knowledge of hospitals and their procedures, the various ways men and women cope with different illnesses, and a self-awareness that manifests itself in patience and understanding, are crucial.

An awareness of hospital procedures and their tendency to depersonalize patients forms the backdrop for ministry during the early stages of the experience. The shock of illness itself together with the sudden separation from all that is familiar fosters uncertainty and a sense of helplessness. Grief and anger may accompany the sense that one has lost control of one's life. A pastoral presence characterized by acceptance of the patient's experience, an earnest effort to understand this experience, and avoidance of the temptation to offer uninformed reassurance or to support various defenses (e.g., denial) can do much to assist the patient in dealing with the fact of illness.

Once the initial shock of illness and hospitalization passes, patients may begin to develop coping strategies to deal with the fact of their illness. Assimilation of the fact of pain and diminished self-esteem fosters despair or the discovery of ways to deal with a new situation. Pastors can be of considerable assistance in this quest. For example, anything a patient can do to assume responsibility for their treatment enhances their self-respect and decreases their sense of isolation and loneliness. Encouragement to request information concerning the procedures being utilized serves to enable the patient to participate in his or her treatment. The opportunity to assess one's illness and to consider possible outcomes also increases one's sense of control. Such occasions also grant patients permission to grieve the possible loss of function or potential as they become aware of the realities of their condition. Such attentiveness may also provide a setting for patients to begin to reflect on the meaning of their illness and to anticipate a future.

A new stage is reached in the life of the hospitalized patient at the point of coming to terms with the meaning of illness and of adjusting to its significance for one's life. The incorporation of the fact of illness into one's self-understanding requires time and patience on the part of both the patient and the pastor. Background, age, religious beliefs, and physical and emotional development all play a part in this quest. Moreover, the general physical and social environment of the patient's life determines in part what is perceived as possible and desirable. Finally, the timing of the illness in the patient's life cycle is significant.

It becomes apparent that the pastor's work with hospitalized patients is not finished when they leave the hospital. In the case of general and acute care facilities, the average length of stay precludes a patient's dealing with all the dimensions of illness described above. Continued attentiveness after the patient returns home and begins to resume his or her former activities assists the patient in coming to terms with both the meaning of the illness and the effect that understanding will have on the subsequent course of their lives.

Bibliography. N. Cousins, *Anatomy of an Illness* (1979). E. Goffman, *Asylums* (1961). J. Katonah, "Hospitalization: A Rite of Passage," in L. E. Holst, ed., *Hospital Ministry: The Role of the Chaplain Today* (1985). R. H. Moos, *Coping with Physical Illness* (1977). S. Sontag, *Illness as Metaphor* (1977).

L. O. MILLS

PATIENCE/PATIENTHOOD; SICK, PASTORAL CARE OF. *See also* CHRONIC ILLNESS; DYING, PASTORAL CARE OF; HEALING.

HOSPITALIZATION, MENTAL. *See* MENTAL HOSPITALIZATION.

HOSTILITY, HOSTILE-AGGRESSIVE PERSONS. *See* RAGE AND HOSTILITY; ANTISOCIAL PERSONS. *See also* AGGRESSION/ASSERTION; ALIENATION/ESTRANGEMENT; CONFLICT AND CONFLICT MANAGEMENT.

HOT-LINE CRISIS MINISTRIES. Established as a preventive service offering counseling and referral information over the telephone to people in crisis in order to avert more severe complications. While many hot-lines offer help to all in crisis, some focus on specific problems such as child abuse, suicide, or substance abuse.

Hot-line services evidenced phenomenal growth from the mid-1960s through the early 1970s but have been on the decline since then. During their growth period, the average hot-line lifespan was two years, giving them a reputation for being unstable and unreliable.

Crisis intervention by telephone holds a precarious position in the mental health field. Many view hot-lines merely as clearinghouses for referral information, providing only minimal, "stop-gap" counseling. Others point out the unique advantages of telephone work and argue that hot-lines can offer viable alternatives to traditional face-to-face psychotherapy.

Hot-lines offer: (1) immediate, personal contact; (2) caller control, giving callers the ability to hang up if they feel threatened; (3) anonymity both for callers and helpers; (4) a bridge over geographical barriers; and (5) access at odd hours. Many are staffed twenty-four hours, and centers with limited hours are often available at night.

Some centers ask for a telephone number in order to provide a few follow-up calls, and find that very few callers are unwilling to provide this information. This suggests that anonymity is less important after the initial contact. In light of consistent findings that only 50–60 percent of the callers act on the referrals given them, follow-up may encourage greater compliance.

The nature and extent of the training provided for helpers varies greatly between centers. In part, this is due to the staffing limitations of many of the agencies. However, much of the variation is reflective of the lack of consensus among professionals regarding the most helpful aspects of hot-line work.

Many centers have trained and evaluated helpers on their capacity to convey warmth, empathy, and congruence, assuming these to be the primary ingredients for any effective helping relationship. Others believe that telephone work requires greater activity and direction from helpers, a notion supported by some early research. Centers with this theory have trained and evaluated helpers on their ability to ask the right questions and offer appropriate, correct information. This disparity highlights the need for convincing evaluative research.

It is clear that the unique aspects of hot-line work prohibit generalization of helpful interventions that have been established by psychotherapy effectiveness research. D. Lester and G. Brockopp (1973) offer a helpful collection of information related to training telephone workers, as well as important issues to consider in establishing and maintaining a telephone crisis service. One agency, Contact Teleministries, has organized a national network of experts and lay people to support Christians involved in hot-line ministries. This is perceived as a method of evangelism as well as a way the church can provide critical care for persons in need.

Bibliography. D. Lester and G. Brockopp, eds., *Crisis Intervention and Counseling by Telephone* (1973).

D. R. GIVEN

CRISIS INTERVENTION THEORY; CRISIS MINISTRY. *See also* REFERRAL; TELEPHONE, PASTORAL USE OF.

HOWE, REUEL (1905–). Episcopal professor of pastoral care. After completing his theological preparation, Howe spent several years in pastoral ministry, but he is best known for promoting clinical training and for advocating dialogue as methods for theological education.

At the Philadelphia Divinity School from 1937–44 Howe was active in establishing the "New Plan of Theological Education." The new feature was the inclusion of full-time clinical training as an integral part of the seminary curriculum. Initially, all students were required to spend ten weeks in each seminary year in clinical experi-

ence, successively in a general hospital, a mental hospital, and a church parish. The program was later altered to a pattern where all students spent a fall semester in clinical training which included all three environments successively.

This plan had only modest success and was abandoned when Howe became James Maxwell Professor of Pastoral Theology at the Theological Seminary of the Protestant Episcopal Church, Alexandria, Virginia. He later became director of the Institute for Advanced Pastoral Studies, Bloomfield Hills, Michigan. In both positions Howe continued to promote clinical experience as a necessary part of ministerial preparation.

Howe has been a vigorous spokesman for a dialogical method in pastoral education, defended in his *The Miracle of Dialogue* (1963). Accordingly, the purpose of education, namely, to release the full powers of persons to participate and grow in their relationships with themselves and others, best occurs in personal encounter; only secondarily is it transmissive (*Man's Need and God's Action*, p. 114). Learning begins in experience; books help persons understand what they have experienced. Hence, teaching and learning should give priority to dialogue in which experience and gospel are brought together, translating traditional into contemporary symbols. In applying the dialogical method to the classroom, Howe has been instrumental in developing an educational philosophy to support CPE.

R. W. CRAPPS

PASTORAL CARE MOVEMENT.

HUBRIS. *See* PRIDE AND HUMILITY.

HÜGEL, BARON FRIEDRICH VON (1852–1925). Writer and spiritual director. His interest in the cultivation of the spiritual life was intensified by his friendship with the noted French spiritual director Abbé Huvelin.

Von Hügel played an important role in the modernist crisis in England, but his firm belief in the transcendence of God kept him from embracing its largely immanentist doctrine. He broke with the modernists after the movement's condemnation by the Vatican in 1910. Von Hügel's most original contribution was his two-volume study *The Mystical Element in Religion* (1908). With a focus on the life of Catherine of Genoa, von Hügel analyzed the nature of mysticism, arguing that authentic religion had to find a creative balance in its mystical, historical, and intellectual elements.

Along with his writing, von Hügel is best known as a teacher of spirituality and as a Christian spiritual director. His spiritual doctrine is best understood by a study of his letters, a selection of which appeared in 1927. In 1928 there appeared an important separate anthology under the title *Letters to a Niece*. His capacity for an open attitude toward all modern developments in culture and his fidelity to institutional Christianity made him a model for many religious searchers in his day.

Bibliography. J. Whelan, *The Spirituality of Friedrich von Hügel* (1974).

L. S. CUNNINGHAM

SPIRITUAL DIRECTOR; SPIRITUALITY (Roman Catholic Tradition).

HUMAN BEING. *See* PERSON. *See also* BIBLICAL, PHILOSOPHICAL, *or* THEOLOGICAL ANTHROPOLOGY, DISCIPLINE OF; HUMANNESS/HUMANISM.

HUMAN CONDITION/PREDICAMENT (Clinical Pastoral Perspective).

In the modern history of pastoral care and counseling, especially in Clinical Pastoral Education, these terms have been a favored way of speaking about what theology calls sin and finitude. Historically, this terminology was the clinical pastoral movement's way of appropriating its dual heritage of psychoanalytic theory and existential theology (e.g., Tillich) during its early heyday in the fifties and sixties. Drawing on Tillich's language and on his insights into the convergencies between theology and depth psychology, the vocabulary of "human condition" allowed the early clinical pastoral leaders to speak of sin and finitude in fresh, seemingly more authentic ways than the legalism and pietism of mainstream religion.

1. **Human "Caughtness."** The continued popularity of this language in the clinical pastoral movement is no doubt due to the fact that it expresses well the experiential realities of human suffering, conflict, and contradiction as these are known intimately in pastoral care and counseling. A "condition" is a "given," one's "destiny" (in Tillich's sense) over which one has no ultimate control, while "predicament" points to its problematic aspects. A predicament is a baffling or inalterable life problem—like an irreversible loss or impending death—which has no real solution and "no exit"; one is caught, trapped, "on the hook."

Equally problematic are those forms of caughtness which humans experience psychologically from within or create in some measure socially for themselves: oppression, conflict, violence, egoism, greed, lust, etc. Certainly some of these patterns can be broken or reformed, at least to some extent, and it is part of the human destiny to be able to take responsible and intelligent action to ameliorate conditions and solve social problems that restrict and destroy. Yet there are also personal and social problems, or aspects of those problems, which human action is incapable of changing, tragic though that fact may sometimes be. There the limits are met; life is experienced in its profound and baffling caughtness as subject to conditions that cannot be changed, controlled, or wished away.

"Caughtness," however, also describes humanity's relation to its higher and better capacities, not only its sin, sickness, and mortality. To be human is also to be "on the hook" as moral agents with freedom and the need to act responsibly; with imagination, creativity and the need to exist culturally; and with other similar propensities including the need for depth relationship with other persons, society as a whole, the cosmos, and God. These higher or "spiritual" capacities also form an ineradicable part of the human condition, its "grandeur" in tension with its "misery."

2. **Clinical Pastoral Significance.** The clinical pastoral tradition has emphasized the importance of encountering and personally coming to terms with "the human condition" as an essential dimension of pastoral care and counseling, and as a critical agenda in the formation of pastoral identity and authority. "Personally coming to terms" means that supervision in Clinical Pastoral Education, for instance, requires the student actually to experience, suffer, and reflect upon the limits of his or her own "human condition," its grandeur and its misery, in whatever ways those limits are encountered in pastoral experience — the limits of one's power to change circumstances or persons, to understand tragedies and absurdities, to love and to care — and the limits of one's ability to escape from moral responsibility, the need for relationship, or the search for God.

What counts—what is fundamentally empowering and creative about CPE—is not, in the first instance, its opportunities for developing pastoral "skills" or engaging in generalized, objective reflection about the human condition, but the direct, searching, struggling experience of encountering it for oneself in the attempt to care meaningfully and effectively for others encountering *theirs*. Given such depth of experience, preoccupation with skill gives way to the cultivation of modes of relationship and presence, and theological reflection becomes personally meaningful in new, more urgent and deeply honest ways.

In larger perspective, this emphasis on the human condition in clinically based pastoral care seems especially important for ministry in contemporary Western culture. American Christianity in particular allies itself with a rational-technical optimism, perpetuating the illusion that the human condition itself can be changed or overcome through scientific (e.g., medical) technologies. CPE students are instead required, at crucial junctures in their training experience, to struggle, with their patients and with themselves, with realities they cannot change. The supervisory hope is that they will thereby learn something of the limits and possibilities of being human. Within that encounter they may learn, as well, something of the meaning of that grace which frees and empowers humans to live in the world as it is, not in the world of their idolatrous, self-serving fantasies, with life-giving faith, hope, and love.

The ability to discern the difference between what can be changed and what must be endured as the "human condition," to avoid mistaking the one for the other, is also of crucial importance. Humans are perhaps always tempted to indulge their godlike fantasies that they can change what cannot be changed, while failing to act where constructive change is really possible. It requires wisdom, courage, faith, and humility to live as men and women and not as gods or demons.

And ultimately, it requires grace, for the deepest form of negative caughtness may well be the bondage of sinful determination *not* to know the difference, to refuse the unique mixture of grandeur and misery that is the human condition. In that sense the old Alcoholics Anonymous prayer may say it best for everyone, especially for those who would lead and minister to others: "God grant me the serenity to accept the things I cannot change, courage to change the things I can, and wisdom to know the difference."

R. J. HUNTER

EXISTENTIALISM AND PASTORAL CARE; FREEDOM AND BONDAGE; HUMANNESS/HUMANISM. *See also* ANALYTICAL(JUNGIAN) PSYCHOLOGY, HUMANISTIC PSYCHOLOGY, *or* PSYCHOANALYSIS, AND PASTORAL CARE; HUMAN NATURE, PROBLEM OF. *Compare* NATURE AND GRACE; REALITY PRINCIPLE; SIN/SINS.

HUMAN CONDITION/PREDICAMENT (Theological Perspective).

The human condition is defined by several interrelated polarities that are united but distinguished in human life. The human predicament is defined by the predilection of human beings to separate or confuse these polarities in their understanding of themselves and others.

1. **Body and Soul.** Human existence is material-physical bodily existence with all the biological determinations that make human beings a part of the natural world. But human beings have the unique capacity to be self-conscious, remember the past, plan for the future, make deliberate decisions, consider consequences of their actions and to some extent be self-determining. This capacity may be called the human "soul" or "spirit." Human beings are not their bodies alone or souls which only incidentally, temporarily, and perhaps unfortunately live in their bodies. They are embodied souls or besouled bodies, bodies and souls in an inseparable interrelationship.

The human predicament is the predilection of people to deny this unity and seek to escape it by trying to be less than human (living only to satisfy their biological instincts) or more than human (trying to transcend bodily limitations, needs and pleasures). This false alternative results in naturalism or materialism on the one hand or idealism or false religious spirituality on the other.

2. **Mind, Heart and Will.** Without presupposing a faculty psychology, it is possible to distinguish three aspects of the inner life of human beings. To be a human being is to a greater or lesser extent to think rationally, to make and execute decisions, and to feel such emotions as compassion, anger, sorrow, joy, regret, hope, love and hatred. Thinking, willing and feeling may be distinguished but are always interrelated in human selfhood.

The human predicament is the predilection of people to distort their own humanity by emphasizing one of these aspects of the human self to the exclusion or neglect of the others. They may emphasize "objective" rationality at the expense of passion, personal involvement and responsibility (rationalism). They may emphasize living by what "feels" good or right or natural at the expense of rational reflection and considered judgment (romanticism). They may irrationally and unfeelingly live by sheer will to self-assertion or self-protection (vitalism).

3. **Individuality and Community.** A human being is a discrete and unique self, but selfhood is identified and realized in community with other selves who are different from "me" and "my kind." In the Judeo-Christian tradition the source and enabling power of this personhood-in-relationship is the creation of human beings in the image of God: as God's deity is not transcendent loneliness and self-serving power but the desire to be the covenant-making partner of God's human creatures, so human beings fulfill their humanity in a relationship to God and fellow human beings marked by listening and speaking, receiving and giving, being helped and helping, being loved and loving.

The human predicament is the predilection of people to contradict their own humanity by seeking self-fulfillment in autonomous self-centeredness, or to contradict it by sacrificing their own and/or others' individuality for the sake of God, another person, some group or institution, or some religious or secular ideology.

4. **Freedom and Limitation.** Human beings have the capacity to decide what they will do and become, and to shape the society in which they live. On the other hand, what they and human society can do and become is limited by all sorts of biological, environmental, economic, political and cultural and historical conditions and circumstances.

The human predicament is the predilection of people to overestimate either their freedom or their limitations. They vacillate between unrealistic expectations about the extent to which change is possible and the despairing or resigned conviction that no change is possible, between false optimism (often involving compulsive activity to bring about change) and false pessimism (usually involving passive acceptance of the way things are).

5. **Being and Becoming.** In both its individual and social dimensions authentic humanity involves both continuity and change. In its individual dimension it involves both preservation of self-identity and growth toward more mature personhood. In its social dimension it involves respect for tradition that preserves enduring truth and reality, and readiness for reformation that brings new truth and reality.

The human predicament is the predilection of people to resist either change or continuity in their own lives and in the world around them. They tend to become fearful, defensive persons who resist all newness, mistaking rigidity for order, repression for stability, adherence to the *status quo* for commitment to reality and truth. Or they become chaotic, irresponsible persons who resist all order, mistaking lack of commitment and discipline for freedom, novelty for creativity, arbitrary rebellion for progress.

6. **Life and Death.** To be a human being is to be born, to live and to die. The human predicament is the predilection of human beings to contradict their own humanity by under- or over-estimating the importance of their own lives and the lives of others as they over- or under-estimate the reality of death. Denying or repressing the reality of death, they may desperately fight to preserve their own and others' lives at the cost of compromising or sacrificing distinctively human life for the sake of maintaining mere physical life. Or, resigned to the shortness of life and the inevitability of death, they may despairingly, apathetically, or hedonistically live as if their own and others' lives were of little value. Some of those who believe in some sort of life after death are also prone either to deny the reality of death or to dismiss "earthly life" as unimportant in light of the "better life" to come.

7. **Human Nature and Human Sin.** Human nature with all its polarities, limitations, and possibilities is the good creation of God. But human beings are sinful. They are unwilling and unable to accept and realize in their self-understanding and in their lives the integration of the polarities, limitations, and possibilities of authentic human existence. Human sinfulness is not to be under-

stood as what people are "by nature" but as their unnatural, self-contradictory, and therefore futile and self-destructive attempt to be what they are not and cannot become. The fundamental issue of human life is not how people can escape their humanity but how they can become the authentic human beings they were created to be and are destined to become.

8. Human Responsibility and the Grace of God. According to the Christian faith, human beings are both responsible for themselves and dependent on the grace of God for the fulfillment of their destiny. But the more human responsibility and ability are emphasized, the more unnecessary seems the help of God's grace. And the more God's grace is emphasized, the more human irresponsibility and passivity seem to be encouraged. Theologians and theological traditions disagree on how to resolve this dilemma. In general the solution lies in understanding God's accepting-forgiving (justifying) and renewing-empowering (sanctifying) grace not as the rival but as the freeing, energizing and guiding source of human responsibility and initiative.

Bibliography. K. Barth, *Church Dogmatics* 3/2 (ET 1956). J. Moltmann, *Theology of Hope* (1965). R. Niebuhr, *The Nature and Destiny of Man* (1941). P. Tillich, *Systematic Theology*, vols. 1 and 2 (1978 [1951]).

S. C. GUTHRIE

PERSON. *See also* BEING/BECOMING RELATIONSHIP; FREEDOM AND BONDAGE; HUMAN NATURE, PROBLEM OF; HUMANNESS / HUMANISM; NATURE AND GRACE; SIN/SINS.

HUMAN DEVELOPMENT. A broad form referring to those areas of psychology which study the psychological, social, moral, and spiritual development of the person throughout the life cycle. Most early researchers focused on the development of personality structures in a child, which were viewed as solidifying by late adolescence. However, more recent researchers have expanded the field to include research in cognitive, social, and moral aspects of child and adult development as well. This article offers an overview of the field and its various studies; other articles pursue these topics individually at greater length.

1. Early Research. Early theorists in human development focused almost exclusively on childhood experiences, theorizing that these early encounters with life determined how the person would develop as an adult. Sigmund Freud, for instance, reduced adulthood to an extension of tensions and problems generated during infancy and early childhood, when the individual has little control over self or environment.

Carl Jung (1933), however, claimed that midlife is the key time in a person's development. He characterized young adulthood as a time of achievement when people are very other-directed as they select a vocation, a career, and a way of relating to others. Middle adulthood, on the other hand, is characterized by introspection, when the individual reassesses past accomplishments, integrates them into a meaningful identity, and develops a deepened philosophy of life, which becomes ultimately a spiritual foundation of personal existence.

2. Contemporary Research. Erik Erikson (1963, 1968) maintained that development occurs throughout the life span and that growth depends on social and cognitive as well as biological factors. He described eight major stages of development in which social, physical, intellectual, and emotional forces interact in a unique way to produce either psychological growth or regression. He referred to these "crisis periods" as extended times of personal vulnerability and malleability, when the personality is subject to change. The result of such growth or regression is the development of specific personality traits. Erikson expresses these in terms of developmental conflicts that occur at a given stage: trust vs. mistrust, (infancy), autonomy vs. shame (early childhood), initiative vs. guilt (play age), competence vs. inferiority (school age), identity vs. role confusion (adolescence), intimacy vs. isolation (young adulthood), generativity vs. self-absorption (adulthood), and integrity vs. despair (mature adulthood).

Subsequent researchers such as Lowenthal (1975), Vaillant (1977), and Levinson (1978) have added significantly to the understanding of adult development. For the most part, they have maintained Erikson's stage theory methodology, focusing on the last four stages of adult development. The main issues during these stages, for males in particular, center on the establishment and ongoing evaluation of one' work, one's significant relationships with a mentor, spouse, and family, and one's vision or "dream" of life.

J. Piaget (1965) devised theories on how moral reasoning develops in children, and L. Kohlberg (1975) has extended that research into adult moral development. Kohlberg proposed six stages, occurring at three levels of moral reasoning. Each level reflects differences in breadth of social perception, in a person's ability to think beyond immediate situations, and in social perspective. Thus in the first two stages (the "pre-conventional level") reasoning is very concrete and is focused on individual persons and events, while at the third and fourth stages (the "conventional level") reasoning involves more abstract thinking and a perception of society as such—its groups.

Kohlberg's theory has been criticized for its monolithic view of moral psychology, for restricting his perspective of moral psychology to the question of what is just, and for doing his research almost exclusively with male subjects. But C. Gilligan (1982), a student of Kohlberg's, has pointed to divergences between men and women's moral reasoning. The central developmental dilemma for women, unlike men, derives from the need to cope with the traditional feminine notion of the good as self-sacrifice (whereas men define the good in terms of justice). The woman's dilemma is between her compassion and her autonomy, and she tries to solve moral problems in such a way that no one is hurt, rather than in terms of abstract justice. Critics charge that Gilligan exaggerates the differences between male and female by failing to control class, race, and religion; that she focuses on issues uniquely affecting women; and that she idealizes women's moral development.

3. Pastoral Applications. *a. Faith development.* Pastoral applications of research in human development have surfaced in several areas. First, in the area of faith development, J. Fowler (1981) has done the most original research. Viewing "faith" in very general terms as a relationship of trust in and loyalty to the transcendent, Fowler utilizes the methodology of Erikson, Piaget, Kohlberg, and others to describe six distinct stages of faith development, ranging from the "intuitive-projective" faith of early childhood to the "universalizing" faith of late adulthood. He does some correlations with Erikson's and Levinson's stages, but notes that development in one area does not necessarily mean development in the other, though he does suggest that being more developed in faith can enhance development in the psychosocial sphere.

b. Religious themes. A second area of pastoral application has been a more general interpretation of Erikson's developmental theory in Christian terms. E. and J. Whitehead (1982) describe Erikson's eight stages of growth and then explore some of the religious dimensions of the final three adult stages. For example, they describe the task of self-intimacy in stage six as necessary for prayer. The task of generativity in stage seven is associated with discipleship and caring for the religious community, while the task of integrity in stage eight is learning to empty oneself. (See Philippians 3.) Other authors such as E. Wright (1982) concentrate on those periods in Erikson's eight stages of development that are especially significant for the religious dimension. While Erikson was not directly concerned with religious issues, Wright maintains that the former's work does allow for the transcendent. D. Capps (1979) has suggested a relationship between each of Erikson's stages and specific theological themes, such as trust and providence, industry and vocation, intimacy and communion, integrity and awareness of the holy. Such interpretations, while helpful to pastoral counselors and spiritual directors, are clearly a second level of interpretation from a theological point of view beyond Erikson's original work.

c. Spiritual development. Other applications include the use of developmental theory to understand growth in the spiritual life. Authors such as B. Groeschel (1983) utilize Freudian developmental theory to explain the traditional Roman Catholic hierarchical three-stage approach to spiritual growth: the purgative, illuminative, and unitive ways. Others like R. Studzinski (1985) incorporate the stage theory of adult development in understanding the pastoral relationship of spiritual direction. W. Johnston (1978, 1981) utilizes Jungian developmental theory to interpret growth toward mystical union in the Carmelite and Ignatian traditions of Roman Catholic theology.

Periodicals like *Human Development* attempt to apply developmental theory in very practical ways to life in Christian communities. Issues such as depression, problems with authority, substance abuse, leadership styles, and organizational theory are discussed within the context of seminary, convent, and church life.

Bibliography. E. Erikson, *Childhood and Society* (1963); *Identity, Youth and Crisis* (1968). J. Fowler, *Stages of Faith: The Psychology of Human Development and Quest for Meaning* (1981). C. Gilligan, *In a Different Voice: Psychological Theory and Women's Development* (1982). For a critique, J. Auerbach *et al.*, "On Gilligan's *In a Different Voice,*" *Feminist Studies* (1985). B. Groeschel, *Spiritual Passages: The Psychology of Spiritual Development* (1983). W. Johnston, *The Inner Eye of Love* (1978); *The Mirror Mind* (1981). C. Jung, *Modern Man in Search of a Soul* (1933). L. Kohlberg,

"The Cognitive-Developmental Approach to Moral Education," *Phi Delta Kappan,* 56 (1975):670–78. For a critique, H. Rosen, *The Development of Sociomoral Knowledge* (ch. 6, 1980). Cf. L. Kohlberg, *Child Psychology and Childhood Education: A Cognitive Developmental View* (1987). D. Levinson, *et al.*, *The Seasons of a Man's Life* (1978); *The Seasons of a Woman's Life* (in press). M. Lowenthal, *Four Stages of Life: A Comparative Study of Men and Women Facing Transitions* (1975). J. Piaget, *The Moral Judgment of the Child* (1965). R. Studzinski, *Spiritual Direction and Midlife Development* (1985). G. Vaillant, *Adaptation to Life* (1977). E. and J. Whitehead, *Christian Life Patterns* (1982). E. Wright, *Erikson: Identity and Religion* (1982). See also the journal *Human Development.*

Q. R. CONNERS

COGNITIVE, EMOTIONAL, FAITH, LANGUAGE, MORAL, PERSONALITY, PSYCHOSOCIAL, *or* SOCIAL DEVELOPMENT. *See also* DEVELOPMENTAL THEORY *or* LIFE CYCLE THEORY, AND PASTORAL CARE; PERSON; SPIRITUAL DISCIPLINE AND GROWTH. *Compare* DEVELOPMENTAL DISORDERS; PILGRIMAGE METAPHOR; PROCESS, CONCEPT OF; SALVATION, HEALING, AND HEALTH; SELF-ACTUALIZATION.

HUMAN NATURE, PHILOSOPHY OF. *See* PERSON (Philosophical Issues); PHILOSOPHICAL ANTHROPOLOGY.

HUMAN NATURE, PROBLEM OF. Human nature is that which essentially or characteristically belongs to the uniqueness of one's existence as an individual person and in relation to other persons. Implied in this definition is a discrimination between human and nonhuman nature as well as between authentic and inauthentic existence. Thus, the problem of human nature is both philosophical and moral. The philosophical problem raises such questions as whether human nature is essential or functional, personal or impersonal, whether it is an immaterial (spirit) or material (body) aspect of the self. The moral problem presents itself as a dilemma when human nature is viewed as both the potential for good and a tendency for evil.

1. The Classical View of Human Nature. The classical view of human nature, shaped by Platonic, Aristotelian, and Stoic concepts, located the uniqueness of human nature in the rational and metaphysical faculty of the self. This resulted in a dualism in which the mind was set over against the body, identified with the divine and immortal aspects of reality, while the body was understood as a mortal and less substantial aspect of human nature. From this perspective, "essence" tends to be determinative of "existence," so that human nature is dissociated from human behavior in its psychical and social manifestation. Consequently, while this view tends to have an optimistic perspective of human nature as essentially immortal and, therefore, virtuous, a melancholy hangs over the actual existence of humanity because of the mortal and, therefore, tragic situation in which this nature exists in the finite and temporal world.

This view of human nature tends to see the body and all of its functions, including sexuality, as intrinsically evil or, at best, a liability to the good. Only death or an extreme asceticism releases one from this dilemma. The inherent dualism between the immortal soul and the mortal body leads also to an ethical dualism, with a consequent alienation of one's physical nature and life from the intellectual or spiritual nature.

2. The Modern View of Human Nature. Beginning with the Renaissance and following the Enlightenment, concepts of human nature turned toward the autonomy and individuality of human nature in the form of both naturalistic and romantic identification of the self with spirit. However, the attempt to ground individuality in either nature or spirit soon failed; idealism and naturalism tended to swallow up the particularity and freedom of the self under the indiscriminate principle of ideal being or under the determinism of natural law. Thus, human nature became dissociated from historical and personal existence and finally lost its status as a criterion for the interpretation of human behavior and ethics.

Following Kierkegaard, existentialist anthropology sought to recover the authentic humanity of the self as an existing individual through a dialectical relation between the infinite and the finite. Human nature no longer was viewed as a metaphysical substance, determinative of the self; rather, the self, in positing personal existence through decision, mediates the eternal moment in time, and so *becomes* human. From this perspective, "existence" tends to be determinative of "essence" with regard to human nature. While the classical view of human nature tended to be essentially optimistic, despite the melancholy of living in a finite and mortal world, the modern existentialist drives the melancholy deep into the very nature of the self in the form of "dread" (angst), with hope and health being potential outcomes rather than causes.

The problem of sin becomes an existential problem rather than a metaphysical or ethical one. While sin is not a necessary or determinative principle of human nature, it is an "inevitable" result of inauthentic decisions of the self. Guilt has existential overtones and cannot be objectified and removed through forensic or sacramental manipulation. Guilt and grace become dialectical movements of the self in its striving for authentic existence.

3. The Biblical View of Human Nature. The Bible does not suggest that human nature exists independently of the creaturely, historical, and social existence of human persons. In the OT, the human person is placed in a context of concrete historical and social existence under the determination of the divine Word, and endowed with the image and likeness of God. The human person is neither the soul in abstraction from the body nor the body as the repository of the soul. As embodied soul and ensouled body, the human person exists as a unique duality of material and nonmaterial being with a positive orientation toward the other, the divine Creator, and the self. Human nature, therefore, is not a blind and deterministic creaturely force that must be tamed and made human, but it is only nature because it is first of all human. And being human, it is essentially personal and spiritual as experienced in a social and historical continuum of creaturely reality.

The problem of evil is not an impersonal and finite condition of creaturely being, but a moral and spiritual failure to exercise freedom and responsibility toward the other, the Creator, and then the self. Viewed in this way, human nature is neither abstract essence nor mere behavior. As distinguished from nonhuman creaturely beings, humans are endowed with a personal and spiritual orientation toward God as Creator, and thus their creaturely nature does not determine their destiny. Created within the time/space structure of this world, human persons have a nature that was originally determined by God to be good and not evil (cf. Gen. 1:31). While sin may be viewed as a radical and even pervasive disposition toward destructiveness and evil, it is not an intrinsic or deterministic aspect of human nature. As the Apostle Paul states, even in his own struggle with sin, "I delight in the law of God, in my inmost self" (Rom. 7:22). This view of human nature breaks the causal connection between nature and sin — a source of hope for those trapped in this vicious circle and a source of encouragement for those who undertake the "cure of souls."

Bibliography. R. S. Anderson, *On Being Human* (1982). K. Barth, *Church Dogmatics*, III/2 (1956). G. C. Berkouwer, *Man: The Image of God* (1962). E. Brunner, *Man in Revolt* (1939). R. Niebuhr, *The Nature and Destiny of Man*, (vols. 1 and 2, 1941, 1943). H. W. Wolff, *Anthropology of the Old Testament* (1974).

R. S. ANDERSON

PERSON; PERSONALITY THEORY; PHILOSOPHICAL *or* THEOLOGICAL ANTHROPOLOGY, DISCIPLINE OF; PHILOSOPHY AND PSYCHOLOGY. *Compare* HUMAN CONDITION/PREDICAMENT; HUMANNESS/HUMANISM; NATURE AND GRACE; PERSONALITY, SOCIETY, AND CULTURE.

HUMAN NATURE AND DESTINY. *See* ESCHATOLOGY; PERSON (Christian *or* Jewish Perspective).

HUMAN POTENTIAL MOVEMENT. *See* HUMANISTIC PSYCHOLOGY (Theories and Research); POPULAR THERAPEUTIC MOVEMENTS AND PSYCHOLOGIES.

HUMAN RELATIONS TRAINING. A general term which includes a wide variety of techniques emphasizing a "here and now" approach in dealing with data generated in a group setting. The training group (T-group), sensitivity training, Gestalt therapy, transactional analysis, and personal growth laboratories are but a few of the many forms of human relations training. The academic roots for these procedures are in the area of social psychology in general, and group dynamics specifically.

The common ingredient for these training programs is the use of what has been called the laboratory method, also termed experiential learning. The group deals with the data that the group generates and does not become involved with history or the "then and there." A wide variety of techniques (e.g., the "Trust Walk"), standard lectures (e.g., the "Johari Window"), and accepted procedures (e.g., group-observing-group exercises) have been developed and are used extensively. The laboratory method designs learning experiences, so that a maximum of learning can occur from a current situation. Critics of this approach claim that the learnings prove not to be permanent.

One of the earliest applications of this method occurred in the early 1930s at Mars Hill College in North Carolina. A Baptist clergyman, Dr. Walter N. Johnson, conducted "Laboratories in Church Revitalization" during summer sessions. These programs were highly praised by those participating and strongly criticized by those not involved. It appears that this training design was developed by Dr. Johnson without reference to other workers, and when he discontinued his summer program, the development of his approach terminated.

Human Relations Training can trace a continuous history from 1946 when, almost by accident, a workshop staff rediscovered the value of letting people interact in a group setting and then taking time to look at that interaction, both the process and the content. The next summer the first T-groups were conducted in Bethel, Maine, by the organization which was to become the National Training Laboratories (NTL). The programs at Bethel expanded to include personal growth, community organization, a behavioral science internship, as well as an expansion into industrial consultation and the provision of training events in other locations. By 1970 many alternatives to NTL began to appear and human relations training became available in a variety of forms and in a wide variety of leadership competence.

Bibliography. L. P. Bradford, J. R. Gibb, and K. D. Benne, *T-Group Theory and Laboratory Method* (1964). D. Cartwright and A. Zander, *Group Dynamics: Research and Theory* (1960). R. T. Golembiewski and A. B. Blumberg, *Sensitivity Training and the Laboratory Approach* (1970).

L. MORGAN, JR.

GROUP COUNSELING AND PSYCHOTHERAPY; POPULAR THERAPEUTIC MOVEMENTS AND PSYCHOLOGIES. *See also* ASSERTIVENESS TRAINING AND THERAPY; GESTALT PSYCHOLOGY AND PSYCHOTHERAPY; GROWTH GROUPS; TRANSACTIONAL ANALYSIS.

HUMAN SPIRIT. *See* PERSON (Christian Perspective).

HUMANISTIC PSYCHOLOGY (Theories and Research). That philosophically rooted orientation within psychology which emphasizes the importance of conscious experience, self-awareness, future-oriented motivation, values, freedom and responsibility, wholism, growth and enhancement, individual uniqueness, and topic-determined research.

Humanistic psychology arose during the 1960s, primarily as a self-conscious protest against the mechanistic determinism of both behaviorism and psychoanalysis. It objected to the extensively used stimulus-response model of American behavioristic psychology and to the biological limitations and "hydraulic pump" image used by the psychoanalytic approach. It was also, in some ways, a part of the counterculture movement of that same time, which objected vigorously to the impersonal and dehumanizing aspects of North American society. It attempted to develop a model of the human being which took greater account of human choice and individual self-determination. At that point it was consistent with a number of trends within the pastoral care movement itself.

Humanistic psychology is not a subject matter specialty within psychology, but an orientation to the whole discipline with certain emphases which distinguish it. It arose in the 1960s, but has historical precedents in some aspects of a number of older philosophical positions, ultimately Aristotelian. It gives a central place to conscious human experience as a necessary starting point and to the uniquely human ability to be aware of one's self. It does not see behavior as largely determined by past events and takes seriously human values and freedom. It emphasizes the importance of self-enhancement and the uniqueness of each individual. It also charges that traditional scientific psychology has too often chosen its research topics to fit available traditional techniques, instead of developing techniques to fit important topics.

Humanistic psychology is often considered together with the existential movement in psychology as a single movement: humanistic/existential psychology. There is much justification for this. The two share a common intellectual ancestry, some major emphases, and many of the same theoreticians. Nevertheless, there are some important differences.

1. **Theoretical Background.** Like any movement, protest or otherwise, humanistic psychology did not arise *de novo*. It had intellectual roots in the past, knowledge of which can be useful to understanding its present concerns. Several philosophers and psychologists are particularly important.

a. Aristotle. Ultimately, humanistic psychology owes a debt to Aristotle (384–322 B.C.), although it shares this with most other approaches in psychology as well. Aristotle, in rejecting Plato's exclusive use of reason as a method of obtaining knowledge, adopted the methodological principle that knowledge building (or research) begins with observation. One does not gain information about the human organism simply by thinking about it; one must observe it as well. Humanists begin with observation, particularly self-observation, and one of their criticisms of other approaches is that they have moved too far away from what is immediately given in such observation.

Aristotle clearly saw the human being as a biological organism, but one with a mind that is largely empty at birth; the contents of consciousness come through experience. Although such a contention may need some modification today, it opened the way for later philosophies of empiricism. The tendency of most psychological humanists to look to the environment for understanding the complexities of human behavior rather than to biology is a descendant of this position.

Aristotle believed also that the soul (*psyche*) is unitary. Although the human organism certainly is made up of a number of different functions, ultimately the essence is one. In this sense Aristotle set the stage for a wholistic emphasis, and this bias is also a part of the humanistic tradition. Moreover, the soul is free. Humanists have found this to be a central point in their view of the human being. They assert that humankind has a much larger share of available freedom than humanity either recognizes or is willing to use.

b. Locke. Trained like Aristotle in medicine, philosopher John Locke (1632–1704) was one of a group of English philosophers whose work dealt with psychological problems. Continuing Aristotle's methodological empiricism, Locke rejected the concept of innate ideas and saw the infant mind as a *tabula rasa* (blank tablet) upon which life writes. The contents of consciousness depend both upon the activities of the mind and upon perceptions or images from the outer world. "Ideas," a term similar to "meanings" or "concepts" today, appeared to be the basic units of the mind to Locke. The importance he gave to the cognitive processes influenced thinking for some time, and is echoed by humanists now.

c. Berkeley. Locke's intellectual successor, George Berkeley (1685–1753), enunciated a "new principle": the only immediate reality is mind itself. It was not well accepted, since it ultimately led to solipsism — a denial that anything except the mind of the person thinking (or speaking or writing) is real. Nevertheless, a descendant of this proposal is found in the point made by many humanists that the phenomenal world of the individual is that person's only reality.

d. Kant. Immanuel Kant (1724–1804), like Locke and Berkeley, maintained a kind of subjectivism which allowed for mental processes which were not reducible to biological processes. He developed the position that the mind itself brings certain categories to the understanding of external reality (whose existence he accepted) without which knowledge would be impossible. In so doing, Kant seems to have provided some early previews of what is now beginning to be explored in regard to the nature of consciousness and alternate states of consciousness.

e. Kierkegaard. Søren Kierkegaard (1813–55) believed that truth about human beings is to be found by individuals looking within themselves. Important knowledge about human beings, then, is not a matter of averages or generalizations, but a matter of knowing intimately and subjectively the unique (isolated) individual. Life is furthermore a matter of constant uncertainty and struggle. Since there is no knowledge apart from the knower, all one can be sure of is one's own existence and this most certainly comes to an end with death.

To Kierkegaard, the process of *searching* for truth was far better than *reaching* objective certainty, because (if such certainty exists) it could finally be reached only by arriving at an understanding of essences — abstractions from the reality which every individual knows. Truth, apart from the individual's commitment to it, is unimportant and perhaps even unknowable. Kierkegaard saw human life sandwiched between the unknown before birth and the unknown after death, with a constant quest for understanding in between. That quest demanded some measure of real personal freedom to be meaningful. His related concern with the inescapable problems of anxiety, guilt, and despair has also influenced those existentialists who came after him and, through them, the humanistic movement.

f. Husserl. After early training and a doctoral degree in mathematics, Edmund Husserl (1859–1938) turned to philosophy. It was he who most clearly established phenomenology as a scientific research method. His starting point was a variation of the view that the only possible beginning point of inquiry for the psychologist is the content of consciousness, which is all that is given directly and all that one can know immediately, although it does presuppose a world to which the content refers. Examining the data or phenomena of consciousness is not easy. To set aside presuppositions, past learnings and present expectations, and to see what is truly presented in experience requires considerable study and courage. Nevertheless, the movement which he began has had considerable impact on both humanistic theory and humanistic psychotherapy.

g. James. The individual who provided the bridge between philosophy and psychology (he excelled in both) was William James (1842–1910). Somewhat younger than Husserl, James is generally considered to be the "Father of American Psychology." Certainly he was not, narrowly speaking, a founder or early proponent of humanistic psychology. But his practical turn of mind, his willingness to use introspection as a research tool, and the breadth of his investigations form an important part of the heritage bequeathed to humanistic psychology. Particularly influential was his description of consciousness as being a basic function of the person, having a focus of some kind, and always changing or moving. James is most closely connected with the phrase, "stream of consciousness."

h. Maslow. The psychologist most responsible for the humanistic movement itself was Abraham Maslow (1908–70). Although his early formal training and thinking were conventional, he soon came to be concerned that psychology as he knew it did not do justice either to the richness of human personality or to the potentialities of human beings. Behaviorism was too closely wedded to a narrow stimulus-response view of human beings; psychoanalysis was too preoccupied with the disabilities and limitations of human beings; academic psychology was investing too much energy in topics that were of little relevance to the massive problems facing mankind. In the late 1950s he decided to make a mailing list of those who shared his concerns, and from this grew the humanistic movement.

i. Rogers. Almost as influential as Maslow, but more of a therapist and less of a general theoretician, was Carl R. Rogers (1902–87). To the general public Rogers probably is the better known. Other psychologists, however, have been important. A little older than Maslow were Gordon Allport and Henry Murray. Others since have included Charlotte Bühler, James Bugental, Rollo May, Everett Shostrom, Sidney Jourard, David Bakan, Amadio Giorgi, and Alvin Mahrer, to name only a few.

2. **Major Emphases.** The humanistic movement developed a number of characteristic beliefs and emphases of which nine are especially important.

a. Conscious experience. A truly human science must begin with the individual's conscious experience. This is a heritage of early English empiricism (Locke and Berkeley) and, particularly, of phenomenology (Husserl). In academic psychology's tendency to model itself after nineteenth century physics, and in behaviorism's early extreme emphasis on the observable, psychology lost sight of the most important aspect of human beings. They experience. They have an inner life. Indeed, from an individual point of view, that is all that an individual knows directly. Humanists point out that any communication, including scientific, presupposes conscious individuals, not automatons ruled only by external stimuli.

Because of this, humanists also hold that scientific understanding must proceed by examining the individual's own experience — what the person feels, thinks, believes, values, fears, is angered by, and the like. It is similar to Rogers' insistence on empathy as a necessary condition for psychotherapy, and is not unrelated to Buber's description of the "I-Thou" relationship in contrast to the "I-It" relationship.

Humanists generally are not willing to say that no other approaches exist or that such approaches have no value in their own right. They do insist that absolute "objectivity" is impossible and that no complete model of a human being can be constructed that does not begin with or make an important place for the individual's conscious experience.

b. Self-awareness. The most important aspect of human awareness is self-awareness. Although there may be some degree of awareness in organisms lower on the phylogenetic scale than the human, it does not reach the level of self-awareness. Somehow, there is a "self" "within" the introspecting self which is able to say: "I am aware that I am aware"; "I know that I know"; "I perceive that I perceive." The nature of this interior "self" or "I" is not altogether clear, but is an undeniable phenomenal fact.

From the existential and the humanistic perspective, it is this capacity which clearly sets humans apart from others. Only humans have the ability to know, to observe, to think about their own mental processes, to know that they are doing so, and to know that they know they are doing so, and so on indefinitely.

c. Proactivity. Humans are proactive; they are concerned with and directed by goals and end states. This affirmation is a reaction against tendencies to find the causes of individual motivation primarily in the person's past. Although the past history of the individual is not unimportant to understanding why that person does what she or he does, this past history should not be thought of as the primary source of information. To explain current experience and behavior in terms of past reinforcements or childhood drives is to miss much of the point, the teleological thrust, of that behavior.

People foresee the consequences of their behavior, and they generally operate in terms of these expected consequences. To be sure, their expectations may be wrong, and they are indeed influenced by their own past; but these are not crucial considerations.

There is an interesting scientific implication in this and the preceding emphasis. In doing research on human motivation, a myriad of indirect measures have often been used. A humanist might suggest, as Gordon Allport once did, that if you wish to know why someone is doing what that person is doing, just ask her or him.

d. Values. The human being is a constantly valuing creature. This is, in part, a natural outgrowth of their ability to be governed by the expected consequences of their actions. When possible alternative outcomes are considered, they are judged not only in terms of their probability, but also in terms of their desirability. Humans constantly are asking themselves such value questions as "Do I want this thing to happen?" or "Is this a good thing to do?"

Not surprisingly, then, if one carefully examines one's own perceptual field, it becomes clear that this field is regularly tinted with value judgments. From early in life individuals come to evaluate all that occurs around to them. The parameters of that evaluation are narrow in childhood and hopefully become more extensive as the individual matures. The process goes on, such that (except in unusual instances) nothing that a person experiences is totally free of some value denotation or connotation.

e. Self-determination. Humans are self-determined to a significant degree. Individuals not only are not completely (or even largely) determined by their past histories, they are also not completely (or even largely) determined by their present environment. Alone among other living beings, humankind is able to mold itself into what it wishes to become. This is not to say that individuals have no limits whatever and are totally free; humanistic psychologists will rarely argue such an extreme position. But it is true that individuals have the freedom and flexibility to choose the ends and goals that significantly influence the course of their own development.

Implied in this is the belief that individuals are also responsible for what they are. With the freedom and opportunity for self-directed change comes also the responsibility for choices and actions. The individual stands, not as the end point of an impersonal, immutable mechanistic process, but as the intersection of a network of forces in which individual choice has played a significant part. The person still has real options at that constantly changing point.

f. Wholism. Individuals always operate as total organisms. In keeping with the anti-reductionistic bias which characterizes them, humanistic psychologists affirm that one cannot understand persons one aspect at a time, or by viewing only one aspect of behavior in isolation from all others. Humans cannot be partitioned; all "physiological" or "psychological" systems ultimately are interconnected. Although viewing different aspects of the individual is at times methodologically defensible, it must never be allowed to obscure the fact that it is only an expedient. Total organisms function totally.

g. Growth and enhancement. Individuals always tend to grow and enhance themselves. There is within each individual an innate drive to become as completely and uniquely human as possible. As an olive tree constantly tends to become the finest olive tree which it can, so do human beings.

This is not to say that this growth process is always fully realized. The reverse is probably the case. In general, the circumstances under which individuals are raised and the social contexts in which they find themselves rarely are nurturing enough to produce optimum development. People are hurtful to each other; they are careless of their own ecological supports; they act in ways that are self-damaging. This does not mean, however, that the process is non-existent, but only that it has become stifled and shows itself in warped ways.

Humanistic psychologists also have a general idea of the form people are likely to take if their growing conditions are the best. Maslow calls such people "self-actualizing"; Rogers refers to them as "fully functioning." They are open, flexible, loving, honest, self-aware, and charitable.

h. Individual uniqueness. Psychology will proceed most productively if it focuses attention on the unique individual. Humanistic psychologists are generally agreed that current scientific psychology has been too much concerned with generalizations, averages, and abstract propositions which rarely describe concrete individuals. The human race is made up of an incredible mix of specifically different people, and psychology needs to turn more of its attention to such specifics.

As one might surmise, humanistic psychologists generally are disenchanted with pieces of research covering large numbers of subjects and which report summary descriptive data for these groups. They believe that more studies should be done involving intense studies of single individuals.

i. Criteria for research topic selection. Finally, humanistic psychologists are insistent that topics selected for psychological study should be determined by their significance and substance. Their belief is that far too much scientific investigation has been determined by the ease with which a method can be applied, not the importance of the subject. This centering on the means of gathering data has produced an incredibly complex and voluminous mass of data, most of which is inconsequential. With some exceptions, such great topics as violence, love, faith, joy, and fear are likely to be skirted, since they do not lend themselves easily to traditional investigative methods.

3. **Research.** Although humanistic psychology has been able to formulate propositions which characterize it, it has been less able to generate a coherent body of supportive research. Not at all satisfied with the traditional scientific research paradigm, it has yet to come up with a thoroughly satisfactory alternative.

The phenomenological method is perhaps the only exception to this. As has been noted, this requires that a subject describe as clearly as possible what she or he is experiencing. Although applicable to many areas, it still does not seem to have been combined with other methods in ways which produce bodies of clearly identifiable humanistic research.

Some attempts have been made to suggest qualities which would tend to make any piece of research more humanistic. Probably the most illuminating is a set of guidelines for research reports which appeared in a 1981 issue of *The Journal of Humanistic Psychology.* In general, research which tends to fit under its umbrella is scattered through a number of professional journals, especially *The Journal of Phenomenological Psychology, The Journal of Humanistic Psychology,* and the annual convention program offerings of Division 32 of The American Psychological Association.

4. **Developing Trends.** Two groups today formally represent humanistic psychology: the Association for Humanistic Psychology (AHP) and the Division of Humanistic Psychology (Division 32) of the American Psychological Association. The former encompasses individuals from all kinds of professional (and nonprofessional) backgrounds; the latter is composed only of psychologists who are also American Psychological Association members. Not surprisingly, AHP is a much larger organization. It maintains a professional staff in San Francisco. Division 32 officers are elected annually without pay, but information on the division can be obtained through the American Psychological Association's offices in Washington, D.C. The two groups have formally cooperated on some projects in the past, and there is

overlap among the membership, though generally not among the officers.

Two general trends seem to be apparent in contemporary humanistic psychology. First, because of its strong influence in the 1960s, much of "mainline" American psychology has incorporated its corrective emphasis. What one sees now is not a sharpening of issues among humanists, behaviorists, and psychoanalysts, but a kind of softening. The battle lines are considerably less distinct than they once were, and one can speculate that a general truce may be setting in.

Second, many members of both Division 32 and AHP are becoming increasingly interested in the transpersonal psychology movement. This loosely defined movement is characterized by its concern for issues and topics which transcend strictly personal emphases: altered states of consciousness, transcendent needs and values, and spiritual and meditative disciplines.

Bibliography. J. Bebout and T. Greening, "Policies for Research Reports," *J. of Humanistic Psychology,* 21:4 (1981), 73–74. E. G. Boring, *A History of Experimental Psychology,* 2d ed. (1957). A. R. Mahrer, *Experiencing: A Humanistic Theory of Psychology and Psychiatry* (1978). A. H. Maslow, *Motivation and Personality* rev. ed. (1970). H. Misiac and V. S. Sexton, *Phenomenological, Existential, and Humanistic Psychologies: A Historical Survey* (1973). J. R. Royce and L. P. Mos, eds., *Humanistic Psychology: Concepts and Criticisms* (1981). J. B. P. Shaffer, *Humanistic Psychology* (1978). C. W. Tageson, *Humanistic Psychology: A Synthesis* (1982).

J. R. TISDALE

PERSON; PERSONALITY THEORY; PSYCHOLOGY, WESTERN. *See also* PHILOSOPHY AND PSYCHOLOGY; POPULAR THERAPEUTIC MOVEMENTS AND PSYCHOLOGIES. *Compare* ANALYTICAL (JUNGIAN) PSYCHOLOGY (Personality Theory and Research); BEHAVIORISM (Theories and Research); CLIENT-CENTERED THERAPY; EXISTENTIAL PSYCHOLOGY; GESTALT PSYCHOLOGY; PHENOMENOLOGICAL PSYCHOLOGY; PSYCHOANALYSIS (Personality Theory and Research); PSYCHOSYNTHESIS; SELF PSYCHOLOGIES; SPIRITUAL PSYCHOLOGIES; TRANSPERSONAL PSYCHOLOGIES. *Biography:* JAMES; KIERKEGAARD; MASLOW; ROGERS, CARL R.

HUMANISTIC PSYCHOLOGY AND PASTORAL CARE.

Humanistic psychology is a movement, primarily within American psychology, that distinguishes itself from behaviorism and psychoanalysis by an emphasis on themes such as the whole person and his or her experience, human creativity, self-fulfillment, human freedom and dignity, human sociability and encounter, and the meaningfulness of personal existence and transcendent experiences.

Humanistic psychology supports the person-centered tradition in contemporary pastoral care, and its promise of growth through human interaction has inspired pastoral leadership of small groups in the life of the church. Pastoral care has also found confirmation for many of its research methods in the research philosophy of humanistic psychology. And the themes that this psychology highlights could well evoke greater appreciation for and attention to the significance of celebration, affirmation, and guidance in pastoral ministry.

Though on the whole its constructive intent has not been informed adequately by an understanding of the reality of evil in human life, humanistic psychology's recognition of human intentionality reintroduces the teleological perspective to modern psychology and thereby enlarges the conversation between theology and psychology, especially on the subject of the centrality of a meaningful outlook in the conduct of life. While various concepts of self-fulfillment may further understanding of how persons realize values, they do not provide understanding of a transcendent reality that frees persons from self-centeredness.

1. **Major Themes of Humanistic Psychology and Their Implications for Pastoral Care.** Humanistic Psychology is a self-grouping of psychologists who differ in theory at many points but who find in one another a commitment to a particular set of values. What are the major themes of their commitment and what are the implications of these themes for the practice of pastoral care?

a. The whole person in his or her subjectivity. Concerned about the depersonalization that permeates modern life and that results from application of the natural science model of research to human beings, humanistic psychologists understand their subject to be the individual as a whole; that is, the complete personality at a given time and the development of the person throughout the life cycle. They contend that one aspect of a person's life cannot be understood fully without reference to all other aspects. Moreover, they contend that human subjectivity is central and essential to any understanding of the human being as a whole person. Thus they are not satisfied to analyze the outwardly observable facts of a life, but insist on exploring the person's self-understanding, unique ways of experiencing life, and basic outlook.

Humanistic psychology's sensitivity to the personal dimension lends support to a tradition of person-centered ministry wherein caring relationships and personal experience are valued more highly than a problem-solving orientation. The whole-person leitmotif also helps pastors to resist tendencies to segregate religious experience from other facets of personal life and provides a perspective for discerning how faith and its struggles organize and give direction to every aspect of daily living. Consequently, in pastoral care and counseling, ministers informed by humanistic psychology can be alert to the ways in which any and all of the experiences and problems people bring to them reflect fundamental understandings and commitments.

b. The value of experiencing. While ministers do well to pay balanced attention to all human experience, there is reason to be especially sensitive and responsive to the heights and depths of the experience people bring to their conversations with pastors, for at these times the light of faith frequently promises to illumine the whole. This pastoral adage concerning the interplay of the individual's unique experiencing of life in all its phases and its most intense moments has guided the pastoral care field since the salient contributions of Anton Boisen.

Humanistic psychology offers a rationale for this bit of pastoral wisdom. According to humanistic psychology, the royal road to discovery of the whole person is the individual's subjective experience of his or her world and self. The focus is not on accumulated contents (the "experienced" person) but on the activity of experiencing itself. The ongoing process of awareness provides the

initial clues to a person's self-image, values, and outlook on life. Not being entirely objective, persons selectively observe and respond to particular facets of reality. This personal experiencing of the world reflects one's basic intentionality in the world. At particular times the patterns that disclose such meaning may become clear, especially when individuals experience their world with greater energy than usual. The child fully engrossed in play is an example of this complete aliveness that can characterize personal experience.

One way to describe variation in the process of experiencing is to say that personal awareness can expand or contract. Humanistic psychologists like to study times of intensified awareness, such as experiences of deep harmony or critical moments when consciousness is expanded, because they promise to disclose with greater clarity the fundamental vision that energizes and gives direction to individuals' lives. This thematic emphasis has been a key source for the springing up of a psychological culture in which the amplification of experiencing and the acquisition of experiences is prized. The accent on experiencing has also served as a catalyst for renewed pastoral interest in human transformation and helps make available experiential referents for symbols of Christian faith. If it is not informed by Scripture and tradition, however, this confidence in experiencing aggrandizes the self in an idolatrous manner.

Humanistic psychology has developed methods for enhancing conscious awareness and studying the inner world of human beings. According to humanistic psychologists the natural sciences do not provide an adequate paradigm for human research. Requiring methods that allow for the participation and involvement of the investigator as well as the research subject and that address significant phenomena, humanistic psychology has looked to philosopher Michael Polanyi and others for a foundation. Given its faith in human rationality, humanistic psychology values the subject's self-report. Humanistic psychologists argue that interviews and case studies are more adequate to human phenomena than is experimentally controlled research and have their own type of validity.

The significance of these claims for pastoral care lies in the weight they give to a broad array of research methods, several of which have been salient in the cure of souls tradition. Reflection and analysis based on journals, diaries, autobiographies, case studies, and verbatim reports of pastoral events are examples. Unfortunately, many ministers have not had a vision of the importance of such data for professional and personal development, and consequently have not contributed to pastoral research.

Humanistic psychologists promote experiential education; that is, learning experiences with a variety of methods for generating feelings and making use of imagination. For example, adults in a seminar on child development may be guided through a relaxation technique and then directed to visualize themselves at a given age in childhood. Through the impact of humanistic psychology and other influences, many church leaders make use of experiential techniques. Walter Wink's approach to Bible study is a popular example.

c. The human potential. In addition to their objections to behaviorists' preoccupation with the measurable externals in behavior and environment, humanist psychologists protest the psychoanalytic suspicion of human motives and its emphasis on the pathological dimensions of human existence. Accordingly, humanistic psychology explores what it envisions to be the best in human life as a corrective to an understanding of human nature that is developed through the study of emotional troubles. In the humanistic account, the individual is motivated to actualize a unique set of potentials to the maximum degree possible under any given set of circumstances. Realizing these potentials, that is, realizing self-fulfillment, is a lifelong task that promotes a meaningful existence. Persons may disregard their potentials, their nature or essence, through fear or social conformity, and consequently experience a weak sense of self or an emptiness. Some humanistic psychologists, however, more decisively influenced by existentialism, do not believe that there is an essence that precedes existence and is to be realized in existence. For them existence precedes essence in that persons create their natures by their choices.

When Maslow studied the lives of persons whom he thought to be models of self-actualization, he described them as decisive and confident, though accepting of limits and weaknesses in self and others; spontaneous and creative, yet realistic; independent and nonconforming, yet open to others' influence and capable of intimate relationships; committed to a worthy and fascinating task or vocation; democratic with a sense of universal identity. This is a representative vision of humanistic psychology's understanding of the good, mature person.

This normative stance and confidence in the human potential raises several issues for pastoral care. How important is the study of the lives of saints and outstanding Christians as a context for effective pastoral care? How do such Christian images of maturity compare with the humanistic vision? With its focus on functions such as healing, sustaining, guiding, and reconciling, has pastoral care paid sufficient attention to the creative dimension in person's lives and to the significance of celebration in the care of persons? How can ministers be genuinely affirmative of persons and their potential in a nonsentimental way that does not neglect the human capacity for evil and self-destruction?

d. Interpersonal experience and encounter. Under the influence of humanistic psychology and the encounter group movement, many churches have incorporated person- centered small groups into their programs. The encounter group movement was a cultural phenomenon of the sixties in which individuals sought personal growth by participation in small groups characterized by high degrees of self-disclosure, support, confrontation, and emotional release. In these churches support groups, growth groups, self-help and Bible study groups that entail significant personal sharing have served as vehicles by which individuals explore their capacities for creativity, love, and honesty. The expressive peer group has also become essential to the methodology of CPE where it develops self-understanding in interpersonal relations and pastoral practice. Such expressive modes of learning are based on the belief that interpersonal experience and intrapersonal experience complement and require each other and are essential to authentic Christian life and ministry.

Humanistic psychology and the encounter group movement demonstrate the value of intense interpersonal experiencing, though it may be questioned whether such experience tends to be prized too highly at the expense of both cognitive integration (for example, of Christian theology and ethics) and a patience to let personal and communal transformation occur at their own pace. While this has sometimes been a problem, churches can surely acknowledge the value of intense, short-term experiences and at the same time incorporate them into the teaching of their historic traditions of meaning and value. And similarly they can incorporate such experiences into a sense of significant community that develops over extended time through a variety of occasions and relationships — a community that is not instantly created and disbanded in a marathon weekend. But this requires an intentional effort to weave such experiences into the wider life and worship of the church, through a rhythmic attention to didactic, liturgical, and missional as well as interpersonal-experiential modes of learning.

e. Nondirective or group-centered leadership. Humanistic psychology has typically promoted a style of group leadership which emphasizes the personal involvement and active participation of the group leader. Sometimes called "nondirective leadership" for its rejection of autocratic or "directive" methods, a better adjective is probably "group-centered." This is because such leaders aim to bring forth the resources and leadership potential of group members and to reach group decision by consensus. Thus they model and promote nondefensive listening, openness, self-disclosure, and caring confrontation. Furthermore, they give direction to the flow of communication, encourage group members to express their immediate feelings and own them personally, block attempts to speak in general terms, protect individuals from invasion of privacy, and in other ways draw group members away from ineffective communication patterns. Humanistic leaders may also introduce verbal and nonverbal exercises in situations where these seem likely to promote learning.

This style of leadership has been widely influential in ministry, where it is often believed to be compatible with the ideal of the church as an egalitarian "priesthood of believers" and the minister as a "servant leader," and because it dignifies and values the contributions of each individual. However, many ministers sense that a more active role is more compatible with their sense of pastoral leadership than is a nondirective or group-centered model, which can easily degenerate into confusion and demoralization. This is especially likely in congregations whose members are not accustomed to participation in decision-making processes or who have strong denominational traditions of more directive pastoral leadership. Possibly some pastors, even under favorable situations, underplay (if not abdicate) their authority too quickly under the influence of the humanistic ideal. On the other hand, some may have a tendency to overplay the leader's modeling role, making group members dependent on them, and to overestimate their own influence on group members as well as the place of structured exercises in the group process. For them, especially, but for all pastors to some degree, the group-centered model offers a helpful reminder of the potential latent in the community and a set of methods for helping to actualize it. If incorporated into a larger pattern of leadership and used flexibly, these methods can enrich and facilitate ministry.

f. Quest for meaning. Viewing persons as agents who value themselves, are purposive, and discover meaning in life, humanistic psychology understands perception itself to be a valuing process. Knowledge, then, derives from valuing: people come to know best what they love best. According to the humanistic vision, a personal quest for meaning in life is an integral dimension of human existence. Everyone has the task of constructing a personal philosophy or faith that is realistic, true to the individual's experiences, and hopeful. A dependency on external or dogmatic sources of meaning, without fully integrating these sources into one's life story or confirming them experientially, inevitably detracts from the authenticity of one's faith.

These principles have spawned a range of practical methods for enhancing the sense of life's meaningfulness, from Viktor Frankl's logotherapy to values clarification exercises. Moreover, humanistic psychotherapists are likely to engage clients in a dialogue about their outlook on life because these therapists believe that no healing process is complete that does not examine the relation of underlying intentionality and the specific concerns that people bring to therapy. While ministers do not require corroboration of the centrality of faith for personal existence, they can be instructed by humanistic psychology's demonstration of the great practical importance of coming to terms with the human condition in an affirmative way. Thus, when individuals struggle to make sense of their experiences and do not have a guiding religious and ethical vision, ministers need not automatically suspect a pathological process. Though alert to such possibilities, the pastor operating on humanistic psychological principles may help such persons engage in a dialogue with Christian faith with the confidence that a search for meaning is central, not peripheral, to psychological welfare. When such an encounter develops out of empathic and affirmative relationship, it does not violate the person's integrity or discount personal experience, but rather enhances and deepens them.

g. Transcendent experiences. For humanistic psychology the patterns of everyday, ordinary consciousness and human development through the life cycle are meaningful and call for reflection. Since intensified experiences may clarify such meanings, some humanistic psychologists see special meaning in those extraordinary moments when people cross the boundaries of ego-regulated consciousness (i.e., the state in which the thought processes that manage and control everyday coping with reality dominate in the person's organization of reality). Mystical states and some conversions are examples of such "peak experiences." Clearly, pastoral ministry is concerned with the meaning and value of such experience and with methods of attending to and possibly promoting them. Prayer, spiritual direction, administration of sacraments, pastoral discussions of the significance of mystical experiences, and guidance during a process of conversion are examples of pastoral ministries that require a knowledgeable appreciation of the meaningfulness of transcendent experiences such as humanistic psychology provides.

2. Conclusion. To date humanistic psychology has not developed a systematic set of constructs that provides a unified theoretical challenge to pastoral care. On the other hand, themes such as personal wholeness, experiencing, self-fulfillment, human love and encounter, and the meaningfulness inherent in the multiple forms of personal experience have evoked constructive and critical responses in current pastoral care. The most promising outcome may turn out to be renewed pastoral research into images of Christian maturity in which the human agency affirmed by humanistic psychology is reconciled with a wisdom to wait before God and an ethical commitment to caring for others.

Bibliography. Association for Humanistic Psychology, "Growth Center List" (1978). M. Bates, *et al.*, *Group Leadership*, 2d ed. (1982). H. J. Clinebell, *Basic Types of Pastoral Care and Counseling*, rev. ed. (1984); *Growth Groups* (1977). B. Hall, *Value Clarification* (1973). M. I. Lieberman, I. Yalom and M. Miles, *Encounter Groups* (1973). T. Oden, *The Intensive Group Experience* (1972). S. Southard, *Religious Inquiry* (1976). W. Wink, *The Bible in Human Transformation* (1973).

R. L. UNDERWOOD

PASTORAL CARE; PASTORAL COUNSELING; PASTORAL PSYCHOTHERAPY. *See also* GROWTH COUNSELING; GROWTH GROUPS; POPULAR THERAPEUTIC MOVEMENTS AND PSYCHOLOGIES; PSYCHOLOGY IN AMERICAN RELIGION; PSYCHOLOGY OF RELIGION (Theories, Traditions, and Issues). *Compare* ANALYTICAL (JUNGIAN) PSYCHOLOGY, NEOFREUDIAN PERSONALITY THEORIES, *or* PSYCHOANALYSIS, AND PASTORAL CARE; BEHAVIOR MODIFICATION AND PASTORAL COUNSELING. *Biography:* CLINEBELL.

HUMANISTIC PSYCHOLOGY AND RELIGION.

The "third force" in psychology which views psychoanalysis as too pessimistic and behaviorism as too mechanistic for a comprehensive understanding of human beings, humanistic psychology is more optimistic about human nature and focuses on such topics as human potential, self-actualization, values, meaning, love, and transcendent experiences.

1. Attitude of Humanistic Psychology Toward Religion. Of the three major movements in psychology, humanistic psychology holds the most positive attitude toward religion and spirituality. The *Journal of Humanistic Psychology* frequently publishes articles on this topic; and the *Journal of Transpersonal Psychology*, which grew out of the humanistic movement, is especially dedicated to the exploration of transcendence. Humanistic psychology has no credo or manifesto and therefore no "official" position in regard to religion. But the writings of Abraham Maslow, who died in 1970, are generally considered to be the theoretical foundations of the movement. Maslow's views on religion and spirituality are found throughout his writings, but his book *Religions, Values, and Peak Experiences* (1964) remains the classic and perhaps most representative statement of humanistic psychology toward religion. This article draws upon the writings of Maslow in its representation of the views of humanistic psychology. It should be understood, however, that the "third force" is characterized by great diversity and that humanistic psychologists hold a variety of attitudes toward religion, from the most conservative to the most liberal points of view.

2. Maslow's Views on Religion. *a. Institutional vs. personal religion.* Maslow made a distinction between institutional, organized religion with its ceremonies, rituals, and dogma and the personal religion and spirituality of the individual. Echoing William James, Maslow believed religion originated in the intense mystic experiences of a charismatic leader whose followers then structured and organized it into more conventional form. Ironically, institutional religion often becomes the enemy of the truly religious person who seeks deeper spiritual experience. Maslow referred to conventional, institutional religion as "big R" Religion and to personal spirituality as "little r" religion. He was clearly more interested in the latter.

b. Religion as a human phenomenon. Maslow, along with John Dewey, believed spirituality is a human phenomenon and that churches and temples do not have a monopoly on it. Because religious experience and spiritual values belong to humanity, they are a legitimate focus of study for psychology. Maslow stated his position as follows: "I want to demonstrate that spiritual values have naturalistic meaning, that they are not the exclusive possession of organized churches, that they do not need supernatural concepts to validate them, that they are well within the jurisdiction of a suitably enlarged science, and that, therefore, they are the general responsibility of all mankind" (1964, p. 33).

c. Personal religion and psychological health. Maslow believed personal religion is essential to health and stated that "the human being needs a framework of values, a philosophy of life, a religion or religion-surrogate to live by and understand by, in about the same sense he needs sunlight, calcium, or love" (1962, p. 206). Rather than pathologizing religious needs, Maslow said that "humanistic psychologists would probably consider a person sick or abnormal in an existential way if he were not concerned with these 'religious questions' " (1964, p. 18).

3. Humanistic Psychology and Religion: Areas of Agreement. *a. Belief humans have a higher nature.* While humanistic psychology and religion differ on some issues, there are several common areas of agreement. First, both humanistic psychology and religion emphasize that humans have a higher, spiritual nature. Traditional behaviorism denied or ignored this higher nature, and psychoanalysis tended to pathologize it. Yet this belief is the very foundation of humanistic psychology.

b. Concern for values and meaning. Humanistic psychology and religion share a deep interest in values and meaning. Maslow believed that valuelessness is the "ultimate disease" of our time and that spiritual distress is at the root of many of the clinical pathologies of our day. In agreement with Viktor Frankl, Maslow believed these "metapathologies" could only be cured by satisfying the existential hunger of people for values and meaning.

c. Concern for human welfare. Humanistic psychologists tend to be caring, compassionate persons who are committed to the alleviation of human suffering and the enhancement of human life. Most humanistic psychologists would agree with the injunctions of Jesus to help the poor, feed the hungry, and clothe the naked. While humanistic psychology and religion often seem to differ in regard to the "vertical" or supernatural dimension, they share a common, intense concern for the "horizontal" or human dimension.

d. Importance of personal spirituality. Humanistic psychology and religion generally agree on the importance of personal spirituality. Maslow believed the "core-religious experience" is the basis of personal spirituality and that these "peak experiences" were a continuing part of the healthy spiritual life. As Allport's research showed, religion can be either extrinsic or intrinsic in nature. Maslow was more interested in intrinsic religion. He identified with the religion of the mystic seer or iconoclastic prophet, believing that conventional religion often becomes the major hindrance to experiential religion. Many pastors, priests, and rabbis have shared Maslow's concerns.

e. Common values in counseling and interpersonal relations. Carl R. Rogers, one of the principle figures in humanistic psychology, was a leading researcher and theorist in regard to the interpersonal conditions which promote healing and growth. His "person centered approach" emphasizes unconditional caring, empathic understanding, and counselor congruence. It would be difficult to name three interpersonal values more in accord with the basic teachings of most religions. Perhaps this is one reason so many pastoral counselors have adopted Rogers's approach to therapy and interpersonal relations.

4. Future Directions. Perhaps because of its roots in humanism and its interest in topics once considered the sole province of religion, humanistic psychology is viewed as a threat by some in religion. Conversely, many humanistic psychologists seem to avoid traditional religion and religious leaders. Because humanistic psychology and religion share so many common values and interests, it seems that increased communication would be mutually enriching. Pastoral counselors will find humanistic psychology to be a gold mine of information for understanding and helping troubled individuals; and members of the "third force" have much to learn from healthy religion and the experience of religious leaders whose roles place them in daily contact with the deepest tragedies and the highest joys of human life. Future efforts should be directed at increased dialogue and communication between humanistic psychology and religion. This is one of the most neglected yet potentially fruitful areas in the interface of psychology and religion.

Bibliography. G. W. Allport, *The Individual and His Religion* (1950). C. Bühler and M. Allen, *Introduction to Humanistic Psychology* (1972). J. Dewey, *A Common Faith* (1934). V. E. Frankl, *Man's Search for Meaning* (1963). E. Fromm, *Psychoanalysis and Religion* (1950). W. James, *The Varieties of Religious Experience* (1902). C. G. Jung, *Psychology and Religion* (1938). A. H. Maslow, *The Farther Reaches of Human Nature* (1971); *Motivation and Personality* 2d ed. (1970); *Religions, Values, and Peak Experiences* (1964); *Toward a Psychology of Being* (1962). C. R. Rogers, *Client-Centered Therapy* (1951); *Counseling and Psychotherapy* (1942). A. J. Sutich and M. A. Vich, eds., *Readings in Humanistic Psychology* (1969).

D. N. ELKIND

PSYCHOLOGY IN AMERICAN RELIGION; PSYCHOLOGY OF RELIGION. *See also* HUMANNESS/HUMANISM; PHILOSOPHY AND PSYCHOLOGY; PSYCHOLOGY, WESTERN; RELIGION; RELIGION AND PSYCHOTHERAPY; SELF-ACTUALIZATION/ SELF-REALIZATION; THEOLOGY AND PSYCHOLOGY. *Compare*

ANALYTICAL(JUNGIAN)PSYCHOLOGY *or* PSYCHOANALYSIS, AND RELIGION. *Biography:* ALLPORT; DEWEY; JAMES; MASLOW; ROGERS, CARL R.

HUMANISTIC PSYCHOLOGY AND THEOLOGY.

An informal definition of humanistic psychology would be that it is that movement within psychology which takes seriously questions of value. Whereas many psychologists espouse a goal of "value free" objectivity, humanistic psychology challenges the (value-laden) assumption that values such as compassion and creativity are something from which the psychologist needs to be "freed."

Questions of value provide a natural way of getting into theology. Beginning with some observation about what is the case, one may ask "Is it right? Is it good?" and then draw on theology for assistance in providing an answer. In this fashion, value questions act as a bridge between common descriptive statements and theological affirmations. This helps clarify why humanistic psychology has been so well received by many pastoral counselors and theologians. It has often served as just such an interpretive bridge, helping people find a religious dimension within their everyday experience.

1. **The Social Context.** To fully understand the impact of humanistic psychology, one must note the social context to which it speaks. If humanistic psychology insists upon conceiving itself as a "third force" pointing beyond the objectivism of both behaviorism and psychoanalysis, it is due to a conviction that such objectivism is not in fact value-neutral, as its advocates claim, but is often quite destructive in its social orientation. For such objectivism contributes to the crucial problem of our time, which is, in the eyes of humanistic psychology, the widespread drift toward a sheerly technological, "one-dimensional" society. In the face of such social reductionism, humanistic psychology insists in a variety of ways that there must be "something more."

It must be said, however, that humanistic psychology's favorite target, technology, is not the only problematic force within contemporary society. In the U.S. a social tradition of narrow individualism, often supported by a religious perspective which focuses upon the individual soul, has increasingly combined with economic consumerism in ways that are deleterious to the larger social fabric. Regarding these tendencies, humanistic psychology's criticism has been muted at best, leading some observers to wonder whether humanistic psychology itself might not be the symptom of a larger problem (cf. Bellah; Slater; Metz).

The argument might run as follows. A society obsessed with the production of material goods will allow technology to dominate the workplace. But it will also realize that people cannot bear to live twenty-four hours a day in such a totally "rationalized" world. Therefore as a pressure valve for the worker, and as an occasion for the economically necessary acts of consumption, the society will encourage certain islands of leisure, isolated moments of fantasy and play. But the true function of these open spaces will be reflected in the fact that they (and the values they represent) will not be taken seriously. Specifically: (1) nothing that occurs within these spheres will affect in any fundamental way the "real" world of production and marketplace; (2) increasingly the open areas themselves will become identified as commodities to be exploited and sold; and (3) since that which is consumable is expendable, there will be constant pressure to keep moving on to the next consumable item of experience (cf. Marcuse; Jacoby).

To what extent does this characterization fit humanistic psychology? In answering, one must distinguish between persons who are genuinely oppressed and those who are relatively comfortable. The oppressed can find in humanistic psychology a means of "conscientization": i.e., an encouragement to trust their own capacities and stand up against dehumanizing forces. For others, it is tempting to focus upon one's own imagined grievances and to make of these an excuse for self-absorption.

2. **Questions of Coherence: Existentialism.** The great strength of humanistic psychology has been its opposition to a reductionistic universe and its active espousal of the human aspiration to "something more." When required to become more specific about that something more, however, the movement sometimes projects mixed messages. Often the confusion is traceable to a conflict among its various historical sources.

The nineteenth century held forth a vision of universal progress. Today there is common agreement that such optimism was naive. But one may question whether so widespread a disposition just suddenly disappeared, as is often implied. Instead it may have performed a mere tactical retreat, withdrawing from the broader sphere of *public* history only to entrench itself as a no less optimistic but now thoroughly privatized *personal* history.

Certainly, optimism regarding "human potential" is one tendency within humanistic psychology. But that tendency stands in ambiguous relationship with other themes drawn from a more distinctly twentieth century source, namely, existentialism. Existentialism itself has two faces, the more positive of which is the "phenomenological" affirmation that, at the deepest level, we may trust our experience. This is to say, for example, that the fact that we experience ourselves as being free is indeed an irreducible fact: it is not to be explained away by some theory of determinism. Not surprisingly, humanistic psychology has embraced this side of existentialism as a weapon against reductionism.

But in classical existentialism such affirmation is held in tension with another, more tragic view. (1) Existentialism recognizes that to be free and thus to be constantly choosing, constantly creating oneself without any guarantees, without any unquestionable certainties, arouses acute anxiety. The result is a "flight from freedom" whereby individuals surrender their freedom to any group which promises to make their choices for them (cf. Sartre). (2) Existentialism further affirms that limitation or finitude is not an incidental but an essential feature of being human. Most pointedly, each of us must die, and the recognition of this fact is part of our very being. Insofar as we transcend the fact, we do so only by an ever more courageous acknowledgment of it (cf. Becker). (3) But if it is true that we tend to avert our eyes from these harsh realities, then it follows that we cannot *simply* trust our experience: we must submit the findings of phenomenology to a certain "hermeneutic of suspicion" (cf. Ricoeur).

It is not clear that humanistic psychology, for its part, has fully confronted this task. There is in the nature of the movement an abiding temptation to make an absolute of one's feelings and of one's freedom.

3. Questions of Coherence: Transpersonal Psychology. More recently, under the heading of transpersonal psychology, humanistic psychology has felt the impact of parapsychology, Eastern religions, and various esoteric practices. For all their oddity, these movements are plausibly presented as the next logical step for humanistic psychology, a further extension of the "something more." But humanistic psychology, in being humanistic, has an abiding stake in the personal. Everything depends, therefore, upon the sense of the ambiguous "trans-."

The issue may be framed as an unclarity about how to relate *humanism* and *wholism*. Humanistic psychology has always aimed to be wholistic, but it has interpreted wholism in a specific way: as the wholeness of the person. Indeed, the (whole) person may be *the* crucial value for humanistic psychology. Obviously, humanistic psychology recognizes that other, larger realities exist (e.g., the group, the nation, the cosmos); but humanistic psychology has insisted that to subordinate the individual to such larger wholes constitutes a virtual definition of oppression.

In contrast, the "trans-" of transpersonal psychology announces that this latter movement accords great value to some larger whole or reality which lies "beyond" the individual. For some movements, e.g., those influenced by Buddhism, it is illusory to regard the particular person as being in any fundamental sense a reality. Others contend that the person is real, but in a manner scarcely imagined hitherto (see Ornstein). Do such assertions preserve and even expand the values of humanistic psychology? Or do they represent a giving up on the true significance of the person?

Throughout history, efforts have been made to reconcile humanism and holism by way of a third "h", *hierarchy*. Humanistic psychology has followed this pattern in arguing that other psychologies have a partial validity, but fail to recognize certain "higher" capacities of the person (see Maslow). Similarly, hierarchy is implicit in humanistic psychology's advocacy of those capacities which remain *distinctively* human. At the same time, however, humanistic psychology has criticized much of religious tradition for falsely spiritualizing the human: that is, for regarding the body, feelings, sexuality, etc., as lower, and therefore as less — and therefore as something to be denied by the truly "spiritual" person.

Many forms of transpersonal psychology are a further extrapolation of the hierarchizing tendency already present within humanistic psychology. A positive place is accorded to the body, for example, but within rather specific contexts; and the movement is generally explicit about championing that which is "spiritual." Thus the question arises whether humanistic psychology's critique of religious hierarchy applies to only one kind of hierarchy, or whether it points to oppressive tendencies in *any* use of hierarchy; and if the latter, how this contention squares with humanistic psychology's own important use of hierarchical imagery. (Chapters 4 and 5 of H. R. Niebuhr, *Christ and Culture* may be read as a critique of the use of hierarchy within theology; more recently the issue has been sharpened by various feminists.)

4. The Soul. In its insistence that there is something more to the human beyond the merely physical, humanistic psychology has generated a secular analogy to the traditional conception of the soul. But the traditional conception bears within itself a certain sense of gracious limit: to take thought of one's soul is to be mindful that there is life after death, but also that one is accountable to one's Judge. The secularized concept of human potential, by contrast, has seldom been comfortable with a sense of limit.

But to minimize the reality of human limit by thinking of the human primarily in terms of possibility may itself become, ironically, a form of confinement. In the language of Kierkegaard, it confines the human to the realm of the "aesthetic." Mesmerized by an ever-receding horizon of possibility, one forgets the reality of the present, the necessary leap of commitment, and the true nature of human incompleteness. The dream of endless possibility becomes interchangeable with the escapist mentality of the modern consumer.

At the same time it must be acknowledged that there is something within the traditional conception which laid it open to psychological translation. For the concept has functioned, especially in Western Christendom, as a key to the *relevance* of Christian teaching, in both the assurance of life and the caution regarding judgment. But once used as a way *into* the gospel, these concerns readily became a virtual definition *of* the gospel; and this was a disastrous distortion. For clearly, the gospel has to do with loving God and loving one's neighbor. But if we set about "loving" in order to save our own skin, then we have not even begun to love. Thus the dialectic which lies at the heart of the best of traditional piety: one may begin by regarding Christianity as a higher form of self-interest, but until one surrenders the logic of self-interest, one remains among the "Pharisees," with no real understanding of what the gospel is about.

At its best humanistic psychology has provided a way for people to turn from religious self-interest to sensitivity and compassion. At its worst it has enshrined self-interest by means of a psychological metaphysic. In any event, the pastoral counselor or theologian who would make use of humanistic psychology will do well to attend particularly to the dialectic of law and gospel. For it is clear from Jesus' teaching that the gospel itself requires a radically self-forgetful love. But to paraphrase St. Paul, the more I struggle to love, the more enmeshed I become in self-concern. To acknowledge this dilemma is one way of confessing one's sin. Now humanistic psychology, for its part, has maintained one notable exception to its general confidence in the resilience of the human subject. It has tended to imply that at the very mention of the word "sin" the human psyche will necessarily collapse into blithering neurosis, and that as a result the word must be withheld from human hearing.

For Christianity, we are freed not from the concept of sin, but from the reality. By grace we are set in that place that St. Bernard described: beyond loving ourselves for our own sake, but also beyond loving God for our own sake, in order that we might love God for God's own sake — and even love ourselves (without hierarchy and without reservations, loving both human potentiality and human fallibility, human freedom and human finitude) for God's sake.

Bibliography. E. Becker, *The Denial of Death* (1973). R. Bellah, *et al.*, *Habits of the Heart* (1985). T. Bernard, *On the Love of God* (1950). R. Jacoby, *Social Amnesia* (1975). S. Kierkegaard, *Either/Or* (1944 [1843]). H. Marcuse, *One-Dimensional Man* (1969). A. Maslow, *Religions, Values, and Peak Experiences* (1964). J. B. Metz, *Faith in History and Society* (1980). H. R. Niebuhr, *Christ and Culture* (1951). R. Ornstein, ed., *The Nature of Human Consciousness* (1973). P. Ricoeur, *Conflict of Interpretations* (1974), pp. 440–67. J. P. Sartre, *Being and Nothingness* (1956). P. Slater, *Earthwalk* (1974).

W. J. LOWE

HUMANISTIC PSYCHOLOGY AND RELIGION; THEOLOGY AND PSYCHOLOGY; THEOLOGY AND PSYCHOTHERAPY. *See also* PASTORAL THEOLOGICAL METHODOLOGY; PASTORAL THEOLOGY; PERSON; PHILOSOPHY AND PSYCHOLOGY. *Compare* EXISTENTIALISM; PSYCHOANALYSIS *or* ANALYTICAL (JUNGIAN) PSYCHOLOGY, AND THEOLOGY; TRANSPERSONAL PSYCHOLOGIES.

HUMANISTIC PSYCHOTHERAPIES (Methods and Research).

An approach to psychotherapy arising out of humanistic psychology. Its main emphases are on the trustworthiness of subjective experience, individual responsibility, the importance of the present, the priority of feelings, therapeutic use of the body, honesty in communication, spontaneity, the equality of client and therapist, the necessity of the therapist's personal growth, and the continuity between the therapeutic context and living itself.

1. History and Background. Humanistic psychotherapies arose out of the humanistic psychology movement of the 1960s and the 1970s. Along with the intellectual protest against behaviorism and psychoanalysis which was taking place came the alternative lifestyle of the counterculture and the encounter group as vehicles of personal change. The counterculture as a self-conscious movement peaked and largely disappeared, leaving behind some new concerns for ecology, alternate states of consciousness, religion (chiefly Eastern), and personal health. The encounter group movement also peaked, but its legacy has been the rise of humanistic psychotherapies and more humanistic emphases within traditional therapies — including pastoral counseling.

2. Assertions About Psychotherapy. Humanistic psychotherapies are diverse, and most individuals discussing them limit their descriptions to one or two specific therapies. It does seem possible, however, to extract ten assertions about the nature of psychotherapy that collectively characterize humanistic therapies and set them apart from other approaches.

a. Subjective experience is primary and trustworthy. The most obvious aspect of this statement is its emphasis on the experiencing individual as the focus or basic unit of therapy. The fundamental "given" for each person is that person's experiencing, and the nature of that experiencing is the key to growth and change. The therapeutic process is, then, essentially a process of exploring one's own experience, whether in a group or individual context. At the point at which formal therapy is terminated, the individual's awareness of self and others should be significantly expanded over what it was at the beginning.

Almost by definition, at the start of therapy significant parts of an individual's total experience are not readily available to awareness. The client has experienced pain or anxiety in connection with certain kinds of experiences or situations. Rather than accept the pain and work through to a new understanding or resolution, the client has avoided it or refused to experience it. Only when the individual comes back to that pain and allows himself or herself to experience it does healing begin.

It is not, however, simply a matter of catharsis, of freeing bound energy. When one knows fully what the pain is, one also knows what needs to be done to use or eliminate it. Often buried, but nevertheless present, in one's experience is the knowledge of what one needs to do to grow. That knowledge is trustworthy. Resources for healing lie within the individual—resources which have been largely untapped up to that point in therapy.

b. The individual is responsible for herself or himself. From existentialism comes this corollary of human freedom: the individual is significantly self-determined and able to change. In extreme instances, some humanists would argue that the individual is *completely* self-determined and that limitations to this are illusory and defensive. Most humanists, however, hold a more moderate position, insisting that, while some limitations are real, they are less important and less determinative than is generally acknowledged. Individuals have freedom enough for choices to be real, and they have responsibility to a commensurate degree.

A clear implication of this is that each individual coming for therapy is also responsible for the predicament in which that person is living. Blaming other people or impersonal circumstances is unhelpful, unrealistic, and counterproductive. The client is having difficulty because the client has created that difficulty. The client is doing what the client is doing because he or she *chooses* to do it, not because the client is somehow being forced to do so. This is true, even (especially) if the client does not perceive it to be true. Learning to accept that responsibility is one of the tasks of therapy.

This assertion carries within it the seeds of an important implication. If the individual has chosen to be this particular kind of person, then the individual also has the opportunity to choose to be something else. In this lies ground for optimism, not pessimism. If a human being's personal history is, indeed, completely determinative, there is no ground for hope in the future. One cannot change if one is only the product of one's prior experiences.

Another corollary is, that since the individual is ultimately responsible for being her or his own change agent, the therapist is not responsible for the change. If the client comes to therapy, as many do, expecting that the therapist will somehow do something ("intervene") that will *make* change, the client is doomed to more frustration. What the client hopefully will understand is that the therapist's respect and concern lead the therapist in a different direction: to help create the conditions in which the client can discover his or her own problems and solutions, and make changes only if he or she wishes to do so.

c. Personal reality is always in the present. Humanistic therapists do not focus much attention on the individual's past history *per se*. If a client is troubled, that person is troubled *now* and wishes to change *now*. If a client is unhappy, this is a current experience, and knowing all about the individual's unhappy childhood is not a precondition of change. This position is usually seen as being pretty directly opposed to the strong genetic emphasis of psychoanalysis.

The individual, then, is encouraged to make more direct contact with what is happening in the present. The client is encouraged to look at his or her present life and present experiences. Indeed, the individual is often encouraged to look carefully at the therapy situation itself, since this will be the most immediate thing which both client and therapist share. To this end the therapist may try to communicate the therapist's own experiences constructively, as both an encouragement to and a model for the client.

What seems to be a radical ahistoricity, however, is not. This assertion does not entirely ignore the fact that the person(s) in the therapeutic relationship has a history. It is quite possible, for instance, that the client is carrying around incomplete events and unresolved feelings from the past which will be part of the client's present and must be attended to as such.

d. Feeling is more important than thinking. Humanists are clear that, for the purposes of therapy, some aspects of the client's perceptual field are more important than others. These are the ones having to do with emotions and feelings. Blocks to growth involve strong affect, and the client in therapy would do well to pay particular attention to these.

There has been a recent upsurge in cognitive therapies, which emphasize the importance of thought processes in determining perceptions and behavior. Humanistic psychologists, however, while agreeing on the respect given to perception and internal processes, are unconvinced that disordered thinking plays the key causal role. Rather, individuals in therapy are encouraged to explore and pay particular attention to their feelings about things. Beginning therapists or individuals learning basic communication skills are taught to be alert to feelings, and to respond by using "feeling words" to improve the communication process.

Humanists also place a higher priority on the individual's feelings than on behavior. Although this is clearly being modified in some systems in the direction of therapeutic setting of measurable goals, even this change is reserved for a later stage in the therapy.

e. The person is a body. While humanistic psychologists are hardly biological determinists, they have developed significant respect for the physical since experience has a bodily referent or aspect. This recognition generally takes either or both of two directions.

In one, attention is paid to the body as the repository of emotional conflicts. In this view, emotional trauma or areas of conflict are reflected in specific areas of dysfunction or tension. These areas are determined either by their symbolic significance or a predisposing system weakness. An individual, for instance, who is afraid of experiencing tenderness and "soft" feelings might have a set of abdominal muscles chronically contracted and tense. Persons with sexual fears may have their pelvic area habitually retracted, with the spinal column showing an exaggerated lumbar curve. Other individuals may note that some areas of their bodies appear to have less sensation than should be expected. Some show easily observable differences in skin tone and coloring in different parts of the body. Such physical symptoms mirror (and help to maintain) emotional disorders.

Thus, clients are often asked to engage in physical "exercises" as a way of making better contact with their own experience. Instead of expressing anger verbally, an individual might beat or attack a cushion. Instead of talking about being lonely, a person might physically isolate herself or himself from other group members. Someone might literally grovel on the floor, the better to experience a sense of sin and guilt.

Because of this concern, humanists are also increasingly interested in wholistic views of health. Believing that behavioral medicine is a step in the right direction, they would go beyond its tenets to include other kinds of emotional "treatment" as part of the treatment of disease (dis-ease). The regular use of guided fantasy to visualize the reduction of a known cancer as part of the treatment plan is an applied example of this kind of approach. Likewise, many humanistic psychologists are concerned about good nutrition and a clean environment as critical factors in maximum human development.

f. Honesty makes better communication. This proposition is by no means the sole property of humanistic psychologists. It is a necessary condition for communication between client and therapist in almost any kind of psychotherapy.

The humanistic application of this principle becomes most conspicuous in the group context. Here all participants (therapist included) are urged to keep their conversations with one another totally honest. Only then can each individual discover the feelings which separate himself or herself from or bind the individual to others. Since humanists believe that our society typically does not function in terms of honest communication, this experience is generally found to be freeing and trust-building.

This principle gives neither client nor therapist license to attack others. "Honesty" here means honesty with responsibility concerning oneself: one's own feelings, perceptions, and attitudes. It is not an encouragement of evaluations and impressions of other people as if they were objectively correct. It is rich in statements which begin with "I . . . ." It is poor in statements which begin with "You . . . ."

g. Spontaneity is important for learning and growth. Humanists hopefully are not skeptical of planning, but they are often wary of attempts to lock events and experiences into prewritten scenarios. Individuals need to be encouraged to put aside rigid scripts and to attempt new behaviors and new ventures in life.

Clients in therapy are often jailed by their own inflexible perceptions and concepts. But as awareness grows and anxieties diminish through therapy, they will be better able to respond inventively to novel situations.

h. Client and therapist are equals. Humanistic therapists do not see themselves as analogous to physicians, to whom one comes with a symptom, who formulates a diagnosis, and prescribes a remedy. The image of therapist as coach or guide is preferable; though perhaps the most appropriate image is the therapist as catalyst, one whose presence allows something to happen that would not otherwise take place.

This does not mean that the therapist has no specialized skills or needs no professional training. As we shall see, the kind of training which is most appropriate may not always be available in graduate school programs, but training *is* in order. If the therapist is to act as a "guide" on a trip it is necessary to know something about the road which is to be taken and those who set out upon it. In general, the more the therapist knows, the better. But this does not make the therapist superior to the client, since the client is the one who actually travels.

i. No client will grow further than the client's therapist. This principle was first present or implied in psychoanalysis' requirement of a "training analysis" as part of the preparation for professional practice, but humanistically oriented practitioners were the first to make it an explicit working principle.

It means that the upper limit of growth, of awareness expansion, of accurate experiencing, for any client is the level reached by the therapist with whom the client is interacting. The reverse, not incidentally, is also true. If the therapist is functioning at a lower level than the client, the client is likely to deteriorate in the relationship rather than grow!

Humanists believe that this principle has important consequences for professional training. In general, they find graduate school programs far too oriented toward cognitive information. If the functioning level of the therapist is an automatic boundary to client growth, then training should be designed to enhance the functioning of the therapist. Typical graduate school courses do not accomplish this. This is also why humanistic psychotherapists are, as a group, less impressed by formal credentials than many other therapists and why they are less excited about the claimed values for clients of most licensing and certification requirements.

j. Therapy and life are continuous. Although formal therapy is a somewhat specialized relationship, it is not different in kind from what other relationships should be. What makes effective communication in therapy makes effective communication elsewhere. What produces more awareness in therapy produces more awareness elsewhere. The mutual trust, respect, and responsibility which exist between therapist and client(s) should be the basis of all human relationships.

Humanistic therapists are pretty clear that the values inherent in their approach to psychotherapy are values which should guide the conduct of nations as well. Thus many of them can be found in social movements. It is probably also for that reason that a high number of articles in the *Journal of Humanistic Psychology* deal with social issues or problems.

Expanding awareness is a process which, once well begun, does not end after one has "worked through" all one's difficulties and is "cured." Therapy as such "stops" when the process is firmly underway. Therapy becomes living.

3. Methods. Humanistic psychotherapy is not a method-centered therapeutic approach, in the sense that behavior therapies are and classical psychoanalysis once was. All kinds of methods are acceptable, provided they involve centering on the experiencing individual in the ways suggested above. It is possible, however, that the humanistic therapist might be more likely than other therapists to use certain kinds of approaches. These include:

a. Meditative techniques. The particular kind of meditative technique used is not important; the therapist will rather be interested in the ways in which the technique, whatever it is, allows the client to contact her or his own experiencing more clearly, to "center," to discover strengths not previously known. It may be suggested that the client learn and practice meditation outside the therapeutic period.

b. Body work. The humanistic therapist may focus on the body in some way. This may be as simple a procedure as helping the client to focus attention on bodily processes, or acting out feelings in the therapeutic session instead of simply verbalizing them. In groups, role plays can help clients to explore a situation as a present happening. Sometimes more structured methods of focusing, such as methods typically used in Gestalt or bioenergentic therapy, might be used: attending to one's breathing, muscular tension, body position, or "mini-gestures." A course of physical therapy or exercise, such as the structural integration of Ida Rolf, might also be included.

c. Fantasy. The use of guided fantasy or imagery is also possible. A client is helped to relax; a topic or setting is then suggested, such as a real situation from the client's experiences or something entirely imaginary. The client is then asked to allow the fantasy to continue and to describe what is taking place. It is allowed to proceed until it reaches a satisfactory conclusion or until the client wishes to "return to normal." This can also be done in a group, in which case all members play a part in shaping the direction of their shared fantasy. Its meaning might or might not be discussed afterward.

d. Artistic media. There is increasing interest in the use of artistic media and expression as part of therapy because they can open up areas for exploration difficult to touch through more exclusively verbal methods. Music, dance or movement, sculpture, drama, drawing or painting, photography, and literature have all been found useful as ways of expanding consciousness. Such methods can be used passively, by observing works and discussing them, or actively, by allowing clients to express themselves through some medium.

e. Appointment flexibility. Although it may seem less important than other items, flexibility in the way therapeutic time is scheduled is an important tool for humanistic therapists. The fifty-minute hour one or more times per week is the traditional unit, but no one has ever proved that it is the optimum unit. The encounter group movement clearly demonstrated that therapy could proceed very effectively using large blocks of time, scheduled less frequently even than once per week.

f. Shared experiencing. More than is true for other therapies, one can expect that the humanistic therapist will share his or her own experiencing as part of the therapeutic process. Open communication is not limited to the client. The therapist will, of course, need to be judicious about exactly how much to share and in what ways, but transparency is an important characteristic.

This is likely to be even more the case in later stages of therapy or at higher levels of client functioning.

4. Research. Psychotherapeutic research in general has been plagued with problems, although it is moving forward. Humanistic research in therapy is doubly plagued, both because of the hardships of such research in general and because of the added difficulty that humanistic psychology has not yet produced a strong research tradition. This, coupled with the pragmatic interests of most humanistic therapists, leaves one with no distinctive body of literature to describe.

To be sure, one study showed that over a recent three-year period, the *Journal of Humanistic Psychology* and the annual program of the American Psychological Association's Division of Humanistic Psychology both devoted about one-third of their space to topics involving psychotherapy and human growth. But the reports did not comprise a coherent opus. They were generally either theoretical, anecdotal, or descriptions of therapeutic method. It is, therefore, difficult to extract any generalizations from this.

5. Relations to Pastoral Counseling. Historically, early American pastoral counseling was strongly influenced by Carl Rogers, perhaps the first and certainly the foremost humanistic psychotherapist. Seward Hiltner and Paul Johnson both show evidence of Rogers's influence. This may not be surprising since there is clear evidence that Rogers's move into counseling was at least partly motivated by religious concerns. Many priests and pastors have since trained with him. Johnson's "responsive counseling" in the context of his dynamic interpersonalism is quite compatible with the "person-centered" approach of today. The second and third generations of people taught by these men are very likely still to show continuity with this tradition. Those who have been trained in traditions strongly influenced by psychiatry's historic preoccupation with psychoanalysis, however, will find less in common with the person-centered approach.

Of all the current approaches to therapy humanism probably offers more to pastoral counseling than other approaches on several counts. Its deep respect for the experiencing individual seems tied to the Judeo-Christian tradition's sanctity of the human personality. While recognizing that individuals often (even usually) fall short of their potential, humanistic psychotherapists still remain confident in the growth processes which individuals have locked within them. The humanistic emphasis on nonverbal modes of communication opens up a number of possibilities for pastoral counseling. There are implications in this as well for the pastoral activities of churches. Role playing, discussion groups, dance, music, and drama within a religious context all take on new possibilities when viewed from this perspective. Finally, of all the "secular" therapies, humanists are most open to the likelihood that healing ultimately requires resources which are transpersonal. That assertion would seem to be an essential cornerstone for pastoral counseling. There appears therefore to be the potential for significant interaction between those interested in these two movements.

Bibliography. R. R. Carkhuff, *Beyond Counseling and Psychotherapy* 2d ed. (1977).

J. R. TISDALE

PSYCHOTHERAPY; PSYCHOTHERAPY AND COUNSELING (Research Studies and Methods). *See also* POPULAR THERAPEUTIC MOVEMENTS AND PSYCHOLOGIES. *Compare* ANALYTICAL (JUNGIAN) PSYCHOLOGY (Therapeutic Method and Research); BEHAVIOR THERAPIES (Methods and Research); CLIENT-CENTERED THERAPY; EXISTENTIAL PSYCHOLOGY AND PSYCHOTHERAPY; EXPERIENTIAL PSYCHOTHERAPY; GESTALT PSYCHOLOGY AND PSYCHOTHERAPY; PHENOMENOLOGICAL PSYCHOLOGY AND PSYCHOTHERAPY; PHILOSOPHY AND PSYCHOLOGY; PSYCHOANALYSIS (Therapeutic Method and Research); PSYCHOSYNTHESIS; RELIGION AND PSYCHOTHERAPY.

HUMANNESS/HUMANISM. Generically understood, *humanness* means revealing the qualities of human being, and *humanism* has more often been understood as denoting a broad philosophical outlook which emphasizes the dignity, freedom, and inherent power of human beings to determine their own existence and solve life's problems out of their own resources. Though not essentially nontheistic, this outlook has often been viewed negatively by religious persons because its emphasis on human capacities has been thought to de-emphasize reliance upon God; however, many Christian theologians have not concurred that the one can be honored only at the expense of the other.

Within the field of pastoral care and counseling the term, "humanness," is not essentially different from this generic understanding, but it takes on a more explicit value. The qualities of human being, even those which have usually been understood as negative, such as finitude, anxiety, and error have been highly valued both in theory and practice. Anton Boisen's insistence that religion study "the living human document," which has been a kind of rallying cry for both theoreticians and the specialized practitioners of pastoral care, is a symbol of the high value attributed to humanness in the clinical pastoral tradition.

The pastoral care movement was strongly influenced, particularly in the 1950s and 1960s, by Carl Rogers (1951) and to a lesser extent by psychologists such as Abraham Maslow (Goble, 1970) who were sometimes identified as being practitioners of a "humanistic" or "third force" psychology. The third force psychology, which emphasized "the positive" in human beings and the primacy of the individual over what was viewed as a repressive and authoritarian society, was so identified because of its contrast with two earlier psychological "forces," behaviorism and Freudian psychoanalysis, which were seen as theorizing about human beings in inappropriately subhuman (e.g., mechanical or biological) terms.

Although the influence of Rogers, particularly his methods of listening, understanding and affirming the other person, has continued to be important to pastoral care and counseling, the philosophical optimism of humanistic psychology has generally been rejected as unrealistic in the light of Christian anthropology and clinical pastoral experience with human beings. Humanness, however, continues to be a central value. CPE focuses on the student's discovery of his or her humanness in pastoral relationships. Pastoral counseling supervision emphasizes "the use of one's person" in the counseling relationship. The understanding of pastoral care and counseling which rejected the exaggerated optimism of humanistic psychology has embraced a more realistic valuing of humanness influenced by psychodynamic psychology and Christian theology. Reinterpretation of the "living *human* document" by Gerkin (1984) in his hermeneutical theory of pastoral counseling and Patton's (1983) identifying a norm for pastoral counseling in "relational *humanness*" are examples of the pastoral care movement's emphasis on humanness as an essential feature of Christian ministry.

Bibliography. C. V. Gerkin, *The Living Human Document* (1984). F. Goble, *The Third Force* (1970). J. Patton, *Pastoral Counseling: A Ministry of the Church* (1983). C. Rogers, *Client-Centered Therapy* (1951).

J. PATTON

ETHICS AND PASTORAL CARE; HUMAN CONDITION/PREDIC-AMENT; HUMAN NATURE, PROBLEM OF; PERSON; PHILOSO-PHY AND PSYCHOLOGY. *Compare* PERSONAL, CONCEPT OF.

HUMILIATION. *See* SHAME.

HUMILITY. *See* PRIDE AND HUMILITY. *See also* VIRTUE, CONCEPT OF.

HUMOR. Humor is a complex behavioral phenomenon considered by many to be fundamental to our well-being. The many forms of humor — antics, puns, jokes, nonsense, cartoons, wit, satire, parody — are ubiquitous in our daily interactions, are triggered by a wide variety of stimuli, and may be used for both malevolent and benevolent purposes. The same humorous remark may evoke both affection and hostility. Whether or not one finds something humorous depends on numerous variables such as personality characteristics, prevailing social attitudes, and one's level of emotional arousal.

Interest in understanding this complex behavior has attracted some of the most creative minds in history (e.g., Plato, Aristotle, Spinoza, Hobbes, Voltaire, and Darwin). Modern psychological studies of humor began in 1905 with Freud's book *Jokes and Their Relation to the Unconscious*. Since the 1940s, social scientists have devoted increasing attention to the empirical study of humor, investigating such issues as the function of humor within social groups, the development of humor in children, the relationship of a sense of humor to creativity and intelligence, and personality dynamics correlated with certain humor responses.

1. **Humor Theories.** Although as many as eighty-one theories of humor have been described, three primary theories have shaped investigations and discussions of humor: superiority theories, incongruity/configurational theories, and release theories. No one theory can account for the variety of forms and purposes of humor.

a. Superiority theories. In much of Greek philosophy the ludicrous is associated with cruelty and disparagement of people. A great deal of present-day humor, including most situational comedies on television, is sparked by people comparing themselves favorably with others who are seen as stupid, ugly, clumsy, and weak. The philosopher Thomas Hobbes, the first to outline the

dynamics behind this superiority theory of humor in the seventeenth century, believed that laughter is an activity of the weak, not the strong. People who are most conscious of their inabilities and who have the greatest need to build up their self-esteem are the ones who are most likely to gloat over the imperfections of others in humor. Hobbes added that we may laugh in superiority at our own past imperfections provided we believe we have successfully mastered those foibles.

b. Incongruity/configurational theories. According to this group of theories, humor is the sudden perception of disjointed ideas or situations that vary from habitual custom (e.g., a bishop falling on a banana peel). Philosophers such as Kant and Spencer have emphasized that humor follows a perception of incongruity only if we perceive the incongruity as innocuous, trivial, or playful (e.g., a princess speaks with egg on her face). Other incongruities may evoke wonder (e.g., a person becomes an angel) or tragedy (e.g., one who has helped others is killed by the mob). Configurational theorists believe that humor arises when the momentary confusion inherent in the incongruity is transformed into a harmonized configuration or meaning. We laugh when the unstable structure in the humor becomes stable and we "get the point of the joke." Appreciating a joke, therefore, is much like creatively solving a complex problem.

c. Release theories. From the view of psychoanalytic theory, humor affords pleasure in two ways. First, in the frivolous, illogical associations of the comic we are given an opportunity to release tension built up in our overly rational, demanding world. The nonsense of humor permits regression to childish ways of thinking and behaving. Second, humor may give release to inhibited fantasies (e.g., sexual or aggressive), which would otherwise be banned from conscious recognition and public communication. Humor like the dream is a camouflage that momentarily deceives the superego as unacceptable impulses are allowed expression in a socially acceptable manner. From this perspective, humor may be compared to art, play, and games. These are socially acceptable and creative channels of liberation from constraints of logic, language, and proper conduct.

2. **Humor and Faith.** When Plato asserted that humor should be debased because of its origin in aggression, envy, or spite, he understood what many others have observed: humor may be a signal of disturbance allowing one to degrade others, escape conflict, avoid intimacy, and resist inward searching. However, because humor generally has been regarded as a supreme coping device and as a bestower of grace, it may be linked with the sacred in terms of the immediate personal benefits it affords. Humor may allow us to have a relaxed, childlike attitude toward the world, momentarily detaching ourselves from the seriousness and cares of reality, thereby enabling us to approach our responsibilities freshly and vigorously. Humor may give us a respectable cover when we momentarily need to mask our pain. Approaching complicated problems with humor may foster flexibility and a willingness to examine multiple sides of an issue. It also has been hypothesized that the positive emotion of laughter may, as faith and hope, reverse serious physiological maladies (Cousins, 1979).

In a more direct bridging of humor and faith, Niebuhr (1949) has commented how both faith and humor reflect one's capacity for self-transcendence: "The intimate relation between humor and faith is derived from the fact that both deal with the incongruities of our existence. Humour is concerned with the immediate incongruities of life and faith with the ultimate ones. Both humour and faith are expressions of the freedom of the human spirit, of its capacity to stand outside of life, and itself, and view the whole scene" (p. 112).

Allport (1950) also claimed that one quality of the mature religious person is self-objectification, which includes having a sense of humor: "The individual with insight sees himself as others see him, and at certain moments glimpses himself in a kind of comic perspective" (p. 60). In the same way as humor helps us to encounter our liabilities and absurdities, says Allport, so also the religious ritual of confession induces self-objectification and a shedding of pretenses. Furthermore, Allport links religion and humor as the best "integrative agents." Both help maintain a person's unity and aspirations in the midst of life's uncertainties. Humor, like religion, may function as a person's "principal technique for getting rid of irrelevancies. . . . Laughter disposes of much that is unpredicted, capricious, and misfit in his life. . . . Humor helps to integrate personality by disposing of all conflicts that do not really matter" (pp. 104–5).

This "purging" of our existential incongruities through humor led Kierkegaard (1941) to postulate that humor is the best way of preparing oneself for the gifts of religion: "An observer who goes out among men to discover the religious individual, would therefore follow the rule of making everyone in whom he found the humoristic the object of his attention" (p. 447). Although humor and faith may have this close affinity, Niebuhr (1949) has underscored the impotency of humor. Laughter is limited to those incongruities of life that do not affect us essentially, while faith is the only effective response to the ultimate incongruities of existence, which threaten the very meaning of life. Thus, "Humour is, in fact, a prelude to faith; and laughter is the beginning of prayer. . . . Laughter is swallowed up in prayer and humour is fulfilled by faith" (pp. 111–12).

Bibliography. G. Allport, *The Individual and His Religion* (1960 [1950]). A. Chapman and H. Foot, eds., *Humour and Laughter: Theory, Research and Applications* (1976); *It's a Funny Thing, Humour* (1977). N. Cousins, *Anatomy of an Illness* (1979). J. Goldstein and P. McGhee, eds., *The Psychology of Humor* (1972). R. Niebuhr, "Humour and Faith," *Discerning the Signs of the Times: Sermons for Today and Tomorrow* (1949).

T. T. WEBER

PLAY; WIT AND HUMOR IN PASTORAL CARE. *Compare* IMAGINATION; RELAXATION, PSYCHOLOGY AND TECHNIQUES OF.

HUNGER. *See* EATING AND DRINKING; MOTIVATION; NEED/NEEDS. *See also* ASCETICAL PRACTICES; OBESITY AND WEIGHT CONTROL.

HUSBAND. *See* MARRIAGE.

HUSBAND, PASTOR'S. The category of pastor's husband is a residue of the time when the wife of a pastor was an identifiable role in parish life. Although that traditional role has been changing, it has not diminished altogether. Men married to pastors may be expected to provide inside information on church matters, exercise informal power in the parish, be a "utility infielder" in the church's work, assume leadership in the pastor's absence, mow the grass in the church yard, or be the pastor's court of last resort.

The emergence of women into the professional work force has already altered the relationship to parish life of couples in which one spouse is clergy. Pastor's spouses of either sex are less available for the activities that characterized the traditional pastor's wife role. The advent of women pastors, and consequently of pastor's husbands, is part of this larger picture of the two-career marriage.

Families in which both husband and wife work outside the home have three basic issues to resolve: linkage between family and occupation, relationships within the family, and involvements with nonoccupational social institutions as well as networks of friendship. The role of the pastor's husband is affected by all three issues.

The survival of a dual-career marriage requires an equity that limits the pastor's freedom of mobility and thereby challenges traditional convictions that movement to a new church assignment is in response to a call that transcends individual choosing. Decisions about moving may be complicated further if the pastor's husband has a larger salary and a position of stability and/or social status but not a "holy calling."

The pastor's husband's involvement in his wife's parish will in part be determined by his interest and available time, but it will be limited by issues of conflict of interest in a way that was not so for traditional pastor's wives, who were already restricted from official boards of the congregation. For that reason, as well as others, a pastor's husband and children may not belong to the church where his wife, their mother, is pastor. Although there is wisdom in that separation even when it is not necessary, it is not easy for couples and congregations who have thought of ministry as a family affair.

It is likely that the pastor and her husband will be unable to afford (or may not choose) child-care assistance. Both of them will therefore need to factor child-rearing responsibilities into their work. If the husband's work is also professional in nature, each is likely to be less available than people expect or the job demands. Organizing the care of children is probably easier, however, than finding prime time to relate as husband and wife, because the rhythm of work and recreation is nearly reversed. When there is time, the needs of the pastor's husband for support because of professional concerns must be balanced by an interest in and support for his wife's work. That is the central agenda for the pastor's husband.

Bibliography. R. and R. Rapoport, eds., *Working Couples* (1978). G. W. Rowatt, Jr., and M. J. Brock Rowatt, *The Two-Career Marriage* (1980). M. Rueschemeyer, *Professional Work and Marriage* (1981).

H. ANDERSON

MARRIAGE AND FAMILY LIFE, PASTOR'S. *Compare* CLERGY COUPLES; WIFE, PASTOR'S.

HUTTERITES. *See* SECTARIAN PASTORAL CARE.

HYPERACTIVE CHILD. *See* BEHAVIORAL DISORDERS OF CHILDHOOD.

HYPERTENSION. *See* BIOFEEDBACK; PSYCHOSOMATIC ILLNESS; STRESS.

HYPNOSIS. A human condition of awareness, usually characterized by a trance-like state of mind and a relaxed body. Hypnosis is an induced state of being, which includes the elements of focused concentration and susceptibility to suggestion. It is neither a form of sleep nor of normal, waking consciousness.

1. Brief Historical Background. Modern concepts of hypnosis are often traced to Frantz Anton Mesmer (1734–1815), who used hypnosis so dramatically that the word *mesmerized* is still commonly used to describe the trance-like state of mind associated with hypnosis. Records reveal, however, that priests in ancient Egyptian, Greek, Persian, Chinese, Hindu, and African civilizations used hypnotic procedures thousands of years ago. It is likely that some of their miraculous cures, particularly of psychosomatic ills, were brought about by hypnosis. Scientific investigation of hypnosis began in Europe (and in India by British colonial doctors such as James Esdaile, 1808–59) in the late 1700s and the 1800s. James Braid (ca. 1785–1860), a Scottish physician and scientist, is considered to be the father of modern hypnosis. He coined the word *hypnosis* from the Greek word for sleep, *nosis*, based on his early misconception that it was a form of sleep.

A French physician, A. A. Liébeault (1823–1904), was actually the real founder of suggestive therapeutics. Hypnosis as therapy suffered decreased acceptance after Sigmund Freud (1845–1939) discarded it as ineffective (after learning the method from French psychiatrist, Jean Charcot). Hypnosis became of interest again during the wars of the twentieth century when it was used effectively to treat war neuroses and for anesthesia during battlefield operations. Professional hypnosis societies have been formed, such as the American Society of Clinical Hypnosis (founded in 1957), and hypnosis was endorsed by the American Medical Association and other groups in the 1950s. Morton (1980) and Wittkofski (1961) give reviews and critiques of hypnosis relevant to pastoral practice. In the 1980s hypnosis made a considerable impact on the pastoral care and counseling community through Ericksonian psychotherapy, particularly in its use of metaphor (Close, 1984; Zeig, 1985).

2. Description. Hypnosis can be induced by oneself (self hypnosis) using an object of attention or by another person, the hypnotist or hypnotherapist. Hypnosis is a natural, common experience of almost all human beings, at least to some degree. The trance, or state of mind, associated with hypnosis can vary from a light to a heavy or deep state that can resemble somnambulism. An example of light hypnosis would be when concentrating on something so intently that one loses track of passing time. An example of deep hypnosis would be induced anesthesia to block what would otherwise be excruciating pain in a normal state of consciousness.

During hypnosis a person is able to focus attention, concentrate intently on a particular subject, and thus expe-rience increased knowledge about the subject being considered, even to (perhaps particularly) those factors in the person's subconscious mind. Also, there is increased suggestibility, with the analytical portion of the thinking process being bypassed to some degree. Thus, critical judgment or so-called "logical" thinking can be bypassed.

3. Delimitations. As noted earlier, hypnosis is not a form of sleep, nor does it cause loss of consciousness. While it is true that a person experiencing hypnosis is more susceptible to suggestion, the consensus of professional opinion is that suggestions must be within the moral value system of the subject if they are to be activated—although this claim remains open to far more experimental evidence than presently exists before it may be counted as a truism. It is also assumed that even hypnotized subjects who manifest unusual or seemingly embarrassing behavior on stage—behavior friends or relatives might judge to be uncharacteristic of them—actually know that they are on stage and are willing to be there and to do what they are doing.

While hypnosis enables a person to remember events that may have been forgotten consciously, hypnosis does not act as a truth serum that causes the subject to give away secrets or tell things against his or her will.

Hypnosis is not something the hypnotist or therapist does to a subject. Instead, the hypnotist guides the subject in experiencing their natural ability to experience a trance. Hypnosis is not magic in any sense of the word. Unfortunately, the relative lack of scientific knowledge about hypnosis and its periodic exploitation by a variety of "healers," entertainers, and manipulative persons through the years have clouded the phenomenon of hypnosis with misconceptions and unfounded fears.

4. Therapeutic Applications. Hypnosis, as a psychological, biological, and perhaps spiritual phenomenon (Francuch, 1981) is able to use the natural ability of the focused mind and relaxed body to effect health. Medical research continues to reveal a growing list of psychosomatic ills brought about by excessive, chronic stress. Also, the body's immune system appears to be affected by one's state of mind. Further, many people are adversely affected psychologically by past traumatic events, some of which are remembered, while others may have been forgotten. Since the hypnotic trance provides access to the subconscious as well as the conscious portion of the mind and can bring about changes in the thinking process, it can be used as follows: to (a) teach a person how to relax quickly and thoroughly; (b) alter automatic responses to previous trauma by restructuring the subconscious reaction to any further "cues" of the trauma; (c) effect anesthesia of pain; (d) reduce or even eliminate phobias; (e) help eliminate unhealthy habits, such as smoking and overeating although the correction of such habits may take considerably more time than other uses of hypnosis; (f) reduce anxiety; (g) alleviate a variety of physical ailments, especially those that have a psychogenic origin; examples include ulcers, colitis, some forms of asthma, some forms of arthritis, dysmenorrhea, and hypertension; (h) enhance healing after medical and dental operations; (i) enhance learning, from memorization to understanding complex insights. Also, test anxiety can be reduced markedly.

The preceding list is not all-inclusive. There are many applications of hypnosis, and much research remains to be done.

5. **Some Contraindications.** While hypnosis can be a powerful tool in the kit bag of persons in the healing professions, and while it is a natural, common experience, there are some contraindications. While most are generally agreed upon among professionals, others are not. (a) Hypnosis should not be used to remove pain that has value. For example, it would be unprofessional and unethical to anesthetize a headache caused by a physiological source, such as a tumor, or to anesthetize back pain caused by a ruptured disc, kidney problems, and so forth. (b) Hypnosis should not be used to remove a psychological defense that has genuine coping value. (c) Hypnosis should not be used if it is likely to cause damaging emotional trauma. In other words, if an abreaction to an event that is buried in the subconscious could be damaging, either hypnosis should not be used or very skillful procedures should be used to avoid or at least control the abreaction. (d) Hypnosis should not be used to suggest possibly embarrassing behavior by the subject. (e) Hypnosis should not be used in an effort to manipulate the subject for the gain of the hypnotist or anyone else except the person who is the subject.

6. **Research Needed.** While hypnosis is ancient as a natural, common experience, one that has been used by persons in the healing arts for centuries, scientific research into hypnosis has been so recent in history and human behavior is so complex and has so many variables that the field of hypnosis is ripe for research. This is especially true in light of recent breakthroughs in brain research.

Bibliography. H. Bernheim, *Hypnosis and Suggestion in Psychotherapy* 2d rev. ed. (1973). H. T. Close, "Metaphore in Pastoral Care," *J. of Pastoral Care,* 38 (1984), 298–316. D. Elman. *Hypnotherapy* (1964). M. H. Erickson, L. Rossi, and S. I. Rossi, *Hypnotic Realities* (1976). P. D. Francuch, *Principles of Spiritual Hypnosis* (1981). W. S. Kroger, *Clinical and Experimental Hypnosis* 2d ed. (1977). R. B. Morton, *Hypnosis and Pastoral Counseling* (1980). H. N. Malony, "Toward a Theology for Hypnosis: A Beginning Inquiry," *J. of Psychology and Christianity,* 2 (1983), 2–11. R. M. Segal and B. Chambers, *Hypnotism Fundamentals* (1982). E. L. Schultz, "Pastoral Hypnosis," *J. of Pastoral Care,* 32 (1978), 256–60. J. Wittkofski, *The Pastoral Use of Hypnotic Technique* (1961). J. K. Zeig, ed. *Ericksonian Psychotherapy,* 2 vols. (1985).

R. R. KING, JR.

PSYCHOTHERAPY. *Compare* FAITH HEALING; MIND-BODY RELATIONSHIP; PAIN MANAGEMENT; RELAXATION; SLEEP AND SLEEP DISORDERS.

HYPOCHONDRIACAL NEUROSIS. *See* NEUROSIS.

HYSTERECTOMY. *See* WOMEN, PASTORAL CARE OF. *See also* SURGICAL PATIENT.

HYSTERIA. A diagnostic category which generally includes (1) histrionic personality disorder (formerly hysterical personality), (2) conversion disorder (previously known as hysterical neurosis, conversion type).

The histrionic personality disorder, as all personality disorders, is a long-standing, deeply entrenched pattern of maladaptive responses, attitudes, emotions, and perceptions which result in impaired interpersonal or occupational functioning. This particular disorder is characterized by such features as: infantile or immature reactions (thus persons with this disorder are sometimes referred to as a "child-woman" or "child-man"); emotional instability manifested in excessive excitability and overreaction; a craving for attention and, along with that, a melodramatic or flamboyant style of expression; an extroversion and charm, yet marked shallowness in interpersonal relationships; and, frequently, a seductiveness which is, in actuality, a defense against underlying ambivalent and conflicting feelings regarding sexuality.

The person with a histrionic personality disorder may also have rapidly vacillating mood swings and, during times of dysphoric mood, suicidal gestures might be made. In addition, such persons will often be manipulative, self-centered, self-indulgent, dependent, and demanding.

In hysteria manifested as conversion disorder, an underlying psychological conflict is unconsciously "converted" into a physical symptom. Conversion symptoms most commonly involve the voluntary muscular system and the special sense organs. Typical conversion symptoms are aphonia (an inability to speak), blindness, deafness, paralysis, and anesthesia (loss of sensation). In all these cases, there is not indication of actual organic, physiological, or neurological cause or involvement.

It is accepted by many that a conversion symptom represents a defense against the anxiety which results from repressed impulses, drives, or fears. Thus, the "primary gain" for a person experiencing a conversion disorder is that an internal conflict is kept out of consciousness and the anxiety, which would ensue if the repressed material were brought to consciousness and acted out, is controlled. An example could be found in the individual who develops hysterical paralysis of the arm and is thus kept from expressing rage by striking someone.

"Secondary gain" from the conversion symptom is found in its providing: increased attention and sympathy from others; a means of avoiding unpleasant situations; an excuse for not doing well; and a way to control or manipulate others. Because of the gain derived from a conversion symptom, some people have "la belle indifference" toward their symptom, meaning that they are blandly unconcerned about it whereas it would normally be very distressing to anyone. This is due to the "pain" being significantly less than the gain or benefit derived from the symptom.

Because the conversion disorder is the result of unconscious processes, it is substantially different from malingering, where the symptom is under conscious, voluntary control. Conversion disorders typically are short-lived with both sudden onset and abrupt termination of the symptoms. Even though there may be considerable resistance, the basic treatment is psychotherapy. Hypnosis is often effective for symptom removal.

A. J. STRAATMEYER

DIAGNOSTIC AND STATISTICAL MANUAL III; NEUROSIS. *See also* ANXIETY; SOMATIZING.

I

I/EGO. *See* EGO, PHILOSOPHICAL CONCEPT AND PROBLEM OF; EGO, PSYCHOLOGICAL MEANINGS AND THEORY OF; PERSON (Philosophical Issues); SELF/SELFHOOD.

I AND THOU. The title of Martin Buber's best-known book and the name of his most noted concept (translated "I-You" in Walter Kaufman's fine [1970] rendering). Buber's account is significant in clinical and religious literature because of the import of what it describes, but also because of productive misinterpretations. I-Thou is sometimes used to name an intimate, personal relationship that is characterized by vulnerability, affirmation, and nonjudgmental affections. Buber, however, uses the concept to name a *non*personal relational state of being that is without intention, conceptualization, subjectivity, or objectivity. It is a "pure" relation in which life occurs without causality or *telos*. I-Thou is disclosure of being with being, an address of same with same. For Buber, deity occurs as this disclosive relatedness.

I-It is the contrasting concept, which refers to relations in which objectification of *any* kind takes place. It thus denotes not only antagonism, but also intention, conceptualization, and all forms of interest, including personal love and affirmation. In principle, an I-It relation can always be understood. I-Thou, on the other hand, is "an unfathomable kind of relational act." It is a *sui generic* event of being in a nonsubjective dimension that cannot be objectified.

In therapeutic relations one might follow Buber's account of I-Thou and expect its occurrence, when it is allowed to happen, to be the experience of greatest significance for profound psychological transformation (as distinguished, for example, from the resolution of transference or the acceptance of archetypal images). Since an I-Thou occurrence is not predictable and since it involves suspension of personal control, identity, and individual efficacy, it can occasion deep anxiety. If Buber is right in his claim that I-Thou names the deepest occurrence of being, then ways of life that resist or close off this dimension are at odds with themselves,

constituting the deepest kind of madness. Types of this madness include obsessive, life-dominating projects that seek self-affirmation, environmental control, or relationship exclusively by knowledge or personal interest.

When one allows the I-Thou event to occur, it can have a pervasive influence in a person's life: an "air" of continuous conversation develops; freedom for otherness and difference emerges; one has a sense of the limits of autonomy and identity; one trusts communication and experiences freedom from the ultimate claims of possessions and possessables. No matter how alienated one feels in the immediate environment, nonalienated trust moves one's soul.

Buber's description of I-Thou means that the psyche is founded in a nonpersonal relatedness that is religious in meaning and that creates psychological well-being through a decentering of the self.

Bibliography. M. Buber, *I and Thou* (1970); *Between Man and Man* (1955). M. Friedman, *Martin Buber* (1955).

C. E. SCOTT

EXISTENTIALISM; PERSON. *See also* PERSONAL, CONCEPT OF; SELF. *Compare* INTIMACY AND DISTANCE; REVELATION. *Biography:* BUBER.

ID. A concept from the Freudian psychoanalytic tradition representing the aspect of the personality that acts in terms of instinctual drives. The id metaphorically represents a pool of energy directed toward the satisfaction of wants, desires, or wishful impulses. The id functions unconsciously, free of the laws governing logical thought, and strives for satisfaction without regard for morality or the appropriateness of expression.

M. ESTELLE

PSYCHOANALYSIS (Personality Theory and Research). *Compare* MOTIVATION; UNCONSCIOUS.

IDEALIST PHILOSOPHY. *See* MATERIALISM; PHILOSOPHY AND PSYCHOLOGY.

IDEALISTIC BEHAVIOR. *See* COMMITMENT; GUILT; MORAL BEHAVIOR AND RELIGION; SACRIFICIAL BEHAVIOR.

IDEALIZATION. *See* DEFENSE AND COPING THEORY; DEFENSIVENESS, PASTORAL.

IDEALS. *See* CONSCIENCE; EGO IDEAL; MORAL BEHAVIOR AND RELIGION; MORAL THEOLOGY; MOTIVATION.

IDEAS. *See* COGNITIVE PSYCHOLOGY AND PSYCHOTHERAPY; FEELING, THOUGHT, AND ACTION IN PASTORAL COUNSELING; PHILOSOPHY AND PSYCHOLOGY; REASONING AND RATIONALITY IN PASTORAL CARE; THEORY.

IDENTIFICATION. A concept in psychoanalytic theory denoting the primarily unconscious defense mechanism in which one defends against anxiety and gains ego strength by assimilating aspects of significant others (e.g., beliefs, values, behavioral styles) into one's self. Identification allows an individual to enhance self-esteem through behaving, in fantasy or actual behavior, as if he or she were, in certain respects, another person, thereby gaining a source of security and an antidote to anxiety. According to Freud, our first relationships with other persons are identifications, and it is through identification that the contents of both ego and superego (internalized moral code operating by emotional compulsion) are established. Freud believed that children identify with their parents as a means of securing love and gaining protection against real or fantasied parental aggression.

M. DOLINSKY

DEFENSE AND COPING THEORY; IDENTITY; OBJECT RELATIONS THEORY. *Compare* INTERPERSONAL THEORY.

IDENTIFIED PATIENT. The member of the family self-designated, or designated by the family, as the cause and location of the family problem. Systemic family theory conceptualizes dysfunctional family transactional patterns as the cause of family problems and therefore views the identified patient only as the family symptom bearer.

B. J. HAGEDORN

FAMILY THEORY AND THERAPY.

IDENTITY. Psychoanalytic theorist Erik Erikson provides the richest and most insightful definition of identity: "The sense of ego identity, then, is the accrued confidence that one's ability to maintain inner sameness and continuity (one's ego in the psychological sense) is matched by the sameness and continuity of one's meaning for others" (Erikson, 1980, p. 94). This awareness is the "accrued experience of the ego's ability to integrate all identifications with the vicissitudes of the libido, with the aptitudes developed out of endowment, and with the opportunities offered in social roles" (Erikson, 1968, p. 261). From the standpoint of adulthood, identity means having a personally satisfying and publicly acceptable answer to the question, "Who are you?" The

following discussion delineates the major features and dimensions of Erikson's theory of identity, which has proved to be of fundamental importance for much contemporary pastoral care and counseling as well as for religious studies and related fields.

1. **Philosophical and Psychological Background.** The concept of identity has assumed an important place in the social sciences as well as popular language since the 1950s. Erik H. Erikson, psychoanalytic pioneer in the study and theoretical interpretation of the life cycle, deserves credit for giving the term its richest theoretical formulations, and for its entry into the vernacular. Prior to Erikson's choice of the term for characterizing the psychosocial crisis which comes to focus in adolescence, the idea of identity had a long and interesting history in the field of philosophy. There it had two principal references: (1) It referred to speculation and criteria for determining the possibility of two or more objects being entirely similar, to the point that they could be determined to be *identical.* (2) It referred to the persistence of sameness and continuity in a person or system over time, in the midst of—or in spite of—changes in the entity and its environment.

In Erikson's influential writings the term identity receives elaboration in relation to a rich confluence of interdisciplinary approaches. Erikson resists the effort to gather into one formulation all of the meanings of this concept. Instead, he has spelled out his characterizations of identity in a variety of places and ways, counting on his readers inductively to construct a complex mental model relating its meanings.

Throughout Erikson's elaboration of identity one consistently finds him integrating the following range of elements and dimensions: (1) Identity is both a *process* and an *accrued condition of integration.* Where it refers to the latter, the phenomenon retains a dynamic quality. Identity is never static or fixed, but represents a kind of personal coherence — recognized by others and sensed and counted upon by the self—which must be maintained and modified in the ongoing interaction of the changing person with changing environments.

(2) Identity always holds together the meanings one has for others and the meanings one has for the self. It integrates one's social "character"—the consistent patterns of attitudes, emotional responses, actions, and physical appearances which make a person both distinctive from others, and recognizable as a person of continuity and sameness over time. At the same time, it refers to the person's sense of internal coherence — his or her ability to recognize consistent patterns in the self and to feel at one with the self. With varying degrees of self-awareness at different points in one's life, identity involves a sense of fit between one's meanings to oneself and one's apparent meanings to those "others" who count.

(3) Always, for Erikson, identity refers to the process of integration, synthesis, and adaptation by which the ego unifies and orders the *evolving configuration* of "constitutional givens, idiosyncratic libidinal needs, favored capacities, significant identifications, effective defenses, successful sublimations, and consistent roles" (Erikson, 1980, p. 125). This process is largely unconscious. Its effectiveness, however, is recognized both by others, who

note the verve, coherence, and sense of energy and direction of a person, and by the self.

(4) In a last dimension of its meaning the idea of identity includes the self's sense of solidarity and belongingness with a determinate reference group or groups. This sense of solidarity may involve familial, gang, societal, ethnic, racial, class, national, professional, or religious identifications. Related to this is the important concept of *negative identity* (see below).

In the concept of identity the "inner" world of the person as well as the "outer" world of society are dynamically joined. Thus Erikson aptly designates his concept as "psychosocial identity," which "depends on a complementarity of an inner (ego) synthesis in the individual and or role integration in his group" (1968b).

2. Identity and Adolescence. Phenomenologically the question of identity emerges at the onset of adolescence when somatic and cognitive advances begin to exert new demands and create new possibilities for the young person. Rapid changes in body-size and structure, maturing sexual organs and drives, and new cognitive capacities for constructing the views that others hold of the self give new force to the reflective and earnest question, "Who am I becoming?" The adolescent's emerging vision of who he or she wants to become needs to be integrated with the images of who he or she has been in the past. In order to forge these different elements into a whole, and to develop an inner sense of consistency and sameness, the range of childhood identifications must give way to a more conscious process of identity choice and formation.

The formulations of the previous paragraph only begin to hint at the complexity of the process of identity formation as Erikson has delineated it. In adolescents' efforts to achieve a lived and conscious sense of the unity of their roles and capacities they must integrate elements both from their personal and familial experiences as well as from the societal and cultural meanings held by the larger groups of which they are part. They bring to the identity struggle the unconscious emotional residue of primary relations in which their feelings of worth and self-esteem were at stake and being formed, as well as the roles they found tolerable or satisfactory in the patterned drama of earlier family and group experiences. They also bring their constructions, partially conscious, of the salient culture's values, beliefs, and images of the good man or good woman.

When we focus on what young persons bring to the struggle for identity we have, for all its complexity, only half the picture. In his interactive, psychosocial account of identity formation Erikson also gives attention to the responses and the resources of the environing societies. The society (often through subsocieties and rituals) identifies the young, recognizing them as being persons who, in some sense, had to become the way they are, and are accepted as such. In turn, the society feels recognized by those youth who care to ask for recognition. It can, by the same token, feel deeply — and vengefully — rejected by the individual who does not seem to care, often forcing such youth toward delinquency.

One of the crucial elements for identity formation and for the strength of *fidelity*, which Erikson sees emerging with it, is the provision of *ideological* resources. Viable

ideologies must offer compelling visions of ideal man-or-womanhood, clear images of good and evil life possibilities, provide orientation, purpose and hope — and a sense of solidarity with worthy others—for young persons standing on the threshold of adulthood in an overwhelmingly complex and ambiguous world.

3. Negative Identity. Coupled with Erikson's conception of identity is the correlative notion of "negative identity." At least two meanings or patterns are united under this one term: First, the term refers to that tendency in all persons to internalize, as a feared, prohibited and yet intriguing "dark side," those qualities which one's primary caregivers warned against, treated as taboos, yet seemed to most fear that one might fall into. Often these are traceable to parental efforts to wall off in their offspring tendencies and patterns which the parents themselves, or other significant members of the extended family, have found difficult to manage. Far more malignant and destructive are the instances when youth feel either that all legitimate avenues toward achievement and recognition for them are blocked, or that no one believes in their worth or the possibilities of their succeeding. Such youth are drawn toward virtuosity in the culture's negative identity roles of delinquency, addiction, and eventually, perhaps, criminal destructiveness.

Second, negative identity refers to the stereotypic group identity forced by dominant majorities upon weaker minorities, as defined by racial, ethnic, religious, or sexual discrimination. This understanding of negative identity correlates with Erikson's discussion of *pseudospeciation*, the apparently universal need in childhood to overprize one's own group and its identity and to make "people of our kind" normative as the standard of humanity. This can be used to justify the vicious or the routine institutional imposition of conditions of subordination upon minorities or outgroups. Negative identity, in this context, refers to the subhuman images of the minority held by the dominant majority, as well as to the personal and group appropriation in the formation of minority group members of the images of their group's inferiority held by the dominant group. One of the most pernicious aspects of a group negative identity as imposed in pseudospeciation is the way in which, in order to achieve personal excellence, a person from a minority group feels pressure to separate the self from, and radically to disvalue, her or his community of origin. When youth experience the double-barrelled impact of racial or ethnic negative identity combined with the kind of personal and familial obstacles described earlier, the thrust toward self-destructive forms of social deviance can be irresistible. W. E. B. DuBois (1908) wrote penetratingly about the experience of "double consciousness" which the members of oppressed visible minorities develop in order to hold together the tensional pulls of identification with the dominant aggressor group, on the one hand, and the continuation of acknowledged membership in the stereotypically negative identity of their racial or ethnic group, on the other.

4. Identity, Moratorium, and Vocation. Erikson has studied the lives of a number of creative and gifted persons whose struggles for identity are both protracted and protected in what he calls a "moratorium." In these studies of prolonged identity crises we see that the identity process of such persons culminates in questions of *vocation* and *faith*. They postpone premature identity foreclosure so as to search for and find what unique task, project, or reason for being calls them toward the devotion and investment of self. They struggle to identify what part of the necessary work of creation or redemption, in a given generation, their unique combination of gifts, drives, experiences, and internal tension makes possible and, in some sense, unavoidable for them. The person asks not only *"Who* am I?" but *"Whose* am I?"

5. Identity, Religion, and Pastoral Care. One of Erikson's keenest insights remains his recognition of the fundamental importance of *ideology* in the formation of identity. In the search for a meaningful existence, including a meaningful identity, people seek to compose a more or less integrated tapestry of meanings, beliefs, and values—a *Weltanschauung*—by which they can make sense of their experience and find guidance, purpose, and hope in their living. Such worldviews—whether found in explicit ideologies such as in organized religions or Marxism, or implicit ones as in "the American way of life"—are usually shared with others and have the power to bind persons to communities of shared interpretation.

In the pluralistic context of modernity many explicit and implicit ideologies compete with each other, such as ideologies in academic fields (philosophy, economics, psychology, and the sciences), or political orientations. The majority of such worldviews, however, either fail to convince concerning the meaningfulness of human existence, or they shift the burden of constituting meaning entirely over to the searching and struggling human, making us responsible for our own "salvation" through self-groundedness. Even our noblest humanisms run out in the face of death. The vacuum of ultimate meanings—and the cultural pressures to ignore the abyss of emptiness—may help explain the alarming proliferation of "addictive" orientations in modern life.

Though he remains oblique and indirect about it, it is clear that Erikson believes that the ultimate guarantor of our human identity—the ultimate significant Other—is God. In his conclusion to *Young Man Luther* Erikson suggests that we perceive God "through a glass darkly" through three dimensions of child-adult experience. On the one hand, our image of God includes the longing and need for the (maternal) face that blesses—the countenance that shines upon us and recognizes us, giving rise to a "separateness transcended and yet also a distinctiveness confirmed," and which thus is the very basis of a sense of "I." "In this symbol," Erikson writes, "the split of autonomy is forever repaired: shame is healed by unconditional approval, doubt by the eternal presence of generous provision." In the second place there is the (paternal) voice of guiding conscience which provides sanction for energetic action, warns of the inevitability of guilty entanglement, and threatens with wrath. Third, there is "the pure self itself, the unborn core of creation, the—as it were, preparental—center where God is pure nothing: *ein lauter Nichts,* in the words of Angelus Silesius. God is so designated in many ways in Eastern mysticism," Erikson continues. "This pure self is the self no longer sick with a conflict between right and wrong,

not dependent on providers, and not dependent upon guides to reason and reality" (Erikson, 1958, p. 264).

It is the special privilege of pastoral care to provide a holding environment where issues of identity can be addressed without ignoring the hunger for relation with that deeper and more transcendent Other who is our ultimate ground and ultimate guarantor of identity. In pastoral care the unfolding, struggling story of the self can find grounding for identity in the larger story of God's loving and redeeming identification with humankind.

Bibliography. W. E. B. DuBois, *The Souls of Black Folk* (1908). E. H. Erikson, *Young Man Luther* (1958); *Childhood and Society* 2d ed. (1963); *Identity: Youth and Crisis* (1968a); "Identity, Psychosocial," in David L. Sills, ed., *International Encyclopedia of the Social Sciences* (1968b).

J. W. FOWLER
N. F. HAHN

EGO, PSYCHOLOGICAL MEANINGS AND THEORY OF; EGO PSYCHOLOGY AND PSYCHOTHERAPY; SELF. *See also* IDENTIFICATION; PERSONAL, CONCEPT OF, IN PASTORAL CARE; SEXUALITY, BIOLOGICAL AND PSYCHOSOCIAL THEORY OF. *Compare* ALIENATION/ESTRANGEMENT; EGO STRENGTH; SELF CONCEPT.

IDENTITY, PASTORAL. The relatively enduring pattern of attachments, behaviors, and values characteristic of persons providing religious ministries, usually but not necessarily referring to seminarians and ordained clergypersons.

Pastoral identity, like all identity formations, presupposes the emergence in adolescence and early adulthood of relatively stable patterns of self-perception that are confirmed by significant others. Professional determinants form in the context of education and induction into leadership of a specific community of faith. Personal factors are primary, however, and must be taken seriously in resolving the ambiguities surrounding efforts to understand and foster pastoral formation.

1. Identity Formation. *a. Personal and professional aspects.* Personal identity forms around one's self-awareness, self-esteem, self-transcendence, and the process of self-actualization. Professional determinants of pastoral identity include individual models and mentors; ecclesiastical structures and role requirements; formal certifications and role designations; and both the private and the normative theological images of God and of the religious community one represents. Multivariant determinants from genetic endowments and family of origin to the impacts of cultural and cosmic realities combine in unique patterns of personal and professional identity.

b. Normative and functional analyses. Contemporary literature of introduction to Christian ministry, and specifically to pastoral care and counseling, typically treats pastoral identity as a central theme. Often these authors concentrate either upon normative images of biblical and historical sources or they focus on functional analyses of contemporary self-perceptions; few, however, give sufficient attention to developing a wholistic view encompassing both psychological and normative aspects of pastoral identity. (But see Arnold, 1982, and Oates, 1982.)

2. Caring and Competence. *a. Being and doing.* Research on pastoral identity in the 1950s found laity and clergy alike focused on the minister's *tasks.* Doing took precedence over being. (See Blizzard, 1956, and Niebuhr, Williams, and Gustafson, 1957). By 1980, however, the emphasis had shifted to "service without regard for acclaim." The top four clusters of value in a study of ministers in forty-seven denominations concerned the clergy's personal commitment and faith, i.e., the minister as a person. Being preempted doing (See Schuller, Strommen, and Brekke, 1980). This issue will undoubtedly receive further consideration as women's experience and feminine meanings of being and doing become more prominent in ministry and in theological education.

b. Attachment and commitment. "Who am I?" is not the only question for one seeking to clarify pastoral identity; another key question is: "To whom do I belong?"—for pastoral identity is also a question of attachment and commitment. Given a basic identification with the church and its ministries, a pastor's commitment is primarily to the community of faith and secondarily to other institutional settings with which she or he may be involved.

c. Authority in identity and competence. Once the question of allegiance is settled, pastoral identity flowers and with it comes the choice fruit of pastoral authority. Authority inheres in a pastor's life of prayer and a clear identification as a representative of God, of a religious tradition, and of a specific congregation. Pastoral authority then permeates one's gestures of caring, the rituals of ecclesiastical functioning, and the specialized services requiring exceptional competence.

3. **Ambiguities and Issues.** Ambiguity surrounds the discussion of pastoral identity at several points. Should professional certification be required to validate pastoral identity and competence or should evidence of spiritual gifts (cf. 1 Corinthians 12–13), as judged by a worshiping congregation, suffice? Should the achievement of a high degree of personal maturity outweigh ecclesiastical endorsement based on role, status, and performance skills? Is ordination a necessary prerequisite or is evidence of an "ultimate concern" enough? How may theological seminaries cultivate a positive pastoral identity, and what weight should be given to research findings relative to the achievement of strong pastoral identity in basic units of CPE?

On issues such as these, main line denominations tend to differ from neo-Pentecostal groups, pastoral specialists from generalists in ministry, and North American pastoral specialists from their international counterparts. Ethnic and educational variables appear with some uniformity as well. Variations on the liberal-conservative continuum are minor compared to these other variables. Clearly the issues related to pastoral identity warrant the investment of large resources both in research and in programs enhancing the formation of pastoral identity.

Bibliography. W. V. Arnold, *Introduction to Pastoral Care* (1982). S. W. Blizzard, "The Minister's Dilemma," *The Christian Century*, 73 (April 25, 1956), 508–10; *The Protestant Parish Minister: A Behavioral Science Interpretation* (1985). H. R. Niebuhr, D. D. Williams, and J. A. Gustafson, *The Advancement of Theological Education* (1957). W. E. Oates, *The Christian Pastor* 3d ed. (1982). D. S. Schuller, M. P. Strommen, and M. L. Brekke, eds., *Ministry In America* (1980). See also *J. of Pastoral Care*, 36:3 (1982).

E. E. THORNTON

PASTOR (Definitions and Functions *or* Normative and Traditional Images *or* Popular Stereotypes and Caricatures). *See also* IDENTITY; CLERGY, EMPIRICAL STUDIES OF. *Compare* AUTHORITY, PASTORAL; RABBI/RABBINATE; *also articles on the pastor's* FAITH AND INTEGRITY; MENTAL HEALTH; MARRIAGE AND FAMILY LIFE; PERSONHOOD; PRAYER AND WORSHIP LIFE.

IDEOLOGY. *See* CRITICAL THEORY; FAITH/BELIEF; MATERIALISM; SECULARIZATION/SECULARISM; SOCIOLOGY OF RELIGIOUS AND PASTORAL CARE.

IDOLATRY. *See* FAITH/BELIEF; SIN/SINS.

IGNATIAN SPIRITUALITY. The unique characteristics of Ignatius of Loyola's relationship to God and the world as revealed in his writings and the testimony of those who knew him, especially the first members of the Society of Jesus (Jesuits). Significant components include: (1) a highly positive view of God's action in the world, coupled with a realistic view of humans that recognizes their ability both to participate in God's activity or to obstruct it; (2) an apostolic perspective essentially oriented toward life in the world "for the greater glory of God," in contrast to monastic retirement; (3) a dialectic of prayer and action, with prayer directed toward finding God in all things, and action for the kingdom as a legitimate and valuable counterpoint to prayer; (4) asceticism oriented toward removing obstructions to interior freedom; (5) a variety of spiritual exercises adapted to unique personalities and states of life; (6) a wholistic notion of prayer employing a spectrum of human faculties, including thinking, imagining, sensing, feeling, and breathing; (7) discernment of spirits as a concrete means to judge one's choices against the norm of God's will in the here and now; (8) a dynamic balance between subjectivity and objectivity, individual and community.

Ignatius's *Spiritual Exercises,* especially the "Rules for Discernment of Spirits," use psychological data interpreted according to a theological worldview common to his time, yet his insights transcend his own interpretive scheme. Although he focuses the conscious elements of decision making within an explicitly Christian context toward the goal of active service of God, the resulting process also deals with unconscious elements. This dynamic relationship appears in the first "Week" of the *Spiritual Exercises,* during which one recalls one's sin in a way that overcomes any rationalizing of its effects and results in a new freedom to live for Christ. The second and third "Weeks" draw one into relationship with Christ, even to participating in his passion and death. In the final "Week" one rejoices with the risen Lord, finding God's love in all things. All of Ignatius's directions for prayer and environment during the *Spiritual Exercises* enhance this progression. For example, one is to repeat the meditations and contemplations in a manner similar to active imagination, a process that moves from the general, abstract, and discursive to the simplified, personal, and affective.

Ignatian spirituality underlies much of the contemporary resurgence and reinterpretation of spiritual direction. His method of discerning spirits is concrete, individualized, and adaptable to group decision making. Both the process of discernment and the responsibility for decisions reside in the discerner rather than the director, (though a director is considered essential to the discipline: individuals should not undertake the exercises alone). In addition, communal discernment according to Ignatius's concepts provides a means based in Christian tradition for groups to address major decisions through prayerful consensus.

Bibliography. J. deGuibert, *The Jesuits: Their Spiritual Doctrine and Practice* (1964). E. Pousset, *Life in Faith and Freedom* (1980). L. Puhl, trans., *The Spiritual Exercises of St. Ignatius* (1951). J. Toner, *Commentary on St. Ignatius' Rules for the Discernment of Spirits* (1982). F. Wulf, ed., *Ignatius of Loyola: His Personality and Spiritual Heritage* (1977). W. Young, ed., *Letters of Ignatius of Loyola* (1959). W. Young, trans., *St. Ignatius' Own Story as Told to Luis Gonzalez de Camara* (1968).

E. LIEBERT

SPIRITUAL DIRECTION; SPIRITUAL DISCIPLINE AND GROWTH; SPIRITUALITY (Roman Catholic Tradition). *See also* DISCERNMENT OF SPIRITS; MEDITATION; PRAYER. *Compare* ASCETICAL PRACTICES; DECISION/INDECISION, PSYCHOLOGY OF; IMAGINATION; RETREATS (Catholic Tradition).

IGNATIUS OF ANTIOCH, ST. *See* CLASSIC LITERATURE IN CARE AND COUNSELING (Roman Catholicism); EARLY CHURCH, PASTORAL CARE AND COUNSELING IN.

IGNATIUS OF LOYOLA, ST. (1491–1556). Born at Loyola Castle in Guipúzcoa, Spain, Loyola was founder of the Jesuits (Society of Jesus). After a career as a courtier he was wounded in 1521 and underwent a religious conversion during his convalescence. He devoted a year at Manresa to prayer and wrote the key parts of his *Spiritual Exercises* (1548). When he returned from a pilgrimage to Jerusalem, he became a student at Barcelona, then at the universities of Alcalá, Salamanca, and Paris. Loyola gathered several disciples at Paris who later helped him found the Society of Jesus, a religious order approved by Pope Paul III in 1540. He spent the last sixteen years of his life at Rome governing the new order and writing its *Constitutions.*

The *Spiritual Exercises* is his chief contribution to pastoral care. It outlines for retreat directors a thirty-day retreat designed to lead persons to reorder and dedicate their lives to God's service. Most of the exercises are meditations on the life of Christ. Several methods of prayer are explained. The *Exercises* assume God's direct inspiration in individual hearts and give profound rules for discerning these inspirations from diabolical suggestions or mere human inclinations. His letters, filling twelve large volumes, are rich in spiritual counsel.

Bibliography. F. Wulf, *Ignatius Loyola: His Personality and Spiritual Heritage, 1556–1956* (1977). H. Rahner, *Ignatius the Theologian* (1968).

J. P. DONNELLY, S.J.

IGNATIAN SPIRITUALITY; SPIRITUAL DIRECTION, HISTORY AND TRADITIONS OF; SPIRITUAL MASTERS AND GUIDES; SPIRITUALITY (Roman Catholic Tradition).

ILLNESS. *See* HEALTH AND ILLNESS; SICK, PASTORAL CARE OF.

ILLNESS, PSYCHOSOMATIC. *See* PSYCHOSOMATIC ILLNESS.

ILLUMINATION. Illumination is an experience in which a person comes to a new awareness or understanding of one or more dimensions of religious faith. (In this article, the focus will be upon the human experience of illumination rather than upon the divine initiative which generates it.) Illumination is experienced as the solution to a problem or as the resolution of conflict with a concomitant sense of closure or completion in perceptual terms. Illumination is accompanied by a number of changes. Some of the more significant changes to be noted are: (1) an increased sense of health and well-being; (2) a deeper sense of certainty and conviction in faith, which is characterized by open-mindedness; (3) an experiential understanding of religious faith, which is seen to have meaning in various events and dimensions of a person's life; and (4) a sense of gratitude which is manifest in one's concern for the well-being of other persons.

When defined in this way, illumination is analogous to several models of insight familiar to pastoral counselors, namely, therapeutic insight. The analogy with insight enables an understanding of the process or stages through which an illumination experience moves. Briefly described, this process begins at the point of a problem or conflict with which a person is struggling, such as the demands of adapting to a new situation — a new job, an illness, or a loss, any of which may generate serious coping difficulties. These conflicts generally include both extra- and intrapersonal dimensions. The person may struggle for a time to resolve the conflict, but finds no resolution and gives up and shifts attention elsewhere. During this struggle, religious faith frequently comes into question and may be found wanting. While the person may shift conscious attention away from the problem, unconscious processes continue to work toward resolution of the conflict. Some time after the person has shifted conscious attention away from the conflict, a resolution breaks into awareness and brings with it a release of tension and a perceptual reconfiguration of the elements of the conflict. The problem comes to be seen in a new light, the person experiences a new sense of direction and awareness of more options than existed before. The last stage of this discovery process is more sober and reflective. It is a time of reality testing, of working through the implications of the new discovery and of integrating the changes with the enduring elements of one's life. A new balance must be found which incorporates the new with the continuity of the old.

The analogy with therapeutic insight offers, in addition, some means of evaluating illuminative experiences. The changes which grow out of the latter reflective stage of the illumination process should be enduring and not temporary changes. These changes should also reflect a strengthening of the ego and contribute to a person's adaptive capacities rather than being defensive in character.

Within the pastoral care setting, illumination can be understood as one of the processes through which persons grow toward mature religious faith. An understanding of the stages and dynamics of this process may enable pastors to assist persons more effectively in working through problems within a theological context.

Bibliography. E. D. Hutchinson, "The Nature of Insight" *Psychiatry,* 4,1 (1941), 31–44. H. Rugg, *Imagination* (1963). D. W. Waanders, *Illumination and Insight: An Analogical Study* (doctoral dissertation, Princeton Theological Seminary, 1973).

D. W. WAANDERS

GUIDANCE, DIVINE; RELIGIOUS EXPERIENCE; REVELATION AND PASTORAL CARE. *Compare* IMAGINATION; INSIGHT; INTUITION; MYSTICISM; DISCERNMENT OF SPIRITS.

ILLUSION. *See* DELUSION; HALLUCINATION; SOCIAL PERCEPTION, JUDGMENT, AND BELIEF.

IMAGE/IMAGERY. *See* IMAGINATION. *See also* BODY IMAGE; GOD, IMAGES AND IDEAS OF; GUIDED IMAGERY TECHNIQUE; INTERPRETATION AND HERMENEUTICS; PASTOR (Normative and Traditional Images) *or* (Popular Stereotypes and Caricatures); PERSONAL STORY, SYMBOL, AND MYTH; PILGRIMAGE METAPHOR; SELF-CONCEPT.

IMAGE OF GOD. *See* IMAGO DEI. *See also* GOD, IDEAS AND IMAGES OF.

IMAGINATION. Imagination traditionally has been defined as the power of forming mental images not directly derived from sensation. In this century imagination has been perceived to be, not a faculty or power, but a posture (imaginativeness) or state of highly ordered, deep feelings exhibited in a variety of activities (e.g., supposing, guessing, planning). This state has been described variously as one of intense absorption and focus; as an altered state of consciousness (the preconscious); and as a poetic, intuitive state, full of wonder. As such, imagination is surrounded by a whole constellation of issues: its relationship to fantasy, reason, truth, make-believe, image, language, and creativity.

1. **Philosophical Aspects.** If there is little agreement as to what imagination is, there is more consensus about what it does. Philosophers and theologians by and large agree that imagination functions in the following way:

Imagination exhibits two movements. First, it analyzes or dismembers elements of experience (often when one's experience is stressed), thus destroying one's previous perceptions. But second, it dissolves a pattern in order to recombine these basic units of experience (most often referred to as images) into coherent, novel wholes. Imagination thus uncovers *new* relationships among old (and new) data. It often joins what previously were thought to be dissimilar experiences or objects to produce metaphors and symbols (thus, a child's block becomes a car; a cross proclaims life everlasting). According to Hart (1969), the analytical-synthetic movement of imagination is the means by which we are capable of putting more meaning into the world than we take out of it.

Imagination is not mere fancifulness, but directed inventiveness. It is disciplined. We train our imagination with the imaginative works of others, and only thereafter give form to human experience. Virtually all commentators notice the intensive, immediate participative quality of imagination. It seems to be a particularly personal kind of knowing. Those captivated by imagination are described by their excitement, their childlike "what if" attitude toward reality in which the normal constraints of life do not seem to apply. Imaginative people are said to see an "inscape" rather than a landscape. Thus, imagination, play, fantasy, and make-believe are often associated with one another.

The most distinctive attribute of imagination is its paradoxical nature. It consistently displays the circularity of one thing leading to its opposite (as when imagination analyzes and dismembers only to associate discrete images into something new). Imagination synthesizes unlike, often unreconcilable, facts (e.g., death as the only avenue to resurrection); it uses material images to speak of immaterial spirit. In short, imagination seems to exist in a middle ground between hard fact and mere fantasy.

2. **Psychological Aspects.** One of the most complete contemporary psychological examinations of imagination is found in the work of D. W. Winnicott, particularly in his writings about play and make-believe (1971). Winnicott "located" imagination in the transitional space between the purely objective world of hard facts and the purely subjective, autistic world of the self. Imagination so placed is quite distinct from fantasy. Fantasies are purely private gratifications. They do not contribute to future actions, nor do they reinterpret past activity; if anything, they impede activity by occupying the present. (One fantasizes eating pizza rather than going to get one.) Fantasies are literal. (The fantasy of eating pizza refers to nothing more than the eating of pizza.) Imagination, on the other hand, emerges from the material (particularly the traditions) of the world and projects its fruits back into the world. It contributes to living by engaging in revisioning and planning. Imagination is never literal: it trades in symbolic, meaningful associations.

Winnicott believed that imagination begins almost immediately upon birth. Out of need, the newborn infant hallucinates the mother's breast. The mother, responding to her child's crying, produces the breast, thus setting off the experience and dynamics of imagination. The breast that was created in hallucination by the infant was simultaneously found in fact. The infant experiences the objective breast as the created, subjective breast; the conjunction of the two is not questioned. These paradoxical subjective objects Winnicott calls possessions — objects that exist in the world (blankets or toys) but which are infused with personal meaning arising out of the private world of the self (the blanket stands in for Mommy when she's gone). These possessions or transitional objects exist in the realm between objective fact and subjective fantasy — in the realm of imagination. In the transitional experience of imagination the infant finds that there is a world that serves personal needs and that there is a place in that world for one's personal contributions (e.g., since the world recognizes that my blanket is important and should not be washed even though it's filthy). Imagination understood as transitional activity thus relates us meaningfully to the world.

As the child becomes an adult, the need for imaginative experience does not diminish. The subjective world of the self as such is autistic; selves have no direct means of communicating with each other. But through transitional activity, through imagination, the self can speak indirectly to other selves using the common material of the objective world. (Thus my private agony of death intersects with the historical fact of the cross; through the cross I can communicate my agony to others.) Culture and cultural objects — art, symbol, poetry, religion — are the means, the only means, for communicating self to self. Only through imagination can we find a legitimate place for our private illusions and only there can the world become significant to us. Imagination thus lies at the heart of community.

3. **Theological Aspects.** Theological explorations of imagination center around two issues: (1) How can finite objects and experiences serve as vehicles for infinite concerns? This is the problem of religious symbol or image (particularly the image of God) and image's extension in sacred narrative. Often the problem of imagination is discussed as an issue of language — language that is not referential or objective, but that filters transcendent experiences through particular materials. (2) The relationship between imagination and revelation; or, how does religious meaning intersect with personal experience and meaning? Theologians speak about religious stories merging with our own stories, or about religion providing the setting for oscillation from reality into our subjective worlds and back again through the aegis of imagination. Others speak of religious imagination providing alternative perspectives (i.e., new relationships) through which we see reality afresh; or about imagination turning a memory into a "paradigmatic event" that keeps on happening and making other events possible. In all of this imagination serves as a bridge, as lived paradox in which the impossible conjunctions of finite and infinite are first believed and experienced and only subsequently explained.

4. **Pastoral Aspects.** Pastoral theologians as well as psychologists have noted the healing capabilities of the imagination. W. Lynch (1965) examines the double analytic-synthetic movement of imagination in the healing process. He notes that imagination first extracts those facts which have caused hurt (e.g., the death of a loved one) and then recontextualizes them into a new story or new perspective which brings meaning and healing to the sufferer. The mentally ill, Lynch says, are those who do not possess imagination; they dwell on particular facts and absolutize them. The synthetic quality of imagination serves as a place where a sufferer can "be" while making the passage through darkness or fantasy on the way to building or discovering a new reality. The ability to envision new combinations of old facts, the ability to envision new realities, is what generates hope.

In a similar vein both Patton (1983) and Gerkin (1984) emphasize the importance of the imagination in pastoral care and counseling. The central concern of pastors — offering a significant relationship to those

within their care — demonstrates an interest in whole persons, not just a concern to solve problems. And the whole person includes the symbols and stories of one's life, past, present and future. The pastor's interest in and facilitation of a parishioner or counselee's sharing a story or symbol which describes something of the character or style of the counselee's life can engage that person's imagination and help the counselee to move from whatever is conceived to be the problem to a new vision of herself or himself as one having value and dignity. Thus, the pastoral use of the imagination can provide a means for seeing the parishioner as the principal character in the story of her or his life, not just the victim of its circumstances.

Bibliography. J. Coulson, *Religion and Imagination* (1981). C. V. Gerkin, *The Living Human Document* (1984). R. Hart, *Unfinished Man and the Imagination* (1968). U. T. Holmes, *Ministry and the Imagination* (1976). W. Lynch. *Images of Hope* (1965). J. Patton, *Pastoral Counseling: A Ministry of the Church* (1983). P. Pruyser, *The Play of the Imagination* (1983). D. W. Winnicott, *Playing and Reality* (1971).

C. WENDEROTH

FANTASIZING; PLAY. *See also* COGNITIVE PSYCHOLOGY; DREAMS (Theory and Research); GUIDED IMAGERY TECHNIQUE; HUMOR; SUBLIMATION; WIT AND HUMOR IN PASTORAL CARE. *Compare* ILLUMINATION; INTUITION; MEMORY.

IMAGO DEI. The divine endowment by which human persons are said to bear the "image and likeness" of God (Gen. 1:26–27). In the Bible, the *imago dei* is specifically taken to represent a qualitative distinction between human and nonhuman creatures, the spiritual basis for human response and obedience to God as Creator, and the ethical basis for respect for human life (cf. Gen. 9:6; I Cor. 11:7; Jas. 3:9).

1. **Biblical Teaching.** There are only three texts in the OT where explicit reference is made to the *imago dei* (Gen. 1:26ff.; 5:1; 9:6) and two in the Apocrypha (Wisd. Sol. 2:3; Ecclus. 18:3). In each of these passages, a special quality of life is attributed to the human person as against nonhuman creatures, described either as being created in the image of God (*tselm*) or after the likeness of God (*demuth*), or both, as in Gen. 1:26. In the NT, reference is made twice to human persons as bearing the divine image (I Cor. 11:7; Jas. 3:9), though the concept of the *imago dei* lies behind more general references, such as Rom. 8:29; II Cor. 3:18; Eph. 4:24; and Col. 3:10. Jesus is seen by NT authors as the original image of God, as well as the one who restores this image through his own incarnate life (Col. 1:15). While the Bible does not contain a well-developed doctrine of the *imago dei*, the *imago* also is the basic presupposition of the scriptural teaching concerning the nature of human existence, including the moral and spiritual dimensions of response to the Word of God.

2. **History of Interpretation.** The earliest significant commentary on the concept of the *imago dei* was done by Irenaeus (ca. 140–202). Based on what is now considered a doubtful exegesis of Gen. 1:26, Irenaeus posited a twofold character to the *imago* based on a distinction between the words *image* (*tselm*) and *likeness* (*demuth*). Image was thought to represent the basic form of the

human, while likeness was taken to mean the material content of righteousness, which was lost or at least interrupted in its development by the Fall. Most scholars today view the two phrases as a construct of Hebrew parallelism, pointing to the single endowment that constitutes the uniqueness of humanity as created by God.

Augustine (354–430) corrected the interpretation of Irenaeus and united the two concepts in an original and perfect attitude of righteousness toward God, which was virtually destroyed in the Fall, leaving no adequate basis for an orientation toward God, either as a rational faculty or spiritual capacity. With medieval theology, and particularly in the thought of Thomas Aquinas (1225–74), the Augustinian concept of the *imago* as knowledge and love of God became more complex as a distinction was once again made between a natural endowment in a formal sense, and a positive disposition toward God in a material sense. The former survived the Fall as an indelible imprint upon the human faculty of reason and became the basis for a natural theology.

Both Luther and Calvin made a radical break with the medieval doctrine. Luther argued that for all practical purposes the *imago* is destroyed by sin, rendering the individual sinner incapable of true knowledge or love of God apart from divine grace. For Calvin, reason continues to reflect the *imago*, but in a negative sense. God has a sovereign hold on the sinner in a relation to Godself (common grace), but this relation has no positive value for the sinner. It does, however, enable Calvin to attribute to the sinner ideas of justice and morality.

The theology of the post-Reformation period contributed little to the development of a doctrine of the *imago dei*. If anything, there was a tendency to return to the earlier conception of the *imago* as an individual, rational, and formal principle of human nature. Particularly following the eighteenth-century Enlightenment the intellect and human spirit became highly individualized and autonomous, with the result that the image of God in human persons became virtually a divine principle in itself.

Recent theology (K. Barth, E. Brunner, G. C. Berkouwer) has interpreted the *imago dei* in a more relational and functional sense, following the text of Gen. 1:27: "So God created man in his own image, in the image of God he created him; male and female he created them." Rather than viewing the *imago* as primarily a formal and critical faculty of reason, these theologians see the openness of the human person to other persons in a relationship of trust, fellowship, and self-communication as constitutive of the image. This view does not eliminate the function of reason from the *imago*, but places reason within the context of love and commitment as that which most clearly reflects the character and being of God. Central to Karl Barth's concept of the *imago dei* as co-humanity is his view that the *imago* also is differentiated as male and female sexuality (cf. G. C. Berkouwer for a contrary view). Because we only experience our humanity as concrete, historical persons, argues Barth, we cannot exclude human sexuality from the *imago*, even though he is careful to point out that this does not entail the view that God is a physical or sexual being.

3. **Implications for Ministry.** The direction in which these more recent theologians have taken the *imago* doctrine — toward a more relational view of the image of God—represents a positive advance in attempts to integrate a theological understanding of the uniqueness of human personhood with sociological and psychological observations on the nature of human beings. Viewing persons as related essentially to one another and to God through a divinely endowed image and likeness gives an objective (ontological) basis for accountability, forgiveness, and restoration to health and wholeness, rather than a merely subjective (phenomenological) basis. If some experience disorder and dysfunction, this need not be taken in a fatalistic or hopeless sense. Because the original divine image continues to be God's gift and purpose through grace, the determining factor in our disordered and destructive lives is not our past but comes to us as an orientation toward a final purpose and destiny—that of sharing God's own wholeness and holiness. Thus the *imago dei* is an orientation toward a goal as much as it is a distinctive mark of our origin. This is a liberating word to those caught in the tyranny of self-contradictory impulses and an encouraging perspective for those responsible for counseling others toward personal and spiritual wholeness.

Bibliography. R. S. Anderson, *On Being Human* (1982). K. Barth, *Church Dogmatics*, vol. 3 (1958). G. C. Berkouwer, *Man: The Image of God* (1962). D. Bonhoeffer, *Creation and Fall* (1959). E. Brunner, *Man in Revolt* (1939). J. Fichtner, *Man, the Image of God: A Christian Anthropology* (1978). H. C. Wolff, *Anthropology of the Old Testament* (1974).

R. S. ANDERSON

PERSON. *See also* BIBLICAL *or* THEOLOGICAL ANTHROPOLOGY, DISCIPLINE OF. *Compare* SELF-TRANSCENDENCE; SPECIALNESS, SENSE OF.

IMITATION OF CHRIST. See CHRISTIAN LIFE; CHRISTOLOGY; LITURGICAL AND DEVOTIONAL LIFE, ROMAN CATHOLIC; SPIRITUALITY; SPIRITUAL DISCIPLINE AND GROWTH.

IMMATURITY. See DEVELOPMENTAL THEORY; LIFE CYCLE THEORY; NARCISSISM; REGRESSION; RESPONSIBILITY/IRRESPONSIBILITY.

IMMIGRANTS. See SOCIAL CHANGE AND DISLOCATION; SOCIAL STATUS AND CLASS FACTORS, *or* CULTURAL AND ETHNIC FACTORS, IN PASTORAL CARE. *See also* MIGRANT WORKERS.

IMMORALITY. See DEVIANT BEHAVIOR; ETHICS *or* MORAL THEOLOGY AND PASTORAL CARE; SIN/SINS. *See also* MORAL BEHAVIOR AND RELIGION; MORAL DEVELOPMENT.

IMMORTALITY. See ESCHATOLOGY AND PASTORAL CARE; PERSON (Philosophical Issues); SOUL.

IMPAIRMENT TESTS, MENTAL. See EVALUATION AND DIAGNOSIS, PSYCHOLOGICAL.

IMPLOSIVE THERAPY. A specific behavioral technique used primarily for reducing the frequency of panic attacks. It involves maintaining immediate, direct exposure of the individual to the fear stimulus until the panic attack peaks and eventually subsides. It is difficult to use because most clients refuse to experience a panic attack voluntarily.

T. J. SANDBEK

BEHAVIOR THERAPIES (Methods and Research). *Compare* AVERSION THERAPY; CONDITIONING.

IMPOTENCE. *See* SEXUAL DYSFUNCTION AND SEX THERAPY.

IMPULSIVENESS. *See* SELF-EXPRESSION/SELF-CONTROL. *See also* RESPONSIBILITY/IRRESPONSIBILITY.

INCARCERATION. *See* PRISONERS AND PRISON CHAPLAINCY.

INCARNATION. *See* CHRISTOLOGY AND PASTORAL CARE.

INCARNATIONAL PASTORAL CARE (Protestantism). A theologically descriptive term utilized by some pastoral care theorists to designate one or more of the following meanings: (a) the intentional effort of the pastor symbolically to embody in the pastoral relationship to persons a relationship analogous to the incarnation of God in the human Jesus; (b) the recognition that pastoral care relationships may on occasion mediate the love of God to the recipient of pastoral care in that the pastor's love speaks of the greater love of God; (c) the care of the entire faithful Christian community for one another and for the world as the response of the people of God to the admonition of Jesus to the disciples to carry on his work in his spirit; (d) pastoral care which seeks to engender in persons the capacity to be open to signs and symbols of God's disclosure in the events of everyday life.

In Christian theological history the doctrine of the Incarnation is closely linked to trinitarian formulations of the nature of God. In trinitarian thought, one of the primary modes of God's self-disclosure was in God's becoming incarnate in fully human form in the man Jesus.

Just as the doctrine of the Incarnation has itself been subject to varying interpretations, so have the implications of the doctrine for formulating practical theologies of ministry, both lay and clerical. During the Reformation, Martin Luther interpreted the implication of the Incarnation to mean that it is the task of Christians to be "little Christs to our neighbors." This has been generally taken to mean that all Christians have the task and calling to emulate and embody, albeit imperfectly, the love of God to others as that love was incarnate in Jesus, the Christ.

A modern pastoral care theorist who clearly articulated a theology of the pastoral care relationship based on Luther's formulation was C. Wise (1966). Wise's definition of pastoral care as "the art of communicating the inner meaning of the Gospel to persons at the point of their need" (p. 8) was built around the understanding of pastoral care as the relational expression of the good news of God's love and care at the point of specific inner need of the person receiving pastoral care. While Wise recog-

nized the imperfection of all pastoral relational communication of that good news, he emphasized the requirement of "a genuine self-giving love, an inner freedom to do or be what is necessary to help another find his [sic] full self-realization" (p. 14). This level of self-giving love, Wise believed, could be communicated only by pastors who had attained a degree of self-awareness that enabled them to be fully empathic in their involvements with those receiving their care.

Gerkin expanded the emphasis on incarnational theology beyond the pastoral relationship itself toward a recognition of the incarnate presence of God in events and relationships in all of human life. This emphasis countered the implicit pietism in Wise's formulation with acknowledgment that both pastor and parishioner are subject to the incarnate activity of God in the world.

Bibliography. C. Gerkin, *Crisis Experience in Modern Life* (1979). W. Oates, *The Christian Pastor* 3d ed. rev., (1982), ch. 2. P. Tillich, "The Theology of Pastoral Care" (1958) in *The Meaning of Health* (1984). C. Wise, *The Meaning of Pastoral Care* (1966).

C. V. GERKIN

CHRISTOLOGY AND PASTORAL CARE; COMPASSION; PASTORAL CARE (History, Traditions, and Definitions); PRESENCE, MINISTRY OF; SYMBOLIC DIMENSIONS OF PASTORAL CARE RELATIONSHIPS. *Compare* AUTHORITY, PASTORAL; IDENTITY, PASTORAL; PASTOR (Normative and Traditional Images).

INCARNATIONAL THEOLOGY AND PASTORAL CARE (Roman Catholicism). Incarnational theology is an approach to theological thinking, as distinct from a theological system, so named because of the central position given to incarnation, understood in two senses: 1) human existence as embodied or incarnated and 2) the doctrine of the Incarnation, that is the mystery of the Second Person of the Trinity's becoming human: Jesus Christ as being both fully human and fully divine.

1. Historical Development. Theological usage of the term *incarnation*, prior to contemporary writings, generally referred to the doctrine formulated by the Council of Chalcedon in 451 after intense christological controversies. The declaration that in one divine person there were two distinct natures set the limits of orthodoxy, but did not give an exact definitive theological position. Subsequent history of the doctrine explored the meaning of and questions associated with the Chalcedonian decree.

Pioneering work in the 1950s among Roman Catholic theologians such as Y. Congar, K. Rahner, and E. Schillebeeckx led to a more encompassing notion of incarnation. Derived from the existential metaphysics of Heidegger, the phenomenology of Marcel and Merleau-Ponty, neo-Thomistic existential philosophy, and modern biblical criticism, the approach led to a view of incarnation as a principle of theological speculation. The Second Vatican Council gave impetus to this now widely accepted approach, used by virtually all leading Roman Catholic theologians.

2. Doctrinal Understanding. That human existence is embodied is a primary datum. An individual does not have a body, but is a body. Bodiliness, as a theological datum, implies that body is a *sacramentum* or sign of all that the person is. Salvation comes through the mystery of redemptive incarnation to enfleshed spirits.

Moreover, revelation is embodied. God's self-communication takes place in the world, in space and time. The relationship of God to the world is *not* found primarily in the doctrine of creation, but is rooted in the history of salvation — an embodied history. The self-communication of God, evident in creation, in the call and mission of prophets, in the history of Israel, reaches its summit in the manifestation of Jesus Christ, incarnate Logos of God. Because this spiritual reality of the God incarnate is received in the world, the world is the place of God's saving presence; its history then is not of perdition, but of salvation. God's self-communication is not mere intellectual speculation, but the result of the salvific presence of God in the created world. It is perceived through historical events, through words, in the person and work of Jesus, in the Church and its sacramental activity. Incarnation, broadly understood, becomes the foundation for theologizing.

3. Implications for Pastoral Care. Pastoral care involves personal relationships of incarnate beings who are oriented toward God and capable of transcendence because of the paradigm of Jesus' incarnation. The caring relationship, thus, attends to bodiliness, rather than to the "soul" as a separate entity: it is ministry to the human spirit enfleshed.

Further, incarnational theology takes the categories of fear, alienation, joy, and fulfillment as important. Because Jesus incarnate shared in humanity and attendant human experiences, life experiences are concrete theological data, demanding attention and reflection. Further, a person's experiences of alienation, pain, grief, death, joy, ecstasy and fulfillment are not alien to Jesus; the life of the incarnate Word becomes a referent for such human experiences and a starting point for theological reflection.

Bibliography. J. Goldbrunner, *Realization: Anthropology of Pastoral Care* (1966). C. F. Mooney, *Teilhard de Chardin and the Mystery of Christ* (1966). L. J. O'Donovan, ed., *A World of Grace: An Introduction to the Idea of Christianity* (1978). K. Rahner, *Foundations of Christian Faith: An Introduction to the Idea of Christianity* (1978). E. C. Schillebeeckx, *Christ, the Experience of Jesus as Lord* (1980); *Christ, the Sacrament of the Encounter With God* (1963); *Jesus, an Experiment in Christology* (1979). B. Tyrrell, *Christotherapy: Healing Through Enlightenment* (1975).

J. A. MELLOH

PASTORAL THEOLOGY, ROMAN CATHOLIC. *See also* HISTORY OF ROMAN CATHOLIC PASTORAL CARE IN THE UNITED STATES; VATICAN COUNCIL II AND PASTORAL CARE. *Compare* SACRAMENTAL THEOLOGY AND PASTORAL CARE, ROMAN CATHOLIC.

INCEST. Sexual activity between persons who are forbidden by law to marry. Its frequency in the general population is higher than many people believe, cutting across all racial, religious, and socioeconomic groups. While sex between siblings may be more frequent, father-daughter and stepfather-daughter contacts are more likely to cause harmful long-term effects, including depression, suicide attempts, sexual dysfunction, low self-esteem, and more frequent marriages to alcoholic or abusive spouses (Meiselman, 1978).

1. Demographics. Usually male-initiated, most identified cases of incest involve an adult (father, stepfather, uncle, grandfather, older brother) victimizing a child or adolescent. However, recent reports identify adolescents as a group amongst whom the perpetration of incest is on the increase. It is estimated that one girl in ten experiences sexual contact with a relative during childhood or adolescence, while one in a hundred has an incestuous relationship with her father. While females are more frequently victimized, there is growing evidence involving adult males and male children. Mother-son and mother-daughter incest have the lowest frequency. Parent-child contacts are considered more taboo than sibling contacts because a generational barrier is violated, but sibling contacts can be potentially harmful the greater the age difference between the parties.

2. Clinical Considerations. Some legal and research definitions of incest require the act of intercourse; others include breast and genital touching, oral-genital contact, and other behaviors. Broader definitions include sexually explicit language, genital display, or voyeurism. Victims in treatment may report damaging effects from even subtle forms of sexual behavior. The term may include sexual activity between a child and any adult in a position of parental authority (mother's boyfriend, for example).

3. Pastoral Counseling Issues. In cases of incest involving a minor, the first response should be to protect the child from further exploitation. All states have laws which require doctors, teachers, or counseling professionals to notify child protective agencies whenever physical or sexual abuse is suspected. These laws supercede any commitment to client or parishioner confidentiality. It is consistent with biblical teaching to approach the offender and express concern that incest is occurring, along with an explanation of the counselor's moral and/or legal obligation to report it. This gives the offender the opportunity to seek help. In many states programs exist, such as Parents United, to help families when incest has occurred.

When counseling an adult offender, it is important to stress the potential damage to the young person involved. The adult is responsible for the relationship, irrespective of provocative or attention-seeking actions by the child. Children seek affection or approval rather than sexual involvement. An adult offender should be counseled to take responsibility for the incest, to ask forgiveness from the victim, and to make a commitment to the victim that incest will cease.

Victims of incest need counseling by someone who will believe them and help them deal with the emotional and behavioral disruptions that often result from incest. Children need to know that incest is a violation of their rights, as well as how to report it. Minors are often coerced into silence with bribes, threats, misrepresentation of the act as normal, or physical abuse.

Adults victimized as children may have unresolved feelings of anger and betrayal along with a variety of residual aftereffects. Many individuals carry their secret for years; until recently, their needs often have been ignored or dismissed by professionals who regarded reports of incest as oedipal fantasies without basis in fact.

An incest case is not always clear-cut. It may involve a relationship between two consenting adults who seek counseling due to feelings of confusion or guilt or a lack of accurate information about incest. States differ in their legal sanction of certain relationships. The pastoral counselor is advised to refer to mental health or social service professionals specializing in incest problems. If there are no incest treatment services available, bibliographic resources will provide useful information on counseling alternatives.

Bibliography. A. W. Burgess, A. M. Groth, L. L. Holmstrom, and S. M. Sgroi, *Sexual Assault of Children and Adolescents* (1978). D. Finkelhor, *Sexually Victimized Children* (1979). H. Giaretto, "The Treatment of Father-Daughter Incest," *Children Today*, 4 (1976). J. Herman, *Father-Daughter Incest* (1981). K. C. Meiselman, *Incest: A Psychological Study of Causes and Effects with Treatment Recommendations* (1978). F. Rush, *The Best Kept Secret: Sexual Abuse of Children* (1980). G. S. Smith, "Incest: The Four Letter Word; A Theological Approach to Therapy," *Pastoral Psychology* 32: (1984) 181–91.

M. L. WINTERSTEIN

FAMILY VIOLENCE; VICTIMIZATION. *See also* LEGAL DIMENSIONS OF PASTORAL CARE AND COUNSELING; SEXUALITY; SOCIAL SERVICES AND PASTORAL CARE; SUPPORT GROUPS. *Compare* RAPE; SEXUAL VARIETY, DEVIANCE, AND DISORDER.

INDECISION. *See* DECISION/INDECISION, PSYCHOLOGY OF; OBSESSIVE-COMPULSIVE DISORDER.

INDEPENDENCE. *See* DEPENDENCE/INDEPENDENCE.

INDIAN PASTORAL CARE MOVEMENT. *See* SOUTH ASIAN PASTORAL CARE MOVEMENT.

INDIANS, AMERICAN. *See* NATIVE AMERICANS; NATIVE AMERICAN TRADITIONAL RELIGION.

INDIGENT PERSONS. *See* MIGRANT WORKERS AND FAMILIES; HOMELESS PERSONS; POOR PERSONS.

INDIRECT SELF-DISCLOSURE (PROJECTION), PASTORAL METHODS AND SIGNIFICANCE OF. Discovering a person's characteristic modes of behavior (attitudes, motivations, or personality traits) by observing his or her responses to relatively unstructured, ambiguous, or vague tasks in which the person's own interests, desires, fears, or expectations, rather than external reality, determine the response. Thus, covert, latent, or unconscious aspects of the personality are disclosed because the individual must impose some internally derived organization onto the unstructured task or stimuli in order to choose one of an infinite number of responses. One is required to "project" internal dynamics and meanings onto external objects or situations.

1. **Projective Techniques.** Although the original concept of projection as a type of defense was developed by Freud, the use of projective techniques such as an inkblot test to study personality differences has been traced to French psychologists Binet and Henri as early as 1895–96. The first attempts to utilize such methods to explore particular dynamics of personality were those of Jung (word-association tests) and Rorschach (inkblots) in the 1920s (Allen). From these early experimental observations, a variety of popular and clinically useful "projective measures" have been developed such as the Rorschach psychodiagnostic method (inkblots), the thematic apperception test (telling stories about characters in pictures), the draw-a-person test (unstructured requests to draw particular persons or things), design completion tests, word-association lists, incomplete sentences, or various forms of psychodrama (Anastasi, Abt and Bellak, Allen). A highly trained, and often highly specialized, psychological test evaluator is required to interpret the results of projective measures.

2. **Pastoral Uses.** Indirect self-disclosure through projective techniques has become a popular and valuable method among pastors and pastoral counselors. It achieves rapid entry into inaccessible or unconscious dynamics of the counselee. It can be used by "normal" as well as distressed individuals to achieve psychological insight into distorting factors of unconscious motivations. It can be a preventive as well as a curative tool. It can be used with individuals, couples, or groups. Rather than using the results of projective techniques to diagnose or categorize persons, pastoral counselors frequently simply confront the individual with his or her own productions and responses. The client and counselor together interpret, organize into patterns, and discuss the significance of the results for the client's past, present, or future.

3. **Pastoral Method.** The principles of indirect self-disclosure are employed in pastoral counseling in a wide variety of ways. (1) *Free association.* The counselee gives an immediate response to each of a series of words designed to elicit emotion-laden, unconscious associations. (2) *Incomplete sentences.* The counselee is presented with the beginning phrase of a sentence and is asked to complete the sentence however he or she chooses. (3) *Draw-a-person.* The counselee is given a blank sheet of paper on which to draw a person (or family, or house, or combination, e.g., a house, tree, person, and animal). (4) *Story-telling.* The counselee is asked to tell a story, with or without a prompt such as a picture or a given set of characters or specific setting. (5) *Guided fantasy.* The counselee (usually in a relaxed state) is started on a fantasy journey and is asked to describe the conclusion of the imagined events. (6) *Dream journals.* The counselee is asked to write down dreams just after waking and bring these to the counselor for exploration. (7) *Biblical episodes.* The counselee is asked to imagine that he or she is participating in a biblical event by choosing a character role (or creating a new one) and describing the outcome of the event for that character. (Other literary episodes may also be used.) (8) *Religious symbols.* The counselee is presented with a religious symbol and asked to respond to it in some way. (9) *Psychodrama.* The counselee (or group) is given a situation or dilemma and asked to play-act the conclusion. (10) *Fantasy dialog.* A counselee is asked to role-play both parts of a dialog with a significant person (or entity such as God, the devil, yourself twenty years from now). (11) *Analogies and metaphors.* The counselee is asked to complete an analogy (Parent is to child as God is to _____) or a metaphor (My mother and I are like _____).

Indirect self-disclosure is best used (and least abused) when the client is maximally involved in mutual and cooperative exploration of the results and the counselor superimposes as little external structure as possible on the stimulus presented or the response of the counselee.

Bibliography. L. E. Abt and L. Bellak, *Projective Psychology* (1950). R. M. Allen, *Personality Assessment Procedures* (1958). A. Anastasi, *Psychological Testing,* 5th ed. (1982). H. Harrower *et al., Creative Variations in the Projective Techniques* (1960). A. Wohl and B. Kaufman, *Silent Screams and Hidden Cries* (1985).

E. S. D. HAIGHT

INDIVIDUAL PSYCHOLOGY. An approach to psychotherapy developed by Alfred Adler (1870–1937) that includes a model of personality, a theory of psychopathology, and the foundation of a treatment method.

Individual psychology is wholistic, underscoring the unity of the person against theories like psychoanalysis that view the person as a collection of drives or instincts divided against themselves. It also places great emphasis on the study of the client's interpersonal transactions (e.g., sexuality, work, and one's sense of belonging to a social group), and is concerned not only with inferiority feelings ("inferiority complex") but also with the individual's struggle for significance or competence. For Adlerians the individual is a creative self and often responds in ways that reflect neither genetic endowment nor social environment; that is, persons are responsible and respond in adaptive, creative ways to the social field in which they find themselves. Finally, individual psychology contends that each individual is striving toward an ideal of significance, a pattern that is evident early in life and runs as the major theme throughout one's lifetime. Adlerians call this the "life-style" of the individual.

Bibliography. A. Adler, *Problems of Neuroses* (1929). R. Dreiburs, *The Challenge of Parenthood* (1948). T. Gordon, *Parent Effectiveness Training* (1970). R. Herink, ed., *The Psychotherapy Handbook* (1980). J. Prochacka, *Systems of Psychotherapy: A Transtheoretical Approach* (1979).

R. E. BUTMAN

PSYCHOLOGY, WESTERN; PSYCHOTHERAPY. *See also* PARENT EFFECTIVENESS TRAINING; SELF. *Compare* PSYCHOANALYSIS (Personality Theory and Research). *Biography:* ADLER.

INDIVIDUALISM. *See* SOCIOLOGY OF RELIGIOUS AND PASTORAL CARE. *See also* ALIENATION/ESTRANGEMENT; COMMITMENT; NARCISSISM; SELF-ACTUALIZATION/ SELF-REALIZATION; SELF PSYCHOLOGIES.

INDIVIDUATION. A process of differentiation having as a goal the development of a conscious, complete, unique individual personality capable of successful outer (social) as well as inner (collective) relationship. In analytical psychology, individuation occurs as the self emerges and the person develops the various functions of personality.

I. R. STERNLICHT

ANALYTIC (JUNGIAN) PSYCHOLOGY (Personality Theory and Research). *See also* PERSONALITY THEORY. *Compare* DEVELOPMENTAL THEORY AND PASTORAL CARE; SELF-ACTUALIZATION/SELF-REALIZATION; SELF.

INDOCTRINATION. This term originally referred to the benign practice of imparting fundamental principles or doctrine. Recently, however, it has taken on a pejorative connotation, having become virtually synonymous with brainwashing and mind control. Indoctrination as defined in this latter sense refers to the utilization of a constellation of techniques in a coercive and/or deceptive manner to alter the attitudes, values, and basic assumptions of the indoctrinee.

The systematic study of indoctrination began in the 1960s with the investigation of the "thought reform" techniques used by the Communist Chinese on political prisoners and POWs. In succeeding decades, a series of events has exemplified the grim reality of indoctrination: ritual murders committed by Charles Manson and his cult family, the kidnapping of Patricia Hearst and her conversion to the Symbionese Liberation Army, and the mass suicide of nine hundred disciples of Jim Jones in the jungles of Guyana. Concurrently, thousands of young people were abandoning homes and families to join cults whose leaders were accused of practicing various forms of mind control in order to gain and hold on to converts. These events, along with well-publicized legal battles over deprogramming, custody rights, and the prosecution of cult leaders, have sensitized laypersons and clergy to the dangers of indoctrination, especially as practiced by numerous cults and cult-like groups.

1. **Misconceptions.** There are a number of misconceptions about cults and indoctrination despite heightened public awareness. One example is the assumption that all indoctrinating cults are religious or pseudoreligious in nature. Some of the most powerful cults are, in fact, psychotherapy cults presided over by mental health gurus who promise their followers mental and emotional well-being. Maurice and Jane Temerlin (1982) examined a number of psychotherapy cults in detail and found their indoctrinating techniques to be as effective and insidious as those of any religious cult.

Another incorrect assumption is that persons are attracted to religious cults for doctrinal or theological reasons. This is rarely the case; inquirers are usually drawn to the group by the constant and generous displays of affection that cult members show toward them. The potential convert is not instructed in the esoteric and often bizarre doctrines of the cult until the indoctrination process is well under way.

A final misconception concerns the belief that all cults engage in some form of mind control. Cults that deviate greatly from societal norms of practice and appearance do not *ipso facto* practice indoctrination. Ash (1984) states that cults lie on a continuum of destructiveness according to the degree to which they utilize indoctrination techniques. Furthermore, a cult's use of indoctrination techniques is not always constant; it may increase or decrease usage, thus varying its place on the continuum of destructiveness.

2. **Techniques.** In counseling cult indoctrinees and/or their families, it is important to understand the techniques used to persuade by coercion and deception.

While these techniques vary, most may be classified within the following six categories. It is unlikely that any single indoctrinating cult would use all of these techniques; however, generally speaking, the more destructive the cult, the more of these techniques it employs.

a. Total milieu control. Recruits are isolated from family members and former friends. Information and access to information from the noncult world are tightly controlled, especially during the early phase of indoctrination. Phone calls and visits from noncult members are restricted. Recruits are forbidden access to information critical of the cult. Information is withheld or distorted to make the cult appear as attractive as possible. The recruits are subject to constant, unwavering peer pressure by indoctrinated members.

b. Dependency cultivation. Recruits are taught that the cult is integral to their entire life; to leave it is to abandon all hope of salvation, or joy. Everyone outside the cult is considered evil or lost. All decisions, however trivial, must be approved by a superior. All earthly possessions are given to the cult or the leader upon joining the group. All money earned or obtained by members is turned over to the leaders to spend at their discretion.

c. Emotional overstimulation. Recruits are showered with nonstop attention and affection. Guilt and anxiety are manipulated via group confessionals in which sins and doubts must be repented of publicly. Deviations from the cult norms are met with harsh, guilt-inducing criticism. Ecstatic singing or chanting often lasts for hours. Sexual excitement is maintained by frequent hugging and patting across sexes.

d. Assault on precult identity. Public renunciation of one's former way of life is required. Members are given a new name, wear unusual clothing, and learn a new language. Previously held goals and values are abandoned as worldly. A person's former religious beliefs are severely criticized as irrational, satanic, or unbiblical.

e. Physical debilitation. Marathon lecturing or singing sessions lead to sleep deprivation. Recruits may be awakened in the middle of the night to engage in group activities. Diets are restricted or radically altered. Members are required to work twelve to sixteen hours per day.

f. Reduction of critical faculty. The value of thinking critically and rationally is demeaned. Doubts or questions about cult doctrine and practice are attributed to evil influences (such as Satan) or to a lack of faith. Jargon phrases are used repeatedly, without elaboration, in answer to questions. Dissociative techniques such as chanting, mind-emptying meditation, and glossolalia are required. Indirect hypnotic induction techniques are used, such as boring, repetitive lectures, use of contradictions, paradoxes, *non sequiturs*, and absurdities in lectures or talks, and inconsistent behavior of leaders toward members without explanation.

It is unlikely that any one of these procedures used in isolation would prove irresistible to a person with normal ego strength who was aware of the intended effect. However, when many of these techniques are intensively applied in a concentrated period of time, the result can be a conversion to the cult without the exercise of free, informed choice.

3. Signs and Symptoms. Since membership in a cult *per se* does not mean that an individual has been indoctrinated, it is important to recognize signs of genuine indoctrination. Richard Delgado (1977) compiled a list of various signs and symptoms of cult indoctrination suggested by a number of mental health professionals: (1) Sudden drastic alteration of the person's value hierarchy, including abandoning previous career or academic goals; (2) reduction of cognitive flexibility and adaptability. This is often revealed by the individual answering questions in a rote, mechanical manner, often substituting cult-specific jargon for individually thought out responses; (3) narrowing and blunting of affect. This can include the restriction of spontaneous expression as well as frantically cheerful, forced ebullience; (4) regression — great difficulty in making even the most simple decisions without guidance and approval from a cult superior; (5) dissociative episodes, commonly called "floating," in which the person's attention wanders. He or she may engage in a fixed stare, and concentration on external stimuli is minimal or absent; (6) physical changes, such as weight loss and deterioration of appearance with mask-like stare or evasive eyes.

4. Counseling Approaches. *a. Reentry counseling.* Counseling with indoctrinated ex-cult members who wish to reenter mainstream society requires sensitivity to the difficulties involved in such a transition. Where the cult demanded absolute obedience, demeaned critical thinking, eliminated all ambiguities and uncertainties, and controlled every aspect of the members' lives, society places a high premium on personal initiative, critical thinking, independent action, and toleration of ambiguity. Because of this, counselees often experience culture shock as they attempt to fit in with the world around them. Counselors need to help such persons learn (or relearn) the ability to act decisively, to take reasonable risks, to think logically and critically, and to tolerate life's ambiguities. Ex-cultists need to come to terms with their former cult involvement and to work though their guilt about being taken in or their anxiety about abandoning the group. They also need to reconnect with their former, precult way of life by interaction with family and friends, as well as talking about what life was like prior to cult involvement.

b. Reevaluation counseling. This term, introduced by Michael Langone (1984), refers to counseling with persons who are still committed to cult membership. The clinical goals are to help clients make or confirm an informed decision to affiliate with the group, to determine whether the cult involvement has impaired their psychological functioning, and to adapt to the world around them regardless of whether they choose to remain in or leave the cult.

c. Family counseling. Parents or siblings of a cultist often need support to deal with problems created by the loved one's cult membership. To avoid misconceptions of the cult, families should be well informed about the group in question. They should also be assisted in examining the alternative attitudes they can adopt in regard to the cult member. These attitudes range from complete acceptance or tolerance to disapproval or disowning the convert. Families, however, should be discouraged from outright rejection of the person; this would reinforce the cult's attempts to isolate and alienate the indoctrinee from his or her prior relationships. Parents may need help in working through feelings of guilt stemming from the belief that they have done something wrong to cause their son or daughter to join a cult.

Bibliography. The seminal works on Chinese Communist indoctrination are R. Lifton, *Thought Reform and the Psychology of Totalism* (1961), and E. Schein, *Coercive Persuasion* (1961). For counseling with cult members see M. Singer, "Therapy with Ex-cult Members," *J. of the National Association of Private Psychiatric Hospitals*, (1978), 15–18; M. Langone, "Counseling Individuals and Families Troubled by Cult Involvement," *American Family Foundation Monograph*, (1984). See also S. Ash, "Avoiding the Extremes in Defining the Extremist Cult," *Cultic Studies J.*, (1984), 36–72; T. Patrick and J. Dulack, *Let Our Children Go* (1976). A negative assessment may be found in A. Shupe, R. Spielmann, and S. Stigall, "De-programming: The New Exorcism," *Conversion Careers*, ed. J. Richardson (1978). For psychotherapy cults see M. and J. Temerlin, "Psychotherapy Cults: An Iatrogenic Perversion," in *Psychotherapy: Theory, Research, and Practice* (1982). J. Hochman, "Iatrogenic Symptoms Associated with a Therapy Cult," *Psychiatry*, (1984), 366–76. For a legal perspective on the issues see R. Delgado, "Religious Totalism: Gentle and Ungentle Persuasion Under the First Amendment," *Southern California Law Review*, (1977), 1–97. On the dangers of indoctrination in preaching see A. Litfin, "The Perils of Persuasive Preaching," *Christianity Today*, (24–77), 14–17. For practical advice see S. Anderson and P. Zimbardo, "Resisting Mind Control," in *Persuasion, Coercion, Indoctrination, and Mind Control*, P. Zimbardo and R. Vallone, eds. (1983), 352–55.

W. G. BIXLER

EDUCATION, NURTURE, AND CARE; NEW RELIGIOUS MOVEMENTS. *Compare* CONVERSION; DEPENDENCE/INDEPENDENCE; DEPROGRAMING; HYPNOSIS; POWER; TEACHING; VICTIMIZATION.

INDULGENCES. Total or partial remissions of the temporal punishment due to sins that have been forgiven. In Roman Catholic theology this belief flows from the principle of solidarity of all Christians within the mystical body of Christ. Even after forgiveness, there remains the obligation to atone for one's offenses. This "temporal punishment due to sin" can be satisfied by one's prayers, virtuous acts, ascetical practices, and willing acceptance of one's trials. Indulgences, granted by the church for the performance of some of these means, apply to the repentant sinner the superabundant merit of Christ and his saints, thus allowing one person to share in the holiness of others.

The official *Enchiridion of Indulgences* lists those prayers and actions to which indulgences are attached and the conditions necessary to gain them. Since interior dispositions (e.g., contrition, fervor) determine one's capacity to gain indulgences, there always remains some uncertainty concerning the efficacy of indulgences in the individual case.

Bibliography. W. T. Barry, ed., *Enchiridion of Indulgences* (1969).

V. B. BROWN

PENANCE, SACRAMENT OF; ROMAN CATHOLIC PASTORAL CARE. *See also* FORGIVENESS; KEYS, POWER OF.

INDUSTRIAL AND BUSINESS CHAPLAINCIES. Industrial and business chaplains are clinically trained ministers, who provide confidential counseling, consultation, and pastoral care to persons in the workplace. The chaplain is employed full-time or part-time and is endorsed by a faith group to serve on a nondenominational basis. In small organizations, this ministry is often performed by volunteer chaplains.

The primary ministry of the chaplain is to employees who bring personal problems to the workplace — marriage and family concerns, alcohol and drug abuse, financial, mental, and job-related stresses. In addition, chaplaincy provides a means of problem *prevention* through voluntary counseling and educational programs; *early intervention* through supervisory training and consultation; and *crisis intervention* through on site accessibility to help.

The earliest reference to industrial ministry in the U.S. is the Saugus Iron Works in Massachusetts in 1644. Modern-day industrial chaplaincy was introduced by R. G. LeTourneau for crews building the roads to Hoover Dam in 1931. In 1941, LeTourneau employed the first full-time chaplain in his Peoria, Ill., plant. A model for pastoral counseling services was initiated when R. J. Reynolds Industries hired its first full-time pastoral counselor in 1949. During the construction of the Alaska pipeline from 1974 to 1977, a unified ecumenical effort by thirteen faith groups successfully provided a chaplaincy staff of eighteen men and two women. Church, industry and union combined efforts to form a chaplaincy in Kenosha, Wis., in 1979. Chaplains are now found in a wide variety of work settings, including airports, motels, and race tracks (serving patrons as well as employees), and most recently are becoming involved with employee assistance programs.

Chaplains are accountable to both church and employer. The chaplain attempts to maintain a neutral and nonadversarial posture. Whether the chaplain's ministry is compromised by obligations to those who pay the bill is a question sometimes asked but the problem is not unique to business or other chaplaincies. As Methodist Bishop Nolan Harmon noted many years ago: "Undue influences can be exerted on any minister by those who control his salary. But this is as true in the local church as anywhere else" (*Charlotte* [N.C.] *Observer*, Dec. 19, 1957, 8A.).

The chaplain does not duplicate the ministry of the local church but extends pastoral care and counseling ministry to the workplace. Studies have shown that the largest segment of people in need first seek the help of clergy. The chaplain is one who is accessible to all—from those needing a sympathetic ear to those who have lost all purpose and hope. Workplace chaplaincy goes beyond employee assistance. As a ministry of faith, chaplaincy represents a perspective of human need that transcends defeat and despair. A chaplain's presence is a reminder to the world of commerce that it, too, is a part of God's world, and that those in the business world have a stake in the divine investment—the human value—as well as in the shareholder's investment—the dollar value. The chaplain's presence is therefore ultimately a reminder of the divine presence, even "in the uttermost parts" (Ps. 139:9; Acts 13:47).

Bibliography. R. C. Brown, "Family and Marriage Counseling in Industry," in D. W. Myers, ed., *Employee Problem Prevention and Counseling* (1985), 49–70. C. H. Peace, "Pastoral Counseling in an Industrial Setting," *Southern Medical J.,* 56 (Sept. 1963), 994–96. RJR Employee Counseling, *Manager's Guide for Helping The Troubled Employee* (1988).

R. C. BROWN

CHAPLAINCY. *See also* SYMBOLIC DIMENSIONS OF PASTORAL CARE RELATIONSHIPS; WORK AND CAREER.

INDUSTRIAL THERAPY. *See* ADJUNCTIVE THERAPIES.

INFANCY/INFANTS. *See* CHILDBIRTH; MOTHER-INFANT BONDING. *See also* LIFE CYCLE THEORY.

INFERIORITY, SENSE OF. *See* SELF CONCEPT; SELF-ESTEEM; SHAME.

INFERTILITY. 1. **Be Fruitful and Multiply.** For one out of six couples, fulfilling God's directive to "be fruitful and multiply" is difficult, if not impossible. It is not a matter of decision, ethical or otherwise. Rather, in the face of their desire to have children, it is a crisis of infertility.

Infertility is defined as the inability to conceive a pregnancy after a year of trying, or repeated failure to carry it to term. (Some authorities add that if one of the couple is over thirty, they should seek help after six months.) Secondary infertility — subsequent to a successful pregnancy—is a more subtle form, but one which affects perhaps half of all infertile couples. Single persons may be affected by infertility, e.g., through an early hysterectomy or adult mumps. Such persons should also be included in a comprehensive understanding of infertility.

The incidence of infertility has nearly tripled in the last twenty years, owing to a variety of environmental, medical, and sociological factors. These include later marriages, postponed attempts to conceive, venereal diseases, and some forms of birth control. Psychogenic explanations are to be rejected, since a physical problem is identified ninety percent of the time.

Of that ninety percent, approximately thirty-five percent of the difficulty can be attributed to the man, thirty-five percent to the woman, and twenty percent to a combined problem. In a deeper sense, of course, it is always a couple's problem. Fifty to seventy percent of infertile couples can be helped to achieve a successful pregnancy. That means the rest must face having fewer children than they wanted, or being involuntarily childless.

To these couples, God's injunction seems cruel. To some others, from the perspective of increasing world competition for limited resources, this injunction is simply poor stewardship. They suggest that to be fruitful now means not to multiply. However, even zero population growth means a couple may choose to have two children. Infertility robs them of that choice.

2. **Give Me Children, or I Shall Die.** There are obviously various motivations for wanting children. And although there may be fewer pressures today to have children, for those who want them but cannot, the prospect can be devastating. "Give me children, or I shall die" was Rachel's response (Gen. 30:1).

A couple exploring their infertility will experience physical, emotional, spiritual, and, perhaps, financial stress. The medical investigation may be protracted, intrusive, and at times like trying to finish a jigsaw puzzle without all the pieces. Each month means a rollercoaster of hope and disappointment. Anger, fear, sadness, failure, helplessness, guilt, embarrassment, loneliness, and envy form a constellation of intense feelings.

So taken for granted by most, conception may become a profoundly traumatic matter for infertile couples. They are subject to remarks which are usually well-meaning, but which are insensitive and often wrong. "Don't you want kids?" "Don't you want another child?" "At least you have one child, be glad for that." "Just relax or adopt, then you'll get pregnant." "God knows best." They may subject themselves to fantasies which are equally unhelpful. "The doctor mixed up my tests with someone else's."

Couples beleaguered by infertility may experience it both running and ruining their lives. Everything else may be put on hold. Or they may pretend that everything is all right, reducing their chances for real help and trapping them in false hope. Special events such as Christmas, and ordinary events such as seeing a pregnant woman, become painful reminders of their situation.

In addition to stress on the individuals, infertility creates great stress on a couple's marriage. Regulated sex, blame, resentment, and fears about the spouse's leaving contribute to the stress. Couples with secondary infertility may experience particular pressures from and on their single child. Accordingly, even when infertility is not conclusively determined, the couple needs to face such issues as doubts about self-worth and sexuality, what parenthood and family mean to them, and how they will work through this experience.

In many ways the process of coming to terms with infertility is one of mourning, and the dynamics are similar. The situation is complicated, however, because there is nothing tangible to mourn, and there are no rituals to facilitate the mourning. But the grief is real: the loss of an image, of a dream, of a family — the joys and trials of parenthood and of genetic continuity—a link with the past and future.

3. **Blessed Are Those Who Mourn.** Coming to terms with infertility confronts people in a unique way with one meaning of being human, *viz.*, the gap between our infinite aspirations and the finite possibilities (Gerkin). They are confronted with examining their pride, their own aging and death, and with giving up illusory bids for immortality.

Depending on their personalities and needs for a child, the couple's struggle around having a child can take on idolatrous proportions (total investment, worship, something that will "save" them). They may want to think of God as Providence, but relate to God as Baal. They may make promises to God as Hannah did (I Sam. 1:11), or feel abandoned and reject God themselves. Often couples, wanting to avoid their pain and the ubiquitous reminders of their situation, will isolate themselves from friends, family, and — worse — each other. In doing this they lose touch with what could be healing.

The pastor can contribute to the healing by helping the couple talk together about the feelings, attributions, and meanings which are a part of their infertility experience. In the process of supporting each other, they may need help accepting their differences as well as sharing their similarities. They may not be informed about medical factors or where to find competent medical help. They may want to discuss the ethical considerations surrounding some of their options. The pastor may help them explore possibilities they might not have considered or have been reluctant to consider. The couple may need encouragement to enjoy and expand other aspects of their lives. They may need support for their decision at any point to continue the process, to take a break, or to say, "That's enough."

The church may be a source of both hurt and help. Churches underscore family structure. Even many Bibles have a "family record" page. For some traditions, the separation of intercourse and the possibility of conception is not acceptable. Barrenness in the OT is viewed as a result of God's disfavor. At one point the NT says, "Women will be saved through bearing children" (I Tim. 2:15).

The church may also be a community of faith where the vulnerable suffering of such couples can be shared in a context of God's incarnate love. This affirms that, as persons with intrinsic worth, they are included in the family of God. The pastor may connect them with people in the community of faith who have experienced their struggle, as well as refer them to resources such as RESOLVE.

It is important to recognize that the pastor may have to take the initiative in talking with these couples, since many will keep the problem hidden, and may even drop out of the church. A pastor who is sensitive both to who these couples may be and to the meaning of their struggle, may help them achieve a new integration of life and faith. Walking with them through the wilderness of infertility, grieving with them, and celebrating their resolution, will be both disturbing and rewarding for the pastor.

Couples who are able to work through this experience, who are able to mourn, are thus able to freely explore alternatives such as adoption, new technologies, or to remain childfree. They emerge with stronger marriages and new ways to express their generativity as a part of the larger family of God.

Bibliography. W. T. Bassett, *Counseling the Childless Couple* (1963). A. J. Cox, "Aunt Grace Can't Have Babies," *J. of Religion and Health*, 25 (1986), 73–85. C. V. Gerkin, *Crisis Experience in Modern Life* (1979). B. E. Menning, *Infertility: A Guide for the Childless Couple* (1977). M. Perloe, *Miracle Babies and Other Happy Endings for Couples with Fertility Problems* (1986). L. P. Salzer, *Infertility: How Couples Can Cope* (1986). J. A. Stigger, *Coping with Infertility* (1983).

R. O. EVANS

FAMILY, CHRISTIAN *or* JEWISH THEOLOGY AND ETHICS OF; INFERTILITY THERAPIES, MORAL ISSUES IN; MARRIAGE. *See also* ADOPTION; FOSTER CHILDREN AND FOSTER PARENTS. *Compare* MISCARRIAGE.

INFERTILITY THERAPIES, MORAL ISSUES IN.

In recent years, several relatively successful therapies have been developed to assist conception by couples, when one or both would-be parents are otherwise infertile. The moral questions associated with such methods arise from the challenges they pose regarding the intrinsic meanings of sexuality, marriage, and parenthood, and from their possible economic and social repercussions. Therapies medically available include: artificial insemination by husband (AIH) or donor (AID); in vitro fertilization (IVF), in which donor gametes may be used; the freezing of embryos conceived in vitro for future use or to avoid the necessity to synchronize the menstrual cycles of donors and recipients; and surrogate motherhood, in which a woman contracts to be artificially inseminated and to carry to birth a child for whom complete responsibility will be assumed by the genetic father and, typically, his infertile wife as the adoptive mother of the child. Key ethical problems are: (1) whether there is a right to have a child, and, if so, how far it extends; (2) the separation of conception from sexual intercourse; (3) the use of donors (nonmarital or extramarital reproduction); (4) the status and rights of the embryos conceived; (5) in addition to the first four issues of intrinsic morality must be added the question of the social consequences of instituting any of the above therapies as general practices.

While both philosophical and biblical (especially OT) traditions portray childbearing as valuable, and as a good legitimately pursued by spouses, it is not an absolute good, that is, a good whose accomplishment overrides all other considerations. The OT (Hebrew Bible) envisions children as a blessing and a gift of God (to Adam and Eve, Abraham and Sarah, Job), not a human achievement, much less a value which supersedes fidelity and obedience to the Lord (Abraham's willingness to yield up Isaac). In the NT, marriage and parenthood are relative to discipleship in a community of faith no longer based on kinship (Mk. 3:31–35; Lk. 8:19–21; Mt. 12:46–50; Mk. 10:29–30; Mt. 10:37; Lk. 14:26). Thus, while children are valued in the Judeo-Christian tradition, the question remains whether any and all means to childbearing are justified, and if not, where the line shall be drawn.

The Roman Catholic tradition, with its emphasis on the morally normative character of human nature has given special consideration to the integrity of the biological processes by which children are produced, as well as to the context of committed marriage presumed to serve their upbringing best. It thus excludes, at least formally, any artificial separation of sexual intercourse and conception, as well as sexual relations and conception outside marriage. Both revisionist Catholic thinkers and many Protestants give greater priority to the procreation of children within a relation of marital love than to the integrity of the physical act by which conception ordinarily occurs, and so justify the technological assistance of conception between spouses, even when that circumvents sexual intercourse (AIH, IVF).

A more controversial matter is the use of donors. While methods employing gametes from unmarried partners certainly lack the intimacy necessary to qualify them as "fornication" or "adultery" in the traditional senses, they do raise the questions of the responsibility a procreator should or should not assume for his or her genetic offspring, and of the relation of shared biological and genetic procreation to the marital union itself. Some Christian authors make the case that the authentic and morally essential meaning of parenthood is to embody, through the creation of and continuing responsibility for a child, a sexually expressed commitment between one man and one woman. Others may admit this as the ideal, but lacking the conditions necessary to it, would allow donorship, provided that both spouses are prepared to accept an imbalance in their respective biological relationships to the prospective child.

The rights of the offspring become an issue at the moment of conception, though most authors agree that at least the very early embryo (prior to implantation) does not have the moral status of the fetus or infant. Thus far, the therapies commonly in use do not appear to damage the embryo or to result in physical harm to the child. Potential for psycho-social risk to the child obviously will increase with the extent to which the circumstances of his or her conception and gestation diverge from the norm. A particularly hazardous—or at least morally complicated and somewhat unpredictable—sort of situation is one in which a surrogate or donor is related to or remains in close contact with the child or the couple who raises him or her.

Even in regard to those infertility therapies not judged intrinsically immoral, it is necessary to consider the moral implications of their widespread use, social acceptance, and cost, which may be supplemented by public funds. One question is whether the *logic* ("the right to have a child") by which a less problematic therapy or practice (AIH, marital IVF) is justified also justifies more questionable practices (donorship, hired surrogate mothers). A further question is whether, even if the appropriate logical lines are clearly drawn around more morally acceptable practices (assisted conception between spouses or use of anonymous donors only), the institutionalization of such practices will create attitudes of public acceptance which can be extended easily to other, morally different, practices. Finally to be considered is the question whether the funding of infertility therapies is a justified and prudent use of scarce economic and medical resources. As with earlier questions, it may be important to make distinctions among types of therapies and to avoid the conclusion that identical ethical and social responses can be given to all.

Bibliography. J. K. Anderson, "Artificial Reproduction: A Biblical Appraisal," *Bibliotheca Sacra*, 143 (1986), 61–67. E. P. Flynn, *Human Fertilization in Vitro: A Catholic Moral Perspective* (1984). P. W. Link and C. A. Darling, "Couples Undergoing Treatment for Infertility: Dimensions of Life Satisfaction," *J. of Sex and Marital Therapy*, 12 (1986), 46–59. J. B. Nelson and J. S. Rohricht, *Human Medicine* (1984). H. Smith, ed., "Biomedical Decision Making: The Blessings and Curses of Modern Technology," *Christianity Today*, 30 (1986), 11–16. H. L. Smith, *Ethics and the New Medicine* (1970).

L. S. CAHILL

INFERTILITY; MORAL DILEMMAS IN PASTORAL PERSPECTIVE. *See also* ETHICS AND PASTORAL CARE; GUIDANCE, PASTORAL. *Compare* MEDICAL-ETHICAL DILEMMAS, JEWISH CARE AND COUNSELING IN.

INFIDELITY, MARITAL. Unfaithfulness or disloyalty to one's spouse in violation of one's marriage vows. Marital infidelity and adultery are traditionally used interchangeably to mean sexual interchange by a married person with someone other than one's spouse (Mowrer). This traditional understanding probably derives from the idea that adultery in the Old Testament was evidence of violation of a man's right to sole possession of his wife sexually. He was thereby assured that indeed their children were his own (Baab). Adultery was prohibited by the seventh commandment. In the NT Jesus upheld the law and extended the meaning of adultery to include a man's looking at a woman lustfully (Mt. 5:28). In addition, he refused to condemn a woman caught in the act of adultery (Jn. 7:53–8:11). The meaning of adultery and marital infidelity were given an understanding which includes the unfaithfulness of a married person against his or her spouse in a broader sense than only sexual intercourse with another. This broader understanding might be described as a disloyalty to one's spouse with regard to the couple's marriage vows. Thus it includes sexual unfaithfulness but recognizes the infidelity of misplaced loyalties as, for instance, to one's family of origin, to children, to work.

The pastor is often expected to use the traditional understanding. However to acquiesce to this expectation may preclude the possibility of reconciliation and set the stage for further difficulty. The alleged unfaithful partner consequently imputes to the pastor and spouse an alliance which prohibits an equitable hearing and thereby limits the possibility for the couple of grasp the fuller meaning of their difficulties.

1. Pastoral Response. Marital infidelity is a complex, multidimensional expression of human alienation. Dynamically it contains intrapersonal, interpersonal, and systemic elements which need to be taken seriously for any viable pastoral approach. The following case illustrates the value of such an approach.

The Dysards had been married for six years and had a two-year-old son. Jeannie, twenty-three, complained that her husband, Jim, twenty-five, was too much like his father and was overly involved in his work. She had discovered that he was engaged in an extramarital affair. They lived in a rural community, within three miles of Jeannie's parents. Yet both worked in a large metropolitan area. Jim complained that Jeannie was still too tied to her parents. They had tried to talk out their difficulties but had only become more frustrated. Neither wanted a divorce. Through a friend's referral Jeannie sought help from a pastoral counselor who encouraged the couple to meet with him initially together.

Had the pastoral counselor responded to Jeannie's request by simply affirming the sin of Jim's infidelity, he would have furthered their alienation and might have promoted their divorce. Or had he met only with Jeannie, he might thereby have encouraged Jim's feeling that his wife and the pastor were in an alliance against him.

A more beneficial approach was for the pastor to withhold judgment and meet simultaneously with Jeannie and Jim. At their first meeting the pastor conveyed to the couple what he had heard from Jeannie in her call. He then gave each an opportunity to express their own views. The pastor gained sufficient information for an evaluation, which indicated that the couple might benefit from appropriate psychotherapeutic help. He also neutralized any attempt by either to gain a supportive alliance against the other. The way was thus set for the couple to begin exploring the meaning of Jim's sexual infidelity as it related to the other difficulties in their marriage. The possibility for reconciliation was thereby enhanced. Such an approach is based on the premise that marital infidelity is not simply the bad behavior of one unfaithful married partner; it is rather symptomatic of a deeper and, likely, unconscious set of difficulties in the couple's relationship and its context.

2. *Dynamics of Infidelity.* Among the many possible perspectives for viewing the deeper meaning of marital infidelity, the following stand out as most useful for understanding the personal, interpersonal, and contextual dynamics which give rise to this problem.

a. The developmental stage of one or both partners. An extramarital affair may be interpreted with regard to the developmental stages of each marriage partner. For instance, it seemed to Jim that Jeannie had been disloyal to him as her husband by remaining too closely tied to her parents, especially to her father. He longed for more intimacy than Jeannie, who kept her distance. Thus each was experiencing difficulties in the developmental conflict between intimacy and isolation (Erikson).

b. The developmental stage of the marital process. A marriage relationship moves through several stages of development. Generally speaking, incidents of marital infidelity occur between the fifth and tenth years of marriage (Whitaker), after the second pregnancy, and/or during the mid-life crisis in the marriage. Jim and Jeannie had been married for six years and had one child. The time was ripe for a crisis to develop in their relationship as a way of raising the sexual temperature. The incident of Jim's sexual infidelity could be viewed as the natural result of the couple's unconscious plan to revitalize their relationship emotionally and sexually.

c. The unconscious collusion between the partners in the marital relationship. The unconscious agreement between a married couple is based on the neurotic needs of each. An extramarital affair often occurs when a couple's marital fit involves anal-sadistic dynamics, according to which one partner becomes the victim (slave) of the spouse's (master's) aggression (Willis). For example, Jim and Jeannie each had unresolved rage from their early life development. Through their marriage each unconsciously hoped to move beyond the developmental blocks which resulted in this rage. But once their marital frustration mounted, they had difficulty dealing with their negative and positive feelings toward each other. Both handled their feelings through obsessive conversations, which resolved nothing and took them further and further apart. Jeannie became victimized by Jim's affair, which was their unconsciously chosen way of attempting to break through their consequent marital impasse.

d. The traditional double standard of sexual fidelity in marriage. In some contexts the double standard of sexual morality for males and females still exists. According to this standard, certain limited concessions are made to males which permit sexual infidelity in marriage so long as it is not excessive or flaunted. This standard is customarily passed from generation to generation in certain communities. For instance, though Jim's sexual infidelity received Jeannie's condemnation, there was a certain recognition that it was not an unlikely occurrence, for Jim's father had engaged in such activities. Thus Jim's identification with his father found expression in his sexual behavior.

e. The dynamics of revolutionized cultural values during the 1960s and 1970s. The cultural changes of the late 1960s and 1970s have revolutionized sexual values resulting in widespread acceptance of marital infidelity as an accepted norm for behavior (Yankelovich). The search for self-fulfillment as a psychological and cultural phenomenon has been a dynamic of revolutionary proportions. The consequences are that marital infidelity now finds general acceptance. It was a testimony to the strength of their marital bond that Jim and Jeannie sought conjoint couple's therapy to deal with their crisis of marital infidelity in such a cultural climate.

Each of these perspectives on the deeper meaning of marital infidelity involves ingredients of the others. Obviously, there are many possible overlaps among them. Therefore each incident of infidelity must be viewed with respect to its own particular character. These perspectives are not offered here as a way of undermining the ethical and moral standards which provide the foundation upon which the pastor is called to function in his or her ministry. Rather they are intended to provide handles for making sense of unfaithful sexual behavior and to help the pastor promote a healthy reconciliation and renewal of the couple's self-chosen obligation to be faithful to one another in their marriage vows.

Bibliography. O. J. Baab, "Adultery," *The Interpreter's Dictionary of the Bible* (1962). E. Erikson, *Childhood and Society* rev. ed. (1978). E. R. Mowrer, "Infidelity," *An Encyclopedia of Religion* (1945). Whitaker, "Existential Marital Therapy: A Synthesis; A Subsystem of Existential Family Therapy," in G. P. Sholevar, ed., *The Handbook of Marriage and Family Therapy* (1981). J. Willis, *Couples In Collusion* (1982). D. Yankelovich, *New Rules Search for Self-Fulfillment in a World Turned Upside Down* (1981).

R. E. JOHNSTON

MARRIAGE. *See also* COMMITMENT; MARRIAGE COUNSELING AND MARITAL THERAPY; RESPONSIBILITY/IRRESPONSIBILITY, PSYCHOLOGY OF; SIN/SINS; VOWS/VOWING. *Compare* APOSTASY; FORGIVENESS; MORAL DILEMMAS IN PASTORAL PERSPECTIVE; TEMPTATION.

INFIDELITY, RELIGIOUS. *See* APOSTASY; BELIEF/UNBELIEF; VOWS/VOWING.

INFLUENCE. *See* SUGGESTION, PERSUASION AND INFLUENCE. *See also* POWER; REASONING AND RATIONALITY; VIPs.

INFORMATION PROCESSING. *See* CYBERNETIC THEORY; *See also* BRAIN RESEARCH; COGNITIVE PSYCHOLOGY AND PSYCHOTHERAPY; COMMUNICATION; DEFENSE AND COPING THEORY.

INHIBITION. Internal constraints or checks on desires, impulses, or instincts with concomitant limitations on behavior and feeling. Unconscious sources and influences, as opposed to conscious restraint or control, are generally implied. However, certain inhibitions, depending on the resulting behavior, are often not judged to need remediation, e.g., inhibitions of sexual expressiveness in a conservative community.

K. P. ROSS

ANXIETY; SHAME; SHYNESS. *See also* NEUROSIS.

INITIATION RITES. *See* RITUAL AND PASTORAL CARE. *See also* SOCIOLOGY OF RELIGIOUS AND PASTORAL CARE.

INITIATIVE AND INTERVENTION, PASTORAL. A significant dimension to the historical and traditional role of the pastor is the access that the pastor has to the congregation. The pastor not only has the right to initiate encounters; he or she is expected to take such initiative and may be criticized when appropriate initiative is lacking. Criticism may occur, also, when the initiative or intervention is too aggressive or lacks awareness of appropriate personal boundaries. Therefore, pastors may feel caught between the varying expectations of others and their own self-concept in ministry.

The advent of psychotherapy and its impact in the counseling role of clergy has further confused the issue. The dominant model presented in the early development of psychotherapy, and remaining in analytically oriented psychotherapy, was one in which the therapist is available to the client at the client's initiative, with no direct intervention outside the sanctity of the therapy hour. Thus, therapy was viewed as a relationship of considerable intensity within the therapy hour and considerable detachment outside that hour. This set up identity diffusion in clergy who adopted the analytical model while remaining in a distinctly pastoral identity.

More recent developments in counseling and psychotherapy are more congruent with the historical role of clergy in terms of initiative and intervention. Caplan and others developed theory and application of crisis intervention techniques that resembled effective pastoral initiative and intervention, even including home visits, an age-old pastoral practice. Behavioral therapists developed approaches that took seriously the environment, current social contacts of clients, and reinforcement strategies which frequently mirrored the traditional procedures of pastors and churches. Marital therapists like Richard Stuart designed short-term intervention strategies that directly relate both to the authority roles and the shepherding roles of the pastor. Virginia Satir has developed a process of family intervention that integrates the use of systems and communication theory with an active relationship approach emphasizing warmth and positive reinforcement. Thus, there exist today abundant models that are congruent with a variety of styles of pastoral intervention. In the 1970s, many professional pastoral counselors actively began to reevaluate their use of initiative and intervention and reclaim the traditional rights and expectations of clergy in this function, informed and enriched by the emerging models from the field of psychotherapy and mental health.

Research into initiative and intervention with alcoholics and their families (Woodruff, 1968) has underscored the pastoral effectiveness of balancing direct initiative with disciplined awareness of the teachable moment in the alcoholic when he or she is open to such intervention. It also emphasized the value of introduction to Alcoholics Anonymous and other community resources as effective channels of pastoral initiative and intervention. Overall, pastors need to be aware of personal strengths and limitations, have a knowledge of community resources, and value their historical roles, while being informed by sound psychotherapeutic theory and practice in regard to initiative and intervention.

Bibliography. G. Caplan, *Principles of Preventive Psychiatry* (1964). V. Satir, *Conjoint Family Therapy* rev. ed. (1967). R. B. Stuart, *Helping Couples Change* (1980). C. R. Woodruff, *Alcoholism and Christian Experience* (1968).

C. R. WOODRUFF

ADVOCACY; ASSERTIVENESS IN MINISTRY; CALLING AND VISITATION, PASTORAL; CRISIS INTERVENTION THEORY. *See also* AUTHORITY, PASTORAL; CONFRONTATION (Pastoral and Therapeutic); PASTORAL COUNSELING; TECHNIQUE AND SKILL IN PASTORAL CARE. *Compare* GUIDANCE, PASTORAL.

INJURY. *See* CRISIS MINISTRY; LOSS OF FUNCTION; TRAUMA.

INJUSTICE. *See* EXPLOITATION/OPPRESSION; SOCIAL JUSTICE ISSUES IN PASTORAL CARE. *See also* VICTIMIZATION.

INK BLOT (Rorschach) TEST. *See* EVALUATION AND DIAGNOSIS, PSYCHOLOGICAL.

INSANE ASYLUM. *See* MENTAL HOSPITAL/MENTAL HOSPITALIZATION. *See also* COMMUNITY MENTAL HEALTH MOVEMENT.

INSANITY. *See* SANITY/INSANITY. *See also* PSYCHOSIS; SCHIZOPHRENIA.

INSIGHT. A personal experience in which perceptions crystallize, and one senses the birth of understanding regarding the new relationship of heretofore seemingly unrelated ideas, conceptions, and experiences. It is a conscious and primarily cognitive experience, which A. Maslow referred to as the "aha" experience. Much like discernment, insight might be contrasted to a "trial and error" process. Insight produces a sense of discovery. The new perception and understanding is sensed to be both meaningful and valid. The term is often used to refer to radical new interpretations of commonly held beliefs such as in the contributions of Newton, Darwin, and Einstein.

Psychotherapeutically, insight refers to the personal awareness of newly established linkages between current behaviors and repressed or forgotten events. One experiences a shift resulting in the reorganization of the meaning of one's experience. Dynamic theorists consider insight necessary but not sufficient for change, the "working-through" process yet being required. Behaviorists see insight as neither necessary nor sufficient, but as a purely cognitive contribution irrelevant to behavior change.

K. P. ROSS

SELF-UNDERSTANDING. See also ILLUMINATION; INTUITION; PERCEPTIVENESS AND SENSITIVITY, PASTORAL.

INSOMNIA. See SLEEP AND SLEEP DISORDERS.

INSPIRATION. See RELIGIOUS EXPERIENCE. See also CHARISMATIC EXPERIENCE; HOLY SPIRIT; ILLUMINATION; IMAGINATION; REVELATION.

INSTINCT. An inborn and predetermined behavior pattern that is not the result of environment or learning. A specific instinct such as nest building in birds may only be seen within species. Other instincts in higher animals and humans, such as aggression, may be predispositions that can be modified through environmental interaction and learning. The concept of instinct plays an important part in the understanding of human behavior for such theories as behaviorism and Freudian psychology.

D. E. MASSEY

MOTIVATION; PSYCHOANALYSIS.

INSTITUTE OF PASTORAL CARE. Was incorporated on January 28, 1944. Rollin Fairbanks became its first executive director. The founding of the institute was the result of concern in New England for over twenty years to provide opportunities for theological students and pastors to encounter human suffering and develop specifically pastoral skills under supervision. Richard C. Cabot, a physician, was an early source of vision, leadership, and financial encouragement to the movement. This resulted in the establishment of the first clinical training center at Worcester (Mass.) State Hospital in 1925 under Anton Boisen and the formation of the Council for the Clinical Training of Theological Students on January 21, 1930, in Boston.

A distinctive clinical training tradition began to emerge when Philip Guiles severed his relationship with the council in 1932. With the help of Cabot and the Earhart Foundation, he began to develop other clinical training opportunities in New England. Massachusetts General Hospital became an important training center with the arrival of Russell Dicks as chaplain in 1933. *The Art of Ministering to the Sick* (1936) by Cabot and Dicks became a standard reference, which reflected the pastoral orientation of the "New England group."

This group emphasized the following things: clinical training as a method of theological education whose primary goal was preparation for the parish ministry, a close relationship with seminaries; the general hospital as the primary place for clinical training, and Dicks's "note-writing" technique (verbatims) as the basic supervisory tool. The "Cabot Club" method, dual calling, and the controlled interview were also developed and used by supervisors.

The New England Theological Schools Committee on Clinical Training was formed in 1938 to foster clinical training in the region. The Institute of Pastoral Care developed six years later because of the desire to expand the work of this committee, including the publication of a journal. This was begun in 1947 as the *Journal of Pastoral Care*. The 1950s were a time of growth, increased cooperation with the Council for Clinical Training, and participation in the Committee of Twelve. By 1960, the institute had thirty-three centers, fifty-one supervisors, and over four hundred summer school students. It had become a national organization.

Paul Johnson, who was involved in establishing the institute, and John I. Smith provided leadership to unify the institute with other clinical training groups in the 1950s and 1960s. By 1966, the institute and council were functionally merged and discussions broadened to include the Southern Baptist and Lutheran groups. This led to the incorporation of the Association for Clinical Pastoral Education on November 17, 1967. The Institute of Pastoral Care officially discontinued on January 1, 1968.

Bibliography. R. Cabot and R. Dicks, *The Art of Ministering to the Sick* (1936). S. Hiltner, ed., *Clinical Pastoral Training* (1945). E. Thornton, *Professional Education for Ministry* (1970). Archives of the Institute of Pastoral Care, Boston University, School of Theology.

M. D. HOUGLUM

ASSOCIATION FOR CLINICAL PASTORAL EDUCATION; HISTORY OF PROTESTANT PASTORAL CARE (United States); PASTORAL CARE MOVEMENT. See also CLINICAL PASTORAL EDUCATION. Biography: BOISEN; CABOT; DICKS; JOHNSON.

INSTITUTIONAL CHAPLAINCY. See CHAPLAIN/CHAPLAINCY.

INSTITUTIONALIZATION. See MENTAL HOSPITALIZATION; PRISONERS AND PRISON CHAPLAINCY. See also HOSPITALIZATION, EXPERIENCE OF.

INSURANCE. See LIABILITY INSURANCE. See also FEES IN PASTORAL COUNSELING; LEGAL DIMENSIONS OF PASTORAL CARE AND COUNSELING.

INTAKE (Pastoral Counseling). See PASTORAL COUNSELING.

INTEGRATION, RACIAL. See RACISM. See also SOCIAL CHANGE AND DISLOCATION; SOCIAL JUSTICE ISSUES.

INTEGRATION OF PSYCHOLOGY AND THEOLOGY. The process of relating psychological concepts as well as the discipline as a whole to theology. As a formally identified task it is of quite recent origin, being a development of the last thirty years.

In a historical sense, the integration of current thought forms with Christianity has been the intellectual task of the Christian theologian and pastor beginning with the apologists in the second century, continuing with Augustine's *City of God*, Thomas Aquinas's *Summa Theologica*, and Calvin's *Institutes*. In the post-Reformation period the task of integration became one of relating the emerging sciences with a Christian theological worldview. The task was continued by Kepler, Newton, and many others with the rapid developments in science. The stress on integrating science and Christianity was particularly strong in such nineteenth century American theologians as McCosh, Porter, and Upham. With the emergence of psychology as a separate discipline at the end of the nineteenth century some integration was incorporated into the early psychology of religion texts of James and Starbuck, although a shift of focus from integration to psychology of religion can be clearly seen. However, the antireligious bias of the early developers of psychology such as Freud and Watson coupled with the strong materialistic and physicalistic emphases of twentieth-century philosophy of science led to an eclipse of the experience-centered areas of study such as the psychology of religion. Shortly after World War II the integration of psychology and theology emerged as an explicit task, in addition to general long-standing talk of integrating science and theology and the more recent study of psychology had become established as a discipline by this point. Integration as an explicit task appears to be one manifestation of what Bloesch has called *The Evangelical Renaissance*, although it has a long root in the clinical pastoral care movement and also in the psychology of religion.

Integration does not imply that psychology and theology are creating a new discipline out of the other two. Rather, it assumes that the phenomena of psychology and theology are not in conflict because they are integral with the unity of truth. This unity is of necessity to God's truth since God is the author of all.

Integration can be conceptualized in terms of the figure of a diamond with three levels. The first level is abstract and conceptual and examines the metaphysical assumptions behind various psychological concepts and theories for this unity with theology. Since truth is one, there is ultimately only one set of explanatory principles, that is, the world and humankind, which science and psychology studies, is in harmony with theology. In theological terms general and special revelation are in agreement because God is the author of both. Integration seeks to discover that harmony. At the second level there is an equal emphasis on both psychology and theology, while their destructive methods are recognized. Psychology tends to be empirical and theology rational in their research. The difference in their content is not fused, nor is one reduced to the other forming a psychologized theology or a theologized psychology. Both are affirmed, including their difference, but the dynamic equivalence of their respective concepts is recognized where it exists. The third level of integration is experience and behavior. Psychology and theology converge at the points of experience because every person thinks, wills, feels, and behaves. The concepts used to explain this process — thought, choice, anxiety, guilt, values, and action — are simultaneously part of psychology and Christian theology, especially pastoral theology, because persons are fundamentally a part of both. Thus the unity or integration appears again as in the first level, but at the third level it is in experience. Finally, the three levels of integration are not separate but form a dynamic whole or gestalt which involves the principles behind both disciplines, study of both disciplines, and awareness of one's experience in psychology as well as one's spiritual context.

Bibliography. L. Aden and P. Homans, eds., *The Dialogue Between Theology and Psychology* (1968). J. D. Carter and S. B.

Narramore, *The Integration of Psychology and Theology* (1979). J. R. Fleck and J. D. Carter, eds., *Psychology and Christianity* (1981). H. N. Malony, ed., *Wholeness and Holiness* (1983).

J. D. CARTER

THEOLOGY AND PSYCHOLOGY; THEOLOGY AND PSYCHO-THERAPY. *See also* EVANGELICAL PASTORAL CARE; PASTORAL CARE MOVEMENT; PASTORAL THEOLOGICAL METHODOLOGY; PASTORAL THEOLOGY; PERSON; PHILOSOPHY AND PSYCHOLOGY; PSYCHOTHEOLOGY; RELIGION AND HEALTH MOVEMENT; RELIGION AND PSYCHOTHERAPY. *Compare* PSYCHOANALYSIS *or* ANALYTICAL (JUNGIAN) PSYCHOLOGY AND THEOLOGY.

INTEGRITY, MORAL. *See* MORAL DEVELOPMENT; *See also* FAITH AND INTEGRITY, PASTOR'S.

INTEGRITY THERAPY. The name given to the therapy based on the theoretical formulations of O. Hobart Mowrer. Integrity therapy is in the tradition of what are sometimes called peer self-help psychotherapy groups, the most notable of which would be Alcoholics Anonymous. Dr. Mowrer once described integrity therapy as "Alcoholics Anonymous in civilian dress." The basic principles of these groups are that they utilize nonprofessional leaders; emphasize personal responsibility; maintain high moral standards; provide a setting for and encourage self-disclosure; use distinctive techniques of teaching, such as songs and slogans; motivate participants into action; and utilize peer group pressures which are both critical and supportive.

1. **Basic Principles of Integrity Therapy.** Integrity therapy rejects all deterministic theories which make a person a victim of heredity or environment. Individuals are responsible for their own lives and exercise their right by making their own decisions. Each individual has a conscience, or value system. When one violates one's conscience, one becomes guilty, a condition which is not a sickness but a result of wrongdoing and irresponsibility.

A common reaction to personal wrongdoing is to cover up and deny its existence. In this secrecy, guilt gives rise to symptoms which may be so severe as to upset life's balance. As secrecy causes one trouble and separates one from his or her fellows, so openness with "significant others" is the road back to normality. Openness takes place with increasing numbers of "significant others" and progresses in ever-widening circles as persons learn to live authentically with their fellows.

By itself, however, openness is not enough. The guilty individual is under an obligation to make restitution appropriate to the acknowledged failure in his or her life. The only way to become a whole person is not only to remain open and make restitution but also to feel a responsibility to carry the "good news" to others.

2. **Characteristic Steps in the Use of Integrity Therapy.** Lead counselees to see the role of personal irresponsibility in their difficulties. After letting counselees verbalize their version of what brought on the malaise, lead them to accept at least a modicum of responsibility. Create an awareness of the self-defeating tendency to ignore and cover up our shortcomings.

Use the distinctive technique of "modeling the role" by which counselors tell of a personal experience in which a violation of values brought on distress.

Pay close attention to a confessional reply. Integrity therapy carefully delineates the nature of confession in this setting. We do not confess for others; confession is not blaming others; confession is not complaining; confession focuses on our weaknesses rather than our strengths.

Introduce the counselee into group therapy. In this situation the leader "models" and the group functions on both a critical and supportive basis. Within the group the client not only becomes open in accordance with integrity therapy principles, but undertakes acts of restitution commensurate with the acknowledged failure. The troubled person moves toward helping other people and hopefully into a leadership role within the group.

The three words Mowrer used most frequently are honesty, responsibility, and involvement; these concepts permeate all the formulations of integrity therapy. From the religious leader's perspective, the theory of integrity therapy has reminded us of a number of basic concepts which include the importance of values, the distinction between scrupulosity and real guilt, the establishment of guidelines for a viable confessional experience, the redemptive power of the small group, the relationship of faith and action, and a technique which is in line with biblical principles.

Integrity therapy's emphasis on lay leaders has probably hindered its wide acceptance by professional psychotherapists, but in many ways it is an ideal counseling method for church life.

Bibliography. J. W. Drakeford, *Integrity Therapy* (1967); *People to People Therapy* (1978); O. H. Mowrer, *Abnormal Reactions or Actions* (1966).

J. W. DRAKEFORD

EVANGELICAL *or* FUNDAMENTALIST PASTORAL CARE. *Compare* PASTORAL COUNSELING.

INTELLECTUAL VIRTUES. *See* MORAL THEOLOGY. *See also* VIRTUE, CONCEPT OF.

INTELLECTUALIZATION. An unconscious defense mechanism, closely akin to rationalization, whereby a person attempts to gain detachment from emotionally threatening situations or undesirable feelings by replacing them with safe intellectual concerns devoid of personal and affective significance. For example, an individual who has endured tremendous personal tragedy may expound every detail while remaining emotionally disengaged.

M. A. WOLTERSDORF

DEFENSE AND COPING THEORY; DEFENSE MECHANISM; REASONING AND RATIONALITY IN PASTORAL CARE. *Compare* COMPASSION; RATIONALIZATION.

INTELLIGENCE AND INTELLIGENCE TESTING. The definition of intelligence and its measurement are extremely complex and often controversial subjects. It is an old adage in this field that there are about as many definitions of intelligence as those doing the defining. Although it seems paradoxical, we do appear to have done a better job measuring intelligence than defining it. The situation, however, is somewhat analogous to electricity, which we are able to use for a variety of practical purposes although we still have trouble defining its precise nature. Lay or colloquial definitions of intelligence typically incorporate such ideas as how smart people are, how much they know, and how fast they are able to learn. The more professional and scientific definitions have emphasized various aspects of this concept depending on the field of endeavor. For example, educators focus on the "capacity to learn," philosophers and mathematicians on "the ability to think abstractly," while comparative psychologists stress "adaptability to new situations."

In the more recent past, the idea of "general problem-solving ability" received considerable attention, culminating in the related but current focus on ideas about "information processing" as being the essence of intelligence. Despite the difference in focus or emphasis, practically all workers in this field agree that intelligence is a hypothetical construct that does not exist as a concrete, physical entity (Conger, 1957).

1. Theories of Intelligence. Although there were no systematic theories available to guide the initial attempts at test construction, we now have a plethora of theories or models of intelligence. Historically, the first group of theories, called the *psychometric approach*, analyzed the data from intelligence tests themselves in trying to figure out the underlying nature of intelligence. The central question in this area has always been whether intelligence is one unified, comprehensive ability or a collection of different specialized abilities. Charles Spearman and Jay Paul Gilford represent the extremes along this continuum, with Spearman stating that intelligence is primarily comprised of a large general factor which he called "*g*," while Gilford has proposed his "Structure of Intellect" (SI) model which now states that there may well be as many as 150 specific abilities comprising intelligence. The research of another pioneer in this approach, L. L. Thurstone, indicated that there were about seven "primary mental abilities."

It is now widely accepted that intelligence is composed of a number of separate but related abilities or components, with the exact number remaining unspecified. Given this multidimensional concept of intelligence, the assessment of intelligence and related research efforts are now much more focused on patterns of ability rather than on a single level of ability, as implied by the IQ.

Another major theoretical approach has been the *biological developmental* view, best exemplified by the work of Jean Piaget, who has produced the most fully specified theory of intelligence, which necessitated an examination of how intelligence actually develops in the individual. He has a very dynamic theory of intellectual development, clearly emphasizing the role of experience in producing qualitative changes in the underlying structures of intelligence as the person develops. He postulated three basic stages of intellectual development, each characterized by a qualitatively different structure of intelligence. In short, Piaget says that intelligence is something qualitatively much different at age two than at age twenty. Furthermore, from this point of view, intelligence could never be represented by a number like IQ, as it is not so much measured as described, since we are talking about a developmental process.

The pervasive use of the *computer analogy* has had a profound impact on the theory and research in the field of intelligence over the last ten to fifteen years. Intelligence is now conceived of in "information-processing" terms. Robert Sternberg (1985) best exemplifies this view, which he calls the computational model. Information processing theory deals with how people attend to, select, encode, and store information, and how they later retrieve it, decode it, and then use it to make decisions and guide their behavior. In addition to focusing on both the processes and content of intelligence, this approach also recognizes that intelligence is truly a dynamic, developmental phenomenon.

2. **Points at Issue.** In discussing theories or models of intelligence, it must be noted that there are those who argue strongly that the notion of intelligence is wholly or partly determined by the nature of the environment in which one lives. In other words, there is no single notion of intelligence that is appropriate for all cultures, since not all cultures view intelligence the same way or consider the same behaviors to be intelligent. These cultural considerations are not dissimilar to the developmental considerations mentioned above, wherein it was noted that the nature of intelligence may also vary over the life span of the individual.

Another related consideration bears mentioning. David Wechsler expanded the notion of general intelligence to include nonintellectual factors, such as personality and motivational variables, which combine with the various abilities in the expression of intelligent behavior. In other words, he maintains that the tests tap these other areas as well, since a test is a behavioral performance. You cannot assess intellectual functions in a vacuum or get a "pure" or "abstract" measure of an ability; the person's personality and motivation interact with his cognitive functions in producing his responses. In essence, the test therefore really gives a measure of a person's "effective" intelligence, which is the product of the interaction of all of these variables.

One of the central issues about the nature of intelligence and its development has been the relative role or contribution of genetic and environmental factors, known in the past as the "nature-nurture" debate. Initially, intelligence was viewed as a static, unidimensional trait that was primarily inherited. Later on, the critical role of the environment and experience in the development of intelligence was stressed. Nowadays, most workers in the field emphasize the interactive effects of genetic and environmental factors, rather than the prominence of either component, since the interaction must occur for any intelligence to be developed and manifested.

3. **Intelligence Testing and IQ.** Although the French Alfred Binet is credited with developing the first successful test of intelligence in the early 1900s, the intelligence testing movement has been primarily an American phenomenon. Lewis Terman from Stanford University translated and applied Binet's procedures in producing the Stanford-Binet test in 1916. The other extremely critical aspect of that introduction was the employment of the IQ index, which had been developed by a German by the name of Wilhelm Stern in 1912. The employment of the Stanford-Binet in 1916 popularized the use of the IQ and

IQ testing in the school system. Shortly thereafter, with the advent of World War I, American psychology was called upon to develop intellectual screening devices that would be useful to the military in the selection of its recruits. The net result of the extensive testing in the military and the schools was that intelligence testing and the IQ were put on the map. Unfortunately, some of the data from the early testing of students and military recruits were inappropriately and erroneously used for sociopolitical purposes that culminated in the sounding of "eugenic" alarms around the 1920s. This was but the start of the misuse and misinterpretation of IQ scores, which has continued to this day.

In 1939 David Wechsler introduced the first of his Wechsler scales. The modern versions are known as the Wechsler Adult Intelligence Scale-Revised (WAIS-R) and the Wechsler Intelligence Scale for Children-Revised (WISC-R). His tests of intelligence employ multiple subscales of specific abilities, which were then summarized into three different IQ scores; namely, a verbal IQ, a performance IQ (dealing with nonverbal material), and a resulting full scale IQ. The tests of intelligence developed by Binet and Wechsler are both composite batteries that are individually administered. For more large scale and screening purposes, particularly in military, industrial, and educational settings, there is now a variety of group tests of intelligence that can be administered. Such devices employ visual and/or verbal materials, often in a simple multiple choice format, and can be given much more quickly and efficiently than the more comprehensive, individually administered tests.

All tests of intelligence have one thing in common: The results are expressed as a quantitative index called the intelligence quotient, or IQ. The IQ summarizes a person's performance, or level of general intellectual functioning, on a given test. It is this index that most people think of and refer to when talking about intelligence. Perhaps no other notion in the field of psychology has engendered so much, often heated, debate.

Much of the controversy concerns interpretation. There are two types of IQ indexes. The first and older type was called the *ratio IQ*, referring to the fact that the rate of intellectual development was expressed as a function of mental age divided by chronological age. Practically all modern revisions of older intelligence tests and new intelligence tests employ what is called the *deviation IQ*. The correct interpretation of the deviation IQ requires a knowledge and understanding of the normal curve and the standard deviation and is based on the assumption that the theoretical distribution of intelligence can be described by the normal curve. Given this assumption, the interpretation of the deviation IQ is quite straightforward. What it tells you is the relative position of the person compared to his or her age peers in terms of standard deviation units. One advantage of the use of the normal curve and standard deviation units is that they have easily understood and interpretable percentile equivalents. Thus, the meaning of the deviation IQ can be thought of in the same terms as SAT (Scholastic Aptitude Test) or GRE (Graduate Record Examination) scores, all of which are expressed in percentile ranks.

In the late 1960s and early 1970s, there was a major controversy regarding the testing of intelligence of racial and ethnic minorities and the resulting differences in mean (average) IQ scores that were variously observed when compared to the white middle-class norm group. While such average differences do exist, many professionals attempted to emphasize that the overlap between the various distributions was considerable. In other words, many people from the various minority groups performed better than the average person in the norm group. The real issue was not with the existence of such average differences, but with the interpretation or explanation of such differences. Suffice it to say that this is an extremely complex question which has not been adequately resolved, partly because of several severe methodological problems.

Bibliography. J. J. Conger, "The Meaning and Measurement of Intelligence," *Rocky Mountain Medical J.*, 54(1957), 570 – 76. R. J. Sternberg, "Human Intelligence: The Model is the Message," *Science*, 230 (1985), 111–18.

M. WARD

COGNITIVE DEVELOPMENT; EVALUATION AND DIAGNOSIS, PSYCHOLOGICAL. *Compare* PERSONALITY, BIOLOGICAL DIMENSIONS OF.

INTENTIONALITY. *See* CAUSALITY IN PSYCHOLOGY, FORMS OF; PARADOXICAL INTENTION; WILL AND WILLING; WILL TO LIVE.

INTERCESSORY PRAYER. *See* PRAYER. *See also* MARY *or* SAINTS, VENERATION OF;

INTERCOURSE, SEXUAL. *See* SEXUAL DYSFUNCTION AND SEX THERAPY; SEXUAL ISSUES IN PASTORAL CARE; SEXUALITY.

INTERDEPENDENCE. *See* DEPENDENCE/INDEPENDENCE.

INTERDICT. A type of Roman Catholic canonical censure, i.e., a penalty depriving breakers of Church law of various ecclesiastical goods until they are restored to full ecclesial communion. Practically speaking, an interdict (canon 1332 of 1983 Code) forbids certain liturgical activities, e.g., ministerial participation in eucharist or other liturgical rites and celebration or reception of sacraments (canon 1331). Unlike excommunication, an interdict does not affect governmental functions or personal prerogatives such as eligibility for church office, nor does it technically deprive one of ecclesial communion.

T. J. GREEN

ROMAN CATHOLIC PASTORAL CARE. *Compare* DISCIPLINE, PASTORAL CARE AS; ECCLESIOLOGY *or* MORAL THEOLOGY, AND PASTORAL CARE.

INTERDISCIPLINARY JOURNALS. *See* JOURNALS IN RELIGION, THEOLOGY, AND THE SOCIAL SCIENCES (Interdisciplinary).

INTERDISCIPLINARY METHODOLOGY. *See* PASTORAL THEOLOGICAL METHODOLOGY; THEOLOGY AND PSYCHOLOGY.

INTERFAITH MARRIAGE. *See* CROSS CULTURAL MARRIAGE AND FAMILY; JEWISH-CHRISTIAN MARRIAGE.

INTERGENERATIONAL CONFLICT. *See* FAMILY, PASTORAL CARE AND COUNSELING OF; FAMILY THEORY AND THERAPY.

INTERMARRIAGE. *See* CROSS CULTURAL MARRIAGE AND FAMILY. *See also* CATHOLIC-PROTESTANT MARRIAGE; JEWISH-CHRISTIAN MARRIAGE.

INTERNAL FRAME OF REFERENCE. The individual's subjective world of perceived or perceptible experience, sometimes called the phenomenal field; more specifically, the total realm of personal perceptions, feelings, and meanings that are experienced by the individual at any given moment and that form the basis on which the individual perceives and acts. Some of the internal frame of reference is unconscious, but most of it is available to awareness when appropriate. It is reality to the individual and theoretically becomes the sole psychological determinant of his or her behavior. The individual never acts on raw data itself. It is a world that is fluid, yet organized; changing, yet consistent.

The phrase "internal frame of reference" is associated with the name of Carl R. Rogers, but the idea behind it is part of a larger trend in psychology that takes the individual's subjective world seriously. It has its philosophical roots in existentialism and phenomenology's concern for the acting person's point of view. It is distinguished from all objective approaches that attempt to understand the individual from an outside observer's point of view. In addition to Rogers, Gordon Allport, Andras Angyal, Arthur Combs, Abraham Maslow, and Donald Snygg are leading proponents of the "internal" approach.

Rogers and others hold that early in human development a portion of the person's internal frame of reference becomes differentiated as the self. The self consists of all those aspects of one's being and functioning that are in awareness and that are identified as "I" or "me." Its various components are invested with negative or positive value and, in turn, it becomes an evaluator of the individual's ongoing experience. It denies or distorts those experiences that are inconsistent with it, causing a basic cleavage between what is owned and what is disowned. The therapeutic and pastoral task, then, is to help the individual become more whole or congruent.

The individual can gain more complete knowledge of his phenomenal field than any outside observer, no matter how sophisticated the external means of investigation may be. This assumption has implications for both research and therapy. It means that to get a detailed and accurate understanding of the person, the observer must get within the person's world and see it and feel it as he or she does.

In recent decades, pastoral care has been heavily influenced by this phenomenological principle, making it less authoritarian and more person-centered. Most important, however, is the fact that person-centeredness becomes other-centeredness. Pastoral focus upon the internal frame of reference of the parishioner can reduce the pastor's need to get across a particular message and free him or her to listen. The key questions then become: How does the parishioner understand and interpret her or his world? Can I as pastor understand that world well enough to communicate care in ways that is understandable within the parishioner's frame of reference?

Bibliography. C. R. Rogers, *Client-Centered Therapy* (1951).

L. ADEN

CLIENT-CENTERED THERAPY; PHENOMENOLOGICAL PSYCHOLOGY AND PSYCHOTHERAPY. *Compare* EMPATHY.

INTERNATIONAL PASTORAL CARE MOVEMENT. The international pastoral care movement has two aspects. It is a kind of invisible community in which there is a constant exchange of persons, methods, and theories. But it is also a kind of structure, an organization, which grows out of this community, organizes meetings, shares news of its work, and thus gradually becomes visible.

1. History of the Movement. *a. Early years.* Although a foundation for the international movement had been prepared by "pioneers" like Weatherhead (Britain), Bovet (Switzerland), Haendler (Germany), and the founders of the St. Luke Foundation (Sweden), the actual beginnings are to be found in the 1960s, when some Americans organized group-tours to Western Europe to visit the European "pioneers." Out of these visits Thomas Klink and Charles Stewart on the American side and Wiebe Zijlstra and Heije Faber on the European side developed a plan for a 1966 meeting between American and Dutch pastoral psychologists. This meeting was preceded by visits to the U.S. by Faber, Willem Berger, and Zijlstra, and a clinical pastoral education (CPE) movement began making headway in Holland. The impact of the American CPE movement was strongly felt, and this impact remained one of the features of pastoral care development in Europe.

In 1972, a larger European conference was held at Arnoldshain, near Frankfurt in West Germany, organized by a committee coordinated by Werner Becher, who had recently studied in the U.S. at the Menninger Foundation. Western Europe and the U.S. were both well represented, and there was a realization that there was already a community of colleagues in the pastoral care field in a number of countries. The need for a better education of ministers, for other methods in pastoral communication, and the concern for the integrity of the minister showed itself present everywhere.

The next international meeting was held in 1975 at Ruschlikon, near Zurich, with Keith Parker, an American professor at the seminary there, as host. This meeting was prepared by a standing committee of representatives from various European countries and the U.S. It was at that conference that the international movement first became consciously self-critical. The group acknowledged the tendency of persons in pastoral care to become so interested in the problems of face-to-face relations that they neglect the social dimension of human problems.

There was a commitment to become more socially oriented in the exploration of pastoral care concerns. Another concern of the group about itself was the international movement's strongly Protestant character. Although there were a few Roman Catholics involved, a real breakthrough into the Roman Catholic world, especially in the countries of Western Europe, was not yet visible.

The German participants in the movement did much to help people from Eastern Germany to attend the meetings. Some of them were in Ruschlikon, and their presence led to the plan to organize a European meeting at Eisenach in East Germany, which was held in 1977. Both Eastern Europe and Western Europe were well represented, and the commitment to bring East and West together has remained a part of the international movement since that time.

b. Edinburgh and the emergence of the modern movement. The first large international meeting was in Edinburgh in 1979. It was prepared by an international committee and a local British one. Denis Duncan, Alastair Campbell, and David Lyall developed a structure in which several hundred participants could effectively encounter one another. The theme of the conference was "The Risks of Freedom." Its proceedings were published in German under the title, "Wagnis der Freiheit." The Edinburgh meeting helped to demonstrate that the movement had an image and a message of its own and an ability to look at itself critically. It was aware of the far-reaching developments in the world of women, of the importance of the theological character of the ministry, of the impact of modern psychotherapy on both church and society, and, finally, of the burning social and cultural issues of today.

The success of the meeting at Edinburgh was also visible in another area. There were representatives of all the continents and even, in often surprising number, of third world countries and of countries behind the (then) iron curtain. In a short time the movement had become genuinely international. Under the leadership of Werner Becher from West Germany, an international committee on pastoral care and counseling was formed as a more or less permanent organization. The committee developed means by which members representing the pastoral care movement in nonrepresented countries could join, and plans for an international newsletter were made, the first issue of which appeared in 1981.

After Edinburgh two regional meetings were held, and a second larger meeting prepared for the conference in 1983 in San Francisco. The first regional meeting was in Europe in 1981 and again in a country then behind the iron curtain, Poland. The host for the meeting was the Catholic University at Lublin. Over a hundred persons from Eastern and Western Europe, plus members of the international pastoral care and counseling committee from non-European countries attended the meeting. Participants in that meeting experienced how pastoral care and counseling are deeply involved in the issues of society. Being in Poland offered a confrontation with the piety of the Roman Catholic church, with the horrors of the Majadanek concentration camp, and with the complexities of the Polish social and political situation. It gave that meeting a width and a depth that went beyond that of former meetings. The second regional meeting was an Asian conference held in 1982 at Manila in the Philippines, which was the first international pastoral care meeting held outside of Europe. Another Asian meeting was held in Tokyo, Japan, in 1984.

c. San Francisco. The second international congress on pastoral care and counseling was held in San Francisco in 1983. In contrast to Edinburgh, it offered few lectures and formal responses but attempted to focus upon the participants themselves, their interactions with one another, and the personal and cultural stories that they brought from their native countries and continents. The theme of the congress was "Symbols and Stories in Pastoral Care and Counseling." It offered dramatic presentations of the character and chaos of the peoples of four continents — Europe, Asia, Africa, and North America — and something of what pastoral caring has meant in these different contexts. As in previous meetings, however, it was the individual and small group encounters among persons who minister in many different contexts that was the real focus of the meeting for most of its participants. And, perhaps most dramatically, the meeting had become more than a meeting of Europeans and Americans with a few from other places; it was genuinely international. Indicative of that was the decision, on a very close vote, by the enlarged international committee that the next congress would take place in Australia in 1987.

2. General Themes and Issues. *a. Psychological influences.* Although in an important sense the story of the international pastoral care and counseling movement is a story of meetings between pastoral carers from different countries and contexts, it may also be viewed in terms of the dynamics of the international community. Its primary sources lie in the CPE movement in the USA, the European involvement in depth psychiatry, and the modernization of pastoral care that resulted. The study of "human documents," as well as written ones, and the principles of learning by doing and of supervision are the main aspects that connect workers the world over. In its first phase the movement was under the influence of the nondirective therapy of Carl Rogers; but in a second phase it learned from psychoanalysis (especially from Freud and his school) and Jung, with his accent on the value of symbols; and now it is influenced by a variety of psychotherapies.

b. Critiques. i. Individualism. Like the pastoral care movement in the U.S., the international movement has had some important blind spots. Pastoral care has been viewed primarily as the care of individual persons or of groups of individuals just like in most psychotherapies. The consequence of this can be a lack of interest for extending pastoral care to conflicts in society or in churches. The structural aspects of personal problems are often overlooked.

ii. Neglect of theology. Another aspect of the movement is that in modern pastoral care much attention is given to the lessons we can learn from modern psychotherapy. Reflection on religious and theological aspects is often neglected. There has been a tendency to see pastoral care more in line with psychotherapy than in continuity with the tradition of the church. There is not enough reflection on the religious problems of secularized modern

society and even less on the reaction to this in a modern radical theology and ministry. Problems of belief and unbelief, of Marxism, of feminism and liberation theology play a marginal role. With its accent on the personal aspects of pastoral care, not only are the social aspects neglected, but pastoral care tends to become in an uncritical way "traditional" also.

iii. Pastoral identity. Yet another problem is the issue of the identity of the minister as seen in the light of his work in the field of pastoral care. Without any doubt, modern developments in this field have extended the range of activities of ministers and priests greatly, but this development accentuates the problem of pastoral identity. What quality or character of pastoral function identifies it as pastoral? This is a problem of the international movement, just as it has been in America and Europe.

iv. Resistance to the movement. Finally, there is the resistance to modern pastoral care among church leaders and theologians. We see this resistance every time the movement reaches new countries. Mostly it becomes weaker and disappears after some time, but in many cases some doubt lingers on. What is the deepest reason for this resistance? In which form does it manifest itself? and How should we handle it? The types of critical statements that some people raise concerning the pastoral care movement are: it is not theology, but psychology; it dilutes the ministry into some superficial kind of therapy; it is an American product; it tends to undermine traditional values. These criticisms are to a great extent rationalizations, because in the depth of our work there is something threatening for a number of people. Open discussion and an honest self-reflection are essential for dealing with the problem as it appears in different countries.

v. Pluralism and cultural differences. Confronting the international pastoral care movement more and more is the issue of understanding the meaning of cultural differences in the practice of pastoral care. That practice is different in the U.S. from the way it is in Europe; different in the Western world than in the East; different among Roman Catholics than among Protestants. There are differences in Europe among the various countries. More differences will emerge, such as those among the first, second, and third world Christians, and among Protestants, Roman Catholics, Orthodox, and Jews. We have a common basis in the openness for the lessons of modern psychology and psychotherapy, and also often for those of modern sociology. These lessons, however, must be integrated in a pluralism of religious and cultural patterns — hopefully a pluralism in which we can learn from one another and enrich one another's work and belief.

Bibliography. W. Becher, A. V. Campbell, and G. K. Parker, *Wagnis der Freiheit* (1981); *Seelsorge in der Oekumene,* (1982). H. Faber, *Pastoral Care and Clinical Training in America* (1961); *Klinische Seelsorgeausbildung* (1972).

H. FABER

PASTORAL CARE MOVEMENT; PASTORAL COUNSELING MOVEMENT. *See also* AFRICAN, AUSTRALIAN AND NEW ZEALAND, BRITISH, CANADIAN, EAST ASIAN, EASTERN EUROPEAN, LATIN AMERICAN, SOUTH AFRICAN, SOUTH ASIAN, *or* WESTERN EUROPEAN PASTORAL CARE MOVEMENTS. *Compare*

ECUMENICAL RELATIONSHIPS IN THE PASTORAL CARE AND COUNSELING MOVEMENTS.

INTERMENT. *See* BURIAL.

INTERPERSONAL DISORDERS. *See* ANTISOCIAL PERSONS.

INTERPERSONAL THEORY. An approach to personality and psychotherapy based upon the seminal formulations of Harry Stack Sullivan, which focuses on the behavior of persons in the context of their interactions with others. Interpersonal theory proposes that (a) self-conceptions are determined primarily by persons' perceptions of what others think of them; (b) people actively and recurrently elicit behaviors from others that confirm their self-conceptions; (c) people affect and are affected by their social environment in a process of mutual influence; and (d) communications, both verbal and nonverbal, make up the essence of human interactions. The emphasis of interpersonal theory on social transactions distinguishes it from other theoretical systems that tend to make the individual their unit of study.

1. **Theory Of Personality.** Sullivan defined personality as "the relatively enduring pattern of recurrent interpersonal situations which characterize a human life." For him, personality is manifest exclusively in interpersonal relationships, though the relations may be with either a tangible "other" or with an imagined person. One's sense of self emerges primarily from the "reflected appraisals" of important others, notably parents. Sullivan taught that interpersonal behavior is directed toward the avoidance of anxiety and maintenance of self-esteem. Anxiety is precipitated by perceived disapproval from the significant persons in one's life, and, in essence, makes up the fundamental core of psychopathology. Although most persons are rarely free from some interpersonal tension, critical levels of anxiety interfere with thought processes, disrupt clear communication, and inhibit interpersonal closeness. Thus, in Sullivan's view, personality may be characterized by the consistent interpersonal strategies and relational patterns that one enacts to minimize anxiety.

Timothy Leary, using an empirically based model of social behavior, was among the first to describe the interpersonal operations of personality in detail. Of greatest importance, he proposed that person A's behavior tends to elicit "complementary" responses from person B, which, in turn, tend to elicit and reinforce person A's original behavior. Specifically, complementarity predicts that friendliness elicits friendliness and hostility elicits hostility, while dominance elicits submission and vice versa. Based upon the work of Leary and Sullivan, interpersonalists hold that social behaviors are proffered in expectation of complementary responses from others, responses that tend to reinforce the initiator's self-concept and personality style.

2. **Theoretical Assumptions and Psychotherapy.** Interpersonal therapy makes at least four assumptions regarding the nature of human beings and mental health. The first three are noted by McLemore and Hart: (a) "People are by nature relational." To be human is to be in relationships with others and to engage in intimate communication. (b) One's capacity for intimacy is a primary criterion of psychological health. And (c) intimate relationships are dependent upon an ability to communicate clearly. A fourth assumption is noted in Sullivan's belief that (d) "Highly developed intimacy with another is not the principal business of life, but is, perhaps, the principal source of satisfactions in life." On the basis of these assumptions, Sullivan proposed that psychological problems result from disordered relationships and are perpetuated by faulty (e.g., indirect, incongruent) communication. Inadequate communications interfere with the individual's ability to sustain intimate, emotionally fulfilling relationships.

Interpersonal therapy posits that the client's problems in living are eventually manifest in all significant relationships, including that of the client and therapist. This often involves the client's attempt to induce responses that reinforce his or her dysfunctional style. For example, the rigidly dependent individual who expresses incompetent, helpless behaviors is likely to inspire reassuring, caretaking responses; such responses simply allow continued helplessness. Interpersonalists thus stress that the therapist's primary diagnostic instrument involves his or her own instinctive reactions to the client. As described by Beier, "the therapist refuses to reinforce the patient's present state of adjustment by refusing to make the response the patient forcefully evokes in him." Rather, the therapist draws the client's attention to the disordered aspects of their mutual interaction and facilitates more flexible and clear communication patterns.

Bibliography. E. G. Beier, *The Silent Language of Psychotherapy* (1966), p. 13. R. C. Carson, *Interaction Concepts of Personality* (1969). D. J. Kiesler, "Interpersonal Theory for Personality and Psychotherapy," *Handbook of Interpersonal Psychotherapy* (1982), pp. 3–24. T. Leary, *Interpersonal Diagnosis of Personality* (1957). C. W. McLemore and P. P. Hart, "Relational Psychotherapy: The Clinical Facilitation of Intimacy," *Handbook of Interpersonal Psychotherapy* (1982), pp. 227–47. H. S. Sullivan, *The Interpersonal Theory of Psychiatry* (1953), pp. 34, 110–11; *The Psychiatric Interview* (1954).

D. BROKAW

NEOFREUDIAN PERSONALITY THEORIES AND PASTORAL CARE; PERSONALITY THEORY (Varieties, Traditions, and Issues); PSYCHOTHERAPY. *See also* ANXIETY; INTIMACY AND DISTANCE. *Compare* OBJECT RELATIONS THEORY; PSYCHOSOCIAL DEVELOPMENT; SELF; SOCIAL PERCEPTION, JUDGMENT, AND BELIEF; SOCIAL PSYCHOLOGY, DISCIPLINE OF; TRANSACTIONAL ANALYSIS. *Biography:* SULLIVAN.

INTERPRETATION AND HERMENEUTICS, PASTORAL. Pastoral interpretation is that process by which the pastor attaches meaning to the events and relationships that occur in any context in which pastoral ministry takes place. Hermeneutics is "the study of the methodological principles of interpretation and explanation; *specifically* the study of the general principles of biblical interpretation" (Webster's *Third International Dictionary*).

Modern usage of *hermeneutics* began in the sixteenth and seventeenth centuries with the post-Reformation need for guidelines for interpreting Scripture. In ancient times the Greek verb *hermēnuein* and noun *hermēneia* were derived from the myth of Hermes, the wing-footed messenger-god. Various forms of the word "suggest the process of bringing a thing or situation from unintelligibility to understanding" (Palmer, 1969, p. 13). In modern usage the discipline of hermeneutics has broadened to include issues related to all processes of human interpretation, understanding, and explanation.

1. General Features. Pastoral interpretation includes both the pastor's activity as interpreter of the faith tradition, particularly the Bible, and the interpretation of present events and relationships. The pastoral hermeneutical task therefore concerns itself with ways of seeing and responding to situations of contemporary life that comport with the vision of life that emerges from Scripture and tradition. The modern context of ministry, however, requires that this Christian vision be supplemented and critically related to the perspectives on contemporary life coming from modern secular thought, especially those coming from the social and human behavioral sciences.

Pastoral interpretation most often involves some practical purpose, for instance the preparation of a sermon addressing a pastoral issue or concern, or the question of appropriate pastoral response to a situation in the life of a parishioner. But in addition it is concerned with the questions of appropriate descriptive language and normative judgments as to what constitutes the good.

Pastoral interpretation likewise goes on at many levels, sometimes formal and explicit, at other times quite informal and unselfconscious. As persons embedded in particular cultural ways of seeing and giving significance to phenomena, pastors are often prone to fall into popular interpretations of common events and relationships. The art of pastoral interpretation involving more critically reflective understanding makes use of theological, ethical, psychological, social scientific, and other languages of interpretation. These more critical understandings, however, can only be acquired by the disciplined process of careful observation and reflection, as well as by the equally rigorous process of learning the appropriate language and conceptual tools provided by the various disciplines applicable to pastoral practice. As a disciplined art pastoral interpretation therefore is inherently an interdisciplinary activity that makes appropriate use of the images, themes, concepts, and descriptive modes of a number of sometimes disparate languages, while sustaining the theological and ethical perspectives central to the Christian vision as normative warrants for pastoral understanding and action. The pluralism of languages by which any event or relational situation may be interpreted in the modern world thus presents an opportunity for enrichment of the pastoral perspective and also the problem of making judgments concerning the most appropriate and helpful languages to be utilized.

A broad interdisciplinary approach to pastoral interpretation or hermeneutics can assist the pastor in avoiding both the superficiality of popular cultural interpretations of the events of everyday life and the tendency toward reductionism—the apparent simplification of explanatory interpretation by reducing explanation to a single set of language images, which are often set in a language of causation. However, an interdisciplinary approach to pastoral interpretation also sets before the pastor the task of determining how to integrate the various available languages, each of which may illuminate a particular facet of meaning and/or explanation of

the problem at hand. The problem of deciding which items among a welter of perceptual data, factual information, and impressionistic notions are to be given significance and how that significance is to be expressed in thought and action cannot be avoided.

2. Practical Implications and Suggestions. Assuming the pastor is confronted with a common human situation of individual, family, or parish community life that demands pastoral interpretation and response, the following set of questions provides the rough outline of a procedure of hermeneutical inquiry that pastors may find useful:

(1) *What has happened or is happening? What is going on here?* Responding to these questions involves the pastor immediately in a choice of language paradigms; more specifically, it requires some designation of descriptive words and association of images from the interpreter's past experience. Some preunderstanding of what is or has happened is immediately brought to bear on *this* happening, designating it as perhaps in some ways like and perhaps in other ways unlike what the interpreter has seen happen before. Evaluative as well as descriptive imagery from prior experience shape this preunderstanding, especially descriptive languages and imagery found useful in previous experience.

(2) *Why did it happen or why is this going on?* Here the interpreter's preimaged notions of causation shape a way of seeing the sequential state of affairs or human predilections that may have brought about the situation at hand. Causal imagery may be influenced by popular psychological notions of causation, most of which tend to be either simplistically reductionistic or in subtle ways moralistically blame-placing. Mature pastoral interpretations will more often recognize the complexity of any human situation and call upon prior experience with use of a variety of psychological, social, and perhaps theological or ethical paradigms to make tentative, heuristic judgments about the possible antecedent causes of present situations. Interpretive judgments concerning causation will have a strong influence over judgments concerning appropriate pastoral response. Thus the richer and more varied the interpretive understanding of causation, the richer and more highly nuanced the response.

(3) *What does it mean that this has happened or is happening?* Here lies a question of significance that is at once a factual question, concerning the meaning being assigned to the situation by its participants, and a moral and theological or religious question. It is important that the pastor seek to understand the significance of whatever has occurred for those who are involved and have a stake in its outcome. But it is also important that the pastor place the situation in some larger theological and ethical context—a context of ultimate meaning. The pastor's interpretive judgments will largely shape the moral and religious climate within which the pastor approaches the situation and, insofar as he or she exercises symbolic power there, will also shape the participants' understanding of it.

(4) *Within the narrative structure of meaning that shapes the self-understanding of the group or community of persons affected by what has happened or is happening, what is now the outcome or direction most desirable or normatively most appropriate or fitting?* Here the pastor's interpretive judgment

takes a teleological turn. Appropriate pastoral response is determined not only by understandings of causation and meaning; it is also influenced by the ends being sought. For example, pastoral response with the intention of reconciliation and movement of life toward wholeness will be substantively different from pastoral response with intention of political change designed to shift power alliances in the group or community.

(5) *Given all of the above considerations, each of which involves interpretation by the employment of one or more hermeneutical keys, what is the appropriate pastoral response in the present time and situation?* The purpose and direction of pastoral interpretation is almost always practical. Pastoral interpretations are therefore most often "action" interpretations or working hypotheses that provide a sufficient framework of understanding and/or explanation to undergird the next step or sequencing of pastoral response. Thus, pastoral interpretation is more appropriately seen as a hermeneutical process of testing and reconsidering tentative interpretations that suggest particular courses of action and response than as prescriptive, definitive diagnosis. The pastoral hermeneutical effort is consistently directed toward bringing the unintelligible elements of a situation or event into a degree of understanding so that a fitting response may be made and then tested in the crucible of ongoing ministry in the situation.

Bibliography. For an introduction to hermeneutics see R. E. Palmer, *Hermeneutics* (1969). Z. Bauman, *Hermeneutics and Social Science* (1978). For pastoral/practical hermeneutics see C. V. Gerkin, *The Living Human Document* (1984) and *Widening the Horizons* (1987); J. Whitehead and E. Whitehead, *Method in Ministry* (1980); C. Winquist, *Practical Hermeneutics* (1980).

C. V. GERKIN

EVALUATION AND DIAGNOSIS; DISCERNMENT OF SPIRITS. *See also* BIBLE, PASTORAL USE AND INTERPRETATION OF; CAUSALITY IN PSYCHOLOGY; CLINICAL PASTORAL PERSPECTIVE; DREAM INTERPRETATION IN PASTORAL COUNSELING; PERSONAL STORY, SYMBOL, AND MYTH, *or* REASONING AND RATIONALITY, *or* RELIGIOUS LANGUAGE, IN PASTORAL CARE. *Compare* CULTURAL AND ETHNIC FACTORS; PERCEPTIVENESS AND SENSITIVITY; PHENOMENOLOGICAL METHOD; PSYCHOLINGUISTIC THEORY; REVELATION AND PASTORAL CARE; VALUES CLARIFICATION.

INTERPRETATION OF DREAMS. *See* DREAM INTERPRETATION.

INTERPRETATION OF SCRIPTURE. *See* BIBLE, PASTORAL USE AND INTERPRETATION OF.

INTERPROFESSIONAL TEAMS AND RELATIONSHIPS. Interprofessional teams are interdisciplinary in practice and involve pastoral care and counseling specialists working together with men and women from various professions and skills for the good of individuals, couples, families, or groups. This kind of practice most commonly takes place in health care delivery systems such as hospitals or clinics, but can also occur in educational institutions, prisons, parishes, mental institutions, the armed services, or denominational judicatories.

Typically, persons in pastoral care and counseling interface with medical personnel. Physicians in a myriad of subspecialties work with nurses, patient care personnel, and clergy to form an interprofessional team. Psychiatrists, family practitioners, internists, and oncologists are probably the most frequently mentioned subspecialists in pastoral care and counseling literature. Other hospital personnel frequently mentioned in the literature are occupational therapists, biofeedback specialists, physical therapists, audiologists, art therapists, and social work personnel. Of all medical personnel, nursing personnel seem to have the greatest amount of interface with clergy.

There are a number of settings outside hospitals where interprofessional teams operate: health clinics, social service centers, mental health facilities, wholistic health centers, pastoral counseling centers, day care centers, and parish or judicatory outreach programs. Other professionals that function outside hospital programs on interprofessional teams are psychologists, social workers, marriage and family specialists, and educators.

Cooperation is the watchword in interprofessional relationships. Each profession represented on the team performs a different function. Thus each presents a different perspective by looking at different aspects of a patient or consumer. This hopefully offers a more well-rounded view of each patient that takes into account physical, emotional and spiritual elements. Clergy are the professionals who demand nothing of patients in the health care setting. While others take blood, administer medication, plan activities, x-ray, test, and monitor calls, the clergy person is available for the patient.

The clergy person provides a link with the community outside the institution as a representative of the church at large. Clergy often have an entrée to the patient unavailable to other team members. If there are patients who do not want to deal with religious professionals they may deal well with other team members.

People still seem to go to clergy more than any other professionals for initial help with personal or emotional problems. One reason is that clergy provide a practical way for people to deal with crisis through the symbols and rituals of the church. Whether a person is facing an operation or the loss of a loved one, when critical changes occur, religious beliefs can help reassure, support, and give needed strength to face whatever difficulty comes.

The religious professional provides this support for both patients and fellow team members. Recent research on hospice teams showed that clergy provided the statistically most significant support to other team members that helps counter burnout. Clergy also report a significant amount of time spent listening to and supporting other team members. Religious professionals often receive support and counsel from other team members, too. The high stress of helping others in crisis requires good support systems for each team member. This sense of fellowship helps forge a team identity that is so essential for the successful function of an interprofessional team.

A good team is built on mutual respect and good communications about team relationships with each other and with the patient. This communication is achieved through writing in a patient's chart, written notes, personal conversations, phone calls, staff meetings, health conferences with the patient present, and sharing times. In this way, team members and patient avoid being isolated from each other, thus reducing loneliness and misunderstandings.

Clergy often play an important role in helping people in crisis understand what is happening to them while encouraging their faith in the type of treatment they are receiving. Again research has shown a significant correlation between belief in a healer, healing team, or an institution and the success of the treatment (Mason et al.; Florell). Religious professionals often take an advocate stance for patients that helps patients have more confidence in their treatment team. Though the clergy person may not be able to answer a patient's questions, he or she may be able to direct them to the appropriate team member who can answer the question.

This referral and consultation function which clergy provide on the team is only one way the religious professional helps people adjust to major changes in life. Pastoral care and counseling specialists also provide rites of passage from one life cycle event to another. Here the clergy use a knowledge of religious fellowship, family systems, and the symbols and sacraments of the church to help people change or recognize a new dimension of life.

The religious professional offers team members and patients his or her services for confession. Because of the meaning many people endow to the office of ministry, many feel they can share their deepest thoughts and feelings without fear of losing confidentiality. The confessional nature of clergy in the team relationship provides an intimacy and closeness that has a very therapeutic effect.

The closeness many interprofessional teams develop is built on a foundation of mutual respect of each discipline. A team must be able to build a sense of fellowship with an identity as a team. To accomplish this, each team member needs to be aware of his or her own needs and what his or her strengths and weaknesses are. Each person must also communicate well within the team. Good listening skills helps team members understand each other and evaluate how effectively they are communicating with patients and each other.

Strong *team spirit* in team members seems to be based on positive self-esteem and esteem of team members and patients. Obviously, lines are not always sharply drawn between professions. Physicians give counsel on emotional and spiritual issues. Psychologists may investigate people's religious beliefs and values as well as their physical well-being. Nurses may pray with patients and care for their medical needs. Pastoral care and counseling specialists frequently counsel about people's emotional traumas and physical lifestyle. The important aspect of team relationships is that all professionals are pulling together for the benefit of the patient, while holding in dynamic tension their being like each other and their being different from each other.

The religious professional also offers the team a person who provides a number of religious services including worship, religious education, being a leader on moral and ethical issues, and an expert on patients' religious backgrounds. These religious services are paralleled by services in medicine, nursing, psychology, etc. provided by other specialists. The interprofessional team sees the patient from many different dimensions and can provide the best overview of the patient and the most supportive environment for professionals to work in.

Bibliography. J. L. Florell, "Crisis Intervention in Orthopedic Surgery," American Protestant Hospital Association *Bulletin*, (1973) 29–36. R. C. Mason, *et. al.*, "Acceptance and Healing," *J. of Religion and Health*, 8 (1969) 123–42.

J. L. FLORELL

CONSULTATION; REFERRAL. *See also* CLINICAL PSYCHOLOGIST; MARRIAGE AND FAMILY THERAPIST; PSYCHIATRY AND PASTORAL CARE; RAPE AND RAPE COUNSELING; SOCIAL SERVICES AND PASTORAL CARE. *Compare* ECCLESIOLOGY AND PASTORAL CARE; MULTIPLE STAFF MINISTRIES AND RELATIONSHIPS; PROFESSIONALISM.

INTERRACIAL MARRIAGE AND FAMILY. *See* CROSS CULTURAL MARRIAGE AND FAMILY.

INTERVENTION. *See* CRISIS INTERVENTION THEORY; INITIATIVE AND INTERVENTION, PASTORAL.

INTIMACY AND DISTANCE. *Intimate* is derived from latin *intimus*, designating the person or thing that is innermost, most familiar, or internal. In relationship it marks one most closely associated or acquainted.

On the opposite end of the scale, *distance* (Lat. *distare*) literally means to stand apart from, to be separate. It is used to measure increments of both time and space.

For the purpose of effective pastoral care and counseling, the pastor does not usually relate as one most intimate to the client or parishioner. Neither is the pastor very often one who stands completely apart.

Usually a pastoral care relationship will take place somewhere between the extremes of intimacy and distance, one being close enough to promote sharing but with enough distance to give the parishioner or client some space if that is needed.

1. The Need for Balance in Pastoral Care Relationships. Too much intimacy puts the minister in the category of close friend. Extreme intimacy either loses some objectivity, or makes the client feel that objectivity is sacrificed, whether or not this is actually the case. The intimate counselor or helper is resented for over-identification with the parishioner or client. The client wants to identify with the pastoring person as a model, not to be made too soon into a model for identification. The distant pastor is resented because this creates barriers to an acceptable identification on the part of the client. The pastor who stands too far on the side of objectivity and distance will often fail to get permission to be a meaningful helper.

2. Factors that Influence Intimacy and Distance. The pastoral role will permit an easier intimacy for persons who have had good relationships to pastors in their own history. The role will give distancing to those whose relations to pastors have been negative or unfruitful. Distance may be used by a client to conceal awkwardness or lack of relational or verbal skills. A psychological factor that creates distance is unresolved childhood pain or grief. These are usually repressed to the degree that the person seeking help has little awareness of their power or even their presence. Crises in relationships such as marriage or vocation can leave a parishioner with a fear of getting too close, or perhaps the inability to do so. Intimacy comes easier where there are parallel areas of interest, common goals, or common frustrations between client and counselor.

3. **Conclusion.** The pastoral counselor is in the paradoxical position of dealing with the most intimate matters of a parishioner's (client's) life without asking to be intimate with the client. It is as though the counselor is allowed to see into the living and intimate space of the client without actually walking into that space. This privilege of seeing without partaking means that an adequate distance needs to be maintained so that the counselor can vacate the intimate zones when this is required. This allows the client the knowledge of having been understood without the feeling of having had one's space violated.

Bibliography. H. G. Zerof, *Finding Intimacy* (1978).

M. C. MADDEN

DEFENSE AND COPING THEORY; GIVING AND RECEIVING; I AND THOU; PERSONAL, CONCEPT OF; SELF-EXPRESSION/ SELF-CONTROL. *Compare* INTERPERSONAL THEORY; LOVE; OBJECT RELATIONS THEORY.

INTIMIDATION. *See* ANGER; ANTISOCIAL PERSONS; FEAR.

INTOXICATION. *See* ALCOHOL ABUSE, ADDICTION, AND THERAPY; ORGANIC MENTAL DISORDER AND ORGANIC BRAIN SYNDROME.

INTROJECTION. In psychoanalytic theory, the superego's incorporation of societal mores through childhood experiences of punishment and reward. Through this process, notions of acceptability or unacceptability are incorporated into two subsystems of the individual's superego: the conscience, which produces guilt at the conscious experience of the unacceptable, and the ego-ideal, which provides self-affirmation at the conscious experience of the acceptable.

Bibliography. S. Freud, *Civilization and Its Discontents* (1961), pp. 70–86.

K. R. KENNEDY

DEFENSE MECHANISMS. *See also* DEFENSE AND COPING THEORY; OBJECT RELATIONS THEORY. *Compare* INTERPERSONAL THEORY.

INTROSPECTION. *See* SELF-EXAMINATION.

INTROVERSION. *See* PERSONALITY TYPES AND PASTORAL CARE. *See also* ANALYTICAL (JUNGIAN) PSYCHOLOGY (Personality Theory and Research); SHYNESS.

INTUITION. The immediate apprehension of reality, without conscious dependence upon reason and the senses. Types of knowledge claimed to be gained by intuition include simple hunches and relationships between data of sense-experience, immediate knowledge of the truth of mathematical propositions and scientific concepts, and unmediated experiences of realities such as time, space, values, persons, and God. There is considerable debate about the origin of intuition, its precise relation to the senses and intellect, and the validity of its claims. Current understanding favors the view that knowledge gained by intuition alone is invalid without empirical verification and logical analysis. In turn, intuition contributes to rational and empirical inquiry by generating hypotheses about possible new relationships between sense data and conceptual understanding.

Intuition has had varied responses in psychology. Freud discounted the validity of knowledge based upon the subjective claims of intuition. Jung understood intuition to be the ego's capacity to place the data of sense experience into larger contexts of meaning from which implications may be drawn and future possibilities derived. Those for whom these intuitive functions dominate he called *intuitive types.* Behavioral theory has made little of intuition because of its apparent affinity with mentalism. Eric Berne's studies of clinical intuition led to the development of his theory of transactional analysis. Humanistic and transpersonal psychology, with support from split-brain research, have regarded intuitive processes as essential for achieving personal integration and higher forms of consciousness. Bruner understands the thinking process itself to begin with an intuitive leap from sense data to an already stored model of the world based upon previous experience.

There is no agreed-upon understanding of intuition operative in pastoral care theory and practice. Its use is mostly subsumed under related concepts such as empathy, "internal frame of reference," "listening with the third ear," and "tuning in to feelings." Intuition plays a central role in these processes and comes to bear in discerning the nature of personal distress, the dynamics perpetuating it, and in identifying new possibilities for healing and growth. Intuition contributes to the pastoral-theological task of creatively relating the religious heritage to specific life situations, and to rethinking the heritage in light of current experience and knowledge. Intuitive sensibility can be developed through supervision and psychotherapy, introspection, imagination and fantasy, cultivating sensitivity to literature and the arts, and involvement in prayer, meditation, and liturgy.

Bibliography. E. Berne, *Intuition and Ego States* (1977). M. Bunge, *Intuition and Science* (1962). J. S. Bruner and J. M. Anglin, *Beyond the Information Given: Studies in the Psychology of Knowing* (1973). K. Pribram *et al.*, "Psychology, Science and Spiritual Paths: Contemporary Issues," *J. of Transpersonal Psychology*, 10 (1978), 93–111.

L. K. GRAHAM

INSIGHT; PERCEPTIVENESS AND SENSITIVITY, PASTORAL. *Compare* COGNITIVE PSYCHOLOGY; GUIDANCE, DIVINE; ILLUMINATION; IMAGINATION; PARAPSYCHOLOGY; SELF-UNDERSTANDING.

INVALIDS. *See* CHRONIC ILLNESS; HANDICAP AND DISABILITY; LOSS OF FUNCTION; NEUROLOGIC ILLNESSES; OLDER PERSONS. *See also* CALLING AND VISITATION.

INVENTORY OF RELIGIOUS ACTIVITIES AND INTERESTS. *See* EVALUATION AND DIAGNOSIS, PSYCHOLOGICAL.

INVOLVEMENT, SELF. *See* COMMITMENT; EXISTENTIALISM AND PASTORAL CARE.

IRENAEUS, ST. *See* CLASSIC LITERATURE IN CARE AND COUNSELING (Roman Catholicism); EARLY CHURCH, PASTORAL CARE AND COUNSELING IN.

IRRESPONSIBILITY. *See* RESPONSIBILITY/IRRESPONSIBILITY; ANTISOCIAL PERSONS.

ISLAMIC CARE AND COUNSELING. Pastoral dimensions of Islam derive from its sacred scriptures, from the evolution of fundamental institutions, notably the mosque, and from a history of syncretic adaption to a variety of societies and cultures. Strictly speaking, Islam rejects the notion of a clergy. Therefore it lacks the formally defined role and conceptually discrete functions of the pastor as found in most Christian traditions. The guidance of the community of believers and the care for individuals beset with difficulties of faith, moral dilemmas, or life crises occur within the framework of an all-encompassing law. However, more recently spiritual reactions have exposed the limits of jurisprudence, and diverse currents of socioreligious reform have shaped responses to modern challenges.

1. Classical Foundations. According to the teaching of Sunni Islam, which accounts for the vast majority of the world's Muslims, the fullness of creation consists in obedience to the divine will as expressed in the Shari'a (literally, "path"). This is a corpus of variegated texts that together make up Islamic law. Its primary sources are the sacred book of the Quran and the Sunna, that is, the words and deeds of the Prophet Muhammad (570–632 C.E.), along with the normative precedent of Islam's generations. The Shi'a tradition adds a reverence for Ali, the husband of Muhammad's daughter. Shi'ites believe that Ali inherited his father-in-law's spiritual charisma, which was then transmitted to his descendants, the last of whom has disappeared but is expected to return in millennial fashion.

Matters of doctrine, worship, personal hygiene, family life, commercial affairs, and government are all treated in the Shari'a. It lays out a totalistic scheme for living as well as the elements of a religion. In principle, therefore, believers who conform to its dictates both achieve merit in eternity and remove obstacles to their prosperity in this world. Within such a system pastoral care is embedded in the prescribed duties incumbent upon all Muslims. However, special responsibilities are defined for those who hold positions of greater influence.

In theory, this single law regulates both personal and public affairs, but in practice the domain of civil enforcement has diverged from specifically religious institutions. Thus a distinctively pastoral authority has emerged which largely coincides with a recognition of superior knowledge in the law. In effect, the exercise of pastoral care has come to be concentrated in a variety of specialists who differ sociologically, according to a broad range of perceptions as to what determines preeminence or learning in the Shari'a. Normally, it is the prerogative of these scholars, known classically as the ulama, to preside at rituals and to preach, while at a practical level they also frequently admonish, issue opinions, give advice, and respond to cases of perplexity or distress.

Islam lacks an explicit theology of sacraments. But it does view such devotions as prayer, fasting, pilgrimage, and almsgiving with a significance that points toward inner transformation and efficacy. The Quran's counsel that "prayer preserves from impurity and evil" (29:44) thus suggests the special symbolic quality of the mosque, the privileged place of prayer. As the scene of regular collective worship, the mosque is a center for the performance of spiritual works, and those who serve there are witnesses to the mercy of God present and active amid human efforts.

2. Sufi Developments. Sufism has its origins in a pious and ascetic reaction against the legalism and materialism that accompanied the consolidation of the Islamic empire. Among its key concepts is "trust in God," which has been variously elaborated into doctrines of pure love and disciplines for attaining inner knowledge and ultimately mystical union. Sufism also encourages a deep attachment to the person of Muhammad as an intercessor and an example of holiness based on the Quranic declaration: "You have in the Apostle of God an excellent model" (33:12). Sufis see their quest as an imitation of the Prophet who enjoyed direct and vivid experiences of God.

Almost from its beginnings a definite pastoral concern has also marked Sufism. What started as devotees gathering around a master later developed into diverse patterns of discipleship, both solitary and communal, eventually involving widespread and sophisticated organizations with pronounced hierarchies. Throughout, however, an interpersonal relationship was considered indispensable. The great medieval theologian al-Ghazali (died 1111) wrote: "The disciple must of necessity have recourse to a director to guide him aright. For the way of faith is obscure, but the devil's ways are many and patent, and he who has no Shaykh to guide him will be led by the devil into his ways."

Sufism has been an important vehicle for the spread of Islam beyond the Middle East to the Indian subcontinent, Central Asia, sub-Saharan Africa, and Indonesia. As a result, aspects of Sufism have fused with many indigenous methods and structures to provide care and counseling. Also, in many cases, the cohesion established through affiliation with Sufi fraternities has helped to balance unequal power relations and to reinforce moral bonds among members of a tribe, a village, a guild, or a military unit. The pastoral component of Sufism also includes a rich ceremonial life, notably, abundant forms of expressive spiritual exercises called Dhikr (literally, "remembrance"). These gatherings often make use of special garments, song, dance, dramatic recitations, and even shamanistic displays.

Although the practice is disparaged by many Muslims, an extensive cult of saints reflects a popular outgrowth of Sufism with clear pastoral features. Tombs and shrines dedicated to holy men or women attract especially the simple people who visit them to perform rituals, to seek favors or guidance. Frequently persons related in some way to the saint reside near such sites, where they may reconcile adversaries or give instruction, advice, or blessings.

Historically parallel to Sufism and matching many of its concerns in a worldly perspective is a movement associated with the concept of Adab (literally, "culture" or "social graces"). Broadly speaking, this repository of teachings deals with character training, the cultivation of virtue, and the pursuit of happiness in a philosophical and ethical context. A sizable literature in many languages and genres presents these ideals of refinement and applies them to particular roles such as rulers, judges, preachers, and teachers.

3. Modern Trends. The encroachment of Western colonialism during the nineteenth century, followed by the rapid penetration of advanced technologies and growing global interdependency, have deeply affected the patterns of society and consciousness in the Muslim world. As a consequence, religious attitudes and institutions are changing under internal and external pressures and tend to reflect conflicting conservative and progressive directions.

Overall, the tendency has been to formalize pastoral care within the context of a nation-state that regards social welfare and the supervision of religion as its official responsibility. Hence bureaucracies, seminaries, and mosque community centers of many types have been established or subsidized. Initiatives have been taken to improve the quality of preaching and generally to professionalize the corps of those identified as representatives of Islam. In many instances, direct or indirect control of mosques and preachers involves their enlistment in campaigns of social reform or political mobilization. The intensity or the ideological orientation of such programs varies depending on differences in motives and available resources.

A strong puritanical strain also characterizes much contemporary Islamic thought. Both modernizers and traditionalists have sought to rid popular piety of practices that diverge from an acceptable range of orthodoxy. The former, which has been more of an elite approach, includes many who are open to Western ideas and are prepared to reexamine classical interpretations. The latter group has resisted intellectual accommodation, although they do embrace many achievements of science that benefit their ministry, such as electronic communication techniques and the study of psychology.

Another prominent current in many Muslim lands appears in movements that oppose the secular state's management of religion. For example, the Jamaat-i-Islami in Pakistan and the Muslim Brothers in Egypt and elsewhere, although they may also contain a political agenda, have their primary impact in the organization of local independent socioreligious societies. Leaders of such associations usually have a modern rather than a traditional educational background. They are nonetheless active in mosques as well as schools and assorted self-help cooperative ventures where the care and counseling of individual members is a priority.

The phenomenon recently described as the "Islamic resurgence" or "revival" epitomized by the revolution in Iran and the resulting Islamic Republic signals a shift in pastoral care as well as politics. Based on the denial of a dichotomy between sacred and secular power, those sharing this militant spirit advocate replacing present-day civil and criminal codes with the implementation of the Shari'a. This implies that religious specialists who are held to be experts in this law become themselves administrators of state authority, thereby conjoining civil and pastoral operations. The unity of these two spheres does correspond to an Islamic ideal. Yet many also argue that the best way to realize it in today's world is to maintain a functional distinction between the mosque and the seat of government.

Bibliography. T. W. Arnold, *The Preaching of Islam* (1913). K. Cragg, *The Call of the Minaret* 2d ed., (1985). H. A. R. Gibb, *Mohammedanism: An Historical Survey* 2d ed. (1957). M. Hamidullah, *Introduction to Islam* 4th ed. (1974). N. Keddie, ed., *Scholars, Saints, and Sufis: Muslim Religious Institutions in the Middle East Since 1500* (1972). B. D. Metcalf, ed., *Moral Conduct and Authority: The Place of Adab in South Asian Islam* (1984). F. Rahman, *Islam* (1966). J. Schacht, *An Introduction to Islamic Law* (1964). E. Sivan, *Radical Islam: Medieval Theology and Modern Politics* (1985). W. C. Smith, *Islam in Modern History* (1959). S. J. Trimingham, *The Sufi Orders of Islam* (1971).

P. D. GAFFNEY

BLACK MUSLIM CARE AND COUNSELING. *Compare* JEWISH CARE AND COUNSELING (History, Tradition, and Contemporary Issues); PASTORAL CARE (History, Traditions, and Definitions); SOCIOLOGY OF RELIGIOUS AND PASTORAL CARE.

ISOLATION, SOCIAL. *See* LONELINESS AND ISOLATION; SOCIAL ISOLATION.

ISRAEL BEN ELIEZER. *See* BAAL SHEM-TOV.

ISRAELI, ISAAC. Born in Egypt around the middle of the ninth century and died in the middle of the tenth century. At the age of about fifty he became the court physician in Karouan. He was a noted and respected theologian and philosopher. He authored medical works on fevers and drugs, among other topics, which were later translated from Arabic into Latin, and was considered one of the great physicians of his generation.

Israeli's best known book is his *Book of Definitions*, which discusses more than fifty categories and has definitions for such items as the intellect, soul, wisdom, and nature. Israeli is also the author of *Book of Substances, Treatise on Spirit and Soul,* and the *Book on the Elements.* He is considered an influential thinker who had great impact on Jewish thinking long after his death. His formulation of the human purpose remains an instructive model for the contemporary context.

R. P. BULKA

THEOLOGY, JEWISH

J

JAMES, WILLIAM (1842–1910). American philosopher and psychologist. After joining the Harvard University faculty in 1872, James became an advocate of philosophical pragmatism and functional psychology.

No philosopher has had greater influence on modern pastoral care traditions, especially in America. His initial contribution to the pastoral theologians was his *Principles of Psychology* (1890), in which James explored the implications of current research in physiology, argued for the interdependence of mind and body, and insisted that the purpose of mental activity was always a bodily change or activity. His conclusions suggested that physical vitality could control psychological dispositions. He illustrated those conclusions in an important chapter on "habit" that impressed American pastoral writers. James defined habits as pathways of neurological discharge formed in the brain, and he described habitual behavior as both an example of the organism's tendency toward action and a consequence of motor activity. Disciplined deeds and useful actions could convert the nervous system into an ally.

Such an idea seemed to have religious and ethical implications. The president of Brown University, W. H. P. Faunce, told a Yale audience in 1908 that the chapter on habit had been "preached in a thousand pulpits." James's voluntarism confirmed the Victorian pastoral commonplace that the secret of character was self-mastery and self-control.

James eventually decided that the accent on the active will needed to be supplemented by an awareness of the need for receptivity and relaxation. In his popular writings, which were indebted to the American New Thought traditions, he advocated a balancing of effort and repose. And in his *Varieties of Religious Experience* (1908), he seemed especially impressed by the possibilities of "letting go" and opening the consciousness to a source of energy beyond itself. Such views helped shape the efforts of Elwood Worcester and the other pastoral writers in the Emmanuel Movement to develop a style of counseling that replaced argumentation with techniques using relaxation and suggestion directed to the subconscious mind. Indeed, James's treatment of that theme remained important even after the Emmanuel Movement collapsed, especially in the writing and counseling of Harry Emerson Fosdick at Riverside Church in New York.

James's *Varieties of Religious Experience* also explored another set of ideas and images that influenced a third group of American pastoral writers. His distinctions between healthy-minded souls, whose temperaments were weighted on the side of cheerfulness, and sick souls, who were intensely aware of the evil lurking around the next corner, accented the turbulence, chaos, and division within the self. Such views were especially important for Anton Boisen, the founder of Clinical Pastoral Education (CPE), whose insistence on the need to study "living human documents" and to recognize the religious implications of psychological turbulence and instability reflected an indebtedness to James's work in the psychology of religion.

And finally, James's functional psychology, as well as his functional understanding of religious belief, had considerable influence on the religious education movement of the 1920s, which helped to elicit within the liberal Protestant seminaries a new interest in methods of pastoral care and counseling.

E. B. HOLIFIELD

HISTORY OF PROTESTANT PASTORAL CARE (United States); PASTORAL CARE MOVEMENT; PHILOSOPHY AND PSYCHOLOGY; PRAGMATISM AND PASTORAL CARE; PSYCHOLOGY OF RELIGION (Theories, Traditions, and Issues).

JANET, PIERRE (1859–1947). French psychologist, neurologist, psychotherapist, and master hypnotist. Janet was a pupil and successor of Charcot and a prolific writer of some ninety clinically-based works, the best known of which is his attempt at classifying the forms of hysteria, *The Mental State of Hystericals* (1892, ET 1901).

Janet played a major role in forging a connection between the academic study of psychology and the clinical treatment of mental disorders. In his investigations of personality dysfunctions, he came to posit psychological origins for neuroses as well as hypnosis. While not entirely abandoning the assumption of a physiological basis of psychoneurotic symptoms, his view of the repression of disturbing experiences constitutes the beginnings of a theory of the unconscious. Through his ongoing research, publications, and lectures on a wide range of subjects, Janet was regarded as the main exponent and dean of French psychology.

N. F. HAHN

HYPNOSIS; HYSTERIA; PSYCHOPATHOLOGY, THEORIES OF; UNCONSCIOUS.

JAPANESE PASTORAL CARE MOVEMENT. *See* EAST ASIAN PASTORAL CARE MOVEMENT.

JEALOUSY. *See* ENVY AND GRACIOUSNESS.

JEANNE FRANCOISE de CHANTAL, ST. *See* WOMEN IN PASTORAL MINISTRIES, HISTORY OF.

JEFFERSON, CHARLES EDWARD (1860–1937). Clergyman and pastoral theologian. For 32 years an influential preacher at New York City's Broadway Tabernacle, Jefferson was author of *The Minister as Prophet* (1905) and *The Minister as Shepherd* (1912).

The latter work reflects the early twentieth century's move away from systematic works in pastoral or practical theology toward literature of the pragmatic assistance type which, however, also stressed the pastor's personal involvement with people. Jefferson analyzed the analogy of the minister as shepherd and the various pastoral functions pertaining to it.

N. F. HAHN

PASTORAL THEOLOGY, PROTESTANT.

JEHOVAH'S WITNESSES. *See* SECTARIAN PASTORAL CARE.

JEROME, ST. *See* CLASSIC LITERATURE IN CARE AND COUNSELING (Roman Catholicism); EARLY CHURCH, PASTORAL CARE AND COUNSELING IN.

JESUIT SPIRITUALITY. *See* IGNATION SPIRITUALITY.

JESUS. Historically, there are two broad ways in which the figure of Jesus has had significance for pastoral care and counseling: (1) As the *"Christ of faith,"* Jesus is understood in terms of his personal significance to the believer, the one to whom the faithful turn for divine care and nurture in the struggles and sufferings of life and for ultimate salvation beyond sin and death in the life of God. Jesus in this appropriation is savior, redeemer, friend of sinners, physician of the soul, and champion of the oppressed. Theologically expressed, Jesus as the Christ, the divine Word of God, is the one through whom the redemptive love and care of God are made known and available to the world. As head of the church which is his body, he is the true sacrament of God and

the primal source of all sacramental and nonsacramental ministries of care. As one with God from the beginning, through whom all things were made, he is the true source and end of all love and acts of care in the world inside or outside the church. (2) *As the "Jesus of history,"* the incarnate Son of God in his "earthly ministry," Jesus has traditionally been regarded as the ideal pastor, the Good Shepherd who, the Gospels tell us, healed the sick, cast out demons, showed compassion to sinners, and preached good news to the poor. His encounters with people portrayed in the Gospels have been taken as ideal instances of care, demonstrating faith in the heavenly Father to meet human need, unbounded compassion, and profound psychological insight into human nature and the ability to become deeply related, at personal levels, to persons who came to him for help. (The latter point appears frequently in contemporary pastoral care and counseling literature.) Until the nineteenth century, these two pastoral appropriations of the figure of Jesus were assumed to be continuous and coherent. The Christ of faith and piety and the Jesus of history were essentially one, and believers could turn confidently to Gospel accounts of Jesus' ministry to provide resources for piety and models of ministry to troubled, sinful, and needy persons.

The advent of historical criticism, however, for those who took it seriously, rendered this unity and this confidence problematic. Criticism made it difficult for thoughtful Christians and pastors to utilize Gospel records of Jesus' life and work in prayer and piety with the former sense of historical reliability, and raised troublesome difficulties for grounding contemporary pastoral care and counseling in Jesus' historical ministry. Though many in the care and counseling movement, following popular piety, have ignored the force of these critical considerations and continue to use the figure of Jesus as an exemplar of contemporary pastoral and psychological ideals, the problem remains and requires a more careful pastoral theological consideration than it has thus far received. Hence the question arises today whether, or in what way, the figure of Jesus in the Gospels can be related to contemporary personal need and piety and to the contemporary caring ministries of the church.

To begin to answer this difficult question it is first necessary to understand the results of modern critical-historical scholarship concerning Jesus, and to consider the diversity of portraits of him that can be distinguished in the Gospel accounts. It may then be possible to envision ways in which these portraits may be able to play a constructive role in the theory and practice of contemporary pastoral care and counseling.

1. Historical Research. In his massive work *The Life of Jesus Critically Examined* (1853), D. F. Strauss concluded that the four canonical gospels were not historical records of factual events but rather the attempts of primitive people to cloak in mythological figures what were essentially religious ideas. Attempts to dispute Strauss's striking claims started the first "quest of the historical Jesus."

a. The "Old Quest." The basic problem underlined so forcibly by Strauss was the nature of the Gospels themselves. Not only do the four canonical Gospels differ in many factual details (e.g., the number of trips to Jerusalem, the names of the disciples, the location of resurrection appearances) but more worrisome still they present four distinct overall pictures of who Jesus was. While still rejecting Strauss's radical position, most scholars must acknowledge that the Gospels are interpretive amalgams of both the message of the historical man Jesus and the continuing revelation of the resurrected, living Lord to the Church, offered in the words of early Christian prophets and preachers—all of whom worked together to speak to the specific problems and experiences of some specific first century Christian communities. Hence, any biography of the historical Jesus cannot be simply read from the text but rather must be reconstructed by peeling away from the Gospel accounts the additions, concerns, and influence of their authors and the early Christian tradition in general.

Such reconstructions, however, produce disappointing results. What can be established with a fairly high degree of historical probability about the man Jesus, as over against the various images of the risen Christ, is meager indeed: He was a Jew born in Palestine toward the end of the reign of Herod the Great (ca. 4 B.C.), raised in Nazareth of Galilee by parents named Mary and Joseph; as a young man he met the apocalyptic preacher John the Baptist, after which he began a brief career as an itinerant preacher in Galilee and Judea, attracting a number of disciples and followers to his message of the coming reign of God. He was crucified for treason by Roman officials in Jerusalem, but his followers, claiming him to be the Jewish Messiah, spread through Palestine and into the major cities of the Greco-Roman world. Clearly, such a brief summary of a man's life provides little support for Christian faith, discipleship, or preaching.

The impossibility of arriving at a full biography of the historical Jesus ended the first quest. Furthermore, in calling a halt to attempts to reconstruct the life of Jesus, Rudolf Bultmann (1951) raised the additional issue of whether or not authentic faith need be based on historical incident at all. Arguing that we are saved by faith and not by history, Bultmann asserted that Christian faith was grounded in the proclamation of the Church's continuing experience of its Lord. Thus, a quest of the historical Jesus was not only impossible but theologically unnecessary.

b. The "New Quest." Pointing to the need for the proclamation of the church to have some relationship to its Founder, in the 1950s and early 1960s some of Bultmann's students announced a new quest of the historical Jesus. While no reconstruction of Jesus' biography was sought, they suggested that it might be possible to glimpse Jesus' self-understanding. Propelled by the insights of both existentialist philosophy and the later Heidegger's work on the power of language, the new quest focused on the language of Jesus' understanding of existence in the world. Yet if it was difficult to determine the actions and words of Jesus from our limited sources, it turned out to be even more difficult to establish his psychological state or view of self or existence. After little more than a decade the new quest also faded away.

2. Narrative Portraits. If the Gospels are not historical biography but rather religious proclamation, how can they be evaluated and appropriated in a modern context? The legacy of the new quest to contemporary scholarship was its concern with the language of the New Testament.

While perhaps not *factual* accounts of the historical Jesus, the Gospels are *faithful* stories witnessing to the Christian proclamation as understood by four different early Christian communities. This diversity of interpretations of who Jesus is and what following him means has been preserved by the Christian canon. Modern Christians, then, do not have *a* model of Jesus, they have at least four (Paul may suggest a fifth), and such diversity need not be threatening but can be creative and helpful. Just as the early Christians understood Jesus according to their own individual experiences and needs, modern Christians may need different understandings of Jesus and Christian discipleship at different points in their lives. Thus, the problem of the Gospels as sources for the historical Jesus may become an asset for creative pastoral appropriations of the various images of Jesus provided in Scripture.

a. Mark. In the Gospel of Mark, Jesus is above all things the Suffering Messiah. He is misunderstood and rebuked not only by his ostensible enemies, the Jewish leaders, but also by his closest friends, the disciples, especially Peter, James, and John. This Gospel presents a dark vision of Christian discipleship as suffering, persecution, and rejection. To follow the Markan Jesus is to follow obediently his way to the cross, expecting all about you to fail and betray you when the crisis arrives.

b. Matthew. The most Jewish of all the Gospels, Matthew presents a Jesus born to be "King of the Jews." Descended from Abraham and David, worshipped by members of the great priestly caste, the magi, announced by a new star in the heavens, from the beginning Jesus is presented as one destined to be the founder of a great, new religion. Like Moses delivering the law from Mount Sinai, Jesus, the Teacher with authority, gives a new instruction for a new community in his Sermon on the Mount. To follow the Matthean Jesus is to learn a new law, as the disciples do, establish a new community, and go forth to teach the rest of the world.

c. Luke. Born in humble surroundings, first worshiped by poor shepherds, descended, as is *all* humanity, from Adam and God, Jesus in the Gospel of Luke is a man for others, whose concern for the poor and marginal members of society all his followers should emulate. While the way of the Lukan Jesus leads to the cross, this cross is only a necessary step to the goal of resurrection and ascension. Hence, it is not alienation and death that define Christian life for Luke but rather communion and the promise of resurrection.

d. John. As the incarnate Word of God present before the creation of the world, Jesus in the Gospel of John is the divine Victor who is "one with the Father." Jesus promises a spiritual kingdom and eternal life to his followers. In long discourses not found in the other three Gospels, the Johannine Jesus reveals his divine nature and his saving presence to any who would see the light. Salvation for John comes not so much from following or emulating Jesus or his teachings but rather from knowing, believing, and confessing who Jesus is.

3. Suggestions for Pastoral Appropriation. The diversity (or even inconsistency) in the portraits of Jesus in the Gospels is sometimes regarded as a threat to faith. However, it is also possible to recognize this diversity as an expression of the inexhaustible richness and mystery of the figure of Jesus, who can be grasped by no single portrait or conception. In this light we may be able to find within the diversity multiple resources for pastoral appropriation.

a. As resources in pastoral situations. Rather than using isolated biblical verses to comfort, counsel, or confront people, pastors aware of the varying narrative portraits of Jesus in the NT and of the deeply theological character of these portraits might consider helping parishioners relate to the distinctive affirmations which they express about Jesus — and ultimately about God — in ways appropriate to the parishioner's immediate concerns. For instance, persons who feel alienated or "marginalized" (prisoners, AIDS victims, persons suffering shame, failure, guilt, or social oppression) may experience the good news of Jesus with particular power and appreciation through Luke's Gospel in which Jesus reaches out to women, Roman soldiers, and robbers in compassion and solidarity. Or again, those struggling with moral confusion and uncertainty — a general sense of lostness or moral nihilism—may find Matthew's Jesus compelling as a figure of loving authority who calls men and women to follow him in a disciplined life of service and responsibility.

Similar points of theological contact are possible with each of the Gospel portraits — e.g., Mark's theme of infidelity and suffering for those who would "walk with Jesus" through difficult situations of service or conflict (the burdened adult child of an aging, chronically ill parent or a burned-out and frustrated public service or church worker), or John's luminous portrait of Jesus the Light and Life of the world for those who must submit to the mysteries of suffering and death.

This is not to suggest that pastors dispense these portraits as magical remedies for human suffering. Rather it suggests that ways can be found by which the figure of Jesus can be made present in situations of personal need with both intellectual honesty and pastoral relevance. This would involve telling and interpreting the stories of Jesus not as historical events to be believed in literal detail, but as diverse expressions of the church's understanding of the love of God in Jesus the Christ for suffering and sinful humankind. The stories should therefore be told and the portraits viewed as the theological affirmations they truly are. This means allowing their theological power to speak in its own unique and saving way to the multifaceted contours of human need.

b. As guiding images for pastoral theory and practice. It is no longer possible, with integrity, to assume that everything believed today about good pastoral care in the contemporary clinical tradition derives directly from the ministry of the historical Jesus. Perhaps there are some continuities, at least of a general sort. Yet it is important to remember that Jesus lived in first century Palestine under very different historical conditions than contemporary "postmodern" pastors, and our concrete knowledge of him is both limited and pervasively colored by the theological affirmations of the early church.

However, the theological themes implicit in the Gospel portraits point to enduring features of the pastoral task. The experience of being misunderstood, betrayed, and persecuted in the service of the gospel (Mark), the gospel's mandate to give priority to the weak, the lost, and the marginal (Luke), the dual obligation to accept discipline and to exercise authority in the church (Matthew), and the need to see beyond the visible order to that which is eternal, to the One who is the Life of the world (John), are all themes relevant and essential to pastoral ministry in any age, however embodied in differing historical epochs.

What is perhaps most important in drawing upon these themes for pastoral theory and practice, however, is precisely their diversity and complementarity. Pastoral care neglects any one of them to its peril, and any adequate theory of care and counseling needs to ponder and appropriate all of them in some fashion. In this way the Gospel portraits can function as a source of critique and guidance for contemporary pastoral practice. It may be asked, for example, whether current pastoral care and counseling in the clinical tradition sufficiently attends to the Matthean themes of discipleship and authority, or to the Johannine themes of belief and spiritual transformation.

In any event, we can appropriate the diverse themes of the Gospel portraits of Jesus for today's pastoral care and counseling with integrity only by searching for forms of implementation appropriate to contemporary culture. Thus, for example, insights from psychology, sociology, psychotherapy and other disciples of culture must be taken seriously in contemporary ministry, however much they may also need to be criticized, selected, or modified in the appropriation. But neither is anything to be gained by romanticizing these contemporary resources as directly derived from or legitimated by the ministry of the historical Jesus. More true to Jesus, and more faithful to the God he proclaimed, are the humility and courage to live faithfully in one's own time. This means seeking to follow Jesus by working out new ways, appropriate to one's time and place, of embodying that to which he witnessed in his life and death, the love of God coming into the world to seek and to save the lost.

Bibliography. G. Bornkamm, *Jesus of Nazareth* (1960). R. Bultmann, *Theology of the New Testament* (1951). H. Conzelmann, *Theology of St. Luke* (1960). R. Edwards, *Matthew's Story of Jesus* (1985). W. Kelber, *Mark's Story of Jesus* (1979). R. Kysar, *John's Story of Jesus* (1984). W. E. Oates, *The Bible in Pastoral Care* (1953); *Christ and Selfhood* (1961); *Pastoral Counseling* (1974). W. B. Oglesby, Jr., *Biblical Themes for Pastoral Care* (1980). A. N. Perrin, *The Resurrection According to Matthew, Mark, and Luke* (1977). J. Robinson, *A New Quest of the Historical Jesus* (1959). A. Schweitzer, *Quest of the Historical Jesus* (1906). D. F. Strauss, *The Life of Jesus Critically Examined* (1835). C. A. Wise, *Psychiatry and the Bible* (1956).

M. A. TOLBERT
R. J. HUNTER

BIBLE, PASTORAL USE AND INTERPRETATION OF; CHRISTOLOGY AND PASTORAL CARE; NEW TESTAMENT, TRADITIONS AND THEOLOGY OF CARE IN. *See also* MINISTRY (Biblical Origins and Principles); REVELATION AND PASTORAL CARE; SALVATION, HEALING, AND HEALTH. *Compare* EXORCISM; FORGIVENESS; FAITH HEALING.

JEWISH CARE AND COUNSELING (History, Traditions, and Contemporary Issues). According to Jewish tradition, the family is the germinal cell from whence come the spiritual and ethical values to shape the Jewish character. This attitude is expressed even in the language, for the Hebrew word for "parents" is *horim*, which comes form the same root as *moreh*, "teachers." The parent, by exemplary deeds, is the primary teacher. The Jewish home is regarded as the *Mikdash Me'at* (miniature sanctuary) where the husband and wife are priest and priestess. This kindred solidarity constitutes the basis of Jewish life and increases in cohesiveness when confronted with adversity and discrimination.

The reciprocal relationship between home and religion is seen in the practice of Judaism. Many of the important religious rituals are home-centered. These rituals are marked not only by extended family visiting, but also by the use of distinctly Jewish foods associated with a particular holy day. Home religious observance requires the recitation of blessings at mealtime and frequently throughout the day. Festivals such as Passover involve extensive participation by family groups in their homes. A family celebration is the climax of the Jewish confirmation ceremony, the Bar or Bat Mitzvah, which takes place in the synagogue when a boy or girl reaches the age of thirteen. Some psychiatrists have noted that Jews, more than members of any other religious group, have reported experiencing their highest religious feelings in a family setting.

In comparison with the first two decades of this century, there has been a marked alteration or abbreviation of home ritual ceremonies on the part of most American Jewish families. However, it is not the content of these ceremonies which is of concern, but their function as a binding influence on the family.

Within the Jewish family setting, healthy attitudes toward sex, education, death, and other aspects of life had helped the family in the past withstand many of the disruptive influences of modern life. By preserving these attitudes and the accompanying religious practices, the Jewish family preserved itself against some of the disorganization that was so currently widespread in other family lives.

1. **A Healthy Attitude Toward Sex.** "It is well for a man not to touch a woman," Paul wrote in the NT (I Cor. 7:1), expressing his fundamental conviction concerning sex. Recognizing immediately that these words were far from the meditations in most hearts, he began to make concessions. "Because of the temptations to immorality," he added, "each man should have his own wife and each woman her own husband" (I Cor. 7:2). Wistfully, Paul then wished that all could be as he was, unmarried and with sexuality thoroughly bridled. Nevertheless he granted that if the "unmarried and the widows . . . cannot exercise self-control, they should marry. For it is better to marry than to be aflame with passion" (I Cor. 7:8–9).

Judaism is not identified with the Pauline concept of sex. Even the sexual aspect of Freud's doctrines, which so alarmed the Christian world, was in harmony with the Jewish viewpoint. Judaism maintains that if people deny themselves the physical enjoyments of love, they also deny the spiritual potential within them. The sexual love relationship is a high adventure of the human spirit, an opportunity for husband and wife to make a oneness of the separateness. In Judaism one does not thwart the body, but rather sanctifies it through love. Voluntary abstinence from sexual relations in marriage is a triple sin—against the health of the body, the fulfillment of soul, and the welfare of society.

The Jewish view is neither hedonism nor prudery. Judaism asserts that there is a middle ground between these two. Jewish proscriptions generally are not against the use of bodily appetites, but rather against the excessive indulgence of such desires.

In the U.S., while it is true that Jews tend to have relatively few illegitimate children, the explanation lies partly in the widespread acceptance by Jews of birth control measures. For example, Kinsey found that American Jews have more marital intercourse than non-Jews at all age levels except the youngest. Even more significantly, Kinsey and his associates reported that Jews talk more freely about sex than their Christian neighbors. Mental health experts are generally agreed that the subject of sex is too seldom discussed by parents and church or synagogue. Consequently, many young people have distorted ideas and information on sex. By allowing a fuller discussion on this vital subject, Jewish parents realize their responsibility to help children obtain more correct information so that their youngsters may develop healthy attitudes toward sex in their youth. They begin to build a way of thinking about marriage which will help them in establishing Jewish homes.

Judaic counseling considers the starting point in the sexual relationship to be the recognition of God as Creator and sovereign Ruler of the universe and all that is in it. In the first chapter of Genesis it says: "So God created man in his own image. . . ; male and female he created them. And God blessed them; and God said to them, 'Be fruitful, and multiply, and fill the earth.' " Jewish tradition maintains that sex is good, not bad, because it is one of God's endowments. Procreation is one of God's commands. Sex is not nasty, but holy; not sordid, but sacred. However, Judaism acknowledges that people can misuse and pervert that which God meant for good, and teaches that sex should not be divested of its dignity and meaning.

The Jew is taught that the sex act has more than biological meaning; a real marriage is a combination of physical attraction plus companionate love. A person's masculinity or feminity makes one look for a person of the opposite sex, but a person's loneliness makes one look for a friend to relieve one's solitariness. When God said, "It is not good for man to be alone," this indicated that God's plan for man and woman was not only for propagation of the race, but also for their mutual welfare, for the well-being of society, and the strengthening of family ties. This Jewish concept of the sexual function is considered by some mental health experts to be less likely to lead to neuroses caused by sexual conflicts than the Pauline concept.

2. **Judaism: A This-Worldly Faith.** Judaism is more than a creed; it is a way of life. One of the distinctive values of the Jewish subculture is that of "life's pleasures" or "nonasceticism"—the belief that "better is one day of happiness and good deeds in *this* world than all the life in the world-*to-come*." Since Jews do not consider their bodily appetites as sinful, their behavior in matters of sex, drink, and food is affected accordingly. This practical, realistic approach of the Jewish concept helps to improve more stable reality testing.

In the view of normative Judaism, the way to God is not through flight from the world or through self-mortification. Holiness, *Kedusha,* while representing a unique category of the spirit, is realizable in one's earthly life. The physical, far from being antithetical to the spiritual, may serve as its vehicle. *Kedusha* is attained through molding the human into the patterns of the divine. *Kedusha* is not in the extirpation of natural instincts and desires, but in their refinement, discipline, and direction toward godliness and social as well as personal welfare.

"And God saw everything that he had made, and behold, it was very good" (Gen. 1:31). So almost with its first words, Scripture states a thesis that echoes and reechoes down the centuries; life is good, and should be treasured and affirmed as a gift from God.

The purpose of this life is the wise, good, and creative enjoyment of the material, intellectual, moral, and spiritual blessings provided for humanity by the Creator. Judaism regards as sinful both *rejection* of the pleasures of life, which is in effect the denial of the wisdom and loving-kindness of a beneficent Provider, and *indulgence* in exclusively material satisfactions which desensitize and make us unconscious of our intellectual or moral-spiritual-aesthetic needs. Each of us is body, mind, and spirit. Denial of any aspect of the self, or failure to satisfy its legitimate needs, rules out maximum self-fulfillment.

Judaism holds that when we are born we are not enchained by original sin. We are inherently good and endowed with a moral conscience that is reinforced by freedom of will. The great Rabbi Akiba said that although everything is foreseen by God, God has given us free will. Maimonides, the medieval philosopher, stated that everyone by free will may be as righteous as Moses or as sinful as Jeroboam, wise or foolish, kind or cruel. Sin exists, and temptation is always with us. But by our own strength we can overcome them. At the very beginning of the Bible story, Cain is told that "sin is crouching at the door, its desire is for you, but you must master it" (Gen. 4:7). We are not doomed to will the good and yet do evil. With goodness, we can and must be the architects of our own lives.

3. Well-Defined Pattern for Meeting Death. While Judaism's major emphasis is thus on life, there are theological beliefs concerning death. Jews understand that the individual is a dying being who, at the same time, must declare: "One world at a time is enough." Judaism does not ignore the mystery of death but is more concerned with the miracle of life. While other religions are, in general, otherworldly, Judaism's concepts of a hereafter are not completely harmonized and integrated.

Although Jewish beliefs about death do not totally center on concepts of a hereafter, Judaic tradition demonstrates a concern for the survivors' reactions to a death. Indeed, the Jewish faith surrounds death with rites that later lay a vital role in the healing work of grief. The bereaved must of necessity realize that a loved one has died and must therefore gradually fill the void in a constructive way. They must not suppress memories or even disturbing, often guilt-producing, recollections which are an inevitable part of all human relationships. The spiritual confusions of shock and grief are structured through definite and solemn procedures.

From the moment that one learns of the death of a dear one, Judaism offers specific religious rituals to be followed, which help to order one's life. Formal mourning periods of diminishing intensity follow death. The Jewish funeral is the rite of separation. The bad dream is real. The presence of the casket actualizes the experience, transforming the process of denial to the acceptance of reality.

In the ritual of bereavement, Jews could well feel that even though they should have done more for the deceased, these ceremonials can be done right. Here they know in clear-cut, unmistakable terms what is expected of them. Perhaps by carrying out the ceremonial, they will regain the love they have lost, the love of their own conscience, which could personify the highest internal ideals.

The first seven-day period following a death is *Shivah,* which tides the mourners over the first dazing shock. The survivors remain at home, receiving a continuous stream of condolence calls. Difficult as this may be, it helps in keeping their minds active and their attentions engaged. Also, it is important because it lends the comfort of the loving concern of family and friends.

Sigmund Freud called *Shivah* the "ties of dissolution." Friends help to review with the bereaved their experiences with the deceased. As each emotion is reconsidered, a pang of pain is felt that the experience will never be repeated. As the pain is experienced, the bereaved are able to dissolve themselves of the emotional ties with the deceased and thus establish new relationships by which they must take an active place in the company of the living.

After this comes the *Shloshim,* covering the following thirty-day period. The mourners resume normal activity, although avoiding places of entertainment and continuing to observe certain forms and prayers. At the end of the thirty days, ritualistic mourning is over except for the reciting of the *Kaddish,* the Jewish prayer for the deceased, daily for an entire year. Through the ancient hallowed tradition of *Minyan* (daily worship), Jews perpetuate the memory of their loved one. Each time they recite the *Kaddish,* they reinforce both the reality of death and the affirmation of life. They publicly display their own needed concern and profound feeling of being a good child, parent, sibling, or spouse.

By participating with others who are also suffering the emotional trauma of bereavement, the mourning Jew belongs to the largest company in the world—the company of those who have known suffering and death. This great, universal sense of sorrow helps unite all human hearts and dissolve all other feelings into those of common sympathy and understanding. Such communal religious rituals create a sense of solidarity, with all the comfort, gratification, pride, and even pain that such a sense brings.

The Jewish ceremonials of *Shivah, Shloshim,* and reciting *Kaddish* communicate the concepts of faith, love, and finality. The event of death is placed in a context greater than that of each individual life. The observance of the Jewish laws and customs of mourning helps one face reality, give honor to the deceased, and guide the bereaved in the reaffirmation of life.

Judaism is strict in limiting mourning to the given periods and the customary observances. Excessive grief is taken as want of trust in God. The faith holds it as natural and desirable that with time the havoc wrought by death should help to repair itself. Though no one is ever the same after a bereavement as before, one is expected, when mourning is over, to take up existence, suppressing for the sake of life itself the remnants of grief. The garment that the pious mourner rends can be sewn and worn again. The mark is there, but life resumes its course.

4. Exalted Position of Learning. For the Jew, education is one of the most effective compensatory dynamisms to meet the inner conflicts of life. Historically, the respect for learning is one of the cornerstones of Judaism. Judaism is the religion of Torah, not alone of the *Chumash* (the five books of Moses) or the written law, nor even of the oral tradition, but of the progressive growth of all religious knowledge and culture. Knowledge is stressed as one of the chief duties which Jews owe not only to themselves but to their God. The *Ethics of the Fathers* states: "*Torah* is the first of the three pillars which support the Jewish world as well as the inspiration and vitality of the other two supports, worship and benevolence." The Hebrew term *Bet Hamidrash* and the Judeo-German *Schul*, which both mean school and learning, are commonly used as a synonym for synagogue.

The ideal of learning kept the Jewish people on a high plane of cultural and intellectual, as well as religious, enterprise. It further provided an ideal occupation and interest for people who were forced to look inward and find a symbolic status gratification. The Jew may attempt to surmount a "handicap," as in the legendary case of Demosthenes who overcame his stuttering and became a famous orator. Feeling that Jews may suffer a handicap, Jewish people often urge their children to study and work harder than their Christian competitors in order to run the unequal race. To be successful, they may point out, a Jew must be better prepared, must have higher academic records, and more experience than the non-Jew. Freud once stated that the one thing that distinguishes the Jews is brainpower, for traditionally they had directed their psychic energies not to athletics but mental gymnastics.

With some other peoples, learning was an afterthought, a by-product of normal living or an entertainment for leisure hours. Historically, for the Jew it was a precondition for a sound mind. Education was revered and respected in that it aided the Jew in looking inward to a life of contemplative content away from the myriad forms of oppression and suggested a belief in the omnipotence of thought.

The importance given to learning and knowledge finds expression among contemporary Jewry in many ways. Students have often been given a higher status in Jewish community life. Settlement workers in immigrant quarters have always noticed the exceptional value which Jewish parents placed on schooling for their children, and this is manifest both in the high figures for Jewish attendance at colleges and universities, and in the grades of Jewish students. In addition, Jews are generously represented in highly esteemed professions, which require the most advanced educational training and intellectual discipline.

5. High Concept of Social Justice. In a graphic statement, Erich Fromm asserts in *The Art of Loving*: "Man is gifted with reason; he is life being aware of itself; he has awareness of himself, of his fellow man, of his past, and of the possibilities of his future. This awareness of himself as a separate entity, the awareness of his own short span of life, of the fact that without his will he is born, and against his will he dies, that he will die before those whom he loves, or they before him, the awareness of his aloneness and separateness, of his helplessness before the forces of nature and of society, all of this makes his separate, disunited existence an unbearable prison. He would become insane could he not liberate himself from this prison and reach out, unite himself in some form or other with other men, with the world outside."

The experience of separateness causes the feeling of anxiety. For Jews, the feeling of separateness may be great. They often feel as marginal beings or, in Sigmund Freud's words, "prescribed from the compact majority." Kurt Lewin likened the lot of the Jew to the condition of adolescents who are never quite certain whether they will be admitted to the dominant adult world. The Jew lives on two levels: as a member of the general community and as "a child of the covenant."

The psychological problem for Jews is to find the relation between their interests and needs and the world in which they exist. These needs, such as the need to love and to be loved, can for a time remain ungratified without disturbing psychological health, but over a longer period of time they create mental distress and may lead to mental disease. Well-being is also disturbed when love is unrequited, curiosity unrelieved, and sympathy unexpressed. And many feel such distress "mentally" even though no bodily ill is noted. Freud, Jung, Adler, and Horney agree that there can be no health for the individual without appreciative and cooperative interaction.

One of the most important Jewish values is *Zedekah*, the Hebrew word for appreciative charity and cooperative social justice. In explaining the continuing solidarity of the Jewish people, Albert Einstein placed the Jewish respect for *Zedekah* above everything else. Although he may have stated the proposition too strongly, there is a partial truth in his claim that "the bond that has united the Jews for thousands of years and unites them today is above all the democratic ideal of social justice, coupled with the ideal of mutual aid and tolerance among all people" (Schmidt).

The strong feeling on the part of the Jewish family created a social consciousness that transcended the solitary demands of the individual. In addition, there were the Jeremiahs, Isaiahs, and Amoses who were not only the teachers of ritualistic religion but were forerunners in the promulgation of a monotheism that was ethical in content. Social legislation was vast and revolutionary, dealing with relief of the poor; protection of the laborer, women, and children; filial duty; charity; hospitality; and relation with one's neighbors. These laws were mandatory because they were the will of God: "Ye shall be holy because I, the Lord, your God, am holy."

The history of the Jewish religion is essentially that of the emergence of ethical ideas and ideals out of a background of purely ceremonial and ritual observance, and the creation of a moral law that declared that God was to be served by means of right conduct. There is the statement of God declaring: "Would that you forsake me but keep my commandments." Today, the Jewish outlook prods Jews constantly to strive for a better world, to be prominently involved in movements for social reform. Even many Jewish radicals who may ignore their Jewishness are the product of this messianic fervor.

There are many reasons which form the basis for Jewish liberalism. Lewis Browne has forcefully stated the proposition that Jews are radicals in politics because they are an urban people. In addition, Jews realize that their security is inextricably interwoven with progressive governments. For example, in Czarist Russia anti-Semitism was the direct result of the interplay of the reactionary regime with a burgeoning liberal movement of the people. When reactionary governments triumphed, the Jew was often the scapegoat in Europe.

The minority-conscious Jews may direct their hostility against the dominant group or the more vulnerable low-status races (projection). But being victims themselves, they often display sympathy rather than aggression for the underdog. These two diametrically opposed reactions may be evident in the same person at different times. Jews are often among the most vigorous workers for liberal causes.

Social justice through the fight against prejudice is a way of sublimation for the Jews and a means for mental health. *Zedekah* is forged as a result of the frustrating outer world and deflected in favor of the cathexis of its substitute, but still showing some of the qualities of the original impulse. Jews are often active in leading protest meetings, raising funds, attempting to persuade friends among the dominant groups to aid in the many liberal crusades. When the neighbor lends support to the Jew, the Jew is not only helped in terms of additional aid for the other minority groups, but is given added ego reinforcement by the non-Jew's concurrence. For while Jews have often achieved a higher economic status, they still find themselves excluded from certain private clubs, organizations, and from high administrative posts in many corporations dominated by non-Jews. Because of this exclusion, Jews have not always developed a true sense of solidarity with the American economic elite and have reacted against the political values of the dominant group.

Jews may throw themselves into the struggle for equality with tremendous vigor, since for every injustice corrected, they experience deeply the satisfaction of a personal wrong redressed. They have handled their own suffering without inflicting suffering in return, and have been instrumental in helping others less fortunate. They have overcome their separateness and have left the prison of their aloneness.

6. **Positive Approach to Medicine.** Judaism derives its optimistic view not from shutting its eyes to evil in all its forms but rather from the conviction that it can be overcome. As a co-laborer with God in the creative task of bringing order out of chaos and of endowing existence with meaning and with value, it is humankind's objective to harness their intelligence, skill, and adventuresome spirit to remove the obstacles that block the road to their physical and mental health and to their full self-realization as moral and spiritual beings.

Judaism is not a system of medicine but a *torat haadam* — a law for the whole person. While the religion has certain therapeutic value for the sick and suffering, it is not confined to healing. The concern is with the enrichment and sanctification of life and with the establishment of society upon the foundations of righteousness. Judaism is not an art of healing but an art of living for the sound and healthy as well as for the ailing. Judaism is the agency of personal and of social morality, of care and counseling.

Some have attributed the Jew's relative acceptance of psychology to the fact that theology and doctrines play a lesser role in Judaism than in Christianity. Emphasis in Judaism is not placed upon creed but deed: reason is of primacy. Medieval Jewish philosophers stressed the idea that all knowledge is vital; it is the pillar of our very being. Faith without reason is mute. Thus a balance is sought and wrought in striving for a synthesis of faith and health, of religion and psychiatry.

4. **The Present.** Roles within the Jewish family are dramatically shifting within the Orthodox, Conservative, and Reform communities. For Jews — as indeed for all Americans—there is the slow but perceptible change to the nonnuclear family. One out of two Jews who married in the 1980s divorced by 1990. One out of every three children born to a Jewish mother or Jewish father will have a non-Jewish parent. One out of every two Jewish college students who married in the 1980s married out of the Jewish faith. Increasing divorce and general dislocation are the emerging facts of Jewish life.

In the past, rabbis were reluctant to enter the area of pastoral counseling. Indeed, in the major Jewish seminaries, the emphasis upon understanding the psychological needs of the congregator was minimal at best.

The needs of the changing Jewish family are no longer being neglected. Efforts are made to sensitize and educate congregational leadership, rabbis, and educators. Within the religious school curriculum, there are developing courses on marriage and the family, sexuality, divorce, and family dislocation. Discussions are held as to who chants the *Kiddish* on Sabbath eve (usually the father) when there is no Daddy at home. At the Bar or Bat Mitzvah ceremony questions are raised as to who brings the youth to the pulpit, who reads, and who blesses (and with the parents, even who pays?). At the wedding, who walks down the aisle; who stands under the *chupah* (marital canopy); and who sits in the front row? Rabbis are now better prepared when to counsel, to advise, and make a referral and how to reach out to the separated, divorced, and widowed families.

The question is how once again to create a *Mikdash me'at* (miniature sanctuary) with a healthier attitude toward sex, a this-worldly faith, an establishment of a well-defined pattern for meeting life and death, an exalted position of learning, a higher concept of social justice, and a positive approach to medicine; how to regain the peculiar and special quality of Jewish family life? There is a reexamination of attitudes, traditions, rituals, and habits. Changing families require changing congregations.

Though many suggestions have been offered, there is one thread that unites all Jews. The agreement is that family life is the cornerstone of Judaism's survival kit.

The thrust for Jewish continuity and affirmation still remains strong. Jews are challenged as never before to forge new combinations of community which continue to provide for the enlarged development of Jewish identity and care, for a *torat laadam*, a law for the whole person.

Bibliography. E. Fromm, *The Art of Loving* (1974). N. S. Goldman, "The Unconscious in Pastoral Psychology: A Rabbinic Perspective," *J. of Pastoral Psychology*, 34 (1968) 193–203. R. L. Katz, *Pastoral Care and the Jewish Tradition* (1984). C. G. Montefiore and H. Loewe, eds., *A Rabbinic Anthology* (1939). H. Schmidt *Judaism*, 8 (1959) 240.

E. A. GROLLMAN

HASIDIC CARE AND COUNSELING; JEWISH HOLY DAYS AND FESTIVALS; JEWISH PRAYERS; JEWISH LITERATURE IN CARE AND COUNSELING; JUDAISM AND PSYCHOLOGY; PERSON (Jewish Perspective); RABBI/RABBINATE; ZADDIK. *See also* EDUCATION, NURTURE, AND CARE; SALVATION, HEALING, AND HEALTH; SOCIAL JUSTICE ISSUES AND PASTORAL CARE. *See also* Jewish articles on CONVERSION, FAMILY, GRIEF AND MOURNING, HAVURAH, MARRIAGE, MEDICAL-ETHICAL DILEMMAS, MENTALLY RETARDED, OLDER PERSONS, PENITENTS, SEXUALITY, SICK AND DYING, SINGLE PERSONS, THEOLOGICAL EDUCATION. *Compare* COMMUNITY, FELLOWSHIP, AND CARE; CULTURAL AND ETHNIC FACTORS IN PASTORAL CARE; ETHICS AND PASTORAL CARE; ISLAMIC CARE AND COUNSELING; MORAL DILEMMAS IN PASTORAL PERSPECTIVE; PASTORAL CARE; PASTORAL COUNSELING.

JEWISH-CHRISTIAN MARRIAGE. Rabbinic organizations have frequently used the term *intermarriage* to refer to couples where the non-Jewish mate converts to Judaism and *mixed marriage* to refer to marriages where there is no conversion. In Jewish sources *interfaith* and *ecumenical* usually emphasize the distinctiveness of the two faiths. Thus, an interfaith or ecumenical ceremony would be one in which a rabbi coofficiates with a minister or priest. This article uses *intermarriage* in its accepted sociological meaning to refer to any marriage between a Jew and a non-Jew.

1. Incidence of Intermarriage. Accurate scientific data on the incidence of intermarriage are rare due to the lack of uniform national statistics. Samplings are most often biased, since data, even in national surveys, are derived from those who are affiliated with or known to the organized Jewish community. The intermarriage rate is always lower for individuals than for couples. For example, if half of all marriages involving Jews are intermarriages, the couple rate is fifty percent but, since one out of three Jews is intermarrying, the individual rate is 33.3 percent. This article uses the couple rate throughout.

The National Jewish Population Study (NJPS) reported an intermarriage rate in the U.S. of six percent prior to World War II, twelve percent in the 1940s and 1950s, and almost fifty percent by 1972. NJPS also found that Jewish males intermarry twice as frequently as Jewish females, but more recent data seem to indicate that the rate is either in the process of equalizing or has already equalized and that the male-female rate differential is now statistically insignificant (I. Fishbein).

Whenever Jews and non-Jews have been free to marry, as in Western Europe during the nineteenth century, the intermarriage rate has reached fifty percent by the third generation. Intermarriage is both symptom and conse-

quence. Before it becomes pervasive, an atmosphere which encourages or permits it must exist.

The intermarriage rate increases with self-selection of mate, the breakdown of ghettoized patterns of living, and the weakening of group cohesion. However, the density of Jews in a given population seems to be important only after group cohesion has been weakened. The intermarriage rate also increases with the removal of economic, social, educational, and political barriers; with acculturation, mobility, and the greater acceptability of Jews as marriage partners; and with children growing up with tenuous ties to the extended family.

Another essential element in an increased rate of intermarriage is the achievement of identification and attitude assimilation. Jews and non-Jews brought up in the same suburbs tend to see themselves in the same way and to share the same values and attitudes. These shared values and attitudes often include an indifference to the theological implications of religion and the minutiae of religious observance, as well as an ability to compartmentalize religion and to view it as just one other difference that has to be recognized and respected. Indeed, if Jewish identity is just another compartment, one can not only tolerate but even welcome the difference as refreshing. Under such circumstances intermarriage is not a rejection of Jewishness or a pathological acting out, but a response to a common environment and a continuation of the assimilative behavior patterns established by prior generations.

Intermarriage may also be looked upon as a way of defusing the emotional intensity of the nuclear family. By choosing a mate who is significantly different, an individual pushes away from the family of origin and can more easily assert independence.

2. Jewish Response. The Jewish community has been slow to respond to intermarrying couples because intermarriage is perceived as a threat to Jewish survival. However, even if there were no intermarriages, assimilation and a low Jewish birthrate would make Jewish survival problematical. A high incidence of intermarriage sometimes serves as a convenient scapegoat for concerns about the future of Judaism.

As the intermarriage rate increased dramatically in the postwar years, the Jewish community steadfastly maintained a commitment to a policy of containment. The last organizational attempt at containment occurred in 1973 when the Central Conference of American Rabbis (CCAR) voted to oppose, but not prohibit, officiating at intermarriage ceremonies by its membership. This policy of containment has gradually been replaced by one of acceptance and accommodation because of a growing realization that responding positively to intermarried couples will strengthen, rather than weaken, the Jewish community.

Jewish communal agencies and synagogues are gradually responding more positively by offering special programs for intermarried couples, like discussion groups, workshops to teach basic Jewish observance, and formal courses in Judaism. While many programs are geared to those who have converted or may soon be willing to convert, they are increasingly reaching out to non-Jews whose sole attachment to Judaism may be a commitment to raise children as Jews. Part of this new approach has been dictated by the pressures of serving a synagogue membership consisting of a significant number of intermarried couples.

Established in 1970, the Rabbinic Center for Research and Counseling (RCRC), Westfield, N.J., has pioneered in serving the needs of intermarried couples. RCRC maintains a list of rabbis who officiate at intermarriages under a variety of conditions, conducts research on intermarriage, and develops programs to help intermarried couples cope with basic issues in their relationship to each other, to family, and to community. In 1981 the Union of American Hebrew Congregations initiated its outreach program for intermarried couples, and in 1984 the Federation of Reconstructionist Congregations and Havurot offered synagogue membership to intermarried couples and endorsed referral of intermarrying couples to rabbis who would be willing to officiate.

3. Conversion. Approximately one out of four non-Jewish females and one out of thirty-five non-Jewish males convert to Judaism either before or after marriage (NJPS). Converts to Judaism are regarded as equal to born Jews in every way but some individual and community resistance often mitigates full acceptance. Conversion of Jews to another religion is rare.

Much concern is expressed over how deeply intermarried couples are committed to Judaism and to what extent the presence of non-Jewish symbols in the home and the very existence of non-Jewish family tend to dilute that commitment. Although two-thirds of the children of intermarriages are raised as Jews and given some kind of Jewish education, a Christmas tree is displayed in almost half of those homes (B. Fishbein).

Acceptance of the children of intermarried couples as Jews is problematical. Reform Judaism and Reconstructionism consider children to be Jews if either parent is Jewish and the children are raised as Jews. Conservative and Orthodox Judaism regard as Jews only children who are born of a Jewish mother. Children of a non-Jewish mother may become Jewish through conversion.

4. The Role of the Rabbi. As the number and percentage of intermarriages rise, there is increasing pressure on rabbis to officiate. Conservative and Orthodox rabbis do not officiate since *halachah* (traditional Jewish law) defines a Jewish marriage as a marriage between two Jews. Consequently, only Reform and Reconstructionist rabbis may officiate without facing the threat of expulsion from their rabbinic organizations. A few Reconstructionist rabbis and one-half of the Reform rabbinate now officiate at intermarriages (I. Fishbein). While not preventing a couple from marrying, a rabbi's refusal to officiate is interpreted by the couple as rejection (T. Lenn).

The average Jewish parents want a rabbi to officiate at their child's marriage. To many Jews a rabbi's officiating represents hope that children born of the marriage will not only be raised as Jews but will also remain close to the Jewish family. However, if the rabbi is to share the ceremony with non-Jewish clergy, the preference would then be for a justice of the peace.

Because of a rabbi's visibility and because intermarriage is legitimately regarded as being within his purview, a rabbi's position on intermarriage is critical in setting the tone for community response. For most rabbis the decision to officiate or not to officiate at intermar-

riages is conflictual. Rabbis want to respond to the expressed needs of the individual but must also take into consideration the needs of family members and the overall welfare of the Jewish community.

5. Understanding Jewish Feelings. The intensity of Jewish feelings toward intermarriage is often puzzling to the non-Jew who tends to measure feelings for Judaism with the same measuring rods that have been traditionally applied to Christians. However, it is just not possible to measure a Jew's commitment as one would measure a Christian's. Jews are the least observant of major religious groups. The existence of secular Jews and secular Judaism is well established and accepted. Strong unconscious forces, such as subliminal experiences of anti-Semitism, are often a cogent and underlying reinforcement of Jewishness.

Historically, Judaism was not always opposed to intermarriage. While patriarchal custom forbade the descendants of Abraham to marry Canaanites, Jacob adopted as his own Ephraim and Manasseh, the two sons of Joseph and his wife, Asenath, the daughter of a non-Jewish priest (Gen. 48:3-5). The biblical books of Esther and Ruth portray a positive attitude toward intermarriage. In contrast, the book of Ezra advocates that intermarriages with non-Jews from idolatrous nations be dissolved.

It was only when Christianity became the dominant religion in the Roman Empire that conversion to Judaism, as well as intermarriage, was prohibited by the church, at times upon pain of death. This attitude, initially imposed upon Judaism from the outside, came in time to be internalized and adopted by the Jewish community as its own.

Bibliography. D. M. Eichhorn, *Jewish Intermarriages: Fact and Fiction* (1974). B. Fishbein, *Attitudes and Practices in the Intermarried Home* (1978). I. H. Fishbein, "Mixed Marriage," *CCAR Journal* Spring (1973), 15–54; "Report of Committee on Mixed Marriage," *CCAR* Yearbook (1973), 59–97; *Male-Female Ratios in Jewish Intermarriage* (1973); *Rabbinic Participation in Intermarriage Ceremonies, Survey #5* (1982); *Rabbinic Participation in Intermarriage Ceremonies, Survey #6*, (1986); "Mixed Marriage, Intermarriage" in *Encyclopedia Judaica*, (1972), 12, pp. 164–69. T. Lenn, *Rabbi and Synagogue in Reform Judaism* (1972). F. Massarik, *National Jewish Population Study* (1972). E. Mayer, *Intermarriage and the Jewish Future* (1979). *Children of Intermarriage* (1983); *Love and Tradition: Marriage Between Jews and Christians* (1985).

I. H. FISHBEIN

JEWISH CARE AND COUNSELING; MARRIAGE COUNSELING AND MARITAL THERAPY. *See also* CULTURAL AND ETHNIC FACTORS IN PASTORAL CARE; DIVORCE AND REMARRIAGE. *Compare* CATHOLIC-PROTESTANT MARRIAGE; ORTHODOX-CATHOLIC MARRIAGE; ORTHODOX-PROTESTANT MARRIAGE; *also* CROSS-CULTURAL MARRIAGE AND FAMILY.

JEWISH HOLY DAYS AND FESTIVALS, PASTORAL DIMENSIONS OF. Integral to Jewish faith and life is a traditionally defined structure of holy days, festivals, and related religious practices. These sacred occasions define and reinforce Jewish identity, nourish a profound sense of community and historical continuity, and provide opportunities for members of the community to care for one another. In order to understand the pastoral significance of these celebrations, each is briefly described. In addition, this article considers the significance of these religious experiences for persons with particular needs and offers suggestions for how non-Jewish pastors, such as hospital and prison chaplains, may extend care to Jews at times of special Jewish observance.

1. **Jewish Celebrations.** *a. Sabbath.* The Sabbath, or Day of Rest, is a regularly recurring holy day in the Jewish calendar. It begins every Friday just prior to sundown and goes on to Saturday, with its termination approximately one hour after sundown. It is not merely a day of rest and cessation from material creativity; it is also a day for concentrating on the human dimension— for husbands and wives to rediscover each other and for children and parents to enjoy one another unencumbered by involvement in the allures of daily life. The Sabbath is ushered in with the lighting of candles, usually by the wife, and the recitation of the sanctification prayer, or the Kiddush, by the husband. A festive meal, accompanied with appropriate Sabbath songs and study of the biblical theme of the week or some other timely topic are usually part of the fare at a Sabbath meal. Sabbath synagogue services include Sabbath prayers, the biblical reading for the week, and a sermon by the rabbi. The Sabbath is perceived in Jewish tradition as one of the essential celebrations in the Jewish calendar. It is a day for intellectual stimulation, emotional and spiritual renewal, and physical reinvigoration through being detached from the fast-paced work schedule of the regular week. The Sabbath is celebrated at its conclusion with a ceremony of ushering out called Havdalah, over a cup of wine, with spices that are inhaled to compensate for the let-down feeling at the exit of the Sabbath, and a torch-like candle, which symbolizes that one can once again make use of fire and engage in work.

b. Days of awe. i. Rosh Hashanah. Rosh Hashanah, literally head of the year, more colloquially referred to as the New Year, is a two-day celebration ushering in the new year with a combination of solemnity and joy. The solemnity inheres in the synagogue worship service, which launches the process of repentance and self-investigation. The essential commandment of this day is the sounding of the ram's horn, with its simple sounds, its sighing sounds, and sobbing sounds. Rosh Hashanah is also a celebrative day, the birthday of the human species, and the day when families come together for the festive meals. The meals themselves contain various symbols indicating the wishes for the coming year, such as honey placed on bread instead of the usual salt; pomegranates and fish, symbolizing proliferation; sweet carrots; and other appropriate foods.

ii. Yom Kippur. Yom Kippur, the Day of Atonement, culminates the ten-day period starting with Rosh Hashanah. Yom Kippur, like Rosh Hashanah, usually falls sometime in September or in the early part of October. It is a day of fasting, with the fasting beginning prior to sundown and continuing to about an hour after sunset of the following day. The total abstinence on Yom Kippur includes no food or drink, no bathing or showering, sexual abstinence, and the wearing of leather-free shoes. The Day of Atonement is spent in the synagogue, reciting confessional prayers and expressing the hopes and desires for a year of peace, tranquility, and sustenance. The memorial prayers for the departed are also an essential component of the Yom Kippur liturgy. Yom Kippur culminates with the sounding of a ram's horn, or shofar, which is the signal for people to return to their homes and to resume eating.

c. Pilgrimage festivals. i. Passover (Pesach). The first of the three pilgrimage festivals is Passover, referred to as Pesach or as Chag Ha'Matzot, the festival of the unleavened bread and the festival celebrating the first yield of the harvest. This festival, which occurs at the beginning of spring, is very much family-oriented. Extended families are likely to come together to celebrate the Passover and most specifically the Passover Seder, which is a special gathering on the first and second nights of Passover. The Seder refers to a special order of service beginning with the sanctification of the festival, and continuing with a reliving of the history of the Israelites in Egypt, their bondage, and the eventual miraculous delivery from slavery into freedom. Passover is identified as the time of freedom, and the Passover Seder reflects on this theme and the gratitude that is owed to God for having delivered the Israelites. The reliving of the Exodus is done verbally and gastronomically. Verbally it is done through telling the story and embellishing it with further insight. Gastronomically it is achieved through eating bitter herbs to feel the bitterness of what must have been the situation in Egypt at that time, and also by eating unleavened bread, which symbolizes the bread of servitude—a slavery so intense that the slaves did not have the time to let their dough rise into bread—and also symbolizes the freedom of the Israelites, who in their rush to leave Egypt were unconcerned about food and instead ate the same unleavened bread. Other foods such as a mixture of nuts, raisins, and wine called charoset, reminiscent of the mortar used for bricks, and salt water symbolizing the tears of the crying Israelites, are employed in the Seder service. Reminiscing on the past moves to celebration of the present, including a festive Passover meal. The Seder concludes with praise and hope for the future. In Israel, Passover lasts for seven days and only one Seder is celebrated. Outside Israel Passover is eight days with two Seders at the beginning. There is an intermediate period that does not have the legal severity of the festival with all of its work prohibitions, and then there follows the concluding day in Israel or two days outside Israel. The first part of Passover celebrates the leaving of Egypt. The last part of Passover celebrates the Israelites winning their final confrontation with the Egyptians at the Red Sea. Memorial prayers are recited in synagogue on the last day of Passover.

ii. Pentecost (Shavuot). This festival, properly called Shavuot, is the second pilgrimage festival and usually comes in late spring. Shavuot is connected to Passover via a counting procedure starting on the second day of Passover, when the forty-nine days leading up to Shavuot are counted in eager anticipation. The festival celebrates the giving of the Ten Commandments to the Israelites on Mount Sinai, as well as the bringing of the first fruits to Jerusalem. In Israel Shavuot is for one day; outside Israel it is a two-day festival. Its major focus is the study of the Ten Commandments, the study of the entire Bible, or any other related study. Shavuot celebrates the receiving of the Commandments of the Torah, showing appreciation by the careful study of them. Traditionally, the image of a mother's milk sustaining her child and nursing it into healthy existence has been seen as a metaphor for the Torah sustaining the Israelite community. This symbolism has given birth to the custom of having dairy products on Shavuot. Cheese cake, blintzes — crepes filled with cheese — and other dairy delicacies are served. In the synagogue the memorial service for the departed also is recited.

iii. Tabernacles (Sukkot). Sukkot, or Tabernacles, is the final pilgrimage festival. In all the pilgrimage festivals, in ancient times, the Israelite community would make a pilgrimage to Jerusalem to celebrate, hence the terminology pilgrimage festival. Today, lacking a temple, this is not done, but "pilgrimage" remains part of the basic terminology. Sukkot celebrates the sojourn of the Israelites in the wilderness for forty years following the Exodus and the protection that was given to them by God. For a seven-day period in Israel and an eight-day period outside Israel, families eat in a booth-like structure called a Sukkah, which is made of wood or canvas walls and a roof of foliage or detached wood. This flimsy structure symbolizes the idea that protection, peace, and harmony come not from living in sheltered homes, but in being able to live in the open without fear. Sukkot is thus a unique pilgrimage festival in that its theme is universal, namely the desire for global peace and harmony. The Sukkot festival comes in the fall and commences four full days after the conclusion of the Day of Atonement. Additionally, the Sukkot festival is distinguished through the practice of taking four different species—the palm branch, three myrtles, two willows, and a citron — and shaking them in all directions, as an expression of our request for a year in which the forces of nature, the winds, and the precipitation will be a blessing and a sustaining force. Sukkot also celebrates the ingathering, the final harvest, and thus, like its counterparts in pilgrimage, Passover and Shavuot, links together religious themes with nature themes. At the conclusion of the pilgrimage festival, on the eighth day, a special festival known as Shmini Atzeret, the eighth day of assembly, is celebrated. In the synagogue memorial prayers for the departed are recited, and in Israel the cycle of biblical readings is completed. Outside Israel the day after is relegated for this purpose. This day is referred to as Simchat Torah, which means the joy at celebrating the conclusion of the Bible, the Five Books of Moses. At that time the synagogue is filled with the rapturous noise of happy congregants who dance around the Scroll of Law, carry it around the congregation for everyone to embrace it, and who conclude and then restart immediately the new cycle of biblical readings from the story of the Creation. Simchat Torah ranks as one of the most joyous and celebrative days in the Jewish calendar.

d. Minor festivals. i. Hanukkah. The Feast of Lights, Hanukkah, is a minor festival in the Jewish calendar. It commences approximately two months after the conclusion of Simchat Torah. It is considered a minor festival since it is not mentioned in the Bible and is a postbiblical celebration of a historical event, the restoration of Jewish autonomy in Israel, and the rededication of the Temple after it had been hellenized by the Greeks (ca. 165 B.C.E.). Hanukkah today can occur any time in the month of December, and though it is a minor festival in

theological terms, its importance for many people has been escalated through its identification, mistakenly so, with the general celebrative atmosphere that prevails in Western society at that time. Being a minor festival, there are no work restrictions on Hanukkah; instead there are celebrative elements superimposed upon the eight-day Hanukkah period. Central to the celebration of Hanukkah is the kindling of the menorah, an eight-pronged candelabra which is lit, either through olive oil or candles, from the first day to the eighth, with each day bringing an additional light on the candelabra so that by the eighth day the entire candelabra of eight is kindled. This kindling is done at the very beginning of the evening by the entire family, and is followed by the singing of songs, the playing of games, and the eating of special Hanukkah delicacies, such as potato pancakes fried in oil. There is a tradition of giving money, called Hanukkah gelt, to the children on Hanukkah. Others give presents to their children, but the emphasis on presents has grown beyond proportion due to the fact that this is gift-giving time in society at large.

ii. Purim. Purim, or the Feast of Lots, is a minor festival occurring approximately one month before Passover, toward the end of the winter season. It celebrates a historical event that occurred prior to Hanukkah, about 450 B.C.E., the redemption of the Jewish community from an edict that would have brought about its total annihilation. The day prior to Purim is the Fast of Esther, a fast which starts in the morning and concludes in the evening and symbolizes the prayers of the Jewish community under seige in that era, prior to its redemption. Purim itself is an exuberant day, commencing with the synagogue reading of a megilla, or scroll, telling the entire Purim story from the very beginning to the exciting redemptive conclusion. Alms are given to the poor in a proportion beyond the normal, and foods of various types are sent from neighbor to neighbor in a spirit of camaraderie and sharing, which serves to project the joy, thankfulness, and gratitude for survival characteristic of this day.

iii. Other celebrations. There are other occasions for celebration in the Jewish calendar including Lag B'omer, the thirty-third day of the counting commencing on the second day of Passover. This day is celebrated as the conclusion of a plague that extracted a heavy toll of lives in the Jewish community in Talmudic times. Another minor festival is Tu B'Shevat, the fifteenth of Shevat, which occurs about a month and a half following Hanukkah. This is the new year for trees, and is celebrated through the eating of different types of fruits, usually at least fifteen, in an atmosphere of joy and thanksgiving for having been blessed with such healthy variety.

e. Fasts. Besides the Fast of Esther and the biblically mandated fast of the Day of Atonement, there are four additional fasts, all related to the destruction of the Temple and the eviction of the Jewish people from their homeland in Israel. The first in historical chronology is the fast of the tenth of Tevet, approximately one week after the conclusion of Hanukkah. Historically, that is the day when Jerusalem came under seige and was cut off from the rest of Israel. This marked the beginning of a long struggle, which was to end in destruction. The second fast, on the seventeenth day of Tammuz, called Shiva Asar B'Tammuz, occurs a bit more than a month after the conclusion of the Pentecost, or Shavuot, and ushers in three weeks of mourning for the destruction. The seventeenth of Tammuz is historically identified as the time when the first breach in the wall of Jerusalem was made, signaling the beginning of the end. The third fast comes at the culmination of the three weeks starting with Shiva Asar B'Tammuz; it is the lengthy fast of Tisha B'Av, commemorating the destruction of the Temple, first in 586 B.C.E. and then in 70 C.E. Like the Day of Atonement, and unlike all other fasts, it commences in the evening and continues for the entire day to an hour after sunset. This twenty-five hours plus fast is characterized by mourning and lamenting, the reading of the scroll describing the destruction of the Temple, and elegiac writings describing the destruction and human havoc that was wreaked. The day of Tisha B'Av is the most depressing day in the Jewish calendar year. Finally there is the Fast of Gedaliah, which occurs the day after Rosh Hashanah, and is historically the commemoration of the murder of the Governor Gedaliah, who had been appointed to administer over Jerusalem after the Babylonian exile. His murder signified the end of any vestige of Jewish rule over Israel and is lamented as placing the mark of finality on exile.

f. Modern celebrations. A few days after the conclusion of Passover there is a commemorative day of collective mourning the world over for the Holocaust, called Yom Hashoah. Commemorative events take place in all Jewish communities lamenting the murder of six million Jews and expressing the hope that the world will have learned the proper lessons from this tragedy so that in the future holocausts will never recur. A few days later, a little less than two weeks following the conclusion of Passover, is the day referred to as Yom Ha'Atzmaut, or Israel Independence Day. This too is celebrated the world over as the day when autonomy was restored to Israel, the land and the people, in 1948. The celebration of independence takes the form of additional liturgy in the synagogue giving praise and thanks, celebrative events in schools and synagogues, and a home atmosphere and celebrative meal expressing gratitude for this fortunate turning of the tide. Approximately one week before Shavuot the celebration of the reunification of Jerusalem, Yom Yerushalayim, is held. It too includes additional liturgy in the synagogue and celebrations in the synagogue, the school, and the home.

2. Implications for Non-Jewish Care of Jewish Individuals and Families. Knowledge of the general pattern of Jewish holy day and festival observances, and the rituals associated with them, as well as the relative importance of these days, is of great value in both active and reactive pastoral care. In active pastoral care, the advance knowledge that these days are approaching is useful information when a non-Jewish clergyperson ministers to a Jewish patient in a hospital that does not have a visiting rabbi. Simply coming in and asking the patient what can be done in order to make the holy day or festival more meaningful can do much to help a patient who may feel lonely and detached in the institution, removed from family and friends.

a. Hospital patients. A major problem facing the hospital or institutional chaplain, relative to the Jewish patient, is the patient's concern about missing an observance or a festival because of being hospitalized. *i. Sabbath.* A patient, such as a woman who has given birth to a child, who must stay in the hospital over the Sabbath, may be concerned about her inability to observe the Sabbath properly. There may be problems related to her desire for meals that accord with the Jewish tradition of dietary regulations. She may feel more comfortable if allowed to kindle the Sabbath candles in her room, assuming appropriate safety precautions are taken. Such a gesture gives the patient, otherwise detached from traditional expression, some anchor and foothold in that tradition, and helps to transform the hospital from four cold walls governed by unbreakable rules into a living, sensitive institution concerned for the entire patient including her (or his) religious needs.

ii. Rosh Hashanah and Yom Kippur. A person who is hospitalized over the period of Rosh Hashanah and Yom Kippur may feel terribly depressed at missing what are considered the highlights of the Jewish festival year. Since a high percentage of Jews attend the synagogue on these days and enjoy their families, these are the most difficult periods to be hospitalized. Pastoral care in the hospital should be sensitive to this and look for means to overcome the sense of deprivation. One way is to encourage the family to bring the meal to the hospital and celebrate it together with the patient in the room, assuming no objection from other patients. Failing that, the hospital may make a room available for that purpose. Additionally, the requirement to hear the sounds of the ram's horn on Rosh Hashanah is very important to some hospital patients, and arranging for a local person who is capable of blowing these sounds to do this in the hospital can be very important to the patient.

In the absence of these compensatory gestures, where the patient is incapable of handling a festive meal or hearing the sound of the ram's horn, or where these resources are not available, and the patient is alone and forlorn, it is important to stress the idea that getting well so that one can live is a very important value in Jewish life. The struggle to regain health so that one can observe next year what one is missing this year is in itself a noble expression of the commitment to life. Impressing the patient with this idea can perhaps mitigate the severity of the bad feeling. As always, simply allowing the patient to talk out what is really bothering him or her and what is really missing, and the hurt that is being experienced at being away from the action, is in itself very useful.

The inability of a patient to fast on the Day of Atonement, because medical reasons (e.g., diabetes) make it dangerous to fast, can present further problems. Fasting on the Day of Atonement is for many Jews the last frontier, that which differentiates between the totally assimilated and Jews who still have some semblance of adherence to tradition. The knowledge that one cannot fast thus comes as a terrible blow. This blow can be blunted, however, with an awareness that Jewish law actually forbids individuals to place themselves in danger; thus fasting on the Day of Atonement would be forbidden for an individual whose life would thereby be put at risk.

iii. Passover, Hanukkah, Purim. Hospitalization can also be distressing for an individual who because of illness cannot join in the celebration of the Passover Seder. The fact that the normal hospital diet includes leavened products such as bread makes this an especially difficult time. Making arrangements for food consistent with the Passover regulations can help. Providing Jewish patients with some form of Passover group Seder is also a possibility. In the case of Sukkot, when it is impractical to think of having the patient go out to sit in a tabernacle or booth, the shaking of the four species can easily be experienced in the hospital if arrangements are made. For celebrative events such as Hanukkah, allowing the patient to kindle his or her menorah in the hospital, and allowing family to join in the kindling, is useful in reducing the pain of being away from the home on this day. Arranging for a private reading of the book of Esther on Purim is also a helpful way of lifting the patient out of the detachment doldrums or depression. In all of these circumstances sensitivity to the religious needs of the patient, and reasonable attempts to satisfy them, can go a long way toward helping the patient feel at ease and spiritually strengthened, perhaps even more responsive to medical treatment.

b. Persons without families. Because most celebrations of Jewish festivals, holy days, and Sabbath are family-oriented, they are particularly trying times for individuals who live alone or for individuals who have recently gone through a traumatic experience like divorce or the loss of a mate. Experiencing these festivals as a single person or as a single parent with a child or children can be anxiety-provoking. In such circumstances there can be different reasons for these fears — various background traumas and hidden agenda that can conspire to create the problem. Here it is important to impress upon the individuals the need to carry on with the important aspects of their tradition in spite of such difficulties. The pastor who counsels persons in such a situation may also have avenues to the community that can be used to help the isolated person experience more social participation and encouragement. Particularly at a time of loss, when people are likely to question the meaning of life and the meaning of all that they have struggled for, it is sometimes difficult to help individuals feel motivated enough to go through such difficulties as preparing for Passover.

c. Prisoners. Those who attend to prisoners doing time in penal institutions can use their knowledge of the significance of the Day of Atonement to open up meaningful possibilities for the Jewish convict. The festival of freedom, Passover, can be celebrated not merely in its prescribed dimensions, but also as a time to become alert to the choice one can make, the choice to shake off the past and prepare for a more socially redeeming future.

d. The poor. Those who cannot afford to buy the extra food and drink to observe the Sabbath, holy days, or festivals properly pose a particular problem for the pastoral counselor. Some will even refuse handouts and prefer deprivation. Helping them feel a part of the community and a part of these special days is not an easy task. At the same time there are those who easily can afford to celebrate these times properly but who question their contemporary significance and value. Sometimes arranging for individuals from these opposite poles to meet, even to get together on these days, can naturally and effectively fill each one's void through the other's strength. The concerned chaplain or pastor with access to the community may arrange for the poor to be invited for festive celebrations or, when this is not possible, may recount some of the numerous tales of poverty confronted by Jews of yesteryear to make present difficulties more bearable.

e. The bereaved. In Jewish law, the seven-day period of mourning following the loss of a relative is abrogated by the Days of Awe or the Pilgrimage Festivals. A family in the midst of mourning is then obliged to radically shift emotional gears, from depression to celebration. This is what the law requires, but it is difficult to translate this into feeling and practice. Pastors involved with such families may empathize with their difficulty while at the same time reflecting on the primacy of community, one of the most deeply cherished values in the Jewish tradition of personal care. It is in community that one finds solace after the hammer blows of death, and if that community is celebrating, one should be part of that celebrating community. The celebrations carry the theme of continuity, a theme central to lifting the mourner out of the rut into a future orientation.

R. P. BULKA

JEWISH CARE AND COUNSELING (History, Traditions, and Contemporary Issues); JEWISH PRAYERS (Significance for Personal Care). *See also* BAR MITZVAH/BAT MITZVAH; CIRCUMCISION; FUNERAL AND BURIAL, JEWISH; REST AND RENEWAL, RELIGIOUS TRADITIONS OF; RITUAL AND PASTORAL CARE; TRADITION AS MODE OF CARE; WORSHIP AND CELEBRATION; WEDDING CEREMONY, JEWISH. *Compare* COMMUNITY, FELLOWSHIP, AND CARE; HOLIDAY DEPRESSION; LITURGICAL CALENDAR; SACRAMENTAL THEOLOGY AND PASTORAL CARE.

JEWISH LIFE. *See* JEWISH HOLY DAYS AND FESTIVALS; JEWISH PRAYERS.

JEWISH LITERATURE IN CARE AND COUNSELING. Counseling and care in the Jewish tradition have always been guided by the traditional literature which included the Bible, Mishnah, Talmud, Midrash, as well as the responsa, codes, and mystical and philosophical writings. The main guidance came from the *halakhic* (legal) literature, which provides a path through life.

Mishnah-Talmud (200–600 C.E.). All counseling efforts were provided with a biblical foundation, although the unsystematic approach of Scripture sometimes made this difficult. The foundation for such care was provided by the simplest and most widely read tractate of the Mishnah, the *Pirgê 'Avot*—the Ethics of the Fathers. In addition to its primary emphasis on learning, this slim book stresses interpersonal relationships as evidenced by such sayings as "Be of the disciples of Aaron, loving peace, pursuing it, loving your fellow creatures and drawing them near to the Torah" (*Pirgê 'Avot* 1.12). "If I am not for myself, who will be for me? But if I am only for myself, what am I? And if not now, when?" (*ibid.*, 1.14). "In a place where no one behaves like a human being, you must strive to be human" (*ibid.*, 2.6). "Those who bring serenity to others please God, but those who do not bring serenity do not please God" (*ibid.*, 3.13). "Do not try to placate your friends at the height of their anger. Do not attempt to comfort them in the first shock of bereavement. Do not question their sincerity at the moment when they make solemn promises. Do not be over eager to visit them in the hour of their disgrace" (*ibid.*, 4.23). Such statements sought mental health and personal guidance.

Counterparts to these statements may be found in virtually every section of the Talmud. Sometimes the emphasis is on *imitatio dei*, i.e., as God visited the sick, comforted mourners, and counseled the troubled, so should human beings (Babylonian Talmud, Shabbat 133b; Sotah 4a, Moed Gatan 27b; Mekhiltá Be Shalah 3.127; Leviticus Rabbah 34).

Specific tractates of the Talmud dealt with every aspect of marriage (*Ketuvot*), divorce (*Gitin*), death and burial (*Semahot*), as well as other critical junctures in the human life cycle.

The medieval codes (1100–1600 C.E.) dealt with many aspects of counseling and psychological/spiritual guidance indirectly. They treated crises of life in sections specifically associated with puberty, marriage, divorce, death, and mourning. The widely used codes, the *Shulhan A`rukh* (1567) by Joseph Caro and the earlier *Mishneh Torah* (1180) by Moses Maimonides, incorporated these concerns when they treated each of these matters, as well as illness. The clear topical arrangement makes such guidance very specific.

Responsa (500 C.E.–present). A clear picture of the problems which troubled Jews and the guidance suggested is provided by the responsa literature. Seven thousand volumes containing approximately 400,000 questions and answers by outstanding scholars from every age form this literature which continues to develop. Although the responsa literature ostensibly deals with issues of religious practice, personal status, and civil law, it frequently touches on issues of counseling (Freehof, 1962; J. Bazak, 1978).

Bibliography. J. Bazak, *Jewish Law and Jewish Life* (1979). S. B. Freehof, *A Treasury of Responsa* (1962). W. Jacob, ed., *American Reform Responsa: Jewish Questions, Rabbinic Answers* (1983). C. G. Montefiore and H. Loewe, *A Rabbinic Anthology* (1963).

W. JACOB

JEWISH CARE AND COUNSELING (History, Traditions, and Contemporary Issues). *Compare* CLASSIC LITERATURE IN CARE AND COUNSELING; JEWISH PRAYERS (Significance for Personal Care); JUDAISM AND PSYCHOLOGY; PASTORALIA.

JEWISH MINISTRY. *See* RABBI/RABBINATE.

JEWISH PRAYERS (Significance for Personal Care). Acknowledge God's majesty, affirm one's covenantal relationship with God, and are conversation with God on one's present state, both in times of crisis and otherwise.

Prayer as a form of request usually addresses itself to situations of need, particularly the need for recovery from ill health, or a spiritual need for God's presence in times of crisis, such as when facing death. The book of Psalms is a rich and much used resource for such prayer.

The major prayer text concerned with request is the *Amidah*, eighteen benedictions recited thrice daily, containing many requests, including a general request-blessing for restoration to health, as well as a more general request-blessing that God heed the pleas of the one praying.

It is common practice to recite public prayers on a sick person's behalf, usually in the form of a special prayer text called a *Mi Shebayrakh*. One directly asks that God who blessed our ancestral parents now bestow recovery on the one named who is ill. Those who hear that others have recited prayers on their behalf feel encouraged by this significant and earnest gesture. Similarly, in Jewish tradition, the ennobled mitzvah (religious fulfillment) of visiting the sick is not complete until the visitor shares the pain and needs of the sick by prayer on behalf of that individual.

The *Blessing of Thanksgiving* is recited within a community of at least ten (a minyan or quorum), usually in the midst of prayer services, by an individual who has recovered from an illness. It involves thanks for God's kindness in making recovery possible. The congregants celebrate the return to health by responding, "May God who has bestowed upon you all this good, continue to bestow good upon you."

The *confession* is appropriate for recitation when a person is clearly nearing death. Appropriate circumspection should be exercised when using this prayer, since the news of possible imminent death can be devastating. Consequently, the sick individual who is asked to recite the confessional is told that many who have confessed have risen up from their illness, while many who have failed to confess die anyway. Thus, confession is appropriate not simply because death could be imminent but because it is an appropriate time to do stocktaking for the life lived and for the life still to come. The official confessional text includes a request for forgiveness of sins of commission and omission, together with a resolution to refrain from future wrongdoing. This is coupled with a request for recovery from illness and a statement that if death is imminent, it should be an atonement for one's sins. If a family is present when their relative passes away, it is proper to rend one's garments and to recite the *blessing*, pronouncing God as ruler of the universe and truthful judge (Dayan haEmet). This is an affirmation of faith and acceptance of heavenly judgment, even in the most painful of situations.

The *Kaddish* or sanctification prayer is recited by close relatives of the deceased, and a quorum during regular prayer services for an eleven-month period following death. The Kaddish makes no direct reference to the deceased but instead speaks of the majesty and glory of God and the hopes for ultimate peace and tranquility. It affirms the unconditional meaningfulness of life in spite of the trying circumstance and serves to bring some spiritual edification and comfort to those mourning the loss of a loved one. The *Yizkor* or memorial prayer directly intercedes on behalf of the deceased by name, and is a traditional text that is recited on major festivals in synagogues. This prayer can also be recited at home if the person memorializing cannot attend synagogue.

Prayer as request, in the context of affirming God's majesty and one's covenantal link with God, is well entrenched in Jewish tradition. The general rule is that one's own prayer is preferable to one recited by others.

R. P. BULKA

JEWISH CARE AND COUNSELING (History, Traditions, and Contemporary Issues); JEWISH LITERATURE IN CARE AND COUNSELING. See also JEWISH HOLY DAYS AND FESTIVALS; PRAYER; RITUAL AND PASTORAL CARE; YIZKOR.

JEWISH RITUALS. See JEWISH HOLY DAYS AND FESTIVALS. See also JEWISH PRAYERS.

JEWISH THEOLOGY. See THEOLOGY, JEWISH.

JOHN XXIII, POPE. See VATICAN COUNCIL II; also HISTORY OF ROMAN CATHOLIC PASTORAL CARE (United States).

JOHN OF THE CROSS, ST. (1542–91). Carmelite reformer, poet, and theologian. Ordained a priest in 1567 after studies at the University of Salamanca (Spain), he was persuaded to join the Discalced ("shoeless") reform of the Carmelite Order by St. Theresa of Avila. In 1571 he became rector of the Carmelite house at Alcala and also served as spiritual director and confessor to the Carmelite convent at Avila. He spent most of 1575 in a monastic prison, incarcerated by friars who resisted the reformation of the Carmelites. When the order was officially divided, he served the reformed branch in a variety of offices until, toward the end of his life, he was banished to the town of Ubeda (where he died) after a jurisdictional dispute in the order.

John of the Cross combined the instincts of a poet and the rigorous training of the scholastic theologian. His most famous works, *The Ascent of Mount Carmel, The Dark Night, The Spiritual Canticle*, and *The Living Flame of Love*, consisted of his lyrical poems (some composed while imprisoned) with prose commentaries. John of the Cross is regarded as one of Spain's greatest poets and an original theologian of spirituality. He was canonized a saint in 1726 and two centuries later, in 1926, declared a Doctor of the Church.

Bibliography. G. Brenan, *St. John of the Cross: His Life and Poetry* (1973).

L. S. CUNNINGHAM

SPIRITUALITY (Roman Catholic Tradition)

JOHNSON, PAUL E. (1898–1974). American Methodist pastor, pastoral theologian, and professor of the psychology of religion at Boston University. Johnson attempted to continue and deepen the tradition of personalist theology at Boston University, where he was trained as a philosopher of religion, completing a doctoral dissertation under Edgar Sheffield Brightman on the topic of Josiah Royce's philosophical idealism. As a professor of psychology and pastoral counseling, he tried to combine personalist thought with dynamic psychol-

ogy. In his *Psychology of Pastoral Care* (1953), he drew on the client-centered therapeutic techniques of Carl Rogers, but by 1967 Johnson had decided that Rogerian methods were unduly individualistic and self-centered. He called his proposed alternative "neopersonalism" or "dynamic interpersonalism." It was a "theology of relationship," reflecting the personalist argument that the external world was the visible expression of an underlying Mind and that the investigation of finite minds could provide evidence by which to derive inferences about ultimate reality. Johnson proposed to enrich personalism by looking closely at unconscious dynamics and interpersonal relationships, hoping that a more adequate psychology might furnish useful images and metaphors for the theologian.

He hoped, as well, that such a synthesis of the personalist and psychodynamic traditions would provide a "theology for the counselor." He sought a theology that could guide a program of "responsive counseling," in which each person in a counseling interview would continually listen and respond to the other. Such a theology was necessary, he thought, to help liberal Protestantism move beyond client-centered therapy. Impressed by both humanistic and interpersonal psychologies, Johnson accented the possibilities of growth within relationships to other persons. He drew on the interpersonal psychologies of Harry Stack Sullivan, Gordon Allport, and Fritz Kunkel; the role-playing theories of Jacob Moreno; the logotherapy of Victor Frankl; and the religious thought of Martin Buber. From such sources, he developed in his *Person and Counselor* (1967) the position that the essential nature of persons was shaped in their encounters with other persons. And he maintained always an optimistic confidence in the capacities of the growing personality.

Having served as a missionary teacher at West China Union University from 1925 to 1927 and as a dean and professor at the Methodist Morningside College from 1936 to 1941, Johnson maintained a strong affection for the church and a deep interest in theological education. He introduced Clinical Pastoral Education (CPE) at the Boston University School of Theology shortly after his arrival there in 1941, and in 1944 he was a co-founder, with Rollin Fairbanks, of the Institute of Pastoral Care, which organized clinical training programs for theological students. He was instrumental also in the merger in 1967 of various clinical programs into the Association for Clinical Pastoral Education. As a clinical educator, he always placed the emphasis on the training of pastors for the church. From 1952 through 1963, he directed the Danielson Pastoral Counseling Service, a center for pastoral counseling in Boston. As a writer, teacher, and administrator of clinical programs, Johnson was one of the half dozen leading figures in the early years of the postwar pastoral counseling movement in the U.S.

E. B. HOLIFIELD

HISTORY OF PROTESTANT PASTORAL CARE (United States); PASTORAL CARE MOVEMENT; PASTORAL THEOLOGY, PROTESTANT; PSYCHOLOGY IN AMERICAN RELIGION; THEOLOGICAL EDUCATION AND THE PASTORAL CARE MOVEMENT, PROTESTANT. See also DYNAMIC INTERPERSONALISM; PERSONALISM AND PASTORAL CARE.

JOKES/JOKING. *See* HUMOR; WIT AND HUMOR IN PASTORAL CARE.

JOURNAL KEEPING. The journal, a personal record of one's thoughts, experiences, and inspirations, may be one of the oldest forms of literature. It records events, activities, ideas, feelings, struggles, and meaning in one's life, and may take the form of art, poetry, prayers, and oral narratives. In the religious sphere the first chapters of Genesis, the prayers of the psalmists, and the poetry of the prophets, all have the character of journal entries. The personal intensity of a journal stands out in the autobiographical writings of Paul, the meditations of the fourth Gospel writer, and the visions of John on Patmos. This tradition of studied, personal reflection on life continues in the *Philokalia* (an anthology of Orthodox spiritual writing compiled by Fr. Nicodemus of the Holy Mountain in 1782) in the East and journals of Wesley (1903), Fox, more recently Dag Hammarskjöld (1965), and a number of others.

Journals may be classified into three forms according to the intention of the writer: historical, psychological, and spiritual. An *historical journal* consists mostly of the recording of events and their meaning. Wesley's journal, for example, records the places he preached, the number of persons present, and their reaction to the message. A typical entry is that of his conversion. "Wed. May 24. I think it was about five in the morning that I opened my Testament on these words, 'There are given unto us exceeding great and precious promises, . . . ' (2 Peter 1:4). . . . In the evening I went very unwillingly to a society in Aldersgate-street, where one was reading Luther's preface to the Epistle to the Romans. . . . I felt I did trust in Christ, Christ alone, for my salvation; and an assurance was given me that he had taken away my sin, even mine, and saved me from the law of sin and death."

The *psychological journal*, or "intensive journal," is a process of journal writing developed by Ira Progoff (1975), a Jungian psychologist. Using the insights of depth psychology, she outlined a procedure for integrating one's life experience through a carefully structured form of journal writing. Progoff invites the journal keeper to write dialogues with wisdom figures, parents, and symbols, etc., akin to Fritz Perl's Gestalt technique (1969). Material for the dialogues is drawn from major events, important persons, dreams, intuitions, imaginative constructions, and the data of social, personal, religious, and bodily existence. The data-gathering suggestions of Progoff as well as the techniques of processing it will be beneficial to the keeper of a spiritual journey. Morton Kelsey (1980) embraces these techniques, but employs them in specifically Christian ways.

A *spiritual journal* intentionally relates the data of one's life to God. Since Progoff's technique suggests a process which permits the religious dimension to surface, it would be a mistake to distinguish completely the psychological and the spiritual journal. The intentions differ: in the former, the writer aims at the actualization of the potential of life — the individuation of self in a wholistic, creative way — whereas the writer of the spiritual journal endeavors to see all of life from God and to relate all of life to God, thus including the wholistic

individuation of the psychological journal, but placing the task within a spiritual (theological) perspective.

The spiritual journal finds theological grounding in the incarnation, presupposing that nature, history, and human relationships can each be a bearer of the divine presence. It takes seriously the actual experience of one's life, the failures to fulfill noble intentions, and reflections on Scripture and offers a place to record dreams and intuitions which may offer guidance for crucial decisions in life and prayers. It provides a matrix to pull together the fragments of a life, a place to reflect intensely upon a single day, to express prayers and ejaculations of praise (Johnson).

The spiritual journal provides a way of in-depth reflection on Scripture (Loyola; Wink). The imaginative projection of oneself into the biblical narrative and the writing of dialogues with Christ provide a fresh existential encounter with Scripture, dimension of self-revelation, and perhaps a revelation of God as well. The journal maintains a record of dreams, intuitions, and hunches which often hold outlines of the future. Recording these data, reflecting on them, and listening to the intuitions which they inspire, shape a perspective. If unrecorded, these images slip easily from consciousness.

The journal is a place for the serious person to record the significant data of his or her life, to seek its meaning, to struggle with self and God, to refine the definition of self, God, and perhaps the meaning of one's life. The intensive spiritual journal appears to be the twentieth century's greatest contribution to the great store of methods of spiritual formation.

Bibliography. D. Hammarskjöld, *Markings* (1965). Ignatius of Loyola, *The Spiritual Exercises* (1968). B. C. Johnson, *To Will God's Will: Beginning the Spiritual Journey* (1987). M. T. Kelsey, *Adventure Inward* (1980). F. Perls, *Gestalt Therapy Verbatim* (1969). I. Progoff, *At A Journal Workshop* (1975). G. F. Simons, *Keeping Your Personal Journal* (1978). J. Wesley, *The Heart of Wesley's Journal* (1903). W. Wink, *The Bible in Human Transformation* (1973).

B. C. JOHNSON

MEDITATION; SELF-EXAMINATION; SPIRITUAL DISCIPLINE AND GROWTH. *See also* FORMATIVE SPIRITUALITY; PERSONAL STORY, SYMBOL, AND MYTH IN PASTORAL CARE.

JOURNALS IN COUNSELING AND PSYCHOTHERAPY. Periodicals, usually published quarterly, sometimes semiannually, containing articles to keep professional and special-interest groups abreast of current developments in their respective fields. The journals are targeted for specific audiences. (1) Those published for practitioners within mental health disciplines, such as clinical psychology, psychiatry, and family therapy. These journals, often the official organs of professional organizations such as the American Psychological Association, contain articles examining the theoretical, empirical, clinical, ethical, and legal issues surrounding each of these counseling fields. (2) Journals targeted for adherents of different theoretical approaches to personality and psychotherapy, such as psychoanalysis, Adlerian psychology, or Rational-Emotive Therapy. Articles in these journals tend to focus upon clinical applications and extensions or revisions of the theory; empirical research is usually a secondary emphasis. (3) Journals directed toward those interested in particular subject areas, such as schizophrenia, alcoholism, or gerontology.

In general, those journals which aim at a more specialized audience assume a greater level of sophistication in their readership. Interdisciplinary journals (for example, see section 2 in the listing below) are directed toward a broad spectrum of readers in several professions, and thus are usually easier for a novice to understand. More specialized journals, targeted for members of a particular organization, or practitioners of particular professions or specializations, may require a prior understanding of the technical vocabulary and theoretical concepts used by persons in that field. Empirical articles, which report the findings of scientific and quasi-scientific studies, require that the reader possess some working knowledge of statistical and research methodology. Clinical articles, while often containing illuminating case studies, are best assimilated by practitioners who are already familiar with the particular syndrome being discussed. A reader interested in a journal should examine a copy to determine if it is suitable for someone of his or her level of training.

Many journals also publish special issues which focus on more narrowly defined topics of interest within the journal's generally broader scope. Thus, a psychotherapy journal may devote an entire issue to the treatment of a particular syndrome. Journals may also publish posthumous memorial issues which review the contributions of key figures in a journal's field. These special issues are usually available for back order from the publisher as single copies, without a subscription.

Below is a selective listing of journals which are directly or indirectly related to the practice of counseling and psychotherapy in a pastoral setting. The list is divided into four sections according to the journals' emphasis or type: counseling psychology, integrative approaches, topical journals, and psychotherapeutic orientations. Not included are journals directly in the fields of pastoral care and counseling and marriage and family therapy, which are surveyed in separate articles. Each journal title is followed by a code letter to indicate the type and balance of articles to be found in a typical issue, as follows:

A = Strong emphasis on empirical research, requiring a higher level of expertise.

B = The journal contains a rough balance of emphasis on theoretical, clinical, and empirical issues.

C = Primarily theoretical and/or clinical; prints empirical articles only occasionally.

D = Little or no empirical content.

N = The journal is new; balance of content unknown.

All journals are quarterly unless otherwise identified.

1. Counseling Psychology.

American Journal of Psychotherapy (D). Association for the Advancement of Psychotherapy.

Journal of Counseling Psychology (A). American Psychological Association. Occasionally prints articles dealing with religious issues.

Psychotherapy (B). The Journal of the Division of Psychotherapy, American Psychological Association, occasionally publishes issues on psychotherapy and religion.

2. Integrative Approaches.
These are interdisciplinary journals addressing the interface of psychology and religion in theory and practice.

Counseling and Values (B). American Association for Counseling and Development. Official journal of the Association for Religious and Value Issues in Counseling, a division of the 56,000 member AACD. Semiannual.

Journal of Psychology and Christianity (B). Christian Association for Psychological Studies. Official journal of CAPS, a multidisciplinary organization of Christians in the helping professions.

Journal of Psychology and Theology (B). Rosemead School of Psychology. Contains extensive reviews of relevant books; also has a helpful "journal file" summarizing articles of interest from other publications.

Journal of Religion and Health (C). Human Sciences Press. Published in cooperation with the Institutes of Religion and Health. More eclectic in orientation than the previous two.

3. Topical Journals.
There are journals for nearly every area of study. Six such areas related to pastoral care are represented below.

Child Abuse and Neglect, The International Journal (B). Pergamon Journals, Inc.

Journal of Chemical Dependency Treatment (N). Haworth Press. "This new journal provides focused thematic issues dealing with practical clinical topics for drug abuse/ substance abuse counselors and treatment professionals." Emphasis upon clinical method with particular problems. Semiannual.

Journal of Divorce (C). Haworth Press. A valuable resource regarding special therapeutic and legal issues surrounding divorce.

Journal of Interpersonal Violence (B). Sage Publications. Focuses on both victims of violence and victimizers.

Journal of Religion and Aging (B). Haworth Press. Addresses issues related to pastoral care of the elderly.

Suicide and Life-Threatening Behavior (B). Guilford Publications. Publication of the American Association of Suicidology.

4. Psychotherapeutic Orientations.
Adherents of particular theories of personality and psychotherapy may wish to examine the following:

Contemporary Psychoanalysis (D). William Alanson White Institute. The Institute offers psychoanalytic training to practitioners from many professions, including ministers.

The Gestalt Journal (D). Center for Gestalt Development. Semiannual.

Individual Psychology: The Journal of Adlerian Theory, Research, and Practice (B). University of Texas Press. Published for the North American Society of Adlerian Psychology.

Journal of Humanistic Psychology (D). Sage Publications. Official journal of the Association for Humanistic Psychology. Co-founded by Abraham Maslow.

Journal of Rational-Emotive Therapy (C). Human Sciences Press. Sponsored by the Institute for Rational-Emotive Therapy. Semiannual.

Transactional Analysis Journal (B). International Transactional Analysis Association.

C. LEE

PSYCHOTHERAPY AND COUNSELING (Research Studies and Methods).

JOURNALS IN MARRIAGE AND FAMILY

COUNSELING. By definition, the field of marriage and family studies is an eclectic discipline. As a result it draws its information and analysis from most of the social and behavioral sciences. However, several journals have emerged that focus primarily on the field itself. Of the many that have emerged, eight are listed here as well as the major inventory in the contemporary field.

(1) *Journal of Marriage and the Family (JMF)*. Published by the National Council on Family Relations, *JMF* is the primary authoritative research publication in the field. Dominated by the discipline of family sociology, its studies are technical in nature, sophisticated in style, and typically difficult for an educated layperson to grasp.

(2) *Family Relations (FR)*. Published by the National Council on Family Relations, *FR* focuses upon both research and application in the field of marriage and family from a less technical perspective. It is especially useful to those who are interested in education and the application of family research to practical settings.

(3) *Family Process (FP)*. This journal was founded jointly by two distinguished institutions in the field of marriage and the family: the Ackerman Institute for Family Therapy in New York and the Mental Research Institute of Palo Alto, California. *FP* provides a broad range of topics written from a wide spectrum of perspectives. Its emphasis upon the family as a system, as suggested by the journal's name, delineates its importance. Although less technical than *JMF*, its topics are often sophisticated and ethereal. *FP* is on the forefront of dialogue in the field.

(4) *Journal of Family Issues (JFI)*. Published by Sage Publications and sponsored by the National Council on Family Relations, this relatively new journal focuses upon issues such as remarriage and power and the family. Although *JFI* reports both qualitative and quantitative research, its editors attempt to provide a broad range of opinion and style for each topic. Typically, research is reported in such a way as to make it understandable and applicable to a lay public.

(5) *Marriage and Family Review (MFR)*. This journal, published by the Haworth Press, typically focuses upon a single topic per issue. Thus, topics such as "obesity and the family" and "women and the family" are covered in relative depth. The style is usually accessible to a layperson.

(6) *American Journal of Family Therapy (AJFT)*. Published in association with the Academy of Family Psychology and the American Board of Family Psychology, this journal focuses upon family therapy as a discipline within the field of psychology. Its topics reflect a broad range of interests and, in the past, also reflected an international perspective. Both the style and content of *AJFT* require some degree of sophistication regarding psychotherapy and relevant research methodologies.

(7) *Journal of Marriage and Family Therapy (JMFT)*. Published by the American Association of Marriage and Family Therapy, *JMFT* purports to be the authoritative publication for the discipline of marriage and family therapy. Its articles are written from a somewhat technical perspective, which makes some knowledge of family psychotherapy desirable. It offers a variety of both broad and more focused articles.

(8) *Journal of Divorce (JD)*. Also published by the Haworth Press, this journal provides an interdisciplinary forum for clinical studies and research in family therapy, family mediation, family studies, and family law. It is relevant to marriage and family counseling in that it provides authoritative articles on issues such as postdivorce adjustment, parent-child relationships, the impact of sex-role attitudes in divorce, and personality issues in marital discord. The articles are technical in nature and usually provide concrete statistical data on each topic.

(9) *Journal of Family Psychology (JFP)*. A recently constituted journal of the Family Psychology Division of the American Psychological Association, *JFP* emphasizes dialogue between different perspectives.

(10) *Inventory of Marriage and Family Literature (IMFL)*. Produced in cooperation with the University of Minnesota, this Sage Publication is an invaluable research tool. As a whole, the inventory classifies research publications in the field of marriage and family from 1900 to the present. *IMFL* is updated every two or three years. Topics are identified by subject, author, and key word in context. It is expensive, but is usually available at major research libraries.

D. GUERNSEY

FAMILY THEORY AND THERAPY; MARRIAGE COUNSELING AND MARITAL THERAPY.

JOURNALS IN PASTORAL CARE AND COUN-

SELING. The article surveys periodicals published regularly in the U.S. and Canada, focusing on the practice of pastoral care, pastoral counseling, Clinical Pastoral Education (CPE), and closely related subjects.

1. Professional Practice and Supervision in Pastoral Counseling and Clinical Pastoral Education (CPE). The oldest journal in pastoral care and counseling and CPE is the *Journal of Pastoral Care (JPC)*, established in 1947 under the editorship of Rollin J. Fairbanks. For three decades this journal has been the most comprehensive and authoritative professional periodical in the field. It is jointly published by the American Association of Pastoral Counselors (AAPC), the American Protestant Correctional Chaplains Association (APCCA), the Association for Clinical Pastoral Education (ACPE), the Association of Mental Health Clergy (AMHC), and the Canadian Association for Pastoral Education (CAPE), the College of Chaplains of the American Protestant Health Association (CC of APHA), the National Association of Catholic Chaplains (NACC), and the National Institute of Business and Industrial Chaplains, Inc. (NIBIC). It is issued quarterly.

In 1947 the Institute of Pastoral Care began publication of *JPC*; that same year the Council for Clinical Training started the *Journal of Clinical Pastoral Work*. In 1950 these groups merged the two publications into one, calling it the *Journal of Pastoral Care*. In 1967 *JPC* became the official publication of ACPE. In 1969 AAPC began offering the journal to its membership, and in 1972 CAPE did the same. During 1983–85 the ownership of the journal was transferred from ACPE to a joint board of managers representing the five groups listed above.

Ernest E. Bruder edited *JPC* between 1950–64. After 1964 publication was directed by an editorial committee chaired by Charles E. Hall (1965), Thomas W. Klink (1966–70), Charles W. Stewart (1970–71), Edward E. Thornton (1971–74), and John H. Patton (1974–83), and Orlo Strunk (1984–present).

Abstracts of Research in Pastoral Care and Counseling is published each spring by the Joint Council on Research in Pastoral Care and Counseling with assistance from the Virginia Institute of Pastoral Care. Issues published 1972–78 were titled *Pastoral Care and Counseling Abstracts*. Member organizations of the Joint Council include AAPC, ACPE, Association of Mental Health Clergy, College of Chaplains, American Protestant Hospital Association, Institute for Research in Pastoral Psychology of Garrett-Evangelical Theological Seminary, U.S. Army Chaplain Corps, and the U.S. Navy Chaplain Corps. Each annual issue reports published, unpublished, and in-progress research for the preceding calendar year. Editors have been John L. Florell (1972–78), Richard E. Augspurger (1978–79), Clinton D. McNair (1980), and W. Victor Maloy (1981–present).

Three other journals representing a smaller professional constituency and circulation can be grouped with the above journals. *Pilgrimage: Psychotherapy and Personal Exploration* was inaugurated by the Pastoral Counseling and Consultation Centers of Greater Washington in 1972 edited by Charles Jaekle. It has given primary attention to the personal experience of the therapist and/or the client. David Barstow succeeded Jaekle as editor in 1976. In 1980 Human Sciences Press assumed publication of *Pilgrimage*.

The *Journal of Supervision and Training in Ministry* first appeared in 1978. Edited by David C. Myler, Jr., published annually, and sponsored by the North Central Region of the AAPC and by the Central Region of the AAPC, its purpose is "to preserve our oral tradition . . . and to extend our knowledge and practice through . . . new approaches to supervision and training." George Fitchett became editor in 1983.

The *Journal of Pastoral Counseling* was started in 1966 as the *Iona Journal of Pastoral Counseling* by the Graduate Division of Pastoral Counseling, Iona College, New Rochelle, New York. The Graduate Division of Pastoral Counseling is staffed primarily by clinical psychologists who supervise graduate students toward an M.S. in pastoral counseling. Editors of the journal have been Vincent S. Conigilaro, M.D. (1966–68), E. Mark Stern (1968–76), Robert A. Burns (1976–84), and Samuel M. Natale (1984–present).

2. Pastoral Care in Parish Ministries. More than any other journal in pastoral care and counseling, *Pastoral Psychology* (PP) has consistently attempted to relate the behavioral sciences and theology to pastoral ministry in the parish setting. *PP* first appeared in February 1950, produced monthly (except July-August) by the Pulpit Digest Publishing Co., with Simon Doniger as editor. Seward Hiltner, influential in the formation of the journal, became its pastoral consultant in May 1950. Charles Wheeler Scott succeeded Doniger as editor in 1969 and remained editor until 1972. James N. Lapsley succeeded Hiltner as pastoral consultant in 1969.

The Meredith Corporation assumed publication of the journal in 1965, but by 1972 decided to discontinue it. Three years later John P. Kildahl facilitated conversations between Behavioral Publications and Seward Hiltner, and James Lapsley of Princeton Theological Seminary. The outcome was a revival of *PP* in the fall of 1975 as a quarterly publication. Human Sciences Press published it and Princeton Theological Seminary provided sponsorship. In the first issue of the revived *PP* the new editor, Liston O. Mills, stated that the journal would maintain the direction of the previous publication with a commitment "to bring psychological and social science wisdom into . . . conversation with the work of ministry and to interpret this relation in pastoral, psychological, and theological terms." Lewis Rambo became editor in 1984.

3. Associations and Societies Related to the Field of Pastoral Care and Counseling. The *Journal of Religion and Health* (*JRH*), published quarterly by the Institutes of Religion and Health, represents professional interests of those who work in the area of religion and health. *JRH* began in October 1961 as a publication of the Academy of Religion and Mental Health (founded in 1954). Its purpose was "to correlate . . . medicine, the behavioral sciences, theology, and philosophy." In 1972 the Academy merged with the American Foundation of Religion and Psychiatry (founded in 1937 and affiliated with the Blanton-Peele Graduate Institute) to form the Institutes of Religion and Health, the present sponsor of the journal. Harry C. Meserve has been editor from the founding of the journal. In 1978 Human Sciences Press assumed publications of *JRH* with the Institutes as a "cooperating agency."

The *Journal of Health Care Chaplaincy* "is devoted to promoting both foundational and applied interdisciplinary research related to chaplaincy as practiced in community hospitals, medical centers, nursing homes, and other health care institutions."

The *Journal for the Scientific Study of Religion* was first issued in October 1961. It is published quarterly by the Society for the Scientific Study of Religion (founded in 1949). The Society's purpose "is to stimulate and communicate significant scientific research on religious institutions and experience." Editors have been Prentiss L. Pemberton (1961–65), Samuel Klausner (1965), James Dittes (1965–72), Benton Johnson (1972–75), Richard L. Gorsuch (1975–79), Phillip E. Hammond (1979–83), and Donald Capps (1983–88).

Human Development is published quarterly by the Jesuit Educational Center for Human Development and is "concerned with interpreting the wealth of information in psychology, medicine and psychiatry impacting on the work of persons engaged in spiritual guidance and counseling." James J. Gill has been editor from the first issue in 1981.

The *Journal of Psychology and Judaism* publishes clinical as well as more philosophical articles on the relationship between psychology and Judaism, with a special interest in the "development of integrated approaches to uniquely Jewish problems in the clinical and meta-clinical realms." Now published by Human Sciences Press, *JPJ* has been edited by Reuven Bulka since its founding in 1976.

4. Pastoral Care and Counseling and Theology. The *Journal of Psychology and Theology*, begun in 1973, published quarterly by the Rosemead School of Psychology, Biola University, is "an evangelical forum for the integration of psychology and theology." It seeks "to place before the evangelical community articles that have bearing on the nature of man from a biblical perspective." Bruce Narramore, editor 1973–77, states that when integrating psychology and the Bible the first essential attitude "is a respect for the complete inspiration and authority of the Scriptures." Narramore was succeeded by J. Roland Fleck (1978–82) and William F. Hunter (1982–present).

Also representing the evangelical community, but perhaps more liberal theologically is the *Journal of Psychology and Christianity*, published quarterly by the Christian Association for Psychological Studies (CAPS). *JPC* is designed to "provide current scholarly exchange among Christian professionals in the Helping Professions." Publication began in 1982, continuing The Bulletin of the CAPS, with J. Harold Ellens as editor (1982–present).

R. L. HESTER

PASTORAL CARE MOVEMENT; PASTORAL CARE (Contemporary Methods, Perspectives, and Issues); PASTORAL COUNSELING MOVEMENT; PSYCHIATRY AND PASTORAL CARE; RELIGION AND PSYCHOTHERAPY. *See also* AMERICAN ASSOCIATION OF PASTORAL COUNSELORS; ASSOCIATION FOR CLINICAL PASTORAL EDUCATION; CANADIAN PASTORAL CARE MOVEMENT. *Compare* JEWISH CARE AND COUNSELING.

JOURNALS IN RELIGION, THEOLOGY, AND THE SOCIAL SCIENCES, INTERDISCIPLINARY. These journals, while not specifically concerned with pastoral care and counseling and therefore directed toward a different audience, have a proven history of publishing quality articles on topics of interest to those involved in pastoral care. While not every issue will have an article of direct relevance to this field, each volume of these journals normally includes one or more articles or reviews that are of significant value to pastoral care and counseling. The following is a selective list of such journals.

1. Journals in Religion. Among journals in religion published in the U.S., probably the most useful to those engaged in pastoral care are the *Journal of Religion*, published by the Divinity School of the University of Chicago; the *Journal of the American Academy of Religion*, the official journal of a professional society comprised of college, university, and seminary professors; and *Soundings*, which is supported by the Society for Values in Higher Education. All three publish interdisciplinary articles in religion and psychology, and also regularly publish articles on ethical issues of direct concern to pastoral counselors and chaplains. Articles on religion and psychology in all three journals tend to reflect the orientation of members of their sponsoring organizations, in that most articles are based on depth or developmental psychology. Articles dealing with Freud, Jung, Hillman, Erikson, and Lifton are the most common. A resurgence of interest in William James is also evident. A fourth journal, *Religious Studies*, published in England and widely circulated in North America, is also of interest to those engaged in pastoral care, because it

addresses interdisciplinary issues and periodically publishes comprehensive articles on the relationship between religious studies and psychology. It reflects the resurgence of interest in psychology of religion in Great Britain.

2. Journals in Theology. Of the many journals of theology published in the U.S., perhaps the most useful to those engaged in pastoral care are *Theology Today*, published by Princeton Theological Seminary, the *Union Seminary Quarterly Review*, the successor to *Religion in Life*, and *Interpretation*, a biblical journal that attempts to relate biblical studies to pastoral practice in the contemporary world. These journals have a seminary orientation in common (unlike the previous group, which are more oriented to the university), and therefore publish articles that are more directly concerned with the church and its ministry. Of the four, *Theology Today* and *Interpretation* are perhaps the most consistently valuable; the former periodically publishes sets of articles on critical pastoral and ethical issues (e.g., religion and pain), and the latter has published articles by pastoral theologians. Many other theology journals could be cited, such as *Andover Newton Quarterly*, *Anglican Theological Review*, and *Word and World* (a Lutheran publication).

3. Social-Scientific Journals. Among journals with a social-scientific orientation, the most valuable for those engaged in pastoral care are the *Review of Religious Research* and the *Journal of the Scientific Study of Religion*. The *Review of Religious Research*, published by the Religious Research Association, contains articles on such topics as the role and gender of clergy in the contemporary church, reasons for church growth and decline, and recent trends in personal religious commitment. Many of its articles are based on empirical research conducted under the auspices of major denominations in the U.S. and Canada, and therefore address issues of church policy. It is a good indicator of what denominational leaders and their staffs are concerned about now and in the near-to-distant future. One of the most valuable features of this journal is its publication of abstracts of recently completed Doctor of Ministry Projects and relevant articles published in other social-scientific journals.

The *Journal of the Scientific Study of Religion*, published by the Society for the Scientific Study of Religion, comprises articles by sociologists, anthropologists, and psychologists of religion. While sociological studies predominate, it is the major journal in the U.S. for empirically oriented studies in psychology of religion, many of which have direct implications for pastoral care. Some examples include articles on death attitudes and personal faith, religious affiliation and psychiatric diagnoses, and attributions of responsibility to God for severe medical problems. This journal also regularly publishes reviews of books in psychology of religion, including books that reflect psychological orientations outside the empirically oriented psychology of religion reflected in its articles. Books on depth and developmental psychology are regularly reviewed.

4. Other Relevant Journals. Other journals that do not fit neatly into one of the above categories, yet are very relevant to pastoral care, are *Religious Studies Review*, *Religious Education*, and the *Journal of Psychology and Theology*. *Religious Studies Review*, published by the Council on the Study of Religion, is a quarterly review journal that attempts to review all recent scholarly books on religion. It includes brief review notes on psychology of religion and some pastoral theology publications. It also has brief review notes on recent publications in theology, biblical studies, ethics, and sociology of religion that are of interest to pastoral care. Those concerned with the relationship of pastoral care to ethics find this an invaluable resource for information on recent publications in religious and social ethics. The *Religious Studies Review* also includes major review articles on topics and figures of interest to pastoral care. In recent years there have been major review essays on William James, Heinz Kohut, James Hillman, Erik Erikson, and others. Annotated bibliographies on conversion and on psychology of religion have also appeared in *Religious Studies Review*. Recent doctoral dissertations in religious studies from all universities and seminaries in North America are listed. Pastoral theology dissertations appear under the heading "Social-Scientific Study of Religion."

Another journal that does not fall neatly into any of the above categories, but is very important to pastoral care, is *Religious Education*, published by the Religious Education Association of the U.S. and Canada and the Association of Professors and Researchers in Religious Education. Given the current interest among religious educators in developmental psychology, and the fact that many of the best articles on this topic are published in *Religious Education*, this journal has particular interest for pastoral care. It demonstrates that the interests of religious educators and pastoral counselors are overlapping ones, and that a common interest in developmental psychology provides a natural bridge between these two practical disciplines.

The *Journal of Psychology and Theology* deserves special mention because it falls between journals specifically concerned with pastoral care and counseling, and the journals we have been reviewing here. This journal has a moderate Evangelical orientation, which is most evident in the articles that develop methodologies for relating theology and psychology. It also includes numerous articles on practical and ethical problems in contemporary life and has a direct appeal not only to pastors but also to Christian social workers, marriage and family counselors, and educators. It has an extensive book review section where a wide variety of psychological texts are evaluated for their use in Christian oriented care and service.

5. Trends in Publication. Unfortunately, the foregoing review deals almost exclusively with journals published in North America. Important work is also being done in religious studies, theology, and the social scientific study of religion by European and Third World authors that is directly relevant to pastoral care, but published in journals that are not readily accessible to pastoral care practitioners in the U.S. Moreover, the work of international authors in these areas is not being published to any significant degree in the aforementioned journals.

A more positive trend is the fact that many authors who regularly publish in pastoral care and counseling journals are also writing for theological journals such as *Theology Today, Union Seminary Quarterly,* and *Interpretation,* and religion journals such as the *Journal of the American Academy of Religion, Religious Studies Review,* and

Journal of the Scientific Study of Religion. This suggests that those who are shaping our thinking about pastoral care and counseling are also seeking to address a wider academic audience than has traditionally been the case with pastoral theologians and pastoral psychologists. The church remains central for these authors, but they also want to speak to and for the interests of religious studies in the university setting. This is a relatively new trend that promises to have important implications for what direction pastoral theology takes in the future. It may, for example, portend a shift from pastoral theologians' traditional desire to dialogue and collaborate with medical and social service professionals to a new interest in communicating with and being numbered among social scientists.

D. CAPPS

RESEARCH IN PASTORAL CARE AND COUNSELING.

JOY. *See* ECSTASY; HAPPINESS.

JUDAISM. *See* CONSERVATIVE, ORTHODOX, RECONSTRUCTIONIST, *or* REFORM JUDAISM. *See also* JEWISH CARE AND COUNSELING *and the Jewish perspective on these more specific topics:* CONSCIENCE; CONVERSION; DIVORCE AND REMARRIAGE; FAMILY; FUNERAL AND BURIAL; GRIEF AND MOURNING; JEWISH-CHRISTIAN MARRIAGE; JEWISH HOLY DAYS AND FESTIVALS; JEWISH LITERATURE IN CARE AND COUNSELING; JEWISH PRAYERS; JUDAISM AND PSYCHOLOGY; MARRIAGE; MEDICAL-ETHICAL DILEMMAS; MENTALLY RETARDED PERSONS; OLDER PERSONS; PENITENTS; PERSON; SEXUALITY; SICK AND DYING; WEDDING CEREMONY; THEOLOGICAL EDUCATION; SINGLE PERSONS.

JUDAISM AND PSYCHOLOGY.

1. The Hebrew Scriptures. The image of the person in the Hebrew Bible is relentlessly monistic. The indissoluble connections between "soul" (*nephesh, neshamah*) and "body" (*basar*) are everywhere evident. *Nephesh* means person and is often translated as *psyche*. It comes from a root which signifies breath or, in other connections, blood. It signifies at once will, an animating principle, and the unity of the organism. The *lev* (heart, mind) is the center of life and the high point of personal identity. *Ruah* (wind, spirit) gives life from a source outside the discreet individual. It is God's gift of life-force, which inspires creativity and "spiritual" accomplishment.

OT anthropology is thoroughly relational. The human being is seen as concrete, imbedded in the natural order and subject to the vicissitudes of aging and death, which is, apparently, quite final. If a human being is the image of God, he or she is also fully part of the animal kingdom and lives utterly in the terrestrial universe.

The OT also raises a number of protopsychological issues, e.g., those of dreams, family relationships, and the prophetic experience. Dreams are at once personal expression and revelations of God's purpose. The human family is the indispensable locus of conflict, development, and self-transcendence. Prophetic experience is seen as both ecstatic and rational, just as soul and body are linked in one fully encompassing entity.

2. Rabbinic Literature. The classical sources of Judaism are imbedded in the Talmud and Midrashic works produced in the land of Israel and in Babylonia during the first five centuries of the Common Era. This voluminous literature is a veritable sea in which the unwary may drown and even the learned require guidance. All kinds of psychological insights and issues emerge from this classical literature, of which we shall discuss some of the most salient.

The doctrine of the two "impulses," *yeser hara* and *yeser tov,* is the most profound and controversial of rabbinic psychological teachings. Human beings have two asymmetrical temperaments: the "evil" is inchoate, primeval, dangerous, but indispensable. The "good" impulse is secondary, rational, superimposed upon and, in some ways, inimical to an original evil which permanently marks the human condition. Only a consistent discipline of Torah study and obedience to God's commandments can tame the impulse to do evil and make it conform more or less to the will of God on the one hand and to the good ego of the human adult, on the other.

The evil impulse is not just evil; it is necessary to a creativity which flows from libidinous energy, but it is not simply equivalent to the Freudian id or, for that matter, to the Christian doctrine of original sin. A dialectic of good and evil, never fully explicated and never fully resolved, is a permanent, sure aspect of mortality. Life is a constant struggle, not so much to destroy the impulse to evil as to turn it into an often unwilling ally in the continuing task of self-transcendence. God made both impulses and knows our united/divided nature without illusion. Like a good psychoanalyst, He is remote, usually silent, and yet continually in decisive dialogue with each of us. His gift of Torah is, as much as anything else, an antidote to our pride and sinfulness and a standard by which to judge how well we have balanced our physical, emotional limitations and our psychic self-unification. Rabbinic literature provides enormous resources of narrative (as does Scripture) called *aggadah,* always in tension with *halakhic* norms, which have legal, transpersonal, consequences.

Rabbinic insistence upon the freedom of human beings to choose good over evil, despite our divided consciousness, emphasizes the need for *t'shuvah,* turning. The process of *t'shuvah* is not quite equivalent to Christian *metanoia,* since it is coterminous with life itself. There is not usually one moment of conversion. Even the unique peak experiences of the Day of Atonement (and the Ten Days of Turning which lead up to it) are only models for a continuing process of sin, repentance, forgiveness, and self-mastery, all in obedience to the Torah. Even Moses was a sinner; no one can exceed his righteousness. But the repentant sinner stands higher than an impossibly idealized, perfect priest. We are made for sin, but we are also capable of a consistent, and consistently necessary, return to God and a recovery of "the pure soul," which he gave us, along with the "impulse to evil."

Rabbinic literature is profound when it deals with death and mourning. A week of fully regressed behavior (*shivah*) follows upon the funeral of a relative, preceded by a brief period of permitted semimadness and followed by a month (*sh'loshim*) of highly restricted obligation. For a full year the deceased is memorialized, after which the anniversary of death (Judaism does not customarily mark birthdays) is an occasion for reciting the Kaddish prayer, a doxology of acquiescence to the inexorable will of God. Grief is appropriate and inevitable. There is no denial of the reality of our beloved's annihilation and no ashamed resistance to the melancholy which accompanies and closely resembles mourning, but the period of grief is self-limiting and precisely specified by an external direction which structures sadness and prevents despair.

The family is a center of rabbinic concern. *Shalom bayit,* the peace and integrity which each home is to strive to create, is a value more prominent than almost any other. Study, charity, prayer are all subject to the family's imperious demands, and if rabbinic literature sometimes seems to place the onus especially upon the woman, men too are required to honor their wives not only with support, but with regular sexual gratification and with a life shared in affection and concern. Sex is a value independent of the commandment to procreate, and its psychological importance has a theological aspect as well. God endorses sexuality.

The resurrection of the human body, a doctrine to which postbiblical Judaism gave great importance, reflects the psycho-physical monism that biblical Judaism implied earlier. Medical ethics is adumbrated in many rabbinic places with deep respect for the function of the physician, always considering the human life as a supreme, architectonic value. Issues of mental competence are discussed in much detail, reflecting serious concern with the psychic aspects of human consciousness, but in a premodern terminology which has consequences for modern, observant Jews among others. Rabbinic Judaism is not so much a monument as a psychological resource and problematic.

3. The Medieval Period. The Jewish Middle Ages lasted from post-Talmudic times through the French Revolution. They take place from Spain to Iran, including most of the important centers of civilization. It would be impossible here to cite more than two examples of medieval Judaism that had a lasting bearing upon psychology. Maimonides in the twelfth century in Egypt is the towering master of philosophic and halakhic literature, but he was also, preeminently, a physician, and his voluminous work includes strictly medical as well as metapsychological material. In general, he is committed to Hellenic/Arabic interpretive modes, but with important ethical and personal variations. For example, though his version of sexual rules tends to be rather puritanical, he cannot deny that any sex act between married Jews is permitted and his physician's frankness avoids many later medical euphemisms.

At the end of the Jewish Middle Ages, Hasidism brought together many dissenting strains in Jewish history, including gnosticism, Kabbalah, post-Sabbateanism, and other forms of subterranean Jewish piety. Especially important is the Hasidic counseling, one which almost uniquely in Jewish tradition emphasizes the pastoral and the mediating role of the "rebbe." Hasidim is both typically Jewish in its obedience to Halakhah and loyalty to the community, and reformist in its sometimes radical theology and in its substitution of emotional for intellectual priorities. It has inspired an enormous literature in its wake, much of which tries to reconstruct older Jewish psychological insights in appropriately modern terms.

4. **Modern Psychology: Movements and Movers and Modern Judaism.** As a glance at the article on psychology in the *Encyclopedia Judaica* (1972) reveals, most of the originating thinkers in modern psychology were Jews. But they were very different kinds of Jews. Max Wertheimer, for example, the founder of Gestalt psychology, was a typical assimilated Western European Jew. Georg Simmel, a Polish Jew from a family converted to Lutheranism, was still considered by everyone, including himself, as a Jew and identified positively with Jewish morality though only loosely with particular Jewish goals like Zionism. He attempted to provide a detached, aesthetic account, not only of social life, but also of private spheres of everyday psychology. Religion, for him, was a purely cultural form with important philosophical implications. Emil Durkheim, the most famous psychologist and sociologist of religion, had an Orthodox Jewish upbringing and identified positively with Jewish morality and community fellow-feeling, leading the pro-Dreyfus forces in France. For him, religion represents a symbolic expression of social solidarity, a sacred communal psychology which prevents personal anomie and dissolution, surely a Jewish emphasis.

Sigmund Freud is the most controversial and important of all pioneers in modern psychology. His deep Jewish roots (Simon) and his hostility to formal religion reflect an ambivalence that proved richly productive, though hardly leading to any univocal conclusions. His was a complex, assimilated, powerfully connected Jewishness which nonetheless saw Judaism, like all other religions, as an illusion (not a "delusion"), an inevitable, universally shared neurosis.

Psychoanalysis, largely a personal creation of Freud himself, tracks many Jewish themes and commitments (Rieff). Freud uncovered the forgotten, recognized that the body is a symptom for the spirit, that mind is a sheath for the body. He asserted that mental illness is basically false reminiscence, a fixation on an unrepeatable past, while remembering and, thus, living out the past is the road to recovery. Neurosis may be unavoidable, but patient talking and relating have their own therapeutic consequences. We are all wounded healers, but our illness can be, if not cured, reduced.

It is impossible to know oneself, as the Greeks believed. There can be no quick conversion, as Christians sometimes assert. "Psychological changes come only very slowly; if they occur quickly and suddenly it is a bad sign." Analysis is, in principle, interminable, since human beings are always caught in a net of contradictions and conceits. Psychoanalysis is the careful interpretation of psychic texts, a taming of "higher" feelings of tenderness and respect, goals which can paralyze and rescind. Jewish to the core, Freud opposes both the orgiastic and the ascetic. The infantile is not our model, as in some versions of Christianity, but our persistent problem.

The ethical question "Am I my brother's keeper?" becomes the question, as for all Jews, "Am I my father and mother's son or daughter?" History is a record of the return of the repressed. Our past (over)determines our future. A truly psychological person, emancipated from commitments to any primitive past by rational analysis, might be autonomously obedient to magisterial commandments like "Thou shalt have no other gods before me," a commandment to which Freud dedicated much of his life. As Rieff says, "Freud retained more loyalty to his Jewishness than his doctrine permits." His revision of Jewish themes was often also a recovery.

Religion is, for Freud, psychologically determined. The question is not whether but what we should worship. "Religion does not overstate the weakness of the human condition, but takes too much pride in it," he said. Even, perhaps especially, in his analysis of (largely Jewish) humor, Freud manifested a thoroughly Jewish system of moral stringency without self-abnegating punishment, a constructive blasphemy which leaves mature religion untouched, a post-Jewish (and pre-Jewish) problematic to which much of modern Jewish thought has attempted to respond. In an unpublished paper, Jacob Taubes wrote:

[A] hundred years after Freud's birth and half a century after he published his fundamental works we are, I think, in a better position to judge his strategic importance for the modern era. He has given to the latent tragic consciousness of post-Christian era a scientific theory; he has developed a method in which tragic man can look for guidance and therapy. For the event of psychoanalysis is not a chapter in the history of medical psychology only, but marks an epoch in human history.

[Had] the Western religions not . . . been reduced to the zero level trying to find support also on the most humiliating terms, they would have recognized that in psychoanalysis a new image of man is born that challenges all presupposition of messianic religion. [Had] the challenge of psychoanalysis . . . been accepted on the level it was posed then we would have been forced to reconsider the fundamental symbols of our faith, we would have learned to spell out what a "new heart" and a "new spirit" means. We would have learned what the fundamental symbol of our messianic existence, the word *novum* means, what hope means.

Surely the psychoanalytic critique of religion can serve as a critical measure to discern all magical element in our eschatological hope. Insofar as religion acts as a magic operation of atonement in which the person seeking reconciliation is not regenerated and transformed, it falls fully under the severest judgment of Freud. In the struggle between the priestly-magical and prophetic-personal element in eschatological religion psychoanalysis can help to unmask the retrogressive form of magic manipulation which replaces the regenerative and transformative human act. But is the eschatological hope in itself an illusion? If the eschatological hope is illusory, then the future itself turns out to be an illusion. This last difference between faith as hope and faith as an illusion cannot be bridged. In the last judgment the supreme question posed to the soul is: hast thou hoped for redemption? Mankind began to suffer *in hope,* and this what we call the new dispensation of Israel, the emancipation from the bondage of blind fate. From this moment on the human soul no longer asks why it is suffering, but trembles whether it is suffering according to [His] will, whether in this suffering it is on the road to a holy mode of existence.

These important transformations in psychology were not without their Jewish effects. Some Orthodox rabbis found modern psychology, in either its psychoanalytic or behavioristic formulations, inimical to Jewish values. Martin Buber, whose intimate contact with the earliest Freudian circles of the turn of the century has not been well known, revised the Freudian model to make unconscious process available to conscious ratiocination, just as the Yeser Ha-ra is said to be amenable to modification by obedience to the Torah and its mandates. Revisionists in modern psychology (Fromm, Rapaport) often emphasized their congruence with Jewish ethical values, though many critics would hold that orthodox Freudian theory is closer to tradition than that of its revisionists. In all of these movements, Jewish theoreticians and clinicians hold a central place. But what Rieff calls "the triumph of the therapeutic," an age of psychological values as the centerpiece of civilization, raises profound challenges to prophetic and Talmudic priorities, which come more directly from Jewish tradition.

5. Issues. A number of conflicts have arisen over panpsychological assertions, especially in the field of human sexuality. Jewish sources have been almost univocal in opposition to male homosexuality (lesbianism is almost unremarked, perhaps because virtually nonexistent), but many psychologists have now come to regard it as simply an alternative lifestyle. More generally, what seems variously to be the determinisms of behaviorism or psychoanalysis stand opposed to the unconditional freedom of choice which Judaism insists upon. Any psychological imperialism, which claims to reduce all other values to its own relatively narrow kind of self-understanding, is incompatible with the wide horizons of Jewish reflection upon life.

The halakhic imperative seems to oppose absolute personal autonomy, the main standard of modern, psychological humanism. Do we do our duty as God commands us in his Torah, or do we obey our own conscience, revealed to us in therapy and experience? Must we do, as a famous New Yorker cartoon of a progressive nursery school once asked, only what we want to do? Science and religion have different trajectories, but modern psychology is indistinctly scientific, and often purports to be an alternative to old-fashioned faith.

In a famous debate with Carl Rogers, Buber (1965) insists that the role of the therapist is not dialogic (or religious) because it is not symmetrical with that of the patient. There can be no fully client-centered therapy nor value-free psychology, since the entire human community is embraced by overarching values and needs. God is a reality beyond our own projections about God or our need for him to be only what we remember or desiderate. The I-Thou dialogue only obtains between equals, never in a situation of the helper and the helped.

Other issues of some importance for the connection between Judaism and psychology include: anti-Semitism and its pathological roots, the value of an ethnotherapy which takes into account the patient's communal roots, medical ethics in the areas of brain death, competence

and responsibility for crime, and the nature of human personality. These and other issues are only beginning to emerge clearly, with more hope of mutual illumination.

6. Review of the Literature. The only continuing publication that tries to deal with these issues is the *Journal of Psychology and Judaism*, published several times each year. Basic descriptions of Jewish anthropology and psychology are found in Bahya's classic *Duties of the Heart*, with a rather ascetic bias, in Urbach and Moore's review of rabbinic material, and in Rubenstein's brilliant and erratic revision of that material (1968). Wolf (1968) and, especially, Katz (1985) offer helpful introductions to Jewish pastoral texts and concerns. Spero offers the only serious attempt to confront traditional Jewish law and informed modern psychology as theory and praxis, and he succeeds beyond any legitimate expectation. An earlier attempt by Liebman to popularize putative connections became a bestseller, but is still useful. Simon's attempt to correlate Freud as a person, a thinker, and a Jew is still the classical place to begin; it continues in the interpretations of Klein, a historian; Rieff, a social scientist; Robert, a literary critic; and Rubenstein (1967) and Wolf (1965), Jewish theologians, as well as by various medical practitioners in Ostow's anthology. Buber's version of Jewish psychology is, in my opinion, one of his supremely valuable books. Bakan's earlier study of Freud and Jewish mysticism is much more nuanced and inclusive in his much more important book of 1966. The most subtle philosophical exploration of the problem of psychological (or, more precisely, phenomenological) ethics and Judaism is in Levinas. One rereads the classic, if also controversial, works of Freud (1927, 1939) with wonder and, inevitably, sometimes dismay. Younger scholars are beginning to make bold connections and reveal serious disjunctions that have so far only been hinted at, and their work promises something very like a revolution to come.

Bibliography. D. Bakan, *The Duality of Human Existence* (1966). Banya Ben Josaph, *The Book of Direction to the Duties of the Heart* trans. M. Mansoor, (1973). M. Buber, *The Knowledge of Man* (1965). A. Cronbach, "New Studies in the Psychology of Judaism," *Hebrew Union College Annual,* 19 (1945–46), 205–73; "The Psychoanalytic Study of Judaism," *Hebrew Union College Annual,* 8–9 (1931–32). S. Freud, *The Future Of an Illusion* (1928); *Moses and Monotheism* (1939); *New Introductory Lectures on Psychoanalysis* (1933). H. H. Hirschberg, "Eighteen Hundred Years Before Freud," *Judaism,* 10 (1961), 129–41. R. L. Katz, *Pastoral Care and the Jewish Tradition* (1985). D. Klein, *Jewish Origins of the Psychoanalytic Movement* (1981). E. Levinas, *Totality and Infinity* (1961). J. Liebman, *Peace of Mind* (1946). G. F. Moore, *Judaism in the First Centuries of the Christian Era* (1944). M. Ostow, ed., *Judaism and Psychoanalysis* (1982). P. Rieff, *Freud: The Mind Of A Moralist* (1959). M. Robert, *From Oedipus to Moses* (1976). R. L. Rubenstein, "Freud and Judaism," *J. of Religion,* 47:1 (January 1967); *The Religious Imagination: A Study in Psychoanalysis and Jewish Theology* (1968). E. Simon, "Sigmund Freud, The Jew," *Yearbook of the Leo Baeck Institute,* 2 (1957), 270–305. M. H. Spero, *Judaism and Psychology: Halakhic Perspectives* (1980). E. E. Urbach, *The Sages* (1975). A. J. Wolf, "Psychoanalysis and Religious Experience," *J. of Religion and Health,* 2 (October 1962), 74–80; *Rediscovering Judaism* (1965); *What Is Man?* (1968).

A. J. WOLF

HASIDIC CARE AND COUNSELING; JEWISH CARE AND COUNSELING; PERSON (Jewish Perspective); RABBIS, EMPIRICAL STUDIES OF; THEOLOGICAL EDUCATION AND THE PASTORAL CARE MOVEMENT, JEWISH. *See also* ANTI-SEMITISM; FREEDOM AND BONDAGE; REPENTANCE AND CONFESSION. *Compare* COUNSELING, ROMAN CATHOLIC; PASTORAL COUNSELING; PASTORAL PSYCHOTHERAPY; RELIGION AND PSYCHOTHERAPY; SPIRITUAL DIRECTION; VALUES IN COUNSELING AND PSYCHOTHERAPY. *Biography:* BUBER; FREUD.

JUDGING/JUDGMENT. *See* SOCIAL PERCEPTION, JUDGMENT AND BELIEF. *See also* CONFRONTATION (Therapeutic); DISCIPLINE, PASTORAL CARE AS; ESCHATOLOGY; PRUDENCE; WISDOM AND PRACTICAL KNOWLEDGE.

JUNG, CARL G. (1875–1961). Swiss psychotherapist and founder of analytical psychology. Born as the son of a Reformed pastor in a small rural town in Switzerland, Jung found little happiness in the church's dogmas and creeds and learned early to rely on his own inner resources. He studied medicine in Basel, psychiatry under Bleuler in Zurich, and psychopathology under Pierre Janet in Paris. Fascinated with the complexes of the mentally ill, Jung began research on the word association experiment. On the basis of this research G. Stanley Hall invited him with Sigmund Freud to lecture and receive honorary doctorates at Clark University in Worcester, Massachusetts, in 1909. Jung and Freud had become collaborators and friends after a substantial correspondence had developed on the subject of dreams. In 1910 Jung became the first permanent president of the International Psychoanalytical Society. Four years later, following the publication of *Symbols of Transformation* (1912), Jung broke with Freud establishing his own theory and practice known as analytical psychology.

After that, Jung's interpretation of the human psyche and theories of therapy, the dynamics of the unconscious, and the definition of the libido differed markedly from Freud. The schism became even more pronounced when Jung published *Psychology of the Unconscious (1917)*, in which the unconscious and its relationship to a person's religious history as a life force diverged from Freud's emphasis on sexuality. Through his travels and study of the indigenous peoples of Africa, America, and India, Jung was impressed by the similarities in the myths and symbols of humankind throughout the centuries and around the world. These common motifs Jung labeled *archetypes.* Out of the congruity of these myths came the theory of the collective unconscious and also the implications of that theory for the study of religion and healing. Jung came to believe that healing and wholeness of the human psyche are a result of returning to one's religious roots and getting in touch with the transcendent element in life.

Jung's most widely known contribution to the field of psychology is his theory of psychological types in which he delineates two attitudinal orientations of the personality, namely introversion and extroversion, published in *Psychological Types* (1921). He also identified four functions of the conscious, two for perceiving the world: sensing and intuition, and two for judging the world: thinking and feeling. Popular instruments have been developed to delineate these dimensions of personality

for the purposes of career development, counseling and interpersonal dynamics of communication.

His most important contribution emerged from consolidating his study and experience of the unconscious and consequently presented the ultimate nature of life in terms of opposites. He contrasted the persona (socially acceptable mask) with the shadow (the rejected counterpart); the anima (the feminine in man) with the animus (the masculine in woman). All the opposites of the psyche are personified in dreams and interpreted in counseling to bring about what Jung called the process of individuation, that is, first recognizing and finally integrating the opposites into the unity called the self, in the psyche's natural drive toward wholeness.

V. deGREGORIS

ANALYTICAL (JUNGIAN) PSYCHOLOGY. *See also* THEOLOGY AND PSYCHOLOGY.

JUNGIAN PSYCHOLOGY. *See* ANALYTICAL (JUNGIAN) PSYCHOLOGY.

JUSTICE. *See* SOCIAL JUSTICE ISSUES IN PASTORAL CARE.

JUSTIFICATION, DOCTRINE OF. *See* CHRISTOLOGY; FAITH AND WORKS; FORGIVENESS; GRACE; RIGHTEOUSNESS/BEING RIGHT.

JUVENILE CRIME AND DELINQUENCY. Juvenile delinquency is behavior that violates cultural norms for juveniles. Juvenile crime is behavior on the part of persons who have not reached the age of majority that violates statutory criminal law.

A wide variety of behaviors is encompassed by the term juvenile delinquency. In practice, virtually all of these activities are unlawful either for all persons or specifically for persons who have not reached the age of legal majority. The first group of offenses is commonly referred to as crimes; the latter are often termed status offenses.

Juvenile delinquency is perceived to be a significant social problem because a large proportion of serious crimes is committed by juveniles. Explanations for juvenile criminality have emphasized either rational choice of criminal behavior or a variety of predisposing factors that are largely beyond the control of the individual. These explanations have been used as the basis for a variety of intervention strategies, but to date there has been little evidence that any prevention or treatment programs are consistently successful in reducing juvenile crime. As a result, the philosophical foundations of the entire juvenile justice system are being questioned, and there is an increasing tendency to respond to juvenile crime in the same manner as adult crime.

1. **Extent and Nature of Delinquency.** *a. Sources of information.* There are three primary sources of statistical information regarding the extent and nature of juvenile crime: official reports, primarily the Uniform Crime Reports (UCR) compiled by the FBI; victimization studies; and self-reports. Because each source of information employs unique criteria for identifying juvenile crimes and unique methodologies for calculating rates of occur-

rence, there is little consistency among them, and none can be accepted as completely accurate or without bias.

b. Scope of juvenile crime. According to official reports, about forty percent of arrests for serious crimes are of persons under the age of eighteen. These youths account for about twenty percent of arrests for violent crime and forty percent of arrests for property crime. Specific crimes for which the proportional juvenile arrest rates are particularly high are burglary, auto theft, arson, larceny (theft of property valued at over fifty dollars), and robbery. These rates are disproportionately high, given that persons between the ages of ten and seventeen constitute less than fifteen percent of the total population.

Not only do juveniles account for a disproportionate amount of crime, but arrest rates suggest that juvenile crime is increasing. Juvenile arrests for serious crimes increased by seventeen percent during the 1970s. Arrests for violent crimes increased forty-one percent; arrest for serious property crimes increased by fifteen percent. During the same period of time the proportion of the population between the ages of ten and seventeen decreased by six percent. The number of adults in the population increased by eighteen percent during that time, while their arrest rates for serious crimes increased by fifty-four percent.

While it is clear that arrest rates are increasing for both juveniles and adults, it is not clear that juvenile crime constitutes a significantly greater threat now than in the past. Some researchers argue that it does. Others disagree, noting that juveniles tend to commit less serious crimes than adults from the standpoint of weapon use, injury rate, and financial loss.

c. Characteristics of offenders. With the exception of age, juveniles arrested for crimes are similar to adult offenders—predominantly white, lower-class, male, urban dwellers. Although the majority of juvenile offenders are white, minorities are overrepresented and account for approximately thirty percent of persons under eighteen arrested for serious offenses. Minorities are also proportionately more likely to be victimized by crime. The association between ethnic background and crime can in part be explained by the lower socioeconomic status of minority groups. High minority arrest rates are also a result of the fact that law enforcement agencies commit a disproportionate share of resources to policing minority communities and are thus more likely to observe minority youth.

Middle-class youth also engage in criminal activities, though they are likely to commit less serious offenses and to receive more lenient treatment by authorities. Likewise, females tend to commit crimes of opportunity related to their sex role, such as prostitution and shoplifting, and in general are less likely to be arrested than are males; however, they are more likely to be arrested for behavior that violates normative expectations for females, such as running away from home, vagrancy, and curfew violations.

Serious violent crime is predominantly an urban phenomenon. Movement from urban, through suburban, to rural areas results in proportionately higher arrest rates for whites but for less serious crimes (*Sourcebook: 1981*).

Relatively few juvenile delinquents become adult criminals. Most simply cease to engage in delinquent behaviors as they take on the responsibilities of adulthood. On the other hand, studies of adult offenders usually indicate a pattern of chronic, serious juvenile crime.

2. Theories of Delinquency. *a. General approaches.* According to the "classical school," human behavior reflects rational choices between alternative courses of action. This school believes that humans, being basically hedonistic, choose the behavior that enhances pleasure or reduces pain. Therefore punishment for crime must be scaled in severity to counteract the presumed pleasure of the criminal act. Exceptions ought to be made for children who are not capable of rational choice and are, therefore, less culpable.

In contrast, scientific (or positivistic) criminology has sought explanations for criminal behavior in a variety of personal and environmental influences that are presumed to be largely beyond the control of the individual. Most of the social scientific theories of crime and delinquency consist of elaborations on the causal relationship between one or more of these factors and criminal behavior. As a group, they suggest that the appropriate remedy for crime consists not of punishment but of alleviating its causal conditions, principally poverty.

b. Specific theories. Psychobiological and psychoanalytical theories of crime assume that antisocial behavior is pathological, resulting from defects in the physical or psychological makeup of the offender, which are either genetically inherited or the result of early childhood experience. Though only a small percentage of delinquents can be termed psychologically disturbed, most social scientists do acknowledge the importance of early childhood experiences, insofar as they contribute to a sense of self-worth, personal efficacy, and self-control.

Sociological and social psychological theories tend to identify delinquency as a lower-class phenomenon and to focus on particular characteristics of lower-class status, such as blocked opportunities for achieving material success, including poor home environment and failure in school; association with delinquent peers; and subcultural norms supporting delinquent behavior.

Most criminologists acknowledge that no single causal factor accounts for all or even most juvenile delinquency. Rather, they assume that a variety of forces interact to increase the likelihood that an individual child will engage in serious criminal activity. The theories simply reflect emphases on different aspects of the juvenile's environment.

Two recent alternative perspectives on juvenile delinquency, critical criminology, and labeling theory, suggest that criminologists ought to pay less attention to individual causation and more to the question of why and how some persons (typically lower-class minorities) are more likely than others to be identified and officially labeled as juvenile delinquents. Critical criminologists argue that the discriminatory treatment of the poor by the criminal justice system is simply one form of the subordination of the lower class by those in power. Labeling theorists maintain that juveniles who come into contact with the criminal justice system are more likely than others to conceive of themselves as criminals and to behave consistently with that self-image (Vold, 1979).

3. **Social Responses to Delinquency.** Strategies for alleviating delinquency typically focus on prevention, rehabilitation, or restraint of offenders through confinement. Specific programs reflect unique characteristics of the geographical setting, target population of juveniles, and philosophy of the sponsoring agency. None has been consistently successful.

The majority of delinquency programs have either an official or unofficial affiliation with the juvenile justice system. In contrast to the adversarial adult criminal justice system, the juvenile court has had broad discretionary powers to act as a "kindly parent" in the best interests of the child. In its parental role the court and other juvenile agencies have implemented each of the following.

a. Prevention. Prevention programs offer the hope of curing the disease rather than treating the symptom. Typical programs include police-sponsored athletic teams, youth employment programs, boys' clubs, and attempts to warn potential delinquents of the consequences of their behavior. Preventive approaches, however, have typically been neither theory-based nor carefully evaluated.

b. Rehabilitation. Rehabilitation efforts have attempted to obtain conforming behavior from delinquents using techniques ranging from nonsupervised probation to incarceration. These expectations are rarely realized because the programs themselves are usually inadequately funded. More importantly, rehabilitation programs focus on the individual offender and leave the conditions producing delinquency untouched—poor education, family neglect, poverty, and racism.

c. Restraint. Although long used as both a preventive and rehabilitative technique for dealing with delinquency, restraint has recently been redefined as an appropriate response in and of itself. While minor criminal offenders are frequently diverted to community supervision programs, the police and courts now attempt to identify and incarcerate serious offenders early in their criminal careers. There is growing recognition that confinement in youth facilities and adult prisons is unlikely to result in rehabilitation. It does, however, ensure societal protection, at least during the period of offender restraint. It also serves to punish the offender.

4. **Current Issues.** *a. Failure of the juvenile justice system.* The juvenile justice system currently assumes responsibility for not only adolescent criminals but also a variety of neglected, abused, and "problem" children. This breadth of jurisdiction has resulted in the creation of programs with competing goals and has overburdened

the resources of the system. Consequently, the system as a whole is perceived as failing.

From the point of view of the general public, the juvenile justice system has failed because it has not reduced the juvenile crime rate, in spite of a declining juvenile population. Minority groups, on the other hand, maintain that the system fails to provide equal protection for them. The bias against minorities is likely to result in harsher treatment of minority youth as reflected in higher rates of incarceration.

b. Changing perceptions of juvenile crime. Public awareness of the extent of juvenile involvement in serious crimes has been heightened by media attention. Consequently, public perception of the nature of juvenile delinquency has changed. There is less inclination to view delinquency as misbehavior on the part of misguided youth and a greater tendency to view it as criminality resulting from willful wrongdoing. There is also less concern with protecting juvenile delinquents from the consequences of their acts and a greater demand to hold them accountable.

5. **Implications for the Pastor/Counselor.** Delinquent behavior usually does not require immediate legal action; it is often a symptom of family problems requiring pastoral attention. If there is any official response to a nonserious juvenile offense, it is likely to be an attempt to divert the juvenile from the justice system. Serious or repetitive delinquency, however, does present cause for concern. Long-term or extensive delinquent behavior usually results in official action, escalating from community supervision to lengthy incarceration. Unfortunately, none of the intervention strategies has been consistently effective. The only sure solution for most serious delinquency seems to be maturation.

Bibliography. L. T. Empey, *American Delinquency* rev. ed. (1987); *Juvenile Justice: Progressive Legacy and Current Reforms* (1979). M. Haskell and L. Yablonsky, *Juvenile Delinquency* 2d ed. (1978). S. Reid, *Crime and Criminology* 3d ed. (1982). U.S. Department of Justice, *Sourcebook of Criminal Justice Statistics — 1981* (1982); "Delinquent Behavior Spawned by 'Traditions of Crime,'" *Justice Assistance News,* 3, 7, 1; "Treatment of Youths in Adult and Juvenile Courts Similar," *Justice Assistance News,* 3, 10, 1. G. Vold, *Theoretical Criminology* 2d ed. (1979).

M. DOYLE
P. M. JOLICOEUR

ANTISOCIAL PERSONS. *See also* ADOLESCENTS; CRIMINAL AND ANTISOCIAL BEHAVIOR, SOCIOLOGY OF; GUIDANCE, PASTORAL; PRISONERS AND PRISON CHAPLAINCY; RESPONSIBILITY/IRRESPONSIBILITY, PSYCHOLOGY OF; VIOLENCE. *Compare* MORAL BEHAVIOR AND RELIGION; MORAL DEVELOPMENT; VALUES RESEARCH.

K

KADDISH. *See* GRIEF AND MOURNING, JEWISH CARE IN; JEWISH CARE AND COUNSELING; JEWISH PRAYERS.

KEBLE, JOHN (1792–1866). Anglican vicar, Oxford graduate, fellow, and tutor. In 1833 his Assize Sermon in Oxford, "National Apostasy," dealing with a growing sense of crisis in the relation of the Church of England to the government, linked him with others of similar concern (e.g., Newman, Froude, Pusey) and marked him as one of the key figures of the emerging Oxford Movement.

Keble's pastoral contributions came in two forms: his religious poetry and his own role model as priest and pastor. *The Christian Year* (1827), intended to raise the thoughts and feelings of readers into unison with the themes of the English prayer book, became immediately popular and was widely reprinted over the rest of the century. This and succeeding poetry offered a different religious tone from the dominant rational or evangelical emphases in the church, calling attention to the mystery as well as the visibility of grace and to the presence of God made manifest in the sacraments, the liturgical life of the church, and the daily rounds of God's holy people. His pastoral life represented a sharp contrast from the typical eighteenth-century country vicar and served as a model for many. He devoted himself to the practice of his calling with seriousness and dedication, advised laity and ministerial colleagues in person and by correspondence on a variety of spiritual matters, and centered his work on the integrity of the historic Church of England and the possibilities for a life of holiness within its ministrations.

D. A. JOHNSON

ANGLICAN PASTORAL CARE.

KELLER, WILLIAM S. (1883–1949). Founder of the summer session for theological students, which later became Clinical Pastoral Education (CPE). Keller, a Cincinnati physician and dedicated Episcopalian, initiated a program in the summer of 1923 by placing five seminar-

ians from Bexley Hall, an Episcopal divinity school then in central Ohio, in several Cincinnati social agencies for the purposes of clinical training.

While this modest program continued for the next few summers, Keller engaged in funding, promotion, and recruitment of students from all Episcopal seminaries. He officially established "The Summer Session in Social Service for Theological Students and Junior Clergy" in 1927, under the auspices of the Diocese of Southern Ohio and the Department of Social Relations of the national Episcopal Church. From 1928 until wartime conditions closed the summer session in 1942, Keller's program usually had twenty to thirty students from ten to twelve Episcopal seminaries. In this period his program gained a national reputation. Annually, Keller visited each Episcopal seminary. His former students, several of whom became bishops or achieved other significant church positions, enthusiastically wrote tracts and delivered speeches in support of the summer session.

On January 4, 1937, after years of planning, Keller inaugurated the Graduate School of Applied Religion, which offered year-round clinical pastoral sessions. His summer session became the graduate school's summer program. Keller persuaded the renowned Joseph F. Fletcher to be the dean of the graduate school.

Keller's constant concern with seminaries was their courses in pastoral theology, which covered only origins and theories of pastoral ministry. Declaring them far too minimal, he strove to provide seminarians with actual pastoral experiences in clinical settings. Keller chose the social agency as the best setting, yet each summer he placed some students in hospital settings. Eventually, CPE would be almost exclusively hospital oriented. However, Keller's program differed little from later CPE programs: the students worked in various social agencies under careful supervision; then all gathered twice weekly for group sessions based upon their clinical experiences.

Today all Episcopal seminaries and most divinity schools throughout the nation require or recommend a summer session of CPE for their students. This in great part is the legacy of Dr. Keller.

R. M. SPIELMANN

CLINICAL PASTORAL EDUCATION; PASTORAL CARE MOVEMENT.

KEMPIS, THOMAS à. See THOMAS À KEMPIS.

KETUBBAH. A Jewish marriage contract. It is written in Aramaic according to a form established in late Roman times. It contains the names of the bride and groom, a declaration on the part of the groom that he is "acquiring" the bride as his wife, stipulations concerning the dowry he receives and the financial obligations owed the wife in the case of divorce, and witnesses' signatures. In medieval times these were often elaborately decorated and displayed prominently in the couple's dwelling.

P. J. HAAS

MARRIAGE (Jewish Theology and Care).

KEYS, POWER OF. (1) Based on Jesus' words of "binding and loosing" to Peter (Mt. 16:19; 18:18), a term for the spiritual authority of the church (in Catholicism, for the papacy also); (2) more specifically, the church's (or priest's) authority to hear confession and pronounce absolution. The penitential meaning, through a variety of interpretations and practices, has had enormous influence in the history of pastoral care, primarily in relation to the sacrament of penance.

R. J. HUNTER

AUTHORITY, PASTORAL; DISCIPLINE, PASTORAL CARE AS; ECCLESIOLOGY AND PASTORAL CARE; MINISTRY; PENANCE, SACRAMENT OF.

KIERKEGAARD, SØREN (1813–55). Born in Copenhagan, Denmark, his brief but highly productive lifetime laid the foundations of modern existentialism. Kierkegaard's sensitivity to the pathos of human existence was shaped by his own experience of suffering. The youngest of six children, he experienced the early deaths of three sisters, his mother, and a brother. His father died in 1838 at age eighty-two, a wealthy but guilt-ridden man under whose dominance Kierkegaard lived most of his life. In September 1840, Kierkegaard became engaged to Regine Olsen. A year later he broke the engagement. This event crystallized his intensive quest for authentic selfhood.

For Kierkegaard, the incarnation underscored the Christocentric focus of human existence, hence his polemic against the "spiritlessness" of historical Christendom and the dispassionate rational analysis of Hegelian idealism. However, he saw in Hegel's "phenomenology of spirit" a conceptual framework for mapping the dialectic of human becoming through the aesthetic, ethical, and religious spheres of existence. In Socrates he found the quintessence of the ironic imagination and a strategy, namely, indirect communication (the maieutic art), which he employed in his pseudonymous works to reinforce the task of self-realization.

Kierkegaard's legacy is his analysis of anxiety (*angst*) and his fundamental thesis that authentic selfhood is made possible not merely by ethical decisiveness but by becoming religious; and even more specifically, by becoming a Christian. To the end he refused to compromise with any attempt to systematize the irreconcilable polarities of existence. Existence is either/or. It presents us with choices that cannot be resolved merely by appealing to reason, hence the "leap of faith."

R. M. MOSELEY

EXISTENTIALISM AND PASTORAL CARE.

KINGDOM OF GOD. See ESCHATOLOGY; NEW TESTAMENT.

KLAUSNER, SAMUEL Z. See RELIGION AND HEALTH MOVEMENT.

KLINK, THOMAS, W. (1920–70). Chaplain supervisor. In 1959 the Menninger Foundation in Topeka, Kansas, invited Klink to become both chaplain and coordinator of its program of graduate studies in religion and psychiatry. He was later promoted to director of the Division of Religion and Psychiatry. Through his teaching and writing Klink worked for understanding between the disciplines. He developed a theory of pastoral care around Freudian conflict theory in *Depth Perspectives in Pastoral Work* (1965) and wrote several articles for *Pastoral Psychology*.

A graduate of Pacific University, Klink studied at the University of Chicago Divinity School as Ford Fellow. During this time he did clinical training with Anton Boisen. Klink pastored a Methodist church in Oregon (1945–49) before serving for two years as chaplain of the Iowa Methodist Hospital in Des Moines and for nine years in a pilot program as chaplain supervisor at the Topeka State Hospital.

Bibliography. R. Preston, "Man of the Month," *Pastoral Psychology*, December (1962).

A. STOKES

PASTORAL CARE MOVEMENT.

KNOWLEDGE. See PHILOSOPHY AND PSYCHOLOGY; REVELATION; WISDOM AND PRACTICAL KNOWLEDGE.

KNOX, JOHN. See REFORMED PASTORAL CARE.

KOINONIA. See COMMUNITY, FELLOWSHIP, AND CARE.

KOREAN PASTORAL CARE MOVEMENT. See EAST ASIAN PASTORAL CARE MOVEMENT.

KOTSCHNIG, ELINED. See NEW YORK PSYCHOLOGY GROUP.

KRONSTADT, JOHN SERGIEFF (1829–1908). One of the classic examples of what the Orthodox church calls "pastor."

Born in northern Russia, he was sent to the parochial school in Archangelsk in 1839, and in 1851, graduating from seminary with honors, was sent to the Academy of St. Petersburg on a scholarship from the state.

All of Father John's temptations and troubles while in school were to be incorporated into his vision of his fifty-three-year-long ministry at Kronstadt, for which he then became famous. The city of Kronstadt was a naval base, festering with immorality and poverty. From early morning until late at night, he ministered by healing, preaching, teaching, and administrating. He founded the House of Industry in 1873, which began for these wayward people a manner for useful contribution to the society. He taught in the municipal school of Kronstadt, talked to the peasants in the fields, and sat with the children in the grass. Many crowds surrounded him as he merely walked down the street, and his fame spread throughout the land as the great pastor of the people, the "Batushka," Father John of Kronstadt.

Bibliography. Bishop A. Semenoff-Tian-Chansky, *Father John of Kronstadt: A Life* (1979). E. E. Goulaff, ed., *My Life in Christ* [extracts from Father John's diary] (1971). W. J. Grisbrooke, ed., *The Spiritual Counsel of Father John of Kronstadt* (1981).

J. L. ALLEN

MINISTRY AND PASTORAL CARE (Orthodox Tradition); PASTOR (Normative and Traditional Images *or* History, Traditions, and Definitions).

KUETHER, FREDERICK K.

KUETHER, FREDERICK K. (1911/12?–71). Clinical pastoral educator. Kuether served as Director of Training at the American Foundation of Religion and Psychiatry, founded by the Rev. Norman Vincent Peale and Dr. Smiley Blanton. Prior to this he was director of the Council for Clinical Training of Theological Students (1947–54), succeeding Robert Brinkman. Kuether was a member of the committee that established national standards for clinical pastoral training and was a moving spirit in the founding of the American Association of Pastoral Counselors (1963).

A student of Anton Boisen's, unlike Boisen, Kuether advocated psychotherapy for the student. He emphasized that the question is not what the student must *do, know,* or *say* to be of help, but what the student must *be*: "Because I bring my self to every human relationship, I must understand and accept my self" (*Pastoral Psychology,* October 1953, 16–20).

Ordained to ministry in the United Church of Christ, Kuether received his B.D. from Eden Theological Seminary in Webster Groves, Missouri. Between 1937 and 1942 he was chaplain supervisor at the Chillicothe Reformatory, designated at the time by the Bureau of Prisons as training center for all chaplains.

A. STOKES

PASTORAL CARE MOVEMENT.

KUNKEL, FRITZ, (1889–1956). Born in Germany, Kunkel came to the U.S. in 1939 to escape conditions in Nazi Germany. While a doctor in World War I, he was wounded and lost an arm. As a result of this trauma Kunkel became a psychotherapist. He studied Freud, Adler, and Jung, and his own psychology is a unique synthesis of the thought of these three men. Like Jung, Kunkel believed personality has two centers: the lesser center of the ego and the greater center of the self. For Kunkel, wholeness emerges when the egocentric ego, through undergoing a series of maturing crises, accepts the primacy of the self. Kunkel saw many comparisons between this process and Christian teaching and conversion. Well known in Germany, Kunkel's reputation was growing in the U.S. when he died. His major works were republished in 1983 under the title *Fritz Kunkel: Selected Writings.*

J. A. SANFORD

ANALYTICAL (JUNGIAN) PSYCHOLOGY; INDIVIDUAL PSYCHOLOGY; PSYCHOANALYSIS.

L

LAICIZATION. A popular term for the process by which a Roman Catholic priest or deacon is returned to the lay state. The official term in canon law is "loss of the clerical state." The process may be initiated either by request of the priest himself or as a disciplinary action by a judicatory of the church. Its execution may involve any of several Vatican congregations.

1. Ecclesiastical Aspects. Conferred by one of the seven sacraments, the priesthood is considered, legally and theologically, to be a permanent state: once conferred it can never be removed. However, a priest can be forbidden to *function* as a priest, and laicization is the process by which this is done. It does not necessarily include dispensation from the obligation of celibacy, which is granted only by a special rescript from the papal office. Dispensation from celibacy, however, always includes laicization.

Until the mid-1960s laicization was rarely requested by priests wishing to resign, since the dispensation from celibacy was seldom granted along with it; worldwide there were about a dozen cases annually. But in 1964 Pope John XXIII initiated a major change in policy, adopting more lenient procedures for laicization, which generally included the celibacy dispensation. His intent was to deal more pastorally with priests who had long since married and were seeking to be reconciled with the church. This stance was continued by his successor Pope Paul VI and, together with the atmosphere of change that surrounded the Second Vatican Council, stimulated unprecedented numbers of requests for laicization in the decades that followed. Between 1963 and 1980 more than eighty thousand priests resigned, over half of whom were granted laicization. Many of the others never requested it, mostly in protest of the celibacy obligation itself.

This era of moderation in the administrative response to petitions for laicization ended with the election of Pope John Paul II in 1979. Disturbed by the large numbers of priests requesting dispensation from celibacy, he published new norms in 1980 that severely limited the conditions under which it could be granted. The number of requests for laicization dwindled imme-diately, and comparatively few were granted in subsequent years.

2. Pastoral Care of Resigned Priests. While pastoral needs of resigned priests vary according to when and how they leave the priesthood, these men almost invariably experience the intense personal pain and life disorientation that such an important change in commitment, lifestyle, profession, and spiritual conviction involves. Many of those who resigned during the 1960s and 1970s saw themselves as gifted and successful clergypersons who were unable to live a celibate lifestyle with integrity as they progressed developmentally. They experienced an excruciating life dilemma: leave the ministry to which they felt called and gifted, or continue to live a lie. They felt betrayed by the church and at the same time a strong attachment to it. Theologically they saw themselves as having received charisma for priestly ministry but not for living celibate lives.

Pastoral counseling of resigned priests has historically been a significant lacuna in the caring stance of the church. While major and expensive efforts are made to assist active priests in dealing with personal problems, once they request laicization the procedures are experienced as more administrative than pastoral and typically quite legal and even penal in tone.

To fill this perceived gap, large numbers of resigned priests in several countries have organized themselves to be of more personal, pastoral, and vocational support to one another and those currently resigning. CORPUS (Corps of Resigned Priests United for Service) is such a group in the U.S. Founded in Chicago in 1976, it now supports an executive secretary, publishes a monthly newsletter, and maintains a network of volunteers in more than one hundred U.S. cities.

3. Emerging Issues. The several changes in the procedures for laicization in the past thirty years reflect an administrative struggle in dealing with the resigned celibate priest, and perhaps the obligation to celibacy itself. Most canon lawyers, however, expect no abolition of the celibacy obligation in the near future. As major forces, such as the rapid development of lay ministry, pressure for ordination of women, and intense shortages of priests in some countries continue to impinge on the Catholic Church, the role of the celibate priest becomes more unclear and increasingly more difficult to live out. Resignations and requests for laicization continue, albeit in smaller numbers. Those resigning continue to exhibit specialized pastoral counseling needs, including that of finding creative ways to utilize their ministry gifts, for which there is little place in current church structure.

Bibliography. J. Coriden *et al.*, eds., *The Code of Canon Law: A Text and Commentary* (1985), 229–39; and "Recent Tendencies in the Field of Pastoral Activity: A Statistical Study of the Overall Trends," in *L'Osservatore Romano*, (1985) 6–8. National Federation of Priests' Councils, *Search and Share Directory II* (1981). E. Kneal, "Laicization: Canon Law Society of America Survey, 1982," *Canon Law Society of America Proceedings*, 47 (1982), 247–50. M. O'Reilly, "Canonical Procedures for the Laicization of Priests," *Canon Law Society of America Proceedings*, 44 (1982), 233–46.

G. HILSMAN

MINISTRY, ROMAN CATHOLIC; PRIEST; VOCATION (Roman Catholicism). *Compare* VOWS/VOWING.

LAITY. *See* ECCLESIOLOGY AND PASTORAL CARE; LAY PASTORAL CARE AND COUNSELING.

LAKE, FRANK (1914–82). The founder of the Clinical Theology Association and author of the monumental book *Clinical Theology* (1966), was born in England, but trained in medicine in Scotland. He served in India for ten years as a medical missionary, an army doctor, and later as medical superintendent of the Medical Training College, Vellore. Returning to England in 1949, he undertook postgraduate training in psychiatry, which prepared him for his major life's work, the founding of an association designed to train the clergy and others in "clinical theology," that is, psychodynamic theology related to pastoral issues. Frank Lake was undeniably a charismatic leader. He set about his chosen task with immense energy and quickly gained the attention of many Anglican bishops who were concerned about the inadequate pastoral training of their ordinands. Study seminars were set up throughout the country, supplied with a stream of literature specially prepared by Lake himself. The seminars were both confrontational and supportive and appear to have had a profound effect on the participants' pastoral understanding. The association went through many revolutions, usually sparked by Lake's powerful and difficult personality and his fascination with new ideas. Thus the early Freudian emphasis of *Clinical Theology* was superseded by LSD work, primal therapy, and finally by an emphasis on very early intrauterine experiences (see *Tight Corners in Pastoral Counselling*, 1981). After its earlier success, the association was viewed with greater suspicion by the churches and theological schools, especially since the latter were developing their own pastoral studies courses. But up to his death, Frank Lake remained a loyal churchman, convinced of the urgency of his message to the churches. Significantly, perhaps, his

last book (*With Respect*, 1982) was a tribute to Pope John Paul II.

A. V. CAMPBELL

BRITISH PASTORAL CARE MOVEMENT; CLINICAL THEOLOGY; PASTORAL THEOLOGY, PROTESTANT.

LAMBOURNE, ROBERT A. (1917–72). Founder and leader of the first university course in pastoral studies in Britain. Lambourne had a lifetime interest in religion and in the interaction between medicine and theology. In his middle years he added to his medical qualification training in psychotherapy and counseling and a degree in theology. The thesis for that degree was subsequently published as *Community, Church and Healing* (1963). A stream of important articles appeared in the remaining years of his life, arguing for a wholistic view of health and challenging pastoral care to become voluntary, lay, and community based, and castigating its "love affair" with psychotherapy. Lambourne remains, despite his premature death, a major influence on pastoral studies in Britain. A selection of his most important papers has been published by Birmingham University (M. Wilson, ed., *Explorations in Health and Salvation*, 1983).

A. V. CAMPBELL

BRITISH PASTORAL CARE MOVEMENT; PASTORAL THEOLOGY, PROTESTANT; WHOLISTIC HEALTH CARE.

LANGUAGE. *See* COMMUNICATION; CONVERSATION, PASTORAL; LANGUAGE DEVELOPMENT; RELIGIOUS LANGUAGE AND SYMBOLISM; SYMBOLISM/SYMBOLIZING. *See also* PASTORAL THEOLOGICAL METHODOLOGY; THEOLOGY AND PSYCHOLOGY.

LANGUAGE, BODY. *See* BODY LANGUAGE.

LANGUAGE, PROFANE. *See* PROFANE LANGUAGE.

LANGUAGE, RELIGIOUS. *See* RELIGIOUS LANGUAGE.

LANGUAGE ANALYSIS. *See* PHILOSOPHY AND PSYCHOLOGY; PSYCHOLINGUISTIC THEORY IN PSYCHOLOGY AND COUNSELING.

LANGUAGE DEVELOPMENT. An aspect of child development referring to speech. Language constitutes a system of signals with socially derived meaning through which individuals represent their world (Bloom and Lahey, 1978). Structure exists at three levels: as sounds that make up words, as words that reflect meaning, and as rules for combining words into sentences. The development of language is intimately tied to the development of thought.

1. **Developmental Milestones. *a. First sounds.*** Infants develop all the basic sounds (phonemes) of their language within the first year. All infants make the same sounds for the first six months; but in the second six months differences emerge that reflect the particular sounds of their native language. By three to four months infants coo and chuckle and by six months babble by combining consonants and vowels. By nine to twelve

months babbling includes the rhythms of speech. Infants begin to understand certain words even while babbling. Words emerge at approximately twelve months (de Villiers and de Villiers, 1979; Lenneberg, 1967).

b. First words. Children say their first word at about one year. By eighteen months most children have vocabularies of approximately twenty words and add new words daily, learning approximately one thousand words by the age of three and from five to ten thousand words by age five.

Articulation errors, common at first, simplify pronunciation by reducing multisyllabic words to repetitions of the first syllable (*baba* for baby), reducing a word to a single consonant and vowel (*wa* for water), or reducing initial consonant clusters to single consonants (*poon* for spoon). Mastery of consonant clusters continues to develop through the preschool years (de Villiers and de Villiers, 1979; Lenneberg, 1967).

First words can communicate a variety of meanings depending on their context. *Milk* might mean *I want more milk, I drank all my milk,* or *I spilled my milk.*

c. First sentences. The syntactic structure to language becomes evident at approximately twenty-four months, when children begin combining words in simple two-word sentences. Early "telegraphic" sentences contain only high-information words and no articles, pronouns, or inflections. These sentences combine words from a small class of frequently used words (e.g., *more* as in *more milk, more tickle*) and a second, larger, and faster growing class of words (e.g. *milk, tickle*). These first sentences allow children to locate or name (*there truck*), demand (*more milk*), negate (*no bed*), describe events (*doggie go*), indicate possession (*Daddy shoe*), modify (*big ball*), and question (*where kitty*) (Slobin, 1971).

Sentences become more complex by children's third year, as they add plurals, articles, and prepositions and inflect verbs for tense; sentences are about three words long. Later they start to modify simple sentences (*I'm not sleepy*), and to ask simple questions. Later still they begin to use clauses and compound and complex sentences (Brown, 1973). By their fourth year, children have a solid understanding of syntax, though mastery of grammar continues to develop through the school years (Chomsky, 1969).

2. **Implications.** *a. Verbal control of behavior.* Verbal control over behavior develops gradually and is usually not complete before the age of five. By two, children can do something asked of them (*Blow the whistle*) but cannot with equal ease stop what they are doing (*Don't blow the whistle*). If anything, telling them to stop may make it more likely they will persist. Three-year-olds can inhibit actions when asked to, but, like four-year-olds, they have difficulty not doing something if they see someone else doing it (Luria, 1961).

b. Communication. Other problems exist because children lack concepts underlying some words. Children may agree to or even repeat warnings (*Stay out of the street because you might get hit*) and then disregard them, because children do not understand the concept of causality until nearly age eight. Similarly, preschoolers may not understand prepositions such as "before" and "after." A child might agree to a parent's "*Do you want a cookie after washing your hands?*" and hold out a dirty hand for the

cookie (order of mention communicates sequence to preschoolers) (Clark, 1971; Kuhn and Phelps, 1976).

c. Discipline. Because verbal control over behavior develops more gradually than speech itself, young children learn best by experiencing the consequences of their actions rather than by hearing rules. Telling them what to do has less effect than building habits. Even toddlers can anticipate the consequences of their actions when these are consistent and predictable. Words alone do not suffice for the very young. Child-proof door handles, a gate to the yard, and holding a hand when crossing the street are simple precautions for early language users, whose age makes external constraints more reliable than internal ones.

Bibliography. L. Bloom and M. Lahey, *Language Development and Language Disorders* (1978). R. Brown, *A First Language* (1973). N. Chomsky, *The Acquisition of Syntax in Children from 5 to 10* (1969). E. V. Clark, "On the Acquisition of the Meaning of Before and After," *J. of Verbal Learning and Verbal Behavior,* 10 (1971), 266–75. J. G. de Villiers and P. A. de Villiers, *Language Acquisition* (1978). D. Kuhn and H. Phelps, "The Development of Children's Comprehension of Causal Direction," *Child Development,* 47 (1976), 248–51. E. H. Lenneberg, *Biological Foundations of Language* (1967). A. D. Luria, *The Role of Speech in the Regulation of Normal and Abnormal Behavior* (1960). D. Slobin, *Psycholinguistics* (1971).

N. J. COBB

DEVELOPMENTAL DISORDERS; SPEECH DISORDERS AND THERAPY. *See also* COMMUNICATION; PSYCHOLINGUISTIC THEORY IN PSYCHOLOGY AND COUNSELING. *Compare* COGNITIVE DEVELOPMENT; DEVELOPMENTAL THEORY AND PASTORAL CARE; PERSONALITY DEVELOPMENT.

LAPSLEY, JAMES N. *See* PASTORAL THEOLOGY, PROTESTANT; THEOLOGY AND PSYCHOLOGY.

LAST RITES. *See* ANOINTING OF THE SICK, SACRAMENT OF.

LATIN AMERICAN PASTORAL CARE MOVEMENT. Although, due to cultural, political, and theological differences among the Latin American countries, there has been no uniform or clearly differentiated pastoral care movement, there are common characteristics of Latin American pastoral care which can be delineated.

1. **The Political and Economic Context.** This has been a major mixed case factor in the recent development of a broader understanding of pastoral care in Latin America. Long-term economic exploitation, by the international economic system or within nationally established political powers, has been a real challenge for pastoralists. The challenge comes from parishioners, nonbelievers, and particularly from the youth who represent a majority of the population: Why is there a predominantly individualist pastoral care if the roots of our individual and family problems, suffering, and poverty are in the macroeconomic and political structure of our society? This is the starting point for the development of the recent pastoral care movement.

2. **Current Understanding of Pastoral Care.** This mixed case is based on the sensibility and particular comprehension of the wider Latin American context.

Most seminaries teach that individual conversion and its accompanying behavior changes are the only means of changing the present situation. Other theological traditions emphasize transformation of societal structures to redeem the millions of Latin Americans.

As a consequence of their philosophical-theological presuppositions, there are denominations which are more involved in the individual dimensions of pastoral care, while other churches are working with the structural aspects. While students do internships in churches or hospitals, increasingly more seminarians are doing internships in Basic Ecclesial Communities (BECs), steelworkers' unions, slums, or in specific pastoral care among, for example, Latin American Indians, homeless children, landless peasants, and campus ministries.

3. **Churches.** *a. The Catholic church.* The Catholic church has historically represented the vast majority of the population and has been more active in the prophetic dimension of pastoral care that addresses structural problems. For example, national conferences of bishops have denounced the injustices of a system that favors the rich to the detriment of the poor, torture carried out by military governments, and the retention of vast portions of uncultivated land by a few landowners while children are dying of hunger.

b. Protestant churches. While some protestant churches (e.g., Methodist and Lutheran in South America; Baptist in Central America) are becoming more involved in the structural dimension of pastoral care, most concentrate their efforts and resources on the individual dimensions.

4. **Major Pastoral Responses.** J. B. Libanio, a Brazilian Catholic theologian, in *Pastoral numa sociedade de conflitos* (1982), identifies three major pastoral responses to the Latin American economic-political situation: psychological, religious, and dialectical-structural. Each of these has its limitations since each brings to pastoral care exclusively the psychological, religious, or sociological aspect of human problems. However, the pastoral care movement in Latin America is moving increasingly toward an integration of these three approaches, building on the specific efficacy of each one.

5. **Basic Ecclesial Communities.** The pastoral care movement in Latin America since the late sixties has been essentially a communitarian as well as a lay movement. This is visible in the thousands of BECs in rural areas or on the outskirts of cities. Pastoral agents trained by theologians and pastoralists have found within their own Christian experience, having themselves been oppressed by the economic-political system, important resources to participate as leaders of the BECs.

The BECs operate similarly to counseling groups, even though the main focus is not on individual needs; nevertheless, in BEC meetings, through common sharing, prayers, biblical study, and mutual support, individual needs are met. The basic methodology of the BECs includes three interdependent steps: see, judge, and act. The first step is to see one's own reality, or to identify one's problem; the second is to judge, or to inquire about the conditions that brought a person into a hopeless, helpless, humiliating, and inhuman situation; the third is to act, or to plan a course of action that will lead to full humanity.

This process is part of the whole liberation process. The Bible, particularly the story of the captivity and the Exodus, had been a decisive resource in the overall process of becoming aware of one's reality, of understanding the development of one's problems, and of taking the risk of acting out one's faith. Most of all, the BECs have been an instrument of empowerment of the poor in their struggles for liberation from the forces of death toward the forces of life.

Bibliography. A. Barreiro, *Basic Ecclesial Communities* (1983). H. C. Clinebell, *Counseling for Liberation* (1976). S. Leas, P. Kittlaus, H. C. Clinebell, and H. Stone, eds., *Pastoral and Social Action* (1981). J. B. Libanio, *Pastoral numa sociedade de conflitos* (1982). W. Oates, *New Dimensions in Pastoral Care* (1970). H. Seifert and H. Clinebell, *Personal Growth and Social Change* (1969). R. Shaull, *Heralds of a New Reformation: The Poor of South and North America* (1984). D. W. Sue, *Counseling the Culturally Different: Theory and Practice* (1981).

R. S. ROSA

INTERNATIONAL PASTORAL CARE MOVEMENT; PASTORAL CARE MOVEMENT. *See also* LIBERATION THEOLOGY.

LATTER-DAY SAINTS. *See* MORMON CARE AND COUNSELING.

LAW. *See* CODE OF CANON LAW; FAMILY LAW; LEGAL DIMENSIONS OF PASTORAL CARE AND COUNSELING. *See also* ETHICS; MORAL THEOLOGY.

LAW AND GOSPEL. *See* FAITH AND WORKS; FREEDOM AND BONDAGE; GRACE; LEGALISM AND ANTINOMIANISM.

LAWRENCE, BROTHER. *See* BROTHER LAWRENCE OF THE RESURRECTION.

LAY CARE AND COUNSELING. *See* LAY PASTORAL CARE; HISTORY OF ROMAN CATHOLIC PASTORAL CARE (United States); ROMAN CATHOLIC PASTORAL CARE.

LAY PASTORAL CARE AND COUNSELING. Pastoral care and counseling which (1) pertains to the laity, as distinguished from the clergy; (2) does not belong to nor is connected with a profession; nonprofessional.

1. **Lay Pastoral Care.** There is a widely held presumption that the congregation's pastoral ministry is the responsibility of the clergy. Visits by laity to fellow members are only infrequently identified as pastoral visits.

When the function of pastoral care is limited to work performed by the clergy, the scope of the pastoral function is also limited. In most congregations, clergy discharge this function through visits to members who are hospitalized or bereaved, and the provision of more or less formalized pastoral counseling. In any event, clergy pastoral care often is limited to crisis response and may exclude any general home visitation.

Shelp and Sunderland (1981) suggest two reasons for this trend. On the one hand, pastoral education in the U.S. has emphasized that clergy have a special function in pastoral care for which specialized training was designed, located almost exclusively in health care settings. On the other hand, opportunities for ministry were surrendered by individual members of congregations and assigned to the professional clergy.

It is regrettable that this development has limited the religious community's perception of pastoral care to response to illness, bereavement, or family crises. The congregation's responsibilities to its members should be perceived in the broadest possible terms, and include such ministries as regular pastoral contacts with each family, with children as well as adults, and on occasions of celebration as well as consolation.

a. The biblical tradition. The emphasis on service (abōdah, diakonia) in the Judeo-Christian tradition indicated that ministry was an obligation expected of believers, who were expected to serve God and, as a corollary, to serve their neighbors. The command to love the neighbor (Lev. 19:18) included readiness for and commitment to service of one's neighbor (Beyer, 1980). Such service was not optional (e. g., Num. 4:27). The verbs used were imperatives: command, charge. The designation of areas of service was the prerogative of the Lord, not of the people, who served at the Lord's command, not of their own volition.

The concept of service delineated in the NT grew out of the Hebraic foundation. The command to love one's neighbor was linked by Jesus with the command to love God. This constituted the substance of the divinely willed ethical conduct of his followers (Beyer, 1980). As in the Jewish Scriptures, Christian writers knew that response to the command of service was obligatory, not volitional. Paul became God's servant because of the task assigned to him by God (Col. 1:25). He perceived his call and assignment as a model for every Christian: "Christ is the master, whose slaves you must be" (Col. 3:24 NEB). It is God who is at work in the Christian, who must be obedient (Phil. 2:12–13). The Christian thus does not volunteer for the service of God, but is called (Eph. 4:1; 2 Tim. 1:9), enlisted, or commissioned to serve.

In the NT community, the sacrament of baptism became both the sign of call to ministry and of the presence of the Holy Spirit. The presence of the Spirit was manifested in part by the receiving of gifts for functions of ministry. These ministries included comforting, showing compassion, or shepherding that constituted key elements of love for one's neighbor (Romans 12; 1 Corinthians 12).

From this theological standpoint, whether one is called to participate in the ministry of pastoral care or that of pastoral counseling, either as a lay minister or an ordained minister, is governed by the determination that one has received these particular gifts of the Holy Spirit. The call to ministry in both Jewish and Christian traditions may be the call to participate in pastoral (caring) functions in the widest sense, or in those of pastoral counseling as a particular ministry — a call that may be addressed to clergy and laity alike.

b. Pastoral theology. Examination of the nature of lay pastoral ministry is a recent phenomenon in the Christian community. Seward Hiltner, for example, when delineating his basic assumptions of pastoral theology addressed only the role of the ordained minister. The topical index of his book *Pastoral Counseling* (1949) did not refer to lay participation. There was no departure from the assumption that it was the ordained minister

who performed pastoral functions. This was due to two factors. First, the tide was only just beginning to turn in the direction of renewal of the life of the congregations through a rediscovery of the role of the laity. Second, the role of the CPE movement in clergy education still had to be defended.

The work of pioneering had begun, but it did not occur to its exponents to extend either training or pastoral functions beyond the ranks of the professional clergy. Hiltner's 1949 statement assumed that pastoral functioning was a professional task, though given the same prerequisites that he applied to ordained ministers — evidence of call, training, and supervision—there was no inherent reason to exclude laypeople from pastoral responsibility.

Hiltner later addressed this issue explicitly in *Preface to Pastoral Theology* (1958). In this book, he developed the concept of pastoral care as *shepherding*, using this term as a "perspective," rather than as a definitive and exclusive stereotype. He proposed that the model of shepherding suggested an identification with pastoral care, as long as that term was seen to be involved to some degree in every act of church and minister, and to be dominantly important in some acts but not in others.

This image was extended to include laypeople — a transition Hiltner believed had not been made previously. He noted that previous discussion of the person in pastoral theology had concentrated on ministers as ordained clergy who had a theological education. He asked whether pastoral theology was a concern only of the clergy: is there not a universal pastorhood to go along with the universal priesthood of Protestantism?

Similar conclusions were reached by Williams (1961), Brister (1964), Oates (1964), and Clinebell (1984). It should be noted that in examining the work of God's people who were called to care for hurt humanity, Brister related caring ministry to the church's public ministry, in which it addressed itself to society's ills. This question was also addressed by Browning (1983), and deserves more careful attention from practitioners and researchers in the field of pastoral care and counseling than it has received.

Despite biblical injunctions and urgings of pastoral theologians, the identification of pastoral care as a congregational function to which both lay and clergy ministers are called, has been slow to emerge. Contemporary authors (e.g., Fenhagen, 1977, 1981; Schillebeeckx (1981a, 1981b), however, are taking up this theme. They suggest that the Christian community needs to develop an overall plan on the basis of which it can discern what kinds of differentiated pastoral teams are indicated for smaller and larger pastoral units in a given area.

It is assumed that the perception of the pastor who is capable of doing everything is clearly out of date. Nevertheless, the issue is not debated on the basis of pragmatic needs, but from biblical and theological images. The ministry Christians have been given in Christ is not a matter of task but of identity. *Ministry* is the word used to describe the way in which they live out the implications of baptism. For some, that will mean preparing for a ministry to people under the pastoral care of the congregation. The term *ministry* is linked to the NT concept of *giftedness*, and both terms are identified as signs of the presence of the Holy Spirit. The Christian community must clarify how gifts are expressed in ministry in both functional and theological terms, if it is to make a useful contribution to the dialogue over the world's future.

Fenhagen noted that the term *laity* comes ultimately from the Greek word *laos,* which means 'people.' The ministry of the laity means the ministry of the people of God exercised in every place where Christian people live and work. He left no doubt that, in his view, that includes the church's ministry of pastoral care (1977, p. 27).

c. Expectations. If it is to be effective, lay pastoral care must be characterized by the same intentionality that religious communities have come to expect of clergy. Expectations of lay ministers include adequate training, a system of accountability, and the provision of support for those people whose pastoral gifts have been recognized and who are called to exercise them in the service of the church. Campbell (1981) noted that the untrained helper's chief distraction is an overwhelming desire to be helpful. Effective ministry will result only when the caring person has accepted the discipline of training.

Second, it is essential that caring ministry be characterized by a level of accountability that reflects a self-consciousness of the importance of the task and the fact that the ministry is offered as an act of the caring community. Third, lay pastoral ministry is likely to be spasmodic and ineffective unless the caring minister receives support that both expresses the community's care for its own ministers and provides oversight, or supervision, by the community of its lay pastors.

2. **Lay Pastoral Counseling.** Pastoral counseling is usually regarded as a professional function requiring of the practitioner a higher level of training and supervision than that expected of ordained and lay ministers who are responsible for the more general ministry of pastoral care. The American Association of Pastoral Counselors has established standards concerning both education and services. Many states require professional counselors to qualify for state licensure before they are permitted to practice. When these standards have been met, pastoral counseling centers may employ social workers, clinical psychologists, and psychiatric nurses whose professional education has equipped them to provide counseling services.

In these instances, the efficacy of lay pastoral counseling will be determined by three factors: evidence of call and gifts for the pastoral counseling ministry, the adequacy of the counselors' training and the quality of supervision, and the degree to which counselors have resolved issues relating to identity and spiritual formation. In pastoral counseling centers which utilize lay counselors under such circumstances, training for the counseling profession and resolution of pastoral identity are the necessary preconditions which must be met for both clergy and lay members of the congregation's staff.

Bibliography. A. H. Becker, *The Compassionate Visitor* (1985). H. W. Beyer, "Diakoneō," *Theological Dictionary of the New Testament,* vol. 3, G. Kittel, ed. (1964). C. W. Brister, *Pastoral Care in the Church* (1964). D. S. Browning, "Pastoral Care and Public Ministry," *Christian Century,* Sept. 28 (1966), 1175–77; "Mapping the Terrain of Pastoral Theology, Toward a Practical Theology of Care," *Pastoral Psychology,* 36:1 (1987), 10–28. A. V. Campbell, *Rediscovering Pastoral Care* (1981). H. J. Clinebell, *Basic Types of Pastoral Counseling* (1984). B. Cook, *Ministry to Word and Sacrament* (1980). J. C. Fenhagen, *Mutual Ministry* (1977); *Ministry and Solitude* (1981). K. C. Haugh, *Christian Caregiving: A Way of life* (1984). S. Hiltner, *Pastoral Counseling* (1949); *Preface to Pastoral Theology* (1958). W. E. Oates, *Christian Pastor* (1964). E. Schillebeeckx, in L. Grollenberg et al., *Minister? Pastor? Prophet?* (1981a); *Ministry* (1981b). E. E. Shelp and R. H. Sunderland, eds., *Biblical Basis for Ministry* (1981). F. Wight, *Pastoral Care for Lay People* (1982). D. D. Williams, *Minister and Care of Souls* (1961).

R. H. SUNDERLAND

COMMUNITY, FELLOWSHIP, AND CARE; MINISTRY. *See also* CHRISTIAN LIFE; CONGREGATION, PASTORAL CARE OF; GROWTH GROUPS; ROMAN CATHOLIC PASTORAL CARE; SUPPORT GROUPS. *Compare* IDENTITY, PASTORAL; JEWISH CARE AND COUNSELING; ORDINATION; PASTORAL CARE (History, Traditions, and Definitions); PASTORAL COUNSELING; RABBINATE.

LAY-CLERGY DISTINCTION. *See* ECCLESIOLOGY; MINISTRY.

LAYING ON OF HANDS. *See* BLESSING AND BENEDICTION.

LAZINESS. *See* SLOTH AND ZEAL.

LEADER, PASTOR AS. *See* PASTOR (Normative and Traditional Images).

LEADERSHIP AND ADMINISTRATION. *Leadership* is the process of influencing the actions and behavior of persons and/or organizations through complex interactions toward goal achievement.

Leadership does not reside in the person of the leader alone. It involves accomplishing goals through persons. Leaders cannot function without the involvement of members. A relationship must be established between the leader and members through an ongoing communication process resulting in a common understanding and commitment as to the goal sought and the actions required for its achievement. Through this interaction, members are influenced to increase their involvement and support toward achieving the desired end.

Administration is a process through which an organization defines its purpose and moves in a coherent and comprehensive manner to plan and implement action through maximizing the utilization of its personnel and resources in achieving its purpose.

Administration, so defined, becomes a means to an end. The word administration is derived from the Latin word *administrare,* meaning to serve. Administration does not exist for its own sake, but as means to achieve the purpose of the institution it serves. Church administration therefore exists to serve the church through providing the processes, structures, and experiences through which the community of faith can accomplish its basic mission, i.e., "to increase the love of God and neighbor" (Niebuhr, 1956).

In this article leadership and administration are approached from the perspective of their relationship to one another as well as to pastoral care and counseling as modes of ministry. This is done from a systems perspective.

1. **Systems Theory and Ministerial Modes.** *a. Vignette of systems theory.* A human organization with an identi-

fied purpose can be viewed as a system. Its purpose defines its identity and distinguishes it from other systems. A system is a set of component parts (or *subsystems*) that work together to achieve a purpose. The subsystems, though distinct, exert interpenetrating impact on one another and the system as a whole, and also interact with relevant outside environmental systems. The components of a system must be mutually compatible if the system is to function effectively.

Functionally this means that a change in one subsystem affects other subsystems as well as the system as a whole. Changes in relevant external environmental systems will also influence the system. To view an organization from the perspective of systems theory requires focusing on the interaction of all the subsystems and their impact on the total system. See Churchman (1968), Lindgren and Shawchuck (1977), Pattison (1977).

b. Modes of ministry as subsystems. Several functional modes of ministry are required for the church to fulfill its purpose. These include worship, preaching, education, evangelism, community outreach, leadership, administration, and pastoral care and counseling. This article will view them as subsystems of the church's ministry. Systems analysis entails relating each ministerial mode to the purpose of the church, examining their individual goals and methodologies, their interaction with one another, and their impact on the church. A systems view is synergistic: individual modes of ministry cannot be seen as independent entities as their impact on the system is more than the sum of the parts.

c. The purpose of the system. The church as a system derives its mission and purpose from an intentional, combined study of at least six factors: Scripture, theological and doctrinal concepts of the church, tradition, the needs of the world and contemporary society, the needs of the local community, and the presence and direction of the Holy Spirit (Lindgren and Shawchuck, 1977). From these elements the overall, ongoing theological-missional purpose of the church is determined, including the church's theological stance in the world and its basic goals and objectives. This understanding of mission provides the standard and direction for each of the individual modes of ministry.

2. Dimensions of Leadership. *a. Goals.* The goal of leadership is to influence the behavior and actions of persons and/or organizations. Leadership is a broader concept than administration, though it is frequently discussed in relation to it. Leadership is involved in carrying out all modes of ministry. Administration is a particular setting through which leadership is expressed to accomplish group or institutional goals. Since leadership is concerned with influencing persons as well as institutions, this takes place in one-to-one settings as well as in groups.

Leadership, administration, and pastoral care and counseling each have distinct goals, but each must be compatible with the church's purpose to increase the love of God and neighbor. Pastoral care and counseling focuses on caring for human needs, usually on an individual basis. Administration, however, focuses on meeting the corporate needs of the community of faith through collective activities. The goal of leadership is to influence the behavior both of individuals and of the institution.

Whether these distinct goals are collaborative or in tension usually depends on the methodologies used to implement each.

b. Key variables. Leadership involves the interaction of a complex set of variable factors that determines its effectiveness. Douglas McGregor identifies four key variables of leadership (Lassey, 1971, pp. 17–25). (1) The characteristics of the leader. These include such qualities as skills possessed, previous experience in similar situations, skill in communicating and relating to persons, and the personal feelings of the leader about self confidence, anxiety, acceptance and hostility. (2) The characteristics of followers or members. These include such factors as their skills related to the task, depth of commitment to the goals, motivation to be personally involved, maturity in assuming responsibilities, relationship to one another, and record of performance. (3) The characteristics of the organization or the group. These factors refer to the group's past history, its expectations, style of operation, performance under pressure, the style of leadership to which it is accustomed, how well members work together, and the interpersonal dynamics of group members. (4) The environmental setting including the social, economic, cultural, and political milieu. Such factors as community history, economic situation, the political atmosphere, and accepted mores all affect organizational and group behavior. Leaders must be aware of these variables and their interaction as they determine what leader behavior will most effectively move a given group toward its particular goals.

c. Leadership styles. The behavior of the leader is the key factor in determining the response of a group. Leaders seek to stimulate group members to become involved in assuming leadership responsibilities themselves toward goal achievement. This style of leadership will seek distribution and sharing of power for motivational reasons. Persons have a stronger feeling of commitment to carry out decisions which they had a part in making.

Leadership styles vary greatly, and social science researchers have analyzed them from several perspectives. One approach measures leadership effectiveness in relation to the use of authority. Rensis Likert (1967) developed a four point spectrum of leader behavior ranging from "exploitative authoritative" on one end to "participative group involvement" on the other. His research indicates that the latter is measurably more effective in achieving the goals of the group, but requires a highly skilled leader and ongoing training of followers in assuming new responsibilities.

Another analysis of leadership style is to measure a leader's degree of concern for task achievement and concern for the needs of persons involved. Blake and Mouton (1969) developed a widely used nine-point grid to measure the concern for each.

Leadership does require a conscious choice as to how authority is to be used, and to the importance given to the needs of persons in the process of task achievement. These decisions must be made in the light of the four key variables identified above. No single leadership style is universally appropriate because of the differences in leaders, members, and situations.

For example, Shawchuck (1981) identifies four possible appropriate leadership styles: *task-oriented*, providing structure and close supervision; *total involvement*, active participation in all phases of the organization with equal attention to relationships, structure, and task; *person-oriented*, more attention to interpersonal relationships than to task; and *passive involvement*, basic withdrawal from active leadership, allowing the group to assume responsibility. The leader's choice of style depends upon the maturity of the group being led; factors in group maturity include degree of independence, flexibility, concern for others, time perspective, depth of interests, and understanding of the purpose, goals, and objectives of the group.

Greenleaf (1977) also maintains that there are two basic stances of leadership — conceptual and operational. The conceptual stance is primarily concerned with planning, defining, and overseeing the mission of the organization. The operational leader carries out the particular tasks as defined by the conceptual person or group. Both types of leadership are needed in any organization; usually one person does not perform both functions, though it is possible that one person may switch from one to the other depending upon the demands of a particular situation.

d. Pastoral theology of leadership. Regardless of the style of leadership used, a biblical and theological understanding of leadership is necessary for effective functioning within the body of Christ. The model of Christ is one of a self-emptying servant (Phil. 2:5–8) whose authority comes from example rather than from coercion or direct assertion of title (Mt. 21:23–27). In church leadership, authority comes from the faithful carrying out of one's call, utilizing gifts which were given by God and confirmed by the community of faith. As such, leadership exists for the sake of the community rather than for the glorification of the leader. Effective leaders are therefore listening proclaimers, wounded healers, and servant rulers (cf. Greenleaf, 1977).

3. **Components of Administration.** *a. Clarification of purpose.* The first function of administration is to clarify the purpose and mission of the institution it serves. Until an organization knows why it exists and the end results it is seeking, no meaningful planning and integrated actions can be initiated. The beginning point for church administration is to establish its purpose and mission and determine the ends toward which it is trying to move. Church administration can thus be described as theology in action, or faith with its sleeves rolled up at work in the church and the world. Before an administrator develops programs, it must first be decided why they are needed and what ends they serve.

The old English word *administry* referred to those tasks which contribute to or lead toward ministry. Through administration, the church as an organized structure is enabled to carry out its ministry and witness. For example, oversight of the Christian education program may be primarily administrative; without such oversight persons could not grow in their faith. Or working with trustees to maintain a church building means that worship, education, and pastoral care and counseling can continue to take place in that building.

Similarly, Seward Hiltner (1958) defined organizing as cognate with the pastoral tasks of shepherding and communicating. For Hiltner, organizing relates to the function of the church as a fellowship, the organic body

of Christ. Organization, or administration, seeks to bring to emergence the focus of the body itself and then attends to the relationships of that body to other bodies (structures, institutions) in the world.

As a primary operation of the pastor, administration, or organization, is also subject to the discipline of pastoral theology, which seeks to develop a theological perspective on all pastoral acts through systematic theological reflection upon those acts. The ministry of organizing requires such a theological perspective in order to maintain its validity as a function of the pastoral office (cf. Oden, 1983, ch. 11).

b. The administrative process. Administration is concerned with developing the means and resources to carry out, through integrated actions, the actualization of the purpose of the organization. Administration must be viewed as dynamic because it works with and through persons and groups in interaction and its subsystems influence one another.

There are five interactive stages in the administrative process: planning, organizing, staffing, implementing, and evaluating. The administrator involves members in developing and carrying out each of these stages, using the appropriate leadership style as delineated in the discussion of leadership. The insights from pastoral care and counseling relative to personality development and interpersonal relationships are also valued resources in working with people (see below). The administrative process seeks to equip the church to minister to the needs of its members and corporately to minister to the needs of society that cannot be done by individual Christians acting independently.

Planning involves identifying areas of need, selecting the best of alternative plans and developing them in detail. Planning, like all other stages, should be a process of shared participation in decision making and developing actions. Such involvement makes administration a context for possible personal growth, developing relationships, and ownership of programs. Within this process personal needs for relationships, mutual stimulation, and a sense of achievement can be met.

Other stages include organizing, to provide for a coherent and comprehensive use of resources; staffing, to secure and train persons for their tasks; implementing, to insure support and supervision in carrying out the planned actions; and evaluating, to check out the degree to which desired ends are being achieved.

Involvement of members at every stage will increase the probability of achieving desired results, personal growth, high morale, and meeting the personal needs of members.

c. Approaches and methodologies. The person of the leader as related to leadership functions is an important dimension of both administration and pastoral care and counseling. An understanding of personality dynamics is also essential for administrators as they continually work with and relate to persons. Sensitivity to personal feelings and needs will give the administrator an awareness of what is happening to persons through their involvement in administrative programs, and add a needed dimension to the evaluative process. Organizational and development skills are basic to administrators as they work with persons in one-to-one settings, with small groups, with interrelationships between groups, and the relationship of groups to the total organization.

4. Tension Areas Between Leadership, Administration, and Pastoral Care and Counseling. *a. Personal and organizational goals.* There is no inherent conflict between the goals of leadership, administration, and pastoral care and counseling as each is a mode of ministry seeking to express the purpose of the church. Tension is experienced, however, when some persons feel that the organizational goals and resulting programs do not meet, or are in conflict with, their personal goals and values. Organizational survival and change goals most frequently produce tensions and thereby increase the need for pastoral care and counseling. The pastor's role as leader and administrator, however, may block some persons from seeking help. Such tension may stem from the style of leadership and administration, how decisions are made, and insensitivity to feelings, and not necessarily from goal conflict.

b. Use of authority. Leaders who take aggressive advocacy positions in planned change, and authoritative administrators making nonparticipative decisions are perceived by some members as being insensitive to their feelings. This undermines a sense of trust, creates resistance and closes the door to a caring ministry. Conversely, a caring pastor in a counseling setting may develop a trust relationship that increases communication and acceptance of the pastor in administrative settings and thus reduces tensions.

c. Role conflicts. Role conflicts may be experienced on three levels: internally by the pastor, among the members and the pastor, and between the members themselves. The multiple modes of ministry require diverse skills and functions of the pastor causing competitive demands for time and energy. This causes tension within the pastor as to how priorities should be determined. Members also may experience these roles as being competitive and hold differing priorities for how the pastor's time should be spent and the ends sought. This not only increases tensions between members and the pastor, but among the members themselves. This frustration and tension as to the emphasis a pastor should give to leadership, administration, and pastoral care and counseling can reduce the effectiveness of each. An overall systems view of the church and ministry as a means through which the church can achieve its purpose is a needed framework for resolving role conflicts.

5. Caring Ministries Performed Through Leadership, Administration and Pastoral Care and Counseling. *a. In individual and group settings.* Caring ministries are experienced in the one-to-one relationship of pastoral care and counseling as well as in the groups and organizational settings of leadership and administration. These different settings meet different personal needs but are mutually supportive caring ministries. When persons need acceptance and support by a group, or to find meaning through involvement with others in a service activity, group settings best meet the need. Individual and group settings for caring ministries are complementary and supportive of each other. The acceptance and fellowship of organized church groups may provide supplementary support needed for persons moving through a crisis ministry in pastoral care and counseling.

b. Through meeting personal needs on different levels. Leadership, administration, and pastoral care and counseling provide caring ministries on different levels to meet the needs of the total person. Needs of particular groups of persons, such as senior citizens, youth, or single adults, are met best by organized programs geared to their concerns through the ministries of leadership and administration. Such groups also provide opportunities for growth, relationships, and self-development that contribute to the well-being and mental health of participants. Pastoral care and counseling provide an individual depth relationship for dealing with exploration of critical concerns in a way not possible in larger groups.

Leadership and administration focus on organizational health by seeking to relate personal and organizational goals in a mutually supportive setting. Pastoral care and counseling focus on personal growth and maturity within the context of the Christian community. Each meets different basic needs and contributes to the maturing of Christian persons.

c. By using divergent and complementary skills. Seward Hiltner (1976, 149–70) maintained that the pastor's role is one role. Even though each mode of ministry has its own special skills, when fully understood they can be usefully appropriated in other modes, but such transfer is neither automatic nor simple.

Skills that enhance all modes of caring ministries include: an understanding of personality development and interpersonal relationships, group dynamics, skills in listening, communication, decision making, counseling, systems theory, theologizing, and many others. The pastor seeks to utilize all appropriate skills in performing the several modes of ministry for the common purpose of increasing the love of God and neighbor. Developing the ability to integrate appropriately these various specific skills will increase the effectiveness of each. Ministry is impoverished if the skills are compartmentalized rather than used to enrich other ministerial modes.

Bibliography. R. Blake and J. Mouton, *Building a Dynamic Corporation Through Grid Organization Development* (1969). C. W. Churchman, *The Systems Approach* (1968). P. Drucker, *Management* (1974). W. B. Eddy, ed., *Behavioral Science and the Manager's Role* (1969). R. Greenleaf, *Servant Leadership* (1977). P. Hersey and K. Blanchard, *Management of Organizational Behavior* 4th ed. (1982). S. Hiltner, *Pastoral Counseling* (1976 [1949]) ch. 7; *Preface to Pastoral Theology* (1958). D. Katz and R. Kahn, *The Social Psychology of Organizations* (1966). W. R. Lassey, ed., *Leadership and Social Change* (1971). P. Lawrence and J. Lorsch, *Developing Organizations* (1969). R. Likert, *The Human Organization* (1967). A. J. Lindgren, *Foundations for Purposeful Church Administration* (1965). A. J. Lindgren and N. Shawchuck, *Management for Your Church* (1977). H. R. Niebuhr, *The Purpose of the Church and Its Ministry* (1956). T. C. Oden, *Pastoral Theology* (1983), ch. 11. E. M. Pattison, *Pastor and Parish: A Systems Approach* (1977). N. Shawchuck, *How to Be a More Effective Church Leader* (1981).

A. J. LINDGREN
G. H. ASQUITH, JR.

MINISTRY; ROLE, MINISTERIAL. See also ASSERTIVENESS IN MINISTRY; AUTHORITY ISSUES IN PASTORAL CARE; BISHOPS; CLINICAL PASTORAL PERSPECTIVE; COMMUNITY, FELLOWSHIP, AND CARE; CONFLICT AND CONFLICT MANAGEMENT; ECCLESIOLOGY AND PASTORAL CARE; STRUCTURING; SYS-

TEMS THEORY. *Compare* DISCIPLINE, PASTORAL CARE AS; EVANGELIZING; LITURGICAL CHANGE AND REFORM.

LEARNING DISABILITY (Theory and Treatment).

Difficulties with reading, writing, arithmetic, and listening characterize learning disabled children; in addition, they often show attentional, behavioral, and social problems. A short attention span, distractibility, inability to follow directions or sequence, poor impulse control, hyper- or hypo-activity, an aversion to academic tasks, and poor social relationships are often associated with academic underachievement. School psychologists refer students to special instruction if they test two years below grade level. This enrichment may involve contained classrooms or pull-out programs, or tutoring in the various subject areas.

Children with impaired cognitive development are called retarded and range from an I.Q. of seventy (moderate) to below twenty (profound). Youngsters with perceptual impairments, blind, deaf, and orthopedically handicapped, require specialized methods of instruction. School districts are mandated by federal legislation to offer classes to all youngsters no matter how severely impaired.

Emotional disturbances can lead to learning disabilities. To master the skills of reading, writing, arithmetic, and listening requires the ability to concentrate and generalize. Varieties of psychotherapy combined with rigorous activities designed to increase attention, develop the ability to follow directions, and control impulsive behavior seem to be the most effective remediation at present.

Dyslexic students have difficulties in reading. They reverse letters, numbers and whole words, and are unable to retain words learned through sight-say or phonetic methods of teaching. Methods of remedying this difficulty include intensive tutoring, speed-reading training, color coding letter combinations, and multimodality experiences.

Developmentally based sensory motor experiences, which increase brain lateralization, effectively remediate most dyslexia. Some special education classes teach compensatory skills such as the use of simply worded newspapers, drills on the shapes of street signs, and taped textbooks.

Aphasic students have difficulty with expressive or receptive language. Treatments involving speech therapy and language saturation attempt to remediate suspected damage to Wernicke's or Broca's areas of the brain. Other modalities of treatment stress auditory-perceptual motor matches and language processing skills to achieve increased cognitive functioning.

Hyperactivity is characterized by developmentally inappropriate inattention, impulsivity, and motion that is not goal directed. Behavior modification techniques have been widely used to settle these children, though with mixed long-term results. Drugs such as Ritalin may help concentration and reduce overactivity. Training in relaxation while problem solving on the motor perceptual or cognitive level have been very successful.

The difficulty inherent in the curriculum of the primary grades for developmentally delayed children may produce hyperactivity to avoid unmanageable tasks.

G. G. RODIGER

COGNITIVE DEVELOPMENT; DIAGNOSTIC AND STATISTICAL MANUAL III; HANDICAP AND DISABILITY. *Compare* DEVELOPMENTAL DISORDERS; MENTAL RETARDATION.

LEARNING THEORIES.

Learning theories have three basic functions. First, they are a way of analyzing, discussing, and doing research on learning. Second, they summarize the laws of learning. Third, they attempt to explain what constitutes learning and why learning works the way it does. In other words, learning theories define and organize knowledge about changes in human thinking or acting.

Learning theories fall into two major categories: stimulus-response theories, which include both contiguity and reinforcement approaches, and cognitive theories. Stimulus-response theories interpret learning as connections between stimuli and responses. A stimulus may be defined as any sensed event, while a response may be any behavior. According to this theory, learning occurs when there is a change in behavior as a result of experience. Cognitive theorists, on the other hand, are concerned with the attitudes, beliefs, and perceptions of the individual about his/her environment, and the ways these cognitions influence behavior. Learning is interpreted as a change in cognitions as a result of experience.

The choice between these two kinds of theories is most often determined by its application. A person most interested in conditioning or in a more precise, behavioristic approach will gravitate toward stimulus-response theories, whereas a person interested in problem-solving and complex intellectual process will find cognitive theories most amenable. The distinction is for classification purposes, but there is often an overlap in practice. The following discussion summarizes the models of learning theory formulated by notable theorists of both traditions.

1. **Stimulus-Response Theories.** *a. Contiguity theory.* John B. Watson (1878–1958) was one of the more colorful personalities in the history of psychology. Although he did not invent behaviorism, he became widely known as its chief proponent. It was Watson who ushered the behaviorist doctrine into the mainstream of American psychology, laying the groundwork for a science of psychology based on objective phenomena.

Watson believed that learning was the most important determinant of everything we are. For Watson, behavior, personality, and emotional disposition are all learned behaviors. Learning occurs as a function of a stimulus and a response occurring close together in time. When this happens, the connection between them is strengthened. How strong the connection becomes depends upon how frequently the stimulus and response occur together.

Another prominent theorist associated with the temporal contiguity theory of learning was Edwin R. Guthrie (1886–1959). Initially his theory was much like that of Watson's, but it evolved over the years and developed unique characteristics. Although his theory has not generated much research since its inception in 1935, its conceptual parsimony and simplicity have made it a popular inclusion in psychology textbooks.

Guthrie's theory was simple. Rather than emphasizing the gradualness of learning and conditioning, he advocated the view that learning occurs all at once. When two behaviors occur together they will automatically remain connected. This is a type of one-trial learning where, after a single connection is made between the stimulus and response, the stimulus will tend to evoke a similar response. Based on this principle, Guthrie maintained that the best prediction of future behaviors is past behavior in similar contexts.

b. Reinforcement theory. Edward L. Thorndike (1874–1949) was the first American psychologist to do learning experiments with animals. In terms of the number of books and papers he published, Thorndike was exceptionally productive. In his famous puzzle-box experiment, Thorndike demonstrated that if a hungry cat is put in a box, the cat can learn to work a mechanical device attached to a latch on the door in order to obtain food placed outside the box. He observed that two features of his experiments were necessary to guarantee learning. First, the cat had to be hungry. This meant that an explanation of learning had to include some motivational factor. Second, food was also necessary: learning would occur if and only if the cat's response had some effect upon its environment. This principle is Thorndike's famous "law of effect," which maintained that if a response had the effect of producing satisfaction, the connection between the stimulus situation and the response would be strengthened.

B. F. Skinner (1904–   ) is best known for the learning experiments with rats and pigeons in his "Skinner Box." His success in developing techniques for analyzing behavior and his ideas about how it should be explained have established him as one of the most prominent and influential theorists in psychology.

Skinner may have been the first to observe that learning is of two types—respondent and operant. Respondent behaviors are elicited by specific stimuli after which the response occurs automatically. These connections are called reflexes, some of which are innate and others the results of conditioning. Increased salivation at the sight of a juicy steak, for example, is a type of respondent behavior. This was demonstrated earlier in the classical experiments on conditioned reflex by Russian psychologist Ivan Pavlov (1849–1936), which had a major influence on the development of stimulus-response theories.

However, although operant behavior relies on a stimulus as a cue, it is not necessarily tied to it. A behavior is learned according to its effectiveness in influencing or "operating" on its environment, either being reinforced by the appearance of a positive result or being terminated by effecting a negative outcome. Buying food is an operant behavior, since the behavior is reinforced positively when the food is received and the negative condition of hunger is terminated. The connection is made not on the basis of what elicited the behavior, but as a result of the effect or consequences of the behavior in the given situation. Therefore, if an operant behavior is followed by reinforcement, the probability of its recurrence is increased.

2. Cognitive Theories. *a. Tolman.* Edward C. Tolman (1886–1959) stood outside the mainstream of behavioristic psychology. He was opposed to the stimulus-response theories and tried to replace them with a theory emphasizing the adaptive, flexible, and creative aspects of behavior. His system was therefore characterized as cognitive.

Tolman advocated the view that behavior is generally goal directed. A hungry cat, for example, directs its behavior toward food. The cat may not have a conscious purpose, but its *behavior* appears to be goal directed. Tolman introduced a new term, *purposive* behavior, to describe this crucial point, and argued that most human behavior is not so much a response to stimuli as a striving toward some goal. Stimuli are used as guides, but the goal gives unity and meaning to the response. If one is to understand and predict behavior, one must also identify the goal to which the behavior is directed.

Tolman posited six kinds of learning: (1) *Cathexis* is the tendency to seek certain goals rather than others when experiencing a specific drive. (2) *Equivalence belief* is a belief that a particular situation is rewarding or punishing in itself. (3) *Field expectancy* refers to ideas describing the way the world is laid out. (4) *Field cognitions* are tendencies to learn some things more easily than others. (5) *Drive discrimination* is what enables one to choose a appropriate goal. (6) *Motor patterns* are the muscular skills used to attain goals.

Tolman's cognitive theory made it impossible for learning theorists to ignore the principles of motivation, expectancy, and adaptiveness. His idea of purposive behavior broadened the conceptual framework in which behavior was understood and opened the way to new research in learning.

b. Gestalt theorists. Wertheimer, Kohler, and Koffka are considered the pioneers of what has become known as the Gestalt theory of cognitive learning. Here, learning is presented in the terminology of perception, or how one has learned to perceive the situation. For the Gestaltists, learning occurs as a result of perceptual reorganization and is therefore a conscious experience. Whereas stimulus-response theories reject the idea of a conscious experience or insight as an explanatory principle, Kohler observed that problems are often solved suddenly after a period of seeming inactivity. He suggested that this occurrence involves the structuring of the cognitive field to correspond with the stimulus field, achieved by grasping the relation of certain aspects of a situation to the whole.

According to Gestalt theorists, learning involves the grouping of elements in the internal or external environment in such a way that they create a consistent and simple whole. This approach has called attention to a number of organizational phenomena that depend on the total configuration of a stimulus rather than on its particular features. To explain these phenomena Wertheimer proposed two laws of perception that Koffka also applied to learning. The *law of proximity* refers to the grouping of objects or ideas as they fall close together in time or space. The *law of closure* states that closed areas more readily form units, gestalts, or wholes. People learn whole events, not specific parts.

Bibliography. G. H. Bower and E. R. Hilgard, *Theories of Learning* 5th ed. (1981). R. M. W. Travers, *Essentials of Learning: An Overview for Students of Education,* 2d ed. (1967).

D. AUFDERHEIDI

BEHAVIOR THERAPIES; BEHAVIORISM; GESTALT PSYCHOLOGY. *Compare* PERSONALITY THEORY.

LEFT BRAIN. *See* BRAIN RESEARCH.

LEGAL DIMENSIONS OF PASTORAL CARE AND COUNSELING.

Legal dimensions of pastoral care and counseling are aspects of the activities in which pastoral counselors engage that may give rise either to legally enforceable duties and liabilities between the counselor and client (obligations of contract and personal injury) or which may be subject to state control and regulation (licensing, communication privileges, and constitutional protections).

1. Overview. The legal dimensions of pastoral care and counseling are as diffuse as the nature of both the activity of counseling and the professional identity of the counselor. Legal aspects of the counseling relationship are derived from two polar extremes. To the extent that counseling is performed as part of a religious activity, the First Amendment of the United States Constitution provides a large degree of independence from legal control and regulation. To the extent, however, that the counseling activity falls within the scope of a socially identifiable secular professional activity, the relationship can and will be subject to a wide variety of laws and regulations.

This article focuses primarily on the legal dimensions of the professional activity engaged in by the pastoral counselor. Such dimensions occur chiefly in two separate aspects of pastoral counseling: the legal identity of the pastoral counselor and possible licensing requirements; and the legal duties, rights, and liabilities concomitant with the professional services provided in the pastoral counseling context. The legal aspects of the concerns presented by the client in the counseling relationship are summarized only for purposes of indicating the breadth of the dimensions in which legal questions may be encountered.

Insofar as the requirements of law vary from state to state, the pastoral counselor is encouraged to consult the specific laws of the jurisdiction in which the counselor is located, and to seek the advice of legal counsel as specific questions arise.

2. Legal Identity of Pastoral Counselors. *a. Religious context.* The specific identity of the pastoral counselor has not been defined by statute or judicial decision, thus there is no clear legal identity. The American Association of Pastoral Counselors, however, defines the *pastoral counselor* as "a minister who practices pastoral counseling at an advanced level which integrates religious resources with insights from the behavioral sciences" (*AAPC Handbook*, 2d ed., 1975, pp. 2–3). Because of this ambiguous and multifaceted integration, it is unlikely that a clear legal definition can be developed.

When the activity of pastoral care and counseling involves a pastor and parishioner in the context of a religious community, a certain degree of legal protection of this activity is provided by the United States Constitution. The First Amendment to the Constitution provides among other things that "Congress shall make no law respecting an establishment of religion, or prohibiting the free exercise thereof." When the relationship between an individual and a counselor is defined solely by the counseling activity rather than a broader religious context, or when the counseling function is offered to the public beyond the religious community, the legal dimensions become far more important, and far more complex. Though the boundary lines between what constitutes a "religion" and what remains a secular activity for purposes of the Constitution have never been clearly delineated, it is clear as a matter of constitutional law that any governmental regulation of religious activity will be scrutinized most closely before it is upheld. The activity of pastoral counseling and the legal identity of professionals engaging in such counseling lie across this uncertain boundary line. To the extent that pastoral counseling is considered primarily to be an activity undertaken within the context of religious activity, then the legal identity of the pastoral counselor may be synonymous with the legal identity of a priest, pastor, rabbi, or minister. To the extent, however, that pastoral counseling is viewed as being undertaken outside of the context of religious activity, then the activity itself and the counselor may be subject to requirements imposed by law. This distinction is vital both to the counselor's self-understanding of professional identity and to the legal requirements applicable to the counseling relationship. As a secular professional activity, pastoral counseling may be subject to governmental licensing requirements, to standards of care imposed by written or oral contracts, and to standards of care for avoidance of personal injury.

b. Licensing and certification. Partially because of the rapid growth recently in related professional associations, in formal education, and in social acceptance of the nature of counseling, governmental entities have begun to enact statutory or regulatory requirements pertaining to counseling in general. Such state regulation usually takes the form of statutes, requiring the counselor to proceed through licensing or certification requirements in order then to have the privilege of holding out to the public as a counselor. Though such statutes will frequently contain a broad exemption for pastoral counseling, or counseling within the context of religious activities, it is possible for an individual who possesses a formal religious affiliation to be subject to state licensing requirements if the individual engages in counseling in a context separate from that of a religious organization. Resting on the uncertain boundary line between a religious and a secular profession, however, the legal identity of the pastoral counselor will always be somewhat uncertain.

The emergence since World War II of several separate professional organizations related directly or indirectly to the activity of counseling has begun to provide one source of specific criteria for the identity of the pastoral counselor. Organizations such as the American Association of Pastoral Counselors, the Association of Clinical Pastoral Educators, and the Association of Marriage and Family Therapists have developed specific standards of professional competency, codes of ethics, and membership criteria. This movement toward professionalization will likely increase the ability and willingness of state and local governments to identify and regulate the delivery of services by this profession.

3. Legal Dimensions of Counseling Relationships. *a. Nature of relationship.* Legal dimensions of the counseling relationship are determined in the first instance by whether the specific activity is merely incidental and casual or is contemplated by the client or the counselor to be within the framework of a professional counseling relationship. In order to have significant legal consequences, it is not necessary that a client agree to pay a fee for the services rendered. All that is minimally necessary is that the client seek the service of an individual who is holding out as a counselor, and receive some degree of counseling from such an individual.

The commencement of any pastoral counseling relationship between a counselor and a client will have numerous possible legal consequences. A pastoral counseling relationship may be of extremely short duration or may extend over a period of months of years. Regardless of the length of such a relationship, an understanding by the counselor and the client of the scope of services to be provided and the anticipated length of the relationship is a prerequisite to the careful handling of legal questions, such as confidentiality, malpractice, payment of fees, and professional responsibility. Whether or not a counselor is able to share information received from the client with other counseling professionals, with members of the client's family, or with state and local agencies will be determined largely by the understanding reached between the counselor and the client. One valuable vehicle for clarifying the scope of services and legal questions from the outset is for the counselor and client, after discussing these issues, to reduce the salient points of the relationship to writing in the form of an "engagement letter." This letter from the counselor to the client could address such questions as the frequency and anticipated length of counseling, the fees associated with the counseling, and the ability of the counselor to share information with others.

b. Confidentiality. With certain exceptions, the relationship between a client and a pastoral counselor is one in which the client expects that all information shared by the client with the counselor will be held confidential by the counselor. This expectation by the client will be protected as a matter of law, and failure to fulfill this obligation will render the counselor liable for damages. If the counselor is a member of a professional counseling association, the breach of this obligation may result in possible professional disciplinary action. Unless the client otherwise agrees in advance, this expectation extends to any written communications between the client and the counselor received after the counseling relationship begins, as well as to any written notes or electronic recordings prepared by the counselor during the course of the relationship. Administrative or office personnel preparing transcripts or other summaries of the counseling sessions at the direction of the counselor are considered to be within the responsibility of the counselor and are held to the same duties protecting a client's rights of confidentiality. Except to the extent agreed upon by the client, preferably in writing in advance, the pastoral counselor is not at liberty to disclose to any third party the substance of the counseling relationship.

Failure to protect a client's rights of privacy and confidentiality may give rise to liabilities on the part of the pastoral counselor. The use of written waivers, releases, or consent forms may avoid this potential liability, but such forms must be understood clearly by the client and be as specific as possible with regard to the permitted forms of disclosure to third parties.

Counseling that takes place in the context of a group setting, or with more than one person present with the counselor, necessarily alters the expectations of the client as to the duty of confidentiality, but it does not eliminate the professional responsibility of the counselor to protect the communications of the client. Marriage and family counseling presents the added legal dimension of the rights of the various family members with respect to intrafamily communications. When a counselor is engaged in working with both spouses, whether separately or together, it is important that the expectations of each person with regard to disclosures made individually and in confidence to the counselor be clearly set forth and understood.

c. Communication privilege. At common law two forms of relationships—the attorney-client relationship and the husband-wife relationship—received certain legal protections from compulsory disclosure of communications within the relationship to third parties. Referred to as "testimonial privilege" or "communication privilege," this right recognizes that confidential information communicated in the course of such relationships belongs to the client or the spouse, and such individual may prevent the unauthorized disclosure of such information to third parties. In many jurisdictions this privilege has been extended in modified forms to other professional relationships such as physician-patient and clergy-communicant relationships.

The clergy-communicant privilege is recognized in a majority of jurisdictions, though the precise scope and requirements for eligibility of this privilege vary from jurisdiction to jurisdiction. A communication privilege, however, has *not* been uniformly accorded to the counselor-client relationship in the context of pastoral counseling. Given the fact that pastoral counseling frequently occurs in the context of a clear religiously affiliated activity, it may be possible that the client would be in a position to claim a "priest-penitent" or "clergy-communicant" privilege to the extent such privilege is recognized within the given jurisdiction. In the event that a communication privilege is not accorded to the pastoral counseling relationship, it is possible that a pastoral counselor may be required, pursuant to judicial authorization, to divulge any written or electronic transcripts of counseling sessions or to offer testimony pertaining to the counseling relationship.

d. Duty to disclose confidential information. Notwithstanding the obligations to protect a client's rights of confidentiality, under certain circumstances a pastoral counselor may have a duty to disclose confidential information to a third party without the consent of the client. One specific situation, for instance, is where the counselor is aware that a client may inflict serious harm upon a third party. One court has held that a therapist, who determines that a client presents a serious danger of violence to a third party, is under a duty to exercise reasonable care to protect the third party (*Tarasoff vs. Regents of the University of California*, 551 P.2d 334 [1976]). Where a counselor is aware of the possibility of a client committing suicide, it is possible that the counselor will be held to have a duty to undertake reasonable efforts to prevent such an action.

e. Malpractice. While most professional service relationships (e.g., attorneys, physicians, psychiatrists) have traditionally enabled clients to sue for failure to provide the appropriate professional services in accordance with accepted standards of care, such personal injury, or malpractice, actions are recent phenomena within the pastoral counseling relationship. In light of the broad deference generally accorded professionals engaged in formal religious activities by virtue of the First Amendment, courts have traditionally been reluctant to sustain a lawsuit against clergy for breaching professional duties. One possible reason for this reluctance has been that such a lawsuit requires a legal decision as to the precise scope of the individual's religious duties.

Notwithstanding this hesitancy to inquire into the scope of a religious counselor's duties, several lawsuits have been filed in recent years seeking to hold clergy liable for actions arising from the counseling relationship (see, e.g., *Nally vs. Grace Community Church,* 253 Cal. Rptr. 948 (1988). Thus far, however, such suits have not resulted in a discernable trend toward the recognition of malpratice actions in the pastoral counseling context. Despite this absence of clear liability, malpractice insurance for pastoral counselors is offered by several insurance carriers, and professional associations offer group insurance plans that include malpractice coverage.

f. Record keeping, tapes, and transcripts. A counselor's duty of confidentiality extends to all of the products of the counseling relationship, including file records, written notes, and tape recordings. The counselor is under a duty to the client to prevent all forms of unauthorized disclosure of such records, and has a duty to ensure the security of such documents or tapes. Descriptions of counseling situations, whether in published form or in oral presentations must not be susceptible to disclosing the client's identity unless the counselor has received the express permission of the client.

Where "verbatims" or typed transcripts of conversations between a counselor and client are prepared for educational or research purposes, such transcripts are subject to the professional and legal duties owed by the counselor to the client. Unless the client has expressly consented to the preparation of transcripts, the transcript should be modified so as to render it impossible for any third party reading the transcript to ascertain the identity of the client. The transcript should be shared with others only to the extent absolutely necessary, and the counselor is advised to destroy all copies other than the counselor's file copy upon completion of use.

4. Legal Dimensions of Client's Concerns. Almost invariably the concerns presented to the pastoral counselor will include a broad range of legal aspects. The counselor needs to exercise caution in not advising or counseling the client as to the specific legal issues which are raised, for this would possibly constitute the unauthorized practice of law.

Being unable as a matter of law to render legal advice, however, does not undercut the counselor's need for awareness of the magnitude of the legal aspects of the client's concerns. For example, marital counseling may well involve the need for the counselor to be aware and have some knowledge of divorce law, marital property laws, and the legal consequences of prior marriages. In family counseling relationships, an awareness of the laws pertaining to reproductive counseling (abortion, contraception), child abuse, and familial duties (child support) will enrich the counselor's abilities.

In such situations the counselor may wish to consult an attorney who specializes in the applicable laws of that jurisdiction in order to gain a general understanding of the laws involved, or the counselor may refer the client directly to an attorney. Permission of the client must always be obtained by the counselor prior to consulting with an attorney on the specific aspects of a client's concerns when that client's identity will be revealed in the process. Similarly, any cooperation, consultation, or "team counseling" by the pastoral counselor with other professionals on a specific matter requires the client's permission in order to protect the client's rights of confidentiality.

5. Summary. The legal dimensions of pastoral care and counseling are broad and uncertain. The legal identity of the pastoral counselor will depend in large measure on the relationship between the counselor and religious organizations and institutions, and on the context of the pastoral counseling activity. The legal aspects, in turn, depend upon these same factors.

As a religious activity, pastoral counseling is likely to continue to rest within the penumbra of legal protections provided by the First Amendment to the U.S. Constitution. To the extent that counseling activities become increasingly detached from religious affiliation, however, the individual counselor and the counseling activity are likely to be subject to state regulation and lawsuits seeking damages for breach of professional duties. The counselor is encouraged to seek the advice of legal counsel concerning any specific question.

Bibliography. American Association of Pastoral Counselors, *Handbook,* 2d ed. (1975). R. E. Augspurger, "Legal Concerns of the Pastoral Counselor," *Pastoral Psychology,* 29 (1980), 109–22. S. Ericsson, "Clergyman Malpractice: An Illegal Theory" (1986). C. E. Funston, "Made Out of Whole Cloth? A Constitutional Analysis of the Clergy Malpractice Concept," *California Western Law Review,* 19 (1983), 507–44. H. N. Malony, T. L. Needham, and S. Southard, *Clergy Malpractice* (1986); "Matters to Which the Privilege Covering Communications to Clergymen or Spiritual Advisor Extends," *American Law Reports Annotated,* 3d series, 71 (1976), 794–838; "Developments in the Law — Privileged Communications," *Harvard Law Review,* 98 (1985), 1450, 1555–62.

F. S. ALEXANDER

CONFIDENTIALITY; COVENANT AND CONTRACT IN PASTORAL COUNSELING; LICENSURE; RECORD KEEPING; STANDARDS FOR PASTORAL COUNSELING. *See also* FAMILY LAW; FEES IN PASTORAL COUNSELING; MALPRACTICE; MENTAL HOSPITAL/MENTAL HOSPITALIZATION; PASTORAL COUNSELING; SANITY/INSANITY. *Compare* ECCLESIOLOGY AND PASTORAL CARE; ETHICS, PROFESSIONAL; MORAL DILEMMAS IN PASTORAL PERSPECTIVE; PROFESSIONALISM.

LEGALISM AND ANTINOMIANISM. The absolute acceptance or rejection of law (*nomos*) as the basis for human behavior. Legalism makes the demands of law determinative in every situation. Antinomianism insists on freedom from any such norms. The terms represent contrasting extremes which both treat law as a set of rules; the one endorsing prescriptive patterns for all human response, the other rejecting them. Both terms frequently carry pejorative weight, with their critical focus on tendencies toward rigidity.

1. Factors in Human Dynamics. Persons are deeply influenced by attitudes to law in relation to decisions. Legalism and antinomianism refer to such attitudes in their inclusive and exclusive extremes.

Legalism exalts conformity, finding rules for everything. It makes every decision an instance of a definite class. The issue for responsible behavior is to determine which class is involved and which rules apply. The diversity of individuals, situations, and consequences are considered insofar as they assist in ascertaining the relevant rule.

Antinomianism—or libertarianism, as it is frequently labeled—rebels against conformity. It rejects the classification of situations and responses. One must decide each case *ex nihilo*. As the rational attempt to classify fades into the background, emotion and affective inclination assume greater roles. Doing what's "comfortable" or what "feels right" replaces other criteria.

Not every appreciation of law is legalism. Neither is every criticism or relativizing of such norms antinomianism. Rules can be appreciated as aids in routine response, without making the charge of legalism appropriate. Everyone develops habits or policies that allow some classification and quick response. Legalism takes this to the extreme, seeking absolute consistency between comparable situations. Antinomianism is the reverse, where no consistency is sought or expected. Every decision must be made from scratch with no guidelines.

The absoluteness of these approaches makes them tempting directions for human self-understanding. They offer such simplistic perspectives on all of life that they are not merely approaches to behavior, but profound ways of conceiving the self in its relationships. They are also unrealistic. As goals for behavior and as foundations for self-understanding, they are substitutes for more responsible human orientation.

Legalism appears first as a rule-oriented ethic where actions are right or wrong, depending on whether or not they conform to general principles. This elevation of rules is seen to apply also to motivation, mind-set, and estimates of the self. The framework of rules becomes the ground for self-acceptance and life orientation.

Antinomianism manifests the opposite of legalism. It is not merely a libertarian approach to behavior. Its rejection of all external authority as a basis for either decision or life orientation is pervasive. In terms of self-worth, it puts the entire burden on the individual's capacity for self-acceptance.

Legalism and antinomianism are mirror images of one another. They both reflect simplistic models of authority. Each reduces law to rigid rules. Each obscures all the other possibilities. Historically, they have usually been seen as distortions of living faith. They have had special prominence as oversimplifications of Jewish and Christian commitments.

2. Biblical and Theological Perspectives. The use of the terms legalism and antinomianism is laden with biblical concerns and theological interpretation. The key here is the centrality of grace. When the mercy of God, forgiveness, and love for the unrighteous are taken seriously, legalism and antinomianism become the obvious modes of rejection of the divine intention. With a dynamic God of love at the center of both Jewish and Christian self-understanding, the place of law must be understood differently than in strict legalism or antinomianism. God's initiative calls for more complex relational views of identity and authority.

The critical perspective on legalism and its mirror twin antinomianism rests on both the Hebrew Scripture and the Christian New Testament. In each of these, law is a much richer term than we often realize. In Jewish Scripture, Torah (law) means the entire revelation of God's relationship to humans, not just the relevant rules. Law is a gift of love, not merely a demand. So also in the NT, terms for law are more varied in their meaning. References to law often point back to the Hebrew usage as an appeal to the entire Torah, not to some set of simplified commandments. Indeed, as in the prophets, law can be written on the heart, making its directive vision compatible with responsible decision.

Thus, the interpretation of Judaism as legalistic needs reconsideration. So does the tendency to see Christianity—including its more Pauline forms—as antinomian and libertarian. Concern with legalism and antinomianism as unhelpful human postures is reinforced both by the Hebrew Scripture and the NT.

Exemplary attacks on both legalism and antinomianism pervade Jesus' ministry. His emphasis on "The sabbath was made for man, not man for the sabbath" (Mk. 2:27) is a key illuminating instance. For Jesus, even the most significant rules had to be treated in the light of broader purpose and perspective. At the same time, Jesus showed persistent respect for the law even as expressed in rules. It was his claim to fulfill, not abolish it. So one can see Jesus as working against legalism and antinomianism. Somehow Jesus represents an appeal to law as a manifestation of God's will that affects our deepest motivation and self-esteem, pointing us to a love that frees us from both our desperate efforts to conform and our frenzied experiments with nonconformity.

Paul's interpretation of Jesus provides much of the theological background for our understanding of legalism and antinomianism. Paul shifts the weight of ethics, as Jesus had done, towards the needs of neighbor, rather than conformity to rules: "'All things are lawful,' but not all things are helpful" (I Cor. 10:23) At the same time, he repeatedly rejects the easy claim that Christians are free of all accountability.

Paul also deals directly with the inadequacy of legalism as a basis for self-worth. He gets at the deepest uses of law as the ground for self-understanding. For him, the law always accuses as human beings seek conformity to standards of perfection. Grace is the alternative where self-appreciation is the gift of God's love. A person's sense of worth is not the result of sheer determination to love oneself either. It rests on an initiative from outside, in love. Such love frees one from the law as a way of salvation, but it also frees people to do what the law requires, serving the neighbor in actual situations. Here there is no room for either legalism or antinomianism—and one can see why these terms have carried so much freight. They represent the perennial alternatives to life understood under the will and mercy of God.

Notice needs to be given to the way the Pauline emphasis has been developed in denominational conflicts in the Christian church. Here the charge of legalism was freely leveled against Roman Catholicism by an emergent evangelical Protestantism. The good news of grace that frees from the bondage of the law led easily to the perception of others as legalistic. Much in the same way, the "liberated" Protestants would be viewed as irresponsible in their neglect of God's will.

This twofold dynamic of charge and counter-charge has also been operative within and between Protestant denominations. Opponents or those misunderstood have frequently been interpreted as blatantly legalistic or irresponsibly situational.

Current trends in ecumenicity have helped greatly on this score. It is now easier to see reductive tendencies toward legalism and antinomianism in all groups, rather than simply noting them in others. This makes the entire discussion of legalism and its reactive libertarian partner a resource for use in the broad concern for personal development.

3. **Practical Considerations** Legalism and antinomianism are widely recognized factors in pastoral care and counseling. If healthy self-acceptance is a goal of such initiatives, then legalistic and antinomian postures are precisely what needs correction. They indicate authority problems in which creative interaction between the inside and outside world of the client is short-circuited by a mind set that shuts one or the other out of the action.

The problem is not properly seen as merely the contrast between external and internal norms. Both legalism and antinomianism result from conflicts and pressures that function internally. In Freudian terms, legalism is the tendency toward domination by the superego. Somehow an idealized self is set as the internal standard of success.

In reaction to frustrated attempts to conform to an ideal self, individuals are often inclined to absolutize their given identity and behavior. Again, the tension between the ideal and the real is not allowed creative interplay, and genuine growth and satisfaction are inhibited.

The effect of legalistic tendencies is oppressive. Should people find themselves worthwhile only when they conform to imposed rules or an absolute ideal, the result is diminishment of the self as an important factor. The very effort to conform increases self-depreciation or equally damaging self-deception. While legalism may be a stage on the way to something better, by itself it is a frustrating dead end.

In a similar way, antinomianism, as rejection of external accountability, or as an internal reaction against the ideals of the superego, makes the development of appropriate self-acceptance a formidable challenge that is ultimately self-defeating. It puts a weight on the shoulders of the individual that is as heavy as any form of legalism. Not needing to conform to given expectations quickly becomes "nobody cares" and "nothing matters." The end result is not a resilient sense of self-worth, but distaste for "total freedom" and sheer fatigue over trying to "love oneself by oneself."

The inner tension between conformity and rebellion also frustrates. When the choice is seen as only between these two (legalism and antinomianism) no healthy

appreciation of the real ambiguities of living relationships and situations can emerge. In this way, both legalism and antinomianism are legal in their orientation. Neither tendency allows the individual to consider both situations and principles, and thus come to conclusions for which responsibility can be taken.

Antinomianism has the special problem that it hides its own assumptions from any criticism or correction. As Seward Hiltner has described it, "The more libertarian the conduct, the greater the chance that compulsion rather than new consciousness is at work."

In pastoral concern, then, the identification of both legalistic and antinomian tendencies is important. Obsession with conformity to ideal expectations is a serious problem. Compulsion to rebel against all standards indicates quite similar difficulties. Recognition of these problems will allow some awareness of alternatives to surface and a strategy for help to develop. So, understanding legalism and antinomianism will drive both client and counselor to fresh understanding of a more viable perspective on identity and authority.

The alternative directions are widely touted in psychotherapeutic literature. Interaction, relationships, and an appreciation of process over time are all important. Trust is the key, so that some relationships of interaction provide a foundation for acceptance that will also allow honesty about ambiguity, dissonance, and growth.

For pastoral care and counseling, the theological grounding of alternatives to legalism and antinomianism is a decisive ingredient both for the one who does the caring and the one who receives it. The radical appreciation of God's initiative of love and acceptance can be a powerful dynamic to help people move beyond the limits of obsessive conformity or narcissistic self-assertion.

Bibliography. S. Hiltner, *Theological Dynamics* (1972), pp. 18–24, 193–95. R. Niebuhr, *The Nature and Destiny of Man*, vol. 2 (1953), pp. 39–41. C. R. Rogers, *On Becoming a Person* (1961), pp. 163–82. P. Tillich, *Systematic Theology*, vol. 2 (1967), p. 81.

L. LUNDEEN

CONSCIENCE; ETHICS AND PASTORAL CARE; FAITH AND WORKS; FREEDOM AND BONDAGE. *See also* ANOMIE/NORMLESSNESS; MORAL THEOLOGY; OBEDIENCE; PERFECTIONISM; RESPONSIBILITY/IRRESPONSIBILITY; PSYCHOLOGY OF; SCRUPULOSITY. *Compare* AUTHORITARIANISM; CASUISTRY; GRACE; HUMAN CONDITION/PREDICAMENT; MORAL BEHAVIOR AND RELIGION.

LEISURE. *See* PLAY; REST AND RENEWAL, RELIGIOUS TRADITIONS OF.

LESBIANISM. *See* HOMOSEXUALITY.

LEUBA, JAMES HENRY (1868–1946). Psychologist of religion. A native of Neuchâtel, Switzerland, Leuba studied under G. Stanley Hall at Clark University and published in the *American Journal of Psychology* some of the earliest articles in the psychology of religion.

A zealous foe of Calvinism, Leuba turned gradually to a purely functional understanding of religion as an activity of a natural organism seeking preservation and enhancement of its life. Through his early studies of the psychology of conversion, he reached the conclusion that a "science of religion" could produce a new form of "soul-midwifery" grounded on positive knowledge (*American J. of Psychology*, 7 [1896], 311). That new style of pastoral care would reflect an understanding of the natural morphology of "regeneration," a movement from a sense of shame and sinfulness (rooted in changes within the physical organism) to a moment of self-surrender through which conflicting impulses coalesced around a new center of unity within the self.

Leuba's materialism limited his influence on pastoral theologians, but he was a pioneer in the study of the psychology of religion, a discipline that deeply informed early twentieth-century revisions in the understanding of pastoral care.

E. B. HOLIFIELD

PSYCHOLOGY OF RELIGION (Theories, Traditions, and Issues). *See also* HISTORY OF PROTESTANT PASTORAL CARE (United States).

LEUKEMIA. *See* CANCER PATIENT.

LEWIN, KURT (1890–1947). Initially represented German Gestalt psychology, founded "field theory" (or topological psychology), and finally founded "action research" and "group dynamics." He left his faculty position at Berlin in 1932, when the Nazi rise to power compelled him to emigrate to the U.S., and served on the faculties at Stanford, Cornell, the University of Iowa, and on the Research Center for Group Dynamics at the Massachusetts Institute of Technology.

Lewin must be regarded as a major systematic psychologist. While he is most often regarded as a social psychologist, he is featured as a personality theorist in C. S. Hall and G. Lindzey's *Theories of Personality* 2d ed. (1970); as a systematic psychologist/learning theorist in S. Koch's *Psychology: A Study of A Science* vol. 2, (1959); as a developmentalist in A. L. Baldwin's *Theories of Child Development* (1967), and as a motivational theorist in B. B. Wolman's *Handbook of General Psychology* (1973).

H. VANDE KEMP

FIELD THEORY; PERSONALITY THEORY (Varieties, Traditions, and Issues).

LIABILITY INSURANCE. The professional practice of ministry can result in charges of alleged malpractice by persons who seek services from the minister. Counseling and advice to others create particular vulnerability to such charges. To cover risk of legal suit, ministers may purchase professional liability insurance coverage, usually through professional associations or denominational judicatories. Such insurance is relatively inexpensive since legal action against ministers, priests, and rabbis has been infrequent.

J. W. EWING

LEGAL DIMENSIONS OF PASTORAL CARE AND COUNSELING; PASTORAL COUNSELING, ECONOMICS OF.

LIBERATION THEOLOGY AND PASTORAL CARE. The mutually critical intersection of a particular (esp. Latin American) theology and a particular (esp. North American) therapy, each of which draws in different ways on the secular disciplines of sociology and psychology as well as from Scriptures and church tradition.

1. Liberation Theology. *a. Development and response.* The critique of domination presented by Latin American Catholic bishops at their meeting in Medellin, Columbia, in 1968 set the stage for what has come to be known as liberation theology. The meeting outlined three fundamental pastoral directions for the church in Latin America, which have come to constitute the core of liberation theology: (a) the formation of basic communities comprising persons from all walks of life for Bible study and worship, (b) becoming a church for the poor, and (c) collaboration with Protestants in the pursuit of justice and freedom for all people. The bishops based these directives on the conviction that the salvific work of Jesus Christ is inextricably bound to the emancipation of the poor and oppressed from the sociopolitical structures of domination, and that God calls Christians to stand in solidarity with all victims of oppression.

Given its revolutionary implications, theology of liberation disturbs those who consider it a threat to ecclesiastical orthodoxy and democratic capitalism. These critics maintain that the gospel is not to be politicized along lines drawn by socioeconomic and class distinctions. Furthermore, liberation theologians express a strong affinity with the Marxist critique of capitalism, a fact often adduced as evidence of their subversive communist-socialist intentions and religious blasphemy. Such charges against liberation theology are simplistic, however: one cannot reduce the emancipatory objectives of liberation theology to an argument between capitalism and communism.

b. Emancipatory praxis. Aristotle's definition of praxis as action governed by intrinsically valuable ends, such as justice and freedom, provides a useful point of departure for explicating the relationship of theory and praxis in liberation theology. Theology as an authentic praxis must be critically informed by the emancipatory ends of its tradition. This means that theology must be committed to interdisciplinary collaboration and must, furthermore, be critical of itself. Its task is to "acutely experience the contradictions—not complementarity—between past and present theories, on the one hand, and the imperatives of authentically transformative praxis on the other" (Lamb 1982, p. 84).

Liberation theology understands itself as critical reflection and action upon the vocation of ministry set forth in the gospel. It reaffirms the gospel's liberation of the poor and the oppressed, it argues that poverty must be examined as a systemic condition involving power relationships, and it asserts that theology must be interpreted in the context of the total society in which the gospel is preached. Succinctly stated, authentic, gospel-centered self-transformation necessitates the transformation of power relationships. Accordingly, liberation theology incorporates a Marxian critique of domination as a method of social analysis.

Following Marx's critique of religion as "the opiate of the people," theologians of liberation have attempted to bring to consciousness the class interests and social domination underlying theological discourse. They challenge any theology that supports any form of oppression to come to terms with the imperatives of freedom and justice. Consequently, liberation theology must necessarily hold together critique (drawing on critical social theory) and crisis (a turning point eventuating from contradictions inherent in a system or situation). Thus, the theoretical project of liberation theology, including critique of domination, relates directly to concrete action—the emancipatory praxis of social transformation. Whether such transformation assumes a specifically Marxist-socialist form of government or democratic socialism is secondary to the goals of justice and freedom. Critique takes precedence over orthodoxy, and theory is not divorced from praxis but is the reflective dimension of praxis.

Without elaborating on the constitutive elements of Marxian analysis of class structure and capitalist production, it is sufficient to point out two aspects of Marxian anthropology relevant to pastoral care: first, the belief that persons create themselves and society through their work; and, second, the claim that the historical material forces of production and the social fabric of human relationships change and are changed by each other over time. These claims help Marx to demythologize all forms of transcendence, which distort the truth that the human condition is the product of material life. He aims to ensure emancipation from all forms of domination and subordination, thereby eventuating in a classless society.

Marx's critique of capitalism is attractive to theologians of liberation who witness the pathological dependence of the poor on the power elite in Latin America and the economic injustice fostered by capitalist-industrialist nations upon the "developing nations." His polemic against individualism resonates with efforts on the part of theologians of liberation to cultivate "basic communities," in which corporate responsibility for social action takes hold at a grass roots level in persons from all walks of life. These "basic communities" are an appropriate location for putting into practice the emancipatory objectives of pastoral care and theology of liberation.

2. **Pastoral Care as Emancipatory Praxis.** From a liberationist's perspective one should conceive of pastoral care fundamentally as the care of society itself. That is, one should understand the needs and hurts of individuals in their primary relationships—the primary focus of pastoral care and counseling—in terms of the macrosocial power relationships of domination and exploitation. For these larger relationships structure selfhood, personal experience, and individual behavior in fundamental, if usually unrecognized, ways. Thus pastoral care must always engage in a mutually critical conversation with theological and social scientific methods informed by an emancipatory praxis.

The therapeutic objectives of pastoral care as ordinarily conceived and practiced span a wide spectrum, including personal adjustment, self-realization, self-acceptance, and emancipation from the quasi-causal power of the unconscious. Especially with respect to the latter objective, Jürgen Habermas's interpretation of psychoanalytic therapy as "an emancipatory science of communicative interaction" (Lamb, 1982, p. 85) offers a bridge between pastoral care and liberation theology. Habermas argues that psychoanalysis *is* praxis-oriented by virtue of its commitment to the elimination of ideological distortion and instrumental rationalism. Although pastoral care is

not psychoanalysis, Habermas's point suggests that pastoral care, like critical social theory, and liberation theology, may have the goal of identifying "possibilities for radical change towards a society in which human beings exercise fully their capacity for self-conscious control over social processes" (Keat, 1981, p. 3). To this extent, pastoral care needs to be informed by critical social theory.

Serious difficulties preclude accepting Habermas's critical social theory in its entirety, however. The theory targets no group for application—no congregation as the locus of communicative praxis. Thus, the imperatives of social justice and undistorted communication, though commendable, remain sterile insofar as passion is divorced from reason, tradition is perceived as an inevitable bearer of distorted communication, and humanity and nature are treated as though ontologically separate. Most importantly, Habermas has no feeling for the nuanced mysteries of theology; hence his project in social transformation lacks any appreciation for divine transcendence, while transcendence is the cornerstone of pastoral care and the theology of liberation.

Liberation theology thus brings to pastoral care the same concerns offered by critical social theory but mediates these concerns theologically through the church, as it struggles to ensure the fullness of life. "Basic communities" express concretely the concern that the political realm is the most comprehensive and decisive arena of praxis (Sölle, 1974, p. 69). Here the emancipatory goals of pastoral care thrust beyond the contours of individual life history and into "the broadest horizon within which human life unfolds and develops" (Fierro, 1977, p. 28).

3. **Conclusion.** The basic premise that liberation theology is guided by faith in the transcendent means that it carries a "surplus of meaning" extending beyond the emancipatory praxis of any particular person or group. This is the same basic premise of pastoral care. In a mutually critical dialogue the theology of liberation challenges pastoral care to resist elevating *techne* (i.e., clinical mastery) over praxis and divorcing the private interior self from public life. On the other hand, pastoral care challenges the theology of liberation to resist being transformed into dogma or identified simply as the manifesto of a particular political party.

Bibliography. C. Davis, *Theology and Political Society* (1980). A. Fierro, *The Militant Gospel* (1977). G. Gutierrez, *A Theology of Liberation* (1973). J. Habermas, *Knowledge and Human Interests* (1971). E. B. Holifield, *A History of Pastoral Care in America* (1983). R. Keat, *The Politics of Social Theory* (1981). R. Kinast, "The Pastoral Care of Society As Liberation" *J. of Pastoral Care,* 34 (1980), 125–30. M. Lamb, *Solidarity with Victims* (1982). D. Sölle, *Political Theology* (1974). S. Torres and J. Eagleson, eds., *The Challenge of Basic Communities* (1981). D. Tracy, *The Analogical Imagination* (1981).

R. M. MOSELEY

CRITICAL THEORY; PROPHETIC/PASTORAL TENSION IN MINISTRY; SOCIAL JUSTICE ISSUES IN PASTORAL CARE; THEORY AND PRAXIS. *See also* ADVOCACY; CONSCIOUSNESS RAISING; EXPLOITATION/OPPRESSION; LIFESTYLE ISSUES IN PASTORAL CARE; PASTORAL THEOLOGICAL METHODOLOGY; PASTORAL THEOLOGY; POWER; SOCIAL CONSCIOUSNESS AND RESPONSIBILITY; SOCIAL STATUS AND CLASS FACTORS IN PASTORAL CARE; THEORY IN PASTORAL CARE AND COUN-

SELING, FUNCTIONS OF. *Compare* BLACK, CONTEXTUAL, EMPIRICAL, FEMINIST, NEO-ORTHODOX, PRACTICAL *or* PROCESS THEOLOGY; EXISTENTIALISM; SOCIOLOGY OF RELIGIOUS AND PASTORAL CARE; THEOLOGY AND PSYCHOTHERAPY.

LIBIDO. A psychoanalytic term for sexual energy; it refers to psychological drives, each representing a biological instinct. Each drive has a distinct origin in a body zone and a distinct target or object; for example, the oral libidinal drive originates in the infant's mouth and aims to contact the mother's breast. All libidinal drives aim for unification in this way; hence, libido fuels all forms of ego integration. Libido opposes those drives that motivate destructive actions and produce ego disintegration.

V. P. GAY

PSYCHOANALYSIS (Personality Theory and Research). *Compare* SEXUALITY, BIOLOGICAL AND PSYCHOSOCIAL THEORY OF.

LICENSURE. The authorization by law to do some specific thing. Professional licensing by the state involves the establishing of examining boards composed of members of the profession being regulated and nonprofessional or public members who are not directly involved in the practice. These boards are responsible for regulating the professional practice by examining persons prior to licensing and disciplining or terminating the license of those who have been proven guilty of unethical practice.

In the field of pastoral care and counseling, the topic of licensure most often refers to the issue of whether or not pastoral counselors should be licensed by the state to practice counseling and psychotherapy. The issue usually takes two forms: (1) whether or not, in the light of separation of church and state principles, it is legitimate or appropriate for the state to license persons as pastoral counselors, and (2) whether or not in the light of the already existing religious authorization of their ministry it is appropriate for pastoral counselors to be licensed to practice as psychologists, marriage and family counselors, etc.

Licensure, on the one hand, is a matter of concern for the clergyperson who specializes in pastoral counseling, because not having a license may allow the state to limit or terminate what the clergyperson views as a ministry authorized by the church. Having a license, on the other hand, may allow the pastoral counselor to receive third-party (insurance) payments for his or her work. Receiving such payments puts the pastoral counselor in the public arena competing for such payments with other health professionals, thus making the licensure issue a controversial one from a self-serving as well as from a theoretical point of view.

It is certainly possible to adopt a position that all persons who do counseling are involved in the practice of health care and therefore should be licensed in order to protect the public. But it is also possible to view the clergyperson's ministry, whatever it is, as exclusively authorized by a religious community rather than by the state. The issue of licensure, however, is obviously more complex than either of these views takes into account and important in the understanding of what ministry may be in today's world. Professional groups, such as the Amer-

ican Association of Pastoral Counselors, governing boards of pastoral counseling centers, religious denominations, and the clergy themselves, all have reason, therefore, to develop a responsible position on the licensure issue.

J. PATTON

LEGAL DIMENSIONS OF PASTORAL CARE AND COUNSELING; STANDARDS FOR PASTORAL COUNSELING. *Compare* ACCREDITATION; CERTIFICATION.

LIFE/ALIVENESS. 1. In humans a period of concrete existence from conception to death; 2. in the Judeo-Christian tradition, a particular quality of existence consistent with God's intention for humankind.

In both the OT and NT life is seen as a divine gift to be valued but not overvalued (Eccl. 9:4; Jn. 15:13). Our appreciation of life often varies depending upon our circumstances, perceptions, achievements, expectations, and sense of self. Meaning for life, however, is not given by our experiences, whether they be full and joyous or empty and joyless. The meaning and value of any life is given by God's purpose and caring for that life.

Human beings are not immortal by nature. Life is lived within limits set by conception and by death. Developments in the biological sciences both affirm and question these limits and give rise to major issues of bioethics. Respect for life requires that it be protected rather than attacked, preserved rather than destroyed. Death is both the end of life and its natural complement but is often experienced as its destroyer. Many of the fears and questions raised for us by death are direct reflections of our concerns about the meaning and quality of our life.

The Bible sees life as fundamentally distorted by sin. Sinners are invited to turn from their evil ways in order to live as God intends (Ezek. 33:11). The NT proclaims that Jesus brought new and true life to the world, which can transcend the limits of natural life (II Tim. 1:10). The person who is not caught up in this new life is spiritually "dead" whereas the true follower of Christ has passed from death into "life" (Jn. 5:24; Eph. 2:1; Col. 2:13; Rev. 3:1). This new quality of aliveness is not something released by our practice of goodness or our overcoming of evil; it is God's gracious gift in Jesus Christ through the Spirit (Rom. 6:23; 8:11; 1 John 5:11–12). This new life is both a present possession and a future hope of eternal life and can be equated with the coming of the kingdom.

Pastoral care contributes to life as it helps people become caught up in, and respond to, God's gift. It increases aliveness to the extent that it encourages people not to see themselves and their own resources as the ultimate source of value or meaning for their lives. That fullness of life which is the goal of pastoral care has discernable shape and form in the NT account of the life of Jesus. Movement toward this goal includes developing existing and new strengths in addition to overcoming weaknesses, cultivating joy as well as relieving distress, and enhancing the welfare of communities as well as of individuals. True life is not the prerogative of any one class, color, race, sex, nation, or culture. It may flourish where survival needs are barely met and be stifled in affluence, or vice versa. We live constantly in the tension between trying to achieve it and learning to receive it.

G. M. GRIFFIN

PERSONALITY, BIOLOGICAL DIMENSIONS OF; CREATION, DOCTRINE OF, AND PASTORAL CARE; WILL TO LIVE. *Compare* ESCHATOLOGY AND PASTORAL CARE; SOUL; SPIRIT; SURVIVAL (Occult).

LIFE, ETERNAL. *See* ESCHATOLOGY; HEAVEN AND HELL, BELIEF IN. *See also* LIFE/ALIVENESS.

LIFE, PHILOSOPHY OF. *See* VALUES RESEARCH; WORLD VIEW.

LIFE CYCLE CONCEPT. The life of the individual viewed as a series of successive psychosocial stages. Each stage of the life cycle has its characteristic developmental tasks. The passage of the individual from one life stage to another is marked by certain transitional or "marker events" which are themselves often acknowledged publicly with certain prescribed rituals.

R. S. SULLENDER

LIFE CYCLE THEORY AND PASTORAL CARE. *See also* DEVELOPMENTAL THEORY AND PASTORAL CARE; PERSONALITY THEORY (Assumptions and Values in).

LIFE CYCLE THEORY AND PASTORAL CARE. The term *life cycle* came into use in the 1950s and is associated with the developmental theories of Erik Erikson. This term is to be distinguished from such other commonly used terms in developmental theory as *life span* and *life course*. *Life span* simply refers to the interval from birth to death. *Life course* refers to the flow of the individual life over time; it concerns the patterning of specific events, relationships, achievements, failures, and aspirations of life. *Life cycle* conveys a more distinctive meaning. It suggests that the life course has a particular character and follows a basic sequence; thus, it is a conception, model, or theory of the life course (Levinson *et al.*, 1978, p. 6).
1. **Erikson's Life Cycle Theory.** *a. The eight stages.* Erik Erikson's theory of the life cycle has been extremely influential in developmental psychology, as well as in pastoral care. His life cycle theory posits eight developmental stages from infancy to old age. Each of these stages involves a focal tension or conflict between a positive, growth-oriented strength and a negative growth-impeding weakness. For healthy growth to occur, an individual needs to achieve a preponderance of the designated strength over the weakness, though the weakness is never entirely overcome. In fact it may actually contribute to development by alerting the individual to hostile forces and agencies in the environments; basic mistrust, for instance, sensitizes one to natural and human evil.

The eight stages and their central developmental conflicts are: basic trust vs. basic mistrust (infancy), autonomy vs. shame and doubt (early childhood), initiative vs. guilt (play age), industry vs. inferiority (school age), identity vs. identity confusion (adolescence), intimacy vs. isolation (young adulthood), generativity vs. stagnation (adulthood), and integrity vs. despair (mature adult-

hood). Each life stage is defined, therefore, by a central psychological dynamic in the form of a dialectical tension or conflict, which functions as a kind of organizing principle for the whole of the individual's experience, pervading and shaping the emotional agenda of everyday events and problems. While many other psychological processes are simultaneously involved in personality development, the focal conflict colors the picture as a whole, as the individual gradually (at times abruptly) attempts to live through its tensions to achieve a degree of resolution and a legacy of permanent psychological strength. Though the process works through ordinary events, at times it becomes focused in specific experiences or crises in which resolution may be achieved or missed. Thus, Erikson describes Martin Luther's anxiety attack while saying his first mass as an "identity crisis", a situation in which problems related to achieving a sense of his unique enduring selfhood were expressed and defined (in this instance without immediate resolution).

These eight stages also describe the *sequence* of the life. This sequence is invariant in the sense that the stages follow the chronology of the life course from infancy to old age, unfolding in every life (and in every culture) in the order stated, according to an inbuilt "epigenetic groundplan." (Each culture has a distinctive way of giving shape and content to the life cycle, and each individual represents a unique variation on the themes of his or her culture. Nonetheless the sequence of the stages itself is invariant and universal).

At the same time, Erikson recognizes that the conflicts of each stage survive in later stages, so that multiple developmental struggles are underway at any given time, though one is usually dominant. He also suggests that later stages have an influence on preceding ones. The human individual is essentially forward-looking, anticipating future developmental issues. In this sense Erikson recognizes the influence of the future on the present. Thus, the infant, in the first stage of life, anticipates the second stage through grasping behavior which is expressive of autonomy. Similarly, Luther is depicted as an adolescent working through identity and intimacy issues but also, within that dynamic, preoccupied with religious questions in anticipation of eighth-stage integrity struggles. Luther also illustrates the continuing effect of earlier stages: basic trust was a relentless life struggle for Luther, woven deeply into his identity, intimacy, generativity, and integrity problems.

b. Cyclical patterns. For Erikson, the stages as a whole represent a cyclical pattern in three important senses. First, the individual life course is itself cyclical. In his discussion of the final stage, for instance, Erikson notes, as shown vividly with Luther, similarities between trust and integrity (the positive poles of the first and final stages). Thus, the developmental process ends where it began—with trust, the most profound (and implicitly religious) issue of human life, now richly elaborated by the cumulative unique learnings of a lifetime.

Second, the process is cyclical in the sense that each generation is interlocked with the preceding and succeeding ones. Erikson refers to this as the "cogwheeling of generations," an image that depicts an interlocking relationship between the generations as each follows its own cyclical pattern. It suggests that there are times when two generations are more closely linked to one another (as when children are growing up and in constant interaction with their parents) and other times when they are quite separate (as when children are grown and living apart from their parents). The infant's need for trustworthy care, for instance, as the emotional cornerstone of a secure and effective personality, is "cogwheeled" into the parents' (seventh stage) developmental task of becoming "generative" (rather than "stagnant"), that is, capable of investing beyond themselves in the welfare of others and the ongoing drama of life that will succeed them. Parents raise their children, but in this sense children also "raise" their parents.

Third, the life course is cyclical in relation to the social context in which the individual life is embedded. Here Erikson uses the image of ever-widening concentric circles, like the ripples produced by throwing a stone into a lake. As the individual matures the circle of significant interaction gradually expands stage by stage, from (1) the maternal person alone to (2) both parents, (3) the whole family, (4) school and neighborhood, (5) groups and outgroups, (6) partnerships, (7) parenthood and enduring social, economic, and civic relationships, and finally (8) the widest circle of all, the sense of participation in and identification with the whole human race across time and culture — the sense that one's unique life history is a part of the universal human story.

c. Schedule of virtues. Erikson's life cycle theory originally consisted of the eight stages with their psychosocial polarities (Erikson, 1950, 1959). But during the 1960s Erikson expanded his theory in two important ways. He developed a "schedule of virtues" to correspond with the eight stages (Erikson, 1964) and also developed a stage theory of ritual engagement (Erikson, 1966, 1977). The schedule of virtues, with a virtue assigned to each of the life stages, holds that individuals are imbued with "strengths" that contribute to growth and health and to the capacity for moral life. These are not static, preestablished traits but inherent strengths that must be cultivated in encounter; they become alive and vital through the individual's interaction with persons and social institutions, and like the schedule of ego dispositions, are never fully achieved. Erikson's psychodynamic principles always point to dialectical, relatively secure levels of attainment. The virtues, in order of their appearance, are hope, will, purpose, competence, fidelity, love, care, and wisdom. For Erikson everyone struggles, more or less successfully, with the tasks of becoming morally "virtuous" in this sense, and these virtues define comprehensively what the ideal of human moral character entails (though recognizing vast cultural diversity in the expression of these human strengths). Clinically, Erikson suggests that these are the strengths that are often present, or beginning to emerge, when a person is beginning to improve during psychotherapy or to evidence signs of significant health and vitality.

d. Ritual engagements. Erikson's theory of ritual engagement is intended to recognize the role of patterned, repetitive interaction or "ritual encounter" in individual development. The mother-infant relationship at the very beginning of life for the infant involves various kinds of ritual encounter, the most notable being the "greeting ritual" through which mother and infant relate to one another each morning. Erikson proposes that such patterned social interaction is crucial in shaping personality through the sequence of stages. Accordingly he identifies specific ritual themes or "elements" for each of the life stages, and suggests that specific social institutions are responsible for sustaining each of these elements. The ritual elements, include, in stage-sequence order, the numinous, judicious, dramatic, formal, ideological, affiliative, generational, and integral. Erikson views religious institutions in particular as protectors and enactors of the numinous element, and thus recognizes parallels between the believer's desire for a face-to-face encounter with God and the "greeting ritual" between mother and infant. Through his theory of ritual process, Erikson has built a conceptual bridge between the individual life cycle and the social system.

2. Contributions to Pastoral Care. The most obvious contribution of Erikson's life cycle theory to pastoral care has been its conceptualization of the individual life cycle. Because pastors work with individuals from infancy to old age, from birth to death, they need some means of conceptualizing the life course: Erikson's life cycle theory has been the most widely used conception of the whole of life. Other theories have been offered to describe faith formation and spiritual development, but Erikson's life cycle theory is virtually the only theory that conceptualizes the life course of the full personality as a whole.

In addition to its value as a conception of the stages of life, Erikson's life cycle theory has also been used as a diagnostic instrument, both at the personal and institutional level.

a. Diagnostic themes. Various authors have recommended the use of theological and biblical themes for diagnostic purposes (Hiltner, 1972; Pruyser, 1976; Oglesby, 1980). As Pruyser puts it, selected themes may be used as "guideposts" for the pastor's "diagnostic thinking" and as "ordering principles" for the "observations" the pastor makes. Pruyser offers seven theological themes for this purpose: awareness of the holy, providence, faith, grace or gratefulness, repentance, communion, and vocation. Likewise, Oglesby offers a set of biblical themes which may also be used diagnostically. These include: initiative and freedom, fear and faith, conformity and rebellion, death and rebirth, and risk and redemption. These themes enable the pastor to assess the parishioner's situation, especially with regard to those life experiences in which relationships between individuals, and between individuals and God, are broken and in need of restoration.

In a similar way, Erikson's life stages, with their psychosocial themes of basic trust vs. basic mistrust, autonomy vs. shame and doubt, and so on, may also be used diagnostically. Technically, they provide psychological, not theological and biblical, interpretation, but they may be used in much the same way as Pruyser's theological themes and Oglesby's biblical themes. When used diagnostically, these psychosocial themes are no longer treated sequentially. Rather, drawing upon Erikson's notion that all of the stage-specific themes are present in some degree in each stage, they are viewed as themes that may be simultaneously operative in a parishioner's life, regardless of that person's age. And, like Pruyser's themes, they may be viewed as interrelated, allowing for a complex multithematic diagnostic assessment. In *Pastoral Care: A Thematic Approach* (1979), Capps proposed that Pruyser's theological themes and Erikson's psychosocial themes have sufficient similarities, dynamically speaking, that they may be correlated in the following manner: trust and mistrust with providence, autonomy vs. shame and doubt with grace or gratefulness, initiative vs. guilt with repentance, industry vs. inferiority with vocation, identity vs. identity confusion with faith, intimacy vs. isolation with communion, generativity vs. stagnation with vocation, and integrity vs. despair with an awareness of the holy. These points of contact between Erikson's psychosocial themes and Pruyser's theological themes indicate that the pastor does not need to decide between psychosocial and theological themes in making a diagnostic assessment of a counselee's situation or problems, but may employ both simultaneously.

b. Psychosocial assessment of church life. Erikson's life cycle theory may also be used in the effort to understand institutional problems and clarify institutional goals. Capps has illustrated the former use of Erikson's life cycle theory in his analysis of a church conflict involving the pastor and the board of elders (Capps, 1979, pp. 53–74). Here, Erikson's psychosocial theme of initiative vs. guilt was used to illumine the nature and causes of the conflict, and to make recommendations for alleviating the crisis. Capps has also proposed the use of Erikson's theory of ritual engagement to clarify the goals of a congregation, using each of Erikson's ritual elements to identify the basic characteristics of the "healthy" and "unhealthy" church (Capps, 1983, pp. 55–80).

c. The pastor's role as moral counselor. Erikson has also developed the negative side of his moral perspective as formulated through his schedule of virtues. In *The Life Cycle Completed* (1982), he develops the "basic antipathies" that oppose the strengths reflected in the eight major virtues. These antipathies include, in order, withdrawal, compulsion or impulsivity, inhibition, inertia, repudiation, exclusivity, rejectivity, and disdain. By formulating these antipathies, Erikson has recognized the need to specify more clearly than he had done previously the forces that impede growth and wholeness.

More recently, Erikson has identified these antipathies as malignant tendencies, and paired them with maladaptive tendencies, including sensory maladjustment, shameless willfulness, ruthlessness, narrow virtuosity, fanaticism, promiscuity, over-extension, and presumption. Malignant tendencies reflect too much of the negative or dystonic pole of a given stage, while maladaptive tendencies reflect too much of the positive or syntonic pole (Erikson, Erikson, and Kirnick, 1986). Joan M. Erikson has expanded on this malignancy/maladaptive schema in her book *Wisdom and the Senses* (1988).

In a similar way, Capps has proposed the use of the traditional classification of the "deadly sins" as diagnostic categories to be used in concert with the schedule of virtues (Capps, 1983, pp. 33–53). The sins and their virtue counterparts are gluttony (hope), anger (will), greed (purpose), envy (competence), pride (fidelity), lust (love), indifference (care), and melancholy (wisdom). As with Erikson's psychosocial themes, these combinations of virtues and sins can be used diagnostically, enabling

the pastor to identify a parishioner's moral strengths and weaknesses. By locating the sins within a psychodynamic framework, there is less danger of a moralistic pastoral approach because the sins are understood dynamically, and not as static traits or as aberrant behaviors only.

3. Implications for Practical Theology and Ethics. In addition to these uses of Erikson's life cycle theory in pastoral care, there have been numerous theological and ethical uses of the theory, many of which have implications for pastoral care. Erikson's life cycle theory has been very influential, for example, in discussions of faith development. Its influence on the faith development theory developed by James Fowler (1981) is widely recognized, even though more attention has been given to the influence of Lawrence Kohlberg and Jean Piaget on Fowler's work. A clear indication of the continuing influence of Erikson's life cycle theory on Fowler's faith development schema is Fowler's recent addition of a new stage of faith development, which he calls *primal faith*. This stage corresponds to the first three stages of Erikson's life cycle theory, and now stands at the beginning of Fowler's faith stages (1984).

Another important use of Erikson's life cycle theory to articulate the meaning of faith and its development is LeRoy Aden's proposal of faith dimensions corresponding to the eight stages of the life cycle (1976). Arguing that "faith as a human response is a dynamic and multidimensional reality rather than a static and monolithic one" and that "faith is also a developmental phenomenon" that "participates in the life cycle of the individual who possesses it," Aden proposes the following correspondences between faith dimensions and life cycle stages: faith as trust (infancy), faith as courage (early childhood), faith as obedience (play age), faith as assent (school age), faith as identity (adolescence), faith as self-surrender (young adulthood), faith as unconditional caring (middle adulthood), and faith as unconditional acceptance (mature age). This model has particular relevance for pastoral care because faith in this conception is a powerful ally in the pastor's caring and healing ministry. As Aden puts it, "The particular development stage in which the individual is immersed influences and in part determines the shape of his response of faith. If this is valid, faith becomes a dynamic and organized pattern of multidimensional elements, but, more importantly, it becomes a healing and fulfilling response that is deeply appropriate to the individual's central organismic struggle. Thus faith is not just a passive reaction to a developmental crisis but is also an active and profound answer to that crisis. It is an answer that heals and transforms, because it is attentive to both God's salutory grace and man's deepest need" (p. 230).

Erikson's life cycle theory has also been employed by Evelyn Eaton Whitehead and James D. Whitehead in their conceptualization of adult Christian development and contemporary spirituality (1982, 1984), and by John G. Gleason, Jr., in his correlation of life stages and Christian doctrines (1975). In Gleason's formulation, the doctrines, in order, include: God, good and evil, redemption, works, humankind, Christology, creation, and eschatology. There has also been some discussion of Erikson's life cycle theory in terms of its ethical norms, with Don S. Browning arguing that Erikson's ethical vision is grounded in the generativity stage (1973) and J. Eugene Wright, Jr., contending that the sixth stage of life, with its virtue of love and emphasis on mutuality, is at least as important to Erikson's ethical vision as the generativity stage (1982).

There is considerable consensus that those involved in pastoral care need to understand the developmental process and to have a working knowledge of the typical problems and crises of each major developmental period or stage. Erikson's life cycle theory has been widely used for this purpose because it is not overly technical and yet not simplistic either. It is also evident that Erikson has deep appreciation for the role that religion plays in human development (cf. 1958, 1968, 1977), and therefore pastors and others involved in pastoral care have been able to adopt his theory without apology.

Bibliography. L. Aden, "Faith and the Developmental Cycle," *Pastoral Psychology,* 24 (1976), 215–30. D. S. Browning, *Generative Man: Psychoanalytic Perspectives* (1973). D. Capps, *Deadly Sins and Saving Virtues* (1987); *Life Cycle Theory and Pastoral Care* (1983); *Pastoral Care: A Thematic Approach* (1979). E. Erikson, *Childhood and Society* 2d ed. (1965); *Identity and the Life Cycle* (1959); *Identity: Youth and Crises* (1968); *Insight and Responsibility* (1964); *The Life Cycle Completed* (1982); "The Ontogeny of Ritualization in Man," in *Psychoanalysis: A General Psychology,* R. M. Loewenstein *et al.,* eds. (1966); *Toys and Reasons: Stages in the Ritualization of Experience* (1977); *Young Man Luther: A Study in Psychoanalysis and History* (1958). E. Erikson, J. Erikson, and H. Kirnick, *Vital Involvement in Old Age* (1986). J. Erikson, *Wisdom and the Senses* (1988). J. W. Fowler, *Becoming Adult, Becoming Christian: Adult Development and Christian Faith* (1984); *Stages of Faith: The Psychology of Human Development and the Quest for Meaning* (1981). J. J. Gleason, *Growing Up to God: Eight Steps in Religious Development* (1975). S. Hiltner, *Theological Dynamics* (1972). D. J. Levinson, *The Seasons of a Man's Life* (1978). W. B. Oglesby, Jr., *Biblical Themes for Pastoral Care* (1980). P. W. Pruyser, *The Minister as Diagnostician* (1976). E. E. Whitehead and J. D. Whitehead, *Christian Life Patterns: The Psychological Challenges and Religious Invitations of Adult Life* (1982); *Seasons of Strength: New Visions of Adult Christian Maturity* (1984). J. E. Wright, Jr., *Erikson: Identity and Religion* (1982).

D. CAPPS

ADOLESCENTS, CHILDREN, MIDLIFE PERSONS, OLDER PERSONS, *or* YOUNG ADULTS, PASTORAL CARE AND COUNSELING OF. *See also* AGING; FAITH/BELIEF; FAITH DEVELOPMENT RESEARCH; PASTORAL CARE; PERSONALITY DEVELOPMENT; PILGRIMAGE METAPHOR; PRACTICAL THEOLOGY; PSYCHOSOCIAL DEVELOPMENT; RETIREMENT. *Compare* PERSONAL STORY, SYMBOL, AND MYTH IN PASTORAL CARE; RITUAL AND PASTORAL CARE. *Biography:* ERIKSON.

LIFE HISTORY. *See* CASE STUDY METHOD; EVALUATION AND DIAGNOSIS; LIFE CYCLE THEORY AND PASTORAL CARE; PERSONAL STORY, SYMBOL, AND MYTH; REMINISCENCE THERAPY.

LIFE REVIEW. *See* REMINISCENCE THERAPY.

LIFE SUPPORT DECISIONS. *See* DYING, MORAL DILEMMAS IN; MORAL DILEMMAS IN PASTORAL PERSPECTIVE.

LIFESTYLE ISSUES IN PASTORAL CARE. Lifestyle refers to a person's or a family's unique way of life. It includes a person's particular blend of priorities, environmental demands, cultural conditioning, and use of resources. These choices reflect certain values or beliefs. Effective pastoral care and counseling includes helping persons to recognize the consequences of their lifestyle choices, to clarify the values and beliefs that underlie them, and to reflect theologically upon these. Dealing with lifestyle issues in the caring process entails finding a balance between the two polarities of acceptance and confrontation.

1. Common Issues of Pastoral Concern. Lifestyle issues of frequent pastoral concern include work patterns, use of leisure time, financial priorities, relative affluence, consumption patterns, religious rituals, marital and child-care patterns, and sexual orientation. Lifestyle hinges both on how a person or a family handles its limited resources, such as time, money, and energy, and on influences outside of free will, such as environment, employment demands, culture, and political systems. There is, however, sufficient freedom for each person to choose a particular lifestyle. Choosing a lifestyle is a process of recognizing, evaluating and affirming one's values and beliefs.

2. An Example: Affluence as a Lifestyle. One of the most subtle and pervasive of lifestyle issues is that of affluence. The majority of people in Western civilization have become increasingly affluent in the last hundred years. With increased affluence comes a certain lifestyle, characterized by increased consumption, concern for things, focus on personal appearance, leisure time, greater mobility, and smaller families. The culture sustains this affluence by promoting the values of acquisition, accomplishment, success, consumption, and instant gratification. Certain subcultures or life stage groups, like the "yuppies" (young, upwardly-mobile professionals) are especially caught up in this lifestyle and its implicit values.

Not all lifestyles are equally healthy—psychologically, medically, or spiritually. While the affluent lifestyle offers tremendous advantages, there also can be certain negative consequences. Increased incidents of family breakdown, heart disease, and drug use may ensue. Spiritually, an affluent lifestyle runs the risk of increased materialism, the love of things, resulting in increased alienation from God and neighbor. Every lifestyle carries with it a relative degree of health or self-destruction. Often, individuals or families come to clergy seeking counseling and guidance, precisely because their lifestyle choices are causing or contributing to their current pain.

3. Pastoral Response. All good pastoral caring begins with the establishment of a trusting, empathetic relationship between pastor and parishioner. One key element in this establishment of trust occurs when the pastor adopts a non-judgmental attitude toward the parishioner, no matter how different the parishioner's lifestyle might be from the pastor's. Pastors must be sufficiently aware of their own biases to avoid judging the parishioner unintentionally and thereby destroying the helping relationship. A common example occurs when a pastor shows a bias toward the married lifestyle. Pastors must be able to understand the single person's situation, without subtly communicating an attitude that everything would improve if the counselee just got married. Other lifestyles may also be offensive to a minister's morals. If a minister is unable to empathize with a person, the troubled individual should be referred to a more suitable professional for counseling.

4. **Lifestyle Values and Consequences.** Each lifestyle has certain built-in consequences which effective pastoral counselors will help their parishioners to face. Whether medical, psychological, relational, or spiritual, the consequences may not be clear to the parishioner. Often it takes the more objective eyes of another person to see the results of one's lifestyle choices. Lifestyle always reflects values. In recent years, there has been a wealth of material on value clarification, to which many schools, churches and religious educators have access. Pastoral counselors may find it useful to be familiar with some of the techniques used. An analogous process involves helping parishioners to clarify the beliefs or meaning that undergird their lifestyle. All lifestyles reflect certain assumptions about what makes one happy, or what the purpose of life is, or what makes one an acceptable person. These questions are essentially theological in nature. Their meanings summarize a person's operational theology, and these beliefs provide the theological rationale for one's lifestyle choices. For example, a workaholic man may compulsively pursue achievement, because he believes that he is a worthwhile person only when he achieves. A death-denying family may avoid funerals, because they believe that grief is a lack of faith. A woman may adopt a rushed, hurried lifestyle, because she believes that death is the end of life, and that she had therefore best make her mark soon. These are examples of theological beliefs that can undergird lifestyle choices.

5. **Reviewing Values and Lifestyles.** Whether one is clarifying values or uncovering operational beliefs, a skillful pastor will help counselees to reflect theologically upon their values and beliefs. Are these values and beliefs true? Are they leading me to an abundant life? Do they fit with my consciously chosen beliefs and values? How can I let the love of God filter through my being, so as to alter any unproductive and self-destructive beliefs and values?

This theological reflection process must be done carefully and with respect. The role of the effective pastoral counselor is to help the parishioner think theologically, not to think for them or to pronounce the correct theology. The most effective approach is to work within the parishioner's religious frame of reference. Sharing beliefs, presenting alternatives, studying religious resources, and praying for guidance are ways of facilitating a person's theological self-reflection process. Such a process can be the beginning of repentance and new life.

In effect, lifestyle issues are interwoven in and through all pastoral care and counseling situations. Attention to lifestyle issues is at the heart of pastoral counseling's uniqueness. The effective pastor is called "to stand with" and "to stand against." Where a person's lifestyle is blocking the fullness of salvation, pastors can facilitate change through the clarification of values and the uncovering of operational beliefs, and through a careful and respectful process of theological reflection. Effective pastoral counseling in situations where lifestyle issues are present involves a careful blending of the polarities of

acceptance and confrontation, a feature that marks the true shepherd of God.

Bibliography. S. Simon *et al.*, *Values Clarification* (1972).

R. S. SULLENDER

ETHICS AND PASTORAL CARE; MORAL DILEMMAS IN PASTORAL PERSPECTIVE; MORAL THEOLOGY AND PASTORAL CARE; PROPHETIC/PASTORAL TENSIONS IN MINISTRY. *See also* ASCETICAL PRACTICES; CELIBACY; CHRISTIAN LIFE; CONSCIOUSNESS RAISING; CULTURAL AND ETHNIC FACTORS IN PASTORAL CARE; EATING AND DRINKING; JEWISH LIFE; LIBERATION THEOLOGY; MORAL BEHAVIOR AND RELIGION; PEACE-MAKING; RESPONSIBILITY/IRRESPONSIBILITY, PSYCHOLOGY OF; SELF-DENIAL; SOCIAL CONSCIOUSNESS AND RESPONSIBILITY; SOCIAL STATUS AND CLASS FACTORS IN PASTORAL CARE; SOCIOLOGY OF RELIGIOUS AND PASTORAL CARE; VALUES. *Compare* FRIENDSHIP; GAMBLING; FAMILY PLANNING; OBESITY AND WEIGHT CONTROL; PHYSICAL FITNESS DISCIPLINES; RICH PERSONS; SOCIAL JUSTICE ISSUES IN PASTORAL CARE; VIPs; WORK AND CAREER.

LIGUORI, ALPHONSO DE (1696–1787). Italian Roman Catholic bishop, casuist, and founder of the Redemptorist Order.

His *Theologia Moralis* remained an authoritative text for Catholic priests, especially in Italy and America, well into the nineteenth century. His "equiprobabilism" was an effort to find a middle course between that of the "probabilists" who permitted Christians facing moral dilemmas to select and act on the less demanding of two generally acceptable opinions, and that of the "probabiliorists" who insisted that the stricter option must always be chosen. When the two conflicting options were nearly equal in moral quality, he said, then either could be chosen. Otherwise, one had to choose the stricter option.

Liguori's position was an attempt to take into account the uncertainties and ambiguities in moral principles. His sensitivity to such ambiguities arose in part from his work among the lower classes of Naples. He founded the Redemptorist Order specifically to serve the poor and the outcast.

E. B. HOLIFIELD

CASUISTRY, ROMAN CATHOLIC; HISTORY OF ROMAN CATHOLIC PASTORAL CARE (United States).

LIGUORIAN (Redemptorist) SPIRITUALITY. *See* SPIRITUALITY (Roman Catholic Tradition).

LIMBO. This term, from the Latin *limbus*, "fringe," denotes the "fringe" of hell occupied by those temporarily or eternally incapable of admittance into the supernatural happiness of heaven, but undeserving of damnation. The concept of limbo arose in the patristic era and has received theological attention both in the medieval period and in contemporary theology. The term *limbo* has been used in two senses: the limbo of the fathers and the limbo of unbaptized children.

The former refers to that state occupied by the souls of the just who died before the resurrection of Christ. Having lived and died in obedience to God's will, they deserved eternal life. However, the gates of heaven had not yet been opened by the redemption, so these souls existed in a state of waiting for the redemptive event of

Jesus' death-resurrection-ascension. It was to those in this limbo that the soul of Jesus "descended into hell" (Apostles' Creed) during the time when His body lay in the tomb. He went to announce to them the glad tidings of their imminent admittance into eternal beatitude.

The limbo of unbaptized children is a hypothesis elaborated principally by St. Thomas Aquinas in answer to the problem of the eternal destiny of those who die unbaptized before attaining the age of moral responsibility. Without baptism in any of its forms, they were deemed ineligible for admittance into heaven. However, innocent of personal sin, they were undeserving of damnation. Thus it was suggested that they would spend their eternity in this limbo of total natural happiness (as distinct from the supernatural happiness of the beatific vision).

This uncertainty about the eternal destiny of unbaptized persons who have not attained moral discretion is one of the reasons why some Christian churches strongly encourage infant baptism.

In dealing pastorally with situations involving the death of unbaptized children, it is well to point out the love that prompts God to create each human being, God's will that all be saved, and the fact that God's power to bestow eternal life is not limited by the sacraments or the lack thereof.

Bibliography. St. Thomas Aquinas, *Summa Theologica,* 3, appendix 1. M. Becque, "Life after Death," *20th Century Encyclopedia of Catholicism* (1960).

V. B. BROWN

EMERGENCY BAPTISM; ESCHATOLOGY AND PASTORAL CARE; HEAVEN AND HELL, BELIEF IN; SALVATION AND PASTORAL CARE; SOUL.

LIMIT SETTING IN PASTORAL CARE AND COUNSELING.

Refers to all efforts of self-definition in which the pastor identifies the boundaries of his or her activity as well as the boundaries of the activities of those with whom the pastor comes into contact.

1. **Pastoral Counseling.** In a counseling relationship, limits refer to all those boundaries which define the relationship. Examples of these boundaries include the length of the session, the amount of the fee, the number of times per week a meeting is held, the type of interaction expected (e.g., the counselor will not answer direct questions, the client is expected to say what comes into his or her mind, there will be no physical or verbal abuse). The clearer the counselor is about the boundaries of the relationship, the clearer the self of the counselor is perceived by the client and the clearer is the therapeutic contract to which the client will either agree or disagree.

Singer summarizes the following rationale for limit-setting: "(1) Limits are designed to facilitate the patient-therapist relationship and to protect the patient's welfare by preventing behavior which entails irreparable and irrevocable harm. (2) In order to be growth-furthering, limits must be rational. . . . (3) The setting of limits has important emotional consequences for the patient. It prevents the development of unnecessary feelings of guilt; it reduces the patient's uneasiness that the therapist might be taxed beyond endurance; and it enhances the patient's sense of reality, helping him or her toward self-definition and awareness by bringing him or her face to face with the reality and definition of another person."

In contemporary psychotherapy, the work of R. Langs has been of extreme importance in this area. By calling attention to the boundaries and ground rules of the psychotherapy relationship, Langs argues that the maintenance of a clear "frame" (clear limits) gives clients a sense of security and trust in the psychotherapist which will help them move into deeper and more relevant material as the psychotherapy continues. The limits and boundaries of the psychotherapeutic relationship are seen by Langs as an extension of the psychic structure of the therapist. Therefore, unclear boundaries (e.g., irregular meeting times, uneven attention to the client's material, nonpayment of fees, lateness to sessions by either client or therapist, physical contact, between-session telephone calls) present to the client a portrait of the therapist as unable to master fundamental self-definition questions, and will therefore compromise the therapist's capacity to be of significant help to the patient.

2. **General Pastoral Availability.** In pastoral care, the question of limit-setting takes on a broader dimension, but the same general issues remain. What are the limits of the availability of the pastor? How are those limits communicated to parish members? Some examples are: Is the pastor on call at all times? Will the pastor marry anyone on the day they present themselves at the door? Is all church business done only with the pastor present? Will the pastor make a home visit on every parishioner? Is the pastor's spouse to be available for auxiliary church activities?

As in the psychotherapy process, the limits which are set by the pastor are an extension of the self-definition of the pastor. How the pastor pictures being a "good pastor" will play a large part in what limits are set or not set.

Following the rationale set out by Singer above, the limits set by the pastor in pastoral care can provide protection for both pastor and parishioner. The pastor is protected in that he or she will not be taxed past emotional or psychological well-being. The parishioner is protected in that he or she will understand what can reasonably be expected of the pastor and what cannot, as well as being given an opportunity to interact with a person who understands and respects boundaries, limits, and finitude.

Limit setting in pastoral care will thus happen, either implicitly (as when the pastor is taxed beyond his or her capabilities and can no longer be available or function effectively), or explicitly by the clear contracting of the pastor with parish and parishioners. In the long run, explicit limit setting by the pastor as a function of his or her self-identity is a more positive and healthful procedure than having the limits explicitly set by circumstance or exhaustion.

Bibliography. R. Langs, *The Bipersonal Field,* (1976). R. Langs, *The Therapeutic Environment* (1979). E. Singer, *Key Concepts in Psychotherapy* (1965).

B. M. HARTUNG

ASSERTIVENESS IN MINISTRY; COVENANT AND CONTRACT; STRUCTURING; TECHNIQUE AND SKILL IN PASTORAL CARE. *Compare* CONFLICT AND CONFLICT MANAGEMENT; CONFRONTATION (Pastoral and Therapeutic).

LIMITS, EXPERIENCE OF. *See* HUMAN CONDITION/
PREDICAMENT; RELIGIOUS EXPERIENCE.

LISTENING. Influenced by prevailing Greek wisdom,
the unknown author of Ecclesiastes says, "Let your words
be few" (5:2). A later NT scribe echoes the earlier wisdom:
"Let every man be quick to hear, slow to speak" (Jas.
1:19). While scattered biblical references allude to the
value of listening as a spiritual reflective discipline, and
numerous texts portray listening as inherent in the nature
of God, little evidence exists to indicate that listening
was practiced in biblical times in the shepherding ministry. Yet the work of deacons with the sick, needy, and
disenfranchised implies a generalized listening ability.
The Gospels assume Jesus' sensitivity to individual conditions. St. Paul, committed to the way of Jesus, suggests his awareness of listening in Gal. 6:2: "Bear [hear]
one another's burdens and so fulfil the law of Christ."
Confession of sin, which became a private practice with
the Irish monks in the seventh century, may have been a
forerunner of pastoral listening. When the reformers
delegated private confession to a secondary practice
because of its degeneration into a mercenary routine,
many confessors nevertheless continued to develop skill
in listening as they participated in and observed the
restoring power of the confessional act.

As listening has been rediscovered in the pastoral
ministry, it is rapidly assuming a responsible and legitimate place in the shepherding work of the Christian
community. Clergy, as they became acquainted with the
diagnostic approach of therapists from other disciplines,
saw the relevance of that approach to their calling. Clergy
also became adept at listening beyond signs, words, and
sounds that mark a concealed condition of the soul. In the
1930s Richard Cabot, a physician, chief of staff at Massachusetts General Hospital, in collaboration with the
hospital's chaplain, Russell Dicks, published *The Art of
Ministering to the Sick*, which offered the first clear statement on the value of listening for the pastoral ministry.
Since that publication various articles by numerous
authors have addressed the theme. Today listening is an
accepted and respected practice with most clergy.

While on the surface listening appears to be a simple
act, when seriously employed, it is a difficult art. In
serious listening the distracting or disturbing noises or
the voice of the listener can cloud the interaction. Lack of
interest and understanding, obsessions, compulsions,
fatigue, and the like can also disable the listener. The
listener's temptation is to resort to anxious activity, control, or fantasy as routes of escape. The capacity to listen
to others depends on ability to listen to the self.

Cabot and Dicks first suggested that listening can be
either passive or active, though in practice it is likely to
combine both forms. In *passive listening* the listener simply avoids intervention in the flow of language, thought,
and feeling. This is not the same as being detached or
remote. Passive listening may be the approach of choice
in the first meeting, but its continued use depends on an
understanding or diagnosis of the condition or situation.
With the deeply troubled, agitated, or dying, quiet
listening is generally the most effective method. In other
situations a heavy reliance on passive listening can be
used as an escape from a responsive relationship. In all

good listening the listener is attentive to words, moods,
body, and affect, and may by a glance or touch communicate a deeper presence.

In *active listening* the pastor, by a quiet question, perceptive comment, or sensitive story, portrays hearing
beyond the overt words in order to engage the other in a
deeper level of the communicative relationship. Overly
active listening can fracture a tentative relationship. It
should always be characterized by caring. Clinical pastoral education usually provides pastors with the foundations necessary for creative listening.

A word of caution: persons with limited personality
development, such as asocial persons, seldom profit from
a listening relationship and may abuse that level of communication.

Bibliography. R. C. Cabot and R. Dicks, *The Art of Ministering
to the Sick* (1936). J. L. Cedarleaf, "Listening Revisited," *J. of
Pastoral Care*, 38 (1984), 310 – 16. R. Dicks, *Pastoral Work and
Personal Counseling* (1949).

J. L. CEDARLEAF

COMMUNICATION; PRESENCE, MINISTRY OF; TECHNIQUE
AND SKILL IN PASTORAL CARE. *See also* EMPATHY; INTERPRE-
TATION AND HERMENEUTICS, PASTORAL; PHENOMENO-
LOGICAL METHOD IN PASTORAL CARE; SILENCE.

LITERALISM, BIBLICAL. *See* BIBLICAL LITERALISM.

LITERATURE, CLASSIC. *See* CLASSIC LITERATURE IN
CARE AND COUNSELING.

LITERATURE, DEVOTIONAL. Literature used to
enhance religious commitment. Throughout history
Christians have produced a variety of writings which
have served this purpose. Broadly speaking, however,
such literature falls into two major categories—
biographical or autobiographical, and directive. In the
first type, writers offer guidance by sharing stories about
the working of grace in human life and experience. In the
second they give more direct instruction. A vast portion
of Christian literature is devotional.

1. **History.** Christianity inherited a corpus of devotional literature in the OT. The first Christians employed
the Psalms in both private and public prayer (cf. Col.
3:16; Eph. 5:19). In addition, apostles and "apostolic
persons" produced gospels, epistles, and other writings
designed to encourage, exhort, and direct the faithful in
their daily walk. Evangelists drew together stories, sayings, and parables of Jesus which could help the devout
to discover the mind of Christ (Phil. 2:5). The Apostle
Paul wrote most of his letters to supply some kind of
spiritual guidance to churches he planted or to individuals to whom he witnessed. Hebrews, I Peter, and the
Revelation rally the faithful in the face of persecution.

During the pre-Constantinian era, Christianity did
not attract a highly literate constituency. Nonetheless,
Christians produced a sizeable body of devotional literature including pious fiction, stories of martyrs and saints,
letters of exhortation and spiritual guidance, and a variety of treatises. *Pious fiction* — gospels, acts of apostles —
did not receive wide approval among early Christians.
According to Tertullian, the priest who wrote the Acts
of Paul and Thecla about A.D. 160 was defrocked. Some

persons, however, may have drawn inspiration from such writings in the way many today find historical novels useful. *Accounts of martyrdoms* presented the martyrs as model Christians and set the tone for Christian piety even after persecution ceased. The first martyrology recounted the death of Polycarp, Bishop of Smyrna, in A.D. 155. One of the most widely read was the account of the martyrdoms of Perpetua and Felicitas in Carthage about A.D. 202. *Letters* served very much as they had in the apostolic age to direct and rally the wavering in different times. Some, like Clement's letter to the Corinthians (I Clement) and Ignatius's seven letters, almost obtained places in the NT canon of certain churches. Cyprian, Bishop of Carthage (248–58), wrote numerous letters of counsel and guidance when he had to hide during the Decian and Valerian persecutions. *Treatises* on spiritual development were not numerous until the third century. Tertullian, who converted around A.D. 195, wrote several treatises on matters of Christian discipline. Clement, head of the school in Alexandria from around 190 until 202, wrote two works largely devoted to spiritual growth— *The Instructor* and *Miscellanies*. Origen, Clement's successor, who later moved to Caesarea in Palestine, used allegorical interpretation of scriptures to prod his hearers and readers to deeper devotion.

Constantine's conversion inaugurated a golden era for Christian devotional literature as many of the brightest minds entered the church. Some of the same types of literature edified the faithful, but some new types also appeared. Although the age of martyrs was over, *memory of the martyrs* was not allowed to fade as the faithful erected martyria and commemorated the lives of the martyrs. When Julian (361–63) ordered removal of the remains of Babylas, Bishop of Antioch martyred under Decius around 250, from a former temple of Apollo in Daphne, a suburb of Antioch, Christians returned them to Antioch with great fanfare. A devoted cult developed around the saintly bishop, and Chrysostom preached two panegyrics in his honor. Recollection of the martyrs inspired much hagiography throughout the Middle Ages.

In the post-Constantinian era monks sought to become the "new martyrs" and did become the models for many. Accordingly, *lives of monks* appeared in some profusion as thousands of bright youth heard the call of the desert. Athanasius, Bishop of Alexandria, wrote a *Life of Saint Antony*, often referred to as the "father" of Christian monasticism, shortly after the latter's death. Admiring followers also wrote lives of Pachomius (ca. 290–346), father of communal type monasticism. Jerome (ca. 342–420) composed a kind of biographical guide to *Illustrious Persons*. Gregory of Nyssa penned a life of his sister Macrina (ca. 327–79), founder of an ascetic community on the family estate, who exerted a strong influence over Gregory and her other brother Basil of Caesarea. A whole row of monastic hagiographers appeared. Palladius and Cassian published collections of stories and quotations from the desert monks. Numerous others crafted lives of saints designed to encourage similar devotion.

Distinctive among devotional literature in this period were Gregory of Nyssa's *Life of Moses*, a treatise on Christian perfection, and Augustine's *Confessions*.

The Middle Ages produced a mountain of devotional literature, especially lives of saints and treatises on spiritual guidance. Many would not have great value for modern persons, but the lives of outstanding figures such as Bernard of Clairvaux and Francis of Assisi still command interest. Classics like Bernard's *Love of God, The Imitation of Christ,* and many other fourteenth century writings also deserve serious attention.

After the Reformation in the sixteenth century, Christians went in different directions concerning devotional literature. The Roman Catholic church reaffirmed its medieval heritage, Protestants repudiated it in favor of a wholly Bible-centered piety. Although they have retained this orientation in theory, however, both have had to make adjustments in practice, Catholic piety becoming more Bible-centered and Protestants relying more on traditional Christian devotional insights. Already in the sixteenth century Protestants began to produce devotional literature to replace what they had rejected. By the seventeenth century Puritans and Pietists self-consciously returned to early and medieval literature and revived and reapplied many of their insights. The corpus of literature which Catholics and Protestants or Anglicans have generated in the modern era is too vast to review. It is important to note, however, that Protestants, Catholics, Anglicans, and Orthodox have been returning together to the same fountains of spirituality in the era since the Second Vatican Council.

2. How to Use Devotional Literature. As this historical review suggests, devotional literature varies widely in content and quality, necessitating care in selecting and using it. The following guidelines may be useful:

a. Choose carefully. It is advisable to select "classics," works which have established a reputation. Some guides to these are available (see bibliography). Once readers have established a basic frame of reference through the classics, they will be able to evaluate contemporary devotional writings.

b. Get acquainted with context. Even classics will reflect the age and circumstances in which they were written. To appreciate them fully, readers should try to learn as much as possible about the author, date, purpose, and context in which they were written. The more readers know about such matters, the greater will be their ability to understand and apply insights from these writings.

c. Read at a leisurely pace. Monks of the Middle Ages developed what they called *lectio divina*, "divine reading," for Scriptures. This approach entailed long pauses after reading a phrase or a sentence to allow the reading to soak in. Hurried reading inhibits serious reflection; more leisurely reading enhances it. The more one can enter into the experience of the author, the more one may gain from the writing. "Reading gives God more glory when we get more out of it," Thomas Merton remarks in *Thoughts in Solitude,* "when it is a more deeply vital act not only of our intelligence but of our whole personality, absorbed and refreshed in thought, meditation, prayer, or even in the contemplation of God."

d. Reread. Readers seldom grasp the profounder insights of what they read the first time. Often after a period of time a second reading will evoke totally different impressions from the same writing. In the seminary at Finkenwalde set up for the training of ministers for the "Confessing Church" in Germany, Dietrich Bonhoeffer required seminarians to meditate on the same passage of Scripture for thirty minutes each day for a whole week.

e. Mark and annotate. Readers will not want to lose track of important discoveries and would thus do well to develop a system for marking. Over a long period of time, most persons will forget what they learned and where they learned it. One good way to avoid this is to make a personal index on blank pages at the front or back of these writings. A few choice words can bring one quickly to the exact passage which meant so much. Another way to conserve highlights to which one will return is to keep a journal in which one can jot down and reflect on insights found in certain writings. A journal allows one to keep an inventory of personal progress.

Bibliography. Athanasius, *The Life of Saint Antony,* R. T. Meyer trans. (1950). St. Augustine of Hippo, *Confessions* (1963). St. Bernard of Clairvaux, *Love of God.* Clement, *The Instructor,* S. P. Wood trans. (1954); *Miscellanies,* F. J. A. Hort and J. B. Mayor, trans. (1987). Gregory of Nyssa, *The Life of Moses,* J. Malherbe and E. Ferguson trans. (1978). E. G. Hinson, *Seekers after Mature Faith* (1968). Jerome, *Illustrious Persons,* E. C. Richardson trans. (1892). F. N. Magill and I. P. MacGreal, eds., *Christian Spirituality* (1988). T. Merton, *Thoughts in Solitude* (1958). Thomas à Kempis, *The Imitation of Christ,* L. Sherley-Price trans. (1418, ET 1952).

E. G. HINSON

MEDITATION; SPIRITUAL DISCIPLINE AND GROWTH. *See also* FORMATIVE SPIRITUALITY; SPIRITUALITY. *Compare* CLASSIC *or* JEWISH LITERATURE IN CARE AND COUNSELING. *Biography:* BERNARD OF CLAIRVAUX; CYPRIAN OF CARTHAGE; FRANCIS OF ASSISI; TERTULLIAN OF CARTHAGE.

LITERATURE, PASTORAL USE OF. The use of literature in pastoral work has been recognized as important in the tasks of preaching, devotions, and religious education. Little recognition has been given to the use of literature in the task of pastoral care and counseling. Emphasis in this area of ministry has been given to the interpersonal process, personal awareness and growth, symbolic processes, and counseling methodologies. Training in pastoral care and counseling has been primarily experiential, with literature used for theoretical orientations in the development of clinical skills, and with minimal focus given to the place of literature in the care and counseling process itself.

The use of literature has a creative and helpful place in clinical pastoral work when discernment and discretion are used in selection of relevant literature and appropriate circumstances for its use. The decision not to recommend literature may be as significant as that of what literature to use in a given situation. It is the intention of this article to raise awareness of the positive and negative consequences of the pastoral uses of literature, as well as to suggest a standard for selection.

1. Selecting Literature. Generally, the clinical use of literature by pastors has been a random process, with little thought given to a strategy for the use of literature or the appropriateness of specific writings for specific persons. Too often literature has been given or recommended as a way for the pastor to avoid personal involvement in a therapeutic relationship or growth process. For example, rather than engage a premarital couple in a conversation about sexuality, a pastor may simply give them a book on sexual relations, with no thought given as to the readiness of this couple to assimilate the information. When literature is recommended, it is important that some criteria for selection have been used. Indiscriminate recommendations can aggravate a problem more than help. Recommended reading can cause unexpected problems even when care in selection has been taken, so this is not a matter to be lightly considered. The following criteria are suggested in the selection process.

a. Relevance. Literature that has meaning in clinical use generally arises out of the process and is immediately relevant to the context of the problem, feeling, or circumstance at hand. Thus, reading that has significant meaning for one person may have little meaning for another. Experienced counselors know that effective counseling requires a strategy. Although the strategy needs to be flexible, the counselor needs to have an awareness of the flow and direction of the process. The counselor needs to own the value of an appropriate directiveness, while giving the client room to initiate and raise issues and feelings. This appropriate directiveness is strategy. When the counselor is in touch with the process and sensitive to the issues, then he or she is able to relate that to relevant reading that can be a further resource to the client for expanded awareness and growth.

The matter of relevance can be deceptive. Persons will sometimes approach the pastoral counselor with a request for something to read on a subject. Whereas this may sound as if the person is highly motivated, the request may be a subterfuge for real change. Reading can set up the pretence for change while not effecting any change at all. Thus there are times when it is best to refrain from recommending any literature until one sees the direction into which the person is moving and understands more about the personality.

b. Comprehensibility. Literature that is beyond the reach of the person to comprehend will obviously be of little use. This may have nothing to do with intelligence. When a person is under significant and prolonged stress, or in the middle of a crisis, the ability to think, reflect, and comprehend is usually impaired. This is not the time to expect someone to make positive use of literature, however relevant it may be. Intelligence and educational level do need to be considered as well, however.

c. Value system. When working closely with a person, it is necessary to have an awareness of the value system of the person. It may be clearly formed or vaguely represented. However it comes across, the value system is related to the integrity of the individual and is a basic consideration for building and deepening rapport. Literature that violates or threatens the person's value system will break or weaken rapport. Special care needs to be taken in regard to literature related to sexuality, often a sensitive issue in regard to values. When a decision is made to recommend reading that is known to challenge or stretch the value system of the client, this needs to be based on a conscious strategy and an open and trusted relationship. The counselor needs to be aware that recommended literature also reflects his or her value system and needs to be congruent with what the client experiences in the relationship.

d. Personal meaning for the counselor. The axiom that a good book is like a good friend is never more true than when a book is recommended to someone who is troubled or distressed. It is like referring someone to a friend who has been meaningful to oneself in times of need. Thus, it is important for a piece of writing to have had significant meaning for the counselor before it is recommended to the counselee.

e. Appropriate timing. In his classic volume, *Human Education and Development,* Robert J. Havighurst describes what he calls the "teachable moment" in human experience. This is the moment when the person is ready and open to learn. It is both spontaneous and planned, voluntary and involuntary. It is an internal readiness to assimilate new awareness and new teaching. To be aware of this moment in another person requires intuitive sensitivity. When reading is introduced at a teachable moment, it has its optimum chance of assimilation and positive impact. Therefore, timing is a crucial factor in effectiveness.

f. Matching and mixing. Richard Stuart, a behavioral marital therapist, cautions against introducing any issue or directive into a counseling session that has the possibility of negative consequences, or cannot be adequately accomplished. This applies to the introduction of literature. In this regard, it may be important that the type of literature introduced match the type of thinking strength of the client. For example, if the client is a very practical thinker who likes facts and specific data, it may be futile, and even negative, to give him or her literature that is heavily theoretical. Likewise, theoretical thinkers may not respond positively to practical literature. They may feel as if they have failed at getting what the counselor wanted them to get from the reading. This further undermines self-esteem and may weaken rapport with the counselor.

Where rapport is deep and the client is willing to work on developing opposite strengths, the counselor may intentionally mix it up. For example, he or she may give practical literature to a theoretical thinker to help the person deal more concretely with reality, or, give a practical thinker theoretical literature to help the person see more options and to gain new ideas. Both matching and mixing require a sensitive awareness of the polar strengths of the individual. *Bi/Polar: A Positive Way of Understanding People* by J. W. Thomas is a helpful resource in gaining this awareness.

2. Case Illustrations. Pieces of literature which the pastor wishes to introduce to counselees may be placed in the waiting room or office. Those for whom it is relevant tend to pick it up and comment on it. Those for whom it is not relevant tend to ignore it. One woman seen in counseling for several months picked up a book on parenting. She brought it into the office, saying that she had wanted to talk about her twelve year old son, with whom she had the kinds of problems that this book seemed to address. The book helped her to disclose the difficulty she was having and her anxiety about being a single parent while her husband was on an extended trip. It was recommended that she buy the book and read it. She did, and the book helped in the design of some effective behavioral strategies for the management of her son at home. By reading the book, she saved time in counseling and increased her awareness.

A couple in counseling for an extended period of time finally became comfortable enough to begin to talk about their rather severe sexual problem. They married young, and after twenty years they felt frustrated by their lack of intimacy, sexual or otherwise. Both of them were sexually naive, especially the wife, and they had difficulty talking together about their sexual relationship. It appeared that they could benefit from some reading in the area of sexuality, but most of the popular literature seemed to be either too licentious for their value system or too simplified for their intelligence. A new book was found which met all of the criteria for selection and seemed to suit them well. They began reading the book together and discussing it chapter by chapter. This process opened up areas of discussion and sharing that gave reliable information and helped to desensitize them to the subject of sex. It should be stressed that the reading was an integrated part of the counseling process. Without the overall process of counseling, the reading would have had little, if any, benefit.

3. Literature and Marital Systems. Literature used in marital counseling is affected by the marital system. Like any other kind of intervention, literature needs to be chosen with an awareness of the system in which persons operate, and awareness of how one might use the literature to reinforce an already negative system of interaction.

For example, a couple had been in conjoint counseling for several months and were making little progress. The only "progress" was that they had not separated, as the wife had fully intended to do after the initial session. In an effort to change strategy and focus more on the internal processes of the husband and wife, it was decided to see them individually for several sessions. While listening to the wife in her session, the counselor began to relate her struggle to a book on personal growth and maturity which he had found meaningful. Without fully considering how this might be used in their marital system, he recommended it to her. She purchased the book within a few days, but she did not read it. The husband, who was grasping for straws to save the marriage, picked up the book and became deeply engrossed in it. In his sessions he discussed how much the book meant to him and how he thought it would help his wife. The counselor reminded him that he had not recommended the book for the marriage but for her personally. Nevertheless, the husband became angry because she would not read the book, accusing her of not trying to do something positive. The content of the book soon became irrelevant; the book had become a pawn in a system bent on self-destruction. The husband's attempts to control and the passive-aggressive behavior of the wife were very evident in this transaction. This was far from the intention of the use of the book and served only to intensify the marital system. This process can happen frequently with popular literature with negative results to the relationship. One uses the literature as a weapon with which to punish or attack the other.

There are times when it is best to refuse to suggest any literature when it is requested, even in regard to religious literature. For example, during the fourth session with one angry and conflicted couple, the wife appeared to be ambivalent and puzzled about the process. The counselor commented on this, and she said she expected something different from counseling, such as use of the Bible and prayer. The counselor responded that he did use such resources when the time was right, but that he would not use such powerful resources until they appeared to be stable enough to make good use of them. They were surprised and even more puzzled, but when reference was made to Scripture and prayer in a later session, they were much more involved and responsive than they could have been at an earlier time. By denying the initial request, this couple's marital system was stretched and began to become more effective.

The clinical use of biblical literature has been adequately discussed by such persons as Wayne Oates, William Oglesby, and Donald Capps, among others, and this article will not attempt to deal with this extensive subject, except to underscore the value of its rich symbolic, metaphorical, and hope-giving imagery and language, when appropriately used.

4. Literature as Self-Disclosure. An interesting way to find out more about a counselee or parishioner is to become aware of what they are reading themselves. It is not unusual for persons to bring in literature that has been significant to them. Reading the literature gives insight into the person that the pastor might not have received otherwise. It is a safe means of self-disclosure, whether unconscious or conscious.

This self-disclosure was apparent in a graduate of a military academy. He had a long-standing problem with self-esteem and assertiveness. Although he had had some success as an officer, he felt like a failure and struggled with depression. He brought a copy of a realistic novel about life at the academy, and said, "When you get to know the plebe in this book, you will know me better." Indeed, the character of the plebe disclosed much about the counselee which he had not otherwise been able to articulate, and the book enriched the counseling process.

Bibliography. D. Capps, *Biblical Approaches to Pastoral Counseling* (1981). R. J. Havighurst, *Human Education and Development* (1961). W. Oates, *The Bible in Pastoral Care* (1953). W. Oglesby, *Biblical Themes for Pastoral Care* (1980). R. Stuart, *Helping Couples Change* (1980). J. W. Thomas, *Bi/Polar: A Positive Way of Understanding People* (1978).

C. R. WOODRUFF

TECHNIQUE AND SKILL IN PASTORAL CARE. *See also* EDUCATION, NURTURE, AND CARE; GUIDANCE, PASTORAL. *Compare* BIBLE, PASTORAL USE AND INTERPRETATION OF; CLASSIC LITERATURE IN CARE AND COUNSELING; FORMATIVE SPIRITUALITY; SELF-HELP PSYCHOLOGIES.

LITURGICAL CALENDAR. From its earliest beginnings the Christian community's worship took time seriously. The liturgical calendar, or "church year," developed slowly in the first three centuries, Christianity having inherited certain feasts and seasons from Judaism. The Passover was foundational to the Christian Pascha or Easter. The feast of weeks (tabernacles), fifty days after the Passover marking the end of the wheat harvest as well as commemorating the giving of the Law on Mt. Sinai, became the Christian Pentecost. These, along with

Epiphany—a festival of Eastern origin focusing upon the incarnation and baptism of Christ—constituted the three principal annual feasts in the pre-Nicene church. The core of the calendar was the Lord's Day, or Sunday, sometimes referred to as a "little Easter." More aptly, Easter was referred to as the "great Sunday."

Beginning with the fourth century, a series of further christological feasts emerged, especially in the church at Jerusalem. Liturgical observance of definitive events in the life and ministry of Jesus was celebrated in the places taken to be the historical sites of such events. From this, Holy Week emerged. Christmas and the two preparatory seasons, Advent (leading to Christmas) and Lent (leading to Holy Week and Easter), developed somewhat later.

In addition to these festivals focusing upon the person and work of Christ, annual commemorations of the deaths of martyrs had developed as part of the liturgical pattern in various local churches as early as the second century. The feast days commemorating the Christ-events are commonly referred to as the "temporal cycle," while those growing out of the remembrance of martyrs are called "the sanctoral cycle." The liturgical year in its historically developed form is a combination of these two cycles.

In recent years major Christian traditions have restored and reformed the basic pattern of the church year with two principal foci: Advent/Christmas/Epiphany, and Lent/Easter/Pentecost. These reforms are based on the early church's practices, seen in light of central theological and pastoral norms. The so-called "liturgical churches"—Roman Catholic, Anglican, and Episcopal in particular—have retained an extensive, though purified, sanctoral cycle while emphasizing the christological meaning of the temporal cycle. At the same time many "free-church" traditions have recovered the pastoral and theological significance of keeping the liturgical year in some minimal form. This is due to ecumenical sharing and to the recognition of the need human beings have for the discipline of keeping ritual time, and of commemorating birth and death and human passages.

Lectionaries, or systems of Scripture readings appointed for use in a pattern over time, are integral to the calendar. From early times, certain festivals and seasons were associated with certain passages from Scripture. The advantages of lectionaries keyed to the principal christological feasts and seasons of the year are three-fold: comprehensive coverage of the whole of Scripture, a disciplined pattern for preaching (avoiding arbitrary or limited subjective choices by preachers), and a christological focus for the community's experience of the word and sacraments. Keeping the structures of time provides the Christian community with its identity in the memories. Appropriating the meaning of the liturgical calendar thus has spiritual and pastoral implications, among which is the symbolic presentation and experience of the worshippers' own temporality. As T. S. Eliot observed, "only in and through time is time redeemed."

Bibliography. A. A. McArthur, *The Evolution of the Christian Year* (1953). J. Talley, *The Origins of the Liturgical Year* (1986). J. F. White, *Introduction to Christian Worship* (1990 [1980]), chap. 2.

D. E. SALIERS

RITUAL AND PASTORAL CARE; WORSHIP AND CELEBRATION. *See also* CHRISTIAN LIFE; JEWISH HOLY DAYS AND FESTIVALS, PASTORAL DIMENSIONS OF; REST AND RENEWAL, RELIGIOUS TRADITIONS OF. *Compare* HOLIDAY DEPRESSION.

LITURGICAL AND DEVOTIONAL LIFE, ROMAN CATHOLIC TRADITION OF.

"Liturgy," the term used in the West to indicate the official worship of God by the church, usually designates corporate sacramental worship, as distinct from other devotions, either practiced by groups or individuals. Pius XII defined it as "the public worship which our Redeemer as Head of the Church renders to the Father, as well as the worship which the community of the faithful renders to its Founder, and through Him to the heavenly Father. In short, it is the integral public worship of the Mystical Body of Jesus Christ, of Head and members" ("Mediator Dei" 20).

1. **Liturgical Practice.** Liturgy comprises sacramental celebrations, the liturgical or church year, and the liturgy of the hours; liturgical arts and music are dimensions of liturgical celebration.

At the Last Supper, Christ instituted the Eucharistic sacrifice of his Body and Blood as a perpetual sacrifice of the cross. The celebration of the Eucharist (the Lord's Supper, the Mass), a memorial of Christ's passion, death, and resurrection, is a sacrament of love, sign of unity, and bond of charity.

Revising the Mass rite, Vatican II simplified its structure to manifest more clearly the inherent connection between its two parts, the Liturgy of the Word and the Liturgy of the Eucharist, and called for the "full, conscious and active" participation of the assembly. The Liturgy of the Word consists of scriptural proclamations, a psalm response, and gospel-alleluia. A homily interprets God's Word and general intercessions petition God for the needs of the world. The Table-Liturgy is a ritual celebration of Jesus' actions at the Last Supper. It consists of a preparation of table and gifts ("he took"), the Eucharistic Prayer, the climactic thanksgiving prayer ("he blessed"), the breaking of bread and pouring of the cup ("he broke"), and a communion rite ("he gave"). "Introductory rites" lead in to the Word-Liturgy and a brief dismissal rite concludes the Mass.

Sacraments of initiation include baptism, confirmation, and Eucharist. Third-century adults prepared for initiation by a period of catechumenal instruction-asceticism, leading to conversion of heart, and were made members of the church in a celebration including water-baptism, confirmation-christmation, and Eucharist. Gradually these rites became distinct celebrations. The revised confirmation rites for adults and children connect confirmation more with the entire process of initiation, as does the restored adult *catechumenate*.

Other sacraments include reconciliation (penance), which restores a Christian to table-fellowship after severance consequent upon serious sin; marriage; initiation into Holy Orders; and anointing of the sick. Significantly, this last rite places anointing within the context of various ministries of pastoral care, for example, visitation and communion of the sick. It is no longer termed extreme unction, "last anointing," a view developed in the medieval period.

The primordial celebration day is Sunday, the Day of the Lord and heart of the liturgical year, restored to its premier place in the revised calendar. The Lent/Easter/Pentecost season, restored as the primary time for pre-baptismal preparation, celebrates the mystery of the passion, death, and resurrection of the Lord; its character is baptismal and penitential. The church year also includes Advent/Christmas/Epiphany season, ending with the Lord's baptism; the season celebrates the mystery of God incarnate.

In addition to the seasonal ("temporal") cycle, there is a "sanctoral" cycle — feasts of Christ, Mary, and saints occurring throughout the year — and certain holy days, determined by each country, are "of obligation," requiring attendance at Mass. A way for Christians to enter into the great mysteries of salvation, the liturgical year memorializes the redemption-mystery, rendering it somehow present.

The Liturgy of the Hours, formerly identified as "the Breviary," originated as daily prayer for Christians; gradually chief "hours" of prayer, Lauds and Vespers, were publicly celebrated morning and evening. Monastic practice influenced the content of prayer, times for celebration, increasing prayer length, and gathering times. The once prayer-of-the-people became the preserve of monastics and clerics.

Vatican II sought to restore public morning and evening prayer as part of parochial life. A means of recalling the Christian mystery, these prayers consist of psalms, hymns, and Scripture readings articulated with the time of day.

The U.S. Bishops' documents on liturgical music and arts are an expansion of the Liturgy Constitution sections and give importance to these sense-perceptible dimensions of worship.

2. **Devotional Practice.** "Devotions," practices of piety, giving concrete expression to one's relationship to God by directing attention to some particular aspect of the Christian mystery, person, or created object, enjoy a lengthy history in the Roman tradition. Originally such pious practices were elements of "popular religion" and many developed to supplement official worship, especially when liturgical celebration was at a low ebb.

Vatican II not only accepted, but recommended such traditional practices, stating they should derive from and lead to liturgical celebration and be drawn up to harmonize with the church year.

The wide range of devotional practices embraces Eucharistic devotions, devotions to Christ (such as the *Imitation of Christ*), Mary and the saints and holy objects ("sacramentals").

Eucharistic devotions focus on the abiding real presence of Christ in the sacramental species, as object of adoration, thanksgiving, petition, and reparation. Benediction, a ritual blessing of the people with the reserved Sacrament, usually placed in a monstrance for viewing, now is done within a context of hymns, scriptural readings, and prayer. Forty hours, associated with the hours of Christ's entombment, was a solemnized reservation of the Sacrament; separated from its original setting, it became an independent petition rite during difficult times. It grew to become a rite celebrating the real, not "symbolic," sacramental presence. Lastly, processions with the Eucharist became a popular expression of piety associated with the feast of Corpus Christi.

Today these devotions are directed to flow from the Eucharistic Liturgy and lead back to it, for Christ's Body and Blood have been given primarily as nourishing food and drink.

Devotions to Christ's passion, especially the Way of the Cross ("Stations of the Cross"), grew out of pilgrimages to the Palestinian holy places. Widespread in the twelfth and thirteenth centuries, these devotions were often promoted by the crusaders, who placed markers at home indicating hallowed places visited. The Way of the Cross, fourteen stations commemorating Christ's way to Golgotha, is a service of meditation on those mysteries, coupled with prayer and song.

Devotion to the Sacred Heart and the celebration of First Fridays of nine consecutive months focus on the humanity of Jesus, the heart understood as seat of the person. A "Holy Hour" of reparation for offences against God, also petitioned God for mercy for sinners. Devotion to Mary, Mother of God, and the saints often takes the form of "novenas," originally nine successive days of prayer, either public or private, for obtaining some special favor. Today novena services take place only weekly. Although novenas began in the early Middle Ages, it was only in the last century that they were recommended by the church.

Underlying novenas is the doctrine of the intercession of saints, which has become popular after the Arian controversy, which, in stressing the divinity of Christ, tended to portray Christ as dramatically transcendent. Consequently saints became popular intercessors for God's people.

The rosary, an expression of Marian devotion, consists of five groups of ten "Hail Marys" ("a decade"), preceded by the Lord's Prayer and concluded with the *Gloria Patri*. Recitation of the same prayer texts is intended to keep the mind free of distraction, as does a mantra, allowing meditation on the mystery of each decade, for example, Annunciation, Visitation, etc. Originally intended for private prayer, this devotion has become popular group prayer.

Holy objects and special blessings, known as "sacramentals," include statues and images of saints and Christ, crucifixes, medals of the saints, especially of Mary (the Miraculous Medal), blessed palm, holy water (Easter water), and holy cards depicting Jesus or a saint. These objects are not venerated, but rather serve to focus attention in religious practice, especially in private prayer. Blessings of persons and objects are included in the new revision of the Roman Ritual.

For the well-disposed faithful the sacramental liturgy and devotions sanctify almost every event of life with divine grace of the paschal mystery—the passion, death, and resurrection of Christ. From this source all sacraments and sacramentals draw their power. There is scarcely any proper use of material things which cannot thus be directed toward people's sanctification and God's praise (*Constitution on the Sacred Liturgy*, 61, adapted).

Bibliography. Bishops' Committee on the Liturgy, *Environment and Art in Catholic Worship* (1978); *Liturgical Music Today* (1982); *Music in Catholic Worship* (1972). C. Dehne, "Roman Catholic Popular Devotions," in *Christians at Prayer*, J. Gallen,

ed., (1977), pp. 83–99. O. P. Flannery, ed., "The Constitution on the Sacred Liturgy," in *Vatican Council II: The Conciliar and Post Conciliar Documents* (1983). R. Guardini, *The Spirit of the Liturgy* (ET 1940). Pius XII, "Mediator Dei," *Official Catholic Teachings: Worship and Liturgy*, J. J. Megivern, ed. (1978), p. 68. J. F. White, *Introduction to Christian Worship* (1980; rev. ed. forthcoming 1990).

J. A. MELLOH

MARY, VENERATION OF; RETREATS (Roman Catholicism); SAINTS, VENERATION OF; SPIRITUALITY, ROMAN CATHOLIC. *See also* ASCETICAL PRACTICES; CHRISTIAN LIFE; SPIRITUAL DISCIPLINE AND GROWTH; WORSHIP AND CELEBRATION. *Compare* PILGRIMAGE METAPHOR.

LITURGICAL CHANGE AND REFORM (Pastoral Issues).

The past quarter-century has witnessed the most widespread reform of Christian worship in the West since the sixteenth century. Every major tradition has produced new service books and new hymnals. Among Roman Catholic and the mainline Protestant churches, extensive reform of the rites of Christian initiation, Eucharist, the liturgical calendar, daily prayer, as well as weddings, funerals, and related pastoral offices have generated a broad range of pastoral issues.

As a consequence of twentieth century reforms, future directions of Christian liturgy require more intentional lay participation in planning worship and the recovery of various lay liturgical ministries. The role of readers, servers, leaders of prayer, cantors, and others brings a new dimension in shared pastoral responsibility for most traditions. A second issue concerns the participation of the whole assembly. The *Constitution on the Sacred Liturgy* of the Second Vatican Council (1963) speaks of the people of God growing into "full, active and conscious participation" in the liturgy. This requires education and faith-formation of the whole church in the meaning and existential dimensions of common prayer and ritual activity. More than simple cognitive learning of doctrine, such mature participation brings the life experience of people to bear directly upon the quality of self-involvement in the liturgical forms. A third and related issue bears upon the catechetical and ongoing educational task of appreciation of the historical and theological development of Christian rites and the human life cycle.

New relationships between sacramental action and forms of healing have emerged as focal points in the reforms. Thus, a fourth pastoral issue focuses on identification and nurture of specific healing and reconciling dimensions of good liturgy, and the tracing of their affective implications in the life of local congregations. This leads to a fifth issue: deepening the relationships between worship and spiritual direction. There are significant relations between pastoral care and counseling outside liturgy in relation to spiritual guidance. Attending to the concrete ways in which liturgy shapes and directs persons' lives is a crucial part of the pattern and process of pastoral care in the community.

A sixth pastoral issue concerns the interrelation between liturgy and ministry to others. Caring for how the Christian assembly perceives its own ministries made audible and visible *within* the liturgy is one side of the matter. Opening up the intrinsic relation between prayer and action in Christ's name in everyday life is the other.

All of these specific pastoral issues require an understanding of the nature of congregational resistance to and acceptance of liturgical change. Understanding the resistance to more frequent celebration of the Eucharist, among Protestants, for example, or to changes in how funerals are conducted discloses the larger arena of ambivalence and growth within the congregation. Within Roman Catholic reforms, for example, the new rites which stress anointing the sick in relation to the whole process of suffering and dying represents a change from the older dramatic rite of extreme unction. Significant changes in the Mass such as the use of the vernacular have required perceptual and affective changes on the part of the assembly. Likewise, practices such as abstinence from meat on Fridays have changed. All of these changes generate some ambivalence, especially among older parishioners.

It is important to remember that deep personal meanings are invested in liturgical practices, changes in which may be confusing and threatening for some even as they may be liberating for others. Thus, liturgical change is best prepared for and supported by a pastorally oriented educational process which encourages the sharing of feelings and concerns about such changes, while teaching the biblical, historical and theological principles involved.

Bibliography. E. Ramshaw, *Ritual and Pastoral Care* (1987). D. L. Vignaud, "The Place of Worship in Pastoral Care," *Pastoral Psychology,* 29 (1980), 99–108. J. H. Westerhoff, *Learning Through Liturgy* (1978). J. F. White, *Christian Worship in Transition* (1976). W. H. Willimon, *Worship as Pastoral Care* (1979). World Council of Churches, *Baptism, Eucharist and Ministry* (1982).

D. E. SALIERS

CONGREGATION, PASTORAL CARE OF; RITUAL AND PASTORAL CARE; TRADITION AS MODE OF CARE; VATICAN COUNCIL II AND PASTORAL CARE; WORSHIP AND CELEBRATION. *See also* ECCLESIOLOGY AND PASTORAL CARE; LEADERSHIP AND ADMINISTRATION; PROPHETIC/PASTORAL TENSION IN MINISTRY. *Compare* SACRAMENTAL THEOLOGY AND PASTORAL CARE; SOCIAL CHANGE AND DISLOCATION.

LITURGY/LITURGICAL THEOLOGY. *See* WORSHIP AND CELEBRATION. *See also* RITUAL; SACRAMENTAL THEOLOGY.

LOBOTOMY. *See* PSYCHOSURGERY.

LOCUS OF CONTROL RESEARCH. Locus of control refers to a generalized expectation that guides behavior. People with an *internal* locus of control perceive events as a consequence of their own behavior and thus controllable; persons with an *external* locus of control view events as unrelated to their behavior, as unpredictable, or as the result of luck, fate, or powerful others, and therefore beyond personal control. Locus of control research began in the late 1950s with studies conducted by Phares, James, and Rotter and gained focus and prominence with the publication of a monograph by Rotter in 1966, which reviewed the work to date and described a twenty-

three-item scale. Locus of control research so proliferated that it gained its own heading in *Psychological Abstracts* in 1971 and peaked in the latter half of the decade. Since then, research has continued at a slower pace as related constructs have gained prominence.

Locus of control has been employed in a wide range of studies involving developmental, demographic, cross-cultural, health, educational, and vocational issues. Internal locus of control has been shown to relate to resistance to influence, achievement, ability to delay gratification, and adaptive reactions to a range of health care issues as well as to success in psychotherapy. More recent research in the areas of attribution, self-efficacy, hope, personal causation, intrinsic motivation, and learned helplessness echo similar concerns.

To some extent, locus of control theory and research reflect American assumptions about self-help and rationality and lend credence to systems urging positive or possibility thinking. Yet there are also limits to this way of thinking, as perhaps best articulated by the Alcoholics Anonymous (Reinhold Niebuhr's) serenity prayer:

God, grant me the serenity
To accept the things I cannot change,
Courage to change the things I can,
And wisdom to know the difference.

It is at this point that locus of control research can help illuminate the process of pastoral counseling. People experiencing crisis of any sort need to have a sense of personal efficacy if they are to take responsibility for their actions, make decisions, learn from their mistakes, and learn to cope effectively with the challenges facing them. On the other hand, there are situations where an acknowledgment of one's finiteness and dependency coupled with faith in God's steadfast love comprise a more appropriate dominant response. Reliance on a loving God, who calls human beings to a responsible, trusting life, is not the same as yielding to chance or fate. Overemphasis on an internal locus of control leads to distorted notions of autonomy and blame, while overemphasis on an external locus of control undermines the individual's sense of responsibility and commitment to change.

Bibliography. R. C. Erickson, "Psychotherapy and the Locus of Control," *J. of Religion and Health,* 22 (1983), 74–81. H. M. Lefcourt, "Locus of control and coping with life's events," in *Personality: Basic Aspects and Current Research,* E. Staub, ed., (1980), pp. 201–35. J. B. Rotter, "Generalized expectancies for internal versus external locus of control of reinforcement," *Psychological Monographs,* 80 (Whole No. 609) (1966), 1–28.

R. C. ERICKSON

RESPONSIBILITY/IRRESPONSIBILITY, PSYCHOLOGY OF; SOCIAL PERCEPTION, JUDGMENT AND BELIEF. *See also* AUTHORITARIANISM; AUTHORITY; MORAL DEVELOPMENT; OBEDIENCE; SOCIAL PSYCHOLOGY. *Compare* PERSONALITY THEORY (Varieties, Traditions, and Issues).

LOGIC. *See* CASUISTRY, PROTESTANT; REASONING AND RATIONALITY IN PASTORAL CARE.

LOGOTHERAPY. An approach in psychotherapy developed by Viennese psychiatrist Viktor E. Frankl shortly after World War II and popularized by Frankl's writings and lecture tours on many university campuses in the U.S. in the 1960s and 1970s. Built upon the foundations of psychoanalysis, but departing from Freud's determinism and reductionism, logotherapy develops a "height psychology" to contrast with a more familiar "depth psychology."

In the term "logotherapy," the "logo" comes from the Greek *logos* ("word"), which Frankl translates as "meaning." Hence logotherapy is the "therapy of meaning." Accenting the capacity of each person to exercise the power of choice, Frankl contrasts his third school of Viennese psychiatry with Freud's first school of "will to pleasure," and with Adler's second school of "will to power," by characterizing his school as the "will to meaning."

Logotherapy is one of the existentialist approaches to psychotherapy. Frankl's best-known book, *Man's Search for Meaning* (1957) is an autobiographical account of his imprisonment in various concentration camps over a two-and-a-half-year period. The original English translation carried the title *From Death-Camp to Existentialism.* Subsequently enlarged and revised, *Man's Search for Meaning* has been a best seller, with translations into more than a dozen different languages. Frankl's emphasis on the will to meaning has had wide appeal in the post-World War II era, especially to lay readers, and has introduced an optimistic philosophy of life that has had significant influence in offsetting the disillusionment of the mid-century. Gordon Allport's preface to *Man's Search for Meaning* added the imprimatur of one of America's top-ranking psychologists and helped to give credibility in the professional world to an approach that was already gaining considerable popularity among lay people. In many ways, Frankl stands in the same tradition as William James and Gordon Allport.

More than most psychological writers, Frankl writes with a pro-religion bias. The first of his many books to be translated into English carried the title *The Doctor and the Soul: From Psychotherapy to Logotherapy* (1955). The publisher's book jacket aptly described it as "A new approach to the neurotic personality which emphasizes man's spiritual values and the quest for meaning in life." Although most of Frankl's writings are directed to a general audience and do not imply the need for religious faith, he is a devout Jew in his basic orientation. He makes it quite clear that what he refers to as "Ultimate Meaning" is interpreted by the religious person as God. His whole point of view is posited on the conviction that there is ultimate meaning, and that persons can be helped to find their own individual meaning. His book, *The Unconscious God,* is very explicit in its affirmation of the place of God in life. He writes: "The religious man experiences his existence not only as a concrete task but as a personal meaning which is given to him by a personal Being" (Wawrytko, 1982, p. 201).

1. The Importance of Meaning. In stressing the importance of personal meaning, Frankl often quotes Nietzsche: "He who has a *why* to live for can bear almost any *how*" (1963). One of Frankl's most helpful therapeutic approaches is in his discussion of how the therapist (or counselor) can help the patient (or parishioner) to discover personal meaning (Nietzsche's *why*). He notes that whereas finding some meaning in life is fairly commonplace, many people seek meaning in too narrow a field.

In distinguishing three arenas for finding meaning, Frankl provides a useful therapeutic tool.

a. Sources of meaning. According to Frankl meaning can be uncovered in three ways: "by doing a deed" (creative values), "by experiencing a value" (experiential values), "and by suffering" (attitudinal values). The problem with creative values is that many people seek all the meaning for their life in their work; and when by reason of retirement or illness or an economic recession they no longer have a job, they lose the sense of meaning. Similarly, people may realize experiential values in the enjoyment of a symphony or in the intimacy of a friendship; but if they become deaf or their friends move away, they, too, are left without meaning.

It is in his writing about attitudinal values that Frankl makes his most significant contribution. Each person can decide how to react to the circumstances that life brings, and in doing so has the potentiality of realizing attitudinal values. Life may bring limiting circumstances but persons must decide how they will respond, and this capacity to respond has no limit. Frankl describes what this means to a person: "In the realization of attitudinal values he is free — free 'from' all conditions and circumstances, and free 'to' the inner mastery of his destiny, 'to' proper upright suffering. This freedom knows no conditions, it is a freedom 'under all circumstances' and until the last breath" (1950).

Frankl's reference to suffering accents the importance of this third pathway to finding meaning. For the pastor, he offers more concrete help in dealing with suffering than any other writer on the therapeutic scene. His insistence on the potential value to be experienced in undeserved suffering reads like the affirmations in Paul's NT letters. "Suffering and trouble belong to life as much as fate and death. None of these can be subtracted from life without destroying its meaning. To subtract trouble, death, fate, and suffering from life would mean stripping life of its form and shape. Only under the hammer blows of fate, in the white heat of suffering, does life gain shape and form" (1973).

b. Freedom and responsibility. A central concept in logotherapy is the joining of freedom with responsibility. Human beings are not only free, Frankl asserts, to decide how to respond to cultural and biological conditioning, but, moreover, they are responsible to do so. More important than *what* has happened to persons is *how* they respond to the circumstances. Tested in the rigors of concentration camp living, Frankl's own witness to the "defiant power of the human spirit" to surmount circumstances and to play a significant role in deciding about personal destiny gives strong support in validating the effectiveness of logotherapy. His approach has had its greatest appeal and its greatest therapeutic success with those who have not been helped by more traditional psychotherapeutic efforts, and who have become disillusioned by the dehumanization of much of current psychological thinking.

2. Therapeutic Methods. In treatment procedures, Frankl employs three distinct approaches: the somatic or organic, the psychic or psychological, and the noetic or spiritual. Like most psychiatrists, he uses drugs where indicated and tries to understand cause and effect in psychological processes; but unlike most psychotherapists he also makes use of the spiritual dimension. Recognizing that many people who seek help for organic and/or psychological distress are really struggling with a sense of existential vacuum, a feeling of emptiness characterized by a lack of any real hold on meaning, Frankl sees the spiritual task as the most essential part of the therapeutic endeavor.

An example is seen in Frankl's description of a highly intelligent schoolteacher who was troubled by recurrent, organically caused depressions. In prescribing a drug for her, he used the somatic approach. In doing psychotherapy he dealt with the psychogenic component: her weeping over the fact that she was so tearful. When she disclosed her low opinion of herself and the almost total absence of any meaning in her life, he turned to logotherapy. "Here was a case where logotherapeutic treatment was necessary. It was the doctor's business to show the patient that her very affliction—these fated recurrent depressions—posed a challenge for her." Frankl's summary of the case is revealing: "After this existential analysis she was able, in spite of and even during further phases of endogenous [i.e., organically induced] depression to lead a life that was more conscious of responsibility and more filled with meaning than before treatment." One day she wrote to Frankl: "I was not a human being until you made me one" (1973).

Logotherapy does not have a neat, systematic treatment approach. Frankl encourages therapists to "improvise," to enter into a responsive relationship with patients and to move freely with intuitive hunches. He does, however, set forth two specific treatment methods: dereflection and paradoxical intention. *Dereflection* involves a recognition of a patient's problems, but a refocusing attention away from the problem to the person's meaning in life. Instead of making the problem central, Frankl helps the patient to see it within the larger perspective of meaning.

Paradoxical intention, the second treatment modality, deals with a problem by encouraging, paradoxically, the very thing that the patient fears. By exaggerating symptoms, the patient is encouraged to objectify the symptoms, often with a touch of humor, so that the symptom no longer controls the person's life.

Logotherapy is still regarded as a novel idea in the Western world, but in Asia the common response is, "How very old." World Congresses of Logotherapy have been held since 1980 and Institutes of Logotherapy are developing around the world as therapists on an international scale are adding logotherapeutic insights to their practices.

Bibliography. R. Bulka, *The Quest for Ultimate Meaning: Principles and Application of Logotherapy* (1979). J. Fabry, *The Pursuit of Meaning* (1980 [1968]). J. Fabry, *et al.*, eds., *Logotherapy in Action* (1979). V. Frankl, *The Doctor and the Soul* (1973 [1955]); *Homo Patiens* (1950); *Man's Search for Meaning* (1963 [1957]), pp. 164, 176. *Psychotherapy and Existentialism* (1967); *The Unconscious God* (1975); *The Unheard Cry for Meaning* (1978); *The Will to Meaning* (1969). R. Leslie, *Jesus and Logotherapy* (1965), reprinted as *Jesus As Counselor* (1982). S. Wawrytko, ed., *Analecta Frankliana* (1982).

R. C. LESLIE

EXISTENTIAL PSYCHOLOGY AND PSYCHOTHERAPY; PSYCHOTHERAPY (Varieties, Traditions, and Issues). *See also* JUDAISM AND PSYCHOLOGY; PASTORAL COUNSELING. *Compare* FORMATIVE SPIRITUALITY; RELIGION AND PSYCHOTHERAPY; SPIRITUAL DIRECTION; VALUES IN COUNSELING AND PSYCHOTHERAPY; WILL THERAPY.

LONELINESS AND ISOLATION. *Loneliness* is an unpleasant affect, combining sadness and anxiety, a felt response to the absence of sufficient relational contact. *Isolation* is the condition of being separated from all important persons, things, or relationships.

The relationship of loneliness and isolation is often stated simply: "If a person is isolated, that person will experience loneliness." The reality is more complex, as different conditions are required to produce loneliness in different people. This article will explore the different ways in which loneliness and isolation are related, and the pastoral responses that those conditions require.

1. Situational Isolation and Transitory Loneliness. This is the most obvious situation. It is the loneliness resulting from life transitions which interrupt relationships. It can produce extreme, though typically temporary, loneliness.

The typical causes of this loneliness are the same as those of grief, of which it is a part. They include death and divorce, vocational changes, geographic moves, major maturational steps that change activity patterns, job promotions and crises that demand intense attention to one area of life to the exclusion of others.

In most cases, this type of loneliness is visible, since the events that bring it on are publicly known and the person affected often needs and wants to speak of them. Its resolution is often delayed by the requirements of the grief process that the loss sets in motion. If a major loss, a period of grieving will precede the individual's readiness for new relationship. Moving too quickly to reduce the loss-induced loneliness will either interfere with the completeness of grieving, or be resisted in a way disruptive to the pastoral relationship.

Pastoral response to this type of loneliness has long been a major priority for clergy. It properly consists of two steps. The first is a personal contact, to assess the nature of the loneliness and its readiness for resolution, plus offering relationship which will mitigate it somewhat. The second step is an environmental manipulation, putting the isolated person in contact with others who are resources for relationship and/or may be similarly afflicted. Funerals, evangelistic calls on move-ins, pastoral visits to a couple whose youngest child has just left home, and the campus minister's contacts with new freshmen are examples; as are self-help groups and newcomers' clubs.

2. Habitual Isolation and Lasting Loneliness. This common type of loneliness often presents itself as situational isolation, but careful inquiry will reveal that this sufferer has often felt a similar pain without apparent life disruption.

This loneliness is characterological, built into the personality of the individual, so that he or she stays isolated most of the time. It is typically the result of the person's anger, suspicion, and anxiety. Such persons, due to their painful experiences in formative relationships, experience others primarily as targets for their anger or as potential sources of danger. They usually avoid others, or when they do offer relationship, they cause enough discomfort for other people that they are often left alone. As a result, they do not develop social skills at the same rate as other people; so even if their fear and hate are resolved, they are still inept in forming relationships.

Situational/environmental manipulation will not be helpful to persons with this loneliness, unless it brings them into contact with someone who can provide the needed therapeutic intervention. A healing action is needed, and needed quickly, because every year that passes in this isolation puts the individual another year behind age-peers in social skill development, increasing the chance of life-long isolation.

The therapeutic intervention must include the following elements: (1) Refusal to be rebuffed, avoided, provoked or discouraged by the behavior that causes the isolation; (2) simultaneous illumination of those behaviors, identifying and describing them; (3) discovery of their motivational roots and goals, and the hopeless or faithless assumptions underlying them; (4) identification of new choice points about those assumptions and about continuing to use those behaviors; and (5) learning to deal with the new situations these new decisions will create.

When this is completed, the environmental manipulation discussed above will be necessary to move the isolated person into social situations.

3. Unnoticed Isolation and Hidden Loneliness. This is probably the most prevalent condition considered here. It prevails when activity, work, concern for appearances, fear of intimacy, and lack of a model for love combine to produce isolated individuals who are so focused on busyness that they do not notice the poverty of their relationships, hence do not feel lonely.

Persons afflicted with this hidden loneliness rarely look for help or welcome it if others offer it, and they typically seek the pastor only in response to a disruption in their lives. Illness, financial reverses, marital crises, drug abuse, and delinquency of their children, force this loneliness into the open. Many "middle-aged" crises are the upsurging of this kind of loneliness.

The most important and difficult pastoral task with hidden loneliness is to awaken the wish for change. Preaching may be the most useful point of leverage, if the pastor preaches a gospel enabling the hearer to grasp something that feels better than the rewards the isolated person has been able to gain in the isolation.

The other crucial pastoral response is crisis intervention when the system begins to break down and the loneliness shows. The opportunity for spiritual and relational growth is best enhanced by pointing out that the crisis is revealing the loneliness and dissatisfaction that has been present all along. It is often necessary to provide support in the face of the panic caused by sudden awareness that the old lifestyle does not work, and then to forthrightly identify the opportunity for growth. Once this is achieved the task is largely the same as the healing interventions described under part 2 above, though the process is usually not as lengthy or as difficult.

4. Apparent Isolation that Transcends Loneliness. Unlike the other conditions, this one is rare. It occurs in persons who have separated themselves from some relationships in order to better focus on other, for them very rich and relational, experiences. In this group are the spiritual adept, the monk, the mourner nearing the end of grief, the terminally ill in the state of acceptance, the analysand late in a fruitful analysis, and the dedicated student who is moved and nourished by that which is studied.

These persons seek a closer tie with something or someone they regard as more important than what they have given up. Some call it God, some self, some knowledge, some "the muse." A well-developed discipline is required to bring this new object into greater focus. Most persons undergo a struggle to resist the temptation to compromise the quest or to use it for other than the intended primary goal.

The required pastoral response to these persons is a species of spiritual direction, requiring an intimate knowledge of the individual's particular quest. Other requirements of such spiritual direction include knowledge of the distractions that disrupt such quests and ability to help the sojourner identify them; the ability to avoid interposing oneself between the other and the quest; and the refusal to become oneself the object of the quest. This is probably the most difficult of all pastoral tasks, because of the temptation to transgress the requirements, the technical difficulties of performing them well, and the importance of a good fit between director and pilgrim.

B. W. GRANT

COMMUNITY, FELLOWSHIP, AND CARE; FRIENDSHIP; PRIVACY AND SOLITUDE; RELATIONSHIP NETWORK; SOCIAL CHANGE AND DISLOCATION.

LONERGAN, BERNARD (1904–84). A Canadian Jesuit philosopher and religious thinker acknowledged internationally for contributions to cognitional theory and theological method. He taught at Collège de L'Immaculée-Conception in Montreal, Regis College in Toronto, the Gregorian University in Rome, and Harvard University, and Boston College in Boston. His major works are *Insight: A Study of Human Understanding* (1957) and *Method in Theology* (1972).

Lonergan's emphasis on technical philosophic issues did not cloud his interest in questions of distinctly pastoral relevance. His doctoral dissertation was a study of operative grace in Thomas Aquinas. He returned to the theme in his late work with penetrating reflections on religious, moral, and intellectual conversion. The authenticity of the human subject emerged as an ever more dominant theme in his writings after 1965. The relation of personal development to social and cultural progress and decline receives extended treatment in *Insight,* and reaches comprehensive articulation in his reflections on the human good in *Method in Theology* and in his subsequent writings on healing and creating in history. "Being in love"—love in the family, love in the community, and the love of God—can justly be considered the dominant motif in much of his later writing.

R. M. DORAN

PASTORAL THEOLOGY, ROMAN CATHOLIC; THEOLOGY AND PSYCHOLOGY. *See also* CHRISTOTHERAPY.

LORD'S PRAYER. *See* PRAYER.

LORD'S SUPPER. *See* COMMUNION/EUCHARIST.

LOSS. *See* GRIEF AND LOSS.

LOSS OF FUNCTION. Refers to the loss of some sensory or physical faculty in the human (e.g., hearing, sight, speech, muscular strength/coordination, or neurological/mental processes) and the accompanying mental and physical privation and crisis. Such loss could occur through accident, illness, genetic abnormality, or normal aging and is a loss of function after this function has developed as opposed to an innate defect or handicap from birth. The crisis accompanying such loss is largely a crisis of self. The personal dynamics and pastoral care issues involved in the immediate crisis surrounding the onset of losses in human sensory and physical functioning are factors affecting the adaptation to such losses, the adjustment process to loss, and theological/religious issues.

1. **Factors Affecting the Adaptation to Loss.** It is helpful to conceive of the various bodily parts and sensory functions as in a more or less intimate relationship with the self. Thus, the self can be envisioned as organizing these various parts and functions in a particular configuration or bodily image which gives more or less importance to some than others.

a. Symbolic significance. The self will attach to some parts and functions a special conscious or unconscious significance. If the loss involves a part which has been given more special significance or is more intimately related to the self, then the reaction to the loss of this sensory or bodily part will be more traumatic than to the loss of another part which is given less significance. For example, for a concert pianist the paralysis in the hand will be more traumatic than the loss of speech. Thus, the adaptation to such a loss will be retarded.

b. Extensiveness. If the loss is partial or only slightly incapacitating, then a person will more readily adapt and the self will usually integrate this loss more easily than if the loss is more extensive.

c. Relation to earlier losses. The loss of some bodily part or sensory function may involve a revival of feelings about a previous significant or symbolic loss. There may also be the presence of unresolved grief over earlier losses or anxiety about additional or future losses. These will all tend to interfere with the adaptive process.

d. Self-integration/differentiation. The degree to which the self is well integrated and differentiated will have a key role to play in the adaptation to losses. If the self is loosely or tenuously integrated and/or enmeshed, then losses can create a diffusion of the self and adaptation will be hindered.

e. Age. The adaptation to losses is usually more difficult at ages where the self is in flux and most vulnerable. Two such ages are adolescence and mid-life when there are developmental crises of identity and direction. Old age is another time when the self concept is more vulnerable and losses may have a more detrimental effect on the self's organization and adaptation processes.

f. Variety of interests. The range of activities and interests which the self integrates and organizes in its concept will affect the adaptation to loss. Usually if the self embraces more options and possibilities for itself,

then it is better able to adapt to the loss of one body or sensory function.

2. **Adjustment Process to Loss of Function.** Although the adjustment process is never orderly or rigidly sequential in terms of stages and although it takes different forms in different persons depending on the previously listed factors, there are several identifiable elements which seem to be commonly present in the adjustment reaction to loss of bodily or sensory functions.

a. Shock is the initial reaction to loss and is physical and psychological in nature. It serves as a massive protective mechanism for the self which provides an immediate numbness and distance from the impact of loss. The shock is usually of short duration.

b. Denial is a more prolonged protective mechanism which buffers the self concept and emotional stability of the self against the devastating effects of loss. This too can be physical and psychological (e.g., "phantom limb" following amputation). Denial can be helpful if it is slowly relinquished in the adaptive process. It serves to sustain hope during a traumatic period. It becomes maladaptive if it interferes significantly with movement. Pastoral interventions to denial should generally move in the direction of listening to but not positively reinforcing unrealistic beliefs and of avoiding confrontation of these beliefs unless the issue is critical or the person evidences a readiness for change.

c. Anger is an emotion which may parallel or follow denial. It is an adaptational response to the physical and psychological hurt of the loss of function. The anger may be symptomatic of feeling of unfairness about the loss and the pain involved in being forced to make significant changes in lifestyle or the way a person looks at life and self. This anger may be projected towards family, friends, fate, or God. Pastoral carers need to be aware of this anger as a part of the adaptive process and not a personal attack. In general, it should be tolerated and listened to as the person's feeling and reaction, but it should not be reinforced.

d. Depression may occur at any point in the process and may arise out of a perception of hopelessness, a guilt about the person's role in contributing to the loss of function, or a guilt about the expression of anger. The pastoral carer needs to be alert to suicidal signals in this depression.

e. Reintegration is the point in the adaptation process where the person engages in positive self-actualizing steps to reorganize the self in light of the loss of function. Pastoral care interventions may include disassociation techniques which foster disengaging the self from the lost function and affirming the value of the self in spite of loss, assistance in the setting of small, concrete goals, and directing the person to support groups, and information sources.

3. **Theological/Religious Issues.** Loss of bodily or sensory function involves a shattering of one's world and the way he or she fits in it. It calls into question one's perception of the meaning of his or her life and the way things are. The person may question God's justice or goodness or even God's power. The age-old problem of evil raised by the loss means the pastoral caregiver will also need to develop a theodicy for loss of function.

A major task for the person in reintegration will be the development of a new understanding of the meaning of life and God's activity in it. The self will need to be reorganized to include a new perspective on God. In the midst of this process, the pastoral carer may find it helpful to discuss with the person the theological affirmations that (1) God does not directly will losses and the suffering which accompanies them even though these things occur by divine permission as a consequence of human finitude and sin and (2) God's power is redemptive and can draw good out of any evil. Rather than presenting these in sermonic form, the pastoral carer can elicit an exploration of these affirmations and the person's feelings about them through questions and dialogue as the person constructs a new worldview in the wake of his or her disability.

Bibliography. F. D. Duncan, "Pastoral Care of Disabled Persons," in W. E. Oates and A. D. Lester, *Pastoral Care in Crucial Human Situations* (1969). K. R. Mitchell and H. Anderson, *All Our Losses, All Our Griefs* (1983). T. Oden, "A Theodicy for Pastoral Practice," in *Pastoral Theology* (1983), pp. 223–48. B. Schoenber, *et al.*, eds., *Loss and Grief* (1970).

C. M. MENDENHALL III

GRIEF AND LOSS; HANDICAP AND DISABILITY; SICK, PASTORAL CARE OF. *See also* BODY IMAGE.

LOVE. A central concept for Judeo-Christian theology and for theories of pastoral care and counseling, yet its meaning is notoriously ambiguous and obscure. Virtually all writers have been obliged to draw distinctions between different types or forms of love and to explain how emotional need and rational decision interrelate in actions determined by love. Love has been used as a description of the nature of God, as an ethical norm, and as a paradigm for the ideal counseling relationship. We may attempt to clarify the obscurities and confusions in this overused and frequently abused concept.

1. The Nature and the Forms of Love. *a. Love as unifying power.* We find in the writings of Paul Tillich a useful discussion of the different forms of love and of its underlying unity. Tillich defines love as the moving power of life that brings about the unity of the separated. Such power is especially significant in human life because each individual must find unity with other selves, but in a way that also retains the integrity or centeredness of each person and which avoids absorption by the other. Tillich discerns four forms of love in human life: *epithymia* (libido or desire), *eros* (the striving for the valuable), *philia* (friendship based on mutual attraction and respect), and *agape* (a giving of self that confers value on the other). He believes that each form is incomplete without the other three. For example, sexual desire (a form of *epithymia*) is necessary in human life, but it requires elements of value, friendship, and self-giving to be fully human. There are no "higher" forms of love that are exempt from the emotional power and biological necessity of *eros* and *epithymia*. All friendship contains elements of need and desire, and even *agape* must still be earthed in human need and emotion. Yet Tillich also gives a special place to *agape*, seeing it as the manifestation of the divine Spirit, which both enters the ambiguities of history and transcends them.

Tillich's exposition of the nature of love is valuable for its coherence and comprehensiveness, but it is by no means noncontroversial. Two contrasting theological views may be briefly referred to: love as mutuality, as this is interpreted in a modern Roman Catholic writer, Martin D'Arcy; and the radical Protestant contrast between *eros* and *agape*, represented especially by Anders Nygren.

b. Love as mutuality. D'Arcy (see *The Mind and the Heart of Love*) concentrates on the notion of *philia*, a natural human capacity to love which is supplemented but not supplanted by grace. Augustine's famous saying, "Our hearts are restless till they find their rest in thee" (*Confessions*, Book 7), forms the basis for a natural theology of love, which regards the individual as participating in the divine through friendship with God. D'Arcy expounds this idea in an original way by contrasting "masculine" principles of self-assertion and rational egoism with "feminine" principles of self-surrender and emotional receptiveness. This polarity (which might now be regarded as somewhat sexually stereotyped) is overcome in the mutuality of *philia*, which is a harmony of giving and getting. Personal friendship leads the way to the perfection of love (*caritas*), which is God. The more God is loved the more the individual is capable of love of self and of others.

c. Eros in opposition to agape. Totally opposed to this synthesis of human and divine love are theological teachings that stress the pervasiveness of sin and the utter dependence of human beings on God's initiative. This view is most clearly represented in Anders Nygren's classic work *Agape and Eros*. Nygren portrays two quite different forms of love: the self-centered and acquisitive love of human beings, even in their highest moments; and the spontaneous, disinterested, and value-conferring love, which comes from God alone. Nygren adamantly denies any synthesis of, or connection between, these two loves. Christian love is possible only when, through grace, human beings become channels for divine love. There are no points of connection between human emotions and God's self-giving. Human beings have nothing to contribute from their nature, which is utterly fallen. The "love of God" is solely the love that *God* offers. Humans cannot offer love *to* God (as D'Arcy, for example, suggests). Only through God's gift of faith are human beings capable of *agape*.

Similar, though less extreme, views are expressed by Karl Barth and Reinhold Niebuhr. Though neither would accept the demotion of human beings to mere "channels" for divine love, both stress the utter dependence of all genuinely loving acts on God's initiative. Niebuhr writes of the "relevance of an impossible ideal" and sees God's love as both judging human history and giving hope. Barth speaks of the "freedom to obey" and argues that it is only in response to the divine self-giving that human beings can be set free to love. Thus, like Nygren, these writers stress the discontinuity between *agape*, as revealed by God in Christ, and all human acts of loving.

d. The emergent issues. Those who follow the synthesis proposed by D'Arcy, or the interdependence described by Tillich, will more readily see a continuity between psychology and theology in dealing with the theme of love. (Thus, for example, they might see the client-centered therapy of Carl Rogers and the injunction of Jesus to love one's neighbor as oneself as saying basically the same thing.) On the other hand, those who reject such "natural theology" will tend to put Christian love into a separate category from human acts of caring and human systems of morality. By discussing these theoretical issues more fully we may gain a clearer view of the practical implications for pastoral care and counseling.

2. Egoism and Altruism. The arguments of Nygren, Barth, and Niebuhr depend, to a large extent, on a radical distinction between self-interested (egoistic) and disinterested (altruistic) love. They appear to support the ethical theory known as Psychological Hedonism, which asserts that all human beings are bound to seek pleasure for themselves and shun pain. All apparently loving actions are, in reality, subtle attempts to gain pleasure for the self. Notable exponents of this view are Thomas Hobbes, Benedict Spinoza, and (of especial relevance to counseling theory) Sigmund Freud, in his formulation of the "pleasure principle." This view of human nature makes it inevitable that the Christian ideal of *agape,* which is a disinterested concern for the welfare of others (even those who are one's enemies), is radically distinguished from ordinary human motivation, or else is rejected as mere illusion.

A contrary view can be defended only if the assumption of Psychological Hedonism is challenged. Erich Fromm represents a modern, psychologically based defense of altruism (see *Man for Himself* and *The Art of Loving*). According to Fromm, a concern for the self (self-love) is not to be confused with a grasping for pleasure for the self (selfishness). Pointing out that the Christian commandment is to love neighbor *as yourself,* Fromm argues that love of self and love of others are not opposed, but complementary. The selfish person does not love self, but anxiously seeks to make up for a lack of self-respect through grasping after material goods. Only if one has a love of self, a true concern for one's own welfare, is one able to love others with equal respect. Fromm's argument assumes the possibility of *agape* while egoism denies this possibility. It is difficult to see how such basic assumptions can be either proved or disproved.

Reinhold Niebuhr's pioneering writings on Christian social ethics (see especially *Moral Man and Immoral Society*) trace the influence of egoism in *all* political and social structures. Niebuhr cannot see how competitiveness and the seeking for advantage can possibly be removed from society. He sees evidence of *agape* only in personal relationships. Fromm sees alienating features but continues to hope for a more humane society, one in which giving is more important than getting and being than doing. Contemporary pastoral theologians (for example, Seward Hiltner and H. Clinebell) have tended to share the more optimistic assumptions of Fromm, describing the releasing of the blocks to inner growth and the heightening of self-esteem as ways of promoting love of neighbor. Perhaps each writer is limited by personal involvement. The sense of harmony between egoism and altruism, which is often gained from the experience of counseling individuals, may not transfer well to the sociopolitical realm, in which human nature is less attractively manifested.

3. The Love of God and Human Love. All theologies of love, whether of the radical Protestant type or of the more naturalistic style of liberal Protestantism and of most Roman Catholic writing, are attempts to explain how God makes genuinely self-giving love possible. The problem is to express this in a way that gives proper weight to human experience (including the physical and emotional aspects of love), which does not reduce the human agent to a mere puppet in God's hands, but which also avoids facile optimism about human behavior. The basic assertion that God is love depends upon supporting insights into God as Spirit and God incarnate. The notion of the "fruits of the Spirit," which recurs throughout Paul's epistles, illustrates that the love which is God is always seen in human acts of purity and caring. This is expressed in Paul's "hymn to love" in I Corinthians 13, and in the challenge in I John to the person who claims to love God but fails to love the "neighbor."

It is in the teaching, life, and death of Jesus, however, that the connection with human relationships is decisively made. The revelation of God in Christ puts divine love into human history, imbues it with human emotion and vulnerability, and locates it with the weak, outcast, and despised. Increasingly, theologians are recognizing that a full understanding of the Incarnation entails a rejection of supernaturalism in favor of a transformation of the natural. Love, personal experience, and the renewal of society are inseparably bound together. Grace does not operate in some private, "spiritual" corner of human experience. Grace becomes the restoration of the courage to love, in both personal and political life, based on the conviction that history is the locus of God's action. (For a recent exposition of this theme see D. D. Williams, *The Spirit and the Forms of Love.*)

4. Love and Ethics. The earthing of God's love in human history has important effects on Christian interpretations of ethics. The philosopher Immanuel Kant was influential in promoting a view of Christian ethics that placed all the emphasis on reason to the exclusion of feeling. He claimed to base ethics firmly on a foundation of laws to which all rational beings could subscribe. The Christian love commandment was to be explained as the universalist principle of respect for all rational beings as ends in themselves and never as mere means. There could be no question of emotion in such love, since emotions cannot be commanded.

Superficially, this Kantian ethic might appear to be a restatement of the Christian norm of *agape,* the disinterested regard for the neighbor, which mirrors God's self-giving love, but it overlooks the incarnate and historical character of Christian love. The two Great Commandments, to love God and to love neighbor (both of which appear first in the OT), demand more than the cool acceptance of the rationally self-evident. This is well illustrated by the teaching of the Sermon on the Mount, which carries commitment to the Kingdom well beyond the relatively easy confines of the Jewish Law. A new heart is sought after, not just a clear conscience.

Thus there is a tendency toward antinomianism in Judeo-Christian ethics. The law may fail to enshrine what love requires. It may elevate the conventional above the more radical demands of devotion to God and neighbor. Recent discussion of this aspect of ethics has tended to focus on the defense of the principle "Love is the only norm" offered by Joseph Fletcher in *Situation Ethics* and other works. But Fletcher's view is little different from that of Kant (although it is presented with less philosophical rigor). *Situation Ethics* is, in effect, a restatement of the Kantian notion of the autonomous moral agent. Each individual is enjoined to "act responsibly in love" and love is distinguished from emotion. Like Kant, Fletcher omits the radical transformation of emotion and attitude which Christian discipleship requires, and Kant's stress on individual autonomy is taken to an extreme by detaching it from any concept of universal law. Each person is treated as an isolated moral agent freely choosing the most loving course of action in the situation.

Against such individualism, some modern theologians emphasize the public and communal aspects of Christian love, arguing that unless theology is expressed in political terms the Christian gospel is reduced to an ideology that protects the rich and powerful. The God of history, it is claimed, is not an impartial God, but a God who is working to liberate the oppressed and who seeks a covenant people who will follow the divine lead. Thus love entails "an option for the poor." (For a valuable survey and critique of this group see A. Fierro, *The Militant Gospel*.)

Such views give a revolutionary edge to Christian love in both the private and the public sphere. Debate will continue about the degree to which love overturns conventional morality and about the correctness of identifying God's action in history with social and political change. For pastoral care and counseling, however, the important point to note is that love is a controversial notion, one that offers challenges to all conventional assumptions and which cannot be easily translated into a rationalistic and individualistic philosophy.

5. Love in Counseling Relationships. It is almost a commonplace of counseling literature that love is a therapeutic force. Freud coined the terms "transference" and "counter-transference" to describe the powerful emotional attachments that can form between analyst and patient. Consistent with his rationalistic emphasis, Freud was concerned to limit the power of these attachments. Countertransference (the emotional attachment of therapist to patient) was to be avoided. Transference was to be encouraged by the analyst's anonymity, which cultivated a fantasy relationship, but cure would come only when the transference was resolved by analytical interpretations. One of Jung's deviations from Freud was to sweep aside this structure and encourage instead a more open, personal, and equal relationship between patient and therapist. (See *Modern Man in Search of a Soul*, ch. 2.) This change is taken further by Carl Rogers in his client-centered therapy. Rogers regards counselor and client as interacting persons in a genuinely human encounter. The empathy, acceptance, and non-possessive warmth of the counselor are what bring about change in the client. (See *On Becoming a Person*, especially ch. 3.)

An emphasis on the healing power of love is found in pastoral counseling literature, notably in the earlier writings of Seward Hiltner, in which he described the shepherding perspective as one of "tender, solicitous concern." Care is necessary, however, in using the word "love" in this context. In warning against counter-transference Freud seemed to be conscious of the destructive force of *eros* in therapy since it can make the patient a victim of the therapist's needs, or *vice versa*. Jung seemed to be advocating a kind of friendship (*philia*), while Rogers apparently aspired to *agape* of a kind. What form of love would characterize pastoral counseling?

Our survey of the Christian concept of love suggests that pastoral counseling based on love has rich resources to draw upon. If Tillich is correct in seeing all the forms of love as interrelated, then pastoral counseling can aspire to be a bodily presence and a simple friendship, as well as a respect for the uniqueness and individuality of the other. But Christian love will also question and confront both counselor and counselee. Pastoral counseling mediates the unsettling force of *agape*, its call for a radical reappraisal. It stimulates an awareness of the prejudice and pride in which counselor and counselee share. This does not imply a return to the moralism and judgmentalism which modern counseling has rejected. It is an opening of awareness, which can transcend the individual counselee's problem without denying its importance. The important emphasis on a love that comforts and sustains in pastoral counseling should be complemented, but not superseded, by a love that challenges and demands.

6. Loving and Caring. Outside the one-to-one counseling relationship, the concept of love has wide relevance to the whole range of groups, structures, and institutions within which pastoral care is provided and to which it must address itself. These may be briefly identified as follows:

a. Love's unity. In personal and family life, the unity and interdependence of the different forms of love require emphasis. Until recently Christian teaching has tended to deny the goodness of the physical and the emotional in the name of an otherworldly, fleshless love. Pastoral care may teach the unity of body and spirit, which opposes both an overestimation of our biological nature and a denial of it. (See Nelson, 1978.)

b. Love's prophetic challenge. Love in the Christian fellowship entails self-giving and respect for others, but also a radical challenge to complacency and privilege. The egalitarian effect of *agape* in its option for the dispossessed reveals much that is wrong in church polity and in the social accommodation of the churches to the rich and the powerful. Pastoral care of church structures requires the prophetic voice of love, as well as its comforting one.

c. Love's search and suffering for the lost. Love inspires fresh initiatives for pastoral care. As the parables of the Good Samaritan (Lk. 10:29–37) and of the Sheep and the Goats (Matthew 25) suggest, *agape* is unselfconscious caring for those whose needs are easily disregarded. Thus pastoral care is never restricted to those safely within the fold, but is a dangerous venture into the wilderness in search of the wounded and lost. In the conditions of modern industrial society, this entails questioning existing political structures and social legislation, seeking to redress injustice. Only a wholly spiritualized and individualized pastoral care can avoid love's Cross, the painful conflict with unjust authority which Jesus faced.

Bibliography. The best general introduction to the topic is: G. Outka, *Agape: An Ethical Analysis* (1972). See also: R. S. Downie and E. Telfer, *Respect for Persons* (1969). M. C. D'Arcy, *The Mind and the Heart of Love* (1962). J. Fletcher, *Situation Ethics* (1966). E. Fromm, *Man for Himself* (1947); *The Art of Loving* (1956). J. McIntyre, *On the Love of God* (1962). J. Nelson, *Embodiment: An Approach to Sexuality and Christian Theology* (1978). A. Nygren, *Agape and Eros* (1937). P. Tillich, *Love, Power and Justice* (1954). D. D. Williams, *The Spirit and the Forms of Love* (1968).

Discussions of the political implications will be found in: R. Niebuhr, *Moral Man and Immoral Society* (1932) and A. Fierro, *The Militant Gospel* (1977).

For love in counseling relationships see: S. Freud, "Observations on Transference Love", *SE*, 12, pp. 157–71. C. G. Jung, *Modern Man in Search of a Soul* (1933). P. Halmos, *The Faith of the Counselors* (1965). C. R. Rogers, *On Becoming a Person* (1961). M. Buber, *The Knowledge of Man,* M. Freidman, ed. (1965), Appendix.

A. V. CAMPBELL

ACCEPTANCE; CARE; COMPASSION; GRACE. *See also* CHARACTER ETHICS; COMMUNITY, FELLOWSHIP, AND CARE; FORGIVENESS; FRIENDSHIP; LUST AND CHASTITY; REASON AND PASSION; SANCTIFICATION. *Compare* COUNTERTRANSFERENCE *or* TRANSFERENCE; EMOTION; I AND THOU; SELF-TRANSCENDENCE; SEXUAL ISSUES IN PASTORAL CARE; SEXUALITY.

LOVE OF SELF. *See* EGOTISM; LOVE; NARCISSISM.

LOVING-KINDNESS. *See* COMPASSION; GRACE.

LOYALTY. *See* COMMITMENT; FAITH/BELIEF.

LOYOLA, ST. IGNATIUS. *See* IGNATIUS OF LOYOLA, ST.

LSD (Lysergic Acid Diethylamide). *See also* PSYCHEDELIC DRUGS AND EXPERIENCE. *See also* DRUGS.

LUST AND CHASTITY (Moral Theology). *Lust,* wholly selfish sexual desire which ignores the person and good of the partner, one of the seven deadly or capital sins. *Chastity,* the virtue opposite to lust, being the attitude in which sexual desire, though present, is in the service of a balanced and committed love of God and the real or potential partner.

The early church, under strong Gnostic and Manichean influence, all but identified sexual passion with the sin of lust; and by medieval times the sin had been identified with specific acts: adultery, fornication, homosexuality, masturbation, etc. The combination of Paul's writings and the establishment of celibate priesthood made all sexual expression suspect, in turn producing the doctrine that intercourse was lawful only for the purpose of procreation.

As Plé points out, the church soon remembered that lust is not the committing of specific sexual acts, but the motive underlying them: a passion in which the primary object is not the partner, but rather the services or pleasure that the partner or the passion itself can provide.

Most post-medieval Christian thinking on lust has emphasized the loss to the partners when the mutual revelation possible between lovers is foregone in favor of a less disclosing and ennobling attention primarily upon the self and physical sensation. It is argued that it is confusing and misleading when an act with that power and potential is taken for less, even by mutual consent. Paul Ramsey observes that sex is an act of procreation whether there is conception or not, because the love relationship itself is further created by the sexual act. To diminish that potential is seen as sinful.

Plé divides critics of the traditional Christian view of sex into sex-mystics and sex-naturalists. Sex-mystics include the Roman Catholic Richard Rohr, and Protestants like James Nelson, who argue the similarity or identity of sexual and spiritual experience, and see the development of full sexual maturity as indispensable to spiritual health. Sex-naturalists take the position that sex is a pleasurable, God-given, natural function, meant to be enjoyed; but most enjoyable in a committed and loving relationship.

Sex-naturalists are skeptical about the separation between love of the partner and enjoyment of the physical pleasure of sex. They see the physical pleasure as a vehicle and avenue for love of the partner, carrying the lover's investment out of self to join with the other. They point out the necessity of fully passionate, physical, investment in the beloved as the release that makes lustful preoccupation unnecessary. It is the sexually unsatisfied who are most likely to be lustful, they contend.

Chastity is a virtue that modern Protestantism is struggling to redefine. In a time when the only sex free from stigmatization as lust was between married partners seeking to conceive a child, chastity could be seen simply as the condition that leads one to abstain from sex motivated by passion. As psychologists and physiologists have increasingly taught us the healthy consequences of passion itself, chastity thus understood lost some of its status as a virtue. "Chastity is its own punishment," became a popular witticism.

Yet chastity can mean something other than to always abstain, though that meaning is not yet taking clear shape in Protestant moral theology. One might suggest that chastity is that condition of spirit that, though movable by sexual passion, invests that passion heartily in one committed and satisfying relationship, seen as a gift of God. Further, that the chaste person is so focused on the partner that the first step beyond rich friendship in the direction of another sexual involvement—the first glance or word—is not taken.

Bibliography. A. Plé, *Chastity and the Affective Life* (1966). P. Ramsey, *Deeds and Rules in Christian Ethics* (1965).

B. W. GRANT

CHARACTER ETHICS AND PASTORAL CARE; CHRISTIAN LIFE; LOVE; SEVEN DEADLY SINS; SEXUALITY. *See also* CELIBACY; MORAL THEOLOGY; SEXUAL ISSUES IN PASTORAL CARE; SIN/SINS; TEMPTATION. *Compare* RESPONSIBILITY/IRRESPONSIBILITY, PSYCHOLOGY OF; SELF-EXPRESSION/SELF-CONTROL.

LUTHER, MARTIN (1483–1546). German theologian, Reformer, pastor, teacher, and prolific writer.

The sermons, letters, and table talks of Luther provide a colorful tapestry of concrete examples of Luther's own acts of pastoral care. In all of them shines through what Luther considers the heart and centerpiece of all soul care: the proclamation of God's promise and God's grace and the unburdening of the troubled and tempted conscience in order to facilitate the beginning of a new, liberated life.

The following examples provide a window into Luther's practice of pastoral care, not a summary of its theory.

In 1519, in response to the severe illness of his prince, Frederick the Wise, and for his comfort, Luther produced the meditation, *The Fourteen of Consolation.* In it, Luther reflects on seven aspects of evil which he juxtaposes with seven goods. Both are manifestations of God's love: the good because it reveals the divine power and mercy, the evil because it drives sinners to seek refuge in Christ's love.

In 1521, a few hours before his appearance at the Diet of Worms, Luther attended to a sick knight, hearing his confession and distributing Holy Communion.

In 1523 Luther dispensed pastoral counsel to two former nuns. One, suffering from melancholia, he encouraged to become a teacher; the other he consoled and urged to seek the Word of God where medication fails.

Luther wrote supportive, faith-nurturing letters to Protestants jailed in Miltenberg, and in 1524, concerning the same matter, an exhortatory letter to Prince Albrecht of Mainz. His pastoral care correspondence further includes letters to soldiers, to his parents, and to a woman wrestling with the issue of predestination.

N. F. HAHN

LUTHERAN PASTORAL CARE; PASTORAL CARE (History, Traditions, and Definitions).

LUTHERAN ADVISORY COUNCIL. This council on pastoral care grew out of a report from the Committee on Institutional Chaplains to the Conference of Lutheran Professors of Theology in June, 1947, requesting that the National Lutheran Council explore possibilities for providing training for Lutheran chaplains. This request reflected two concerns. First, the historic Lutheran investment in hospital chaplaincies was being threatened by the growing acceptance of clinical training standards. Second, there was suspicion that clinical supervision was anti-seminary and undermined students' theology.

This report set in motion a series of discussions co-convened by Clarence Krumholz of the National Lutheran Council and Henry Wind of the Lutheran Church-Missouri Synod which resulted in the formation of the Lutheran Advisory Council on Pastoral Care by the Division of Welfare, National Lutheran Council on February 28, 1950. It was an *ad hoc* committee whose purpose was to encourage clinical training as a dimension of theological education, to assist seminaries in identifying and establishing training centers and securing supervisors, and to recommend standards and accreditation procedures. As a consultive committee to the seminaries, it also provided bibliographies and developed clinical course materials and curricula. Edward Mahnke, Frederick Norstad, Carl Plack, and Granger Westberg were among those who made important contributions to its formation and subsequent work.

The Lutheran Advisory Council sent representatives to the Second National Conference on Clinical Pastoral Education in Boston in 1951. In addition, it formally invited the Institute of Pastoral Care and the Council for Clinical Training to meet together to discuss ways to coordinate their activities, to adopt national standards, and to accredit students completing training at approved centers. These groups accepted the Lutheran invitation and were later joined by the Association of Seminary Professors in the Practical Fields to form the group later known as the Committee of Twelve. The initiative in proposing this meeting and its ongoing concern for a close relationship between clinical training and theological education were significant contributions Lutherans made to joint discussions which led to the formation of the Association for Clinical Pastoral Education in 1967.

Throughout this period, the Lutheran Advisory Council stimulated interest and provided support for clinical training in Lutheran seminaries and among chaplains. This eventuated in the appointment of Henry Cassler to a full-time staff position with responsibility for clinical pastoral education by the National Lutheran Council in 1962. The Department of Institutional Chaplaincy and Clinical Pastoral Education assumed this responsibility when the Lutheran Council in the U.S.A. replaced the National Lutheran Council as the national Lutheran coordinating body in 1967.

Bibliography. C. Plack, "Report on the Lutheran Advisory Council on Pastoral Care to the Division of Welfare Committee, National Lutheran Council", mimeographed manuscript; Archives of the Lutheran Council, U.S.A. (1953). D. Sandstedt, "The Lutheran Church and Clinical Pastoral Education," *Lutheran Theological Seminary Bulletin,* 50 (3) (1970), 4–17. E. Thornton, *Professional Education for Ministry* (1970).

M. D. HOUGLUM

ASSOCIATION FOR CLINICAL PASTORAL EDUCATION; HISTORY OF PROTESTANT PASTORAL CARE (United States); PASTORAL CARE MOVEMENT. *See also* CLINICAL PASTORAL EDUCATION.

LUTHERAN PASTORAL CARE. Lutheran pastoral care began with Luther. Because of his own anguished spiritual journey, pastoral care became a significant part of Luther's ministry, both as a Reformer of the church, and as a parish priest. His *Letters of Spiritual Counsel,* for example, shows the wide range both of his pastoral concerns as well as of the persons who received his counsel.

1. Pastoral Emphasis in the Lutheran Tradition. Luther's emphasis on pastoral care has continued in the Lutheran Church. The importance of the German word *Seelsorge* — taken over untranslated into English — to the Lutheran ministry, illustrates this emphasis. In his textbook *The Lutheran Pastor,* G. H. Gerberding notes that seelsorge means "the cure and care of souls," which is the pastor's purpose — to be a seelsorger.

Pastoral care or seelsorge is shaped in the Lutheran Church by three factors. (1) *The role of the pastor.* In the Lutheran Church the pastor is not only a priest before the altar or a preacher in the pulpit but a strong influence in the homes of parishioners, an authority figure and friend in and part of the family structure. (2) *A focus on theology.* The Lutheran Church's major characteristic is its theological emphasis, especially concerning the Word and Sacraments as means through which God works and which he gave to his church for the ministry of reconciliation. (3) *An approach to life in the world based on the doctrine of the two kingdoms.* Although not specifically a confessional teaching of the Lutheran Church but rather a teaching of Martin Luther, this doctrine has nonetheless strongly influenced the church's life. The kingdom on the right hand is the kingdom of the Spirit in which God rules by grace. The kingdom on the left hand is this fallen world in which God rules ambiguously by law. We are called by God in the kingdom on the right hand to live out our calling in the kingdom of the left hand. God calls us not only to the office of the ministry but to all lawful occupations as well. Although the kingdoms are distinguished, they are not separated, and God is ruler of both.

2. **Pastoral Care and Pastoral Theology.** Lutheran pastoral care is in mutual dialogue with pastoral theology. The centrality of forgiveness in this theology is the basis for the dynamics of reconciliation in pastoral care. Repentance as a change of mind is a way of receiving this forgiveness; together they constitute the agency of change in human behavior. Repentance as sorrow *with* hope is differentiated from remorse, which is sorrow *without* hope. Remorse is the result of bondage to the law while repentance is the result of freedom in the gospel.

The process of the law at work within the individual provides preparation for forgiveness, but the Lutheran emphasis is on the gospel. It assumes that the process of the law is already at work and does not necessarily need to be initiated by the pastor. The freedom of the gospel, therefore, is freedom from the judgment of the law. The law in this sense is a "tyrant" (Luther) enslaving us to unresolved guilt or, in more contemporary terms, to a low self-image. This tyranny is overcome by Christ in his crucifixion and resurrection.

The centrality of forgiveness and the "leap of faith" that claims it, is developed as a pastoral theological dimension by the Lutheran theologian and philosopher Søren Kierkegaard in his covertly autobiographical book, *The Sickness unto Death* (1954), a classic in Lutheran pastoral theology and care. "Christianity," he writes ". . . is in this case [forgiveness] as paradoxical as possible; it works directly against itself when it establishes sin so securely as a position [the law that accuses] that it seems a perfect impossibility to do away with it again — and then it is precisely Christianity which, by the atonement, would do away with it so completely that it is as though drowned in the sea [grace]."

The law is thus transcended by love, a process that brings a new way of perceiving. Liberated from the narrow blinders of the knowledge of good and evil, which is a legacy of the Fall, one receives the liberated vision of unconditional love of God, who through Christ accepts us as we are regardless of inward or outward behavior. Now one can "see" in descriptive rather than judgmental terms and thus is open to appreciate what heretofore was not in one's line of vision. This is the potential of the new nature born out of forgiveness—the new creation of personhood in Christ Jesus, which makes possible the new community. For Luther it was a newness of life communicated and sealed by the sacrament of baptism.

In dialogue with this pastoral theological base, Lutheran pastoral care has the ambience of Good News in which forgiveness (hope) precedes repentance (sorrow), making possible the change that remorse would inhibit. This ambience is embodied in the approach and attitude of the pastor. He or she may also verbalize the Good News (God language) in a dialogical manner appropriate to the concerns of the other.

Distinct pastoral resources in pastoral care in addition to this dialogical use of God language are Scripture, prayer, meditation, and the Sacrament of the Lord's Supper. The latter, pastorally speaking, is a multisensory participatory reassurance of God's accepting presence.

Despite its heavy theological base, Lutheran pastoral care provides more than an intellectual understanding of how God's love is relevant to the needs of the moment. It is also a personal encounter in which one is inspired by this ambience of Good News to feel better about oneself, about life, and about God. Through the medium of a personal relationship, Christ is revealed through his body, the church, and one's perception is changed. This change in perception is the basis for a subsequent change in behavior.

3. **Corporate Agencies for Pastoral Care.** Besides being a ministry within congregations, Lutheran pastoral care is also a ministry through agencies and institutions, such as Lutheran Social Service and Lutheran Hospitals. Lutheran Social Service consists of multiservice agencies sponsored by local congregations throughout the U.S. and Canada. The name of William Passavant stands out as a nineteenth-century pioneer in these ministries in his founding of eleven hospitals and other "institutions of mercy."

The wholistic approach of these ministries is shown in three recent developments. (1) *Lutheran General Hospital, Park Ridge, Illinois.* This hospital was founded on the principle of human ecology in which patients and their families and the interdisciplinary staff, which includes the chaplain, consult together for the total health— physical, mental, spiritual — of these patients and their families. (2) *Wholistic health centers.* Founded by Granger Westberg, these centers or clinics are sponsored by and housed in churches and employ a team approach consisting of physician, nurse, pastor, and other health care professionals. Their work is focused in joint interviewing of patients and consultation regarding their treatment. (3) *Clinically-oriented pastoral care and counseling departments in most Lutheran seminaries.* Utilizing the ministries of Lutheran Social Service and the chaplaincies of Lutheran Hospitals and similar institutions, theological students from Lutheran seminaries are educated not only in the classroom but also in the healing institutions of society, where they learn by supervised doing. (4) *The Lutheran Council.* Both Lutheran Social Service and Lutheran Hospitals were from the beginning natural settings for Clinical Pastoral Education (CPE). The CPE movement was warmly endorsed by Lutherans. The Lutheran Council was organized to work along with the two original accrediting and training agencies of CPE— the Institute of Pastoral Care and the Council for Clinical

Training. Edward Mahnke of the Lutheran Church-Missouri Synod, Fritz Norstad of the American Lutheran Church, and Granger Westberg of the Lutheran Church in America were pioneers in the Lutheran CPE movement.

The Lutheran Council along with the other groups sponsoring CPE participated in the founding of the Association for Clinical Pastoral Education (ACPE). The Inter-Lutheran Coordinating Committee for Specialized Pastoral Care and Clinical Education now maintains files of Lutheran clergy aspiring to be chaplains and chaplain supervisors, and oversees an interview process for denominational endorsement to supplement the certification process of the ACPE.

Bibliography. G. H. Gerberding, *The Lutheran Pastor* (1902). S. Kierkegaard, *The Sickness unto Death* (1954). G. Kraus, "Luther the *Seelsorger*," *Concordia Theological Quarterly*, 98:2–3 (1984), 153–63. M. Luther, *Concerning the Ministry*, J. Pelikan, ed. (vol. 40 of *Luther's Works*, 1953); *Letters of Spiritual Counsel* (1955). J. T. McNeill, *A History of the Cure of Souls* (1951). A. Nebe, *Luther as Spiritual Advisor* (1894). E. Plass, ed., *What Luther Says: An Anthology*, 3 vols. (1959). E. E. Thornton, *Professional Education for Ministry* (1970). G. Tinder, "Luther's Theology of Christian Suffering and Its Implications for Pastoral Care," *Dialog*, 25:2 (1986), 108–13.

W. E. HULME

HISTORY OF PROTESTANT PASTORAL CARE; PASTORAL CARE (History, Traditions, and Definitions); PASTORAL CARE MOVEMENT. *See also* CLINICAL PASTORAL EDUCATION; FAITH AND WORKS; PASTORAL THEOLOGY, PROTESTANT; SACRAMENTAL THEOLOGY AND PASTORAL CARE, PROTESTANT; SEELSORGE; WHOLISTIC HEALTH CARE. *Compare* ECCLESIOLOGY AND PASTORAL CARE; PIETISM AND PASTORAL CARE; TRADITION AS MODE OF CARE.

LYING. Telling an untruth with the intention of deceiving another.

1. Truth. Our philosophical understanding of lying is tied to our understanding of truth. One cannot be guilty of lying until one can recognize truth. Recent psychology, however, has added some useful insights.

a. Moral development. Lawrence Kohlberg's theory of moral development suggests that all people move through stages of moral reasoning that are hierarchical, sequential, and invariant in the order of emergence. Moral judgments are active rather than passive reflections of external facts or internal emotions. For Kohlberg there is no stable category "truth," but a variety of truths based, in part, on the individual's cognitive abilities. This idea is particularly evident in children whose grasp of truth varies noticeably with development and whose immature understanding "justifies" both their own lying and lying to them. For example, in the first or heteronomous moral stage, moral life is perceived in terms of reward and punishment. A person of this stage, seeing a lie go undetected and unpunished, might conclude that lie to be truthful. By the second stage, that of instrumen-

tal hedonism in which instrumental exchange and purpose ("an eye for an eye") predominate, a person may consider a lie told in retaliation for a previous lie to be fair, and therefore right or true. A person in the third stage, in which truth resides in mutual interpersonal expectations rather than abstractions (e.g., laws, rights of society), might well accept paternalistic lying (when, for example, a parent tells a frightened child "everything's all right" during an emergency). In short, in evaluating and counseling liars, the counselor must consider the grasp of truth available to the persons involved.

b. Imagination. The relationship of truth and imagination bears directly on the issue of lying (Eck). Is a novel a lie (to "tell a story" often means to lie in English)? Do children lie when they play and make-believe? Do parents lie about Santa Claus? We often excuse the child-related untruths of make-believe, play, and fantasy because we are convinced of their positive developmental role (Piaget), but we are harsher in our judgments concerning adults. Erikson suggests that before we condemn adults we may need to reevaluate the role of play and imagination in individual and communal adult life. Of particular importance is the relationship of religion and its symbols and stories to lying.

2. Social Dimensions. *Subject-object relationship.* Lying is a relational activity in that the intention to deceive is usually considered a necessary component. Lying cannot occur until, developmentally, a person is aware of "self" and of "other." Thus, to deal effectively with the liar, the counselor must understand the community in which lying occurs. The cultural context of lying includes unspoken norms of a given society and the influence of loyalties and covenants (e.g., the Hippocratic Oath, family secrets).

3. Pathological Lying. In cases of pathological lying, there is no discernible conscious or premeditated intention to induce another into error. There are at least three types of pathological lying: hysterical lying (in which the liar believes the lie); sociopathic lying (in which the liar deceives for personal gain without a sense of guilt); and mythomaniac lying (in which the liar fabricates a complex, coherent story he or she tries to make others believe. This can be on the cultural or individual level.)

Bibliography. S. Bok, *Lying* (1978). M. Eck, *Lies and Truth* (1970), pp. 126–43. E. Erikson, *Toys and Reasons* (1977). M. Furse, *Nothing But the Truth?* (1981). L. Kohlberg, *Essays on Moral Development* (1981, 1984). J. Piaget, *Play, Dreams and Imitation in Childhood* (1962).

C. WENDEROTH

ANTISOCIAL PERSONS; MORAL DEVELOPMENT; RESPONSIBILITY/IRRESPONSIBILITY, PSYCHOLOGY OF. *See also* CONSCIENCE; MORAL DILEMMAS IN PASTORAL PERSPECTIVE; SIN/SINS; SOCIAL PERCEPTION, JUDGMENT, AND BELIEF; SOCIOPATHIC PERSONALITY. *Compare* MALINGERING; MANIPULATION; TRUTH-TELLING.

M

MacLACHLAN, ARCHIE. *See* CANADIAN ASSOCIATION OF PASTORAL CARE; CANADIAN PASTORAL CARE MOVEMENT.

MACRINA. *See* LITERATURE, DEVOTIONAL; WOMEN IN PASTORAL MINISTRIES, HISTORY OF.

MAGIC/SORCERY. *See* CULTURAL ANTHROPOLOGY OF RELIGION; SPIRITUALISM; WITCHCRAFT.

MAGICAL THINKING. Belief that one's thoughts, words, or actions have power to influence external events by means apart from culturally acknowledged laws of cause and effect. Magical thinking is a recognized characteristic of various mental disorders. Thus, its prominence may indicate the advisability of psychological evaluation.

1. **Description.** The individual who engages in magical thinking believes that there is a causal relationship between events which, according to conventional standards, do not or cannot occur without mediating action. For example, a mother believes that if she has an angry thought her child will become ill. Magical thinking is also said to occur when a person's words or actions are believed to alter events to which they bear no logical relation. For example, a person spins around three times before entering the house in order to keep the roof from falling in.

Magical thinking is said to occur in primitive cultures, in children, and in certain mental disorders. It is a major component in the primitive practice of voodoo with its hexes, for example. In children, it is common and considered normal during certain stages of cognitive development. Children may believe they become invisible by covering their eyes, for instance. Psychoanalytic thought, a major source of literature on magical thinking, posits that an infant believes its needs can be met solely by wishing. But it soon realizes that the sensation of hunger, for example, does not disappear with a wish; gratification requires an external object or action. In normal development the infant learns the distinction between internal and external, that "I want" is not a synonym for "I have" (Eidelberg, 1968,

p. 283). Primary thought processes, including magical thinking, gradually yield to more logical "secondary" thought processes.

Magical thinking may be considered pathological when it continues beyond the expected age of occurrence due to a problem in psychological development or later regression to primary thought processes. The latter may occur when tested means of handling reality have failed: "When reality is too unpleasant, or one is unable to influence it, one regresses again to the magical method" (Fenichel, 1945, p. 50).

Magical thinking may be manifested apart from any pathology, as in persons who are tired, intoxicated or under unusual stress. Also, the common defense mechanism of undoing is predicated on magical thinking. Such instances rarely indicate pathology and may be argued to have psychotherapeutic value.

2. **Theological Concerns.** Theorists who disallow the supernatural have used magical thinking to explain belief in God, prayer, and the miraculous. Thus, Freud writes, everything is "exactly as we are bound to wish it to be" (Freud, 1961, p. 33). From this antireligious perspective, magical thinking encompasses a broad spectrum.

Allowing for a personal God, however, narrows the scope considerably. Belief in events which transcend natural laws may be considered a component of authentic faith, not magical thinking, though what is considered magical thinking may vary according to theological perspectives and dogmas: a healthy expression of faith in one camp may be deemed a sign of pathology in another.

3. **Practical Aspects.** Magical thinking is a recognized component of several mental disorders. According to the American Psychiatric Association, these include schizotypal personality disorder, obsessive compulsive disorder, and certain phases of schizophrenia. In evaluating the presence and role of magical thinking, careful consideration must be given to differences in cultural and religious values. When the problem appears significant nonetheless, and if it lies outside one's expertise, prayerful referral to an appropriate mental health professional is advisable.

Bibliography. American Psychiatric Association, *Diagnostic and Statistical Manual of Mental Disorders*, 3d ed., (1980). L. Eidelberg, *Encyclopedia of Psychoanalysis* (1968). D. Benner, ed., *Baker Encyclopedia of Psychology* (1985). O. Fenichel, *The Psychoanalytic Theory of Neurosis* (1945). S. Freud, *The Future of an Illusion* (1961 [1927]). M. Eckblad and L. Chapman, "Magical Ideation as an Indicator of Schizotypy," *J. of Counseling and Clinical Psychology*, 51 (1983), 215–25.

R. A. NEWMAN

PRIMARY AND SECONDARY PROCESS; OBSESSIVE-COMPULSIVE DISORDER; SUPERSTITION. *See also* PSYCHOPATHOLOGY AND RELIGION; SHAMAN; SPIRITUALISM; WITCHCRAFT. *Compare* PARAPSYCHOLOGY; POWER; REALITY PRINCIPLE; RITUAL AND PASTORAL CARE; SPECIALNESS, SENSE OF.

MAIMONIDES (MOSES BEN MAIMON) (1135-1204).

Jewish philosopher popularly referred to as Rambam, an abbreviation for *Rabbi Moses ben* Maimon. Born in Cordova, Spain, Maimonides was the most outstanding Talmudic scholar of his time, a prolific writer, a philosopher of note, and leader of the Jewish community. His "Guide for the Perplexed," a classic formulation, in philosophical terms, of Jewish thinking and practice, was written to help those who, though well versed in Jewish categories, were confronted with contemporary philosophical and theological notions which made it difficult to fully comprehend Jewish thinking and law. Maimonides remains, to this day, probably the most influential Jewish philosopher.

In addition to the Guide, Maimonides also authored a monumental work, entitled *Mishneh Torah*. A freeflowing codification of Talmudic discourse in clear, concise legislation, this work has become a standard legal text for application to Jewish life.

Maimonides was also an outstanding physician, and the author of many works on the treatment of medical problems, which include his medical aphorisms, a work on hemorrhoids, another on sexual intercourse, a treatise on asthma, and one on poisons and their antidotes. In his philosophical and religious works, as well as in his medical practice, Maimonides was ever the rationalist, emphasizing reason and reality, using logic and strict discipline, thorough, comprehensive, and deeply sensitive to the totality. His religious affirmation, in the context of respect for the sciences, is an approach that is particularly instructive for the pastoral situation.

R. P. BULKA

JEWISH CARE AND COUNSELING; THEOLOGY, JEWISH.

MALE MENOPAUSE. *See* AGING; MIDLIFE PERSONS.

MALINGERING.

The voluntary production and presentation of false or exaggerated physical or psychological symptoms "motivated by external incentives" (*Diagnostic and Statistical Manual III*) that are obviously recognizable, such as to avoid work or military service, to gain financial advantage, to elude criminal prosecution, or to obtain drugs. It differs from neurotic production of false or exaggerated symptoms by its voluntary character and by the obvious, realistic advantages it seeks.

Although the phenomenon of malingering was identified and defined as early as the eighteenth century, it was introduced into the psychiatric diagnostic nomenclature only recently, with the third edition of the *Diagnostic and Statistical Manual of Mental Disorders* (*DSM-III*, 1980), though it is not considered a mental disorder.

The actual incidence of malingering in contemporary society is unknown, but there is a growing consensus that it constitutes a serious social problem. The issue is raised with regard to both criminal and civil litigation, especially worker's compensation cases. Clinical psychologists and psychiatrists increasingly are called upon as "expert witnesses" to assess the validity of alleged psychological and/or neurological impairment and thus to make a determination regarding malingering.

A. GLASSER

ANTISOCIAL PERSONS; EVALUATION AND DIAGNOSIS, PSYCHOLOGICAL. *See also* CHARACTER ETHICS AND PASTORAL CARE; DIAGNOSTIC AND STATISTICAL MANUAL III; MORAL DEVELOPMENT; MORAL THEOLOGY AND PASTORAL CARE; RESPONSIBILITY/IRRESPONSIBILITY, PSYCHOLOGY OF. *Compare* CHARACTER AND PERSONALITY (Comparative Concepts); LYING; PERSONALITY DISORDER; SECONDARY GAIN.

MALLEUS MALIFICARUM. *See* WITCHCRAFT.

MALPRACTICE.

The failure by a professional to conform to a standard of care, imposed by the law to protect those who use the professional's services from unreasonable risk, which failure causes the one who is protected to be injured and to suffer damages as a consequence of the injury.

Bibliography. H. N. Malony, T. L. Needham, and S. Southard, *Clergy Malpractice* (1986).

J. J. ROGGE

LEGAL DIMENSIONS OF PASTORAL CARE AND COUNSELING. *See also* ETHICS, PROFESSIONAL; LIABILITY INSURANCE; PROFESSIONALISM.

MAN. *See* PERSON. *See also* BIBLICAL, CULTURAL, *or* THEOLOGICAL ANTHROPOLOGY, DISCIPLINE OF; HUMAN NATURE, PROBLEM OF; MEN.

MANAGEMENT. *See* LEADERSHIP AND ADMINISTRATION; CONFLICT AND CONFLICT MANAGEMENT.

MANIC-DEPRESSIVE (BIPOLAR) DISORDER.

A major affective disorder in which the person is in (1) a manic episode, (2) a major depressive episode having previously been in a manic phase, or (3) an episode with both manic and major depressive characteristics, in either intermixed or alternating fashion.

The manic phase (in its less severe form known as hypomanic) is marked by such features as: (1) hyperactivity manifested in an increase of excited psychomotor behavior which can reach the point of violence and aggression in acute mania; (2) speech which is rapid, loud, and pressured, usually with little hint of what all these words mean to the person on an emotional level; (3) a mood which is characterized by elevation, euphoria, and expansiveness recognized to be excessive, and sometimes easily interrupted by an underlying irritability; (4) a significantly decreased need of sleep; (5) attention which is easily distracted, accompanied by difficulty in concentration; (6) a grandiose view of self and a confidence in self which are unlike the same person when not manic; and (7) gross rashness and reckless abandon resulting in such behaviors as self-defeating financial ventures or atypical promiscuous sexual activities. Manic episodes usually have an acute onset and may last anywhere from a few days to several months. They are typically briefer and end more abruptly than the depressive phase of the bipolar disorder.

The depressed phase in a bipolar disorder is differentiated from a major depression by the fact that the person has previously experienced a manic episode. Other than that, with almost everything being the converse of the manic phase, any of the usual signs of major depression may be present including such features as: feelings of hopelessness and helplessness, social isolation, negative evaluation of self and of accomplishments, reduced concern over personal appearance and hygiene, diminished interest in sex, changes in eating patterns resulting in either weight gain or loss, difficulty in remaining asleep with early morning awakening, lethargy and easy fatiguing, and a characteristic dysphoric mood. Suicidal ideation may also be present. Depressive episodes tend to be longer with advancing age, but are briefer in the bipolar disorder than in a major depression.

In the bipolar disorder, either the manic or depressive phase is usually present to the apparent exclusion of the other, but in rare cases they may be intermingled. Typically, the two phases alternate with the mood swings often being so drastic that the person appears to have had a complete personality change. In between these phases there may be periods of normal functioning, sometimes lasting for years. The manic episode is often considered to be a mask for or a running away from an underlying depression. In severe forms of the bipolar disorder hallucinations and delusions may occur (which are usually consistent with the prevailing mood).

The bipolar disorder is serious and ordinarily requires professional intervention. A combination of pharmacological and psychotherapeutic treatments is deemed to be the most effective.

Bibliography. American Psychiatric Association, *Diagnostic and Statistical Manual*, 3d ed. (1980).

A. J. STRAATMEYER

PSYCHOSIS; SADNESS AND DEPRESSION. *See also* DIAGNOSTIC AND STATISTICAL MANUAL III; EMOTION; EVALUATION AND DIAGNOSIS, PSYCHOLOGICAL; MENTAL HEALTH AND ILLNESS; PSYCHOPATHOLOGY, THEORIES OF. *Compare* HOPE AND DESPAIR.

MANIPULATION. The use, control, or exploitation of persons; manipulating is considered to be a psychologically self-defeating behavior. It is not to be confused with the simple influencing of behavior or situations. In everyday life experience we influence other persons, as well as our environment, in a variety of ways that are essential to our existence. The child must learn to use the environment in order to survive, and the mature person must influence the environment as well as other persons in such activities as earning a living. The minister also influences parishioners in many ways in the promotion of the activities of the church.

The nature of manipulation becomes clearer when contrasted with self-actualizing behavior. Where the manipulator seeks to gain control and power over others, either consciously or unconsciously, to use them to gain personal ends, the self-actualizer enters into relationships from a quite different perspective. The actualizer is one who trusts personal feelings, claims present experience in an open way, and offers a relationship that is honest in terms of personal desires and needs. By contrast, the manipulator's behavior is not honest, and real feelings and desires are usually hidden. Since authentic living can not occur when the relationships a person offers are characterized by manipulation, it is considered to be self-defeating. The process of counseling in this perspective may be seen as essentially helping a person move from manipulation to self-actualization.

Manipulation reflects the value system which is influenced in part by society's dominant values, and our social system conveys many values that encourage or legitimate manipulative behavior. The basic moral thrust of Christianity, however—its emphasis on loving the neighbor as oneself—is anti-manipulative. For Christian faith a full acceptance of self, including the frailties of human nature, results in authentic rather than manipulative behavior.

In the biblical literature one illustration of conscious manipulation may be seen in the actions of Rebekah (Genesis 27). Here, through deceptive manipulation, Rebekah controls the situation in such a way that Jacob receives the blessing that rightly belonged to Esau. She has taken advantage of her dying husband, Isaac, to achieve her own ends in a premeditated way. Not all manipulation is so overtly conscious, however, and the Apostle Paul echoes the dilemma of discovering our unconscious manipulations when he comments, "For the good I would I do not: but the evil which I would not, that I do" (Rom. 7:19 KJV).

Bibliography. A. H. Maslow, *Toward a Psychology of Being* (1982). C. Moustakas, *Creativity and Conformity* (1967). E. L. Shostrom, *Man, The Manipulator* (1967). V. Van De Riet, *et al.*, *Gestalt Therapy* (1980).

W. A. KNIGHTS

CONFRONTATION (Pastoral and Therapeutic); ANTISOCIAL PERSONS; LIMIT SETTING IN PASTORAL CARE AND COUNSELING; POWER. *Compare* AGGRESSION AND ASSERTION; COMPETITIVENESS; DOMINEERING PERSONALITY; LEADERSHIP AND ADMINISTRATION; SUGGESTION, PERSUASION, AND INFLUENCE.

MARATHON GROUPS. *See* GROUP COUNSELING AND PSYCHOTHERAPY.

MARCELLA. *See* WOMEN IN PASTORAL MINISTRIES, HISTORY OF.

MARIJUANA. *See* DRUG ABUSE, DEPENDENCE, AND TREATMENT; DRUGS.

MARILLAC, ST. LOUISE DE. (1591–1660). Foundress of the Sisters of Charity. The natural daughter of a minor aristocrat, she was educated by Dominican sisters in her youth. Married in 1613, she bore one son but was widowed in 1625. Shortly after, she met and was profoundly influenced by St. Vincent de Paul. She worked as a part of his circle of ladies of charity. In 1633 she started a training center for young women who wished to do charitable work. From that beginning grew the congregation of the Sisters of Charity although the new order did not get full church approval until 1655. She wrote a rule of life for these women in 1634 and at least four of them took private religious vows in 1642.

The foundation of the Sisters of Charity was a revolutionary step in the charitable work of vowed women religious in the Catholic Church. They were the first sisters not bound by the strict laws of monastic enclosure. They worked actively with the poor, sick, mentally ill, derelict, and convicts outside the confines of their own proper cloister. In a famous formulation of Vincent: their cell was to be the sickroom; their cloister the streets of Paris; their chapel the local parish church. The Sisters (or Daughters) of Charity were the forerunners of those many active congregations of religious women who served the world by the works of charity. Louise de Marillac was canonized a saint in 1934; she was named patroness of social workers by Pope John XXIII in 1960.

Bibliography. J. Calvet, *Louise de Marillac: A Portrait* (1959).

L. S. CUNNINGHAM

ROMAN CATHOLIC PASTORAL CARE; WOMEN IN PASTORAL MINISTRIES, HISTORY OF.

MARRIAGE. A central feature of all human societies is an institution composed of a culturally accepted union of a man and a woman in husband-wife relationship as well as roles that recognize an order of sexual behavior and legalize the function of parenthood. Most modern definitions tend also toward a dynamic description of marriage as process (Carl Rogers) or as companionship (Ernest Burgess).

In time of marital instability, sociologists and marriage counselors have sought more exact, value-laden definitions of the categories within marriage. Thus Lederer and Jackson (1968) designated four: the stable satisfactory, the stable unsatisfactory, the unstable satisfactory, and the unstable unsatisfactory marriages. Cuber and Harroff (1977), on the other hand, have divided marriages into the total, the vital, the passive-congenial, the conflict-habituated, and the devitalized. Their study forced them to "the extremely depressing conclusion" that few good marital relationships exist among upper middle-class Americans, but instead that there are numerous *sub rosa*, extramarital relationships in which the communication is more satisfying than that in marriage.

The reasons people marry vary widely and cover a spectrum. In a stable, rational society, marriage is valued for its ordering of relationships. Through it property is allocated and passed on to heirs. By it intimate companionship between a man and a woman is defined, progeny are provided for and protected, and families are organized. Historically marriage has also regulated sexual intercourse, a regulation once again vigorously challenged by many, and certainly not for the first time.

This article discusses the history, sociology, and theology of marriage and current issues of significance for pastoral care and counseling. For specific methods of marital care and counseling see "Marriage Counseling and Marital Therapy" and such articles as "Marriage Communication," "Marriage Enrichment," "Premarital Counseling," and "Divorce (Care and Counseling)."

1. Forms of Marriage. Despite the universality of marriage throughout all societies, its forms are numerous and are becoming still more varied.

a. Universal types. Monogamy appears as the most common type of marriage throughout history and in the world's current societies. This long-established pattern of wedding one woman to one man has no end of variations and violations and yet serves as the model by which other forms are judged and adjusted. Polygamy, the union of one man to several wives, has survived centuries of custom; it is to be found in biblical literature (e.g., Solomon in I Kings) and throughout much of Africa and the Near East today. Polyandry, the union of one woman to several husbands, has always been a rarer phenomenon and remains so, although its vestiges can be located in areas of India and Polynesia. Group marriage, the union of plural husbands and plural wives with open sexual access, has been traced at least in theory to early human history as the norm for earliest humanity (see Engels, 1942; Briffault and Malinowski, 1956; Westermarck, 1922) and is to be found today in some communes. Promiscuity, for which no regulations are imposed, and therefore different from the standards within group marriage, is that form of total license to sexual unions that recognizes no necessary continuation of relationships; it is rare as a socially accepted form.

b. Social classifications. These cut across the five universal types cited above. *Endogamy,* for example, operates within a society's governance to influence marriage within the general group. This serves to keep language, custom, and property within the social structure. It was brought to bear on Isaac's choice of Rebekah (Genesis 24), but can also be seen in contemporary practice of families who introduce and nudge their children into social contacts and associations within the same class structure.

Exogamy, on the other hand, is an emphasis upon marriage outside the immediate group. It serves to offset incest and to enlarge the contacts of a family line and its holdings, a frequent situation within the history of royal families. That endogamy and exogamy are compatible can be seen in the expectation that a marriageable person will seek a mate outside immediate relationships but still well within the confines of faith and custom.

Hyperogamy is the term given to upward marrying in those cases where one betters oneself through matrimony with a person of superior rank or caste. A standard example is the morganatic marriage of a commoner to a noble.

Homogamy is the practice of persons marrying similar persons regardless of whether they are from the same social group, although the chances are greater for them to be found there. Like interests and compatibility are the common features of such mating.

c. Alternative styles. In recent years alternatives to conventional marriage have proliferated. The practice of couples living together without marriage has, as one style, spread throughout North America. It is estimated that at any one time more than four percent of all households are of this description; they include not only young persons of college age but also middle-age divorced people and even the elderly.

So-called trial marriages, companionate unions, and "two-step marriages," once advocated by Margaret Mead (1966), are among these alternatives. In Mead's plan a young couple would enter a first step of marriage with minimal commitment and no pledge of permanence, but would cement this relationship at a later time if they planned to be licensed to bear children. Most of these ideas for probationary or apprenticeship marriages appear to have been superseded by actions of couples themselves. A social climate of minimally coercive relationships appears to have paved the way for open marriages with permission to add temporary partners, for mate swapping, and now for homosexual unions as well. In addition, the continuing high divorce rate has led to what some observers dub serial monogamy.

2. **Demographics and Statistics** (U.S.A.). In the U.S. there are nearly two-and-one-half-million weddings annually. At the same time there are close to one-and-one-quarter million divorces each year, making a ratio of two to one. By age fifty, ninety-three percent of the population has been married. The marital life cycle has been affected by a series of changes: the average age at marriage is advancing into later years; women now spend less of their lives in raising children; greater marital satisfaction is reported by couples once their children are grown and gone from the home; and the remarriage rate after divorce has risen in recent years.

Despite the high divorce rate, discontinuities in parental care are no greater now than they were in the past; and the number of children affected by parental disruption has actually decreased in the past century (see Bane, 1976) because the death rate is significantly lower.

3. **Regulation of Marriage.** This varies from culture to culture, but tends to hold some standards in common. Through custom and religion societies seek to govern marriage, its ceremonies, sexual practices, child rearing, and family property. Everywhere cultures enact legal restrictions on who may marry, how and when. These prescribe such regulations as blood tests, licenses, registration, and witnesses. Although in the U.S. the separate states determine marital laws, the "full faith and credit" clause of the U.S. Constitution serves to homogenize these laws to the extent that what is legal in one state is respected in the others.

Rules of consanguinity are all but universal; thus a society protects against incest and disallowed genetic relationships. In some situations affinity, the relationship between persons and their spouses' blood relatives, has been ruled outside the possibility for marriage by canon law. However the regulations that work social constraints are fewer than they once were. Both consanguinity and affinity are viewed as having movable boundaries in civil and in canon law, a historic sign that such laws are in the midst of dynamic change. Miscegenation is yet another factor considered in permitting or prohibiting marriage; but the U.S. Supreme Court has opposed laws that rule against marriage for reasons of

race. The statutes that declare marriages void or voidable grow fewer with the passing years. Society's insistence on regulating marriage and marrying, however, continues.

4. **History of Marriage.** Debates over the issue of whether human marriage began with a period of group promiscuity have largely subsided as evidence mounts that the norm has been monogamy from the start. Arguments on behalf of the promiscuity theory by Lewis P. Morgan and Robert Briffault have gone down under the logic of Bronislaw Malinowski. It appears likely, instead, that the earliest age produced an experimental form of marriage that was unregulated, but that this soon gave way to a legal stage in which property rights governed marital standards; and that, in turn, to the long period of monogamy in which we now live. The current standard is monogamous marriage based on companionship and mutual consent, with rights and duties protected by law, the sanctions being imposed by family and society. Although there are notable exceptions to this standard (Murdoch in 1949 still reported 193 polygynous societies, sixty-five promiscuous, and only forty-three monogamous), and although contemporary conformity is sometimes lax, monogamy is the norm of even primitive cultures.

An economic interpretation of marriage, emphasizing property rights and labor (Friedrich Engels) has been argued as a standard of marital history. But, like a religious or a psychological interpretation, its cogency lies in features that are selectively compared and combined with other data. It is observable, for example, that marriages of persons in lower economic levels have widely separated sex roles as compared to those in other classes. Moreover it is obvious that marriage does serve to protect property, persons, and society, also to protect the rights of women and the formation of family; yet these functions are not purely economic and do not support a dominantly economic interpretation of marriage.

5. **Theology and Marriage.** Theological considerations play a major role in Christian marriage even though the institution of marriage is not intrinsically Christian, and its presence throughout time and space has been recognized quite apart from any theological considerations.

In Christian doctrine marriage fulfills God's plan of creation; for we were created in the image of God, and blessed as male and female (Gen. 1:27). Moreover the doctrine of Christian marriage is so integrally built into existence that it provides a paradigm for God's relation to humanity. In a cosmic analogy, God is to us as a loving husband to a wife (Jer. 31:32; Isa. 54:5) and this ratiocination is echoed where Christ is pictured as the bridegroom in the Synoptic Gospels as well as in the writings of Paul (II Cor. 11:2). From these and similar passages, Christians may deduce that the mystical wedding of God-in-Christ to the church is an archetype for human marriage.

Throughout the Bible, marriage is considered a covenant (*berith*) whose very nature is fidelity. The covenant is not only between husband and wife but also between that couple and God. Unlike a legal contract whose agreement may be broken when conditions change, this covenant is binding for better, for worse, for richer, for poorer, in sickness and in health. It partakes of the age-old covenantal characteristics; that is, it is a freely made promise that will involve an obligatory task, and it is negotiated for permanence. It includes witnesses and social/family support; it can be renewed, and it enjoys the blessing of God whose promise seals it.

The once-heated debate between Protestant and Roman Catholic Christians over whether marriage is a sacrament has been subsiding. It stemmed from a Tridentine dogma, which had been based on a translation of *mysterion* (Eph. 5:32) as *sacramentum*. This complex doctrine from Paul's metaphysical concept of psycho-physical bonds was seen at the Council of Trent as a mystical union. As regulated by the Roman Catholic Church, marriage is conferred on one another by a baptized woman and a baptized man marrying in the presence of witnesses. With Christian faith present, this sacrament of marriage mediates a means of divine grace.

The Protestant Reformers, on the other hand, contended that *mysterion* had been wrongfully translated, that marriage is not a sacrament as are Baptism and the Lord's Supper, but that it is a vocation. For them marriage remains a holy estate, blessed by God, and an imitation of Christ's relation to the church; this, they insisted, was the higher doctrine of marriage.

Consensus now is growing in Christendom that there is a "sacramental quality" about Christian marriage. Roman Catholics since Vatican II view a sacrament as not simply material, but as a personally dynamic act. In this concept faith, hope, and love impart a religious character to marital mutuality (Schillebeeckx).

a. Marriage in ancient Israel. Marriage in ancient Israel was decidedly endogamous; Hebrews were enjoined to marry only their own kind, and heavy pressures enforced this standard. The marriage estate operated as sanctification affecting tribe and nation. For them marriage was seen not only as a one-flesh relationship but also as a means of survival for their system. It involved a betrothal ring, a *mohar* payment by the groom to the bride's father as well as a dowry, a religious blessing, a procession to the couple's tent, and often a week's celebration of eating and drinking.

b. Marriage in NT times. Marriage in NT times continued many of these customs but redefined the relationship in terms of Christ and the church. Marriage now had become a symbol of the Kingdom of God. We have little extant evidence of any nuptial rite except that it gradually evolved into an adaptation of contemporary customs that featured the presence of a bishop and a Eucharist. Mutuality in the Lord was the key element (Eph. 5:21); tenderness to one another was enjoined (I Pet. 3:7); and the unitive relationship was emphasized (Mk. 10:8). Nowhere in the NT is sexual intercourse understood to be exclusively for the procreation of children; the one-flesh bond of marriage is normative.

By this time polygyny had been superseded by monogamy: a higher place was accorded to women (Gal. 3:28); and both husband and wife are considered joint heirs of the grace of life. The commitment to fidelity in the relationship and the expectation of its permanence are stressed: "What God has joined together let not man put asunder" (Mk. 10:9).

c. Henosis. A more dynamic concept of marriage has been growing in recent years. The purpose of marriage is seen in *henosis,* that one-flesh relationship of cohumanity,

with all other ends as secondary. Just as Vatican II avoided ranking mutuality and procreation as respectively primary and secondary ends, so a reawakened theology has been moving to view Christian marriage more in interpersonal than in functional terms. This has enabled couples to see their marriages as a process of growing relationship, their failures as potentially forgivable, and their life together as pilgrimage.

6. **Contemporary Issues in Marriage.** It is impermanence and instability that concern most observers of the marital scene today. The ratio of one divorce decree to every two marriage licenses is but one indication. To that must be added the annulments, the "emotional divorces" of those who remain together in the same house but without intimate relationship, and those whose recurrent strife makes a mockery of their matrimony. The ubiquitous breakdown of marriage shows up some couples who are individually well adjusted but wed in combinations that are maladjusted, some persons who lack marital aptitude, and others who view marriage as a temporary connection. Thus many divorces may represent unions that had been stable for a time but were incapable of so continuing.

Changing roles of women and men around the world have profoundly altered marital expectations. The struggle between a new sexual egalitarianism and an older double standard promotes strife in numerous couples. Power equalization is counterbalanced by a traditionalism (Parsons and Bales, 1955) and complicated by resentment and communication failure. The interweaving of habit systems in marital relations traditionally interlocks our customs by cross-influence and continuity (Waller and Hill, 1951). Roles are changing, but they change gradually.

The conflict issues at stake are difficult to rank as they change both in year and in area. Yet among the problems that stand out will usually be found control issues, fear of abandonment, discipline of children, sexual disappointment, spending of money, relations with in-laws, lack of consideration, infidelity, and violence.

Today's major marital differences tend to include fewer of the social distinctions over which past generations fought: ethnic, religious, class, and cultural issues. The increasing number of mixed marriages across such lines is clear indication of our growing pluralism and toleration. As marriage changes from institution to companionship to system, it moves also to a desacralized secular status and demands a more highly adaptive family system than any we have seen in the past.

Researchers, seeking clues for stabilizing marriage, have investigated the congruence of satisfaction between husbands and wives, their assumption being that like interests hold a couple together. But the hypothesis could not be verified by evidence. Others, with a diametrical assumption, have supposed that complementarity by attracting opposites could keep marriage alive through the mutual fulfilling of needs. But research evidence fails also to substantiate this theory. Similarities and differences between the sexes are important in the ways they are perceived by the persons. Larger differences emerge from the changes that mates experience through development and their interactive relationships in those passages.

A gradual decline in marital satisfaction can be measured in most couples over a period of time. Although there are wide variations in the trend (e.g., lower economic classes exhibit the sharper decline according to Komarovsky), the tendency is marked, and disillusionment can result.

Deterioration in marital stability prompts all the helping professions to seek methods of education and enrichment that enable couples to survive their changes in role and development and to persevere through periods of adjustment. Imaginative and varied programs have been devised from written contracts to behavioral modification in order to arrest the breakdown of marriage; for it is widely recognized that our society is not so vigorous that it can forego the ideals and values that uphold marital permanence and family life.

7. The Future of Marriage. In time it is to be expected that the divorce rate will level off, that equality between the sexes will improve, that sexual fidelity and monogamy will be the norm, though with a concurrent pattern of alternative styles in marriage.

The divorce rate is likely to continue at a high figure; for the countervailing social and spiritual forces are not organized to reverse it. Indeed the trend is abetted by the ready availability of divorce, the approbation of friends, and the economic situation that now allows both sexes to achieve financial independence.

The proliferation of alternative marital styles is certain to expand beyond the living-together arrangements, group marriages, and serial marriages of today. With the measurable increase of households among single persons, single parents, child-free marriages, homosexual unions, and smaller families, it is predictable that new patterns will also emerge even from these.

Inevitably, though slowly, a new sex symmetry is replacing male domination in society. Dual employment of couples, their separate careers, and the liberated political awareness of women contribute to this expectation. Gradually the tension felt among older husbands will subside and a stronger relationship of marital equality will emerge. Though still at a disadvantage in career and status, women are advancing to a place of parity.

Although premarital sexual activity is now institutionalized through much of our culture, and a greater quantity of sexual activity is measurable both within and outside marriage, most sexual contact remains contained within marriage. Dissatisfactions with sexual freedom, attested by experienced persons, often lead to recommitments toward sexual exclusivity in marriage. Though clearly not the preference of a significant minority, fidelity does however establish the norm.

Despite the spread of alternative marital styles and the notable toleration of these, monogamy will continue to be the standard by which all forms of marital relationship are evaluated. A conventional expectation of weddings, fidelity, child rearing, and mutuality will prevail. Even in the face of shorter contracts for marriages, the ideal of marital stability will obtain for the majority, and remain as a societal standard.

Bibliography. D. S. Bailey, *The Mystery of Love and Marriage: a Study in the Theology of Sex and Religion* (1952). M. J. Bane, *Here to Stay: American Families in the Twentieth Century* (1976). R. Briffault and B. Malinowski, *Marriage Past and Present* (1956). E. W. Burgess and H. J. Locke, *The Family from Institution to Companionship* (1945). M. E. Cavanaugh, "The Impact of Psychosexual Growth on Marriage and Religious Life," *Human Development*, 4:3 (1983), 16–24. H. Clinebell and C. Clinebell, *The Intimate Marriage* (1970). J. F. Cuber and P. B. Harroff, *Sex and the Significant Americans: A Study of Sexual Behavior Among the Affluent* (1977). W. J. Everett, *Blessed Be the Bond: Christian Perspectives on Marriage and Family* (1985). F. Engels, *The Origin of the Family, Private Property and the State* (1942 [1884]). M. Komarovsky, *Blue-collar Marriage* (1964). W. J. Lederer and D. D. Jackson, *The Mirages of Marriage* (1968). M. Mead, "Marriage in Two Steps," *Redbook* (1966). L. H. Morgan, *Ancient Society, or, Researches in the Lines of Human Progress from Savagery Through Barbarism to Civilization* (1877). G. P. Murdoch, *Social Structure* (1949). T. Parsons and R. F. Bales, *The Family, Socialization and Interaction Process* (1955). C. R. Rogers, *Becoming Partners: Marriage and Its Alternatives* (1972). J. Sandler, M. Myerson, B. Kinder, *Human Sexuality: Current Perspectives* (1980). E. Schillebeeckx, *Marriage: Secular Reality and Saving Mystery* (1966). W. W. Waller and R. Hill, *The Family: A Dynamic Interpretation* (1951). E. Westermarck, *The History of Human Marriage* (1922). J. C. Wynn, ed., *Sex, Family and Society in Theological Focus* (1966).

J. C. WYNN

For marital care and counseling see MARRIAGE COUNSELING AND MARITAL THERAPY *and related articles on* CROSS-CULTURAL MARRIAGE AND FAMILY; DIVORCE; FAMILY; HOMOSEXUAL MARRIAGE; MARRIAGE; MATRIMONY, SACRAMENT OF; PREMARITAL COUNSELING; REMARRIAGE; WEDDING CEREMONY. *See also* COMMITMENT; JEWISH-CHRISTIAN MARRIAGE; SEXUAL DYSFUNCTION AND THERAPY; SEXUALITY; STEPFAMILIES; VOWS/VOWING. *Compare* COHABITATION; MEN; SINGLE PARENTS; SINGLE PERSONS; WOMEN.

MARRIAGE (Jewish Theology and Care). Marriage creates the basic social unit of family, community and society.

1. The Meaning of Marriage in Judaism. Biblical literature ascribes to marriage a twofold purpose: procreation (Gen. 1:28) and companionship (Gen. 2:18). To these two purposes the Talmud adds a third, the fulfillment of oneself as a person. "He who has no wife is not a proper man" (Yev. 63a); he lives "without joy, blessing, goodness . . . protection . . . and peace" (Yev. 62b). Jewish tradition regards marriage as the ideal human state. While celibacy was advocated by the Essenes, the mainstream of Jewish thought looks upon it with disfavor since it does not permit the individual to procreate and thereby fulfill one's basic obligation to society.

Although the Talmud refers to the sexual urge as *yezer ha-ra* (lit., "the evil inclination"), it is basically not regarded as evil. Because the sex drive is such a powerful force in human life, it must be contained within the bounds of marriage and controlled by limitations on permissibility even within that framework. When thus moderated, it is a powerful motivating force which serves good ends. "Were it not for the *yezer ha-ra* no man would build a house, marry a wife or beget children (Gen. R. 9:7)."

While polygamy was permissible during the biblical period and until the *takanah* (a decree for the betterment of society not based upon traditional Jewish law) of Rabenu Gershom around the year 1,000 C.E., it was practiced primarily by the upper classes. Even in biblical times the norm was that a man had only one wife. This is corroborated by the prophetic use of marriage as a metaphor for the relationship between God and Israel and by the metaphorical interpretation of the Song of Songs. While polygamy was still possible in Talmudic times, it was almost unknown.

Marriage was prohibited among close relatives. The biblical laws of incest were supplemented and expanded in the Talmud and became the basis of incest laws throughout Western civilization. During the biblical period endogamous marriages were encouraged while exogamous marriages were opposed in order to protect the community from idolatry and to preserve Jewish identity.

Although marriage is not a sacrament in the Christian sense of the word and can be dissolved by divorce (Deut. 24:1–4), it is considered a sacred relationship. The Hebrew word for marriage is *kiddushin* (lit., sanctification). In marriage the wife is consecrated or set apart to her husband. While the legal obligations of husband and wife and their respective families were traditionally defined in the *ketubah* (marriage document), the couple also had the moral obligations of love, honor and respect for each other.

2. The Jewish Marriage Ceremony. The traditional marriage ceremony has two parts: *erusin*, the betrothal, and *nissu'in*, the marriage proper. In Talmudic times the two ceremonies could be separated by as much as a year. Although the couple was considered married after *erusin*, cohabitation could not take place until *nissu'in*. This posed many practical and legal difficulties for the couple as well as for the Jewish community. Consequently, in post-Talmudic times the two ceremonies were combined into one. This has been the accepted practice since the twelfth century except in a few Oriental communities.

A marriage ceremony may be performed in any location, since sanctity in Jewish tradition resides not in a place but rather in the purpose for which a place is used. It may be held on any day of the week except for the Sabbath or a festival when the signing of a legal document is prohibited in traditional Judaism. While technically this prohibition does not apply in Reform Judaism, the custom of not holding a wedding on the Sabbath or a festival is so rooted in tradition that it is almost uniformly adhered to. Traditional Judaism also does not generally permit a marriage ceremony between Passover and Shavuot, except for Lag Ba-omer (thirty-third day after Passover), or during the three weeks between the seventeenth of Tammuz and the ninth of Ab (July/August). There are many differences of opinion in traditional sources concerning these prohibited days. The restrictions are not observed by Reform Judaism.

There are no specific dress requirements for the bride and groom. Traditionally the bride wears white and has both a headdress and a veil. The bridegroom may sometimes wear a *tallit* (prayer shawl), as may the officiating rabbi.

The essential elements of the marriage ceremony are: (1) the groom's giving the bride a ring and reciting to her the words: "With this ring you are consecrated to me as my wife according to the traditions of Moses and Israel." In most Reform and Conservative ceremonies there is an exchange of rings with the bride repeating the traditional formula or another selection such as "I am my beloved's and my beloved is mine" (see Song of Sol. 2:16); (2) the

reading of the *ketubah* in the traditional ceremony but not in Reform and some Conservative ceremonies; (3) the recitation of the seven marriage benedictions. In the Reform ceremony these benedictions are usually modified and abbreviated; (4) the drinking of two glasses of wine in the traditional ceremony and one in the Reform ceremony; (5) the breaking of the glass; and (6) the priestly blessing (Num. 6:24–6). The noise made by the breaking of the glass harks back to a primitive attempt to ward off the evil spirits from the bride and groom. Its specific Jewish interpretation is as a sign of mourning for the destruction of the Temple, to be remembered by the bride and groom on the happiest day of their lives.

The rituals and prayers outlined above form the framework of most Jewish marriage ceremonies, even when the bride and groom contribute to the creation of their own ceremony. Under such circumstances one or more of the customary rituals is sometimes omitted. This is more likely to occur in a ceremony conducted by a Reform rabbi.

The wedding ceremony is traditionally held under a *huppah* (canopy) which in ancient times referred to the room in which the groom and bride consummated the marriage. (See Joel 2:16 where *huppah* is in synonymous parallelism with *heder*, the common Hebrew word for room.) The custom of a symbolic *huppah*, festively decorated and held up by four poles, derives from the late Middle Ages. The bride, groom, and their parents stand under the *huppah* during the ceremony.

In Orthodox and some Conservative ceremonies the ring is placed on the forefinger of the bride's right hand. In Reform and many Conservative ceremonies, the ring is placed on the ring finger.

Customarily the bride and groom do not see each other immediately prior to the ceremony. The actual duration of time depends upon the particular community and may vary from a week to the day of the ceremony itself. Fasting for the bride and groom on the wedding day dates from Talmudic times and is still observed among the Orthodox. It is also customary among the Orthodox for the bride to go to the *mikveh* (ritual bath) following the last menstrual period prior to the wedding ceremony. The custom of examining the sheets on which the bride and groom spend the first night for spots of blood as proof of virginity was widespread during the Middle Ages but is practiced today primarily in Oriental communities.

There were three traditional ways to effect a marriage. In the presence of two witnesses: (1) the groom gives the bride either money or its equivalent, today usually a ring and recites the formula—"With this ring you are consecrated unto me as my wife according to the law of Moses and Israel"; (2) the groom gives the bride a document which delineates the conditions of the marriage and recites the same formula as above, substituting "document" for "ring"; (3) The groom recites the same formula to the bride but substitutes "cohabitation" for "ring" and then takes the bride into a private room for the purpose of consummating the relationship. All three ways have been incorporated into the modern marriage ceremony with the exchange of rings, the signing of the marriage document, and the cohabitation of the wedding night. In the traditional ceremony the bride and groom are ushered into a room where they can be alone for a few moments immediately after the ceremony.

3. Jewish Law and Tradition Governing Marriage. Marriage can be entered into only if both parties are adult and have legal capacity. Marriages are prohibited between relatives within the forbidden degrees of kinship (Lev. 18:6ff; Kid. 67b). Traditionally marriage between a man and a married woman was prohibited since that was considered an adulterous relationship, but the reverse was not true. Reform Judaism regards a marriage between a Jew and non-Jew as a Jewish marriage but traditional Judaism does not. However, all branches of Judaism recognize the validity of a civil marriage. In fact, many couples opt for a civil ceremony when, for instance, because of failure to obtain a *get* (Jewish divorce — not required by Reform Judaism) or because of intermarriage, the kind of Jewish ceremony they want is not available to them. A civil ceremony is often the ceremony of choice for many couples caught in the web of conflicting traditions.

Prior to the emancipation of women, Jews tended to marry early. The divorce rate was low because of the pressures exerted by a self-contained Jewish community to work out conflict within a marriage and because of less emphasis on personal happiness and fulfillment. Although divorce was not difficult to obtain, it was looked upon as a stigma for both men and women and, therefore, resorted to only rarely. Starting with the emancipation of women, Jews tended to marry late. The frequency of divorce, as well as of intermarriage, drastically increased due to the loss of power of the organized Jewish community.

4. Jewish Marital Care. Synagogues and other Jewish organizations provide a limited number of programs for married couples. Sermons, lectures, workshops, and discussions focus on various aspects of the marriage relationship. Some of the most popular programs help couples establish a Jewish home by acquainting them with Sabbath, festival, and life cycle observances. While such programs tend to emphasize ritual practice, an increasing amount of attention is being given to discussing practical issues, e.g., Jewish identity, the impact of Christmas, Jewish education, minority issues, anti-Semitism, etc. There are few programs focusing on the marital relationship either prior to or following marriage. What programs there are tend to be sponsored by Jewish Family Service agencies rather than by synagogues and staffed by social workers rather than by rabbis. The Sabbath Couples Groups, sponsored by the Rabbinic Center for Research and Counseling, Westfield, N.J., is a notable exception. Once a month on a Friday evening couples come together to talk about relationship issues with a clinical social worker and a rabbi who is a pastoral psychotherapist. While such a program is not possible among synagogue members who see each other socially or at synagogue functions, it is possible in the larger Jewish communities.

Jewish Marriage Encounter, modeled after its Christian namesake, provides some communications skills to many couples. However, it tends to operate on the periphery of Jewish life and is usually not sponsored or encouraged by Jewish community organizations. A limited number of programs have been developed by synagogues and community centers in response to the needs of specific groups, e.g., groups of intermarried couples.

Programs directed toward helping couples develop a more caring relationship tend to depend on the initiative and training of individual rabbis. As more rabbis, trained as social workers and pastoral psychotherapists, approach the Jewish community with acceptable secular credentials, both the synagogue and Jewish Family Service agencies are becoming more sensitized to the need for providing programs to deal with marital issues.

At the present time rabbis usually meet privately with a couple for one or more premarital sessions. The extent to which these sessions are devoted to relationship issues rather than to the details of the ceremony or to encouraging the couple's home observance, depends upon the training and sensitivity of the individual rabbi. The lack of premarital counseling programs for couples may be attributed to the fact that most synagogues do not have at any one time a sufficient number of couples to form a group. Consequently, premarital meetings tend to be on an individual rather than on a group basis. Most rabbis require that a couple see them only once prior to the marriage ceremony while some require six or eight premarital counseling sessions.

I. H. FISHBEIN

MARRIAGE; DIVORCE AND REMARRIAGE (Judaism); FAMILY, JEWISH CARE AND COUNSELING OF *or* JEWISH THEOLOGY AND ETHICS OF; PREMARITAL COUNSELING; REMARRIAGE (Issues in Pastoral Care). *See also* JEWISH CARE AND COUNSELING (History, Traditions, and Contemporary Issues); JEWISH-CHRISTIAN MARRIAGE; JEWISH HOLY DAYS AND FESTIVALS, PASTORAL DIMENSIONS OF; SEXUAL ISSUES IN PASTORAL CARE; SEXUALITY, JEWISH THEOLOGY AND ETHICS OF; WEDDING CEREMONY, JEWISH. *Compare* CROSS-CULTURAL MARRIAGE AND FAMILY; SINGLE PERSONS, JEWISH CARE AND COUNSELING OF.

MARRIAGE, CATHOLIC-ORTHODOX. *See* ORTHODOX-CATHOLIC MARRIAGE.

MARRIAGE, CATHOLIC-PROTESTANT. *See* CATHOLIC-PROTESTANT MARRIAGE.

MARRIAGE, COMMON LAW. *See* COMMON LAW MARRIAGE.

MARRIAGE, INTERFAITH. *See* CROSS CULTURAL MARRIAGE AND FAMILY; JEWISH-CHRISTIAN MARRIAGE.

MARRIAGE, ORTHODOX-CATHOLIC. *See* ORTHODOX-CATHOLIC MARRIAGE.

MARRIAGE, ORTHODOX-PROTESTANT. *See* ORTHODOX-PROTESTANT MARRIAGE.

MARRIAGE, PASTOR'S. *See* MARRIAGE AND FAMILY LIFE, PASTOR'S.

MARRIAGE, PROTESTANT-CATHOLIC. *See* CATHOLIC-PROTESTANT MARRIAGE.

MARRIAGE, PROTESTANT-ORTHODOX. *See* ORTHODOX-PROTESTANT MARRIAGE.

MARRIAGE, SACRAMENT OF. *See* MATRIMONY, SACRAMENT OF.

MARRIAGE AND FAMILY LIFE, PASTOR'S. The minister's family specifically encompasses a nuclear family where one of the members is a functioning, usually ordained, clergyperson. For both Protestants and Jews this normally means a spouse. For Catholics the clergyperson is usually an adult child in the family system. Benefits and stressors are experienced in both contexts though in different ways. Ministry-related issues exert force on the family homeostasis. However, more generally, the minister's family encompasses the wider circle of the expanded family such as siblings, grandparents, grandchildren, aunts, and uncles, though the issues in the larger family diminish in both intensity and clarity.

Specific agendas for the minister's family vary with sociological factors including ethnic background, economic standards, educational levels, geographical region, and social class. Denominational traditions and a specific congregation's expectations further impact the clergy's family. Nevertheless, a cluster of significant elements remain common, if not universal, in the family system of persons set aside for professional service in religious institutions.

1. **Benefits of Clergy Life.** Benefits felt by clergy families focus around status and resources. The minister's parents receive praise and enjoy special recognition within the religious community. Siblings likewise benefit but to a lesser extent. A spouse and children are most aware of the extent of this status because of the opportunities afforded them—such as acceptance into social gatherings, positions of community and organizational leadership and for some, extra economic considerations. Throughout life, clergy's offspring gain attention as a special subgroup.

In addition to general social status, the status within a specific parish looms high. Instant introductions and immediate attention come with each new assignment or calling. Invitations arrive for attendance at "all of the right places." The minister's family gets elevated to a position of importance within the congregational structure. Special recognition adds to their self-esteem.

The minister's spouse and children enjoy certain resources due to their position within the congregation. They enjoy unique opportunities to meet visiting political and ecclesiastical dignitaries. The physical facilities of the church are often available for their personal use, such as for entertaining or for recreation. The programs of the wider denominational group often open up to the whole family of the minister, such as conferences, rallies, and conventions. Travel becomes more possible for the minister's family.

Specific internal resources strengthen the clergyperson's family. One, a common sense of calling, places extra demands on the spouse, but often gets reported as a major sense of satisfaction. Another, an awareness of a common spiritual formation, comes to any devout religious family. However, this is a unique strength for fervent ministers and their immediate families. They report a sense of dedication

to a single cause and an awareness of spiritual strength for and from that dedication.

2. **Stressors in Clergy Life.** Stressors upon the nuclear family often outweigh these benefits according to self-reports from ministers' mates and children (Mace and Mace, 1980, p. 37). Although studies differ over the order of importance, research suggests several common pressures.

Living under excessive expectations from their congregation and of the community ranks high as a frustration for clergy families. Their family life may be watched as an ideal or model. Spouses live under a locally defined role and their offspring face a code of how they "ought to behave." In one unpublished student study supervised by the author, pastors projected higher expectations than the congregations actually reported. This may be related to excessive approval needs on the part of ministers.

A second major stressor, common to service-oriented professionals, is time pressure from a heavy work schedule and from "on call" expectations. A minister's work has no defined ending. Crises that demand immediate attention arise at inopportune times. This pressure intensifies for the clergy family because weekends and religious holidays require even more time away from their families.

Closely related to the time stress is the fact that a minister's work is emotionally depleting. Even when a minister makes time for the family, there may be little emotional energy available. The minister often turns to the family for emotional replenishment.

As with other public figures, the minister's family household may be open for public inspection. The general community knows everything that transpires in the parsonage. A mistake there becomes newsworthy material for private and media publication. The pressure of "living in a fishbowl" seems to be felt more by the clergyperson than by the spouse and children. However, public attacks on the minister inflict deep wounds on their mates and older children (Mace and Mace, 1980, p. 38). Church staff persons, denominational workers, and institutional ministers such as chaplains, pastoral counselors, and social workers report to this author less stress than pastors in the area of living under public scrutiny.

Financial stress burdens a majority of American clergypersons. They are expected to maintain a lifestyle respected by their congregation but on the average are compensated less than persons in other vocations with similar education and training. The minister's family is expected to lead a simple life without frills or extras. This seems to be especially hard for their adolescent children. Few ministers are content to live out their life in the parsonage; they desire their own home, especially at the time of retirement. In one study, only three percent of pastors and five percent of wives felt that it was an advantage for housing to be provided (Mace and Mace, 1980, p. 36).

Some ministers report stress from loneliness and social isolation. Their family gets set apart, albeit elevated, and thus suffers from a lack of external emotional support. This is aggravated by frequent geographic moves. Ministers and their nuclear families also tend to become isolated from their extended families. The minister may not have close friends within the church because of fear of rejection and pressure against favoritism within the congregation; this further segregates the minister's family. Clergy and family support groups that frequently cut across denominational lines can help to relieve this isolation.

3. **Factors in Coping.** As the benefits and stressors balance in a minister's household, a few factors determine the overall success and strength of the unit. The key appears to be the compatibility of the clergy couple. As goes the marriage so goes the family and to a large extent the vocation. Furthermore, ministers with one or two offspring report less stress than those with larger families. As could be expected, special-needs and handicapped children are complicating, but not insurmountable factors for stability in clergy homes. In fact, clergy couples like other persons need open communication, effective conflict resolution models, mutual commitments, and reciprocal positive regard in order to maintain family happiness and stability. The divorce rate for clergy couples continues to be lower than the national average, though it is rising (Goodling and Smith, p. 277). Clergy offspring achieve at higher levels than their school peers. Ministers' families experience some unique pressures, but due to their special resources, appear to fare better than average.

The family system's homeostasis revolves around six factors that redistribute in a clergy setting. Nathan Ackerman notes that three of these, individual identity, couple identity, and family identity, interrelate. He further postulates that capacity for change, control of conflict, and the continuity of identity over time also impact the family system.

(1) Pastoral identity significantly interrelates with a minister's individual identity. Becoming a minister alters one's self-image. Pastoral identity reshapes one's understanding of personal history and family background. It further develops a sense of personal self-worth and perhaps aids in a person's claim of individual authority. As a set-apart servant of the religious community, the personal commitments of a minister lie in tension between giving to the immediate family and giving to the family of God. In general, pastoral identity focuses individual identity so narrowly that other family members also find their individual identities defined by the minister's role. Unless the minister is sensitive to these issues the family balance becomes distorted.

(2) Consequently, couple identity gets defined by the calling into ministry of one of the spouses. Pastoral identity often affects the minister's sense of sexuality, the attitudes toward negative emotions, and the freedom to face marital failure. Pastoral identity may carry a denial of personal sexuality that inhibits the clergy couple's sexual expressions and satisfaction. However, overreaction to such pressures can lead to sexual acting out or a need to prove oneself as sexually powerful. For some ministers, negative emotions like fear, anger, and guilt cannot be faced. Repression and refusal to deal with negative feelings create enormous destructive pressure on the family system. Social pressure to be a model family contributes to this denial and results in fear of facing marital difficulties. Ministers stay in unfulfilling marriages in order to avoid the professional consequences of divorce.

(3) Pastoral identity further reaches out to influence the identity of the whole family. The idealized minister's family has no room for failure and little space for offspring to experience their personal identity apart from the clergy system. Although they experience a bit more freedom than the minister's spouse, the children feel external and parental expectations constricting their individuality. Moreover, the family rules about sexuality, emotions, and failure get passed down to them as norms. Unless their parents protect their right to self-expression, they face the alternatives of strict compliance or some form of rebellion. The minister's family identity, marriage dyad identity and personal identity either balance with each other or create family discord.

(4) Capacity for change is a further factor in coping. Ministry can constrict or empower a family system's capacity for change. Religion as a social restraint pulls back from change and embraces history. The norms are to be maintained at all cost. However, when religion provides a faith that looks to the future, change can be embraced as creative potential. The minister's family hinges on how their faith views change.

(5) Control of external conflict varies inversely with the capacity for change. If one chooses no change, conflict with society increases. If one adjusts with society, external pressures decrease. The reverse is true with internal conflict. If one compromises with others, internal conflict increases. For the minister's self-identity, marriage, and larger family, the control of conflict becomes a major issue. For those who choose a lifestyle different from community norms, conflict increases. The same is true for those who desire to change society by social action.

(6) The continuity of identity over time may also be cited as a coping factor. Continuity strengthens whatever patterns arise in the personal, marriage, and family areas and stabilizes the patterns of change and conflict. If a minister stands in a succession of generations of clergy families, these patterns are more deeply ingrained. If a person is the first family member to embrace ministry as a calling, the adjustments increase. This seems especially significant for families that have a parent who enters ministry in mid-life. A lack of continuity creates confusion and magnifies the change as a crisis. For example, if a man has been primary wage-earner in the family and enters ministry at mid-life at a reduction in pay, the resulting economic crisis can substantially change the family's lifestyle.

The role changes for both men and women entering ministry at mid-life also create stress for the family. In a study of fifteen married, mid-life women entering ministry, Guy Mehl found that entrance into seminary was a major turning point for their marriages and that serious conflict erupted in eight of the fifteen marriages, with five ending in divorce. Marital stress points while the women were in seminary included use of time, care of home and children, and sharing and communication patterns. Once in ministry, marital stressors included time management, household chores, the husband's relationship to the church and the validity of the husband's work (Mehl, 1984, pp. 293–6).

4. **Conclusion.** The unique struggles of clergy families require the pastoral attention of seminary and judicatory

officials. In many cases, pastoral counseling, marriage and family therapy, or career development centers would provide helpful resources in dealing with these pressures. Both denominations and congregations can provide important financial and emotional support in times of crisis.

Clergy families are complex systems that on the one hand appear similar to all professional families; on the other hand, they experience unparalled forces that create matchless experiences for all family members.

Bibliography. N. Ackerman, *The Psychodynamics of Family Life* (1958). W. V. Arnold, *Introduction to Pastoral Care* (1982). S. Barber, "Comparing the Marital Satisfaction of Clergy and Lay Couples," *J. of Pastoral Counseling*, 19 (1985 [1984]), 77-88. M. L. Bouma, *Divorce in the Parsonage* (1979). J. Conway and S. Conway, "What do you Expect from a PK?" *Leadership*, 5:3 (1984), 84-5. W. Denton, *The Role of the Minister's Wife* (1962). W. Douglas, *Ministers' Wives* (1965). J. J. Gleason, Jr., "Perception of Stress Among Clergy and Spouses," *J. of Pastoral Care*, 31 (1977), 248-51. R. A. Goodling and C. Smith, "Clergy Divorce: A Survey of Issues and Emerging Ecclesiastical Structures," *J. of Pastoral Care*, 37 (1983), 277-91. D. and V. Mace, *What's Happening to Clergy Marriages* (1980). L. G. Mehl, "*Marriage and Ministry in Midlife Women,*" *J. of Religion and Health*, 23 (1984), 290-8. W. Oates, *The Christian Pastor*, 3d rev. ed. (1982). J. Warner and J. D. Carter, "Loneliness, Marital Adjustment and Burnout in Pastoral and Lay Persons," *J. of Psychology and Theology*, 12 (1984), 125-31.

G. W. ROWATT

CHILDREN, PASTOR'S; CLERGY COUPLES; DIVORCE, PASTOR'S; HUSBAND, PASTOR'S; WIFE, PASTOR'S. *See also* CLERGY, EMPIRICAL STUDIES OF; PASTORS, PASTORAL CARE OF.

MARRIAGE AND FAMILY THERAPIST. A person certified by the American Association for Marriage and Family Therapy and/or licensed by the state to function as marriage and family therapist. As such he or she is one who has been trained in theory and practice to view health and illness more in terms of family function than in terms of individual health and pathology. The professional association and the states which license such therapists require both academic and clinical education as well as regular continuing education for original certification and/or licensure and for maintaining one's status as a marriage and family therapist. The usual components in a program designed to prepare a person for becoming a marriage and family therapist are studies in: human development; marital and family studies; marital and family therapy; professional ethics; supervised clinical work; and research methodology.

Although the strategy of the American Association for Marriage and Family Therapy has been to insist that the practice of marriage and family therapy is an identifiable profession, in fact, members of several professions, including the ministry, practice this type of therapy. Ministers who choose, by license or certification, to become identified as marriage and family therapists are saying publicly that they have taken on a secular identity as well as an ecclesiastical one. How that identity is related to their role and function as minister is dependent upon the minister and the particular ecclesiastical structure to which he or she is accountable. Ministers who have functioned in the dual role of minister and marriage

and family therapist and have chosen to be licensed by the state have often justified their decision to be licensed by the state on the grounds that they cannot in good conscience allow the state to prevent them from carrying out what has been an historic function of the clergy — offering appropriate care and counseling for families.

J. PATTON

FAMILY THEORY AND THERAPY; INTERPROFESSIONAL TEAMS AND RELATIONSHIPS; MARRIAGE COUNSELING AND MARITAL THERAPY. *See also* CONJOINT MARRIAGE AND FAMILY THERAPY; PSYCHOTHERAPY. *Compare* CLINICAL PSYCHOLOGIST; PSYCHIATRIST/PSYCHIATRY; PSYCHOLOGIST; PSYCHOTHERAPIST; SOCIAL WORKER.

MARRIAGE COMMUNICATION. The nature, patterns, skills, and quality of communication between married persons. A clear relationship has been found to exist between reported marital satisfaction and effective communication skills. Marriage communication has come to refer to patterns and skills commonly used by couples rated as satisfied in their marriage relationship. Because communication skills are so important in marital satisfaction, they are an important focus for ministers dealing with couples needing counseling or for couples wishing to prepare themselves for marriage.

Areas of marriage communication are conflict resolution, relationship-building communication, and primary-group communication.

1. **Conflict Resolution.** The ability to deal with differences and conflict is an essential part of successful marriage. Conflict-resolution communication skills involve message-sending and listening skills as well as attitudes and approaches deemed desirable in marriages.

a. Message sending. Message-sending skills include the ability to focus, the ability to send clear, direct messages without blaming or accusing, the ability to be specific and stay away from global requests or observations, the ability to know and share one's feelings in an appropriate manner, and the willingness to stay in the here and now as opposed to bringing up old issues from the past. In addition, effective message sending involves being brief, taking personal responsibility for one's choices and feelings, and being able to consider the listener while clearly disclosing one's own feelings and positions. An attitude helpful in message sending involves a belief that in marriage there is never a winner or a loser — only two winners or two losers.

b. Listening skills. Listening skills include the ability to set aside one's own feelings, positions, and perceptions in an intent to hear another person's feelings, positions, and perceptions even though they may differ. Effective listening usually involves a restatement process; feeding back both the content and the emotional level of the message to check out understanding and to reassure the speaker that he or she is being understood. Effective listening also often involves a willingness and ability to be clear about areas of agreement and common ground held by the sender and listener.

Effective listeners avoid such negative behaviors as assuming, accusing, and sabotaging.

c. Attitudes and approaches. Couples who are effective in dealing with conflict have developed certain attitudes about conflict and have specific approaches in dealing with conflict. In successful couples conflict is seen as normal rather than pathological. There is also a commitment to dealing with the conflicting issues rather than ignoring them or coercing the other. Attempting to reach an agreement where both partners win is a desirable attitude in successful marriages.

Many effective couples have specific approaches or tools in helping deal with the conflicts. These may be rules such as talking over any persisting negative feelings before a week goes by. Or the approaches may be specific and formal such as writing out specific agreements or contracts.

2. Relationship-Building Communication. Successful marriages foster the kinds of communication that nurture the partner and the relationship. *a. Affectionate communication.* Both verbal and nonverbal affectionate communication that does not lead to sexual contact is seen as invaluable in successful marriages. Effective couples daily share appreciations for small behaviors and tend to minimize faults and weaknesses. Troubled couples tend to minimize appreciations and focus on faults and weaknesses.

b. Sharing and self-disclosure. The private sharing of feelings, dreams, weaknesses, daily activities, successes, and failures is a kind of communication observed in couples who are satisfied with their marriages. Self-disclosure is related to the reported feeling of closeness and warmth in intimate relationships. Troubled couples do not self-disclose because of a perceived lack of safety. Happy couples disclose comfortably and regularly.

3. Primary-Group Communication. Because marriage is a primary group, communication patterns that exist in primary groups will also exist in successful marriages. Talking over pleasant and unpleasant things that happen during the day, talking about things both spouses are interested in, talking over difficulties in the relationship, adjusting to the mood or present feelings of the spouse, recognizing feelings from facial or bodily gestures — all these are present in effective marriages.

G. BRAINERD

MARRIAGE COUNSELING AND MARITAL THERAPY. *See also* COMMUNICATION; DOUBLE BIND; MEDIATION/CONCILIATION. *Compare* CONFLICT, MARITAL; GROWTH COUNSELING; HUMAN RELATIONS TRAINING.

MARRIAGE CONFLICT. *See* MARRIAGE COUNSELING AND MARITAL THERAPY.

MARRIAGE COUNSELING AND MARITAL THERAPY. Counseling and therapy that are directed toward improving a couple's relationship, primarily involving approaches, techniques, and methods designed to modify the non-functional or enhance the functional aspects of the couple's relationship.

Couples seek marriage counseling or therapy when their relationship has reached a state of unhappiness and dysfunction that is intolerable to one or both of the partners or when they desire the greater enrichment of a marriage that is functioning well. The setting may be the pastor's office, a clinic or agency, or the private office of a marriage counselor or therapist, pastoral counselor, social worker, psychiatric nurse, psychologist, psychia-

trist, or other mental health worker who has been trained in marriage counseling/therapy.

The terms, "marriage counseling" and "marriage therapy" are currently used interchangeably. They may be seen at the two ends of a continuum, with a strictly cognitive, problem-solving approach at the counseling end and a psychodynamic approach with an emphasis on the unconscious at the therapy end. For the purposes of this article, the term "therapy" will be understood to include counseling, and the term "therapist" will be understood to include counselor.

1. Models of Marriage Therapy. The following six models have been selected from reviews of the preferred or most frequently practiced forms (see Cookerly, 1976; Greene, 1970; Humphrey, 1983).

(1) *Individual.* In this early model of marriage therapy a husband and wife each have a separate therapist. Here the focus is on the intrapsychic material underlying the relationship. Today, such therapy is usually not considered marriage therapy. (2) *Collaborative.* In collaborative marriage therapy, both partners are seen individually during the same period of time by different therapists. With the clients' permission the therapists consult or collaborate about the therapies, preferably at regular intervals. (3) *Concurrent.* Concurrent therapy is the model in which the same therapist sees both spouses in individual therapy only. (4) *Conjoint.* In conjoint therapy the marital partners are seen together in the same session by the same therapist(s). (5) *Tandem.* In tandem therapy (see Murphy, 1976) individual therapy sessions and conjoint marriage therapy sessions are held alternately by the same therapist. (6) *Group.* There is an increasing use of couple group therapy combined with other models of therapy.

2. Profession of Marriage Counseling and Therapy. Marriage counseling and therapy as a distinct professional discipline began to emerge in the 1920s and 1930s. To develop criteria for the training and functioning of marriage counselors, the American Association of Marriage Counselors was established in New York City in 1942. The organization was later designated the American Association for Marriage and Family Therapy (AAMFT), having a program of accreditation for training programs in marriage and family therapy (see Humphrey). AAMFT draws its membership from a number of therapeutic professions, including pastoral counseling.

3. Theories of Marriage Therapy. As the marriage therapy field developed, it adopted aspects of various therapeutic theories to inform the marriage therapy process. The three major approaches today are those based on the psychoanalytic, the behavioral, and systems theories (see Paolino and McCrady, 1978).

a. Psychoanalytic theories. The psychoanalytic approach addresses itself to understanding the unconscious conflicts that affect the sense of self, which in turn affects the marital relationship (see Meissner, 1978). There is an emphasis on the concept of transference, which can be explained as the reaction of the spouse that is similar to the way the spouse reacted as a child to his or her parent. Psychoanalytic theory also emphasizes the meaning of levels of individuation in mate selection. Meissner postulates that couples "tend to choose partners who have achieved an equivalent level of immaturity, but who have adopted opposite patterns of defensive organization" (p. 43).

b. Behavioral theories. Behavior theory operates on learning principles, is outcome-oriented, and is directed to positive behavioral change, to problem solving, and to the accomplishment of tasks. Originally, its major emphasis was on building positive interactions through a social reinforcement reward system, but recently the emphasis has shifted to problem solving and communication training (see Weiss, 1978).

c. Systems theories. In general, the term "systems" is applied loosely to a variety of theories addressing themselves to the interaction of the couple as a unit. The systems approach highlights the organization of the parts within the whole of the relationship, the patterned rather than the linear interaction and the importance of the context. Of prime significance are the concepts of homeostasis and feedback (see Steinglass, 1978).

4. Clinical Practice of Marriage Therapy. *a. Reasons for seeking therapy. i. Complaints.* Couples present many complaints when they begin marriage therapy. B. L. Greene's study (1970) with 750 couples indicated that lack of communication was at the top of the list of complaints. In addition Greene listed constant arguments, unfulfilled emotional needs, sexual dissatisfaction, financial disagreements, in-law trouble, infidelity, conflicts about children, a domineering spouse, a suspicious spouse, alcoholism, and physical attack (p. 33).

ii. Marital life cycle problems. Couples may seek help when a crisis occurs because of a new development in the marital life cycle (see Singer and Stern, 1980), regarding the birth of a child, a change of job, children leaving home, and so forth.

iii. Enrichment. Couples who experience their marriage as reasonably satisfactory at times request help in actualizing a more fulfilling relationship. Frequently such couples select marriage enrichment programs rather than a marriage therapist (see Mace and Mace, 1977).

b. Role of the therapist. i. Perspective. Couples seeking therapy are usually experiencing one or more of the following feelings: pain, anger, disappointment, disillusionment, anxiety, and depression. It is important for the therapist to perceive that beyond the feelings of the moment are two individuals who have the potential for being healthy and loving. The perspective is crucial in order that the therapist may view the couple nonjudgmentally and with compassion and may be enabled to offer hope that at some point, if they so desire, they may reconnect with their wholeness (see Satir, 1972).

ii. Establishing an alliance. Usually couples who come for therapy are under pressure from their relational conflict and from the threat to their self-esteem of exposing their relationship to a third party, the therapist. A step in the restoration of their self-esteem is the experience of knowing they are heard. To listen empathically to each individual's presentation of his or her perception without agreeing or disagreeing and to ask questions for clarification are the beginning tasks of the therapist. The importance of establishing a therapeutic alliance cannot be overestimated. "Therapist relational skills have a major impact on the outcome of marital therapy regardless of the 'school' orientation of the clinician" (Gurman, 1978, pp. 550–1).

iii. Authority of therapist and autonomy of the couple. The therapist is responsible for structuring the scheduling of sessions, for example, individual, conjoint; for structuring the format and ground rules of the conjoint sessions; for setting the fee; for discussing confidentiality; and for intervening to facilitate the process. For example, when the couple addresses the therapist, the therapist will actively intervene and will encourage the couple to talk directly to one other in the session. The couple is responsible for autonomously bringing to the sessions what each wants to understand and for making their own life decisions. It is crucial that the therapist avoid telling the couple what to talk about or what to do about their personal choices.

iv. Process versus content. Couples in marriage therapy tend to present the content of their problem and then want to deal with specific issues in relation to finances, in-laws, child rearing, and so forth. In order to resolve such issues, the therapist helps them to focus on the process of the interactive system. Interaction can be understood in terms of sequences of behavior that occur over a period of time (see Minuchin, 1974). For example, if on Wednesday the husband were unresponsive to his wife's decision concerning vacation next summer, on Thursday she may be unresponsive to his sexual initiative. The therapist can assist the couple in recognizing their reactive patterns and in taking responsibility for more immediate expression of feelings, needs, wants, and expectations. By focusing on the interaction, the therapist offers an opportunity for the couple to observe their interactive behavior more objectively, to become aware of their feelings, to recognize differences in perception and to explore alternative approaches to the situation.

c. Methods and techniques. No clear-cut, agreed-upon procedure for the conduct of marriage therapy exists. From a variety of methods and techniques the author has selected those that are most frequently emphasized in the literature and about which there seems to be a consensus concerning their usefulness in marriage therapy.

i. Reframing the problem. Frequently couples in marriage therapy want to blame the partner and enlist the therapist as judge (see Lasswell and Lobsenz, 1976). It is essential that the therapist resist accepting that role. One way to approach the blaming is to intervene in the process and reframe the problem in terms of the system of interaction. Lasswell and Lobsenz, using the term "no-fault" marriage, indicate the individuals are not at fault but that their system of relating with each other is not working. The therapist can emphasize the responsibility each partner has in creating the problem. For example, if the wife complains that the husband does not take care of her needs, the therapist can assist the wife in taking responsibility for expressing her needs to her husband. A question for each individual spouse is "In what way am I contributing to the problem?"

ii. Clarifying expectations. One cannot overestimate the significance of the expectations that individuals bring to a relationship. These expectations culminate in a contract with a partner, some of which is conscious and verbalized, some of which is conscious and unverbalized, and a large part of which is unconscious (see Sager, 1976). One task of therapy is assisting individuals to become aware of and integrate the various levels of the contract.

iii. Clarifying perceptions. Frequently spouses perceive that the other is intentionally behaving in a displeasing manner. Ables and Brandsma suggest the importance of helping "spouses to learn to separate feelings and intentions from behavior and outcomes" (1977, p. 204), and thus to avoid blaming the spouse or thinking that he or she behaved in a manner that was deliberately provocative. T. Hora (1977) emphasizes the importance of "seeing" the spouse as a "loving" individual who lives and moves and has his or her being in God (Acts 17:28). To clarify and change the way spouses see each other from a negative perception to a more realistic and usually more positive and accepting one allows for a climate in which the relationship can be nurtured.

iv. Expressing feelings. "It is only by acknowledging feelings and their intensity that spouses can indicate to their mates the importance of issues and their need for change" (Ables and Brandsma, 1977, p. 153). The expression of feelings includes negative feelings of annoyance, anger, pain, and positive feelings such as love, tenderness, and caring. In the expression of negative feelings it is crucial to focus on the communication of a message about the issue and the desired change and to avoid labeling or denigrating the partner (see Bach and Wyden, 1969).

v. Training in communication and negotiation. Establishing functional communication includes a variety of skills: listening; making statements that begin with the pronoun "I"; referring to specific behaviors; distinguishing between and stating wants, needs, and expectations; separating issues and addressing one issue at a time; avoiding abstractions; avoiding "why" questions; completing communication; giving feedback; and recognizing nonverbal messages (see Ables and Brandsma, 1977; Lasswell and Lobsenz, 1976; Jackson, 1968; Satir, 1967). By utilizing communication skills and considering the possibilities of making choices and having options, couples can learn to negotiate conflictual issues. Throughout, there is an emphasis on increasing positive verbal interactions (see O'Leary and Turkewitz, 1978).

vi. Therapy of sexual dysfunctions. Due to the work of investigators W. H. Masters and V. E. Johnson (1970) and others, tremendous advances have been made in the understanding of human sexuality. H. S. Kaplan (1974) has used research on human sexuality as a basis for a comprehensive description of the process of therapy of sexual dysfunctions, integrating psychoanalytic concepts and behavior sex therapy approaches. She indicates that usually, though not always, problems in the couple's relationship need attention prior to their being able to benefit from sex therapy techniques.

vii. Developing empathy. One of the obstacles to the growth of a relationship is the inability of one or both partners to show empathy in relation to the other, that is, to participate in the other's feelings and ideas. This lack of empathy can have a variety of meanings. It can indicate a threatened self-esteem (see Satir, 1967) or a developmental failure in the process of individuation (see Meissner, 1978). Or, it may be due partially to a deficit in learning how to relate to another individual.

d. Re-education. i. Challenging beliefs. A significant part of marriage therapy consists of the challenging of long-held and inappropriate views of the marriage rela-

tionship. Lasswell and Lobsenz suggest one obstacle is the notion that what is comfortable in marriage should never change or be changed. Believing that truly loving mates know what the partner wants and should satisfy those wants is another unrealistic obstacle. (Ables and Brandsma, p. 211).

ii. Exploring perspectives. New and more appropriate concepts that can be introduced for a couple's consideration include, among others, the following: a key aspect in a harmonious marriage is the couple's ability to make the most of the assets and to minimize the liabilities (Lederer and Jackson, 1968, p. 198); marriage is a process in which individuals change, and one helpful change is the shift from being "in love" to being "loving"; and growth in a relationship is based on a couple's respect for each other's differences of feelings, ideas, and opinions.

e. Therapy impasses. When a couple have reached an impasse in the marriage therapy, many therapists (except those who work only with current behavior) find it helpful to explore with each partner, individually, what emotions and beliefs from their early personal histories are being activated in the current relationship (see Ables and Brandsma, 1977; Humphrey, 1983; Meissner, 1978). To this end, the therapist may find it useful to bring into the individual's awareness unconscious aspects of life scripts, beliefs, and modeling from their families of origin (see Dixon-Murphy, 1981). In addition, the examination of the projection of unexpressed and unaccepted aspects of the self usually assists in the clarification of the impasse (Dicks, 1967).

5. Training of the Marriage Therapist. Two aspects of training considered essential by a majority of clinicians in the training of the marriage therapist are clinical work with couples under the direct, one-to-one supervision of a qualified supervisor and academic qualifications that guarantee that the therapist is adequately informed about the theories, methodologies, and techniques of marriage therapy. A number of therapists consider personal therapy and/or relational therapy essential in the training of the marriage therapist (see Berman and Dixon-Murphy, 1979). Standards of training have been designed and programs accredited by AAMFT for the marriage therapist and by the American Association of Pastoral Counselors for therapists who work with both individuals and with couples.

6. Spiritual Dimensions. H. J. Clinebell and C. H. Clinebell (1970) describe the various ways in which a couple can grow into their God-given potentialities within the marital relationship. One aspect of that growth is the transcendent quality of spiritual intimacy, which they describe as a "relationship with the realm of values and meanings . . . and with that 'ultimate concern' [Tillich] which we call God" (p. 179–80). A. Linthorst refers to the harmonious marriage as one in which the couple participate together in the spiritual qualities of love, intelligence, beauty, harmony, peace, joy, and so forth (1979, p.35). In the opinion of the author, it is the task of the marriage therapist to assist the couple to reach new levels of awareness in their spiritual development. Further, the major factor in this process is the therapist's own level of spiritual awareness. Such awareness enables the therapist to see the couple as individuals created in the image of God and, therefore, whole. It also enables the therapist to posit sources of healing in a frame of reference that is beyond the therapist or couple and to experience the grace of God in the healing process.

7. Conclusion. Research in the field of marriage therapy is in the early phases of its development. However, some conclusions are emerging: there is a greater rate of improvement when both spouses are involved in therapy together than when only one spouse is involved (see Gurman, 1978, p. 550); the relationship with the therapist is crucial in the therapeutic process (see Gurman, 1978, p. 550); and structured communication training is an indispensable part of effective marriage therapy (see Jacobson, 1978, p. 440).

In the author's opinion, the spiritual dimensions are profoundly significant in helping couples become aware of their potential for being loving individuals in a marriage relationship. As the therapist is aware of and trusts the transcendent power of God, the source of Love, the couple in marriage therapy will have increased possibilities of recognizing themselves as spiritual beings with the goal of reflecting that Love within the marriage relationship.

Bibliography. B. S. Ables, in collaboration with J. M. Brandsma, *Therapy for Couples* (1977). G. Bach and P. Wyden, *The Intimate Enemy: How to Fight Fair in Love and Marriage* (1969). E. Berman and T. F. Dixon-Murphy, "Training in Marital and Family Therapy at Free-Standing Institutes," *J. of Marital and Family Therapy,* 5 (1979), 29–41. H. J. Clinebell and C. H. Clinebell, *The Intimate Marriage* (1970). J. Cookerly, "The Outcome of the Six Major Forms of Marriage Counseling Compared: A Pilot Study," *J. of Marriage and the Family,* 35 (1973), 608–11. H. V. Dicks, *Marital Tensions* (1967). T. F. Dixon-Murphy, "Couple Therapy Resistance Based on Early Developmental Patterns," A. Gurman, ed., *Questions and Answers in the Practice of Family Therapy* (1981). B. L. Greene, *A Clinical Approach to Marital Problems* (1970). A. S. Gurman, "Contemporary Marital Therapies: A Critique and Comparative Analysis of Psychoanalytic, Behavioral and Systems Theory Approaches," T. J. Paolino and B. S. McCrady, eds., *Marriage and Marital Therapy* (1978). T. Hora, *Existential Metapsychiatry* (1983) and *In Quest of Wholeness* (1972). F. G. Humphrey, *Marital Therapy* (1983). D. D. Jackson, ed., *Communication, Family, and Marriage* (1970). Jackson was one of a group at the Mental Research Institute in Palo Alto who did initial research on communication. Major contributors in the group included G. Bateson, J. Haley, C. E. Sluzki, V. Satir, P. Watzlawick, and J. Weakland. N. S. Jacobson, "A Review of the Research on the Effectiveness of Marital Therapy," T. J. Paolino and B. S. McCrady, eds., *Marriage and Marital Therapy* (1978). H. S. Kaplan, *The New Sex Therapy* (1974). M. Lasswell and N. M. Lobsenz, *No-Fault Marriage* (1976). W. J. Lederer and D. D. Jackson, *The Mirages of Marriage* (1968). A. T. Linthorst, *A Gift of Love: Marriage As a Spiritual Journey* (1979). D. Mace and V. Mace, *How to Have a Happy Marriage* (1977). W. H. Masters, and V. E. Johnson, *Human Sexual Inadequacy* (1970). W. W. Meissner, "The Conceptualization of Marriage and Family Dynamics from a Psychoanalytic Perspective," T. J. Paolino and B. S. McCrady, eds., *Marriage and Marital Therapy* (1978). S. Minuchin, *Families and Family Therapy* (1974). J. M. Murphy, "A Tandem Approach: Marriage Counseling As Process in Tandem with Individual Psychotherapy," *J. of Marriage and Family Counseling,* 2 (1976), 13–22. C. E. Obudho, *Black Marriage and Family Therapy* (1983). K. D. O'Leary and H. Turkewitz, "Marital Therapy from a Behavioral Perspective," T. J. Paolino and

B. S. McCrady, eds., *Marriage and Marital Therapy* (1978). C. Sager, *Marriage Contracts and Couple Therapy* (1976). V. Satir, *Conjoint Family Therapy,* 3d ed. (1983) and *Peoplemaking* (1972). L. J. Singer and B. L. Stern, *Stages: The Crises That Shape Your Marriage* (1980). R. F. Stahman, and W. J. Hiebert, eds., *Klemer's Counseling in Marital and Sexual Problems,* 2d ed. (1977). P. Steinglass, "The Conceptualization of Marriage from a Systems Theory Perspective," in T. J. Paolino and B. S. McCrady, *Marriage and Marital Therapy* (1978). P. L. Weiss, "The Conceptualization of Marriage from a Behavioral Perspective," in T. J. Paolino and B. S. McCrady, eds., *Marriage and Marital Therapy* (1978).

T. F. DIXON-MURPHY

MARRIAGE. *See also* COMMITMENT; CONJOINT MARRIAGE AND FAMILY THERAPY; CROSS-CULTURAL MARRIAGE AND FAMILY; DIVORCE; MARRIAGE COMMUNICATION; PREMARITAL COUNSELING; REMARRIAGE (Issues in Pastoral Care); SEXUAL DYSFUNCTION AND THERAPY. *Compare* COHABITATION; FAMILY, JEWISH *or* PASTORAL CARE AND COUNSELING OF; JOURNALS IN MARRIAGE AND FAMILY COUNSELING.

MARRIAGE ENCOUNTER, Roman Catholic. A program of marriage enrichment with an explicit spiritual component. Marriage Encounter (ME) had its genesis in the Roman Catholic community through the work of Father Gabriel Calvo in Spain in 1962. Since then eight versions of ME have developed in the U.S. representing various ecumenical and interfaith perspectives. ME has had an enormous following, though there has been a sizeable falling off of support for all marriage enrichment programs within religious institutions during the 1980s.

Methodologically, ME has a couple focus and uses a reflection, writing, and dialogue process. The evolving content of an ME weekend includes: (1) encounter with self, i.e., "Who am I and what are my strengths and weaknesses?" (2) encounter with one's partner, i.e., "Who are we and where are we in our marital journey?" (3) encounter with God, i.e., "What is God's plan for me and for us, and how are we called to and equipped for mutual love, sacrifice, and service?" Scriptural resources are used, and couples are encouraged to deepen their involvement in their individual faith communities. After completing a weekend couples are invited to participate in a monthly couples group that emphasizes inter-couple sharing and continued faith development.

Bibliography. L. Hof and W. Miller, *Marriage Enrichment: Philosophy, Process and Program* (1981). J. Moss and R. Basher, "From the Editors: Special Issue on Family Life Education," *Family Relations,* 30 (1981), 491–2.

P. R. GIBLIN

MARRIAGE ENRICHMENT. *See also* ENGAGED ENCOUNTER; MARRIAGE COMMUNICATION. *Compare* ENCOUNTER GROUPS; HUMAN RELATIONS TRAINING; RETREATS.

MARRIAGE ENRICHMENT. Both an approach to relationship enhancement for couples and a movement.

1. The Marriage Enrichment Movement and Methodology. The movement began in Spain in January, 1962 under the leadership of Father Gabriel Calvo, and in the U. S. this program became known as Marriage Encounter. David and Vera Mace began marriage enrichment retreats with Quaker couples in October, 1962, and by 1973 they had organized the Association of Couples for Marriage Enrichment (ACME); within a decade several thousand lay and professional couples in all fifty states held membership in ACME. In the U. S. the movement has been closely associated with religious faith groups, and some fifteen national programs are directly connected to an established religious organization.

Many programs are localized but some of the more prominent national programs are: Marriage Encounter (ME), Marriage Communication Labs (MCL), Relationship Enhancement Programs (RE), Couples Communicational Program (CCP), Training in Marriage Enrichment (TIME), Listening and Loving, Practical Application of Intimate Relationship Skills (PAIRS), and the Association of Couples for Marriage Enrichment (ACME). In 1975 the Council of Affiliated Marriage Enrichment Organizations (CAMEO) was formed with a major concern to establish standards for leadership training, but a system of national certification of leaders and accreditation of training centers is yet to be developed.

The stated aim is to "make good marriages better," and implicitly, the goal is to foster personal growth and mutual fulfillment in enough marriages that the public image of marriage as a fulfilling relationship will be enhanced. A growth-oriented, potential-oriented perspective of the individual and a dynamic view of the marital system are employed to promote an intentional companionship model of marriage in the varied programs. Experiential, relational, inductive methods of education are employed to enhance communicational skills and alter behavior of individuals with the primary objective of enriching the marital relationship. But prevention of marital dysfunction is also perceived to be as important as intervention or correction.

Methodologically, the programs focus on the couple relationship through self-disclosure of feelings and thoughts, concentrate on the present tense and the positive strengths of the mates, teach communicational skills, accept conflict positively and resolve it creatively, seek behavioral and attitudinal change, advocate a companionship model of marriage, and enable the renegotiating of commitments and the reforming of contracts.

2. Critique. There are some indications that the movement has contributed significantly to the stabilizing of marriage and that the programs have enhanced marital relationships in middle-class America. Sufficient research data has not been collected to verify either the types of individuals served or to identify the specific relationship changes that have been produced or the stability of the changes over a period of time. Also, some questions about the movement have been raised from both clinical and theological perspectives. Among the clinical concerns are these: the lack of selectivity or screening of the participants, the seeming little appreciation of the power of resistance and anticipatory grief in the promulgation of instant intimacy, the assumption that enhancement of a relationship follows better communication, the arrested focus on intimacy between equal, self-fulfilled individuals, and the lack of structured aftercare and/or sufficient attention to the reentry of participants following their weekend retreat high. (Marriage Encounter, however, has developed a follow-up structure involving a monthly couples group.) Theological concerns have been related to the movement's concept of time, its understanding of commitment, its implicit humanism, and its implicit promotion of a "new church" mentality.

From a sociological viewpoint, the movement's emphases may be digestible for that educated, equal, ego-strong husband or wife who realizes that he or she does not have to stay married. But some people have dependency needs and find satisfaction in more provider/dependent type relationships because they do not function on the level of Maslow's "self-actualized" individual. The quest for intimacy among equals is endemic to upper-middle class, white-collar, upwardly socially mobile Americans. Intrinsic values and belonging needs are acclaimed and proclaimed by the movement, but utilitarian concerns and security needs are ignored or assumed. Most retreat formats remove the couple from the real world of distractions and duties to a brief world of intimacy and ecstasy, but the tasks of Monday and the squeeze of inflation and taxes have to be faced. Productive work, good citizenship, and middle-age generativity can be meaningful to intimates too, and they must be attended to by most people regardless.

Theologically, along with enticing persons to make their marriages more perfect by mastering skills of sharing feelings, the movement might also give greater acknowledgment to the ambiguity, the frailty, and the incompleteness of human existence. Otherwise it may be in danger of implicitly encouraging persons to be committed to little more than instant gratification of immediate, impulsive feelings within the closed system of the couple.

Bibliography. H. A. Otto, ed., *Marriage and Family Enrichment: New Perspectives and Programs* (1976). L. Hof and W. R. Miller, *Marriage Enrichment: Philosophy, Process and Program* (1981).

J. N. KEITH

MARRIAGE COUNSELING AND MARITAL THERAPY; MARRIAGE COMMUNICATION. *Compare* GROWTH COUNSELING; GROUP COUNSELING; HUMAN RELATIONS TRAINING; RETREATS.

MARRIAGE THERAPY. *See* MARRIAGE COUNSELING AND MARITAL THERAPY.

MARRIAGE TRIBUNAL. The popular name given to an ecclesiastical court established by the diocesan bishop, administered by his judicial vicar, assisted by others also trained in canon law. A tribunal judges matters concerning Catholic Church law (e.g., an individual's status in the church) that have no bearing in civil courts. Tribunals often study broken marriages, hence the appellation. Previously married Catholics or persons of other denominations desiring to marry in a Catholic ceremony may ask for such a study. *The Code of Canon Law,* Book 7 (1983) describes tribunal operation and organization.

Bibliography. G. Taylor, *Catholic Marriage Tribunal Procedure* (1981). J. Young, ed., *Divorce, Ministry and the Marriage Tribunal* (1983).

J. MILLER

DIVORCE AND REMARRIAGE (Roman Catholicism). *See also* CANON LAW SOCIETY OF AMERICA.

MARRIAGE AND FAMILY COUNSELING. *See* FAMILY THEORY AND THERAPY; MARRIAGE COUNSELING AND MARITAL THERAPY.

MARTIN OF TOURS, ST. (ca. 316–97). Monk and bishop, among the first non-martyrs honored as a saint in the West. Born in Pannonia (present-day Hungary), the son of a Roman army officer, Martin became a Christian after serving as a conscript in the Roman army. He founded the first organized monastery in Gaul on land donated by his spiritual master, Hilary of Poitiers. Elected bishop of Tours by popular acclamation in 372, he continued his monastic life in Tours and later in a nearby area called Marmoutier, where he founded a monastery. His episcopate in Tours was marked by his keen interest in evangelizing the *pagani* of the still unchristianized countryside. His custom of visiting each church and village in his jurisdiction on an annual basis later became the norm for all episcopal visitations in the Western church. Martin was also one of the first bishops to insist on formal intellectual and spiritual training for the clergy of his area. He was best known in the later tradition of the church as a miracle worker and an ascetic.

The prodigious cult of Martin of Tours in the Middle Ages rests partially on the *Vita Martini*, the elegant biography written by his friend Sulpicius Severus.

Bibliography. C. Stancliffe, *St. Martin and His Hagiographer* (1983).

L. S. CUNNINGHAM

MEDIEVAL CHURCH, PASTORAL CARE IN; PASTOR (Normative and Traditional Images of).

MARTYR COMPLEX. *See* SELF-DESTRUCTIVE BEHAVIOR.

MARXISM. *See* CRITICAL THEORY; LIBERATION THEOLOGY; MATERIALISM; SOCIOLOGY OF RELIGIOUS AND PASTORAL CARE; THEORY AND PRAXIS.

MARY, VENERATION OF. The recognition of the preeminence of Mary, the mother of Jesus, within the Christian community and the principal consequences of that recognition: filial devotion to her, invocation of her maternal intercession, and imitation of her as the outstanding exemplar of Christian life.

Veneration of Mary belongs to the wider practice of devotion to all the saints. In theological terms, it is called *hyperdulia* to distinguish it from the veneration of other saints (*dulia*), and from the adoration due to God alone (*latria*).

1. History. The tradition of Marian veneration begins in the Bible itself. Although some scholars interpret Lk. 11:27–28 as a warning against the veneration of Mary, other scholars, particularly in the Roman Catholic tradition, draw heavily on other scriptural messages to support the belief; e.g., the archangel salutes Mary (Lk. 1:28) as "favored one"; Elizabeth calls her "blessed among all women" and is honored that "the mother of

my Lord should come to me" (Lk. 1:42–43). Mary herself realizes that "all generations shall call me blessed" (Lk. 1:48). In the Gospel of John it is at her request that Christ's first "sign" is performed (Jn. 2:5). The dying Christ gives her and his beloved disciple to one another as mother and son (Jn. 19:26); the Roman Catholic tradition sees in the disciple a representative of all humanity receiving Mary as spiritual mother.

Second century writers speak of Mary as "the new Eve"—companion of the new Adam, Christ. Baptismal creeds of that century describe Jesus as "born of the Holy Spirit and the Virgin Mary." By the fourth century she is seen as the exemplar of Christian chastity and consecrated virginity.

The definition of Mary as *Theotokos* (Mother of God) at Ephesus in 431 gave impetus to her veneration. Churches were dedicated to her; prayers offered in her praise. By 450 Marian feasts had begun, e.g., the Annunciation on March 25. Dating from the sixth century is her commemoration in the canon of the Mass. Feudal court structure is reflected in the veneration of Mary as "our Lady," the mother of the Lord. The high Middle Ages focused attention upon her compassion (her sharing in the redemptive suffering of Jesus) and honored her sinless conception.

2. Devotional. The rosary, a very popular Marian devotion, originated in the thirteenth century. The advent of printing brought a proliferation of Marian literature. New religious communities were founded with special devotion to her, and Renaissance art extolled her privileges and dignity.

Her alleged apparitions at Lourdes (1858) and Fatima (1917) have occasioned widespread popular devotion. Pope Pius IX solemnly defined her Immaculate Conception in 1854, Pius XII her Assumption in 1950; and the Second Vatican Council included in its dogmatic constitution on the church a section on the cult of Mary within the believing community.

Mariology has found its way into pastoral psychology and the psychology of religion in a variety of ways, but particularly as a notion which demonstrates (1) the integral part the feminine plays in God consciousness (Harding, 1971); (2) the way in which religion takes the ordinary (Mary as "handmaiden of the Lord") and transforms it into the extraordinary (Mary as "Mother of God") (P. Pruyser, 1968, p. 224); and (3) how love (*eros*) is lifted to the heights of spiritual devotion (C. G. Jung, 1964).

Bibliography. J. B. Carol, ed., *Mariology*, 3 vols. (1964). E. R. Carroll, "Mary, Devotion to," *New Catholic Encyclopedia*, 9 (1967), p. 364. "Lumen Gentium" (Dogmatic Constitution on the Church), ch. 8, *Second Ecumenical Council of the Vatican* (1964). M. E. Harding, *Woman's Mysteries: Ancient and Modern* (1971). P. A. Harrington, "Mary and Femininity: A Psychological Critique," *J. of Religion and Health*, 23 (1984), 204–17. P. W. Pruyser, *A Dynamic Psychology of Religion* (1968), pp. 222–4. M. L. von Franz, "The Process of Individuation," in C. G. Jung, *Man and His Symbols* (1964), ch. 3.

V. B. BROWN

LITURGICAL AND DEVOTIONAL LIFE, ROMAN CATHOLIC TRADITION OF; SPIRITUALITY (Roman Catholic Tradition). *See also* PILGRIMAGE METAPHOR; SAINTS, VENERATION OF; SHRINES.

MASCULINITY. *See* MEN; SEXUALITY, BIOLOGICAL AND PSYCHOSOCIAL THEORY OF.

MASLOW, ABRAHAM (1908–70). Considered one of the founders of the humanistic movement in psychology. Maslow obtained his degree in a behavioral program at the University of Wisconsin, and in reaction to the mechanistic determinism he discovered in both behaviorism and the psychoanalytic movement he attempted to transcend these major forces in psychology. Because Maslow's humanistic theories offered an alternative approach to psychoanalysis, they have been referred to as the "third force" in psychology. He began with a new set of foundational premises that were specifically person oriented and emphasized the capacity for goodness, creativity, and freedom within people, for he recognized people as spiritual, purposeful, autonomous beings.

Maslow hypothesized that there are five broad categories of basic needs, and a person must be able to obtain the lower needs on the scale before advancing to the next level. The scale begins with physiological needs or deficits such as hunger, thirst, and fatigue. The next level contains the safety needs: the need to avoid pain, feel secure, be free from chaos, and the need for structure. Maslow describes the third level as belongingness and love, followed by the need for esteem and self-respect, adequacy, and competence. Finally, the highest level in the hierarchy is the need for self-actualization, understanding, and aesthetic pleasure.

Maslow focused much of his work on people society considers healthy. Self-actualized people were those persons thought to be in a state of exemplary psychological health, those who embodied the values embraced by humanism. Maslow perceived these persons as having characteristics such as self-acceptance and acknowledgment of others, openness, autonomy and independence, and compassion with strong moral and ethical convictions. In essence, the self-actualized person embodies secular humanism's ideals as Maslow perceived them.

Bibliography. A. Maslow, *Motivation and Personality*, 2d ed. (1970). J. Lowry, *Dominance, Self-Esteem, Self-Actualization* (The Germinal Papers of Abraham Maslow).

B. HOUSKAMP

HUMANISTIC PSYCHOLOGY; PERSONALITY THEORY (Varieties, Traditions, and Issues); PSYCHOLOGY, WESTERN; PSYCHOLOGY OF RELIGION (Theories, Traditions, and Issues); SELF-PSYCHOLOGIES. *See also* PEAK EXPERIENCE; SELF-ACTUALIZATION/SELF-REALIZATION.

MASOCHISM / MASOCHISTIC BEHAVIOR. *See* SELF-DESTRUCTIVE BEHAVIOR; SEXUAL VARIETY, DEVIANCE, AND DISORDER.

The MASS. *See* MINISTRY (Roman Catholic Tradition); ROMAN CATHOLIC PASTORAL CARE; SACRAMENTAL THEOLOGY AND PASTORAL CARE, ROMAN CATHOLIC. *See also* LITURGICAL AND DEVOTIONAL LIFE, ROMAN CATHOLIC; LITURGICAL CHANGE AND REFORM (Pastoral Issues).

MASTERS, SPIRITUAL. *See* SPIRITUAL MASTERS AND GUIDES.

MASTURBATION. Sexual arousal caused by self-stimulation. A compound from the Latin roots *manus* (hand) and *stuprare* (to defile), the term has a pejorative connotation. Attempts to coin value-neutral terminology have not been successful. "Automanipulation" is too mechanical and vague; "autoerotism" is too broad, for it can also describe, for example, one's response to sensuous works of art; and "auto-orgasm" incorrectly assumes that orgasm is always the aim of this endeavor.

1. **Traditional Attitudes.** Masturbation is not mentioned in the Bible. Even so, in medieval Judaism and Christianity masturbation came to be regarded as a grave offense. In the Talmud it is associated with Onan who, according to Gen. 38:8–10, was slain by God for spilling his semen on the ground. Onan's sin was actually *coitus interruptus* which resulted in his failure to fulfill his levirate responsibilities. In the eleventh century, Pope Leo IX held that masturbators should not be admitted to sacred orders. Aquinas classified masturbation as an unnatural sin more deserving of damnation than the natural sexual sins of rape, incest, and adultery, where procreation was a possibility.

In the eighteenth century, Catholic neurologist Samuel Tissot wrote a widely circulated treatise entitled *Onania* which claimed that masturbation causes an excessive blood flow to the brain that can result in impotence and insanity. A fallacy in inductive reasoning was responsible for the easy acceptance of Tissot's view. Since the insane are less inhibited with respect to open practice of what is not in conformity with social standards, attendants of the insane observed with comparative ease that most of them masturbated during periods when they were institutionalized and deprived of sex partners. However, there were few opportunities for observing whether or not most of the sane indulged in masturbation in similar circumstances.

Tissot's views had an impact on medical spokesmen in subsequent centuries. In the first psychiatric text published in the U.S., mania, seminal weakness, dimness of sight, epilepsy, loss of memory, and even death were ascribed by Benjamin Rush to masturbation. Sigmund Freud championed the usual Victorian outlook on masturbation. He warned that it "vitiates the character through indulgence" and that it might result in "diminished potency in marriage." Masturbation was, according to Freud, the cause of a neurosis characterized by fatigue, worry, and lack of physical and mental alertness.

Through much of the twentieth century, Christian clergy have also terrorized youth by attributing acne, stuttering, sallow complexion, lethargy, cowardice, and selfishness to masturbation. Some Protestant theologians have condemned it because it is not altruistic. In 1975, Pope Paul mandated a "Declaration of Some Questions of Sexual Ethics" that unhesitatingly asserted that "masturbation is an intrinsically and seriously disordered act."

2. **Current Clinical Outlook.** During the past generation there have been conclusive sociological and medical studies showing the harmlessness of masturbation. The Kinsey researchers have shown that approximately three-fourths of Americans have experienced masturbation and that it is frequently practiced by the majority of the total population. Masturbation statistics for European and Middle Eastern peoples are about the same. The natural-

ness of this behavior is also attested to by its being found among some other mammals, with greater incidence among males.

There is no evidence that masturbation, regardless of frequency, leads to physical or mental disorders. The physiological system has its own controls, so there is as little point in warning about the dangers of masturbation as about the dangers of sneezing. Both are usually orgasmic experiences in which tensions are relieved. The data regarding masturbation prompt the generalization that never has a more harmless activity provoked more harmful anxiety.

Masturbation can be therapeutic for tense persons. Some women find it a relief for menstrual cramps. For men as well as for women, masturbation can transform a restless night into quiet sleep. Rather than draining off vital potency, it can be an aid to restoring physical energy. Case studies show that neurosis, rather than being caused by masturbation, can be caused by attempting to live without masturbation.

Premarital masturbation may assist in developing orgasmic relations in marriage. By contrast, the repression of masturbation, especially among women, contributes to marital frigidity. The fact that female masturbation increases throughout the years of greatest coital activity shows that the two sexual expressions are compatible. When there is a disparity between the sexual drives of partners, masturbation can help to ease the situation so that unpleasant heavy demands need not be made. Both inside and outside marriage it is a cathartic safety valve in that it releases pent-up emotions and thereby protects against exploitative and violent sexuality.

3. **Religious Values.** Since the most widespread of all sexual activities for youth is masturbation, a culture's attitude toward it significantly affects its outlook toward all sexual expressions. Parental contempt of masturbation is a main cause of guilt feelings over sexual pleasure. When authority figures treat masturbation as repulsive and dirty, youth tend to evaluate all genital expressions in a similar manner. For wholesome growth it is important for children to learn to understand their own bodies and to accept the ways in which they respond to stimulation. The adolescent is absorbed in establishing his or her psychosexual identity and is curious about erogenous areas, sensitive swellings, and seminal emissions. If she or he is encouraged to appreciate these things, many lasting difficulties can be avoided. Autogenital manipulation provides a laboratory situation in which bodily functions and pleasures can be experienced under controlled circumstances. In that situation there is no need for anxieties over venereal infection, conception, or social detection. Out of these experiences youth can understand better that sex has both recreational and procreational purposes.

From the standpoint of the prevailing religious outlook on sexuality, masturbation can be given a comparative evaluation. To follow the thought of the apostle Paul regarding marriage, it may be better to masturbate than to be "aflame with passion" (I Cor. 7:9). Yet it has been generally acknowledged that sex has the more fundamental purpose of expressing a depth of relationship between companions. Even as composing poetry for one's own reading is usually not as enjoyable as its use as a means of communicating one's intimate feelings to others, so masturbation is a lesser good than sexual intercourse by partners. By the same token it seems apparent that there are circumstances, such as those of the unmarried or separated from spouse, those confined in prisons or hospitals, and of those with certain handicaps, in which masturbation may be considered an appropriate and enjoyable expression of sexuality.

Bibliography. A Kinsey, *et al.*, *Sexual Behavior in the Human Female* (1953). W. F. Kraft, "A Psychospiritual View of Masturbation," *Human Development* 3:2 (1982), 39–45. R. Masters, *Sexual Self-Stimulation* (1967). W. Phipps, "Masturbation: Vice or Virtue?" *J. of Religion and Health*, (1977), 183–95. W. Stekel, *Auto-Erotism* (1950).

W. E. PHIPPS

SEXUALITY. *See also* PLAY; SEX RESEARCH; SEXUAL VARIETY, DEVIANCE, AND DISORDER. *Compare* FANTASIZING; LUST AND CHASTITY.

MATERIALISM. The name given to a family of interpretive doctrines that accord primacy to matter and a secondary position to mind (spirit), if it grants any position at all. The preoccupation with material goods and values, so evident in late twentieth-century Western (bourgeois) societies, is a variant of materialism. This popular meaning of "materialism" is more adequately understood when placed in the context of its formative influences.

1. **Classical Materialism and the Rise of the Modern View.** Materialism has been a persistent theme of Western speculative thinking. Following Thales, Ionian philosophers attempted to construct comprehensive interpretations of the world in terms of fundamental substances and their changes. Empedocles organized such substances into four elements: earth, air, fire, and water. The Stoa (Xeno and followers) accorded primacy to fire, interpreting it as a tensional motion or holding power. From this one principle, it was possible to account both for a physics and for the communal character of human relationships. Epicurus taught materialism as the sole foundation for a good life — calm, serene, and free from superstition. To accept this world as one of the infinite, inevitable arrangements into which atoms fall and to appreciate its marvels and beautifully organized living bodies were the cornerstones of his view.

Between the close of classical thought and the emergence of Renaissance thought, materialism was almost wholly obscured by variations of Aristotelian and Thomist philosophies. But when in the seventeenth century Thomas Hobbes developed a polemical discourse against the feudal hierarchies he associated with Aristotelianism, the basic structure that he appropriated was derived from the materialistic teachings of the Stoa. Concerned to develop a comprehensive physics and viable civil philosophy, Hobbes claimed that the force of self-preservation could account both for laws of uniform physical motion and for principles of political organization. He viewed individuals apart from a teleological framework; in the absence of some preestablished end toward which human striving aims, the individual is instead obliged to move from work to work. Restless in its striving, the individual is never more than the sum of its work — a view that tends to emphasize the empirical content of the work.

2. Enlightenment and Nineteenth-Century Perspectives.

In the following century, d'Holbach developed another speculative philosophy of materialism that had far-reaching effects on the Continent. He claimed that nothing exists outside nature. Humans, as a part of nature, and as in nature, act according to natural causes. Moreover, intellectual faculties, passions, and thoughts are merely ways of construing inner motion. What therefore is required is a system of classification for a comprehensive interpretation of life.

What d'Holbach called for, Diderot championed in the development of the French Encyclopedia (Encyclopédie). A source book and symbol of Enlightenment thought, the Encyclopedia drew upon the collaborative efforts of d'Alembert, d'Holbach, Voltaire, and others, under the direction of Diderot. As in the earlier instances of prominent materialist thought — Greek, English (Hobbes), and German (d'Holbach), the materialism of the Encyclopedia inveighed against religious metaphysics. The encyclopedists laid great emphasis upon experience, and still more, the scientific character of experience, thereby laying the foundation for the view that the only valid form of knowledge is scientific, and that the only objects of knowledge are facts — a view that has come to be known as positivism. Indeed, the prominence of the physical sciences continued to flourish under the sway of such materialists as La Mettre, who sought to explain mental activity in terms of neural changes; Lavoisier, who held that chemistry was strictly a matter of the natural interactions of material substances; and Boscovitsch, who claimed that matter is points of force. At the same time, Saint-Simon galvanized interest in the science of human behavior and the conviction that such a science could be deployed in the effort to reconstruct society — an interest that would be developed encyclopedically by his secretary, Comte.

By the nineteenth century, Marx observed that French materialism of the preceding century had developed into two branches—natural science and the social sciences — and he called for a new materialism (historical or dialectical materialism) to revolutionize human life. Following lines of thought suggested by Feuerbach, Marx construed historical materialism as the affirmation of "the real," the "empirical," and as the rejection of speculative idealism. He also thought that the recognition that different social laws belong to different historical epochs could contribute to overcoming the social repression of instinct and natural desires. Thought and action, similarly, were no longer viewed as antithetical; in Marx's view, scientific advance and practical improvements are in principle bound up with one another. And Marx thought, as had Hegel before him, that social development takes place through struggle and opposition. Along with the development of historical materialism, medical materialism continued to flourish. Bolstered by Darwin's publications, physicochemical explanations in the natural sciences achieved ascendency.

At the end of the nineteenth century, Sigmund Freud offered still another turn to materialism, holding that thoughts and actions are affected by forces which may not be amenable to structures of conscious life; insofar as these forces are amenable to the structures of conscious life, they are so only indirectly, as for example, in the case of dreams.

3. Late Twentieth-Century Materialism.

The meaning of the term "materialism" as we now use it thus appears to be a multidimensional confluence of several lines of thinking. The role of Stoic materialist theory in the formation of modern discourses (law, physics, economics, ethics, political science, and history) doubtless disposes us to uses of language that embody materialist assumptions, as does, no doubt, the inheritance of the specifically Hobbesian view that we are the sum of our works, with particular attention to the acquisition of empirical goods. Similarly the devaluation of idealistic patterns of thought in favor of a more realistic interpretation of life continues to enjoy currency. "Realistic" in this sense more nearly favors knowledge confirmable by facts and accordingly classifiable, a view that bears the imprint of our Enlightenment heritage. Finally, the unchallenged proprietary role of physicochemical explanations in the natural sciences reinforces our sense that materialism has brought us to our current state of scientific understanding.

But where today's materialism differs from previous forms is in its apparent adoption of a view that holds that life directed to reason and self-determination is an illusion. This is evident, in part, in the rising emphasis upon "pharmacotherapy" in psychiatric circles, and, in part, in the new prominence of "behaviorism" and "empirical method" in psychology, especially in the fields of cybernetic and systems models research. But perhaps most paradoxical of all is the seeming adoption of the values of self-determination in the popular psychological culture of "self-help": the appropriation of the language of self-determination as the legitimation for the practices of material acquisition scarcely veils the contempt the "self-help movement" harbors for communal freedoms and responsibilities.

This turn in the outlook of contemporary materialism is more readily understood when one of its foundational elements is brought into view. This foundational element is a form of nihilism, which directly attacks convictions about human life as meaningless, a sham, and therefore worthy of dissolution. In celebrating the finite subject and its possessions at the expense of the world, the nihilistic penchant of contemporary materialism poses a more serious threat than is ordinarily reckoned. For in showing that our ideals are frequently illusory, nihilistic practices show themselves to have a firm interpretive foundation.

4. Pastoral Implications.

Pastoral care and counseling with individuals who have appropriated the materialist bent of our culture, especially its "popular" form, needs to take seriously the power of the interpretive foundation of this outlook. Indeed, only by loosening and ultimately removing that foundation can nihilism lose its legitimating force. Awakening individuals to a range of spiritual values to which they are heir is a prospect that appears to be intimately linked to acknowledgment of and insight about the unknown. Since the unknown cannot be shown to be illusory, the psychoanalytic insight that there are forces which operate upon us which are not amenable to consciousness (Freud), coupled with the religious insight about the unknowability of God (Luther, Calvin, Barth), may intimate a distinctive path for contemporary pastoral care and counseling to follow in unseating the nihilistic penchant of contemporary materialism.

Bibliography. D. M. Armstrong, *A Materialist Theory of the Mind* (1968). D. Henrich and D. S. Pacini, "The Contexts of Autonomy," *Daedalus* 112:4 (1983), 355–77. D. S. Pacini, *The Cunning of Modern Religious Thought* (1987).

D. S. PACINI

VALUES; WORLD VIEW. *See also* PHILOSOPHY AND PSYCHOLOGY; SOCIOLOGY OF RELIGIOUS AND PASTORAL CARE. *Compare* MONEY; SECULARIZATION/SECULARISM; POOR PERSONS; RICH PERSONS.

MATERNAL BONDING. *See* MOTHER-INFANT BONDING.

MATERNAL DEPRIVATION. A syndrome of developmental deficits in infants who are reared without adequate mothering. Symptoms of deprivation include intellectual impairments, disturbances in socio-emotional relations, and delays in psychomotor behavior and physical growth. The greatest precipitant is the mother's inability to convey love and warmth to her infant, and thus give it a sense of security, value, and worth. Studies show that the physiological state and emotional needs of infants require this special nurturing interaction from their caregivers (Brazelton, 1963; Winnicott, 1960; Stern, 1977).

1. History of Research. Research studies of infants reared in institutions led to the discovery of maternal deprivation (Spitz, 1945; Rheingold, 1956). These infants exhibited a pattern of apathy, withdrawal, and delay in attaining developmental milestones. All had received excellent physical care along with proper nutrition. The fallacy of the care related to the impersonal relations between staff and infants. It was found that infants had no single caregiver with whom they could bond or attach. As a result, these infants had no interest in the social pleasures, in exploration of the environment, or in developing affectionate ties.

Ainsworth's (1977) theory of attachment further explained the "deprivation" phenomenon. Infants progress from a state of undifferentiated attachment (0–3 months) toward a caregiver to a stage of extreme attachment (7–8 months) where they prefer the mother figure over all others, experience stranger anxiety when approached by unfamiliar individuals, and use the mother as a secure base from which to explore their environment. The mother becomes associated with pleasure, comfort, and reduction of tension.

2. Causes of Deprivation. These include: (1) intrapsychic dysfunctions (e.g. psychoses and depression); (2) substance abuse; (3) insufficient child development knowledge on the part of the mother; (4) multiple caretakers (infant unable to attach to a single mothering figure); and (5) infant characteristics, that is, difficult infants who consistently need extraordinary amounts of stimulation (Thomas, Chess, and Birch, 1963).

3. Profile of Deprivation Behavior. In a deprivation situation, infant and mother have little or no social engagement or physical contact. A bond has generally not been formed (see Ainsworth, 1977). Maternal feedings are performed unaffectionately. Emotionally, the mother resents her parental responsibilities and/or is unable to cope with the infant's dependency upon her.

Some mothers are more covert in their deprivation style. Though emotionally distant they make efforts to disguise their disinterest and dislike of the infant, and they engage in more passive forms of deprivation such as withdrawing from the infant or isolating the infant for long periods of time, (but *only* during times when they are not likely to be observed).

4. Failure-to-Thrive Syndrome. One of the most severe forms of maternal deprivation is associated with the non-organic failure-to-thrive syndrome. Infants measure below the third percentile in height and weight (on Stuart Growth Scales) in the absence of medical cause and appear apathetic and withdrawn.

It is hypothesized that as the mother deprives her infant of her emotional investment, the infant will react by refusing to eat or by regurgitating its food.

5. Maternal Deprivation and Child Abuse. Emotional detachment may be concomitant with abuse or neglect. It signals danger to the infant's safety, survival, and emotional well-being.

Bibliography. M. Ainsworth, "The Development of Mother-Infant Attachment," in Caudill, ed., *Review of Child Development Research* (1977), vol. 4, 1–94. T. B. Brazelton, "The Early Mother-Infant Adjustment," *Pediatrics*, 31 (1963), 931–37. S. Fraiberg, "Intervention in Infancy: A Program for Blind Infants," *J. of the American Academy of Child Psychiatry*, 10 (1971), 381–405. M. Lamb, "Paternal Influences and the Father's Role," *American Psychologist*, 34 (1979), 938–43. M. Lewis and L. Rosenblum, eds., *The Effect of the Infant on Its Caregiver* (1974). H. Rheingold, "The Modification of Social Responsiveness in Institutional Babies," in *Monographs of the Society for Research in Child Development*, 21 (1956), No. 63. R. Spitz, "Hospitalism: An Inquiry Into the Genesis of Psychiatric Conditions in Early Childhood," in A. Freud, ed., *Psychoanalytic Study of the Child*, vol. 1 (1945). D. Stern, *The First Relationship: Mother-Infant Interaction* (1977). A. Thomas, S. Chess, and H. Birch, *Behavioral Individuality in Early Childhood* (1963). D. Winnicott, "The Theory of Parent-Infant Relationship," *International J. of Psychoanalysis*, 41 (1960), 585–95.

G. ROWLAND

PARENTS/PARENTHOOD; PERSONALITY DEVELOPMENT, BIOLOGICAL AND SOCIALIZING INFLUENCES IN; PERSONALITY THEORY (Varieties, Traditions, and Issues); PSYCHOSOCIAL DEVELOPMENT. *Compare* DEVELOPMENTAL DISORDERS; FOSTER CHILDREN AND FOSTER PARENTS; MOTHER-INFANT BONDING.

MATRIMONY, SACRAMENT OF. One of the seven sacraments of the Roman Catholic and Eastern Orthodox churches. Unlike the other sacraments, it is the bride and groom themselves, and not a cleric, who are the ministers of the sacrament of matrimony in the Western churches. The marriage rite presumes that it is the couple who marry each other and that the church's function is to witness and bless the union. Although marriage is also an important liturgical action in the Protestant churches, the Reformers denied the historic link to the words and actions of Jesus necessary for standing as a sacrament.

To speak of matrimony as a sacrament is to set the marriage relationship within the context of the whole work of God in salvation history. Matrimony is considered a sign of the bond between Christ and the church, a great "mystery" (Eph. 5:32), and is understood as a call to holiness wherein the couple works out their salvation through the grace of God by following Christ and serving God's people. In the matrimonial covenant the couple establishes a partnership with each other and with Christ for the whole of life — a covenant characterized by unity, fidelity, and indissolubility reflecting Christ's love for the church (Eph. 5:25).

Ideally, preparation for matrimony deepens the faith given at baptism and nurtured by Christian upbringing. Pastoral care should focus on the couple's maturity, intention, freedom to marry, and understanding of the sacrament of matrimony. In the Catholic Church the Engaged Encounter program is widely used as an effective means of preparation for matrimony.

Bibliography. Documents of Vatican II, "Gaudium et Spes" (Pastoral Constitution on the Church in the Modern World) (1966), pp. 47–52; *Vatican Council II: More Postconciliar Documents,* "The Christian Family in the Modern World" (1982). M. Lawler, *Secular Marriage: Christian Sacrament* (1985).

J. MILLER
S. J. WHITE

MARRIAGE; WEDDING CEREMONY, CHRISTIAN. *See also* BLESSING AND BENEDICTION; RITUAL AND PASTORAL CARE; SACRAMENTAL THEOLOGY AND PASTORAL CARE, ROMAN CATHOLIC; VOWS/VOWING. *Compare* CATHOLIC-PROTESTANT MARRIAGE; JEWISH-CHRISTIAN MARRIAGE; ORTHODOX-CATHOLIC MARRIAGE; SACRAMENTS, ORDINANCES, AND RITES, TERMINOLOGY AND CONCEPTS OF.

MATURITY. *See* DEVELOPMENTAL THEORY AND PASTORAL CARE; INDIVIDUATION; PERSONALITY THEORY.

MATURITY, PASTOR'S. *See* MENTAL HEALTH, PASTOR'S. *See also* FAITH AND INTEGRITY, PASTOR'S; PERSONHOOD OF THE PASTOR, SIGNIFICANCE OF.

MAY, ROLLO (1909–   ). With interests in art, philosophy, and theology, this American-born psychologist has been a major influence in the development of existential psychology and psychotherapy. Initially a student of art, and then a pastor, May eventually moved into the field of psychology. As a student at Union Theological Seminary he was first exposed to existential thought by Tillich. He became enamored with the ideas of Kierkegaard and Heidegger. His books *The Meaning of Anxiety* (1950), and *Man's Search for Himself* (1953), detail his theory of personality and existential development. His writings and theories have become foundational in the development of humanistic psychology and the practice of existential therapy. While May is not antithetical to religion or spirituality, his writings have done little to bring together the religious nature of persons and their phenomenology of existence.

S. C. WILLIS

EXISTENTIAL PSYCHOLOGY AND PSYCHOTHERAPY; NEW YORK PSYCHOLOGY GROUP.

MBTI (Myers-Briggs Type Indicator). *See* EVALUATION AND DIAGNOSIS, PSYCHOLOGICAL.

McCOMB, SAMUEL. *See* EMMANUEL MOVEMENT.

McKNIGHT, EARLE. *See* CANADIAN ASSOCIATION OF PASTORAL CARE; CANADIAN PASTORAL CARE MOVEMENT.

MEANING. *See* INTERPRETATION AND HERMENEUTICS, PASTORAL.

MEANINGLESSNESS, SENSE OF. *See* ALIENATION/ESTRANGEMENT; EXISTENTIALISM; HOPE AND DESPAIR.

MEDIATION/CONCILIATION. Mediation is a dispute-resolution process in which an independent third party helps disputants to settle a conflict in a mutually acceptable fashion. The disputing parties, whether individuals or nations, are active participants. A goal-directed, problem-solving process, mediation occupies a position midway between self-help approaches and formal third-party decision-making processes. Mediation differs from formal litigation in that the process is voluntary; the mediator has no coercive power or authority to impose a settlement on the parties.

Conciliation is a term often used interchangeably with mediation; at other times, it is used to refer to a more unstructured process of facilitating communication between estranged parties.

Mediation and conciliation are perhaps best distinguished historically. In the family sphere, *conciliation* arose when the Los Angeles Family Conciliation Court was established in 1939, the first of a whole movement of conciliation services associated with domestic relations courts which grew up around the country; these affiliated in 1963 as The Association of Family and Conciliation Courts, an international association concerned with the provision of family counseling as a complement to judicial procedures. Family *mediation* developed as a broad movement in the 1980s, most significantly in the divorce mediation movement.

Along with ombudspersons, arbitration, and consumer complaint agencies, mediation has gained currency as there has been growing recognition of the difficulties and deficiencies involved in the heavy reliance in American society on the formal adversarial court system to handle disputes and to provide for social ordering. Proponents of mediation argue that among the benefits of the process are its privacy, informality, convenience, timeliness, lack of expense, and effectiveness. As Folberg (1984) comments: "It is ideally suited to polycentric disputes and conflicts between those with a continuing relationship, since it minimizes intrusion, emphasizes cooperation, involves self-determined criteria of resolution, and provides a model of interaction for future disputes" (p. 13). Research indicates that family mediation is effective in achieving higher levels of satisfaction and compliance with the agreements reached and in limiting the adverse impact of the conflict (Pearson, 1982).

1. Mediation: Limits and Issues. The very aspects of mediation that constitute its advantage over the adversarial system also embody its problematic areas. Since mediation is a private, informal process less controlled by statutory law, precedent, and rules of procedure, many people have raised concerns about its capacity to ensure a fair process and a just settlement. Many question whether mediation is not unduly subject to the unequal bargaining power of the respective parties involved.

There are other problems and limits to mediation. Some *disputes* are not amenable to mediation. "One cannot negotiate everything. Deeply cherished beliefs and values are simply not negotiable . . . Either we believe in God, capital punishment, and a woman's right to have an abortion or we do not. These views may change, but they are not negotiable" (Rubin, 135 – 6). Some *disputants* are unwilling or unable to employ mediation to resolve their conflict (e.g., the ideologically committed, the mentally ill, substance abusers). Mediation normally involves dealing directly with the other party. Some people find this too compromising, difficult, frightening, or painful and cannot or will not have their case mediated. However valuable, mediation is *one* form of dispute resolution, and it does not replace the need for a formal system of justice.

As a new field, family mediation lacks licensure or registration. Some people question whether it is or ought to be regarded as a separate profession. Turf questions abound. There is much debate about how to ensure adequate quality control. More broadly, there are questions about the ethics of bargaining and negotiating and about how to make mediation services available to people at all income levels.

2. Divorce and Family Mediation. The major American organization of neutrals, SPIDR (Society of Professionals in Dispute Resolution), includes mediators working in labor, community, and environmental mediation. In the context of the social revolution in which American society averages one million divorces a year, however, the most rapid expansion of mediation services and the area most relevant to pastoral care is that of divorce and family mediation. (Prior to 1981, the Family Mediation Association had one hundred members nationally; by the mid-1980s, several thousand divorce mediators had been trained.)

Conducted by mediators with training in family law, the divorce process, conflict management and family systems and therapy, divorce mediation deals with family disputes relating to a decision to separate or divorce. Its end product is a memorandum of agreement, a written document detailing the agreements reached with regard to the division of marital property, spousal and child support, and child custody and parental access.

3. Mediation and the Church. The history of religious involvement in family dispute processing is inadequately documented. However, examples include the *bet din*, Jewish courts which date back to biblical times. A broadscale contemporary expression of church involvement in family mediation is the evangelical Christian Conciliation Service, a ministry of the Christian Legal Society, organized in 1961, and now a national network which attempts to offer mediation and arbitration of disputes "based upon a biblical mandate and spiritual principles."

The modern pastoral care movement, however, has involved itself only minimally with mediation. The tendency of the church to view conflict as a negative phenomenon to be avoided contributes to this reluctance. This seems unfortunate since there appears to be not only historical precedent but also theological rationale for such activity. An examination of the biblical concept of *shalom* and the Christian doctrines of reconciliation and forgiveness would seem to give warrant to the claim that conflict resolution and mediation represent two contemporary forms of reconciliation and healing as expressions of the classic mission of the church and the work of the pastor (cf. II Cor. 5:17–20; Mt. 18:15–17; 5:22–24; I Cor. 6:1–5; Eph. 2:13–17).

Pastors ought not to assume, however, that they can do mediation without special training. Specific skills are necessary. When referrals are to be made, mediators may often be located through local or state (family) mediation councils or through such national organizations as the Academy of Family Mediators (for family mediation) and SPIDR (for other forms of mediation).

As American society seeks more effective and informal means of social ordering and dispute resolution, pastors have an opportunity to involve themselves in mediation as a significant mode of ministry: Lon Fuller (1971, p. 328) speaks of this opportunity in his description of the "central quality of mediation, namely, its capacity to reorient the parties toward each other, not by imposing rules on them, but by helping them to achieve a new and shared perception of their relationship, a perception that will redirect their attitudes and dispositions toward one another."

Bibliography. L. Buzzard and R. Kraybill, *Mediation: A Reader* (1980). L. Buzzard and L. Eck, *Tell It to the Church* (1982). R. Fisher and W. Ury, *Getting to Yes* (1981). J. Folberg and A. Taylor, *Mediation* (1984). L. Fuller, "Mediation: Its Forms and Functions," *Southern California Law Review*, 44 (1971), 305–39. J. Haynes, *Divorce Mediation* (1981). R. Kraybill, *Repairing The Breach* (1980). S. Leas and P. Kittlaus, *Church Fights* (1973). J. Pearson and N. Thoennes, "The Benefits Outweight the Costs," *Family Advocate* (1982), 26 – 32. J. Rubin, "Negotiation," *American Behavioral Scientist* (1983), 135 – 6. D. Saposnek, *Mediating Child Custody Disputes* (1983).

C. D. SCHNEIDER

CHRISTIAN CONCILIATION MOVEMENT; CONFLICT AND CONFLICT MANAGEMENT; RECONCILING. *Compare* DISAGREEMENT, DIFFERENCE, AND CONFLICT IN PASTOR-PARISHIONER RELATIONSHIPS; DIVORCE (Care and Counseling); FAMILY VIOLENCE; FORGIVENESS; PROBLEM SOLVING.

MEDICAL-ETHICAL DILEMMAS. *See* MORAL DILEMMAS IN PASTORAL PERSPECTIVE. *See also* DEATH, MORAL DILEMMAS IN; INFERTILITY THERAPIES.

MEDICAL-ETHICAL DILEMMAS, JEWISH CARE AND COUNSELING IN. Jewish medical ethics includes both soft (psychosocial) and hard (medical) issues of the physician-patient relationship and their decision-making process. The soft issues reflect the dignity of all persons *qua* human beings regardless of their socio-economic status or quality of life. The dignity of the individual is beautifully summarized in the physician's prayer attributed to Moses Maimonides (1135–1204):

> . . . Inspire me with love for my art and for Thy creatures. Do not allow thirst for profit, ambition for renown and admiration, to interfere with my profession, for these are the enemies of truth and of love for mankind and they can lead astray in the great task of attending to the welfare of Thy creatures. Preserve the strength of my body and of my soul that they ever be ready to cheerfully help and support rich and poor, good and bad, enemy as well as friend. In the sufferer let me see only the human being . . . (*The Bulletin of the Johns Hopkins Hospital,* 28 [1917] pp. 256–61).

The hard issues require an analysis and ultimately a resolution among contrasting religious and secular value systems.

1. Major Principles. Three major principles, based on biblical statements, underlie Jewish responses to issues in medical ethics: (1) Gen. 1:27 states that God created the human being in the image of God, thus differentiating human life from all other living matter. This uniqueness of persons is the basis of the major Jewish principle that human life has *infinite* value. Since infinity is indivisible, even an infinitesimal fraction of a person's life is also of infinite value. Nor is human life or the value of human life dependent on any external criterion. Human life is an absolute value.

(2) The *aging* process, from birth to death, represents a normal, non-pathological unfolding of human development. Although physiological and other psychological and sociological factors change with time, aging is not a disease. A ninety-year-old woman has the same right to life as someone aged nine or nineteen. Indeed aging is the anticipated blessing and reward for living an ethical and pious life (Exod. 20:12). Respect for the aged is prominently commended (Lev. 19:32) and rabbinic sages are frequently referred to as "elders." The Talmud (Kiddushin 32b) understands the word "aged" or "elderly" to epitomize mature wisdom of life experience. The absolute value of human life is not predicated on one's age, pragmatic utility, or even upon the potential for service to fellow human beings.

Similarly, the inevitability of *illness* is a basic assumption of life. The Bible places double emphasis on the necessary safeguards that one should take in caring for oneself (Deut. 4:9, 15). Whenever illness occurs, Judaism requires the patient to seek medical assistance. Although the proper observance of all the Jewish laws, such as fasting on Yom Kippur (Day of Atonement) or the observance of the Sabbath is very important, proper care of one's physical and mental health always has priority when a person's health is threatened. Avoidance of the harmful becomes a religious commandment subsumed under the guiding principle of taking good care of oneself (Deut. 4:15). The Code of Jewish Law (Joseph Karo, Orah Hayyim 329:3) summarizes this thesis by stating that all laws of the Torah (except the cardinal three of idolatry, murder, and forbidden sexual relations) are suspended when the possibility arises that one's life is in danger. Even hesitation in evaluating whether the danger to life is significant or not is deemed inappropriate.

The Bible grants specific permission and indeed mandates the physician to heal (Exod. 21:19; Lev. 19:16, 18;

25:35; Deut. 22:2). In this manner physician and patient become "partners with God" in attempting to conquer illness. At the end of the creation story (Gen. 2:3) God ceased from all his work which he had "*created to do.*" The Midrash (homiletical Biblical commentary, Gen. Rabbah 2:3) asks what is meant by the phrase "*created to do.*" The Midrash replies that God created the world with much more left to do. The work of creation is in a continuous process. When one creates by conquering illness such as curing infections one becomes a partner with God. According to Jewish tradition, the human response to illness is to be responsible for oneself and for one's neighbor. Health care was placed first by Maimonides among the ten important communal services that had to be offered by a city to its residents (Mishnah Torah, Sefer Hamadda 4:23).

(3) Although the reality of *death* destroys the individual physically, the idea of death confers meaning on life. An awareness of death moves one away from trivial preoccupations and concerns and provides life with a sense of depth, substance, and perspective. Death itself is considered to be "good." "And God saw everything that he had made, and behold, it was very good" (Gen. 1:31). The Midrash comments that the phrase "very good" includes death (Gen. Rabbah 9:5). Indeed, the dying process begins with birth. Rabbi Eliezer states (Mishnah, Avot 2:10): "repent one day before your death," to which the Talmud comments (Shabbat 153a): "Rabbi Eliezer's disciples asked him, 'Does one know when one is going to die?' He said to them, ' No, then certainly one should repent today, because maybe one will die tomorrow, thus, one will always be in the process of repenting.' "

Even when one is healthy one can and should be aware that life is finite. A healthy awareness of life's finiteness should constantly lead one to search for a meaningful existence. A terminal illness only accentuates the reality and imminence of death and urges a more acute focus on the duration of time left before one dies. If there were no death, there would be no illness or aging. Succinctly stated, without death there is no life.

The exact time of one's death is not known beforehand. This fact is part of the gift of life and gift of death. It is both the known and the unknown which together endow life with the potential for finding meaning. The known aspect is that death is the common denominator of all of humankind; the unknown is the exact time of death. Together these allow death continually to endow life with meaning.

The Bible states the reason why life is finite: "And God said: My spirit shall not abide in man forever, for he is flesh; and his days shall be a hundred and twenty years" (Gen. 6:3). God specifically created human beings with diametrically opposed entities, spirit and flesh, which cannot coexist eternally. God created people who would ultimately die. Death is the natural outgrowth of the lack of compatibility of flesh and spirit; death is the natural outcome of life.

One of the goals of the practice of medicine is constantly to improve the patient's quality of life. Human beings are given the choice to choose between life or death, blessing or curse, good or evil. The Bible commands that people should "choose life" (Deut. 30:15–19). Jewish medical ethics is rooted in the doctrine of human responsibility. Within the limitations of heredity and environment, everyone is a free agent to choose order over chaos, homeostasis over disequilibrium, and family over a life of solitude. In Hebrew the word for life (*Hayyim*) is always in the plural, representing the ultimate goal of life which is living in tranquility with others.

Despite the fact that medical and mental health professionals strive for the improvement of the patient's life, quality of life is never a factor in determining whether a patient should live or die. The sanctity of life is inviolable. Subjective considerations, either by the patient, physician, or family cannot allow either homicide, suicide, or fratricide (Gen. 9:6). The reality of pain, suffering, and anguish requires compassion, support groups, pain medication, and whatever else may ameliorate the patient's condition, but not the termination of the life. Naturally, this does not preclude the patient's choice to refuse further treatment if the risk-benefit ratio is not favorable and may hasten the patient's death.

2. *Implications.* Every medical-ethical dilemma requires its own analysis and resolution. However, based on these three major principles of Jewish medical ethics, two examples, one from the beginning of life and one from the end of life, will be offered on how these principles are reflected in actual situations.

An *abortion*, the killing of potential human life, is allowed and even mandated if the life or health of the mother is gravely threatened. However, for most other reasons, an abortion is prohibited. The stated rationale for this ruling (Mishnah, Oholot 7,6) is that the mother's actual life takes precedence over the *potential* human life of the fetus. This overriding concern for the welfare of the mother is prior to the birth of the fetus. From the moment of birth, the life of both the infant and the mother is absolute.

Since the human being is created in the image of God, it is sacred. It may not be terminated because of considerations of the patient's suffering. *Suicide* and *euthanasia* are both prohibited under the category of homicide. A physician is committed to prolong the life of a patient and to try to cure the patient. It makes no difference whether the life prolonged is of long or short duration. An exception is made (permitting passive euthanasia) only for the case of a person who is defined by Jewish law as a moribund patient and the death process has actually begun. Euthanasia, even when it is motivated by compassion (designed to put an end to unbearable pain), is tantamount to murder (Gen. 9:6). Naturally, everything should be done to alleviate the patient's suffering (Lev. 19:18), but not at the sacrifice of the sanctity of life.

Bibliography. J. D. Bleich, *Contemporary Halakhic Problems*, 2 vols. (1977–1983). D. M. Feldman, *Health and Medicine in the Jewish tradition* (1986). I. Jakobovits, *Jewish Medical Ethics*, 2d ed. (1975). L. Meier, *Jewish Values in Bioethics* (1986). F. Rosner, *Modern Medicine and Jewish Ethics* (1986). R. Schindler, "Truth Telling and Terminal Illness: A Jewish View," *J. of Religion and Health*, 21 (1982), 42–48.

L. MEIER

ETHICS AND PASTORAL CARE; JEWISH CARE AND COUNSELING; MORAL DILEMMAS IN PASTORAL PERSPECTIVE. *See also* ABORTION; FAMILY PLANNING; INFERTILITY; SICK AND DYING, JEWISH CARE OF. *Compare* CONSCIENCE (Jewish); GUIDANCE, PASTORAL; VALUES IN COUNSELING AND PSYCHOTHERAPY.

MEDICINE, RELIGION, AND PASTORAL CARE. *See* HEALING. *See also* HEALTH AND ILLNESS; RELIGION AND HEALTH MOVEMENT; SALVATION, HEALING, AND HEALTH, THEOLOGY OF; WHOLISTIC HEALTH CARE.

MEDIEVAL CHURCH, PASTORAL CARE IN. The care of souls (from Latin: *cura animarum*) as exercised by Christian pastors in the Middle Ages (ca. A.D. 500–1500) in Western Europe. Four general types of activity are encompassed by the term: healing, sustaining, teaching (later guiding), and reconciling.

The care of souls, like all human activities, is done by individuals acting within a specific social context. The actions themselves are motivated by similar desires and goals throughout human history, but they take very different forms as individuals attempt to heal, sustain, teach, and reconcile within the particular social milieu which constitutes their world. We improve our own pastoral abilities in so far as we can appreciate the ways in which other pastors in other historical circumstances chose to exercise the care of souls.

1. **The Early Middle Ages (500–1000).** By the sixth century, the urban-oriented civilization of Rome was being rapidly displaced in Western Europe by groups of people whose primary loyalties were to their individual tribes, and whose values were shaped by family traditions and the exigencies of a rural life. The methods of patristic soul care developed under the Empire had to be adapted to meet the expectations and requirements of this changing society.

A medieval writer at the end of this early period described his society as comprising three groups: those who pray, those who fight, and those who farm. Each group had its own needs and interests with respect to pastoral care. Those who pray were the secular clergy of the cathedral centers and the monks in monasteries being founded throughout Europe. Pope Gregory I (d. 604), wrote his *Pastoral Care* for the former, and Benedict of Nursia (d. ca. 550) wrote his monastic *Rule* for the latter. These works and the pastoral activities they inspired remained normative throughout this period for the education of those whose primary function was to preserve their society through prayer.

Those who fight were the tribal and feudal leaders whose skills-at-arms were highly prized in a society where physical security as well as economic well-being often depended on them. One of their interests was to make available the best religion possible for themselves and for the people under them. Each individual, of course, had his or her own notion of what constituted the best religion, but in general they were interested in a religion which would sanctify the land and the people, and intercede with God for divine aid in times of war and peace. To attain this they turned increasingly from their old religions and embraced the pastoral care of the Christians, establishing churches and chapels on their own land (*Eigenkirchen*), and encouraging monks to establish communities there.

Those who farm constituted the bulk of the population in this period. For them, as for their leaders, religion was not a separate facet of their lives. Pastoral care was inextricably interwoven with their daily activities. As their existence was closely bound to the land and the natural cycle of the seasons, the church calendar took on great importance. The rhythms of pastoral care, with its saint's days and seasonal fasts, its greater festivals, and its rituals of tithes, blessings, and sacraments, reflected this life.

The most striking characteristics of pastoral care in this period are those which tended to fall out of favor during the modern age. For example, soul care was directed less toward personal conversion and internal self-examination than toward the safeguarding of God's presence among the faithful. This was done primarily through rites and rituals, many of which were Christianized consolidations of pre-Christian practices. To dismiss these as "empty" and "superstitious" is to ignore some of the most common ways that God has acted in human history, and to mistake the purposes of pastoral care in this period. The goal of most Christians was not to become holy, but to be in contact with the holy. Even monks and priests saw themselves as ministers of holy things rather than as holy men. In our own concern with internal states of holiness we often tend to overlook the actions of God which are independent of our intellectual comprehension and our particular emotional receptivity. The following brief survey will illustrate some of the ways by which soul care brought Christians into contact with the Holy.

a. Healing. Early medieval healing took three basic forms, all of them closely tied to pastoral care. The actions performed were not viewed as magical but as normal or natural rites of healing. The implicit pastoral concern was to point individuals to the true sources of healing power inherent in the created world, in sacred objects, and in words which mediated divine power. One type of healing was through Christianized folk medicine — the use of oils, holy water, herbs, stones, the sign of the cross, incantations—to restore health to the sufferer. A second method involved contact with relics known to have been closely associated with divine activity in the past. A third, the use of prayers and exorcisms which could invoke a panoply of divine powers, from God, Mary, and the angels, down to the saints and protectors of the local community. That such powers were efficacious was a matter of personal experience to many, and was reinforced by innumerable stories beginning with those of Jesus' own ministry.

b. Sustaining. The work of sustaining was the primary activity of "those who pray." The wealth, authority, and prestige of monasticism in this period testifies to the high value placed on the regular life of prayer as a means of sustaining the whole population. In addition to relying on the vicarious prayers of monks and clergy, people could turn to a wide range of sacramental rites and rituals for sustenance in every conceivable aspect of their existence. There were blessings for all of the community's produce, for important staples such as salt, butter, and cheese, for eggs at Easter, gold at Epiphany, candles on various feasts, and seed at planting time. So too, God's power was brought to bear at all the stages of one's life, from before birth, through the first haircut and the first shave, in marrying and establishing a new household, in caring for the dying and for the dead.

c. Teaching. The ability to read and write was not a highly prized skill in this period. Books were more important as repositories of holy writ (relics in their own right) than as educational tools. Pastoral teaching and guidance took place, instead, through recurrent ritual actions, through art, and especially through the oral traditions of poetry and storytelling. The Bible played a central role. It was a health-giving relic of great power. It was learned by heart through liturgical repetition in the monasteries and churches. Its stories were translated into artistic images, and incorporated into the oral traditions at every level of society. The representations of tribal life in Genesis, Joshua, Judges, etc. were especially meaningful to the tribal peoples of Western Europe, and as they, like the Israelites, developed stronger monarchies, the Books of Kings and the Prophets became crucial to their own self-understanding. The stories of Jesus, of creation, and of apocalypse proved to be of timeless interest, and were adapted and used throughout the period. Pastoral teaching consisted less in explaining or interpreting the Christian tradition than in illustrating through ritual and example how God had acted in history, and how one should act toward God.

d. Reconciling. Reconciliation of individuals to God and to each other took place in many ways. In a society that emphasized the separateness and uniqueness of different tribes and people, pastors were able to find a common ground for reconciliation in the shared Christian faith. Individuals, too, were reconciled with each other and with their community through pastoral mediation. This was a period when God could still be asked to judge directly concerning an individual's guilt or innocence through ordeals and other judicial proceedings supervised by the clergy. The rite of public penance was also used to reconcile notorious criminals or sinners to God and to the community. But it was the invention of private penance — a secret confession of sins to a priest— that was to prove one of the most potent methods of reconciliation (the Penitential Tradition). Such a confession required individuals to take responsibility for their actions, and to perform a penance which would reestablish them in a right relationship to the holy powers at work in their community and in the world.

2. The Later Middle Ages (1000–1500). For many people living in isolated rural areas the requirements and provisions of pastoral care remained much the same, even into the nineteenth and twentieth centuries. But as medieval society changed, a new shape and direction was given to pastoral care. The division of society into those who pray, those who fight, and those who farm, was being supplanted by the more familiar hierarchy of the Three Estates: the clergy (i.e. the ecclesiastical nobles), the nobility (the secular nobles), and the bourgeoisie (the important townspeople). This last group was quite new as a powerful and respectable force in society, and many of the new directions in pastoral care were taken with them in mind.

Two new sources of pastoral care emerged in this period. On the one hand were the networks of new religious orders—the Cluniacs, Cistercians, and Regular

Canons during the eleventh and twelfth centuries, and the Mendicant Orders (Franciscans, Dominicans, etc.) in the thirteenth. Each provided new perspectives on pastoral care, and the Regular Canons and Mendicants in particular tended to focus their attention on meeting and shaping the pastoral needs of town dwellers. A second source of pastoral care which came into prominence in this period was the parish priest. This individual came to be seen as the primary provider of soul care throughout Europe. He was expected to exercise a number of pastoral functions such as preaching, teaching, and disciplining, which had previously been expected only of bishops and learned members of monastic communities.

Most striking in this period is the emergence of "scientific" or learned approaches to soul care. When the Fourth Lateran Council (1215) described soul care as "the art of arts," it was suggesting that this activity was the most important of all the liberal arts and sciences which were being studied in the schools and universities springing up throughout Europe. This marks the beginning of the modern expectation that all pastors, even the local priest, should ideally receive formal academic training for exercising the functions of soul care.

a. Healing. Two types of trained healers emerged in this period: medical practitioners for treating physical ailments, and pastors for spiritual ones. Concerning physical diseases, people began to distinguish more sharply between natural and supernatural (miraculous) healings, the latter being unusual and noteworthy, but seldom subject to pastoral intervention. Priests concentrated instead on healing ailments of the soul. One of their most successful diagnostic tools was the list of the seven vices—pride, envy, wrath, sloth, avarice, gluttony, and lust—which infect the soul and impede healthy human actions.

b. Sustaining. Modern notions of Word and Sacrament as the two primary ways of sustaining the faithful emerged in this period. The sermon became, for the first time in centuries, a popular and widely exercised form of pastoral care. Much attention was paid in the schools to the most effective ways of preaching to the many different kinds of audiences (clerics, nobles, citizens, merchants, even prostitutes) which the pastor might encounter. The myriad sacramental rites and rituals of the earlier period also were studied carefully, and seven major sacraments—baptism, confirmation, penance, Eucharist, Holy Orders, marriage, and Extreme Unction—were distinguished as the sources and archetypes of all the others. In keeping with the academic interests of the period, pastors were expected not only to administer the sacraments correctly, but also to understand and to be able to explain as accurately as possible the ways in which God's sustaining grace was mediated through these sacramental acts.

c. Teaching. As formal education and book learning became more prestigious, simple priests and, eventually, the laity began to desire a learned understanding of their faith. Only at the end of this period did lay people begin to attend the schools and universities themselves, but they increasingly required that their pastors should share with them some of the fruits of the new learning. Two sources of pastoral teaching were most important. The first was the Bible. In the schools of theology all of the academic resources, from grammar and logic to physics and philosophy, were brought to bear on understanding and elucidating the Scriptures. Making this learning available to non-scholars was one of the most widely pursued pastoral activities of the period. A second source of pastoral teaching was the Law. The study of ancient Roman law and Canon or Church Law (which includes the decisions of Church Councils, the writings of the Fathers, and the teaching of the Bible) enabled pastors to apply the accumulated wisdom of the natural world, of Christian tradition, and of revelation to guiding human actions in the new circumstances of a changing society.

d. Reconciling. Private penance became, in this period, the primary means of reconciling Christians with each other and with God. The particular appeal of this personal admission of sins to a priest lay, at least in part, in allowing ordinary Christians to participate actively and intellectually in this reconciliation. The act of penance was analyzed into three constituent elements, each of which required a conscious exercise of intellect and will on the part of the person confessing. First was contrition, a genuine remorse for injuries done to God, to neighbor, and to self. Next was confession, a full and ingenuous admission of one's personal responsibility for these injuries. Finally came satisfaction, the acts one undertook to make amends for the damage done by sinning. The priest, as spiritual guide and judge, found one of his most challenging tasks in the administration of this sacrament of reconciliation.

Bibliography. K. Bosl, *Regularkanoniker (Augustinerchorherren) und Seelsorge in Kirche und Gesellschaft des europäischen 12. Jahrhunderts* (1979). W. Clebsch and C. Jaekle, *Pastoral Care in Historical Perspective: An Essay with Exhibits* (1964). J. T. McNeill, *Medieval Handbooks of Penance* (1965). For a more immediate experience of medieval soul care consult the monastic *Rule* of St. Benedict, Gregory the Great's *Pastoral Care*, and Chaucer's "Parson's Tale" in the *Canterbury Tales*.

J. GOERING

PASTORAL CARE (History, Traditions, and Definitions). *See also* CARE OF SOULS (*Cura Animarum*); ETHICS AND PASTORAL CARE; PHILOSOPHY AND PSYCHOLOGY, WESTERN; ROMAN CATHOLIC PASTORAL CARE. *Compare* EARLY CHURCH, PASTORAL CARE AND COUNSELING IN; ISLAMIC CARE AND COUNSELING; JEWISH CARE AND COUNSELING (History, Traditions, and Contemporary Issues); MINISTRY AND PASTORAL CARE (Orthodox Tradition).

MEDIEVAL JEWISH CARE AND THEOLOGY. *See* JEWISH CARE AND COUNSELING; JUDAISM AND PSYCHOLOGY; JEWISH LITERATURE IN CARE AND COUNSELING.

MEDITATION.
Exercises for concentrating upon objects of devotion, for example, a verse of Scripture, an attribute of God or a divine name. Meditation is the "laboratory work" in which persons can come to know themselves in relation to the divine. Prerequisites include proper preparation of the body and a relaxed yet concentrated mind. Prayer as the meeting of persons with God is a form of meditation. Secularized forms of meditation are used in contemporary society for therapy and relaxation.

Psychologically, there are two general types of meditation. (1) *Concentrative meditations* seek to restrict awareness by the focusing of attention on an object (e.g., a cross) or a word (e.g., "Jesus"). (2) *External awareness meditations*, on the other hand, aim at a deliberate "opening-up" of one's awareness of the external environment. Some Eastern religions teach a third type — so-called "middle way"—which focuses on a mental state emptied of all thoughts or perceptions (e.g. the objectless *samādhi* of Patanjali's *Yoga Sūtras*).

1. **Concentrative Meditation.** This type has appeared in a variety of forms. In visual meditation, the meditator gazes at the object continually; in auditory meditation, the sound, chant, or prayer is repeated either aloud or silently. If physical movement is involved, the movement is continually repeated. In each case, awareness is concentrated on the movement, the sound, or the visual object as a means for making contact with the divine.

Sensory deprivation and environmental manipulation have been used to help achieve the required single-pointed mental focus. Following the Syrian desert fathers, many Christian meditators have sought out a solitary existence as hermits in order to better concentrate their minds upon God. At times the results border on hallucination and delusional states, perhaps due to the severity of their self-imposed deprivations. Manipulation of the environment occurs in Ignatius Loyola's *Spiritual Exercises* in which the retreat master, in a series of systematic meditations, urges the meditator to imagine as vividly as possible the excruciating sufferings of Jesus at various stages of the cross and to identify with Jesus' agonies until they are "lived" within one's own experience. The simplicity of monastic cells, the maintenance of silence, the lack of personal property and restrictions upon visits from family are all aspects of the traditional monastic rule aimed at shifting the center of gravity within one's personality from the individual ego to God. The psychological process involves both reduced sensory stimulation and a concentrated focusing of thoughts.

In meditative prayer the same concentrative process is observed. The postures assumed, the setting chosen (e.g., "the privacy of one's own closet"), the closing of the eyes and folding of hands all function to reduce distracting external stimuli and promote a focused mind. The use of set opening phrases and patterns of praying (e.g., adoration, confession, thanksgiving, etc.) help to induce the desired mental state until the prayer becomes spontaneous and totally absorbing. Sometimes single-word prayers are employed so that the various mental images created by many words do not distract the mind from worship. In this approach the use of a single word such as "Jesus" keeps the mind concentrated. The Prayer of the Heart in the Orthodox tradition is a method for keeping one's entire self attentive to Jesus. Meditative breathing is also prescribed. The mind is concentrated and led along the path of the breath until the breath and mind are said to enter the heart together. There the "Jesus prayer," "Lord Jesus Christ, Son of God, have mercy upon me," is constantly repeated.

Jacob Böhme and St. John of the Cross prescribed concentrative meditative exercises very similar to those of Eastern yoga. Böhme practiced fixing his gaze on a spot of sunlight on his cobbler's crystal. He then carried this image with him mentally. John of the Cross taught the withdrawal of thoughts from outward and material things, including the body and its five senses. Memory

and all forms of knowledge are to be negated until the soul is left bare, ready for communion with God.

The common element throughout these various concentrative practices is the active restriction of awareness to a single unchanging process, and the withdrawal of attention from ordinary thought. The psychological state achieved is characterized by non-responsiveness to the external world as a result of the continuous recycling of the subroutine in the nervous system.

2. **External Awareness Meditation.** Opposite to concentrative meditational exercises are those forms which seek to open up one's awareness and put one more intensely in contact with God as manifested in the external environment. Rather than isolating one from ordinary life, opening-up exercises directly involve the everyday in the training of awareness. An example is the Benedictine discipline of "listening" to the world. Benedictine listening is based on the belief that God speaks through nature and history, and the human heart is called to listen and to respond. Listening in this sense involves the whole personality — senses, thoughts and emotions — and the monk attempts to experience every event as a Word of God to be heard and responded to in obedience. The attentive peeling and eating of an orange, for example, can bring awareness of God's sustaining stewardship; the taking of a friend's hand pledges a relationship in which love's sacrifice and celebration may be called forth. Even calamity and tragedy are to be listened to as God's word. Such sincere listening is promoted by the silence and simplicity of monastic life. In the Benedictine view, this kind of responsive listening will bring life into harmony with the divine rhythm of seasons—with God's time rather than our time. Through such opening-up comes the understanding of oneself as a word spoken out of the Creator's heart and at the same time addressed by the Creator.

Another Christian form of this "listening with the heart" meditation is the Quaker practice of individual and congregational silence, which would seem to be a Protestant version of Benedictine spirituality. Such Christian forms of "opening-up meditation," it may be added, bear many formal similarities to Buddhist Zen practice.

3. **Religious Understanding and Appropriation.** In Christian theology meditation is understood to depend for its result on the action of God's grace. It is the action of the Holy Spirit within the soul and the presence of God in the external world which, theologically, give both types of meditation their transforming or enlightening power. Moreover, biblical support for meditation can be found in Jesus' regular withdrawal to go into the hills. After being alone with the Father he then returned refreshed to meet the challenge of the crowds.

Recognizing the need for such practices in the stress and strain of modern life, secular psychology has recently produced a variety of therapies (e.g., Gestalt Therapy) that represent secularized versions of classical religious meditative disciplines; for example, certain forms of humanistic and transpersonal psychology have championed the expansion of human potential through meditative techniques like biofeedback.

There is little doubt that everyone from Olympic athletes to business executives can obtain practical benefits from secularized versions of meditation. However, relaxation and therapeutic benefits are side effects, not the essential purpose of meditation. The removal of meditative practices from their traditional religious contexts robs them of their most significant power—the unifying of life with ultimate truth. Furthermore, the modern tendency to graft the meditative practices of one tradition onto another (e.g., yoga onto Christianity) will likely produce more confusion and distortion of religious traditions than spiritual benefit. Yoga, for example, is a meditative practice that presupposes a metaphysical world view fundamentally different from that of the Western biblical tradition.

A more integrated experience may be achieved if Christians and others adopt and develop meditative practices native to their own religious tradition. Christians in Western culture are looking to Eastern religion or to the secularized meditations of modern psychology in order to fulfill a need in their own practice of faith. Thus, there is a need for the development of Christian meditative disciplines in the Western world.

Bibliography. H. Coward, "Jung's Encounter With Yoga," *The J. of Analytical Psychology,* 23 (1978), 339–57. H. Coward and T. Penelhum, eds., *Mystics and Scholars* (1977). J. Davidson and R. Davidson, eds., *The Psychobiology of Consciousness* (1980). D. A. Helminiak, "Meditation—Psychologically and Theologically Considered," *Pastoral Psychology,* 30 (1981), 6–20. W. Johnson, *Silent Music* (1974). C. Jung, *Letters,* G. Adler, ed. (1973). C. Naranjo and R. Ornstein, *On the Psychology of Meditation* (1971). J. Needleman, *Consciousness and Tradition* (1982). R. Ornstein, *The Psychology of Consciousness,* 2d ed. (1977). J. Woods, *The Yoga System of Patanjali,* 3d ed. (1977).

H. COWARD

PRAYER; SPIRITUAL DISCIPLINE AND GROWTH; PSYCHOLOGY AND PSYCHOTHERAPY (East-West Comparison); WORSHIP AND CELEBRATION. *Compare* JOURNAL KEEPING; PRIVACY AND SOLITUDE; RELAXATION, PSYCHOLOGY AND TECHNIQUES OF; REST AND RENEWAL, RELIGIOUS TRADITIONS OF; SILENCE.

MEDIUMS/SORCERERS. *See* PARAPSYCHOLOGY; SPIRITUALISM; SURVIVAL (Occult); WITCHCRAFT.

MEEKNESS. *See* ANGER AND MEEKNESS.

MELANCHOLY. *See* SADNESS AND DEPRESSION.

MEMORIAL SERVICE. A service marking a death without the body of the deceased present; an alternative to the funeral. Usually in this pattern the body is cremated or buried shortly after death, and a memorial service is held a week or more later.
1. **Motivations.** A memorial service can reduce the emotional stress of mourners by delaying the public service until acute grief has subsided and by avoiding the emotional stimulation of the presence of the body of the deceased. However, the delay can also simply serve the utilitarian purpose of allowing family and friends at a distance to gather at a convenient time.

Because of the immediate disposition of the body of the deceased no expense for embalming or other preparation of the body is incurred, and inexpensive, utilitarian coffins can be used. Other economies are achieved by having no viewing, no floral tributes, no funeral procession. In a number of communities memorial societies will assist in making arrangements.

The memorial service places emphasis on life rather than on the conjunction of life and death. The physical is deemphasized in favor of an approach that is more intellectual and spiritual.
2. **Pastoral Responsibilities.** The same objectives for ministry are present in the memorial service as in the more traditional funeral service. The memorial service, like the funeral, is an integral part of the mourning process. The service enables effective mourning by reinforcing the reality of the loss, supporting the remembering process, facilitating the expression of feelings, providing community support, and relating the experience of loss to the meanings that the faith community has given to death and its consequences.

Memorial services should be conducted in ways that acknowledge candidly the fact of mortality. A brief committal service with the family present at the time of burial or cremation helps this process. It is important that death not be ignored but be seen as a part of life.

Because the service is planned without the presence of the body of the deceased, it is helpful to include in the service appropriate personal references to the life *and death* of the individual. Display of a picture of the deceased helps support the remembering process. Special attention should be given to providing adequate community support during the privatized period of acute grief as well as during and after the memorial service. Mourners should be assured of the naturalness of their grief and given permission to express themselves autonomously.

The pastor should assess from family contacts the major reasons for planning a memorial service. When strong intentions for avoiding grief work or evading the reality of death are present, the pastor will want to plan the memorial service to redirect mourners toward more therapeutic goals.

Bibliography. P. E. Irion, *The Funeral: Vestige or Value?* (1977 [1966]). R. M. Harmer, "Funerals, Fantasy, and Flight," *Omega,* 2 (1971) 127–35. E. Morgan, *A Manual for Death Education and Simple Burial,* 8th ed. (1977).

P. E. IRION

FUNERAL. *See also* CREMATION; MOURNING CUSTOMS AND RITUALS; WORSHIP AND CELEBRATION.

MEMORIAL SOCIETY. Usually an organization of people who choose for themselves a limited form of ceremonial process at the time of death. This is usually done to reduce expense and to limit the forms of acting out that are considered to be undesirable and unnecessary. A questionnaire of memorial society members showed that they were well educated, apt to be affluent, and less inclined to believe in immortality. They organize and bargain collectively with funeral directors to provide services usually at less than cost. Proponents claim a more rational approach to death and grief with an escape from morbidity and an opportunity for a less emotional and more intellectual attitude.

E. N. JACKSON

FUNERAL. *See also* BURIAL; CREMATION.

MEMORIES, HEALING OF. *See* HEALING OF MEMO-
RIES.

MEMORY. The re-expression in consciousness or
behavior of previous experiences or learned associations.
We remember persons, events, verbal statements, ideas
and images, autonomic (visceral) responses, and motor
skills. The following description will focus on what is
known as episodic memory, that is, memory for life
events. However, many of the principles apply equally
well to motor and visceral memories.

There are three commonly recognized forms of memory that are differentiated from one another by their
duration in time. (1) *Sensory Memory* is very brief (less
than one second). It preserves an exact replica (a visual
"icon" or auditory "echo") of sensory experience in the
nervous system long enough to be scanned and processed
in such a way as to bring only certain aspects of sensory
experience into conscious attention. (2) *Short-Term Memory* (STM) is the immediate awareness of what just
happened—the consciousness of the last few minutes of
experience. STM is also considered by some to be the
working space of the conscious mind (much like the
working registers in a computer), where information
from past experience is brought from permanent memory
into consciousness for thinking and problem solving.
(3) *Long-Term Memory* (LTM) is what we typically refer to
as "memory" (e.g., remembering an old friend's name,
even though one has not seen or thought of him or her for
ten years).

For a past event to be remembered, it must not only
have been perceived and stored originally, but it must
also be re-expressed in some form in consciousness. Thus,
there are two equally important processes in LTM: registration in the memory store, called *encoding,* and *retrieval*
of the item from the memory store.

1. Short-Term Memory. STM has both time and quantity limits. Items cannot stay in STM for more than a few
minutes without being consciously rehearsed or otherwise maintained in attention. One experiences the necessity for attention and rehearsal when one tries to remember a new phone number just received from the operator
long enough to dial it. Shifting attention to another task
(e.g., trying to remember the name of the person you
wish to speak to) causes the original information (the
telephone number) to be lost from STM, since it is
replaced by the information necessary for the new task
(recalling the name). Only that which has entered more
permanent memory can be recalled later. Only about a
half-dozen items can be kept active simultaneously in
STM. However, the capacity of STM, called *memory span,*
can be extended by encoding items in such a way as to
make each item carry many specific details. This process
is called *chunking.* This is commonly done when remembering telephone numbers.

2. Long-Term Memory. *a. Encoding.* Experiences that
are held for a long enough period in STM have strong
enough emotional impact, demand extensive cognitive
processing, are repeated often enough, are consciously
rehearsed, or are given elaborate mental associations, can
be recalled after relatively long intervals and are thus said
to have been encoded in LTM. Encoding involves inclusion of the to-be-remembered event into a network of
associational cues and paths by which memory is
searched for the retrieval of the information at a later
time. Encoding strategies are means of increasing the
richness of associations surrounding an item in memory
and have much to do with the facility with which information can be retrieved from LTM. Encoding strategies
are normally unconscious, but can be consciously augmented by what are commonly called "mnemonic
devices." An example of a mnemonic device is "A Walk
Through the Bible," where the entire history of biblical
events is learned by associating each event with a unique
single phrase and gesture. These phrases and gestures are
learned and the biblical events remembered as a sequence
of images denoted by the words and motions.

Old memories sometimes interfere with our ability to
form new memories (a phenomenon called "proactive
interference"). Similarly, new memories may interfere
with our ability to remember old events ("retroactive
interference"). Anything that increases the distinctiveness of the items currently being experienced decreases
the interference from old items in memory.

Rehearsal and repetition of events or information generally increase memorability. However, the effect is not
due to the mere strengthening of already existing associations by the repetition itself, but to an increased opportunity to elaborate the network of associated ideas. Repetition increases the number of contexts associated with
the to-be-remembered item and allows new associations
to be formed. In both cases the memory is stronger
because there is a greater number of cues that can serve
to elicit memory.

b. Retrieval. Retrieval of information from LTM is an
active reconstruction process. Thus, remembering is a
cognitive skill in which an individual unconsciously
makes inferences about "what must have been" based on
a general scheme implied by the few specific details
retrievable from memory. Reconstruction proceeds from
the deeper levels of the meaning or significance of the
event being remembered to the more surface detail. The
result is well-remembered meaning, but less accurately
recalled detail. However, surface detail is well recalled
when it was particularly distinctive. A good example is
the "flashbulb effect" in which very specific (even irrelevant) details of highly emotional events, or events with
far-reaching impact, are remembered.

The number and salience of available cues at time of
recall is important in this reconstruction process. For
example, our ability to remember a specific item is often
highly context-dependent because contexts provide
many of the important cues for memory retrieval. Similarly, we can often recognize the item we are trying to
remember when it is produced by someone else (as in a
multiple-choice test question) even when we can't freely
recall it (as in completing a fill-in test item).

3. Amnesia. Beyond normal failure of memory, or forgetting, amnesia refers to particularly marked cases of
memory failure, where a significantly large span of experience is almost totally unavailable to memory. Difficulty in remembering events that occurred before the
onset of the amnesia is called *retrograde amnesia;* failure of
memory for events subsequent to onset is referred to as
anterograde amnesia. Amnesia is generally associated with
some form of brain trauma or neuropathology. It is

usually not complete but patchy, in that some events are remembered and others are not.

Similar loss of memory occurs with electroconvulsive shock treatment (ECT), used in psychiatry as a treatment for severe depression. Memory loss is also the primary symptom of Korsakoff's syndrome. In Korsakoff's syndrome neural degeneration has taken place as the result of thiamine deficiency caused by malnutrition associated with alcoholism. Although these patients are generally alert and have relatively normal IQs, they have a severe and irreversible anterograde amnesia.

In the annals of the neuropsychological literature, there is a single outstanding case of surgically caused anterograde amnesia from which much has been learned. The patient, known as H. M., had the hippocampus, a structure deep within the temporal lobe of the brain, removed on both sides to prevent epileptic seizures. The result, surprising at the time, was complete amnesia for virtually all events since the day of the surgery. Although, his intelligence was above average, his experience was constantly that of a person just awakening from sleep, having no recollection of immediately preceding events or experience. The case of H. M. illustrates an important aspect of memory, that is, the distinction between the processes of memory retrieval (intact in H. M. as evidenced by his ability to recall memories for events prior to the surgery), and the encoding of new memories (completely absent in H.M.). This case also dramatizes the critical role of the hippocampus in memory encoding.

4. Neurophysiology of Memory. For nearly a century there has been an intensive search for the neurophysiological basis of memory. Scientists studying the nervous system have attempted to find the neural processes that underlie both STM and LTM. It is currently felt that STM is the product of reverberating electrical impulses within recursively active neural circuits. For some period of time after an event, the neural units involved in mental processing of the event remain activated by continuously looping electrical currents. During this period of time, memory can be disrupted by anything that disrupts the electrical activity of the brain, for example, electroconvulsive shock, head trauma, or other states of unconsciousness, like sleep.

If not abnormally terminated, the reverberating neural circuits eventually produce more permanent structural changes in the neurons involved. This structural change most likely occurs at the synapse (the point of intersection between nerve cells). It is this structural change in the neuron that permits LTM. The process of establishing this long-term memory trace is referred to as *consolidation*. Mental activities, such as rehearsal, which increase the amount we remember, apparently prolong activation within reverberating neural circuits long enough to allow for greater structural change.

5. Pastoral Implications. (1) Recent memories are vulnerable and easily lost. Cognitive psychology suggests that the best way to enhance one's ability to remember something is to increase the amount of other information associated with it. This has implications for preaching, where redundancy within new and enriched context will aid the memory of those listening. (2) Loss of the ability to store new memories, as in Alzheimer's Disease, is

devastating to one's ability to function normally. One becomes perpetually perplexed by not being able to keep track of events that have recently occurred. Even the normal elderly suffer somewhat from this problem. (3) Finally, old memories are relatively resistant to interruption. This has implications for counseling in that some past experiences will be difficult to *forget*. However, there is some evidence that old memories can be modified by restoring them within new associational contexts via a process of remembering and reanalyzing the meaning of the memory.

Bibliography. J. R. Anderson and G.H. Bower, *Human Associative Memory* (1973). R. G. Crowder, *Principles of Learning and Memory* (1976). M. W. Eyseuck, *Human Memory: Theory, Research, and Individual Differences* (1977). J. Piaget and B. Inhelder, *Memory and Intelligence* (1973). J. A. Deutsch, ed., *The Physiological Basis of Memory*, 2d ed. (1983). R. Kail, *The Development of Memory in Children*, 2d ed. (1984). U. Neisser, ed., *Memory Observed: Remembering in Natural Contexts* (1982). D. Rapaport, *Emotions and Memory*, rev. ed. (1972). R. W. Houdar, "The Amen Corner: To Recall and Renew the Ancient Memories", *Worship*, 60 (1986), 246–54. J. Wilhoit, "Memory: An Area of Difference Between Piaget and Goldman," *J. of Christian Education*, 2 (1982), 11–14. K. I. Pargament and D. V. DeRosa "What Was the Sermon About: Predicting Memory for Religious Messages from Cognitive Psychology Theory," *J. of the Scientific Study of Religion*, 24 (1985), 180–93.

W. S. BROWN

MIND; TIME/TIME SENSE. *See also* ANNIVERSARY DEPRESSION; HEALING OF MEMORIES; PERSON (Philosophical Issues); REMINISCENCE THERAPY. *Compare* CONSCIOUSNESS; IMAGINATION; LITURGICAL CALENDAR; REPRESSION; SELF-TRANSCENDENCE.

MEN, PASTORAL CARE OF. The care and counseling of men from the Judeo-Christian perspective of human wholeness, which contrasts with common and entrenched views of male roles in Western culture. Its goals are (1) to help men liberate themselves and transcend traditional, stereotypical, and commonly held images and models of masculinity that frustrate and block their growth and the growth of others, and (2) to help men adopt more androgynous images of selfhood that assist them and others to become whole persons.

The contemporary women's liberation movement has forced men to examine the patriarchal, hierarchical, and domineering dimensions of masculinity and how these have frustrated the fulfillment of women's full possibilities. The women's movement has also provided a model for men to discover how stereotypical images and ideals of masculinity are preventing them from becoming whole persons who are related to their bodies and feelings, to others, to the environment, and to God.

The changing relations between women and men and the discovery that masculine stereotypical images are frustrating to men's growth raises anxiety and confusion that may lead men to seek emotional help and support. Pastoral care and counseling should envisage this contemporary male identity anxiety and role confusion as a growth opportunity. It should utilize a variety of therapeutic and educational approaches to help men become free from growth-blocking images of masculinity in order to become whole persons committed to the growth of others. The growth counseling perspective offers pastoral counseling of men a creative, eclectic approach which draws on individual, marital, and family counseling as well as educational methods and consciousness-raising growth groups.

1. Pastoral Care and Counseling. *a. The problems that bring men to counseling.* Traditional male-female relationships have often made women satellites and derivatives of male identity, and these derivative identities have been relegated to an inferior status by society. Women have been openly and quietly rejecting these satellite identity extensions and are revising their self-understanding as separate, independent, and autonomous whole persons. This has led to a crisis for the men and for many male-female relationships and has presented an opportunity for men to examine carefully how their own identities are tied to the subjugation of women.

The following list includes many presenting problems that men are bringing to pastoral counseling: (1) uncertainty about their function and role as husbands and fathers, (2) anxiety about their wives' growing autonomy, (3) needing to update their self-perception as men, husbands and fathers, (4) anxiety caused by identity revision struggles, (5) escalating marital conflict as women demand a more rapid change toward equality, (6) fear of having more to lose than gain in changing roles, (7) grief over losing roles that guarantee automatic superiority, (8) inability to cope with chronic hostility of women because of gross inequity, (9) emotional struggles because of realistic guilt over inequities, (10) lack of guidelines for being fathers and husbands in egalitarian marriages, (11) loss of security from relying on traditional norms of effective manhood, (12) double bind pressure from society to achieve as well as to be caring husbands and fathers, (13) psychological, spiritual and psycho-physiological problems caused by chronically repressing "unmasculine" feelings and their need for nurture, and (14) awareness of living half-lives or being truncated persons because of their adoption of narrow images of masculinity (H. Clinebell, pp. 141–5).

b. The traditional male. Stereotypical images of masculinity emerge out of the dominant social philosophy in a capitalistic America associated with John Locke, John S. Mill, and Adam Smith (M. F. Fasteau, pp. 2–16). It emphasizes the arena outside the home and lifts up values such as competition, seeking one's own self-interest, denying the importance of feelings and relationships, valuing the market place over the home, talking rather than listening, open conflict rather than behind the scenes negotiation, self-confidence without humility, quick decision making without thoughtful pondering, charisma and dynamism rather than long term credibility, struggling for power and achievement, business as an end in itself rather than human concern, aggressiveness rather than soft persuasive approaches, and external rewards at the expense of inward satisfaction for contributing to the good life.

This masculine value system has led to incompetence in interpersonal relationships—not relating through one's vulnerable and feeling side and condescending to women who are deemed inferior because they are labeled unfairly as illogical and impractical. Men have become slaves to the cult of masculinity and suffer from work

addiction and compulsive desire to achieve, overstressing competition, ignoring one's warmth and tenderness, sacrificing the present moment of fulfillment for future economic reward and refusing to take time for relaxation and enjoyment. As a result men are increasingly realizing how they are trapped by social and cultural expectations and how they are alienated from their bodies and feelings, from others, from the environment, and from their spirituality.

c. Growth opportunities. The effort of women to extricate themselves from derivative identities and men's discovery of the limits and costs of their traditional role are opportunities with which the pastoral counselor can work to help males to grow. The crisis is an opportunity to help husbands to learn to relate to wives as authentic growing persons, to develop marital skills that enrich marital relationships, to provide avenues for helping men to become part of rearing children, and to develop an androgynous self-perspective where the so-called feminine and masculine traits are combined in the same person. In summary, the crisis of changing sex roles is an opportunity for liberation from the traditional male role.

d. Growth counseling methods. The goals of pastoral counseling with men can be accomplished through a variety of counseling methods, drawing on resources from traditional psychoanalytic therapies, contemporary human wholeness models, and consciousness raising, educational and growth group resources. Whatever growth resource one utilizes — e.g., individual, marital, family, or network therapies, or growth group resources—four core dimensions must be present in one's intervention with men. These dimensions are care, confrontation, coaching, and modeling. The counselor must communicate an accepting attitude to the male counselee through recognizing the feelings and difficulty that the male is having because of role changes. However, the male needs to be confronted with the ways he resists liberation from the traditional male models. He needs coaching in developing interpersonal skills as well as to see them modeled by the counselor. Women pastoral counselors can help the male in all four core dimensions including modeling, as well as a male pastoral counselor who is himself growing toward liberation from the traditional male role, and moving toward androgynous self-identity. Similarly helpful are groups of men so committed.

How the pastoral counselor helps to develop the structure and goals of the counseling relationship is very important. At the outset the male counselee may not be able to envisage the relationship of his presenting problems to the general male predicament discussed here. The male model as a source of identity is typically held firmly, unreflectively and not really open to challenge. Interpreting these more general issues must be done gently in ways that stimulate exploration, not imposed in ways that enhance resistance.

2. Theological Foundations. The major goal of pastoral counseling with men is to help them become liberated from the stereotypical images of masculinity that block growth. This may be understood as an expression of God's intention to free all persons from limiting bondages imposed by a distorted and distorting human condition. Single-minded reliance on achievement, control, and other characteristics of the traditional role is a futile trust that is regarded, theologically, as idolatrous. Traditional "manhood" can become a norm at the center of a person's life which can block growth toward wholeness. In this theological formulation of the problem, the task of the pastoral counselor is to facilitate through care, confrontation, coaching and modeling an environment where God can assume God's place at the center of the person's life and release the hold of the idol.

Bibliography. H. J. Clinebell, "Creative Fathering: The Problems and Potentialities of Changing Sex Roles," in *Fathering: Fact or Fable,* E. V. Stein, ed. (1977), pp. 139–59; *Contemporary Growth Therapies* (1982), pp. 237–62. J. E. Dittes, *The Male Predicament* (1985); *When Work Goes Sour* (1987). M. F. Fasteau, *The Male Machine* (1974). D. J. Levinson, *et al., The Seasons of a Man's Life* (1978) E. P. Wimberly, *Pastoral Counseling and Spiritual Values: A Black Point of View* (1982), pp. 33–8.

E. P. WIMBERLY

CULTURAL AND ETHNIC FACTORS IN PASTORAL CARE; LIFE CYCLE THEORY AND PASTORAL CARE; PASTORAL CARE (Contemporary Methods, Perspectives, and Issues). *See also* CONSCIOUSNESS RAISING; IDENTITY; SEXISM; SEXUAL ISSUES IN PASTORAL CARE; SEXUALITY. *Compare* WOMEN, PASTORAL CARE OF.

MEN, PSYCHOLOGY OF. The psychological processes that are involved in a given culture's definition of masculinity depend on the particular values and meanings which that culture ascribes to being masculine. Thus any discussion of the psychology of men must simultaneously entail a description and analysis of cultural definitions of masculinity.

In the following discussion, a dominant contemporary image of masculinity is described and critiqued. As a definition of masculinity, this image dominates modern society, though in individual human lives it assumes varied forms and emphases in relation to variables of individual experience, family life, subculture, race, socioeconomic status and other factors. Because of its particular psychological dynamics, however, it creates a major issue for the mental and physical health of men, for the quality of male-female relations, for family life, and for society at large. In *the new male,* (Goldberg) masculinity is termed "a blueprint for self-destruction."

1. Characteristics of Masculine Defenses. Masculine defenses are tenacious and powerful. The male resists changing or letting go of them because he fears that to do so will mean that he will lose his manliness. This is particularly threatening because masculinity is a powerful reaction formation against man's deeper identification, which is actually female. That is, most boys are brought up by and identify with women. It is mother primarily, and other women such as grandmothers, nursery school teachers, and babysitters who feed, hold, interact with, comfort, and teach boys right from wrong. Particularly in the crucial early years of life, father traditionally is largely an absent parent. He "plays" with the children for a short time in the evening after work or on the weekend. However, his participation is usually tangential and minimal compared to the mother's. Masculinity, therefore, is an unconscious process designed to convert this feminine imprint into its extreme opposite and to "make a man out of him."

a. Autonomy versus dependency. Dependency, for example, is considered feminine. Therefore, the masculine defense produces an intense striving for autonomy. As a boy, his heroes are the likes of the Lone Ranger, James Bond, John Wayne, to name a few—men who are supposedly totally independent. They lean on no one.

The defensive reaction against dependency creates many life problems for the man. He resists acknowledging need, and in particular, resists asking for help. Men suffer from almost all major diseases leading to death at significantly higher rates than women; have a life span that is almost ten years shorter; commit suicide at a rate at least three times higher; are alcohol and drug dependent at considerably higher rates than women; and they make fewer visits to doctors, dentists, and psychotherapists. In times of disturbance and distress, they tend to turn inward, to "steel" themselves, rather than to open up, expose, explore, and reach out for help.

A man is particularly resistant to and threatened by psychotherapy because it gives no immediate, clear-cut answers or actions that can quickly remedy or change his life. Psychotherapy requires some willingness and capacity to be dependent; to acknowledge the inability to do it oneself; to express feelings; to be intimate; and to reveal "weaknesses." All of these are anathema to the masculine-defensive male and also have implications for a man's relationship to religion and religious practices.

b. Activity versus passivity. Passivity, for example, is considered feminine. In unconscious reaction, therefore, the male becomes driven to be ever-active and productive; to feel he is wasting his time unless he is doing something; and to resist acknowledging fatigue and the need for sleep. He prides himself on his ability to continue his usual schedule with little sleep, or to recuperate from major surgery and illness rapidly. This repression of passivity, coupled with an overly active lifestyle, prevents appropriate attention to fatigue and the need for recuperation, and is a key factor in "sudden" and premature death.

c. Rationality versus emotionality. Emotions also are considered feminine. Therefore, the defensive masculine reaction against them results in a coldly logical, rational style. He is "out of touch" with his feelings and tends therefore to be uncomfortable in close, intimate human interaction with his wife, children, friends, or people in general. Instead, he relates most comfortably to his machines. He can tinker and endlessly enjoy playing with his automobile, computer, boat, or motorcycle. Or he might stay glued to a television, endlessly watching sports, while he gets "bored" with people.

The repression of emotions also makes him a "victim" in his intimate male-female relationships. That is, he cannot recognize and understand emotional cues, and is "surprised" when a relationship he is heavily involved in falls apart, and he is "suddenly" abandoned. "I thought we were getting along fine; I don't know what went wrong," is a common reaction.

d. Denial of fear. Of all the emotions, the defensive compulsion to repress and deny fear is perhaps the most destructive to a man, as well as to others. He will go to great lengths to avoid the feeling of being a "coward," or a "sissy," and to prove that he is brave and fearless. This defensive reaction often produces what is termed "macho psychotic" behavior. This involves irrational or objectively "crazy" things that are done to prove one is not afraid. The compulsion to deny fear thus supersedes his instinct to survive. He would rather die like a man than to risk being labeled a coward.

Examples of "macho psychotic" behavior are seen daily. Men who are total strangers will fight, sometimes to the death, for seemingly minor reasons, such as when an obscene gesture or threatening remark was made, a parking spot was taken, or a woman was insulted. Even in battles that result in injury or death, nothing objectively is at stake except the masculine ego, or the need to prove "I am a man," or "I am not a sissy." Any man could choose to walk away instead of fight but usually is unable to do so.

e. Control versus submission. Masculinity also produces a powerful reaction against submission or loss of control and creates a counterpart striving to control everything and everybody he is close to. Unfortunately, this need to control severely limits his life because he avoids situations or events where he cannot control or triumph. In addition, he tends to be resented and even hated by those who are close to him and dependent, such as wife, children, employees, and so forth, who feel oppressed by his endless need to have his way.

2. **Self-destructive Effects.** Specific self-destructive ramifications of masculine defenses can be seen clearly in various areas of life.

a. Health. In physical health matters, a man learns as a little boy not to cry and to equate his capacity to take pain and not give in to it with manliness. The acknowledgment of pain is perceived by men as weakness. Therefore, instead of acknowledging pain as a signal to pay attention to a cue for adjusting to bodily distress, he tends to deny and disregard these signals as long as possible. Consequently, as an adult male, he may "suddenly" become severely ill or die of a heart attack even though he was "feeling great" just the day before.

Because of the endless need to prove his manliness in every way, he even equates his masculinity with what he eats and drinks. Salads, wine, and yogurt, for example, are considered women's food. Steaks and liquor are "masculine" foods, though both are known carcinogens, and damaging to the body, particularly in large quantities.

b. Sexuality. Masculine defenses drive a man to prove himself by his sexual performance and to experience his sexual response in a depersonalized way. He perceives his penis as a tool that is either working well or not; he refers to his penis as "it." He becomes panicky at any deterioration in or loss of performance ability. He does not view his sexual response as a changing expression and barometer of his feelings, his assumptions and self-image, or the state of his relationship.

The traditional medical language describing sexual dysfunction is a sexist outgrowth of this distortion. Terms such as "impotence" and "premature ejaculation" imply a performance standard a man must live up to in order to be "normal." When he fails at it, he is considered to have "a problem" that requires treatment and puts his manliness in jeopardy and doubt.

His masculine defenses also isolate him from close relationships with other men. To relate to other men aggressively and competitively is masculine. To feel affection, to touch, or to love another man, however, makes him suspect homosexuality.

3. **Conclusion.** "Men's liberation" is the attempt on the part of men to break through their self-destructive, macho compulsions and to find ways to reown and redevelop their repressed tender, feeling, relational side. Such breakthroughs, which will reverse the powerful, self-destructive, masculine defense processes, are crucial if men are to survive and participate in a fulfilling, nourishing life. This and other efforts at self-awareness will enable men to affirm the positive qualities of the masculine, while at the same time allowing "feminine" qualities to bring them toward growth and wholeness.

Bibliography. J. E. Dittes, *The Male Predicament* (1985). H. Goldberg, *The Hazards of Being Male* (1976); *The New Male* (1979); *The New Male-Female Relationship* (1983). E. Neumann, "Fear of the Feminine," *Quadrant,* 19:1 (1986), 7–30. See also "Race, Socioeconomic Status, and Age: The Social Context of American Masculinity," *Sex Roles,* 11 (1984), 639–56.

H. GOLDBERG

IDENTITY; SEXUALITY. *See also* DEFENSE AND COPING THEORY; DEPENDENCE/INDEPENDENCE; PERSON. *Compare* PERSONALITY, BIOLOGICAL DIMENSIONS OF; FEMINIST ISSUES IN PSYCHOLOGY; WOMEN, PSYCHOLOGY OF.

MENNINGER, KARL (1893–   ). Psychiatrist, psychoanalyst, psychiatric administrator. Menninger is often referred to as the "Dean of American Psychiatrists." Together with his father, C. F. Menninger, and his brother, William C. Menninger, he founded the Menninger Clinic in Topeka, Kansas. His medical education at Harvard, followed by psychiatric training with such figures as Smith Ely Jelliffe and Ernest Southard, and then by his own psychoanalyis, prepared him for a unique career.

The clinic, which later became the Menninger Foundation, flourished under his leadership. His particular genius was the uniting of a highly disciplined understanding of psychoanalytic theory with a determined pragmatism willing to experiment and to adopt "whatever works." The result was a series of therapeutic successes—some with well-known figures who publicly gave the clinic credit—which brought both the clinic and Menninger considerable fame.

These practical successes were matched by lively theoretical interests. Menninger's publication list includes psychiatric studies such as *Theory of Psychoanalytic Technique, Man Against Himself, Love Against Hate, The Vital Balance.* It also includes approaches to a number of major problems tangentially related to psychiatric concerns: *Whatever Happened to Sin?* raised the question of evil in a fresh way when evil was not a popular topic, and *The Crime of Punishment* reflected Menninger's long and deep concern for the way in which prisoners are treated in this country. *A Psychiatrist's World* is a rich collection of clinical, theoretical, historical, and personal material.

A Presbyterian ruling elder, Menninger welcomed and fostered religious concerns at the Menninger Foundation at a time when psychiatry and religion were deeply suspicious of each other. He brought Thomas W. Klink to the Foundation as chaplain, and encouraged Klink in the formation of the Division of Religion and

Psychiatry. Menninger collaborated with Seward Hiltner in the writing of *Constructive Aspects of Anxiety*.

It is difficult to assess which of the facets of Karl Menninger's life and thought had the most impact on our thinking. Perhaps in the long run the most profound impact will be seen to have come from his willingness to swim against the stream. He made practical adaptations of psychoanalytic theory; he championed the unpopular cause of prisoners, insisting that our treatment of them was as much a crime as the offenses they had committed; he welcomed religious concerns to his clinic when psychiatry and religion were antagonists; angry at what he thought was slipshod work, he was a vociferous critic both of *DSM-III* and of *Webster's Third Edition*. In any case, he changed the face of American psychiatry more than any one other person.

K. R. MITCHELL

HEALTH AND ILLNESS; MENTAL HEALTH AND ILLNESS; MENTAL HEALTH MOVEMENT; PSYCHOPATHOLOGY, THEORIES OF.

MENNINGER, WILLIAM C. *See* RELIGION AND HEALTH MOVEMENT.

MENNONITES. *See* SECTARIAN PASTORAL CARE; SIMONS, MENNO.

MENOPAUSE. The cessation of menstruation. Menopause is often a misunderstood and misused term. In both medical and psychological literature there is little consensus on when it begins or ends and what are its definitive signs. In popular usage, the phrase "going through menopause" is usually understood as beginning with a woman's first menstrual irregularities and ending when menses stops completely and her body adjusts to estrogen level changes. This process may begin as early as the late thirties for some women, and physical manifestations may be felt into the late sixties for others. The median age at the actual cessation of menstruation in industrial societies is now fifty years (Notman).

1. **Physical Manifestations.** *a. Menstrual changes.* There are three basic physical signs that are attributable to the change in estrogen production that results in menopause. The first is changes in the menstrual cycle. The particular changes vary from woman to woman. Some menstruate more often, while others find their periods coming less frequently. Sometimes periods are shorter and lighter, and other women have episodes of heavy bleeding with clots. The premenstrual time may manifest changes as well. Only one out of five women experiences no changes in menstruation until it suddenly stops (Clay). Menstrual flow may stop for several months and then return. Women are advised that they should consider themselves able to become pregnant until they have not had a period for two years.

b. Vasomotor disturbance. Most commonly referred to as "hot flashes" or "flushes," this phenomenon is a result of blood vessels irregularly dilating and constricting. It varies among women in its intensity, duration, and frequency. Most medical professionals would agree that stress and diet can affect these dimensions. Descriptively, the woman feels heat sensations in the upper half of her body; sweating, feelings of suffocation, and chills may follow. The physiological reason for this disturbance is unclear.

c. Vaginal changes. The different level of estrogen production during the menopause process may result in vaginal changes. Possible changes include: thinning of the vaginal walls, loss of elasticity, flattening of ridges, shortening or narrowing of vagina, and dryness and itching. These conditions can make intercourse uncomfortable or painful, and subsequently result in irritation and higher vulnerability to infection.

2. **Treatment Approaches.** *a. Surgery.* Irregular or heavy menstrual flow is a warning signal to medical personnel to look for possible cancer. Surgeons will often perform biopsy surgery to confirm or disconfirm this and often a hysterectomy will follow confirming results. However, hysterectomies are sometimes recommended and chosen simply to relieve a woman of the source of disruption in her social and work life that menopausal "symptoms" may cause. The decision to have a hysterectomy should be made carefully and after alternative treatment approaches have been attempted.

b. Estrogen replacement therapy (ERT). Menopausal "symptoms" are sometimes treated by prescribing estrogen to replace that which the ovaries are no longer producing. Two possible benefits of this treatment are the relief of vasomotor disturbance and vaginal dryness. ERT is still a controversial treatment approach. There are several contraindications to taking estrogen. In addition, ERT may increase the risk of breast and endometrial cancer, intensify growth of fibroid tumors, and create vitamin deficiencies. For vaginal dryness, estrogen creams or suppositories may not be as risky.

c. Sexual activity. With regard to the problem of decreased vaginal lubrication, regular intercourse or engaging in any sexually arousing activity has been found to help improve a woman's ability to lubricate. Vaginal dryness has not been found to be an irreversible condition, although a woman may take longer to become lubricated. Lubrication can also be provided "artificially" by applying a topical substance.

Various nonmedical treatments for the physical manifestations of menopause include: regular moderate exercise, a balanced diet high in certain vitamins and minerals, herbal teas, and relaxation techniques.

3. **Psychological Considerations.** The process of menopause has been blamed for a variety of somatic and psychological symptomology in middle-aged women that cannot be substantiated in the research. The symptoms have included insomnia, irritability, apathy, depression, diminished sexual interest, weight increase, headaches, dizzy spells, palpitations, and hypertension. Obviously, menopause is a major life event for a woman, and as such may affect her psychologically. This transition is also taking place in the midst of her unique cultural and psychosocial situation and at a certain developmental period of her life. Problems arise in understanding the multifaceted nature of this phenomenon when only one facet, either the psychological ("It's all in your head") or the biological ("It's simply a physical change, it shouldn't affect you in any other way") is emphasized.

Research does indicate a rise in minor psychological and somatic symptomology among women in the general population in the menopausal years. Menopause has often been blamed for this, but the question remains open. Other factors may be involved in this rise.

Depression is the most popular psychological dysfunction assigned to menopause, although research links depression more with psychosocial variables in these women than with hormone changes, and statistical evidence indicates that menopause does not increase rates of depression (Notman). Research evidence does suggest that estrogen influences emotional behavior, but exactly how and to what extent is unclear. Notman cites studies indicating that women with low self-esteem, women who have heavily invested themselves in the role of mother, women of lower social status with fewer opportunities open to them, and women in a culture that devalues middle age and does not provide a clear role for them are more likely to experience depression in the menopausal years.

Atchison and el-Guebaly have identified several factors that may predispose a woman to psychological dysfunction during menopause. These include: previous history of psychiatric illness, painful menstruation, limited education, previous adjustment difficulties, sexual and marital problems, and low sociocultural expectations. They conclude that, "the evidence supporting social and psychological factors as involved in the onset of psychiatric disorder during the menopause is stronger than the biological evidence" (p. 641).

Menopause occurs at a specific developmental phase of life, known as middle age, that psychologists have only begun to research for women. What is more, with women's roles changing and more opportunities open to them, women's lives do not tend to follow patterns as predictably as they have in the past. Some of the major life events that often occur in middle age include: illness and death of parents, spouse's mid-life issues, and children reaching adolescence and leaving home. Cooke and Greene have found that psychological and somatic symptoms experienced during menopause were due more to experienced life stress than to menopause itself. Their study points to the importance of a social support system in providing assistance in times of crisis and transition to avoid the development of psychological and somatic symptomology.

4. **Implications for Pastoral Counseling.** In counseling with women who are experiencing difficulties in mid-life, several things are important to keep in mind. Referrals to competent, sensitive, well-informed medical personnel should be made when physical complaints are a part of the presenting problem. A woman should not be viewed primarily from her reproductive functions. Menopause is an important experience for a woman, but it is best understood in the context of her entire life, her particular adaptive and response style, and her sociocultural environment with its value systems. In individual counseling with these women, issues of competence, anger, locus of control, attribution, social networks, and identity apart from childbearing roles may need to be explored. In addition, marital counseling and support groups made up of women in similar life situations may be appropriate.

Bibliography. B. Atchison and N. el-Guebaly, "The Joint Mature Women's Clinic or Menopause Revisited," *Canadian J. of Psychiatry*, 28 (1983), 640–45. Boston Women's Health Book Collective, *The New Our Bodies, Ourselves* (1984). A. M. Brodsky and R. Hare-Mustin, *Women and Psychotherapy* (1980). V. Clay, *Women: Menopause and Middle Age* (1977). D. J. Cooke and J. G. Greene, "Types of Life Events in Relation to Symptoms at the Climacterium," *J. of Psychosomatic Research*, 25 (1981), 5–11. A. Lake, *Our Own Years* (1979). E. Markson, ed., *Older Women* (1983). M. Notman, "Midlife Concerns of Women: Implications of the Menopause," *American J. of Psychiatry*, 136 (1979), 1270–74. J. Porcino, *Growing Older, Getting Better* (1983). J. Posner, "It's All in Your Head: Feminist and Medical Models of Menopause," *Sex Roles*, 5 (1979), 179–90. R. Reitz, *Menopause: A Positive Approach* (1979). L. Rose, ed. *The Menopause Book* (1977). A. M. Voda, M. Dinnerstein, and S. R. O'Donnell, eds., *Changing Perspectives on Menopause* (1982).

C. E. SCHULER

AGING; MEN; WOMEN. *See also* PERSONALITY, BIOLOGICAL DIMENSIONS OF; BODY; MIDLIFE PERSONS. *Compare* LOSS OF FUNCTION.

MENSTRUATION/PREMENSTRUAL SYNDROME. *See* PREMENSTRUAL SYNDROME; WOMEN, PSYCHOLOGY OF.

MENTAL DEFICIENCY. *See* MENTAL RETARDATION.

MENTAL DISORDERS. *See* MENTAL HEALTH AND ILLNESS. *See also* ORGANIC MENTAL DISORDER AND ORGANIC BRAIN SYNDROME; OLDER PERSONS, MENTAL DISORDERS OF; PSYCHOPATHOLOGY, THEORIES OF.

MENTAL HEALTH. *See* MENTAL HEALTH AND ILLNESS.

MENTAL HEALTH, PASTOR'S. The psychological well-being and adequate adjustment of the pastor to his or her role. The pastoral ministry is fraught with high expectations, emotional hazards, and role conflict. Donald Smith notes that "there are few professions, if any, that demand as broad a range of different skills and styles of action as the ministry" (Smith, 1973, p. 71). Like many other helping professions, it is a drain on ministers to work continually with people in need or conflict. Ministers often begin their careers with inadequate training in handling conflict situations, difficult personalities, and communication problems. Coupled with the voluntary structure of the church, these factors contribute greatly to the development of emotional and physical problems (Hart, 1984, p. 117).

Research on the pastor's mental health has either been primarily anecdotal or it has suffered from poor experimental design. A few studies (Jud, *et al.*, 1970; York, 1982; Congo, 1983) have attempted to document the unique emotional hazards of the pastoral ministry empirically, but these studies have been plagued by poor response rates, limited subject pools, or confinement to a single denomination. Blackmon and Hart (1984) have attempted to obtain a broader base of data that would allow comparisons across denominations, but even this study has limited application outside of California. This is an area of research that needs more systematic study within and between denominational and regional differences.

To cope with these unique demands and to maintain adequate mental health, ministers must not only develop spiritual strengths and resources but also healthy psychological attitudes and adequate psychological coping skills. Among these skills should be the ability to be self-reliant and self-directing; to take responsibility and make needed adjustments with flexibility and resiliency; to be persistent through difficult and stressful times; to get along with others and resolve interpersonal conflicts; to show respect and provide unconditional acceptance of others; to tolerate delays and frustrations without undue hostility; to be generous with forgiveness without harboring resentment for the many hurts that "people-helping" professions commonly experience.

Fundamental to the pastor's mental health ought to be a highly developed self-awareness and insight into the unique way he or she utilizes defense mechanisms or is prone to emotional pitfalls. One major conflict with much potential for undermining mental health arises between the demands of being human and the idealization of being a representative of godliness. Margaretta Bowers says that "all through the ages the clergy have suffered from the insurmountable contrasts between their very real humanity and the transcendent requirements of their symbolic representation as the priest, the Incarnate Christ" (Bowers, 1963, p. 9). This conflict often leads pastors to deny aspects of their humanity and to ignore basic faults in their personalities or coping styles.

Many theological seminaries do not place enough emphasis on the development of emotional and interpersonal skills. This neglect of the "person" of the minister in professional training may predispose pastors to greater stress and depression during the first five years of ministry.

The work of the ministry is conducive to the experience of many losses and frustrations. The voluntary structure of the church causes problems that require specialized abilities to resolve, including organizational and motivational skills. Many pastors do not master these skills and consequently suffer from loss of self-esteem and self-confidence. The threat of failure and the constant feeling of loneliness and isolation add to the burden. The work of the ministry also has no clear boundaries, so that there is always a sense of incompleteness, and work accomplishment cannot always be measured because the criteria are too subjective.

To remain psychologically healthy, therefore, the pastor must develop strategies for coping with these deficiencies in the structure of pastoral work. Some resources for growth and self-understanding include support groups, clinical pastoral education, psychotherapy, career counseling, spiritual direction, and continuing education for a variety of skills.

Bibliography. R. Blackmon and A. Hart, *The Hazards of Ministry* (1984). M. Bowers, *Conflicts of the Clergy: A Psycho-Dynamic Study with Case Histories* (1963). D. Congo, *The Role of Interpersonal Relationship Style, Life Change Events, and Personal Data Variables in Ministerial Burnout* (1983). E. Grider, *Can I Make It One More Year? Overcoming the Hazards of the Ministry* (1980). A. Hart, *Coping with Depression in the Ministry and Other Helping Professions* (1984). G. Jud, E. Mills, and G. Burch, *Ex-Pastors: Why Men Leave the Parish Ministry* (1970). C. Rassieur, *Stress Management for Ministers* (1982). D. Smith, *Clergy in the Cross-Fire: Coping with Role Conflict in the Ministry* (1973). D. York, *Relationship Between Burnout and Assertiveness, Aggressiveness, Styles of Relating, and Mental Adjustment with Pastors* (1982).

A. D. HART

CLERGY, EMPIRICAL STUDIES OF; PASTOR, PASTORAL CARE OF; PERSONHOOD OF THE PASTOR, SIGNIFICANCE OF. *See also* BURNOUT; CAREER DEVELOPMENT AND GUIDANCE (For Pastors); THEOLOGICAL STUDENTS, EVALUATION AND EMPIRICAL STUDIES OF. *Compare* AUTHORITY *or* IDENTITY, PASTORAL; FAITH AND INTEGRITY, PASTOR'S; MARRIAGE AND FAMILY LIFE, PASTOR'S.

MENTAL HEALTH MOVEMENT. A broad spectrum of community, professional, and scientific groups committed to promoting mental and emotional well-being and improving the care and treatment of the mentally ill. The founding of the contemporary mental health movement is widely attributed to Clifford Whittingham Beers, a former mental patient, whose autobiographical account of his experiences in three Connecticut asylums was published in 1908. A classic in the literature of social reform, Beers' book, *A Mind That Found Itself,* called for a national movement of citizens and professionals dedicated to improving the care of the mentally ill and preventing mental disorders. In 1908 Beers organized the first state society for "mental hygiene" in Connecticut, and less than a year later founded the National Committee for Mental Hygiene. Attracting strong support from such eminent leaders as William James and Adolf Meyer, Beers remained a zealous advocate of the movement until his death in 1943.

With the appointment of Thomas Solomon as medical director of the National Committee in 1912, the movement broadened its focus to include gathering uniform statistical information about patients in mental hospitals, upgrading the training and credentialing of psychiatrists, encouraging the development of child guidance clinics, and educating the general public. Supportive links were forged with major disciplines involved in treating the mentally ill, as well as with related professions—family physicians, teachers, and clergy—whose work brought them into daily contact with the emotionally troubled. During the 1940s, "mental health" replaced "mental hygiene" as the movement's preferred designation. Widespread acceptance of psychodynamic perspectives and the presumption of environmental influences in mental illness soon extended the scope of "mental health" to almost undefinable limits. In 1950, the National Committee merged with two related organizations to form the National Association for Mental Health, which now has over a million volunteers in 850 local associations and divisions. Counterpart organizations exist in many countries of the world.

Recent developments often subsumed under the umbrella of the mental health movement include the introduction of psychotropic drugs during the mid-1950s, efforts to provide "close-to-home" treatment through community mental health centers and psychiatric units of general hospitals, emphasis on patients' "right-to-treatment" in least restrictive settings, and the rapid deinstitutionalization of the chronically mentally ill to community-based facilities. In addition, promising research is under way in the areas of psychopharmacology and neuropsychiatry. Lately formed support and advocacy groups include the National Alliance for the Mentally Ill and the American Mental Health Fund.

Age-old problems of fear, stigma, and lack of scientific knowledge remain as significant barriers to adequate public support for mental health services. The large number of mentally ill among the nation's homeless is a stark reminder of reforms still needed.

Bibliography. C. Beers, *A Mind That Found Itself* (1908). A. Deutsch, *The Mentally Ill in America* (1938). D. Martindale and E. Martindale, *Mental Disability in America Since World War II* (1985). N. Ridenour, *Mental Health in the United States: A Fifty-Year History* (1961).

C. S. AIST

COMMUNITY MENTAL HEALTH MOVEMENT; MENTAL HOSPITAL/MENTAL HOSPITALIZATION. *Compare* PSYCHIATRY AND PASTORAL CARE.

MENTAL HEALTH AND ILLNESS. *Mental health* is a condition of well-being in relation to self and others characterized by such qualities as (a) positive self-acceptance, (b) accurate perception of others and the world, (c) stability and appropriateness in mood, (d) balance and purposiveness in behavior, (e) dependable sense of identity and values, (f) adaptability to one's environment, (g) ability to engage in productive work and fulfilling love, and (h) commitment to a source of devotion beyond oneself. As such, mental health is an active process, not merely the absence of illness. Nor are its characteristics optimally present at all times; at best they represent general norms within which there is considerable variation. The term "mental health" also connotes rehabilitation of the mentally ill, prevention of mental and emotional disorders, and efforts to promote social-environmental conditions in which individuals can function according to their highest mental and physical potentials.

Mental illness refers to a variety of enduring or recurrent disturbances in patterns of an individual's thinking, mood or behavior that are typically associated with painful distress and/or impairment of social, occupational or leisure functioning. Severity of symptoms may range from mild annoyance to extreme discomfort, from little or no violation of conventional norms to floridly deviant behaviors, and from minor distortions of reality to significant impairment in reality testing. The concept of "illness" is important in order to distinguish the condition from social deviance or moral corruption and to assure a response by society of diagnosis, treatment and follow-up in light of known or suspected causes.

Taken together, mental health and illness implies a continuum between gross pathology and psychological perfection, with most people most of the time occupying a broad mid-range between the two extremes. Everyone experiences transient thought disturbances, periods of depression, unexplained fears, and outbursts of unjustifiable behavior; it is when these "symptoms" persist and interfere significantly with one's daily living, either without apparent precipitating cause or as an exaggerated response to untoward events, that one may infer some type of mental illness.

1. Historical Background. The health or sickness of the mind has been a perennial concern of human societies throughout the centuries. In most ancient cultures, madness was attributed to possession by supernatural spirits. Caregivers were usually priests or shaman-type religious functionaries who appeased the gods or exorcised demons. Torture was often a "treatment of choice," as epitomized by the practice in Neolithic cultures of drilling holes in the skull to allow evil spirits to escape (trepanation). Healthy-mindedness was assured by participation in sanctioned rituals, observance of taboos, and the use of magical devices (amulets, talismans, and fetishes). These measures not only protected from demonic forces, but conveyed solidarity with one's community and favor with its gods.

Biblical references to insanity include King Saul, whose shifting moods, suspicious brooding and eventual suicide suggest a disabling psychosis, and King Nebuchadnezzar whose ". . . mind was made like that of a beast and his dwelling was with the wild asses" (Dan. 5:21), a condition known as lycanthropy. In Deuteronomy, mental aberrations ("madness and blindness and confusion of mind") are manifestations of divine retribution for violating Yahweh's commandments, while prosperity and personal fulfillment are rewards for faithful obedience (Deut. 28).

As medicine began to emerge as an art distinct from religion in Classical Greece, mental illness was increasingly attributed to natural causes. Led by Hippocrates (460–375 B.C.) and Galen (A.D. 130–200), both of whom believed madness was an imbalance among bodily humors which affected the sufferer's brain, the naturalistic movement in medicine exercised considerable influence during the Greco-Roman era.

With few exceptions, however, superstition and magic prevailed in the treatment of mental disorders during the Middle Ages. One development of note was the establishment of hospitals for the care of the insane in centers like Valencia in Spain, Gheel in Belgium, and Bethlehem in London. During the fifteenth century, the infamous *Malleus Maleficarum (The Witch's Hammer)* linked witchcraft and mental illness. Within two centuries, this unfortunate confluence resulted in the torture and execution of perhaps two hundred thousand demented persons in France and Germany.

It was not until the eighteenth century Enlightenment that medicine as a whole and the treatment of insanity in particular became stripped of supernaturalism and infused with the spirit of scientific inquiry. The mentally ill became wards of the state and their treatment was placed in the hands of physicians. Under such leaders as Pinel, Tuke, and Chiarugi, treatment became increasingly humane and optimistic in terms of outcome. Many new hospitals for the insane were built in Europe and America during the 1800s.

By the first decade of the twentieth century, psychiatry, greatly aided by Kraepelin's system of classification, had become firmly established as a specialty of medicine. At the same time, Freud's revolutionary concepts about unconscious determinants of deviant behavior and treatment by psychoanalysis were slowly winning adherents. The two world wars brought vivid attention to the effects of stress and other socio-environmental factors on individual and community mental health. The introduction of phenothiazines and antidepressant drugs in the 1950s not only aided the treatment of many "hopeless" patients, but set the stage for two future developments: (a) the controversial movement over the past two decades to deinstitutionalize the nation's chronically mentally ill, and (b) new advances in research regarding the neurological, genetic, and biochemical factors that influence mental health and illness.

2. **Theoretical Models.** Many theoretical models have been advanced in efforts to organize the vast amounts of data about mental health and illness into coherent explanatory frameworks and strategies for ameliorative intervention. Five models, or families of models, are important today.

a. Biological. Genetic defects, biochemical imbalances, nutritional deficiencies and infections (along with toxins, trauma, tumors, etc.) are believed to be the underlying causes of the functional or structural abnormalities in the central nervous system which appear to be associated with many if not all mental illnesses. Life experiences may have relevance as possible contributors to organic dysfunction or as precipitating factors of illness. Typical interventions include chemotherapy, hospitalization when needed, supportive therapy, and for certain patients dietary regulation or electroconvulsive therapy.

b. Psychodynamic. Unconscious conflicts between desires and prohibitions are thought to generate anxiety which is defended against by various mechanisms (denial, projection, etc.). When defenses prove unsuccessful, pathological conditions occur. Therapeutic intervention seeks to modify behavior by providing insight into the relation between symptoms and underlying conflicts through exploring the patient's dreams, free associations, and interactions with the clinician.

c. Behavioral. Pathologic symptoms are perceived as learned responses or as deficits or distortions in learning. Treatment defines the problem behavior and analyzes its frequency and circumstances. Modification is effected through such methods as desensitizing the patient to problem-producing stimuli or by pairing that stimuli with stronger competing stimuli (e.g., images that prompt fear of heights with muscular relaxation). New behaviors are acquired through various reinforcement techniques.

d. Family. The main source of dysfunction presented by "identified patients" is said to be located in family transactions. Treatment helps family members communicate more clearly and openly, prize differences, and achieve differentiation.

e. Social and community. The principal source of many mental illnesses is conceived as residing in the community. Treatment is geographically defined, system focused, delivered by natural caregivers when possible, and targeted to populations at risk.

No single model, regardless of how compelling in a given sphere, is universally applicable in all circumstances. In practice, the helping person, within the domain of his or her competence, synthesizes elements from those models that best fit the situation.

3. **Types of Mental Disorders.** A valid and reliable classification of mental disorders is needed to ensure clarity in communication, consistency in diagnosis, and comparability in treatment. In the U.S. the most widely used and authoritative resource for this purpose is the revision of the third edition of the *Diagnostic and Statistical Manual of Mental Disorders* of the American Psychiatric Association (*DSM III-R*). Recognizing competing conceptual and therapeutic views, its nosology is atheoretical, heuristic, and subject to change in response to new research and clinical knowledge. The descriptions which follow in this section have been adapted primarily from the *DSM-III*.

a. Disorders usually first evident in infancy, childhood or adolescence. Disorders in this class usually appear in infancy, childhood, or adolescence and may or may not persist into adult life. Types include: (i) a cluster of *developmental disorders*—various levels of mental retardation, autism, and non-neurologic disorders related to specific developmental skills (language, speech, academic and motor); (ii) *disruptive behavior disorders*—attention-deficit hyperactivity, extreme oppositional patterns, and conduct disturbances; (iii) *anxiety disorders*—focused on separation, avoidance of unfamiliar people, and patterns of excessive worry or anxiety; (iv) *eating disorders*—Anorexia Nervosa and Bulimia Nervosa; (v) *gender identity disorders*—disturbance associated with incongruence between assigned sex and gender identity; (vi) *tic disorders*—motor and vocal; (vii) *elimination disorders*—functional enuresis and encopresis; (viii) *speech disorders*—stuttering and cluttering; and (ix) a group of other disorders assoicated with identity uncertainty, attachment deficits, and refusal to talk (elective mutism).

b. Organic mental disorders. This is an extremely varied and difficult to characterize collection of disturbances which are diagnosed on the basis of (i) the presence of one of several organic brain syndromes, and (ii) the demonstrated presence of some organic condition judged to cause the abnormal mental state. These are the only disorders for which etiology is presumed.

Organic brain syndromes are clusters of psychological or behavioral abnormalities associated with dysfunctions of the brain. Some types involve relatively global cognitive impairments (delirium and dementia) while others involve more selective spheres of abnormality (amnesia and hallucinations). Still others resemble schizophrenic, mood, or personality disorders. The underlying causes of these organic syndromes, however, can range anywhere from psychoactive substance intoxication and withdrawal (like alcohol, PCP, or hallucinogens) to Alzheimer's and Pick's diseases. Other causes of organic syndromes include brain tumor, vitamin deficiency, Huntington's Chorea, cerebral arteriosclerosis, (now called multi-infarct dementia), and encephalitis.

c. Psychoactive substance use disorders. These disorders focus on maladaptive behaviors associated with regular use of a given substance, as distinguished from its effects on the central nervous system (see above). A diagnostic distinction is made between *psychoactive substance abuse* (very excessive substance use for at least one month accompanied by impairments in social or occupational function) and *psychoactive substance dependence* (increased intake to maintain desired effect and a substance-specific withdrawal syndrome following cessation). Five classes of substances are covered: alcohol, barbiturates, opiates, amphetamines, and cannabis.

d. Schizophrenic disorders. Criteria used to define schizophrenic disorders are psychotic manifestations during some phase of the illness, deterioration from previous levels of functioning before and after onset, and a continuous duration for at least six months.

Psychotic symptoms characteristic of schizophrenia include bizarre delusions often involving persecutory or messianic themes; thought fragmentation associated with rapid, unconnected shifts in subject, or in severe instances, gross incoherence; perceptual disturbances in the form of hallucinations (voices, sounds, visual images); blunted affect which is discordant with thought content; impairment in capacity to initiate goal-directed behavior; and various psycho-motor imbalances characterized by lack of spontaneity, rigid posturing, or excitement. The definitive symptom in all psychotic behavior is gross impairment in reality testing.

There are four major sub-types of schizophrenia: (i) *disorganized* — extreme incoherence and silly affect, marked social impairment and peculiar mannerisms; (ii) *catatonic* — stupor, rigid posturing and mutism which often alter- nates with states of excitement; (iii) *paranoid* — persecutory or grandiose delusions; and (iv) *undifferentiated* — psychotic symptoms without the predominant features of the other types.

e. Mood disorders. The essential features of these disorders are a disturbance of mood, accompanied by a full or partial manic or depressive syndrome. Symptoms of a manic episode are a distinct period when the person's predominant mood is euphoric, expansive, and flamboyantly excessive. A major depressive episode is manifested by feelings of intense sadness and hopelessness accompanied by an inability to experience pleasure, disturbances of appetite and sleep, agitation, and social withdrawal. Suicide is the most serious danger associated with a major depressive episode.

Diagnostic criteria for *mood disorders* include (i) *bipolar disorder, mixed* — current disturbance involves both manic and depressive symptoms intermixed or alternating every few days; (ii) *bipolar disorder, manic* — current disturbance is a manic episode; (iii) *bipolar disorder, depressed* — has had one or more manic episodes but the current disturbance is depression; and (iv) *major depression* — has never had a manic episode but the current disturbance is a first time or recurrent depression. Less severe mood disturbances include *cyclothymia,* identified by recurrent episodes of mood elevation and expansiveness (hypomania) followed by periods of mild depression, and *dysthemia* (formerly depressive neurosis) which is manifested by intense sadness or loss of pleasure in usual activities. Sometimes present is loss of appetite or overeating, sleep disturbance, social withdrawal or suicidal ruminations.

f. Delusional (paranoid) disorder. The criterion for this condition is a persistent, nonbizarre delusion that is *not* caused by other mental disorders (such as schizophrenia or a mood disorder). Five types are commonly seen: *erotomanic* (delusion that a person, usually of higher status, is in love with the subject); *grandiose* (delusion that one possesses some great, but unrecognized, gift, talent or special relationship); *jealous* (delusion that spouse or lover is unfaithful); *persecutory* (delusion that one is being spied on, conspired against, poisoned, or otherwise malevolently treated); and *somatic* (delusion that one has some physical defect, disorder or disease). Impairment is primarily to social and marital functioning.

g. Neuroses. Neurotic disorders are a class of disturbances in which a symptom or group of symptoms is distressing to the individual and is recognized by him or her as alien to self. Although painful and quite disabling at times, capacity for reality testing remains intact and behavior usually conforms to social convention.

Four categories of disorder constitute neurotic-type disturbances. *Anxiety disorders* consist of conditions like phobias, panic attacks, generalized anxiety states, obsessive thoughts and compulsive behaviors, and stress related to re-experienced trauma. *Somatoform disorders* feature physiological symptoms without any organic basis and include chronic somatic complaints, loss or change in physical functioning (such as paralysis) due to inner conflicts, pain disturbances, and unfounded fear of having a physical disease. *Dissociative disorders* are characterized by mental alterations related to consciousness (amnesia), identity (multiple personality, depersonalization) or motor behavior (unexpected travel and lack of recall, e.g., psychogenic fugue).

h. Psychosexual disorders. This category comprises sexual disturbances which are predominately psychological, and not organic in origin. *Gender identity disorders* are characterized by feelings of discomfort with one's anatomical sex and a wish to get rid of one's genitals and/or live as a member of the other sex. The *paraphilias* refer to a cluster of disorders featuring a need for unusual or bizarre imagery or acts to experience sexual excitement (fetishism, transvestism, sexual activity with children or animals, etc.). The *psychosexual dysfunctions* refer to specific inhibitions in some phase of the sexual response cycle (e.g., inhibited sexual desire, premature ejaculation, etc.).

i. Personality disorders. When personality *traits* are sufficiently inflexible and maladaptive so as to cause either significant functional impairment or subjective distress, they constitute *personality disorders.* Manifestations of these patterns are usually recognizable by adolescence and continue through most of adult life.

Personality disorders may be grouped in three congruent clusters, the first of which includes the paranoid, schizoid, and schizotypal personality disorders. Individuals with these disorders often appear "odd," eccentric, and lacking in humor. The second cluster includes the histrionic, narcissistic, anti-social and borderline personality disorders. Persons with these disorders will often seem overly dramatic, self-preoccupied, lacking in genuineness, irresponsible, or unstable. The third group consists of avoidant, dependent, compulsive, and passive-aggressive personality disorders. Individuals with these disorders frequently appear overly anxious, fearful, emotionally constricted, overly sensitive, and perfectionistic.

j. Other DSM-III-R categories. Includes such conditions as (i) atypical psychoses, (ii) disorders related to impulse control (gambling), adjustment to stress, inaccurate reporting of symptoms without motive, and (iii) non-pathological life problems.

6. Issues Regarding Etiology and Treatment. It is estimated that between one-third and one-fourth of all

Americans will be treated for a mental disorder during their lifetime. Aside from a few disorders where precise etiological factors are presumed, the ultimate causes of most mental illnesses are not known. The introduction of symptom-suppressing medications, however, has led to important research into the effect of these drugs on particular brain sites and on specific neurotransmitters (chemical substances which convey messages between nerve cells). Researchers now have evidence for hypothesizing that an excess of certain brain chemicals (such as dopamine) is associated with schizophrenic-like symptoms while a deficiency in others (serotonin and norepinephrine) is connected with depression. Studies using computerized tomography (CT) have shown a number of structural abnormalities in the brains of persons with schizophrenia, while twin studies have demonstrated a definite but imprecise genetic involvement in the development of this disorder. These and other findings have convinced many investigators that manic-depressive disorders and some types of schizophrenia are genetically influenced diseases of the brain.

Treatment outcome studies, however, point to the important influence of psycho-social factors, especially in rehabilitation. Medication plus supportive therapies have been shown significantly superior in treating chronic mental patients than intervention alone. Moreover, a recent multi-site study has shown either of two forms of psychotherapy (interpersonal and cognitive/behavioral) to be as effective as standard drug treatment with severe, non-psychotic depression. These studies suggest that the brain is more malleable and susceptible to the environment than once thought.

In decades to come, research knowledge will significantly modify present understandings of mental health and illness. Some disorders now of unknown etiology will be found to have biological causes, others to have psycho-social origins, and still others a complex interplay of psychological, environmental,and biological determinants. The more treatment is based on etiology, however, the greater the prospect that treatment will cure, and that what cannot be cured may be prevented.

7. The Role of Religious Communities. Over the centuries, religious communities have assumed many roles in relation to mental health and illness. During the asylum era, religious groups sponsored chaplains and devoted untold hours in sharing friendship and concern through volunteer activities. In recent years, they have endorsed highly skilled pastoral care and counseling ministries in hospitals and other settings along with programs of clinical pastoral education. Perhaps their most constant contribution has been the enrichment of human life, in both health and illness, through communicating faith, hope, and a deep sense of belonging — a considerable gift to a lonely, recovering mental patient or to a world menaced by the possibility of nuclear holocaust.

A current challenge to religious congregations nationwide is the human and spiritual care of persons recovering from mental illnesses in the community. These persons, most of whom are poor and many of whom are black, are returning to neighborhoods already underserved in terms of mental health resources. All too often, they live in sub-standard housing or swell the ranks of the street population.

What can churches and temples do? The following are approaches of demonstrated effectiveness:

(a) Development of volunteer-led aftercare programs for former and about-to-be-discharged patients which provide opportunities for recreational activities, socialization, and supportive counseling.

(b) Acquisition and management of apartment housing for persons recovering from mental illnesses which feature accessibility of essential support services, opportunities for self-help and socialization, and options for various degrees of supervision.

(c) Management and operation of shelters for the homeless mentally ill (perhaps by a consortium of congregations) where minimum standards of health, nutrition and human dignity are assured pending placement in more permanent accommodations.

(d) Organization of work opportunities and small business ventures which employ recovering mental patients.

(e) Intentional incorporation of formerly hospitalized persons into the normal religious group activities of the congregation after careful education of the constituent members.

(f) Use of pastoral counseling facilities and trained pastoral counselors to provide skilled supportive counseling to the chronically mentally ill and their families in collaboration with psychiatric consultants. (Ideally, pastoral counselors might consider devoting a percentage of their caseloads to this service.)

(g) Use of new or established clergy councils, networks and coalitions to advocate adequate funding for services to the chronically mentally ill and to promote programs to help diminish the stigma associated with mental illness.

It remains true that religious groups and institutions are the community's greatest untapped resource for helping the mentally ill and promoting positive mental health.

Bibliography. For further information see American Psychiatric Association, *Diagnostic and Statistical Manual of Mental Disorders* (1980). H. Kaplan and B. Saddock, *Comprehensive Textbook of Psychiatry*, IV (1985). L. Kolb and K. Brodie, *Modern Clinical Psychiatry* (1982). F. Torrey, *Surviving Schizophrenia* (1983), especially for families. P. Hollinger, *Pastoral Care of Severe Emotional Disorders* (1985).

C. S. AIST

EVALUATION, PSYCHOLOGICAL; HEALTH AND ILLNESS; SALVATION, HEALING, AND HEALTH. *See also* EVIL; HEALING; MENTAL HOSPITAL/MENTAL HOSPITALIZATION; NEUROSIS; PSYCHOPATHOLOGY AND RELIGION; PSYCHOPATHOLOGY, THEORIES OF; PSYCHOSIS; RELIGION AND HEALTH; SIN AND SICKNESS. *Compare* ADJUSTMENT DISORDERS; BORDERLINE PERSONALITY; DEVELOPMENTAL DISORDERS; MENTAL RETARDATION; PERSONALITY DISORDERS; OLDER PERSONS, MENTAL DISORDERS OF; ORGANIC MENTAL DISORDERS; PSYCHOSOMATIC ILLNESS.

MENTAL HOSPITAL/MENTAL HOSPITALIZATION. A *mental hospital* is a hospital specifically designated for the treatment of severe mental and emotional disorders in a residential setting. Legal responsibility for treatment is vested in one or more physicians, although teams of professionals from a variety of disciplines actually carry out treatment plans. Such hospitals may be privately funded or tax-supported at any level of government. *Mental hospitalization* is the state of being an in-patient in a hospital designated for the treatment of persons with mental and emotional disorders. A patient's status may be voluntary or involuntary. In general, voluntary patients have the right to terminate treatment at any time without legal prejudice, provided that notice is given in writing the required number of days prior to leaving the hospital. Involuntary patients may not leave until certain requirements are satisfied.

1. **Brief History and Current Practices of Mental Hospitals.** In America, Benjamin Franklin and Benjamin Rush were responsible for the founding of the first hospital with specific facilities for treating persons "distempered in Mind and deprived of their rational Faculties," which opened in Philadelphia in 1752 as the Pennsylvania Hospital. Kindness toward such people was urged by the Quakers, but was often understood to mean inflicting pain in an attempt to induce a return to normal living.

In the 1800s "moral treatment" was developed, consisting of humane treatment, kindness, pleasant surroundings, few restraints, and structured activity. As state-supported institutions evolved, demand for treatment became so overwhelming that many hospitals were overcrowded, and moral treatment, geared to small groups, became almost impossible.

The first psychotropic drug, chlorpromazine, was introduced in 1954, and the character of mental hospitals changed radically. By 1969, about 850 medications of this type had made it possible to reduce emotional disturbance, thus making treatment possible.

In many ways, mental hospitals have become analogous to medical hospitals as society's concept of mental illness has changed. Where once people were "sent away" to an asylum to be held for the rest of their lives, today hospitalization is often understood to be a temporary necessity, brought on by emotional crises. Many patients are admitted for brief periods in order to be helped through difficult times, then released to continue recuperation in the community. If similar problems arise in the future, return to the hospital for additional help is possible. Much of the stigma of mental illness is becoming a thing of the past.

2. **Admission Procedures.** Hospitalization laws and procedures vary from state to state. The best practical source of specific knowledge is the admissions office of the hospital being considered.

a. Voluntary admissions. It is becoming a common practice for mental hospitals, both state-run and private, to require a referral from a community mental health center or physician in private practice (usually a psychiatrist) in order to admit a voluntary patient. Persons who suffer from mental or emotional disorders seem to benefit most if treatment is possible on an out-patient basis in the community. A person will be admitted for treatment in a hospital setting only when a professional person or team judges that out-patient treatment will be not sufficient.

Generally speaking, hospital treatment teams prefer voluntary admission because it is believed that persons who recognize their own mental illness are likely to participate actively in their treatment. In most states, the voluntary patient does not lose civil rights, but rather retains the right to vote, to sign personal papers, and to continue the management of property. In addition, a voluntarily admitted patient may obtain a discharge upon written notice to the superintendent.

b. Involuntary admissions. There are several reasons for involuntary hospitalization, all of which recognize the patient's inability to perceive the need for treatment. In some cases, a person may be too ill to act to obtain help, or too indecisive to meet mental health needs. In others, there may be irrational and impulsive behavior which is beyond the individual's ability to control, and it is essential for a second party to take the necessary action. All states make provision for a process to make this possible, sometimes requiring a court order, sometimes not.

In any case, there must be a written application by a person authorized by law; these range from almost any interested friend or citizen to spouses only. Following receipt of the application, there must be an examination of the patient's mental status conducted by a qualified person as specified by statute, within an established time limit.

There is an increasing tendency to recognize the need for determinate (time-limited) hospitalizations intended for observation, diagnosis, and/or short-term therapy. The maximum amount of time varies from state to state, but in no state does it exceed six months; it is typically found to be around sixty days.

All states provide a procedure for the indeterminate hospitalization of patients after a formal judicial hearing. In such cases, when there is a finding of "mentally ill" or its equivalent, the court may commit a patient to a mental hospital for treatment until the hospital administration initiates discharge. At this point, state statutes vary as to whether or not the patient must be returned to the court for a final decision (See *Harvard Law Review*).

3. **Treatment and Daily Living.** Because of the advent of community mental health centers, conditions in mental hospitals are no longer as crowded as they were as recently as the 1950s and 1960s. Many patients who would previously have been admitted for in-patient treatment are now able to receive the needed care on an out-patient basis. Consequently, mental hospitals have been able to utilize space efficiently, including effective use of interior decoration to provide pleasant surroundings. Mental hospitals are rapidly becoming places where people are accorded dignity during treatment. Many living quarters are pleasant, bright, and open, and judicious use of medication allows physicians to make use of a wide range of treatment approaches, including milieu therapy, individual and group psychotherapy, family therapy and guidance, and education in the tasks of daily living. Unfortunately, the type of treatment that is available across the country is not consistent in quantity or quality. However, it is rare today to find a psychiatric facility which is merely a "holding area" for chronically ill patients.

The backbone of any treatment program is the corps of nurses and aides who are with patients around the clock. Registered nurses provide supervision for other mental health workers, who are licensed as "mental health technicians" or other designations. Whatever they are called, however, these ward staff members are responsible for the day-to-day management of the patients, and must assure that basic needs are met (food, clothing, comfort, and security). Often they must also teach social skills, arbitrate disputes, prevent excessive friction, and help motivate patients to participate in treatment.

Most states require that a physician be legally responsible for the treatment of mentally ill persons. A physician (usually a psychiatrist) must diagnose illness, prescribe medication, and oversee the work of the entire treatment staff. Much of the actual treatment is carried out by other trained personnel.

Psychological testing is a standard procedure in most mental hospitals, with trained psychologists administering, scoring, and interpreting them. Test results often form the core of the treatment plan, and aid team members in understanding the needs of patients. In addition, psychologists frequently utilize their skills as therapists for individual patients or groups.

Social workers are responsible for liaison between patients and their home communities, and for helping to make discharge plans. Sometimes they also conduct family therapy within the context of the hospital, using various approaches depending on the patients' needs and the training of the individual social worker.

Activities therapists plan and conduct a wide variety of specialized programs for hospitalized patients, including music, occupational, horticultural, industrial, and drama therapies. All of these are seen as integrally related to treatment, with specific purposes and methodologies; they are not simply "activities" designed to keep people busy.

A patient's day in a mental hospital includes much time for "normal" activities. Nutritious meals are served, usually in a cafeteria-style dining room. Most wards enforce a rest hour in the middle of the day, and evenings are often free for reading, card-playing, watching television, and similar activities. In some places there are hospital-wide leisure programs which provide a relaxed atmosphere for music, dancing, and socializing. On weekends, religious services are usually provided for those who desire them.

4. Pastoral Care. a. Chaplaincy services. Many mental hospitals have on the staff a clinically trained chaplain whose responsibility is to minister to patients and to assure that their religious needs are met. Most chaplains function in a nondenominational capacity, often acting as facilitators for community pastors and religious groups.

b. Community pastors. Mental hospital patients retain their need for contact with familiar people and groups in their lives. For many, a relationship with the church and/or a pastor back home fulfills this need. Mental hospitals are increasingly aware that community pastors can be powerful allies in the treatment of mental illness.

The chaplain and the community pastor can work together to promote maximum benefit from a patient's religious background and interest. Often, the pastor who wants to visit a parishioner in the hospital can arrange to do so through the chaplain; or a patient who wants to see

a particular pastor may communicate that wish through the chaplain. Later in the patient's stay, the pastor may work with a social worker to make plans for the parishioner's return to the community. After discharge, the community minister may consult with the chaplain for clearer understanding of the needs of the parishioner. Together, they can work to provide a continuity of pastoral care for mentally ill persons.

Bibliography. S. Hamilton, "The History of American Mental Hospitals," in *One Hundred Years of American Psychiatry* (1944). M. Marguerite, *Psychiatric Nursing,* 9th ed. (1973). P. W. Pruyser, "Religion in the Psychiatric Hospital: A Reassessment," *J. of Pastoral Care,* 38 (1984), 5–16. J. A. Talbott, *The Death of the Asylum* (1978). "Developments in the Law: Civil Commitment of the Mentally Ill," *Harvard Law Review,* 87 (1974), 1202.

B. P. BOGIA

HOSPITALIZATION; MENTAL HEALTH AND ILLNESS; MENTAL HEALTH MOVEMENT; PSYCHOSIS. *See also* ELECTROCONVULSIVE THERAPY; EVALUATION AND DIAGNOSIS, PSYCHOLOGICAL; MILIEU THERAPY. *Compare* COMMUNITY MENTAL HEALTH MOVEMENT; LEGAL DIMENSIONS OF PASTORAL CARE AND COUNSELING.

MENTAL HOSPITAL CHAPLAINCY. The chaplaincy department of a mental hospital contains one or more clergy who are attached in an official way to the institution. Ordination and/or endorsement by a recognized religion or denomination is required by most institutions, as well as additional training in clinical practices. An understanding of the particular needs of mentally ill persons is essential to the position, as well as expertise in the interrelationship between religion and psychiatry. The chaplain is expected to work effectively with patients of a wide variety of religious beliefs, and is usually charged with the responsibility of seeing that their religious needs are met, either through direct ministry or through referral to clergy of the patient's religious persuasion.

1. History. The word "chaplain" derives from the Latin "cappella" meaning "cloak." In Christian legend, St. Martin divided his cloak with a beggar—sometimes thought to be Christ in disguise. That small cloak became a famous relic, guarded by a group of priests who called themselves "cappellani." Later, "cappellani" was used to designate clergy who were not attached to a church but who had other specified duties. Dictionaries usually define a chaplain as one who offers a religious ministry to a special group, such as a military unit, a ship, a lodge, or a hospital.

Early mental hospitals had no need for separate chaplaincy services, since the whole approach to treatment was dominated by religiously oriented persons. For example, in America, the Quakers were largely instrumental in the establishment of the Pennsylvania Hospital in 1792.

Although chaplains had been familiar figures in the military services and in some other institutions, it was not until the early 1900s that the concept was applied to mental hospitals. In 1924, the Rev. Anton Boisen became a full-time chaplain at Worcester State Hospital, Worcester, Massachusetts. Boisen was a minister with a troubled history, having been hospitalized himself for mental difficulties. During his hospitalization he became convinced that he had conceived a breakthrough in the wall between medicine and religion, and dedicated the rest of his life to developing this concept. In so doing, he laid the groundwork for specialized training for chaplains and emphasized the contributions which may be made to medicine by theology (see Boisen, 1936).

2. Training. Standards for the training of mental hospital chaplains are not universally accepted; criteria are usually established by each hospital according to guidelines developed by its personnel office or board of directors. In general practice, however, most mental health facilities expect at least six months of clinical training (such as that offered by the Association for Clinical Pastoral Education, ACPE), in addition to college and seminary degrees. Thus a high degree of importance is placed on training in a clinical setting, over and above education gained in an accredited theological school.

Such clinical education has a double focus: (a) the acquisition of knowledge about mental illness and treatment, and (b) the growth of understanding of the use of self as a pastoral tool in ministry. These goals are accomplished through experiential means, with much emphasis placed on writing and presenting verbatim accounts of pastoral visits, recording significant learning incidents, preparing pastoral case studies, examining worship and preaching, small group interaction, and individual supervisory sessions. While didactic input and required reading are utilized, they are of less importance than the exploration of the meanings of experiences of pastoral care.

Obviously, individual hospitals may choose to accept as chaplains ministers whose training has not been done through the ACPE, but who are considered to have equivalent credentials, either certified by another organization (such as the National Catholic Chaplains Association or the Association of Mental Health Clergy), or obtained by academic degree in a related field. A few mental hospitals still have established no standards of their own for chaplaincy training, and will accept any ordained minister or professed religious, depending on the orientation of the hospital. In these places, chaplaincy services are usually seen as "added-on" rather than as professionally integrated with the treatment program.

3. Functions. Chaplains in mental hospitals are, first of all, pastors. Their primary job is to see that patients receive pastoral care. In order to accomplish this task, however, chaplains must function in a variety of roles.

a. Ecclesiastical services. Most mental hospitals provide their residents with regular chapel services, usually on Sunday mornings. As representatives of the church, chaplains conduct worship in the hospital chapel and, where indicated, on wards where there are patients who are restricted from off-ward activities. Catholic services normally include confession and the celebration of the Mass, and Protestant services often include weekly Communion.

Other sacraments are available from the chaplains, as needed. Baptisms are rare, since chaplains usually prefer to act as a liaison with a community pastor so that baptism will be performed within the context of a worshiping community.

Religious education and nurture is provided for patients through Bible study, discussion groups, and individual teaching and training as the need arises.

b. Professional services. As hospital staff members, chaplains frequently serve as members of one or more treatment teams, acting as an interpreter to the staff of the religious ideation of the patients, and being available for religious counseling.

Specific pastoral counseling may be done with patients who are struggling with religious issues. This can be at the patient's initiative, in response to a concern on the part of the chaplain, or by referral from the staff.

In many hospitals, value is accorded to religious evaluations prepared by chaplains. These are not attempts to diagnose illness but are assessments done from a religious point of view. The chaplain's contribution is sometimes an important element in the team's understanding of patient needs.

Chaplains are included on many hospital committees as one way of sharing their particular perspective. These may include committees on quality assessment, research (especially as pertaining to the use of patients in research projects), professional library, and employee wellness.

Occasionally, chaplains may acquire additional training in order to become therapists, but this is usually understood to be outside the scope of the hospital's expectations.

c. Community relations. An important function of the chaplaincy department is to act as a liaison with patients' home churches and pastors. Some care must be exercised here, since an occasional patient may prefer that news about hospitalization not reach the home community; but a chaplain's offer to initiate a contact is often met with gratitude. As a patient's stay progresses, the chaplain's relationship with a home pastor may develop into interpretive functions.

Local congregations also may call upon a mental hospital chaplain to provide interpretation of the whole field of mental health and illness, as well as the kind of work which is being done in a particular hospital. It is not unusual to find chaplains speaking to various church-related groups, or preaching in local pulpits.

d. Educational services. Many mental hospitals provide educational opportunities for local pastors through their chaplaincy departments. These are often one-day workshops on a specific topic, such as "Stress Management" or "The Church and Mental Health." Sometimes chaplains act as consultants to individual pastors or to small groups, dealing with topics of particular interest.

Some mental hospitals are accredited centers for CPE, and may offer either academic credit through a nearby seminary or continuing education units.

e. Research. This area may be the most neglected one, for the duties of the hospital pastor leave little time or energy for writing. However, in recent years chaplains have been contributing in increasing numbers to professional journals, documenting styles of pastoral care and wrestling with theological concerns in practical terms.

Bibliography. A. T. Boisen, The Exploration of the Inner World (1971 [1936]). R. Dayringer, Pastor and Patient (1982). K. R. Mitchell, Hospital Chaplain (1972). R. Powell, Anton T. Boisen

(1976); *Fifty Years of Learning Through Supervised Encounter With Living Human Documents* (1975).

B. P. BOGIA

CHAPLAINCY; INTERPROFESSIONAL TEAMS AND RELATIONSHIPS; MINISTRY. *See also* PASTORAL CARE MOVEMENT; SALVATION, HEALING, AND HEALTH. *Compare* CLINICAL PASTORAL EDUCATION; MENTAL HEALTH MOVEMENT.

MENTAL HYGIENE. *See* MENTAL HEALTH MOVEMENT.

MENTAL ILLNESS. *See* MENTAL HEALTH AND ILLNESS; PSYCHOPATHOLOGY, THEORIES OF.

MENTAL PATIENT. *See* MENTAL HOSPITAL/MENTAL HOSPITALIZATION.

MENTAL PHILOSOPHY. *See* PSYCHOLOGY IN AMERICAN RELIGION.

MENTAL RETARDATION. The American Association on Mental Deficiency defines mental retardation as "subaverage intellectual functioning which originates during the developmental period and is associated with impairment in adaptive behavior." Accordingly, three factors must be considered in deciding that a person is retarded: measured IQ, level of social adaptation, and onset of difficulties before adulthood. Approximately three percent of the population are considered to be mentally retarded.

1. **Levels.** Four levels of retardation are recognized, referring to a specific range of IQ scores. *Mild mental retardation* (IQ level 50−70) comprises about 86 percent of the retarded population. This level of retardation includes individuals considered to be "educable" who usually can achieve social and vocational skills in adulthood that are adequate for minimum levels of self-support. As children they are eligible for special classes for the educably retarded and may obtain academic skills up to the sixth-grade level by late adolescence. Few individuals at this level of functioning are institutionalized unless they have severe behavioral or emotional problems in addition to their retardation.

Moderate mental retardation (IQ level 35–59) includes about 10 to 12 percent of retarded individuals. They are considered to be "trainable" and may profit from social and vocational training. Communication and self-help skills such as bathing, toileting, and feeding are generally adequate though they usually develop slowly and require special training. As children they are placed in classrooms that emphasize social and practical skills. Few progress beyond second-grade levels of academic achievement. As adults these individuals continue to remain in a dependent relationship to society. Few hold jobs except within sheltered workshops or family businesses, though they can contribute to their own support by performing unskilled or semi-skilled work under supervision. Many are institutionalized or live dependently within their families. Coordination is poor and awareness of social conventions is limited.

Severe mental retardation (IQ level 20−34) comprises about 4 to 7 percent of retarded individuals. During early years motor development and speech are impaired. Communication and elementary hygiene skills require prolonged training. Vocational training is unlikely to be profitable. As adults these individuals require continued intensive supervision and most are institutionalized. They engage in little independent activity.

Profound mental retardation (IQ level below 20) applies to less than one percent of the retarded population. Minimal capacities for learning are evidenced, and few skills beyond walking, feeding, toileting, and limited utterances are ever acquired. Constant aid and supervision are lifelong requirements. Many have severe physical and neurological deformities so that nursing care also may be necessary.

These diagnostic categories are difficult to apply, due in part to the fact that many retarded individuals are difficult to test using standard measurement instruments. Tests measuring the degree to which individuals are capable of functioning and maintaining themselves independently in daily living should be included in any determination of level of retardation, however, and periodic reassessments are also necessary to allow for the possibility of shifts in level of functioning.

The social implications of labeling a child as mildly, moderately, or severely retarded must also be considered and may often be of pastoral concern. Social agencies make decisions about specialized services for a child in part depending upon the level of retardation evidenced, so that once placed, the child may not have the opportunity to achieve beyond that level. However, new technologies and teaching principles such as operant training have been used to help retarded children acquire skills that they were previously considered incapable of learning.

2. **Causal Factors.** The causes of mental retardation are diverse but fall into two major categories: cultural-familial retardation and organic retardation. The former is assumed to account for most mild retardation, while the latter is thought to be the cause of most moderate, severe, and profound retardation.

Cultural-familial retardation is thought to be caused by environmental factors. No identifiable physiological damage is apparent, and other family members also are observed to have subaverage intellectual abilities. Often this form of retardation is not discovered until the child enters school. A disproportionate percentage of such persons come from lower socioeconomic families. Inadequate nutrition, poor medical care, lack of intellectual stimulation, and inadequate social support are often part of the home environment (Hurley).

The moderate, severe, and profound types of retardation are considered to be caused by a single pathological organic factor, such as a defective gene or a brain trauma. Individuals who sustain organic forms of retardation are evenly distributed throughout all socioeconomic, ethnic, and racial groups and comprise approximately 20 percent of the retarded population. Organic retardation is caused by one of three mechanisms: genetic, infectious, or traumatic. *Genetic disorders,* including Down's syndrome, phenylketonuria (PKU), Klinefelter's syndrome, cretinism, Tay-Sachs's, and others are determined at conception by an aberrant chromosome or the pairing of two defective genes, one from each parent. Of these, Down's syndrome (formerly called Mongolism) is the most common and is caused by the presence of an extra chromosome. Down's syndrome individuals are recognizable by their slanted eyes, broad flat faces, overly large and fissured tongue, and stubby fingers. The chances of having a Down's syndrome child increase dramatically with the age of the mother, especially after age 35.

Infections that cause retardation can affect the child both before birth, through contagion of the mother, or after birth. The most common form of infectious retardation is rubella or German measles, contracted during early pregnancy, which can result in both mental and physical defects, very often including blindness. Syphilis, also an infectious cause of retardation, is no longer as common as it once was, due to routine blood testing in marital licensing and prenatal clinics. Usually the child is immediately affected and often dies *in utero*. After birth, the infectious disease childhood meningitis can lead to retardation and other physical disabilities such as deafness, paralysis, and epilepsy.

Traumatic causes of retardation can occur prenatally, through delivery complications, or in childhood. They include lead poisoning, over-exposure to x-rays, malnutrition, oxygen deprivation, head injury, and certain drugs.

3. **Prevention.** There are no "cures" for mental retardation, though prevention is becoming more effective with new technologies and improved methods of prenatal care. Particularly with regard to cultural-familial retardation, early intervention, which includes improved medical and nutritional care and psycho-social stimulation, may help to alleviate the degree of retardation. With regard to organic causes of retardation, genetic counseling, the elimination of maternal diseases such as rubella and syphilis, and parental education in regard to the effects of poisoning and accidents can help to reduce the incidence of mental retardation. Amniocentesis, a technique of testing the fluid in a woman's uterus, can reveal whether a fetus is affected by some forms of organic retardation. The development of this technique, in conjunction with the availability of therapeutic abortions, opens the possibility of further limiting the number of retarded individuals. This prospect is accompanied by heated debates over right to life and the value and rights of retarded individuals which will not be readily resolved.

4. **Related Needs.** In addition to the problems that are faced as a direct result of mental retardation, other difficulties are also indirectly associated. Behavioral and emotional problems may be observed in individuals who are retarded, just as in normal persons, and should be treated with equal priority. Socially, the acceptance of the retarded individual into the family, church, and community constitutes a continuing problem to be addressed by both public and private social service agencies and by the church. The effect of the birth of a retarded child into a family is traumatic, and sensitive counseling can often contribute substantially to family adjustment. The role of the pastor as advocate, counselor, educator, and emotional-supportive presence can be invaluable to retarded individuals and their families.

Bibliography. J. M. Hunt, *Intelligence and Experience* (1961). R. L. Hurley, *Poverty and Mental Retardation: A Causal Relation-*ship (1969). H. B. Robinson and N. M. Robinson, *The Mentally Retarded Child: A Psychological Approach* (1965). S. B. Sarason and J. Doris, *Psychological Problems in Mental Deficiency* (1968).

L. MANS-WAGONER

INTELLIGENCE AND INTELLIGENCE TESTING; MENTALLY RETARDED PERSONS, JEWISH *or* PASTORAL CARE AND COUNSELING OF. *See also* DIAGNOSTIC AND STATISTICAL MANUAL III; DOWN'S SYNDROME; EXCEPTIONAL CHILDREN AND THEIR FAMILIES; HANDICAP AND DISABILITY. *Compare* PERSONALITY, BIOLOGICAL DIMENSIONS OF; DEVELOPMENTAL DISABILITIES; LEARNING DISABILITY; ORGANIC MENTAL DISORDERS.

MENTAL STATUS (In Diagnosis). That component of a psychological-psychiatric evaluation which is aimed at detecting the extent to which organic factors (head injuries, brain tumors, etc.) are involved in a mental disorder. Factors considered include: orientation to reality, memory, concentration, abstract thinking ability, intelligence, judgment, affective level, sensory and perceptual functioning, thought processes and content, and general behavior.

A. J. STRAATMEYER

EVALUATION AND DIAGNOSIS, PSYCHOLOGICAL.

MENTAL TELEPATHY. *See* PARAPSYCHOLOGY.

MENTALLY RETARDED CHILD AND FAMILY. *See* EXCEPTIONAL CHILDREN AND THEIR FAMILIES.

MENTALLY RETARDED PERSONS, JEWISH CARE OF. The obligation of Jews to show compassion and provide service to the unfortunate should apply fully to retarded persons. Yet, as has been true for other faiths, until recently, Jews have tended to neglect this group and failed to meet the responsibility for providing the special education necessary for meaningful religious participation.

This failure in a faith so dependent on the written Word and cognitive learning, stems in part from the nature of the disability. Retardation is a chronic condition usually present from birth, characterized by impairment both in intellectual functioning and in the capacity to respond to daily environmental demands. While intellectual development does occur, it is slower and peaks later at a lower level. Retardation is also frequently accompanied by physical characteristics that make the individual appear different. Often, the presence of a retarded member may create marital and family tensions.

The incidence of retardation among Jews is probably the same as for the population as a whole — approximately 3 percent. The occurrence of retardation tends to be higher in large families. While 4 percent of the retarded (profound and severe, with IQs ranging from 0 to 35) require full-time care, and 11 percent (moderate, with IQs from 36 to 51) can learn only limited self-care and basic communication skills, the large majority are capable of learning both academically (many to the sixth-grade level) and socially to meet basic standards of behavior. Whatever his or her handicaps, the retarded person remains an individual with a distinctive personality needing love, identity, connection, and recognition.

Judaism is in a particular position to meet those needs. The retarded person suffering often from a sense of difference with resulting rejection and isolation can use Judaism's values, special calendar, rituals, and customs to bring meaning into his or her life with a sense of belonging to a larger, caring universe. No less than the "normal" individual, the retarded person can utilize faith in God to deal with aspirations as well as with the uncertain and unpredictable in life.

The challenge to the rabbi, teacher, communal worker, and parent is to find the means to reach the retarded individual at his or her level through simplified methods and materials, accompanied by sympathy, patience, and understanding. Expectations and goals are important, but they must be formulated according to individual capacity. Experience has shown that the retarded person can learn the Jewish calendar, observe and understand holidays and festivals, learn simple prayers, observe rituals, and participate, at a simple level, in religious services.

Family, school, and synagogue must work together cooperatively. Careful planning and skilled teaching can prepare the retarded person, albeit at an older age than usual (about 16 or 17), for Bar or Bat Mitzvah. He or she can be helped to assume a rightful role in Jewish communal life. Wherever programs have been established, retarded persons and their families have responded positively. Provision of such programs can enrich Judaism and its institutions as well as the lives of retarded people.

Bibliography. S. Hofstein, "Giving Jewish Retarded a Chance to Be Individuals," *J. of Psychology and Judaism,* 5 (1981), 116–132.

S. HOFSTEIN

MENTAL RETARDATION. *See also* EXCEPTIONAL CHILDREN AND THEIR FAMILIES; FAMILY, JEWISH CARE AND COUNSELING OF; HANDICAP AND DISABILITY; PERSON (Jewish Perspective).

MENTALLY RETARDED PERSONS, PASTORAL CARE OF.

Persons are considered mentally retarded if, during their first eighteen years, they score significantly below average on a standard intelligence test and are also unable to meet the standards of behavior appropriate for their age and cultural group.

1. **Classification and Causes.** Mental retardation is classified according to severity as mild (IQ 52–67 on the revised Stadford-Binet scale), moderate (36–51), severe (20–35), and profound (19 and below). Persons mildly retarded are considered educable, those moderately to severely retarded trainable, and those profoundly retarded custodial. Approximately three percent of the population is thought to be mentally retarded. Of this group, eighty to eighty-six percent is mildly, ten to twelve percent moderately, and four to seven percent severely to profoundly affected.

Among the causes of mental retardation are prenatal infections, injuries to the brain during birth, metabolic and nutritional disorders, brain tumors early in life, chromosomal abnormalities, and environmental influences. Seventy-five to eighty-five percent of mental retardation is attributed to environmental or unknown causes.

2. **Care of the Family.** Many parents respond to the discovery that their child is retarded with behavior and feelings normally associated with bereavement, such as sorrow, anger, and guilt. In some cases the retarded child may be rejected, in others, overprotected. Parents must be helped to knowledge the loss of the wished-for "normal" child, to express the painful feelings that accompany that loss, and to reinvest their love by seeking appropriate help for the retarded child.

Parents often struggle to find an acceptable religious meaning for their child's condition. Although some are comforted by the belief that the handicap was willed by God, others vigorously reject this notion. Few parents today seem willing to believe that they or their child are the objects of divine punishment. The majority struggle to affirm that God is present in their suffering and will help bring some good out of their pain and loss.

Feelings of shame or inferiority are common in these families. Parents may be highly sensitive to the curiosity, condescension, or pity shown by others. A trusted pastor may serve as a bridge between the family and congregation or community, to enhance mutual acceptance and understanding.

Parents need considerable support for the difficult task of raising a retarded child. Many children need extensive professional help to achieve their full potential, and make heavy demands on parental time, patience, and resourcefulness. Parents may find it difficult to set realistic goals for their retarded child, or to balance their concern for that child with the well-being of non-retarded siblings. Difficult decisions can arise over education, medical care, or institutionalization. Some families will require referral to other professionals or helping agencies. Finally, parents need encouragement to affirm the unique gifts and joys they find in their retarded youngster.

3. **Care of the Individual.** Ministry to the retarded person is partly governed by the severity of the handicap. Most profoundly retarded persons cannot understand the spoken word, yet they appreciate attention and respond to touch, gesture, taste, and smell. Many enjoy music. Their families and caregivers especially deserve pastoral support.

Mildly to severely retarded persons have needs and feelings similar to those of non-retarded persons, and can benefit from pastoral understanding, acceptance, and honest, warm caring. They need help dealing with experiences of failure and loss, and in developing a life-affirming trust in the goodness of God. Their intellectual limits must be kept in mind, however. Moderately to severely affected persons have difficulty recognizing social and moral consequences of behavior and require firm guidance. The capacity of mildly retarded persons for insight is limited by their inability to handle abstract concepts; therefore, they need assistance to solve problems in step-by-step fashion.

Perhaps the most important thing a pastor can do for the retarded persons or their families is to be an agent of inclusion, seeking to broaden the boundaries of congregation and community and to enable their active participation in the family of God. The greatest need of retarded persons is not for a highly specialized ministry, but for the love and respect of their fellow humans.

Bibliography. P. Chinn, C. Drew, and D. Logan, *Mental Retardation: A Life Cycle Approach,* 2d ed. (1979). W. Gaventa, "Religious Mainstreaming of Retarded Persons," *Bulletin of the American Protestant Hospital Association,* 44:2 (1980), 35–40. G. W. Paterson, "Ministering to the Family of the Handicapped Child," *J. of Religion and Health,* 14:4 (1975), 165–76. J. L. Philpott, "By the Waters of Babylon: The Experience of Having a Down's Syndrome Child," *Pastoral Psychology,* 27:3 (1979), 155–63. D. Schurter, "Jean Piaget and Counseling the Mentally Retarded," *Bulletin of the American Protestant Hospital Association,* 44:2 (1980), 39–42. H. Stubblefield, "On Being a Pastor to the Mentally Retarded," *J. of Pastoral Care,* 24 (1970), 98–108.

G. W. PATERSON

MENTAL RETARDATION. *See also* EXCEPTIONAL CHILDREN AND THEIR FAMILIES; FAMILY, PASTORAL *or* JEWISH CARE AND COUNSELING OF; HANDICAP AND DISABILITY; PERSON.

MERCY KILLING. *See* DEATH, MORAL DILEMMAS IN; MEDICAL-ETHICAL DILEMMAS, JEWISH CARE AND COUNSELING IN; MORAL DILEMMAS IN PASTORAL PERSPECTIVE.

MERCY. *See* COMPASSION; FORGIVENESS; GRACE.

MERIT. *See* FAITH AND WORKS; PENANCE.

MERTON, THOMAS (1915–68). Trappist monk, theologian, poet, and author whose interest in and works on various aspects of Christian spirituality made him a celebrity and a magnetic figure for many great people, a process which tested his commitment to the monastic life. Later in life, he became interested in Far Eastern spirituality. His life and deliberations, which have found expression in many writings, have served, and still serve, to spur the imagination of many contemplative persons as well as an inspiration for much secondary literary reflection.

Merton's significance for pastoral care is rooted, first, in his stature as one of the great spiritual masters, perhaps the greatest one, of the second half of the twentieth century. Second, Merton was one of few in his time who espoused the twin emphases of profound personal spirituality and, flowing from it, deep social concerns and action. Thus, Merton anticipated, and perhaps provided a model for, the dilemma and agenda of the field of pastoral care in the future: the coupling of care for (hurting) individuals with care for the common good with the aid of spirituality rather than at its expense as in earlier social action movements.

N. F. HAHN

SPIRITUALITY (Roman Catholic Tradition).

MESMER, FRANZ ANTON (1734–1815). Austrian physician. In trying to open the way for the study of neuroses, Mesmer originated the practice of "mesmerism," which led to the discovery of the psychological phenomenon that later came to be known as "hypnosis."

In pursuing the traditional idea that heavenly bodies influence health and disease, an idea he had already pursued in his medical thesis, Mesmer performed many experiments with "animal magnetism." After achieving some initial popular fame, his work was not taken seriously until it became integrated, and thereby validated, in the psychological and neurological work of the French psychiatrists Pierre Janet and Jean-Martin Charcot.

In a historical period deeply steeped in the Enlightenment belief about the foundational function of reason for all belief and conduct and in which scientific advances, therefore, did not include the study of the nervous system and its psychology or physiology, Mesmer's work occupies an important position in the shift toward greater awareness of the interaction between mind and body, and anticipated the modern disciplines of psychopathology and psychotherapy.

N. F. HAHN

MIND-BODY RELATIONSHIP; HYPNOSIS.

METANOIA. *See* REPENTANCE AND CONFESSION.

METAPSYCHOLOGY. *See* PSYCHOANALYSIS (Personality Theory and Research).

METHODIST PASTORAL CARE. Pastoral care in the Methodist tradition has two noteworthy features: a central focus on "the path to perfection," whereby the Christian is nurtured and impelled by grace to a maturity of discipleship; and the practice of mutual accountability, primarily through the weekly class meeting.

1. The Path to Perfection. *a. Catholicity of grace.* Integral to the Methodist concept of pastoral care is the doctrine of grace which Wesley derived from the Anglican theological tradition. The English Reformation had resisted the extremes of continental theology by plotting a middle way between the doctrines of creation and salvation, thereby avoiding the Protestant disjunction between nature and grace. Every human being was perceived to have a measure of the grace of God, and every aspect of human existence was perceived to be under the governance of God.

Methodists view Christian discipleship, therefore, as a dynamic of constant divine initiative and developing human response. The freedom of the human will lies not in a choice between good and evil, but in resisting or not resisting the gracious initiatives of the Holy Spirit. With sensitive pastoral care, these initiatives can be discerned by the believer and accepted in a progressively obedient discipleship.

There is, however, a critical point of surrender which marks the inception of mature discipleship, and which is accompanied by a regeneration of the will. Theologically this is, of course, the doctrine of justification by faith. But pastorally, Wesley describes it as a new birth in which the Christian, experiencing a new relationship with God through Christ, receives the grace of God in a critical new dimension.

b. Christian maturity. The surrender of the will to justifying grace is not final, however, nor yet is it irresistible. The immediacy of this new dimension of grace must be worked out in a transforming discipleship of obedience, which proves to be a two-fold struggle: against a world which is manifestly resistant to the will of God; and against residual resistance in the individual Christian. The regenerative grace of God will increasingly prevail, however, in a developing acceptance of the divine initiatives—a pattern of spiritual perception which reflects Wesley's knowledge of the Eastern Fathers. The goal of this progression is Christian perfection, though the more helpful (and more accurate) translation of the NT word *teleiosis* would be *maturity*.

In response to the many personal accounts of society members, Wesley acknowledged that this maturity could be experienced as clearly and even as dramatically as the new birth, leading him and many others in the various Methodist traditions to declare it as a "second blessing." Yet he was careful to affirm that the transforming relationship with God was limitless, "grace upon grace," and while the faithful disciple should aim for and expect a maturity of obedience, this should not be restricted to a special experience. Christian maturity was a consistent submission of every thought, word, and deed to the will of God, the token of which was a pervading sense of divine love in every dimension of life.

c. Pastoral care and the path to perfection. Methodist pastoral care was thus perceived as the nurture and guidance of persons at varying stages of surrender to God's gracious initiatives. Borrowing language from the Moravians, who greatly influenced Wesley for a number of years, Methodists were classified as "awakened," those who "professed justification," and those who "professed the perfect love of God." Those who "fell from the faith" were classified as "penitents," and were given special instruction and advice. Those who "recovered the ground they had lost" proved even stronger in the faith. But always the goal was a maturity of obedience in a loving relationship with God.

2. **Mutual Accountability.** *a. The class meeting.* During the early years of the Methodist movement, Wesley borrowed another concept from the Moravians, and divided the societies into small intimate groupings known as *bands*. Their purpose was intensive self-examination, so the path to perfection might be followed by each person more rigorously. But the *bands* proved neither appropriate nor effective for the majority of ordinary people who became Methodists. Intensive mutual confession was found to require a degree of spiritual perception and, perhaps more important, a level of education, which could not be presupposed in eighteenth-century England.

Wesley's solution, by his own account, was a practical means of pastoral oversight which he discovered almost by accident. In an attempt to resolve a building debt in the Bristol society in 1742, he appointed a number of members as *leaders* to collect a weekly contribution from the others, whom he grouped into *classes* of twelve. The weekly round proved to be an immediate and welcome means of pastoral care, and within a year had evolved into a weekly meeting together at which the leader, beginning with him or herself, called upon the members in turn to give an account of their discipleship during the past week.

This direct and matter-of-fact procedure avoided the intensity of the bands, and at the same time engendered a mutuality of pastoral care which addressed the pragmatic concerns of daily living. As Wesley put it, the class members began to "watch over one another in love." But it was love with a purpose. The fellowship and the mutual care were the blessings they received as they pursued their prior objective of faithful discipleship. They did not make the mistake of seeking fellowship for its own sake—the chronic error of some later experiments in small group dynamics, and the most persistent historiographical misreading of the early Methodist class meeting.

b. Works of obedience. Because Christian discipleship was viewed as the development of obedient response to the divine initiative, practical good works featured prominently in the weekly catechesis of the class meeting. While there was no prerequisite for joining a Methodist society other than a "desire to flee from the wrath to come," in order to *remain* a Methodist there were rules to be observed. The first of these was a commitment to resist the temptation of sinning against God and one's neighbor; and the second was to do every possible good in the service of God and one's neighbor. Methodism affirmed that the cure of the soul was inextricably bound up with practical good works, and in the Minutes of the Methodist Conferences, begun in 1744, it is stated quite clearly that, without the intentional practice of Christian service, faith is at risk, and can even founder. A concept of pastoral care which ignores the present obligation to do one's best as a Christian disciple has no place in the authentic Methodist tradition.

c. The means of grace. The third general rule of the Methodist societies was that every member should be faithful in observing the time-honored ordinances which the church had found to be efficacious across the centuries. A Methodist could not expect to sustain discipleship, nor yet to grow in grace, without using the "means of grace," which Wesley identified under the categories of "instituted" and "prudential." The instituted means of grace were: prayer—private, family and public; searching of the Scriptures; public worship; the ministry of the Word, read or expounded; the Sacrament of the Lord's Supper; temperance and fasting; and Christian conference, or conversation. The most important prudential means of grace was the class meeting, where Methodists held one another accountable each week for their discipleship. And close to this in importance was their singing of hymns, in which they not only expressed their faith, but evinced a mutual concern. This is very clear in the subject headings of *A Collection of Hymns* (1780), which more than any prayer book forged their liturgical identity.

d. Wesley's episcopate. Perhaps most significant about the Methodist model of pastoral care is that, even though his preachers and class leaders were as skilled a group of pastoral mentors as the church has ever produced, Wesley regarded it of paramount importance that his pastoral office as an ordained clergyman be acknowledged as the pivotal link with the visible church, without which no pastoral care in the true sense of the word could be effected. He maintained this link at every level of the connectional structure of Methodism.

Bibliography. F. Baker, "The People Called Methodists: 3. Polity," in *A History of the Methodist Church in Great Britain*, vol. 1, R. E. Davies and E. G. Rupp, eds., (1965), pp. 213–55. R. E. Cushman, "Salvation for All—John Wesley and Calvinism," in *Faith Seeking Understanding* (1981). F. Hildebrandt and

O. A. Beckerlegge, eds., *The Works of John Wesley, vol. 7: A Collection of Hymns for the People Called Methodists* (1984). A. C. Outler, ed., *The Works of John Wesley, vol. 1: Sermons I: 1–33*, (1984), intro., pp. 55–96.

DAVID LOWES WATSON

HISTORY OF PROTESTANT PASTORAL CARE (Canada *or* United States); PASTORAL CARE (History, Traditions, and Definitions). *See also* COMMUNITY, FELLOWSHIP, AND CARE; ECCLESIOLOGY AND PASTORAL CARE; EVANGELICAL PASTORAL CARE; PERFECTIONISM; PIETISM AND PASTORAL CARE; SANCTIFICATION/HOLINESS. *Biography:* WESLEY.

METHODOLOGY, THEOLOGICAL. *See* PASTORAL THEOLOGICAL METHODOLOGY; THEOLOGY AND PSYCHOLOGY.

METHODS OF CARE AND COUNSELING. *See* PASTORAL CARE (Contemporary Methods, Perspectives, and Issues). *See also* PASTORAL COUNSELING; PSYCHOLOGY AND PSYCHOTHERAPY (East-West Comparison); SPIRITUAL DIRECTION; TECHNIQUE AND SKILL.

MIDDLE AGE. *See* MIDLIFE PERSONS. *See also* LIFE CYCLE THEORY.

MIDDLE AGES. *See* MEDIEVAL CHURCH, PASTORAL CARE IN.

MID-LIFE PERSONS. Mid-life is the life stage that begins at approximately the mid-thirties and runs through the mid- to late fifties. Value redefinition, reaffirmation of personal identity, and a large number of major change events are outstanding features of the mid-life era.

Within this broad time span there are subdivisions with unique characteristics. The traits in *early mid-life* (mid-thirties through early forties) for most men are strength, vigor, and a clear sense of direction. Women at this time, however, often are beginning a phase of personal evaluation that can develop into a crisis. The *middle* division of mid-life (forties) is characterized by a serious reconsideration of values and a decline in life satisfaction by most men. Many women, who have generally clarified their values and direction in life by their forties, experience a growing assertiveness and focus of energy. *Late mid-life* (end of forties into the late fifties) is usually a period of productivity resulting from accumulated wisdom, value clarification, and access to resources. The productivity of late mid-life is marked by generativity, which is a willingness to teach and train the younger generation, in contrast to late young adulthood productivity, which has a dimension of self-aggrandizement and a willingness to sacrifice personal values for cultural standards of success.

1. Characteristics. Mid-life adults are developmentally different from young adults in the following ways.

Physically, some decline in physical functioning is experienced in mid-life. Body movement is slower; sleep is shorter; hearing, vision, and sense of smell are reduced. Weight tends to shift from the limbs to the torso. Fat composition in the skin is reduced, allowing bones and muscles to become more visible. Although there are physical losses at mid-life, they are not massive and generally do not impose restrictions on productivity. In fact, the senses of touch and taste are more sensitive through mid-life, and the reflex response to stimuli is equal to that of adolescence.

Socially, the early mid-life adult is very relational but often uses people to advance personal goal aspirations. During the mid-life evaluation period there is frequently a retreating from friends and especially from perfunctory social obligations. The late mid-life person who has refined his or her value direction may have fewer friends, but the friendships are truer and not used for political advantage.

Vocationally, the early mid-life male attempts to complete goals set in young adulthood before he enters a plateau of achievement in the forties. There is a focused direction and great energy expenditure—an upward vocational thrust. But the forties often are years of vocational trauma for a man as he feels he has leveled off and may never reach his vocational goals. Even if he has achieved his goals, he may feel, because of the new value structure he now has, that he has wasted his life on a meaningless career. Vocational readjustments, continued education, and job skill development are common for men in their forties. If career learning and adjustment adequately fit the man's new value structure, his productivity and sense of fulfillment likely will be high during his late forties and continue to retirement.

About 50 percent of women are working by early mid-life. Many are working only for financial reasons, however, rather than for the fulfillment of a career. As women reevaluate who they are during early mid-life, their work shifts more toward their career motivations and abilities. Their value clarification and psychological growth will generally cause them to be vocationally productive and satisfied with life during their forties and fifties.

Emotionally and attitudinally, the early phase of mid-life for men generally is marked by optimism. During the forties they often take a depressive downturn, but the latter part of mid-life is again optimistic. Women tend to be more emotionally unstable during the early phase of mid-life, but they are more optimistic and productive during their forties and fifties, except for those who experience hormone imbalance due to menopause. The sense of self-esteem in both men and women tends to follow the patterns of optimism or depression.

In early mid-life, men are generally very assertive and aggressive. In their forties—as they are confronted with the realities of aging, vocational limitations, and family change events—they begin the process of value redefinition. When they have completed the process, they generally are less aggressive and more affiliative, generative, and mellow.

A woman in early mid-life exhibits insecurity as she wrestles with the questions of life. After she passes through her value redefinition period, she tends to be more assertive and goal-oriented. She may be a late bloomer, now living out the dreams she had envisioned in her young adulthood.

Intellectually, tests indicate a high degree of stability between ages twenty and fifty. Adults who continue to be stimulated intellectually tend to perform better in learning experiences than those without stimulation. Although an adolescent has a higher capacity for memorization, a mid-life adult has a greater capacity to synthesize, to put things into perspective, and to make sense out of facts and experience.

The mid-life adult's capacity to learn is not related to intellect so much as it is to the educational process itself. Adults learn in order to use the information in their current life. (Therefore, educational systems should provide adults with relevant, need-related learning experiences rather than simply providing information for future use.)

Maritally, even though a couple survives the first two "eras" of high divorce potential (the first three years and the seventh through tenth years of marriage), their marriage may be severely tested in mid-life. This is caused by two major factors, the first of which is neglect. Neglect occurs when either of the spouses becomes preoccupied with other matters. The husband often is willing to sacrifice everything else, including a healthy marriage relationship, to arrive at his career aspiration. The wife may be consumed with caring for children and an ever-expanding involvement in community and church activities, or she may be combining child rearing and housekeeping with a career.

The second stress factor is the value redefinition period through which each spouse goes. Women on the average are in their late thirties and men generally are in their forties when they seriously consider issues such as "Who am I?" "What is the meaning of life?" "What shall I do with the rest of my life?" "To whom do I want to relate?" "Whom do I really love?" and "How does God fit into my life?"

A younger couple tends to believe that marital difficulties will eventually be ironed out in the future. However, mid-life brings an immediate time orientation, and there is impatience with unresolved matters. If the marriage has not been positive, the couple tends to look for a quick solution through divorce or affairs. Married persons who realize that their marital problems can be resolved, however, may be able to use the mid-life evaluation time to make their marriage stronger. Marriages that survive the value redefinition period experience a growth in satisfaction that continues to increase into old age.

Morally and spiritually, mid-life adults are more inclined to see ambiguities than young adults, who tend to have more neatly defined moral concepts. In addition, the process of value redefinition in mid-life seems to move in one of two possible directions. One group progresses to higher moral stages characterized by flexibility and the acceptance of differences in moral perspective, while the other group becomes entrenched in or regresses to a stage where moral actions and attitudes are defined by outside authorities, and one assumes little personal responsibility for thinking through ethical principles.

Participation in the church tends to be high and family-centered during the thirties. During the reevaluation time of the forties, church involvement is generally at a lower level, with some adults going through a sharp withdrawal. The fifties are marked by a participation that involves meeting personal spiritual needs as well as training a younger generation to be the next leaders.

2. Mid-Life Change Events. During mid-life, couples with children will experience the "empty nest" as children leave home for college, to start a career, and/or to marry. Thus, they also may become in-laws and grandparents. Many will work through some major career adjustments or be involved in continuing education. There will likely be a decline in their parents' health and independence, and many will experience the death of one or both of their parents. In addition, mid-life adults also may experience some degree of "mid-life crisis."

3. Mid-Life Crisis. Every mid-life adult goes through the transition from young adulthood to mid-life adulthood. Some make the move gradually over a period of years so that they do not experience the change as a crisis; however, about 75 percent experience a moderate to severe crisis. Mid-life crisis happens when a person is forced to redefine in a short period of time his or personal identity and goals because of an aging body, a growing awareness of death, an unsatisfying marriage, the realization of limited career achievements or opportunities, the illness or death of parents, or the emerging independence of children.

Because there are so many issues to rethink at once, the psyche seeks a moratorium while the person wrestles with value concerns. This preoccupation is sometimes demonstrated by withdrawal, anger, and irritability with people and with life, self-centeredness, a pleasure-seeking lifestyle, or a strong desire to escape. A person commonly will feel that he or she needs more space and time to think and that life doesn't make sense. Drastic lifestyle changes are common, such as a new wardrobe, new time schedules, different groups of friends, and different attitudes toward family and work. Often there is withdrawal from church and social activities. It is a period of testing new lifestyles caused by a need to set new priorities and redefine life values.

The processing of values at mid-life can be more successfully handled by reading information about mid-life, taking time for personal reflection, holding discussions with friends and confidantes, having depth interaction with God, and confronting the psychosocial and spiritual tasks to be accomplished, perhaps through psychotherapy or pastoral counseling. Tasks to be accomplished include such matters as accepting one's aging, including coming to terms with failures and the realization that one will not achieve all of one's earlier goals and hopes, and that future possibilities are limited and gradually narrowing; facing the reality of death of self and loved ones; strengthening and deepening relationships with family and friends; re-aligning career with abilities and interests; and reassessing life values and meanings.

Bibliography. C. Aslanian and H. Brickell, *Americans in Transition* (1980). J. Conway, *Men in Mid-Life Crisis* (1978). S. Conway, *Your Husband's Mid-Life Crisis* (1980, 1987). J. Conway and S. Conway, *Women In Mid-Life Crisis* (1983). E. Erikson, *et al.*, *Adulthood: Essays* (1978). A. B. Knox, *Adult Development and Learning* (1977). L. Kohlberg, "Continuities and Discontinuities in Childhood and Adult Moral Development Revisited," in *Moralization the Cognitive Development Approach* (1974). D. J. Levinson, *The Seasons of a Man's Life* (1978). R. D. Chassick, "Mental Health and the Care of the Soul in Mid-Life," *J. of Pastoral Care,* 37 (1983), 5–12. D. J. Maitland, *Looking Both Ways: A Theology of Mid-Life* (1985). S. D. Sammon, "Life After

Youth: The Mid-life Transition and Its Aftermath," *Human Development*, 3 (1982), 15–25. J. R. Zullo, "The Crisis of Limits: Midlife Beginnings," *Human Development*, 3 (1982) 6–14.

J. CONWAY
S. CONWAY

LIFE CYCLE THEORY AND PASTORAL CARE; MORAL DEVELOPMENT; PERSONALITY DEVELOPMENT. *See also* PARENTS / PARENTHOOD; WORK AND CAREER. *Compare* OLDER PERSONS; YOUNG ADULTS.

MIGRAINE. *See* PAIN MANAGEMENT/PAIN CLINIC. *See also* BIOFEEDBACK; PSYCHOSOMATIC ILLNESS.

MIGRANT WORKERS AND FAMILIES. The needs of migrant agricultural workers are many, largely the result of their lifestyle, the weather patterns, and injustices suffered at the hands of employers and society. Thanks to the hard and ongoing work of numerous benevolent religious and secular agencies during the last fifty years, working conditions for migrants have improved somewhat. Although not dramatic, some significant steps have been taken to improve their lot, particularly on the West Coast, through the historic work of Cesar Chavez. His clear articulation of the problems of migrants and steadfast efforts to improve their social and economic condition brought about the United Farm Worker's Union in 1966. But significant as this may be, much more work remains to be done. And there is much the church can and should do through the ministries of pastoral care and advice, social service, and political advocacy.

1. The Needs of Migrants. Because most migrants live at the poverty level and are frequently displaced, it is common to encounter entire family units without proper medical, mental, and spiritual care. Thus, it is not surprising to find that migrant life expectancy is forty-nine years. Adequate housing is a constant problem as well. Dwellings are often substandard, lacking the amenities of the average American home and deficient in facilities for proper personal hygiene and sanitation. Migrants are frequently found living in old dormitories, shacks, or even in vehicles.

Migrants are also at an educational disadvantage because of language; many speak only their native language and very rarely attain a functional mastery of English. Since permanent employment is contingent on speaking English, most migrants are relegated to picking seasonal crops. This cycle adversely affects their aspirations and hopes for the future. In addition, the constant displacement of their children from public schools breaks up learning patterns and adversely affects the development of academic skills and proper work habits. Consequently the message conveyed to the migrant children is that migrant lifestyle is not temporary but permanent. The problem, however, is not only a matter of academic deficiencies but a question of negative values that must be arrested and dealt with in order that more positive values may be established and prioritized to the migrant's advantage.

2. Ministry to Migrants. Pastoral care for migrants is a very complex and difficult task. It requires having available a stock of biblical stories, themes, and images along with practical and informed advice. In proclaiming the gospel of Jesus Christ, the pastor may refer to Israel's exodus from Egypt and Israel's migration to the Promised Land as biblical stories of special relevance. One may emphasize, for example, that God had a *permanent* goal for Israel—that God's people should arrive at a *permanent* destination—the Promised Land—and that God *organized* Israel during their migration in order to prepare them to take and keep that land and prosper in it. While other lessons can be learned from this biblical story, these two points offer a beginning basis for addressing in a biblical manner the migrant's pattern of constant displacement.

Pastors should be acquainted with the wandering pattern of migrant people in order, if possible, to recommend a series of churches where migrants can be oriented to their surroundings as they follow seasonal crops. Churches finding themselves in a migrant "stream" can provide spiritual, moral, and in some cases even emergency financial support. These churches also may be in contact with other legal, medical, and welfare agencies that specialize in migrant care; it is important to remember that migrants are often not educated about the community agencies and public resources at their disposal. Some pastors in agricultural areas have started emergency funds or "helping hands ministries" for financial and social aid when inclement weather ruins crops that migrant laborers have traveled long distances to pick.

Migrants often impress the pastor as nervous, insecure people who are attracted to a life of frequent displacement or, conversely, as people who have *become* nervous and insecure through a lifetime of dislocations. In either case special patience and sensitivity are called for. When communicating with migrants, the pastor should encourage their aspirations to a better life. A good beginning is to provide education in stewardship, including learning to live within a limited budget. Migrants should also be encouraged to set a goal of becoming permanent residents in a town of their choosing and members of a church that meets their family needs. Another goal should be to learn English so that they might locate permanent employment. Migrant parents should be advised that permanence is also vital to their children's future.

Pastoral care of migrant families is a formidable challenge. But the rewards of watching migrant families settle, sink roots, and develop long and lasting friendships are worth the efforts of wise and informed pastoral care.

Bibliography. R. Coles, *Migrants, Sharecroppers, Mountaineers* (1972). J. Levy, *Cesar Chavez* (1975).

I. CANALES

CULTURAL AND ETHNIC FACTORS *or* SOCIAL STATUS AND CLASS FACTORS, IN PASTORAL CARE; POOR PERSONS; SOCIAL CHANGE AND DISLOCATION; SOCIAL JUSTICE ISSUES IN PASTORAL CARE. *See also* ADVOCACY; EXPLOITATION/OPPRESSION; LIBERATION THEOLOGY AND PASTORAL CARE; PROPHETIC / PASTORAL TENSION; SOCIAL SERVICES AND PASTORAL CARE. *Compare* WORK AND CAREER.

MILIEU THERAPY. The manipulation of the environment of a mental patient as an aid toward the patient's recovery. The creation of a therapeutic environment in a hospital or other institutional setting is vital to healthy adjustment of people with emotional or mental problems. Much research suggests that the family and home environments are the primary therapeutic milieus. Intervention in these settings is exemplified by work with families of schizophrenics, where family members are trained to meet special needs of the patient for containment, support, and structure. Examples of other types of milieu therapies include token economy behavior modification programs for the mentally retarded and the confrontational Scared Straight approach to dealing with juvenile delinquents. Some religious institutions, like Oral Roberts University's City of Faith Medical Center, include spiritual assessment, counseling, and prayer partners in their milieu therapy. Although varied in design and philosophy, three common denominators have been found by Gunderson (1983) in the majority of successful milieu therapies: distribution of responsibilities and decision-making power; clarity in treatment programs, role, and leadership; and a high level of patient-staff interaction.

Bibliography. J. Gunderson *et al.*, *Principles and Practice of Milieu Therapy* (1983).

S. ALLISON

COMMUNITY, FELLOWSHIP, AND CARE; COMMUNITY PSYCHIATRY/PSYCHOLOGY; PSYCHOTHERAPY; THERAPEUTIC COMMUNITY. *Compare* THERAPEUTIC CONDITIONS.

MILITARY SERVICE AND MILITARY CHAPLAINCY.

Military service denotes participation as a uniformed member in one of the armed forces: Army, Navy, Air Force, Marine Corps, Coast Guard. Military chaplaincy is a cooperative arrangement between religious faith groups and the government to provide ministry to persons in the military environment.

1. **The Experience of Military Service.** Persons in military service are under obligation to defend the nation and its way of life. Their oath of service sets them apart from the larger civilian society. This separation is necessary because of the requirement for combat readiness. Unlike civilian life, the military is organized around those hierarchical values of control, discipline, and obedience that are essential to success in armed conflict. Military units also serve the nation in disaster relief, rescue missions, and international peacekeeping operations. As public servants, military people, like law enforcement officers, live with the possibility that the performance of duty may require the supreme self-sacrifice.

Persons entering military service make a transition into a new way of life. This transition begins with the oath of office and is followed by a rigorous period of basic training. By the end of basic training new members will have made the initial adjustment to military life. They are then sent to service schools or to operational units where the transition continues.

New members soon learn that military life offers both worthwhile opportunities and personal challenges. The skills taught in service schools, for example, often transfer easily into civilian occupations, and educational programs are offered on military posts by colleges, universities, and vocational schools. These opportunities, and the promise of travel, are available to all.

However, young people in military service, like all young people, inevitably face conflict, anxiety, and questions of personal identity, though military people must face these issues in ways that do not interfere with their military responsibilities. Conflict may arise between personal desires and the requirement of military duties. A service member will get help from superiors and colleagues in meeting this challenge, but the management of personal conflict is the individual's responsibility.

Anxiety may be high in the new member. The new person must adjust, show ability, and establish rapport with leaders and peers. All service people share the anxieties of unexpected transfers, high-tempo military operations, potential dangers, and physical separation from families.

Questions of personal identity are often intense. Service life brings together persons of varied backgrounds. Duty in other lands exposes one to unfamiliar cultures and practices. These experiences force service members to draw on their inner resources and to make choices between competing values and lifestyles.

Since those entering military service will naturally seek role models, parish ministry can help prospective service members by drawing on the military expertise of the congregation to prepare them for the experience. In addition to spiritual formation, such preparation should also include an emphasis on coping skills, and an introduction to the work and ministries of military chaplains.

2. **Military Chaplaincy.** *a. Origins.* The roots of the military chaplaincy go back to the fourth century, to the soldier who later became St. Martin of Tours. While traveling on a winter night, Martin met a freezing beggar. Having no money, he divided his cloak with his sword and gave half of it to the beggar. Later he had a vision of Jesus Christ wearing the half-cloak. The vision led to Martin's baptism. He finally left military service and devoted his life to the church. By the Middle Ages St. Martin was revered as the patron saint of French kings, and his half-cloak was preserved as a sacred relic of the church.

The church permitted the kings to carry the cloak into battle. But, because it was a relic of the church, it was cared for by a priest. The priest, who also served as the king's pastor, was called "capellanus," which means "keeper of the cloak." From his title comes the English word "chaplain."

b. Characteristics. The medieval *cappellani* and contemporary military chaplains share two important characteristics. First, in the medieval arrangement, neither the priest nor the cloak belonged to the king. Both were loaned him by the church. A similar arrangement exists in the military services. The armed forces do not create their own ministry. They receive ministries from the religious bodies of the nation. The second characteristic involves accountability. In the performance of their duties the original *cappellani* were accountable to both bishop and king. In similar fashion, the military chaplain is answerable to both ecclesiastical and military authority. These two characteristics constitute what R. G. Hutcheson calls the chaplain's "institutional duality." This duality is evident both in the appointment and the ongoing accountability of military chaplains.

c. Endorsement and commissioning. Prior to appointment as a military chaplain, a clergyperson must be certified for this special ministry by his or her religious body. This certification, called "ecclesiastical endorsement," is the responsibility of the religious body. When accepted by the military for appointment as chaplain, the endorsed clergyperson is given military officer status. The conferring of military status, called "commissioning," is the responsibility of the military.

Endorsement and commissioning symbolize the chaplain's ongoing accountability to two institutions. As a commissioned officer, the chaplain serves as a special assistant to a military commander. Because the commander has total responsibility for the military unit, the chaplain, like other unit personnel, is accountable to that officer. Likewise, as an endorsed clergyperson, the chaplain is a full member of his or her religious body. Like other clergy, the chaplain is accountable to the religious body for a faithful representation of its beliefs and practices.

d. Distinctive features. The sacramental, liturgical, and pastoral work of military chaplains is identical to that of civilian clergy. Where the military ministry is different, it reflects the following unique features of the military environment:

(1) *Mobility.* Worldwide involuntary mobility is routine for military people. A significant part of the military population is always in transit. Chaplains often work with people who face impending transfers or deployments. Long-term relationships are the exception.

(2) *Young adults.* The military's large young adult population, busy meeting the challenges of service life, seeks the chaplain's counsel on a wide variety of concerns. Chaplains spend much of their time listening to, advising, and encouraging young adults.

(3) *Field operations.* The chaplain goes where the unit goes and shares its hardships and dangers. Lacking a permanent chapel, the work of ministry becomes non-building centered, portable, and highly relational.

(4) *Religious pluralism.* The most distinctive aspect of the chaplain's ministry is the religious pluralism of the military unit. The unit chaplain must be concerned for the religious needs of all personnel, not just those of his or her faith group. A Roman Catholic chaplain, for example, would not be expected to conduct Protestant, Jewish, or Muslim services. But he would be expected to work with others to provide whatever ministries are needed. In this larger context, the chaplain facilitates the constitutional right of military people to the free exercise of religion.

Military chaplains have a long history of assisting one another in providing for the spiritual needs of their units. This arrangement among chaplains acknowledges pluralism while allowing for cooperation.

(5) *Institutional concerns.* In addition to serving people as individuals or groups, chaplains can also exercise their ministry by influencing the function of the larger organization. The placement of the chaplain within the military staff allows opportunity for significant influence on policy decisions. Chaplains may contribute to decisions that ensure that the rights and needs of people are respected. They also may function, in a variety of ways, as advocates for the people they serve.

e. Religious and civil cooperation. First authorized by the Continental Congress in 1775, the American military chaplaincy is now in its third century. In light of the evolutionary and radical changes in American life over the past two centuries, the military chaplaincy represents an enduring area of cooperation between government and religious institutions. The constant factors undergirding this cooperative effort are: (1) the nation's concern for professionally trained religious leadership in the armed forces, and (2) the willingness of American religious bodies to provide it.

Bibliography. C. L. Abercrombie, *The Military Chaplain* (1977). J. S. Boozer, *Edge of Ministry . . . The Chaplain Story* (1984). H. G. Cox, Jr., ed. *Military Chaplains* (1973). C. M. Drury, *The History of the Chaplain Corps, United States Navy: 1778–1939* (1948). R. A. Gabriel, *To Serve With Honor* (1982). R. G. Hutcheson, Jr., *The Churches and the Chaplaincy* (1975). Official Department of Defense Publication, *The Armed Forces Officer* (1975).

I. C. STARLING, JR.

CHAPLAINCY; MINISTRY. *See also* SPECIALIZATION IN PASTORAL CARE. *Compare* POLICE OFFICERS AND POLICE CHAPLAINCY.

MIND. That which is possessed by a creature who has the ability to think, feel, and will, to be aware of its environment and, in highly developed minds, to be aware of itself. The questions which are posed by the concept of mind are among the most vexed issues in philosophy and psychology. It is of course the nature of human minds that is the focus of attention, although the nature of God's mind and the minds of animals are also worthy of inquiry. The mind may have both conscious and unconscious elements. Though initially the concept of an unconscious mind seemed to some philosophers to be a contradiction in terms, the concept is now well accepted.

1. Denial of Mind: Behaviorism. A good deal of philosophical discussion has focused on two questions: "What kind of entity is the mind?" and "What is the relationship of the mind to the body?" However, a more fundamental question is whether the mind should be regarded as an *entity* at all. Philosophical *behaviorism* is the denial that the mind is an entity or object; to speak of the mind for the behaviorist is not to speak of an *entity* but of the capacities an organism has to behave in various complicated ways. Philosophical behaviorism must be distinguished, however, from methodological behaviorism, which holds that the mind can only be studied or investigated in terms of behavior. A behavioristic analysis of a mental activity attempts to analyze that activity in behavioral terms. For example, "learning" would be seen not as an event occurring "in the mind" but as a new pattern of behavior produced by interaction with the environment.

Philosophical behaviorism runs up against two problems. First, there is the phenomenon of introspection, in which people seem to be aware of distinctively mental activities and operations which are not reducible to externally observable behavior. Second, since the mind is analyzed in terms of behavior, it cannot be seen by behaviorists as a cause of behavior. Yet people often do seem to behave the way they do because of their inner beliefs and emotions.

2. Affirmations of Mind. Of those views which see the mind as an entity, the oldest is *dualism,* which regards the mind as a distinct immaterial entity or substance, which is usually viewed as interacting with and united to the body. Dualism's most illustrious philosophical representatives are Plato and Descartes. Dualism's strengths are its ability to explain the relative autonomy of mental processes, the ability of the mind to govern the body, and, especially from traditional theological perspectives, its evident compatibility with life after death. Major problems include a difficulty in explaining the interaction between mind and body and in showing how the emerging scientific understanding of brain functions fits in with dualistic views of the mind or soul.

Non-dualistic views are called *monisms,* of which there are three main types. *Idealism* denies the existence of the physical and regards the spiritual mind alone as real. Much more popular today is *materialism,* which has been given much impetus by the development of brain science to view the mind as simply the brain and central nervous system. A weakened form of materialism, *functionalism,* holds that mental states are in fact physical states, but that these states are picked out and described as mental by virtue of their functions, instead of some physical feature they possess.

Neutral monism holds that the mind and body are in some way a single unified entity, with two distinct aspects, one mental and one physical. Neutral monism is attractive to many theologians since it appears to avoid the problem of dualism without leading to a reductionistic view of the mind. However, it is difficult to explain clearly the nature of the "neutral stuff" which makes up the mind on this view.

In facing this issue Christians should recognize the theological implications of each position. For example, the traditional belief in an "intermediate state" of continued existence between death and the resurrection is only compatible with dualism. Also, it should be recognized that many variations on each view are possible. Specifically, Platonic dualism is not the only form of dualism. One could hold that human minds are not *separate* from the body in this life, except perhaps in the functionalist sense, and yet still hold that minds are distinct because they are *separable.*

Bibliography. J. Eccles and K. Popper, *The Self and Its Brain* (1977). C. S. Evans, *Preserving the Person* (1977). H. D. Lewis, *The Elusive Self* (1982). D. M. MacKay, *The Clockwork Image* (1974). B. Reichenbach, *Is Man the Phoenix?* (1978). G. Ryle, *The Concept of Mind* (1949). J. B. Watson, *Behaviorism* 3d ed. (1930).

C. S. EVANS

PERSON (Philosophical Issues); PHILOSOPHY AND PSYCHOLOGY. *See also* CONSCIOUSNESS; EMOTION; INTELLIGENCE AND INTELLIGENCE TESTING; MEMORY; REASON AND PASSION; WILL / WILLING. *Compare* PERSONALITY THEORY.

MIND-BODY RELATIONSHIP. The relationship existing between such events as thinking, willing, conceiving, and perceiving, usually conscious, and those physical events, usually unconscious, occurring within the body of the thinking person. This relationship became problematic beginning in the seventeenth century with the rise of modern natural science, when what occurred to a body or within a body was taken to be explainable in terms of matter in motion.

For Plato, Aristotle, and most medieval philosophers, mind (*nous*) was a part or aspect of the soul (*psychē*), which was the internal principle of motion for the body and was the source of locomotion, nutrition, growth, and perception, as well as thinking. In the seventeenth century, Descartes developed a conceptual revision in order to accommodate the new physics arising at the time. He accepted the new physical principle that matter in motion in space is explainable by matter in motion. The old concept of the *psychē,* the principle of motion for the body, disappeared and was replaced by *nous,* or the mind. Descartes defined "mind" as a thinking thing, unextended in space, and "body" as an extended thing moving in space, but unthinking. Such activities as conceiving, perceiving, and willing were all modes of thinking. Descartes was himself an interactionist, maintaining that there was a causal relationship between these two different kinds of things, minds and bodies. After all, our body needs water (material state); we have a sensation of thirst (mental event); we decide to go to the water fountain (mental event); and our body moves to the water fountain (material event). There are, however, two major difficulties in conceiving of the relationship as one of causal interaction. (1) What kind of causal relationship could this be between something moving in space according to its own physical laws and something which is not in space and thinking? (2) Did this not violate the basic principle of the new natural science in which the motions of one's body (matter) were completely explainable in terms of other matter in motion? These two problems of causal interaction gave birth to a plethora of theories concerning the mind-body relationship.

The idealist's solution was to characterize material objects as ideas in the mind (Berkeley); the materialist's was to characterize thought as matter in motion in the brain (Hobbes). These two solutions avoided the problems of causal interaction, but they ran up against the difference between the private nature of ideas in conscious minds and the public nature of unconscious material objects. The ideas in my conscious mind are my ideas and the ideas in your conscious mind are your ideas; yet there is only one public material chair and it is apparently unconscious and unthinking. The two realms are so different that it appears as difficult to assimilate one to the other as to explain how they can causally interact. This fact gave rise to the conceptualization of two distinct realms which do not causally interact, the positions of psycho-physical parallelism and occasionalism. The parallelist sanctioned no causal relationship between the two realms, but each realm had its own internal type of causal relations which were synchronized by God like two clocks so that what appeared to be a causal relation between the realms was no more than God's synchronization of the causal relations within the two realms (Leibniz). The occasionalist sanctioned no causality but the causality of God, so that an event in the material realm was only the occasion for God to cause an event in the mental realm, and vice versa (Malebranche). These solutions retained the distinctiveness of the two realms and avoided causal interaction between them, but at a very high price, a divine pre-established harmony or constant divine intervention. Another solution was Spinoza's neutral monism, where there was only one substance which in itself was neither mental nor material, but it could be conceived of as mental or conceived of as material. Spinoza's solution avoided assimilation and kept the two realms distinct, while avoiding causal interaction and *ad hoc* divine intervention, yet it raised a problem: What would a neutral substance, which was neither mind nor body, be?

Contemporary theories of the mind-body relationship tend to reflect these earlier views. There are a few contemporary interactionists (H. D. Lewis) who would still hold the mind-body relationship to be a causal relation between two different kinds of entities or events. But the same problems which plagued Descartes also plague contemporary interactionists. There are very few Berkeleyan idealists today; however, contemporary sense-data theorists (E. Mach, A. J. Ayer) historically can be traced back to Berkeley. They prefer, however, to speak of sense data, rather than ideas, and tend to consider sense data as neutral with reference to the mental-physical distinction and to construct (define or analyze) both mental operations and physical objects (including the body) in terms of sense data. Yet no philosopher has ever constructed a single physical object, for example, solely from sense data, or as most would prefer to say, completely analyzed a single statement about a physical object into statements solely about sense data. The task appears to be monumental, if not impossible.

The contemporary descendants of Hobbes are generally called physicalists or identity theorists (J.J.C. Smart, H. Feigel). They tend, however, to shy away from merely defining thought as matter in motion in the brain, as Hobbes appears to do, and to say that the identity of mental events and physical events is something that is known empirically, much as we know, not by definition but from experience, that the morning star is identical to the evening star. Although contemporary identity theorists avoid Hobbes' apparent justification of his theory by a stipulative, or unconventional, definition, they are nevertheless hard pressed to present empirical evidence for their own identity; also, it is difficult to take consciousness as a property of physical events, given our ordinary understanding of "consciousness" and "physical." Few, if any, philosophers, however, hold an occasionalist or a parallelist view as espoused by the philosophers of the modern period. The *deus ex machina* character of their solutions tends to repel most contemporary philosophers.

A. N. Whitehead can be thought of as holding a double aspect view somewhat like Spinoza, but with important differences. All actual entities, according to Whitehead, have both a mental aspect (pole) and a physical aspect (pole). His neutral element is feeling which can have both aspects. Every actual entity is a synthesis of both physical and conceptual (mental) feelings. That a physical object, such as a chair, is made up of feelings and that an electron, for example, has conceptual feelings, has been very hard for a non-Whiteheadian to accept.

One contemporary theory of the mind-body relationship which does not appear to have attracted adherents in the modern period is epiphenomenalism. Epiphenomenalism (Santayana, Russell) holds a causal relationship between minds and bodies, but it is a one-way causality: bodies influence minds, but minds do not influence bodies. The main points in favor of this theory are that mental events and physical events are not assimilated and physical events are explainable in terms of physical events. It is left, however, with a peculiar kind of causality whereby bodies can affect minds, but minds cannot affect bodies. This is certainly not like the kind of causality whereby physical objects affect physical objects. Also, the only apparent reason for not allowing mental events to affect bodily events by this unique causal relation is that the epiphenomenalist wishes to hold on to physical determinism.

The average Westerner's view of the mind-body relationship is probably basically Cartesian, but embellished with elements from the Greek and Judeo-Christian traditions. And it is this conceptual heritage, along with the rise of modern natural science, which underlies this plethora of theories of the mind-body relationship. There is probably no clear and consistent characterization of this relationship which fits all the elements in this diverse conceptual heritage.

Bibliography. R. Descartes, *Meditations* (1964). G. Berkeley, *The Principles of Human Knowledge* (1965). C. Broad, *The Mind and Its Place in Nature* (1925). A. N. Whitehead, *Science and the Modern World* (1928).

B. L. CLARKE

PERSONALITY, BIOLOGICAL DIMENSIONS OF; BRAIN RESEARCH; PERSON (Philosophical Issues). *See also* BIOFEEDBACK; BODY; EMOTION; HYPNOSIS; PAIN; PHILOSOPHY AND PSYCHOLOGY; PSYCHOSOMATIC ILLNESS; PSYCHOSURGERY; SENSORY DEPRIVATION RESEARCH; SLEEP AND SLEEP DISORDERS; THEORY AND PRAXIS. *Compare* FREEDOM AND DETERMINISM.

MIND CONTROL. *See* INDOCTRINATION; MEDITATION.

MIND-CURE MOVEMENT. A predominantly American popular religious movement emerging in the nineteenth century out of the Protestant tradition, especially in New England. Its appearance has been linked to the inability of established ideas and institutions, i.e., doctors and pastors, to provide health and peace of mind. Human life was identified with mind, and God was understood as Universal Mind. Thus discontent and illness were the fruit of wrong belief while health and happiness resulted from displacing individual consciousness with thoughts of God, with living in oneness with Infinite Power. Suggestion served as the vehicle of cure. Persons were to relax, be passive, and surrender, aligning themselves with Universal Consciousness and sharing its essence. Spirit was the only reality; evil and matter were either neglected or considered "a lie." Phineas Quimby is regarded as the fountainhead of the movement. Its best-known expressions are found in Christian Science, the Unity School, and New Thought. More recent examples include Norman Vincent Peale and Charles Schuller, though the influence of the movement may be seen in some current psychologies and approaches to pastoral care.

Bibliography. W. James, *The Varieties of Religious Experience* (1902), lect. 4 and 5. D. Meyer, *The Positive Thinkers* (1965). A. Stokes, *Ministry After Freud* (1985).

L. O. MILLS

CHRISTIAN SCIENCE; HISTORY OF PROTESTANT PASTORAL CARE (United States); PSYCHOLOGY IN AMERICAN RELIGION. *Compare* POPULAR THERAPEUTIC MOVEMENTS AND PSYCHOLOGIES.

MINIMAL BRAIN DYSFUNCTION. A syndrome with multiple etiologies and clinical symptoms which affects over five percent of school-aged children, most of whom are boys. Often there are no conclusive neurological signs on medical examination, or very minimal indications. Manifestations of MBD include the following: hyperactivity; perceptual motor impairment (auditory and visual); distractibility; learning disorders; impulsiveness; poor interpersonal relationships; dysphasia; EEG irregularities; and equivocal neurological signs.

L. V. MAJOVSKI

ORGANIC MENTAL DISORDERS. *Compare* BRAIN RESEARCH; LEARNING DISABILITY.

MINISTER. A religious functionary, commonly a person ordained to officiate in a Christian church.

While concepts and roles of the minister vary considerably, most are rooted in the image of servant (L. *minister*, Gr. *diakonos*). Servanthood expresses the concrete and constant commitment of a person to God and humanity, participating in God's mission in the world and attending the world's people. Throughout the Bible authentic leaders are also characterized paradoxically as servants and slaves: "He who is greatest among you shall be your servant" (Mt. 23:11). In this contradictory paradigm ministers partake of both the authority and the suffering servanthood of Christ.

Tension persists in the identification of the minister. Contemporary American descriptions tend to stress the minister's multiple, competing functions such as preaching, evangelism, prophecy, caring, administration, celebration, education, discipline, social reform, and reconciliation. This task-oriented approach to ministry is also reflected in the pattern of curricular and faculty growth in seminaries. Attempts to simplify (by the development of integrating roles) or diversify (by the assignment of roles to other church members) the burgeoning functions expected of an ordained minister have not been notably successful. In the strain of role conflict many ministers today suffer from exhaustion and uncertainty regarding the point and effect of their vocation. While considered spokespersons for grace, ministers tend to understand their own calling according to their works.

Four recent approaches to clarifying the vocation of the minister have sought to understand dimensions of ministry other than its tasks.

1. The Character of the Minister. The Readiness for Ministry project of the Association of Theological Schools in the U.S. and Canada examines priorities that different denominations give to qualities in the style of ministers. By providing a profile of attributes most desired by a church, and an instrument by which these characteristics might be measured in an individual, the project intends to aid the selection, education and self-understanding of the minister.

2. Ministry Theory. Substantially greater sensitivity to the divergent worldviews present in pluralistic denominations is sought through ethnographic analysis by several centers for ministry in the U.S. Instead of examining denominational preferences, this approach studies the individual congregation as a peculiar culture which in each case constructs a specific understanding of the world and maintains a particular theory of ministry in consonance with that understanding.

3. The Ministry of the Congregation. Arising in part from earlier discussions regarding the ministry of all Christians, wide attention is given today to the systemic nature of ministry within a congregation. Such disciplines as social psychology, sociology, and organization theory and development are used to envision and enable ministry as the activity of an entire local church.

4. Minister as Symbol. Explorations, using phenomenological, ethnographic, and psychological methods, probe the manner in which the minister serves symbolically in representing both the community of believers and also that which is believed. Such focus upon the expressive nature of the minister may lessen general preoccupation with her or his instrumental tasks.

Bibliography. R. Anderson, ed., *Theological Foundations for Ministry: Selected Readings for a Theology of the Church in Ministry* (1979). C. Dudley, *Building Effective Ministry: Theory and Practice in the Local Church* (1983). U. Holmes, *The Priest in Community: Exploring the Roots of Ministry* (1978); *Spirituality for Ministry* (1982). H. Nouwen, *The Wounded Healer: Ministry in Contemporary Society* (1972). E. Schillebeeckx, *Ministry: Leadership in the Community of Jesus Christ* (1981). D. Schuller, M. Strommen, M. Brekke, eds., *Ministry in America* (1980).

J. F. HOPEWELL

MINISTRY. *See also* CHAPLAIN; DEACON; ELDER; PASTOR; PRIEST. *Compare* CHRISTIAN SCIENCE PRACTITIONER; RABBI/RABBINATE; SPIRITUAL MASTERS AND GUIDES.

MINISTERIAL CALL. *See* CALL TO MINISTRY. *See also* CALLING AND VISITATION.

MINISTERIAL CANDIDATES. *See* THEOLOGICAL STUDENTS. *See also* READINESS FOR MINISTRY STUDIES.

MINISTERS, EMPIRICAL STUDIES OF. *See* CLERGY, EMPIRICAL STUDIES OF.

MINISTRY (Biblical Origins and Principles). In the early church there were some clearly recognized leadership roles that, when named, carried a clear identity and were recognized as essential for the functioning of the church. These roles were rooted in and derived from the public ministry of Jesus Christ.

1. Ministry in Origin. The roles given the general title "ministry" (*diakonia*) carry the fundamental understanding that they are services within the life of the church and community (I Cor. 12:5, 28; Eph. 4:12). Literally, ministry (*diakoneō*) is feeding care for guests (Lk. 8:3; 10:40; 17:8; Acts 6:2). It further describes employing the various gifts (*charismata*) which God bestows (I Cor. 12:5; I Pet. 4:10) as well as referring to specific acts such as an offering (II Cor. 8:19–20), personal help to one in prison (Philemon 13), apostleship (Rom. 11:13), and aid to a congregation (I Cor. 16:15). In fact, all members of the church have their own gifts of grace to exercise in ministry to others (I Cor. 12:7–11, 14ff).

All forms of service are ministries of Jesus Christ and derive their authority from him. Jesus' whole life, especially at the cross, is interpreted as an act of ministry (Mk. 10:45). The servant style of Jesus contrasts with the Greek depreciation of the servant which regards the one served as great. Jesus rejects lording it over others and affirms, "I am among you as one who serves" (Lk. 22:24–7; Mk. 10:42–4; Mt. 20:25–8). In his teaching this style of ministry includes caring for the hungry, the thirsty, the stranger, the naked, the sick, and the prisoner (Mt. 25:44).

In the Gospels Jesus is also pictured as performing all the clearly defined leadership roles that the early church later identifies as central in its life (I Cor. 11:28; Eph. 4:11). He is sent (apostle), prophet, teacher, pastor-shepherd, and priest (in Hebrews). Since specific persons can be identified with all these roles (except priest), they represent defined functions rooted in the ministry of Jesus Christ. The role is never limited, however, but on specific occasion can be filled by all sorts of individuals. The function performed never becomes the possession of those in that ministry. Nor is there any evidence that persons having a role protect or guard that function from being exercised by the membership of the church.

The role seems to derive its authority in the reverse direction. Because prophecy, for example, is a function of the whole church, the church identifies individuals as prophets so that the function may be responsibly performed. This guarantees the integrity of the community, but the community does not thereby abrogate its prophetic responsibility. However, while priestly imagery can be used to describe the community, a priestly office for individuals other than Jesus Christ is not identified in the NT.

As Christ is the source of all ministries in the NT, so OT offices are traced from and dependent on Moses who is designated by scholars as the covenant mediator. Moses authorizes judges (Exod. 18:13–27), priests (Exodus 28, 29), prophets (Deut. 18:15–18), and kings (Deut. 17:14–20). These offices are given authority in the Mosaic tradition.

The offices serve and develop the life of the faith community. Each one serves the power and will of God in a unique way: the king is God's anointed agent in the arena of public power to see that justice is done, especially toward the weak who cannot fend for themselves; the priest maintains the community in the presence of God's holiness, providing a perspective from which public power can be established or critiqued; the prophet calls the people and nation to live by faith in the face of public issues so that nation and king will not submit to habits of oppressive rule that are visible in culture; the wisdom teacher examines life out of common experience and discerns what is universal and practical.

All these functions are related to historical life which can both shape and pervert them. Only God is sovereign, and all ministries are provisional and tentative for the pursuit of God's purpose in history. Perversion occurs when they are used for self-serving and self-centered ends, rejecting the authority of faith in God.

2. Leadership Roles. Elements that are identifiably clear in these ministerial roles include: (1) the source of authority, (2) a life setting for exercising the role, (3) a way for performing the task, (4) a content of faith related to the function, (5) the desired result or goal.

The leadership functions specifically identified in the early church are four: apostles (evangelists), prophets, teachers, and pastors (cf. Ephesians).

a. Apostles. The very word, apostle, (from Greek *apostellein:* to send away) carries with it identity in ministry. First, an authoritative sender is implied. One goes on another's behalf. Second, "being sent" implies some sort of mission or goal. One is to accomplish something for the sender. Third, "being sent" implies a destination. There is a clear and identifiable group within the earliest church, that Paul identifies as apostles (Gal. 1:17–19; I Cor. 9:1) as well as a function that Paul labels as apostleship (Rom. 1:5; I Cor. 9:1–2; Gal. 2:8). Paul sees himself within this group, though at times he may act like a teacher, prophet, or pastor.

The apostle's authority lies in the divine calling. Apostles are God's first appointment in the church ("appointment" indicates the creation of a new role by God).

The primary commission of an apostle comes through a resurrection appearance. After citing the kerygmatic formula (I Cor. 15:3–5), Paul immediately starts talking of his apostleship and its meaning. Fuller (pp. 32–49) finds the persons named either as being church-founding appearances (Peter, the Twelve, the Five Hundred) or mission establishing (James, all the apostles, Paul). Following the listing of appearances, Paul immediately starts talking of his apostleship, indicating the close proximity of these two.

The content of the apostle's ministry is the Christ-event, that is, the saving act of God wrought in Jesus Christ, for it is this story that the apostle is to preach. The hard work of the apostle is preaching the Gospel so that persons might come to *faith.* They know of the action of God *for* them, and of the relation of the risen Lord *with* them. So faith's increase is the purpose of apostolic ministry.

The apostle tells the story, not as a personal story, but as an authoritative testimony by which the person is claimed. So the story of God's gracious activity belongs, not to the apostle, but to the church. Paul roots the Gospel in history and tradition, both in reciting the words of the supper (I Cor. 11:23f) and in the preaching formula (I Cor. 15:3–5).

Consequently, the formation of a new congregation is evidence that the work of an apostle has been faithfully performed, and is the human sign of the apostle's authority (I Cor. 9:1–2). The Corinthian church is the "seal of my apostleship in the Lord."

The work of the apostles, as a result, is foundational. Probably for this reason the title, *apostle*, gets reserved for the first generation eventually, and the function continues under the new title, "evangelist" (Eph. 4:11).

In the Gospels of Matthew and Mark the disciples are called "apostles" only when they are sent out on mission by Jesus, two by two, with authority to preach the Kingdom of God and to work its signs by healing the sick, etc. (Mt. 10:1–2, 5, 7–9; Mk. 6:7, 30; Lk. 9:1–2; 10:1, 9). Several important conclusions come from this: (1) the role of the apostle is traced back to the historic act of Jesus' sending, (2) "sending" is distinct from the general meaning of discipleship, (3) such "sending" involves the full authority of the sender, (4) the apostle proclaims the Kingdom of God and does the signs of the apostle which are identified with overcoming evil powers and healing, (5) since they are persons sent by the authority of another, they must return and give account of what they have done (Mk. 6:30; Lk. 9:10; 10:17), (6) how one treats a person Jesus sent, also determines how one responds to Jesus since his authority is fully shared with the apostle (Mt. 10:40).

In Ephesians, "apostles" refers to a time-honored role in the church that honors the first generation (2:20). "Evangelists" seems to be the new term taken from the content of what the apostles preached (the evangel), and these persons carry on the function of the apostles in the church. Evangelists are preachers of the Gospel with full authority and power (Acts 8:4, 12–14).

b. Prophets. A second focus of ministry lies in the persons called prophets. This function is rooted deeply in the classical Hebrew tradition but with some interesting NT emphases. NT prophets, in contrast to apostles, function primarily in the local congregation. Prophecy is contrasted with tongues (I Cor. 14:1–5) because it is the highest gift that is characteristic of the local church and its life. Prophecy is desirable, not because it is more spiritual, but because it builds up the congregation's life (I Cor. 14:3, 4, 12). Yet it is not prophecy that abides; it, too, will pass away. Only the love (which builds up — I Cor. 8:1–3) that is embodied in it abides (I Cor. 13:8).

The prophet brings a revelation to the congregation gathered in worship (I Cor. 14:29–30). It is a word from the Lord that enables one to see in a new way (i.e., gain an alternative view of reality). In this way they continue the function of Hebrew prophets in creating the possibility of a new order (see Brueggemann). The authority for the revelation lies in the Spirit of God. Prophets reshape life under the authority of this new age of the Holy Spirit. So the phrases belong together, "Do not quench the Spirit, do not despise prophesying" (I Thess. 5:19–20). Furthermore, any member on occasion in public worship might become an agent of the Spirit and prophesy (cf. I Cor. 3:12–13).

Since the Spirit is the Spirit of God's Reign, prophets are the agents of *hope* as they reveal the eschatological purpose of God. The prophet reveals what is always a mystery, namely what God is doing in an old age toward shaping that which is new (Rom. 16:25; cf. Eph. 3:3–5). Prophets, therefore, are called to create an "awake" or resurrection people who are already living out of the reality of this new age. Ezekiel's model of the prophet as watchman (33:1–16) is fulfilled when NT prophets create a watchful people (Eph. 5:14).

Since the Spirit is the authority of the prophet, prophets in the church are a sign of the Spirit. However, prophecy is always a precarious thing as persons are tempted to try to manipulate the Spirit. So false prophecy is a worry throughout biblical history. Consequently, the community and other prophets, as co-bearers of the Spirit, must always test the works of the prophets. For the prophet the fundamental issue is: Who or what is worshiped? Who or what is served? The issue in worship is that of Lordship, and it is only by the Holy Spirit that one can truly worship, confess "Jesus is Lord" (I Cor. 12:3). Prophets then seek to discern the true object of the community's worship as well as discern the special gifts that persons are given by God so that in identifying them, they may serve the common good.

The book of Revelation is the clearest literary deposit of one who is identified as a prophet in the work itself. The prophet, John, apart from the apocalyptic style, functions in the way Paul discusses prophets. His purpose is to disclose the mystery of what God is now doing in an old world that is riddled with evil. The symbolic communication makes no sense in the old world, but makes powerful sense to a community of faith where God makes all things new, very much even as Isaiah gives new vision to a despairing people. John's purpose is to bring encouragement and strength to beleaguered congregations addressed by name. John knows that a community that seeks to live by the new age is always in tension and struggle with the old and needs constantly to be built up so that its vision of history might remain new.

John speaks with authority in the congregations addressed (Rev. 21:5; 22:6). Readers are not to modify or subtract anything from the prophetic word (Rev. 22:18–19). But while authoritative, John is also aware of the danger of putting a false value on the messenger's words, so that twice the messenger reproves him, "I am a fellow servant with you and your brethren who hold the testimony of Jesus, worship God" (Rev. 19:10; 22:8–9).

Central to John's functioning is the inspiration of the Spirit. The revelation, the seeing of God's mysterious purpose in history, becomes possible only through the Spirit (Rev. 1:10; 4:2; 17:3). Yet the *context* for the Spirit's presence is the community at worship on the Lord's Day and the book itself resounds with communal hymns and prayers, liturgical symbols and themes. Christian prophecy becomes possible in the community before God and song break the oppressive rule.

In the Gospel of John the Spirit gets a personal name, the Paraclete, the Encourager, whose function is the prophetic one of making the words and teaching of Jesus present. This is a revelation that the world cannot receive. The Paraclete continues the function of prophecy in the church.

In Luke-Acts the context for the life of Jesus is the witness of the prophets, Simeon, Anna, and John the Baptist. During his life Jesus is filled with the Spirit and hence is identified in prophetic ways which are not characteristic of the other Gospels. Above all, the Spirit is creator of a new community with a new life on Pentecost. In his Pentecost speech Peter makes clear that prophecy is the sign of the Spirit in the new age (Acts 2:17). This is especially clear when Peter adds, "and they shall prophesy" to the quote of Joel (Acts 2:18) later on.

Prophets discern the Spirit in the community and encourage and strengthen it (Acts 15:28, 32).

A prophet, then, is primarily a leader related to a local congregation, who in watching and praying (communal worship), receives revelations in the Spirit (Acts 13:1; I Tim. 1:18; 4:14). They point to the signs of the new age that is coming into being and create an awake or resurrection people.

c. Teachers. The teacher is also a leader who functions in the local church and has close relationship with the prophets (Acts 13:1; cf. I Cor. 14:6). There is a sense of inherited and accumulated knowledge which has been passed on in the church (Rom. 6:17; 16:17), which is the fruit and deposit of the teachers. This is most clearly seen in the ordered sermons in Matthew, which through the words of Jesus address the needs of the ongoing Christian community.

Teachers were those who sought the embodiment of the Gospel in day-to-day life, and the single word that might best affirm the nature of that life was *love*. Teachers faced the problem of structuring the Gospel in such a way that it might have an impact on daily life. The focus on love lies in all the larger catechetical pieces (cf. Lk. 6:27–36; Mt. 5:43–48; Rom. 12:9–21; I Pet. 3:8–12; I Thess. 5:15).

The real concerns of the teachers are that: (1) the love command be made operative in concrete situations like factions and vegetarianism at Rome (Romans 14–15) or weak conscience (Romans 10) and tongue-speaking in Corinth (I Cor. 12–14), (2) the motivation for the command be rooted in the heart of the Gospel, lest the command be seen merely as legalism, (3) the relationship with God be the fundamental reality (cf. Lk. 6:36; I Pet. 3:12, 15; Mt. 5:8). Teaching is not informational; rather it involves the hearer in the will of the one in whom the believer trusts and hopes. The work of the teachers is always undergirded by that of apostles and prophets. The teaching catechisms ground their claims within the framework of the eschatological hope which this present life already seeks to embody. So Romans climaxes its catechetical instruction with ". . . salvation is nearer to us now than when we first believed . . . The day is at hand. Let us then cast off the works of darkness and put on the armor of light" (13:11–12). A like context climaxes the ethical forms in Ephesians (6:10–20, directly rooting the catechism in the prophetic discernment, "watch and pray"; cf. I Pet. 4:7–11; I Thess. 5:1–11; Mt. 5:48; 7:21–3). The battle language reflects the awareness of the toughness required for living the new life already in the midst of the old age.

Baptism and clarity in worship provide the essential realities and authority in which the ethical appeal is rooted as reflected in the ethical phrase, "in the Lord." Their appeal to baptism focuses in the call "to put off" and "to put on" (Col. 3:5–17; Eph. 4:17–32) which is the call to a transformed life (Rom. 12:2; I Pet. 1:14–15). The kerygmatic formulas of the apostolic preaching, finally, provide the basic motivation for the teacher's appeal: "walk in love as Christ loved us and gave himself for us" (Eph. 5:2), "for to this you have been called, because Christ also suffered for you" (I Pet. 2:21).

In the Gospel tradition it is Jesus who is first of all, teacher. His authority is rooted in his relation to God as reflected in the intimate worship-prayer address—"Abba," as well as in the remembered speech form which arises out of that relationship—"Amen, I say to you." The decisive authority for Jesus' teaching lay in his embodying the presence and the will of God in his person. This accounts for the surprising fact that the disciples are never accorded the title *teacher* in the gospels. They can witness, be sent, but they are always disciples (learners) in relation to Jesus.

It is in the risen Lord's commission in Matthew that the disciples are commissioned to teach. The teachers of the church draw deeply on the OT and its teaching tradition as well as on the commands of Jesus. These latter are authoritative now since the Jesus of history is now the worshiped risen Lord. So in the catechisms a phrase such as, "in the Lord," "in him," etc. shows the covenant binding in which the command finds inherent meaning.

d. Pastors. The function of pastor is ultimately in the Hebrew king. The image of kingship was derived from the shepherd—even as the shepherd boy David was made king (I Samuel 16). Yet Israel's kings never fully actualized their shepherding function in relation to the people. In Ezekiel 34:3–4 there is a vivid description of the abuses of shepherd-kings: "You eat the fat and clothe yourselves with the wool . . . . The weak you have not strengthened, the sick you have not healed, the crippled you have not bound up, the strayed you have not brought back, the lost you have not sought, and with force and harshness you have ruled them." The result is that the sheep are scattered. In contrast, the true shepherd is to gather and feed the sheep, caring for the weaker.

As the OT develops, God not only calls the false shepherds to account (Zech. 13:7; 10:3) but promises to become the true shepherd who will gather and feed the sheep (Zech. 11:7–17; Jer. 50:19; Isa. 40:11; Ps. 23).

In the Gospels, Jesus himself fulfills the shepherding role. He sees the multitude as sheep without a shepherd and feeds them, first by teaching and then with bread (Mk. 6:30–45). Drawing heavily on the Exodus imagery, he commands the people to sit by hundreds and fifties, thus gathering and ordering the chaotic crowd. Teaching is part of his pastoral office as well as healing the sick (Mt. 14:14; 20:34), raising the dead (Lk. 7:14–15), or acting in forgiveness (Mt. 18:27).

Disciples are called into this feeding ministry, but they cannot believe in the divine resources. They fail to comprehend or believe in their role in the face of the incomprehensible vastness of the task as they face the hungry multitude. So when they want to dismiss the crowd and avoid responsibility, Jesus rebukes, "You give them something to eat" (Mk. 6:37).

The most complete picture of Jesus as shepherd is found in John 10. The true shepherd is contrasted with false leaders "who do not know by name" (cold professionalism), who rob the sheep (consumers rather than feeders), and who act as hirelings (profit-motive) in contrast to the shepherd who "lays down his life" for others.

Both bishops and elders are described in the later NT books in the same word sets as shepherds. Common words are used for caring rule or "looking over" (overseeing) of people for their gathering and growth. So these titles express also basic meanings of pastoral ministry.

The unification of shepherd and bishop is clearly seen when the ministry of Jesus is patterned after the suffering servant of Isaiah in the hymn in I Pet. 2:22–5, which climaxes in "the Shepherd and 'episkopos' of your souls." It is likewise manifest in the interplay of elder, shepherd, and overseeing (*episkopeo*): "So I exhort the elders among you . . . shepherd the flock of God, exercising oversight" (*episkopeo*) (some manuscripts only, I Pet. 5:1–4) and "Take heed to yourselves and to all the flock, in which the Holy Spirit has made you overseers (*episkopos*) to shepherd the church of God" (Acts 20:28).

This identification of functions goes back to the use of *episkopeo* in the Greek OT as a description of true shepherding (Jer. 23:2; Zech. 11:16). The Lord God is to "look out for" a person who will lead the flock in and out, lest they be as sheep without a shepherd (Num. 27:16). Shepherding and supervision have a long history of relationship. God's visiting the people can mean supportive love, but God's supervising, overseeing presence also means examination and judgment on those who are alienated from God (Zech. 10:3; Ezek. 33:6–8).

Overseeing with the appropriate sense of care and discipline is reflected in Moses' decision to visit (*episkopeo*) his brethren in Egypt (Acts 7:23) and in Paul's and Barnabas' visit to determine how the churches are (Acts 15:36). All this is patterned in ministry after the God who "watches over," "guards," and "visits" his people for their salvation.

The antithesis to the true shepherding rule is described in words like "lording it over" (Lk. 22:25), which is the unacceptable style of rule characteristic of society at large and which had also tempted the kings of Israel to corruption. When shepherding (teaching and nourishing) is absent, then domineering results.

Finally, the word "minister" (*diakonos*) gathers the same identity as pastor. Its literal image of "serving," rather than sitting at the table (Lk. 22:27), moves to giving one's life as a ransom for many (Mk. 10:45), to caring for and feeding neglected widows (Acts 6:2). All of these terms designate pastoral "administering, caring for, managing, and watching over" that is the NT understanding of pastor.

The function of pastor-minister was essential to congregations and was exercised by persons bearing different titles or no title. Such functions had the peculiar temptation of appropriating status. Hence, they need to be clearly designated as "service" or the "elder" must become as the "younger," etc. Yet, rightly interpreted they were absolutely essential to the community. Shepherds feed, watch over, stand before congregations (*proistemi* — Rom. 12:8) that they might mature — grow in the Lord. It is this function of nurture that causes the role of teacher and pastor to merge in the early church as the list in Eph. 4:11 already suggests.

3. The Human Authorizing Function. We have suggested the authority of each function as follows: apostles —having seen the risen Lord; prophets—the call of the Spirit; pastors—caring rule given for nourishing the people; teachers—the interpreted words of the historical Jesus, now risen.

Yet there is always the human community's verification of that authority. The faithful community can discern the calling and action of God and so authorize the appropriate function. In so doing the temptation to self-centered claim and false functioning is countered. So Moses is also designated by the people (Exod. 20:18–20). Apostolic ministry is verified by the formation of a congregation. The Spirit among other prophets and congregations tests the utterances of prophets at worship since false prophecy is always a danger. Pastoral ministries are designated by the congregation in worship with the laying on of hands.

Bibliography. R. Brown, "Episkopē and Episkiopos: New Testament Evidence" *Theological Studies*, 41 (1980), 322–38. W. Brueggemann, *The Prophetic Imagination* (1978). H. Campenhausen, *Ecclesiastical Authority and Spiritual Power in the Church of the First Three Centuries* (1969). R. De Vaux, *Ancient Israel* (1961). R. H. Fuller, *The Formation of the Resurrection Narratives* (1980). D. Hill, *New Testament Prophecy* (1979). J. Kirk, "Apostleship Since Rengstorff: Towards a Synthesis" *New Testament Studies*, 21 (1975), 249–64. R. Schnakenberg, "Apostles Before and During Paul's Time" in *Apostolic History and the Gospel* (1970). J. Panagopoulos, ed., *Prophetic Vocation in the New Testament and Today* (1977). E. Schweizer, *Church Order in the New Testament* (1961).

E. S. WEHRLI

NEW TESTAMENT *or* OLD TESTAMENT AND APOCRYPHA, TRADITIONS AND THEOLOGY OF CARE IN. *See also* BISHOP; DEACON; ELDER; JESUS; RABBI/RABBINATE.

MINISTRY (Jewish Tradition). *See* JEWISH CARE AND COUNSELING; RABBI/RABBINATE.

MINISTRY (Orthodox). *See* MINISTRY AND PASTORAL CARE (Orthodox).

MINISTRY (Protestant Tradition). As a consequence of different approaches to the reform of the church, the Reformation of the sixteenth century resulted in a variety of concepts and forms of ministry. The Church of England (in the U.S. the Episcopal Church) diverged little from the medieval Catholic church. Luther introduced potentially radical changes with his restoration of the priesthood of all believers, but, after significant alterations in the first few years of the reform, Lutheran churches reverted to earlier ideas and patterns connected with the territorial system in Germany. By virtue of their insistence on reforming the churches according to what Scriptures enjoin or exemplify, Zwingli and Calvin were responsible for more decisive shifts, but they also did not fully implement Luther's idea of a universal priesthood. That remained for radical reformers such as Anabaptists and Spiritualists, who virtually eliminated altogether distinctions between clergy and laity.

All four traditions have undergone significant modifications as they have evolved in different branches and contexts. By the twentieth century, while retaining many of their traditional features, all have assumed characteristics common in an ecumenical setting and imposed by prevailing social models.

1. Anglican or Episcopal Tradition. Anglicans or Episcopalians differ among themselves in their conception of ministry. Anglo-Catholics hold a high view of ministry similar to that held by Orthodox or Roman Catholics. In this view sacerdotal or priestly roles are emphasized. Ordination or Holy Orders confers special gifts of the Spirit which raise the priest to a different level from that of the unordained and transmits authority for spiritual direction and discipline. Evangelicals, on the other hand, more strongly influenced by the Protestant Reformation, accentuate the preaching function of ministers. In their view, accordingly, ordination does not create so wide a gap between clergy and laity.

In the Anglican tradition episcopacy has usually been seen as the key to continuity and stability in ministry. Consecrated only by other bishops, bishops are viewed as successors of the apostles charged with the authority to ordain, teach sound doctrine, assure proper worship, and administer discipline in their dioceses. In councils they frame rules and establish discipline for both clergy and laity. They are responsible for the formation and guidance of priests (presbyters) and deacons and other subordinate ministers. Bishops normally confirm members of their communion by the laying on of hands.

Responsibility for ministry in parishes rests upon the shoulders of priests or presbyters. Ordained by bishops and fellow priests, they serve as rectors in local parishes, baptize, preside over the liturgy, preach, administer communion, counsel, and exercise discipline. In the work of the parish they receive assistance from wardens, who are charged with oversight of church records and the collection of alms; vestrymen, who control church property; lay readers, and deacons or deaconesses.

Although Methodism originated from the Anglican tradition, the Methodist understanding and practice of ministry differ significantly from it. The founder of Methodism, John Wesley, died in communion with the Church of England as an Anglican priest. By reason of their involvement in the eighteenth century evangelical revivals, however, Methodists soon found it necessary to modify the episcopal structures they inherited and to develop those which could assist them in their exuberant evangelistic enterprise. Quarterly, annual, and general conferences play key roles in governing Methodist churches. Presided over by district superintendents, quarterly conferences fix salaries of pastors, set budgets, elect church officers, and select delegates to send to annual conferences. Presided over by bishops, annual conferences ordain and admit ministers to the ministry, vote on constitutional questions, supervise pensions and relief, assign ministers to their churches, and elect lay delegates to general conferences. General conferences held every four years under episcopal direction legislate for the Methodist churches.

2. Lutheran Tradition. Martin Luther opened a wide chasm between Protestant and medieval conceptions of ministry when he declared that "the only real difference between lay persons and priests is one of office and function, and not of estate; they are all priests, though their functions are not the same" (*Appeal to the German Nobility*, 1520). The functions of ordained ministers are chiefly two: to preach the Word and to administer the sacraments, which Luther reduced to two, baptism and the Lord's Supper. Other vocations are also ordained of God.

Luther severely restricted the power of bishops and other clergy. According to the Augsburg Confession (1530), they have a right to maintain order within the churches, but they should not assume authority in the temporal realm unless commissioned to do so by secular authorities nor lay down an endless number of human ordinances. Christians should have the liberty to do what the Word of God dictates. As Luther spoke of the freedom of Christians, however, he had in mind the aristocracy and not the masses on the verge of revolt. He vigorously sustained the princes in opposition to rebellious peasants and scathingly denounced visionaries and enthusiasts. At Augsburg in 1555 a territorial settlement was arranged according to the principle that the religion of the ruler would determine the religion of an area. Although Lutherans had initially replaced bishops with superintendents, they soon reverted to the traditional terminology.

In the Lutheran tradition the basic office is that of pastor. Pastors are usually ordained at annual meetings of synods composed of the pastors and lay representatives elected by the congregations, but they are elected, called, or recalled by the congregations they serve. Lutherans place much stress on "calling" and on seminary training. In congregational ministry pastors receive assistance from several elected lay officials, usually called elders, deacons, and trustees. The chief pastoral duties include preaching, leading worship, administering the sacraments, visitation, and counseling.

Synods play a major role in the ministry of Lutheran churches. Some are legislative, some consultative. Synods supervise the work of congregations in worship, education, publication, charity, and missions. Superintendents or bishops act as executive officers at this level. As the ecumenical movement has progressed, however, their roles have undergone changes which will bring them more in line with traditional roles of bishops in the Catholic tradition.

3. Reformed Tradition. John Calvin defined the concept and established the general outlines for ministry in Reformed and Presbyterian churches, and the United Church of Christ (which came into being as a result of a merger between the Congregationalists and the Evangelical and Reformed Church in 1957). To a lesser extent, Baptist, Disciples or Christian churches descended from the Reformed tradition. Calvin looked upon the ministry as "the chief sinew by which believers are held together in one body" (*Institutes* 4.3.2.). Ministers should receive both an "inward" and an "outward" (church) call, being chosen "by the consent and approval of the people" (4.3.15).

In Geneva, Calvin established four offices: presbyters, deacons, pastors, and teachers. Presbyters (who could also be called "bishops") were to exercise supervision over the morals of the people and to govern the churches, deacons were to administer the affairs of the poor and to care for them, pastors to govern and care for local congregations, and teachers to train the entire constituency. To assure integrity in governance of the churches, which he regarded as their key role, Calvin separated the presbytery from the churches themselves. Laying on of hands in ordination, restricted to the presbytery, was a "sort of sign" that the person ordained was no longer acting independently "but bound in servitude to God and the church" (*Institutes* 4.3.16).

In Reformed and Presbyterian churches presbyteries examine, ordain, and install ministers with the consent of congregations. Synods supervise presbyteries, review their records, hear complaints and appeals from them, organize new presbyteries, and perform other administrative duties within their districts. Above the synods stands the general assembly composed of clerical and lay delegates elected by the presbyteries on a proportional basis. This assembly settles matters of discipline and doctrine referred to it by lower bodies, establishes new synods, appoints boards and commissions, and reviews appeals.

The United Church of Christ (UCC), Baptist, and Disciples or Christian churches place much greater stress upon local congregations and think of authority as gravitating upward rather than downward. Congregations exercise authority to ordain ministers, to "call" or dismiss them, and even to define their roles. Although congregations are interconnected through associations and conventions, none of these bodies exercises authority over the congregations. Rather, they discharge tasks such as evangelism, missions, social service, and publication which are decided on by representatives of the congregations. Historically, all three groups have regarded the "inward" call as primary and the "outward" call and ordination as secondary. They have also viewed preaching as the ministers' most important function. Baptism and the Lord's Supper are usually called "ordinances" rather than sacraments, although ecumenical contacts have caused some changes in attitude here. The participation of the United Church of Christ and the Disciples in the Consultation on Church Union, which projects a merger of ten Protestant denominations, has necessitated major shifts in their understanding of ministry.

4. **Free Church Tradition.** The radical reformers — Anabaptists, Spiritualists, Rationalists — opted for much simpler concepts and forms of ministry which would permit restitution or restoration of primitive Christian concepts and forms. Repudiating all connections between church and state, they insisted on the autonomy of local congregations or "gathered churches" and thus a strictly local ministry exercised with the concurrence of the congregation. They deemphasized or abandoned ordination and heightened the role of lay persons.

Anabaptist or Mennonite churches recognize three types of ministers: bishops or presbyters, ministers, and deacons or almoners. Nearly all ministers pursue other vocations. Traditionally they exercise substantial authority. The Schleitheim Confession of 1527, one of the most definitive documents for Anabaptism, listed the duties of "pastors" as "to read, to admonish and teach, to warn, to discipline, to ban in the church, to lead out in prayer for the advancement of all the brethren and sisters, to lift up the bread when it is broken, and in all things to see to the care of the body of Christ, in order that it may be built up and developed, and the mouth of the slanderer be stopped." However, congregations may discipline their ministers. Deacons and deaconesses discharge chiefly charitable ministries. Ministers are ordained by the laying on of hands by other ordained persons, but this is viewed as a confirmation of gifts already perceived rather than as a means of conferring them.

No sixteenth century Spiritualist group has survived, but the Quakers, who emerged during the mid-seventeenth century, have exhibited some of the same attitudes toward ministry. George Fox (1624–1691), originator of the Friends' movement, criticized clergy of the Church of England severely and repudiated ecclesiastical ordination. He stressed instead the leading of the Spirit or "the Inner Light" as the chief qualification for ministry. Although the Friends, from the beginning on, recognized some persons, women and men, as "ministers," they did so on a basis of spiritual endowment rather than through a formal rite of ordination. Some tension, however, has existed throughout the history of this movement relative to the extent to which the Friends should rely on guidance of the Spirit through silent meetings or call forth more formal leadership. In recent decades some groups in the Midwest have elected to train ministers in a more formal way and changed the ministers' rules to be somewhat like those assumed by other Protestant ministers. They are not ordained, however, and the Friends still seek to carry out their ministry corporately and individually under guidance of the Spirit.

5. **Women in Ministry.** Woman have played leading roles in Protestant churches from the Reformation on, but they have not been accorded equal status or recognition. The Friends were the first to recognize a partnership of women and men in ministry. The next person after George Fox to receive a call to ministry in the Friends was a woman, Elizabeth Hooten. The fact that the Friends stressed spiritual endowment rather than ordination assisted in the extension of equality. Other Protestant groups did not ordain women until the nineteenth century. The Disciples ordained women from their beginnings in the early 1800s on. British and American Baptists ordained women in the nineteenth century, Southern Baptists not until 1964. The Congregationalist Church ordained its first woman minister, Antoinette Brown (later Blackwell) on September 15, 1853. Universalists ordained several women in the next half century. Although Methodists licensed women to preach from an early day, they did not remove barriers to women's ordination until 1956. United (Northern) Presbyterians began ordaining women also in 1956, U.S. (Southern) Presbyterians in 1964. Lutherans in the Scandinavian countries opened the way for women's ordination between 1958 and 1964, the Lutheran Church of America and the American Lutheran Church in 1970. The Episcopal Church ordained eleven women in 1974, but the Anglican Church is still debating the issue. By the 1980s most Protestant denominations were ordaining women. In 1982 the Faith and Order Commission of the World Council of Churches completed a study of *The Community of Women and Men in the Church,* however, which indicated that all of the churches have a long way to go before genuine partnership in ministry is effected.

6. **Education for Ministry.** Protestants continued initially to educate ministers in the universities as had been done during the late Middle Ages. So long as the universities remained close to the churches, this caused no problem. As they became more secularized and lapsed into a Protestant scholasticism, however, it caused alarm in the churches. In response Pietists followed the exam-

ple of Roman Catholics at Trent in establishing seminaries, the first founded in 1868.

In North America the first colleges (Harvard, Yale, and others) were established by the churches for the purpose of training ministers. As they broadened their curricula to educate a broader constituency, training of ministers was relegated first to departments of theology and then to seminaries. Initially the seminaries were more or less strictly denominational. During the twentieth century, however, education for ministry took on an ecumenical cast and, while retaining features distinctive to certain traditions, became more uniform. In the 1980s Protestant ministers were receiving basically the same type of training in biblical, historical, theological, and practical studies. The Association of Theological Schools in the United States and Canada (formerly The American Association of Theological Schools) was establishing guidelines and monitoring degree programs in member schools, thus assuring some standardization. This body has commissioned numerous studies which have resulted in changes in the shape of ministry in America (see Schuller, et al., 1980).

Education for ministry has experienced significant changes since the Second Vatican Council (1962–65) as Roman Catholics have joined Protestants and Orthodox in common educational efforts. By 1970 theological institutions were freely sharing library and other resources, exchanging students and faculty, and participating in consortia in which ministers would receive an ecumenical education. Catholic seminaries added a special concern for spiritual formation.

7. **Ecumenical Trends.** From the outset Protestant ministry tended toward proliferation of concepts and patterns. The four major traditions took separate paths. Then in North America all Protestant groups experienced significant alterations under the impact of a highly diversified culture. Since the nineteenth century, however, ecumenical trends have reversed the earlier tendencies and caused some movement in the direction of common understanding and practice of ministry. Protestant cooperation in revivals, missionary endeavors, and social service or action led the way toward structuring of efforts to promote Christian unity. As the churches confronted common problems together, they exchanged ideas and customs which prepared for more formal mergers.

At the Second Vatican Council, Roman Catholics inaugurated a new era of ecumenical reflection by their rethinking of Catholic concepts of church and ministry. Although the Council introduced no radical changes, its emphasis upon the church as the People of God rather than the mystical Body laid foundations for some important shifts. Ministry is now perceived as the task of the whole People of God. Thus the role of lay persons within the churches has been brought into closer proximity to the Protestant concept of a universal priesthood. In addition, although the Council kept the sacraments at the center of the churches' ministry, it restored preaching to the place of importance it held in ancient Christian times.

Ecumenical developments have forced most Protestant churches to reassess thoroughly their understanding of ministry. This has certainly been the case for the ten denominations participating in the Consultation on Church Union, a plan for reunion first proposed in 1962 by Eugene Carson Blake. Broader in scope even than that Consultation's document on ministry is a consensus statement on *Baptism, Eucharist and Ministry* adopted at Lima, Peru, in January, 1982, by the Faith and Order Commission of the World Council of Churches and approved at Vancouver in July, 1984, by the Sixth Assembly of the Council. This document has been circulated among member churches of the World Council for their "acceptance."

The Lima statement affirms that ministry in its broadest sense is the task of the whole People of God. Within this larger calling the chief responsibility of an ordained ministry is "to assemble and build up the body of Christ by proclaiming and teaching the Word of God, by celebrating the sacraments, and by guiding the life of the community in its worship, its mission and its caring ministry" (13). Ordained ministers do not hold authority independent of the whole body. They may be called "priests" insofar as they contribute to the upbuilding of the priestly ministry of the whole.

Ordained ministry, according to the *Baptism, Eucharist and Ministry* document, may take a variety of forms, but the historic threefold pattern of bishops, presbyters, and deacons is to be preferred. What is needed, however, is not a particular form, even episcopacy, but *episkopé* or "oversight." Whatever the form, ministry should be exercised in "a personal, collegial and communal way" (26). If early Christian practice is followed, bishops and presbyters would have leading roles, deacons subordinate ones.

Steering around the question of the validity of non-episcopal ordinations, the document accentuates continuity in handing on the apostolic faith rather than episcopal succession from the apostles. Ordination is described as "a sign of the gift of the Spirit" (39) rather than as a "means." It is, above all, a prayer for the Spirit to give gifts to the person ordained and an acknowledgment of the gifts which that person manifests. The document notes that the churches set various conditions for ordination but states a clear preference for inclusiveness in ministry, women as well as men. It closes with a plea for mutual recognition of ordained ministries. Protestant ministry can expect continuous changes with few resemblances to what it was in the sixteenth century.

Bibliography. J. Calvin, *Institutes of the Christian Religion*, J. T. McNeill, ed. (1960). Consultation on Church Union, *A Plan of Union for the Church of Christ Uniting* (1970). L. T. Howe, "Theology in the Practice of Ministry," *J. of Pastoral Counseling*, 19:2 (1984), 128–35. M. Luther, *Appeal to the German Nobility* (1520). F. S. Mead, *Handbook of Denominations of the United States*, 4th ed. (1965). H. R. Niebuhr and D. D. Williams, eds., *The Ministry in Historical Perspective* (1980). D. S. Schuller, M. P. Strommen, and M. L. Brekke, eds., *Ministry in America* (1980). E. E. Thornton, *Professional Education for Ministry* (1970). World Council of Churches, *The Community of Women and Men in the Church* (1982); *Baptism, Eucharist, and Ministry* (1982).

E. G. HINSON

VOCATION (Protestantism). *See also* BISHOP; CALL TO MINISTRY; CAREER DEVELOPMENT AND GUIDANCE (For Pastors); CLERGY COUPLES; DEACON; ELDER; WOMEN IN PASTORAL MINISTRIES, HISTORY OF. *Compare* ECCLESIOLOGY AND PASTORAL CARE; PERSONHOOD OF THE PASTOR, SIGNIFICANCE OF; RABBI/RABBINATE. *Biography:* CALVIN; FOX; LUTHER; WESLEY; ZWINGLI.

MINISTRY (Roman Catholic Tradition). The dimension of service proper to Christian life and to positions of public office within the church community. Also, the positions of service themselves. In the Catholic community after Vatican II, the term has gained new currency for both the ordained (bishops, priests, deacons) and the un-ordained (various lay ministers). This signals a shift away from a pre-conciliar mindset that viewed bishops and priests in terms of prestige and power. Moreover, it restores to all the baptized an active responsibility for the life and mission of the church, and opens to lay men and women positions of public service previously reserved to the clergy. The Christological model operative in this shift is that of the human Jesus who came "not to be served, but to serve."

Christian ministry is a function of the mission of the church, which remains a twofold task: to proclaim the Good News of what God has done in Christ, and to continue the saving works of Christ until he comes again. It is also a function of church order. Ministry is not simply an attitude of mind but determines the way a community structures its life, its prayer, and its network of interactions, both within itself and of itself toward society at large. It pertains to the actions of individuals, to be sure, but also to the public and the corporate nature of the church. Finally, ministry is a function of the Incarnation. In Christian ministry flesh and blood is given to the mystery of Jesus Christ present in the church, who is, in the power of the Holy Spirit, the source of all its effectiveness.

1. The Mission of the Church. Jesus of Nazareth appeared in history to announce and make present the Kingdom of God. In his life, death, and resurrection, that Kingdom is established in a definitive way. It is named by Paul (Rom. 8:22–3) as a deep yearning in creation to be free from all destructive forces and to achieve its full destiny intended by God. It is named in more personal terms by Jesus as a conversion of heart and a life lived in obedience to the creative plan of God (Mk. 1:15).

The church is established by the Holy Spirit poured forth in the resurrection of Jesus Christ. It is comprised of all who have heard the word of Christ and allowed that word to lead them into the mystery of his own dying and rising. Entrusted to the people of the church is the mission to teach and call to conversion, to baptize and gather into unity, to remember, to hope, and to work for the coming of God's Kingdom in its fullness. All Christian ministry is an expression of one or several of these tasks.

The church's task of teaching or evangelization is to announce to human life and society the way revealed by Jesus Christ, and to display by its own life both the possibility and the value of following Christ's way. Christian initiation, which is both the fullness of baptism and the call to participate in the Eucharist, is the lifelong process of drawing people into the way of Christ. One is always initiated into a living community. It involves learning to believe, to pray, to relate, and to serve by entering into its fellowship of shared belief, prayer, relationship, and service (Rite of Christian Initiation of Adults).

Remembrance lies at the heart of Christian life and prayer. In essence it is the constant proclamation to the church of all that God has done and promised in Christ so that the people may actively seek God's deeds and promise. Hope is the other side of remembrance. It names the expectation of God's firm fidelity to all who follow Christ's way, even as God is proclaimed to have been faithful to Jesus.

Finally, in the time between, the church is to work so that both in human lives and in human history the way of Christ may take flesh and blood. One principal name for this activity is humanization. Another, which stresses the communal dimension of human life, is reconciliation. Such activity involves discerning and doing what is given us to do, and trusting still in the face of what we cannot and are not given to do. It is therefore both incarnational and eschatological.

2. Historical Overview. *a. Key biblical texts.* Because of its strong sacramental self-identity, the Roman Catholic sense of ministry has been shaped primarily by texts of sacramental institution. The mandate to teach and baptize (Mt. 28:18–20) is foundational. The commission to forgive (Jn. 20:22–3), often taken to name the power of priests to absolve from sin, names also the mandate to the whole church to be ministers of reconciliation (II Cor. 5:19–20). Finally, the command to share in the Eucharist in I Corinthians and Luke, which is classically interpreted to mean repetition of Jesus' own actions in obedience to his word, embraces even more the commission to remember, to hope, and to act toward the Kingdom's fulfillment.

The stress on sacramentality has also nurtured a sense of Christian ministry as action that embodies the personal presence of Christ. A key text that has shaped the personal dimension of this task is the description of the compassionate and humanly empathetic Christ in Hebrews (4:15).

b. Development in understanding and practice. In the early church the development of ministry was fluid and varied, following different patterns in the Gentile and Jewish-Christian communities. Specific tasks within the community, such as leadership (presbyter-bishops) and proclamation (prophets and teachers), were assigned to individuals according to both talent and need. Other tasks, such as intercession, reconciliation, initiation, and care for the members, belonged to the entire community. In general, the domestic or synagogue model governed the organization of these early churches and hence of the ministries that they developed.

From the fourth century on, as church life and prayer became more organized and structured, a shift to temple imagery for the church brought with it a separation of ministers (*cleroi*) from the people (*laos*), and eventually a reduction of ministries to the triptych: bishop, priest, and deacon. By the Middle Ages, offices such as reader, tableserver (acolyte), and doorkeeper (porter), once ministries in their own right, had become clerical orders open to and mandated for only those who were moving toward priesthood. With the exception of a few ministries reserved to the bishop alone, the variety of ministries in and for the church were funneled into the role of the priest. The people became recipients of the priest's ministry, no longer proper ministers themselves.

Vatican II, with its accent on the church as the whole people of God, radically reversed this pattern. Concretely, it restored the office of deacon as a true and proper ministry and opened up the liturgical ministries of reader and acolyte to the laity. More significant, however, has been the restored sense that all of the baptized actively share in the worship of God, in the responsibilities of the community, and in the saving mission of Christ.

3. Elements in Christian Ministry. The scope of Christian ministry may be analyzed according to structure (Tavard), content (Cooke), or relational pattern.

a. Structure. Tavard's theological reflection on the actual functions of Christian ministers reveals four essential structures to Christian ministry. The first is *mediation,* which unfolds principally in the arena of prayer. Presidency of the liturgical assembly and the life of contemplative religious communities exemplify this structure of ministry. The second is *proclamation.* Preaching, spiritual direction, and confessional counseling are three of its expressions. The third is *service;* under this heading is included a whole array of activities, from personal care of the sick and the aged to pursuits of social justice in society. Finally, there is *education,* embracing the twofold task of Christianizing the church and humanizing the world. These are essentially four Gospel responsibilities, which may be distributed variously among different offices and communities. None of them can be neglected or absorbed by the others.

b. Content. Cooke explores the scope of Christian ministry under five headings: formation of community, the word, service, judgment, and sacramental ministry. The first is that kind of *koinonia* desired by the Lord, which is the goal of the Eucharistic action and indeed of the church's mission to the world. Ministry of the word embraces preaching, prophecy, and service—the various helping ministries that arise as needs dictate. Judgment is discernment in matters that are moral and spiritual. The sacrament of penance is a prime arena of this ministry. Ministry of sacraments includes both the liturgical enactment of sacraments and a variety of ministries required to set the proper life context for sacraments to be true and effective. In all Cooke insists that these five ministries belong to the entire community even where special ministers are appointed to orchestrate and lead them.

c. Relational patterns. Ministry may also be analyzed according to relational patterns that it establishes. There is first the one-to-one pattern where intimacy, presence, and personal vulnerability are paramount. This is most frequent where human fragility is at stake, such as sinfulness, sickness, and spiritual growth. There is also the one-to-many pattern, typical of prayer leadership and proclamation. A third is the many-to-one, as in Christian initiation and reconciliation, where the community itself provides the context for personal journeys of faith and healing. Finally, there is the many-to-many, as illustrated by the American bishops' *Pastoral Letter on Peace.* This last is the rule for the church's corporate service in shaping a just and humane society.

4. Episcope, Presbyterium, Diakonia. Pastoral leadership, wise counsel, and service lie at the heart of this ministerial triptych, which has found expression in the office of bishop, priest, and deacon.

a. Ministry of bishop, priest, deacon. The bishop is the primary pastor of a local church or diocese. His ministry is that of overseer or elder responsible for the faith and prayer of his diocese. A member of the College of Bishops, he is also a sign and symbol of the universal communion of churches, and the primary link establishing that communion. Several bishops from other local churches are called upon to administer his ordination.

The presbyterium is the college of ministers ordained to assist the bishop in his pastoral ministry to the diocese. They are pastors in parish communities and preside at the Eucharistic assembly, thus sharing the *episcope* of the bishop. They likewise serve in diocesan councils to advise the bishop in his spiritual ministry. The presbyterium comprises diocesan or secular priests, ordained for service in a particular local church, and priests of religious communities assigned for a time to a diocese.

The deacon, according to the revised rite of ordination, assists the priests and bishops in ministry to word and sacrament. Deacons preside at some liturgical functions and likewise preach and proclaim the gospel.

b. Emerging ministries in the church. In the years since Vatican II, a growing number of lay men and women have taken seminary education and have entered the public ministry of the church as what is sometimes called "non-ordained ecclesial ministers." These laypersons serve as members of parish pastoral teams, chaplains in hospitals and educational institutions, and directors of diocesan pastoral projects. They are appointed, not ordained, though their status as public church ministers places them in a different category of service from the ordinary laity.

c. Ministry of the laity. The prime ministry of the laity is to take the gospel and its values into secular society. The accent here is on the Christian mission given in baptism. The laity also have an essential liturgical ministry more far reaching than the roles of reader and auxiliary Eucharistic minister which they have recently been given. Liturgy demands full and active participation of all the faithful to be true liturgy. Intercession is the highest act of the priesthood of the baptized, and consent to the faith enacted in the liturgy (Amen) constitutes their own necessary completion of the church's worship of God.

5. Appointment of Ministers. *a. Baptism and confirmation.* All Christians are established as agents in the church's mission by baptism and its complementary anointing. Placed with Christ, they are consecrated by God and commissioned to call all men and women into God's *koinonia.*

b. Installation and dedication. Special ministers are appointed in liturgical assembly. While not ordinations with the traditional laying on of hands, these are public commissioning ceremonies, presided over by bishop or pastor, including acts of dedication and willingness on the part of the minister and prayers of intercession on the part of the assembly. Official liturgies have been established for the ministries of lector and acolyte, and the way has been opened for the development of other "lay ministries."

c. Ordination. This liturgical action with the laying on of hands and solemn prayer of consecration establishes one as deacon, priest, that is, in the presbyterium, or as bishop. Symbolically it links the new minister with the apostolic church, and sacramentally it commissions the minister to act on behalf of the church. The laying on of hands is an invocation of God's Spirit and the consecration prayer an entrustment of both the minister and the ministry to the Spirit's power. While ordination is one of the ministries reserved to the bishop, it remains a liturgical action, with other ministers, and indeed the whole assembly, assuming an important role. Ordination to the presbyterate is required to preside at the Eucharist and to proclaim sacramental absolution. Ordination to the diaconate is for preaching and gospel proclamation.

6. **Attitudes and Dispositions in Ministry.** Christian ministers ought to be possessed to an exemplary degree of such basic Christian virtues as compassion, kindness, meekness, and patience (Col. 3:12–14). Whether dealing with an individual or with an assembly, the proper disposition to exhibit is that which Christ would display in the situation. While Christian ministers do have an obligation to preserve the traditions and laws of the community they represent, the commission to embody Christ for others is their highest obligation.

There is a peculiar vulnerability to the gospel, whether proclaimed in word or enacted in sacrament, which is required of Christian ministers. In order to speak and embody Christ's word for the human life of others, they need first to have heard that word with power in the depth of their own human life. They need also to trust firmly that God's power will indeed be made manifest in their own ministry.

7. **Questions of Current Concern.** *a. Church and culture.* Vatican II let down the barriers between church and culture that were established firmly in the nineteenth century and opened the door both to adaptation in the liturgy and to inculturation of the gospel message. This shift marks a transition from a dominantly European church to what Rahner calls "a world Church" ("Significance of Vatican II"). Questions of identity, fidelity, continuity, and the freedom to create new forms of faith are of central concern in this transition. Evolution of radically new expressions of Christian ministry is inevitable (see Donovan).

b. Women in ministry. The Catholic Church has held fast in its conviction that women cannot be admitted to the ministerial priesthood (1977). Arguments in support of this position are assessed variously among Catholic theologians. Nonetheless, the church insists that all discrimination against women be eliminated and that they be welcomed into positions of authority and responsibility.

The fact is that a large number of the laypersons entering public ministry on parish teams, in retreat work, in hospital chaplaincies, and the like, are women, some of whom have been appointed pastoral administrators of parish communities in the absence of priests. The issue may well be one of inculturation rather than precise theological argument and will no doubt be significantly advanced as women in ministry become more pastorally visible.

c. Ministry of the papacy. The ministry of the papacy is interpreted differently in the two ecclesiologies that sit side by side in the post-conciliar Catholic consciousness. The strict hierarchical or "pyramid" model names the pope "Supreme Pastor," and sees all bishops, and hence all local churches, directly subject to his pas-

toral authority. The second places the local bishop as head of the local church related in the communion of faith and commitment to the primatial Roman See. This second is closer to the Orthodox position that the See of Peter ranks first among equals, though Roman Catholics generally do not accept that articulation.

d. Relation to other Christian churches. The document on ministry from the World Council of Churches called for respect for the different church orders that exist and for recognition of the different ministries within each church order. The principal issue for Roman Catholics concerns only those ministries that it holds to require validly ordained priests and bishops, namely the Eucharist, reconciliation, ordination. This hurdle gets lessened as the church begins to recognize the truth of other communities' Eucharist. It is yet another issue that may well be decided on the pastoral front before it reaches adequate theological resolution.

Bibliography. J. Barnett, *The Diaconate* (1981). T. Clarke, "To Make Peace, Evangelize Culture," *America* (1984), 413–17. B. Cooke, *Ministry to Word and Sacraments* (1976). V. Donovan, *Christianity Rediscovered* (1978). F. Eigo, ed., *Ministering in a Servant Church* (1978). B. K. Estadt, "The Lay Ministry Megatrend," *J. of Pastoral Care*, 40 (1986), 292–96. L. Gilkey, *How the Church Can Minister to the World Without Losing Itself* (1964). R. Hovda, *Strong, Loving, and Wise: Presiding in Liturgy* (1980). H. Kung, ed., *Papal Ministry in the Church* (1971). N. Mitchell, *Mission and Ministry* (1982). T. O'Meara, *Theology of Ministry* (1983). D. Power, *Gifts that Differ* (1980). J. Provost, ed., *Official Ministry in a New Age* (1981). K. Rahner, "The Lasting Significance of Vatican II," *Theological Digest*, 28 (1980), 221–25 and *Bishops: Their Status and Function* (1964). J. Rigel, *Ministères dans l'Eglise* (1980). E. Schillebeeckx, *Ministry* (1981). G. Tavard, *A Theology for Ministry* (1983). P. E. Fink, "The Sacrament of Orders: Some Liturgical Reflections," *Worship*, 56 (1982), 482–502.

P. E. FINK

ROMAN CATHOLIC PASTORAL CARE; VOCATION (Roman Catholicism). *See also* BISHOP; CALL TO MINISTRY; DEACON; HOLY ORDERS; ORDINATION AND CERTIFICATION IN PASTORAL COUNSELING; PASTOR (Normative and Traditional Images); PERSONHOOD OF THE PASTOR, SIGNIFICANCE OF; PRIEST; VATICAN COUNCIL II; WOMEN IN PASTORAL MINISTRIES, HISTORY OF. *Compare* ECCLESIOLOGY AND PASTORAL CARE; LAICIZATION; RABBI/RABBINATE; RELIGIOUS LIFE.

MINISTRY AND PASTORAL CARE (Orthodox Tradition).

To understand how pastoral care is administered in the Orthodox Church, one must first understand the nature of the people who are cared *for*. This means, of course, to understand the church itself since the people of God *are* the church.

1. **The Orthodox Church.** Although many persons in "Western" society have come into the Orthodox Church through conversion, the influential roots of the Orthodox people remain "Eastern," that is, the ethos of the Eastern Orthodox Church is distinguished by those groups who emigrated from Greece, Russia and the Ukraine, the Middle East (Syria and Lebanon), Serbia, Romania, and other Eastern European countries. Although they very often know themselves to be "American and Western," those elements that distinguish them as Greeks, Russians, Antiochians (Syrian-Lebanese), and so forth, are clearly maintained.

For the Orthodox priest who must pastor them, this is at once a blessing and a problem. It is a blessing inasmuch as many of the customs brought with them from these lands serve to maintain and even transmit the Tradition (what the Orthodox know as the Great *Parádosis*), although the customs of those lands and the tradition of the faith are never to be confused. At the same time it presents a problem.

The priest finds himself dealing with persons who are being subjected to secular influences, which are often in conflict with the values of the Orthodox subculture. Such a "tension" is no small problem for the Orthodox priest.

The Orthodox pastor's activity is one of total *care;* it is never reduced to any one aspect, for example, counseling, administration, liturgies, teaching, and so forth, although such care would *include* each of these. (St. Basil calls this "total care" an *epiméleia.*) He is, in fact and in deed, "the shepherd" (*poiménos*) and "overseer" (*epíscopos*) of which I Pet. 2:25 speaks when referring to Our Lord Himself. The pastor lives with his flock in all the intimacy of one who "calls them by name . . . and the sheep follow him, for they know his voice" (Jn. 10:2–4, KJV).

There are three major areas in which the Orthodox pastor realizes such inclusive care: in the *ministry of the sanctuary,* in the *ministry of the word* and in the *ministry of spiritual counsel;* each is crucial to his pastoral ministry and has roots in the Orthodox faith.

2. The Ministry of the Sanctuary. Here the pastor sees himself directly related to the priesthood of Christ. For the Orthodox, Christ is the only *Leitourgós* ("the leader of our worship"), that is, he is "the minister of the sanctuary, and of the true tabernacle, which the Lord has pitched, and not man" (Heb. 8:12, KJV). Jesus is the sole priest, the sole celebrant, and those serving in this ministry of the sanctuary are making *him* present; the priest does nothing by himself, but is "presentifying" him who is *always* present as the "Eternal Priest" (Heb. 10:15–16, KJV). In this case, this is how the Orthodox understand the word "represent," precisely as re-*presenting* Christ who is always there. Liturgically, the priest is thus not an "officer" who is acting *in persona ecclesiae,* but only *in persona Christi.*

The Orthodox never forget the centrality of this action, and for this reason, the liturgy is the true binding center of their identity as a people. From this center they make their way through life, knowing that they have touched the Kingdom, brought by Christ's presence, and which eternally "resides" by the power of the Holy Spirit. In the end, the church remembers that we offer ourselves to the Lord, and yet it is not *we* who offer, but Christ who has offered himself for us and who *is* our offering.

To see Christ in this way, as "the One who offers and is offered," is to understand his "priesthood" proper; it is never reduced to being merely a teacher or a worker of good deeds, although these are included. Rather, his priesthood is the *core* of his ministry, because it is defined in what he is and does, that is, in the offering of himself, in his "self-oblation."

As the pastor of his flock (cf. Lk. 12:32, KJV), Christ cares by such a total offering of himself; those in his priesthood do likewise. In the Orthodox ministry of the sanctuary, then, this function of pastoral care is evident.

3. The Ministry of the Word. *a. Kerygma.* Proper caring within the pastoral ministry includes the *kerygma* (the proclamation). The Word of God is proclaimed basically, but not solely, within the liturgy. It is always the gospel (the "good news") that is proclaimed, and it is proclaimed in total cooperation with God: "It is not you who speak, but the Holy Spirit" (Mk. 13:11, KJV). It is certainly not without the input—the prayer, struggle, intent—of the one whose human words carry the message; but the human effort cooperates in the dynamic of *synergía* (synergy) with God's grace. The pastor preaches out of an *assimilation* to God; this is as deeply organic as Ezekiel, who "consumes the word of God" who is "written on a scroll" (Ezek. 3:1–2, KJV).

The message of the gospel is always the *same:* Jesus is Lord. It is this gospel which is thus "assimilated" and out of which the *kérygma* comes. The pastor is to be a collaborator of all those who have, and who will, preach that same gospel within the catholicity of the church. (*Katholikí* here means an "inner wholeness," or *Kat'olos* "according to the whole"—and not a geographical or worldwide designation). This is precisely what St. Paul understood as being "received" by him first, then being "delivered" to others (I Cor. 15:3, KJV). The ministry of the word is continuous with that gospel delivered to the church (I Cor. 15:11, KJV).

b. Particular application. However, also like St. Paul, "a lateborn Apostle," and also like the Fathers to whom the Orthodox have always turned, the one eternal Word must be applied, appropriated, and delivered differently; there is a need to move out of the same basic message toward the "particular." This Word, eternally the same, is addressed to the circumstances and predicaments of each day and era. In all such situations we see a true divine—human synthesis, a true *synergía*—in which all human words are spoken to facilitate, to prepare the soil of the soul, to cause the *heart* to be receptive and responsive to the one Word of God (*Lógos tou Theoú*).

For the Orthodox pastor, then, it is never a question of mere human "technique," or of human absence (i.e., God does it all, the human playing no part). It is *always* up to the pastor to give the distinct human form to the proclamation, by prayer, study, and even planning, which in itself is part of the cooperation with the Holy Spirit (cf. II Tim. 2:2; I Tim. 4:13). Yet it is always God who lifts up the effort (cf. I Cor. 2:4).

How do the Orthodox see this as a distinct "ministry"? And how is it pastoral care? It is ministry, first of all, because its intent is *to serve,* and ministry *means* to serve: For I came "not to be ministered unto [to be served], but to minister" (*diakoneésai,* "to serve", Mt. 20:28, KJV). When the pastor preaches it may be to *lead* the community (St. Basil calls the pastor *proestós,* the "leader") but even at that, that leadership is still one of *service.* Secondly, preaching is ministry because what is spoken is done so verbally and powerfully, in order to *change* people, to *convert* people's lives, to *move* people closer and closer to Jesus Christ. And it is pastoral care because the "pastor" who "cares" is interested, always and only, in *touching and stretching* persons.

When God speaks the "Word," something is created, things change, people change, something happens; this we see both at Creation and in the Incarnation. God's Word is a manifestation of both, the One who speaks the word, and God's intent in its "spokenness." When the preacher speaks his *human* word, likewise, the intent is that an event also happens in which the same revelation is realized in which creation and change can take place. Of course, this implies a congruence of the human word with the Word of God (the preacher *never* preaches *himself*)! All this means that no mechanical process, no factual information, no essay, no composition, is being here developed: it is a true *kérygma* of the *Evangélion,* a true proclamation of the gospel, which rests on the original meaning of *the* Word, and upon the intent of the one who ministers by that Word (I Cor. 2:4).

4. **The Ministry of Spiritual Counsel.** *a. The Orthodox approach.* The third area in which the Orthodox pastor cares for the flock is in ministry of spiritual counsel. There are various sources to which the Orthodox turn in considering this area. When such sources are considered, a very distinct approach is taken, which fits solidly within the understanding of true pastoral care. The pastor is there to touch and to stretch the persons of his flock. If the pastor does not touch them first, he will not be able to stretch them. If the pastor has no intent of stretching them, his touch has no ultimate purpose, no spiritual intent.

It is in such a dynamic that a clear distinction is seen between the various secular approaches that abound today, and a more Orthodox Christian approach (see Leech, 1977). This distinction is first marked by certain ethical imperatives. This does not mean that ethics is applied in a perfunctory or facile manner such as, "do this, do that." It means that the pastor remains aware of the danger of removing the stretching element of the "ought" or the "should" (what the Fathers knew as the *télos,* the "final goal" or "meaning" toward which one moves), which would finally end in mere "adjustment."

The ethic, in a sense, "tugs" at the pastor's counsel; the "should" remains in tension with the "is," pulling persons from where they are to where the Christian gospel is attempting to call them. This tension is required even for the proper *study* of pastoral care (as a subject), since without it we create a false polarity between ethics and pastoral care in our curricula. If we maintain the "touch and stretch" dynamic, however, pastoral care remains related to both — the "is" (i.e., where the pastor finds the parishioner, counselee, person) and the "should," which ethics brings to the situation.

Secondly, the Orthodox pastor has many examples in the tradition which serve to guard him or her from the naive *application* of this ethical "should;" there is much more to it than applying it "by pronouncement" or "moralizing," and much more than the pharisaical arrogance, which leaves no room for forgiveness and repentance. The *Sayings of the Desert Fathers* are full of examples warning of this. The theme is clearly, "To the weak I became weak, that I might win the weak" (I Cor. 2:3). Here is the paradoxical reality of a "strong weakness," which allows the "touch and stretch" dynamic to operate in spiritual counsel: "For we do not have a high priest who is unable to sympathize [*sympathé*] with our weakness" (Heb. 4:15).

b. Presuppositions. There are various presuppositions, of course, which allow such a "touch and stretch" dynamic to lead to healing; they are solidly related to the theology and tradition of the Orthodox Church, and they clearly inform this area of spiritual counsel.

The first presupposition is the constant remembrance that "the sin is to be hated, but never the sinner." The theological roots of this distinction (of being and act) are found in the writings of the Fathers. For example, St. John Damascene says that humans are created sinless "by nature" (*kata phy'sin*) and that we sin only "by choice" (see Allen, 1981). This understanding gives a very positive orientation to Orthodox counseling, because it implies that the human being, created in God's image has "by nature" the capacity and inclination to grow, to move in his or her acts and choices toward God, unless blocked by sin. Thus, the Damascene (in *De Fide Orthodoxa*) says, "we must remove the rust from the steel" to see its shine, and Nyssa says "the athlete must throw off all undue weight to compete" (in *Life of Moses*).

The pastor's hope, in light of this, is to help persons "remove the rust," and to "throw off the undue weight," which comes by way of their wrong choices and actions, and which they have, in a sense, "attached" to their being. There is, however, never a time when persons cannot make such a correcting, freeing choice, even if they do not realize that they can make it, and even if it means their own martyrdom. The pastor's vocation as a shepherd is to stand and walk with such persons, and against their wrong choices and actions, reminding them that Christ has truly freed us, even if the truth is painful. This is a true spiritual freedom, not a political or social freedom; it is rather a freedom to grow toward Christ through all of life's crises and dilemmas, and to do this by coming to the knowledge of truth. This is part of *théosis* (deification) to which the Orthodox point, but now seen through a "pastoral" eye as applied to the life of every Christian.

c. The Stáretz. Spiritual counsel in the church has always been connected to a special relationship with the "elder" (the *stáretz* or *géron*), one's spiritual father. The *stáretz* has traditionally been older (although this is not always so today) because through life experience he could see the "larger pictures" of life, delineate this from that with wisdom, and help persons to become "seers." This is done by "pushing the person back on himself" (or herself), by helping the person separate things that seem murky, by challenging the person to move toward freedom. But always this is done with love and care; it is never done as a "sheriff," but always as a true shepherd, though it may indeed be straight and hard, an *epitémisis* (a rebuke). Its intent is nevertheless to lead the person toward spiritual healing and growth. This same *stáretz* may at other times be most tender, especially when persons are wrongly punishing themselves, or assuming guilt that is not theirs to assume. (Perhaps the person is even suffering from "self-pity," which may be a source of pride!) His spiritual counsel is as broad as this because the elder is concerned about the whole life of the person, not only particular problems or emotional and physical difficulties, and with what the person will make of them. He is precisely concerned about the direction in which the person is going, despite such difficulties. In fact, such difficulties themselves are to be used to grow; the old ascetic saying (which has come down even in modern Greek) is that "every obstacle is for the good!"

Such spiritual counsel in the Orthodox Church, however, never ends with "insight"; it may begin there, but insight by itself is never enough. Insight is of the mind, but the mind must always be taken down into the heart; in a like manner the heart is to be brought up to the mind. The unity of mind and heart, which is to say in this case of insight and Christian action (or charity), are what the Orthodox believe comprise the *being* of a person. The counsel of the pastor is to lead from insight to Christian action, and to work precisely at this "being-level" of the counselee.

d. Relation to sacramental life. The spiritual counsel of the Orthodox pastor is also related to the sacramental life. The sacraments are neither magic nor a "form without content." They are related to the person's condition, to what the person is doing (or not doing), to how he is struggling, to the individual's relationship with others, and so on. The pastor will not arbitrarily give the Holy Eucharist without considering this entire range of the Christian life. He may, in fact, instruct the person in the sacrament of repentance (*Exomológesis* or *Metánoina*) *not* to approach the sacrament until the sin and/or spiritual problem is resolved. (Here it must be remembered that the sacrament of repentance is not limited to spiritual counsel, although it may include it; repentance, in the Orthodox Church, is an initiation, a "baptism of tears." To receive the Holy Eucharist means to enter into "common union" (communion) with God and God's church; it is receiving "unto condemnation" if through the person's unresolved and unconfessed sin, he or she is in fact not truly *in* "common union." In one's life and acts he or she often breaks such communion, and spiritual counsel is there to lead the person toward reconciliation and true union with God and the church through repentance.

e. Healing aim. In the Orthodox perspective, spiritual counsel is not "merely" counseling, helping, or offering sound advice for betterment and peacefulness. Anybody can do that—and in fact, should do that. But the pastor's aim is a true healing, a true wholeness: both healing and wholeness are from the same root, *hólos,* a "holding together." His counsel is to help persons "hold together" their lives with God, with their neighbors, and within themselves (in the mind and heart). Each of these relationships is crucial for the Christian, and each is a part of the pastor's concern for the whole life of his flock.

The pastor, then, when counseling, is the *true* "therapist," for the original meaning of this term is from the ancient *therápon* or *therapía theón* (the "Godly servant"). The secular therapist may hardly care about God, about seeing Christ in the sick or naked, about the sacramental life, about the mind *and the heart,* about the ethical dimension; the Orthodox pastor has no choice. As the Godly Servant, his "therapy" is truly "spiritual," since what is spiritual (*pneumatikó*) is not, as some think, opposed to what is "material," but indicates the total directivity of one's life, including all that one is (the existential) and all that one can do (the teleological).

5. **Care of the Sick.** *a. Physical healing and pastoral care.* In the Orthodox Church the service of anointing is a distinctly pastoral function. It must be dealt with separately because it is related to each of the aforementioned areas of pastoral care, and yet does not belong *solely* to any one of them.

In the early church the sacrament of oil was administered with seven clergymen, each of whom read an Epistle and Gospel, then the prayer, then the anointing proper. Thus, there were seven Epistles readings, Gospel readings, and prayers. The entire community gathered around the sick person and, led by the pastor, anointed him or her. Today this is usually done by one priest in either the home or the hospital. The prayers of the entire community are embodied in the identity of the priest as the shepherd. The service usually includes the distribution of the Eucharist after the person is "anointed unto the healing of body and soul."

What is important pastorally is precisely how such healing is to be understood. For the Orthodox, healing is understood in terms of "wholeness," as previously noted. The implication is that without such wholeness we have "dis-ease" (or *asthénia*). Healing has to do with restoration to such wholeness.

Three dimensions of this healing service, however, require special comment.

b. The petitionary prayer. Christian prayer, even in this case, is never "demanding"; it is always supplication or doxology. For the Orthodox Christian this means that it is never a case of whether or not "I get what I want," or even "what *I* think I need." Christian faith is not there *because* of what happens, but *in spite of* what happens. As the church has learned from the Psalms (used in every liturgical service), God knows even better than we do what we should or should not have. This is the great discovery of Job, who was an upright and God-fearing man. He lost everything: his cattle and asses, his servants and camels, his children, and he was even physically afflicted with "sore boils from the sole of his foot unto his crown" (Job 2:7, KJV). Is God unjust? Not understanding, his wife and curious "friends" become sarcastic: whoever *did* suffer being innocent? Job discovers in God's answer, however, the deepest meaning: "Where were you when I laid the foundation of the earth?" (Job 38:4). His response, remembering that "man is born to trouble" (5:7), that is, in no sense removed from disease and sin, is that of the Christian in this circumstance: "Behold I am of small account; what shall I answer thee? I lay my hand on my mouth!" (40:4). In such a way, it is *faith* in God which cuts into such suffering.

c. Theology of healing. This faith in which the healing prayer and anointing take place reminds all those present of that which St. Paul well knew: "For our light affliction, which is but for a *moment,* worketh for us a far more exceeding *and* eternal weight of glory" (II Cor. 4:17, KJV). Each particular ailment can be a way to connect our present experience with the meaning of our *total* existence as humans before God.

Even in the case of a "cure"—now in the narrow sense of the word—other meanings must *still* be kept alive: *God* heals, even if through the mediation of other persons and/or medicines. The principle is the same: in the middle of my *problem* I come to terms with the meaning of my existence. In either case one's relationship to God is not arbitrary when physical illness strikes; it is essential, and for the Christian, is the very foundation of one's search for the ultimate healing and wholeness.

d. The nature of anointing. The anointing, thus, is never to be understood so narrowly that it has the implication of "curing," for example, as medicine cures a skin rash. Furthermore, the anointing has a clear "consecratory" meaning which remembers that the body is the "temple of the Holy Spirit" and that it too, along with the soul, is created in God's image. This is true regardless of any somatic disease.

Our hope is always to be one with God, whether we live or die, whether in pain or not; it is this by which the experience is interpreted. Obviously, how we interpret the experiences of illness or misfortune is itself *part* of that experience. "Rabbi, who sinned, this man or his parents? . . . Jesus answered, It was not that this man sinned, or his parents" (Jn. 9:2–3, KJV). Sin and disease, which are related in the cosmic sense, that is, in a fallen world, have broken in upon all of life; our hope, however, lies in our faith that, because Christ has become like us in everything (but sin), he has assumed even our pain and mortality. The Orthodox constantly live by this axiom: "What is not assumed, cannot be saved." Such a faith interpretation is related to the healing in the service of anointing: "Though he was in the form of God, [Christ] did not count equality with God a thing to be grasped, but emptied himself, taking the form of a servant, being born in the likeness of men" (Phil. 2:6–7).

Bibliography. K. Leech, *Soul Friend* (1977). H. Waddell, trans., *The Desert Fathers* (1957). J. L. Allen, ed., *The Orthodox Synthesis* (1981).

J. L. ALLEN

MINISTRY; PASTORAL CARE (History, Traditions, and Definitions). *See also* SACRAMENTAL THEOLOGY AND PASTORAL CARE, ORTHODOX; STARETS. *Compare* EARLY CHURCH, PASTORAL CARE IN; EASTERN EUROPEAN PASTORAL CARE MOVEMENT; ECCLESIOLOGY AND PASTORAL CARE; TRADITION AS MODE OF CARE.

MINISTRY STUDIES. *See* CLERGY, EMPIRICAL STUDIES OF; READINESS FOR MINISTRY STUDIES; THEOLOGICAL STUDENTS, EVALUATION AND EMPIRICAL STUDIES OF.

MINNESOTA MULTIPHASIC PERSONALITY INVENTORY (MMPI). *See* EVALUATION AND DIAGNOSIS, PSYCHOLOGICAL.

MINORITIES. *See* CULTURAL AND ETHNIC FACTORS; RACISM; SEXISM; SOCIAL JUSTICE ISSUES.

MIRACLES. *See* PROVIDENCE. *See also* FAITH HEALING; HOPE AND DESPAIR; MAGICAL THINKING; SHRINES.

MISCARRIAGE. Colloquially refers to any unsuccessful pregnancy. Medical language speaks of *spontaneous abortion* which is defined as the unintended delivery of a human fetus before it can survive, even with medical intervention. Pastorally, the issues and needs resemble those of stillbirth and neonatal death. The dynamics of bonding mean that grief is usually intense, yet these events are commonly ignored or minimized to the detriment of those who grieve, including the mother and her partner, children, grandparents, and medical personnel, especially the doctor and/or midwife. Many cities now have parent support groups which assist during bereavement and resolution of grief. An increasing interdisciplinary body of literature written by parents, medical staff, and clergy suggests strongly that resolution of grief is facilitated by (1) clear, person-centered communication, (2) access to medical information as it becomes available, (3) access to the body, (4) some record of the birth/death, (5) the option to plan a simple memorial service, and (6) follow-up support.

1. Medical Data. Spontaneous abortions are believed to occur in fifteen to twenty percent, or three hundred thousand, of all pregnancies in the U.S. each year. Congenital and placental abnormalities account for the majority of spontaneous abortions but the underlying causes are not fully understood. Genetic factors, serious disease, infection, and malnutrition are implicated as are exposure to radiation, toxic chemicals, and drugs, including alcohol and nicotine. Most miscarriages occur within the first twelve weeks of pregnancy. Viability for the human fetus ranges between twenty and twenty-eight weeks. After thirty-five to forty weeks, death usually occurs due to oxygen insufficiency caused by tangling and constriction of the umbilical cord or by separation of the placenta from the uterus before birth; *stillbirth* replaces the term miscarriage in both medical and common vernacular.

2. Bonding and the Meaning of Pregnancy. Those who work with women who are pregnant and their families witness the emotional bonding process, which almost always begins before the birth of the baby. This bonding happens gradually, intensifying at rather predictable points. As the new being makes itself known with certain size, activity, and sleep rhythms, the anticipated baby begins to take shape in the imagination. Family characteristics, desired traits, positive and negative experiences during the pregnancy, and plans for the future contribute to the bonding process. Bonding may be more problematic when there are strong ambivalent feelings about the arrival of the baby due to social and material factors. While some ambivalence is probably usual, severe negative feelings appear to impede bonding after birth of a healthy baby and to increase guilt if miscarriage or stillbirth occur.

It is critical to allow individuals to talk about their experience of pregnancy, their feelings of attachment and ambivalence and to discover what the pregnancy means to them. For some the baby means someone who will need them or someone who will "really love" them. Some believe a baby is a way out of a troubled family of origin or proof they were loved or evidence that their marriage might last. Many see a baby as a symbol of being "a woman" (or "a man"). For some miscarriage will be the first significant "failure" of their lives.

3. Grief: Feelings and Issues. Bonding and the meaning that people attach to pregnancy contribute to the intensity with which they respond to miscarriage and stillbirth. The experience, often exhausting and frightening, may strain relationships and faith in one's body, medical care, and God. The state of shock which usually follows the announcement of fetal death or the sudden experience of spontaneous abortion should not be misinterpreted as nonchalance, or evidence of superb coping skills. A few individuals may resolve wounds without outward tremors. Others may maintain defenses which reduce emotional expressiveness. But most women and their partners move through a process of bereavement and resolution.

Miscarriage and stillbirth mean death in the midst of a process we expect to bring forth new life: birth and death in intimate connection. We need to pay more attention to events which connect two of the most ritualized moments in life within the Judeo-Christian tradition.

Pastoral tasks include giving permission to vent strong feelings, assisting communication as needed and assuming appropriate roles within the health care team. In many places the hospital staff have developed *standard procedures* which, for *spontaneous abortion* and *stillbirth,* may include (1) footprint, weight, length and photograph; (2) cuddling and looking time as desired; (3) extra time before removing the body from the nurses' station in case someone wants more time for contact; and, (4) notification of the chaplain or family pastor.

Such protocol develops from the belief that records and firsthand experience are objective data which help people to grieve and then to heal. Families will ask the clergy to pray for a variety of needs; they often request some sort of "blessing for the baby" and may want to explore the possibility of a simple memorial service. Naming and honoring the unique though brief relationship and realizing both the loss and the community recognition and support help persons resolve grief. It is important to involve any who wish to contribute to the plans.

As with all pastoral counseling, clergy may have the opportunity to assist persons to bring the events of their lives into contact with the symbols, images, and promises of faith. It is by respecting their feelings and by entering into dialogue with those in grief that the gaping wounds of this loss begin to heal and new tendrils of life emerge from the devastation.

Bibliography. S. Borg and J. Lasker, *When Pregnancy Fails* (1981). R. Case, "When Birth Is Also a Funeral," *J. of Pastoral Care,* 32(1978), 6 – 21. S. Hunt, "Pastoral Care and Miscarriage," *Pastoral Psychology,* 32 (1983), 265–78. E. Kirkley-Best, *et al.,* "On Stillbirth: An Open Letter to the Clergy," *J. of Pastoral Care,* 36 (1982), 17–20. M. Klaus and J. Kennell, *Maternal-Infant Bonding* (1976). H. Pizer and C. Palinski, *Coping with a Miscarriage* (1980). H. S. Schiff, *The Bereaved Parent* (1977).

R. CASE

CRISIS MINISTRY; GRIEF AND LOSS; PREGNANCY. *See also* FAMILY, JEWISH *or* PASTORAL CARE AND COUNSELING OF; WOMEN, PASTORAL CARE OF. *Compare* ABORTION; CHILDBIRTH; CHILDLESSNESS; PREMATURE BIRTH.

MISHNAH. *See* JEWISH LITERATURE IN CARE AND COUNSELING.

MISSIONARIES, PASTORAL CARE OF. A missionary is one who lives in a country other than one's own, representing a religion, usually a Christian denomination or sect, and who is engaged in the propagation and support of that religion and its organizational structures (ecclesiastical, educational, medical, agricultural and social services).

Although it is dangerous to put great confidence in generalizations, those who have worked extensively with missionary personnel would probably agree that missionaries are: (1) idealistic, i.e., both guided by ideals such as ecumenism, compassion, service, and often sacrifice; and deemphasizing the importance of material possessions. Their idealism may also be accompanied by a critical attitude toward the prevailing values of their homeland; (2) adventurous, and curious about unknown places and people. Some are unusually resourceful in adapting to difficult circumstances; (3) individualistic, with a significant number having difficulty with authority, preferring to live and work in isolated areas rather than in situations that require cooperation; (4) theologically more conservative and pietistic than their sponsoring constituencies, but sometimes more liberal regarding social issues such as racial equality. They often possess a more cosmopolitan outlook than the religious denominations they represent.

1. Sources of Stress. Isolation is inherent in living in a foreign country, and is especially significant for those who live in remote areas with few opportunities to be with compatriots. Speaking a second language learned as an adult, especially a non-European language, requires more energy than one's own language. Similarly, the effort to learn and to adapt to a different culture is also energy-consuming. In some areas health hazards require special attention and political tension may pose a threat to stability or even to life.

The failure to realize idealistic goals exacerbates tension. Some missionaries expect initially to transcend massive cultural barriers readily through religious faith, so that they would receive primary support and nurture from their adopted religious communities. (Since World War II, this expectation has been inadvertently encouraged by some major sponsoring agencies through their missiological shift, i.e., from conceiving of mission in patronizing terms, toward an ideal of partnership and equality with receiving bodies.) Some are painfully disillusioned when they cannot achieve such a goal. Many encounter disillusionment and feelings of powerlessness when they fail to make the impact they had expected. Reactions to such stresses and disappointments are of a broad range, from a healthy resiliency to crippling guilt and despair, but no one is immune. In one way or another, all are affected.

Children of missionaries, having spent a major part of their lives in a foreign culture, often present special needs when they reach adolescence and/or must stay in their homeland for their education while their parents return to their assignment. Some present major adjustment problems such as depression or acting out in various ways. They experience reverse culture shock on entry into a homeland that is not in fact their own. Often they suffer, in addition to loneliness, damage to self-image and self-esteem. Sometimes they feel resentment and anger toward their parents; frequently they have difficulty establishing peer relationships; usually they are homesick. Because of the increased facility of travel and communication and the "shrinking" of the world, such problems are not as frequent or severe as they were a generation ago, but they persist nevertheless.

2. **Pastoral Care.** The development of the modern pastoral care movement since World War II has introduced new concepts and has heightened the consciousness of missionaries' needs for care. Efforts are directed toward providing care both in the field of assignment and in the homeland during furlough. The former is the more difficult because resources are limited and because of language barriers. One approach is the encouragement of periodic conferences and retreats for missionaries. Occasional visits from administrative personnel and/or pastoral care experts from the home office are effective.

The identification of available pastoral care and mental health experts, as well as of lesser qualified persons, leads to the identification of a network of caregivers. While the need for ordinary support and nurture may be possible to meet in most situations, there is in most areas a lack of availability of persons with specialized training who are qualified to offer counseling in the missionary's language.

For pastoral care in the homeland, regular furloughs of from six weeks to one year (sometimes longer) offer the opportunity for renewal. A relationship with a local congregation can be nurturing, if the pastor and others are sensitive to special needs. Pastoral counseling may take the form of supportive counseling, or career counseling for those who need to reconsider their vocation.

Several considerations are relevant for those who wish to move to a deeper level than supportive counseling. Most denominations maintain a somewhat paternalistic structure for the financial support of missionaries, i.e., support is provided according to need, without any differential based on performance. The structure has clear advantages but it encourages the dependency and compliance that breed anger and hostility. These feelings are often in conflict with religious beliefs about the expression of anger. Pastoral counseling, then, involves a focus on this complex, often with an exploration of its genesis in early life.

Another common issue is disillusionment. Here pastoral counseling involves a reassessment of religious ideals in the light of present reality, and includes a consideration of the common phenomenon of middle-age disappointment in what one has achieved in comparison with earlier goals. More often than not, mild to serious depression is involved in all of these problems. The outcome of pastoral counseling, with its emphasis on awakening of initiative and on taking responsibility for one's own life, may sometimes be the termination of missionary service. While this may be inevitable, it is important for the counselor to examine his or her own biases in an effort not to encourage termination covertly because he or she may personally question the value of the missionary enterprise, or discourage it for the opposite reasons.

Bibliography. F. J. White, "Some Reflections on the Separation Phenomenon Idiosyncratic to the Experience of Missionaries and Their Children," *J. of Psychology and Theology,* 11 (1983), 181–8,

and other articles in that issue. See also *J. of Psychology and Christianity* 2:4 (1983).

W. P. BOYLE

CLERGY, EMPIRICAL STUDIES OF; MENTAL HEALTH, PASTOR'S. *See also* CALL TO MINISTRY; EVANGELIZING. *Compare* PASTOR, PASTORAL CARE OF; RELIGIOUS, PASTORAL CARE OF; VOCATION; WORK AND CAREER.

MISSIONARY PASTORAL CARE. *See* CROSS CULTURAL PASTORAL CARE; EVANGELIZING.

MISTRUST. *See* SUSPICIOUS AND PARANOIA. *See also* TRUST IN PASTORAL RELATIONSHIPS.

MITZVAH/MITZVOT. Literally "commandment" (Mitzvot is the plural). The term in its narrow sense refers to the norms given by God to the community of Israel at Sinai. By extension it has come to mean any obligation in Judaism. In common parlance the word is often used to refer to any good deed.

P. J. HAAS

JEWISH CARE AND COUNSELING; JEWISH LITERATURE IN CARE AND COUNSELING. *See also* BAR MITZVAH/BAT MITZVAH. *Compare* RITUAL AND PASTORAL CARE.

MIXED MARRIAGE. *See* CROSS CULTURAL MARRIAGE AND FAMILY. *See also* CATHOLIC-PROTESTANT MARRIAGE; JEWISH-CHRISTIAN MARRIAGE.

MMPI (Minnesota Multiphasic Personality Inventory). *See* EVALUATION AND DIAGNOSIS, PSYCHOLOGICAL.

MODELS IN PSYCHOLOGICAL AND PASTORAL THEORY. In general usage in pastoral care and counseling, a model is a design or pattern for working with persons or, more specifically, a particular theoretical approach to the understanding of persons and the implications of such an approach for the practice of pastoral care and counseling.

In psychology models may have a similar meaning when personality theories are applied to counseling and psychotherapy, but the primary meaning of model is the systematic representation of a part of a theory or an aspect of behavior being studied in order to contribute to the development of theory and research. A computer simulation of a cognitive process, for example, may be helpful in stimulating further reflection and research. After the cognitive process has been studied a model is generated to interpret what is known and to suggest what might also be occurring. The model may remain as a series of carefully developed theoretical statements or it may be translated into mathematical or structural form or a computer simulation. Sometimes the model may be developed from another discipline or area of study as an analogy to the behavior being investigated. In the process of knowledge-building models are closely related to theories, conceptual frameworks, and paradigms.

The understanding of the use of models in knowledge-building is important for the development of theory and research in pastoral care and counseling. In the U.S., however, there has been a strong emphasis on the development of practice in these fields making use of models from other disciplines or helping professions. The development of training in pastoral care and counseling in clinical settings has meant that patterns or designs for practice have been influenced by medicine, psychology, and social work. The theoretical bases for practice have been drawn largely from theories of personality and healing developed by psychologists and psychiatrists. Such borrowing is a common part of the model-building process and may provide helpful analogies, but such models usually lack adequate understanding of the spiritual dimensions of life and reflect the biases of European and American (and masculine) views of personality. The development of appropriate models requires taking the word "pastoral" in pastoral care and counseling seriously. This means that issues such as those listed below need to be considered in the development of models for the practice of pastoral care and counseling: (1) the pastor's identity as "minister" in the context of a religious community; (2) theological understandings of the nature and growth of persons; (3) the relevance of the resources of a religious community and its ministry for the healing and growth of persons; (4) the influence of culture and sexual identity on the understanding of persons and the patterns of working with persons in a particular cultural context.

Bibliography. A. J. Chapman and D. M. Jones, eds. *Models of Man* (1980), esp. P. B. Warr, "An Introduction to Models in Psychological Research." A. Clark, *Psychological Models and Neural Mechanisms* (1980). I. T. Ramsey, *Models and Mystery* (1964). M. B. Turner, *Philosophy and the Science of Behavior* (1965), esp. ch. 9, "Theories and Models."

H. L. JERNIGAN

PERSON (Philosophical Issues); PERSONALITY THEORY (Varieties, Traditions, and Issues); PHILOSOPHY AND PSYCHOLOGY; PSYCHOLOGY AND PSYCHOTHERAPY (East-West Comparison); PSYCHOLOGY; THEORY IN PASTORAL CARE AND COUNSELING, FUNCTIONS OF. *See also* CAUSALITY IN PSYCHOLOGY, FORMS OF; COMPARATIVE PSYCHOLOGY; CYBERNETIC THEORY IN PSYCHOLOGY; DEPTH PSYCHOLOGY; DEVELOPMENTAL THEORY AND PASTORAL CARE; DYNAMIC PSYCHOLOGY; GROWTH COUNSELING; PROCESS, CONCEPT OF; TRANSACTIONAL ANALYSIS. *Compare* BLACK *or* FEMINIST ISSUES IN PSYCHOLOGY; MYTHOLOGY AND PSYCHOLOGY; THEOLOGICAL METHODOLOGY.

MODERN SOCIETY, PASTORAL CARE IN. *See* PASTORAL CARE (Contemporary Methods, Perspectives, and Issues); SOCIOLOGY OF RELIGIOUS AND PASTORAL CARE.

MONASTICISM/MONASTIC PASTORAL CARE. *See* EARLY *or* MEDIEVAL CHURCH, PASTORAL CARE IN; RELIGIOUS LIFE.

MONEY. Money is thought to have originated from religious and social custom and only later evolved into an economic instrument. It still carries immense psychological and social significance—even sometimes being regarded theologically as a sign of grace—which probably far outweighs its economic functions. At the same time that money has become a source of personal self-esteem and security, of social cohesion, and of other individual and group values, its significance can be exaggerated and distorted to the point of neurotic fixation or social manipulation in ways that are theologically regarded as idolatrous or evil.

Money seems to have evolved from the use of commodities as ransom, bride-price, ceremonial offering, or means of ostentation. The practical application to economic ends generally developed out of this earlier discharge of religious, legal, and ritualistic uses. Because the commodities system lacked proper standards to value each object, an instrument called money gradually evolved to standardize exchanges. A normal attitude toward money as an economic instrument is therefore to regard it as a means to an end and not as an end in itself. Money enables one to acquire certain things that are needed or desired.

The neurotic and morally distorted meanings and uses of money, however, are far more familiar to most pastors. Irrational and destructive uses of money are frequently evident in church and family conflicts; individual hopes and fears, strengths and weaknesses, are commonly expressed through financial concerns (whether realistically justified or not); and money functions as a multivalent symbol of personal as well as collective meaning, power and worth. It also plays a significant role in structuring pastoral counseling and psychotherapy relationships, where the question of fees often evokes significant feelings and therapeutic issues requiring careful examination. In all of these contexts money conceals, and sometimes reveals, basic attitudes, meanings and values.

Thus it is important for the pastor to understand the deeper social and psychological meanings of money beyond its practical function, and likewise its deeper theological significance beyond simple moralism. From a pastoral standpoint this means being able to "hear" these meanings in everyday situations and to respond to the larger pastoral issues they present with perceptiveness, wisdom, and informed moral perspective.

1. Social Psychological Meanings. Money is also a symbol of the emotional relations between an individual and the other members of the group. It represents a complex system comprising rights and promises arising out of human actions in the past and human faith in the future. Money thus becomes a record of interpersonal promises. As a symbol, money is a seal of good faith, marking society's indebtedness to an individual for services to the community.

Since one of the deepest of human longings is to enter fully into a shared life with others, money symbolizes the loving, giving and receiving that gives individuals a feeling of emotional rootedness in their community. This longing for mutual devotion is basic within the heart of every person, and the history of money is the story of the forms that this yearning has taken.

There is substantial anthropological evidence that money increased social cohesion and was a useful check on aggressive and exploitive behavior. Yet in extreme form, such control becomes exploitive and manipulative itself. The proper uses of money give the individual a sense of well-being and emotional security, while inappropriate uses may create, as well as grow out of, deep emotional conflicts. Research has substantiated the observation that the development of sound attitudes toward money does not depend so much on the amount of income as on how the individual uses the income.

2. Depth-Psychological Dimensions. *a. Anxiety and security.*

The power, prestige, social status, and freedom which money offers are obvious to all. One may be less aware of the powerful effect money has on inner feelings of security. In a world of turmoil and sudden change, the quest for money is motivated greatly by the desire to find something akin to a magical charm for attaining emotional security. The quest then moves the individual into competitive struggles where success becomes the form of self-validation. Individual competitive success is given top priority as a cultural value because it is identified with self-esteem and self-worth.

The competitive striving for success also involves a serious effort to triumph over others, thus augmenting intrasocial hostility and interpersonal isolation. Since one's own success is relative to that of others, such a cultural value is insatiable. A person's failure to achieve competitive success not only earns social contempt but, more importantly, self-contempt and feelings of worthlessness.

Students of human behavior see widespread anxiety about money in almost all types of people and age groups. Perhaps this anxiety is related to some more or less universal experience of privation in childhood.

b. Power and self-regard. The "will to power" is related to the quest for a high level of "self-regard." Thus acquiring wealth appears to be a means of increasing or maintaining the level of one's self-regard. Such a goal has its origin in the fact that young children think they are omnipotent, and that throughout their lives a certain memory of this omnipotence remains, with a longing to recapture it. This need for high self-regard can also be looked on as a derivative of the primitive form of regulation of self-regard in which the individual feeds the ego from the environment in the same way in which he or she, as an infant, required an external supply of food. Money, then, is an ego supplement, and the possibility of getting rich, the idea of being wealthy, becomes an ideal. The attainment of wealth is fantasied and worked for as something bound up with an enormous increase of self-regard.

Thus, the original and basic aim is not for money but for power and respect among one's fellow humans or within oneself. In our society, power and respect are mostly based on the possession of money; this makes the need for power and respect a need for money. For many people, the full actualization of their potentialities means becoming a financial success.

c. Overcoming fears of loss. The struggle to accumulate money, beyond one's reasonable needs, may be an effort to neutralize and escape a pathologic fear of impoverishment, growing partly out of a sense of isolation in today's fragmented society. An analysis of the fear of impoverishment reveals that the loss of possession and the loss of love that are feared, mean a loss of self-regard, a diminution of power, and a return to the status of a helpless, hungry child. The Lebanese poet and artist, Khalil Gibran, has asked the crucial question in his book *The Prophet*: "Is not dread of thirst when your well is full, the thirst that is unquenchable?" A person who is isolated or alienated finds it difficult to share money (or self)

but will guard and keep it, as though it were the essence of one's life that is being guarded and kept.

3. Distortions.

Both the biblical record and psychoanalytic writing testify to humankind's distortions of the real value of money. *Filthy lucre* in the Bible (I Tim. 3:8, Tit. 1:7, 11; I Pet. 5:2 KJV) refers to "base gain," or to the fact that money is often the means of prostituting human personality. William Tyndale's translation of the NT rendered "base gain" as *filthy lucre,* and the Authorized (King James) Version retained it. The implication is not that money is filthy or evil in itself; the filthiness or evil is in the misuse of it. The Bible warns: "The love of money [not money itself] is the root of all evil" (I Tim. 6:10). Similarly, psychoanalytic writings on attitudes toward money have emphasized the unconscious relationship of money and excrement.

In most national studies where people are asked to name their biggest worry, "money" and "making ends meet" are the predominant answers. Clergy report that seventy-five percent of couples with marital problems mention money as an important factor. Likewise, it does not take physicians long to learn that many of their patients' aches and pains are caused by financial stresses. Thus, money as symbol, reality, or camouflaged force becomes a major factor in our lives as it moves between the two extremes of its role as servant or as master.

4. Norms for Use of Money.

The promise of money is freedom; the threat of money is domination. When money is kept in the role of servant, one is free to use it as a symbol of grace and as an empathic instrument. Where there is empathy, there is real understanding of others as persons and of their suffering in relationship to their personal and social world.

Money is a part of wholistic stewardship. When God created humans, they were given dominion over the earth — dominion in the sense of responsibility and not in the sense of domination or exploitation. God created humans as stewards of the world's resources which they were to develop and to share with one another in justice, gratitude, and love. Thus, stewardship refers to the way people conduct their lives, their being in the world.

Bibliography. E. Bergler, *Money and Emotional Conflicts* (1959). J. C. Haughey, *Personal Finance in Light of Christian Faith* (1986). J. A. Knight, *For the Love of Money* (1968). B. N. Nelson, *The Idea of Usury* (1969 [1949]). P. G. Schurman, *Money Problems and Pastoral Care* (1982).

J. A. KNIGHT

POWER; SOCIAL STATUS AND CLASS FACTORS IN PASTORAL CARE. *See also* ANXIETY; COMPETITIVENESS; COVENANT AND CONTRACT; FEES IN PASTORAL COUNSELING; GIVING AND RECEIVING; PERSONAL, CONCEPT OF, IN PASTORAL CARE; VALUE, CONCEPT OF.

MONGOLISM. *See* DOWN'S SYNDROME.

MOOD/MOODINESS/MOOD SWINGS. *See* EMOTION; TEMPERAMENT.

MOONEY PROBLEMS CHECK LIST. *See* EVALUATION AND DIAGNOSIS, PSYCHOLOGICAL.

MOONIES. *See* NEW RELIGIOUS MOVEMENTS.

MOORE, THOMAS VERNER. *See* COUNSELING, ROMAN CATHOLIC.

MORAL BEHAVIOR AND RELIGION. There are complex psychological and social factors involved in the gap that separates our beliefs about ourselves as religious and moral persons from our actual behavior. For example, if moral behavior appears to be profoundly influenced by religion and yet nonreligious persons often behave better morally than do believers, how is moral behavior to be understood? And what is religion? Is the relationship of moral behavior to religion to be understood logically, causally, motivationally, or in some other way? As long as the issues and their relationship are discussed using differing basic assumptions and descriptions, the issue will remain a complex one.

There are three main kinds of moral behavior that may be affected by religion: (1) judgments; (2) attitudes, emotions, and dispositions; and (3) actions.

1. **Moral Judgments.** They are constitutive elements of moral "behavior," because it is by means of such inner evaluations that we identify what is morally right or wrong and attempt to conduct ourselves accordingly. A moral judgment is never a mere expression of emotional approval or disapproval, but rather involves giving or being ready to give reasons that explain, as mere personal tastes do not, why an action is right or wrong or a state of affairs desirable or undesirable. These reasons are invariably connected to the welfare of human beings, as individuals or members of groups.

Today most ethicists as well as an increasing number of psychologists (e.g., Lawrence Kohlberg) insist upon the logical autonomy of moral judgments from religious beliefs. The primary concern of those who take this position is with the general normative principles that inform moral judgments, like keeping promises and telling the truth, and the evidence that they are not logically derivable from religious propositions. The following reasons are commonly offered in support of the logical autonomy of moral principles from religion: First, insofar as theological claims are descriptive of the ultimate nature of reality, they are similar to other factual statements and no evaluative conclusions can be logically deduced or induced from an "is"; second, the claim that morality must be derived logically from religion implies that atheists and other religious skeptics cannot justify moral standards, though this appears to be patently incorrect, as the writings of secular ethicists attest. Even if morality is developmentally an offshoot of religion in the sense that all children pass through a stage of morality when principles are legitimated by sacred authority, this fact does not show that there is any *necessary* logical connection between religious and moral judgments; third, the autonomy of morality is often brought out by religious discourse itself, as, for example, when religious apologists argue for theological beliefs on the grounds that they have ethically desirable consequences. Kohlberg's (1981) research supports these logical arguments by showing that our most general normative principles are developed independently of religious beliefs or affiliations.

How then do we account for the widespread conviction among believers that moral judgments are derived from, or at least enormously influenced by, faith commitments? A partial explanation is that religious persons, like most others, are often confused about matters of logic. But in addition, religious traditions commonly provide overlapping—religious *and* moral—justifications of the same judgment (see Gustafson, 1975, p. 175; Wallwork, 1972, p. 286). Believers thus often find themselves confusing the two types of reasoning.

The conviction that morality depends on religion also derives from the fact that conclusory moral judgments about particular issues involve knowledge of a lot more than abstract principles alone and these additional considerations are typically influenced by religious beliefs. These further factors that we normally take into account in arriving at a moral decision include basic assumptions about (a) the context(s) in which moral action is contemplated, (b) the nature of the persons affected, their basic needs and interests, (c) the likely consequences of alternative courses of action, given the ways in which persons and institutions can be expected to behave, and (d) the actor's own previous loyalties, commitments, and conception of personal integrity. From this wider perspective on moral judgments, it is understandable how persons with identical moral principles, but differing religious convictions, are likely to arrive at very different conclusions about practical questions, such as whether a war is just or an act of civil disobedience warranted.

2. **Attitudes, Emotions, and Dispositions.** A second broad category of moral behavior affected by religion includes the attitudes, emotions, and dispositions that agents bring to moral situations as aspects of their personalities. These moods and motivations affect judgments, as well as the discernment of situations as moral in the first place, and the spirit with which a judgment is carried into action. A person who profoundly cares about other persons, for instance, is more disposed than others to see a need to reach a moral judgment that is based on vivid awareness of that need, and to carry out the decision in a manner that conveys sympathy and respect, as contrasted with a mere duty perfunctorily performed.

There are two opposing schools of scientific thought about the origins of personality traits that speak to the role of religion in the formation of attitudes and dispositions. According to the environmentalist or social learning approach of Durkheim and Skinner, our personalities are largely the by-product of social forces. Here religion is important for personality formation to whatever extent it is a significant aspect of the social environment in which the person is conditioned. The alternative, maturational school, which descends from Freud's psychosexual model, sees our distinguishing emotions, attitudes, and dispositions as developing in connection with the unfolding of biologically triggered stages of growth. In this view, appropriate stimulation is needed at each stage to elicit, support, and maintain behavior patterns, but the stimulations do not create these patterns, which are more or less wired into the organism. Religious convictions or institutions may be important either negatively, by inhibiting maturation (Freud, 1927), or positively, by supporting the attitudes of parents, as they respond to the stage-specific needs of their children in ways that allow the children's personalities to mature (Erikson, 1963 pp. 247–51; Wallwork, 1973 pp. 322–61).

Most recent social psychologists combine these opposing approaches in theories that are "interactional." These newer theories assume that our basic moods and motivations are the result of interactions between the maturing organism and the socio-cultural environment rather than directly reflecting either innate patterns in the organism or patterns of events in the environment. Interactional theories—like those of Kohlberg, Kegan, and Fowler—indicate that the same religious symbols, narratives, and rites may have widely differing effects on the attitudes and dispositions of participants, depending on their age, stage, and psychosocial condition. To this interactionist perspective, we need to add the obvious point that persons are agents and as such possess the capacity, however circumscribed, to shape their own characteristic responses and dispositions, first by recognizing them as their own, even when they are not consciously intended, and then by "leaning into" alternative descriptions and possibilities for action.

3. The Role of Religion in Actual Moral Behavior. Research on religious affiliation and prejudice (Allport and Kramer, 1946; Gorsuch and Aleshire, 1974) indicates that people who attend church services are more racially and ethnically prejudiced than people who do not go to church. This is presumably not a direct consequence of their religious beliefs or the attitudes their churches are trying to inculcate, but, rather, of the extrinsic motivations churchgoers often bring with them (Allport and Ross, 1967; Paloutzian, 1983, pp. 135–51). As for the ability of religious institutions to influence moral behavior positively, Hartshorne and May (1928–30) found that participation in Sunday school fails to lead to any improvement in moral character as measured by experimental tests of whether subjects will cheat or not.

Obviously, our actual moral behavior is not always consistent with our moral judgments, attitudes, and dispositions. Sometimes this is because cognitive moral judgments about issues, like the equal worth of persons, are not supported by emotions, attitudes, and dispositions. Cognitively, a person may believe in the equality of the races, but in practice he or she may make disparaging remarks about blacks or Mexicans, feel uncomfortable around them, and oppose racial integration. Novels, films, and role-playing exercises may aid in the extension of empathy, thereby assisting the process of bringing attitudes and dispositions in line with judgments, but such procedures may not always be adequate. If unconscious motives lie at the root of the problem, in-depth clinical exploration of what Jung calls the *shadow* and Erikson *negative identity* may be necessary to overcome this kind of intrapsychic inconsistency.

Sometimes the unconscious meaning of moral ideals themselves may be a source of the difficulty in acting morally. As Freud (1921, 1930) observed long ago, religious persons may take narcissistic pleasure in simply belonging to a group, like the church, that possesses high moral ideals, like the love commandment. The unwitting behavioral consequence is often not love, but hostility toward outsiders, who are self-righteously condemned as religiously or morally inferior.

Conflicting unconscious motivations undoubtedly account in part for the disheartening results of so much empirical research on the relationship between religious affiliation and actual moral behavior. However, the explanations briefly surveyed here only hint at the complex psychological and social factors that cause the disparity between our beliefs about ourselves as religious and moral persons and our actual behavior.

Bibliography. G. W. Allport and B. M. Kramer, "Some Roots of Prejudice," *J. of Psychology*, 22 (1946), 9–39. G. W. Allport and J. M. Ross, "Personal Religious Orientation and Prejudice," *J. of Personality and Social Psychology*, 5 (1967), 432–43. E. Erikson, *Childhood and Society* (1978). D. Evans, *Struggle and Fulfillment: The Inner Dynamics of Religion and Morality* (1979). J. Fowler, *Stages of Faith* (1981). S. Freud, *Group Psychology and the Analysis of the Ego* (1960 [1921]); *The Future of An Illusion* (1975); *Civilization and Its Discontents* (1963 [1930]). R. L. Gorsuch and D. Aleshire, "Christian Faith and Ethnic Prejudice: A Review and Interpretation of Research," *J. for the Scientific Study of Religion*, 13 (1974), 281–307. J. Gustafson, *Can Ethics Be Christian?* (1975). H. Hartshorne and A. M. May, *Studies in the Nature of Character*, vols. 1–3 (1928–1930). R. Kegan, *The Evolving Self* (1982). L. Kohlberg, *The Philosophy of Moral Development* (1981). R. Paloutzian, *Invitation to the Psychology of Religion* (1983). E. Wallwork, *Durkheim: Morality and Milieu* (1972); "Erik Erikson: Psychological Resources for Faith," in R. Johnson and E. Wallwork, *Critical Issues in Modern Religion* (1973), pp. 322–61; "Morality, Religion, and Kohlberg's Theory," in B. Munsey, ed., *Moral Development, Moral Education, and Kohlberg* (1980), pp. 269–97; "Thou Shalt Love Thy Neighbor as Thyself: The Freudian Critique," *J. of Religious Ethics*, (1982), 264–319.

E. WALLWORK

CULTURAL ANTHROPOLOGY OF RELIGION, DISCIPLINE OF; SOCIOLOGY OF RELIGION. *See also* GUIDANCE, PASTORAL; LIFESTYLE ISSUES; MORAL DILEMMAS IN PASTORAL PERSPECTIVE. *Compare* CHRISTIAN LIFE; FAITH AND WORKS; GRACE; GRATITUDE; RELIGIOUS BEHAVIOR.

MORAL DEVELOPMENT. Refers to: (a) changes in moral judgment that occur during childhood, adolescence, and adulthood in the formulation and resolution of ethical dilemmas; (b) a subfield of developmental psychology concerned with stages of ethical reasoning.

1. Psychology of Moral Development. From the Holocaust to the tragedies of everyday life, there is ample evidence that a fundamental dimension of being human is the inevitable necessity of making moral judgments.

a. Jean Piaget. The pioneering work in the psychology of moral judgment development is Piaget's, *The Moral Judgment of the Child* (1932). There, Piaget refocused his concern with cognitive development to consider the development of children's moral reasoning. He distinguished two types of moral reasoning, based on their different understandings of respect, fairness, and punishment.

i. Heteronomous morality is based on unilateral respect for authorities and the rules they prescribe. From a heteronomous perspective, fairness is understood as obedience to authorities and conformity to their sacred rules; consequences are understood as concrete objective damage, which is more relevant than intentions; expiatory punishment is favored as a way of making atonement.

ii. Autonomous morality is based on mutual respect, reciprocity, and equality among peers. From an autonomous perspective, fairness is understood as mutually agreed upon cooperation and reciprocal exchange; intentionality is understood as relevant—both intentions and consequences can be kept in mind concurrently; punishment by reciprocity is favored.

b. Lawrence Kohlberg. Kohlberg's (1958) original dissertation extended Piaget's typology beyond childhood. He found that six forms of reasoning could more accurately describe moral phenomena than Piaget's two. Until his death in 1987, Kohlberg continued to explore the way people interact with their social environment in increasingly more adequate ways of resolving social-moral dilemmas. Kohlberg has suggested that children, adolescents, and adults are all concerned with some of the same ideas and problems that concern moral philosophers. The success of his work has been due in part to his adaptation of the basic norms and issues of ethics as the focus of his developmental study.

The six stages of moral judgment, as defined by Kohlberg (1981, 1984), are as follows:

i. Obedience and punishment orientation. What is moral is to avoid breaking rules, to comply for obedience's sake, and to avoid doing physical damage to people or property. "Stage 1 justifications" for being moral include avoidance of penalties and the superior power of authorities.

ii. Instrumental purpose and exchange. What is moral is following rules when it is in the person's immediate interest, especially in terms of an equal exchange, a good deal. A "Stage 2 justification" for being moral is to serve one's own needs in a world where one must recognize that other people have their own interests, too.

iii. Mutual interpersonal expectations, good relations. What is moral is conforming to what is expected by people close to you or what people generally expect of people in one's role as son, sister, pastor, and so on. "Stage 3 justifications" for being moral focus on the desire to be seen as a good, nice, and caring person. It is vitally important to maintain interpersonal trust, loyalty, and appreciation.

iv. Social system and conscience maintenance. What is moral is fulfilling the actual duties to which one has agreed. Laws are to be upheld except in extreme cases in which they conflict with other fixed social duties. This is a social-maintenance rather than an interpersonal-maintenance perspective; being moral involves contributing to one's own society, group, or institution. "Stage 4 justifications" for being moral are to keep the institution functioning, to maintain self-respect for having met one's defined obligations, and to avoid setting a socially disruptive precedent.

v. Prior rights and social contract. What is moral is being aware that many values and rules are relative to one's group and subsuming these culturally relative values under fundamental human rights, such as the rights of life and liberty, that are logically prior to society. Such nonrelative rights are inviolable and should be built into and upheld in any society. This is a society-creating rather than a society-maintenance point of view. A social system is understood, ideally, as a social contract freely entered into. Persons at "Stage 5" justify upholding the social contract because it preserves one's own rights and

the rights of others, assures impartiality, and promotes the greatest good for the greatest number.

vi. Universal ethical principles. Deciding what is moral is guided by self-conscious universal ethical principles that generate decisions by which human dignity is ensured and persons are treated as ends in themselves rather than simply as means. Beyond the importance of a social contract, "Stage 6" also focuses on the process by which a social agreement is reached. This is a moral-justice point of view, involving the deliberate use of justice principles, which centers on the equality of human rights and respect for the dignity of all human beings as free and equal autonomous persons. The "Stage 6 justification" for being moral is the belief, as a rational person, in the validity of universal moral principles and a self-conscious commitment to these principles.

2. Empirical Research Findings. After an initial period of acclaim, Kohlberg's model was severely criticized, primarily because of inadequate empirical research. Subsequently, however, hundreds of reliable studies were conducted, and, during the last decade, several systematic evaluative reviews of the research were published, which have drawn the following conclusions:

a. Developmental sequence. Developmentally, moral stage change among individuals is invariant in sequence and proceeds one stage at a time (Kohlberg, 1984).

b. Cross-cultural inclusiveness. Cross-culturally, the first four stages are found in virtually all cultural groups and the highest measured level (Stage 5) is found in all complex cultural groups (i.e., societies with elaborate systems of education) like India, Japan, and Taiwan. There is also evidence, however, that there are genuine ethical principles, besides those addressed by Kohlberg's model, in other cultural groups. In particular, collective or communalistic principled reasoning is missing from Kohlberg's model and is misunderstood by his scoring manual (Snarey, 1985).

c. Gender inclusiveness. Despite the controversy regarding possible gender differences in moral judgment, the current empirical evidence indicates that there are no significant differences between males and females in moral development when measured by the current standardized scoring system. Women seem to use Kohlberg's ethic of justice as well as men; however, evidence also suggests that an ethic of care is present among both women and men, but that it is inadequately represented in Kohlberg's model (Gilligan, 1982; Walker, 1984).

d. Moral behavior. Moral behavior and moral reasoning are positively and significantly associated. In both laboratory and real-life settings, moral reasoning predicts moral action, including honesty, altruistic behavior, resistance to temptation, and nondelinquency. For instance, persons at higher moral stages are significantly more likely to help a stranger who needs medical attention (Blasi, 1980; Kohlberg, 1984).

e. Moral education. Pedagogically, Kohlberg's dilemma discussion approach has been shown to produce modest but definite educational effects upon moral development, while other types of intervention programs produce smaller effects, and individual academic courses in the humanities and the social sciences produce even weaker effects (Schlaefli, Rest, and Thoma, 1985).

3. Religion and Moral Development. The book of Genesis portrays humanity as facing a moral dilemma symbolized by the tree of the knowledge of good and evil. The way we make sense of "the tree," however, is not static across the life-span. "When I was a child," explains the Apostle Paul, "I spoke like a child, I thought like a child, I reasoned like a child; when I became a man, I gave up childish ways" (I Cor. 13:11).

a. Kohlberg's contribution. While Kohlberg's own work focused primarily on a person's moral structuring of the social environment, he also hypothesized that a similar model may characterize the development of religious moral reasoning about one's ultimate environment (Kohlberg, 1981).

b. Contributions of others. A developmental perspective on religious moral reasoning has been elaborated by others. Oser (1985) has pioneered the empirical validation of a developmental perspective on religious moral reasoning. Clouse (1986) has demonstrated that church conflict may be attenuated by a pastor's sensitivity to parishioners' stages of moral judgment. Pressau (1977) has applied moral development to the doctrine of salvation as exhibited in various religious groups. Munsey (1980) has edited a volume that includes Jewish and Christian perspectives on religious moral education. The field of moral development appears to have great potential for advancing the development of an effective critical dialogue between psychological and theological perspectives on pastoral care.

Bibliography. A. Blasi, "Bridging moral cognition and moral action: a critical review," *Psychological Bulletin,* 88 (1980), 1–45. B. Clouse, "Church conflict and moral stages," *J. of Psychology and Christianity,* 5(3) (1986), 14–19. C. Gilligan, *In a Different Voice* (1982). L. Kohlberg, "The development of modes of moral thinking and choice in the years 10 to 16," unpublished doctoral dissertation, University of Chicago (1958); *Essays on Moral Development I: The Philosophy of Moral Development* (1981); *Essays on Moral Development II: The psychology of moral development* (1984). B. Munsey, ed., *Moral Development, Moral Education, and Kohlberg: Basic Issues in Philosophy, Psychology, Religion, and Education* (1980). F. Oser, "Religious Dilemmas: The Development of Religious Judgment," in C. Harding, ed., *Moral Dilemmas: Philosophical and Psychological Issues in the Development of Moral Reasoning* (1985), pp. 174–90. J. Piaget, *The Moral Judgment of the Child* (1932). J. Pressau, *I'm Saved, You're Saved, Maybe* (1977). A. Schlaefli, J. Rest, and S. Thoma, "Does moral education improve moral judgment?" *Review of Educational Research,* 55:3 (1985), 319–52. J. Snarey, "The cross-cultural universality of social-moral development: A critical review," *Psychological Bulletin,* 97:2 (1985), 202–32. L. Walker, "Sex differences in the development of moral reasoning: A critical review," *Child Development* 55, (1984), 677–91.

J. SNAREY

CHARACTER ETHICS AND PASTORAL CARE; CONSCIENCE; RESPONSIBILITY/IRRESPONSIBILITY, PSYCHOLOGY OF. *See also* PERSONALITY DEVELOPMENT, BIOLOGICAL AND SOCIALIZING INFLUENCES IN; PRUDENCE; STRUCTURALISM; VALUES RESEARCH. *Compare* COGNITIVE DEVELOPMENT; LOCUS OF CONTROL RESEARCH; RELIGIOUS DEVELOPMENT; FAITH DEVELOPMENT RESEARCH; EVALUATION AND DIAGNOSIS.

MORAL DILEMMAS IN PASTORAL PERSPECTIVE. Problems perceived by pastoral caregivers and receivers to involve ethical decisions as an important component are the focus of this article. The term "pastoral perspective" is broader than pastoral care, as there is, or may be, a pastoral perspective on all that goes on in the churches, wherever the personal dimension of lives is in focus. This article focuses only on those moral dilemmas arising in pastoral care and its special form of pastoral counseling, since in the direct care of individuals and groups a pastoral approach to moral problems can best be seen. Only a few of the most common and pressing such dilemmas will be treated explicitly, mainly as a means of exemplifying the principles and processes of pastoral care through which moral dilemmas of all kinds may best be approached. For more detailed discussions of these and other moral dilemma topics, such as vocational, lifestyle, and sex preference issues, the reader is referred to specific articles on those topics.

1. Reflective Principles. These principles are intended as guidelines for preparation for pastoral encounters with persons troubled by moral dilemmas or thought by the caregiver to have moral dilemmas.

a. Basic principles of pastoral care apply. The focus on moral questions is set within the context of sound pastoral care. Pastoral care, by whomever initiated, takes a basic phenomenological approach mediated by empathic responsiveness to the center of the care-receiver's communication—both verbal and nonverbal. Although many relational modalities may be employed as a part of pastoral care, all are adjunctive to basic empathy communicated by the caregiver and its healing and liberating effects on the care-receiver. Focus on moral dilemmas, among other conscious concerns with cognitive components, is thus set within the continuity of an empathic "bass" over which various "melodies" may be played.

b. Caregiver has a considered position on ethical issues. Those offering pastoral care to morally perplexed persons need an acquaintance with some fundamental issues in theological ethics, although they do not necessarily need to be experts. A basic distinction exists, for instance, between positions which begin with universal principles, such as equality, justice, or the command of God, and try to deduce correct applications (deontological positions), and positions which view the *consequences* of action as being of greatest import, as in utilitarianism and the ethics of virtue or character (Hauerwas). Many hold a mixed view, weighted one way or the other (Frankena).

As an illustration, one may hold such a mixed view weighted toward utilitarianism (the greatest good for the greatest number of persons) and agree with Frankena that sometimes the principles derived from these two positions are in conflict without any *a priori* way of reconciling them. This makes one finally an existentialist—emphasizing decision and risk. One may further hold that all human action entails loss, at least potentially, as well as gain. The relational matrix of human life means that there are no exclusively private or public moral questions, but some decisions impact more directly on one of these spheres than they do on the other.

c. Timing is crucial. Explicit attention to the resolution of ethical issues in pastoral care requires careful timing. Some pastoral caregivers tend to attempt resolution before the matter is sufficiently clarified, while others may postpone attention too long or avoid it all together. Whether a resolution is imposed by the caregiver prematurely, or the matter is allowed to "resolve itself," the outcome will be less than optimal and often disastrous.

d. The influence of the caregiver should be overt, not covert. Complete neutrality in ethical matters arising in pastoral care is impossible. At the proper moment (Section 2) the caregiver should make known his or her opinion and how strongly it is held. Otherwise the care-receiver is subject to non-verbal suggestions and guesses about the opinion, which is usually being actively sought and hence all the more subject to distortion if not carefully stated.

2. **Procedural Principles.** In order to make these sequential principles as clear as possible, the form of pastoral care presupposed is pastoral counseling — pastoral care extended by agreement or "contract" over a period of time with a relatively definite goal.

a. Respond first to emotions and "control damage." Persons with moral dilemmas are usually rather anxious even if they do not appear to be excited on the surface. An initial response to anxiety and other emotions is needed before the problem which the care-receiver perceives can be clearly communicated. At the same time enough information usually emerges to signal the caregiver if some kind of action may be warranted to control damage already under way or about to occur. Violence that the care-receiver is contemplating or perceives that others are about to commit, either toward the care-receiver or others, is, for a prime example, a signal for further inquiry which can usually be pursued with a few well chosen questions. Clinical signs of depression are another indicator for further inquiry, as they may indicate suicidal thoughts or increasing dysfunction. In such cases the caregiver may suggest remedial action on the part of the care-receiver, make a referral, or in rare instances, take direct action.

b. Clarify issues. Clarification proceeds along with continued attention to the feelings of the person or persons. It includes attention to history of the person and the kind of ethical thinking which has characterized his or her background and present context (Browning, 1976). The understanding of the moral dilemma brought to the pastoral encounter by the care-receiver must be clarified, and perhaps altered. In some instances the character of the dilemma as a moral one, as well as a personal or family problem, will need to be pointed out. The possible solutions entertained by the care-receiver must be identified, and the felt reservations about carrying each of them out, explored. In this way the nature of the conscience will to some extent become known. In some instances the early beginnings of the conscience of the person in intense relationships with parents or parenting figures will have to be explored to gain adequate knowledge of the way the moral dilemma is being experienced. In other instances no conscience will be immediately visible and some digging into both past and present relationships may be needed to find what still may be a primitive "super-ego" which has been overlaid with various rationalizations against the felt oppressiveness of early training. In rare instances little or no conscience can be found; the task then becomes that of moral

upbringing and belated development — a task beyond pastoral care alone. In achieving the degree of clarity needed, the schemas of moral development proposed by Piaget and Kohlberg may be of use if they are adapted to the context, and to the person who is receiving the pastoral care, and if the schemas are not taken too literally.

c. Reflect together on the possibilities. The careful examination of the possibilities which lie before the care-receiver when the issues have been sufficiently clarified is always central to pastoral counseling, and especially so when moral dilemmas are in focus. These possibilities are examined in the light of a broad vision of the Christian faith and life, but the emphasis is on examining *all* the possibilities that can reasonably be seen, even though some of them may be partially or totally off known Judeo-Christian "maps." This examining of possibilities gives the care-receiver a sense of being able to influence (although not to completely control) his or her life, identifies live options, and those options, which though theoretically possible in some sense, are actually impossible for the care-receiver because of his or her character, context, and beliefs. In this process the caregiver responds carefully to tentative and often vague directional signals offered by the care-receiver in an effort to clarify them, as well as raising questions and suggesting directions for exploration. The interpersonal bond of trust between caregiver and care-receiver is now well established, but needs to be maintained by the caregiver through continuing empathy.

d. Offer guidance, interpretation, confrontation, opinion as required. This is the stage in the process that is often mistakenly identified as the whole of pastoral care focused on the moral problems. But, if the foregoing steps have been adequately carried out, it may receive little emphasis. The only element that is always, or almost always, required is the *opinion* of the caregiver (Section 2, d.). "As required" here means as required by the caregiver's now informed perception of the care-receiver and his or her real possibilities, and the caregiver's own ethical position. The possibilities may be many or few. Some may be more attractive than others on a graded scale. Usually the caregiver's understanding of these gradients needs to be communicated, unless the care-receiver has already communicated a decision that seems to be a "right" choice for him or her.

Confrontation occurs when the care-receiver makes, or is about to make, what the caregiver perceives as a "wrong" ethical choice, if that choice is seen as clearly dangerous to the care-receiver and/or other persons. Reasons for the confrontation are given, although they do not need to be heaped up into a homily. Time always should be allowed for response and working through after a confrontation. Thus they should not be offered at or near the end of a counseling session. A risk that the care-receiver may withdraw from the relationship following confrontation is always present, and the likelihood of withdrawal is one factor that must be weighed before confronting a care-receiver. Even if the care-receiver does withdraw, however, he or she may return, or find that the confrontation becomes the touchstone of future reflection and action.

e. Move toward resolution. Optimally, a firm decision about the resolution of the dilemma that is acceptable both to the care-receiver and to the caregiver should be made before the pastoral counseling is terminated. In practice such a firm resolution may be only in view before termination. This may be due to a variety of factors, such as circumstances that either have proved more intractable than was earlier supposed, or new circumstances, as well as to the difficulty that the care-receiver has in making such a decision.

f. Partial exceptions to the foregoing five steps. In many situations in the life of the churches it will not be possible to carry out all five of the steps in pastoral counseling presented above. First, there are emergencies in which the clergyperson may be called only at the last minute, for example, before a wife finally decides to leave her husband after months of considering such a move. Although further pastoral care may be possible, it may not be, and in this sense the situation differs from the "damage control" problem outlined in Section 2a. The caregiver has to do what can be done on the spot. In other situations, which may be called contextually limited encounters, there may be no emergency and follow-up pastoral care may be encouraged, but the caregiver does not know whether it will be pursued by the care-receiver — especially if the latter is not a part of the church community, or a marginal member of it. Such encounters are relatively frequent — at the church door, at a social gathering, or in public places.

In both kinds of situations the caregiver may decide to omit steps "b" and "c," and to proceed to step "d" after responding directly and empathically to the person's distress signals. This is a relatively high risk procedure, as either undue dependency or rejection of further help may result. But in many cases it is better than leaving the moral dilemma unattended or not taken seriously.

In family and group counseling most pastoral theologians agree that the basic principles undergo a shift of focus from individual to the "system" comprised of interacting persons. Although systemic issues are also present in pastoral work with individuals, and even those convinced of the efficacy of systems approaches cannot totally neglect individuals, the differences are important. There is also a question about whether a family or group can be a moral agent with all that that implies. For our purposes it is sufficient to note that moral dilemmas are frequently a part of the discussion in the pastoral care of families. Insofar as these issues become a focus of the care being offered, the systems analogue for the first step, response to emotions and damage control, is appropriate, and steps "b" and "c" are needed in some form. The last two steps can usually best be carried out in relation to one or more individuals in the family (spouses when divorce is the issue), since clarification usually will reveal who has been making which decisions, and who is ready in the present to make them. In some instances the family as a whole should participate in the decision, and most members need to participate in working through the resolution.

3. **Problem Areas.** The problem areas chosen for discussion are those deemed most frequent in the churches or those presenting particular difficulties, though relatively infrequent. The categories chosen for grouping these problems represent common contexts of discussion of these issues. However, other groupings are possible, since there is considerable overlap. For instance, both abortion and sexual issues could be treated as family matters, even though the specific questions often arise outside any immediate family context.

a. Marriage and family. i. Betrayal issues: adultery, incest, child and spouse abuse. In these matters the moral dilemma is not whether the actions in question are ethically correct or permissible, for in almost all ethical views none of them is possible. (A possible exception for adultery may obtain in "open marriage" theories, but then betrayal is not an issue.) Rather, these matters present the basic issue of betrayal of trust and promise, either explicit or implicit (in the instances of incest and child abuse). The questions the caregiver has to deal with are who shall know and what shall be done after the facts are clarified as much as possible. In ethical terms the deontological claims of retributive justice demand punishment for the offending parties in the name of a universal principle in which both the church community and society as a whole have a stake, for without punishment, it is argued, the cosmic scale of justice is out of balance. Punishment is also required in the view of some utilitarians who argue that without punishment for such universally acknowledged offenses, insufficient fear will lead to their becoming increasingly prevalent. This position leads to the conclusion that everyone shall know and that the offenders shall be punished according to the degree of heinousness of the offense. Such punishment usually includes imposed separation. Most would agree that adultery, a consensual act, is less offensive than exploitative and violent acts.

In practice very few clergy would hold the unmodified position outlined above, but it nevertheless underlies the *dilemma* character of trying to assist the victims of betrayal. In the context of the family, the forgiveness and reconciliation path will be seen by many as the better one, partly because it is a prominent Christian theme (deontological), but even more importantly, because it leads to a continuation of the family relationships, a utilitarian value, but one also with the status of a command for many, and often desired by the victim(s). Sometimes a compromise is attempted with the family continued (perhaps after a "damage control" period of enforced separation) but with the offending member engaging in rehabilitation procedures, which are at least covertly viewed by all as partly punishing, since they involve self-examination, which is regarded as painful and may publicly signal a character defect. Sometimes the entire family engages in the rehabilitation procedures, at least in part, thus spreading the sense of responsibility and guilt.

These considerations indicate something of the range of possibilities about who shall know and what shall be done, some of the ways that various components may be recombined, and also why no solution will be felt to be very satisfactory — at least in the present. In the author's view there is no quick or easy resolution to betrayal problems. Caregivers best serve families presenting these problems by being prepared to sustain them over rather long periods of time, while the various issues and values are being explored and attempts at rehabilitation are made. The one exception is the case of secret adultery, where the question of whether the spouse shall know can sometimes best be resolved by individual pastoral counseling in the light of all the consequences that can be foreseen, especially the character and attitude of the care-receiver and that of the spouse.

ii. Separation and divorce. Although many people in our culture have come to regard these matters as essentially private in character, scarcely any human act except marriage has a greater impact on society than divorce and to a lesser extent, separation. Conjoint counseling of the spouses is much more likely to lead to a constructive resolution when separation and divorce are seriously contemplated, although not necessarily when they are only being entertained as a possible option — one which may fade with further clarification. Both divorce and the continuation of marriage can be defended on both deontological and utilitarian grounds, depending upon which visions of the good are employed. Divorce is contrary to the traditional interpretation of Scripture and to the traditions of all the churches, but it can, and has, been defended and allowed on the ground of equal justice (as seen in adultery, cruelty, and abandonment) and more recently on the ground of the right to personal fulfillment. On the other hand, the consequences of divorce are seen as involving pain, loss, and suffering for the families directly involved, as well as the sought freedom from intimate relationships, and, when divorces occur in great numbers, disruption for society.

Ministers thus have a responsibility to help the couple reflect on *all* consequences of their contemplated action. Mutual decision is, of course, at least a minimal goal of such counseling, and forgiveness and personal reconciliation is a further goal where divorce is the outcome. (For a case study focused on these issues employing an "ethics of character" model similar to that of Hauerwas, see Poling, 1984.)

b. "Quality of life" issues. These are the issues that have come to full bloom in the late twentieth century, although they have a long history in the idea of human rights—the rights to "life, liberty and the pursuit of happiness," for instance. The "quality of life" is, with increasing frequency, seen by many as clashing with the value of life itself (Section 1b.).

i. Care of the dying. Sometimes these are called the "right to die" issues, but that is an overstatement unless the sanctioning of suicide on a universal basis is in view, which it is generally not in these discussions. Rather, the issues concern the question of the dying person's desire and perhaps the family's desire to influence the time and mode of death, when the person is regarded as dying by all or some of those involved. Often the question comes to the caregiver in an emergency situation (Section 2f.), but sometimes counseling on a sustained basis is possible. Assisting the person and the family to clarify the consequences as much as possible — including the personal, family, and economic consequences—is optimal, but in emergencies much will depend upon the caregiver's grasp of the total situation and his or her communicated opinion. As medical technology continually advances, all rules related to specific techniques for sustaining life and even definitions of death tend to become rapidly obsolete. Thus opinions must be formed in relation to basic ethical principles (Section 1b.). (For a summary of the facts, issues, and some recommendations, see

Summing Up, the report of a Presidential Commission, 1983.)

ii. Abortion and birth control. Almost all ethicists are in substantial agreement about abortion: it is morally problematic. The differences, and these are substantial, occur over the question of under what kind of circumstances abortion is to be permitted. Allegiances to different deontological principles—the right to life of the fetus (on the assumption that the fetus is a *human* life) versus the rights of the woman to personal fulfillment or the pursuit of happiness — and to different utilitarian principles— the need of the community for children and the lack of fulfillment for the fetus versus the impediments to "quality of life" presented by unwanted infants to the mother, her family, and the community — are the basis of controversy among ethicists. Care-receivers, and often caregivers, seldom see all these dimensions of the problem when initially confronting the question as a moral dilemma, so an important element in the caregiver's task is to present to the care-receiver other important dimensions of the problem than those initially perceived (Section 2c.). Of equally great importance is attention to the personal perceptions of the care-receiver (Sections 2a. and 2b.) or else information about other dimensions and the opinion of the caregiver will likely fall on deaf ears or add to the care-receiver's confusion. Time is also obviously of the essence in pastoral care and counseling of persons contemplating abortion.

Although much less emotionally laden than abortion in our culture, birth control and family planning present many of the same issues. Some birth control techniques are probably abortions (e.g., the intrauterine device) and all have the intended effect of preventing the procreative consequence of sexual intercourse in an early phase, the same intent as abortion. It is then not surprising that some Christians hold birth control to be on the same, or only a slightly lower, level of reprehensibility than abortion.

Bibliography. D. S. Browning, *The Moral Context of Pastoral Care* (1976). D. S. Browning, ed., *Practical Theology* (1983), chs. 1, 5, 9, and 10. W. K. Frankena, *Ethics* 2d ed. (1973), 43 – 61. C. Gilligan, *In a Different Voice* (1982). J. M. Gustafson, "The Minister as Moral Counselor," *J. of Psychology and Christianity,* 3 (1984), 16 – 22. S. Hauerwas, *A Community of Character* (1981). J. C. Hoffman, *Ethical Confrontation in Counseling* (1979). H. A. Katchadourian and D. T. Lunde, *Fundamentals of Human Sexuality* 3d ed. (1980). B. M. Kiely, *Psychology and Moral Theology* (1980). L. Kohlberg, *The Philosophy of Moral Development* (1981). T. W. Ogletree, "The Activity of Interpreting in Moral Judgment," *J. of Religious Ethics,* (1980), 1–26. J. Piaget, *The Moral Judgment of the Child* (1948). J. N. Poling, "Ethical Reflections and Pastoral Care," Part 2, *Pastoral Psychology,* (1984), 160 – 70. E. S. Shneidman, *Death: Current Perspectives* 2d ed. (1980). *Summing Up: Final Report on Studies of the Ethical and Legal Problems in Medicine and Biomedical and Behavioral Research* (1983).

J. N. LAPSLEY

ETHICS AND PASTORAL CARE; GUIDANCE, PASTORAL; MORAL THEOLOGY AND PASTORAL CARE; VALUES CLARIFICATION. *See also* ABORTION; DEATH AND DYING; DIVORCE; FAMILY PLANNING; HOMOSEXUALITY; INFERTILITY; LIFE-STYLE ISSUES; MEDICAL-ETHICAL DILEMMAS; JEWISH CARE AND COUNSELING IN; SUICIDE (Ethical Issues). *Compare* CASUISTRY; CHARACTER ETHICS; CONFRONTATION; CONSCIENCE; DECISION/INDECISION, PSYCHOLOGY OF; DISCI-

PLINE, PASTORAL CARE AS; ETHICS, PROFESSIONAL; LEGAL DIMENSIONS OF PASTORAL CARE AND COUNSELING; MORAL BEHAVIOR AND RELIGION; PASTORAL COUNSELING; RESPONSIBILITY/IRRESPONSIBILITY, PSYCHOLOGY OF; TIMING; VALUES IN COUNSELING AND PSYCHOTHERAPY.

MORAL GUIDANCE. *See* MORAL DILEMMAS.

MORAL INTEGRITY/MATURITY. *See* MORAL DEVELOPMENT; FAITH AND INTEGRITY, PASTOR'S.

MORAL THEOLOGY AND PASTORAL CARE. As a formal discipline, it may be defined as that discipline concerned with evaluating behavior in the light of Catholic doctrines on the origins and the purpose of human life. As such, it comprises both general ethical reflections and reflections of a more specifically Catholic nature, for example, on the proper use of the sacraments. As a formal discipline, moral theology first emerged in the Middle Ages. However, this term is generally used more broadly to refer to any reflections on the ethical significance of a Christian commitment carried on within a Catholic context. So understood, moral theology can be traced to the earliest days of the church.

Throughout its history, moral theology has been closely connected with penitential practices and pastoral care generally. As a result, it has been shaped by the tension between perfectionism and inclusiveness that has always characterized the church's pastoral practice. The perfectionist strand in Catholicism has been expressed in the institutionalized ideal of life in accordance with the evangelical counsels (poverty, chastity, and obedience), and in the tendencies toward rigorism and legalism that recur periodically in Catholicism. But on the whole, the inclusive strand in Catholic thought has tended to dominate, expressing itself again and again: in repeated affirmations of the basic goodness of marriage and business; correlatively, in an openness toward taking common morality into account in formulating the moral duties of the Christian; and in a general posture of liberality, verging sometimes on laxity, in admitting people to the sacraments.

1. Key Themes and Concepts. The organization of moral theology as a formal discipline was set in the late sixteenth century by the *Institutiones morales,* which were manuals designed primarily to train seminarians to be confessors. In their theoretical introductions, these manuals followed the organization of the moral treatise in Thomas Aquinas's *Summa Theologiae,* briefly discussing the nature of human action, conscience, virtue, and sin, and law as the norm of action. They then proceeded to the study of particular cases under the headings of (a) the commandments of God and the church; (b) the Sacraments; (c) censures. This plan was followed by most manuals of moral theology up until Vatican II, and even today, its key concepts still inform much of the work of Catholic moralists.

Note that this plan of study is not meant primarily to address the question of the ethical duties of the Christian — that was assumed to be settled, at least in principle — but to prepare the confessor to judge the state of the penitent's soul. Hence, traditional moral theology is heavily oriented toward moral psychology, and its key concepts are concerned with persons and their actions rather than with moral rules. Human actions are analyzed in terms of the conditions for freedom and the impediments to responsibility (chiefly ignorance and fear), in a way that is dependent on Thomas Aquinas (who, in turn, drew heavily on Aristotle). The virtues are analyzed as principles operative within the person, enabling him or her to live a morally good life (the cardinal virtues) and even to participate in God's life through the Holy Spirit (the theological virtues). Sins, understood as deliberate transgressions of the commands of God or the church, either impeded or completely destroyed the individual's participation in God's life through charity (venial and mortal sins, respectively). When the manuals turn to the discussion of specific actions, they do so through analyzing the principles involved in particular cases, and showing how to resolve moral dilemmas.

It would be misleading to suggest that Catholic moral theology had no concern at all for the Christian's development from minimal virtue to the higher stages of charity. To the contrary, theologians have generally recognized that charity, or the love of God and the neighbor for God's sake, is the root of the Christian life in all its stages. The formal study of the stages of the growth of charity through maturity to near-perfection (ascetical and mystical theology) has usually been thought to be closely allied to, or even a part of, moral theology. Nonetheless, moral theologians have devoted most of their attention to the needs of beginners in charity, no doubt because there are so many of them. If this attitude has sometimes done little to encourage moral and spiritual maturity on the part of Catholic laity, at its best it reflects the inclusiveness and concern for the spiritually weak that lie at the heart of Catholicism.

2. History. *a. Late antiquity.* In late antiquity, the nascent Christian community struggled with, and eventually resolved, the most fundamental issue for Christian moral reflection: To what extent does Christianity call for a distinctive way of life, and to what extent is it compatible with the ordinary customs and obligations of family and society? The widespread practice of extreme asceticism and monastic withdrawal from society, and the recurrent suspicions of marriage and procreation in both Gnostic and orthodox circles, testify to the widespread sense that Christian life, and ultimately salvation, are incompatible with life "in the world." Nonetheless, the Christian community gradually articulated a more inclusive view, which affirmed the goodness of the created order and the possibility of living a Christian life within the structures of family and society, even while it held out monastic withdrawal as a higher Christian ideal to be pursued by a chosen few. As a result, the church fathers, most notably Augustine (d. 430) and Gregory the Great (d. 604), draw freely on the popular moral writings of the late Roman empire when instructing those under their care.

b. The Middle Ages. In the West, this era was characterized by the struggles of an expanding church to maintain its own integrity while providing a decent modicum of care for its people.

One of the earliest results of this struggle was the development of an important new genre of religious writings, the penitentials, which originated in the British missions. These manuals attempted to correlate penances with sins for the benefit of an often poorly trained clergy. As such, they helped to tether moral reflection firmly to sacramental and pastoral practice; unfortunately, they also paved the way for abuses of penitential practices such as the sale of indulgences.

As the power of the institutional church increased, so did its conflicts with secular governments and its own vulnerability to corruption. In response to these problems, theologians and jurists began to hammer out a political theory which, drawing heavily on the natural law theories of late antiquity, made reasonableness and justice the touchstones of all authority, ecclesial as well as secular. Eventually, these discussions led to the first collection and systematic analysis of the church's legal canons in 1139 by Gratian, the father of canon law.

At the same time, dissatisfaction with the church's worldliness led to the foundation of religious communities devoted to renewal through witness and preaching. The two most notable of these were the Franciscans, devoted to a life of witness through radical poverty, and the Dominicans, who were organized to combat heresy through preaching. These communities quickly began to take over much of the church's pastoral care, and so it is not surprising that they formed a number of notable men and women who carried on the patristic traditions of moral guidance and reflections on the soul's growth in holiness.

Perhaps the single most important work in the development of moral theology as a formal discipline was the *Summa Theologiae* of the Dominican Thomas Aquinas (d. 1274). Using Aristotle's *Nicomachean Ethics* (recently rediscovered in the West) as a rough framework, Thomas begins the first part of the second book of the *Summa Theologiae* by articulating a distinctively Christian concept of happiness as the vision of God to which, he asserts, all are called. He goes on to set forth a fairly detailed psychology of motivation and action, and ends by examining the principles for action contained in the natural law, positive legislation, and grace. In part two of the same book he takes up a consideration of specific precepts. In this book he relies much less on Aristotle and much more on traditional moral teachings, for example on the cardinal and theological virtues, the gifts of the Holy Spirit, and the works of mercy. Moreover, his massive treatise on justice owes far more to the natural law tradition of late antiquity than it does to Aristotle. Finally, in this book he considers the special precepts appropriate to those who are called to the priestly ministry, or to religious life in accordance with the evangelical counsels.

The period just before the Reformation was characterized both by serious abuses of penitential practice, most notoriously the sale of indulgences, and by a growing hunger for a renewed spirituality. Luther's insistence on salvation by faith alone was anticipated by the Italian evangelicals, who continued to be a force in Catholicism through the Council of Trent. The humanism of this era is exemplified in the writings of the layman Erasmus (ca. 1466–1536), who emphasizes Christ's presence in family life, society, and even in the best of pagan culture.

c. From the counter-reformation to the nineteenth century. Moral theology as a formal discipline took its modern form in this period, amid a general hardening of doctrinal and institutional lines within Catholicism. The Council of Trent called for a deepening of the study of moral theology. At the same time, by insisting on the necessity of private confession to a priest, and further specifying that grave sins must be confessed by kind and number, it inevitably led to a juridical focus among moral theologians that was to remain until well into the twentieth century.

Theologians responded to the Council's invitation from within the context of a Thomistic revival that had been under way since the early sixteenth century. These theologians included both Dominicans and members of the newly formed Society of Jesus (the Jesuits); the latter were to play an increasingly important role in the development of moral theology. The greatest thinkers of this period took Thomistic principles as the basis for independent thought. At the same time, their use of the basic outline of Book II of the *Summa Theologiae* set the plan for most manuals of moral theology until Vatican II.

By the end of the sixteenth century, modern moral theology was beginning to grapple with the difficult question of how to judge the uncertain or erring conscience. Discussions of this issue focused increasingly on the question of whether it is permissible to act on a less than certain moral belief. The Jesuits Vasquez (d. 1604) and Suarez (d. 1617) argued for probabilism, the view that one may act on an opinion that is only probably true (and not certain). But many later Jesuits took probabilism to the extreme of laxism, so much so that one of them, Juan Caramuel y Lobkowitz (d. 1682) received the dubious honor of being dubbed "Prince of Laxists."

The alleged laxism of the probabilists led to a storm of controversy within Catholicism that included the rigorist (and heretical) Jansenists in France, the Dominicans, more than one branch of the Jesuits, and at least three Popes, who confined themselves to condemning extremes on both sides. (It is noteworthy that Blaise Pascal published an attack on Jesuit laxism, the *Provincial Letters,* in 1656). Finally, out of this controversy came a voice of common sense in Alphonsus Liguori (1696–1787) whose own system (equiprobabilism) was ultimately less important than the common-sense opinions he offered on a multitude of specific topics. A pastoral bishop in the best Catholic tradition, he also attempted to improve the training of confessors, and established a new religious community, the Redemptorists, especially to provide pastoral care in the rural districts. For these accomplishments, he is still referred to as "Prince of Moral Theologians."

d. From the nineteenth century to Vatican II. Under the influence of German romanticism, a number of moral theologians, most notably Sailer (d. 1832), and Hirscher (d. 1865), attempted to lay the foundations for a moral theology that emphasized the individual's growth in holiness, rather than the juridical needs of the confessional. They were followed by the Tübingen school, which argued that grace, seen as a call to perfection, is the ground of moral theology. In their concern for holiness rather than minimal standards of conduct, and in their reaction against legalism, these theologians anticipated the dominant themes of contemporary moral theology.

e. Vatican II to the present. There can be little doubt that the Second Vatican Council is a major turning point in the life of the Catholic Church. At the same time, much of its significance lies in the fact that it validated and institutionalized developments that had already taken root in the life of the church, including a new independence on the part of the laity, greater openness to modern thought, and increased receptivity to Protestantism. All these developments have had a major impact on moral theology.

3. **Modern Developments.** Perhaps the single most important development for moral theology since Vatican II is the growing independence of the laity. In this country, at least, the autonomy of the laity has been accompanied by a decline in the use of the sacrament of penance, and an increased willingness on the part of both priests and laity to allow persons of uncertain ecclesial status (for example, divorced and remarried Catholics) open access to the sacraments. Practically, this means that moral theology can no longer focus on the juridical judgments of the priest in the confessional. Instead, moral theologians are attempting to understand the variety of ways in which a person's actions reflect his or her stance in relation to God and neighbor, and to formulate these linkages in a more flexible, less legalistic way.

A second key development has been the greater openness to modern thought and correspondingly, greater reluctance to appeal to authority and tradition. The majority of moral theologians still look to Thomas Aquinas as their primary inspiration, but the Thomas they have in mind is decidedly not the Thomas of the Counter-Reformation; he has been reinterpreted in the light of contemporary philosophy. Moreover, the role of the magisterium in moral discernment is increasingly subject to scrutiny and revision on the part of these theologians.

Thirdly, an increased ecumenical receptivity on the part of both Catholics and Protestants has led to an exchange of themes and emphases between Catholic moral theologians and Protestant Christian ethicists. While Protestants are discovering the natural law and the virtues, many Catholics are reaffirming the scriptural bases of moral theology.

Finally, the continued presence of individual Catholics and the institutional church in public life, combined with the above mentioned trends, has led to a renewal of Catholic political theory. Liberation theology is perhaps the best known example of this renewal, but the recent statements of the U.S. Catholic bishops on public policy matters are also attracting a good deal of attention.

Bibliography. C. Curran, "Discipleship: The Pastoral Minister and the Conscience of the Individual," *Clergy Review*, 68 (1983), 271–81. L. Gillon, *Christ and Moral Theology* (1967). B. Häring, *The Law of Christ*, vol. 1 (1963). H. Jedin, *A History of the Council of Trent*, vols. 1 and 2 (1957–61). B. M. Kiely, *Psychology and Moral Theology: Lives of Convergence* (1980). K. E. Kirk, *The Vision of God* (1931). A. Koch, *A Handbook of Moral Theology*, vol. 1 (1925). J. T. McNeill, *A History of the Cure of Souls* (1951). T. C. Oden, *Care of Souls in the Classic Tradition* (1984). G. Peterson, *Conscience and Caring* (1982). E. Troeltsch, *The Social Teachings of the Christian Churches*, vols. 1 and 2 (1931).

Various authors, "Moral Theology," *New Catholic Encyclopedia*, vol. 9, pp. 1109–25 (1967).

J. PORTER

CASUISTRY; DISCIPLINE, PASTORAL CARE AS; ETHICS AND PASTORAL CARE; MORAL DILEMMAS IN PASTORAL PERSPECTIVE; PASTORAL CARE (History, Traditions, and Definitions); PRUDENCE. *See also* CHARACTER AND PERSONALITY (Comparative Concepts); CONSCIENCE; GUIDANCE, PASTORAL; LIFESTYLE ISSUES; INTERPRETATION AND HERMENEUTICS, PASTORAL; PENANCE, SACRAMENT OF; SEVEN DEADLY SINS; SIN/SINS; SOCIAL JUSTICE ISSUES. *Compare* MORAL BEHAVIOR AND RELIGION; PASTORAL THEOLOGY; PRACTICAL THEOLOGY, PROTESTANT; SACRAMENTAL THEOLOGY *or* SPIRITUAL THEOLOGY, AND PASTORAL CARE; VALUES.

MORAL VIRTUES. *See* MORAL THEOLOGY; VIRTUE, CONCEPT OF.

MORALE. *See* ATTITUDE; MENTAL HEALTH AND ILLNESS. *See also* BURNOUT; HOPE AND DESPAIR; SELF-ESTEEM; WILL TO LIVE.

MORALITY. *See* ETHICS AND PASTORAL CARE; MORAL BEHAVIOR AND RELIGION; MORAL DEVELOPMENT; MORAL DILEMMAS IN PASTORAL PERSPECTIVE; MORAL THEOLOGY AND PASTORAL CARE. *See also* CHARACTER ETHICS; ETHICS, PROFESSIONAL; LIFESTYLE ISSUES; SOCIAL CONSCIOUSNESS AND RESPONSIBILITY; VALUES.

MORALIZING. In clinical pastoral usage, the inappropriate expression of praise or blame, often done, without conscious awareness of motive, for purposes of winning affection or approval, defending oneself, venting hostility or anger, or establishing superiority over another. Moralizing is regarded as antitherapeutic, and is distinguished from situationally appropriate moral reflection undistorted by defensive motivation or other personal needs of the pastor.

R. J. HUNTER

DEFENSE MECHANISMS; DEFENSIVENESS, PASTORAL. *See also* DEFENSE AND COPING THEORY; MORAL BEHAVIOR AND RELIGION; VALUES IN COUNSELING AND PSYCHOTHERAPY. *Compare* COMPASSION; INTELLECTUALIZATION; MORAL DILEMMAS IN PASTORAL PERSPECTIVE.

MORAVIANS. *See* SECTARIAN PASTORAL CARE; PIETISM AND PASTORAL CARE.

MORMON CARE AND COUNSELING. Pastoral organization, beliefs and practices of the Church of Jesus Christ of Latter-day Saints (also known as Mormons or Latter-day Saints). Through its lay, male priesthood and its lay, female Relief Society, the church provides for every member's household to be visited at least every month by pairs of priesthood "home teachers" and Relief Society "visiting teachers." Home and visiting teachers provide the conduit for most pastoral care, acting on behalf of the "ward" (parish) bishop and the ward relief society president.

1. **History, doctrine, and values.** To understand Mormon care and counseling, one must have some acquaintance with Mormon history, doctrine, and values. Since

its founding in 1830, the Church of Jesus Christ of Latter-day Saints has had to rely upon itself. In 1844 Joseph Smith, the first president of the church, was martyred. The resultant unrest provoked his successor, Brigham Young, in 1847 to lead thousands of the "Saints" out of the Midwest to the Great Salt Lake valley, where they hoped to find geographic insulation from further conflict. Mormons retain today a sense of being apart from the larger culture.

The Mormon church bases all doctrines, policies, procedures, and structure upon acceptance of Jesus Christ as Savior and Redeemer. Mormons rely heavily upon the King James Bible but also believe *The Book of Mormon* (subtitled *Another Testament of Jesus Christ*) to be the word of God. *The Book of Mormon* succinctly expresses Mormon theology: "We talk of Christ, we rejoice in Christ, we preach of Christ, we prophecy of Christ" (2 Nephi 25:26).

Mormon doctrine about the family views marriage as an eternal covenant when performed by proper priesthood sanction within a Mormon temple. This has considerable relevance to care and counseling, as, for example, in counseling an unwed mother and father or a married couple in distress. In the first instance abortion receives no consideration; and in the second, divorce becomes a choice of extreme last resort. Mormons consider child abuse not only an antisocial aberration but also a gross assault upon one's eternal progeny and a violation of divine trust.

Latter-day Saint families are taught self-sufficiency and take most seriously Paul's admonition: "But if any provide not for his own, and specially for those of his own house, he hath denied the faith, and is worse than an infidel" (I Tim. 5:8 KJV). Mormons also believe that the Lord wills that the widowed and homeless have a claim upon the church.

As a consequence of Mormon history and doctrine, Mormonism holds central the values of caring and nurturing through an almost paradoxical mixture of individual initiative and institutional structure. When asked how he governed such a diverse and rapidly expanding society, Joseph Smith responded, "I teach them correct principles and they govern themselves." Thus as an example, a Mormon or non-Mormon marriage counselor serving a Latter-day Saint couple would be well-advised to collaborate with the bishop, *if the couple authorised it.* Such collaboration ties the counseling in with the person who has primary pastoral responsibility, as well as tapping into various priesthood and Relief Society resources. More commonly, the couple will seek marriage counseling from the bishop himself or from someone within their church called to assist the bishop in counseling people with such needs.

A fundamental value underlies baptism. As administered in the church, this ordinance, symbolic of cleansing of sins, requires complete immersion. Confirmation for admittance into the church, by laying on of hands by priesthood holders, immediately follows. Thus "born again," the new member is addressed as "Brother" or "Sister." This familiar form of address implies acceptance into a fellowship of responsibility for the well-being of others. *The Book of Mormon* prescribes that persons should submit to the nurturant ordinance of baptism when they are "willing to bear one another's burdens, that they may be light; yea, and are willing to mourn with those that mourn; yea, and comfort those that stand in need of comfort."

2. Structure and Function. The Mormon Church has developed a geographical and administrative structure to support and enhance the individual and the family. Approximately four hundred to six hundred members usually constitute a ward. The ward bishop, a layman, gives overall direction to priesthood and Relief Society activities. He deals with matters such as serious marital discord or spouse or child abuse.

The priesthood comprises six quorums, each with a president. As support to parents or adults in their own households, home teachers carry various messages and doctrinal instruction, hold prayers, and minister to the ill and distressed. They also report needs to the bishop or quorum president. Home teachers and quorum presidents also attend to matters of educational or remedial concern, such as financial counseling, career guidance, and church doctrine.

The Relief Society functions as one body. Relief Society visiting teachers address themselves specifically to women. The ward relief society president works with the bishop to provide care.

3. Care and Counseling. The Mormon church emphasizes prevention of overwhelming need through support of individuals and families. Church resources serve as a cushion when needs exceed family resources.

a. Personal and family preparedness. Every household is expected to set aside a "family home evening" to enhance their lives through recreation, study of the Scriptures and arts, and activities that develop relationship skills. Sabbath services that complement family home evening include Sunday School, sacrament meeting (a worship service), and meetings of the priesthood, Relief Society, youth, and children's groups.

Further preventive efforts center on six foci that permeate church literature and programs: (1) literacy and education; (2) career development; (3) financial and resource management; (4) home production and storage of food, clothing, fuel, and other essentials; (5) physical health; and (6) social-emotional and spiritual strength.

b. Bishops resource system. If needs exceed family or individual resources, the church makes use of the "bishops resource system," funded by "fast offerings" and staffed by employees and volunteers. (Members abstain from at least two meals each month and donate, as a fast offering, the equivalent or more in cash for care of the needy.) The system consists of the following: (1) *Employment services* help people search, qualify, and apply for jobs. (2) *Production projects* either grow, assemble, or manufacture food or other commodities for the needy. (3) Local, church-owned *canneries* can food under government license, and *local storehouses* disperse these products as recommended by the Relief Society president and authorized by the bishop. (4) *Social services* provide licensed services in adoptions, foster care, and assistance to unwed parents (abortion being proscribed except to save a mother's life), and church-employed or community professionals provide counseling. (The Association of Mormon Counselors and Psychotherapists (AMCAP) publishes its own journal.) (5) *Deseret Industries*, a system of sheltered workshops and thrift stores, employs and trains handicapped people to refurbish and sell goods donated by members through "ward drives" throughout the year.

Each member receiving assistance is expected in turn to assist others for the sake of personal dignity. The person receiving food from the storehouse might help can food for the storehouse. The small business owner might financially advise the dentist in exchange for needed dental work. Entire families help mend secondhand clothing for sale by Deseret Industries.

4. **Conclusion.** As pastoral leader the bishop has the responsibility for evaluating spiritual, emotional, and material needs. In addition, the bishop is expected to develop an intimate relationship with the Holy Spirit in which to receive guidance for offering welfare services. Family, priesthood, and Relief Society caring are thus coordinated. From rudimentary frontier survival efforts and neighborly nurturance has developed an extensive pastoral system. Repeatedly, though, Mormons remind themselves that their mission is personal, devoted to succor of the individual and family. Principles undergirding this mission include self-sufficiency, strengthening nuclear and extended families, service to neighbors, and creation of church-sponsored welfare resources. Coordinating the care and counseling prompted by these principles and values, the church defines basic helping roles and relationships for its members. What illuminates the entire undertaking is faith in the redemption and love of Jesus Christ and a personal responsibility to act as his pastoral servant.

Bibliography. The Book of Mormon (1830). The Doctrine and Covenants (1978).

V. L. BROWN, JR.

PASTORAL CARE (History, Traditions, and Definitions); HISTORY OF PROTESTANT PASTORAL CARE (United States). *Compare* ECCLESIOLOGY AND PASTORAL CARE; SECTARIAN PASTORAL CARE; SOCIAL SERVICES AND PASTORAL CARE.

MORTAL SIN. That sin whereby one is deprived of saving grace and alienated from God, an idea supported by biblical references to sins that exclude one from the Kingdom (e.g., Gal. 5:19, I Cor. 6:9, Eph. 5:5). More technically, mainly in Roman Catholic tradition, an act or state of disobedience to God so grave as to forfeit justification. One guilty of such sin is obliged to sacramental confession, but the essential condition of its forgiveness by God is wholehearted contrition. Recent Roman Catholic theologians tend to be diffident about the practical identifiability of mortal sins.

J. GAFFNEY

SEVEN DEADLY SINS; SIN/SINS. *Compare* UNPARDONABLE SIN; VENIAL SIN.

MORTICIAN. *See* FUNERAL DIRECTOR.

MOTHER / MOTHERING. *See* PARENTS/ PARENTHOOD; WOMEN; *see also* PREGNANCY; CHILDBIRTH.

MOTHER, GOD AS. *See* GOD, IDEAS AND IMAGES OF.

MOTHER, PASTOR AS. *See* PASTOR (Normative and Traditional Images); WOMEN IN PASTORAL MINISTRIES.

MOTHER-INFANT BONDING. The mother-infant bond is an intense relationship of unparalleled human affection. It serves as the very foundation of the infant's emotional and physical survival. As the more mature member of the dyad, the mother must assume responsibility for initiating the love, physical contact, and communication with her newborn.

The mother engages in behaviors which join her to the infant as a viable unit. She extends the warmth, gives the sense of security, and investigates the infant's every need to insure it adequate provisions. The infant's early bonding-like efforts consist of crying, clinging, smiling, rooting, and sucking.

Throughout the first year of life, infants develop progressively differentiated forms of attachment to the mother. The attachment behaviors include following and proximity-seeking behavior, exhibiting preference for the mother over others, utilizing the mother as a secure base from which to venture out to explore the nearby environment, and displaying stranger-anxiety when unfamiliar individuals approach.

The infant's attachment indicates that it associates the mother with feelings of pleasure, contentment, and relief of distress. Much of the infant's later social development and interaction with other people results from the generalization of positive feelings toward the mother onto others.

Mothers who prove most effective in establishing a bond between their infants and themselves express warmth and positive feelings toward their children; see things from the infant's point of view, providing prompt and appropriate reinforcement and feedback; provide frequent and sustained contact; give stimulation appropriate to the child's developmental level; help the infant develop the feeling of having some control over what happens; and express feelings of mutual delight between themselves and their infants (Ainsworth and Wittig, 1972).

Some theorists believe that there is a critical period for the mother's ability to be sensitive to her infant and for the development of the mother-infant bond (Klaus and Kennell, 1976).

Infants born of normal and unmedicated delivery are in an alert state for a period of forty-five minutes immediately following birth. This unique time can be used for skin-to-skin contact and for first breastfeeding. In longitudinal studies, mothers who experienced such early contact were deemed to be more attached to their infants and maintained greater proximity, while their infants reportedly developed better social and intellectual skills than did a comparison group.

Mother and infant behaviors complement each other in ways that seem innately programmed to start the process of bonding. Several avenues of communication that seem essential to the process of bonding include vision (eye-to-eye contact and holding the infant at an exact distance of twelve inches, the distance at which infants can best focus on an object); hearing (hunger cries increase the blood flow to mother's breasts, prompting her to nurse and thus maintain contact; the mother's (often) high-pitched voice is adapted to the infant's acute auditory sensitivity to speech in the high frequency range); and touching, which stimulates important maternal hormones.

Bibliography. M. Ainsworth and B. Wittig, "Attachment and Exploratory Behavior of One-year-olds in a Strange Situation," in B. M. Foss, ed., *Determinants of Infant Behavior*, vol. 4 (1969). M. Klaus, and J. Kennell, *Mother-Infant Bonding* (1976).

G. ROWLAND

CHILDBIRTH. *Compare* ADOPTION; MATERNAL DEPRIVATION; OBJECT RELATIONS THEORY.

MOTHER TERESA OF CALCUTTA (1910–).

Turkish-born Catholic nun and teacher living in India. Founder, and since 1980 mother, of the worldwide order, Missionaries of Charities. In 1948 Teresa moved into the slums of Calcutta to minister to the poor, the sick, and the outcasts of Indian society.

Grounded in a strong sense of a calling, a regular prayer and worship life, and a willingness to see God in everyone she meets, Mother Teresa embodies the universal compassion of Christ probably more powerfully, more radically, and more consistently than any other individual in this century.

Her life, work, philosophy, and spirituality have two implications: one, as a way of raising consciousness about the plight of the world's poor; and two, about the importance of a personal response by those who can help. At the same time, however, her almost exclusive stress on a personal, one-on-one ministry coupled with her unwillingness to address the systemic (social and political) conditions that cause such of the ills and suffering she is trying to relieve has, perhaps unwittingly, produced false consciousness concerning possible remedies for the conditions of dire misery worldwide.

N. F. HAHN

ROMAN CATHOLIC PASTORAL CARE; SPIRITUALITY (Roman Catholic Tradition).

MOTIVATION. The forces that arouse and direct

human behavior. Motivation is similar to learning because it influences the direction of both thought and behavior. However, while learning emphasizes events in the past (experience), motivation emphasizes factors that influence present behavior. Also, learning tends to be long-term while motivation is not.

1. The Development of Motivational Concepts. Long before contemporary psychologists became interested in motivation, philosophers had developed elaborate theories regarding what it is that makes animals and people move. In his early writings, Plato, for instance, already familiar with a pleasure/pain explanation of humankind's drives, tended to assign that principle to "things of the body" that disrupt a person's contemplation of the Good and the works of the rational mind. Later, however, Plato modified his views and noted that some pleasures—such as aesthetic joy—may be viewed as healthy. He speculated that humans have within them a stream of passionate desire, which may be channeled into the search for physical pleasures, the state of honor, or the acquisition of philosophical knowledge and virtue.

Thus, like some contemporary motivational theories, drives may motivate either transitory pleasure *or* "higher" forms of expression or goals.

Following Plato, Aristotle's views on motivation tended to be conceptualized around the notions of *appetite* (rooted in immediate pleasure and characteristic especially of animals) and *wish* (desires for good and long-term benefits, characteristic of humans), a theory expanded much later by Aquinas in his explorations of "faculties of estimation and appetite."

In the seventeenth and eighteenth centuries, philosophers suggested that some actions arise from internal or external forces over which persons have no control. Hobbes, for example, held that regardless of the reasons persons give for their conduct, the underlying causes of behavior are the tendencies to seek pleasure and avoid pain.

2. Instincts, Needs, Drives, and Incentives. *a. Instincts.* When this pleasure/pain view is taken to the extreme it is known as the theory of instincts. An instinct is an innate biological force that predisposes a person to act in a given way. Since animals are without ethical volition, instincts have been attributed to animal behavior for hundreds of years, but it was not until Darwin that the door was opened for instincts to explain human behavior. William McDougall, a psychologist, was the strongest advocate of the instinct theory. He believed that all thoughts and behavior were the result of inherited instincts. It should be noted that Freud's psychoanalytic theory also advanced an instinctual concept of behavior against the rationalist tradition.

The instinct theory is therefore diametrically opposed to a rationalistic view of human behavior. According to this point of view, instead of choosing goals and actions, a person is at the mercy of innate and unconscious forces that motivate behavior. People work because they have an instinct for survival; they learn because they have a curiosity instinct; marriage was instituted because there was a sex instinct. Not until more than a thousand instincts could be listed from the literature did psychologists begin to question whether instincts explained *anything* as far as human beings were concerned.

b. Needs and drives. It soon became clear that there were too many instincts; an instinct could be found for almost any imaginable behavior. It was also discovered that to call a particular action instinctive did not really explain it. Anthropologists learned that many instincts were not found in every culture. For example, in some societies, people found no need to fight.

Therefore, during the twenties, the instinct theory was replaced by the concept of drives. A drive is an aroused state resulting from a biological need, such as a need for food, water, or oxygen, which motivates a person to reduce the drive and satisfy the need (the "drive-reduction theory of motivation"). Although "need" and "drive" are similar concepts, they differ in that "need" refers to a physiological state of deprivation whereas "drive" refers to the psychological consequence of a need.

c. Incentives. During the fifties psychologists began to question the drive-reduction theory of motivation as an explanation of all types of behavior. It became apparent that people are not pushed into action solely by internal drives. They learned that external stimuli ("incentives") are also important. For example, a delicious-looking pizza in a TV commercial may arouse the hunger drive of a person who is not hungry. In this case, the incentive (pizza) activates hunger rather than reduces it. The motivation here is not an internal drive, but an external event. Thus, more recent approaches to a theory of motivation have focused on the interaction of environment and particular physiological states.

3. **Maslow's Hierarchy of Needs Theory.** Many theories have been proposed to explain human motivation, but as yet there is little consensus. Abraham Maslow (1954) proposed a theory of motivation integrating several motivational concepts. Maslow thus described his theory as a fusion or synthesis theory, and as a wholistic-dynamic one.

Maslow proposed a hierarchy of motives (or needs), ascending from the basic biological needs present at birth to more complex psychological motives that become important only after the more basic needs have been satisfied. According to Maslow, if a person is going to live and thrive, his or her needs must be met. Some needs are natural or innate and others are acquired or learned. Needs vary from person to person, from time to time, and from place to place. The theory explains why needs shift from a responsive orientation to a personal growth orientation.

Maslow categorized human needs in a hierarchy of five levels:

a. *Physiological needs.* Physiological needs, the first low-level needs, must be satisfied if life is to continue (food, water, oxygen, activity, rest, and protection from extreme temperatures). These are basic or "prepotent" needs for Maslow in the sense that prior to their satisfaction the higher level needs do not serve as motivators.

b. *Safety needs.* When physiological needs are satisfied, a person acquires a new set of needs which Maslow calls safety needs. An understanding of these needs is seen in infants and children in their reaction to threat or danger. According to Maslow, adults in our society have been taught to inhibit their reaction to danger.

Safety needs, however, function beyond childhood. Many sociologists have attributed youth rebellion to arrested development at the safety level. In adulthood, safety needs will be met by competence, self-discipline, and the wisdom acquired through experience. When an adult cannot seem to satisfy safety needs, he or she may amass a substantial savings account, purchase extensive insurance against various potential disasters, constantly prefer the familiar and routine to the unknown, or try to force the mystery of God or the universe to fit a single and easily comprehensible scientific theory or personal philosophy. Societies have sought safety by means of customs and laws.

c. *Belongingness and love needs.* If the previous two needs are fairly well met, the needs for love, to love, to belong, and to be accepted will then emerge as motivators. At this time, the individual hungers for affectionate relationships and intensely feels the pangs of loneliness resulting from the lack of friends. To Maslow, love consists of feelings of tenderness, affection, elation, yearnings for the loved one, and sexual arousal. He views our desire to receive love from others as a relatively selfish

deficiency need (since it may involve defensive and manipulative efforts to win the affection of another). When this need is satisfied, a growth-oriented or "being" love, which is nonpossessive, unconditional, and giving, will emerge.

d. *Esteem needs.* When needs for being loved and loving others have been satisfied, they move toward a higher level of motivation. Maslow calls this the esteem need.

At this level in the hierarchy, persons need to be appreciated. They must be persons of worth because of their competence. In contrast, at the love level, persons need approval because of whatever they are (mother, student, athlete). At the esteem level however, one seeks to be a good mother, a knowledgeable student, or a superior athlete. A person at this higher level of need motivation is striving for self-confidence, mastery, and recognition and appreciation from others. However, Maslow argues that these esteem needs normally act as motivators only if the three lower types have been satisfied to some degree.

e. *Self-actualization needs.* Few people meet the highest level of motivation, self-actualization, which consists of discovering and fulfilling one's innate potentials and capacities.

Some individuals spend their time and energy seeking to satisfy physiological, safety, love, or esteem needs. It must be remembered however, that self-actualization becomes more prominent with increasing age; the young are more concerned with issues like education, autonomy, identity, love, and work, which Maslow regards as merely "preparing to live." In fact, the specific needs of those rare individuals who achieve this highest level differ in quality from the lower needs. Maslow sees their needs as a love of beauty, truth, goodness, justice, and usefulness for their own sakes.

Maslow's hierarchy provides an interesting look at the relationships among motives and the opportunities afforded by the environment. Although many theories have been proposed to explain human motivation, Maslow's theory has the virtue of attempting to capture the importance of both the physiological and the sociological, the intrinsic and the extrinsic, in a single theory.

4. **The Variety of Basic Motivations in Humans.** Among the human motives often proposed as basic today, singly or in combination, are: a. *Hunger.* The body needs an adequate supply of the essential nutrients to function efficiently. Depletion of these nutrients brings about a release of food that has been stored in the body. For example, the liver releases stored sugar into the bloodstream. This process enables a person to continue to function even after a limited fast. When the stores of nutrients are diminished, however, the entire organism becomes mobilized toward food.

Eating behavior is motivated by a number of variables. External stimuli can influence feelings of hunger. The odor or sight of food can arouse hunger even when there is no physiological need. For example, after a full meal, one may still desire a delicious dessert.

b. *Thirst.* The thirst drive is controlled by delicate biochemical balances within the body and has been linked to the level of salt in the bloodstream. When the level of blood salt reaches a certain point, the brain is stimulated and activates the thirst drive. As with hunger, however, thoughts and attitudes can affect thirst.

c. Sex. Nearly everyone discussing biological motivation includes the sexual drive but adds that it is different from the other biological drives. While it is necessary for the survival of the species, it is not vital to the survival of the individual and it uses energy rather than restores it. Cultural conditioning and moral implications guide its satisfaction.

d. Competence motivators. Whereas the survival motives are shared by humans and other animals, the competence motives are more distinctly human. Robert White (1959) suggests that the "master reinforcer" that keeps most of us motivated over long periods of time is the need to confirm our sense of personal competence. These motives are not rooted in specific physiological needs.

e. Curiosity. In the first few months of life a baby learns to manipulate objects, apparently out of interest. A plastic rattle can be fascinating to an infant at this stage. As the child grows, he or she will begin to look behind or beneath things. In fact, according to developmental psychologist Jean Piaget, much of what we call "play" in infants and children is part of the enterprise of exploring the environment. Whether one is a scientist probing the inner workings of the atom, or a child learning through play, the curiosity motive is a necessary part of becoming a competent and effective person.

f. Cognitive consistency. In addition to a desire to explore, people have a need to experience a world which makes sense. We have a need to believe that our own attitudes and behaviors are consistent with one another. The term "cognitive dissonance," coined by Leon Festinger (1958), refers to the state of unease when we perceive inconsistencies between our own attitudes and/or behaviors. Festinger saw cognitive dissonance as being an unpleasant feeling operating very much like a drive (as hunger motivates us to eat). Cognitive dissonance motivates us to change our opinions or behavior to restore consistency, thus reducing dissonance. People have a predisposition to understand their world in predictable terms, and the search for these consistencies plays an important part in human motivation.

g. Control. Another important human motive is the desire to be in control of one's life and future, rather than to remain at the mercy of external forces. We may enter the world in a helpless state, but as we grow we are continually motivated to gain more control over our environment and our lives.

This desire for control provides an explanation for the effectiveness of so-called "reverse psychology": If you want someone to do something, tell them that they *must* do the opposite. The individual may be so eager to reassert control that he or she will do what you really want.

Bibliography. L. Festinger, "The Motivating Effect of Cognitive Dissonance," in G. Lindzey, ed., *Assessment of Human Motives* (1958). J. L. Fuller, *Motivation: A Biological Perspective* (1962). R. C. Teevan and R. C. Birney, eds., *Theories Of Motivation In Learning* (1964); *Theories Of Motivation In Personality And Social Psychology* (1964). A. H. Maslow, *Motivation and Personality* (1954). C. L. Stacey and M. F. DeMartino, *Understanding Human Motivation* rev. ed. (1965). R. W. White,

"Motivation Reconsidered: The Concept of Competence," *Psychological Review*, 66 (1959), 297–333. H. R. Arkes and J. P. Garske, *Psychological Theories of Motivation* (1982).

L. PARROTT

PERSONALITY THEORY. *See also* CAUSALITY IN PSYCHOLOGY, FORMS OF; COGNITIVE/CONATIVE PROBLEM; COGNITIVE DISSONANCE THEORY; NEED/NEEDS; PHILOSOPHY AND PSYCHOLOGY; WILL / WILLING.

MOURNING. *See* GRIEF AND LOSS; GRIEF AND MOURNING, JEWISH CARE IN.

MOURNING CUSTOMS AND RITUALS. Secular or religious activities and practices repeatedly carried on in a social group following a death by which persons and groups who mourn call attention to the death and the reorientation it requires in the lives of the survivors. Although mourning customs may have ancient origins, there is value in understanding their present functions as integral parts of the mourning process. Most of these customs and rituals in contemporary American culture are seen in the first few days and weeks following a death, losing the value of having a structure of custom which is operative for a longer period.

1. **Purposes of Mourning Customs.** From prehistoric times individuals have confronted death with patterns of responsive action. Assuming that what was useful to others will be helpful now, these patterns are repeated, providing reassurance in time of distress.

Mourners often feel restless and confused as they face accepting their loss, dealing with their potent feelings, and radically restructuring their relationship to the one who died. Often, having difficulty completing meaningful activities, they turn to custom which promotes a kind of standardized behavior. This simplifies the decision-making process, trading the necessity and the freedom to innovate for the reassurance and efficiency of the familiar.

Custom presents group norms for acceptable grieving, guiding the behavior of mourners and educating others for a time when they too will be bereaved.

Although anthropology shows religious roots for many mourning customs in contemporary America, apart from the funeral itself, most mourning customs show little direct connection with Judeo-Christian belief.

2. **Main Types of Mourning Customs.** *a. Gift giving and receiving.* Earliest forms of gifts to the deceased are seen in providing proper burial and grave goods. These may have been responses to needs of the dead or were to protect the living by appeasing the spirits of the dead. Now, gifts to the deceased include a casket and funeral service which reflect the family's estimation of the social status of the deceased, attendance at the visitation or funeral to "pay respects" to the deceased, decorating graves, and establishing memorials.

Gifts to a bereaved family include flowers, sympathy cards, visits, memorial gifts, food, or the flag following a military funeral. Attendance at visitations and funerals is a supportive gift to the family.

Gifts to funeral guests were once very common to induce community support and respect, or as mementos of the occasion. Now such gift giving is largely token:

memorial cards and orders of service from the funeral or the refreshments which are sometimes served following the funeral.

b. Feasting. In many communities it is the custom to serve refreshments or a meal to funeral guests after the service or to eat and drink at the wake prior to the funeral. The act of eating together expresses community solidarity and is a demonstration that life, for the survivors, goes on. The emotional context for such events offers alternation from unrelieved grieving.

c. Kinship affirmation. The disruption of a family by death calls for reenforcing kinship patterns, affirming that the family will endure, even without the deceased. By custom those most closely related learn of the death directly from next of kin and those more distantly related are notified indirectly. Obituaries outline family relationships. Those who belong to the inner family circle participate in the decision-making surrounding the death. Seating at the funeral denotes closeness of relationship to the deceased. Distribution of the estate further confirms that pattern.

d. Social solidarity affirmation. The style of the funeral, the number or status of persons who participate, newspaper obituaries, and lasting memorials are testimonies to the identities of the deceased and the mourners and the esteem in which they are held. Public announcement informs the community of the death and is a general invitation for persons beyond the family to respond to the loss. Social solidarity is affirmed by the participation of religious groups, lodges, or veteran organizations. The Jewish custom of sitting Shiva is an expression of family and community solidarity. The procession to the cemetery was once a parade of all those who mourned the death. Mourning customs, such as the settling of an estate, mark the redistribution of social roles within a family or business.

e. Supporting/shielding mourners. Mourning customs demonstrate the ambiguity of the situation of many bereaved persons: their hurt and loneliness cause them to draw close to others for support and, simultaneously, to need some distance from others. Some customs draw persons to support mourners, while other customs mark them as persons set apart for protection. This was once seen in special mourning dress and periods of curtailed social activities. Most such customs are no longer generally observed, reflecting perhaps the extent to which anonymity, depersonalization, and mobility have accomplished isolation, but not protection.

f. Relating to deceased. All cultures have customary patterns for treatment of the body of the deceased. In American culture embalming, cosmetic preparation for viewing, and placing in a casket are most common, although variations are possible. Markers and memorials signify that the person is remembered as dead.

g. Closure. A crucial feature of mourning custom and ritual is dramatizing separation from the deceased, demonstrating that life goes on without the deceased. Ways of saying farewell include: passing the property of the deceased to heirs, or changing residence or lifestyle to represent a new beginning.

h. Relating to property of the deceased. In early times personal property, sometimes even family members and servants, was destroyed or buried with the deceased, perhaps to prevent the return of the dead. Present day customs more frequently redistribute property informally or legally through a will. Either destruction or redistribution of property can be an element of grief work, acting out the changes brought about by death.

i. Termination of mourning. One of the goals of mourning customs is to move through a period of grief work to a time when mourning can end. Some cultures provide a final death ceremony to indicate the end of structured mourning. The Jewish Jahrzeit has something of this function. But for most Americans there is no period of patterned mourning following the funeral, leaving the legal mechanism of settling the estate as the only mark of the ending of the time of transition. Customs need to be recovered to guide persons through an extended period of mourning to a structured terminus.

3. Custom and Pastoral Care. The functions of mourning customs and rituals can be consistent with many of the goals of pastoral care of the bereaved. Customs should be seen as potential avenues for grief work and judged by our best knowledge of the psychodynamics of grief. Pastors can be helpful by supporting customs that serve the needs of mourners.

Mourners should not be obligated to follow customs which are clearly irrelevant to their needs. At the same time they should be free to turn to familiar ways that have helped those who encountered bereavement in the past.

Bibliography. P. Ariès, "The Reversal of Death: Changes in Attitudes Towards Death in Western Societies," in D. Stannard (ed.), *Death in America* (1975). E. Bendann, *Death Customs* (1930). N. Cassem, "The First Three Steps Beyond the Grave," in V. Pine, *Acute Grief and the Funeral* (1976). I. Crichton, *The Art of Dying* (1976). J. Farrell, *Inventing the American Way of Death* (1980). R. Haberstein and W. Lamers, *Funeral Customs the World Over* (1960). P. E. Irion, *The Funeral: Vestige or Value?* (1977 [1966]). C. Jackson, *Passing* (1977). R. Kalish and D. Reynolds, *Death and Ethnicity* (1976). P. Rosenblatt, *Grief and Mourning in Cross-Cultural Perspective* (1976). J. Whaley, *Mirrors of Mortality* (1982).

P. E. IRION

COMFORT/SUSTAINING; COMMUNITY, FELLOWSHIP, AND CARE; RITUAL AND PASTORAL CARE. *See also* FUNERAL; GRIEF AND LOSS; GRIEF AND MOURNING, JEWISH CARE IN; YAHRZEIT; YIZKOR. *Compare* CULTURAL AND ETHNIC FACTORS IN PASTORAL CARE.

MOVEMENTS AND CULTS, RELIGIOUS. *See* NEW RELIGIOUS MOVEMENTS.

MOWRER, O. HOBART (1907–82). An American psychologist and founder of Integrity Therapy. Mowrer is well-known for his work in learning theory but holds special significance for pastoral counselors because of his emphasis on the moral and social nature of persons. He claims that American psychology is moving away from psychoanalysis, with its emphasis on amorality, toward a psychology that is in harmony with religion. He sees great curative value in this combination of psychology and religion. The two central elements of Mowrer's Integrity Therapy are confession and restitution. Through confession the client begins to accept personal responsibility, and through acts of restitution the guilty conscience can be relieved.

Bibliography. O. H. Mowrer, *The Crisis in Psychiatry and Religion,* (1961). O. H. Mowrer, ed., *Morality and Mental Health,* (1967).

S. C. WILLIS

INTEGRITY THERAPY.

MUHAMMAD. *See* ISLAMIC CARE AND COUNSELING.

MUHLENBERG, HENRY MELCHIOR. *See* PIETISM.

MULTIPLE AND DISSOCIATIVE PERSONALITY. A category which includes those disorders in which there is an alteration in consciousness, personal identity, or behavior patterns.

Strictly speaking, present nosology includes multiple personality under the broader classification of dissociative disorders. The latter also includes such diagnoses as: (1) psychogenic amnesia (certain experience or periods of time blotted out of memory), (2) psychogenic fugue (sudden, unexplained travel to another locale accompanied by amnesia regarding the journey and past life along with a partial or total manifestation of a new personal identity), and (3) depersonalization disorder (an unwanted change in perception of self such as the experience of seeing one's own body from some distance away, involving substantial difficulty or deterioration in occupational or social functioning). Although somnambulism (commonly known as "sleepwalking," during which the person arises from sleep and accomplishes a particular act or series of acts without a memory of such after awakening) is essentially a mild form of a dissociative disorder, it is now categorized under, "Disorders Usually First Evident in Infancy, Childhood, or Adolescence."

The multiple personality disorder has at times been confused by many people with schizophrenia, giving to the latter the wholly inadequate definition of "split personality." The common example of a "Dr. Jekyll and Mr. Hyde" is then typically proffered as an instance of a split personality. Although in schizophrenia, there may indeed be the hearing of and talking to other personalities and be a confusion of identity, the psychotic disorder manifests other significant symptomatology which rather readily distinguishes it from the multiple personality disorder.

In actuality the multiple personality disorder is exceedingly rare. Even though it is observable in childhood, it is more apt to be seen emerging in late adolescence or early adulthood. It is believed by some that extreme emotional trauma in childhood, e.g., physical abuse, may predispose an individual to the multiple personality disorder. This particular dissociative condition is considered to be serious and chronic, with total remission difficult to achieve.

In the multiple personality disorder, the basic or original personality and one or more subpersonalities exist in the same individual with any one of these personalities being uppermost at a given time. The subpersonalities may be of the opposite sex, or of different age, ethnic background, or parentage from the original personality.

Each of the personalities appears to be autonomous and well integrated within itself, including its own characteristic behavior patterns, attitudes, cognitions, and style of interpersonal relationships. It is believed by some authorities that the basic, original personality will have no knowledge of any of the subpersonalities, but that the latter may have some awareness of each other. All of the personalities appear to be aware of blocks of time for which they cannot account.

The switching from one personality to another is usually abrupt and is ordinarily precipitated by stress or anxiety or the anticipation of such. The personalities may or may not have their own names, talk with one another, and participate together in certain activities.

The various personalities may be quite incompatible and disparate from one another, e.g., the basic, conscious personality is spared from the conflict and anxiety which would be manifest if the unacceptable, repressed elements of the person were allowed to enter awareness. Many view this as one of the unconscious etiologies of the multiple personality phenomenon.

Another suggested causative factor is what has been called a lack of "psychic cohesion," a term originally used by Pierre Janet (1859–1947). By this is meant the absence of a solid, coherent core of personality which is integrative of the myriad experiences, cognitions, and feelings typical of every life. Instead, these elements are "loose" and split (dissociated) from one another and from the basic conscious personality.

The possibility of a "secondary gain" or unconscious benefit derived from the subpersonalities might be viewed as reinforcing their existence as well as being etiological. Such secondary gain might be seen in the attention, the compassion, and the "pleasure" provided by the disorder.

The treatment for the dissociative disorders ordinarily includes intensive psychotherapy. Hypnosis and narcosynthesis (intravenous injection of sodium Amytal or sodium Pentothal to achieve a high degree of relaxation) are frequently a part of the therapeutic program, with both being aimed at accessing repressed materials.

It is deemed beneficial to bring resolution to any stress which may have precipitated a dissociative episode. As preventative of recurrence, coping measures which are more adaptive in dealing with stress should be taught.

A. J. STRAATMEYER

DISSOCIATION. *See also* DEFENSE AND COPING THEORY; PERSONALITY DISORDERS; PSYCHOPATHOLOGY, THEORIES OF; PSYCHOSIS.

MULTIPLE STAFF MINISTRIES AND RELATIONSHIPS. Those patterns of service and leadership in a local congregation or other setting in which two or more persons share pastoral responsibility and authority. Although in some settings the multiple staff is thought of as comprising all employed persons, the term *multiple staff ministry* (MSM) is usually used only in congregations employing two or more persons in pastoral roles.

MSM may be organized along a variety of lines. Important organizational models include: (a) the *staff,* in which one person, called senior pastor or simply pastor, is the "head of staff," with others — associate or assistant pastors or directors of education—accountable to that one person; (b) a *collection,* distinguishable from a staff in that while there may be a senior pastor, each person's ministry is relatively independent and unconnected with other ministries; and (c) a *team,* which attempts to see all pastoral activities as aspects of one whole ministry exercised by the team. These three models represent three differing views of authority and responsibility. In a staff, authority belongs to the senior pastor and is delegated to others by that "head of staff." In a collection, authority and responsibility are seldom defined, leaving each minister with independent personal authority. In a team, authority and responsibility rest with the team as a whole.

A *co-pastorate* exists where, in terms of the polity of the denomination, two or more pastors are given absolutely equal authority and responsibility. Co-pastorates often grow out of the hope of exercising a team model, but many co-pastorates are essentially organized as collections. Co-pastorates are sometimes imposed by judicatories in order to solve a problem. True co-pastorates seldom exist. However, this model is increasingly being employed by clergy couples serving a single parish.

An MSM is most frequently found in large congregations, where one person could not effectively exercise all the leadership required. It may provide richness by adding to a working group persons with specialized training in education, pastoral care, or other areas. An MSM may also provide opportunities for mutual support, education, and challenge within the group.

1. **Problems and Challenges.** The MSM may involve significant problems. Questions of the extent of a particular person's authority and responsibility seem to arise with great frequency. The fact that one person does a major share of the preaching may leave others with a sense that their ministry is unnecessarily limited. Theological education tends to prepare ministers to work alone rather than to function effectively in shared tasks. Patterns of congregational life in most churches dictate that the "head of staff" should also be the minister who preaches most often, thus giving a senior pastor two tasks that have little relation to each other and are based on quite different sets of skills.

Many factors, but particularly the relative intimacy of close working relationships and the powerful emotions unleashed in religious contexts, create dynamics in an MSM that resemble the dynamics at work in families. Staff members who explore their families of origin often report that the social and psychological roles assigned to them and accepted by them are usually reproduced in their team behavior. The child used as a conflict resolver in a family of origin is likely, as an adult, to become a pourer of oil on troubled waters in a staff. Such a working style, though useful in some situations, may prevent important conflicts from being recognized and resolved.

Some MSMs in the U.S., and an even greater number in Canada, have experimented with team models. Their aim has been to create as strong as possible a sense of shared ministry. In some experiments, the team as a whole writes the sermon for the coming Sunday after a study of congregational life and biblical materials. Leadership is not fixed in a given person but rotates on a planned basis. Some Canadian experimenters have

reported positive results, but on the whole such experiments in "teaming" have been disappointing. The most powerful factor seems to be a form of transference; one member of the team is almost invariably, though without its being acknowledged, identified by team and congregation alike as the "real" leader.

Participation in an MSM often provides an opportunity for the minister to specialize in a particular area of interest. Such specialization is not without difficulties; the parish ministry is unique among educated professions in that specialization usually involves a reduction in income and lowered influence in judicatories. Nevertheless, pursuing specialized knowledge in pastoral care, education, or administration and finance exerts a powerful pull on many clergy, and draws them into an MSM. Specialists in pastoral care have sometimes avoided the problems implied by specialization by joining the staffs of counseling centers. By and large, all the dynamics, advantages, and problems inherent in the multiple staff in a parish are replicated in counseling centers, as well as in judicatory staffs, denominational agencies, and other settings where clergy work together with some form of shared responsibility.

2. **Criteria for Health and Effectiveness.** There are few if any generally agreed upon criteria for measuring the "health" of a particular staff. Although the dynamics of staffs and teams resemble those of families, comparisons with families have limited value in evaluating the functioning of a staff; the major aims of the family, such as launching offspring and providing deep emotional satisfactions, are too far removed from the aims of a group working together in ministry. Broadly speaking, we may use three major criteria: effectiveness, satisfaction, and longevity. Effectiveness: Does the team accomplish a defined and agreed upon set of tasks with regularity? Satisfaction: Are the members of the group, as well as the recipients of their services, receiving satisfaction from their work and their relationships? Longevity: Is staff turnover infrequent enough that the population served has a sense of object constancy?

Analysis of reports from more than 150 functioning teams suggests that certain factors do mark the effective, satisfied, and stable team or staff. Staffs seem to experience greater measures of these qualities when staff members' *primary* social relationships are not with other staff members. Attempting to secure one's principal social satisfactions from relationships with others on the team reduces both effectiveness and satisfaction. Job descriptions are seldom reported as significant by participants in teams. Reports indicate that job descriptions meet the needs of congregations rather than the needs of clergy. The stability provided by a written job description is usually achieved at the cost of flexibility, creativity, and initiative.

The single factor reported as having the most positive impact on the functioning of a team is *a faithful commitment to meetings*. Those staffs which meet regularly, with attendance by everyone required or strongly expected, and with understood purposes and clear agendas, are also the staffs that appear healthiest in terms of the criteria mentioned above.

Each staff member almost invariably develops a personal constituency; exceptions occur only in the case of extreme incompetence or unpopularity. Teams reporting the most effective, stable functioning tend to be those teams in which each individual's constituency is openly recognized and perhaps formalized in an advisory group. Factionalism, probably the most feared phenomenon in the MSM, is reduced when the fact of personal loyalties to a particular staff member is frankly admitted.

Bibliography. M. T. Judy, *The Multiple Staff Ministry* (1969). K. R. Mitchell, *Multiple Staff Ministry* (1988). K. R. Mitchell, "Implications of Pastoral Theology for Intraprofessional Relationships," in W. B. Oglesby, ed., *The New Shape of Pastoral Theology* (1969). L. Schaller, *The Multiple Staff and the Larger Church* (1980). H. J. Sweet, *The Multiple Staff in the Local Church* (1963).

K. R. MITCHELL

LEADERSHIP AND ADMINISTRATION; SPECIALIZATION IN PASTORAL CARE. *Compare* CONGREGATION, PASTORAL CARE OF; INTERPROFESSIONAL TEAMS AND RELATIONSHIPS.

MURDER. *See* VICTIMIZATION; VIOLENCE. *See also* ANTISOCIAL PERSONS; DEVIANT BEHAVIOR.

MURRAY, HENRY A. (1893–). Influential psychologist known for developing the *Thematic Apperception Test* (TAT), a series of ambiguous pictures intended to draw out a person's unconscious thoughts and feelings as he or she engages in a storytelling task.

The hypothetical construct of need occupies a central place in Murray's theories. He perceived "need" as a central organizing force that works to draw together different aspects of the personality, such as perception, intelligence, and behavior, in order to work toward a desired goal or outcome. Murray distinguished between viserogenic or biological survival needs and psychogenic needs—needs that are the outcome of a socialization process. The striving to satisfy the psychogenic needs forms the foundation of personality. The individual works to meet these psychological needs until they have been filled. Personality is the composite picture of the many means of meeting these needs.

The psychogenic needs have differing intensities and effects. Murray distinguished between "latent" needs that are subtly hidden within the individual's unconscious and needs that were "manifest" or more openly apparent. He designed his TAT to specifically tap those latent needs.

Bibliography. H. Murray, *Explorations In Personality* ([1938] 1985).

B. HOUSKAMP

PERSONALITY THEORY (Varieties, Traditions, and Issues).

MUSIC AS A MODE OF CARE. Music may serve as a mode of care both for the listener who hears it and for the musician who who makes it. "David took the lyre and played it with his hand; so Saul was refreshed, and was well, and the evil spirit departed from him." (I Sam. 16:23b). The qualities of music which contribute to this caring function are its structure and mathematical order which address the disorder in persons' lives. Participating in a musical experience, such as singing, can contribute to personal integration—bringing together body, mind, and spirit. For the singer in a group it provides a type of intimate, emotional communication between the leader and individual group members and between the members themselves which takes place even when interpersonal relationships are limited and/or broken. Music can unify a diversified group of persons into a functional unit, demonstrating in surprising ways what they, who are so far apart, can do together. Music's caring function may also be seen in the way it may be experienced as a gift from persons who seem to have nothing to give.

1. **Music as Therapy and Care.** The use of music as a mode of care and as an adjunctive therapy to pastoral counseling involves the integration of several historic disciplines: music education, music ministry, and music therapy. Music therapy is the youngest of these three fields and the one most directly related to the clinical application of music.

The word "therapy" in this context means more than "the healing of disease." Rather, in this day of stress, ambiguity, divisiveness, despair, and defeat, that may be called therapeutic which stimulates, restores, enlivens, unifies, sensitizes, channels, and frees. Music therapy has a unique and well-established capacity to effect these profound changes.

Music is one of the temporal arts, that is, it exists in time like dance and drama. It involves the systematic, purposeful ordering of the various sound components—rhythm, melody, and harmony—for the purpose of repeated performance and enjoyment. Music, like all other art forms, is stylized expression. It involves skillful organization of the artistic material so that it represents or communicates a certain thing, idea, or state of feeling.

Music may be considered from several points of view: historical, theoretical, philosophical, aesthetic, or functional. Music whose primary function is sociological or psychological rather than purely aesthetic is functional music. In other words, whenever music is used primarily for extra-musical purposes, it is being used functionally. The aesthetic use of music, on the other hand, is "music for music's sake" or "music for artistic gratification." Actually most music serves both purposes to some degree, so that an exact classification is sometimes difficult.

A distinction should be made between the therapeutic use of music in an informal or unstructured way and the use of music therapy as a specific dimension of an integrated therapeutic regimen. In the first instance musical experiences can be self-selected by the patient or suggested by the therapist, and might include such activities as participation in a church choir or community chorus, attending a concert, taking music lessons, and so on, whereas formal music therapy makes frequent use of simple rhythm and percussion instruments (also known as Orff instruments) which can be played by virtually everyone.

In a clinical setting one might also have musical experiences with "therapeutic value" which would not constitute formal music therapy. Examples might be participating in a community sing-along, listening to a recording of inspirational music, or singing hymns at the bedside of a sick person.

On the other hand, music therapy, as a scientific discipline, involves the careful and intentional utilization of all the subtle and potent dynamics related to the musical experience, including selecting, rehearsing, and performing the music itself, as well as the relationships and interactions between the therapist and the participant (and *among* the participants when a group is involved).

In this more formal sense music therapy can be prescribed as a general group activity of the therapeutic milieu in the form of group sing-along, choral or instrumental ensemble, and music appreciation classes, or it can be individually prescribed for particular patients, on the basis of their unique therapeutic needs and/or their personal interests and abilities in the form of vocal or instrumental coaching and music theory and composition lessons.

The choice of musical material, musical medium, level of complexity, and therapeutic goal is a collaborative decision involving the primary therapist, the music therapist, and the patient. As in all therapeutic regimens, music therapy involves individual patient assessment, activity prescription (including goal setting), therapeutic experience, and evaluation.

At times, music therapy can be effectively combined with other creative art activities, for example, dance, psychodrama, poetry and creative writing, painting and sculpting, and various forms of occupational therapy (arts and crafts, carpentry, and horticulture). Moreover, each of these adjunctive therapies can be a distinctive therapeutic modality in its own right with its unique capacity for stimulating and actualizing the creative potential within each individual.

Psychologically, all forms of artistic expression have the capacity to gratify the fundamental ego needs of the individual, namely, to belong, to achieve, to excel, to revere, to dream, to love and be loved, and to develop a positive self-image.

Music therapy occupies its prominent position among the creative art therapies for several reasons. In the first place, music has traditionally and correctly been called the "universal language." Every culture has its musical tradition which pervades all areas of life — religious, social, aesthetic, and commercial. Secondly, music is the ultimately versatile and accessible art form. Almost everyone is capable of engaging in some musical activity at some level of competence. Finally, music — especially vocal music—with its wedding of music and poetry, is capable of expressing and evoking the whole gamut of human emotions, values, aspirations, and experiences.

2. **Music as Behavioral Therapy.** Music therapy then is more than entertainment; it is more than an educational experience or a social activity, although it may, to some degree, serve entertainment, educational, and social purposes. Technically speaking, music therapy has been defined as "a highly developed system for stimulating and directing behavior for the purpose of achieving clearly delineated therapeutic goals." One of the best and most concise presentations of this conceptual framework is that of William Sears:

a. Music provides experience within structure. Goals are to lengthen commitment to the activity, to vary the commitment, and to stimulate awareness of benefits to be gained. Music demands, in a non-threatening way, behavior that is time ordered, reality ordered, ability ordered, and affect ordered. Music evokes extra-musical ideas and associations.

b. Music provides experience in self-organization. Experience influences a person's attitudes, interests, values, and meaning. Goals are to provide satisfaction so that a person will seek more such experiences, and to provide an experience which is safe, good and pleasurable. Music provides occasion for self-expression and for the gaining of new skills which enhance self-image (especially for the handicapped).

c. Music provides experience in relating to others. Music is the occasion for group encounter in which the individual willingly subordinates his own interests for the sake of the group. Goals are to increase the size of the group, increase range and variety of interaction, and provide experiences that will facilitate adaptation to non-institutional life. Group experience allows sharing of intense feelings in socially acceptable ways; music provides entertainment and recreation, necessary to the general therapeutic environment. Experience aids in development of realistic social skills and personal behavior patterns acceptable in institutional and community peer groups.

Obviously, professional music therapy is most effectively practiced by a person specifically trained in this discipline. A registered music therapist (RMT) has a balanced orientation in the various fields of music education, the humanities, and the behavioral sciences, plus a music therapy internship in an accredited clinical training center. Utilizing the creative arts in this innovative way presents a new and urgent challenge to ministers, musicians, and therapists of all sorts—to all three groups the challenge is the same, to become more person-centered and more psychologically aware of the rich nature of their professional roles, the complex needs of the people whom they serve, and the depth dimensions of all artistic media (especially music, dance, and drama).

These new developments also suggest that the structure of institutional ministry needs to be expanded and enriched. There needs to be in the institutional setting an equivalent of the "multiple ministry concept" found in the local parish. Religious observance and music making have always been closely related. The objective, rational, conceptual quality of theological discourse has always been elaborated and intensified by the subjective, relatively non-rational, and emotive quality of music and dance.

In the institutional setting both the religious "professional" (chaplain, pastoral counselor) and the musical "professional" (music minister, music therapist) are learning to view and do their respective tasks as unique but constituent parts of a total treatment regimen. This multidisciplinary, wholistic approach is becoming the hallmark of institutional care at its best. Moreover, these innovative concepts are being applied in the local parish setting with the same positive results.

Bibliography. D. C. Houts, "The Structured Use of Music in Pastoral Psychotherapy," *J. of Pastoral Care,* 35:194–203. W. W. Sears, "Process in Music Therapy" in E. T. Gaston, ed., *Music in Therapy* (1968), pp. 30–44.

J. N. SIMS

ADJUNCTIVE THERAPIES; RITUAL AND PASTORAL CARE; WORSHIP AND CELEBRATION. *Compare* DRAMA *or* TRADITION AS MODE OF CARE.

MUSIC THERAPY. *See* ADJUNCTIVE THERAPIES.

MUSLIM CARE AND COUNSELING. *See* BLACK MUSLIM CARE AND COUNSELING; ISLAMIC CARE AND COUNSELING.

MYERS-BRIGGS TYPE INDICATOR (MBTI). *See* EVALUATION AND DIAGNOSIS, PSYCHOLOGICAL.

MYSTERY, SENSE OF. *See* DOUBT AND UNBELIEF; The HOLY; RELIGIOUS EXPERIENCE.

MYSTICAL THEOLOGY. *See* SPIRITUAL THEOLOGY.

MYSTICISM. Dictionaries usually define mysticism (1) within a religious frame of reference as a spiritual discipline aiming at union with the divine, or (2) in a popular sense as "confused and groundless speculation," undoubtedly to emphasize its contrast with "scientific" theorizing (a contrast which must be questioned in light of much contemporary theory building in the physical sciences, particularly physics).

But generic dictionary definitions, and even phenomenological descriptions, are of limited value in view of the bewildering variety of meanings that this term actually has. Like "love" or "truth," mysticism escapes the usual denotative nets and is further confounded by the fact that it is highly contextual, being understood somewhat differently when viewed from a religious, philosophical, aesthetic, literary, theological, or epistemological stance, or simply as a way of life, a form of experience, or the like.

For this reason it may be helpful to get a sample overview of the varieties of ways mysticism has been treated in modern times, especially in religion and psychology, before turning to its possible importance in praxis, particularly in pastoral care and counseling. Though such a survey can provide only a general characterization, it can assist in appreciating the complexity and profundity of the topic and may yield useful hints for assessing its contemporary pastoral significance.

1. Mysticism and Religion. The critical and formal study of religion is divided into a variety of categories or dimensions — comparative, historical, aesthetic, existential (Kaufmann, 1987). Some scholars (e.g., Streng, Lloyd, and Alben, 1973) have been able to demonstrate eight different ways of being religious when religion is seen as a *"means* toward ultimate transformation." Whether it is formal areas of study or classifications of religious expressions, mysticism usually finds a place in all such schemata. Taxonomically, it often finds its niche within an existential dimension or at least within a category stressing experience and a wholistic view of the religious condition or sentiment. The notion, for example, that mysticism is a means toward ultimate transformation which rests heavily on *discipline* and *union* is quite evident in the religious studies literature.

At the same time, it is often argued that mysticism is not simply another dimension of religion but rather an integral and pervasive force in all the various expressions of religion. This argument is usually based on the historical contention that the origin of all world religions focuses on some person's extramundane experience — an experience defying the usual, rational explanations and one so powerful that it furnished the energy for the founder to attract and maintain the necessary devotees for the establishment of the faith. The basic thesis here is that the mystic experience *precedes* the other aspects of religion; e.g., theologies and doctrines. In William James's (1902) words, "The mother sea and fountainhead of all religions lie in the mystical experience of the individual, taking the word mystical in a very wide sense. All theologies and all ecclesiasticisms are secondary growths superimposed."

Although this traditional scenario has never been completely accepted as the authentic place of mysticism in the evolution and development of religion, the claim holds a rather firm place in the literature. Whether very modern expressions of religion — e.g., humanism, communism, technocracies — can fit a similar pattern remains even more problematic.

2. Mysticism and Psychology. *a. Types of research.* It is not surprising that the modern human sciences of psychology and psychiatry sooner or later should turn their conceptual notions and their methodological tools to the study of mysticism, particularly the mystical experience. There is a general sense in which all science, especially the behavioral and social sciences, has as its goal the naturalizing of spirit, just as religion has as its goal the spiritualizing of nature. It is in this general, often unspoken or unrecognized cauldron that psychological science has approached mysticism, usually religious mysticism. And the specific field of inquiry has been the psychology of religion.

In this regard, the turn-of-the-century work of the American philosopher-psychologist, William James, must be counted as prototypic of the psychology of religion's treatment of mysticism. In his classic *Varieties of Religious Experience* (1902) James identified four characteristics of the mystical experience: (1) its ineffability (it defies verbal expression); (2) its knowledge-producing power (it leads to authoritative realness); (3) its transiency (it fades quickly into our paramount, everyday reality); and (4) its passivity (it is received rather than achieved). Although psychologists of religion since James have elaborated on these characteristics, they remain fairly well intact and are foundational for understanding the mystical experience from a psychological perspective, if not mysticism in all its forms.

In more modern times, research into human consciousness, particularly right brain/left brain studies, has produced a slightly different explanation of the mystical experience. Based partly on the hemispheric division of the brain, the thesis is that the left hemisphere is predominantly involved with analytic, logical thinking, primarily linear in its operation, whereas the right hemisphere specializes in a variety of wholistic mentation such as orientation in space, artistic endeavors, relational propensities, etc. It is easy to see how such a physiological perspective could lend itself to a variety of hermeneutical exercises where, for example, the mystical experience may be viewed more as an unusual mode of perception rather than an experience necessarily stimulated by an external object (Deikman, 1966).

This line of understanding stresses the nature of human consciousness (Ornstein, 1972), not in itself a novel approach (e.g., Bucke, 1951) except in its demonstrated rootage in physical reality.

This modern stress on seeing mysticism, or the mystical experience, as an internally produced phenomenon was dramatized in the 1960s when research linking psychedelic drugs with religious and mystical experiences was at its peak. It had been observed that mystical experiences are often preceded by certain conditions or situations such as nature, solitude, music, or exhaustion (Laski, 1961). Stace (1960) elaborated on a principle of "causal indifference" in which he essentially claimed that mysticism is not to be identified by that which causes it but by the nature of the experience. Thus it was argued that one could study mystical experiences "artificially" induced. Psychedelic drugs provide one such inducement or "trigger"; others may include aesthetic experience (especially certain kinds of music), and states of solitude and exhaustion.

Needless to say, Stace's principle was not unanimously accepted and produced a heated and animated debate regarding artificially induced states of consciousness which researchers called "mystical." Although that research has subsided in recent years, the philosophical, ethical, and theological communities still can be readily ignited whenever the relationships between drugs and mysticism are discussed.

b. Mysticism and psychopathology. Not quite as dramatic as the drug/mysticism debate, though perhaps equally problematic, has been psychology's concern over the relationship between mysticism and psychopathology. Within the psychology of religion this always has been a topic of interest; and it is particularly consequential for those involved in praxis, especially those in the pastoral care and counseling fields.

In 1976 the Group for the Advancement of Psychiatry released its study, *Mysticism: Spiritual Quest or Psychic Disorder?* In many respects, this document identifies the innate complexity involved in interfacing mental health categories with religious categories, particularly when one "system" attempts to comment normatively on the other. Despite excellent background material on mysticism and fascinating depictions of the mystical experience, the committee's conclusions do not help a great deal in resolving this age-old tension. The epilogue of this study contains a paragraph which depicts not only the committee's frustration in dealing with the mysticism and psychopathology topic but portrays as well the state of the art regarding this exploration:

> The inability of this Committee to make a firm distinction between a mystical state and a psychopathological state may be due, in part at least, to more fundamental theoretical problems in psychiatry. The many ways in which human behavior and thought can be perceived make numerous points of view inevitable. For example, there are those who draw fine lines between various psychiatric disorders and, on the other hand, those who regard all psychiatric diagnoses

as irrelevant and who perceive in schizophrenia a manifestation to be prized as a way toward better adaptation. Pathology may be uncovered in the nature of—and the method of resolution of—the conflicts in someone who seems to be brimming over with mental health, while the thought and behavior of the most disturbed patient may be viewed as a contribution to his well-being. Therefore we should not expect to be able to reach a consensus on the line distinguishing mysticism from mental disorder. From one point of view all mystical experiences may be regarded as symptoms of mental disturbances, and from another, they may be regarded as attempts at adaptation (Committee on Psychiatry and Religion, 1976, pp. 815–16).

Although such a perspectival conclusion may be unsatisfactory to those in need of closure or those wishing an olympian judgment on the issue, it is probably the most realistic assessment of the relationship between mysticism and psychopathology.

Even the perspectival resolution, however, is frequently seen as a form of reductionism, a term itself as esoteric and as elusive as mysticism. For no matter what the intricacies of the philosophical doctrine of reductionism, in essence there must be some sort of hierarchical given or doctrine or assumption before one can talk meaningfully about reduction. It seems ludicrous to talk about reducing something to something else unless one already holds to a vision of reality which places things or ideas or disciplines in some sort of graded series. When, therefore, psychiatry (or sociology or medicine or psychology) attempts to understand mysticism utilizing its own concepts and theories, it engages in reductionism *only* if one assumes that a particular religious experience stands above such intellectual and conceptual armamentaria. Thus it is that a perspectival position seems more probable and more productive whenever the interpretative systems of psychiatry, psychology, sociology, physiology, etc. are employed.

3. Mysticism and Pastoral Care. *a. General issues.* The meaning of mysticism within the pastoral care and counseling movement is an important yet elusive topic. The presence and significance of mysticism within religious and theological frameworks varies greatly, and such degrees of presence undoubtedly have great impact on the hermenutic of the praxis. One might assume, for example, that the Eastern Orthodox tradition would place considerably greater emphasis on mysticism than would a Universalist-Humanistic tradition. It would not be unreasonable to assume also that pastoral caregivers from these traditions would differ in the importance assigned to mysticism. Added to this is the fact that modern pastoral care and counseling draws its theories and concerns largely from the behavioral and social sciences which themselves differ as to the attention given to mysticism — even as a topic worthy of empirical research. The behavioristic school, for instance, tends to ignore or at least minimize the mystical, whereas transpersonal psychology is more apt to integrate the mystical into its total meaning system.

b. Significant findings. Despite these varieties of perspectives and emphases, there are at least two empirical findings which have significance for the development of pastoral care and counseling. The first has to do with the clear fact that a significant number of persons report having had mystical experiences. In Andrew Greeley's (1974) general population survey, for instance, over twenty percent reported having had a mystical experience. "What is surprising about contemporary North American culture is not that there is less mysticism than allegedly exists in the East," Greeley wrote, "but that there are so many people who experience mystical interludes as apparently do. The twenty percent of the American population that reports frequent ecstatic experiences does so despite immense obstacles. In a culture without silence, where only technical reason is valued, where the educational system conspires to turn everyone to a prosist, and where the mystical interlude is equated with mental illness, it is not easy to be an ecstatic . . ." (Greeley, 1974, p. 59).

The other finding, of perhaps no less significance, is that most of those reporting mystical experiences interpret such phenomena as a way of *knowing*; that is, they see cognition at the core of the experience. At a time when cognitive systems of counseling and psychotherapy are on the upswing, this would argue for greater attention being paid to this epistemological dimension of mysticism. And although such is not evident in mainstream pastoral care and counseling literature, it would appear that this absence may be more in accordance with the movement's general mind-set (theologically liberal, enamored with a nineteenth-century scientism, and a penchant for psychoanalytic musings) than with the full range and reality of what people are experiencing.

c. Larger implications. Mysticism is an important topic for pastoral care and counseling, primarily because certain forms of mysticism have the potential of providing the pastoral movement with a richer way of understanding and interpreting human experience. Even if the field is encapsulated in scientism — as much psychotherapeutic literature, from which it draws its principal understandings, seems to be — room can and should be made for the nuances and poetic picturing of reality implicit in a mystical way of perceiving and knowing. Psychology and pastoral care ought to reflect seriously on the fact that a vast segment of modern science, particularly physics, leads to a worldview similar to the view of the world held by mystics of all ages and traditions. Physicist David Bohm, for instance, points to the need for a more complete understanding of the realm of the spirit — what he has termed the holomovement—the universe as "undivided wholeness in flowing movement" (Bohm, 1978; Schmidt, 1983).

In any case, it is clear that pastoral care desperately needs a cosmological foundation for its praxis. The literature on foundational topics has tended to be adversarial and constricted — often with theological categories set over against psychological and psychiatric ones. What this has accomplished — other than at times turning hermeneutics into politics—remains doubtful. But it just may be that given the richness and complexity of the "living human document," the pastoral care movement stands in need of a new order of fundamental concepts, an order which is more inclusive conceptually than has so far generally been true.

Such considerations, however, would require pastoral theologians and pastoral caregivers to develop a high tolerance for ambiguity, for epistemologies often fraught with uncertainty, for ineffability, for the imaginative, and for a willingness to enter into what philosopher Gaston Bachelard has phrased the "domain of the superlative" (Bachelard, 1969, p. 89). It requires, in other words, a desire to develop a sense of being which is inclusive of, if not completely in accord with, mysticism.

Bibliography. G. Bachelard, *The Poetics of Space* (1969). D. Bohm, *Wholeness and the Implicate Order* (1980). R. M. Bucke, *Cosmic Consciousness* (1951). W. H. Clark, *Chemical Ecstasy* (1969). A. J. Deikman, "Bimodal Consciousness," in R. E. Ornstein, ed., *The Nature of Human Consciousness* (1968), pp. 67–86. A. M. Greeley, *Ecstasy: A Way of Knowing* (1974). Group for the Advancement of Psychiatry, *Mysticism: Spiritual Quest or Psychic Disorder?* (1976). W. James, *The Varieties of Religious Experience* (1902). W. Kaufmann, *Religions in Four Dimensions* (1976). M. Laski, *Ecstasy: A Study of Some Secular and Religious Experiences* (1968). R. E. Ornstein, *The Psychology of Consciousness* (1972). W. S. Schmidt, "Toward a Cosmological Foundation for Pastoral Care," *J. of Pastoral Care*, 37 (1983), 207–16. W. T. Stace, *Mysticism and Philosophy* (1960). F. J. Streng, C. L. Lloyd, Jr., and J. T. Allen, *Ways of Being Religious* (1973).

W. H. CLARK
O. STRUNK, JR.

ECSTASY; PEAK EXPERIENCE; RELIGIOUS EXPERIENCE; SPIRITUALITY. *See also* The HOLY; MEDITATION; PSYCHOLOGY OF RELIGION. *Compare* BORN-AGAIN EXPERIENCE; CHARISMATIC EXPERIENCE; ILLUMINATION; PSYCHEDELIC DRUGS AND EXPERIENCE; TRANCE; VISIONS AND VOICES.

MYTH, PERSONAL. *See* PERSONAL STORY, SYMBOL, AND MYTH IN PASTORAL CARE.

MYTHOLOGY AND PSYCHOLOGY. Mythology is the body of sacred tales that provide people with a vision of the cosmos and a set of ultimate values. A myth is held to reflect "the real," displayed in the paradigmatic acts of gods and heroes. Myth in this sense is not "falsehood," contrary to popular usage.

Depth psychologists have been fascinated by mythology and are eager to interpret myths. Their main questions have been: how can we account for the similarity of myths produced by dissimilar peoples? What are the psychic sources for common mythic motifs? What value, if any, does mythic thought have today? A second relationship between psychology and mythology interprets psychology itself as a new myth, a set of sacred tales for twentieth-century persons, similar to the tales of religious traditions.

1. Depth Psychological Interpretation of Mythology. *a. Freudian.* This perspective holds that the same unconscious wishes and anxieties found in dreams also appear in myths, folktales, and legends. All depend on primary-process thought, rather than the reality principle. Hence comes the fantastical quality of myths and their seeming disregard for the law of nature and logic. Like dreams, myths are said to depict the basic conflicts of childhood in disguised form, especially the Oedipus complex. The universal appeal of myth is due to the universality and primordiality of these childhood concerns.

b. Jungian. Jung and his followers have been even more fascinated by mythology than psychoanalysts. Jung too held that myth originates in the deepest level of the psyche, and that it depends on mental processes very different from those of the rational ego. Jung relied on the parallel between myth and dream, often allowing each to interpret the other. However, he denied the link between myth and childhood experiences and saw myths (particularly hero-myths) as expressions of the individuation process. He stressed the numinous and impersonal qualities of mythic figures and events, labeling them "archetypal." Myths arise from the collective unconscious —a universal storehouse of wisdom repressed by our post-Enlightenment rationalism. Mythology, for Jung, is a human necessity; its loss in the lives of many modern persons is a major disaster. In Jungian writings, myth always carries this highly positive connotation. In fact, myth as "sacred tale" is broadened so that it becomes equated with religion or a transcendent perspective.

Many non-psychological scholars of myths have been skeptical of these interpretations, particularly of the Freudian. There are surely other determinants for mythology than those cited by depth psychology, and the universality of archetypal patterns is an assumption rather than a fact.

2. Psychology as Mythology. A major debate among scholars of mythology centers on the question of "modern myth": is there a direct parallel in contemporary culture for the myths of traditional peoples? For those whose answer is yes, depth psychology itself is one source of sacred tales and functions just as previous mythologies did. It gives order and meaning to the individual's life, identifies prototypical human situations, and offers a set of ultimate values. Depth psychology, so this argument claims, may or may not be a science, but it has become a mythology for post-traditional persons in search of a replacement for religious faith. This perspective has been held by both critics such as Rieff and supporters of psychological myth, especially Hillman. Once again, it is important to distinguish this usage of myth from the derogatory view whereby myth would be equivalent to false story.

To view psychology as modern myth has an important consequence: it now appears in direct competition with all alternative mythology. This prevents an easy division of labor whereby the theologian asks and answers ultimate questions while the psychologist as empirical scientist is restricted to non-ultimate claims. Such a division, although extremely convenient, is ruled out if psychology sees itself as myth, charged with the task to create and retell its own set of sacred tales.

Bibliography. J. Campbell, *The Hero with a Thousand Faces* (1949). S. Freud, *The Interpretation of Dreams, SE,* (1958 [1900]). J. Hillman, *The Myth of Analysis* (1972). C. G. Jung, *Archetypes and the Collective Unconscious, Collected Works* 91, 2d ed. (1968). C. G. Jung and C. Kerenyi, *Essays on a Science of Mythology* (1971 [1949]). H. Murray, ed., *Myth and Mythmaking* (1960). P. Rieff, *The Triumph of the Therapeutic* (1966).

L. BREGMAN

PERSONAL STORY, SYMBOL, AND MYTH IN PASTORAL CARE; PSYCHOLOGY OF RELIGION. *See also* ANALYTICAL (JUNGIAN) PSYCHOLOGY *or* PSYCHOANALYSIS, AND RELIGION. *Compare* MODELS IN PSYCHOLOGICAL AND PASTORAL THEORY; PHILOSOPHY AND PSYCHOLOGY; SYMBOLISM /SYMBOLIZING.

N

NARCISSISM/NARCISSISTIC PERSONALITY. By common definition, love of one's own body, hence inordinate love of self, narcissism is a psychological term that has come to enjoy far-reaching popularity, meaning variously: self-absorption, grandiose self-love, a retreat to privatism, asocial individualism, and bourgeois acquisitive individualism. What these meanings hold in common is that the narcissist is more involved with self-love than love for others. In clinical circles, as well, the meanings of "narcissism" have so proliferated that they have come to encompass the "border-line personality," prompting recent researchers to call for a moratorium on the use of the term.

Clearly, theoretical precision about the term is important, not only because the term is susceptible to inflation and moral platitudes, but also because many of the uses to which it is put today are inaccurate and further blur the very real conceptual, theoretical, and clinical issues that surround it. Moreover, theoretical precision is of pressing concern, owing to its widespread application to contemporary North American culture (e.g. Lasch, 1978), and its emergence in many circles as a model character type; hence, it has become a matter of general importance not only for specialized disciplines of therapy and counseling, but also for ministries that seek to interpret the relation between faith and culture.

1. **Freud and Psychoanalysis on *Narcissism*.** The term narcissism was first chosen in 1899 by Havelock Ellis to denote the psychological attitude of auto-eroticism. In a classic paper published in 1914, Sigmund Freud sought to deepen and to reposition the significance of narcissism. Departing from the modern premise that self-preservation is a universal tendency of living matter toward objects that sustain and away from those that imperil, Freud claimed instead that self-preservation impels a being into the world even though it is perilous, and that only in its engagement with the world does a being learn what sustains and what imperils it. Moreover, a being *internalizes* sustaining objects, *identifying* them with pleasure and gratification, and thus transforming them into love objects.

Since self-preservation is closely linked with auto-eroticism, desired objects are transformed so that they conform to the inner desires of the person: in a word, desired objects are robbed of their "otherness." The child does not distinguish between itself and the world, but the world is an extension of itself. Freud surmises that this "presumption" of an original unity between the individual and the world is an extension of the primordial experience of the womb, reinforced by parental attention and hopes.

On the basis of these insights Freud proposed that human relationships with other persons and things ("object choices") are of fundamentally two types: the "anaclitic," in which auto-erotic tendencies are united with self-preservation, and the "narcissistic," in which auto-erotic impulses alone hold sway. The potential for taking oneself as object choice is inherent in all individuals at birth and is what Freud calls "primary narcissism."

Where primary narcissism is aggravated, "disturbed" (Freud) or "injured" (Kohut), anaclitic object choice becomes subordinated to the narcissistic type. Whether through the effects of "failure to thrive" (Spitz), the absence—"death"—of the mother (Winnicott), or "pathogenic repression of narcissistic gratification" when confronted with the ideals of its culture (Freud), the individual's primary narcissism reconfigures to repair the wounds and deprivations of the ego. This reconfiguration, referred to in more recent clinical literature as "secondary narcissism," is a defense against overpowering rage (Klein) and the basis for a "blind optimism" (Kernberg) that protects the narcissist from developing dependencies on others. Far from being content with himself or even infatuated with himself, the individual who employs narcissistic object choices is actually desperate for and frightened by love. Indeed, bereft of a strong sense of himself, this individual fashions ideal self-images which conform to the highest standards of society. Owing to the public approbation of this "ideal person," the individual identifies himself with the ideal and directs his love toward it. The ideal self thus functions to represent the lost perfections imagined to have been associated with childhood. At the same time, the ideal functions as parental and societal conscience to check the rage that the narcissistic individual harbors in consequence of its disappointments in being loved.

The forming of the ideal self is consuming of the narcissistic individual, entailing both mental exultation and aggrandizement; desire for sexual gratification is either aggravated to the degree of promiscuity (Freud) or altogether suspended (Kohut), although in each case the actual gratification derives from maintaining the ideal. But failing to discharge gratification outwardly, the narcissistic individual becomes dammed up, accepting sensory renunciation for the sake of adherence to the moral principles of the ideal self. Increasingly inaccessible, the narcissistic individual retreats further into the realm of ideas, bestowing almost talisman-like power upon words. However much the narcissistic individual appears to be in command of the course it pursues, a greater measure of faltering marks the narcissist's soul than is outwardly evident. Despite strong and independent intellectual acts, the narcissistic individual remains tied emotionally to few others, extending no more love to them than is necessary to retain them in the service of his or her own interests. Longing for omnipotence, the narcissist is dogged by a nagging awareness of necessity, of reality. And the more the narcissist struggles to fend off the exigencies of necessity and external reality, the more the narcissist actually bends moral ideals he or she represents to serve his or her own ends: the consolidation of the ideal self progresses only proportionally with indifference to the external world.

With the recognition that the ideal self is derived largely from the external, social world, the narcissist withdraws from that world as well, while simultaneously carrying the guilt that the real social community will now inflict in condemnation, owing to this failure, this withdrawal. Driven again to the most primordial of his or her own conflicts, in pursuit of the excellences, which, if possessed, would finally effectuate the gratifications of love, the narcissist strives relentlessly to shore up his or her own world. Shorn of the magnanimity of earlier accomplishments, the narcissist's nihilistic penchants manifest themselves in the act of regarding and rejecting those around him or her as mere parasites. Annihilating their otherness, in the ever-recurring primordial act of incorporation and transformation of objects, the narcissist loves only those perfections in others that are desired but not possessed.

The narcissist thus becomes unreachable, inhabiting a world of ideas that may become virtually unintelligible to others. In desperate search of love but terrified of the pain of its loss, as well as of the pain of exposing the rage over its loss, the narcissist becomes steeped in language, ineluctably traveling the most primitive route of ego- formation—the acquisition of self-objects—thereby assuring the fate of lovelessness. Recognizing the near-inchoate character of this penchant, Freud deemed this disorder virtually untreatable: in his view, the predominance of narcissistic over anaclitic object-choices in the narcissist rendered the prospect of transference relationships with the therapist, and thus successful treatment, unlikely.

2. **Recent Clinical Literature.** More recent clinical literature, namely, that of object relations theorists and of

Heinz Kohut, has presented more hopeful appraisals of the treatment of narcissistic personality disorders, but these hopes have been both modest and guarded. Building more nearly on Freud than has been recognized, Kohut (1971, 1977, 1978) discovered that despite their vulnerability and lack of cohesiveness, narcissists do in fact enter into transference relationships with their therapists. The character of the transference differs, however, from Freud's expectations: rather than psychosexual transferences, narcissists transfer the dynamics of their inner fragmentation. Thus Kohut stressed the need for empathic encounters with narcissistic patients, mirroring their intellectual or physical achievements back to them, accepting their desire to merge with their idealization of the therapist, and permitting the narcissist to appropriate the therapist as an alter ego, thereby being part of a larger community of like-minded and like-spirited individuals. Moreover, in keeping with the distinction between anaclitic and narcissistic object choices, patients must gradually be brought into awareness of the kinds of transference they operate under (narcissistic) as opposed to their own presumption of their "normal" (anaclitic) character. Above all, empathic encounters have as their ultimate objective self-love and love of neighbor: the realization of a central tenet of the Judaic-Christian traditions.

3. **Critical Reservations.** Despite the recognition of the prevalence of narcissistic personality disorders in late twentieth-century therapeutic practice, much remains unclear about this "disorder." Social therapists, such as Adorno and Sennett, have been critical of Freud for his seeming disregard of the sociological factors involved in the formation of this disorder, as have such analysts as Fromm and Horney. But a careful review of Freud's own writings only partially supports this claim: Freud knew only too clearly that the formation of the ideal self was both a familial and a cultural phenomenon. What has only begun to enter into theoretical and clinical discussions is the extent to which the way in which Freud formulated the problem remained fundamentally oriented to a philosophical conception of the mind that accords primacy to the reflecting self (neo-Platonic and Kantian views). The presumed self-reference of self-preservation and auto-eroticism in Freud's theory clearly adhere to this philosophical model of mind. Yet when self-reference is not interpreted in terms of an ego's knowledge of itself, but instead as a secondary trait of perception (awareness of awareness does not equal awareness of an "I") or as a reflexive feature of language (self-reference is a feature of the first person pronoun "I"), the way to construe the relation between auto-eroticism and self-preservation is subject to numerous other interpretations. This observation alone raises the prospect that the clinical interpretation of "narcissism" may serve as a foil for certain moral values associated with modern philosophies of the "self" (e.g., Kant). These philosophies may be "read into," but not necessarily derived from empirical observations of character formation.

In line with this observation are the interpretations of Freud by the French analyst Jacques Lacan (1977), and the philosophical and theological investigations of the limits of Kantian moral discourse by Ludwig Wittgenstein and Karl Barth. According to these views, the narcissistic personality is a consequence not of disrupted patterns of object cathexes (emotional attachments to persons), but a direct outcome of certain ways of speaking and thinking derived from Kantian moral philosophy — which emphasizes autonomy of the self and renounces radical otherness and empathic feelings — and their embodiment in institutional practices. These critiques remain in their nascency. But they, together with the recognition of the formative role of allegedly narcissistic practices in the development of Western culture (Paul Zweig, 1968) offer some of the more promising leads for the ongoing interpretation of this peculiar configuration of human personality. So, too, do further explorations into the materialist character of Freudian theory, particularly as it pertains to the seemingly acquisitive character of the narcissistic personality. As such studies gain greater currency in clinical and therapeutic circles, the often facile and misleading characterizations of narcissism as egoistic self-preoccupation may finally be upended.

Bibliography. R. Chessick, "The Problematical Self in Kant and Kohut," *Psychoanalytical Quarterly,* 49 (1980), 456–73. S. Freud, "On Narcissism: An Introduction," *SE* 14. H. Kohut, *The Analysis of the Self* (1971); *The Restoration of the Self* (1977); *The Search for the Self,* (1978). O. Kernberg, *Borderline Conditions and Pathological Narcissism* (1975). M. Klein, *Envy and Gratitude and Other Works* (1975). J. Lacan, *Ecrits* (1977). C. Lasch, *The Culture of Narcissism* (1978). D. Pacini, "Metamorphosing Narcissus' Mirror," *The Cunning of Modern Religious Thought* (1987). J. Perry and G. L. Klerman, "The Borderline Patient: A Comparative Analysis of Four Sets of Diagnostic Criteria," *Archives of General Psychiatry,* 35 (1978), 141–50. D. Winnicott, *Collected Papers Through Pediatrics to Psychoanalysis* (1958). P. Zweig, *The Heresy of Self-Love* (1968).

D. S. PACINI

PSYCHOANALYSIS (Personality Theory and Research); SPECIALNESS, SENSE OF. *Compare* BORDERLINE DISORDER; EGOTISM; OBJECT RELATIONS THEORY.

NARCOTICS. *See* DRUG ABUSE, DEPENDENCE, AND TREATMENT.

NARCOTICS ANONYMOUS. *See* ALCOHOLICS ANONYMOUS; DRUG ABUSE, DEPENDENCE, AND TREATMENT; SUPPORT GROUPS.

NARRATIVE / NARRATIVE THEOLOGY. *See* INTERPRETATION AND HERMENEUTICS, PASTORAL; MYTHOLOGY AND PSYCHOLOGY; PERSONAL STORY, SYMBOL, AND MYTH IN PASTORAL CARE.

NATION OF ISLAM. *See* BLACK MUSLIM CARE AND COUNSELING.

NATIONAL ASSOCIATION OF CATHOLIC CHAPLAINS. *See* COUNSELING, ROMAN CATHOLIC.

NATIONAL CONFERENCE OF CATHOLIC CHARITIES. *See* COUNSELING, ROMAN CATHOLIC.

NATIVE AMERICAN TRADITIONAL RELIGION, PERSONAL CARE IN. Early Western observ-

ers reported that American Indians lived their lives within cultural contexts formed by sacred powers which transcended the human world. These powers appeared in their dreams and visions as luminous human, animal, or plant beings. Special relations with transcendent powers were established and maintained through the activities of persons who occupied specific social roles. Interpreters referred to such persons as shamans or medicine men or women. In this context a more general term will be applied: persons of medicine power. Furthermore, the term *medicine* should be understood in the general sense of *sacred.*

Persons of medicine power often served both as "doctors" and as "priests." An examination of their role shows how they performed some functions which may be compared with certain dimensions of practice within contemporary pastoral care.

1. **Health and Healing.** Aboriginal peoples on the North American continent were divided into hundreds of tribal groups exhibiting great linguistic and cultural diversity. For this reason it is difficult to generalize about their relations with transcendent powers. Perhaps the clearest case, however, appears in tribal views of health and healing. These views embody diagnoses of disease which required spiritual as well as physical therapy. Persons of medicine power functioned at both of these levels.

Some tribes believed disease arose as a consequence of sorcery or witchcraft. Others attributed disease to a lapse in behavior which offended transcendent powers. Still others believed disease arose because a foreign object or spirit intruded into a person's body. And some tribes understood disease to be caused by the theft of an individual's soul or personality by a malevolent spirit or power. Among other tribes, notably those of Iroquoian ancestry, unfulfilled dreams or desires were understood to cause physical or psychological disorders.

2. **Ritual and Life Crises.** Persons of medicine power engaged in symbolic action believed to be appropriate to crises in individual or tribal life. If the cause was sorcery, then a ritual of power might be directed against the offending being; if difficulties arose because taboos had been violated, then appropriate restitution was accompanied by special ritual processes; if an object or spirit had entered the person's body, then specific acts, such as sucking and other manipulations, along with appropriate rituals, were necessary. In other cases, such as on the Plains, the opening of a bundle, containing various sacred objects, might be at the center of the ritual process. Sometimes these techniques were combined with herbal remedies drawn from the stock of folk tradition.

Disorders of the personality, such as soul loss, were addressed by persons of medicine power in a variety of ways. Among the Eskimos, for example, the medicine person would enter the spirit world, there to seek for the lost soul, often doing combat with powers which held it in bondage. When the ailment was caused by unfulfilled dreams or desires, as in the Iroquoian case, then both the medicine person and the community may have been involved. In addition to rituals of healing led by the person of medicine power, the patient may have been treated to communal feasts, dances, and gifts.

3. **Other Functions.** Persons of medicine power related to tribal life in a more general manner as well. Such

persons were repositories of ritual knowledge, keepers of sacred objects, and often occupied priestly roles in tribal societies. In such roles, these persons surrounded critical events, such as birth, death, marriage, and puberty, with important ritual processes. In addition, persons of medicine power had a central place in tribal rituals of social and world renewal.

In their more general role, medicine persons in Indian societies served broad therapeutic purposes within religious contexts. As compared with contemporary pastoral care, the role of medicine persons was certainly broader. But whether the issue was physical illness, delirium consequent upon soul loss, or important individual and tribal life crises, the role of the medicine person was central. It is also clear that success or failure was dependent not only upon appropriate rituals, but also upon confidence in the medicine person and sharing his or her religious worldview. These features indicate some general kinship between modern pastoral care and the wisdom of aboriginal tribal peoples.

Bibliography. J. Brown, *The Sacred Pipe* (1953). M. Eliade, *Shamanism: Archaic Techniques of Ecstasy* (1964). J. H. Howard, *Oklahoma Seminoles: Medicines, Magic, and Religion* (1984). D. Sandner, *Navaho Symbols of Healing* (1979). J. Vogel, *American Indian Medicine* (1970).

H. L. HARROD

SOCIOLOGY OF RELIGIOUS AND PASTORAL CARE. *Compare* AFRICAN *or* WEST INDIAN TRADITIONAL RELIGION; CULTURAL ANTHROPOLOGY OF RELIGION, DISCIPLINE OF; SHAMAN.

NATIVE AMERICANS, PASTORAL CARE OF.

The great majority of counseling techniques and therapeutic methods used with Native Americans have proven sympathetic but ineffective. Much of the problem lies in a lack of cross-cultural understanding, coupled with a predominance of mass stereotyping, media-created images, and romantic projection. Having experienced two hundred years of a government's unconscious and, at times, conscious attempts at political genocide, Indian people's historical and ongoing resistance to be accommodated, healed, and acculturated by a more pervasive, sophisticated social system is a testament to their remarkable status as unique survivors. In 1900 the U. S. Department of the Census estimated Indian peoples to number fewer than 200,000. In 1980 the figure stood at 1,400,000. The current birth rate of this one-time "vanishing race" is double that of the national average. Reminding us of our own history, and the blemished, often brutal effects of national policy, they refuse to disappear. An encounter with groups or individuals of Native American descent warrants sensitivity, caution, and the deepest respect.

1. **Questions of Identity.** Indian people represent some 516 federally recognized tribes in the U.S. They find themselves in any one or a combination of the following groupings, each one, in turn carrying distinct characteristics: (a) Reservation, (b) Urban, (c) Traditional, (d) Assimilated, and (e) Militant.

Reservation and rural populations make up approximately 48 percent of Native Americans. Two hundred and six reservations were historically established by treaty agreements and currently are coordinated and work in cooperation with the Bureau of Indian Affairs, an office of the Department of the Interior with the U.S. government. Due to complex historical factors, tribal governments are often riddled with conflict. The sporadic and inconsistent support of treaty rights by federal agencies has frequently contributed to the violence and cyclical poverty so reflective of much reservation life.

Urban Indian people live in metropolitan areas, usually in clusters or neighborhoods; they tend to be mobile, and often constellate around urban Indian centers. *Traditional* native people, living on and off reservations, carry certain long-cherished values that include a political conservatism rooted to the concept of consensus, a respect for diversity, non-competitiveness, and a relative understanding of the importance of material wealth. *Assimilated* Indian people, although in many instances still committed to traditional roots, are those who have identified and adapted to the dominant culture in terms of goals and expectations, many of them having reached positions of social power and influence. *Militant* native groups, typified by the American Indian Movement (A.I.M.), are media conscious, politically organized, and popular among the press.

Each of the above mentioned groups reflect differing expectations and experiences which need to be respected. The terms "Native American" or "Indian" are interchangeable among most Indian people, with the exception of the Eskimo, who are very determined in distinguishing themselves from other land-based tribes. A clue in approaching groups and individuals is how they choose to identify themselves. In dealing with native people, it is wise to make as few assumptions as possible.

2. **Contrasting Values.** Working with Native Americans often entails an encounter with a subtle but intricately defined value system that is frequently troublesome and frustrating for the therapist and/or counselor. Several of these values warrant special mention.

a. Time. Attitudes toward time among Native American subcultures frequently pose a marked contrast to more dominant and pervasive understandings. Appointments, meetings, and organizational concerns find their significance in light of basic tribal understandings of what is important. From the outside this may appear as a casual disregard for more normative time structures. From the inside, it is simply a deeper respect for the seasonal and more natural unfolding of events and situations.

b. Materialism. Material goods, including money, carry a relative sense of value among most native communities. There is an emphasis on sharing, not saving. What may appear to be a disrespect for material things is frequently a more community-oriented, utilitarian understanding of possessions. Gift-giving remains a strong tradition among many native cultures and holds a central place in the psychological language, the *lingua franca* of tribal peoples.

c. Respect for diversity. Respect for another person's philosophy or opinion is a characteristic inherent in most Native American belief systems. Embracing apparently contradictory ideas and experiences is common among Indian people. One uses "what works" with an emphasis on the experiential rather than the dogmatic.

d. Family. Loyalty to family and clan is held in high regard by native people and in a counseling situation should be sensitively explored and honored. Many Indian people have been raised by members of extended families, and so it is common to hear individuals refer to grandmother or sister to designate any one of several persons. Children and animals are traditionally understood to carry special power. At most meetings, and frequently in therapeutic situations, it is not unusual for Indian people to bring their children with them. This may prove to be disruptive or uncomfortable for the pastoral counselor and needs to be dealt with in a sensitive and affirming manner.

3. Therapeutic Relationship and Intervention. In initiating relationships and responding to Native American persons, it may prove helpful to consider the following suggestions. (a) When Indian people become nervous, they frequently become quiet. In similar situations non-Indians generally talk more. This reflects an underlying commitment to non-interference that is characteristic of many native groups and individuals.

(b) Confrontation is usually not helpful. Indian people carry a strong sense of an inner world and will withdraw and appear passive to the outside observer. It is, has been, and continues to be a part of cultural survival. To enter another's inner world, one must be invited; one does not break in. This is a difficult but important concept for all who share a part of reinforcing more dominant aggressive social norms.

(c) There is often an unspoken understanding that patience and nature will heal. Pacing with an Indian client is extremely important. There is a seasonal quality to any pastoral interaction that Native American people are often more in touch with, and implicitly express through behavior and patterns of communication.

(d) The intuitive edge of native peoples has been traditionally more nurtured in the development of their communities. This is a kind of "trump card" in relationships between Indian and non-Indian persons that needs to be given appropriate consideration. It can also prove helpful in distinguishing what is a specifically native problem dealing with culture and identity, and that which may be identified as a more trans-cultural issue regarding interpersonal relationship or psychodynamic concern.

To enter into a pastoral relationship with Native American peoples is a great gift, as it is with any people, but in the Indian world it is also an invitation into a rich but dark history of institutional racism, community violence, and deep personal wounds. It is a journey of shadows, of mystery, courage, and soul. It is a good place to test one's own identity and begin to examine the ambivalent values which have so threatened the Indian people and defined non-Indians on this continent as a dominant people of conquest and power.

Bibliography. M. Craven, *I Heard the Owl Call My Name* (1973). V. Deloria, Jr., *Custer Died for Your Sins* (1969). R. Mazur-Bullis, "Pastoral Care in a Native-American Context," *J. of Pastoral Care*, 38:4 (1984), 306–9. D. McNickle, *Native American Tribalism* (1973). M. Momaday, *The Way to Rainy Mountain* (1969).

J. W. MAGNUSON

CROSS-CULTURAL PASTORAL CARE; CULTURAL AND ETHNIC FACTORS IN PASTORAL CARE. *Compare* EXPLOITATION/OPPRESSION.

NATURAL LAW. *See* MORAL THEOLOGY AND PASTORAL CARE.

NATURAL THEOLOGY. *See* EMPIRICAL THEOLOGY; PROCESS THEOLOGY.

NATURE AND GRACE. In Roman Catholic theology a distinction is commonly drawn between the situation and capacities of the human person considered as the actual or potential recipient of God's election in Christ, and the human condition as it would be if God had not called us to share in God's own personal life. In other words, the condition of the human person as actually or potentially enjoying grace is contrasted with what that condition would have been had we been left to develop our natural potentialities without supernatural intervention.

Generally, this distinction has been regarded as a theoretical distinction only. Since God first offered a share in God's own life to our first parents, human life and history has been radically shaped by the reality of that offer and humanity's refusal, in our first parents and then again in the sins of each individual. Thus, pure human nature has never in fact existed. Modern Catholic theologians, while often deemphasizing the universality of the effects of original sin, tend to place even greater emphasis on the ubiquity of the grace of Christ than did their predecessors.

Nonetheless, the distinction is significant for two reasons. Most importantly, it helps to delineate the concept of grace. Catholic theology has generally insisted that sanctifying grace brings the recipient into direct, personal fellowship with God, in the process transforming him or her into the divine likeness of God in Christ. The distinction between nature and grace underscores the fact that this transformation is not merely a development of the innate capacities of the human person, resulting in his or her perfection as a creature. Correlatively, the distinction between nature and grace serves to recall the complete gratuity of God's call to share in the divine life. Because grace goes beyond the exigencies of human life, it would not have been required for our natural perfection, and thus God cannot be said to somehow "owe" it to us. Had God not chosen to enter into our history, we would have developed in accordance with the capacities for life and happiness built into us as a natural species, in all probability without even imagining the possibilities of the life of sin and grace.

Although the distinction between nature and grace is a purely theoretical one, it seems to this author to have contributed to a distinctive set of emphases and assumptions within Catholic pastoral practice. Perhaps the most significant of these is the understanding of the sacraments as means of grace that can have a transforming effect on persons outside the usual psychological channels. This understanding has been modified, but by no means denied, by the more personalist conceptions of the sacraments that have evolved since Vatican II. Also, it should be noted that this distinction was at one time applied to the situation of children who died without baptism, and therefore, it was feared, could not enter into the direct fellowship enjoyed with God in heaven. Many theologians speculated that these children enter into a condition of natural happiness, deprived of the direct vision of God, but without any sense of loss on that account. (This was the condition often referred to as *limbo*.) However, speculations along these lines are not common today.

Bibliography. J. Alfaro, "Nature," in *The Concise Sacramentum Mundi* (1975) pp. 1028–38. H. de Lubac, *The Mystery of the Supernatural* (1967). P. Donnelly, "St. Thomas and the Ultimate Purpose of Creation," *Theological Studies*, 2 (1941), 53–83. K. Rahner, *Nature and Grace* (1964). P. Sherry, *Spirit, Saints and Immortality* (1984).

J. PORTER

GRACE AND PASTORAL CARE; HOLY SPIRIT, DOCTRINE OF AND PASTORAL CARE; HUMAN NATURE, PROBLEM OF; PERSON (Christian Perspective); SANCTIFICATION/HOLINESS. *See also* FAITH/BELIEF; INCARNATIONAL THEOLOGY AND PASTORAL CARE (Roman Catholicism); LOVE; PASTORAL THEOLOGY; SACRAMENTAL THEOLOGY; WILL/WILLING. *Compare* FREEDOM AND BONDAGE; HUMAN CONDITION/PREDICAMENT; PHILOSOPHY AND PSYCHOLOGY; SELF-TRANSCENDENCE.

NAZARENES. *See* SECTARIAN PASTORAL CARE.

NEAR-DEATH EXPERIENCE. A transcendent alteration of consciousness, similar to religious mystical states, occurring in a significant minority of persons close to death. The common pattern of near-death experiences (NDEs) includes one or more elements: ineffability; an out-of-body episode; movement through a dark void or tunnel; encounter with a sometimes-personified light of indescribable radiance; meeting "spirits" of loved ones; a feeling of encompassing all knowledge; life review; sense of boundary; decision; return to the physical body.

1. **History.** Although NDEs were known in antiquity, (cf. Book X of Plato's *Republic* and the Tibetan *Book of the Dead*), recent centuries have dismissed them as occult phenomena. In the early 1970s they were brought to public attention by Drs. Elisabeth Kübler-Ross and Raymond Moody, and have since received serious study as a legitimate area of consciousness research.

2. **Research Findings.** Systematic studies by Ring, Sabom, Gallup, and others indicate that 35–40 percent of persons who come close to death report NDEs; eight million adult Americans may be experiencers. The NDE occurs across categories of age, sex, race, education, religious belief, national origin, and precipitating clinical event. The studies substantiate earlier reports of differentiation from dreams or hallucinations, and document profound aftereffects. There is no generally accepted theory of causation or explanation for the nonreporting of NDEs by a majority of persons near death.

3. **Aftereffects.** Immediate aftereffects vary widely, including anger at being "brought back," euphoria, or anxiety about insanity. Many experiencers are unable to talk about the NDE at first for fear of being thought insane, because it seems too sacred, or because "no one could understand."

Permanent aftereffects include: (a) Loss of the fear of death; (b) pronounced shifts in values from materialistic striving toward agape, service, and acceptance of others;

(c) increased interest in spirituality, though not necessarily in formal religious observances; (d) psychic abilities; (e) a powerful sense of life purpose.

4. **Counseling Implications.** Many who have had an NDE become more self-actualizing, interpreting the experience as a powerful personal revelation of God's loving purposefulness. Those who have attempted suicide appear less likely to repeat the attempt. Conversely, as values shift, lifestyles and relationships are often disrupted. Families may need help; divorce is not uncommon. Many are bewildered by the advent of psychic phenomena or worried because their "mission" is unclear. A sense of deep isolation is frequent.

Counseling interventions may be needed for these issues, for continuing anger, and to discover new perceptions of religious belief. Careful, receptive listening is important in enabling the person to assimilate this powerful experience and to understand its implications for relationships and future decisions. After an NDE, persons often develop intuitive gifts for parish visitation or counseling, especially with the sick, the dying, or the bereaved.

Bibliography. G. Gallup, Jr., *Adventures in Immortality* (1982). C. R. Lundahl, *A Collection of Near-Death Research Readings* (1982). D. M. Moss, III, "Near-Fatal Experience, Crisis Intervention and the Anniversary Reaction," *Pastoral Psychology*, 28 (1979), 75–96. R. Moody, Jr., *Life after Life* (1975). K. Ring, *Life at Death* (1980). M. Sabom, *Recollections of Death* (1982). See also publications of International Association for Near-Death Studies.

N. E. BUSH

DEATH RESEARCH AND EDUCATION; DYING, PASTORAL CARE OF. *See also* DEATH, BIOMEDICAL DEFINITION OF; DEATH, MEANING OF; PARAPSYCHOLOGY; SURVIVAL (Occult). *Compare* DYING, MORAL DILEMMAS IN; ESCHATOLOGY AND PASTORAL CARE.

NECROMANCY/SORCERY. *See* MAGICAL THINKING; SPIRITUALISM; SURVIVAL (Occult); WITCHCRAFT.

NEED/NEEDS. Those motives which serve to maintain life; they come to the fore when one is deprived and recede when one is satisfied.

1. **Bodily Needs.** In response to a pronounced state of need-deprivation, Jesus quoted Scripture, "Man does not live on bread alone" (Lk. 4:5, Deut. 8:3, Jerusalem Bible). Many social scientists, on the other hand, have tended to exaggerate the importance of biological needs in human motivation. Freud, for example, focused much thought on the interpersonal and self-transcendent (art, religion, civilization) dimensions; yet as a reductionist he considered all behavior to be derived from bodily needs—the sources of the life and death instincts (Hall and Lindzey, pp. 39–43). Drawing upon anthropology as well as animal and human psychology, O. Klineberg (p. 164) concluded that the "absolutely dependable" motives consisted of hunger, thirst, rest and sleep, elimination, and breathing—plus the less obvious needs for activity and for sensory stimulation. He found gregarious behavior to be universal yet left it off his "absolutely dependable" list because it had no known physiological basis (1954, p. 160).

2. Broader Needs. Less concerned with biology and more interested in the variability in human motivation, H. Murray developed a list of twenty social needs (Hall and Lindzey, pp. 218–19). Included are such obvious and well-researched ones as affiliation, sex, and achievement, but also less popular ones like infavoidance (to avoid failure, shame, or embarrassment). A grouping of needs common to all organisms is inherent in R. Plutchik's (pp. 144–45) functional terms for eight "basic emotions": incorporation, rejection, destruction, protection, reproduction, reintegration, orientation, and exploration. Very popular and useful is A. Maslow's (pp. 80–92) hierarchy of needs: physiological, safety (including "a predictable, orderly world"), belongingness and love ("not synonymous with sex"), esteem, and self-actualization ("to become everything that one is capable of becoming"). Maslow also contributed the concept of "meta-needs"—those for justice, goodness, beauty, etc. He suggested that just as prolonged deprivation of the basic needs leads to physical or psychological illness, failure to meet metaneeds leads to unhealthy states such as alienation, anguish, apathy, and cynicism.

3. Needs and Religion. Psychologists of religion have sought to delineate how much of religious belief and practice can be understood as serving needs like protection, affiliation and group identity, consolation, and understanding the world. A. Godin (p. 51) notes that such "functional religion" may actually impede a person-transforming encounter with God. Yet he does not oppose religion and revelation; he argues, instead, that we all come to God with needs, but that attachment to, and identification with, Christ can take us beyond them (Godin, pp. 52, 224–30).

Bibliography. A. Godin, *The Psychological Dynamics of Religious Experience* (1985). C. S. Hall and G. Lindzey, *Theories of Personality*, 3d ed. (1978). O. Klineberg, *Social Psychology*, 2d ed. (1954). A. H. Maslow, "A Theory of Metamotivation," *J. of Humanistic Psychology* (1967), 93–127. R. Plutchik, *Emotions* (1980).

P. KELLY

MOTIVATION; PERSON. *Compare* CAUSALITY IN PSYCHOLOGY, FORMS OF; EATING AND DRINKING; HUMAN CONDITION/ PREDICAMENT.

NEEDS, PASTOR'S. *See* PASTOR, PASTORAL CARE OF. *See also* FRIENDSHIP, PASTOR-PARISHIONER; MARRIAGE AND FAMILY LIFE, PASTOR'S; MENTAL HEALTH, PASTOR'S; PRAYER AND WORSHIP LIFE, PASTOR'S.

NEO-EVANGELICAL PASTORAL CARE. *See* EVANGELICAL PASTORAL CARE.

NEOFREUDIAN PERSONALITY THEORIES AND PASTORAL CARE. In a departure from traditional Freudian psychoanalytic theory, the neofreudians emphasized the sociocultural and interpersonal aspects of personality development and structure.

The neofreudian movement developed out of tensions and dialogue with traditional Freudian psychoanalytic theory. Believing humans to be more than biophysical, closed systems, these theorists moved towards understandings grounded in the social sciences. Utilizing concepts of Alfred Adler (1870–1937), Erich Fromm (1900–80), Karen Horney (1885–1952), and Harry Stack Sullivan (1892–1942), the neofreudians have greatly influenced pastoral care, particularly in America, between the fifties and the late-seventies. While only Sullivan was American born, the others arrived in America in the early to mid-thirties, bringing with them the beginnings of a social analytic approach as an alternative view of the human person. Each theorist contributed uniquely to pastoral theology, yet some common themes emerged.

The cultural, academic, and clinical milieu provided the context for this alternative perspective which had as its most consequential difference from psychoanalytic theory a predominant consideration of the dynamics of culture in personality. Following Adler, these theorists viewed with unprecedented earnestness the human being as a social creature who developed in the midst of a culture which impacted, influenced, and shaped life. It is this element which attracted pastoral theologians such as Seward Hiltner and Wayne Oates. The neofreudians initiated a radical shift in pastoral care as Hiltner and Oates began to look beyond the traditional psychoanalytic perspectives of the human to the person as a social creature.

Anxiety was understood as the negative outcome of the human attempt to deal with tensions in society. While there were individual differences in their perceptions, the neofreudians agreed that a major source of anxiety was the incongruency between individual striving for health and the alienation present in society. Karen Horney and Erich Fromm provided the most helpful insight for those within the pastoral community. Pastoral care attempted to address the anxiety of individuals by attending to the social environment.

The neofreudians considered not only the way in which culture impacted human personality, they actively participated in efforts to alleviate social anxiety and create a cultural environment for positive mental health. Utilizing Fromm's *The Sane Society* and *Escape From Freedom*, Horney's *Neurotic Personality of Our Time*, and Sullivan's activity in the "World Federation for Mental Health," the neofreudians sought to positively affect culture and its power in shaping human character. These ideas were embraced by pastoral theologians as they encountered structures in society and the institutional church. From this orientation pastoral care began to concern itself with institutional evil as well as social alienation.

The humanistic tendencies of the neofreudians fostered a renewed sense of optimism and concern for holistic growth. Pastors encouraged persons toward optimal growth as part of the care-taking of self and others. This emphasis reached its climax in the human potential and self-realization movement of the sixties and seventies.

The neofreudian influence was also apparent in the praxis of pastoral care and counseling via the therapeutic process itself. Harry Stack Sullivan provided the greatest impact in this arena as pastoral theologians began to link the interpersonal approach and Sullivan's conception of the process of counseling with the practice of pastoral care and counseling. His knowledge that development occurred in interaction with others has continued to be an important motif within the pastoral care and counseling literature. Sullivan's seven life periods, however, were of somewhat less import. Here glimpses of the emerging importance of developmental theory for pastoral care can be seen.

The influence of the neofreudians has been quite significant in pastoral care in America. Their reframing of the human creature as a social being, their more optimistic understanding of humanity, and their concern and critique of the social context of one's life have been integrated in the literature of pastoral care. At the same time critics claim that neofreudians sacrifice a profound view of human life when they set aside Freud's insights into the unconscious bases of human action and substitute superficial views of wholeness which lack clinical depth.

Bibliography. E. B. Holifield, *A History of Pastoral Care in America: From Salvation to Self-Realization* (1983).

J. L. MARSHALL

INTERPERSONAL THEORY. *Compare* EGO PSYCHOLOGY AND PSYCHOTHERAPY; HUMANISTIC PSYCHOLOGY *or* PSYCHOANALYSIS AND PASTORAL CARE; SELF PSYCHOLOGIES. *Biography:* ADLER; FROMM; HILTNER; HORNEY; OATES; SULLIVAN.

NEOORTHODOX THEOLOGY AND PASTORAL CARE. *Neoorthodoxy* identifies a broad theological movement which began in 1918 with Karl Bath's commentary on Romans and continued to dominate the theological scene until the sixties. The movement included Karl Barth, Emil Brunner, Rudolph Bultmann, Paul Tillich, Dietrich Bonhoeffer, Reinhold and H. Richard Niebuhr, and others less influential in the U.S. These theologians had in common the conviction that the idealistic liberalism that prevailed in the nineteenth century was unable to explain or deal with the brutal realities of the twentieth century. They believed that only a return to the theology of the Reformation and the Bible could offer a realistic and authentically Christian understanding of God and human life in a time characterized by the dehumanizing consequences of the industrial revolution, World War I, the Great Depression, World War II, and the ideological clash between Marxist East and capitalistic West.

Neoorthodox theologians differed, however, in the extent to which they rejected liberal theology and in their interpretation of Reformation and biblical theology. All of them respected scientific-historical views of the Bible, and agreed with the liberal conviction that the Christian faith has to do with the meaning of history rather than with impersonal theological truths and propositions. But they differed in their evaluation of other fundamental presuppositions of liberalism. Moreover, for some of them "return to the Reformation" meant return primarily to the theology of Luther, while for others it meant return primarily to the theology of Calvin. These differences led to significant disagreements within the movement and make it impossible to speak of a single neoorthodox answer to theological questions.

People responsible for pastoral care today are still challenged by some critical issues that emerged from the neoorthodox criticism of liberalism and from the differences within the neoorthodox movement itself.

1. **Human Potential and Divine Potential.** Liberal theologians had great confidence in the ability of human beings to achieve self-fulfillment and to improve the world. They justified this confidence by appealing to the immanent presence of God in human rationality, religious intuition, pious self-awareness and moral sensitivity. Neoorthodox theologians, accusing liberalism of confusing the divine and the human, emphasized the finitude and sinfulness rather than the godlikeness of human beings. The hope of neoorthodoxy for individual and social life was not hope in the help God-in-dwelled human beings can give themselves and others but in the judgment of God against all the pretensions of human wisdom, power, virtue, and piety; and in the grace of God that does indeed work in and through human beings but is not to be confused with their own capacities and achievements. The insights of neoorthodoxy continue to contribute to pastoral care that seeks both to be an instrument of God's healing grace and to be realistic about the limited ability of pastors to enable, and recipients of their care to achieve, human wholeness.

2. **Revelation and the Knowledge of God.** Emphasis on the transcendent hiddenness of God led all neoorthodox theologians to insist that God is known only through God's self-revelation. They disagreed, however, in their convictions about how and where this revelation takes place. Some (like Barth and Bultmann) insisted that while God is present and at work everywhere, we can recognize and know God only through Christ and the revelatory events of Scripture. Others (like Brunner, Tillich, and the Niebuhrs) believed that there is a partial, preparatory "general" or "natural" revelation of God in the order of the natural world, in history in general, and in the structures of human life and society. Whether and to what extent there is a general or natural revelation, and if so how it is related to specifically biblical-Christian revelation, continues to be an important issue for theologians and pastors today as they seek to find the right "point of contact" for thinking and speaking about God in relation to human life in the world.

3. **Truth and Relevance.** Like all theologians before them, neoorthodox theologians sought both to preserve biblical-Chrisitan truth and to show its relevance for the thought and life of their time. But, like theologians before them, they found it difficult to fulfill both tasks at the same time. Some (like Barth and Brunner) had more affinity for protestant orthodoxy, which in its attempt to preserve "objective" Christian truth tended to ignore questions about the relevance of traditional Christian teaching. Others (like Tillich and Bultmann) had more affinity for liberalism, which tended to compromise distinctive Christian truth in the attempt to make it compatible with the knowledge and subjective experience of "modern man." The strengths and weaknesses of these theologians continue to help pastors today who seek to make sense to people in contemporary society without simply supporting whatever happens to be their psychological and cultural presuppositions and their personal and social goals.

4. **The Addressees and Language of Theology.** Neoorthodox theologians concerned especially about the relevance of the Christian faith believed (following Schleiermacher) that theology must be addressed to the

"cultured despisers of religion" and that traditional theological language must therefore be translated into philosophical, psychological, or cultural language that is meaningful to such "outsiders." Those especially concerned about the preservation of biblical-Christian truth believed that the task of theology is first of all to reinterpret and correct classical theological language and concepts to enable Christians "within the theological circle" to be faithful witnesses to the Christian gospel in the twentieth century. Although the shape of the debate between apologetic and kerygmatic theology has changed, pastors today still struggle with the advantages and dangers of these fundamental alternatives as they were developed by neoorthodox theologians.

5. **Interpersonal Relationships and Life in Community.** Neoorthodox theologians believed that human selfhood is realized in human relatedness. Some (like Bultmann), depending on the categories of existentialist philosophy, emphasized the fulfillment of authentic human existence in personal "I-Thou" relationship with God and other human beings. Others (like Barth, Brunner, Tillich, Bonhoeffer, and the Niebuhrs) emphasized the fulfillment of authentic human existence in responsible participation in human community—in the church and in the political and economic structures of civil society. Especially in the context of American religious and secular individualism, the question of the relationship between individual self-fulfillment and social solidarity remains a critical problem.

6. **God's Grace as Acceptance and as Transformation.** Neoorthodox theologians of the Lutheran tradition (like Bultmann) emphasized that God's grace accepts us just as we are and frees us from the necessity of having to do or achieve anything to make ourselves worthy of God's and other's love and acceptance. Neoorthodox theologians influenced by the Calvinistic tradition (like Brunner, Barth, and Bonhoeffer) also knew about this "justifying" grace of God but believed that it leads to passivity, self-centeredness and irresponsibility unless it is complemented by an emphasis on the "sanctifying" grace of God that confronts and exposes human sinfulness and requires and enables changed lives. The neoorthodox revival of this classical Lutheran-Calvinist debate still reminds pastors of the danger of emphasizing one form of grace without the other, and of the importance of both "being" *and* "becoming" for authentic human existence.

Bibliography. A. I. C. Heron, *A Century of Protestant Theology* (1980). H. Zahrnt, *The Question of God: Protestant Theology in the 20th Century* (ET 1969). M. E. Marty and D. G. Peerman, eds., *A Handbook of Christian Theologians* (1965).

S. C. GUTHRIE

PASTORAL THEOLOGICAL METHODOLOGY. *See also* REVELATION AND PASTORAL CARE; THEORY IN PASTORAL CARE AND COUNSELING, FUNCTIONS OF. *Compare* EMPIRICAL THEOLOGY, EXISTENTIALISM, LIBERATION THEOLOGY, *or* PROCESS THEOLOGY, AND PASTORAL CARE; PSYCHOANALYSIS AND THEOLOGY; THEOLOGY AND PSYCHOTHERAPY. *Biography*: BARTH; BONHOEFFER; BRUNNER; BULTMANN; NIEBUHR, H. RICHARD; NIEBUHR, REINHOLD; TILLICH.

NEOPLATONISM. *See* MEDIEVAL CHURCH, PASTORAL CARE IN; PHILOSOPHY AND PSYCHOLOGY, WESTERN.

NERI, ST. PHILIP (1515–95). Roman Catholic priest, spiritual leader, provost of the Church of the Roman Oratory.

Ordained in 1551, he shared, for several years, with other priests the ministry at the Church of S. Girolano della Carita, where he instituted an innovative form of pastoral care: he augmented his excellent ministry of confession with informal talks, discussions, prayers, and fellowship events for the further instruction and sanctification of the penitents.

In addition to his humility, gaiety, personal attractiveness, and fervent commitment to Christ, his spiritual leadership seemed of such quality that several of his followers organized a religious community for prayer, lecturing and preaching, Holy Communion, and fellowship. Now known as the Oratory because of its high musical productivity, Neri served as its first provost. He continued to maintain a high spiritual profile attracting many advice-seeking visitors, including cardinals and others influential in church government. In this position, Neri is credited with exerting significant influence during the Counter-Reformation.

N. F. HAHN

SPIRITUALITY (Roman Catholic Tradition).

NERVOUS BREAKDOWN. *See* PSYCHOSIS. *See also* DEFENSE AND COPING THEORY; MENTAL HEALTH AND ILLNESS.

NERVOUS SYSTEM. *See* BRAIN RESEARCH.

NETWORKS. *See* RELATIONSHIP NETWORK.

NEUROLOGIC ILLNESSES, PASTORAL CARE IN. Neurologic illness refers to an organic insult to the central nervous system resulting in physical and/or mental impairment. This may be the consequence(s) of an infectious disease as in the case of a brain abscess; the progressive effects of a degenerative disease such as Alzheimer's, Parkinson's, or Huntington's Chorea; or, the presence of a cerebrovascular disease as might be manifested through a stroke. Although widely varied as to causation, neurologic illnesses present a common cluster of behavioral symptoms that are dependent upon the intensity, progression, and nature of the particular diagnosis. Such effects as the following are observed: memory disturbances, demanding behaviors, aphasia and other difficulties with communication, suspiciousness, depression, anger, refusal to eat, wandering, inappropriate sexual behavior, poor hygiene, and physical violence. The impact of these diseases reaches beyond the patient to family members, who frequently become the primary caregivers.

1. **Stroke.** *a. Symptoms and consequences.* Not all neurologic illnesses are easily diagnosed in their early stages. Frequently symptoms "look like" something less serious and may be ignored. However, one of these, the stroke, provides a good reference point for appreciating the impact on patients and families. According to the National Stroke Association, every year more than half a million people suffer a stroke in the United States. One

third of these will die within a month. The other two-thirds will have some degree of permanent impairment. There are approximately two million persons living with stroke sequelae in this country. It is the third leading cause of death, and the number one cause of adult disability.

Since the majority of strokes occur to those over age sixty-five, they frequently are found along with other illnesses and complications associated with the aging process. A stroke (also called cerebrovascular accident or CVA) occurs when the flow of blood to the brain is interrupted by either a blockage (clot) or rupture (aneurism) in the vessel. The affected part of the brain begins to die. The extent of the damage and the area impacted determine the symptoms. Frequently these are paralysis, speech and language deficits, memory loss, perceptual difficulties, and behavioral changes. These symptoms may be transient or permanent. The first six months following a stroke are crucial in determining what "losses" can or cannot be recovered.

b. Psychological reactions. During the immediate period following the onset of a stroke, especially when there is loss of speech or sensory functions or massive paralysis, the patient is likely to experience deep fear, bewilderment, and anxiety about the future. Those who begin to experience early recovery, on the other hand, may experience euphoria, often while still hospitalized.

The reality of what has happened awaits discharge to either home or a rehabilitation center. Of primary importance in providing pastoral care is the recognition of the psychological concerns secondary to the physical impairments. What is the general meaning of the disease to the patient? How does the patient understand the specific physical losses and their day-to-day consequences? What are the effects on body image? How has status and role within the family and community been altered? The patient's physical and emotional health prior to the illness will provide a clue to the illness-related behaviors. However, impairment in brain functioning may cause the person to act in ways beyond his or her ability to control. These behaviors must be understood by the family as symptoms of the disease itself and not as intentional behavior by the patient. In many ways, stroke patients are persons who have been victimized by their own bodies.

c. Family reactions. This victimization extends beyond the patient to the family. Studies have found a number of problems present in the family-as-caregiver: anger, physical exhaustion, depression, guilt, grief, accusations toward and from relatives, a more restrictive lifestyle, and a sense of being trapped. The neurologic illnesses that are degenerative will rapidly introduce grief and bereavement issues. For example, the premature mental deterioration of Alzheimer's disease has a quality of fear, hopelessness, and helplessness attached to it that is difficult to manage. There is no chance that the patient will improve. Increasingly regressive and frequently dangerous behaviors characterize both the present and the future. Death usually occurs in seven to ten years. However, the disease can progress more rapidly (three to four years), or more slowly (up to fifteen years). Institutionalization is frequently the only "treatment" available.

d. Pastoral care. Although pastoral care will begin at the time of the initial crisis, its value will become more evident as the patient *and* family learn to cope with small changes and long-term hopes. The needs of the family cluster around its role as caregivers. First, they will need accurate information as to the nature of the illness and its present and future consequences. Second, being linked up with other families in similar situations will provide an invaluable network of peer support. Third, the presence of medical support for both the routine and for emergency situations is essential. Fourth, the inevitable need for respite care can be met through the recent development of organizations providing day care for adults. Fifth, there will need to be professional input from outside the immediate context. The suddenness and/or apparent irreversibility of the illness may make it difficult for the family to assess the situation accurately. Because of this, the patient can easily become the entire focus of the family. Accurate information about family relationships prior to the illness is invaluable.

As a rule, the needs of the recovering patient will, to a great degree, be consistent with those of the family. (1) The patient needs to know the exact diagnosis and, if possible, the prognosis. (2) The patient needs to know that treatment is available and how "successful" this has been in others with similar diagnoses. (3) Since disablement can be a time of reassessment, the patient needs to believe that each therapeutic intervention is a symbol of hope, a statement of faith about the future. (4) With present-day skills in rehabilitation, the patient must not be allowed to remain isolated and alone in front of a TV set. Solitude and boredom are two major enemies in "recovery" for the chronically ill person. Both feed into the depression that can be as crippling emotionally as the illness is physically. Even seriously handicapped stroke patients can make significant progress toward becoming self-sufficient. (5) The patient will need assistance in adjusting to the numerous specialists that will become a part of the routine — neurologists, neurosurgeons, physical therapists, occupational therapists, and other specialists in rehabilitation. The needs of the particular patient must be considered very carefully. What does the patient want most? Is it realistic? If not, is there an alternative that fits into the patient's worldview?

Effective ministry will involve: (1) An understanding of the disease itself. Check with the appropriate organizations. Be sure the parishioner has up-to-date and accurate information. Read what the patient reads. These illnesses will bring many families and patients into contact with medical and religious "quacks." (2) An understanding of the person who is now sick. What was she or he like prior to the illness? How well did she or he cope with routine crises? What was your prior relationship? Minister? Friend? Stranger? This will matter greatly. (3) An understanding of the family dynamics. The minister is in a unique position to have access to this information. (4) A theological "understanding" as to how major illnesses may be viewed in relation to God's intentions for creation.

Catastrophic illnesses like strokes are painful reminders of human finitude and frailty. Reactions to the loss of sensory capacities and motor function become intermingled with experiences of confusion, terror, helplessness, and anxiety over potential non-recovery and/or death. Normal patterns of relating to the world are compromised. Faith perspectives are radically altered. Pastoral care requires a focused and intentional presence of the caregiver, including the physical presence of the minister and the symbolic presence of the community of faith. The "tactile" nature of many religious rites and rituals can have major impact on the ones who are struggling with recovery or even anticipating death. For example, the human touch in the "laying on of hands," or the fragrance of the oil used for anointing become powerful and adjunctive reminders of the presence of God. And God's grace is indeed a major dynamic in the entire process of recovery, both physically and spiritually, as this "changed" person learns to reclaim his or her place in life.

2. **Degenerative Diseases.** The crippling effects of a diseased brain are especially devastating as the person deteriorates faster than his or her "physical" organism. Degenerative brain disorders, such as Alzheimer's and Huntington's, are particularly insidious in their impact on patient and family. Their major characteristic is dementia. Dementia is an acquired syndrome that produces a significant decline in intellectual functioning and compromises such essential mental activities as language, memory, visuospatiality, abstracting abilities, and judgment.

In their *early phase,* signs of beginning dysfunction may be so subtle as not to be noticed even by family members. Memory gaps, for example, may be attributed to a preoccupation with other matters. Those around him or her may "compensate" for these developing deficits. The *middle phase* intensifies the symptoms so that they can no longer be ignored. The person may become disoriented and confused. Anxiety and frustration increase as wider areas of life become more unmanageable. With the *final phase* the person loses the ability to care for self. All of the behaviors and idiosyncrasies by which he or she has been identified are lost to the degenerative processes.

a. Alzheimer's disease is one of the four major causes of death (the others being heart disease, cancer, and stroke) in the American adult population. Although it seems to have a direct correlation to aging, the disease has been found among persons in their forties. The earlier it appears, the more virulent its effects. The character of the symptoms reveals the unique crises inherent in the diagnosis. *Early on,* the patient will experience memory loss, lack of initiative, and a general difficulty in coping with the most routine tasks. In the *middle phase* there will be an increase in memory loss, passivity, wandering, incontinence, severe problems in communicating, etc. With the *final phase* the person becomes bedridden, requiring constant care. Even though plateaus may occur in which there seems to be improvement, this "terrible thief of minds" will continue unabated. The average life span from diagnosis to death is seven to nine years.

b. Huntington's disease has triadic clinical picture of chorea, dementia, and a history of family occurrence. This idiopathic disorder appears in the fourth and fifth decades of life. In contrast to Alzheimer's, deterioration is seen more in the emotional and social behaviors. The impact on cognitive functioning is typically slower and less dramatic. Although apathy may characterize the *early phase,* emotional instability, impulsivity, and explosive outbursts are frequently observed. The usual

presence of a depressive illness correlates with the high rate of suicide and suicide attempts found among those with this diagnosis. Personality changes may "mimic" psychiatric disorders. Persecutory delusions are common. Unique choreiform movements give this disease a distinctive description: jerky and bizarre movements of head and limbs, involuntary contortions of facial muscles giving an appearance of grimacing or "leering," rolling of eyeballs. Each of these are intensified with stress or excitement. As with other degenerative diseases of the brain and central nervous system, there will be a steady decline in the ability to deal with day-to-day life. Death usually occurs within fifteen years of onset.

The suggestions for pastoral care as discussed in the first part of this article are also applicable here. However, the major difference is that these patients will die from an incurable disease. Thus, issues in grief, bereavement, and loss become paramount. There are six additional interventions that must be made. First, although the disease cannot be cured, the symptoms and "suffering" can be treated. Be sure that the patient has a thorough neurological workup. Second, pay close attention to those providing primary care. They need to be actively involved in each step of the treatment, assessment, and planning. With Huntington's, genetic counseling is recommended. Third, take particular note of the emotional devastation that may occur in the family members: bitterness, grief, anger, shame, disgust, hopelessness. Fourth, the patient may not initially appear "sick" to those outside the immediate environment. Supportive counseling will be essential. Fifth, an anthropology and theology that incorporates the diseases that rob one of his or her humanness will be required for the pastoral caregiver. Sixth, the recognition of the phases of the diseases will be the key to appropriate pastoral responses.

Bibliography. I. S. Cooper, *Living With Chronic Neurologic Disease* (1976). J. K. Glickstein, *Therapeutic Interventions in Alzheimer's Disease* (1988). J. Lavin, *Stroke: A Family Guide from Crisis to Victory* (1985). N. Mace and P. Rabins, *The 36-Hour Day: A Family Guide to Caring for Persons with Alzheimer's Disease* (1981). R. Moos, ed., *Coping With Physical Illness: New Perspectives* (1984). National Stroke Association, *The Road Ahead: A Stroke Recovery Guide* (1986). R. Rabin, *Six Parts Love: A Family's Battle with Lou Gehrig's Disease* (1985). G. D. Weaver, "Senile Dementia and a Resurrection Theology," *Theology Today,* 42 (1986), 444–56. J. W. Worden, *Grief Counseling and Grief Therapy* (1982).

G. BROCK

LOSS OF FUNCTION; SICK, PASTORAL CARE OF. *See also* HEALTH AND ILLNESS; MEMORY; PATIENCE/PATIENTHOOD; PRESENCE, MINISTRY OF; SUFFERING. *Compare* CHRONIC ILLNESS; HANDICAP AND DISABILITY; MENTAL HEALTH AND ILLNESS; MENTALLY RETARDED PERSONS; MIND-BODY RELATIONSHIP; PERSONALITY, BIOLOGICAL DIMENSIONS OF.

NEUROPSYCHOLOGY. *See* BRAIN RESEARCH.

NEUROSIS. A somewhat outmoded diagnostic term that designates varying combinations of behavioral, emotional, and cognitive features considered intermediately severe in the range of psychological disturbances. While this term once was assumed to denote a specific entity, today it is considered ambiguous, and its usefulness is widely questioned. Various attempts to explain a common causation have proven either too inclusive or too restrictive to gain general agreement. Clinically, the term is now used to indicate a condition that distresses the affected individual but does not totally disrupt functioning or thinking. Contact with reality remains intact, and behavior is fairly reasonable. Anxiety is an important feature of the condition, but anxiety may or may not be in evidence depending upon measures taken by the individual to prevent its appearance. These measures often consist in behaviors that by their presence determine the type of neurosis diagnosed.

1. **History.** By the onset of the twentieth century, medicine, following the discovery of the infectious causation of many diseases, was making great strides in classifying illnesses according to the causative agent responsible. Psychiatry had hopes of doing the same. The search developed along two lines: (1) to define clinical syndromes that appeared with regular features, (2) to search for causes common to all cases of a defined class. It became clear that a group of disorders did not have an obvious biological cause. This group was called "functional" because the disorders within it were felt to result only from psychological causation. Contained in this group was a collection of disturbances that while distressing to the individual left the person reasonably able to relate and to carry on daily activities. These became known as the neuroses.

Freud, still hoping that someday a biological defect would prove decisive in defining these disorders, nonetheless undertook to define their cause. He postulated that the root of the problem was a conflict between an impulse to do something and an injunction not to. He felt that the offending impulse occurred in the context of an experience reminiscent of childhood and was largely outside of conscious awareness. Such conflicts, he believed, resulted in anxiety. Either the anxiety itself or measures taken by the individual to avoid it were seen as constituting the behavioral manifestations labeled "neurotic."

2. **Current Diagnostic Usage.** Freud's explanation of the condition became virtually synonymous with the term "neurosis" but was universally accepted for only a brief period. Soon others became impressed with its *adaptive* significance: neurotic behaviors as efforts to change something in one's environment. By the time current diagnostic categories appeared (as those found in the Diagnostic Statistical Manual of Mental Disorders— DSM III), the term had become limited, descriptively, to conditions that: (1) are distressing to the affected individual, (2) leave the person in touch with reality, (3) are enduring or recurring, (4) are not necessarily connected with immediately identifiable stressors, (5) include behaviors that are not terribly bizarre, (6) are not demonstrably organic in nature.

The severity of a condition may be determined on the basis of two factors: how much disruption occurs in the individual's life and how long the condition lasts. The degree of disruption is judged by the condition's effect upon work, play, and relationships. Obviously, a condition may effect any one or all of these in any combination; thus the degree of disruption is a sum of these changes in relation to the condition. One's judgment must, of course, be relative to what one normally expects to see in life. If a person has experienced a major, recognizable, recent source of stress (e.g., moving, death in the family, new baby), we can say that the present distress is a normal "adjustment reaction." If, however, the stressor is small and the reaction is more disruptive, the condition is more appropriately termed a "neurotic disorder"; and if the condition results in totally disrupting almost everything, it is probably a "psychotic" disturbance. Thus current usage suggests a spectrum of degrees of severity with the neurotic conditions occupying a central position.

Duration of disturbance also is considered in the total picture. As a rule, the briefer the disorder, the lesser the seriousness. However, a history of similar episodes in the past is suggestive of a neurotic condition.

Crown (1976), in his survey of neurosis, still treats the term as descriptive of a defined class of disorders. He specifies the types as anxiety, depressive, phobic, obsessive-compulsive, hysterical, depersonalization, and hypochondriacal. The label of each type indicates the disordered behavior predominantly observed. Treating each of these types as "classical," the following description correlates Crown's typology with current categories in DSM III:

Anxiety neurosis is a condition satisfying the general characteristics of neurosis. Behavior is dominated by the presence of anxiety, which the individual reports as a feeling of nervousness, fright, panic, or a sense of dread. The anxiety may be experienced relatively constantly or intermittently and is considered distressing to the individual. DSM III classifies this condition under "anxiety disorders."

Depressive neurosis is a condition, again satisfying the general characteristics of neuroses, which is dominated by reported feelings of depression, sadness, unhappiness, disinterest, lethargy, or dissatisfaction. However, one may use clinical judgment in the absence of such reports to determine that clients who have histories of lethargy, loss of interest, trouble sleeping, loss of appetite or irritability are depressed, for these are considered common symptoms of the condition. DSM III classifies this state as "dysthymic disorder."

Phobic neurosis is a neurotic condition in which an individual unreasonably fears one or more things and seeks to avoid them. The avoidance usually causes a problem in functioning and results in further distress. The prevalence and visibility of this disorder make it vulnerable to publicity, and it is reported with greater frequency when receiving attention in the media. It is classified in DSM III as "phobic disorder," one of the anxiety disorders.

Obsessive-compulsive neurosis occurs rarely without some degree of disruption, suggesting a more serious condition than simple neurosis. It is dominated by ritual-like behavior in thought or action that the individual reports as the problem. The performance of the ritual is felt to be out of one's control, exerts great pressure to be performed, and is felt to recur without meaning. Often these behaviors have a quality of doing and undoing. It is possible that the condition is not as "fashionable" as it once was and is now seen less frequently. It is classified as "obsessive-compulsive disorder" in DSM III.

Hysterical neurosis as a designation is rarely used in current practice. It used to indicate a group of conditions characterized by what appears to be a medical problem but does not have a demonstrable medical cause. .The problem is reported as a medical disorder by the affected individual (e.g., a paralyzed limb, no feeling in part of the body, blindness, loss of memory, headache, and so forth), and medical attention is sought. While the cause of this condition is understood to be psychological, the individual with the complaint usually must be confronted with a medical opinion that the condition is not biological. Even then this may not be accepted, and the search for a doctor who will treat the condition as organic continues. DSM III now classifies this group of disturbances as "somatoform disorders" and "dissociative disorders."

Depersonalization neurosis is a condition that is rather rare. Since the symptom occurs so often in conjunction with anxiety, the affected individual is usually diagnosed as having an anxiety disorder. In its pure form, the disturbed individual simply reports feeling strange, different, or changed. The body or self-experience of the individual is perceived in an unusual way (e.g., some portion of the body may be felt to be abnormal in size or in its characteristics of movement). DSM III retains this diagnosis under dissociative disorders as "depersonalization disorder."

Hypochondriacal neurosis is a condition in which an individual is overly concerned with bodily disease. The appearance of this condition often indicates other more serious psychological disturbances or even real and serious physical disease. It is now classified under "somatoform disorders" in DSM III.

Bibliography. S. Crown, "Neurosis: General Survey," in S. Krauss, ed., *Encyclopaedic Handbook of Medical Psychology* (1976). American Psychiatric Association, *Diagnostic and Statistical Manual of Mental Disorders* DSM III (1980). R. R. Grinker, "Neurosis, Psychosis, and the Borderline States," in A. M. Freeman, H. I. Kaplan, and B. J. Sadock, eds., *Comprehensive Textbook of Psychiatry* 2d. ed. vol. 1 (1975). L C. Kolb, *Modern Clinical Psychiatry* 9th ed. (1977). L. S. Kubie, "The Nature of the Neurotic Process," in S. Arieti, ed., *American Handbook of Psychiatry* 2d. ed. vol. 3 (1974). J. Menninger, M. Mayman, and P. Pruyser, *The Vital Balance* (1963). J. D. Page, *Psychopathology* (1975).

H. A. SELVEY

MENTAL HEALTH AND ILLNESS. *See also* ANXIETY; DIAGNOSTIC AND STATISTICAL MANUAL III; EVALUATION AND DIAGNOSIS, PSYCHOLOGICAL; HYSTERIA; OBSESSIVE-COMPULSIVE DISORDER; PSYCHOPATHOLOGY AND RELIGION; PSYCHOPATHOLOGY, THEORIES OF; SADNESS AND DEPRESSION. *Compare* ADJUSTMENT DISORDERS; BORDERLINE PERSONALITY; PSYCHOSIS.

NEW AGE RELIGION. *See* FAITH HEALING; NEW RELIGIOUS MOVEMENTS.

NEW RELIGIOUS MOVEMENTS. Sometimes called cults, refer to various religious and quasi-religious groups and movements that have developed significant followings among predominantly white middle-class youth of America since the mid-sixties. Some are communal, some resemble more traditional congregational forms, and some are more like practitioner-client relationships. Although the Jesus Movement groups have developed variations on Christian theology and practice, some significant new religions derive their major impetus from Eastern traditions, from other sources outside the Christian tradition, or a combination of these sources. Most have developed on the West Coast of America, and then spread eastward across America, some even into other countries. Some scholars claim that as many as 2,500 new religious groups of various types have developed in America within the past two decades, and that hundreds of thousands of young Americans have participated in them, at least for a short time. Some of them have developed large memberships or clientele, and collect large amounts of money, but most are relatively small and have meager resources. Some of the more prominent (and at times controversial) new religions include the Unification Church ("Moonies"), the Children of God/Family of Love, the Hare Krishna, Scientology, Transcendental Meditation, the Divine Light Mission, the Way International, and Rajneeshism.

Considerable controversy has surrounded new religious movements (NRMs), focusing on recruitment methods, ways they raise and spend money, and some of their beliefs and practices. These controversies have resulted in the development of a strong reactionary movement referred to as the anti-cult movement, and to the development of a questionable tactic of rigorous resocialization, deprogramming, used by some trying to extract a person from a new religion and return him or her to a more normal and acceptable lifestyle. Because of the controversy a number of levels of government and the courts have become involved in monitoring and attempting to control the new movements.

1. Why People Join the New Movements. The new religions should be viewed within the context of the American historical pattern of great general interest in religion, and the waves of revivalism that have occurred sporadically throughout American history. Particularly during times of social stress, Americans have often sought solutions to personal and social problems by turning to religion. The present rapid growth of interest fits this pattern, with some significant modifications, including the number of the major newer religions which draw their inspiration from outside the dominant American culture, and the attraction of many of the relatively affluent young in our society to the movements. Many commentators have suggested that the movement of large numbers of the most educated young people into new religions is in part a rejection of American cultural values by these youth. This view seems reasonable, even if other factors are operating, and even if the rejection is usually only temporary and partial.

During the sixties, when media first began attending to newer religions, the largest generation of American young people in both absolute and proportional terms came of age. These people were reaching adulthood in a society torn by racism, the Vietnam War, and assassinations of several heroic figures. Drug use and other types of social experimentation were prevalent. Many of the young were actively seeking answers to questions of cultural legitimacy, and some decided to affiliate with groups that appeared to offer a new interpretation of life. Thus, many of America's most educated and affluent youth experimented with the new religions, even if most left them after a relatively short time.

The fact that this type of person has joined in large numbers has led some to claim that they must have been "brainwashed" or are suffering from some sort of "mind control." Such pseudo-scientific terms have been used as "social weapons" against new groups with practices and beliefs markedly different from those of traditional churches. Most social and behavioral scientists who have researched new religions reject claims that brainwashing or mind control takes place and instead suggest that fairly normal social processes are operating. People who are dissatisfied with their lives are looking for alternatives to furnish them with a human community or surrogate family and a different set of beliefs and practices. Often a more authoritarian living situation is chosen, in reaction against the more libertine lifestyle that many have been living in terms of their sexual and drug-related behaviors. Communal groups offer a totalistic lifestyle and thus have appeal to those more estranged from normal society.

2. **The Nature of Conversion to NRMs.** This recognition that most who join the movements are searching young people has led to a new understanding of conversion to the new groups. Social scientists now stress the transitoriness of affiliation with such religious groups, and use such terms as *conversion careers* to refer to the pattern of trying out several different groups for shorter periods of time. There is recognition that attrition rates are high for nearly all the groups, and that a very small proportion of youth are affiliated at any one time, even if a significant number of young people have participated at one time. Although emotion may well enter into the decision to join a certain group, it appears that most people are making rational decisions to try out a new lifestyle. They are "shopping around," and the group is "on trial," as the person negotiates with the group and its leaders about what must be done to be a member in good standing.

One key conclusion of a number of social scientists who have studied this process concerns the relationship of beliefs and behavior. A traditional view of conversion includes the idea that significant cognitive change occurs initially, and then behavioral changes follow. However, many of those who are trying out the new religions apparently have *decided to behave* as new members to "try out" the group, and, if they like what they find, then a more gradual shifting of beliefs and behaviors occurs. Although there are some "true believers" in newer movements, it now appears that most of those who "flow through" the new movements are not of this type, even if they act like fully committed members by being involved in proselytizing and fund-raising for the groups.

3. **What Happens to Those Who Join.** As just indicated, most who join leave after a few weeks or months in the groups and move back into conventional life, or they join yet another group or movement. However, some do stay for lengthy periods of time, and considerable attention has focused on these long-term members, often to the exclusion of the others aforementioned. Social and behavioral scientists who have used standardized instruments of personality assessment on group members along with other researchers who have done survey and participant observation on the new groups, are nearly unanimous in concluding that being in the groups has ameliorative effects on most members. Data are accumulating which indicate that most groups are effective in relieving drug and alcohol addition, and in solving sexual-related problems. Many are searching for something different when they contact the groups, and they are coming from lives that evidence considerable personal disorganization. The groups furnish these individuals with a structure, a community of others, and a set of beliefs that provides new meaning to the members. Marc Galanter, a psychiatrist who has done a number of studies on members of various new religions, has focused especially on what he calls the "relief effect" of joining these groups, and has speculated about why such groups are so effective in modifying behavior. His interest derives from a desire to apply to the therapy situation knowledge gained about how new religions so effectively modify behavior.

Some sociologists have focused on the reintegrative function of new religions, pointing out that many of the groups serve as "halfway houses" for people returning to normal society. Some of the new groups and movements do attempt to isolate their members and protect them from outside influences, but even in those instances the long-term effect of joining the groups for many people may be to learn discipline, some job skills, and gain a new perspective on life.

4. **Problems With New Movements.** Not everyone gains materially or is made into a better citizen through the experience in the new movements, and not everyone who joins gains self-confidence and job skills. But no systematic research has demonstrated that membership fosters mental illness and that members cannot function as normal human beings. A minority of members do have difficulty readjusting to normal society when they leave the groups. This seems to be the case particularly with some who have been "deprogrammed." The forced extraction of a person from one of the new groups is a risky action because it may have long-lasting negative effects, particularly on those estranged from the ones responsible for the deprogramming effort. Caution should be taken in trying to extract a person from one of the new religions. Some youths may be using the new religions as a way of expressing independence from family, and to use mental or physical coercion in such situations could have lasting negative impact.

5. **Ministering to Families of Members.** Related problems concern the impact on families of having a family member join the new movement. Although many parents accept this action, some do not, and this can lead to a crisis within the family unit. Pastors and therapists may be required to counsel with the family members on how best to respond to this situation. Extreme care is needed in this situation because of possible negative reactions on the part of those who have joined to strong pressure from parents. Efforts should be made to discuss more general issues such as the freedom of religion of the member, while at the same time expressing sympathy and offering guidance about responding to the immediate "problem" of the family having "lost" a member to a new religion. Remind the family that attrition rates for such groups are high, and their own loved one will probably leave the group within the foreseeable future. Encourage them to maintain contact with the family

member, and always communicate that the member is loved and is welcome if he or she wants to return home.

Bibliography. D. Bromley and J. Richardson, *The Brainwashing/Deprogramming Controversy* (1988). D. Bromley and A. Shupe, *Strange Gods* (1981); *The New Vigilantes* (1980). R. Ellwood, *Alternative Altars* (1979); *Religious and Spiritual Groups in Modern America* (1973). M. Galanter, *et al.*, "The 'Moonies': A Psychological Study of Conversion and Membership in a Contemporary Religious Sect," *American J. of Psychiatry*, 136:2 (1979), 165–69. C. Glock and R. Bellah, *New Forms of Religious Consciousness* (1976). J. G. Melton and R. L. Moore, *The Cult Experience* (1982). J. Richardson, *Conversion Careers* (1978). J. Richardson and B. Kilbourne, "Cults Versus Families: A Case of Misattribution of Cause?" *Marriage and Family Review*, 3/4 (1982), 81–100; "Psychotherapy and New Religions in a Pluralistic Society," *American Psychologist*, 39 (1984), 237–51. T. Robbins and D. Anthony, *In Gods We Trust* (1981). S. Tipton, *Getting Saved from the Sixties* (1982). J. T. Ungerleider and D. Wellisch, "Coercive Persuasion (Brainwashing), Religious Cults, and Deprogramming," *American J. of Psychiatry*, 136:3 (1979), 279–82. R. Wuthnow, *The Consciousness Reformation* (1976); *Experimentation in American Religion* (1978).

J. T. RICHARDSON

CONVERSION; DEPROGRAMMING. *See also* CULTURAL ANTHROPOLOGY OF RELIGION; PSYCHOLOGY IN AMERICAN RELIGION; PSYCHOLOGY OF RELIGION; RELIGION; RELIGIOUS BEHAVIOR; SOCIOLOGY OF RELIGION. *Compare* CHURCH-SECT DIFFERENCES IN PASTORAL CARE; COMMITMENT.

NEW TESTAMENT, TRADITIONS AND THEOLOGY OF CARE IN.

The NT for the most part consists of writings aimed at the moral, religious, and theological formation of people relatively young in the faith. The pastoral methods in these writings were indebted to Jewish and Graeco-Roman traditions. The latter were highly developed and widely used in the culture of the time. The Gospels describe the ministry of Jesus in a manner that relates him to the church's needs; Paul's letters are themselves forms of pastoral persuasion; and Paul's successors to various degrees adapt his practice to the needs of the consolidating church.

1. **The Context of NT Practice.** *a. Jewish.* See OLD TESTAMENT AND APOCRYPHA, TRADITIONS AND THEOLOGY OF CARE IN.

b. Graeco-Roman. Pastoral care in the Graeco-Roman tradition was part of a rich and wide-ranging enterprise known as psychagogy, which also included what we mean by spiritual exercises, psychotherapy, and psychological and pastoral counseling. Developed by philosophers concerned with human moral formation, psychagogy aimed, through character education, at the attainment of virtue and happiness, an achievement of which one could justly be proud. Elements of the endeavor are found as early as Socrates, but a more highly developed system was created by Epicurus (fourth century B. C.), and by the first century A. D. was in common use by philosophers of all persuasions.

Moral philosophers were viewed as physicians of sick souls, and their goal was to benefit their hearers by bringing them to their senses. This they sought to accomplish by frank speech, with which they laid bare the human condition and pointed to the rational life as the way to attain fulfillment of one's potential as a human being. These philosophers performed their tasks in public and in private, in the marketplaces and in homes, schools, philosophical communities, aristocratic salons, and the imperial court. The topics that occupied them ranged as widely as human experience, including such concerns as marriage, the rearing of children, old age, death, happiness, grief, anger, joy, modesty, pride, dissipation, and self-control. While the content of what they said remained quite traditional, responsible philosophers adapted themselves to the social circumstances and emotional conditions of the persons they sought to help, and gave serious attention to the approaches and methods most likely to result in their benefit.

The forms in which they engaged themselves in others' lives extended from private sessions with individuals through talks with small groups, to letters to individuals or larger groups, open letters, and tractates. In addition, they often spoke and wrote of their understanding of the enterprise itself and their role in it. This tradition of pastoral care was therefore not confined to private contexts, nor was it the province of one professional class. The moral philosophers developed the manner in which such care was exercised, and it is their writings which reflect at greatest length on it, but there is ample evidence that they also served as models whom non-philosophers emulated.

2. **Jesus.** *a. The Gospels as evidence.* Modern critical study of the NT has established that, before the Gospels were written, the traditions about Jesus which they employed had already been adapted to the church's needs. The Gospels therefore reflect, in the first instance, the church's conceptions of Jesus rather than that of Jesus himself. Nevertheless, the church continued to be challenged by Jesus, and the Gospels are themselves evidence of the church's constant effort to conform to the person and teaching of its Lord, and of the restraint with which it worked on the Jesus traditions. The multiple sources of the Gospels contain sufficient evidence to allow us a picture of some characteristics of Jesus, that of the church's Pastor or Shepherd (Jn. 10:11–12, 16; I Pet. 2:25, 5:4).

b. Jesus' goal. The center of Jesus' concern was not human moral education, as it was with the Greeks, but the Kingdom of God. Jesus acted with an authority that set him apart from other people (Mk. 11:27–33) and was not shared even with his disciples (Mt. 23:8–12). As the recipient of divine revelation, he proclaimed the good news of the Kingdom, the message of God's active, concrete ruling in human affairs (Mt. 12:28), known primarily in God's forgiveness of sins (Lk. 15:11–32). His emphasis on God's initiative and action did not minimize human responsibility, but threw new light on it. Confronted by God's invitation, listeners could no longer rest secure in their presumed personal relationship with God, nor might they delay decision, but had to respond instantly (Mt. 22:1–14). Acceptance of the good news of the Kingdom entailed a change in values and a rejection of attempts to hold onto both human merit and divine mercy (Mt. 20:1–16). It required confidence in God (Lk. 11:5–10) and a perspective which conceived of the Kingdom as both a present and future reality

(Lk. 17:20–21; Mk. 9:1; Lk. 13:28–29). Jesus' pastoral approach was informed by this message.

c. The compassion of Jesus. In some of his parables Jesus drew attention to God's mercy that attends the coming of the Kingdom (Mt. 18:23–35; Lk. 10:29–37, 15:11–32). The Gospels describe Jesus as the exemplification of that compassion. In response to the objection that he associated with tax collectors and sinners, he replied, "Those who are well have no need of a physician, but those who are sick. Go and learn what this means, 'I desire mercy and not sacrifice.' For I came not to call the righteous but sinners" (Mt. 9:12–13, cf. 12:7, 23:23). Thus, what determined Jesus' relationship with people, even those whom he called to form the inner circle of his disciples, was not scrupulous legal interpretation that might separate him from outcasts, but mercy and compassion that recognized their need.

According to the Gospels, Jesus' compassion was manifested in a variety of ways in his ministry. Because he viewed the throng of people around him as sheep without a shepherd, out of compassion he taught them (Mk. 6:34), and for the same reason he sent the twelve on their limited mission to preach the message of the Kingdom (Mt. 9:36–38). Jesus' compassion also led him to meet the physical needs of those who came to him, as when he fed the four thousand (Mt. 15:32–39; Mk. 8:2–10), and when he healed the sick (Mt. 14:14). When a leper expressed his trust in Jesus' power to heal him, Jesus compassionately did so (Mk. 1:41). Mark is explicit that a plea for compassion must issue from faith in Jesus (Mk. 9:21–23).

It is especially in Matthew that the mercy of Jesus comes to the fore and that he is presented as a model of compassion to the believing community. As the Suffering Servant who takes infirmities and diseases upon himself, Jesus exorcizes demons and heals the sick (Mt. 8:17). As the Servant who gives his life for many, he provides an example to those who would be leaders (Mt. 20:20–28). A practical demonstration of what it meant for Jesus to be the Suffering Servant is provided by the story of the healing of the two blind men, which immediately follows the discussion of leadership. When the blind men ask him for mercy, Jesus out of pity restores their sight (Mt. 20:29–34).

Compassion is also an essential quality in the relationships between members of the community. In chapter 18, Matthew describes Jesus as discussing the community's responsibility to its offending members and stressing the need to forgive them (see f., below). By way of elaboration, the parable of the unmerciful servant (18:23–35) then makes the point that forgiveness does not depend on calculation of someone else's obligations, but on a deep awareness of one's own forgiveness by God. The experience of God's mercy, which is beyond calculation, should enlarge the disciples' capacity to forgive each other (cf. Lk. 6:36). Rather than self-vindication, the appropriate response to a petition for patience is not calculated postponement of the day when impossible obligations are to be met, but compassion that forgives.

d. Jesus' methods of communication. Jesus performed mighty deeds, taught, preached, and polemicized, but did not engage in pastoral care narrowly con-

ceived. Yet some characteristic ways in which he communicated are of interest to us.

i. Parables. Jesus frequently used parables to bring about a change in people's normal perceptions. In their present form, parables sometimes deliver a moral lesson, but their original function can still be discerned. Luke 12:13–21, for example, contains a lesson against greed, but Jesus places the vice in the perspective, not of legal rights, but of one's relationship with God and his actions. The parables contain strong elements of surprise, as when they deal with the unexpectedly imminent Kingdom (Mk. 13:28–29), or the capacity for growth (Lk. 13:18–19), or joy (Lk. 15:3–32). They were frequently used by Jesus to reverse people's values (Lk. 10:30–37, 16:19–31), but not to the degree that human responsibility was removed (Mt. 22:1–14). They call for decision (Mt. 25:1–30; Lk. 14:28–32), but conceive of human action as grounded in the nature of God, who is ready to heed human needs (Lk. 11:5–8, 18:2–5).

ii. Questions. Jesus was Socratic in that some of his questions drew correct answers from his listeners, thus impressing the answers more effectively on them (Mt. 17:24–27, 21:28–32), but the authority that he claimed for himself and with which he spoke set him apart even from Jewish teachers (Mt. 7:28–29). Jesus frequently responded to hostile questions with questions of his own to show up his opponents' inconsistency (Mk. 2:24–26, 12:13–17) or the weakness of their case (Lk. 5:29–32). Confronted by a hostile attitude not expressed in questions, Jesus himself might, with questions of his own, focus the issue (Lk. 14:1–6). Of perhaps greater importance to his pastoral method was his use of questions when he was confronted by what he considered inappropriate. In replying to an inappropriate request, he might reject it with a question which embodied his reason for doing so, continue with a warning that revealed the real, ignoble reason for the request, and tell a parable to amplify his response and bring about a change in perspective (Lk. 12:13–21). In such an instance, his question sharply lodged his point and formed the transition to his treatment of the deeper problem. Related to this use of a question is Jesus' response to a request made with the wrong attitude. In the parable of the Good Samaritan, for example (Lk. 10:29–37), the parable exposes the self-righteousness of the lawyer, and Jesus' concluding counter-question (vs. 36) reformulates the issue. His rhetorical questions frequently were designed, not to evoke a verbal response, but to express his exasperation (Mk. 9:19), add weight to what he was saying (Mt. 5:13, 7:9–10), or to secure his listeners' assent (Mt. 7:16; Lk. 15:8).

e. Jesus and the Individual. The story of Jesus and Zacchaeus (Lk. 19:1–10) illustrates one way in which he fulfilled his mission in his encounter with an individual, and the story may have served the church as a paradigm of pastoral care. As in stories of other encounters (e.g., Mk. 10:17–22; Lk. 7:36–50), it is not Jesus who first takes the initiative. Zacchaeus has to overcome social, religious, and physical difficulties in order to see Jesus (cf. Mk. 2:3–5). He was not motivated by faith, but by simple curiosity about Jesus (vs. 3). Jesus initiates the actual encounter and invites himself into Zacchaeus's house, thus underlining the unusual nature of his mission. His action meets with the disapproval of the self-righteous crowd (vss. 5–7). What is noteworthy in this encounter is that it is not Jesus' words, but his actions which transgress against the conventional understanding of religious law and result in a response that transcends the strict requirements of that law (vss. 8–10).

Jesus' encounter with the Samaritan woman (Jn. 4:7–30) is a classic example of his dealing with a hostile person whom he wishes to benefit. Unlike the incident with Zacchaeus, here it is Jesus who initiates the encounter and relentlessly pursues his goal by engaging her in a dialogue. The evangelist recounts the story to say something about Jesus' self-disclosure to and acceptance by the Samaritans. From the perspective of pastoral care, however, the story is instructive for the way in which it presents Jesus as overcoming the woman's defenses in his goal to help her attain her own spiritual good. The dialogue is occasioned by a simple request for a drink of water (vs. 7), which the woman cuttingly rejects on the basis of race, religion, sex, and social convention (vs. 9). Jesus refuses to be deflected by these barriers, but replies by speaking of the gift of God (vs. 10). The woman then raises a practical objection (vs. 11), and again turns *ad hominem*. Undaunted, Jesus enigmatically offers *her* the water of eternal life (vss. 13, 14). She now turns sarcastic, daring him to give her that water (vs. 15). Finally, Jesus focuses on her (vs. 16), and her evasive reply (vs. 17) does not turn him from revealing his knowledge of her personal circumstances (vss. 17, 18). She acknowledges that Jesus is a prophet (vs. 19), but tries once more to divert him by now introducing a religious issue (vs. 20). Jesus replies by asserting that a new order of things is at hand, which renders her objection irrelevant (vss. 21–24). When she retorts that it is the Messiah who would reveal all things (vs. 25), Jesus claims to be the Messiah (vs. 26). It is not explicitly said that the woman believed his claim, but it may be implied in her announcement to the people of what Jesus had disclosed about himself, which then brings about their faith (vss. 29, 39). Eventually, however, they believe because of what they themselves hear (vs. 42).

f. Jesus and the community. Matthew 18 reveals how one writer, and perhaps the church with which he was associated, understood how Jesus' pastoral concern was to be expressed in the Christian community. Jesus is presented as beginning the discourse by stressing the need for humility rather than a concern about prominence in rank (vss. 1–4, cf. 20:20–28, 23:1–12). Probably with church leaders in mind, responsibility towards members of the community is asserted (vss. 5–9), particularly toward individuals who may be held in low esteem (vss. 10–14). The integrity and value of the individual are also the theme in the discussion of the community's discipline. The primary concern should be to preserve the offending member, and to bring this about, a procedure along Jewish legal lines (cf. Deut. 19:15–21; I QS 5:25–6:1) is to be followed which requires private (vs. 15) and semi-private (vs. 16) steps before the entire community becomes involved (vss. 17–20). Nevertheless, Jesus' message of forgiveness remains the guiding principle: in spite of the concern to maintain group boundaries by the disciplining procedure outlined, Matthew concludes the discourse by stressing the

need to forgive offending members of the community as God has forgiven all (vss. 21–35).

3. **Paul.** *a. Paul's goal.* Paul has a view of Christian formation that is quite unlike the Graeco-Roman one with its understanding of character education. He does not think that the Christian progresses to virtue as innate human potential is fulfilled through reason and self-discipline. He rather views Christian existence from different, interrelated theological perspectives. He believes that God predestined those whom he called to be conformed to the image of his Son (Rom. 8:29). This formation requires an intellectual transformation which rejects conformity to the world and aims at discerning the will of God (Rom. 12:1–2). In addition to these theological and christological dimensions, there are others. The Holy Spirit is active in this transformation (II Cor. 3:18), which takes place within an eschatological perspective (II Cor. 4:16–18). There is, furthermore, an ecclesial dimension, for Paul does not conceive of personal growth as separable from membership in the Christian community. The called share collectively in a partnership with Christ (I Cor. 1:9) and the Holy Spirit (II Cor. 13:14), in grace (Phil. 4:14), and sufferings and comfort (II Cor. 1:7). Paul considers his own function to be the upbuilding of the body of Christ, that is, the nurture of the church in Christ (II Cor. 10:8, 13:10, cf. 12:19), or, as he exclaims in Galatians 4:19, using the image of a pregnant mother, "My little children, with whom I am again in travail until Christ be formed in you!"

b. Paul's method: in person. While Paul's letters primarily witness to his pastoral method when he was separated from his churches, they do provide glimpses into his life and approach when he was with them. Among his letters, I Thessalonians may serve as our main source, for it was written to people who had been Christians for only a few months and in whose minds Paul's sojourn was fresh, and whose circumstances called for pastoral exhortation and comfort rather than doctrinal explication or correction.

i. Founding the church. Paul's opponents did not think highly of his oratorical ability (II Cor. 10:10), and he seems to have agreed that he was not a skilled speaker (II Cor. 11:6). He rather stressed the content of his preaching (II Cor. 4:5; I Thess. 1:9–10) and his conviction that God through the Holy Spirit was active in bringing his listeners to faith (I Cor. 2:1–5; I Thess. 1:4–5, 2:13). The theological perspective for his later nurture of his converts was thus already formed as people accepted the message. It should be appreciated what becoming a Christian meant to people like the Thessalonians. In addition to the religious and theological reorientation they underwent, they experienced social dislocation and, in many cases, psychological trauma, with a pervading sense of isolation or, in the language of Jewish proselytes, a feeling of having been orphaned from their families, friends, patriarchal traditions (cf. I Pet. 1:18), as well as rejection by the society in which they had been reared. These were also the experiences of converts to Judaism, and it is not surprising that Paul's letters and the methods of care they represent betray an awareness of them.

ii. Nurturing the church. As important as Paul's initial missionary preaching and his continuing theological instruction were, it is striking how frequently he gives indications that in establishing a church he equally stressed behavior. Intellectual reconstruction was an ongoing process, but it was engaged in as part of the total process of forming the behavior and growth of the individual and the community. At the center of the effort stood the person and example of Paul.

Paul's demeanor did more than provide a concrete example of what he taught, in the manner of moral philosophers who required that one's deeds conform to one's words. Paul describes the Holy Spirit as active in both his preaching and his hearers' acceptance of it, and in making them joyful in their afflictions. In this they became imitators of Paul and the Lord (I Thess. 1:5–7). It was more than a practical method to organize the church around himself, for to Paul it was theologically unthinkable that his converts might be independent of him (cf. I Cor. 4:14–21). Yet Paul stresses, and the mood of I Thessalonians confirms it, that in drawing the converts into a community around himself, he did so with gentleness rather than on the basis of his prerogatives as an apostle (I Thess. 2:6–7; cf. II Cor. 10:1), and that, although his demeanor was designed to offer them an example to follow (II Thess. 3:6–9), it was equally designed not to burden them or impede the progress of the gospel.

In describing his original pastoral work with his converts, Paul repeatedly makes use of Graeco-Roman psychagogic traditions, and there is no reason to assume that his comments are due to literary convention and do not reflect his actual practice.

In the first century, scores of individuals took up the role of the moral guide whose frank speech would heal the masses. Some of them saw the essence of that frankness in brutal excoriation of all human shortcomings, and considered any gentleness in a speaker a sign of weakness or lack of integrity. In response, more humane philosophers reflected at length on the proper nature of courageous outspokenness. Plutarch, for example, agreed that frankness is salutary and necessary, but insisted that it be applied properly, and in his discussion used the image of the nurse to illustrate his point that frankness should be modulated and used at the correct time. "When children fall down," he wrote, "the nurses do not rush up to berate them, but pick them up, wash them, and straighten their clothes and, after all this is done, then rebuke them and punish them" (*How to Tell a Flatterer from a Friend*, 69 B.C.). Paul uses the technical language of such discussions when he refers to his courageous outspokenness in Thessalonica (I Thess. 2:1–2), and also uses the image of the gentle nurse who croons over her charges instead of being rough with them (I Thess. 2:6–8). This was the correct psychagogic approach to his converts. Paul differs from his contemporaries, however, not only in the way he introduces his relationship with Christ and the gospel of God into the discussion, but especially in his perception of his method as a giving of himself to his converts.

Another aspect of the philosopher's care is also reflected in Paul. The true philosopher was more kindly disposed toward those he would benefit than even to a father, brothers, or friend. He would nevertheless not shrink from admonishing or exhorting them. On the other hand, he would be discriminating in deciding when to speak and what speech would be appropriate.

While the responsible philosopher would always safeguard his own integrity, he would give attention to individuals and vary his speech according to the conditions of the persons he addressed. He would lead people to virtue by adopting different means of persuasion, "on some occasions persuading and exhorting them, on others reviling and reproaching them, . . . sometimes taking an individual aside privately, at other times admonishing them in groups" (Dio Chrysostom, *Discourse* 77/78.41–42). Paul, too, had a special relationship with his converts which led to similar personalized care: ". . . you know how, like a father with his children, we exhorted each one of you and encouraged you and charged you to lead a life worthy of God, who calls you into his own kingdom and glory" (I Thess. 2:11–12). Again Paul's psychagogic method is the same as that of the genuine philosopher, but his goal is not virtue, rather a life worthy of God, which is placed within an eschatological perspective. This preparedness to adapt himself to people whom he attempted to gain for the faith was characteristic of Paul (cf. I Cor. 9:19–23), despite the charges of his opponents that he was inconsistent and without integrity (II Cor. 10:1–2, 10; Gal. 1:10).

The Thessalonians had suffered for their new faith (I Thess. 1:6, 2:14), and in addressing this issue Paul in at least one respect is like the philosophers. Seneca writes repeatedly on the proper attitude toward hardships. One remedy that he stresses is that one should not be surprised by misfortune. "What, have you only at this moment learned that death is hanging over your head, at this moment exile, at this moment grief? You were born to these perils. Let us think of everything that can happen as something which will happen" (*Moral Epistles* 24.15). "Therefore, nothing ought to be unexpected by us. Our minds should be sent forward in advance to meet all problems, and we should consider, not what is wont to happen, but what can happen. For what is there in existence that Fortune, when she has so willed, does not drag from the very height of its prosperity?" (*Moral Epistles* 91.4). Affirming that misfortunes were in the very scheme of things and were due to arbitrary fate, and that one way to vanquish them was to anticipate them, was a standard part of consolation.

Paul had also prepared the Thessalonians for the hardships that they would endure. Having heard that they were again suffering, he had sent Timothy to establish them in their faith and exhort them not to be moved by their afflictions. "You yourselves know that this is to be our lot. For when we were with you, we told you beforehand that we were to suffer affliction; just as it has come to pass and as you know" (I Thess. 3:2–4). Once again, Paul's psychagogic technique has affinities with those of the philosophers, but the theological framework within which it is applied is radically different. Paul does not attribute Christian experience to arbitrary fate, nor does he advise stoic impassivity or think that victory over the difficulties is purely an attainment of the rational person. On the contrary, it is God, who has their salvation in mind, who has a hand in their affairs (cf. I Thess. 5:9). That is why he is so concerned about their faith. For Paul it is faith that makes a new relationship with God possible and allows us to perceive a significance in our sufferings that results in joy (cf. Rom. 5:1–5; I Thess. 1:6). In his own experience, it was the comfort he had experienced when in dire straits, that enabled him to comfort others (II Cor. 1:3–11).

Such features in Paul's work allow us to see how he as an individual worked with his converts and how he understood that work. But a major thrust of his work was to form a community which exemplified the principles he taught and would continue his work of pastoral care. Thus, after their conversion he taught them to love one another in obedience to God, who had loved them (I Thess. 4:9, cf. 1:4). It is striking how often Paul's instructions have to do with relationships within the church. Even sexual morality is discussed as it relates to the rights of others in the community (I Thess. 4:6). That formation of a strong sense of community would foster a feeling of belonging in those converts who had been wrenched from their former security is understandable. Paul, however, was equally concerned that Christians not form a ghetto (cf. I Cor. 5:9 – 10), but that their love for one another provide the basis for their relationship to the larger society (I Thess. 4:9 – 12, cf. 3:12).

c. Paul's method: in his letters. Paul was frequently forced to leave his newly founded churches before they were firmly established (cf. Acts 13:42–52, 17:5–8, 13–14), and sometimes was prevented from returning to them later to continue his work (I Thess. 2:17–18). Such separation weighed heavily on Paul (e.g., II Cor. 10:2, 11; Gal. 4:20; Phil. 1:27, 2:12; cf. II Cor. 11:28) and sometimes caused strained relations with the churches (e.g., II Cor. 1:15–2:4). One way in which he attempted to overcome the problem was through the use of his co-workers as intermediaries (e.g., I Cor. 4:16–17; Phil. 2:19–24), another was through letters. Letter writing was a well-established means of communication, and was self-consciously discussed by writers. A letter was defined as one half of a dialogue, regarded as a substitute for one's physical presence and expected to be written in a style appropriate to the aim the writer sought to achieve. Letters had come to be used in the psychagogy of individuals by writers like Seneca, and of his communities by Epicurus. Although Paul in many ways is unique as a letter writer, there were therefore precedents to his use of letters as instruments of pastoral care. First Thessalonians is the best example of such a Pauline letter, and shows how in the letter Paul built on his previous experience with the Thessalonians.

The first striking thing about the letter is the ways in which Paul stresses personal relationships. He refers to himself as an apostle only once, and then to disavow any special standing which apostleship might confer on him (2:6). Rather, he is a nurse (2:7), father (2:11), or orphan (2:17; RSV: "bereft"), who yearns to see them as they do him (3:6, 10). The heavy use he makes of personal pronouns, frequently in conjunction with each other, further demonstrates that Paul views his role as pastoral director as one that is formed by the intertwining of his and his converts' lives. The family language extends further. The Thessalonians are called brethren eighteen times in this short letter, and God is called father four times. They are, further, imitators of Paul (1:6), his hope, joy, glory, and crown of boasting (2:19–20). The combination of this emphasis on relationships rather than authority or hierarchical positions with the affective

language throughout the letter and the many different terms for varieties of exhortation sets the tone for the letter and is precisely what one would expect in an ancient (and modern) pastoral letter to a situation like that in Thessalonica.

The manner in which Paul exhorts his readers by way of reminder (2:9, cf. 3:6), or to references to what they already know (1:5, 2:1, 5, 3:4, 4:2, 5:2), or by saying that they need no further instruction (4:9, 5:1), but only need to continue in what they are already doing (4:1, 10, 11), is part of the same pastoral style which assumes a warm relationship between the two parties and seeks to strengthen confidence. It, too, is the style frequently adopted by moralists. Pliny (*Epistle* 8.24.1) provides an example: "The love I bear you obliges me to give you, not indeed a precept (for you are far from needing a preceptor), but a reminder that you should resolutely act up to the knowledge you already have, or else improve it." But once again, while Paul adopts the style from his contemporaries, he puts it to service in the expression of his conviction that the behavior he inculcates is pleasing to God, and that his precepts are given through Christ (e.g., I Thess. 4:1, 2, 9). And when he gives directions on marriage, his stress is not on the concrete behavior he demands, with which many moralists would agree, but on sanctification, which frames his advice, and on other theological motivations for Christian behavior (4:3–8).

Paul's religious and theological perspective thus informs his pastoral care and marks the difference between him and his contemporaries. This is nowhere so clear as in his prayers. Four prayers punctuate I Thessalonians. The first two are thanksgivings which set the tone of the letter. In 1:2-3 he expresses genuine thanks for the Thessalonians' faith, hope and love, but in doing so introduces themes to which he returns later in the letter. It is thus clear that the prayer itself performs a hortatory function. To slightly different degrees this is also true of the other three prayers which occur at strategic points in the letter (2:13, 3:11–13, 5:23, cf. 3:9–10). The pastoral care in which Paul engages in the letter is not only couched in a style that conveys a sense of immediacy to his readers; it is offered in the presence of God, to whom Paul turns in thanksgiving and petition.

d. The Christian community. Paul feels a special responsibility to his converts, but as during his time with them he had been at great pains to develop a community, so in his letter he continues to foster that communal sense and to impress on them their responsibilities to each other. For Paul the community is not simply a social entity, but is a creation of God's love (1:4–5) which will continue to the parousia and beyond (3:11–13). It is noteworthy, then, that each time Paul takes up a specific matter, he discusses it in terms of the Christians' concern for each other (4:6, 9, 17–18, 5:11).

His final directions of this nature (5:12–515) are particularly significant for our interest. Whereas elsewhere he had engaged in pastoral care, here he treats the way members of the congregation should be responsible for each other. In the preceding verse, already he had directed them to encourage one another and build one another up (5:11). The moralists' and his own interest in the individual is thus also laid on the congregation. So is the concern with the proper relationship between those extending and those receiving pastoral care (5:13), and especially his urging that the treatment be appropriate to the conditions they aim to better: "And we would urge you, brothers, to admonish the careless, encourage the faint-hearted, support the weak, and to be very patient with them all" (5:14 NEB). Just as Paul describes his own pastoral care in terms of relationships, so does he theirs. There is no interest here in any particular office, but rather in functions that are performed by persons who continue Paul's pastoral activity.

4. Paul's Successors. The later writings of the NT generally do not reflect, as clearly as Paul's letters do, the church's actual practice of pastoral care. Increasingly confronted by doctrinal crises, the church in defense became more highly structured and tended to relegate certain functions to particular offices in the church. While an overstatement, it is true to say that these writings represent greater interest in doctrinal, institutional and moral consolidation than in the pastoral care that we assume continued to take place.

Acts 20:17–35 provides a view of Paul's pastoral work that contains some of the elements that characterized Paul, but also marks changes characteristic of the later period. First, the apostolic farewell address is a charge to the church leaders who are called elders (vs. 17) and bishops (vs. 28; RSV: "overseers"), appointed by the Holy Spirit to pastor (vs. 28; RSV: "care for") the church. This function is confined in these writings to apostles (Jn. 21:15–17) and elders or bishops (I Pet. 5:1–2). The apostolic paradigm that Luke sketches, and that the leaders are to follow, is familiar: Paul had been outspoken in public, in homes, and to individuals, and had provided them with an example of self-sacrifice of which he could remind them. The entire discourse, however, is shaped by the expectation of the imminent arrival of heretics, and we gain little information on exactly how the leaders are to feed the flock.

The Pastoral Epistles, despite their traditional nomenclature, offer a very similar picture. Beleaguered by heresy, the church is structured as the supporter and defender of the truth with no regard for the appropriateness of when the message should be preached or convincing, rebuking or exhortation be engaged in (II Tim. 4:2), and, even when the responsibilities of Timothy (I Tim. 4:11–16) and Titus (Tit. 2:7–8), or their gentle demeanor (I Tim. 6:11; II Tim. 2:24–26) is described, the author has the battle against heretics in mind. There are exceptions in this literature, which do reflect on the pastoral care of the congregation (e.g. Heb., 13:7, 17; I Pet. 5:1–5), but the main tendency is to make the traditions of pastoral care that we have discovered serve the developing ecclesiological interests and needs.

Bibliography. F. W. Beare, "St. Paul as Spiritual Director," *Studia Evangelica* II, F. L. Cross, ed. (1964), 303–14. R. Bärenz, ed., *Gesprächs-Seelsorge* (1980). T. Bonhoeffer, *Ursprung und Wesen der christlichen Seelsorge,* Beiträge zur evangelischen Theologie, 95 (1985). D. Capps, *Biblical Approaches to Pastoral Counseling* (1981). E. W. Chadwick, *The Pastoral Teaching of St. Paul* (1907). S. Dill, *Roman Society from Nero to Marcus Aurelius,* 2d ed. (1956). I. Hadot, *Seneca und die griechisch-römische Tradition der Seelenleitung* (1969). A. J. Malherbe, "Gentle as a Nurse," *Novum Testamentum,* 12 (1970), 203–17; "Medical Imagery in the Pastoral Epistles," *Texts and Testaments,* W. E. March, ed. (1980), 19–35; "Exhortation in First Thessalonians," *Novum Testamentum,* 25 (1983), 238–56; "In Season and Out of Season," *J. of Biblical Literature,* 103 (1984), 235–43; *Paul and the Thessalonians: The Philosophic Tradition of Pastoral Care* (1987). N. Perrin, *Rediscovering the Teaching of Jesus* (1967). P. Rabbow, *Seelenführung* (1954). E. E. Shelp and R. Sunderland, eds., *A Biblical Basis for Ministry* (1981). R. S. Sullender, "Grief and Growth: Perspectives from Life-Span Psychology and Pauline Theology," Ph.D. Diss., Claremont, 1978; "Saint Paul's Approach to Grief," *J. of Religion and Health,* 20 (1981), 63–74.

A. J. MALHERBE

JESUS; MINISTRY (Biblical Origins and Principles). *See also* BIBLE, PASTORAL USE AND INTERPRETATION OF; BIBLICAL ANTHROPOLOGY, DISCIPLINE OF; COMPASSION; PASTORAL CARE (History, Traditions, and Definitions); *also* CHRISTOLOGY; CREATION; ECCLESIOLOGY; ESCHATOLOGY; GOD; PROVIDENCE; SALVATION, HEALING, AND HEALTH. *Compare* JEWISH CARE AND COUNSELING; OLD TESTAMENT AND APOCRYPHA; *also* EDUCATION, NURTURE, AND CARE; PSYCHOTHERAPY.

NEW THOUGHT. *See* MIND-CURE MOVEMENT; HISTORY OF PROTESTANT PASTORAL CARE (United States); JAMES, WILLIAM.

NEW YORK PSYCHOLOGY GROUP. A group of eminent theologians and psychotherapists which met monthly in Manhattan during World War II to discuss the relationship between religion and mental health. Calling themselves "the New York Psychology Group" (NYPG) and keeping their by-invitation-only meetings confidential, they met to exchange ideas in an intellectual forum. Erich Fromm, Seward Hiltner, Rollo May, David Roberts, Carl Rogers, and Paul Tillich were the most prominent members. Others included Ruth Benedict, Harry Bone, Gotthard Booth, Violet de Laszlo, Harrison Elliott, Elined Kotschnig, Otis Rice, and Frances Wickes.

Particularly important for vital dialogue was the intentional mix of persons: Freudian and Jungian, American-born and European-immigrant, Christian and Jew, professor and student, male and female. During a time of global warfare what they shared in common was a conviction about the critical importance of their conversations. They studied theoretical issues in theology and psychology with a practical objective: human progress. Each academic year the program committee chose a theme and members presented formal papers to focus discussion: the Psychology of Faith (1942), the Psychology of Love (1942–43), the Psychology of Conscience (1943–44), and the Psychology of Helping (1944–45). The seminar met under the auspices of the National Council on Religion in Higher Education.

The NYPG is of incalculable importance for the development of pastoral care and counseling, which blossomed in the postwar era partly as a result of the influence of its members.

Bibliography. A. Stokes, *Ministry After Freud* (1985).

A. STOKES

PASTORAL CARE MOVEMENT; PSYCHOLOGY IN AMERICAN RELIGION. *Biography:* FROMM; ELLIOTT; HILTNER; MAY; ROBERTS; ROGERS; TILLICH.

NEW ZEALAND PASTORAL CARE MOVEMENT. *See* AUSTRALIAN AND NEW ZEALAND PASTORAL CARE MOVEMENTS.

NIEBUHR, H. RICHARD (1894–1962). American theologian. H. Richard Niebuhr has proven to be one of the most durable and influential of twentieth-century American theologians. Each of his seven major books remained in print in the eighties, more than twenty-five years after his death. In 1988 an eighth book, *Faith on Earth,* was posthumously published. Niebuhr taught and influenced more persons who are and have been influential in North American theological education than any other American theologian. He served on the faculty of Eden Theological Seminary (1919–22) and as its academic dean (1927–31), as president of Elmhurst College (1924–27), and as professor of ethics at Yale Divinity School (1931–62). At Yale he became director of Graduate Studies in Religion in 1953 and received the Sterling professorship in Christian Ethics (1954). From 1954–56 Niebuhr headed the American Association of Theological Schools' study of theological education in the U.S. and Canada.

The principal hallmark of Niebuhr's theological thinking is its way of holding together and in tension a powerful insistence upon the sovereignty of God, on the one hand, with sustained illuminative inquiry into the texture of human personal and corporate experience, on the other. In this regard he can rightly be described as working theologically "between Schleiermacher and Barth." Niebuhr utilized the work of philosophical, sociological, and psychological interpreters of human experience. He anticipated a great deal of contemporary work in critical social theory, hermeneutics, and structural developmental theories in psychology. But he kept his use of these perspectives and methods under the control and in the service of theological commitments. In many ways he is a precursor of what, in the eighties, has come to be called practical theology.

The themes of Niebuhr's theology that have central importance for pastoral and practical theology include the following: (1) the effort to characterize, through metaphor and imagery, the action and being of God as the fundamental reality in the processes of nature and history, and therefore, in human personal and corporate experience; (2) the development of a theological anthropology focused on human interpretation of and responsiveness to the totality of action impinging upon us, and centering in faith as a dynamic relation of trust in and loyalty to those causes or realities that have "God-value" for us; (3) a view of revelation as the experience of "paradigm shift"—the dissolution of one set of images by which to interpret and respond in life, and the appropriation of the gift of new images through which unity, grace, and meaning derive from God's reality and power; (4) a view of the church as a community of interpretation grounded in a normative story, called to grow in faithful union with the story that comes to expression in Jesus' proclamation of the inbreaking and already actual Kingdom of God; (5) a rich set of typologies for sorting out various patterns in the church's responses to and engagement of culture, and for characterizing various patterns of personality integration in relation to a center or centers of value and power.

J. W. FOWLER

NEOORTHODOX THEOLOGY AND PASTORAL CARE; PSYCHOLOGY IN AMERICAN RELIGION. *See also* FAITH/BELIEF.

NIEBUHR, REINHOLD (1892–1971). Although his major contributions were in the fields of Christian ethics and theology, Reinhold Niebuhr, longtime faculty member of Union Theological Seminary in New York, contributed indirectly but significantly to the pastoral care field through the theologically critical method he employed in his writings.

In spite of the horrors of World War II, postwar America still believed strongly in human potential and the power of positive thinking. Modern pastoral care and counseling had, almost uncritically, embraced psychological knowledge as being able to alleviate pain and contribute to human happiness. Niebuhr approached this panacea as he did others with what has been called "Christian realism," radically questioning modern psychology's optimistic view of human being. His psychologically sophisticated reminder of the seriousness of sin and the empirical fact of human brokenness was one of the most important challenges to the enthusiasm with which pastoral care and counseling had embraced psychotherapeutic wisdom. His work in Christian anthropology and ethics helped to make the pastoral care movement more theologically critical in its approach to psychology and its own methods of care.

Less important but still significant for the pastoral care movement was Niebuhr's application of his theologically critical principle to his own pastoral work. The central focus of CPE has been the sharing, reflection upon, and interpretation of one's efforts in ministry. In his book, *Leaves From the Notebooks of a Tamed Cynic,* Niebuhr provided a theologically informed model of reflection on ministry based upon his pastoral work in a Detroit parish in the teens and twenties of this century. Toward the end of the book Niebuhr becomes more generally philosophical than reflective upon particular acts of ministry; nevertheless, what he has done is still useful and challenging to those who are willing to look critically at their work in ministry.

Bibliography. R. Niebuhr, *Leaves From the Notebooks of a Tamed Cynic* (1957); *The Nature and Destiny of Man* (1955).

J. PATTON

NEOORTHODOX THEOLOGY AND PASTORAL CARE; PSYCHOLOGY IN AMERICAN RELIGION; SOCIAL JUSTICE ISSUES IN PASTORAL CARE.

NIGHT SHELTER MINISTRIES. *See* HOMELESS PERSONS.

NIGHTMARES. *See* ANXIETY DISORDERS; DREAMS (Theory and Research).

NIHILISM. *See* HOPE AND DESPAIR; MATERIALISM.

NONCHRISTIANS. *See* CROSS-CULTURAL PASTORAL CARE. *See also* CROSS-CULTURAL MARRIAGE AND FAMILY; EVANGELIZING.

NONCHRISTIAN-CHRISTIAN MARRIAGE. *See* CROSS-CULTURAL MARRIAGE AND FAMILY.

NONDEFENSIVENESS. *See* DEFENSIVENESS, PASTORAL; INTIMACY AND DISTANCE; PHENOMENOLOGICAL METHOD IN PASTORAL CARE.

NONDIRECTIVE COUNSELING. *See* CLIENT-CENTERED THERAPY.

NONVERBAL COMMUNICATION. *See* BODY LANGUAGE; COMMUNICATION. *See also* PRESENCE, MINISTRY OF; RITUAL AND PASTORAL CARE; SILENCE; SYMBOLIC DIMENSIONS OF PASTORAL CARE RELATIONSHIPS.

NORMLESSNESS. *See* ANOMIE/NORMLESSNESS.

NOTES AND RECORDS. *See* CONFIDENTIALITY; LEGAL DIMENSIONS OF PASTORAL CARE AND COUNSELING; VERBATIM.

NOUTHETIC COUNSELING. *See* EVANGELICAL *or* FUNDAMENTALIST PASTORAL CARE.

NOVENA. *See* LITURGICAL AND DEVOTIONAL LIFE, ROMAN CATHOLIC.

NOVICE/NOVITIATE. *See* RELIGIOUS, PASTORAL CARE OF.

NUCLEAR FAMILY. *See* FAMILY, HISTORY AND SOCIOLOGY OF; FAMILY THEORY AND THERAPY.

NUCLEAR THREAT. *See* PEACE-MAKING AND PASTORAL CARE. *See also* DEATH AND DYING, PSYCHOSOCIAL THEORIES OF; ESCHATOLOGY.

NULLITY, DECREE OF. *See* DECREE OF NULLITY.

NUNS. *See* RELIGIOUS.

NURSING HOME. *See* CHAPLAIN/CHAPLAINCY. *See also* CHRONIC ILLNESS; HANDICAP AND DISABILITY; NEUROLOGIC ILLNESSES.

NURTURE. *See* EDUCATION, NURTURE, AND CARE.

O

OATES, WAYNE E. (1917–   ). Baptist pastor, chaplain, pastoral theologian, and clinical educator. Oates taught pastoral theology at Southern Baptist Theological Seminary and serves as professor of psychiatry and behavioral sciences at the School of Medicine, University of Louisville, Kentucky.

A product of a South Carolina mill town, Oates remained sensitive throughout his career to the problems of pastoral care in the rural South. He also maintained a strong interest in the "symbolic role of the pastor" as the representative of a specific community and tradition. The result was a conception of pastoral counseling as "spiritual conversation," a dialogue between a pastor and a parishioner marked by trust, understanding, covenantal engagement, and concern for persons within community. In his *Protestant Pastoral Counseling* (1962), he attempted to define the precise character of pastoral care within the Protestant free church tradition and found its defining marks to be theological: an affirmation of the lordship of Christ, of the personal dialogue between Creator and creature, of the priesthood of believers, and, above all, of the power of the Spirit. Such criteria enabled Oates to draw on modern psychotherapeutic theories, but to modify them in the light of the specific social and ecclesiastical setting within which the pastor worked.

Using a notion of "social role" derived in part from the social psychology of Gardner Murphy, Oates urged ministers to be sensitive to a community's ways of expressing its expectations of the clerical role. He thought that ministers could learn to use communal expectations in understanding why people would come to them in search of aid, rather than to other counselors. He also felt that the ministerial "role" properly affected the minister's method of counseling. On occasion, the minister might well simply help men and women interpret their feelings, but ministers should also acknowledge certain broad objectives and therefore assume a measure of initiative in counseling.

As a theologian, he stood in a neo-Orthodox tradition that reasserted the importance of Christology as the clue to understanding human existence. In his *Christ and Selfhood* (1961), he argued that "the claim to uniqueness of the Christian understanding of the personality resides wholly in the Person of Jesus Christ." He also shared the prevailing neo-Orthodox fascination with the destructive power of "idolatry," the misdirected focusing of ultimate loyalties on conflicting finite values. And he worried that psychology itself could become still another idol, so he warned against the tendency of pastoral counselors to seek a "borrowed identity" derived from psychotherapy. He always maintained a deep interest in psychoanalytic traditions, developmental psychologies, and social psychology, but he also wanted pastors to find within their own religious traditions the imagery and language to guide their pastoral practice.

Oates helped to introduce Clinical Pastoral Education (CPE) into the South. He had undergone clinical training at Elgin State Hospital under the auspices of the Council for Clinical Training, but he eventually founded his own clinical program at Kentucky State Hospital in Danville and forged links with Southern Baptist Theological Seminary.

A prolific writer, Oates has published dozens of books and hundreds of articles on theology, pastoral care, and pastoral theology. He was one of the leading figures of the postwar pastoral counseling movement in the U.S.

E. B. HOLIFIELD

HISTORY OF PROTESTANT PASTORAL CARE (United States); PASTORAL CARE MOVEMENT; PASTORAL COUNSELING MOVEMENT; PASTORAL THEOLOGY, PROTESTANT; PSYCHOLOGY IN AMERICAN RELIGION; THEOLOGICAL EDUCATION AND THE PASTORAL CARE MOVEMENT, PROTESTANT. *See also* PSYCHOPATHOLOGY AND RELIGION. *Compare* NEO-ORTHODOX THEOLOGY AND PASTORAL CARE.

OATHS. *See* PROFANE LANGUAGE; VOWS/VOWING.

OBEDIENCE (Roman Catholicism). Strictly speaking, a vow the religious and clergy make to follow the authority of their religious superior. Like the vows of poverty and chastity, it is modeled upon the life of Christ. More expressedly, it signifies oneness with Christ in obeying the Father's will as a selfless expression of faith. It embodies Christ's response to the Father, from his baptism, in his life of teaching, preaching, and healing, and in his death on the cross. In this sense, obedience must be freely given on the individual's part in seeking a closer identification with the life of Christ.

In the church, obedience allows the religious to put his or her life in the service of the church as guided by a religious superior, whether that superior be the local bishop, abbot, or head of a religious order. It allows for service to be directed in two senses: first, to the betterment and work of the local community, and second, to the continued task of the church's apostolate.

However, religious obedience has never meant the renunciation of one's own conscience. It is not a flight from mature, reasonable responsibility. If a person is commanded to do what is sinful or is contrary to what the individual discerns as God's will for himself or herself, then that person may not obey. Conscience has long been regarded as the measure by which the individual may question authority. In Catholic tradition, it is the nearest available norm for knowing what is right or wrong and the criterion by which God judges the human soul. Blind obedience to authority is not a valid reason for doing what is sinful, unjust, or morally wrong.

At the same time, the test of conscience does not allow an individual license to disregard the command of legitimate authority. Authority and obedience are complementary ideas that promote the religious life and are two aspects in living the life of Christ. The individual has the responsibility of understanding authority's aims, values, and purposes, so that obedience may be freely granted. Likewise, authority has the responsibility of helping the individual in this understanding. An individual can thus disagree with his or her religious superior if that individual considers a particular command to be misguided, misinformed, or detrimental to his or her person, the community, or the church.

A. W. R. SIPE

AUTHORITY; COMMITMENT; RESPONSIBILITY/IRRESPONSIBILITY, PSYCHOLOGY OF. See also CONSCIENCE; GOD'S WILL, ACCEPTANCE OF; VOWS/VOWING. Compare LOCUS OF CONTROL RESEARCH; PATIENCE/PATIENTHOOD.

OBEDIENCE, CHILDREN'S. See ADJUSTMENT DISORDERS; PARENTS/PARENTHOOD.

OBESITY AND WEIGHT CONTROL. It is estimated that between forty million to eighty million Americans are obese. Although the need for more refined diagnosis and treatment remains critical, no one theory has been able to isolate the cause or causes of overeating and/or underexercising in the obese. Among the numerous theories, a few are dominant, however.

The "psychosomatic" position emphasizes internal, emotional factors. Bruch (1957, 1961) first suggested that the obese confuse hunger with other negative emotions and that individuals overeat in response to emotional arousal. Extension of this viewpoint suggests that eating, when used as a way to cope with anxiety, results in stress reduction. Other researchers now are looking also at how thoughts and feelings of failure (e.g., "I blew

it again; I might as well give up") affect increased emotional arousal and can result in the frantic irrationality of binge eating.

In direct contrast to Bruch's hypothesis, Schachter (1971) and associates have compared the eating behaviors of obese and normal-weight individuals in the presence of a wide variety of environmental settings. Their findings suggest that the eating responses of the obese are especially sensitive to environmental (external) factors rather than internal control. The obese are not only more likely to report greater hunger, but also to eat more than their normal-weight counterparts when food-relevant cues, such as the sight and taste of food, are made salient.

A third major position, commonly called the "set point" theory, agrees that the obese may be externally responsive but primarily as a direct result of chronic physiological hunger. Nisbett (1972) reported that the body is programmed, possibly genetically, to carry a certain amount of fat. An individual may learn, as a result of social pressures, to decrease weight below a biological set point; but there is always a "biological pull" to fill up empty fat cells. Thus, maintenance of a "statistically normal" weight level may be even biologically abnormal and constitute semi-starvation for a given individual. Only through constant vigilance can a slim appearance be accomplished. Most recently, there has been some evidence that the set point can be decreased and that consistent exercising may play a key role.

Increasing attention has been focused upon the role that exercise plays in balancing caloric intake with energy output. It appears that exercise may be critically important in helping many individuals maintain their weight goals. If exercise is adapted to the normal daily routine, there is a greater chance that exercising will become a more permanent lifestyle change.

Bibliography. H. Bruch, *Eating Disorders* (1973). N. Kiell, *The Psychology of Obesity* (1973). R. E. Nisbett, "Hunger, Obesity, and the Ventromedial Hypothalamus," *Psychological Review,* 79 (1972), 433–53. S. Schachter, "Some Extraordinary Facts about Obese Humans and Rats," *American Psychologist,* 26 (1971), 129–44. E. Walkenstein, *Fat Chance* (1982).

J. J. FOG

BODY IMAGE; BULIMIA; EATING AND DRINKING; GLUTTONY AND TEMPERANCE (Moral Theology); HEALTH AND ILLNESS. See also PERSONALITY, BIOLOGICAL DIMENSIONS OF; LIFESTYLE ISSUES IN PASTORAL CARE. Compare ANOREXIA NERVOSA; ASCETICAL PRACTICES; PHYSICAL FITNESS DISCIPLINES.

OBJECT RELATIONS THEORY. A theory within the field of psychoanalysis which postulates that as the self develops it internalizes its early object relations, particularly those between the self and the mother, and that these internalized relationships determine the quality of the self's relationships in adulthood. Based upon this hypothesis, object relations theory studies what happens between the self and its early caretakers, in normal and abnormal development, and how these relationships become internalized into the self. It also seeks to understand how these early internalized object relationships become re-enacted in psychoanalysis, and how the internal world of the self may be modified through psychoanalytic treatment.

1. **Historical Survey.** While Freud focused more upon the instinctual life of the person than upon its object relationships, he is generally regarded as having introduced object relations theory. He developed the tripartite theory of the personality, where the personality is divided into the id, ego, and superego, and where both the ego and superego are understood as developing, at least in part, through the internalization of object relationships. Thus, Freud stated that the ego develops in part through identification, where an external object is "taken into the ego" (as in the process of mourning). That process, Freud said, is especially present in the early phases of development, "is a very frequent one, and it points to the conclusion that the character of the ego is a precipitate of abandoned object-cathexis and that it contains a record of past object choices." Freud also considered the superego to be the heir to the Oedipus complex, meaning the superego resulted from an internalization and identification of the self with the father, in the case of the boy, and the mother, with the girl, as a result of the Oedipal situation and its resolution. Freud's conceptualizations of object relations and their internalization was far from complete, however, and it remained for later theorists to develop the theory.

This development came about because of a need to understand conflicts within the self originating earlier in life than the Oedipus complex, which was understood to occur between the third to the fourth year and the fifth to the seventh year in the life of a girl or boy respectively. Freud concentrated his efforts on the neuroses originating from the Oedipus complex, noting that the narcissistic neuroses, meaning those disorders which arose because of difficulties prior to the Oedipal period, would have to be studied by others.

The first object relations theorist after Freud was Melanie Klein. She was pushed to understand the development of the self during the years prior to the Oedipal period because she undertook the psychoanalytic treatment of children whose difficulties clearly originated in the first to third years of life. Klein theorized that the disturbances she was seeing were based upon internalized object relations that developed during the first year of life, that the Oedipus complex began during the first year, and that psychological development was essentially complete by the age of three. While most object relations theorists now disagree with Klein's squeezing the psychological development into the first two years of life, her work remains foundational for all other object relations theories.

Two other object relations theorists who, along with Melanie Klein, have become known as the British school of object relations theory, were W. R. D. Fairbairn and C. W. Winnicott. Fairbairn believed that all psychopathology originated in the first year of life, when the self developed a schizoid condition because of the internalization of bad object relationships. That caused the ego to relate more to the world of internal objects than to the external world. Fairbairn's work, while interesting and innovative, has not been followed by many modern object relations theorists because he did not take into account the importance of internalizing good object relations in addition to the bad relationships. Winnicott, however, developed a theory, based on Freud, Klein, and Fairbairn, which asserts what most object relations theorists believe today.

In the U.S., object relations theory has been integrated into psychoanalytic ego psychology. Of the many writers, perhaps the most important are Edith Jacobson, Otto Kernberg, and Heinz Kohut. Jacobson's book, *The Self and the Object World,* is essential for the study of modern object relations theory. Kernberg has developed an object relations theory which comes out of his psychoanalytic treatment of borderline and narcissistic patients. He presents a useful summary of the development of object relations theory, and addresses most of the crucial arguments currently taking place in this school. Kohut focused primarily on his clinical work with the narcissistic character disorders, developing what is called self psychology. Kohut and his colleagues have claimed that self psychology is a movement beyond ego psychology and object relations theory, and that self psychology will eventually become the dominant theory in psychoanalysis. While that may occur, it is more likely that self psychology will continue to be seen as an object relations theory that is specifically applicable to the narcissistic disorders.

2. **The Development of the Self.** In general, object relations theorists describe the development of the self as occurring in three phases.

a. Symbiosis or fusion between the infant and the mother. In this phase, which lasts from birth until the sixth to eighth month of life, the self moves from complete fusion to an awareness of the mother as a whole person separate from the self. At first self and object images are fused and all experience is felt as coming either from the self or from the outside. The self also experiences things as either all bad or all good, and develops good and bad self and object image units. At first these object relations units are kept separate from one another. Gradually the self begins to differentiate experience and by the end of this period is able to differentiate self and object, good self and bad self, and good object and bad object. The primary mechanisms for dealing with reality during this stage are splitting, projection, and introjection. When the environment is basically positive during this stage the good self and object images predominate over the bad and the self begins to develop a belief in the goodness of itself and the world. The self also begins to internalize the soothing or holding function which the mothering persons provide so that it begins to provide that function for itself. Frustration is, of course, a necessary and important part of the process, and the internalization of bad self and object images that results leads to the self's beginning to discriminate between good and bad, and between self and non-self.

b. Separation-individuation. Winnicott calls this the stage of relative dependence,' meaning the period between absolute dependence and independence, and between the self's being able to differentiate between inner and outer reality. This phase lasts from the sixth to eighth month and the eighteenth to thirty-sixth month. During this stage the self moves to integrate the good and bad self and object images to form a realistic self-image in relationship to a realistic object image. This will occur in an optimal environment, and the self will then emerge with sufficient internal structure to perform for itself those functions which the environment was previously required to perform. These functions are those of soothing or comforting itself, expressing feelings of love and anger, and the beginning of a belief system which directs the self toward realistic goals and ideals. When the environment is not optimal, either because of too much or too little frustration, the self does not become separate, inner structure does not develop, and borderline and narcissistic disorders occur.

c. The Oedipal phase. This is seen as building on the previous phases and results in the self's developing the familiar ego-id-superego structure, and is where the self has a realistic image of itself and of reality. Difficulties during this stage of development, which come about when the parents and child are unable to deal with their sexual relationships, result in the neuroses. It should be said, however, that object relations theorists tend to believe that most psychopathology originates in the years prior to the Oedipal period, and that neuroses that do not also involve issues having to do with symbiosis and separation-individuation do not exist.

Overall, object relations theorists emphasize that the self must internalize realistic self and object images, but that no self is complete. In every person's unconscious there reside primitive positive and negative self and object images which may become activated under varying circumstances, and which influence behavior in many ways.

3. Object Relations Theory and Pastoral Care. Object relations theory has influenced pastoral care in several ways. First, many, if not most, pastoral counselors are using object relations theory as the primary psychological theory which informs their work. Second, object relations theory has been integrated into the literature of pastoral care and counseling. Merle Jordan (1965) considered the development and psychopathology of the self using the object relations theory of Fairbairn and the concept of idolatry from theology, particularly as that concept is elaborated in the writings of Paul Tillich. More recently, Donald Ziemba (1986) presented a theory of pastoral counseling based upon an integration of the psychology of Fairbairn and the theology of Karl Rahner.

While traditional Freudian and ego psychology has been integrated into the formal literature of pastoral care and counseling for many years, only recently has object relations theory been introduced into that literature. Charles Gerkin (1984), for instance, uses object relations theory to develop a hermeneutical theory of pastoral counseling.

A third way in which object relations theory is important to pastoral care is emerging in the understanding of the development of faith. John McDargh (1983), for example, uses object relations theory to show how faith development is linked to the development of a "god image" in the self, and that the "god-image" is itself linked to the self and object images that are internalized in the self's early years.

Bibliography. W. R. D. Fairbairn, *Psychoanalytic Studies of the Personality* (1952). S. Freud, *The Ego and the Id* (1950), pp. 35 – 41. C. Gerkin, *The Living Human Document* (1984). H. Guntrip, *Schizoid Phenomena, Object-Relations and the Self* (1969). E. Jacobson, *The Self and the Object World* (1964). M. Jordan, "The Idolatry of a 'Bad' Parental Image as a Frustration to Becoming a Whole

Person," doctoral dissertation, School of Theology at Claremont (1965). O. Kernberg, *Object-Relations Theory and Clinical Psychoanalysis* (1976). H. Kohut, *How Does Analysis Cure?* (1984). J. McDargh, *Psychoanalytic Object Relations Theory and the Study of Religion* (1983). A. M. Rizutto, *The Birth of the Living God* (1979). H. Segal, *Introduction to the Work of Melanie Klein* 2d ed. (1974). D. Winnicott, *The Maturational Processes and the Facilitating Environment* (1965). D. Ziemba, "A Model for Pastoral Counseling: An Essay in Pastoral Counseling Using the Theology of Freedom of Karl Rahner and the Object Relations Theory of W. Ronald D. Fairbairn," doctoral dissertation, Emory University (1986).

C. KROPP

EGO PSYCHOLOGY AND PSYCHOTHERAPY; PSYCHOANALYSIS; SELF. *See also* BORDERLINE DISORDER; NARCISSISM/NARCISSISTIC PERSONALITY; NEUROSIS; SCHIZOPHRENIA. *Compare* I AND THOU; INTERPERSONAL THEORY; SELF PSYCHOLOGIES; TRANSACTIONAL ANALYSIS.

OBJECTIVITY, PROFESSIONAL. The ability of professionals to conceive of people, relationships, and themselves as objects that are external to their minds in contrast to internal mental and emotional processes. On the other hand, subjectivity is a perception of reality that is conditioned by personal mental characteristics and past personal experiences. In subjectivity the perceptions arise from conditions within the brain and sensory organs and are not directly caused by external stimuli.

In recent years, particularly with new developments in the philosophy of science, the objective/subjective dichotomy has been severely challenged, especially in the areas of scientific research. The works of scholars such as M. Polanyi (1985) and T. Kuhn (1970) have gone a long way to demythologize the notion that a scientist is purely objective. And this growing recognition has found its way into the psychotherapeutic movement, challenging especially those forms of counseling and psychotherapy claiming the necessary condition of objectivity on the part of the therapist.

Still, objectivity tends to counteract biases, prejudices, illusions, or distortions that may result from subjectivity. Pastoral counselors are trained to give attention to countertransferences, which are a special type of distortion in which psychotherapists' childhood perceptions of members of their families of origin are transferred to those with whom they do therapy. Pastoral counselors may acquire and maintain greater objectivity by engaging in supervision, consultation, training in psychotherapeutic skills, continuing education, study of tape recordings of sessions, and personal therapy. What appears essential is that the pastoral counselor be *aware* of these forces and utilize them in assisting the client or the parishioner. The modern emphasis thus moves away from the establishment of a radical objectivity toward a recognition and therapeutic use of the inevitable presence of countertransference. There are a variety of clues to the presence of countertransference (e.g., Searles, 1979; MacKinnon and Michels, 1971), and these may be used as therapeutic tools.

Pastors' sensitivity and personal concern for people may be combined with an enlightened objectivity so that their caring is both warm and emotional and also intelligent and effective.

A high degree of objectivity is necessary for empathy, which is a mode of perceiving people. Empathy means "emotional knowing" in contrast to intellectual understanding. It involves a partial and temporary identification with another person. It is a way of seeing the world through the other person's eyes so as to understand, as nearly as possible, what it is like to be the other person, a condition essential in the counseling relationship.

Bibliography. T. Kuhn, *The Structure of Scientific Revolutions* (1970). R. A. MacKinnon and R. Michels, *The Psychiatric Interview in Clinical Practice* (1971). M. Polanyi, *Personal Knowledge* (1985). H. F. Searles, *Countertransference and Related Subjects: Selected Papers* (1979).

J. M. MURPHY

INTERPRETATION AND HERMENEUTICS, PASTORAL; PHENOMENOLOGICAL METHOD IN PASTORAL CARE. *See also* COUNTERTRANSFERENCE; TRANSFERENCE. *Compare* CLINICAL PASTORAL PERSPECTIVE; ETHICS, PROFESSIONAL.

OBLIGATION, SENSE OF. *See* CONSCIENCE; RESPONSIBILITY/IRRESPONSIBILITY, PSYCHOLOGY OF.

OBSCENITY. *See* PORNOGRAPHY; PROFANE LANGUAGE.

OBSESSIVE COMPULSIVE DISORDER. Disturbance of thought and behavior which may present itself in three forms: (1) recurring, persistent, unwelcome, invasive, and ego-dystonic thoughts; (2) repetitive, stereotypical, seemingly irresistible, and ostensively purposeful behaviors which usually provide no genuine pleasure; and (3) a combination of both such obsessive thoughts and compulsive acts.

The full obsessive compulsive disorder sometimes develops in individuals with underlying compulsive personality traits. Such persons are preoccupied with concerns such as neatness, orderliness, punctuality, efficiency, hard work, and adherence to rules, social customs, and moral codes. In many settings, these traits and behaviors are viewed as admirable and are accordingly rewarded. In the obsessive compulsive disorder, however, the above-mentioned tendencies become distressing, unwanted, and are sometimes significantly debilitating or disabling.

Thoughts in the obsessive compulsive category are often of the kind which are totally repugnant and frightening to the persons entertaining them, for example, killing a member of the family or committing suicide. Unless the person with such thoughts is suffering from schizophrenia, these feared behaviors will usually not materialize. Other common obsessional thoughts revolve around irrational doubts such as whether the front door has been locked when it has already been carefully checked. Even though obsessional ideation is horrifying, cumbersome, and would lead to actions completely unlike the person, these thoughts continue to intrude upon consciousness and remain there despite efforts at suppression or expulsion. It should be noted that a person might be preoccupied with certain thoughts which do not rank as obsessive ideation because these thoughts are neither repugnant nor unwanted, like thinking

almost constantly of a new job, or of members of the opposite sex.

Compulsive acts may consist in a single act or a ritualistic combination of behaviors. One of the most common compulsions is repetitive handwashing sometimes to the point where the hands become extremely raw. Compulsive behaviors are frequently done an arbitrary or superstitious number of times such as seven, twenty-six, or the person's age. Although seemingly purposeful at times, the compulsive behavior usually accomplishes nothing that is rationally or consciously meaningful.

Compulsive behaviors are sometimes called "obsessions in actions," indicative of how intertwined obsessional ideation and compulsions may be. An example of such an interrelationship is found in the obsession of being contaminated by dirt or germs associated with compulsive handwashing. This particular obsessive compulsive combination has been known to lead to an avoidance of touching doorknobs altogether, resulting in the person's resorting to climbing through windows unless someone opens the door.

It is believed that both obsessions and compulsions are unconscious ways of coping with underlying anxiety, tension, anger, or guilt. Evidence for this is found in the fact that these feelings frequently surface when the person is restrained from completing a compulsive act. Obsessions and compulsions are often a substitution for or symbolic of another more anxiety-producing thought or feeling which is thereby kept out of consciousness for the time being.

A. J. STRAATMEYER

NEUROSIS; REPETITION COMPULSION; UNDOING. *See also* DIAGNOSTIC AND STATISTICAL MANUAL III; EVALUATION AND DIAGNOSIS, PSYCHOLOGICAL.

OCCULT PHENOMENA. *See* PARAPSYCHOLOGY; SPIRITUALISM; SURVIVAL (Occult); WITCHCRAFT.

OCCUPATIONAL THERAPY. *See* ADJUNCTIVE THERAPIES.

ODEN, THOMAS C. *See* PASTORAL THEOLOGY, PROTESTANT.

OEDIPUS COMPLEX. *See* PSYCHOANALYSIS (Personality Theory and Research). *See also* MYTHOLOGY AND PSYCHOLOGY.

OFFICE. *See* PASTORAL OFFICE.

OIL, HOLY. *See* ANOINTING OF THE SICK, SACRAMENT OF.

OLD TESTAMENT AND APOCRYPHA, TRADITIONS AND THEOLOGY OF CARE IN. While there is no single theology of pastoral care in the OT and the Apocrypha there is evidence of considerable concern with the subject. In general, the goal of care according to the OT is the maintenance and restoration of relationships among human beings, between human beings and God, and of human beings with the world. The evidence reflects a wide diversity of responses to situations of human need that evoke care. These responses emerge from fundamental biblical perspectives on human life, the world, and God, and for the most part stress the corporate and communal aspects of care. Nevertheless, there were in ancient Israel a number of specialized religious roles concerned directly with the care of individuals and groups. The most important of these roles were those of the priest, the prophet and the sage. A review of diverse OT perspectives on the matter reveals the main characteristics of the biblical response to situations of human need and suggests possibilities for reflecting on some of the central issues of a contemporary theology of pastoral care.

Since the OT is both a collection of documents from antiquity and the sacred scriptures of communities of faith, our topic can be considered both descriptively and normatively. Our immediate goal is descriptive, that is, to analyze and characterize the OT views themselves, for if the biblical approach is to have any normative force it must first be understood on its own terms. However, the selection of topics to treat descriptively is shaped by modern concerns with the theory and practice of pastoral care. The concluding section of this article will suggest some of the implications of the OT for such theory and practice.

1. **The Sources.** The primary sources for an understanding of the OT theology and traditions of care are, obviously, the texts of the biblical books themselves. Here the longer canons are considered, either the OT of the Roman Catholic Church or the Protestant OT plus the so-called Apocrypha. These two include the same books but their orders are different. Other ancient Near Eastern texts from Mesopotamia, Syria-Palestine, and Egypt at points provide important information on the background of biblical perspectives and practices, as well as archaeological evidence.

The OT reflects a wide diversity of responses to situations of human need that evoke care because of (a) the long and complex oral and literary develoment of which the OT is but the final stage; (b) the circumstances of the long history of Israel and Judah, related to that literary history; (c) the everchanging complexity of social situations, social structures, and social roles reflected even in a single layer of literature or period of history; and (d) religious, theological, political, and other conflicts in ancient Israel and early Judaism, many of which are expressed in the OT itself. These last include disagreements and even outright conflicts between priests and prophets, prophets and prophets, different groups of priests, wisdom teachers and pious priests, various political factions and religious sects, among others. Such disagreements, as well as historical developments, stand behind the fact that there are different schools of thought concerning some of the most fundamental questions of theology, including "care." Even when such schools and traditions are not in conflict they may represent very different perspectives on particular issues.

Moreover, at no point do the OT texts articulate a theology of care as such, nor do they provide us with an explicit structure for organizing such a theology. On the other hand, they express various perspectives or allude to numerous practices that relate to issues of care. However, while there is not a single thelogy of care, there are limits beyond which the thought of the OT does not go, and assumptions shared by virtually all levels and layers of its thought so that certain pre-understandings, issues, and themes emerge that give shape to a distinctly biblical understanding of care. But we must deduce the shape and contents of those OT views of care from sources that at times are indirect, and acknowledge that the data could legitimately be organized in various ways.

For the most part, and certainly in its final form, the OT has come down to us from the representatives of the dominant and central religious institutions of ancient Israel. Thus the officially sanctioned institutions such as the priesthood, the monarchy, and the temple practices loom large, as do the dominant theological perspectives, such as those of Deuteronomy and the deuteronomic tradition. But there were small or primary group practices, ideas and traditions as well. These never disappeared even after the large and even bureaucratic institutions emerged. Among these were the family, the clan, the town, and the neighborhood group. The traditions of such primary groups, difficult as they are to discover, are important to a full picture of care in the OT.

2. **General Assumptions.** Any understanding or practice of care, or even the perception of the situations that evoke it, is shaped by a worldview, a theology, and epecially by an anthropology. It is worth emphasizing that the worldview, theology, and anthropology of the culture that produced the OT was different in important respects from those of the modern world. What modern Western cultures call madness, for example, other cultures — especially those of antiquity — understood as the effects of possession by evil spirits, or the power of curses, or even divine inspiration. It is essential, therefore, to set the OT traditions of care in the framework of ancient Israel's most fundamental convictions about the world, God, and humanity.

a. God, history, and the world. Expressed or assumed in virtually all layers of OT tradition is belief in Yahweh, the God of Israel, ultimately understood as God of all peoples. In a genuine sense, the leading theme of the OT is God's care for a people and for the world. This observation must be qualified only by pointing out that God's care takes place within the limits of the actualities of history, and that the divine purpose is not unaffected by human activities. Nevertheless, at the heart of virtually all OT traditions lies the conviction that Yahweh cares for his people and his world. Moreover, the care of human beings for one another is derived from that divine care.

Two sides of Israel's fundamental assumptions about God should be noted in this regard. On the one hand, ancient Israel recognized Yahweh as the one who established and maintained the possibilities and limits for all human life. This is affirmed in the accounts of creation (Genesis 1–3), in the Psalms that sing the praises of God by cataloguing the works of creation (e.g., Psalms 100; 104; 135; 147; 148), and taken for granted in virtually all layers of the tradition. This means, of course, that life exists because of God, but it also means that life has its limits, including physical limits, because of the freedom of God. Even where objections to these realities arise, e.g., in Ecclesiastes and Job, the basic notions about divine freedom and human limits are assumed to be facts.

The questions concern either the justice of God or the appropriate human response to those limits. There is, in short, a sober realism in the recognition that God has made the world as it is, including setting the boundaries for human life. In most traditions, those limits are understood in terms of Yahweh's justice. Those who violate the limits of justice, especially within the covenant community, are subject to punishment as Yahweh balances the scales.

On the other hand, ancient Israel knows her God to be one who is vulnerable. Even in creating the world and all who dwell in it, God acted to establish the possibility of relationship with others. The biblical tradition understands that God in absolute freedom chose to limit himself, to make room for human and other creatures. Then by making promises and by electing a particular people, Yahweh binds himself in covenant. Sometimes those promises and covenants are viewed unconditionally and sometimes conditionally. Fundamentally, the covenant relationship is a pledge of mutual loyalty, of God to people and people to God (cf. Josh. 24:1–28). Over and over again it is Yahweh who takes the initiative, who acts and then calls for response (cf. Exod. 20:1ff.) and who gives another chance to those who trespass.

Utterly remarkable in this regard are the not infrequent references to Yahweh's capacity for and willingness to "repent," to change his mind, and almost invariably to act in grace when judgment would be called for. A classic example is the bone of contention between Jonah and his God. After the prophet announces judgment upon Nineveh and all the people sincerely repent, "God repented of the evil which he had said he would do to them; and he did not do it" (Jonah 3:10). This is no isolated instance, for the OT often reports, particularly through the use of anthropomorphic metaphors and images, that God's will be directly affected by human actions (cf. Joel 2:12–19). Perhaps the most powerful expression of the vulnerability of God is found in Hosea 11, in effect a divine soliloquy in which Yahweh first recalls the deep relationship with Israel—like a mother with a child—then remembers how the people had constantly been unfaithful and therefore deserve to be punished through military defeat and exile. But then comes Yahweh's astounding vow:

"My heart recoils within me,
    my compassion grows warm and tender.
I will not execute my fierce anger, . . .
for I am God and not man . . ." (Hos. 11:8–9).

That capacity to repent, to be vulnerable, is to Hosea what distinguishes God from human beings, and it stands at the heart of Israel's theology.

Israel's experience with and understanding of her God is directly related to her views of the world and of history. The conditions of life in space and time are taken to be trustworthy, for they were created by a just God and entrusted to humanity. "And God saw all that he had made, and behold, it was very good" (Gen. 1:31). Ultimately—that is, in terms of both the beginning of history and its destiny—the world and history are in God's hands. But in that framework human beings understand themselves as stewards of a world that does not belong to them, and history is experienced and must be lived as the interaction of the divine and human wills.

God's will is seen to be active in various ways, ordinary and extraordinary, but above all through human individuals and groups. Abraham, Moses, the Davidic kings, and the prophets are called to be agents of the divine will. God establishes a covenant with Israel, setting stipulations that prescribe and proscribe their definition as a chosen people. But whether the future will bring good news or bad is contingent upon human actions. To be sure, disaster often is understood as divine judgment upon sin and prosperity as divine reward for right behavior, but the link between human and divine wills is deeper. When the question comes to the surface, the answer would be: Everything that transpires emerges from the web of divine and human interaction.

All of this means that history is to be taken with utmost seriousness, that the individual and specific moments in time are alive with potential for both blessing and curse. History, like the world, is the sphere of divine activity.

b. The human situation. The most explicit OT reflections on "anthropology" are found in the creation stories in Genesis 1–3. At the beginning of the older Yahwistic document's account of the creation and "fall" of the first human beings there is this observation: "Then the Lord God formed man [better, "the human"] of dust from the ground, and breathed into his nostrils the breath of life; and man ["the human"] became a living being" (Gen. 2:7). While this is a singular narrative statement about human nature, it is fully consistent with what is assumed throughout the OT. It means: Human beings are ordinary created matter ("dust") that is alive ("breath of life"; cf. Ezek. 37:1–14). They do not consist of some two- or three-part union of, e.g., body, mind, and soul, for this "breath of life" does not exist independently of the physical matter. Life is a divine gift. The human being is embodied life, or animated earth. Moreover, there is no belief whatsoever in immortality. It is highly doubtful that this initial part of the story considered such a possibility, but if it did that possibility was cut off when the original pair was driven from the garden (Gen. 3:22–24). Consequently, death to the ancient Israelite was real and it was final (cf. Psalm 49). Only two very late passages consider the possibility of life beyond the grave (Dan. 12:1–3; Isa. 26:19; cf. also Isa. 25:6–8), and that in terms of resurrection.

The crux of the later Priestly writer's account of creation concerns not so much human nature as the role of human beings in relationship to God and the world: "So God created man [better, "humanity"] in his own image, in the image of God he created him; male and female he created them" (Gen. 1:27). This "image" is no spark of divinity in the human creature, nor even a single quality or characteristic, such as free will. The terminology is concrete, specific, and even plastic. "Image" and "likeness" refer to visible representations, such as idols, and the metaphor is a royal one that alludes to the practice of conquering kings who set up their standards, emblems, or even images in a territory to indicate that it was theirs. Moreover, given OT anthropology, such an image of God here will mean the whole: the physical body, the alive, willfull, physical human being. The instructions that follow in the account (Gen. 1:28–30) make it clear that human beings are the creatures responsible for acting on behalf of God as stewards for the rest of creation (cf. Psalm 8).

If life is experienced as a good gift — and that certainly is the case — it is also known to be imperfect. One aspect of that imperfection, human finitude, has already been noted. In addition to the sober awareness of death as the end the OT speaks in various ways of the brokenness of life itself. Rarely is the language as strong as that in Job (e.g., "but man is born to trouble . . . " 3:7), but there is a rich vocabulary to characterize evil, pain, suffering and sin. The classic interpretation of the human predicament is the Yahwistic account in Genesis 3. Such sad facts of human life as shame (3:7); fear and guilt (3:10); estrangement from one another, from the rest of nature and from God (3:12–13); the domination of women by men (3:16); work filled with frustration (3:17–19a), and an awareness of death that cripples life (3:19b) are seen to be the effects of sin as disobedience. Thus the children of God face their lives with broken bearing.

One other facet of the OT understanding of human life should be emphasized, namely, its corporate and communal character. Certainly there is a concern with the individual and the individual's responsibilities and problems, particularly in the wisdom literature and in the numerous complaint songs of the individual (e.g., Psalms 3–7), and the laws have in view individuals as well as the people as a whole. Especially some of the later literature focuses more directly upon individual accountability, but some of that concern is directed against a misuse of older traditions about corporate responsibility (e.g. Ezekiel 18), and in any case it is against the background of a long tradition about corporate sin, guilt, and punishment. The dominant language is that of the people, the nation, the group. The covenant is a relationship established between God and people, and thereby of the people with one another. The legal stipulations of the covenant thus concern the response of the people to God and the regulation of their just relations with one another. The early prophets announce judgment on the nation as a whole, knowing that not all members of the community were equally guilty. In fact, some were victims of others. Nevertheless, all stand or fall together. In the historical books it is clearly stated that the nation as a whole suffers because of the sins of the kings. Moreover, the corporate body extends in time, for "the iniquity of the fathers" is visited "upon the children to the third and fourth generation . . ." (Exod. 20:5). To be human is to exist in communal interdependence.

c. Terminology. The OT has no specific term for care in the more or less specialized sense of the term in contemporary pastoral circles. On the other hand, pastoral images abound. Especially since the understanding of the care of human beings for one another is derived from convictions about God's care, it is particularly important that OT texts frequently characterize Yahweh as a shepherd, and the people as his flock. Psalm 23, an affirmation of utter trust in the Lord's care, is only the most famous example. Others include Ps. 80:1; Gen. 49:24; and numerous allusions to God as the one who leads, guides, and provides for his flock (Isa. 40:11; 49:10; Ezek. 34:31; Ps. 68:7–10; Jer. 23:3; 50:19; etc.). The title "shepherd" is applied to kings, usually in a positive sense (Jer. 23:4; Ezek. 34:23–31; 37:22, 24), but the

prophets also know that political leaders can be "bad shepherds" (Zech. 10:3; 11:4–17).

Most of the terms that define the attitudes and actions of care are directly or indirectly related to covenant, and thus can refer to both divine and human care. One of the most important of these is *hesed,* variously translated as "steadfast love," "lovingkindness," "kindness," "goodness," or "loyalty." Perhaps the awkward expression "covenant loyalty" best captures its meaning, for it presumes a covenant relationship under God, and emphasizes the solidarity of that relationship in both disposition and action. Those who observe *hesed* also practice *mishpat* ("justice") and *sedeqah* ("righteousness"); their loyalty to the covenant is enacted in obedience to the laws that are meant to maintain the rights of all members of the community.

d. The goal of care. Any act or institution of care presumes both that human life — individually or corporately — is either actually or potentially broken and that it can be maintained or restored. While the particular goal of care depends upon the problem, or the perception of the problem, its general purpose is the maintenance or restoration of relationships between God and people or among people. Its goal may be understood appropriately as establishing or contributing to *shalom,* "peace" in the sense of wholeness, well-being, and security.

Care also presumes postures of responsibility, and in some cases of authority. But here one must be cautious. The story of Cain and Abel (Gen. 4:1–16), for example, frequently is misinterpreted to argue that human beings are supposed to be "keepers" of one another. Cain's defensive response to Yahweh's question about his brother, "Am I my brother's keeper?" demands a negative answer. Nowhere are people expected to be keepers of one another. Roles and responsibilities have their limits. As a "watchman" for the people of Israel, Ezekiel was to discharge his duty faithfully and leave the response to those he warned (Ezek. 33:1–16; 3:16–21).

In view of the anthropology reflected in such texts as Gen. 2:7, which see human beings as a unity of body and life, it is not surprising that care is directed to the whole, living person in community. It is, in short, wholistic. Peace does not mean first of all "peace of mind," but such matters as a family, food to eat, a place to live, freedom from domination or oppression, and living in covenant with God. Emotional factors, as modernly defined, seldom are addressed explicitly or in isolation from other factors such as physical well-being. Sin and even guilt are not viewed as simply internal feelings, but appear as more or less objective realities that will have their effects if they are not forgiven or taken away.

3. The Understanding of Care in Different Roles and Literature. One important way of viewing the understanding of care in the OT is to consider the functions of various roles, especially those of religious specialists, and the perspective of various bodies of literature that to some extent reflect the perspectives of distinct functionaries. However, two qualifications should preface this summary. First, since one of the distinctive characteristics of the biblical view is the corporate and communal sense of responsibility, care was by no means limited to official or even quasi-official roles. In many situations care could be and was provided by any individual or group. Second, the modern category of "professional ministry" is hardly appropriate for ancient Israel. To be sure, some roles—such as that of the priest and even in many cases the prophet — amounted to full-time occupations that provided a person with a livelihood, and some required specialized training. However, these functions are better understood in terms of divine vocation or designation.

a. Priests and cultic literature. The priesthood was by no means a static institution throughout the history of Israel, and even in any given period various groups existed side by side. In particular, the relationship between "priests" and "levites" changed several times. In some early traditions, the two seem to be synonymous (Judg. 17:13), in others they are responsible for the law (Deut. 17:18), but later levites are not considered legitimate priests in the temple. In the late post-exilic period "levite" is a general term for all temple personnel descended from Levi, the brother of Moses, and sacrificial functions are limited to certain of the levitical families.

Religious ritual stabilizes life, relates it to transcendent realities, and through its enactment of mysteries locates people in relation to the divine. In ancient Israel, regardless of the historical developments, priests implemented the purposes of ritual in two ways. First, and most obviously, they were responsible for the sacrificial worship, eventually limited to the temple in Jerusalem. There is a great body of literature, especially in the Priestly document in the Pentateuch, that spells out the detailed instructions for various sacrifices and offerings, and gives the requirements for the priesthood. Priests themselves were to be holy (Lev. 19:1–2; 21:1–9) and unblemished (Lev. 21:16–24). The function of the sacrificial priesthood is not easy to state briefly, since various rituals served different specific purposes. On the one hand, the ancient Near Eastern background of offerings as the care and feeding of the gods is visible in some texts (Ezek. 44:15–16). Deuteronomy tends to historicize the rituals, e.g., viewing the Passover sacrifice/meal as a remembrance of the exodus. There is more emphasis in Priestly texts, however, on sacrifices as atoning for or removing the effects of sin (Leviticus 16). In general, the priestly role is to preserve the proper relationship of people to God, and that by maintaining the distinction between holy and profane (Lev. 10:10).

A second priestly function was that of instruction, since in various ways religious ritual extended to all of life. The levitical priests, according to Deuteronomy, are specifically charged with teaching the law (Deut. 17:18; 33:10). Hosea holds the priests responsible for the apostasy and therefore the punishment of the people, for they failed to teach the law (Hos. 4:4–10). Particularly important in priestly tradition was instruction of the laity concerning the distinction between sacred and profane: "You are to distinguish between the holy and the common, and between the unclean and the clean; and you are to teach the people of Israel all the statutes which the Lord has spoken to them by Moses" (Lev. 10:10–11). Thus the main priestly functions relate to what we have defined as the goals of care, the maintenance or restoration of relationships, particularly between God and peo-

ple. In these ways, as well as explicitly, the priests blessed the people (Num. 6:22–26).

The literature of the cult, mainly the lyrical poetry of the Psalms, is related directly or indirectly to religious functionaries as well. Here several types of literature and thus various religious ceremonies come into view. Hymns or songs of praise, as parts of communal worship, both celebrate and establish solidarity in the community and with God. They express the sense of the goodness of the created order and the graceful will of God in history. There were also laments or complaints of the community (e.g., Lamentations) which were used when the life or well-being of the group was threatened, in order to present the case before God and ask for help.

The largest single group in the Psalter, the complaints or laments of the individual, call for special attention in the consideration of OT traditions of care. These prayers concern most of the major human difficulties that evoke care: sickness, impending death, estrangement, conflict with enemies, and the sense of being abandoned by God (Psalm 22). Typically they are in the first person singular. Someone in trouble presents the case to God, describing the problem in detail, confessing sin or innocence (Psalm 17), complaining — often in angry terms—that God has not responded, asking for help, and sometimes making a vow to be kept if God will listen. It has been recognized in recent years (Gerstenberger) that even these highly personal prayers reflect communal activity, a prayer service for the individual that included both religious specialists—priests or other worship leaders — and the troubled individual's primary group such as family and neighbors. The purpose of the service was the restoration of the individual to health in the fullest possible sense of the term, including physical well-being and renewal of relationships. These songs demonstrate some of the most fundamental perpsectives of the OT on human care: first, no attitude or emotion was inappropriate before God. The ancient Israelite could freely express not only gratitude but also anger and frustration in prayer and within the community. Thus Job's angry and passionate complaints and questions were part of a broad and deep tradition. Second, there were structures for the corporate expression of and response to the person in trouble. The suffering individual did not want to be left alone, and did not have to be.

b. Prophets and prophetic literature. While Israel's prophets performed many different functions, including intercession (Amos 7:2, 5; Isa. 6:11) and occasionally calling for repentance or change (Amos 5:4–7, 21–24; Isa. 1:16–17), their most fundamental and distinctive role was to proclaim the word of God for the future. They were mediators whose words came from God and therefore set into motion the events they announced (Amos 1:2; Jer. 1:10). Their speeches were not predictions, then, but announcements, either of punishment or salvation. Generally, the announcements of punishment gave the reasons for the impending disaster (Amos 4:1–3) in terms of the sins of the people. Amos cites social injustice and religious arrogance, Hosea stresses religious apostasy and attendant sins such as political strife, and Isaiah emphasizes a failure of faith leading to corrupt political alliances. Announcements of salvation, mainly but not exclusively from the exilic and post-exilic periods, tend to locate the reasons for the good news not in the behavior of the people but in the graceful will of God (Isaiah 40–55). In short, the prophets saw their roles primarily in terms of the divine purpose, to set history on its right course, even if that meant the end of the covenant people.

It is easy to see an interest in "care" in the announcements of salvation, for they set that saving future into motion in part by empowering the people with hope. But what of the other side, the proclamations of judgment? In most instances, the indictments mean to make the disaster understandable, reasonable. In some cases such punishment is viewed as purging (Isa. 1:18–20; Hos. 2:1–15; 3:1–5). At least in some cases, while the prophetic purpose was to bring about punishment, the effect could be repentance and thus avoidance of the disaster. That is the situation with Jonah, whose message was the announcement of judgment upon Nineveh (Jonah 3:4), but first the people and then God repented (3:6–10). In the exilic and post-exilic periods, the earlier prophetic words of judgment were reinterpreted as warnings (see the prose speeches in Jeremiah). Ezekiel appears to have seen his role in such a light (Ezek. 3:16–21; 33:7–16). In fact, some blamed the disaster of the exile on prophets who had not told the truth, and thus failed in their duty to "restore the fortunes" of the people:

"Your prophets have seen for you
    false and deceptive visions;
they have not exposed your iniquity
    to restore your fortunes,
but have seen for you oracles
    false and misleading" (Lam. 2:14).

Moreover, it was the pre-exilic interpretations of the national disaster as the result of sin that laid the basis for a hopeful future. The exile did not mean that history was meaningless or chaotic, but it was Yahweh's reaction to the failures of the covenant people. So the old prophetic indictments could serve later generations as confession of sin and thus the basis for a new covenant.

Whether before groups or individuals, the prophetic role involved confrontation. This was even the case in many of the announcements of salvation, such as those of II Isaiah, which ran against the popular expectations. A classic but typical instance of prophetic confrontation is the response of Nathan to David's adultery with Bathsheba and his murder of her husband Uriah (II Samuel 12). Uninvited, the prophet condemns the king's actions and announces the death penalty. When David confesses and repents, the sin still has its effects, but the punishment is modified.

c. Sages and wisdom literature. If priests were responsible for ritual and instruction and prophets for the Word of God, sages were responsible for "wisdom" or "counsel" (cf. Jer. 18:18). There is relatively little direct information in the OT concerning the role until the second-century B.C. book of Ecclesiasticus. It is known that as early as the time of David such figures served in the court of the king alongside prophets, priests and generals (cf. II Sam. 17:1–14). They were teachers and scholars, the predecessors of later scribes. Jesus Ben Sirah had a school (Ecclus. 51:23), and his book is a collection of his teachings. Like the priests, the role of the sages concerned stability, but based on wisdom derived from experience and tradition instead of ritual.

The "wisdom" of the sages, included in the books of Proverbs, Ecclesiastes, Job, Ecclesiasticus, and Wisdom of Solomon, covers a broad range of subjects. It is simple practical knowledge, good manners, specialized skill, knowing how to raise children (Prov. 23:13), and it is also reflection upon the meaning of life (Eccl. 1:3; 2:1–26). While the wisdom writers make no appeals to revelation, they finally conclude that piety and wisdom begin and end at the same point (Prov. 1:7).

With regard to care, two trends can be identified among the sages and in the wisdom literature, one direct and another indirect. The direct form of care is advice and instruction. Through the transmission of proverbial wisdom as well as their own compositions, the sages tell others how to live. Numerous speeches are exhortations or admonitions in direct address form (Prov. 1:8–19; 2:1–22; 3:1–12). Even the writer of Ecclesiastes cannot leave his readers without recommendations about how to live their sad lives (Eccl. 3:22; 5:1–2, 18–20). Generally, this advice is cautious and prudent, favoring the status quo (Prov. 17:14; 26:17), but the sages also expressed concern for the same social justice seen in the prophets (Prov. 20:10; 22:22–23). There was a deep concern for the establishment of norms for behavior, defined in terms of "wisdom." The advice was based on the assumption that there is a more or less direct relationship between works and rewards: the righteous prosper and the wicked suffer. That view is challenged by the authors of Ecclesiastes, who know that both the righteous and the sinner come to the same end, and Job, who knows that the righteous suffer.

Indirectly, the wisdom teachers presume that it is helpful to make sense of life, and to transmit one's analysis and conclusions to others, including in writing, so they can even deal playfully with life's enigmas (Prov. 30:18–19, 24–31). Wisdom attempts to make sense of life and the world, to bring all things into and under the purview of human thought. The main tradition is optimistic: it is possible to know what one needs to know. But even when the thinkers confront the limits of human understanding — Ecclesiastes and Job — they see value in presenting their reflections to others. If life is tragic, its tragic power is diminished by seeing it as such. Of course, reflection upon the meaning of life is not always the most helpful form of care for persons in crisis. When Job needed a friend, those who came to visit him gave him theology instead (cf. Habel).

4. **Situations That Evoke Care.** Any society that persists through history, as ancient Israel's did, will have developed structures for the care of its members, as care has been defined here. Those structures, which include institutions, specialized roles, rituals and routines, were related both to everyday life and to crisis situations.

a. Everyday life. While crisis situations and the structures that developed in response to them are perhaps more obvious, the structures for care in the ordinary day-to-day life of individuals and groups are at least as important. In ancient Israel these included rituals and routines of various kinds, whether directly related to the cult or not, more or less stable social patterns such as family, tribe and—sometimes—state, and the transmission of conventional wisdom about life. All such structures established and maintained identity for individuals and groups. In the patriarchal family structure the place of all persons in relationship to others was clear. Rituals marked one's place in relation to both others and to God, and assured the safe passage from one stage of life to another. The function of the law and its transmission and interpretation was to enable people to define themselves. The covenant affirmed that they were Yahweh's people; the law defined what that meant. Everyday wisdom in the form of proverbs or even cliches taught one practical matters and morals. The recitation of the tribal and national traditions located persons in relation to time and the divine purpose, and could enable a people to see themselves as either fulfilling or failing to fulfil their destiny.

Ordinary life, almost without exception affirmed as good, was attended from the cradle to the grave by rituals and practices concerned with care. The circumcision of male children marked their membership in the covenant community. Sexuality was understood as natural and good (Gen. 1:28; 2:22–25; Song of Songs). Structures of authority in the patriarchal family were very clear and seldom challenged. Rights, responsibilities, and behavior in general within the family were geared to maintain stability. Laws concerning family relationships ranged from prohibitions of adultery to taboos concerning sexual relationships with family members to provisions for the care of widows and orphans. Aging as such was not viewed as a crisis situation at all. To the contrary, age brought distinction, honor, and authority. The "elders" in effect ruled the society at the local level.

b. Crisis situations. There can hardly be a more serious crisis than death, including the pain, suffering, and fear that precedes it and the grief that follows it. Such certainly was the case in ancient Israel, where death was perceived as the final boundary, the end of life without hope for resurrection or immortality. To live, especially in the land that the Lord gives (Deut. 30:16), was a blessing; to die young was a tragedy and a curse. Two features stand out in Israel's typical reactions in the face of death. The first is its openness, reflected especially in the Psalms of individual complaint discussed above. Many of these Psalms describe death in effect as a process, with the gradual loss of mobility, light, and community (cf. Psalms 6; 13; 22; 30; 38; C. Barth). The second is the reliance on the community. To die alone and forsaken was the most painful death.

This corporate solidarity is all the more striking given the fact that in priestly tradition, contact with a corpse rendered one unclean (Num. 19; 31:19–24; Lev. 21:1–12). Thus the funeral was not conducted in the sacred precincts of the temple, but would have been a ritual of the primary group. There are allusions to more or less professional mourners (Amos 5:16), and to some other rites for burial. Above all, the body should not be dishonored (I Sam. 31:8–13), but a person should be buried in his or her homeland (Genesis 23; II Sam. 21:12–13). The most important texts for understanding grief in ancient Israel are the dirges or funeral songs. The most poignant of these is David's lament over Saul and Jonathan (II Sam. 1:19–27), but its elements are typical and instructive: consistent with Israel's willingness to express the deepest possible feelings — even anger and outrage — to God in prayer and worship, the expression of grief is not

only allowed but encouraged. Thus mourning is articulated openly (vs. 26), and the community is called to join in (vs. 24). The grieving one recalls the previous times of joy with the departed (vss. 22–23), and expresses reluctance to accept the fact that the final blow has fallen. There is a call to remember, at the same time expressing the seriousness of the loss. Such ritual patterns enabled ancient Israelites to come to terms with grief.

In many respects the perception and care of illness in ancient Israel was similar to what has been said about death. Along with pain and suffering, one who is ill has diminished capacity and therefore — at least potentially — approaches death. The desire of the sick person and the goal of those who care for him or her is the restoration of the previous condition of health (Seybold and Mueller, p. 11), the re-establishment of *shalom*.

The OT reports or alludes to instances of what we would call mental as well as physical illness. A classic example of what may be the former is the case of Saul. The OT interpretation of his malady, linked with the account of the transfer of kingship from him to David, is quite explicit: "Now the Spirit of the Lord departed from Saul, and an evil spirit from the Lord tormented him" (I Sam. 16:14). Therapeutic steps were taken by the king's servants: they called in a musician — David — who would play when the spirit tormented him and make him "well" (I Sam. 16:16). Although the playing "refreshed" him (I Sam. 16:23), the symptoms eventually worsened and contributed to Saul's conflicts with David and his eventual downfall.

Illness would have been viewed from various perspectives, including those of the sick individual and of the ones charged with providing care, but it clearly was both a corporate and a religious concern. One finds instances of miraculous healing by prophets (e.g., I Kings 17:17–24), always as testimony to the power of God, but by and large both sickness and death are recognized as inevitable. The health of the individual was directly related to the health of the community, and in relationship to Yahweh. This is especially clear in the priestly interpretation and response to particular illnesses, especially visible afflictions such as skin diseases. Such illnesses were viewed as pollution with the potential to pollute the people as a whole. The concern for contagion was not fundamentally medical but religious. Therefore detailed procedures were prescribed by means of which the priests could diagnose the illness—such as skin ailments incorrectly understood as leprosy — and implement proper responses (Leviticus 13). Such diseased persons were ostracized, but there were also ritual procedures for cleansing them and returning them to the community (Leviticus 14).

Many crisis situations that called for care were explicitly public and corporate. These were the obvious national disasters such as military threat or defeat and natural disasters such as drought or pestilence. The most persistent responses were cultic: times of national trouble called for prayer services that included mourning, confession, petition, and expressions of confidence in God (see the book of Joel, especially 2:12–17). There were also corporate crises of meaning and faith, such as the one evoked by the Babylonian Exile. With the loss of the land promised to the ancestors, the destruction of the temple and the disruption of all the major institutions, many obviously asked whether Yawheh had abandoned them, or if the gods of the Babylonians were in control. Among the many reactions to this crisis, none is more significant than the works of the scholars and scribes who both collected and recorded the ancient traditions and interpreted the present in terms of the past. One of the aims of the large history work that reaches from Deuteronomy through II Kings was to account for the disaster as punishment for a history of sin. Remarkably, such a recital — as well as the words of the old prophets of judgment — could serve as confession of sin and therefore as the basis for a new future and a new covenant.

5. **Contemporary Implications.** The implications of OT traditions and theology of care for contemporary pastoral care may be considered from several perspectives. First, understanding the biblical traditions enables one to comprehend more fully the context of care in modern culture. This is so because biblical views—their intepretation and even misinterpretation—have contributed to the Jewish and Christian understandings of life, and to cultures such as ours with deep roots in those traditions. Much of the modern language of self-understanding depends heavily on the Bible, including the OT. It is not self-evident except on the basis of biblical faith, for example, that the interpretation of human life and its problems should depend so directly upon the language of sin, guilt, and forgiveness. Nor would it be so generally taken for granted that human beings are created by God and accountable to God except for the influence of the Bible.

Second, the OT theology and traditions may function critically with regard to modern views. At the simplest level the OT may be a mirror to self-understanding, an essential conversation partner for those who see themselves as part of that biblical tradition. Through the reading and interpretation of the texts we understand ourselves both by means of identification and dissonance, by seeing ourselves and others more deeply reflected in the stories and the poetry, and by recognizing the sometimes sharp contrasts between our understandings and those of ancient Israel. At the very least, one's horizons can be expanded. More than that, one can objectify experience and examine it, to be in dialogue beyond oneself. In another way — at the level of normative theological reflection—the biblical traditions may serve to affirm or deny the claims or assumptions that particular perspectives are in fact biblical. For example, the widely held view that death and disasters are "the will of God" obviously has some affinity to certain biblical traditions. Biblical theological reflection on this assertion, however, reveals that this is only one view among others in the OT tradition, and that in the last analysis it is contrary to the most fundamental assumptions about God, humanity, and history: historical events are the result of the interaction of human beings with the vulnerable and graceful will of God.

Third, an approach to pastoral care that is attentive to the OT will be guided by the following basic perspectives: (1) One should neither take for granted nor overlook the obvious theocentric character of biblical thought. Thus any biblical understanding of care will be founded on the conviction that God is active in human life and history, and that any concern for the care of others will be lived out in the context of divine care. (2) Human beings are not only creatures but children of God, and destined for covenantal relationship with God. On the one hand, as children of God they have within themselves the resources necessary for life. On the other hand, human lives are characterized by finitude, sin and brokenness. (3) Biblical care is communal and corporate, not individualistic. The health and peace of individuals is both affected by and affects the community as a whole. Those who recognize such facts live in covenant with one another and with God. (4) Given the historical and even physical concreteness of biblical thought, care is neither abstract nor general nor merely "spiritual." Rather, life in its historical particularity is taken with ultimate seriousness. (5) OT thought knows of a relationship between God and people that allows for the free and full expression of all feelings—however negative they may appear— even in the life of prayer and worship. Confrontation has a place, both in the suffering individual's confrontation of God and the prophet's confrontation of the people or specific individuals. (6) Biblical means of care are by no means limited to one form of response but are diverse. These means include the work of religious specialists of various types and institutions that range from the cult to the state, but above all the people as a whole participate in the care of one another.

Bibliography. L. Bailey, *Biblical Perspectives on Death* (1979). C. Barth, *Die Errettung vom Tode in den individuellen Klage- und Dankliedern des Alten Testamentes* (1947). W. Brueggemann, "From Hurt to Joy, From Death to Life," *Interpretation,* 28 (1974), 3–19; *In Man We Trust* (1972); "The Formfulness of Grief," *Interpretation,* 31 (1977), 263–75. D. Capps, *Biblical Approaches to Pastoral Counseling* (1981); *Pastoral Care and Hermeneutics* (1986). B. H. Childs, *Old Testament Theology in a Canonical Context* (1985). R. E. Clements, *Old Testament Theology* (1978). J. L. Crenshaw, ed., *Theodicy in the Old Testament* (1983); *A Whirlpool of Torment* (1984). P. A. H. De Boer, "The Counsellor," in *Wisdom in Israel and the Ancient Near East,* M. Noth and D. W. Thomas, eds. *Supplementis to Vetus Testamentum,* 3 (1955), 42–71. G. Fohrer, *History of Israelite Religion* (1972). T. E. Fretheim, *The Suffering of God: An Old Testament Perspective* (1984). E. Gerstenberger, *Der bittende Mensch: Bittritual und Klagelied des Einzeln im Alten Testament* (1980). E. Gerstenberger and W. Schrage, *Suffering* (1980). N. Habel, "'Only the Jackal is my Friend': On Friends and Redeemers in Job," *Interpretation,* 31 (1977), 227–36. W. Harrelson, "Wisdom and Pastoral Theology," *Andover Newton Quarterly,* 7 (1966), 6–14. A. R. Johnson, *The Vitality of the Individual in the Thought of Ancient Israel* 2d ed. (1964). O. Kaiser and E. Lohse, *Death and Life* (1981). W. E. Oates, *The Bible in Pastoral Care* (1953) W. B. Oglesby, Jr. *Biblical Themes for Pastoral Care* (1980); "Pastoral Care and Counseling in Biblical Perspective," *Interpretation,* 27 (1973), 307–26. G. von Rad, *Old Testament Theology,* vol. 1 (1962), vol. 2 (1965); *Wisdom in Israel* (1972). J. W. Rogerson, "The Hebrew Conception of Corporate Personality," *J. of Theological Studies,* 21 (1970), 1–16. K. Sakenfeld, *Faithfulness in Action: Loyalty in Biblical Perspective* (1985). K. Seybold and U. B. Mueller, *Sickness and Healing* (1981). E. E. Shelp and R. Sunderland, eds., *A Biblical Basis for Ministry* (1981). S. Terrien, *The Elusive Presence: Toward a New Biblical Theology* (1978). W. S. Towner, *How God Deals with Evil* (1976). G. M. Tucker, "The Role of the Prophets and the Role of the Church," *Quarterly Review,* 1:5 (1981), 5–22. C. Westermann, *Blessing in the Bible and the Life of the Church* (1978); "The Role of the Lament in the

Theology of the Old Testament," *Interpretation*, 28 (1974), 20–38. C. A. Wise, *Psychiatry and the Bible* (1956). W. W. Wolff, *Anthropology of the Old Testament* (1974). W. Zimmerli, *Old Testament Theology in Outline* (1978).

G. M. TUCKER

JEWISH CARE AND COUNSELING; MINISTRY (Biblical Origins and Principles); PSALMS, PASTORAL USE OF; TEN COMMANDMENTS; WISDOM TRADITION, BIBLICAL. *See also* BIBLE, PASTORAL USE AND INTERPRETATION OF; BIBLICAL ANTHROPOLOGY; PASTORAL CARE (History, Traditions, and Definitions); PERSON; SHEPHERD/SHEPHERDING. *Compare* NEW TESTAMENT, TRADITIONS AND THEOLOGY OF CARE IN; *also* EDUCATION, NURTURE, AND CARE; PROPHETIC/PASTORAL TENSION IN MINISTRY; RITUAL AND PASTORAL CARE; SOCIOLOGY OF RELIGIOUS AND PASTORAL CARE; WORLD VIEW.

OLDER PERSONS, JEWISH CARE AND COUNSELING OF.

Respect for the aged is deeply rooted in Jewish tradition as is the related concept of honoring father and mother (Ex. 20:12, Lev. 19:32). However, caring for the aged as a group apart from the poor and the downtrodden is a comparatively modern concept.

1. **History.** The Bible usually regards longevity as a reward for righteousness. The commandment to honor father and mother is the only commandment that proffers longevity for those who keep it. A more balanced approach is contained in Ecclesiastes (12:1–6). Respect for the aged was not only part of the biblical tradition but also the custom throughout the ancient Middle East (Ahikar 2:61). Disrespect for the aged was looked upon as a sign of barbarism.

In ancient Israel the elderly were highly regarded and served in leadership roles within the Jewish community (Num. 11:16). When they were no longer able to function in that capacity, they were absorbed into their extended families. In the Middle Ages persecutions and massacres, which were often followed by migrations and the breakup of families, brought additional suffering to the elderly. While those who were separated from their families received charity from the Jewish community, no specific institutions yet existed to care for the aged.

Communal institutions for the aged were developed during the eighteenth century in response to the disintegration of the extended family. As a result, there was less family cohesiveness and increased generational estrangement. These are essentially the same conditions that have shaped the caring for the aged in contemporary society. The Sephardic community of Amsterdam built a home for the aged as early as 1749. By the end of the nineteenth century most large Jewish communities in Europe had established an old-age home among their other welfare institutions, had clearly accepted responsibility for the elderly, and had come to see aging and the aged as a social issue distinct from poverty.

2. **Contemporary Approaches.** The twentieth century has brought a new understanding of the social and psychological needs of the aged and an increasing realization that society must take some responsibility for providing for the elderly. At the same time the dramatic increase in life expectancy and the ability of modern medicine to prolong life have created a new set of problems.

Increasingly, a variety of alternative lifestyles exists for the elderly. Those who are able to remain in their own homes or with their families and to care for themselves with limited professional assistance can avail themselves of many programs sponsored by the Jewish community, for example, a hot kosher meal served at the local synagogue or Jewish community center, or delivered to the homes of shut-in persons. Those who live in senior citizen housing may avail themselves of amenities that make life for the elderly more pleasant. For those who cannot take care of themselves, almost every large Jewish community has a Jewish home for the aged. These homes often evoke in the elderly warm memories of the past with the serving of special foods and the planned observance of Jewish customs and holidays. Many large Jewish communities also have senior citizen housing that incorporates transitional care and nursing home facilities.

The traditional Jewish concern for the elderly reflects itself in the fact that some of the leading and most respected institutions for caring for the elderly and the infirm are Jewish. Many of the pioneers in geriatric psychiatry are also Jewish.

3. **The Role of the Rabbi.** The role of the rabbi in caring for the elderly is a significant one from a pastoral, as well as from a communal, perspective. The rabbi customarily visits not only the hospitalized elderly but also attends to the needs of the shut-in persons. However, regular home visitations for those who are not housebound are not the norm except in response to specific requests. In addition, the rabbi is involved in creating community infrastructures and fostering family settings where care for the elderly can be enhanced.

Bibliography. *Encyclopedia Judaica*, vol. 2, "Age and the Aged" (1971). M. Berezin and S. Cath, *Geriatric Psychiatry* (1965). D. Clingan, *Aging Persons in the Community of Faith* (1980). Synagogue Council of America, *Guide to Aging Programs for Synagogues* (1975).

I. H. FISHBEIN

AGING; LIFE CYCLE THEORY AND PASTORAL CARE. *See also* JEWISH CARE AND COUNSELING (History, Traditions, and Contemporary Issues). *Compare* MIDLIFE PERSONS.

OLDER PERSONS, MENTAL DISORDERS OF.

The mental disorders of late life encompass both organic and functional conditions. The organic conditions include Alzheimer's disease and related disorders while the principle functional disorders are depression and paranoia. Symptoms are not exclusively associated with one condition or another, so diagnosis must be thoroughly accomplished by competent practitioners.

The incidence of mental disorders probably increases across the life span, principally due to the increased incidence of cognitive disturbances and depression. In 1975 persons over sixty-five represented twenty-eight percent of all mental hospital patients, while they constituted less than eleven percent of the population.

1. **Functional Conditions.** The category of functional disorders which is termed affective disorders includes depression and mania (elation). These are primarily disorders of *mood* rather than thinking process as in schizophrenia. The symptoms include dysphoria (sad mood), somatic symptoms (sleep and appetite disturbances), reduced social contacts, psychomotor retardation or agitation, and suicidal ideation. Hypochondriasis and physiological signs are common. Mild cognitive symptoms of

disorientation and memory loss may sometimes accompany depression and are referred to as pseudodementia.

It is difficult to identify the precise cause of depression, although there are often stressful life events, including significant and multiple losses which may be contributing factors. It is also suspected that chemical changes in the brain may be a factor. Depressive reactions often occur along with physical diseases involving incapacity and chronic pain. Many drugs taken by the elderly, such as hypertensive and cardiac medications, may cause depression.

Treatment of depression in the elderly includes psychopharmacology, electroconvulsive therapy, and psychotherapy (Busse and Blazer, 1980). Research has shown cognitive and behavioral approaches to psychotherapy to be the most effective in reducing the feelings of depression in the elderly (Gallagher and Thompson, 1981). Dynamically, depression in the elderly is more a function of feelings of inferiority and loss of self-esteem than guilt surrounding unacceptable impulses (Busse and Blazer, 1980).

Paranoia (suspiciousness and persecutory delusions) is disturbing to all who have contact with an older person suffering from it. If the onset is in later life it is usually in the context of social isolation exacerbated by sensory losses, most commonly vision and hearing loss. It may also accompany dementia. In other instances it is consistent with a lifelong pattern which becomes exaggerated as the losses of aging are experienced. Schizophrenia in older people may be the continuation of an early adulthood chronic condition or more rarely may begin late in life as an acute condition. Therapy is largely symptomatic and includes social interventions, substitution of losses, and antipsychotic medication.

2. Organic Conditions. Delirium specifies an acute (rapid) onset syndrome with attentional, memory, and orientation deficits. This can result from a wide variety of physical disorders and toxic conditions. It is imperative to distinguish delirium from the more chronic senile dementias.

Impairment of previously acquired intellectual functions such as memory and orientation are the most prominent features of senile dementia. The most common dementia is Alzheimer's disease, a progressively degenerative condition which on post-mortem reveals atrophy of the frontal and temporal lobes of the brain cortex. The life expectancy is about five years (Busse and Blazer).

Multi-infarct dementia is responsible for ten to twenty percent of the dementias. A step-wise deterioration is seen in the context of hypertension. Other causes of dementia include Parkinson's disease, normal pressure hydrocephalus, Huntington's chorea and Creutzfeldt-Jacob disease.

Treatment of the patient is generally symptomatic but will need to include family consultation. Psychotropic medications may be used to control agitation and some psychotic-like symptoms. Strategies which focus on structuring the environment and reality-orienting interventions can maximize functioning. Questions regarding safety in the home and placement will need to be considered by the family.

Bibliography. E. W. Busse and D. G. Blazer, *Handbook of Geriatric Psychiatry* (1980). D. Gallagher and L. W. Thompson, *Depression in the Elderly* (1981). A. L. Meiburg, "Understanding Senile 'Confusion': Sources and Stages," *Pastoral Psychology,* 31 (1983) 161–69. G. D. Weaver, "Senile Dementia and a Resurrection Theology," *Theology Today,* 42:4 (1986) 444–56.

C. Z. BENSON

AGING; EVALUATION AND DIAGNOSIS, PSYCHOLOGICAL; ORGANIC MENTAL DISORDER AND ORGANIC BRAIN SYNDROME.

OLDER PERSONS, PASTORAL CARE AND COUNSELING OF. In this article, "older persons" refers to persons over age fifty-five. With ever-increasing longevity, this developmental stage can constitute up to one-third of the total life span. This has resulted in two generations of older persons: the "young old" (those 55-74) and the "old old" (those seventy-five and over). It is estimated that, in the year 2000, forty-four percent of older persons will be over seventy-five (Meiburg, 1985). Therefore, the following themes regarding the pastoral care and counseling of older persons must be viewed with their relative applicability to the varying phases of this stage.

1. Theological Issues. Of prime concern for older persons is the meaning of *vocation.* Studies have shown that workers in the U.S. tend to endow their jobs, regardless of their nature, with a profound sense of vocation. This attachment of theological and ethical values to one's work gives a sense of meaningful participation in society which is often lost upon retirement. Loss of work thus can result in a loss of a primary source of meaning, identity, and (according to Freud) mental health (Pruyser, 1975).

Thus a spiritual task for the older person is to reframe the sense of self apart from work role (Meiburg, 1985). In a society replete with "works theology," this involves a personal integration of the fundamental meaning of justification by faith (Rom. 5:1; Eph. 2:8–10)—the acceptance of self, others, and God for who one *is* rather than for what one *does.* Vocation can then be seen as the appropriate, focused investment of one's life energy in contrast to simply one's paid occupation (Hiltner, 1975). In the Jewish tradition, for example, the older years are regarded as the sabbath of one's life; the meaning of the word sabbath does not imply complete inactivity but rather an opportunity to do that which one could not do before, such as a more intensive study of Scripture or attention to important moral and ethical concerns of society. A disabled person living in a nursing home may discover a vocation in visiting and encouraging other residents of the home.

Another primary theological issue is that of *finitude.* As a person ages, he or she is faced with the gradual limitation of life choices and options. The seemingly boundless opportunities of youth become increasingly narrow, so that one is forced toward either acceptance or rejection of the major life directions which were decided upon in earlier years. This involves a fundamental confrontation with the physical, financial, social, vocational, and spiritual limits with which one is faced in older age. The spiritual task is to achieve faith and values which enable one to transcend the immediate limits of the self.

Related to finitude is the anxiety of *nonbeing*. Paul Tillich (1952) defines anxiety as "the state in which a being is aware of its possible nonbeing." The aging process, combined with the death of persons close to us, make us existentially aware of the certainty of our own death. The threat of nonbeing calls forth the spiritual task of a deeper understanding of the meaning of resurrection and eternal life (I Cor. 15:51–58) and the unchanging love of God (Rom. 8:35–39).

2. **Developmental Issues.** Erik Erikson has identified the primary developmental task of older persons as "integrity vs. despair." The positive resolution of this task results in wisdom, which Erikson defines as "informed and detached concern with life itself in the face of death itself" (1982). The negative counterpart of wisdom is despair and disdain, which is basically a bitter rejection of one's place in life — a rejection of the self as finished and helpless.

The struggles of this stage prompt a natural activity for older persons—the remembrance of significant past events in their life and the retelling of those stories to the self and others. While this kind of reminiscence is often dismissed as a sign of senescence or "living in the past," such a review of one's life can be a very positive and integrating activity. For some, it is an adaptive response which enables an older person to cope with physical disability by recalling stories from his or her youthful past which demonstrated physical prowess, recovery from illness or escape from danger (McMahon and Rhudick, 1967).

Robert N. Butler (1963) noted that realization of approaching death prompts a natural, progressive return to consciousness of past experiences and, particularly, unresolved conflicts which are surveyed and reintegrated. The older person may reveal to significant others previously undisclosed qualities or truths about the self which can change the quality and intimacy of lifelong relationships. In the life review, a substantial reorganization of the personality can occur which contributes to the evolution of wisdom and serenity.

Randall (1986) applies Kohut's self-psychology to the life review in noting that "self-narratives" provide older persons with a sense of continuity or consistency in the face of disturbing life changes. The recall and affirmation of the achievements in one's life help to create and preserve a sense of personal significance and meaning; this review also becomes a source of hope for the future.

Lewis Sherrill (1951) noted that the primary task of the older person is achieving simplification of the physical, social, material, and spiritual aspects of one's life. The older person is faced with the loss of many important aspects of life — status, home, material possessions, physical health and agility, and important relationships. These multiple losses in a relatively short period of time can result in a telescoped and nearly chronic grief reaction which tests the faith issues of basic values and philosophy of life. If one has primarily found meaning and identity in accumulated wealth and status, the simplification process is devastating. On the other hand, if the core qualities of relationships with self, others, and God are given primary importance, simplification is received more graciously and perhaps even welcomed.

C. G. Jung (1933) also noted that the afternoon of life "means the reversal of all the ideals and values that were cherished in the morning." In the first half of life, one follows the purposes of nature — development of the individual, establishment of career and place in society, reproduction and raising of children. The meaning and purpose of the second half of life, however, lie in culture; one's primary focus turns from the outer world to the development of the inner world — a deeper understanding and apprehension of spiritual, aesthetic, and cultural values.

While it is often natural for a person approaching the threshold of old age to look backward with regrets over unfulfilled potential and unsatisfied demands, Jung asserts that "it is better to go forward with the stream of time than backwards against it." The promise of eternal life enables one to view death not as a cruel end but as a transition—"as part of a life process whose extent and duration are beyond our knowledge" (1933, p. 402).

3. **Pastoral Care and Counseling.** Meiburg (1985) asserts that "the aim of pastoral care is to challenge senior adults to discover their unique growth possibilities and to sustain and encourage them to use the resources of their faith" (p. 95). This implies that pastoral care and counseling of older persons is not just what is done *for* persons who are unable to assume their own responsibility and initiative; it is rather ministry *with* persons— "among people who are in a dynamic and evolving relationship together" (Clements, 1981).

Thus, the church's pastoral care of older persons includes providing a place for ministry. This might include volunteer service in the church or community, consulting work for special projects, preparing an oral or written history of the congregation, record keeping or financial accounting, assisting in day care of children, or ministry to the ill or disabled. In all, personal and pastoral relationships are more important than the mere provision of activity.

Another important aspect in care and counseling is family relationships, especially between adult children and their parents. As older persons are involved in major life decisions regarding health care, finances, and living arrangements, open and accepting relationships are needed in order to enable the older person to make the right choices with dignity and as much autonomy as possible. Adult children need to be able to confess feelings of guilt, anger, and frustration without allowing their own needs for control to override their parents' right of self-determination (see Lester and Lester, 1980).

Religious rituals are also of prime importance in ministry to the elderly. The sacraments, traditions, and music in worship take on deeper meaning and significance as a person grows older and has lifelong memories associated with these practices. Religious rituals represent continuity and the steadfast presence of God in the midst of loss and change. For the disabled and homebound, home communion and regular pastoral visits are important reminders of both the caring community and the grace of God.

Finally, at a deeper level, effective ministry to older persons requires coming to terms with the "elderly stranger" within ourselves (Nouwen, 1976). Avoidance of a deep pastoral relationship with the elderly can be due to a denial of our own aging process and the fear of what older persons represent. As young and old are able to meet in the common bond of the human condition, a most important aspect of ministry may occur. The younger person may be able to learn of and accept the meaning of growing old, and the older person may be able to give the redemptive gift of wisdom by representing faith and courage in the midst of suffering or loss. As these precious gifts are shared in the midst of ministry, both the minister and the older person may experience the kind of hope expressed in the Song of Simeon:

> "Lord, now lettest thou thy servant depart in peace, according to thy word; for mine eyes have seen thy salvation which thou hast prepared in the presence of all peoples, a light for revelation to the Gentiles, and for glory to thy people Israel" (Lk. 2:29−32).

Bibliography. R. N. Butler, "The Life Review: An Interpretation of Reminiscence in the Aged," *Psychiatry,* 26 (1963), 65–76. W. M. Clements, ed., *Ministry With the Aging* (1981). E. H. Erikson, *The Life Cycle Completed* (1982). S. Hiltner, "Discussion and Comment," in S. Hiltner, ed., *Toward a Theology of Aging* (1975). C. G. Jung, "The Stages of Life," *Collected Works* 8 (1960 [1933]), 387–403. A. D. Lester and J. L. Lester, *Understanding Aging Parents* (1980). A. W. McMahon and P. J. Rhudick, "Reminiscing in the Aged: An Adaptational Response," in S. Levin and R. J. Kahana, eds., *Psychodynamic Studies on Aging* (1967). A. L. Meiburg, "Pastoral Care with the Aged: The Spiritual Dimension," in G. L. Borchert and A. D. Lester, eds., *Spiritual Dimensions of Pastoral Care* (1985). H. J. M. Nouwen and W. J. Gaffney, *Aging: The Fulfillment of Life* (1976). P. W. Pruyser, "Aging: Downward, Upward, or Forward?" in S. Hiltner, ed., *Toward a Theology of Aging* (1975). R. L. Randall, "Reminiscing in the Elderly: Pastoral Care of Self Narratives," *J. of Pastoral Care,* 40 (1986), 207–15. L. J. Sherrill, *The Struggle of the Soul* (1951). P. Tillich, *The Courage to Be* (1952).

G. H. ASQUITH, JR.

AGING; LIFE CYCLE THEORY AND PASTORAL CARE; RETIREMENT; VOCATION. *Compare* MIDLIFE PERSONS.

ONLY CHILDREN. In the early part of this century G. Stanley Hall suggested, "being an only child is a disease in itself." He continued, "Because of the undue attention he [or she] demands and usually receives, we commonly find the only child jealous, selfish, egotistical, dependent, aggressive, domineering, or quarrelsome."

1. Theoretical Conceptions. Adler (1927) suggested that the location of one's birth order within the family had an impact upon the personality. Because the one-child family was seen as unusual, even abnormal, and the parents in such a family as unconventional, most conceptions of a child raised in that atmosphere include the assumption that a negative impact occurs. Description of the only child's nature include: maladjusted, self-centered, self-willed, spoiled, unlikeable, attention seeking, temperamental, expecting to be supported, indulged, protected, dependent on others, demanding, and generally unhappy. Less frequently, perspectives occur that suggest the only child may develop confidence and other desirable characteristics. Perhaps the desire to please adults, who are such a significant part of the only child's

world, facilitates greater achievement motivation. The only child also may display a strong sense of autonomy and independence because of the increased rates of divorce, separation, and difficult births, which may account for the lack of siblings.

2. Research Findings. Research literature reveals few findings that set only children apart. Those findings that suggest differences are also contradictory. On one hand studies have found that only children more frequently seek psychiatric help, use more drugs, report having fewer friends, are more conceited, more maladjusted, and experience greater unconscious feelings of guilt than non-onlies. Other studies suggest they differentiate emotional expressions more successfully, are more sociable, self-confident, resourceful, independent and assertive, achieve greater educational attainment, are more trusting, and more intelligent than children with siblings. The relative lack of studies available accompanied by small sample sizes, questions of methodology, and conflicting findings make it difficult to draw any definite conclusions about the only child. Certainly the research does not support the view of the only child as a "monster." Despite these inconclusive findings the popular belief continues that children who grow up without siblings are at a disadvantage.

3. Practical Applications. The pastor may be influenced in his or her view of the parishioner or counselee by the critical stereotypes of only children. Unfortunately, in counseling or psychotherapy, this contamination can become a stumbling block to the therapy process and play a part in the diagnosis and outcome. It is important to move beyond existing portraits of the only child to a less judgmental attitude. The psychological realities, as determined by the counselees definition of the impact of being an only child, are more important issues than the generally unsupported theoretical descriptions of only children.

Bibliography. A. Adler, *Understanding Human Nature* (1927). J. Almodovar, "Is There An Only Child Syndrome?" *Enfance,* June (1973). T. Falbo, "The Only Child: A Review," *J. of Individual Psychology,* 33 (1977), 47–61. G. S. Hall, *Aspects of Child Life and Education* (1921).

R. D. BERRETT

BIRTH ORDER; CHILDREN; PARENTS/PARENTHOOD.

OPENNESS. *See* EXISTENTIALISM AND PASTORAL CARE; INTIMACY AND DISTANCE; PHENOMENOLOGICAL METHOD IN PASTORAL CARE.

OPERANT CONDITIONING. *See* BEHAVIORISM; BEHAVIOR THERAPIES; CONDITIONING.

OPPRESSION. *See* EXPLOITATION/OPPRESSION.

OPTIMISM. *See* HOPE AND DESPAIR; WILL/WILLING. *See also* MIND CURE MOVEMENT.

ORDERS. *See* HOLY ORDERS; RELIGIOUS, PASTORAL CARE OF; RELIGIOUS LIFE.

ORDINANCES. *See* SACRAMENTS, ORDINANCES, AND RITES, TERMINOLOGY AND CONCEPTS OF.

ORDINATION AND CERTIFICATION IN PASTORAL COUNSELING.

Ordination refers to a faith community's designation of a person as having special responsibilities and functions which are carried out in a representative capacity for the community, usually following evidence of special gifts and calling and often the completion of educational requirements of a general, theological nature. *Certification* here refers to the endorsement given to a specialized professional practitioner, such as a pastoral counselor, by a professional organization such as the American Association of Pastoral Counselors (AAPC) upon completion of advanced education and the demonstration of specialized competency. Both ordination and certification confer the right to practice specialized functions and responsibilities and some form of ongoing accountability to the endorsing body. Ordination's rights and responsibilities are broad and tied to the church or religious community; certification is specialized and tied primarily to the professional organization.

The emergence of pastoral counseling as a specialized ministry with its own standards of competence and its own certifying organizations and procedures inevitably raises the question how the criteria and structures of accountability of the profession relate to those of the church. Generally, professional organizations involved in ministry, like AAPC, require ordination or its equivalent of their members and view certification as an indication of specialized competency within ordained ministry, establishing specialized structures of accountability for the pastor in addition to denominational authority (not in place of it).

1. **Ordination.** Ordination conveys authority which is granted to the clergyperson by a faith group to preach and teach the Word of God, to administer the sacraments, to conduct worship, to evangelize, to engage in pastoral care and counseling with those persons entrusted to his or her care, and to participate in some fashion in the governance of the church. Similarly, the ordaining faith group has the authority to hold the clergyperson accountable in his or her representative capacity.

Alongside this general meaning of ordination, each faith group determines its own designations and qualifications for ordination, and there is variety concerning precise procedures and requirements. For some faith communities, ordination becomes an inherent dimension of the clergyperson's life and ministry which is never abrogated. For others, ordination is effected for only so long as the person continues to meet the prerequisites, perform the appropriate duties, and remain committed to the ordination vows. Should any or all of these be relinquished or abandoned, or should the person be found guilty of a breach of commitment or experience a radical change in his or her vowed beliefs, then the ordination is withdrawn and the person returns to the general lay status as defined by each faith group. With respect to the specialized pastoral care ministries, differences arise as to the meaning or necessity of ordination. All faith groups recognize that certain members of the groups perform competent and constructive functions in the bearing of human burdens, the easing of human suffering, and the providing of guidance and nurture. While caring for the people of God is the gift of God to the entire faith community, ordination identifies persons who may be designated as functioning for the entire faith group rather than as individual members of the faith group. Thus, even though nonordained persons provide valuable services in the alleviation of human stress, only those persons who are ordained or designated by the faith group for a particular ministry are generally understood at this point in time to function on behalf of the people of God.

2. **Certification.** The fact that there is a variety of definitions, procedures, and requisites for ordination constitutes a critical problem for the certification of persons as pastoral counselors by recognized professional groups such as the AAPC. Since the term "pastoral" connotes a corporate, ecclesial dimension, then by definition all pastoral counselors represent a faith community and do not function independently. At the same time, certain faith communities have strictures against the ordination of certain categories of persons (e.g., the Roman Catholic Church does not ordain women). In such cases, certifying organizations pay attention to the "core" of the ordination process, the concept of appropriate accountability. This means seeing evidence that through such rites as consecration or equivalent means, the person has been endorsed by his or her faith community and has established lines of accountability with it. The intent of ordination has then been fulfilled for the purposes of pastoral counseling specialization and certification. This practice is not generally true for persons who belong to faith communities where ordination is possible, as certifying groups have no interest in defining requisites for ordination or consecration for any faith group. The variety of forms of ordination or consecration are seen also in the fashion by which the faith communities exercise ecclesiastical supervision of the persons ordained or consecrated. In some faith communities considerable attention is given to the requisite for endorsement but scant attention to a continued practice of accountability. As a consequence, the basic purpose of ordination may be abrogated in practice. Ordinarily, the certifying groups have nonetheless given attention to the persons certified maintaining good standing in the faith community which effected the endorsement. In this sense if the good standing ceases to exist, the certification is ordinarily withdrawn.

Bibliography. Consultation on Church Union, ch. 7, "Ministry," *The COCU Consensus: In Quest of a Church of Christ Uniting* (1984). B. Cooke, *Ministry to Word and Sacraments: History and Theology* (1976). E. Schillebeeckx, *The Church with a Human Face* (1985). World Council of Churches, *Baptism, Eucharist and Ministry,* Faith and Order Paper No. 111 (1982).

S. R. BROWN

PASTORAL COUNSELING. *See also* CALL TO MINISTRY; IDENTITY, PASTORAL; MINISTRY; RABBI/RABBINATE; THEOLOGICAL STUDENTS, PASTORAL CARE OF; VOWS/VOWING. *Compare* CAREER DEVELOPMENT AND GUIDANCE (For Pastors).

ORDINATION. *See* MINISTRY.

ORDINATION, SACRAMENT. *See* HOLY ORDERS.

ORGANIC MENTAL DISORDER AND ORGANIC BRAIN SYNDROME. In psychiatric diagnosis, organic mental disorder (OMD) refers to forms of brain dysfunction in which the etiology (causation) is suspected or known, as distinguished from "organic brain syndrome" (OBS) in which no reference is made to etiology. Both terms describe a cluster of psychological or behavioral manifestations of brain dysfunction; the distinction between them pertains solely to the issue of etiology.

In the diagnosis of mental illness a distinction is made between organic and functional impairment. It is assumed that all human psychological processes are related to brain functioning, whether normal or abnormal. However, the term "organic" is used when a suspected or confirmed abnormality of brain *structure* is regarded as the major contributor to a person's mental condition. The term "functional" is used when the main contributor is a person's response to psychological or environmental factors without evidence of structural impairment of brain functioning.

Organic mental disorder (OMD) is a relatively new term in mental health. Prior to 1980, organic brain syndrome (OBS) was used diagnostically to describe a single type of brain dysfunction with limited manifestations. However, because of the difficulty in diagnosing etiology in cases of mental dysfunction, and because of the limitations of current knowledge of these conditions, the third edition of the *Diagnostic and Statistical Manual* (DSM-III, 1980) introduced the additional term OMD to allow for more accurate description.

The addition of the OMD category was not intended to suggest that non-organic (or functional) mental disorders are unrelated to brain processes, but merely to recognize a distinction between conditions in which etiology could be determined or suspected and those in which it could not. The distinction between dysfunction due to known organic etiology and dysfunction more adequately attributed to psychological or social factors is not always clear, however. In some cases, the dysfunction may be due to a combination of organic and non-organic factors or to as yet unknown organic factors, as for example in schizophrenia.

1. Organic Brain Syndrome. All OBS categories, regardless of their course and severity, are associated with impairment of orientation, memory, intellectual functioning, judgment, and affect. The psychophysiologic functions of attention, perception, and memory (cognitive functioning) must be intact for a person to appreciate relations with time and place, one's own identity, and the identities of those in the world around one. A significant amount of OBS variability can be noted among individuals as well as within one individual over a period of time.

DSM-III identifies seven categories of OBS, the most common of which are delirium and dementia. (Other categories include amnestic syndrome, organic hallucinosis, organic delusional syndrome, organic affective syndrome, and organic personality syndrome. An extensive diagnostic description for each category is provided in the DSM-III.) The major characteristics of *delirium* are a clouded state of consciousness with difficulty in sustaining attention, disturbed sensory awareness, and disturbed thought processes. *Dementia's* major characteristics include impairment in job or social functioning due to loss of intellectual abilities (i.e., memory, judgment, abstract thought and other higher cortical functions) and changes in personality and behavior.

2. Organic Mental Disorder. OMD includes a heterogeneous group of disorders, making their description as a group difficult. However, disorders that are related to either aging of the brain or to ingestion of an identifiable substance are classified in this category. In the various disorders related to aging of the brain the accompanying features include delirium, delusions, or depression. Disorders related to ingestion of an identifiable substance are categorized by reference to the ten classes of most commonly taken substances: alcohol, barbiturates, opiods, cocaine, amphetamines, PCP, hallucinogens, cannabis (marijuana), tobacco, and caffeine. *Intoxication* is described in terms of the recent use and presence in the body of any of these classes of intoxicating substances together with associated maladaptive behaviors (the latter to distinguish pathological from recreational use). Specific clinical manifestations are determined by the substance but commonly include disturbances of perception, sleep, attention, thinking, judgment, impulse control, and psychomotor behavior. The major characteristics of *withdrawal* include a residual substance-specific syndrome following the cessation of or decrease in consumption of substance used previously to induce intoxication. Specific clinical manifestations tend to be substance specific, but commonly include anxiety, restlessness, irritability, insomnia, and impaired attention.

The primary characteristics of the OMDs is an abnormality of psychological or behavioral features associated with either short-term or permanent dysfunction of the brain. According to DSM-III, the OMD diagnosis is made by recognizing: (1) the presence of one of the OBSs or a functional disturbance (or both), and (2) identifying through the person's history, physical exam, laboratory tests, or neurological evaluations an organic factor specifically implicated in the dysfunctional mental status. Differences in a person's clinical manifestation, determined by a physician or medical team, reflect differences in the localization, mode of onset, progression, duration, and nature of underlying etiological process. Organic factors may include either a major illness which in turn affects the brain, or a disease of the brain itself. In addition, the presence of a substance or toxic agent in the body that is still actively affecting brain functioning can cause OMD. Even after the substance or toxic agent is no longer in the body, OMD can be attributed to long-lasting affects. A wide range of emotional, motivational, and behavioral abnormalities are associated with OMD for which many explanatory theories have been proposed.

3. Diagnostic Issues and Care. The proper identification of OMD and OBS is extremely important for both medical and psychological reasons. Symptoms of OMD and OBS can resemble other diseases. Therefore, the skills of medically trained professionals are required for proper diagnosis and medical treatment. Referral to an internist or neurologist is recommended. Psychological problems accompanying OMD and OBS can include emotional reactions to the loss of cognitive skills and the disruption of work performance, personal relationships, and self-esteem; thus psychological assessment may be needed to more accurately describe the personality and behavioral manifestations of OBS and OMD. More specific assessments also may be indicated in the cases of suspected cognitive impairment. Such information can be used as baseline against which recovery is plotted.

The families and friends of persons diagnosed as OMD and OBS invariably need support, which can be provided and facilitated by hospital chaplains, pastors, congregations, neighbors, and friends. Often help is needed in modifying living situations or environments and in adjusting to the patient's limitations, which can produce stress on themselves and others. Support groups in the local community can be tapped for both patients and family members. Meaningful daily activities also need to be arranged. While OMD and OBS usually require the involvement of specialized professionals, pastors and congregations can provide significant help to family and friends.

Bibliography. American Psychiatric Association, *Diagnostic and Statistical Manual,* 3d ed., rev. (1987).

L. F. MAJOVSKI

DIAGNOSTIC AND STATISTICAL MANUAL III; EVALUATION AND DIAGNOSIS, PSYCHOLOGICAL; MENTAL HEALTH AND ILLNESS; PSYCHOPATHOLOGY, THEORIES OF. *See also* ALCOHOL ABUSE, ADDICTION, AND THERAPY; PERSONALITY, BIOLOGICAL DIMENSIONS OF; BRAIN RESEARCH; CHRONIC ILLNESS; DRUG ABUSE, DEPENDENCE, AND TREATMENT; HANDICAP AND DISABILITY; MIND-BODY RELATIONSHIP; OLDER PERSONS, DISORDERS OF. *Compare* MENTAL RETARDATION; MINIMAL BRAIN DYSFUNCTION; NEUROLOGIC ILLNESSES.

ORGANISMIC THEORY. *See* PERSONALITY THEORY.

ORGANIZATION DEVELOPMENT. An organization is an administrative and functional structure, usually for the purpose of achieving a specific goal. Normally this will involve a hierarchical structuring of responsibility, a division of labor and an internal system of communication. The complexity of the organization varies with its size and the scope of its mission or goals, ranging from a simple primary grouping like the family to the international conglomerate.

Organizational development is a process which includes seven basic functions: planning, organizing, staffing, leading, controlling, deciding, and communicating. Each of these functions is equally important; the breakdown of an organization will usually be the result of failure to devote enough attention to one of these seven operations.

1. Planning. Planning is the management process of identifying the goals of the organization and intentionally moving the organization toward the achievement of those goals. Planning involves (1) the review of the organizational mission—the purpose which brings the organization into being; (2) the identification of goals—the major events, activities or directions that define the shape of the organization in line with its purpose; (3) the establishment of objectives—the specific measurable results that the organization wants to accomplish

within a determined time frame; (4) the allocation of resources—the human, physical, and financial support necessary to attain the objectives; and (5) the development of an action plan—the individual tasks that must be performed by a given date, by a specified person, to implement the plan. It is this last step that becomes the point of failure for many plans. An effective planning process must include the plan for implementation, detailing who will do what, by when, and how it will be reported and evaluated (see Controlling, below).

The planning process normally includes at least three basic levels. Strategic planning sets the long-range directions for the organization in light of the mission. Medium or short-range planning establishes the goals and objectives for the next three to five years. Annual planning identifies the objectives and tasks to be completed this year as the organization moves to carry out its mission.

2. Organizing. This is the management process of providing the structure and resources to implement the organization's plan. Organizing includes (1) the identification and grouping of tasks to be completed, (2) the assignment of each task to a specific person or group of persons, and (3) the acquisition, distribution, and control of human, physical, and financial resources to provide effective attainment of the objectives.

3. Staffing. This management process provides the human resources needed to implement the plan. Staffing involves (1) human resource planning—identifying the organization's needs for people to carry out its activities; (2) personnel policy development—setting up the procedures for the care and nurture of the organization's human resources; (3) employment—the recruitment, selection and orientation of persons; (4) performance appraisal—the evaluation of employees to enable them to grow in their work performance and in their lives; (5) career development—the support and training of persons to enhance their personal and vocational development; and (6) compensation administration—the provision of wages and benefits to the employee in return for his or her work and commitment.

Many organizations, especially Christian organizations, utilize volunteers as a significant part of their human resources. Each of the six components of staffing applies to the volunteer as well as the paid employee. This is often overlooked by organizations with the result that volunteer resources "burn out" much more rapidly than they need to. The "rights of volunteers" should include as a minimum (1) a written description of the task to be undertaken; (2) a stated period of time for which the volunteer contracts to perform the task; (3) the training and resources necessary to accomplish the assignment; (4) evaluation and feedback on the volunteer's performance; and (5) compensation, in terms of periodic and appropriate recognition of the service rendered.

4. Leading. This is the management function of providing direction in each area of the organization's development. Leading includes (1) vision—the understanding and articulation of the goals of the organization; (2) delegation—the assignment of responsibility and authority to persons in the organization; (3) motivation—the inspiration and encouragement of people to accomplish their assignments; (4) coordination—maintaining the network of relationships between persons within the organization; (5) communication—the dissemination of information needed for the effective operation of the organization; and (6) service—a commitment to the well-being of the organization, the achievement of its mission, and the development of its people.

The appropriate leadership style has been a much debated topic. Leadership style ranges from autocratic to democratic. Most management authorities now agree that an effective leader will utilize a variety of leadership styles depending upon the situation at hand. While a democratic style of leadership receives the most support from management consultants, there are situations in every organization's development when an autocratic approach or a consultative style of leadership will be most effective.

5. **Controlling.** This is the management process of assessing and monitoring the progress and completion of organizational objectives. Controlling includes (1) the development of standards for performance of tasks in the organization; (2) the measurement of performance and results; (3) the appraisal of performance against standards; (4) the correction of performance deviation; and (5) the reinforcement of performance up to standard. Controlling is a function of human resource management, looking at individual employee performance in the staffing process.

Organizations use two basic types of controls: feedback control and "feedforward" control. Feedback control uses information from activities that have already occurred to correct errors in the system. "Feedforward" control predicts problems before they occur and makes the necessary adjustments. The two most common control systems are the budget and the management information system. The budget details the resources needed for a particular set of tasks or objectives and provides feedback control to the organization's management process. The management information system produces the information needed at each level of the organization to take corrective action, make planning decisions, and manage the daily operations of the organization.

6. **Deciding.** This management function occurs in each of the processes above. Deciding involves (1) a stimulus event making the decision necessary; (2) an information search to understand the problem; (3) formulation of the problem; (4) evaluation of alternatives; and (5) implementation of the choice. The top management personnel will tend to make strategic decisions with long-range impact on the organization. Middle managers make more administrative decisions that coordinate the operations of the organization or handle exceptions. Lower level employees are most occupied with operational decisions of a routine nature.

7. **Communicating.** This is another continuous management function that permeates all areas of organizational development. Within and between levels and divisions of the organization communication takes place daily. It is the vital link relating the people and processes to the purpose and tasks of the organization. Management consultants recognize that it is frequently poor communication processes that reduce the effectiveness of the organization. Communication is never exact since it is the process of recreating an idea or image from one person's mind in the minds of others.

The church as the continued incarnation of Jesus' ministry to the world seeks to be a Christian organization by gathering believers in the name of Christ so that they might be empowered with his spirit to carry out his mission in the world. The Church seeks to manage itself responsibly, operating with methods compatible to its message and its Christian ethics. Any other organization calling itself Christian has the church as its model.

W. C. WRIGHT, JR.

CONGREGATION, PASTORAL CARE OF; LEADERSHIP AND ADMINISTRATION. *Compare* COMMUNITY, FELLOWSHIP, AND CARE; ECCLESIOLOGY AND PASTORAL CARE; VOLUNTEERS, PASTORAL CARE OF.

ORIENTAL RELIGION, SOUL CARE, AND PSYCHOLOGY. *See* PSYCHOLOGY, EASTERN; PSYCHOLOGY AND PSYCHOTHERAPY (East-West Comparison). *See also* NEW RELIGIOUS MOVEMENTS.

ORIENTAL AMERICAN PASTORAL CARE. *See* ASIAN AMERICAN PASTORAL CARE.

ORIENTATION, RELIGIOUS. *See* RELIGIOUS ORIENTATION.

ORIENTATION, SEXUAL. *See* HOMOSEXUALITY; SEXUALITY.

ORIGEN. *See* EARLY CHURCH, PASTORAL CARE AND COUNSELING IN.

ORIGINAL SIN. *See* SIN/SINS. *See also* BIBLICAL ANTHROPOLOGY, DISCIPLINE OF.

ORPHAN/ORPHANAGE. *See* CHAPLAIN/CHAPLAINCY; GRIEF AND LOSS IN CHILDHOOD AND ADOLESCENCE. *See also* FOSTER CHILDREN.

ORTHODOX-CATHOLIC MARRIAGE. There is a special affinity and relationship between the Orthodox and Roman Catholic churches because of their fidelity to the great catholic tradition of Christianity and the proximity of doctrine and practice. Both churches see marriage as a sacrament through which Christ unites a man and woman in mutual love for their ultimate salvation; a permanent commitment to personal union reflecting the mystery of Christ and his church; a consecration by divine grace in the dignity and duties of the married life. This sacrament, modeled after the two great evangelical sacraments of Baptism and the Eucharist, is one of the significant moments or states in the dynamic life of Christians as they progress toward the eternal Kingdom.

Marriage is celebrated in a liturgical rite, as a symbol of the close relationship between this sacrament and the church. It evidences the willingness of the couple to be in union with the community, to abide in it, and to accept responsibility for building it up. The church also has a responsibility for the married couple and for the development of the children.

There are difficulties, however. Particularly in the Catholic conception of sacrament there exists a complicated history of terminology and usage which relies upon legal and juridical insights. This has sometimes led to artificial and even contradictory practices. The separation of the marriage rite from its earlier eucharistic setting, the gradual desacralization of marriage, and the recent ecumenical encouragement of "intercommunion" between separated Christians have contributed to the usual sociological and psychological objections to so-called "mixed" marriages. The issue of the spiritual formation of children is of primary concern.

Even the ecclesial rite of matrimony raises ecclesiological, sacramental, and canonical issues. In Orthodox teaching the role of the priest is theologically necessary as is the marriage rite proper. Normally, the sacrament of marriage takes place only between Orthodox faithful. To be in proper canonical and spiritual standing, an Orthodox Christian must be married in the Orthodox church by an Orthodox priest. By application of the principle of "economy" the Orthodox sacrament of marriage between an Orthodox and a Christian baptized in the name of the Trinity may be performed as prescribed in the service book.

Recent recommendations of the joint Orthodox-Roman Catholic Consultation in the U.S. propose a temporary solution in which Orthodox-Catholic marriages take place in the Orthodox church, as a normative practice, because in the Orthodox view the priest is the minister of the sacrament. Ultimately, it is hoped that the solution will be based on the reciprocal recognition of the ecclesial reality of both churches and of the true sacramental character of their actions.

Counseling by pastors of both churches is very desirable. In it the religious convictions of each partner must be respected and the teachings and practices of both churches honored. Particularly in the case of the spiritual formation of children, joint recommendations of Orthodox and Roman Catholic theologians propose pastoral counseling by both priests, the active involvement of both parents in their children's spiritual formation through prayer, study, and perhaps a fuller participation in the life and traditions of both churches.

R. G. STEPHANOPOULOS

CROSS-CULTURAL MARRIAGE AND FAMILY; MARRIAGE. *Compare* DIVORCE AND REMARRIAGE.

ORTHODOX JUDAISM.

The most traditional branch of contemporary Judaism. It regards the Sinaitic revelation to be accurately preserved in two forms: a written form, namely, the Old Testament, and an oral form which was written down later with the Talmud as its principal document. These, as well as the rabbinic interpretations which logically follow from them, are regarded as eternally true and valid. Unlike conservative Judaism, Orthodoxy regards Jewish law as independent of the community's historical experience. About ten percent of Jews in North America are identified as Orthodox.

P. J. HAAS

JEWISH CARE AND COUNSELING (History, Traditions, and Contemporary Issues).

ORTHODOX TRADITION.

See MINISTRY AND PASTORAL CARE (Orthodox Tradition). *See also* DIVORCE AND REMARRIAGE (Orthodoxy); LITERATURE IN CARE AND COUNSELING (Orthodoxy); ORTHODOX-PROTESTANT *or* ORTHODOX-CATHOLIC MARRIAGE; SACRAMENTAL THEOLOGY AND PASTORAL CARE, ORTHODOX; SPIRITUALITY (Orthodox Tradition).

ORTHODOX-PROTESTANT MARRIAGE.

Christian marriage and family life is regarded as a sacred and creative calling by all Christians, since this is a basic biblical teaching. Marital union "in Christ" appeals to divine grace for support and fulfillment of a natural union of a man and a woman. Whereas the Orthodox teaching and practice of marriage is understood in sacramental terms, emphasizing the ecclesial, salvific, and eschatological dimensions of the married life, most Protestants find other expressions and concepts to describe the marital union. Although unwilling to formulate marriage and family life in precisely sacramental terms, Protestants generally stress that this union is a profound spiritual commitment and covenantal relationship. The biblical teaching and the church's participation in assisting the Christian couple to preserve and complete their marriage are held by all as basic. Most Protestants tend to limit the role of the clergy and of the church in marriage, as contrasted with the Orthodox teaching, since for them marriage is not constituted by the marriage rite. The blessing of the clergy is declaratory and an assurance of God's grace fulfilling the vocation of the couple to glorify God in their marriage. The exclusion of any sacramental significance to marriage runs the risk of depriving this sign of its spiritual content, in the Orthodox view.

Orthodox Christians may be married sacramentally in the Orthodox church. The Orthodox teaching emphasizes the positive aspects of marriage and family, stressing mutual spiritual growth through love and respect, divine grace, and the eternal Kingdom. To be in proper ecclesial and canonical standing, an Orthodox Christian must be married in the Orthodox Church by an Orthodox priest according to the "Rite of Crowning."

It is customary, however, to celebrate marriages between Orthodox and Protestant Christians by application of the principle of "economy." More specifically, the Orthodox sacrament of marriage may be performed in the manner prescribed in the service book between an Orthodox Christian and another Christian baptized in the name of the Holy Trinity. The Orthodox marriage rite is not permitted in the case of two non-Orthodox Christians or in the case of an Orthodox and an unbaptized person. Thus, care is taken to procure the baptismal records of those who come to celebrate marriage in the Orthodox church. Those few "Christian" communions which do not practice Trinitarian baptism are not recognized as Christian by the Orthodox church for the purposes of marriage.

Orthodox priests are encouraged to meet with the clergy of other communions to explain the theological and pastoral reasons for the Orthodox church's canonical regulations on marriage, and, at the same time, to become familiar with the marriage regulations of others. Confessionally mixed marriages usually place unusual burdens and demands upon those involved. This presents an occasion for pastoral counseling and teaching regarding the true nature of marriage as a preparation for the Kingdom, the joys and duties of family life, and the relationship of the family to the community of faith. Pastors should admonish the couple on their obligations as parents to nurture their children in all things. With respect for conscience, every reasonable effort should be made to raise the children as Orthodox Christians.

Should a Protestant minister be invited to an Orthodox ceremony, he may pronounce a benediction and/or address the couple at the conclusion of the ceremony.

R. G. STEPHANOPOULOS

CROSS-CULTURAL MARRIAGE AND FAMILY; MARRIAGE. *Compare* DIVORCE AND REMARRIAGE (Orthodoxy *or* Protestantism).

ORTHOPSYCHIATRY. A cross disciplinary approach to the problems of children, adolescents, and near normal persons of all ages. Typically the disciplines of psychiatry, developmental psychology, sociology, medicine, and family studies are included. The discipline is conceived as a prophylactic psychiatry, and the prefix "ortho-" was originally intended to connote "right development." More recently the focus of orthopsychiatry has been on the total life span issues as well as those of pre-adult development.

Bibliography. The American J. of Orthopsychiatry.

H. N. MALONY

PSYCHIATRIST/PSYCHIATRY; PSYCHOTHERAPY.

OSTEOPATHIC HEALING. Osteopathy is an alternative system of medical care based on the philosophy that the person is a unique individual with a dynamic unity of structure and function. This means that the person, as integrally unified body and mind, has all the necessary resources within for a continuous monitoring and shifting of bodily functions in the optimal direction at any moment, and thus the inherent ability to maintain health. Thus the person essentially heals from within. The osteopathic physician is trained to support the whole person and to intervene for that person by stimulating the inherent healing resources and removing obstacles to their function.

Osteopathic medicine utilizes all modern medical modalities incorporated into this philosophical approach to the patient. Medicines, surgery, nutrition, counseling and manipulation of the physical structure are tools to improve the body's functions, prevent disease or dysfunction, or dis-ease of structure in order to optimize health.

The physician must address each component of the person, and the person as a totality. Healing progresses in a continuing process as the person accepts his or her own unique wholeness.

L. M. DICK

HEALING. *Compare* CHIROPRACTIC HEALING.

OTTO, RUDOLPH (1869–1937). Philosopher of religion and theologian. Otto published numerous works on theology, the philosophy of religion, and the relationship of Hindu and Christian thought. His most influential work, *Das Heilige* (1917; ET, *The Idea of the Holy*),

was an analysis of religious experience as contrasted with aesthetic or other emotional experiences of the sublime. According to Otto, the genesis of religious feeling comes from contact with a totally other (*ganz anderem*) *mysterium* which, simultaneously, inspires awe and fear. Otto called that experience a numinous one and named its object and source the *mysterium tremendum et fascinans*. When that *mysterium* can be more clearly schematized with an appeal to categories like goodness, substantiality, necessity, and the like, the numinous experience becomes a holy one. To deepen this model of religious experience Otto utilized both Eastern and Western sources that describe religious experience. According to Otto, the *mysterium* is experienced as something outside the person who has the experience and, as a consequence of that assertion, Otto avoided any kind of reductionistic analysis since the *mysterium* was *a priori*.

Otto's work on the nature of religious experience had a lasting effect on the later course of the study of religion. He shifted attention away from the study of the external phenomena of religion toward a consideration of religion as something experienced. That shift in focus had ramifications both for phenomenologists of religion and theologians.

Bibliography. P. C. Almond, *Rudolf Otto: An Introduction to his Philosophical Theology* (1984).

L. S. CUNNINGHAM

The HOLY; PSYCHOLOGY OF RELIGION (Theories, Traditions, and Issues); RELIGIOUS EXPERIENCE.

OUT-OF-BODY EXPERIENCE. *See* PARAPSYCHOLOGY.

OUTCOME STUDIES. *See* PSYCHOTHERAPY AND COUNSELING (Research Studies and Methods); EMPIRICAL RESEARCH IN PASTORAL CARE AND COUNSELING.

OUTLER, ALBERT C. (1908–89). American Methodist pastor and historical theologian. As Dwight Professor of Theology at Yale Divinity School and as professor of historical theology at Perkins School of Theology, Southern Methodist University, Outler explored the relationships between theology and psychological theory.

After combining study of historical theology with work in the Yale Institute of Human Relations and the William Alanson White Institute of Psychiatry, Outler published his *Psychotherapy and the Christian Message* (1954), in which he sought areas of agreement between psychotherapy and theology but also insisted on the need for Christian theology to call into question the naturalistic presuppositions that often characterized an uncritical psychotherapeutic "faith."

E. B. HOLIFIELD

PASTORAL THEOLOGY, PROTESTANT. *See also* HISTORY OF PROTESTANT PASTORAL CARE (United States); PSYCHOLOGY IN AMERICAN RELIGION.

OVEREATERS ANONYMOUS. *See* ALCOHOLICS ANONYMOUS; SUPPORT GROUPS.

OVERWEIGHT PERSONS. *See* OBESITY AND WEIGHT CONTROL. *See also* GLUTTONY AND TEMPERANCE.

P

PACE, EDWARD A. *See* COUNSELING, ROMAN CATHOLIC.

PAIN MANAGEMENT/PAIN CLINIC. Pain Management is the systematic application of therapies for the reduction of pain perception and suffering. These therapies treat pain as a unique illness or set of behaviors rather than a symptom of some underlying tissue damage.

A brief survey of pain therapies through history indicates a plethora of different strategies including the ancients' use of sorcery, charms, diet, and purgatives. Pain relieving substances or sedating drugs like opium have been used in Western civilization since the first century and even earlier in China. A number of "sleeping draughts" were known throughout the Middle Ages but usually were rejected by physicians because of their association with witchcraft. Alcohol or the addition of special herbs to alcoholic beverages such as wine has been used by almost all cultures (Longhurst, 1983). Unfortunately, the bold, intrusive remedies of the physician and surgeon were often worse than the pain and led to drug addiction, disfigurement, toxic poisoning, and even death.

As medicine became more scientifically based in the eighteenth and nineteenth centuries, advances in treatment were made possible by the discovery of general anesthetics such as chloroform and ether. More recently the study of pain and its neurological mechanisms has generated a number of new medical approaches which attempt to relieve pain by analgesic medication, local anesthetic blocks, electrical stimulation, and even neurosurgery. These treatments all have one important thing in common. They are aimed at reducing the patient's perception or reaction to pain rather than removing the cause (Houde, 1980).

Added to the medical management of pain has been the rapid growth of psychologically based treatments, which emphasize the role of central nervous system functioning in pain perception. Of particular import is the patient's past conditioning, anxiety, and stress, and the meaning or value of the pain experiences. Psychological approaches used include hypnosis, operant conditioning, biofeedback, cognitive restructuring, and dynamic psychotherapy. Most of the methods are used in pain clinics and are made available to patients along with medical interventions. Most of the patients referred to a pain clinic have an identifiable chronic pain syndrome as opposed to acute pain.

The first pain clinic started approximately twenty-five years ago. Since then, pain clinics have proliferated throughout most of the Western world and can be classified into three types depending on their staff, facilities, and treatment philosophy. (Gerbershagen, 1980).

(1) Modality oriented pain clinics use only one approach, such as nerve block clinics run by anesthesiologists or acupuncture clinics. These clinics usually only treat outpatients and are limited in their focus. (2) Syndrome oriented pain clinics provide treatment usually of an interdisciplinary nature for a particular chronic pain syndrome. The most common are back and headache clinics. (3) Comprehensive pain centers have the broadest scope. Their staffs utilize multidisciplinary diagnostic and treatment approaches. They treat a variety of pain syndromes and have both inpatient and outpatient programs. They routinely do psychological evaluation and treatment (Ng, 1981).

Criticisms have been leveled against the highly intrusive, single-minded drug and surgical treatments in face of research which emphasizes the complexity of pain and suffering (Shoemaker, 1982).

The noted neurologist, Dr. Silas Mitchell, said seven years before the discovery of aspirin that humanity's tolerance for pain has decreased in the process of being civilized (Illich, 1976). One possible explanation offered by Illich is that people take offense at being ill, growing old, and dying, and see pain as an unnatural part of life. Another explanation may be the eroding of spiritual values in modern persons that often give meaning to unavoidable suffering (Lewis, 1962). These values have been replaced by hedonism and a narcissistic concern for the body, which is devoid of any intrinsic pain coping mechanisms.

Bibliography. D. de Moulin, *Bulletin of the History of Medicine,* 48 (1974), 540–60. H. U. Gerbershagen, "Pain Clinics," in H. W. Kosterlitz and L. Y. Terenius, eds., *Pain and Society* (1980), pp. 403–14. R. W. Houde, "Principles of Clinical Management," in H. W. Kosterlitz and L. Y. Terenius, eds., *Pain and Society* (1980), pp. 383–402. I. Illich, *Medical Nemesis* (1976). C. S. Lewis, *The Problem of Pain* ([1940] 1962). M. Longhurst, "Pain: History, Theories, Therapies," *British Columbia Medical Journal,* 25:4, 194–7. L. K. Y. Ng, eds. *New Approaches of Treatment of Chronic Pain: A Review of Multidisciplinary Pain Clinics and Pain Centres,* NIDA Research, Monograph 36 (1981). I. Pilowsky, "Abnormal Illness Behaviour and Sociocultural Aspects of Pain," in H. W. Kosterlitz and L. Y. Terenius, eds., *Pain and Society* (1980), pp. 445–60. M. E. Shoemaker, "Psychological Aspects of Back Pain," a paper presented to the Low Back Pain Symposium, Vancouver, B. C., (September 9, 1982). D. C. Turk, D. Meichenbaum, M. Genest, *Pain and Behavioural Medicine* (1983).

M. E. SHOEMAKER

BIOFEEDBACK; PATIENCE/PATIENTHOOD. *See also* CHRONIC ILLNESS; DYING, PASTORAL CARE OF; SICK, PASTORAL CARE OF. *Compare* HEALING; SUGGESTION, PERSUASION, AND INFLUENCE.

PAIN THEORY AND RESEARCH. Originally from the Greek word *poinē,* meaning penalty, and later merged with the Latin word *poena,* which meant punishment, pain in modern usage has come to mean mental and/or physical distress or suffering, but most commonly a sensation of discomfort felt in the body.

1. History of Theory of Pain. The history of the concept of pain may be traced from primitive religious belief systems through philosophical inquiry to contemporary scientific conceptions derived from the disciplines of neurophysiology and psychology. In primitive cultures, pain was believed to be caused by "evil fluids" entering the body through the intrusion of an object (like an arrow or a demon). Specific treatments were applied to release or drive out the intruder (Keele, 1962). The concept of pain as an "evil spirit" was a theme in many ancient religions and merged with the more abstract ethical concept of sin in Western culture. Often, in this context, pain was conceived as punishment or tribulation meted out by God for human wickedness or to bring about obedience (Procacci, 1979).

Greek and Roman cultures minimized religious explanation, turning instead to philosophical speculation based on the observation that pain was a product of sensation related to touch. Galen, the famous Roman physician, made the first scientific contribution to the anatomy of pain, linking it to the central nervous system and to brain function. After Galen, however, anatomical inquiry lay dormant for over a thousand years and was not revived until the Renaissance studies of scientists like da Vinci, Descartes, and Vesalius.

2. Modern Research. The first scientific theory of pain emerged in the middle of the nineteenth century when the discovery of electrical energy was incorporated into nerve physiology. The resulting theory, often referred to as the "specificity theory of pain," postulated specific pain receptors that transmitted pain sensations through the nervous system to the brain. More recently, however, improved neurophysiological research techniques, espe-

cially the development of sophisticated biopsy experimentation on skin tissue and the central nervous system, have challenged the simplicity of specificity theory. In recent decades, for instance, both pattern theory (Wendell) and gate-control theory (Keele; Melzack; Wall) have attempted to incorporate a growing body of research evidence emphasizing the complexity and differentiation of the receptors that transmit pain. These theories also emphasize the influence of higher central nervous system functioning on pain sensation. Other recent discoveries include "natural pain killers" called endorphins, secreted within the body, which have powerful analgesic effects. These endogenous, opiate-like chemicals are thought to provide a possible explanation for the pain control mechanism of acupuncture. (See Melzack, Kosterlitz and Terenius for excellent reviews of this research.)

Recent research has also shown considerable interest in the role of learning and psychological functions on pain perception, tolerance, and expression. Such environmental factors as parenting patterns, modelling, and reinforcement have been identified as important determinants of pain expression and tolerance. Equally so are cognitive factors such as expectation, meaning, and perceived locus of control, which can be manipulated under experimental conditions to alter pain tolerance. Anxiety and depression have been shown both experimentally and clinically to lower pain thresholds and, paradoxically, to increase endorphin levels (Bakal, 1979). Zborowski's classic study (1969) of ethnic differences in pain expression among surgical patients has stimulated interest in cultural differences. Recent investigation of the role of meditation, hypnosis, and biofeedback in pain control has again emphasized the brain's potential to be the dominant structure in pain perception. (Bakal, 1979).

3. Basic Concepts in Pain Theory Today. From this definition and brief summary of relevant research, three conceptual levels are needed to understand pain. At its most basic or rudimentary level, pain is a sensory-discriminative capacity of human beings and animals most probably related to the reflexive avoidance of noxious stimuli. Higher mental functions are not required but may affect this level. The second, or motivational-affective level, is generally accepted as an important component in pain and refers to the unpleasant emotional quality that differentiates it from all other sensations. The third, most complex level is the cognitive-evaluative, which is influenced by many environmental and situational variables and a score of higher intellectual functions. All of these levels are connected and interact or influence each other to produce the total pain experience.

So conceived, the experience of pain requires theories delineating a complex interaction of physical, mental and spiritual factors, though no scientific theory can express the unique anguish of pain for the sufferer or speak to the ultimate questions of meaning that it raises. The symbolization of pain in the various religious traditions may seem irrelevant to scientific theory, but religious symbols provide an important cultural setting through which the individual can endure and articulate the moral mystery of pain in a meaningful way.

Bibliography. C. S. Lewis, *The Problem of Pain,* ([1940] 1962). J. H. Fichter, *Religion and Pain* (1981). International Association for the Study of Pain, "Pain Terms: A list with definitions and notes on usage," *Pain*, (1979), 249–52. K. D. Keele, "Some historical concepts of pain," in C. A. Keele and R. Smith, eds., *The Assessment of Pain in Man and Animals* (1962). P. Procacci, "History of the pain concept," in H. W. Kosterlitz and L. Y. Terenius, eds., *Pain and Society* (1980). R. Melzack, *The Puzzle of Pain* (1973). D. A. Bakal, *Psychology and Medicine* (1979). M. Zborowski, *People in Pain* (1969).

M. E. SHOEMAKER

BIOFEEDBACK; HEALTH AND ILLNESS; MIND-BODY RELATIONSHIP. *Compare* EVIL; SUFFERING.

PANIC. Panic attacks are discrete episodes of apprehension or fear, accompanied by symptoms of somaticized anxiety. Should such attacks occur as frequently as three times in three weeks, a panic disorder can be suspected. The most common manifestation of panic disorder is agoraphobia, that is, fear of leaving one's home. Treatment typically consists of psychotherapeutic techniques like flooding and systematic desensitization and/or medications.

S. ALLISON

DECOMPENSATION; FEAR; NEUROSIS; PSYCHOPATHOLOGY, THEORIES OF. *Compare* CRISIS MINISTRY.

PAPACY. *See* MINISTRY (Roman Catholic Tradition).

PARADOX. *See* WIT AND HUMOR IN PASTORAL CARE; IMAGINATION.

PARADOXICAL INTENTION. A psychotherapeutic technique, also known as "symptom prescription," which involves directing the client intentionally to exaggerate the symptom. For example, a client who worries excessively is told to worry at least one hour each night and to record all the worries in detail. Paradoxical intention has been especially successful in the treatment of phobias, obsessive-compulsive disorders, and anxiety states.

T. T. WEBER

DOUBLE BIND.

PARALYSIS. *See* HANDICAP AND DISABILITY; LOSS OF FUNCTION; NEUROLOGIC ILLNESSES.

PARANOIA. *See* SUSPICIOUSNESS AND PARANOIA.

PARANORMAL PSYCHOLOGY. *See* PARAPSYCHOLOGY.

PARAPSYCHOLOGY. The study of mental phenomena that are not explainable by the generally accepted principles of science, using scientific discipline in the investigation of paranormal and supernormal phenomena, especially the study of *psi communications,* that is, behavioral or personal exchanges with the environment that are extrasensorimotor—not dependent on the senses or muscles. Narrowly defined, parapsychology includes the study of extrasensory perception (ESP) and psychokinesis (PK). Extrasensory perception (ESP) involves the ability of one individual to receive, know, and/or respond to knowledge (past, present, or future) from objects or events in the outside world or from other persons' minds without the aid of the bodily senses as normally understood. ESP includes: *clairvoyance,* the extrasensory perception of a physical object or event; *telepathy* (mental telepathy), the extrasensory perception of another person's thoughts or mental state; *precognition,* the prediction of a future event, the occurrence of which cannot be inferred from present knowledge. Psychokinesis (PK) involves the direct influence of mental activity upon physical objects or processes exerted without the use of direct physical contact.

Most areas of paranormal experience can be studied within these defined areas, and done so in a manner that eliminates the carnival and spiritualistic overtones that are generally considered incompatible with scientific inquiry, Thus, "mindreading," "fortune telling," "déjà vu," and "premonitions" can be studied as instances of ESP, while faith healing and spoon-bending are studied as instances of PK.

1. **Related Phenomena.** Some peripherally related subjects are: (1) *Auras.* This word is used in at least two ways: (a) as implying a physical energy emanating from an individual that is detectable under some conditions through the use of electromagnetic sensing devices or photosensitive chemicals (as in Kirlian photography). This type of aura is believed to be a bioenergy detectable through physical means, not an extrasensory phenomenon; (b) as a "psychic" aura, an emanation of the mind or spirit, not physical in nature, and detectable by "sensitives" or mediums. (2) *Automatic writing.* The process whereby the mind or spirit of another individual in another place and/or time communicates to an individual or group by using another person as a mechanical instrument of written communication. (3) *Out-of-body experience.* Reports of the mind or soul leaving the body and traveling independent of it, as in near-death experiences, in which an individual later reports leaving his or her body and viewing the sick room scene from outside of the body; reports of the mind leaving an otherwise healthy body (often during sleep) and traveling unimpeded by space or time to other locations and then returning. This kind of experience is sometimes called astral body projection. (4) *Poltergeists.* Disturbances such as spontaneous and unexplainable rapping noises in a house, flying pots and pans, dishes crashing to the floor, and similar experiences that are attributed to and used as evidence for the activity of spirits or ghosts. (5) *Reincarnation.* The occupation by a soul of a new body after the death of a previous one; used to explain the availability of information from the past to individuals who are said to regress to a former life under hypnotically induced regression ("past life regression"). (6) *Transpersonal psychology.* An extension and outgrowth of humanistic or third-force psychology that has a special interest in the ability and experiences of humans that transcend their personal physical and limitations of body, therefore, emphasizing the activity of the mind or soul; study of the miraculous, the esoteric, the parapsychological, and the occult.

2. **Experimental Research.** Parapsychology is comparatively modern as a scientific discipline, having its inception with the founding of the Society for Psychical Research in London in 1882. In 1885 the American

Society for Psychical Research was founded in Boston. The early efforts of these societies attempted to dissociate physical phenomena from spiritualism and superstition and the general carnival atmosphere that surrounded individuals who practiced them. They did, however, especially in London, investigate mediums and their claims to invoke spirits or apparitions. They also studied automatic writing, levitation, and poltergeists.

Modern parapsychology in the U. S., and legitimate scientific parapsychology in general, began with the work of J. B. Rhine, founder of the parapsychology laboratory at Duke University. His work was mainly focused on rigorous studies of ESP through a technique in which subjects "guessed" the order of cards in a deck (consisting of five different cards in random order), or in which the subject guessed a target object that an experimenter was looking at at a specified time in some room at a distant location on the campus. With hundreds of repeated trials, the experimenters sought to show, and often did, that the subject could guess the objects or the order of the cards at greater than chance levels of probability. Thus, the experimenters could reject the null hypothesis that the guesses were strictly chance and lend support to the conclusion that the subject had some form of knowledge of the cards or of the target objects. Since there was no sensory access to that knowledge, the experimenters concluded that the knowledge was acquired through extrasensory perception.

Another modern center for parapsychological research using a different methodology is the Stanford Research Institute, where Russell Targ and Harold Puthoff conducted a now famous series of remote viewing experiments. Twelve target locations were preselected. At the outset of each experiment, five to seven envelopes, each with one of the locations sealed inside, were randomly selected. An experimenter traveled to each location, and at a predetermined time spent twenty minutes viewing the location while at that exact time the subject in the laboratory described the location as he imagined it. Then, an independent judge took the descriptions of the locations and associated them with the target location (either through photographs or through actual visitation of the site). In this type of experiment, rejection of the null hypothesis is based on the number and order of matches being greater than expected through chance. Targ and Puthoff preferred the phrases "remote viewing" or "remote sensing" to the less scientific and more suggestive or biased terms ESP, clairvoyance, and telepathy. In their experiments, the positive results that they reported could be attributed to either clairvoyance or telepathy.

3. **Anecdotal Reports and Popular "Proofs."** For the unsophisticated individual with an interest in the paranormal, the most compelling evidence for parapsychological phenomena is the plethora of anecdotal reports of dramatic personal experience of "skeptical" individuals who have had completely unexpected experiences of ESP. There are also stage performers, such as Uri Geller, famous for bending keys and other metal objects, who do amazing and unexplainable feats, suggesting or directly claiming the use of parapsychological powers. And there are reports of scientific experiments that claim to demonstrate beyond any doubt the existence of special mind

powers, though often these "experiments" are poorly controlled and do not deserve serious scientific consideration. In the case of these more popular "proofs" for parapsychological phenomena, the results can always be duplicated through simple or professional techniques (e.g., magicians bending spoons) that do not require any paranormal powers.

4. **Criticisms and Issues for Research.** These anecdotes and poorly controlled studies aside, a skeptical approach to the more scientific studies is required. There has been admitted fraud in a number of the landmark studies. Fraud and trickery charges, made by the critics of parapsychological research, demonstrate how a fraud could have been perpetrated but do not directly disprove the results of any particular study. Although these critiques may be unfair due to the spirit in which they are undertaken, they do offer alternative, more traditional explanations.

Some criticisms are important when considering parapsychology as a science and must be kept in mind by professional counselors working with individuals who report paranormal experiences. First, if parapsychological phenomena are factual, then parapsychological experiments and observations should be replicable by individuals not committed to their existence. Most evidence suggests that individuals must *expect* to find a paranormal manifestation in order to find it "scientifically." Second, many apparently decisive experiments have been found to have methodological flaws—and some have been simply fraudulent. Generally, with improved experimental methods in science, results are stronger and more reliable, but this has not been the case in parapsychological investigations.

Third, there is a basic lack of consistency in the phenomena under investigation. Some people seem to have psi abilities, and others do not. In those who do, there is a U-shaped curve in most studies of their abilities. Even in these "sensitives" there seems to be an increase in their accuracy in psi tasks over time in initial experimental trials, with a trailing off of results and a return to chance or almost chance levels after several trials. Not only are some people not good at psi tasks, but those who are have great fluctuations in their ability. Most have much greater difficulty exhibiting their ability under scientifically controlled conditions than they report experiencing in everyday life.

Fourth, it is crucial to remember that the explanations of the paranormal require change in the basic assumptions of natural and physical science. Thus, in a particular instance, an explanation in terms of psi may seem simple and most convincing, but requires a reopening of basic questions about the nature of science and a reconsideration of all the theories and laws that have been based on those assumptions. An apparently simple explanation may therefore not be parsimonious. The laws of science should not be put aside for a few isolated demonstrations that cannot be generalized.

The fundamental problem, then, in dealing with parapsychological phenomena from a rational and traditional scientific standpoint is that there is no logical way to test the validity of the claims except to rule out all possibility of sensory communication. The so-called psychic processes behave in an erratic manner, apparently without lawlike consistency, and are therefore not testable or refutable on traditional scientific grounds. What we are left with is a definition of paranormal as something that cannot be explained through extant scientific principles. This leaves the door open for the possibility, which indeed seems to be the case, that the strong belief in parapsychology leads to all sorts of intellectually irresponsible claims. Once one steps outside consensually defined reality, it is easy to entertain any number of ideas that are neither scientifically acceptable nor verifiable (flying saucers from other planets, communication from other worlds, reincarnation, etc.).

Dealing with individuals who hold beliefs in parapsychological experiences is made especially difficult by the strong emotional attachment to those beliefs. This is because the paranormal explanation answers questions that have been difficult for the individual to deal with through rational processes. Furthermore, events tend to validate themselves subjectively; a person expects something to happen, it does, and this is seen as validation of the hypothesis on which the expectation was based. It fails, however, to take into account the random likelihood of the event occurring, the fact that other events have also occurred but not been attended to, or the hundreds of other expectations that have not been verified. Finally, a person may have an increased emotional attachment due to the special nature of the psi ability that he or she possesses which others do not, and, in fact, do not understand or believe.

Parapsychology poses special problems for the religious person, and especially for the religious person involved in counseling other religious persons. Faith claims and personal belief systems do not ordinarily claim to be verifiable through scientific means. While it is assumed that science will not directly contradict the claims of religion, neither is it equipped to validate those claims. Parapsychology, on the other hand, seeks to be accepted as science and contributes to the scientific understanding of the universe. Therefore, its claims must be objectively verifiable through scientific methods. So, while the psychic phenomena must be integrated into science, religion is outside of, but conceivably not inconsistent with, science. This is an important distinction since religion, as a valuing system, must stay independent of science to critique science and to assess its progress.

The pastor therefore is wise to take a position of rational skepticism with tolerance for the possibility of paranormal experiences. Whatever the parishioner's or counselee's experience, it is part of his or her reality and therefore important and must be taken seriously, though not necessarily agreed with. The counselor can suggest other, more psychologically defensible explanations and should keep in mind the possible diagnostic value of these experiences. It is also important to question or explore the tendency to use convictions about psi to excuse an inability to live effectively with other individuals in the consensual world. Even if an individual has great psi ability, it is still expected that one will relate appropriately with employers, friends, and family members.

Bibliography. J. Ludwig, ed., *Philosophy and Parapsychology* (1978). D. Marks and R. Kammann, *The Psychology of the Psychic* (1980). J. Randall, *Parapsychology and the Nature of Life* (1975).

See also *The Journal of Parapsychology.* J. J. Heaney, *The Sacred and the Psychic: Parapsychology and Christian Theology* (1984). For a critical review of ESP and paranormal research see D. G. Myers, *The Inflated Self* (1981).

R. PONSFORD

PSYCHOLOGY; SURVIVAL (Occult); WORLD VIEW. *See also* FAITH HEALING; NEAR-DEATH EXPERIENCE; PHILOSOPHY AND PSYCHOLOGY; SPIRITUALISM. *Compare* MAGICAL THINKING; PSYCHOLOGY, EASTERN; TRANSPERSONAL PSYCHOLOGIES; WITCHCRAFT.

PARDON. *See* FORGIVENESS; PENANCE, SACRAMENT OF.

PARENT EDUCATION. A term that refers to various methods of increasing the parent's knowledge and understanding of self, child, and the forces operating in family relationships. The concept has emerged along with interest in psychology and human potential and parallels a growing self-consciousness about relationships with others.

1. **Definitions and Objectives.** The term denotes general study of the parent's role in child development as well as specific instructional programs aimed at training parents in communication skills, family management, and cognizance of parenting issues. It connotes the usefulness of developing knowledge and parenting skills to supplement one's own childhood experience, in contrast to the belief that parenting is instinctive, innate behavior that is best left to its natural expression. Many parents need support, information, skills, understanding, and often remedial help that intuition and experience do not adequately provide. Societal expectations for family, children, and parents have dramatically changed, creating new requirements of the parent-child relationship, and altering the parent's traditional resources. Many parents want to avoid imitating the child-rearing practices of their parents, and are looking for new methods of parenting. At its best, parenting requires merging two histories and two personalities into a partnership.

Some persons may seek parent education as early as the time when they consider whether or not to have children. Others may require particular knowledge for parenting under special conditions. Parenting begins for most people when they first experience the major responsibility for an infant, and they seek to care for their child in the best way possible. Parents want to learn how to gain their children's cooperation, how to avoid or reduce conflicts within the family, and how to develop good relationships with their children. They seek education to enable them to adapt to or to make decisions regarding personal and social crises. Parent education is a useful adjunct to psychotherapy and counseling, offering new perspectives and alternative ways of dealing with children, ways that may improve family relationships and alleviate crises. Schools and religious congregations may incorporate parent education into their educational programs. Couples who learn together can modify their individual perspectives into compatible strategies and common goals of parenting. Single parents may find it especially helpful in working out effective family systems.

2. **Literature and Programs.** Traditionally, the experts to whom parents have turned for education are pediatricians, who have training and practical experience with children and are accessible to parents. Benjamin

Spock's handbook, first published in 1945, is a classic in educating parents about the care of infants and children. T. Berry Brazelton, also a pediatrician, has written books directed toward helping parents appreciate the wide range of normalcy in children and the individuality in rate and style of their child's development.

Research institutions that specialize in child development sometimes publish their data in a form that parents can utilize. In *Child Behavior*, the Gesell Institute of Child Development describes the stages of behavioral growth in children, with the aim of preparing parents to respond to the needs of their children at various ages and stages of growth. Recently the Princeton Center for Infancy, a parent-based research and education group, has compiled a parenting guidebook covering a wide range of information.

Psychotherapists who work with children are an important source for understanding the emotional and psychological world of the child. Selma Fraiburg describes personality development during the first five years and offers insight into the imagination and fears of the typical child. Haim Ginott's therapeutic work with children and guidance groups for parents led to a practical guide written for parents, which offers specific advice about common situations and problems as well as basic principles for parent-child relationships based on mutual respect. Ginott's approach epitomizes a new emphasis in parent education, in which parents learn communication skills that facilitate the development of a cooperative relationship between parent and child. Parents who participated in his workshop for several years have written about their experiences applying Ginott's teachings in their own families (*Liberated Parents — Liberated Children*). Rudolph Dreikurs, a child psychiatrist, extends the concept of the societal change from autocracy to democracy to the parent-child relationship. *Children the Challenge* presents a program of parent education based on balancing freedom with responsibility in the democratic family. His program offers specific suggestions for effective parenting and is based on a consistent philosophy of mutually respectful relationships.

Thomas Gordon's *Parent Effectiveness Training* course (PET) is one of the first step-by-step courses aimed at developing open communication and mutual problem solving, avoiding both authoritarian and permissive parenting. Professional leaders and a group context are characteristic of this program.

Groups have proven useful for providing mutual support and the opportunity for sharing experiences, as well as for efficiently disseminating information. *Systematic Training for Effective Parenting* (STEP) and *How to Talk So Kids Will Listen and Listen So Kids Will Talk* are programs designed to be used by groups without professional leaders. Handbooks, workbooks, and visual aids provide a self-teaching method. *Better Parents, Better Children* is an individual workbook of exercises with similar goals— teaching parents how to communicate with their children to develop cooperative relationships and to promote responsibility without using punishment.

Reaction against permissiveness in child rearing has promulgated parent education programs and books that emphasize the need for parents to assert control over their children. In *Dare to Discipline*, psychologist James Dobson

combines methods for achieving firm control with his interpretation of the goals of the Christian home. John Rosemond's *Parent Power* presents methods of taking charge of children and setting guidelines.

Ourselves and Our Children is the outcome of discussions between parents compiled by the Boston Women's Health Book Collective. It considers several parenting issues not usually discussed in other sources, such as being a parent of grownups. Like *Kids Day In and Day Out,* this collection of essays, written from a socially liberal point of view, by parents rather than experts, is not intended to present a system of child rearing, but emphasizes individuality in parenting style.

3. Pastoral Considerations. Pastors or religious educators who are advising parents or who are considering offering a parent education program in their congregation will find that there are programs with a declared Christian orientation. Typically these programs promote an authoritarian relationship of parent to child. Many church groups have found programs encouraging family democracy and cooperation between family members, such as those based on the writings of Dreikurs and Ginott, to be consistent with Christian family values although not directed toward any specific religious view.

It is advisable to review several parent education viewpoints before selecting a program. A course package, including books, workbooks, tapes, and films, has the advantage of convenience and consistency. On the other hand, there are useful ideas to be gathered from various perspectives. Primary is the attitude that parent education is a process of learning and adapting with the needs and experiences of the family, rather than being a program or a book.

Bibliography. Boston Women's Health Book Collective, *Ourselves and Our Children* (1978). T. Brazelton, *Infants and Mothers* (1969). D. Dinkmeyer and G. McKay, *Systematic Training for Effective Parenting* (1976). J. Dobson, *Dare to Discipline* (1970). R. Dreikurs, *Children: the Challenge* (1964). A. Faber and E. Mazlish, *Liberated Parents — Liberated Children* (1974); *How to Talk So Kids Will Listen and Listen So Kids Will Talk* (1980). S. Fraiburg, *The Magic Years* (1959). H. Ginott, *Between Parent and Child* (1965). T. Gordon, *Parent Effectiveness Training* (1970). F. Ilg and L. Ames, *Child Behavior* (1955). B. Marshall and C. Marshall, *Better Parents, Better Children* (1979). Princeton Center for Infancy, *The Parenting Advisor* (1977). J. Rosemond, *Parent Power* (1981). E. Scharlatt, ed., *Kids Day In and Day Out* (1979). B. Spock, *Baby and Child Care* (1945).

P. P. SHROPSHIRE

PARENT EFFECTIVENESS TRAINING; PARENTS/PARENTHOOD. *See also* CHILDREN; EDUCATION, NURTURE, AND CARE; FAMILY, JEWISH *or* PASTORAL CARE AND COUNSELING OF; TEACHING. *Compare* SEX EDUCATION.

PARENT EFFECTIVENESS TRAINING. A nationally offered training program, also called PET, developed by psychologist Thomas E. Gordon, designed to teach parents to relate more effectively with their children. The program focuses upon skill development in four areas: responsive listening, nonjudgmental self-expression, changing children's behavior by changing the environment, and "no-lose" conflict resolution.

Gordon's approach combines Rogerian principles of empathy, understanding, and positive regard with

Adlerian notions of the importance of power in selfhood. PET language addresses the child as a moral equal, encouraging responsible participation and decision making.

PET is perhaps most helpful when read for its attitudes toward children and the qualities of personhood implicit in them. A pastor recommending PET might encourage attention to the development of self-understanding, wholeness, and maturity as the emotional context for the appropriation of PET's techniques.

Bibliography. T. E. Gordon, *Parent Effectiveness Training* (1970).

C. A. VAN WAGNER

PARENT EDUCATION; PARENTS/PARENTHOOD.

PARENT-CHILD CONFLICT. *See* FAMILY; FAMILY THEORY AND THERAPY; PARENTS/PARENTHOOD.

PARENTS/PARENTHOOD. Although parenthood is one of the most important, demanding, and complicated long-range tasks known to human society, there are no criteria for qualification whatsoever (Kliman and Rosenfeld, 1980, p. 11); no formal training, no license, no experience, or character references. Yet parents become "trustees for the future" by virtue of their self-appointment to the job and are responsible for the physical and emotional well-being of their children. Thus parenting can be viewed as "voluntary procreative responsibility, a consciousness raising on behalf of the future" (Kliman and Rosenfeld, 1980, p. 12). In this context, it is the responsibility of the church and the pastor to provide appropriate pastoral care and family ministry to assist parents to become more effective.

1. **Reasons for Parenting.** Persons become parents for a variety of reasons, but motivation often determines the quality of parenting. Over the years, through cultural adaptation and medical advances, many persons, especially women, have been guided in their child-conceiving decisions less by biological instinct than by cultural expectations. Procreative decisions are much more deliberate. Yet the biological and psychological developmental tasks of young and middle adulthood include "generativity," or the decisions to produce and procreate.

One of the most significant motivations for parenting is the opportunity to give love to another human being. The process of creating another human through birthing a child calls forth a profound emotional involvement. In return, parents also have the opportunity to receive love from children. The ongoing giving and receiving of love throughout parenthood provides rich sources of meaning for living.

The charge to "be fruitful and multiply" (Gen. 1:28) is the blessing from God for human beings to join in creating new life. Just as God created persons and "saw that it was good," so the divine mandate invites us to affirm life and the future by participating in the procreation of new life. One of the motivations for devoting significant time and energy to parenting is the desire and hope of enhancing the quality of life for one's own children and for all the world.

In addition to the more positive motives for parenting, there are several potentially destructive reasons why people become parents. Many become parents accidentally or because they have little motivation to do anything else. Others become parents with the unrealistic hope that parenthood will provide sufficient meaning for their lives when they have no other reason for living. Some couples in dysfunctional relationships decide to become parents with the hope that a child will become the necessary bond to hold the relationship together. Many become parents because they feel an obligation to satisfy a spouse, a parent, or cultural expectations. Such reasons for becoming parents place burdens on parents and children and lead to ineffective parenting.

2. **Timing for Parenthood.** Another factor influencing quality parenting is the issue of when to have children. Although persons can have good reasons for becoming parents, they must also take into consideration the timing of having children. Several issues determine this decision.

One of the most important factors in readiness for parenthood is maturity of individuals and couples. One is more prepared for the pressures of parenthood after having differentiated, or become one's own self, in relation to parents and other significant persons. Being self-reliant, independent, and autonomous creates the climate for effective parenting. Having healthy self-esteem prepares one to enhance the self-esteem of children. Likewise, maturity in a marriage relationship fosters interdependence and bonding that allow a couple to interact and make decisions mutually.

Although many couples now recognize the need for premarital preparation, very few actively participate in it. Such preparation could begin with a young couple's "experimenting" by taking care of children on a temporary basis, providing an opportunity for them to discover their parenting styles. Reflecting deliberately on parenting styles and parent role models and reading books on parenting help couples to prepare for parenting.

The church has an opportunity and a responsibility to assist potential parents by providing classes to help couples "grow up" and learn about the dynamics and skills of parenting.

Although it is impossible to be completely ready, more effective parenting is likely to take place when a couple's life is stable and secure. Because of the time and energy required for parenting, parents need to be free of the burdens of multiple jobs and financial pressures to devote themselves wholeheartedly to the task. The spacing of children is another factor in parental decision making, since brief time between births tends to increase the stress level immediately, as well as financial obligations later on.

Of course, secure and stable living is an ideal which is often unrealistic in the lives of young families. Nevertheless, the optimum hope is for children to be brought into families where persons are able to provide for their needs. The pastor and the church have the opportunity to "coach" parents in their decision making concerning the timing of children.

If parenting is an opportunity to be co-creators with God, then the decision to become parents has spiritual dimensions. Wholeness and maturity suggest a spiritual as well as an emotional readiness. Christian couples have the responsibility of seeking the right time spiritually to give birth to a child of God.

3. A Theology of Parenting. The family is a "human being garden," and the parent-child relationship is the basis of human existence within the garden (Anderson and Guernsey, 1985, pp. 55–65). What are the biblical/theological implications of parenthood?

a. The parenthood of God. According to Karl Barth, parenthood is accountability to the command of God to fulfill history. Thus, we are called to honor our parents because they bear the commandment and the promise of life. The relationship of parents and children is one of the central focuses of the Bible. In the scriptural concept of God as Israel's parent, and in the relationship of Jesus Christ to "Abba," Father, human parents find the paradigm of their own parent-child relationships (Barth, 1969). God functions as a heavenly Parent serving both to nurture and to discipline.

b. Cohumanity. The theological affirmation of the Bible is that we experience our full humanity, our personal selfhood, in relation to another in cohumanity. The being of one is opened up and affirmed by the being of the other (Anderson and Guernsey, 1985). Therefore, parenthood is the humanization process in which selfhood of both parent and child develops in their relationship. Love is given and experienced and thus awakens the parent's and child's response to the love of God. The cohumanity of the parent-child relationship is designed by God to allow both parent and child to experience the openness of being and the distinctions that reflect the divine image.

c. Love. The primary theological purpose of parenting is to fulfill the law of love. Christian parents are called to teach their children the greatest commandment—to "Love the Lord your God with all your heart, with all your soul, with all your mind"—and the second greatest commandment—to "love your neighbor as yourself" (Mt. 22:36–40, NEB). Love for God, neighbor, and self is the guiding principle for Christian parenting.

Self-esteem is the starting place for loving others. Thus, the crucial assumption of value formation is loving one's self with the love of God. Often parents attempt the difficult task of trying to create self-esteem in their children without having adequate self-esteem themselves. The parent-child bond that is trusting, dependable, and loving allows the child to develop higher self-esteem, thus creating the potential for esteeming others and God.

Because of the grace of Jesus Christ and the help from God in loving unconditionally, Christian parents have the opportunity and responsibility to convey the grace of God to children through unconditional loving. Therefore, parents participate with God in the process of creating children of God.

4. The Tasks of Parenting. Parenthood involves many tasks that foster the development of the child's fully mature self. Deliberate and intentional parents have the opportunity to guide their parenting by the images and concepts of what they wish their children to become. The biblical admonition to train children in the way they should go, so that when they are old they will not depart from it (Prov. 22:6), calls for parents to develop a long-range plan for their parenting. There are certain crucial tasks or gifts that parents can give to assist children in developing helpful life characteristics.

a. Trust. The first developmental task identified by Erik Erikson is the task of learning to trust. Through attachment with a primary parent, the infant is able to cope with the anxiety of being totally dependent on another for all needs. The infant's vulnerability is met by a warm, affectionate, and caring parent, and thus the basic ability to trust others and life is developed. Through touching and talking, parents assure the child that the world is a safe place. When a child's fears and anxieties are taken seriously, he or she does not have to swallow them and create the mistrust that life and people are not dependable to meet one's needs. A positive experience of trust-building allows a child to develop a trusting and trustworthy attitude and lifestyle. Jesus provides a parenting model in the question he used with his disciples in the midst of the storm, "Why are you afraid?" (Mt. 8:26). Such trustbuilding opens the possibility for a child to begin to have faith in God and life.

b. Autonomy. Simultaneous with the process of bonding in the parent-child relationship is the process of differentiation. The child not only learns to depend on parents but also soon has to learn to relate to the larger world of person and things. As the world begins to take on more significance, the child learns ways to make decisions and become self-reliant. This process often becomes quite traumatic in the "first adolescence" of the "terrible two's" and the next adolescence of the teenage years.

Becoming responsible for oneself is necessary for living in the world, and therefore healthy parents raise their children not to need them too much. Separation and individuation allow the child to fail and to realize that failures are ways to learn about living. Sometimes children experience separation anxiety when they fear they will be abandoned in this world. At these times children may need more reassurance that the caregiver will be a steady source of support and encouragement.

Parents can assist their children in developing a sense of autonomy by giving them opportunities to make decisions. Children can be encouraged to become more independent by being allowed to develop their own thoughts and plans. Encouragement is a continuous process aimed at giving the child a sense of self-respect and a sense of accomplishment (Dreikurs, 1964, p. 39). At the age of twelve Jesus was "about his Father's business" in the temple, and "Jesus increased in wisdom and in stature, and in favor with God and man" (Lk. 2:41–52).

c. Belonging. Ultimately the task of parenting is to teach children how to get along with others in the world. The family is the first school of those social virtues that every society needs (McGinnis and McGinnis, 1981, p. 1). To become a mature adult, a child needs to learn the relational skills to belong, to manage interpersonal conflict, and to experience intimacy. These skills create the possibility for community.

Parents need to devote time and imagination to developing these skills in children, primarily through marriage and sibling relationships. By observing parents manage anger and love, children learn how to relate. By having to share and negotiate conflict with a sibling, children develop skills for belonging. Through family stories and traditions, children learn the importance of belonging and caring. Through shared responsibilities, children learn to work together. Through caring for others, children learn the importance of ministry to persons in need.

Trust, autonomy, and belonging become the shaping guidelines for parenting. When these have been developed, children will have the skills and attitudes for living in the world successfully. For most parents the struggle is how to develop these in children.

5. Issues in Parenting. Many parents agonize over the issues of limits, control, discipline, and punishment. The search for appropriate and effective parenting methods may lead to frustration and confusion: parents are often overwhelmed with the issues and are perplexed by the array of approaches offered by specialists. The Christian approach to parenting calls for a balance between judgment and grace, between control and love, and between dominion and service.

a. Authority. The book of Genesis provides a picture of humanity's ruling task. True biblical authority calls for dominion and service to go hand-in-hand. Dominion involves making decisions, taking initiative, setting and enforcing limits. It may well include the use of power and coercion (Stehouwer and Stehouwer, 1983). Many parents, however, tend to become authoritarian and overuse their right to dominion: they are rigid and controlling; they demand much and have very high expectations. Such parenting is inadequate and nonbiblical.

Service describes the biblical model for understanding the very nature of God, who in the form of Jesus Christ became the "suffering servant" to redeem humanity. Parents are called to embody this self-sacrificial service with their children. This usually includes evaluating parental behavior, asking the questions, "What is of best service to my child? What will allow him or her to develop fully?"

b. Discipline. The biblical meaning of discipline is taken from the word "disciple," which means pupil. Therefore, the Christian approach to discipline involves the dynamics of learning, of growth and maturation, rather than revenge and penalty (Narramore, 1979, p. 263). The purpose of discipline is to guide a child to internalize and follow the teacher's values. Ultimately, the teacher's task is to aid the child in developing skills and attitudes for functioning in the world. It is a process of teaching the child self-regulation (Dodson, 1970, pp. 217–238). When a child moves outside the limits of acceptable behavior, the parent's responsibility is to view the episode as an opportunity for growth toward the future. While punishment tends to involve hatred, anger, and retribution, discipline involves love, nurturance, and future growth.

c. Relational parenting. The focus of effective parenting is the parent/child relationship. Four critical dimensions emerge from this analysis of a Christian approach to authority and discipline, namely, control, warmth, involvement, and instruction (Stehouwer and Stehouwer, 1983, p. 344). The relationship is guided by mutual care, understanding, time together, dialogue, and acceptance. Problems are dealt with by all persons involved through mutual problem-solving, which calls for sharing of feelings, "active listening," and "win-win"

negotiations (Gordon, 1970). Parents have the responsibility for understanding the developmental dynamics of the child's particular situation (Dodson, 1970 and 1974). Through regular family meetings, matters of importance can be discussed together, and future directions can be determined mutually.

The techniques and methods for parenting are crucial issues. Much responsibility rests on parents because they are the child's first conceptualization of God. Through parenting they have the responsibility/opportunity to become the incarnation of God for the child.

6. Changing Patterns of Parenting. In contemporary society several parenting patterns are in transition. These are important, as they affect parenting dynamics and the growth of children as well as parents.

Traditionally, the mother has served the role of primary parent, while the father has often been the protector/provider/disciplinarian. With the impact of the women's liberation movement and changing economic forces, both mother and father roles have changed. As women are working outside the home, both parents are now assuming shared responsibilities for parental duties. Dual-career marriages have called for the institution of child-care facilities that in turn introduce "hired" parental figures into the life of the child. Such a transition can be an excellent opportunity for the church to provide quality child-care facilities.

With the changing culture also comes the possibility of persons to be more deliberate about their decisions concerning parenthood. Consequently, many are deciding not to have children but rather to devote their time and energy to other priorities.

Due to the high divorce rate and decisions by single persons to have children, parenting does not always involve "teamwork." Many persons are having to take on the major responsibilities of serving as both mother and father. These single parents face major stresses as they attempt the tremendous task of parenting.

The divorce rate has placed many persons in second marriages, thus creating a stressful situation with stepchildren and stepparents. Both children and parents are placed in the often awkward role of learning to relate in new and different family relationships. These complicate the already difficult dynamics of authority and discipline within the parent-child relationship. Adequate time and energy need to be given to developing the love relationship. The church has the opportunity to offer important learning experiences for these blended families.

As persons continue to have children without having the desire or ability to provide parenting, there are opportunities for adoption, though less frequently than in the past. There are also many parents who are both willing and able to take on the responsibility of adoptive children, especially hard-to-place children. Churches and other institutions are taking on the responsibility of creating parent-child relationships with these adoptive children.

Economic forces, educational opportunities, and perhaps other causes have created a situation in which children are remaining in or returning to the home beyond the traditional time of dependence. These young adults often continue to rely on their parents for financial and emotional security. Such adult parent-child relationships become the basis of much role confusion, as well as family dysfunction. Often these families need special care dealing with the unique stresses of this situation.

A unique transition in our current culture is the opportunity and responsibility for adult children to provide parenting for their own parents. As medical science and good nutrition have progressed, persons are now living longer. Many who are still actively involved in parenting their children are called to provide the same basic parenting skills for their own parents. Many aging persons return to a dependent situation where they need both control and love of a parent figure. Working out this complicated reverse relationship often creates stress for all involved. Churches have the opportunity of offering education and experiential learning for this precarious transition.

7. **Parent Education.** Throughout the course of the parent-child relationship, there are many ways in which the church and the pastor can provide care. Because of the theological implications of parenting, it is imperative that the church do all in its power to enhance this significant task. The church needs to be visionary in its care by providing educational and enrichment experiences for the many aspects of parenting.

Bruno Bettelheim, a child psychologist, believes that successful child rearing means raising a child who may not necessarily become a success in the eyes of the world, but who is satisfied with himself or herself. God can empower parents with the grace and love to raise children who are at peace and can create a world for peace.

Bibliography. R. Anderson and D. Guernsey, *On Being Family* (1985). K. Barth, *Church Dogmatics* III/1 (1969). F. Dobson, *How To Parent* (1970). R. Dreikurs, *Children: The Challenge* (1964). T. Gordon, *Parent Effectiveness Training* (1970). G. Kliman and A. Rosenfeld, *Responsible Parenthood* (1980). K. and J. McGinnis, *Parenting for Peace and Justice* (1983). B. Narramore, *Help! I'm a Parent* (1972); "Discipline's Divine Design," *J. of Psychology and Theology*, (1979). J. and M. Siler, *Communicating Christian Values in the Home* (1984). N. and S. Stehouwer, "A Christian Approach to Authority and Discipline in The Family: Theological-Theoretical Issues and Research Findings," *J. of Psychology and Theology*, (1983).

J. M. HESTER

FAMILY; FOSTER CHILDREN AND FOSTER PARENTS; SINGLE PARENTS; STEPFAMILIES. *See also* ADOLESCENTS; ADOPTION; CHILDBIRTH; CHILDLESSNESS; CHILDREN; FAMILY PLANNING; GODPARENTS; MATERNAL DEPRIVATION; MIDLIFE PERSONS; PREGNANCY; SEX EDUCATION; YOUNG ADULTS. *Compare* EDUCATION, NURTURE, AND CARE.

PARENTS ANONYMOUS/PARENTS UNITED. *See* INCEST; SUPPORT GROUPS.

PARISHIONER. *See* COUNSELEE /CLIENT/PARISHIONER TERMINOLOGY. *See also* DISAGREEMENT, DIFFERENCE, AND CONFLICT IN PASTOR-PARISHIONER RELATIONSHIPS; FRIENDSHIP, PASTOR-PARISHIONER.

PARISH PASTORAL CARE. *See* CONGREGATION.

PARKINSON'S DISEASE. *See* NEUROLOGIC ILLNESSES.

PAROLEES AND EX-CONVICTS. These persons experience rejection and loss of self-respect to a degree unimaginable to most pastoral counselors. They have contended with shame, insecurity, degradation, hopelessness, and helplessness, with a sense of failing not only in society but even in their criminal enterprise. They may have experienced physical and sexual assault in prison. Lifelong anger and the accompanying depression may be assumed. They have intense needs for acceptance, concern, genuineness, warmth, respect, and empathy, and opportunities to express their feelings. Many have become law-breakers as an attempt to overcompensate for feelings of powerlessness, for a sense of special vulnerability of psyche and spirit to be protected and denied, and for the inaccessibility of those things upon which society has placed such high value—money, prestige, education, and power.

Many who have ended up serving prison terms have come from impoverished backgrounds in which they have had little opportunity to acquire an adequate range of social skills and a good social network, no sense of faith in themselves and in others, and no hope of fairness or of change. Pastoral care needs to acknowledge this extreme frustration, depression, and resentment and aim at helping to restore faith in God, in themselves and in others.

Parolees and ex-convicts face with fear the practical daily problems of living, reentering society, the job market, and family or dating relationships. Besides hope and acceptance, they need to have some success in life. While traditional pastoral counseling—which deals with questions of morality, shame, guilt, and repentance — is relevant, far more is demanded here: practical lessons related to results in the real, not just the spiritual, world. They will look for practical "proof" of others' acceptance and forgiveness of them in their being able to get and keep a job and in being given a chance to prove themselves and to be trusted as good citizens. These conditions must be met before parolees and ex-convicts can fully trust and accept themselves. Anything short of this will be viewed as holy but empty words and promises. Halfway houses or other group settings assist in making these practical transitions.

Developing the following insights has been found helpful for parolees and ex-convicts: (1) One can learn to be humble but not self-reproachful, industrious but not avaricious, and willing to start work at modest wages rather than immediately seeking and demanding sudden wealth; (2) Not having all that one might desire in life is not due to a special curse from a non-loving God or a cold world of faceless others; (3) In their frustration, criminal offenders have struck out in anger against others who now fear and distrust them, and as parolees and ex-convicts they need to learn to accept others' frailties, sins, and errors and to forgive other people; (4) Expecting an all-loving and all-giving world on this present earth is a misleading and frustrating myth which can only lead to a sense of failure; and (5) Persons can rely on God's strength rather than their own to get them through difficult times.

C. A. RAYBURN

COMMUNITY, FELLOWSHIP AND CARE; GUIDANCE, PASTORAL; SUPPORT GROUPS. *See also* ADVOCACY; RESPONSIBILITY/

IRRESPONSIBILITY, PSYCHOLOGY OF; SOCIAL JUSTICE ISSUES; SOCIAL STATUS AND CLASS FACTORS. *Compare* POOR PERSONS; PRISONERS AND PRISON CHAPLAINCY.

PAROUSIA, BELIEF IN. *See* ESCHATOLOGY.

PASCAL, BLAISE (1623–62). French Catholic mathematician, physicist, inventor, and Christian apologist.

In addition to his authentic and humble lifestyle, Pascal's significance for pastoral care consists in his personal and literary witness to the compatibility of reason and religion, once the limits of reason, the need for a religious domain, and the necessity and validity of revelation are acknowledged. Thus, science and metaphysics become separated, though not hostile. In his adherence to the thought of Port-Royal and his fervor for Augustine, he anticipates (Protestant) insights of the twentieth century which downplay rigid theological propositions in favor of an emphasis on grace and love. This position is reflected in his attack on the casuistry of the Jesuits of his *Provincial letters.*

After a miraculous mid-life conversion in 1654, which brought to a climax a gradual, ten-year process of distancing from worldly values, the already accomplished and famous Pascal wrote the *Pensées,* a rough draft for an apology against Cartesian rationalism and Montaigne's scepticism.

N. F. HAHN

SPIRITUALITY (Roman Catholic Tradition).

PASSAGES. *See* RITUAL AND PASTORAL CARE.

PASSION OF CHRIST. *See* CHRISTOLOGY.

PASSION/THE PASSIONS. *See* EMOTION; REASON AND PASSION.

PASSIVE-AGGRESSIVE PERSONALITY. A personality disorder in which anger and hostility are expressed in a subdued (passive) manner, thus veiling or discounting their actual intensity. Instead of anger being directly revealed, it is manifested in more generally acceptable ways such as forgetting, procrastinating, "misunderstanding" expectation, sarcastic humor, and deliberate inefficiency.

A. J. STRAATMEYER

AGGRESSION AND ASSERTION; ANTISOCIAL PERSONS. *Compare* SELF-EXPRESSION/SELF-CONTROL.

PASSOVER. *See* JEWISH HOLY DAYS AND FESTIVALS.

The PAST. *See* MEMORY; REMINISCENCE THERAPY; TIME/TIME SENSE.

PAST LIFE REGRESSION. *See* PARAPSYCHOLOGY.

PASTOR (Definition and Functions). A minister, particularly one whose actions show care for an individual or group.

Pastor is the Latin word for *shepherd,* and conveys the image frequent in both the OT (Ps. 80; Isa. 40:11; Jer. 23:1–4; Ezekiel 34) and NT (Heb. 13:20, I Pet. 2:25) which discloses through the work of the sheepherder God's loving protection and guidance of God's people, the flock. Jesus Christ, the good shepherd (Jn. 10:1–18), apparently preferred this metaphor as a figure of self-designation (Mk. 6:34, 14:27; Mt. 25:32; Lk. 12:32; Jn. 21:16). The warrant and standard for the later pastoral ministry of the church is derived from the nature and quality of his pastorate.

While *pastor* may refer to the minister of a congregation and, hence, to all functions of that position, the term is also used more specifically to designate the caring aspects of ministry in distinction to its modes of administration, celebration, proclamation, and teaching. That differentiation is seen in the traditional fourfold pattern of ministry which claims as distinct offices for the church the priestly, prophetic, kingly, and pastoral gifts of Christ. In like manner the lists of ministries in I Cor. 12:28 and Eph. 4:11 distinguish pastors from such roles as apostles, prophets, evangelists and teachers. The OT also contrasts the sage, whose counsel is similar to the work of the pastor, to the priest and the prophet. In all of these typologies the pastoral mode emphasizes the integrative nature of ministry. Whether by ritual, hospitality, consolation, or advice, the pastor tries to make matters whole: to give integrity to lives, solidarity to groups, to mend broken relationships, to heal, accept, restore. The work of the pastor is thus analytically distinct from the governing and ordering activities of the administrator, and from the primarily expressive activities of the priest and prophet.

Clebsch and Jaekle describe four basic functions of the pastor: (1) healing, which is both a restoration to a state of wholeness and a deepening of spiritual awareness; (2) sustaining, which, in cases where healing is improbable, seeks endurance and access to the redemptive life of suffering; (3) guiding, which, by listening and advice, helps perplexed persons make confident decisions; and (4) reconciling, which, by forgiveness and discipline, enables persons to gain deeper relationships with God and neighbor. Implied in all these activities are two characteristics which may distinguish the work of the pastor from that of other helping professions. The pastor acts, first, as the representative of the church, the community made whole by God, which authorizes the pastor to convey in its behalf its redemptive experience to persons in trouble. Like that of the other offices of ministry, the work of the pastor is fundamentally a corporate undertaking, rooted in the message and mission of the church and seeking the *shalom* of the community which those in the pastoral situation share. Second, the pastor acts theologically to uncover the particular meaning in the crisis at hand. Not only does the pastor provide instrumental help; he or she also works with those involved to interpret the present situation according to their ultimate concerns.

Bibliography. W. Clebsch and C. Jaekle, *Pastoral Care in Historical Perspective: An Essay with Exhibits* (1964). R. Johnson,

Congregations as Nurturing Communities (1979). E. M. Pattison, *Pastor and Parish: A Systems Approach* (1977).

J. F. HOPEWELL

CHAPLAIN/CHAPLAINCY; CONFESSOR; MINISTER; PRIEST; SPIRITUAL DIRECTOR. *Compare* CHRISTIAN SCIENCE PRACTITIONER; IDENTITY, PASTORAL; RABBI/RABBINATE; SHAMAN; WOMEN IN PASTORAL MINISTRIES, HISTORY OF.

PASTOR (Normative and Traditional Images).

Images through their appeal to the imagination have both affective and cognitive power. While concepts are the material of logical argument of the "linear" type, images are "lateral," associative rather than derived from a theoretical perspective. (This difference may correspond to the different functions carried out by the left and right hemispheres of the brain.) Images may be represented by words, but these words evoke sensory experience — visual, auditory, olfactory, and tactual— thus creating a response that arouses memory and provokes emotional reaction. For this reason, images have a particular power to influence people's attitudes, though this is often not consciously perceived. Images can lose this power, and the perpetuation of the words representing them then leads to confusion and misunderstanding.

Images also become distorted, in the sense that over time the primary reference of an image may be obscured and new associations take its place. Thus *pastor* (Latin: *grazier* or *shepherd*) has gained leadership and institutional associations only distantly related to the original imagery of shepherding. We may note three aspects of pastoring: leading, healing, nurturing. Each aspect has images other than *shepherd* associated with it. For Christians the concept of Jesus as the Good Shepherd provides a unifying theme, but the shepherd image may no longer be a normative one. Jesus as servant, as brother, and as companion probably have greater power at the present time.

1. Leading and Guiding. This aspect is prominent in both OT and NT references to shepherding. In the poor pastureland of Palestine, shepherding was an arduous and dangerous task. The shepherd walked at the head of the flock seeking and guiding it to good grazing, water, and shade, and watching out for wild beasts and robbers. Death may lurk in the shadows of valleys (Ps. 23:4) and stragglers must be restored to the flock (Mt. 18:12). The shepherd is courageous and tough (see David's boasting in I Sam. 17:34–37), not always trustworthy, especially if only a hired hand (Jn. 10:13), perhaps more like a cowboy or drover than the modern shepherd. In the Bible such courageous leadership is applied chiefly to God or to God's Chosen One (Ps. 23; Isa. 40:11; Ezek. 34; Mt. 18:12–14; Jn. 10:1–16; Heb. 13:20; Rev. 7:17), only rarely to leaders in the congregation (Acts 20:28; Eph. 4:11; I Pet. 5:2). But subsequent church tradition (e.g. Chrysostom, *De Sacerdotio;* U. Zwingli, *Der Hirt;* R. Baxter, *The Reformed Pastor*) has equated the flock with the congregation and the shepherd with the minister or bishop. The result has often been a blunting of the "trail-blazing" (Heb. 2:10) aspects of the image and a paternalistic approach to the "ordinary" Christian's service of the Great Shepherd (Heb. 13:20). In recent times S. Hiltner's writing has recovered the notion of shepherding as a "perspective," not a clerical function, but the

pioneer aspect of the original image is still muted. A more vivid image (also with biblical roots) for this leadership aspect is that of the "comrade in arms." Here a greater equality between helper and helped is evident, but the courage of the comrade in combat situations and his or her trustworthiness is also of critical importance. Pastoral care in personal crisis situations (e.g., impending death, suicide attempts, facing grievous loss) and pastoral care under political or social oppression requires the "standing beside" that the comrade provides.

2. Healing and Restoring. A second feature of the image of pastor is tenderness toward the weak and wounded (Isa. 40:11; Ezek. 34:4) and even self-sacrifice to save those being cared for (Jn. 10:15). In Revelation the shepherd and the sacrificial Lamb are one (Rev. 7:17). The ministry of Christ is portrayed in the Passion narratives as that of a suffering servant (Isa. 53:5), whose vulnerability saves others when he cannot save himself (Lk. 23:35). The image of the pastor as a "wounded healer," helping at personal risk, is easily lost when organizational questions predominate. It is present, in a sense, in the martyrs of the church throughout history, but often such acts are merely self-aggrandizing, not of direct benefit to others. The rise of sacramentalism in the Middle Ages produced a different image, the "physician of the soul," dispensing the "medicine of the sacraments" and acting as a father confessor. Although undoubtedly a powerful source of healing, this image also acted as the justification for a priestly elite, in opposition to which the Reformers stressed the "priesthood of all believers." Modern Roman Catholic and Protestant thought is returning to the notion of human vulnerability as a medium for God's healing power (H. Nouwen and J. Hillman), emphasizing that each Christian, by freely acknowledging weakness and mortality, can be a tender and empathetic wounded healer. The more intimate images of father, mother, sister, brother, lover, all have a part to play in this healing or restorative aspect of pastoring. Because they are closer to everyone's personal experience they can be both more powerful and more easily distorted. The problem of transference in pastoral situations is very often embodied in such images, material from the person's own life history providing the motive and the style of both seeking and offering help. Such images are helpful, however, when the personal associations are recognized and then used creatively by both helper and helped. For example, a pastor may for a time be a "good" father/mother or loving brother/sister for a person in distress, provided the symbolic character of the relationship is not denied. Often the greatest risk comes when the image of lover is also allowed a place.

3. Nurturing and Sustaining. The shepherd is also a source of strength to the flock, providing rest and nourishment. Jesus instructs Peter to "feed my lambs" as a proof of his love (Jn. 21:15). The pastor feeds with the Word, and so pastor and teacher become equated. (See the list of ministries in Eph. 4:11.) But though a real shepherd knows well what will nourish the sheep, the authority of the teaching pastor is not so secure. Cleverness is not to be equated with wisdom, for, to the clever, the Gospel is folly (I Cor. 1:18–25). Thus the figure of the wise fool or the tragi-comic clown lurks behind that of the pastor. Authority is always under question by simplicity, and human order is threatened by divine freedom. It is perhaps especially the folly of the Cross that protects the pastoral image from a tendency toward paternalism and pomposity. To be a fool for Christ's sake demands humility above all. Those called "pastors" are just as frequently the lost sheep, wandering far from home, in need of the Good Shepherd. The courageous shepherd, the trustworthy comrade, the weak fool, and the vulnerable brother or sister all belong to pastoring. But stereotypes of the pastor or minister frequently obscure this rich diversity and complementarity. Unlike the image, which creates fresh understanding and emotional development, the stereotype prevents the evolution of ideas, giving a one-dimensional and unalterable shape to the word used. Here the loss of the original meaning of *minister* as *servant* is a serious loss. The servanthood of Christ calls into question all triumphalist and manipulative approaches to pastoring. It leaves open the question whether pastoring is itself really a professional activity, since professionalism implies superior knowledge and power. The normative image of servant requires that fresh images of pastoring be created from contemporary experience, that the weakness of the helper be acknowledged, and that mutual companionship and friendship in a servanthood for the one Lord become the primary motivating powers in all helping acts.

Bibliography. S. Hiltner in *Preface to Pastoral Theology* (1958) and *The Christian Shepherd* (1959) initiates the contemporary discussion of shepherding. T. Oden, "Recovering Lost Identity," *J. of Pastoral Care*, (1980), 4–19, warns of a dangerous neglect of classical sources. A. V. Campbell, *Rediscovering Pastoral Care* (1981) discusses images of shepherd, wounded healer, and wise fool; see also his *Professionalism and Pastoral Care* (1985). For the pastor as healer see J. Hillman, *In search: Psychology and Religion* (1967); H. Nouwen, *The Wounded Healer* (1972); and J. A. Knight, "The Minister as Healer, the Healer as Minister," *J. of Religion and Health*, 21 (1982), 100–14. For the pastor as fool, see H. Faber, *Pastoral Care in the Modern Hospital* (1971); and J. Saward, *Perfect Fools* (1980).

A. V. CAMPBELL

AUTHORITY, PASTORAL; IDENTITY, PASTORAL; MINISTRY; PASTOR (Definitions and Functions); PASTORAL CARE (History, Traditions, and Definitions); SHEPHERD/SHEPHERDING; SYMBOLIC DIMENSIONS OF PASTORAL CARE RELATIONSHIPS. *See also* COMFORT/SUSTAINING; CONFESSOR; EVANGELIZING; GUIDANCE; HEALING; LEADERSHIP AND ADMINISTRATION; *Compare* SHAMAN; SPIRITUAL MASTERS AND GUIDES; WOMEN IN PASTORAL MINISTRIES, HISTORY OF.

PASTOR (Popular Stereotypes and Caricatures).

The images of clergy, held by receivers of pastoral care, that distort the reality of the presently involved minister; a major source of resistance, typically stemming from transference and other forms of stimulous generalization.

There are a number of widely held ministerial stereotypes: that pastors never get angry or have any strong feeling; that pastors are not sexual; that pastors are legalistic and/or moralistic; that pastors are naive and impractical; that pastors do not understand money or business; that pastors will always try to convert you; that pastors are ultimately after your money; that pastors raise children poorly; that pastors are dishonest about spiritual matters, though scrupulously honest about other things; and that pastors are all men.

These stereotypes create barriers between clergy and receivers of care. The minister may become aware of them when the receiver enters the relationship with a strong feeling toward the minister that is not based on prior experience of this particular individual: as when a hospital patient refuses to let the chaplain "or any minister" into his or her room, or when the counselee says that he would not have come to this place if he had known it was a *pastoral* counseling center.

There are also positive stereotypes that make the pastor's job easier, if they are held in moderation. Many people believe that ministers are able to speak directly for God; that they are kind, honest, and committed; that they have legitimate authority by virtue of their ordination.

It is important for the minister to be aware of the operation of both positive and negative stereotypes in pastoral relationships. Though very intensely held images often proclaim themselves blatantly, more silent prejudices can as effectively undermine care. The signs that these are in operation include the awareness that one is not being taken seriously, that the other is polite but not acting on what is said, or that the other seeks almost anyone else's input first. It is as though whatever the minister says or does is being perceived through the filter of the other's inaccurate expectations, which function to disqualify the clergyperson.

When the pastor notices that, it is important to say so. A direct but polite observation of the other's behavior can begin a stereotype-altering conversation. "You're very polite, but you don't seem to hear what I say." Often that will elicit some information about the other person's past experience of ministers. If not, it can be useful to ask if they have had unpleasant dealings with clergy before. If so, one might say something like, "I'm sorry to hear that, but it's possible that we're not all alike. Could you tell me more about the problem you had with Rev. So-and-so?"

The minister's intention is to get the care-receiver to link specific data to the caricature, so he or she can see that it represents too general a conclusion. It is important for the pastor to recognize that such caricatures usually begin with a real, unpleasant experience; and to empathize with the person about that event. It remains wise for the pastor to concede that there may be truth in the receiver's view, but to add that this pastor knows the importance of not falling into the error that offended in the past. One way to do that is to contract with the person to tell you if he or she notices you beginning to get close to the offending behavior.

Later in the relationship it may be feasible to interpret the former minister's actions in a more favorable light — once you believe you understand them—but at the beginning it is important to disassociate yourself from their more offensive elements, if they are things you can appropriately separate yourself from.

The more clearly and accurately the pastor is perceived as an individual, and the less that perception is bound to others' prior expectations, the more likely the pastor can represent God faithfully and be an instrument of the divine will.

B. W. GRANT

AUTHORITY, PASTORAL; IDENTITY, PASTORAL; *Compare* PREJUDICE; TRANSFERENCE; WOMEN IN PASTORAL MINISTRIES, HISTORY OF.

PASTOR, AUTHORITY OF. *See* AUTHORITY, PASTORAL. *See also* AUTHORITY ISSUES IN PASTORAL CARE.

PASTOR, CALLING AND VOCATION OF. *See* CALL TO MINISTRY; MINISTRY.

PASTOR, CARICATURES OF. *See* PASTOR (Popular Stereotypes and Caricatures).

PASTOR, CHILDREN OF. *See* CHILDREN, PASTOR'S. *See also* MARRIAGE AND FAMILY LIFE, PASTOR'S.

PASTOR, DEFINITION OF. *See* PASTOR, (Definitions and Functions).

PASTOR, DIVORCE OF. *See* DIVORCE, PASTOR'S.

PASTOR, EMPIRICAL STUDIES OF. *See* CLERGY, EMPIRICAL STUDIES OF.

PASTOR, ETHICS OF. *See* ETHICS, PROFESSIONAL; FAITH AND INTEGRITY, PASTOR'S.

PASTOR, FAITH AND INTEGRITY OF. *See* FAITH AND INTEGRITY, PASTOR'S.

PASTOR, FAMILY OF. *See* MARRIAGE AND FAMILY, PASTOR'S.

PASTOR, FUNCTIONS OF. *See* PASTOR (Definitions and Functions).

PASTOR, HOMOSEXUAL. *See* HOMOSEXUAL PASTOR.

PASTOR, HUSBAND OF. *See* HUSBAND, PASTOR'S.

PASTOR, IDENTITY OF. *See* IDENTITY, PASTORAL.

PASTOR, IMAGES OF. *See* PASTOR (Normative and Traditional Images); PASTOR (Popular Stereotypes and Caricatures).

PASTOR, INTEGRITY OF. *See* FAITH AND INTEGRITY, PASTOR'S.

PASTOR, LAY. *See* PASTOR (Definitions and Functions).

PASTOR, LEGAL OBLIGATIONS OF. *See* LEGAL DIMENSIONS OF PASTORAL CARE AND COUNSELING.

PASTOR, MARRIAGE OF. *See* MARRIAGE AND FAMILY LIFE, PASTOR'S.

PASTOR, MATURITY OF. *See* MENTAL HEALTH, PASTOR'S. *See also* FAITH AND INTEGRITY, PASTOR'S; PERSONHOOD OF THE PASTOR, SIGNIFICANCE OF.

PASTOR, MENTAL HEALTH OF. *See* MENTAL HEALTH, PASTOR'S.

PASTOR, PASTORAL CARE OF. Historically, the church has a weak and inconsistent record in providing pastoral care for pastors. Certain aspects of caring have sometimes been evidenced through the structure of the disciplined orders of clergy and through the various types of appointive systems. Security needs, for instance, have frequently been addressed, often as a partial inducement to "give up the world" and entrust one's future to hierarchical authority. (Likewise, religious orders have frequently cared for the needs of their members for retirement, treatment of alcoholism, and mental illness.) These efforts have typically been inadequate and have normally been grossly underfunded, understaffed, and peripheral in planning and contracting. The judicatory system itself has often aggravated problems of pastoral morale, rather than effectively alleviating known stressors. Too often, the pastor has been scapegoated as lacking in commitment or as being too self-serving—thus helping to deny ongoing systemic dimensions of the problem.

One might assume that there would be vast differences in the pastoral care needs of priests, rabbis, and Protestant clergy. There is as yet no compelling data to support this view since very little research data is yet available. The author's own direct experience has been primarily with Protestant clergy in the Midwest, although ecumenical contacts have seemed to verify these impressions across a wide spectrum of clergy.

1. **The Needs of Pastors.** To deal more helpfully with the pastoral needs of pastors, one must assess the actual unmet needs as experienced by large numbers of reporting pastors. These problems may be as endemic to presuppositions about themselves as to the failures of the peculiar judicatory structures in which they function. Significant numbers of pastors seem to hold unconscious or subliminal presuppositions which tend to help them deny their own need for pastoral care. Some of the most common presuppositions are as follows: Some feel that they should not get any personal gratification from their work. Others feel that they must be on duty twenty-four hours a day. Many seem to derive much of their sense of self-worth from "helping others," and appear to be motivated more by ego deficits than by the overflow of their own self-actualization. Many seem to feel that their religious calling permits no negative feelings. Thus they limit the range of their expressed emotions rather severely. Some seem to need to project an image of being able to cope perfectly with all situations at all times. Whether this attitude is a way of inviting others to lean on them or an inadvertent response to such dependency is unclear.

In addition to the unconscious presuppositions hypothesized above, there are some frequent complaints and deficits which are often spoken of. The first of these is personal *loneliness;* whether it is from a sense of being the outsider who does not quite fit into the community into which they have entered, or whether it is a matter of status boundaries, professional choices, or a combination of several factors, varies from person to person. It does seem clear that pastors who spend a great deal of energy caring for the needs of other lonely people are often very lonely people themselves. Their spouses and their children frequently report feeling social separation from others and great frustration and confusion about how to legitimately bridge such isolation. Church rubrics often severely limit fraternization with parishioners, and may thus compound the conflict.

Imprecise competence is a second source of great concern for many clergy of all faiths. The work of a pastor — particularly a parish pastor — requires many varied and contrasting skills. Few are equally adept at preparing good sermons, delivering sermons well, fund raising, group facilitation, organization and planning, bedside pastoral care, marriage and family crisis counseling, conducting liturgy, and community involvement, to name a few examples. Since the pastor is a generalist, it is extremely difficult to measure competence and success except in terms of worship attendance, budgets, and new members. If the pastor chooses instead to pursue goals for deepening the spiritual lives of the congregation or involving laity in responsibility for mission, those goals are often not fully understood or shared by denominational superiors and influential laity.

Spiritual malaise may be seen as the third most common source of internal stress among clergy. It is akin to the feeling of fraud and emptiness, where the message proclaimed is not consonant with their own internal experience. This mood is very characteristic of clergy in their peak years, many of whom were once "on fire" with their message. Much chronic low morale is mistaken for depression when it is more clearly an issue of internal integrity.

Clinical depression is certainly not unknown among pastors. At the same time, the incidence of pastors plagued with the internal conflict between their anger and their guilt is a much more common phenomenon. Actually, such a condition is easily treatable and with a high rate of success.

Conflict over meeting the *varied expectations* of many persons is likewise frequently reported. Many pastors are particularly disturbed over the conflicting expectations of parish, parsonage family, and a third force (such as a theological seminary, an advanced degree program, or community and connectional responsibilities). It is very difficult for a pastor who needs the gratification of so many different commitments and yet feels continually pressed by such competing demands. *Overextension* of energy, time, and ability is therefore often related to such internal conflicts as well as to low salaries, low autonomy, unfair expectations by others, and unrealistic expectations of themselves.

Most Protestant pastors are married and have families. Hence, the stresses of modern life have similar effects on their families as on those of the general population. Higher expectations based on double standards and a continuing "goldfish bowl" existence may therefore serve to further aggravate their defensiveness or anxiety about admitting and dealing with their own marriage and family problems. While the divorce rate among clergy families is certainly on the increase, it is still very much below the national average. These data may be interpreted to mean better management of domestic problems, more passive and acquiescent spouses, denied feelings, or simply a shift toward less punitive response by the church to clergy divorce.

One final suggestion might be made about common and observable clergy needs for emotional and spiritual support. The hearing of confessions of others may build both an inhibition and a reluctance to admit similar foibles, conflicts, and sin. Many pastors seem able to deal with intimacy only in a formal structured role and need skilled help in learning how to deal with emotional intimacy without confusing it with sexual intimacy.

2. **Career Support.** Within the last twenty years, several new career support models have emerged which have sought to take the realities of pastoral needs more seriously. While these models are still the exception and not the rule, they are nonetheless suggesting a more realistic grasp of and commitment to clergy needs.

The most common form of judicatory career support for the pastoral needs of pastors has been funding through group insurance policies or through allocated funds for partial support of counseling services to clergy. While there are many variations in this pattern, it is the one most frequent type of support available across many denominational lines. Such a pattern quickly evidences concern for gross pathology, but hardly addresses the systemic and personal causes of such breakdown, or the preventive dimensions of routine nurture and growth-oriented ministries.

A number of denominations use existing committees which normally screen clergy for admission to attempt modest symbolic caring ministries, usually in the form of periodic retreats, continuing education opportunities, transition seminars, etc. Frequently, the services seem tainted to some pastors because there is an implicit "big brotherism" related to the double function of such committees. A similar problem is often found in the pastoral care given by judicatory authorities, who are sometimes compromised by their disciplinary, appointive, and congregational interests. Even support by fellow clergy, while certainly present throughout the history of religious leadership, sometimes threatens individual clergy with potential future exposure.

The model of delivery of pastoral care services of pastors best known is one predicated on certain presuppositions: an orientation toward growth, balance between clinical rehabilitation and a comprehensive preventive program, diversity of therapeutic options, a relationship between responsibility and authority, development of clergy initiative, and an attempt to better prepare persons for constant change.

The scope and priority of such a program may include crisis intervention services, consultation, continuing education, career assessment, pilot programs, supervision and research, pastoral retreats, and a variety of informal support projects which are ongoing, undramatic, and highly individualized.

Crisis intervention services might include one or more persons trained in both theology and in one of the helping professions, preferably in pastoral counseling. Such persons should be highly qualified by the highest professional standards so that their credibility as both pastor and psychotherapist is unquestioned. In some geographical areas where transportation is easy and direct, one person may serve an entire judicatory from a particular office, to which others come for diagnostic evaluation, marriage counseling, assistance in a family crisis, assessment of depressive symptoms, exploration of crippling emotions and/or counterproductive behavior, and occasionally for long-term therapy. In a large geographical area, satellite centers might be developed to bring such clinical services close to constituent users. This may be feasible when adjunct clinical resource persons are available or when there is a multiple staff.

Consultation about continuing conflicts or relational problems in ministry, other career options, continuing education, clinical training opportunities, and about the pastor's own parish caseload are important services which are much needed. The establishment of regular hours for a telephone consultation service is one way of making such consultation viable and realistic. Consultation with local churches regarding their plans for weekend marriage enrichment retreats, conflict resolution, etc., is another possible service.

Continuing education opportunities in marriage and family counseling, premarriage consultation, grief and bereavement, and the whole range of pastoral care and counseling skills is another aspect of the total career support concept. Such events give opportunity to integrate cognitive understandings, clinical skills, peer support, and personal affective conflict. In addition, the development of training programs and events for multiple-staff clergy, for single clergy, for two-clergy couples, for pastor-parish relations committees, etc., is also feasible.

Training and research related to judicatory systemic problems, morale, and specific supervision of clergy in special kinds of needs are also possible foci for a supportive nurturing and preventive ministry. Interviewing committees often need training to provide an effective and sensitive process for new entrants into the ministry. Pastoral retreats which combine spiritual refreshment, resocialization with colleagues, and biblical studies, often provide the initial contact from which later requests for specific counseling and psychotherapy emerge. Many informal support projects which are ongoing, undramatic, and highly individualized are possible within such a model. Attention to the transitions of clergy, individual letters of pastoral care, and immediate responsiveness to reported needs, e.g., a called consultation for clergy in their middle years, are feasible. Part of the effectiveness of such interventions inheres in flexible programming, change of priorities, and autonomy of function.

For such a model to be viable, the pastoral care office must stand independent from the power structures within the denomination. There must be autonomy of function and minimization of vulnerability to power groups within the judicatory system—particularly regarding accountability, control, and financing. Clear contracts of relationship between the confidentiality of the counseling experience and the appointive or disciplinary authority are pivotal in the prediction of success of a new program.

Bibliography. D. C. Houts, "Pastoral Care for Pastors," *Pastoral Psychology,* 25:3 (1977), 186–96. D. Mace, ed., "Clergy Families Today," a thematic issue of *Pastoral Psychology,* 30:3 (1982), 139–97. D. Mace and V. Mace, *What's Happening to Clergy Marriages?* (1980). J. Patton, "The Pastoral Care of Pastors," *The Christian Ministry* 11:4 (1980), 15–18.

D. C. HOUTS

BURNOUT; DIVORCE, PASTOR'S; FAITH AND INTEGRITY, PASTOR'S; MARRIAGE AND FAMILY LIFE, PASTOR'S; MENTAL HEALTH, PASTOR'S; PERSONHOOD OF THE PASTOR, SIGNIFICANCE OF; PRAYER AND WORSHIP LIFE, PASTOR'S. *Compare* CLERGY COUPLES; CLERGY, EMPIRICAL STUDIES OF; ECCLESIOLOGY AND PASTORAL CARE; HOMOSEXUAL PASTOR; MISSIONARIES, PASTORAL CARE OF; RELIGIOUS, PASTORAL CARE OF; THEOLOGICAL STUDENTS, PASTORAL CARE OF.

PASTOR, PERSONALITY OF. See CLERGY, EMPIRICAL STUDIES OF; PERSONHOOD OF THE PASTOR, SIGNIFICANCE OF. *See also* MENTAL HEALTH, PASTOR'S.

PASTOR, PRAYER AND WORSHIP LIFE OF. See PRAYER AND WORSHIP LIFE, PASTOR'S.

PASTOR, ROLE OF. See PASTOR (Definitions and Functions); ROLE, MINISTERIAL.

PASTOR, STEREOTYPES OF. See PASTOR (Popular Stereotypes and Caricatures).

PASTOR, WIFE OF. See WIFE, PASTOR'S.

PASTOR, WOMAN. See MINISTRY; WOMEN IN PASTORAL MINISTRIES, HISTORY OF.

PASTOR-PARISHIONER FRIENDSHIP. See FRIENDSHIP, PASTOR-PARISHIONER.

PASTORAL AUTHORITY. See AUTHORITY, PASTOR. *See also* AUTHORITY ISSUES IN PASTORAL CARE.

PASTORAL CALLING AND VISITATION. See CALLING AND VISITATION, PASTORAL.

PASTORAL CARE (Contemporary Methods, Perspectives, and Issues). For the present purpose, *contemporary methods* means pastoral care methods that are in use now, regardless of their length of service in pastoral care. Therefore, in this exploration of contemporary methods there is a distinction between neo-traditional methods of pastoral care and twentieth century influences on pastoral care. Neo-traditional methods refer to those classical approaches which have been characteristically used throughout the Hebrew-Christian era but are being given new forms and meaning for this present era.

1. **Neo-traditional Methods.** *a. Scriptural instruction, interpretation, proclamation.* A constant responsibility of pastors has been to teach, interpret, and take an ethical stand on what the Bible says. In contemporary pastoral care since the work of Anton Boisen, this has been one of the methods of pastoral care. Boisen gave his cases such names as *A Modern Jonah* and spoke of him and other mental patients as being on a 'journey into the wilderness.' The psychosocial principle of development was used by Harry Emerson Fosdick in his book, *A Guide*

to Understanding the Bible. Russell Dicks's vital contribution was his sensitive blend of the art of ministering to the sick with the "patience and comfort of the Scriptures." In 1953, Wayne Oates published a small volume recording his use of *The Bible in Pastoral Care.* Carrol Wise wrote of his own integration of the wisdoms of *Psychiatry and the Bible* (1956). The diagnostic and therapeutic value of religious ideation is prominent in Edgar Draper's *Psychiatry and Pastoral Care* (1968). William Hulme relates Job's *Dialogue in Despair* (1968) to the care of souls today. Jay Adams published his book, *Competent to Counsel* (1974), using the Bible as a blend of Hobart Mowrer's "moral model" of psychotherapy with a confrontational use of Scripture in a nouthetic form of pastoral counseling. William Oglesby relates the *Biblical Themes for Pastoral Care* (1980) to past issues of initiative and freedom, fear and faith, conformity and rebellion, death and rebirth, risk and redemption. Most recently, Donald Capps has identified the structure and function of Scripture in his book, *Biblical Approaches to Pastoral Counseling* (1981).

b. Preaching and pastoral care. Twentieth-century methods of pastoral care may accurately be interpreted as having their broadest and deepest roots in the preaching of early twentieth-century preachers. Nineteenth-century preachers of the frontier revivals and even earlier in the Great Awakening were far more concerned about the care of souls than popular stereotypes lead us to believe. Wesley's "classes" began as fund-raising efforts and flowered into life-support groups for persons dogged by economic necessity, marital conflict, alcoholism, and the rest of the gamut of pastoral care needs. Jonathan Edwards did not employ "the sawdust trail" of the invitation. People came to his study "enquiring." The "after-meeting" was used extensively when questions and concerns could be voiced. In the twentieth century, preachers use these as methods of pastoral care with a new sophistication as to developmental tasks, problems such as grief, divorce, retirement, etc. A defensible thesis could be written to demonstrate the ways in which the preaching of Leslie Weatherhead, Norman Vincent Peale, Harry Emerson Fosdick, George Buttrick, Ralph Sockman, Monsignor Fulton J. Sheen, John Sutherland Bonnell, George W. Truett, and Paul Scherer was the forerunner of a distinctly person-centered pastoral care of individuals, families, and small groups. They sensitized people to the intimately personal involvement of God in Jesus Christ in the crucial human situations that make them feel alien from the starched-stiffness of formal church propriety.

Preaching shaped by the methods of pastoral care in the last half of the twentieth century has been evident in Charles Kemp's *Life-Situation Preaching* (1956), David McClelland's *Pastoral Preaching* (1955), John Claypool's *Tracks of a Fellow Struggler* (1982), and Wayne Oates's book, *The Revelation of God in Human Suffering* (1959). The innovative preaching of John Killinger, "feedback sessions" after sermons, and the distinct literary form of the "dialogue sermon" are neo-traditional forms of pastoral care.

c. The pastoral use of initiative. In the Hebrew-Christian tradition God takes initiative toward human beings in a spirit of fellowship and redemptive concern.

God walks with *ish* and *ishah,* man and woman, in the garden. God visits Moses at the burning bush. God speaks to Elijah in the wilderness cave. God intervenes in corporate and personal histories. God, in the fullness of time, visited the world fully and completely, becoming flesh in Jesus Christ (Jn. 1:14; Heb. 1:1–4).

Pastors as undershepherds of Jesus Christ have traditionally emulated this initiative. In the fifties and sixties an increasing passivity and lack of initiative became the staple diet of theological students in pastoral care. Meanwhile, however, in Clinical Pastoral Education (CPE) these passive methods were being dissonantly interposed upon a traditional pastoral task—the visitation of the sick. Much was learned in this contrast of new and old. Emerging from this in the seventies and eighties have been neo-traditional expressions of pastoral initiative in the use of marketplace social action ministries. In the revived use of the letter or the pastoral epistle, pastors in the clinic and in the parish are finding access to people who are too depressed, too withdrawn, or too alienated to reach out for help. Crisis intervention is the new name for the aggressive use of the telephone, the letter, and the pastoral visit as well as the more passive "wait-until-they-ask-for-help" approach of the formal psychotherapist. The pastor is always ambiguously involved in balancing the healing power of distance with the redeeming power of intimacy in the critical situations of pastoral care. To make an either/or of one or the other of these is to miss the essential calling of being a pastor.

d. Prayer, contemplation, meditation, and spiritual direction. The mode, mood, and matter of prayer is as old and diverse as the forms of pastoral care can get. Yet, contemporary pastoral care has not until recently—in the seventies and eighties—become articulate and consciously purposive in fully drawing upon this modality. Russell Dicks very early stuck closely to the centrality of prayer in the minor miracles of pastoral care. The main thrust of the pastoral care movement, however, was intensely involved in secular explorations of the mechanism of miracle and how to reproduce the miracle again and again in psychotherapy and/or social action. The competitive spirit of sibling groups within the movement also short-circuited attention to the ultimate concern for God — who is also the ultimate authority who loves siblings even when they compete to the point of forgetting *whose* sons and daughters they are.

Since 1975 the pastoral care movement has come to a new and exhilarating level of maturity. In a part this is due to Vatican II which opened up fellowship with Roman Catholics in a way not known before. The work of Henri Nouwen has given new strength to a "reaching out" of "wounded healers" for a life of prayer that infuses pastoral care with a more than analytical understanding of "the way of the heart." In addition, the influence of increasing numbers of women in pastoral care has challenged men's "taboos on tenderness" that often prompt men to adopt a new hypocrisy of *appearing* less spiritual than they really are.

Furthermore, a matured discipline of altered states of consciousness, appropriated through a transpersonal approach to pastoral care, has prompted a fresh use of the methods of meditation, contemplation, and prayer. These methods are eventuating in a re-evaluation of spiritual direction as an aspect of pastoral care, as evident in Kenneth Leech's *Soul Friend* (1980) and *True Prayer: An Invitation to Spirituality* (1980), and Gerald D. May's *Care of Mind—Care of Spirit: Psychiatric Dimensions of Spiritual Direction* (1982).

2. **Twentieth Century Influences.** The foregoing discussion of neo-traditional methods points up ways in which old methods are taking new shape in contemporary pastoral care. Yet specific *new* forms of pastoral care have also come into general use in the twentieth century.

a. Longer term psychotherapeutic approaches to pastoral counseling. This has finally "come into its own" in recent decades. Its extensive practice is attributable to several forces. First, the training of ministers in pastoral counseling is elaborately intensive for those who subscribe to the standards of the American Association of Pastoral Counselors (AAPC), the Association for Clinical Pastoral Education (ACPE), and the American Association for Marriage and Family Therapy (AAMFT). Many ministers are now qualified in all three of these national regulatory bodies. Supervision by certified supervisors is widely available and, in many instances, is superior in quality and intensity to that done in social work, clinical psychology, and psychiatry.

Second, several cognate professions have abdicated positions they once held as major providers of psychotherapy. Many social workers have abandoned psychotherapy in favor of administrative positions in governmental agencies. In medical education psychotherapy has suffered severe attrition as psychiatry has moved closer to neurology, internal medicine, and biochemistry under the impact of the biochemical and genetic breakthroughs, evolving away from psychotherapy toward psychopharmacology. Psychoanalysis, for its part, translated itself into arcane medical categories and became a highly expensive, indefinitely lengthy form of training and therapy available only to a few, and severed from a humanistic concern for the 'soul' in order to gain acceptance by the scientifically self-conscious medical profession. (See Bettelheim, *Freud and Man's Soul*, 1983.) Today, many physicians simply repudiate psychotherapy, especially in psychoanalytic forms, while, on the other hand, a few pastoral counselors are beginning to rework its methods, restoring some of its original concern for the masses.

Another reason for the effective flourishing of pastoral counseling is the administrative and organizational skill of pastors, who by and large are more aware and skilled in relating to the roots of a community than physicians (with notable exceptions in each case) and have been remarkably successful in developing pastoral counseling centers. (See John C. Carr, John E. Hinkle, and David M. Moss III, *The Organization and Administration of Pastoral Counseling Centers*, 1981.) Local churches are sponsoring such centers in increasing numbers, and many multiple staff churches are employing associate pastors whose sole function is pastoral care and counseling. Major denominations are also establishing counseling centers, sometimes on a statewide basis, and some denominations have established specialized career guidance centers. In almost all of these counseling centers ecumenical service to people of all faiths is characteristic, and is no doubt an additional reason for their striking success.

b. Retreat centers. Another new form of pastoral care is the retreat center. Recognizing the need for dramatic interruption of the stress syndrome, many pastoral counselors have either established or become leaders of already established retreat centers. These centers combine intensive personal counseling with group therapy and set both in a context of worship and physical outdoor activity. An example is the Yokefellows Centers, where the Society of Friends has brought the wisdom of their quest for the "Inner Light" to bear upon people's personal and social needs for care.

The retreat center has a longer history than the pastoral counseling center, having deep roots in the Catholic and the Quaker traditions. (It was also presaged earlier in this century by Gandhi's ashrams and the ashrams of E. Stanley Jones.) Yet the new dimension is that many retreat centers today are being led by persons with long experience and intensive, supervised training in contemporary therapeutic skills and understandings.

The retreat center is being widely expanded on an ecumenical basis for coeducational groups in Catholic facilities maintained and supervised by various orders of priests and nuns. The OT "city of refuge" (Num. 35:6–32), the medieval tradition of the cathedral as a place of "sanctuary," and the contemporary retreat center have all served to halt the unremitting stress of life and insert creative parentheses into human existence. This enables persons to gain a new perspective on old issues, to make more spiritually reflective and less impulsive decisions, and to discover more free and less compulsive behaviors. In short, it enables the person to put away idols and find a center for living in the true and living God.

e. New psychologies and pastoral care. Pastoral care in the first half of the twentieth century was heavily influenced by psychoanalysis and clinical psychiatry. The pervasive frames of reference of these disciplines—their "mythologies"—left few if any parts of American society (not just pastoral care) untouched. Yet by the time of the Vietnam war the assumptions, orthodoxies, and methods of both psychoanalysis and psychiatry had been shaken severely both within and without. From within, the psychopharmacological revolution and the federal funding of comprehensive mental health centers throughout the country, staffed by people of non-medical as well as medical training (at pitifully low incomes), brought a new order of treatment modalities—and a new chaos—into the professions of psychoanalysis and psychiatry. Some psychiatrists, noting these changes, have feared that their whole profession was at "high risk." Radical non-psychiatrists such as Thomas A. Szasz spoke of *The Myth of Mental Illness* (1961), and E. F. Torrey predicted *The Death of Psychiatry* (1974). Perry London (*Behavior Control*, 1969) and William Glasser (*Reality Therapy*, 1965) offered a calmer assessment, separating out the personality disorders for a more reality-oriented, here-and-now form of treatment. Psychiatry was not dead or even dying, but was undergoing a revolution from within.

From without, the steady, persistent voices of Gordon Allport, Abraham Maslow, Fritz Perls, and Eric Berne began to be heard at last. Whole new therapeutic approaches were devised out of the more human potential movement. Pastoral counselors, accustomed to riding the waves of therapeutic popularity, flocked to transactional analysis, Gestalt therapy, and various growth-oriented therapies. Howard Clinebell's, *Contemporary Growth Therapies* (1981), documents the fresh angles of vision that these therapies brought to pastoral counseling. His 1984 revision of *Basic Types of Pastoral Care and Counseling* also reflects these new forms of pastoral care.

3. Emerging Issues. Important issues abound in contemporary pastoral care. While it is difficult to make an unbiased selection, there is probably general agreement among leaders of the field that the following issues are among the most important:

a. Leadership. Contemporary leadership in pastoral care has literally come of age. Pastoral care has moved out of the era of a few maverick 'pioneers' and 'founders' into a time when men and women of demonstrated competence are deeply rooted in advanced pastoral practice all over the country. They have become durably related to schools, churches, denominations, business communities, and political structures as well as to hospitals and physicians. The earlier founders, like Boisen and Dicks, were solely related to hospitals. The prevailing pattern was the World War II social identity of 'the chaplain.' Leadership was predominantly charismatic in that the vivid or forceful personalities captivated the imagination of students. To a great extent, the leadership was also itinerant; there were few specific, enduring institutions carrying on the work of the leaders in particular places. Yet, these leaders sowed seeds of wisdom, inspiration, and motivation that produced the leaders of today, whose main characteristics are clinical competence, rootedness in local culture, and skill at designing and building institutional structures capable of providing high quality pastoral care. The field now faces the need to reproduce this. A certain blend of genetics, social conditions, hard work, and a yearning for excellence produced the present leadership. Out of an incredibly wide diversity, this leadership produces a quality of pastoral care that is competent, maintains close ties with its ecclesiastical constituencies, and has, by and large, hewn jobs out of the hard rock of remote possibility. Few of their jobs were handed to them, ready-made, fully approved and financed. Will the replacements for these persons take this for granted? Will the surplus of persons being educated in pastoral care be able to find work in an economy of scarcity rather than abundance? It remains to be seen. No dependency upon ready-made positions is a safe stance for new young aspirants to work in pastoral care. They, too, will necessarily face the organizational and administrative task of forming their own positions with encouragement from present mentors, but with independence of mentors as well.

b. Variety and uniqueness in ministry. Training bodies such as the AAPC, the ACPE, and the programs in pastoral care and counseling in theological schools have been intensely engaged in *regulating* the quality of persons aspiring to specialized ministries in pastoral care and counseling. They have invested enormous amounts of unpaid volunteer time in the accreditation of training clusters and centers, in the certification of persons supervising and practicing the arts of pastoral care, and in refining standards for these accrediting and certifying committees to follow. A side effect of this effort, how-

ever, can be an iatrogenic *sameness* in the end product. A critical issue is how to use the established facts of demonstrated performance of candidates for certification to offset these "cookie cutter" results of sameness. A strange footnote of historical fact is that Anton Boisen and Russell Dicks were *never* certified pastoral counselors nor clinical supervisors. Many of the present leadership described above were certified on demonstrated performance only and never met with a certifying committee. In the military, this is known as a "battlefield" promotion. Such persons have proved their leadership ability in combat. This is a crucial issue in pastoral care in the nineties.

c. Women specialists in pastoral care. The ethos of pastoral care specialization today is certainly attractive to women entering the ministry. In many respects, women are superior to men in the caring ministry. Yet the network of women who have become established in pastoral care positions of influence and ecclesiastical power is very new and very sparse. Even social work, an historically feminine profession, has fallen on hard times for the employment of qualified persons (dwindling governmental funds having hit social work especially hard). An emerging issue of great consequence therefore is: "What are the ethical issues involved in educating large numbers of women for positions that do not or may not exist?" Or, to state it in another way: "How can the vast resources of *older* women in this country's private sector be mobilized to create positions of ministry for *younger* women equipped for the ministry of pastoral care?"

d. Spiritual balance. Balance is needed between the regulatory functions of pastoral care organizations and the spiritual fellowship function of these organizations. No doubt the regulation of *who* shall be certified to render a service of pastoral care and *who* shall be certified to teach pastoral care has to this date resulted in a superior level of care and teaching. Yet this may be factorially related not to the regulation of certifying bodies but to the simple matter of *numbers* being taught. The standard ratio is six students to one supervisor. This ratio has been a direct contravention of mass methods endemic to American education. Couple this with the centrality of face-to-face encounters with people in need and collaboration with other professional persons, and one has a teaching relationship that is regulated better at the point of *selection* of students than at the point of certification. The heavy emphasis upon regulatory certification work needs to be balanced with an equally important emphasis upon spiritual fellowship among people who are committed to the clinical approach to education for professional ministry.

e. Responsibility and financial support. The pastor in all tasks is ultimately responsible first and always to God. Yet the pastor is susceptible to temptations to idolatry. The exhortation of I John 5:21 is always an urgent appeal to the pastor at work amid the ambiguities and contradictions of institutions in the *saeculum* of his or her contemporaneity. The church itself, a hospital, a particular organization such as the ACPE, AAPC, or AAMFT can indeed become idols to the pastor.

Most alluring of idols for the pastor is the source of his or her income. The sources of financing of pastoral care are a rather precise index to our responsibility. In the specialized pastoral counseling done by pastors today, the sources of income for the time and energy used in the work for the support of the pastor are varied. In some instances, churches provide support with a subsistence budget and expect fees from counselees to complete the budget. In other instances associations, synods, conferences, dioceses, etc. provide the support on a similar basis. In a few cases the programs are endowed in perpetuity and/or are supported by renewable grants from foundations or individual wealthy benefactors. Today, widespread concern about support for pastoral counseling, both in counselees and counselors, focuses on "third party payments" from health insurers. In an earlier era the hope of national health insurance loomed large in some policy-making in pastoral counseling centers and to some extent in regional and national meetings.

All of this impinges heavily on the question: "To whom is the pastor answerable?" The sources of funds will not only shape the nature of the care given but form the center of the pastoral counselor's attention. Basic to this is the pastor's sense of relationship to his or her ordination, participation in the ongoing life of the faith group, and, more profoundly, his or her personal commitment to the love of God and neighbor and a feeling of responsibility for nurturing that commitment to his or her counselees.

This is not to say that simple ecclesiastical connectionism and participation in every theological rectitude is possible only if one is paid by the church. To the contrary, secular funds *may* grant a kind of freedom to represent God more accurately. It is to say, however, that the sense of belonging to a community or Christian fellowship is integral and not optional if the care given is indeed pastoral. Biblically, the agrarian metaphor of "pastor" invariably implies a "flock." That "flock" is not only a band of followers, but also a "network," a "system of support," or even a "resource." The reality is in the need for such in our care of others, and in being explicit about our reliance prophetically on the *other* seven thousand whose knees "have not bowed to Baal" and whose "mouth has not kissed him" (I Kings 19:18).

f. Pastoral identity. The previously discussed issue of responsibility leads to the crux of who the pastor perceives himself or herself to be before God. "In whose name" do we extend care to other persons? If we are called of God, what do we *call* ourselves as God's representatives in order to let people know who we are, whom we represent, and to whom we give the glory for any results of our caring? Repeatedly in the New Testament, both Jesus and his disciples stated "in whose name" they did their works of therapy. (See Mt. 7:22; Mk. 9:38; Lk. 10:17–20.) The clergyperson always sees God as an Eternal Thou in the caring relationship, characteristically seeks divine guidance in his or her pastoral care of others, and feels hesitant to the point of refusing to attribute to his or her own efforts whatever success may be achieved in pastoral care. To the contrary, the "wounded healer" is more likely to feel that both he or she and those being cared for have been sustained, healed, redeemed, and loved together by God.

Bibliography. J. Bowlby, *Attachment and Loss* (1969). E. B. Holifield, *A History of Pastoral Care in America* (1983). W. E. Oates, *Pastoral Counseling* (1982); *The Christian Pastor*, rev. 3d.

ed. (1982). A. Stokes, *Ministry after Freud* (1985). E. Thornton, *Professional Education for Ministry*, (1970).

W. E. OATES

For articles related primarily to practical methodology see: COMFORT/SUSTAINING; CONVERSATION, PASTORAL; GUIDANCE; HEALING; LISTENING; PERCEPTIVENESS AND SENSITIVITY; HERMENEUTICS AND INTERPRETATION; PHENOMENOLOGICAL METHOD; REFERRAL. *See also* BIBLE, PASTORAL USE AND INTERPRETATION OF; CONFLICT AND CONFLICT MANAGEMENT; EVALUATION AND DIAGNOSIS; FAMILY; MARRIAGE; PRAYER; THEORY IN PASTORAL CARE AND COUNSELING, FUNCTIONS OF. *For major theoretical issues see:* PASTORAL THEOLOGICAL METHODOLOGY; PASTORAL THEOLOGY. *See also* BLACK, FEMINIST, *or* LIBERATION THEOLOGY; CROSS-CULTURAL PASTORAL CARE; DISCIPLINE, PASTORAL CARE AS; ECCLESIOLOGY; ETHICS; LEGAL DIMENSIONS; MORAL DILEMMAS; RITUAL; SACRAMENTAL THEOLOGY; SALVATION, HEALING, AND HEALTH; SOCIAL JUSTICE ISSUES; SPIRITUAL THEOLOGY; TRADITION AS MODE OF CARE. *Compare* EMPIRICAL RESEARCH IN PASTORAL CARE AND COUNSELING; PHILOSOPHY AND PSYCHOLOGY; PRACTICAL THEOLOGY; *also* ANALYTICAL *or* HUMANISTIC PSYCHOLOGY AND PASTORAL CARE; PSYCHOANALYSIS AND PASTORAL CARE. *For specialized pastoral care see primarily:* PASTORAL COUNSELING; PASTORAL PSYCHOTHERAPY; *also* COUNSELING, ROMAN CATHOLIC; JEWISH CARE AND COUNSELING; LAY PASTORAL CARE AND COUNSELING; SPIRITUAL DIRECTION; SUPERVISION. *For the relation of pastoral care to other functions of ministry see:* MINISTRY; *also* EDUCATION, NURTURE, AND CARE; EVANGELIZING; LEADERSHIP AND ADMINISTRATION; PREACHING; PROPHETIC/PASTORAL TENSION; SOCIAL JUSTICE ISSUES; TEACHING; WORSHIP. *For practical education in care and counseling see:* EDUCATION; *also* CLINICAL PASTORAL EDUCATION; SPECIALIZATION IN PASTORAL CARE.

PASTORAL CARE (History, Traditions, and Definitions).

Pastoral care derives from the biblical image of *shepherd* and refers to the solicitous concern expressed within the religious community for persons in trouble or distress. Historically and within the Christian community, pastoral care is in the cure-of-souls tradition. Here cure may be understood as care in the sense of carefulness or anxious concern, not necessarily as healing, for the soul, i.e. the animating center of personal life and the seat of relatedness to God.

Designating this care as pastoral may refer either to the person of the religious leader or to the motivation/attitude characterizing the caregiver. In the first instance, pastoral care refers to ordained or acknowledged religious leaders who bring the resources, wisdom, and authority of the religious community to bear on human distress. But pastoral care may also be understood to be provided by any representative of the religious community who is perceived to stand for or reflect the values and commitments of the group.

Just as *pastoral* may reflect different understandings, so *care* has both broad and narrow meanings. It may refer to any pastoral act motivated by a sincere devotion to the well-being of the other(s). In this sense liturgical forms and ritual acts may reflect care as may education and various forms of social action. Usually, however, pastoral care refers to the more intensive dimension of the larger tasks of ministry, to conversation with persons or groups who seek interpersonal, moral, or spiritual guidance. Seward Hiltner (1958) and Clebsch and Jaekle (1964) suggest that the content of care includes the pastoral functions of healing, sustaining, guiding, and reconciling, and specify a precise content to the care. They also limit pastoral care to instances in which there is some sense of individual need and willingness to accept help. Further, Clebsch and Jaekle insist that the care must include matters of "ultimate concern," i.e. the troubles must be meaningful in relation to Christian faith in that they foster a deeper faith and relation to God. To follow these writers leads to the conclusion that not all helping acts of mercy, love, and charity are pastoral care.

What becomes apparent rather quickly in any survey of the history of pastoral care are the diverse understandings of the endeavor. Simply stated, what constitutes pastoral care is rooted in the basic religious convictions of the community. But it is also rooted in the historical, political, and social fabric of a given time and place. Thus christological, soteriological, and ecclesiological convictions define our sense of obligation for each other and to some degree determine what constitutes helping. Even so, the political climate, cultural values and ideals, economic factors, and various forms of secular knowledge enter to determine in part the shape and intent of pastoral care.

Only a few efforts have been made to trace this history. Apart from McNeill (1951), Clebsch and Jaekle, Kemp (1947), and, to a lesser degree, Oden (1983) and Hiltner, the history of pastoral care is largely unclaimed and unknown. Yet members of religious communities have always sought out those whom they perceived as wise or mature or holy for assistance in life. And the perplexities, uncertainties, and efforts to understand, which plagued the caregivers, are recorded in a rich treasure of literature on the human quest for relatedness to God and the successes and failures of those seeking to help.

The purpose of this essay is to offer a glimpse of this history and its varied understandings of pastoral care.

1. **From Beginnings to Establishment.** Any definition of pastoral care has at its core a way of understanding our relatedness to God and the ingredients or acts which may serve to enhance or detract from that relatedness. Despite its diversity, the NT reflects a view of Christian life rooted in an inner transformation resulting from faith in Christ as God and as the inaugurator of a new age. In the Gospels and Letters, the task of the shepherd is "to create an atmosphere in which the intimate exchange of spiritual help, the mutual guidance of souls, would be a normal feature of Christian behavior" (McNeill, p. 85).

Paul reflects this concern when he confesses his "daily anxiety" for the churches. He seeks to express the meaning of the Christian life and to have the churches reflect this meaning. The form his anxiety takes is first instruction, then rebuke, later exhortation, and always encouragement and compassion. He guides the churches in disputes, answers questions about marriage, and wants them to settle disagreements among themselves. He wants sinners restored, the weak strengthened, and love to prevail. He reminds them of his weakness while seeking their prayers and encouraging them to utilize their gifts for the welfare of the community and as a sign of faithfulness.

This quest for mutual edification and care has both individual and corporate dimensions. They should live quietly, bearing one another's burdens without shirking responsibility for themselves. Anxiety about themselves should foster contemplation about what is honorable and true and of good report. At the same time they should wait on and encourage each other with "brotherly affection." The needs of the saints should be attended to, especially the need for mutual confession, prayers and visitation for the sick, and contributions to the homeless, hungry, and destitute.

By the close of the first century the emphases in care within the church began to change. Second and third generation Christians sought to preserve the genius which had sustained them while at the same time attempting to come to terms with themselves as a separate community. The results were a somewhat different view of the Christian life which placed more emphasis on its form than its content.

The Shepherd of Hermas reflects this shift. The overriding concern of Hermas is sin committed after baptism. Baptism remitted sin, but since Christ's return was delayed, Christians began to question whether there could be a second repentance. In the vision which constitutes this book, Christ as grace and forgiveness falls into the background before the demands for moral conduct on the part of the believer. What is stressed is the laxness of the church in its attachment to the world, the ambition, discord, and misconduct of church leaders, and a representative table of virtues and vices. Hermas paves the way for the strong ascetic tendency in the early church. He begins to exchange the Pauline emphasis on justification for moralism and legalism. Finally, he concludes that one additional repentance is possible for less grievous sins provided the believer demonstrates true repentance and has paid for his or her error. Pastors, in turn, are to regulate both repentance and penance.

The shift to reconciliation became a dominant theme of pastoral care during the persecutions (c. 150–300 C.E.). Questions as to what kinds and degrees of renunciation of the faith were forgivable led to strife in the church over efforts to reconcile apostates. The controversy, finally resolved by Cyprian, led to the definition of bishops as the determiners of church membership and served to standardize the practice of one penance even for those guilty of the three capital sins of murder, unchastity, and idolatry.

Although this debate dominated the time of the persecutions, care continued to be exercised in other modes in the church. For example, Augustine suggested a list of pastoral duties: "Disturbers are to be rebuked, the low-spirited to be encouraged, the infirm to be supported, objectors confuted, the treacherous guarded against, the unskilled taught, the lazy aroused, the contentious restrained, the haughty repressed, litigants pacified, the poor relieved, the oppressed liberated, the good approved, the evil borne with, and all are to be loved" (McNeill, p. 100). Another example of other modes of care is seen in the continuation of the consolation literature of the classical era. Cyprian reworked topics from pagan treatises adding Christian doctrine to support those undergoing persecution and reminding them that "Christ was the companion of his soldiers in flight and hardship and death." Others such as Gregory of Nazianzus, Jerome, and Ambrose addressed letters to individuals for sympathy and consolation. The Christian faith, said Ambrose, will only be discredited by excessive sorrow so the grief-stricken should allow themselves to be comforted.

When Constantine converted to the Christian faith in 313 C.E., the focus of the church's pastoral energies shifted once more. Two early church fathers reflect the pastoral effort to assume their place as "semiofficial educators, as dispensers of state welfare funds, as leaders of an imperially endorsed religion, [and as interpreters] of the troubles that beset people" (Clebsch and Jaekle, p. 19). In his *Treatise on the Priesthood*, John Chrysostom described the mark of the true pastor as his readiness to perish for his sheep. In caring for souls, Chrysostom presented himself "as a physician dispensing medicaments to those who voluntarily submitted to his art and of the church as a hospital whither the sinner might have to repair for more than one serious sin" (Niebuhr and Williams, p. 70). Perhaps his most important pastoral contribution was his search for an alternative to the humiliating act of public penance. His understanding of inward sinfulness caused him to advocate the iteration of penance in a diversified fashion. "It is not right to take an absolute standard and fit the penalty to the exact measure of the offense, but it is right to aim at influencing the moral feelings of the offenders, [since] no one can, by compulsion, cure an unwilling man" (Niebuhr, Williams, p. 70).

In the West, Ambrose was Chrysostom's counterpart. His *On the Duties of Clergy* was also published in 386 C.E., and exemplifies efforts to accommodate lofty pagan virtues with the spirit of Christianity. Relying upon Cicero, he found biblical examples of the classical virtues of prudence, justice, fortitude, and courage and joined them with Paul's faith, hope, and love.

2. From Gregory to the Renaissance (500–1300 C.E.).

The soul care of the church fathers was codified and transmitted by Pope Gregory the Great. The invasion by the Slavic and Teutonic peoples and the collapse of Roman society left the church, its priests and monasteries, as the primary vehicle for order. Gregory's *Book of Pastoral Rule* became the guide for centuries of priests in their attempts to provide care. It is without question among the most valuable classics in the cure of souls.

Gregory regarded the "government of souls [as] the art of arts." Priestly authority should be exercised with humility by one who acts as a compassionate neighbor. In the midst of social and political transition Gregory sought order by guiding troubled souls into faith and moral uprightness. By encouraging the distraught to bring their concerns to the church, he was able to introduce the Christian tradition and to impose rites and practices on the nature-paganism of the folk cultures.

Part III of the book might prove the most interesting to today's pastor. Gregory sought to adapt his advice to individual cases, all the while assuming that care provided in depth would invariably involve deeper spiritual issues. He noted different personality types, e.g. the simple and the insincere, the impudent and the bashful, as requiring special concern and called attention to situational differences affecting persons. With each type he enumerated the particular temptation to which they were subject and sought to strengthen their resolve. Later he spoke more carefully of different treatments for sins of intention and of impulse, for sins abandoned as opposed

to those one clings to, etc. Physicians of the soul must be discerning and have medicine "to meet moral diseases by a varied method."

The Celtic penitential literature represented another source of guidance for the medieval priest. One of these, *Corrector et medicus*, explained: "The book is called 'the Corrector' and 'the Physician' since it contains ample corrections for bodies and medicines for souls and teaches every priest, even the uneducated, how he shall be able to bring help to each person, ordained or unordained; poor or rich; boy, youth, or mature man; decrepit, healthy, or infirm; of every age; and of both sexes" (Clebsch and Jaekle, p. 24). A vast array of this literature was in use offering instruction on every aspect of soul care. The literature's attention to detail, to modes of interviewing, to penances prescribed for various sins, to exceptional cases, etc., meant that the priest could provide guidance on life as the church saw it in every circumstance.

By 1200 the church had codified the sacramental system and essentially standardized pastoral care practices. The parish priest, as the most educated person in the community, was regarded as counselor, lawyer, teacher, doctor, and friend. His foremost function was the provision of the sacraments, for therein lay the cure for human disease and distress. Thus baptism was essential for salvation and removed the taint of original sin. The other sacraments came as propitious events in the life cycle. Confirmation sanctioned the move to adulthood, holy matrimony the joining with a mate, and unction vouchsafed one's death.

For adults, however, the two great sacraments of healing were the Mass and penance. The Mass provided a dependable grace during the common ventures of life. Here the faithful partook of the very life of God, strengthening them to endure and withstand temptation, illness, bereavement, indeed every joy or vicissitude of life. The penance, involving as it did contrition, confession, and satisfaction, offered the priest opportunity to conduct a thorough spiritual examination. No one escaped faultless, yet hope, not despair, was the outcome. Penitents emerged with clean slates and an assured relation to God.

3. The Reformation.

John McNeill begins his chapter on the Reformation with the statement: "In matters concerning the cure of souls the German Reformation had its inception" (p. 163). The sale of indulgences aroused Luther's indignation; simple people were deceived to believe that the purchase of the certificates assured salvation. Luther himself had undergone a long and arduous personal conflict over repentance and justification. For him repentance meant "coming to one's sense," "a change in our heart and our love" as response to God's grace. Thus Luther's objection was not against either confession or absolution but against the notion that the remission of sins depended on confession and not the goodness of God. He objected, secondly, to the authority to bind and loose sin being restricted to priests. All Christians, he said, have authority to hear confessions and absolve; we share a common priesthood just as we share our spiritual gifts. Thus to Luther only two things mattered: "the Word of God and faith." Or as he put it: "The sum of the Gospel is this: who believes in Christ, has the forgiveness of sins" (Niebuhr and Williams, p. 111).

The key to relatedness to God, then, is a trusting faith in God's mercy. For Luther "spiritual counsel is always concerned above all else with faith—nurturing, strengthening, establishing, practicing faith" (Tappert, p. 15). Luther's pastoral practice is characterized by warmth, conviction, and identification with the distressed. At Worms, a few hours before his second appearance before the Diet, he went at dawn to the bedside of a dying knight to hear his confession and administer the Sacrament. The *Table Talk* shows him conversing in a friendly fashion and asking questions about the state of body and soul of his companions. His letters of consolation, his concern for the young women who had left the nunneries, his correspondence with friends, and his response to plague and persecution reveal him as always attentive to the distressed. And he took his own advice. When his beloved thirteen-year-old daughter was near death, he comforted his wife with the words, "I rejoice in the spirit, but sorrow in the flesh" (McNeill, p. 172).

John Calvin shared Luther's concern for justification by faith, the priesthood of all believers, and his commitment to the cure of souls. But Calvin's emphasis on repentance was broader than Luther's, and this was reflected in his pastoral approach. Calvin's repentance "embraces the soul's progressive appropriation of the obedience, holiness, and goodness that mark the restoration of man's lost or obscured image of God" (McNeill, p. 198). Thus he, like Luther, has a place for confession and absolution. But the fruit of this confession is transformation. There was no requirement for private confession but ministers were encouraged to interview each communicant prior to communion. Here the power of the keys was exercised by Christ's ambassador and the grace of the gospel was confirmed and sealed.

Calvin's genius at organization also influenced his pastoral care. The elders watched carefully over the citizens of Geneva and sought to protect and to correct them. Ministers met regularly to admonish and sustain each other. Deacons visited the sick, the imprisoned, the widows and orphans and were charged to catechize the children. And Calvin himself by means of a voluminous correspondence sought to strengthen, encourage, and embolden the persecuted and comfort the bereaved.

Neither Luther nor Calvin wrote specifically on the care of souls. However, two prominent Reformation figures did. Ulrich Zwingli in *Der Hirt (The Pastor)* distinguished between the true and false shepherd. Proclamation, he said, must be followed by instruction and service, since the sheep that are healed should not be allowed to fall again into sickness. In love pastors do everything to upbuild the people. In *On the True Cure of Souls*, Martin Bucer describes a fivefold ministry in soul care. In public and by visitation ministers draw the alienated to Christ, lead back those drawn away, restore those who fall into sin, strengthen weak and sickly Christians, and preserve those who are whole and strong (McNeill, p. 192).

Reformation pastoral care may be characterized in several ways. The confessional as institution was abandoned and the pastor emerged as a central figure. However, the pastor's ordination did not set him apart. A married clergyman emphasized his identification at every point with his people. Moreover, though the primary acts of care were preaching and the communion, the message of reconciliation symbolized in these events was felt to be central to the life of the entire community. Pastors and laypersons alike were mutually to comfort, correct, and sustain each other. The mark of a transformed life lay in mutual ministry with the end of being reconciled to God and to each other.

4. Traditions. Until the Reformation the course of pastoral care followed a well-marked path in the Roman Catholic church. Disagreements were always present but the tradition itself was clear. Since the Reformation a number of somewhat different understandings of relatedness to God have fostered a variety of traditions of pastoral care. Brooks Holifield in *A History of Pastoral Care in America* enumerates four: Roman Catholic, Anglican, Lutheran, and Reformed. To these one might add the Congregational or Free Church tradition. These same traditions existed in Europe although they assumed a particular shape in America. It is impossible to trace these streams in any detail, but it is informative to attend individual representatives of each.

a. Roman Catholic. Roman Catholic pastoral care continued to revolve around the sacramental system after the Reformation. The Council of Trent in 1552 sought to correct the abuses of the penitential discipline and made great strides in that regard. Thus penance was defined as a sacrament for the baptized and consisted of contrition, confession, and satisfaction. But an *entire* confession was required by Christ for *all* sins after baptism. This of course emphasized sin as an act of transgression and reflected the conviction that original sin was covered by baptism. Mortal sins, then, must be confessed and the confession of venial sins was commended. The confession was to priests and bishops only. They alone could remit sins and their absolution was effected by the Sacrament. Penalties and penance remained both as remedy and as "an avenging and chastisement for past sin" (McNeill, p. 288).

This careful redefinition of sacramental penance fostered an immense literature on problems of conscience. The Jesuits were among the more attentive to these matters of casuistry and, when they were suppressed, a Redemptorist priest, Alfonso de Liguori, took up some of their tasks in moral theology and ascetic piety. A confessor, he said, must be a father, physician, teacher, and judge. "Confession must be: vocal; secret; true; and integral" (McNeill, p. 292). He sought particular remedies for various faults and warned confessors that to hear confessions without sufficient knowledge (of laws, bulls, decrees, other opinions) is to be subject to damnation. Liguori became the accepted authority for confessors so that by 1831, all priests were advised or permitted to follow his opinions.

In the seventeenth century the vocation of spiritual director emerged. This role was distinct from that of confessor in that the goal was the pursuit of higher spiritual attainments. St. Francis de Sales, St. Vincent de Paul, and St. François Fénelon provide a treasure of correspondence on the spiritual life. Fénelon urged the quest for a pure and disinterested love reflected in quietism. His letters are replete with a subtle awareness of the capacity for self-deceit, the exhortation to attend devotions, and a rare courage to remind court figures of their worldliness. All, he said, need to be humiliated by their faults, to lose hope in themselves, without losing hope in God.

Undergirding the sacramental system was, as Holifield notes, a metaphor of growth. Salvation is achieved in ascending stages and the sacraments nurture this process. The process is reminiscent of Benedict's *Twelve Step Ladder of Humility* that began with fear and culminated in a life of love. Such notions of growth had long since set the standards of morality for priest and laypersons. And though the laity could not attend the ascent as did priests and religious, the aspiration permeated the church. In this context, then, the sacraments provided the means, the grace, to feed the soul and to foster love of God for God's sake.

b. Lutheran. Throughout the seventeenth and eighteenth centuries Lutheran pastoral care was characterized by a formal orthodoxy on the one side and a pietistic reaction to it on the other. A voluminous pastoral literature appeared during this time, but it viewed the cure of souls narrowly and placed emphasis on confession to the pastor. Scholarly literature neglected pastoral care in the name of belief and behavior, and pastoral literature recommended limited visitation, a mechanical view of confession based on the catechism, and absolution by the pastor. Critics said, "The binding key is quite rusted away while the loosing key is in full operation" (McNeill, p. 182).

Pietism under the direction of Philipp Jacob Spener turned away from the scholastics and invited Christians to personal religion. Spener stressed regeneration and the cultivation of the religious life, utilizing small conferences as vehicles for mutual edification. Christian faith meant accepting responsibility for a spiritual priesthood which included sacrifice, prayer, and the word. By the word persons were empowered to teach, exhort, rebuke, and console others who gathered to study Scripture and for mutual encouragement.

Pia Desideria (Pious Longings) was regarded as the text of the movement. Here and in *The Spiritual Priesthood Briefly Set Forth*, Spener expressed his wish that every Christian stand in a special friendship with their pastor or another Christian. He stressed individual conferences and private conversations, visiting in homes, and calling on the sick. Moreover, such work did not belong to the pastor alone. Lay persons were to engage in mutual correction and encouragement. "The sum of Christianity," he said, "is penitence, faith, and a new obedience; true, inner, spiritual peace" is its fruit (McNeill, p. 184).

For the generation after Spener, August Hermann Francke and his associates at the University of Halle became leaders among the Pietists. Franke's experience of anguish and conversion caused him to value despair as the prelude to rebirth. Indeed, this agony, this "feeling of repentance," constituted the difference between the true believer and others. Personal interviews became an important pastoral mode so as to discern despair and to lead one through these negative feelings to hope. Preparation for the Lord's Supper frequently involved such conversations.

This stream of Pietism flowed into America through many channels. It influenced Zinzendorf and Wesley, New England Puritanism, and British and subsequently American Baptists. Among Lutherans Pietism came to the U.S. through Henry M. Muhlenberg and Theodore Freylingshuysen. It sought to turn persons away from controversy to fellowship and from scholastic argument over faith to faith itself. Muhlenberg brought with him the ideals of Halle and records in his journals the spiritual guidance he sought to provide. His psychological insight convinced him that a "sick body produces a sick soul," so that he frequently cooperated with physicians. He sought to institute a clear discipline in his congregation and, like his predecessors, examined candidates before communion.

c. Anglicans. Winthrop Hudson remarks that the Reformation in England was both less drastic and less systematic than on the Continent. The structure of the church was largely unchanged so that its dioceses, parishes, bishops, and priests remained. And the theological statement, the Articles of Religion, "avoided precise definition." Despite this lack of drastic reform, the view of ministry in Anglicanism was altered. "Formerly the clergy had been 'priests,' finding their primary responsibility at the altar; now they were 'ministers,'] with preaching and pastoral care as their preeminent duties" (Niebuhr and Williams, p. 180).

During the seventeenth century the distinction between even Puritans and Anglicans was not great as regards pastoral care. Their differences were more of mood and temperament than theology. The Puritan wanted reform and was more eager to obey God than men. "The Anglican was more cautious and moderate; more aware of the power of habit and custom. . . . [remembering] Paul's counsel that due regard must be given constituted authority" (Niebuhr and Williams, p. 181).

These tensions seem important if one is to understand the Anglican tradition in pastoral care. No one represented the cautious and moderate mood better than George Herbert. His classic volume *A Priest to the Temple or, The Country Parson* presents the ideal pastor as devout, competent, gracious, and holy. On Sundays he preached in the morning and catechized in the afternoon. The rest of the day he reconciled quarreling neighbors, visited the sick, sometimes attempting to persuade them to confess, or exhorted those in his flock "his sermons cannot or do not reach." On weekdays he engaged in systematic parish visitation to examine and advise, to counsel, admonish, and to exhort. Mornings were for reading and mealtimes for inviting parishioners to dine so that within a year he had been with them all. He offered advice to pastors for assisting those in good spiritual condition and for those in despair of God's grace. The goal of this activity, according to Henry Scougal, was "to advance the divine life in the world. . . . The world lies in sin, and it is our work to awaken men out of their deadly sleep" (Niebuhr and Williams, p. 184).

Throughout the seventeenth and much of the eighteenth centuries, an extensive literature on the cure of souls emerged among Anglicans. Jeremy Taylor's *Holy Dying* and Gilbert Burnet's *Discourses of Pastoral Care* are among the most important. Some, such as William Law, reflected a higher view of the authority of priests as guides of conscience. Law placed great emphasis on daily self-examination and confession of sins to God as a means of growth. It was this emphasis on an awakened conscience and the work of grace in the hearts of believers, together with the evangelical revivals personified in George Whitefield, that led finally to despair of reform of the church among Puritans and an affirmation of the sacraments among Anglicans. The Puritan strain appears in the Reformed and Free Church traditions. The Anglicans emphasized the Eucharist and the sacramental efficacy in the life of the community of the prayers and worship of the church.

It seems fair to observe that in the balance between tradition and experience, Anglican pastoral care finally leaned towards the tradition. The Evangelicals were an exception to this, but the Oxford Movement, as represented by Edward Pusey and John Keble, reacted to this strain with an emphasis on the confessional and spiritual direction that was finally persuasive. Yet in the midst of these differences, an enormous importance was attached to the cure of souls and an impressive literature on conscience and casuistry resulted. In the U.S. Philips Brooks personifies this devotion to pastoral guidance and spiritual intimacy between priest and people.

d. Reformed. Although a historical distinction must be made among Presbyterians, Puritans, and the continental Reformed traditions, their pastoral care orientation reflects a common source. The source, according to Holifield, was John Calvin and his emphasis on the disobedience of an idolatrous heart as the core of human distress. What their physicians of the soul sought to cure was the idolatrous heart. What they sought to insure was exemplary conduct. Their theology was rooted in experience, but their insistence upon constant and effective discipline and their watchful care to protect the communion from scandalous offenders gave this tradition a distinct character.

Scottish Presbyterian and continental Reformed churches each reflected this orientation. The Discipline of the Reformed Church of France, for example, contained exacting codes of behavior for ministers, elders, deacons, and members, providing procedures for suspension and excommunication for those who refused to repent "after many admonitions and entreaties" (McNeill, p. 209). Although it was difficult to maintain order during the persecutions, elders were instructed to "teach, reprove, and comfort." Dutch ministers were to provide guidance for elders, deacons, and members, and elders were to visit so as to "instruct and comfort the members in full communion as well as to exhort others to the regular profession of the Christian faith" (McNeill, p. 210).

The Reformed Church in Scotland also placed great emphasis on discipline as pastoral care. John Knox's *Book of Discipline* carefully outlines the procedures for dealing with offenders. He intended to insure a watchful firmness with patient consideration for human frailty, a desire "rather to win our brother than to slander him." Yet the discipline was difficult to maintain at a high level and frequently deteriorated to simple legalism. The purity of the congregation was carefully guarded by means of examinations by the elders prior to communion

and by their general oversight of congregational life. At the same time, ministers and elders were enjoined to visit the sick, distribute goods to the poor, and to insure that Bibles and other literature were available so that faithfulness could be engendered.

The record would be incomplete, however, if one neglected those seventeenth century pastors whose efforts went beyond discipline. In Scotland, David Dickson tried to be a "prudent friend" to those caught up in doubt, depression, and temptation; he wanted to lead them to repentance, never despair. In the Netherlands, Gijsbert Voet prescribed mental prayer and solitary devotion to strengthen the soul and restricted excommunication even for grave sins. Beyond question the Swiss Reformed pastor Alexander Vinet personifies most clearly this movement in the Reformed church. His *Pastoral Theology* became immensely influential and can be read with profit today. Vinet manifests great empathy for his friends and parishioners and cautions against too much "direction" and too little regard for liberty and responsibility in pastoral work. After visiting Vinet one parishioner told her pastor, "you judge me from above, but he . . . as my equal" (McNeill, p. 215).

Over the next two centuries Reformed churches relaxed discipline and placed more emphasis on the reclamation of souls and personal religion. The evangelical revivals influenced this change as did the secularization of certain of the church's functions, e.g., the Poor Law in England in 1845. Vinet exemplifies this shift on the Continent. In Great Britain John Watson ("Ian Maclaren") wrote *The Cure of Souls* (1896) and emphasized visitation and private conversation, offering guidelines for interviewing and keeping confidences. A few years earlier Patrick Fairbairn in *Pastoral Theology* described the difficulty of knowing where discipline should begin and encouraged the cultivation of spiritual enlightenment and conviction as an alternative.

Reformed pastors in the U.S. adapted their pastoral practices to different conditions than those of Europe. Their convictions were the same and may be traced to their Scottish, continental, and Puritan forebearers. However, the absence of settled communities and parish structures made the institution of the procedures difficult. Trinterud (1949) notes, for example, that though "experimental religion" was the foundation, Gilbert Tennant insisted that "a continual renewal of repentance was . . . utterly essential" for Christian life. And William W. Sweet (1936) describes later Presbyterian congregations on the frontier seeking to enforce discipline and insure church purity by examinations of conscience and "fencing the table." Seward Hiltner (1958) examined the work of the nineteenth-century Presbyterian pastor, Ichabod Spencer, as he sought through diligent visitation to lead anxious men and women to repentance and faith. Spencer possessed a keen sense of responsibility to guide persons in distress yet reflected genuine compassion for their anguish.

English Puritanism's contribution to pastoral care in this tradition was extensive. They shared the basic theological ground with their colleagues and so emphasized codes of behavior and concern for offenses. However, since they never attained the status of an organized church, they lacked the institutional structures to enforce a discipline. Their pastors turned instead to casuistry and to the guidance of individuals and families. William Perkins expressed this goal of awakening and guiding conscience when he said, "As the lawyer is [a counselor] for their estates and the physician for their bodies," so the minister is the "counselor for their souls," who "must be ready to give advice to those that come to him with cases of conscience" (Niebuhr and Williams, p. 196). The fruition of this emphasis on conscience was an extensive literature on casuistry best represented in the works of William Ames, Jeremy Taylor, and Richard Baxter.

There is no doubt that the most important contribution to pastoral care in this era was Richard Baxter's *Reformed Pastor*. The volume places great demands on pastors and suggests that for Baxter, care consisted of two concerns. First, it must reveal to persons that happiness or good which is their ultimate end. Second, it must introduce them to the right means to attain this end, help them to utilize these means, and discourage any contrary efforts. His practice was to spend 15–16 hours each week instructing families in the faith, "searching men's hearts and setting home the saving truths." He also visited the sick and the dying "helping them prepare for a fruitful life or a happy death." Care also involved counseling, and lest unskilled counselors aggravate problems, he advised such persons "to have a care to qualify themselves." A host of manuals gave instruction on approaches to various questions of conscience and states of anxiety and depressions. A good counselor, it was said, would bear with peevishness and with "disordered and distempered affections and actions." He would share sorrows and tears, listen well, guard secrets, and not be censorious when conscience was "unduly disturbed." According to Baxter, the pastoral office was more than those "men have taken it to be, who think it consists in preaching and administering the sacraments only."

In summary, it may be observed that established groups within the Reformed tradition were somewhat more compulsory in their emphasis on discipline in pastoral care than were the Puritans, at least for a time. At the same time, the continental and Scottish groups also placed more responsibility on lay participation through elders and deacons. The entire tradition reflects the extension of the goal of preaching to pastoral care. Private interviews, consultations, corrections, and admonitions became extensions of the call to repentance and uprightness of life. The relief of anxiety and guidance to one's true destiny were the goals of both.

e. Congregational. One tradition emerged in Great Britain in the seventeenth and eighteenth centuries which has been prominent in the U.S. McNeill describes it as non-Anglican British churches and their daughter communions. The theological roots of these groups were in Anabaptism, pietism, and puritanism, so that without exception they sought conversion and insisted on an upright life among their members. Life, they said, was a brief interlude, a battleground in which the forces of evil seek to divert the believer from God and eternal rest. Their distinction was their emphasis on congregational care. In itself this was not new; "mutual edification" and "fraternal correction" served to characterize most Protestant congregational life. But the shift to a congregational church polity by Baptists and Congregationalists and

geographical circumstances among Methodists meant that the laity assumed a larger role in pastoral care.

Such generalizations certainly appear true for British Baptists. With roots in puritanism and pietism, they maintained strict membership standards. Their small congregations provided a setting for intimate relations of watchful care both with their pastors and each other. John Bunyon was the best known representative of the era which continued until the Act of Toleration (1689) precipitated a diminution of discipline and communal life before these were renewed by the Evangelical revivals.

In the U.S. Baptist life is linked with New England Congregationalism and frontier revivalism. Few of these churches had regular pastors, so the responsibility for pastoral care fell to the congregation. These groups were held together by covenants wherein they agreed to "watch over each other in brotherly tenderness, each endeavoring to edify his brother; striving for the benefit of the weak of the flock . . . (and) to bear each other's burdens" (Sweet, 1931). The records of early Baptist churches are largely a record of this care. Discipline was prominent, frequently over matters now regarded as trivial, but so was concern for the sick, widows, families, and the troubled.

British Independents also adopted a congregational polity after the Act of Toleration, though never so completely as the Baptists. Isaac Watts and Philip Doddridge, two of their best known leaders, maintained an extensive correspondence reflecting spiritual guidance and concern for personal and family religion. Doddridge emphasized private religious exercises and directions for the spiritual life. As pastor, he put elders to work visiting prisoners and those in spiritual distress. They were to reprove wrongdoers and not to spare their pastor for offensive temper and behavior.

The American Puritans as successors to these British Independents are best known through the works of Cotton and Increase Mather and Jonathan Edwards. Like their British mentors, conscience was the theme of their preaching, conversation, and concern. Edwards encouraged his members to give themselves to mutual care and admonition and not simply to be preoccupied with their own souls. Neglect is "a failure of our duty of love and charity." Cotton Mather felt the personal care of souls neglected and instructed fellow ministers to visit, catechize, and distribute literature so as to enhance piety, aid in reproof, and provide consolation. By the end of the nineteenth century, Washington Gladden's *The Christian Pastor and the Working Church* revealed just how far Congregationalists had moved from these roots. He advised pastors that "the one thing needful is for them [parishioners] to know that he loves them and wants to do them good" (McNeill, p. 278). At the sickbed he suggested "a few pleasant and sympathetic words with the patient."

From the beginning John Wesley organized Methodism in groups intended for mutual confession and discipline. His societies were subdivided into classes of some twelve persons according to sex and marital status. Together with their leader they were to "help each other to work out their salvation." They should bear one another's burdens and "do good of every possible sort"; they should feed the hungry, clothe the naked, visit or help the sick or imprisoned and "instruct, reprove, and exhort" (McNeill, p. 279). They should do business with each other, practice frugality, and attend worship. Wesley's groups owed much to pietism and would have delighted Spener.

Wesley himself was a model for his followers. He talked constantly to the anxious, perplexed, and distressed, visited the sick, and attended prisoners condemned to death. His correspondence was voluminous but its constant theme was the spiritual needs of persons. He wanted conversions, to be sure, but he was equally concerned to encourage the pursuit of holiness and to reclaim the lapsed.

In the U.S. Francis Asbury was Wesley's heir. He too traveled constantly, always ready to engage in personal counsel and guidance out of his evangelical faith. Asbury insisted on maintaining the standards of the *Discipline*. "Our society," he wrote, "may be considered a spiritual hospital, where souls come to be cured of their spiritual diseases" (Mills, 1965). Basic to this cure was conversion. But the prospect of relapse demanded striving for "full salvation" and Wesley's class structure was the vehicle for this care.

It is apparent that certain theological assurances underlay the pastoral care practices of each of these traditions. Foremost among them was that persons were created in the image of God and that their true destiny was a meeting with God. In between preparation was to be made for that meeting, and pastoral care was endemic to that process. By the end of the nineteenth century these affirmations were not so widely shared. The winds of secularism and technology offered the symbols of science as alternative understandings of both human distress and care and set the stage for the particular problems and possibilities of pastoral care in the twentieth century.

5. The Twentieth Century. Beyond question the single most important influence of the twentieth century on pastoral care was the emergence and prominence of the psychological sciences. On the one hand, their influence fostered an emphasis on pastoral care which led H. Richard Niebuhr to describe it in 1955 as the most important movement in theological education. On the other hand, their presence symbolized the diminution of theological understandings of human life and offered alternative, and at times competitive, conceptions of human distress and its alleviation. The efforts of pastors and theological educators to make their way amidst uncertain theological affirmations and the secularization of care have shaped pastoral care's recent history.

Pastors and theological educators were quick to discern the significance of psychology and psychotherapy for ministry. Following the initiative of Anton Boisen in 1925, it took only two decades for most of the major theological seminaries to appoint full-time faculty versed in these disciplines to teach pastoral care, and a substantial literature began to appear.

These teachers and authors undertook a difficult task. At the same time they sought to reinterpret the work of ministry as illumined by various psychological theories, especially by Carl Rogers, *Client-Centered Therapy*, and to maintain a tie to the traditions by defining ministry and pastoral care as distinct from other professions and forms of care. The literature reveals an interest in all the human dilemmas that have served as a focus for pastoral concern. Its distinction lay in the tentativeness of its normative theological judgments and in its misgivings about confrontation and discipline. Holifield describes this shift as occurring over three centuries and suggests it to be a move from the theological notion of salvation to the cultural ideal of self-realization as the goal of pastoral care. However, this assessment may be too easy. For to survey this literature certainly shows the leaders, e.g., Anton Boisen, Seward Hiltner, Carroll Wise, Wayne Oates, Paul Johnson, Ruell Howe, William Hulme, Howard Clinebell, struggling with the issue of theological understanding. In any event, the practice flourished, producing specialists in clinical education (Association for Clinical Pastoral Education), pastoral counseling (American Association of Pastoral Counselors), and graduate programs in theological seminaries.

With the exception of the Roman Catholic church and conservative Christian groups, these developments seem to have characterized pastoral care until 1970. More recently an increasing number of persons, such as Don Browning, Edward Farley, and Charles Gerkin, suggested that pastoral care was too dependent on its auxiliary discipline, psychology, and had lost its theological mooring. The Roman Catholic tradition, contrary to the others, resisted the incursions of psychology and maintained itself until Vatican Council II. The work of this council laid the foundation for a broadened understanding of care and a reinterpretation of the sacramental tradition and has made possible an increasing participation by Roman Catholics in the broader understanding of pastoral care. Conservative Christians and groups tended to view the shifts in pastoral care with caution. They voiced concern that the innovators were forsaking the Bible and setting aside a proper understanding of Christian faith and life. In recent years these same voices have begun to articulate an evangelical pastoral care and to produce a significant literature.

When one inquires about the present state of pastoral care, several observations are in order. First, despite the uncertainties of definition, pastoral care continues as an essential activity of ministers and laypersons. The perennial concerns of illness, death, family conflict, and depression are now supplemented with divorce and a host of complex moral and ethical questions surrounding abortion, live-in mates, prolongation of life, and aging. Second, the emerging consciousness of the Black Church and the increasing participation of its leaders in specialized pastoral care introduces new dimensions to pastoral care's self-understanding and definition. *Pastoral Care in the Black Church* by Edward Wimberly offers a sample of the contributions that may be anticipated. Also, an increasing number of women are finding their vocation in ministry in pastoral care. Literature by women is just beginning to appear but it promises to have a significant effect on the conceptualization and practice of pastoral care.

Finally, there appears to be a growing sense that pastoral care neglects its theological roots and intent to its peril. Serious efforts by Don Browning, Charles Gerkin, John Patton, James Lapsley, Don Capps, James Poling, and a host of others seek to attend the theological character of the endeavor. It seems that concerted efforts are under way to reclaim pastoral care's place in the cure of souls tradition and to understand its tasks as intrinsically theological. The hard-won gains of association with the psychological sciences are not being set aside, but these gains are being placed in relation to the heritage in the church. Thus pastoral care seeks its roots in a theological world view at the same time that it comes to terms with the forces and contending voices of the contemporary scene. What is reflected in these more recent enterprises is a continuation of a long and honorable tradition. For the commitment to persons which pastoral care's history reveals and the effort to discern the meaning of life in relation to God remain as fundamental ideals in those who would care for souls.

Bibliography. R. Baxter, *Reformed Pastor* (1656). M. Buer, *On the True Cure of Souls* ( ). W. Clebsch and C. Jaekle, *Pastoral Care in Historical Perspective* (1964). G. Herbert, *A Priest to the Temple or, The Country Parson* (1632). S. Hiltner, *Preface to Pastoral Theology* (1958). E. B. Holifield, *A History of Pastoral Care in America* (1983). C. Kemp, *Physicians of the Soul* (1947). J. T. McNeill, *A History of the Cure of Souls* (1951). L. O. Mills, "The Relation of Discipline to Pastoral Care in Frontier Churches," *Pastoral Psychology,* (December, 1956). H. R. Niebuhr and D. Williams, *The Ministry in Historical Perspective* (1956). T. Oden, *Pastoral Theology* (1983). P. J. Spener, *Pia Desideria* (1675); *The Spiritual Priesthood Briefly Set Forth* (1677). W. Sweet, *Religion on the American Frontier: The Baptists* (1931); *The Presbyterians* (1936). T. Tappert, *Luther's Letters of Spiritual Counsel* (1955). L. Trinterud, *The Forming of An American Tradition* (1949). A. Vinet, *Pastoral Theology* (1853). J. Watson, *The Cure of Souls* (1896). E. Wimberley, *Pastoral Care in the Black Church* (1979). U. Zwingli, *Der Hirt* (1524).

L. O. MILLS

For biblical and early pastoral traditions see: OLD TESTAMENT AND APOCRYPHA; NEW TESTAMENT; EARLY CHURCH; MEDIEVAL CHURCH; *also* CASUISTRY; CLASSIC LITERATURE; MINISTRY; SPIRITUAL DIRECTION; WOMEN IN PASTORAL MINISTRIES. *Compare* ISLAMIC CARE AND COUNSELING; JEWISH CARE AND COUNSELING. *For histories of more recent pastoral care see:* HISTORY OF PROTESTANT *or* ROMAN CATHOLIC PASTORAL CARE (Canada *or* United States); PASTORAL CARE MOVEMENT; PASTORAL COUNSELING MOVEMENT; THEOLOGICAL EDUCATION AND THE PASTORAL CARE MOVEMENT; WOMEN IN PASTORAL MINISTRY, HISTORY OF; *also* INTERNATIONAL PASTORAL CARE MOVEMENT. *For denominational traditions see:* ANGLICAN, BAPTIST, LUTHERAN, METHODIST, REFORMED, *or* ROMAN CATHOLIC PASTORAL CARE; MINISTRY AND PASTORAL CARE (Orthodox Tradition); *also* CHRISTIAN SCIENCE, QUAKER, UNITARIAN-UNIVERSALIST PASTORAL CARE; CHARISMATIC, EVANGELICAL, *or* FUNDAMENTALIST PASTORAL CARE; PIETISM AND PASTORAL CARE. *Compare* AFRICAN, NATIVE AMERICAN, OR WEST INDIAN TRADITIONAL RELIGION, PERSONAL CARE IN; *also* HASIDIC *or* MORMON CARE AND COUNSELING; PSYCHOLOGY, EASTERN. *For ethnic and racial traditions see:* ASIAN AMERICAN, BLACK AMERICAN, HISPANIC, *or* NATIVE AMERICAN PASTORAL CARE. *Compare* BLACK MUSLIM CARE AND COUNSELING; ISLAMIC CARE AND COUNSELING; JEWISH CARE AND COUNSELING. *For cultural and theological traditions see:* ETHICS AND PASTORAL CARE; MORAL THEOLOGY; PASTORAL THEOLOGY; PRACTICAL THEOLOGY; PSYCHOLOGY IN AMERICAN RELIGION; THEOLOGY AND PSYCHOLOGY. *Compare* PHILOSOPHY AND PSYCHOLOGY; PSYCHOLOGY AND PSYCHOTHERAPY (East-West Comparison).

PASTORAL CARE, ANGLICAN. *See* ANGLICAN PASTORAL CARE.

PASTORAL CARE, ASIAN AMERICAN. *See* ASIAN AMERICAN PASTORAL CARE.

PASTORAL CARE, BAPTIST. *See* BAPTIST PASTORAL CARE.

PASTORAL CARE, BIBLICAL ORIGINS AND PRINCIPLES OF. *See* BIBLICAL ORIGINS AND PRINCIPLES OF PASTORAL CARE.

PASTORAL CARE, BLACK AMERICAN. *See* BLACK AMERICAN PASTORAL CARE.

PASTORAL CARE, BLACK MUSLIM. *See* BLACK MUSLIM PASTORAL CARE.

PASTORAL CARE, CHARISMATIC. *See* CHARISMATIC PASTORAL CARE.

PASTORAL CARE, CHRISTIAN SCIENCE. *See* CHRISTIAN SCIENCE PASTORAL CARE.

PASTORAL CARE, CLASSIC LITERATURE OF. *See* CLASSIC LITERATURE IN PASTORAL CARE.

PASTORAL CARE, CROSS CULTURAL. *See* CROSS CULTURAL PASTORAL CARE.

PASTORAL CARE, ORTHODOX. *See* MINISTRY AND PASTORAL CARE (Orthodox Tradition).

PASTORAL CARE, EDUCATION IN. *See* EDUCATION IN PASTORAL CARE AND COUNSELING.

PASTORAL CARE, ETHICS AND. *See* ETHICS AND PASTORAL CARE; MORAL DILEMMAS IN PASTORAL PERSPECTIVE. *See also* ETHICS, PROFESSIONAL.

PASTORAL CARE, EVANGELICAL. *See* EVANGELICAL PASTORAL CARE.

PASTORAL CARE, FUNDAMENTALIST. *See* FUNDAMENTALIST PASTORAL CARE.

PASTORAL CARE, HISPANIC AMERICAN. *See* HISPANIC AMERICAN PASTORAL CARE.

PASTORAL CARE, HISTORY OF. *See* PASTORAL CARE (History, Traditions, and Definitions). *See also* HISTORY OF PROTESTANT *or* ROMAN CATHOLIC PASTORAL CARE (Canada *or* United States).

PASTORAL CARE, JEWISH. *See* JEWISH CARE AND COUNSELING.

PASTORAL CARE, JOURNALS IN. *See* JOURNALS IN PASTORAL CARE AND COUNSELING.

PASTORAL CARE, LAY. *See* LAY PASTORAL CARE AND COUNSELING.

PASTORAL CARE, LEGAL DIMENSIONS OF. *See* LEGAL DIMENSIONS OF PASTORAL CARE AND COUNSELING.

PASTORAL CARE, LUTHERAN. *See* LUTHERAN PASTORAL CARE.

PASTORAL CARE, MEDIEVAL. *See* MEDIEVAL CHURCH, PASTORAL CARE IN.

PASTORAL CARE, METHODIST. *See* METHODIST PASTORAL CARE.

PASTORAL CARE, METHODS OF. *See* PASTORAL CARE (Contemporary Methods, Perspectives, and Issues); TECHNIQUE AND SKILL IN PASTORAL CARE.

PASTORAL CARE, MORMON. *See* MORMON PASTORAL CARE.

PASTORAL CARE, NATIVE AMERICAN. *See* NATIVE AMERICAN PASTORAL CARE.

PASTORAL CARE, PATRISTIC. *See* EARLY CHURCH, PASTORAL CARE AND COUNSELING IN.

PASTORAL CARE, PIETIST. *See* PIETIST PASTORAL CARE.

PASTORAL CARE, PRESBYTERIAN. *See* REFORMED PASTORAL CARE.

PASTORAL CARE, PSYCHOLOGY OF. *See* PASTORAL CARE (Contemporary Methods, Perspectives, and Issues); PASTORAL PSYCHOLOGY, DISCIPLINE OF; The PERSONAL, CONCEPT OF, IN PASTORAL CARE. *See also* ANALYTICAL (JUNGIAN) PSYCHOLOGY, PSYCHOANALYSIS, *or* HUMANISTIC PSYCHOLOGY, AND PASTORAL CARE.

PASTORAL CARE, QUAKER. *See* QUAKER PASTORAL CARE.

PASTORAL CARE, REFORMED. *See* REFORMED PASTORAL CARE.

PASTORAL CARE, RESEARCH IN. *See* EMPIRICAL RESEARCH IN PASTORAL CARE AND COUNSELING.

PASTORAL CARE, ROMAN CATHOLIC. *See* ROMAN CATHOLIC PASTORAL CARE.

PASTORAL CARE, SECTARIAN. *See* SECTARIAN PASTORAL CARE.

PASTORAL CARE, SOCIOLOGY OF. *See* SOCIOLOGY OF RELIGIOUS AND PASTORAL CARE.

PASTORAL CARE, SPECIALIZATION. *See* SPECIALIZATION IN PASTORAL CARE.

PASTORAL CARE, THEOLOGICAL EDUCATION AND. *See* THEOLOGICAL EDUCATION AND THE PASTORAL CARE MOVEMENT. *See also* EDUCATION IN PASTORAL CARE AND COUNSELING.

PASTORAL CARE, THEOLOGY OF. *See* PASTORAL THEOLOGY; PASTORAL THEOLOGICAL METHODOLOGY.

PASTORAL CARE, TRAINING IN. *See* CLINICAL PASTORAL EDUCATION; EDUCATION IN PASTORAL CARE AND COUNSELING.

PASTORAL CARE, UNITARIAN/UNIVERSALIST. *See* UNITARIAN-UNIVERSALIST PASTORAL CARE.

PASTORAL CARE, WOMEN AND. *See* WOMEN, PASTORAL CARE OF; WOMEN IN PASTORAL MINISTRIES.

PASTORAL CARE AND COUNSELING (Comparative Terminology). In contemporary American usage *pastoral care* usually refers, in a broad and inclusive way, to all pastoral work concerned with the support and nurturance of persons and interpersonal relationships, including everyday expressions of care and concern that may occur in the midst of various pastoring activities and relationships. *Pastoral counseling* refers to caring ministries that are more structured and focused on specifically articulated need or concern. Counseling always involves some degree of "contract" in which a request for help is articulated and specific arrangements are agreed upon concerning time and place of meeting; in extended counseling a fee may also be agreed upon, depending on the institutional setting and other considerations.

Counseling generally implies extended conversation focused on the needs and concerns of the one seeking help. *Care* in many of its expressions is also conversational though briefer and less therapeutically complex than counseling, as in supportive or sustaining ministries like visiting the sick. The term is also applied to nonconversational ministries in which a significant caring dimension may be present, as in administering communion, conducting a funeral, or pastoral teaching.

In earlier, postwar pastoral literature *care* and *counseling* were often used synonymously; their gradual distinction no doubt reflects the emergence of pastoral counseling as a specialized ministry. Today there is a question as to what extent, and in what respects, the general ministry of care should be guided by the methods and principles of specialized counseling, which have heavily influenced its modern development.

R. J. HUNTER

PASTORAL CARE (History, Traditions, and Definitions); PASTORAL COUNSELING. *Compare* COUNSELEE/CLIENT/PARISHIONER TERMINOLOGY.

PASTORAL CARE MOVEMENT. A twentieth-century movement, prominent especially in Protestantism within the U.S. after 1945, which attempted to refine ministry by drawing upon the findings of modern medicine, psychotherapy, and the behavioral sciences. It produced innovative forms of pastoral practice, created new institutions, generated theological reflection, and influenced the training of ministerial students.

1. **Historical Background.** The reliance on secular wisdom in the modern pastoral care movement is no innovation. From the beginnings of church history, Christian theologians have enriched pastoral care by exploiting the resources of Western philosophy, medicine, and psychology. Even the letters of St. Paul reflect the philosophical tradition of "psychagogy" that defined pre-Christian Western methods of spiritual direction. Sixteenth-century casuists appropriated innovations in Renaissance philosophy and logic in much the same way that twentieth-century pastoral theologians read Freud, Adler, and Jung. Earlier pastoral writers also studied medical treatises to enrich their practice of the pastoral arts, as when seventeenth-century English Calvinists incorporated in their pastoral handbooks the standard medical analysis of such ailments as *melancholia*. From one perspective, the pastoral care movement simply represented a significant twentieth-century form of this time-honored practice of appropriating secular psychological and medical wisdom for a ministry of healing.

As early as 1808, moreover, when American Protestant seminaries began to offer lectures in "pastoral" or "practical" theology, these courses included attention not only to preaching but also to standard forms of pastoral counsel and visitation, as codified in such classics as George Herbert's *Country Parson* (1652), Richard Baxter's *Reformed Pastor* (1658), and Gilbert Burnet's *Discourse of the Pastoral Care* (1713). The pastoral theology lecturers hoped to help young ministers engender and recognize the marks of rebirth, partly by teaching them the categories of English and Scottish "mental philosophy"—the early nineteenth century's version of what we call psychology. This tradition of pastoral theology continued through the later nineteenth century, introducing ministerial students not only to customary methods of exhortation and advice but also to changing conceptions of human nature formulated by philosophers and psychologists.

By the late nineteenth century, pastoral writers displayed an increasing awareness of the ways in which knowledge of psychology and medicine could instruct the pastor. In part this awareness reflected the influence of liberal theologians, whose doctrine of divine immanence assumed that God was manifest in the highest cultural attainments. Further stimulus for a new awareness came from innovations in medicine and the academic disciplines.

2. **Psychology of Religion and Psychotherapy.** One such new discipline was the psychology of religion. Its seminal figure, G. Stanley Hall at Clark University in Worcester, Massachusetts, emphasized the functional value of religious experience as a means of nurturing the development of the personality. When William James wrote *The Varieties of Religious Experience* (1902), he expanded this notion by arguing that religious experience put men and women in touch with a "wider self" through which they could be transformed. A few of the early psychologists of religion used these insights to promote methods of pastoral care designed to respect the natural processes of human growth. They also stimulated interest in notions of the unconscious or subconscious

and deepened within the seminaries a growing interest in the practical applications of psychological research.

Equally important for pastoral practice was the expanding critique of medical materialism. After the English translation in 1905 of the *Psychic Treatment of Nervous Disorders* by Pierre DuBois, a professor of psychotherapy at the University of Bern, a few American physicians began to acknowledge the possibility of a "scientific mind cure." In 1906 the American index of medical papers listed *psychotherapy* as a separate topic, and in 1909 Sigmund Freud attended the first American Conference on Psychotherapy. The National Committee for Mental Hygiene, also founded in 1909, soon was attempting to apply the new understandings of psychotherapy to the reform of hospitals and the creation of institutions to advance mental health.

Both the psychologists of religion and the psychotherapists displayed a special interest in notions of subconscious or unconscious mental processes. By 1905, a few American pastoral writers began to explore those notions, some favoring a Freudian notion of the unconscious as a source of internal conflict, others preferring theories that attributed to the subconscious mind both rationality and creativity. Both ideas found proponents among the pastors, who in 1905 organized in Boston the Emmanuel Movement, whose founders, especially the Episcopal priest Elwood Worcester, argued that the cure of souls within the church should be guided by science, not tradition. Their journal, *Psychotherapy*, helped to popularize themes that would reappear in the later pastoral care movement.

3. **Religious Education.** Even more important than the Emmanuel pioneers in laying the groundwork for the pastoral care movement were the religious educators. In 1903 they formed a Religious Education Association, which became a channel for communicating to the churches many of the latest developments in psychological theory and research. Agreeing with George Albert Coe that religious education should be a "forming of the whole self," they taught some of the earliest pastoral counseling courses in Protestant seminaries. As early as 1921 Harrison Elliott taught such a course at Union Seminary in New York; Gaines Dobbins at Southern Baptist Theological Seminary made similar efforts to "capture psychology for Christ" in the heartland of southern religious conservatism.

In the thirties, religious educators and pastoral theologians began to publish guidebooks instructing pastors how to apply twentieth-century psychological theory to their pastoral conversations. In *The Cure of Souls: A Socio-Psychological Approach* (1932), Charles Holman of the University of Chicago, drawing partly on John Dewey's definitions of adjustment, described "soul-sickness" as inadequate religious or moral adaptation. In *Pastoral Psychology* (1932), Karl Stolz of the Hartford School of Religious Education also argued that the pastor's responsibility was to help persons adjust themselves to reality. John Sutherland Bonnell, a Presbyterian minister in New York, drew the ideas in his *Pastoral Psychiatry* (1938) from both Sigmund Freud and Alfred Adler, though he too contended that the goal of pastoral counseling was to help people make a right adjustment to God. The most influential book written during the thirties came from the physician Richard Cabot and the hospital chaplain Russell Dicks, who published in 1936 *The Art of Ministering to the Sick,* which depicted the pastor's task in the hospital room as the discerning and nurturing of the patient's "growing edges."

4. Clinical Pastoral Education. It would not have been possible to refer during the thirties to a pastoral care "movement." Interest in the newer understandings of pastoral care were still too diffuse and unorganized. But a few innovators in theological education had begun as early as 1923 to create new patterns of ministerial training —and some new institutions—that made it possible for a genuine movement to develop.

The Episcopal physician William S. Keller in 1923 founded a summer school in social service in Cincinnati, designed to deepen theological education by having students do casework in social agencies. Keller thought that the students would learn best through engagement in the practice of ministry with persons in need, followed by periods of reflection.

In 1925, Richard Cabot, a Boston neurologist and cardiologist, published a "Plea for a Clinical Year in the Course of Theological Study," arguing that the exposure of theological students to people suffering in hospitals would enhance their capacities for ministry. Before the end of the year, the hospital chaplain Anton Boisen began, with Cabot's blessing, to train a handful of students at Worcester State Hospital. Boisen viewed clinical training as an occasion for introducing students to "living human documents" from whom they might derive insight into sin, salvation, and religious experience. His *Exploration of the Inner World* (1936) argued that mental illness represented a chaotic encounter with God, which could lead either to a new integration of the personality or a fall into total inner disarray.

In 1930, Cabot, Boisen, and others joined in the formation of the Council for Clinical Training of Theological Students, designed to make possible a long-term supervised encounter with men and women in crisis in hospitals, prisons, and social agencies. Known later as Clinical Pastoral Education (CPE), this new form of theological education was destined to alter dramatically the prevailing conceptions of pastoral care.

Almost from the beginning, the clinical pastoral educators split into two groups. Under the leadership of the psychiatrist Helen Flanders Dunbar, the Council for Clinical Training favored mental hospitals as training sites and tried to give students a clear conception of the place of psychoanalysis in psychotherapy. When Robert Brinkman became director in 1938, he turned to psychoanalytic doctrine not only to provide the students an understanding of "deeper motivation" but also to interpret traditional Christian images. Richard Cabot, scornful of psychoanalysis and skeptical of other forms of psychotherapy, then joined with Philip Guiles of Andover Newton and David R. Hunter, chaplain at Massachusetts General Hospital, in the formation of the New England Theological Schools Committee on Clinical Training.

The Theological Schools Committee lasted only a short time, but in 1944 Rollin Fairbanks, a professor at the Episcopal Theological Seminary in Cambridge, led in the organization of an Institute for Pastoral Care, which developed close relationships with seminaries in the Boston area. In contrast to the Council, which preferred mental hospitals and prisons as training sites, the Institute initially preferred general hospitals. While the Council was sometimes perceived as interested mainly in educating chaplains, the Institute emphasized its interest in training the parish minister. The Council viewed itself as a focus of rebellion against rigid and oppressive moral conventions and religious legalism; the Institute did not share that self-understanding.

The tensions between the two clinical programs dissipated slowly, but in 1967 they joined in a new organization: The Association for Clinical Pastoral Education, a group that also encompassed denominational clinical programs founded by Lutherans and Southern Baptists.

In 1932 Austin Philip Guiles had broken away from the Council for Clinical Training of Theological Students and established a program in clinical education at Andover Newton Theological Seminary. Within the next thirty years, clinical supervisors developed alliances with more than forty other theological schools; they also organized at least 117 regular centers for CPE, linked closely to medical centers and other institutions. By 1955 more than four thousand Protestant students had undergone some form of CPE, and the National Council of Churches was offering scholarship aid for parish ministers who wanted the training. By this time, moreover, Anton Boisen, Russell Dicks, and the Presbyterian theologian Seward Hiltner had refined the pedagogical methods that would mark education in the centers: case studies, and "verbatims" or word-for-word transcriptions of pastoral conversations.

5. Pastoral Counseling Centers. The expansion of CPE paralleled and stimulated a gradual proliferation of pastoral counseling centers staffed by ministers, psychiatrists, and social workers. Austin Philip Guiles typified the leadership of clinical educators in the formation of such centers: He opened one at the Wellesley Hills Congregational Church and another at the Old South Church in Boston. Other counseling centers came into existence independently of both the Council for Clinical Training and the Institute for Pastoral Care. The Religio-Psychiatric Clinic of Marble Collegiate Church in New York, founded in 1937, gradually developed into an extensive center for pastoral counseling, especially after 1951, when it was renamed as the American Foundation of Religion and Psychiatry. In 1950 there were ten such centers; in 1963, by one count, there were 149.

The emergence of the pastoral counseling centers helped to sharpen a new distinction between pastoral care and pastoral counseling. Some of the centers offered specialized training programs in counseling. For instance, shortly after Frederick Kuether, one of Boisen's early students, assumed responsibility for the clergy training program of the American Foundation of Religion and Psychiatry in 1954, he inaugurated such a program. The Institute of Religion in the Texas Medical Center in Houston became another popular center for the training of pastoral counselors.

6. Seminaries and Chaplaincies. Prior to the Second World War, few theological seminaries offered courses in counseling. During the war, however, the Chaplain's School at Harvard discovered that counseling skills were essential for military chaplains. The clinical programs and counseling centers also helped convince the seminaries to take counseling seriously, and during the fifties almost all the North American theological schools developed counseling courses. Over eighty percent offered additional courses in psychology, and over eighty percent listed at least one psychologist on the faculty.

Such courses proved especially enticing for students planning for institutional chaplaincies, and the post-war economy permitted increasing numbers of hospitals to hire full-time chaplains. In 1940, few openings were available. By the end of the fifties, almost 500 full-time chaplains served in general hospitals, and at least 200 more worked in mental hospitals. In the hospitals of the Veterans Administration alone 240 clergy served in chaplaincy posts. As early as 1946, John M. Billinsky, who taught pastoral care at Andover Newton, and Russell Dicks, who would soon begin teaching at Duke Divinity School, formed a Chaplain's Section of the American Protestant Hospital Association. Two years later, Ernest Bruder, a chaplain at St. Elizabeth's Hospital in Washington, D. C., led in the formation of the Association of Mental Hospital Chaplains. Because hospital chaplains spent most of their time visiting and counseling patients and their families, the expansion of hospital openings deepened interest in counseling issues.

The new literature of the pastoral care movement reflected this interest in counseling. Clinical pastoral educators founded in 1947 the *Journal of Pastoral Care* and the *Journal of Clinical Pastoral Work*. In 1950, Simon Doniger became the first editor of *Pastoral Psychology*, which soon had over 16,000 subscribers, most of them ministers. A small group of pastoral theologians assumed a position of intellectual leadership. Seward Hiltner, who had been associated with the Federal Council of Churches before joining the faculty of the University of Chicago, drew on social and cultural anthropology in preparing his *Pastoral Counseling* (1949), in which he proposed "eductive" methods of counseling that tried to elicit solutions out of the creative potentialities of the person needing help rather than offering advice and direction. Carroll A. Wise, a professor of pastoral psychology and counseling at Methodist Garrett Biblical Institute, based his *Pastoral Counseling* (1951) on personalist theology, dynamic psychology, and the non-directive theories of the therapist Carl Rogers. In *The Christian Pastor* (1951), Wayne Oates, a professor of pastoral care and the psychology of religion at Southern Baptist Theological Seminary, attempted to combine traditional Protestant language with a theory of "psychosocial role behavior" taken from the social sciences. Paul Johnson, a Methodist professor of psychology at Boston University, drew on the methods of Carl Rogers, interpersonal psychiatry, and personalist theology for his *Psychology of Pastoral Care* (1953).

The surge of interest in counseling stimulated reflection on the broader meaning of pastoral care. A few pastoral theologians reemphasized the distinction between pastoral care, the whole range of clerical activity aimed at guiding and sustaining a congregation, and counseling, a more narrowly defined relationship between a pastor and a person in need. Some argued that pastoral counseling was merely one dimension of pastoral care and that it made sense only within the context of the church. In 1955 a Commission on the Ministry sponsored by the New York Academy of Sciences observed that a minister's work was always "distinguished by the religious setting in which it is done."

7. American Association of Pastoral Counselors. By 1961 a number of leaders in the pastoral care movement began to call for pastoral counseling specialists to work in counseling centers or even to carry on private pastoral practice. In 1963 Frederick Kuether and Arthur Tingue convened a conference in New York City that resulted in the formation of the American Association of Pastoral Counselors, a group designed initially for specialists in pastoral counseling. The conference, which elected Howard Clinebell of the Claremont School of Theology in California as its chairperson, generated controversy within the larger pastoral care movement. When Kuether challenged the idea that pastoral counseling belonged exclusively in the churches, both Seward Hiltner and Wayne Oates of Southern Baptist Theological Seminary criticized the Association, arguing especially that the notion of private pastoral practice, which Kuether thought might sometimes be appropriate, was a contradiction in terms and a violation of the character of ministry. In 1964, however, the Association, meeting in St. Louis, decided to admit parish ministers as members. It soon opposed any notion of private practice that failed to ensure some measure of accountability to an ecclesiastical judicatory.

The interest in pastoral care and counseling had other institutional consequences. By the end of the fifties, at least seven universities offered advanced graduate programs in personality and theology, pastoral psychology, pastoral theology, or pastoral counseling. And pastors could also find resources at more than thirty-five institutes and seminars, such as Reuel Howe's Institute for Advanced Pastoral Studies, located in a suburb of Detroit, or Thomas Klink's Program in Religion and Psychiatry at the Menninger Clinic in Kansas.

The movement during the fifties invested heavily in the nondirective methods of the American psychologist Carl Rogers, but during the sixties the Rogerian style came under attack. Clinebell and Johnson began to argue that the presuppositions of Rogerian counseling were too individualistic, and Clinebell called in his *Basic Types of Pastoral Counseling* (1966) for a "relationship-centered counseling" aimed at enhancing a person's ability to form satisfying relationships with other people, and advocated an eclectic array of alternative pastoral counseling methods. Hiltner and Oates warned against the tendency of pastoral writers to seek a borrowed identity from psychotherapy, emphasized the importance of the church as the setting for pastoral care, and accented the distinction between pastoral care and pastoral counseling.

By the late seventies, theologians of pastoral care were seeking greater clarity about the theological underpinnings of their discipline. Such theorists as Don Browning of the University of Chicago and Charles Gerkin at Emory University proposed new ethical and theological models for pastoral care. Gerkin's *The Living Human Document* (1984) drew on theological hermeneutics to reinterpret pastoral counseling, and Browning's *Religious*

Ethics and Pastoral Care (1983) related psychology and the social sciences to moral theory.

The pastoral care movement flourished especially in America. This was owing partly to the profound influence of psychotherapy in American culture, partly to the strength of the institutional network established by clinical pastoral educators, who created and nurtured in theological students an interest in counseling issues, and partly to the capacity of the American economy to sustain a host of chaplaincy positions in hospitals and other institutions. The expansion of the movement also depended heavily on financial support from private foundations. The William C. Whitney Foundation gave the Council for Clinical Training its start; the Earhart Foundation provided the initial money for the rival clinical program in New England; a foundation funded by insurance magnate W. Clement Stone supported the American Foundation of Religion and Psychiatry and provided most of the initial money to start the American Association of Pastoral Counselors; the Old Dominion Foundation backed the new program in psychiatry and religion at Union Theological Seminary; and the Lilly Endowment undergirded a similar program at the University of Chicago.

8. European Movements. By 1963, Europeans had also developed their own revised views of pastoral care and counseling. In England, Leslie Weatherhead began as early as 1922 to encourage ministers to learn from psychotherapists, and the former medical missionary Frank Lake began seminars in 1958 that introduced depth psychology to many English pastors. During the twenties in Berlin, the "Doctor and Pastoral Counselor" group began conversations between ministers and psychoanalysts, and Otto Haendler introduced a later generation of German theological students to the writings of Freud, Adler, and Jung. In 1944, Gute Bergsten in Stockholm founded an Institute for Spiritual Counsel and Psychological Treatment under the auspices of the St. Luke's Foundation.

In 1966, Dutch and American pastors met together in Holland, with the result that the American CPE movement soon gained strong adherents in that country. Six years later, Werner Becher in Germany, who had studied at the Menninger Foundation, led in the organization of a European conference on "Clinical Pastoral Education for Pastoral Care and Counseling" at Arnoldshain, the first of several such gatherings that preceded the first large international meeting at Edinburgh in 1979. Out of that meeting came not only an International Committee on Pastoral Care and Counseling but also a new consciousness of what came to be called the International Pastoral Care and Counseling Movement. This was the first international meeting in which there was significant Third World participation, with representatives from Africa, Asia, and Latin America.

Europeans who founded national organizations tended to follow the nomenclature that became standard in the international movement, which linked pastoral counseling closely to pastoral care. When the English, for instance, founded in 1972 their own Association for Pastoral Care and Counseling, they tended not to encourage a view of counseling as an autonomous activity. And the American debates over the accreditation of counselors

and organizations, the nature of pastoral counseling centers, and the practice of pastoral psychotherapy have not attracted significant attention in Europe. In Third World countries the movement has developed indigenous forms emphasizing the force of social, political and economic circumstances on human development and fashioning new forms of pastoral education and care in response to them.

Bibliography. R. Baxter, *Reformed Pastor* (1658). A. Boisen, *Exploration of the Inner World* (1936). G. Burnet, *Discourse of the Pastoral Care* (1713). J. S. Bonnell, *Pastoral Psychiatry* (1938). D. Browning, *Religious Ethics* (1983). H. Clinebell, *Basic Types of Pastoral Counseling* (1966). R. Dicks, *The Art of Ministering to the Sick* (1936). P. DuBois, *Psychic Treatment of Nervous Disorders* (ET 1905). C. Gerkin, *The Living Human Document* (1984). G. Herbert, *Country Parson* (1652). S. Hiltner, *Pastoral Counseling* (1949). E. B. Holifield, *A History of Pastoral Care in America: From Salvation to Self-Realization* (1983). C. Holman, *The Cure of Souls: A Socio-Psychological Approach* (1932). W. James, *The Varieties of Religious Experience* (1902). P. Johnson, *Psychology of Pastoral Care* (1953). W. E. Oates, *The Christian Pastor* (1951). A. Stokes, *Ministry After Freud* (1985). K. Stolz, *Pastoral Psychology* (1932). E. E. Thornton, *Professional Education for Ministry* (1970). C. A. Wise, *Pastoral Counseling* (1951).

E. B. HOLIFIELD

CANADIAN PASTORAL CARE MOVEMENT; HISTORY OF PROTESTANT PASTORAL CARE (United States); INTERNATIONAL PASTORAL CARE MOVEMENT; PASTORAL COUNSELING MOVEMENT. *See also* AMERICAN ASSOCIATION OF PASTORAL COUNSELORS; ASSOCIATION FOR CLINICAL PASTORAL EDUCATION; CLINICAL PASTORAL EDUCATION; COUNCIL FOR CLINICAL TRAINING; ECUMENICAL RELATIONSHIPS IN THE PASTORAL CARE AND COUNSELING MOVEMENTS; EMMANUEL MOVEMENT; INSTITUTE OF PASTORAL CARE; JOURNALS IN PASTORAL CARE AND COUNSELING; LUTHERAN ADVISORY COUNCIL; NEW YORK PSYCHOLOGY GROUP; PASTORAL CARE (History, Traditions, and Definitions); SOUTHERN BAPTIST ASSOCIATION FOR CLINICAL PASTORAL EDUCATION; THEOLOGICAL EDUCATION AND THE PASTORAL CARE MOVEMENT. *Compare* GENERAL *or* MENTAL HOSPITAL CHAPLAINCY; PERSONALISM *or* PRAGMATISM, AND PASTORAL CARE. *Biography:* BOISEN; BONNELL; BRINKMAN; CABOT; CLINEBELL; COE; DICKS; DONIGER; DUNBAR; ELLIOTT; FAIRBANKS; FLETCHER; GUILES; HALL; HILTNER; HOLMAN; HOWE; JAMES; JOHNSON; KELLER; KLINK; KUETHER; OATES; SEXTRO; SHERRILL; STOLZ; WISE; WORCESTER.

PASTORAL CONVERSATION. *See* CONVERSATION, PASTORAL.

PASTORAL COUNSELING. A specialized type of pastoral care offered in response to individuals, couples, or families who are experiencing and able to articulate the pain in their lives and willing to seek pastoral help in order to deal with it. A pastoral counselor is a person with commitment to and education for religious ministry who is functioning in an appropriate setting for ministry and accountable to a recognized religious community. Most pastoral counseling in the U. S. is provided by ordained clergy as a part of the ministry they perform in parishes, hospitals, and other authorized settings for ministry. Certain religious groups, due to shortage of clergy or special understandings of what constitutes the appropriate clergy function, authorize nonordained persons for the ministry of pastoral counseling. In all cases the criteria for what pastoral counseling is have more to do with the person and accountability of the counselor than with the methods adopted for the counseling. The primary criterion for method is that it be consistent with what ministry is and appropriately related to the need of the person seeking counseling.

1. **Definitions and Distinctions.** *a. The meaning of "pastoral."* The term "pastoral" means relationship both in the sense of responsibility and of attitude. Pastoral counseling is a specific sub-type of the larger ministerial function of pastoral care, originally (and still sometimes) referring to the ministerial oversight of the total area or group for which one is responsible, such as a parish. In twentieth-century usage the term more often refers to a pastor's responsibility for one or more persons who are in some way estranged, by illness or other life circumstance, from a group to which they usually belong. The biblical image most often used for this function is the shepherd's seeking the one sheep who is lost, while maintaining administrative responsibility for the ninety-nine who are not.

Because it is a type of care offered by the religious community, pastoral counseling is not a profession but a function performed by persons in the profession of ministry. It may be one of many functions in a person's ministry or the primary function performed in ministry by one who specializes in pastoral counseling. The term "pastoral psychotherapy" is most accurately understood as a more narrowly focused type of pastoral counseling that has been structured for the achievement of personality change and growth, not just the addressing of situational problems in living.

b. The distinctiveness of pastoral counseling. What distinguishes pastoral counseling from other forms of counseling and psychotherapy is the role and accountability of the counselor and his or her understanding and expression of the pastoral relationship. Pastoral counselors are representatives of the central image of life and its meaning affirmed by their religious communities. Thus pastoral counseling offers a relationship to that understanding of life and faith through the person of the pastoral counselor. This emphasis upon a relationship to the religious community through a representative person distinguishes pastoral counseling both from religious counseling in general and from certain types of secular psychotherapy. Whereas religious counseling and some secular therapies commonly teach particular practices and/or systems of belief, pastoral counseling is identified by its representation of the community that authorizes it, through a relationship to a pastor accountable to that community.

One of the ongoing problems for and debates within the pastoral counseling field has centered upon this distinguishing point—the nature of accountability to the religious community. Some pastoral counselors and religious groups have simply not dealt seriously with this pivotal issue. Any counselors who identified themselves as members of the religious group were viewed uncritically as pastoral counselors, and the problem of whether or how those counselors were accountable was simply avoided. Other religious groups have insisted upon the accountability of the counselor in an administrative way, but have not concerned themselves with what theological accountability might mean.

One way of conceptualizing both the administrative and the theological accountability of the pastoral counselor is through the image of a continuing dialogue with those elements within the religious community that have authorized the pastoral counselor's ministry. Patton (1983) identified three such dialogues: (1) with the story of the faith as received through the religious community; (2) with the role, function, and identity of a minister of that faith; and (3) with the specific religious community that nourishes that faith.

i. Dialogue with the faith tradition. The first dialogue is an expression of the pastoral counselor's theological accountability. To be a pastoral counselor one's experience with the story of faith must be in the present as well as the past. A theological education is not enough. One is a pastoral counselor because one continues to be committed to and involved with what the story that "chartered" the religious community means. The Christian pastor, for example, continues to study, question, and witness to the meaning of the Christ event. He or she continues to study the best in traditional and recent theological formulation as well as psychotherapeutic theory and to practice the reinterpretation of the faith in the light of what pastoral counseling experience reveals about human life. The so-called religious counselor, "Christian psychologist," *et al.*, may do something like this as a part of personal faith, but the pastoral counselor is committed to do so at a level of professional competence and as an expression of accountability to the community of faith that authorizes his or her ministry.

ii. Dialogue with ministerial role, function, and identity. The second dialogue, with the role, function, and identity of a minister, expresses both theological and administrative accountability. It is theological in that it requires an ongoing consideration of what representative ministry means in terms of historical and contemporary understanding. It is also theological in a more personal sense because it raises the existential question, "Do I still feel called to this ministry, and do I have the gifts and graces for it?" It is administrative in the institutional sense of response to a particular religious structure, and theological in its question to the pastoral counselor of how it "feels" to be identified as a minister. How does the pastoral counselor handle his or her embarrassment and/or feeling of power in being a minister? Is there an ongoing pastoral identity which can be expressed naturally, without conscious effort?

iii. Dialogue with the specific religious community. The pastoral counselor's ongoing dialogue with the religious community involves participating in that community as it celebrates and interprets its faith, thus maintaining a common experience with all members of that communion. Here the pastoral counselor and religious counselor are alike. They differ, however, in that the pastoral counselor is administratively responsible for reporting and interpreting his or her ministry as ministry in terms that can be understood by the authorizing body. Religious counselors have no comparable responsibility for interpreting their function. The pastoral counselor, as a representative member of the religious community (ordained or commissioned for special function), is com-

mitted to cope with and even take responsibility for modifying the doctrinal and administrative peculiarities of his or her particular denomination or religious structure in the light of his or her ministry of pastoral counseling. Moreover, this function, as a part of the ministry of the authorizing religious group, contributes (at least indirectly) to the pastoral counselor's particular ministry of counseling.

2. **History of Modern Pastoral Counseling** Although at least one interpreter of modern pastoral counseling (Oden, 1984) sees its roots in the church fathers, the historical foundations of pastoral counseling can more clearly be seen in later centuries. Historian Brooks Holifield (1983) has identified four post-Reformation traditions of pastoral care: Roman Catholic, Lutheran, Anglican, and Reformed. He notes their differences and the common theme among all four — the ascent toward holiness. He traces some of the theories and practices used by pastors to guide this "ascent" from the sixteenth century to the end of the 1960s. Moreover, he examines modern pastoral themes, such as self-expression, secularization, and conversational style (in contrast to rhetorical style) as they emerged in the late nineteenth and early twentieth centuries prior to the advent of dynamic psychology. Throughout his discussion one can see both the implicit and explicit use of psychology in the counsel offered by pastors (cf. Clebsch and Jaekle). This development culminated in the psychological fascination of the twenties, thirties, and forties, as illustrated by John Sutherland Bonnell's influential book, *Pastoral Psychiatry* (1938).

a. The use of psychology by pastors. In the late 1940s and on into the 1960s, clinical pastoral education (CPE) was the most significant influence on the development of pastoral counseling as it is known today. CPE made extensive use of psychological theory and psychotherapeutic technique, and most often took place in non-ecclesiastical, interdisciplinary settings which were often dominated by health concerns and psychiatry. Therefore theological students, as part of their training for ministry, had direct experience of the interpretive power of psychological theory and the life-changing influence of psychotherapeutic techniques; and they developed a strong interest in both. This development initiated and shaped the modern pastoral care movement.

b. The four pioneers. Seward Hiltner, whose early work was with the Council for Clinical Training and the Federal Council of Churches Commission on Religion and Health, represented both the influence of clinical training for clergy and the concern for the relation of religion and health. Hiltner's first book, *Religion and Health* (1943), expressed both of these formative concerns of the pastoral counseling movement. His second book, *Pastoral Counseling* (1949), was both an announcement that the modern day of pastoral counseling had dawned and, for many years, pastoral counseling's most authoritative document.

Hiltner was joined, in the modern development of pastoral counseling, by three other "gospel writers": Carroll Wise, Paul Johnson, and Wayne Oates. In the fifties and sixties each had a significant professorship in a theological seminary which graduated both practitioners and professors of pastoral counseling. Hiltner had, per-

haps, the broadest following because of his regular editorials and articles in the popular monthly journal, *Pastoral Psychology*. During the fifties and early sixties pastoral counseling was the "glamour discipline" of theological education, and pastoral care, in contrast to the more carefully distinguished definitions of today, was popularly viewed as a type of counseling.

Although there were significant differences in the theories and methods among the four modern pioneers of pastoral counseling, all were concerned with making a sharp distinction between counseling and the advice-giving and didactic instruction which had long been associated with pastoral ministry to individuals. Hiltner advocated what he called "eductive" counseling which emphasized "calling forth" the concerns and problem-solving resources of the counselee and facilitating the counselee's "working them through" rather than the pastor's telling the counselee what to do. Hiltner's method was often identified with Carl Rogers's "non-directive" (and later, "client-centered") therapy, but Hiltner insisted that his theory developed independently of Rogers.

Hiltner, Wise, Johnson, and Oates were all significantly influenced by psychoanalytic theory and practice, although Wise exhibits this influence most explicitly. He focused on the importance of the counseling *relationship* and described *insight* as its goal (1951). Johnson and Wise were both significantly influenced by philosophical personalism, but in Johnson (1953) the personalist influence is more evident. He advocated what he called "responsive counseling" and made more use of interpersonal theory of a Sullivanian type than of psychoanalysis. Oates (1974), on the other hand, like Wise (though in a different way) focused on the importance of pastoral identity and relationship as the key emphases of method. He used the free church tradition as an argument against pastoral dogmatism and in favor of responsiveness to the counselee's concerns, which brought him close to the other pioneers in methodological outcome, though he took a different route to get there.

c. The AAPC and recent theorists. The emergence of the American Association of Pastoral Counselors (AAPC) in 1963 was a significant factor in the further development of modern pastoral counseling (Van Wagner). Although Hiltner and Oates were publicly skeptical and critical of the new organization, it has served both as a context for the development of new leadership in the pastoral care movement and as a forum for discussion and debate about the nature of pastoral counseling and its relationship to religious groups and to secular psychotherapy.

Howard Clinebell, the first president of AAPC, emerged as a new leader in the pastoral counseling movement in the mid-sixties. Clinebell's published "debates" with Hiltner, his organizational leadership, and his enthusiastic carrying of the "gospel" of pastoral counseling to countries outside the U. S. all established him as the pastoral counseling leader of the late sixties and seventies. The first edition of Clinebell's *Basic Types of Pastoral Counseling* (1966), broadened the understanding of pastoral counseling to include a variety of psychological procedures and (probably unintentionally) raised the question which became pervasive in the field: "Is there no critical principle to distinguish what is and what is not pastoral counseling?" Certainly the pioneers had dealt with this question in their constructive efforts, but Clinebell's multiplication of "types" and the development of pastoral counseling training programs and certification procedures within AAPC raised it even more persuasively.

Recent efforts to discuss pastoral counseling systematically (Patton, 1983, and Gerkin, 1984) have returned to some of the old ground plowed by the pioneers while also breaking new ground, both theoretically and practically. Patton has attempted to develop a theory of pastoral counseling based on a normative concept of the pastoral relationship—"relational humanness." Gerkin has made use of hermeneutical theory from philosophy and biblical studies to develop an image of the pastoral counselor as interpreter—one skilled at discerning the story within "the living human document" and its relation to the larger story of the tradition of faith.

The emergence of books on pastoral counseling by Roman Catholic authors (e.g., Natale, Estadt) has underscored for the first time some of the Protestant assumptions of the pastoral counseling movement. The differences between Protestant and Catholic approaches to pastoral counseling have not been systematically discussed, perhaps because of an overconcern for ecumenical cooperation within the pastoral care professional organizations. However, discussion of these differences represents one of the growing edges of the pastoral counseling movement. The focus of that discussion is on the relationship of the pastor's personal and professional identity and how the central image of ministry in each tradition is related to the practice of counseling.

3. Basic Elements in Pastoral Counseling. Pastoral counseling uses both psychological and theological resources to deepen its understanding of the pastoral relationship. Although there is no one method to be mastered, the norm of the relationship to the "person" of a pastoral counselor, related to and representative of the religious community, is influential in all elements of the counseling process.

a. Initial structuring and evaluation. i. Intake and referral. Seward Hiltner (1949) used the term "precounseling" for what is here referred to as "structuring" and in many mental health settings as the "intake" process. Whatever the terminology, it is one of the most important and most frequently neglected elements in the pastoral counseling process. The emphasis in a great deal of counseling training upon what is and is not a good verbal response to what a counselee says has contributed to this neglect. Structuring and evaluation, which are done early in the counseling process, are intended to broaden the focus of the counseling or develop the context in which it takes place. They help to determine whether the counselee's concern is one which can best be addressed with the pastor or with another helping person. The pastor may simply not be able to offer what is wanted or needed. Moreover, the way the pastor understands the counselee may suggest that there needs to be a referral to another helping person because of the pastor's lack of time, limited training, or the nature of his or her relationship to the counselee within the parish or other institution (Oglesby).

As the term suggests, structuring emphasizes the structure or context of the pastoral counseling; i.e., it emphasizes developing the relationship within which the problem is shared, more than identifying a problem to be solved. In structuring, the pastor is also assisting persons in recognizing their need for help and affirming their humanness in asking for it. This recognition helps to shift the focus of the counseling from the problem to the relationship.

ii. "Magic questions." Perhaps the most useful structuring tools for the pastor are what have been called the "magic questions" (Patton, 1983). These questions, used in some form by all the mental health disciplines, are: "What are you looking for?" "Why now?" and "Why me?" The pastor needs to give the parishioner or counselee an opportunity to ventilate his or her concerns and thereby reduce the anxiety associated with them; but in order to understand how those concerns might be dealt with, the "magic questions" are necessary for ordering the data in an understandable way. Briefly described, the function of the first question is to allow both parties in the relationship to deal, not with everything, but with something in particular. The second question can enable the counselee to focus the concern further. The problem probably did not always exist but began at some time and therefore can end. The third question emphasizes the importance of the relationship in pastoral counseling but also begins to put realistic limits on what might be expected of the pastor.

iii. Unit of care. Another significant dimension of structuring is determining the unit of care. Can the concern which the counselee brings be dealt with most effectively individually, with both husband and wife present, or with all those present who live in the household? The pastor is generally better equipped to determine this than the person asking for help. Clinical training and supervision can assist the pastor in taking responsibility for this dimension of structuring. Having the appropriate persons involved in the counseling process is often more important than what is said in the interview.

Evaluation or diagnosis in pastoral counseling is also a contextual issue. Most importantly it means not losing touch with the larger issues in the lives of persons in the process of attending to their specific concerns. Certainly pastors who specialize in counseling and psychotherapy need the understanding of diagnosis offered by the mental health disciplines; but all pastoral counseling involves maintaining an awareness of the picture a person paints of him or herself and finding appropriate ways to share that awareness in the counseling process. The pastor has a special interest in and commitment to religious concerns (Pruyser). Yet his or her ongoing diagnostic concern is to formulate ways to allow persons to see the larger picture of themselves in relation to religious and other issues, not to classify them in a particular way.

b. Pastoral relationship. The most important ability of a pastoral counselor is the capacity to offer an honest, caring relationship. The relationship itself provides the counselee a direct and personal connection to the religious community and the values it represents. The pastor may or may not know a great deal about the problem that the counselee presents. In most cases, the counselee has

enough knowledge to deal with the problem. What he or she usually needs, therefore, is a context (relationship) within which the resources necessary to deal with the problem can be mobilized. Normatively, pastoral counseling offers a relationship to a person, the pastoral counselor, who represents religious faith and who is disciplined and honest in his or her caring.

The pastoral counseling relationship offers experience with a person who represents maturity in the faith and who has the emotional capacity to be a parent. Whatever the chronological age, the pastoral counselor needs to be emotionally and spiritually "middle-aged," having the capacity to facilitate the development of another rather than needing to do something to prove his or her own adequacy. Pastors receive more anger and more affection than they deserve because, inevitably, they represent other important persons in the lives of their parishioners and counselees (the "transference" phenomen). Learning to deal with this phenomenon in a way appropriate to the context for one's ministry is a major concern in any adequate education for pastoral counseling.

The other "most important" ability of the pastoral counselor is the capacity to care in a disciplined and honest way. The caring is disciplined in the sense that the pastor must be personal but have his or her personal needs met in other relationships. It must be honest in the sense of genuinely offering to the counselee an example of what it is to be human.

c. Pastoral counseling process. Broadly speaking, what happens in pastoral counseling is the telling of stories, genuinely understanding them as they are presented, and interpreting them in the light of the religious community's larger story of life's meaning. It usually involves assisting the counselee to experience and interpret new possibilities of selfhood, relationship and behavior. It is the pastoral relationship, however, which is basic in enabling counselees to move toward the fundamental humanness of telling their stories rather than presenting all the bad things that have happened to them.

The pastor's skill as a counselor is expressed primarily through the ability to be significantly related to the counselee. Relatedness is expressed in the pastoral counseling process through the counselor's skill in hearing and accurately understanding the story as it is presented, and in beginning to reinterpret it in terms that present the counselee as one with significant responsibility for the events of his or her life. Both dimensions of the process are equally important. What the counselee says must be understood accurately enough to affirm the value of who he or she is as a person, but it must also be enriched through the communication of the pastor's understanding of the counselee. Moreover, the pastor's role and function as representative of the story of faith enables him or her to reinterpret the counselee's story in the light of the faith's understanding of who a person related to God really is. The interpretive function in pastoral counseling is clearly relational. It is not bringing symbols and stories from outside, but as Gerkin (1984) suggests, it represents a "fusion of the horizons" of pastoral counselor, counselee, and community of faith.

d. Termination. As with any process, the process of pastoral counseling involves termination, sometimes before there has been any effective resolution of the concern which originally brought the counselee to the pastor. Premature termination usually occurs because the counselee is unable to generate a realistic hope that the counseling process can relieve the pain for which the counselee sought help. Termination when the counseling has been useful to the counselee most often occurs at two points: (1) when the presenting problem has in some way been "solved," the pain of the situation relieved and the counselee decides that is all that he or she wants; (2) when the counselee has dealt with both the presenting problem and the related "larger" issues of life and faith. In the latter case, when the result has been more satisfying both to counselee and counselor, termination in pastoral counseling is less decisive and less important than in other types of psychotherapy. Because the pastoral counselor, more clearly than other therapists, represents an ongoing community and belief system which claims relevance for all of life and not just its crises, it is sometimes difficult to identify just when termination occurs. Pastoral counselees can maintain at least a symbolic relationship to the counselor through their relationship to the religious community, and they are more likely to return, not inappropriately, to their pastoral counselor for further consultation regarding subsequent events in their lives.

4. **Education for Pastoral Counseling.** Pastoral counseling education is provided through seminary courses that deal with the pastor's broad ministry of pastoral care and the more specific ministry of pastoral counseling. Because pastoral counseling is primarily the offering of a relationship, however, whatever level of competence the pastor seeks in his or her counseling ministry education for it is more interpersonal than didactic, involving at least as much personal struggle and growth as academic training. Pastoral role, function, and identity may be explored in CPE under the auspices of the Association for Clinical Pastoral Education (ACPE). One's own personal style, ability to relate to others, personal story, and strengths can best be explored with a competent psychotherapist who may or may not be a pastor. Specialized education in pastoral counseling beyond the seminary course level may be obtained in training centers accredited by the AAPC, many of which are related to theologically based graduate programs.

Bibliography. American Association of Pastoral Counselors, *Handbook.* J. S. Bonnell, *Pastoral Psychiatry* (1938). W. A. Clebsch and C. R. Jaekle, *Pastoral Care in Historical Perspective* (1964). H. Clinebell, *Basic Types of Pastoral Care and Counseling* (1966). B. K. Estadt, *Pastoral Counseling* (1983). C. V. Gerkin, *The Living Human Document* (1984). S. Hiltner, *Religion and Health* (1943); *Pastoral Counseling* (1949). S. Hiltner and L. G. Colston, *The Context of Pastoral Counseling* (1961). E. B. Holifield, *A History of Pastoral Care in America: From Salvation to Self-Realization* (1983); P. Johnson, *Psychology of Pastoral Care* (1953). S. Natale, *Pastoral Counseling: Reflections and Concerns* (1977). W. Oates, *Pastoral Counseling* (1974). W. B. Oglesby, *Referral in Pastoral Counseling* (1968). T. Oden, *Care of Souls in the Classic Tradition* (1984). J. Patton, *Pastoral Counseling: A Ministry of the Church* (1983), "The New Language of Pastoral Counseling," in G. L. Borchert and A. D. Lester, eds., *Spiritual Dimensions of Pastoral Care* (1985). P. Pruyser, *The Minister as Diagnostician* (1976). C. Schneider, "Faith Development Theory and Pastoral Diagnosis: Promise and Problems" in C. R. Dykstra and S. Parks eds., *Faith Development and Fowler* (1986). C. Schneider, C. A. Van Wagner, "The AAPC: The Beginning Years, 1963–65," *J. of Pastoral Care* (1983), 163–79. C. A. Wise, *Pastoral Counseling: Its Theory and Practice* (1951).

J. PATTON

PASTORAL CARE (History, Traditions, and Issues); PASTORAL COUNSELING MOVEMENT; PASTORAL COUNSELOR; PASTORAL PSYCHOTHERAPY; SPECIALIZATION IN PASTORAL CARE. *See also* CHRISTOTHERAPY; COUNSELING, ROMAN CATHOLIC; ECUMENICAL RELATIONSHIPS IN THE PASTORAL CARE AND COUNSELING MOVEMENTS; EDUCATION FOR PASTORAL CARE AND COUNSELING; EMPIRICAL RESEARCH IN PASTORAL CARE AND COUNSELING; JOURNALS IN PASTORAL CARE AND COUNSELING; PASTORAL THEOLOGY; *also* CONSULTATION; FEELING, THOUGHT, AND ACTION IN PASTORAL COUNSELING; FEES; LEGAL DIMENSIONS; SUPERVISION; REFERRAL. *Compare* COUNSELING AND PSYCHOTHERAPY (Comparative Concepts); JUDAISM AND PSYCHOLOGY; LAY PASTORAL CARE AND COUNSELING; PSYCHOLOGY AND PSYCHOTHERAPY (East-West Comparison); PSYCHOLOGY IN AMERICAN RELIGION; PSYCHOTHERAPY; RELIGION AND PSYCHOTHERAPY; SPIRITUAL DIRECTION; THEORY AND PSYCHOTHERAPY. *Biography:* BONNELL; CLINEBELL; HILTNER; JOHNSON; OATES; WISE.

PASTORAL COUNSELING, CERTIFICATION IN. *See* CERTIFICATION.

PASTORAL COUNSELING, ECONOMICS OF. In the early 1960s, a major shift occurred in the thinking about the funding of pastoral counseling centers and the financial support for pastoral counselors.

Prior to 1960, pastoral counseling was carried on largely in local parish settings by clergy who comprised the staffs of those institutions and by chaplains at various mental and physical health facilities. Counseling was provided to persons free of charge; that is, the church or health institution itself paid all remuneration received by the counselor. In the late 1950s and early 1960s, some pastoral counselors began to charge fees to those who made use of their services. Roman Catholic and Jewish congregations continued to follow the practice of meeting the needs largely of parishioners and not asking them for additional contributions, while a theological debate about the charging of fees was waged mainly in the Protestant community. Some argued that the churches should not charge fees to anyone who sought pastoral counseling (Seward Hiltner; Ernest Bruder), while others argued that pastoral counseling could not be funded solely by the existing sources being utilized by the churches (Carroll A. Wise; Charles R. Jaekle), In the mid 1960s, the American Association of Pastoral Counselors adopted a code of ethics that permitted the charging of fees to those who made use of pastoral counseling services while requiring members not to turn anyone away because of inability to pay. The trend toward financial support for pastoral counseling programs being shifted from the institution to the consumer of the services was influenced by three factors: the trend toward specialization in ministry; the increasing professionalism and subsequent improved training of clergy/counseling specialists; the demand from the general public for increased mental health services under religious auspices.

Pastoral counselors are generally paid in one of two ways: a fixed salary and benefits package; or, a percentage of the fees charged and collected; or some combination of these two. Each plan has practical and theological disadvantages and drawbacks.

The fixed salary and benefits package plan offers an institution the advantage of planning a fixed budget for a particular fiscal year. In addition, this plan helps to avoid any temptation on the part of the counselor to see only those that can afford to pay a higher fee or the additional temptation of putting in too many clinical hours. Theoretically, this model provides a clear way to see persons from all income levels and receives little theological criticism. Practically, however, such a payment model has resulted in a fixed budget which then has to be met during any particular year regardless of income generated from client fees. This model has necessitated finding other funding sources. On the other hand, remuneration derived from a percentage of the fees charged has solved the practical problem of a large budget with deficits to be made up at the end of the year. Since payment is only made on a percentage of that fee which is collected, theoretically there are no deficits at the end of any particular budget year.

The shortfall in any particular institutional or counseling center budget is usually made up from several sources: grants from foundations and individuals; direct solicitation from interested individuals in a community; financial contributions from church members; and services volunteered by interested parties and persons who are unable to pay a full fee. Occasionally, some counseling centers have used special fund-raising events and direct mail solicitation in order to enhance their revenues. However, the largest contribution seems to be in terms of the space and related facilities provided by host churches for counseling centers or for individual pastoral counselors. This "subsidy" has resulted in widespread use of a sliding fee scale where a fee a counselee has to pay is based on family size and income. Fees often range from as low as one dollar to a fee equal to that being charged for counseling or psychotherapy services in the private sector of a given community. Some have argued that this sliding fee approach should be altered in order to meet the objection from certain sectors that high-fee clients are being asked to make an involuntary contribution in the form of a subsidy to low fee-paying clients. Some organizations have instituted a variation of the sliding fee scale. A calculation of the actual cost of delivering a unit of service is made. A voluntary fund is established from sources other than fees to subsidize any fees charged which are lower than the actual cost of delivery.

Bibliography. J. C. Carr, J. E. Hinkle, D. M. Moss, III, eds., *The Organization and Administration of Pastoral Counseling Centers* (1981).

A. R. GILMORE

COVENANT AND CONTRACT IN PASTORAL COUNSELING; FEES IN PASTORAL COUNSELING. *See also* LEGAL DIMENSIONS OF PASTORAL CARE AND COUNSELING; PASTORAL COUNSELING CENTER. *Compare* ETHICS AND PASTORAL CARE.

PASTORAL COUNSELING, EDUCATION IN. *See* EDUCATION IN PASTORAL CARE AND COUNSELING; SPECIALIZATION IN PASTORAL CARE.

PASTORAL COUNSELING, ETHICS OF. *See* ETH-ICS, PROFESSIONAL; ETHICS AND PASTORAL CARE.

PASTORAL COUNSELING, FEES IN. *See* FEES IN PASTORAL COUNSELING.

PASTORAL COUNSELING, JEWISH. *See* JEWISH CARE AND COUNSELING.

PASTORAL COUNSELING, JOURNALS IN. *See* JOURNALS IN PASTORAL CARE AND COUNSELING.

PASTORAL COUNSELING, LAY. *See* LAY PASTO-RAL CARE AND COUNSELING.

PASTORAL COUNSELING, LEGAL DIMEN-SIONS OF. *See* LEGAL DIMENSIONS OF PASTORAL CARE AND COUNSELING.

PASTORAL COUNSELING, METHODS OF. *See* PASTORAL COUNSELING.

PASTORAL COUNSELING, PSYCHOLOGY OF. *See* PASTORAL COUNSELING; PASTORAL PSYCHOLOGY, DISCIPLINE OF; PASTORAL PSYCHOTHERAPY.

PASTORAL COUNSELING, RESEARCH IN. *See* EMPIRICAL RESEARCH IN PASTORAL CARE AND COUNSEL-ING.

PASTORAL COUNSELING, ROMAN CATHO-LIC. *See* COUNSELING, ROMAN CATHOLIC; ROMAN CATHOLIC PASTORAL CARE.

PASTORAL COUNSELING, SOCIOLOGY OF. *See* SOCIOLOGY OF RELIGIOUS AND PASTORAL CARE.

PASTORAL COUNSELING, SPECIALIZATION IN. *See* SPECIALIZATION IN PASTORAL CARE. *See also* PASTORAL COUNSELOR.

PASTORAL COUNSELING, STANDARDS FOR. *See* STANDARDS FOR PASTORAL COUNSELING.

PASTORAL COUNSELING, THEOLOGY OF. *See* PASTORAL THEOLOGY; THEOLOGY AND PSYCHOTHER-APY.

PASTORAL COUNSELING, TRAINING PRO-GRAMS IN. *See* CLINICAL PASTORAL EDUCATION; EDU-CATION IN PASTORAL CARE AND COUNSELING; SPECIAL-IZATION IN PASTORAL CARE.

PASTORAL COUNSELING CENTER. A setting or context in which pastoral counselors engage in the spe-cialized ministry of pastoral counseling, pastoral psycho-therapy, and other work of personal healing or growth, often in collaboration with other mental health profes-sionals, utilizing the insights and principles from the disciplines of theology and the behavioral sciences. A

pastoral counseling center is an institutional extension and an expression of the healing and therapeutic ministry of the church. The American Association of Pastoral Counselors (AAPC) has noted that the historic roles of pastoral counseling centers have been to serve as "pri-mary sources of prevention, education, evaluation, appropriate referral, and psychotherapy in the field of wholeness in personal and interpersonal relationships."

1. **Organizational Models of Pastoral Counseling Centers.** There is a diversity of styles in the organization and administration of pastoral counseling centers. Even within the same model there can be significant differ-ences and relative uniqueness. There is also considerable overlap among the various models, and the following list of models developed by Carr and Hinkle (1981) is not exhaustive.

(1) Parish staff counselor. The professional pastoral counselor is a member of the parish staff with the constit-uency being primarily the members of the church.

(2) Parish-based pastoral counseling service. This model has an ecumenical outreach to the community, usually with an autonomous board of directors and a mental health advisory committee.

(3) Community-based pastoral counseling center. This service is organized on an ecumenical basis utilizing varied ecclesiastical and mental health organizations and professionals. A representative board of directors and a professional advisory committee are usually involved.

(4) Pastoral counseling group practice. In this model two or more pastoral counselors work together in a church or private office in a collegial relationship which they define in a variety of contractual ways. Administra-tive and clinical responsibilities are determined by the people involved in the group practice.

(5) Satellite pastoral counseling service. An existing pastoral counseling center makes a contractual arrange-ment with a church, group of churches or a judicatory for the counseling services of one or more of its staff members for a determined amount of time each week outside of the central office.

(6) Seminary and university counseling services. In one type of this model the pastoral counselor serves only those who hold membership in the seminary or univer-sity community in some manner. A second type, which is often involved with training programs within the center, reaches out to the larger community beyond the educational institution.

(7) Hospital outpatient pastoral counseling services. This center may be directly connected with the pastoral care department or chaplaincy of the hospital as an extended ministry to the community served by the hos-pital on a fee-for-services-rendered basis. Other hospitals have a completely separate arm for the pastoral counsel-ing center which can offer pastoral psychotherapy to the community at large, various educational programs for clergy and others, and in-house educational experiences for various professionals.

(8) Judicatory counseling service. Various church judicatories have organized pastoral counseling centers and services for clergy and other church leaders and their families to deal with their psychological and spiritual problems.

855

(9) Denominational social service agency. Pastoral counselors have sometimes been added to the staffs of denominational social service agencies. Marital and family therapy are often central to the service provided by a pastoral counselor in this context.

(10) Pastoral counseling in church information centers. Some denominations have included a pastoral counselor in their centers where the major context for the pastoral counselor would be in education, prevention and referral. Usually there is little or no long-term pastoral psychotherapy done in this context.

(11) Association-based pastoral counseling service. Some pastoral counselors function in a private practice setting but are accountable for their ministry of pastoral counseling to the local association of the denomination. The practices of such ministries and the procedures of accountability for them are agreed upon by the association and the pastoral counselors.

2. Accreditation. There are numerous ways by which quality control in pastoral counseling centers is handled. However, the AAPC is the major professional organization responsible for quality control of pastoral counseling centers in the U.S. In order to become an accredited service center of the Association the following standards have to be met: (1) The pastoral counseling center must be responsible to a board representing primarily the religious community and others committed to the work of the center, and the board must establish a general policy for the center. (2) There must be multiple staff members, including at least two pastoral counselors, with each staff member certified by his or her professional discipline. (3) The director must be a diplomate or fellow of the AAPC. (4) The center must demonstrate responsible policies and practices in its professional and administrative work (such as personnel, record keeping, fees, referral, supervision, confidentiality, etc.). (5) The counseling center staff should not work in isolation, but they should be involved in regular consultation with other qualified psychotherapeutic professionals. (6) The center should have a sound financial structure and a plan for long-range financing. (7) The center should have appropriate fee scales and provision to subsidize the counseling of persons unable to pay. (8) The center should commit itself to the standards and code of ethics of the AAPC.

Accreditation of a center involves an extensive self-study according to the guidelines of the AAPC as well as a rigorous site visit of the center by three well-qualified pastoral counseling specialists. Full accreditation to a pastoral counseling center is given for a seven-year period with annual reports about the center to be filed with the Centers and Training Committee of the Association. Renewal of the accreditation after the seven-year period is dependent upon satisfactory completion of another self-study and a new site visit.

3. Training Opportunities in Pastoral Counseling Centers. Pastoral counseling centers offer varied training and educational opportunities for their constituencies. Training is usually offered for three groups, including seminarians and parish ministers, specialists in pastoral counseling, and laity. Education and training for seminarians and parish ministers are often focused on enhancing the pastoral care and counseling skills of those persons by offering such things as case conferences,

supervision, consultation groups, and continuing education events. Persons preparing for specialized ministries in pastoral counseling may find supervised internships and graduate training offered through pastoral counseling centers. Pastoral counseling centers also may offer workshops and seminars for laypersons, often with the goal of enhancing the ministry of care by laity in the parish.

Some pastoral counseling centers seek accreditation for their training program from the AAPC. In addition to meeting the accreditation standards for service centers, they must have an interdisciplinary faculty of at least three persons, a minimum of three students, a supervisory program that guarantees quality control, periodic review of the trainees and the program, plus a broad and deep program of instruction in personality theory, counseling methodologies, assessment skills, implications of religious experience for pastoral counseling, etc. Site visits for training programs in pastoral counseling centers are conducted under the auspices of the national Centers and Training Committee of the AAPC. Accreditation is for a seven-year period.

Training programs and pastoral counseling centers wrestle with a wide variety of issues in preparing pastoral counselors, including the integration of theology and the behaviorial sciences, and the integration of prophetic and social justice concerns.

4. Selected Administrative Issues. Pastoral counseling centers are usually directed administratively by a person who has been clinically and theologically trained but who often has little prior experience in management and administration. However, there is a growing group of professional administrative leaders in pastoral counseling centers who are seeking to bring the best knowledge from the world of sound management practices to bear upon their administrative roles and functions.

Among the more common administrative issues are: (1) Developing a sound financial base for the establishment and long-range growth of the center, involving the management and securing of fees, third party payments, gifts, and grants; (2) the evolving size and pace of development of a center, sometimes including the growth of satellite centers; (3) the recruitment, cultivation and nurturing of a creative board of directors; (4) personnel decisions for clinical and non-clinical staff; (5) establishment and expansion of training programs; (6) public relations to inform the church and the community of the center's ministry; (7) research and evaluation of services provided; (8) the quality of life within the center itself and among the staff members.

5. Center for Evangelism Incognito. The pastoral counseling center has been a key institutional development of the ministry of the church during the past three decades. Since there were only ten pastoral counseling centers before 1950, James Lapsley has called the mushrooming of the pastoral counseling movement since that time a "mid-century phenomenon." The phenomenal growth of the number of centers established and the number of staff members employed is an indication of the tremendous need for this ministry of the church in our communities. The growth of such centers has led Carroll Wise to note in his foreword that "clearly a new arm of the church is being established" (in Carr, Hinkle, and

Moss, 1981). While many pastoral counselors and church leaders would not identify the development of pastoral counseling centers as part of the mainstream of the evangelistic thrust of the church, nevertheless evangelism incognito has been taking place in the various expressions of the good news that emanate from the ministries performed in pastoral counseling centers. John Patton (1983) speaks of the pastoral counseling center as a "halfway house" where people can carry out their search for meaning and healing in a spiritual context without "having to identify with a particular religious community." The pastoral counseling center has provided a locus for persons inside and outside of the institutional church to discover life-giving and transforming relationships and experiences in the course of their journey. "Thousands of persons who go to pastoral counseling centers would not go near a parish church. For thousands of others the pastoral counseling center is an intermediate church structure that can be used as an entryway to a more traditional form of Christian community" (Patton, 1981). As the pastoral counseling movement continues to come of age, the healing, transforming, and therapeutic dimensions of the ministries in pastoral counseling centers move from evangelism incognito to an established role as an extension ministry of the church itself.

Bibliography. J. C. Carr, J. E. Hinkle, and D. M. Moss III, eds., *The Organization and Administration of Pastoral Counseling Centers*, 11(1981), pp. 24–37. C. Hathorne, "A Critical Analysis of Protestant Church Counseling Centers," unpublished Th.D. dissertation, Boston University (1960). J. N. Lapsley, "Pastoral Counseling Centers: A Mid-Century Phenomenon," *Pastoral Psychology*, 13:2 (1963), 43–52. J. Patton, *Pastoral Counseling — A Ministry of the Church*, (1983); "Pastoral Counseling Comes of Age," *Christian Century* 98(1981) 229–31.

M. R. JORDAN

PASTORAL COUNSELING; PASTORAL COUNSELING, ECONOMICS OF; PASTORAL COUNSELING MOVEMENT. *See also* ECUMENICAL RELATIONSHIPS IN THE PASTORAL CARE AND COUNSELING MOVEMENTS. *Compare* ECCLESIOLOGY AND PASTORAL CARE.

PASTORAL COUNSELING MOVEMENT.

A twentieth century development which has made the use of counseling and psychotherapy by clergy an increasingly prominent aspect of their work. This development began and has had its major expressions among Protestant ministers in North America. The movement has had two major dimensions—the increasing practice of and competence in counseling by generalist clergy, and the emergence and flourishing of a new speciality within the ministry called "pastoral counseling." This innovative movement has produced a vital new expression of the century-spanning heritage of the cure of souls ("cure" meaning both care and healing).

1. **Background.** As with any complex social development, a variety of interrelated factors contributed to the emergence and shaping of the pastoral counseling movement. These factors (with names of persons associated with them) include: The growing interest since about 1870 in applying psychology to the work of ministry (e.g., Elwood Worcester and the Emmanuel Movement); the flowering of psychology of religion in the early decades of this century (E. D. Starbuck, William James, J. H. Leuba, G. S. Hall, Sigmund Freud); the increasing use of psychological and counseling insights by religious education teachers and writers during the post-World War I surge of interest in psychology (George Albert Coe, Harrison Elliott); the use of psychological and counseling approaches in ministry by prominent liberal pastors (Harry Emerson Fosdick, John Sutherland Bonnell, Norman Vincent Peale, Leslie Weatherhead) beginning in the 1920s and 1930s. Courses in pastoral counseling were taught in some seminary religious education departments as early as 1921. Several pioneering books on the subject appeared in the 1930s — e.g. Charles Holman, *The Cure of Souls: A Socio-Psychological Approach (1932); Karl Stolz, Pastoral Psychology* (1932); J. S. Bonnell, *Pastoral Psychiatry* (1938); Richard Cabot and Russell Dicks, *The Art of Ministering to the Sick* (1936). Rollo May's *The Art of Counseling* (1939) grew out of lectures given to pastors.

2. **Beginnings.** The immediate precursor and launching pad of the pastoral counseling movement was the Clinical Pastoral Education (CPE) movement beginning in the mid-twenties with the pioneering work of Richard Cabot, Anton Boisen, Philip Guiles, and Russell Dicks. This training in ministering to persons in crises under intensive supervision gradually had a transforming impact on the theory and teaching of pastoral psychology and counseling. America's surging interest in psychology and psychotherapy during World War II (including the discovery by some eight thousand chaplains of their pressing need for counseling skills) continued after the war, providing a fertile social context within which pastoral counseling flowered in the late forties and fifties. Intrigued with the power of psychology, Americans sought counseling, including help from clergy, in increasing numbers.

Major books shaping this formative period of the movement included Dicks's *Pastoral Work and Personal Counseling* (1944); Hiltner's *Pastoral Counseling* (1949), Wise's *Pastoral Counseling: Theory and Practice* (1951); Oates's *The Christian Pastor* (1951); and Johnson's *Psychology of Pastoral Care* (1953). These intellectual leaders of the new movement reflected the influence of Carl Rogers (*Counseling and Psychotherapy*, 1942) and Freud, and in varying degrees, Fromm, Horney, and Sullivan.

3. **Development.** The movement flourished with increasing vigor through the fifties and the sixties, fed by the abundance of new therapies, the encounter group and human potential movement, and most importantly, the new generation of CPE-trained teachers of pastoral care who brought depth psychology and clinical methods of counseling into seminary classrooms. Articles and books on pastoral counseling proliferated, including two thriving professional journals — *Pastoral Psychology* and *The Journal of Pastoral Care*. Increasing numbers of seminarians and clergy were receiving CPE and instruction in pastoral counseling. Findings of a national survey published in 1957 revealed that forty-two percent of Americans who had sought help with personal problems had turned to clergy for that help. (A comparable study two decades later found that thirty-nine percent still reported seeking pastoral counseling, in spite of dramatic increases

in community mental health facilities during that period).

In the sixties and early seventies there was a broadening of the earlier Rogerian and psychoanalytic models of pastoral counseling with the introduction of resources from ego psychology, crisis intervention methods, the newer nonanalytic therapies, group therapy, and role-relationship couple counseling (e.g. C. W. Stewart's *The Minister as Marriage Counselor,* 1961; Clinebell's *Basic Types of Pastoral Counseling,* 1965; Robert Leslie's *Sharing Groups in the Church,* 1971). It had become clear that most counseling by parish pastors is short-term crisis help and not depth psychotherapy.

4. Emergence of Specialty. The specialty of pastoral counseling grew out of two interrelated developments during the psychological "boom" of the post-World War II period. One was the establishment of graduate programs in pastoral psychology and counseling with rigorous academic and clinical components—e.g. by Johnson at Boston University School of Theology; Wise at Garrett; Hiltner at Chicago Divinity School and later at Princeton; Oates at Southern Baptist Theological Seminary in Louisville; and David Eitzen at University of Southern California's graduate department of religion (which became the School of Theology at Claremont). An influential, psychoanalytically oriented program in pastoral counseling was established by the American Foundation of Religion and Psychiatry with Fred Kuether as director of training. Clergy trained in these graduate programs developed both depth psychological understanding and psychotherapeutic skills.

The second factor in the emergence of specialists was the burgeoning development of church-related counseling centers in the fifties and sixties. The establishment of the American Association of Pastoral Counselors (AAPC) in 1963 was a response to a pressing need to develop practice standards for the nearly one hundred centers and training standards for the pastoral counselors who helped staff them. Graduate programs and CPE had created a pool of clergy with advanced clinical and academic training. This undoubtedly encouraged the development of new centers. Many of the centers established training programs which both helped increase the counseling competencies of parish clergy and train more specialists. The existence and growth of AAPC has stimulated and guided the development of the new specialty by providing rigorous standards, professional networking and identity undergirding.

5. Broader Developments. American CPE centers and pastoral counseling graduate programs have attracted many clergy-trainees from Europe and other parts of the world during recent decades. Many of these have returned to their homelands to establish training programs similar to American models. Thus the pastoral counseling movement has gradually become internationalized.

The pastoral counseling emphasis has developed much more slowly in Roman Catholic and Jewish than in American Protestant seminaries. But several Catholic authors have written on this subject (e.g., M. J. O'Brien, *An Introduction to Pastoral Counseling,* 1968). Training clergy as psychologists rather than integrating this training with theological disciplines in seminary graduate programs has been the most common Catholic approach.

6. Present Trends — Future Directions. The pastoral counseling field is in ferment. A variety of trends have emerged within the past decade. Some of these may point to directions in which the movement will continue to evolve. Contemporary trends include: a lively interest in discovering and developing the potentialities of the spiritual center and the ethical, theological, ecclesiological, and pastoral care context of pastoral counseling, including the ancient traditions of spiritual direction and healing; an increasing interest in systems- and relationship-oriented ways of understanding human problems and facilitating healing and growth; a determination to bridge the chasm between personal and societal healing by using counseling methods (individual and group) to empower people to correct the social injustices which are the hidden roots of many personal problems; a growing commitment to transcend the middle-class, Protestant, Caucasian, North American, largely male origins and limitations of the movement by becoming more intercultural in perspective; efforts to train more women clergy in pastoral counseling and to balance the field's masculine orientation with insights from feminist theology and psychotherapy; a trend toward broadening the conceptual maps of the field by drawing on newer therapies including the "right brain" and body therapies; efforts to make pastoral counseling more wholistic by aiming at the healing and growth of *all* dimensions of human beings, not just their minds and spirits; and a commitment to strengthen the empirical research base of the pastoral counseling movement.

A final trend with sweeping implications for the future of pastoral counseling aims at incorporating such high-tech communication instruments as computers, videocassettes, cable TV, teleconferencing, and satellite communication networking in all dimensions of pastoral counseling — clinical services, training, preventive education, research, and interprofessional collaboration. Developments within the pastoral counseling movement since 1945 are remarkable indeed. Yet future potentialities for developing new springs of healing in the desert of personal and social brokenness far transcend the achievements of the past.

Bibliography. E. B. Holifield, *A History of Pastoral Care in America: From Salvation to Self-Realization* (1983). E. E. Thornton, *Professional Education for Ministry: A History of Clinical Pastoral Education* (1970). C. A. Van Wagner, *The AAPC: The Formative Years* (1986).

H. CLINEBELL

AMERICAN ASSOCIATION OF PASTORAL COUNSELORS; HISTORY OF PROTESTANT PASTORAL CARE; INTERNATIONAL PASTORAL CARE MOVEMENT; PASTORAL CARE MOVEMENT; RELIGION AND HEALTH MOVEMENT. *See also* COUNSELING, ROMAN CATHOLIC; ECUMENICAL RELATIONSHIPS IN THE PASTORAL CARE AND COUNSELING MOVEMENTS; EMMANUEL MOVEMENT; JOURNALS IN PASTORAL CARE AND COUNSELING; PASTORAL COUNSELOR; PSYCHOLOGY IN AMERICAN RELIGION. *Biography:* BOISEN; BONNELL; CABOT; COE; DICKS; ELLIOTT; FOSDICK; GUILES; HALL; HILTNER; HOLMAN; JAMES; JOHNSON; KUETHER; LEUBA; MAY; OATES; PEALE; ROGERS, CARL R.; STARBUCK; WEATHERHEAD; WISE; WORCESTER.

PASTORAL COUNSELING PROGRAMS. *See* EDUCATION IN PASTORAL CARE AND COUNSELING.

PASTORAL COUNSELOR. The term pastoral counselor is understood primarily in two ways. It refers in a generic sense to the professional role of the person offering counseling. Thus, a pastoral counselor is a pastor who, as a part of his or her ministerial responsibility, offers counseling to persons in need. In a more specific and important sense it describes the function of a pastor who practices pastoral counseling at a level of competence beyond that of the general practice of ministry and who skillfully integrates religious resources with insights from the behavioral sciences.

Four general qualifications are commonly accepted for the more specific view of the pastoral counselor: validation and accountability to the religious group which authorizes the person for such ministry, education in theology and behavioral science, professional skill in counseling/psychotherapy, and awareness of one's own personality functioning.

Validation and accountability are granted by the person's religious group. Most Christian and Jewish groups ordain persons for ministry; however, other processes are often employed to designate pastoral counseling as a specific ministry, both for ordained and nonordained persons.

Education in theology and behavioral sciences is conferred through academic degrees, usually master of divinity, master of arts, master of science, doctor of ministry, and/or doctor of philosophy.

Professional skills in counseling/psychotherapy are confirmed through supervised practice of pastoral counseling. Supervision is provided by advanced pastoral counselors as well as qualified persons in other mental health professions.

Awareness of one's own personality functioning is accomplished through psychotherapeutic investigations as well as self-learning from life experience.

A pastoral counselor integrates the general qualifications in the course of practice and continued education of ministry. The definition, standards, and review of pastoral counselors are functions of the American Association of Pastoral Counselors (AAPC), which serves as a certifying and accrediting agency for individuals and institutions that practice and teach pastoral counseling.

Bibliography. H. H. Clinebell, *Basic Types of Pastoral Care and Counseling* rev. ed. (1984). W. E. Oates, *Pastoral Counseling* (1974).

J. W. EWING

PASTORAL COUNSELING. *Compare* CHRISTIAN PSYCHOLOGIST; CHRISTIAN PSYCHOTHERAPIST; CONFESSOR; COUNSELOR; LAY PASTORAL CARE AND COUNSELING; PASTOR; SPIRITUAL DIRECTOR; SPIRITUAL MASTERS AND GUIDES.

PASTORAL EFFECTIVENESS STUDIES. *See* PASTORS, EMPIRICAL STUDIES OF; EMPIRICAL RESEARCH IN PASTORAL CARE AND COUNSELING.

PASTORAL EPISTLES. *See* NEW TESTAMENT.

PASTORAL GUIDANCE. *See* GUIDANCE, PASTORAL.

PASTORAL IDENTITY. *See* IDENTITY, PASTORAL.

PASTORAL OFFICE. A term having a broad and a narrow meaning. Both utilize the shepherding motif to illumine the nature of ordained Christian ministry.

In its broader sense pastoral office refers to everything the minister represents and does. It designates the pastor's unique public status and responsibility. Traditionally, the office has three corollaries: (a) a special calling, (b) the personal embodiment of Christian ideals, and (c) devotion to a distinctive work—the care of Christ's flock through preaching, teaching, sacramental administration, and discipline.

Since the Reformation the term has frequently been used in a narrower sense to indicate ministerial duties other than preaching. Usage has been ambiguous, and during the nineteenth century several Protestant theologians appeared to limit it specifically to pastoral care as a function distinct from preaching, religious instruction, and worship.

Current thinking manifests a decline in the notion of pastoral office. It has generally been displaced by the ascendancy of the professional model.

Bibliography. W. E. Oates, *The Christian Pastor* 3d ed. (1982), chs. 2–4. T. C. Oden, *Pastoral Theology* (1983). S. Hiltner, *Preface to Pastoral Theology* (1958).

B. VAUGHN

ECCLESIOLOGY; MINISTRY; PASTORAL CARE.

PASTORAL PERSPECTIVE. *See* CLINICAL PASTORAL PERSPECTIVE.

PASTORAL PRAYER. *See* PRAYER IN PASTORAL CARE.

PASTORAL PREACHING. *See* PREACHING.

PASTORAL PSYCHIATRY. The title of a book by John Southerland Bonnell (1938). Bonnell defined psychiatry on the basis of the primary lexical meaning of the Greek term *psyche*. He states: "Psychiatry . . . means primarily 'the healing of the soul of man,' as opposed not only to the body, but also to the mind, reason, and understanding." The term pastoral psychiatry never gained significant usage.

R. L. HESTER

PSYCHIATRY AND PASTORAL CARE; CARE OF SOULS. *Biography:* BONNELL.

PASTORAL PSYCHOLOGY, DISCIPLINE OF. A body of knowledge about human behavior which views religious beliefs and practices as integrative forces in the psychological and social dimensions of human experience.

In the U.S. and Western world the relationship between religion and psychology, up to about 1950, was one of adoption and antagonism. It was a period when clinical pastoral work was often judged according to the standards of psychology. As a result, some virtually abandoned the religious and pastoral dimensions of their work and were seen as pastoral ministers in name only. Psychologists were making progress in their attempt to be legitimized by a technological society. In this society, science assumed godlike status and those in pastoral ministry envied psychology as a science which appeared more capable of meeting human needs. In reaction to this tendency there were some who rejected psychological principles completely and claimed that pastoral psychology was, in reality, the clinical application of theological and religious truths. In between have been those who struggled with the ambiguity in search of a new methodology and a more creative approach.

One specific expression of dialogue was the emergence, during the 1950s and 1960s, of the journal *Pastoral Psychology*. Specifically aimed at the professional ministry, this journal reflected the burgeoning trend of utilizing the insights of modern psychologies in improving pastoral skills in specific areas of routine ministry. For example, care for the dying and bereaved was examined in light of new insights into the dying and grief processes, while ministry to the young, middle-aged and elderly gained from studies in human development.

The dialogue and collegiality between psychology and ministry has continued to develop. Within religious studies there is the profound impact of process and humanistic theologies with their focus on co-creatorship between God and human beings. Within psychological studies there is an increasing interest in human development and stage theory, as well as humanistic psychology with their focus on life drama as a process which unfolds from birth to death. Both of these major developments were reinforced by the gradual shifting in Western society from a world view overwhelmingly technological and scientific to a more humanistic and social-interpersonal awareness. Pastoral psychology aims at maximizing the usefulness of an ontology of the human which is shared by psychology and theology.

Contemporary pastoral psychology is making its own contributions to psychological theory most often in applied and clinical areas. For example, much creative development in pastoral psychology is seen in the area of marriage and family studies. Cooperative possibilities seem evident in combining the church's expertise with the meaning, value, and religious significance of interpersonal experience with new methodologies for exploring marriage and family which are being developed in psychology.

Pastoral psychology is providing those practitioners who specialize in the ministry of pastoral counseling with their own unique and legitimized body of knowledge. Utilized appropriately, it provides the pastoral caregiver with a more holistic or transcendent perspective. Life is seen within a larger, integrating context of purpose, meaning, and value.

E. A. HOOVER

PASTORAL CARE; PASTORAL COUNSELING; PASTORAL THEOLOGY. *See also* PSYCHOLOGY AND JUDAISM; PSYCHOLOGY IN AMERICAN RELIGION; PSYCHOLOGY OF RELIGION (Theories, Traditions, and Issues); RELIGION AND PSYCHOTHERAPY. *Compare* PASTORAL SOCIOLOGY; THEOLOGY AND PSYCHOLOGY.

PASTORAL PSYCHOTHERAPY. Psychotherapy is defined by the American Psychiatric Association as "the treatment of mental and emotional disorders based primarily on verbal and nonverbal communication with the patient"; the descriptive adjective "pastoral" denotes a

formal office of leadership in the church, usually achieved by ordination or consecration.

1. Psychotherapy. L. Wolberg's definition of psychotherapy still remains perhaps the most complete: "Psychotherapy is the treatment by psychological means of problems of an emotional nature, in which a trained person deliberately establishes a professional relationship with the patient with the object of (1) removing, modifying or retarding existing symptoms, (2) mediating disturbed patterns of behavior, and (3) promoting positive personality growth and development."

At one time it may have been appropriate to identify the use of the word psychotherapy only with forms of patient-therapist relationships that had insight-oriented and depth-psychological goals, such as classical psychoanalytic treatment (see Clinebell). More recently, however, the use of the term psychotherapy has broadened by much popular and professional usage to include, as Meissner and Nicholi suggest, "a wide variety of therapies that differ in intensity and duration" (see Strupp, Wise). It is no longer possible to identify the term psychotherapy with a particular psychological school or therapeutic methodology or treatment, although there may be such associations with the use of the term still prevalent in both popular and professional usage.

2. Religious Roots of Psychotherapy. C. Wise suggests that in the use of the term psychotherapy a religious practitioner is "returning to the roots of our religious tradition." Both of the Greek words which combine to make the word psychotherapy, *psyche* and *therapeuo*, are NT words. *Psyche* includes meanings of life-principle, earthly life, and soul (both as the center of the inner life of the person and as the center of life that goes beyond the earthly—see W. F. Arndt and F. Gingrich). According to N. Porteous, the NT usage "continues the old Greek usage by which it means 'vitality, life,'" and is sometimes translated as "soul" and sometimes as "life" in the KJV. *Therapeuo* is, according to H. Beyer, not used in the NT in the sense of service, but rather "in the sense of 'to heal,' and always in such a way that the reference is not to medical treatment, which might fail, but to real healing." Such healing is a demonstration of the power of the ultimate rule of God—"victory in the conflict with forces which struggle for mastery over the cosmos." If the Greek words were to be combined in this NT sense, a meaning would emerge centered around the healing of the life-force which is central to humankind both in earthly existence and beyond.

3. Pastoral. *Pastor* is seen in the NT only once, a Latin translation of *poimen* in Eph. 4:11. Opinion is divided on whether that term already implied a formal ecclesiastical office (see Throckmorton, Jeremias for differing views). *Pastoral* as an adjective generally has referred to a person who holds a formal ecclesiastical office, who then is engaged in whatever the adjective modifies. Pastoral administration, care, counseling, psychotherapy, and the like all have implied a person who holds the ecclesiastical office of pastor while doing the activity (see Hiltner and Colston).

The American Association of Pastoral Counselors has historically accepted this view of *pastor*, in that its accredited membership is open only to those persons who are "authorized by a denomination or faith group through ordination, consecration, or equivalent means to exercise specific religious leadership and service within and on behalf of the denomination or faith group."

4. Questions About Usage. As the term psychotherapy has gained in popularity among counselors in general, it has also gained in popularity among pastoral counselors. For instance, in C. Wise's 1951 book *Pastoral Counseling: Its Theory and Practice,* psychotherapy is not even listed in the index. In his 1980 book *Pastoral Psychotherapy: Theory and Practice,* the term counseling is abandoned except as a kind or type of psychotherapy, and psychotherapy becomes the normative word. A comparison of the definitions of counseling in the first book and psychotherapy in the second give credence to the hypothesis that the usage of the two words in the two books is parallel, both having to do with a process (rather than a static definition) which has the characteristics of psychotherapy as listed above. In this sense the use of psychotherapy represents an accommodation to the cultural popularity of the term, as well as a possible sense of the word having more meaningfulness in its etiology. Since in the professional literature psychotherapy has lost its narrow meaning bound by certain canons of theoretical and methodological dogma, it is a word that can be used more broadly, even allowing for the reality that its popular meaning may not be as broadly based as its meaning within the professional community. Additionally, since counseling has also expanded its base to include such things as nutritional, vocational, and financial counseling, a term which signifies a professional relationship entered into for the healing of a person's psyche, such as psychotherapy, has much to commend it. Its problem in usage might very well also be the other side of its strength, in that it does imply a formal relationship that exists in a therapist-patient sense, which might not be consistent with a particular pastor's understanding of the nature of his or her relationships with people or pastoral task.

A second current issue has to do with the definition of "pastoral." Can pastoral psychotherapy be done by people who are not in a formal office of leadership in the church, as that office is designated by ordination or consecration? There are academic programs in pastoral counseling or psychotherapy which offer an advanced degree (often two years after an undergraduate degree) with no formal seminary or theological training, and no official office of pastor in the church. In this sense, *pastoral* seems to represent an orientation to the psychotherapy process rather than a definition of the role and status of the person who is doing the psychotherapy. As to a formal office in the church, these psychotherapists are almost "para-pastoral," which is perhaps a better, although cumbersome, term. The relevant issue is whether "pastoral" signifies an office in the church or whether it signifies an attitude and orientation toward psychotherapy. In the former case, only people who are set apart in some way by the church into a formal office of the church are pastoral psychotherapists, with others forming a para-pastoral service. In the latter case, anyone who is sensitive to spiritually or theologically oriented matters could be a pastoral psychotherapist. The issue is not easily resolved, but without a resolution the nature of the formal identity of the pastoral psychotherapist will remain confusing both to the therapist and to those the therapist wishes to serve.

Bibliography. American Association of Pastoral Counselors, *Handbook* (1986). American Psychiatric Association, *A Psychiatric Glossary* (1975). W. Arndt and F. Gingrich, *A Greek-English Lexicon of the NT and Other Early Christian Literature* (1957). F. Beyer, "Therapeuo," *Theological Dictionary of the NT,* G. Kittel and G. Friedrich, eds., vol. 3 (1976), pp. 128–32. E. Beyreuther, "Shepherd," *Dictionary of NT Theology,* C. Brown, ed., vol. 3 (1976) pp. 564–69. H. C. Clinebell, Jr., *Basic Types of Pastoral Counseling* (1966). B. Grant, "Pastoral Psychotherapy and the Jesus of Q," *J. of Pastoral Care,* 34 (1980), 244–53. R. Harper, *Psychoanalysis and Psychotherapy: 36 Systems* (1939). S. Hiltner and L. Colston, *The Context of Pastoral Counseling* (1961). J. Jeremias, "Poimen," *Theological Dictionary of the NT,* G. Kittel and G. Friedrich, eds., vol. 6 (1976), pp. 485–502. J. D. Jeske, "Varieties of Approaches to Psychotherapy: Options for the Christian Psychotherapist," *J. of Psychology and Theology,* 12 (1989), 260–69. R. Langs, *Psychotherapy: A Basic Text* (1982). W. Meissner and A. Nicholi, Jr., "The Psychotherapies: Individual, Family, and Group," *The Harvard Guide to Modern Psychiatry,* A. Nicholi, Jr., ed. (1978). D. M. Moss III, "Priestcraft and Psychoanalytic Psychotherapy: Contradiction or Concordance?" *J. of Religion and Health,* 18 (1979), 181–88. N. Porteous, "Soul," *The Interpreter's Dictionary of the Bible,* G. Buttrick, ed., vol. 4 (1962), pp. 428–29. H. Strupp, *Psychotherapy and the Modification of Abnormal Behavior* (1971). B. Throckmorton, Jr., "Pastor," *The Interpreter's Dictionary of the Bible,* G. Buttrick, ed., vol. 3 (1962), p. 668. C. Wise, *Pastoral Counseling* (1951); *Pastoral Psychotherapy* (1980). L. Wolberg, *The Technique of Psychotherapy,* 2d ed. (1967).

B. M. HARTUNG

PASTORAL COUNSELING; PSYCHOTHERAPY. *See also* COUNSELING AND PSYCHOTHERAPY (Comparative Concepts); CARE OF SOULS; PSYCHOTHERAPY AND COUNSELING (Research Studies and Methods); RELIGION AND PSYCHOTHERAPY; THEOLOGY AND PSYCHOTHERAPY. *Compare* CHRISTIAN PSYCHOLOGIST; COUNSELING, ROMAN CATHOLIC; JUDAISM AND PSYCHOLOGY; SPIRITUAL DIRECTION.

PASTORAL RESPONSE. *See* CONVERSATION, PASTORAL; LISTENING; VERBATIM.

PASTORAL SOCIOLOGY. A seldom encountered term in North America, has no broadly recognized definition or use. In Europe the term generally refers to religious sociology and is closely linked to ecclesiastical data formulated in terms of statistical analysis carried out to advance the cause of the church. Roman Catholic institutions have been founded for sociological research and European Protestant churches have held conferences focusing on pastoral sociology with an empirical emphasis.

Although there is no developed discipline of pastoral sociology within the U.S., there is much evidence of sociological influence on the pastoral perspective of a number of major historical figures of the care and counseling movement. The writings of A. Boisen, S. Hiltner, and W. Oates have demonstrated the importance of approaching the pastoral task with a sociological as well as psychological and theological framework. It has been suggested by recent sociologists that a pastoral perspective informed by sociology can serve as a necessary corrective to the widespread adoption of the medical paradigm for conceptualizing pastoral situations. Such a model provides a contextual hermeneutic for critiquing what is often a reductionistic rationale and individualistic ethic in pastoral psychology.

While the term pastoral sociology has no defined position within the field, there are ample signs of an expanding sociological viewpoint within all phases of contemporary pastoral work. Theologically correlated family systems theory as employed by J. Patton and B. H. Childs offers one example of the increasing use of sociologically related perspectives for clinical pastoral understanding. Important theological questions are raised when the human condition is conceived as being largely determined through the dynamic balance of an intricate web of social interactions. Traditional theological categories such as sin and grace are reshaped within a perspective that interprets an individual life as a harmony of influences within an encompassing collective. Expanded beyond the existential particulars of the moment, temporal, social, and economic dimensions of life become significant contributors to pastoral reflection and theological understanding.

Bibliography. J. Patton and B. H. Childs, *Christian Marriage and Family* (1988). W. Swatos, Jr., ed., *Religious Sociology* (1987).

P. J. JOHNSON, III

SOCIOLOGY OF RELIGIOUS AND PASTORAL CARE; SOCIOLOGY OF RELIGION. *Compare* PASTORAL PSYCHOLOGY, DISCIPLINE OF; PASTORAL THEOLOGY.

PASTORAL STEREOTYPES AND CARICATURES. *See* PASTOR (Popular Stereotypes and Caricatures).

PASTORAL SUPERVISION. *See* SUPERVISION, PASTORAL.

PASTORAL TECHNIQUE. *See* TECHNIQUE AND SKILL IN PASTORAL CARE.

PASTORAL THEOLOGICAL METHODOLOGY. The critical evaluation of the procedures for arriving at theological judgments, proposals, or assertions. Thus it is derivative from theology, which has the task of explicating and critically appropriating the language of faith. The "language of faith" includes all of a community's religious phrases, gestures, narratives or rituals. The focus of this article, however, is on the special task and context of *pastoral* theological reflection—the *process* of theological reflection or "theologizing" in the pastoral context or from a pastoral perspective.

We may employ the following distinctions. *First order religious language* will designate the collection of phrases (e.g., God loves me, God is punishing me), narratives (e.g., remembered biblical stories), and liturgies (prayers, hymns, gestures) which are employed to give expression to the way in which a person or community's life is related to God.

Second order religious language (theology) is the explication and critical evaluation or appropriation of their basic meaning, with the more or less provisional result yielding a theological judgment or proposal. When an entire community of faith attains or accepts the same judgment, the result is a doctrine.

Theological method, including pastoral theology, is a *third order reflection* upon the way in which such judgments are made and a critical evaluation of the appropriateness of such procedures. Thus theological method is concerned with an evaluation of the sources, norms, and procedures of theological judgments.

1. Pastoral Care Itself as Theological Reflection. *a. Explicating religious meanings.* A frequently neglected dimension of pastoral care and counseling is that of assisting the person who comes for help to explicate and critically evaluate assumptions concerning the meaning of faith and the life of faith. Yet this is certainly a crucial aspect of pastoral counseling. Much of the work of counseling involves assisting persons to formulate explicitly what may have been only tacitly or subconsciously assumed, such as evaluations and expectations of self and of others, in order that they may be consciously elaborated, explained, evaluated, and possibly altered. If one supposes that a person's tacitly held religious assumptions are of comparable significance, then pastoral care must include assisting the person to expose, elaborate, and so to give some account of these assumptions.

Of course, this must be distinguished from simply encouraging persons to employ (first order) religious language and from employing it oneself in the counseling situation. For theology is not the uncritical or superficial use of a particular (religious) vocabulary, but an attempt to understand the meaning and/or truth of that language. Theological reflection may begin by drawing attention to the religious language, imagery, and gesture employed and by teasing out its connections to other religious and nonreligious articulations of experience. This process assembles the data of theological reflection which may then inquire about the fundamental meaning or generalizable significance of such first order discourse. It is only in this process that underlying or tacit assumptions are made explicit and can thus be formulated and examined.

b. Evaluating religious meanings. But theological reflection is not only the explication of religious language in terms of meaning and significance. It also entails the evaluation of such explicit meanings in terms of their truth. That is to say, theology is a normative endeavor. This may at first seem inappropriate in a counseling situation in which, to be sure, the task of attentive and sympathetic listening is of paramount importance. Yet pastoral care necessarily entails the facilitation and application of normative judgments. Where one engages in a process which seeks not merely to maintain a given situation or pattern of behavior, but to transform it, then one is engaged in the application of normative or evaluative judgments, e.g., is this conducive to growth or decline, to healing or injury, to freedom or bondage, to maturity or infantilization, to integrity or fragmentation? The case is much the same with respect to matters of faith and to the theological judgments which explicate the language of faith.

With respect to the question of the truthfulness of a theological judgment, several kinds of tests may be employed: (a) Is it coherent? That is, is it intelligible, understandable, or is it confused or self-contradictory?

(b) Is it consistent with other aspects of one's faith? e.g., does what I say about life after death seem compatible with what I say about the nature of God, or my body? (c) Does it correspond to what I or we actually experience? (d) How does it relate to formulations which I take to be especially reliable (e.g., the doctrine of my community, the Bible)? These tests do not provide an automatic checklist to determine truth or falsity but indicate possible directions of reflection.

The task of theological reflection within the pastoral situation must be prosecuted with great care and sensitivity. It is not a substitute for but an instrument of the attentive and compassionate regard for the other which is at the heart of pastoral care. Thus it cannot be the goal of such a reflection to impose upon the other a vocabulary or conceptuality which is alien or heteronomous. Instead, the goal is that persons be able to speak more accurately, truthfully, and responsibly of their own pilgrimage as persons of faith.

2. Theological Reflection upon Pastoral Care. The development of a genuinely pastoral theology (that is, a theology rooted in and tested by pastoral practice) is crucial for the development of pastoral care and counseling as an activity of the church and as a discipline in the school of theology. This task has been often hindered by a division between practitioners of academic theology and practitioners of pastoral care. An appropriate pastoral theology will be the result of a collaboration between these disciplines, which will explicate and test the pertinence of theological proposals for pastoral care and test the theological insights generated from pastoral practice by the general canons of adequacy of theological inquiry generally. The development of pastoral theology consists then of a two-way movement between (theological) theory and (pastoral) practice.

a. From practice to theology. Pastoral theology does not consist merely in the employment of a first order religious discourse as an alternative vocabulary for psychological or experiential insight. While insights gained through pastoral practice may be initially couched in religious, psychological, or experiential terminology, their theological significance appears only through the transition to a critically reflected or second order religious discourse. Thus the pastoral counselor may ask of a particular episode, insight, or counseling practice concerning its theological appropriateness.

The first step is that of explication: what are its implications for an understanding of human nature and transformation; for an understanding of priestly or ecclesial office and role; for an understanding of divine agency and purpose? Once their theological relevance is carefully explicated it is possible to inquire whether these implications are consistent with aspects of the Judeo-Christian tradition to which one or one's community is committed. Normally, this entails careful attention to biblical, confessional, and other sources and norms of theological formulation. Again the emphasis is not upon these as first order discourse, but upon the basic or fundamental meaning of this discourse.

As a consequence of this procedure one may discover a mutually illuminating and confirming relationship between practice and theology. On the other hand, one may find it necessary to relinquish or revise the initial interpretation or practice as incompatible with one's theological position. So, for example, some therapeutic practices may be avoided or modified because they appear to contradict a theologically appropriate emphasis upon human freedom and responsibility, or because they fail to take with adequate seriousness the forces and structures which diminish or corrupt responsible freedom. If one concludes that it is the theological tradition itself which must be revised in the light of pastoral practice, then the latter becomes a *norm*.

b. From theology to practice. Pastoral practice provides a norm as well as a source for theological reflection and formulation. Theological or doctrinal assertions regarding the structure and dynamics of human brokenness and bondage (e.g., formulations of original and actual sin), as well as those concerned with the basic process and goal of transformation and growth (e.g., justification, reconciliation, sanctification), must be tested in clinical or pastoral contexts. Only if they prove to be actually illuminating of such contexts do they retain the general interpretive power which is necessary for second order discourse. Thus with respect to a particular proposal or doctrine it is appropriate to inquire whether it has implications for understanding of or intervention in situations of pastoral care and counseling.

Once these implications are understood, it is then appropriate to inquire whether the situation is in fact clarified or the indicated intervention commensurate with pastoral experience. Where it is not, then the theological formulation may require revision or may be abandoned for an alternative formulation. It is important in the process to keep clear the distinction between first and second order religious discourse. It is quite possible that first order language (e.g., talk of sin) may be employed in ways which conceal rather than clarify the situation, or hinder rather than assist transformation, without thereby entailing that the second-order (reflective-critical) use of such terminology is similarly impaired.

The development of a pastoral theology may be greatly enhanced by paying attention to the way many doctrines of the church have been generated from and tested by pastoral practice. Many formulations of the doctrine of sin, for example, serve to diagnose underlying structures which produce experiential and relational conflict, boundness, or brokenness. Thus an inability to trust (unbelief), inordinate self-preoccupation (pride, despair, the heart turned inward), and the compulsive acquisition of things, persons, and symbols of value (concupiscence) are often elaborated with rich pastoral detail. Similarly corresponding categories explanatory of healing or transforming processes (justification, sanctification, election, etc.) are also often developed in the theological tradition in ways which clearly demonstrate their basis in and testing by pastoral insight. Thus contemporary pastoral practice may serve as a powerful heuristic device for interpreting past doctrinal formulations and thus for enriching the domain of contemporary pastoral theology.

c. Liturgical reflection. In so far as pastoral care and counseling is understood to be an exercise of priestly or ministerial office, a reflection upon pastoral care as a direct application of the ministry of word and sacrament (and thus of the liturgical structure and foundation of pastoral care) may be an especially fruitful approach to the development of a pastoral theology. Certainly Catholic traditions have an advantage here in the application of the sacrament of penance as such a pattern while a Protestant bias in favor of word (preaching and teaching) has inhibited the development of such a pastoral/liturgical theology. As is true of any theological inquiry today, pastoral theology must be ecumenical.

3. **Theology and the Human Sciences.** *a. The need for dialogue.* Pastoral care turns not only to theology for theoretical generalization and illumination but also to the human sciences. Indeed many practitioners of pastoral counseling may find themselves more at home within the realm of psychological or psychotherapeutic theory than in the sphere of theology. In extreme cases psychological theory may be the only second-order conceptuality with which the practitioner has any familiarity. In such cases religious language may be regarded only as data to be explained or understood in some other (e.g., psychological) terms. The existence of such cases makes especially urgent a critical dialogue between theology and the human sciences.

Such a dialogue has a strong precedent in the more familiar history of a dialogue between theology and philosophy, a dialogue which has enriched both disciplines. Theology has appropriated philosophical categories and methods to develop trinitarian and christological doctrines in the early church and to develop understandings of the being and attributes of God, the relation of God to the world and notions of freedom and responsibility in theological ethics. Philosophical discourse has likewise been enriched through the development of theories of transcendence, relations, and language.

b. Conditions for fruitful dialogue. A dialogue between theology and the human sciences is likely to be fruitful where (1) both are regarded as second order discourses and (2) the discussion is focused upon the common subject matter of human nature and transformation.

One factor which blocks significant dialogue is the tendency to regard all religious language as first order discourse for which it is the task of the human science to give some explanation. This tendency is reinforced by the observation of ways in which first order religious discourse may be employed so as to prevent the person from obtaining a realistic or truthful perspective upon their actual situation, or in ways which are destructive to possibilities for creative or healing transformation. Thus, for example, people may use talk of God's will to deny grief or anger, or they may use talk of sin in ways which increase a sense of hopelessness and powerlessness. Of course any vocabulary and conceptuality may be employed in the aid of sickness rather than health. As the jargon of psychology becomes more widespread, it too is often employed in such ways. For genuine dialogue to occur it is important that each discipline take seriously the other's claim to be not only a first-order discourse but also a theoretical, reflective, and thus second-order language, whose clarity and general applicability and power of illumination it is then possible to discuss.

If dialogue between theology and the human sciences is to be fruitful it should also be directed toward a common subject matter. The subject matter common to both is not the existence or nature of God but the nature and possible transformation of human existence. Too

often dialogue is blocked by excessive preoccupation with the categories of the theism-atheism debate. This preoccupation may prevent the discovery of important areas of shared interest and possibly fruitful discussion.

c. Further considerations. The range of dialogue between theology and the human sciences is inordinately restricted when it is limited to representatives of the human sciences who appear to have a positive regard for the religious life and its vocabulary (so Jung vs. Freud) or to theologians who have appropriated some of the conceptuality of the human sciences (e.g., Tillich vs. Barth). But this overlap of vocabulary and conceptuality is by no means a prerequisite to dialogue and may even prevent dialogue by the reduction of both sides of the discussion to areas of explicit agreement. Thus one side is but the echo (or translation) of the other.

A useful test of the seriousness and fruitfulness of such a dialogue is whether the conceptuality and vocabulary of both sides is altered and enriched through the process. The reduction of different discourses to a table of equivalences (neurosis = sin, wholeness = salvation, acceptance = justification, etc.) is certainly *not* an enrichment of insight but the reduction of one discourse to another or of both to a lowest common denominator. The sign of a mature, responsible, and fruitful dialogue is that both sides come to require revision in the light of the discussion. Thus we should expect that theological discourse, especially as it seeks to illumine the human predicament, will be transformed by such a dialogue. Indeed the theological vocabulary has been formed in just this way—as a result of dialogue with other disciplines and discourses. But if pastoral theologians do their work properly, they will also succeed in enriching and correcting the conceptuality of the human sciences. Again, this does not mean that the human sciences will adopt a theistic or religious paradigm, but rather will understand ordinary human existence, its predicaments and possibilities, more clearly, incisively, and accurately.

Bibliography. J. Cobb, *Theology and Pastoral Care* (1977). G. Ebeling, *Introduction to a Theological Theory of Language* (1973); *The Study of Theology* (1978). W. W. Everett and T. J. Bachmeyer, *Disciplines in Transformation: A Guide to Theology and the Behavioral Sciences* (1979). E. Farley, *Ecclesial Man* (1975). D. Gelpi, *Experiencing God* (1978). L. Gilkey, *Message and Existence* (1979). S. Hiltner, *Preface to Pastoral Theology* (1958). T. W. Jennings, *Introduction to Theology* (1976). G. Kaufman, *An Essay on Theological Method* (1975). B. Lonergan, *Method in Theology* (1972). J. Metz, *Faith in History and Society* (1980). A. C. McGill, *Suffering: A Test of Theological Method* (1982 [1968]). L. Monden, *Faith: Can Man Still Believe* (1970). A. Nygren, *Meaning and Method* (1972). W. Pannenberg, *Theology and the Philosophy of Science* (1976). K. Rahner, *Foundations of Christian Faith* (1978). F. Schleiermacher, *Brief Outline on the Study of Theology* (1970 [1830]). D. Tracy, *The Analogical Imagination* (1981).

T. W. JENNINGS, JR.

PASTORAL THEOLOGY; PRACTICAL THEOLOGY, PROTESTANT; PSYCHOANALYSIS AND THEOLOGY; THEOLOGY, CHRISTIAN; THEOLOGY AND PSYCHOLOGY; THEOLOGY AND PSYCHOTHERAPY. *See also* JOURNALS IN RELIGION, THEOLOGY, AND THE SOCIAL SCIENCES, INTERDISCIPLINARY. *Compare* INTEGRATION OF PSYCHOLOGY AND THEOLOGY; PSYCHOTHEOLOGY.

PASTORAL THEOLOGY, GRADUATE EDUCATION IN.

Graduate education refers to advanced education, i.e., postbaccalaureate education, usually in specific subject matters. Claude Welch describes the goal of such education as competence judged by a sophisticated knowledge of a given field or area, a capacity for critical judgment, the knowledge and ability to utilize appropriate methods of investigation, and integrity in the use of these methods. Efforts to achieve a consensus as to what constitutes graduate education in pastoral theology are often frustrated by lack of agreement on the nature, subject matter, goals, and methods of the area. To be sure, pastoral theology has accrued many of the characteristics of an academic or scholarly discipline, i.e., literatures, methods, designations, and professional organizations. But differences of opinion on the basic nature of the area creates dilemmas in describing its relation both to the behavioral sciences and to other areas of theological inquiry. To appreciate these issues is to grasp the complexities and the possibilities of advanced education in this field.

1. Background. When the designation first appeared ca. 1750, pastoral theology was not understood as a discipline or subject matter. Instead it referred to certain activities or practices, first in the church and later specified as pastoral. Usually the reference was to what we call the pastoral care functions of ministry, and these, along with education, homiletics, worship, church government, and occasionally missions, constituted the practical field of studies. In some circles, e.g., Roman Catholic, and at different times among Protestants, e.g., in the nineteenth century, pastoral theology has been employed in the same manner as practical theology, as a generic term embracing a number of specific studies pertaining to the tasks of ministry.

Advanced study in pastoral theology as graduate education was therefore unknown prior to the appearance of dynamic psychiatry, psychotherapy, and personality theory. Insofar as advanced study was present at all it fell under the rubric of what we would describe as professional education. It consisted of instruction in the pastoral care tasks of ministry. Theology was essential to these tasks in that it served to define who the pastor was, determined the tasks, provided rules for their proper performance, and suggested the intent of the acts. But pastoral theology was not a discipline, a subject matter. It relied on classical studies for its substance and gave its attention to pastoral acts of care.

With the appearance of dynamic psychology came the prospect of a redefinition of pastoral theology both in its graduate and professional dimensions. The initial inroads of these studies were in the psychology of religion, i.e., Hall, Coe, Leuba, Starbuck, James. But the immediate relevance of dynamic theory for the pastor's relations with distressed and suffering persons, both in terms of understanding and of relief, made these disciplines seem important for intense study. When these concerns began to appear in seminary curricula, pastoral theology was only one of a number of designations used to describe the work. Others included: psychology of religion and pastoral care, religion and personality, pastoral psychology and counseling, Christian psychology and counseling, pastoral theology and pastoral counseling, clinical training for pastoral ministry, pastoral counseling, psychiatry and religion, and religious experience and pastoral counseling.

2. Emergence of Advanced Study. Graduate programs in pastoral care began to emerge in the 1930s and 1940s. Among the pioneers were Paul Johnson of Boston University School of Theology, Harrison S. Elliott of Union Theological Seminary in New York, and David Eitzen at Southern California. During this era and into the 1950s and 1960s, a substantial number of such programs appeared. Records are scarce, but in 1954 the *Journal of Pastoral Psychology* began a series which listed the institutions "offering graduate programs of study and clinical experience leading to Master's degrees or doctorates in one of the following fields or combinations of fields: pastoral theology, pastoral counseling, clinical psychology, and guidance." Between 1954 and 1965, the number of programs reported rose from seven to forty-two in Association for Theological Education related institutions. In 1961 the articles included a list of completed doctoral dissertations. This number rose from twenty to forty by 1971. The schools involved in doctoral study varied, but among those listed more frequently and consistently were Boston University School of Theology, Harvard (prior to 1965), Southern Baptist, Union (New York), Chicago, Garrett, Southwestern Baptist, Princeton, and Claremont.

Reading these program descriptions leaves certain impressions about the nature of advanced study in the field during the post-World War II era. First, it was a vigorous enterprise. In 1956 H. Richard Niebuhr described the work in pastoral theology as one of the most important movements in theological education. Second, regardless of how the area was designated, there seems to have been general agreement that it was in the pastoral care tradition. In this sense the focus was on the pastoral care *acts* of ministry. Third, a shift occurred in that the subject matter of the discipline was increasingly funded by the psychological sciences. In a sense, as Edward Farley notes, the area's existence was maintained by its relation to its auxiliary discipline rather than by its relation to the theological sciences (p. 33). Fourth, although the work was obviously advanced and rigorous, the area was more closely identified with professional than graduate education. The field's possibilities were not perceived to lie in the expansion of knowledge; they were instead understood to reside in the prospect of enriched understandings of persons and enhanced ability to deal with suffering and distress.

These generalizations should not be construed to mean that there were no theological concerns reflected and addressed in these programs. To the contrary, work in psychology raised a multitude of theoretical and theological issues which found expression in doctoral dissertations and in an expanding literature. One focus of this literature was the pastoral care work of ministry, especially as counseling, and the import of psychological theory for this work. Another focus was on the relation of theological and psychological theory. Not only pastoral theologians but persons such as David Roberts, Albert Outler, Daniel Day Williams, and Paul Tillich entered this conversation. But the premise of this work seems to have been that religion, theology, and ministry refer to one thing, and psychology and psychotherapy to another. The crucial task for the pastoral theologian is to discern their relation, i.e., to discover the ways in which psychological understanding may inform and contribute to theological understanding, to critique psychology out of a theological orientation, and to utilize the work of psychology to enrich the practice of ministry. Thus the distinctiveness of the pastor and of a theological orientation was the subject of much debate.

As the discipline matured in the late 1950s, two of its leaders, Wayne Oates and Seward Hiltner, began to wonder, in the words of Brooks Holifield, whether "the field had not taken a wrong turn." They acknowledged its value in the education of clergy and affirmed efforts to relate theology and psychology. But, returning to the emphasis of Anton Boisen, they proposed a pastoral theology grounded in the concrete data of the minister's practice. Boisen, who was regarded as the "father of pastoral theology" in its revived form, had insisted that attention to the "living human document," i.e., the persons themselves with their histories of conflict, defeat, and victory, provided a method for the study of theology. The development of pastoral care sensitivities was an important dimension of the field's contribution, but its primary value was as a mode of theological inquiry.

The significance of Boisen's work for gradate education went unattended for some thirty years. But in 1959 Hiltner published *Preface to Pastoral Theology* and argued that the pastor's practice itself was a source for the writing of theology. Pastoral theology, he said, was theology done from the "shepherding perspective." Its focus was the healing, sustaining, and guiding ministries of the pastor and the church. Thus by reflecting on pastoral operations from a shepherding perspective, pastoral theology could become a disciplined inquiry into the healing, sustaining, and guiding ministries of the pastor and the church. This, in turn, would lead to a separate branch of theology, a "theological wisdom that could illumine all the church's functions."

Hiltner's definition necessitated a new turn in graduate education in pastoral theology. His proposal made possible a shift in the self-understanding of the area by designating the activities with which pastoral theology was concerned and which included attention to method and the prospect of theory construction. Yet this understanding did not capture the day. Many, perhaps most, of the graduate programs understood advanced work in the area, however designated, as essentially the enhancement of the pastoral care and counseling functions of ministry.

3. Current Status. What becomes clear in this brief survey is that advanced study in pastoral theology takes at least two forms. It is also clear that many persons consider themselves pastoral theologians who do not utilize the term either to describe their programs of study or as an institutional title. In 1980 Rodney Hunter summarized the discussion at a symposium honoring Seward Hiltner by distinguishing between two ways in which a discipline may be defined and described. (He defines a *discipline* as any "ongoing, corporate inquiry with more or less agreed upon topics of investigation and principles of research.") He suggested, first, that a discipline may

be understood "humanly and descriptively in terms of its social task and function, institutional location, what its practitioners do, and so forth." Second, it may be defined "ideally in terms of its intellectual problematic and principles of procedure."

Although it would be unfortunate to draw the lines between graduate programs in pastoral theology too sharply, it does seem that Hunter's distinction helps to clarify their foci. His first definition reflects a professional service orientation located in relation to the church. Some advanced programs perceive this task as the fundamental one and so emphasize clinical competence within a theological orientation as the goal of their work. Despite the fact that the contours, requirements, and theological orientations of the studies differ, programs at Boston, Fuller, Claremont, Rosemead, Loyola of Baltimore, and Southwestern Baptist are among those which exemplify this orientation. Proficiency in psychological theory and psychotherapy, the distinctiveness of the pastoral counselor, the relation of psychology and theology, and the place of specialization in ministry are among the concerns addressed. Usually it is expected that graduates will receive certification by one or another professional group as an aspect of the study.

The institutions which reflect Hunter's second definition are more clearly in the Hiltner tradition. Such programs do not neglect the professional task. Each in some fashion acknowledges the vocational heart of pastoral theology to be the clinical case or pastoral event and each, in varying degrees, expects some measure of clinical competence in its students. But the primary agenda of programs at schools such as Chicago, Emory, Princeton, and Vanderbilt is to establish the field of pastoral theology in the world of scholarship and research. Their concerns are reflected in efforts to come to terms with pastoral theology as a discipline in quest of knowledge. Thus questions of definition, subject matter (what is the area trying to discover), method (by what means), and the nature of the knowledge discerned constitute its concerns. The task is understood as theological inquiry, utilizing psychological and behavioral science data and theory, but culminating finally in theological statement. The recently constituted Society of Pastoral Theology serves as a forum for the pursuit of these issues.

It is evident, then, that advanced study in pastoral theology reflects the quandries not only of the field in its historical manifestations but of theology generally. The place of situations, experience, etc., in theological reflection and the relation or place of secular knowledge in theological study are brought to the foreground in the effort. The resurgence of interest in practical theology by such persons as Edward Farley, Thomas Ogletree, David Tracy, Don Browning, *et al.* suggests that the issues which seem to be endemic to pastoral theology are becoming a concern to the entire theological community. Such a development offers promise of enrichment of theological study in general and pastoral theology in particular.

Bibliography. D. Browning, *Practical Theology* (1983). E. Farley, "Theology and Practice Outside the Clerical Paradigm," *Practical Theology*, D. Browning, ed., (1983), pp. 21–41. S. Hiltner, *Preface to Pastoral Theology* (1958). E. B. Holifield, *History of Pastoral Care in America* (1983). R. J. Hunter, "The Future of

Pastoral Theology," *J. of Pastoral Psychology*, 29:1 Fall (1980), 58–69. L. Mudge and J. Poling, *Formation and Reflection* (1987). T. Oden, *Pastoral Theology* (1983). W. Oglesby, *The New Shape of Pastoral Theology* (1969). C. Welch, *Graduate Education in Religion* (1971).

L. O. MILLS

EDUCATION IN PASTORAL CARE AND COUNSELING; SPECIALIZATION IN PASTORAL CARE. *See also* THEOLOGICAL EDUCATION AND THE PASTORAL CARE MOVEMENT.

PASTORAL THEOLOGY, JEWISH. *See* JEWISH LITERATURE IN CARE AND COUNSELING; JUDAISM AND PSYCHOLOGY; THEOLOGY, JEWISH.

PASTORAL THEOLOGY, PROTESTANT. The word *pastoral* derives from the biblical word for shepherd, and pastoral theology has traditionally referred to the theology of shepherding, the pastor's oversight of the people of God. There is no consensus on the precise meaning of the term in contemporary Protestantism, however, and at least three definitions may be discerned:

(1) Traditionally, the branch of theology which formulates the practical principles, theories, and procedures for ordained ministry in all of its functions (though in the nineteenth century often excluding homiletics).

(2) The practical theological discipline concerned with the theory and practice of pastoral care and counseling. In addition to a study of methods of helping and healing, this includes studies of moral and religious life and development, personality theory, interpersonal and family relationships, and specific problems like illness, grief, and guilt.

(3) A form of theological reflection in which pastoral experience serves as a context for the critical development of basic theological understanding. Pastoral theology in this sense generally focuses on topics like illness, death, sexuality, family, and personhood, though in principle any theology topic may be considered from a pastoral perspective — faith, hope, love, salvation, and God, for example. Here pastoral theology is not a theology *of* or *about* pastoral care but a type of contextual theology, a way of doing theology *pastorally*. Pastoral theology in this sense is complementary, not competitive, with definitions 1 and 2.

This article surveys recent Protestant pastoral theology in the senses of definitions 2 and 3, which are the meanings current in the American clinical pastoral context. An accompanying article, PASTORAL THEOLOGICAL METHODOLOGY, considers detailed methodological questions involved in reflecting theologically in pastoral situations.

1. Disciplinary Distinctions and Relationships.
a. Theology and ethics. In any of its forms pastoral theology emphasizes the understanding of concrete human experience and problems with the explicit intent of developing practical principles and methods of ministry. It is distinguished from systematic theology and ethics with regard to both concreteness and practicality, for systematics and ethics are primarily concerned with articulating and critically developing general meanings and principles. In all of its forms pastoral theology, however, also involves the articulation and application (if

not critical development) of normative meanings and principles, though defining abstract moral and religious visions is not usually its primary focus.

Within pastoral theology in any of its forms there is little consensus about how normative visions relate to practical and empirical analyses. In general, pastoral theology concerns itself with relatively specific kinds of human problems, often in empirical detail, and adopts a variety of disciplinary perspectives to understand them, including nontheological disciplines (e.g., psychology, sociology). The issue in question is the degree of centrality given to the normative perspectives, principally theology and ethics. Don Browning (1983) views pastoral theology as a branch of ethics. Empirical analysis in Browning's approach is important but primarily as a means to normative construction. James Lapsley (1983) and other disciples of Seward Hiltner, on the other hand, feel that this approach overstresses normative reflection at the expense of the analysis of actual human dynamics, the discipline's most distinctive and valuable point of contribution.

b. Practical theology. For many years practical theology has been mainly an umbrella term for the multiple practical fields of ministry, within which pastoral theology is one component along with homiletics, liturgics, religious education, church administration, social ministry, evangelism, etc. It has never been clear whether practical theology in this sense is or might become a discipline in its own right. Thus its relationship to pastoral theology has been either ambiguous or inconsequential.

Recent proposals by various American pastoral theologians, ethicists, and systematic theologians, however, have attempted to reconfigure the relationship (Browning, 1983). In these proposals practical theology becomes a substantive theological discipline with a basic methodology, within which pastoral theology focuses on issues of care and thus becomes a "practical theology of care." Such practical theology is also concerned with the whole of the church's life in the world, not the functions of clergy alone as was the case with most traditional pastoral theology.

c. Pastoral psychology and psychology of religion. Pastoral psychology is the traditional term for the attempt to apply secular psychology and psychotherapy to pastoral practice. The term does not ordinarily imply the need for a uniquely religious or theological psychology in ministry (though some conservative Protestants advocate developing a "Christian psychology"); it only asserts that pastoral care can be performed more effectively if psychology and other secular knowledge are employed. The term was especially popular through the fifties and sixties but is still widely used. From an academic perspective pastoral psychology and pastoral theology are sometimes regarded as a branch of the psychology of religion on grounds that caring acts done from a religious perspective constitute a form of religion.

Critics of the pastoral movement contend that the secular disciplines, especially therapeutic psychology, have so dominated modern pastoral theology that theological concerns have become peripheral (Oden, 1967). In recent years, however, there has been a growing awareness of the problem and a new affirmation of *pastoral theology* as the appropriate, comprehensive term for the discipline, as evidenced by the founding of the Society for Pastoral Theology in 1985.

d. Psychology and theology, and personality and theology. Among evangelical Protestants the term *pastoral theology* is not as common as among liberals. However, an intense interest in the relation between psychology and theology has developed among "neo-evangelicals," sometimes under the banner of "integrating" psychology and theology (Carter and Narramore, 1979). This movement is largely unrelated to the mainline pastoral care movement though increasingly conversant with it. Generally, conservatives attempt to distinguish practical methods and empirically verifiable theories from the deeper philosophic and value assumptions of contemporary psychology, adopting the former and rejecting aspects of the latter; and they try to combine psychology with a dualistic nature-supernature world view and an emphasis on the authority of Scripture.

The liberal counterpart to this movement, predating it by a generation or more, is usually referred to as the field of "personality and theology" or "religion and personality," and is primarily associated with Seward Hiltner's pioneering program at the University of Chicago in the 1950s. Personality and theology has historically oriented itself heavily to the depth psychological traditions of Freud and Jung and to certain strands of humanistic psychology (e.g., Rogers), in contrast to the more empirical, cognitive, and behavioral orientation of the conservative movement. Liberals have generally sought to rethink theological doctrine in light of these theories and to apply them to pastoral practice under the heading of "pastoral theology." Thus "personality and theology" has designated the anthropological foundation of liberal pastoral theology. Today the concept of "personality" is often considered too narrow for the field, though the appellation "personality and theology" continues in use, especially in settings influenced by the Chicago-Hiltner tradition.

2. History. *a. Early Protestant pastoral theology.* In one sense, pastoral theology is as old as the Christian church; in a more restricted sense it is a modern creation whose origins reflect the specialized and fragmented character of theology since the Enlightenment.

In the wider sense, all traditional and modern literature pertaining to the "cure of souls"—so-called "pastoralia"—including letters of consolation and spiritual counsel, penitential and confessional handbooks, treatises on casuistry, and the infinite proliferation of modern practical religious literature, constitute a kind of pastoral theology, an attempt to relate the meanings and requirements of faith to concrete human problems and situations.

Protestant pastoral theology became recognized as a formal theological discipline only after publication of German theologian Claus Harms's *Pastoral-Theologie* in 1830, though books on pastoral theology had been appearing in Germany for nearly a hundred years (Hiltner, 1958, pp. 43, 225). Later pastoral theologians like J. J. Van Oosterzee and W. G. T. Shedd referred to the field as "poimenics" (Greek for shepherd, neatly matched with "homiletics," "catechetics," etc.), and wrote voluminous treatises that made use of current psychology (Holifield, 1983). While these efforts appear ponderous

and overly systematized today, they did give the church a comprehensive, ordered grasp of pastoral problems and methods.

Clebsch and Jaekle (1967) are correct in noting that our own century has not been able to achieve a comparable systematic pastoral theology, despite (or because of) its immense variety of theoretical perspectives and resources. On the other hand, the older pastoral theologies, like many today, failed to engage their topics in theologically creative ways and tended to advocate methods of practice ("hints and helps") unrelated to fundamental theory (see Hiltner, 1958, ch. 3 and p. 226f.).

b. American clinical pastoral theology. As Holifield (1983) shows, there was intense interest in psychology, psychology of religion, religion and health, and the nascent discipline of psychotherapy among religious people in the United States, including pastoral theologians, around the turn of the century. Out of this ferment emerged the clinical pastoral care movement of the 1930s and later, pioneered by Anton Boisen, Richard Cabot, Russell Dicks, and others, giving practical expression to this lively interest in the relation between religion and health. In particular, the movement sought a cooperative relation between ministry and medicine and soon began to reorient the field of pastoral care itself toward a therapeutic, especially psychotherapeutic, self-understanding.

The movement produced a deluge of practical and psychological literature on pastoral care and counseling employing these new ideas, as well as books and articles attempting to give theological form to the burgeoning field (e.g., Outler, 1954; Roberts, 1950). The principal pastoral theologians drew on Tillichian, process, and personalist theologies—Tillich himself was a major contributor (Tillich, 1984)—though some were sympathetic with aspects of neo-Orthodoxy when modified to accommodate the new psychological insights. American pastoral theology, however, never embraced neo-orthodox theology in the strong form in which it was so influential in German pastoral theology of the same period. Eduard Thurneysen, the principal advocate of Barthian pastoral theology on the continent, is little known and generally disliked by American pastoral care leaders, who have tended to view him as the antithesis of the clinical tradition (e.g., E. Thornton, 1964).

i. Empirical theology (Boisen, Hiltner). There is room for debate as to whether Anton Boisen, the principal founder of clinical pastoral education (CPE), is properly considered a theologian; some would contend that his work lay closer to the psychology of religion. In any case, out of his own profound personal and emotional struggles Boisen fashioned a theory with deep theological significance. For Boisen, mental crisis and religious experience are dynamically indistinguishable. Each involves a struggle with ultimate issues of value and loyalty—one's moral solidarity with one's fellow humans—and can be distinguished only retrospectively in terms of ultimate outcome (whether constructive or destructive). This revolutionary thesis meant that "living human documents," especially those suffering profound mental or emotional disorders, could become the source of significant, authoritative religious insight and thus ought to be utilized in theological education and studied by theologians.

Boisen's research agenda for CPE never caught on in the pastoral movement, and his direct influence on pastoral theology was remarkably slight. His student Seward Hiltner, however, elaborated Boisen's thesis about learning theology from living human documents into a major theory of pastoral theology. Hiltner's proposal gave the discipline systematic, abstract form and an emphatically empirical, operational focus. Pastoral theology, said Hiltner, is an "operation-centered" form of theology (in contrast to classical or "logic-centered" kinds). It is "that branch of theological knowledge and inquiry that brings the shepherding perspective to bear upon all the operations and functions of the church and the minister, and then draws conclusions of a theological order from reflection on these observations" (1958, p. 20). Hiltner distinguished pastoral theology from other "operation-centered" forms of theology by its angle of vision or "perspective." This he proposed to call "shepherding" (meaning essentially "caring"), which he distinguished from "organizing" and "communicating." Shepherding in turn was perceived to entail three aspects: "healing," "sustaining," and "guiding," terms that have become standard in American pastoral care. Hiltner has been criticized for employing the traditional rural metaphor of the shepherd, for unclear or underdeveloped theological premises (related to pragmatism and process thought), and for appearing to advocate a kind of pragmatic activism (which was not, however, the case).

Nonetheless Hiltner remains the major architect of the discipline of American Protestant pastoral theology. While details of his proposal have not been widely adopted, his work encouraged the notion that pastoral care provides an important context for critical theological reflection and the belief that pastors can participate significantly in theology precisely in their role as pastors. Hiltner's work stands behind the contributions of several of the leading contemporary figures as well (see below).

ii. Revelation theology (Oates, Oden, E. Thornton). While Hiltner and his students blended psychology and theology rather easily on the foundations of liberal process theology, others representing evangelical and neoorthodox theology have attempted to establish a more sharply defined distinction between faith and psychology, while nevertheless attempting to interrelate them. While not necessarily using the term "pastoral theology" for their efforts, they have viewed their task as that of formulating a distinctively theological conception of pastoral care.

The leading figure in this group is Southern Baptist clinical pastoral pioneer Wayne E. Oates, who represents the free church evangelical tradition emphasizing biblical revelation, personal experience, and the mutual ministry of the whole people of God, but enhanced by psychiatric and psychological wisdom. Oates (1962, 1982) advocates the critical use of social scientific perspectives and encourages empirical research, but also strongly emphasizes the theological and historical identity of pastoral care and the symbolic role of the pastor. He has also made significant contributions to the dialogue between religion and psychiatry and mental health. Oates generally does not use the term "pastoral theology," however, and has not focused his work on the theory of the discipline as such.

Among others seeking a more explicit rapprochement between kerygmatic theology and therapeutic psychology are Thomas Oden and Edward Thornton. Oden (1966, 1967) proposed that the *kerygma* is "implicit" in the empirical conditions of effective psychotherapy (essentially, "acceptance") but can only be clearly known and understood through revelation. While Oden did not spell out a theory of pastoral theology as such, it seems clear that for him pastoral theology would provide authoritative interpretation, on the basis of biblical revelation, of pastoral practices and presuppositions found to be truly life enhancing, finding in them a deep wisdom and faith, which only need to be rightly named and fully appreciated theologically.

Edward Thornton (1964), on the other hand, operating within a broadly neoorthodox framework (via Bonhoeffer), proposed a more reciprocal relationship between psychology and theology. In Thornton's view, "Health is potential in salvation and salvation is potential in health." Therapeutic psychology in particular "prepares the way for divine-human encounter," yet ultimately such encounter occurs only at God's initiative and in God's good time. This formulation sets up a problem suggesting that pastoral theology's task is to work out the theoretical and practical details of their mutual potentiality.

iii. Personalist theology (Johnson, Wise). The pastoral theologies of Paul Johnson and Carroll Wise were deeply influenced by Boston personalism. Johnson (1953, 1967) was perhaps more explicit about it, though he preferred the term "dynamic interpersonalism" to avoid the individualistic and rationalistic bias he found in classic personalism (see Strunk, 1973). Johnson was concerned that unconscious and interpersonal processes be taken seriously, and regarded the pastoral relationship as the key element in pastoral care. While he did not elaborate his theology extensively or formulate an explicit theory of the discipline, his "dynamic interpersonalism," like Oates's work, understands pastoral theology mainly in terms of the second definition.

Carroll Wise was perhaps more cautious about theology than the other "pioneers" noted here, being keenly aware of the ease with which theological thinking becomes divorced from experience, i.e. from the deep human realities with which theology is concerned. Nevertheless, Wise (1966) articulated his concept of pastoral care theologically, proposing that "pastoral care is the art of communicating the inner meaning of the Gospel to persons at the points of their need" (1966, p. 8). The "inner meaning of the Gospel" is a certain "quality of being" characterized by inner freedom and love. Rooted in Boston personalism, this conception draws on a radically personalistic or "incarnational" understanding of faith (and of pastoral care), and implies a belief (without developing it) that there is an experiential "core" to the gospel which takes precedence over theological formulations. This does not mean that theology is rejected in principle. For Wise, authentic (i.e., loving and free) personhood functions as a sort of hermeneutical principle, the perspective necessary for truly understanding and speaking the essence or "inner meaning" of the gospel. By implication, pastoral theology would appear to become the attempt to speak the gospel authentically out of the crucible of pastoral experience (a form of definition), though Wise did not develop this possibility.

iv. Recent major figures. More recent American pastoral theology has taken diverse directions. Howard Clinebell has greatly revised and expanded his influential, eclectic model of pastoral care and counseling (1966, 1984), developing a "holistic liberation-growth model" that expresses a quintessentially liberal Protestant standpoint without the Hiltnerian methodology of developing theological insights from pastoral practice.

James Lapsley, Charles Gerkin, and John Patton, on the other hand, represent a more Hiltnerian understanding of pastoral theology, each developing his position in close engagement with pastoral practice. Lapsley (1972) has developed a theory of pastoral care based on the complex interrelationships of salvation and health understood as life processes. Gerkin (1984) has focused on the recovery of religious meanings as the central concern of pastoral care, drawing on hermeneutical theory in tension with the field's psychodynamic and therapeutic orientation, and has developed the theology of providence in relation to crisis experience (1979). Patton (1983) has advanced a notion of "relational humanism" as key to pastoral care and counseling, and has developed a variety of theological insights out of his pastoral counseling practice, particularly concerning guilt, shame, and forgiveness (Patton, 1985).

In a quite different vein Don S. Browning (1976, 1983) has sought to recover the "moral context of pastoral care," emphasizing the role of ethics in pastoral theology in contrast to its recent psychotherapeutic emphases and historic neglect of ethics in favor of theology. Browning's theory relates ethics to pastoral care through five hierarchical levels of analysis, and is linked closely to a sophisticated conception of practical theology.

The recovery of traditional aspects of pastoral care has also been proposed by some recent writers, principally Donald Capps, who has sought to recover the pastoral use of the Bible (1981), the practice of moral guidance, and the role of ritual (1983), and Thomas Oden. Whereas Capps seeks to integrate modern psychology with traditional practices and functions, Oden (1983) appears largely to favor traditional methods and theories over contemporary ones. Oden advocates a recovery of classical (i.e., patristic and premodern) literatures and styles of pastoral care and largely views the modern pastoral care movement as impoverished by comparison, caught in the secular superficialities of modernity.

c. British pastoral theology. British pastoral theology, as well as that of the continent, has taken its own distinctive course. An early, ground-breaking effort was Clement Rogers's (1912) attempt to establish pastoral theology as an inductive, empirical science concerned to discover the laws of spiritual life and human relationships in that light. More recent developments have taken both clinical and spiritual directions.

i. Clinical orientation (Lambourne, Lake). A pair of British physicians, Robert Lambourne (1963) and Frank Lake (1966, 1987), are perhaps the most widely known figures in twentieth century British pastoral theology. Both have focused on the relation of religion to health and have proposed distinctive styles and methods of pastoral care. Lambourne (1963) advocates an incarnational

and sacramental understanding of the healing ministry, a thoroughly communal understanding of illness and health, and a strongly wholistic understanding of salvation. His conception of pastoral theology includes the task of working out biblical and theological bases for pastoral practice, critiquing current healing theory and practice in their light, and integrating them with the best contemporary medical and psychological wisdom.

The massive work of Frank Lake (1966, 1987), by contrast, draws heavily on the object relations psychology of Melanie Klein and others, focusing in depth upon individual dynamics and their infantile and childhood origins. Lake's massive *Clinical Theology* details a theory of the dynamics of various types of defensive closedness to relationship and to experience, and their implications for pastoral practice. His theory evidences a deep continuity between psychiatric and spiritual processes, and is suffused with a mystical, Christocentric piety. It implies a view of pastoral (or "clinical") theology as a religiously framed attempt to understand the deepest dynamics and struggles of the soul, and to draw out its spiritual insight and practical pastoral implications.

ii. Spiritual orientation (M. Thornton). Anglican cleric Martin Thornton's pastoral theology is tied to the spiritual tradition rather than to clinical theory or health concerns. In Thornton's (1968) view pastoral theology is one of the basic methodological phases or moments of the theological enterprise as a whole, in which the pastor attempts to grasp the meaning of the theological tradition from the standpoint of the immediate questions or needs of a pastoral situation. The pastoral theologian attempts to think back across the tradition of Christian theology and spirituality for insights and wisdom, synthesizing the tradition anew from a pastoral perspective. Thornton regards this work as essential to theology but differing from its other forms by its synthetic nature, combining theology with concrete experience in a pastoral context. Thornton's idea of pastoral care is heavily oriented toward spiritual growth and direction and very little related to practical, interpersonal, and therapeutic problems. At the same time his conception of pastoral theology, despite its radically different ethos, bears interesting resemblance to Hiltner's, insofar as both exemplify definition 3, pastoral theology as the attempt to rethink theology itself—to "do" theology—pastorally.

d. German pastoral theology. Despite the pathbreaking contributions of Oskar Pfister (1927) relating psychoanalysis to ministry, clinical and psychological interests did not become a major influence in Continental pastoral theology until well after the Second World War. Prior to that time the Barthian theology of Eduard Thurneysen was the dominant influence. In recent decades, however, the clinical psychological emphasis has had wide influence in Europe, having made its way there from North America to Finland and Norway in the 1950s and Germany and the Netherlands in the 1960s. Clinical pastoral education and the work of Carl R. Rogers were the principal conveyers of this influence. The following discussion focuses on Germany, since developments in German pastoral theology have been most accessible to English speaking pastoral theologians.

i. Neoorthodox theology (Thurneysen). German pastoral theologians were decisively influenced by Karl Barth and neoorthodoxy for most of this century, particularly through the work of Eduard Thurneysen (1946; ET 1962). This approach, which may be termed "proclamatory pastoral care," attempted to make use of social science and psychology while maintaining a sharp distinction between these human "words" and the Word of God. Communicating the Word of God is the fundamental aim of pastoral care and counseling, just as it is for preaching and for the whole life of the church. In contemporary terms, Thurneysen advocated a pastoral method in which the pastor seeks, on the one hand, to be phenomenologically empathic and sensitive, while on the other hand continually reframing the interpretative context from human-centered meanings to gospel-centered (i.e., forgiveness-centered) meaning. He urged pastoral care to keep the radically relativizing Word of divine judgment and grace (or forgiveness) central, allowing it to liberate persons from false, self-centered striving. Psychology, shorn of alien philosophies and values, can help describe the fallen human condition but cannot speak the liberating Word which can only come from beyond the human sphere. A sort of "spiritual listening" or frame of reference is thus critical to the pastoral task.

For Thurneysen pastoral theology was equivalent to the theology of pastoral care, a field derivative from more basic dogmatic principles and not fundamentally informed by pastoral experience. At the same time, however, Thurneysen (like Barth) believed that the Word of God, heard primarily in Scripture, is only fully and rightly heard in relation to the concrete life situation; it is not abstract. Thus there is a sense in which pastoral care hears the Word concretely, in its fullness; and while this does not entail an empirical epistemology, it does suggest (beyond Thurneysen's explicit articulation) that a fresh hearing or being grasped by the Word can come through pastoral experience. Thurneysen speaks of a "deepened" understanding of sin, for example.

ii. Clinically oriented neo-orthodoxy (Haendler, Uhsadel, Thilo). Other twentieth century pastoral theologians like Otto Haendler, Walter Uhsadel, and Hans-Joachim Thilo have made more use of psychology and psychotherapy than Thurneysen, though they too have sought to maintain a basic distinction between Word and words. Something — a revelation from outside the person — must be offered to persons; something which they cannot bring out from within themselves. For Haendler, psychology can be helpful in understanding the process of "working through" (in the psychoanalytic sense) the message of the gospel, and appropriating it personally over and over through a variety of life circumstances. Both Uhsadel and Thilo have also emphasized the potential of nonverbal (especially artistic) communication of the gospel. Thilo in particular broadens the scope of pastoral care from justification and forgiveness to the spiritual and moral formation of the person, and Uhsadel develops the pastoral significance of the liturgical calendar in his attempt to understand how the gospel can speak to the "image layer" of the psyche.

iii. Clinical pastoral theology (Piper, Stollberg). After ground-breaking work by Joachim Scharfenberg, a pastor-psychoanalyst, "therapeutic" pastoral care arrived on the scene in Germany in the mid-1960s with the appearance of works by Hans-Christoph Piper and Dietrich Stollberg. Piper said that the task facing the church is to understand its mission not as one of converting its people, but of going to them and standing beside them, listening to their needs, reservations, doubts, and difficulties. Client-centered ministry, he argued, is not an evasion of the gospel but a means to its proper expression. The first article of the creed teaches that God is concerned about the small, everyday things of life, not just the great religious problems; thus the pastor does not come as an authority from "another world" (à la Thurneysen) but as a neighbor who does not have the salvation of God at his (or her) disposal any more than anyone else.

Dietrich Stollberg's (1969) pastoral theology is constructed around a fundamental distinction between the "general proprium" (essence) of pastoral care, meaning the generic human activity of caring and its various laws and dynamics, and a "specific proprium" that occurs in communities explicitly responsive to the unconditional love of God (the church). In the former, pastoral care draws freely on psychology and psychotherapy and utilizes general laws of human interaction and development (though Stollberg is keenly aware of the tendency of all caring acts to subvert care into subtle forms of control and enslavement). The specific proprium cannot escape these human tendencies either, but it is grounded in the encompassing, gracious love of God which continually frees and renews the community to comfort, exhort, and encourage one another in freedom and love. Stollberg insists that the general and special propria belong together paradoxically like the two natures of Christ in the Chalcedonian formula; the laws of communicating and care giving stand side by side with the free grace of an accepting God, and both are necessary. Thus Stollberg (and Thilo as well) sees a paradox in the new therapeutic pastoral care. While it represents a genuine advance in freedom for the church, it cannot eliminate the danger of legalism and pharisaism; the new pastoral care can bring its own rigidity. The task of pastoral theology in any case is to ponder and clarify such issues as these, which is to say to develop a theology of pastoral care in the sense of definition 2 above.

3. Disciplinary Status and Future Prospects. *a. Theological method.* Clearly, pastoral theology is in a time of uncertainty and ferment. Its varied and partially conflicting self-understandings lead some to ask whether pastoral theology is a viable "discipline" at all. Questions generally revolve around (a) how broadly or narrowly "pastoral" is to be taken, i.e., whether in the narrow sense pertaining to the work of clergy or pastors (the so-called "clerical paradigm") or broadly as the work of the whole church, individually or corporately; (b) whether the ministry involved is limited explicitly to care and counseling or understood in some larger sense; and (c) how the discipline interprets its claim to being a form of theology.

The latter issue is perhaps the most important. The question is whether pastoral theology will see its task primarily in traditional terms as one of applying theology to pastoral situations and developing theories of pastoral care — essentially regarding the discipline as a branch of ecclesiology or ethics — or that of doing theology itself, contextually, out of the pastoral situation, in a pastoral mode or perspective. The question is whether the discipline entails doing a theology *of* something, or doing theology *pastorally*.

b. Particular topics and approaches. Many other issues crowd the future of this discipline in either event. Today the perspectives of feminist, liberation, black, and third world theologies challenge the comfortable clericalism and professionalism of the traditional discipline and open up new vistas of understanding and challenge. Related to this is the need to develop relationships between the understanding and care of individuals (and families) and the needs of the larger society that bear upon personal difficulties. Issues of race, sex, and social justice in general, and of corporate, congregational life and worship, must be integrated with the field's more individualistic, therapeutic concerns.

Similarly, there is a need to attend to the considerable gulf between the mainline liberal side of the field, with its particular psychological and theological traditions, and recent evangelical, Catholic, and Jewish pastoral theorizing. Lying behind these differences are larger problems of basic relevance to contemporary pastoral theology related to psychology itself: psychology's emerging function as a species of religion in late twentieth century culture, its particular philosophical origins and issues, which are often unrecognized or inadequately critiqued in contemporary enthusiasms for particular theories, and problems such as the relation between psychologies that consider the self or personality as primary and those that emphasize behavioral process and social systems.

The field today also stands in need of developing better historical perspective on itself and its favored (or rejected) psychologies. Oden's recent work (1983), for example, challenges the current field to identify the distinctive elements of modern psychology in relation to its predecessors and to appropriate premodern psychologies and forms of care and spirituality. A further set of issues has to do with how behavioral scientific research methodology should function in pastoral theology (if at all). Are these methods too narrow, superficial, or "objective" to speak to theological and spiritual questions, to give voice to women's, minority, and oppressed perspectives, or to inform an essentially practical theological discipline?

In any event it seems likely that the church will continue to need something like pastoral theology by whatever name. The need will always exist to bring religious and moral meanings into relationship with the needs, problems, and activities of everyday human experience and care, both to interpret their significance and to guide ameliorative interventions. This work can be done only by forms of theology which interrelate normative vision, concrete understanding of human beings, and practical wisdom about care — which is generally what Protestant pastoral theology has attempted to achieve through its long history, varied traditions, and innovative modern developments.

Bibliography. H. Amme *et al.*, *Handbuch der Praktischen Theologie* (1975). A. T. Boisen, *The Exploration of the Inner World* (1971 [1936]). D. S. Browning. *The Moral Context of Pastoral Care* (1976); *Religious Ethics and Pastoral Care* (1983); D. S. Browning, ed., *Practical Theology* (1983). J. R. Burck, "A Critical and Constructive Consideration of Representative Prot-

estant Seelsorge (Pastoral Care) Literature, 1946–73," unpublished doctoral dissertation, Princeton Theological Seminary (1976). D. Capps, *Biblical Approaches to Pastoral Counseling* (1981); *Life Cycle Theory and Pastoral Care* (1983). J. D. Carter and B. Narramore, *The Integration of Psychology and Theology* (1979). W. A. Clebsch and C. R. Jaekle, *Pastoral Care in Historical Perspective* (1964). H. Clinebell, *Basic Types of Pastoral Care and Counseling* (1966; rev. ed. 1984). H. Gastager *et al.*, *Praktisches Wörterbuch der Pastoral-Anthropologie* (1975). C. V. Gerkin, *Crisis Experience in Modern Life* (1979); *The Living Human Document* (1984). O. Haendler, *Grundriss der Praktischen Theologie* (1957). C. Harms, *Pastoral-Theologie* (1830). S. Hiltner, *Preface to Pastoral Theology* (1958). E. B. Holifield, *A History of Pastoral Care in America* (1983). P. E. Johnson, *Person and Counselor* (1967); *Psychology of Pastoral Care* (1953). C. F. Kemp, *Physicians of the Soul* (1947). F. Lake, *Clinical Theology* (1966; abridged ed., 1987). R. A. Lambourne, *Community, Church, and Healing* (1963). J. N. Lapsley, *Salvation and Health* (1972). J. T. McNeill, *A History of the Cure of Souls* (1951). W. E. Oates, *The Christian Pastor* 3d ed. (1982); *Protestant Pastoral Counseling* (1962). T. C. Oden, *Contemporary Theology and Psychotherapy* (1967); *Kerygma and Counseling* (1966); *Pastoral Theology* (1983). W. B. Oglesby Jr., *The New Pastoral Theology* (1969). A. C. Outler, *Psychotherapy and the Christian Message* (1954). J. Patton, *Is Human Forgiveness Possible?* (1985); *Pastoral Counseling: A Ministry of the Church* (1983). O. R. Pfister, *Analytische Seelsorge* (1927). H. C. Piper, *Gesprächsanalysen* (1973). E. Pond, *Lectures on Pastoral Theology* (1847). D. E. Roberts, *Psychotherapy and a Christian View of Man* (1950). C. F. Rogers, *An Introduction to the Study of Pastoral Theology* (1912). D. Rössler, *Der ganze Mensch* (1962). J. Scharfenberg, *Pastoral Care as Dialogue* (ET 1987 [1972]); *Sigmund Freud and His Critique of Religion* (ET 1988 [1972]). F. Schleiermacher, *Brief Outline of the Study of Theology* (ET 1966 [1811, 1830]); *Die Praktische Theologie nach den Grundsätzen der Evangelischen Kirche* (1983 [1850]). W. G. T. Shedd, *Homiletics, and Pastoral Theology* (1867). D. Stollberg, *Seelsorge durch die Gruppe* (1972); *Therapeutische Seelsorge* (1969). O. Strunk, Jr., ed., *Dynamic Interpersonalism for Ministry* (1973). H. J. Thilo, *Beratende Seelsorge* (1971); *Der ungespaltene Mensch* (1957). E. Thornton, *Theology and Pastoral Counseling* (1964). M. Thornton, *The Function of Theology* (1968); *Pastoral Theology: A Reorientation* (1956). E. Thurneysen, *A Theology of Pastoral Care* (ET 1962 [1946]). P. Tillich, *The Meaning of Health: Essays in Existentialism, Psychoanalysis, and Religion*, ed. P. LeFevre (1984). W. Usadel, *Praktische Theologie*, vol. 3: *Evangelische Seelsorge* (1966). J. J. Van Oosterzee, *Practical Theology* (ET 1878). A. Vinet, *Pastoral Theology* (1853). D. D. Williams, *The Minister and the Care of Souls* (1961). C. A. Wise, *The Meaning of Pastoral Care* (1966).

J. R. BURCK
R. J. HUNTER

PASTORAL THEOLOGICAL METHODOLOGY; PRACTICAL THEOLOGY, PROTESTANT; THEOLOGY AND PSYCHOLOGY; THEORY IN PASTORAL CARE OF COUNSELING, FUNCTIONS OF. *See also* JOURNALS; PASTORAL CARE (Contemporary Methods, Perspectives, and Issues); PSYCHIATRY AND PASTORAL CARE. *Compare* CLINICAL THEOLOGY; EMPIRICAL RESEARCH IN PASTORAL CARE AND COUNSELING; GRACE AND PASTORAL CARE; MORAL THEOLOGY; PASTORAL PSYCHOLOGY, DISCIPLINE OF; PASTORAL SOCIOLOGY; POIMENICS; RELIGION AND PSYCHOTHERAPY; SACRAMENTAL THEOLOGY AND PASTORAL CARE, PROTESTANT; THEOLOGY AND PSYCHOTHERAPY; VALUES IN COUNSELING AND PSYCHOTHERAPY. *Biography:* BOISEN; CABOT; CLINEBELL; DICKS; HARMS; HILTNER; JOHNSON; LAKE; LAMBOURNE; OATES; OUTLER; PFISTER; ROBERTS; SCHARFENBERG; SEXTRO; SHEDD; TILLICH; THURNEYSEN; VAN OOSTERZEE; WISE.

PASTORAL THEOLOGY, ROMAN CATHOLIC.

The use of theological sources to ground, interpret, and guide the activity that constitutes the pastoral life of the church. This activity is customarily divided into preaching and teaching, sanctifying — especially through the sacraments — and pastoring. All three activities are exercised both internally, toward members of the Roman Catholic church, and externally, toward members of other churches, religions, and society at large. The activity of ordained ministers is given special attention in discussions of pastoral theology. In fact, prior to the Second Vatican Council the focus of pastoral theology was almost exclusively on the activity of the priest. Pastoral theology was essentially an application of church doctrine and discipline to the circumstances of parish life. Vatican II broadened the pastoral focus from the clergy to the church and adopted an open, reciprocal attitude toward modern society. Since Vatican II, pastoral theology has been developing as a theological reflection drawn from the lived experience of the church. In this development the role of the laity and the place of social analysis have been prominent.

1. **Pre-Vatican II.** Before the Second Vatican Council, pastoral theology focused almost exclusively on the life and work of the parish priest. The primary theological sources for pastoral theology were (a) official church teachings, catalogued in manuals that incorporated biblical references; (b) catechisms and books of instruction for converts; (c) the sacramental rites and liturgical rubrics; (d) the code of canon law; (e) moral theology guidebooks; (f) practical manuals with recommendations for administering a parish. The overall aim of pastoral theology was to apply these sources to parish life where the priest ministered.

This type of pastoral theology was consistent with the general structure and emphasis of Roman Catholicism, especially as it had taken shape in the nineteenth and early twentieth centuries. Priests were the primary pastoral agents; parishioners were for the most part recipients of the priest's pastoral care, although there was a variety of organizations, led by lay persons, which had either spiritual or apostolic goals. On the whole, pastoral activity was oriented inward, toward the organization and maintenance of the parish so that it might contribute to the spiritual well-being of the parishioners. Outreach consisted mostly of charitable works to the needy and some limited efforts to attract converts.

The goals and structure of pastoral theology were clearly stated in the source books mentioned above. Within this structure there was room for creativity and individual initiative, expressed primarily in the way the priest carried out the church's expectations. In this respect priests used various pedagogical and communication techniques, as well as the insights from psychology, group dynamics, and the behavioral sciences. At the level of application and in the hands of individual priests, pastoral theology was interdisciplinary. Also at the level of application, ethnic customs were very influential in translating the general pastoral theology of the church into effective practice.

Pastoral theology before Vatican II provided a secure and stable pastoral care for parishioners, but it also tended to exaggerate the role of the priest and to restrict the contributions of parishioners to secondary activities. It likewise tended to confine pastoral life to the parish, sometimes isolating it from the larger social environment and even from other parishes.

2. **Vatican II.** The Second Vatican Council is the decisive turning point in Roman Catholic pastoral theology. The council was convened as a pastoral council, and it set in motion changes that have affected every aspect of church life. Two changes in particular have had a great impact on pastoral theology: (a) a shift in focus from the clergy to the church as a whole, and (b) a shift of attitude toward the modern world from suspicion and hostility to respect and reciprocity. As a result of these two shifts, the scope of the word pastoral has broadened so that it now has more of an ecclesial and societal reference. In keeping with this development, the sources of pastoral theology have expanded, leading to a new designation for pastoral theology itself—theological reflection.

3. **Post-Vatican II.** *a. Theological reflection.* The term theological reflection refers to a group process that begins with an actual, pastoral situation; correlates theological resources with this situation; and aims at an informed course of action, "praxis," as a result. This process of theological reflection differs from pre-Vatican II pastoral theology in several ways.

First, it is more inductive than deductive. Theological reflection begins with a specific situation of pastoral care rather than with generic formulations or hypothetical cases. This means that pastoral care experience initially takes precedence. Theology's contribution to pastoral care is sought out rather than pastoral care being fit into a predetermined theological framework.

Second, the traditional disciplines of theology are correlated with the pastoral care situation. This means that pastoral care functions as a criterion in determining the specific relevance of theology in a particular instance. In addition pastoral care can contribute to a reformulation of theology, thereby serving as a source of theological insight and not merely as a field of theological application.

Third, theological reflection ordinarily occurs in a group in order to utilize the different vantage points and experiences of the reflectors. In this way it seeks to overcome anonymous or privatized pastoral theology and to foster creativity from the beginning of the process, not just in its application.

Fourth, theological reflection is multidisciplinary. It continues to utilize insights into individual behavior from psychology and behavioral science as pre-Vatican II pastoral theology did, but theological reflection also draws upon insights into corporate dimensions of human life from the social sciences, especially techniques of structural analysis.

Pastoral theology understood as theological reflection is not confined to the activity of the priest. However, the priest's activity remains a special example of pastoral theology as theological reflection. As such, it is an important contribution to the church's total pastoral theology. Theological reflection is also more contextual than pre-Vatican II pastoral theology. For this reason, it can give the misleading impression of being only a collection of diverse reflection models with illustrations rather than a coherent theological interpretation of pastoral care practice.

b. Contribution of theology. The key issue in contemporary Roman Catholic pastoral theology is the contribution of theology to pastoral practice. It is clear that the traditional disciplines of theology do not simply predetermine pastoral practice; practice requires supplementary principles and the analysis of specific contexts. It is also clear that pastoral practice and reflection on the concrete situations of ministry partially shape and develop the content and method of theological disciplines. This interaction between theology and practice makes it difficult to define precisely what role theology plays and how pastoral theology is to be defined as a discipline. At the present time, however, theology seems to contribute to pastoral practice in at least three ways:

i. Situation analysis. Theology helps to analyze pastoral situations by providing categories and themes which parallel those derived from psychology and other helping disciplines. The traditional theological disciplines best suited for this type of contribution are fundamental and systematic theology. These disciplines already entail a theological analysis of the human condition and the faith experience; indeed theology can sometimes describe a life situation more accurately and perceptively than secular disciplines, and can make the traditional resources of pastoral care — prayer, Scripture, sacraments — more accessible and harmonious. In this role theology aims at discerning where God is present in life situations, how that presence is experienced, where it may lead, and what difference it makes.

ii. Narrative interpretation. Theology helps to interpret the meaning and value of pastoral situations and thereby enables people to share their meanings more consciously. Christian meaning and values, in particular, are expressed most poignantly in narrative. The traditional disciplines of biblical and historical theology contain the normative Christian story and therefore are the disciplines most conducive to interpreting pastoral situations. These formal sources are always supplemented, however, by a strand of charismatic witness and evangelical testimony that proclaim in autobiographical fashion the meaning and value of a person's faith.

Narration invites sharing, and sharing leads to celebration. In the Roman Catholic tradition of pastoral care, sacraments have been the primary form of sharing and celebrating the faith proclaimed in narrative. Since Vatican II sacramental practice has become more integrally related to the Word of God. Now, both Word and sacrament can be integrated more effectively into pastoral care by a pastoral theology that interprets the meaning of situations in a narrative way.

iii. Critical corrective. In addition to analyzing and interpreting what is already in a pastoral situation, theology can and sometimes must bring a critical or prophetic statement *to* the situation. Theology as a whole represents a tradition of experience, critically reflected upon and tested by time. The theological disciplines that serve the pastoral purpose best in this regard are the prayer and worship life of the church and the practical moral life of the church. In these forms especially, theology has a message apart from any particular situation. In this sense theology can expand, question, challenge, open, and define the present situation in relation to the larger church experience. Thus, theology can keep a

given situation from becoming isolated or from asserting an independence which is ultimately self-destructive. At the same time theology tries to remain selfcritical, especially in dialogue with pastoral practice, and so avoid an apodictic or dogmatic role.

c. Practical theology. In the Roman Catholic church after Vatican II pastoral theology has developed a variety of meanings and has had a somewhat uncertain status and location among theological disciplines. On one hand the question has been raised whether pastoral theology is an autonomous or even a definable theological discipline, while in Europe, under the influence of Karl Kahner, the autonomy of pastoral theology has been argued, though under the name "practical theology." Practical theology is understood as a theological analysis of the total social situation in which the church finds itself, in order to plan for the enactment of the church's nature in that precise social situation. This orientation has been taken a step further in Latin American praxis theology, which utilizes social analysis and seeks to structure the pastoral activity of the church as a preferential option for the poor; in praxis theology a commitment to social transformation is regarded as the first indispensable step toward an effective and integral pastoral care. In the U.S., however, pastoral theology is still chiefly oriented toward parishes, relies primarily on psychology rather than social science, and aims at the spiritual development of individuals rather than the social praxis of communities.

Nonetheless, there is an emerging awareness of the public implications of the pastoral work of the church. As theological reflection continues to occur on a wide scale in many types of faith communities, it engages social questions and thus may be expected to feed into the resurgence of the discipline of practical theology.

Pastoral (or practical) theology will no doubt continue to struggle with its identity. In this respect, however, it is consistent with the total life of the Roman Catholic church since Vatican II, as indeed with the worldwide Christian church. In the midst of confusion and uncertainty about the future, there is confidence that pastoral theology, in an enlarged ecclesial context and fueled by theological reflection and practical theology, will continue to ground, interpret, and guide the activity that constitutes the pastoral life of the church.

Bibliography. E. K. Braxton, *The Wisdom Community* (1980). R. F. Collins, *Models of Theological Reflection* (1984). R. A. Duffy, *A Roman Catholic Theology of Pastoral Care* (1983). B. K. Estadt et al., *Pastoral Counseling* (1983). T. H. Groome, *Christian Religious Education* (1980). James E. Hug, *Tracing the Spirit* (1983). R. L. Kinast, "How Pastoral Theology Functions," 37 *Theology Today*, (1981), 425–38; "A Process Model of Theological Reflection," *J. of Pastoral Care*, 37 (1983), 144–55. National Conference of Catholic Bishops, *As One Who Serves* (1977); *The Program of Priestly Formation* 3d ed. (1981). H. J. M. Nouwen, *Creative Ministry* (1971). K. Rahner, *Theology of Pastoral Action* (1968); "The New Claims Which Pastoral Theology Makes upon Theology as a Whole," *Theological Investigations,* 11 (1974), 115–36. J. L. Segundo, *The Hidden Motives of Pastoral Action* (1978). J. Shea, *Stories of God* (1978). J. D. Whitehead and E. E. Whitehead, *Method in Ministry* (1980).

R. L. KINAST

PASTORAL THEOLOGICAL METHODOLOGY; THEOLOGY AND PSYCHOLOGY; THEORY IN PASTORAL CARE AND COUNSEL-

ING, FUNCTIONS OF; VATICAN COUNCIL II. *See also* ECCLESI-OLOGY AND PASTORAL CARE; ROMAN CATHOLIC PASTORAL CARE; SPIRITUAL DIRECTION, HISTORY AND TRADITIONS OF. *Compare* CASUISTRY, ROMAN CATHOLIC; GRACE AND PASTORAL CARE; INCARNATIONAL THEOLOGY AND PASTORAL CARE (Roman Catholicism); LIBERATION THEOLOGY; MORAL THEOLOGY; PASTORAL PSYCHOLOGY; PASTORAL SOCIOLOGY; SACRAMENTAL THEOLOGY; SPIRITUAL THEOLOGY. *Biography:* GODIN; RAHNER; LONERGAN.

PASTORAL THEORY. *See* THEORY IN PASTORAL CARE AND COUNSELING, FUNCTIONS OF. *See also* PASTORAL THEOLOGY; PRACTICAL THEOLOGY.

PASTORAL/PROPHETIC TENSION. *See* PROPHETIC/PASTORAL TENSION IN MINISTRY.

PASTORALIA. The term *pastoralia* is used to describe a genre of literature that treats the professional and personal life of the ministry in a practical and devotional manner. Unlike theological writing about the nature of ministry or the nature of the church, pastoralia concentrated on such practical matters as the preparation of children for communion, the enlistment of lay persons in benevolence or education, and the personal piety of the ministry. By 1900, although such practical advice to pastors continued to be published, pastoralia had largely been replaced by the emerging technical fields of modern practical theology.

The origin of pastoralia can be traced back to the ancient church, especially to John Chrysostom's *On the Priesthood* and Gregory the Great's *Treatise on Pastoral Care (Liber regulae pastoralis)*. In the medieval period, the demands of the sacrament of penance produced a number of penitential books that examined explicitly a variety of sins and carefully catalogued them according to their seriousness and their appropriate penalties. Such writings influenced relatively few priests before the Council of Trent (1545–63), since few priests were educated and books were expensive. After Trent pastoralia became more influential. Printing and the improvement of the formal education of the ministry produced a significant body of such literature. The Jesuits, who were known as confessors, were famous for their guides to confession, and the Society of St. Sulpice, established by J. J. Olier in 1642, and the Lazarists, established by Vincent de Paul in 1642, made pastoral formation the heart of their program of priestly education.

The basic shape of medieval ministry was determined by the sacramental system and tradition. When Protestantism was established, however, these benchmarks were removed, and little was done to replace them. The confessions of faith defined ministry in terms of the preaching of the Word and the administration of the sacraments, and the various legal definitions of the office by the Protestant states did little to clarify further the pastor's role. Visitations by church officials, such as the Saxon Visitation of 1527–28, revealed serious weaknesses in ministerial practice and concept. Pastoralia literature was an attempt to define the office and its duties in an extra-confessional and extralegal fashion.

Among Lutherans, the pastoralia tradition began with such works as Luther's *Large Catechism,* designed to train the pastors in the fundamentals of the new faith, and was often continued in the *Tröster* literature. A *Tröster* book was a book that provided spiritual consolation in such areas as sickness, death, and dying. The most influential of such works were those by John Bugenhagen (1485–1558) and John Arndt (1555–1621).

The classical Reformation writer on the work of the ministry was Martin Bucer (1491–1551) who ministered at Strasbourg and served as Regius Professor of Divinity at Cambridge. In addition, Bucer was an important influence on John Calvin (1509–64) during his period of exile in Strasbourg (1538–41).

Although Bucer was concerned with the classical Protestant doctrines of justification and scriptural authority, the focus of his advice to the ministry, contained in his *Pastorale,* was his belief in the community as the dwelling place of the Spirit. The cleric was to assist the Spirit by pursuing pastoral visitation, the personal instruction of believers, the organization of small groups for prayer and edification as well as through his labors to support and establish means of benevolence. Above all, Bucer argued that the minister was to be a model of faith to the pious, and this personal faith was the source of his efficiency in the accomplishment of his objectives.

Little significant pastoralia was written by the more scholastic Protestant theologians. The religious wars that gripped Europe until 1648 and the vitality of Catholicism in the period directed much energy into polemics. In addition, the orthodox faced a staggering educational task. Protestantism had inherited its clergy from the medieval church, and its theologians had to reeducate existing ministers as well as train new preachers. In some countries, a century was required to replace the adherents of the old church with advocates of the new.

The Puritan-Pietist emphasis on conversion and religious experience produced the classical age of Protestant pastoralia. There were two aspects of the reform of the ministry that the Puritans and Pietists hoped to effect. The first was a shift away from either the heavily doctrinal preaching favored on the continent or the more ornate preaching popular in England toward a style of preaching that put personal religious needs at the center of the sermon. The second was the advocacy of a pastor with many different areas of his parishioner's life.

The activist interpretation of ministry was elaborated by theologians at the University of Cambridge, where Bucer had taught earlier. William Perkins (1558–1602) and his student, William Ames (1576–1633), who later taught in Holland, were important figures in the development of a form or genre of pastoralia called "cases of conscience." In this type of literature, ethical and religious situations were analysed abstractly so that the minister could recognize the same or a similar situation in the life of his people and give appropriate advice. Such *pastoralia* stressed the role of the minister as a physician of the soul who was guided in his own practice by his own apprehension of grace. Jonathan Edwards (1703–58) drew heavily on this tradition in his *Treatise on Religious Affections* (1746), in which he attempted to establish criteria for distinguishing between various emotional apprehensions of God's saving grace.

The author who most ably represented Puritan and Pietist beliefs about the ministry was Richard Baxter (1615–91) whose *Gildas Silvianus: The Reformed Pastor* has been the most frequently reprinted pastoral manual in English. Baxter envisioned a ministry in which the pastor's study was the fulcrum of his professional life. The minister entered his study to prepare himself for a two-fold witness: preaching to the public and private ministration to individuals. The work needed to prepare for both was similar in nature, involving prayer and Bible study, and symbolically the minister left his study to go to pulpit or home. As in the case of Bucer, personal piety was stressed. The High Church or Laudian party of the seventeenth century maintained a similar ideal of the union of piety and learning. George Herbert (1593–1633), in his *A Priest to the Temple; or the Country Parson* (1652), gave the High Church version a classic expression.

Other Puritan and Pietist ministers maintained similar ideals in their pastoralia. In Germany, Spener and Francke developed the same basic model, although they placed far greater emphasis on the education of the young. Largely as a result of their writings, confirmation became part of the ritual of most Lutheran churches on the continent.

The pastoralia ideal of a union of piety and learning remained normative until the nineteenth century. The last great examples of the genre were Alexandre Vinet's (1797–1847) *Pastoral Theology* and Washington Gladden's (1836–1918) *The Christian Pastor and the Working Church*. Both works, however, were transitional with many elements more characteristic of modern practical theology than of the previous tradition.

Pastoralia declined for a number of reasons. At least from the time of George Whitefield and John Wesley, some Protestant ministers were becoming specialists in certain forms of service, such as evangelism. Second, in the nineteenth century the parish was transformed. Whereas the traditional parish had been a community organized around Word and sacrament, the new parish was more a confederation of organizations that shared a common building and common worship. Naturally, ministry also changed. Third, in the nineteenth century, various branches of pastoral theology became university or seminary disciplines and moved into an academic environment. Fourth, the social scientific revolution of the late nineteenth century and early twentieth century had its impact on the practice of ministry. While this impact began in the area of benevolence, it quickly spread to include education and counseling as well as administration. In this new world, pastoralia had a far less significant role to play in the training of ministers.

Bibliography. R. Baxter, *Gildas Silvianus: The Reformed Pastor* (1766). J. Edwards, *Treatise on Religious Affections* (1746). W. Gladden, *The Christian Pastor and the Working Church* (1898). G. Herbert, *A Priest to the Temple; or the Country Parson* (1652). A. Vinet, *Pastoral Theology* (1853).

G. T. MILLER

CLASSIC LITERATURE IN CARE AND COUNSELING; LITERATURE, PASTORAL USE OF.

PATIENCE/PATIENTHOOD. The terms patience and patienthood are derived from the Latin word meaning to suffer or to endure. Both words are important in describing the essential features of a good pastor. Pastoral care and counseling both involve a significant degree of

patience. One of the warmest expressions of appreciation for a pastor's care comes in the parishioner's memory that "he or she never seemed to be in a hurry."

Listening to many of those in the pastor's care requires a great deal of patience. Older parishioners are those who most often seem to require patience, but there are many others who seem to demand this capacity. Perhaps the most useful skill for pastors in facilitating patience is active listening. Certainly the major portion of a pastoral interview involves quietly listening to what the parishioner says in his or her own way. A significant minority of the time may be spent in trying to put the parishioner's story in the pastor's own context of understanding. Attempting to find ways to reconceptualize what is being said can help to avoid boredom and facilitate patience with the other person. A more active means of listening involves the asking of questions about particular issues of interest in the parishioner's story, thus bringing that story into more dialogical form. This pastor demonstrates patience through listening and interpreting what he or she has heard.

Perhaps the most important use of patience in pastoral counseling concerns the pastoral counselor's dealing with resistance. James Dittes (1967) has persuasively demonstrated how an understanding of and skill in dealing with resistance is important in general pastoral leadership, but in pastoral counseling the ability to handle resistance is one of the competencies that distinguishes the professional therapist from the helpful amateur. The skilled pastoral counselor does not need the "quick cure" to improve his or her self-esteem and can, therefore, tolerate and patiently comment on the counselee's avoidance of what seem to be the central issues in his or her life. Such a counselor has enough understanding of the depths of human nature that getting quickly to the central issue in a person's life is more of a surprise than an expectation.

The concept of patienthood is related to the quality of patience in a number of ways. Most simply, to be a patient requires patience. One must be able to wait for those from whom assistance has been asked. More importantly, pastors are able to be patient with the patients or parishioners they care for when they recognize the patient in themselves. Patience is more likely to be achieved when one recognizes one's likeness to the other in terms of the common human need for care. Another way of expressing this is in terms of the mutuality of care. We can care for others when we have been cared for ourselves and when, in the moment of giving care, we are able to receive it (Tillich). Virtually all skilled pastoral counselors have received counseling or psychotherapy (i.e., have been patients) in the process of learning their specialty in ministry. It is essential, not only for the specialists, but for all who care for others to be aware of their own "patient" needs in order for them to be able to give.

Bibliography. J. E. Dittes, *The Church in the Way* (1967). P. Tillich, "The Theology of Pastoral Care," *Pastoral Psychology,* 10:97 (1959), 21–26.

J. PATTON

GOD'S WILL, ACCEPTANCE OF; SUFFERING. *See also* HANDICAP AND DISABILITY; HEALING; HOSPITALIZATION; EXPERIENCE OF; CHRONIC ILLNESSES. *Compare* ACTING OUT; PAIN MANAGEMENT/PAIN CLINIC.

PATIENT, HOSPITAL. *See* HOSPITAL VISITATION; HOS-PITALIZATION, EXPERIENCE OF. *See also* CANCER, HEART, *or* SURGICAL PATIENT; MENTAL HOSPITAL/MENTAL HOSPITALIZATION; SICK, PASTORAL CARE OF.

PATRISTIC SOUL CARE. *See* EARLY CHURCH, PAS-TORAL CARE AND COUNSELING IN.

PATTON, JOHN. *See* PASTORAL THEOLOGY, PROTES-TANT.

PEACE. From scriptural times, *peace* has been understood within the Judeo-Christian tradition to imply much more than the absence of conflict. In the Hebrew Scriptures, peace can mean a state of rest and well-being, physical as well as spiritual, or it can refer to a state of concord among individuals and communities. Finally, peace can be equivalent to salvation, although not in any theologically precise sense; so understood, peace is necessarily God's gift (Kittel, pp. 401–8). In the NT, peace is again understood as rest, or as reconciliation with God. Most fundamentally, it is equated with the eschatological salvation of the whole person, or indeed of creation itself, wherein we will be restored to the state of well-being that God intends for us. When Paul urges those within the churches to live at peace with one another, his exhortations are colored by the religious connotations of peace. Repeatedly, he calls for a harmony of persons that goes beyond mere absence of conflict, to approach the integrity of a community that is called by God to peace, and shares the mind of Christ (Kittel, pp. 411–17).

In the early centuries of the church, the idea of peace as the harmony of believers who are of one mind in Christ was associated with the concept of *communio*, the bond that unites the bishops and the faithful within local communities and throughout the church. In this context, to be at or in peace became synonymous with "to be in communion with the church." The bond of *communio* was originally seen as being both effected and signified by common participation in shared beliefs, practices, sacraments, and above all, in the Eucharist. The custom among Catholic and some Protestant congregations, of exchanging some sign or greeting of peace during a worship service, should be seen in this light. Properly understood, this gesture is not merely a sign of good will, but an affirmation of the unity of the people as a church recreated by their common worship.

Recently, the concept of peace has also assumed great importance in social ethics. The insecurities of the nuclear age have generated much interest in identifying the political conditions for peace, the state of mind and spirit of peaceableness, and the religious imperatives to be peacemakers. At the same time, a number of churchmen and theologians have insisted that on the political level, true peace cannot be equated with the absence of strife. Rather, it necessarily requires justice and the good order that flows from right relationships among persons.

Bibliography. J. Gremillion, *The Gospel of Peace and Justice* (1976). L. Hertling, *Communio: Church and Papacy in Early Christianity* (1972). G. Kittel, ed., *Theological Dictionary of the New Testament*, vol. 2 (1964) 400–20.

J. PORTER

FORGIVENESS; LOVE; RECONCILING. *See also* HOLY SPIRIT, DOCTRINE OF AND PASTORAL CARE; SALVATION AND PAS-TORAL CARE. *Compare* CONFLICT AND CONFLICT MANAGE-MENT.

PEACE-MAKING AND PASTORAL CARE. A movement among persons in specialized ministries of pastoral care to use the resources of their training and professional roles to work for peace based on justice. The movement is based on a conviction that socially responsible, "prophetic" pastoral care and counseling must address the eco-justice issues which are the underlying societal causes of individual and family problems. It focuses on what its proponents regard as the most urgent moral and spiritual issue of our times—the threat of nuclear holocaust.

A group of pastoral counselors with this concern met during the national convention of the American Association of Pastoral Counselors in April 1983 and organized a nuclear peacemaking group called "Pastoral Counselors for Social Responsibility." At the International Congress on Pastoral Care and Counseling (1983) this group became an international peacemaking network when pastoral care specialists from nineteen countries joined. In November 1984, a peacemaking federation was created of persons from all eight pastoral care associations in America, called the "Pastoral Care Network for Social Responsibility" (PCNSR). In June 1989, the PCNSR co-sponsored (with the Christian Peace Conference) a theory-building conference in Czechoslovakia of forty-five pastoral theologians and psychologists from Eastern and Western Europe and North America on "Developing Resources for Justice-Based Peacemaking."

The purposes of PCNSR are the following: (1) To provide a federation of specialists in pastoral care which will support and empower one another to respond to the nuclear crisis by working for peace with justice. (2) To promote increasing awareness among such specialists of the impact of this crisis on the lives of the persons and institutions with whom they work; to provide pastoral care and counseling to persons experiencing anxiety and stress from the crisis; and to develop a variety of healing responses to the crisis using the insights and skills of specialized training in pastoral care. (3) To support the development of peacemaking groups and activities within and among all pastoral care associations. (4) To reach out to specialists in pastoral care in other countries for cooperation and mutual support of peacemaking activities across national boundaries. (5) To cooperate with other professional groups committed to nuclear peacemaking, e.g., Physicians (Psychologists, Teachers, etc.) for Social Responsibility.

Some of the contributions to peace which persons with advanced training in pastoral psychology and counseling can make include: (1) Utilizing their dual psychological-theological training and research skills to increase understanding of the fundamental ethical, spiritual, and psychosocial causes of intergroup and international conflict, and the "nuclear insanity" characterizing the thinking and behavior of the leaders of the political superpowers. (2) Employing clinical insights and therapeutic methods to help heal the widespread despair, denial, and "psychic numbing" which block constructive responses to the nuclear threat; this includes helping people in pastoral counseling and education to do their "despair work" (Joanna Macy), so as to move through and beyond paralyzing, suppressed terror, and anticipatory grief about the death of the biosphere, to empowering hope and change-producing action. (3) Utilizing theological and psychological resources to generate in oneself and others images of a transformed future, and to nurture a deepening reverence and love for the planet and for humankind. (4) Creating small study-action groups, to provide the mutual support and caring that are essential for thinking about the unthinkable and acting together effectively for peace. (5) Developing and testing new methods for doing these peacemaking actions in relationships with parishioners, clients, patients, students, colleagues, and family, beginning with oneself.

Bibliography. J. R. Macy, *Despair and Personal Power in the Nuclear Age* (1983). K. McGinnis and J. McGinnis, *Parenting for Peace and Justice* (1981).

H. CLINEBELL

PROPHETIC/PASTORAL TENSION IN MINISTRY; CONSCIOUSNESS RAISING; LIFESTYLE ISSUES IN PASTORAL CARE. *Compare* CHRISTIAN CONCILIATION MOVEMENT; CONFLICT AND CONFLICT MANAGEMENT; MEDIATION/CONCILIATION; VIOLENCE.

PEAK EXPERIENCE. A term coined by A. Maslow to depict the climax of an individual's self-actualization process. Persons undergoing such experiences report feeling deeply at peace with themselves, others, and their world; more aware, spontaneous, and integrated; and more focused and less bound by time and space. Religion, according to Maslow, can yield a type of peak experience in such individuals, especially in its more mystical expressions.

Peak experiences, according to Maslow, cannot be willed or forgotten. They merge subject with object, value and emotion, without the loss of self. They are a type of altered state of consciousness, perceived as pleasant and desirable by those open to such deepening and stretching experiences. Recent authors (e.g., Foster, 1978; Fowler, 1981) have considered such experience in the context of their theories of spiritual growth and development.

Bibliography. R. Foster, *Celebration of Discipline* (1978). J. Fowler, *Stages of Faith* (1981). A. Maslow, *The Psychology of Science* (1966); *Toward a Psychology of Being* 2d ed. (1968).

R. E. BUTMAN

MYSTICISM; RELIGIOUS EXPERIENCE. *See also* HUMANISTIC PSYCHOLOGY (Theories and Research); PSYCHOLOGY OF RELIGION. *Compare* ECSTASY; ILLUMINATION; TRANCE.

PEALE, NORMAN VINCENT. (1895–). Has become synonymous with the words "positive thinking" and "art of living." An author, pastor, lecturer, preacher, and media celebrity, Peale has been minister of the Marble Collegiate Church (NYC) since 1932, teaching a lively blend of religion and psychology, which takes the form of workable techniques for living happy and successful lives. His main emphasis is on affirming hope over despair and the ability and responsibility of each person to do something tangible about making his or her situa-

tion better. Though criticized for his view of human existence, Peale's popularity through radio, television, books, and *Guideposts* magazine has contributed to the wide acceptance of the use of practical psychological principles in religious living. His most significant contribution to pastoral counseling has been the American Foundation for Religion and Psychiatry, which he formed with psychiatrist Smiley Blanton in 1937. This foundation was an early training center for pastoral counselors and a guiding force in bringing pastoral counseling specialists together in the American Association for Pastoral Counselors in 1963.

C. M. MENDENHALL, III

MIND-CURE MOVEMENT.

PELAGIANISM. *See* FREEDOM AND BONDAGE; WILL/ WILLING.

PENANCE, SACRAMENT OF (SACRAMENT OF RECONCILIATION). The Roman Catholic sacrament in which sins committed after baptism are forgiven through the absolution of a priest.

1. **History.** The biblical text usually cited as the scriptural basis for the sacrament of penance is Jn. 20:22–23: "Receive the Holy Spirit. If you forgive the sins of any, they are forgiven them; if you retain the sins of any, they are retained." The text does not indicate who is to do the forgiving or how it is to be done, but the fact that the text is there at all indicates that the forgiveness of sins was part of the ministry of the early church.

By the fourth century a clear pattern had evolved, whereby one could receive sacramental forgiveness of sins, or "second baptism," only once in a lifetime. Furthermore, the sacrament was reserved for serious sins of a public nature (apostasy, murder, heresy, adultery). The penitent was in a sense excommunicated. Only after a long period of public penance did the penitent receive absolution and reconciliation with the community in a public ceremony presided over by the bishop.

After the barbarian invasions, the European continent was to a great extent re-Christianized by Celtic monks, who brought with them customs that had evolved in the Irish monasteries. One such custom was the practice of private confession, originally a form of spiritual direction that eventually evolved to include the sacramental confession of even minor faults. A relatively minor penance of a private nature was imposed, and absolution was granted even prior to the performance of the penance. It was at this time that the use of penitential books also appeared. These books contained lists of various sins with an appropriate penance attached. The spread of the practice of private confession, which could be made as often as one wanted, gradually submerged the notion of sacramental confession being a reconciliation with the larger Christian community.

Although the practice of private confession was resisted by many regional councils of bishops as an unacceptable innovation, the practice eventually became the norm, although the practice of public confession still continued to coexist in various places. Finally, the Fourth Lateran Council (1215) introduced the precept of confession at least once a year. This precept tacitly accepted the full validity of private confession and effectively eliminated the practice of public confession.

During the Middle Ages the essential elements of the sacrament of penance were more clearly delineated. These elements include contrition with an accompanying resolution not to sin again, oral confession to a priest, acceptance of a penance including reparation and restitution, and absolution by the priest. As soon as the penitent is contrite, his or her sins are, of course, forgiven, but implicit in the contrition is the intention to confess at least all grave sins to the community as represented by the priest. To this extent the notion of reconciliation with the larger Christian community still survived even in private confession. In response to the controversies of the Reformation, the Council of Trent (1545 – 63) simply reaffirmed this understanding of the sacrament of penance, which remained the normative understanding of the sacrament until the Second Vatican Council (1962 – 65).

2. Second Vatican Council Reforms. The Second Vatican Council called for a revision of the rite for the sacrament of penance, so that the communal aspect of sin and reconciliation with the larger Christian community would both again be stressed. What resulted were three separate rites. The "Rite of Reconciliation of Individual Penitents" is the rite most commonly used. The penitent confesses his or her sins privately to a priest. The anonymity of the confessional booth remains an option. A new option is face-to-face confession to a priest in a "Reconciliation Room," which lends itself potentially to an in-depth discussion of the penitent's spiritual growth.

Pastorally disastrous were the changes in the responses that the penitent was to make in the course of his or her confession. Even though these responses were minimal, they constituted a "new way of going to confession." The old way, though difficult enough for some, was at least familiar. Undoubtedly, the fact that there was now a new way of going to confession partially explains the decline in the number of confessions. Many confessors simply began to tell their penitents to confess the old way or "the way you were taught."

The other two rites are the "Rite for Reconciliation of Several Penitents with Individual Confession and Absolution" and the "Rite for Reconciliation of Penitents with General Confession and Absolution." The latter rite is to be used only in emergency situations when there are not sufficient confessors available to hear all the individual confessions within a reasonable period of time. After Vatican II many priests artfully arranged for such emergency situations to occur by advertising a "Penance Service" without really explaining what a penance service is.

3. Factors in Decline. A penance service is essentially the Rite for Reconciliation of Several Penitents with Individual Confession and Absolution. A common period of preparation precedes the individual confessions. Without an explanation beforehand that individual confession is integral to the rite, the penance service sometimes attracts penitents who are expecting general absolution. Priests are sometimes intentionally vague about whether or not there will be general absolution, because they want to create a situation where general absolution would be the only reasonable alternative, and because they want to attract penitents who would other-

wise stay away. Although priests who resort to this subterfuge are undoubtedly well-intentioned, such casuistry is not pastorally effective in the long run. Pastorally, such policies have resulted in confusion about the need for individual confession. This confusion is also a partial explanation for the decline in the number of confessions.

Another reason for the decline is a more scriptural understanding of grave sin as being the breaking of a covenantal relationship with God rather than the commission of specific sinful acts. It is not that specific sinful acts are meaningless, but they have to be placed within the context of the overall orientation of the penitent's life. What fundamental option either for or against a relationship with God has the penitent made, and how do these acts support, alter, or rescind that fundamental option? In this way of thinking only a decisive breaking of the covenantal relationship with God would constitute a grave or mortal sin. Specific sinful acts, even though very seriously wrong, would not necessarily indicate that this decisive break has taken place. Mortal or grave sin is certainly still possible and undoubtedly common enough, but in this more scriptural view of sin, mortal or grave sin is much less common than previously perceived. Since strictly speaking only mortal sins must be confessed, a more scriptural view of sin lessens those occasions when confession would be required.

The confession of nonmortal or venial sins is not required, although it is recommended. Such confessions are called "confessions of devotion." After Vatican II many confessors discouraged penitents from making confessions of devotion. The confessors evidently thought that the frequent recital of "a grocery list of sins" was not particularly conducive to spiritual growth. Such confessors may well have been correct in their thinking, but their approach to their penitents was often harsh and abrupt. Pastorally they often created further confusion about the need for individual confessions. This additional confusion is yet another factor explaining the decline in the number of confessions.

Another factor explaining the decline is an increased social consciousness concerned about issues of war and peace, racism, and sexism. Catholics who are passionately concerned about the social sins imbedded in our culture sometimes have difficulties relating to a sacrament that is still primarily concerned about the personal sins of the individual.

Furthermore, ecumenism has highlighted the fact that Rome has always acknowledged the validity of Orthodox sacraments. In most branches of Orthodoxy, however, the communal confession of sins at the beginning of the Eucharist is considered sacramental reconciliation. For the Orthodox the Eucharist is the primary sacrament of the forgiveness of sins. Private confessions are still heard, but they are accompanied by little of the legalism that has characterized Western Christianity. An ecumenical awareness about the practice of the Orthodox churches raises further questions about the need for the private confessions of individuals.

Finally, it can be argued that the birth control issue caused many Catholics to stop going to confession. A great many Catholics formed their own conscience in opposition to official church teaching. On the church's part there was no consistent pastoral approach for Catholics who could not accept papal teaching on this point. Going to confession became a form of roulette. One could encounter everything from affirmation to outright condemnation. After a while it became easier simply not to go to confession at all.

Whether or not people go to confession has a lot to do with the kinds of priests available to hear them. Some parishes still have a considerable number of penitents; other parishes have next to none. Some priests are pastorally inept; others have pastoral sensitivity. Nevertheless, it is clear that Catholics are going to confession less frequently. This may well be desirable, especially if these less frequent confessions manifest a deeper level of conversion and a more mature effort at Christian growth.

Bibliography. P. DeClerck, "Celebrating Penance or Reconciliation?" *Clergy Review*, 68 (1983), 310–21. B. Häring, *The Sacrament of Reconciliation* (1980). M. Hebblethwaite and K. Donovan, *The Theology of Penance* (1979). M. Hellwig, *Sign of Reconciliation and Conversion* (1983). J. Martos, "Penance" in *Doors to the Sacred* (1981). L. Orsy, *The Evolving Church and the Sacrament of Penance* (1978). E. Schillebeeckx, ed., *Sacramental Reconciliation* (1971).

G. McCARRON

CONSCIENCE; DISCIPLINE, PASTORAL CARE AS; REPENTANCE AND CONFESSION; RITUAL AND PASTORAL CARE; ROMAN CATHOLIC PASTORAL CARE. *See also* ASCETICAL PRACTICES; CASUISTRY, ROMAN CATHOLIC; ECCLESIOLOGY AND PASTORAL CARE; FORGIVENESS; GRACE AND PASTORAL CARE; GUILT; LITURGICAL AND DEVOTIONAL LIFE, ROMAN CATHOLIC; MORAL THEOLOGY AND PASTORAL CARE; RECONCILING; SIN/SINS; SPIRITUALITY, ROMAN CATHOLIC; VATICAN COUNCIL II. *Compare* UNDOING.

PENITENCE. See PENANCE, SACRAMENT OF; REPENTANCE AND CONFESSION.

PENITENTIAL TRADITION. See PASTORAL CARE (History, Traditions, and Definitions); PENANCE. *See also* CASUISTRY; EARLY CHURCH, PASTORAL CARE AND COUNSELING IN.

PENITENTS, JEWISH CARE AND COUNSELING OF. Judaism teaches that human beings are endowed with the potential for both good and evil and that life is a continuing struggle between forces that make for decency and drives and emotions that are self-destructive. Jewish tradition categorized these forces as the *Yetzer Tov*, the impulse to do good, and the *Yetzer Ra*, the impulse to do evil. At times they even complemented one another. For example, were it not for the sexual impulse, whatever its negative side, marriages would not take place and children would not be brought into the world.

Judaism holds out the opportunity for forgiveness and the promise of a second chance for those who are genuinely penitent. The Hebrew word for repentance is *Tshuvah* derived from the root, *to return*. Individuals who are successful in changing their behavior are called *Baalei Tshuvah* (plural) or *Baal Tshuvah* (singular), literally, *masters of repentance.*

The holiday and life cycles of Judaism are replete with liturgical and ritual themes focusing upon penitence.

Foremost among them is the High Holiday season—*Rosh Hashanah*, the Jewish New Year, and *Yom Kippur*, the Day of Atonement, which follows ten days later. Jews recognized that it was necessary to create a mood and a tone in anticipation of these events. Therefore, during the 30 days prior to the onset of the High Holidays, special penitential prayers are recited in the synagogue. The *Shofar*, or ram's horn, is always sounded daily, its call is a reminder that worshipers must ready themselves for the coming season of soul searching and introspection.

The ten day period between *Rosh Hashanah* and *Yom Kippur* is known as "the ten days of Penitence" and the intervening Sabbath is called "the Sabbath of Repentance." On that day, special selections are read from the prophet Hosea. The imagery here is significant. The people of Israel are compared to Hosea's wife, Gomer, a wayward woman. Atonement will be followed by forgiveness. Rejection is never immutable. The liturgical call is clear: "Repentance, prayer, and righteousness avert the sincere decree."

Judaism stresses that prayer, however important, is only a beginning. Wrongful acts against another individual can only be forgiven through deeds and not through words. Each person is accountable both to God and to those who have been wronged.

Although deathbed confessions are not only accepted but encouraged, Judaism is well aware of the limitations of this form of penitence. Certainly, for those whose lives have been steadfastly evil or who wish to salvage their consciences before death, it is an important cathartic. Still, repentance during one's active lifetime is far more desirable since it allows for the opportunity to make amends and reparations. It is the latter which is constantly emphasized. That emphasis commences during the early years of a child's religious education and remains an all pervasive theme.

There are penitents whose intentions to change are blocked by deep seated psychological difficulties which they cannot resolve by themselves. Judaism urges such persons to seek guidance and counseling. Rabbis are prepared to provide insights and to be supportive. When the occasion requires it, rabbis will refer such men and women to others who are therapeutically trained to handle more complex situations.

Traditionally, Jewish sages were leery of persons who repeated the same transgressions again and again followed by repeated repentance. Today, it is clear that the need to repeat patterns of misbehavior is a manifestation of deep seated conflicts. Such individuals require appropriate interventions by a trained therapist who can help uncover the factors thwarting the person's wish to become whole once more. The capacity to understand the motivations behind one's behavior will lead to genuine penitence. Psychological understanding can be an important tool in the service of achieving religious ideals.

Bibliography. J. D. Soloveitchik, *On Repentance* (1984).

S. SELTZER

CONSCIENCE (Judaism); JEWISH CARE AND COUNSELING (History, Tradition, and Contemporary Issues); REPENTANCE AND CONFESSION. *See also* FORGIVENESS; GUILT. *Compare* CONVERSION (Jewish Care and Counseling); PENANCE, SACRAMENT OF.

PENTECOST. *See* JEWISH HOLY DAYS AND FESTIVALS; LITURGICAL CALENDAR.

PENTECOSTALISM. *See* CHARISMATIC EXPERIENCE; CHARISMATIC PASTORAL CARE.

PERCEPTION. *See* PERCEPTIVENESS AND SENSITIVITY, PASTORAL; PHENOMENOLOGICAL METHOD IN PASTORAL CARE; PHENOMENOLOGICAL PSYCHOLOGY AND PSYCHO-THERAPY; SOCIAL PERCEPTION, JUDGMENT, AND BELIEF.

PERCEPTIVENESS AND SENSITIVITY, PASTO-RAL. *Pastoral perceptiveness* is the well developed ability to take in data about human situations and to draw accurate inferences from that data when practiced by a pastor or a person acting pastorally. *Pastoral sensitivity* is the capacity for having a keen and delicate responsiveness for the range of feelings generated by persons and their interactions, coupled with the ability to let that awareness inform care-giving action as practiced by a pastor or pastoral person.

1. **Distinctions.** Perceptiveness and sensitivity are overlapping but not identical qualities. Perceptiveness typically denotes use of a more active than passive process, and one which operates on discrete and tangible, if subtle and easily missed, sources of data. It also suggests an ability to cognitively combine the data thus garnered to draw conclusions most people would fail to reach. Sensitivity suggests a more passive openness to being affected by emotional stimuli, an absence or defendedness against feelings. Its data are generally understood to be more visceral, less cognitive, and less available to be measured. It partakes more of Whitehead's mode of causal efficacy, whereas perceptiveness stresses presentational immediacy. Sensitivity also implies that a relationship of vulnerability to the other's feelings exists between sender and receiver, and that that relationship exerts a governing influence over the receiver's response. Perceptiveness suggests no such mutuality, though it does not preclude it.

"Pastoral" in this usage suggests, in addition to the office of the person described, a normative quality of investment in the deeper well-being of the other; so the phrase could properly be used about someone who is not formally a pastor.

2. **Development.** Perceptiveness can be greatly enhanced by learning the signs and symbols that convey meaning in different groups and situations. A pastor's broad grasp of the resources of a culture's literature, music, art, and language directly increases perceptiveness, as it alerts him or her to layers of encoded meaning that would otherwise be missed. Similarly, specialized knowledge of the lifestyle of a given region or vocation, or of the data peculiar to a pastoral specialty (i.e., pastoral psychotherapy), will multiply the meanings the skilled pastor can glean from any human exchange.

Sensitivity is more likely to be improved by identifying and reducing the pastor's own internal barriers to feelings. CPE and the pastor's own psychotherapy are the typical structured routes to that improvement, though it is generally understood that the pastor's own experience of intense pain and/or joy increases the ability to respond to it in others. It is also probable that an increase in

sensitivity produces an increase in perceptiveness, in that it reduces the defense against recognizing certain classes of data.

3. **Limits.** There are finite limits to the expansion of both qualities, though none of us ever reaches their full potential. Perceptiveness is limited by the intellectual capacity of the pastor and by the sharpness of his or her senses. Sensitivity's potential limits are set by the early life experiences of the pastor. Those who develop the capacity for intense feeling as children maintain a life-long advantage, though major increases in this capacity can be cultivated successfully.

B. W. GRANT

CLINICAL PASTORAL PERSPECTIVE; LISTENING; PHENOME-NOLOGICAL METHOD IN PASTORAL CARE; PRUDENCE (Moral Theology). *Compare* INSIGHT; INTERPRETATION AND HERME-NEUTICS, PASTORAL; INTUITION; PRESENCE, MINISTRY OF; SELF-UNDERSTANDING; SOCIAL PERCEPTION, JUDGMENT, AND BELIEF.

PERFECTIONISM. Behavior or belief that is governed by standards that would commonly be recognized as unrealistically high. Often paradoxical, it appears as unforgivable guilt and inability to receive grace in the apparently upright, or as continual striving and dissatisfaction with oneself in the outwardly successful. In these forms it is a distortion in self-evaluation and thus in self-transcendence. Narcissistic perfectionists, who demand that others be perfect for them, have a flawed view of what the world can provide for them.

Perfectionism appears, for example, in (1) the attitude, "It's better to do it myself, then I know it's done right"; (2) the demands of wounded church members that others validate their ideas, include them in decision making, and the like; (3) the inability to organize ideas clearly, despite good knowledge of a subject; (4) the belief that only one way will do, when several means are feasible; (5) the tone of moral perfection that is intolerant toward others' faults; and (6) constant searching for the "perfect" church. Among professionals, perfectionism abounds in many unexamined assumptions about obligations to persons and in compulsive obedience to procedure, without regard to its contribution to others' well-being.

1. **Psychological Interpretations.** Commonly associated with obsessive-compulsive disorders, perfectionism can be understood as a reaction-formation to the self-reproaches that Freud identified as the material from which obsessional ideas come. It is also similar to the ritualistic, anxiety-reducing behavior of compulsions. Some traits of the obsessive personality also characterize the perfectionist: emotional constriction, obstinacy, perseverance, rejection of others, rigidity, self-doubt, strong superego (Lazarre).

Psychoanalytic psychology assigns perfection, understood as primary narcissism, a crucial role in human development. Under favorable conditions in the parent-child relationship, one line of the child's early experience of perfection ("I am perfect") later powers "ego-syntonic ambitions and purposes," enjoyment, and self-esteem. The other line, ("You are perfect, but I am part of you") leads to ideals for the personality. Residual perfectionism in adults, at least in the narcissistic personality disorders, expresses archaic perfections that have remained "untamed" and unintegrated into the adult personality, owing to less than optimal parent-child relationships (Kohut, 1971). Psychoanalysis helps account for the suffering that some perfectionism brings to those around the perfectionist, as well as for the suffering of this person himself or herself.

Beyond these two views, perfectionism is a useful "perspective" on all human experience and pathology. For example, the hopelessness of depression can be seen as perfectionism: the unattainable ideal leads to the inevitable conclusion, "There is no value in doing anything at all."

From the psychoanalytic perspective, an overactive superego or ego-ideal produces "chronic feelings of unworthiness, or low self-esteem, depression, or self-dejection" (Pruyser, 1968). Here perfectionism stands within the framework of shame and guilt, which can be linked to the framework of vocation, i.e., to the fault and the exposure that result from employing one's energies in a calling. Under vocation, perfectionism appears as "unproductiveness, ungenerousness, controlling behavior, and the warding off of much of life, experience and feeling" (Pruyser, 1976). Jungian thought links it to procrastination, impatience, and the inability or refusal to commit oneself to something and to follow through (Woodman, 1982; von Franz, 1981). The forces of duty and control stifle the forces of life (Leonard, 1977–79), but the controlling behavior provides only a false security and cuts persons off from other inner resources.

Pruyser (1968) believes that perfectionism may not originate in invalid standards, but in an atmosphere of blame in which standards are communicated to children. Children learn to associate the standards with aggression toward themselves, rather than to anticipate recognition and admiration. Misseldine (1963) traces perfectionism to the parents' withholding of affection and acceptance until the child's achievements are superior. These children belittle their efforts rather than appreciate what they have achieved. Existential theology views perfectionism as a normal response to guilt and condemnation. The resulting striving for moral perfection becomes pathological only if the "risk of imperfection is avoided" (Tillich, 1952). Still, in all the various terms that describe it, perfectionism is heteronomous: persons lose themselves to external standards of achievement, to unintegrated grandiose expectations of themselves or others, or to harsh, often unjustified expectations of the consequences of falling short.

However, cultural standards of achievement and striving support perfectionism (Misseldine, 1963). Ideas of progress and of individual responsibility also support it. In addition to scrupulosity, strivings for spiritual flawlessness, and schismatic demands that others be perfect, perfectionism now takes the form of striving for one's "personal best." Each of the modern therapies has its own ideas of human perfection, e.g., the ability to love and work in an illusionless acceptance of reality, or the acceptance of one's own power, rather than the granting of it to others through projection. The effort to attain these secularly recognized states consumes energy and resources comparable to those required to produce a monk, mystic, or sage in the past.

Perfectionism thus is commonly associated with a number of pernicious values. Paramount among them is a loss of vitality, courage, and power to affirm oneself (Tillich, 1952). It also inhibits the development of community.

2. **Theological Understandings.** The critique of perfectionism raises the question, What does it mean to be a perfect human being? Theology has not treated the question as oxymoronic, but meaningful. It is a way of asking what the benefits of grace are for this life and how persons are to live in light of their faults and capacity for good. The primary biblical words for "perfect" do not describe an ideal condition, but have such meanings as "whole," "sound," or "mature," and the Latin root means "thoroughly made or done." Where perfection appears as an ideal (Mt. 5:48), it represents an aspiration, not a standard (Campbell). Even if one disagrees, one's assumptions about how to read NT ideas of perfection must come under scrutiny.

For R. Niebuhr (1949) the original perfection of humanity entails the creaturely as well as the self-transcendent aspect, thereby removing the justification for perfectionist rejection of the body. Tillich views perfection as unattainable in this life, but as a sanctifying process leading toward maturity. It consists of four elements: increasing awareness, increasing freedom, increasing relatedness, and increasing transcendence.

Perfectionism also takes specific social forms. Franciscan perfectionism delivered hope to the Renaissance and helped fuel its belief in the possibilities of the human being (Niebuhr). It is found in ideas of progress, utopias, evolution, even development. Despite the risk that these ideas will fail, leaving behind them cynicism and conservative reaction analogous to the loss of vitality in individual perfectionists, they probably have more to contribute than the personal form.

3. **Pastoral Approaches.** Perfectionism poses many pastoral problems. The main prescription is to learn survival skills, beginning with the nondespairing recognition that perfectionism is here to stay. That established, pastors will see some perfectionism yield to the various skills and experiences that aid coping. A disorganized teacher may learn to set objectives and consider the audience. A person who sees only one means to an end may benefit from some general teaching about substitutability of means in practical reason. With the less tractable, pastors may make more use of their authority ("go to confession no more than every six months" or "name at least one positive thing you've done or experienced each day and celebrate it"). Pastors may need to become reconciled to persons' seeking help from other pastors and be attentive to persons who bring repetitious complaints. Pastors should also be able to answer the question, "Who is suffering primarily—the perfectionist or others?" If others are suffering primarily, then the pastor may need, in addition to skills of referral, some skills or consultation in group dynamics and intervention with those who are lacking in insight.

Perfectionist persons may present a particularly difficult problem to pastoral counselors who themselves come from faith traditions where perfectionism in its many guises is preached or implied. Thus beside the innate psychotherapeutic difficulties of getting and keeping perfectionistic persons in counseling, the added possibility of countertransference forces which may threaten the thin line between assisting persons in softening their superego demands and at the same time appreciating the values and standards of one's faith commitments has to be taken into consideration.

Bibliography. S. M. Burgess, ed., *Reaching Beyond: Chapters in the History of Perfectionism* (1984). J. Y. Campbell, "Perfection," *Interpreter's Dictionary of the Bible* (1962). S. Freud, "Further Remarks on the Neuro-psychoses of Defense," *SE,* III, pp. 162–89. H. Kohut, *The Analysis of the Self* (1971). R. D. Laing, *The Politics of Experience* (1967). A. Lazarre et al., "Oral, Obsessive, and Hysterical Personality Patterns," *J. of Psychiatric Research* , (1970), 275 – 90. L. Leonard, "Puer's Daughter," *Psychological Perspectives,* 8:1 (1977), 22–31; "Puella Patterns," *ibid.,* 9:2 (1978), 127 – 43; "The Puella and the Perverted Old Man," *ibid.,* 10:1 (1979), 7–17; "Amazon Armors," *ibid.,* 20:2 (1979), 113–30. W. H. Misseldine, *Your Inner Child of the Past* (1963). R. Niebuhr, *The Nature and Destiny of Man* (1949). P. Tillich, *The Courage to Be* (1952); *Systematic Theology,* vol. 3 (1964). M. L. von Franz, *Puer Aeternus* 2d ed. (1981). M. Woodman, *Addiction to Perfection* (1982).

J. R. BURCK

CONSCIENCE (Protestantism); LEGALISM AND ANTINOMIANISM; OBSESSIVE-COMPULSIVE DISORDER; RIGHTEOUSNESS/BEING RIGHT. *See also* GUILT; PRIDE AND HUMILITY (Moral Theology). *Compare* CASUISTRY; SANCTIFICATION; SCRUPULOSITY.

PERKINS, WILLIAM (1558–1602). English Puritan theologian and casuist. As the celebrated lecturer at Great St. Andrews in Cambridge, Perkins helped to initiate and to shape the Puritan preoccupation with introspective piety, innovative pastoral methods, and "case divinity."

Known for pulpit oratory that "left a doleful echo in his auditors' ears a good while after," Perkins developed a rigorously logical method of resolving pastoral dilemmas (Thomas Fuller, *The Holy State,* 1648, p. 81). "Amongst other things which he preached profitably, he began at length to teach, How with the tongue of the Learned one might speake a word in due season to him that is weary . . . by untying and explaining diligently Cases of Conscience (as they are called)" (William Ames, *Conscience with the Power and Cases thereof,* 1643, p. 2).

Perkins appropriated the dialectical methods of the French logician Petrus Ramus to unravel moral and spiritual dilemmas. His *Discourse of Conscience* (1597) and *Whole Treatise of the Cases of Conscience* (1606) therefore popularized a style of pastoral conversation marked by intensive questioning, biblical citations, and syllogistic reasoning. He was equally important for a style of preaching designed to elicit anxiety, conviction, hope, and assurance. His influence was pronounced in the American colonies, where his texts were read in the colleges throughout the seventeenth and eighteenth centuries.

E. B. HOLIFIELD

CASUISTRY, PROTESTANT; HISTORY OF PROTESTANT PASTORAL CARE (United States). *See also* REFORMED PASTORAL CARE.

PERLS, FRITZ (1893–1970). The founder of Gestalt Therapy, a major theoretical orientation that stresses life as experiential. Perls came from a family of German Jews and was raised and trained in medicine in Berlin. He served as a medic for the German army during World War I and, after training in psychoanalysis, emigrated to South Africa, where he worked as an analyst. In 1946 he moved to America, initiated the original framework for his Gestalt Therapy, and established the New York Institute or Gestalt Therapy. Throughout the remainder of his career he founded additional Gestalt Therapy Institutes and promoted his theories through his writings and lectures.

Perls wove together strands from psychoanalytic psychology, existentialism, and previous work in Gestalt Psychology to form his Gestalt Therapy. He recognized his psychoanalytic roots, but expanded them and classified himself as an existentialist rather than an analyst. Perls stressed the necessity of acting out experience using a variety of techniques such as the empty chair, in order to experience fully the whole or "Gestalt" of life.

Bibliography. F. Perls, *Gestalt Therapy Verbatim* (1969); *In and Out of the Garbage Pail* (1969).

B. HOUSKAMP

GESTALT PSYCHOLOGY AND PSYCHOTHERAPY.

PERSECUTION. *See* ANTI-SEMITISM; HOLOCAUST; VICTIMIZATION; WITCHCRAFT. *See also* EARLY CHURCH, PASTORAL CARE AND COUNSELING IN; PASTORAL CARE (History, Traditions, and Definitions).

PERSON (Christian Perspective). The notions of the person and the personal have had an important place in the history of Christian thought and in contemporary discussion. Whether applied to the human individual or to God, they have been used to point to a reality which is rational, relational, self-conscious, free and responsible. In contemporary discussion the terms are used both descriptively and normatively. By examining the parallels to these terms in the Bible and reflecting on their use in the history of Christian thought, we can approach more meaningfully their use in contemporary Christian anthropology and in pastoral care.

1. **Biblical Understandings.** The terms *person, personal,* and *personality* do not have an exact equivalent in biblical thought, but in so far as these terms express the contemporary attempt to distinguish the distinctively human from other forms of individuality or to speak of God by using the human being as a basic metaphor or model, there are biblical parallels. The Hebrew words *ruah* (spirit), *nephesh* (soul), and *leb* (heart) in a number of their usages express something of the distinctiveness of the human individual which modern use of the term person is meant to express. Moreover, the reality of God, even apart from the anthropomorphic language often used to characterize God, is in a variety of senses understood metaphorically and perhaps literally in personalistic terms.

Biblical scholars have long argued over the degree to which there was a vital sense of individuality within Hebrew patriarchal culture. Ideas of corporate personality have been held to be characteristic of Hebrew moral, religious, and legal thought. It now seems probable that

883

corporate moral responsibility may have marked Hebrew life, but it is not clear how such thinking may have modified the sense of individuality. Certainly, by the time of Jeremiah and Ezekiel there was a clear and strong emphasis on the responsibility of the individual. The extent to which women and children would qualify as persons in the modern sense during any period of Hebrew history is uncertain.

2. **Historical Development.** In the NT and the Septuagint the term *prosopon,* which becomes the Latin *persona* in the early church, was usually understood to mean face or countenance, but it could mean simply a human being. In Greek usage the term also meant a "mask" worn by an actor, since the mask resembles the human face. Derivatively, it could mean the part played by the actor as well. In time *prosopon* or *persona* came to be used in Trinitarian discussions to distinguish between Father, Son, and Spirit as persons, while affirming that they shared one substance. Hippolytus and Tertullian spoke of persons in relation to the manifestation of God in the order of revelation. Later, the term came to be applied to the Son and the Spirit as immanent in God's eternal being. But, writes J. N. D. Kelly, "in neither case . . . was the idea of self-consciousness nowadays associated with 'person' and 'personal' at all prominent" (*Early Christian Doctrines,* p. 115).

In christological discourse the term person came to be used to affirm that in Christ one person united two modes of being, human and divine, even as one being united body and soul in the human person. Within both trinitarian and christological thinking the conception of the person underwent development and debate. From denoting a mode of God's being, the notion of person, under the influence of increasing emphasis on the human person as a center of self-consciousness and freedom, has been used to develop a social conception of the unity within the Trinity.

The basic definition of the human person which was to shape Christian thinking for centuries was offered by Boethius: a person is an individual substance of rational nature; (*persona est naturae rationalis individua substantia*). As interpreted by Richard of St. Victor this meant that the three basic elements of personal being were singularity, incommunicability, and the dignity which belongs to reason. These mean that as person the individual is not simply part of a whole, but the person is a subject who is free and responsible. Such an understanding of the person could and did lead to thinking of the person as constituted by self-consciousness and to identification of *person* with such terms as *ego* and *subject.*

Apart from the use of the term person to refer to the members of the Trinity, God's unity has been understood or modeled as that of a personal being. One of the distinctive modern forms of such thinking is to be found in the theological versions of philosophical idealism associated with the Boston University school of personalism (Bowne, Brightman, Bertocci), but it is widely present in other forms of theology and in popular thought. One of the debates in the theology of the last half century has centered on the applicability of the terms *person, personality,* and *personal* to the being of God. Some have held that while God enters into personal relations with human beings, God is not a person. Others have held that God is "super-personal," that the notions of person or personality are not adequate to express the reality of God. Still others have insisted on the symbolic and metaphorical character of all speech about God and have argued that the reality of God, while transcending all categories of thought, must be spoken of using both personal and impersonal metaphors.

3. **Contemporary Meanings and Questions.** Contemporary religious thought about the person, the personal, and personality has greatly deepened and extended the meaning of these terms. In general, the deepening and expansion is both a creative and constructive development and a reaction to the rationalistic reduction of the human to the knowing subject. Culturally it reflects a reaction against the depersonalizing and dehumanizing forces of technology and of political totalitarianism. While there have been a variety of movements of thought and a number of religious thinkers who reflect this concern for the person and the personal (Mounier and French personalism, the Scottish philosopher John Macmurray, the philosopher of science, M. Polanyi, the symbolic interactionism of George Herbert Mead, etc.), the most important influences have grown out of the existentialist thought of Kierkegaard, the dialogical philosophical theologies of Buber, Berdyaev, Marcel, *et al.* and out of various developments in modern psychology — contemporary studies of personality, psychologies of development, and the various depth psychologies. The understandings of the person and the personal derived from these sources have been both descriptive and normative.

a. Descriptive. It is not possible to review the contributions of each of these thinkers or of the various disciplines to the contemporary notion of the person, but in summary form several of the major characteristics of the person and of personal existence can be described:

i. Multidimensionality and unity. A person is multidimensional, constituted as a biological organism, a self in a body, related to a world and others beyond self. The person is not simply consciousness or self-consciousness. The person includes the vital emotional ground from which self and the self-consciousness arise in dialogue with others. What depth psychologists have called the unconscious is an integral aspect of the person.

The person is a unity, a centered self. The person has coherence, consistency, identity through time. A person is a whole, having a distinctive life and integrity, yet related to others. Persons are not simply parts in relation to some other whole. In this sense persons are separate and singular, finally impenetrable by the other. The coherence, consistency, and identity of the person through time is a part of what is meant by the term self. But the self is not a simple unity. Rather the self is reflexive. It has the capacity of self-transcendence in the sense that it can stand apart from itself and enter into dialogue with itself. It can also transcend itself by reaching out to others, entering imaginatively into their lives and into dialogue with them as persons.

ii. Sociality and temporality. A person is a person in community. Though in some final sense singular and impenetrable by the other, the person has been formed and shaped by social interaction, by dialogue with others, in and through communication with others and with the "generalized other" (G. H. Mead), which is the voice of its community. Not only has the person been formed and shaped by the exchange with others, but its ongoing life is social through and through. Personal existence is life together. The person is an interpersonal reality.

The person's being is a becoming. Personal existence is historical and temporal. Change, movement, development, growth, and decline in and through time are marks of personal life. Moreover, it is characteristic of personal existence that such development is phased. It is structured both by biological and cultural factors so that there are stages on life's way which may be universal as well as others which are shared by persons in a given culture or community. Personal existence is historical and temporal also in that the past and the future are dimensions of the person's being and becoming. Memory and imagined futures qualify personal becoming. The past and the future, grasped in memory and imagination, function in the living present, and presentness or the decisiveness of the now, of decisions made or refused in the present moment, constitute lived time as personal.

iii. Freedom and language. Persons are free. They have the capacity to resist complete determination by their causal pasts, to say yes, to say no, to inject new reality into the mix coming out of the past. Freedom is freedom of the person acting as a whole, not of some part—the mind, the will, the feeling. It is grounded in the existence of real possibilities, genuine alternatives which can be perceived, imagined, and chosen on the basis of intelligent judgment founded on memory, imagination, and rational understanding. Personal freedom is self-formation and self-determination at the same time that it is a selective response to possibilities and meanings emerging from the world beyond the self. In this sense it is both creativeness and choice. Freedom is freedom to be as well as to create and to choose. As Kierkegaard put it, the self is its freedom. The self has its being and becoming in the power of self-transcendence.

Persons are beings who shape themselves and their world through language. Language makes possible the dialogue which gives birth to mind, self, and society. Language makes possible the distancing and the use of memory and imagination which grounds freedom. Language makes both the experience of meaning and the communication of meaning possible, and thereby is related to every aspect of the emergence of the personal within a natural or not yet personal world. Language, of course, is more than words, and the communication of meaning more than speech.

b. Normative. i. Multidimensionality and unity. Contemporary Christian anthropology is not simply descriptive in its account of the person and the personal. Personal existence has its own dimensionality. It exists on a continuum. An individual may be more or less a person. The personal might be said to vary in range and depth. Personal existence has gradations. For someone like Kierkegaard, to become a person or to actualize personal existence is to move toward faith as a mode of existence. It is to move toward becoming a Christian, and human lifestyles or forms of personal existence can be arranged hierarchically as they are closer to or farther from existence in faith. Not all normative interpretations of the personal are as hierarchical or structured as Kierkegaard's. For some the hermeneutical principle is

to be found in the christological norm or in some understanding of the image of God. For others a more universal norm (though itself definable in christological terms) might be love, where love is understood both as a form of being and a form of relating. Whatever the normative principle, each of the aspects of the personal can be seen in relation to the norm.

Thus the individual may be more or less a unity or the unity may be disrupted. Inner division or inner conflict, imbalance between the dimensions may characterize the being and the becoming of the individual. Or the unity may be of many different kinds. One kind of personal unity may be rigid and closed, unable to grow or to respond to others. The conflict or disunity may be sufficient to distort or arrest the individual's growth of freedom and the possibility of love. The disunity or the kind of unity present may produce alienation from others. Such alienation can be expressed in diverse ways—through hostility, self-encapsulation, flight, dependence, rejection, etc.

ii. Sociality and temporality. By contrast there may be the degree and kind of inner personal unity to allow the individual to move toward full mutuality, to be able to accept and confirm the other and to share being and becoming with the other. Such a sharing of the hopes and fears, joys and sorrows, such a mutual giving and receiving of the very persons we are, is the fulfillment of the meaning of the personal.

Though no person can escape the historical-temporal character of existence, a person may live too much in the past or in the future. Memory and imagination may be paths of escape from the present moment, from the basic decisions which form the self and the self's relation to the other and which constitute the personal reality of the present moment.

iii. Freedom and language. So too human freedom can be turned into bondage. Freedom can be used both to destroy itself and others. Or freedom may be limited or arrested by the distortions of perception, imagination, or judgment which are rooted in the conflicts and rigidities of the inner life of the self or the self's relations to the body or to others. At the other extreme there can be a freedom to love and to care, a freedom of a self, sufficiently secure that it is not burdened by itself but is free to be for others. The self which is available for others is the self which is free indeed.

Language may be a defense against personal growth and development. It may be the means of arresting or destroying the personal through self-deception or the deception of others. Language may be a means of promising or of communicating truth, including the truth of one's own being, or language may be the means of lying and deceit, of hiding oneself and of dissembling.

4. **Conclusion.** In the normative sense human beings are persons to the extent they are moving toward becoming centers of freedom and love, to the degree they are realizing a christological mode of existence, or are actualizing the image of God in their personal being and becoming. But the personal is more than the person. Persons are social beings and the life together of persons transmutes community into communion. It makes what would otherwise be only a sociological community a caring community. Care and mutuality are the form of

the personal at the level of community. So too at the societal level, the personal emerges and is sustained to the degree that the society embodies or is moving toward justice. Justice is the form of the personal at the level of society. The personal is not individual human existence at all. It is the eschatological existence of Christ's community of being and becoming. It is life in the Spirit.

The implication of such an understanding of the person and the personal is that becoming a person and actualizing personal existence at the individual, communal, or societal level are not simple possibilities. There is evidence in our own lives and ample evidence in history that the transformation of life toward the personal cuts across the grain of individual life and that of society and history as well. Where the personal emerges it appears to come as a gift. Perhaps we can provide conditions for the emergence of the personal and then say yes to life when it comes.

Bibliography. G. Allport, *Personality* (1937). M. Buber, *Between Man and Man* (1947); *I and Thou* (1970). J. N. D. Kelly, *Early Christian Doctrines* (1958). P. LeFevre, *Understandings of Man* (1966). J. Macquarrie, *In Search of Humanity* (1983). G. H. Mead, *Mind, Self, and Society* (1934). W. Pannenberg, *Anthropology in Theological Perspective* (1985). P. Tillich, "The Idea and Ideal of Personality," in *The Protestant Era* (1948). *Systematic Theology,* III (1964).

P. LeFEVRE

PHILOSOPHY AND PSYCHOLOGY; PSYCHE; SELF; SOUL; THEOLOGY AND PSYCHOLOGY; TRINITY AND PERSONHOOD. *See also* CONSCIENCE; I AND THOU; IMAGO DEI; HUMAN CONDITION/ PREDICAMENT; HUMAN NATURE, PROBLEM OF; MIND; PERSONAL, CONCEPT OF, IN PASTORAL CARE; PERSONALISM AND PASTORAL CARE; PERSONALITY; SELF-TRANSCENDENCE. *Compare* BIBLICAL *or* THEOLOGICAL ANTHROPOLOGY, DISCIPLINE OF; CHRISTOLOGY; ESCHATOLOGY; EXISTENTIALISM AND PASTORAL CARE; FAMILY; HUMANNESS/ HUMANISM; SEXUALITY.

PERSON (Jewish Perspective). Person refers to human individuality, especially as distinct from inanimate objects and lower orders of animate beings. The Jewish perspective is based upon the Hebrew scriptures, the Midrashim (rabbinic expositions of scriptures), the Mishna (the authorized collection, ca. 200 C.E., of extrascriptural legal traditions), the Talmudim, two (a Babylonian and a Palestinian) wide-ranging collections of traditional materials organized around the Mishna. It reflects, in large measure, traditional attitudes but also attends to the adaptations of these exhibited in modern movements of the post-Enlightenment period.

1. The Divine Image. For Jewish tradition the essential characteristic of personhood is its having been formed in the divine image. Simeon ben Azzai (early second century, C.E.) commenting on Gen. 5:1, "when God created Adam, he made him in the divine image," declared the verse to be the root principle of human conduct. His contemporary, Rabbi Akiba, commenting on Gen. 9:6, is more cautious, for he does not treat "divine," that is, implying God as the modifier of "image." For him, Adam was created according to an image (ikon), perhaps a Platonic idea. The specific nature of the image or likeness, however understood, is not indicated in the biblical text, yet as interpreted in the

Mishna (Sanhedrin 4:5), it is seen as indicating both the unity and the diversity of humankind. "Man stamps many coins with one die and they are like one another. The King of kings has stamped every person with the seal of the first man, yet not one of them is like its fellow." There is little doubt that because of certain linguistic usages in some passages dealing with the creation of Adam (= humankind) open to anti-Judaic polemics, rabbinic Judaism did not dwell upon the concept at length. At most it was suggested that the likeness was moral, although in hellenistic Judaism it was taken to be a reference to the immortal, intellectual soul. Nonetheless, although direct reference was seldom made, the implications of the concept played a significant role in the development of Jewish thought. Among the ideas thus derived, three in particular may be underscored:

(a) Every human being is of value to God, irrespective of sex, class, nation, and race, and thus has a derived self-worth. "Only a single person was created in the world, to teach that if any person has caused a single soul to perish . . . Scripture imputes it as though that person has caused a whole world to perish; and if any person saves alive a single soul . . . Scripture imputes as though that person had saved alive a whole world" (Mishna, Sanhedrin 4:5).

(b) To be in God's image is the source of ethical requirements. One is called upon to imitate God as the ethical model, walking in the "ways of God." "The Holy One, blessed be he, visited the sick . . . so do you also visit the sick. The Holy One, blessed be he, comforted the mourner . . . so do you also comfort the mourners" (Babylonian Talmud, Sotah 14a).

(c) Being made in God's image invests humankind with active partnership with God. Since it is a representation of God, it has the responsibility of acting for God in creation *(sittûf ha-Shem).*

2. The Human Self: Body and Soul. *a. Unity in life.* The biblical person is monistic; it is a *nefesh,* a living self of which rûah (breath, spirit) is a manifestation. Bodily organs are expressive of the whole being. *Leb* (heart) is a comprehensive term for rational and volitional activity, while *kelayim* (kidneys) are the seat of emotions. Thus, the self is considered to be a psychophysical organism. Rabbinic thought, although linked to Scriptures, moved toward a dualistic interpretation of the person. Influenced by observation of human life and by hellenistic thought, it saw the person as composed of various parts, some given by the father, some by the mother, some by God. It is this latter endowment, the intellectual and emotional parts, that is understood to survive when the self disintegrates in death. Thus the biblical *nefesh* is viewed as a component, that is, the soul, not the entirety of the person. The body, coming from the parents, is inferior to it. The soul is joined to the body at the moment of conception (b. Niddah 31a). A similar idea of duality is expressed in a statement that unlike other creatures formed either from celestial stuff (angels) or terrestrial (animals, etc.), humankind is formed from both. While there is an occasional tendency to downgrade the body, in large measure its partnership with the soul is viewed positively. The person is seen as a microcosm, reflecting, in its totality, the whole of creation. "All that the Holy One, blessed be He, created upon earth, He created in man." The *nefesh,* too, is seen related to person as God is related to the world. "Just as the Holy One, blessed be He, fills the whole world, so the soul *(nefesh)* fills the body. Just as the Holy One, blessed be He, sees but is not seen, so the soul sees but itself is not seen" (b. Berakhot 10a). In the second half of the third century, some Palestinian teachers began to emphasize the distinction between body and soul through the idea of the preexistence of the latter. The words from Deut. 29:14, "with him who is not here with you today," were understood to refer to souls already in existence, which, though disembodied, were destined to become embodied. This idea influenced the judgment about the relationship between body and soul, with the latter bearing major responsibility for behavior, since it had dwelt in the celestial realm before becoming embodied and hence should govern the body, coming from the terrestrial sphere.

b. Death and resurrection. The monistic biblical view of person saw death not as the opposite of life but as its feeble, shadowy continuation. *Sheol* is the shadow of the world in which this takes place. This continued existence is provided for through the individual's role in the corporate personality of the family. The individual is a member of a community so that as the latter exists, so does the enfeebled self that continues to be part of it. It may be, too, that the continued existence of some part of the body, for example the bones, guarantees the existence of the shadow of the self. The more dualistic view of rabbinic Judaism modified this considerably. Emphasis on the distinction between body and soul had two results: death was seen as a severing of the two but the relation between them was seen as renewable. As a mirror reflection of the idea of the preexistence of the soul there developed the belief in the continued existence of the soul after death. As the soul resided in the "Treasure House" before birth, so too will it dwell in a "Habitation" after death. This, however, is not to be understood as immortality if by that is meant the perpetual existence of the soul in a disembodied state. It is to be understood in connection with the doctrine of the resurrection of the body. The traditional position, expressed in the Mishna (Sanh. 10:1), is that the doctrine of the reanimation of the dead is scriptural. Modern scholarship, however, sees it as having developed, perhaps under Iranian influence, during the postexilic period. It has been suggested that it arose as a solution to the problem of divine providence and as a provision for the renewal of lives unjustly terminated. The doctrine received particular impetus during the Maccabean period. In either case, the souls of the righteous and of the wicked—whose situation in the interim period is not clearly defined other than that the abode of the righteous is the "Treasure-house," while the wicked are cast to the ground—will be reunited with the body, and the person, again the biblical psychosomatic self, will be judged. The doctrine of the resurrection has been rejected in nontraditional sectors of contemporary Judaism in favor of that of the immortality of the soul. This position slights the traditional stress upon the totality of the individual as ultimately a unit.

3. The Person in Relation to God. The human individual is a moral being, responsible to God, the source of morality. There are several principles crucial for Jewish ethical motivation.

a. Sanctification and profanation of the name. The twin principle of *qiddûsh* and *hillul ha-Shem,* sanctification and profanation of God's name, is a universalistic rubric in Jewish ethics. The latter refers, in general, to acts that are intrinsically profane but have the added consequence of publicly defaming, that is, bringing into disrepute, the divine nature. Further, acts in themselves that are not reprehensible, or indeed may be permitted, may yet, in a particular circumstance, reflect negatively on God as the source of the commandments and may also fall into this category. The former refers to such acts that pristinate the divine nature either by their performance, behavior beyond the requirements of Torah, or by their rejection. In the latter instance, Jews are enjoined to endure martyrdom rather than commit murder, idolatry, or sexual offenses. Failure to do so constitutes profanation of the name. The individual's behavior is understood to uphold respect and reverence for or to denigrate God both within and without the community.

b. Free will. The person is endowed with free will. Deut. 30:15–18 speaks of the human ability to choose between good and evil and to act upon that choice. In rabbinic thought freedom is not regarded as incompatible with divine sovereignty: "All is foreseen but freedom is given" (Mishna, Abot 3:16). God is seen, however, as the aider and abettor of the choice of the good.

c. The evil and good inclinations. Judaism does not have a doctrine of Original Sin, understood as an inherited curse or defect infecting the person. Adam's sin, some teachers taught, brought death into the world, but Adam is not thought of as responsible for each individual's death. Sin is a personal, subjective, negative response to the divine will. Human nature is frail and liable to succumb to temptation. The dynamics of human response to God's will are explained in rabbinic Judaism by the dual concept of the evil inclination *(yeṣer ha-râ)* and the good inclination *(yeṣer ha-tôb).* These are understood to be two contrary psychological drives that are part of human endowment from creation. They represent the capacity to choose between right and wrong and are often personified in the discussions. The evil inclination seems comparable to the idea of libido, the drive to satisfy the self. It is thought of as having a constructive possibility, but as it goes out of control, it causes harm and destruction. The good inclination is seen as a countervailing force that seeks to keep the evil inclination within constructive bounds. Perhaps the term evil must be thought of not as moral evil but as a destructive possibility within the person.

d. Repentance. The rabbinic Hebrew word *tesûbâh,* often translated "repentance," properly means "turning" or "return." It indicates the possibility that sin in its various forms is not irreparable and expresses this by use of the concrete act of turning about, that is, away from the negative to the positive response to the divine will. Involved in it are recognition of one's wrongdoing, the turning of the whole self God-ward and the sincere intention not to repeat the act. These taken together and expressed in prayer are the means by which humanity atones for transgression and is received with love by God.

4. The Person in Relation to Others. Great stress is laid upon responsibility to and for one's fellows. The biblical phrase: "Love your neighbor as yourself" (Lev. 19:18) is seen as the great principle of the Torah. Hillel, at the turn of the era, paraphrased it: "Whatever is hateful to you, do not do to your neighbor: that is the whole Torah, the rest is commentary. Go now and learn." The medieval philosopher Maimonides expounded it: "All the things you wish others to do to you, do to your brothers." Transgressions against God are forgiven by turning; those against a fellow, only when there has been reconciliation. Much of the legal structure of rabbinic Judaism is concerned with the establishment of affirmative relationships of justice and equity within society. Obedience to negative commandments is insufficient; there are positive obligations as well.

5. The Person in Relation to the World. The world is understood in Judaism to be the realm in which obligations are to be fulfilled. The individual's concerns are with others in the context of daily living, with life in all its forms, and with the environment. It is in the world that one is called upon to perform the commandments as a partner of God (*ittuf ha-Shem*) in the upbuilding of existence. A correlative of *qiddush ha-Shem* (the sanctification of God's name) is *qiddush ha-Hayyim* (the sanctification of life). Holiness is not thought of as a quality of life outside the world but within the everyday activity of individual and community.

6. Pastoral Reflections. Distinctive emphases in Jewish belief about the person, which are relevant to the pastor, are the wholistic view of the person, self-affirmation, and world-affirmation. The body and soul constitute a composite being whose total needs and capabilities are to be respected. The person, made in the divine image by the divine craftsman, is of infinite worth. God cares how the individuals live and what they do with their lives. This quality of worth should be reflected in one's view of oneself and of others. The world and its material properties are to be enjoyed as gifts of God and as a setting of honorable and self-giving service. Above all, life need never be characterized by despair; it has a purpose, living for God, which supremely means to walk within reasonable parameters of behavior revealed of God, with the consciousness that God is one's helper in this endeavor.

Bibliography. Relevant biblical studies are W. Eichrodt, *Man in the Old Testament* (ET, 1951). H. W. Wolff, *Anthropology of the Old Testament* (ET, 1974). The standpoint of rabbinic Judaism is reflected in G. F. Moore, *Judaism in the First Centuries of the Christian Era* (1947). W. Hirsch, *Rabbinic Psychology: Beliefs About the Soul in Rabbinic Literature of the Talmudic Period* (1947). S. Belkin, *In His Image: The Jewish Philosophy of Man as Expressed in Rabbinic Tradition* (1960). E. E. Urbach, *The Sages: Their Concepts and Beliefs* (1975). The translation used for the Mishnah is H. Danby, *The Mishnah* (1933). That used for the Talmud is *The Babylonian Talmud*, I. Epstein, ed. (1948). Surveys of the whole history of Jewish concepts are to be found in *Encyclopaedia Judaica* (1971), especially such articles as "Man, the Nature of," "Body and Soul," and "Soul, Immortality of". See also L. Baeck, *The Essence of Judaism* (1948) and *God and Man in Judaism* (1958).

L. C. ALLEN
L. H. SILBERMAN

JUDAISM AND PSYCHOLOGY. *See also* CONSCIENCE (Judaism); FAMILY, JEWISH THEOLOGY AND ETHICS OF; I AND THOU; IMAGO DEI; SEXUALITY AND SEX COUNSELING (Jewish Perspective). *Compare* HUMAN CONDITION/PREDICAMENT; HUMAN NATURE, PROBLEM OF; PERSONALITY; PSYCHE; SELF/SELFHOOD; SOUL; SPIRIT, HUMAN; THEOLOGICAL ANTHROPOLOGY, DISCIPLINE OF.

PERSON (Philosophical Issues). A general term used primarily though not exclusively to refer to human beings to demarcate their special status when compared to inanimate objects and lower species of animals. To call someone a person is to emphasize that this individual is not a mere "thing" or "object," but is in some sense a subject or self.

The term *person*, however, is not restricted in its application to human beings. Traditionally, theologians have understood God as a person, not to mention angelic and demonic powers. The discovery of extraterrestrial beings who are entitled to be regarded as persons seems clearly possible, and serious questions have been raised about whether it could ever be necessary to regard artificially intelligent beings as persons. One can even ask whether some of the higher animals are sufficiently like human beings to be regarded as "quasi-persons." However, the existence of intermediate cases between the personal and the nonpersonal order by no means shows that the distinction between persons and nonpersons is unimportant or meaningless.

Philosophers, theologians, psychologists, and other social scientists have, of course, developed many alternative ways of characterizing what is distinctive about persons. This article will attempt to describe some of the different ways the concept has been understood and the continued contemporary debate as to the status of human persons.

1. Alternative Uses of Concept. It is important to distinguish different senses in which something may be a person. There is first what may be termed the dramatic sense, in which a person is a "part" or "role." Though not common today, this usage may be the oldest etymologically, since the English term *person* is thought to have been derived from the Latin *persona,* a theatrical term that referred either to the mask worn by an actor who assumed a particular part or to the actor himself.

Secondly, there is what may be termed the legal sense, which can be seen in the designation of corporations as persons. A legal person is an entity with some standing before the law, a potential bearer of rights and obligations.

The third and most significant sense of *person* is the moral sense. Morally, to regard people as persons is to think of them as beings entitled to respect, bearers of moral rights and obligations. This moral sense is clearly reflected in Immanuel Kant's famous dictum that persons are "ends-in-themselves" who ought never to be treated as "mere means." Though the legal and moral senses must be distinguished, they are closely related, as is shown by the contemporary debate as to what the legal status of human fetuses should be.

Since our concept of humans as persons is intimately tied up with our belief that humans are worthy of consideration and respect, it is obviously a concept with practical as well as theoretical importance. Theoretically, there is rough agreement about the qualities persons normally have that make them special. These would include the ability to act responsibly and freely, self-consciousness, the potential for knowledge, and the ability to respond to other persons and situations. To question whether human beings have such qualities is not merely to raise abstract concerns; it is to threaten the self-understanding that is embodied in countless human institutions and practices.

2. History of the Concept. *a. The ancient and medieval emphasis on rationality.* The medieval concept of the person, Aristotle's classical definition of a human being as a "rational animal," emphasized rationality. Aristotle did not, however, seem to think of human beings in terms of the distinctive category of personhood, as he regarded some humans as "natural slaves" who were not fully personal. The conviction that all human beings are persons seems to be rooted in the Christian belief that all humans are created in God's image, especially as this notion was blended with the Stoic concept that human beings should think of themselves as "fellow-citizens of the universe." The most famous medieval definition of a person was Boethius's view that a person is "an individual substance of a rational nature."

b. The modern classical emphasis on self-consciousness. While the concept of rationality was by no means dropped in the modern classical period, a much greater emphasis was placed on consciousness and self-consciousness. Thus John Locke says that a person, in addition to being rational, must possess the kind of consciousness that enables one to understand oneself to be the same being at different times and places. A similar emphasis is found in Leibnitz, where consciousness of one's identity over time is a necessary condition for holding someone responsible for actions performed.

c. The contemporary emphasis on action and choice. The contemporary period has seen a greater emphasis on the person as a dynamic, developing reality. This is seen perhaps most clearly in the existentialist view of the person as one who decides the meaning of his or her life through creative choices, though this emphasis is not limited to existentialism. Psychologists who are not existentialists, like Gordon Allport, have also emphasized personhood as something that is achieved. Many contemporary analytic philosophers also view the concept of action as the key to an understanding of persons. From this perspective, the doings of persons are not mere events or happenings but actions that must be understood with reference to their meanings and purposes. Actions here become both the expression of our emotions and caring concerns and the ways in which these are formed.

This emphasis on freedom of choice and action is also related to the concept of humans as responsible beings. The notion that people are not responsible for what they cannot help doing is deeply embedded in Western thought. Our desire to hold each other responsible for our behavior toward each other provides a powerful motive for believing that we are free beings; this belief is a central feature of our understanding of ourselves as persons.

Of course, the concept of personhood includes a great deal more than the capacity to act freely. The earlier emphases on rationality and self-awareness over time

seem to be presupposed for free action. Also, a full account of human persons must include some account of those emotions which shape our character as persons: particularly our loves, hates, fears, and anxieties. Our relations with other persons, which both shape and are shaped by individual actions, are also central to the understanding of human persons.

3. The Threat of Reductionism. *a. Philosophical materialism and naturalism.* The idea that persons are free, creative centers of action is troubling to many who hold to a materialistic or naturalistic worldview. Such a worldview sees all of reality as stemming from matter and ultimately understandable in physical terms. To see persons as free and responsible beings is to introduce a mysterious element into nature that is difficult to analyze in a naturalistic manner. It is hard to see how such beings could arise in a purely natural way from the evolutionary process. For this reason there is a powerful tendency on the part of naturalists and materialists to reduce or eliminate the differences between persons and the subpersonal order. The attempt to deny that human beings are unique or qualitatively different from the rest of the natural order may be termed reductionism, since the aim is to reduce humans to the status of other animals.

b. Reductionism in psychology. Also influenced by a naturalistic or materialistic worldview, contemporary psychology contains powerful reductionistic tendencies. This can be seen most clearly in the popularity of determinism, the tendency to view human beings as natural organisms which can be completely explained as a result of genetic and environmental forces. Although there are important countertrends in psychology, in general there is still a good deal of suspicion of the concept of free choice. This reductionistic tendency is clearly visible in both classical Freudian and in behavioristic theories.

The classical Freudian theory accepts a strict psychic determinism in which every event in the mind has a determining cause. The person is seen not as a unified center of actions but as a battleground of opposing forces. The key Freudian concepts, such as instinct, repression, and object-cathexis, are all derived from either biology or mechanics. Although it is evident that many of Freud's key structural constructs are heavily anthropomorphic— the id and superego are often talked about as if they were persons in their own right—the overall thrust seems to be toward seeing the person as a product of forces and mechanisms that are not of his or her own making. This reductionistic element has, however, much less prominence in subsequent developments of Freudian theory, particularly ego psychology and object-relations theory.

Behaviorism is more relentlessly reductionistic in its basic thrust. Early behaviorists like Watson were explicit in their desire to understand humans in the same way as other animals are understood. B. F. Skinner has argued that science always moves from personalistic to mechanistic types of explanation; thus a truly scientific psychology must reject categories like "freedom," which are intrinsic to personhood. These reductionistic tendencies are of course not universal, and some recent behaviorists have sharply modified Skinner. Nevertheless the behavioristic image of human beings as products of their environment has penetrated popular culture to a remarkable degree.

4. Responses to Reductionism. Both inside and outside of psychology, responses to reductionism fall into three categories. These responses can be described by referring to a particular view of science that has influenced psychology greatly: the view that science consists in the search for causal generalizations that correlate observable variables. Such generalizations are empirically verifiable, since they concern observables, and they make possible both explanation and prediction of particular phenomena. This view of science presupposes a deterministic view of reality as completely law-like. Given such a conception, it is inevitable that "scientific" psychology would develop a mechanistic understanding of human beings viewing them not as free and autonomous but as products of causal chains. A scientific view of people in this conception of science is in tension with the traditional view of persons. Three sorts of responses to this situation are possible.

a. Reinterpreters. The reinterpreter accepts this situation as inevitable. The traditional view of the person is a prescientific one that cannot survive. Our human self-understanding must be revised or reinterpreted accordingly, as must our institutions and practices. Specifically, human freedom is either rejected or reinterpreted in a manner that makes freedom consistent with determinism.

Christians who are attracted to this option generally attempt to argue that the traditional Western view of the person is more Greek than Hebraic. They claim that the concepts of freedom and autonomy reflect humankind's attempt to deify itself, and that the biblical emphasis on the sovereignty of God lends itself well to seeing human beings as fully determined creatures. This view is well presented in the work of David Myer.

b. Limiters of science. The second possible response to the threat of reductionism is one that would emphasize the inherent limits of science. This strategy does not question the view of science outlined above or its implications for a scientific psychology, but it questions the ultimacy of a scientific perspective. While a scientific account of human beings is both legitimate and valuable, it is not the only perspective from which human behavior can be viewed. To claim otherwise is to commit the fallacy of *scientism,* which is to assume that science gives the whole and complete truth about reality. When the limits of science are properly understood, it is possible to view the scientific image of human beings and the traditional personalistic model as complementary views.

It is important to recognize that science is not here being limited in some arbitrary, irrational manner. Rather, the limits are internal, grounded in the nature of the scientific method itself. Science searches for the causal principles to which empirical entities conform. It necessarily restricts itself to what is objective, observable, and repeatable. It would be a fallacy to conclude from this that what is subjective, unobservable through empirical methods, and unique does not exist, or even that such things cannot be apprehended; it simply is not the job of science to apprehend such things.

The writings of Donald M. MacKay, the British brain researcher and communications theorist, illustrate many aspects of the "limiter of science" view. Though acknowledging many unanswered questions, MacKay claims that science seems to be making progress by looking at human beings in a mechanistic manner. Christians and others who are concerned about reductionism should not fear such scientific progress, however. Only if we commit the fallacy of thinking that the scientific perspective is the only possible one, will we succumb to the threat of reductionism. Such reductionism MacKay calls "nothing-buttery." In actuality, the scientific story about human beings must be combined with a more personal subjective perspective, the "I-story," which is the perspective that an agent takes on himself or herself. This subjective perspective deals with human actions and thoughts in terms of their *meanings,* a perspective that is legitimate but not one proper for science. MacKay insists that a relationship of complementarity exists between these two perspectives.

c. Humanizers of science. A more radical response to the threat of reductionism is found in the work of psychologists and philosophers whom we might term humanizers of science. The humanizer is not content to accept a mechanistic view of human beings as even scientifically adequate and challenges the view of science as mainly concerned with prediction and control. If we begin by assuming that science can only assume that reality is determined by mechanistic laws, then a scientific view of human beings will inevitably be machine-like. The humanizer of science, however, holds that science properly conceived aims at understanding, not just prediction and control. True science must adapt its methods to its subject matter. If human beings are to some degree free and responsible beings, then psychology must use methods that allow it to observe and understand free and responsible actions.

Much of humanistic and "third-force" psychology, including such writers as Carl Rogers, Rollo May, and Abraham Maslow, attempt to "humanize" psychology in this way, as do existential and phenomenological approaches to psychology and psychotherapy. The existential analyst, for example, sees the clinical situation as a potentially meaningful encounter between two persons rather than as a scientific expert analyzing a "case." Mary Stewart Van Leeuwen would be an excellent example of a Christian psychologist who has attempted to integrate psychology and theology by transforming psychology in a humanizing or personalistic manner.

A legitimate concern that has been voiced most vigorously by Paul Vitz is whether such personalistic psychologies do not commit the opposite error of reductionism. Vitz says that instead of denying our personhood, these theorists come close to deifying the human self, making the self the ultimate end of life and the source of meaning and value. Vitz's concern is one that must be respected; the Christian must always understand human personhood as a gift from God. Personal characteristics are grounded in God and are only fully developed when received from God in faith and gratitude. But these concerns should not lead us to deny or minimize the unique qualities of human persons as creatures made in God's image.

5. Unresolved Problems. Although there are notable exceptions (e.g., the humanizers of science) contemporary psychologists have not made much use of the concept of person or self. Psychologists have focused more on personality than on personhood, but the two are evidently not the same. A person can change personality dramatically without ceasing to be the same person, and a person can have a rather fully formed personality and yet in one sense not be a fully developed person. Gordon Allport came close to developing a theory of the person with his concept of the "proprium," which he developed in *Becoming*. However, even Allport stops short of a full-fledged theory of the person, apparently in the belief that the concept is not necessary for psychology (though he says it may be indispensable for philosophy and theology). In the absence of sustained attention by psychologists, therefore, the problems associated with personhood have been largely left to philosophers and theologians. Three major problem areas will be considered.

a. Mind and body. Philosophers and theologians have traditionally thought of persons as substances or entities — real objects. A question naturally arises as to what kind of an entity a human person is. The *dualist* answer is that a person is a composite of a material body and a nonmaterial soul or mind. *Monistic* theories deny this and claim that human persons are unitary substances.

The most popular form of monism is materialism, which views a person as identical with his or her physical body; its opposite is idealism, which identifies the person with a spiritual entity. Both materialism and idealism can be seen as reductionistic views, one reducing the spiritual to the material, the other reducing the material to the spiritual.

Although Christian theology has traditionally accepted a dualistic or even tripartite view of the person (body, soul, spirit), recent theologians have moved in the direction of monism (often called "holism" by its proponents). Dualism is criticized as a non-Hebraic intrusion from Greek philosophy, better fitted for a philosophical doctrine of the immortality of the soul than a Christian hope for bodily resurrection. The biblical view of the person is seen as one that focuses on the unity of the person as a responsible being in relationship with others. The thrust is not toward either materialism or idealism but toward a nonreductive "neutral" monism which sees physical and mental and spiritual characteristics as fundamental features of the unified person. P. F. Strawson has developed neutral monism from a secular, philosophical perspective.

Although neutral monism is an attractive option, it too has problems. One is a difficulty in specifying the nature of the "neutral stuff" of which both mind and body are supposed to be aspects. (For this reason there is a tendency for this view to collapse into materialism.) Theologically, neutral monism leads to the rejection of the idea of an "intermediate state" of continued existence between death and the resurrection. Rather, either the resurrection occurs immediately at death or persons temporarily cease to exist. For these and other reasons, dualism still has able defenders, such as H. D. Lewis.

b. Personal identity over time. It was noted earlier that a crucial aspect of the concept of personhood is that a person is a being who may be held responsible or accountable for his or her actions. It follows that psychological theories lacking a concept of person or self have difficulty with the concept of responsibility. It is no accident, for example, that behaviorists have replaced traditional concepts of rewards and punishments, which

are logically tied to the concept of just deserts, with less personal concepts of positive and negative reinforcers.

It is obvious that people change enormously over the course of a lifetime, both physically and psychologically. In what sense then can a person be the same person as he or she was at earlier times? Unless there is an answer to this question, it would appear wrong for anyone, even God, to reward or punish a person for past actions.

Two main theories of personal identity have been developed, memory theory and bodily continuity theory. The memory theory, developed by John Locke, holds that a person is identical with a past person if he or she has memories of that person's actions and experiences. Yet this theory faces severe difficulties. What about large gaps in memory? And I can only truly remember my *own* past actions and experiences, so that an *apparent* memory of someone else's behavior would not be deemed valid, no matter how much knowledge of details was present. Saying that I remember past events seems to *presuppose* my identity with the subject of those events, rather than accounting for that identity.

The bodily continuity theory holds that having the same body makes a person the same over time. Aside from the problems of specifying what it means to "have the same body," this theory seems to rule out the possibility of bodily transfers and exchanges. Such cases are common in fairy tales and literature. Even if in fact a person never gains a new body, such an event seems to be possible or conceivable. Christians who believe literally in the resurrection of the dead believe that human persons not only can gain new bodies, but that they will in fact do so.

One possible solution to this dilemma for a Christian is to hold that a person's identity rests completely on his or her relationship to God. God creates each individual as an individual and always has a clear conception of who a person was, is, and what the person could become. This synthesis of past, present, and future actualities and possibilities is the person as he or she is truly known by God and held in being by God. If God chooses to maintain the person in existence after death or to re-embody the person, the continuity is found in God's continuing knowledge and creative power.

c. Freedom and determinism. A third problem area, which has been of concern to philosophers, theologians, and psychologists, is that of freedom and determinism. Central to the concept of personhood is the notion that persons are responsible agents who deliberate and make choices. A person is not merely a battleground of competing forces or an arena through which causal lines flow but an originating cause. This conviction appears to conflict with the belief, often claimed to be central for science, that every event is causally determined by some set of antecedent conditions.

Those who abandon belief in freedom are usually referred to as determinists. In general, determinists appeal to the predictability of human behavior to support their view, as well as to the *a priori* conviction that all events simply must have a cause. The explanation that God determines the outcome of every event is theological determinism.

Those who reject determinism are usually referred to as libertarians, a term that must be understood in a different sense than it carries in social and political thought. Libertarianism is a position often caricatured by its opponents. Responsible libertarians such as C. A. Campbell or Peter Bertocci concede that much human behavior is determined and even that free behavior is subject to causal influences that "weight" a choice in one direction. Free behavior is also grounded in the past in the sense that the limited options that are present in a free decision are the outcome of the past. Free actions are not seen as random or totally unpredictable but meaningful behavior done for a reason. The reason for an action is not seen, however, as a determining cause.

A popular compromise between determinism and libertarianism is the position of compatibilism. The compatibilists argue that if proper definitions of freedom and determinism are given, both are true. The compatibilist understands freedom as lack of external coercion. The opposite of freedom is not determinism but coercion. The opposite of determinism is not freedom but chance. If freedom is understood as a person's ability to act in accordance with his or her own desires or wants, then it is compatible with determinism, for it will be possible to view those desires as *caused.*

The compatibilist views the celebrated "ability to do otherwise," which is a crucial element in freedom, as a hypothetical or conditional quality. A person who is free to do something different is one who has other options that could be actualized *if* the person so desires. No external force compels the individual to do what will be done, but rather the person's own internal wishes constitute the moving force.

Libertarians retort that the ability to do otherwise must be categorical and not hypothetical in a case of genuine free action. They claim that since our internal desires are ultimately caused by external factors, the *ultimate* responsibility for an action, even in cases of uncoerced actions, always lies outside the individual. An individual can only be held responsible for doing what he or she could not help doing when the inability is itself grounded at least in part in the individual's past free choices.

In the face of a problem as difficult as this one, some Christians have simply concluded that the question of human freedom is an ultimate mystery. Such a conclusion is not necessarily to be despised, so long as it is not an excuse for avoiding the struggle to understand the issues. However, at the very least, it can be argued that one must ultimately live *as if* libertarianism were true. When faced with decisions that must be made, a person cannot believe that it is already determined what he or she will do, and that the task is only to guess or predict what will inevitably happen. The decision is one that must be made; a presupposition of the agonizing process of deliberation is that there are real possibilities that confront the individual. This is true whether the individual is struggling with the issue of eternal life and death or with the more mundane questions of life. Determinism is a doctrine that can be adopted only when one takes the role of a spectator of human life.

6. **Practical Implications.** C. S. Lewis has explored some of the practical implications of abandoning the belief that we are persons in the full sense of the word. In *The Abolition of Man,* Lewis showed that education inev-itably degenerates into indoctrination when children are viewed as objects to be molded instead of as developing persons to be prepared for full participation in a community of subjects. In "The Humanitarian Theory of Punishment" Lewis explored the devastating implications of discarding the traditional view that humans are free and responsible agents who sometimes should be rewarded or punished because they deserve rewards or punishments. An apparently more humane view says that people should not be punished on the basis of desert but rather "helped" or "treated" to behave better in the future. This "humanitarian" view ultimately dehumanizes the individual who is helped by viewing such persons solely as *objects* for treatment, treatment which will be just as compulsory as the old-style punishments but which will not be limited by the deserts of the individual.

The concept of personhood is so central to human life that there is scarcely an area that would not be transformed if the concept were to be abandoned or significantly modified. Within Christian faith, areas such as evangelism, Christian education, and counseling are especially critical. If human beings are persons, then the evangelist dares not think of potential converts simply as objects to be manipulated, or as "consumers" of a product that must be "sold" in a polished manner. This is not to say that an evangelist should not seek to appeal to emotions. Human persons are not mere thinking machines; a person who does not care deeply about righteousness cannot be brought to faith. It does mean that the evangelist strives to present the gospel honestly and truthfully, so that the Spirit of God can empower the individual to make a genuine decision.

Christian counselors of many persuasions agree that a crucial element in a process of counseling or therapy is the dignity and respect which the counselor or therapist accords to the person being helped. The individual must never be viewed simply as a case to be manipulated by the scientific expert but as a responsible participant in the process. The therapeutic importance of recognizing the personhood of individuals confirms and strengthens the theoretical case that, however shrunken and atrophied their powers, however badly they may have misused their status as persons, human beings remain persons. For the Christian, being a person is not simply a fact; it is a calling, a task rooted in the personal God who stoops to address us as the very personal, incarnate Word of God.

Bibliography. Classical passages dealing with the concept of personhood include Boethius, *Contra Eutychen et Nestorium,* sec. III. J. Locke, *Essay Concerning Human Understanding,* Book II (1690). G. W. Leibnitz, *Theodicy* (1980 [1879]). I. Kant, *Foundations of the Metaphysics of Morals* (1969). Also see the articles on "Persons" and "Personal Identity" in *The Encyclopedia of Philosophy* (1967). One of the best contemporary treatments of personhood is P. Bertocci, *The Person God Is* (1970), which deals with personhood in both psychological and theological contexts.

Classical examples of reductionism are J. B. Watson, *Behaviorism* 3d. ed. (1930). B. F. Skinner, *Beyond Freedom and Dignity* (1972). C. S. Evans, *Preserving the Person* (1977), analyzes alternative strategies to reductionism. D. M. MacKay, *Human Science and Human Dignity* (1979), illustrates the "limiter of science" approach. M. S. Van Leeuwen, *The Sorcerer's Apprentice* (1982), illustrates a "humanizer of science" alternative. For the opposite danger of self-deification, see P. Vitz, *Psychology as Religion: The*

Cult of Self-Worship (1977). G. Allport, in *Becoming* (1955), contributed toward a revival of the concept of the self in psychology. The revival and development of the self in psychoanalysis is described in H. Guntrip, *Psychoanalytic Theory, Therapy, and the Self* (1971).

On the mind-body problem see H. D. Lewis, *The Elusive Self* (1982). See J. Eccles and K. Popper, *The Self and Its Brain* (1977), for contemporary defenses of dualism. Materialism is advocated by D. M. Armstrong, *A Materialist Theory of the Mind* (1968), and by a variety of people in C. V. Borst, ed., *The Mind-Brain Identity Theory* (1970). P. F. Strawson, *Individuals* (1959) is a classical defense of nonreductive monism. B. Reichenbach defends a Christian materialism in *Is Man the Phoenix?* (1978). J. Shaffer gives a good overview of the contemporary debate in *Philosophy of Mind* (1968).

On freedom and determinism see B. Berofsky, ed., *Free Will and Determinism* (1966), which contains many classical arguments on both sides of the issue. D. Myer in *The Human Puzzle* (1978) sees determinism as a viable option for Christians, though problems remain.

C. S. Lewis's classical essay "The Humanitarian Theory of Punishment" can be found in *God in the Dock* (1970). Lewis's most extended treatment of personhood is *The Abolition of Man* (1947).

C. S. EVANS

PHILOSOPHICAL ANTHROPOLOGY, DISCIPLINE OF; PHILOSOPHY AND PSYCHOLOGY; PSYCHE; SELF, PHILOSOPHY OF; SPIRIT, HUMAN; SOUL; THEOLOGY AND PSYCHOLOGY. *See also* FREEDOM AND DETERMINISM; HUMAN NATURE, PROBLEM OF; I AND THOU; IDENTITY; MATERIALISM; MIND; PERSONAL, SENSE OF; REASON AND PASSION; RESPONSIBILITY; SELF-ACTUALIZATION; SELF-TRANSCENDENCE. *Compare* HUMANNESS/HUMANISM; INTERPERSONAL THEORY; JUDAISM AND PSYCHOLOGY; MODELS IN PSYCHOLOGICAL AND PASTORAL THEORY; MYTHOLOGY AND PSYCHOLOGY; PERSONALITY THEORY. *Compare also* ANALYTICAL (JUNGIAN) *or* PSYCHOANALYTIC PERSONALITY THEORY; BEHAVIORISM; EXISTENTIAL, GESTALT, HUMANISTIC, INDIVIDUAL, PHENOMENOLOGICAL *or* SELF PSYCHOLOGIES.

PERSONA. In analytical psychology, the psychological mask an individual unconsciously adopts; an assumed set of attitudes to meet the circumstances perceived in the outer world. The term is derived from the masks worn by actors of antiquity to identify the role performed. It represents one's projected image in and defense against the external world.

I. R. STERNLICHT

ANALYTICAL (JUNGIAN) PSYCHOLOGY; SELF CONCEPT. *Compare* PERSONAL, CONCEPT OF.

The PERSONAL, CONCEPT OF, IN PASTORAL CARE. While pastoral care has always been concerned with ministry to individuals and thus been a personal form of ministry, the modern pastoral care and counseling movement has heavily emphasized certain notions of what is truly personal. These have become distinctive features of its style and method, and have tended to make earlier, more ritualized and rational forms of care seem comparatively "impersonal."

The contemporary pastoral meaning can be seen through a series of contrasts. (1) *Uniqueness and Freedom.* Personhood is irreducibly unique and free, whatever general theories or outside forces may be brought to bear.

Thus contemporary care and counseling sharply contrasts its concern for persons with any approach that stereotypes individuals as types or cases, failing to experience and "hear" persons in their full uniqueness, or that subjects them to coercive techniques. (This theme was especially emphasized in Seward Hiltner's concept of "shepherding.") (2) *Intimacy and Interiority.* The true person is distinguished from the public mask or "persona," and is identified with that which is internal, emotional, private, and accessible only through intimate self-disclosure. (3) *Emotional and Imagistic Self-Expression.* The truly personal is assumed to be expressed more through feelings and fantasy (e.g., dreams and images) than through rational thought or public action. Feeling and fantasy are believed to be closer to the "core" of the "true person." (4) *Social Need and Vulnerability.* Pastoral relationships become truly personal when and to the extent to which they reveal the deep need human beings have for one another, their sense of common humanity, vulnerability in relationships, and need for mutual trust and care.

The sense of the personal that emerges from this series of contrasts has defined much of the style and "feel" of contemporary pastoral care and counseling, and accounts for much of its special depth and value for persons. Individuals who receive such care experience an intimate attentiveness to their subjectively felt experience, which is often unique in their social experience and profoundly meaningful to them. Frequently also they find unexpected resources for healing and strength in such deeply personal ministry.

At the same time, this understanding of what is truly personal is highly focused and, arguably, overly narrow. The emphasis on interiority and intimacy may lead pastoral care to neglect *public* identity, responsibility, and action. One's public persona, political and institutional praxis, and rational thought also constitute important dimensions of personhood though relatively neglected in this understanding. Should they not also be the focus of personally focused pastoral care at times? And must such care be less intimate or personal in the narrow sense if it expands its concern to include, say, the "public self," the "political-institutional self," or the "rational self"?

Bibliography. S. Hiltner, *Preface to Pastoral Theology* (1958). W. E. Oates, *Pastoral Counseling* (1974). A. Smith, Jr., *The Relational Self* (1982).

R. J. HUNTER

PERSONHOOD OF THE PASTOR, SIGNIFICANCE OF. *See also* BODY; I AND THOU; IDENTITY; INTIMACY AND DISTANCE; SELF CONCEPT. *Compare* CLINICAL PASTORAL PERSPECTIVE; HUMANNESS/HUMANISM; SOUL; SOUL (Black Church).

PERSONAL STORY, SYMBOL, AND MYTH IN PASTORAL CARE. The use of story, symbol, and myth in pastoral care is one of the more useful ways in which a pastor may assist persons to achieve an understanding of themselves and their problems. They may be used in brief encounters in pastoral care as well as in longer-term pastoral counseling relationships. A personal story relates something specific and significant about how the person understands his or her life. A personal symbol is a specific object or action that reminds one of who he or she is. A personal myth is a similar explanation, inherited tradition, image, or story. An example which has elements of symbol, story, and myth is the biblical image, "a wandering Aramean was my father" (Deut. 26:5), which presents a specific visual image, calls to mind the early history of the Hebrew people, and can give persons a sense of who they are and to what they belong.

A personal story, symbol, or myth is a means of communicating who one is, who one is identified with, and how one functions. These may appear in the pastoral conversation in a number of ways, usually in something specific that the parishioner or counselee says about himself or herself, which a carefully attentive pastor notices. This specificity is important. Persons who share themselves with a helping person most often communicate two kinds of material: (1) what they think is wrong with their present situation or with themselves, and (2) generalizations about the kind of persons they are, i.e., a general statement about themselves, such as "I am often depressed" or "I procrastinate a lot."

Although the following generalization cannot be universally applied, it is a useful guideline: *Pastoral care involves assisting persons to move from talking generally about themselves and specifically about their problems to talking specifically about themselves and generally about their problems.* Many persons seen in pastoral care and counseling hide from themselves and others through generalizations. A major pastoral task, therefore, is to assist them in talking concretely about themselves by finding some of the symbols, stories, and myths in their lives.

In doing this, the pastor makes use of all that he or she has learned about empathic listening and reflection of feelings. Equally important, however, is an active search for anything in what the person is sharing that captures the pastor's imagination, and using that symbol or story in his or her own mind as a new way of thinking about that person. This can enable the pastor to have an image of the person which transcends his or her problem. The problem is not ignored but is put in a perspective that sees it in relation to other dimensions of a person's life. While the unconscious dynamics of pastoral relationships are also important, the discovery of symbol, story, and myth does not negate but complements pastoral understanding.

Underlying the use of story, symbol, and myth is modern pastoral care's coming of age in seeking a relational model of the pastor-parishioner relationship apart from the traditional image of doctor-patient. Certainly, persons come to pastors for help with specific problems which are not limited to medical or psychiatric traditions of meaning and care. So-called "personal work" with individuals is a centuries old Christian tradition (Holifield). The fact, however, that most CPE has taken place in healthcare institutions in which pastors have had to demonstrate their usefulness to the health of the patient is a major factor in pastors' willingness to be identified as healers and problem solvers.

Stories and symbols give the pastor a way of seeing the dignity and humanity of a person in situations where dignity and humanity seem almost lost. The pastor who visits an elderly person struggling with disease and aging, for instance, may be able to see much more than that if he or she can elicit or discern that person's story,

find an appropriate symbol for the person's life, or hear a myth about their family history or practice. Deciding when, if, and how to share that image depends primarily on the development of a trusting and respecting relationship with that person and whether or not the symbol discerned seems more supportive or confrontive. Both can be valuable when appropriately used.

Bibliography. C. V. Gerkin, *The Living Human Document* (1984). S. Hauerwas, "The Gesture of a Truthful Story," *Theology Today*, 41 (1985), 181–89; *Truthfulness and Tragedy* (1977). J. R. Haule, " 'Soul-Making' in a Schizophrenic Saint," *J. of Religion and Health*, 23 (1984), 70–80. E. B. Holifield, *A History of Pastoral Care in America* (1983). M. Jensen, "Some Implications of Narrative Theology for Ministry to Cancer Patients," *J. of Pastoral Care*, 38 (1984), 216–25. S. B. Kopp, *Guru: Metaphors from a Psychotherapist* (1971). J. Patton, *Pastoral Counseling: A Ministry of the Church* (1983). C. E. Winquist, *Practical Hermeneutics: A Revised Agenda for Ministry* (1980).

J. PATTON

INTERPRETATION AND HERMENEUTICS, PASTORAL; PASTORAL CARE (Contemporary Methods, Perspectives, and Issues). *See also* LIFE CYCLE THEORY AND PASTORAL CARE; MYTHOLOGY AND PSYCHOLOGY; PASTOR (Normative and Traditional Images); SYMBOLISM. *Compare* DREAM INTERPRETATION IN PASTORAL COUNSELING; FEELING, THOUGHT, AND ACTION IN PASTORAL COUNSELING; RELIGIOUS LANGUAGE IN PASTORAL CARE; WIT AND HUMOR IN PASTORAL CARE.

PERSONALISM AND PASTORAL CARE. Personalism is a philosophical perspective for which the person is the ontological ultimate and for which personality is the fundamental explanatory principle. Its moral correlate is the affirmation of the ultimate and irreducible worth of the person. In a general sense, therefore, any religious care-giver or pastoral counselor is a personalist if the person in his or her care is the main focus of concern, is understood in essentially personal terms (not primarily in terms of subpersonal, nonmental forces or processes), and is regarded as of supreme value for his or her own sake — or, as one personalist has put it, if one holds to the conviction that truth is of, by, and for persons.

Undoubtedly personalism in this general sense has been widely espoused in the contemporary practice of pastoral care and counseling, even by many pastors who may never have studied personalist philosophy as such or thought of themselves as "personalists." But personalism is also a formal philosophy, and in terms of the relationship between personalism as a *formal philosophy* and pastoral care as a *movement*, the issue is a bit more complex.

1. **Philosophical Personalism.** Personalism is a species of idealism and as such has a long and distinguished history, which may be traced from Socrates and Plato through Kant and Hegel to recent Neo-Thomism (e.g., Etienne Gilson), absolute idealism (e.g., Josiah Royce), and process thought (e.g., Alfred North Whitehead). In recent times Polish philosopher Karol Wojtyla (Pope John Paul II) has embraced a form of personalism called Lublin Thomism (Woznicki, 1980).

The American school of personalist philosophy, with which this article is concerned, originated after the Civil War under the influence of George Homes Howison of St. Louis (though the term *personalism* was first used by the poet Walt Whitman in 1867). In 1908 Bordon

Parker Bowne of Boston University, the father of one major form of personalist philosophy, published his major work, *Personalism,* which contains most of the philosophy's tenets.

Like all idealist philosophy, personalism represents an affirmation (against materialism) of the ultimacy of mind or spirit. Personalists, however, emphasize its personal character in contrast, for example, to the "impersonalism" of the absolute idealists (e.g., Hegel), for whom the individual person is not ultimate but subordinate to universal Mind or Spirit, and against similar tendencies in recent existential theology (e.g., Tillich's "Ground of Being" and Macquarrie's "Being") and process thought. Personalism and process philosophy (and theology) are nevertheless very similar. In the judgment of some personalists, process thought tends to give insufficient support or clarity to the irreducible nature of personhood, giving a greater role to lower orders of subjectivity in the universe and tending, in theology, to subordinate God as person to an impersonal notion of Process or Creativity.

In relation to psychology, personalism emphasizes the irreducible nature of the person against the tendencies of behaviorism, psychoanalysis, and social psychology to identify or confuse the true person, the ontological agent, with the learned characteristics of the person known as "personality." Personalism is thus a natural ally of "humanistic" psychology (e.g., Allport, Maslow), though it is not necessarily incompatible with other psychologies of the person (e.g., Eriksonian ego psychology) if this distinction is maintained.

2. **Personalism and the Pastoral Care Movement.**
Although there are many streams of personalism in the history of philosophy, it is Boston personalism that needs to be highlighted in considering its impact on pastoral care. It was at Boston University that the many strands of personalism were dialectically reconstructed and where its project penetrated the education and training of a significant number of pastoral care and counseling students who later became leaders in the Clinical Pastoral Education Movement. Four generations of personalists in this tradition may be noted: The first generation was led by Borden Parker Bowne; the second generation included Edgar S. Brightman, Albert C. Knudson, Francis J. McConnell, and George Albert Coe; in the third generation were Peter Bertocci, L. Harold DeWolf, Georgia Harkness, John Lavely, Walter Mueder, S. Paul Schilling, and Paul E. Johnson. The fourth (contemporary) generation includes Martin Luther King, Jr., who explicitly identified himself with the personalist tradition (King, 1958, p. 100).

These personalists, teaching in such areas as philosophy, theology, biblical studies, and social ethics, undoubtedly influenced many pastors and pastoral counselors who trained at Boston University during the present century. One can perceive their influence, for example, on Carroll A. Wise, one of the pioneering figures and significant theorists of the Pastoral Care Movement. Though Wise was sharply critical of formal philosophizing as narrowly intellectualistic, the personalist influence of his Boston teachers is evident in his stress on the personal nature of all true communication of the gospel and the importance of the personhood of the pastor in authenticating Christian ministry, especially in pastoral care (Wise, 1966).

It is Paul E. Johnson, however, who must be singled out as the individual with root systems deep in the Boston personalist tradition who had the most direct impact on the development of pastoral care in the early years of the movement. Yet there is also a sense in which Johnson's critical *response* to personalism and his proposed *revision* of it were as influential as his fundamental commitment to it.

> Paul Johnson became increasingly convinced that personalism received via Bowne, Knudson, and Brightman could not account for what he called the dynamics of interpersonal relations—between mother and child, between members of a family, between persons in their encounters with each other in social contexts, between counselor and patient, and between man and God (Bertocci, 1973, p. 33).

It was Johnson's constant struggle for a synthesis of philosophical, theological, ethical, and scientific data, which led him away from personalism—as he understood it—to what he came to call dynamic interpersonalism. "The philosophy of personalism," he wrote in his later years, "is an organic pluralism of persons united by a Cosmic Person. This has been called personalism, but to accent the social relations of our universe we call it *interpersonalism*" (Johnson, 1966, p. 752).

It is important to note that some personalists have found such a development unnecessary, claiming that philosophical personalism, rightly and fully understood, contains all that is necessary to account for the dynamic and interpersonal nature of the person (Bertocci, 1973). Nevertheless Johnson's thirst for a more systemic way of viewing persons within helping contexts—particularly in the areas of pastoral care and counseling—led him away from a perspective that seemed to overstress the factors of unique individuality and conscious intentionality and to underestimate the power of unconscious process and the potency of community and interpersonal factors. Johnson's stress on the systemic nature of the person is best seen in his last published volume (coauthored with Lowell G. Colston) in which the following definition of personality is offered:

> *Personality is the dynamic mutual interaction of all systems which comprise and affect the organism.* Among these systems are physical, social, economic, political, ecological, etc., which are held together in a total organization known as *personality* (Colston and Johnson, 1972, p. 22).

This formulation best captures the philosophical foundation of the particular emphasis in pastoral care and counseling found in Boston personalism. Whether it may be seen as an authentic expression of philosophical personalism remains a question for scholarly research.

The broader question, however, is the extent to which *any* formal philosophy has been influential in the development of modern pastoral care and counseling. Certainly the pastoral literature suggests that psychology and theology have been more evident as intellectual influences than have philosophical systems; for the most part the leaders of the Pastoral Care Movement have gotten their intellectual bearings from other sources.

This seems equally true in the case of personalism, despite the explicit use made of it by Johnson and certain other theorists. The personalist philosophers themselves have not considered pastoral care and counseling a significant sphere of influence (e.g., Deats and Robb, 1985).

Yet it may be that formal philosophies exert an *indirect* influence on ministry through their role shaping social scientific theories and theology, and by influencing (and reflecting) the cultural ethos of church and society. Personalism (especially its emphasis on the worth of persons) and other idealist philosophies, have influenced the development of American education, psychology, and counseling (e.g., humanistic psychology), which in turn have influenced contemporary pastoral care and counseling at many points.

Bibliography. O. Strunk, Jr., ed., *Dynamic Interpersonalism for Ministry* (1973) contains essays on personalism and pastoral care focusing on Paul Johnson; see also *Psychology of Pastoral Care* (1953) and *Psychology of Religion* rev. ed. (1959). See also: B. P. Bowne, *Personalism* (1908). L. G. Colston and P. E. Johnson, *Personality and Christian Faith* (1972). P. Deats and C. Robb, *The Boston Personalist Tradition in Philosophy, Social Ethics, and Theology* (1985). P. E. Johnson, "The Trend Toward Dynamic Interpersonalism," *Religion in Life*, 35 (1966), 751–59. M. L. King, Jr., *Stride Toward Freedom* (1958). C. A. Wise, *The Meaning of Pastoral Care* (1966). A. N. Woznicki, *A Christian Humanism: Karol Wojtyla's Existential Personalism* (1980).

O. STRUNK, JR.

PASTORAL CARE MOVEMENT; PHILOSOPHY AND PSYCHOLOGY. *See also* HISTORY OF PROTESTANT PASTORAL CARE; PASTORAL CARE (History, Traditions, Definitions); PERSON. *Compare* PROCESS THEOLOGY AND PASTORAL CARE. *Biography:* JOHNSON; WISE.

PERSONALITY, BIOLOGICAL DIMENSIONS OF.

The genetic, hormonal, metabolic, and neural factors influencing the regulation and expression of emotional and interpersonal behavior. Biology effects personality in many ways and in many degrees. Short-term biological changes such as fatigue, hunger, or sickness affect transient aspects of personality like irritability and depression. More permanent are the personality traits we inherit genetically (as opposed to environmentally) from our parents. Sexual identity, both physical and psychological, is influenced in strong but not necessarily unchangeable ways by hormonal balances, particularly during prenatal development. The effects of some kinds of brain damage on an individual's personality traits are remarkable and permanent. The major psychotic disorders (schizophrenia and manic-depressive psychosis) involve relatively enduring personality abnormalities, which are most likely the result of neurochemical dysfunctions.

1. **Inheritability of Personality.** Identical (monozygotic) twins have nearly identical personalities. Under normal circumstances the relative importance of their common genetic makeup and environment in creating similar personalities is uncertain. However, when one studies monozygotic twins who were adopted by different families at an early age and raised apart, the strong influence of genetic endowment on very subtle and idiosyncratic aspects of personality becomes apparent. Lykken (1982) has brought together and studied nearly fifty pairs of monozygotic twins raised apart (MZA).

When studied, most of these twin pairs were together for the first time since infant separation.

Of course the MZA twins looked alike and had very similar measurable intelligence. We are all accustomed to the idea that physical appearance and native intelligence are largely under genetic control. Yet the remarkable aspect of this research was the degree of personality similarity they manifested despite different home environments. MZA twins were more alike than dizygotic twins raised *together* (DZT) on all scales of a personality inventory. MZA twins were particularly alike in social potency (i.e., charisma) and positive affect, where correlations exceeded 50 percent in the MZA group and were near zero in the DZT group. Also, measures of recreational interests were more strongly concordant for the MZA group than the DZT, suggesting that there is genetic influence on the kinds of hobbies and sports to which one is attracted.

Most interesting and surprising were the similarities found for very idiosyncratic aspects of personality. One MZA twin pair found that they both had a habit of wearing seven rings. Another pair both compulsively counted things, and another had independently developed a "talent" as a raconteur. Although Lykken reports that such similarities were the rule among the MZA twins, he had thus far found no such similarities in the DZT twins, despite encouraging the DZT twins to find them.

Lykken theorizes that these similarities are "emergenetic" traits in that they are the expression of specific configurations of many genes, as opposed to a single gene. Thus, these traits are highly concordant in MZA twins who have exactly the same genetic makeup, but are often unrelated in DZT twins, who share only part of their genetic endowment. Lykken argues that since such "emergenetic" traits involve the configural interaction of many genes, they will likely not run in families. The statistical probability of passing on an exact complex of a large number of genes to an offspring is very small. Thus, even what appears to be an environmentally determined idiosyncratic personality development within a family may, in fact, be an "emergenetic" trait, which is the expression of a unique confluence of genes.

2. **Hormonal Determinants of Sexual Identity.** After the genetically determined development of the ovaries or testes in the fetus, the remainder of sexual differentiation is under hormonal control. That is, hormones determine the development and differentiation of internal and external sex organs. During critical intrauterine periods, male and female hormones (androgens and extrogens, respectively) also exert a strong influence on the organization of the brain, setting up the neural systems which will, in adolescence, regulate specific patterns of male or female hormonal flow.

Intrauterine hormones during this critical period (approximately three to four gestational months in humans) appear to affect more than just sex organ development and hormone release in later adolescence. The brain is differentiated, in ways not yet fully understood, to predispose individuals to behaviors and cognitive abilities which are gender typical, though not necessarily gender specific. Girls exposed to high levels of prenatal androgen, though considered normal, describe themselves as tomboys, preferring boys as playmates and enjoying more typically boy-type play. Similarly, prenatal exposure to high levels of estrogen in boys may produce a bias toward less assertive and aggressive behavior and less prowess in athletic activities.

Though biological factors appear determinant for gender specific behavior in animals, there is evidence that psychosocial environment may play at least as strong, if not stronger, a role in the gender identity of humans. An anecdotal example of the strength of this influence has been reported of normal twin boys, one of whom at the age of seven months accidentally lost his penis via a surgical accident. The parents, after much deliberation, decided to raise him (her) as a girl. Further surgical change was performed and hormonal supplements given later, during adolescence. Mostly, the parents began dressing and treating their "daughter" like a girl. The subsequent behavior of the twins was remarkably different, the "daughter" showing clear feminine behaviors and preferences, while the son was clearly male. In humans at least, the biological influences on gender identity can be overridden to some degree by psychosocial environment.

3. **Brain Damage.** Perhaps the most famous single case in all of neurology is the case of Phineas Gage. In 1848, Gage, a responsible, quiet, efficient railroad worker, had a tamping iron blown through the frontal lobe of his brain by an accidental dynamite discharge. Remarkably, he was not killed, at least not physically. After recovery, Gage was able to function normally, his intellectual abilities having been little affected. However, his personality was very different. He was now loud, ebullient, occasionally prone to violent outbursts, and irresponsible. His personality was so changed by the frontal lobe damage that his physician remarked that Phineas Gage was no longer Phineas Gage. The case of Gage is famous because of the bizarre nature of the accident, but the personality change that resulted from the extensive frontal damage is not uncommon.

Although frontal lobe damage generally lessens control and regulation of behavior, the effects of left and right frontal damage on personality generally differ. Individuals with right frontal damage manifest an unconcerned, optimistic, almost euphoric outlook, reminiscent of Gage, whose primary damage was on the right side. Those with left frontal damage react to situations (particularly their own disability) with much anxiety and frustration, a syndrome often referred to in neurology as a "catastrophic reaction."

The frontal lobes are not the only brain area where damage or malfunction will impact personality. Longstanding temporal lobe epilepsy has been associated, in various studies, with changes in affect, behavior, and thought. Bear and Fedio (see Bear, 1979) studied the personalities of individuals with temporal lobe epilepsy. They found that the interictal (i.e., between seizure) personalities of these patients had very strong similarities. They were generally seen by others as circumstantial (i.e., they never got to the point in conversation), having a strong philosophic interest, and angry. These individuals consistently reported that they had little sexual drive. They rated themselves as more humorless, dependent, and obsessional than nonepileptic individuals rated

themselves. When the seizure focus was on the right side of the brain, the individuals tended to be emotional (i.e., anger, aggression, and sadness), while those with left temporal epilepsy were more ideational (i.e., philosophical concern, religiosity, humorlessness, a sense of personal destiny, and hypergraphia). Thus, a long-standing seizure disorder of the temporal lobe has predictable effects on personality, though it is sometimes less dramatic than that which results from frontal lobe damage.

The relationship between temporal lobe seizures and violent behavior is discussed under psychosurgery. Briefly, episodic outbursts of violent, aggressive behavior with minimal provocation may (in some undetermined percent of individuals manifesting this behavior) be the result of undetected abnormal electrical activity in the limbic nuclei underlying the temporal cortex. Unprovoked fear and aggression can be produced in an animal by injecting substances into the amygdala (a subcortical nucleus of the temporal lobe), which causes abnormal physiological activity in the nucleus.

4. **Psychosis.** Schizophrenia and the affective disorders (i.e., manic-depressive psychosis and psychotic depression) are clinically defined by severe abnormalities in personality. There is currently little doubt that both of these categories of psychosis are the manifestations of physiological abnormalities, likely in neurochemical systems, although environmental factors may play some triggering or modulating role.

Both schizophrenia and affective disorder have been shown to have weak but statistically significant genetic links. The incidence of psychosis runs between ten and twenty percent in those with psychotic relatives. The coincidence of psychosis is particularly high for monozygotic twins, whether raised together or apart, that is, a greater than fifty percent chance of one twin becoming schizophrenic if the other twin is schizophrenic. Thus, these psychotic conditions, which severely impact personality, are behavioral manifestations of neural disease.

One of the current theories of schizophrenia is that it is a defect specific to the brain subsystem of neurons that uses dopamine as its neurotransmitter. The antischizophrenic drugs (i.e., phenothiazines) appear to operate by blocking (therefore desensitizing) dopamine receptors. Similarly, drugs that increase the activity of the dopamine system, that is, amphetamine, cocaine, L-DOPA and methylphenidate (Ritalin), are all capable of producing psychotic symptoms in normal persons or exacerbating symptoms in schizophrenics. The dopamine system of the brain, among other functions, interconnects the brainstem arousal areas and the frontal lobe cortical areas involved in regulating attention. The clinical description of schizophrenia as a hyperattentive state (i.e., unable to filter out the insignificant information and focus attention on the important stimuli) is concordant with the neurophysiology of the dopamine system.

There are two varieties of major affective disorder—manic-depressive psychosis and depression. The manic phase of the manic-depressive condition is rather dramatically relieved by the administration of lithium, which also usually eliminates the ensuing depression. The condition of psychotic depression (as opposed to manic depression or more normal neurotic depression) is relieved rather effectively by two types of drugs. Inhibitors of the enzymes that get rid of excess dopamine and chemically similar neurotransmitters (serotonin and norepinephrine) are effective in relieving depression, but have undesirable side effects. A group of drugs called tricyclic antidepressants, which also seem to produce their effects by increasing the amount of the same three neurotransmitters, alleviate psychotic depression.

5. Summary. Four areas have been discussed that illustrate rather strong biological effects on personality. In all cases, though the effects of biological factors are rather striking, it must be remembered that environmental and psychosocial factors also play some role. In the more dramatic cases of personality change with brain damage or psychosis, we are dealing with a malfunctioning system. These conditions can be viewed as producing individuals who are *less* responsive to normal environmental influences, that is, these individuals are abnormal for the very reason that their personalities are overdetermined by biological factors. Brain disease and damage generally affect personality by reducing behavioral flexibility, thus restricting the range of response possibilities.

Whether normal or abnormal, the concept of biological determinism is generally objectionable to Christians, even many who study brain-behavior relationships. But it is difficult from the point of view of the scientific literature to know where biological influences give way to psychological, social, or spiritual ones. Even learning, the central pillar of theories of environmental influence on personality, has its biological constraints and determinants. Free will and personal responsibility are factors that must be considered in light of biological influences.

Bibliography. D. Bear, "The Temporal Lobes: An Approach to the Study of Organic Behavioral Changes," in M. Gazzaniga, ed., *Handbook of Behavioral Neurobiology:* vol. 2, *Neuropsychology* (1979), pp. 75–98. D. D. Kelly, "Sexual Differentiation of the Nervous System," in E. R. Kandel and J. H. Schwartz, *Principles of Neural Science* (1981), 533–46. B. Kolb and I. Whishaw, *Fundamentals of Human Neuropsychology* (1980). D. T. Lykken, "Research with Twins: The Concept of Emergenesis," *Psychophysiology*, (1982), 361–73. E. J. Sachar, "Psychobiology of Schizophrenia," in E. R. Kandel and J. H. Schwartz, *Principles of Neural Science* (1981), pp. 599–609.

W. S. BROWN

BRAIN RESEARCH; MIND-BODY RELATIONSHIP; PERSON; PERSONALITY THEORY; SOCIOBIOLOGY. *See also* BEHAVIOR; BIORHYTHM RESEARCH; BIOFEEDBACK; DRUGS; EPILEPSY; INTELLIGENCE AND INTELLIGENCE TESTING; MANIC-DEPRESSIVE (BIPOLAR) DISORDER; ORGANIC MENTAL DISORDER; PSYCHOSURGERY; SCHIZOPHRENIA; SEXUALITY, BIOLOGICAL AND PSYCHOLOGICAL THEORY OF; SOMATOTYPE; TEMPERAMENT. *Compare* HOMEOSTASIS; SENSORY DEPRIVATION RESEARCH; SLEEP AND SLEEP DISORDERS.

PERSONALITY, CONCEPT OF. *See* CHARACTER AND PERSONALITY (Comparative Concepts); PERSONALITY THEORY; PERSON (Philosophical Issues).

PERSONALITY, PASTOR'S. *See* PERSONHOOD OF THE PASTOR, SIGNIFICANCE OF; MENTAL HEALTH, PASTOR'S.

PERSONALITY, SOCIETY, AND CULTURE. The primary units of study for the disciplines of psychology,

sociology, and anthropology respectively. Briefly defined, *personality* consists of the pattern of dispositions to behave in certain ways which characterizes an individual; *society* consists of the patterns of social structure and relationships between a people who think of themselves as one united people; and *culture* consists of the way of life of a people.

Whereas personality has an individual base, that is, it refers to that which exists within the individual, society and culture both have a collective base, meaning that they exist not in any one individual, but in a people as a whole. Because society and culture share a collective referent, they are sometimes used interchangeably as if to represent "two sides of the same coin." On one side is society, which has a structural connotation, in that it refers to the structural arrangements of social institutions and the positions people occupy in these social structures. On the other side is culture, which has a normative connotation, referring to the norms that govern the social-structural positions, the values they share, and behavior of individual participants. Personality is a quality which makes it possible for individuals to occupy positions in society and to behave or play their role according to culturally defined norms.

1. Personality Formation. A personality is formed within a society according to cultural expectations. Personalities are formed through the process of socialization, whereby certain aspects of culture (values, beliefs, attitudes, preferences, etc.) become an internalized part of the individual. Cultural determinism is a position which seeks to explain all of human personality in terms of cultural conditioning. Critics of this extreme view argue that much of modern social science has an over-socialized view of the development of the human personality. Sociobiology is a recently emergent point of view which attempts to explain human personality in terms of genetic composition. Most social scientists hold to a middle position, critical of cultural determinism as representing an over-socialized view of human behavior, but equally critical of sociobiology as ignoring the vast evidence which points to the importance of cultural conditioning in personality formation.

Although most social sciences consider cultural conditioning more important than genetics in their relative contributions to personality formation, both factors are seen as interacting with each other in contributing to personality formation. A recent trend in personality theory has been toward viewing the individual as actively involved in selecting from the offerings of culture. Although cultural conditioning is not unimportant, individuals are seen as actively involved in creating their own personalities.

2. Subculture and Subsociety. One of the results of the diverse complexity of modern society has been the development of a multitude of subcultures and subsocieties. All members of a society share a common culture. However, every member of modern society is also a member of various subsocieties, each of which provides a subculture for its members which is not shared by others in the wider society. As an example, members of a local church together constitute a subsociety in that they are part of the social structure of the church. Although these congregational members are also members of the wider society, and probably a number of other subsocieties also, only the members share in the congregational social structure. Members of this church also share a common subculture — the religious beliefs, attitudes, norms, values, etc. of the church. This religious culture which is shared is a *sub*culture because it is not shared by all persons in society as a whole.

Some subsocieties seek to have total control over their members, which they seek to accomplish by isolation from the influences of the wider society. Religious cults can be thought of as subsocieties which are seeking to become total societies. When a total society has achieved its goals, such as in the case of the People's Temple in Jonestown, Guyana, in reality a new society has been formed. In such a society only one cultural version of life is tolerated, with little chance for subcultural views to emerge. Not surprisingly, a high degree of homogeneity among individual personalities will result in such societies. Personality diversity will be greatest in secular modern societies in which many subsocieties exist.

3. Breakdown and Disorder. Societies, as well as personalities, break down and enter into states of disorder. This is especially true in modern secular societies where social change has been extremely rapid. Due to the interdependence of personality, society, and cultural systems, personality disorder is likely to be low in slowly changing societies and high in rapidly changing societies. In the rapid change of modern society, alternative values and beliefs compete for acceptance, personal values and beliefs are challenged and often discarded, and personality disorder is common.

Inversely, traditional societies are characterized by cultural systems which comprise a unified whole, relatively free of internal contradictions. Individuals residing in these societies can be expected to have integrated personalities because they are rarely exposed to cultural discontinuity or contradiction. Given that personality, societal, and cultural systems are highly interrelated, conflict in one can be expected to result in conflict in the others.

4. Therapeutic Change. Attempts to change a personality, a society, or a culture must take into account the interdependence between each of these three systems. Pastoral care and counseling is by its very nature focused upon the personality system, and most attempts at therapeutic change are directed at the individual rather than the societal or cultural level. However, attempts at individual change should take into account the fact that an individual personality is formed and maintained within social and cultural systems if it is to be fruitful. Attempts to bring about personality change may be futile if not accompanied by corresponding attempts to address or change social structures. This fact can most easily be appreciated by considering the importance of the family to a family member. Personal problems are usually identified as personality problems — a rebellious child, a depressed wife, an alcoholic husband. However, during the last twenty years therapists have decreasingly understood personality problems strictly in terms of a medical model (as sick personalities), and increasingly as by-products of social structural dysfunctions (unhealthy family or community relationships). Likewise, some therapists have come to believe that personality change

can most effectively take place when the focus of therapeutic change is upon the social system and not the individual personality only. This is not to negate the continued usefulness of individual counseling and therapy, but rather to point out the wisdom of looking beyond the individual to social structural systems. Whereas pastoral care and counseling is most sharply focused upon caring for individuals, in a wider sense it should culminate in helping to foster a caring and serving congregational community. This is to say that the fruits of pastoral care and counseling should be evident in a congregation at the personality, subsocietal, and subcultural levels.

Bibliography. D. Augsburger, *Pastoral Counseling Across Cultures* (1986). D. Browning, *Pluralism and Personality* (1980). H. J. Eysenck, *Personality, Genetics, and Behavior* (1982). C. Kluckhohn and F. Kluckhohn, *Man, Society, and Social Order* (1965). R. Niebuhr, *Moral Man and Immoral Society* (1932). T. Parsons, *The Social System* (1963). E. Sapir, *Culture, Language, and Personality* (1962). V. Satir, *Conjoint Family Therapy* 3d ed. (1983). B. F. Skinner, *Beyond Freedom and Dignity* (1971). P. Tillich, *Theology of Culture* (1959). R. M. Williams, *American Society* (1957).

J. BALSWICK

HUMAN NATURE, PROBLEM OF; PHILOSOPHICAL ANTHROPOLOGY. *See also* CHARACTER AND PERSONALITY (Comparative Concepts); CULTURAL AND ETHNIC FACTORS, *or* SOCIAL STATUS AND CLASS FACTORS; IN PASTORAL CARE; ROLE; SOCIOBIOLOGY. *Compare* SOCIOLOGY OF RELIGIOUS AND PASTORAL CARE.

PERSONALITY AND THEOLOGY. *See* PASTORAL THEOLOGY, PROTESTANT; THEOLOGY AND PSYCHOLOGY.

PERSONALITY DEVELOPMENT. *See* LIFE CYCLE THEORY; PERSONALITY DEVELOPMENT, BIOLOGICAL AND SOCIALIZING FACTORS IN; PERSONALITY THEORY. *See also* ANALYTICAL (JUNGIAN) PSYCHOLOGY, PSYCHOANALYSIS, *or* HUMANISTIC PSYCHOLOGY (Personality Theory and Research); COGNITIVE, EMOTIONAL, LANGUAGE, MORAL, *or* PSYCHOSOCIAL DEVELOPMENT.

PERSONALITY DEVELOPMENT, BIOLOGICAL AND SOCIALIZING INFLUENCES IN. Personality is the organized and distinctive pattern of behavior, thought, and feelings which characterize a person's adaptations to various situations, and which endure over time and set persons apart from each other. In another sense, personality is that which organizes and directs responses to a wide variety of somatic and environmental demands, for example, an angry boss, a dissatisfied customer, an unhappy child, or an excited co-worker. Although personality endures over time, most persons experience some change in attitudes and actions over the years. This article notes a few of the biological and social factors that are known to affect personality development.

1. Prenatal Factors. Recently researchers have been able to identify factors which may have dramatic effects upon the unborn child. Some of these factors may have long-term effects on personality development.

Historically, the unborn child (called a fetus) was assumed to be parasitical. It was believed that regardless of the mother's condition the child received all the nourishment it needed. Further, the umbilical cord was thought to act as barrier between mother and infant, shielding the infant from potential harmful agents entering the infant through the mother.

Some rather significant events have, however, exposed the true relationship between the fetus and mother. During the early and mid-sixties, many children were being born with defective or absent limbs. Research revealed that the fertility drug thalidomide had been responsible. Here was clear evidence that a drug ingested by the mother had found its way into the developing fetus.

More recently, researchers have identified effects on children of maternal use of alcohol, barbiturates, heroin, tobacco, and even aspirin. For example, women who are chronic smokers have a much higher incidence of premature deliveries, low birthweight infants, and spontaneous abortions, and heavy aspirin users are more likely to bear children who have various blood disorders.

The emotional condition of the mother also contributes significantly to prenatal development. Emotionally disturbed and chronically anxious mothers are more likely to produce emotionally disturbed children. Further, anxious mothers have also been found to have higher incidences of premature deliveries, spontaneous abortions, and other delivery complications. Anxious mothers are also more likely to have infants who are hyperactive, irritable, cry more, and have more problems feeding and sleeping.

The significance of these relationships on personality development is twofold: First, prematurity and low birthweight, in and of themselves, are associated with a number of adjustment problems, such as intellectual impairment and poor social development. Premature infants are more likely to have difficulty in school (in reading, arithmetic, and spelling) and are more likely to become dropouts. Second, prematurity and low birthweight are associated with infants who are more difficult to care for, in that they are active, irritable and irregular in feeding schedules.

The reasons for these outcomes are unclear. Perhaps neurological or brain damage occurs as a result of the poor prenatal environment and directly affects intellectual and social ability. Perhaps the effect is mediated by the parent-child relationship. For example, a child who is difficult to have, or who is frail or demands a great deal of attention, is generally irritable, and does not seem to enjoy his or her parents, sets into motion a pattern of parent-child interactions that are generally unpleasant and full of conflict.

2. Hereditary (Genetic) Influences. *a. Physique.* The influence of genes upon virtually every area of human behavior has long been of interest to psychologists. E. Kretschmer and W. Sheldon were two twentieth-century psychologists convinced that one's body type (or physique) was ultimately responsible for one's personality. Sheldon examined this relationship by classifying persons according to their body type and then testing the basic personality of each type. Sheldon found that muscular people, called mesomorphs, had aggressive personalities. Persons with rounded body lines (chubby), called endomorphs, were friendly and jovial. Angular, thin persons, ectomorphs, were shy and deceitful.

Later research has revealed that the relationships described by Sheldon are too simplistic and inaccurate. It is now known that a person's physique does not singularly determine personality, although it may have a rather significant impact because of the interaction between physical characteristics and social environment. For example, a large muscular male who observes that others allow him to have his own way when he makes threatening gestures may learn a more aggressive and intimidating conflict style than a slightly built child for whom threats do not result in positive outcomes.

Parents and friends who downplay the importance of physical characteristics while nurturing inward qualities play an important role in helping their children develop positive feelings about themselves. Additionally, parents who maintain a realistic awareness of the teasing and unkind remarks that their children may experience at the hands of their schoolmates or siblings and who strive to instill an assurance of parental love and acceptance can nurture a positive acceptance of one's physical characteristics, an important personality component.

b. Temperament. A. Thomas and S. Chess have examined those aspects of personality which appear at birth and that remain consistent over the years. In their original research more than two hundred children were examined, from infancy through adolescence, for characteristics such as activity level, regularity in biological functioning (e.g., eating, sleeping, and bowel movements), ease in accepting new people and situations, adaptability to changes in routine, sensitivity to noise, bright lights, and other sensory stimuli, mood (cheerful or unhappy), intensity of responses, degree of persistence, and distractibility. They called the combination of these characteristics "temperament" and discovered that infants differed tremendously on these dimensions almost immediately after birth.

Thomas and Chess also found consistent patterns of characteristics. For example, some children had regular biological functions, adjusted easily to new situations and schedules, had moderate response patterns, and were generally cheerful. These children were called "easy" children and accounted for about forty percent of the infants examined. "Difficult" children, about ten percent, tended to have intense reactions, did not adjust well to changes in routine or people, were restless, irregular in biological functioning and were generally unhappy. The third group, called "slow to warm," which included about fifteen percent, were mild in their responses, and while they did not initially respond positively to change, if allowed repeated exposure usually adjusted well.

Such temperamental differences can directly affect personality development. For individuals who are constantly active, who seem to have unlimited energy and need little sleep to replenish spent resources, such an elevated activity level may translate into any one or more personality characteristics associated with heightened energy level, such as aggressiveness, gregariousness, or thrill-seeking. Individuals who have a lower activity level might come to prefer activities or occupations which allow them to work at their own pace, out of the spotlight.

Temperamental differences also affect personality through interaction with the environment. An "easy" child adjusts well to parental control and fits into the parents' idea of what a child is supposed to be like. A "difficult" child is a candidate for a great many more confrontations with parents. It is likely that these different relationships with parents will generate differing personality characteristics. But much depends also on parental temperament, whether easy or difficult.

c. Abilities. A third area where heredity and personality interact is in the limitations that heredity places on abilities, such as intelligence. Given an enriched positive environment, a person might reach the upper bounds of ability, while a depressed environment may stifle whatever genetic ability had been present. One way by which differences affect personality development is that they are related to the success and failure experiences which a child has. Success increases both a desire to achieve and feelings of self-worth, while failure has the opposite effect. Parental reactions also play an important role. A child who fails in an area where the parent has invested much emotional energy may suffer damage to feelings of self-worth if the parent does not convey feelings of acceptance.

3. **Socialization Factors.** Socialization is the process whereby an individual learns what the culture expects from him or her. Parents are the primary socializing agents, although other individuals play important secondary roles. Parents may significantly influence their children through child-rearing techniques, modeling and imitation, or incidental learning.

a. Parental influence. i. Child-rearing techniques. D. Baumrind has identified and compared three basic parenting styles: authoritarian, permissive, and authoritative. Authoritarian parents attempt to control childrens' behavior by demanding unquestioning obedience and adherence to strict behavioral codes. Their children tend to be discontent, withdrawn, and distrustful. Permissive parents are nondemanding and noncontrolling. They rarely punish but take care to explain the reasons for rules. Their children tend to be discontent, immature, have poor self-control, and poor self-reliance. Authoritative parents attempt to direct action by focusing attention on issues rather than punishment. They are firm and will use punishment, if necessary. They structure the household such that each person knows what is expected. In that regard, they make an attempt to be respectful of their children's opinions and feelings. Discipline and a recognition of authority is mixed with warmth and love. Their children tend to be self-assured, confident, and generally well-adjusted.

Typically, authoritarian parents who demand strict adherence to rules have children who obey the rules when they are likely to be discovered, but who break rules and experiment with forbidden alternatives when discovery is unlikely. They are significantly less likely to trust their parents with sensitive information, especially if parents tend to condemn rather than listen. They are also less likely to disclose feelings with others, including friends. Permissive parents are more likely to have children who have difficulty controlling impulses. They tend to be selfish, demanding and immature. With the authoritative style, discipline is tempered with love and implemented through dialog; the child learns rules, but also

learns that parents are flexible and willing to dialog. Trust becomes an important context for mature personality development and an important trait of the developing personality.

ii. Modeling. Learning by observation, or modeling, is also an important factor in personality development. Because children admire their parents so much, they seek to be like them. For example, in situations where parents verbally teach sharing and then are observed actually sharing, children are much more likely to share themselves. If parents words are not accompanied by actions, children are likely to verbalize that sharing is good, but not practice it themselves. Parents who have shown children affection and a genuine enjoyment of their company, tend to have children who model that behavior themselves; they are more tolerant of others, and more likely to show distress at others' misfortunes. Children who grew up in homes where they were considered a nuisance tend to be less tolerant of others and to respond negatively to others' distress. Although children do not model everything parents do, there is a significant part of children's personality which results directly from modeling.

b. Peers. A secondary social influence on personality development is the peer group. For most children, peers, though important, rank a distant second to parents in influencing choices in areas such as occupation, marriage, religion, and moral values. In other areas, however, particularly where the behaviors are related to popularity and acceptance, peers can exert a powerful influence. Peer group influence centers around engaging in similar behaviors in exchange for mutual support and friendship. Overall the peer group serves many useful functions and provides acceptance in ways that parents cannot. Peers allow for exchange of information, friendship and fellowship, and comparison of the self with others.

Bibliography. D. Baumrind, "Child Care Practices Anteceding Three Patterns of Preschool Behavior," *General Psychology Monographs*, 75 (1967), 43–88. E. Kretschmer, *Physique and Character* (1925). W. Sheldon, *The Varieties of Human Physique: An Introduction to Constitutional Psychology*, (1940). E. Straub, ed., *Personality: Basic Aspects and Current Research* (1980). A. Thomas, S. Chess, and D. Birch, *Behavioral Individuality in Early Childhood*, (1963).

K. A. HOLSTEIN

LIFE CYCLE THEORY AND PASTORAL CARE; PERSON; PERSONALITY THEORY. *See also* COGNITIVE, EMOTIONAL, LANGUAGE, MORAL, *or* PSYCHOSOCIAL DEVELOPMENT; BIRTH ORDER; HUMAN DEVELOPMENT; SELF-ACTUALIZATION/SELF-REALIZATION.

PERSONALITY DISORDERS. The concept of personality disorders dates back to ancient Greek classifications of temperamental types. Pathologies of personality reflect developmental deficits and may involve biological differences or vulnerabilities.

The concept of personality is abstract and interrelated to other attributes of person. *Character* is defined as the personal qualities that represent an individual's adherence to the values and customs of society. *Temperament* refers to the energy level, emotions, and moods of a person. *Self* refers to the cognitive recognition and naming of one's own being. *Identity* is the content of self-reference as to who I am. *Personality* is defined as the complex patterns of psychological organization, largely unconscious, which result in relatively endurable and consistent styles of behavioral responses to life events. Clinically, we might describe a person with a compulsive personality style, who may have a sanguine, explosive, or taciturn temperament, who might exhibit noble or ignoble character traits, with either little or extensive awareness of self in action, with any degree of a defined identity.

1. **Personality Organization.** Personality organization is a developmental process. It follows that the more primitive the level of personality organization, the more pervasive will be the adverse consequences for mature expressions of character, temperament, self-awareness, and identity formation. Thus we can order personality disorders along a developmental continuum. The most immature personality disorders reflect primitive, even infantile, coping patterns in life, lacking autonomy of self-direction. Whereas the mature "neurotic personality disorder" has considerable effective adult coping repertoires and substantial self-direction, but manifests some stereotyped dysfunctional personality traits.

We can subdivide psychopathology into three major domains: *Personality patterns* are behaviors reflective of deeply embedded and pervasive dysfunctional lifestyles. *Behavior reactions* are transient dysfunctional responses to ambient life stress. *Symptom disorders* are in between, reflecting intensification or disruption of behavior in response to life events where the personality style is particularly vulnerable.

All persons have a personality, which for most is a set of relatively effective coping styles combined into a repertoire of potential behavioral responses. Pathologies of personality have four dysfunctional attributes: (1) Lack of autonomy. The person responds in stereotyped or automated fashion without the sense of personal choice, will, or direction. It is reflexive behavior. (2) Adaptive inflexibility. The person does not consider, evaluate, or select among alternative responses. This person is considered rigid. (3) Repetitive dysfunctional behavior. The person does not learn from experience, or consider the consequences of his or her behavior. (4) Tenuous stability. The person exhibits fragility and lack of resilience in response to stress. He or she is overwhelmed by anxiety if stereotyped behavior is not effective, or the person resorts to more regressive and infantile responses. He or she lacks the capacity for innovation and adaptive creativity.

2. **Personality Disorders.** In the 1980 third edition of the *Diagnostic and Statistical Manual of Mental Disorders (DSM-III* and *DSM-III-R)*, a diagnostic class of eleven major personality disorders is described. A diagnosis of personality disorder can be made as a primary mental disorder, or as an underlying predisposing disorder. The work of Theodore Millon (1982) affords an empirical descriptive organization of these eleven disorders by combining two dimensions of interpersonal styles of behavior. First is a dimension of dependent-independent-ambivalent-detached relationships combined with either an active or passive mode. The eleven clinical syndromes are defined in terms of these interpersonal dimensions, with the official *DSM-III* diagnostic label.

a. The passive-dependent pattern (DSM-III, Dependent disorder). Characterized by a search for relationships where one relies upon others to supply security, affection, direction, and leadership. A passive role is assumed and others are expected to provide comfort and support. There is acquiescence and passive submission to the demands of others in order to maintain a supply of dependent gratification.

b. The active-dependent pattern (DSM-III, Histrionic disorder). Here one demonstrates an insatiable and indiscriminant search for stimulation and affection. Although sociable and gregarious, there is lack and fear of autonomy, along with an intense need for social approval and support.

c. The passive-independent pattern (DSM-III, Narcissistic disorder). This pattern is marked by egoistic self-involvement. There is overevaluation of self-worth, overwhelming sense of superiority, and exploitation of others to aggrandize self-worth. There is the sense of entitlement to be served by others.

d. The active-independent pattern (DSM-III, Antisocial disorder). There is a mistrust of others, desire for autonomy without autonomous capacity, and a sense of entitled retribution for perceived past injustices. There is indiscriminate striving for power, in which others are used and abused. There is little impulse control with short-term need for immediate gratification, while the person lacks a mature moral sense and does not learn from experience.

e. The passive-ambivalent pattern (DSM-III, Compulsive disorder). There is approach-avoidance conflict. The person desires acceptance and approval from others but has intense anger and fear of closeness to others. The ambivalence is resolved by suppression of the conflict with overconformance and overcompliance, often accompanied by erratic outbursts of hostility. The overcontrol of self is extended to attempts to overcontrol others.

f. The active-ambivalent pattern (DSM-III, Passive-aggressive disorder). Here the ambivalence toward others is relatively conscious and erratically expressed in everyday life. Behavior fluctuates between conformity and deference, and aggressive negativism. Anger and stubbornness evoke subsequent guilt and shame, thence remorseful penitence, and then anger, in a vicious cycle.

g. The passive-detached pattern (DSM-III, Schizoid disorder). This is noted by social impassivity. There is deep repression of emotional needs and strivings reflected in an observer role of most social relations.

h. The active-detached pattern (DSM-III, Schizoid disorder). This person fears and mistrusts others. He or she longs for affection but fears repeated pain and anguish of prior conflictual relations. Active withdrawal and denial of feelings is used to protect oneself from possible painful relations.

i. The cycloid pattern (DSM-III, Borderline disorder). There are intense attachments to others, which rapidly fluctuate between ardent affection and vicious hostility. There is an obvious demand for affection and closeness that brooks no frustration, so that minor disappointments precipitate rage.

j. The paranoid pattern (DSM-III, same). Here there is vigilant mistrust and suspicion of others. Self-worth is aggrandized by projection of faults and failures onto others. There is intense fear of loss of autonomy reflected in insensitivity to others, aloofness, and coldness toward others.

k. The schizotypal pattern (DSM-III, same). There is severe lack of integrated behavior leading to eccentric patterns of life, deliberate isolation from others, and lack of interest in others.

Most people exhibit mild and mixed variants of all the above patterns of interpersonal relations, which we term personality traits. The diagnosis of a personality disorder would be made when the traits are relatively fixed, are obdurate to change, and result in subjective distress and/or significant impairment in social and vocational function.

Bibliography. T. Millon, *Disorders of Personality, DSM-III: Axis II* (1982). D. B. Rinsley, *Borderline and Other Self Disorders* (1982). D. Shapiro, *Autonomy and Rigid Character* (1981).

E. M. PATTISON

DIAGNOSTIC AND STATISTICAL MANUAL III; EVALUATION AND DIAGNOSIS, PSYCHOLOGICAL; MENTAL HEALTH AND ILLNESS; PSYCHOPATHOLOGY, THEORIES OF. *See also* AMBIVALENCE; ANTISOCIAL PERSONS; BORDERLINE DISORDER; DEPENDENCE/INDEPENDENCE; NARCISSISM/NARCISSISTIC PERSONALITY; OBSESSIVE COMPULSIVE DISORDER; PERSONALITY TYPES AND PASTORAL CARE; SUSPICIOUSNESS AND PARANOIA.

PERSONALITY THEORY (Assumptions and Values in). How we ask our questions regarding personality shapes the nature of our answer. Heschel (1963) has suggested that if we ask the question "What is wo/man?" We obtain a very different view of personality than if we ask the question "Who is wo/man?" The first tends to lead to a focus on the nature of "being" in human being. Humaneness and personality is then a subset of that which is natural. The second question emphasizes the quality of the "human" in being human. The empirical approach to understanding personality emphasizes the former and will be delineated first. Two alternatives that focus on the second question will be explored thereafter.

1. The Empirical Tradition. The empirical tradition of studying personality obtains its impetus from Aristotle's concern (in contrast to Plato) with the concrete. It receives further support from Locke's assumption that the method so successfully applied by the physical sciences to nature should be applied also to human nature. In the twentieth century, the scientific approach to personality tends to predominate. Scientific studies of the psyche have acquired the force of certainty by virtue of the development of personality inventories used in business, education, and welfare institutions.

The nature of the knowledge of personality produced by the scientific method understands the self in terms of operations, behaviors, or simply what is observable. Anxiety may then be defined as high blood pressure (physiological), tics (behavior), or as comments about the fear of rejection (self-report). It is assumed that the more complex units of behavior should be broken down into and understood by the more simple elements. Further, the focus of analysis is not experience but behavior. The work of the social learning theorists, trait theorists, and, in a limited way, the psychoanalysts falls into the empirical tradition in understanding personality.

The empirical approach is concerned to obtain reliable information. The variables, operationally defined, are studied through experimental manipulation. An example would be the question whether anxiety is related to factors such as age, gender, or education. The data collected becomes the basis of generalizations (e.g., there is a curvilinear relationship between anxiety and learning). Knowledge so gained is viewed as objective, ahistorical, and propositional.

The purpose of this approach is to test both tradition and common sense. Virtually every introductory psychology text contrasts the reliability of the results of the scientific method with the unreliability of common sense understandings. Furthermore, the express purpose of this procedure is to discover order in human nature as the natural sciences have in physical environment. It is hoped that the result will be reliable information that can be the basis of action more productive than that built on the vagaries of intuition and arbitrary revelation.

Several images and metaphors of the person emerge from this approach. The individual may be compared to a reflexive organism conditioned to respond to stimuli. The mind might be described as a computer processing input, organizing memory, and directing output. Or the self is seen as functioning in society as part of a magnetic field with a variety of boundaries, valences, and forces. For Freud, the psyche was an energy system where the kind and amount of tension was transferred from one location to another.

When this approach is used in pastoral counseling, it is assumed that there is an objective standard for human nature with which one can compare any given individual. For example, a counselee with wide mood swings may be suffering from a hormonal imbalance. Furthermore, personality inventories use the statistical average as the point of comparison even though such a person does not exist in reality. Identity is viewed as sameness over time. In each case it is assumed that there is a norm given in the nature of reality whereby one can judge a particular instance.

A variety of concerns has been raised regarding empirical approaches to understanding personality. (1) The application of natural science methods to personality fundamentally disregards the difference between nature and human nature—self-reflexivity. Hence, method appears more important than the object of inquiry. (2) The commitment to the observable produces only knowledge that deals with behavior and physiological processes. It fails to consider intangibles such as meaning, purpose, and feeling. (3) Science tends toward ethical positivism. Since it separates description and prescription, reality as it is tends to become normative. Because it seeks to be apolitical, it becomes *de facto* politically conservative. (4) Some would argue for an approach to personality research that seeks not only to test tradition but to renew it. (5) Others argue that the aspiration to universality is doomed from the start. What is needed is particular knowledge, not universal knowledge. (6) The knowledge produced tends to be discrete facts without historical interpretation. (7) There appears to be a commitment only to one approach to understanding personality. (8) It tends toward reductionist explanations that fail to appreciate multiple ways of understanding human life. (9) The researcher (*qua* scientist) of personality tends to be less aware of the impact of the intervention of the researcher on the subject and the subsequent knowledge. The approach is too static. (10) This approach tends to reinforce (unintentionally perhaps) deterministic views of human life. (11) The scientific approach tends toward atomistic explanation rather than integrative, holistic ones.

2. The Humanistic Approach. In contrast to the experimental tradition, a more idealist, social, and hermeneutical approach has a different methodology and thus has different implications for the understanding of personality and for pastoral care and counseling. It finds its support in the work of theorists such as Dilthey, Wundt, James, Rogers, George Herbert Mead, Van Kaam, and Giorgi.

The goal of this approach is not to test tradition against an objective reality but to renew tradition. Its focus is on understanding personality rather than experimental manipulation. The model for understanding comes from the humanities rather than the sciences.

The shift to a *human* science places emphasis on the study of lived experience in contrast to inanimate objects. How the subject perceives the world and situates the self in the larger social world is of major interest. The whole rather than the parts is the object of study. The concern is more to retool the stories (cultural objectifications) that shape the psyche than to discover the order that constitutes the psyche *a priori* or through social conditioning. The modalities of understanding tend to be more varied than the scientific approach. The critical concern is the constellation of images and metaphors that create a sense of continuity and direction for the psyche. The internationality of the subject is highlighted.

The critical metaphors of the self that emerge in this perspective include agency, intentionality, decision, significance, freedom, actualization, reference group, and the significant other. Consequently, this approach is more open to understanding the particular stories that shape individuals, whether or not they are religious. Rather than focusing on independent units, there is a concern to establish the nature of the relationships between events. The self-report of the subject is considered the primary datum. This approach is found more among the existentialist-humanists and the Jungian analysts.

In pastoral counseling with this approach, one begins with the perceived world of the counselee. It is assumed that it is unique but comprehensible. Personal meanings are understood against historical and cultural backgrounds. The ability of the counselee to choose is assumed and critical to growth.

The limitations of this approach are: (1) From the perspective of the logical positivists, it is too subjective. The "information" it produces is not sufficiently reliable. (2) This approach also can be seen as apolitical and hence conservative. By virtue of not specifying a normative social and a political context, it unwittingly supports existing political arrangements. If the scientific tradition can be criticized because it assumes an order in nature, this tradition can be criticized in that it assumes, in a pluralistic world, a consensus on what it means to be human.

3. The Ethical Approach. To meet the objections of both methods, a third approach to understanding personality has emerged. The goal of research on personality here is neither to describe nor to understand but to liberate. It takes as its point of departure a clear statement of the normative self and the good society. Neither of the first two perspectives is sufficiently sensitive to the ethical contexts of research. Sexism, racism, ageism, and nationalism, it is argued, must be dealt with before one engages in research. The purpose of research is to provide the data that enables one to see the present situation as oppressive and to explore liberating alternatives. Its most pressing concern is that the "knowledge" produced by the other two approaches is ideological.

The metaphors of the self that emerge from this approach tend to be more historical. The self is an actor in history. The social environment is the shaper of personality and is shaped by individuals. The future is open to the acting agent.

This approach is implicit in the pastoral approaches of Charlotte Clinebell, Rubem Alves, and Archie Smith. The relevant biblical images for understanding the self are the Exodus, the life of Christ, the Crucifixion, and the Resurrection.

The limitations of this approach from the perspective of the other two are its lack of objectivity and its commitment to a specific cluster of values.

4. Summary. The nature of authority, the role of order, and the nature of the good differ in each of the three approaches. The first assumes that objective reality accurately described is the locus of authority. The second assumes that the interpreter of the human speech is the center of authority, while the third locates it in the ethical vision that precedes research. The first assumes that order is discovered, the second that order is interpreted, that is, created through meaning-making, and the third that it is created in concrete social and institutional terms. And in terms of the nature of the good (person or society), the first two approaches assume that a consensus is either irrelevant or that it already exists, while for the third approach it is in need of being created.

Bibliography. R. Alves, "Personal Wholeness and Political Creativity: The Theology of Liberation and Pastoral Care," *Pastoral Psychology*, 26 (1977), 124–36. R. Cattell, *The Scientific Analysis of Personality* (1965). C. Clinebell, *Counseling for Liberation* (1976). A. Giorgi, "Psychology: A Human Science," *Social Research* (1969), 412–32. A. Heschel, *Who Is Man?* (1968). H. Hodges, *The Philosophy of Wilhelm Dilthey* (1952). W. Wundt, *The Elements of a Folk Psychology* (1916). A. Smith, *The Relational Self: Ethics and Therapy from a Black Church Perspective* (1982). A. Van Kaam, *Existential Foundations of Psychology* (1966).

A. C. DUECK

PERSON (Philosophical Issues); PSYCHOLOGY AND PHILOSOPHY. *See also* MODELS IN PSYCHOLOGICAL AND PASTORAL THEORY; MYTHOLOGY AND PSYCHOLOGY; PSYCHOLOGY, EASTERN *or* WESTERN *or* EAST-WEST COMPARISON.

PERSONALITY THEORY (Varieties, Traditions, and Issues). Personality theories are efforts to bring order to the vast compelxity of human behavior and human personality. Moving inductively from concrete and specific observations, the theorist draws generalizations about the makeup and operations of personality. These generalizations are linked and made meaningful by a set of assumptions, inferences and constructs that account for the behaviors observed. Thus, personality theories are seen as interpretations of people's makeup and behavior.

A good theory *describes* persons and their behavior. It also helps to *explain* and *understand* behavior and the inner processes related to that behavior. And, perhaps most important of all, a good theory enables us to *predict* future thoughts and feelings which the personality will exhibit and experience.

1. **History.** While the roots of personality theorizing extend back to the personality types and character sketches of earliest literature, modern personality theory has emerged from nineteenth-century psychiatry and the study of mental illness.

Medical models of personality have long since replaced the crude biochemical theory of Hippocrates, who linked personality to body fluids or "humors." Humors have given way to hormones, and the pioneering efforts of nineteenth-century France (Janet, Charcot, Liébault, Bernheim), devoted to studies of neurosis, have paved the way for contemporary theorizing.

Personality theory's roots are also empirical. From Franz Joseph Gall's attempts to assess "mental faculties" by examining bumps on a person's skull to present-day assessments of traits and interests and aptitudes, empirical observation and measurement have continuously been a part of theory formulation and hypothesis testing.

2. **Major Traditions.** There are five categories within which personality theories may be grouped:

a. Trait theory. Trait theorists view personality as a set of stable and enduring traits: inner dispositions causing individuals to act and react in particular ways. A trait is a measurable characteristic that influences the perception of incoming information (stimuli) and lends consistency to the person's responses. Trait psychologists view traits either as motivational (e.g., hard-driving, caring) or stylistic (e.g., cheerful, independent).

Gordon Allport (1961), considered by many as the dean of American personality psychologists, stressed that the trait is more generalized than a mere habit, and that it exists as a neuropsychic structure within the personality. He labeled "central" those traits that pervade much of a person's behavior, and "secondary" those more superficial or less prominent.

Raymond Cattell brought a different approach to trait study and theory. Using the complicated statistical technique of factor analysis, Cattell sought to identify the minimum number of separate and nonoverlapping factors (traits), which would account for the variability observed in behavior. He developed a test to measure sixteen relatively independent dimensions of personality. The profile of a person's scores on these scales can be compared with those of other persons.

There is popular appeal in being able to describe human beings in terms of such general characteristics. This approach, however, has been criticized on the grounds that traits that supposedly are within the persons observed may be mostly "in the eye of the beholder" instead. Furthermore, being able to describe a person in terms of traits is considered by many as not very useful: putting on labels does little to explain or understand the individual as a person. Trait theory does not seem to do a particularly effective job of predicting behavior except in broad generalities. Despite these limitations, the trait approach has proven useful in assessing pathological tendencies, in measuring self-reported personal adjustment, and in detecting growth and change in personality.

b. Psychodynamic/psychoanalytic theory. This view originates in the psychoanalytic approach to psychotherapy developed by Sigmund Freud. Freud likened the personality to an iceberg. Above the surface is the conscious part but below is the vast domain of the unconscious: urges (especially sex and aggression), passions, conflicts, repressed ideas and feelings — a great underworld of vital, unseen forces exercising control over conscious thoughts and action.

Freud structured the total personality in terms of the *id* (the instinctual, selfish, pleasure-seeking component), the *ego* (the partly conscious, rational, reality-oriented, organizing "executive" of the personality), and the *superego* (the internal representation of traditional values, ideals, and taboos of society as interpreted through parents, functioning with the force of unconscious instinctual id energies).

Conflicting demands of the id and superego, as well as their collusion, the unconscious and impulsive push of the id for conscious expression, and demands and limits of the outside world — all produce internal battles and outer threats which, in turn, give rise to anxiety with which the ego must deal. However, defense mechanisms (repression, projection, rationalization, reaction formation, sublimation, etc.) are employed to keep this anxiety manageable, the ego more or less in command, and the personality intact.

Freud's followers did not always agree with his opinions. Carl Jung rebelled at Freud's emphasis on sex and gave greater importance to the work of the conscious ego. At the same time he saw evidence for a collective (racial, common) unconscious in all human personalities, which profoundly shapes experience and action. He also posited the capacity for an integrated, teleologically oriented self. Alfred Adler, also opposing Freud's pessimism, saw the human personality as creative, as capable of surmounting inferiority in striving for mastery, and as essentially social by nature.

Later psychoanalytic theorists emphasized further the social nature and needs of humankind: Erich Fromm's humanistic psychoanalysis stressed love of humankind and our interdependence on one another; Karen Horney taught the importance of human relationships — especially early relationships — in healthfully overcoming existential anxieties; Harry Stack Sullivan looked at personality as a pattern of interpersonal behavior.

The most influential psychoanalytically oriented personality theorist today is Erik Erikson, who has outlined the psychosocial development of the individual across the entire life span through a series of formative transition experiences or "crisis," with the development of identity as a central theme.

The heaviest criticism of the psychodynamic/psychoanalytic view of personality has been leveled against

Freud. He based his personality theory on his analyses with turn-of-the-century, neurotic, upper-class Viennese housewives, taking at face value their self-reports, and not even taking notes to refer to until later. His "explanations" of personality development and dynamics were always *post hoc*, working backward from the present to see what in the past would account for the present. this makes a weak theory when it comes to predictive validity and developing testable hypotheses to confirm its accuracy. Freud is generally criticized for having emphasized the biological and hereditary roots of personality to the neglect of social influences and the present situation, and for overemphasizing sex.

However, Freud's view of the unconscious, the role of early childhood in personality formation, and the importance of sexuality did provide a significant foundation for later psychoanalytic theories, which have a more empirical basis. Contemporary psychoanalytic approaches provide great potential for insight, growth, and change when skillfully applied in longer-term psychotherapy.

c. Learning-behavioral theory. This approach focuses on *behavior,* not on personality's inner states, events, or processes. It stresses *learning* as the means by which personality is formed and maintained. Personality is seen as patterned behavior; the person *is* his/her behavior. Conditioning shapes behavior and personality, and reinforcement is an especially powerful force.

The radical behaviorist view (e.g., B. F. Skinner) rejects inferred motives and similar dynamics behind behavior; it omits cognitive processes such as perceiving, thinking, judging, choosing, and reasoning. Behavior is determined by previous conditioning and is lawful, predictable, and controllable; therefore, personality is totally malleable and is acquired and maintained through reinforcement and punishment.

More prominent among learning-behavioral theories of personality are those of the social learning theorists (e.g., Bandura, Rotter, Mischel) who have admitted *cognitive processing* to the conditioning-learning paradigm. These theorists see there as being more to the learning involved in personality development than basic conditioning. Persons learn through observing others and through vicarious reinforcement as well. Based on their experiences and observations, persons develop expectancies of what the outcome of certain behaviors is likely to be and shape their own behaviors and tendencies according to the value of those outcomes. Perception, thinking, and judgment produce a self-regulation and self-control that permit persons to shape their own personalities, as well as to be shaped by external reinforcement contingencies.

Much of our behavior and the habits and traits of our personality are shaped through learning. Yet this approach to personality is also limited. There is inadequate accounting for such aspects of personality as traits, attitudes, values, beliefs, and the self. Nor is adequate consideration given to the crucial motivational and emotional dimensions that appear to be essential forces in personality. However, recent movement among the social learning theorists has been in the direction of recognizing that inner functions and processes provide the uniquely human qualities of personality.

d. Humanistic (phenomenological) theory. This view of personality arose partly in protest against the tenets of psychoanalysis and the determinism of behavioristic thinking. It placed more emphasis on the distinctively human qualities in personality and on the phenomenological or personally experienced dimensions of personality. This view provides a wholistic look at the total personality, which emphasizes the uniqueness, worth, dignity, and integrity of the individual. These theorists see the healthy personality as their model and as the appropriate focus of study. The person is seen as having a basic, natural tendency toward growth, creativity, health, and realization of potential. We make our own personality in the sense that this approach stresses self-determination, freedom, choice, and responsibility. Human nature is viewed as essentially good or having possibilities for both good and evil. The experience and the perceptions of the person are seen as the keys to understanding the inner workings and states of personality.

Abraham Maslow, the "founding father" of the humanistic psychology movement, made good the aims of a humanistic study of personality by studying a number of "self-actualizing" personalities, both historical and living (e.g., Eleanor Roosevelt, Albert Schweitzer, Abraham Lincoln). He found them to display such characteristics as efficient and unclouded perception, freshness of appreciation of the miracles of life, an ethical awareness of intrinsic right and wrong, mystic peak experiences, freedom to be spontaneous, an objectivity that could simply let things be as they are, creativity and inventiveness, a naturalness totally without pretense, and a deep trust of self, others, and the world.

Maslow constructed a hierarchy of needs that provide the basic motivations in life. First the physiological or survival needs, next the safety/security needs, then love and belongingness needs, fourth the esteem needs (both for esteem of others and for self-esteem), and finally the need for self-actualization—the need to realize and become what we are potentially capable of as full persons.

Carl Rogers also believed that the master motive in all of life is an inborn urge toward growth, health, and self-actualization. Believing that human nature is essentially good and that everyone is guided by these healthy inner motivations, Rogers says that only the person himself or herself knows what is good and true and authentic. If the personality is given a climate of "unconditional positive regard," it will develop a sense of worth, dignity, and integrity and follow the path to responsible conduct and the emergence of a healthy, consistent self. Rogers's description of such a "fully functioning" person is similar to Maslow's description of the self-actualizing person.

Critics of the humanistic theory say that it is too fuzzy and that one finds it too difficult to draw hypotheses to test its validity. Others mistakenly link humanistic theories of personality with humanistic philosophy and see it as a godless, narcissistic, and totally permissive view of how a healthy personality evolves. Some critics believe that human nature and the inner self cannot be trusted because it is self-serving or sinful at its root.

These theories may also be limited in application to Western, middle-class values. Persons in lower socioeconomic groups find it hard to "self-actualize" when they are still primarily concerned with Maslow's first two levels of need. Rogers's theory also seems to apply more fully to articulate, self-motivated people than to those who have been culturally or educationally deprived.

While humanistic theory may not sufficiently consider the negative aspects of personality and human experience, it does present a positive, healthful view of human personality that gives persons dignity and worth. As such, it provides a helpful corrective to the unconscious determinism of the psychoanalyst or the mechanistic conditioning view of the behaviorist.

e. Eastern theories. Recently, increasing attention has been given to Eastern philosophy and theories about personality. Eastern ideas stress transpersonal experience and growth (beyond the ego, self, personality). They also focus a great deal on morality and values, on the relationship between religious practice and everyday life, and on the advisability of living in accord with "cosmic" spiritual standards. The individual is seen as an aggregate of intellect, emotions, and body, and since free will is very much a part of human nature, development of the intellect is critical in becoming a full human personality.

Disciplined control of mind and thought permits the mind to be calm and thus clearly to reflect and realize the self. This self-realization means the removal of delusive understanding, the reduction of distortion, seeing clearly with a full grasp of reality, and the attainment of spiritual illumination and enlightenment. The basic idea is to experience the inner workings of one's being in the most direct way. The wise person knows and molds himself or herself through direct, undistorted awareness.

The body is viewed as the vehicle for one's pursuit of truth and for service to others. While there are obstacles to growth (e.g., greed, hate, pride), everyone is believed to have the capacity to attain full awareness, to transcend the lesser ego, and thus to be a part of all humanity and, ultimately, of the universe.

3. **Major Issues.** *a. Motivation.* Central to most theories about human personality is the concept of motivation. For at the core of our being lie biological drives, psychological and social needs, and other life forces that arouse, sustain, and direct our activities. In addition to such "pushing" forces, however, it is equally important to look at the "pulling" or goal-oriented forces: short- and long-term goals, intentions, strivings, wishes, hopes, and dreams. It is arguably just as valuable to know where persons are headed and what they wish to become as it is to know what drives them "from behind." It is all part of motivation.

b. Consciousness and unconsciousness. Personality theorists have provided varied views of consciousness—from the psychoanalyst's ego, through the cognitive mediation processes of the social learning theorists, to the choosing, willing, self-determining consciousness of the humanistic theorists. Most contemporary psychologists would agree that conscious mental life is crucial to understanding personality and that it is continuous with subconscious mental life. Conscious awareness of self and the surrounding world, perceptions and judgments, thinking and reasoning, choosing and deciding, are all states and processes that instigate and channel behavior.

Freud and Jung, however, have provided important insight into the unconscious forces that influence behavior. While Freud stressed dark, animalistic impulses and the conflict between personality components, Jung expanded the focus beyond the self to include the collective unconscious. Each self is an individual entity, but there are unconscious images of the whole of human experience and racial awareness that connect these individuals at the unconscious level.

Trait theorists, social learning theorists, and humanistic theorists tend to give little attention to the unconscious. Since by definition we cannot know the unconscious directly, these theorists prefer to work with introspective self-reports and conscious states and processes, including only such unconscious material as can be raised to consciousness. There seems, however, in any case, to be a need for including both conscious and unconscious processes in any attempt to understand personality.

c. Development. Any adequate theory of personality must deal with the issue of development. How does the personality form?

There is clearly a natural process of maturing and unfolding (natural propensities, the anatomical, the physiological, the neurological), and there is also a shaping by environmental (especially social) forces. This socializing of the person to be an accepted, independent, functioning member of society is an important part of the developmental process. The individual is the product of interplay of the hereditary *and* the environmental, of the biological *and* the social, of learning *and* maturation.

Theories vary on the emphasis given one or the other of these pairs of concepts and in the precise way they are formulated and interrelated. Psychoanalysts give great attention to the description of developmental stages, especially those early in life. Learning-behavioral theorists see personality always as the result of basic conditioning and learning, giving environmental shaping the predominant role. Humanistic theorists stress the interaction of the natural needs and propensities of the person with the social environment—whether it is nurturing or stifling.

Most important is the fact of *interaction*, which produces the human personality as we know it. One factor in development cannot be thought of as operating independently of other factors.

d. Person vs. situation controversy. Theorists who stress traits, habits, genetics, or unconscious mechanisms note the personality's consistency in similar situations: for example, the honest person is honest in most situations; the aggressive person is aggressive in a variety of activities. Although most personality theorists see consistency in personality and attempt to account for it, recent research indicates that human behavior is not as consistent as traditionally assumed. It varies considerably from situation to situation and even from time to time. This has raised controversy over which is *more* important: the inner person or the situation.

e. Determinism vs. choice, responsibility, self-direction. Some say personality is determined by forces and events beyond voluntary control; others say that we make our own personality because we have free choice and self-determination. Since it is impossible to know all the influences acting upon an individual at any given time, this is a moot question. Even those favoring the deterministic view recognize that predictions about behavior and personality are probabilistic at best.

The classical psychoanalyst would see personality as largely determined by the primitive drives of the id, the demands of the superego, and as these impact present experience through the developmental history of early childhood experience. Radical behaviorism sees personality in a deterministic and reductionist way: personality is the sum of past conditioning and shaping. Social learning theory implies more control over our process of becoming by emphasizing cognitive processes—following a line of deduction such as "I can control my thoughts; my feelings come from my thoughts; therefore, I can control my feelings." The humanistic theorist reaches the ultimate in terms of choosing, deciding, responsibility, and self-direction. The person must take full responsibility for all aspects of one's personhood and existence in the here and now.

f. Pathology. The psychoanalyst sees disintegration or decompensation in personality as due to internal conflict (mostly unconscious) and to ineffective attempts to deal with anxiety. Learning-behavioral theorists interpret psychopathology as deviant behavior, the result of inappropriate or inadequate socialization understood as conditioning. The humanistic theorist sees pathology as coming from some thwarting or distortion of the natural propensities toward health.

All viewpoints may help us to understand the personality difficulties of the deviant or "mentally ill" person. Research is also providing new insights into genetic and biochemical factors that play a role in psychopathology.

g. Health. While a definition of "mental health" or the healthy human personality will reflect the views, preferences, and values of the theorist and the theorist's culture, there are some criteria for which a good deal of agreement can be found in Western professional circles. Among these are: (1) realistic orientation to the world (both social and physical environments); (2) patterns of behavior and conduct that are productive and efficient; (3) self-awareness or absence of self-deception; (4) adaptive dealing with frustrations and conflicts; (5) realization of one's potential; and (6) productive and satisfying relationships with other people.

h. Assessment. For the study of personality to be systematic and empirical there have to be ways of measuring it. Again the assessor's own approach to personality will dictate his or her methods and techniques for making such assessments. Trait theorists employ objective personality tests and self-inventories designed to describe the person on various dimensions or dispositions, relative to other populations. Psychoanalysts rely heavily on the analytic interview or projective personality tests to tap the deeper levels of unconscious motive and conflict. The learning-behavioral theorist uses systematic observations and records of behavior for making assessments. Humanistic theorists rely heavily on first-person documents and verbal reports.

4. **Future Trends.** In the years ahead there will probably be increased study of the healthy personality: not only persons free from abnormalities, but persons exhibiting high levels of health, productivity, and creativity.

More and more attention will also be given to the physiological (biochemical) and neurological underpinnings of personality and to personality change and development with advanced aging. Theories pertaining to the latter part of the life span have been notably few and weak.

Bibliography. G. W. Allport, "The Historical Background of Social Psychology," in G. Lindzey, ed., *Handbook of Social Psychology* (1954); *Pattern and Growth in Personality* (1961). D. S. Cartwright, *Theories and Models of Personality* (1979). H. Chiang and A. H. Maslow, *The Healthy Personality: Readings* 2d. ed. (1977). N. S. Di Caprio, *Personality Theories: A Guide to Human Nature* 2d ed. (1983). C. S. Hall and G. Lindzey, *Theories of Personality* 3d ed. (1978). B. R. Hergenhahn, *An Introduction to Theories of Personality* 2d ed. (1984). L. A. Hjelle and D. J. Ziegler, *Personality Theories: Basic Assumptions, Research and Applications* 2d ed. (1981). W. James, *The Varieties of Religious Experience* (1902). R. Lazarus and A. Monat, *Personality* 3d ed. (1979). S. R. Maddi, *Personality Theories: A Comparative Analysis* 4th ed. (1980). A. H. Maslow, *Motivation and Personality* 2d ed. (1970). L. A. Pervin, *Current Controversies and Issues in Personality* 2d ed. (1984). C. Rogers, *On Becoming a Person* (1961). R. M. Ryckman, *Theories of Personality* 2d ed. (1982). E. Erickson, *Childhood and Society* 2d ed. (1963). B. F. Skinner, *Beyond Freedom and Dignity* (1971). R. Cattell, *The Inheritance of Personality and Ability* (1982); *Personality and Mood by Questionnaire* (1973). S. Freud, *The Ego and the Id* (1957). C. G. Jung, *Analytical Psychology* (1968).

L. BEACH

PERSON; PSYCHOLOGY AND PHILOSOPHY; PSYCHOLOGY. *See also* ANALYTICAL (JUNGIAN) PSYCHOLOGY *or* PSYCHOANALYSIS (Personality Theory and Research); COGNITIVE, EXISTENTIAL, GESTALT, HUMANISTIC, INDIVIDUAL, PHENOMENOLOGICAL, *or* SELF PSYCHOLOGIES; *also* CAUSALITY IN PSYCHOLOGY, FORMS OF; CONSCIOUSNESS; DEVELOPMENTAL THEORY; DEVELOPMENTAL PSYCHOLOGY; EVALUATION AND DIAGNOSIS, PSYCHOLOGICAL; FREEDOM AND DETERMINISM; HEALTH AND ILLNESS; MOTIVATION; PSYCHOPATHOLOGY, THEORIES OF; The UNCONSCIOUS. *Compare* BEHAVIORISM; CHARACTER AND PERSONALITY (Comparative Concepts); MODELS IN PSYCHOLOGICAL AND PASTORAL THEORY; MYTHOLOGY AND PSYCHOLOGY; PSYCHOLOGY, EASTERN; THEOLOGY AND PSYCHOLOGY. *Biography:* ALLPORT; ERIKSON; FREUD; FROMM; HORNEY; JUNG; MASLOW; ROGERS; SULLIVAN.

PERSONALITY TYPES AND PASTORAL CARE. Personality differences or "types" inherent in each person's temperament or constitution have preoccupied scholars since recorded history began. In Christian theology prior to the scientific depictions of personality types, the concern for inherent differences between individuals was worked out in doctrines of creation and sin. The image of God in humankind, male and female, has always been a poetic commentary on two personality types—the inherent differences between male and female.

In psychological discussions of personality types the Christian pastor as theologian may ask, "What are the changeable and unchangeable dimensions of these various types of personality? By what means can they be transformed? What is the shape into which they are to be transformed and to what end?" These questions may be correlated with the empirical data upon which various thinkers and clinicians in the behavioral sciences have based their conceptions of personality types.

1. **Physical Morphology of Personality Types.** In ancient Greek medicine, Hippocrates made one of the earliest empirical attempts at a typology of personality.

He postulated that the humors (blood, phlegm, black bile, and yellow bile) resulted in different kinds of personalities prone to different kinds of diseases. Also, he suggested a twofold classification of physiques and divided subjects into those who were short and thick (prone to apoplexy) and those who were long and thin (prone to tuberculosis). The humoral theory prevailed for many centuries. Galen (A.D. 130–200) identified four types of human characters in terms of the humors: (1) the sanguine, buoyant type; (2) the phlegmatic, sluggish type; (3) the choleric, quick-tempered type; (4) the melancholic, dejected type. Robert Burton (1577–1640) in his *Anatomy of Melancholy* provided the most elaborate example of the humoral theory. These personality types are no longer taken seriously from a scientific point of view, but their names persist in our language.

Specific linkage of personality types to different shapes of bodily makeup has been proposed by Ernst Kretschmer (1888–1964) in his book *Physique and Character* (1936, p. 21). He posited four types of personality or temperament: (1) *The asthenic type:* a lean, linear, frail physique, very small of growth, and not prone to gaining weight even with overeating. These persons are by heredity and life experience "schizothymic," which does not necessarily mean that they become psychotic. (2) *The athletic type:* "tall, wide projecting shoulders, a superb chest, a firm stomach, and a trunk that tapers in its lower region." These persons too represent a variation of the schizothymic temperament. One wonders if the *Diagnostic and Statistical Manual III* (Revised) classification of the schizo-affective personality would not be relevant to Kretschmer's athletic typology. (3) *The pyknic type:* a tendency to breadth, softness, and rotundity, with an overlay of fat. Kretschmer identified it with the cycloid or manic-depressive, bipolar temperament. (4) *The dysplastic type:* striking digressions from the three "standard" types are "morphologically very closely related to the clear cases of dysglandular syndrome in endocrine pathology."

Somewhat contemporary in time with Kretschmer was the work of William Sheldon, *The Varieties of Temperament* (1942, pp. 7–8, 31–95.) He, like Kretschmer, was intrigued with the physique of human beings. He engaged in meticulous research which he called *somatotyping*. A somatotype is a series of three numbers, each representing the degree to which an individual conforms to one or the other of three pure body types: (1) *Endomorphy,* in which "the digestive viscera are massive and highly developed, while the somatic structures are relatively weak and undeveloped." (2) *Mesomorphy,* in which "the somatic structures (bone muscle and connective tissue) are in the ascendancy." (3) *Ectomorphy,* "fragility, linearity, flatness of chest, and delicacy throughout the body" are characteristic.

The personality type correlative with endomorphy is the *viscerotonic:* a person who is relaxed in posture and movement, loves physical comfort, loves to eat, eats in company with others, has good digestion and pleasure in it, is even in emotional flow, is easy-going and tolerant, complacent, and is generally like untempered metal.

The personality type correlative with mesomorphy is *somatotonic;* a person who is assertive in posture and movement, loves dominating and having power, loves risk

and chance, has a bold directness of manner, and the physical courage for combat. He or she is characterized by extroversion or a honozastal mental cleavage.

The personality type correlative with ectomorphy is the *cerebrotonic.* The characteristics of cerebrontonia are restrained, tight posture and movement, physiological over-response, overly fast reactions, and love of privacy. The cerebrotonic personality temperament is characterized by introversion and a vertical mental cleavage. Sheldon was a multitalented, multieducated, and experienced person. He was a clinical psychologist, a clinical psychiatrist, and a psychoanalyst by credentials and experience. The imaginativeness of his interpretation of somatotypes was informed and enriched by all of this plus a remarkable native intuitiveness about human nature.

2. Psychological Approaches to Personality Types. Probably the most influential psychological assessment of personality types has been done by C. G. Jung in *Psychological Types* (1971). Jung describes two types of personality—introvert and extrovert. These two "attitude-types" are "distinguished by their attitude to the object. The introvert's attitude is an abstract one; at bottom he is always intent on withdrawing libido from the object as though he had to prevent the object from gaining power over him. The extrovert, on the contrary, has a positive relation to the object. The object can never have enough value for him and its importance must always be increased" (p. 330).

This sounds simple enough, but Jung classifies four different subtypes of each of these two types, and things become much more complex. These subtypes are: (1) The extroverted thinking type, whose every activity is dependent on intellectual conclusions based on objective data. (2) The extroverted feeling type, whose feelings must be right before he or she acts. (Jung overidentifies this type with women.) (3) The extroverted sensation type, for whom true, concrete enjoyment is oriented, with its own moderation, lawfulness, unselfishness, and willingness to make sacrifices. (Jung overidentifies this with men.) (4) The extroverted intuitive type, who is never found in the world of accepted reality values, but is always searching out anything new and in the making. (5) The introverted thinking type, who restricts himself or herself to ideas, critical thinking, and subjective thinking. (6) The introverted feeling type, who is silent, inaccessible, hard to understand, and shows little effort to respond to the emotions of the other person. (Jung again overidentifies this type with women.) (7) The introverted sensation type, who is oriented primarily by events that happen and not by rational judgment. (8) The introverted intuitive type, who is the mystical dreamer and seer on the one hand, and the artist and crank on the other hand. Perception and the shaping of the perception is his main problem.

Jung's description of these eight types of personality has been elaborated even further by Isabel Briggs Myers in her book, *Gifts Differing*. She separates Jung's eight types into two further subtypes of judging and perceiving. She devised the Myers-Briggs type indicator to measure personality preference. Each of the sixteen types has test items which, when scored, reflect an individual's personality profile, its capacities and limitations. Her belief is that each type has its own strengths. Understanding and using these can lead to individual fulfillment and improved communication with others. Pastors and teachers can productively use this with functioning adults as both a teaching and a therapeutic instrument.

A recent approach to the behavioral analysis of personality types is found in *The Diagnostic and Statistical Manual III* (Revised), which describes eleven personality disorders. These are arranged in three clusters. In cluster A are people who appear odd and eccentric: (1) paranoid, (2) schizoid, (3) schizotypal. Cluster B describes those who appear dramatic, emotional, or erratic: (4) antisocial, (5) borderline, (6) histrionic, (7) narcissistic. Persons in cluster C appear anxious, fearful, and fretful: (8) avoidant, (9) dependent, (10) obsessive-compulsive, (11) passive-aggressive.

Millon (1981) historically analyzes the literature on each of these disorders. However, he emphasizes the cultural reinforcement of "blessing" of these types of social behavior that not only blesses but takes the style of life as a norm. In this sense he makes the typology relevant to religious behavior and the pastoral care of people in the religious community. Oates (1987) has pinpointed the ways in which personality disorders appear in religious behavior wherein people use religion as a vehicle of expressing essentially pathological behaviors against the "common good" of the community. In doing so, they appear to themselves as doing God a service.

Millon's most crucial distinction throughout his book is the differences between the *active* and *passive* forms that the behaviors take. For example, the dependent person clings passively to others whereas the histrionic person grabs actively at others. The antisocial person is actively aggressive against others and the passive aggressive person does so by the things he or she does not do.

The distinctions between active and passive personalities and extrovert and introvert personalities both point to the essential paradox in religious faith between community and solitude, social action and personal piety, fellowship and loneliness. In response to stress, even individuals in early infancy can be classified as tending to express stress reactions either outwardly or inwardly, either actively or passively, either in behavioral difficulties of an overt type or in somatic internalization.

In summary, however, typing personalities emphasizes the differences between individuals. The vital *balance* of the contrary traits within an individual enables him or her to have a wide repertoire of responses instead of being "stuck" with any one response. The Greek word for righteousness, *dikaiosyne*, comes from a classical Greek word, *dike*, meaning "nothing short of what is fitting." The balanced personality is one who responds to and receives responses from others in a way that is "nothing short of fitting," appropriate, and edifying of the common good a well as of himself or herself.

Bibliography. The American Psychiatric Association, *Diagnostic and Statistical Manual of Mental Disorders,* 3d. ed. rev. (1987). C. G. Jung, *Psychological Types,* rev. by R. F. C. Hull (1971). E. Kretschmer, *Physique and Character: An Investigation of the Nature of Constitution and of the Theory of Temperament* (1936). T. Millon, *Disorders of Personality: DSM III, Axis II* (1981). I. B. Myers, *Gifts Differing* (1980). W. E. Oates, *Behind the Masks:* *Personality Disorders in Religious Behavior* (1987). W. Sheldon, *The Varieties of Temperament: A Psychology of Constitutional Differences* (1942).

W. E. OATES

EVALUATION AND DIAGNOSIS; PERSONALITY THEORY (Varieties, Traditions, and Issues). *See also* ANALYTICAL (JUNGIAN) PSYCHOLOGY *or* PSYCHOANALYSIS (Personality Theory and Research); BODY IMAGE; SOMATOTYPE; TEMPERAMENT. *Compare* HUMAN NATURE, PROBLEM OF; PERSON.

PERSON-CENTERED THERAPY. *See* CLIENT-CENTERED THERAPY.

PERSONHOOD. *See* PERSON (Philosophical Issues); The PERSONAL, CONCEPT OF, IN PASTORAL CARE; TRINITY AND PERSONHOOD.

PERSONHOOD OF THE PASTOR, SIGNIFICANCE OF. Clinical pastoral education and the pastoral care movement have accented the significance of the personhood of the pastor as a unique and crucial vehicle through which the ministry of personal care finds expression and achieves effectiveness (e.g., Wise, 1966). While in no way seeking to minimize the importance of the pastoral role, contemporary pastoral care has refocused attention on the central importance of anthropology understood in a wholistic biblical sense. Effective and creative pastoral care and counseling, not only for those who receive pastoral care but also for those who provide it, requires an adequate self-understanding involving attention to all the dimensions of personhood —physical, mental, emotional, and social—in the context of a centering relationship with God.

The complex interaction of the person of the pastor with the filling of the pastoral role has been the subject of a growing body of empirical research. For example, studies utilizing such instruments as the Myers-Briggs Type Indicator suggest that the kinds of ministry that a pastor finds attractive, the way one's ministry is carried out, and the vulnerability of the pastor to such problems as stress and burnout are all related to personality factors. Career services specializing in evaluating candidates for ministry have reported similar interconnections between person and ministerial role.

As important as personality is, however, it is not everything. Neither research nor experience has demonstrated that any one personality type necessarily makes a more effective or faithful pastor than another. What seems to be crucial is whether a match exists between the personal gifts of the pastor and the special needs of the ministry context. These findings appear to support those traditional theologies of the "call to ministry" which include a calling to a particular ministry at a particular place and time, thus understanding the personhood of the pastor in the larger context of the providence of God.

In addition to the "fit" between person and context there are also symbolic dimensions of the pastoral role that transcend individual personhood. Regardless of the personal characteristics of the pastor, the pastor is a representative person whose ministry communicates an ultimacy that goes beyond the personal. This representative role may contribute to the difficulty people have if the pastor behaves in ways they believe to be inconsistent with the pastoral role. Related to this representative character of the pastor is a psychological "attribution" process whereby people ascribe an authority and power to the person filling the pastoral role that cannot be justified on personal grounds alone. The significance of the pastor, both as a representative person and as one to whom attributions are made, thus goes beyond the personal.

Nevertheless, the pastor's personhood is an important component of ministry, and additional research is needed into the ways in which the personhood of the pastor affects a person's ministry. A theology of gifts based on such passages as Psalm 130, Jeremiah 1, Romans 12, I Corinthians 12, Ephesians 4, and I Peter 4 requires that the church not underestimate the significance of the interrelationship between a person's particular gifts and graces and God's call to a particular ministry.

Bibliography. H. Clinebell, *Basic Types of Pastoral Care and Counseling* rev. ed. (1984). G. L. Harbaugh, *Pastor as Person* (1984); *God's Gifted People* (1988); "The Person in Ministry: Psychological Type and the Seminary," *J. of Psychological Types* (1984), 23–35. G. L. Harbaugh *et al., Beyond the Boundary* (1986); *Pastor as Person* (1984). W. Hulme, *Your Pastor's Problems* (1966). W. Hulme *et al., Pastors in Ministry* (1985). W. Oates, *The Minister's Own Mental Health* (1955). R. Oswald, *Crossing the Boundary Between Seminary and Parish* (1980). C. A. Wise, *The Meaning of Pastoral Care* (1966).

G. L. HARBAUGH

CLERGY, EMPIRICAL STUDIES OF; FAITH AND INTEGRITY, PASTOR'S; MENTAL HEALTH, PASTOR'S; MINISTER; MINISTRY; PASTOR; ROLE, MINISTERIAL; SYMBOLIC DIMENSIONS OF PASTORAL CARE RELATIONSHIPS; THEOLOGICAL STUDENTS, EVALUATION AND EMPIRICAL STUDIES OF. *See also* AUTHORITY *or* IDENTITY, PASTORAL; CALL TO MINISTRY; PASTOR, PASTORAL CARE OF; PERSONAL, CONCEPT OF, IN PASTORAL CARE. *Compare* AUTHORITY *or* SEXUAL ISSUES IN PASTORAL CARE; THERAPEUTIC CONDITIONS.

PERSPECTIVE, PASTORAL. *See* CLINICAL PASTORAL PERSPECTIVE.

PERSUASION. *See* SUGGESTION, PERSUASION AND INFLUENCE. *See also* REASONING AND RATIONALITY IN PASTORAL CARE.

PERVERSION. *See* SEXUAL VARIETY, DEVIANCE, AND DISORDER.

PFISTER, OSKAR ROBERT (1873–1956). A Swiss pastor and educator. He was a follower of Freud and utilized psychoanalysis in his pastoral work with children and adolescents. The correspondence that developed between Pfister and Freud led to a deep and sincere friendship that lasted from 1909 until the time of Freud's death. He published many books and papers including *The Illusion of a Future* (which was a response to Freud's *The Future of an Illusion*) and *The Psychoanalytic Method,* which helped to introduce psychoanalysis to Switzerland. Pfister was a warm, loving, and enthusiastic person who was devoted to Christ and sought to develop psychoanalysis as a method of fulfilling his pastoral care duties. His attempt to merge the cathartic powers of the psychoanalytic method with the healing powers of religion led

him to believe that a healthy religion can be of great benefit to human development.

Bibliography. H. Meng and E. L. Freud, eds., *Psychoanalysis and Faith: The Letters of Sigmund Freud and Oskar Pfister* (1963). H. N. Malony and G. North, "The Future of an Illusion and the Illusion of the Future: The Freud-Pfister Debate," *J. of the History of Behavioral Science* (1979).

S. C. WILLIS

PSYCHOANALYSIS AND PASTORAL CARE; PSYCHOANALYSIS AND RELIGION.

PHARMACOTHERAPY. *See* DRUGS; MEDICATION; THEORY AND PRAXIS.

PHENOMENOLOGICAL METHOD IN PASTORAL CARE. An approach to ministry that focuses on the person being cared for in a disciplined, empathic, nonjudgmental fashion, by seeking to enter into his or her "internal frame of reference." As a caring method it embraces overt judgments about reality, truth, and moral values, tolerates ambiguity and complexity, and deeply values the life experience of persons. It can therefore be equated with an attitude of wonder and empathic, inquisitive respect.

1. History. Phenomenology is a complex philosophical movement variously defined by different proponents, but fundamentally concerned with describing the world as it *appears*. Phenomenological method in pastoral care is allied to philosophical phenomenology in seeking to describe rather than to explain, in valuing interpretation rather than "objective truth," in opposing reductionism while focusing on intentionality, coherence, and intelligibility, and in assuming a fundamental prereflective, nonrational part of experience, which is consciously available to the person. Thus, it seeks to understand individuals from the perspective of their "moving historical fields of lived existence" (Husserl).

The phenomenological method entered contemporary American pastoral care primarily through the influence of psychologist Carl R. Rogers, who used the terms *empathy* (later, *accurate empathic understanding*) and *client-centered therapy* to describe the phenomenological entrance of the therapist into the world of the client. Eventually, he came to regard empathy as one of six necessary and sufficient conditions for therapeutic change, claiming that a phenomenological approach is essential to any successful therapeutic endeavor, because it facilitates internal "congruence" with the depths of one's experience, thus helping the client become a more unified and authentic person.

The phenomenological method has influenced recent Protestant pastoral care and counseling profoundly. Especially in the decades of the 1950s through the 1970s, through the influence of pastoral theologians like Seward Hiltner, Wayne Oates, Carroll Wise, and later Don Browning and Thomas C. Oden, the phenomenological method became the preferred (if not normative) approach to pastoral ministry. Its chief effect was to make pastoral care less authoritarian, that is, less inclined to impose predetermined values and preconceived solutions onto individuals seeking help. In doing so it intended to encourage greater individual initiative, insight, and responsibility in the solving of life problems and the attainment of healing on the part of the person seeking help.

2. Use in Pastoral Care. At its best, the phenomenological method serves as a basic approach in pastoral care but not as a specific methodology. It clarifies the stance of the pastor toward needy persons but does not prescribe particular or preset ways to respond to them. On the level of principle, then, it is constant in its focus on the person, but on the level of application it allows for a wide variety of response.

Pierre Thevanaz has observed that "phenomenology is description, but it is more than that: It is radical searching for foundations." The same can be said of the phenomenological approach in pastoral care. It has been a way of relating to persons on their own terms, but it has been more than that: it has been seen as a vital part of the healing process. As such, its significance has sometimes been extended to include the belief that the solution to an individual's plight comes from his or her own inner resources. Theologically, this assertion may be considered true in one sense but false in another. It is true in the sense that if one is to find an answer to a situation, it must be one's own answer existentially discovered and owned, and not imposed by external authority. But it is theologically false if it means that individuals possess within themselves the ultimate answer to their plight. For this reason, pastoral care and counseling cannot be simply a phenomenological act of drawing out what is there all along. It must also help the individual receive and accept healing as an unearned gift from beyond the self.

The most thoroughly developed and critically appropriated use of the phenomenological method in pastoral care has been proposed by Thomas Oden. Using the phenomenological approach to illuminate human existence in relation to being and time, Oden examines our relation to the temporal categories of past, present, and future and to the being categories of God, self, neighbor, and world. His study is a landmark in the use of the phenomenological method in pastoral care for several reasons: (1) He uses the method as a descriptive (not therapeutic) tool. (2) He makes a clear distinction between phenomenological and theological analyses of the human situation. (3) He maintains that a phenomenological analysis is incomplete for pastoral purposes if not correlated with theological inquiry.

Oden is representative of current assessment. The phenomenological method makes a significant contribution to contemporary pastoral care and counseling, but it must be supplemental by theological affirmations.

Bibliography. D. S. Browning, *Atonement and Psychotherapy* (1966). S. Hiltner, *Pastoral Counseling* (1949). W. E. Oates, *Pastoral Counseling* (1974). T. C. Oden, *The Structure of Awareness* (1969). C. R. Rogers, *The Therapeutic Relationship and Its Impact* (1967), pp. 97–108. P. Thevanaz, *What is Phenomenology?* (1962), p. 91. C. A. Wise, *The Meaning of Pastoral Care* (1966).

L. ADEN

LISTENING; PERCEPTIVENESS AND SENSITIVITY, PASTORAL. *See also* INTERNAL FRAME OF REFERENCE; PASTORAL CARE MOVEMENT; INTERPRETATION AND HERMENEUTICS, PASTORAL; PASTORAL COUNSELING; THERAPEUTIC CONDITIONS. *Compare* CLIENT-CENTERED THERAPY; CLINICAL PASTORAL PERSPECTIVE; COMPASSION; EXISTENTIALISM AND PASTORAL CARE; OBJECTIVITY, PROFESSIONAL; PHILOSOPHY AND PSYCHOLOGY; TECHNIQUE AND SKILL IN PASTORAL CARE.

PHENOMENOLOGICAL PSYCHOLOGY AND PSYCHOTHERAPY.

Phenomenological psychology is psychological research using a phenomenological method; phenomenological psychotherapy is psychotherapy based on views of human consciousness and human being developed in the existential/phenomenological tradition.

1. Phenomenology. The word *phenomenology* comes from *phos*, "light," *nomos*, "law" or "rule," and *logos*, "account." It names a descriptive method designed to give an account of how things come to light, that is, how things are disclosed and made apparent. Emphasis is placed on descriptive, structural accounts of how people and things occur together in ways that allow expression and development of human being, and on descriptive accounts of ways of being that are self-restrictive and oppressive. Particular attention is usually paid to spatial and temporal structures of pathological and nonpathological human experiences. Experiences are characteristically viewed in terms of meanings rather than in terms of material or behavioral patterns.

Phenomenology, like its close associate, existentialism, developed a broader conception of experience than those that characterized most other sciences and philosophies. People in both movements, which count Husserl and Kierkegaard respectively as their founders, turned toward the ways things are present and the ways human experience occurs as their fields of work. In both movements description is the primary mode of thinking, although Kierkegaard was more dialectical and reflexive in his descriptive thinking than Husserl. Both founders reinstated the importance of intuitive states of mind as sources for descriptive, experiential evidence, and both made consciousness, now experientially broadened, the center of philosophical reflection. Kierkegaard, however, placed much greater emphasis on emotion, feeling, and mood in his accounts of human existence than Husserl, who considered primarily non-affective states of mind in his account of consciousness.

The combined interests in description, human experiences, and consciousness are the primary bridge between phenomenology/existentialism and psychology and psychotherapy. Since phenomenology/existentialism includes all manner of religious, anthropological, and social positions, we may assume that we are dealing with an approach that is centered on human consciousness without a specific commitment to any one claim about the nature of human consciousness.

2. Phenomenological Psychology. In a phenomenological approach one's understanding of "scientific" is changed from accounts based on linear causation, mathematical measurements, and laboratory-oriented perceptions to a method of description in which the intentional spacio-temporal structures of the presence of things, as well as of approaches to things, is taken centrally into account. States of mind and states of objects are experientially inseparable. Therefore research in this area can include Gestaltist accounts of the structures of phenomena or studies of perception in which the intrinsic involvement of world and consciousness in the perceptive occurrence is delineated and detailed, for example, studies of body consciousness (Husserl, Scheler, Sartre), imagination (Sartre, Casey), abnormal psychology (Scheler), and the relation of consciousness and brain processes (Ey). These studies have in common an effort to understand with methodological rigor the essential inter-penetration of consciousness and world and to develop a broadened interpretation of how human alertness occurs and can be occluded. This orientation attempts to develop methods and vocabularies in which the subject under study is not abstracted from its lifeworld; thus research does not culminate in mathematical formulations. Rather, a disciplined phenomenological approach shows how something lives or is lived in relations of meaning, how it is available or self-presented for relation, how certain experiences or perspectives occur, and how things constitute our consciousness. The phenomenological motto, "to the things themselves," is thus carried out in psychology by descriptive studies of specific relational states or of structures of consciousness essential for all experiences.

The word *intention,* which is closely associated with phenomenology, refers to the fundamental and irreducible coherence between human awareness and things that are experienced. An intentional analysis in this context thus does not mean a study of motivation or personal intent, but an attempt to clarify structures of consciousness, or structures of meaning, as they are presented in experience, as characteristic either of consciousness as such or of specific types of consciousness.

3. Phenomenological Psychotherapy a. *Martin Heidegger.*

Heidegger's influence has dominated contemporary phenomenological psychotherapy. In order to begin with a thorough involvement of human beings in the world of human life, Heidegger developed the German word *Dasein* (literally 'being there'), which is usually the word for existence, to name human being. A synonym for *Dasein* in his work *Being and Time* is *being-in-the-world.* With this beginning point he was able to avoid the separation of subject and object which has characterized academic disciplines and to avoid as well an emphasis on consciousness and subjectivity, which characterized earlier phenomenological and existential thinking. *Dasein* is the nonreducible occurrence of human-world. People are human-world events composed of such factors as language in its rich and often obscure history, everyday involvements, nonpersonal possibilities (such as the capacities to decide, to die, and to change nonvoluntarily), understanding intrinsic to cultures and societies, and the ability to be alienated or appropriate in relation to its own event. If a person's way of living is profoundly attuned to human being (*viz., Dasein*), that person may be said to be authentic, that is, to live individually in ways that are open to and fully responsive to the limits and powers of the human occurrence.

Human being as described by Heidegger is a disclosive event, that is, a presenting event, in which things are self-disclosed rather than being produced by subjectivity. The joint emphasis on the presentational structure of human being and on its disclosive nature, which may be open with itself or at odds with itself, marks the direction of Heidegger's influence in psychotherapy.

b. Ludwig Binswanger. Binswanger called his approach *Daseinsanalysis.* Its goal, with the bases for psychotherapy primarily in mind, is to describe how human being is experienced—to discern its experiential structures in its health as well as in its pathologies. He judged Freud's work, which exercised a continuing influence on him, to be based on an inadequate, "naturalistic" anthropology. Rather than seeing human existence as a "natural" reality that is best approached by the natural sciences, he found Husserl's account of consciousness and Heidegger's description of *Dasein* to lead to the conclusion that we are in fact worldly, spiritual occurrences whose being is fulfilled through living relationships. What prevents people from fulfilling relations? Husserl gave him a method and Heidegger gave him the basis for an anthropology in his effort to answer that question. His rendering of Heidegger was, in fact, closer to Husserl's acceptance of transcendental subjectivity and to Kierkegaard's development of existential subjectivity than to Heidegger's understanding of *Dasein,* but Binswanger called the interpretative error a productive one and developed an impressive account of structures of human experiences. His procedure was to look for the essential structures of given experiences, namely, of ways of being-in-the-world, such as the structures of time, space, personal relations, relations with nonhuman things, with one's own body, and so forth in, say, compulsive-obsessive ways of being, and thereby to provide a definitive account of this way of existing. Such an account provided a descriptive basis for diagnosis and treatment of a way of being as distinct from a "natural" pathology conceived on a medical model of the human body.

A key to phenomenological thinking is an emphasis on the self-disclosure of persons and things. All beings occur in and as self-revealing events, as "words" in the Hebraic understanding. Binswanger placed emphasis on the self-disclosive nature of dreams, for example, which means that one's task is to listen to them with as little interpretative interference as possible, to learn their language and ways of being, and to let the dreams themselves develop insights as one lives with them and heeds them. How a person reports a dream, how he or she experiences uncertainty, hesitancy, irritation, and pleasure, to name a few, in relation to the dream is the person's own disclosure in the presence of the disclosing dream.

On Binswanger's terms, when a patient and therapist experience each other in deep mutual acceptance, in an occurrence of "we together," space is no longer defined in terms of mine and yours, and time has a quality of "ever" to it, in striking contrast to experiences of mere endurance of temporal separation. In that situation a fulfillment of human being takes place that is intrinsically healing.

c. Medard Boss. His work has exercised a particularly strong influence on American humanistic psychology because of his emphasis on the primary importance of the therapeutic relation for understanding psychological issues. Whereas Jung, and to a certain extent Binswanger, used speculations concerning drives, archetypes, and *a priori* structures of consciousness to explain psychological phenomena, Boss deals primarily with how a human being presents itself in well or ill states of existence.

With careful reliance on Heidegger's work, Boss interprets human being as disclosive world-openness, namely, as an occurrence that reveals itself in how it relates to all the humans and things in its environment. When human being fights its own disclosure — when, for example, it tries to live as though it had no possibility for intense hostility or vulnerable, loving intimacy—it reveals itself as being at odds with itself through dreams, lifelessness, phobias, compulsions, and the like. The therapist notices that this person is attuned to hostility everywhere, that people and things stand out in their potentiality for opposition and resistance, or the therapist finds another person attuned to defenses against loving interaction, that the world occurs for this person bereft of loving mutuality. The therapeutic goal in all cases is freedom for one's being and for the self-disclosures of all things. As one becomes freer for the full range of given human-world possibilities, one is able to make decisions and generally to live as he or she allows beings to be, without fearful distortion, denials, fixations, and separations. One finds that being well is direct and full encounter with whatever is given in one's world in acceptance of one's own being.

Boss's therapeutic practice is an existential/phenomenological version of psychoanalysis. It is based on a descriptive account of human being (analysis of *Dasein*) and on the therapist's openness to human being however it occurs. It is a totally nonjudgmental relatedness in which one experiences the conditions in which a person may reestablish the lost openness with being, a lostness that he or she has been living as closure to fundamental human possibilities and to the presence of things as they are. In therapy the closures may cease with impunity and a freer way of being may be experienced.

d. Carl Rogers and Eugene Gendlin. Although Rogers has not developed a theoretical position that could be called, in any careful sense of the word, phenomenological, his work is aligned with aspects of the existential/phenomenological movement. Self-discovery by means of unconditioned acceptance by the therapist is the keystone in Rogers's edifice. His practice is focused on counseling, not analysis, and short-term "client-centered" work is emphasized. The therapist's acceptance enables the client to accept him or herself more thoroughly and to allow greater differentiation in what he or she perceives in the world. This approach suggests tacit agreement with the phenomenological claim that human being is being-in-the-world and that liberation for open acceptance of being-in-the-world is the primary therapeutic goal.

The therapist is also to enter the client's perceptive world to experience as he or she does the emotional and objective manner of other people and things. As in phenomenological psychotherapy, experience, not observation, provides the primary basis for understanding and interpretation. This empathy, combined with unconditional positive regard and the therapist's own psychological congruence with him or herself and with the client, creates the conditions for the client's psychological development.

Eugene Gendlin has developed most thoroughly the phenomenological dimension of the Rogerian direction.

Gendlin uses an explicitly phenomenological approach to show how experiencing and conceptualizing interplay. He also has applied his theoretical work to practice in an approach he calls focusing.

Bibliography. L. Binswanger, *Being-In-The-World* (1963). M. Boss, *Psychoanalysis and Daseinsanalysis* (1963); *A Psychiatrist Discovers India* (1965). E. Casey, *Imagining* (1976). E. T. Gendlin, *Experiencing and the Creation of Meaning* (1962); *Focusing* (1978). A. Giorgi, *Human Science: A Phenomenologically Based Approach* (1972). M. Heidegger, *Being and Time* (1962). M. Merleau-Ponty, *Phenomenology of Perception* (1962). R. May, ed., *Existence* (1958). C. Rogers, *On Becoming a Person* (1961). J.-P. Satre, *The Emotions* (1948); *Being and Nothingness* (1956). H. Spiegelberg, *Phenomenology in Psychology and Psychiatry* (1972).

C. E. SCOTT

CLIENT-CENTERED THERAPY; EXISTENTIAL PSYCHOLOGY AND PSYCHOTHERAPY; EXPERIENTIAL PSYCHOTHERAPY; PERSONALITY THEORY; PHILOSOPHY AND PSYCHOLOGY; PSYCHOLOGY, WESTERN; PSYCHOTHERAPY. *See also* EXPERIENCE; INTERNAL FRAME OF REFERENCE. *Compare* GESTALT PSYCHOLOGY AND PSYCHOTHERAPY; HUMANISTIC PSYCHOLOGY *or* PSYCHOTHERAPIES.

PHENOMENOLOGY. *See* THEOLOGY AND PSYCHOLOGY.

PHENOMENOLOGY OF RELIGION. *See* RELIGIOUS EXPERIENCE.

PHILIPPINE PASTORAL CARE MOVEMENT. *See* EAST ASIAN PASTORAL CARE MOVEMENT.

PHILOSOPHICAL ANTHROPOLOGY, DISCIPLINE OF. Philosophical study of the nature of human being. Since the modern period inquiry has focused on philosophical interpretation of the data provided by the natural and social sciences, especially biology and psychology. Speculations have also begun from intuitions and extrasensory perceptions.

A second use of the term refers to philosophical movements concerned more with humanity and human freedom than with nature and scientific causality. Examples are existentialism, phenomenology, personalism, and *Lebensphilosophie.*

Usually, the term designates a school of German philosophy, dominant since the 1940s, which has absorbed elements from the movements noted above, but has not displaced them.

A history of German philosophical anthropology begins with Hobbes, Locke, Hume, and Mill, who desired to study humanity from an empirical biological perspective. On the Continent, Kant's positing of an unbridgeable gap between the phenomenal world of the senses and the noumenal world of essences, between facts and values, was accepted as basic. Herder was the first German philosopher to synthesize the study of biology and human nature. Theories of alienation from Hegel through Marx and Feuerbach made humanity the standard of judgment. Philosophical anthropology thus replaced theology. Others from whom later philosophical anthropology drew conceptions of humanness include Kierkegaard, Nietzsche, and especially Pascal.

The goal of philosophical anthropology is to study humans as both creatures and as creators of cultural values. It therefore rejects methods of mechanical determinism and employs the nonempirical phenomenology developed by Edmund Husserl and employed by Max Scheler. Phenomenology involves a direct, intuitive grasp of essences which claim to be presuppositionless and to precede the natural sciences.

The essence of humanity remains an open question. Humans, however, are believed to have creative freedom and an infinity of choices. An optimum of social organization would provide a maximum of free choice and a minimum of limitation of individual liberty.

Major Applications of philosophical anthropology are found in biology, cultural anthropology, pyschology, and theology. Psychological-philosophical anthropology is the most notable post-Freudian development in psychiatry on the Continent. Leading exponents include Binswanger, Strauss, and Boss. Erich Fromm, Rollo May, and R. D. Laing show similarities. Existential psychologists resist the dominance of empirical methods of experimental psychology and seek to augment them with philosophical or phenomenological approaches.

Theological philosophical anthropology stresses the relationship of dialogue between humans and God. Martin Buber, Emil Brunner, and Dietrich Bonhoeffer represent this movement. An intellectual grasp of truth is insufficient. Humans need an existential I-Thou relationship with God to be authentically human. This approach dominated European and American theology from the 1930s until the mid 1960s.

Bibliography in English includes: G. Bryson, *Man and Society* (1945). R. D. Laing, *The Divided Self: A Study of Sanity and Madness* (1960). R. May, ed., *Existence* (1958). H. O. Pappé, "Philosophical Anthropology," *The Encyclopedia of Philosophy*, P. Edwards, ed. (1967). J. W. S. Pringle, *The Two Biologies* (1963). E. Rosenstock-Huessy, *The Christian Future* (1946). S. Strasser, "Phenomenological Trends in European Psychology," *Philosophy and Phenomenological Research*, vol. 18 (1957), 18–34.

J. R. ROGERS

HUMAN NATURE, PROBLEM OF; PERSON (Philosophical Issues); PHILOSOPHY AND PSYCHOLOGY. *Compare* HUMAN CONDITION/PREDICAMENT; PERSONALITY, SOCIETY, AND CULTURE; THEOLOGICAL ANTHROPOLOGY; THEOLOGY AND PSYCHOLOGY.

PHILOSOPHY AND PSYCHOLOGY, EASTERN.

See PSYCHOLOGY, EASTERN, PSYCHOLOGY AND PSYCHOTHERAPY (East-West Comparison).

PHILOSOPHY AND PSYCHOLOGY, WESTERN.

From its beginnings, Western philosophy has had as one of its central preoccupations questions about the nature of mind, that is, questions concerning the ultimate nature and basis of psychological reality. Yet despite its long-standing interest in the questions related to psychology, Western philosophy has found it very difficult to develop a satisfactory theory of mind—whether mind is conceived in terms of "soul," "self," "experience," or "consciousness."

The quest has led to a variety of philosophies of mind in Western intellectual history. These traditions provided the fund of basic ideas — and unsolved problems—from which contemporary Western psychology and psychotherapy, and their pastoral derivatives, arose. Thus, achieving clarity about these traditions and the ongoing issues and questions they present is essential for enabling pastoral care and counseling to relate critically and constructively to contemporary psychology.

1. **Basic Questions.** Western philosophy of mind has taken three fundamental forms: Stoicism, Aristotelianism, and Platonism. Each emerged in classical culture and underwent significant transformation in the modern period. The whole tradition, however, has struggled in various ways with two basic questions. These questions continue today and form the underlying problematic of all forms of Western psychology.

a. Questions about knowledge versus questions about consciousness. In Greek philosophy the first questions concerning philosophical psychology evolved out of an attempt to understand the nature of human knowing. This is because the act of knowing implies a knower and thus raises the question of who or what the "knower" is, and how it might be possible for the knower to obey the Delphic Oracle's injunction to "Know Thyself!" Following Anaximander, Athenian philosophy plumbed the question of self-knowledge and sought to define the oneness or unity of the mind. Yet even Plato, who discovered the structure of conceptuality (the theory of forms), was not able to delineate a concept of mind able to explain the paradox of self-knowledge — how (or whether) it is possible for the mind to understand *itself* (and its place in the world).

In modernity, this approach to philosophical psychology, by way of epistemology, underwent a fundamental shift. Questions about knowledge gave way to questions about consciousness—the nature of awareness, and of "awareness of awareness." Yet paradoxes and ambiguities abound in this problem, and the single greatest difficulty in Western theorizing about mind continues to be how to express the *reflexivity* of the mind, the possibilities and limits of its self-knowing, and the peculiar unity of the mind that can be defined in terms of such reflexivity.

b. Questions about "subject" versus questions about "person." As intended here, the concept of "person" refers broadly to the observable, functioning social being, as one of a class of such beings identifiable by certain characteristics which can be described in a more or less objective or third-person manner, such as the ability to use language, act responsibly, and so forth. By contrast, "subject" refers to the "I," the "first person," which is, in some sense, "private" or separated from the social world, and which experiences various states of awareness. Owing to the inaccessibility of the "subject," it is frequently said to enjoy a "privileged position."

Western theories of philosophical psychology have differed widely in their accounts of the relation between "person" and "subject." The problem also runs deep in contemporary psychology: witness the gulf between, say, behaviorism and psychoanalysis, or between neurophysiological and humanistic psychologies. Historically, the three most prominent approaches have been: (1) the thesis that personhood derives from subjectivity (Stoicism); (2) the thesis that personhood and subjectivity are equiprimordial (Aristotle); and (3) the thesis that subjectivity is derivative from personhood (Plotinus). The following discussion of classical philosophical psychology is organized around these three fundamental traditions.

2. **Classical Thought.** *a. Personhood derived from subjectivity: Stoicism.* The Stoa taught that there is in every individual something of the original creative fire. All form and shape, life and reason in the arrangement of the world have grown out of this original fire or spirit, which functions also to hold everything together, preventing its disintegration into the void. In holding the individual together the original fire also makes the individual familiar with or well disposed toward itself (*oikeiosis*) and simultaneously on bad terms with, or alienated from, what is not itself (*allotrios*). To the extent that individuals are familiar with themselves, they are also aware of potential self-alienation and the possibility of resisting it. Thus *oikeiosis,* the subjective state of well-being, gives rise to the notion that all beings are caught between being well disposed toward and alienated from themselves.

In a novel move, the Stoa linked *oikeiosis* with the doctrine of self-preservation. Because a being is already well disposed toward itself it can preserve itself. Conversely, only insofar as a being preserves itself can it remain familiar with itself; if it fails to preserve itself adequately it falls into a state of alienation from itself (*allotrios*). Though aware of their distinctive character, beings also become aware that they, like all other beings, are engaged in self-preservation.

The key to what is proper for a being stems from its *oikeiosis.* Thus the perception of external objects is impossible without perception of oneself, but as an individual becomes more explicitly aware of itself, it becomes increasingly independent of externals, thereby learning to develop more clearly its own powers of reason. This deepening awareness culminates in being well disposed toward others of the same species—first family and then community—because the way in which one relates to oneself is at the same time the way in which one is related to the world. In this way, according to the Stoa, an individual moves from the privacy of subjectivity to the social reality of personhood. Stoic self-awareness is thus not an achievement but an innate subjective state or disposition. Sustained introspection on this state yields progressive insight, disclosing the powers of reason and making possible a community of persons constituted in unity with the world.

b. Personhood and subjectivity equiprimordial: Aristotle. Well before Xeno and his followers began to teach in the porticos of Athens, Aristotle had offered an approach of a very different sort to the interpretation of mental life. He attempted to explain self-reference in two ways, using completely different frameworks. The first is self-reference in *perception;* the second is self-reference in *thinking.* The latter Aristotle attributed to God, and devoted only a single paragraph to a consideration of the kind of self-cognizing humans might have.

i. The nature of life. To understand these two theories of self-reference, one must know Artistotle's thinking about the nature of living things in general. For Aristotle

all life is motion, a complex but determinate power to act in definite, discoverable ways. To understand how the power of life operates one must see through and beyond particular instances to its "nature." For example, we understand the power of sight in terms of the activity of seeing, and also in terms of the means by which vision operates—its instrument, the eye. In a similar way, we think of the power of thinking (*nous*) in terms of the activity of thinking, and in terms of the instrument by which thinking operates—images. Moreover, Aristotle teaches us to think of seeing and thinking also in terms of the objects (what he called "correlative objects") to which seeing and thinking are directed, or to which they are a response. Aristotle was convinced that to understand life as a complex determinate power of motion we must understand the behavior of an organism as a whole in its environment: sight is not simply the activity of seeing, or the activity of the eye, but also what is seen—the visible. Sensing and knowing are thus a matter of *motion,* which Aristotle divided into the categories of the mover, that which is moved, and that by which something moves. Humans alone, however, have the power of responding to universals and meanings (*nous*), of acting with deliberation and conscious forethought, and of acting rationally.

ii. Self-reference in perception. The implications of this threefold division for Aristotle's theory of sensing are interesting if strange to modern ways of thinking. Sensing for Aristotle is an activity characteristic of all organisms possessing the *power* of sensing or perceiving. Existing potentially in some organisms, this power may be set into motion or "actualized" by some sensible object in the environment. Once actualized, the functioning of the sense organ becomes in a certain respect "like" the sense object, impacted or shaped by the object insofar as it shares the object's universal qualities (the "whiteness" of a white object, for instance). Sensing, in other words, is a being acted upon, so that in sensing one becomes like the object. Similarly, the potential qualities of the object become actual in the sensing activity of the organ. To put the matter technically, the activity of the mover (the sense organ) has its locus in the thing moved, and not in the mover itself.

Following this line of reasoning, it becomes clear that to each sense there corresponds an appropriate object: color for vision, sound for hearing, and the like. Yet there are also objects that are sensed by *every* sense: motion, rest, figure, magnitude, number, and unity. Aristotle was at pains to point out that there is not another sense or special sense by which these "objects" are apprehended. Instead, he held that they are "common sensibles" of which there is a "common sensing," that is, an area of overlap, a sensing which the senses share. This teaching of the "common sensing" or *sensis communis* enabled Aristotle to explain a number of particular problems such as how several senses can have the same apprehension of one object.

When Aristotle sketched out his theory of the *sensis communis* in *De Anima,* he denied for logical reasons any special, separate sense for apprehending common sensibles, stating instead that whenever we perceive, we are aware that we have perceived. He wanted to avoid the conclusion that awareness of perceptions was a second "seeing," and so claimed that this awareness belonged to the same faculty as perception (thus relating it to each of the senses separately). Yet in his later treatise, *On Dreaming*, Aristotle refined his position, noting that when we wake up, we do not wake up sense by sense, with a different self-awareness for each sense. Instead, there is only one act of waking up. Self-awareness is now linked with the *sensis communis,* and not with each individual sense: the underlying unity of sense perception relates different awarenesses to one another. This is the first theory of self-reference in Aristotle.

iii. Self-reference in thinking. On this topic Aristotle occupies himself primarily with the problem of the First Mover (God) who is The Best, and as The Best, must *think* (*nous*). Of course the Prime Mover can only think that which is best—which is to say, itself. Therefore Aristotle's First Mover contemplates ideas which are identical with itself, making the First Mover the pure presence of what is thought; as some later philosophers construed it, the Prime Mover is pure self-reference (e.g., Hegel). But thinking at this level is appropriate only for the Prime Mover and cannot be linked with Aristotle's theory of perception, which always requires an object. Humans cannot think in this way but must be satisfied with a half-glimpse of this kind of thinking.

In only one instance (in his *Nichomachean Ethics*) did Aristotle make reference to what his second theory of mental self-reference implied: we not only think, but know that we can think. But here Aristotle suggests that in fact we *perceive* that we think, we do not *think* that we think. Thinking becomes once again dependent upon the *sensis communis,* and the highest faculties of the mind remain ultimately dependent upon sensation.

What these complex considerations yield is a notion of subjectivity defined in terms of perception and not in terms of references by the first person "I" to itself. At the same time, self-perception is always primordially linked with the social world through the *sensis communis,* making it in principle a public (third person) reference and not a private (first person) reference. Thus mental self-reference in Aristotle is entirely independent of reliance upon an "I" that is aware of itself.

c. Subjectivity derived from personhood: Plotinus. Plotinus's theoretical efforts, which can be construed as Neoplatonic attempts to overcome the difficulties in the Stoic and Aristotelian theories, led him to an entirely new way of interpreting mind. Plotinus taught that the first principle is the One or the Good, which is above being. Of the One, nothing may be directly predicated, although in contrast with the world, the One is infinite, unchanging, and the highest Power or Force. The power of the One is so great that it overflows, yet the overflow in no way diminishes the One. But as the overflow of divine power becomes more distant from its source it changes character, becoming more imperfect, culminating in the complete loss of the Good, and so, in its opposite, evil.

i. Products of the One. The first product of the One's overflow is Mind (*nous*), which is self-thinking. The appearance of Mind is simply spontaneous: it is not the result of deliberate planning, willing, or action on the part of the One. Plotinus describes the One's production of mind as "sight not yet seeing," which looks back upon the One, thereby assuming content as Intellect and Being. Plotinus also speaks of the appearance of Mind in terms of a kind of self-assertion oriented toward independence. Whatever the manner of Plotinus's descriptions, the characterization of Mind as life—Being and Thought—is constant.

From Mind proceeds Soul, again by a kind of self-assertion, a desire for a life different from Mind. Just as Mind divides into Being and Thought, Soul divides into a higher soul (*psyche*) which stands nearer to Mind and contemplates Mind's ideas, and a lower soul (*physis*), furthest from the One, which acts upon matter. Whether contemplating or acting, Soul is not itself the realm of Ideas. Because Ideas belong to Mind alone, the soul's contemplation and subsequent action have to do with reflections of the ideas (*logoi spermatikoi*).

From Soul, both universal order and individual souls proceed. Individual souls have the same division within them as does Soul: one part directed to intelligible realities, another to the world of matter. Plotinus also states that the individual soul may direct its attention to either the higher or lower part, clearly suggesting a "middle" between higher and lower components of the soul.

ii. Union with the Good. To be raised to union with the Good—to attain intuitive, contemplative knowledge—the individual soul must direct its attention upwards, gaining freedom from irrational passions and affections. And to so free itself, the individual soul must engage in disciplined conduct, a process Plotinus calls moral progress.

Plotinus maintained that the soul's right direction of attention to the Good is an activity proper to its nature (i.e., the nature of the *psyche*). Hence the soul's return to its source is dependent upon nothing other than its own structure and is not necessarily conscious, in the sense of being aware of itself as properly directed. Such consciousness, as Plotinus explains it, is a secondary effect, an epiphenomenon. Thus self-awareness, the soul's awareness of its distinctive individual character, is parasitic upon an underlying structure or nature that defines what a person related to the total social order of being is. Subjectivity is dependent upon the prior and more fundamental structure of persons.

d. Classical Christian appropriations: Augustine and Aquinas. Throughout the formation of classical Western philosophical psychology, and in Christian theology as well as philosophy, one or another of these three strategies tended to predominate. Thus it is a part of conventional wisdom to hold that with Augustine the Neoplatonic formulation of Plotinus achieved prominence; with Thomas Aquinas, the Aristotelian formulation. And there are obvious senses in which this is so: Augustine tended to adopt the language of Neoplatonism, Aquinas the language of Aristotle. Yet there is also a sense in which the languages of self-relatedness that these thinkers exploited do not accord at the deepest levels with their own theoretical formulations, which tend, more surprisingly, in the direction of the Stoic formulation. As this tendency has important ramifications for the development of modern theories of mind, it deserves some amplification.

Stoic doctrines entered Christian teaching through St. Paul, whose Hellenistic apostleship made such appropriation inevitable. What St. Paul left to the imagination, however, Clement of Alexandria traced out in greater detail in his reflections upon the nature of mind and its relation to God. Indeed, Clement may have been the first to transform the Stoic language of self-relatedness into a rudimentary theory explaining how the individual soul, through linkage with the being of God, comes into knowledgeable relatedness with itself and with God.

Augustine deepened Clement's theoretical reflections by claiming not only an ontological but also an epistemological link between the individual soul and God. Augustine held that the source of the being and unity of the created order is at the same time the source of the being and unity of the individual mind, a principle which may be discovered through introspection. The individual mind discovers its own nature only because it is also in relation to the author of its being; the mind knows itself as created. Yet given the insufficiency of the mind to direct its attention properly, without confounding itself with God, the perfect form of the mind must be represented to the individual. This is the pivotal role of Christ. As Word, Christ restores right knowing about the ongoing relationship between Creator and creature. The formidable problem of directing one's attention rightly, however, more nearly favors the Stoic teaching than the Plotinean. Indeed, Augustine was sharply critical of the Neoplatonists for dropping the role of individual consent from their teachings.

Aquinas, too, taught that the correlation of self-knowledge and the knowledge of God has its locus in self-consciousness. According to Aquinas, the individual is placed at the meeting point of the world of spirit and the world of bodies where the powers of both are combined. Each power, moreover, is defined *as such* by reference to its object—in this Aquinas follows Aristotle. The human intellect knows itself in the same way that it knows other things—as it passes from potency to act. Owing to its position as the highest being in the realm of bodies and as the last being in the realm of intellect, the human intellect must exercise its many mental properties and powers to achieve its proper good. To know the good is to participate in the actuality of the divine light that is in all creatures as a potency. As creatures who are in relation to God their preservation begins with an act of God toward us: God's eternal law that reflects God's intentions for the Creation to preserve life, to propagate and to preserve truth and peaceful society. Hence, we are directed to come into awareness of ourselves as creatures dependent upon the Creator whose light and law within guide us to our proper end. In this, however, Aquinas more closely resembles the Stoic teaching than the Aristotelian: one moves from original familiarity with oneself (subjectivity) to a knowledge of one's right relation to and position in the social world (persons).

Given the pervasive influence of the Stoic teaching upon the formulations of Augustine and Aquinas (and upon those in the Pauline tradition who followed them — Bernard of Clairvaux, Bonaventura, Nicholas of Cusa, Luther, and Calvin), it is not difficult to imagine the potential attractiveness of this way of thinking for many modern theories of mind.

3. **Modern Thought.** Whereas classical philosophical psychology developed theories of the mind by reflecting on the nature of knowledge, the modern discussion has characteristically focused on the problem of consciousness. By examining the features of self-consciousness, modern thinking became convinced that the limits and finitude of the subject mark the real boundaries of all possible knowledge. This led to a dethroning of the role that the self-referential character of God had played in classical theories of mind. It also led to the abandonment of the Platonic and Aristotelian insistence upon insight into the nature of laws, since that was inconsistent with the individual search for new strategies of self-maintenance.

a. Hobbes, Descartes, Fichte. Thomas Hobbes created the first modern systematic philosophy built around the empirical contents of self-consciousness. Hobbes taught that the basic drive of all individuals is self-preservation. Even human passions and virtues amount to little more than varying intensities of self-maintenance. In Hobbes's teaching, self-preservation has a profoundly anti-teleological character: individuals find themselves in an unknown and thus hostile world, whose origins and end (or *telos*) remain hidden. Though they do not know what the world is about, they are nonetheless driven to explore the world in order to find themselves, for one cannot preserve oneself if one cannot distinguish oneself from that which is other. Because self-preservation is their basic drive, individuals live, in principle, in a state of mutual antagonism, requiring moral law and the body politic to effect mutual peace. The function of the body politic is thus not to fulfill some cosmic plan, but to consolidate and support "persons" as self-related beings engaged in the drive for self-preservation. Thus with the concept of self-preservation, the language of "self" emerged.

Whereas Hobbes took for granted the privileged, private features of self-consciousness (subjectivity), *René Descartes* made subjectivity the focus of his concern by analyzing the peculiar first-person claim, "I think." His celebrated formulation, "I think, therefore I am," appears to move from a claim about thinking to a claim about being. Doubting, he argued, involves a mental transition from conceiving the *idea* (or proposition) that "I do not exist" to actually assenting to it; doubting implies a prior act of conceiving ("cognizing")—a point he took as intuitively certain—and cognizing in turn refers immediately to a "cognizer." Descartes concluded his argument at this point, convinced that his argument had proved the essence of the "I" to be a "thinking substance" that is "really distinct" from the body or anything physical (whose existence *can* be doubted). This was Descartes's much noted and criticized "mind-body dualism."

Controversy over the nature of the existence Descartes claimed in his famous proposition, continues today. Set in the context of methodological doubt—Descartes' determination to arrive at certain knowledge by systematic doubting—his proposition may actually succeed in making a different point. Rather than establishing the existence of the "I" as "thinking substance," it may only argue a necessary relation between assenting and conceiving; the argument's further steps, which Descartes regarded as intuitively certain, may be doubted.

Whereas Hobbes constructed an entire political philosophy from an analysis of the self and its drive for self-preservation, and Descartes argued a distinctive kind of existence for the "I" by analyzing thinking itself, both redirected Western philosophy of mind toward the enticing possibilities — and significant theoretical difficulties — entailed in the attempt to understand self-consciousness. The problem, essentially, is whether it is possible to develop a comprehensive definition of the person, the publicly observable socially related individual, from an examination of subjectivity, the self-relating structure of consciousness, the "I." David Hume was intrigued with the question, but equally convinced that it is impossible to develop such a theory. Yet the idea persisted.

Johann Gottlieb Fichte was the first to achieve its realization. Fichte's principal insight was that the mind cannot be understood as a simple unity but must be understood as fundamentally oppositional. The opposition is between two elementary activities: the mind's need to "position itself" (when it says "I" it "takes up a position" that is simultaneously not other positions) and its need to interpret itself through some particular description. These two activities are not the same; the inevitable distance between them constitutes a basic tension or opposition in every act of self-consciousness. This circumstance permits the mind to recognize the limited character of its own self-description, which it must then oppose in order to interpret itself more adequately. In Fichte's account, which cannot be fully traced here, these opposing actions provide the basis for a knowledge of the world and for a knowledge of oneself as both "I" (subjectivity, the encounter of consciousness with itself in the world) and "person" (the course of descriptions under which I have interpreted these encounters). Fichte's theory thus embraces both "I" and "person" and in a manner reminiscent of the Stoa, making personhood contingent upon subjectivity.

b. Kant. Immanuel Kant's thinking was fundamentally in the Platonic tradition in contrast to the Stoic structure of Fichte's thought (though it was Kant's theoretical fragments about the nature of mind in his *Critique of Pure Reason* that prompted Fichte to undertake his bold theory about the self-related character of consciousness). Kant taught that the mind's capacity to know itself is the highest principle to which all other knowledge must conform. By this he meant that it is necessary for the "I think"—the consciousness I have of my own thoughts—to accompany all my thoughts about everything else; otherwise, I could not have these thoughts as *mine*. But this means that my other thoughts must be compatible or consistent, in basic *form*, with the form or structure of the fundamental act of self-knowing. The structure of self-knowing therefore governs (is the criterion for) the knowledge we have of other things.

More precisely, the formal structure of our knowledge of the world consists of mental categories like space, time, and causation by which sense data are meaningfully organized. Through an elaborate analysis Kant attempted to show that, at bottom, these categories must be the same as the formal structure of our knowledge of ourselves (the elementary "I think"). This insight led Kant to claim that we do not know the world as it is in itself, but only as it appears to us through the categories of our own thinking, categories which are determined not by lower forces or individual preference but by necessary, universal laws of concept formation. The concept

of self-consciousness is thus the point of departure for defining our relation to the whole world of appearances, including ourselves as physical and social "persons." What was novel in Kant's teaching was his claim that the conformity of all our knowledge with the form of self-consciousness is the condition of our having any knowledge whatsoever.

To this fundamental (or "transcendental") analysis of knowledge Kant added another, concerning action and moral life. Human beings are free. We are not entirely bound by Newtonian action and reaction. And our freedom, said Kant, like our knowledge, is rooted in reason; or, more accurately, in reason's capacity to "determine itself" and thus to become the sole incentive to action, the basis of moral conduct. Kant's insight cannot be adequately expounded here, but it may suffice to say that the self-determining character of reason, which Kant called the "moral law," makes it possible to act out of genuinely principled motives not driven by considerations of pleasure or happiness. And since the moral law, as pure form, is universal, it obliges all who adhere to it to follow the same moral course of conduct.

Despite the intuitive correctness of Kant's insights into the role and character of self-knowledge, there is something oddly empty — even plaintive or melancholy — in his whole conception of the individual's relation to the world. The mind in Kant's theory is without a home, neither fully belonging to the realm of ideas (we cannot think form apart from sensory content) nor to the sensory realm (no sense data without organizing categories or form), though moral action, at least in principle, begins to make the world a "home." Even fundamental self-knowing—the "I think"—turns out to be more questionable than it first seems. Because it is purely formal, without sense data, we cannot really *think* this idea; we only, as it were, catch a glimpse of it "transcendentally." Like Descartes, Kant wants to move from the "I think" to the "I am." But he is far more circumspect in making claims concerning subjective existence. At best, Kant thinks, we assume that we are more than an empty thought, especially in moral matters, because we can have some impact on what is given to us.

c. Brentano, Husserl, James. In the wake of Kant and Fichte, some theorists attempted to move away from what they considered the failure of theories anchored in the idea of the ego. In their place, such theorists proposed theories of self-relatedness that were ego-less.

In an effort to retrieve the insights of Aristotle from Kantian neglect, *Franz Brentano* developed a complex theory of mental acts that could account for the self-referential character of consciousness without recourse to an "I," or to the problem of the "subject-object" relationship that he thought riddled Kantian theories. He also claimed that it was possible to develop from such a theory an entire psychology — a view that many in the phenomenological school have since attempted to maintain as basic.

Brentano's student, *Edmund Husserl,* attempted to recast the issue of awareness in terms of time-consciousness. By this he meant that mental acts pass from the present to the past, but in distinctive ways. For example, a sound may be heard simultaneously with its physical occurrence or heard even after it has ceased sounding, the second kind of presence being a matter of "longitudinal intentionality." This staying of the mental perception seemed to Husserl to be an extension of the *same* perception, and *not* a second or new mental act. Moreover, longitudinal extension implicitly entails self-reference for Husserl, insofar as it continues to hold the perception in place after its external stimulus has ceased. Thus the temporary of experiences in consciousness is primary and precedes what can be said about subjectivity.

Husserl was well aware that these claims invoked overtones of a "subject" who does the attending and was willing to explore the idea, but many of his followers were not. Principal among these was *William James,* who argued that to talk of a transcendental self was to replace a description of facts with an unjustified explanatory conceptual scheme. What we encounter in consciousness are thoughts, together with a quality of warmth or intimacy among them, which arises from their relation in a stream of thought. Within the stream, specific relations emerge among thoughts: a present thought may, for example, appropriate past thoughts randomly or as a whole. As James sees it, this amounts to thought thinking itself. It accounts for the unity of the stream of thought, but thoughts thinking themselves are not "selves." The idea of the self refers empirically, according to James, to a speaker, and distinguishes a speaker from others. The distinction between "self" and "others" occurs continually, but the distinction is empirical only.

The approaches of Brentano, Husserl, and James each provide ways to conceive of the equiprimordiality of subjectivity and personhood without reference to an "I." Each nonetheless provides, implicitly, some basis for "privileged consciousness" (e.g. James's notion that thoughts are related to one another in terms of their "warmth" and "intimacy") and public "person." Owing to their distinctness from ordinary ways of thinking, these philosophies present initial difficulties, but their insights are often instructive. They bring into view the force of ordinary language patterns in shaping how we understand subjectivity and personhood. They also help us see how ordinary patterns of discourse tend to mask certain operations of mental life.

4. **Implications for Understanding Contemporary Psychologies.** The Stoic, Aristotelian, and Platonic approaches to the philosophy of mind and their modern psychological derivatives are not exhaustive of Western methods of philosophical psychology, but they have nonetheless had the most far-reaching effect upon the psychologies that predominate in contemporary culture. It is doubtless true, for example, that the Platonic stream, and its modern Kantian reformulation, has enjoyed the greatest currency, funding psychoanalytic, object relations, developmental, and self-psychology theories, all of which hold some form of the basic idealist conviction of a transcendental mind or self. But the Aristotelian stream, and its modern phenomenological reformulation, has given impetus to phenomenological and gestalt psychology, systems theories, cybernetics, and various forms of behaviorism. And the Stoic stream, especially with its modern Fichtean reformulation, has inspired Jungian thought, existential psychotherapy, and the so-called post-structuralist psychoanalytical

school (including "feminist" and "deconstructive" approaches).

Contemporary psychologies have greatly elaborated the insights of these philosophers but they continue to encounter seemingly insuperable historic difficulties in developing an adequate theory of mind. Indeed, in more recent philosophy, prominent figures like Heidegger and Wittgenstein have devoged considerable energy to the task of unseating theories about consciousness, arguing in various ways that the problems of these theories are actually problems with language. While criticisms of this kind are applicable to all theories of consciousness, they have been aimed with particular urgency at the Platonic and Kantian traditions.

The import of these criticisms is unsettling, for they question the very tenability of (for instance) psychoanalytic theory and its derivatives; Freudian psychology devolves ultimately from Kant's model of the mind. Indeed, even as he was developing his ideas Freud drew sharp rebuke both from his teacher, Brentano, and his classmate, Husserl.

At the very least, this survey of the history of the problem of mind points to the importance of being clear about the theoretical foundations of any psychology, as a basis for discriminating between competing schools and theories. It also ought to caution against the uncritical acceptance of psychological theories in pastoral care and counseling and in theology, which have often attempted to bring psychoanalytic or humanistic psychologies (for instance) into constructive relation with themselves. Only through efforts at conceptual clarity can superficiality in these matters be avoided and hope offered for a deeper understanding of ourselves.

Bibliography. C. D. Broad, *The Mind and Its Place in Nature* (1937). E. E. Harries, *Nature, Mind, and Modern Science* (1954). D. Henrich, "Self-consciousness: A Critical Introduction to a Theory," *Man and World,* 4 (1971), 3–28. N. Malcolm, *Problems of Mind: Descartes to Wittgenstein* (1972). G. H. Mead, *Mind, Self, and Society* (1962). E. Neumann, *The Origins and History of Consciousness* (1954). D. S. Pacini, *The Cunning of Modern Religious Thought* (1987). J. Piaget, *Insights and Illusions of Philosophy* (1971). G. Ryle, *The Concept of Mind* (1949). J. Wisdom, *Philosophy and Psychoanalysis* (1964).

D. S. PACINI

For philosophic discussions of the person see PERSON (Philosophic Issues) *and related articles* HUMAN CONDITION/PREDICAMENT; HUMAN NATURE, PROBLEM OF; I AND THOU; PSYCHE; SELF-TRANSCENDENCE; SELF-UNDERSTANDING; SOUL. *See also* PERSONALITY THEORY (Varieties, Traditions, and Issues) *and* PHILOSOPHICAL ANTHROPOLOGY, DISCIPLINE OF. *For specific topics in philosophical anthropology see* CAUSALITY IN PSYCHOLOGY, FORMS OF; CONSCIOUSNESS; CRITICAL THEORY; EMOTION; EXPERIENCE; FREEDOM AND DETERMINISM; MEMORY; MIND; MIND-BODY RELATIONSHIP; NEED/NEEDS; REASON AND PASSION; TIME / TIME SENSE; WILL / WILLING. *See also* ACTION/BEING RELATIONSHIP; BEING/BECOMING RELATIONSHIP; DEVELOPMENTAL THEORY AND PASTORAL CARE; PROCESS, CONCEPT OF. *For philosophic topics related to therapeutic care and counseling see* CARE; CONCEPT OF; ACTION/BEING RELATIONSHIP; BEING/BECOMING RELATIONSHIP; PROCESS, CONCEPT OF; PRUDENCE; SELF-UNDERSTANDING; THEORY AND PRAXIS; VALUES IN COUNSELING AND PSYCHOTHERAPY; WISDOM AND PRACTICAL KNOWLEDGE. *For philosophic discussions of pastoral care and counseling see* EXISTENTIALISM AND PASTORAL CARE; HUMANNESS/HUMANISM; INTERPRETATION AND HERMENEUTICS, PASTORAL; PERSONALISM

AND PASTORAL CARE; PHENOMENOLOGICAL METHOD IN PASTORAL CARE AND COUNSELING; PRAGMATISM AND PASTORAL CARE; REASONING AND RATIONALITY IN PASTORAL CARE. *See also* EMPIRICAL, PROCESS, *or* NEOORTHODOX THEOLOGIES AND PASTORAL CARE; PASTORAL COUNSELING; PASTORAL PSYCHOTHERAPY; PASTORAL THEOLOGICAL METHODOLOGY; THEORY IN PASTORAL CARE AND COUNSELING, FUNCTIONS OF.

PHILOSOPHY OF HUMAN NATURE. *See* HUMAN NATURE, PROBLEM OF; PERSON (Philosophical Issues). *See also* HUMAN CONDITION/PREDICAMENT; PHILOSOPHICAL ANTHROPOLOGY, DISCIPLINE OF; PHILOSOPHY AND PSYCHOLOGY.

PHILOSOPHY OF LIFE. *See* VALUES RESEARCH; WORLD VIEW.

PHILOSOPHY OF PASTORAL CARE AND COUNSELING. *See* PASTORAL CARE (History, Traditions, and Definitions); PASTORAL COUNSELING; PHILOSOPHY AND PSYCHOLOGY.

PHOBIA. *See* ANXIETY DISORDERS; NEUROSIS.

PHYSICAL FITNESS DISCIPLINES. Fitness disciplines may be classified from a pastoral perspective as an ascetical practice with the potential for cultivating a higher moral and spiritual existence.

Once the almost exclusive domain of competitive athletes, physical fitness has become a popular movement cutting across boundaries of generation, social class, and culture. The fitness disciplines include aerobic or endurance exercise, optimal diet, and moderate lifestyle. Americans have heeded the call for a change in lifestyle with a sense of moral obligation. Few movements in our pluralistic society have come as close to creating a moral consensus as has the physical fitness movement.

Medicine, psychology, religion, and even large corporations enthusiastically proclaim the benefits of physical fitness to the public. Its promises include improvements in physical and mental health, a hedge against aging, an enhanced spiritual life, and increases in employee productivity. Recent neurophysiological research finds that the fitness of our bodies influences the ways in which we experience and think about ourselves, others, and our physical environment (Appenzeller, 1983, p. 141).

While pastoral care has ample theological warrant for affirming the psychophysical unity implied in these values, its specifically pastoral focus has been upon the connection between the physical condition of the body and the moral development of the whole person. Pastoral counseling specialists have found that the fitness disciplines provide a way for people to bring order and limit to their lives. The discipline of fitness requires an exercise of the will to overcome the inertia of sedentary life and limits tendencies to eat beyond nutritional need. The practice of this discipline may become a paradigmatic action that guides subsequent moral decisions. Making moral choices about the use of what lies closest to hand, the body, may, for some, be the most available starting place for moral development. Many who suffer from various personality disorders find it difficult to exercise

self-restraint or take initiative for the sake of a good that may be realized only in a future that is based upon a history of sacrifice and hard work. The fitness disciplines activate their self-reporting neural pathways and thereby reaffirm their sense of self and its continuity through time. Although we must critique narcissistic preoccupations with fitness and stop short of placing ultimate value upon physical fitness disciplines, they have served many as an introduction to rituals of self-transcendence.

Bibliography. O. Appenzeller, "Exercise and Mental Health," *Encyclopedia Britannica*, 1983 Medical and Health Annual. Compare E. B. Holifield, *A History of Pastoral Care in America* (1983), p. 189.

G. E. MYERS

ASCETICAL PRACTICES; HEALTH AND ILLNESS. *See also* BODY IMAGE; LIFESTYLE ISSUES IN PASTORAL CARE; OBESITY AND WEIGHT CONTROL. *Compare* POPULAR THERAPEUTIC MOVEMENTS AND PSYCHOLOGIES; RELIGION AND HEALTH; SELF-HELP PSYCHOLOGIES.

PHYSICAL SUPPORT. *See* TOUCHING/PHYSICAL SUPPORT.

PHYSICAL THERAPY. *See* ADJUNCTIVE THERAPIES.

PHYSICIAN OF THE SOUL. *See* PASTOR (Normative and Traditional Images).

PHYSIOLOGICAL PROCESSES AND DISORDERS. *See* PERSONALITY, BIOLOGICAL DIMENSIONS OF. *See also* BODY; HEALTH AND ILLNESS.

PIAGET, JEAN. *See* DEVELOPMENTAL THEORY AND PASTORAL CARE.

PIETISM AND PASTORAL CARE. German Pietism began in the late seventeenth century as a reaction against intellectualism, churchly formalism and ethical passivity in Protestant Orthodoxy. The term "pietism," however, refers not only to Philipp Jakob Spener's (1635–1705) German separatist movement but also to a score of related traditions. Characteristically, Pietism emphasizes "heart religion," the centrality of the Bible for faith and life, the royal priesthood of the laity, and strict morality. These foci are applied to religious experience so that faith becomes a personal attitude based on repentance, forgiveness, and changed lives.

Critics of Pietism oppose its subjectivism, separatism, and encouragement of legalistic moralism. Pastoral care influenced by Pietism historically involves the nurture of prayer with devotional readings and the maintenance of "conventicles" or small religious groups. A premium is placed on preaching as a tool for guidance, admonishment, and encouragement. Formal liturgies are discouraged. Pietism aims at building up lay spirituality, applying the gospel to life and urging the pursuit of holiness. **1. Historic Pietism.** There is no systematic treatment of Pietism's influence on pastoral care. Spener's pastoral methods reveal some consistent patterns. Spener wanted pastors to raise the issue of salvation with their parishioners. By the examination of the felt experience of "new birth," pastors could help their people practice the "godly life." Clergy were to be "shepherds of souls." They were to preach for conversions, to diligently instruct confirmands and to vigorously catechize their flocks. Spener discouraged the much-abused use of private confession. He defended the role of the laity in caregiving, regular household devotions, extempore prayer, daily Bible readings, and strict Sabbath observance.

Pietists largely adopted these pastoral approaches; especially pastors educated at the University of Halle and later in Württemberg. August Hermann Francke (1663–1727) dominated the Halle school after Spener. Francke taught that real "conversion" demanded a conviction of sin and a personal spiritual regeneration. Under Francke's direction graduates of Halle became quite narrow in their judgments of the "unconverted."

By the mid-eighteenth century Lutheran Pietists in America had advanced a distinctive form of pastoral ministry. Henry Melchior Muhlenberg of Pennsylvania believed pastoral visits were never to be merely social calls. During visits Muhlenberg spoke to the "condition of the soul" looking for "evidences of God's grace working in people." He also used such occasions to reconcile, advise, and admonish. He chastised parishioners and maidservants alike for offences ranging from Sabbath swimming to attending "Christian drinking parties." His aim was to produce a consciousness of sin culminating in repentance and a holy life.

Special attention was given to the sick and dying. Illness was interpreted as a visitation from God to punish sins, convert the unbelieving or warn the afflicted. A typical visit included a type of "soul analysis" learned at Halle. Muhlenberg's purpose was to discover hidden "signs" of sinfulness concealed by deadened spirits. He would read Scriptures, exhort the sufferer, pray and sing hymns to "awaken" the impenitent and provide biblical consolation to the penitent. Halle graduates even offered a medical diagnosis complete with prescriptions.

Other colonial Pietist groups modified these practices. Schwenckfelders concentrated on inner spirituality, so that faith became almost a mystical experience. The Church of the Brethren (Dunkers) included in pastoral duties footwashings, a "holy kiss" after communion, and the love feast. The Moravian Brethren under Count Nicholaus Ludwig von Zinzendorf emphasized spiritual growth through devotional literature. Moravian hymnody, replete with sentimental images, focused on pastoral evangelism and personal salvation.

Pietist influences were also seen in early Methodism. John Wesley organized "bands" for "mutual confession, edification and fraternal correction." Wesley wrote many pastoral letters on spiritual matters urging regular devotions. George Whitefield's Great Awakening preaching included the Pietist's conviction that Christianity is a life lived, not a creed. Francis Asbury advocated use of the Prayer Book in pastoral work. For Asbury pastoral calls were a surrogate form of the confessional; thus they were intended for "thorough religious conversation." While Pietism and Methodism eventually took different directions, a disciplined piety and earnest pastoral visits remain important for Wesley's heirs.

2. **Modern Applications.** *a. Scripture.* Pietism stresses the importance of Scripture. Since Dicks's (1936) obser-

vations on the role of the Bible in hospital ministry, the place of Scripture as a spiritual aid has been discussed by clinicians and pastoral theologians. Hiltner (1949) argued that the Bible be used in ways consistent with appropriate counseling techniques — avoiding moralism, coercion or undue directiveness. Oates (1953) also cautioned against the abuse of the Bible in pastoral care. Instead of limiting Scripture to an aid for consolation, Oates valued the diagnostic and instructional insights available to clergy through a disciplined application of texts to lives. Wise (1956) described the relation of biblical concepts to dynamics of psychological illness. In the 1960s Europeans like Faber, van der Schoot, and Thurneysen remained advocates of the Bible as a major resource for pastoral care. More recently, Collins (1972) rejoined the appeal for the judicious use of Scripture for pastoral work. Meanwhile Adams (1970) rejected psychologically based pastoral care proposing that Scripture alone be the guide for pastoral caring. Capps (1981) summarizes these developments and offers pastoral counseling approaches that are consistent with biblical forms. Few of these authors wrote from a Pietist perspective; yet, their mutual concern that pastors use the Bible for pastoral care has Pietist antecedents.

b. Techniques of care. i. Growth counseling. An expectation of religious growth permeates Pietist models of pastoral care. By moving from an awareness of sin to a change of heart, Pietists seek higher levels of holiness. Clinebell (1979) advocates wholistic approaches to pastoral care whose hope-filled, spiritually centered theologies are consistent with Pietism. In *Contemporary Growth Therapies* (1981) Clinebell offers a helpful review of pastoral care theorists influenced by the human-potentials movement.

ii. Groups. Intimate religious fellowships are a standard mark of Pietism. Oden (1972) identifies similarities between small group encounters in Protestantism and Judaism and the secular encounter culture. Both Spener's *collegia pietatis* and Jewish Hasidic groups, place high valuations on immediate experience. In Protestant and Jewish Pietism the key is an intensely felt present transformation of spirit. Judeo-Christian Pietism underscores intensive small groups; honest confession of sin; experimental mysticism; mutual pastoral care; and the operation of the Spirit. Oden finds these themes largely repeated by the encounter culture of Perls, Rogers, and Maslow.

iii. Spiritual discipline. Spener's methods for "practical Christian living" included prayer, meditation, and fasting. These spiritual disciplines continue to reappear in contemporary pastoral care literature such as E. Thornton's *Being Transformed: An Inner Way of Spiritual Growth* (1984). Thornton calls for being transformed by experience, "spontaneity-in-love," and spiritual journeying. In this material relaxation exercises, centering and contemplation are put in the service of achieving deeper states of spiritual development. The goal remains the personal fulfillment of dynamic spiritual potentials.

iv. Lay caregiving. Pietism promotes lay ministry while discounting clericalism. Visitation teams, sharing groups, and enrichment fellowships are all ways by which lay spirituality can grow. Though these groups may not necessarily be of a Pietist orientation, they are often logical refinements of conventicles and holiness clubs. Pastoral care resources such as Detwiler-Zapp's and Dixon's *Lay Caregiving* (1982) overlook this rootage.

Bibliography. J. Arndt, *True Christianity* (1720). D. Brown, *Understanding Pietism* (1978). D. Capps, *Biblical Approaches to Pastoral Counseling* (1981). H. Clinebell, *Growth Counseling* (1979); *Contemporary Growth Therapies* (1981). G. Collins, *Fractured Personalities: The Psychology of Mental Illness* (1972). D. Detwiler-Zapp and W. Dixon, *Lay Caregiving* (1982). R. Dicks, *The Art of Ministering to the Sick* (1936). S. Hiltner, *Pastoral Counseling* (1949). E. B. Holifield, *A History of Pastoral Care in America: From Salvation to Self-Realization* (1983). J. T. McNeill, *A History of the Cure of Souls* (1951). W. Oates, *The Bible in Pastoral Care* (1953). T. Oden, *The Intensive Group Experience: The New Pietism* (1972). J. Spener, *Pia Desideria* (1675). F. Stoeffler, *The Rise of Evangelical Pietism* (1965). E. Thornton, *Being Transformed* (1984). C. Wise, *The Meaning of Pastoral Care* (1956).

G. S. ELLER

PASTORAL CARE (History, Traditions, and Definitions). *See also* LAY PASTORAL CARE AND COUNSELING; RELIGIOUS EXPERIENCE; SPIRITUAL DISCIPLINE AND GROWTH. *Compare* CHARISMATIC, EVANGELICAL, FUNDAMENTALIST, QUAKER, *or* SECTARIAN PASTORAL CARE; EXPERIENCE; PRAYER AND WORSHIP LIFE, PASTOR'S; PRAYER IN PASTORAL CARE; SPIRITUALITY (Protestant *or* Roman Catholic Tradition). *Biography:* ZINZENDORF, COUNT NICOLAUS LUDWIG VON.

PIETY. *See* CHRISTIAN LIFE; JEWISH HOLY DAYS AND FESTIVALS; JEWISH PRAYERS; LITURGICAL AND DEVOTIONAL LIFE, ROMAN CATHOLIC; SPIRITUAL DISCIPLINE AND GROWTH; SPIRITUALITY. *See also* FAITH AND INTEGRITY, *or* PRAYER AND WORSHIP LIFE, PASTOR'S.

PILGRIMAGE METAPHOR. A pilgrimage is a journey to a holy place undertaken for devotional purposes. Common reasons for going on a pilgrimage are to receive healing from physical or emotional distress, to gain deepened religious insight by drawing near to tangible symbols of one's faith, to express thanksgiving to God for some benefit, and to undertake penance for wrongdoing. The practice of pilgrimage is common in many of the world's "higher" religions and has been an important motif in Christian piety and theology.

1. **History.** The term "pilgrimage" appears relatively few times in the OT and not at all in the NT. The closely related term "pilgrim" only appears in certain English translations of the NT, notably the Authorized (King James) Version (Heb. 11:13 and I Pet. 2:11). The Greek term in both places is *parepidemos*, which other translations render "exiles" (RSV), "refugees" (TEV), and "aliens" (NIV). The term connotes one who is staying for a short while in a strange place, a sojourner.

In both Hebrews and I Peter, the dominant emphasis is on how Christians' loyalty to God through Jesus Christ places them in a tension with the world as it is. The church and its members live between the already of Christ's first coming and the not-yet of his final coming in glory. In this context, *parepidemos* — pilgrim, sojourner, exile — connotes two basic ideas: the provisional and temporary nature of a Christian's relationship to the world in the present age, and the Christian life as a journey toward the Kingdom of God as its final destination.

These themes have been reworked in various ways throughout the church's history. Augustine gave them classic expression in *The City of God*, portraying the Christian life as a pilgrimage from the earthly city to the heavenly city of God.

But during the Middle Ages the eschatological underpinnings of pilgrimage were dropped. The idea became closely associated with penance, and frequently the penitents were directed to go on pilgrimages as a way of doing penance for wrongdoing.

Luther's critique of the theology and practice of penance during the Reformation had the effect of diminishing the importance of the pilgrimage motif in Protestantism. It is thus ironic that this theme has reemerged in recent Protestant thought. This is due, in part, to a recovery of the eschatological dimensions of Jesus' proclamation.

2. **Contemporary Uses of the Metaphor.** The pilgrimage metaphor is sometimes used to give expression to the modern experience of ongoing change and the subsequent awareness of historical relativity. It attempts, however, to transform the experience of historical relativity by grounding it in a sharpened awareness of the sovereignty of God. According to this line of thought, Christians need not fear historical relativity for it simply reflects the fact that God and God alone has absolute knowledge (H. R. Niebuhr). An understanding of the church as engaged in an ongoing pilgrimage emerges. The greatest temptation facing the church is to "pitch its tents" and settle down in some idolatrous form of faith.

The metaphor is also often used, especially by specialists in pastoral care and Christian education, to express their heightened awareness of human development as a life-long process. Acknowledging the fact that adulthood no longer means the entrance into a period of stability, these persons have described the need to move through life stages in ways that enhance the Christian's faith (Sherrill; Whitehead and Whitehead). Interest in faith and moral development also has led some to portray the Christian life as being like a pilgrimage, offering a normative series of stages which lead to a more universalizing form of faith (Westerhoff, Fowler).

This metaphorical use of the pilgrimage theme to bring into focus the developmental dimensions of faith can be helpful to the extent that it is used to highlight certain themes that have been lost in recent discussions of sanctification. Too frequently, however, pilgrimage has served as a simplistic affirmation of psychological growth toward wholeness which is understood in utilitarian or therapeutic terms (Bellah *et al.*), losing the eschatological and moral dimensions of this concept as used in Scripture and early Christian thought. Practitioners of pastoral care and Christian education would do well to keep the theme of pilgrimage under theological control, especially when their use of this idea is, in part, an effort to give expression to some dimension of modern thought.

Bibliography. St. Augustine, *The City of God* (1972). R. N. Bellah, *et al.*, *Habits of the Heart* (1985). J. W. Fowler, *Stages of Faith* (1981). R. Greer, *Broken Lights and Mended Lives* (1986). S. Hauerwas, *Character and the Christian Life* (1975). A. Kendall, *Medieval Pilgrims* (1970). H. R. Neibuhr, *The Meaning of Revelation* (1941). L. J. Sherrill, *The Struggle of the Soul* (1961).

J. Westerhoff, *Will Our Children Have Faith?* (1976). E. White-head and J. Whitehead, *Christian Life Patterns* (1979).

R. R. OSMER

RETREATS; SAINTS, VENERATION OF; SHRINES; SPIRITUAL DISCIPLINE AND GROWTH. *See also* CHRISTIAN LIFE; LIFE CYCLE THEORY AND PASTORAL CARE; PASTORAL CARE (History, Traditions, and Definitions); SPIRITUALITY, ROMAN CATHOLIC. *Compare* DEVELOPMENTAL THEORY AND PASTORAL CARE; PROCESS, CONCEPT OF; SELF-ACTUALIZATION/SELF-REALIZATION.

PINEL, PHILIPPE

PINEL, PHILIPPE (1745–1826). French physician who originated the concern for moral treatment of the mentally ill. He headed two of France's largest insane asylums during his career, and his work during those tenures set the standard for a reform movement whose effects reverberated throughout Europe and the U.S. for the next century.

Pinel directed his efforts toward promoting humane care for the insane; care that included clean quarters, food, and freedom from chains. He was the first to alter the prevailing "warehousing" structure of insane asylums and actively promoted a search for mental healing of patients. He became an influential figure through his writings as well as through the practical applications of his theories. Pinel believed that mental illness contained both physiological and environmental components, and he incorporated treatment within a psychological orientation in his primary discussion of mental illness, *Medico-Philosphical Treaties on Mental Alienation or Mania*. In it he advocated the positive approach he initiated in his facilities and encouraged replacing some of the medical techniques with care, concern, and interpersonal relationships.

B. HOUSKAMP

MENTAL HOSPITAL/MENTAL HOSPITALIZATION.

PIPER, HANS-CHRISTOPH. *See* PASTORAL THEOLOGY, PROTESTANT.

PITY. *See* COMPASSION.

PIUS XII, POPE. *See* COUNSELING, ROMAN CATHOLIC.

PLACEBO EFFECT. *See* MEDICATION; SUGGESTION, PERSUASION, AND INFLUENCE.

PLANNING. *See* CONGREGATION; LEADERSHIP AND ADMINISTRATION.

PLATONISM. *See* PHILOSOPHY AND PSYCHOLOGY.

PLAY. Play is many things: an activity engaged in for the sake of relaxation or refreshment; what we do to get rid of excess energy in an acceptable manner; what children are supposed to do naturally when they are sent outside.

1. Developmental and Ritual Aspects. Play is also a dimension of human development. Erik Erikson regards play as a characteristic of the stage in the human life cycle during which the child develops initiative. The child uses play in order to relive, correct, and recreate past experiences or to anticipate future events and roles.

Play is not limited to development in childhood. At every age, it has a transitional function. Play helps to effect a transition between one's inner universe and a complex, changing outer environment. It provides a connection between the dread of inner boredom and imagined possibilities. Play is the wedding of imagination and factual reality in ordinary, everyday interactions. Playing video games or contract bridge or even watching pro football games are efforts to make a transition or achieve a balance between the seemingly ordinary present and "something more." That "something more" may be a dream of what might have been or a pleasurable alternative in the present or a future vision.

Ritual is one of the manifestations of playfulness throughout life. Most rituals ensure the availability of significant individuals in the interest of community. At its best, ritual deepens communality, mediates a sense of the numinous, and helps to consolidate a shared vision. When Christian worship is able to be playful enough to be that kind of ritual, it becomes a resource for the care of those who are lonely and bereft of ways to transcend their plight or who are consumed by a private vision of the world.

2. Therapeutic Uses. The psychotherapeutic use of play has traditionally been diagnostic. One can often clearly understand a child's inner conflict more quickly through play than through conversation. Erik Erikson broadened Freud's belief that play construction in clinical work revealed inner conflict to include "interplay" between the child's inner world and the evolving external social world. Play has not been commonly used in pastoral care for diagnostic purposes except insofar as there might be occasions in ordinary pastoral work to observe parishioners at play. Whether we play and how we play are both self-revelatory. When play has been a part of pastoral care, it has been used particularly by hospital chaplains in the care of children.

The use of metaphor in work with families has introduced play into therapeutic practice in ways that will undoubtedly influence pastoral work. Playfulness in the helping process is a powerful means for effecting change. The introduction of playfulness into an intense family system can suggest new behaviors that in turn bring about new alternatives. Metaphoric interventions that may appear to disregard the grimness of the situation depend on the belief that non-seriousness is the highest seriousness.

3. Larger Meanings. Play is more than something to do. It is a way of being that is open to encounters with God. If the essence of the religious person is to celebrate change and be open to mystery, then playfulness is a way of being religious. The playful, religious person is creative, passive, innocent, and capable of being receptive. And if play is the mark of being religious, then it might also be said that being religious includes a recognition that fiction is the highest truth, change is the highest stability, and purposelessness is the highest purpose.

The place of play in pastoral work is also more attitudinal than programmatic. It is the ability *not* to take one's self or one's ministry too seriously. To be playful is to have the kind of imagination that sees life through a child's eyes. To be playful about life is both liberating and a little unsettling. Acting in faith as if it were true is risky. It could lead, however, to a discovery of the graciousness of God.

Bibliography. E. H. Erikson, *Toys and Reasons* (1977), connects playfulness with the inner ordering and ritualization of everyday life. See also his *Life Cycle Completed* (1982). J. Huizinga, *Homo Ludens* (1955) contends that play is the basis of culture. Activities such as law, war, education, philosophy, and art have their basis in play even though the players pretend to be workers. R. K. Johnston, *The Christian at Play* (1983) proposes that Christian theology needs a fuller understanding of the person at play for a proper balance between work and play in a leisure oriented society. J. B. Reeves, "The Leisure Problems and the Role of the Clergy," *Pastoral Psychology*, 29:123–33, and G. L. Wright, "Spirituality and Creative Leisure," *Pastoral Psychology*, 32:192–203 examine the relation of play to ministry and the minister's spirituality. D. L. Miller, *Gods and Games* (1973) is a playful book suggesting a theology of play in which the medium is as gracious as the message. J. Moltmann, *Theology of Play* (1972) profoundly interprets play in terms of grace and the Christian hope. R. E. Neale, *In Praise of Play* (1969) considers play from the perspective of psychology of religion. Neale's vision is that play is irreverent, irrelevant and ultimately surprise. V. Turner, *The Ritual Process* (1969) sees an element of play or "antistructure" at the core of ritual activity and social process.

H. ANDERSON

HUMOR; IMAGINATION; RELAXATION; REST AND RENEWAL, RELIGIOUS TRADITIONS OF; WIT AND HUMOR IN PASTORAL CARE. *See also* CHRISTIAN LIFE; RITUAL AND PASTORAL CARE; SEXUAL VARIETY, DEVIANCE, AND DISORDER; STRESS AND STRESS MANAGEMENT; WORSHIP AND CELEBRATION. *Compare* WORK AND CAREER.

PLAY THERAPY. *See* ADJUNCTIVE THERAPIES.

PLEASURE. *See* HAPPINESS.

PLEASURE PRINCIPLE. *See* REALITY PRINCIPLE.

PLURALISM. *See* HERMENEUTICS AND INTERPRETATION, PASTORAL; SOCIOLOGY OF RELIGIOUS AND PASTORAL CARE; WORLD VIEW.

POETRY THERAPY. *See* ADJUNCTIVE THERAPIES.

POIMENICS. From Gk. *poimēn*, shepherd. A term once employed to designate the study of pastoral care as a formal branch of theology. Apparently introduced into English usage with the translation of J. J. Van Oosterzee's *Practical Theology* (1878), the term rarely appears after World War I. During this period it served as a synonym for pastoral theology which, alongside homiletics, liturgics, and catechetics, was considered a subcategory of practical theology.

Poimenics was generally understood as: (a) a body of knowledge pertaining to pastoral care as separate and distinct from other ministerial functions, (b) a field of study for the training of clergy (pastoral care being regarded as solely a clergy responsibility), and (c) a discipline dedicated to applying the truths of revelation to specific situations. Poimenics was typically divided into a general branch, concerned with care of the whole congregation, and a special branch, organized around types of individual cases. It embraced tasks as varied as church administration, congregational discipline, pastoral visitation, and individual counseling.

Bibliography. S. Hiltner, *Preface to Pastoral Theology* (1958). J. J. Van Oosterzee, *Practical Theology* (1878).

B. VAUGHN

PASTORAL THEOLOGY, PROTESTANT; SHEPHERD/SHEPHERDING.

POLICE OFFICERS AND POLICE CHAPLAINCY.
A police chaplain is an ordained person who functions as a minister to police officers, their families, and citizens in crisis situations to which the police are called. As an ecumenical and interfaith ministry it offers religious and moral guidance, pastoral care, counseling and referral, and various forms of worship services. While the police chaplain is not intended to be a substitute for an officer's local religious leader or congregation, he or she is often specially trained for the problems and stresses peculiar to the work of law enforcement. Though most police chaplains work on a part-time and volunteer basis, those who are salaried often have responsibility for the organization and oversight of a network of volunteer chaplains in addition to their regular chaplaincy duties.

1. **History.** Chaplaincy originated with clerics who followed the military into battle, carrying a relic (piece of the cape or "capella") from the martyr St. Martin of Tours. Police chaplaincy is not entirely modeled after its military antecedent, but also draws on the experience of hospital and university chaplaincy. The oldest police chaplaincy in the U.S. began in New York City in 1906. While a few others followed between the 1930s and 1950s, it was during the unrest and social upheaval of the 1960s that most chaplaincies were formed. In October 1973, the International Conference of Police Chaplains was organized to address the qualifications, credentials, training, appointment, responsibilities, and ethics of chaplains and to support chaplains by providing literature and further training and education in the field.

2. **The Nature of Police Work.** Police work includes dealing with accident and trauma victims, facing violence and danger, encountering corruption, and dealing with criminals and victims of crime. Shift work disrupts an officer's personal life and participation in other support structures, e.g., church and synagogue. Often racial and political tensions within police departments add to the stress of the work, as do the complexities of the law itself and a felt lack of support from the criminal justice system.

There is also a subtle psychological ambiguity to the nature of police work. While an officer functions as a protector of society and a bulwark against chaos, he or she must also intimately know and understand the antisocial personality and criminal substructure of society. The officer may in addition experience hostility from the public, a hostility often reflecting ambivalence toward authority rather than a rejection of the work that police do, and this may leave the officer feeling isolated.

925

3. Emotional and Psychological Responses of Officers. Displacement, an unconscious transference of emotions from their original object to another, is the primary psychological defense found among police officers. For example, an officer who is fearful and angry about a situation of violence and danger may repress these feelings in order to function effectively, and later on take out the anger on someone or some situation which has nothing to do with the original occasion. One's family, colleagues or even oneself may become the target for these displaced feelings. Internalization, i.e., making oneself the target of displaced anger, often results in irrational self-denigration, depression, unreasonable guilt, and even suicidal impulses. Such stresses may result in burnout, the symptoms of which include boredom, cynicism, fatigue, bitterness, and loss of values. Dealing with burnout requires some distancing from the demands of one's work, rest, and an opportunity to regain some sense of reward from the work itself. Both burnout and displacement often find expression in financial difficulties, family conflict, divorce, and alcoholism.

4. Pastoral Response. Police chaplaincy work is to a great extent a ministry of listening, and may allow simple ventilation on the part of officers, or demand more sophisticated pastoral care and counseling. At times, care also entails referral to a specialist. A police chaplain is also an advocate for and supplier of continuing education for officers and their families on topics ranging from child abuse or grief response to family communication counseling. The chaplain may visit sick members of the police department and sometimes assist at funerals.

Visibility and accessibility may be the police chaplain's most difficult problem. Upon consent of the officers involved, chaplains may accompany police in patrol cars, allowing them to experience police work directly and demonstrate their solidarity with police officers. Otherwise, chaplains are available in department headquarters, at special departmental functions, or are on call for emergencies.

The ambiguities of the police chaplain's position, between the institutions of law enforcement and those of religion, require that she or he both identify with the realistic "street values" of police officers and also hold to the values of faith. While this can enable and support the distance that is required and appropriate for a chaplain in a listening ministry, it may also occasionally bring about a conflict of values when a chaplain needs to take a more prophetic stance as moral guide. Thus, the chaplain's chief concern must be compassion, for there is a unique kind of suffering involved in police work which calls for a caring, compassionate pastoral friend in the person of the chaplain.

In theological terms, it is thus the task of the police chaplain to name the conflict of good and evil, restore an eschatological vision of hope and reconciliation, and help the officer to realize the value of both protecting the innocent and the weak and defending the structure and order of society. The chaplain reminds others of the equality of all persons before God and their consequent right to equal respect.

Bibliography. R. Baldwin, *Inside a Cop* (1977). W. Haynes, Stress Related Disorders in Policemen (1978). W. Lyons, "A Family Recruit Program for the Anne Arundel Co. Police Department Introducing the Problem of Stress and Resultant Anxiety in the Police Officer," D. Min. thesis, Drew University (1981). T. Norton, "The Police Chaplaincy, a Ministry of Listening," D. Min. thesis, Drew University (1983).

H. E. KENNEDY
A. R. OSTROM
E. SPRINGMAN

CHAPLAINCY. *Compare* MILITARY SERVICE AND MILITARY CHAPLAINCY.

POLITICAL DIMENSIONS OF PASTORAL CARE. *See* AUTHORITY; ECCLESIOLOGY; LIBERATION THEOLOGY; POWER; SOCIAL JUSTICE ISSUES; SOCIOLOGY OF RELIGIOUS AND PASTORAL CARE.

POLTERGEIST. *See* PARAPSYCHOLOGY; SURVIVAL (Occult).

POND, ENOCH (1791–1882). American Congregationalist pastor and pastoral theologian at Bangor Theological Seminary.

He represented the early American pastoral theology tradition, which offered practical advice about preaching, public worship, marriages, funerals, revivals, and reform. But his *The Young Pastor's Guide* (1844) emphasized also the minister's "more *private* intercourse" with parishioners. He encouraged pastors to become adept at visitation and in small groups, to keep written notes on their visits, and to learn to classify the variety of spiritual conditions in order to respond appropriately.

E. B. HOLIFIELD

PASTORAL THEOLOGY, PROTESTANT.

POOR PERSONS. (Lat. — *pauper*; Heb. — *anaveem*; Gk. — *Ptōchos*; Span. — *Los Pobres*). A class of people of any age and in any country, designated as living below a certain set of visible and spiritual standards. Historically, there have always been persons who were destitute and considered part of the "underclass" (D. Moynihan). Slaves, indentured servants, the uneducated, beggars, the unemployed, the racial and ethnic minorities, the unmotivated, the dependent, the helpless, the indigent, the handicapped, the elderly, and those who need financial assistance from others such as the state and/or federal government to survive. The poor are not confined by geography, race, or sex. Poverty cuts across and transcends all lines of definition. There are the collective poor, the situational poor, and the individual poor.

Collective poor are those considered to be of a certain group with certain common traits such as the black poor; the Appalachian poor; the unemployed; the migrant workers. Anyone who lives below an economic level and whose lifestyle limits him or her from moving away from the group can be viewed as part of the collective poor. For example, in the U.S. there are twenty million persons who are termed "functionally illiterate" which means their future is bleak and their hopes are limited. They are confined within the framework of poverty.

Situational poor are those who become poor at a certain time and because of situations over which they have or had little control. For example, the worldwide depression caused significant poverty, the results of which were reflected in the lives of certain individuals. Other situational poor would include substance abuse victims, the chronically mentally ill, the criminal offender, dependent children, and other persons who have experienced semi-permanent hardships, resulting in the loss of income, loss of expectancy, and the loss of hope.

Individual poor are those persons who lack the ability to obtain the basic necessities for survival at any given time or place. An individual who is poor becomes poor whenever earnings are not regular or substantial enough to purchase food, clothing, and shelter.

While being poor has long been a common experience of human beings, in a wealthy society the state of being poor is a contradiction. Poverty is a degrading and harsh event for those who are caught in its vice. One of the problems in examining the poor is that it is difficult to know how many poor people there are in any area at any time. Statistics are not absolute because someone is being born into a poor condition daily.

The poor in the U.S. may be seen as having some general formula. A person runs the risk of being poor if the following conditions apply: (1) He or she is non-white, (2) belongs to a family of non-earners, (3) belongs to a female-headed household, (4) belongs to a family of more than four persons, (5) is between fourteen and twenty-five or over sixty, (6) lives in a populous urban area or a deprived rural area, (7) has a minimal education.

The poor live in specific geographic areas. In a 1968 survey fifteen percent of the poor lived on farms and twenty-five percent lived in the inner cities. The rest of the poor—sixty percent live in rural non-farm areas and in the outlying areas of large cities.

Pastoral care and counseling with the poor is a call for a special challenge and opportunity. Jesus announced in the Gospel of Luke that he was anointed to "preach the gospel to the poor." This statement and the ones that follow in Lk. 4:16–21 are an adaptation of Isaiah 61. There is a theological concern for the poor getting out of their condition both from the OT's point of view and from that of the NT. It was continued into the early church when a dispute was settled between the Jewish Christian leaders (Peter, James, and others) and the Apostle Paul and his followers who were evangelizing the Gentiles. In Gal. 2:9–10, it is recorded that the two opposing camps agreed to "remember the poor."

Preaching the gospel to the poor suggests that pastors and pastoral counselors think through their own attitudes and feelings toward the poor. If the gospel is "good news" and preaching and pastoral care are functions of the ministry, then pastoral care and preaching may need to take on the form of liberation theology, a theology that seeks to free the poor from their bondage and release them from their "stigmata" of helplessness, dependency, and hopelessness.

The traditional European-American style of counseling may or may not liberate the poor. If tradition means, as is often suggested, acceptance of the situation as it is, then other methodologies should be considered. Such methods of counseling as behavioral therapy, motivational therapy, educational counseling, Gestalt therapy and action-directed counseling may be more helpful and may get the poor

actualized and energized for goal-directed and hope-oriented plans to alleviate their suffering.

Pastoral counselors and pastoral caregivers may need to see themselves as educator/mentor counselors to the poor. It should be clear to the pastoral counselor that poverty, or "being poor" is not an acceptable way of life, except as a chosen religious vocation. The goal of pastoral counseling with the poor is to empower the poor with changed attitudes about God, about themselves as people of God, and about their circumstances.

Poor people probably have the same dreams as other people. However, these dreams get repressed, denied, and deferred. Pastoral care and counseling should take on the form of dream resurrection, dream nurturance, and dream fulfillment. For example, in a tenement housing development in St. Louis, Missouri, pastoral care took on the form of Gestalt counseling. A group of concerned persons transformed the blighted area. After ten years, the *U. S. News and World Report* magazine (August 4, 1986) reported that "the secret of the Cochran Public Housing Project is re-education—we changed people's attitudes."

Appalachia has its share of the poor, primarily "poor whites." The U. S. government spent five billion dollars within twenty years in an effort to change the poverty situation. The geographic, economic, and cultural isolation spans thirteen states and suffers all the indignities listed in the studies as bondage factors: economic hardships, hopelessness and helplessness. A poor resident is reported to have said, "We don't have an easy time here. I don't like this place . . . but I guess I'll be here til I die." The mountain areas of Appalachia have a fifty percent school dropout rate and one third of the people are functionally illiterate — a mark of poverty. Teenagers account for one out of five pregnancies in Kentucky and in 1983 Kentucky had the highest rate of births to white teenagers in the country. Poverty cuts across racial and cultural lines. Poverty is no respecter of persons. Children born into mountain poverty find it equally hard to escape as do children born into an inner city environment.

In working as a counselor with the poor one should expect hesitation and resistance (C. Kemp). The reasons for this resistance are: (1) distrust of the helping persons; (2) lack of patience; (3) need for immediate gratification; (4) poor educational background; (5) pessimism about the future; and (6) disvaluation of goal-directed plans. The poor have varying degrees of motivation and may have difficulty using traditional structures of counseling. The pastoral caregiver needs to be aware of these dynamics and work within the framework of the poor person's world view.

Traditional counseling modalities are generally seen as "middle-class," primarily of an unreachable value system and offered to those who can pay a consistent and long-term fee for the service of "talking." Pastors who serve inner city parishes . . . may discover that "methods and goals of pastoral counseling are usually ineffective with people suffering from the pains of poverty" (H. Clinebell).

The pastoral counselor or pastoral caregiver will need to make some alterations and some modifications in counseling procedures including time, fees, process, and methods. Pastoral presence is acutely important to the poor. It becomes a part of "incarnational theology" associated with liberation theology—a theology of action and location. The *praxis* of pastoral care and counseling should not be confined to a designated office space. It should be flexible, mobile, and need-focused. It takes a dedicated caregiver with a willingness to reach out and go "the second mile," in order to work creatively, meaningfully, and relevantly with the class of people in our societies classified as "the poor."

Bibliography. H. J. Clinebell, *Community Mental Health: The Role of the Church and Temple* (1970). P. Freire, *Pedagogy of the Oppressed* (1970). M. Harrington, *The Other America: Poverty in the United States* (1962). C. F. Kemp, *Pastoral Care with the Poor* (1972). R. L. Kinast, "The Pastoral Care of Society as Liberation," *J. of Pastoral Care* (1980). G. Seldes, *The Great Quotations* (1967). A. Simon, *Faces of Poverty* (1968). H. Thurman, *Jesus and the Disinherited* (1959). E. P. Wimberly and A. S. Wimberly, *Liberation and Human Wholeness* (1986).

G. POLK

SOCIAL SERVICES AND PASTORAL CARE; SOCIAL STATUS AND CLASS FACTORS; HOMELESS PERSONS. *See also* ADVOCACY; EXPLOITATION/OPPRESSION; PROPHETIC/PASTORAL TENSION; SOCIAL JUSTICE ISSUES. *Compare* LIBERATION THEOLOGY AND PASTORAL CARE; RICH PERSONS.

POPULAR THERAPEUTIC MOVEMENTS AND PSYCHOLOGIES. New therapies and personal growth methodologies have proliferated and gained widespread popularity in the U.S. and, to a lesser extent, in other Western countries, since the mid-1940s. This dynamic social phenomenon, and the cultural forces that feed it, have profound implications for pastoral care and counseling, as well as for ministry and organized religion in general. These popular psychologies and therapies offer pastoral care and counseling many useful, though potentially hazardous, resources for enhancing the ministry of care and counseling.

1. The Variety of Movements. Popular therapeutic movements in contemporary society are abundant and varied. New approaches are constantly emerging, enjoying a "time in the sun" of popular interest and then declining, to be supplanted in the popular imagination by other "in" psychologies and therapies. In the 1940s and 1950s, psychoanalysis was a popular therapeutic movement whose theories influenced our culture's thinking, self-understanding, and language (as evidenced by the widespread though often inaccurate use of terms such as "repression," "sublimate," "neurotic," "phobia," etc.). The same has been true to a lesser degree of the Jungian and the Adlerian schools of therapy. The Freudian and Jungian therapies are examples of theories of personality and methodologies that have been widely used by many therapists long before and after the peaking of their popularity in the wider society.

Some of the newer therapies that have attracted sizable followings and, to some extent, generated "movements," are: Eric Berne's Transactional Analysis; Fritz Perls's Gestalt Therapy; the body therapies, including Alexander Lowen's bioenergetics; and Ida Rolf's Structural Integration ("Rolfing"); the human potentials psychologies and growth approaches derived from them (reflected in the Association of Humanistic Psychology); the transpersonal therapies that focus on the spiritual dimension of

therapy with strong Eastern influences; the cognitive therapies, including Albert Ellis's RET (Rational Emotive Therapy); William Glasser's Reality Therapy; various self-help crisis approaches; behavioral and learning theory therapies, including systematic desensitization, aversion therapy, operant conditioning, and a variety of do-it-yourself approaches derived therefrom; the radical therapies, including feminist therapy; EST (Erhard's Seminar Training by Werner Erhard); Arthur Janov's Primal Therapy; rebirthing therapy; the art therapies, including dance therapy and poetry therapy; psychodrama (Joseph Moreno); hypnotherapy, including self-hypnosis; meditation therapy and Transcendental Meditation; biofeedback therapy; relaxation and imaging methods of healing and therapy; co-counseling (Harvey Jackin); a wide variety of group therapies and growth group approaches (including the encounter group and National Training Lab movements, and the widespread networks of self-help/growth groups, such as Alcoholics Anonymous and the many other group approaches modeled on AA); various marriage enrichment programs, of which Marriage Encounter is the most widespread.

2. The Cultural Context. The sociological revolution that has generated popular therapeutic movements like flowers in a spring meadow was described in the 1960s by sociologist Philip Rieff as "the triumph of the therapeutic." This term referred to the emergence of "psychological man" (*sic*) as the dominant character type of the twentieth century. The increasingly pervasive influence of psychoanalytic thought was the dominant factor in producing this profound metamorphosis in our culture. In the surge of interest in psychology following the World War I, and the greater flowering of psychology, counseling, and psychotherapy during and after the World War II, psychological and psychotherapeutic categories and modes of thinking have reshaped the corporate identity of our society. The seeds of all manner of psychological theories and movements have taken root and flourished in the receptive soil of contemporary Western culture.

In Rieff's interpretation these changes represented a process of "deconversion" from a culture in which religious categories drawn primarily from the Judeo-Christian faith shaped, at deep levels of psychic life, the dominant self-understanding of most persons. The gradual decline in power of this century-spanning religious identity has left a sociocultural vacuum. The new identity based in psychological theories is the most common means of seeking to fill this lacuna. It is within this new cultural identity that individuals form their personal identities and organize their world of experience to give it meaning. The plethora of psychological theories and therapies, and the popular movements growing up around them, are expressions of this basic transformation of our culture's guiding images and beliefs. These movements are perceived by their disciples as offering paths to the ideal human condition of well-being—secular, psychological paths to salvation.

3. Characteristics. Although there are many methodological and anthropological differences among the popular psychotherapies, the vast majority of them share certain characteristics that are potentially problematic:

(1) They focus primarily or exclusively on individual healing and well-being, deemphasizing or ignoring the sources of individual sickness or health that may be found in the social context (the radical and feminist therapies being striking exceptions).

(2) They tend to be highly optimistic in their view of the human situation and the possibilities of self-help, emphasizing the accessibility of well-being to those who take the initiative in using the recommended self-care or self-cure methods. They, however, also place a healthy emphasis on personal responsibility.

(3) They flow, in many cases, from the seminal thought and writings (frequently in best-selling books) of a creative theoretician-therapist, who is perceived as a kind of therapeutic guru by those who become disciples and thus generate a "movement."

(4) The "true believers" tend to regard their approach as *the* most effective path to wholeness, ignoring or favorably comparing themselves to older, more established therapies, while ignoring their debt to these therapies. Often they highlight their distinctiveness by creating neologisms to describe their understanding of personality and therapy. There often is a strong in-group awareness that approaches a cult-like mentality in some movements.

4. **Evaluation and Appropriation.** In spite of their problematic characteristics, many of these therapeutic schools or movements have produced valuable insights about human personality and innovative therapeutic methods that are valuable resources for counselors, therapists, and educators, including counseling pastors and pastoral counseling specialists.

In deciding how to use resources from any psychology or therapeutic movement, it is important for those who do counseling and therapy with a Judeo-Christian orientation to evaluate these psychologies and therapies from a theological perspective. This means examining their assumptions about the nature of persons and human transformation in light of the Judeo-Christian understanding of the human situation and the role of the Divine in healing and wholeness. In using resources from popular contemporary therapies, it is important also to critique them from the perspective of the depth psychologies and psychodynamic therapies and from the perspective of radical, feminist, and social-systems therapies.

From the perspectives of the Judeo-Christian heritage and the systemic and radical therapies, the hyperindividualism and the exclusive emphasis on enhancing personal consciousness in many popular therapies must be balanced by an equally robust emphasis on enhancing relationships and changing social systems. The tendency to psychologize societal and institutional problems needs to be corrected by emphasizing the prophetic dimension of pastoral care and counseling. This involves recognizing the social-economic-political context of all individual problems and, therefore, the need to include in counseling the goal of empowerment for changing relationships and oppressive systems.

The overly optimistic view of human beings and their transformation must be corrected and balanced by the kind of realism about human evil and resistance to constructive change found in both the Judeo-Christian view of persons and in the depth psychologies and the psycho-

analytically oriented therapies. The appropriate emphasis on the importance and effectiveness of self-help methods, found in many popular therapies, needs to be balanced and complemented by a clear awareness of the need for professional therapeutic expertise in resolving some types of problems. The emphasis on the capacity of the conscious mind to effect desired changes must be balanced by a realistic awareness of the limitations and difficulties of this process as illuminated by ego psychology and depth psychology's understanding of the power of the unconscious mind.

A strong case can be made for the view that the most effective counselors, therapists, and educators are those who draw selectively on various psychologies and therapies to develop a pattern of integrated eclecticism in their theory and methodology, an eclecticism that utilizes their own unique personality resources. To use creatively the rich resources that are available in many of the popular psychologies and therapies it is important also to avoid the exclusivistic mentality that characterizes some of these movements. Furthermore, it is essential to use a comprehensive understanding of personality (e.g., drawn from depth psychology or learning theory) as a core around which these resources are utilized in a coherent manner.

Through the centuries pastors have drawn on the popular psychologies of their day, adapting them by exposing them to the light of the Judeo-Christian wisdom, and then using them in the ministry of pastoral care. The unprecedented richness of the resources from the wealth of psychologies and therapies in our day makes the continuation of this practice a particularly vital way of strengthening and enriching our work with hurting, burdened, wholeness-seeking people.

Bibliography. H. Clinebell, *Contemporary Growth Therapies* (1981). L. Bregman, *The Rediscovery of Inner Experience* (1982). R. A. Harper, *The New Psychotherapies* (1975). J. Kovel, *A Complete Guide to Therapy* (1976). R. D. Rosen, *Psychobabble* (1977). P. Rieff, *The Triumph of the Therapeutic* (1966). E. Schur, *The Awareness Trap, Self-Absorption Instead of Social Change* (1976).

H. CLINEBELL

PSYCHOLOGY IN AMERICAN RELIGION; PSYCHOTHERAPY; SOCIOLOGY OF RELIGIOUS AND PASTORAL CARE. *For specific popular psychologies see:* ADJUNCTIVE THERAPIES; ASSERTIVENESS TRAINING AND THERAPY; BEHAVIOR THERAPIES; BIOFEEDBACK; BODY THERAPIES; ENCOUNTER GROUPS; FEMINIST THERAPY; GESTALT PSYCHOLOGY; GROUP COUNSELING AND PSYCHOTHERAPY; GROWTH GROUPS; HUMAN RELATIONS TRAINING; HUMANISTIC PSYCHOLOGY; HYPNOSIS; MARRIAGE ENCOUNTER *or* ENRICHMENT; MEDITATION; PRIMAL THERAPY; RATIONAL-EMOTIVE PSYCHOTHERAPY; REALITY THERAPY; RELAXATION; SELF-HELP PSYCHOLOGIES; SPIRITUAL PSYCHOLOGIES; SUPPORT GROUPS; TRANSACTIONAL ANALYSIS; TRANSPERSONAL PSYCHOLOGIES.

PORNOGRAPHY. A term denoting "that which exploits and dehumanises sex, so that human beings are treated as things, and women in particular as sex objects" (Longford). Research supports the value of this restrictive definition, rather than "anything sexually explicit." Explicit sex may be presented educationally or to arouse sexual desire (erotica) without denying its humanness.

Criteria for pornography change with time and across cultures because pornography challenges social taboos. By violating taboos for a given society, sexual gratification can be generated among those willing to see others as sex objects. While erotica can generate tenderness and love in a sexual context, pornography requires a victim, either explicitly, as in physically aggressive portrayals, or more subtly in the messages conveyed about relationships and sex roles.

Pornography characteristically aims at a male market, exploiting women and children in its intentional promotion of lust. While many suppose it may overcome unhealthy sexual inhibitions, scientific evidence fails to confirm any personal or social benefits, while indicating a development of dangerously disinhibited behavior and calloused attitudes (Malamuth, 1984).

In the early 1970's, it was widely publicized that pornography is benign or beneficial. Following a massive increase in its availability, and the appearance of new forms (e.g., violent and child pornography), further research has shown the earlier optimism to be misplaced (Scott, 1986).

The development of a social insensitivity to sexual violence against women has been linked to pornography by scientific evidence and by the women's movement. Its addictive attraction and its negative impact on marriage is widely recognized.

With its widespread dissemination and efforts to achieve glossy respectability, pornography was estimated to be a five-billion-dollar business in the U.S. in 1982. Instead of being a fringe influence on society, its values are increasingly absorbed, especially through technological developments such as cable TV and videocassettes.

The counselor can expect to find pornography to be a significant factor in shaping the sexual mores and attitudes of teenagers, usurping healthy development with disturbing deviant themes. In adult life, in marriage, men may turn hopefully to pornography for novelty, often with negative consequences for their wives, while the lonely or angry single male often feeds his imagination on pornographic materials, only to increase his alienation. Several lines of evidence show that in many sex crimes, pornography has been among the triggering influences — especially in relation to rape (Court, 1984).

While the Supreme Court has refused to give it First Amendment protection, pornography still flourishes, with strong commercial and ideological support, thereby becoming entrenched against legal or moral opposition.

A solid moral stance in response to pornography has been made difficult due to problems of clear definition, its changing expression, and the difficulties among religious groups in expressing a coherent moral position over public representations of sexuality. Rational evaluation requires the following features to be considered.

Pornography is nihilistic and reductionist, focusing sexual desire at the level of lust. It promotes sexual activity as behavior regardless of relationship; it ridicules love and marriage, while promoting promiscuity.

It denies humanness. Preoccupied with anatomy, it reduces sex to the level of animal copulation. It is outstandingly chauvinistic, degrading and humiliating of women, and treating them as disposable objects for male gratification. It also challenges the taboos against child sexual abuse and incest.

Pornography is paradoxically anti-sex, robbing it of its privacy and intimacy. It has become antisocial by overturning relationships of trust. Violent pornography especially glorifies the violation of others, physically and sexually, with impunity.

By its desensitizing pervasiveness, pornography has made people less sensitive to the heinous character of sexual offences, and it even raises the threshold of willingness to commit such offences (Malamuth and Donnerstein, 1984).

Bibliography. J. H. Court, *Pornography: A Christian Critique* (1980). Lord Longford, *Pornography: The Longford Report* (1972). N. Malamuth and E. Donnerstein, eds., *Pornography and Sexual Aggression* (1984). Especially good sources are: J. H. Court, "Sex and Violence," and N. Malamuth, "Aggression Against Women: Cultural and Individual Causes," D. A. Scott, "How Pornography Changes Attitudes," in T. Minnery, ed., *Pornography: A Human Tragedy* (1986).

J. H. COURT

SEXISM; VIOLENCE; VICTIMIZATION. *Compare* EXPLOITATION/ OPPRESSION; PROFANE LANGUAGE; SEXUAL VARIETY, DEVIANCE, AND DISORDER.

POSITIVE REGARD. *See* CLIENT-CENTERED THERAPY; THERAPEUTIC CONDITIONS.

POSITIVE THINKING. *See* MIND-CURE MOVEMENT.

POSITIVISM. *See* PHILOSOPHY AND PSYCHOLOGY; THEORY AND PRAXIS.

POSSESSION, SPIRIT. *See* CHARISMATIC EXPERIENCE; CULTURAL ANTHROPOLOGY OF RELIGION, DISCIPLINE OF; EXORCISM.

POSSIBILITY THINKING. *See* MIND-CURE MOVEMENT.

POSTPARTUM PSYCHOSIS. *See* CHILDBIRTH.

POST-TRAUMATIC STRESS DISORDER. An anxiety disorder characterized by a pattern of symptoms attributable to the experience of a traumatic event. The symptoms of PTSD include (1) reexperiencing of the traumatic event, (2) emotional numbing, and (3) any of a variety of autonomic, cognitive, or behavioral symptoms. PTSD can occur at any age. While preexisting psychopathology appears to enhance the likelihood of developing PTSD, even otherwise well-adjusted individuals may develop this disorder following a major trauma. Symptoms may begin immediately following the trauma or may not emerge until months or even years later. Natural disasters such as earthquakes or floods may produce PTSD, as well as human actions, both those that are *accidental* (e.g., airplane crashes, major traffic accidents) and those *deliberately* inflicted (e.g., rape, incest, military combat, concentration camps). Although the adverse and persistent psychological influence of traumatic events has been recognized in the past, it was the frequency of these symptoms among Vietnam combat veterans that led to its formal identification as a disorder.

1. **Symptoms.** The traumatic event may be reexperienced in a number of ways that vary in intensity. At a minimum, recurrent, intrusive, and painful recollections of the event are present; recurrent dreams related to the event are also common. Less frequently, an individual may experience dissociative-like states, lasting from a few minutes to several days, during which the traumatic event is vividly relived. Such "flashbacks" appear to be more common in combat veterans than in survivors of other intense, stressful experiences. These flashbacks may superficially resemble hallucinations but can be distinguished from hallucinations by their link with an actual historical event as well as by the individual's awareness that they are not a present reality. During these episodes the person may behave unpredictably; violent outbursts occur in some cases.

The emotional numbing of PTSD usually begins soon after the traumatic event and may be marked by diminished interest in once-valued activities, decreased interpersonal involvement, and impairment of the ability to feel emotions of any kind. In particular, an individual may report difficulty experiencing tender, intimate feelings; sexual desire may be impaired as well.

A variety of psychophysiological, cognitive, and behavioral symptoms may occur in PTSD. Autonomic symptoms include sleep disturbances and hyperalertness or an exaggerated startle response and may contribute to a diminished sense of personal control. There also may be difficulties with concentration and memory. A preoccupation with themes of guilt is often associated with PTSD, often concerning behaviors that had been necessary for survival, or perhaps regarding personal survival when others perished. Behaviorally, PTSD may be expressed by the avoidance of activities reminiscent of the traumatic event, or an intensification of symptoms during unavoidable participation in such activities.

2. **Treatment and Prognosis.** Given the complex range of PTSD symptomatology, a successful treatment program will address not only the emotional issues that characterize the disorder but also its psychophysiological, cognitive, and interpersonal processes and existential meanings. First, an assessment of psychophysiological function should be conducted and treatment of autonomic symptoms considered. This is important not only in order to obtain symptomatic relief, but so that the individual can begin to reestablish a sense of personal, physical control. A variety of well-established relaxation techniques exist which are likely to be effective in reducing the autonomic arousal associated with the experience of anxiety.

It is essential that the individual have the opportunity to ventilate his or her feelings about the traumatic event. Only after a thorough and emphatically accepting exploration of such feelings should cognitive distortions regarding responsibility and guilt in relation to the traumatic event be addressed. Cognitive restructuring strategies are often helpful at this point; for Christian counselees who have approached clergy for help, a pastoral and biblical perspective on God's grace in extremity can inform such therapeutic cognitive restructuring. In particular, inappropriate perceptions are common regarding personal culpability and guilt, as well as concerning the uselessness and risk of interpersonal relationship. Such perceptions can be powerfully countered for Christian counselees by making sensitive therapeutic use of their religious beliefs.

The promotion of adaptive social behaviors should be an important aspect of treatment as well. Research on the severity of PTSD symptomatology in Vietnam veterans has noted the negative influence of socially isolating patterns of behavior in conjunction with correspondingly minimal levels of social support. This research underscores the clinical importance of assessing social network functioning and the counselee's ability to elicit appropriate supportive resources. If social skills training and/or increased social involvement is indicated, selective participation in the varied activities of a church community may become an important part of an overall treatment plan.

In its milder forms, PTSD may be ameliorated by supportive pastoral counseling, although careful consideration should be given to each symptom area as described above. In more severe cases of this disorder, collaboration with or referral to a mental health professional experienced in treating PTSD is advisable.

The prognosis for an individual with PTSD depends on a variety of factors, including the presence of physical injury secondary to the traumatic event as well as pre-existing or concurrent psychopathology. When symptoms of PTSD become evident within six months of the trauma and are of less than six months' duration (PTSD, acute subtype), the prognosis is generally better than when symptoms emerge more than six months following the trauma (PTSD, delayed subtype) or when the symptoms are of greater than six months' duration (PTSD, chronic subtype).

Bibliography. American Psychiatric Association, *Diagnostic and Statistical Manual* 3d. ed. rev. (1987). R. J. Lifton, *Death in Life* (1976).

N. C. BROWN

CRISIS MINISTRY; SURVIVOR PSYCHOLOGY; TRAUMA; VICTIMIZATION. *See also* HOLOCAUST; RELAXATION, PSYCHOLOGY AND TECHNIQUES OF; STRESS AND STRESS MANAGEMENT.

POVERTY. *See* EXPLOITATION AND OPPRESSION; HOMELESS PERSONS; SOCIAL STATUS AND CLASS FACTORS; POOR PERSONS. *See also* RELIGIOUS LIFE.

POWER. The ability to act or to be acted upon. A psychologically, socially, philosophically, and morally necessary part of our personal and social experiences, it is also open to great abuse.

Awareness of the fact of power has existed since ancient times. Anthropologists sometimes named it "Mana" (Melanesia), but it has more generally been referred to as *magic* (Malinowski, 1954). Almost all religions impute power to the gods, to priests, events, and social relationships (Schmidt).

The Greeks, especially Aristotle, both contributed to and spawned a long and rich tradition of political thinkers, foremost among them Locke, Hobbes, Rousseau,

Hume, and the amazingly clear and pragmatic approach to power by Machiavelli in *The Prince*.

A more variegated understanding of power has emerged in recent social science, particularly with Comte, Spencer, Sumner, Ward, and especially Gumplowics through his idea of *domination*. Political scientists focused mainly on power in the process of government (the distribution of power) while sociology was concerned with interpersonal and institutional power, and psychology has focused on subjective feelings and dynamics (McClelland, Winter).

Institutional settings such as politics (McClelland) are one area in which power is particularly prominent. Among ideological systems, Marx's is premised on classes and power domination. "The proletarians have nothing to lose but their chains. They have a world to win" (*Communist Manifesto*). Another powerful system is Freudian psychoanalysis, which projects societal power in the form of the superego over the "normal" expression of the self (Brown). Other systems, such as Buddhism, emphasize the renunciation of desire, which includes the desire for power.

1. Definition of Power. (1) *Physical power* (might) is the ability of one agent to act upon another object, or the ability to be acted upon (Aristotle, *Metaphysics*, viii. ix. I). (2) The *psychological* definition of power almost always slips into discussions of "Social Power" (Raven). McClelland states that the psychological function of power is "to feel stronger" either by "strengthening myself" (Stage I, 1975), or being strengthened by others (Stage II). Stages III and IV are actually sociological power which have as their object the influence of others.

(3) The generally accepted *sociological definition*, is "Power *(Macht)* is the probability that one actor within a social relationship will be in a position to carry out his own will despite resistance, regardless of the basis on which the probability rests" (Weber, p. 152). This definition has been shortened to: "the determination of the behavior of others in accordance with one's own ends."

The sociological approaches to power have included *magnitude* (how much?), *scope* (how broad is the power?), the *domain* (in which areas does the person have power?), *distribution* (who has power?) and the *permanence* of power (how long does the person retain power?).

2. Bases of Power. The controller has power when he or she (1) has information needed by the controllee (information power); (2) can punish the controllee if he does not respond positively (coercion); (3) can provide rewards which the controllee desires (reward); (4) has the *right* to demand responses. This right derives from political, religious, economic or other type of institutional status (Weber's legal and traditional types of authority); (5) is able to move others by virtue of personality or psychological factors (charisma); (6) can expose or otherwise embarrass the controllee so that the social costs of noncompliance are too great (blackmail).

Institutionalized class power derives from group or class membership. An illustration would be the poor and impoverished in Latin America. The impersonality of this kind of power, also exemplified in the modern corporation and state, makes the question of justice and ethics of power very complex (Tillich, vol. 3). Some ethicists in fact claim that organizations cannot act morally (Ladd). This perspective

helps explain how individuals in institutional or political structures (e.g., Nazi Germany) could use power in the most brutal ways with seeming impunity.

3. Forms of Power. (1) *Coercion* is compliance achieved by physical means, either potential (threats to hurt, shoot, maim, etc.) or kinetic, actually carrying out the threats. However, there is power on both sides, because the recipient of coercion has the power to resist being acted upon (Aristotle).

(2) *Manipulation* is achieving the conscious or unconscious compliance of the controllee through forces which do not involve physical means (or threats).

(3) *Influence* and *domination* are forms, where the controllees are in varying degrees able and willing to be influenced or dominated. Influence by advertising is an example.

(4) *Authority* is power which is recognized as legitimate by the controllee(s) and can involve voluntary or eager compliance (cf. Tolstoy's account of the French armies under Napoleon, *War and Peace*).

4. The Motivation for Power. The drive to power has been assumed to be universal (Adler; Tillich, vol. 3, pp. 350 ff.), and many philosophers have built systems on the desire for power (Machiavelli, Nietzsche, Carlyle, Bismarck, Marx, etc.). Newborn babies and the handicapped and weak usually have power in societies which have developed a "humane" moral system.

Psychologically, the drive for power has developed numerous theories — compensatory theories, frustration theories, fear of weakness, deprivation theories, neurotic needs, and others. Obtaining power has normally been assumed to result in desired status, but self-denial of power and giving of self to others (altruistic love) has helped to confound these theories (Sorokin).

Most theories of psychological power drives basically transform into sociological motivations where power is a means of achieving some form of advantage or status with significant others. But basic forms of power motivations are institutionalized value systems which place highest prestige on certain forms of domination through wealth, property rights, status allocations, political position, etc.

5. Theories of the Consequences of Power. One of the most abiding sociological concerns has been the relative or absolute powerlessness of societal classes. Numerous scholars have stated that anomie results from powerlessness —not having the power to influence or direct one's own life in any sense (Marx; Mills; Moore).

a. Psychologically. "Power asymmetry" has produced a number of theories. In Freudian psychoanalytic thought, the individual is caught in an irreconcilable conflict between his instincts and social restrictions, especially sex inhibitions, but above all the power of death (Brown, p. 81). Neo-Freudians of various persuasions have focused on the neuroses and psychoses resulting from the frustration of drives, dynamics, needs, and urges, etc. (Sullivan; Maslow; Erikson). Maslow's "self actualization" theory, for example, is an attempt to bypass this power vacuum.

Psychological therapy systems themselves assume a lack of power to achieve the "reality principle" (Freud). To work through or around guilt, repression, or self-defeating neuroses and psychoses demands outside assistance — the therapist. Psychotherapy, in its various forms, is a culturally defined way to assist individuals (and groups) to achieve inner states which they lack the power to achieve by themselves (Brown, p. 246).

b. Social power. Psychologists have realized that individual neuroses and psychoses are often socially and culturally determined (May; Fromm). Social scientists have long assumed that power in society is asymmetrical —some individuals are vested with more power than others. This asymmetry is presumed to reflect the evolutionary process of developing statuses with rights and obligations—which is a central element or factor in social order without which a society could not exist (Maduro; Marx; Moore).

Asymmetry of power is a necessary fact of social life. But when a challenge to the distribution of power emerges, social structure is changed. For example, women's power has been asymmetrical in most cultures (Pescatello). In relatively recent times, women are demanding and achieving more power. To be equal, or to be considered a fellow human being demands the source of that equality and humanness, which *includes* power. To be human and social means possession and exercise of power by *everyone* (Tillich). The really interesting question is why power asymmetries have developed, become accepted, and why they have not been challenged. Sociology, especially, has been evasive of this fact, and Marxist and critical sociology have alerted us.

One final locus of asymmetry involves the domination and subordination of ethnic groups, cultures and nation-states. Liberation from oppression is a modern password for the desire of small groups and weak nations to achieve freedom from oppression and to develop their own autonomy (Moore).

Cultural asymmetry refers to the way in which some cultural systems overpower others ("cultural determinism," Malinowski, 1961, p. 64 ff.)

6. The Ethics of Power. Most systems of power analysis do not address the central moral and ethical issue: "How and when is power used correctly?" But it is the moral-ethical dimensions of power which seem to have the best potential for solving personal, interpersonal, institutional, and political problems of power. Thus the discussion of power remains largely academic which is probably why society(ies) have not been able to solve issues such as the military arms race which is threatening at this point to misuse power in a final, blasphemous, and obscene cataclysm. (This personal analysis of the ethics of power derives from a Christian value and moral system, and more specifically an Anabaptist-Mennonite one.)

a. Personal misuse of power. A person can misuse power by suppressing legitimate urges and desires; he can also demand more of himself than he is able to achieve. The former is expressed in unnecessary guilt or self-condemnation for his own acts and desires, the latter in self-denigration for failure to achieve goals or objectives. More obvious misuses of power include obsessive actions toward self-enhancement and self-service which, when expressed in overt manner, conflict with social norms and become social misuse of power (Erikson).

One dimension which has not been fully developed in psychotherapy is the misuse of the power *not to be acted upon.* The contemporary scientific paradigms which focus on causality may be downgrading the other side of power (Aristotle)—"other directed" in distinction to "inner direction" (e.g., Riessman). The Christian religion, however, refers to this as "resisting the devil," "temptation," or "not letting the world squeeze one into its mold." Christianity has maintained the idea of the "responsible individual" who is in charge of his or her life, and who has a "free will." Psychology, along with psychotherapy, has tended to deny that humans have the power to be in charge of their actions, and has rather assumed that behavior is caused by forces outside a person. This has had the profound consequence of encouraging people to *believe* that they are powerless victims of their environments. But if power is by definition two-faced—on the one side the ability to exert force, and on the other, the ability to resist force—then individuals are never powerless. "We are suspicious of the very word 'instinct'; it suggests an unalterable biological datum, and therefore seems to deny man the power to alter himself. . ." (Brown, p. 77). According to Christian belief, what a person is emotionally, sexually, etc., is to a degree within his or her own power to decide.

b. The social misuse of power. The social misuse of social power is ultimately based on a moral or value system which stipulates what is correct social behavior. In the case of a society dominated by Christian values, the misuse of power can thus be squarely defined as all those expressions of power, which: (1) cause the controllee to act against his or her own will; (2) limit the freedom of the controllee to act as an autonomous individual; (3) diminish or destroy the controllee's humanness, which means the freedoms to enjoy life in all its aspects; (4) uses other people for the controller's own benefit without their express and free desire; (5) refuses the controllee the chance to reciprocate by using *his* or *her* power on the controller; (6) exploit other people's power, i.e., in a dependency relationship with a weaker person, a handicapped person, or a neurotic person, who can evoke sympathy power which can become a *coercion.*

c. Institutional misuse of power. All institutions exert tremendous power, be they religious, economic, political, familial, etc. It is through institutional power that individuals are most often dehumanized. The institutional misuse of power becomes an almost impossible phenomenon to evaluate from a moral/ethical point of view, because it is so difficult, if not impossible, to ascribe moral aspects of power to individuals.

Removing moral ethical responsibility from individuals and positing it in the organizational structure, then makes power become a "systems process." This may be what the Apostle Paul meant by "principalities and powers" and "spiritual wickedness," and thus he could say, "None of the rulers of this age understood this [hidden wisdom of God]; for if they had, they would not have crucified the Lord of glory" (I Cor. 2:8). A recent flurry of theological writings has a new appreciation of the "principalities and powers" (Berkhof; Miguez; Gutierrez, etc.).

From psychological, sociological, philosophical, and moral standpoints therefore, power is a given, necessary for human life. *How* it is applied is the crucial issue, and health and harmony depend upon its moral application. Most societies may have solved the use of power much better than our contemporary Western society. Could one assume that it is the *misapplication* of Christian faith which has resulted in such a tragic misuse of power? Some writings suggest that biblical teachings, especially those of Jesus (Phil. 2:5–8), state that the end of power is to "give it away" by empowering others (Tillich, vol. 3, p. 388; Redekop), whereas liberation theology proposes "action in the present, in favor of the oppressed, . . ." (Miguez Bonino, p. 77; Gutierrez). The *misuse*, not the use, of power may be the most serious issue in human existence.

Bibliography. A. Adler, *Understanding Human Nature* (1927). Aristotle, *Metaphysics* W. D. Ross trans., (1908). H. Berkhof, *Christ and the Powers* (1977). R. Bierstedt, "An Analysis of Social Power," *American Sociological Review,* (1950), 730–8. P. M. Blau, *Exchange and Power in Social Life* (1964). Miguez Bonino, *Doing Theology in a Revolutionary Situation* (1975). N. O. Brown, *Life Against Death* (1959). D. Cartwright, "Influence, Leadership and Control," in J. G. March, ed., *Handbook of Organizations* (1965). E. Erikson, *Childhood and Society* (1964). S. Freud, *Basic Writings of Sigmund Freud* (1938). E. Fromm, *Escape from Freedom* (1941). G. Gutierrez, *A Theology of Liberation: History, Politics and Salvation* (1973). F. Hunter, *Community Power Structure* (1963). J. Ladd, "Morality and the Ideal of Rationality in Formal Organizations," in Donaldson and Werhane, eds., *Ethical Issues in Business* (1979). J. Locke, "Of Power," in *Essay Concerning Human Understanding* (1952). N. Machiavelli, *The Prince* (1952). D. C. McClelland, *Power in the Inner Experience* (1975). O. Maduro, *Religion and Social Conflicts* (1982). B. Malinowski, *Magic, Science and Religion* (1954); *The Dynamics of Culture Change* (1976). K. Mannheim, *Systematic Sociology* (1957). K. Marx and F. Engels, *Basic Writings on Politics and Philosophy* (1959). A. Maslow, *Motivation and Personality* (1954). R. May, *Power and Innocence* (1972). C. W. Mills, *The Power Elite* (1959). B. Moore, Jr., *Injustice: The Social Base of Obedience and Revolt* (1978). A. M. Pescatello, *Power and Pawn* (1976). B. H. Raven, "The Comparative Analysis of Power and Power Preferences" in J. T. Tedeschi, ed., *Perspectives on Social Power* (1974). C. Redekop, "Institutions, Power and the Gospel," in J. R. Burkholder and C. Redekop, eds., *Kingdom, Cross, and Community* (1976). W. Schmidt, *The Origin and Growth of Religion* (1972 [1931]). P. A. Sorokin, *Altruistic Love* (1950). H. S. Sullivan, *The Interpersonal Theory of Psychiatry* (1953). J. T. Tedeschi, ed., *Perspectives on Social Power* (1974). P. Tillich, *Systematic Theology* (1967). J. Veroff and J. B. Veroff, "Reconsideration of a Measure of Power Motivation," in *Psychological Bulletin*, 78 (1972), 279–91. M. Weber, *The Theory of Social and Economic Organization* (1947). D. G. Winter, *The Power Motive* (1973). B. B. Wolman, "Power and Acceptance as Determinants of Social Relations," *International J. of Group Tensions*, (1974), 151–83. E. M. Woodward, "The Uses of Power in Community," *Human Development*, 4:2 (1983), 24–32.

C. REDEKOP

CONFLICT AND CONFLICT MANAGEMENT; DISCIPLINE, PASTORAL CARE AS; INDOCTRINATION; LOCUS OF CONTROL RESEARCH; MONEY; SELF-EXPRESSION/SELF-CONTROL; SOCIAL STATUS AND CLASS FACTORS. *See also* ADVOCACY; AUTHORIZATION; EXPLOITATION/OPPRESSION; LIBERATION THEOLOGY; RICH PERSONS; VIPs. *Compare* AGGRESSIVE/ASSERTION; AUTHORITY; COMPETITIVENESS; SUGGESTION, PERSUASION, AND INFLUENCE; RAGE AND HOSTILITY; VIOLENCE.

POWER OF THE KEYS. *See* KEYS, POWER OF.

POWERFUL PERSONS. *See* VIPs.

PRACTICAL KNOWLEDGE. *See* WISDOM AND PRACTICAL KNOWLEDGE; PRUDENCE.

PRACTICAL METHODS OF CARE. *See* TECHNIQUE AND SKILL.

PRACTICAL THEOLOGY, JEWISH. *See* JEWISH CARE AND COUNSELING; JEWISH LITERATURE IN CARE AND COUNSELING.

PRACTICAL THEOLOGY, PROTESTANT. (1) A field of study in clergy education covering the responsibilities and activities of the minister and usually including preaching, liturgics, pastoral care, Christian (church) education, and church polity and administration. (2) An area or discipline in clergy education whose subject matter is the life and activity of the church as it exists in the present. (3) An area or discipline of theology whose subject matter is Christian practice and which brings to bear theological criteria on contemporary situations and realms of individual and social action.

The three definitions indicate that practical theology is now being used in more than one sense. The first definition is the standard and traditional meaning which was more or less in place in European universities at the beginning of the nineteenth century. Although the other two definitions are similar to certain pre-modern views, they essentially represent the contemporary attempt to correct and expand the traditional concept.

1. **The Traditional Concept.** Practical theology was a term in theology long before it came to mean a discrete field of clergy studies. It initially expressed the almost universal conviction that theology itself is a "practical" type of knowledge or discipline because it concerns the human being's salvation. After the seventeenth century, there was an interim period when practical theology began to name that area of theology especially concerned with human good, the area of moral theology, but also including the means of obtaining that good which occur in the church and which are assisted by the clergy.

Throughout the two-thousand year history of the church, there have been occasional writings on the nature and duties of the priesthood or ministry. Works of this sort continued to appear after the Reformation, for instance, Zwingli's *The Shepherd*. In eighteenth century Europe, some of these works began to be entitled Pastoral Theology, and in England and America, a number of pastor's manuals were written, many modeled on Richard Baxter's *The Reformed Pastor*. In the second half of the eighteenth century in Europe, a development occurred which shaped the future of practical theology. This was the organization of theological studies in the German university of the Enlightenment. The result was the four standard disciplines of biblical, dogmatic, church historical, and practical theology. At this point, practical theology obtained the status of a "science," an area of inquiry and teaching in the university. It is thought of as the fourth theological science, the applied science which mediates the three theoretical sciences to matters of Christian ministry. Once this four-fold structure is in place, we have the conditions for the nineteenth century consensus on practical theology.

Practical theology consists of five prominent activities of the minister: preaching, liturgics, catechetics, pastoral care, and church polity. In the U.S., subjects like preaching and church polity were taught at Harvard in the mid-nineteenth century, but not under the rubric of practical theology. As the century progressed, homiletics was an important part of the curriculum of seminaries, but it was not until the turn of the century that new courses in practical theology began to be added. By the twentieth century, the European model had exercised sufficient influence on the seminaries to produce practical theology as the fourth area.

2. Contemporary Correctives. The nineteenth century German view of practical theology as the fourth theological science has continued in Protestant theological education into the present. It does not appear to have obtained the status of a single, clearly defined "science" either in Europe or in the U.S., but rather names an area of clergy education whose specific undertakings (e.g., homiletics) have taken on some of the marks of an academic discipline. It might be argued that the North American form of practical theology has a more concrete and functionalist character than the European form.

The traditional view of practical theology as a generic name for a number of relatively independent pastoral sciences has had some unfortunate consequences. Most of these consequences are due to practical theology being construed as a discipline separated from other theological disciplines, and to the fact that each of its subdisciplines works without being subject to an overall theory or theology of church and ministry. The fact that practical theology existed only in the form of relatively independent areas of inquiry and teaching had the following results: First, little or no place was provided in clergy education for full treatment of the church and the ministry as such, the very presuppositions of the specific areas. Second, even though practical theology was thought of as the application of the theoretical disciplines, its independent subdisciplines tended to sever their connections with biblical, historical, and theological work. These severances from both general theological and ecclesiological considerations had their own set of consequences. The first is that each area becomes vulnerable to being transformed into a mere technology, a how-to or skill-oriented undertaking. The second is that each subdiscipline is forced to consider some auxiliary discipline or science as that which gives it academic or scholarly respectability. Accordingly, the auxiliary science moves into the center of the subdiscipline and tends to become both its norm and content. Thus, psychology controls pastoral care; development theory controls Christian education; rhetoric controls homiletics. Because practical theology names an area of clergy education, and not an aspect of theological thinking itself, its context is the seminary and not church education as such.

These consequences have not gone unnoticed. And although practical theology as an area pertaining to clergy activities remains fairly much in place in current theological curricula, this concept has been severely criticized in recent decades. Initiating the criticism were European Roman Catholic theologians such as Karl Rahner

and Heinrich Schuster. They attempted to broaden the Roman Catholic "pastoral theology" to a discipline having to do with the church in its totality and its concrete situation in the present. (The relation between practical theology and *pastoral theology* has a complex history. Until recently, pastoral theology has been the preferred term in Roman Catholic circles. In the eighteenth century and in occasional nineteenth century Protestant authors, e.g., Vinet, the two terms name roughly the same thing. More typical, however, is the usage of practical theology as a term to include all disciplines of church or ministerial activity and pastoral theology as a narrower term for studies pertaining to pastoral care or *Seelsorge*.) So dominant is this corrective in the European Roman Catholic literature that it is virtually a consensus. European Protestant theologians such as G. Ebeling, W. Pannenberg, and F. Mildenberger have followed suit. In the 1980s, a similar criticism of the traditional view which has the effect of broadening practical theology from a clerical to a churchly undertaking has been explored by North American theologians.

Recently, a second type of corrective of the traditional view has occurred. The first type of corrective proposed practical theology as an area of studies or discipline which made the contemporary situation and action of the church an object of inquiry. The second type moves practical theology out of the context of clergy education and therefore out of the genre of an academic science and regards it as a dimension of theological thinking itself. Proposed here is not just the importance of thematizing *church* activity but of thematizing Christian action as such. Many factors are operative in the background of this second corrective: the amorphous state of ethics as an aspect of theology, the stringent criticisms of academic theology by liberation theology, and the corporate hermeneutic of post-Marxist ways of relating theory and practice. Gerd Otto, Norbert Mette, and Johann Metz in Europe and David Tracy in the U.S. describe practical theology as a dimension of theology focused on *praxis* itself and not just on ministerial action or ecclesiastical activities. The first corrective tends to resurrect the earlier nineteenth century definition of practical theology as a "science of the church's life and action." The second corrective is reminiscent of the pre-eighteenth century insistence that all theology is practical.

3. Persisting Issues. The situation of practical theology in this last quarter of the twentieth century is clearly one of turmoil, ambiguity, and explorations of new paths. Several problems are especially prominent. The first is the problem of the genus or genre of practical theology. Is practical theology a term for a teaching area in clergy education or is it an immanent aspect of all theological thinking? To state the question differently, in what sense is practical theology *theology*? "Theology" itself is not a self-evidently clear genre. If it refers to the actual process of interpreting, thinking, and judging which faith itself engenders and is not simply a term for a cluster of academic disciplines, practical theology is an aspect of that thinking. It would seem to be, accordingly, that aspect of theological thinking in which the thinking is focused on a situation, an event, or a practice. It is theological thinking outward on the world and not simply on the texts and symbols which constitute the

inherited tradition. The issue posed by this genre question is how to relate practical theology in this sense of a dimension of theological thinking to the valid task of thinking about the church, the ministry, preaching, worship, etc.

A second issue emerges as a discerned need. Granting that clergy education unavoidably includes focused attention on such primary areas of responsibility as pastoral care and worship, how can the unfortunate consequences of the traditional approach be overcome? The need in question is the need to restore both a comprehensive treatment of church and ministry to that education and to approach the activities of ministry by relating them both to general theological criteria and to a comprehensive interpretation of church and ministry.

A third issue is the lacuna discerned by those who criticize the isolation of the church and the acts of ministry from a general theory and method of Christian practice, individual and social. Theological education has yet to develop an area of study which asks how faith and its criteria relate to situations and practice as such. In other words, practical theology as a general theory of Christian practice involving a theological hermeneutic of situationism is rarely taken up in clergy and church education. It would be such a theological hermeneutic of practice which would provide some guidelines as to what occurs in proclamatory communication, pastoral diagnosis, counseling of the aged, etc. It would also offer a way to place the activities of the church and its ministries in political and social settings, thus correcting the parochialism of separated disciplines by relating each one to various contexts of practice.

These three issues may express a single issue. The question remains as to how the two major types of correctives offered in recent decades, the ecclesiological and the social-hermeneutical, can be incorporated into a comprehensive undertaking called practical theology which would address the unfortunate consequences of the traditional view.

Bibliography. E. A. Achelis, *Praktische Theologie* 2 vols. (1890). F. X. Arnold, N. Greinacher, and R. Zerfass, eds., *Handbuch der Pastoraltheologie* (1964). D. Browning, ed., *Practical Theology: The Emerging Field in Theology, the Church, and the World* (1983); various volumes in *Pastoral Psychology*, 29:1 (1980). G. Ebeling, *The Study of Theology*, ch. 9 (1975). N. Greinacher and R. Zerfass, eds., *Einführung in die praktische Theologie* (1976). C. Harms, *Pastoraltheologie*, (1847). L. T. Howe, "Theology in the Practice of Ministry," *J. of Pastoral Counseling*, 19 (1985), 128–35. F. Klostermann, and R. Zerfass, eds., *Praktische Theologie heute* (1974). G. Krause, ed., *Praktische Theologie* (1972). D. P. McCann, and C. R. Strain, *Polity and Praxis: A Program for American Practical Theology* (1985). F. Mildenberger, *Theorie der Theologie*, (1972) pp. 131–41. A. Müller, "Zur Geschichte der Disziplin," in N. Greinacher and R. Zerfass, eds., *Einführung in die praktische Theologie* (1976). C. Nietzsche, *Praktische Theologie* (1847). J. J. van Oosterzee, *Practical Theology* (1972 [1878]). W. Pannenberg, *Theology and the Philosophy of Science* (1976), pp. 423ff. K. Rahner and H. Schuster, eds., *The Pastoral Mission of the Church* (1965). D. Tracy, *The Analogical Imagination* (1981) pp. 69ff. A. Vinet, *Pastoral Theology* (1907). G. Winquist, *Practical Hermeneutics* (1980). O. Zöckler, ed., *Handbuch der theologischen Wissenschaften*, 4, (1883) pp. 3–15.

E. FARLEY

PASTORAL THEOLOGICAL METHODOLOGY; THEORY AND PRAXIS. *Compare* EXPERIENTIAL, MORAL, *or* PASTORAL THEOLOGY; PRUDENCE; WISDOM AND PRACTICAL KNOWLEDGE.

PRACTICAL THEOLOGY, ROMAN CATHOLIC. *See* PASTORAL THEOLOGY, ROMAN CATHOLIC.

PRACTICAL WISDOM. *See* PRUDENCE; WISDOM AND PRACTICAL KNOWLEDGE.

PRACTICE. *See* PRAXIS/PRACTICE (Terminology).

PRACTITIONER, CHRISTIAN SCIENCE. *See* CHRISTIAN SCIENCE PRACTITIONER.

PRAGMATISM AND PASTORAL CARE. Pragmatism is a theory of truth developed in the latter part of the nineteenth and early twentieth centuries principally by American philosophers Charles Peirce, John Dewey, and William James, and the British philosopher F. C. S. Schiller. It asks, as a criterion of "truth," whether an idea is useful for the benefits it confers on human life. Pragmatism has historical roots in Kant's "practical reason" and utilitarianism. It also has affinities with aspects of existentialism, for example, Kierkegaard's criticism of the speculative system of Hegel, which James also criticized.

In the American pastoral care movement there has long been a question whether or to what extent contemporary theories and methods of pastoral care entail an essentially pragmatic theory of truth, implying a loss of theological and/or scientific objectivity (e.g., Oden, 1967, pp. 81–5).

1. The Philosophic Meaning of Pragmatism. As a theory of truth pragmatism gives a particular interpretation to the commonsense notion that truth refers to the *conformity* or *agreement* of an idea, a notion, a theory, or a belief with reality. In pragmatism, the crux of the truth question is what is meant by "to agree" or "to fit." For James an idea or belief must prove itself useful or valuable; it must *prosper* human beings. True ideas guide or lead us into the presence of the reality to which they point. Their leading is useful for any number of benefits they may bequeath, such as consistency, stability, peace, joy, satisfaction. The pragmatic test is: Is the idea useful? Does it pay? Does it lead to the elevation of life rather than to its mere imitation or duplication?

It is important to understand that this notion of pragmatism, as a sophisticated theory of truth, differs from the common misunderstanding that pragmatism means simply that if something "works" it has met the pragmatic test. Pragmatism is more sophisticated; it emphasizes the criterion of prospering or enhancing of human life in distinction from the narrow (and often self-interested) notion that "what works is true." In this respect some of the criticism of American pastoral care may have been based on a misconception of the meaning of pragmatism. Nonetheless the issue is an important one for the theory and practice of any essentially practical discipline like pastoral care and counseling.

2. Pragmatism and Pastoral Care. Pragmatism has nothing to do with "flying by the seat of one's pants," as some pastors have admitted they do. It is erroneous to call the results pragmatic merely because in a particular case they have turned out well.

Behind pastoral care there is no psychological theory, therapeutic in nature, which is avowedly pragmatic. Yet every theory of healing is empirical (that is, derived from experience) and every theory uses some pragmatic testing, whether or not the theorist is conscious of the process.

There is also no pastoral care theory that is avowedly pragmatic. Yet the history of pastoral care in the twentieth century is in part a history of pragmatic testing of several theories to enhance the skills and the art of pastoral caring. The pragmatism implicit in these theories lies in the testing of these ideas in actual practice to see how well they operate in resolving individual or group emotional or spiritual problems or crises. There must be a theory to test and it must be tested by how well it leads up to problem resolution. Such theories may be informed biblically and theologically, as well as psychologically; but they must also face the pragmatic test: do they *agree with, or fit*, the therapeutic (or redemptive) needs of the client?

An example is the theological idea that God is omnipotent. Put with that the psychological and theological assumption that the parishioner or counselee has some responsibility for actualizing himself or herself into a different state of being so that the presenting problem, say, depression, is at least better managed if not alleviated. There seems to be an inconsistency between the belief in an omnipotent God and God's requirement that a human being be self-actualizing and therefore responsible. The pastor, concerned with helping the parishioner or client to solve his or her problem, will need to examine carefully the complex idea which pragmatically does not fit, or agree, with reality. The reality in this case is a certain kind of God — one with all power — and a finite being who is responsible for changing. Pragmatism tests the idea of omnipotence (or responsibility) and finds it wanting. Then the carer must go back to the drawing board to work over the idea or theory so that it better fits the reality of God and human beings in relation to each other.

Bibliography. D. S. Browning, *Pluralism and Personality: William James and Some Contemporary Cultures of Psychology* (1980). W. James, *Pragmatism and Four Essays from The Meaning of Truth* (1955). T. C. Oden, *Contemporary Theology and Psychotherapy* (1967). J. Wild, *The Radical Empiricism of William James* (1970).

G. E. JACKSON

PASTORAL CARE (History, Traditions, and Definitions); PASTORAL THEOLOGY, PROTESTANT; PHILOSOPHY AND PSYCHOLOGY. *See also* ETHICS AND PASTORAL CARE; FEELING, THOUGHT, AND ACTION IN PASTORAL COUNSELING; HISTORY OF PROTESTANT PASTORAL CARE (United States); PASTORAL CARE MOVEMENT; PROBLEM SOLVING; THEORY AND PRAXIS; WISDOM AND PRACTICAL KNOWLEDGE IN PASTORAL CARE. *Compare* PROCESS THEOLOGY AND PASTORAL CARE. *Biography:* DEWEY; JAMES.

PRAISE. *See* PRAYER; WORSHIP AND CELEBRATION. *See also* EARLY CHURCH, PASTORAL CARE IN; MORAL BEHAVIOR AND RELIGION.

PRATT, JAMES BISSETT (1875–1944). A psychologist of religion who received his Ph.D. from Harvard in 1905, with a dissertation on "Historical Illustrations of the Psychology of Religious Belief." He later served on the faculty at Williams College and was a proponent of pragmatism in the tradition of William James. He authored three major books in the area of psychology of religion—*The Psychology of Religious Belief* (1907), *The Religious Consciousness* (1920), and *The Pilgrimage of Buddhism and a Buddhist Pilgrimage* (1928)—and numerous journal articles.

Pratt was also a major philosophical psychologist in the personalist tradition, authoring many articles and three major books: *What Is Pragmatism?* (1909), *Matter and Spirit* (1922), and *Personal Realism* (1937). Pratt was an apologist for the philosophical position known as critical (or dualistic) realism and the theological stance of absolute theistic personalism.

H. VANDE KEMP

PERSONALISM AND PASTORAL CARE; PSYCHOLOGY OF RELIGION (Theories, Traditions, and Issues).

PRAXIS. *See* THEORY AND PRAXIS; WISDOM AND PRACTICAL KNOWLEDGE.

PRAXIS/PRACTICE (Terminology). In clinical pastoral usage, "practice" basically connotes professional role performance (which need not exclude theoretical understanding and existential commitment). "Praxis," following liberation theology, connotes the practice of ministry (or a way of life) emphasizing critical social consciousness, questioning its own power interests and those of others.

R. J. HUNTER

THEORY AND PRAXIS. *See also* PRACTICAL THEOLOGY.

PRAYER. Generally viewed as a dynamic form of communion of the religious person with the deity or transcendent Other. True prayer involves articulation of that which is deepest in human life, often at an unconscious or nonverbal level. Prayer thus distinguishes living religion from a purely intellectual view of the world and from philosophical interpretations of human nature and destiny. Prayer presupposes a responsiveness in that which transcends the human. The "Other" is not only friendly, not only worthy of commitment; the Other can respond.

1. **Understanding Prayer.** Prayer may well be the primordial human language. Caught in a situation of fundamental insecurity, aware of the disjunction between what is and what might be, the human being utters a cry of anguish or of joy, a cry of terror or of wonder. This cry is the primal religious act arising out of the search for, or affirmation of, whatever can help in living with the insecurity of human existence. The one who prays seeks what is trustworthy and dependable in the face of the human existence situation. Ultimately, the concern is for the one who is unconditionally trustworthy. Prayer is rooted in this existential question of trust. The history of religions and each of our personal religious histories is the story of the human response to

this existence question. As Luther said, "faith is prayer and nothing but prayer, for prayer is the very heart of religion."

The character of prayer in the life of a religious community or person will be shaped by the understanding that the community or the individual has of the human condition and of what is ultimately trustworthy. As that understanding changes, so will the understanding and practice of prayer. Human existence is fundamentally ambiguous, for gain and loss, joy and sorrow, hope and despair are strangely mixed. The forms of prayer reflect this fundamental ambiguity of the human situation. The experience of need, of loss, of impoverishment on the one hand, and the experience of abundance, gain, or gift on the other are reflected in the community's and in the individual's prayer. The experience of lack or need is expressed in petition, confession, and intercession, and that of joy in adoration, thanksgiving, and praise.

2. Prayer in Christian Faith. For the Christian, both the form and content of prayer are governed by a christological norm. All Christian prayer is social or communal whether the prayer itself is congregational or personal, for Christians understand human existence as shared in Christ. Human beings are one body, linked together through their relation to Christ who is the form of God's own being and becoming. The content of Christian prayer is also christological. What Christians are to pray for is governed by Jesus' teaching in the Lord's Prayer. To pray in Jesus' name means that what one prays for is fit to be coupled with his name. It means to bring one's needs and joys into relation to that vision of human becoming which is consonant with the Kingdom of God—that persons might move toward becoming centers of freedom and love, that communities might become caring communities, and that society might embody structures of increasing justice.

Christian prayer may be voiced or silent, active or contemplative, expressive or meditative. The fundamental initiative, however, is seen to be God's. Whether the one who prays appears to be a seeker, to take the initiative in petitioning God, or whether one despairs of being able to pray or even doubts that there is a God to whom one can pray, the initiative which moves an individual to pray or to struggle toward prayer is God's. The Spirit prays in us and through us in both our doubts and hopes, our petition and our praise. Conscious prayer is our attempt to respond to the one who responds to us, to bring our lives into harmony with God's intentions. Prayer is thus the means by which God's possibilities become a lure for human transformation. Prayer is God's power to transform the human world through human freedom.

3. Prayer in the Twentieth Century. In the pre-critical era, prayer was popularly understood to be a kind of speaking to God conceived of as a personal being. God could and did intervene in the course of historical events and personal life. Conceptions of God's perfection and unchangeability and scientific views which no longer allowed or required supernatural intervention or explanation of historical or natural events raised critical questions about petitionary prayer. Prayer as petition was diminished in importance and reinterpreted by such theologians as Schleiermacher and Ritschl. Prayer as

thankful response to God's reconciliation and providential care was emphasized. Such views, together with the enduring problem of unanswered prayer diminished the importance of prayer for many critical theologians.

Nevertheless, twentieth century theologians continued to ponder such problems. Reinterpretations of the nature of God and of God's relation to human existence have made possible fresh approaches to the problem of petition and intercession. In process theology, for example, the perfection of God is understood in a new way. God is not unchangeable, but rather is present in every event even as every event is present in God. This means that God is influenced by human action even as God influences all events. What human beings do, whether they pray and how they pray, will make a difference not only to God, but to the way in which God is able to influence the present and the future.

In the theology of Paul Tillich, God's creativity does not interfere with or manipulate human freedom. It is not an additional factor entering into ongoing reality. Rather, it qualifies every constellation of conditions. Prayer is part of the situation. It makes a difference. God's creativity can function differently when faith and prayer transform the existential situation. Karl Rahner holds a similar view. God does not interfere in or alter the causal processes which science sees as operative in the object world. Rather, God is the transcendental ground of the world which must be taken into account in understanding both the existence of the old and the emergence of the new.

a. Psychological understanding. Just as philosophical and scientific conceptions seemed to undercut the traditional understanding and practice of prayer, so psychological and psychoanalytic understandings of the unconscious led many to the conclusion that our gods were illusory projections. Prayer was thought to be a matter of wish fulfillment and the mechanisms of defense. Theologians have now come to recognize that locating the roots of prayer in primary process thinking may, on the contrary, provide one of the keys to understanding its power and importance. As Kierkegaard thought, the efficacy of prayer lies in the inner transformation of the one who prays. It is only superstition, he said more than a century ago, to believe that God acts on human beings in an external way. God is spirit. God acts on human inwardness. Prayer is what we do so that God can do something to us and with us. The hate, anger, despair, fear, pride, self-trust, and the desires which are part of us are to be drawn into the open in prayer. They are to be probed and acknowledged so that we can come to see ourselves as we really are. Only in the face of such honesty about ourselves and about the projections we make into God can the spirit begin to transform us.

b. Prayer and liberation. The hermeneutic of suspicion growing out of psychological understanding and applied to human praying has been enlarged and deepened through the work of the liberation theologians. The language and content of prayer have been seen to reflect class, racial, and gender interests. The cultivation of the inner life and the self-centeredness of much traditional prayer have been criticized as privatistic and ideological. Such criticisms have been launched not simply out of Marxist, feminist, or black perspectives but in the name of the gospel itself which shatters all human pretensions and relativizes all human language. Constructively, the liberation perspective has begun to face in fresh ways the relevance of prayer to the struggle for justice. Just as with regard to the condition of the individual, the darker side of hate and pride, of lust and ambition are to be taken into our prayers and faced honestly, so too the social injustice, the oppression of one human group by another, the common need for bread, for work, for political freedom become the very stuff of prayer. The journey inward is balanced by the journey outward. Contemplation and action are fused in one action, and the action is that of love seeking justice.

c. Language. If our changing understanding of the nature of God and of individual and social existence has brought about a reinterpretation of the meaning of prayer, so too has our changing view of the nature of religious and theological language. Prayer is a human language. As religious and theological language it is fundamentally metaphorical. The debate over whether God is a personal being capable of entering into dialogue with human beings become reformulated when this is understood. The question is no longer whether God *is* a personal being, but whether language utilizing the metaphors of the person and of dialogue are appropriate for carrying and expressing the interaction between human beings and that which is unconditionally trustworthy.

A further issue is whether other metaphors and models may also be important for prayer and for understanding what happens when human beings pray. Our language may be subject to the hermeneutic of suspicion because it is ideologically tainted or embodies projections but even more important, all our language is relativized by the very nature of the reality it attempts to express or reflect. At the same time, it is realized that language is a powerful carrier of meaning and is the most fundamental shaper of *human* being and becoming. Contemporary interpretations of prayer are, therefore, attentive in new ways to the character of prayer as human language.

Bibliography. D. Capps, "The Psychology of Petitionary Prayer," *Theology Today,* 39:2(1982), 130–41. F. Heiler, *Prayer* (1932). P. LeFevre, *Understandings of Prayer* (1981); *Radical Prayer* (1982).

P. LeFEVRE

MEDITATION; SPIRITUAL DISCIPLINE AND GROWTH; SPIRITUAL THEOLOGY AND PASTORAL CARE; WORSHIP AND CELEBRATION. *See also* ILLUMINATION; JEWISH PRAYERS; PRIVACY AND SOLITUDE; RELIGIOUS EXPERIENCE; RELIGIOUS LANGUAGE; RITUAL AND PASTORAL CARE; SPIRITUALITY.

PRAYER BOOK. *See* ANGLICAN PASTORAL CARE.

PRAYER AND WORSHIP LIFE, PASTOR'S. The image of the minister as one who preaches and looks after the pastoral needs of the congregation has been replaced by one based on the reality of the demands made by the contemporary church. The pastor today is expected to administer the institution, raise funds to meet the budget, direct a complex committee system, participate in community activity, develop and promote a comprehensive church program, and provide extensive counseling services. As the demands on the pastor's time increase,

prayer and devotion tend to be relegated to a position of low priority. It is not that the pastor regards such things as less important. Rather, more immediate drains on energy and time cause prayer and devotion to be neglected. The expectations of church members put institutional matters in the forefront of the pastor's work schedule to the neglect of personal spiritual growth and development.

However, if one of the pastor's basic tasks is to help people discern a Divine Presence in their lives, the prayer and worship life must be given more serious and disciplined attention. Pastoral counseling, as opposed to purely secular counseling, assumes that the work and will of God have some relevance to the resolution of the counselee's problem. The pastor, then, must have a deep sensitivity to the presence and activity of God in human affairs. The same is true of the pastor as a leader of worship.

1. **Principle of Balance.** In the Christian Benedictine tradition the monk's life involves a balance of prayer, study, and work. Those elements must also be kept in balance in the pastor's own life. Pastoral work is always at the forefront of a minister's attention, but that work must be fed by study and prayer. The study of classical and contemporary spiritual writers whose religious experience was very deep is helpful in understanding and verbalizing one's own experience. Generally, the best devotional writers are those who have struggled with doubt and spiritual aridity prior to arriving at a mature faith.

Ideally, the Christian life should include a balance of contemplative and active elements. In reality, most personalities are inclined toward one or the other and must make a serious effort to develop the neglected aspect. Each pastor will have to develop his or her own style of devotion.

2. **Resources for Solitary Spiritual Discipline.** Introverted personalities tend to be attracted to solitary prayer. The Christian contemplative tradition has developed a plethora of approaches and methodologies, all of which have attempted to bring a sense of discipline into one's devotional life. Some of these may serve as helpful models for the pastor seeking to develop a more organized approach for his or her prayer life. The second-century *Didache* suggested fasting on Wednesdays and Fridays and praying the Lord's Prayer three times a day. The medieval development of the Breviary for praying the Psalms at stated times throughout the day was an effort to create within the Christian's life a rhythm of prayer and work. Aelred of Rievaulx's *Rule for the Life of a Recluse*, written in the twelfth century, prescribed the use of a variety of contemplative activities in order to avoid weariness or boredom with any one approach: praying the Psalter, reading, meditation, physical labor, and examination of conscience.

One of the finest literary examples of a regulated devotional life is the seventeenth-century *Private Devotions of Lancelot Andrewes*. This book contains the daily devotional routine of an Anglican bishop and is a literary jewel. It outlines a personal liturgy for morning and evening prayer, with prayers appropriate for each: confession, intercession, praise, and petitions for grace. A similar but longer and more detailed system is William

Law's *A Serious Call to a Devout and Holy Life* (1792). It suggests five major times of prayer during the day with themes for each. Morning prayer should focus on thanksgiving, mid-morning on humility, midday on intercession, mid-afternoon on conformity to God's will, and evening on examining one's conscience. Pope John XXIII's *Journal of a Soul*, selections from his diaries, contains outlines of his own devotional procedures developed at different points in his life.

Each minister should develop his or her own methodology. Traditional elements to be included are Scripture reading, prayer for one's own ministry and spiritual growth, prayer for parishioners, examination of conscience, and confession. The most important form of prayer, however, may be a simple listening. The deepest form of prayer is nonverbal. Many pastors today find journaling a fruitful devotional activity and a valuable means of reflection on what is happening in one's ministry. Some form of meditation should also be cultivated. Ignatius Loyola's *Spiritual Exercises* of the sixteenth century is an example of directed meditation on Scripture. Others may be attracted to Eastern forms that emphasize silence and the absence of mental images.

3. Resources for Social-Activist Spiritual Discipline. People with more extroverted personalities will tend to find a Divine Presence not in solitude but in interaction with others. Martin Luther King, Jr.'s *Stride Toward Freedom* (1953), Dag Hammarskjold's *Markings* (1964), Dietrich Bonhoeffer's *Letters and Papers from Prison* (1953), Simone Weil's *Waiting for God* (1951), and Dorothy Day's *The Long Loneliness* (1952), as well as her articles in the *Catholic Worker*, describe the spiritual lives of these social activists. They were sensitive to the presence of God at work in the lives of other people and events in history. Some of them had the gift of discerning God's presence in the poor, the suffering, and the hopeless. Yet, they also saw a need to withdraw inwardly from time to time as a means of renewal.

4. Current Issues. There is a growing interest in Protestantism today in the ministry of spiritual direction, a ministry of helping others discern what God is doing in their lives. The field assumes that such a minister will also be under direction. Understanding the work of God in one's own life is essential to discerning that in the life of another person or the parish as well as for effective counseling that is based on religious assumptions.

As leaders of worship, many pastors are often so overwhelmed with liturgical mechanics and concerns that the service flows smoothly that they are unable to engage in the act of worship themselves. The solution to this problem is to be found not in the techniques of leading worship but in the pastor's own relationship with God. When private worship becomes a more natural part of one's life there is a carryover into the way one leads public worship. Private prayer is an important part of the minister's preparation for conducting a public service and for other ministerial activity, such as counseling.

Finally, the depth of a pastor's prayer and worship life will depend in large measure on that person's understanding of the purpose of ministry. One may see it as a helping profession in a humanistic sense, or one may see it as leading people to an encounter with Transcendence, which will influence the way they face human problems.

In the latter the pastor's own prayer life and religious experience will be the foundation of ministry.

Bibliography. U. T. Holmes, *Spirituality for Ministry* (1982). H. J. M. Nouwen, *The Way of the Heart* (1981). J. Dalrymple, "Some Reflections on Spiritual Direction for Priests," *Circuit Rider*, 70 (1985), 307–10.

W. O. PAULSELL

FAITH AND INTEGRITY, PASTOR'S; PRAYER; WORSHIP AND CELEBRATION. *See also* AUTHORITY, PASTORAL; IDENTITY, PASTORAL; SPIRITUAL DIRECTION; SPIRITUAL DISCIPLINE AND GROWTH. *Compare* MENTAL HEALTH, PASTOR'S.

PRAYER HEALING. *See* FAITH HEALING.

PRAYER IN PASTORAL CARE. Prayer is communication with God. Prayer in pastoral care is assisting people to communicate with God in their time of need. In the Christian tradition, prayer in pastoral care is usually coupled with the reading of Scripture. This expands the concept of communication as God also speaks through Scripture. Prayer, then, is listening as well as speaking. Prayer in time of need is in response to divine invitation: "Call upon me in the day of trouble; I will deliver you, and you shall glorify me" (Ps. 50:15). In pastoral care, this divine invitation is reinforced by the pastor's invitation to pray or by a request to the pastor for prayer.

1. Mediating, Symbolic Role. Prayer in pastoral care is based on the pastor's symbolic role. As a "called and ordained servant of the Word" he or she is a mediator between the world of nature that is limited to sense and time and space, and the world of the Spirit that is not bound by these limits.

This symbolic role of the pastor as a "person of the cloth" buttresses his or her pastoral acts, placing them within the context of a "bridge between the worlds." As ministers of Christ, pastors thus continue the incarnational character of Christ's ministry. As Christ is the incarnation of God, so the church is the incarnation of Christ and the church's clergy are appointed representatives of this incarnational function. Prayer in pastoral care is one of the ways in which pastors carry out this function. The pastoral prayer in the corporate ministry of worship is another manifestation of this same representative office.

The pastor's use of prayer is a particular expression of his or her caring. The fact that a pastor visits with those in need is the initial expression of this caring. The pastor prays with and for those in need because he or she senses that they need or could be helped by assistance in formulating and articulating their concerns to God and in experiencing the community of which they are a part—the body in which they are members.

Prayer in pastoral care can be abused. The pastor may resort to it as a way of avoiding the anxiety that may come from talking about painful, threatening issues. "Shall we pray?" can be a convenient escape for the anxious pastor —and the parishioner's "Will you pray?" can serve the same purpose. Pastors often are susceptible to this manipulation. Instead of immediately going into prayer, the pastor could say, "Yes, but first I would like to visit with you," or "I would like to know how you are feeling so I *can* pray for you."

2. Purpose of Prayer. One purpose of prayer in pastoral care is to facilitate healing—in body, mind, spirit, and in marital and family relationships. Prayer is one of the means of God's healing.

A second purpose is also to support a context of meaning in affliction, when a sense of meaning is often lost or threatened. The anxiety of meaninglessness is intensified by the trials and tribulations of life. In the "day of trouble" we chafe at the limits of the world of nature, feeling cramped by the confines of sensory perception. Doubts about providence plague the believer, "Where is God in all of this pain?" Prayer is an exercise in the belief in providence. It supports our search for meaning in suffering, especially if it is recognized that God feels our pain even as Jesus endured it on the cross. Though God may not will pain, Christian faith holds that there is a redemptive potential in suffering. Prayer is a way of actualizing it.

A third purpose in prayer is to direct us to the Source and Center of our identity as sons and daughters of God. Prayer assists us to be still—comforted and secure—in the knowledge of God's Being and Presence (Ps. 46:10). It is an antidote to stress in highly stressful situations.

A fourth purpose is to energize one's faith. Prayer is an expression of faith, and faith is a way of receiving. Thus, when ending a prayer the pastor may add the petition, "Help us to be open to receive that for which we pray." Psychologically, prayer in pastoral care can stimulate this picture of receiving in one's mind.

3. Style and Content of Prayer. The style of one's prayer depends to a great extent on one's religious orientation and tradition. Perhaps the chief difference lies in the degree of liturgical formality that people are used to, though for all Christians the repetition of the Lord's Prayer can be a meaningful part of the prayer experience. When the pastor and the recipients of his or her care are of the same religious orientation, the familiar and shared style of prayer is especially supportive. Where they differ, however, the pastor's style can hinder the recipient's participation. When the pastor does not know the background of the persons involved, he or she needs to discuss their religious history, so that some adaptation can be made. In a pre-surgical visit, for example, one chaplain asked the patient if he would like him to pray with him. Evidently the patient thought the chaplain had asked *him* to pray for he said, "I only know one prayer." The chaplain assumed it was the Lord's Prayer, but nevertheless inquired as to which it was. The patient repeated the serenity prayer of Alcoholics Anonymous. The chaplain then used this prayer, with adapted petitions in regard to the upcoming surgery, as his prayer with and for the patient.

The content of prayer in pastoral care comes from the needs of the moment revealed in the pastoral visit. The visit and the prayer are "of one piece." Both are means through which the Holy Spirit works. This connection is more apparent if God language is part of the visit. Praying and visiting go together because both are functions of a ministry based on the conviction that God both exists and cares for the individual. This conviction expands the dialogical concept of the visit. Inherent in the dialogue between pastor and people is the awareness of the Other. When the pastor prays he or she is directing

this awareness into petitions for help. The content of the visit enables the pastor to make these petitions specific and personal.

In the Christian tradition one prays in Jesus' name, though the words need not always be spoken to communicate their spirit. They should be used neither as a magical formula nor as a way of excluding people, but as an expression of inclusion. They affirm that through Jesus' mediation all obstacles to our prayer are removed and we stand "before the throne of grace" (Heb. 4:16).

4. Prayer as Human Responsibility. Americans tend to bring a Western scientific orientation into our religion in a simplistic way. For every effect, we say, there is a cause. We might say, "I prayed for healing and was healed; therefore prayer was the cause of my healing."

The Eastern concept of synchronicity may actually be closer to reality. According to this understanding there are many factors involved in healing, and each of these needs to come together—to synchronize—to make healing a reality. Prayer is one of these factors.

It is our responsibility to pray. According to the Scripture, God wants to work with and through us and not in spite of us. What happens following our prayers is not our responsibility; after making our petitions—even repeatedly—we commit the situation to God. Prayer is not a form of magic by which we attempt to control the Deity. In praying we are using a means given to us by the Deity to be used in the milieu of trust.

5. When to Pray. If the content of the pastoral conversation has included important life issues, prayer is often appropriate. But there may be times in pastoral care when prayer is not fitting. How can the pastor know? Some simply rely upon intuition—a pastoral sense—in determining when the other is receptive to prayer. But probably the best way to know is to ask. The response is usually clear. For example, a response like, "If you want to," is not really an assent but a deference to the pastor's role and indicates the need for further dialogue about the person's *own* interest in prayer. Prayer should not be forced on one, and a negative response needs to be accepted. The pastor can pray for the person in his or her own intercessory prayers, a ministry not observed by others but nonetheless important.

Since praying confronts one with the presence of the living God, emotions often come to the surface. Moist eyes and quivering lips may be due to feelings as diverse as joy and guilt or gratitude and hurt. Only their verbal expressions will reveal their identity. The pastor may need to encourage this verbalization to bring about a helpful closure to the visit. It is not unusual for the most authentic dialogue to occur after the prayer. Even when the emotions are those of hurt or guilt their verbal expression in the pastoral dialogue prepares the way for reconciliation and healing.

Bibliography. J. R. Finney and H. N. Maloney, "Contemplative Prayer and Its use in Psychotherapy: A Theoretical Model," *J. of Psychology and Theology*, 13:3 (1985), 172–81 and "An Empirical Study of Contemplative Prayer as an Adjunct to Psychotherapy," *J. of Psychology and Theology*, 13:4 (1985), 284–90. G. M. Furniss, "Healing Prayer and Pastoral Care," *J. of Pastoral Care*, 38 (1984), 107–19. S. Hiltner, *Pastoral Counseling* ch. 9 (1949). W. E. Hulme, *Pastoral Care and Counseling* ch. 7 (1981). K. W. Keidel, "Prayer with Patients: Whose Will Be

Done?" *American Protestant Hospital Association Bulletin*, 47:3 (1983), 11–16. M. A. Lange, "Prayer and Psychotherapy: Beliefs and Practice," *J. of Psychology and Christianity*, 2:3 (1983), 36–49. M. A. Lucas, "Praying with the Terminally Ill," *American Protestant Hospital Association Bulletin*, 43:2 (1979), 35–40. N. Thayer, *Spirituality and Pastoral Care* (1985). R. L. Underwood, "The Presence of God in Pastoral Care Ministry," *Austin Seminary Bulletin*, 101:4 (1985), 5–14. *See also* S. Carney, "God Damn God: A Reflection on Expressing Anger in Prayer," *Biblical Theology Bulletin*, 3 (1983), 116–20.

W. E. HULME

JEWISH PRAYERS; RELIGIOUS LANGUAGE IN PASTORAL CARE; RITUAL AND PASTORAL CARE. *See also* DYING, PASTORAL CARE OF; GOD'S WILL, ACCEPTANCE OF; GUIDANCE, DIVINE; MEDITATION; SICK, PASTORAL CARE OF; SPIRITUAL DIRECTION AND PASTORAL CARE. *Compare* BLESSING AND BENEDICTION; PASTORAL CONVERSATION.

PRAYER MEETING. *See* PIETISM AND PASTORAL CARE.

PRAYERS, JEWISH. *See* JEWISH PRAYERS.

PREACHING. The proclamation of the good news of God's grace toward all persons. While in theory this proclamation may be by anyone to any group of auditors, in practice most preaching is done by ministers to the congregations to which they have been called or appointed to give spiritual oversight. This means that the preacher who regularly delivers a sermon as a more-or-less formal address in the context of an assembly structured for worship and fellowship is also the pastor who regularly ministers to these people in settings quite often informal, personal, and conversational. If it is the case that the minister as preacher regards the message as primary while the minister as pastor regards the parishioner's needs as primary, then the possibilities for confusion, misunderstanding, and tension within ministers and among parishioners are increased. But the dual roles of preacher and pastor have not been uniformly experienced as problematic. Responses have varied from being comfortable with both to subordinating one to the other to rejecting one for the other to struggling for integration and mutual enrichment.

1. **Preaching with Pastoral Care: A Matter of Perspective.** *a. The biblical tradition.* That the believing community experiences the same person as both preacher and pastor is not a modern phenomenon; it is as old as the church itself. In fact, the church inherited from Judaism the image of the bold proclaimer with the heart of a shepherd and of the gentle pastor who announces the word of the Lord. Sharp distinctions among prophets, priests, and pastors are more the work of modern commentators than descriptions of the tasks and roles of religious leaders as presented in the Hebrew Bible. Their functions were defined by their understanding of God who not only "roars from Zion" (Amos 1:2) but who "will feed his flock like a shepherd, he will gather the lambs in his arms, he will carry them in his bosom, and gently lead those that are with young" (Isa. 40:11). The Servant of the Lord of whom Isaiah sang had a mouth like a sharp sword (49:2) but knew "how to sustain with a word him that is weary" (50:4). This Servant would

proclaim justice to the nations but would be so caring as not to break a bruised reed nor quench a dimly burning wick (42:1–3). Drawing heavily upon these passages, NT writers portrayed Jesus as a preacher of repentance and the approach of the kingdom (Mk. 1:14–15) and at the same time a compassionate shepherd (Jn. 10:1–16). The apostle Paul understood his vocation as that of one sent to preach (I Cor. 1:17) but faithfulness to that calling included relating to the churches as a father to children (I Cor. 4:14–15), as a woman in the pains of childbirth (Gal. 4:19), and gentle as a nurse (I Thess. 2:7). Likewise, in the Pauline tradition and in Paul's name, the next generation of ministers was instructed to preach the word and pastor the flock of God (I Tim. 2:1–6:16). There is no hint that the one task negated, weakened, or subsumed the other.

b. The post-biblical tradition. Editors of anthologies of sermons from St. Augustine to the modern period have been hard pressed to find appropriate classifications for these classics: doctrinal, devotional, exegetical, apologetic, polemical, expository, topical, and so forth. These and other such terms are only partially appropriate. A reading of these sermons reveals clearly that they were all pastoral in perspective. They were preached with a mind to nourish, guard, comfort, inform, warn, encourage, heal, or renew the flock of God. Of course, these sermons are finished products, reflecting a high degree of harmony between proclaiming and pastoring but not revealing the tensions suffered in the process. One can be sure that if only in terms of demands upon time, most if not all found it difficult to be both preacher and pastor. In his lecture on preaching given at Yale in 1877, Phillips Brooks insisted that the work of the preacher and the pastor belong together. But he acknowledged that due to multiple demands, "you may come to believe that it would be good indeed if you could be one or other of two things and not both; either a preacher or a pastor but not the two together. But I assure you you are wrong" (*Lectures on Preaching*, p. 76). Brooks spoke his word of assurance to ministers beleaguered primarily by pressures of time. On the horizon were other factors that would argue more strongly that one be either preacher or pastor.

2. **Preaching as Pastoral Care: A Matter of Content.** Early in the twentieth century a number of factors combined to alter the relationship between preaching and pastoring. For many practitioners of both it would no longer be enough that a pastoral involvement with the parishioners would give flavor and perspective to preaching. Now pastoral care, and pastoral counseling in particular, would give sermons their subject matter.

a. Growing discomfort with "preaching the Bible." In the American church, preaching the Bible has most generally referred to a kind of sermon called expository. Simply stated, an expository sermon explains a biblical text in its own historical and cultural setting, draws out the central lesson or meaning of that text and urges its application in the lives of the hearers. The certainties and clear continuities upon which such preaching was based were disturbed, however, by the methods of biblical criticism moving through the seminaries and into the pulpits. Lacking a way of preaching the Bible congenial with the newer approaches to the Scriptures, some ministers rejected biblical criticism while others moved the Bible to the margins of their sermons while searching elsewhere for central content. Preaching on topics of the day became quite popular, but it was the growth of the pastoral psychology movement in the first half of the twentieth century that offered a new and exciting alternative.

b. H. E. Fosdick and life-situation preaching. The most influential figure in the shift from expository preaching to life-situation preaching was Harry Emerson Fosdick, pastor of Riverside Church, New York City, from 1926 until 1946. Fosdick rejected expository preaching not solely because he embraced the methods of biblical criticism but also because he believed that the personal problems of his parishioners were the central concern of the pulpit. As he phrased it in his now famous expression, "Only the preacher proceeds still upon the idea that folk come to church desperately anxious to discover what happened to the Jebusites" (*The Living of These Days,* 1956, p. 92). When he became convinced that the most vital dimension of his ministry was personal counseling, Fosdick developed his preaching so as to make it group counseling. He called the messages life-situation or counseling sermons. The problems and needs of the listeners provided the subjects and themes and the personal conversation method of the counseling session provided the style. The Bible, the classics, and reading in many fields nourished the messages, which reached wider and wider audiences through print and radio.

c. Appraisal. It is beyond question that the problem-solving format gave new life to preaching, not only among listeners but also among pastors whose sermons had become to them stale, flat, and tasteless. The immediacy of addressing felt needs, the style of speaking as to one person, the rapport between preacher and listeners in both sympathy and understanding, and the greater respect for the hearers who were treated not as the destination but as the source of sermons all contributed to a kind of success for the pulpit. Fosdick spoke not only of the immediate responses to his sermons but of the increased numbers who made appointments for further counseling. But did the pulpit lose anything in the process? The best answer lies, of course, with each preacher. In the case of Fosdick, personal skills, depth of understanding, disciplined study, and knowledge of the biblical tradition probably made his counseling preaching a far greater gain than loss for the listeners. In some sermons he likely was more biblical than in his early efforts to be biblical. However, in lesser hands life-situation preaching produced losses both for the preacher and the pastor. Among these were: absence of real struggle with biblical texts; loss of substantive continuity with the tradition and the nourishment it provided; treatment of apparent rather than real needs; facile use of psychological answers that had never been in dialogue with Christian theology; erosion of community by privatizing religion; and failure to treat matters of ultimate relevance because they seemed not to be of immediate relevance.

Exceptions notwithstanding, in many churches pastoral care, and especially pastoral counseling, was radically affecting not only how the pulpit served its fare but also the content of what was served. In fact, so strong was the shift of attention to pastoral care, so much to be preferred over the old homiletics was the personal, conversational, client-centered, problem-facing style of the counselor, that by the 1960s the next question was seriously raised: Is there any further need for preaching? Is it not an exercise in obsolescence?

3. Preaching or Pastoral Care: A Matter of Choice. During the sixties and early seventies many young ministers no less dedicated than their predecessors were opting for forms of ministry that were non-traditional and which excluded the pulpit. While preaching maintained its strong advocates, the new atmosphere was one of freedom to choose one's style and direction, even within a vocation as traditional as ministry. Seminaries responded by reducing requirements and increasing alternatives. Preaching, long a requirement of all ministerial students, became one of a number of options in many schools. Those moving away from the pulpit went primarily in one of two directions: to the streets as agents of social change or to the privacy of an office as counselors.

a. Reasons for the debate. The issues between preaching and pastoral care were real ones: the locus of authority in the Christian faith, modes of communication, a person's right to self-determination, the role of tradition in achieving freedom and maturity, the ethics of manipulation, personal versus institutional values, the gospel as content or as relationship, and a bundle of questions having to do with the matter of what constitutes Christian ministry. However, while these issues were being discussed and debated, in some quarters the gulf between preaching and pastoral counseling was widened by less than responsible arguing. Readers and audiences were treated to messianic claims for one or the other form of ministry and to false contrasts between the best of one and the worst of the other. On one hand, some gave the impression that the alternative to lively preaching of the good news of God's grace was the passive pastor posing as a psychologist, relishing all the intimate details of the parishioners' private lives. On the other, the alternative to empathetic ministry in a therapeutic relationship was imaged as a droning pulpit, full of authoritarian harangues, moralistic scoldings, creedal conformities, denominational loyalties, and promotional trivia. And all this was occurring within a society caught up in the winds of change. All religious, political, and social institutions and traditions were being questioned and called to account. Authority could not be assumed, and values were given full examination. It was a time of freedom and experimentation.

b. European reactions. The situation described in the paragraph above prevailed primarily in America and has more slowly and with modifications been descriptive of the religious scene in Europe. In fact, the major theological and ecclesiastical influences in Europe in this century, Catholic and Protestant, have been reaffirmations of the importance of preaching. Vatican II called for an increased role for preaching and the implementation of Aquinas's insistence upon proclamation as a primary task of the priest. In Protestant circles, the two most significant figures in this century have been Karl Barth and Rudolf Bultmann. Both their programs, the one in church dogmatics and the other in existential exegesis, have been intended as efforts in the service of the sermon.

This is not to say that the concerns of pastoral care and counseling have been untouched. These have been growing areas of practice and reflection as evidenced by books, articles, and reports of conferences and institutes. But even so, the conversation between preaching and pastoral care is still governed by the focus on the pulpit. The proclamation of God's care precedes, inspires, and informs all other expressions of care, and God's saving act in preaching is prior to all therapeutic ministries. As long as "preaching the word of God *is* the word of God" holds as the definition of the pulpit's place in the church, preaching will sit in the host's chair entertaining other forms of ministry. This is not to say by any means that preaching is not to be pastoral. Karl Barth's sermons were widely regarded as strongly pastoral in the sense of being directed to individual as well as communal needs, deeply empathetic and addressed to human grief, suffering, and sin. But in his mind, the listeners were always the recipients and not the source of the sermon. It is understandable that with this background, Dietrich Bonhoeffer would find American preaching generally non-substantive, highly subjective, and quite humanistic.

4. Preaching and Pastoral Care: A Matter of Mutual Enrichment. Since the mid-1970s a number of changes have occurred in both preaching and pastoral care and in their relationship. These changes are in the main positive, having been purchased at the price of painful listening to one another and continued exercises of self-criticism.

a. In perspective. It is probably fair to say that pastoral care has had greater influence upon preaching than preaching has had upon pastoral care. However, it is not necessary to identify which influenced the other in order to recognize the mutual enrichment if not integration of the two tasks of ministry. After all, it is still the case that most ministers do both preaching and pastoring. But in situations where the two modes of ministry are performed by different persons, there is growing mutual respect. Preaching and counseling are different forms of ministry and both have limitations; neither is a cure-all. Just as there are varieties of gifts for ministry so there are varieties of human needs to be addressed, and the modes of ministry for addressing those needs differ in their appropriateness from case to case. However, all forms of ministry are doubly authorized by the tradition of the Christian faith and the needs of the parishioners. The Incarnation makes possible both preaching and pastoral care. The Divine Son dwelling among us enables our understanding that a caring presence can be the presence of Christ; the Word made flesh enables our understanding that a human word spoken can be the Word of God. And at a time when pastoral care is being de-clericalized in the sense of equipping the whole church to be a community of caring and healing, preaching is giving a larger role to the congregation. This is not in the sense of proclaiming what the people want to hear but rather what they want to say. After all, it is the church's faith, the church's tradition, the church's message that is being spoken and not a private word that arrived with the preacher.

b. In method. As stated earlier, it is more the case that pastoral care has influenced preaching than vice versa. Some of this influence has been direct and some indirect, and all of it has improved as pastoral care has matured in its methods and goals. For example, preaching early sought to be pastoral counseling by having the listeners provide the questions to be treated and the Bible provide the answers. Now pastoral preaching better understands that the Bible as often questions its reader as it offers an answer. Pastoral preaching has also recognized that the relationship between speaker and listener need not be very different from that between a pastor and a parishioner who has come for counsel. Trust, empathy, and mutuality in strength and weakness, faith and doubt, sin and grace do not destroy the effectiveness of preaching. If the preacher does not indulge week after week in unbridled subjectivity, some self-disclosure can be healthy. Of course, total identification with parishioners, whether as preacher or pastor, can emotionally consume the minister and create loss of perspective. Without critical distance, helpfulness dissolves into a pool of pity.

Whether directly or indirectly influenced by pastoral care, or as a result of a hard look at itself, preaching today is more pastoral in both preparation and structure. More and more sermons bear evidence of preparation, which includes careful listening to the people as well as the text. Exegesis of the congregation does not replace but joins exegesis of Scripture in the creation of the message. In the matter of sermon structure, while there have been efforts to apply principles of counseling directly to sermon formation, more importantly an increasing number of preachers are attempting to implement the priesthood of all believers in the way sermons unfold. This is to say, listeners are permitted to assume some responsibility beyond agreeing or disagreeing. Sermons that arrive at conclusions rather than starting with them evoke in the hearers thinking, feeling, reflecting, recalling, and finally, owning the message. This respect for listeners is far more pastoral than tossing into the sermon a few life-situation illustrations. Forms for such sermons have many sources, but prominent among them are the Scriptures. Literary critical studies have quickened new interest in the form as well as content of a text, offering the preacher clues as to what a text does as well as says. Some of these forms, especially parables and narratives, have been found congenial not only to preaching but also counseling. In these models our stories and the divine story intersect most revealingly. At points such as this, preaching and pastoral care not only enrich each other but experience genuine integration.

c. In content. Recent books and articles indicate that both preaching and pastoral care have experienced an increase in the size of their subject matter. Problems, issues, and questions, whether originating in biblical texts, in culture, or in the lives of parishioners, are always there to be dealt with, but not those matters alone. In the sanctuary or in the pastor's study, persons often need to dip into the tradition and into their own lives to enjoy, to celebrate, and to give thanks. Health as well as illness belongs on the agenda of pastoral preaching. There are also occasions when more important than attention to an immediate felt need is attention to the larger context of the life of faith. This context is not only congregational or denominational or even ecumenical; it is historical. Faith needs and has a past. The Christian life is in one sense an exercise in memory, and it makes a qualitative difference in one's life to remember that we are children of Abraham and Sarah, Isaac and Rebekah, Jacob and Rachel. Pastoral preaching always contains a yes, but sometimes it also contains a no. A call to repentance may be pastoral, just as it is also pastoral to take the parishioners by the hand and let them step off the size of their inheritance as children of God. Spoken or unspoken, the gospel of God's grace is the subject matter of ministry, and preaching is pastoral if it creates in the listener a sense of the presence of the unconditional care of God.

Bibliography. For the history of the conversation between preaching and pastoral care, the journal *Pastoral Psychology.* Most volumes since inception (1950) have articles on preaching. For Fosdick's method, E. H. Linn, *Preaching as Counseling* (1966). For contrasts between early and more recent application of pastoral care and counseling to preaching, E. N. Jackson, *A Psychology for Preaching* (1961); D. K. Switzer, *Pastor, Preacher, Person* (1979); T. C. Oden, *Pastoral Theology* (1983), ch. 9. To see changing views of pastoral preaching, C. F. Kemp, *Pastoral Preaching* (1963) and G. D. Stratman, *Pastoral Preaching* (1983). For theological and methodological attempts at integration see T. C. Oden, *Kerygma and Counseling* (1966); D. Capps, *Pastoral Counseling and Preaching* (1980); J. R. Nichols, *Building the Word: The Dynamics of Communication and Preaching* (1981). F. B. Craddock, *Preaching* (1985). For European reactions R. Bohren, *Preaching and Community* (1965) and J. J. Von Allmen, *Preaching and Congregation* (1962).

F. B. CRADDOCK

COMMUNICATION; INTERPRETATION AND HERMENEUTICS, PASTORAL; MINISTRY; ROLE, MINISTERIAL; WORSHIP AND CELEBRATION. *See also* IMAGINATION; NEO-ORTHODOX THEOLOGY AND PASTORAL CARE; NEW TESTAMENT, TRADITIONS AND THEOLOGY OF CARE IN; REVELATION AND PASTORAL CARE. *Compare* EVANGELIZING; TEACHING.

PRECEPT (Moral Theology). In Roman Catholic morality, a command binding in conscience, given by a legitimate ecclesiastical superior to a subject or a community. The precept must be moral and promulgated by legitimate authority. Its binding force lasts only during the regime of the one who issued it. Ecclesiastical law binds in conscience but is of a general nature and for an indefinite period of time, whereas a precept is given by superiors to subjects for a limited period of time. The "precept" is obsolete today since superiors rarely issue orders binding their subjects in conscience.

Bibliography. D. Prümmer, *Handbook of Moral Theology* (1957).

W. M. NOLAN

GUIDANCE, PASTORAL; MORAL THEOLOGY AND PASTORAL CARE. *Compare* CASUISTRY.

PRECOCIOUSNESS. *See* LIFE CYCLE THEORY; PERSONALITY DEVELOPMENT, BIOLOGICAL AND SOCIALIZING FACTORS IN.

PRECOGNITION. *See* PARAPSYCHOLOGY.

PREDESTINATION. *See* PROVIDENCE.

PREDICAMENT, HUMAN. *See* HUMAN CONDITION/PREDICAMENT.

PREFRONTAL LOBOTOMY. *See* PSYCHOSURGERY.

PREGNANCY. Research on pregnancy, which has historically focused on the physiology of the unborn baby and of the mother, recently has shifted to pregnancy's psychological components. An authoritative "psychology of pregnancy" has not been established but there is a body of research concerning the complexity of responses to pregnancy, both planned and unplanned.

Emotional Responses to Pregnancy. A common emotional response to pregnancy is ambivalence. Even the woman who has planned her pregnancy is uncertain at times about whether or not she wants to be a mother. Some studies suggest that this ambivalence can produce physical symptoms, most commonly nausea. Newton (1955) found a relationship between negative attitudes toward pregnancy, lack of interest in breast feeding, and very limited physical contact with the infant. Extreme ambivalence is expressed through denial of the pregnancy and/or refusal to receive medical care. Frequently such women have also been found to later abuse their children physically.

Another common response to pregnancy is a preoccupation with the growing, unborn baby. Winnicott (1965) says that a "well enough" woman "surrenders to motherhood," becomes closely identified with the baby, develops strong feelings of love for it during pregnancy, and at birth knows how to care for it. In the healthy mother this identification and preoccupation continue for a few months until individuation gradually begins to occur. In the pathological mother this preoccupation either continues too long and is evidenced by overprotection, or it stops too abruptly and the mother switches to a new preoccupation. Anxiety, a third common response to pregnancy, has also been well-researched. Most women experience some anxiety, but extreme anxiety has been associated with obstetrical problems and excessive crying and restlessness in infants. Davids's (1968) research suggests a relationship between anxiety and unfavorable attitudes toward children as well as slower emotional and intellectual development in infants.

While not conclusive, these studies point to a possible relationship between a woman's emotional response to pregnancy and to her view of, and later interaction with, her baby. Although the traditional psychoanalysts recommended termination of therapy during pregnancy, important therapeutic work can be done during this period. Pastoral care and counseling can offer help with the ambivalences, preoccupations, and anxieties of pregnancy realizing that the greater possibility for a healthy birth and healthier relationship between the mother and her child comes with resolution.

While counseling can be useful for the woman whose pregnancy is planned, it is more important for the woman whose pregnancy is unplanned. The options of keeping the baby, giving it up for adoption, or abortion are all complex, both emotionally and morally.

Women who choose abortion often suffer much guilt, the magnitude of which is underplayed in the literature. This guilt is often long-lasting, even in the woman who, years after the abortion, is convinced that having the abortion was her best option.

Just as difficult emotionally is the option of placing the baby for adoption. Many Roman Catholics in particular see this as the only option. At the time of the pregnancy, adoption may seem easier, but in middle or late years it often becomes difficult. Knowing one's child is alive and wanting to make contact, yet having no legal rights, is problematic for both mother and father as well as the adopted child.

The complexities with adoption may be one of the factors in today's teenage mothers choosing to keep their babies. In Chicago, for example, eighty percent of the unwed mothers have kept their babies in recent years; whereas as recently as the 1960s only twenty percent kept them.

Whether a pregnancy is planned or unplanned, it is complex and often reaches crisis proportions. More counseling is needed to help both mothers and fathers face these problems earlier, thereby preventing later and even more difficult problems.

Bibliography. A. Davids, "A Research Design for Studying Maternal Emotionality Before Childbirth and After Social Interaction With the Child," *Merrill-Palmer Quarterly*, 14 (1968), 345–54. E. Heffner, *Mothering: The Emotional Experience of Motherhood After Freud and Feminism* (1978). N. Newton, *Maternal Emotions* (1955). D. W. Winnicott, *The Maturational Process and the Facilitating Environment* (1965).

L. S. GROH

CHILDBIRTH; MARRIAGE; PARENTS/PARENTHOOD; WOMEN. *Compare* FAMILY PLANNING; MISCARRIAGE; MORAL DILEMMAS IN PASTORAL PERSPECTIVE.

PREJUDICE. Unfounded hostile attitudes—suspicion, dislike, disparagement, rejection—directed toward members of a group identifiably distinguished by religion, race, occupation, nationality, gender, age, region, sexual orientation, height, weight, physical handicap, social class, dress, hair style, membership in labor unions, personal habits such as smoking, or presumably any other identifiable characteristic. Typically prejudice is directed toward persons distinctly different from oneself, but self-disparaging attitudes toward groups with which one identifies can also be regarded as prejudice. Increasingly, largely as a political strategy, specific terms are used to identify prejudice directed toward particular groups; thus, anti-Semitism, racism, sexism, ageism, and the like.

1. **Nature of Prejudice.** As the literal meaning of the term implies—pre-conceived judgment (perhaps such a relatively bland term is used as a euphemism for the powerfully disruptive force it names)—the prejudiced attitude is held without regard for objective data about the targeted group, its characteristics, or its impact on society and on the person expressing the prejudice; the prejudice is not usually modified by education or challenge which arrays such facts. Prejudice imposes a pre-cast stereotype on the facts, selecting and interpreting them to buttress the hostile attitudes.

Prejudiced attitudes, behavior, and decisions are often demonstrated, not only in the presence of contradictory information, but also in the presence of consciously and genuinely professed attitudes of tolerance and non-prejudice (e.g., persons consciously and publicly committed to affirmative action remain, in their actual employment practice, party to persistent exclusionist decisions). This fact leads some to conclude that prejudice is rooted in the structures of society, impervious to changes in personal attitudes, and responsive only to legally enforced changes in that structure. It leads others to conclude that prejudice is immune to conscious attitude change because it is rooted in unconscious scenarios and fears which must be countered or exposed before prejudice can be modified.

Although groups that are victims of prejudice have a legitimate stake in isolating the prejudice directed toward themselves as an urgently distinct social problem —in the form, e.g., of anti-Semitism or racism or sexism— prejudice is, in fact, a highly generalized personality characteristic, displayed against any recognizable "out-group" including fictitious groups such as "Pireneans," invented by social psychologists for questionnaires intended to illustrate just this point.

More generally, prejudice is correlated with conservative attitudes toward social issues such as capital punishment and rehabilitation of criminals; war, militarism, and colonialism; abortion and sexual practices; public responsibility for the homeless, unemployed, ill, and aged.

Still more generally, prejudice is correlated with constrictive styles of personal relationships, and is part of a personality marked by rigidity, intolerance of ambiguity and of change, and defensiveness, that is, a personality type which has come to be called the "authoritarian personality." The portrait of the prejudiced personality is, generally, the portrait of a person with a highly structured and compartmentalized view of life, with tight boundaries drawn between the familiar, which is deemed good, even to the point of over-idealization (as in super-patriotism) and the unfamiliar, which is *ipso facto* viewed as threatening and evaluated negatively.

The minister may be concerned about the dehumanizing effects of prejudice both on the targets of that prejudice, with its resultant injustices and barriers to community, and also on the conveyers of that prejudice, with their constricted, fearful, and joyless outlook on life. The minister will also necessarily and personally be distressed by the constricting and obstructionist effects which the prejudiced/authoritarian personality exerts on the immediate community and often on the minister's own hopes and programs for that community.

2. **Prejudice and Religion.** Empirical research conducted for half a century by many different investigators, using many different groups in many countries, has demonstrated a fact disconcerting to many religious leaders: In general, members of Christian churches are more prejudiced than non-members; orthodox believers are more prejudiced than less faithful adherents. While the data, of course, reveal many individual exceptions, the general tendency is firm: religious adherence appears associated with prejudice. The only systematic exception is the discovery that church attendance has a complicated "curvilinear" relationship with prejudice: Although attenders are more prejudiced than non-attenders, the most faithful attenders, those who attend church at least

weekly, are less prejudiced than those who attend often but not quite every week.

This finding is disconcerting because prejudice contradicts essential religious proclamations about the oneness of the human race and the fullness of life; about the sovereignty of God, as contrasted with the sovereignty of some groups over others; about the casting out of fear, on which prejudice breeds; and about the foolishness of trusting idols, which prejudice exalts and protects. It also may be discouraging for ministers to realize that the church lags rather than leads society on this fundamental issue of individual and communal wholeness.

Probably the best interpretation of this association between prejudice and church adherence is to perceive each as a very understandable reaction to the feeling of precariousness of life. This is not inconsistent with the church's self-understanding. The Bible proposes that its message and the fellowship of the church is for those who experience themselves as outcasts and exiles, in despair, hungry, lonely, in sin, and in every way needy. Such a psychological portrait of the roots of religious quest is probably also an accurate portrait of the roots of prejudice: Prejudice displays a defensive posture against what is perceived as the threat of the alien and unfamiliar, and its bravado in fact betrays a fundamental sense of insecurity, expressed often as a fear of being socially "marginalized."

Put in more Jungian terms, both much religious practice and prejudice show how the fearful ego excludes the alien, the shadowy elements of life, as threatening and tries to live in a world constructed of the more familiar, and therefore more limited and limiting dimensions of life. Much religion has this one-sided quality of "healthy-mindedness" or of "positive thinking," and groups which differ ethnically, racially, in sexual practice, etc., could all trigger this deeply held mistrust of the alien and provoke exclusion, which occurs in the form of prejudice, converting unacknowledged archetypes into stereotypes.

3. **Pastoral Care of the Prejudiced.** Prejudice and the prejudiced personality pose the classic confrontation between two types of strategies: one regards the prejudice itself as the primary object of pastoral (or "prophetic") attention; the other regards the prejudice as derived and symptomatic of deeper distress which becomes the primary object of pastoral care.

a. Challenge to prejudice. The first strategy emphasizes that the prejudice is wrong, factually wrong (almost always) in its portrayal of target groups, and morally wrong, destructive in its impact on the quality of life, both for the targets and the prejudiced persons. (1) Misstatements of fact can be challenged and corrected ("Property values do *not* decline"); (2) Appeals to values transcending the prejudice can be made ("Even so, don't they deserve a chance?"); (3) Authority can be appealed to, especially the authority of the group: the prejudiced person can be "resocialized" by being surrounded with a group of respected persons whose social attitudes are relatively unprejudiced. The prejudiced/authoritarian personality is presumably especially vulnerable to suggestion and authority; (4) Behavior inconsistent with the prejudice can be induced or coerced, as for example, in national civil rights legislation, in court-enforced social

change, and in local community programs, all encouraging behavior of integration and non-discriminatory, respectful treatment by those not intrinsically disposed to grant it.

This last behavioral modification strategy, like any behavioral therapy, promises a double gain: (1) It reduces the troubling symptoms, especially in this case mitigating the unjust impact of prejudice on target groups; (2) it also can be an effective strategy for modifying the underlying attitudes themselves; behavior change can induce attitude change, not just vice versa. Research studies and actual experience demonstrate that behaving "as though" one believes or feels something enhances the likelihood of that belief or feeling — as response to an altar call may, for example — being the first step more often than the final step toward religious conversion and adherence. (The James-Lange theory of emotions, the cognitive dissonance theory of attitude change, and behavior modification theories of therapy are some of the better known rubrics under which this principle has been discussed in psychology.)

However, these symptom-challenging tactics of persuasion and coercion have limits. Like a cancerous growth, prejudice reduced at one point tends to recur, often to the pastor's dismay, at another point. Further, there is the real risk that assertive and judgmental tactics against the prejudiced person may only enhance the sense of precariousness and threat in which the prejudice is rooted.

b. Undermining the prejudice. If prejudice is understood as a defensive response to fundamental needs and fears, what are they? What is the function of prejudice? Can pastoral care and community meet those needs and fears in a way that makes prejudice less necessary? If prejudiced put-down of others makes one feel more status and esteem, less insecure and vulnerable, can religious faith and community provide that sense of status and security? If prejudice draws social boundaries that deal with one's sense of loneliness and isolation by manufacturing the experience of membership in an "in" group, can religious community meet the same need? If prejudice is an attempt to cope with a terrifying world, can pastoral care make life seem less terrifying? If prejudice is an attempt by persons to arrange and guarantee their own well-being, can pastoral care help them discover that they cannot and need not save themselves, but rather find that they are saved?

Bibliography. G. W. Allport, *The Nature of Prejudice* (1954). B. Bettelheim and M. Janowitz, *Dynamics of Prejudice* (1950). E. B. Brody, "Psychiatry and Prejudice", in *American Handbook of Psychiatry*, S. Arieti, ed., (1974). J. E. Dittes, *Bias and the Pious* (1973).

J. E. DITTES

ANTI-SEMITISM; RACISM; SEXISM. *See also* HOLOCAUST; SOCIAL PERCEPTION, JUDGMENT, AND BELIEF. *Compare* ANTISOCIAL PERSONS; AUTHORITARIANISM.

PREMARITAL COUNSELING. Premarital counseling most often refers to the ministry offered by a pastor to a couple prior to officiating at their marriage. It is more often a type of pastoral care, guidance, and interpretation rather than counseling because the majority of couples who come to the pastor have no awareness of "having a problem"—the condition presupposed by the concept of "counseling." In fact, the time immediately prior to the marriage, when most couples receive premarital pastoral care is likely to be a time of denial of problems and the negative side of their ambivalence about the marriage.

1. **Purpose.** The primary value in premarital pastoral care is in assisting a couple to surface assumptions about themselves, their families of origin and the religious community which—at least through the minister—they are asking to bless their marriage. Its secondary value is to provide the couple with an opportunity to develop a significant relationship to the minister and thence to the religious community. Premarital pastoral care may become counseling, and is most likely to, when one or both persons in the couple have been previously married, when the couple has had a long relationship, perhaps having been living together, when one or both are resistant to marriage, or when at least one person fears that a past individual experience may influence the relationship in a negative way. Under such circumstances premarital work is not focused upon preparing for a marriage for which a date already has been set but upon examining some of the areas of concern which the couple has acknowledged.

It can be argued that premarital pastoral care developed more out of the church's concern to preserve the institution of marriage than from a pastoral concern for individuals. Its identification of this ministry as "counseling"—in addition to the popularity which the word, "counseling," developed in the 1950s—may be attributed to the church's preference to locate the problem of marriage in the couple rather than in its view of marriage or its effectiveness in blessing it.

2. **Origins and development.** As an accepted form of ministry, premarital counseling had its beginning in the U. S. during the 1920s. The earliest literature which provided guidance to pastors on this topic was published by the Federal Council of Churches. Premarital counseling literature prior to 1950 encouraged ministers to believe that if they did effective premarital work, the divorce rate could drop dramatically. Although this concern diminished in later literature, there seems to have been a continued assumption that effective premarital care coupled with faithful church attendance could help reduce the divorce rate. The procedure that ministers were to follow was largely instruction addressed to the major problem couples were assumed to have: lack of information on what constituted a successful marriage, and the steps they as a couple could take to ensure its maintenance (Nease).

A noticeable shift in the emphasis of the literature occurred during the decade of the 1950s when, due to the strong influence of pastoral psychology with its heavy emphasis upon counseling and psychotherapy, premarital pastoral care began to focus more upon the nature of the relationship which marriage involved rather than the information necessary for successful marriage. Premarriage ministry was to help a couple achieve an intense interpersonal involvement and exchange through open and free communication of feelings. The major purpose

for meeting with couples was to prepare them for marriage by anticipating various aspects of the relationship.

The view of human nature implicit in most writers of premarital counseling literature has tended toward a kind of theological optimism and works righteousness, i.e., with proper premarital counseling, and sufficient effort on the part of the couple, marriage could be freed from the presence and influence of sin and human frailty, and divorces would be reduced (Nease).

In contrast to these assumptions, the point of view of this article is that the function of premarital, counseling, like human nature, is considerably more limited. The role of the pastor in carrying out these purposes is interpretive and consultative: interpretive, in the sense of reviewing the data of the couple's lives and interpreting them from a mature religious and psychological perspective; consultative, in that the acceptance of the pastor's interpretations and suggestions are not required. They may be used, rejected or deferred for use until a later time.

3. **Approaches.** Mitchell and Anderson have argued that the most important task of premarital care is assisting the couple in appropriate disengagement from their family of origin. "You must leave," they say, "before you can cleave" (1981). Couples intent on being married may be reluctant to examine their own relationship. Discussing their families of origin is less likely to produce resistance and more likely to yield fruitful results for the couple; therefore, it is also an effective means of surfacing assumptions about what marriage is and what their particular marriage is likely to be. Adapting the work of family system theorists, such as Bowen (1978) and Framo (1982) to their purposes, Mitchell and Anderson describe their family system approach to premarital pastoral care and suggest a variety of methods of implementing it. Preparing and interpreting genograms, examining triangles within the families of origin, discussing family myths and traditions as well as the role of various family members and the explicit and implicit rules for family behavior are among the suggestions made for the structure of the interview.

Consistent with such an approach, a couple might be asked to write a story about the past, for example, the myth of their parents' marriage or some other significant marriage; a story that characterizes their present relationship and a story about the future. In the telling and interpretation of these stories there is practice in the use of the imagination needed for creating a life together. Moreover, these efforts also help put this particular couple's story into the historical context of other stories —with those who have taken similar vows—and to help suggest the common story of those who are seeking a Christian blessing for the journey they are undertaking.

4. **Exploring Religious Tradition.** Related to this is the discovery or rediscovery of the story of the religious tradition from which they come and of the one which they are asking to bless their marriage. As is often the case even with couples from the pastor's own parish, assumptions about their religious tradition are not what one might expect. In order to bring together couple and tradition in an honest and meaningful wedding service, religious assumptions and traditions need to be explored and interpreted. It is the minister's responsibility to

interpret what the religious community has said and is saying about marriage in the wedding service. Most often there needs to be an interpretation of the history of the various elements, their meaning and how that might be related to the couple to be married. Optimally, this interpretation may elicit dialogue about the couple's view of the elements in the marriage service, sometimes re-stating them so that they may be participated in with honesty and conviction.

The minister's responsibility in pre- or postmarital pastoral care might be described as providing a hermeneutical bridge between the couple's present life situation, their families of origin, and the way that the church has historically offered blessing to a marriage. That bridge or relationship, which can seldom be used for counseling prior to the marriage, may be an important basis for the establishing of a counseling relationship later on when the circumstances of life and marriage make the couple aware of their need for such a ministry.

Bibliography. M. Bowen, *Family Therapy in Clinical Practice* (1978). W. J. Everett, *Blessed Be the Bond,* (1985). C. A. Gallagher, G. A. Maloney, M. F. Rousseau and P. E. Wilczak, *Embodied in Love: Sacramental Spirituality and Sexual Intimacy* (1983). J. L. Framo, *Explorations in Marital and Family Therapy* (1982). R. Haughton, "Marriage: An Old, New Fairy Tale," in J. J. Burtchaell, ed., *Marriage Among Christians* (1977). W. J. Lederer and D. D. Jackson, *The Mirages of Marriage* (1968). D. R. Mace, *Getting Ready for Marriage* (1985). T. S. Nease, *Premarital Pastoral Counseling Literature in Protestantism, 1920–71,* Ph.D. dissertation, Princeton University, University microfilms (1973). K. R. Mitchell and H. Anderson, "You Must Leave Before You Can Cleave: A Family Systems Approach to Premarital Pastoral Work," *Pastoral Psychology,* 30:2 (1981), 71–88. T. K. Pitt, *Premarital Counseling Handbook for Ministers* (1985). D. J. Rolfe, "Developing Skills and Credibility in Marriage Preparation Ministry," *Pastoral Psychology,* 33:3 (1985), 161–72. C. J. Sager, *Marriage Contracts and Couple Therapy* (1976).

T. S. NEASE
J. PATTON

MARRIAGE. *See also* COHABITATION; CROSS-CULTURAL MARRIAGE AND FAMILY; REMARRIAGE; WEDDING CEREMONY.

PREMATURE BIRTH. Especially for mothers, the sight of the premature nursery signals the end of a fantasy. The middle-class pregnancy myth is sentimental and joyful: mother and child bond during gentle stretches of time together. By contrast, a mother entering the neonatal unit is confronted with bright lights, noise and frenetic activity. Tiny two-pound bodies are sustained and strengthened through a maze of wires, tubes, and monitors. Rather than immediately experiencing intimate closeness with her child, she is told that she must scrub, gown, and mask before brief visits. Holding her newborn is more like embracing an apparatus than a child; tubes and monitors entangle and separate. At the medically appointed time she is instructed to go home while her newborn remains in the hospital. The old dream is shattered and the mother must necessarily deal with the new reality.

In the interminable hours of separation the mother may experience both frustration and guilt. Why could *I* not finish what I had started? What is it about *me* that could not sustain this relationship to term? Why am *I* weak and not like other women? Residual self-doubts may again come to the surface and natural post-partum depression may be intensified. Frequently, husbands and in-laws also experience such feelings, as well as feelings of blame and judgment. If not resolved, these feelings can take the form of overt hostility or over-solicitousness. In either case, the mother's unrealistic guilt is exacerbated.

Pastors need to be clear in this circumstance that they are the *family's* minister and that this is a *family* problem. The premature infant is special in many ways and has a profound effect on the family. The infant lives separately from the others; an air of uncertainty surrounds the new life; and the mother may be apart from her older children and husband for inordinate amounts of time. And the child is costly. In emotional terms the price is obvious, but the financial cost is equally important. Intensive neonatal care costs hundreds of dollars per day, and no family can help but feel the impact of this new financial burden. The family's entire standard of living is affected, and there are no guarantees that the costs will ensure a normal, healthy life. Pious sentiments not withstanding, most families entertain the fleeting question: Is this child worth it?

The pastor who would work well with the family of the premature child must be prepared emotionally and intellectually in certain specific ways. For instance, being aware of times in one's own life when one was not ready, but had to act or choose *anyway,* will help the pastor understand the family's experience of the premature birth of their child. Intellectually, it is important to ask oneself such questions as: What do I know about the ways this family works? In what way, or to what extent, can I use my pastoral authority to advise and encourage them? What are the emotional and functional resources of this family? Can the husband be less threatened by this new mother-child attachment? Can this wife realize that she is more than a mother? Can siblings be less afraid that they will lose both parents to this unseen stranger? The pastoral task may include helping to clarify options, establish priorities, and accept compromises. In so doing the pastor can fill a tremendously important role that no family member can be expected to play.

Medical research has established a relationship between premature birth and later child abuse. The very young and the very poor are at the highest risk of delivering premature infants. Along with these births one can expect complication, expense, and frustration. It is easy to understand how quickly immature parents in deprived situations can turn to abusive behavior. The pressures of dealing with a premature child, however, can place stress on even the most intact of families. Thus pastoral care of any family in this circumstance, during the early days especially, should be alert to ways of enabling parents to accept their confusing and frequently hostile feelings, and to reach an emotionally honest and mature acceptance of their difficult situation.

P. C. TEMPLE

CHILDBIRTH; MOTHER-INFANT BONDING. *See also* CRISIS MINISTRY; FAMILY, PASTORAL *or* JEWISH CARE AND COUNSELING OF; PARENTS/PARENTHOOD; WOMEN, PASTORAL CARE OF.

PREMATURE EJACULATION. *See* SEXUAL DYS-
FUNCTION AND SEX THERAPY.

PREMENSTRUAL SYNDROME. The cyclic recurrence in the luteal phase of the menstrual cycle (ovulation
to menstrual flow) of a combination of physical, psychological and/or behavioral changes of sufficient severity to
result in deterioration in interpersonal relationships and/or
interference of normal activities. The symptom-free time
coincides with the follicular phase of the cycle (beginning
of menstrual flow until ovulation) (Reid).

It has been estimated that thirty to forty percent of
women of reproductive age experience premenstrual
symptomatology significantly troublesome to provoke a
temporary deterioration in interpersonal relationships
and effectiveness on the job. Only five percent of reproductive age women experience symptoms severe enough
to disrupt family and social relationships, however
(Reid).

1. Diagnosis. The clinician must be careful when diagnosing premenstrual syndrome (PMS) that it is not
merely a late luteal phase exacerbation of another disorder
such as major depression, panic disorder, dysthymia, or
significant personality disorder.

To date as many as 150 symptoms have been catalogued and attributed to premenstrual syndrome. At
least five of the following symptoms must be present
during the luteal phase, including at least one of the
symptoms from categories one through four: (1) marked
affective lability, e.g., feeling suddenly sad, tearful,
irritable, or angry; (2) persistent and marked anger or
irritability; (3) marked anxiety, tension, arousal, or
"edginess"; (4) markedly depressed mood, feelings of
hopelessness, or self-deprecating thoughts; (5) decreased
interest in usual activities; (6) easy fatigability or marked
lack of energy; (7) subjective sense of difficulty in concentrating; (8) marked change in appetite, overeating, or
food cravings; (9) disturbed sleep; (10) other physical
symptoms, such as breast tenderness or swelling, headaches, joint or muscle pain, feeling "bloated," weight
gain (DSM-III-R).

If PMS is suspected, confirmation is provided by a
calendar. Published forms are available (Haskett and
Stein; Harrison, Sharpe, and Endicott). The patient
should then be referred for medical evaluation by a psychiatrist and gynecolgist.

2. Counseling Interventions. Validations of the reality of PMS are helpful in reducing associated distress.
Women report that guilt, self-blame, feeling of failure,
and fears of going crazy are reduced when a diagnosis of
PMS is made. While it is widely believed women use
PMS as an "excuse," data suggests that many increase
self-expectations to compensate for perceived decrements. Sufferers should be encouraged to reduce stress by
shifting tasks to other times, decreasing expectations of
perfection, and making anticipatory plans with family
for increased support. Stress management techniques
(physical exercise, relaxation) may be beneficial also.
Lifestyle interventions should be initiated only during
the follicular phase. Negative responses occurring in the
luteal phase should not be discredited as "only PMS."
Genuine emotional responses must be discriminated

from premenstrual affect. Responses must be used as
information to be evaluated in the follicular phase.

3. Conclusion. Data indicates that intermittent hormonal activity is the *sine qua non* of PMS. A pathophysi-
ological theory to relate the clinical manifestations to
neuroendocrine function is needed. A disservice is done
to patients when it is assumed that this syndrome is
motivated totally psychologically. The symptoms are
clearly tied to ovarian function and the cyclical nature of
the illness.

Bibliography. American Psychiatric Association, *Diagnostic and
Statistical Manual III-R* (DSM III-R) (1987) pp. 367–9.
R. Haskett, M. Steiner, "Diagnosis of Premenstrual Syndrome," *Hospital Community Psychiatry,* 37 (1986), 33–6.
W. Harrison, L. Sharpe, and J. Endicotte "Treatment of Premenstrual Syndrome," *J. of General Hospital Psychiatry,* 7
(1985), 54–65. R. Reid, *Current Problems in Obstetrics, Gynecol-
ogy and Fertility* (1985).

S. B. BROWN
S. MATHIS-HARTLEY

WOMEN, PASTORAL CARE OF; WOMEN, PSYCHOLOGY OF. *See
also* SEXUALITY, BIOLOGICAL AND PSYCHOSOCIAL THEORY OF.

PREMONITION. *See* PARAPSYCHOLOGY.

PRESBYTERIAN PASTORAL CARE. *See* REFORMED
PASTORAL CARE.

PRESCHOOLERS. *See* CHILDREN; PARENTS/PARENT-
HOOD.

PRESENCE, MINISTRY OF. The ministry of presence
has come to mean a form of servanthood (*diakonia*, ministry) characterized by suffering, alongside of and with
the hurt and oppressed—a *being*, rather than a doing or
a telling. The articulation or celebration of faith goes on
within the individual or community that chooses these
circumstances, but does so in the form of *disciplina arcani,*
the "hidden discipline," with no program of external
testimony. Further, Christian presence is sometimes contrasted to Christian social action—suffering with the
victim rather than seeking to alter the circumstances by
systemic change. However, there are examples of the
fusion of the ministries of presence and action, and also
proclamation, as in the Taizé Community.

The ministry of Christian presence is grounded in the
doctrine of the Incarnation, sometimes in its kenotic
form, and/or the doctrine of the Atonement, especially
the priestly office. The identification of the ministrant
with the condition of those in need is viewed as a continuation of the ministry of Christ who "emptied himself,
taking the form of a servant. . . . and became obedient
unto death" (Phil. 2:7a–8a). This ministry of participation follows that of Christ, who "partook of the same
nature, that through death he might. . . . be made like
his brethren in every respect, so that he might become a
merciful and faithful high priest in the service of
God. . . . For because he himself has suffered and been
tempted, he is able to help those who are tempted" (Heb.
2:14a, 17a, 18). The ministry of presence can be volun-

tary or involuntary, as when verbal proclamation in the public sector is forbidden.

The ministry of presence in the pastoral office means vulnerability to and participation in the life-world of those served. The sharing of existence, satisfactions, and burdens may take the specific form of silent witness, as in the vicarious involvement of the counselor in the joys and pains of the counselee, or the change agent in the circumstances of the victim of poverty and injustice.

Another usage of the phrase is appearing in movements encouraging the ministry of the laity. Here Christian presence refers to the exercise of ministry by the people of God in the secular world, preeminently the workplace. Just as the clergy continue the prophetic, priestly, and royal work of Christ in their preaching and teaching, liturgical and pastoral acts, and leadership role in the church, so the laity carry forward this "threefold office" in the secular setting by their solidarity with the needs therein and their ministry of deeds thereto (not precluding, however, a verbal witness when appropriate). In counseling, for example, exponents of the ministry of the laity would view the arena of secular therapy as an opportunity for the continuation of Christ's priestly work through a lay ministry of presence, complementary to the pastoral exercise of the priestly office in the church.

Bibliography. J. F. Six, ed., *Spiritual Autobiography of Charles de Foucauld,* J. H. Smith, trans. (1964). J. V. Taylor, *The Go-Between God* (1973). B. B. Zikmund, "Christian Vocation—in Context," *Theology Today,* 36 (1979), 328–37. G. Fackre, "Ministries of Identity and Vitality," *Theology Today,* 36 (1979), 375–82.

G. FACKRE

MINISTRY; INCARNATIONAL PASTORAL CARE. *See also* ACTION/BEING RELATIONSHIP; BEING/BECOMING RELATIONSHIP. *Compare* EMPATHY; LISTENING; SILENCE; SYMBOLIC DIMENSIONS OF PASTORAL CARE RELATIONSHIPS.

PRESENTING PROBLEM. Refers to the originally stated concern which the parishioner or counselee brings to the pastor. There may be a deeper or more important issue related to the presenting problem, but pastoral responsibility requires that a careful and understanding hearing be given to the presenting problem even when the pastor suspects that there is a more important concern.

J. PATTON

PASTORAL COUNSELING. *See also* INTERPRETATION AND HERMENEUTICS, PASTORAL; SYMBOLISM/SYMBOLIZING. *Compare* CLINICAL PASTORAL PERSPECTIVE; PROBLEM SOLVING.

PRESURGICAL PATIENT. *See* SURGICAL PATIENT.

PREVENIENT GRACE. *See* GRACE.

PRICE, JOHN. *See* BAPTIST PASTORAL CARE.

PRIDE AND HUMILITY (Moral Theology). (1) *Pride.* Traditionally the first of the seven deadly or capital sins, pride is defined as self-exaltation in contempt of God. In theology it is often known by its Greek and Latin originals, *hubris* and *superbia.* (2) *Humility.* The

virtue opposite to pride, humility is self-forgetfulness that exalts the glory of God.

Pride has regularly appeared at the head of the list of sins, reflecting the church's judgment that the other sins spring ultimately from pride and are not possible until pride has first established itself. The soul without pride remains focused on God and the creation, knowing and loving its own place within it, hence incapable of sin. It is when the attention swings to self in preponderance over God and world—the beginning movement of pride —that the distortion that allows the other sins to enter is under way.

Metaphors of height have often been linked to pride, stemming in part from the literal meaning of *hubris* and *superbia,* "to fall upwards" as in Augustine's classic discussion in which pride is described as "inordinate exaltation . . . when the soul cuts itself off from the very Source to which it should keep close and somehow makes itself and becomes an end to itself" (*City of God,* 14:13). The proud person sees self as above the other, even on a par with or above God. One of the symptoms of this elevation is the refusal to take the other into account, to hear or respect that person as of equal importance as oneself.

Modern writers have been at pains to differentiate pride as sin from healthy self-respect and self-love. A key point in that distinction is that a positive self-evaluation is not necessarily a mark of pride, even a self-evaluation that assesses one's performance as superior to others' performances. The slip into pride occurs at the point where one concludes, on the basis of such an evaluation, that one should be treated differently than others, that one has less need for reverence for God or creation.

Pride has recently been linked with narcissism, a clinical phenomenon in which the self is unable to attend to the other's feelings and perceptions because of the desperate and usually unsuccessful attempt to reach a good feeling about the self. Hence sinful pride is most often present in those who have the greatest difficulty respecting either self or creation.

The successful, accomplished, and righteous are seen as the most vulnerable to pride, which is often termed "the sin of the first person singular." Most people experience enough failure in the normal course of things to keep pride within moderate bounds, but those who consistently outdo others in good works or visible achievements are thereby in a more dangerous position.

The long-range costs of pride center in personal isolation and social disorganization. As the prideful person's circle shrinks from the exclusion of first one and then another as unworthy of equal consideration, the individual is left more and more with only self as a fitting companion. This destroys the social links of communities, making distrust and retaliation more likely.

Humility too is often misunderstood as the equivalent of holding a low opinion of oneself. Yet the tradition has consistently held that humility has more to do with one's esteem toward God and others than toward oneself. The truly humble person is, therefore, not a cringing and ineffective weakling, but a vital, engaged individual who passionately invests in relationships with God and humanity. The decisive characteristic of true humility is a constant awareness of the infinite mystery and greatness of God and the immensity of God's creation, within which one shares with many others a finite though honored place. It has been written that the greatest humility is to remember always that while one is not the king, one *is* a prince or princess, the child of the Great King.

Bibliography. H. Fairlie, *The Seven Deadly Sins Today* (1979). B. W. Grant, *From Sin to Wholeness* (1982). S. M. Lyman, *The Seven Deadly Sins: Society and Evil* (1978). The classic theological discussion of pride is Augustine's *City of God,* 12:6, 14:13–14; cf. R. Niebuhr, *The Nature and Destiny of Man,* pt. 1, ch. 7 (1949).

B. W. GRANT

CHRISTIAN LIFE; SELF-ESTEEM; SEVEN DEADLY SINS. *See also* CHARACTER ETHICS AND PASTORAL CARE; MORAL THEOLOGY AND PASTORAL CARE; SIN/SINS; TEMPTATION. *Compare* NARCISSISM/NARCISSISTIC PERSONALITY; RIGHTEOUSNESS/ BEING RIGHT.

PRIEST. One who functions officially to establish or preserve contact between the human community and the Deity; thus, a mediator between God and humankind. In Roman Catholic theology, Christ is the sole priest of the New Covenant. However, Christ instituted the Sacrament of Holy Orders, whereby he chose to associate with himself those who would carry on within his church the roles of teaching, ruling, and sanctifying (the functions of prophet, king, and priest).

During the development of ministry in the early church the distinctions among bishop, priest, and deacon became clearer. By the second century, the three were fixed. Priesthood, or the presbyterate, is conferred upon a candidate by the Sacrament of Holy Orders, which is administered by a bishop.

In Roman Catholic practice, a priest may be taken from the ranks either of the laity or from a religious community of men. A layman who becomes a priest is called a *diocesan* or *secular priest;* he is incardinated into the diocese in which he will serve and is subject to its bishop as his religious superior. A member of a religious order (monk, friar, canon regular, etc.) who is ordained to the presbyterate is known as a *regular* or an *order priest.* He retains membership in his religious community and is subject to its superiors regarding his personal life, and to the bishop of the diocese where he may be assigned regarding his ministry to the laity there.

The Second Vatican Council devoted one of its documents to the training of priests ("Optatam Totius"; Oct. 28, 1965). After making general recommendations concerning care in the choice of candidates, the organization of seminaries, and the spiritual formation of the seminarians, it becomes more specific, calling for "that literary and scientific education which is prerequisite to higher studies in their country" and a knowledge of the Latin language for the understanding of church documents in their original texts.

A philosophical understanding of the human, the world, and God is also necessary, as well as some knowledge of contemporary trends in philosophy and science. Theological principles are to be taught in the light of faith and under the guidance of the church, based principally upon biblical themes. Patrology, the history of dogma, systematic theology, especially that of Aquinas,

and the liturgy are singled out for special emphasis. Finally the training of the modern priest is to include those secular disciplines that can assist him in the exercise of his ministry: psychology, sociology, counseling, homiletics, and the details of pastoral practice.

Bibliography. P. F. Palmer, "Priest and Priesthood, Christian," *New Catholic Encyclopedia* vol. 11, (1967), p. 768. "Lumen Gentium" (Dogmatic Constitution on the Church), no. 28, *Second Ecumenical Council of the Vatican* (1965). "Optatum Totius" (Decree on Priestly Formation), *Second Ecumenical Council of the Vatican* (1965).

V. B. BROWN

MINISTER; PASTOR; SACRAMENTAL THEOLOGY AND PASTORAL CARE. *See also* ECCLESIOLOGY AND PASTORAL CARE; HOLY ORDERS, SACRAMENT OF; MINISTRY; PASTORAL THEOLOGY, ROMAN CATHOLIC; THEOLOGICAL EDUCATION AND THE PASTORAL CARE MOVEMENT, ROMAN CATHOLIC; VOCATION (Roman Catholicism). *Compare* CONFESSOR; LAICIZATION; RELIGIOUS LIFE; SPIRITUAL DIRECTOR.

PRIEST, PASTOR AS. *See* PASTOR (Normative and Traditional Images).

PRIESTHOOD. *See* MINISTRY (Roman Catholic Tradition).

PRIESTLY TRADITION, OLD TESTAMENT. *See* OLD TESTAMENT AND APOCRYPHA.

PRIESTS, EMPIRICAL STUDIES OF. *See* CLERGY, EMPIRICAL STUDIES OF.

PRIMAL THERAPY. Introduced by Arthur Janov, primal therapy offers a view of emotional turmoil which is dynamic while emphasizing the "here and now." Conflict derives from the aggregate of painful experiences (minor "primal scenes") resulting in a major "primal scene" (neurosis). By weakening defenses, the patient re-experiences primal pain and releases it in the primal scream (anguished summation of major primal scene).

K. P. ROSS

POPULAR THERAPEUTIC MOVEMENTS AND PSYCHOLOGIES; PSYCHOTHERAPY.

PRIMARY AND SECONDARY PROCESS. In psychoanalysis, names given to the ways of thinking characteristic of two structures of personality, the id and the ego. The id, governed by the "pleasure principle," seeks immediate gratification ("I want it now"). It uses primary process thinking, which is essentially *wishing* (equating desire with reality). Its ideas are concrete, sensory *images* connected by *association* rather than logic or realistic relationship. Dreams are an example of primary process thinking. The ego, on the other hand, is governed by the "reality principle" and is willing to delay gratification, distinguishing wish from reality. It uses secondary process thinking, which is conceptual, realistic, and logical.

H. M. GIRGIS

PSYCHOANALYSIS (Personality Theory and Research). *See also* DREAM THEORY AND RESEARCH; FANTASIZING; IMAGINATION; MAGICAL THINKING.

PRIMITIVE RELIGION. *See* CULTURAL ANTHROPOLOGY OF RELIGION, DISCIPLINE OF; SOCIOLOGY OF RELIGIOUS AND PASTORAL CARE. *See also* AFRICAN, NATIVE AMERICAN, *or* WEST INDIAN TRADITIONAL RELIGION, PERSONAL CARE IN.

PRISONERS AND PRISON CHAPLAINCY. The function of the prison chaplaincy is to provide pastoral care and related ministries in the unique parish of a prison. In this environment the chaplain ministers to the entire prison community — prisoners, officers, and staff. Prison ministries tend to focus on pastoral and liturgical functions but may also include evangelism, religious education, assistance with social and legal services, and a concern for prison policies and management. Many prison chaplains also become pastorally involved with the families of prisoners, work to establish community involvement through visitation programs and support for parolees and ex-convicts, and assist in developing community understanding and concern for the prison and for the criminal justice system.

Within the institution, prison ministry may be thought of as including: (1) *General ministry,* the inclusive work of religious leadership and care, including visitation, conducting Bible classes, leading worship, and coordinating religious functions; (2) *Counseling and related ministries,* including the care and counseling of particular individuals and families, leadership of small groups, and training of volunteers; (3) *Crisis ministry,* the care of prisoners during special times of personal or family crisis; and (4) *Structural ministry,* pastoral concern directed toward the institution as a system so as to effect positive changes in policy or administration and to serve as the voice of conscience for the institution.

1. Social Profile of Prisoners. Prisoners represent a diversity of social backgrounds and histories often at odds with popular stereotypes of criminals. In outward appearance they often cannot be distinguished from ordinary citizens. Before incarceration they may have lived, worked and dressed according to common standards and even been active in church and community organizations. In every prison there are inmates with respectable backgrounds, and some with unusual musical, artistic, or other talents, as well as those with well developed intellectual interests. Some manage to earn high school diplomas or college degrees while imprisoned. The industrious, self-taught "jailhouse lawyer" is a familiar prison figure.

Nonetheless prison populations are unrepresentative of society at large. More than half of all prisoners in the U. S. come from homes where one parent has been significantly absent; many have histories of family conflict and childhood abuse and neglect. Many have suffered economic and cultural deprivation, educational failure, and chronic unemployment. A lack of employable skills, illiteracy and histories of drug dependency are common. Racial and ethnic minorities are disproportionately represented.

Moreover, prisoners represent only a small portion of society's law breakers. The more "successful" criminals escape apprehension or have enough resources to outmaneuver the criminal justice system. The great majority of persons arrested for crimes are never prosecuted, and only a small portion of those convicted are ever actually imprisoned. Many who end up in prison are therefore the "unsuccessful" ones, usually poor, undereducated, and powerless.

Many prisoners are repeat offenders, having failed to cope successfully with parole or release. Rates of recidivism vary widely depending on age, nature of offense, type of institution from which the prisoner is released, and the release plan. (The release plan and community support are often crucial factors in achieving satisfactory reintegration into society.) A criminal lifestyle often develops in which the prison becomes a revolving door for some and, for all too many, a factory manufacturing criminal lifestyles and careers; prisoners teach one another antisocial attitudes and skills despite rehabilitation programs.

2. Psychological and Pastoral Needs. While the "atmosphere" of penal institutions varies widely, all of them, however progressive, impose involuntary restrictions on individual behavior and are fundamentally coercive in nature. Psychologically, this means that themes of law, force, authority, status, fear, threat, and violence are pervasive psychological facts of prison life and relationships (for staff as much as for inmates). In addition, the institution's enforced isolation of prisoners from family and friends creates intense emotional concerns about sex, love, family and marital relationships, and loneliness. Boredom and the passing or "doing" of time are of course major problems as well; many prisoners calculate the time remaining on their sentences to the day, though the practice of indefinite sentencing and the uncertainties of parole often inject great anxiety into the struggle to endure the slow passing of time.

Given the background social factors and the coercive nature of the prison itself, it is not surprising that many prisoners suffer poor self-images ("I feel like dirt" is a common expression), tend to view the world as untrustworthy and threatening, regard other persons as alien "others" to be used or manipulated for selfish purposes or to be defended against, and have chronic difficulty establishing and maintaining favorable interpersonal relationships. Typically, prisoners compensate for sharply felt inadequacies by bragging, engaging in bodybuilding exercises, wearing uncommon attire, or flaunting themselves before others.

Some — perhaps many — inmates, especially those with multiple incarcerations, appear to have strong unconscious dependency needs. These persons value and seek the structured security of the prison environment where food and shelter are guaranteed, where decisions are made for them, and where they are protected from the consequences of their own impulses. Initially they may vehemently deny wanting to be in prison, but when confidence is established many will discuss honestly their ambivalence about life outside prison. However, many psychological and social factors are involved in histories of repeated incarceration. Failure to "make it" on the outside is often related, for instance, to inadequate education, lack of marketable skills, deficient family and community support, and drug addiction.

These themes and problems obviously present important issues for pastoral care. Given the atmosphere of the prison, it is especially challenging to know how and when to encourage trusting forms of personal relationship, a realistic sense of hope, psychologically healthy self-esteem and ways of relating to law and authority, and understandings of religious faith and life in which religion's themes of authority and responsibility are appropriately interpreted and constructively related to love, forgiveness and grace.

3. **History of Prison Ministry.** Following the apostolic injunction to "remember those who are in prison, as though in prison with them" (Heb. 13:3), Christian pastors and lay persons have exercised a ministry of visitation and compassion in prisons for centuries. An important institutional step was taken in the early 1800s, however, when the Quakers of Philadelphia established the concept in the U.S. of isolating offenders to encourage reflection, meditation, and penitence — the source of the word *penitentiary*. More recently Christians were influential in the formation of the American Correctional Association in 1892 and have promoted prison reform and the establishment of rehabilitation programs.

Until the 1920s and 1930s the prison chaplain was often the only professional person employed full-time by the prison (except the warden). But gradually educators, social workers, psychologists, medical personnel, and recreational specialists were added to prison staffs and began to take over functions for which the chaplain had been responsible. The change forced a reexamination of the clergy's role. Attention got focused specifically on doing pastoral functions. In the mid-1930s the Federal Bureau of Prisons asked the Protestant churches (the then Federal Council of Churches) to endorse the maturity and quality of training of prison chaplains. CPE, although in its infancy, became a requirement of endorsement, and the prison chaplaincy thus became the first established chaplaincy to require CPE in the training of its candidates.

As years passed many states also set standards, and the major denominations established departments of pastoral care and standards for endorsement of prison chaplains. Nonetheless, high standards for readiness to minister in prisons and jails have not been accepted by some fundamental, evangelistic, and independent church groups. Some state and local authorities have not been concerned, and early in 1982 the Federal Bureau of Prisons retracted its position with the churches and moved to do its own screening of chaplain candidates, calling upon church representatives only when needed. Today much prison and jail ministry is done by part-time persons and volunteers who have not been trained in the available body of knowledge regarding the understanding of persons, relationship skills, organizational structure, and pastoral care.

Bibliography. H. H. Cassler and G. C. Kandle, *Ministering to Prisoners and Their Families* (1968). S. Chaneles, *Prisons and Prisoners: Historical Documents* (1985). W. R Graham and B. A. Carlson, "The American Protestant Correctional Chaplains Association," *J. of Pastoral Care*, Fall (1988). A. Hanson, "Prison Outreach Ministry," *Theology Today*, 39:4 (1983), 395 –

401. D. A. Phillipy, "Hearing and Doing the Word: An Integrated Approach to Bible Study in a Maximum Security Prison," *J. of Pastoral Care*, 37 (1983), 13–21.

W. R. GRAHAM

ANTISOCIAL PERSONS; CHAPLAINCY; DEVIANT BEHAVIOR, THEORY OF; JUVENILE CRIME AND DELINQUENCY. *See also* BLACK MUSLIM CARE AND COUNSELING; HALFWAY HOUSE. *Compare* PAROLEES AND EX-CONVICTS.

PRIVACY AND SOLITUDE. Privacy is a necessary condition for the cultivation of a healthy sense of self. Jesus described privacy when he spoke of the need to go into our closet when we pray, shut the door, and "pray to our Father who is in secret" (Mt. 6:6). Everyone needs some time and some sense of a space where he or she will not be observed or intruded upon. Children need privacy in order to cultivate those gifts of fantasy and imagination that open them to the movement of their own inner lives. Adults need privacy if they are going to develop the inner strength necessary to live without overdependence on outside stimulation and the approval of others—to live from "inside out" rather than from "outside in."

Privacy is not easily gained. Indeed, for many it must be carved out and defended, though the barriers to privacy are internal as well as external. When we are not comfortable with ourselves, privacy can be experienced as threat, driving us compulsively to seek the company of others. Privacy demands that we say "no" to others, in order to say "yes" to ourselves.

Privacy leads either to solitude or to loneliness. Paul Tillich once pointed out that loneliness expresses the pain of being alone; solitude expresses the glory of being alone. The *glory* of solitude is experienced when it is freely chosen. The *pain* of loneliness, however, is experienced when privacy is forced upon one, either by circumstance or by the fear of encounter with others. There are, of course, times when being alone produces feelings of loneliness simply because those who are close to us are not available. But loneliness, however, can be chronic and not circumstantial, produced by internal feelings of isolation, disconnectedness, a diminished sense of self, and an inability to experience intimacy with others. Such chronic loneliness generally requires therapeutic help if one is to be sufficiently free of self to experience the sought-for closeness with others and with life.

Solitude is loneliness freely chosen. It involves being connected to what often is referred to as "our center"— that metaphysical point within the self from which a sense of wholeness and well-being comes. Solitude is a way of being alone that involves a sense of being open to those intuitive and reflective processes that come from within and that ultimately connect us with others, below the level of consciousness; hence it is also a way of being intuitively or potentially present with others.

Although we can pray publicly or in the company of others, the practice of prayer at times demands the experience of solitude. In deep silence we can enter into the rhythm of the spirit of God praying within us. In solitude we are able to experience the God who is beyond human definition, the God who simply is. Solitude is the crucible in which prayer is nourished and God is known.

Bibliography. W. C. Bier, ed., *Privacy: A Vanishing Value?* (1980). J. S. Dunne, *The Reasons of the Heart* (1978). R. E. Neale, *Loneliness, Solitude, and Companionship* (1984).

J. FENHAGEN

MEDITATION; REST AND RENEWAL, RELIGIOUS TRADITIONS OF; RETREATS. *Compare* COMMUNITY, FELLOWSHIP, AND CARE; PERSONAL, CONCEPT OF; SPIRITUALITY; LONELINESS AND ISOLATION.

PRIVILEGED COMMUNICATION. *See* CONFIDENTIALITY.

PROBLEM CHILD. *See* BEHAVIORAL DISORDERS OF CHILDHOOD; CHILDREN; FAMILY THEORY AND THERAPY; JUVENILE CRIME AND DELINQUENCY; PARENTS/PARENTHOOD.

PROBLEM SOLVING. Problem solving is seldom the major focus of pastoral care and counseling, but the pastoral relationship offers a context of affirmation and support within which persons may address their problems. Because pastoral care is the care of the whole person in relationship, concern with specific problems is never completely separated from the broader issue of what a particular problem means for a person's life. Nevertheless, as persons ask for help with particular problems, they develop a relationship with a helping person; by so doing they may get in touch with the more profound religious issues in their lives of which they were only vaguely aware.

Certainly problem solving *per se* has significant value, and several types of psychotherapy may be accurately described as "problem solving therapies." The most obvious of these is behavior therapy which is based upon the principles of conditioning. Problems such as phobias, lack of assertiveness, or sexual dysfunction result, according to this theory, from an individual's being punished for behavior resulting from a bodily need or drive. Anxiety and fear arise as a result of such punishment and accompany the behavioral problem. Treatment involves the learning of techniques that reduce anxiety and conditioning which reverses the original association of the problem behavior with punishment (Wolpe, 1982).

Aaron Beck (1976), who was trained in psychoanalysis, became dissatisfied with its complexity and abstractness and developed a method of cognitive analysis of the problems of his patients. Although he was interested in behavior therapy, Beck felt it was limited because it ignored patients' thinking about themselves. His cognitive therapy attempted to correct faulty interpretations of reality and faulty reasoning. He emphasized solving problems rather than changing personal defects. Jay Haley (1976), one of the pioneer family therapists, is like the behavioral therapists in not being concerned with developing insight and understanding or providing an experience of personal growth. The focus of his concern is not the individual but the family and its social situation. He attempts to approach each problem with special techniques for the specific situation. The therapist's task is to design an intervention in the client's social situation which will solve the presenting problem.

An awareness of each of these types of therapy, and their assumptions and techniques, may be quite useful to pastors. Pastoral care and counseling, like the behavior therapies, involves assisting persons in reducing their anxiety about a variety of concerns. It may involve consulting with parishioners and counselees about ineffective ways of thinking about their problems. On occasion it may involve an intervention into a family's social situation, e.g., suggesting changes in the rules which govern a particular activity in the home. These problem-solving efforts, however, take place in a relational context of care for all the persons involved. Furthermore, they are carried out with the assumption, at least by the pastor, that although one is constantly tempted to seek appreciation as a problem solver, the fundamental issues of life are not solvable, only livable — in the context of significant human relationships. The problem-solving pastor can usefully remember the aphorism, "Life is not a problem to be solved, but a mystery to be lived."

Bibliography. A. Beck, *Cognitive Therapy and the Emotional Disorders* (1976). J. Haley, *Problem Solving Therapy* (1976). J. Wolpe, *The Practice of Behavior Therapy* 3d ed. (1982).

J. PATTON

PASTORAL COUNSELING; REASONING AND RATIONALITY IN PASTORAL CARE. *See also* FEELING, THOUGHT, AND ACTION IN PASTORAL COUNSELING; PRAGMATISM AND PASTORAL CARE; TECHNIQUE AND SKILL IN PASTORAL CARE. *Compare* PRESENTING PROBLEM.

PROCESS, CONCEPT OF. A concept used to point to change, coming to be, flux, and interaction in contrast to permanence, fixity, being, and substance. The term has a formal and precise meaning in the schools of process philosophy and theology which have influenced contemporary pastoral theory in indirect ways. The concept and the term itself are also widely and directly employed in a more popular sense in pastoral counseling and CPE, where its meaning is both indebted to, yet different from its formal articulation in philosophy and theology.

1. **In Philosophy and Theology.** The formal concept is frequently used to group together the thoughts of such a diverse group of thinkers as C. S. Peirce, William James, John Dewey, A. N. Whitehead, Henri Bergson, H. N. Weiman, Charles Hartshorne, and John Cobb, because they emphasize the characteristics of change, coming to be, flux, and interaction as comprising the most concrete aspects of experience. Enduring objects, such as a table or chair, are generally taken to be abstract patterns, forms, properties, or structures repeated in a process and abstracted from the process. The degree to which things are caught up in process varies from Dewey's heraclitean flux, in which mathematics and the laws of logic seem to evolve, to Whitehead's process of coming to be, in which a platonic realm of eternal objects and their relation to God remains fixed throughout. Process thinkers also tend to reject the "spatialization" of time (Bergson), which is the viewing of time as a fixed series with the present sliding along it from the past to the future. In contrast they argue for a radical difference between the past and the future relative to a given present. The past is settled; the future is always open. There is real freedom, or chance (Peirce; James), in the present,

so that the future can take alternative courses depending upon the free choices in the present.

In applying the concept of process to God there are divergencies. For Whitehead God is nontemporal and does not change. God is everlastingly in the process of becoming and embraces the immediate present of each temporal creature in an everlasting present. For Hartshorne God does change. God is a temporal sequence of presents with each one more inclusive of value than the previous ones. Thus for Hartshorne temporality enters into the characterization of God in a way in which it does not for Whitehead. In either case, God is a becoming God in contrast to the fully actual and impassive God of classical theism. This conception of a becoming God makes possible a greater sensitivity on the part of God to the free choices of the creatures than appears to be the case in classical theism. All reality, from God to electrons, is essentially social. And the extension of freedom, in some degree, to the lowest creature provides for a possible solution to the problem of evil.

2. In Pastoral Counseling and Clinical Pastoral Education. Not inconsistent with the philosophical understanding of process but of a quite different order is the way that the term is used in a psychotherapeutic or clinical pastoral setting. Here process refers, in the first place, to the verbal and nonverbal interaction itself which takes place within the bi-personal field of psychotherapy (Langs, 1976). Most significant in this is the "trust" by both patient and therapist that the emerging, interactive "process" of interpersonal relations making up the therapy is effective and can relieve the patient's pervading sense of demoralization (Frank, 1973).

For many therapists, however, learning to "trust the process," while emotionally threatening, is also an important *goal* of psychotherapy as well, inasmuch as it entails a deepening of trust, a loosening of defensive rigidities, and the emergence of a more vital, spontaneous, and creative style of personal and interpersonal existence. For these therapists "trusting the process" usually refers also to a certain *style* of therapeutic care. This involves the discipline of a sensitive, nuanced listening that "follows" the emergent and half-emergent tendencies of the therapeutic interaction and gradually evolves a sense of "who this person is," "who this person is becoming," and "what the deeper issues are" in the evolving process of his or her healing and growth.

Bibliography. J. Cobb, *A Christian Natural Theology* (1965); *Theology and Pastoral Care* (1977). J. Frank, *Persuasion and Healing* rev. ed. (1973). C. Hartshorne, *A Natural Theology for Our Time* (1967); *The Divine Relativity* (1948). R. Langs, *The Therapeutic Interaction*, vol. 2 (1976). A. N. Whitehead, *Process and Reality* corrected ed. (1978 [1929]).

B. L. CLARKE

BEING/BECOMING RELATIONSHIP; PHILOSOPHY AND PSYCHOLOGY, WESTERN. *See also* MODELS IN PSYCHOLOGICAL AND PASTORAL THEORY; PILGRIMAGE METAPHOR. *Compare* DEVELOPMENTAL THEORY AND PASTORAL CARE.

PROCESS STUDIES (Psychotherapy). *See* PSYCHOTHERAPY AND COUNSELING (Research Studies and Methods).

PROCESS THEOLOGY AND PASTORAL CARE. Process theology is a theological system based largely upon the metaphysical vision of Alfred North Whitehead, mathematician, scientist, and philosopher who in the mid-1920s at Harvard University described reality as a process of becoming. God is both changeless and changing, absolute and changeless in love, but precisely because of that love is affected constantly by experiencing the world which is ever-changing in response to new possibilities luring it forward. The human being, as the highest form of life in creativity's ladder, is constantly responding to its past, to new beckonings from a future infinite with possibilities, and from God whose lure of the present is by way of the most relevant possibility appropriate to each person in his or her moment of becoming. What each person does with this rich offering of multiplicity is his or her responsibility. Thus in the final analysis all of us determine what we become as we put our lives together for better or for worse.

Pastoral care, within this framework, will seek to help each person to become a thing of beauty; that is, a whole person born of harmony and richness instead of a truncated being born of disharmony and trivia. So pastoral care emerging out of the process theology vision has a spiritual and aesthetic goal as its ultimate *telos*.

Four basic realities form the conceptual vision of what has come to be called process thought. They are: (1) causal efficacy, or the way the past is a given for each present moment; (2) eternal objects, or the infinity of possibilities which constitute the future and make their demands for novelty on the present; (3) God, whose omniscience knows all the past everlastingly and the eternal objects in their infinitude, and whose love is ever luring the present moment into the novel unity it can become, and whose love also experiences the becoming of the world in both its beauty and its evil. This means that God is directly affected by the world and, at the same time, God affects the world; and (4) concrescence, which is the growing together of each actual occasion out of what causal efficacy, the eternal objects, and God provide as the environmental conditions for its moment of becoming.

These four realities directly affect pastoral care, as they do preaching and the other forms of ministry, because ministry is involved with persons concrescing or growing together out of the givens of their lives. For the sake of analysis the realities will be dealt with separately even though they never exist alone. Process thought sees everything related to everything else.

1. Causal Efficacy. This would be roughly equivalent to Aristotle's efficient causation. The past is efficaciously or effectively present to us all the time. It might be as remote as a decade or two millennia ago, or as recent as a tenth of a second ago, but is always a given to which we must respond. We respond by conforming to it. That is the way we bring the past into the present.

Freud's creative work on the superego is an illustration of the past residing in the present. Parents, whether dead or alive, continue to reside in their children both as ego ideal and as conscience, as their parents lived on in them. This is a part of the biblical truth that the sins of the parents are visited unto the third and fourth generations. But it is not only sins out of the past that are present to be dealt with. It is the total past, positive and negative, good and bad, large and small. Jung wrote of the past in terms of memory traces: ". . . everything that will be happens on the basis of what has been, and of what—consciously or unconsciously—still exists as a memory trace" ("The Archetypes and the Collective Unconscious," *Collected Works,* vol. 9, pt. 1, p. 279).

The empirical way of understanding the massive power of the past is through our present experience. What is available to us is our own experiencing. The past is an important given in that experiencing. A vignette from pastoral care illustrates the role of causal efficacy in a case of depression. A forty-year-old, depressed woman seeks out her pastor who gets her to talk about her present feelings and the events surrounding the onset of this depressive period. As she talks, she offers the observation that throughout her life she has felt depressed. She was an only child. Her mother could let her do no wrong. If she came home with a report card of four As and one B, the question came forth immediately, "Why the B?" Her father who "always" sided with her against her mother, died when she was twelve. As she talked her eyes began to flash. Suddenly she cried out, "Here it comes again. That old anger."

This woman for nearly forty years had responded angrily to her perceived world. Anger fed anger until anger became the dominant chord in her life. She felt anger toward her mother who demanded that she be perfect; toward her father for "leaving me when I needed him so"; toward God for making her mother "that way," for "taking" her father, for not protecting her better. And she hated herself for being the failure her mother "told" her she was and for being so filled with negative feelings.

Her defining characteristic was anger. Most of the time other emotions were crowded out by the dominance of anger. In effect, she factored out or excluded moments of love, tenderness, joy. She held on to the negative feelings of anger until she became stuck on that response and it defined her mode of being. In effect, her becoming through the myriad experiences of her forty years was shaped by a chain of angry responses to the stuff of her life. She was actually pressed down by her anger. This was her depression. She had built up an internal habitual response: anger was the habit of her soul, to borrow from Plato. As her past increased by a multiplicity of new experiences, e.g., marriage, motherhood, her responses continued to conform to older responses. She projected onto her husband, her children, her friends anytime they failed her the anger which dominated her. Then she felt guilty sensing that what she was doing came from other times. The past was viciously in her by the way she grasped it in her fixated responses of anger.

Process thought takes very seriously the massiveness of the past. It is a given to which we *will* respond. *How* we respond constitutes largely *who* we are.

2. Eternal Objects. These are roughly equivalent to Plato's Realm of Ideas. Eternal objects compose the future. They are the multiplicity of possibilities which lie ahead of us, possibilities that are inert and static waiting to be actualized. True to the ontological principle in Whitehead's thought, which is the principle that everything must reside somewhere, the eternal objects reside in God. God envisages all possibilities. This is God's omniscience of the future: knowing all the possibilities that lie ahead but not how they will be actualized in a particular moment of becoming.

Not all the infinitude of possibilities located in the mind of God are relevant to any one occasion of becoming; relatively few are. Causal efficacy, or the past of each of us, limits drastically which possibilities are relevant. Possibilities obviously vary greatly for a teenager and a person of seventy, for a male and a female, for an Asiatic and an Occidental. But they also vary greatly for this teenager as an only child and that one who learned to fight among six siblings. They also vary within the unique history of each of us. Decisions made today may rule out one set of eternal objects or possibilities and offer another set as on a wedding day.

One of the functions of God is to try to match causal efficacy and the most relevant possibility that will produce value for each occasioning of experience. God knows everlastingly every iota of experience which has been ours. What any given person was doing twenty years ago at precisely this moment measured in clocktime that person cannot know. But such knowledge is part of God's present experience. God's treasury contains in vivid awareness the total flow of causal efficacy. Consequently, God can match the most relevant possibility to produce good precisely where each of us is in the flow of our lives. In theological language this matching would be the will of God for us at that precise moment in our becoming.

The tragedy of many lives is that there seems to be so little real future in the sense of new possibilities. So stuck are those lives in their compulsion to repeat old patterns that symbolically they appear to be backing into the future. Not even God seems able to break through their fixations to lure them toward a future pulsating with new life. Erikson's seventh stage descriptive of mid-adulthood—generativity versus stagnation—aptly pinpoints where so many are: stagnating. It is as though they are afraid of adventure, to reach beyond themselves. Process thought raises Erikson's insight into a metaphysical dilemma. The so-called mid-life crisis is composed largely of stagnation and regression. Possibilities for continual transformation and growth, which is the yearning of God for every person, fall so often on ears and eyes closed by fear. This condition, issuing in ennui and boredom, would seem to be life without spirit.

Process theology would view this situation as pastoral care's superb opportunity to help stagnating people grasp the future by living toward fresh possibilities through which God beckons. Pastoral care might then be seen in the model of a Socratic midwife helping people toward a birth of new life. Process theology would see God's using the pastoral career to help actualize the divine vision which directs people to reach beyond themselves through spiritual renewal.

3. God. Already God has entered the picture of reality envisaged in process thought. That suggests the critical place God occupies in this metaphysical vision. Now it is necessary to describe formally the reality, God, within process categories. Whitehead writes about the primordial and consequent natures of God. Loosely they can be equated with the transcendent and immanent categories of traditional theology. The primordial nature is God's eternal envisagement of the eternal objects or possibilities. These are ordered in the mind of God into a realm so that there is not chaos among the infinitude of possibilities. A chart of colors in which the hues and shades all relate into an aesthetic whole would be an illustration of this ordering. There is an order to possibilities!

But God as primordial is deficient without the consequent nature. It is in the consequent nature that God is affected by the world. We have already touched upon the consequent nature when we talked of causal efficacy, or the past as a given for each present moment, and noted that God carries the past everlastingly in the divine memory. The importance of every bit of life is that nothing is lost. God experiences us experiencing! The total flow of our histories are in the treasury of God's memory. God enjoys in the profound sense of prehending or feeling us in our prehending the world about us — causal efficacy and eternal objects — and what we make of all the offerings of those environments. What each of us is, he or she is for God to experience, for good or for bad. Thus, every happening in each concrescence, to which we turn next, is a happening God will experience. That is the nature of reality. Every happening from the growth of a blade of grass to a scene of lovemaking affects God. God is both changeless, the primordial nature, and changing, the consequent nature. Each event brings to God a new experience. The form may be the same, but never is the content the same. Marriage is a form with a long history. But no two marriages are identical. This woman with her history and this man with his bring their uniqueness together into a unity that God has never before enjoyed. So each marriage, beginning with the wedding and continuing throughout its blissful and stormy history, adds to the experience of God.

In this very profound sense God's enjoyment — a technical word in process language meaning experience — is consequent upon the world's actions which become part of God's personhood. The world does not add to God's divinity but to the constantly growing value-filled experience of God. A careful analysis of the love of God would understand that love somewhat in these terms. For love to have meaning it cannot be unilateral. Charles Hartshorne and Daniel Day Williams, both major process thinkers, have done much to reclaim the bilateral or multilateral dimensions of God's love.

God's being acted upon by the world gives to God direct, intuitive knowledge of what every iota of the world needs at each moment of its becoming. So God can bring to each of us in every concretion of ourselves just that possibility most relevant to where we are. God lures us, to borrow a choice Whiteheadian term, to reach toward a new vision of what we can become. God's joy is to set before us the best possibility for that moment and to have us become congruent with the divine vision.

This activity of God is constant. It does not depend upon a religious vision at all, although a religious vision helps us to be more aware of, and more faithful to, the vision God has for us. Rather, in the very nature of reality this is the way God acts. God wants the best for every situation, receives the responses of the world, and comes back again with another aim for us to conjure with. Even if the client is atheistic, the ontological structure holds: God aims at the best possible vision for her or him.

This means that in every caring or counseling situation there are always three parties at work: the client (or group), the pastor, and God. The pastor can count on the constantly redemptive activity of God struggling to bring a new vision to the client. The silences during a caring or counseling session, the intervening days between appointments, the internal struggles of the person seeking health are opportunities for God to focus in upon the client. This insight releases the pastor from undue burden bearing, as it points to the Source of Hope, the Cosmic Ally who labors constantly to redeem both pastor and client that each might become a thing of beauty.

4. Concrescence. A growing together — concrescence — is the way process thought sees every occasion taking place. An actual occasion is the smallest bit of experiencing imaginable, whether an iota of a puff of cloud in the atmosphere, a sub-atomic particle of the blood system having its "moment" within the wholeness of the organism, or a minute, discrete part of the soul enjoying with its equally tiny brothers and sisters the aha-experience of the macrocosm we call soul. The point is that any organism, e.g., a human being, is a nexus or many nexuses of atomic bits of experiencing. What we see through the senses is the system spread out. But the real life is happening within the smallest centers of experiencing we can imagine. Process thought is atomic in structure. An actual occasion is a subjective center of experiencing. A molecule is made up of many such occasions. In turn, a molecule becomes part of a larger nexus. So there are systems of togetherness within systems within systems. The importance of this vision is that sense experience, viz., seeing a person or hearing a person, is missing the amazing richness of what is really happening within the myriad actual occasions that are making up, or constituting, that person. The mystery of each is incredible and unfathomable.

What does an actual occasion experience? It starts with its birth. The whole of the past — causal efficacy — is a given for each new occasion. We are not born ex nihilo. Rather, we conform to the past in some measure and that very conforming is part of our birthing. God, too, is part of that birthing. God knows what the past is offering to the new present. But God—who loves novelty because one good custom can corrupt the world and an evil custom corrupt it more corruptibly—brings to the nascent occasion a new possibility. Perhaps it is taking the anger of the previous one tenth of a second with a twist of humor. Otherwise the old would simply repeat itself. Born out of the givens of a massive past and the vision of God of what is best for it, the new occasion responds to these givens with an aim or a goal of its own. Respond it will. Aim it must. Then ensues the intense struggle to put it all together. Now and then we sense the struggle: competing feelings of joy, pain, guilt, humor, excitement, dullness. Most of the time the struggle is below the level of consciousness like the iceberg, only the tip of which is showing.

The concrescence is how each actual occasion puts it all together into a thing of beauty or ugliness, the two opposing outcomes. We are ultimately our own final causes; we cause, or constitute, ourselves. A favorite Whiteheadian word for this is: *causa sui*. Out of the very rich environments—causal efficacy, eternal objects, God—we actualize ourselves.

Bernard Loomer, a key philosopher/theologian in the process tradition, has set the human task in these words: "The aim of life, at the human level, is to create people of greater stature" (unpublished paper). Pastoral care and counseling within the framework of process theology is to help the concrescing subject to become a person of greater stature. In aesthetic terms, it is to help the other to create herself or himself a thing of beauty. To enable the other to do this, pastoral care and counseling must listen *into* the other, into the hidden depths of the other where the subjective aims are taking place and the self-actualizing is going on. Facile diagnosis and advice-giving will usually fail to meet the other where he or she really is, so great is the wonder and mystery of the other. Only God knows the other in that way. Pastoral care and counseling have a humbler task. That is to help the other to get unstuck, to become free enough to entertain God's vision for her or him, and so to encourage the divine-human dialogue through which a person of greater beauty can emerge. The emergence will be toward dynamic wholeness which is the gift of peace, as though bestowed. Ultimately this is the peace which Jesus Christ both exemplified and promised. Its bestowal is the crown of the metaphysical vision known as process thought.

Bibliography. H. J. Cargas and B. Lee, eds., *Religious Experience and Process Theology* (1976). J. B. Cobb, Jr., *A Christian Natural Theology* (1965); *Theology and Pastoral Care* (1977). J. B. Cobb, Jr., and D. R. Griffen, *Process Theology: An Introductory Exposition* (1976). C. Hartshorne, *Man's Vision of God* (1941); *Reality as Social Process* (1953); *The Divine Relativity* (1948). G. E. Jackson, *Pastoral Care and Process Theology* (1981). C. Jung, "The Archetypes and the Collective Unconscious," *Collected Works*, vol. 9, pt. 1 (1968), 279. R. L. Kinast, "A Process Model of Theological Reflection," *J. of Pastoral Care*, 37 (1983), 144–55. N. Pittenger, *God in Process* (1967); *Process Thought and Christian Faith* (1968). A. N. Whitehead, *Adventures of Ideas* (1933); *Process and Reality* (1929); *Religion in the Making* (1930). D. D. Williams, *The Minister and the Care of Souls* (1961); *The Spirit and the Forms of Love* (1968).

G. E. JACKSON

EMPIRICAL THEOLOGY AND PASTORAL CARE; THEOLOGICAL METHODOLOGY. *See also* PASTORAL THEOLOGY; PHILOSOPHY AND PSYCHOLOGY, WESTERN; THEORY IN PASTORAL CARE AND COUNSELING, FUNCTIONS OF. *Compare* EXISTENTIALISM, EXPERIENTIAL THEOLOGY, LIBERATION THEOLOGY, *or* NEOORTHODOX THEOLOGY, AND PASTORAL CARE; PERSONALISM AND PASTORAL CARE; PRAGMATISM AND PASTORAL CARE; THEOLOGY AND PSYCHOTHERAPY.

PROCRASTINATION. *See* ANTISOCIAL PERSONS; DECISION/INDECISION, PSYCHOLOGY OF.

PROFANE LANGUAGE. Words or phrases considered impolite, too intense for ordinary use, or defiant of the strictures of church or family. Such language is usually either an expression of anger or a sign that a given experience is too intense to be encompassed in ordinary language.

Since the pastor is stereotyped as neither using nor approving of such language, its use toward him or her must be understood in light of that expectation. On first meeting or otherwise early in the relationship, profanity is typically a sign of defiance or disdain—not solely or even primarily of the pastor, but of the world in general and what the pastor stands for in particular. Further along, but still before the heart of pastoral work is reached, it is testing the expansion of the style of expression between server and served, to see if the pastor can hear and accept the other in his or her full intensity. In the maturity of the relationship, profanity is a sign of trust and intimacy; an indicator that the other no longer feels required to censor speech, but is free to use the full range of his or her language tools.

More than very sparing and moderate use of profanity in the first few minutes of a pastoral contact requires special attention. It may be an element of the "generalized transference," an indication that the other's stance toward the world at the moment is angry, disdainful, and pained. If so, it immediately suggests the importance of ascertaining the roots of the anger, and modifying it if possible. On the other hand, if the other's affect is intense and covers the full range of emotion, strong profanity usually indicates intense stress, anxiety, or panic. It is the pastor's clue that a crisis intervention response may be helpful. In yet other situations, abundant profanity in the absence of apparent strong feeling, or generalized disdain, is often a sign that the other does not perceive social limits and boundaries well and may have wide-ranging difficulties with reality perception.

From the pastor's side, profanity needs to be governed by three variables: the other's use of such language, the stage of the relationship, and the pastor's typical language patterns. Pastors should not introduce it. Only in the mature stages of a relationship, and one in which the other has demonstrated comfort with strong language, can pastors safely give vent to their own profaneness; and then only to an extent consistent with their typical personal style.

B. W. GRANT

SELF-EXPRESSION/SELF-CONTROL; VOWS/VOWING. *Compare* ANGER; PORNOGRAPHY; RAGE AND HOSTILITY; RELIGIOUS LANGUAGE AND SYMBOLISM, PSYCHOLOGY OF.

PROFESSIONAL, PASTOR AS. *See* INTERPROFESSIONAL TEAMS AND RELATIONSHIPS; PROFESSIONALISM.

PROFESSIONAL ETHICS. *See* ETHICS, PROFESSIONAL.

PROFESSIONALISM. A profession is a calling, vocation or employment that requires specialized knowledge and skills, is characterized by and conforms to technical and ethical procedures and standards that have been established by a group of peer professionals, and is both the principal occupation of and source of financial gain to those who practice it. In the ministry, professionalism means that clergy develop a specialized knowledge of the scriptures, theology, history of religion, worship and liturgy, preaching, and pastoral care and counseling; establish and maintain standards of professional competence, ethics, and morality; promote the advancement of religious belief; express loving concern for those who receive their ministries, and function consistently with the mission and purposes of the church.

Ministers may professionalize the function of preaching by aquiring specialized knowledge and skills in the use of language, voice, and public speaking. They may professionalize the function of pastoral care and counseling by pursuing advanced studies in psychotherapy so as to be more helpful to those who are in crisis, faced with difficult decisions, troubled with emotional or mental problems, or involved in unsatisfactory relationships. They may develop expertise in relating to counselees, in the use of psychotherapeutic techniques, and in the use of conversation and listening to understand the unconscious forces operating in an individual's personality and the psychodynamics that impell current adult behavior and, thus, help counselees change their thinking, feeling, and behavior. Such specialized techniques have been strongly shaped by the theories and techniques of Sigmund Freud and the psychoanalytic movement, and by other contemporary theories and techniques of helping people, such as behavior modification and gestalt therapy. In doing pastoral counseling with more than one individual, such as in marital, family, and group counseling, ministers may become knowledgeable and skilled in systems theory, interpersonal relationships, family and small group dynamics, and various techniques designed to change patterns of interaction in these relationships.

In the performance of a task, professionalism goes beyond technical skill and craft. The professional has the ability to apply general principles to individual situations, assess novel and ambiguous situations, and make educated judgments about them (see Schön). Although professionals receive pay or remuneration for their services, professionalism carries with it a clearly delineated ethical obligation to act and make judgments in the best interests of their clients.

The inspired, dedicated, and sacrificial expressions of ministry, deeper religious authority, and the empowerment that results from special or personal religious experiences may motivate ministers to professionalize their work in order to be of greater service to God and to the people they serve.

Unfortunately, the term *professionalism* may also have acquired negative connotations, based partly on the incompetence, unethical behavior, and abuse of power and authority by certain members of every profession. Expertise provides the professional with power that can be misused in ways that do *not* serve the best interests of clients. By virtue of his or her position, a professional may become authoritarian and pressure clients to accede to inappropriate demands. Here power is applied irrationally or self-interestedly. In contrast, a professional may use power appropriately—based on the authority of expertise—to make suggestions and recommendations that are received or rejected voluntarily.

The expertise and resulting power and authority of ministers who professionalize ministerial functions may be questioned in Protestantism, which evolved from a protest against clerical position and power. The Protestant position holds that all individuals are equal before God and have direct access to God, and conceives of the church as a "priesthood of believers." Moreover, in America the equality of all citizens before the law, the guaranteed freedoms including religious freedoms of individuals to make their own decisions, and the belief in democracy, that the majority has the collective power to rule, have created a climate in which the power and authority of professionals may be questioned.

In some Christian faith groups, the professionalization of ministerial functions is viewed as contrary to the inspiration and workings of the Holy Spirit. Against a background of religious thinking that sees science as contrary to religion, sickness as the result of sin, and sexuality as contrary to spirituality, professionalism in pastoral counseling may be viewed as a secularization of ministry.

Thus, professionalism in ministry and in pastoral care and counseling raises many polity and theological questions about the definitions and functions of the faith group, the religious community, the concept of ministry, the meaning of ordination, the role of laity, and the status of specializations within both ordained and lay callings.

Bibliography. A. V. Campbell, *Professionalism and Pastoral Care* (1985). D. Capps, *Pastoral Care and Hermeneutics* (1984). J. W. Carroll, *Ministry as Reflective Practice: A New Look at the Professional Model* (1986). J. M. Murphy, "Ministry to the Total Person," *J. of Pastoral Care*, 34 (1980), 234–43. D. A. Schön, *The Reflective Practitioner* (1982).

J. M. MURPHY

ETHICS, PROFESSIONAL; INTERPROFESSIONAL TEAMS AND RELATIONSHIPS; MINISTRY; VOCATION. *See also* CALL TO MINISTRY; CONFIDENTIALITY; CONSULTATION; COVENANT AND CONTRACT; FEES IN PASTORAL COUNSELING; LEGAL DIMENSIONS OF PASTORAL CARE AND COUNSELING; REFERRAL; SOCIOLOGY OF RELIGIOUS AND PASTORAL CARE; WORK AND CAREER. *Compare* ADVOCACY.

PROJECTION. A defense mechanism in which one unconsciously attributes one's own unacceptable feelings, desires, thoughts, and impulses to another person. This removes the responsibility for unacceptable qualities or feelings from oneself, thus protecting the ego. An example is a husband who is barely able to control his anger toward his spouse and subsequently becomes suspicious that *she* is angry.

J. ESTELLE

DEFENSE AND COPING THEORY; DEFENSE MECHANISMS.

PROJECTIVE TESTS AND TECHNIQUES. *See* EVALUATION AND DIAGNOSIS, PSYCHOLOGICAL.

PROMISCUITY. *See* SEXUALITY, CHRISTIAN *or* JEWISH THEOLOGY AND ETHICS OF; SEXUAL ISSUES IN PASTORAL CARE; SEXUAL VARIETY, DEVIANCE, AND DISORDER.

PROMISING. A promise is an assurance given by one party to another that specifies a future way of being or acting. As a declaration made by one person to another it states what one will do or refrain from doing, or how one will be for the other or what one will bestow upon the other.

As the roots of the word (*pro* and *mittre*) indicate, promising sends oneself forth or ahead. By promising one states one's intention—but a promise is more than an intention. It involves a "promisor" telling a "promisee" not only his or her intention but his or her intention not to change the intention. A promise therefore describes one's decision about the future, and implies that one can foresee, choose, and to a certain extent determine not only one's present but one's future.

1. **Forms of Promising.** Promises can be formal or informal depending on the degree to which their fulfillment is expected or demanded as well as in the depth of subjective commitment given to them. Formal promises can take the form of vows, pledges, oaths, treaties, covenants, contracts, and deeds, some of which may have legal sanctions attached to their fulfillment. The object of the promise can be a single action ("I swear to tell the truth, the whole truth, and nothing but the truth, so help me God") or a series of actions ("to love, honor, and obey"). Some promises are contingent on certain circumstances being fulfilled; others are unconditional. Some promises are mutual, others unilateral. Promises also possess different degrees of solemnity, depending on the form they take, what is promised, and to whom. A promise made to God involving one's whole self is notably different than a promise made about an insignificant particular to someone with whom one is casually associated.

2. **Psychology of Promising.** Promising has a prior psychological history in those who make promises. Developmental psychologists, such as Jean Piaget and Herbert Schlesinger, have been particularly insightful on the pattern of promising that develops in the young.

Early promising is notable for its underdeveloped sense of time. Time in the young is connected to observable events, not to abstract measurement. Thus the child promises: "When the big hand of the clock moves to here I will go to bed," or "After this program I will pick up my toys, I promise." Such statements do not realistically pledge the future. They do, however, win love in the present or at least the approval of the parent, and to neglect to fulfill such promises jeopardizes the bonds the child enjoys or would enjoy. Love and promising are connected at an early age.

Adult promising takes place with a clearer notion of time. The promise is made about the future, at times the whole of one's future, notwithstanding the unpredictable character of future contingencies. As with early promising, "being valued" remains a main motivation of the adult promisory pattern. For the adult, however, instead of only the parents valuing the promisor's promise, there are now usually many who value the promise. Even the larger society is ordinarily perceived as valuing the socially articulated promise (in witnessing marriage vows, for example). The community expresses its approval of promises and its disapproval of breaking promises in the customs, traditions, and laws it articulates and enforces.

Breakdowns in adult promising or failure by adults to keep promises can be traced to many causes, several of which relate to too great a rootage in early promising patterns. An insufficiently developed appreciation of the time component of the promise is one cause of breakdown; another is too much reliance on approval for perseverance in keeping the promise. There is also a general erosion today of the importance of perseverance in keeping formal promises in the valuing community itself (e.g., regarding marriage).

There is some dispute in the literature about adult promising. The dispute is about the psychic structures that operate in the promisor. Those who are pessimistic or suspicious of them see promises as too often mired in the dynamics of infantile or adolescent promising, functioning even as substitutes for action at times. These psychologists usually employ a Freudian grid for their reading of behavior. This theory would see maturity as a movement away from an ego held in the sway of drives and stimuli compulsively responded to, toward ego autonomy. Among other things, ego autonomy entails a capacity to take action on the basis of the "reality principle." This means that the person has psychologically sorted out the difference between the nonself and the self, word and action, wish and reality. The reason for suspicion about promises is the likelihood that promises have more to do with words than with actions, with wishes than reality. If this were the case, even ordinary promises would represent a regression back to an immature stage of ego development. Autonomy would be forfeited by a reluctance to deal with reality, and the ego would be in servitude to the promise, vow, or commitment.

This analysis is only as good as the theory on which it rests. It can be helpful in explaining some promisory behavior, but it will be misused if it attempts to read all promisory behavior as ego regression. The theory is much better at explaining unconscious drives, compulsions, and psychic structures than it is at assessing intentions and motives. Moreover, the theory seems deficient in its evaluation of promises as future-oriented thoughts or wishes.

A more positive line of explanation of promises has been taken by others, for example Rodney J. Hunter, who locates promises under the general rubrics of creativity and risk taking. While there is always a risk in making a promise or a commitment, he observes that this risk also brings about new possibilities. A new social network, howsoever small, is created by every promise.

Hunter employs the Freudian model of ego autonomy in a different and more optimistic way than the classical theory. The promise or commitment comes about partly through a loosening of the ego's controls, but the loosening is followed by a realistic, constructive integration. The ego is flooded by data from the unconscious, requiring it to regroup itself and its sense of rationality. While there is some regression in this, it is a regression "in the service of the ego." The step backward makes a step forward possible, one that can be creative and constructive because the now enlarged ego has appropriated data from the unconscious hitherto unavailable to it.

This theory is based on post-Freudian ego psychology, which sees the ego as not only controlling or repressing the drives but also as an integrating mechanism, taking in and creatively synthesizing data both from inner, unconscious sources and from external sources — events, experiences, and socially mediated influences. It sees a healthy ego as one that is capable of a dialectic, now taking charge and yet leaving itself open to an invasion from outside and below.

According to this school, new promises and new commitments come about because of a positive response to the invasion. A negative response to the new data can be motivated by a sense of fidelity to prior promises or by a perception of the incongruity between one's past sense of self and the beckoning one.

3. **Moral Aspects.** A promise must be entered freely by both the one promising and the one receiving the promise in order for it to have moral quality. Conversely, the moral quality of a promise lessens to the degree that the promise is made unfreely or in a state of psychological incapacity or developmental immaturity. Since a promise involves the commitment of oneself to something in the future, the act of promising presumes a continuity between the present self and the future self. It presumes, furthermore, that by the word one gives one can be relied upon in the future to be what one is expressing about oneself in the present. The act of promising also presumes that a person may impose on him or herself an obligation where none existed before, and that one has something to put at the disposition of another (a possession or some aspect of oneself).

The moral aspects of promising can also be looked at in terms of the one receiving the promise. Promising appears to invoke a universal social convention that creates a legitimate expectation in the person to whom the promise is made. The person receiving the promise is given reason to expect that the promised performance will occur and can be counted upon. The *promisee* has the right to expect fulfillment of that which has been promised and therefore can be said to have a claim over the one making the promise.

The act of promising both deepens and presumes community. It *deepens* community by creating new bonds between those making promises and those who rely on the promises being kept. It *presumes* community insofar as those relying on the keeping of the promises take for granted that those making them live more or less in the same value world. Recipients of promises are invited to trust. Because community or society is only as strong as the bonds of trust that have been created over the course of time, the fabric of community and of society is weakened to the extent that giving one's word or making promises proves unreliable. At the heart of trusting is the assurance that each member will keep his or her promises.

4. **Theological and Pastoral Aspects.** For Jews and Christians the act of promising is undertaken ideally within a historical and theological context of a God who promises. Early in the Hebrew scriptures Yahweh manifests Himself and His love for Israel by promising to Abraham that he would be the father of many nations (Gen. 12:1). This promising was subsequently reinforced by themes of covenant and fidelity. The necessity which society has that promises made by its members be kept is reinforced by a religious tradition that sees the human being as made in the image of a God who makes and keeps promises. The fidelity of God undergirds the faithfulness of human beings to their word and their promises and is most deeply and fully expressed in redemptive grace when human promising fails.

One of the most difficult pastoral theological questions involved in appropriating this covenantal tradition in contemporary society is the issue of freedom, which appears to many people to be antithetical to the claims and obligations involved in promising. The question concerns the true nature of freedom and its relation to obligation. Freedom has to be addressed because the general image that is conveyed by the contemporary culture is that "freedom" means keeping one's options open. If this image is taken uncritically, then freedom and commitment would be seen as incompatible. Freedom would increase by every increase in one's capacity for having things one's way. If freedom is the capacity for indefinite revision or for always doing something different, then one is not justified in making promises that specify one's future and limit one's options.

The options-open image of freedom neglects several important considerations. It confuses freedom with indetermination. The attempt to live in a state of permanent indetermination can hardly be enlightened, for such indeterminacy would render one socially unconnected. Commitments, on the other hand, make communities; they make for relationships one can count on. Moreover, as Gabriel Marcel has shown better than any other, it is only by the exercise of freedom that we determine our lives, making them concrete and specific; and such freedom is always enjoyed within a history of previous choices and inevitably limited circumstances.

The German Jesuit theologian Karl Rahner pithily encapsulates the anthropological point about how freedom functions in a person: "Freedom is not the capacity for indefinite revision, for always doing something different. It is rather the capacity that creates something final, something irrevocable and eternal" (Rahner, 1969, p. 80).

Freedom is integral to commitment, in other words, not the enemy of commitment. Freedom is the right condition for making promises. Furthermore, promises made specify the parameters within which freedom is exercised.

Bibliography. For a general discussion see J. C. Haughey, *Should Anyone Say Forever?* (1975). See also P. Atiyah, *The Rise and Fall of Freedom of Contract* (1979). C. Fried, *Contract as Promise* (1981). N. MacCormick, "Voluntary Obligations and Normative Powers," in *Proceedings of the Aristotelian Society*, supp. vol. 46 (1972). D. Locke, "The Object of Morality and the Obligation to Keep a Promise," *Canadian J. of Philosophy*, 135 (1972). D. Hume, *A Treatise of Human Nature* (1888), pp. 516–25. R. J. Hunter, "Commitment as Psychological Process: Theory and Pastoral Implications," *Pastoral Psychology*, 24:3 (1976), 190–205. G. Marcel, *Being and Having* (1965), *Homo Viator* (1952). K. Rahner, *Grace in Freedom* (1969). H. J. Schlesinger, "Mature and Regressive Determinants of the Keeping of Promises," in *The Course of Life: Psychoanalytic Contributions*, S. J. Greenspan and G. H. Polloch eds., vol. 3 (1980); "Developmental and Regressive Aspects of the Making and Breaking of Promises" in *The Human Mind Revisited*, S. Smith ed. (1978).

J. C. HAUGHEY

COMMITMENT; VOWS/VOWING. *See also* COVENANT AND CONTRACT; FREEDOM AND BONDAGE; MORAL DEVELOPMENT; RELIGIOUS LIFE; RESPONSIBILITY/IRRESPONSIBILITY, PSYCHOLOGY OF; TRUST.

PROPHETIC TRADITION. *See* OLD TESTAMENT AND APOCRYPHA, *or* NEW TESTAMENT; PROPHETIC/PASTORAL TENSION IN MINISTRY.

PROPHETIC/PASTORAL TENSION IN MINISTRY. *Prophetic* is that dimension of ministry which more confrontationally seeks improvement in large groups and systems. *Pastoral* places more emphasis on personal health and growth, including intimate interpersonal relations with family and other small groups.

Past practice reflected a sense of conflict between prophetic and pastoral. Deeper exploration suggests not contradiction but mutual reenforcement. Recognition of this interdependence modifies the practice of both functions and has implications for total congregational programs.

1. **Aspects of the Tension.** The pastoral has often been directed toward adaptation to existing society, and the prophetic toward social disruption and change. Pastoral types often spoke soothingly, while prophets might abrasively have proclaimed revolutionary change. Caring and confronting have frequently appeared to be contradictory approaches. Comfort and challenge were regarded as discrete functions of ministry.

The rich literature on pastoral care includes little publication about the prophetic function of the counselor. Prophetic emphases have too often been less effective because they neglected basic insights from pastoral care. The two emphases often became rivals for the time of pastor or priest, and for budgets and program priorities of religious groups.

Resolution of the tension might be pursued in four possible directions. One could concentrate rather completely on nurturing individuals on the theory that enough changed individuals would automatically improve society. One could concentrate on the prophetic in the confidence that a better social environment would allow the natural flowering of personal capabilities. One could continue the rivalry between the two approaches, hoping that out of the dialogue would emerge tolerable compromises. Or specialists in both areas could develop a wider consensus which more harmoniously integrated the two concerns. Prophetic pastors and pastoral prophets would then be supporting each other.

2. **Biblical and Theological Norms.** Along with examples of tension between pastoral and prophetic, our biblical and theological tradition also points toward a closer relationship. The recorded message of the OT prophets was emphatic in forthright condemnation of the immorality of the nation. Yet they also shared God's compassionate concern for the people they exhorted (see Jer. 4:19; Hos. 11:8). Jesus comforted his hearers with assurance of God's love, and confronted them with radical requirements for discipleship. Because of his great concern for persons, he vigorously opposed evil. He joined social responsibility and personal growth by seeing service as the path to self-realization, whereas self-centered seeking of personal enhancement became self-defeating (Mt. 16:25).

Theologically, we recognize that the purposes of God include both personal growth and social improvement. Devotion to God unites both emphases in a more inclusive vocation. Ministry then goes beyond the therapeutic techniques of psychologists and the social strategies of sociologists to a more unified and greatly expanded task. Furthermore, we view God as the source of both challenge and comfort. God demands radical repentance. God also becomes the source of hope for forgiveness and deliverance.

Theology provides a wholistic view of the person as a totality of body, mind, and spirit — of attitudes, feelings, and actions. Faith is the complete response of our total beings in all our relationships. Being created in community, our choices inevitably become political and economic, as well as more intimately interpersonal. Our environment includes all the created universe, the world of nature, and all our interrelated social institutions. We are faithfully to cooperate with God's continuing creative activity in this total environment.

The goal of the gospel is full liberation of individual potentialities in a world of justice and opportunity for all. Both pastoral and prophetic then become authentic aspects of the mission of the church. Each emphasis can be enriched by the other. The full purpose of neither can be realized without the other.

3. **Contributions of Pastoral to Prophetic.** *a. Persuasive appeal.* Pastoral approaches could increase the persuasive power of prophetic voices. If prophets dealt with their own unrelated frustration and hostility, they might reduce the counterproductive results of belligerent attack. Excessive threat can lead hearers to counterattack, close minds, and avoid communication. Unless accompanied by strong evidence of caring, confrontation is experienced as rejection, to be met with defensiveness.

Instead of threatening postures, pastorally oriented prophets aim at a climate of security and acceptance. Establishing interpersonal trust gains a more receptive hearing for unpopular opinions. The pastor responds to both thinking and feeling of those who disagree. Giving up long-held convictions or behavior patterns is always experienced as loss. Helping persons through this feeling is comparable to caring for those bereaved by the death of a loved one. Especially, the members of a defeated group in a controversial decision require pastoral care.

Instead of simply giving answers, pastoral prophets are willing to raise questions for exploration. If an issue is presented as a shared dilemma, the method for decision more easily becomes participatory problem-solving instead of debate. This also points toward supplementing mass communication with one-to-one and small group discussion. All of these pastoral insights suggest unilateral initiatives available to prophets for reducing hostile resistance — even though crucifixion of prophets is never entirely eliminated.

b. Quality of consensus. Combining pastoral and prophetic skills can improve the quality of any consensus reached. Hopefully the conclusion which emerges is enriched by the perspectives of all participants. The two-way communication encouraged in counselor-client relationships is also productive between change agent and citizen audience. In social debate also, others are less likely to listen to us if we do not listen to them. At their best, reciprocal openness and collaborative problem solving are more conducive to valid conclusions.

c. Growth of participants. Introducing the pastoral dimension into prophetic ministry encourages growth of all participants toward emotional maturity and deeper insight. Personal problems often block social vision. Individual counseling then becomes prerequisite to social discovery. Supportive group experience can contribute to wholesome self-esteem, without severe feelings of guilt or fear. By reducing defensiveness and inflexibility, participants are freed to act in life-enhancing ways, with less need to cling to outmoded opinions and habits. Prophetic spirits become more aware of their temptation to exhibitionism or playing God.

Sustaining prophetic outcomes in society requires such personal growth toward wisdom and altruism as will support improved institutions. Ideal structures will collapse without enough honest, dedicated people to staff them. The importance of this is underscored as we now see the economic havoc which can be wrought by officials of vast corporations or labor unions, and the peril to civilization in irresponsible political leaders with access to nuclear weapons.

d. Group building. A pastoral approach also contributes to stronger groups. Beyond mere intellectual agreement, deeper relationships of trust, empathy, and solidarity can emerge. Debilitating conflicts are more easily avoided. Group participation, motivation, and influence are increased.

Groups so empowered can become more effective in prophetic witness. A notable illustration is the World Council of Churches' "Family Power for Social Change Project." Initiated in 1974, this international project aimed to strengthen families for both personal nurture and change in social structures which handicap women, men, and children.

Qualities of mutual caring and common action which are helpful to small groups are also important for society as a whole. Especially when emerging problems approach crisis, the ability to make rapid change without destructive schism is essential if we are to avoid totalitarianism and collapse.

4. Contributions of Prophetic to Pastoral. *a. Social systems.* If pastoral purposes are to be accomplished, pastors must deal with social systems as well as personal problems. If counselors are to serve where people hurt, they will do something about unemployment, nuclear threat, and ethnic and sex discrimination. Many existing social conditions stymie rather than stimulate personal growth. Threats of war, competition for wealth, and rapid technological change produce insecurity and anxiety. Stress leads to both psychological and physical illness.

Damaging social conditions often are produced by organized groups, including mass media, governments, and economic agencies. Such social structures also need pastoral care. Unless the clergy works at improving structures, they are neglecting their pastoral duties as much as when they refuse to counsel the troubled or visit the dying. The task is to reverse the vicious cycle of individual and social problems, turning it into an ascending spiral in which personal growth will energize social change, and social change will nurture personal growth.

Social action can become a therapeutic resource for personal change. Working on a social welfare project is one treatment for the major modern malady of frustration and powerlessness. Psychic numbing and maladaptive behavior result from trying to deny the existence of overpowering social threats. More realistic meaning, self-esteem, and personal power can be released through the hope in prophetic vision and action.

b. Confrontation. Both for personal growth and social change it is necessary to confront as well as to care. Confrontation can be defined as calling attention to dissonance within the value systems held by individuals or society, or between values held and actual behavior, or between values previously accepted and new experiences of reality. Confrontation is not blaming, or unceasing criticism, or self-righteous gloating. When accompanied by acceptance and caring, confrontation is not to be shunned or feared, but to be examined and appreciated as an expression of concern and a contribution to growth. One does not fully affirm and respect another person unless one is willing to speak to that person whatever is likely to be helpful. At the same time, our honest sharing is not complete until we have also expressed the love we feel for the other.

Until there is a recognition of dissonance there is not likely to be major change. Our history is a story of controversy from Moses to the latest social stands of the World Council of Churches. The prophets denounced those who "have healed the wound of my people lightly, saying, 'Peace, peace,' when there is no peace" (Jer. 6:14, 8:11). To break through the complacency of their people they were impelled to announce powerfully the doom that was at hand—coupled always with an energizing vision of a new day possible with God.

c. Skill training. The prophetic approach would emphasize training both clients and therapists in the neglected skills of a social change agent. Pastoral care is not complete until persons are competent not only in resolving marital conflict, but also in political campaigning and influencing legislation. Individuals are to be empowered to make responsible personal decisions and adequate contributions to social improvement.

Pastoral care includes working with power structures as well as referring to welfare agencies. The skills of the pastor include not only counseling and church administration, but also social analysis and community organization. To supplement biblical and theological resources, pastors need essential psychological knowledge about personality development and basic sociological knowledge about social structures.

Lest their practice contradict their teaching, pastors must model a socially creative lifestyle. As individual citizens they then become actively involved in political and economic change. As society confronts dangerous social threats, pastoral specialists might well adopt appropriate resolutions at their professional meetings. They might well join groupings such as the "Pastoral Care Network for Social Responsibility." Organized in 1983 in response to the nuclear weapons crisis, this network affirms, "Pastoral counselors are the mental health professionals directly concerned with moral integrity and social justice as integral parts of personal well-being." Their purpose includes "to encourage and empower one another in our mutual and individual responses to this spiritual and political crisis of our time."

d. Preservation of future. A prophetic approach to pastoral ministry is now essential for the preservation of both human life and an authentic church. We face not only God's call to liberate the full potentialities of each of God's children within a creative community. We also face the calling to preserve God's Creation in order that all its unrevealed possibilities may continue to unfold through the centuries ahead.

God's gift of freedom now appears even more awesome than we once realized. It is possible that our rebellion may defeat the purposes of God on this present planet by bringing history to a premature close. This is a predictable consequence of military weaponry even more destructive than the nuclear and deployed beyond the earth into space, of exhaustion of irreplaceable natural resources, or of a continuation of such glaringly unequal opportunities for rich and poor as intensify a holocaust of revolution and war.

Even if civilization should continue, the future of an authentic church is at stake. Disastrous decline awaits the church in which pastoral care becomes what James Luther Adams called "the opiate of the pious." (Adams and Hiltner, eds., 1970, p. 216.) The church denies its own function when it contributes to apathetic resignation or adaptation to social injustice where it is called to protest and reconstruction. Religion then becomes an instrument in the hands of those who profit from exploitation —a way of co-opting those who suffer to support the system which causes their suffering. When the great majority of the earth's residents who suffer from social oppression wake up to discover this effect of the church's work, they may be expected to become anti-ecclesiastical.

Unless the church acts prophetically for social justice it may well deserve the judgment Paul leveled against an early congregation: "Your meetings for worship actually do more harm than good" (I Cor. 11:17 TEV). Paul's illustration suggests a form of perpetuating social inequality, because when eating together each ate his or her own meal "so that some are hungry while others get drunk" (vs. 21). By such conformity with social evil, the church contributes to the defeat of God's purposes, and at the same time contributes to its demise.

5. **Implications for Ministry.** The interrelationship of the pastoral and prophetic is such that neither is complete without the other. Pastoral emphases are necessary for effective prophetic witness, and prophetic elements are necessary for wholistic pastoral care. While professional specialization is appropriate, the practice of the specialists is modified. This interpenetration has been emphasized in preceding sections for counseling and social witness. Other aspects of ministry would also be altered.

The recognition that personal health and social improvement are interdependent —and that both require reform of social systems as well as relief of sufferers —demands balanced prominence for all of these elements in preaching, worship, and educational programs. In an exaggerated deference to tradition, churches are tempted to do a better educational job on details of Hebrew history than on details of decent housing for the poor. We easily spend more time on balancing the church budget than on training parishioners for hospital calling. A recall to the pastoral/prophetic function of the church often requires a revolution in curriculum and a reordering of administrative priorities.

Adequately dealing with a complex problem, like personal sexuality or world poverty, requires an entire sermon or a series of classes devoted to that single topic. The widespread practice of using only brief references or occasional illustrations can be worse than useless since it easily leads to misunderstanding and needless rebellion by those who disagree. Generalizations do not effectively change attitudes since they are easily interpreted to mean what the hearer already believes.

On controversial issues collaborative problem solving requires enough time to present fairly the chief arguments of the other side, as well as stating one's own conclusions. This suggests that preachers will listen as well as speak. Education will become more dialogical than authoritarian. Preaching, uninterrupted on Sunday, needs to provide for feedback from laity either in helping prepare sermons or in talkback sessions afterward.

Care and confrontation can both be included in each sermon, worship service, or class. For example, if the dominant sermon theme is a controversial social topic, the worship service might well include emphatic thanksgiving for a vital personal relationship to God. Or, since ours is a total gospel, a class emphasizing the inexhaustible love of God might well include an evangelistic challenge to share one's experience of God with others.

Such insights are especially helpful in dealing with serious controversy in the congregation, whether over theology, church architecture, personal growth, or social change. A church is more likely to avoid damaging conflict if it has developed among members an understanding of the purpose of the church as both caring and confronting. And if it comes to conflict, those educated in democratic process are not disturbed by vigorous debate. They see differences of opinion as valuable to learning. Nurturing loving relationships among parishioners helps to sustain acceptance of opponents during disagreements. Our agreement on superordinate goals (like the loving nature of God, the value of prayer, or the general principles of the Bible) is much more important than matters on which we disagree. Wider agreement is possible insofar as groups take historically validated norms of their religious faith more seriously. During controversy, leaders can facilitate discussion, emphasizing a problem solving approach with a data base, and remaining alert for compromises or new approaches which will incorporate the best insights and legitimate concerns of both sides.

The entire church program also shares the pastoral/prophetic purpose of presenting the whole gospel to persons with a great variety of differing needs. Educationally, this means beginning where people are in all their diversity, and then moving to deeper individualized understandings through a wide range of elective offerings. In worship this suggests recognizing that different worship styles have meaning to different people, and therefore providing within the congregation all possible pluralism in worship experience.

Church programs need to create profound dissatisfactions within each unique individual and social group. At the same time these programs can offer an encouraging message of hope. Unless there appears to be a way out of personal and social difficulties, the reaction is likely to be inaction and depression. Beyond study in sanctuary or classroom, church programs need to include a variety of direct action opportunities. Perhaps in the narthex following worship or in specialized task forces, we can encourage acting on new resolves as soon and as often as possible.

The evangelistic appeal of the church is enhanced as we become person-centered and life-related, offering programs which attract persons because deeply felt dilemmas are helpfully addressed. Persons tend to drop out when they no longer find personal meaning in church attendance. Church representatives abroad also report that missionary outreach becomes more attractive as the church works at liberation from injustices suffered by the majority of people. A rapprochement between prophetic and pastoral thus becomes essential to our total witness.

Bibliography. J. L. Adams and S. Hiltner, eds., *Pastoral Care in the Liberal Churches* (1970). R. H. Bonthius, "Pastoral Care for Structures—As Well as Persons," *Pastoral Psychology,* 18 (1967), 10–19. H. Faber, "Prophetic Role in Pastoral Care," *Pastoral Psychology,* 29 (1981), 191–202. S. Leas and P. Kittlaus, *Pastoral Counselor in Social Action* (1981). W. Oates, *Pastoral Counseling in Social Problems* (1966). E. M. Pattison, "Systems Pastoral Care," *J. of Pastoral Care,* 26 (1972), 2–14. H. Seifert and H. Clinebell, *Personal Growth and Social Change* (1969).

H. SEIFERT

MINISTRY; PASTOR; PASTORAL CARE; SOCIAL JUSTICE ISSUES. *See also* ADVOCACY; AUTHORITY, PASTORAL; AUTHORITY ISSUES IN PASTORAL CARE; CONFRONTATION (Pastoral and Therapeutic); CONSCIOUSNESS RAISING; LIFESTYLE ISSUES; PEACE-MAKING. *Compare* BLACK, FEMINIST, *or* LIBERATION THEOLOGY, AND PASTORAL CARE; OLD TESTAMENT AND APOCRYPHA, TRADITIONS AND THEOLOGY OF CARE IN; SOCIOLOGY OF RELIGIOUS AND PASTORAL CARE.

PROSELYTIZING. *See* CONVERSION (Jewish Care and Counseling); EVANGELIZING; NEW RELIGIOUS MOVEMENTS.

PROTESTANT TRADITION OF CARE. *See* PASTORAL CARE (History, Traditions, and Definitions). *See also* CLASSIC LITERATURE IN CARE AND COUNSELING (Protestantism); HISTORY OF PROTESTANT PASTORAL CARE (Canada *or* United States); PASTORAL CARE MOVEMENT; PASTORAL THEOLOGY, PROTESTANT; THEOLOGICAL EDUCATION AND THE PASTORAL CARE MOVEMENT, PROTESTANT.

PROTESTANT-CATHOLIC MARRIAGE. *See* CATHOLIC-PROTESTANT MARRIAGE.

PROTESTANT-ORTHODOX MARRIAGE. *See* ORTHODOX-PROTESTANT MARRIAGE.

PROVERBS. *See* OLD TESTAMENT AND APOCRYPHA; WISDOM TRADITION, BIBLICAL.

PROVIDENCE, DOCTRINE OF, AND PASTORAL CARE. The belief that God sees all things, governs over all things, and cares for all things, so as to work out the ultimate divine purposes for creation. Neither the

OT nor the NT uses a term for divine providence, but the idea of providence pervades the Bible (Kittel, 1985).

1. The Doctrine of Providence. *a. Classical definitions.* In the development of the theology of the church many definitions of providence have been offered. The Heidelberg Catechism express it experientially:

[Providence is] the almighty and ever-present power of God whereby he still upholds, as it were by his own hand, heaven and earth together with all creatures, and rules in such a way that leaves and grass, rain and drought, fruitful and unfruitful years, food and drink, health and sickness, riches and poverty, and everything else, come to us not by chance but by his fatherly hand.

Calvin points to some of the issues quite vividly: "Providence means not that by which God idly observes from heaven what takes place on earth, but that by which, as keeper of the keys, he governs all events. Thus it pertains no less to his hands than to his eyes."

A contemporary Roman Catholic discussion in *Sacramentum Mundi* (1975) puts it this way: "The notion of providence sums up God's relationship to the world as he knows, wills, and executes his plan of universal salvation and leads the world to the end decreed by him."

The simple classical definition of the doctrine of providence is given in the Westminster Shorter Catechism: "God's work of providence are his most holy, wise, and powerful preserving and governing all his creatures and all their actions."

b. Two elements: preservation and governance. In classical theology, *preservation* refers to the way in which God upholds and directs the natural order of the created universe as an inherent part of divine creative activity. God may be seen as preserving the created order or as continuously giving the created order its shape and being. In any case, God as creator does not simply initiate creation but maintains it.

Governance refers to the way in which God directs the activities of creatures and the historical order of events. Most of the theological and pastoral issues of providence have to do with the relation of God to the lives and histories of human beings. The questions raised for theology and for pastoral care by natural disasters, illness, and death are basically human questions, and to these we now turn.

2. Some General Principles in Thinking About Providence. In thinking about providence, certain theological principles need to be kept in mind in order to avoid difficulties in interpretation. The first of these principles is to keep clear the distinction between *time and eternity.* All language about God and God's activity is conditioned by the temporariness of human existence. So the very term providence has within it the notion of fore-seeing and often involves fore-ordaining on the part of God. But God acts out of eternity, which characterizes the being of God and which is understood by classical theology as a different dimension of being from the temporal.

The providential action of God, what Tillich calls God's "directing creativity," is to be understood not as the action of an impersonal cause, acting mechanically in the manner of physical causes. Rather, God's providence is *teleological,* purposeful, understood in the manner of intelligent and intentional causes. Providence involves neither a mechanistic fate or destiny, often since the seventeenth century called "natural law," nor blind chance or randomness, which is the twentieth-century scientific principle of understanding the physical universe.

Furthermore, the providential activity of God is to be understood not by the use of mechanistic models or symbols (as in fatalism) but by models or symbols that may be called *political*. God does not deal with humans as if they were inanimate objects but recognizes that human creatures have a God-given power to initiate and respond.

Misunderstandings can also be avoided by keeping clear the relationship between *providence and eschatology*. On the one hand, providence is distinguished from eschatology, for providence is a way of looking at what God has done, while eschatology looks ahead to what God will do. On the other hand, providence and eschatology must never be separated from each other, for what God has done and what God will do are both part of the single will of the one God.

Interpreting providence will be more accurate and pastorally helpful if one keeps in mind *the whole Christian theological story*. God's providence begins with Creation and continues through the whole dreary history of human rebellion and sin. God's providence is also expressed in God's saving acts and reaches its climax in the fulfillment of God's purposes in the end. One goes astray if one sees providence only as God's power over creation or in God's judgment against sin.

A final principle of interpretation for the doctrine of providence is that providence is the expression of *God's justice and God's love*. In the Bible God's justice is expressed in the overthrow of evil, in the punishment of disobedience, and in setting free those who are oppressed. God's love is expressed in giving good things to the faithful and in sharing the sufferings of the oppressed.

3. Some Major Problems About Providence.
a. Providence and scientific understanding: miracles. Since the seventeenth-century and the rise of modern science, there has been a struggle about interpreting the providence of God in a world which is increasingly explained by scientific principles. The modern worldview denies any recourse to God as the explanation of ordinary events and relegates the activity of God to the unusual or the "miraculous." Christian theology has often gone along with this view.

Contemporary theology, however, has come to recognize that it is wrong to say that God is at work only in the extraordinary or unpredictable, in what insurance policies and courts of law call "acts of God." God is at work in the regular, usual, ordinary, predictable events as well as in the unusual (Tillich, 1951). Seedtime and harvest are also signs of God's providence according to Scripture.

Miracles are not denials of the power of finite natural causes but are *signs* of the action of God. A miracle is an event that one finds oneself led to interpret by reference to God's action rather than in terms merely of finite acts or causes (Kaufman, 1968). God's healing power, for example, is exercised through the agency of the healing

arts and sciences regularly and expectedly; but God's power may also be unexpectedly made evident.

b. Providence and human freedom and responsibility. In creating human persons, God gave them relative independence, expressed as freedom. Freedom in this sense is the power to choose, i.e., to deliberate, to decide, to take responsibility for actions. Human freedom is never absolute but is always in relation to constraints and in polarity with destiny (Tillich). There is no freedom without destiny. The question is always about the nature of destiny, the dimensions or extent of destiny, the source or "author" of destiny. There is no destiny without freedom, or else human beings are simply the pawns of fate or chance, mechanically determined not destined.

All Christian thought has connected God with the destiny pole. The classical Augustinian/Calvinist tradition, where the action of God is primary, speaks of the independence of "second causes." The Pelagian tradition, where freedom of the human creature is primary, speaks of the divine "concurrence." Contemporary process tradition speaks of the divine aim. All the traditions affirm both God's providential direction and human independence and freedom expressed as choice.

In Christian theology there is another sense of freedom besides the sense of freedom as relative independence and choice: the freedom to love and obey God. That freedom is not one's possession, for in sin one does not love and obey God. That freedom is the gift of God's grace.

Both freedom as independence and freedom as the gift of obedience before God are important for pastoral care. The former makes it possible to deal with persons as persons, able to respond and to change their lives. The latter offers the hope and possibility of newness of life.

c. Providence and the reality of evil. The sharpest theological problem about providence has to do with the existence of evil in the face of God's sustaining and governing activity. Christian thinkers have offered explanations of the presence of evil in the world which a loving and powerful God has created and sustains and governs in one of two ways: either evil is instrumental to the attainment in freedom of human good, or it is finally an ingredient in the totality of God's good purpose (Hick, 1966).

Two important principles lie behind any adequate Christian exploration of providence and evil. One is that evil is what God opposes. The old phrase was "God is in no way the author of evil," but the more adequate phrase is "God always acts to overcome evil." The second is that God has shared the human suffering in the world and continues to share that suffering. Jesus Christ endured the pains that evil brings, including death itself, and showed the suffering love of God.

4. Providence and Pastoral Care. For the person providing pastoral care, the doctrine of providence and the issues discussed have two outcomes. On the one hand, the claims of providence often give rise to the expression of problems about the love and power of God. So one is confronted by people who ask, "Why has God done this?" On the other hand, the doctrine of providence is a great resource to offer hurting people to whom one can present the reality of God's presence and loving care.

a. Dealing with the problems raised by God's action. The issue of providence for people today, as for those in the Bible, arises out of the discrepancy between the revealed character of God and the circumstances or events of life. One form of this questioning comes, as the title of Harold Kushner's book suggests, *When Bad Things Happen to Good People.*

For theological and pastoral reasons some temptations must be avoided. One temptation is to try to turn off the angry accusation of God as unworthy or irreligious. Another is to let the person asking the question take the blame or seek some sinful reality in life. Yet another is to attempt a defense of God by explaining how some natural forces or some sinful acts of others have caused the event. And still another is to insist that while God has indeed done this act, it will turn out for good.

Another form of the questioning comes in the opposite situation, when good things happen to bad people. This is the frequent biblical question, "Why do the wicked prosper?"

Again, for sound pastoral and theological reasons, one must avoid the temptation to explain the evil away or defend God by denying it. And one must not deny the complaint against moral inequities.

What pastors are called upon to do is to affirm what they can affirm about God. They are to continue to hold on to the reality that God is at work in the natural order in its regularity. They are to continue to affirm that human agents have independence and responsibility. They are to continue to acknowledge that God is always opposed to evil, and that God shares the suffering and pain of human life.

b. Calling on the reality of God's care. The doctrine of providence is also a resource for the pastoral care of persons. Providence affirms the reality of the goodness of God as expressed daily in the world and the life of persons. The natural order is an expression of God's care. And history is the arena of God's working to achieve through human beings and for human beings the good fulfillment of God's purposes for all humankind. The world is not subject to blind necessity or chance, but is in the hands of a just and loving God.

Such an understanding sustains the pastor and the people in the living out of life and in the offering of care and love and justice to people. Providence is not in the first instance for the Christian a doctrine that explains the past. It is rather the basis for a trust about the future. There may be little help in the doctrine of providence at the moment of pain for the question, "Why is this happening? Why is my child dying?" But there is very great help for the haunting cry, "I am afraid! How can I face the future?" Providence points to a present and a future that are securely in the hand of God (cf. Rom. 8:28ff.).

Finally, providence offers the basis for serious endeavor to change the world and the situation. The doctrine shifts one's attention from "What will happen to me or to the world?" to "What is God's purpose for me and for the world?" Providence leads one to care for others and to take action to change the concrete situations in the world.

Bibliography. J. Calvin, *Institutes of the Christian Religion*, bk. I, ch. 16 (1953). J. Hick, *Evil and the God of Love* (1966). G. D.

Kaufman, *Systematic Theology: A Historicist Perspective* (1968). G. Kittel, ed., "pronoia," in *Theological Dictionary of the New Testament*, IV (1985), pp. 1009–17. H. Kushner, *When Bad Things Happen to Good People* (1981). E. Niermann, "Providence," in K. Rahner, ed., *Encyclopedia of Theology: The Concise Sacramentum Mundi* (1975). P. Tillich, *Systematic Theology*, vol. I (1951). *Heidelberg Catechism*, QQ.26–28. *Westminster Shorter Catechism*, Q.11.

C. B. KLINE

ESCHATOLOGY; CREATION; GOD; SALVATION. *See also* EVIL; FREEDOM AND DETERMINISM; GOD'S WILL, ACCEPTANCE OF; GUIDANCE, DIVINE; SALVATION, HEALING AND HEALTH; SUFFERING.

PRUDENCE (Moral Theology). In classical and medieval Christian moral theory, prudence ("practical wisdom") is that virtue denoting the habit or disposition to exercise rational, intelligent judgment in particular situations, hence the disposition to discern good moral ends in specific circumstances and appropriate means for achieving them (Aquinas). For Augustine, prudence denoted the disposition to distinguish rightly between what hinders love and what helps it. In modernity, by contrast, prudence has acquired the meaning of rational calculation of self-interest, connoting caution and self-control. In the modern conception, prudence tends to oppose or stand in tension with truly moral life, while in the earlier meaning it provided the necessary element of intelligent judgment for enactment of other virtues.

Though the term is not employed in clinical pastoral care and counseling today, the earlier concept of prudence is implicitly present and potentially of value to counseling theory and practice. It describes, at one level, the ability—that is, the developed habit or disposition—of effective counselors to exercise care or love wisely and intelligently, with an insightful sense of what constitutes truly helpful involvement with particular persons in particular situations. This is not a matter of the deductive application of rules nor, on the other hand, merely being sincere, empathic, or "congruent." It requires specific knowledge (e.g., of psychology) combined with an intelligently implemented, well-timed and proportioned exercise of care (doing neither too little nor too much) expressed in ways that fit the uniqueness and particular complexity of each situation. It is a quality (or "virtue") only developed over time by learning from experience and from participation in a community of similarly disposed (or "virtuous") counselors.

From another perspective, the development of prudence can also be seen as one of the appropriate *aims* of pastoral counseling. While the goals of counseling are today commonly described in such terms as healing, reconciling, improved psychological functioning, individuated selfhood, a deepened sense of meanings and values, and the like, it may also be useful to consider the importance of prudence in this connection. One of pastoral counseling's implicit if not explicit goals is to develop the capacity to distinguish intelligently between what *helps* and what *hinders* love (as in sexual desire or child raising) or the other virtues (e.g., courage, as in conflicts of trust, decision, and commitment). Mature love is wise, not blind; true courage is intelligent, not impulsive or reckless. The qualities of personhood (or "strengths of character") sought in pastoral counseling require an element of intelligent discernment and good judgment; thus one of the aims of pastoral counseling is the cultivation of "practical wisdom" or "prudence."

Bibliography. G. C. Meilaender, *The Theory and Practice of Virtue* (1984). D. M. Nelson, *The Priority of Prudence* (1986). J. Pieper, *Four Cardinal Virtues* (1964).

R. J. HUNTER

INTERPRETATION AND HERMENEUTICS, PASTORAL; PERCEPTIVENESS AND SENSITIVITY, PASTORAL; WISDOM AND PRACTICAL KNOWLEDGE. *See also* MORAL THEOLOGY AND PASTORAL CARE.

PRUYSER, PAUL (1916–86). Psychologist. A native of the Netherlands who emigrated to the U.S. after World War II, Pruyser spent most of his career on the staff of the Menninger Foundation in Topeka, Kansas. During the Nazi occupation of his country, Pruyser was a courier for the Dutch underground. After emigrating, he took his Ph.D. at Boston University. He joined the Menninger Foundation as a clinical psychologist, and served for many years as director of the foundation's department of education. At the time of his death, he was the foundation's Henry March Pfeiffer Professor.

Pruyser was an elder in the Presbyterian church, and deeply interested in theology. The department of education at the Menninger Foundation included the division of religion and psychiatry, in whose affairs he took an active part. He served as vice-president of the Society for the Scientific Study of Religion. He was a guest professor in the religion and personality field of the Federated Theological Faculty at the University of Chicago, and lectured at Princeton Theological Seminary, Boston University, and many other schools.

An expert in psychiatric nosology, he was coauthor with Karl Menninger and Martin Mayman of *The Vital Balance* (1963), an innovative approach to understanding mental illness. Although he continued to write a huge number of psychological monographs on a variety of subjects, most of his publications had to do with the psychology of religion. They included *A Dynamic Psychology of Religion* (1968), and *Between Belief and Unbelief* (1974).

Perhaps his best-known book was *The Minister as Diagnostician* (1976). It was an expansion of his 1975 Lowell Lectures at Boston University, and dedicated to the memory of Thomas W. Klink. Though believing strongly in educating ministers in the human sciences, Pruyser was dismayed to discover that such training often led clergy to abandon their theological roots. He wrote *The Minister as Diagnostician* to reverse that trend, and to insist that ministers should use their theological knowledge and training to assess the problems of help-seekers.

Pruyser exercised a strong influence upon such pastoral theologians as Seward Hiltner, Thomas W. Klink, and Kenneth Mitchell. He took an active part in teaching pastoral care and counseling skills to a large number of the Menninger Foundation's students, many of whom are now active as educators and counselors.

K. R. MITCHELL

PSYCHOANALYSIS AND RELIGION; PSYCHOLOGY OF RELIGION (Theories, Traditions, and Issues).

PSALMS, PASTORAL USE OF. In general, the psalms are used in situations where the pastoral objective is to offer comfort. This means they are employed for ministering to the sick, the infirm, the dying, the bereaved, and to persons who for various other reasons are frustrated or discouraged.

The psalms lend themselves to this pastoral use for two significant reasons. First of all, among the various types of psalms, the personal lament is the most common. At least one third, or some fifty psalms, are personal laments. Persons who are troubled or distressed find that these laments capture their own feelings and express them more profoundly than they themselves are capable of doing.

Second, these personal laments are nonspecific about the original causes or circumstances behind the lament; this makes it possible for readers of these laments to apply them to their own special circumstances without doing violence to the biblical text. Even in ancient Israel, the psalm lent itself to use in situations not immediately envisioned by the original lamenter.

Therefore even though the original circumstances of the psalmist are inaccessible to us, (and we do not even know whether this plea is to be taken literally or metaphorically), we may use psalms of personal lament for certain specific pastoral situations. For example, Psalms 6, 23, and 139 are applicable when death is imminent; Psalm 41 for terminal illness; Psalm 42 for an uncertain future; Psalm 90 in instances of bereavement; Psalm 102 for premature death; Psalm 71 for victimization in old age; Psalm 55 for grief over severed relationships; Psalm 38 for grief over past mistakes; Psalm 62 for grief over loss of personal dignity; and Psalm 73 for grief over personal failure.

Because of the great popularity of Psalm 23, with its reference to the "valley of the shadow of death," the psalms have been very closely linked to grief counseling. Recent efforts by biblical scholars to identify the basic structure of the personal lament are especially relevant to the pastoral use of psalms in grief counseling. The structure of the typical lament has these six stages: (1) address to God; (2) complaint; (3) confession of trust; (4) petition; (5) words of assurance; and (6) vow to praise God (Anderson).

This six-stage structure is applicable to the grief process; the pastoral objective is to facilitate movement through the process, helping the bereaved to fully experience each phase of the lament (Capps, 1981; Peterson). In contrast to bereavement practices in modern societies, psalms of lament express frustration, anger, and vindictiveness as fully and passionately as verbal language permits; they make very specific requests and even demands of God for concrete help; and they promise in turn that they will do their best to praise God in spite of the pain endured. In effect, the deeper the grieving, the more profound the confidence that God has not abandoned the lamenter, but actually shares in the lament (Westermann, 1974).

This lament structure has value for pastoral work with the bereaved, because in modern societies grief tends to be a very diffuse, meaningless experience (Brueggemann). The lament structure does not reduce the pain of bereavement, but it enables the bereaved to give a meaningful shape or pattern to their experience of loss.

Bibliography. W. Anderson, *Out of the Depths: The Psalms Speak for Us Today* (1974). W. Brueggemann, "The Formfulness of Grief," *Interpretation*, 31 (1977), 263–75. D. Capps, *Biblical Approaches to Pastoral Counseling* (1981). M. E. Marty, *A Cry of Absence* (1983). H. J. M. Nouwen, *In Memoriam* (1980). W. E. Oates, *The Bible in Pastoral Care* (1953). E. Peterson, *Five Smooth Stones for Pastoral Work* (1980). C. Westermann, *The Psalms: Structure, Content and Message* (1980); "The Role of the Lament in the Theology of the Old Testament," *Interpretation*, 28 (1974), 20–38.

D. CAPPS

BIBLE, PASTORAL USE AND INTERPRETATION OF. *See also* OLD TESTAMENT AND APOCRYPHA, TRADITIONS AND THEOLOGY OF CARE IN. *Compare* INTERPRETATION AND HERMENEUTICS, PASTORAL; LITERATURE, PASTORAL USE OF; RELIGIOUS LANGUAGE IN PASTORAL CARE.

PSI PHENOMENA. *See* PARAPSYCHOLOGY.

PSYCHE. The human soul, breath, vital force, life, mind, true self, or personality, as variously rendered (1) in classical and Hellenistic Greek usage, (2) in Greco-Roman mythology, and (3) in psychoanalytic theory.

1. Classical and Hellenistic Greek. For Homer (tenth century B.C.) the term *psychē* denotes the *vital force* within the body that comes to expression in breath (Greek *psychō*, "to breathe") and that leaves the body at death. By the sixth century B.C., however, the term comes to denote an inner self that is held captive in the body (*sōma*), thus generating the notion of a mind-body split, an idea that spreads to Hellenistic Jewish literature (e.g., *Apocrypha, Pseudepigrapha,* Philo, LXX), superseding the earlier Hebrew conviction that body and soul constitute an undifferentiated unity (Hebrew *nephesh*).

In the NT the term *psychē* occurs 105 times, in some instances serving simply as a synonym for "life," but in others designating that quintessential, "true self" (Mk. 8:36 NEB) of which Christ is shepherd and guardian (I Pet. 2:25). Paul, however, disuses the term, emphasizing instead the *pneuma* (the God-given "Spirit"), anticipating the later Gnostic ranking of the pneumatic (spiritual) over the psychic (vital) and hylic (somatic) person.

2. Greco-Roman Mythology. The myth of Eros (Cupid) and Psyche reported in *Metamorphoses (The Golden Ass)* of Apuleius (ca. A.D. 250) provides an allegory on the life of the soul with four prime characters: the beautiful Psyche, a jealous Aphrodite, her son Eros (Cupid) who falls in love with Psyche contrary to Aphrodite's wish, and Zeus (Jupiter) who finally admits the loving pair to Mount Olympus. The story suggests that the full value of the psyche, though beautiful, cannot be reached until it has endured trials and realized its need to be assisted by love (Eros). Elsewhere in Greek thought psyche is portrayed as a butterfly, symbol of immortality, or as a young woman with butterfly wings.

3. Psychoanalytic Theory. Though frequently defined as "mind" or "personality," "psyche" in psychoanalytic theory denotes the totality of all the psychic processes, conscious and unconscious, with cognitive, conative, and affective dimensions.

For Freud the primary dynamic components of the psyche are the id, ego, and superego, with the unconscious conceived of as a repository of repressed, instinctual elements in need of integration with consciousness. Jung sees the dynamic components of the psyche as ego (the center of personal consciousness), shadow (the personal unconscious), persona (one's psychic attitude or "mask" toward the outside world), and animus/anima (the "soul-image" or inner personality expressed in contrasexual images). The unconscious for Jung consists of both personal and collective dimensions functioning within a self-regulating psychic totality aimed at individuation, that is, the achievement of the Self, which is the original wholeness out of which personality is formed as well as that which the psychic process seeks to bring to expression.

Bibliography. J. Jacobi, *The Psychology of C. G. Jung*, 7th ed. (1971 [1942]) pp. 5–51. G. Kittel, *Theological Dictionary of the New Testament*, 9 (1974), p. 608ff. P. Grimal, *The Dictionary of Classical Mythology* (1987), 396–7.

W. G. ROLLINS

PHILOSOPHY AND PSYCHOLOGY; SELF, PHILOSOPHY OF; SOUL. *See also* ANALYTICAL (JUNGIAN) PSYCHOLOGY (Personality Theory and Research). *Compare* EGO, PSYCHOLOGICAL MEANINGS AND THEORY OF; MIND; PERSON; THEOLOGY AND PSYCHOLOGY; THEOLOGY AND PSYCHOTHERAPY.

PSYCHEDELIC DRUGS AND EXPERIENCE. Psychedelic is the name given to a class of consciousness-altering drugs and plants that, when ingested, bring about intense experiences. Among the more powerful psychedelics are LSD, psilocybin, and hashish (mescaline); marijuana is a milder and more widely used psychedelic drug that, studies have shown, may be more deleterious over a long period of use. The experiences these drugs produce are often gratifying but sometimes exceedingly frightening and occasionally dangerous, and should therefore be undertaken only with proper supervision. Though legally interdicted for general use, psychedelics continue to be used socially; their professional use is tightly restricted by government controls. However, psychedelic drugs have proved to be valuable psychiatric and psychotherapeutic tools, and they have been used religiously since ancient times as a means of attaining mystical experience and spiritual transformation.

1. Psychedelic Experience. Psychedelic drugs do not directly produce these extraordinary experiences but rather act to trigger or release what is already present in one's psyche, bringing buried memories and capacities to the surface of consciousness. This experience nearly always is felt to be religious in whole or in part, though there also may be vivid aesthetic and extrasensory (e.g., out of the body) aspects as well as illusions of approaching death. Though frightening and painful, the relief that follows the facing of death in a psychedelic experience may indicate a deep release of energies normally tied up in holding death-fear from consciousness.

2. Therapeutic Uses. Marijuana has been found useful in suppressing the nausea that often accompanies treatment for cancer, and dying patients have been helped to face death by use of LSD-like drugs. The stronger drugs, like LSD, have been useful in treating alcoholics and have also been used as an adjunct to depth- and insight-oriented psychotherapy, where they are able to facilitate intrapsychic conflict resolution and produce deep, religious, life-changing transformations.

However, the so-called "bad trip" is also a possibility. In a "bad trip" one is confronted by frightening ideas from the unconscious of which one had previously been but dimly aware. Fears of a "bad trip" seem to have been exaggerated by the mistaken notion that the drugs remain in the bloodstream permanently and accumulate from one experience to the next. There is no evidence that this is so, and little evidence that psychedelic experiences promote repetitions of themselves any more than other equally intense emotional experiences.

Nonetheless, psychedelic drugs *are* dangerous and should only be used with proper supervision. Those who are severely neurotic or on the brink of a psychotic episode should certainly not use them. Others are well advised to avoid them except under the supervision of an experienced "guide." As with all intense experiences, common sense should rule.

3. Religious Use and Significance. Psychedelic drugs remain a subject of ignorance and uncertainty for many religious persons. Nevertheless the power and depth of these experiences, their life-changing potential, and their capacity to stimulate a sense of transcendent reality all continue to fascinate and puzzle some religious theorists. For though most ignore or devalue psychedelic experience as a source of religious understanding, some, following William James (1902), have seriously entertained the possibility that psychedelic drugs can disclose higher (or deeper) levels of reality.

James proposed that the brain, far from being the originator of all thoughts and mental activity, acts more like a "reducing valve," protecting the individual from unnecessary stimuli — cosmic influences — while admitting only those impressions that are of value to the physical preservation of the person. Psychedelic drugs loosen the hold of the brain in its efforts to keep out the awareness of eternal matters in favor of the more practical and mundane, allowing supramundane influences to enter.

Most religious theorists sympathetic with such views probably would agree that psychedelic drugs should not be seen as the exclusive way to deepen one's religious life; they are only one way, and not necessarily the best way for all. Nonetheless, like the initiates in the Eleusinian mysteries of ancient Greece, there will no doubt always be persons who will find the controlled use of psychedelics a valuable means of intensifying or even beginning the spiritual life.

Bibliography. W. H. Clark, *Chemical Ecstasy* (1969). L. Grinspoon and J. B. Bakalar, *Psychedelic Drugs Reconsidered* (1979). S. Grof, *LSD Psychotherapy* (1980). W. James, *The Varieties of Religious Experience* (1902). H. Smith, "Appendix," in *Forgotten Truth* (1976). G. Wasson, A. Hofmann, and C. A. P. Ruck, *The Road to Eleusis* (1978).

W. H. CLARK

DRUGS; ECSTASY; MYSTICISM; RELIGIOUS EXPERIENCE. *See also* DRUG ABUSE, DEPENDENCE, AND TREATMENT; RELIGIOUS LANGUAGE AND SYMBOLISM, PSYCHOLOGY OF; SYMBOLISM/SYMBOLIZING. *Compare* ILLUMINATION; PSYCHOPATHOLOGY AND RELIGION; SENSORY DEPRIVATION RESEARCH; DISCERNMENT OF SPIRITS; TRANCE.

PSYCHIATRIC EVALUATION. *See* EVALUATION AND DIAGNOSIS, PSYCHOLOGICAL.

PSYCHIATRIST/PSYCHIATRY. A psychiatrist is a physician who practices psychiatry. Psychiatry is that branch of medicine which involves the study of the mind and the prevention and healing of mental disorders.

The training of a psychiatrist includes completion of medical school and completion of training in a psychiatric residency program. Subspecialization in child psychiatry or psychoanalysis requires additional training. Certification by the American Board of Psychiatry and Neurology may be obtained but is not required for practice.

Training in psychiatry involves study of the anatomy, biochemistry, and physiology of the brain; study of the theories of normal and abnormal functioning of the mind; and study of the disease processes of the brain that affect behavior. It also includes study of other organ systems that affect or are affected by the individual's emotional state. It includes the study of the effects of medications, drugs, chemicals, vitamins, and hormones on the brain.

The practice of psychiatry involves the evaluation of the patient for the presence of physical and/or mental disorders, and the establishment of a treatment program based upon the evaluation. Evaluation of the patient includes: (1) the history of the presenting problem; (2) the history of any present or past mental or physical problems; (3) the mental status examination; (4) a physical examination including laboratory tests as indicated; (5) psychological testing. In the mental status examination the examiner should determine the presence or absence of abnormalities in behavior, affect, thought, memory, orientation, judgment, and reality contact.

The treatment program includes the use of psychologists, social workers, nurses, clergy, and other mental health professionals. Individual counseling, ECT (shock therapy), medication therapy, group therapy, family therapy, adjunctive therapies (occupational, recreational, movement) may be part of the psychiatric treatment program.

The modes of therapy include crisis intervention, medication therapy, consultation, supportive counseling, behavior therapy, "long-term" insight-oriented psychotherapy, psychoanalysis, partial hospitalization and in-patient hospitalization.

Psychiatrists treat a wide range of emotional problems including: transient adjustment reactions, family dysfunctions, organic brain syndromes, depressions, psychotic illnesses, anxiety states, sexual disorders, and childhood and adult conduct disorders.

A. J. ROOKS

INTERPROFESSIONAL TEAMS AND RELATIONSHIPS; PSYCHOTHERAPY; RELIGION AND PSYCHIATRY (History and Issues). *Compare* ANALYST; CLINICAL PSYCHOLOGIST; CLINICAL PSYCHOLOGY; MARRIAGE AND FAMILY THERAPIST; PASTORAL

PSYCHIATRY; PSYCHOANALYST; PSYCHOLOGIST; PSYCHO-
THERAPIST; RADICAL PSYCHIATRY; SOCIAL WORKER; SOCI-
OLOGY OF RELIGIOUS AND PASTORAL CARE.

PSYCHIATRY, COMMUNITY. See COMMUNITY PSY-
CHIATRY.

PSYCHIATRY, PASTORAL. See PASTORAL PSYCHIA-
TRY.

PSYCHIATRY AND PASTORAL CARE. Healers of
primitive societies were the "priest-physicians"—the
shamans or witch doctors. In their cosmologies the
human was a unitary being and sin was sickness and vice
versa. Healing involved mind and brain, soul and body,
spiritual and corporeal. The healer embodied religious
and medical roles and tasks in one person. Contemporary
indigenous healers in non-Western societies exhibit the
continuance of this unitary healer role where "wholeness
is holiness."

Gradual separation of the two functions of the priest-
physician occurred in Western cultures. In medieval
times, the priest offered confession, penance, absolution,
and exorcism, while the first psychiatric textbook in
1530 argued the distinction between spiritual malaise
and mental disorder. From 1750–1850 the Christian
humanism of the Enlightenment fortified development
of mental hospitals as humane refuges, termed "moral
treatment of the insane." But after 1850 the debate
between science and religion drove a wedge between
psychiatry and the church and a rigid dualism ensued.
Psychiatry addressed human behavior as a deterministic
biological process while the church cared for the ephemeral soul. Since 1900 a series of different relationships
have developed.

In the era from 1900 to 1920, the scientific study of
religion emerged. High interest between psychiatrists
and clergy in separate but collaborative roles was
reflected in spiritual support and uplift, moral enlightenment, and church participation, all respected as part of
comprehensive psychiatric treatment.

From 1920 to 1940, logical positivism and materialistic empiricism ruled out religion. Psychoanalysis
defined religion as immature and neurotic. Sin was redefined as ill health. Anton Boisen pioneered in the role of
mental health chaplain, but most clergy viewed psychiatry with suspicion.

In the 1940s psychiatrist-theologians addressed a new
synthesis. Pastoral care and counseling training was initiated to prepare clergy for ministry to the mentally ill.
In the following decade joint psychiatry-clergy organizations were formed to promote clinical collaboration and
distinctive skills were emphasized.

In the 1960s the U.S. Joint Commission on Mental
Health reported that forty percent of emotionally disturbed persons first seek help from a pastor. The community mental health movement embraced the church and
clergy as major mental health resources. Clergy moved
from parish ministry into specialized and secularized
pastoral counseling. Since 1970 there has been a reem-
phasis on wholistic health care. Pastoral care is being
redefined as part of whole-person health and spiritual

care, and psychiatrists initiate religiously oriented psychotherapy.

Clergy-psychiatrist relations, however, remain varied
and complex. Among psychiatrists in the U.S., about
fifty percent are theists, thirty percent agnostic, and
twenty percent atheistic; twenty percent regularly provide clinical services to religious institutions; and fifteen
percent have theological training. Among clergy, the
conservative-fundamentalist sector make few psychiatric
referrals, and emphasize specialized pastoral counseling
skills. The orthodox-sacramental sector emphasizes skills
in pastoral care expressed through generic pastoral roles.
Nevertheless, the old separatism is being eroded by
renewal of whole-person care, generating new roles for
healers in both the psychiatric and church domains.

Bibliography. E. M. Pattison, *Clinical Psychiatry and Religion*
(1969); "Psychiatry and Religion Circa 1978: Analysis of a
Decade," *J. of Pastoral Care,* 27 (1978), 8–25, 119–41.

E. M. PATTISON

INTERPROFESSIONAL TEAMS AND RELATIONSHIPS; RELI-
GION AND HEALTH MOVEMENT. See also ANALYTICAL PSY-
CHOLOGY, HUMANISTIC PSYCHOLOGY, or PSYCHOANALY-
SIS, AND PASTORAL CARE; EVALUATION AND DIAGNOSIS,
PSYCHOLOGICAL. Compare PSYCHOTHERAPY; RELIGION AND
PSYCHOTHERAPY; SALVATION, HEALING, AND HEALTH.

PSYCHIATRY AND RELIGION. See PSYCHIATRY
AND PASTORAL CARE.

PSYCHIC DETERMINISM. See PSYCHOANALYSIS
(Personality Theory and Research).

PSYCHIC ENERGY. Refers to attempts, numerous
and sundry from earliest times to the present, to understand that which is both fundamental to and produced by
the mind (or soul). A mechanistic, physical conception
of that which is amorphous and ethereal, it nevertheless
is used to contrast mere biochemical activity of the brain
with unknown mental potentials; e.g., Freud's libido
theory.

K. P. ROSS

ANALYTIC (JUNGIAN) PSYCHOLOGY (Personality Theory and
Research); PSYCHOANALYSIS (Personality Theory and Research).
Compare COGNITIVE/CONATIVE PROBLEM IN PSYCHOLOGY
AND COUNSELING.

PSYCHIC HEALING. See FAITH HEALING.

PSYCHICAL RESEARCH. See PARAPSYCHOLOGY.

**PSYCHOANALYSIS (Personality Theory and
Research).** To Freud, who created it, psychoanalysis
was: (1) "*a procedure for the investigation* of mental processes
which are almost inaccessible in any other way," (2) "a
method (based upon that investigation) *for the treatment* of
neurotic disorders," and (3) "a *collection of psychological
information* attained along those lines, which is gradually
being accumulated into a new scientific discipline"
(1923, p. 235; my italics). Although psychoanalysis
originated in the attempt to treat severe functional psychiatric disorders, Freud ultimately emphasized its pre-

eminence as an investigative method. Indeed, he ended life on a sober, even pessimistic, note about its therapeutic value (Freud, 1937).

1. Origins and Core Concepts. Sigmund Freud (1856 – 1939), undoubtedly the most influential physician of all time, began work as a neuroanatomist and neurologist firmly committed to the mechanistic materialism of latter nineteenth century German science. Although he gradually abandoned neurology, his loyalty to the mechanistic teachings of his revered mentor Brücke always conflicted with his clinical appreciation of the meaningful and symbolic aspects of human experience and behavior. Freud was never comfortable acknowledging that his psychological truths had cracked their biophysical mold; psychoanalytic propositions were treated as a theoretical-therapeutic Brest-Litovsk, a temporary concession to psychology of a domain that would ultimately be wrested by neuroscience and neurology.

Nevertheless, however much Freud longed to theorize in neuroanatomic-physiologic terms, the impotence of neurological approaches to his patients' largely hysterical problems was a major factor in compelling him toward psychological concerns. Another determinant, beyond the scope of this article, was the direct and indirect impact of prior workers in the domain of dynamic psychology, unconscious mental life, and childhood sexuality (Ellenberger, 1970; Sulloway, 1979); like Newton and Darwin before him, Freud was in part the synthesizer of the ideas and concepts of others.

The early 1890s were the watershed. Freud reluctantly relinquished tonics, electrotherapy, and the theory that hysteria resulted from cerebral degeneration for a psychological approach. He formulated, partly with the assistance of Breuer (Breuer and Freud, 1895), the theory that his patients' apparent somatic symptoms (blindness, paralysis, anesthesias, and so forth) were the effect of strangulated *affect* associated with the warding off ("repression") of painful *ideas* and *memories* deriving from traumatic events. The therapy, initially largely hypnotic, consisted in making the patient consciously aware of the split-off, hitherto unconscious, ideas and memories related to the traumata, and of facilitating his or her abreaction of the dammed-up feelings associated with them.

Freud eventually discovered that his patients were quite capable, in waking consciousness, of eventually arriving at repressed mental content through the free association method—the relentless and painful reporting of their stream of thoughts and feelings. By 1893–95 the only remnant of the earlier hypnotic phase was Freud's continued use of the couch.

From focus on the traumata of adulthood Freud moved to emphasize their presumed childhood antecedents. In short, it was largely because of the latter that the adult was vulnerable to whatever current stressors precipitated his or her illness. Moreover, Freud shifted the accent from the "actual reality" of the traumatic events (i.e., those aspects which, in principle, could be reported by indifferent third-party witnesses) to their particular meaning for the individual patient ("psychical reality"). In this regard, the patient's *fantasies* about the event were considered the prepotent pathogens. A number of recent writers, such as Masson (1984) and Miller (1986), have charged that Freud's accent on psychical reality promotes ignorance of the extent to which actual traumatic events, such as incest, occur. Even so, in many cases it hardly seems possible, theoretically or therapeutically, to dispense altogether with the patient's particular fantasies and interpretations about the episodes. (See the discussion of "intersectional causation" in Section 3.)

In any event, from 1895 to 1912 Freud hammered out the core concepts of psychoanalysis: the preeminent role of *unconscious mental life* in normal and pathological mental functioning; the place of *unconscious intrapsychic conflict* in symptom, character, and dream formation (*compromises* between the forces of drive and defense); the key role of *intrapsychic conflicts over sexuality and aggression* in psychopathology; the *developmental stages of psychosexuality* (oral, anal, phallic, latency, genital); the impact of *childhood experience* on adult personality and psychopathology; the *primary and secondary processes* of mental functioning (prelogical, pictorial, wish-dominated of unconsciousness and childhood, versus logical, verbal, reality-oriented of consciousness and adulthood); the *pleasure-constancy principle* (the *ur*-drive to reduce the intraorganismic tension associated with unfulfilled strivings to a minimum, tension discharge being experienced as satisfaction); the *transference* as the patterned repetition of historically determined motives, defenses, anxieties, and interpretations in the patient's relationship with the analyst; and, at the therapeutic level, insight into historically determined anxieties and conflictual motivations, rather than simple catharsis, as curative (the patient's *free associations and anamnesis* and the analyst's *interpretations* being the primary vehicles).

2. Freud's "Metapsychology" and Later Work. From 1914 to 1926 Freud developed key elaborations and modifications of analytic theory—what could be called his *metapsychology* (higher order attempts to explain clinical observations), as opposed to his clinical theory, which continued to center around historical and drive-defense analysis (though with some change in emphasis as well).

a. The topographic approach. The first (1900) of the six, ultimately complementary, metapsychological approaches was the *topographic*. This divided the mind or "psychical apparatus," into three systems: "*conscious*," "*preconscious*," "*unconscious*." The first is the locus of those day-to-day operations with which we become intimately familiar; the second of mental content not now conscious though, with appropriate direction of attention, to varying degrees possible of becoming so; and the third is the seat of mental activities which no amount of conscious effort can bring to awareness. Conflict was generally considered to operate between the systems unconscious and preconscious, with the decisive repression barrier being the door to the latter.

b. The structural approach. Freud divided the mind into three "compartments" (*id, ego,* and *superego*), with consciousness, preconsciousness, and unconsciousness no longer systems, but qualities associated with the mental content of these new structures. Each of these "structures" is best considered as an organization of psychical functioning with a slow rate of change. The ontological status of these structures is debated, though factor analytic studies (Kline, 1981) and clinical and personal experience of the discontinuities and fragmentation in mental life and motivation suggest they are more than merely scientific fictions or operational constructs. Structural theory grew out of Freud's clinical appreciation that both components of conflict—drive and defense—could be unconscious, as well as the anxieties and moral injunctions that motivate defense.

The *id* (*Es*, "it") is the mental organization of powerful aggressive, sexual, and egoistic strivings originating in childhood and persisting, with the force of infantile urgency, throughout life. Id operates in accord with primary process. In the normal individual, id content is deeply unconscious, although its disguised derivatives appear in dreams, symptoms, and waking fantasies; direct representations of id are found only in psychosis and anxiety dreams (nightmares). The *superego* (*Überich*, over-I or I-above) is the individual's partly conscious and preconscious, mostly unconscious, moral demand system. Formed largely by the internalization of parental and societal injunctions, interdictions, reinforcements, and punishments, it is an important source and component of intrapsychic conflict; in melancholia its self-punitive tendencies can assume life-threatening proportions. The *ego* (*Ich*, "I") mediates among the demands of id, superego, and human and non-human environment. Many ego functions are secondary processes, logical, and adaptive reality-oriented activities. Large aspects of ego functioning are preconscious or unconscious. Both highly complex and reality-oriented and defensive ego functions can occur outside awareness. Defense itself is thought to be motivated by the ego's generation of "signal anxiety" at the prospect of emergence of warded off id content. Analysis would now move to a focus on these defensive maneuvers and the apperceived danger situations and anxieties motivating them, rather than on direct interpretation of id strivings. When the former are dealt with the latter will, in any event, emerge as a matter of course.

c. The economic approach. Economic theory refers to the drives (*Trieb*), their vicissitudes, and relative intensities. Although in theory Freud treated the drives as wholly determined by their presumed somatic sources, viewing wishes and mental images as their derivative representations, in clinical practice his concept of motivation was teleological and symbolic—affect-laden wishes, goals, purposes. Freud's last (1920) instinct theory stressed sexuality and aggression, whereas earlier ones had emphasized self-preservation and sexuality, object and ego libido. The place of instinct theory is currently one of the most controversial in psychoanalysis. (See Gill and Holzman, 1976).

d. The dynamic approach. This refers to the *currently operative unconscious mental forces* said to motivate all behavior. These mental forces may converge in complement or diverge in conflict; almost invariably each behavior is the effect of several operating concurrently ("overdetermination"). The *genetic* perspective addresses the origin of these currently operating mental tendencies in the history of the individual's fantasies and interpersonal relations.

e. The adaptational approach. The last of the six modes to be developed, the adaptational approach, is adumbrated in Freud but formulated by Heinz Hartmann (1939) and other "ego psychologists." It refers to the personality's aim to maintain an optimum adjustment or fit with the environment. This is achieved through *alloplastic* (environmental manipulation) or *autoplastic* (changes in self) means. Psychopathology can be understood, among other ways, as miscarried attempts at adaptation.

In his last years (1927 to 1939) Freud made no fundamental alterations in psychoanalytic theory—though erstwhile disciples such as Adler, Jung, Rank, and Ferenczi were departing from the basic analytic canon in irreconcilable ways. During this period Freud indulged the cultural and philosophical interests against which he had so long struggled—*Future of an Illusion* (1927), *Civilization and Its Discontents* (1930), and *Moses and Monotheism* (1938). *Totem and Taboo* had appeared in 1913. Freud's *Introductory Lectures on Psychoanalysis* (1915–17), *Outline of Psychoanalysis* (1938), and Brenner's *Elementary Textbook of Psychoanalysis* (1973) remain the best presentations of classical analytic theory.

3. Developments Since Freud. Since Freud the ranks of analysts and scholars have divided along divergent lines on each of these features, as well as upon such issues as whether psychoanalysis is art (Reik, 1949), rhetoric (Lacan, 1968), hermeneutic discipline (Ricouer, 1970; G.S. Klein, 1975; Schafer, 1976), natural science (Hartmann, 1964; Brenner, 1973; Hanly, 1979); "crypto-biology" (Sulloway, 1979); semiotic science (Lacan, 1968); phenomenological enterprise (Guntrip, 1971; Atwood and Stolorow, 1984); a "philosophy" in the manner of the classical Greeks (Ellenberger, 1970); or a hybrid natural science-humanistic discipline (Rubinstein, 1975; Meissner, 1984; Wallace, 1985). Clearly one's decision about the nature of the discipline powerfully determines one's delineation of its central epistemological issues.

Various interpretations and emphases have radiated from the core concepts and principles (below) of psychoanalysis, the most important of which are: the *interpersonal* or *dynamic culturalist* school, as best represented by Horney, Fromm, Kardiner, and, preeminently, Sullivan; *ego psychology*, as adumbrated by Freud and developed by Anna Freud, Hartmann, Kris, Arlow and Brenner, and many others; *object relations* theory, as initiated by Melanie Klein, Winnicott, Fairbairn, Jacobson, and developed by Kernberg, and others; and, finally, *self psychology*, as inaugurated by Kohut and carried forward by followers such as Goldberg and Basch. Space does not permit detailed consideration or bibliographic citation of these orientations (see Wyss, 1973; Greenberg and Mitchell, 1983 for the latter). Suffice it to say that many aspects of these perspectives are in fact compatible with one another. Indeed, many believe that a truly comprehensive and broadly based dynamic psychiatry must take account of all of them. It is easy to see, for example, how interpersonal and object relations approaches complement one another. Self psychology has alerted us to a whole area of character structure and pathology hitherto neglected; it places emphasis on the role of empathy in human development, psychopathology formation, and the psychotherapeutic enterprise, and does not necessarily contradict much of traditional psychoanalysis.

4. Core Principles of Psychoanalysis. It is by now common knowledge that psychoanalysis is no monolithic affair. It is composed of a number of interlocking and interdependent axioms, hypotheses, and methods; moreover, there have been many theoretical and therapeutic innovators working within the "psychodynamic tradition" as broadly defined. Although there have been considerable elisions, emendations, and enrichments of analysis since Freud, virtually all dynamic schools of thought agree on the following four core principles:

a. Exceptionless psychical causality. This means that all psychological events have determinative psychological antecedents. The "causes" which psychoanalysis asserts to operate exceptionlessly (and, moreover, in large measure unconsciously) are purposive ideas, affect-laden fantasies, intentions, goal-oriented strivings—"wishes" in short (Wallace, 1985). No position is taken on the manner in which these determinative purposive ideas themselves arise (presumably from the interaction between those two species of matter-energy—body and world); they are simply treated as emergent properties whose organization and course must be comprehended psychologically (as opposed to neurobiologically or physicochemically). To assert that behavior is "psychically caused" is simultaneously to insist that it is "meaningful": to know the "meaning" of a behavior is to discern its motivation, its intentionality, and its place in a complex causal nexus comprising, preeminently, the unconscious, current and historical interpersonal context of the individual's desiring and fearing. Although the causes with which psychoanalysis is most concerned are motives, it recognizes that nonmotivational causes—cognitive structures, nonsymbolically mediated physiological processes, and so forth—are important as well. Finally, the psychoanalytic concept of causation is neither purely internal ("immanent") nor external ("transeunt"), but *intersectional.* In short, it recognizes that the determinative motivations, anxieties, defenses, and interpretations arise at the interface between the events in the current environment *per se* and the historically-constitutionally determined mental set of the individual (Wallace, 1985, pp. 193–200; 1989a).

b. Historical determinism. This means that the present day configuration of the personality—including one's conscious and unconscious interpretations of self and world and one's desires, fears, inhibitions, and observable behavior patterns—is a function of the history of the individual's actual and fantasied interpersonal relations. This principle is the bedrock of the psychoanalytic theory of character and pathology formation and the theoretical foundation for the central activity of the psychoanalytic therapeusis—the interpretation of transference. "Character" is a more or less adaptive, and "psychopathology" a more or less maladaptive, way of dealing with unconscious intrapsychic conflict. Both the conflicts and the means of handling them arise from the interaction between the child's biological endowment and nascent personality structure on the one side and the environment on the other. Pathological modes of coping with conflict are instances of *atavism*—the persistence of once adaptive, historically determined modes of behavior into the present, where they are no longer useful. The analyst's task, as Freud (1915–17, p. 270) said, "is then

simply to discover in respect to a senseless idea and a pointless action, the past situation in which the idea was justified and the action served a purpose." Adult neuroses and character styles are thus conceptualized as the effects of historically conditioned conflicts, behaviors, and interpretations of reality. *"Transference,"* the most clinically useful concept in psychoanalysis, is the patterned manifestation of the patient's historically determined motivations, fears, expectations, and interpretations in his or her relationship with the analytic clinician. Facilitating the patient's awareness of these experiences and behaviors, and resolving them through elucidation of their historical roots, is the bedrock of analytic treatment.

c. Unconscious mentation and motivation. Psychoanalysis emphasizes the impact of unconscious processes on conscious experience and behavior. The concept of unconscious motivation and mentation was extant for centuries before Freud. There is by now such an abundance of everyday, clinical, and experimental support for the idea that it is seldom questioned by serious scientists and scholars (see Kline, 1981; Fisher and Greenberg, 1977; Bowers and Meichenbaum, 1984). Although in actual clinical practice the attribution of unconscious motives is a largely inferential affair, hypnosis demonstrates the existence of unconscious mental processes, and post-hypnotic suggestion provides direct evidence of their causal impact on conscious behavior, as do a number of subliminal perceptual studies (see Kline, 1981). It is axiomatic, in psychoanalytic circles, that *all* experience and behavior begins unconsciously and rises to consciousness only if unopposed by powerful contravening unconscious motives and defensive maneuvers. This is not to deny the causal efficacy of conscious mentation, as ego psychology stresses; it is merely to assert a proposition regarding the *origin* of these conscious mental processes themselves. The free association method is considered to be the cardinal means of attaining a knowledge of hitherto preconscious and unconscious motivation.

d. Conflicting unconscious motives. The mind, or "psychic apparatus," is comprehended as a system of complementary and conflicting unconscious motivations and psychic organizations which play an etiologic role in character and psychopathology formation. Analysis concerns itself with the latter and with symptomatic and characterological attempts to resolve or reconcile them. Conflicting motives give rise to anxiety, which itself functions as a motive for defending against one or more of the contending strivings. This process is carried out largely unconsciously; we are, for the most part, consciously aware of only the *derivatives* and *compromise formations* of our unconscious motives. For clinical examples of unconscious intrapsychic conflict see Nemiah (1961), Brenner (1976), and Wallace (1983). Much of analysis is concerned with elucidating the specific anxieties that motivate the patient's defensive avoidance of awareness of his or her conflicting unconscious intentions (*analysis of resistance*).

5. Critique and Evaluation. There are many overlapping tasks within the epistemological assessment of psychoanalysis. The first concerns the *logical* structure of psychoanalytic theory—such issues as its internal consistency and coherence; the ordering of its concepts and theorems; and the demarcation between its propositions, assumptions, and data. The second concerns its *empirical* warrant—the extent to which its constructs correspond veridically to the phenomena under consideration, the predictive power of its hypotheses, the nature of the evidence alleged to motivate and support its theories, and so forth.

a. Logical analysis. There is now a growing literature concerned with the logical analysis of psychoanalysis (Hook, 1959; Hanly and Lazerowitz, 1970; and Wollheim, 1977). An important wing of controversy centers around whether psychoanalysis is a natural science or a hermeneutic discipline. Promoting an acausal, hermeneutic perspective are G.S. Klein (1976), Schafer (1976), and, in places, Ricoeur (1970). Such authors regard analysis as a purely idiographic discipline and eschew any search for covering laws. They distinguish sharply between "reasons" and "meanings," which they consider the proper explanatory category for human behavior, and "causes," which are allegedly appropriate only to the natural science realm. Such authors have found a large following among the humanistically and religiously inclined, though a number of writers have mounted strong criticisms of their acausal approach (Blight, 1981; Grünbaum, 1984; Wallace, 1985); it is noteworthy that Ricoeur (1981) himself appears to have returned to a causal framework.

Properly construed as working within the hermeneutic tradition is Spence (1982). Like Feyerabend (1975) in the philosophy of science, Spence adopts a radical relativism, subjectivism, and idealism. Correspondence truth criteria are jettisoned in favor of "aesthetic" (the artistry and coherence of the narrative) and "pragmatic" (whether the patient buys the story and profits therefrom) desiderata. The notion of objective reality is abrogated to the point that, for epistemic purposes, the existence of the patient himself or herself is effectively denied: "As an analyst one empathizes with *one's idea of the analysand* [my italics]" (Schafer, 1976, p. 73).

In the past three decades an enlarging coterie, from within both history and psychoanalysis, has been mining the ore embedded in the many parallels between the historiographic and the psychoanalytic enterprises. The methodological-epistemological issues involved in attempting to reconstruct the past from its traces in the present are basic to both history and psychoanalysis (Wallace, 1985).

Recently a number of scholars have recognized the relevance of phenomenological philosophy to the analyst's task. In psychoanalysis this is often referred to as the "psychology versus metapsychology" or the "clinical language versus metapsychology" debate (see Guntrip, 1971; Gill and Holzman, 1976). Phenomenologically oriented psychoanalysts deride metapsychology as mechanistic and emphasize explanation (or "understanding", as they are more apt to put it) in the experience-near language of motives and meanings rather than in terms of instincts, energies, and the principle of constancy. Atwood and Stolorow (1984) draw on Sandler and Rosenblatt's (1962) concept of the "representational world" and on Husserlian philosophy to produce a seminal monograph on psychoanalytic phenomenology. They emphasize the complementarity of many of the ostensibly incompatible perspectives of Freud, Jung, Rank,

Reich, and Adler, and foresee the day of a unified dynamic psychiatry. Nissim-Sabat (1986) is a gifted recent worker in the attempt to carry Husserlian insights to psychoanalysis; indeed, she regards psychoanalysis as *the* quintessentially phenomenological discipline and, as such, the queen of the social sciences. May, Ellenberger, and Angel (1958), Boss (1963), and Weisman (1965) attempt to meld existentialist and psychoanalytic insights.

Sherwood (1969), Cheshire (1975), and Farrell (1981) have done splendid work on the logical structure of psychoanalytic theory. Popper (1968) argues that psychoanalysis is nonfalsifiable and hence a pseudoscience. Kline (1981) and Fisher and Greenberg (1977) underline the fatuity of any attempt to treat psychoanalytic theory as a monolith; these writers, as well as Grünbaum (1984) and Salmon (1959), point, contra Popper, to the falsifiability of a number of the component hypotheses. Logical analyses of key concepts such as "transference" have been undertaken by Szasz (1961), Greenson (1967), and Gill (1982); many important concepts, such as "narcissism" and "self," cry out for similarly painstaking treatment.

A sensation has been stirred by the work of Adolf Grünbaum, a leading American philosopher of science. Grünbaum (1984) argues that psychoanalytic hypotheses cannot be tested in the clinical setting because the data are irremediably contaminated by the therapist's witting and unwitting suggestions. Moreover, the failure of psychoanalysis to demonstrate that its therapeutic results are consistently superior to those of other psychotherapies vitiates, asserts Grünbaum, its claim to be arriving at veridical causal formulations. He argues, as well, that the free association method cannot yield reliable information about psychological causes. While Grünbaum's erudition is impressive, he has been criticized on a number of grounds: that he treats the alleged thoroughgoing suggestiveness of psychoanalysis as a given, that he exhibits little familiarity with the psychoanalytic method as actually practiced, that he pays virtually no attention to the extensive experimental literature on psychoanalysis, that ways of knowing and testing other than controlled experimentation are paid short shrift, that he gives little heed to the testing possibilities inherent in audio-visual taping of analytic sessions, and that he ignores the nettle of confounding issues involved in psychotherapy outcome research (see Wallace, 1986, 1989, and the June, 1986 issue of *Behavioral and Brain Science,* devoted to a number of critiques of Grünbaum's position).

b. Empirical analysis. There is now an extensive experimental, epidemiological, and cross-cultural literature on psychoanalytic concepts and hypotheses. Fisher and Greenberg's (1977), Kline's (1981), and Masling's (1983, 1985) exhaustive compendia present the methods and findings of hundreds of empirical and statistical studies of psychoanalysis. Space hardly permits adequate presentation of their conclusions though, on balance, the studies provide impressive support for psychoanalytic thinking on repression, sexual symbolism, the Oedipus complex, the oral and anal personalities, and important aspects of dream theory (although, in regard to this last, they suggest that a simple wish-fulfillment theory of dreaming is inadequate). Particularly noteworthy are the perceptual defense and subliminal psychodynamic activation studies of Dixon *et al.* (see Kline, 1981) and Silverman and associates (see Masling, 1985).

Longitudinal and infant observation studies are making important strides. Some of these call into question traditional positions on aggression, primary narcissism, the status of the early infant's representational world, the resolution of the male Oedipus complex, the instinctual need gratification theory of the origin of object relations, and the principle of constancy (Lichtenberg, 1983). Longitudinal studies of verbatim transcripts and videotaped interviews are allowing for predictive tests of clinical hypotheses (the deduction of a class of observable consequences and determining whether they are present or not); rating instruments are being designed (Dahl, 1972; Luborsky, 1984). Sophisticated epidemiologic studies are examining the impact of factors such as the loss of a parent in childhood on depression proneness in adulthood (see Wallace, 1986). Cross-cultural studies examine the oedipal and other theorems (Whiting and Child, 1953; Stephens, 1967; Rohner, 1975).

While not explicitly epistemological, works such as Rieff's (1966) and Browning's (1987) examine the metaphysical and moral dimensions of the psychodynamic theories and therapies and are hence indispensable to the student of religion.

6. Conclusion. Despite all the activity, the scientific assessment of psychoanalysis is yet in its infancy. When one considers that the bulk of the logical and empirical work lies ahead, and that generations will likely transpire before we have sufficient returns from the requisite clinical, epidemiological, experimental, and longitudinal tests, then the dynamic clinician or investigator must possess considerable patience, tolerance of ambiguity, and that peculiar combination of commitment to the value of theorizing and humble skepticism best exemplified by the classic Greeks. The pastor and theologian is advised to keep this in mind and to recognize that the analysis-religion interface presents him or her with the ambiguities inherent in each party to the interaction, as well as with those arising in the interaction itself.

Bibliography. G. Atwood and R. Stolorow, *Structures of Subjectivity: Psychoanalytic Phenomenology* (1984). J. Blight, "Must Psychoanalysis Retreat to Hermeneutics?" *Psychoanalysis and Contemporary Thought,* 4 (1981), 147–205. M. Boss, *Psychoanalysis and Daseinsanalysis* (1963). K. Bowers and D. Meichenbaum, *The Unconscious Reconsidered* (1984). C. Brenner, *An Elementary Textbook of Psychoanalysis* (1973); *Psychoanalytic Technique and Psychic Conflict* (1976). D. Browning, *Religious Thought and the Modern Psychologies* (1987). N. Cheshire, *The Nature of Psychodynamic Interpretation* (1975). H. Dahl, "A Quantitative Study of a Psychoanalysis," *Psychoanalysis and Contemporary Society,* 1 (1972), 237–57. H. Ellenberger, *The Discovery of the Unconscious* (1970). B. Farrell, *The Standing of Psycho-Analysis* (1981). P. Feyerabend, *Against Method: Outline of an Anarchistic Theory of Knowledge* (1975). S. Fisher and R. Greenberg, *The Scientific Credibility of Freud's Theories and Therapy* (1977). S. Freud, *Introductory Lectures on Psycho-Analysis,* SE 15, 16; "Two Encyclopedia Articles (A. Psychoanalysis; B. Libido theory)," *SE* 18; *The Ego and the Id, SE* 19; *Inhibitions, Symptoms, and Anxiety, SE* 20; *Analysis Terminable and Interminable SE* 23. M. Gill, *The Analysis of Transference* vol. 1 (1982). M. Gill and P. Holzman, eds., "Psychology versus Metapsychology," *Psychological Issues Monograph* no. 36 (1976). J. Greenberg and S. Mitchell, *Object Relations in Psychoanalytic*

Theory (1983). R. Greenson, *The Technique and Practice of Psychoanalysis* (1967). A. Grünbaum, *The Foundations of Psychoanalysis: A Philosophical Critique* (1984). H. Guntrip, *Psychoanalytic Theory, Therapy, and the Self* (1971). C. Hanly, *Existentialism and Psychoanalysis* (1979). C. Hanly and M. Lazerowitz, eds., *Psychoanalysis and Philosophy.* H. Hartmann, *Essays on Ego Psychology* (1964). S. Hook, ed., *Psychoanalysis, Scientific Method, and Philosophy* (1959). G. S. Klein, *Psychoanalytic Theory: An Exploration of Essentials* (1976). P. Kline, *Fact and Fantasy in Freudian Theory* (1981). J. Lacan, *Speech, Language, and Psychoanalysis* (1968). J. Lichtenberg, *Psychoanalysis and Infant Research* (1983). L. Luborsky, *Principles of Psychoanalytic Psychotherapy: A Manual for Supportive-Expressive Treatment* (1984). R. May, H. Ellenberger and E. Angel, eds., *Existence* (1958). J. Masling, ed., *Empirical Studies of Psychoanalytic Theories* 2 vols. (1983, 1985). W. W. Meissner, *Psychoanalysis and Religious Experience* (1984). J. Nemiah, *Foundations of Psychopathology* (1961). M. Nissim-Sabat, "Psychoanalysis and Phenomenology: A New Synthesis," *Psychoanalytic Review,* 73 (1986), 273–99. K. Popper, *Conjectures and Refutations: The Growth of Scientific Knowledge* (1968). J. Reik, *Listening with the Third Ear* (1949). P. Ricoeur, *Freud and Philosophy* (1970); *The Conflict of Interpretations* (1974). P. Rieff, *The Triumph of the Therapeutic* (1966); *Freud: The Mind of the Moralist* 3d ed. (1979). R. Rohner, *They Love Me, They Love Me Not: A Worldwide Study of the Effects of Parental Acceptance and Rejection* (1975). W. Salmon, "Psychoanalytic Theory and Evidence," in S. Hook, ed., *Psychoanalysis, Scientific Method, and Philosophy* (1959). J. Sandler and B. Rosenblatt, "The Concept of the Representational World," *The Psychoanalytic Study of the Child,* 17 (1962), 128–145. M. Sherwood, *The Logic of Explanation in Psychoanalysis* (1969). W. N. Stephens, *The Oedipus Complex Hypothesis: Cross-Cultural Evidence* (1962). F. Sulloway, *Freud: Biologist of the Mind* (1979). J. Szasz, "The Concept of Transference," *International J. of Psycho-Analysis,* 44 (1963) 432–43. E. Wallace, *Dynamic Psychiatry in Theory and Practice* (1983); *Historiography and Causation in Psychoanalysis: An Essay on Psychoanalytic and Historical Epistemology* (1985); "The Scientific Status of Psychoanalysis," *J. of Nervous and Mental Disease,* 175 (1986) 379–86; "Toward a Phenomenological and Minimally Theoretical Psychoanalysis," *Annual of Psychoanalysis,* 17 (1989a) 17–69; "Pitfalls of a One-Sided Image of Science," *J. of the American Psychoanalytic Association,* 37 (1989b) 493–529. A. Weisman, *The Existential Core of Psychoanalysis: Reality Sense and Responsibility* (1965). J. Whiting and I. Child, *Child Training and Personality* (1953). R. Wollheim, ed., *Philosophers on Freud* (1977). D. Wyss, *Psychoanalytic Schools from the Beginning to the Present* (1973).

E. R. WALLACE, IV

PERSONALITY THEORY; PSYCHOLOGY, WESTERN. *See also* DREAMS (Theory and Research); EGO PSYCHOLOGY AND PSYCHOTHERAPY; OBJECT RELATIONS THEORY; PSYCHOANALYSIS AND THEOLOGY. *Compare* ANALYTICAL (JUNGIAN) PSYCHOLOGY (Personality Theory and Research); BEHAVIORISM *or* HUMANISTIC PSYCHOLOGY (Theories and Research); MYTHOLOGY AND PSYCHOLOGY; PSYCHOSYNTHESIS.

PSYCHOANALYSIS (Therapeutic Method and Research).

A conscious effort on the part of the analyst and patient to induce an unconscious process, the gradual dissolution of neurotic structures. Such therapeutic technique is an intensely studied topic in all branches of analysis. It pertains to the curative techni-ques and the psychological science developed by Sigmund Freud (1856–1939).

1. General Remarks: the Analytic Hour. From the beginning, Freud claimed that his techniques gave rise to new insights, and that these insights, in turn, validated the techniques employed to find them. It is far easier to describe psychoanalytic theory than it is to describe psychoanalytic technique. This is true for two major reasons. First, psychoanalytic theory is a set of claims made about human experience. Theory exists in the realm of public discourse, while therapeutic method refers to the privacy of the analytic hour. It is easy to read theory, it is hard to comprehend analytic technique. Second, technique grows out of the intense, non-intellectual, relationship that obtains between analyst and patient. Technique, or therapeutic method, consists of the actions undertaken deliberately by the analyst to promote cure. These actions induce the curative process, for example, the recovery of repressed memories, or mourning for lost ideals.

We confront a paradox when evaluating psychoanalytic technique: we can report what the analyst says he or she does in the hour, but this self-conscious report is always less than complete. Even in recorded hours, there is an inherent gap in our record. No videotape can record also the interior experience of both participants. To understand those internal events we ask the participants to reflect upon nonverbal feelings, sensations, fleeting fantasies, etc., and then to convey them to us using language. Yet only gifted poets can do this adequately. Most of us cannot. Our inability to say entirely what occurs in the analytic hour does not signify failure; it demarcates the limits of speaking about "technique."

This real barrier to a completely intellectualized portrayal of technique means that reports of what occurs in the analytic hour are suspect. Indeed, with each development of psychoanalytic theory and with the widening scope of analytic therapy, analysts have reexamined classic case histories and found there numerous hitherto invisible features. Freud's great case studies have been thus reinterpreted for some sixty years.

2. Pre-psychoanalytic Method: Hypnosis and the Pressure Technique. Both the *zeitgeist* and Freud's own predilections, enhanced by his training in neurology, led him to use hypnosis in his early attempts to cure neuroses. Inspired by J. Breuer's report of the spectacular case, Anna O., treated in 1882, but reported publicly in 1893, Freud tried to repeat Breuer's success at "chimney-sweeping" using hypnosis. Freud found that some patients did not respond to hypnotic suggestion. As early as 1893, Freud no longer required hypnotic sleep. Instead, in a calm and authoritative way, he pressed his patient's forehead, telling the patient that upon feeling that pressure, repressed memories would emerge. Often this worked. From this success, Freud deduced that his external pressure overcame an internal, psychological pressure, generated by repressed ideas.

3. Early Analytic Method: Dream Interpretation and Free Association. By 1895 Freud was deeply involved with his revolutionary study of dreams, published as *The Interpretation of Dreams* in 1900. In that text and in his unpublished comments to his colleagues, Freud altered his technique. He now used methods of dream interpretation to interpret his patient's manifest actions and no longer forced the pathogenic ideas from his patients. Also, Freud found that he could discover the source of his patient's thoughts by listening with great

care. He urged his patients to speak to him without censoring themselves and to report to him what they said, privately, to themselves. The entire range of feelings, twinges, thoughts, fantasies, etc., thus reported made up "free associations." Such reports were "free" to the degree they were not consciously controlled or censored by the patient. They are "unfree" to the degree they represent neurotic processes, themselves caused by previous conflicts. Without free associations interpretation is impossible and without interpretations, the pattern latent within free associations cannot emerge. These two methods, promoting free associations and interpreting their unconscious meaning, combined with the interpretation of resistances to free association, define classical analytic technique.

4. Analytic Method: Transference and Transference Neurosis. In the year he published his study of dreams, Freud treated a young woman now immortalized as "Dora" (in his "Fragment of an Analysis of a Case of Hysteria" [1905] *SE,* 7). In this much discussed case history, itself the subject of novels and plays, Freud described a therapeutic failure but theoretical success. For reasons that are obvious now, Dora came to hate Freud, her therapist, with passions that derived in part from her feelings toward her father and other persons responsible for her suffering. This shift of feelings from one person onto another Freud termed "transference." It quickly became the center point of analytic reflection on technique. For in transferring past feelings and fears onto the therapist, the analytic patient brings that past to life. This is both a great danger and a great advantage to the treatment.

The danger is that, like Dora, the patient will not be able to distinguish the analyst's good will from the malign forces in the patient's past. This makes the analytic relationship potentially another source of trauma. The advantage is that, with good technique, the analyst can revive ancient hurts, reveal the patient's original efforts to contain those hurts, and then help the patient discover better ways to solve these deep problems. This is all accomplished through the evocation of the transference, its preservation, and, according to classical terms, the creation of a "transference neurosis." As Freud put it, in therapy, the original neurosis is dissolved and replaced with the transference neurosis. It is the latter that is analyzed and ultimately cured. The neurosis cannot be slain in effigy; it is reanimated by good technique.

With these central issues at the forefront, classical technique understands impediments to the formation of the transference neurosis as resistances which must be analyzed.

5. Later Freudian Developments: the Analysis of the Ego. Freud's thought is extremely compact; he rarely abandoned an idea he liked. Rather, he found ways to integrate it later into a more complex theoretical structure. This is true of the concepts of defense and ego which appear in Freud's preanalytic papers, all but disappear in his early analytic essays, and then return, full force, in his essays on the ego in the 1920s. There Freud laid out new concepts that altered technique: analysts were to focus their attention not merely on uncovering hidden feelings and wishes. Rather they should alter, through interpretation, the structure of the mental agency, the ego, responsible for repression itself. This shift from "id psychology" to "ego psychology" had already occurred in practice and many early analytic authors, like Sandor Ferenczi, addressed themselves to the "ego" qualities of the patient's experience.

Ego analysis gained ground in the late thirties, especially with the publication of Anna Freud's classic, *The Ego and the Mechanisms of Defense* (1936), and similar works by H. Hartmann, Ernst Kris, Erik H. Erikson, and later, David Rappaport, and Roy Schafer.

6. **The Analysis of Sicker Patients, the Analysis of Children.** Analytic techniques were applied early to the treatment of children. Freud's daughter, Anna, opened a nursery school in Vienna; there she trained future colleagues in the fields of educational and developmental psychology, including Erik Erikson. In Berlin, and later in london, Melanie Klein made major contributions to the theory of infantile development and theories of child analysis, especially to the interpretation of play as the child's form of free association. As new populations of patients entered analysis new insights emerged and these, in turn, influenced technique. For example, the works of David Winnicott (e.g., 1971) and Heinz Kohut (e.g., 1977) whose focus on the "analysis of the self" and the curative qualities of empathy have altered dramatically many customary features of analytic style.

7. **Further Studies and Reading.** The effectiveness of analytic therapy has long been studied and debated. A classic review of nearly four hundred studies on therapeutic effectiveness is "Meta-Analysis of Psychotherapy Outcome Studies," published in *American Psychologist,* September, 1977 by M. L. Smith and G. V. Glass. They argue that many forms of psychotherapy, from analysis to behavioral therapies to Rogerian counseling, had similar rates of efficacy. For a detailed review of hundreds of scientific studies on psychoanalysis, see also S. Fisher and R. P. Greenberg, *The Scientific Credibility of Freud's Theories and Therapy* (1985).

Bibliography. M. F. Basch, *Doing Psychotherapy* (1980). P. Gay, *Freud: A Life for Our Time* (1988). R. Greenson, *The Technique and Practice of Psychoanalysis* (1967). E. Jones, *Life and Work of Sigmund Freud* 3 vols. (1953; 1955; 1957). H. Kohut, *The Restoration of the Self* (1977). J. D. Lichtenberg, *The Talking Cure: A Descriptive Guide to Psychoanalysis* (1985). J. Reppen, ed., *Analysts at Work* (1985). D. Winnicott, *Playing and Reality* (1971).

V. P. GAY

PSYCHOTHERAPY; PSYCHOTHERAPY AND COUNSELING (Research Studies and Methods). *See also* DREAMS (Theory and Research); PHILOSOPHY AND PSYCHOLOGY, WESTERN; PSYCHOANALYSIS AND THEOLOGY; RELIGION AND PSYCHOTHERAPY. *Compare* ANALYSTICAL (JUNGIAN) PSYCHOLOGY (Therapeutic Method and Research); BEHAVIOR THERAPIES (Methods and Research); EGO PSYCHOLOGY AND PSYCHOTHERAPY; HUMANISTIC PSYCHOTHERAPIES (Methods and Research); OBJECT RELATIONS; PSYCHOSYNTHESIS.

PSYCHOANALYSIS AND PASTORAL CARE. Psychoanalysis, as explained more fully in related articles, is a system of theories and methods originating in the work of Sigmund Freud for investigating mental processes and treating disorders of the mind. Modified and developed by Freud and his successors, psychoanaly-

sis in its present form consists of: (a) theories concerning the relation of conscious and unconscious psychological processes; (b) developmental theories that relate early childhood experience to present behavior and interpersonal relationship patterns; and (c) practical procedures for investigating mental phenomena and diminishing the suffering caused by neurotic conflicts.

As both a therapeutic procedure and a body of theory about human beings, psychoanalysis has had an immense impact on American thought and culture in the twentieth century, including religious and moral life, theology, and, in a variegated but very significant way, pastoral care and counseling. In fact, its impact on the pastoral care movement was one of the major means by which psychoanalysis entered American (especially Protestant) religious life. This article attempts to trace the broad as well as more specific nature of that influence as well as to identify its principal contributions to contemporary pastoral care. For present purposes, pastoral care will be understood as a function of professional ministry focused on the care and nurture of persons as individuals and in their family and other personal relationships; pastoral counseling is its more specialized, structured form.

1. **History of the Relationship.** *a. General levels of interaction and influence.* In broad cultural terms, both psychoanalysis and pastoral care have contributed to the increasing preoccupation of American culture with individual self-realization, particularly during the middle decades of this century. During this period psychoanalysis came to be viewed as the paradigmatic model of the professional caring relationship, capable of engaging both specific and profound aspects of individual need. At the same time, clinically informed pastoral care and counseling emerged with specialized standards of expertise which, at least initially, were influenced heavily, in some quarters, by the psychoanalytic model. Although even then the actual roles of psychoanalyst and pastoral care specialist differed considerably, in popular culture their images tended to blur together. The psychoanalyst became the secular "priest," keeper of the confessional and esoteric expert in the secrets of abundant life, while the pastoral care specialist became (or appeared to become) something of a religious psychoanalyst — a perception that inevitably evoked vigorous criticism (Mowrer, 1961).

Undeniably, however, at another level of interaction and influence, a number of psychological ideas that have become influential in clinically based pastoral care can be traced to the impact of psychoanalysis. One is developmentalism, the notion that the dynamic causes of present problems of living (as well as strengths) can be derived from an evolving sequence of events and experiences in the life history of the individual. This notion found its way into both popular and technical psychology from psychoanalysis. The modern clinically educated pastor takes the concept of psychological development for granted, not only in his or her work with troubled individuals and families but also in the task of Christian nurture through the educational and community life of the church. Other such concepts derived from psychoanalysis include intrapsychic conflict, unconscious motivation, and the symbolic character of human thought and behavior. These ideas are all widely understood to be pertinent to the caring work of the pastor today, though precisely how much and in what way they actually affect pastoral observation, decision and action is less well known. Their importance, however, is commonly accepted.

It does seem, however, that pastoral knowledge concerning unconscious motivation, intrapsychic conflict and the like has often been rather vague in both concept and application, a fact that has probably led to a mixed effect upon the quality of everyday pastoral care in the parish. For some, it seems, this general knowledge has brought participation in what philosopher Paul Ricoeur called a "hermeneutic of suspicion" concerning everyday conversation and behavior: "Things are not always as they seem to be on the surface;" "There is more going on here than meets the eye;" What is this person *really* saying?" Such comments, common to the pastor who has been exposed to psychoanalytic ideas, often express both an awareness of the reality of these phenomena and an inability to make effective use of such knowledge in pastoral decision and response. For many pastors, psychoanalysis has simply meant participation in the popular culture's psychoanalytic jargon without professional understanding or expertise. For others, however, educational experiences like CPE have made possible a more disciplined, insightful, and effective use of the observational and interpretive tools of psychoanalysis and psychoanalytic ways of thinking about human relationships.

b. Influence on pastoral care specialists. The first attempt to incorporate Freud's insights into ministry, especially counseling and education, was made in Europe by several pioneers including Paul Blau, Martin Schian, Otto Baumgarten, Horst Fichtner, but especially by Oskar Pfister, a Swiss pastor and personal friend of Freud. Pfister believed it possible for religious care and counseling to adopt most of Freud's insights and methods with certain modifications — about which he and Freud maintained a cordial and respectful, but sharp, disagreement (S. Freud and Pfister, 1963). Pfister's correspondence with Freud was not translated and published until years afterward and had little influence on the American pastoral care movement.

Following this initial positive appropriation the European response to Freud became far more cautious. German pastoral care, for instance, developed a "proclamatory" model following the work of Karl Barth's friend, Eduard Thurneysen (ET 1962). In this model psychoanalysis was most often employed to illuminate the darker depths of personality and human sinfulness but not as a major constructive component of pastoral theory and practice, though the work of Otto Haendler and others provided some exceptions. This situation did not fundamentally change, however, until pastors like Dietrich Stollberg and Joachim Scharfenberg developed "therapeutic pastoral care" in the late 1960s, a radically contrary movement that made major appropriations of psychoanalysis for theology and biblical interpretation as well as for pastoral counseling and supervision.

In the U.S. the chief influence of psychoanalysis came through the clinical pastoral training programs, where its impact varied from direct and substantial to very little. From the 1940s to the 1960s, some programs,

notably those affiliated with the Council for Clinical Training headquartered in New York, were heavily involved in teaching psychoanalytic theory and its practical use in pastoral relationships. Other programs, generally those affiliated with the Institute of Pastoral Care centered in Boston, were much less engaged in appropriating psychoanalytic insight. The psychologies informing these programs were more apt to be those of Gordon Allport, Carl Rogers, and other phenomenological psychologists academically influential at the time.

Throughout this period of rapid development, however, many pastoral care specialists availed themselves of personal psychoanalysis or psychoanalytically oriented psychotherapy as preparation for their work as pastoral counselors or clinical pastoral supervisors. Thus many techniques of psychoanalytic therapy found their way directly, with personal and experiential authority, into pastoral care and counseling. Some, of course, adopted these methods in enthusiastic but unexamined ways, virtually identifying pastoral care and counseling with psychoanalytic psychotherapy. But others acknowledged differences as well as similarities and reflected more critically on the relationship.

c. Psychoanalysis in pastoral literature. The pastoral care literature of the modern period beginning in the 1930s likewise evidenced a somewhat mixed picture of engagement of psychoanalytic concepts. Some writers of the 1930s, at the beginning of the pastoral care movement, evidenced both interest in and knowledge of what was then popularly called "depth psychology." (Cf. J. G. McKenzie, 1981; K. Stolz, 1932; R. May, 1939; A. Boisen, 1936.) In popular usage "depth" came to be applied to Freudian as well as Jungian psychology primarily in two senses: the "depth" of unconscious intrapsychic process and the "depth" of historical-developmental dynamics in their impact on present relationships and behavior. Later the term became associated with psychoanalytic theory influenced by existentialist thought. Other pastoral texts of the 1930s, such as Cabot's and Dicks's *The Art of Ministering to the Sick* (1936), express little interest in psychoanalysis and even caution pastors to eschew all appearance of involvement with psychotherapeutic techniques.

By the late 1940s, when the modern pastoral care movement began to flourish, the literature continued to give attention to psychological insights drawn from the Freudian tradition. By this time, however, the impact of "neo-Freudian" revisionism (K. Horney; H. S. Sullivan; E. Fromm) and Rogerian phenomenological theory was more directly apparent than was that of classical Freudianism. Seward Hiltner, in his classic 1949 text *Pastoral Counseling,* footnotes the neo-Freudians a total of twenty-five times; Freud only eight times; Paul Johnson's popular text, *The Psychology of Pastoral Care* (1953), was greatly influenced by Henry Stack Sullivan's neo-Freudian interpersonal theory. In terms of practical method, both of these standard texts were heavily dependent upon Rogerian non-directive, client-centered approaches, as was *Pastoral Counseling: Its Theory and Practice* (1951) by Carroll Wise, another leader of the movement in this period. Wise, an early student of Anton Boisen, carried on a life-long dialogue with Freudian psychoanalytic theory while largely embracing a Rogerian approach to methodology. In his later career, however, Wise renewed his methodological interest in psychoanalytically oriented psychotherapy (*Pastoral Psychotherapy*, 1980). Similarly Wayne Oates, the other major pastoral care theorist of the 1950s and 1960s (*The Christian Pastor*, 1951; *Protestant Pastoral Counseling*, 1962), evidenced a thorough knowledge of psychoanalytic concepts but showed much less interest in appropriating psychotherapeutic techniques drawn from the Freudian and neo-Freudian traditions.

An interesting, additional point of psychoanalytic influence occurred in the late 1950s when pastoral care literature became heavily concerned with grief and bereavement. Virtually all of these pastoral studies drew upon Freud's classic essay, "Mourning and Melancholia," and the equally classic psychoanalytic study by psychiatrist E. Lindemann, "Symptomatology and Management of Acute Grief" (1944). (Cf. P. Irion, 1956; and E. Jackson, 1958.)

An important, somewhat later pastoral care text that presented a theory of pastoral work directly influenced by Freudian conflict theory was Thomas Klink's *Depth Perspectives in Pastoral Work* (1965). Klink drew his primary insights from psychoanalytic theory, modified by the eminent psychoanalytic psychiatrist Karl Menninger, with whom Klink was closely associated.

Of a rather different kind but also an important source of psychoanalytic influence during the 1950s and 1960s was the rich and sustained dialogue with psychoanalytic thought that developed among several major theologians of the time, notably Paul Tillich and Reinhold Niebuhr. Tillich, in particular, was widely read by both pastoral care theorists and practitioners, in part because of his existentialist interest in the mysteries of the unconscious. For many pastors as well as pastoral specialists, books like *The Courage To Be* (1952) and Tillich's numerous articles in *Pastoral Psychology* spoke equally to psychological and theological interests, legitimating and integrating psychoanalytic ideas theologically and underscoring their importance for the work of ministry.

In the late 1960s pastoral care literature began to break away from the dominance of Rogerian methodology. Howard Clinebell in his widely used text, *Basic Types of Pastoral Counseling* (1966), presented a broad spectrum of methodological approaches from which the pastor could choose, depending upon the presenting problem and need of the parishioner. Among these "tools" of pastoral care and counseling, Clinebell included "Depth Counseling," a form of ministry drawn directly from psychoanalytically-oriented psychotherapy. Clinebell was, however, careful to discourage pastors from attempting work at this level without the benefit of extended advanced training in the techniques it involved.

The 1970s saw a full flowering of this eclecticism and pluralism in approaches to pastoral care and in the variety of pastoral concerns addressed by the literature, including dying and bereavement, drugs, alcohol, suicide prevention, needs related to particular periods of the life cycle, and care of the parish as a community. Although, generally speaking, the influence of psychoanalysis on pastoral care theory declined during this period, some writings on these specialized topics drew upon one or another aspect of it. For example, Donald Capps employed Erik Erikson's psychoanalytic ego psychology of the stages of the human life cycle for interpreting the specialized needs of persons at various times and structuring the purpose of the pastoral relationship (cf. D. Capps, 1979 and 1983). Charles Gerkin's *Crisis Experience in Modern Life* (1979) also drew upon psychoanalytic ego psychology for a theory of pastoral care in crises such as death, bereavement, identity confusion, marital and intergenerational conflict, and the like. In a less systematic but sophisticated fashion, George Bennett made use of psychoanalytic insight in exploring the nuances of everyday pastoral relationships in parish life (1978).

2. **Relevance to Contemporary Pastoral Care.** Certain methodological concepts of psychoanalysis have emerged through this history as particularly significant for the work of the parish pastor as much as for the pastoral counseling specialist. They include the following:

a. Historical-development perspective. Although the parish minister is seldom in a situation appropriate for taking an extended social history such as might be done in a clinical context, psychoanalysis has emphasized the importance of understanding present human relational problems in terms of life process and history. In psychoanalytic theory, patterns of stressful relationship not only tend to repeat themselves, but relationship "templates" formed in the crucible of early family life have a strong tendency to influence (if not determine) characteristic modes of relationship in later life. Questions such as: "Have you ever felt this way in a relationship before?" or "Does what has happened remind you of anything that has happened to you earlier in your life?" will often evoke memories that can both clarify present stress and provoke self-examination in terms of life themes important to the person. In pastoral care and counseling the purpose of such inquiry is not to look for chains of causation so much as to help the person place the present stressful situation in a narrative structure of meaning that holds self-identity together. This creates the possibility of finding solutions to present stress that have continuity with the self's deepest needs and intentions.

b. The technique of free association. Freud based much of the technique of psychoanalysis on the process he called free association. In the Freudian theory, if an individual brings to verbal expression whatever comes to mind, no matter how absurd or disconnected the chain of thought may seem at first to be, and if the articulation is attempted without conscious censorship either by the patient or the analyst, the chain of association will unwittingly reveal the unconscious thought processes underlying the difficulty and will lead inevitably to the core of the problem, understood historically and in terms of unconscious dynamics.

Like history taking, the technique of inviting free association has limited but important usefulness for the pastoral counselor and even for the parish pastor, if applied in a limited way in certain situations. For example, if a parishioner reports feeling vaguely depressed much of the time or being short-tempered with his or her children or spouse, it is often useful simply to ask, "What comes to mind when you think of being depressed or of being short-tempered?" Careful listening to the associations that are expressed not only in immediate response to the question, but also over the ensuing moments of conversation, will often provide a clue to the source of the stress. The father of a ten-year-old boy, for instance, mentions a recent family incident in which the boy's disobedience to his mother provoked him to angry and excessive punishment, which was followed by feelings of remorse. The pastor asks what comes to mind when he thinks of these feelings. "Believe me, I jumped when *my* mother spoke to me!" he says, seeming to evade the question. The pastor then recalls an earlier comment complaining that he is now required to report to a female supervisor at work. Such a pattern of associations would suggest that these recent incidents may be stirring deeply buried childhood conflicts concerning authority and obedience, especially to women (and mother).

c. Symbolic communication. Despite the famous quotation from Freud concerning his penchant for smoking long cigars—"Sometimes a cigar is only a cigar!"—Freud and his followers truly believed that virtually all human communication and behavior are symbolic. By this he meant that even ordinary or seemingly trivial actions are rich in multiple unconscious meanings which sometimes get expressed in what Freud called "the psychopathology of everyday life." Certainly in fifty years of CPE countless groups of fledgling pastors have played the game of identifying one another's unconscious symbolic communication through slips of the tongue, temporary memory loss, unconscious gestures, and the like!

In its more serious application, however, the technique of attending to the symbolic communication through talk and relational gesture that goes on in any parish community is an irreplaceable tool of the psychologically sensitive pastor. One is more deeply cognizant of the relational needs and symbolic meanings of events and problems in the lives of parishioners if a finely disciplined sensitivity to this level of communication—what psychoanalyst Theodor Reik nicely termed "listening with the third ear"—is cultivated. As is the case with all helping techniques appropriated from psychoanalysis, this sensitivity must be tempered with wisdom and common sense. The pastor who goes about pointing out the possible symbolic meanings of his or her parishioners' conversational sharing and gestures will soon be in more relationship difficulty than might reasonably be anticipated! But the pastor who quietly hones the ability to hear and see beneath the surface to the symbolic level will be rewarded by recognition from parishioners that this pastor somehow "understands."

d. Transference relationships. Early in his work Freud began to focus attention on the excessive or irrational emotional attachments (positive or negative) that each of his patients seemed inevitably to form with him. Rather than ignoring or suppressing these tendencies, he came to view them as providing valuable clues to the patient's distress. In essence, he became convinced that in every instance patients were "transferring" emotional features of earlier significant relationships, often with parents and siblings, onto himself, thus unconsciously reliving the childhood conflicts directly with him—conflicts Freud believed to be the core of the current neurosis. Such "transference neuroses" themselves could then be analyzed, that is, brought into the therapeutic arena where new resolutions might be found to the core

conflicts, modifying their determinative influence over contemporary relationship patterns. The Freudian analyst therefore seeks to invite transference (by remaining relatively silent and ambiguous) and to "manage" its appearance therapeutically.

In its more general significance the theory of transference suggests that individuals give form and meaning to all new relationships by stamping them with the template of earlier significant relationships. Thus broadly conceived, transference is regarded as a universal phenomenon in human relationships in psychoanalytic theory. In particular, relationships with spouses, peers, and authority figures are fraught with symbolic transference meanings.

It is in this general sense that an understanding of transference phenomena is most useful to the parish pastor. As a commonly recognized authority figure in the religious community, the pastor is subject to considerable transference of authority feelings of all kinds. Some parishioners become deeply dependent upon the pastor's approval. Others struggle against the authority of conscience, personified in the pastor as surrogate for a demanding or persistently evaluative parental figure. Still others feel compelled to resist pastoral authority at every turn. Awareness of these common transferences can greatly illuminate some of the often difficult demands, expectations, and distortions into which parishioners can entangle themselves in their relationship with the pastor. The fact that for many unsophisticated parishioners the pastor is in a peculiar sense the transference surrogate for God, the ultimate parent, can at times further complicate an already over-determined relationship as well as endowing it with more profound pastoral possibilities.

The wise pastor will, of course, be careful not to fall into the pattern of manipulating parishioners through the transference relationships, for example, by exploiting a parishioner's tendency to idealize, antagonize, or sexually seduce the pastor. Also, it is not wise to invite a quasi-therapeutic transference relationship with parishioners beyond that which the context of a parish pastoral relationship can usefully contain. A deep, intentional transference relationship should only be undertaken in a carefully defined and controlled therapeutic context. Such relationships require a highly skilled therapist such as a clinically trained pastoral counseling specialist or other psychoanalytically oriented professional helper.

Pastors would, however, do well to be aware when parishioners are overloading their relationship to him or her with transferred feelings and expectations in order that reality boundaries may be maintained and, on occasion, be pointed out directly. In addition, sensitivity to transference in pastoral relationships can help the pastor perceive deeper life issues and levels of need in otherwise puzzling or difficult parishioner behavior, opening up avenues for more significant pastoral relationships.

e. The concept of resistance. This idea came into being out of Freud's early discovery that, without deliberately intending to do so, his patients tended to set up barriers to his efforts to be of help by "forgetting" appointments, coming late, exhibiting excessively cooperative or antagonistic attitudes, and so on. It seemed that the attainment of new and potentially transforming insights into the dynamic meaning of their behavior, and the awareness of their own participation in bringing about their suffering, had to be achieved, as it were, under protest, in the midst of subtle, pervasive and largely unconscious counterforces. At first this frustrated both Freud and his patients. But Freud learned to interpret these "resistances" themselves as manifestations of the very problems that both therapist and patients were attempting to bring to consciousness and new solution. Like transferences, they could be analyzed and become part of the constructive work of the therapy. Resistance in psychoanalysis thus became a valued and important phenomenon that could be utilized to mobilize the patient's psychic energies for change that penetrated to the level of the unconscious.

In *The Church in the Way* (1967) James E. Dittes has utilized the psychoanalytic concept of resistance as an applicable psychological tool for assisting pastors in both coping with and capitalizing upon the resistance of congregations and individuals to change and transformation. Dittes proposes that such resistance be viewed not as a sign of apathy or simple opposition to ministry, but as a sign of vitality. By interpreting behaviors such as reluctance, subtle no-saying, ambivalent support of new ideas, and the like as phenomena analogous to resistance in psychotherapy, Dittes offered pastors significant and illuminating new ways to respond to these phenomena in pastoral practice.

As is the case with other key psychoanalytic concepts, the concept of resistance is one that must be utilized with care and wisdom. Not every disagreement with the pastor by a parishioner can be rightly said to involve the parishioner's psychological resistance. Nevertheless, careful appropriation of this interpretive tool can assist the pastor in making creative use of the often frustrating encounters with negativism and subtle no-saying that frequently occur in pastoral work.

3. The Evolving Relationship and Emerging Issues. Psychoanalysis, once a dominant influence in most therapeutic helping disciplines, is now less in the forefront of popular interest among helping professionals. Family systems theory, behaviorism, transactional analysis, and a plethora of other systems both popular and academic vie for professional attention and thus compete indirectly or directly for dialogue with pastoral theory and practice. Some pastoral counselors, eschewing the psychoanalytic model as too "medical" or too concerned with psychopathology, have moved on to conversations with humanistic, structural, or cognitive psychologies. Others have become conversant with ego psychology, object relations theory, or self psychology, psychologies which, while rooted in psychoanalysis, greatly modify classical Freudian theory.

The theory and practice of pastoral care itself are likewise undergoing considerable change. In recent years there has been a renewed concern for issues of pastoral theology, the loss of a consensual moral context in Western culture, and the search for community as a central—perhaps *the* central—agency in the religious care of persons. It is just at these growing edges of the discipline, however, that potentially fruitful opportunities lie for a resurgence of conversation with psychoanalysis. Each of these concerns reflects a growing dissatisfaction in American culture with thirty years of overweening

emphasis on self-realization and the identification of freedom with the reduction of moral commitments and obligational bonds. The evidence mounts that the actualization of human potential must require something other than unlimited possibilities for growth and creativity, that personality, society and culture flourish only when certain ideals and limitations—"moral demand systems" (in Philip Rieff's pointed phrase)—are acknowledged by individuals and communities and appropriately sustained by authority.

This is not to plead for social or political convervatism, however. It is rather to recognize the contemporary relevance of the insights into human nature that lay at the heart of Freud's tragicomic vision of the human condition. Social limitation and moral order, and the emotional energies of love and aggression by which they are empowered, were among Freud's most passionate concerns; he was, as Rieff has nicely put it, at least as much a "moralist" as a healer. Thus the current disillusionment with the naive dream of having creativity and fulfillment without limit, power without conflict, and happiness without suffering seems precisely suited to a recovery of classical psychoanalytic themes, perhaps nowhere more appropriately than in pastoral care and counseling.

At the same time it is also clear that classical Freudian theory requires revision at many points. In light of pastoral care's emerging agenda, the most important of these may have to do with reconceiving psychoanalysis to fit more accurately the pluralistic and narcissistic features of contemporary culture. Today, social structures and their intrapsychic counterparts (ego, superego, id) cannot be taken for granted as easily as when psychoanalytic theories were created; the deepest ongoing psychic tasks have as much to do with finding or creating limits as obeying or imposing them. Recent developments in psychoanalytic object relations and self theory, however, hold much promise for reconstructing classical analytic theory and show the continuing vitality and resilience of the psychoanalytic tradition. Charles V. Gerkin's *Living Human Document* (1984) illustrates the potential of these newer forms of psychoanalytic theory for pastoral theory and practice.

Though Freud and his psychoanalytic followers were generally hostile to religion and, at best, indifferent to theology, psychoanalysis, because of its depth, richness and realism about the human condition continues to offer challenging and potentially fruitful possibilities of dialogue with pastoral care theory and practice. Their relationship has been varied and not without difficulties and shortcomings to this point. But it seems likely that pastoral theory and practice will continue to appropriate and struggle with the insights of psychoanalysis for some time to come.

Bibliography. G. Bennett, *When They Ask for Bread* (1978). A. Boisen, *Exploration of the Inner World* (1936). S. H. Brown, "A Look at Oskar Pfister and His Relationship to Sigmund Freud," *J. of Pastoral Care*, 35 (1981), 220–33. D. Capps, *Pastoral Care: A Thematic Approach* (1979); *Life Cycle Theory and Pastoral Care* (1983). H. Clinebell, *Basic Types of Pastoral Counseling* rev. ed. (1984). J. E. Dittes, *The Church in the Way* (1967). S. Freud, "Mourning and Melancholia," *SE* 14, 243–60. S. Freud and O. Pfister, *Psychoanalysis and Faith* (1963). S. Hiltner, "Religion and Psychoanalysis," *J. of Pastoral Care*, 4:1

(1950), 32–42; *Pastoral Counseling* (1949). E. Jackson, *Understanding Grief* (1951). P. Johnson, *The Psychology of Pastoral Care* (1953). T. Klink, *Depth Perspectives in Pastoral Work* (1965). E. Lindemann, "Symptomatology and Management of Acute Grief," *American J. of Psychoanalysis*, 101 (1944), 141–49. J. Maes, "Weighing Psychoanalytic Theory for Pastoral Counseling and Clinical Pastoral Education," *J. of Pastoral Care*, 27 (1974) 196–202. R. May, *The Art of Counseling* (1939). J. G. McKenzie, *Nervous Disorders and Religion: Souls in the Making* (1981 rep.). W. Oates, *Protestant Pastoral Counseling* (1962); *The Christian Pastor* (1951). A. Stokes, *Ministry After Freud* (1985). K. Stolz, *Pastoral Psychology* (1932). P. Tillich, *The Meaning of Health: Essays in Existentialism, Psychoanalysis, and Religion*, P. LeFevre, ed., (1984). E. Thurneysen, *A Theology of Pastoral Care* (ET 1962). C. Wise, *Pastoral Counseling* (1951); *Pastoral Psychotherapy* (1980).

C. V. GERKIN

PASTORAL CARE (Contemporary Methods, Perspectives, and Issues); PASTORAL CARE MOVEMENT; PSYCHOANALYSIS; PSYCHOLOGY IN AMERICAN RELIGION. *See also* DREAM INTERPRETATION IN PASTORAL COUNSELING; INTERPRETATION AND HERMENEUTICS, PASTORAL; OBJECT RELATIONS THEORY; RESISTANCE; SYMBOLIC DIMENSIONS OF PASTORAL CARE RELATIONSHIPS. *Compare* ANALYTICAL (JUNGIAN), HUMANISTIC, *or* NEOFREUDIAN PSYCHOLOGIES, AND PASTORAL CARE. *Biography:* BOISEN; CLINEBELL; HILTNER; JOHNSON; KLINK; MOWRER; OATES; STOLZ; WISE.

PSYCHOANALYSIS AND RELIGION. No interface better embodies the issues inherent in the theism-secularism encounter than that between psychoanalysis and religion. There is by now so large and complex a literature on the topic that this brief essay can offer no more than the barest outline of this rich and problematic dialogue.

1. Psychoanalytic Interpretations of Religion.
a. Freud. Religion was foremost among the cultural concerns that occupied Freud for much of his later career. In a number of provocative and controversial writings Freud used the psychological mechanisms he had encountered in his work with patients to elucidate religious behaviors. In *The Psychopathology of Everyday Life* (1901), he introduced his conceptualization of religion as a projective system in which God, Satan, and the spirit world were held to be personifications of projected unconscious fears and fantasies. In his famous essay, "Obsessive Actions and Religious Practices" (1907), Freud explained religious ritual on the model of obsessive-compulsive symptomatology. The religionist's rituals, like the obsessional's symptoms, were viewed as compromise formations between a repressed impulse, and repressing forces, as simultaneous defenses against unconscious strivings and disguised gratifications of them.

The omnipotence of thoughts, a mechanism particularly favored by obsessive-compulsives, was recruited to explain animism and religion in *Totem and Taboo* (1913). The omnipotence of thoughts is the unconscious presupposition that the wish is equivalent to the deed and therefore that wishing alone can effect changes in one's environment independently of any realistic or practical action. Freud believed that in the animistic-magical stage of cultural history, human beings ascribed omnipotence to themselves, while in the religious stage they

transferred it to a deity and yet retained the idea that they could influence the god, through prayer and ritual, according to their wishes.

Freud believed that one's attitude toward God (assumed to be masculine) derives from one's childhood attitude toward one's father; the heavenly Father is conceptualized as an exalted version of the earthly one. Not being content to account for this with individual or "ontogenetic" factors alone, however, Freud introduced "phylogenetic" ones as well. In this construction human beings, at the dawn of their evolutionary history, were said to have lived in a horde, dominated by a tyrannical "primal father" who maintained jealous possession of the women and excluded the sons, subjecting them to a life of celibacy and impotence. One day the young men, overcome with dissatisfaction, united, and slew and ate the primal father. But no sooner was this accomplished than remorse and longing for the father set in. The unconscious memory of this deed and guilt over it were genetically transmitted to succeeding generations where they became institutionally embodied in religion and morality, determining the inner dynamic of each subsequent historic religion, including Judaism and Christianity. Religious rituals as diverse as the totem meal and the Eucharist were explained as the simultaneous reenactment of the eating of the primal father, and expressions of remorse over this original crime and its continuing unconscious motivations.

In *The Future of an Illusion* (1927) Freud developed his thesis of religion as infantile dependency and illusion or wish fulfillment: "When the growing individual finds that he is destined to remain a child forever, that he can never do without protection against strange superior powers, he lends those powers the features belonging to the figure of his father; he creates for himself the gods whom he dreads, whom he seeks to propitiate, and whom he nevertheless entrusts with his own protection. Thus, his longing for a father is identical with his need for protection against the consequences of human weakness" (p. 24).

Elsewhere Freud emphasized the role of primary process in myth and religion, comparing them to dreams. He conceptualized religious behaviors as sublimations of sexual and aggressive drives. Religious mysticism was explained as a reactivation of the infant's experience of oceanic oneness with its mother's breast.

b. Freud's successors. Subsequent psychoanalytic treatments of religion have consisted, by and large, of elaborations and exemplifications of Freud's original insights. Nevertheless, the dynamic culturalists such as Kardiner (1939, 1945); ego psychologists such as Erikson (1958), Arlow (1961), and Loewald (1978); and psychoanalytic anthropologists such as Spiro (1965) and Levine (1973), have offered models and analyses that give greater attention to the "ego" and to the adaptive aspects of religious behavior than did Freud's. Particularly important is Winnicott's concept of "transitional experience" as "an intermediate area of experiencing, to which inner reality and external life both contribute" (1958, p. 230). Pruyser (1974), Rizzuto (1979), and Meissner (1984) have applied Winnicott's thinking to the understanding of both religious experience and the concept and representation of God itself (as "transitional object"). (See Wallace, 1985a for criticism of these views.)

2. Critique and Appropriation. *a. Psychological and methodological issues.*

Freud's original work on religion can be criticized on several grounds (Wallace, 1983a, 1984). (1) There is a good deal of personal bias implicit in his characterizations of religion as infantile dependency and in his many comparisons of it to psychopathology. References to religion as "neurotic relics," "mass delusions," and "blissful hallucinatory confusion" evidence the presence of hidden moral judgments. (2) Freud's treatment of religion ignores questions of history and sociocultural context. (3) His theory draws no distinction between the concept of the individual and that of the institution, presupposes the existence of a mass mind, relies on an exaggerated concept of psychic unity, and gives insufficient attention to the conscious aspects and phenomenology of religious behavior and experience. (4) Freud pays insufficient attention to adaptiveness as a point of differentiation between psychopathology and religious behavior. (5) His concepts about religion were derived not from analytic work with religious persons themselves, but from a speculative transfer of psychoanalytic ideas to groups of people (and whole cultures) whom he had never analyzed. He thus failed to use his most powerful tool—the clinical method of psychoanalysis. (6) Freud presumed to give "scientific" answers to metaphysical questions.

To conclude from these speculative excesses and methodological weaknesses that Freud makes no contribution to the psychology of religion would be disastrous indeed. However, it is in his psychological writings, rather than those specifically addressed to religious issues, that we find the greatest contribution.

b. Hermeneutical issues. In the debate on psychoanalysis and faith we encounter at least two basic dichotomies involving the proper interpretation of Freud and psychoanalysis. The first is a conflict between the view that Freud's (largely negative) attitudes toward religion derive logically from the premises of psychoanalysis and are essential and integral to its theory and practice, and, on the other hand, the notion that his opinions are merely idiosyncratic and personal, on a par with his passion for cigars and mushrooms. The second is a division between the conceptualization of psychoanalysis as a theoretical, indeed philosophical, system with ethical implications of its own, and the idea of psychoanalysis as a philosophically and ethically neutral instrument or tool. Each side of these two dichotomies is consistently associated with a certain type of answer to the particular questions under consideration. Furthermore, both dichotomies are, interestingly enough, present within Freud himself.

To Pfister, for instance, Freud wrote that psychoanalysts "need not be doctors and *should not* be priests" (Meng and E. Freud, 1963, p. 123, [italics mine]). He contrasted psychoanalysis, as the moral treatment without illusions, to religious treatment as a "crooked cure" *"Schiefheilung"* promoting illusion and childish dependency. Indeed, at times Freud treated psychoanalysis as if it were virtually a *"Weltanschauung"* (Wallace, 1984). On the other hand, Freud was quite capable of treating analysis as theory and technique only, rather than

worldview or "secular religion." He admitted that merely because religious beliefs correspond to our most infantile and deeply cherished wishes does not mean they are false. Writing to Pfister he declared that the opinions in *Future of an Illusion* "form no part of analytic theory" and were his "personal views." Yet in that very polemic against religion, Freud also asserted that "psychoanalysis is a *method of research, an impartial instrument,* like the infinitesimal calculus, as it were; [and] defenders of religion will by the same right make use of psychoanalysis in order to give full value to the affective significance of religious doctrines" (1927, pp. 36–37; [italics mine]).

Among his successors and critics, Pfister (1928), Zilboorg (1962), and Linn and Schwarz (1958) adopt a similar position. Maritain (1957), Fromm (1972), Dalbiez (1941), Dempsey (1956), and Hiltner (1956), however, distinguish between Freud's empirical findings, his treatment methodology, and his metapsychological and cultural writings, and contend that it is only the last of these that are irreconcilable with religious belief and practice. Stern (1951), Küng (1979), Tillich (1957), Pattison (1978–1979), and Meissner (1984) are other psychiatrists and theologians who consider the psychoanalytic and religious enterprises as compatible in large measure. Pfister even maintained, as have the theologians Lee (1948), White (1952), DeLuca (1977), and the philosopher Ricoeur (1970), that the application of psychoanalysis to religion can lead to greater maturity and purification in religious practices.

On the other side of the issue stands Philip Rieff, one of Freud's most brilliant exegetes, who views religion and psychoanalysis as two "inherently antagonistic legacies" (1966, p. 92): "Confronting religion psychoanalysis shows itself for what it is—the last great formulation of nineteenth-century secularism, complete with substitute doctrine and cult." Allers (1940) and LaPiere (1960) draw similar conclusions. And Wallace (1983b, 1984) has elaborated upon Rieff's suggestion that psychoanalysis owes its rise to the decay of religious communities and belief systems, which formerly operated as (in the psychoanalytic sense) socially constructed vehicles for compromise formation, conflict expression, and conflict resolution.

c. Ethics, illness, and epistemology. When one turns to ethics, one encounters divided opinions as well. Mowrer (1961) and Buber (1965) accuse Freud of undermining the traditional religious sense of guilt, and emphasize the need for a category of "real," "existential," or "ontic" guilt alongside neurotic guilt. Menninger (1973) and others point out the considerable gray zone between what the pastor conceptualizes as sin and the analyst as psychopathology. Wallace (1985b, 1986) has addressed the impact of psychoanalytic determinism on moral evaluation. Another crucial issue is the relationship between the psychoanalytic-psychiatric *summum bonum* of adaptation and the religious emphasis on goodness, holiness, and transformation. On the other hand, Hartmann (1960) argues that psychoanalysis is not incompatible with traditional moral reasoning and judgment.

Another area of overlap requiring clarification includes that between the religious and psychoanalytic categories of sickness, health, and cure. Szasz (1961) and others have shown that much that the analyst treats is by no means "illness" in the strictly medical sense of the word and that the term in psychoanalysis has only metaphorical significance at best. Freud (1926) conceptualized the analyst as a lay "curer of souls" or "secular pastoral worker" *(Seelesorger)* and fought strenuously against the monopoly of psychoanalysis by doctors. The issue is further complicated by the fact that the clergy have used medical metaphors as well, for example, the "sick soul," the "cure of souls," the confessor as the "physician of souls," and so forth. There is need for a parallel analysis of the concepts of sickness and healing in medicine and religion, for the implications of such words are far from merely academic. In practice, there is as little doubt that religion cures some "neuroses" as there is that psychoanalysis functions for some as a "religion" (Wallace, 1983b).

Finally, any attempt at reconciliation between psychoanalysis and theology must recognize that each one possesses numerous unresolved and unclarified epistemological issues. The logical and ontological status of both disciplines and their propositions is open to question. The relationship of "evidence" to "theory" in both is inadequately elucidated. Within psychoanalysis itself there is disagreement over the relationship between the clinical and metapsychological "languages" and over whether psychoanalysis is a hermeneutic or natural science discipline. One's decision on these and many other vital philosophical matters could profoundly affect one's conclusions about the compatibility of psychoanalysis with religion (Wallace, 1985c).

3. Conclusion. There is a great deal that psychoanalysis can contribute to the elucidation of religious phenomena. It can clarify the relationship between religious belief and the rest of one's psychical structure, including the quality of the integration with the rest of the personality. It can disclose conflicts for which religious convictions and practices serve as the vehicle of expression or defense, or in which they lend force to one side or the other. It can uncover the history of each individual's religious beliefs, the childhood object representations and identifications that are associated with these beliefs and which help determine their final form. It can comment on the role of religion in one's overall adaptation (or maladaptation) to the internal and external environments. Finally, it can contribute to the ethical sphere of religion: broadened awareness of one's motivations and enhanced ego strength can lead to a more realistic sense of responsibility, the avoidance of easy rationalizations, and a more subtle form of self-control.

In short, psychoanalysis is on most solid ground when it investigates the psychological meaning of the religious beliefs of an individual. Only from the cumulative results of such laborious, clinically based studies can psychoanalysis make meaningful statements about religion and religionists in general. What Freudian psychology can never do of course is determine whether, after all the psychodynamic factors are removed, there is a transcendental justification for religious faith; such a question remains forever beyond the range of a theoretical and empirical psychology.

The interface between religion and psychoanalysis is but one of the many intersections between religion and modern secular culture. To avoid confronting modernity is to subject Judaism, Christianity, and the other great world religions to stagnation, atavism, and irrelevance. And yet to embrace secular thinking and morality too readily, to precipitously reframe religious categories in terms of their secular counterparts, to justify religious practices on the grounds of psychosocial adaptation or mental hygiene, and to be overawed by the scientific pretensions of psychodynamics and the social sciences is to subject the spirit of religion to equally catastrophic results.

Bibliography. R. Allers, *The Successful Error* (1940). J. Arlow, "Ego Psychology and the Study of Mythology," *J. of the American Psychoanalytic Association,* 9 (1961), 371–93. M. Buber, *Between Man and Man* (1965). R. C. Dalbiez, *Psychoanalytic Method and the Doctrine of Freud* (1941). A. DeLuca, *Freud and Future Religious Experience* (1977). P. Dempsey, *Freud, Psychoanalysis, Catholicism* (1956). E. Erikson, *Young Man Luther* (1958). S. Freud, "The Psychopathology of Everyday Life" in *SE* vol. 6 (1901); "Obsessive Actions and Religious Practices" in *SE* vol. 9 (1907); "Totem and Taboo" in *SE* vol. 13 (1913); and "The Future of an Illusion" in *SE* vol. 21 (1927). E. Fromm, *Psychoanalysis and Religion* (1972 [1950]). V. Gay, *Reading Freud: Psychology, Neurosis, and Religion* (1983). H. Hartmann, *Psychoanalysis and Moral Values* (1960). S. Hiltner, "Freud, Psychoanalysis, and Religion," *Pastoral Psychology* 7, (1956) 9–21. A. Kardiner, *The Individual and His Society* (1939); *The Psychological Frontiers of Society* (1945). H. Küng, *Freud and the Problem of God* (1979). R. LaPiere, *The Freudian Ethic* (1960). R. Lee, *Freud and Christianity* (1948). R. Levine, *Culture, Behavior, and Personality* (1973). L. Linn and L. Schwarz, *Psychiatry and Religious Experience* (1958). H. Loewald, *Psychoanalysis and the History of the Individual* (1978). J. Maritain, "Freudianism and Psychoanalysis: A Thomist View" in B. Nelson, ed., *Freud and the Twentieth Century* (1957). W. Meissner, *Psychoanalysis and Religious Experience* (1984). H. Meng and E. Freud, eds., *Psychoanalysis and Faith: The Letters of Sigmund Freud and Oskar Pfister* (1963). K. Menninger, *Whatever Became of Sin?* (1973). O. H. Mowrer, *The Crisis in Psychiatry and Religion* (1961). E. M. Pattison, "Psychiatry and Religion Circa 1978: Analysis of a Decade, Part I," *Pastoral Psychology,* 27 (1979) 8–25; "Part II," *Pastoral Psychology,* 27 (1979) 119–141. O. Pfister, *Psychoanalyse und Weltanschauung* (1928). P. Pruyser, *Between Belief and Unbelief* (1974). P. Ricoeur, *Freud and Philosophy* (1970). P. Rieff, *Freud: The Mind of the Moralist* (1959); *The Triumph of the Therapeutic* (1966). M. Spiro, "Religious Systems as Culturally Constituted Defense Mechanisms" in M. Shapiro, ed., *Context and Meaning in Cultural Anthropology* (1965). P. Stern, *Pillar of Fire* (1951). T. Szasz and N. S. T. Thayer, "Merton and Freud: Beyond Oedipal Religion," *J. of Pastoral Care,* 35 (1981) 36–41. P. Tillich, *The Dynamics of Faith* (1957). E. Wallace, *Freud and Anthropology* (1983a); "Reflections on the Relationship Between Psychoanalysis and Christianity," *Pastoral Psychology,* 31 (1983b) 215–243; "Freud and Religion: A History and Reappraisal" in L. B. Boyer, W. Muensterburger, and S. Grolnik, eds., *The Psychoanalytic Study of Society* vol. 10 (1984), pp. 113–53; "Further Reflections on the Relationship Between Psychoanalysis and Religion," *Listening: J. of Religion and Culture,* (1985a); "Determinism, Possibility, and Ethics,"; *J. of the American Psychoanalytic Association,* (1986); "Freud as Ethicist," in P. Stepansky, ed., *Contributions to Freud Studies* vol. 1 (1985b); *Historiography and Causation in Psychoanalysis* (1985c). V. White, *God and the Unconscious* (1952). D. W. Winnicott, "Transitional Objects and Transitional Phenomena," in D. W.

Winnicott, ed., *Collected Papers* (1951). G. Zilboorg, *Psychoanalysis and Religion* (1962).

E. R. WALLACE, IV

PSYCHOANALYSIS AND PASTORAL CARE *or* THEOLOGY; PSYCHOLOGY OF RELIGION. *See also* PHILOSOPHY AND PSYCHOLOGY; PSYCHOLOGY IN AMERICAN RELIGION; THEOLOGY AND PSYCHOLOGY. *Compare* ANALYTICAL (JUNGIAN) *or* HUMANISTIC PSYCHOLOGY, AND RELIGION; MYTHOLOGY AND PSYCHOLOGY; OBJECT RELATIONS THEORY. *Biography:* BUBER; ERIKSON; FREUD; FROMM; MOWRER; PFISTER; PRUYSER.

PSYCHOANALYSIS AND THEOLOGY. The term psychoanalysis variously refers to (1) a particular method of long-term, individual psychotherapy, (2) that therapeutic practice as a general research instrument for the study of the psychic life of individuals, or (3) a family of related theories of human personality that may be generalized into a theory of culture and society. Psychoanalysis had its origin in the work of Sigmund Freud (1856–1939). Though Freud himself was a professed atheist and negative critic of religion, and though his theories have been the object of much subsequent revision and development, his insights into personality, religion, and culture continue to draw serious, often constructive attention from theologians.

The specific focus of this article is on the enduring significance of psychoanalysis as a resource for theological reflection. The article first sketches ways in which Catholic and Protestant responses to psychoanalysis have historically reflected underlying theological concerns related to the general problem of continuity and discontinuity between the human and the divine, then asks how contemporary developments within psychoanalysis may be opening up new possibilities for the constructive task of theology.

1. Theological Response to Psychoanalysis. All Christian theology has been faced with the common problem of how to think credibly and faithfully about the nature of the human person in an age in which the categories of thought have been increasingly formed by the assumptions of the social sciences, in particular psychology. Two styles of theological response can be identified as "Catholic" and "Protestant," which approach the same common problem from two different apologetic concerns.

a. Catholic responses. One may generalize that in their dealings with psychoanalysis Catholic theologians have more typically been concerned with the problem of the diminishment of the human. From the ancient scholastic dictum that *gratia perficit naturam* — grace builds upon nature — to Karl Rahner's assertion that the minimal but indispensable affirmation of Catholic Christianity is *homo capex infiniti* — the human has the capacity for the infinite or transcendent—the Catholic preoccupation has been with defending the continuity between the human order and the divine. Hence it has typically sought in psychoanalysis evidence for the *conatus* or intentionality toward the transcendent, and rejected and opposed those psychoanalytic accounts of human motivation that have appeared to deny this capacity or reduce it to something else.

It is frequently observed that historically Catholic writers have been more favorably inclined to the work of Freud's brilliant dissenting disciple, Carl Jung, than have Protestant theologians — a sympathy that has sometimes been attributed to Jung's own more appreciative understanding of the psychic value of imagery, symbolism, and sacrament. On balance, however, for Catholic intellectuals as well as Protestants Freud has remained the more influential thinker. For the former, psychoanalysis' greater religious usefulness has been laid to its relatively more rigorous and straightforwardly scientific approach, and appropriately its greater concreteness with respect to the actual life histories of individuals. Particularly in Europe, from the forties into the sixties, Catholic psychologists and theologians like Albert Plé, Louis Beirnaert, Marc Oraison, Ignace Lepp, Maryse Choisy, and Roland Dalbiez variously argued that psychoanalysis was an invaluable instrument for the spiritual director, confessor, and moral theologian. Psychoanalysis, they urged, uncovered the mixed motivations and the constraints on human freedom and self-disposition which must be understood if we would wisely discern the difference between authentic and inauthentic prayer, mystical experience, and moral action. To approach psychoanalysis in this way obviously required that all of these Catholic writers share in some measure the conviction of Neo-Thomist philosopher Jacques Maritain that the theologian critically distinguishes between "Freudian therapy and psychology" (which he endorsed) and "Freudian philosophy" (which he regarded as flawed and inadequate).

Catholic fundamental and systematic theologians have been slower to engage the psychoanalytic perspective explicitly in their work, yet the influence of psychoanalytic ideas can be tracked here as well. In the work of Karl Rahner, for example, one finds the sense for the multivalent, multilayered human psyche that is so much a part of modern psychoanalytic consciousness. It expresses itself in his understanding of the "fundamental option," the recognition that the self-disposing character of human beings toward good or evil can be operative even below the level of awareness. This consciousness is also behind Rahner's notion of concupiscence as the fracture between human nature and the human person manifest in our inability fully to intend and enact what we desire.

b. The Protestant response. By contrast, the Protestant response has generally been interested not so much in the problem of the impoverishment of the human as with the psychological diminishment of the divine, that is, the collapse of the transcendent into the temporal and the mundane by any of the strategies of psychological analysis that reduce the divine to "nothing but" a projection of human wishes or a functional aspect of cultural adaptation. The Protestant style has been characterized by the effort to employ psychoanalytic categories in such a way as to make clear the *discontinuity* between what is properly styled the human or psychological and what can only be accounted for by reference to that which exceeds us utterly, the reality of God.

Protestant systematic theologians, particularly in the neo-Reformation tradition, have been much more willing than their Catholic counterparts to take seriously both Freud the philosopher and Freud the clinician as a contributor to theology's understanding of the human condition before God. Freud's Stoic pessimism about human beings and their capacity for cruelty and endless self-deception suggests what many of these theologians found most significant in the psychoanalytic diagnosis of human culture, namely its unmasking of the true character of sin, idolatry, and alienation. Paul Tillich was perhaps the most influential Protestant theologian to appropriate psychoanalytic ideas to forward this analysis. Tillich perceived in psychoanalysis the continuation and, in some respects, the "re-discovery" of fundamental spiritual perceptions which Christianity had always known but had forgotten how to identify in common human experience. Tillich's method of correlation called for critical passage back and forth between the data of human life experience as might be interpreted by psychoanalytic thinking, and the insights and understandings into faith that are cast in the language and story of Christian revelation and traditional doctrinal formulations. The method is "critical" precisely because Tillich was not willing to say that psychoanalysis could render a whole and adequate account of the full development of faith. Psychoanalytic theory could describe the structure and etiology of human mistrust and unfaith, and psychoanalytic psychotherapy might even be able to lift some of the psychic blocks to the development of faith, but psychology cannot trace the movement of the human being into the realm of graced living. By this understanding, then, psychoanalysis functions, in the words of German Protestant theologian Jürgen Moltmann, as a "bulldozer to clear the way for the gospel."

2. **The Future Dialogue Between Psychoanalysis and Theology.** It is fair to observe that both the "Protestant" and the "Catholic" appropriations of psychoanalysis have their strengths and their limitations, but a common limitation has been the general failure of most theological discussion of psychoanalysis to stay current with progressive developments within the psychoanalytic community of investigation and discourse. Some developments, of course, have already made their theological mark, for example, the use, particularly by pastoral theologians, of the psychosocial theories of Erik Erikson. There are other theoretical innovations more fundamental than Erikson's, however. These developments are significant because they promise to move the theological dialogue with psychoanalysis into new territory precisely because they address some of the traditional theological concerns with the reductionism of Freud's original formulations.

a. *New developments in psychoanalysis.* The classical Freudian understanding of the motive force behind human action was a model in which the drive for individual self-preservation, often in conflict with sexual and aggressive instincts, is determinative in shaping human consciousness. Freud identified the crucial early arena in which these instinctual desires encounter their most decisive social frustration as the family romance, the triangular relationship of child to parents, which assumes critical importance during the phase of early development known as the oedipal period. Over the last forty years, under the impact of new clinical data as well as the influence of studies of mother-child interaction and ethological studies of attachment and separation among high

primates, many psychoanalytic theorists have seriously questioned the adequacy of Freud's instinctual drive model and the primacy of the oedipal conflict. The "oldest, strongest and most urgent" wishes of human beings have been re-identified by some psychoanalysts as the foundational desire of the human person from birth for the affirmation and confirmation of the self by the relationship to the other. Human beings, in other words, are primally and irreducibly "object (or relationship) seeking" from infancy. This paradigm shift within the basic psychoanalytic model, often identified as "object relations theory" and associated with such theorists as W. R. D. Fairbairn, D. W. Winnicott, Margaret Mahler, and George Klein, has a number of attendant implications. Pre-oedipal (primarily mother-child) experience gets raised to greater significance in this model. So, too, does lifelong importance for health of the psychic process by which the solacing and confirming memories of significant relationships are maintained and renewed. Indeed the whole vital function of the imagination and the symbolizing process attains a new theoretical dignity and centrality in this psychoanalytic model.

b. *Implications for theology.* The full meaning of these developments within psychoanalysis has yet to be adequately explored by Christian theologians; nevertheless, the potential lineaments of such a theological dialogue are clear. Closest to the concerns of pastoral theory and practice, the emergent psychoanalytic model of an "inner representational world" crucial for the life of the self is also highly relevant to an understanding of the formation and transformation of an individual's image or representation of God. Research already begun in this area suggests that the capacity for "illusion" is not resigned in maturity but persists as a vital factor in maintaining a sense of wholeness, well-being, and empathic connection with others. At the level of systematic theological reflection, this enlarged psychoanalytic model of the self also has clear soteriological significance, for it powerfully names both the fundamental human orientation toward relationship to "the Other" as well as those inevitable traumas of early life that cause persons to retreat in fear and mistrust from a liberating relationship to themselves, to others, and to God.

Bibliography. W. Birmingham and J. Cunneen, eds., *Cross Currents of Psychiatry and Catholic Morality* (1964). R. Dalbiez, *Psychoanalytic Method and the Doctrine of Freud* (1941). M. Eagle, *Recent Developments in Psychoanalysis* (1984). R. Fine, *The Development of Freud's Thought* (1973). S. Freud, *Future of an Illusion* (1927). J. Greenberg and S. Mitchell, *Object Relations in Psychoanalytic Theory* (1983). P. Homans, *Theology After Freud* (1970). M. Jahoda, *Freud and the Dilemmas of Psychology* (1977). J. McDargh, *Psychoanalytic Object Relations Theory and the Study of Religion* (1983). W. Meissner, *The Birth of the Living God* (1979). R. Munroe, *Schools of Psychoanalytic Thought* (1955). R. Niebuhr, "Human Creativity and Self-Concern in Freud's Thought," in B. Nelson, *Freud and the Twentieth Century* (1957). P. Pruyser, *The Play of the Imagination* (1983). P. Rieff, *Freud: The Mind of the Moralist* (1961); *The Triumph of the Therapeutic: Uses of Faith After Freud* (1966). A. Rizzuto, *The Birth of the Living God* (1979). P. Tillich, *Systematic Theology*, III (1963). D. Wyss, *Depth Psychology: A Critical History* (1966). E. Zetzel and W. Meissner, *Basic Concepts of Psychoanalytic Psychiatry* (1973). G. Zilboorg, *Psychoanalysis and Religion* (1967).

J. McDARGH

PERSON; PASTORAL THEOLOGICAL METHODOLOGY; THEOLOGY AND PSYCHOLOGY. *See also* OBJECT RELATIONS THEORY; PASTORAL THEOLOGY, PROTESTANT; PHILOSOPHY AND PSYCHOLOGY; RELIGION AND PSYCHOTHERAPY. *Compare* ANALYTICAL (JUNGIAN) PSYCHOLOGY AND RELIGION *or* THEOLOGY; JUDAISM AND PSYCHOLOGY; PSYCHOANALYSIS AND RELIGION; PSYCHOTHEOLOGY. *Biography:* RAHNER; TILLICH.

PSYCHOANALYST. A person, ordinarily a psychiatrist, who has completed rigorous professional education beyond psychiatric residency in the theory and practice of psychoanalysis. Psychoanalysts also may be qualified persons from other disciplines. Psychoanalysts work primarily with individuals in long-term therapy toward a goal of characterologic change.

S. A. PLUMMER

PSYCHIATRIST/PSYCHIATRY; PSYCHOANALYSIS (Therapeutic Method and Research). *Compare* ANALYST; CLINICAL PSYCHOLOGIST.

PSYCHOANALYTIC EGO PSYCHOLOGY. *See* EGO PSYCHOLOGY AND PSYCHOTHERAPY.

PSYCHOANALYTICALLY - ORIENTED PSYCHOTHERAPY. A type of psychological therapy aimed at the modification of repressed and suppressed unconscious conflicts and the ways these determine everyday life patterns.

Psychoanalytically oriented psychotherapy can be contrasted with psychoanalysis and the non-psychoanalytic therapies. Two factors which separate this treatment approach from its parental source, psychoanalysis, are the greater significance of the client-therapist relationship and the emphasis on discussion of everyday life events. While unconscious and preconscious material is still of central significance it emerges from the conversations about work, family, friendships, self-image, religious experiences, etc. The therapist makes connections between repetitive issues, and between current patterns and the client's life history. The former bring unconscious determinants of behaviors into awareness for modification. The latter facilitate insight about historic developmental conflicts which continue to be repeated with final resolution being the goal. Usually the frequency of sessions is limited to one meeting each week though, in certain situations, this may be extended to twice a week.

Since the therapist-client relationship takes on much greater significance, there is diversity of style in this therapeutic approach. The therapist's personality is apparent and influential on the therapy relationship. This also is one of the major strengths of this approach in that it fully utilizes the client-therapist relationship. This can enhance the client's interpersonal sensitivities and skills as well as serving as the doorway through which the client's unconscious issues and unresolved familial conflicts can emerge.

In contrast to non-psychoanalytic therapies, there are several distinguishing features of psychoanalytically oriented psychotherapy. First, it is intrapsychically oriented in contrast to social, interpersonal, systems, and group process therapies. Second, it is clearly psychologically oriented in contrast to biological or biochemical therapies. Third, it views pathology as the symptom of the repressed and suppressed unconscious conflicts, wishes, and fantasies in contrast to the behavioral and humanistic therapies.

Bibliography. R. Blanck and G. Blanck, *Ego Psychology: Theory and Practice* (1974); *Ego Psychology II: Psychoanalytic Developmental Psychology* (1979). R. Langs, *The Technique of Psychoanalytic Psychotherapy I, II* (1973–74). R. Langs, ed., *International J. of Psychoanalytic Psychotherapy.* D. M. Moss III, "Priestcraft and Psychoanalytic Psychotherapy: Contradiction or Concordance?" *J. of Religion and Health,* 18 (1979), 181–8.

E. A. HOOVER

PSYCHOANALYSIS (Therapeutic Method and Research); PSYCHOTHERAPY.

PSYCHOBIOLOGY. *See* PSYCHOLOGY, WESTERN.

PSYCHODRAMA. *See* ADJUNCTIVE THERAPIES.

PSYCHODYNAMICS. A generic term describing any psychological theory or therapeutic method which explains and approaches psychological processes in terms of motives and drives. There is an attribution of causal efficacy to most if not all psychological processes. Literally translated "the mind in action," it assumes there is never a static moment within even the mature individual.

M. A. WOLTERSDORF

ANALYTICAL (JUNGIAN) PSYCHOLOGY *or* PSYCHOANALYSIS (Personality Theory and Research). *See also* COGNITIVE/CONATIVE PROBLEM IN PSYCHOLOGY AND COUNSELING; MODELS IN PSYCHOLOGICAL AND PASTORAL THEORY.

PSYCHOHISTORY. The application of psychology to the study of history, particularly to the study of historical individuals. As a method, psychohistory is most frequently associated with psychoanalytic and neo-Freudian psychologies; it focuses on the role of an influential individual's personality in relation to his or her cultural achievement and childhood experience.

1. **Erikson's Work.** A well-known example of psychohistory is Erikson's *Young Man Luther,* published in 1958. This work was not, however, the first attempt to apply psychoanalysis to famous, yet long-dead, subjects; an earlier example is Freud's study of Leonardo da Vinci. However, Erikson's work overcame the most serious defects of many previous efforts: lack of attention to cultural context and reductionistic use of psychiatric labels. Erikson's Luther study depended on the concept of identity and was intended as a study of identity crisis and its resolution.

Identity develops as the individual integrates childhood experiences with prevailing models and ideologies of society at large. Religion has always been a key provider of ideologies and functions as an aid or obstacle to identity formation. An innovator such as Luther could use his childhood conflicts constructively, so as to forge a new ideology and fresh role models. Erikson's goal was to plumb the sources of Luther's religious creativity, not to overemphasize his neurotic qualities or denigrate his thought. Other examples of psychohistorical studies follow the *Luther* pattern, including Erikson's study, *Gandhi's Truth*.

2. **Evaluation.** Psychohistory has been extensively criticized (cf. R. Johnson, 1975). It seems to rest on a "great man" theory of historical change. Moreover, few individuals have left the kind of information about themselves upon which psychoanalytic interpretations must rely—for example, information about early childhood. The actual data used by Erikson about Luther's early life, for example, was both scanty and suspect, if not entirely discredited. A long-dead subject is unable to challenge specific interpretations, however arbitrary these may be. Finally, psychological theories, such as Erikson's, rest on models of human personhood derived from Western culture and are difficult to apply to non-Western individuals.

These criticisms can be answered. Some persons from the past have left behind detailed personal information, covering those topics psychoanalysis deems important. The problem of arbitrary interpretation is endemic to any historical reconstruction, psychological or otherwise. The criticism of "Western bias," however, is the most interesting and has led to studies of cross-cultural biography and life-patterning, as well as detailed investigation of Erikson's own moral and religious assumptions. Such studies demonstrate the crucial role of cultural, religious, and traditional patterns in the formation of individual character and the self-interpretation of life history.

Bibliography. D. Capps, W. H. Capps, and M. G. Bradford, eds., *Encounter with Erikson* (1977). E. Erikson, *Young Man Luther* (1958); *Gandhi's Truth* (1969); *Life History and the Historical Moment* (1975). S. Freud, *Leonardo da Vinci and a Memory of His Childhood*, SE vol. 11 (1910). R. Johnson, ed., *Psychohistory and Religion* (1977). F. Reynolds and D. Capps, eds., *The Biographical Process* (1976).

L. BREGMAN

PSYCHOLOGY OF RELIGION; PSYCHOLOGY, WESTERN. *See also* NEOFREUDIAN PERSONALITY THEORIES; PSYCHOANALYSIS (Personality Theory and Research). *Biography:* ERIKSON.

PSYCHOKENESIS. *See* PARAPSYCHOLOGY.

PSYCHOLINGUISTIC THEORY IN PSYCHOLOGY AND COUNSELING. Psycholinguistics is a field of study that grows out of the marriage of the concerns of both psychology and linguistics. Psychologists attempt to understand, control, and/or predict human behavior, while linguists attempt to understand and describe the structure of language. Within the broad field of psychology, psycholinguists have traditionally focused on two primary questions: (1) How do children acquire language? and (2) How is language encoded and decoded, produced, and understood? (DeVito, 1971). More recently, however, Bandler and Grinder (1975) have ventured into application of psycholinguistic theory for counseling.

Because of the questions that psycholinguists have generally addressed, the field has not yet had a major impact on individual counseling, Bandler and Grinder's work notwithstanding. It should be noted, however, that the theories and research findings within the field of psycholinguistics have found application in several widespread areas including the treatment of the following problems: disorders of first language development in otherwise normal children, language development of the mentally retarded, infantile autism, language development in the deaf, difficulties with reading and writing, and adult aphasia, to name a few.

A Brief History of Psycholinguistics. While it is nearly impossible to get scholars to agree on where a history of modern American psycholinguistics should begin, almost everyone points to the linguist Noam Chomsky as the pivotal figure in that history. As Palermo (1978) aptly points out, Noam Chomsky started a revolution in 1957 with the publication of his little book entitled *Syntactic Structures*. In this book Chomsky detailed the inadequacy of a behavioral model to fully explain the phenomenon of speech in human behavior. He argued that the number of novel sentences that a person could produce is infinite. He went on to explain that this fact would militate against the notion that the child learns language solely through the process of making connections between stimuli and responses.

Chomsky proposed instead what has been called a "transformational grammar." He asserted that a "grammar" is a set of linguistic rules for generating sentences in a particular language and that a transformational grammar represents the actual operations used by a speaker to produce sentences (Greene, 1972). The reason this conceptualization was considered revolutionary was that it heralded a new willingness to focus once again the study of psychology of language on mental processes. When Chomsky wrote his book, the behaviorism of Watson and Skinner had for years made the practice of postulating mental processes seem unscientific within both linguistics and psychology.

Bandler and Grinder (1975) have since come along as key figures in the attempt to apply the structural principles of Chomsky's transformational grammar to the therapeutic environment. Central to their work are the convictions that (1) transformational grammar is a model of how humans represent their world, and (2) effective therapy involves helping people change their model of their world. Therefore, Bandler and Grinder use the structural principles of psycholinguistic theory to isolate and formalize the basic mechanisms of change in therapy.

The term psycholinguistics actually first gained widespread popularity in the early 1950s when psychologists like George Miller began to integrate the work being done in linguistics into their own research and writing (Aaronson, 1979). In the mid-1960s the work of researchers like Miller prompted Chomsky to broaden his theory to include an interpretative or semantic component (Baker, 1983). While modern psycholinguistic theory is not unified or monolithic, Chomsky still seems to be the major voice.

Bibliography. D. Aaronson and R. Rieber, eds., *Psycholinguistic Research* (1979). W. Baker and L. Mos, "Mentalism and Language in (and out of) Psychology," *J. of Psycholinguistic Research*,

12, 397–406. R. Bandler and J. Grinder, *The Structure of Magic* (1975). N. Chomsky, *Syntactic Structures* (1957). J. DeVito, *Psycholinguistics* (1971). J. Greene, *Psycholinguistics* (1972). D. Palermo, *Psychology of Language* (1978).

K. POLITE

COMMUNICATION; PSYCHOTHERAPY AND COUNSELING (Research Studies and Methods). *Compare* COGNITIVE PSYCHOLOGY AND PSYCHOTHERAPY; CYBERNETIC THEORY IN PSYCHOLOGY; LANGUAGE DEVELOPMENT; SPEECH DISORDERS AND THERAPY.

PSYCHOLOGICAL EVALUATION AND DIAGNOSIS. *See* EVALUATION AND DIAGNOSIS, PSYCHOLOGICAL.

PSYCHOLOGICAL MODELS. *See* MODELS IN PSYCHOLOGICAL AND PASTORAL THEORY.

PSYCHOLOGICAL TESTING. *See* EVALUATION AND DIAGNOSIS, PSYCHOLOGICAL.

PSYCHOLOGIES, POPULAR. *See* POPULAR THERAPEUTIC MOVEMENTS AND PSYCHOLOGIES; PSYCHOLOGY IN AMERICAN RELIGION.

PSYCHOLOGIST. Person who specializes in the science of human and animal behavior. A psychologist's area of study or practice may extend to anything a person or animal does that can be observed in any way, including bodily movements and mental processes such as thoughts and feelings. Psychologists engage in experimentation and other empirical research methods to develop a body of knowledge used to describe, explain, predict, and influence behavior.

A psychologist is generally recognized as an individual who has completed graduate study in specific aspects of human and animal behavior, such as sensation and perception, biological bases of behavior, learning and environmental influences, processes of human development, theories of personality, behavior disorders, and patterns of social behavior.

In the application of psychology, a psychologist is to be distinguished from other, related professionals. A *psychiatrist* is a physician who undergoes a period of supervised experience in the diagnosis and treatment of mental disorders. Psychiatrists prescribe drugs, while psychologists cannot. A *psychoanalyst* is a person who uses the psychotherapeutic techniques developed by Sigmund Freud and his followers. A psychoanalyst may be a psychologist, a psychiatrist, or neither. *Counselor* is a term that does not denote any particular level of training in the behavioral sciences.

The American Psychological Association has advocated the completion of doctoral level training as a minimum requirement for the independent practice of psychology. Almost all states in the U.S. have certification or licensing laws that generally require a doctoral degree and additional supervised experience for a person to qualify as a practicing psychologist. It should be noted, however, that licensure generally applies to the practice of psychology as a whole, rather than to the practice of a specialty such as clinical psychology.

A psychologist may specialize in any of the components of behavior mentioned above, or in the application of psychological principles to specific types of individuals or in specific settings. For example, a school psychologist specializes in evaluation and intervention with individual students. A physiological psychologist studies the brain as it relates to behavior. An industrial and organizational psychologist makes applications to management, work behavior, and other human factors in organizations. A community psychologist makes applications to social problems and human adaptation to the larger environment.

C. P. RAGAN

INTERPROFESSIONAL TEAMS AND RELATIONSHIPS. *See also* SOCIOLOGY OF RELIGIOUS AND PASTORAL CARE. *Compare* CHRISTIAN PSYCHOLOGIST; CLINICAL PSYCHOLOGIST; MARRIAGE AND FAMILY THERAPIST; PSYCHIATRIST/PSYCHIATRY; PSYCHOTHERAPIST; SOCIAL WORKER.

PSYCHOLOGIST, CHRISTIAN. *See* CHRISTIAN PSYCHOLOGIST.

PSYCHOLOGIST, CLINICAL. *See* CLINICAL PSYCHOLOGIST.

PSYCHOLOGISTS, EMPIRICAL STUDIES OF. Illuminating empirical observations have been made regarding professional psychologists. Deliberate attention is given to those who function as psychotherapists.

(1) No clear connection exists between the personality of the psychologist and his or her therapeutic orientation (Geller and Berzins, 1976). There are as many personality differences among therapists who share the same orientation as between therapists of different persuasions. In some cases, more personality differences exist within schools than between schools (Lazarus, 1978; Loew, Grayson, and Loew, 1975). In one important study, extreme differences in personality, temperament, and style were found among three behavior therapists and among three psychoanalysts (Sloane, *et al.*, 1975). Individual behavior therapists, in some respects, were more similar to their psychoanalytic counterparts than to each other.

(2) The person of the therapist is more critical to therapeutic effectiveness than the endorsed orientation or specific techniques employed (Bergin and Lambert, 1978; Garfield, 1980; Luborsky, *et al.*, 1971; Strupp, 1960). The therapist's own emotional well-being is the most consistently important variable contributing to positive treatment outcome (Luborsky, *et al.*, 1971). Therapists with poor emotional adjustment can produce deterioration among their patients (Bergin and Lambert, 1978). On the other hand, clients of less pathogenic therapists develop more foresight in planning, show less cognitive disorganization, and are psychologically more healthy upon the termination of treatment (VandenBos and Karon, 1971). Hostile and competitive therapists tend to provoke reciprocal client behavior, while supportive therapists elicit support-seeking and low levels of hostility from their patients (Mueller and Dilling, 1968).

(3) Few psychologists endorse a "pure" therapeutic orientation. Most disavow any systematic, organized articulated theory (Sundland, 1977). In fact, the majority of clinical psychologists have identified themselves as "eclectic" (Garfield and Kurtz, 1974).

(4) At an unprecedented rate of growth, psychologists more recently have been involved in private care delivery (Dorken, 1977). Most psychotherapists whose primary affiliation is not private practice engage in some sort of part-time private practice (Garfield and Kurtz, 1974). Psychologists who work as independent practitioners are more likely to be older, more experienced, work fewer hours, engage in marital therapy, and find more satisfaction with psychotherapy as a career than their colleagues in institutional settings (Norcross and Prochaska, 1983).

Bibliography. A. Bergin and M. Lambert, "The Evaluation of Therapeutic Outcome," in S. Garfield and A. Bergin, eds., *Handbook of Psychotherapy and Behavior Change* 2d ed., (1978). H. Dorken, "The Practicing Psychologist: A Growing Force in Private Sector Health Care Delivery," *Professional Psychology,* 8 (1979), 269–74. S. Garfield, *Psychotherapy: An Eclectic Approach* (1980). S. Garfield and R. Kurtz, "A Survey of Clinical Psychologists: Characteristics, Activities, and Orientations," *The Clinical Psychologist,* 28 (1974), 7–10. J. Geller and J. Berzins, "A-B Distinction in a Sample of Prominent Psychotherapists," *J. of Consulting and Clinical Psychology,* 44 (1976), 77–82. A. Lazarus, "Styles not Systems," *Psychotherapy: Theory, Research and Practice,* 15:4 (1978), 359–61. C. Loew, H. Grazson, and G. Loew, eds., *Three Psychotherapies* (1975). L. Luborsky, M. Chandler, A. Auerbach, J. Cohen, and H. Bachrach, "Factors Influencing the Outcome of Psychotherapy: A Review of Quantitative Research," *Psychological Bulletin,* 75 (1971), 145–85. W. Mueller and C. Dilling, "Therapist-Client Interview Behavior and Personality Characteristics of Therapists," *J. of Projective Techniques and Personality Assessment,* 32 (1968), 281–8. J. Norcross and J. Prochaska, "Psychotherapists in Independent Practice: Some Findings and Issues," *Professional Psychology: Research and Practice,* 14:6 (1983), 869–81. R. Sloane, F. Staples, A. Cristol, N. Yorkston, and K. Whipple, *Psychotherapy versus Behavior Therapy* (1975). H. Strupp, *Psychotherapists in Action: Explorations of the Therapist's Contribution to the Treatment Process* (1960). D. Sundland, "Theoretical Orientations of Psychotherapists," in A. Gurman and A. Razin, eds., *Effective Psychotherapy: A Handbook of Research* (1977). G. VandenBos and B. Karon, "Pathogenesis: A New Therapist Personality Dimension Related Therapeutic Effectiveness," *J. of Personality Assessment,* 35 (1971), 252–60.

C. R. RIDLEY

PSYCHOTHERAPIST. *Compare* CLERGY *or* RABBIS, EMPIRICAL STUDIES OF; THERAPEUTIC CONDITIONS; VOCATION.

PSYCHOLOGY. *See* PSYCHOLOGY, EASTERN *and* WESTERN; PSYCHOLOGY AND PSYCHOTHERAPY (East-West Comparison); PSYCHOTHERAPY. *See also* JUDAISM AND PSYCHOLOGY; MYTHOLOGY AND PSYCHOLOGY; PERSONALITY THEORY; PHILOSOPHY AND PSYCHOLOGY.

PSYCHOLOGY, CLASSICAL. *See* EARLY CHURCH, PASTORAL CARE AND COUNSELING IN; PHILOSOPHY AND PSYCHOLOGY, WESTERN.

PSYCHOLOGY, COMMUNITY. *See* COMMUNITY PSYCHOLOGY.

PSYCHOLOGY, CONTEMPLATIVE. *See* SPIRITUAL PSYCHOLOGIES.

PSYCHOLOGY, EASTERN. The psychology of the East is very diverse; therefore the use of some ordering framework is required in constructing a brief summary. The framework adopted must be broad enough to include all the viewpoints to be surveyed. Accordingly, three "pegs" of human experience are isolated from which to "hang" our survey. They are: (1) Transcendent Consciousness, (2) Egoic Consciousness, and (3) Shadow Consciousness.

1. **Transcendent Consciousness.** This is the level of pure mystical awareness in which all duality, all sense of subject-object separation has been overcome. This is the aspect of our human nature which, in ordinary life, gives us those brief moments of being taken out of our own small egos and being caught up into a larger experience. For example, in listening to a piece of good music or while watching a drama we may have the experience of being so completely involved that only later do we "come back to ourselves," as it were, and say, "I was really caught up in that." These are our moments of high aesthetic and religious experience, or creative scientific insight. In Yoga psychology, this aspect of human nature is technically termed *samadhi*; in Western thought, *spirit* or *intuition*. It is through this aspect of human nature that experiences of separation and alienation are seen to be overcome through unification or communion with the divine or absolute—variously described as "the All," Brahman, God, Allah, Sunyata, Tao, etc. Experience on this level is non-conceptual and non-dualistic; it is immediate and intimate. It is knowing by being one with. . . This level of human awareness is timeless, spaceless and objectless—there is a sense of supreme unity between oneself and the greater universe.

2. **Ego Consciousness.** This encompasses what we usually call normal experience. In contrast to the non-duality of transcendent consciousness, egoic consciousness is characterized by its strong sense of "I-ness" as existing apart from everything else. "I" am subject, all else is object, to be described, examined, and manipulated. This split between subject and object, between person and the rest of the universe brings with it both the anxiety of separation (and its inevitable consequence, death) and the power of science to create and control. Rather than identifying with realities greater than themselves, humans identify with their egos, their own self-images. We know things not immediately, but mediately —through observation, description, and rational inference. Not only is any identification with the greater universe repressed in the egoic mode of consciousness, but also those unwanted or unrecognized aspects of one's own psyche. These repressed aspects of one's nature are then hidden in the unconscious or projected onto the surrounding environment creating the third aspect of human nature, the shadow.

3. **Shadow Consciousness.** This is the unconscious aspect of our human nature which contains our unwanted tendencies and unrealized potentials. Often we are unaware of this aspect of our nature, or we may actively try to disown it. Nevertheless, it stays with us like a shadow.

Since most Westerners view the East as being totally idealistic in its thought, it is perhaps surprising to find a traditional Eastern view of human nature that is totally materialistic. According to the Cārvākas, all of human nature is derived from material elements (*mahābhūta*), which are judged to possess their own immanent life force (*svabhāva*). Intelligence, thought, language, and aesthetics are all seen as derived from these material elements. There is no God, no supernatural, no immortal soul, and the only aim of life is to get the maximum of pleasure. The Cārvākas, like present day positivists and empiricists, argue that we know only what we perceive, and not what someone else says we have perceived. In this view, the capacity of human nature for knowing is restricted to material objects, and direct sensory perception of such material referents is the only valid knowledge of reality.

Like the *tabula rasa* or "blank slate" view of American behavioristic psychology, the Cārvāka position locates human experience dominantly within the level of egoic consciousness. Little recognition seems to be given to the possibility of unconscious processes, and the notion of a transcendent level of consciousness is seen as unwarranted inference resulting from supersensuous suppositions which are unsupported by direct sensory perception.

Although the Cārvāka school has been present in the East for a very long time (dating back to 640 B.C.), it has exerted a relatively minor influence in Eastern thought. The Yoga school of thought has been far more dominant and widely accepted. Within Indian thought, for example, it seems clear that just as certain conceptions such as *karma* and *samsāra* are taken as basic to all Jaina, Buddhist, and Hindu schools, so also there are certain common conceptions about the psychological processes of human nature (e.g., the existence of cognitive traces or *samskāras*) which are seen to exist in and through the specific differences of the various schools. Jadunath Sinha supports this contention in his finding that the psychological conception of yogic intuition (*pratibhā*) is found in all schools with the exception of the Cārvāka and the Mīmāmsa. The eminent scholar Stcherbatsky observes that yogic trance (*samādhi*) and yogic courses for psychological training toward the achievement of freedom or enlightenment (*yoga-mārga*) appear in virtually all schools of thought—be they Hindu, Buddhist, or Jaina. Mircea Eliade states that Yoga is one of the four basic motifs of all Indian thought. Probably the most complete presentation of this traditional Indian psychology is to be found in the *Yoga Sūtras of Patanjali*, and it is from this source that the following exposition is taken.

Yoga starts with an analysis of ordinary experience. This is characterized by a sense of restlessness caused by the distracting influences of our desires. Peace and purity of mind come only when our easily distracted natures are controlled by the radical step of purging the passions. But if these troublesome passions are to be purged, they must be fully exposed to view. In this respect, Yoga predated Freud by several hundred years in the analysis of the unconscious. In the Yoga view, the sources of all our troubles are the karmic seeds of past actions or thoughts, heaped up in the unconscious or storehouse consciousness, as it is called in Yoga, and tainted by

ignorance, materialistic or sensuous desire, and the clinging to one's own ego. Thus, it is clear that Yoga psychology gives ample recognition to the darker side of humans—the shadow consciousness.

At the egoic level of consciousness, Yoga conceives of human cognition on various levels. There is the function of the mind in integrating and coordinating the input of sensory impressions and the resurgent memories of past thoughts and actions (*samskāras*). These may all be thought of as "learned" if we use behavioristic terminology. But, then there is the higher function of the mind in making discriminative decisions as to whether or not to act on the impulses that are constantly flooding one's awareness. This discriminative capacity (*buddhi*) is not learned, but is an innate aspect of our psyche and has the capacity to reveal our true natures. This occurs when, by our discriminative choices, we negate and root out the polluting passions (*klista karmas*) from the unconscious until it is totally purified of their distracting restlessness—their "pulling" and "pushing" of us in one direction and then another. Once this is achieved by disciplined self-effort, the level of egoic consciousness becomes transcendent, since the notion of ego, I or me, is also ultimately unreal, it is simply a byproduct of my selfish desiring. Once the latter is rooted out, the former by necessity also disappears and the final level of human nature, transcendent consciousness, is all that remains.

According to Yoga, transcendent consciousness is not immaterial, but is composed of high quality, high energy luminous material (*sattvic citta*). Since all egoity has been overcome, there is no duality, no subject-object awareness, but only immediate intuition. All experience is transcendent of individuality, although this is described differently by the various schools of thought. The Hindus, for example, overcome the subject-object duality by resolving all objectivity into an absolute subject (i.e., *Brahman*). The Buddhists seem to go in the opposite direction and do away with all subjectivity, leaving only bare objective experience (i.e., *Nirvana*, which may be translated "all ego and desiring is blown out"). For our present purpose, the metaphysical speculation, although interesting, is not important. What is significant is that Yoga psychology finds the essence of human nature to be at the transcendent level of consciousness, where ego and unconscious desires have been excised.

The various kinds of yogic meditation are simply different practical disciplines or "therapies" for removing conscious and unconscious desires, along with the accompanying ego-sense from the psyche. Again, let us stay with Patanjali's *Yoga Sūtras*, although there are many other yogic techniques from which one could choose (e.g., Tantric, Hatha, Jaina, Taoist, Zen, etc.). There are five prerequisite practices and three ultimate practices. The prerequisite practices include: (1) self-restraints (*yamas*) to get rid of bad habits and achieve non-violence, truthfulness, non-stealing, celibacy, and absence of avarice; (2) good habits (*niyamas*) to be instilled (washing of body and mind, contentment with whatever comes, equanimity in the face of life's trials, study and chanting of scriptures, meditation upon the Lord; (3) body postures (*āsanas*) such as the lotus position to keep the body controlled and motionless during meditation; (4) controlled deepening of respiration (*prānāyāma*) to calm the mind; and (5) keeping senses (e.g. sight, hearing, touch, etc.) from distracting one's mind (*pratyāhāra*) by focusing them on an object or point of meditation.

The ultimate practices are: (1) beginners spend brief periods of fixed concentration (*dharana*) upon an object (usually an image which represents an aspect of the divine that appeals to one, e.g., Īsvara, Shiva, Krishna, Kali); (2) as one becomes more expert, concentration upon the object is held for longer periods (*dhyāna*) and the sense of subject-object separation begins to disappear from one's perception; (3) *samādhi* occurs when continuous meditation upon the object loses all sense of subject-object separation—a state of direct intuition or becoming one with the object.

Through these yogic practices one has weakened the hold of the egocentric memories and desires (*karmas*) from the conscious and unconscious levels of one's psyche, and the discovery of the true self has begun. Four levels of *samādhi*, each more purified than the last, may be realized through repeated practice of yogic meditation. The final state (*nirvicāra samādhi*) occurs when all obstructing egoic desires have been purged from the psyche which is now like a perfectly clear window to the aspect of the divine (e.g. Shiva, Krishna, Buddha, Jesus) which has served as the object of meditation. According to the *Yoga Sūtras*, any image will do. The divine image is only an instrument to aid in the direct experience of the transcendent—at which point the image is no longer needed.

Meditation of the sort prescribed by the *Yoga Sūtras* is esoteric in nature, requires the supervision of a teacher (*guru*) who has achieved perfection, and is a full-time occupation which, even in traditional India, was not possible for most people until the final stage of life—retirement from worldly affairs. Another and much simpler Yoga was and still is practiced by the masses—the Yoga of the word. In Eastern psychology it is generally accepted that the chanting of a special scriptural word or phrase (*mantra*), chosen for one by one's teacher (*guru*), has power to remove the obstructing egoic desires until the transcendent stands fully revealed. The Yoga of the word assumes that the scriptural word and the divine are mutually intertwined—very much as stated in John's Gospel 1:1, "In the beginning was the Word, and the Word was with God, and the Word was God." The word is therefore filled with divine power and when meditated upon by repeated chanting is able to remove obstructions of the shadow and egoic levels of consciousness. The *guru* chooses the scriptural word best suited to remove current obstructions (*karmas*) in the mind of the devotee. The power of the chosen *mantra* to remove obstructions is enhanced by the intensity and duration of the chanting. Chanting may be either aloud or silent. As the first obstructions are removed, the *guru* prescribes a new *mantra* better suited to tackle the remaining, more subtle obstructions. The more obstacles in the mind to be overcome, the more repetitions are needed. When the chanting removes the final obstacles, the psyche is like a purified or cleaned window fully revealing the divine as a direct intuition to the devotee—a vision of the Lord is experienced. *Samādhi*, or union with the transcendent, is

realized. With proper Yoga, words are experienced as having the power to remove ignorance (*avidyā*), reveal truth (*dharma*) and realize release or salvation (*moksa*). It is this traditional Eastern psychology of the word that is behind the *mantra* chanting, common throughout traditional Hinduism and Buddhism, and today encountered in North America in the chanting of "Hari Krishna" . . . and the teaching of meditation *mantras* by Transcendental Meditation.

Jacob Needleman has identified much of the current American fascination for the East with this much expanded view of human nature. This, he argues, is what is felt to be lacking in contemporary Judaeo-Christian religion. It is also this larger experience of human nature that is glimpsed in the psychedelic drug experience or perhaps in the present day interest in sensitivity training (Needleman). The fascination of these fads is that they provide a technique which enables one to break out of the too-narrow Western rational-empirical view of human nature into which the whole society has been conditioned. But there are dangers here for the freeing of a person from his or her rigid ego encapsulation is only beneficial if the shadow or unconscious dimension of his or her nature is also known and controlled. As the history of sensitivity training indicates, this latter aspect has usually been ignored, often with disastrous results. The person is "freed" from his rational encapsulation, only to be made captive to the darker side of his animal passions.

Another perceptive analyst of the pluralistic intermixing of Eastern and Western psychology is R. C. Zaehner, who has pointed to even more serious dangers that are sometimes involved. The radically transcendent Eastern view of human nature is open to the misinterpretation that "All is One" means nothing is good or evil, love equals hate, life equals death, in the hands of one who is still immersed in the shadow and egoic levels of consciousness. The esoteric knowing of the transcendent mystical vision is open to dangerous distortion when placed in the hands of one who has not yet controlled her darker animal desires and power-hungry ego, and who is not under the supervision of a *guru*.

The critique of Eastern psychology for modern life is that if the transcendent is not seen as absolute then humankind is no longer being seen as splendid or divine, but as simply "raw nature"—on a par with minerals and rocks—to be manipulated for purposes of economic, political, and personal selfishness. Of course this need not necessarily happen if Gandhi's warning is taken seriously. First a human being's lower nature must be controlled and his higher nature actualized, and then when the power of science and technology is placed in his hands, it will not enslave him in the endless attempt to satisfy his lower desires as clearly has happened in the West.

As usual a middle road between the extremes seems indicated. A human being is neither all spiritual nor all animal desires, but a psychosomatic unity of the two. Two Western scholars attempt to champion such a balanced approach to psychology. Rudolf Otto argues for an analysis of humans which would include their feelings, rationality and supra-rationality or transcendent consciousness. And the Harvard philosopher F.S.C. Northrop finds that the reason of the West and the intuition of the

East must be complementary in any workable scientific or humanistic enterprise. Finally, mention may be made of Carl Jung whose insights seem to be able to encompass most of the Eastern and Western psychologies without committing the academic sin of reductionism on one side or the other. Although a thoroughly Western psychologist, he is acclaimed by many from the East as expressing their understanding of human experience.

Bibliography. G. Coster, *Yoga and Western Psychology* (1934). H. G. Coward, "The Meaning and Power of Mantras in Bhartṛharis," *Vākyapadīya Studies in Religion* (1982), 365–75; *Jung and Eastern Thought* (1985). M. Eliade, *Yoga: Immortality and Freedom* (1970). C. G. Jung, *Psyche and Symbol* (1958). J. Needleman, *The New Religions* (1972). R. Otto, *The Idea of the Holy* (1958). *The Yoga System of Patanjali*, J. H. Woods, trans. (1966). J. Sinha, *Indian Psychology: Cognition* (1958). Swami Akhilananda, *Hindu Psychology* (1946).

H. COWARD

MEDITATION; PSYCHOLOGY AND PSYCHOTHERAPY (East-West Comparison); SPIRITUAL MASTERS AND GUIDES. *Compare* ILLUMINATION; PERSONALITY THEORY (Varieties, Traditions, and Issues); PHILOSOPHY AND PSYCHOLOGY, WESTERN; PSYCHOLOGY OF RELIGION; SPIRITUAL DISCIPLINE AND GROWTH; SPIRITUAL PSYCHOLOGIES; SPIRITUAL THEOLOGY AND PASTORAL CARE; SPIRITUALITY; TRANSPERSONAL PSYCHOLOGIES.

PSYCHOLOGY, PASTORAL. See PASTORAL PSYCHOLOGY, DISCIPLINE OF. *See also* ANALYTICAL (JUNGIAN) PSYCHOLOGY, PSYCHOANALYSIS, *or* HUMANISTIC PSYCHOLOGY, AND PASTORAL CARE; PASTORAL CARE (Contemporary Methods, Perspectives, and Issues); PASTORAL COUNSELING; PASTORAL PSYCHOTHERAPY.

PSYCHOLOGY, PHILOSOPHY AND. See PHILOSOPHY AND PSYCHOLOGY, WESTERN; PSYCHOLOGY, EASTERN.

PSYCHOLOGY, POPULAR. See POPULAR THERAPEUTIC MOVEMENTS AND PSYCHOLOGIES; PSYCHOLOGY IN AMERICAN RELIGION.

PSYCHOLOGY, WESTERN. Views European-American psychology as a modern academic discipline. Rooted in Western philosophy and the developing natural sciences, it has many branching theories and applied areas. The psychological laboratory established at Leipzig University by the physiologist Wilhelm Wundt in 1879 dates the beginning of the modern discipline.

1. Structuralism. Wilhelm Wundt, the father of experimental psychology, tried to explore the science of the mind by examining the structure of experience. Through guided introspection on experience, he researched for people's mental chemistry to discover the elements of experience.

Structuralism combined associationism with St. Augustine's meditative idealism, Kantian phenomenology (only conscious phenomena are known), H. L. F. von Helmholtz' physiology, and Gustav Fechner's psychophysics.

E. B. Titchner popularized structuralism in America, but even as structuralism made psychology more attractive, conflictual results from different laboratories plus many criticisms caused its demise.

2. Functionalism. Functionalists were early critics of structuralism, because to study psychology as a natural science would follow the evolutionary model regarding various adaptive functions of the mind in relationship with the environment. William James, the pragmatist, and John Dewey, the philosopher-educator, were leading functionalists.

James's pragmatism advocated that the value of any viewpoint is its practical consequences. Dewey's progressive education, analysis of the reflex arc, and teaching the mind as a functioning brain (monism) influence today's theories.

3. Behaviorism. Behaviorism defines psychology as the study of behavior. Behaviorism is linked to similar predecessors as functionalism, plus the positivism of Auguste Comte, Edward L. Thorndike's reinforcement/habits research, and Ivan Pavlov's classical conditioning.

Clark Hull and his students, like Kenneth Spence, sorted the many factors influencing stimulus-response (S-R) learning (e.g., habit strength, reinforcements, trials, and motives). A. Hullian, Neal E. Miller, with John Dollard (an anthropologist interested in culture and personality) attempted to translate Freudian theory into a behavioristic framework (e.g., intrapsychic conflicts are incompatible response tendencies), but were criticized by both camps. O. Hobart Mowrer, also a Hullian, showed how Pavlovian conditioning and instrumental conditioning are two sides of the same learning process.

Edwin R. Guthrie saw contiguity (simultaneous pairing of stimulus and response) as the main learning factor. Edward Tolman elaborated purposive behaviorism, with more cognitive variables (as intentions) influencing behavior.

The most influential radical behaviorist is B. F. Skinner. His animals dramatized differences when reinforced by various schedules of reinforcement—labeled the functional analysis of behavior.

Neo-behaviorism has successfully applied learning principles into a new industry—behavior modification. Families, schools, penal institutions, and clinics use learning techniques to more precisely manipulate participants.

Social learning theorists magnify the influence of social models on behavior. Albert Bandura has incorporated scores of precise variables at different levels of the imitative processes (attention, retention, reproduction, and motivation) which suppress or magnify modeling, including more physiological (e.g., arousal) and cognitive (e.g., vicarious reinforcement) variables than stressed by purely reinforcement behaviorists.

4. Psychobiology. Psychobiology explores the relationships between psychological and physiological variables. Better instrumentation (e.g., Pavlov's methods and Fritsch-Hitzig brain stimulation methods) plus clinical evaluations of brain-damaged people (e.g., the Paul Broca speech area) expanded the field. Karl S. Lashley's evidence of mass action (an entire cortical site involves a function) and equipotentiality (all of a site works for that site's function), plus precise readings on brain cells (e.g., some cells fire to straight lines, others to curves or angles) and Donald O. Hebb's theory of reverberating circuitry —all point to extreme psychoneurological complexity.

This complexity adds to the philosophical mind-brain debates and provokes research. Parallelists (like John Dewey's monism) conflict with interactionists (like Nobel laureate Sir John Eccles, who finds the self-conscious ego to be qualitatively different than the physical brain—but egos interact with brains). Karl Pribrim sees the brain functioning like a hologram (a three-dimensional picture made and seen in laser light but meaningless in sunlight), and Roger Sperry found split-brain patients functioned differently from each hemisphere, so mind-brain complexity is multiplied.

Behavioral genetics examines the relationships between genes and behavior, primarily by looking at correlations between identical twins reared differently and other related/unrelated people.

5. Psychometrics. Measuring psychological phenomena more objectively than subjective essay tests, interviews, or tribal screenings has its roots in Gustav Fechner's psychophysics, Herman Ebbinghaus's records of memorizing nonsense syllables and his sentence completion method, and Francis Galton's sensory-motor devices.

When the Paris government wished to determine the most educable public school students, Alfred Binet developed the first useful intelligence test. The Binet test and translations, like the American Stanford-Binet by Louis M. Terman, were privately administered; but the World War I emergency soon spawned group tests, like the Army Alpha for recruits and the Beta for nonliterates. Increasingly more objective, reliable (consistent), and valid (truthful) tests were developed for achievement, aptitude, clinical, and placement purposes. The Minnesota Multiphasic Personality Inventory is an example of a popular clinical test to evaluate various abnormal populations. Computer and statistical advances (like multivariate analyses) and scaling methods (like the Thurstone and Likert scales) helped pollsters, experimentalists, and clinicians.

6. Developmental Perspectives. Psychological development is so closely linked to physical development that it was often labeled genetic psychology. Based on evolutionary theory (including Darwin's record of his son's baby-biography) and Galton's attempt to link simple psychophysiological measurements and eugenics (breeding for "good" genes), G. Stanley Hall, the father of genetic psychology, taught that normal psychological growth follows evolutionary stages (ontogeny recapitulates phylogeny). Hall's student, Arnold Gesell, and his colleagues accumulated specific behavioral norms expected of children at different ages.

A highly cross-culturally researched developmental theory is Jean Piaget's cognitive theory. A trained biologist, he started developmental research by analyzing mistakes youth make on the Binet intelligence test, which reflects cognitive capabilities. Lawrence Kohlberg's moral development theory, based on Piaget's research and Kant's epistemology, has been widely influential in educational and religious circles.

An influential developmental theory is Freud's psychosexual stage theory. Over- or under-gratification at either the oral (incorporating or aggressing), anal (hoard-ing or squandering), or phallic (Oedipus/Electra conflict) period of development leads to fixation of personality at that level and reflects abnormality. Basic personality is set by the age of five.

Erik Erikson expanded Freud's psychosexual theory into eight psychosocial crises throughout life—e.g., the infant learns to trust or mistrust caregivers, whereas the aged encounter integrity or despair. Overcoming one's identity crisis is most important for youth, being rooted in beneficial resolutions of earlier crises and foundational for positive resolutions of future ones.

All areas of experimental psychology (e.g., sensation-perception, psycholinguistics, and learning) have refined understanding of developmental processes. Information theories, like cybernetics (the science of control and communication in organisms and machines—following Norbert Weiner), and ethology (applying animal observations to humans, as did Nobel laureate Niko Tinbergen) have refined the discipline.

7. Communication Views. All social theories assume communication which requires a source (encoder), channel (communication method), and receiver (decoder) plus noise. Epistemologists have long explored verbal communication, but psycholinguists have dissected its nature and magnified the influence of paralinguists (qualities accompanying verbal communication, like pitch) and nonverbal gestures. Ray Birdwhistle has refined the science of kinesics (gestures). Charles E. Osgood's psycholinguistics colleagues showed that cross-culturally all languages use words with three dimensional connotations of: value, power, and activity. Similar to cybernetics, general systems theory explains broad multidimensional communications parallels (e.g., homeostasis in the inorganic, biological, psychological, and social worlds).

8. Phenomenological Views. Phenomenologists study the appearances (interpretations) of phenomena by observers. Reacting against structuralism and associationism, Gestalt psychology holds that the whole of one's perception is different than the sum of its parts, (e.g., its founder, Max Wertheimer, demonstrated the phi phenomenon—lights' off-on patterns seem to move). Gestaltists explored perceptual principles (like similarity, proximity), productive thinking, and insight learning (by Wolfgang Kohler), which supplements behaviorists' theories.

Kurt Lewin and Fritz Heider developed field theories which tied action to the person's view of oneself and others in the environment. Lewin saw behavior as a function of one's life space (personal processes and the perceived whole environment). Lewin's applications included social power analyses, cooperative/competitive behavior, and other group dynamics.

Heider's field theory focused on interpersonal relationships from a common-sense perspective. Perception of self and environment affect behavior, but it especially affects others' perception of the observer. Heider's attribution of responsibility views showed how one attributes the cause of success or failure differently for oneself versus others.

9. Other Cognitive/Social Perspectives. Social psychologists study the influences of groups on individuals and persons on groups. Much of their empirical research is interpreted around minitheories, like cognitive consistency.

A popular consistency theory was Leon Festinger's cognitive dissonance theory, where dissonance exists if one holds to two or more inconsistent cognitions. This dissonance pressure forces a change (behavioral or psychological) toward consistency, although it is difficult to exactly predict the nature of the dissonance reduction (e.g., Darryl Bem's self-perception interpretations).

Equity processes appear similar to consistency pressures, where a group tends to allocate proportionate rewards based on input into the group. Although most people try to maximize their own gain, group commitment pressures toward equity restoration, as discussed by moral philosophers and cultural anthropologists (e.g., George P. Murdock's work on cultural universals), who have observed cross-cultural values including distributive justice and truthfulness.

The sociobiologist Edward O. Wilson hypothesizes that there are altruistic genes which evolved up the phylogenic scale to their most magnified appearance in humans, explaining the similarity of cross-cultural values.

Group dynamics are the processes existing between groups as they start, develop, become productive, and degenerate. Kurt Lewin started research in the field and fostered applications for families, schools, industries, and governments. He started the oldest training organization for group dynamics, the National Training Laboratories.

10. Personality and Clinical Systems. *a. Ancient views.* Western personality theory is still influenced by two ancient clinical traditions. The Judaeo-Christian view sees humans created in God's image (healthy interpersonal qualities) and developing differing types and numbers of gifts (abilities). Abnormality appears due to modeling evil (good's distortion), choosing bad behavior, demonic influences, and/or God's permission to allow the ill/evil to pressure those involved to reflect God's character by need-meeting through available gifts.

The other tradition grew from Hippocrates (the father of medicine, circa 400 B.C.) who labeled four different fluids influencing bodily functions: blood, black and yellow bile, and phlegm. Galen, five hundred years later, labeled people with excesses of each fluid with a personality temperament: sanguine (warm-hearted), melancholic (sad), choleric (hasty), and phlegmatic (apathetic). Still popular categories, they are seen in Hans Eysenck's typology by combining the extremes of stable-neurotic and introversion-extroversion.

b. Psychoanalysis. i. Freudian. Besides Sigmund Freud's psychosexual stage theory of development, he theorized a complete unconscious structure and functioning (psychically determined and conflictual) of personality. Psychopathology appears from the ego's poor defenses against libidinal (sexual) energy of the id's desires, superego's oppressive values, and world-pressures. Psychoanalysis involves examining ego-weakness and strengthening defense mechanisms (e.g., repression) by using unconscious-tapping methods (e.g., free association) and sexual-symbolic interpretation. Therapeutic goals include enabling the patient to work and to engage in heterosexual relationships.

ii. Early deviates. Although president of the International Psychoanalytic Association, Carl Gustav Jung's ideas increasingly conflicted with Freud's theory. For him, libido is a general life-force, partially sexual; the unconscious has personal complexes and collective archetypes (evolved predispositions); and personality grows throughout life. His mystical ideas were attractive to some counterculture groups.

Alfred Adler conflicted with Freud over social influences on personality (e.g., family constellation) and optimistic teleological goals people strive for (fictional finalisms) motivated by the only inborn drive—that for superiority. His counseling was friendly and directive.

iii. Ego/social analysts. Other Freudian revisionists magnified greater social- and ego-control over personality. A feminist version came from Karen Horney. Abnormal families cause basic anxiety which leads to neurotic ingratiating, aggression, or isolation (normal persons use these appropriately with a high degree of congruency between the real self and ideal self).

Erich Fromm entered psychoanalysis through his sociological training and still influences sociology (e.g., David Riesman). He finds the average person cannot develop real humanity in evil Western culture with unmet needs, and thus experiences alienation. Most people develop unproductive personalities, but a few become productive, which result is especially produced in humanistic communitarian socialism.

Harry Stack Sullivan's interpersonal theory sees humans developing dynamisms (habits) around good/bad experiences with significant others. These personifications make personality never private but always interpersonal.

iv. Object relations. Object relations analysis focuses on symbolisms of significant objects (e.g., breasts, clothes) arising from early mother-child conflictual relations. Concepts from Sullivan's dynamisms, Melanie Klein's ungratified needs of children, M. S. Mahler's destructive symbiotic relations, and Heinz Hartmann's values-adaptations sample their concerns.

c. Trait/need theories. i. Physique. Stature and shape (e.g., phrenology) and sensory-motor prowess (e.g., graphology) were popular attempts to measure personality. William H. Sheldon (after Ernst Kretschmer) developed a three somatype measurement framework: endomorphy (round), mesomorphy (muscular), and ectomorphy (thin), plus mixed forms. Sheldon's measurements found high correlations between the somatypes and certain temperament and clinical measures, but others found less stable relationships.

ii. Gordon Allport. As the dean of American personologists, Allport's heuristic realism pictures personality as a dynamic unity, continually developing. Humans react, but also proact—create their own environment. The proprium (ego) is constantly changing and functions complexly with the multifunctional self.

iii. Henry Murray. A congruent multi-need theory to Allport's trait theory is that of his Harvard colleague, Henry Murray. Structure of personality is similar to Freud's, but the id, ego, and superego all appear more acceptable than Freud showed. He listed over twenty common needs, like needs for affiliation, power, and achievement (especially explored by David McClelland).

Murray measured them by the Thematic Apperception Test, a projective that measures motives through people's stories.

iv. Factor structures. Charles Spearman developed factor analysis to find groupings of variables which correlate together. Raymond B. Cattell designed a trait theory rooted in factoring and a psychodynamic energy system. By factoring observer and self-ratings with objective tests, Cattell discovered about twenty different personality traits (factors) among people. Most are measured in the Sixteen Personality Factor (16PF) Questionnaire, which has been translated into many different cultures.

Before Cattell's work, the ten-factor Guilford-Zimmerman Temperament Survey was analyzed from several popular personality scales in the 1940s. Structures of many other personality, attitude, and aptitude tests are determined by factor analysis. J. P. Guilford hypothesizes at least 120 factors reflecting intelligence.

d. Culture and personality. Cultural anthropology magnified how all peoples are alike in some ways, each is similar to some others and yet each is unique (after Ralph Linton). Humanity's unity is seen in our common biological and sociopsychological needs and processes, and in cross-cultural values (e.g., justice, truth, and respect). Research on "national character" and "modal personality" explicated different cultures' magnification of some values over others. Irving Goffman's impression management theory sees people as actors playing out their various roles in society. Following similar role requirements creates similar traits, yet different roles show varied traits.

11. **Humanistic Views.** Humanism, psychology's "third force" after behaviorism and psychoanalysis, sees constructive forces in people toward potential-realization. Carl Rogers's non-directive (client-centered) counseling theory became widely accepted by helping professions for it was rooted in his humane personality theory. The client-centered counselor reflects aloud on the clients' feelings and ideas, assuming that restatement of these observations in a warm, accepting atmosphere will climatize problem self-solution.

Although trained a behaviorist, counseling and teaching moved Abraham Maslow toward other humane concerns about humans' self-actualizing tendency. His hierarchy of needs theory assumed that lower survival needs (deficiency motives of physiological, safety, belongingness, and esteem) must be met before self-actualization (being values) is reached.

Psychological existentialism stresses existence before essence — seeing each existing person in an entire context rather than subdividing anyone by tests and other scientific abstractions. Although not a systematic personality theory, existential concerns filtered into humanistic (e.g., Charlotte Bühler), psychoanalytic (e.g., Ludwig Binswanger), and religious (e.g., Adrian van Kaam) traditions. Existentialism stresses human freedom and choice, future orientation, and creating one's own world, even of evil—but each is responsible for this creation. Anxiety reflects pressures toward authenticity, aided by awareness of death ("nothingness" for some) and transcendence (transpersonal, mystical or interpersonal).

12. **Multidisciplinary Approaches.** A student of Raymond B. Cattell, Joseph R. Royce of the University of Alberta's Center for Advanced Study in Theoretical Psychology factored about 250 measurements of people around his individuality theory. This incorporating philosophy of psychology integrates multimethods (of all behavioral sciences), multivariate (e.g., factor analysis), multiepistemic (empiricism, rationalism, metaphorism), multiworldviews, multisystemic (sensory, motor; cognitive, affective; style, value), multiparadigmatic (explicit theories), multitheoretic (e.g., integrate cognitive and humanistic), and multidisciplinary (all behavioral sciences and humanities with an expert staff).

13. **Prospectives.** Since few psychological theories are abandoned, revisions will increase with more congruencies and a few maxitheories (e.g., Royce's individuality theory) will tie idiographic to nomothetic research. Conflict between theorists will continue but interdisciplinary research will grow. Experimentalists will mostly work from minitheory interpretations, requiring absorption into maxitheories. Refined applications of therapeutic measures (e.g., cognitive vs. behavioral) will progress with better diagnostic-prognostic tools. Social forces will push the discipline to more activism and values commitment. Better psychometric measures (e.g., culture-fair tests and curvilinear factor analysis) may create more confidence in psychology, but forensic (legal) psychology's limitations will still create conflict (e.g., predicting abnormal behavior and the John Hinkley, Jr. affair). Psychohistories analyzing the famous from more varied theories will increase along with more refined psychology of religion and values research.

Bibliography. A. J. Chapman and D. M. Jones, eds., *Models of Man* (1980). E. G. Boring and G. Lindzey, eds., *A History of Psychology in Autobiography* 6 vols. (1967). C. Hall and G. Lindzey, *Theories of Personality* 3d ed. (1978). S. Koch, ed., *Psychology* 6 vols. (1959). G. Lindzey and E. Aronson, eds., *Handbook of Social Psychology* 2d ed. 5 vols, (1968). M. H. Marx and W. A. Hillix, *Systems and Theories in Psychology* 3d ed. (1979). M. E. Shaw and P. R. Costanzo, *Theories of Social Psychology* 2d ed. (1982). D. L. Sills, ed., *International Encyclopedia of the Social Sciences* 18 vols. (1968). R. I. Watson, *The Great Psychologists* 4th ed. (1978). G. Zilboorg, *A History of Medical Psychology* (1967).

R. W. WILSON

FAMILY THEORY AND THERAPY; MENTAL HEALTH AND ILLNESS; PERSON; PERSONALITY THEORY; PSYCHOLOGY OF RELIGION; PSYCHOPATHOLOGY, THEORIES OF. *See also* ANALYTICAL (JUNGIAN) PSYCHOLOGY; BEHAVIORISM; COGNITIVE PSYCHOLOGY; HUMANISTIC PSYCHOLOGY; PSYCHOANALYSIS. *Compare* BLACK *or* FEMINIST ISSUES IN PSYCHOLOGY; CRITICAL THEORY; JUDAISM AND PSYCHOLOGY; MYTHOLOGY AND PSYCHOLOGY; PARAPSYCHOLOGY; PHILOSOPHY AND PSYCHOLOGY; POPULAR THERAPEUTIC MOVEMENTS AND PSYCHOLOGIES; PSYCHOLOGY AND PSYCHOTHERAPY (East-West Comparison); PSYCHOLOGY IN AMERICAN RELIGION; THEOLOGY AND PSYCHOLOGY. *Biography:* ALLPORT; DEWEY; ERIKSON; FREUD; FROMM; HORNEY; JAMES; JUNG; LEWIN; MASLOW; MURRAY; ROGERS; SKINNER; SULLIVAN.

PSYCHOLOGY AND JUDAISM. *See* JUDAISM AND PSYCHOLOGY.

PSYCHOLOGY AND MYTHOLOGY. *See* MYTHOLOGY AND PSYCHOLOGY.

PSYCHOLOGY AND PSYCHOTHERAPY (East-West Comparison).

This comparison of Eastern and Western psychologies and psychotherapies seeks to recognize the limitations of such a project while pointing out in broad terms the uniqueness of the two perspectives and their possible points of compatibility. "Eastern," for the purposes of this article, refers to that broad spectrum of thought and practice grounded in the religious and philosophical traditions of the Hindu Vedas and Yogas, Taoism and the numerous branches of Buddhism. As religious traditions, these spiritualities have been formative of Oriental life and thought and offer more than the social regulation of practical Confucianism and Shinto. They offer relief from the suffering of the world. Though differing in emphasis, they manifest a generally common view of the human situation, as well as what would be therapeutic in it. "Western" refers to the common cultural heritage of Europe and the Americas which, for all of its diversity, is basically rational, scientific, and humanistic, attempting to bring these cultural traditions to bear on improving the historical lot of the individual.

A comparison of psychology and psychotherapy in the East and West is complicated by a lack of congruence between the two vast cultures in which these psychologies are embedded. Though perhaps complementary, the experiences of East and West are not directly comparable, neither in their understanding of the human situation, nor in their methods of addressing it. The East, believing in no *psyche*, until lately has had no psychology as such, holding its psychology in the form of its religions, which were interested in therapeutic methods leading to enlightenment. In the modern West questions of health and salvation have been sharply distinguished and assigned to different cultural spheres (science and religion). Western psychology shows much concern for the health of the psyche understood historically and naturalistically, but little for enlightenment or salvation of the soul as a transcendent reality. Indeed, as an alternative to salvation, secularized views of health in the West have produced a psychological culture with many of the features of religion. Yet, though difficult, a comparison is worthwhile for, despite instructive differences and contrasts, both cultures have developed methods whereby human consciousness is changed and persons are freed of some of their antagonistic relationships to personal and social realities.

1. **Comparative Meanings of Psychology and Psychotherapy.** An East-West comparison of psychology and psychotherapy begins in the recognition that two different worldviews naturally lead to divergent psychologies and therapies. The Western mind as evidenced in its psychologies appears dominantly scientific, rational, and bound to the phenomenal world. From such a mindset grows a psychology and therapy focusing on understanding and accentuating the human in the context of the phenomenal. (The theories of transpersonal psychologists, such as Charles Tart, and "spectrum psychologist" Ken Wilbur are countercultured exceptions.) By contrast, however, the Eastern mind, which is more relational, wholistic, intuitive, and given to looking beyond phenomena, has seen in its psychology and therapy a vehicle for liberation and for a transcendence of the historical human situation, rather than an improvement of it.

It is noteworthy that neither psychology nor psychotherapy in their Western forms were to be found in the East until quite recently when, as in Japan, therapeutic goals have been separated from religious ends, so that questions like personal adjustment and adjustment to the social world could be pursued in their own right (as in psychotherapies such as Morita, Naikan and Shadan; see Reynolds, 1980). But the East has had its own psychology and therapy in religious form. On a sophisticated level, Hinduism, Taoism, and most radically Buddhism, are not so much interested in religion defined as the worship of deities, as in understanding the human situation so as to offer a therapeutic course that will free human beings from suffering (*dukkha*), illusion or ignorance (*maya*), and the cycles of birth and death (*samsara*).

In Western psychologies and therapies, on the other hand, the focus is on understanding and ameliorating the historical predicament of the individual, a predicament perceived with a diversity that makes comparison difficult between East and West, or even among Western psychologies, which are as varied as psychoanalysis, behaviorism, and existentialism. Yet, insofar as both cultures exhibit an interest in the function and structure of human personality and its vicissitudes, however conceived, both have psychologies; and insofar as each offers an ordered method by which to modify personality, so that it is more in keeping with reality, however conceived, each has a psychotherapy.

2. **The Psychology-Religion Relationship.** The turning point in the comparison of East and West lies in the relationship between psychology and religion in the two cultures. Eastern psychologies are invariably and in their own ways religious, for they are concerned with bridging the gap between the phenomenal and temporal, on the one hand, and the ultimate contexts of life, on the other. Eastern psychology and attendant therapies are not interested in amelioration and adjustment focused on the phenomenal world.

On the other hand, Western psychologies are fundamentally secular and this-worldly. With the exception of third and fourth force psychologies (humanism and transpersonalism), Western psychologies assume that the world as it appears is the proper human context, and humanity's proper end is within it (Rieff; Schaer). But in the East, where psychology is held in the form of religion, the therapeutic is designed to alter consciousness in the service of transcendence, assuming that the final human context stretches beyond the world of appearances and utterly transcends it.

3. **Therapeutic Aims.** The basic orientations and mindsets of the East and West are reflected in the comparative values and assumptions that define the aims of their psychologies and therapies. In the West the psychological focus is on the formation, maintenance, and healing of the individual. Therapy tries to enable the individual to accommodate to, and live fruitfully in, the world. One's ability to do so is a sign of health and sanity. Even Western psychologies such as Jung's analytical psychology, Assagioli's psychosynthesis, and the many forms of systems theory that have a synthetic Eastern bent still focus on the adjusted, synthesized *individual*.

They assume that separateness and individuality are ontologically given and that the proper therapeutic outcome is individual identity and development.

By contrast, Eastern psychology and therapy have radically different assumptions about the end of the psychotherapeutic enterprise. In their own way the Eastern therapies are based upon a radical belief in the essential unity of all phenomena. Individuality — even the apparent existence of objects in an objective world—is the product of the ways in which the human mind *divides up* the world. The separateness of things — even the ultimate existence of "things" themselves—is fundamentally illusory. Liberation, which frees one from bondage to the phenomenal world, shows individuality to be a misperception. Therefore, Eastern psychologies require the relinquishing of what in the West is dearest of all: the ontological individual. This liberation is variously referred to as enlightenment (*satori*) or deliverance (*moksha*).

4. **Therapeutic Methods.** Both East and West offer a plurality of therapeutic methods for dealing with the human situation. In the West, therapeutic method on the concrete level is tied to the different schools of psychology and therefore varies widely from the psychoanalytic couch to the gestaltist hot seat. Yet all Western therapeutic methods are fundamentally social. Basic to Western psychotherapy is an interpersonal encounter, varying from a dyadic to a small group format. But interestingly, while its methods are social, the Western therapeutic outcome is ultimately some variation of individuation.

While Eastern methods are likewise variable, their ways of liberation are, in their more sophisticated expressions, strikingly individual. This is true of the Hindu Yogas, the sitting meditation of Zen Buddhism (*zazen*), and of Vajrayana (Tibetan) Buddhism (*samatha-vipassana*). While the settings in which meditation for liberation is practiced may be variously social and are almost always in relation to a teacher (*guru, roshi*), the therapeutic work, which involves "seeing through" in order to give up one's illusions, is done individually. There are reasons for this. Fundamentally, the shared belief is that one already has or is what one seeks. One need only uncover the goal by eliminating delusory activity. Not only is there no need of a social situation to do this, but social relationships serve to reinforce the common bonds of illusory social reality, especially the rudimentary social fiction that the subject of therapy is an *individual* subject.

5. **Comparison by Levels.** In an attempt to organize and interrelate the various psychologies of the two cultures, psychologist Ken Wilber has proposed a suggestive integration of Eastern and Western perspectives in what he calls a "spectrum psychology," which it may be helpful to cite in this context. In Wilber's view psychological reality—that which is the object of psychological inquiry and therapy—is not one-dimensional and unitary, but multidimensional, various, and subject to hierarchical classification in terms of degrees and kinds of complexity. The various schools of Western psychology —behaviorist, psychoanalytic, cognitive-structuralist, humanistic, etc.—may thus be regarded as addressing different levels of psychic reality and, rather than being competitive, may be shown to be frequently complementary. Each of these theories is simply understood to be

addressing different orders of psychic life—some, like behaviorism, closely tied to the person's interaction with material and social environment, others, like Jungian theory, focusing on higher levels of psychic process. Further, Wilber attempts to synthesize the language and mythos of Western psychotherapies and Eastern religions and philosophies in order to address both "lower" and "higher" developmental tasks. He suggests that Western psychology (other than the transpersonal psychologies) address the psychosocial stages of development spanning the period from infantile symbiosis to the emergence of mature ego, while Eastern philosophy and religion speak to the subsequent transcending movement of the soul from the individual ego to union with Being (*Atman*). Wilber states that this latter movement is frustrated, especially in the West, because Western culture is dominated by individualism, and because its psychologies treat mystic experience reductionistically. Finally, embracing Eastern mythology, Wilber insists that human development from the symbiosis of infancy through the mature ego stage and on to self-transcendence and union with Being is a process of remembering one's origins rather than creating one's future.

While Wilber's spectrum psychology is a helpful attempt at relating Eastern and Western perspectives, it too eventually faces the problem posed by the cultural embeddedness of each of the psychologies. Can elements of a particular psychology be extracted from its culture of origin—the whole connecting web of ideas, meanings and values—without altering or distorting these elements in subtle but significant ways? And are the profoundly different worldviews implicit in these psychologies sufficiently compatible to permit even the very general synthesis Wilber seeks for their psychologies?

6. **Normative Perspective and Issues.** It is difficult to draw comparisons between Eastern and Western psychologies without being misleading or inaccurate, given their profound and subtle differences and their cultural embeddedness. It is even more risky to attempt normative judgments. At the very least it is necessary to recognize that any assessment will entail some system of presuppositions and values. At the same time it is not possible to suspend or avoid at least tentative normative assessments once one has encountered — or been encountered by—the challengingly different world of Eastern spirituality. This is an issue for increasing numbers of Western Christians and Jews as Eastern religions become more and more prominent in Western societies. It is especially pressing for pastors and pastoral counselors and even secular psychologists, for all of whom Eastern practices represent tempting or threatening alternatives to fundamental psychological presuppositions and methods, alternatives about which some normative decisions become inescapable. Given this situation, a few critical issues need to be raised.

Eastern thought, in a way that is significantly different from, but nevertheless sympathetic with, Christianity, questions and challenges humanity's self-understanding. It therefore also interested in human destiny and the issue of transcendence which bridges the everyday and the ultimate, however considered (Altizer). This is an emphasis almost totally lacking in Western psychology and psychotherapy which, while making their metaphysical assumptions (e.g., the phenomenal world is "real"), largely eschew questions of ultimate meaning and salvation. Certainly from a religious and pastoral perspective, Western psychology's disinterest in, or rejection of, these questions points to a deficiency: Can any psychology be considered adequate that fails to allow for, or give an account of, dimensions of human being transcending phenomenal reality? Both Eastern and Western religions point to the ultimate in ways that challenge Western psychologies. At the same time, some Christian theologians, e.g., Karl Barth, suggest that it is perhaps quite appropriate that Western psychologies limit themselves to describing the phenomenal, since human understanding and reason are limited to the finite created world and distorted by sin.

Second, from their origins in the Christian doctrine of incarnation and its consequent high valuation of historical reality, Western psychologies embody a deep concern for concrete, everyday historical reality and have much to commend them from a moral point of view. At the same time, their ethical thrust suffers from the rationalism and materialism of post-Enlightenment thinking, which have limited their sense of how the historical world may be the arena of divine action (i.e., the transpersonal and transhistorical) and how human moral action may participate in this action. Eastern psychologies, on the other hand, with their emphasis on the illusory nature of human history and the world, can work to devalue or even undermine everyday moral responsibility and social action. From the Christian perspective, these are essential to spiritual welfare.

Finally, there is the question of the ontic status of the human individual. In Eastern thought, the individual is not primary but is a part of a larger whole. Such a view may function as a corrective to the ethical egoism of the West by throwing into sharper relief the underlying individualism of Western psychologies of the self, including those that entail a social view of the self, and opening new possibilities for psychological theorizing. Such a corrective need not lead to the theoretical abolition of the individual, however, so much as a relativizing and reinterpreting of the absolutistic claims made for the individual, explicitly or implicitly, in Western culture.

Though Western pastors may well choose to remain loyal to their own traditions of faith and psychology, it may be hoped that the continuing encounter with Eastern traditions will broaden and deepen the concern for transcendent, "spiritual" dimensions of human being and therapy and the profound interrelation of all things. In a highly rationalistic, materialistic and pragmatic culture, whose psychologies largely embody and implement its dominant values, this may be regarded as a salutary and hopeful prospect, stimulating the Western pastoral tradition to rediscover its own spiritual heritage.

Bibliography. T. Altizer, Oriental Mysticism and Biblical Eschatology (1961). E. Fromm, et al., Zen Buddhism and Psychoanalysis, (1960). D. Reynolds, The Quiet Therapies (1980). P. Rieff, The Triumph of the Therapeutic (1968). H. Schaer, Religion and the Cure of Souls in Jung's Psychology (1950). C. Tart, Transpersonal Psychologies (1975). A. Watts, Psychotherapy East and West (1961). K. Wilber, The Atman Project (1980); The Spectrum of Consciousness (1977).

S. M. ANDERSON

PSYCHOLOGY, EASTERN; PHILOSOPHY AND PSYCHOLOGY; PSYCHOLOGY, WESTERN; PSYCHOTHERAPY. See also JUDAISM AND PSYCHOLOGY; PASTORAL COUNSELING; PASTORAL PSYCHOTHERAPY; PSYCHOLOGY OF RELIGION; SOCIOLOGY OF RELIGION AND PERSONAL CARE; SPIRITUAL DIRECTION; SPIRITUAL THEOLOGY AND PASTORAL CARE.

PSYCHOLOGY AND THEOLOGY. *See* THEOLOGY AND PSYCHOLOGY; THEOLOGY AND PSYCHOTHERAPY. *See also* ANALYTICAL (JUNGIAN) PSYCHOLOGY, HUMANISTIC PSYCHOLOGY, *or* PSYCHOANALYSIS, AND THEOLOGY; PASTORAL THEOLOGICAL METHODOLOGY.

PSYCHOLOGY IN AMERICAN RELIGION. The term "psychology" became common in America only during the 1840s, but psychology and religion have been intertwined in America from the seventeenth century onward, partly because psychological reflection permeated the scholastic theological heritage that shaped early American religious thought and partly because psychological preoccupations were ingredients in the introspective piety that marked early American religious experience. One might well argue that the popularity of psychology in subsequent American religion — and in American culture — was a residue of the experiential piety of the early Puritan, Pietist, and revivalist traditions that helped form the culture. America became a nation of psychologists partly because it once had been a nation of Pietists. In any case, psychological reflection, especially since the early eighteenth century, has deeply informed theology and religious life in America, and religious concerns have shaped a substantial portion of that reflection.

1. Psychology and Colonial Piety. In the seventeenth century, the theologians were the "psychologists," and their forays into psychological theory were intended to clarify Christian doctrine or enhance Christian piety. They drew on medieval and scholastic traditions that described the soul as a gradation of higher and lower powers: each person was a body, a "vegetative soul" (hence able to grow), a "locomotive soul" (hence able to move), a "sensitive soul" (hence able to perceive, think, remember, and feel), and a "rational soul" (hence able to know, judge, and choose). Hierarchically organized, each higher power both transcended and integrated the lower ones. Thus, the rational soul, perched atop the biological ladder, rightly assumed command and government over the other powers, especially over the body and the affections. Colonial theorists often used social and political metaphors to describe the relations among the powers of the soul.

Reason normally maintained its hegemony by using its two faculties—the understanding and the will. Beyond this the various theorists often disagreed. Intellectualists claimed that the will followed the last dictate of the understanding, while voluntarists insisted that the will could control the intellect (as it did, for instance, when it directed attention to a specific object). Everyone agreed that the sanctified life required an inner harmony of the faculties, especially of the reason and the affections, and that the universal fall into sinfulness had disrupted that harmony, partly by unleashing inordinate passions. However, some theologians believed that divine grace restored harmony primarily by informing the intellect; others assumed that grace transformed the soul mainly by altering the will; and still others believed that will and intellect were so intertwined that grace had to operate on both of them at the same time in order to effect a true restoration of the original inner harmony. Those theoretical differences had important implications for ministry.

The implications became manifest especially during the Great Awakening of the early eighteenth century. Both the revivalists and their critics agreed that the renewal of the soul began with the illumination of the understanding, but they disagreed in their evaluations of the faculties. For the critics of the revival, the understanding seemed to be more exalted and more important and valuable than the will or the affections. For the revivalists the understanding was of only preliminary importance, and the will and affections were the deeper powers of the self. Hence Charles Chauncy, an opponent of the revival, thought that the revivalists failed to encourage the proper subordination of the affections. In contrast, Jonathan Edwards argued that true religion consisted "chiefly in affections," precisely because the affections were the hidden source of all human action. His *Treatise on Religious Affections* (1746), a masterpiece of psychological observation, proposed that the affections were the deepest impulses of human nature, though Edwards also insisted that in true religious knowledge the understanding and the affections (or the will) were inseparably united. Religious affections constituted a perception of the soul that was cognitive and conative at the same time. Such an understanding permitted him to draw careful distinctions between true and false religious experience and therefore to criticize the excesses of the revivals without dismissing their fruitful effects.

The debates over the revivals thus intensified the theological interest in psychology, as did the disputes that followed the publication of Edwards's massive treatise on the freedom of the will in 1754. In that book, Edwards argued that men and women bore the responsibility for their inevitable misdeeds, even though they were enmeshed in a chain of causes. They were unable to choose the motives that elicited their acts, but they were free to act (and an act implied consent and responsibility). His tightly woven arguments occupied theologians and mental philosophers for over a century. One important result of the debate was a tendency to distinguish carefully — as Edwards had not done — between volitions and affections. By the late eighteenth century, a number of theologians were insisting on a tripartite psychology of the will, the understanding, and the affections, in contrast to the Edwardian (and Lockean) tendency to assume a bipartite psychology of will and understanding. One consequence of the change was increasing attention to "sentiment" in both formal psychology and evangelical Protestant piety. The affections and passions also came to be regarded as trustworthy guides to benevolent activity. Ethicists spoke of a "moral sense," and revivalists claimed that mental philosophy confirmed their insistence on the need for a transformed heart.

2. The Tradition of Mental Philosophy. Theologians did not limit their attention to problems of volition and affection. The publication of John Locke's *Essay Concerning Human Understanding* (1690) had intensified interest in epistemology and cognition. Such topics became especially pertinent for theologians after David Hume, who, seeming to accept Locke's premises, reached skeptical conclusions that were devastating to traditional theology. In their eagerness to overcome Hume's challenge, the American theologians turned to the work of the Scottish philosophers, particularly Thomas Reid and Dugald Stewart, whose epistemological Realism appeared to refute Hume's arguments. Stewart's *Elements of the Philosophy of the Human Mind* (1792) became a standard text in the colleges, and the Scottish methods stimulated an outpouring of such treatises in "mental philosophy" as the celebrated *Elements of Intellectual Philosophy* published in 1827 by a Congregationalist minister named Thomas Upham. By 1840, when the German Reformed theologian Frederick Rauch published his *Psychology: or, A View of the Human Soul,* mental philosophy was coming to be known as "psychology."

The Scottish philosophers argued that one could refute epistemological skepticism by means of a detailed introspective examination of mental activity. Such an investigation, they wrote, was the task of "consciousness," which Reid defined as the faculty of discerning the operations of our minds. The appeal to consciousness thus became the hallmark of Scottish philosophy and the heart of American mental science. The method soon proved useful not only for narrow epistemological questions but also for wide-ranging descriptions of all the powers of the mind: perception, sensation, conception, abstraction, judgment, reasoning, taste, volition, instinct, habit, appetite, desire, affection, and moral sensibility. The mental philosophers, trying to follow the example of Sir Francis Bacon, attempted to use inductive methods to discover the minute differences that distinguished sensations and perception; or emotions, desires, and volitions; or feelings of revenge, envy, and jealousy; or penitence, discontent, sadness, mournfulness, and grief; or pride, conceit, vanity, and haughtiness; or similar mental states.

The most prominent mental philosophers were clergy, who naturally advertised the value of their work for ministerial labors. They claimed to teach pastors how to understand and appeal to the mind in each of its various states, how to make pastoral diagnosis of mental states, how to discover the laws that governed spiritual growth, how to understand the stages of grief or the permutations of guilt, how to discern the inward springs of action, and how to make proper distinctions when dealing with theological topics like regeneration, conversion, and the freedom of the will. The theologians of the period regularly lectured on mental philosophy in their courses on systematic theology, and the earliest texts in "pastoral theology" were written by such men as Ezra Stiles Ely, Enoch Pond, and Heman Humphrey, who also wrote or edited textbooks in mental philosophy.

The prevailing mental philosophy had its critics. Benjamin Rush of Philadelphia expounded an early version of a materialist medical psychiatry in his *Diseases of the Mind* (1812), arguing that most mental abnormalities had physical causes and that proper medication could cure even distorted religion. And the phrenologists hoped to unlock the secrets of the mind by exploring the bumps on the skull. But most of the clergy found mental philosophy more appealing, partly because its accent on the power of the will and on the harmony of will, understanding, and affection seemed to undergird the evangelical piety of the revivalist era.

3. **The New Psychology.** By the late nineteenth century, however, psychology was attempting to break free from its theological associations. Devoted to the scientific psychology of Wilhelm Wundt, who had established the first of the European psychological laboratories in Leipzig in 1879, the American "structural" psychologists constructed galvanometers, oscillographs, and recorders to measure degrees of attention and levels of sensory awareness. Theologians had little interest in their experiments.

The "functionalist" revolt against structuralism, however, promised a new understanding of the concrete world of human relationships and purposive activities. The functionalists, led by William James and John Dewey, were interested in the way organisms survived and flourished; they were concerned more about the mind's adaptations than about its isolated elements. Hence they studied actions, habits, attention, and purposes. Theologians immediately began to explore both the way that mental adaptations—such as habits—contributed to religious growth and ethical character and the way in which religion itself functioned to aid the individual and the group.

A preoccupation with the function of religious experience marked the emergence in the 1880s of a new discipline—the psychology of religion. Stimulated by the work of G. S. Hall, James Starbuck, and James Leuba, the psychologists of religion initially devoted their energies to the study of religious conversion, which they interpreted as a natural occurrence that usually accompanied the physical and emotional changes of adolescence. Subsequently they expanded their research in an effort to learn not only how religion helped adolescents pass through crises of growth but also how it helped adults find inner unity or nourish the development of the personality or how it helped social groups maintain inner stability.

James's *Varieties of Religious Experience* (1902) was the masterpiece of this tradition. In this classic work James contended that the conscious self is in touch with a source of salvation outside itself. He speculated that such a source—which he called "the More"—might be simply each person's own subconscious energies. However, it might also be more than that and, he thought, in any case it was real, for it produced real effects, unifying and enhancing the divided self.

By the time that James wrote, the psychotherapeutic movement that had begun in Europe in the 1860s was attracting attention in America. By 1905 the English translation of Swiss psychotherapist Pierre Dubois's *Psychic Treatment of Nervous Disease* helped to convince the medical public that there was such a thing as "scientific mind cure." While Dubois argued that healing occurred

through rational instruction of the patient, others called for the use of hypnotism, suggestion, creative assertion, or psychoanalysis. In 1908, Sigmund Freud argued the case for analysis at Clark University in Worcester, Massachusetts, and his views immediately attracted attention in the church.

Though the church has often expressed distaste for Freudian theory, it was one of the first American institutions to give Freud a serious hearing. A. A. Brill, the early translator of Freud's works, quickly found himself in demand as a lecturer in fashionable Episcopal churches in Boston, and in 1909 Elwood Worcester, the rector of Emmanuel Episcopal Church there, announced that he and his fellow ministers had aligned themselves with Freud. (In fact, they had only a partial understanding of Freud, holding notions of the subconscious and unconscious that stood in conflict with Freud's views.)

As early as 1905, Worcester and his assistant Samuel McComb had begun an "Emmanuel Movement" with the intent of harnessing the new interest in psychotherapy for the ministry of the church. The movement spread from coast to coast and by 1908 had its own journal, *Psychotherapy,* devoted to the application of psychological principles to problems of religion and ministry. Its adherents sponsored new forms of group therapy and individual counseling, designed largely to effect personal change by tapping the resources of the subconscious, primarily through techniques of relaxation and suggestion. By the 1920s the Emmanuel Movement was moribund, but it had represented an important institutional response to the new psychotherapeutic interests.

4. **A Psychology of Adjustment.** World War I stimulated public interest in psychology, partly by introducing millions to psychological testing. By the 1920s popular journals were writing of a "psychological revival" in American culture, and Freudians competed for attention with functionalists and behaviorists. But the theme that increasingly attracted the attention of the educated public was the notion of psychological "adjustment," a notion that combined European psychotherapeutic interests with American functionalism. Indeed, by the 1920s the National Committee for Mental Hygiene had spawned a movement that popularized the theme of adjustment throughout American institutions, including the churches.

The distinctive locus for psychological reflection in the churches was the Religious Education Movement. In the 1920s, the leaders of the movement, inspired especially by George Albert Coe, a professor at Union Theological Seminary in New York, were arguing that modern psychology could transform Sunday schools into resources for adjustment to God and neighbor and for self-realization. Long before there were any chairs of pastoral counseling in seminaries, religious educators like Harrison Elliott at Union Seminary (New York) or Gaines Dobbins at Southern Baptist Theological Seminary (Kentucky) began introducing students to the writings of Freud, Alfred Adler, Carl Jung, and Otto Rank, usually filtering their ideas through the lenses of an educational psychology that emphasized the plasticity of human nature and the possibilities of intelligent self-direction and adjustment.

The vocabulary of adjustment gradually influenced not only the practitioners but also the academic systematic theologians. The emergence of a theology of adjustment can best be dated from the appearance in 1919 of Douglas Clyde Macintosh's *Theology as an Empirical Science*. Psychological notions of adjustment increasingly influenced theologians like Henry Nelson Wieman at the University of Chicago, who defined religious experience as a process of continuing adjustment to the ultimately real and valuable for the sake of self-fulfillment. By 1931 Walter Marshall Horton of Oberlin could argue in his *Psychological Approach to Theology* that the "central religious problem" was "the psychological problem—how may personality be unified, energized, and directed to worthful ends?"

The metaphor of adjustment also guided the Protestant pastoral theologians who published texts on the cure of souls in the early thirties. Charles Holman at the University of Chicago and Karl Stolz of the Hartford School of Religious Education appealed frequently to the psychoanalysts, especially to Carl Jung and Alfred Adler, but their main debt was to the older psychologists of religion, the religious educators, and the liberal theologians who had written about "adjustment" to reality. J. S. Bonnell's *Pastoral Psychiatry* (1938) exhibited a far greater debt to the European psychoanalytic tradition, but even he was inclined especially toward the emphasis on "adjustment" in Adler's "individual psychology."

By 1939, however, the theological realists, especially Reinhold and H. Richard Niebuhr, were raising questions about the metaphor of adjustment, and the publication of Rollo May's *Art of Counseling* in that year marked his first steps toward an existential psychology that accented the unending tension between anxiety and freedom. By that time, moreover, the movement for Clinical Pastoral Education, begun in the 1920s, had also stimulated a quest for alternative metaphors. The movement's indebtedness to the liberal theologian Anton Boisen, whose *Exploration of the Inner World* (1936) advanced the notion that emotional collapse was a chaotic encounter with God that could lead either to a new integration of the personality or to a fall into inner disarray, stimulated a new openness to dynamic psychologies that accented inner turbulence, even though Boisen felt uneasy about Freud. Under the guidance of Helen Flanders Dunbar, the Council for Clinical Training regularly introduced ministerial students to the place of psychoanalysis in psychotherapy, and the other clinical organization, the Institute for Pastoral Care, while more inclined to emphasize the positive capacities of the self, also provided theological students an introduction to dynamic psychology. By 1955, about four thousand Protestant ministers had learned something about psychological theory in clinical settings. And by that time, they rarely spoke about "adjustment."

5. **Religion in the "Age of Psychology."** World War II and the subsequent affluence in American society helped stimulate a second renaissance of psychological interest in the culture. By 1957 *Life* magazine concluded that Americans were living in the "age of psychology," and the popular religious revival of the 1950s rested in large part on the reinterpretation of religion as "God's psychiatry." Rabbi Joshua Loth Liebman's *Peace of Mind* (1946)

and Norman Vincent Peale's *Power of Positive Thinking* (1952) both stimulated and reflected the popularizing of psychology in the religious communities. But the psychological revival also influenced the seminaries and universities: by the 1950s all mainline Protestant and most Catholic seminaries taught courses in counseling that introduced students to the newest psychological theories; over eighty percent of the Protestant theological schools offered additional courses in psychology and had at least one psychologist on their faculties. In 1955, the Jewish Theological Seminary in New York inaugurated courses taught by psychiatrists to acquaint future rabbis with psychotherapeutic methods. By the end of the 1950s, moreover, clinical educators had established 117 regular centers for Clinical Pastoral Education. Other religious leaders had established at least thirty-five institutes and centers (like the program in Religion and Psychiatry at the Menninger Clinic) to expose ministers to the latest psychological wisdom. Also at this time, Protestants established at least eighty-four counseling centers that were deeply influenced by psychotherapeutic theory, following the example of the American Foundation for Religion and Psychiatry in New York, which in 1937 created a counseling center connected to the Marble Collegiate Church. The founding of the journal *Pastoral Psychology* in 1950 symbolized the interest in psychology that could be found among the parish clergy, and the writings of such pastoral theologians as Seward Hiltner, Carroll Wise, Paul Johnson, and Wayne Oates—writers thoroughly grounded in dynamic psychologies—also exercised immense influence among Protestants.

Roman Catholics remained cautious until after World War II, and conservatives like Bishop Fulton Sheen frequently criticized modern psychology. However, in 1953 Pope Pius XII gave the church's official approval to psychoanalysis as well as to other forms of psychotherapy, so long as their use remained consonant with Christian teaching. By 1957 more than one hundred priests belonged to an American Catholic Psychological Association, and such writers as Charles Curran, Gregory Zilboorg, and J. Vanderveldt had reinterpreted traditional Catholic notions of the cure of souls in the light of modern psychotherapy. By the end of the 1950s, such Catholic schools as Fordham, Woodstock, St. John's, and Loyola regularly offered training in "pastoral psychology."

Among the Protestant pastoral theologians, the dominant authority during the 1950s was the psychologist Carl Rogers, whose notions of "client-centered" therapy seemed to counter the moralism and authoritarian disposition of earlier pastoral counseling. The pastoral writers also drew heavily on the social psychology of Erich Fromm and Karen Horney, who found Western culture oppressed by bureaucratic authoritarianism. By the mid-1960s, however, when popular psychologies that promised to counter false authority and bureaucratic order permeated American culture, the pastoral writers turned their attention to such psychologists as Kurt Lewin, H. S. Sullivan, and Erik Erikson, who emphasized interpersonal relationships and structured patterns of human development. One consequence was enthusiastic interest in group dynamics and group therapy within the church.

By the 1950s, moreover, systematic theologians found themselves increasingly influenced by psychological conceptions. David Roberts's *Psychotherapy and a Christian View of Man* (1950) urged a synthesis of theology and psychotherapeutic theory to redefine traditional notions of sin and guilt. Other writers—like Albert Outler—were more cautious about the benefits of redefinition, but clearly the dominant theologian in America during the 1950s was Paul Tillich, whose method of correlation offered a way to interpret theological theories in psychological terms, as Tillich did when he reinterpreted the traditional doctrine of justification in the light of the "acceptance" that a therapist offered a client. Some strong neo-orthodox currents flowed against the tendency to translate theology into psychological categories, but the psychological turn in theology maintained its force well into the 1970s and will probably continue to influence American theologians.

The proliferation of departments of religious studies in American universities during the 1960s led to a growing interest in understanding religion as a general human phenomenon, and scholars found psychology to be a useful tool. Joseph Campbell, for instance, drew upon Jung in his studies of myth and symbolism; Mary Douglas used psycholinguistics to study symbol systems; Mircea Eliade cited the usefulness of depth psychology for the understanding of religious symbols; and Paul Pruyser attempted to reinvigorate the psychology of religion as a means of studying religious experiences and beliefs. The older psychology of religion now seems moribund, but American students of religion have by no means abandoned psychological approaches to the topic.

Critical observers of modern America have described it as a "therapeutic culture" thoroughly governed by psychological modes of interpreting reality. They also have argued on occasion that modern religion has attempted to survive in a secular culture by grabbing the coattails of psychology and claiming to share its therapeutic powers. Whatever the accuracy of such claims, it is clear that the close alliance of religion and psychology in America is no sudden innovation. From seventeenth-century casuistry to twentieth-century pastoral counseling, from Edwards's analysis of the affections to James's study of sick and healthy souls, from the church's appropriation of mental philosophy to its interests in dynamic psychology, religion in America has exhibited continuing and complex relations with psychology. The psychological preoccupations of American religion are clearly an inheritance from its past.

Bibliography. A. Stokes, "Bibliographies of Psychology/Religious Studies," *Religious Studies Review*, 4 (1978), 273–79. E. B. Holifield, *A History of Pastoral Care in America: From Salvation to Self-Realization* (1983). R. C. Fuller, *Americans and the Unconscious* (1986).

E. B. HOLIFIELD

HISTORY OF PROTESTANT *or* ROMAN CATHOLIC PASTORAL CARE (Canada *or* United States); JUDAISM AND PSYCHOLOGY; PASTORAL CARE MOVEMENT; PASTORAL COUNSELING MOVEMENT; POPULAR THERAPEUTIC MOVEMENTS AND PSYCHOLOGIES. *See also* COUNSELING, ROMAN CATHOLIC; PSYCHIATRY AND PASTORAL CARE; RELIGION AND PSYCHOTHERAPY; THEOLOGICAL EDUCATION AND THE PASTORAL CARE MOVEMENT. *Biography:* BOISEN; BONNELL; COE; DEWEY; DUNBAR; EDWARDS; ELLIOTT; ERIKSON; HALL; HILTNER; HOLMAN; JAMES; JOHNSON; LEUBA; MAY; NIEBUHR, H. RICHARD; NIEBUHR, REINHOLD; OATES; OUTLER; PEALE; POND; ROBERTS; STARBUCK; STOLZ; TILLICH; WISE; WORCESTER.

PSYCHOLOGY OF PASTORAL CARE AND COUNSELING. *See* PASTORAL CARE AND COUNSELING. *See* PASTORAL CARE (Contemporary Methods, Perspectives, and Issues); PASTORAL COUNSELING; PASTORAL PSYCHOTHERAPY; The PERSONAL, CONCEPT OF, IN PASTORAL CARE. *See also* ANALYTICAL (JUNGIAN) PSYCHOLOGY, PSYCHOANALYSIS, *or* HUMANISTIC PSYCHOLOGY, AND PASTORAL CARE; PASTORAL PSYCHOLOGY, DISCIPLINE OF.

PSYCHOLOGY OF RELIGION (Empirical Studies, Methods, and Problems). The psychology of religion offers observations and explications of the phenomenon of religion, using the terminology of psychological theories. Strictly speaking, all studies of religion within the framework of psychology are "empirical" (even clinical case studies, in terms of their source of data), but normally the term "empirical" is used for studies that follow the logic and the methods of conventional academic psychology.

1. **Subject, History, and Method.** One question that the psychology of religion attempts to answer is that of religious motivation; that is, why people engage in religious acts. Empirical studies of religion ask questions about (1) the nature and origins of religious beliefs, and (2) the correlates of religious beliefs. The majority of the studies in the literature of academic psychology deal with questions of the second variety.

The history of the psychological study of religion is complex and paradoxical. Freud (1927), Hall (1904), James (1902), Maslow (1964), Watson (1925), and Wundt (1916) all gave considerable attention to the subject matter of religion. Early in the 1880s Calvin Hall began lecturing and writing on the "moral and religious training of children and adolescents" as part of his general interest in developmental problems; this marked the beginning of the new field. Hall's interest in adolescence brought about empirical studies of religious "conversion," which became the most popular subject for such studies (Leuba, 1896; Starbuck, 1901). Edwin Starbuck (1866–1947) was stirred in 1890 by Max Müller's (1870) "Introduction to the Science of Religion" and decided to begin studying the area systematically. At Harvard, in 1893, he circulated two questionnaires—one on "conversion" and the other on "gradual growth."

This early study, the first to use a questionnaire dealing with religious behavior, led to the adoption of questionnaire surveys as the most common method in the empirical psychology of religion. The preferred methodology in academic psychology is that of the laboratory, but the subject of religion is too complex and too soft for that method. For example, imagination and feelings are two topics that academic psychology finds hard to approach. Experimental studies of religion also present ethical and practical problems, and only little "experimental" or "quasi-experimental" work has been done in the psychology of religion, using the dominant laboratory model in psychology (Deconchy, 1977; Osarchuk and Tate, 1973).

Religion lends itself easily to analysis in the subfield of social psychology, which is concerned with concepts such as beliefs, attitudes, values, and norms. Social psychologists, with a few notable and commendable exceptions (Bem, 1970; Festinger, Riecken, and Schachter, 1956; Rokeach, 1968), have not used religious beliefs often as the subject matter for their research and theorizing. Bem (1970) presents a penetrating discussion of religious beliefs in a textbook that deals with beliefs and actions "in the real world." A unique study by Fishbein and Ajzen (1974) used religious attitudes and activities to test the question of the relationship between attitudes and behavior. Most empirical studies in the psychology of religion are done by psychologists who are interested in the topic, and not because they are asking questions of general interest to psychological theory.

2. Findings, Generalizations, and Theoretical Questions.

In the language of academic psychology, "findings" are the results of conventional psychological research. More detailed reports of these findings, summarizing the research literature, are found in Dittes (1968), and Argyle and Beit-Hallahmi (1975). These studies all belong to the social psychology of religion, that is, the effort to find behavior and social background correlates of religiosity and religious affiliation. While these results provide answers to some interesting questions about religion, they are often the product of a theoretical research. Some of the findings, however, give partial answers to some of the "classical questions" in the psychological study of religion.

a. The consequences of religiosity. Glock (1962), in one of the best-known and most frequently used formulations in social science literature on religion, proposed the following five dimensions of religiosity:

(1) ideological, covering religious beliefs

(2) intellectual, covering religious knowledge

(3) ritualistic, covering participation in religious rituals

(4) experiential, covering intense religious experiences

(5) consequential, covering the consequences of religiosity in non-religious activities.

Later, as the result of further research, the consequential dimension was dropped because, they said, such consequences in nonreligious behavior could not be found (Glock and Stark, 1965). One problem in the study of consequences is logical and methodological. It is always safer to assume that secular factors lead to secular behavior, but, traditionally, religion is tied to the expectation of consequences in the secular sphere. The main reason for the expectation of consequences is that religious traditions quite explicitly predict those consequences. Religion exists for many believers as a prescriptive behavior system, containing specific moral injunctions. For many believers, religion is a proscriptive, not a prescriptive, system, which from the psychological viewpoint is concerned mainly with impulse control. Other findings (Argyle and Beit-Hallahmi, 1975), however, indicate that religion does have a considerable effect on secular behavior in two areas: sexual behavior and the use of drugs, though these effects exist only where a specific proscription exists.

The expectation that religiosity would lead to some kind of a general social attitude in response to the traditional moral exhortations of religious representatives has not been supported by research. Religious people are not more likely to engage in positive social actions, to be more honest, or to be more generous (Argyle and Beit-Hallahmi, 1975). The well-known findings about the positive correlation between religiosity and prejudice have been mentioned often, but it is hard to view them as specific consequences of religiosity. The best explanation for the correlation between religiosity and prejudice, authoritarianism and conservatism may be social rather than psychological. Religious people tend to be conservative in their general worldview and to support the traditional beliefs of their cultures in nonreligious areas.

b. The search for the "religious personality." The question of consequences can be pursued in another related way, which is the search for an individual, religious type of personality. Something that laity expect of psychologists studying religion is a psychological description of the religious person. Laity may ask, with some justification, what the religious person is like, and how that person is different from the nonreligious person. Religion itself expects religious persons to be different. Thus, one natural task of the psychology of religion is to develop a psychological profile of the religious person, but there have been many obstacles to the completion of this task. Numerous studies have tried to contribute to such a profile (see Beit-Hallahmi, 1973; Brown, 1973), but so far the results have been limited. Western psychologists have generally concluded today that the religious person is likely to be more conventional, authoritarian, dogmatic, and suggestible than is the nonreligious person. James Dittes (1968) adds that "psychological research reflects an overwhelming consensus that religion (at least as measured in the research, usually institutional affiliation or adherence to conservative traditional doctrines) is associated with awareness of personal inadequacies, either generally or in response to particular crisis or threat situations; with objective evidence of inadequacy, such as low intelligence; with a strong responsiveness to the suggestions of other persons or other external influences; and with an array of what may be called desperate and generally unadaptive defensive maneuvers" (p. 616).

Yet attempts to relate personality variables and religiosity have been largely unsuccessful. One reason is the complexity of variables and measurements used. When this complexity is involved in studying religious behavior, which is in itself complex and over-determined, the difficulty in arriving at any easy generalizations is obvious. There is also an historical reason for the difficulty. On the psychological level, "secularization" means that there is a less detectable influence of religion on individual personality and behavior than in earlier eras. Indeed one may ask whether religion, in our secularized society, makes a difference in anyone's life. One researcher (Bouma, 1970) concluded that in fact psychology is able to prove only a marginal influence of religion in any area of modern life.

c. Social-psychological findings. It is possible to summarize social-psychological findings on a number of points (cf. Argyle and Beit-Hallahmi, 1975):

(1) Religious behavior is obviously culturally and socially conditioned. This is an important and elementary truth that often tends to be neglected. Social learning, despite its seeming simplicity, and maybe because of it, remains the best explanation for most religious actions. The more unusual and "esoteric" religious actions are socially learned, just like the less "esoteric" ones. To the question: "Why do people believe in God?" the best answer remains: "Because they have been taught to believe in God."

(2) The effects of parental beliefs are more important than any other factor in determining individual religiosity.

(3) Unmarried individuals are likely to become more involved in religious activities than married individuals.

(4) Adolescence is the period of religious "conversions," which are experiences of personal recommitment to a familiar religious tradition, and differ from true conversions, which refer to the change from one religious tradition to another, or from nonreligion to religion.

(5) There is a decline in religious involvement during the third decade of life.

(6) There is a rise in religious involvement after age thirty to old age.

(7) Women are higher than men on every measure of religiosity and religious involvement.

(8) There is a slight negative correlation between religiosity and I.Q.

(9) Religiosity is correlated with the traits of authoritarianism, dogmatism, and suggestibility.

(10) Religiosity is positively correlated with ethnocentrism and political conservatism.

(11) Religiosity does not affect suicidal behaviors.

(12) Religiosity is negatively correlated with sexual activity, as measured by "total sexual outlet" (number of orgasms per week).

(13) Religiosity is positively correlated with better adjustment in marriage and a lower frequency of divorce.

3. Conclusion. The criticism that may be directed at the empirical psychology of religion stems from two sources: dissatisfaction with the theoretical achievements of the field in explaining religion from a psychological point of view, and dissatisfaction with the methods of psychology, which limit the possibilities of any theoretical progress. The empirical psychology of religion has barely scratched the surface of religion as a living institution in human society. What is needed for future progress in the field is more sophisticated work, tied in turn to related and parallel theoretical progress.

Bibliography. M. Argyle and B. Beit-Hallahmi, *The Social Psychology of Religion* (1975). B. Beit-Hallahmi, *Research in Religious Behavior: Selected Readings* (1973). D. J. Bem, *Beliefs, Attitudes, and Human Affairs* (1970). L. B. Brown, *Psychology and Religion* (1973). J. P. Deconchy, "Regulation et signification dans un cas de 'compromis' idéologique (ecclésiastiques catholiques et propositions 'marxistes') *Bulletin de Psychologie,* 30 (1977), 436–50. J. E. Dittes, "Psychology of Religion," in G. Lindzey and E. Aronson, eds., *The Handbook of Social Psychology* vol. 5 (1969, 1985). L. Festinger, H. W. Riecken and S. Schachter, *When Prophecy Fails* (1956). M. Fishbein and I. Ajzen, "Attitudes Towards Objects as Predictors of Single and Multiple Behavioral Criteria," *Psychological Bulletin,* 81 (1974), 59–74. S. Freud, *The Future of an Illusion, SE* vol. 21 (1961 [1927]). C. Y. Glock, "On the Study of Religious Commitment," *Religious Education,* 57 (1962), S98–S109. C. Y. Glock and R. Stark, *Religion and Society in Tension* (1965). G. S. Hall, *Adolescence: Its Psychology and its Relations to Physiology, Anthropology, Sociology, Sex, Crime, Religion, and Education* 2 vols (1904). W. James, *The Varieties of Religious Experience: A Study in Human Nature* 2d ed. (1902). J. H. Leuba, "A Study in the Psychology of Religious Phenomena," *American J. of Psychology,* 7 (1896), 309–85. A. H. Maslow, *Religions, Values, and Peak Experiences* (1964). M. Müller, *Introduction to the Science of Religion* (1870). M. Osarchuk and S. J. Tate, "Effect of Induced Fear of Death on Belief in Afterlife," *J. of Personality and Social Psychology,* 27 (1973), 256–60. M. Rokeach, *Beliefs, Attitudes, and Values* (1968). B. Spilka, R. W. Hood, Jr., and R. L. Gorsuch, *The Psychology of Religion: An Empirical Approach* (1985). E. D. Starbuck, *Psychology of Religion* (1901). J. B. Watson, *Behaviorism* (1925). W. Wundt, *Elements of Folk Psychology,* E. L. Schaub, trans., (1916 [1912]).

B. BEIT-HALLAHMI

FAITH DEVELOPMENT RESEARCH; RELIGION. *See also articles describing empirical studies of* CLERGY; RABBIS; RELIGIOUS; *and* THEOLOGICAL STUDENTS; *articles on* RELIGIOUS BEHAVIOR, EXPERIENCE, *or* LANGUAGE; SECULARIZATION/SECULARISM. *Compare* JOURNALS IN RELIGION, THEOLOGY, AND THE SOCIAL SCIENCES (INTERDISCIPLINARY); RELIGION AND HEALTH; PSYCHOPATHOLOGY AND RELIGION; RELIGION AND PSYCHOTHERAPY. *Compare also* CULTURAL ANTHROPOLOGY *or* SOCIOLOGY OF RELIGION; RESEARCH IN PASTORAL CARE AND COUNSELING.

PSYCHOLOGY OF RELIGION (Theories, Traditions, and Issues).

Religion was a central concern to a number of the founders of scientific psychology. Wilhelm Wundt (1916), G. Stanley Hall (1917), and William James (1902), among others, recognized the significance of faith in the lives of those they studied. Interest in religion flourished until the 1920s, when it receded into the background of "respectable" psychology. Though many factors can be called to account, none were more influential than psychoanalysis and behaviorism. The former derived religion from human weakness; the latter's positivistic emphasis simply had no place for a consideration of faith. Because of this troubled history, the psychology of religion finds itself struggling to find a home within the mainstream of scientific psychology while embracing the humanistic ideals of religion. The origins of this identity struggle are found in the traditions underlying both the psychology of religion and general psychology.

1. Traditions. *a. The subjectivist tradition.* To early scholars, religion often meant intense mystical experience. This was usually identified with conversion and adolescence. In this tradition, experience is usually regarded as phenomenologically indivisible; it is conceived as a gestalt that must be taken as an unanalyzable whole. This approach represents what can be termed the subjectivist tradition in the psychology of religion. Its essence is that religion is a deeply felt personal matter, the core of which is experiential. Individuality is stressed, and the dominant method utilizes case histories. The writings of William James (1902), Anton Boisen (1936), and Evelyn Underhill (1910) exemplify this outlook.

This classic orientation gained support from a parallel development within mainstream psychology, which was termed the idiographic approach. This method emphasized clinical work and sought depth understanding of the internal dynamics of the individual rather than concern with what were designated as surface behaviors.

The force of these developments within psychology and the psychology of religion has been most fully expressed by those who employ the theories of Freud, Jung, Erikson, and existential thinkers. It naturally followed that a version of clinical practice representing this tradition was applied to the realm of religion. The use of such techniques in the pastoral context reflects not only strong trends in psychology but the equally important pastoral functions of institutional religion. From this grew the Pastoral Psychology movement. Since pastoral psychologists are concerned with personal and spiritual conflict, religious meaning and experience on the phenomenological level are of prime interest (Oates, 1973). The emphasis is wholistic, humanistic, individualistic, and, in the main, represents cooperation between psychology and religion.

b. The objectivist tradition. Concurrent with the development of the subjectivist tradition, much of professional psychology sought to identify itself as "objectivistic" or "scientific," using the physical and biological sciences as models. Religious thinking and behavior were now to be studied by psychologists using forms of measurement that were apparently independent of the researcher. Attention was initially directed away from the "soft" content of experience to the "hard" data provided by questionnaires and behavioral observations. The orientation was nomothetic: individuality became submerged in statistical averages and relationships among variables on data gathered from large numbers of people. Lawfulness and order were and are the goals of this research, hence objectivity, reliability, and validity become of prime concern in order to establish the public nature and reproducibility of findings. Growing sophistication has resulted in efforts to develop single-person research paradigms (Malony, 1977). These methods have not yet gained wide acceptance in the field.

Unlike the compatibility of religion with psychology that seems to exist within the subjectivist tradition, the potential for conflict between these realms appears to be much greater with objectivist ideas and methods. Psychologists may be perceived as "passing judgment" on religionists and their doctrines and institutions. In contrast, religionists might claim that the more basic philosophical-theological premises of their field should permit them to be the final evaluators of truth.

c. Coordinating the traditions. This subjective-objective controversy is basically spurious. Theories derived from individual-phenomenological study must be evaluated in general behavioral terms in order to determine their validity and generalizability. In like manner, relationships, similarities, and differences observed in nomothetic work have to be brought to the level of the individual to determine their validity and generalizability. Neither perspective can exist meaningfully without including the other. Hanford (1975) has proposed a synoptic approach to resolve differences between advocates of the subjectivist and objectivist tra-

ditions in which ideas from one domain would be assessed in the other. Though this has often been undertaken, both satisfaction and integration have been hard to achieve.

The complementary nature of these two traditions may also be seen in research. As already noted, the subjectivist theoretical position of William James (1902) and early writers on religious experience suggested the unitary nature of such phenomena. In addition, subjectivist concepts such as ineffability implied that reductionistic analyses of experience were not possible. However, more recent thinking and research of an objectivist character has shown that such experience is multidimensional and a function of situational and personality factors (Hood, 1974, 1977, 1978).

2. Theory. a. The defensive-protective approach. This outlook has its modern origins in Darwinian functionalism and has found psychological expression in the theories of Freud, the behaviorists, and social psychologists who treat religion as functionally utilitarian and necessary to both physical and psychological survival. Here faith is an outgrowth of human inadequacy and weakness. People are said to need religion to alleviate their fears, particularly of death, but also because of a wide range of physical, psychological, and moral shortcomings. Identification with an omnipotent deity is said to endow the believer with protection and power (Freud, 1957).

These views are often convincing as they are based on parallels between religion and aspects of everyday life, particularly from one's early years in a traditional home (Casey, 1938). Probably the most famous specific inference concerns generalization from images of the father to God. Research on this problem has not been conclusive, and it may never be satisfactorily resolved; however, the weight of some objective evidence is against the psychoanalytic position (Spilka, Addison, and Rosensohn, 1975; Vergote and Tamayo, 1980).

In a similar defensive-protective approach, Glock (1964) hypothesized economic, social, organismic, ethical, and psychic forms of group and individual deprivation as motivating religious activity. Though this goes far toward providing a heuristically useful framework for research assessment of the functional utility of religion, little work has been directed toward such a goal.

b. The growth-realization approach. This perspective sees faith as fostering enhancement of the individual —emotionally, cognitively, totally (Adler, 1964; Fromm, 1950; Jung, 1938). Religion is viewed as a striving to locate oneself in the scheme of things with ever-broadening horizons. Elkind's (1970) theory of the origins of religion in the child, in which religious and cognitive growth parallel each other, is an excellent developmental illustration of this outlook. Allport's (1959, 1966) concept of "intrinsic" religion as a search for truth may be included here. Those who identify religious maturity with Maslow's concepts of self-actualization and growth motivation also utilize this framework (Fleck and Carter, 1981).

c. The mechanical-habitual approach. In this approach the basic assumption is that one's faith is learned like any other complex human behavior. Implied is the notion that most people in a religiously oriented society simply assent to anything that refers to God or institutional religion. Robert Bellah's (1967) notion of civil religion, in which a superficial, generalized religious atmosphere pervades national life, provides one example. Strommen's (1963) "general religion" and what Allport and Ross (1967) refer to as "religious muddleheadedness" may also be examples of this kind of faith. It is an indiscriminately pro-religious tendency that expresses itself as automatic habit.

3. Current Theoretical Frameworks. The foregoing metatheoretical perspectives are part of the assumptive foundations of all the major approaches currently utilized in the psychology of religion. To date, however, theory has usually been restricted to the treatment of specific problems within the overall field, and there has been little integration of these various domains. Each subfield appears to be developing its own conceptual framework to handle the problems with which it is concerned.

a. The developmental psychology of religion. Those who study religious development most often utilize Piaget's structuralist theory of cognitive development (Elkind, 1978). This formulation has been applied to changes that occur in concepts of God, the meaning of prayer, biblical figures and stories, religious maturity, and moral understanding. Elkind (1970) further suggests that the development of faith itself is a normal and natural result of cognitive development, an idea subsequently developed in detail, with empirical research, by James Fowler (1981, 1984). Fowler's developmental theory combines structuralist and dynamic psychologies with theology in describing an invariant sequence of six formal, purportedly universal, "stages of faith."

b. Religious experience. Psychologists have viewed religious experience as both positively and negatively motivated. Ralph Hood (1976) has criticized as "regressive" those defensive explanations claiming that religious expressions reflect childish and neurotic motives. In much of his work, Hood (1977) embraces a view closer to a growth-realization perspective. He also has constructed measures of religious experience, shown that persons with certain religious propensities are more likely to have such encounters, and has even undertaken to produce conditions that stimulate these phenomena.

c. Religion, personality, and abnormality. Psychoanalytic views have had the most appeal to those who study the relationship of religion to personality and abnormality (Beit-Hallahmi, 1984). Emphasis is on the nature of motivational characteristics believed to have developed in childhood. These have been used primarily to explain religious experiences and ritualistic behavior. Most of these discussions employ *post hoc* interpretation rather than empirical assessment.

d. The social-psychological basis of religion. For approximately a decade, the psychology of religion has resided within social psychology (Dittes, 1969). Among efforts to apply formulations from this domain to religion, the most successful appear to be derived from attribution theory (Proudfoot and Shaver, 1975; Spilka and Schmidt, 1983). Predictions from this framework contend that religious belief, experience, and behavior are a function of the causal attributions or interpretations people make under various conditions. These seem to occur because of the characteristics of situations and the tendencies of people to perceive and act in patterned ways. Currently much research is being conducted utilizing these views.

The role of cognitive dissonance, with its stress on inconsistencies among attitudes, expectations, environmental events, and behavior has also been examined. These show that religious activity, especially conversion and commitment, may involve dissonance within the person (Festinger, Riecken, and Schachter, 1964).

Social-psychological theory seems to have much potential for the psychology of religion. To date, however, little programmatic research using these ideas has been undertaken. There are, however, signs of growing attention to this domain, particularly with respect to social influence and cognition.

4. Issues. *a. Theory, theology, and psychology: separation and integration.* A number of scholars have suggested that theology and psychology may be more fundamentally integrated than is immediately apparent. Hiltner (1958), for example, feels that a "psychological language may also be a theological language" (p. 26). Aden (1968) and Pruyser (1960) point out that theologians have always been quite psychological in their pronouncements.

Efforts to integrate psychology and theology have encountered a number of difficulties, however. In addition to the usual weaknesses of practitioners in one or the other of the disciplines, there has been a tendency to remain abstract rather than to become involved in substantive matters (Collins, 1981). The only exception has been with regard to pastoral counseling and psychology, and here pastoral counselors often seem to desire identification with psychology rather than with religion (Hulme, 1970).

It also has been suggested that theology might serve as a theoretical basis for work in the psychology of religion (Carter and Narramore, 1979; Hodges, 1974). Some efforts have been made to develop and employ these ideas (Spilka, 1976).

b. The operational complexity of personal religion. i. Forms of personal faith. It has often been assumed that religiosity is a single dimension, with those expressing a negative outlook at one end and the orthodox at the other. Most theoreticians feel that the complexity of religion defies this kind of easy simplification. Even though most research has treated religiosity in terms of elementary indicators, such as church attendance or personally rated importance of faith, many feel religion is multidimensional in nature. One of the earliest multiform schemes was advanced in 1902 by William James, who denoted religions of "healthy-mindedness," and "sick souls." The 1950s saw a number of similar dichotomies advanced by Erich Fromm (1950) and Gordon Allport (1954, 1959). Others have proposed systems with anywhere from three to thirteen forms of religious expression (Batson and Ventis, 1982; Glock, 1962; King and Hunt, 1972).

Most of these systems have been essentially undeveloped. A notable exception is the intrinsic-extrinsic dichotomy of Allport (1959, 1966), which dominated research and theory for about two decades. Intrinsic religion "regards faith as a supreme value in its own right . . . a religious sentiment of this sort floods the whole life with motivation and meaning" (Allport, 1966, p. 445). In contrast, extrinsic religion is described as "strictly utilitarian: useful for the self in granting safety, social standing, solace and endorsement for one's chosen way of life" (Allport, 1966, p. 455). The meaning of these forms of personal faith has been amply demonstrated in their differential associations with measures of interpersonal relations, prejudice, God images, death perspectives, creativity, and self-esteem, among a host of other social and psychological expressions (Batson and Ventis, 1982; Paloutzian, 1983).

ii. Images of God. Multidimensionality in religion has been demonstrated also in the images of God that people hold. One investigation revealed up to twelve different concepts of God (Spilka, Armatas, and Nussbaum, 1964). Further research suggested eight basic patterns, six of which combined to produce two higher-level configurations (Gorsuch, 1968). Various God images also have been associated with different forms of personal faith and ways of looking at oneself and the world.

iii. Religious experience. The notion that religious experience is a unitary phenomenon has been increasingly questioned. James even suggested four major expressions of such phenomena. One unpublished survey of thinking and research suggested up to seventeen possible features. This work also indicated seven different kinds of intense spiritual experience.

iv. Religion and mental disorder. Pastoral psychologists must consider five possibilities in the relationship of religion to mental disorder: (1) religion may be an expression of abnormality, (2) it may act as a socializing agent to suppress aberration, (3) it can function as a haven, an escape from life for the troubled person, (4) it has the potential of being therapeutic, and (5) it may be a hazard to the person by exacerbating personality problems.

v. Issues for further research. Anton Boisen (1936) noted that mental disorders have a religious dimension if they lead to a new level of awareness and commitment. Oates (1955, 1970) concluded that while religion is never the sole cause of mental illness, it is more likely to become a contributing factor when it is an externalized object used as a defense. While religious development has been coordinated with psychological knowledge in cognition, little is yet known about patterns of relationships within the home and how they affect one's faith; religious change, conversion, and commitment, though studied for almost a century, are far from being satisfactorily understood; and the most fundamental of questions regarding the influence of faith in everyday life, in interpersonal relationships, and on moral thinking and behavior are only beginning to be researched. What *is* unquestionably clear is the enormous complexity of religion and the need for an overriding and coordinating theoretical perspective that defines the place and role of psychology and religion in the psychology of religion.

Bibliography. L. Aden, "Pastoral Counseling as Christian Perspective" in P. Homans, ed., *The Dialogue Between Theology and Psychology* (1968). A. Adler, *Social Interest* (1964). G. W. Allport, *The Nature of Prejudice* (1954); "Religion and Prejudice," *Crane Review*, 2 (1959), 1–10; "The Religious Context of Prejudice," *J. for the Scientific Study of Religion*, 5 (1966), 447–57. G. W. Allport and J. M. Ross, "Personal Religious Orientation and Prejudice," *J. of Personality and Social Psychology*, 5

(1967), 432–43. C. D. Batson and L. Ventis, *The Religious Experience* (1982). B. Beit-Hallahmi, "Psychology and Religion," in M. H. Bornstein, ed., *Psychology and Its Allied Disciplines* (1984). R. Bellah, "Civil Religion in America," *Daedalus*, 96:1 (1967), 1–21. A. Boisen, *The Exploration of the Inner World* (1936). J. D. Carter and B. Narramore, *The Integration of Psychology and Theology* (1979). R. P. Casey, "The Psychoanalytic Study of Religion," *J. of Abnormal and Social Psychology*, 33 (1938), 437–52. G. R. Collins, *Psychology and Theology* (1981). J. Dittes, "Psychology of Religion," in G. Lindzey and E. Aronson, eds., *The Handbook of Social Psychology* vol. 5, 2d ed. (1969), 602–59. D. Elkind, *The Child's Reality: Three Developmental Themes* (1978); "The Origins of Religion in the Child," *Review of Religious Research*, 12 (1970), 35–42. L. Festinger, H. W. Riecken, and S. Schachter, *When Prophecy Fails* (1964). J. R. Fleck, and J. D. Carter, eds., *Psychology and Christianity* (1981). J. Fowler, *Stages of Faith* (1981); *Becoming Adult, Becoming Christian* (1984). S. Freud, *The Future of an Illusion*, SE vol. 21, (1927). E. Fromm, *Psychoanalysis and Religion* (1950). C. Y. Glock, "On the Study of Religious Commitment," *Religious Education, Research Supplement*, 57 (1962), 98–110; "The Role of Deprivation in the Origin and Evolution of Religious Groups," in R. Lee and M. E. Marty, eds., *Religion and Social Conflict* (1964). R. L. Gorsuch, "The Conceptualization of God as Seen in Adjective Ratings," *J. for the Scientific Study of Religion*, 7 (1968), 56–64. G. S. Hall, *Jesus, the Christ, in the Light of Psychology* (1917). J. T. Hanford, "A Synoptic Approach: Resolving Problems in Empirical and Phenomenological Approaches to the Psychology of Religion," *J. for the Scientific Study of Religion*, 14 (1975), 219–27. S. Hiltner, *Preface to Pastoral Theology* (1958). D. L. Hodges, "Scientific Theory and the Supernatural, *J. for the Scientific Study of Religion*, 13 (1974), 393–408. R. W. Hood, Jr., "Psychological Strength and the Report of Intense Religious Experience," *J. for the Scientific Study of Religion*, 13 (1974), 65–71; "Conceptual Criticisms of Regressive Explanations of Mysticism," *Review of Religious Research*, 18 (1976), 264–70; "Differential Triggering of Mystical Experience as a Function of Self-Actualization," *Review of Religious Research*, 18 (1977), 264–70; "Anticipatory Set and Setting: Stress Incongruities as Elicitors of Mystical Experience in Solitary Nature Situations," *J. for the Scientific Study of Religion*, 17 (1978), 279–88. W. E. Hulme, *Pastoral Care Comes of Age* (1970). W. James, *Varieties of Religious Experience* (1902). C. G. Jung, *Psychology and Religion* (1938). M. B. King, and R. A. Hunt, "Measuring the Religious Variable: Replication," *J. for the Scientific Study of Religion*, 11 (1972), 240–51. H. N. Malony, "N = 1 Methodology in the Psychology of Religion," in H. N. Malony, ed., *Current Perspectives in the Psychology of Religion*. W. E. Oates, *Religious Factors in Mental Illness* (1955); *When Religion Gets Sick* (1970); *The Psychology of Religion* (1973). R. F. Paloutzian, *Invitation to the Psychology of Religion* (1983). W. Proudfoot and P. Shaver, "Attribution Theory and the Psychology of Religion," *J. for the Scientific Study of Religion*, 14 (1975), 317–30. P. W. Pruyser, "Some Trends in the Psychology of Religion, *Journal of Religion*, 40 (1960), 113–29; *A Dynamic Psychology of Religion* (1968); *Between Belief and Unbelief* (1974). B. Spilka "The 'Compleat Person': Some Theoretical Views and Research Findings for a Theological Psychology of Religion," *J. of Psychology and Theology*, 4 (1976), 15–24. B. Spilka and G. Schmidt, "General Attribution Theory for the Psychology of Religion: The Influence of Event-Character on Attributions to God," *J. for the Scientific Study of Religion*, 22 (1983), 326–39. B. Spilka, J. Addison, and M. Rosensohn, "Parents, Self and God: A Test of Individual-Religion Relationships," *Review of Religious Research*, 16 (1975), 154–65. B. Spilka, P. Armatas, and J. Nussbaum, "The Concept of God: A Factor-Analytic Approach," *Review of Religious Research*, 6

(1964), 28–36. M. P. Strommen, *Profiles of Church Youth* (1963). E. Underhill, *Mysticism* (1910). A. Vergote and A. Tamayo, *The Parental Images and the Representation of God* (1980). W. Wundt, *Elements of Folk Psychology* (1916).

B. SPILKA

ANALYTIC (JUNGIAN) PSYCHOLOGY, HUMANISTIC PSYCHOLOGY, *or* PSYCHOANALYSIS, AND RELIGION *or* THEOLOGY; PSYCHOLOGY AND PSYCHOTHERAPY (East-West Comparison). *See also* FAITH DEVELOPMENT RESEARCH; JOURNALS IN RELIGION, THEOLOGY, AND THE SOCIAL SCIENCES; MORAL BEHAVIOR AND RELIGION; MYTHOLOGY AND PSYCHOLOGY; PSYCHOLOGY, EASTERN *or* WESTERN; PSYCHIATRY AND PASTORAL CARE; PSYCHOPATHOLOGY AND RELIGION; RELIGION AND HEALTH; RELIGION AND PSYCHOTHERAPY. *Compare* CULTURAL ANTHROPOLOGY; PASTORAL THEOLOGY; PHILOSOPHY AND PSYCHOLOGY; SOCIOLOGY; THEOLOGY AND PSYCHOLOGY; THEOLOGY AND PSYCHOTHERAPY. *Biography:* ADLER; ALLPORT; BOISEN; ERIKSON; FREUD; FROMM; GODIN; HALL; JAMES; JUNG; KUNKEL; LAKE; LAMBOURNE; LEUBA; MASLOW; MOWRER; OATES; PFISTER; PRUYSER; REICH; REIK; SCHARFENBERG; STARBUCK.

PSYCHOMETRICS. *See* EVALUATION AND DIAGNOSIS, PSYCHOLOGICAL; PSYCHOLOGY, WESTERN.

PSYCHONEUROSIS. *See* NEUROSIS.

PSYCHOPATHIC PERSONALITY. *See* ANTISOCIAL PERSONS.

PSYCHOPATHOLOGY, THEORIES OF. Presumptions about the origin and appearance of abnormal human behavior. Proposed definitions of what is normal or abnormal must necessarily be prefaced with the statement that what is considered to be pathological will vary from one culture to another. One definition which is accepted by many is that behaviors, thinking, affect, and perceptions may be considered pathological when they are dysfunctional, self-defeating, or maladaptive for the individual and thus contribute to a lack of (a) personal comfort, happiness, and well-being, (b) satisfaction in interpersonal relationships, and (c) fulfillment and actualization of personal potential.

The cause or precedent of psychopathology may be found in either the remote past or the immediate present. That which is pathological, as well as that which is normal, must be viewed within the context of a given person's own unique complex of attitudes, memories, expectations, behaviors, perceptions, and interpersonal experiences. The individual's unique personal history, physical composition, intellectual capacity, interpersonal relationships, and cultural environments, are all seen as contributing to either pathology or normality. However, certain general features of these dynamics have been determined as the discussion of the several themes will demonstrate.

1. **Genetic.** Is the development of schizophrenic psychosis somehow controlled by inherited, predispositional— i.e. genetic — factors? In his classic study involving 691 schizophrenic twin-index families, noted researcher Franz Kallman and associates (1964) found morbidity rates as follows: 1.8 percent for step-siblings; 2.1 percent for marriage partners; 7.0 percent for half-siblings; 14.3 percent for full siblings; 14.7 percent for dizygotic co-twins; and 85.8 percent for monozygotic co-twins. The difference in morbidity rates between dizygotic and monozygotic co-twins was found to be that of one to six. Such studies are posited as evidence for the genetic component in the etiology of psychopathology while others say that the fact that not all monozygotic twins were concordant for schizophrenia is an argument *against* the genetic factor in psychopathology.

Some (e.g. Kety, 1983) believe that hereditary elements are responsible for a predispositional "susceptibility to psychopathology" in addition to the possible role of environmental factors. In addition, a confusion of "ego identity" on the part of monozygotic twins may also be involved as a non-genetic factor in the development of psychopathology in twins. This issue revolves around the assumed close association and identification between the monozygotic twins. Thus, after one twin has developed a particular psychopathology, the co-twin may be more vulnerable simply because the latter fears (or even anticipates) that he or she too will develop a similar disorder.

In summary, because of genetic predispositions, an individual may develop a particular psychopathology more readily than someone without the same hereditary vulnerability even though both are subjected to similar environmental stresses and pressures.

2. **Biochemical.** Closely related to the genetic factors in psychopathology is another biological component, namely, the biochemical one. This is a factor which has long been considered to be implicated in the causation of pathology. As far back as Hippocrates who posited four body fluids (phlegm, blood, black bile, yellow bile), there have been those who have advocated that biochemical factors are the key to our understanding of "mental disorders." Questions which need to be pondered throughout this discussion is: (1) Do biochemical factors *cause* psychopathology, (2) change *concurrently* with the disorders or (3) *result* from preceding psychological-emotional problems?

Among the biochemical factors which have been implicated in the etiology of mental disorders is one referred to as the "plasma factor." The hypothesis here is that there is some blood-borne factor present in persons suffering from schizophrenia which is not found in blood of normal subjects.

Another hypothesis is that a particular biochemical imbalance affects the cellular function of the brain and thus creates a physiological disorder which produces behavioral symptoms.

One biochemical factor which has received a great deal of attention in the past is dimethoyphenylethylamine (DMPE) which when placed on a paper chromatogram leaves a pink spot. It is alleged that this DMPE is found more frequently in the urine of schizophrenics than in that of others although it is also found in the urine of others occasionally.

The biogenic amine hypothesis holds that there is an excess of such neurotransmitters as epinephrine, norepinephrine, and dopamine in the manic and schizophrenic disorders and that there is an inadequate supply of these same transmitters in the case of depression.

Countless other biochemical factors have been posited as perhaps involved in the causation of psychopathology such as cerebral serotonin, disturbances in lipid metabolism, hyperglycemic factors, and histamine.

Although the issues are still unclear, it is generally accepted that chemical imbalances are involved in the schizophrenic and more serious affective disorders. The question of whether they are the cause, the effect or the concomitant of psychopathology is still being debated.

3. Psychoanalytic. Basically, the psychoanalytic explanation of the etiology of psychopathology is that the individual has not successfully passed through the stages of psychosexual development. The roots of such psychopathology as depression are seen in the very earliest stage of psychosexual development, that is, in the oral dependent stage. In the psychoanalytic view, the obsessive concern with neatness, cleanliness, and parsimoniousness, and an inability to live with confusion or ambiguity are believed to have their roots in the anal retentive stage. Likewise, the superego which is the incorporation of societal and, in particular parental, values is believed to develop in the phallic stage (probably beginning in the third year of life and extending through the fifth year) and where this superego development has been weak, such things as antisocial behavior often result in later life.

Many forms of aberrant behavior and symptomatology result from the attempt to deal with anxiety which comes from being threatened by the real world, by the id, and by the superego. In order to deal with this anxiety, numerous defense mechanisms may be employed by the ego, such as repression, displacement, reaction formation, intellectualization, projection, denial, rationalization, and regression. Because these defense mechanisms are used to deal with the threat coming from unconscious material, the strictures of the superego, and the demands of the outside world, a great deal of psychic energy is consumed which could be spent much more productively. All of the defense mechanisms are not viewed as being undesirable but are generally seen as less than a realistic means of dealing with the demands imposed upon the ego.

4. Behavioral-Social Learning. The behavioral perspective on psychopathology is that both normal and abnormal behavior develop according to the very same principles of *learning*, with the particular behavior in focus being specified in exact, observable, and measurable terms. Where problem behaviors exist, they can be changed by manipulating certain variables, reinforcing appropriate behaviors, and extinguishing maladaptive ones. Nonempirical factors such as unconscious material, disease processes, and existential phenomena are thus avoided by the behaviorists.

One of the names most prominently mentioned in the initial work done in the area of behaviorism is that of John Broadus Watson (1878–1958) who worked primarily within a Pavlovian model of conditioning (classical or respondent). Within this conceptualization, phobias, for example, are the result of some stimulus (conditioned stimulus) having been associated with a frightening object or experience (unconditioned stimulus). The conditioned stimulus then develops the power to elicit the same emotional response as the unconditioned stimulus. This response is involuntary, autonomic, automatic, and reflexive. Such responses can be extinguished if the conditioned stimulus is presented frequently enough without being associated with the original unconditioned stimulus with which it was paired.

The second major trend in the behavioral approach to psychopathology centers around the name of B. F. Skinner and the model which has come to be known as operant learning. According to this position, behaviors are emitted because of the consequences which will ensue from the environment. Behaviors, both normal and abnormal, tend to be strengthened when they receive a reward or positive reinforcement or when they result in the avoidance of punishment or other aversive consequences. Abnormal behaviors may thus be seen as initiated and maintained because they are rewarded with such things as attention and monetary gain, or because they represent a way of avoiding or escaping something undesirable or unpleasant.

The social learning approach which is closely related to the behavioral perspective is exemplified in what is known as "modeling." The name most prominently associated with this is that of Albert Bandura. Whereas in operant conditioning, a response, once it is emitted, is either rewarded or punished, in social learning (modeling), an entirely new response may be learned simply by observing another person emitting the behavior and receiving the consequences of it. Both normal and abnormal behaviors can be learned by watching a model. Some particular behaviors may be inhibited in the future because the subject has seen the model receiving the aversive outcomes of that behavior.

5. Cognitive. The cognitive perspective on psychopathology emphasizes the importance of an individual's lack of ability to interpret information properly and to use it in solving vital problems. Thus irrational or erroneous thinking is seen as both precipitator and maintainer of psychopathology. Psychological disorders are seen as resulting from failing to attend properly to the things, events, or persons in the environment and to use realistic and available information. Because of this, the individual misperceives reality and thus misinterprets what is going on in the world.

One of the names which is usually mentioned in the cognitive approach to psychopathology is Aaron Beck who claims that psychopathology, and depressions in particular, result from errors in cognition such as arbitrary inference (conclusions of a negative nature from situations that are essentially neutral or impersonal), selective abstraction (focusing on a small piece of evidence taken out of context and exaggerated), over-generalization (drawing a far-too-general conclusion on the basis of a single incident or experience), and other thinking of a similar nature.

Another leading proponent of the cognitive approach to explaining psychopathology is Albert Ellis, who in 1956 began to develop what is known as Rational-Emotive Therapy (RET). The cardinal point in RET is that one feels and acts the way one thinks. If thinking is irrational, illogical, or unrealistic, one will experience distressing uncomfortable emotions and/or will engage in maladaptive and self-defeating behaviors. A foundational point in RET is that an activating event or experience in the life of the individual does not directly cause the emotion or behavior, but is rather the result of how that experience is mentally processed by the individual. In RET, it is held that emotional distresses and maladaptive behaviors are often originally learned or aggravated through the early inculcation of irrational beliefs by significant others but these irrationalities are not automatically sustained over the years unless the individual actively and creatively reinstills them. It is the repetition of such irrational thinking that sustains and perpetuates distress and self-defeating behaviors. The individual is thus seen as responsible for the continuation of irrational thinking and as needing to accept responsibility for emotional discomfort and maladaptive behavior.

6. Social Influence. The social influence perspective of the etiology of psychopathology is based on community psychology. There are primarily two explanations given. The first of these is the theory of *social causation* which views such things as poverty, crime, inadequate housing and education, and prejudices which tend to be found in certain clusters or neighborhoods as increasing the stress which is felt by people living there. These social factors are thought to provoke psychopathology. The second theory is that of social *selection* which states simply that people who are unable to deal effectively with the demands of their environment tend to gravitate downwards into so-called lower classes and that this therefore increases the number of people at the lower socio-economic stratum which will manifest psychopathology.

7. Interpersonal. The interpersonal approach to explaining psychopathology states that most behaviors, thoughts, affects, and perceptions are the result of ineffective or detrimental relationships with others. Virginia Satir (1972, 1975), for example, holds that behavior results from "interactional experiences," not from "psychic forces." In 1948 Frieda Fromm-Reichmann coined the term "schizophrenogenic mother" to describe overprotective and controlling women who keep their children from developing as independent, self-confident individuals.

Gregory Bateson and associates (1956) have proposed a concept which has become important in the interpersonal approach to explaining the etiology of psychopathology, namely, the "double bind." In this "double bind" conflicting messages are received, one being on a verbal level, and the other often non-verbal. As a result of these double messages the individual feels "damned if she/he does and damned if she/he doesn't." Because of the extreme difficulty in knowing what the expectations are, the individual receiving the double bind messages will tend to be withdrawn and regressive. In the process, significant, healthy interpersonal relationships are not developed and the result is what has been called the "burnt-child reaction."

In 1967 Theodore Lidz began to talk of marital schism and marital skew as interpersonal factors involved in development of psychosis (1976). By "marital schism," Lidz means that the child is drawn into the conflict between the parents, both of whom seem to need having the child allied with them in the marital battle, which results in much "tearing" for the child. In the "marital skew" situation, significant psychopathology is demonstrated or modeled particularly with regard to marriage and parenthood, the consequence being the child's accepting such a distorted presentation of marriage and parenthood as "normal."

8. Existential-Humanistic. In the existential explanation of the etiology of psychopathology the emphasis is placed on the fact that people have had a choice in which they could have chosen authentic living but have instead elected to live inauthentically. Rollo May (1977), prominent existentialist, sees anxiety as the result of making a forced choice which would imply movement either forward or backward; when anxiety is not used constructively, the result is guilt. Anxiety for May is further seen as representing the "threat of imminent non-being."

R. D. Laing (1969), an English existential psychiatrist, sees schizophrenia as representative of the splitting between the facade which the person tries to present to the world and that real or true inner self which is not expressed. Laing believes that the strange behaviors which are witnessed in the case of schizophrenia are basically the result of the false facade being stripped away and the individual's fears and distortions being directly exposed. In this way, Laing sees serious psychopathology as a positive experience because at last a truer "outer self" is manifested.

Another prominent person in the existential approach is Carl Rogers (1959, 1961). He believes that in striving to fulfill the "conditions of worth" which have been imposed upon the individual from childhood, the person will filter out those things which come from within (the organismic valuing process) which do not conform to those conditions which need to be met in order to feel personal worth. Consequently, there is a conflict between "the self" that is fashioned by what the person perceives others want him or her to be and the *organismic* self. Essentially then, this means that others are allowed to "define one's self." In all of this, there is a distortion or denial of the person's own experiencing and a blocking of self-actualization. This conflict between the self and the organism is termed by the Rogerians as incongruence and, in cases where that conflict is great enough, an individual may become immobilized by the resulting anxiety. For the person who is functioning in a healthy fashion, there has been the experience of unconditional positive regard from significant others and no conditions of worth have been imposed. Consequently, a state of congruence exists as the person is aware of the organismic valuing process and does not have to distort or defend it in any way. In essence, such a healthy person is free to respect and value all the manifestations of himself or herself.

Abraham Maslow (1987), another existentialist, believes that if the environment is without adequate love or stability, people will need to spend most of their time in satisfying the needs which are lowest on the hierarchy of needs and never be able to devote themselves to gratification of higher needs, in particular that of self-actualization. Maslow speaks of abnormal behavior as, in a sense, never getting beyond the "normal behavior" of holding a job, taking care of the children, and keeping self physically clean and healthy. Such persons, even though quite "normal" will very likely still be lonely and unfulfilled. Maslow speaks of such people as manifesting "the psychopathology of the normal."

Victor Frankl (1985), the Viennese psychiatrist who survived the concentration camps of World War II, speaks of abnormal behavior as resulting from existential frustration of the "will-to-meaning." When the meaning to life, or the purpose to life, is not found, "a person will tend to drift aimlessly like a ship without a rudder." Frankl believes that people need something to live for, something to look forward to, something that transcends themselves to which they can give themselves. According to Frankl, meaning to life can be found in creative values (such as experiencing the achievement of a task that establishes a person in the world), experiential values (experienced through the appreciation of the good and beautiful in the world and in the loving of another person), and in attitudinal values (experienced through dealing with one's suffering).

Still within the general existential camp is the Gestalt approach which emphasizes that if a person has "unfinished business," which refers to unresolved issues in the past, there will be an interference with growth and development, and stagnation and regression will result. In the presence of unfinished business, awareness is blocked, need cycles cannot be completed, tension remains at a high level, and emotions rise but are left unexpressed. In all of this, the natural flow of behavior is clogged or stopped and the person is constricted and frustrated. In this state, the result is despair, boredom, lack of autonomy, lack of spontaneity, and lack of intimacy. At best, life is bland and unfulfilled. Psychopathology is seen as too much experiencing in the "there and then" (past or future) instead of the "here and now." Persons who are experiencing almost any kind of psychopathology are viewed as having not been aware of their present feelings and the options available to them and as failing to take responsibility for their own behavior, thoughts, and feelings.

9. **Multimodal-Interactional.** In this perspective on psychopathology, a multiplicity of factors is seen as being potentially involved. Any one or all of them may be involved in the disorders at hand. Arnold Lazarus (1976) has been a pioneer in what is called Multimodal Behavior Therapy. Although the approach leans heavily on behavioral and cognitive principles it also goes beyond those. Lazarus includes seven vantage points on psychopathology: *behavior* patterns (such as compulsions, habits, mannerisms); negative *affect* or emotions (anxiety, depression, etc.); unpleasant *sensations* (aches, pains, dizziness, etc.); undesirable *images* (such as disturbing memories of unpleasant events or scenes); faulty *cognitions* (self-defeating beliefs and attitudes); *interpersonal* shortcomings (overcompetitive striving, aggressiveness, childish demands); and physiological factors which may influence all six of the above.

Theodore Millon (1974) has attempted to integrate the various intraorganismic and environmental factors which may contribute to psychopathology in what he has termed an interactional approach. In this approach, there is a "reciprocity and circularity of influence" among these forces through a multidetermined developmental process.

The multimodal-interactional approach to the etiology of psychopathology is deemed eclecticism in the best sense of the word in that it allows for and considers many potential factors as apt to be involved. None of the approaches discussed in this article can be quickly or automatically ruled out; instead each is seen as important. In addition, there is an openness to the possibility that there are factors involved in the etiology of psychopathology which are not yet known but which may well be added to the factors which are already believed to be causative or, at the least, concomitant. In its most simplified form the multimodal-interactional approach might be stated as considering the interaction between predispositional factors, precipitating life-experiences, and individual personality composition.

Realizing that psychopathology is a multifaceted and interwoven entity, clergypersons need to assess their expertise as well as limitations to determine when to work with the troubled person and when to refer to a mental health professional.

Bibliography. A. Bandura, *Social Learning Theory* (1977). G. Bateson, *et al.*, "Toward a Theory of Schizophrenia," *Behavioral Science*, 1 (1956), 251–64. A. T. Beck, *Cognitive Therapy and the Emotional Disorders* (1976). A. Ellis, *Reason and Emotion in Psychotherapy* (1963). V. Frankl, *Man's Search for Meaning* rev. ed. (1985). A. Freud, *The Ego and the Mechanisms of Defense* (1937). F. Fromm-Reichmann, *Principles of Intensive Psychotherapy* (1950). H. Hartmann, *Ego Psychology and the Problem of Adaptation* (1958 [1939]). F. J. Kallman, *et al.*, *Schizophrenia* (1964). S. S. Kety, *Genetics of Neurological and Psychiatric Disorders* (1983). R. D. Laing, *The Divided Self* (1969). A. A. Lazarus, *Multimodal Behavior Therapy* (1976). T. Lidz, *The Person* rev. ed. (1976). A. Maslow, *Motivation and Personality* (3rd. ed., 1987). R. May, *The Meaning of Anxiety* rev. ed. (1977). T. Millon and R. Millon, *Abnormal Behavior and Personality* (1974). C. R. Rogers, "A Theory of Therapy, Personality, and Interpersonal Relationships, as Developed in the Client-Centered Framework," in S. Koch, ed., *Psychology*, vol. 3 (1959); *On Becoming a Person* (1961). V. Satir, *Peoplemaking* (1972); *Helping Families To Change* (1975). B. F. Skinner, *Science and Human Behavior* (1953); *Upon Further Reflection*, 1987). J. B. Watson, *Behaviorism* (1930).

A. J. STRAATMEYER

MENTAL HEALTH AND ILLNESS; PSYCHOPATHOLOGY AND RELIGION; SIN AND SICKNESS. *See also* PERSONALITY, BIOLOGICAL DIMENSIONS OF; BORDERLINE PERSONALITY; DIAGNOSTIC AND STATISTICAL MANUAL III; EVALUATION AND DIAGNOSIS, PSYCHOLOGICAL; NEUROSIS; PERSONALITY DISORDERS; PSYCHOSIS; PSYCHOSOMATIC ILLNESS (Somatoform Disorders). *Compare* DEMONIC; PHILOSOPHY AND PSYCHOLOGY; SALVATION, HEALING, AND HEALTH.

PSYCHOPATHOLOGY AND RELIGION. The relationship between religious and abnormal behavior. Since religions typically offer socially constructed and supported interpretations of the self and the world, their imagery and language are often adopted when the self is deranged or its views of or relations to the world go awry. As Boisen has demonstrated, profound psychological upheaval as well as serious religious malcontent with the self — both crisis situations — operate at a level of experiential or existential depth at which primitive emotions, thoughts, and action tendencies are released from their customary rational control. The person who feels disintegrated or "falling apart" tends to fall back at first on primitive coping devices so as to achieve some tolerable equilibrium; if this regressive process is not stemmed, a more or less widespread primitivization of the inner life and/or overt behavior results. And since religion is usually a combination of creed and cult, religious thoughts and acts influence each other: an irrational belief may lead to an irrational ritual and vice versa.

Freud held that religion begins with the infantile needs of dependent children to see their parents as strong protectors with whose powers it is prudent to be aligned, so that parental benevolence will outweigh their malevolence. According to Freud, religion begins by granting people, through its God concepts, some indulgence in fantasizing about a heavenly protector; it does not insist on an *a priori* renunciation of such wishful fantasies and is therefore not a sublimation, no matter what sophisticated superstructure might be built upon this original indulgence.

Throughout the history of psychiatry evidence has accumulated indicating that serious mental disorder often derives some of its ideational or behavioral content from the patients' religious traditions and practices. Delusions of being a Messiah, the Christ, or Satan, or of being a priest or prophet are not rare, though they may be kept secret for a long time. Conversely, the history of religions shows that deranged persons were often seen as hallowed and sometimes set apart for cultic office, or else were exorcised.

The term "religious psychopathology" is ambiguous. In psychological perspective it refers to mental disorders with significant religious content, in religious perspective it refers to creedal or cultic aberrations that seriously curtail the person's own well-being or thwart his relations to other people, while markedly deviating from the standards of the person's tradition. In most flagrant cases expert psychological and expert religious judgment converge, but in some cases there is room for divergent diagnostic conclusions. The term "religion" covers so much that distinctions must be made between primitive and developed, rational and irrational, confining and liberating, healthy and sick religion, no matter how difficult it may be to distinguish clearly among these sub-groupings.

Pastors may in their counseling and caring roles adopt —among other perspectives—a *functional* view of their clients' religious thoughts, feelings, acts, and values, seeing these as coping devices for dealing with life's stresses in order to reestablish a workable psychological equilibrium. Praying, worshiping, confessing, whether done privately or corporately, can also acquire a defensive meaning for holding excessive anxieties or guilt feelings at bay; the conviction of being unforgivable, having committed an unpardonable sin, or being singled out for punishment by life's adversities can give a quasi-religious rationale to states of puzzlement or depression.

By using the term *disorder* in a broad sense, not confined to recognized psychiatric syndromes, the following groups of religious psychopathology may be arranged:

1. **Narcissistic Disorders.** These are distinguished by conspicuously unrealistic self-regard in either an over-inflated or a self-deprecating direction. In the first case, grandiosity may lead to attributing to oneself superhuman powers and divine or demonic attributes, such as foreknowing the future, penetrating into other people's motives, and displaying conspicuous disregard for reality. In the second case, self-abasement or self-hatred may make one feel damned beyond rescue, perhaps engaged in a pact with the devil.

2. **Thought Disorders.** These include delusional ideas, such as being mistress to the Pope, or of being destined by divine plan to undergo a sex change; paranoid schemes of being singled out to execute God's retributional plans or judgments, of being persecuted, destined for martyrdom, or carrying the burden of all humanity's guilt; magical thoughts of having been immaculately conceived and earmarked for divine favor, often leading to obsessional engagement in praying and other rituals with the utmost perfectionism lest their outcome be spoiled or entail boomerang effects; and preoccupation with hyper-symbolic cosmic ideas such as the all, God, good and evil, male and female, salvation and damnation—often with the utmost polarization between these notions—with conspicuous absence of common sense and awareness of gradations.

3. **Mood and Affect Disorders.** These are indicated by unmodulated and immoderate emotions incommensurate with precipitating events or stimuli. In depression the self is held to be despicable, sinful, unworthy, disloyal, and sometimes unable to receive any forgiveness or grace. The somber person also tends to be preoccupied with past misdeeds or evil thoughts to the extent of not being able to even imagine a different, let alone hopeful, future. In elated states, such as religious ecstasy or frenzy, the self becomes the pivotal point of the universe, grandiose, magically omnipotent, and often overbearing or meddlesome in relation to others; in such a condition some patients become zealous soul winners, proclaimers, evangelists, or founders of some sectarian movement. Mood varies with energy level such that the depressed are lethargic and the elated are hyperactive and ebullient.

4. **Moral Disorders.** The link between religion and ethics, as well as the frequency of moralistic indoctrination in religious education, predispose some believers to a singular preoccupation with right and wrong, virtue and vice, righteousness and sinfulness, and to an overactive or punitive conscience. Excessive, irrational feelings of guilt do not only pertain to deeds, but to unexpressed thoughts as well, with the result that such people find much to condemn in themselves, though by comparative social standards they may appear to be quite upright to others. Some patients even go so far as to confess repeatedly to imagined or imaginary sins (scrupulosity) under the whiplash of their severe conscience, resisting all proclamations of absolution. Others experience their religion in legalistic terms exclusively, holding self or others culpable, demanding retribution, and devoting themselves to finding fault. Somewhat rarer is the blithe absence or denial of any feelings of guilt in people who have clearly transgressed and should seek some expiation or redress. In such cases the laxness of conscience may barely mask an excessive demandingness, arrogance, or grandiose claim of being a favorite child of God.

5. **Behavioral Disorders.** These involve ritual acts that may resemble or abuse sacramental practices. Excessive ritualization of action, accompanied by perfectionism, fear of spoiling, and often with exhaustive preparatory movements and postures is found in compulsions, which are frequently used in the service of warding off some imagined or real threat of evil, contamination, or danger. Persons may pray, cross themselves, reiterate religious phrases, or cleanse themselves compulsively with an apprehensive belief in the magical power of such acts, if done precisely in all prescribed minutiae, to bring

about the desired result and with the counter-fear that a marred performance will bring personal or cosmic disaster. Such persons tend to swing ambivalently between belief and doubt, between praying and blaspheming, between hypercontrol and dyscontrol of their acts. Sudden and conspicuous engagement in acts not customary to the patient's religious tradition, for example, glossolalia, footwashing, or ecstatic shouting for a Presbyterian can be seen as behavioral manifestations of inner turmoil and may be a pious form of acting out against the person's religious affiliates.

A noteworthy sign of brewing religious malcontent, disaffiliation, or alienation is "church hopping," i.e., moving from one denomination to another in a frantic search for external control in compensation for the person's failing inner control over his or her life and actions. Not infrequently, such moves are from liberal to strict denominations or sects which offer clear rules for living and simple interpretations of right and wrong and often provide or encourage direct but solicitous confrontations between the members.

6. Other Disorders. A special group may be earmarked for seeing religious visions and hearing voices, taken as hallucinations, i.e., subjectively sensed as if coming from outside (and thus felt as "real") but without verifiable external stimulus. Some patients will seek to add an objective, message-type character to these utterly subjective experiences. In this they may be supported by their community or tradition, either by offering encouraging responses to their reports, or by the supernatural thrust of the tradition's theology.

Bibliography. A. T. Boisen, *The Exploration of the Inner World* (1952 [1937]) S. Freud, *The Future of an Illusion* (1928); *Civilization and Its Discontents*, (1930). P. W. Pruyser, *A Dynamic Psychology of Religion* (1968).

P. W. PRUYSER

PSYCHOLOGY OF RELIGION; RELIGION AND PSYCHIATRY (History and Issues); RELIGION AND PSYCHOTHERAPY. *See also* EVALUATION AND DIAGNOSIS; JOURNALS IN RELIGION, THEOLOGY, AND THE SOCIAL SCIENCES, INTERDISCIPLINARY; RELIGIOUS BEHAVIOR; RELIGIOUS EXPERIENCE; SALVATION, HEALING, AND HEALTH; SIN AND SICKNESS. *Compare* RELIGION AND HEALTH.

PSYCHOPHYSIOLOGIC DISORDERS. *See* PSYCHOSOMATIC ILLNESS.

PSYCHOSEXUAL DEVELOPMENT. Psychological growth stimulated and shaped by stages of sexuality through which each individual passes from birth to adulthood. It is the experiential impact of sexuality, not genitality, upon personality via the impetus provided by the libido, or psychic energy. Specifically Freudian in origin and content, the order of the stages is oral, anal, phallic, latency, and genital.

M. A. WOLTERSDORF

PSYCHOANALYSIS (Personality Theory and Research); SEXUALITY, BIOLOGICAL AND PSYCHOSOCIAL THEORY OF. *Compare* EMOTIONAL DEVELOPMENT; PERSONALITY DEVELOPMENT.

PSYCHOSIS. The most severe of mental disorders encompassing a heterogeneous group of conditions in which adaptive function is largely lost, relatedness to the environment is at best haphazard, and behavior, including thought and feeling, is disorganized. The psychotic state may be temporary, intermittent, or constant. Different types bear little resemblance to each other except for the seriousness of the disruption they cause in the lives of the affected individuals. Observable behaviors may appear unpredictable, unrealistic, erratic, and often bizarre. It is usually assumed that the affected individual has little control over the condition or resulting behaviors.

Psychosis is divided into two types—organic and functional. Organic psychoses are classified according to causation or similarity of biological damage. Functional psychoses are divided into three categories: affective, schizophrenic, and paranoid.

1. Organic Psychoses. All of these conditions include varying degrees of loss of ability to regulate one's contact and interaction with the environment; there is always a "clouding of consciousness" to some degree. In all cases there is a demonstrable organic defect, either anatomical or chemical. Organicity, that is, the effect of an organic defect in the central nervous system, results in a reasonably coherent clinical appearance. While severe clouding of consciousness is manifest as confusion, stupor, or coma, minimal degrees produce less severe disorientation. An individual may not be able to orient herself or himself in time, to location, or to identifiable people. Loss of function usually progresses in that order— disorientation with regard to time, location, other persons—until orientation in all areas is lost. One's emotions become labile, that is, characterized by intense feelings that shift rapidly. One's judgment appears compromised; the person does not appear to plan ahead or to be aware of the consequences of behavior. Memory defects appear, recent memory often showing considerably greater impairment than memories of events of long ago. In some states, made-up events may replace lost memories—so-called "confabulation."

All of the above symptoms and signs of organicity may exist in varying degrees of severity and, simply or together, may not constitute a psychotic state. The diagnosis of psychosis depends upon a clinical determination of severity and a judgment as to the individual's loss of adaptive capacity ("being in touch with reality").

2. Functional Psychoses. *a. Affective psychoses.* The primary defect noted in this group of disorders is an intense, unrelenting mood that so dominates an individual that all behavior and thought is congruent with the emotion and is relatively unresponsive to the environment. The affective psychoses include depression and mania (elation). These two intense affects sometimes alternate, giving the classic picture of manic-depressive psychosis (or "bipolar disorder," in current terminology).

There are obvious biochemical changes associated with affective disorders, and since there is evidence also of a genetic contribution to the condition, many believe the biological defect is primary. While this is not necessarily the case (the biochemical changes could be secondary to the depression or elation), the presence of an identifiable biochemical defect allows medical intervention. Such treatment has proven reasonably successful. It is probably not coincidental that the diagnosis of "affective psychosis" is made more frequently now that effective treatment is available.

Depressive psychosis appears as an extravagant exaggeration of what is normally recognized as depression. The affected individual is immersed in a dismal world of self-recrimination and self-hatred. Relative immobility, loss of appetite, interest, desire, and sleep, as well as self-preoccupation leave one inaccessible to those in the environment. The condition may be recurring, and if untreated, each episode may last six months or more. Suicide, malnutrition, and dehydration are all complications of the disorder.

Manic psychosis involves the feeling of elation. The affected individual is driven endlessly in a frenzy of action, speech, and thought. Extravagant excesses of expansive ideation (grandiosity) may leave one behaving as if he or she owned the world. Spending sprees are common. As in depressive psychosis, episodes may recur, but, unlike depressive psychosis, the episodes rarely last long before exhaustion, depression, or hospitalization supervene.

b. Schizophrenic psychosis. This is considered the most severe of functional mental conditions. It comprises a group of disorders characterized by personality disorganization, bizarre behavior, functional incapacity, and unrelatedness to the environment. The classic "thought disorder" merely represents the individual's use of language in which content appears of little consequence; communication is not constantly logical. There may be extreme deviant behavior, which includes hearing or seeing things that others do not hear or see (hallucinations) or having fixed ideas that others find unbelievable (delusions). All such symptoms indicate that the individual is isolated from the environment—there has been an abdication of contact with reality.

Of all disorders known to humankind this one has probably engendered more awe, more speculation, and more disparate beliefs than any other. Biochemical, behavioral, genetic, and social theories of causation abound but create no consensus.

The condition seems to exist in two forms: an acute psychosis or a chronic condition. This author believes that the acute form is an entity characterized by an altered state of consciousness where experience is largely managed intuitively within a logical system that is emotional rather than rational. The chronic condition is an adaptive lifestyle incorporating the capacity to experience the acute state, but more often, simply utilizing behaviors learned from the acute state to appear psychotic. Most people, however, believe that the affected individual has no control of behavior. This belief has far-reaching consequences that may further support the condition.

c. Paranoid psychosis. In this disorder we may not be dealing with a psychotic state as much as a restitution of, means of recovery from, or avoidance of (defense against) a psychotic state. Nevertheless, the affected individual has in varying degrees forsaken contact with reality and become preoccupied with an internal belief system, perhaps behaving in accord with it also. The internal belief system is inaccessible to change as a result of lost contact with reality, and is thus a delusion. The belief system usually contains elements of persecution, grandiosity,

and egocentrism, portraying the individual as someone special whom others are out to "get." A common form within this group of disorders that is otherwise relatively rare is paranoid jealousy. The individual becomes convinced that his or her spouse is involved with someone else. Individuals affected by a paranoid condition are designated psychotic depending upon the degree of their loss of contact with reality and the degree of functional impairment. Often intellectual and occupational functioning remain reasonably intact while social and intimate interpersonal functioning are severely disrupted.

Clinical experience has taught that this condition, more obviously than many other mental conditions, involves an environmental complicity. The affected individual often *is* persecuted, although the source may not be obvious. Usually the persecutor is very close to the individual and is adept at lying. The affected individual has a commitment to believe the persecutor and requires an illogical belief to explain his or her experience of persecution.

3. **Social Dimensions.** "Psychosis" has in recent times taken on some of the pejorative connotation formerly held by the term "crazy." As such, even as used by professionals, it indicates a social sanction of the affected individual. Psychotic individuals often appear willfully manipulative, perverse, and devious—simply interested in obtaining gratification of their desires, unusual though they may be. Society grants considerable reinforcement (reward) for this state, especially by considering the affected individual not responsible for his or her behavior and entitled to support and care, exemption from the usual sanctions for misbehavior, release from work, and deserving of unusual attention. A care-taking establishment depends upon these individuals as the means of its employment. All depend upon the psychotic state as one possible way out of situations that seem impossible. The appearance of the psychotic state itself may be therefore seen as a cry for rescue.

Bibliography. S. Arieti, "Affective Disorder," in S. Arieti, ed., *American Handbook of Psychiatry*, 2d. ed., vol. 3 (1974). American Psychiatric Association, *Diagnostic and Statistical Manual of Mental Disorders* 3d. ed., rev., (1987). R. R. Grinker, "Neurosis, Psychosis, and the Borderline States," in A. M. Freeman, H. I. Kaplan, and B. J. Sadock, eds., *Comprehensive Textbook of Psychiatry—II* 2d. ed., vol. I (1975). L. C. Kolb, *Modern Clinical Psychiatry*, 9th ed., (1977). J. Menninger, M. Mayman, and P. Pruyser, *The Vital Balance* (1963). J. D. Page, *Psychopathology* (1975). M. Sim, "Psychosis," in S. Krauss, ed., *Encyclopaedic Handbook of Medical Psychology* (1976).

H. A. SELVEY

MENTAL HEALTH AND ILLNESS; MENTAL HOSPITAL/MENTAL HOSPITALIZATION; PSYCHOPATHOLOGY, THEORIES OF. *See also* DIAGNOSTIC AND STATISTICAL MANUAL III; EVALUATION AND DIAGNOSIS, PSYCHOLOGICAL; MANIC-DEPRESSIVE (Bipolar) DISORDER; MULTIPLE AND DISSOCIATIVE PERSONALITY; ORGANIC MENTAL DISORDER; PSYCHOPATHOLOGY AND RELIGION; SCHIZOPHRENIA; SUSPICIOUSNESS AND PARANOIA. *Compare* BORDERLINE PERSONALITY; DEMONIC.

PSYCHOSOCIAL DEVELOPMENT. One aspect of personality development that is usually distinguished from physical and cognitive development. Psychosocial development consists of some aspects of both psychosexual and ego development. Psychosexual development explains the individual's major drives and impulses, interpersonal issues, and adjustment to the demands of the social order. Ego development describes the style of impulse control, interpersonal manner, and conscious preoccupations that clarify the person's understanding of self in relation to the social environment. Together psychosocial and ego development focus on the individual's interaction with the social environment and on social role identity and performance.

1. A Psychosexual Model. *a. Assumptions of the model.* Psychosexual development posits sequential stages in life in which maturation and/or social demands differentially impact the individual. As one matures, both changes in one's body — such as puberty — and changes in social demands force new adjustment tasks. No matter how well or poorly a particular stage is managed, changing circumstances, external and internal, bring the next one.

b. Erikson's psychosexual model. This model theorizes eight stages: (1) *Trust versus mistrust.* The infant undergoes an intense emotional conditioning toward life. Sufficient predictability and concern for the child's well-being allow the infant to see itself as acceptable and the universe as kind. Such trust, necessary for the religious ethos, makes possible the experience of reverence and surrender to Providence.

(2) *Autonomy versus shame and doubt.* To maintain self-esteem, the now active child must not be given self-control problems that are too difficult. Shaming may lead to later self-consciousness. Doubt may produce uncertainty about ability to manage oneself. In this stage appreciation of law and order, rights and obligations, privileges and limitations, is established.

(3) *Initiative versus guilt.* Self-guidance and self-punishment become possible. If too much of a child's enjoyment of new mental and motor skills is interpreted as bad conduct, initiative may be crushed and children may consider any enjoyment of themselves to be evil. Religious rituals help shape the child's self-image and suggest behavior to imitate.

(4) *Industry versus inferiority.* Education into the culture's technology begins. When one's skills seem inadequate, discouragement may lead to becoming a "drop-out" from society. Cooperative participation in religious ritual begins. A sense of stewardship and seeing oneself as a "tool" for God's purposes may develop.

(5) *Identity versus role confusion.* Body changes raise identity concerns. Adolescents cluster with similar others to understand themselves. Sometimes they make premature commitments—to persons, an ideology, or a career—to solve identity problems. Initiating adolescents into religious adulthood is thus questionable on developmental grounds.

(6) *Intimacy versus isolation.* Young adulthood is the time for personal, ideological, and vocational commitments, though many people are poorly prepared for this. Dangers during this stage are estrangement or inadequate relationships. A major task is development of the ethical strength to abide by one's commitments.

(7) *Generativity versus stagnation.* During middle adulthood one should learn to care for and establish the fruits of one's commitments: children, products, or works. It is the time for full ripening of one's capacity for love of neighbor. Failure to acquire this attitude leads to increasing self-preoccupation and self-indulgence.

(8) *Integrity versus despair.* In old age, one completes the trust task begun in infancy. Those who achieve ego integrity are not afraid to die. Those who fail suffer many regrets and disgusts with life. Personal integrity should be the mainstay of one's entire life.

2. An Ego Development Model. *a. Assumptions of the model.* Stages occur in a fixed order, and none can be skipped. One cannot move to a higher stage until satisfactory completion of earlier ones. Each stage will be the terminal one for some people, and some adults will remain at relatively low levels of development.

b. Loevinger's ego development model. This model also proposes eight stages: (1) *Impulsive stage.* This stage is appropriate to early childhood. Actions are seen as bad only when punished. Interpersonal relations are exploitive, with others seen as sources of supply. Temper tantrums and running away are common ways of managing problems. Adults at this level see responsibility as a burden, and believe that troubles rest in places (the bar on the corner) rather than situations (my drinking).

(2) *Self-protective stage.* These individuals have an expedient morality and observe rules only to gain advantage. A simple hedonism governs their lives. They see others' gain as personal loss. Power and advantage are very important to the adult at this stage. They tend to be prejudiced, to have a hostile sense of humor, and to retaliate for hurts suffered.

(3) *Conformist stage.* This level is appropriate to the elementary school years. Conformists obey existing rules simply because they are the rules. Disapproval is a potent sanction for them. They tend to moralize, judge others by rigidly absolute standards, and strongly disapprove of deviation from conventional social and gender roles. They frown on ingroup hostility, but may scapegoat others outside their family, religious, or political groups.

(4) *Self-aware level.* Though appropriate to late adolescence, this is the most common terminal level of development. One recognizes one's own deviations from conformist norms. This brings ability to see multiple possibilities in situations, to recognize exceptions to rules, and to evaluate conduct according to context.

(5) *Conscientious stage.* For those developing this far, the college years are the modal age for conscientiousness. Morality is internalized, and is defined more by consequences and motives than by rules. The greatest self-criticism occurs at this stage where idealism and achievement motivation are high. Interpersonal relationships are based on shared values rather than shared social activities. The conscientious may try to impose their self-chosen values on others.

(6) *Individualistic level.* Tolerance for oneself and others increases, as does awareness of inner conflict. Preoccupations include social problems and personal development (as opposed to simple achievement). Interpersonal relationships become more intensive.

(7) *Autonomous stage.* Impulse control ceases to be a problem. Moral concern is with appropriateness and priorities. Inner conflict is acknowledged and managed.

Personal ties are cherished, and one values one's own and others' autonomy. Self is seen in a broad social context.

(8) *Integrated stage.* This rare level of development is very similar to Erikson's idea of ego integrity.

3. **Usefulness of the Models.** The *psychosexual model* informs us of the expected life tasks and problems of different times of life. It makes us aware of the consequences of inadequate solutions to these issues and shows ways in which religion can foster or impede development. The *ego development model,* on the other hand, offers a way of discerning the relative maturity of individuals. By understanding the unique constellation of psychological characteristics that define each stage, we can assess how closely one matches any given stage. Knowing what the next expected signs of development should be helps one become aware of the signs of its appearance.

4. **Cautions in Using the Models.** Most people can understand levels beyond their own, and it is easy to mistake such understanding as an indication that one is actually functioning at that higher level. One will almost inevitably overestimate one's own level. Sometimes distinguishing preconformists from postconformists is difficult. Social protestors fall on both sides of conformity. Though the difference between a Gandhi or Martin Luther King, Jr., and those who burn and loot is obvious, such distinctions are not always so easy. It should also be noted that one's conversation often reflects principles and understandings that are not manifest in behavior. Quite often actual behavior indicates a lower level of psychosocial development than does verbalization.

Bibliography. E. H. Erikson, *Childhood and Society* 2d ed. (1963) and *Toys and Reasons: Stages in the Ritualization of Experience* (1977). J. Loevinger, "The Meaning and Measurement of Ego Development," *American Psychologist,* 21 (1966), 195–206; *Ego Development* (1976).

M. J. MEADOW

HUMAN DEVELOPMENT; LIFE CYCLE THEORY AND PASTORAL CARE; MORAL DEVELOPMENT; PERSONALITY DEVELOPMENT; PSYCHOSEXUAL DEVELOPMENT. *See also* CONSCIENCE; DEVELOPMENTAL THEORY AND PASTORAL CARE; EGO PSYCHOLOGY; FAITH DEVELOPMENT RESEARCH; SELF-UNDERSTANDING. *Compare* INTERPERSONAL THEORY; SOCIAL CONSCIOUSNESS AND RESPONSIBILITY; SOCIAL ISOLATION; SOCIAL PSYCHOLOGY.

PSYCHOSOMATIC ILLNESS. From *psyche* (soul) and *soma* (body), psychosomatic illness is a term currently used to describe those disorders of human beings which are considered to be especially due to complex mind/body/spirit interactions, including reactions to stress. The term "psychosomatic," as now used in medicine and psychology, is intended to convey the idea that all health disorders result from a complex interaction between heredity and environment, nature and nurture. Indeed, it is difficult to think of a disease or health problem that is *entirely* physiological or *entirely* mental. In this sense all diseases are "psychosomatic."

1. **General Concept.** In current thinking illness is understood as a complex interaction of physical and physiological, psychological, sociological, and spiritual factors. Such factors include the personality of the patient, built-in (genetic) abnormality, environment, stress, and lifestyle. For instance, it is now becoming clear that a large number of physical disorders are related to deficiencies in the immune system and that the effectiveness of this system is reduced by psychological and social factors such as stress. (The most common bodily systems involved in stress-produced reactions are the pulmonary, cardiovascular, gastrointestinal, genitourinary, and immune systems.) Even contagious diseases need a fertile soil in which to grow; such soil can often be created by psychological factors like disappointment, anxiety, and feelings of rejection.

Over the years certain specific disorders came to be designated as psychosomatic because psychogenic factors were suspected of playing a prominent role in their etiology. These included peptic ulcer, colitis, asthma, hay fever, arthritis, hypertension, amenorrhea, enuresis, paroxysmal tachycardia, migraine headache, sexual impotence, insomnia, alcoholism and drug addiction. There remains considerable debate and uncertainty in scientific research, however, concerning the relative importance of psychological and physical factors in these conditions taken as generalized categories, and the etiology of particular cases may vary. Thus it is probably wise not to form dogmatic or generalized opinions about particular disorders.

2. **Suggestions for Prevention and Treatment.** The materialistic slant of our culture and recent dramatic advances in medical technology have made it difficult for many today to appreciate the psychological and social components of illness. This may be seen especially in the fact that the use of drugs (both prescription and over-the-counter) for the management of human disorders of all kinds has become pervasive in our society. Such an exclusive reliance on medication is questionable; many believe it excessive and undesirable. Besides often creating troublesome side effects (like restlessness, drowsiness, loss of sexual drive, depression, diarrhea, apathy, and insomnia), drug therapy taken by itself, as a primary or singular response to health problems, fails to respond to the full meaning and complexity of illness and its multiple interacting determinants.

Thus it has become important to cultivate a broader public understanding of medical disorders and to develop strategies and techniques of health care that relate to the whole person and to the complexity of health and illness. Following are a few suggestions for non-drug approaches to the prevention and management of the psychosomatic complexity of illness:

a. Supportive social contexts. Studies of communities throughout the world support the view that the nature of the interaction between lifestyle and social support systems will determine to a large measure the health and longevity of the individual. Psychosocial factors even influence both the time and nature of dying. A loving and forgiving neighborhood can help the person live a longer and healthier life. So can other supportive groups such as those of a church, a club, a school, children and grandchildren, and friends. It should be pointed out here that adversity is not uniformly destructive.

Today it is abundantly clear that marriage, positive religious attitudes, feelings of usefulness and well-being, and mental and physical activities, are all major influences in managing pathology and disease. Body, mind, and spirit operate together to affect resistance to disease and to promote healing of damages done. Genetic and biological factors always play a role in disease and death, but their precise expression can often be significantly modified by psychosocial factors.

b. Meditation. It is important to distinguish between meditation as used here and the common mental activities of contemplation, rumination, thinking, and self-induced lethargy. The process of meditation as a therapeutic factor attempts to gain mastery over attention and quiet the insistent activity of the mind. When the mind is still, we will experience that aspect of our being which is prior to and distinct from our focused thoughts and attention. This state may be described as transcendental consciousness. With practice and patience persons can learn to eliminate the mind's powerful tendency to produce thinking and related activities.

Meditation has been found to be effective in reducing stress and in establishing a favorable guiding belief system for living. When authentic meditation is achieved, it is not unlike an experience of religious conversion. Dramatic lifestyle changes may occur, leading to better health practices and to the elimination of sickness. Such psychosomatic disorders as asthma, hypertension, headaches, colds, and insomnia have been successfully treated by meditation. Reductions in the usage of alcohol, cigarettes, coffee and other drugs have been reported as a result of meditation programs.

c. Relaxation and visualization. Basic to many therapeutic approaches is relaxation. The best way to attain a relaxed state is to let the sensations of ease and peace come and take over while avoiding active *striving* for relaxation. Agreeable feelings of warmth and love should be welcomed. Out of this soil of physical and mental well-being the act of visualization can be cultivated to picture the defeat of any and all destructive forces within the body. The patient visualizes his or her disorder as the heat and noise of a battle between opposing forces within, the structures and functions of his or her own good body and the invaders, the bad ones, bent on destruction. One imagines a great army and navy of good fighters (white blood cells) killing the foreign invaders and/or insurgents (bacteria, cancer cells . . .) and carrying them off through the blood to be disposed of by the kidneys. The swelling or fever or pain is then visualized as disappearing with the end of the battle. Peace is restored and all is well again.

These suggestions for managing psychosomatic disorders are certainly not all that is needed. It is especially important not to engage in these activities as a magical flight from reality, reducing the organic aspects of illness to nothing but psychological processes and neglecting or repudiating other forms of treatment. On the contrary, it is important to recognize the complexity of illness and treat it accordingly. Thus medical treatment, surgery, various forms of psychotherapy and biofeedback will remain as powerful tools in the treatment of all human ills. However, it is also important to note that psychosocial factors such as group support, emotions and imagery can have profound impacts upon the complicated neurophysiological and immunological systems of the body.

Bibliography. A. Anderson, "How the Mind Heals," *Psychology Today*, (Dec. 1982). H. B. Benson, *The Mind/Body Effect* (1979). L. H. Evans, Jr., *Creative Love* (1977). K. R. Pelletier, *Mind As Healer Mind As Slayer* (1977); *Longevity, Fulfilling Our Biological Potential* (1981). J. A. Sanford, *Healing and Wholeness* (1977). A. T. W. Simeons, *Man's Presumptuous Brain* (1961). O. C. Simonton, *Getting Well Again* (1978). O. C. Simonton and S. Simonton, "Belief Systems and Management of the Emotional Aspects of Malignancy," *J. of Transpersonal Psychology*, 7 (1975), 29–47. R. L. Taylor, *Mind or Body* (1982). C. W. Wahl, *New Dimensions in Psychosomatic Medicine* (1964). N. B. Woods, *The Healings of the Bible* (1958).

L. E. TRAVIS

MENTAL HEALTH AND ILLNESS; MIND-BODY RELATIONSHIP; PSYCHOPATHOLOGY, THEORIES OF. *See also* COMMUNITY, FELLOWSHIP, AND CARE; EVALUATION AND DIAGNOSIS, PSYCHOLOGICAL; HEALTH AND ILLNESS; MEDITATION; RELAXATION, PSYCHOLOGY AND TECHNIQUES OF; SUPPORT GROUPS.

PSYCHOSURGERY. The neurosurgical treatment of disorders whose primary manifestation is psychological or behavioral. Many would reserve the term "psychosurgery" to situations in which no organic pathology can be demonstrated and the principle goal of surgery is the modification of behavior.

The most widely known example of psychosurgery is the prefrontal lobotomy (or leucotomy) first performed by the Portuguese neurosurgeon Egas Moniz and used extensively with chronic psychiatric patients in the 1940s and 1950s. Here the major pathway to and from the prefrontal area of the cerebral cortex was surgically severed, generally leaving the patient less anxious and concerned, more emotionally "flat," and certainly more manageable. Although there was little effect on intelligence, prefrontal lobotomy had unfortunate side effects in many cases, such as diminished social sense, distractibility, inability to plan ahead, and changes in the finer aspects of personality. Prefrontal lobotomies were largely discontinued when pharmacological treatments for mental disorders were discovered and became widely used.

Psychosurgery, however, has not been abandoned. Currently there are two principal uses. First is the surgical treatment of habitually violent individuals ("episodic dyscontrol syndrome") whose symptoms are sometimes very similar to psychomotor epileptic seizures. Some of these individuals suffer from undetected seizure activity within brain areas involved in initiating and regulating emotional and aggressive behavior and have unprovoked outbursts of violent and physically destructive behavior of which they later have little or no memory and for which they feel much remorse. Surgical lesion of the amygdaloid nucleus of the limbic (emotional) system of the brain has been successful in ending the violent behavior in some cases. It must be emphasized that few persons with epilepsy are violent, and few habitually violent individuals are so because of a seizure disorder. Brain disorder is not a major source of social violence or crime.

The second current use of psychosurgery is in the treatment of extreme depression, anxiety, or obsessive-compulsive states, or for the relief of intractable pain. These disorders are treated with lesion of the cingulate cortex, another part of the limbic system. The surgical treatment of pain and depression are relatively successful, with equivocal results in the treatment of the other disorders.

Psychosurgery has been an issue of great social debate because of the irreversibility of the treatment, effects on personality, uncertain effectiveness in treating some disorders, the problem of obtaining informed consent for treatment, and the uncertainty of deciding between environmental and biological causes of behavior. Some are concerned about the possible social-governmental misuse of psychosurgery to "eliminate troublemakers." Many automatically consider any procedure that might be labeled "psychosurgery" as crude, inhumane, or immoral. Although much research has yet to be done, including some serious thinking regarding the medical ethics of the treatment, psychosurgery will likely have some minor place in the future battery of neuropsychiatric procedures.

Bibliography. V. Mark and F. Ervin, *Violence and the Brain* (1970). E. S. Valenstein, *Brain Control: A Critical Examination of Brain Stimulation and Psychosurgery* (1974).

W. S. BROWN

MENTAL HEALTH AND ILLNESS; PSYCHOPATHOLOGY, THEORIES OF; *See also* PERSONALITY, BIOLOGICAL DIMENSIONS OF; BRAIN RESEARCH; EPILEPSY; MIND-BODY RELATIONSHIP; PSYCHOSIS. *Compare* ELECTROCONVULSIVE THERAPY.

PSYCHOSYNTHESIS.

PSYCHOSYNTHESIS. A comprehensive psychology which blends Western and Eastern thought with an emphasis on spiritual development. Psychosynthesis first became widely known in North America with the publication of *Psychosynthesis: A Collection of Basic Writings,* by Roberto Assagioli, in 1965. It reflected a growing interest in Western culture for a psychological theory which was innovative, wholistic, and incorporated the transcendent as well as the human dimensions of the person. It has since developed into a viable alternative to psychoanalysis and behaviorism.

Assagioli, the founder of psychosynthesis, was born in 1888 in Venice, Italy. Educated as a medical doctor and as a psychiatrist, he studied and learned the new psychology of his day, psychoanalysis. He felt that Freudian theory provided only a partial description of the human personality. In 1910 he began to formulate the concept of psychosynthesis and spent the rest of his life developing this comprehensive psychology of the human subject that includes the higher self (soul) as well as the libido, the imagination as well as the neurotic complexes, and the will as well as the lower unconscious (id).

Assagioli was influenced by a tremendous breadth of learning, including classical Greek thinkers and Eastern psychology. Consequently, he has not only written a Christian psychology *per se,* but he has produced a work which can deeply enrich the minister in his/her theologizing, preaching, healing and counseling. Psychosynthesis is a series of practical, working techniques which include many approaches to personal and spiritual growth such as the use of affirmations, positive thinking and the will; meditation, prayer, visualization, guided imagery, and journal keeping. These techniques are unified by the concept of a self at the core of every person which can direct the harmonious development of all facets of the personality. Beyond this personal harmony lies access to the more expansive realms of the higher self,

such as creativity, transpersonal experience, intuition, and spiritual development.

Psychosynthesis provides theoretical and practical insight on the integration of theology and psychology, or of faith and practice. It appears to have developed concepts and techniques that many Christians would find useful in developing unconditional love, forgiveness, and spiritual gifts.

Bibliography. R. Assagioli, *Psychosynthesis: A Collection of Basic Writings* (1965). Further resources are found in the *Journal of Transpersonal Psychology* and the *Psychosynthesis Digest.*

D. L. STOLTZFUS

PERSONALITY THEORY (Varieties, Traditions, and Issues); PSYCHOTHERAPY. *See also* PHILOSOPHY AND PSYCHOLOGY, WESTERN; PSYCHOLOGY AND PSYCHOTHERAPY (East-West Comparison); RELIGION AND PSYCHOTHERAPY. *Compare* FORMATIVE SPIRITUALITY; HUMANISTIC PSYCHOTHERAPIES; NEOFREUDIAN PERSONALITY THEORIES AND PASTORAL CARE; POPULAR THERAPEUTIC MOVEMENTS AND PSYCHOLOGIES.

PSYCHOTHEOLOGY.

PSYCHOTHEOLOGY. A system and perspective which views a synthesis between theology and psychology as a necessary and authentic project. Built on the belief that both religion and psychology deal with similar topics and concerns — especially in such areas as guilt, sexual love, and social conscience — this bridging discipline endeavors to build a viewpoint from which experience and behavior can be understood without losing the conceptual strengths of either theology or psychology. As a convergent approach, psychotheology explicitly works at seeing psychology and theology participating in a project of understanding rather than being set over against one another. In its first systematic usage (Stern and Marino, 1970), the perspective was heavily weighted with Christian notions and concepts and drew mostly on psychoanalytic psychology.

Bibliography. B. Narramore and J. D. Carter, *The Integration of Psychology and Theology* (1981). E. M. Stern and B. G. Marino, *Psychotheology* (1970).

O. STRUNK, JR.

INTEGRATION OF PSYCHOLOGY AND THEOLOGY. *See also* PASTORAL THEOLOGICAL METHODOLOGY; PSYCHOANALYSIS AND THEOLOGY; PSYCHOLOGY OF RELIGION; THEOLOGY AND PSYCHOLOGY.

PSYCHOTHERAPIST.

PSYCHOTHERAPIST. An individual acting alone or with others who is considered qualified to affect beneficially the emotional, mental, or behavioral distresses and aberrations of another person or persons through planned nonphysical ministrations.

Any instance of *therapy* assumes the interaction of two parties—the party requiring healing and the party expected to aid a healing process. These two parties conform to roles designated by the terms *sick role* and *healer role.* The roles and the interaction of the parties in the roles are established by convention within the surrounding society. How a society understands the etiology of a given kind of sickness determines how it expects that sickness to be treated. Thus, for example, if the sickness is felt to be caused by invading foreign organisms, then the destruction of these organisms is understood to affect a cure. The title of a particular healer specifies what kind of sickness he or she is to treat and what kind of treatment is expected to be performed.

Two basic requirements govern the role of a psychotherapist: (1) that he or she treat mental, emotional, or behavioral disorders, and (2) that the treatment does not directly affect the physical body.

In order to be recognized by society as qualified to treat mental conditions, an individual must complete an indoctrination period (training) designed specifically for this role. Depending upon the intensity and the length of time spent in such training, as well as on how the program itself is recognized as preparing one for the role, different levels of expertise are recognized. In North American society this generally requires the attainment of an academic degree at the masters level or higher in a mental health field, the role designation being determined by the kind of training. Of those who treat mental conditions, society designates healing power and status in a descending order, according to the amount of training: psychotherapist, counselor, advisor. The individual healer, however, is also a member of society and plays a part in determining his or her designation. Since experience in the role often serves as qualifying expertise, increasing one's status without additional formal training is often recognized — and is often abused.

There is no standard nonphysical treatment of the emotionally disturbed that is recognized by all of society, and there is also very little agreement concerning the etiology of these conditions themselves. However, all treatments depend upon three factors: (1) the disordered individual's interest in changing (society may help to promote this by the application of sanctions), (2) an expectation that the interaction of healer and "sick" party will affect beneficial change, and (3) the interest of the therapist in promoting healing. Generally the interaction concentrates on establishing a bond of mutual cooperation between involved parties, then upon performing some kind of ritual (which always involves the use of a hermeneutical theory interpreting the nature and etiology of the condition) understood to promote cure. Persuasion to become "well" is usually included. Generally speaking, the more complex the ritual and hermeneutic used, the higher the status and designation of both therapy and therapist.

H. A. SELVEY

INTERPROFESSIONAL TEAMS AND RELATIONSHIPS. *Compare* CHRISTIAN PSYCHOTHERAPIST; CLINICAL PSYCHOLOGIST; MARRIAGE AND FAMILY THERAPIST; PSYCHIATRIST/PSYCHIATRY; PSYCHOLOGIST; SOCIAL WORKER; SPIRITUAL MASTERS AND GUIDES.

PSYCHOTHERAPIST, CHRISTIAN. *See* CHRISTIAN PSYCHOTHERAPIST.

PSYCHOTHERAPY. *Psychotherapy* comes from the Greek words *psuche* (mind or soul) and *therapeuo* (one who serves the gods or heals) and denotes attempts to heal the human mind or soul. The first use of the term *psychotherapy* was in 1803 in an article by J. C. Reil. "Since then," Daniel Hogan (1979) writes in his three-volume work on the regulation of psychotherapists, "the term psycho-

therapy has become a lexicographer's nightmare. Definitions abound, though few have much in common with each other and many are antithetical."

Given the state of theory and practice in modern psychotherapy, it is tempting to conclude that there are as many psychotherapies as there are psychotherapists. Such a view is not all hyperbole. A sober review of the psychotherapeutic literature reveals a labyrinthian assortment of theories and practices that transcend even the most outlandish of religious denominationalism. When one realizes, however, that contemporary psychotherapy has deep roots in at least three significant traditions—the Judeo-Christian, the Greco-Roman, and the Anglo-Saxon (Reusch, 1961)—it is possible to appreciate why it is that much of modern psychotherapy appears unsystematic, diffuse, and pluralistic. Nor should this state of affairs be surprising when one examines the inflationary projects too often claimed by psychotherapeutic movements and compares them with the rather conservative expectations of Sigmund Freud (1962)—often considered the founder of modern psychotherapy—who felt that a successful psychoanalysis might be expected to help a person make what is basically an intolerable existence a mite more tolerable.

Nor is the theoretical and technological diffusion of modern psychotherapy difficult to appreciate when one realizes that a great deal of its praxis grows out of a modern field of inquiry which is itself fraught with complexity and division—psychology. Add to this the fact that modern psychotherapy's roots extend as well into medicine, magic, and religion (Ehrenwald, 1976) and it is not difficult to see how vagueness, mystery, and pluralism dominate precision and direct simplicity.

Still, out of this swirling confusion of patterns and propensities it is possible to detect major and visible forms of psychotherapy that tend to persist over time.

1. **Fundamental Features and Variables.** Though its etymology evokes religious, perhaps mystical, images, today's healer is usually an authorized clinician who holds at least one graduate-level degree. The many models of effective therapeutic practice vary because they are based on different theories of human normality and of the origins of personal difficulty. And, though on one level, intellect, emotions, and behavior are inseparable in human beings, most psychotherapeutic approaches emphasize one or another of those avenues in treating people.

In spite of differences in psychotherapeutic methods, several significant features are present in any healing relationship. The first is persistent, structured interaction with the therapist. The other features describe the client's attitude: trust and belief in the therapist's competence and integrity, a perception of the therapist as an empathic and caring human being, a desire to change, and hope that change for the better can occur.

Some psychologists have attempted to classify therapies as either traditional or modern. The former are communal, and ritual and symbolic processes and the power of suggestion play a large role in them. The latter tend to be more individual and rational and claim a basis in more scientific principles. However, many kinds of subtle persuasion play a role in modern therapeutic settings, while traditional therapies may utilize a good deal of rational insight. It is impossible to make a precise, unambiguous distinction between traditional and modern therapeutic approaches.

2. **The Three Major Psychotherapeutic Traditions.** It seems reasonable — though not without serious problems — to view the psychotherapies in broad clusters: the psychoanalytic/psychodynamic therapies, which include all those psychotherapies dominated or strongly influenced by traditional Freudian psychoanalysis and expressing a primary concern with the unconscious; behavioristic/cognitive psychotherapies, which are traceable to the scientific laboratories and rooted deeply in learning theories and in epistemological appreciations; the existential/humanistic/transpersonal psychotherapies, which tend to be based in philosophical, cultural, and religious meaning systems (both West and East), and, although highly pluralistic in terms of methods, hold to serious attempts to be wholistic in both theory and praxis; the eclectic psychotherapies, which often struggle to synthesize a variety of psychotherapeutic approaches and to honor systemic notions; and, finally, the specific psychotherapies, which focus on some rather idiosyncratic cultural or subcultural phenomenon.

In explicating this clustering approach, problematics soon become manifest. The demarcations often become blurred and at times overlap severely. Still, the organization may hold some didactic value and provide at least a set of handles to identify the array of psychotherapies existent today.

a. Psychoanalytic/psychodynamic psychotherapies. Freudian psychoanlaysis, often viewed as the foundational therapy for all psychodynamically oriented psychotherapies, rests on two key notions—psychic determinism and the unconscious (Chessick, 1974). Basically, psychoanalysis is a procedure designed to assist a patient to deal more effectively with unconscious, unacceptable wishes, which tend to produce guilt, somatic symptoms, and disruptions in interpersonal functioning. As a process originally designed to treat the "neuroses," it proceeds in the following stages (Cashdan, 1973):

(1) *Free association*—a stage in which the patient engages in a one-way type of communication that exposes an assortment of fantasies and private thoughts unrestricted by the ordinary controls of logic, syntax, and social strictures.

(2) *Procedure frustration*—a stage in which the patient begins to resist this one-sided process, thus allowing the analyst the opportunity to analyze the various resistances in hope of assisting the patient to begin to see how unconscious forces are roadblocks to change.

(3) *Repression*—a developmental phase in which the patient's unwitting tendency to cast the therapist in the role of a parental figure, thus recapitulating past experiences and behaviors and creating a "transference neurosis."

(4) *Transference insight*—a stage at which the analyst attacks the various distortions implicit in the transference neurosis in an attempt to reveal to the patient how his or her behaviors are not based on anything the therapist has said or done but, instead, on early relationships with parental figures.

(5) *Insight proper*—a stage of analysis where the patient begins to see and understand causal connections between his or her present behavior and attitudes toward the therapist and similar reactions to significant others from the past, thus achieving the basic goal of treatment; that is, making conscious what has been unconscious.

(6) *Working through*—a final phase when a patient takes these newfound insights and relates them to her or his contemporary life, particularly to those troublesome areas fraught with conflict and unhappiness. Armed with a new tool of analysis, the patient is encouraged to use it on his or her own without the need of the analyst.

Historically, it was from these and other psychoanalytic principles that the so-called neo-Freudian approaches were spawned; that is, the theories and therapies of Alfred Adler, C. G. Jung, Otto Rank, Karen Horney, Erich Fromm, and Harry Stack Sullivan (Mullahy, 1948). Essentially, these school psychotherapies, along with the more contemporary psychodynamically oriented psychotherapies such as object-relations theory (Hartmann, 1958; Winnicott, 1958) and the later self-psychology of Heinz Kohut (1977), were and are formulations that stem from reactions and modifications of the parent system.

Psychodynamic psychotherapies remain the bedrock (or quicksand, depending on one's convictions) of much contemporary psychotherapy as practiced in the mainstream of the mental health movement, although its position is constantly being challenged by a variety of pressures and as the result of growing research findings.

b. Behavioristic/cognitive psychotherapies. Whereas psychoanalytic and psychodynamic psychotherapies have tended to have their origins in the clinic and within a medical framework, the behavioristic and cognitive therapies are expressions of the psychological laboratories and the theories of learning tested experimentally within them. Modern behavioral-directed therapies have conceptual roots in magic, religion, and science — as do all forms of psychotherapy—but their central contemporary *raison d'être* is the conviction that so-called emotional problems are really problems of learning; and treatment therefore is in essence a project of relearning. Partly an expression of the turn-of-the-century philosophical writings of the American philosopher John Dewey (1933), the massive attempt to make the stimulus-response (S-R) bond the paradigm of modern psychological science, and the research and speculations of B. F. Skinner, the various behavioral-directive therapies tend to stress problem-solution, not person-change. In these psychotherapies, the therapist is usually actively engaged in attacking the *observable* source of the problem. Conceptually she or he avoids an understanding or insight-slanted approach, emphasizing instead the undoing of inadequate habits and patterns.

In Kovel's (1976) survey of the behavioral-directed therapies he lists the *somatic therapies,* which include all treatments that implicitly or explicitly assume a biological rootage, including the many drug-related therapies; *sex therapies,* which have mushroomed into an objective approach of immense and problematic proportion since the original Masters and Johnson studies; *directive therapies,* which are based primarily on suggestion and would include such strategies as contained in hypnotherapy, Glasser's reality therapy, and Ellis's rational-emotive therapy; and *behavior therapy* proper, a strictly psychological approach that has found wide acceptance in the mental health community (Wolpe, 1958). Indeed, as Kovel notes, "Behavior therapy is definitely the choice of the psychiatric and psychological establishments as the alternative to the psychodynamic treatment informed by the psychoanalytic principles."

Behavior therapy is characterized by its preoccupation with what is observable, testable, quantifiable, reproducible — what is, in short, "objective." Its praxis project therefore is deeply ingrained in a problem-solving mode. In general, effective psychotherapy from this perspective will include the following sequence of operations (Urban and Ford, 1971, p. 9): (1) the systematic and detailed analysis of the presenting problem, (2) the concrete specification of the objectives to be obtained, (3) the selection of procedures in terms of the nature of the problem, (4) orderly and systematic operations to implement the objectives, (5) efforts to obtain an objective verification of the extent to which the goals have been achieved.

This sort of psychotherapeutic approach is utilized by a variety of psychotherapists, many of whom would not ordinarily think of themselves as behavioral therapists.

A more expansive and realistic notion of behavioral therapy is particularly evident when one includes within its perview the so-called cognitive therapies, which began to assume considerable importance in the 1960s. Two examples are the cognitive therapy of Aaron T. Beck (1979) and the rational-emotive therapy of Albert Ellis (1962).

Beck's cognitive therapy is an active, directive, time-limited, structured approach used to treat a variety of psychiatric disorders, particularly depression. The model postulates three specific concepts to explain the psychological substrata of depression: (1) the cognitive triad (negative views of self, negative interpretations of ongoing experiences, and negative views of the future); (2) schemas (relatively stable cognitive patterns which house a group of stimuli); and (3) cognitive errors (faulty information processing). It is from this model that the cognitive psychotherapist attempts to understand the patient and to offer a variety of active techniques designed to alter the essentially defeating kinds of cognitive strategies that bring patients to the therapist in the first place.

Although Albert Ellis's rational-emotive therapy (RET) has been seen, especially by Ellis himself, as a humanistic therapy, many of its technical operations are rooted in a learning paradigm. Its philosophical assumptions are closely aligned to a form of hedonism that is operationalized through cognitive restructuring processes. Conceptually, RET is based on what Ellis has called the ABC theory of learning, where A represents the activating event in the life of client, B is the belief or opinion the client has of that event, and C is the reaction resulting from B. Thus it is that B, not A, becomes the focal point of the therapeutic intent since it is these "irrational ideas" that lead to the psychological pain described by patients. The task of the therapist is to assist the client in recognizing the irrational ideas that are leading to the client's difficulties. This is usually accomplished by a variety of techniques with confrontation being an exceedingly important one.

c. *Existential/humanistic/transpersonal psychotherapies.* If the psychodynamic psychotherapies tend to have roots in medicine and the clinic and the behavioral-cognitive therapies in the scientific laboratory and in learning theories, then the existential-humanistic-transpersonal psychotherapies reach far back into philosophic and literary traditions, and, at the same time, draw from many surface roots that are cultural and even political in nature. In part, these therapies are an expression of a particular *Zeitgeist* — a spirit that is impregnated with the notion of the supreme importance of the human person and his or her potentialities. Within the psychological community, this spirit was personified in an assortment of American psychologists but particularly by the late Abraham Maslow (1962), often viewed as the father of the modern humanistic movement as expressed in the psychological community. Partly stimulated by his writings and presence, a so-called "Third Force" in American psychology was formed, taking particular expression in the founding of the American Association for Humanistic Psychology. The movement's various philosophical postulates gave rise to a variety of expressions in education, political life, institutional forms, and psychotherapy. Often the overall movement has been designated as the existential-phenomenological alternative (Valle and King, 1978), and its praxis has frequently manifested similar terms in psychotherapy. However, the hyphenated designation tends to hide as much as it explains; and it is necessary to see such psychotherapies as more of an approach, or even a spirit, than as "schools" of psychotherapy. Yalom (1980), for instance, defines existential psychotherapy — often influencing these other forms — as a "dynamic approach to therapy that focuses on concerns that are rooted in the individual's existence." His characterization of the stance is both picturesque and accurate:

> Existential psychotherapy is rather much a homeless waif. It does not really 'belong' anywhere. It has no homestead, no formal school, no institution; it is not welcomed into the better academic neighborhoods. It has no formal society, no robust journal . . . , no stable family, no paterfamilias. It does, however, have a genealogy, a few scattered cousins, and friends of the family, some in the old country, some in America (Yalom, 1980, p. 14).

Its European genealogy includes such names as Søren Kierkegaard, Martin Heidegger, Jean-Paul Sartre, Albert Camus, Miguel de Unamuno, and Martin Buber. Transporting these philosophers to American soil and into the psychological community has been carried out by such persons as Viktor Frankl (1963), Rollo May (1958) and Adrian Van Kaam (1966). Their attempts to introduce existential notions into mainstream American psychology have met with mixed results, although *as an approach* existential psychotherapy has had a marked influence on the psychotherapeutic community, particularly among those therapists who work with persons within a "growth motivation" framework. Indeed, James Bugental, one of the leading practicing existential psychotherapists in America, has suggested that such a form of therapy might better be seen as "evocation" rather than therapy, since it deals more with emancipation and transcendence issues than with adjustment and coping types of problems (Bugental, 1978).

Essentially, then, existential psychotherapy is much more an approach and a general stance than it is a systematic theory with specific therapeutic techniques attached to it. In this sense, a Gestalt therapist or a Rogerian or a Freudian might embrace its perspective and still utilize the particular techniques developed by their own therapeutic "school."

Phenomenological psychotherapy has an equally problematic place as one of the psychotherapies being practiced today. Deeply rooted in European phenomenological philosophy, phenomenological psychology was brought into American psychology by Robert B. MacLeod (1947), who considered it to hold great potential for social psychology, which had become chained to a rather positivistic bias. As a perspective or orientation phenomenological psychology concentrates on an unbiased exploration of consciousness and experience. Although such an introduction was aimed at complementing the dominant behavioristic stance of much of American psychology at the time (Giorgi, 1970), its implications for counseling and psychotherapy soon became evident, and the phenomenological method soon became the most acceptable way of relating to clients for humanistic and existential psychotherapies. Much of Rogerian psychotherapy, for instance, is phenomenological in its spirit and approach (Rogers, 1942, 1980), although Rogerian therapy is usually considered a complete representation of the humanistic approach (Kovel, 1976).

Although the humanistic-existential psychotherapies tend to offer an amazingly comprehensive view of the human condition, one of its outgrowths, transpersonal psychology, has developed an even wider mélange of perspectives and psychotherapeutic modes. Often a mixture of humanistic therapy and various Eastern spiritual practices, the "technologies" and praxis of this group defy classification and description. Psychosysthesis, for example — a form of therapy originated by the Italian psychiatrist Roberto Assagioli (1971) — may utilize such techniques as guided imagery, disidentification, dance, dreams, and all varieties of Gestalt methods and tends to see itself as going beyond the personal to what is called spiritual psychosynthesis. As already noted, Bugental (1978) has suggested that such approaches might better be classified as "evocation" rather than therapy in that their intentions are tied to growth motivation, to "inner vision" types of projects, to nonattachment, and to an openness to ultimate awareness. At the same time, their tendency toward what Kovel (1976) calls "totalization" moves very close to such ancient practices as spiritual direction and to the spiritualities often associated with many of the world's major religions.

3. **Eclectic and Specific Developments.** Alongside of these three major psychotherapeutic developments, another grouping of psychotherapies has evolved—the eclectic attempts and the specific therapies. Although often quite similar in their intentions, they deviate significantly enough from the more formal "schools" to constitute legitimate developments that have come to have importance in the practice of psychotherapy.

a. Eclectic psychotherapies. Given the varieties of psychotherapies existing within the three general groupings already noted, it is not surprising that attempts at synthesis and consolidation have increased in recent years. In research conducted in the early 1980s, the trend toward some type of eclecticism became evident. After surveying a random sample of clinical and counseling psychologists who were members of the American Psychological Association, Smith (1982, p. 808) concluded:

The heyday of schools of psychotherapy has passed. Psychoanlaysis remains the most preferred among the schools of therapy but continues to decline in popularity. Even with the steady decline of the psychoanalytic orientation as observed in this and previous studies, however, Sigmund Freud is perceived as still having a strong impact on counseling and therapy.

Eclecticism is clearly the preference of the largest number of psychologists. Yet, there seems to be a dissatisfaction with the term *eclecticism per se*. Concepts such as multimodal, creative synthesis, emerging eclecticism, integration, and systems theory appear to be most descriptive of the current trend toward broad spectrum approaches to counseling and psychotherapy. . . . No single theme dominates the present development of professional psychotherapy. Our findings suggest, however, that cognitive-behavioral options represent one of the strongest, if not *the* strongest, theoretical emphases today. There seems to be a greater interest at this time in therapy systems that emphasize the integration of affect, cognition, and behavior and stress intervention strategies more than heavily theoretical approaches.

The desire for psychotherapy to become more eclectic without at the same time falling prey to what the late Gordon Allport called "bitter eclecticism" constitutes a major thrust in contemporary psychotherapeutic literature. The notion of "prescriptive eclecticism," for instance, is characteristic of such projects. While trying to retain a dynamic model of personality, prescriptive eclecticism at the same time attempts to take into account the many environmental factors that play themselves out in the person seeking help, and to form theory and techniques that are just as appropriate for group psychotherapy and community psychology as for individual psychotherapy, which has tended to dominate the psychotherapeutic movements generally. Although such a synthetic task is just beginning, the vigor of the eclectic movement is powerful enough to carry it well into the next century.

b. Specific psychotherapies. At the same time such eclectic and synthetic projects are going on, a host of specific-type therapies continues to proliferate. Some of these are clearly within traditional psychotherapeutic streams. The short-term and time-limited therapies, for instance, have challenged a variety of myths and offer promise for a whole new assortment of psychotherapeutic services to consumers long thought to stand beyond the long-term, uncovering types of psychotherapies. Although many of the brief psychotherapies—for example, those of Sifneos, Mann, Malan, Davanloo, and Wolberg — carry radically different operational procedures, they remain essentially analytically oriented (Flegenheimer, 1982). Their implications, however, are particularly important in terms of the populations they may service, including the poor and those on the other end of what Goldstein (1971) has called the YAVIS population (young, attractive, verbal, intelligent, successful).

Even more dramatic are those psychotherapies that are aimed at specific social, ethnic, or gender groupings. Family therapy, for example, is a massive and complex assortment of psychotherapeutic modes that moves through and beyond the three traditional developments (Gurman and Kniskern, 1981). In a very real sense, family therapy is more a redefinition of the therapeutic task—a project that attempts to shift the "object" of therapy from the individual to the family. Although the many leaders of the family therapy movement often differ considerably in their theoretical formulations and in their operational procedures, they hold firm to the great importance of the ecological or systems points of view (Gray *et al.*, 1969).

Feminist therapy is another dramatic expression of a form of therapy that has evolved out of a complex of cultural realities. Partly a reaction to the fact that much traditional psychotherapy has been constructed on male models, the feminist movement has addressed as one part of its much broader concerns the psychotherapeutic community. From this critique has come a variety of feminist therapies and educational approaches. But, like family therapy, feminist therapy redefines the object of therapy itself—in this case concentrating on the conviction that sexual oppression is the basis of all other repressions and that one of the major responsibilities of feminist therapies is to attack the core causes of sexual oppression (Mander and Rush, 1974).

Pastoral psychotherapy is another example of a therapeutic movement that has evolved from a particular community of meanings—in this instance, the religious. An extension of pastoral counseling (the two terms are not clearly distinguishable in the literature and frequently are used interchangeably), the movement has a full-blown professional association and training requirements. It has a lengthy history traceable to the "cure of souls," long a central concern in many religious traditions. Although its theoretical task has been one of relating or even integrating theological and behavioral science categories in ways that might enlighten praxis, it has not developed a systematic conceptual schema that gives it a clear identity. For the most part, pastoral counselors and/or pastoral psychotherapists have borrowed heavily from the three psychotherapeutic developments covered in this article, paying special homage to the psychodynamic and humanistic tendencies with less attention being given to the behavioral-directive ones. In all of this, the writers and clinicians in the field have tended to add numinous qualities to traditional and mainline psychotherapeutic categories and practices (Patton, 1983; Wise, 1980).

The list of psychotherapies that have evolved out of cultural and culturally specific phenomena could be greatly extended, of course. Counseling and psychotherapeutic modes have been developed for blacks, homosexuals, the aged, divorced, alcoholics, the religious, the young, mid-lifers, and so forth. All of these therapeutic varieties draw upon one or a combination of the three developments already noted or they make use of eclectic stances.

4. Concluding Notes. That such a colorful array of psychotherapies is confusing scarcely needs elaboration. If the technical literature is perplexing — which it surely is—imagine what faces the consumer whose images of psychotherapy are often conditioned more by its depiction in TV soap operas than by any enlightened investigation. Indeed, when one stands on tip-toes to get an overall view of the psychotherapeutic terrain, it is easy to see that the "freight" psychotherapy carries is much too weighty, much too grandiose for any one profession or "science" or "art" to hold. At least we might consider with sobriety Kovel's warning:

"Therapy has to be taken most seriously within the terms of the neurosis it addresses. When, however, therapy begins to acquire a superordinate value—that is, when the treatment promises liberation, transcendence, or the answers to the riddles of life; indeed, when it becomes an end *in itself* offering the hope of happiness— then we may know we are being duped, and distracted from more valid goals."

Bibliography. R. Assagioli, *Psychosynthesis* (1971). A. T. Beck, A. J. Rush, B. F. Shaw, G. Emergy, *Cognitive Therapy of Depression* (1979). G. S. Belkin, *Contemporary Psychotherapies* (1980). J. F. T. Bugental, *Psychotherapy and Process: The Fundamentals of an Existential Humanistic Approach* (1978). S. Cashdan, *Interactional Psychotherapy: Stages and Strategies in Behavioral Change* (1973). R. D. Chessick, *Techniques and Practice of Intensive Psychotherapy* (1974). J. Dewey, *How We Think* (1933). J. Ehrenwald, *The History of Psychotherapy: From Healing Magic to Encounter* (1976). A. Ellis, *Reason and Emotion in Psychotherapy* (1962). W. V. Flegenheimer, *Techniques of Brief Psychotherapy* (1982). V. Frankl, *Man's Search for Meaning: An Introduction to Logotherapy* (1963). S. Freud, *SE* (1962). A. Giorgi, *Psychology as a Human Science: A Phenomenologically Based Approach* (1970). A. P. Goldstein, *Psychotherapeutic Attraction* (1971). W. Gray, F. J. Duhl, and N. D. Rizzo, *General Systems Theory and Psychiatry* (1969). A. Gurman and D. P. Kniskern, *Handbook of Family Therapy* (1981). H. Hartmann, *Ego Psychology and the Problem of Adaptation* (1958). D. B. Hogan, *The Regulation of Psychotherapists: A Study in the Philosophy and Practice of Professional Regulation* 2 vols. (1979). H. Kohut, *The Restoration of the Self* (1977). J. Kovel, *A Complete Guide to Therapy: From Psychoanalysis to Behavior Modification* (1976). A. V. Mander and A. K. Rush, *Feminism as Therapy* (1974). A. H. Maslow, *Toward a Psychology of Being* (1962). R. May, ed., *Existence: A New Dimension in Psychiatry and Psychology* (1958). R. B. MacLeod, "The Phenomenological Approach to Social Psychology," *Psychological Review*, 54 (1947), 193–210. P. Mullahy, *Oedipus: Myth and Complex* (1948). J. Patton, *Pastoral Counseling: A Ministry of the Church* (1983). J. Reusch, *Therapeutic Communication* (1961). C. R. Rogers, *Counseling and Psychotherapy* (1942); *A Way of Being* (1980). B. F. Skinner, *Science and Human Behavior* (1953). D. Smith, "Trends in Counseling and Psychotherapy," *American Psychologist*, 37:7 (1982), 802–9. H. B. Urban and D. H. Ford, "Some Historical and Conceptual Perspectives on Psychotherapy and Behavior Change," in A. L. Bergin and S. L. Garfield, eds., *Handbook of Psychotherapy and Behavior Change: An Empirical Analysis* (1971). R. S. Valle and M. King, *Existential-Phenomenological Alternatives for Psychology* (1978). A. Van Kaam, *Existential Foundations of Psychology* (1966). D. W. Winnicott, *Collected Papers* (1958). C. A. Wise, *Pastoral Psychotherapy: The-*

ory and Practice (1980). J. Wolpe, *Psychotherapy by Reciprocal Inhibition* (1958). I. D. Yalom, *Existential Psychotherapy* (1980).

O. STRUNK, JR.

For principal varieties and traditions of psychotherapy see ANALYTICAL PSYCHOLOGY (Therapeutic Method and Research); BEHAVIOR THERAPIES; GROUP COUNSELING AND PSYCHOTHERAPY; HUMANISTIC PSYCHOTHERAPIES; PSYCHOANALYSIS (Therapeutic Method and Research); PSYCHOANALYTICALLY-ORIENTED PSYCHOTHERAPY; TRANSACTIONAL ANALYSIS; COGNITIVE, EGO, EXISTENTIAL, GESTALT, *or* PHENOMENOLOGICAL PSYCHOLOGIES AND PSYCHOTHERAPIES; FAMILY THEORY AND THERAPY. *See also* ADJUNCTIVE, EXPERIENTIAL, FEMINIST, PRIMAL, RATIONAL-EMOTIVE REALITY, *or* WILL THERAPIES; ASSERTIVENESS TRAINING AND THERAPY; CLIENT-CENTERED THERAPY; INDIVIDUAL PSYCHOLOGY; LOGOTHERAPY; PRIMAL THERAPY. *Compare* POPULAR THERAPEUTIC MOVEMENTS AND PSYCHOLOGIES; SELF-HELP PSYCHOLOGIES. *For pastoral and religious forms of psychotherapy see* PASTORAL PSYCHOTHERAPY; PASTORAL COUNSELING; COUNSELING, ROMAN CATHOLIC; JUDAISM AND PSYCHOLOGY; PSYCHOLOGY, EASTERN; SPIRITUAL DIRECTION. *See also* CHRISTIAN PSYCHOTHERAPIST; CHRISTOTHERAPY; FORMATIVE SPIRITUALITY; PSYCHOLOGY AND PSYCHOTHERAPY (East-West Comparison); SPIRITUAL PSYCHOLOGIES; TRANSPERSONAL PSYCHOLOGIES. *Compare* COUNSELING AND PSYCHOTHERAPY (Comparative Concepts); ETHICS AND PASTORAL CARE; FAITH HEALING; INTEGRITY THERAPY; PHILOSOPHY AND PSYCHOLOGY; RELIGION AND PSYCHOTHERAPY; THEOLOGY AND PSYCHOTHERAPY.

PSYCHOTHERAPY (East-West Comparison). *See* PSYCHOLOGY AND PSYCHOTHERAPY (East-West Comparison).

PSYCHOTHERAPY, JOURNALS IN. *See* JOURNALS IN COUNSELING AND PSYCHOTHERAPY.

PSYCHOTHERAPY, PASTORAL. *See* PASTORAL PSYCHOTHERAPY.

PSYCHOTHERAPY, VALUES IN. *See* VALUES IN PSYCHOTHERAPY AND COUNSELING.

PSYCHOTHERAPY AND COUNSELING. *See* COUNSELING AND PSYCHOTHERAPY (Comparative Concepts).

PSYCHOTHERAPY AND COUNSELING (Research Studies and Methods). Research in the area of psychotherapy and counseling is a relatively recent development. Most of the early significant figures were psychoanalysts who followed the theoretical views of Freud or who had somewhat related views. These individuals were not researchers and, in fact, saw little need for research investigations of psychotherapy. Consequently, until about forty years ago, there were practically no systematic research studies evaluating psychotherapy and counseling.

Several factors appear to have influenced the subsequent interest in research. Carl Rogers, the founder of client-centered therapy, and his students made the first recordings of actual counseling sessions as a means of studying the processes involved. This was an important advance. A second factor of significance was an article published in 1952 by Hans Eysenck, a British psycholo-

gist. In this article, Eysenck reviewed twenty-four studies of outcome in psychotherapy and concluded that there was no evidence to support the view that psychotherapy was effective! A third possible factor was the increased involvement of psychologists in the area of psychotherapy in the period following the Second World War. Trained in research methods, psychologists have played a leading role in research on counseling and psychotherapy.

1. Types of Research. Two broad categories of research in psychotherapies can be designated — outcome and process research. The first designation refers to research that attempts to evaluate the outcome or effectiveness of psychotherapy. In essence, clients are evaluated before treatment is begun and again at the end of therapy, or some estimate of improvement is made at the termination of therapy. Process research, on the other hand, is concerned with certain events, behaviors, or interactions that take place during the therapy session. Attention is focused on the process of therapy rather than on its outcome. Depending on the theoretical orientation of the investigator, a variety of different process variables may be investigated, for example, negative or positive self-statements by clients, affective responses, silences, therapist reflective statements, interpretations, and the like.

Clearly, both types of research are important and required if we are both to understand and evaluate psychotherapy. Furthermore, the most desirable research would be that which studies both process and outcome. Unfortunately, the great majority of studies have focused on one or the other. Although studies of outcome are crucial for appraising the effectiveness of psychotherapy, such research alone will not provide information concerning the processes that are responsible for the outcomes secured. On the other hand, studying process in isolation and apart from outcome does not provide much useful information, even though some researchers have appeared to be interested only in the process of psychotherapy.

2. Factors in Research. *a. Basic research variables.* In planning or evaluating research in psychotherapy, certain basic variables and research procedures need to be considered. In any given research study, the variables that conceivably may influence the results are the following: the type of client, the particular therapist, the interaction between the two, the criteria used to evaluate the therapy, and the type of therapy or counseling. Thus, it is important to be able to describe these variables clearly. Generalization from a research study to the clinical or counseling situation depends on how comparable the clients and procedures in the study are to the situation in which one works. Results obtained from studies of highly motivated, intelligent, and mildly disturbed clients may not necessarily apply to unmotivated and generally more difficult clients.

It is obvious that investigations comparing two forms of therapy should have comparable conditions for both of the therapies. Both patient groups need to be comparable, as do the therapists, if we are to draw reasonable conclusions. If one of the therapies to be evaluated has less disturbed or "better" clients and more experienced therapists, it would be impossible to draw valid conclusions as to the relative efficacy of the two forms of therapy. The results might be due to the clients and/or the therapists and not to the form of therapy. It is, of course, difficult to match patients precisely, for they can differ on so many attributes, for example, age, sex, education, social class, motivation, type of problem, chronicity, degree of disturbance, intelligence, and the like. However, serious attempts should be made to equate groups as closely as possible on variables of potential importance. Again, if this is not done, it is difficult to draw valid conclusions. The usually preferred method is to use cases that are randomly assigned to the two treatment groups. In this way, assignment to treatment is left to chance, and there is no overt bias. The two groups also can be matched on variables of importance.

b. Client and therapist variables. Although more could be said about the basic research variables already mentioned, we shall limit further comments to essentially two of them. Client and therapist variables have received a moderate amount of investigation (Garfield, 1978; Parloff, Waskow, and Wolfe, 1978). However, the interaction between these two principal participants in psychotherapy, because of its complexity in terms of appraisal, has received less attention. Nevertheless, it would appear to be of great importance for both the study of process and the outcome in psychotherapy. At least clinically, it is believed that certain therapists work better with some clients than others, and vice versa. Such interactional aspects, therefore, might help explain to some degree the limited findings frequently secured by studying client and therapist variables separately or in isolation.

c. Outcome criteria. The criteria used to evaluate outcome are also of great importance. In the past, most estimates or ratings of outcome were made by the therapist at the completion of therapy. This was usually done on the basis of some brief rating scale. This has been criticized on two counts. The therapist is not an unbiased or objective observer, and judgments made at the end of therapy may be overly influenced by the patient's overall adjustment level. That is, patients who initially are minimally disturbed and improve slightly may be judged as more improved at the end of therapy than those who were more severely disturbed at the outset of therapy and have actually changed more, but are not yet at the level of the less disturbed patients.

Patients' ratings of outcome have also been used. Although patients, too, are not objective observers, they are the consumers of counseling, and thus their appraisal is worth considering as one measure of outcome. More recently, expert clinicians have been used to evaluate the patient before and after therapy as a means of securing more objective appraisals. Psychological tests administered before and after therapy have also been used to evaluate possible changes resulting from psychotherapy. Although this procedure does pay attention to the actual change produced by means of psychotherapy, there are also some problems associated with it. The difference in the two sets of scores does not take into account the level of the patient at the beginning of therapy. Patients who have relatively high scores have less chance of showing significant improvements. Also, there is a statistical phenomenon called regression to the mean, whereby low and high scores may move to the mean or average score. There

are, however, statistical procedures to control such problems. Consequently, most studies today use a variety of procedures, including behavioral or performance measures to overcome the limitations of any single measure. However, if the various measures of outcome do not agree, then personal judgment may enter into the overall appraisal.

d. Control groups. Finally, control groups are a very important consideration. For example, if outcome is evaluated in a particular form of counseling and there is no control group, there can be no firm conclusions concerning the effectiveness of the counseling. If seventy percent of the clients improve, there is no way of demonstrating clearly or convincingly that the changes were actually due to the counseling, for it is possible that these individuals would have improved over time without such help. A control group represents an attempt to resolve such a problem. If the control group does as well as the treated group, one cannot say the treatment was effective. However, if the treated group does significantly better than the control group, there can be more confidence in the effectiveness of the treatment. Controlled studies thus are potentially much more definitive than uncontrolled ones.

3. **Research Findings and Debates.** A moderate number of studies have been reported in the past thirty years, even though many forms or types of psychotherapy have not been evaluated adequately. Furthermore, the studies conducted vary in their general quality, as well as in the types of clients and therapists used, and also in the criteria of outcome employed. As a result, there are conflicting findings in the literature. In addition, reviewers of the existing research may also reach different conclusions about the research as the following summary indicates.

In 1961 and 1966, Eysenck reviewed a number of studies and concluded that there were no adequate data to demonstrate the effectiveness of psychotherapy. According to him, psychotherapy was no more effective than no therapy. Meltzoff and Kornreich (1970) later reviewed 101 studies and stated that eighty percent of the studies reviewed showed positive results for psychotherapy. They also stated that Eysenck had not made a careful enough search to find studies in the literature that were positive toward psychotherapy. Bergin (1971) also disagreed with some of Eysenck's interpretations. He evaluated forty-eight studies and concluded that psychotherapy had a modestly positive effect. Rachman (1971, 1973), a colleague of Eysenck, in turn was critical of Bergin's appraisal and agreed essentially with Eysenck. The critical point of contention was the differing estimates of what is termed "spontaneous remission"—the percentage of clients who improve without therapy. Eysenck and Rachman stated that about sixty-five percent of clients improve without therapy, the same percentage of improvement that is secured by therapy clients. Bergin, on the other hand, basing his estimate on an analysis of selected studies, offered a spontaneous remission rate of thirty-one percent, which was distinctly less than the estimated therapy improvement rate of sixty-five percent. Later Bergin and Lambert (1978) revised Bergin's original spontaneous remission estimate to forty-three percent, although they emphasized that this rate varied noticeably from study to study.

Drawing upon the earlier studies of Eysenck (1952) and Truax and Carkhuff (1967), Truax and Mitchell (1971) concluded from both process and outcome studies in a variety of settings that the effectiveness of psychotherapy was more dependent upon the personality of the therapist than upon particular techniques. After defining and measuring therapist interpersonal skills, which were important for therapeutic relationships (cf. Rogers, 1957), Truax and Mitchell stated that the "inherently helpful" therapist-as-person possessed qualities of accurate empathy, nonpossessive warmth, and genuineness. These qualities were seen as enhancing the effectiveness of any technique when used at levels appropriate for a given therapeutic situation.

Three other important research reviews also deserve mention here. Luborsky, Singer, and Luborsky (1975) examined thirty-three selected studies and concluded that most of the psychotherapies studied were effective and that their results were comparable. Smith, Glass, and Miller (1980), in the largest review, analyzed 475 published and unpublished controlled studies of counseling and psychotherapy, using a new procedure, called meta-analysis, which enables the reviewer to combine and analyze studies in a more objective and systematic manner. These reviewers concluded that psychotherapy was indeed an effective treatment and, also, that the major types of therapy obtained essentially comparable results. Their procedures and conclusions, however, have been challenged by a number of individuals, including Rachman and Wilson (1980). The criticisms of the review by Smith and her colleagues (1980) include the following: the average age of the subjects evaluated being only 23 years, the use of volunteer and solicited subjects in many of the studies, the use of inexperienced therapists, a preponderance of individuals with phobias, and limited representation of other disorders. Rachman and Wilson (1980), on the other hand, in their review found no evidence to support the efficacy of psychoanalysis, only limited evidence on behalf of psychotherapy, but stronger evidence for behavioral and cognitive therapies. Thus, it is apparent that very different interpretations of the existing research literature have been forthcoming, and that individuals with differing orientations tend to view the findings in different ways.

4. **Conclusions.** It is difficult to draw firm conclusions from the various reviews that have been summarized briefly here. Many of the reviewers find some support for the efficacy of psychotherapy, but the credibility of the evidence varies, and there are critics of both the research studies and the literature reviews. At best, we can state that there is some moderate evidence supporting psychotherapy, but many questions remain. Future research clearly will have to pay more attention to the important variables that conceivably may affect outcome in research on counseling and psychotherapy and attempt to discover those factors which are potentially crucial for affecting positive change. This will be no easy task, but it is one that is essential for advancing the fields of psychotherapy and counseling. Furthermore, there are many groups in society who are demanding satisfactory evidence that psychotherapy is indeed effective and who are reluctant to accept the opinions of therapists. Large-scale studies such as that which the National Institute of Mental Health has organized and funded on depression, in which two forms of psychotherapy are being compared to pharmacotherapy, may shed additional light on the issue of the efficacy of psychotherapy.

Bibliography. A. E. Bergin, "The Evaluation of Therapeutic Outcomes," in A. E. Bergin and S. L. Garfield, eds., *Handbook of Psychotherapy and Behavior Change* (1971). A. E. Bergin and M. J. Lambert, "The Evaluation of Therapeutic Outcomes," in S. L. Garfield and A. E. Bergin, eds., *Handbook of Psychotherapy and Behavior Change* 2d ed. (1978). H. J. Eysenck, "The Effects of Psychotherapy: An Evaluation. *J. of Consulting Psychology,* 16 (1952) 319–24; "The Effects of Psychotherapy," in H. J. Eysenck, ed., *Handbook of Abnormal Psychology* (1961); *The Effects of Psychotherapy* (1966). S. L. Garfield, "Research on Client Variables in Psychotherapy," in S. L. Garfield and A. E. Bergin, eds., *Handbook of Psychotherapy and Behavior Change* 2d ed. (1978). L. Luborsky, B. Singer, and L. Luborsky, "Comparative Studies of Psychotherapies, Is It True that 'Everyone Has Won and All Must Have Prizes' "? *Archives of General Psychiatry,* 32 (1975), 995–1008. J. Meltzoff and M. Kornreich, *Research in Psychotherapy* (1970). M. B. Parloff, I. E. Waskow, and B. E. Wolfe, "Research on Therapist Variables in Relation to Process and Outcome," in S. L. Garfield and A. E. Bergin, eds., *Handbook of Psychotherapy and Behavior Change* 2d ed. (1978). S. Rachman, *The Effects of Psychotherapy* (1971); "The Effects of Psychological Treatment," in H. J. Eysenck, ed., *Handbook of Abnormal Psychology* (1973). S. J. Rachman and G. T. Wilson, *The Effects of Psychological Therapy* 2d ed. (1980). C. R. Rogers, "The Necessary and Sufficient Conditions of Therapeutic Personality Change," *J. of Consulting Psychology,* 21 (1957), 95–103. M. L. Smith, G. V. Glass, and T. I. Miller, *The Benefits of Psychotherapy* (1980). C. B. Truax and R. R. Carkhuff, *Toward Effective Counseling and Psychotherapy* (1967). C. B. Truax and K. M. Mitchell, "Research on Certain Therapist Interpersonal Skills in Relation to Process and Outcome," in A. E. Bergin and S. L. Garfield, eds., *Handbook of Psychotherapy and Behavior Change* (1971).

S. L. GARFIELD

For research in major schools and forms of psychotherapy and counseling see ANALYTIC PSYCHOLOGY; BEHAVIOR THERAPIES; HUMANISTIC PSYCHOTHERAPIES; PSYCHOANALYSIS. *See also* FAMILY THEORY AND THERAPY; GROUP DYNAMICS, PROCESS, AND RESEARCH; JOURNALS IN COUNSELING AND PSYCHOTHERAPY; PSYCHOLOGISTS, EMPIRICAL STUDIES OF; RESEARCH IN PASTORAL CARE AND COUNSELING. *For empirical and practical research see* CATHARSIS; CONDITIONING; DREAM THEORY AND RESEARCH; EVALUATION AND DIAGNOSIS, PSYCHOLOGICAL; GROUP DYNAMICS AND RESEARCH; HEALING; HYPNOSIS; LOCUS OF CONTROL RESEARCH; THERAPEUTIC CONDITIONS; VALUES IN COUNSELING AND PSYCHOTHERAPY. *For related theoretical issues see* COGNITIVE/CONATIVE PROBLEM; CYBERNETIC THEORY; LEARNING THEORIES; MODELS; PSYCHOLINGUISTIC THEORY. *See also* ETHICS AND PASTORAL CARE; PHILOSOPHY AND PSYCHOLOGY; RELIGION AND PSYCHOTHERAPY; THEOLOGY AND PSYCHOTHERAPY. *Compare* HEALING; INTERPRETATION AND HERMENEUTICS, PASTORAL; PSYCHOPATHOLOGY, THEORIES OF.

PSYCHOTHERAPY AND RELIGION. *See* RELIGION AND PSYCHOTHERAPY. *See also* PSYCHOLOGY AND PSYCHOTHERAPY (East-West Comparison).

PSYCHOTROPIC DRUGS. *See* PSYCHEDELIC DRUGS AND EXPERIENCE.

PUBERTY. *See* ADOLESCENTS; LIFE CYCLE THEORY; PERSONALITY DEVELOPMENT, BIOLOGICAL AND SOCIALIZING FACTORS IN; SEXUALITY, BIOLOGICAL AND PSYCHOSOCIAL THEORY OF.

PUBLIC EMERGENCY. *See* DISASTER, PUBLIC; EMERGENCY, PSYCHOLOGY OF PASTOR IN.

PUBLIC/PRIVATE INTERFACE. *See* PERSONAL, SENSE OF. *See also* PROPHETIC/PASTORAL TENSION IN MINISTRY; SHAME.

PUNISHMENT. *See* BEHAVIOR THERAPIES; DISCIPLINE, PASTORAL CARE AS; PARENTS AND PARENTHOOD. *See also* AVERSION THERAPY; GUILT.

PURGATORY. *See* ESCHATOLOGY; HEAVEN AND HELL, BELIEF IN; MEDIEVAL CHURCH, PASTORAL CARE IN.

PURIM. *See* JEWISH HOLY DAYS AND FESTIVALS.

PURITANS. *See* CASUISTRY, PROTESTANT; HISTORY OF PROTESTANT PASTORAL CARE (United States); REFORMED PASTORAL CARE; SPIRITUALITY (Protestant Tradition).

PURPOSIVENESS. *See* WILL/WILLING. *See also* CAUSALITY IN PSYCHOLOGY, FORMS OF; COMMITMENT; WILL TO LIVE.

QUAKER TRADITION OF CARE. The Quaker tradition seeks to promote openness to the divine transforming activity of the Spirit of God at the very center of life. There is also an emphasis on mutual lay ministry and on practical Christian living.

1. **History.** George Fox, a "seeker" after spiritual truth and inward peace in mid-seventeenth century England, failed to find what he was looking for among the various churches of his day or in the pastoral ministry of the clergymen to whom he turned for help. "When all my hopes in them and in all men were gone," wrote Fox in his *Journal*, "so that I had nothing outwardly to help me, nor could tell what to do, then, oh then, I heard a voice which said, 'There is one, even Christ Jesus, that can speak to thy condition,' and when I heard it my heart did leap for joy."

Fox's message of the contemporaneity of the living Christ with the believer of every age, and his experiential emphasis on the present working of the Spirit of God, found a hearing among religiously sensitive men and women of his day who were making this same discovery for themselves. Despite strong opposition and periods of fierce persecution, the movement grew into what became the Religious Society of Friends.

Turning aside from the outward forms and ceremonies practiced by other Christians of their day, they simply gathered in homes, barns, fields, and later in unadorned "meetinghouses" to wait in silent worship, seeking to find God's will for their lives, both singly and corporately. Any who felt moved might rise to speak or lead in prayer.

They deeply distrusted the "hireling ministry" of the times and, quoting Mt. 10:8, refused to pay tithes to support the state church. Care of members (both in the spiritual and material senses) was seen as the responsibility of the entire group under the direct guidance of the Spirit of God. As early as 1653 monthly meetings of all Friends in a given area were established "to look after the poor and to see that all walked according to the Truth." Later, structures of quarterly and yearly meetings were added, periodically bringing Friends together from successively larger geographic areas. However, the local monthly meeting is still the basis of membership in the Society of Friends and has primary responsibility for the care and discipline of members and for the extension of Quaker witness.

With no formal paid clergy, ministry was seen as the task of all members of a local meeting, following his or her gifts. Through participation in the life of the meeting, members were expected to kindle in one another a deep inner life of devotion, a strong integrity of character, moral sensitivity and concern, seriousness of purpose, and to show mutual encouragement toward practical Christian living.

Within this system of mutual ministry, some Friends felt a special call to take up a ministry of counseling, though always under the recognition that the living Spirit of God is the primary counselor and strengthener of God's people. Stephen Crisp, convinced to Friends in 1655, writes: "The more I came to feel and perceive the love of God and his goodness to me, the more was I humbled and bowed in my mind to serve him and to serve the least of his people among whom I walked . . . so I became a counselor of those that were tempted in like manner as I had been; yet was kept so low, that I waited to receive counsel daily from God, and from those that were over me in the Lord."

Friends whose gifts in ministry had become evident over a period of time were "recorded" as ministers by their local meeting. Such ministers included women as well as men. With the approval of their meeting, they might travel "in the ministry" to other Friends meetings and to isolated worship groups. Such travels in the ministry often took months and sometimes years to complete. It entailed visiting in Quaker homes and raising pastoral concerns, as well as speaking when moved in the meetings for worship. Unlike ministers in the more clerical traditions, the classical Quaker minister had no scheduled duties to perform, no rites or ceremonies to preside over, no marriages or funerals at which they had to officiate. They were free to engage in ministry as they felt the Spirit leading them.

Other forms of lay leadership which have emerged in the Quaker meeting have been the "elder" and the "overseer." Though originally not clearly differentiated from the role of minister, nor from each other, eventually the name of elder was given to those who took special responsibility for the spiritual vitality of the local meeting, while those known as overseers had a more general care for the meeting and its needs. Again, women regularly served in these leadership capacities along with men.

In modern times the official recording of ministers has been dropped in some Friends groups, and the function of the elders in the local meeting has been taken over by committees on "worship and ministry" or "ministry and counsel." In other Friends groups, particularly under the pressure of caring for the many new members who joined Friends on the American frontier or in mission fields, as well as in response to patterns of worship and ministry brought by the great revival movements of the last century, there has developed a pastoral system not unlike that of many rural American Protestant churches.

2. **Special Contributions.** Friends' regular use of prolonged periods of quiet meditation, both corporately in their gathered meetings for worship as well as privately in a daily time of "inward retirement," suggests that a wider use of silence may prove helpful for nurturing a centered and integrated lay spiritual life. Home visits from ministers and elders also traditionally included a period of silent waiting on God, before probing into the spiritual state of the family and its members, and perhaps such silent worship together may still find a place in deepening experiences of pastoral calling and pastoral counseling today.

Certainly Friends' historic emphasis on lay ministry, and on mutual ministry as the responsibility of all members of the congregation, is one which is widely echoed in current pastoral care literature. It remains to be seen to what extent the presence of a paid professional in the Christian community proves to be either an aid or a hindrance in helping each member of the community to discover their own ministry.

A related area in which Friends have pioneered, despite much opposition from other Christians, has been in accepting and encouraging the ministry of women. As Quaker ministry was assumed to arise out of a response to the "Inward Light of Christ" operating in the heart of all persons, regardless of sex, the Society defended sharply the right of women to enter upon ministry equally with men.

The Quaker tradition, with its emphasis on the present leading of the Spirit of God, has also placed a peculiar emphasis on openness to divine guidance and to the concerns that spring from it. Much of Friends' well-known work in the antislavery movement and prison reform, their early experiments with humane treatment for the mentally disturbed at York Retreat in England and Friends Hospital in Philadelphia, their concerns in the fields of education, women's rights, race relations, and international peace, as well as many lesser known philanthropic and humanitarian undertakings, can be traced to the persistence of individual Friends and small Quaker groups in seeking out what new things God may be requiring of them in their own day.

The Quaker mode of reaching group decisions by waiting to achieve a common "sense of the meeting," rather than by voting, may also be of value to others. According to the Quaker understanding, the whole truth of a situation is likely to transcend the fragmentary insights of various individuals or factions. As each contributes their insights and listens for the insights others bring, these partial insights supplement one another. The resulting resolution is not so much a compromise, as a "new creation" aided by the working of the Spirit among them. Voting, on the other hand, may emphasize rather than remove an existing division of opinion, and can result in a disgruntled minority hindering the further functioning of a religious community.

Two lesser known Quaker practices which may have wider relevance are the Quaker committee on clearness and Quaker queries. The former consists of a group of seasoned and caring Friends appointed to help someone who is facing a major life decision (such as marriage) sort through the inner conflicts and tensions they may be feeling, help discern what possible results the contemplated action may entail and help determine whether it seems in "right ordering." The latter are a series of questions designed to direct the thinking of members of the Society of Friends towards their daily conduct of life, the quality of their meeting as a worshiping and caring community, and their faithfulness to Quaker testimonies such as nonviolence and simplicity. Used both personally and corporately, the queries perform a role parallel to that of the "examination of conscience" in other traditions of pastoral care.

Bibliography. H. Barbour, *Quakers in Puritan England* (1964). R. Barclay, *Apology for the True Christian Divinity* (1678). S. Bownas, *Descriptions of the Qualifications Necessary to a Gospel Minister* (1750). W. C. Braithwaite, *Beginnings of Quakerism* 2d ed. (1955); *Second Period of Quakerism* 2d ed. (1961). H. Brinton, *Quaker Journals* (1972). E. T. Elliott, *Quakers on the American Frontier* (1969). G. Fox, *Journal* (1952 [1694]). J. W. Frost, *Quaker Family in Colonial America* (1973). R. Jones, *Later Periods of Quakerism* (1921). L. S. Kenworthy, *Quakerism: A Study Guide* (1981). J. D. Marietta, *Reformation of American Quakerism 1748–1783* (1984). M. J. Sheeran, *Beyond Majority Rule* (1983). Society of Friends, London Yearly Meeting, *Christian Faith and Practice* (1960). D. V. Steere, *Quaker Spirituality: Selected Writings* (1984). J. Woolman, *Journal* (1971 [1774]).

K. W. HENKE

MINISTRY (Protestant Tradition); PASTORAL CARE (History, Traditions, and Definitions); HISTORY OF PROTESTANT PASTORAL CARE (United States). *See also* COMMUNITY, FELLOWSHIP, AND CARE; GUIDANCE, DIVINE; SILENCE; WOMEN IN PASTORAL MINISTRIES, HISTORY OF. *Compare* LAY PASTORAL CARE AND COUNSELING; PIETISM AND PASTORAL CARE; SECTARIAN PASTORAL CARE; TRADITION AS MODE OF CARE. *Biography:* FOX; WOOLMAN.

QUALIFICATIONS FOR PASTORAL COUNSELING. *See* STANDARDS FOR PASTORAL COUNSELING.

QURAN. *See* ISLAMIC CARE AND COUNSELING.

R

RABBINIC CARE AND COUNSELING. *See* JEWISH CARE AND COUNSELING.

RABBI/RABBINATE. The title *rabbi* (my master, my teacher) was not used before the destruction of the Temple in A.D. 70. Earlier sages (like Hillel the Elder) were quoted without honorific. Rabbinic ordination is a ceremony of doubtful antiquity, though tradition holds that there was a successive laying on of hands, unbroken since the time of "Moses, our Rabbi." In the NT, particularly in the book of John (e.g., 1:49), Jesus is called "Rabbi," but Matthew, in particular, is eager to distinguish Jesus from "the scribes and the Pharisees" who like to be "called rabbi by men" (23:2, 7).

1. The Classical Talmudic Rabbinate. During the classical Talmudic period, rabbis performed the crucial function of (re-)creating the religion of Judaism. During the first four or five centuries of our era, they taught, judged, interpreted Scripture, fixed holy seasons, supervised Diaspora communities from the land of Israel, and permanently determined canonical structures. They created the liturgy of the synagogue, which in earlier generations still had a spontaneity that became less and less possible. Included in their new formulations was a "blessing" against dissidents (Christians, Gnostics, heretics) whom the rabbis termed *minim*.

Talmudic rabbis were professional wood-choppers, farmers, shoemakers, shepherds. The rabbinate was, in that period, an important avocation, but in the Middle Ages (beginning somewhat earlier and ending somewhat later than the Christian medieval period), the rabbinate was decisively professionalized. Despite Maimonides's explicit opposition, the hired rabbi was an almost universal phenomenon. Some rabbis had written contracts; others lived on fees for services like marriage and divorce, or the sale of ritual objects and kosher meat. Imitating the Christian "doctor," the Jewish leadership insisted on religious preeminence over merely lay officials. A collision course was inevitable, with the result by no means determined in advance. Rabbis could excommunicate in extreme cases, a weapon more commonly sheathed than

employed. But they were often torn between lay factions and had to face dismissal or diminution of authority.

The civil government regularly intervened in rabbinical placement and function as early as the time of the emperor Justinian. Some princes tried to control ordination, others were the rabbis' main support. The Jewish community slowly but steadily achieved autonomy, but lay leadership continued to manipulate and control its internal agenda.

Nonetheless, the rabbis were usually honored and respected during the Middle Ages. They controlled the judiciaries and authorized the publication of books; they were the spiritual center of an essentially egalitarian Jewry. They circumcised newborn boys. They preached at least twice a year and, in some communities, regularly. They studied and raised up disciples. Some were proud or irresponsible; many were addicted to intricate Talmudic interpretations, ignoring personal needs. Some led an entire community. All symbolized to Jew and Gentile alike what the Jewish community intended to be. The medieval rabbi was often an isolated, beleaguered prince, but still a prince of the spirit.

2. The Modern Rabbinate. In modern times the professional rabbinate became universal, and in Britain, France, and Eretz Yisrael, even a chief rabbi was named by the government. Since Emancipation, at the beginning of the nineteenth century, all uniformity was lost. The Hasidic *rebbe* became a pastor and wonderworker. The university-trained scholar of Western Europe led a dignified and sometimes assimilated congregation from a distance. The older functions (judging, teaching, "learning") remained crucial in Orthodoxy and neo-Orthodoxy, but the sage gave way typically to an administrator, a fund-raiser, a political spokesperson, a speaker, and ambassador to the Gentile world.

In America rabbinic education has been fragmented by denominations. Orthodox yeshivot (rabbinical schools) teach Talmud almost exclusively with traditional commentaries. It is taught to a population of which most will not occupy pulpits but will be learned, observant, professional and business men. The Conservative Movement teaches Talmud in a more critical spirit and adds elements of Jewish history and literature. Reform seminaries train rabbis in an eclectic, frequently elective manner with emphasis on Bible and Jewish creativity. Reconstructionist rabbis study the epochs of Jewish history consecutively and rather rapidly. In each of the three last movements women are found in almost equal numbers to men, a development that suggests a growing feminization of the rabbinic role.

The contemporary rabbi suffers a clear crisis of authority. In an educated democracy with secular values, it is not clear where he (more recently, also, she) can derive status. Rabbis now serve at the pleasure of their lay leadership, as many did centuries ago. They are employed leaders. Still, the rabbinate has not only survived but also has flourished. The rabbinate may be a terminal profession, but it is more likely a symptom of present-day Jewish ambivalence and a challenge to a Jewish future of promise and mystery.

Bibliography. S. W. Baron, *The Jewish Community,* 2 (1942). A. J. Wolf, ed., "The Future of Rabbinic Training in America," *Judaism,* 18 (1969), 386–420.

A. J. WOLF

JEWISH CARE AND COUNSELING (History, Traditions, and Contemporary Issues); MINISTRY (Biblical Origins and Principles). *See also* HASIDIC CARE AND COUNSELING; JEWISH LIFE; RABBIS, EMPIRICAL STUDIES OF; THEOLOGICAL EDUCATION AND THE PASTORAL CARE MOVEMENT, JEWISH; ZADDIK. *Compare* JUDAISM AND PSYCHOLOGY; MINISTRY; OLD TESTAMENT AND APOCRYPHA (Traditions and Theology of Care); PASTOR (Definition and Functions); ROLE, MINISTERIAL.

RABBIS, EMPIRICAL STUDIES OF. This article concerns studies of Jewish clergy and seminarians in the Orthodox, Conservative, and Reform branches of Judaism, which are based on data derived from surveys, interviews, and psychological testing.

In a study originally commissioned by the Board of Theological Education of the Lutheran Church in America and in another one commissioned by the Research Council of the Ministry Studies Board, R. J. Menges and J. E. Dittes, originally working independently, eventually crossed paths and decided to pool their efforts. The results of their survey yielded a work containing abstracts of over seven hundred empirical studies of clergy in all denominations. A tabulation of the studies by denomination reveals that nearly all involve Protestant and Catholic clergy with only nine dealing with Jewish clergy. Others who have done research in this field have noted the paucity of published studies of the rabbinate by comparison with the Christian clergy. Not only are there very few studies dealing with psychological aspects of the rabbinate, but there is also a dearth of sociological studies as well. In addition, few articles concerning the rabbinic vocation are based on actual empirical research. The comparatively few studies of the rabbinate that have been done fall into three categories: the training of American rabbis; role differences, role conflict, role ambiguity, and personality issues; and stresses in the rabbinate.

1. The Training of American Rabbis. An extensive study of the rabbinical training programs in the three largest seminaries that prepare rabbis for the three branches of Judaism in America was done by C. Liebman in 1968. The study not only provided an in-depth analysis of the program of studies, but also analyzed the demographic and educational background of the student bodies and their attitudes toward the institutions where they were receiving their training. In connection with the training of American rabbis, the study found that American rabbinical seminaries are neither vocational nor professional institutions but are closer in character to graduate schools of arts and humanities. The emphasis in the training is primarily on developing a thorough familiarity with Jewish textual material and secondarily on basic skills in preaching and officiating at religious functions. Third in importance is an ability to do minimal counseling.

2. Role Differences, Role Conflict, Role Ambiguity, and Personality Issues. One of the earliest studies of the rabbinic role was done by S. Goldstein, whose research revealed that the rabbinate was a multirole profession that required competence in as many as eight or more roles. The rabbi is expected to be a teacher, scholar, educator, preacher, prayer leader, pastor, organizer, and administrator. The rabbi must constantly make decisions as to the relative priorities of each, and his priorities are not always the same as his congregants' priorities, which often leads to strife and misunderstanding.

Another study by J. E. Carlin and S. H. Mendlovitz examined the changing roles of the American rabbi as the older European-born clergyman was replaced by an American-born counterpart. They suggested that the frustrations and dissatisfactions of the American rabbi can best be understood as an attempt to cope with changes in the Jewish community, which have seriously undermined traditional authority structures and the legitimations and value systems upon which these authority structures relied. A similar study of the changing roles of the American rabbi was done by B. J. Bamberger, who pointed out the conflicting demands on today's rabbi.

A study of the differing role perceptions in the rabbinate contrasting those of the synagogue membership with those of the rabbi was done by S. Greenberg, involving 403 Jewish families and eight rabbis representing the three major branches of Judaism. It was found that rabbis stressed scholarship as the most essential element of their service, although the term had different meanings for each denomination. For the Orthodox and Conservative rabbis, the term meant religious studies, while for the Reform rabbi it meant secular studies. One study by J. Schnitzer examined the rabbi's role as a counselor, and another by M. Sklare concerned itself with the rabbi's role in the Conservative movement. Sklare came to the conclusion that the philosophy of the Conservative movement is not clearly defined, and as a result, "ten different Conservative rabbis will have ten different ideas of Conservative Judaism."

By far the most ambitious project in this area was a self-study commissioned by the Reform movement entitled, "Rabbi and Synagogue in Reform Judaism." The study done by T. I. Lenn and his associates focused on the roles of the Reform rabbi as perceived by the rabbi and the conflicting views of the rabbis and the memberships, as well as the possible causes of vocational dissatisfaction among Reform rabbis and their families. The data indicated that a great deal more is expected in most of the specific rabbinical roles than the extent to which the rabbis perform these roles. In the roles assigned to the rabbinical vocation, which generally include religious teaching, Jewish communal activity, rabbinical scholarship, counseling, preaching, and visiting the sick and the bereaved, the greatest degree of dissatisfaction among Reform congregants involved the rabbi's role as a pastor. In the area of religious beliefs only forty-one percent of the congregants felt that their rabbi believes in a personal God; the rest disagreed or did not know. On their part, eighty percent of the Reform rabbis expressed varying degrees of satisfaction with their professional careers and fifty-four percent would choose the rabbinate again if given the opportunity. Sources of dissatisfaction stemmed mainly from lack of a systematic arrangement for sabbaticals and the need for better arrangements for equitable salary schedules, pay raises, and tenure. Some nineteen percent were dissatisfied with the religious indifference of their congregants.

A number of studies involving the psychological aspects of the rabbinical roles were done by J. H. Blass. One study found that individual preferences for certain roles in the rabbinate were significantly related to specific psychological needs that vary in strength from one individual to another. The data also gave evidence that rabbis manifest psychological need patterns and role preferences according to the denominational group to which they belong. Members of each group have common psychological need patterns and role preferences that are unique to the group as a whole. In another study of role preferences among Jewish seminarians, Blass found that Orthodox seminarians demonstrated the greatest preference for the spiritual guide role, which involves assisting people to develop a deeper faith. The Conservative group preferred the teacher role, while members of the Reform group demonstrated the greatest preference for the counselor role. In contrast to Catholic and Protestant seminarians who rank some form of preaching as among their most preferred activities, Jewish seminarians of all three denominations relegated the preaching role to the lowest position of interest.

Another study by the same researcher involving personality correlates of religious orientation among rabbis concluded that there were significant differences in personality according to the position of the rabbis on a theological continuum from conservative to liberal. A study by M. Greenfield dealt with the personality traits of rabbis and their persistence or nonpersistence in the rabbinic vocation. The data suggested that those who persist and remain in the rabbinate tend to be extroverted while the nonpersisters are generally more introverted.

3. **Stresses in the Rabbinate.** With increasing interest in the subject of occupational stress, a study by L. R. Freedman, involving a total of 1,342 Conservative and Reform rabbis, measured the level of stress in the rabbinical profession and sought its origin in the psychological demands that the profession makes on its members, as well as the psychological conflicts that are related to their work.

To promote more effective placement of rabbis, further research might focus on the role preferences of synagogue memberships or their governing bodies as a means of achieving more harmony between rabbi and congregation. The result may be more persistence in the rabbinate and less stress for the rabbi. Further research may also reveal psychological patterns that are more predictive of success in the field. Finally, a better under-standing of rabbinic role preference may also lead to better ways of lessening ministerial dissatisfaction.

Bibliography. B. J. Bamberger, "The American Rabbi: His Changing Role," *Judaism,* 3 (1954), 488–97. J. H. Blass, "The Relationship of Psychological Values and Needs to Vocational Role Preferences Among Jewish Seminarians," unpublished doctoral dissertation, Fordham University (1975); "Role Preferences Among Jewish Seminarians," *Sociological Analysis,* 38 (1977), 59–64; "Some Personality Correlates of Religious Orientation Among Jewish Seminarians," *J. of Psychology and Judaism,* 4 (1979), 68–77. J. E. Carlin and S. H. Mendlovitz, "The American Rabbi: A Religious Specialist Responds to Loss of Authority," in M. Sklare, ed., *The Jews: Social Patterns of an American Group* (1958). L. R. Freedman, "Role-Related Stress in the Rabbinate: A Report on a Nationwide Study of Conservative and Reform Rabbis," (1984). S. Goldstein, "The Roles of an American Rabbi," *Sociology and Social Research,* 38 (1953), 32–7. S. Greenberg, "The Contemporary Synagogue: A Study of Eight Congregations," unpublished dissertation (1965). M. Greenfield, "Typologies of Persisting and Nonpersisting Jewish Clergymen," *J. of Counseling Psychology,* 16 (1969), 368–72. T. I. Lenn et al., *Rabbi and Synagogue in Reform Judaism* (1972). C. S. Liebman, "The Training of American Rabbis," *American Jewish Yearbook* (1968). R. J. Menges and J. E. Dittes, *Psychological Studies of Clergymen: Abstracts of Research* (1965). J. Schnitzer, "Rabbis and Counseling," *Jewish Social Studies,* 20 (1958) 131–52. M. Sklare, *Conservative Judaism: A Sociological Analysis* (1955).

J. H. BLASS

RABBI/RABBINATE. *See also* CLERGY, EMPIRICAL STUDIES OF; ROLE, MINISTERIAL; THEOLOGICAL STUDENTS, EVALUATION AND EMPIRICAL STUDIES OF. *Compare* JUDAISM AND PSYCHOLOGY; PERSONALITY THEORY (Varieties, Traditions, and Issues); PSYCHOLOGY OF RELIGION (Empirical Studies, Methods, and Problems); RELIGIOUS, EMPIRICAL STUDIES OF; SOCIOLOGY OF RELIGIOUS AND PASTORAL CARE.

RACIAL DISCRIMINATION. *See* RACISM.

RACIAL IDENTITY AND CONSCIOUSNESS. *See* BLACK IDENTITY AND CONSCIOUSNESS.

RACIAL INTEGRATION AND PASTORAL CARE. *See* RACISM. *See also* PROPHETIC/PASTORAL TENSION IN MINISTRY; SOCIAL CHANGE AND DISLOCATION; SOCIAL JUSTICE ISSUES.

RACISM. The term *racism* is not easily defined. The most common (and common sense) definition—racism as a scheme of oppressive social classification based on physical features, mainly skin pigmentation—suggests that its roots are in the biological realm where classifications based upon physical distinctiveness can be made. There is a history of scientific attempts to define races on the basis of such distinctions. Related to this is the history of defining races on the basis of blood, or at least along certain "blood lines." Literature, as well as popular language, is filled with references to this notion. Kings and queens have "royal blood" and aristocrats are said to possess "blue blood." In the U.S., laws have been passed to insure against the mixing of bloods. For many years an accepted definition of a black person was anyone who had a "quantum of Negro blood." The effects of this law still linger on in some parishes. The key here was the contention that certain hereditary characteristics were transmitted through the blood (Haller, 1971). The actual definition or meaning of racism, however, is far more differentiated and complex.

1. **Meanings of Racism.** *a. Relation to nationalism.* Racism is also related to certain theories of nationalism. Here the definition often shares certain pseudoscientific opinions about racial characteristics or potentials with theories about the role or calling of particular people. Here racism functions as part of an ideology, and seen in this light has been most fully developed by Western societies. When it functions as part of a political system racism becomes a significant part of the ideology of white supremacy. As such it developed as part of a colonialist rationale in the mid-eighteenth century (Arendt, 1968).

The theory that some races are inherently inferior to others was deemed a necessary support for colonial exploitation on the part of European powers. As an ideology, racism functions as an official position by which people and their governments arrange their societies and policies to further their self-image and vested interests. When combined with religion, the ideology of white supremacy becomes a powerful civil religion in which God or the gods are said to be the source and protector of such a system. Logically, such a system, so conceived, could not be opposed. The most blatant expressions of this nationalist ideology in the past fifty years are Nazism in Germany and the current government policy of apartheid in South Africa. Both systems share the same view of nationhood: a theory of ancestry based upon blood, reinforced with religion. These views are buttressed by or interpreted through the application of selected Scripture references which seem to offer divine sanction for racialist practices.

b. Relation to white supremacy. It is important to distinguish between racism and white supremacy. The latter has become official doctrine in some countries, whereas it is possible for a person to be a racist without having developed a systematic supremacist rationale. Racism, at a popular level, is rarely subjected to the rigors of rationality. This attitude, often unconscious and always undisciplined by reference to facts, is based upon erroneous assumptions about others. Walter Lippman referred to them as "pictures in our heads." These mental attitudes can easily be translated into forms of discrimination. Nevertheless, some form of official sanction for racialist attitudes is necessary if personal hostility toward others based upon racial characteristics is to become institutionalized. The most recognizable forms by which racism expresses itself are patterns of segregation, attitudes of stereotyping, and ordinances of discrimination.

c. Racism as attitudes and values. Racism can be defined in terms of the attitudes and actions of persons or institutions towards others based upon color or ethnic origin with a view to depriving them of access to the rights and privileges of those holding this view. Central to this definition is the issue of power. In order to maintain a racialist position over others, the racist must have some access to power. Or if lacking power, must manipulate the system so as to give the oppressed the impression that such power is possessed. To be successful in either case, a racist must be able to manipulate the image-building apparatus of a society. "Reality" must be carefully managed by those in power.

Thus education, politics, the arts and sciences, and even religion constitute the multiple ways in which a given culture expresses its fundamental values, serving as channels for its reigning ideology. It has been demonstrated, for instance, that the dictionary can be used to reinforce the values of the dominant group, or conversely, to reinforce the dominant group's negative images of the subgroup. References to "black" or "blackness" are associated with negative qualities whereas "white" or "whiteness" are associated with characteristics of a more positive nature. By this means language serves as the chief conveyor of a nation's cultural values.

These values (held as early as the sixteenth century by some Europeans), when wedded to Scripture which seems to identify whiteness with salvation and cleansing (e.g., Isa. 1:18), became the basis for racial discrimination anchored in Holy Writ and the divine will. Later, an elaborate theology developed which sought to base discrimination and segregation on God's "curse" upon Ham. This theology, though long discredited by both science and responsible exegesis, still persists among supremacists in the Christian community (Buswell, 1964).

2. **Effects of Racism on Persons.** Minorities within racist societies, to the extent they are exposed to the majority culture, are systematically exposed to negative images of themselves, which become internalized. Such exposure is the chief source of various forms of self-abnegation on the part of minorities. Self-doubt, self-hatred, and "compensatory grandiose behavior" are only several ways in which negative self-image is internalized and acted out in minority behaviors.

The effects of racism in any society are too numerous to mention, but it is important to appreciate the ways in which persons have come to terms with this reality in the society. For many of the victims of racism in American society (who are usually people of color), it is all too easy to internalize the definitions, explanations, and expectations of the majority. Their hard work in school or the working place often yields disproportionate benefits compared to the efforts of their white counterparts (Loehlin *et al.*, 1975). It is all too easy, when confronted by daily reminders that one's efforts are not good enough for even a modicum of success, to assume that the fault lies within oneself. This is often followed by harder work, and if this proves unfruitful, the resultant despair often leads to alcoholism, violence toward loved ones, or various forms of dropout.

For others, adaptation takes the form of accommodation, the acceptance of the values, styles, and behaviors of the dominant culture. The price of such an accommodation has often been a form of ethnic schizophrenia, or at least a struggle for an identity which could no longer be defined internally or in terms of one's cultural heritage. W. E. B. DuBois referred to this as the black person's attempt to mediate between "is-ness" and "two-ness," what one knows oneself to be as a black person and the definition of identity pressed upon one by the oppressing culture, a wrenching split which produces rage and violence in the victim. Violence is the consequence of this prolonged loss of well-being in powerless persons. Thus violence is not an expression of power, but of powerlessness. Its source is in frustration, impotence, and an inability to assert oneself in human relations.

It is important to keep in mind, however, that power in the service of racialist attitudes is not merely personal and private in its expression. It is also institutional (Knowles and Prewitt, 1969). It is in its institutional forms that the minority person is most likely to encounter repeated denial aimed at his or her personhood. The school room, the court room, the factory, and the corner store can exhibit attitudes that tend to reinforce majority attitudes of superiority and power. Hence in the riots which shook American cities in the late sixties, neighborhood "mom and pop" stores were torched because they were perceived as perpetuating powerlessness in those neighborhoods. Churches have also contributed to the climate of racism in the society by remaining segregated, often by the simple device of moving when people of color occupied the same neighborhoods. Thus is communicated to the community that Christianity is incapable of relieving racialist attitudes. The aim of the civil rights movement was not revolution, let alone secession. It was integration.

3. Coping with the Power of the Oppressor. The issue in the conflict between victim and oppressor is power. Oppressed persons are typically powerless. They lack the ability to say "no" or "yes" to their oppressors. Power, as Rollo May has reminded us, is derived from the Latin *posse*, meaning "to be able," and connotes the ability to effect change in one's life or in the lives of others. It is crucially related to a sense of being, and it is the legacy of racism that its victims are denied the right to be.

The oppressor is also oppressed by the power he or she assumes. This is not always perceived by the oppressed. There is something illusory about power also. It promises more than it can deliver to those who possess it. It can be likened to a prison-house syndrome: those who keep others imprisoned are themselves incarcerated. Thus the genius of the civil rights struggle was Dr. King's realization that the oppressor must be set free if the oppressed were to be liberated (see Roberts, 1971; King, 1958).

a. Separatism. Many victims of discrimination have found recourse in various forms of separatism. For some, this has taken the form of self-imposed segregation, e.g. the refusal to have any more social intercourse with the majority than necessary, and the refusal to cooperate in any political options such as holding political office. This is a form of self-determination and in its most extreme expression was championed by the former black Muslims in the decade of the sixties, when demands of land grants were made to further secure a status of independence from the oppressor.

b. Integration. Another attempt at coping with racism on the part of its victims has been integration. The strategy carries with it certain assumptions about the good-will of the oppressor and confidence in the oppressor's willingness to abide by the laws of the land where those laws seem to provide equal protection for all its citizens. Experience has shown, however, that people who have power over others rarely live up to their stated values unless it can be shown that it is clearly in their best interests to do so. For this reason integrationists have taken care not to appear too aggressive in the pursuit of equality while pressing claim to the benefits of the legal system. The civil rights movement changed even this strategy in the main when nonviolent confrontation forced the issue of power and vested interests to the fore, and the white majority was made to see that its interests were clearly in jeopardy if they refused to live up to their laws.

Integration, as an experience, has proven to be illusory for many. At best it holds out the prospect of resolving racial conflicts in the most radical way — by getting the victims and victimizers together, or at least within proximity. Attempts have been made to integrate neighborhoods, schools, and work places. Pressure has been applied to effect changes in the image-making industries such as those responsible for writing text books and television commercials. But after years of legislation, busing of children, and multicolored images on TV screens, integration has achieved only a modest success.

Integration is limited in its ability to effect the necessary resolutions between antagonists. The chief shortcoming is that integration requires that the victims make most of the adjustments. When this is resisted by minorities the majority has only to recall its good will. Or when the majority feels they have gone as far as they can, they suspend the arrangement. They simply walk off or change the rules of the game. This can be done legally by outvoting or outspending the minority. These are expressions of majority power.

It may be true, as Fred Harris, former senator from Oklahoma, has claimed, that racism is America's number one mental health problem. Many victims of racism in our society would agree. Such a mentality, if unchecked, would have profound influence in all our domestic relations, especially in urban life, and in foreign affairs as well.

4. Pastoral Care and Counseling of Racists. Racism is, more often than not, irrational. It is based upon images in the mind. But these images, given enough time, can become reality. As a first step in helping the person afflicted by these images, it is important to help him or her trace the origins of these images. In a pastoral conversation with the author a professional football player, upon hearing the OT story of the tower of Babel, recalled another story, "something about a curse" on "somebody." I recalled the story of Noah's "curse" of Canaan. I could tell he was trying to find a connection between that dimly recalled story and race relations on the team. "Where did I hear that story?" he asked. I inquired where he was from, and he mentioned a Southern state. When I asked him if he had ever attended church, he replied that he had gone to Sunday school as a boy. It became clear as we talked that his earliest recollection of teaching about the supposed inferiority of black people came from his religious teachings in Sunday school.

Related to these mental images about others is fear, and help is needed to identify these fears. Often they are grounded in the person's own sense of guilt for past failures in human relations. "I know how I'd behave toward people who have done me wrong if I had the chance" (the chance, of course, to get even). Such a person needs to realize that not everyone who has been wronged as a result of racist actions or policies wants to get even. Black Americans, for instance, have generally not sought to get even but to catch up in the arena of opportunity. But then, that may be another fear — that if given opportunity, "they" will take over. This needs careful analysis, for this fear may mask the real issue, that of a pervasive sense of powerlessness in the racist. The issue may never have been racial in nature, but embedded in deep personal, family, and social inequities. A classic illustration is the emergence of the doctrine of apartheid in South Africa. When the budding Afrikaner nation severed itself from Holland in 1806 the issue was not racialist hostility toward the neighboring Xhosa people to the east. Rather it was an understandable reaction to an alien British administration bent on Anglicizing them. This was the beginning of an intense struggle for self-definition on a national scale. Only later did a native *herrenvolk* nationalism develop into an official ideology of apartheid aimed at native Africans. The origin of the ideology was fear and a deep-seated sense of national insecurity.

Racialism of the right and left seem related to the need to be in control, especially when social circumstances suggest that others, unlike themselves, threaten to supplant or marginalize their social position. Here it is important to assist racists to see that by surrendering stereotypes and relinquishing the need to dominate others, they are acting in their own best interest. This suggests that, finally, the best way to deal with racism is to expose racists to their victims. If part of the problem is ignorance — "being down on what you're not up on" — and social isolation, then ways must be structured to expose people who fear others to those very people whom they fear. Assistance must be given to assure that "the enemy" has a face, a name, an identity. One way to do this is to identify a task or problem which affects a plurality of people, the solution to which is not possible except in a cooperative effort. United by such a problem-solving venture, people often discover that past feelings of animosity and stereotypical thinking do not hold up under the dynamics of cooperation.

Bibliography. H. Arendt, *Imperialism, Part Two: The Origins of Totalitarianism* (1968). J. O. Buswell, *Slavery, Segregation, and Scripture* (1964). J. S. Haller, *Outcasts from Evolution: Scientific Attitudes of Racial Inferiority 1859-1900* (1971). M. L. King, Jr., *Stride Toward Freedom* (1958). L. L. Knowles and K. Prewitt, *Institutional Racism in America* (1969). J. C. Loehlin, *Race Differences in Intelligence* (1975). R. May, *Power and Innocence: A Search for the Sources of Violence* (1972, 1981). J. D. Roberts, *Liberation and Reconciliation: A Black Theology* (1971).

W. PANNELL

EXPLOITATION/OPPRESSION; PREJUDICE; SOCIAL JUSTICE ISSUES IN PASTORAL CARE. *See also* BLACK IDENTITY AND CONSCIOUSNESS; BLACK ISSUES IN PSYCHOLOGY; BLACK THEOLOGY AND PASTORAL CARE; CONSCIOUSNESS RAISING; CULTURAL AND ETHNIC FACTORS IN PASTORAL CARE; SOCIAL CONSCIOUSNESS AND RESPONSIBILITY; SOCIAL PERCEPTION, JUDGMENT, AND BELIEF. *Compare* AUTHORITARIANISM; SEXISM; SOCIAL STATUS AND CLASS FACTORS IN PASTORAL CARE.

RADICAL PSYCHIATRY. A movement repudiating the medical dominance of psychiatry and asserting that social alienation is the essence of all psychiatric conditions; hence individual pathology reflects social pathology and requires social solutions through consciousness raising, developing cooperative social relationships, and political action.

Bibliography. R. D. Laing, *The Politics of Experience* (1967). C. Steiner, *Readings in Radical Psychiatry* (1975).

M. DOLINSKY

PSYCHIATRIST/PSYCHIATRY. *Compare* LIBERATION THEOLOGY AND PASTORAL CARE; POPULAR THERAPEUTIC MOVEMENTS AND PSYCHOLOGIES; POWER.

RADICALS AND EXTREMISTS. *See* COMMITMENT; POWER; SOCIAL JUSTICE ISSUES IN PASTORAL CARE.

RAGE AND HOSTILITY. Rage is most often understood as furious, uncontrolled anger, usually of brief duration. Hostility, derived from the Latin word for enemy, *hostis,* is a motivating force — a conscious or unconscious impulse, tendency, intent, or reaction — aimed at injuring or destroying, and usually accompanied by the feeling or emotion of anger (Saul). Rage has some kind of obvious, behavioral expression, whereas hostility involves a strong element of calculation and control. Related concepts that are important in the understanding of rage and hostility are *anger,* a feeling, more controlled than rage, of displeasure resulting from real or imagined injury, and *cruelty,* the actual behavior of inflicting suffering on another, usually without just cause or the expression of mercy. The adjective *aggressive,* usually modifying behavioral nouns, and the noun *aggression* itself are often used in discussions of rage and hostility. Aggression is understood as the energetic pursuit of one's own ends; when used negatively, it means a ruthless desire to dominate and, when used positively, it refers to vigorous initiative in the pursuit of one's goals. The importance of understanding rage and hostility in the field of pastoral care and counseling becomes clear when one examines their origin, function, and significance in human life, and what seem to be some of the appropriate ways of dealing with them.

1. **Theories.** There are a number of important theories about the origin of rage and hostility, which may be divided into two basic categories: biological and psychological. Konrad Lorenz argues that aggressive behavior of human beings is based in their evolutionary kinship to lower animals and that the laws derived from the study of the instincts of animals are applicable to humans. There is evidence, according to Lorenz, that the first inventors of tools used them to kill not only game, but fellow members of their species. Cultural anthropologist M. F. Ashley Montagu (1968) argues against Lorenz's biological instinct theory, claiming that for both animals and humankind learning and experience are the key factors. Unrewarded and unrewarding aggressive behavior, he says, is minimally if at all evident in human societies.

It is psychoanalysis, however, which has dealt most extensively with aggression. In Freud's earlier views (1915) human beings are driven by two basic instincts, the sexual and the aggressive, which are normally intermixed. According to this theory, the most violent fantasy or act also possesses a sexual meaning, and the most tender and loving act, an aggressive element. Rage and hostility, however they are expressed, are based in these instinctual drives. In his later writings, however, Freud argued that aggression was an independent energy source in its own right (Freud, 1920). Melanie Klein, who in her earlier writings was an instinct theorist like Freud, later expanded Freud's views in a more psychological and relational direction. The Oedipus complex for Klein was not a struggle over pleasure and fear of punishment but a struggle for power and destruction and the fear of retaliation. Aggression in her theory is not a directionless destructive energy but an informed, personal, and purposive hatred involving relationships with specific others. According to Klein, the child rages against the imagined mutual gratifications of his parents in the face of his frustration and exclusion and fantasizes a spiteful revenge and triumph.

More recently, Heinz Kohut (1972) deviated from Freud and argued against the instinctive origin of aggression and for its understanding as a psychological phenomenon. In the prototypical situation of early life, the self asks for care and for one reason or another fails to receive it or receive enough of it. The result of this is shame at one's vulnerability and at the strength of one's need for care by the other. The first line of defense against this vulnerability is what Kohut calls "narcissistic rage," recognized by the need for revenge, for righting a wrong, for undoing a hurt by whatever means. Those who are in the grip of such rage show total lack of empathy toward those who have offended them and it is overcome only indirectly, through empathy, which eventually strengthens the self and allows the person to develop "maturely modulated aggressions" used in the service of cherished values.

2. Psychological Functions. As suggested above, the major function of rage, understood psychologically, is the defense of the vulnerable self from shame. Hostility, as compared to rage, extends that defense beyond the initial rageful impulses to a long-term, calculated aggression. It may become a major organizing principle of a person's life, replacing more constructive values such as care and purposive cooperation with others.

It is less well known about rage than about anxiety that its major function is a signaling one. When rage is present, the self is threatened. Whatever issue or circumstance triggered the rage has, by the time rage is felt, become secondary to dealing with the security needs of the person or persons exhibiting it. A secondary significance of rage is its intensity, its association with self-righteousness (Horowitz), and its function of extricating persons from apathetic dullness. Stated simply, persons often feel better being angry than depressed, particularly if they can convince themselves that the rage they feel is justified (Patton). Thus, rage may be unconsciously chosen by a person as an alternative to painful self-doubt and the depression that often accompanies it.

In contrast to rage, which is too physically exhausting to last for long periods of time, hostility is "colder" and more calculating and may be maintained indefinitely. Its significance lies in its having captured the person's overall view of the world and, therefore, his or her perception of particular situations so that rational and constructive actions, untainted by hostility, are precluded.

3. Pastoral Response. Although rage has been touched on in several helpful books on anger by pastoral care specialists (Augsburger, 1979; Grant, 1982; Lester, 1983), appropriate response to rage is a somewhat different matter. The destructiveness of rage lies in its "feeding on itself" rather than in responding to an external stimulus. Many of the

negative things that persons have been inappropriately told about anger may be appropriately said about rage. Whereas it can be a constructive experience to find ways of expressing anger, this is not the case with rage. The source of rage is not an issue or circumstance but the self's sense of impotence; therefore discovering the ability to control it contributes more to the self's security than anything resembling uncontrolled expression.

An appropriate response to one's own rage is an attempt through self-reflection and/or counseling and supervision to understand its sources and to develop enough security in significant relationships so that it becomes unnecessary. The response to the rage of a child is the setting of clear limits on potentially destructive behavior and the offering of an empathetic (knowledgeable) support to the child's developing his or her own controls for rage. The appropriate pastoral response to the rage and hostility in an adult parishioner or counselee is understanding that the rage or hostility probably results more from a threat to that person's self than to the specific circumstance which triggered it.

In the rather common circumstance of the conjoint pastoral counseling of a couple, it is important for the pastor to be willing to stop rageful outbursts and escalating arguments in the counseling hour by firmly labeling them as unproductive and as wasting the time of all those involved in the counseling. Moreover, when rage and hostility have been evidenced in the counseling process, a pastor can often be helpful by suggesting that the couple avoid the open and intense conflicts which can make matters worse. This usually can be done by helping the counselees differentiate between the assertiveness and situational anger which may result from discussing differences and the feeling of irrational rage with the desire to hurt the other at all costs. This type of calm, interpretive intervention, coupled with empathic understanding and an attempt to offer a dependable and secure pastoral relationship, are the most desirable and appropriate responses which a pastor can make to rage and hostility.

Bibliography. D. Augsburger, *Anger and Assertiveness in Pastoral Care* (1979). S. Freud, *Civilization and Its Discontents* (1930). E. Fromm, *The Anatomy of Human Destructiveness* (1973). B. W. Grant, *From Sin to Wholeness* (1982). M. Horowitz, "Self-Righteous Rage and the Attribution of Blame," *Archives of General Psychiatry,* 38 (November 1981). A. Lester, *Coping with Your Anger* (1983). K. Lorenz, *On Aggression* (1966). H. Kohut, "Thoughts on Narcissism and Narcissistic Rage," *Self Psychology and the Humanities,* (1985), 124–60. R. May, *Power and Innocence* (1972). M. F. A. Montagu, ed., *Man and Aggression* (1968). J. Patton, *Is Human Forgiveness Possible: A Pastoral Care Perspective* (1985). L. J. Saul, *Psychodynamics of Hostility* (1976).

J. PATTON

AGGRESSION AND ASSERTION; ANGER; VIOLENCE. *See also* ANTISOCIAL PERSONS; CONFLICT AND CONFLICT MANAGEMENT; FAMILY VIOLENCE; SELF-EXPRESSION/SELF-CONTROL. *Compare* POWER.

RAHNER, KARL (1904–84). German Roman Catholic dogmatic theologian and Jesuit priest. He taught theology at the University of Innsbruck from 1937 to 1964 (except for the war years), held the chair of Christian Weltanschauung at the University of Munich 1964–67, and finally moved to Münster to teach dogma and the history of dogma from 1967–71. Over four thousand publications have appeared with Rahner's name on them, with the sixteen volumes of his *Schriften zur Theologie,* 1954–84 (ET: *Theological Investigations*), offering the most comprehensive presentation of his thought, and *Grundkurs des Glaubens,* 1976 (ET: *Foundations of Christian Faith*), the fullest summary. He also made major contributions to pastoral theology, both inside Roman Catholicism and in dialogue with the Reformation churches. Reconceiving theology anthropologically according to a twofold transcendental and historical method, Rahner dedicated himself to a lifelong correlation between the secular situation of the Christian life and the mystery of God as its ultimate horizon. He saw the divine self-communication to history as doubly mediated, through the Spirit poured forth among human beings that they might truly seek God and through the living Word of Jesus in whose death and resurrection humanity is irrevocably united with God. Many essays in the *Schriften* and elsewhere stress the dignity of freedom and the unique individuality of human choice; the church as a sacrament of gracious reconciliation between God and humanity and as the place of the Spirit's ever new gifts; and Christianity's vocation to be a credible sign in the world that God is its absolute future. In addition to essays on the basic "existentials" of human life (responsibility, transcendence, historicity, subjection to guilt, death) and on the most ordinary of experiences (sleep, sickness, laughing, walking, age), he wrote frequently and movingly on the theological and moral virtues. Of enduring importance were his editorial contributions to the *Handbuch der pastoraltheologie* (5 vols., 1964–72), with its insistence on the need for contemporary theological analysis of the situation to which the whole church should seek to respond with pastoral care.

L. J. O'DONOVAN

PASTORAL THEOLOGY, ROMAN CATHOLIC.

RAJNEESHISM. *See* NEW RELIGIOUS MOVEMENTS.

RANK, OTTO (1884–1959). A member of Freud's original inner circle of colleagues who became a prominent psychoanalyst in his own right. An uneducated youth when first introduced to Freud, Rank earned his way through school as the secretary for the Psychoanalytic Society. He was seen as Freud's prodigy and greatly enhanced psychoanalysis through his expanding practice and his writings. In 1924, after moving further away from Freud's theories, he wrote *The Trauma of Birth,* which drove a wedge between himself and Freud and ended their close relationship. Rank eventually moved to America where he was warmly welcomed by the growing field of social work. He settled at the Pennsylvania School of Social Work, where he published and taught for many years.

Rank's theories center around the critical importance of guilt in leading to neurosis. He portrayed the therapeutic process in artistic terms and rested many of his conclusions upon his concept of the soul and the will. Although Rank was a Jewish atheist, he recognized the validity of religion as a dynamic force, and many of his theories provide framework for integrating psychological and theological concepts of persons.

B. HOUSKAMP

WILL THERAPY. *See also* BIRTH TRAUMA; NEOFREUDIAN PERSONALITY THEORIES AND PASTORAL CARE; PSYCHOANALYSIS.

RAPE AND RAPE COUNSELING. 1. Sexual intercourse achieved or attempted with a woman by a man without her consent and chiefly by force or deception. 2. Unlawful sexual intercourse by force or threat of bodily harm other than by a man with a woman, for example, sexual contact between males (homosexual rape), between members of one's family (incest), or between adults and minors (statutory rape). Contact need not be made between penis and vagina in order for rape to occur, though in some states archaic laws still define rape this way. Forced oral or anal intercourse, penetration with objects, or forced contact with animals are included under a broader definition. After an attack, physical evidence of violence may not be present. Many victims are too frightened or unable to resist and therefore escape visible injury. Use of a weapon and threats of harm are common.

Rape is thought to be the world's most hidden crime. It is estimated that only one in ten is ever reported to the authorities. The incidence is higher in urban areas and during the summer months. There are no accurate statistics as yet for the incidence of sexual abuse of children, since these are the most under-reported. However, it is thought that each year more than 100,000 children are raped.

Marital rape (forced sexual intercourse within marriage) is only beginning to be recognized legally as a crime, is often hidden within a generally abusive relationship, and is seldom reported to police, no doubt because abused women fear retribution from their husbands. Significant factors working against the recognition of its importance and frequency are the social and legal traditions that marriage confers on men a right of sexual dominance over their wives and that private relationships lie outside the domain of public law.

1. **Myths and Facts About Rape.** It is a common myth that rapists are overcome with sexual desire and commit rape in a fit of passion. The fact is that rape is a violent crime of aggression motivated by the desire to humiliate and injure. Rapists usually plan their rapes, often choosing victims who appear vulnerable, particularly young single women, children, and the elderly. In over one-third of reported cases, the rapist was an acquaintance, neighbor, friend, or relative. Research has further established that rapists are generally men who feel powerless and humiliated elsewhere in their lives. Often they are immature, hostile, sexually disoriented, and believe they cannot have sexual satisfaction without an atmosphere of coercion or violence. Many show sexual dysfunction such as impotence or retarded ejaculation during the attacks.

Many people, including many victims, mistakenly believe that women can resist rape if they want to, and that they "ask for it" by their independent behavior or provocative appearance. Though widely believed, this is one of a number of gross falsehoods or myths about rape. Others include the popular suspicion that women lie about rape in order to get revenge for being slighted, or really do want sex and say "no" when they mean "yes." Clinical experience and numerous studies have shown, however, that such popular beliefs, which depict the woman as temptress, deceiver, and desiring to be sexually victimized, are objectively without foundation. They persist, despite educational programs, as expressions of our culture's images of men, women, and sex, and are focused in the mistaken belief that rape is an act of erotic passion and that violence is somehow manly and sexy. It is scarcely necessary to add that such myths impose an additionally cruel burden of suffering on rape victims who must bear the stigma and blame for the violence perpetrated against them.

2. **General Principles of Care.** *a. Basic needs.* When a rape is reported, loving, emotional support is needed. The victim may act differently for a while — withdrawn, fearful, highly emotional, or unsure. It is also not uncommon for rape victims to fear being alone for a time after the rape. Family and friends can be particularly helpful in providing simple presence and companionship. Because the victim's family and friends may also feel angry, hurt, or upset, their needs also should be addressed by pastors and counselors.

Psychologically the victim needs assurance that those whom she trusts to tell about the incident care about *her*, and not primarily about the rape, though family and friends should encourage the victim to talk about the rape if she so desires. Many women feel guilty or ashamed and worry that they did not fight hard enough, or blame themselves for being in the wrong place at the wrong time. The victim should be reassured that she did the right thing to report the rape and that she did whatever was necessary to survive. It is important that the victim not be viewed as "sick," but rather as someone whose psychological and behavioral equilibrium has been severely shaken.

It is also important, however, in all situations of rape that the victim contact the police. This may be socially and emotionally difficult for the woman to do; many rapes go unreported for this reason. However, by not reporting the crime to authorities victims contribute to possible assaults on others and perhaps invite a second assault on themselves; a rapist, if not caught, will rape again.

b. Wholistic care and counseling. Although the victim's momentary focus is fixed on the rape incident, it is important to remember that she experiences the impact of the rape in every aspect of her life. Thus it becomes especially important for counseling to be available that allows her to work through the experience in all its dimensions. In addition to pastors and pastoral counselors, many communities have rape hotlines with twenty-four hour service staffed by volunteers, as well as local psychotherapists, police specialists, and hospital emergency room personnel who may provide counseling and supportive services. A specialist rape counselor or pastoral counselor can offer the victim a wholistic form of care, providing emotional support, help with practical decision-making, and an opportunity to focus on the victim's concerns about such matters as health, safety, family relationships, employment, or school. Supportive and insightful counseling can enable the victim to make an easier, more direct resolution of the crisis than if she or he had struggled with the problem alone. The pastoral counselor, in particular, can offer, at appropriate times later in the recovery process, opportunities for reflection on the meaning of the event in relation to the victim's faith, and a means of struggling with the deeper existential and religious issues involved in this frightening encounter with human evil.

In any case, the ability to deal with the victim as a whole person is what broadly differentiates a specialized rape counselor or pastor from police officers, examining physicians, and district attorneys who can be supportive and sensitive, yet must carry out their specific duties. Such specialized rape counseling or pastoral counseling is particularly important during the period of crisis, but often is helpful if continued over an extended period of time. If this is not possible, the counselor may be able to help by referring the victim to appropriate professionals or agencies once the immediate crisis has passed.

3. **Specific Phases of Care and Counseling.** Research describes four overlapping phases of stress reaction to rape, which have been identified as the Rape Trauma Syndrome (Burgess and Holmstrom, 1974). Each phase suggests the need for somewhat different care and counseling emphases within the general approach cited above.

a. The anticipatory phase includes the background "worry work" or "what if" form of psychic preparation that assesses the danger and helps a woman become aware of the strengths and resources she can muster in a crisis. Such anticipatory awareness can be helpful in mobilizing psychic resources in the event of an actual rape. Rape education, self-defense training, and "what if" discussions with family and friends can contribute to the kind of psychic preparedness that facilitates a successful psychological adjustment should a rape subsequently occur. More commonly, many women assume an illusion of invulnerability which, though potentially misleading, is in fact useful in protecting her from unduly limiting her life or living in constant fear.

b. The impact phase, immediately after the rape, may bring forth reactions of shock and disbelief followed by fear, anger, and anxiety. Expressed behavior may include sobbing, agitation, tension, short attention span, or sometimes an apparent lack of emotional response. Effective counseling allows the victim to talk about what happened, cry, and express emotions such as rage and shame, and at an appropriate time guides the victim into purposeful activity that will help her adapt, reduce her anxiety, and restore feelings of self-control. Support can be given for decisions regarding such tasks as telling loved ones, seeking medical treatment, reporting to the police, and reassuming family and work responsibilities.

c. The recoil or adjustment phase may come within days or weeks of the attack. This is when the victim shows outward adjustment as she begins to resume emotional expression and daily activities. Physiological reactions, such as tension and a loss of appetite and sleep, diminish. However, the victim may become hyperactive in an attempt to normalize and reorganize her life; she may, for instance, change her living arrangements, school, or job. Maladaptive behavior such as severe agitation or depression, excessive self-blame, or an inability to resume regular activities or relationships should be assessed to decide if continued counseling or psychotherapy is indicated.

d. As the victim enters *the posttraumatic phase* or integration phase, she may feel the need to be alone as she attempts to reconcile her thoughts and feelings about the rape. Counseling may be ended at this time only to be resumed if additional problems arise. Sometimes depression and anxiety can be temporarily reactivated when emotional situations such as other losses, the anniversary of the rape, or the time for the rape trial approaches. Victims who have not sought counseling previously often do so at this time.

4. **Pastoral Theological Dimensions.** *a. Rage, revenge, and guilt.* Though theological reflection is likely to be appropriate with rape victims only at later phases of their recovery, it is important for pastors to be aware of the religious dimensions of the experience and be able to assist the victims with questions of faith, meaning, and moral life that may arise in the wake of rape trauma. In particular, the feelings of rage and revenge may call for compassionate religious understanding and interpretation, especially in light of traditional moralistic injunctions against anger and the religious ideal of forgiveness. While each pastor must work out his or her own theology through experience, it may be helpful to consider such rage not as sinful vindictiveness in essence, but as an appropriate existential expression of the value, goodness, and moral integrity of one's bodily and personal existence and as a justifiable, even necessary, moral protest against its violation. In this light, feelings of rage, hatred, shame, and fear testify passionately, if indirectly, to the created goodness of the human person and the sanctity of personal existence. Similarly a rape victim's guilt feelings, however unjustified in reality, may be regarded not simply as an emotional problem to be overcome but also as an expression, however misdirected, of the inherently moral nature of human beings, an expression of the indelible human quest for moral integrity and right relationship.

b. Forgiveness. The further question of forgiveness may well be more difficult to answer existentially for both pastor and victim. Certainly care should be taken to avoid untimely moralistic demands that one forgive one's attacker out of Christian duty. Such expectations, however well-intended, may in fact result in a forced, self-deceptive, psychologically repressive pseudosolution that dynamically and morally caricatures rather than actualizes true forgiveness.

Nonetheless, the question of forgiveness, to some degree, in some form, at some appropriate time, remains an ultimate concern of Christian ministry and constitutes one of the most sensitive and challenging pastoral problems in situations of genuine victimization like rape. The subject cannot be addressed at length in this context, but it may be helpful, pastorally and theologically, to consider J. Patton's suggestion (1985) that forgiveness becomes humanly possible to the extent that one can courageously identify elements of common humanity between oneself and one's "enemy," without being false to oneself or to the moral seriousness of the wrong that has been committed. As Patton shows in considerable detail, there are ways that this difficult, painful, transformative work can be understood and facilitated psychologically. At the same time, in its depths, the ability to forgive, like forgiveness itself, is ultimately also a gift of God, liberating the hurt and rageful soul for a renewed life of trust, hope, and faith. Such an affirmation of grace need not lead to pastoral passivity. Rather, it suggests that pastors actively seek, for themselves and for their parishioners,

the personal transformation that forgiveness entails and that grace enables. This requires all the psychological skill and personal sensitivity at their disposal, while yet being mindful and trusting of the mysterious depths of spirit with which they and those in their care are involved, and in which, as pastors, they are called to participate redemptively and creatively.

Bibliography. Training materials and helpful articles for rape counselors can be found in L. Brodyaga *et al.*, *Rape and Its Victims* (National Law Enforcement and Criminal Justice, U.S. Department of Justice, 1975), pp. 285–309. Other helpful works include: M. Amir, *Patterns of Hope* (1971). S. Brownmiller, *Against Our Will: Men, Women and Rape* (1975). A. W. Burgess and L. Holmstrom, "Rape Trauma Syndrome," *American J. of Psychiatry,* 131 (1974) 981–86. S. Fox and D. Scherl, "Crisis Intervention with Victims of Rape," *Social Work,* 17 (Jan. 1972), 37–42. A. N. Groth and A. W. Burges, "Sexual Dysfunction During Rape." *New England J. of Medicine,* 297 (1977), 764–66. U.S. Department of Justice, Office of Justice Assistance, Research and Statistics, *How to Protect Yourself Against Sexual Assault* (1979). See also J. Patton, *Is Human Forgiveness Possible?* (1985).

L. S. BRAKENSIEK
R. J. HUNTER

CRISIS MINISTRY; VICTIMIZATION; VIOLENCE. *See also* ANGER AND HOSTILITY; ANTISOCIAL PERSONS; CRISIS INTERVENTION THEORY; POST-TRAUMATIC STRESS DISORDER; POWER. *Compare* INCEST.

RAPPORT. *See* COMPASSION; EMPATHY; THERAPEUTIC CONDITIONS.

RASHI (RABBI SHELOMAH YITZHAKI) (1040– 1105). Author of outstanding commentaries on the Bible and the Talmud. The former makes much use of rabbinic sources but does not quote them at length. Instead, Rashi sifts out from the rabbinic sources a phrase or sentence that sheds light on a specific word or idea. The pointedness and terseness of the commentary is probably a result of Rashi's assuming that the reader of the Bible is conversant with the text. He often adds a word or phrase to guide the reader past difficulties. Rashi's commentary on the Babylonian Talmud, most of which is still extant, is a massive achievement. Opening up the Talmud as a work that can be comprehended, Rashi's commentary is an insightful, ingenious explication of difficult, even incomprehensible dialogue, and remains a most indispensable guide to these basic texts of Judaic law and lore. Through Rashi one is able to properly grasp wisdom in applying its insights to human concerns.

R. P. BULKA

JEWISH LITERATURE IN CARE AND COUNSELING.

RATIONAL-EMOTIVE PSYCHOTHERAPY. One of the best known cognitive therapies, in which irrational ideas are considered to be the cause of emotional disturbance. Originated by Albert Ellis, rational-emotive psychotherapy (RET) shares with other cognitive therapies the assumption that maladaptive feelings are often caused by maladaptive thoughts. However, RET helps individuals challenge the core of irrational ideas which all troubled individuals are assumed to hold, whereas other cognitive therapies focus on an individual's idiosyncratic thought patterns.

L. R. PROPST

COGNITIVE PSYCHOLOGY AND PSYCHOTHERAPY; PSYCHO-THERAPY. *See also* COGNITIVE/CONATIVE PROBLEM IN PSYCHOLOGY AND COUNSELING. *Compare* REASON AND PASSION; REASONING AND RATIONALITY IN PASTORAL CARE.

RATIONALITY. *See* REASON AND PASSION; REASONING AND RATIONALITY IN PASTORAL CARE. *See also* FEELING, THOUGHT, AND ACTION IN PASTORAL COUNSELING.

RATIONALIZATION. A reasonable justification given for some attitude, intended action, or completed behavior that wins the approval of self and others but actually masks one's true motivations. If recognized, these motivations would produce anxiety, embarrassment, or other painful affects. Rationalization preserves self-esteem and softens the impact of failure, deprivation, or feelings of guilt.

D. HICKEL

DEFENSE AND COPING THEORY; DEFENSE MECHANISM. *Compare* INTELLECTUALIZATION; REASONING AND RATIONALITY IN PASTORAL CARE.

RAUSCHENBUSCH, WALTER (1861–1918). Baptist pastor and theologian and advocate of the Social Gospel. In his *Christianity and the Social Crisis* (1907), Rauschenbusch expressed a vision of ministry that he had learned as the pastor of a struggling Baptist congregation in the Hell's Kitchen area of New York City. He believed that pastors should serve human need as heralds of a coming Kingdom of justice and righteousness. He criticized an individualistic conception of pastoral ministry that ignored superpersonal forces of evil and corporate forms of justice.

E. B. HOLIFIELD

SOCIAL JUSTICE ISSUES IN PASTORAL CARE.

RAUTENSTRAUCH, FRANZ S. (1734–85). Austrian-Hungarian Roman Catholic abbot and seminary dean. Author of several works, Rautenstrauch made his mark in 1774 with his *Entwurf einer besseren Einrichtung theologischer Schulen*, which led to the inclusion of pastoral theology in the university canon of theological disciplines. His *Entwurf* suggested a threefold didactic and methodological renewal of the study of theology: (a) the inclusion of a correlation between the theological sources and the empirical pastoral problems of the times; (b) the adoption of critical sciences for the study of source documents, a didactic pragmatism, and the study of pedagogy and methodology; (c) the intensification of the practical pastoral education with a special emphasis on the functions of instruction and proclamation.

N. F. HAHN

PASTORAL THEOLOGY, ROMAN CATHOLIC.

REACTION FORMATION. An unconscious defense mechanism whereby unacceptable attitudes and feelings are replaced with socially and personally acceptable attitudes and emotions. This mechanism typically yields exaggerated and rigid beliefs that serve to detain the unacceptable material from conscious awareness. For example, unconscious hate may be supplanted by tremendous kindness or unconscious criminal intent may be replaced by persecutory zeal toward lawbreakers.

M. A. WOLTERSDORF

DEFENSE MECHANISMS. *See also* DEFENSE AND COPING THEORY; NEUROSIS.

READINESS FOR MINISTRY STUDIES. Readiness for ministry is a concept that denotes the qualities, abilities, and knowledge of the beginning professional minister which enable him or her to do the work of ministry acceptably. Readiness for ministry is to be distinguished from the larger concept of effectiveness in ministry. The latter has meanings that vary at different stages of a person's career, with readiness to begin professional ministry being one of those stages. Readiness for ministry studies are research and development projects aimed at identifying competencies for the professional practice of ministry.

The two major examples of ecumenical readiness for ministry studies using survey methods occurred in 1956–59 and 1973–79. The former popularly called "The Ministry Study," identified goals, personal traits, and activities of ministry as criteria, and led to the eventual development of the Theological School Inventory (TSI). The latter, much more extensive project, popularly called "The Readiness for Ministry Study," identified criteria common to forty-six denominations, as well as specific criteria for each of fourteen denominational families in North America.

1. **The Ministry Study.** Three approaches marked early readiness for ministry studies: survey, role definition, and mental testing. A National Council of Churches Consultative Conference in 1955 recommended research via psychological tests as predictors of performance in Protestant ministry. With funding from the Lilly Endowment, Inc., a large "Study of Testing as Related to the Ministry" (later to be called "The Ministry Study") was begun the next year at Educational Testing Service. Though the project was never completed as designed, five groups of personal characteristics, three types of goals, and four constellations of activities were identified as criteria for effective ministry from a survey of seventeen theological schools, 545 ministers, and 520 lay people in thirteen representative Protestant denominations. The Theological School Inventory for assessing motivation of theological students in all denominations was an eventual product of this work.

2. **The Readiness for Ministry Study (RfM).** This refers to a project begun in early 1973, entitled "The Assessment of Readiness for the Professional Practice of Ministry Project," sponsored by the Association of Theological Schools in the U.S. and Canada (ATS). A parallel but somewhat smaller project called the Lutheran Seminarian Project (LSP) of the Lutheran Council in the USA began just six months later. Search Institute, (formerly Youth Research Center) of Minneapolis, Minnesota, pro-

vided research expertise and used essentially the same methods for both. Criteria for readiness to minister common to the participating denominations were identified, and representative sets of tools for assessment were developed in both projects, but initially only for graduating seniors in Rf M, and only for entering students in the LSP.

Rf M involved seminaries and congregations of the forty-six denominations represented in the ATS as well as nondenominational seminaries in the developmental processes. Attention was concentrated initially on evaluation of the outcomes of theological education and thus on assessment of the readiness of graduating seniors. Rf M was funded by the Lilly Endowment, Inc., entirely for a three-year developmental period and partially for a three-year implemental period. The LSP involved only the three largest Lutheran church bodies in the U.S. (LCA, ALC, LC-MS), concentrated on providing seminaries with profiles of their entering classes in order to improve the match of curricula to student needs, and was funded by Aid Association for Lutherans. (The LSP eventually merged into the Rf M Program for financial reasons.)

The assessment services provided by Rf M for schools and students include: casebook, interview, and field observation measures with technical and administrator's manuals; a computerized system for continuous data collection and preparation of group and individual profiles on each school's schedule; interpretative workshops and manuals; interview coding as well as training, certification, and monitoring of interview coders; workshops and manuals for Rf M coordinators; and counseling on use of Rf M criteria (those common to all denominations in North America, to each of fourteen denominational families, or to clinical pastoral educators) in relation to curriculum and faculty development. An assessment service called "Ministry: a professional and personal profile" has also been developed by the ATS for practicing clergy and other pastoral ministers.

a. Criteria. The study used statistical methods to identify the criteria that people affiliated with church bodies in North America believed should be used to assess readiness to minister. From more than two thousand descriptions of activities, roles, and qualities found in existing taxonomies and lists, and from more than one thousand two hundred critical incidents collected from across the denominations, a criterion-rating survey of 444 statements describing characteristics and behaviors of ministers was developed. This survey was submitted to random samples of five evaluator groups (seminary faculty, seniors, denominational executives, lay people, and clergy) from each of seventeen denominational families judged to be represented in the ATS (seventy-eight schools and 5,169 people responded). A core set of criteria common to all denominations, and fourteen sets of criteria specific to each of fourteen denominational families, were identified empirically using cluster and factor analyses with equal weighting given to the ratings of each evaluator group and denominational family.

From the core clusters, eleven major themes in ministry expectations were developed. Of these, seven were rated across the entire sample as "quite important" qualities for ministry. These included (in rank order) open, affirming style; caring for persons under stress; congregational leadership; theologian in life and thought; minis-

try from personal commitment of faith; development of fellowship and worship; and denominational awareness and collegiality (Schuller *et al.*, 1980, p. 25). For a comprehensive description of the methods, criteria, and expectations, see *Ministry in America* or *RfM(I): Criteria* concerning Rf M, and *Ten Faces of Ministry* concerning the LSP.

b. Assessment tools. Three kinds of measures were developed: (1) a *casebook* measure, which requires the assessee to give paper and pencil responses to verbal descriptions of actual opportunities for ministry to indicate the likelihood that he or she will choose certain goals, rationales, and courses of action in corresponding real-life situations; (2) an *interview* measure, which requires the assessee to respond orally to open-ended questions as an indication of beliefs, values, attitudes, opinions, judgments, and past or probable behavior; and (3) a *field observation* measure, which requires other people, on the basis of their past observations of the assessee, to estimate the likelihood that the assessee will act in specific ways.

Psychometric methods and conventions including empirical scaling and estimates of reliability were used to develop all measuring instruments including the interview. All measures were reviewed and revised in 1979 after careful monitoring of their psychometric properties during the first three years of use. These were further revised in 1985 in the *Profiles in Ministry* materials.

Whether Rf M provides assessment tools that are truly indicative of competency has been debated. If giving evidence of knowing and intending to do what is defined as preferred behavior under specific hypothetical circumstances is measurement of competency, then Rf M assessment measures competency. If a representative sample of actual performance under a variety of real-life conditions is required, then Rf M does not meet this standard. The predictive validity of the Rf M tests, that is, the correlation of the test scores with subsequent professional behavior, has not yet been established, although one study (Majovski and Malony, 1983) developed a ministerial effectiveness inventory based on Rf M criteria.

Bibliography. For a comprehensive description of how the tests were developed and interpretative guidelines, see *RfM (II): Assessment, The Technical Manual,* and the *RfM Interpretative Manuals.* See also M. Brekke, *RfM Technical Manual* (1976). M. Brekke *et al.*, *RfM Advisor's Manual* (1979); *Ten Faces of Ministry* (1979). M. Harrower, "Psychological Tests in the Unitarian Universalist Ministry," *J. of Religion and Health,* 2 (1963), 129–42. F. Kling, "A Study of Testing as Related to the Ministry," *Religious Education,* 53 (1957), 243–48. L. F. Majovski and H. N. Malony, "The Role of Psychological Assessment in Predicting Ministerial Effectiveness," *Review of Religious Research,* 28:1 (1986), 29–39. D. Schuller *et al.*, *RfM I: Criteria* (1975); *RfM II: Assessment* (1976); *Ministry in America* (1980). D. Schuller and M. Strommen, *Expectations of Ministry: The View of Clinical Pastoral Educators* (1981). G. Stern, *Methods in Personality Assessment* (1956). S. Webb, "A Summary of Research Activities of the Ministry Study During the First Year 1956–57," Unpublished, Educational Testing Service. D. Williams *et al.*, *RfM Interpretative Manual for Graduating Seminarians* and *RfM Interpretative Manual for Entering Seminarians* (rev. eds., 1979). G. W. Rowatt, "What Does the ACPE Expect of Ministry?" *J. of Pastoral Care,* 36 (1982), 147–59.

M. L. BREKKE

See articles describing empirical studies of CLERGY, RABBIS, RELIGIOUS or THEOLOGICAL STUDENTS. See also MINISTRY; ROLE, MINISTERIAL; THEOLOGICAL EDUCATION AND THE PASTORAL CARE MOVEMENT. Compare PSYCHOLOGY OF RELIGION (Empirical Studies, Methods, and Problems).

READING MATERIALS, PASTORAL USE OF. See LITERATURE, PASTORAL USE OF.

REALITY PRINCIPLE. One of two principles that for Freud regulate mental function. (The other is the pleasure principle.) The reality principle represents a person's capacity to postpone immediate pleasure in order to assure satisfaction or avoid pain at some future time. It is not an innate function, but an ability which develops during childhood and marks a maturing individual.

In Freudian theory the reality principle corresponds to the conversion of freely moving energy into bound energy, belonging to the level of preconscious-conscious operations. Consequently, the psychoanalytic perspective views the intervention of the reality principle as a specific type of instinctual energy as a service for the ego's development. For example, when an infant attempts to find an avenue for discharging instinctual energy, it may hallucinate the object of its desire. When real gratification then does not occur, or when it produces pain, these hallucinatory attempts are relinquished, and a sense of external reality is substituted, even if such "reality" proves disagreeable. In the mature person the pleasure principle is not fully suppressed, but governs other psychical activities, like fantasies and the unconscious.

According to depth psychology, the agent that assumes the task of insuring the authority of the reality principle is the ego. The ego mediates between instinctual demand and the world. It controls the operations necessary for satisfying cravings through thought and action modified by present reality, as well as the memory of that person's prior experiences. Estimating consequences of immediate satisfaction, postponement, or abandonment of the attempt for satisfaction is the chief task of the reality principle.

The reality principle acquires an additional dimension for the pastor: as clergy assist persons with many of the same problems other therapists deal with, the pastoral counselor also addresses an individual's concept of ultimate reality and how such faith functions in personal life. The minister sees the person's ideas about external reality as a reflection of their inner world and its spiritual concerns. This dimension can be severely distorted, indicating religious beliefs that may be pathological. However, it may also reflect a vital spark of hope and inner strength. The personality of the perceiver — that person's feelings, attitudes, and way of responding — can have a powerful influence on the quality of perception. The pastoral counselor is not primarily called upon to "theologize" with a person in intense need, except to guide that person toward understanding of how his or her religious beliefs might be stunted. Such a professional is committed to affirm the reality and potential health of the psyche, the "self" or "spirit".

Bibliography. A. Freud, *The Ego and the Mechanisms of Defense* (rev. ed. 1966), pp. 59, 61. S. Freud, "Beyond the Pleasure Principle," *SE* 18; "Formulations on the Two Principles of Mental Functioning," *SE* 12.

D. M. MOSS

HUMAN CONDITION/PREDICAMENT; PSYCHOANALYSIS. See also PHILOSOPHY AND PSYCHOLOGY, WESTERN. Compare CONFRONTATION; MAGICAL THINKING; PRIMARY AND SECONDARY PROCESS; REASON AND PASSION; SPECIALNESS, SENSE OF.

REALITY TESTING. The process of comparing fantasized behavior or relationships with actual consequences by performing the fantasized act. It is testing the idea against the reality of the world and others. For example, the idea that one can solve every problem is tried by the "reality" of one's ability or failure to master each problem experienced.

Q. L. HAND

PSYCHOANALYSIS (Personality Theory and Research). Compare MAGICAL THINKING; PRIMARY AND SECONDARY PROCESS.

REALITY THERAPY. A present-oriented therapy originated by William Glasser which asserts that the patient is responsible for all of his or her difficulties. According to this model the common cause of maladjustment is the inability to fulfill one's needs, which include loving and being loved and feeling worthwhile to oneself and others. Reality therapy construes the failure to fulfill these needs as being due to the irresponsible denial of reality and the refusal to execute responsible behavior for their fulfillment.

L. R. PROPST

PSYCHOTHERAPY. See also LIMIT-SETTING; RESPONSIBILITY/ IRRESPONSIBILITY, PSYCHOLOGY OF; THERAPEUTIC CONDITIONS.

REASON AND PASSION. In classical Christian understanding, reason and love, when properly functioning, are inseparable and positively related. The passions (destructive emotions, states of mind, or behavior) obscure reason and prevent or corrupt love. How to embrace reason and govern the passions without denigrating love and other emotions has been a persistent tension in Christian life and thought.

The patristic way of understanding the relationship between reason and the passions was based on the Platonic insight into the way the Good and the True are inseparably linked in reality. Much of patristic thought also assumed a generally Platonic psychology: a human personality is likened to a chariot drawn by two horses. When reason is the driver and the two horses, anger and desire, provide the energy, the person functions properly. If the horses overthrow the driver, however, they assume a destructive character and become the passions.

In patristic theology, reason is the most important part of the image of God in human beings. It has two functions: seeing reality and God as they truly are, and making moral choices. The reality reason sees, however, is not neutral. Since it is an expression of God the Logos, it reveals to human rationality the Creator who is visible in creation as love. According to Irenaeus, God is present and visible symbolically to us even in the four directions which form the shape of a cross as surely as God is in the crucifixion. An ability to love and reason functioning as it ought are therefore closely related.

By reason we were meant to know God in creation; however, this knowledge is obscured by sin and the passions. Part of the work of Christ is to help us conquer the passions so that reason may function to enable us to truly see God and God's love within creation. Certain physical conditions which affect our ability to see reality and love were also called passions, though they are not considered to be sins unless they are overindulged; these include a need for sleep and food, death, and certain kinds of physical suffering.

The passions cloud our reason and produce an inability to love. These passions are destructive emotions, attitudes, or even objects, which take away our freedom to make real choices. As specified by Evagrius Ponticus, the passions develop into what the Middle Ages were to call the seven deadly sins. Evagrius's list includes gluttony, lust, avarice, restless boredom (acedia), anger, depression, inordinate love of praise, and pride. Talking too much, judgmentalism, and overreligiosity were also considered to be passions in the early monastic literature.

Emotions and states of mind do not become passions until they distort their sufferer's ability to relate to reality for what it is. Generosity, pity, and hospitality, for example, are not passions because they are naturally associated with reason and love. Even these, however, can be experienced in a way that perverts love and reason. While anger, on the other hand, is considered by some always to be a passion, others would believe that there are circumstances in which it is anger itself which allows a person to see a situation for what it is.

In later theology, Aquinas, though wanting to show how all of human experience reflected divine love and order, focused more on reason as the primary reflection of the divine, and was more concerned with the dynamics of faith and reason than those of reason and the passions, which he took to be quite complex but less problematical. Since the time of the Enlightenment, all human emotion, including love and its expressions as well as the passions, have often been thought to be merely destructive to the functioning of reason. Such a view sees reason in logical or even mechanical terms and reality as neutral in value rather than revelatory of God's love, with love for God itself becoming a kind of abstract asset of reason.

Such Enlightenment views have become deeply embedded in subsequent Western culture, including much of its secular and pastoral psychology, though they are clearly ill-suited to a pastoral care that aims to integrate body, mind, and soul while respecting the provenance of each. Contemporary pastoral care could no doubt benefit from critically reviewing its Enlightenment assumption of an adversarial relationship between reason and love (and the other emotions), in order to reappropriate the patristic notion of the way in which reality is truly seen only through the eyes of love — while love is known and nourished only through a proper relationship with reality — with God revealed in the ordered structure of creation.

Bibliography. T. Aquinas, *Summa Theologicae 1a 1ae: The Emotions*, Blackfriars ed. (1967). Athanasius, *On the Incarnation* (1953). E. Ponticus, *The Praktikos* (1970). Gregory of Nyssa, *The Life of Moses*, vol. 2 (1978), par. 63–129. Irenaeus, *Proof of the Apostolic Preaching* (1952), par. 34. I. Kant, *Religion Within the Limits of Reason* (1960). B. Ward, trans., *The Sayings of the Desert Fathers* (1975).

R. C. BONDI

COGNITIVE/CONATIVE PROBLEM IN PSYCHOLOGY AND COUNSELING; EMOTION; MIND. *See also* CHARACTER ETHICS AND PASTORAL CARE; EMOTION; HUMAN CONDITION/PREDICAMENT; LOVE; SEVEN DEADLY SINS. *Compare* FEELING, THOUGHT, AND ACTION IN PASTORAL COUNSELING; EARLY CHURCH, PASTORAL CARE AND COUNSELING IN; PERSON (Christian Perspective); PHILOSOPHY AND PSYCHOLOGY; RATIONAL-EMOTIVE PSYCHOTHERAPY.

REASONING AND RATIONALITY IN PASTORAL CARE.
Reasoning is the drawing of conclusions and inferences from observation, fact, hypothesis, and doctrine. *Rationality* is the quality of being able to reason.

Reasoning is the key method for appealing to the rationality of other persons, but it is less effective in appealing to their will or their feelings. The place of reasoning and rationality in pastoral care is dependent on which of the three — rationality, will, or feeling — is deemed most important to address.

From the beginning Christian pastors used reason and rationality in pastoral care. Two of the major sources for the NT and early Christian writings, the Wisdom literature of the OT and Stoic philosophy, highlighted reason's importance. Following the example of Jesus and Paul, the early church devoted a significant portion of its energy to teaching (e.g., the catechumenate). During the Middle Ages the sacramental system, which appealed to the affections, and church discipline, which appealed to the will, became central in pastoral care. The Reformation, however, with its program of Scripture reading, preaching, teaching, and rationalizing the sacraments, restored the importance of reason and rationality to pastoral care.

From the seventeenth to the mid-twentieth century, American pastoral care shifted its focus from reason, to will, to the irrational forces and affections. In the seventeenth century most pastors assumed that reason and revelation were complementary; therefore, reason was their primary tool. These pastors understood the will to be the handmaiden of reason; pastoral care consisted in aiding the mind, with the cooperation of the will, to establish order among the unruly affections. During the eighteenth and nineteenth centuries there was emphasis on the appeal to sentiment and to will, as well as to mind — American pastors moved from a purely rational psychology to a more balanced one. In the early part of the twentieth century this balance was destroyed by Freud's theories of the unconscious. At mid-century, the nondirective methods of Carl Rogers intensified the attention given to feelings. Pastoral care through the clinical movement adapted the new emphasis on the unconscious and the affections which drew attention away from both reason and will.

Pastoral care, by becoming identified with dynamic psychology, distanced itself from behavioral psychology, which had begun to dominate academic departments by the middle of this century. Cognitive counseling, a new rational psychology closely allied to behaviorism, arose in the 1960s and 1970s under the leadership of Albert Ellis

(Rational Emotive Therapy [RET]) and Aaron Beck (Cognitive Therapy). Cognitive counselors postulate that disordered thoughts cause troubled affections and unhelpful behavior; therefore feelings and behavior can be changed by changing the thoughts that underlie them. This approach reestablishes the place of reason and rationality in counseling because its central method is the reasoned appeal to the client's rationality.

This new rational psychology does not have a solid place in the literature of pastoral care yet, though it could become important. It makes use of training in reasoning and belief that is central to the theological education of many pastors. Moreover, because cognitive theorists conceive of the therapist as teacher, they have developed theories and methods that can be used helpfully in doing the educative counseling (e.g., premarital, baptismal, referral, vocational, divorce), in classes and groups that make up a large part of pastoral care. It could also help pastors develop the skill of "wise pastoral reasoning" with suffering parishioners on questions such as theodicy, as practiced in the early church and advocated in recent years by Thomas Oden (1983, p. 232).

Bibliography. A. Beck, *Cognitive Therapy and the Emotional Disorders* (1976). A. Ellis, *A Guide to Rational Living* (1961). P. Hauck, *Reason in Pastoral Counseling* (1972). E. B. Holifield, *A History of Pastoral Care in America* (1983). T. Oden, *Pastoral Theology* (1983).

C. W. TAYLOR

FEELING, THOUGHT, AND ACTION IN PASTORAL COUNSELING; PROBLEM SOLVING; PRUDENCE; SUGGESTION, PERSUASION, AND INFLUENCE. *See also* HISTORY OF PROTESTANT *or* ROMAN CATHOLIC PASTORAL CARE (United States); JEWISH CARE AND COUNSELING; PASTORAL CARE (History, Traditions, and Definitions); PHILOSOPHY AND PSYCHOLOGY; TECHNIQUE AND SKILL IN PASTORAL CARE. *Compare* COGNITIVE/CONATIVE PROBLEM IN PSYCHOLOGY AND COUNSELING; COGNITIVE PSYCHOLOGY AND PSYCHOTHERAPY; GUIDANCE, PASTORAL; INTELLECTUALIZATION.

REBAPTISM. The practice of repeating baptismal rites for an individual. Generally disallowed or discouraged by most churches, this practice becomes a pastoral concern in several instances. One typical situation is when a person, baptized as an infant, has doubts about the validity of his or her baptism and asks to be baptized again as an adult believer. The question also arises when persons who have been baptized as infants wish to join a church which practices believer's baptism.

Historically, this issue has most critically arisen in questions of apostasy, when a person has renounced the church for a period of time, disavowing the meaning of baptism, and then wishes to be reinstated into the fellowship of faith. Such a request for rebaptism may be accompanied by a religious conversion experience in which the person has come into a full awareness of sin, has gone through a time of confession and repentance, and has experienced a radical change of direction in life. For such a person, rebaptism would indeed be seen and experienced as a rebirth in which one is baptized into the death of Christ and raised with Christ to "walk in newness of life" (Rom. 6:4).

Consent for rebaptism depends largely upon a particular church's theology of baptism. Many churches view baptism as a human act in which one responds to God's grace with an outward demonstration of faith; this may allow for its repetition, especially if one has been baptized as an infant. The majority of churches, however, view baptism as a once-and-for-all act of God's grace, permanently incorporating one into the body of Christ, thus making the act unrepeatable. This is based in part on exegesis of passages such as Jn. 13:1–11 and Heb. 10:26 (see Gilmore, 1959).

Gilmore (1966) and others suggest that in churches with this theology the felt need for rebaptism may be addressed pastorally through a liturgy or ritual during Holy Communion or the baptism of others. Requests for rebaptism often come at times of major transitions in life and may express developmental concerns or other feelings such as guilt for which an open-ended, sensitive pastoral conversation may be helpful. The religious significance of these feelings should also be taken seriously, however, and some liturgical response may be appropriate. A service of repentance and reaffirmation of faith may enable persons to express liturgically the feelings of death and rebirth accompanying these transitions and allow the pastor and congregation to affirm the work of the Holy Spirit in individual lives while honoring the unique significance of baptism.

Bibliography. J. Baillie, *Baptism and Conversion* (1964). A. Gilmore, *Baptism and Christian Unity* (1966). A. Gilmore, ed., *Christian Baptism* (1959). World Council of Churches, *Baptism, Eucharist and Ministry* (1982).

G. H. ASQUITH, JR.

BAPTISM AND CONFIRMATION. *See also* ECCLESIOLOGY AND PASTORAL CARE; LIFE CYCLE THEORY AND PASTORAL CARE; RITUAL AND PASTORAL CARE. *Compare* BORN-AGAIN EXPERIENCE; EMERGENCY BAPTISM.

REBELLIOUSNESS. *See* AUTHORITY ISSUES IN PASTORAL CARE.

REBIRTH. *See* BORN-AGAIN EXPERIENCE; CONVERSION; EVANGELICAL PASTORAL CARE.

REBIRTHING THERAPY. *See* POPULAR THERAPEUTIC MOVEMENTS AND PSYCHOLOGIES.

RECEIVING AND GIVING. *See* GIVING AND RECEIVING; GRACE; GRATITUDE.

RECONCILIATION, SACRAMENT OF. *See* PENANCE, SACRAMENT OF.

RECONCILING. Pastoral acts that "call back together" the estranged. Broad usage recognizes reconciling as the establishment of harmony with one's world, one's destiny, or oneself. In pastoral theology, Clebsch and Jaekle defined it as that function of pastoral care which "seeks to reestablish broken relationships" with others, including God. Added to healing, sustaining, and guiding — which were already considered aspects of pastoral care (Hiltner) — reconciling seemed to these authors the most promising pastoral function. Reconciling operates through both forgiveness and discipline: forgiveness, which restores relationships through proclamation, confession-absolution, and the like, and discipline, which reviews behavior and places persons in situations that can lead to restored relationships.

Bibliography. W. A. Clebsch and C. R. Jaekle, *Pastoral Care in Historical Perspective* (1964). S. Hiltner, *Preface to Pastoral Theology* (1958).

J. R. BURCK

CHRISTOLOGY AND PASTORAL CARE; FORGIVENESS; PENANCE, SACRAMENT OF. *See also* CONGREGATION, PASTORAL CARE OF; FAMILY THEORY AND THERAPY; MARRIAGE COUNSELING AND MARITAL THERAPY; MEDIATION/CONCILIATION. *Compare* ALIENATION AND ESTRANGEMENT; HEALING OF MEMORIES; SHEPHERD/SHEPHERDING.

RECONSTITUTED FAMILIES. *See* STEPFAMILIES.

RECONSTRUCTIONIST JUDAISM. A movement within Conservative judaism which established its own institutional identity in the 1930s. Like Conservative judaism, Reconstructionism pays close attention to the historical development of Jewish law and custom. It differs by claiming that Judaism is not primarily a religion, but a culture of which religion is but one part. Thus observance of the Sabbath, which is a religious obligation for Conservative Jews, is regarded as an expression of Jewish cultural and ethnic identity by Reconstructionists. Although growing, Reconstructionism does not yet claim a substantial following.

P. J. HAAS

JEWISH CARE AND COUNSELING (History, Traditions, and Contemporary Issues).

RECONSTRUCTIVE SURGERY. *See* SURGICAL PATIENT.

RECORD KEEPING. Four types of records are kept in connection with pastoral care and counseling: (1) dates and times of meetings; (2) specific data about parishioners and counselees; (3) notes about what took place during meetings; and (4) if contributions or fees are involved, records of account.

Records are needed for many purposes. They contain information needed to aid in reflection, recollection, supervision, consultation, and peer review. They may form the basis for research, needed to aid in decisions about professional concerns and social policy. Ethics or legal proceedings may hinge upon their contents.

Record-keeping practices are intended to protect the interests of those who seek the pastor's care or counsel. They also reflect the pastor's sense of legal, professional, and social responsibilities. This gives rise to competing interests. A pastoral approach seeks to differentiate between these, meeting each as best can be.

Practically, this means that the pastor approaches the conflicts inherent in developing record-keeping practices by making separations. Financial records are kept completely separate from records containing other information. Primary records concerning parishioners and counselees are broken down by the use which will be made of them, and separated from secondary research material.

It is important to develop an information control code with which to coordinate records containing information, and to keep it in a safe place. A simple numbering system will do. Code designations should be used in appointment books and to identify files. Books and files should be kept in locked cabinets when not in use.

Parishioner and counselee identifying information, such as names, addresses, dates of birth, social security numbers, should be separated from appointment books and other records and kept in separate files.

Official files need to be separated from work files. Parishioners and counselees may be entitled to access to the former, which may be susceptible to subpoena. Specific information in these should be minimal. The date of the meeting, its duration, and a brief summary in general terms of what was considered and accomplished will usually do.

In the separate, detailed work files, there should not be identifying information, as they may contain much specific data about parishioners or counselees. They are not always immune from legal process and should be routinely destroyed after a reasonable period. A lawyer can advise as to what period is reasonable in particular locations.

Information for use in research should be kept in separate files. There should be no identifying information in these or cross references in them to other files unless there is a compelling reason to do so. If there is such information, the information control code should be used: it should be entered so that it can be separated from research files when cross reference is no longer needed.

The accounting code should also be separate and not cross referenced to the information control code.

J. J. ROGGE

CONFIDENTIALITY; LEGAL DIMENSIONS OF PASTORAL CARE AND COUNSELING.

RECREATION. *See* PLAY.

RECREATIONAL THERAPY. *See* ADJUNCTIVE THERAPIES.

REDEMPTION. *See* CHRISTOLOGY.

REDEMPTORIST SPIRITUALITY. *See* SPIRITUALITY (Roman Catholic Tradition).

REDUCTIONISM. *See* THEOLOGY AND PSYCHOLOGY; PASTORAL THEOLOGICAL METHOD.

REFERRAL. In ancient times, care for persons was ordinarily provided by persons who were variously identified as witch doctors, shamans, holy men or women, and who seemed to possess special powers of healing. This led to the often noted fact that the priest and the physician were one person dealing, however primitively, with the entire gamut of needs of the individual.

Gradually through the years, and especially following the Enlightenment, there was an advance in the knowledge of human suffering and in the gaining of particular skills for meeting human needs. This refinement of knowledge and skill led to a diversity of persons identified as care deliverers. While until the twentieth century it would be inappropriate to speak of specialties as the term is known today, it was true nonetheless that a division of labor increasingly occurred. This factor, as is usually true with any transition, was accompanied by both gain and loss. The gain was an increase in the quality of care in particular areas of human suffering whether physical, emotional, or spiritual. Physicians learned new ways to deal with illness, broadly defined. Counselors assisted in wrestling through personal problems and in discovering the most appropriate responses to human vicissitude. Clergy provided nurture and guidance in enabling persons toward deeper faith and greater awareness of the power of reconciliation and forgiveness as well as the moral context in which life is lived.

The corresponding loss, however, lay in the increasing tendency to overlook the wholeness of the person as care delivery was reposited in one group or another depending on the nature of the need. Increasingly, the specialities emerged, not only in the general spheres of need, but also within the broad categories of the helping professions. In the twentieth century this shift toward specialization has enabled care delivery to become highly skilled in the several caring professions; so much so that persons are often at a loss as to where they shall seek help when faced with a particular trouble or distress.

As a means for attempting to offset part of the loss, the concept of the healing team began to emerge where persons with particular skills and understanding could join forces with those having other skills and knowledge. Particularly true in institutional settings, the team approach was also evident among persons who functioned more or less independently. The process of referral took shape as a means for bringing to bear upon the situation every resource available. Gradually, responsible principles were developed a guidelines for when to refer, how to refer, and where to refer. Although applicable to all the helping professions, the procedures for referral by pastoral counselors have become increasingly clear.

1. **Timing of Referral.** The question of when to refer is approached by an assessment of one's own resources and a knowledge of the resources available in the community. Referral is indicated when the caregiver recognizes an inadequacy in any one of three areas. The first of these is *time,* as the pastoral counselor assesses whether or not he or she can devote sufficient attention to the needs of the person or persons requiring assistance. Many parish ministers discover that they cannot give time to long-term counseling without neglecting crucial dimensions of the work for the faith community.

Alongside assessing adequate time, the pastoral counselor evaluates possession of *skill* sufficient to deal with the intricacies of the human predicament. Although the minister may have sufficient time to devote to the caring situation, he or she may be appropriately aware of the fact that his or her past experience of study, supervision, and consultation is inadequate to provide that which is needed to be of greatest help to the parishioner.

In the third place, even though the minister may have adequate time and appropriate skill for the assisting of the parishioner, it is clear that on occasions she or he may, for a variety of reasons, find it impossible to provide the *emotional*

presence and support needed. For whatever reason including personal struggle or the bearing of many burdens, the "wounded healer" will from time to time be too wounded to be of help. Ordinarily such times are temporary, but when they occur, referral is clearly indicated.

In light of these three basic assessments two dangers face the pastoral counselor in reaching the decision to refer. On the one hand, referral may be made too quickly, thus depriving the parishioner of skills and knowledge possessed by the minister. Correspondingly, the pastoral counselor may be too slow in referral, thus depriving the parishioner of needed skills and knowledge possessed by colleagues in the helping professions. The first ordinarily arises out of an inadequate assessment of the self and an unwillingness to affirm genuine strength. The second usually arises out of inordinate pride, which deludes the minister into thinking that she or he can indeed be all things to all people.

2. **Process of Referral.** Care should be taken that the parishioner does not experience the process of referring as rejection. Thus, partnership is affirmed as pastor and parishioner work together to find the assistance the parishioner needs. The paradigm sentence, whether or not spoken in so many words, is "Let us join in discovering the best resource available to assist in your particular circumstance."

Ordinarily, there are two models which obtain most frequently in referral. In the first, the referring person relinquishes responsibility for the care-receiver until such a time as the referral resources have been effectively utilized. This does not mean that the person referring ceases to be concerned for the person referred; it is designed to assure that there be no confusion or cross purposes encountered by the care-receiver with particular reference to the source of assistance. In addition, such a model removes the opportunity for the care-receiver to pit one resource against another in the process of avoiding the pain which may be necessary in the healing experience.

The second model, one that has increasingly emerged in contemporary family practice of medicine, occurs when the caregiver retains overall responsibility for the care-receiver but calls on colleagues as needed to provide particular and specific services. In this model the wholeness of the person is always in focus and the several areas of need are seen in the context of the unity of the individual or family. This model may be helpful for the parish minister who continues to relate to the parishioner in varieties of ways along with particular services being temporarily utilized from persons with special skills and knowledge.

3. **Resources for Referral.** The question of where to refer turns on the resources available in any community or situation which is the locus of the care delivery. For many localities outside urban areas the choices are limited. In most urban communities there are a variety of different types of services and resources requiring only that the pastoral counselor continually keep abreast of the ever changing array of persons and organizations which address some aspect of human need. The pastor should have some personal awareness of the competence and quality of care which is given by various professionals and agencies.

The basic principle in any and all referral is the well-being of the care-receiver. This principle offsets any tendency toward a grandiose assumption that the care-deliverer is omnicompetent and needs no assistance on the one hand, and the tendency to downplay one's own resources and healing abilities on the other. When the care-receiver is kept in focus as the primary concern of the caregiver, then appropriate utilization of the community of helpers can make for fullness of life.

Bibliography. H. C. Clinebell, *Basic Types of Pastoral Care and Counseling* (1984), ch. 12. W. B. Oglesby, Jr., *Referral in Pastoral Counseling* (1978).

W. B. OGLESBY, JR.

INTERPROFESSIONAL TEAMS AND RELATIONSHIPS; PASTORAL CARE (Contemporary Methods, Perspectives, and Issues). *See also* GUIDANCE, PASTORAL; PROFESSIONALISM; TECHNIQUE AND SKILL IN PASTORAL CARE. *Compare* CONSULTATION.

REFLECTION. *See* PASTORAL THEOLOGICAL METHODOLOGY. *See also* CASE STUDY METHOD; CRITICAL THEORY; THEORY IN PASTORAL CARE AND COUNSELING, FUNCTIONS OF.

REFORM, LITURGICAL. *See* LITURGICAL CHANGE AND REFORM; VATICAN COUNCIL II.

REFORM JUDAISM. The most liberal branch of contemporary Judaism, having its roots in nineteenth-century Enlightenment Germany. It is based on the doctrine that only the ethical norms given at Sinai are eternally valid, all other traditional laws and customs being historically contingent. Accordingly, Reform Judaism maintains the right to recast or discard any traditional practice not in line with modern, enlightened sensibilities. The last few decades have seen a reappropriation of traditional practices among Reform Jews. About forty percent of affiliated Jews in North America are Reform.

P. J. HAAS

JEWISH CARE AND COUNSELING (History, Traditions, and Contemporary Issues).

REFORMED PASTORAL CARE. That tradition of Protestant pastoral care originally shaped by the Reformation in Switzerland under Ulrich Zwingli, Henry Bullinger, and John Calvin, as well as John Knox in Scotland and other Calvinist reformers throughout Europe (especially the Netherlands) and North America. Today the Reformed tradition encompasses a worldwide family of churches, variously called Reformed or Presbyterian. In North America, the pastoral style and emphasis of the Reformed churches, especially Presbyterianism, has blended into mainstream Protestantism to a large extent, having contributed significantly to and been heavily influenced by the pastoral care and counseling movement.

1. **Historic Themes and Emphases.** Much of the early understanding of pastoral care in the Reformed tradition may be summed up under the rubric of discipline — the spiritual discipline of the pastor and the discipline of the flock. The seriousness with which this tradition has viewed sin has influenced the emphasis on discipline in pastoral care, but sinfulness was also seen to lie at the very root of the human dilemma, thereby necessitating reconciliation with God.

Related to each of these themes was the emphasis upon correct teaching and preaching of the Word. Hearing clearly the Word of God convinced persons of their sinful condition, thereby leading them to repentance and reconciliation with God. Following upon regeneration and reconciliation, the Word was seen as a guide to faith and a continuing source of nourishment for the soul. As Calvin wrote: "The office of a true and faithful minister is not only publicly to teach the people over whom [one] is ordained pastor, but as far as may be, to admonish, exhort, rebuke and console each one in particular" (McNeill, p. 177).

2. **The Early Reformers.** *a. Zwingli.* As the Reformation began in Switzerland, Zwingli was concerned with abuses which affected the pastoral office. Using the language of the prophets and apostles, he described the marks of "the true shepherd" and attacked the "false prophets" who must be recognized and corrected or else expelled. Zwingli stressed faithful preaching which would lead to repentance and emphasized that proclamation must be followed by pastoral instruction and devoted service to the people. Pastors were to stand on guard for the people of God, exercising discipline in love toward the increase and upbuilding of the flock. Since the secular governments in Switzerland assumed responsibility for maintaining and supporting Christianity, there was close cooperation with the church in the discipline and punishment of offenders. In 1525, for example, Zwingli wrote the Marriage Ordinance, which was adopted by the Council of Zurich establishing a court of six judges to meet twice a week to handle offenses and complaints. The primary means of discipline used by the church was to exclude offenders from the sacrament of Holy Communion; moreover, the state contributed to the enforcement of this disciplinary action.

Confession of sin was one of Zwingli's chief means of discipline. Christians were urged to confess directly to God, but if that proved difficult they were encouraged to unburden their consciences "to a wise counselor, a Minister of the Word."

b. Bullinger. Henry Bullinger was Zwingli's able successor in the church in Zurich. In the Second Helvetic Confession, Bullinger placed a strong emphasis on repentance and confession and on the office of the minister. Persons overwhelmed by their sins and temptations were encouraged to seek pastoral counsel. Bullinger identified a number of specific duties of the minister, and pastoral care is prominent in this list. It included "comforting the faint-hearted, rebuking offenders, restoring the wanderers, raising the fallen, catechizing the ignorant, providing for the poor, visiting the sick and those entangled in temptation" (McNeill, p. 194).

Bullinger is reported to have listened with great patience and attention to persons in need, serving as a trusted and sensitive confessor and a skillful minister to their suffering. His house was open to all and he provided both spiritual and material aid to many refugees from persecution.

c. Calvin. As pastor, Calvin functioned as a "director of souls." He would call parishioners to repentance, exhort them to read the Scriptures, comfort them in their suffering, and guide them in responsible Christian behavior; his correspondence is full of such "personal guidance" or "spiritual direction." He also wrote to kings and queens and other prominent persons encouraging them to be faithful Christians and urging their protection and advocacy of the church. His letters reflect deep care for persons who were ill or bereaved and patience with political complexities. He wrote to prisoners soon to die during the persecutions of Henry II of France, seeking political means to secure their release, but he also inquired after their souls.

In his theological writings, Calvin's doctrine of repentance and his description of the process of salvation, which included a succession of stages, are significant in shaping Reformed pastoral care. He saw the doctrine of election as a comfort for Christians, removing the struggle to earn salvation through good works. He also sought to shift the Christian's focus from subjective, inward searching or pulse-taking to a more objective faith in Christ, i.e., a trust in divinity rather than in oneself.

d. Knox. In Scotland John Knox further developed pastoral discipline by emphasizing church order and liturgy, and by providing strict guidelines for moral behavior. He was concerned to preserve the purity of the congregation as well as to secure the repentance of guilty persons. Serious offenses required public discipline by the church, whereas private admonition was sufficient for lesser offenses. Excommunication was the most severe punishment administered to those who were unrepentant, but this was intended to be a careful and deliberate process exercised only in the most severe situations.

3. The Puritans in America. Pastoral care of penitents and the understanding of the process of salvation took new forms in the Puritan churches in America. Discipline continued as a central theme in Reformed pastoral care in America but the focus shifted, as it had done earlier in England and Scotland, from church order and collective discipline to a dealing with specific cases by the pastor.

In New England, "Puritan pastors became masters of introspection, cartographers of the inner life, adept at recognizing the signs of salvation" (Holifield, 1983, p. 27). Their pastoral methods were built upon the Reformed theological heritage of Europe, a carefully reasoned system of logic and a psychology of the inner life, which described how persons acquired knowledge of God and how the competing forces of reason and the passions were governed by the will.

The rigorous Puritan emphasis upon righteousness and the elaborate focusing upon the complexity of the salvation/sanctification process left numerous "anxious souls" in its wake. One of the most common pastoral care problems was the reassurance of these sensitive individuals. Using Ramist logic, a method of "questioning" was developed which would lead troubled persons through a carefully reasoned process to an answer drawn from Scripture, which was intended to convince, to confront, and eventually to reassure the person.

4. Recent Developments. Increasing urbanization in North America at the turn of the century created a challenging new context for pastoral care. In the late nineteenth and early twentieth centuries a surge of interest developed in human personality and the psychological disciplines, together with a hope that "ministry to personality" could be "at once scientific and religious." Out of this ferment came the pastoral care and counseling movement, among whose leaders were Reformed pastors like Anton T. Boisen and Seward Hiltner. While these leaders undoubtedly brought a theoretical and intellectual emphasis to the movement characteristic of their Reformed heritage, they also introduced new clinical insights and liberating principles into Reformed pastoral care and counseling. These developments have heavily influenced Reformed ministry, especially among Presbyterians, and have brought Reformed pastoral care more and more into the mainstream of pastoral care in America. They have undoubtedly also contributed to a general shift in focus from "salvation" to "self-realization" in this tradition as in mainline Protestantism in general (Holifield, 1983). At the same time, the tradition's distinctive focus on discipline and the centrality of the Scriptures for faith, worship, and practice have remained prominent features of Reformed ministry. Moreover, the new clinical emphases in its care and counseling, and the shifts of focus they entail, may be consistent in certain ways with Reformed theology's interest in sanctification or "growing in grace" and with the Puritan interest in the inner workings of the mind.

It is interesting to note that recent voices have been calling American pastoral care back to a serious consideration of sin, the moral dimensions of pastoral care, and the need to recover a disciplinary emphasis, as well as emphasizing congregational care, spiritual direction, and spiritual growth or sanctification. These are all themes much in evidence in the Reformed tradition. Thus the Reformed pastoral tradition may still be very much alive and have much to contribute in the years to come.

Bibliography. R. Baxter, *The Reformed Pastor,* J. T. Wilkinson, ed. (1939 [1655]). J.-D. Benoit, *Calvin, directeur d'âmes* (1947). W. A. Clebsch and C. R. Jaekle, *Pastoral Care in Historical Perspective* (1964). S. Hiltner, *Preface to Pastoral Theology* (1958). E. B. Holifield, *A History of Pastoral Care in America* (1983). J. T. McNeill, *A History of the Cure of Souls* (1951). J. J. Van Oosterzee, *Practical Theology* (1878). A. Vinet, *Pastoral Theology* (1853).

D. W. WAANDERS

PASTORAL CARE (History, Traditions, and Definitions); HISTORY OF PROTESTANT PASTORAL CARE (Canada *or* United States). *See also* DISCIPLINE, PASTORAL CARE AS; ECCLESIOLOGY AND PASTORAL CARE; PSYCHOLOGY IN AMERICAN RELIGION. *Biography:* BAXTER; BOISEN; BUCER; BUNYON; CALVIN; HILTNER; PERKINS; ZWINGLI.

REGENERATION. *See* CHRISTIAN LIFE; SANCTIFICATION/HOLINESS.

REGRESSION. Most often used within the framework of psychoanalytic thought, regression refers to a return to more primitive patterns of coping (associated with an earlier phase of development) to avoid the challenges of the higher forms of behavior. Regression is a defense mechanism that operates outside of awareness and is used to protect the ego from excess stress and anxiety. When the present appears too overwhelming, the person resorts to behaviors that once gained ego-gratification or provided psychological security. For example, a child whose sense of importance is threatened by a new arrival may regress to bed-wetting, thumb-sucking, or infantile temper tantrums. Such use of regression may range from the frustrated adult's pouting and inappropriate childish behavior to the assumption of the fetal position by a person diagnosed as schizophrenic.

Freud likened the process of regression to an army that has left some of its number (cathected libido) at rear bases and in the face of a strong enemy (psychic conflict) is retreating to those previously established strongholds at the rear.

The concept of regression is central to the classical psychoanalytic understanding of psychopathology. In this framework, psychopathology is thought to result from the ego's regression to various points of fixation. In fact, the severity of psychopathology is in part due to the degree of regression. While neurosis represents regression at an Oedipal level, psychosis is thought to result from regression to pre-Oedipal points of fixation.

Not all forms of regression are necessarily pathological. Many authors view some regression as normal and even healthy or creative ("in the service of the ego") under certain conditions (Kris, 1964, pp. 312–14). For example, organic disease may produce regression which, with its increased narcissism, may assist in the healing process. Object loss (death of a loved one, separation, etc.) often produces regression, which may aid in the mourning process and the preparation for subsequent object relationships. In these examples, however, the ego of the individual is not overwhelmed as in the case of psychosis.

Since regression always carries back characteristics of the present level to an earlier level, it may allow reworking of an earlier conflict by a more mature ego organization. In fact, this often happens in psychotherapy.

Bibliography. G. Blum, *Psychoanalytic Theories of Personality* (1953). C. Brenner, *An Elementary Textbook of Psychoanalysis* rev. ed. (1974). S. Freud, *An Outline of Psychoanalysis* (1949). C. Hall, *A Primer of Freudian Psychology* (1954). H. Kohut, *The Restoration of the Self* (1977). E. Kris, *Psychoanalytic Explorations in Art* (1964 [1952]).

H. M. GIRGIS

DEFENSE AND COPING THEORY; PSYCHOANALYSIS (Personality Theory and Research); PSYCHOPATHOLOGY, THEORIES OF.

REHABILITATION. *See* VOCATIONAL REHABILITATION; JUVENILE CRIME AND DELINQUENCY.

REICH, WILHELM (1897–1957). Reich, who died in a federal prison because of his communist sympathies and his controversial "orgone biophysics," contributed substantially to personality theory and psychoanalytic method through his *Character Analysis* (1933/1945). His "character armoring and character resistance" are classic descriptions of defense mechanisms, accompanied by sound techniques for the interpretation of resistance and transference. Similarly, his descriptions of the hysterical, compulsive, and phallic-narcissistic characters provided the basis for David Shapiro's *Neurotic Styles* (1965).

Reich ventured into the psychology of religion in his later orgonic writings on "the emotional plague of mankind." The person afflicted with this biopathic character structure is characterized by prejudice, action under strict structural compulsion, and sexual lasciviousness accompanied by sadistic moralism — all resulting from the killing of the emotional/libidinal life-force in the person. For Reich, the story of Christ epitomizes the human condition: Christ, because he represents life and good, must be [continually] murdered/denied because he confronts humans with their personal responsibility for evil and death.

H. VANDE KEMP

DEFENSE AND COPING THEORY; PASTORAL CARE MOVEMENT. *See also* PSYCHOANALYSIS.

REIK, THEODOR (1888–1969). An early member of the Vienna Psychoanalytic Society, founded the [American] National Psychological Association for Psychoanalysts in 1948. Reik developed "archaeological psychoanalysis," his label for "the branch of analytic research dealing with reconstruction of prehistoric myths, customs and history." This exegetical method emphasized that phylogenetic (species) development retrospectively can be understood as vulnerable to the same unconscious defensive maneuvers as ontogenetic (individual) development. Reik applied this exegetical method to a number of biblical passages and themes in his six books on the psychology of religion.

H. VANDE KEMP

MYTHOLOGY AND PSYCHOLOGY; PSYCHOLOGY OF RELIGION (Theories, Traditions, and Issues); PSYCHOANALYSIS.

REINCARNATION. *See* PARAPSYCHOLOGY; PSYCHOLOGY, EASTERN.

REINFORCEMENT. *See* CONDITIONING. *See also* BEHAVIOR THERAPIES; BEHAVIORISM.

REJECTION. *See* CRUELTY AND SADISTIC BEHAVIOR; GRIEF AND LOSS; SOCIAL ISOLATION.

RELATIONSHIP NETWORK. The constellation of important relationships surrounding and informing a person.

Each person has a set of relationships which provide primary emotional satisfaction, guidance for living, personal assistance, and an opportunity for giving and self-expression. The cohesiveness, volume, flexibility, permeability, and dependability of that network are crucial variables for the viability of each individual within them. The resources they provide and the burdens they bring with them are central determinants of the quality of life for all persons, and in emergency can literally be the difference between life and death.

The networks of both parishioner and pastor are important elements in any pastoral transaction. For instance, the quality of the network in which each is embedded has an important bearing on whether the new pastoral relationship will occur and at what level of intensity and usefulness it will function. Pastors and others who are not well linked in their own network will typically not link well with each other.

It is important for the pastor to assess the relative connectedness and/or isolation of each person served. That information reveals a great deal about the likelihood of the individual to bond dependably and usefully with the religious institution, with a new spouse, or with growing children. It gives an indication of the person's likelihood of developing significant physical and psychological problems, since there is a strong correlation of personal isolation and major illness, especially, but not solely, psychological. It also may indicate how vulnerable the person is to suicide, psychosis, and violence. All these circumstances are more likely for isolated persons.

The pastor's relationship network also enters this equation. A large, available, harmonious, and strongly invested relationship network is the pastor's best immunization against misuse of those whom she or he serves. Furthermore, it is a resource that enables the pastor to continue giving in situations that do not provide much intrinsic satisfaction. It is thus a buffer against burnout, stress, and fatigue. God's grace is mediated through human relationships, and the pastor's need for it is great if he or she is to continue mediating it to others.

B. W. GRANT

COMMUNITY, FELLOWSHIP, AND CARE; CONGREGATION, PASTORAL CARE OF; FRIENDSHIP. *See also* HAVURAH; SUPPORT GROUPS. *Compare* LONELINESS AND ISOLATION; SOCIOLOGY OF RELIGIOUS AND PASTORAL CARE.

RELATIONSHIPS, INTERPROFESSIONAL. *See* INTERPROFESSIONAL TEAMS AND RELATIONSHIPS. *See also* RELIGION AND HEALTH MOVEMENT.

RELATIONSHIPS, PASTORAL. PASTORAL CARE; PASTORAL COUNSELING; SUPERVISION. *See also* AUTHORITY ISSUES; SEXUAL ISSUES; CONGREGATION, PASTORAL CARE OF; DISAGREEMENT, DIFFERENCE, AND CONFLICT IN PASTOR-PARISHIONER RELATIONSHIPS; FRIENDSHIP, PASTOR-PARISHIONER; MULTIPLE STAFF MINISTRIES AND RELATIONSHIPS; SYMBOLIC DIMENSIONS OF PASTORAL CARE RELATIONSHIPS.

RELATIONSHIPS, PERSONAL. *See* COMMUNITY, FELLOWSHIP, AND CARE; HUMAN RELATIONS TRAINING; I AND THOU; INTERPERSONAL THEORY; RELATIONSHIP NETWORK; TRANSACTIONAL ANALYSIS.

RELATIONSHIPS, THERAPEUTIC. *See* PASTORAL COUNSELING; PASTORAL PSYCHOTHERAPY; PSYCHOTHERAPY. *See also* THERAPEUTIC CONDITIONS; TRANSFERENCE *and* COUNTERTRANSFERENCE.

RELAXATION, PSYCHOLOGY AND TECHNIQUES OF. A tranquil state of being characterized by diminished physiological arousal and the absence of troubling or worrisome thoughts. Relaxation functions as a homeostatic mechanism which promotes restorative processes which counteract stress arousal.

The physiological functions which accompany relaxation are mediated by the parasympathetic branch of the autonomic nervous system and hormonal activity both under the control of the hypothalamus. Among others, these functions include reduced muscular tension, reduced metabolism and oxygen consumption, slowed heart rate, lowered blood pressure, dilation of the peripheral vasculature resulting in warmer skin temperature, and increased alpha brain wave activity.

The phenomenon of relaxation is an intrinsic component of the human being, which is capable of being elicited from birth. It has been observed to have analgesic, antianxiety, and antidepressant effects. The inhibition of the relaxation response and the prolonged activation of sympathetic autonomic nervous system arousal is the critical factor in the development of stress related diseases. Relaxation training is an important component in the treatment of any of these conditions, which include migraine and tension headaches, hypertension, ulcers, and chronic anxiety.

Many techniques have been utilized to help individuals elicit relaxation including yoga, meditation, progressive relaxation, hypnosis, autogenic training, and biofeedback. Whatever technique is used, the cultivation of a passive effortless attitude is essential. One does not make relaxation happen, but rather allows it to take place by creating the right conditions. Of primary importance is a sense of safety, security, and freedom from threat.

The use of a mental device such as a fixed gazing on an object or image or the repetition of a sound or phrase is helpful in inhibiting negative evaluative thought processes. The assuming of a comfortable posture in a quiet environment can further facilitate the emergence of the state of relaxation.

Relaxation is distinct from simply being at rest, which may or may not be accompanied by a state of relaxation. Similarly, involvement in such activities as leisure recreation, hobbies, and reading can help elicit relaxation to the extent that they foster the above conditions.

The Christian tradition has a rich background where the involvement in a passive receptive meditative prayer not only results in a meaningful spiritual experience but also yields the health benefits of relaxation. This is in contrast to the contemporary popular practice of prayer which is active, expressive, and goal-oriented.

For a given person, the relaxation strategy which is most helpful and favored reflects individual differences in personality and the physiological systems which are most stressed. Objective confirmation that relaxation is actually taking place requires the use of biofeedback or some other method of direct physiological monitoring. Specialists in relaxation training can be of value in selecting and utilizing an appropriate strategy. A mental health agency would be a source of referral to these individuals.

Bibliography. H. Benson, *The Relaxation Response* (1975). W. Edmonston, Jr., *Hypnosis and Relaxation* (1981). A. Sugarman and R. Tarter, *Expanding Dimensions of Consciousness* (1978).

P. J. PETERSON

STRESS AND STRESS MANAGEMENT. *See also* HUMOR; PLAY. *Compare* ANXIETY; REST AND RENEWAL, RELIGIOUS TRADITIONS OF.

RELICS. *See* MEDIEVAL CHURCH, PASTORAL CARE IN.

RELIGIO-PSYCHIATRIC MOVEMENT. *See* RELIGION AND HEALTH MOVEMENT.

RELIGION. The task of constructing a definition of religion that is both internally consistent and takes account of all ordinary usage of the word is very difficult. Ninian Smart has suggested that no single feature binds together all its manifestations, from Buddhist meditation to Neolithic rain dances, but only what may be called "family resemblances." Similarly, William James argued that religion "cannot stand for any single principle or essence, but is rather a collective name" for ideas, acts, and attitudes that in reality are quite diverse.

Nonetheless, humans must have some reason for labeling the many entities of this vast collection with the same term. One peculiarity that makes religion stand out from the rest of human life, and so ask for a special name, is that it possesses the quality Mircea Eliade has spoken of as the religious person's "non-homogeneous" experience of reality. She or he experiences certain times, places, ideas, attitudes, or states of consciousness as *other* than the ordinary and different in the sense that they are better aligned than ordinary life to transhuman powers, planes of being, or centers of meaning. The "other" involved may be no more than finite nature or ancestral spirits, or it may be the ultimate, unconditioned Reality of the Buddhist Nirvana or the Judeo-Christian God. It may have either objective or subjective existence, or it may be beyond subject-object distinctions. Nevertheless, it stands in a nonhomogenized relation to the ordinary human realm, which has none of that power or meaning, and has therefore been spoken of as the Numinous, the Transcendent, or the Sacred as opposed to the profane.

A major point for religion is that it seeks to provide access to these "other" realms of the cosmos. Religion is predicated upon the assumption that the Transcendent can be known, or makes itself known, in certain definable ways in this world, and that there are ways in which persons can address it or even become more fully assimilated into it. This commerce is the distinctive work of religion, though it may produce other effects based on its view of reality, such as a model of an ideal social order and sanctions for ethical behavior.

Religion, as a general human phenomenon, is by no means wholly inward but is a cultural and social reality. It sees specific ideas, stories, practices, and groups as highly discrete, tangible portals between humanity and the Transcendent; while these vary from one religion to another, none is without its set of forms of expression. Joachim Wach has depicted three such forms, which may be thought of as vehicles by which the Transcendent is communicated to humans, and conversely by which we may be brought into alignment with it. These are (1) the theoretical: significant beliefs and narratives; (2) the practical: "practices" such as public and private worship; and (3) the sociological: religious groups and social institutions. To these might be added other forms of expression, such as (4) art forms: including painting, sculpture, music, and literature; and (5) morals and ethics: norms of behavior sanctioned by the faith together with its canons for value judgments.

The main consideration in that which is called religion is an awareness of the Transcendent *together with* expression of that awareness through forms that give it conceptual, cultural, and social shape. Bare awareness of the Transcendent is not religion in the full historical sense, for without expression it would be known only to the recipient of the experience and have no visible impact on history. Nor is only one or two of the forms of expression sufficient; each requires the others and cannot stand alone as religion. Mere ideas and theories, however much about the Transcendent, would be philosophy rather than religion; practices involving the Sacred by themselves, without adequate sociological and theoretical undergirding, would be only private magic. Religion, in the full sense, is a rich and complex reality that links humans, in their complete being as thinking, feeling, doing, social, and cultural creatures, to Ultimate Reality.

Bibliography. M. Eliade, *Myth and Reality* (1963); *A History of Religious Ideas* (1978). W. James, *The Varieties of Religious Experience* (1978 [1902]). N. Smart, *Beyond Ideology: Religion and the Future of Western Civilization* (1987). J. Wach, *Types of Religious Experience: Christian and non-Christian* (1951).

R. S. ELLWOOD

RELIGIOUS BEHAVIOR; RELIGIOUS EXPERIENCE; RELIGIOUS LANGUAGE AND SYMBOLISM; FAITH/BELIEF; The HOLY; RITUAL AND PASTORAL CARE. *See also* NEW RELIGIOUS MOVEMENTS; RELIGIOUS AND UTOPIAN COMMUNITIES; AFRICAN, NATIVE AMERICAN, *or* WEST INDIAN TRADITIONAL RELIGIONS. *For social scientific studies of religion see* CULTURAL ANTHROPOLOGY, PSYCHOLOGY, *or* SOCIOLOGY OF RELIGION. *Compare* THEOLOGY; SPIRITUALITY.

RELIGION AND HEALTH, THEORIES OF. *See* FAITH HEALING; HEALTH AND ILLNESS; PSYCHOPATHOLOGY AND RELIGION; SALVATION, HEALING, AND HEALTH, THEOLOGY OF; SIN AND SICKNESS; WHOLISTIC HEALTH CARE.

RELIGION AND HEALTH MOVEMENT. (1) Originally, an early twentieth-century movement, also referred to as the "Religio-Psychiatric Movement" (Klausner), which sought to recover Christ's healing ministry by using the tools of depth psychology. (2) More broadly and generally, the wide range of subsequent developments (including the pastoral care and counseling movement) which developed and greatly expanded the founders' original ideas through a plethora of publications, programs, and institutes that have had a powerful, pervasive influence on twentieth century American religion and health care. The movement as a whole is characterized by a concern to promote the convergence of religious and health concerns in ministerial practice as well as in social scientific theory and research.
1. **The Early Twentieth Century.** The nature of the relationship between religion and health first became a subject of modern interest and investigation in the late nineteenth and early twentieth century. During this time of rapid development of the human sciences and increased understanding of the human person, there began to be a growing conviction about the wholeness of human life: physical, psychological, spiritual. In fact, as people came to view mind/body dualism as being unhelpful, if not destructive, and experienced the benefits of wholistic attitudes and thought, a fascination with the relation of religion to health became a hallmark of the twentieth century.

Prompted in large part by the enormous popular interest in faith healing, mind cure, and Christian Science, professionals charged with the cure of souls and the cure of bodies—clergy and physicians—began to come together in conversation and working partnerships. The earliest of these was between the Rev. Dr. Elwood Worcester, the Rev. Dr. Samuel McComb, and Isador Coriat, M.D., at a consultation clinic at the Emmanuel Episcopal Church in Boston. Their effort to bring together sound religion and sound science in healing ministry sparked what became known as the "Emmanuel Movement," which reached thousands as it spread to cities in the U.S. and abroad. Its story is told in the collaborators' book, *Religion and Medicine* (1908), and also in *New Ideals in Healing* (1909) by contemporary journalist Ray Stannard Baker. The work of Emmanuel continued for several decades, and Worcester and McComb updated their thinking in 1931 in the highly popular *Body, Mind and Spirit*.

The early twentieth century movement may be understood as constituting in American liberal Protestantism a parallel to the Social Gospel, which sought to recover Christ's social ministry by using the tools of sociology. But unlike the Social Gospel the religion and health movement was not originally conceived as a movement; thus, its various aspects are seen in their unity only in retrospect and through a conceptual framework which understands the liberal enterprise to be the key.

2. The Thirties and Forties. A kind of successor to Emmanuel was established in 1939 when the Rev. Norman Vincent Peale reached out in partnership to Smiley Blanton, M.D., a man who had his training analysis with Sigmund Freud. Together Blanton and Peale established the Religio-Psychiatric Clinic at the Marble Collegiate Church in New York City. This enterprise, too, grew phenomenally as the world learned of it. In 1948 *Newsweek* reported that more than ten thousand persons had come for help. When the free clinic began to strain the church's budget, in 1951 Peale and Blanton established the American Foundation of Religion and Psychiatry as a successor organization.

The year that Peale and Blanton began their collaboration, the Federal Council of Churches of Christ in America organized a Commission of Religion and Health and within a few months appointed Seward Hiltner as executive secretary. This commission actually took up the work begun much earlier by a Joint Committee on Religion and Health of the Federal Council and the New York Academy of Medicine. The Joint Committee was directed by Helen Flanders Dunbar, M.D., pioneer in psychosomatic medicine. An important research project that came out of Dunbar's work for the Committee was the massive bibliography, *Emotions and Bodily Changes* (1935). This was a standard reference work, considered authoritative in medical circles, which Dunbar updated several times. Crucial financing and support came from Ethel Phelps Stokes Hoyt and (through the Josiah Macy, Jr., Foundation) Kate Everit Macy Ladd.

In 1943 while directing the Religion and Health Commission, Seward Hiltner undertook a comprehensive survey of religion's relationship to health in his first book, *Religion and Health*. It opens with a discussion of what mental hygiene teaches the church, followed by a balancing discussion of some contributions of religion to mental health. Included are sections on mental health

and religion education, pastoral counseling, and pastoral work and community resources. When in 1945 Paul Tillich gave a lengthy paper to the Religion and Health Seminar at Columbia University, he made many references to Hiltner's study, acknowledging appreciation for the practical matters he said he learned from it. In his own treatment of religion and health, however, Tillich took exception to some of Hiltner's interpretations. Tillich's paper, "The Relation of Religion and Health: Historical Considerations and Theoretical Questions" (1946), is unsurpassed in its clear rendering of elusive philosophical material.

At the time Hiltner was writing his book, a colleague in the pastoral counseling field, Carroll A. Wise, was at work on *Religion in Illness and Health* (1942). Hiltner found it to be one of the most helpful statements available on several aspects of the field—including psychosomatics and religion, and religious symbolism and health—and regretted that it did not appear before his own inquiry was completed.

3. The Fifties and Sixties. During the decade of the fifties research and writing in religion and health flourished. In February 1950 Simon Doniger launched *Pastoral Psychology* with the help of Seward Hiltner as pastoral consultant. The eminent clergypersons, psychiatrists, and psychologists represented in that first issue—John Sutherland Bonnell, Russell L. Dicks, William C. Menninger, and Carl E. Rogers—signalled the high quality of articles offered throughout the next twenty-two years. Doniger articulated the objective behind the planning of *Pastoral Psychology:* "One comes to the basic similarity between the profession of the ministry and that of dynamic psychology—the goal of helping man to strengthen or rediscover his essential relatedness to himself, to his fellow man, to the universe, and to God," (*Pastoral Psychology*, 1 (1950), 6) a fourfold focus often cited by religion and health writers. Over the years Doniger edited several collections of journal articles, among them *Religion and Health* (1958).

In 1952 Russell L. Dicks founded *Religion and Health*, a periodical based on the conviction that "there is a force operating within the human creature that makes for health. Some call this force *nature*, others call it *God*. When this force is blocked, either consciously or unconsciously, illness results" (*Religion and Health*, 1 (1952), 4). Bulk distribution in churches and hospitals accounted for half the magazine's circulation. After four years publication ceased; unfortunately, energies and expenditures to maintain regular operation had kept the editor from necessary promotional efforts.

That religion and health had matured as a field of inquiry became apparent when the academy legitimated it. In 1956 the University of Chicago appointed Granger E. Westberg as associate professor of religion and health in the School of Medicine and Federated Theological Faculty.

An Academy of Religion and Mental Health, an educational venture, was established by the Rev. George Christian Anderson in 1954. Beginning in 1957 members of the Academy conducted regular symposia devoted to subjects engaging persons at work promoting human physical, mental, and spiritual health. In the fifth symposium in 1961 theologians, psychologists, and psychiatrists met to discuss significant areas of research in order to give specific practical guidance to the Academy's research program. The Rev. William C. Bier, Samuel Z. Klausner, and the Rev. Harry C. Meserve edited their proceedings and, with the help of the Josiah Macy, Jr., Foundation, published them in 1963 in *Research in Religion and Health*. Topics included methods of data collection, religion and social attitudes, selection of personnel for the clergy, and psychopathology in religious experience.

By mid-century the various religion and health enterprises and the literature of religion and health was sufficiently established to have a distinctive history, indeed, to be seen in retrospect as a movement. Sociologist Samuel Z. Klausner began an extremely important sociological study in 1956 of the relationship between the social positions of ministers and psychiatrists involved in what he named the "Religio-Psychiatric Movement" and the ideals they espoused. He found that these persons were innovators, disenchanted with their respective institutional traditions of healing, and they were located in industrialized and scientifically oriented milieus, i.e., urban centers of Western countries. Klausner's fascinating findings are succinctly summarized in a valuable article about this movement in the *International Encyclopedia of Social Science* (12: pp. 632–38). A full study, which contains a history of the Blanton-Peale Religio-Psychiatric Clinic and a description of the religio-psychiatric literature, may be found in Klausner's *Psychiatry and Religion* (1964). The investigator estimated that perhaps 2,500 items were published in the religion and health field between 1900 and 1962. Stages in the growth of the literature are reflected in its shifting thematic emphases.

4. **Subsequent Developments.** The Institutes of Religion and Health—representing a merger between the American Foundation of Religion and Psychiatry founded by Blanton and Peale and the Academy of Religion and Mental Health founded by Anderson—came into being in 1972. The Institutes comprise an interfaith network of clinical service, as well as educational and research programs, supporting churches, synagogues, and communities across the country. Its training arm is the Blanton-Peale Graduate Institute. A grant of more than half a million dollars from the National Institute of Mental Health in 1975 for the establishment of ten pastoral counseling centers across the country guaranteed the mainstream legitimacy of the enterprise.

The *Journal of Religion and Health*, begun in 1961, has been published quarterly by the Human Sciences Press since 1978 in cooperation with the Institutes. Intended "for all who are interested in the indivisibility of human well-being: physical, emotional, and spiritual" (title pages), its purpose reflects the wholistic persuasion that has been the driving force of religion and health partnerships, writing, and research from the beginning.

Bibliography. R. S. Baker, *New Ideals in Healing* (1909). W. C. Bier, S. Z. Klausner, and H. C. Meserve, eds., *Research in Religion and Health* (1963). S. Doniger, *Religion and Health* (1958). H. F. Dunbar, *Emotions and Bodily Changes* (1935). C. A. Kemp, *Physicians of the Soul* (1947). S. Klausner, *Psychiatry and Religion* (1964). A. Stokes, *Ministry After Freud* (1985). P. Tillich, "The Relation of Religion and Health: Historical Considerations and Theoretical Questions," *Review of Religion*, 10 (1946), 348–84. C. A. Wise, *Religion in Illness and Health* (1942). E. Worcester and S. McComb, *Body, Mind and Spirit* (1931). E. Worcester, S. McComb, and I. Coriat, *Religion and Medicine* (1908).

A. STOKES

PASTORAL CARE MOVEMENT. *See also* EMMANUEL MOVEMENT; MIND-CURE MOVEMENT; NEW YORK PSYCHOLOGY GROUP; PSYCHOLOGY IN AMERICAN RELIGION. *Biography:* BLANTON; BONNELL; DICKS; DUNBAR; HILTNER; PEALE; ROGERS; TILLICH; WESTBERG; WISE; WORCESTER.

RELIGION AND MORALITY. *See* MORAL BEHAVIOR AND RELIGION.

RELIGION AND PERSONALITY. *See* PERSON (Christian *or* Jewish Perspective); PSYCHOLOGY OF RELIGION.

RELIGION AND PSYCHIATRY. *See* PSYCHIATRY AND PASTORAL CARE.

RELIGION AND PSYCHOLOGY. *See* PSYCHOLOGY OF RELIGION; RELIGION AND PSYCHOTHERAPY. *See also* ANALYTICAL (JUNGIAN) PSYCHOLOGY, PSYCHOANALYSIS, *or* HUMANISTIC PSYCHOLOGY, AND RELIGION; PSYCHIATRY AND PASTORAL CARE; PSYCHOLOGY, EASTERN; PSYCHOLOGY IN AMERICAN RELIGION.

RELIGION AND PSYCHOPATHOLOGY. *See* PSYCHOPATHOLOGY AND RELIGION.

RELIGION AND PSYCHOTHERAPY. Religion is any complex of interlocking beliefs, explanations, symbols, and behaviors to which an individual, community, or society appeals, for the most part unconsciously, in order to understand itself ultimately. Psychotherapy is any treatment or course of treatment conducted by one or more trained or initiated persons for the benefit of a patient or group of patients with the goal of improving the quality of the patients' lives in a primarily mental or spiritual, rather than physical, sense.

1. **Cross-Cultural Overview.** Both terms belong to modern Western culture, *religion* being a word and concept without a directly corresponding notion in any other culture (Islamic, Hindu, etc.,) and *psychotherapy* being only about a century old. In other cultures, religious and therapeutic activities, beliefs, and expectations appear ubiquitous and are by no means as distinct from one another as might be expected. A historical, cross-cultural overview shows that psychotherapy has become differentiated from religion only rather recently and that each realm still has much to contribute to the other.

a. Undifferentiated trance. In the simplest of known societies, nomadic hunter/gatherers such as the !Kung Bushmen, it appears that religious and healing activities are one and the same. The community sings, drums, and dances until various members attain a state of trance, a state which virtually all adults are considered capable of achieving. Trance, believed and felt to be contact with the energetic foundations of human life, makes the tranced individual a conduit to restore the cosmic balance of those in the community who are ill. Activities believed and experienced as transferring energy from the trancer to the patient include touching, holding, and rubbing with bodily fluids such as sweat, saliva, and blood.

b. Shamanism. In more differentiated societies, the ability to enter trance becomes the specialty of the shaman, who, through election by the spirits and initiation at the hands of experienced practitioners, becomes a familiar visitor to the one or several invisible spirit worlds, especially to the celestial world and the underworld. Shamans are experts in the human soul. Sickness being an affliction of soul, they typically retrieve lost souls that have wandered off or have been stolen by malignant spirits or other shamans. To effect the retrieval, the shaman passes into trance and pursues the soul in the spirit world, where familiarity with its "geography" and inhabitants is essential for success. The shaman, therefore, cures by means of intimate knowledge of and experience with the symbol system (especially cosmology), which expresses the community's concern with ultimacy, as well as by close psychological contact with the patient.

c. Priesthood. In the much more hierarchically ordered societies characteristic, in the first instance, of the ancient city-states, religious specialization devolves upon a priesthood, the typical four-caste structure including priests, warriors, merchants, and peasants. Unlike shamans and undifferentiated trancers, priests require no personal intimacy with the gods or spirits; their position is rather an institutional office attained by liturgical consecration. Insofar as the individual's psychological difficulties stem from loss of a living connection with ultimacy, the priest's mediation of the symbol system may, in fact, be psychotherapeutic. Priestly psychotherapy may utilize either theology (as in preaching and teaching, whereby the patient may be led to conscious insights that reconnect daily experience with symbols of ultimacy) or liturgy (as in public prayer, laying on of hands, anointing, confession, or exorcism).

d. Alternative religions. Priesthood is therapeutically effective when it mediates a "living" (i.e., experientially gripping) symbol system. As societies become more complex, and particularly as they approach crises requiring structural renewal or revitalization, more and more individuals are apt to find themselves unmoved by traditional symbols of ultimacy. When they are few, they may judge themselves as suffering from psychological problems. When they become more numerous, however, they may gather to experiment with alternative symbols, explanations, and behaviors. Some of these will be alternative sects of the same mainstream religion. Others may become new religious movements that differ widely from the mainstream and in which, typically, an inability to adjust to the "godless" mainstream society (experienced, e.g., in fainting spells, anxiety-depression, or lethargy) becomes a sign of election by the powerful and secret gods of the cult. Membership in the movement may, in itself, be therapeutic. If so, religion and psychotherapy have again become one, as in the undifferentiated trance of the very simplest societies.

e. Mediumism. Worldwide surveys have shown that belief in spirit possession is a factor of central importance in about three-fourths of all societies. Leaders in such cults are often called mediums because through their ecstasy they mediate the more significant invisible world

for their less gifted followers in the visible world. Like shamans, they have their position in virtue of their ecstatic talents. Unlike shamans, however, they do not enter the spirit world but call the spirits into the visible world, where they allow themselves to become possessed by them. Consequently, insofar as they rely on the words of these spirits rather than their own initiative, their methods resemble those of the priests.

2. Emergence of Secular Psychotherapy. Through the scientific revolution, beginning in the seventeenth century, theological explanations were progressively reduced in scope. Witch-hunting and -burning became the activities by which the theological mainstream "cast out" potential founders and members of new cults and healed those thought to be possessed of evil spirits. Subsequently, the symbols and explanations of science became alternate means to validate dissent.

a. Hypnosis. Anton Mesmer's rediscovery of hypnosis is an example of scientific-seeming explanations replacing theological ones. Although the phenomenon had already been known in shamanism, yoga, and elsewhere, Mesmer's contribution was to make it acceptable in a secular context by developing analogies with electromagnetism and the tides. Nevertheless, the apparent reason hypnosis succeeded for Mesmer lies in its reliance upon many of the ingredients that had already contributed to the influence of shamanism and exorcism: confession, catharsis, human relationship, and submission to a stronger will. It is dubious, however, whether its muddled theory offered any symbol of ultimacy, except possibly its allusions to cosmic harmony.

b. Psychiatry. While the hypnotists dealt primarily with neurosis, another development was taking place in the sanatoria, which housed those suffering with psychosis. Under the influence of the humanitarian and scientific ideals of the Enlightenment these patients were sorted out, the ill separated from the criminal and impoverished, and the various psychotic and organic conditions categorized. Although these developments were far more descriptive than therapeutic, they laid the foundations for a thoroughly nontheological understanding of psychopathology and ultimately of treatment.

c. Experimental psychology. Another strand of secular psychotherapy emerged from the empirical study of perception, learning, and memory, advancing theories based on Newtonian mechanics and Darwinian biology. In behaviorism, which has produced the most important therapeutic applications, empiricism has dominated to such an extent that the phenomena of consciousness were ignored in favor of precisely measurable actions. Behavior modification therapies operate without any reference to symbols of ultimacy.

d. Psychoanalysis. Consciousness, soul, and even religion have regained importance in Freud's psychology, which is a theory of culture as well as of the human mind. The models, however, are essentially biological. Religion is deemed an "illusion," appropriate to an immature stage of human development. If anything has attained a position of quasi-ultimacy in psychoanalysis, it is scientific investigation itself and the Freudian insistence upon the demands of "reality."

3. Psychotherapy's Rediscovery of Its Religious Foundations. Dissatisfaction with scientism and materialism in the second half of the twentieth century has generated several alternate trends in psychotherapy. These are not so much distinct methods of therapy as worldviews within which psychological insights are given context.

a. Jung. Already in the second decade of psychoanalysis, dissenting voices were heard. Instead of reducing religious phenomena to manifestations of psychopathology, C. G. Jung broadened psychology's conception of its field by taking the data uncovered by anthropology and the study of religion, particularly mythology, as descriptive of the human psyche. Jung believed the crux of most psychological problems to be religious.

b. Third force. In recent years, *humanistic psychology* and *transpersonal psychology*, each a loose fellowship of therapists for several different traditions, have declared themselves alternatives to behaviorism and psychoanalysis. Their interests include consciousness here and now, mystical experience, sacralizing of everyday life, cosmic awareness, spirituality, and meditation. Studies of psychedelic experience and non-Western religions have been formative influences.

The new field of *Ethnopsychiatry* has approached the basic issues of psychology by cross-cultural comparisons of psychopathologies and methods of treatment. Although many of these studies are not aware of the religious implications of their findings, they have revealed the provincialism of Western scientism and materialism. Therapists working with immigrants from other cultures or with members of well-established cults have discovered that cooperation with the patient's religious expectations often affords the best results. If so, whether the therapist knows it or not, psychotherapy is serving the patient's quest for ultimacy.

4. Religion's Rediscovery of Psychotherapy. After decades of fear that psychology was a tool of atheists and libertines, religion has begun to accept psychology as a method and body of knowledge that can be employed in the service of ultimacy.

This is evident in both the so-called *new religions,* which borrow syncretistically not only from non-Western religions but also from several of the psychological traditions, particularly humanistic and transpersonal, and in traditional *pastoral counseling.* Pastors have always had to be counselors as well as theologians and liturgists. In recent decades, however, pastoral counseling has become a widespread emphasis in theological education, as well as a professional specialty in its own right. The pastorate thus has begun to recover some of the functions that previously belonged to other experts in the symbols of ultimacy. The pastoral counseling movement, along with what some define as pastoral psychotherapy (Wise), represents a major factor in the reconnection of religion and psychotherapy.

Likewise, the renewed interest of psychotherapists in integrating religious concerns into the therapeutic process (Lovinger, Stern) is further evidence of the return of these two fields to their original synthesis.

Bibliography. R. N. Bellah, "Religious Evolution," in W. A. Lessa and E. Z. Vogt, eds., *Reader in Comparative Religion*, 2d ed. (1965), pp. 73–87. E. Bourguignon, "World Distribution of Patterns of Possession States," in R. Prince, ed., *Trance and Possession States* (1968). V. Crapanzano and V. Garrison, eds.,

Case Studies in Spirit Possession (1977). M. Eliade, *Shamanism* (1964); *Yoga* (1969). H. F. Ellenberger, *Discovery of the Unconscious* (1970). S. Freud, *Future of an Illusion, SE,* 21 (1927), 3–58. D. A. Halperin, ed., *Psychodynamic Perspectives on Religion, Sect, and Cult* (1983). J. R. Haule, "Psychology and Religion," *Religion* (1982), 149–65. P. Janet, *Psychological Healing* (1976). C. G. Jung, *Psychology and Religion, Collected Works,* 11 (1938). R. Katz, *Boiling Energy* (1982). A. Kiev, *Transcultural Psychiatry* (1972). I. M. Lewis, *Ecstatic Religion* (1977). R. Lovinger, *Working with Religious Issues in Therapy* (1984). M. Stern, ed., *Psychotherapy and the Religiously Committed Patient* (1985). P. Tillich, *Dynamics of Faith* (1958). A. F. C. Wallace, "Revitalization Movements," *American Anthropologist*, (1956), 264–81. I. I. Zaretsky and M. P. Leone, eds., *Religious Movements in Contemporary America* (1974). G. Zilboorg and G. W. Henry, *History of Medical Psychology* (1941).

J. R. HAULE

PASTORAL COUNSELING; PASTORAL PSYCHOTHERAPY; PSYCHIATRY AND PASTORAL CARE; PSYCHOPATHOLOGY AND RELIGION; THEOLOGY AND PSYCHOTHERAPY; VALUES IN COUNSELING AND PSYCHOTHERAPY. *See also* ANALYTICAL (JUNGIAN) PSYCHOLOGY, HUMANISTIC PSYCHOLOGY, *or* PSYCHOANALYSIS, AND RELIGION; JUDAISM AND PSYCHOLOGY; PSYCHOLOGY OF RELIGION; SALVATION, HEALING, AND HEALTH; SOCIOLOGY OF RELIGIOUS AND PASTORAL CARE. *Compare* INTEGRATION OF PSYCHOLOGY AND THEOLOGY; INTERPRETATION AND HERMENEUTICS, PASTORAL; JOURNALS; NEW RELIGIOUS MOVEMENTS; PSYCHOLOGY AND PSYCHOTHERAPY (East-West Comparison); RITUAL AND PASTORAL CARE; SHAMAN. *Biography:* BLANTON; CLINEBELL; FRANKL; FREUD; JUNG; KUNKEL; LAKE; MAY; MOWRER; PFISTER; RANK; ROBERTS; SCHARFENBERG; TILLICH; WISE.

RELIGIONS, TRADITIONAL. *See* AFRICAN, NATIVE AMERICAN, *or* WEST INDIAN TRADITIONAL RELIGION.

RELIGIO-PSYCHIATRIC MOVEMENT. *See* RELIGION AND HEALTH MOVEMENT.

RELIGIOUS, EMPIRICAL STUDIES OF. In its precise sense, the term *religious* refers to those men and women who are members of specific religious orders of the Roman Catholic church. For the purpose of this article, the term *religious* has been employed to designate Roman Catholic seminarians and priests in general. An investigation of the bibliography of Weisgerber's (1977) review of the research on the assessment of Roman Catholic seminarians, yields approximately 240 substantive references. Much of this research has dealt with the development of assessment batteries and criteria (Bier, 1965; Carroll, 1970; Herr, 1970; Herr, Arnold, Weisgerber, and D'Arcy, 1964; Kolber, 1964), while other research has focused on the personality characteristics of seminarians throughout seminary training (Carroll, 1967; Lonsway, 1969; McCarthy, 1942, 1970; Murray, 1958; Vaughan, 1970).

1. Psychological/Emotional Maturity of Seminarians. A number of researchers have developed lists of those positive characteristics (i.e., traits and qualities) that are most desirable in seminarians (Carroll, 1970; Coville, 1968; Whealon, 1962). By far the most comprehensive treatment in this area is that of Coville (1968), who lists the characteristics of spirituality, motivation, emotional stability, capacity for effective interpersonal relations, and intelligence. In addition, the trait of psychological maturity, explicated by Carroll (1970), substantiates Coville's (1968) emotional stability characteristic and further emphasizes the importance of the dimension of psychological/emotional maturity.

Parrot and Romain (1958), as cited by Liebert (1974), consider emotional maturity to be a major requirement for the effective undertaking of the priestly vocation. Specifically, they define emotional maturity as characterized by the traits of personal autonomy, dominance of reason, sociability, sexual integration, and balance. Once again, this description is similar to that proposed by Carroll (1970) in defining the emotionally balanced and mature seminarian as one who possesses "a personality in which reason and emotions are well developed and wisely blended" (p. 165).

2. Personality Characteristics of Seminarians. Research on the personality characteristics of seminarians tends to reveal that the traits of dependence, submissiveness, passivity, insecurity, and conformity predominate. McCarthy (1942) found higher than average submissiveness for both a major and minor group of Roman Catholic seminarians. Cattell, Eber, and Tatsuoka (1970) report that both Roman Catholic priests and seminarians exhibit tendencies toward dependence, overprotectedness, and sensitivity. Liebert (1974) in commenting on this personality profile hypothesizes that "one effect of seminary training could be the development of dependence in seminarians [and that] it is also possible that independent students drop out before completion of training" (pp. 19–20). Research by Lee (1968) tends to support the latter section of this hypothesis. Lee found that those Roman Catholic seminarians who exhibit greater conformity in both attitude and behavior in social interactions are more likely to complete seminary training than those who are less conforming.

Finally, Strom (1981), in attempting to establish the validity of her construct of obedience, found significant interrelationships between higher agreement with the hypothesized functional characteristics of obedience and higher "principled reasoning" scores (Rest, 1979a, 1979b), liberal attitudes concerning Roman Catholic ghetto mentality (Coursey, 1971, 1974) and greater agreement with the hypothesized functional characteristics of obedience, and greater dominance (Mehrabian and Hines, 1978) and higher self-ratings on the hypothesized functional characteristics of obedience for two major seminary samples.

3. Personality Characteristics of Priests. Greeley (1972a, 1972b) and Kennedy and Heckler (1972) have focused on the personality characteristics of Roman Catholic priests in the U.S. These data, although confused by the interaction of training, lifestyle, progressive attrition, and initial selection, yields significant information concerning the personality characteristics of U.S. Roman Catholic priests.

Employing the Personal Orientation Inventory (POI), developed by Everett L. Shostrom (1966) and purported to measure Maslow's concept of self-actualization, Greeley (1972a, 1972b) found no appreciable difference between priests and other American males of the same age category. Further, evidence indicating tendencies toward passive-aggressiveness (rather than passive-dependency), assertion of self-worth in the face of weakness and diffi-

culties, and the inclination to take a constructive view of the nature of humanity was also found. Kennedy and Heckler's (1972) findings tend to substantiate those of Greeley (1972a, 1972b). In addition, their findings, with reference to priests and authority, are most illuminating.

They found little indication that American priests would exercise more freedom in any impulsive and/or destructive manner. In reference to those priests described as "underdeveloped," they found a preponderance of ambivalent attitudes toward authority — wanting its direction and protection on the one hand and resenting and using it in order to externalize their own troubles and conflicts on the other hand. In addition, Kennedy and Heckler discovered that although these men perceive their lives as defined and circumscribed by authority, they also report few practical, day-to-day encounters with persons who exert controlling authority over them. In short, these "underdeveloped" American priests do not, in general, exhibit a consistent pattern of attitudes and responses to authority and hence waver between dependency and independency in relationship to it. Kennedy and Heckler close their discussion of American priests and authority with a most interesting comment: "Authority, if it is a major problem, may be such because it does not seem to be a fully realized value on the part of those who exercise it or those who are subject to it. There is some evidence to suggest that priests are becoming increasingly indifferent to it" (p. 16).

Kennedy and Heckler (1972) conclude that, as a group, American priests are bright, able, and dedicated. However, a large number are "underdeveloped" (i.e., not fully grown as opposed to being sick), and there is a need for a broader and freer experience of life in order to facilitate personal growth in these "underdeveloped" priests.

Bibliography. W. C. Bier, S.J., "Testing Procedures and Their Value," in J. E. Haley, C.S.C., ed., *Proceedings of the 1959 Sisters' Institute of Spirituality* (1960), 263–95; "Selection of Seminarians;" in J. M. Lee and L. J. Putz, C.S.C., eds., *Seminary Education in a Time of Change* (1965). D. W. Carroll, S.J., Initial Psychological Prediction as Related to Subsequent Seminary Performance (1967), *Dissertation Abstracts International,* 28 (1968), (10–18), 4292B; "A Follow-up Study of Psychological Assessment," in W. C. Bier, S.J., ed., *Psychological Testing and Ministerial Selection* (1970). R. B. Cattell, H. W. Eber, and M. M. Tatsuoka, *Handbook for the Sixteen Personality Factor Questionnaire* (1970). R. D. Coursey, "The L-C Scale Measuring Liberal-Conservative Religious Attitudes Among Roman Catholics (1971), *Dissertation Abstracts International,* 32 (1971), (3–B), 1819B; "Consulting and the Catholic Crisis," *J. of Consulting and Clinical Psychology,* 42 (1974), 519–28. W. J. Coville, "Basic Issues in the Development and Administration of a Psychological Assessment Program for the Religious Life," in W. J. Coville, P. F. D'Arcy, M.M., T. N. McCarthy, and J. J. Rooney, *Assessment of Candidates for the Religious Life: Basic Psychological Issues and Procedures* (1968). A. M. Greeley, *The Catholic Priest in the United States: Sociological Investigations* (1972a); *Priests in the United States: Reflections on a Survey* (1972b). V. V. Herr, S.J., *The Personality of Seminarians: A Study Guide and Reference Work* (1970). V. V. Herr, S.J., M. B. Arnold, C. A. Weisgerber, S.J., and P. F. D'Arcy, M.M., *Screening Candidates for the Priesthood and Religious Life* (1964). E. C. Kennedy and V. J. Heckler, *The Catholic Priest in the United States: Psychological Investigations* (1972). F. J. Kolber, "Screening Applicants for

Religious Life," *J. of Religion and Health*, 3 (1964), 161–70. J. L. Lee, "An Exploratory Search for Characteristic Patterns and Clusters of Seminary Leavers and Persisters" (1968), *Dissertation Abstracts International*, 29 (1968), (3 – A), 816A. J. L. Liebert, "Personality Profiles of Students in Two Differentially Oriented Roman Catholic Seminaries" (1974), *Dissertation Abstracts International*, 35 (1975), (9-A), 5818–19A. F. A. Lonsway, "Personality Characteristics of Seminarians," *Vocational Guidance Quarterly* 18 (1969), 133–36. T. N. McCarthy, "Personality Traits of Seminarians," *Studies in Psychology and Psychiatry, Catholic University of America*, 5 (1942), 4, "Testing for the Roman Catholic Priesthood," in W. C. Bier, S.J., ed., *Psychological Testing for Ministerial Selection* (1970). A. Mehrabian and M. Hines, "A Questionnaire Measure of Individual Difference in Dominance-Submissiveness," *Educational and Psychological Measurement*, 38 (1978), 479 – 84. J. B. Murray, C. M., "Personality Style of Priests and Seminarians, *Homiletic and Pastoral Review*, 59 (1958), 443 – 47. P. Parrot and R. P. Romain, "Maturité Affective et Vocation Sacerdotale," *Via Spirituelle*, 11:46 (1958), 307–22. J. R. Rest, *Revised Manual for the Defining Issues Test* (1979a); *Development in Judging Moral Issues* (1979b). E. L. Shostrom, *EITS Manual for the Personal Orientation Inventory (POI): An Inventory for the Measurement of Self-Actualization* (1966). A. J. Strom, "The Development of a Construct of Obedience for Roman Catholic Diocesan Seminarians," (1981), unpublished doctoral dissertation, Fuller Theological Seminary. R. P. Vaughan, S.J., "Seminary Training and Personality Change," *Religious Education*, 65 (1970), 56 – 59. C. A. Weisgerber, S.J., *Testing the Seminarian: A Review of the Research* (1977). J. F. Whealon, "Judging the Character of a Seminarian," *National Catholic Educational Association Bulletin*, 59 (1962), 103 – 9.

A. J. STROM

PERSONALITY THEORY *or* PSYCHOLOGY OF RELIGION (Empirical Studies, Methods, and Problems). *Compare* CLERGY *or* RABBIS, EMPIRICAL STUDIES OF; THEOLOGICAL STUDENTS, EVALUATION AND EMPIRICAL STUDIES OF.

RELIGIOUS, PASTORAL CARE OF. *Religious* in Roman Catholic tradition refers to men and women who are members of a religious community approved by the church and who are usually bound by vows of poverty, chastity, and obedience. Diocesan clergy generally are not included within the term *religious*, because of their individual responsibility to a bishop. Therefore, the pastoral care of religious applies to a way of life within a religious community.

1. Historical Background and Model. Communal religious life—a way of taking care of the physical, spiritual, and emotional needs of its members—precedes the Christian era. One such example in Judaic tradition is the Essene community. Inspired by a belief system, it had a highly regulated mode of living into which religious practices were integrated. The result was a total way of life that fostered the human person. Within the Christian tradition, religious communities (as considered in this article) existed by the fourth century A.D. Religious life was designed to imitate the earliest Christian communities as idealized in the NT. Early founders asserted that only in community could believers fulfill the double obligation of love of God and love of neighbor.

The idea of pastoral care of religious men and women living in community found its formulation with the growing popularity of organized religious communities,

for example, monasteries and convents. These formulations for the conduct of a religious life are generally known as "rules." Some of the early community rules include the rule written by St. Basil who lived A.D. 330 – 79 and the rule practiced by Pachomius who died A.D. 346. The most influential code was the rule of St. Benedict (A.D. 529). Benedict had established his rule as a guide for Christian living by religious, especially those who gathered around him in Montecassino. It encapsulated the basic elements of pastoral care of religious. All subsequent writings or thinking about pastoral care down to the Reformation developed from this Benedictine model. For example, it furnished Pope Gregory the Great with a basis for his *Liber regulae pastoralis* (Book of Pastoral Care, 591). Gregory's *Regulae* proposed norms for pastoral care by secular clergy just as Benedict's Rule established the pattern of conduct for life within religious communities.

2. The Structure of Pastoral Care in Religious Life. All rules for religious, such as Benedict's as well as the thirteenth-century rules of the poverty movement exemplified by St. Francis of Assisi and St. Dominic and the 1558 constitutions of St. Ignatius Loyola, address three areas of communal life: a member's relation to the community, psychological needs, and spiritual development. The components of any such rule or guide for the care of men and women in religious communities has to be concerned with these essential features.

a. Relation to the community. Within the community a member's *physical needs* are cared for. He or she receives sufficient food, clothing, medical attention, and rest, according to individual needs. A member engages in meaningful *work*, which nurtures a positive attitude toward useful activity. Such work oftentimes relates to the material sustenance of the whole community. A member of the community finds an *order* to life's many activities, both daily and seasonal.

b. Psychological needs. In addressing psychological needs, the pastoral care of religious looks to developing certain attitudes that allow the member to be a whole person, who is integrated into the life of the community. Thus, a member develops a sense of *bonding* to the community. There is a shared sense of belonging to the group and of durable and permanent relationships among its members. A member comes to respect the pursuit of *learning*, whether it be practical or for its own sake. Learning is recognized as having an important place in a person's daily life and life development. A member recognizes the necessity of *service* to others, whether it be the poor, persons in the local or extended community, or each other. It engenders a sense of purpose and a way of seeing Christ in those who are served. A member also derives a sense of *security* in being able to integrate the religious life with human life and in enjoying the benefits of a regular rhythm and stability to life itself.

c. Spiritual development. The religious life is pursued above all because the individual recognizes the spiritual dimension of human life. Thus, a member needs to develop *interiority*, which is fostered by a life of prayer, recollection, and silence. These activities allow the individual to be in touch with him- or herself, the world, and God. A member comes to appreciate *moderation* through the interplay of both religious and secular aspects of the communal life, balancing basic needs and spiritual strivings, gratifications and ascetic discipline, individual and communal goals. A member becomes sensitive to *beauty,* which in turn permeates the individual's life. The spiritual security fostered in this hospitable environment is conducive to the expression of beauty as something natural and necessary. To some extent, the religious vows of poverty, chastity, and obedience free the religious man or woman from mundane concerns and thus allows for the expression of a person's spirituality.

3. **Contemporary Issues.** Modern pastoral care of the religious is less restricted to the confines of the religious community, although it must still incorporate the elements listed in the above section. It admits that all the pastoral needs of the religious man or woman cannot (and need not) be satisfied by life within the community. Thus, there is a lesser reliance upon self-sufficiency than in an earlier age. This realization, however, as with so much of modern pastoral care, has come about in the past several decades, which have seen important developments in the social sciences, especially psychology and psychiatry, and in historical events themselves. Four movements can be singled out as particularly influential. They are: the mental health movement, the Second Vatican Council, the charismatic movement, and the feminist movement.

a. The mental health movement. With the development of mental health care by secular institutions, those within religious communities find that certain benefits of psychological care can best be obtained from experts outside the religious community. In one particular way, religious communities have come to realize that the promises of a spiritual or religious life do not prevent an individual from succumbing to mental illness of some sort. They employ the tools of modern psychological testing to screen prospective members and some even offer psychotherapy for longtime members who encounter self-doubts and psychological problems. They even recognize that alcoholism touches men and women within religious communities. In fact, they have drawn upon programs originally designed for nonreligious men and women.

b. The Second Vatican Council. A key issue raised at the Second Vatican Council was the renewal of religious life in the modern world. As a result, the council encouraged religious communities to reexamine their constitutions and to revise and adopt them to the conditions of the present era. This decision has had important implications for the organizational aspects of religious life and its pastoral care. While they have retained the essence of their traditions and basic principles, renewed communities are aware of basic changes in the relationship between themselves and the larger world, and in the life within the community and among its members. Many communities have become more engaged in the issues of the contemporary world, have modified the strictures of their earlier codes, and have even drawn upon developments in psychology and psychiatry for the care of members.

c. The charismatic movement. The charismatic movement of the 1960s and 1970s rekindled interest in spirituality, and its impact has even been felt among members of religious communities, most significantly in their spiritual development. For many, charismatic prayer groups offered an alternative to prayer and spiritual support derived from the religious community alone. This new interest in spirituality fostered an attitude of openness within the church such that religious women and even laypersons have become accepted as spiritual directors, a role traditionally limited to ordained clergy.

d. The feminist movement. The assertive presence of the feminist movement, with its origins in secular society, has affected the organizational, spiritual, and psychological dimensions of community life among religious women in particular and within the church in general. Accepting the principle that women have a role in society which is not subordinate to that of men, many religious women have assumed new leadership roles within the church, their religious communities, and even in the secular world. Religious women now participate significantly in the administration and key decision making of their communities, thus affecting the kind of pastoral care found within these communities. They find they are accepted in a greater variety of jobs and roles previously unavailable to them, such as pastoral counseling and spiritual direction. They are much more conscious of the need to develop themselves as whole and integrated human persons. To be sure, these changes in the role of women (both religious and lay) in the church has necessarily altered the way men view themselves and their call to a religious life.

These contemporary issues only point to the fact that the pastoral care of religious will continue to be influenced by the world in which religious men and women find themselves. The roles for men and women will continue to change as the different functions and needs are identified and explored. Still, although the responses of this pastoral care of religious may differ according to changing situations, the essentials of that care, as outlined above, will persist.

Bibliography. RB 1980: The Rule of St. Benedict in Latin and English with Notes (1981). O. Engels, "Religious Orders," in K. Rahner, ed., *Encyclopedia of Theology,* (1975), pp. 1406 – 26. A. W. R. Sipe, "The Psychological Dimensions of the Rule of St. Benedict," *American Benedictine Review* (1983), 424 – 35.

A. W. R. SIPE

RELIGIOUS LIFE. *See also* CELIBACY; OBEDIENCE; RELIGIOUS AND UTOPIAN COMMUNITIES; ROMAN CATHOLIC PASTORAL CARE; SPIRITUAL DIRECTION AND PASTORAL CARE; VOWS/VOWING. *Compare* PASTOR, PASTORAL CARE OF; MISSIONARIES, PASTORAL CARE OF; THEOLOGICAL STUDENTS, PASTORAL CARE OF.

RELIGIOUS, RESEARCH ON. *See* RELIGIOUS, EMPIRICAL STUDIES OF.

RELIGIOUS AFFECTIONS. *See* RELIGIOUS EXPERIENCE; PSYCHOLOGY IN AMERICAN RELIGION.

RELIGIOUS AND UTOPIAN COMMUNITIES. *Religious community* refers to any group of individuals living together for religious purposes and practicing the same rule of life. *Utopian community* refers to any group of persons living together for the purpose of creating and participating in an ideal existence.

Utopia is a Greek term coined by Sir Thomas More (1516) in his literary work, "On the Highest State of a Republic and on the New Island Utopia." It is derived from *ou-topos* (no place) and is a pun on *eu-topos* (good place). As generally used, utopia has come to refer to those ideal states which are impossible of actualization. However, a focal point of More's work was that the ideal society he described was realizable if people wanted it. Religious and utopian communities generally are dedicated to this same optimistic pursuit. Their desire is to make idealized kingdoms earthly realities. Other common factors often include: emergence following periods of social unrest, communal sharing of material resources, commitment to fellow members, and simple, orderly, daily routines. A primary distinction between these two types of communities is whether their idealized kingdom is overtly defined with religious ("the kingdom of God") or socio-political language.

The Christian church offers a rich history of communal practices. The earliest picture is presented in Acts 2:42–46 and 4:32–35. Here Christians are described as sharing their material possessions as part of their life of prayer and brotherhood. By the fourth century the monastic way of life was fully established with its primary structure being the communal group. These groups were "monos" in their existences outside the bounds of normal society. The Reformation preceded a burgeoning of communal groups both within the Catholic church (e.g., the Society of Jesus) and within the Protestant tradition. The communal model as a way of living was embraced by such notable Protestant groups as the Hutterites, Diggers, and Shakers.

From Plato's "Republic" to Skinner's "Walden Two," secular utopian thinkers have sketched ideal societies. The classical utopian believed that societies could be built free from human imperfections. Although religious groups have been more active in the establishment of communities, many secular communities have been established. One of the first was founded by the British manufacturer, Robert Owen. His New Harmony was established in Indiana in 1825 as a cooperative colony. The Shaker communities, Clarence Jordan's *Koinonia Farm,* Jewish Kibbutzim, and the communes of the 1960s and 1970s are other examples of communities founded to varying degrees on utopian ideology.

Sociological theory suggests various functions of community living. Primarily, communes provide a means of strengthening and supporting minority views against the pressures of conformity to a larger society. Additionally, they are seen to serve as vehicles of retreat from the pressures of a complex world. It is, therefore, not surprising that the proliferation of communal ideology and development has so closely followed times of societal upheaval and unrest.

There are many potential dangers inherent to the communal lifestyle. (1) Especially for religious communities, there exists the danger of an exclusivism and perfectionism that leads to the creation of a little church for the perfect within the church at large. This can lead to a distortion of, if not a contempt for, the sacramental understanding of Creation. (2) The German church historian, Ernst Troeltsch, illuminates another potential danger in his classic distinction between church and sect.

According to Troeltsch, the more sectarian a religious group or organization becomes, the more likely its membership will be motivated by anger and openly challenge church and secular powers. Sects, like separatist communal groups, often attract individuals who feel particularly deprived and alienated from society. Often lacking is the system of checks and balances offered through the complex and formalized structure of the church. (3) Communal groups can be at risk for giving over much control to an authoritarian leader.

However, religious and utopian communities provide settings for much potential good: they can provide hope in times of chaos; religious communities offer an alternative view of the loss of self in order to grow in the reality of relationships in the love of Christ; and they present an expansion of alternatives for future living.

Bibliography. C. Andrews, *Famous Utopias* (1937). R. Fogarty, *Dictionary of American Communal and Utopian History* (1980). A. Lockley, *Christian Communes* (1976). L. Mularkey and D. J. Marron, "Evaluating Community Interaction," *Human Development,* 3:3 (1982), 17–24. E. Troeltsch, *The Social Teaching of the Christian Churches,* 2 vols. (1931). B. Ward, "Monastic Spirituality," in *A Dictionary of Christian Spirituality,* ed., G. S. Wakefield (1983). L. Wrightsman, *Social Psychology in the 70s* (1972).

G. MOON

COMMUNITY, FELLOWSHIP, AND CARE; RELIGIOUS LIFE. *See also* SOCIOLOGY OF RELIGION. *Compare* CONGREGATION, PASTORAL CARE OF; NEW RELIGIOUS MOVEMENTS; POPULAR THERAPEUTIC MOVEMENTS AND PSYCHOLOGIES; THERAPEUTIC COMMUNITY.

RELIGIOUS BEHAVIOR. (1) The individual's practice of activities, such as church attendance, prayer, or giving of money, that are commonly associated with a religious tradition; (2) individual beliefs about and interpretations of these activities and relationships assumed to involve religion in any way; (3) any activity or belief that individuals associate with religion, the supernatural, or high intensity values in some way.

In North America since the late nineteenth century, psychologists of religion have sought to describe a taxonomy of religious behavior and how these behaviors are related to other areas of life, both empirically and theoretically. The earliest attempts were by E. D. Starbuck and William James.

1. **Taxonomies of Religious Behaviors.** Early students of religious behavior attempted to define religion as a single unitary variable consisting of beliefs and activities that the researcher and/or respondents identified as "religious." As early as 1939, L. L. Thurstone and E. J. Chave had developed a wide variety of measures of religious belief and behaviors. Since the 1940s, however, most investigators have refined definitions of religious behaviors along several dimensions.

a. Religion and community. Emile Durkheim (1947) distinguished between "beliefs," "rites," and "community" as elements of religious behavior. Joachim Wach (1944) divided religious expressions into theoretical (belief), practical (ritual), and sociological (fellowship). Gerhard Lenski (1961) described religious behavior as "associational" (such as church attendance) and "communal" (such as proportion of relatives and friends in the same religious tradition). He also used two measures of religious orientations: belief (doctrinal orthodoxy) and frequency of prayer.

b. *Inner and outer directedness.* Gordon Allport (1950) distinguished between "institutionalized" and "interiorized" motivations to religious behaviors. He later revised these to "extrinsic" (religion used for instrumental, self-serving, utilitarian purposes) and "intrinsic" (religion as the ultimate end in itself). Bernard Spilka and R. O. Allen (1967) used "consensual" (conventional conformity in the acceptance and practice of religious behaviors) and "committed" (flexible, open religious practice by personal choice) in ways similar to Allport.

c. *Dimensions of religious behavior.* Charles Y. Glock (1962) proposed five major dimensions of religious commitment and behavior, which Joseph Faulkner and Gordon DeJong (1966) then developed into measuring scales. These five dimensions are: ideological (beliefs about God's will, control, purpose, etc.); ritualistic (practice such as prayer, attendance at worship, reading of scriptures); experiential (feelings of ecstasy, trust in or fear of the Divine, inner personal experiences); intellectual (knowledge about one's religious traditions and practices); and consequential (effects of these dimensions on behavior, ethical and moral principles derived from the other dimensions).

d. *Religious practice and spiritual growth.* Morton King and Richard Hunt (1975) built on the work of Glock in their development of scales to measure creedal assent, devotionalism, church attendance, organizational activity, financial support, and religious growth. These scales can be combined to measure individual social involvement in religious groups (how often one attends church, shares faith with another, talks about religion) and personal meanings of religion (belief in God, personal meanings, trust in God).

e. *Religion and ultimate concern.* Thomas Luckmann (1967) and Milton Yinger (1970) represent approaches to understanding religious behavior by expanding the definition to include any behavior, institutional or personal, that expresses an individual's ultimate concerns. This approach helps to transcend biases from a specific religious tradition or country in order to measure positive responses to pervasive human concerns such as suffering, violence, injustice, and death. Charles Morris (1956) used a similar approach in describing thirteen "ways to live" that seem to transcend nationalities and religious traditions. These ways include traditional religious behaviors, socially sensitive humanism, and personally pragmatic life-styles.

f. *Alternate sources of religious behavior.* Robert Bellah (1970) suggests that in addition to traditional religious dimensions there is a dimension of civil religious behavior and belief in the U.S. Robert Wuthnow (1976) also postulates four alternative meaning systems that tend to affect behavior: theism (emphasis on God's involvement with self and world); individualism (emphasis on isolated personal responsibility unrelated to other factors); social science (emphasis on sociological factors producing behavior); and mysticism (emphasis on nature, cosmic harmony, the arts, and inner personal experiences). Studies of nonconventional religious groups and of persons who do not participate in any religious group do find

differences in the reported ethical standards and behaviors, but these differences are often not as extreme as the content of the different religious belief systems might suggest.

2. Relationships Between Religious Behaviors and Other Measures. In considering how religious behaviors are related to other personal characteristics, attention must be given to the types of persons included in a given sample and the ways that variables are measured. When a research sample is heterogeneous, including both persons who are highly committed and others who are not committed to a particular perspective measured, then it is likely that a general religious factor or dimension will cause most of the measures of religious behaviors to be closely correlated. When a sample is homogeneous with respect to religious perspective, age, sex, or other characteristics, then differences among measures of religious behaviors are more likely to appear.

The other major consideration in seeking relationships between other measures and religious behavior is the type of measures used and the settings in which the data are obtained. Most studies of religious behavior use paper and pencil self-report measures that ask the subjects to introspect or to describe what they perceive themselves to do under certain circumstances. Various response biases and inaccuracies may affect individuals' responses to these measures. These cautions are essential in interpreting data on religious behaviors.

a. *Traditional religious practices.* Most studies indicate moderate to high positive correlations between church attendance, involvement in other activities of a religious group, and financial support of that group. Creedal assent (i.e., agreement with specific creedal statements) and devotionalism (prayer, reading of Scriptures) tend to have lower relationships with religious practices, as does factual information about the religious group (denomination or tradition). Thus participation in a religious group is likely to be related to factors in addition to religious knowledge and personal beliefs.

b. *Belief in God.* How beliefs about God are related to other behaviors depends heavily upon the content of the belief. Although most national surveys indicate that fewer than ten percent of the U.S. population does not believe in God, there is evidence that another twenty to forty percent of the population is uncertain about whether they believe in God or which type of deity, if any, they choose. Among the remaining who "definitely believe" in God, those who feel distant or remote from God are much less likely to be actively involved in the activities of a religious group. Those who have an image of God as being actively concerned and caring for them personally and /or being actively involved in the social order are more likely to participate regularly in religious activities such as attendance at church and regular prayer.

c. *Religion and personality.* Relationships between religious beliefs, religious behaviors, and measures of personality depend heavily upon both the type of religious beliefs of the individual and the type of measurement of these beliefs. Some studies suggest that persons with more traditional, literal, simplified religious belief systems tend to have lower self-esteem and confidence, increased guilt feelings, less education, greater submissiveness, increased dependency, and more constricted personalities. By contrast, persons who hold more flexible, moderate religious beliefs, with more room for uncertainty, tend to have higher self-esteem, greater independence, less prejudice, and greater sense of social responsibility.

Since these types of studies only measure correlations between variables, it is not clear that traditional, literal, or simplistic belief systems produce (or are produced by) these less desirable personality characteristics. One hypothesis is that other factors, such as socialization, type of education, and cognitive complexity produce both the type of religious beliefs and personality qualities. It is relatively clear, however, that the meanings one attaches to religious beliefs are associated with religious behaviors such as participation in church worship and activities. Persons who report feeling a more personal relationship with God are more likely to report regular attendance in church activities. (See Piazza and Glock, "Images of God and Their Meanings," in Wuthnow, 1979).

d. *Religion and socialization.* Religious behaviors, both verbal (beliefs) and lifestyle (church attendance, prayer, etc.) are probably related to the socialization history and current group participation of the individual. Thus factors such as the roles one had in his or her childhood family and the perceived rewards one experiences from significant others probably greatly influence these religious behaviors. Increasingly, research suggests curvilinear relationships between religious behaviors and other attitudes and life-styles. For example, persons who are very involved in a traditional religious group or are not involved at all tend to have fewer ethnic prejudices than persons who are nominally involved.

e. *Other factors.* Religious beliefs and behaviors are related to a wide variety of other variables, although cause-effect relationships are unclear. Approximately forty percent of the U.S. population report attending church two or three times per month, but this percentage varies widely according to age, ethnic origin, type of religious group, socioeconomic status, and other factors. Greater commitment to religious beliefs and higher participation in church, in turn, tend to be positively related to lower delinquency, greater satisfaction in marriage, and socioeconomic achievement. Religious beliefs and behaviors are significantly related to many other variables, but the exact nature of these relationships depends upon the meanings and experiences of the individual involved.

Bibliography. R. O. Allen and B. Spilka, "Committed and Consensual Religion," *J. of Scientific Study of Religion,* 6 (1967), 191–206. G. Allport, *The Individual and His Religion* (1950). R. Bellah, *Beyond Belief* (1970). J. E. Dittes, "Psychology of Religion," in G. Lindzey and E. Aronson, eds., *Handbook of Social Psychology,* 2d ed. vol. 5 (1968), pp. 602–59. E. Durkheim, *The Elementary Forms of Religious Life* (1976 [1947]). J. Faulkner and G. DeJong, "Religiosity in 5-D," *Social Forces,* 45 (1966), 246–54. C. Y. Glock, "On The Study of Religious Commitment," *Research Supplement to Religious Education,* 57 (1962), 98–110. W. James, *The Varieties of Religious Experience* (1902). R. Kenthnow, *The Consciousness Reformation* (1976). M. King and R. Hunt, "Measuring the Religious Variable: National Replication," *J. of the Scientific Study of Religion,* 14 (1975), 13–22. G. Lenski, *The Religious Factor* (1961). T. Luckmann, *The Invisible Religion* (1967). C. Morris, *Varieties of Human Value* (1956). E. D. Starbuck, *The Psychology of Religion*

(1899). M. P. Strommen, *Research on Religious Development* (1971). L. L. Thurstone and E. J. Chave, *Measure Religion: Fifty-two Experimental Forms* (1939). M. Yinger, *The Scientific Study of Religion* (1970).

R. A. HUNT

RELIGION. *See also* CULTURAL ANTHROPOLOGY OF RELIGION; PSYCHOLOGY OF RELIGION (Empirical Studies, Methods, and Problems); SOCIOLOGY OF RELIGION; SOCIOLOGY OF RELIGIOUS AND PASTORAL CARE. *Compare* ASCETICAL PRACTICES; COMMITMENT; MORAL BEHAVIOR AND RELIGION; RELIGIOUS EXPERIENCE; PSYCHOPATHOLOGY AND RELIGION; WORLD VIEW.

RELIGIOUS BELIEFS. *See* FAITH/BELIEF.

RELIGIOUS CARE AND COUNSELING. *See* PASTORAL CARE; PASTORAL COUNSELING; SOCIOLOGY OF RELIGIOUS AND PASTORAL CARE.

RELIGIOUS COMMUNITIES. *See* RELIGIOUS AND UTOPIAN COMMUNITIES.

RELIGIOUS DEVELOPMENT. *See* FAITH DEVELOPMENT RESEARCH; LIFE CYCLE THEORY; SPIRITUAL DISCIPLINE AND GROWTH; SPIRITUAL THEOLOGY AND PASTORAL CARE.

RELIGIOUS EDUCATION. *See* EDUCATION, NURTURE, AND CARE; TEACHING.

RELIGIOUS EDUCATION MOVEMENT. *See* HISTORY OF PROTESTANT PASTORAL CARE (United States); PASTORAL CARE MOVEMENT.

RELIGIOUS EVALUATION AND DIAGNOSIS. *See* EVALUATION AND DIAGNOSIS, RELIGIOUS.

RELIGIOUS EXPERIENCE. A person's responses, primarily in terms of cognitions and feelings, to whatever he or she considers divine. Though there is no consensus among modern investigators in the definition of religious experience, this definition is probably typical in incorporating some conceptualization of a deity as essential. Less typical are definitions focusing upon a person's ultimate concerns, whether centered upon a deity or not. Such definitions attempt to avoid the difficult issue of the interface between theology and psychology. However, especially in dealing with the Judeo-Christian tradition, explicit consideration of some conceptualization of the Divine is essential in any definition of religious experience. In this sense, religious experience is best conceived as the totality of responses to one's conception of the Divine. This definition is congruent with the classic definition of religious experience offered by William James: "The feelings, acts, and experiences of individual men [persons] in their solitude, so far as they stand in relation to whatever they may consider the divine" (1961 [1902], p. 42). Similar experiences without consideration of the Divine are best viewed as analogous to, rather than as instances of, religious experience proper.

The infinite variety of religious experiencing is evident throughout the history of the world's major religious traditions. Classifications of particular types of religious experiences are always tentative and incomplete. Any experience can be religiously interpreted, either simultaneously with its initial occurrence or retrospectively. A large part of the psychology of religion is concerned with identifying motivations, situations, and settings within which experience is defined as religious. Specific instances can range from simple acts of prayer, to conversions, to times of special inspiration or illumination, to a wide variety of experiences that defy conventional mores. From a purely psychological perspective the issue is simply whether the phenomenon in question is defined in religious symbols or meanings, centering on the Divine. If so, whatever other properties are present, the experience itself is religious. Ultimate judgments as to the truth quality of religious experience must be made within particular theological traditions, a fact many psychologists would like to avoid. Ultimately, in many instances, only theological criteria can distinguish religious experiences from otherwise merely pathological experiences.

1. **Descriptive and Explanatory Approaches.** The definition herein proposed for religious experience has been central in the work of two major traditions whose approach to religious experience has been either purely descriptive (in the case of phenomenology) or purportedly explanatory (in the case of psychoanalysis).

a. Phenomenology. Phenomenological confrontations with religious experience have tended to identify it as qualitatively unique. Schleiermacher (1799) located this uniqueness in persons' awareness of their utter dependency and finitude, while Otto (1923) identified the uniqueness of religious experience in the fascination and awe of the numinous. While such phenomenological descriptions are valuable, they tend to lack consensus and to limit the range of experiences empirical psychologists identify as religious.

b. Psychoanalysis. Psychoanalysts have tended to provide purely naturalistic reductive interpretations of religious experience. Freud's claim that religious experience is but a disguised reappearance of unconscious parent-child conflicts is one example. Jung's efforts to provide a naturalistically based alternative to established theological interpretations is another. Psychoanalytic views have not tended to generate much empirical work and are formulated such as to be essentially nonfalsifiable by contemporary empirical methodologies. As such they are essentially alternatives to established theological systems for confronting and explaining religious experiences. Their early acceptance has been tempered by recent theological criticisms of purely naturalistically based efforts to confront religious experience. For instance, Freud's claim that theistic belief is merely a projection fails to confront the conceptual claim that projections of parent-child relationships may nevertheless foreshadow objectively real God-person relationships as explicated in various religious traditions.

2. **Empirical Research.** Dissatisfaction with phenomenological and psychoanalytic traditions has led the contemporary empirical psychology of religion to focus upon more narrowly defined issues, especially on factors contributing to the common report of religious experience among normal populations. Four major research areas have emerged with some degree of clarity and independence.

a. Altered states research. This rubric includes a rather divergent array of studies united by their common effort to provide empirically based, nonreductive descriptions of modes of experiencing, many of which are religious (Tart, 1960). Of particular importance is the empirical verification that there are modes of experiencing the world that vary radically among themselves, and that the presumption of a single "normal" mode of experiencing the world is unwarranted. This fact promises to link altered states research with classic research on religious conversion. The latter research has long established that new modes of experiencing the world can follow from religious conversion and in fact often are the major indicators of such conversion.

b. Psychedelic drugs. Research with psychedelic drugs has verified that many historically identified modes of religious experiencing can be elicited with some degree of predictability with a wide variety of natural and synthetic drugs. Such drugs tend to elicit imagery and feelings long associated with religious experience (Leary, 1964). Such research suggests that some forms of religious experience can be facilitated deliberately, especially when linked with historical and ethnographic studies documenting the use of drugs in religious ceremonies. However, drug ingestion *per se* produces no identifiable religious experience. Rather, set and setting unite with belief commitments to determine religious experiences. In this sense, whether or not a drug will facilitate a religious experience is not simply a drug-specific property, but a complex interaction between physiological arousal, situational context, and belief commitment.

c. Imagination and religious experience. Especially among Catholics and certain Protestant Evangelical groups the frequent report of imaginative experiences, religiously interpreted as revelation or inspiration, is common. In the past visual and auditory experience, especially when apparently spontaneous, has been rather casually dismissed by psychologists as instances of hallucination. Yet recent research documents both the normalcy of supposedly hallucinatory phenomena in normal populations (Al-Issa, 1977) and the religious relevance of the elicitation of such experiences in controlled laboratory settings (Hood and Morris, 1981). The necessity for psychology to reconceptualize imaginative phenomena in terms more congruent with theology is evident from such research (Volken, 1961).

d. The personal dimension of religious experiencing. Contemporary research has clearly documented the tremendous relevance of the personal dimension to religious experience. A large number of persons, perhaps a majority, experience their God in intimate personal terms. Stark (1968) has proposed a typology of religious experience based upon a continuum of the personal along which experiences can be ordered, including experiences in which the person is aware of a divine presence as well as those in which a divine presence acknowledges the person. A crucial implication of this research is that personal experiences of the Divine are not only normal, but also require reconceptualization of many of the fundamental assumptions of modern psychology (Hillman, 1975).

3. **Higher Order Conceptual Integration.** The search for higher order integrating concepts to confront the empirical data concerning religious experience has led to two major contemporary conceptualizations of religious

experience: motivational and limit theories. Both these theories have been largely based upon empirical research on mysticism.

a. Motivational theories. One fruitful classification of the endless variety of religious experiences is to identify two major motivations for such experiences: deficiency and growth. Under deficiency motivations are included all conditions of deficiency or lack relative to some standard. Here, troubled souls find consolation and resolution in experiencial confrontations with the Divine. Within the deficiency category are persons who if assessed prior to their religious resolutions would appear troubled and psychologically disturbed. Yet the crucial issue is that genuine religious experiencing can and often does provide resolutions for these troubles; hence religious experiencing is to be at least partly evaluated by its consequences over a period of time. The empirical fact that religious experiences resolve otherwise troublesome situations is one criterion for distinguishing neurotic distortions of religion from its mature expression (Boisen, 1936).

On the other hand, religious experience can be sought for growth motives among persons otherwise identified as fulfilled. This view, most associated with the work of Abraham Maslow (1964), suggests that religion can be an active quest for spiritual fulfillment occurring in otherwise psychologically adequate lives. It suggests that religious experiencing can be found among the most healthy in any society, and especially among those whose religious motivations are intrinsic rather than extrinsic and who are likely to seek experiential fulfillment within the bounds of their particular faith (Hood, 1973).

b. Limits and transcendence. The focus upon deficiency and growth motivations meshes nicely with efforts to link theological and psychological perspectives in broader conceptualizations of religious experience. For instance, Hood (1978) has argued that any confrontation with limits suggests the possibility of transcendence, and that it is precisely in such experiences of transcendence, divinely interpreted, that religious experience lies. Hence, almost any activity, process, or awareness can be religiously experienced. The crucial issue lies in the elicitation and religious resolution, sudden or gradual, of one's awareness of what were previously perceived as limits, but are now transcended. This awareness of transcendence, rooted in the Divine, makes religious experiencing a continual human potential, regardless of its otherwise purely contingent eliciting circumstances or any of its other objectively desirable properties.

This discussion should not mask an often overlooked fact that religious experience need not be dramatic or extreme. Many persons within particular faith traditions experience the world continually in a religious mode. It is suggestive to note that insofar as religious views dominate one's life, life itself becomes an integrated religious experience. In this sense, it is difficult for some to select out from their own experiences those that are uniquely religious. It can be the mark of a mature religiosity simply to live one's religion in a continual fulfillment of personal, experiential religiosity.

Bibliography. I. Al-Issa, "Social and Cultural Aspects of Hallucinations," *Psychological Bulletin*, 84 (1977), 570–87. A. T. Boisen, *The Exploration of the Inner World* (1971 [1936]).

A. Godin, *The Psychological Dynamics of Religious Experience* (1985). J. R. Hillman, *Revisioning Psychology* (1975). R. W. Hood, Jr., "Religious Orientation and the Experience of Transcendence," *J. for the Scientific Study of Religion*, 12 (1973), 441–44; "Anticipatory Set and Setting: Stress Incongruities as Elicitors of Mystical Experience in Solitary Nature Situations," *J. for the Scientific Study of Religion*, 17 (1978), 279–87. R. W. Hood, Jr. and R. J. Morris, "Sensory Isolation and the Differential Elicitation of Religious Imagery in Intrinsic and Extrinsic Persons," *J. for the Scientific Study of Religion*, 20 (1981), 261–73. T. Leary, "The Religious Experience: Its Production and Interpretation," *Psychedelic Review*, 1 (1964), 324–46. J. E. Loder, *The Transforming Moment* (1981). W. James, *The Varieties of Religious Experience* (1961 [1902]). A. H. Maslow, *Religions, Values, and Peak Experiences* (1964). R. Otto, *The Idea of the Holy* (1923). F. Schleiermacher, *On Religion: Speeches to Its Cultured Despisers* (1958 [1799]). R. Stark, "A Taxonomy of Religious Experiences," *J. for the Scientific Study of Religion*, 5 (1965), 97–116. C. T. Tart, *Transpersonal Psychologies* (1975). L. Volken, *Visions, Revelations and the Church* (1963).

R. W. HOOD, JR.

CHARISMATIC EXPERIENCE; CONVERSION; MYSTICISM; PSYCHOLOGY OF RELIGION. *See also* BORN-AGAIN EXPERIENCE; ECSTASY; The HOLY; PEAK EXPERIENCE; PSYCHOANALYSIS, ANALYTICAL (JUNGIAN) PSYCHOLOGY, *or* HUMANISTIC PSYCHOLOGY, AND RELIGION; SELF-TRANSCENDENCE; TRANCE; VISIONS AND VOICES. *Compare* GUIDANCE, DIVINE; ILLUMINATION; PHENOMENOLOGICAL PSYCHOLOGY AND PSYCHOTHERAPY; PSYCHEDELIC DRUGS AND EXPERIENCE; PSYCHOPATHOLOGY AND RELIGION; RELIGION; REVELATION AND PASTORAL CARE; SPIRITUALITY.

RELIGIOUS FEELINGS. *See* RELIGIOUS EXPERIENCE; The HOLY.

RELIGIOUS LANGUAGE AND SYMBOLISM, PSYCHOLOGY OF. Religious language uses a vocabulary which is often quite ordinary, but employs it in special ways to articulate religious truth. Symbols are often distinguished from signs on the ground that they resonate more deeply with the mind than more abstract language. They may be verbal or nonverbal. Skepticism about the adequacy of religious language may result in the feeling that God cannot be characterized and is therefore impersonal or remote. Conversely, the absolutizing of certain selected symbols or privileged models can lead to serious distortion in an individual's view of God, the self, and the world.

1. The Operative Basis of Religious Language.
a. Analogy. The problem posed by the fact that God transcends human language has long been recognized. Quite apart from appeals to special revelation, two ways of approach were distinguished in medieval Christian theology. The *via negativa* allowed characterization of God by negative contrast: God is invisible, immortal, and infinite. The second way, *via eminentiae,* ascribes to God the highest degree of certain qualities which may be found in the world, such as wisdom, power, and love. These approaches together amount to a theory of analogy. Language about God does not correspond exactly in meaning with the application of the same words to persons or to objects. But neither is the meaning unrelated. To call God "Father" is to use language neither equivocally nor univocally, but analogically.

b. Models and qualifiers. Though broadly correct, there are some difficulties in the traditional doctrine, including its alleged dependence on a particular metaphysic and its overexclusive concern with the cognitive aspect of religious language. In modern times Ian Ramsey suggested an approach which took account of these two problems. He observed that scientists construct models in order to understand complex aspects of the world. Similarly, models are also needed for the articulation of religious truth. This may include personal models (e.g., father), mechanical models (e.g., cause), or spatial models (e.g., high, above). But each model needs an appropriate qualifier. God is not simply Father, but heavenly Father; not simply cause, but First Cause. Indeed one important way of qualifying models is through the mutual interaction of a plurality of models. If God is above, God is also beyond and within. To see the "point" of the model now becomes a more than purely cognitive or intellectual exercise. A disclosure situation is set up in which understanding dawns at a deeper level.

c. Language and life. The operation of religious language also transcends the purely cognitive realm in another respect. Most, or at least much, religious language commits the speaker to certain attitudes or patterns of behavior. To say "God has forgiven me," or "I repent," is to commit oneself to a practical stance in the absence of which the utterance begins to lose credibility, and ultimately, meaning. In more positive terms this interrelationship between language and life is what gives language, in Wittgenstein's words, its "backing." Jesus gave backing, currency, and credibility to the language of divine grace by eating with the irreligious and the outcasts.

d. Cultural relativity. A monarchical society may call God King; a pastoral community may speak of God as Shepherd. But this obvious point does not justify a reductionist approach to religious language. Such models may retain a normative significance within a religious tradition, provided that their status as models is appreciated. Often such models articulate foundational truths of the tradition, and constitute language paradigms. The task of interpretation is not to reduce them, but only to identify and exclude those aspects which are inapplicable to the religious reality.

2. **Implications for Pastoral Psychology.** *a. Over-preoccupation with selected models.* Some individuals tend uncritically to absolutize certain selected models, giving them privileged status as controlling "keys" for understanding God, themselves, or the world. Models lose their appropriate and necessary qualifiers. For example, an individual's entire experience, good and bad, of a human parent may be read into the term "father" and applied to God without qualification. The model is no longer understood as analogy, image, or metaphor. The other problem is that when such a model is accorded this privileged status, other balancing and complementing models tend to be crowded out and lost from view. For example, a person obsessed with the problem of guilt may see God exclusively as Judge. The way forward is to explore the value of other models, and this will have the automatic effect of de-absolutizing the previously dominant model.

b. Devaluation of religious language. Other individuals may dismiss models and analogies as "merely" imperfect symbols, and attempt to restrict themselves to more abstract modes of thought about God. Such a strongly intellectualist approach, however, deprives the individual of linguistic resources which may resonate with the emotions and engage the will. A sense of trust toward, and intimacy with, God becomes increasingly difficult. Further, in seeking to move beyond traditional linguistic formulations, the individual may also invite a sense of estrangement from the religious community. Confidence needs to be restored in the possibility of using a plurality of models with honesty and integrity. In the Christian tradition Christology is also fundamental, since Jesus himself is the Word made flesh.

3. **Symbol, Myth, and Story.** *a. Symbol.* Symbols are said to resonate with the human mind at a deeper and less intellectual level than more discursive or abstract language. Jung, Jaspers, and Tillich stress the value of symbols as bridges between the conscious and unconscious. Symbols, they argue, are not artificially contrived, but well up from the springs of the unconscious to meet situations of need or action. Paul Ricoeur also stresses that symbols give rise to thought rather than merely expressing it. They remain suggestive and open-ended.

If this less cognitive account of symbols is accepted, the two major problems already outlined reappear in greatly intensified form. On the one hand, symbols remain necessary for integration and a grounding in reality which is more than purely intellectual. The place of the sacraments in the life of the Christian church witnesses to this recognized need. On the other hand, symbols may also set up unwanted and destructive resonances in the mind, which are all the more dangerous because they operate at a level often beneath that of conscious critical control. Even normally positive objects may, for some minds, become invested with sinister or frightening significance. Thus the interpretation of symbols must be checked against the understanding of the wider community, and especially against its sources of theology.

b. Myth and demythologizing. Rudolf Bultmann's work on myth raises a special aspect of the problem of projection or objectification. He argues that the NT employs a mythology which presents aspects of human experience as if they were external realities. Thus the last judgment is to be interpreted as a myth of human responsibility. Language about demonic agencies and cosmic forces externalize human conflicts. Bultmann was unable to prove his case and his views are vulnerable to severe criticisms. But he succeeded in showing that those who find themselves preoccupied with questions about angels and demons, or about happenings at the end of the world, largely misconstrue the point of the language concerned. These are not foci of attention in their own right. They serve primarily to point to the scope of Christ's victory and lordship, and to the Christian's consequent experience of deliverance and freedom.

c. Myth, story, and narrative. More broadly, myths denote stories which embody symbols of God or the otherworldly, and involve the hearer as participant and not merely as observer. The Adam story speaks of innocence, of guilt, of paradise, of temptation, of fall, and of promise, but not merely as remote phenomena of the past. The hearer is drawn into the narrative world as participant, not as spectator. A sense of community based on common memory and experience is also generated. But the cognitive dimension should not be overlooked. Some narratives are confessional history. In this case cognitive truth-claims are made, and in the corporate testimony and memory of the believing community the individual finds some guard against the fear of illusion or self-deception.

Bibliography. I. G. Barbour, *Myths, Models, and Paradigms* (1974). P. van Buren, *The Edges of Language* (1972). G. Cope, *Symbolism in the Bible and the Church* (1959). F. W. Dillistone, *Traditional Symbols and the Contemporary World* (1973). M. Douglas, *Natural Symbols* (1970). M. Durrant, *The Logical Status of 'God'* (1973). D. D. Evans, *The Logic of Self-Involvement* (1963). T. Fawcett, *The Symbolic Language of Religion* (1971). R. S. Heimbeck, *Theology and Meaning* (1969). D. M. High, *Language, Persons, and Belief* (1967). S. Hook, ed., *Religious Experience and Truth* (1961) pp. 3–89. W. Hordern, *Speaking of God* (1965). C. G. Jung, *Man and his Symbols* (1968 [1964]). R. May, ed., *Symbolism in Religion and Literature* (1960). S. McFague, *Metaphorical Theology* (1982). J. Macquarrie, *God-Talk* (1967). E. L. Mascall, *Words and Images* (1957). A. M. Olson, *Myth, Symbol, and Reality* (1980). H. Palmer, *Analogy* (1973). I. T. Ramsey, *Religious Language* (1957); *Models and Mystery* (1964). P. Ricoeur, *The Symbolism of Evil* (1967). A. C. Thiselton, *The Two Horizons* (1980), 252–92; "Language and Meaning in Religion," in C. Brown, ed., *New International Dictionary of N.T. Theology*, 3 (1978), pp. 1123–46. P. Tillich, "The Religious Symbol," in S. Hook (1961), pp. 301–21. D. Tracy, *Blessed Rage for Order* (1975). A. Vergote and A. Tamayo, *The Parental Figures and the Representation of God* (1981).

A. C. THISELTON

SYMBOLISM/SYMBOLIZING. *See also* COMMUNICATION; CULTURAL ANTHROPOLOGY OF RELIGION; INTERPRETATION AND HERMENEUTICS, PASTORAL. *Compare* BLESSING AND BENEDICTION; PSYCHOLINGUISTIC THEORY; RELIGIOUS BEHAVIOR; RITUAL AND PASTORAL CARE.

RELIGIOUS LANGUAGE IN PASTORAL CARE.

Religious language conveys that which is holy through thoughts which are expressed (as in Paul Pruyser's *The Minster as Diagnostician*), in thoughts of God that are beyond expression (as in the introduction to Martin Buber's *Between Man and Man*), and in all the expressions of the self that take place in a consciousness of a Being beyond self (as in Rudolph Otto's explanation of Isaiah 6 in *The Idea of the Holy*).

Pastoral counseling has placed special emphasis upon an awareness of the self in religious language. In the tradition of Søren Kierkegaard, counselors assist clients to express the tension between being someone and knowing about something. The experience of the holy is given more attention than concepts of the Holy One. The former is involvement; the latter is detachment. Language must formulate awareness of the self and others rather than recite formulas for acceptance. The theory of the unconscious, attention to body language, and awareness of subliminal responses are some of the counselor's resources in developing deeper expressions of the self.

To express the self-before-God, both counselor and counselee must participate in the specialization and the specificity of religious language. The former was defined

by James Gustafson in *Treasure in Earthen Vessels*. Knowledge of a special language and facility of its use are two marks of belonging to a nation, a profession, a church. Verbal symbols provide identity.

Sociologically, religious language defines the "reference group" of a pastoral counselor. This may also be the reference group of a counselee, in which case the words of the faith connect them and allow investigation of feelings that both understand through common symbols.

However, language may distort as well as clarify. There must be a specificity as well as specialization to know what religious phrases mean to counselor and counselee, and to other significant persons in the life of the counselee. When feelings relationships are specified, the self is made known through language.

When self, feelings, and relationships are related, then language facilitates the psychological process of individuation, the sociological requirements of socialization, and the religious expectation of salvation. Salvation, as Jonathan Edwards wrote in the eighteenth century, comes about when a person is no longer lost in words that have no meaning. Evangelism for Edwards was a challenge for the head to be brought down into the heart, so that the godly words of grace, sin, repentance, and faith could be experienced by every hearer. When the Word of God became personal feeling, salvation had occurred.

Pastoral counseling aids this type of communication in several ways. One is through an awareness of the ways in which language may conceal rather than reveal. Therefore, whenever "God-talk" occurs, the counselor seeks authentic evidence that the person is speaking from the heart rather than through rationalization of the head. Another contribution is through attention to signs of the unconscious, such as body language which conveys defensiveness or hostility while the counselee verbalizes love or forgiveness.

A very specialized contribution of pastoral counseling is the balancing of the concrete with the symbolic in the religious life of schizophrenics (Carroll Wise, *Religion in Illness and Health*).

Bibliography. M. Buber, *Between Man and Man* (1965). F. W. Dillistone, *Christianity and Communications* (1956). J. Gustafson, *Treasure in Earthen Vessels* (1976). H. N. Malony, "Godtalk in Psychotherapy," *Wholeness and Holiness* (1983). J. L. Moreau, *Language and Religious Language* (1961). S. Nichols, *Words on Target* (1963). R. Otto, *The Idea of the Holy* (1968). P. Pruyser, *The Minister as Diagnostician* (1976). C. Wise, *Religion in Illness and Health* (1942).

S. SOUTHARD

INTERPRETATION AND HERMENEUTICS, PASTORAL; PERSONAL STORY, SYMBOL, AND MYTH IN PASTORAL CARE; PRAYER IN PASTORAL CARE. *Compare* RELIGIOUS BEHAVIOR; RITUAL AND PASTORAL CARE; SYMBOLIC DIMENSIONS OF PASTORAL CARE RELATIONSHIPS.

RELIGIOUS LIFE (VOWED LIFE). Originating in fourth-century monasticism and based on the three "evangelical counsels," religious (vowed) life is distinguished by profession of "simple" or "solemn" vows. Most vow chastity, poverty, and obedience; others, "conversion of morals" (Benedictines) and "obedience to the pope" (Jesuits). Religious life is considered an intensifi-

cation of baptismal commitment and witnesses to the church's true nature, a community of radical discipleship. This, however, does not imply superiority or privilege, but charisms and service. Traditionally found in Roman Catholicism, recent years have seen a revival of religious life in Anglicanism and Lutheranism. An ecumenical religious community flourishes in Taizé, France.

S. BEVANS

VOCATION (Roman Catholicism); VOWS/VOWING. *See also* CHRISTIAN LIFE; RELIGIOUS AND UTOPIAN COMMUNITIES; SPIRITUALITY, ROMAN CATHOLIC. *Compare* COMMUNITY, FELLOWSHIP, AND CARE; MINISTRY (Roman Catholic Tradition).

RELIGIOUS MATURITY. *See* FAITH DEVELOPMENT RESEARCH; LIFE CYCLE THEORY; SPIRITUAL DISCIPLINE AND GROWTH; SPIRITUAL THEOLOGY AND PASTORAL CARE.

RELIGIOUS MOVEMENTS. *See* NEW RELIGIOUS MOVEMENTS.

RELIGIOUS ORDERS. *See* RELIGIOUS LIFE (VOWED LIFE); RELIGIOUS AND UTOPIAN COMMUNITIES.

RELIGIOUS ORIENTATION. Typically, intrinsic and extrinsic religiosity as operationally defined by Gordon Allport. Best understood as motivational variables, extrinsic religiosity refers to the pursuit of religion as a *means* to other ends, while intrinsic religiosity refers to the pursuit of religion as an *end* in itself. Consistent relationships have been found between religious orientation and a number of other religious and personality variables, most notably racial prejudice.

Bibliography. G. W. Allport and J. M. Ross, "Personal Religious Orientation and Prejudice," *J. of Personality and Social Psychology,* 5 (1967), 432–43. M. J. Donahue, "Intrinsic and Extrinsic Religiousness: Review and Meta-Analysis," *J. of Personality and Social Psychology,* 48 (1985), 400–19.

G. D. VENABLE

RELIGION. *See also* ATTITUDE; FAITH/BELIEF.

RELIGIOUS SYMBOLISM. *See* RELIGIOUS LANGUAGE AND SYMBOLISM, PSYCHOLOGY OF; SYMBOLISM/SYMBOLIZING.

REMARRIAGE. Pastoral care of those seeking remarriage involves a look backward and a look forward. Guilt, grief, and the need for reintegration are three foci around which the pastoral dimensions for remarriage may be understood. Whereas early approaches to remarriage focused almost totally on the couple or the individual who was divorced, twentieth-century developments have come to be aware of the place of the pastor, the community, and society in general.

1. Guilt. The historic and perhaps still most pronounced area of pastoral concern centers on guilt. The experience of divorce leads to questions of failure, unhappiness with oneself, anger, and anger at one's own anger. There is a pastoral need to be aware of the feelings of the self, guilt, anger, depression, affection, love-hate. There

is then also the need to learn how to deal appropriately with these feelings.

Scripturally and pastorally, the realization of forgiveness is a key response to the experience of guilt. It is in the context of forgiveness that a person becomes free to see the nature of the personal feelings, to "own" them, and to deal with the feelings appropriately so as not to be bound by them. Failure to make such forgiveness leads to projection of hates, fears, and anger on the new spouse.

2. Grief. The grief dimension of divorce was identified by John Calvin, who spoke of circumstances in which, after divorce, a person could remarry as though the spouse were dead. Originally, the analogy of grief related only to the death of a spouse. Now, studies of developmental psychology lead us to see the grief dynamic related to any matter of separation. Physical death is but one form of separation. Movement from one stage of life to another requires separation from a previous stage. The previous stage has to "die" in order for the new stage to be reached.

From a pastoral standpoint, the care and counseling of a couple planning remarriage operates on several levels. One level concerns the first marriage, which has to be "let go." The hurts, ties, and scars from that break need to be healed in order to move on to the next stage of life, and an assessment should be made as to whether grief work from divorce has been successfully completed (Rolfe).

Another level involves the concerns, problems, and factors that the individual carried into the prior marriage that may have helped cause the break. What was not dealt with from the time before the marriage must be dealt with now if there is to be hope for moving on to a new stage of life. The pastoral context is one that brings to the individual an opportunity to deal with these aspects. Attention to these "early" factors may be difficult because renewed awareness may imply that the individual must accept some responsibility for the divorce that he or she does not want to take. Judgment becomes part of the process—not because the counselor judges, but because judgment in the situation comes to conscious awareness. Pastorally, the interaction between care and forgiveness along with separation and judgment become central issues.

3. Reintegration. In remarriage, the "look forward" requires letting the past go. Pastorally, attention must be given to the questions of purpose, meaning, and direction in a new marriage. Yet the thrust to the new stage of life in the developmental process, the new meanings that can help with a sense of direction, the purpose in the new life that will give life meaning reflect this forward direction. The question of one's calling or vocation in life is called the "future cause." It is as much a part of the pastoral concern in the developmental process as those matters that dealt with the past.

Letting go of the past and looking forward to the future requires a new integration of the person. The integration which results from this forward thrust is variously described as healing, wholeness, completeness. The biblical word *Shalom* encompasses the result of this integration.

In remarriage, this pastoral concern is for wholeness at the areas of the inward system, the nuclear system of the new intimate relationship, the wide community system, and the cosmic system. There is an interrelationship amongst these different systems and each has a certain unique identity. In general, the dynamics of preparation for a new marriage must be blended with each partner's process of adaptation to divorce (Rolfe).

Inwardly, there is the need to develop a sense of wholeness of the ego. "Awareness of soul" and the work of the personal are other ways of describing this "wholeness of ego." The ability to "own" one's self, feelings, and experiences, and to recover a sense of one's being of worth are part of this new wholeness. Integration allows for pulling together all those internal systems of the personality wherein there comes a new sense of being—being who we are, being a man, being a woman, being a person, being a soul.

Those in the nuclear system of family life include the children of the previous marriage, the children of the new spouse, and children that may come from the new marriage. This task of reintegration must take place with others in the network. Children may be living with one of the formerly divorced people and visiting the other. Children may be in church school two weekends a month and at the "other home" two weekends a month. Children may live with the new family. The pastoral concern relates, then, not only to the individuals immediately involved in the divorce but to those who are in the network or system of the nuclear family as a whole.

The social system of which a person is a part, in going through the experience of remarriage, includes the church as a community and the local society as a community. How does a new couple become part of a community? What of the former spouse? And how does the group itself adjust to the new spouse?

In the instance of church groups, the group may itself have an investment in the couple. When a couple breaks up, the feeling may be not unlike that of a child who loves both parents, who no longer love each other. The group will need pastoral care in dealing with its own pain as will the individual in the divorce. In remarriage, the approach to the group will be as important as the approach to the couple. As the group is helped to deal with anger, bewilderment, loss, and new relationships, the group then becomes free to help the couple deal with the same feelings.

The cosmic system is the system of the universe that can seem terribly cold and uncaring in the midst of personal pain. The Christian message is that nothing can separate one from the love of God. The pastoral task is to help mediate that sense of love to the individual and to the couples and to bring it to their awareness.

4. The Remarriage Service. Throughout the experience of remarriage, the pastor is dealing not with a static event but a continuing process. Symbols that help make real the new relationships must be discovered. The marriage service itself has a pastoral function in providing those symbols. Other symbols — e.g., the sacraments — must be found as the "process" continues.

Planning a remarriage service with a couple requires sensitivity to their particular needs and situation. This might include a liturgy for confession and assurance of God's grace, recognition and participation of the supportive community of faith, and the possible involvement of children of previous marriages in the service (Morgan).

Bibliography. S. Brown, "Clergy Divorce and Remarriage," Pastoral Psychology, 30: 3 (1982), 187–97. J. G. Emerson, Jr., Divorce, the Church, and Remarriage (1961). H. K. Hoster, To Love Again: Remarriage and the Christian (1985). M. and R. Kysar, The Assundered: Biblical Teachings on Divorce and Remarriage (1978). L. Messinger, Remarriage: A Family Affair (1984). R. L. Morgan, "A Ritual of Remarriage," J. of Pastoral Care, 37, 4 (1983), 292–301. D. J. Rolfe, "Preparing the Previously Married for Second Marriages," J. of Pastoral Care, 39: 2 (1985), 110–19. G. S. Twomey, When Catholics Marry Again (1982).

J. G. EMERSON

DIVORCE AND REMARRIAGE; PREMARITAL COUNSELING; STEPFAMILIES. See also DIVORCED PERSONS; MARRIAGE COUNSELING AND MARITAL THERAPY; MORAL DILEMMAS IN PASTORAL PERSPECTIVE.

REMARRIED PARENTS/REMARRIED PERSONS. See DIVORCE (Care and Counseling); PARENTS/PARENTHOOD.

REMINISCENCE THERAPY. A form of psychotherapy designed for use with the elderly which seeks to foster personality reorganization through recalling and resolving past experiences.

Reminiscence as a therapy tool with the elderly is based on Butler's observation that a specific form of reminiscing called "life review" spontaneously occurs in the later years of life. The assumption is that life review takes place because there is a natural, universal propensity among the elderly for past conflicts, regrets, and experiences to surface so that they may be resolved and reintegrated into the present personality structure of the individual. In relation to Erikson's developmental stage theory, life review is seen as a mechanism by which the elderly deal with the crisis of integrity vs. despair, and either conclude that life has been satisfactory and worthwhile or despair over the inadequacy of the life lived.

Reminiscence therapy has been practiced in varied settings, such as senior adult centers and housing projects, in age-integrated psychotherapy groups, and inpatient geripsychiatric wards. Clinicians observing the reminiscence process in the aged have noted that it is useful for catharsis, provides coherence in the face of "life's accidents," offers a personal mythology and thus a valued sense of identity, and improves self-esteem. Other possible outcomes are reduced death anxiety, a feeling of meaningful continuity between one's past and present, assistance in dealing with depression, and an ability to live in the present, called "elementality." Reminiscence group therapy has been judged superior to traditional group therapy with severely regressed geriatric patients because the reminiscing led to increased social interaction and alertness. However, research has not adequately demonstrated reminiscence therapy's utility with the elderly since the literature is mostly anecdotal, with few controlled studies.

Reminiscence therapy holds promise as a tool for ministering to the psychological needs of the elderly. The techniques can be flexibly applied in various settings, can be used both individually and in a group, and its use is not restricted to highly functioning persons. Also, since the life review process is self-initiated and can be successfully completed without the aid of highly trained professionals, lay church members can be provided with the necessary focused training so they may promote the life review through their active and concerned listening.

Besides the practical considerations, reminiscence therapy is theologically compatible with pastoral care for the aged. The assumption in reminiscence therapy that each person is of worth and is able to develop and grow during any stage of life is parallel with the Judeo-Christian tenet that people are made in the image of God. Reminiscence therapy also emphasizes reconciliation between the individual and past life choices as well as the mending of broken relationships from the past.

Bibliography. R. N. Butler, "The Life Review: An Interpretation of Reminiscence in the Aged," *Psychiatry*, 26 (1963), 67–76. W. M. Clements, "Reminiscence as the Cure of Souls in Early Old Age," *J. of Religion and Health*, 20 (1981), 41–47. E. Erikson, *Identity and the Life Cycle* (1980). M. Lewis and R. Butler, "Life-Review Therapy: Putting Memories to Work in Individual and Group Psychotherapy," *Geriatrics*, (November, 1974), 165–73. R. L. Randall, "Reminiscing in the Elderly: Pastoral Care of Self-Narratives," *J. of Pastoral Care*, 40 (1986), 207–15. M. H. Spero, "Death and the 'Life Review' in Halakhah," *J. of Religion and Health*, 19 (1980), 313–19.

R. GEORGEMILLER

HEALING OF MEMORIES; MEMORY; OLDER PERSONS, PASTORAL CARE AND COUNSELING OF; PERSONAL STORY, SYMBOL, AND MYTH IN PASTORAL CARE. *See also* INTERPRETATION AND HERMENEUTICS, PASTORAL; TIME/TIME SENSE. *Compare* FORGIVENESS; PASTORAL COUNSELING; REPENTANCE AND CONFESSION.

REMORSE. *See* GUILT; REPENTANCE AND CONFESSION.

RENEWAL MOVEMENTS AND PROGRAMS. Reactions to the perceived one-sidedness or lack of life in organizations or environment. Generally not separatistic, such movements intend to bring new life and traditional values into their denominations or groups, and eventually to society. While renewal movements may result in schism, they do not intend it. Examples of renewal movements include the Brethren of the Common Life, a reaction against clerical abuses in the medieval church; Pietism, a reaction against "dead orthodoxy" in Lutheran and Reformed churches; and Methodism, a reaction against aridity in the Anglican Church.

Renewal programs tend to emphasize personal (and, to a lesser degree, corporate) piety, small groups, deep devotion to God, and an equally profound concern for the spiritual and physical well-being of one's neighbor. Theologically conservative, their proponents stress morality and hold a personalistic rather than a psychological, rationalistic, or primarily doctrinal understanding of faith. They perceive faith as an interpersonal relationship between the living God and the believer, visibly manifested in new ways of being, consonant with their concept of biblical or "true" Christianity. Emphasis on the ministry of the laity means that laypersons assume leadership roles, particularly in teaching and facilitating small groups for prayer, study, and personal growth.

Renewal movements tend to start with the individual. Through renewed individuals acting in consonance with each other and the will of God as revealed in Scripture and understood by the leadership of the movement, the parent organization, its corresponding institutions, and eventually all of society will be transformed.

A typical renewal program within a church context begins with the leadership (lay and ordained) through retreat and small-group experiences intended to bring individuals into a more vigorous and emotionally satisfying relationship with God. This "renewed" leadership then extends the renewal through programs and events similar to those in which they found their faith reawakened. Normally, renewed church members not only will become more active within their own congregations but will also share their experience and renewed faith with "nominal" believers (renewal) and with nonbelievers (evangelism). The renewed person finds nurture for his or her faith and enthusiasm in worship and in ongoing small groups whose primary concerns are prayer, study of Scripture, mutual encouragement and correction, and the recounting of personal experiences with God.

In recent history, renewal programs have tended to address primarily spiritual needs and issues. Genuine renewal within the Christian tradition, however, has most often reawakened a love for both God and one's neighbor, leading not only to widespread revivals and evangelism but also to a concern for the physical well-being of the poor and oppressed, the ill and the disenfranchised. Renewal movements have seen social involvement as a logical or natural consequence of being renewed by the Spirit of God who cares about the spiritually and physically poor and lost.

Bibliography. D. R. Mains, *Full Circle* (1971). J. T. McNeill, *A History of the Cure of Souls* (1951). R. C. Stedman, *Body Life* (1972). J. F. Westerhoff, *Inner Growth, Outer Change* (1979).

G. R. SATTLER

REST AND RENEWAL, RELIGIOUS TRADITIONS OF; RETREATS; SPIRITUAL DISCIPLINE AND GROWTH.

REPARATION. *See* PENANCE, SACRAMENT OF; REPENTANCE AND CONFESSION.

REPENTANCE, SACRAMENT OF. *See* MINISTRY AND PASTORAL CARE (Orthodox Tradition).

REPENTANCE AND CONFESSION. Confession, repentance, penance, forgiveness, and reconciliation are words and experiences that must be seen together. The focus of this article is on the first two. Reconciliation is the goal of the first four. Reconciliation with God, others, and self requires forgiveness — God's forgiveness for us and our forgiveness for each other. Penance is a link between confession-repentance and forgiveness-reconciliation.

1. The Relation Between Confession and Repentance. The specific relation between confession and repentance is not always clear. In some instances, confession is seen as part of the act of repentance, and in others, confession is seen as the more encompassing category.

The root meaning of confession is to "speak with." Negatively, the word carries the view of avowal of sin or human failing. Positively, confession carries the view of affirming a reality — a faith, a relationship. Whereas *Webster's Unabridged Dictionary* reflects the common parlance that places the negative emphasis first, writings on church doctrine generally place the positive, affirmative view first. That change of emphasis has both a theological and psychological assumption. Theologically, the assumption is that it is only in the praise of what God has done that one can be free to look at one's sin. Psychologically, there is the assumption that only in the loving context can one look at the unloving aspects of one's life.

There is likewise a divergence in the view of repentance. Where the word is taken from the Greek, *metanoia*, repentance emphasizes the positive. It speaks of new direction. It relates to a "repointing." Where the word is taken from the Latin, *penitentia*, repentance emphasizes the negative. It then speaks of what must be done to redeem or satisfy the sin or failure.

As both a doctrine and an area of pastoral care, confession and repentance began as dynamic experiences in the Christian faith. John the Baptist called people to repent their sins. The capacity for that repentance, however, depended on the awareness that the Kingdom of God was at hand and confession of a need to repent. Both the positive aspect of the confession—"the Kingdom of God is at hand" (Mt. 3:2)—and the negative—"therefore, repent"—are necessary.

2. The Early and Medieval Church. In the early church, confession and repentance were seen as part of the corporate or pastoral experience. Sins were confessed in the presence of the congregation and forgiveness was affirmed through the congregation. If one was sorry for sins, one could come to the Lord's table. Those who were in the greatest state of repentance sat toward the front—during one stage of the early church—and those less ready were toward the back. Thus, the group dimension in confession and repentance was real and important.

As time passed, the public aspect of confession and repentance became somewhat abused. There is evidence that pride developed in the confession of some great sin, and problems developed when public confession implicated others in the community—rightly or wrongly. By the time of the fifth and sixth centuries, confession and repentance as a meaningful part of the Christian experience lessened. The experience was real in the monastic orders and the life of the hermits, but in the church at large, confession-repentance had lost the dynamic, healing quality.

The role of those who heard confession (confessors) developed early in the life of the church (although the title came much later). Paul saw himself as a spiritual father to Timothy. Especially with the development of the monastic orders, the position of one who could help an individual or group realize confession and repentance became important.

According to McNeill—the chief authority in this field of history—it was in the Celtic Penitentials (books on the practice of penance) that confession and repentance took on a new dimension that informs pastoral care today. Through the orders, clergy developed an understanding of penance which enabled them to hear confessions and to lead people in repentance in such a way as to allow for the value of each. The idea of penance as a means of "paying for sins" when Christ had already "paid the price" was not part of the early experience. Rather, the Celtic Penitentials were practices to help the repentant

deal with his or her sense of guilt and find new directions. The use of the penitential allowed the repentant to sense that the forgiveness was indeed real.

Further, a system of "contraries" proved an early form of behavioral modification for sins committed. If one confessed to gossip, for example, and repented of the sin, the confessor prescribed the opposite (the contrary)—silence. By such practice, the theory went, the habit would be broken.

The difficulty of the time was that the experience of working with trained confessors who could help a confession be effective and make the forgiveness real was outside the experience of the parish itself. Thus, the sense of care from the parish—central in the early church—was lost. In fact, the private confessors became so popular that bishops found the flock going to the experts rather than staying with the church. The resolution was to bring the confessors into the established church. Confession was still private, however. The parish aspect of pastoral care was not recovered.

3. The Reformation. The Reformation sought to correct this error. In the Middle Ages, penance had become so central that the dynamic role of confession and repentance was lessened. As a correction, the Reformation recovered the corporate aspect of the confession, placed emphasis on individual repentance, but lost the dynamic of the place of penance.

From the Reformation on, there was a tendency for confession and repentance to be interpreted so doctrinally and juridically that the experiential quality became lost. Religious movements such as those associated with Christian Science, the pastoral care development, as well as the charismatic and pietistic thrust of the church have served as a countermovement to the intellectualistic and doctrinaire approaches.

The model for understanding the dynamic is found in Luke 5:8 when Jesus approaches Peter in the boat and helps with a great catch of fish. Overwhelmed, Peter replies, "Depart from me for I am a sinful man, O Lord." In this biblical "case study," we hear the confession of Peter, "I am a sinner." We see that the dynamic which made that confession possible was the context of the presence of Christ.

The nature of that context has been subject to debate. One side, represented by Luther, holds that the context in which one can see one's sin—and thus confess—is the law. This point of view argues that as the law is proclaimed (Paul's "school master"—Gal. 3:24), a person sees the sinful way and then confesses. In the biblical model, Jesus, then, would be seen as incarnating the law. The other side, represented by Calvin, holds that the context in which one sees the need to confess is love—or the grace of God. Only through love—only in a nonthreatening moment of concern—is one free to see one's true self, confess it, and repent. For Calvin, the nature of humankind is such that our failures so warp us that we cannot see the reality of our need and make a "true confession" except by the grace and love of Christ. Only then can the law be helpful as a teacher.

4. Contemporary Uses and Pastoral Practice. Whichever approach is taken, this dynamic aspect of both Calvin and Luther is largely lost today (with notable exceptions in people such as Richard Baxter and Jonathan

Edwards). The psychological sciences have recovered tools for the understanding of human relations and human thought. Today, whether one speaks of confession within the service of worship or the moment of private confession (whether in Roman Catholic or Protestant circles), there is awareness of a pastoral context and a need of help in response.

As a result, today's pastor is again seeking to allow for the experiential aspects of confession and repentance. In the liturgy or the counseling room, tools are sought to allow a person to lift to conscious awareness what in fact must be confessed, and what must be done about the repentance as a means of acting appropriately upon the confession. Theologically and liturgically, repentance is usually characterized by contrition and sorrow. From the standpoint of pastoral care, there is a concern that such repentance may be as neurotic or as much in need of healing as the original confession—which itself may have been quite healthy. Whether in the liturgy or in the counseling room, the task of repentance is to allow for that letting go which puts the confessed act so in the past that one no longer feels a need to overreact to a failure or engage in massive denial. The task is to clarify the new direction and move ahead.

Repentance is thus related to penance, yet it is not the same. It is related in that both respond to that which is confessed. Repentance, however, focuses on the attitude to that which is confessed and penance (in its dynamic and not legalistic form) focuses on making real the forgiveness of the failure.

The total identification of confession with the negative is not consistent with experience or doctrine. Confession may be of sin, and confession may be of faith. In the former, I confess my sin and then repent. In the latter, I repent, and then affirm the experience by confessing the faith that I have indeed been forgiven.

In pastoral care, therefore, attention must be given both to facilitating the confession of what is wrong and to the confession of what is right. Therein lies true healing, wholeness, and reconciliation.

Those counseling methodologies that most relate to the point of view expressed here are seen in the work of Carl Rogers and Fritz Perls. The former emphasizes acceptance and trust. The latter adds emphasis on behavior that expresses the inner feelings or experiences that have helped rediscover the meaning of confession and repentance.

As to what happens in the dynamic relationship that allows for the confession-repentance act to heal, this is subject to debate. The differences between the Freudian and Jungian views of transference, the role of archetypes, the place of culture and society are but a few of the areas of difference of opinion. These psychological theories have their counterparts in the differences among those who emphasize the "inner light" (Society of Friends), substitutionary or moral influence or ransom views of the atonement, and so on.

Tension continues among those who see confession and repentance as a private issue and those who regard it as a corporate matter. When Calvin's wife was dying, he ministered to her and sought the state of her soul. She assured him, according to his letters, that all was well. Despite this private act by the great Reformer, most Protestant practice emphasizes confession and repentance as an act that is public. Frequently, a prayer of confession is part of the liturgy.

Particularly with charismatic groups, the public act emphasizes the laying on of hands, healing prayers, and exorcism all of which stress the awareness that we are not people in isolation, that there is an interpersonal dimension to personality, and that we are what we are in relationship to others. The danger is that the nature of these dynamics and the uniqueness of the individual dynamic often get lost. Group tyranny, unfortunately, may also come into play. The point of agreement among the modern views is on the fact of experience: confession-repentance is a matter not of legalistic action, but deep personal and interpersonal experience.

The Roman Catholic church has vastly altered the place and practice of auricular confession to deal with the dangers and misuse of the experience. Rather than the secret and private booth, the face to face counseling approach is more and more in evidence. The public confession is also in the liturgy. Since the priest, doctrinally, represents the church, he symbolizes the relationship to the fellowship as a whole. Yet in both Catholic and Protestant uses of confession, the danger remains. Confession and repentance may become isolated. The interpersonal nature of confession and repentance too easily becomes privatized.

On the basis of the experience in the early church and the modern knowledge of field theory and interpersonal dynamics, the pastoral care of confession and repentance needs the balance of the private and the public experience.

Bibliography. W. Clebsch and C. Jaekle, *Pastoral Care in Historical Perspective* (1964). E. B. Holifield, *A History of Pastoral Care in America* (1983). J. McNeill, *A History of the Cure of Souls* (1951); *The Celtic Penitentials and Their Influence on Continental Christianity* (1923). J. D. Solveitchik, *On Repentance* (1980).

J. G. EMERSON

CONSCIENCE; FORGIVENESS; GUILT; PENANCE, SACRAMENT OF; PENITENTS, JEWISH CARE AND COUNSELING OF. *See also* BORN-AGAIN EXPERIENCE; CONVERSION; HEALING OF MEMORIES; MORAL BEHAVIOR AND RELIGION; RESPONSIBILITY/IRRESPONSIBILITY, PSYCHOLOGY OF; SALVATION AND PASTORAL CARE.

REPETITION COMPULSION. In psychoanalytic theory, the tendency to repeat earlier experiences, especially actions that first led to one's psychological illness. In *Beyond the Pleasure Principle* (1920) Freud attributed the phenomenon to a universally inherent death instinct. Later theorists have explained repetition compulsion more as a progressive attempt to master or assimilate negative experience.

J. Z. CLARK

DEFENSE AND COPING THEORY; DEFENSE MECHANISMS; OBSESSIVE-COMPULSIVE DISORDER. *Compare* UNDOING.

REPRESSION. A technical concept in Freud's theory and a general one in many other psychologies. In Freud it refers to automatic processes in which the ego distorts systematically the appearance of ideas the recognition of which would bring psychic pain. Freud used its German equivalent, *Verdrängung,* in his early essays on hysteria (1893–95). There it is nearly identical to the concepts of *defense* and *fending off.* All three are notions with which he and Breuer attempted to classify hysteric behavior. In these texts repression is not necessarily unconscious; hence, Freud speaks of "intentionally repressed ideas" (*SE* 1, p. 208).

These terms ceased to be interchangeable when Freud recast his explanatory theory in the second great epoch of his work, the so-called metapsychological period of 1911–19. In his essay, "Repression," written in 1915 (in *SE* 14), he links repression systematically with the notion of the unconscious. This established the psychoanalytic definition of the concept. Like the theory of Oedipal conflict, it has become part of the psychoanalytic shibboleth.

The concept of repression as a split in the psyche, or as one part of the self warring against another, is much older than Freud. It figures in both Augustine's and Luther's accounts of their spiritual conflicts. These accounts are primarily phenomenological; their authors aim to describe their suffering and to evoke similar experiences in their readers. They and contemporary phenomenological psychologists believe this is part of the curative process; exposing one's inner suffering aids in its elimination.

Freud, in contrast, uses the technical term *repression* to refer to unconscious actions by which the ego avoids some form of psychic pain, like guilt or shame, but at the cost of discarding its ability to employ the memories and feelings associated with that painful event; e.g., a young woman molested in a clothing store "forgets" the incident but subsequently is terrified of clothing stores. In addition to this phobia, she finds her daily life full of sexualized encounters, and her sexual life full of frustrations and unnameable terrors. Repression seals off memory of trauma but at great cost; it engenders unending future conflicts the causes of which will remain unknown as long as the original act of repression remains in force. Neurotic suffering is a sign of prior repression. Cure can come about only by removing (undoing) the effects of that cause.

Both Freud and theologians seek to heal a split in the psyche, to remove the source of psychic pain, and to unify the self. Freud sought to do this by interrogating the past and locating that moment when the ego disowned part of itself through the unconscious act of repression. Theologians seek it in the future, when the suffering of the present will yield to the intervention of a divine Other in whom all things come together. According to Freud repression amounts to a denial of the truth about oneself; for theologians it is a denial of the truth about oneself in relationship to another.

Bibliography. J. Breuer and S. Freud, *Studies on Hysteria, SE* 2. A. Freud, *The Ego and the Mechanisms of Defense* (1966 [1937]). P. Madison, *Freud's Concept of Repression and Defense* (1961). G. Mahl, *Psychological Conflict and Defense* (1971).

V. P. GAY

MEMORY; PSYCHOANALYSIS (Personality Theory and Research); The UNCONSCIOUS. *See also* DEFENSE AND COPING THEORY; PSYCHOPATHOLOGY, THEORIES OF. *Compare* ALIENATION/ ESTRANGEMENT; DENIAL; HUMAN CONDITION/PREDICAMENT; PHILOSOPHY AND PSYCHOLOGY, WESTERN; SUPPRESSION.

RESCUE REQUESTS, PASTORAL. *See* EMERGENCY, PSYCHOLOGY OF PASTOR IN.

RESEARCH IN PASTORAL CARE AND COUNSELING. *See* EMPIRICAL RESEARCH IN PASTORAL CARE AND COUNSELING; PASTORAL THEOLOGICAL METHODOLOGY; PASTORAL THEOLOGY; THEOLOGY AND PSYCHOLOGY. *See also* JOURNALS.

RESENTMENT. *See* WILL/WILLING.

RESISTANCE. In psychoanalytic therapies, an unconscious force within an individual's personality that opposes the making conscious of early memories and their painful affects, the repression of which has led to the development of some emotional and/or behavioral disorder. An unconscious force within an individual's personality which leads to any behavior that is in contradiction to that person's consciously experienced and often stated goals, intentions, commitments, etc. in regard to any aspect of that person's life.

Resistance is not only a significant factor to be taken into consideration in pastoral counseling and other forms of pastoral care, but in all aspects of church life and in all relationships between the minister and members of a congregation. Critical to effective ministry is the sensitivity of the minister to signs of resistance, the pastor's attitude toward resistance (whether an opportunity for ministry or an impediment), and his or her skill in relating to persons in ways that facilitate the understanding and reduction of resistances.

1. Historical Development. *a. Freud.* Freud's identification of resistance, its unconscious sources, and the ways in which it manifests itself in the psychoanalytic process are among his main contributions. The first reference to resistance in Freud's writings appeared in 1893, though it was not until 1926 that he formulated his insights into a fully developed theory. Freud's scheme attributes resistance to five possible sources, three of which arise from the activity of the ego: (1) *Repression resistance* refers to the ego's perception of threat, which triggers and maintains the repressive mechanism, eliminating from unconsciousness the threat-producing situation; it continues to maintain the repression in the face of therapeutic attempts to make the unconscious conscious. (2) *Transference resistance* is the action of the ego in maintaining a repression by reacting to the analyst in the present as if the analyst were a parent in the past. (3) *Secondary-gain resistance* grows out of the ego's awareness of the secondary psychological advantages accompanying an illness and the desire to continue these benefits which the ego believes would be lost if the person became well. (4) The *id* is the source of a fourth type of resistance. Even when a resistance from another source is recognized and interpreted, the id may continue to repeat its resisting functions for a period of time. (5) The *superego* is the source of resistance when it has produced guilt so powerful that it dominates the ego and requires continual punishment. When this happens the superego interferes with any movement toward success, including successful therapy.

b. Menninger. Karl Menninger has made significant additions to Freud's work. He renames "transference resistance" and calls it "frustration" or "revenge resistance," and sees it as a function of the patient's resentment at not getting desired responses from the analyst, who is the representation of an earlier parental figure. There is mounting anger on the part of the patient, which is a barrier to open participation in the relationship and the therapeutic process. Menninger also describes what he calls "erotization resistance," a particularly pernicious kind because some of its expressions involve temptations to collusion on the part of the analyst. Such behavior may attempt to influence the analyst through bribery, seduction, or anger, interfering in the analytic process by threatening to contaminate the therapeutic relationship. Interestingly, Menninger also warns the helping person of *counter*resistance. If the therapist's own repressed past begins to be activated, then the ego of the therapist begins to resist the process. The therapist's resistance is just as unconscious as the analyst's and/or client's. Thus, the therapist blocks the process and is in danger of not knowing that it is she or he who is doing it.

c. Beavers. W. Robert Beavers adds an interpersonal dimension to the understanding of resistance (a particularly useful perspective for the minister), pointing out that any power differential in a relationship *encourages* resistance. He views the intensity of resistance in a relationship as related to the degree of affiliation versus opposition, and egalitarianism versus authoritarianism, with the former in each case decreasing resistance and the latter increasing it. Beavers believes that the root of resistance is the need to maintain a coherent identity, a basically positive motivation. However, fear of the unknown leads one to maintain oneself as one is. Beavers's position suggests that resistance is minimized when all behaviors of the therapist encourage an eqalitarian relationship.

2. Application to Ministry. *a. Pastoral care and counseling.* The most obvious application to ministry is the pastor's recognition of resistance in people with whom he or she is engaged in pastoral care and counseling. The best response to such resistance may be an egalitarian rather than an authoritarian relationship between pastor and parishioner, it being the responsibility of the pastor to function in ways that communicate most clearly the essential conditions of the helping process which lead to such a relationship. It is just as important, however, for a minister to be aware of his or her own resistance in the helping process, what Menninger called *counterresistance.* There certainly are times when pastors have their own unconscious past stimulated in a present relationship, leading to behaviors that impede the helping process. It is essential that ministers be attentive to such behaviors in themselves, perhaps consulting with their own counselor or supervisor about the meaning of such behaviors, such as forgetting pastoral appointments, not wanting to see particular persons, and boredom with or anger at the person with whom they are engaged in pastoral care. Certainly if ministers are not aware of or cannot resolve their own resistance in pastoral care situations, they cannot assist parishioners in resolving theirs.

b. Preaching. Relatively few writers have explicitly dealt with resistance as a potent influence upon the way in which persons in a congregation give selective atten-

tion to preaching and their degree and forms of responsiveness and nonresponsiveness. (But see Dittes, pp. 178–80, 246–50, Switzer, chs. 3, 4; Hunter). Awareness of possible resistance in the hearers of a sermon should lead a minister to go beyond the usual methods of sermon preparation and presentation to reflect seriously upon its possible sources. She or he then would properly give attention to the specific wording of the gospel proclamation so that it will also communicate those relational conditions and situational understandings that support affiliation and egalitarianism and thus reduce unnecessary or distracting resistance. This level of preparation contributes to the sermons being accurately heard as the Word of God to *these* people at *this* time.

c. Administration. Every minister has known enigmatic persons on administrative and program committees who agree to function in a particular way and then do not attend meetings, are always late, disrupt the meeting process in a variety of ways, oppose every suggestion, or unpredictably oppose a particular individual for no apparent reason. While there may be other interpretations, the theory of resistance offers itself as a possible way of understanding such behavior and finding significant opportunities for ministry in relating to it. Since moralistic or disciplinary responses, direct attack, and other authoritarian moves increase such resistance, the key to effective ministry generally involves discovering the nature of a parishioner's resistance and responding in ways which diminish it by addressing its underlying meanings and motives. In church meetings it is also important to remember that resistance is increased or decreased depending upon whether the whole meeting process is primarily directive and authoritarian, or open, encouraging the expression of feelings as well as ideas, and promoting the idea of the equal value of every person to the process.

Taking the reality of resistance seriously into account by seeking to understand it and to relate to individual persons and groups in ways that help to reduce it contribute to the quality of congregational life and the effectiveness of ministry. Rather than forming a *barrier* to ministry (as it is so often experienced to be), resistance in fact offers an *opportunity* for ministry. If it is not *attacked* but *understood* as playing some vital maintenance role in the lives of persons, its power can be utilized, individually and corporately, for growth in faith and mission.

Bibliography. W. R. Beavers, *Psychotherapy and Growth* (1977). J. Dittes, *The Church in the Way* (1967), deals with the issue of resistance in the life of the church and the practice of ministry — cf. R. J. Hunter, "Ministry — or Magic?" *Princeton Seminary Bulletin*, 1 (1977), 61–67. S. Freud, "Fräulein Elisabeth von R." [1893], *SE*, 2:21–47; *Inhibitions, Symptoms, and Anxiety* [1926], *SE*, 20:77–174. K. Menninger, *Theory of Psychoanalytic Technique* (1958). D. K. Switzer, *Pastor, Preacher, Person* (1979).

D. K. SWITZER

PSYCHOANALYSIS (Therapeutic Method and Research); PSYCHOANALYSIS AND PASTORAL CARE. *See also* DEFENSE AND COPING THEORY; LEADERSHIP AND ADMINISTRATION; PREACHING. *Compare* AMBIVALENCE; DECISION/INDECISION, PSYCHOLOGY OF; FREEDOM AND DETERMINISM; HUMAN CONDITION/PREDICAMENT; SIN/SINS; WILL/WILLING.

RESOURCES, COMMUNITY. *See* SOCIAL SERVICES.

RESPONSA. Rabbinic essays dealing with exegetical, legal, or moral questions. Responsa first appear in the ninth century as brief guidelines issued by the deans of the Babylonian Talmudic academies. In the Middle Ages questions were usually addressed to local rabbis, who often wrote answers of several pages in length. Responsa continue to be written today by rabbinic scholars in Israel, America, and Europe, representing all major branches of Judaism.

A responsum usually consists of three parts: a question, a discussion of the issue in light of Scripture and other religious literature, and a conclusion. They generally contain detailed analyses of the moral or religious implications of a question. Thus a responsum on abortion might consider the status of the fetus as human life and the relevance of the pursuer argument before rendering a decision. Modern responsa deal also with such contemporary issues as organ transplants and Jewish military ethics.

P. J. HAAS

JEWISH LITERATURE.

RESPONSE, PASTORAL. *See* COMMUNICATION; CONVERSATION, PASTORAL; LISTENING; VERBATIM.

RESPONSIBILITY/IRRESPONSIBILITY, PSYCHOLOGY OF. The definition of responsibility is threefold: (1) the social moral status of a person, (2) the personal experience of being a responsible agent, (3) the ability to engage in personal processes leading to moral actions (being response-able).

1. Social Dimensions. Cultures are organized in accord with the moral expectations we place on each other to act responsibly toward ourselves and toward others. Irresponsible action toward oneself (such as suicide or self-neglect) brings social condemnation. Irresponsible action toward others brings social punishment and/or demand for just recompense. It is assumed that societal members possess an inherent capacity to act in accord with implicit social moral expectations, though these are variously defined by cultures. In some, the infant may be held responsible (the crying baby is punished); in others the child is not held responsible until pubescent initiation rites. In current western culture there is ambiguity about when and how one assumes the status of morally responsible adult (Nader). Only recently have male versus female concepts of responsibility been addressed (Melton).

Western philosophy has long dealt with responsibility as an implicit issue: the question of accountability for one's beliefs and actions, and the imputability of moral praise or blame. But it was not until 1884 that the concept of responsibility *per se* was considered (McKeon). In turn, jurisprudence considered all adults to possess the capacity to act as responsible persons. In legal history, informal allowances were made for children and for the physically and mentally ill, but irresponsible action was generally viewed as both sinful and criminal. It was not until 1800 that English law first entertained situations where responsibility was absent, impaired, or diminished. The landmark M'Naughten case (1843) held that responsibility devolved on the cognitive capacity to discriminate between right and wrong actions. Alternate

legal theory depends upon intentionality or motivation, the capacity to resist an impulse to action, or the ability to appreciate the consequences of one's actions. Although such *single trait* concepts are psychologically inadequate, they underscore the fact that responsibility is a core social concept, for a society is created out of a social contract to hold ourselves accountable to each other. Responsibility is preeminently a concept of social relationships (Agich).

2. The Development of the Experience of Responsibility. The personal sense of responsibility is the product of complex ego operations. Here we trace an idealized developmental pathway.

a. Causality, connections, and boundaries. The key to responsibility is the perceived causal linkage between the self-as-agent and actions of that person. The infant possesses no sense of self and cannot differentiate the boundaries between self and others. There is no causal linkage because one is part of all. A sense of self emerges by twenty-four months along with differentiation between self and others. But the boundaries of self are diffuse (all these toys are mine). There is the sense of causal connection to other objects, but the direction of cause is confused (the child kicks the table for bumping him). By age four the child experiences self-as-agent, but the potency of self is variable. As impotent self, the child says: I want to eat but I can't lift the fork; while in grandiose self, the child says: I can knock you to pieces with my fist. During latency the child refines his/her perception of a causal chain. I am affected by an object, I respond to that object, and my response affects that object. (You took my marble, I am mad at you and hit you, then you give me my marble back.) Here responsibility is my perceived capacity to change my relationship to the object world.

b. Intention and motivation. To external stimulus and response we now add internal stimuli: wants, desires, oughts, and shoulds. The internalization of parental objects produces two powerful but primitive sources for responsible behavior. The ego ideal demands behavior, which if achieved produces a sense of self-esteem and righteous self-satisfaction, but if not achieved produces shame and a sense of failure. The superego prohibits behavior, which if avoided produces self-approbation, but if indulged produces self-deprecation and guilt. These primitive affects form the bulk of motivation for responsible action in the latency age child. Only in adolescence does the capacity for personal choice emerge. Now, self-as-agent, driven by oughts/ought-nots, shoulds/should-nots, musts/must-nots is transformed into "I may or may not as I so choose." Self-as-agent is not merely reactive but can be proactive and self-determinative. I can now be responsible for creating my own intentions and motivations.

c. Conscience, values, and commitments. The capacity for choice of action, however, does not necessarily lead to responsible moral action. This requires the development of a self-model of desired behavior based on consciously chosen values. Ego ideal and superego are not abandoned, but superseded and modified to fit an adult moral code. This is mature conscience and mature self identity. It requires a commitment to act toward oneself and others with integrity to one's chosen self-model of behavior. I am now responsible to maintain the moral integrity of my self-model.

d. The will to action. One may choose, intend right action, and hold integrity, but not act so. Responsibility finally involves the process of action-inhibition and action-activation. One must be able to delay response and inhibit impulses, and then appropriately activate an external response. A weak-willed person is vulnerable to simple stimulus-response, while a strong-willed person is able to self-direct appropriate action. Thus *will* may be considered the process of translation of internal understanding of responsibility into externally responsible action.

e. The process of responsible action. Responsibility is a bridging concept that represents a chain of psychic events. The person receives internal and external stimuli, holds onto those stimuli without action, assesses the meaning and value of the stimuli, evaluates the range of possible responses in terms of a mature self-model of moral valuation, estimates the consequences of alternative actions, chooses the most reasonable option, and then acts accordingly. To act as a mature responsible person, then, requires the development of self-differentiation, an internal locus of control of self-as-agent, the maturation of discriminative ego operations, the development of a mature self-model, the acquisition of mature moral principles, and mature acceptance of the consequences of one's actions.

3. Distortions of Responsibility. These occur due to psychological immaturity, ego maldevelopment, neurotic processes, mental illness, and sociocultural influence.

a. Distortion of inability. The developing child has variable capacity for responsibility. So too, the mentally retarded, the brain damaged, and psychotics. It is rare that such inability is total; rather responsibility capacity is variable.

b. Distortions with ego maldevelopment. The severe personality disorders present major responsibility deficits in accord with the level of ego maturation. First, autistic, schizotypal, and borderline personalities lack a sense of self-other boundaries, and do not experience a connection to either self or other. Thus they do not experience the sense of being a responsible agent of action. Second, the dependent personality experiences the other as responsible for them. The passive-aggressive personality attempts to make others responsible for self. Third are the impulsive, aggressive, and acting out personalities who experience an external locus of control—from internal drives and impulses or external agents. Typical of alcoholics and drug abusers, they experience no sense of control over their actions. They blame others and assume no responsibility for their own inner stimuli. Fourth, is the sociopath, for whom self is agent, but others are impersonal objects. Hence they are responsible only to their amoral self and hold no responsibility to others. Finally, the narcissist demands that others act responsibly to meet his or her demands, without a commitment to reciprocal responsibility with others.

c. Distortions of neurotic development. The immature person fails to engage in self-conscious reflection and evaluation. There is little experience of self-as-agent. Their unexamined ego-ideal and superego form most of an unconscious self-model. They live unchosen, undirected lives in accord with their unconscious socializa-tion. They are typically conventional moral persons, but ill-equipped for moral struggle. They represent pseudomaturity, pseudomorality, and pseudoresponsibility.

Roccoco neurotic processes distort responsibility. The paranoid sees self as only good and disavows responsibility for the bad in self. All bad action is projected onto the persecutory other. The histrionic disavows bad in self or other and only sees pollyanna goodness in all. The histrionic avoids responsibility for negative actions. The obsessive-compulsive is exquisitely sensitive to good and bad, feels responsible for everything but equivocates on responsible action. Persons with scrupulosity syndrome seek forgiveness for alleged sins, but can accept no absolution. The schizoid-avoidant fears responsibility for anything and hence withdraws from all possible action.

d. Distortions from the socio-cultural milieu. Membership in subcultural groups, whether the Mafia, a religious cult, or political cell, may evoke highly responsible in-group behavior that appears immoral and irresponsible in terms of higher social moral principles. (A Nazi death camp supervisor was highly responsible.) Second, responsibility may be construed in terms of immature faith development. Here there is responsibility to rules and regulations but neglect of higher moral responsibility. Such is the case of pharisaism (Fowler). Third, much conventional responsibility is framed in terms of current social conventions that allocate different senses of responsibility to men and women as culture-bound gender roles, which again ignores higher precepts of responsibility (Ramsey).

4. The Limits of Responsibility. The concept of responsibility is an ideal, never attained fully by any human. As "response-able", all persons vary in their ability to act responsibly. One can possess the proper values and motivations, yet experience limited will and capacity to achieve proper action. In neurotic responsibility, the person may experience self as acting responsibly, yet the observer sees irresponsibility (a righteous child-abuser). Or a person may experience more responsibility than it is humanly possible to achieve (the grandiose person or the pietist). In fact, the ideal concept of responsibility is too rational and humanistic. It fails to apprehend the human condition of distorted self-awareness, of inaccurate self-evaluation, of limited knowledge, and of compromised self-direction. The best of intention and motivation are loosely linked to our actions. ("I do not understand my own actions. For I do not do what I want, but I do the very things I hate"— Rom. 7:15.) Thus, the limits of responsibility are the limits of the human condition.

5. Clinical Interpretations. No definitive psychological model of responsibility has been developed. Brickman *et al.* (1982) describe four current clinical models: the *compensatory* model, where people are not responsible for problems, but only for solutions; the *enlightenment* model, where people are responsible for problems, but not for solutions; the *medical* model, in which people are responsible for neither problems nor solutions; and the *moral* model, where people are responsible for both problems and solutions.

Both behavioral and psychoanalytic theory follow a strict deterministic medical model in theory, but in practice use the compensatory model (Schoeck and Wiggins).

Therapeutic realists assume a legalistic moral model. So, O. Hobart Mowrer averred that psychotherapy should make people confess to their real sins, while in the reality therapy of William Glasser the problem is that people know better, but refuse to act better. The humanistic therapies emphasize responsibility to self as primary. For A. H. Maslow, self-actualization is almost a preemptory narcissism, while the Gestalt therapy of Fritz Perls assumes that responsibility to others is incidental. The only consistent explication of responsibility in a moral model is found in phenomenological psychology (Straus and Griffith), and in existential psychotherapy (Farber).

6. The Core Problem: Determinism vs. Free Will. The issue is ontological: are humans created with the capacity for moral choice (Niebuhr)? If our actions are causally determined, how can we hold people responsible for illusionary moral choice? If there is no moral human agent, then there can be no evil human action. Here we can come perilously close to moral anarchy (Pattison, 1984). At the other extreme, Jean-Paul Sartre asserts that since God does not exist, humans are responsible for everything, and life is rendered absurd.

Each core position assumes a different view of the human in the causal linkages of behavior. The free-will assumption is that self-as-agent is the initiator of acts, for which one is wholly responsible. The deterministic assumption is that action is the end-response to internal stimuli (psychoanalysis) or external stimuli (behaviorism). Neither assumption incorporates our phenomenological experience of intending, willing, and choosing, while observing that action does not necessarily follow volition. In the existential view of responsibility, the experienced self-as-agent is neither at the beginning nor the end, but in the middle of the causal process. Our conscious experience of those ego operations we shall term the executive choosing actions, are conducted within the constraints of prior contextual stimuli and subsequent action alternatives. In this sense, all choice is existentially determined, but not caused by antecedent or consequential variables (Wallace). Both psychoanalytic and behavioral theory view causality as a linear sequence, whereas in existential terms, our conscious ego operations of choice operate in an open system of purposeful data processing that is self-determinative (Ackoff and Emery). As the Freudian aphorism puts it: our lives are more determined than we want to admit, and we have more capacity for choice than we want to accept!

7. Toward a Psychology of Responsibility. The contribution of behavioral psychology is public, universal determinants of action. The contribution of psychoanalytic psychology is private, universal determinants of action. But neither addresses the person-as-agent. Here we must address those ego operations of personal awareness, personal being, and personal choice (Loevinger). These are conscious experiences—the name we give to the experience of executive synthesizing ego operations. We experience the focusing of awareness, of attending to stimuli, of directing cognitive evaluation, and of willing action. Such experiences produce the sense of "owning" personal awareness, personal being, and personal choice. The personalized owning we term the "I" experience. Thus "I" as personal being am connected to what "I do." In turn, the experience of "self" may be defined as a

consciously constructed model-for-being. Thus "I" choose my actions in accord with "my self-model" (Pattison and Kahan). In this process of choosing, I assume responsibility to act in accord with my self-model, while acknowledging my own multiple motivations and intents (Thalberg). To be responsible does not mean that I fully apprehend all of the causes and consequences of my choices (Erikson). Rather, to be responsible is to assume the imputation that I am the agent who chooses by acting and accepting the consequences thereof (Beals). Thus the psychology of responsibility is ultimately the existential declaration of myself as agent-in-the-world.

8. Implications for Pastoral Care. There are obvious theological parallels to the core problems: the Calvinist tradition of election and determinism versus the Arminian emphasis on free will, or religious legalism versus antinomianism. Pastoral care must transcend such antinomies with an appreciation for the actual human complexity of responsibility.

Second, a moral model of responsibility must distinguish between blamability and responsibility. Blame justifies punishment, retaliation, or just retribution, but does not change the person. Blaming of self or other evades self-responsibility, whereas being responsible evokes resolution and reconciliation.

Third, pastoral care must incorporate grace, forgiveness, and absolution as the corollary to accountability and obligation. All of us demonstrate daily our limits in "ableness to respond." Since all of our actions are overdetermined and multidetermined, every piece of behavior is imperfectly responsible. Therefore, as Tillich observed, no one can justify any action as righteous. To be responsible implies that we accept, forgive, and are reconciled to our own irresponsibility and that of others. We live in, through, and by grace, rather than responsible action *per se* (Pattison, 1965).

Fourth, responsibility is ontologically grounded in our acceptance of our relationship to God. ("Against thee, thee only, have I sinned"— Ps. 51:4.) In turn, to be responsible to God implies a responsibility to self and others (Hiltner).

Bibliography. R. L. Ackoff and F. E. Emery, *On Purposeful Systems* (1972). G. J. Agich, ed., *Responsibility in Health Care* (1982). L. W. Beals, "An Imputation Theory of Free Will," in G. E. Myers, ed., *Self, Religion and Metaphysics* (1961). P. Brickman *et al.*, "Models of Helping and Coping," *American Psychologist*, 37 (1982), 368–84. E. H. Erikson, *Insight and Responsibility* (1964). L. H. Farber, *The Ways of the Will* (1966). J. W. Fowler, *Stages of Faith* (1981). S. Hiltner, "Clinical and Theological Notes on Responsibility," *J. of Religion and Health*, 2 (1962), 7–20. J. Loevinger, *Ego Development* (1976). R. McKeon, "The Development and the Significance of the Concept of Responsibility," *Revue Internationale de Philosophie*, 2 (1957), 3–32. G. B. Melton, ed., *The Law as a Behavioral Instrument* (1986). L. Nader, *Law in Culture and Society* (1969). H. R. Niebuhr, *The Responsible Self* (1963). E. M. Pattison, "On the Failure to Forgive and to Be Forgiven," *American J. of Psychotherapy*, 19 (1965), 106–15; "Psychoanalysis and the Concept of Evil," in M. C. Nelson and M. Eigen, *Evil, Self and Culture* (1984). E. M. Pattison and J. Kahan, "Personal Experience as a Conceptual Tool for Models of Consciousness," in B. B. Wolman and M. Ullman, *Handbook of States of Consciousness* (1986). P. Ramsey, *Deeds and Rules in Christian Ethics* (1967). H. Schoeck and J. W. Wiggins, *Psychiatry and Responsibility*

(1962). E. W. Straus and R. M. Griffith, *Phenomenology of Will and Action* (1967). I. Thalberg, "Motivational Disturbances and Free Will," in H. T. Engelhardt and S. F. Spicker, eds., *Mental Health: Philosophical Perspectives* (1978). E. R. Wallace, *Historiography and Causation in Psychoanalysis* (1985).

E. M. PATTISON

COMMITMENT; CONSCIENCE; OBEDIENCE; SELF-EXPRESSION/ SELF CONTROL; SOCIAL CONSCIOUSNESS AND RESPONSIBILITY; WILL/WILLING. *See also* ANTISOCIAL PERSONS; DECISION/ INDECISION, PSYCHOLOGY OF; GUILT; IMPULSIVENESS/ SPONTANEITY; LEGALISM AND ANTINOMIANISM; LOCUS OF CONTROL RESEARCH; SHAME; TEMPTATION. *Compare* APOSTASY; AUTHORITARIANISM; DEPENDENCE/INDEPENDENCE; GRACE; INFIDELITY, MARITAL; RIGHTEOUSNESS/BEING RIGHT; SIN/SINS; WORKING THROUGH.

RESPONSIBILITY, SOCIAL. *See* SOCIAL CONSCIOUSNESS AND RESPONSIBILITY.

REST HOME. *See* CHAPLAIN/CHAPLAINCY. *See also* CHRONIC ILLNESS; HANDICAP AND DISABILITY; NEUROLOGIC ILLNESSES.

REST AND RENEWAL, RELIGIOUS TRADITIONS OF. Rest commonly refers to a suspension of activity following physical or mental exertion. Renewal implies a re-creation or recuperation of energies and capacities. Religious understandings of rest and renewal are shaped by the foundational theological metaphors and the sociological context of the interpreting tradition. Sacred stories of divine activity provide religious frameworks for the establishment of meaningful rhythms of work and rest within corporate and individual life. Jewish and Christian understandings have been largely informed by biblical accounts of persons who withdrew from their regular patterns of life for periods of rest, reflection, and renewal. Even more significant has been the tradition of Sabbath observance originating from the suspension of activity by God on the seventh day of Creation.

Other religious traditions also attribute a divine significance to the cycles of rest and renewal in human life. The Hindu tradition regards play as an efficacious activity related to the creation of the cosmos. Krishna, the popular blue-skinned god of the Hindu pantheon, is paradigmatic for the believer as a symbol of renewal and new creation. He is portrayed in sacred art and text as a dancing, playful deity imparting positive value to activities that are not related to work. Recent investigation of play as a philosophical concept supports a thesis of play as a meaning-making activity of the human spirit. J. Hans (1981) understands play as a value-generating activity which serves a renewing, restoring purpose for its participants. Zen Buddhism emphasizes spontaneity as the way of enlightenment. Purposeless activity is extolled as the path toward true understanding. Goal directed striving is a knotted obstacle to awareness that must be loosened.

1. Rest, Renewal, and Leisure. Both rest and renewal can be placed under the concept of leisure, a philosophical ideal first debated by the Greeks who defined it as a spiritual capacity for freedom. From such lofty beginnings leisure shifted across a spectrum of understandings, moving in the Christian tradition toward more

narrow pastoral meanings of idleness, waste, and sin. In the Puritan tradition especially, any activity without extrinsic purpose or reward became an offense against proper piety.

Widespread leisure, the opportunity for rest and renewal, is a recent sociological development. Made possible by the industrial and agricultural revolutions of the last two hundred years, leisure is no longer the restricted possession of a privileged elite. It is now a part of the daily lives of a majority of the population of Western industrialized societies and a growing proportion of persons worldwide. The tremendous growth of leisure time has been accompanied by modern philosophical and theological reflection.

For all religious traditions the concept of leisure raises theological questions related to the use of time. How is unobligated, discretionary time to be theologically understood? The Catholic tradition has long upheld the value of contemplative time as intrinsically meaningful. The activity of contemplation with its praxis toward God is acknowledged as a good. Protestant traditions have tended toward more utilitarian values, viewing discretionary time as a useful preparatory period renewing the individual for return to productive labor.

J. Pieper's (1963) views of leisure establish it as an essential element in the creation of culture. For Pieper, leisure serves as an attitude of the soul, an attitude of inward calm which fosters a capacity for true apprehension of the world's reality. Pieper begins his essay with a verse from Psalm 46 translated from the Septuagint: "Have leisure and know that I am God." The ultimate justification for leisure is its service as an activity of worship linking humanity in a contemplative, celebrative encounter with the divine. Pieper traces the development of cultic feast days into their modern counterparts. Ancient "holy days" once set aside for purposeful turning toward God have become "holidays" in which time is no longer the bracketed context for divine encounter but an aimless circumstance for boredom.

Modern culture has constructed a huge leisure industry centered about activities which provide rest and renewal from labors of production. Recreational play and relaxation are promoted as meaningful ends in themselves. Limitless leisure time is fantasized as a desirable goal of life. From a religious perspective leisure has degenerated into a gold ring to be grasped, whose value-laden promises will always prove empty. Separated from its spiritual context leisure is deprived of the power engendered by the divine-human encounter and tumbles into meaningless tedium. Secular understandings of rest and renewal tend toward the fragmentary division of life into overvalued spheres of work and nonwork. Religious traditions seek to blend the two together, dissolving the dichotomy into a unified vision of all life as illumined and revealed by the light of God.

2. Withdrawal and Return Motif. R. Brown (1988) emphasizes the nature of scriptural accounts narrating journeys of "withdrawal and return" on the part of biblical characters. The withdrawal from workaday life is temporary and is always carried out for the purpose of return. Jesus withdraws to the wilderness. Elijah retreats to a cave. Both return to their working lives with new insight with which to carry on the tasks given them by

God. Withdrawal is never portrayed in the Bible as an end in itself. Rather it provides the context for an encounter with the divine that will alter former perceptions of life and bring about transformative change.

N. Kazantzakis makes reference in his fiction to Byzantine mystics whose writings express similar understandings. Since we cannot change reality, let us change the eyes which see it. This is the religious function of all rest and renewal, to provide the requisite conditions for a true perception of life experience unencumbered by our enslavement to the demands of daily activity. E. O'Conner similarly captures the exercise of such activity in her book *Journey Inward, Journey Outward*. In contrast to popular conceptions of a leisure lifestyle in which the pursuit of leisure is viewed as an end in itself, O'Conner expands upon Christian perspectives which recognize the necessity of return to the regular rhythms of life to put into action the discernment and new energy that withdrawal has made possible.

3. **The Sabbath.** The most powerful Western religious understandings of rest and renewal have their source in Jewish and Christian conceptions of the Sabbath. The tradition of the Sabbath may date to prebiblical cultic patterns but its mature development as a religious institution of rest and renewal begins with the OT. The Sabbath's insistence on rest reminds its keepers of the senselessness of uninterrupted, unreflected work and experience. Its universal character affirms a divine dominion over all Creation and a unity within the creatures of that Creation. Sabbath time is hallowed, liberating time in which master and slave, rich and poor, male and female are all teased into a remembrance of their common reliance upon an ultimate meaning of life greater than themselves.

Medieval Jewish mystics deepened classic views of the Sabbath by expanding its symbolic meaning beyond a seventh day of rest. The Sabbath was understood as feminine, embodying the spirit of a mystical marriage ceremony which nurtures and restores the worn spirit of men and women who enter into its atmosphere. Christian metaphors of the Middle Ages celebrated the Sabbath as "the Marketday of the Soul," a time for restoration and connection. Many European churches preached a practical Sabbatarianism seeking to compromise the secular spirit with theological doctrine. The open spaces of the churchyards became the local fairgrounds of leisure activities and holidays. The tension between strict and flexible interpretations of the keeping of the Sabbath have persisted to the present.

A. Heschel stresses the meaning of the Sabbath as the celebration of time rather than space. As a symbol of the sanctification of time, the Sabbath releases men and women from the tyranny of production-oriented activity. The keeping of the Sabbath is not an activity but an attitude of the soul. One does not so much keep the Sabbath as one is joined to its keeping of us. For Heschel, the Sabbath may be understood as a "Sanctuary in Time" representing the ideal state of Creation and of the relationships within that Creation. As a symbol of rest and renewal, the Sabbath signifies an inner serenity of the spirit providing the context for a timeless apprehension of the eternal within the bounds of time.

Bibliography. N. E. Andreasen, *Rest and Redemption* (1978). R. M. Brown, *Spirituality and Liberation* (1988). E. K. Ginsburg, *The Sabbath in the Classical Kabbalah* (1985). J. S. Hans, *The Play of the World* (1981). A. J. Heschel, *The Sabbath: Its Meaning for Modern Man* (1951). T. M. Kando, *Leisure and Popular Culture in Transition* (1975). D. R. Kinsley, *The Divine Player* (1979). E. O'Conner, *Journey Inward, Journey Outward* (1975). J. Pieper, *Leisure: The Basis of Culture* (1963).

P. J. JOHNSON, III

CHRISTIAN LIFE; JEWISH HOLY DAYS AND FESTIVALS; OLD TESTAMENT AND APOCRYPHA, TRADITIONS AND THEOLOGY OF CARE IN; RENEWAL MOVEMENTS AND PROGRAMS; RITUAL AND PASTORAL CARE; WORSHIP AND CELEBRATION. *See also* LITURGICAL CALENDAR; MEDITATION; TRADITION AS MODE OF CARE. *Compare* PLAY; RELAXATION, PSYCHOLOGY AND TECHNIQUES OF.

RESTITUTION. *See* PENANCE, SACRAMENT OF; REPENTANCE AND CONFESSION.

RESURRECTION. *See* CHRISTOLOGY; CROSS AND RESURRECTION; ESCHATOLOGY.

RETARDATION, RETARDED PERSONS. *See* MENTALLY RETARDED PERSONS. *See also* EXCEPTIONAL CHILDREN AND THEIR FAMILIES; MENTAL RETARDATION.

RETIREMENT. Detachment from the work force as a full-time employee. According to this definition, nine out of ten men and women aged sixty-five and older in North America are retired.

1. **When Do People Retire?** In 1884 German Chancellor Otto von Bismarck arbitrarily set the age of sixty-five for receiving pension benefits, and his model has been followed in much of the Western world. The same age for receiving benefits — and therefore being a candidate for forced retirement—was embodied in the U.S. social security system when it was established in 1935. Almost all private pension plans which sprang up after World War II adopted the same eligibility age.

The U.S. Congress subsequently extended the mandatory retirement age from sixty-five to seventy and in 1986 abolished it altogether. The research of the Senate Committee on Human Resources estimated that only two-tenths of one percent of the total labor force would choose to work full-time beyond sixty-five if given the opportunity. Those who choose to do so tend to be in the ranks of professional, executive, and highly technical workers. In the largest U.S. corporations many workers are encouraged or forced to retire at a much earlier age, in spite of the law. It is estimated that not more than ten percent of blue collar workers will stay on the job until sixty-five.

As many as fifty percent of male workers retire because of poor health and most of the remainder for such voluntary reasons as desire for leisure, dissatisfaction with the job, being needed at home, or opportunities for rewarding part-time work (Steiner *et al.*). Whatever the reasons for retirement, voluntary or compulsory, the retiree often enters a new world, a new lifestyle.

2. **Losses and Gains in Retirement.** In retirement one enters a transition period characterized by the loss of

an assumptive world. Familiar practices and relationships can no longer be taken for granted. The amount of stress experienced depends on the personal meaning of retirement and one's perceived resources—financial and personal—for the new state of affairs (Lazarus and DeLongis). Retirement is a highly personalized process and can be anticipated as benign, threatening, or challenging. The majority of retirees do not experience the dreaded negative consequences which are a part of modern American folklore. A major study of occupational retirement concluded that while there was usually a sharp reduction in income in the impact year of retirement, there was no increase in worry about money, no sharp decline in health, feelings of usefulness, and satisfaction in life for most retirees (Streib *et al.*).

Ordinarily, retirees experience both losses and gains in the process of retirement. One of the first recognized losses is a *loss of power* as one moves from the working to the nonworking world. The power that was manifest in one's decision-making, in having influence in one's work environment, in the ability to be productive and to win respect for the symbols of one's position, may no longer be available. When one is no longer productive, influential, consulted, or needed at the workplace, self-esteem can suffer if no substitutes are found.

The loss of work is more than a matter of economics; it is the *loss of a social world*. For most people employment provides a social anchorage, a community of associates, friends, and enemies with whom one interacts at the workplace and perhaps beyond it. Work also provides a framework of reality-testing that forces one into contact with the nonfantasy world of things and materials, ideas, processes, and people. Work structures time into distinct and helpful periods of action and relaxation, work and play. It structures space in terms of home and office or shop. One may not discover until late in retirement what one misses most. But something is lost, and grief work, with its anger and sadness, may need to be encouraged for the person who has invested himself or herself in a career, who comes to possess it, or be possessed by it, and who suffers on leaving it.

There are numerous gains in retirement, one of which is the *freedom to reshape aspects of one's identity*. Work is usually a crucial ingredient of one's self-identity and, in retirement, cannot be the sole ingredient. The idea that retirement and aging can be the occasion for *individuation* was introduced by C. G. Jung more than sixty years ago. Formerly defined by one's occupation, income, and social approval for "making it," the retiree may begin to define himself or herself in terms of personal criteria, recognizing what one really wants to do that tallies with one's natural bent and with working or playing at it without the pressure of time and social expectation.

Freedom from time constraints and obligations is one of the rewards of retirement. The pleasure of slowing down, of cultivating friendships, of volunteer service, of savoring the delights of life, of release from feverish expectations and deep worries about one's work are cited by the majority of retirees in industrial societies as key retirement benefits.

Bernice Neugarten's longitudinal study of adult life in Kansas City disclosed patterns of personal response to retirement which tended to reflect the person's earlier lifestyles (Neugarten). The majority of the two thousand seventy-year-olds in her study were well integrated and satisfied with their lives. They fell into three general patterns:

The *reorganizers* are those who substituted new activities for lost ones; who, when they retired from work, gave time to community affairs or to church or other associations. They reorganized their patterns of activity.

The *focused* gained satisfaction by selecting one or two areas of activity, often one aspect of their work experience, to center upon. They tended to withdraw from many former activities and memberships and spend more time with their families, their friendship groups, and their hobbies.

The *disengaged* were happy to abandon most of the former community obligations and commitments and become "homebodies." Neugarten found them to be self-directed persons, not shallow, having an interest in the world but an interest that avoided the social networks of that interest. They had chosen what might be called a "rocking chair" approach to old age.

A minority of the two thousand persons in Neugarten's study showed less adaptive patterns of response which led to less life satisfaction: the *defended* were striving, ambitious people who tried to overcome their anxiety about aging by clinging to the lifestyles of their middle age; the *passive-dependent*, constantly sought succorance and got along with fair satisfaction as long as they had someone to lean on; the *apathetic* clung to long-standing patterns of passivity which fed their inertia and prevented them from doing much beyond their daily routines; the *unintegrated* were personalities with such disorganization that they could neither control their emotions nor think clearly.

Along with her classifications, Neugarten offers this general conclusion: "[In retirement] there appear to be two sets of values operating simultaneously. . . . On the one hand, the desire to stay active in order to maintain a sense of self-worth; on the other hand, the desire to withdraw from social commitments and to pursue a more leisurely and more contemplative way of life" (Bradbury).

3. **Women and Retirement.** The significance of retirement for women, as compared with men, has not been systematically explored and remains a matter of conjecture. Longitudinal studies of adults seem to conclude that continuities or sameness of lifestyle from young adult to old age are much more apparent among men than women. Women apparently experience many more role changes in occupational, marital, and parenting areas of life, and these are highly influential on how they live their daily lives, even in retirement (Maas and Kuypers).

One contemporary phenomenon that requires study is the discrepancy between many husbands and wives on the anticipation of retirement. For the wife who has been chiefly a homemaker, her "retirement" may mean very little change. For the woman who enters the work force after the children have grown, a dilemma presents itself. She may be well settled in her career about the time her husband—after thirty or forty years of work—intends to retire. These late-entry workers have no intention of retiring or moving away from the vicinity of their work. Such marriages must reconcile the "coming" and "going" cycles of the mates into a satisfactory individualized lifestyle.

4. Implications for the Pastoral Care of Retired Persons.
Three especially important tasks for the pastoral care of retired persons can be suggested.

First, pastoral ministry can *foster awareness of the need to grieve* the loss of work life where it has been a crucial aspect of identity and, for some workers, an addiction. If sorrow is not embraced and expressed adequately, the ground is being prepared for future bouts of depression.

Second, the church or religious community can *foster an awareness of "vocation"* which is far richer and deeper than the kind of work in which one has been engaged. One's primary vocation from a Judeo-Christian standpoint is that of serving God by contributing to wholeness, love, and justice in the world; no one need be out of work in that calling.

Third, the religious community can help retired persons *become aware of new and heroic goals* in the years that remain to them. Instead of reducing their demands upon one another, husbands and wives and members of the religious community can come to see retirement as an occasion for adventurous challenges. The risk of failure matters least now; significance and meaning matter most.

Bibliography. W. Bradbury, *The Adult Years*, in *Time-Life*, (1975), p. 144. R. W. Fairchild, *Finding Hope Again: A Pastor's Guide to Counseling Depressed Persons* (1980). R. S. Lazarus and A. DeLongis, "Psychological Stress and Coping in Aging," *American Psychologist*, (March 1983), 245–53. H. S. Maas and J. A. Kuypers, *From Thirty to Seventy* (1974). B. L. Neugarten, "Grow Old Along with Me!" *Psychology Today*, (Dec. 1971). P. O. Steiner and R. Dorfman, in Neugarten, *Middle Age and Aging* (1968), p. 355. G. F. Streib and C. J. Schneider, *Retirement in American Society* (1971), 163.

R. W. FAIRCHILD

AGING; LIFE CYCLE THEORY AND PASTORAL CARE; OLDER PERSONS, PASTORAL CARE AND COUNSELING OF. *Compare* WORK AND CAREER.

RETIREMENT HOME. *See* CHAPLAIN/CHAPLAINCY; OLDER PERSONS. *See also* CHRONIC ILLNESS; HANDICAP AND DISABILITY; NEUROLOGIC ILLNESSES.

RETREATS (Protestantism). To retreat is to withdraw from the distractions of the world and self in order to renew one's self (soul) with the personal redeeming power of God. Retreat is a spiritual exercise, and the ingredients facilitating retreat are solitude, simplicity, stillness, and spiritual reflection.

The practice of retreat is based on a theological belief that oneness with God and the Holy Spirit is a continuing possibility and necessity. It incorporates a dynamic incarnational viewpoint. Retreat is only a discipline and a medium to know God better and to continue an inward spiritual journey seeking God at the center of all of life.

Retreat and withdrawal are very much a part of the biblical record as evidenced by the depictions of Jesus, Moses, Deborah, Elijah, Amos, Isaiah, and Paul. The symbolism of the desert and wilderness in both the Old and the New Testament clearly highlight the importance of "getting away" for renewal, a fresh perspective, and a more personal confrontation with God. Noted religious leaders in all branches of Christendom have practiced retreat and spiritual reflection. Jesus encouraged retreat for his disciples (Mk. 6:30–31; Lk. 10:42) and he regularly withdrew for renewal and re-centering.

It is believed that more formal and organized retreats began with the influence of the Counter-Reformation (St. Ignatius Loyola), and the Jesuits were the first order to require retreats.

In Protestantism, the Oxford Movement in England promoted the retreat practice, and by the twentieth century the idea of retreat and retreat centers had grown significantly.

Douglas Steere is a Protestant pioneer in promoting, interpreting, and leading retreats in the renewal movement in America. Steere wrote a definitive treatise on retreat and described some of the early Christian retreat communities in Protestantism.

Formal retreat usually involves planning, escaping into a quiet environment, and days of reflection, but retreat can also be practiced by going inward and communing for short periods of time in any physical surrounding.

Planned retreats include emphases on prayer, meditation, Bible study, and complete solitude. Other focused retreats may guide persons to consider marriage enrichment, spiritual growth, spiritual struggle, spiritual journaling, dreams and revelation, etc. Retreat schedules vary from carefully guided formats to completely open agendas and leaderless reflection time.

It is usually considered that all aspects of retreat have a spiritual emphasis and symbolism. Therefore, the food eaten, fasting, manual labor, exercise, no exertion at all, where one stays, and how one communicates are all part of the intentional planning and reflection of retreat.

Paradoxically, to retreat is to withdraw to the real strength and renewal of the spiritual sanctuary which the outer world cannot continually provide.

Bibliography. D. Steere, *Time to Spare* (1949). J. Townroe. "Retreat," in Jones, Wainwright, Yarnold, eds., *The Study of Spirituality* (1986). J. Wareham, *The Conducting of Retreats* (1950).

T. DOUGHERTY

PILGRIMAGE METAPHOR; RENEWAL MOVEMENTS AND PROGRAMS; REST AND RENEWAL, RELIGIOUS TRADITIONS OF; SPIRITUAL DISCIPLINE AND GROWTH; SPIRITUALITY (Protestant Tradition).

RETREATS (Roman Catholicism). A period of time set aside from the normal day-to-day activity which is devoted to prayer, reflection, and examination of one's religious and spiritual life. It may range from a day, to a few days, to a month, as with some religious orders, and is usually guided by a retreat director, who may be a religious, clergy, or layperson. Many religious orders, and some diocesan and religious organizations, support retreat centers which provide individuals and groups with facilities and programs for making a retreat. Formal retreats for large groups can focus on Scripture, a particular contemporary church issue, or a recurrent religious theme. Retreats for individuals tend to be less structured because these are made on a personal, one-to-one basis usually with a retreat master or spiritual director. Common features for personal or group retreats include periods for prayer, personal reflection, and sharing of insights from such self-examination. Individuals are encouraged to incorporate into their daily lives this self-knowledge and insight into their faith life.

In the Roman Catholic church, retreats have a long tradition. It has its scriptural basis in the many references to Jesus drawing away for prayer, for example, his forty days in the desert fasting and praying. Especially in Christian Egypt, Africa, and areas of the Near East, ancient monastic and hermitic life actively followed Christ's example by setting aside long periods for self-examination and spiritual development. These practices continued into medieval and early modern Europe. The *Spiritual Exercises* of St. Ignatius of Loyola (1548), a thirty-day program for individuals, is one of the most influential examples of retreat-making. Today many religious orders and clergy make frequent retreats to sustain their spiritual lives. Increasingly, lay people, who have always turned to clergy and religious for spiritual direction, are participating in private and group retreats that are sponsored by parish, diocesan, or other religious organizations.

Individuals often consider making a retreat during Advent or Lent, the traditional seasons of the liturgical year when the church encourages its members to be more reflective about their lives as Christians. Those who face important life decisions or who consider their present life unsatisfying frequently find the retreat opportunity especially valuable. Most men and women use it as a time for personal spiritual renewal and enrichment.

A. W. R. SIPE

PILGRIMAGE METAPHOR; REST AND RENEWAL, RELIGIOUS TRADITIONS OF; SPIRITUAL DISCIPLINE AND GROWTH; SPIRITUALITY, ROMAN CATHOLIC. *See also* FORMATIVE SPIRITUALITY; LITURGICAL AND DEVOTIONAL LIFE, ROMAN CATHOLIC; RENEWAL MOVEMENTS AND PROGRAMS; ROMAN CATHOLIC PASTORAL CARE.

REVELATION AND PASTORAL CARE. Revelation is the theological category used to describe what is known about God and how that knowledge occurs. Hence revelation often serves as the epistemological basis for theological claims about God.

1. The Structure of Revelation. *a. Revelation, grace, and faith.* Revelation has been an important topic in the history of Christian thought and doctrine because many Christians have held the conviction that knowledge of God is not finally a matter of human discovery. The reasons for that conviction vary. Some philosophers and theologians have argued that because God is beyond the limits of human reason, Christian claims about God are not the discovery of human reason, but are rooted in an event of grace in which transcendent reality discloses itself to human experience and knowledge. Consequently, revelation refers primarily to the self-disclosure of ultimate reality and only secondarily to the human apprehension of that reality.

In Christian experience and discourse and in the fabric of theology, the concepts *revelation, grace,* and *faith* are tightly interwoven. For many theologians the gracious character of revelation is a correlate of faith. Faith is a human act, but in the most important and profound sense faith is also a gift. Just as revelation refers to the

unveiling or disclosure of transcendent mystery, so, too, faith is not primarily an act of human will and intellect, but a reality Christians believe has been given to them.

b. The objective and subjective poles. Because revelation describes what is known about God and how that knowledge occurs, it has both objective and subjective poles. The objective pole is what is known or disclosed in revelation, and it has been interpreted by theologians in various ways. For example, the objective pole can be interpreted as propositions revealed in Scripture, in the traditions of a particular community, or in the teaching office of the church. Or the objective pole can be interpreted as knowledge of God which is derived directly from human experience of the holy or indirectly from human relationships which mediate God.

In the same manner, the subjective pole of revelation —how knowledge of God occurs — also assumes various forms. Revelation can be described as an event in which the mind is illumined and knowledge of God disclosed. Or the subjective pole can be described in terms which refer less to the cognitive and more to the affective dimension of human being. That is, the subjective pole can be described as a religious experience in which one's understanding of self and world is altered and transformed.

In most descriptions of revelation, there is an important connection between the content of revelation—what is revealed — and how revelation is understood to occur. Although some interpretations of revelation may emphasize one pole at the expense of the other, the interpretation of one pole weighs heavily on the interpretation of the other pole. If the content of revelation is interpreted in terms of God's self-disclosure, it is not surprising that the description of how revelation takes place is more likely to appeal to interpersonal than to propositional categories.

2. Models of Revelation. *a. Classical models.* The Christian tradition has been dominated by two models of revelation. The first model trades heavily on the concept of illumination, and the second model is based on the relation between Word and Spirit.

In ancient and medieval theology, different forms of the illumination model can be found in Augustine, Bonaventure, and Thomas Aquinas. Forms of this model of revelation are especially common along theologians influenced by Platonic thought. When revelation takes place, the intellect is illumined and enabled to know those truths which are beyond the limits of human reason. This classical model gave rise to the discussion of the relation between reason and revelation. Thomas Aquinas, for example, proposed a synthesis between what can be known by reason and what can be known only by revelation. Thomas argued that reason can know the existence of God, but knowledge of the Trinity and the resurrection of Jesus Christ must be revealed to the intellect by God.

In the Reformation, a second model of revelation emerged. Martin Luther and John Calvin argued that reason may be able to discern something about God, but reason is of no use whatsoever in discerning what matters —namely, God's will toward the world. God's will, they argued, can be known only by means of Jesus Christ. What God wills is disclosed in God's Word, and that Word is incarnate in Jesus of Nazareth and witnessed to by the Bible. While the illumination model emphasized God's enlightenment of the intellect, the Reformers' interpretation of revelation—a model of Word and Spirit—stressed the Word, incarnate in Jesus and written in Scripture, as the content and medium of revelation. Furthermore, the Reformers insisted that no one can know the Word simply by means of an exercise of the will and the intellect. The hearing of the Word is an event of grace, and as such the Spirit must open human hearts and minds, closed by sin, in order for God's Word to be heard.

b. Contemporary models. In the seventeenth and eighteenth centuries these two classical models of revelation were subjected to extensive criticism. Many deists argued that revelation was superfluous. They claimed to know that those truths on the basis of revelation were simply a "republication" of what could be known by reason. With the rise of modern science, the collapse of established forms of authority, the Enlightenment's emphasis on reason unhindered by superstition and tradition, and the turn to the self as the starting point for what can be known, the classical models of revelation suffered a severe blow. Both classical models of revelation presupposed a supernatural interpretation of God's relation to the world and God's activity in the world, which was rejected by many Enlightenment theologians.

The history of nineteenth- and twentieth-century theology is to a considerable extent the struggle to formulate an adequate interpretation of revelation in response to the criticisms of the Enlightenment. No typology can do justice to the many different interpretations of revelation that have been proposed, but it is possible to identify four different interpretations of revelation in contemporary theology.

First, there are those interpretations which focus either on historical events or history as a whole as the content and medium of revelation. For G. W. F. Hegel in the nineteenth century and for Pannenberg in the twentieth century, the whole of history or "universal history" is the arena in which God is known and the disclosure of the nature of God. Other theologians have emphasized particular historical events or series of events as the activity and revelation of God.

Second, other theologians have argued that revelation should be interpreted in terms of human experience and the structure of human existence. Schleiermacher argued that the essence of Christianity is the experience of redemption as that is mediated by the life of the community and interpreted by means of the biblical image of Jesus Christ. In the twentieth century, some theologians have employed contemporary forms of existentialism and phenomenology in order to identify what it is in the structure of human existence that enables human beings to experience transcendence. For Karl Rahner, it is the openness of humanity to being itself which is the foundation for the possibility, if not the reality, of revelation.

Third, the theological movement known as "neo-orthodoxy" and usually associated with theologians such as Karl Barth and Emil Brunner described revelation as God's self-disclosure in Jesus Christ. For Barth, Jesus Christ is God's Word and as such is the disclosure of God's being. Revelation, therefore, is the first and decisive form of the Word of God. Scripture and proclamation are human words which become revelatory when God's grace enables them to become events in which God's Word is heard and believed.

Fourth, in the last half of the twentieth century several theologians have shifted their attention to the category of "narrative" or "story" as an interpretation of revelation. H. Richard Niebuhr first proposed that revelation be described as an event of disclosure in a person's internal history. For Niebuhr, revelation was not primarily a matter of propositions but the confession of the heart, "Thou art my God." The recent work of Paul Ricoeur also describes revelation in terms of the confession of faith which assumes the form of "testimony."

3. Issues for Pastoral Care. While the topic of revelation has significant implications for the interpretation and practice of pastoral care, it is surprising that so little attention has been given to the subject by scholars in the field. A survey of recent literature in pastoral care and counseling leaves the impression that the interpretation of revelation, questions of epistemology, and other such "foundational" matters have not been a primary concern of those who think and write about the discipline of pastoral care. The failure to attend to these issues is surprising because so many of the unresolved questions in the contemporary discussion of revelation have obvious significance for the practice of pastoral care and could perhaps be illumined by some of the insights of pastoral counselors.

a. Truth and meaning. One example of an important issue in the discussion of revelation that is relevant to the practice of pastoral care is the question of truth and meaning. What is meant when what is believed to have been revealed is said to be "true"? In part, that depends on what it is that has been revealed and how that revelation is supposed to have taken place. If what has been revealed is a series of propositions, then the criteria for assessing the truth of those propositions are determined by what the propositions assert. If what has been revealed is a historical assertion (for example, having to do with the crossing of the Red Sea or the significance of the cross), then the truth of the assertion is dependent on what historical research can determine. On the other hand, if what has been revealed is a personal relation to transcendent mystery, then historical considerations may no longer be relevant.

The practice of pastoral care provides an important focus for some of the issues that surround the topic of revelation. The initial problem in a counseling relationship may take the form of a narrative, and while the truth of that narrative may be finally a major issue, the initial narrative, no matter how disconnected and incoherent, provides the raw material for analysis. While the deeper challenge may be to unravel the true narrative hidden in the initial one, the latter offers its own perception of truth.

b. Hermeneutics. Recent discussions of revelation and pastoral care recognize the importance of hermeneutics. If revelation is understood as the indirect disclosure of divine mystery in the symbols and myths of the Christian tradition, then an important issue is how those symbols and myths function in order for disclosure and healing to occur. Charles Gerkin (1984), for example, has attempted to describe how the use of parable and metaphor in pastoral counseling may allow the true story hidden in the initial narrative to emerge, and how parable and metaphor may evoke transformation.

Pastoral care is a hermeneutical task. It necessarily involves making judgments about the proper and improper use of Christian symbols to interpret life. Furthermore, pastoral care is a hermeneutical and confessional task in that the counselor interprets life stories as a representative of a community which has experienced particular symbols and myths to be disclosive of ultimate reality. The symbols to which the pastoral counselor appeals have their meaning and their revelatory power in the life and history of the religious community which he or she represents. The pastoral counselor, therefore, not only listens to narratives but interprets them by means of the revelatory symbols and myths of the Christian tradition.

Bibliography. J. Baillie, *The Idea of Revelation in Recent Thought* (1956). K. Barth, *Church Dogmatics, I/1* (1975). E. Brunner, *Revelation and Reason* (1946). R. Bultmann, "The Concept of Revelation in the New Testament," in *Existence and Faith* (1960). F. G. Downing, *Has Christianity a Revelation?* (1964). S. J. A. Dulles, *Revelation Theology: A History* (1969); *Models of Revelation* (1966). A. Farrer, *The Glass of Vision* (1948). C. Gerkin, *The Living Human Document* (1984). R. Hart, *Unfinished Man and the Imagination* (1968). J. E. Loder, *The Transforming Moment* (1981). H. D. McDonald, *Ideas of Revelation* (1959); *Theories of Revelation* (1959). H. R. Niebuhr, *The Meaning of Revelation* (1941). W. Pannenberg, ed., *Revelation as History* (1968). K. Rahner, *Hearers of the Word* (1969). P. Ricoeur, "Toward a Hermeneutic of the Idea of Revelation," in *Essays on Biblical Interpretation* (1980).

G. W. STROUP

GUIDANCE, DIVINE; ILLUMINATION; RELIGIOUS EXPERIENCE. *Compare* CHRISTOLOGY, GOD, HOLY SPIRIT, *or* SALVATION, AND PASTORAL CARE.

REVENGE. *See* RAGE AND HOSTILITY.

REVERENCE. *See* THE HOLY; RELIGIOUS EXPERIENCE.

REVIVAL SERVICE. *See* EVANGELICAL PASTORAL CARE.

RICE, OTIS. *See* NEW YORK PSYCHOLOGY GROUP.

RICH PERSONS. This article offers a broad definition of the rich, describes a few of their identifying characteristics, outlines their main problems, discusses difficulties encountered in ministering to them, proposes a way of dealing with these, and suggests a brief bibliography.

1. **Definition.** How one defines the rich depends a great deal on one's position in the socio-economic spectrum. To the poor a middle class person would appear wealthy. To the upper middle class only those with millions would qualify. Complicating these perceptions are factors of class and status, for example, how one's position is measured by income, education, family background, social prominence, political and economic power, and achievement (Fussell). One can be quite wealthy and have low status (drug trafficker) or have comparatively high status and not be so well off financially (impoverished descendant of famous family). The complexity of the class structure and its relative flexibility in the U.S. make it difficult to define with any precision which group constitutes the upper class. It is therefore better to speak of upper classes.

Usually having money, high status, and being of the upper classes go together. Rich people encompass several subgroups, such as those who were born into families of wealth, those with recently acquired prosperity through entrepreneurial or scientific acumen, and those professionals whose earnings put them in the upper income brackets. Only the top five percent of U.S. families are considered well-to-do, that is having incomes of $100,000 or more. Of these only a fraction of one percent are very wealthy with incomes in the millions.

2. **Characteristics.** Social and economic background effect everyone's personality development, the quality of education one gets, the kind of family life one is exposed to, the opportunities one has for advancement, and the views of life and the world one develops. It is often forgotten that this also holds true for the rich, and especially for those who are born to wealth. Their single most important personal characteristic is a pervasive sense of entitlement, a feeling of assurance about one's place in the social order, one's right to be there, the certainty that one will receive what one needs, and the trust that one can make things happen to accomplish one's ends (Coles). In an emotionally healthy person of means this can result in self-confidence and productivity. In a wealthy person who is troubled, the feeling of entitlement can exist alongside with, or even hide, fears, self-doubt, depression, and despair.

A well-to-do person learns at an early age to be socially, and to a degree personally, confident. Such an individual can therefore easily appear to others of lesser means and status to be demanding, intimidating, or even imperious. The casual attitude toward money and expenditures, the facile use of power and influence, the cosmopolitan taste and outlook that money and frequent travel make possible, the ignorance and naiveté about what life is like for most people in this world, particularly for those who are economically and socially deprived, only serve to reinforce the impression of superiority or snobbishness. Wealth can shield one from many troubles and deprivations and cause one to be distanced from common life. The wealthy can be quite insular and therefore can also, strange as that may seem, be intellectually and culturally deprived.

Private education which plays such a crucial role in the socialization of the rich limits the interaction with others who are economically, culturally, or ethnically different, and may offer an educational experience which for all its academic excellence does not do much to challenge values and assumptions. Not surprisingly, this can contribute to the transmission of a self-serving ideology for the upper classes, but can also make for a stifling homogeneity of the like-minded and the equally privileged. For the more independently thinking and socially aware students in such schools this can become an issue.

The single most striking family characteristic is a strong sense of historical continuity, of belonging to an exclusive and larger intergenerational kinship network, a knowledge and pride of being descendant from persons of consequence and accomplishment, frequently the founder of the clan or dynasty to which one belongs. For many people of class and wealth their family history is a legacy to be proud of, to be intimately acquainted with and talked about, to be loyal to, to perpetuate. The ancestral home or mansion, even when no longer extant, can serve as a powerful symbol and organizing metaphor, in the sense of *noblesse oblige* of counting for something, of having a certain set of shared hopes, values, norms, and sentiments.

The rich are usually surrounded by servants and helpers of all kinds, by nannies, who frequently play a crucial role in the rearing of their children, by maids, cooks, butlers, gardeners, chauffeurs, but also by lawyers, accountants, and bankers. The job of all these people is to do those things that the wealthy do not want to do or cannot do for themselves. This easily fosters an attitude that anyone not of their social set, including teachers, clergy, physicians, and mental health professionals, is of inferior social status (which they commonly are), can be hired (which they usually can be), and are to be treated as employees (which may be inappropriate). Dealing with so many people who are employed to help them, trains the rich to keep a certain social distance, to retain control, and to always, no matter how gently, be the ones giving the orders.

These relationships, on the other hand, often become very important, close and intimate and long-lasting (as with nannies), or quite dependent (as with professionals). Nowhere is this more evident than in the relation of so many heirs, and in our androcentric society particularly of heiresses, to the lawyers and trust officers who are appointed to administer their inheritances. The paradoxical effect of these complicated legal and fiscal arrangements can be to infantilize the rich. This can result in a significant loss of autonomy and a vulnerability to being exploited.

3. **Problems.** There is a cost to riches, to success, and to the lifestyles that often go with these. The most obvious is the problem of not knowing whether one is liked or accepted for oneself or for one's position and wealth. When one's identity is shaky, and close and trusting relationships are lacking, the results can be disastrous, as is shown by the great incidence of failed marriages, alcoholism, drug addiction, acting-out behavior like running away and self-destructive rebelling, promiscuity, and severe psychiatric disorders. Even in the best functioning family of means it can be a problem to come to the realization that one cannot measure up to the accomplishments of one's family and forebears, to avoid a failure of nerve when such high standards have been set, and to battle the resulting self-doubt; to have the emotional wherewithal to persevere in attaining career goals that require denial of immediate gratification when the latter is so easy to come by; to discover that one's privileged position in society is not the result of one's own efforts or, worse, may have been gained at the expense of others; to achieve the necessary maturity to avoid inadequate solutions to the resolution of personal or relational problems, short cuts that money can so easily provide; or to struggle with the boredom that often results from a life in which challenges are more an option than an inevitability.

In dysfunctional wealthy families these problems are greatly intensified. Being raised by servants, especially when no close bond can be developed with a caring parental substitute, can cause severe developmental difficulties and chronic emotional deficits, loneliness, not knowing who one really is, and an inability to establish emotionally satisfying relationships (Vanderbilt).

4. **Pastoral Care.** Not much is written on pastoral care of the rich. This appears to be a puzzling omission. Many denominations and faith groups have wealthy members, and throughout its history the church has been the recipient of largesse from benefactors, as can be gleaned already from the letters of Paul (Meeks), and as can be seen in the many buildings and memorials of all kinds that bear their names. Granted that such contributions usually arise from mixed motivations, including needs for power and control and ostentation, these people must have had sufficiently close and meaningful relations with representatives of the church to want to contribute at all. There are many prosperous people who do not give ever or much and, if they do, not to a religious organization. One also has to assume that the clergy and laypersons involved in any contact or ministry with wealthy believers would be aware of their personal distresses and concerns. So the curious fact emerges that a whole group of Christians, namely, those who are rich, is and has been presumed to be insufficiently important or special to warrant study and description from the perspective of pastoral care.

Why is this? Four reasons suggest themselves. First, the strong emphasis in both the OT and NT on the dangers of hubris and the obvious temptation of the rich and powerful to imagine themselves above the created order and to regard fellow humans as lesser and exploitable. The ethical indignation of a prophet like Amos against those "who oppress the poor" and "crush the needy" (Amos 4:1) and the sobering admonition of Jesus that the little money the widow gave counts for more than the easy donations of those who are well-off (Lk. 21:1-4) are but two examples of many that could be used to illustrate this important theme. Jesus' humble birth, his ministry to the down and out, his insistence that "as you did it to the least of these my brethren, you did it to me" (Mt. 25:40), his self-definition as one who was anointed "to preach good news to the poor. . . . to proclaim release to the captives and recovery of sight to the blind, to set at liberty those who are oppressed" (Lk. 4:18), his repeated demonstration in parable after parable that the Kingdom of God manifests itself in the small and the commonplace, and his final rejection and execution by the religious and secular authorities of his time have not only powerfully shaped our understanding of the gospel and our practice of pastoral care, but have also introduced a suspicion against those with money, power, and authority. Our awareness of the degree to which the church has been coopted by national, economic, and ideological interests and thereby has colluded in political oppression and economic exploitation has been recently heightened by liberation movements of various kinds. This has only increased the tendency to think negatively about those with wealth and power, and positively about those who are poor and down and out.

A second reason has to do with issues of class and social status, and the conflict of allegiances which these can create in a person of faith. Most clergy in this country are middle-class people and upwardly mobile. With this goes an inevitable sensitivity to social class and status, and a usually unwitting subscription to the prevailing societal values. These values, among which the equation of goodness and wisdom with economic success is an influential one, are often in direct conflict with the Christian ethos. This results in much ambivalence. From the perspective of the gospel and the prevailing historic Judeo-Christian view, the rich and well-to-do are under suspicion. From the perspective of contemporary American culture they are looked up to and esteemed, for they embody the values our culture prizes: achievement, competition, and success. So it is difficult not to envy the rich for their wealth and position, even when one looks down on them for theological or ideological reasons.

Our own ambivalent feelings toward persons who are more wealthy, successful, or powerful than we are constitute a third reason why the needs of the rich have not been studied to any degree. It is difficult to see the distress in a person whom one looks up to, or fears, or takes an aversion to.

Finally, another reason why so little has been done to study the special distresses and concerns of wealthy persons is that the rich do not like to be the subject of any kind of investigation and know how to protect their privacy. The reasons for this neglect also suggest the difficulties faced when ministering to the rich.

First, it is much easier to be helpful to persons who are below one in class, status, emotional maturity, and education. Clergy are almost always parental children or caretakers in their families of origin and find it natural to take a parental position toward those in need. That is not easy to do in ministering to the rich. It is difficult to avoid strong transference reactions to those of wealth and higher social status, such as feeling envious and resentful, less able, vulnerable, childlike, incompetent, or overawed.

Second, the financial conditions of the church and its ministry being as unstable as they usually are, it is hard to minister without an ulterior motive to someone with money to give. This only serves to reinforce the distrust of the rich toward expressions of love and caring. Conversely, it can be equally difficult when a church becomes too dependent on the largesse of a wealthy church member, especially when it is necessary to go against the views of that parishioner. Third, it is easy to be drawn into a relationship with a needy rich person in which one begins to function as a personal caretaker or private chaplain, especially when the short-term rewards of such a ministry can be gratifying.

In summary, the peculiar dangers of ministering to the rich are twofold: the many strong unresolved conflicted feelings that can be activated in the pastor or counselor, and the pull to take either a covert one-down (childlike) or one-up (parental) position. Either of these will soon, or in the long run, derail efforts at helping. Only by being able to maintain explicit personal and professional boundaries, a sufficient sense of one's strengths and weaknesses, enough differentiation from one's family and culture of origin to have arrived at a point of acceptance of oneself, and a theology and psychology which seek the good and bad in everyone and which seek to understand all persons in their context, can

one hope to be of responsible help to the rich (Friedman). In that sense ministry to the wealthy can be a litmus test of one's readiness and maturity as a clergyperson to engage in responsible pastoral care to anyone.

Bibliography. R. Coles, *Privileged Ones* (1977). E. H. Friedman, *Generation to Generation* (1985). P. Fussell, *Class* (1984). W. A. Meeks, *The First Urban Christians* (1983). G. Vanderbilt, *Once Upon a Time* (1985).

A. J. VAN DEN BLINK

CULTURAL AND ETHNIC FACTORS IN PASTORAL CARE; LIFESTYLE ISSUES; PROPHETIC/PASTORAL TENSION IN MINISTRY; SOCIAL STATUS AND CLASS FACTORS; VIPs, PASTORAL CARE OF. *See also* POWER; SOCIAL JUSTICE ISSUES; SOCIOLOGY OF RELIGIOUS AND PASTORAL CARE. *Compare* EXPLOITATION/OPPRESSION; POOR PERSONS.

RIGHT BRAIN. *See* BRAIN RESEARCH.

RIGHTEOUSNESS/BEING RIGHT. Although frequently used in biblical and theological writing, the term *righteousness*, which describes the quality of being right and doing the right thing, is used infrequently in everyday speech. In fact, it is often used ironically or negatively, suggesting that a particular person's righteousness is more self-righteous than genuine. It is an important concept in pastoral care and counseling because it is so often used naively and defensively. A person who feels lonely, rejected, or shamed quite frequently defends himself or herself against those painful feelings by focusing attention upon what is "right" in a particular situation.

In contrast to this common understanding, in the OT righteousness is not "being right" according to an ethical, legal, or religious norm. It is, rather, the fulfillment of the demands of a relationship, whether that relationship is with other persons or with God. The covenant relationship was prior to all law and demands. Faith is the fulfillment of the relationship to Yahweh and, thereby, is righteousness. The righteous person is one who acts in love, which means maintaining of the covenant relationship (Pedersen). The concept has a similar meaning in the NT. Those acts which preserve a covenant relationship between God and human beings and between human beings are righteous, while those acts which break the relationship are unrighteous (Achtemeier).

A familiar experience in the pastoral care of a couple is hearing the "righteousness" of the spouses—how if only the other spouse had not done such and such everything would be all right and how the spouse who is telling the story has been terribly wronged. Persons who question a significant other's caring for them are quite likely to retreat into being right, dealing with their shame by searching for the other's guilt. Persons who see themselves as in the right, place whatever problems that exist outside themselves, blaming others for whatever has happened (Kaufman). Another expression of righteousness or being right is perfectionism, which, according to Karen Horney (1950), is less a claim of superiority than an effort to control one's life and find a way to deny the fact that life is not "fair."

The important thing for the pastor in his or her pastoral work is to be aware of the protective function of a person's claim of being right. Judged from some objective point of view the hurting person may indeed be right or righteous. The pastor may need to acknowledge that judgment or fact to herself or himself and to the counselee or parishioner, but at the same time be aware that this is not the main issue for pastoral care. The pastoral care of the "righteous" person involves being aware of the hurt, probably the shame, underneath the insistence upon being right and offering an empathic relationship in which the injured person can feel affirmed in spite of what has happened.

In the situation of a pastor's seeing both spouses at the same time, it is important that he or she hear and respond to the hurt expressed — probably in differing degrees — by each of the spouses and suspend all judgments of rightness. Because of the church's own shame and defensiveness about divorce, the pastor often has difficulty in not being a judge about who is the righteous party. Many denominations have in the past and, to some degree in the present, instructed their pastors to do just this. This makes it difficult for pastors to avoid the role of the judge in favor of the more important one of the pastor. Nevertheless, it is possible. Sometimes it is helpful for a pastor to say to a troubled couple that he or she recognizes the ultimate importance of being and knowing what is right, but that in the present conflict deciding who is right is considerably less important than dealing with the feelings that affect the concern for righteousness.

The defensive use of righteousness/being right is less obvious in the pastoral care or counseling of an individual, but it is quite often a part of the counseling relationship. Again, the most important thing is for the pastor not to be misled by the fact that being right *is* important, but it is not *most* important for a person who seems to need his or her righteousness. The "not good enough" mother may indeed have been wrong in what she did or did not do, but more important in the counseling relationship is the counselee's awareness of the hurt and moving on to find relationships, like the one with the pastor, which are good enough to affirm and sustain the counselee in living like an adult. He or she may find it helpful sometimes to confront the inadequate parent with some of his or her old disappointment, but not in an effort to seek justice. The pastor's most effective care is in supporting the parishioner in getting to know the parent as one adult relating realistically to another, not as an angry child seeking to right an old wrong.

Thus in pastoral care and counseling and in Scripture, one's righteousness or being right is more likely to be found in a dependable, covenant-like relationship than in a judgment of who is more right than another. A good pastor is more likely to be the one who can provide such a relationship than the one who most effectively discerns who is in the right.

Bibliography. P. J. Achtemeier, "Righteousness in the NT," *Interpreter's Dictionary of the Bible* (1962). K. Horney, *Neurosis and Human Growth* (1951). G. Kaufman, *Shame: The Power of Caring* (1980). J. Patton, *Is Human Forgiveness Possible?* (1985). J. Pedersen, *Israel: Its Life and Culture* (1926).

J. PATTON

CONSCIENCE; GRACE AND PASTORAL CARE; PRIDE AND HUMILITY (Moral Theology); SPECIALNESS, SENSE OF. *See also*

PERFECTIONISM; SCRUPULOSITY. *Compare* CHRISTIAN LIFE; RESPONSIBILITY/IRRESPONSIBILITY, PSYCHOLOGY OF.

RIOT. *See* DISASTER, PUBLIC.

RISK-TAKING. *See* COURAGE. *See also* COMPASSION; GAMBLING; SELF-DESTRUCTIVE BEHAVIOR.

RITE OF CHRISTIAN INITIATION OF ADULTS (RCIA). *See* BAPTISM AND CONFIRMATION; PASTORAL THEOLOGY, ROMAN CATHOLIC; VATICAN COUNCIL II.

RITES. *See* SACRAMENTS, ORDINANCES, AND RITES, TERMINOLOGY AND CONCEPTS OF.

RITES OF INITIATION AND PASSAGE. *See* RITUAL AND PASTORAL CARE. *See also* CULTURAL ANTHROPOLOGY OF RELIGION, DISCIPLINE OF; SOCIOLOGY OF RELIGIOUS AND PASTORAL CARE.

RITUAL AND PASTORAL CARE. *Rituals* are repeated, normative, symbolic, and functional behaviors often associated with religious expression. The technical and popular uses of related words are imprecise. *Rites* are formal, institutionally sanctioned, religious rituals, while *customs* are informal rituals associated with secular social experience. *Rites of passage* are informal but culturally recognized patterns through which the individual moves during stages of the life cycle. *Ritualizations* may be defined as informal rituals associated with secular individual experience.

Contemporary interest in ritual and pastoral care focuses on three fundamental questions: (1) How do ritual and pastoral care together participate in the larger dynamics of human society and religion? More specifically, how do ritual and pastoral care together contribute to cultural stability and change? (2) What is the relationship between ritual practices and modern, psychologically rational pastoral counseling? (3) What is the relation of ritual and pastoral care in promoting the health or pathology of individual experience?

1. The Relation of Ritual and Rational Methods of Care. Underlying the contemporary experience of tension between ritual and psychotherapeutic care — for example, between congregational or individual worship and therapeutic self-understanding—lie divergent social processes, the classic formulations of which were given by sociologists Max Weber and Emile Durkheim.

Durkheim (1915) describes how the rituals of primitive culture produce cohesion in the community, creating a moral order. He identifies the two distinguishing features of religion as rites and belief. Religious rites aim at helping individuals move from the profane to the sacred world. This movement is achieved by negative and positive "ritual attitudes." Negative rituals restrain ordinary activities such as physical contact, looks, words, and sexual activity, and prepare a person for the rite of initiation into the cult. Positive rituals, on the other hand, are the foundation of the great religious institutions of civilization. Positive rituals primarily center around a sacrificial meal, which signifies abundant food production. Rather than being an act of renunciation, the common sacrificial meal reinforces kinship among human beings and renews the natural kinship between humans and their god. The cycle of ritual feasts creates interdependence between the individual, society, and their god and provides the rhythm of social life.

In addition to rituals of sacrifice, "rites of imitation" solidify the community by creating identity between the members of the tribe and their god or totem animal. Rites of imitation impose an "invisible action over the mind." They become a source of social authority as they regulate social conformity. "Commemorative rites" create community by recollecting the past and making it present by dramatic representation. Commemoration "awakens certain ideas and sentiments which attach the present to the past or the individual to the group." "Piacular rites" are organized around sorrow. Rather than being focused on individual, spontaneous acts of mourning, piacular rites impose a moral duty on the community to mourn together, through which collective sentiments are renewed.

In some contrast to Durkheim, Weber (1922) noted an evolutionary process in the understanding of the ritual sacrifice. Beginning as a magical attempt to coerce the gods or to absorb their potencies, ritual sacrific gradually evolved into the communion of humanity with gods. The development of the moral order in religion depended not on ritual *per se* but on beliefs about ritual and on the rejection of ritual by the ethical prophets. Primitive rituals gave rise to an ever-broadening thinking about the god concept and about the relationship of the human and the divine. According to Weber, the initial meanings of ritual receded in light of this rationalization, giving way to a negation of ritual by the ethical prophets: the God of the Israelite prophets required not burnt offerings but obedience to the commandments. Thus an ethical type of congregational religion arose which created a moral power through preaching and rational pastoral care. Pastoral care, rather than priestly ritual, became the priests' real instrument of power. Priestly ritual reified social structure, but pastoral care as exercised by the ethical prophets enabled the restructuring of society. Thus, Durkheim and Weber demonstrate a clash between the power of ritual to create moral order in community and the power of pastoral care to create change.

In contemporary cultural anthropology Victor Turner (1969) offers an example of how ritual and pastoral care need not clash but stand in creative tension with one another. Ritual, Turner says, creates change within the community through "liminality" and "communitas," intense experiences of social intimacy which temporarily reverse social status and roles, reminding the exalted person of his or her bondedness to common humanity when he or she assumes the power of a higher status, for instance.

E. Norbeck (1961), like M. Gluckman (1962), identifies a relationship between social stability and change through "rites of rebellion." Rites of rebellion offer a contained, socially sanctioned opportunity for aggressive or hostile behavior. By providing a safe space for unacceptable behavior they stabilize those social orders which are unquestioned. In a social order such as ours which is questioned, however, no such rites exist. Rather, alternative, unsanctioned rituals arise and challenge the existing order, with the capacity to create social and cultural change.

2. Ritual, Health, and Illness. Does ritual express or contribute to pathology, or does it foster health, for example, by creating stability and identity throughout the life cycle? Sigmund Freud was perhaps the original advocate of the view that ritual acts express psychic processes that are either identical with or very close to pathological conflict. Connecting cultural and social experience to the family and the individual, Freud (1907, 1909, 1913) understood the religious ritual of sacrifice to be derived from the incest taboo and the Oedipus complex, the source of psychopathology for Freud. Their origins, he believed, lay in a violent family feud in which the patriarch of the primal horde was killed by his jealous sons so that they could have access to the horde's females. After killing the patriarch they ate him in order to absorb his powers, and protected themselves from being similarly killed by limiting sexual relations to those women outside the immediate family. In order to commemorate the "awful deed," ritual sacrifice arose as the foundation of religious ritual. Freud also noted that some individuals express the pathology of their personality through private ritualizations which are expressions of unresolved conflicts, principally obsessive-compulsive personality disorders. Ultimately, Freud believed that religion and ritual were expressions of cultural and individual pathology for which psychoanalysis sought to become the cure.

V. Gay's (1979) recent interpretation of Freud's 1907 essay on ritual provides a bridge from Freud to later psychoanalysts who suggest that religious ritual is ego-enhancing. Gay claims that Freud misinterpreted his own metapsychology when he disdained all religious ritual. Rather, Freud's 1907 essay implied that religious rituals are founded on the nonpathological defense of "suppression" rather than the frequently pathogenic defense of "repression," thus aiding intrapsychic balance by assisting the ego to suppress dangerous id impulses and further the cause of adaptation.

E. Erikson (1972) has emphasized the healthy aspects of ritual and ritualization, pointing to the relationship between ritual and play. Ritualization becomes "creative formalization which helps to avoid both impulsive excess and compulsive self-restriction, both social anomie and moralistic coercion." Ritualization helps the ego orient itself within the worldviews which compete within a culture. In psychopathology, ritualizations have fallen apart, leaving the individual isolated. Ego-enhancing ritualizations allow for a mutuality of recognition, the overcoming of ambivalence, the transcendence of separateness, and the affirmation of distinctiveness. The ritualizations of the individual correlate with the rituals of religious institutions by providing the individual and the community with "faith in a cosmic order, a sense of justice, a hierarchy of ideal and evil roles, the fundamentals of technology, and ideological perspectives." Erikson recognizes the pathological distortion of ritual which Freud discovered, but he emphasizes the connection between the healthy structuring of the individual and of culture through rituals and ritualizations, which Freud negated.

3. Religious Ritual and Contemporary Pastoral Care. The clinical pastoral care and counseling movement of the later twentieth century arose out of the critique of mass culture (Holifield, 1983). As interest in pastoral care and counseling proliferated, and as counter-cultural criticism yielded the disdain of social institutions of the 1960s, many churches became skeptical of traditional ritual practices.

The countercultural critics of the 1960s developed hierarchy and formalism and emphasized equality and inclusiveness. These changes brought new trends in ceremony and ritual. Feminists challenged the hierarchy and formalism of patriarchy and popularized gender- and image-inclusive language. Their concern for inclusive language in worship resounds with Durkheim's assumption that ritual exercises invisible action over the mind. Laity demanded that their ministry be valued equally with the ministry of the clergy. Just as Luther's protest against the Vatican's abuses of ritual power initiated the modern meshing of the sacred and profane realms, the present emphasis on the ministry of the laity further obscures those neat distinctions, creating renewed discussion of the meaning and practices of baptism, Eucharist, and ordination. Blacks reclaimed African rituals and brought the music of slavery and oppression into liturgical renewal. After Vatican II Roman Catholicism introduced the vernacular Mass and communion in two kinds, significant signs of the permanent modernization of religious ritual. The movement from deconstructing some values through the denial of ritual to the restructuring of culture by incorporating new values into ritual life recalls Weber's observation that a prophetic message must be "routinized," or incorporated into the orthodox life of the church, for permanent change to occur.

Alternative rituals which have rarely been routinized by religious institutions, eg., the merger of African naming rituals with Christian baptism, covenant ceremonies for homosexual couples, or overt politicizing of ritual in base Christian communities, are forms of "rituals of rebellion." Such rituals function simultaneously as expressions of aggression against the ruling social order, and /or as transformations of aggression into identity and integrity within a marginalized space at the edge of the social order, and /or as syncretic merger of cultural and religious rituals through which one claims plural identities.

Substantial changes in family structure have created renewed debate over the rituals of the life cycle, particularly the rituals which solidify adult commitments like marriage in a changing culture — adult commitments which were once considered permanent but now, at least in practice, are no longer irrevocable. Turner helps us understand how rituals have moved persons from a status the community has accepted as lower to one the community deems higher. Attempts to incorporate in ritual the reversal of that process, eg., releasing persons from marriage or religious vows, have floundered. Instead, the reversal of that process most often involves formal or informal shunning, banning, or exiling, as in the case of laicized priests or divorced pastors. The successful reentry into the community by persons formerly married or formerly ordained occurs most often through the process of rational (i.e., psychological) pastoral care and counseling.

At best, psychological pastoral care and counseling and ritual practices remain in creative tension with one another, holding together mind and body, word and

action, logic and drama. E. Ramshaw (1987) suggests that both attend to the intrapsychic need for holding together ambivalent emotions. Together they provide nurture and signification for the passage through the stages of the life cycle, and locate people in social institutions and in culture.

In terms of pastoral practice, this means that ritual will continue to have a significant pastoral role to play in individual pastoral care, especially at the crisis and transition points of life like illness, accident, death, marriage, and birth. And rituals, formal and informal, will continue to be essential components in the life of communities of faith where they both express and form common vision, uniting individual and community, and nourishing individuals through their common life. The wise and caring pastor therefore is one who can discern when creative ritualizing is pastorally appropriate for individuals and for communities, when more rationally oriented forms of care are indicated, and how the two can be most artfully and gracefully combined.

Bibliography. W. Clebsch and C. Jaekle, *Pastoral Care in Historical Perspective* (1964). R. Duffy, *On Becoming A Catholic: The Challenge of Christian Initiation* (1984). E. Durkheim, *The Elementary Forms of the Religious Life* (1915). E. Erikson, *Toys and Reasons: Stages in the Ritualization of Experience* (1972). R. Fenn, "Recent Studies of Church Decline: The Eclipse of Ritual," *Religious Studies Review*, 8 (1982), 124–28. S. Freud, "Obsessive Actions and Religious Practices," *SE* 9 (1907); "Notes Upon a Case of Obsessional Neurosis," *SE* 10 (1909); *Totem and Taboo* (1913). V. Gay, *Freud on Ritual: Reconstruction and Critique* (1979). M. Gluckman, *Essays on the Ritual of Social Relations* (1962). E. B. Holifield, *A History of Pastoral Care in America* (1983). K. R. Mitchell, "Ritual in Pastoral Care," *J. of Pastoral Care*, 43 (1989), 68–77. E. Norbeck, *Religion in Primitive Society* (1961). E. Ramshaw, *Ritual and Pastoral Care* (1987). R. R. Ruether, *Women-Church* (1985). V. Turner, *The Ritual Process* (1969). United Methodist Church, *Ritual in a New Day* (1976). M. Weber, *Sociology of Religion* (1922).

P. COUTURE

ANOINTING OF THE SICK, SACRAMENT OF; BAPTISM AND CONFIRMATION; BLESSING AND BENEDICTION; COMMUNION (EUCHARIST); JEWISH HOLY DAYS AND FESTIVALS; LITURGICAL CALENDAR; PENANCE, SACRAMENT OF; PRAYER IN PASTORAL CARE; SACRAMENTAL THEOLOGY AND PASTORAL CARE; SOCIOLOGY OF RELIGIOUS AND PASTORAL CARE; WORSHIP AND CELEBRATION. *See also* COMMUNITY, FELLOWSHIP, AND CARE; CONGREGATION, PASTORAL CARE OF; JEWISH CARE AND COUNSELING; LIFE CYCLE THEORY AND PASTORAL CARE; LITURGICAL CHANGE AND REFORM; MOURNING CUSTOMS AND RITUALS; OLD TESTAMENT AND APOCRYPHA, TRADITIONS AND THEOLOGY OF CARE IN; PASTORAL CARE; REST AND RENEWAL, RELIGIOUS TRADITIONS OF; SOCIOLOGY OF RELIGION. *Compare* SYMBOLISM/SYMBOLIZING; TRADITION AS MODE OF CARE.

ROBERTS, DAVID E. (1911–55). Professor of systematic theology and of the philosophy of religion at Union Theological Seminary (New York). As a Presbyterian minister, Roberts sought ways in which psychological understanding could deepen theological doctrine. His participation in the Columbia University seminar on religion and health provided insights that appeared in his influential and widely read *Psychotherapy and a Christian View of Man* (1951). He was also active in the movement for clinical pastoral training and served on the Commission on Religion and Health of the National Council of Churches.

E. B. HOLIFIELD

PASTORAL THEOLOGY, PROTESTANT; PSYCHOLOGY IN AMERICAN RELIGION; RELIGION AND PSYCHOTHERAPY *or* THEOLOGY. *See also* NEW YORK PSYCHOLOGY GROUP.

ROGERIAN COUNSELING. *See* CLIENT-CENTERED THERAPY.

ROGERS, CARL R. (1902–). American psychologist. Rogers formulated the theories of client-centered counseling that dominated the American pastoral care movement for roughly two decades. His *Counseling and Psychotherapy* (1942) became a standard text among Clinical Pastoral Education (CPE) groups and in Protestant theological seminaries. His was the first systematic theory of psychotherapy that attracted widespread support among the liberal Protestant clergy.

Rogers had studied briefly at Union Theological Seminary in New York, where Harrison Elliott and others introduced him to theories of counseling. He left Union, however, to study clinical psychology at Columbia Teacher's College. But it was his work at a children's clinic in Rochester, New York, which convinced him that a supportive environment could release an inner "drive to health" and that any "coercive" relationship in counseling was never more than superficially effective. By the time he moved to Ohio State, where he published *Counseling and Psychotherapy,* he had decided that the counselor's "acceptance" of the client's impulses provided the setting for self-acceptance and growth.

Rogers believed at the time that the counselor was to respond not so much to the substance of what the client said as to the feelings that the client expressed. He hoped therefore that a "non-directive" form of counseling would enable the client to achieve an insight that would issue in growth. Part of the appeal of his program was his seeming success in presenting scientific evidence that the counselor's acceptance of unacceptable impulses in persons seeking aid would open the way to their self-acceptance and self-realization.

By 1951 Rogers was arguing that even the explicit clarification of feelings in counseling implied a subtle imposition on the autonomy of the client, and he urged that the counselor simply try to adopt the client's "frame of reference" through an attitude of "empathy." In his *Client-Centered Therapy* (1951) Rogers spoke of client-centered rather than of nondirective counseling, signaling the change from a preoccupation with a "method" to an interest in a warm personal relationship. The counselor was to mirror the feelings of the client, thereby helping the client achieve self-understanding and self-acceptance on the client's own terms.

Rogerian ideas began to influence pastoral counseling especially after the publication in 1949 of Seward Hiltner's *Pastoral Counseling.* Hiltner had developed his own ideas of "eductive counseling" independently of Rogers, but both men discouraged advice-giving and exhortation by counselors, and Hiltner's extensive footnotes provided a brief introduction to Rogers's theories. Carroll Wise further popularized the Rogerian style in

his textbook on *Pastoral Counseling* in 1951, and Paul Johnson based much of his *Psychology of Pastoral Care* (1953) on Rogers's *Client-Centered Therapy.*

By the 1960s, when Rogers became widely admired as a founder of humanistic psychology, the pastoral writers were becoming increasingly critical, especially of what they now viewed as Rogers's excessively individualistic conception of growth. A new interest in the interpersonal and theological context of growth within specific traditions and communities led to a growing inclination to push beyond Rogers, though without adopting coercive and moralistic alternatives.

E. B. HOLIFIELD

CLIENT-CENTERED THERAPY; HUMANISTIC PSYCHOLOGY; PASTORAL CARE MOVEMENT; PASTORAL COUNSELING MOVEMENT; SELF PSYCHOLOGIES.

ROGERS, CLEMENT. *See* PASTORAL THEOLOGY, PROTESTANT.

ROLE, MINISTERIAL. The concept of *role*, as used here regarding the ordained minister, is a construct referring to the expectations concerning attitudes, knowledge, emotions, and behavior appropriate to a socially recognized position. These expectations are held by others in reciprocal positions and also by the individual incumbent of the position. Individuals engage in roles by acting in accord with their understanding of the role expectations. Some roles are only minimally defined in terms of expectations; others, such as the role(s) of the ordained minister, are well defined and institutionalized. Actual definition of the ministerial role varies in content and degree of institutionalization in different historical periods and among different religious traditions.

Role and the self should be distinguished. Most selves occupy a number of social positions at any given time and throughout their life span. In so doing they engage in multiple roles.

This article focuses on the ministerial role in parish ministry. Nonparish ministerial roles that have emerged in modern times, for example, teaching roles and institutional chaplaincies, have their own peculiar histories and role dynamics that lie beyond the scope of this article.

1. Historical Development of the Ministerial Role. In the earliest NT documents, ministry was not a specialized position or role, but rather the service of God and neighbor to which all Christians were called. The entire Christian community had a priestly ministry (I Pet. 1:5). As the churches grew in size and complexity, distinctive leadership functions emerged and were institutionalized into positions and roles—for example, bishops, assisted by presbyters and deacons, became responsible for community building and presiding at the Eucharist. By the thirteenth century, the ordained clergy had become a priesthood, taking over the priestly role that had belonged to the community. Further, they were viewed as possessing a special sanctity that set them apart from laity in spiritual status.

The Reformers' teachings about ministry, and more recently those of Vatican II, reduced the distinctions between clergy and laity and reemphasized the clergy's community-building roles—preaching, teaching, and pastoral care. Nevertheless, with few exceptions, formal ministerial roles continue to be recognized as necessary for the church's functioning.

From the mid-nineteenth century on, especially within Protestantism, ordained ministry became professionalized in the peculiarly modern sense of the word, implying expertise based on scientific knowledge and norms. Theological education incorporated the historical-critical approach to Scripture and social science and management theory were applied to parish and community life and pastoral counseling based on psychological and psychoanalytic theory. Ministers became a self-conscious occupational group, and their expertise set them apart from laity, much as had the earlier emphasis on their special sanctity.

Concomitant with professionalization has been a narrowing of the scope of clergy roles. Rather than functioning broadly within society in representative roles, clergy have come to define their roles—and to have their roles defined by laity—in terms of more specifically religious tasks within the congregation. Ministerial roles in predominantly black churches are an exception to this general narrowing of scope.

2. Contemporary Ministerial Role Analysis. *a. Types of clergy roles*. Since the 1950s, numerous social scientific studies of ordained ministry have been undertaken, many of them indebted to the work of S. W. Blizzard, who identified three categories of roles among Protestant parish ministers. First are the "practitioner roles"—for example, administrator, organizer, pastor, preacher, priest, and teacher—which describe the means by which ministers accomplish their goals and indicate the categories of work across which they apportion their time. There are also "integrating roles," defining the ends toward which ministers work in practitioner roles in professional relationships with parishioners and others. Integrating roles may be traditional in character, such as believer-saint, evangelist, father-shepherd; or they may be contemporary, such as parish promoter, community problem solver, or church politician. Finally, there is the minister's "master role," the image by which a minister conceives of the ministry as an occupation distinguishable from other occupations. Some ministers describe their master role ideologically, such as mediator or servant of God; others do so functionally in service oriented or inspira- tional images. The importance of Blizzard's work is in providing ministers and others with analytical tools for examining and reflecting on everyday dynamics of ministerial practice. Additionally, the degree of integration between the three types of roles in any minister's experience, and the relative agreement between a minister's definition of her or his role and that of laity, are significant issues in the study of ministerial role conflicts.

b. Role conflicts of ministers. The role concept is useful in illumining various conflict experiences of ministers and churches. By viewing conflicts in terms of roles (which, as noted, are not identical to the self), the tendency to overpersonalize some conflict situations may be reduced. Furthermore, understanding and management of the conflicts may be facilitated. Several types of role conflicts may be noted.

i. Conflicts among several roles associated with a single position. Blizzard's research showed how the actual time allocated to the various practitioner roles by ministers conflicted sharply with their sense of the normative importance of the roles and their enjoyment of them. The administrator role took the majority of time but was rated least important normatively and in enjoyment.

ii. Conflict built into the normative expectations for a single role. The role of minister may carry with it seemingly contradictory expectations that create difficulties for ministers and parishioners. For example, ministers are counseled to treat parishioners according to universalistic criteria ("don't play favorites") and standards of affective neutrality ("don't become emotionally involved with parishioners"). At the same time, however, they are expected to be sensitive, warm, compassionate, and caring in interpersonal relationships with parishioners.

iii. Lack of consensus among relevant others regarding role expectations. Sometimes ministers and those in reciprocal roles lack consensus regarding appropriate ministerial behavior. The minister may act in one way—for example, taking a controversial stand on an issue of social injustice—in opposition to lay members' expectations regarding appropriate behavior (although it would be wrong always to assume a consensus among laity about expectations for their minister). Furthermore, there are others, in addition to lay members, in reciprocal role relations with clergy—for example, denominational officials, family or other clergy—who may hold differing expectations for the ministerial role. Ministers may, therefore, be caught in contradictory expectations about their role, including their own normative beliefs about appropriate behavior, the expectations of diverse groups of lay members, and those of other significant individuals or groups. This problem was dramatically illustrated in a classic study by Campbell and Pettigrew, who used ministers' responses to these conflicting "reference groups" in analyzing the actions of ministers during the Little Rock racial crisis.

iv. Conflicts from involvement in multiple positions. Individual clergy not only function in the position of minister, they also are incumbents of other positions—for example, as spouse, parent, citizen, or, in the case of military chaplains, as military officers. Individuals may experience conflicting role expectations for these various positions. Conflict may come over time allocation, as in the case of demands of parenting versus parish responsibilities, or in the difficulty of separating one's behavior as citizen from that of a congregation's pastor; or, in the case of the military chaplain, in separating values and behaviors related to ministry from those expected of a military officer. Various strategies for managing these conflicts are possible, including establishing priorities among roles, role compartmentalization, eliminating conflicting roles, rationalization, or denial.

c. Roles and identity. While self and role are not identical, important roles often shape an individual's sense of identity or self-definition in all aspects of life. People "become" their roles as they deeply internalize the attributes, attitudes, emotions, and behaviors expected of the role. Ordained ministers are no exception. Ministerial and personal identity are often merged. Indeed this is one of the functions of socialization into the ministry.

On the one hand, such internalization has its liabilities. Ministers come to act in stereotypical ways and are treated stereotypically by others. This reflects what sometimes has been called "bad faith," that is, the denial of the reality of one's self apart from one's roles, as well as the inability to see possibilities for change. Persons who leave the ministry frequently have great difficulty separating their identity from the ministerial role. On the other hand, deep internalization of the ministerial role is salutory, not only for facilitating predictable role behavior, but more important for developing lasting commitment to the role—precisely because it makes leaving difficult. Those who provide counsel and support systems for ministers need to be aware of both the liabilities and assets of the tendency to merge the ministerial role and identity.

Bibliography. S. W. Blizzard, "The Minister's Dilemma," *Christian Century*, 73 (1956), 508–10; "The Protestant Parish Minister's Integrating Roles," *Religious Education*, 53 (1958), 374–80; "The Parish Minister's Self-Image of His Master Role," *Pastoral Psychology*, 9(89) (1958), 25–32. D. P. Boyd, "Stress Diagnosis and Clerical Careers," *J. of Pastoral Counseling*, 17 (1982), 61–68. W. Burchard, "Role Conflicts of Military Chaplains," *American Sociological Review*, 19 (1954), 528–35. E. Campbell and T. Pettigrew, *Christians in Racial Crisis* (1959). B. Cooke, *Ministry to Word and Sacrament* (1976). N. Gross *et al.*, *Explorations in Role Analysis* (1958). G. Jud *et al.*, *Ex-Pastors* (1970). E. Mills, ed., "Role Conflicts Among Clergy," *Ministry Studies*, 2(34) (1968). H. R. Niebuhr and D. D. Williams, eds., *The Ministry in Historical Perspectives* (1956). A. Russell, *The Clerical Profession* (1980). R. Schoenherr and A. Greeley, "Role Commitment Processes and the American Catholic Priesthood," *American Sociological Review*, 39 (1974), 407–26. D. Scott, *From Office to Profession* (1978).

J. CARROLL

MINISTRY; PASTOR (Definition and Functions); SOCIOLOGY OF RELIGIOUS AND PASTORAL CARE. *See also* ECCLESIOLOGY AND PASTORAL CARE; PASTOR (Normative and Traditional Images); PASTOR (Popular Stereotypes and Caricatures); PERSONHOOD OF THE PASTOR, SIGNIFICANCE OF. *Compare* RABBI/RABBINATE.

ROLE CONFLICT IN MINISTRY. *See* ROLE, MINISTERIAL; PROPHETIC/PASTORAL TENSION IN MINISTRY.

ROLE PLAY. Role play has its roots in psychodrama which was created by Jacob Moreno in 1925 for use in group therapy. Psychodrama would have remained just another attempt to increase personal insight if it were not for the contributions of assertion training and behavior therapy. In comparison to psychodrama, behavioral role play is less formal (no requirement for a stage or specially trained people) and more structured (specific personal and interpersonal behaviors are taught).

Contemporary role play is more concerned with teaching than insight. It is a technique used to show people how to change self-defeating behaviors and how to learn more adaptive behaviors. It has also moved out from the clinical domain into educational and industrial settings. For example, it is used extensively in management training and teaching children to improve their social skills.

Role play is used with people other than just psychiatric inpatients. It can be a valuable tool for family and couple counseling both diagnostically as well as thera-peutically. Retarded people have gained valuable personal and social skills through the use of role play. The therapist in private practice can also use this technique for teaching a client how to be more assertive. The immediacy of the counseling context is a constructive source of feedback and learning for the client.

Role play has a wide range of applications. It can be used for teaching social and personal skills, conflict management, vocational skills, communication skills, basic living skills for the handicapped, and anxiety reduction. Role play has even been used to teach young children how to deal with potential child molesters.

Experience has shown that effective role play follows a basic set of guidelines. The first step is to clearly identify the target skill. The counselor can utilize a behavior inventory to help facilitate this process. Target behaviors are then divided into small steps through a task analysis.

Second, the skill must be modeled for the client. It is important that the modeled behavior be suitable for the behavioral level of the client. The more realistic the situational aspects of the modeling, the more effective it will be.

Next, the counselor needs to give instructions for the new behavior in terms the client can understand. Each step must be spelled out and verified for client understanding. As the client begins each step, verbal and behavioral prompting can enhance the learning process.

Reinforcement for successfully completing each step is crucial. As each substep in the behavior becomes learned, the prompting should be faded so that the natural environment will begin to cue the behavior. The final stage of role play is to assign homework for the client. In this way the new behavior can be practiced and mastered in the client's natural environment. The client needs to be encouraged to practice slowly and keep written records of progress and setbacks.

Bibliography. D. Bissett and C. Edgley, *Life as Theater: A Dramaturgical Sourcebook* (1974).

T. J. SANDBEK

TEACHING. *See also* ADJUNCTIVE THERAPIES; BEHAVIOR THERAPIES; GROUP COUNSELING AND PSYCHOTHERAPY. *Compare* CONSCIOUSNESS RAISING; HUMAN RELATIONS TRAINING.

ROLFING. *See* BODY THERAPIES; POPULAR THERAPEUTIC MOVEMENTS AND PSYCHOLOGIES.

ROMAN CATHOLIC PASTORAL CARE. The various ordained and nonordained ministries by which the church assists its members to continue to walk together in the way of conversion and to share in the work of the gospel. Although the classical *cura animarum* (the care of souls) usually referred to the sacramental ministry, pastoral care within the Roman church has historically been exercised in several areas: parish life, sacramental ministries, and various social ministries. Within the Roman Catholic tradition, it is necessary to discuss pastoral care against the background of ordained and nonordained ministries and their consequent complementarity and dissonance.

1. Teaching of Vatican II. Vatican II's teaching on pastoral care appears in several conciliar documents, either directly in treating the mission of the church or indirectly in its discussions on ministries. There is an underlying tension in these statements between ordained and nonordained ministries within the church. The ordained are reminded that Christ did not restrict "the entire saving mission of the Church toward the world" to them (*Lumen Gentium*, 30). As a result, there is "no member who does not have a part in the mission of the whole Body" (*Presbyterorum Ordinis*, 2). At the same time, the council reiterated the distinction between the general priesthood of the faithful and the ministerial priesthood (*Lumen Gentium*, 10).

The unique charism of the laity, according to the council, lies in "the distinctively secular quality" of their situation (*Apostolicam Actuositatem*, 29). When the wider mission of the church to the contemporary world is taken seriously (*Gaudium et Spes*), then the complementary ministries of all Christians are needed (*Lumen Gentium*, 32). These teachings reflect a compromise between a clericalized ecclesiology and a more scriptural approach to mission and ministry. The ultimate challenge of the council "of scrutinizing the signs of the times and interpreting them in the light of the Gospel" (*Gaudium et Spes*, 4) remains a normative guide to pastoral care.

The postconciliar effort to realize this broader ideal of pastoral care has had mixed success. Although there have always been nonordained ministries of pastoral care, the postconciliar sacramental reforms extended limited roles to the laity: lectors, lay preaching in some countries, eucharistic ministers, and the permanent diaconate. The active recruitment of the laity to work with religious communities in domestic and foreign missions has had some success. These modest advances, however, have been paralleled by a considerable diminution of priests and religious who have traditionally done a major part of the pastoral care within the Roman Catholic church.

2. **Parish Life.** Vatican II proposed the classical image of the parish as a center for priests and laity to work together, "bringing to the church community their own and the world's problems as well as questions concerning human salvation" (*Apostolicam Actuositatem*, 10). This ideal has been made difficult to realize within the rapidly changing sociology of local community. The parish is no longer the unique center of neighborhood activity which it was for ethnic immigrant Catholics in the early part of this century. The traditional devotional, counseling, and social life of parishes has been significantly affected by the work lives of commuting parishioners and by a sometimes hostile urban environment. The large size of many Catholic parishes with reduced parish staff as well as other complex sociological factors conspire to make pastoral care within traditional structures more challenging than ever before.

In response to this situation, there has been a trend toward shared ministries in several forms. Within traditional parish structures there has been an expansion of staff to include religious and lay people who have been professionally trained in religious education, theology, counseling, or other pastoral care skills to assume responsibility for certain areas of parish life usually reserved for priests. Parish councils, where they have been successfully implemented, have also shared some of the administrative tasks associated with pastoral care. The effect of

this expanded approach to ministry has been a revision, on the praxis level, of the parameters and style of pastoral care.

A second important development to meet the changing pastoral situation has been team ministry. The model was originally developed in post-war France in parishes such as St. Séverin in Paris. Although team ministry has been implemented as an organizational model in some places, the more authentic understanding is a core gospel community of ministers who invite commitment and service from the larger parish community. On a practical level, team ministry permits expanded pastoral care. On a theological level, the team models the very commitment which it attempts to engender in the larger community. According to the sparse testing that has been done on this model, there is a correlation between team effectiveness and ministerial effect.

Within the parameters of traditional pastoral care, there are two groups in the parish whose needs have received renewed attention. Youth has always been a particular concern of pastoral care. In the pre-Vatican II era this commitment was expressed by a strong emphasis on parochial education and the Catholic Youth Organization (CYO). Viewing the social unrest of youth in the sixties Vatican II described them as "rebels in distress" (*Gaudium et Spes*, 7) who have experienced "a complete change in the circumstances of their lives, their mental attitudes, and their relationships in their own families" (*Apostolicam Actuositatem*, 12).

The council drew a positive pastoral implication from this: contemporary youth has a greater responsibility for the active apostolate. Bishops were encouraged to take a more active and personal role in pastoral care of youth. Adults were urged to open a more sensitive dialogue with young people. In more dynamic parishes, response to the conciliar challenge has taken two forms. There has been a renewal of retreat models in the form of "search" or "discovery" weekends in which young people learn to reexamine their experience and its implicit values in the light of the gospel message. Second, in some parishes the pastoral care staff has been expanded to include a youth minister.

The pastoral care of the elderly has become a major concern of many parishes because of increased life expectancy and psychosocial factors that tend to isolate them from the rest of society. The social dimensions of the problem have been addressed more easily by pastoral care than the religious issues. While outreach services are a regular part of the pastoral care of the elderly in many parishes, their isolation from other age groups and the fear of growing old in a youth-oriented culture are not so easily solved. Eschatological issues are the ultimate concern of the elderly and one may doubt whether Roman Catholic pastoral care has adequately dealt with such issues.

Pastoral care has also been expanded to include groups that were formerly treated as marginal: the divorced and remarried, and unmarried young adults. With the revision of canonical praxis, there has been an effort to reexamine the situations of the divorced and, where no canonical solution is currently available, to explore the ways in which they might be still reinserted into the life of the church. Pastoral care of singles takes into account the difficulty of clarifying vocational ideals and choices in a society where professional and financial pressures are more intense and where a healthy affective life requires greater effort.

3. Sacramental Ministries. Within the Roman Catholic tradition sacramental ministries have always occupied a privileged place in pastoral care. In line with the classical image of Christ as *medicus* (doctor), the sacraments continue to be spoken of as *medicamenta* (medicine) in theological writing well into the medieval period. Vatican II reiterated the biblical reminder that liturgy presumes that participants "must be called to faith and conversion," (*Sacrosanctum Concilium*, 9) and that honest liturgical participation must be knowing, active, and fruitful (*ibid.*, 11). The pastoral importance of liturgy is described as "the outstanding means by which the faithful can express in their lives and manifest to others the mystery of Christ and the real nature of the true Church" (*ibid.*, 2). The post-conciliar reform of the liturgy was to concretize these pastoral ideals.

The norms for revision of the sacramental rites were pastorally motivated: restoration of the Word of God in sacramental celebrations, active participation of all, cultural adaptation, an intimate connection between ritual words and actions, simplicity, sensitivity to liturgical tradition and to the contemporary needs of the faithful (*ibid.*, 21–46). Externally the liturgical restoration has been generally successful within the limits set by the council. From the viewpoint of pastoral care, however, the more complex task within the intensely sacramental tradition is the liturgical internationality of ecclesial communities and individual participants. Liturgical intentionality refers to the operational motives and values that participants assign to their ritual activity. When liturgical intentionality is ignored in pastoral care, liturgical consumerism is always a danger.

A major pastoral innovation was the restoration of the catechumenal process (The Rite of Christian Initiation of Adults, 1988). The catechumenate is, in effect, an overall plan of pastoral action within a community since it ideally requires the involvement of the parish as well as a catechumenal team. The successful implementation of the process also entails a reassessment of pastoral commitments, priorities, and tasks within a community, and implies a model of continuing religious education for both candidates and baptized. Thus, a major task of pastoral care in the catechumenal context is the evocation of ecclesial responsibility of all Christians for the mission of the church. The sacrament of confirmation as reseen within the catechumenal model implies a pastoral reconsideration of how and when the appropriation of initiation by young people is achieved.

The restoration of the sacrament of penance and reconciliation has been pastorally the least successful. Penance in its various historical forms has always been considered a major task of pastoral care. Traditionally it provided the possibility for Christian self-awareness and some spiritual direction. The new ritual attempted to restore public celebrations of reconciliation at the same time that it allowed the penitent the option of face-to-face or anonymous confession. Some of the pastoral problems that have plagued the new forms of penance are the question of the use of general absolution without the confession of the particulars of serious sin, the effectiveness of some confessors in the new ritual forms, and a changing mentality

on the part of some Catholics on certain questions of conscience. The International Synod of Bishops in 1983 devoted itself to a reexamination of the pastoral implications of the current troubled praxis of penance.

Finally, the restoration of the anointing of the sick in both public and private celebrations has helped pastorally to interpret sickness within a Christian context and to make the ecclesial community aware of its responsibility to suffering humankind. The appointment of nonordained persons to visit the sick and to bring them the Eucharist has vividly concretized this responsibility.

4. Social Ministries. Historically pastoral care has always included the care of the sick and orphans, education, and the fostering of skills and crafts to assist people in their economic situation. These traditional pastoral ministries have become transformed with the professionalization of such skills. Since Vatican II many Roman Catholic pastoral ministers have been trained in the CPE model, and pastoral care has become a major component in the theoretical and practical training of seminarians.

Even before Vatican II pastoral counseling and psychology had received a more professional impetus from the writings of French priest psychologists such as R. Hostie, M. Oraison, and A. Godie, as well as that of J. R. Cavanagh and C. A. Curran in the U.S. In the sixties and seventies this trend continued with the work of C. Rogers and S. Hiltner exercising a wide influence among Roman Catholics.

Social justice issues also occupy an important place in current pastoral care. Under the leadership of the bishops, there has been a strong impetus to educate Catholics on the moral implications of nuclear defense, of consumerism, of the needs of the poor in an affluent society, and the worldwide problems of famine and disregard of human rights. These forms of pastoral care are among the most demanding because they have not been considered personal concerns in the traditional formation of many Catholics.

Bibliography. W. Abbott, ed., *The Documents of Vatican II* (1966). F. X. Arnold *et al.*, eds., *Handbuch der Pastoraltheologie* (1972). B. Cooke, *Ministry to Word and Sacraments* (1976). R. Duffy, *On Becoming a Catholic: The Challenge of Initiation* (1984). *A Roman Catholic Theology of Pastoral Care* (1983). E. Echlin, *The Deacon in the Church* (1971). A. Greeley *et al.*, *Parish, Priest and People* (1981). F. Klostermann, ed., *Lexikon der Pastoraltheologie* (1972). P. Murnion, *The Catholic Priest and the Changing Structure of Pastoral Ministry* (1978). D. Power, *Gifts that Differ: Lay Ministries Established and Unestablished* (1980). V. Schurr, "Pastoral Ministry," *Sacramentum Mundi*, 4 (1969), 359–64. H. Schuster, "Pastoral Theology," *Sacramentum Mundi*, 4 (1969), 365–68.

R. DUFFY

COUNSELING, ROMAN CATHOLIC; HISTORY OF ROMAN CATHOLIC PASTORAL CARE (Canada *or* United States); MINISTRY (Roman Catholic Tradition); PASTORAL CARE (History, Traditions, and Definitions); PASTORAL THEOLOGY, ROMAN CATHOLIC; THEOLOGICAL EDUCATION AND THE PASTORAL CARE MOVEMENT, ROMAN CATHOLIC; VATICAN COUNCIL II. *See also* CASUISTRY, ROMAN CATHOLIC; EARLY CHURCH, PASTORAL CARE AND COUNSELING IN; INCARNATIONAL THEOLOGY AND PASTORAL CARE (Roman Catholicism); MEDIEVAL CHURCH, PASTORAL CARE IN; RELIGIOUS, PASTORAL CARE OF; RETREATS (Roman Catholicism); SACRAMENTAL THEOLOGY AND PASTORAL CARE; SPIRITUAL DIRECTION; SPIRI-

TUAL THEOLOGY AND PASTORAL CARE. *Compare* CARE OF SOULS; CONGREGATION, PASTORAL CARE OF; ECCLESIOLOGY AND PASTORAL CARE; MORAL THEOLOGY AND PASTORAL CARE; SOCIAL JUSTICE ISSUES; TRADITION AS MODE OF CARE.

RORSHACH INK BLOT TEST. *See* EVALUATION AND DIAGNOSIS, PSYCHOLOGICAL.

ROSH HASHANAH. *See* JEWISH HOLY DAYS AND FESTIVALS.

ROSARY. *See* LITURGICAL AND DEVOTIONAL LIFE, ROMAN CATHOLIC.

RULE. *See* OBEDIENCE (Roman Catholicism); RELIGIOUS, PASTORAL CARE OF; RELIGIOUS LIFE (VOWED LIFE). *See also* BENEDICTINE SPIRITUALITY.

RUNAWAYS. Minors who leave home without parental permission, often judged by the courts to be guilty of a status offense, i.e., an offense (like truancy) applicable only to minors.

The National Program Inspection Report conservatively estimates that 1.3 to 2 million youth run away from home each year. One would reach a more accurate picture by multiplying those figures by four and realizing that many "missing" children in reality have run away from home in response to situations and forces they feel powerless to affect.

1. **Demographic Picture of Runaways.** Runaways are extremely vulnerable to victimization on many levels. It appears that a high percentage of runaways, particularly girls, have histories of physical or sexual abuse at home. A high proportion come from families below the poverty line, many from single-parent homes. Many report regular use of alcohol or drugs and come from families where substance abuse is a problem. Large numbers have attempted suicide. On the streets, runaways are prime targets for prostitution (male and female), health problems, legal troubles, and addiction. In response to concern over victimization of the increasing number of runaway youth, Congress passed the Runaway and Homeless Youth Act of 1974.

The courts and families often view running away as a control issue. A family systems perspective, however, suggests that running away is the flight of a powerless person. Perhaps half the runaways leave home because of long-standing family problems often related to divorce, new parent figures, new foster family placements, or some other family realignment. In light of frequent victimization by their families, running away can seem an eminently sane response. One can also see it as response to typical ambivalence over how to respond to family and life pressures within bounds of the adolescent's decreased dependence on parents and family.

2. **Opportunities for Care and Prevention.** Running away implies the absence of nurturing structures in society. With significant changes in the past decades in family and neighborhood school structures, few places provide adolescents a strong mooring. The vacuum of available support systems presents a rich opportunity for effective pastoral care. First, pastors can listen to the runaway's story and take it seriously, insisting on investigation of alleged physical or sexual abuse, and querying about drug or alcohol abuse by both the runaway and the parent(s). Second, unless adolescence is their area of expertise, pastors can refer the runaway to a local runaway shelter, if one is available, or encourage reconnection with the parents, seeking to refer all for family therapy. Third, pastors can seek to make churches and synagogues places of alternative activities and forums for expression and listening. Pastoral leadership can help make the faith community a place of stability where taboos are lifted from discussion of sexuality, abuse, and addiction, and where alternative behaviors can replace the dangers of running away.

Bibliography. C. Chapman, *America's Runaways* (1975). L. Schaffer and K. Meyne, "Youth on the Run," *Engage/Social Action*, 13 (September 1985), 10–15. R. J. Stout, "Homes for the Unwanted," *Christian Century*, 94 (September 28, 1977), 849–50.

G. A. VOGELPOHL

ADOLESCENTS; CHILDREN; FAMILY. *See also* ADVOCACY; ALIENATION/ESTRANGEMENT; FAMILY LAW; FAMILY THEORY AND THERAPY; FAMILY VIOLENCE; SOCIAL SERVICES AND PASTORAL CARE. *Compare* JUVENILE CRIME AND DELINQUENCY; LONELINESS AND ISOLATION; POOR PERSONS; SOCIAL JUSTICE ISSUES.

RUSSIAN ORTHODOXY. *See* MINISTRY AND PASTORAL CARE (Orthodox Tradition).

S

SABBATH. *See* Jewish Holy Days and Festivals. *See also* Rest and Renewal, Religious Traditions of.

SACRAMENT OF RECONCILIATION. *See* Penance, Sacrament of.

SACRAMENT OF REPENTANCE. *See* Ministry and Pastoral Care (Orthodox Tradition).

SACRAMENTAL THEOLOGY AND PASTORAL CARE, ORTHODOX. The Orthodox church is a liturgical church *par excellence*. As such, it lives primarily through its liturgical and sacramental life and expresses itself through them. Quite naturally, sacramental and liturgical theology also have a central position in the church's theology as a whole. In fact, the very distinction made today between various aspects of theology, whether liturgical, systematic, pastoral, or biblical, is quite foreign to the Orthodox tradition.

The primary locus of the church's existence is the Sunday eucharistic assembly. Here all are united to form the Body of Christ. Here, in the *epiclesis,* the Holy Spirit is invoked upon the entire community. At the Eucharist, the local church is realized as the church universal; individual persons enter into communion with Christ, and thus with the church and with one another. Here individuals become what they are meant to be—divinized persons in communion with God and one another. All the other sacraments, baptism-chrismation, marriage, ordination, anointing, and repentance, reach their fulfillment in the Eucharist. From the Orthodox understanding and experience of the Eucharist flow its ecclesiology, pneumatology, and anthropology. This close connection has been amply demonstrated in the works of such major Orthodox theologians as N. Afanassiev, A. Schmemann, J. Meyendorff, and J. Zizioulas.

The very purpose of the church, then, is to restore the communion between God and humanity—a communion broken by sin and restored in Christ. Only within the church, and particularly within its sacramental life can this communion be fully established. Of course, the final realization will come only at the Parousia, but the church's sacraments are "windows" through which this communion can already be seen and experienced in the present. The Eucharist is *already* our sharing in the banquet of the Kingdom, in that joy which is yet to come.

In a very real sense for the Orthodox, therefore, the sacraments are the most perfect expression of the pastoral care of the church. In and through the sacraments, human existence is brought into contact with the divine and thus transcends its own, fallen nature. Through baptism, Christians are made members of the church, the redeemed People of God. In the Eucharist, this new, human nature is nurtured and realized. Through repentance/confession, the person who has succumbed to sin is readmitted into the communion of the church. Through anointing, the suffering of the sick is joined to the suffering of Christ on the cross—and is thus transformed from a defeat into victory.

Evidently, the life of the church is not limited simply to the sacraments. Rather, within the church, all life is transformed into "sacrament"—into a means of communion with God. The sacraments are signposts, which guide and provide reference points. Everything the church does must be consistent with them, and must be aimed at restoring the image of God within humanity.

All the various aspects of pastoral care, then, must be guided by these same criteria. The tools of modern science, psychology, and medicine may, and certainly should, be used, but only insofar as they do not contradict the model presented by this sacramental view of the church and of humanity. In particular, this implies the adoption of a *theocentric* anthropology, a view which contrasts sharply with modern society's prevalently secular, humanistic approach. The primary goal of pastoral care must be to reintegrate the person into communion with God, into the church, which is the body of Christ.

Bibliography. J. Meyendorff, *Byzantine Theology: Historical Trends and Doctrinal Themes* (1974). A. Schmemann, *For the Life of the World: Sacraments and Orthodoxy* (1973). J. Zizioulas, *Being as Communion* (1985).

P. MEYENDORFF

ORTHODOX MINISTRY AND PASTORAL CARE; PASTORAL CARE (History, Traditions, Definitions). *See also* COMMUNION (EUCHARIST). *Compare* TRADITION AS MODE OF CARE.

SACRAMENTAL THEOLOGY AND PASTORAL CARE, PROTESTANT.

In the celebration of the sacraments, the church intends both the adoration of God and the edification (upbuilding) and empowering of Christians. God acts in the sacraments as ecclesial instruments in gracious and efficacious ways to cleanse, nurture, heal, restore, and unite. For centuries, the Church's calling to pastoral care was exercised primarily through the sacraments.

Sadly, but perhaps understandably under the circumstances, the sacramental tradition of pastoral care was disrupted by the Reformation of the sixteenth century and only rediscovered among non-Roman Catholic western Christians in recent times. Prompting this disruption were the decay into which the sacramental system had fallen, the intense clericalization of the church's whole liturgical life, and the need for the restoration of liturgical preaching (seen by some as a "replacement" for sacramental practice) in order to instruct as well as edify the people. The rediscovery, on the other hand, of the legitimate relationship of pastoral care and the sacraments is due in large measure to increasingly strong ecumenical understanding and exchange, the recognition by the churches of a common liturgical heritage, the growing awareness of the powerful role played by ritual sign-acts in the life of humankind, and, more particularly, the role particular sign-acts (sacraments) play in the spiritual development and well-being of Christians.

To the extent that pastoral care is understood to be individual care, and to the extent that the meaning of pastoral care is captured in the older phrase, "the cure of souls," the most obvious locus for the coincidence of pastoral care and sacramental practice is the sacrament of penance (confession, reconciliation). The *Lutheran Book of Worship* (1978) and the Episcopal *Book of Common Prayer* (1979) contain rites for the reconciliation of penitents. In each case, although some measure of counseling might be associated with the event, the rite of reconciliation intends sacramental as well as therapeutic efficacy, the gracious accomplishment of forgiveness and reconciliation through absolution.

When pastoral care is given a broader, more obviously communal character, the relationship of pastoral care and the corporate liturgical sacraments is clearer. This is evident only if the sacraments are viewed as corporate ecclesial actions, actions whose proper theological setting is the church, yet whose effect is appropriated in specific and particular ways. The recovery of this connection, in turn, depends in large measure on our ability to understand and experience corporate sacramental actions as "personal" in an age which glories in the privatization of religious experience. Ironically, seeing the sacraments as occasions of pastoral care, moments in which God (through the church) acts faithfully to upbuild, sustain

and nurture, provides a basic enrichment of the notion of pastoral care itself.

For some, the rediscovery of the sacraments and Christian ritualization as healthful and health-giving dimensions of the Christian life is most likely to occur in the midst of the typically Protestant concern for education. Understood more as nurture or formation, and fashioned with regard to stages of psychological and spiritual development, the process of Christian religious education provides not only a continuum for growth in Christian life and responsibility, but also a series of moments which invite sacramental ritualization. Be they moments of initiation and growth (baptism/confirmation, adult affirmation of faith and commitment), moments of crisis (sickness), moments when new responsibilities are undertaken (marriage, ordination), moments for the acknowledgment of alienation and the need for restoration and forgiveness (reconciliation), or those regular moments when nourishment for the journey is needful (Eucharist), it is in each of these that one sees the theological convergence of pastoral care, Christian nurture and the sacramental life.

Bibliography. R. L. Browning and R. A. Reed, *The Sacraments in Religious Education and Liturgy* (1985). C. Hyde, *To Declare God's Forgiveness* (1984). R. Jensen, *Visible Words: The Interpretation and Practice of Christian Sacraments* (1978). J. T. McNeill, *A History of the Cure of Souls* (1977 [1951]). E. Ramshaw, *Ritual and Pastoral Care* (1987). J. Westerhoff and W. Willimon, *Liturgy and Learning through the Life Cycle* (1980). J. F. White, *Sacraments as God's Self-Giving* (1983). W. H. Willimon, *Worship as Pastoral Care* (1979). *Lutheran Book of Worship* (1978). *Book of Common Prayer* (1979).

W. S. ADAMS

MINISTRY, PROTESTANT; PASTORAL CARE (History, Traditions, Definitions). *See also* BAPTISM AND CONFIRMATION; COMMUNION (EUCHARIST); ECCLESIOLOGY AND PASTORAL CARE; LITURGICAL CHANGE AND REFORM (Pastoral Issues); RITUAL AND PASTORAL CARE; SYMBOLISM/SYMBOLIZING. *Compare* JEWISH HOLY DAYS AND FESTIVALS, PASTORAL DIMENSIONS OF; PASTORAL THEOLOGY, PROTESTANT.

SACRAMENTAL THEOLOGY AND PASTORAL CARE, ROMAN CATHOLIC.

Theology of Christian worship (also, liturgical theology) brought to bear on the care of individuals and of local communities. Understood variously in history as *mystery, sign, ordinance*, etc., sacrament is here understood as an action of the assembled church expressing and manifesting Christ's saving action (*Constitution on the Sacred Liturgy* p. 2), made effective by signifying Christ's meaning and intention for human life and relationship, thus serving to alter one's image of certain human situations, and one's affection and behavior toward those situations.

Sacraments can be grouped under three headings: *initiation* (baptism, confirmation, Eucharist), which provide resources for entrance into the church community, growth in Christian life, and approach to Christian death; *healing* (anointing and reconciliation), which guide a Christian response to human sickness and sinfulness; and *vocation* (marriage and ordination), which nurture human love, family, and ministry within the church community. Sacraments serve to identify Christ's meaning for these human realities, and to invite people to choose that meaning over other, less creative and nourishing meanings that are possible.

1. Principles. Vatican Council II identified several major principles to guide the practice of Christian sacraments. Sacraments are named liturgical actions in which full and active participation of all the people is of major importance (CSL, p. 14). The point of this participation is that, by actively engaging in the liturgical action, people can come to experience in their lives the saving action of Jesus Christ. Sacraments achieve this effect by signification, a process which is more than cognitive (CSL, p. 7). It allows the participants to "put on" for a moment the way of Jesus Christ, with the specific affections and behavior patterns (e.g., trust, caring, friendliness) which the way of Christ involves (CSL, p. 2).

2. Sacramental Ritual. The primary enactment of sacraments is their ritual expression. Each ritual includes as a necessary first ingredient the proclamation of the word, as it is only in response to, and under the influence of, the world proclaimed that the assembly is empowered to act. The response to the word, in each case, is a threefold movement that closely parallels the tryptich of rites of passage (separation, liminality, reaggregation). The human reality is placed with Christ in offering so that through God's Spirit it may be transformed into a reality that expresses and manifests God's active presence in Christ. All in the assembly receive back what was offered and consecrated, now possessed of the new meaning and power that the church's faith proclaims upon it.

The response of initiation is enacted in three sacraments: baptism (which places the person with Christ), confirmation or chrismation (which signs God's transforming consecration of that person), and Eucharist (which incorporates the newly initiated into Christ's table fellowship). It is this same initiation, continued and deepened throughout life in the Eucharist itself, that is the primary proclamation at the liturgy of Christian burial, and the primary resource to help Christians in the face of death. In the healing sacraments, sickness and sin are offered in the hope of healing, though this seldom involves removal of the sickness or the effects of sinful choices. The primary aim is to open up for all involved the life-giving possibilities in the negative, and to urge all to choose those life-giving possibilities. In the vocation sacraments, the human realities of love and service are entrusted to God's Spirit in order to allow the assembly to see God's love in human love, and receive God's service in human service. These sacraments also aim to instill a confident boldness in both love and service for those over whom the assembly prays.

3. Context for Their Enactment. Sacraments do not take place in isolation from life. At the heart of each sacrament is a life reality which is given new meaning, purpose, and status by the word proclaimed upon it. The transformation of that reality is always a gradual transformation. Ministry to the sacraments is, therefore, not restricted to liturgical ministry, but includes a variety of ministries within the life of the assembly. The context in which sacraments are enacted is all important for their effectiveness.

The primary context for Christian sacraments is the universal faith of the church and the living community of believers who, by their common life and worship, keep alive the *remembrance* of God's action in Christ. It is their rehearsal of God's commitment to bless, heal, and consecrate that enables individuals within the community to seek such blessing, healing, consecration. It is likewise their commitment to endorse and embody God's ways for each other that authenticates and completes what is enacted in the sacramental ritual (*Amen*).

The life process of individuals in the community is an equally important context for sacraments. The ritual gathers and seeks to deepen the faith convictions already present in the person (CSL, p. 59). Initiation sacraments, for example, properly occur when the catechumenate has brought the individual to an appropriate awareness of the power and summons of Christ's word. All other sacraments presume the growing conviction of God's faithfulness which is the primary fruit of ongoing initiation. Initiation trains one to live in faith, hope, and love with God and one's sisters and brothers. All sacraments tap and deepen that faith, hope, and love.

4. Pastoral Care *for* Sacraments. In preparation for the enactment of sacraments, ministers will serve well to help individuals identify and bring into focus the faith convictions they already have about the reality in question, be it sin, sickness, love, service, life, or death. Such is the purpose of the catechumenate for those preparing for initiation sacraments. Something parallel to the catechumenate is appropriate for both the healing and the vocation sacraments. More delicacy is of course required to present the life-giving possibilities in sin and sickness than in love and service. Identification with Christ is easier to name in the positive than in the negative. It is essential, however, in both.

The primary liturgical ministry is to embody for those ministered to the revealed affections of Jesus Christ. These include tenderness and compassion for the sick, forgiveness and understanding for the sinner, welcome to the newcomer, and a profound joy in the face of love and service. It also involves trust in the power of ritual and care in the ritual enactment. Sacramental ritual properly enacted allows people the freedom to meet their God and be drawn where God wills to draw them. It is a poetic rather than a didactic ministry, inviting not imposing.

5. Pastoral Care *Flowing from* Sacraments. Sacramental ministry does not stop when the ritual is concluded. The community continues as *the* sacramental reality. The sick need the continued support and witness of the community that enacted the anointing. Sinners need people to embody the proclaimed reconciliation, and to help undo the damages wrought by sinful choices and actions. Both married and ordained need continued support to help them grow in love and service. Pastoral care is needed to realize in life what is proclaimed by faith in sacrament.

Bibliography. W. Bausch, *A New Look at the Sacraments* (1983). B. Cooke, *Sacraments and Sacramentality* (1983). F. Eigo, ed., *The Sacraments: God's Love and Mercy Actualized* (1979). C. Gallagher, *The Marriage Encounter* (1975). B. Haring, *The Sacraments in a Secular Age* (1976). R. Hoeffner, "A Pastoral Evaluation of the Rite of Funerals," *Worship*, 55 (1981), 482–99. A. Kavanagh, *The Shape of Baptism* (1978). *New Catholic World*, (Jan. 1984), issue devoted to "Reconciliation." M. Searle, "New Tasks, New Methods: The Emergence of Pastoral Liturgical Studies," *Worship*, 57 (1983), 291–308. M. Taylor, ed., *The Sacraments: Readings in Contemporary Sacramental Theology* (1981). U.S. Catholic Conference, *Pastoral Care of the Sick* (1983). Vatican Council II, *Constitution on the Sacred Liturgy* (CSL) (1963).

P. E. FINK

LITURGICAL AND DEVOTIONAL LIFE, ROMAN CATHOLIC TRADITION OF; MINISTRY (Roman Catholicism); PASTORAL CARE (History, Traditions, Definitions); RITUAL AND PASTORAL CARE; ROMAN CATHOLIC PASTORAL CARE; VATICAN COUNCIL II AND PASTORAL CARE. *See also* INCARNATIONAL THEOLOGY AND PASTORAL CARE (Roman Catholicism); LITURGICAL CHANGE AND REFORM (Pastoral Issues); SPIRITUAL DISCIPLINE AND GROWTH; WORSHIP AND CELEBRATION. *Compare* ECCLESIOLOGY AND PASTORAL CARE; JEWISH HOLY DAYS AND FESTIVALS, PASTORAL DIMENSIONS OF; MORAL THEOLOGY AND PASTORAL CARE; PASTORAL THEOLOGY, ROMAN CATHOLIC; SPIRITUAL THEOLOGY AND PASTORAL CARE.

SACRAMENTS, ORDINANCES, AND RITES, TERMINOLOGY AND CONCEPTS OF.

Typically, *sacrament* is defined as an "outward and visible sign of an inward and spiritual grace." For Augustine, for instance, a sacrament is a sacred sign that represents what it signifies, e.g., bread and wine as body and blood. Thus a sacrament is a "visible form of an invisible grace" or, put more actively, an effective sign that causes what it signifies. For centuries, the sacraments have been the church's primary forms of pastoral care, and for much of Christianity today they remain the basis of its caring ministry.

The term *ordinance*, used by some free church traditions in place of the term *sacrament*, refers to institutions of the gospel relating to the worship of God, such as prayer, thanksgiving, and singing. *Rites*, in the broadest sense of the term, include the whole body of ceremonies, liturgies, and external signs and actions (such as laying on of hands) employed in a particular religious ceremony (such as baptism or the Eucharist).

The number of sacraments was not precisely defined until the late Middle Ages. Peter Lombard's twelfth-century list of seven (baptism, confirmation, Eucharist, penance, extreme unction, ordination, and marriage) did not include many other actions which at times were called sacraments. Lombard's list became dogma for Roman Catholics. Five of these seven were challenged by the Reformers on the grounds of insufficient scriptural evidence for any but baptism and the Eucharist. In fact, Quakers question the need of outward sacraments for truly spiritual worship. Recent theology is less concerned with rigid enumeration.

Scholastic theology developed precise sacramental terminology, some of which is considered irrelevant today. However, requisites for sacraments included: "matter" (objects such as water), "form" (words defining the action), and a designated "ministrant" with the proper "intention" of carrying out what the church effects.

Sacraments can be "valid" (if they fulfill all these requisites) or "invalid." But "efficacy" is a much more subjective quality. As a minimum, recipients must have the proper "disposition," i.e., they must not impose an "obstacle" to receive the designated grace. Sacraments are considered "regular" (legal, licit) if conducted according to church law; otherwise they still may be valid but irregular. The concept of *ex opere operato* refers to the doctrine that God works through the performance of the sacrament whose efficacy is not dependent on the celebrant. By contrast, "sacramentals" (such as prayers of

intercession) are pious acts of indeterminate number and *do* depend on the piety of the person performing them. Baptism, confirmation, and ordination impose an "indelible character" on the recipient and hence are not repeatable.

Recent sacramental theology bypasses many of these distinctions and places more emphasis on sacraments as signifying grace rather than causing it. Christ is seen as the primordial sacrament from whom the church's sacramentality derives. Christ acts in individual sacraments according to human stages of life and needs. Sacraments are often called "sign-acts" and recognized as Christ's love made visible. Accordingly, more concern is shown with the quality of celebration and the communal nature of these actions.

J. F. WHITE

ECCLESIOLOGY AND PASTORAL CARE; MINISTRY; SACRAMENTAL THEOLOGY.

SACRED AND PROFANE. *See* RELIGION; SECULARIZATION/SECULARISM; The HOLY.

SACRIFICE. The simple definition of "sacrifice" is the offering of anyting to a deity as a propitiation or homage. The word comes from *sacrificium*, which denotes a victim killed and consumed on an altar or at a sacred place. The object or animal is held to be *sacer* (holy).

1. Sacrifice in General. Sacrifice is the means by which one contacts the unseen and feared spirit world that influences everyday life in many ways. Sacrifice is virtually a universal phenomenon through which the two worlds are kept in balance. Reciprocity is a first law of sacrifice. The giving of something of value will be rewarded, in turn, by good from the god or gods. This voluntary gift of value will, however, obtain something of greater value. The sacrifice may be offered as a gift or for the purpose of atonement or communion. But the purpose of sacrifice is constant. It is an act that acknowledges humanity's dependence on the supernatural and assures continued benevolence. Sacrifices are offered in a variety of sacred places such as caves, trees, hills, and even water. With urbanization, the centers for sacrifice became located in temples, and altars in these temples were considered the actual dwelling of the gods. Open to personal and communal rituals, these temples provided regular nourishment and honor to the gods through sacrifice.

2. Sacrifice in Israel. In ancient Israel sacrifice fell into two broad classifications: (1) the covenant sacrifice, celebrated as a sacred meal, symbolized Jehovah as the Host while the head of the house and his family were the guests. Through the process of eating together the covenant bond between the people and their god was renewed. (2) The second was the redemption of tithe sacrifice whereby all natural goods, grains, or animals must symbolically be returned to God. The underlying principle of sacrificing the firstfruits or the firstlings of the flock was to remove the restrictions placed on the whole, all of which belongs to God. The remaining part was thereby redeemed for ordinary use. The person offering the redemption sacrifice was not allowed to eat any of the sacrifice itself. It was either burned completely on the altar, or a small portion was burned, and all that remained was given away. No wild animals, fruits, or grains could ever be used for sacrifice, since the principle of worth and personal cost to the sacrificer was always of highest importance.

3. Christian Sacrifice. The requirements of God's holiness contrasted to humanity's sinful nature required an offering after the model of the OT. Jesus personifies God's righteous servant being led to the slaughter as a sacrifice. In this way the most valuable gift God can give bears the sins of many (Isa. 53:7). Jesus' death, therefore, conforms to the Israelite prototypes. The universal adequacy of Christ as sacrifice is central to the Christian faith, both Catholic and Protestant. When Christians celebrate the Eucharist they confess together that there will never be another sacrifice for sin. The offering of greatest value has been given in the person of the divine servant of God.

This understanding of the Judeo-Christian tradition of sacrifice is helpful in pastoral care and counseling. The meaning of sacrifice might be considered an archetype in the Jungian sense. Persons dealing with idolatry or guilt over loss or broken relationships often need to find ways to atone; this often happens outside of the person's awareness. As in ancient Israel, the ritualization of this atonement involves giving up something of great personal value in order to gain the favor of God. A woman carrying guilt over the accidental death of a child may give up all pleasurable activities, for instance.

For Christians, the theological heresy in such acts is the inability to acknowledge the sacrifice of Christ as the ultimate atonement for sin. It is a form of pride to assume the role of God in prescribing one's own atonement. Part of the sin in this is the unwillingness to let go of that which cripples one in order to avoid responsibility. In such situations, the pastor steadfastly represents a gracious God who provides forgiveness through faith in the atoning Christ. The use of liturgy and the ritual of the sacraments can be a concrete reminder of the action of God's grace in one's life.

Bibliography. W. R. Smith, *The Religion of the Semites* 3d ed. (1927). G. B. Gray, *Sacrifice in the Old Testament* (1925). C. F. D. Moule, *The Sacrifice of Christ* (1956).

D. GILLILAND

CHRISTOLOGY AND PASTORAL CARE; COMMITMENT; GIVING AND RECEIVING; RELIGIOUS BEHAVIOR. *Compare* ASCETICAL PRACTICES; COMMUNION (EUCHARIST); GUILT; OLD TESTAMENT (Traditions and Theology of Care); SYMBOLISM/SYMBOLIZING.

SACRIFICIAL BEHAVIOR. Etymologically, sacrifice means "to do/make what is sacred," and contemporary usage retains metaphorical overtones of the original sacral meaning: sacrificial behavior involves the relinquishing or destroying of something of value to oneself or one's group in order to achieve or affirm a greater value.

This definition immediately suggests the problematical character of all sacrificial behavior, namely its deep moral and psychological ambiguity: value is destroyed for the sake of value. Perhaps for this reason psychological and social psychological analysis of sacrificial behavior discloses considerable complexity of meaning; the motivational and social dynamics are seldom as simple as they seem. For purposes of analysis, however, it is possible to distinguish two fundamental forms of sacrificial behav-

ior: sacrifice of another and sacrifice of self. In both instances, though especially with regard to sacrifice of self, the larger question arises whether any sacrificial behavior can be morally and motivationally authentic, that is, unconditioned by selfish or egoistic motives.

1. Sacrifice of Another. An unfortunately common form of sacrificial behavior is that which takes another as it object, as in scapegoating. Analysis of this kind of sacrificing almost always reveals elements of self-aggrandizement and is therefore to be understood, psychologically and theologically, as narcissistic and sinful. It is motivated essentially by concern for oneself. It also has elements of both aggression (or violence) and anger insofar as the sacrifice of others represents an attempt to assert or restore one's own autonomy, pride, and integrity by attacking others rather than oneself. In this kind of action anger and aggression become necessary for self-definition, and the act of violence toward another is an attempt to defend the attacker from a sense of vulnerability, pain, anxiety, or annihilation. Thus the sacrifice of others is an attempt to overcome what is perceived as evil or threatening in order to establish the victimizer's survival and/or superiority. Typically, it also requires the distancing and depersonalization of the other, as studies of the attitudes of soldiers toward their enemies or of criminals toward their victims have shown.

One common form of the sacrifice of others is scapegoating. Onto the scapegoat (a child, a spouse, a group, or a whole class of people) is projected the fault of many. A sense of exoneration is bought at the price of blaming the victim, trading ambiguity and shared guilt for a false but reassuring simplicity. Scapegoating, understood from the perspective of individual psychology, is usually understood as the product of projection. On the other hand, scapegoating can be understood systemically as the sacrificing of weaker members or a minority group for the sake of stronger members and/or the majority of a particular group. This becomes a pastoral concern in the guidance of groups and the counseling of families, requiring the pastor to look behind an easy solution to a problem in order to discern its true complexity.

While the sacrifice of another most often entails selfish or hostile motives or grows out of unresolved conflicts in family or group life, it is also important to consider the possibility that this form of sacrificial behavior may occur under certain circumstances without such morally disqualifying considerations. This can occur especially in situations where a leader or parent must make difficult decisions involving the welfare of others — individuals or groups — which may be in conflict with the welfare of the group as a whole or with ethical principles and values that are judged to be of superior worth. Decisions about stopping life-support systems for the terminally ill, abortion, disciplinary decisions concerning morally deviant individuals, and acts of sacrificial offering in worship all involve a significant element of presumably altruistic sacrifice. In specific cases one can never rule out the possibility of ignoble (perhaps unconscious) motivations or group pressures in such situations, but the possibility that such decisions may be reached with a minimum or absence of such forces must be considered seriously at least from a theoretical point of view. In such situations the sacrificial behavior would be judged as morally noble. To the extent that such decisions are forced by circumstance, they would appear to reveal an ultimately tragic conflict in values — that not all values can be actualized, and some must be sacrificed for the benefit of others who are somehow judged more worthy.

2. Sacrifice of Self. *a. Pathological dimensions.* The second form of sacrifice takes oneself as its object. This also can have considerable motivational ambiguity. Psychoanalytically understood, the motivation for self-sacrificial behavior can be self-seeking and manipulative. Self-sacrifice may also be hostile, involving internalized aggression and/or sublimated rage, as well as pride and idolatry or cowardice. Scapegoating oneself, for example, may be evidence of severe narcissistic injury that allows one to define oneself masochistically in terms of one's deficits. When displayed in a family or marriage context, such "martyring" behavior can be a strategic move to gain sympathy and passively dominate a situation, or it may betray a failure of nerve which signals one's inability to sustain a struggle. In this latter instance, a person may be experiencing a sense of despair or hopelessness, unable to imagine a positive or psychically livable future (as in suicide). While this may express an attempt to transform the situation, it is done at the cost of the objectification of the self (Lifton).

"Throwing oneself to the wolves" is either done quite publicly, in which case it is clearly self-aggrandizing, or it may be a well-intentioned but failing effort to solve a problem by allowing others to absolve themselves from any participation in it. In either case one has given oneself over for reasons that are either self-serving or delusory.

b. Ethnic, racial, and sexual dimensions. Where Christianity is the socially dominant religion, self-sacrifice is generally acknowledged as one of the highest virtues. In situations of systemic cultural oppression, however, this valuing of self-sacrifice can be used manipulatively to motivate sacrificial behavior and/or to justify and rationalize behavior that is required by the dominant group of those who are the victims of prejudice and exploitation. Within oppressed groups, those who are less powerful, e.g., women, racial minorities, and the poor, are doubly targets of this kind of manipulation, for both members of the socially dominant group and persons of their own group may demand self-sacrificing behavior of them.

As members both of a particular subgroup and of the larger society, persons of racial and ethnic minorities may be best understood as being bicultural. In societies which are hostile to certain subgroups, members of these groups tend to exhibit a kind of dual character formation in response to the prejudice and injustice of the larger society. Within one's own subculture, it is the essential and universally human aspirations, qualities and rights that inform one's positive, "transcendent" character. At the same time, a negative, "depreciated" character functions as a defense against the prejudices of the larger society by appearing to act out all those prejudices with a vengeance. The two sides of the character are to be understood as functioning together for the wholeness and well-being of the individual. The depreciated character is a positive adaptation in response to a hostile environment (Chestang). Thus, the depreciated character is to be distinguished from the masochistic personality in that it serves primarily to defend the transcendent character

from the assault of the larger society, rather than expressing the fundamental orientation of one's personality. The above has a direct impact on our understanding of ethnic and racial dimensions of self-sacrifice.

In contexts that are oppressive, a person of a racial or ethnic minority may be acting primarily out of such a depreciated character, in such a way that the transcendent character is protected and also served. In such a situation, self-sacrificing behavior may quite wittingly express hostility toward the oppressors as well as an affirmation of one's own inherent value and goodness. It seems to prove the superiority of the victim of injustice while at the same time giving evidence of the ignorance and moral corruption of the oppressor. This becomes a pastoral concern when a person appears to be acting more out of the depreciated than the transcendent character. Self-sacrificing behavior that expresses vengeance and vindication more than benevolence and virtue is evidence of the pain, distrust, and outrage that result from victimization. The same behavior that expresses superiority and pride more than generosity and free self-giving betrays an underlying sense of inferiority that may result from the internalization of the prejudices of the oppressing group.

This understanding of dual character formation may apply also in a general way to women, especially to the extent that a woman is conscious of the double standard of sexist society and is also assured of her own value as a human being. In addition to this, women face a more pervasive, psychological challenge.

Some theorists recognize that the conventional mode of moral reflection into which women are socialized in Western, Judeo-Christian culture is based on the sacrifice of women's autonomy and selfhood. While it may be an essential aspect of all care-giving to bracket one's own concerns in the interest of another's well-being, it is a precocious and immature form of self-sacrifice if a woman lacks true autonomy and adult identity.

This has psychological roots in the relationship of an infant with its primary caretaker, most often a woman. While boys early on experience themselves as different and separate from their mothers, thereby beginning to develop a sense of autonomy while they are very young, girls tend to experience themselves as similar to and connected with their mothers, developing a sense of identity based on relationship (Chodorow). Social conditioning, meanwhile, reinforces a man's sense of autonomy as he matures, while it frustrates a woman's later development of autonomy. Therefore, an "ethic of care" (Gilligan) may or may not be based on a mature sense of self-sacrifice, depending on a woman's sense of autonomy and identity.

The pastoral concern that is at stake here is the integrity and psychological maturity of women. A woman who is generous with her person, her time, and her resources, while at the same time appearing to be parasitically dependent for her sense of identity on those to whom she gives, may very well be self-sacrificing in a way that is immature and precocious. Rather than mocking or taking advantage of the conventional female "martyr," however, it is important to affirm her as an individual and support her developing sense of personal identity.

3. The Question of Genuine Sacrifice. While all sacrificial behavior is morally ambiguous and at least open to question psychologically, genuine self-sacrifice may be

a human possibility, assuming a high level of psychological and religious functioning (or, as in the case of inhabitual and heroic self-giving, a momentary transcendence). In such a case one would find deep, empathic identification with the needs of others and a willingness to place their needs before one's own, rather than a hidden agenda of self-aggrandizement or manipulation. A model for such behavior which transcends self-interest can be accounted for by reference to the transpersonal, to Christian *agape*. Unlike counterfeit or pathological forms of sacrificial behavior, this comes from a position of strength and not weakness; it is a matter of choice, not of self- or other-imposed necessity; it is in the service of truth and not of delusion; and it is an expression of free self-giving rather than compensation or compulsion. While in a logical sense it may be that no sacrificial behavior transcends the ambiguity of making the most effective choice as to goal and method (the real vs. the possible), in rare instances — a Schweitzer, a Mother Teresa, or an individual whose life is lost while saving another — sacrificial behavior can utterly transcend ordinary human motives. Certainly, for Christians, the life and death of Jesus is the supreme instance of mature self-sacrifice, simultaneously revealing sacrificial love or the highest human possibility and the deepest truth of the divine nature, that "God is love."

Bibliography. G. Allport, *The Nature of Prejudice* (1958). L. Chestang, "Character Development in a Hostile Environment," Occasional Paper, School of Social Service Administration (1972). N. Chodorow, *Reproduction of Mothering* (1978). J. Cobb, *The Structure of Christian Existence* (1979). C. Gilligan, *In a Different Voice* (1982). S. Kierkegaard, *Fear and Trembling* (1954). J. Lapsley, *Salvation and Health* (1972). R. J. Lifton, *The Broken Connection* (1979), K. Menninger, *Love Against Hate* (1942); *Man Against Himself* (1938). N. Shainess, *Sweet Suffering* (1984). P. Tillich, *Systematics,* vol. 3 (1978). A. Wilson-Schaef, *Co-depence* (1986).

S. M. ANDERSON
A. R. OSTROM

GIVING AND RECEIVING; MORAL BEHAVIOR AND RELIGION. *Compare* ASCETICAL PRACTICES; CROSS AND RESURRECTION; SELF-DESTRUCTIVE BEHAVIOR; *also* FAMILY THEORY AND THERAPY; IDENTIFIED PATIENT; MASOCHISM; SADISM.

SADISM/SADISTIC BEHAVIOR/SADOMASOCHISM. *See* RAGE AND HOSTILITY; SEXUAL VARIETY, DEVIANCE, AND DISORDER; VIOLENCE.

SADNESS AND DEPRESSION. *Sadness* is (1) a feeling state characterized by sorrow, dejection, or unhappiness; (2) a dispirited mood, varying in intensity, which is ordinarily related to the loss of valued persons, objects, or values. *Depression* is (1) a complex mood disorder involving the entire psychobiological organism and characterized by persistently negative views of the self, the world, and the future; (2) a clinical syndrome, or collection of signs and symptoms, in which a slowing down of the whole organism — emotional, intellectual, and physical — predominates.

Although no rigid line of demarcation can be drawn, sadness differs from depression in a number of ways. Depression is characterized by a significant loss of self-

esteem and is considered a complex pattern of psychological and physical symptoms. Sadness is primarily an emotional state triggered by the loss of something important to the individual's well-being; research has revealed a close relationship between sadness, loneliness, and boredom. In religion, classical mysticism's "dark night of the soul" is considered a form of sadness (rather than clinical depression) in current thinking.

Depression, as a clinical syndrome, involves a slowing down of the entire organism as well as lowered self-esteem. The severity and duration of the symptoms, ranging from constant tiredness to attempts at suicide, must be understood by pastors in order to facilitate appropriate treatment and care. Even when physical treatment (drugs or electro-convulsive therapy) is indicated, pastoral care and psychotherapy are needed to ameliorate the psychological and spiritual factors in depression. In particular, forms of pastoral care that depend upon a caring community and a biblical understanding of hope can be effective in dealing with five elements common to depression: negative views of one's future, guilt, anger, paralysis of will, and unfinished mourning.

1. The Relation of Sadness to Depression. Sadness is often a part of the depressive disorder, but sadness need not lead to clinical depression, nor does depression always manifest conscious sadness. Sadness is a healthy reaction to life situations that represent loss and disappointment. It is closely related to grief. One mourns for the loss not only of a valued person but also of health, employment, parts and functions of the body, valued objects, ideals, lost social roles and status, relationships, and opportunities. Freud (1917) says that in sadness and grief one's world becomes poor and empty. While one does not ordinarily lose perspective when one is sad over things going wrong, in depression self-doubt and low self-esteem predominate. Pastors need to listen carefully to how a sad person thinks and talks of herself or himself in order to make the distinction between sadness and depression. Schoenberg and associates (1970) report a young adult victim of myasthenia gravis, a degenerative disease of the muscles, commenting:

> I feel so sad when I think of how I am, I could cry. I think of all the things I could do before. Then I look around me and see all the healthy people my age, and get jealous and begin to hate them. But then I get to feeling guilty because they've never done any harm to me, and I'm overwhelmed by a blue feeling. (p. 189)

Here we see a progression from grief to depression, from sadness about her illness to a rage and jealousy she cannot tolerate and about which she feels overwhelmed with guilt. She illustrates negative feelings about herself, her world, and her future. She is depressed.

It should not be assumed, however, that loss always leads to depression, even though the victim might feel deep sorrow and loneliness. One study (Schoenberg *et al.,* p. 283) shows that only twenty-five percent of cancer patients manifest marked depression although all showed signs of grief. The significant factors in depressive patients were feelings of hopelessness, the inability to visualize a future, and a belief that control had passed from the patient's hands. This study also suggested that in eighteen percent of suicides, the principle cause was physical illness, frequently cancer. More accurately, however, the cause was the patient's *internal* thoughts and beliefs about his or her despair.

The distinction between sadness and depression is important in pastoral care. If sadness and sorrow predominate, "grief work" is indicated. If self-depreciating depression is present, medical treatment and more specialized therapeutic approaches are called for.

2. **Sadness, Loneliness, and Boredom.** When people who are studied in research label themselves as "lonely," the feelings they mention most often are sadness, boredom, and self-pity. Such "sad passivity" is most frequently found among young people. This state of lethargic self-pity contributes to their social isolation and often is expressed in crying, oversleeping, overeating, doing nothing, watching TV, or drinking and "getting stoned." While loneliness may lead to self-blame and depression, the most usual feeling is that of social dissatisfaction and isolation (Peplan and Perlman, 1982, pp. 211, 215).

A prime goal for the pastor should be to alleviate the isolation of lonely persons by encouraging them to (a) share their feelings and life stories more openly (Fairchild, 1980); (b) learn to listen attentively to others; (c) cultivate the art of creative solitude (Nouwen, 1975, pp. 13–44); and (d) develop the courage to create actively, even if the mental and physical products are modest (Fried, 1970; May, 1975).

3. **Spiritual Sadness.** What has been described in classical spiritual literature as "desolation" or "dark night" experiences are often confused with clinical depression. There are many depictions of the dark night, and spiritual guides view it in different ways (John of the Cross, 1958; Squire, 1976). The most important features are: (a) a sense of God's absence when presence has been an important experience of one's life; (b) a frightening sense of losing many of the familiar anchor points in one's life, for example, gratifications, faith understandings, ideals, and self-image; (c) a sense of sadness about one's persisting sinfulness or failure to grow spiritually. This latter sensation, if it is not accompanied by an awareness of God's graceful acceptance, can lead to clinical depression. Dark night experiences have been interpreted as unconscious resistance to a total reliance upon God.

Some of the differences between responses to experiences of the dark night and clinical depression have been noted by psychiatrist Gerald May (1982, p. 90): (a) Dark night experiences are not usually associated with a loss of effectiveness in life or work as are clinical depressions. (b) A sense of humor is usually retained through the experience. (c) There is a sense of rightness about one's awareness of spiritual poverty. (d) There is little of the tendency to plead for help, which one finds frequently in depression. (e) Unlike one's pastoral work with clinically depressed people, the pastoral guide seldom feels frustrated, resentful, or annoyed when working with someone experiencing the dark night. Often the pastoral encounter develops into a prayerful awareness of a graced relationship.

4. **Depression: Its Signs and Symptoms.** The signs of depression include not only a low mood, as in sadness or sorrow, but many physical, intellectual, emotional, and spiritual symptoms as well. A partial listing would include: low energy level and constant tiredness; sleep disturbances, especially insomnia; decreased effectiveness at school, work, or home; anxiety and irritability; inability to concentrate; loss of interest in sex; loss of appetite; loss of involvement in formerly vital activities; feelings of guilt and self-condemnation; and social withdrawal from groups and friends (Paykel, 1982). A depressive disorder is not just a collection of symptoms, however, there is a coherence among them, a pattern which is frequently dominated by lowered self-esteem.

Pastors will not ordinarily need to know the many classifications of depressive disorders (Paykel, 1982). However, pastors ought to be aware of two factors that will determine how helpful they can be: the severity and duration of the symptoms. In the severely and acutely depressed, three symptoms are clearly present: a deeply depressed mood, feelings of guilt and unworthiness, and suicidal thoughts or plans. Suicidal thoughts ought always be probed by the pastor before referral (Fairchild, 1980, pp. 95–99). Suicide is the great danger to depressives, and fifteen percent ultimately kill themselves (although many more make attempts). In less depressed parishioners, the most common symptoms seem to be physical complaints, such as loss of energy, lack of appetite, fatiguability, the lack of emotional feeling and interest in ongoing activities, and preoccupation with negative thoughts about self, world, and future. Initially, such parishioners are likely to share with their pastors rumination over their deficiencies and "what might have been," minor moral lapses, and self-reproach for neglect and unkindness to their families.

It is important to note how recently signs of depression have developed in a person's life and whether there seems to be a precipitating cause, for example, serious losses, disputes, or transitions; a series of major life changes; physical illness; or the prescription of drugs that produce depression as a side effect (Fairchild, p. 45; U.S. Pharmacopeial Convention, 1981). If the person seems to have been chronically depressed over much of her or his lifespan, or if no triggering cause is apparent, the person may be suffering from "endogenous" depression (arising from within). In endogenous depression, especially, there may be a genetic vulnerability in the family line and/or an abnormality in the neurochemical and endocrine balance in the body, which bring about the symptoms in a unipolar or bipolar depression (reflecting mood shifts). In these kinds of depressive disorders, antidepressant drugs (of which there are scores now with different functions) and electroconvulsive "shock" therapy often prove helpful. The use of drugs in the treatment of depression is now in the ascendency in psychiatric circles but their effectiveness is still being critically evaluated (Paykel, 1982).

It would appear that however effective drugs may be in removing some of the symptoms of depression (for instance, low mood, sleep disturbance, inability to communicate), they will not constitute the exclusive treatment of depression. It has been demonstrated that while chemical imbalances create moods and influence thoughts, thinking can influence the body's chemistry as well (Pelletier, 1977). Depression probably always includes psychological and spiritual factors which increase one's vulnerabilty to it. Thus psychotherapy or pastoral care will still be needed even when a part of the treatment of the depressed person includes physiological modalities.

5. Pastoral Care in Depression. Many books on pastoral care have helpful suggestions for counseling in situations of grief and depression (Fairchild, 1980; Oates, 1976). Two often overlooked resources of pastoral care, however, are (1) the community of believers and (2) biblical images of hope. Today pastoral care is seen increasingly as the "pastorhood of all believers," the mutual care of members for one another. The concept of "hope in the Lord" implies that reality is open-ended, that God always has options for persons that cannot at first be perceived. Hope is imagining another way (Fairchild, pp. 46–58).

When care-giving persons encounter a depressed person, once the trust level has been built up by attentive, "care-full" listening, one of the following themes usually emerges in the conversation or behavior: negative views of one's future, guilt, anger, paralysis of will, or unfinished mourning. How can the caring party increase the options and hope when these themes arise? In addition to excellent resources for activating hope in the therapeutic field (e.g., Rush, 1982), the following suggestions are pertinent.

a. Negative views of one's future. Unlike persons in grief, depressed persons may generalize that negative events or losses mean that life will always go badly. Depressed persons often label themselves as "helpless" or as "losers" and tend to overlook positive strengths and experiences that can arm them for a changed future. An inner critical voice tells them they cannot go into the future confidently because they are defeated, defective, deserted, or deprived (Beck, 1972). Pastoral care must first help the person to monitor this fear-ridden, internal dialogue and debate with these negative voices (Burns, 1980). Second, a life review can be prompted that reminds the depressed of times when she or he did come through hard situations well. Third, depressed religious persons may not feel alone in their struggle if they are reminded of the stories of biblical people in which the battle between fear and hope is prominent, such as the Israelites in the Exodus, or if they are encouraged to reflect on the Psalms, particularly the "psalms of lament" (e.g., Psalms 6, 22, 28, 31, 51, 55, 63, 69). (See Capps, 1981.)

b. Guilt. Dr. Aaron Beck's research (Beck, pp. 17–23) reveals that eighty percent of depressed patients express self-dislike and low self-esteem, much of which is related to a sense of failure to be the person that they felt they ought to be. This is particularly true of religious people. A healthy reaction to such failure might be expressed in honest confession, in restitution, or in the Catholic rite of reconciliation (sacrament of penance), in which forgiveness is realized and a new beginning is made. When a parishioner is unable to gain release from guilt in these time-tested ways, one can suspect a perfectionist self-ideal or a neurotic need for self-punishment. It is important to differentiate between normal and neurotic guilt (Stein, 1968; Tournier, 1962).

Where erroneous theological views have contributed to depression, religious reeducation is required. For example, some religious people equate strength of faith with good health: "If I am good or have enough faith, I (or my loved ones) will not get sick." This false equation and self-deception often leads to self-condemnation and guilt—to a feeling that sickness is the punishment of God. In many cases of neurotic guilt leading to depression, persons must be helped to reevaluate their values

and "shoulds" and get distance from uncritically accepted standards which they have introjected from significant people over the course of their lives.

c. Anger. In many people there is a strong connection between anger and depression. While depressed, they seldom show direct hostility to others, but their irritability can be detected by the discerning pastor. One can notice passive aggression in sulking, forgetting, and self-isolation, for instance, insofar as these behaviors seem calculated to make sure other persons are affected by their suffering. Because of fear, the depressed person may not be able to express his or her anger toward the source of frustration but instead turns it toward the self, engaging in minor or serious self-destructive acts. These persons may not be convinced that anger is a normal part of life, including religious life. They often need assurance that honest anger is acknowledged and accepted in the Bible, for example, in Psalms, Job, and certain passages of the NT (Mt. 23:23–36, Mk. 3:5, Jn. 2:13–17, Eph. 4:26–27.) When a person is helped to express anger to the appropriate person, even to God, in an appropriate way, a lifting of the depressive mood often follows (Flatch, 1974; Wolff, 1979).

d. Paralysis of will. D. Burns (1980) claims that "do-nothingism" is a frequent consequence and cause of depression. In its mildest form this malady takes the shape of procrastination toward disliked chores. In more serious depression it may be expressed in extreme passivity such as staying in bed. Because one accomplishes so little, self-hatred is aggravated, resulting in further isolation and incapacitation. The majority of depressed persons improve substantially if they can be helped to cut through their apathy and passivity by taking small, manageable steps to accomplish something useful. This can be taught (Burns, pp. 75–118). Always there is great need in any congregation to which the depressed person can contribute if encouraged and helped to find positive feedback. In his work with terminally ill children, Dr. Gerald Jampolsky enables them to lift their depression and self-pity by showing them that "to give is to receive," and so to engage in ministry to one another (Jampolsky, 1979).

e. Unfinished mourning. Depression is often the result of unresolved grief from the past. When a pastor discovers that fairly small losses or disappointments are leading a person to self-accusation, guilt, or severe depression, he or she must entertain the possibility that these are actually symbolic of earlier, greater disappointments and losses for which genuine mourning has not been done. The sorrow has remained unprocessed; grief work, with all of its conscious suffering, has not been completed. Often, for instance, a child is not helped to adequately mourn the loss of a parent, and later deaths may reactivate all of the mourning left unfinished in the earlier event. The pastor must be aware that the crucial problem may lie in the inability of the depressed person to sustain the "work of sorrow" after such an early loss. Psychiatrist Silvano Arieti further maintains that those who cannot finish their mourning remain excessively vulnerable to the normal disappointments and losses which are a part of human destiny (Arieti and Bemporad, 1978). Thus a knowledge of the parishioner's early losses is required whenever a depression seems disproportionate to its precipitating event.

6. Religious Significance. Depression is a condition in which life on all fronts seems to be blocked. Often it is a signal that directs our attention to a way or style of life that needs to be changed. In this sense, depression is a painful spiritual condition out of which significant growth can come. To use a biblical metaphor, depression can be conceived as a wilderness journey — the experience of being lost in a desert place, lonely, without the water of life, and in great danger from thorns and beasts. Yet it is a place where angels can minister and where distraught persons have found transformation, new identity, direction, and hope.

Bibliography. R. Fairchild, *Finding Hope Again: A Pastor's Guide to Counseling Depressed Persons* (1980). See also: S. Arieti and J. Bemporad, *Severe and Mild Depressions* (1978). A. Beck, *Depression: Causes and Treatment* (1972). D. D. Burns, *Feeling Good: The New Mood Therapy* (1980). D. Capps, *Biblical Approaches to Pastoral Counseling* (1981). R. Fairchild, *Lifestory Conversations* (1977). F. F. Flach, *The Secret Strength of Depression* (1974). S. Freud, "Mourning and Melancholia" in *SE* 14 (1917). E. Fried, *Active/Passive: The Crucial Psychological Dimensions* (1970). G. G. Jampolsky, *Love Is Letting Go of Fear* (1979). John of the Cross, *The Ascent of Mount Carmel* and *Dark Night of the Soul* (1958). G. May, *Care of Mind/Care of Spirit* (1982). R. May, *The Courage to Create* (1975). H. J. M. Nouwen, *Reaching Out* (1975). W. E. Oates, *Pastoral Care and Counseling in Grief and Separation* (1976). E. S. Paykel, ed., *Handbook of Affective Disorders* (1982). K. R. Pelletier, *Mind as Healer, Mind as Slayer* (1977). L. A. Peplau and D. Perlman, *Loneliness: A Sourcebook of Current Research and Therapy* (1982). A. J. Rush, ed., *Short-Term Psychotherapies for Depression* (1982). B. Schoenberg et al., *Loss and Grief* (1970). A. Squire, *Asking the Fathers* (1976). E. V. Stein, *Guilt: Theory and Therapy* (1968). P. Tournier, *Guilt and Grace* (1962). United States Pharmacopeial Convention, *The Physicians' and Pharmacists' Guide to Your Medicines* (1981). P. Wolff, *May I Hate God?* (1979).

R. W. FAIRCHILD

HOPE AND DESPAIR; MANIC-DEPRESSIVE (BIPOLAR) DISORDER. *See also* ANGER; BIBLE, PASTORAL USE AND INTERPRETATION OF; COMMUNITY, FELLOWSHIP, AND CARE; EMOTION; FEELING, THOUGHT, AND ACTION IN PASTORAL COUNSELING; GRIEF AND LOSS; GUILT; PSALMS, PASTORAL USE OF; RAGE AND HOSTILITY. *Compare* HAPPINESS; SELF-DESTRUCTIVE BEHAVIOR.

SAGE. *See* JEWISH CARE AND COUNSELING; RABBI/RABBINATE; SPIRITUAL MASTERS AND GUIDES; WISDOM TRADITION, BIBLICAL; ZADDIK.

SAILER, JOHANN M. (1751–1820). German professor of theology and bishop, Sailer sought to move beyond the narrowly moral and rationalistic approach to pastoral theology and care characteristic of much of Enlightenment Catholicism. Pastoral theology became the science of bringing human beings, separated from God and one another, into communion in Christ and in the church. In the training of the clergy the focus is on the salvation-historical content of pastoral activity and on the dynamics of incarnation. He gives particular emphasis to the formation of the personality of the priest. He strongly influenced the Catholic Tübingen School. Cf. his *Vorlesungen aus der Pastoraltheologie* 4th ed. (1820–21).

W. McCONVILLE

PASTORAL THEOLOGY, ROMAN CATHOLIC.

SAINTS, VENERATION OF. In Catholic tradition, devotional practices which honor and seek the intercession of deceased believers who are recognized by church authority as eminent examples of Christian holiness and who now live in full union with Christ in glory.

1. History and Practice. The practice of venerating saints has its origins in the fact of martyrdom in the first three centuries of Christianity. To the Christian assembly the martyr ("witness") represented the fullest possible identification of a believer with Christ. Conformed to the likeness of his death (Rom. 6:5) the martyr shares Christ's risen life fully. The body of the martyr was buried with honor, and the grave, carefully tended, often became a shrine. Oil lamps or candles placed at the grave symbolized the honor shown to the martyr, a custom that continued in the lighting of candles before images of saints. Each year the Christian community celebrated at the grave the anniversary of the martyr's death as the *dies natalis,* the day of his or her birth into glory. As Christians travelled to attend these anniversaries the practice of pilgrimage arose.

When the age of martyrs ended, other believers, called "confessors," were also honored after death in similar ways. These included church leaders, teachers, and ascetics. Mary, as the mother of the Lord, has received special veneration since at least the fourth century A.D. Since the early fifth century both martyrs and confessors have been designated with the official title "blessed" or "saint."

Since the early Middle Ages certain saints have been identified as patrons, or especially important helpers, for specific needs: St. Anthony of Padua as a helper in finding lost valuables; St. Jude Thaddeus as helper in impossible cases; St. Joseph as the patron of a peaceful death. Mary has been regarded as a comforter and helper in any circumstance, and as a patroness in diverse cultural areas — at Lourdes in France, Fatima in Portugal, Guadalupe in Mexico. The most common devotional practice honoring Mary is the recitation of the rosary.

2. Pastoral Significance. Christians who are accustomed to the veneration of saints will frequently invoke their help in times of personal need. Those who minister in the field of pastoral care will recognize symbols of such devotion — a medal, rosary, small picture, or statue. At times the role of the saint or the saint's image may be exaggerated or distorted by elements that appear superstitious or even magical. While not encouraging such exaggerations, the pastoral minister can, with sensitivity and understanding, emphasize the saint's role as a fellow member of the body of Christ, as one who offers companionship that transcends the realities of solitude, illness and death. An appreciation of the saints' sharing in Christ's constant intercession can portray the saint as an ally in a process of growth or healing, or as a help and comfort to those experiencing grief or loss, discouragement or confusion.

An informed understanding of the veneration of saints will emphasize their union with believers as fellow members of one body of Christ. Their role as intercessors in no way denies Christ's unique role as the only mediator between God and humanity (I Tim. 2:5). Rather, their role reveals the sharing of the body's members in the life of the head, who is Christ.

Bibliography. P. Brown, *The Cult of the Saints* (1981). H. Delehaye, *Sanctus: Essai sur le culte des saints dans l'antiquité* (1927); *The Legends of the Saints* 3d ed. rev. (1962). P. Molinari, *Saints: Their Place in the Church* (1965). P. Sherry, *Spirits, Saints, and Immortality* (1984).

W. J. SHORT

LITURGICAL AND DEVOTIONAL LIFE, ROMAN CATHOLIC TRADITION OF; SPIRITUALITY, ROMAN CATHOLIC. *See also* MARY, VENERATION OF; PILGRIMAGE METAPHOR; SHRINES.

SALVATION, HEALING, AND HEALTH, THEOLOGY OF.

The focal question of this article is the relation of the great ends or purposes of the church, connoted by salvation, and the goal of health and the processes of healing that move toward it, as these are found both inside and outside the contemporary life of the churches. The question has always been present in the life of the church, but it has been raised to a more acute form by twentieth-century developments.

1. Salvation and Health. *a. Old Testament.* In the OT salvation was primarily corporate and this-worldly in character, based upon the remembered experience of deliverance from Egypt recorded in the book of Exodus. It applied to the people of Israel as a whole, although in the Wisdom Literature (Job, Proverbs, Ecclesiastes) and some of the Psalms, it took on a more individual, but still this-worldly, coloring. Health and healing in the OT were applied to individuals, except for some metaphorical use by the prophets to describe the "healing" of the nation of Israel. They were seen as evidence of God's power and compassion for his people along with the blessings of flocks and herds. Sickness, on the other hand, was regarded as punishment in the Deuteronomic paradigm of blessing and cursing (Deuteronomy 7–8). This view was challenged later, particularly in Job, and questioned in some of the Psalms, (for example, Psalm 73) but remained an important part of the OT legacy regarding sickness.

b. New Testament. The NT conceptions of salvation were radically affected by the rise of apocalyptic thinking during the intertestamental period and, of course, by the central vision of Jesus Christ as both divine agent and exemplar of salvation. In the letters of Paul individual salvation from sin through faith in Christ in the context of the community of believers, culminating in the resurrection of the dead in the final inbreaking of God into human history, was the focal idea. In the synoptic Gospels Jesus Christ is depicted as bringing in the messianic Kingdom, with salvation viewed as participation in it through faith in him. Both present and future dimensions are emphasized. Healings done by Jesus, and subsequently by the apostles, as recorded in the book of Acts, are regarded as signs of the arriving Kingdom along with other mighty works, and also as the compassion of Jesus toward human suffering. In the synoptic Gospels these are signs that the full power of God in the apocalyptic inbreaking will soon be felt, and in the

Gospel of John that it has fully arrived in the coming of Jesus. In some synoptic accounts healing and saving come close to meaning the same event, as in the use of the verb *sodzo* to denote healing in Mk. 5:23 and Lk. 8:36, even though it usually is translated "to save." In Mk. 5:34 it appears to have had the double meaning of both saving and healing in the story of the woman healed of a flow of blood. Healing is thus close to the center of the synoptic meaning of salvation, although it can never be said to exhaust the meaning of salvation, or to be indispensable to it. In Paul's writings healing has a much less important place, viewed as one spiritual gift among others possessed by believers (I Cor. 12:9). In the NT as a whole healing is one among several signs of the new age, which taken together indicate the arrival of God's Kingdom and of its full appearance in the near future.

c. History of the church. In the patristic period healing continued to be an important part of the life of the church as one of the apostolic gifts. In the West during the Middle Ages healing declined as an official part of church life, even though it continued in practice. This seems to have been due to the rise of Augustinian views of the salvation of the individual soul in the next life (even though Augustine himself had not opposed healing). In the East a more Johannine emphasis on growth toward Godlikeness, beginning in this life and continuing into the next, was more compatible with a healing emphasis. The split between body and soul, an outgrowth of Neoplatonic strands in the theology of Augustine and others, was continued in the West in the later Middle Ages in the Aristotelian based theology of Thomas Aquinas, and sickness took on a central meaning of punishment or testing reminiscent of the OT emphasis. This attitude toward sickness, which viewed it at best as a matter of little importance in relation to salvation, and at worst as a sign of divine displeasure, carried over into the period of the Reformation, when healing by spiritual means was also under a cloud.

Beginning in the late nineteenth century several factors changed the attitude of the churches in the West to a more open and constructive one toward health and healing as integral to their mission. Among the most prominent of these are the rise of dynamic psychology, which has called into question the split between body and soul, the challenge of Christian Science and its establishment as a church of the middle class, and the emergence of Pentecostalism and its charismatic offspring in the mainline churches, both of which have emphasized healing in the context of worship. In the late twentieth century various forces coalesced to form the wholistic health movement, which, though loosely structured, put added pressure on both medicine and theology to deal with human beings as wholes rather than parts.

2. Contemporary Views of Salvation. Prominent contemporary theologies contain both corporate and individual dimensions of salvation but tend to emphasize one or the other. Conservative evangelical theology, for example, has focused on the individual in its emphasis on the saving power of the atoning work of Christ, although an eschatological theme of judgment and corporate redemption is also present. As the body-soul split has waned as a basic assumption, the salvation-health relationship has increased in importance in this group. On the other hand, liberation theology, with the exception of some feminist theologians, such as Letty Russell and the Latin American Juan Segundo, has tended to emphasize the corporate liberation of the oppressed with little attention to individuals. Process theology has tended to emphasize individual salvation through relationships with both human beings and God, but recently has tried to balance this with ecological and social emphases. The health question remains, however, as a central issue because of the view of individuals as internally related to the human and nonhuman environment in process theology.

All of these contemporary viewpoints have connections and resonances with various strands of the biblical materials. Conservative evangelicals look to the emphasis on justification through the atoning work of Christ in Paul's writings for their roots. Liberation theologians stress the deliverance motifs in the exodus from Egypt and the salvation of the poor and oppressed in the synoptic Gospels. Process theology, though closely related to the metaphysical response to the rise of modern physics found particularly in A. N. Whitehead, stresses relational and corporate themes that resonate with these basic themes in both the OT and the NT.

3. Contemporary Views of Health. *a. Minimal or average views.* This is the most common meaning of the term health. Health is seen by many clinicians and laypersons as being essentially the absence of illness and the symptoms of illness. Although we may term this a minimal view, its presence is determined primarily by observations focused upon the statistically average range of expectations of structure and function for a particular person. The vital signs of temperature, pulse, and respiration are well-known examples, but much more obscure structures and functions that require very sophisticated devices to detect are viewed in the light of the same principle. The basic model in this view of health is that of a finely tuned machine. Health and illness tend to be dichotomous. The presence of one implies the absence of the other, at least in the region or part of the organism being observed.

b. Coping or adaptation views. In these views the individual is seen primarily in relation to his or her human and nonhuman environment. A person may be healthy in one culture or work environment and very unhealthy in another. The ability to cope and adapt, including the ability to adapt the environment to oneself by influencing it, may be considered as primarily the function of the internal strengths of the individual, as in psychoanalysis. Or it may be considered as a function of the relative "fit" of individual environment, even though from a more ideal point of view (see below) neither may be considered to be optimal. The context of family life is widely regarded as a powerful environmental influence on the ability of persons to cope and adapt, but the wider social and cultural context can never be ignored.

c. Ideal views — health as fulfillment of potential. All of these views have at their core a vision of what a human being should be like, although these visions differ widely. The self-actualization model, now associated with the human potential movement, is one such vision. The wholistic health movement represents another variant, which places emphasis upon unity of the person as an organism. Apart from such twentieth-century health

movements, many clinical decisions made by physicians and other health care professionals imply some kind of ideal vision of what the particular person might or should be like. The clinicians' own values inevitably enter into the decision making along with whatever limits and possibilities they perceive. Hand surgery for a violinist is viewed differently from such surgery proposed for a radio announcer, for instance.

d. Health as a value among others. In this view health is conceptualized as a quality or qualities of the human organism, which provides the potential for the realization of other values. That is, it is primarily viewed as providing the possibility for other desired human values or relational connections. Health is necessary at least in some degree and in aspects of the organism for the realization of faith, hope, and love, for instances of values held central in the Christian tradition. Viewing health as a basic value incorporates attention to all three of the views stated above. For instance, statistical, coping, and ideal viewpoints must be taken into account, but they are seen as less than a complete conceptualization. Rather, health is a potential for appropriate functioning which an individual possesses at any given time. This definition emphasizes the understanding of health as an enabling value and its changing character.

4. **Health and Healing in Relation to Salvation.** In the following discussion the different kinds of views of salvation and of healing and health presented above are significant and sometimes control influences in the various positions taken about the relationship between salvation and health. Thus it is important to ask which concept seems to be the more significant in defining the relationship between them.

a. Exclusionist and random views. Although there have been few published expositions of this view in recent years, it still exercises considerable influence in the churches. The controlling idea is that God, through direct or indirect action through word and sacrament, or both, is the sole initiator of salvation and is not dependent upon human factors such as health. The work of Eduard Thurneysen, quite influential in the churches in the 1960s, exemplified this position. Thurneysen emphasized the direct word of forgiveness in pastoral care as the vehicle of salvation. He viewed psychotherapy as a kind of secular analogue for this forgiving work, but without salvatory power. He recognized that psychotherapy might precede the word of forgiveness offered through the church by a minister. The random character of the relationship between salvation and healing is seen in the position that healing may or may not be present for salvation to occur.

b. Inclusionist views. These views are comprised basically of two groups: those positions which have broadened the understanding of salvation to include healing in its many forms, and those in which a particular view of healing and health has come to influence or control the conception of salvation.

i. Broadened views of salvation. Those who seem to have taken this position did not abandon central tenets of the Christian faith regarding God's action in the salvatory process, but they were inclined to see these actions in a wider context of human relationships. David E. Roberts was one of the earlier writers to urge that salvation always includes healing, setting his position against some narrow interpretations of the Protestant, and particularly Calvinist, views of salvation in the 1940s.

Carroll A. Wise, in his earlier writings emphasizing the human relational character of pastoral care, also seems to have broadened his approach to salvation to include all dimensions of such relationships. (Later Wise came to emphasize a psychotherapeutic model, but without abandoning his relational emphasis.) Some liberation theologians who have given some attention to the health question, such as Juan Segundo, also view it as one of the human values to be enhanced by corporate liberation.

ii. Health as controlling concept. In these views some vision of human health derived from the personality disciplines, usually of the self-realization type, has come to exert a controlling influence on salvation. Many of those writing from a Jungian perspective seem to have almost equated the Jungian concept of individuation with salvation. These writers include Morton Kelsey and John Sanford in the Anglican tradition, and to a lesser extent Ann B. Ulanov. In all these writers the idea of the progressive emergence of the self as the unification of personality has primary healing and salvatory significance.

c. Dialectical views. These views try to take seriously the integrity of both understandings of salvation and of health, and to address the question of their relationship by finding some points of contact while acknowledging differences.

i. Mutual potential. Edward Thornton has been the primary proponent of this view. He held that both salvation and health are potential to one another, using a psychotherapeutic model for healing and health and an existential-encounter model for salvation. Although mutually potential, salvation is seen as an ultimate concern while healing is penultimate.

ii. Analogical models. Thomas Oden and Don Browning, both working with a psychotherapeutic model of health based on the work of Carl R. Rogers, proposed different kinds of analogies in the late 1960s. Focusing on theories of atonement, Browning argued that psychotherapy of the type he was examining, and theories of the Atonement, especially the classical theory, were mutually illuminating. Oden, on the other hand, saw the grace of God illuminating the psychotherapy by an ontology of acceptance, but not the other way around. More recently, John D. Carter, writing from the perspective of conservative evangelicalism, has proposed what he terms an "integrated" model of the relation of theology and psychology, which is based upon partial analogies between concepts and processes in psychotherapy and growth in the Christian life as he understands it. For instance, he sees an analogy between actualization and congruence processes in personality theory and maturity in the Christian life, but also sees differences in content, particularly in motivation and dynamics.

d. An "interlocking" view. Although the dialectical views described in the foregoing section have much to commend them, they focus too much on the individual's sense of acceptance or forgiveness and growth in grace (sanctification) on the one hand, and rely too much on self-realization health models on the other. What is needed is a model that takes better account of God's action in corporate and even cosmic perspectives on salvation in which the individual participates, and a better account of the emphases in the different models of health presented earlier.

The term *interlocking,* proposed by Lapsley (1972), indicates that the participatory processes of salvation and the focally individual and organic processes of health do not occur separately and are mutually dependent in some respects. Health in differing degrees is comprised of enabling processes that make participation in salvatory processes and the creation, enhancement, and preservation of Christian values possible. (See section 3 d.) Health does not guarantee participation in salvatory processes, however, for factors of human intentionality, including sin at conscious and unconscious levels as well as external social and other structures of finitude play limiting roles.

In Lapsley's model dynamic factors, such as development and the need for individuals to maintain themselves through various compensatory devices, as seen in the interplay of ego defenses that may result in the distortion of reality, play both limiting and enabling roles within the general sphere of health. That is, those whose development has progressed to greater levels of complexity are capable of greater salvatory participation, but various compensations may shape the kind of participation possible and limit it. In such cases health viewed as coping and adaptation comes into focus. All persons, no matter how impaired their health (as in severe illness), are capable of participating in salvatory processes to some degree.

Health, as ideal or as the realization of personal possibilities, comes into focus when development is more full or complete, but not all possibilities can be realized in any person. Choices must be made to actualize those values which are linked to participation in the salvatory process, even though tragic loss of unactualized potential is inevitable in such choices. Every possibility chosen means the loss of others. But those which are actualized, even on the basis of minimal health or health only adequate for coping, are preserved in the life of God through the participation of God in the processes of the world, including especially the interhuman processes. This interlocking view of the salvation and health relationship is also dialectical in the sense that it views the two processes as separable perspectives on human life in constant dynamic interaction, but which are not directly analogous or necessarily mutually potential.

In Lapsley's view healing usually increases the potential for participation in the salvatory process, since it increases health. In some instances partial healing may decrease the potential for salvation, as when the meaning of the symptom or illness is not understood to be the result of underlying conflict inhibiting participation in salvatory processes. In these instances the limited light of the traditional view of sickness as punishment, testing, or education may be discerned. But this understanding is never to be seen as a first principle of the relation of salvation and health, even though the suffering of illness may be the occasion of the refinement of the human spirit.

Bibliography. D. Browning, *Atonement and Psychotherapy* (1966). J. H. Ellens, *God's Grace and Human Health* (1982). J. R. Fleck and J. D. Carter, eds., *Psychology and Christianity* (1981); see especially chapters 5, 6, and 10 by J. D. Carter alone or in collaboration. M. Kelsey, *Healing and Christianity* (1973). J. N. Lapsley, *Salvation and Health* (1972). T. C. Oden, *Kerygma and Counseling* (1966). D. Offer and M. Sabshin, *Normality* rev. ed. (1974). D. E. Roberts, *Psychotherapy and a Christian View of Man* (1950). L. M. Russell, *Becoming Human* (1982). H. W. Sanborn, *Mental-Spiritual Health Models: An Analysis of the Models of Boisen, Hiltner, and Clinebell* (1979). J. A. Sanford, *Healing and Wholeness* (1977). J. L. Segundo, *Evolution and Guilt* (1974). K. Seybold and U. B. Mueller, *Sickness and Healing* Biblical Encounters Series, (1981). E. E. Thornton, *Theology and Pastoral Counseling* (1964). E. Thurneysen, *A Theology of Pastoral Care* (1962). P. Tillich, *The Meaning of Health: Essays in Existentalism, Psychotherapy, and Religion* (1984). A. B. Ulanov, *The Feminine* (1977). C. A. Wise, *The Meaning of Pastoral Care* (1966).

J. N. LAPSLEY

CHRISTOLOGY AND PASTORAL CARE; FAITH HEALING; HEALING; HEALTH AND ILLNESS; PROVIDENCE, DOCTRINE OF, AND PASTORAL CARE; SICK, PASTORAL CARE OF. *See also* PROCESS THEOLOGY AND PASTORAL CARE; RELIGION AND HEALTH. *Compare* SIN AND SICKNESS.

SALVATION AND PASTORAL CARE.

Salvation may be broadly understood as the divine life impinging upon the world to deliver it from the effects of sin and finitude. Hence, it is a principal doctrine of the Christian faith. The theoretical relationship of this doctrine to pastoral care, understood as those acts of ministry which focus upon the personal dimension of the lives of individuals and groups, is the concern of this article. It must be noted at the outset, that there is either no direct correlation, or a weak correlation, between the pastoral care practice of most ministers and the kind of doctrine of salvation they hold. Their practice of pastoral care is influenced by many factors, perhaps most strongly by the kind and degree of training and the models of helping to which they have been exposed. What can be discussed here are the theoretical understandings of pastoral care specifically advocated by pastoral theologians and those suggested by others hold different doctrines of salvation and who have linked their understanding of pastoral care to these doctrines in some identifiable way.

1. **Contemporary Understandings of Salvation and Pastoral Care.** There appear to be four principal understandings of salvation in North American churches in the late twentieth century. These understandings are not completely discrete, and they have had varying relations to pastoral care though all are of importance in the pastoral care movement. Each of these understandings includes both individual and corporate components, but each tends to emphasize one as a focal concern.

a. The Western tradition. Developing from Pauline and Augustinian roots, the emphasis has been on justification and reconciliation of the individual to God through the atoning work of Jesus Christ, and on sanctification as a succeeding lifelong process. (Some important thinkers, such as Luther and Barth, have not viewed sanctification as a distinct phase succeeding justification.) This emphasis is shared by Roman Catholics, Protestants, and many in the free churches. Controversies have been mainly about the means of grace or salvation, whether sacramental or by faith alone, or combined with particular experience or behavior, rather than about its essential character. Pastoral theologians who draw on this

formulation of salvation tend to view pastoral care as intrinsically salvatory in intent, though varying in degree of centrality, and most make some use of secular models of healing and helping as well.

Since the early 1950s, when the modern pastoral care movement began to develop a theological interest, a number of thinkers have participated in the discussion of theology in general and salvation in particular, especially in the mainline Protestant churches. An emphasis on forgiveness of sins in pastoral care has characterized the work of William E. Hulme from a Lutheran perspective, as it did that of Eduard Thurneysen earlier from a Barthian perspective. Thurneysen was the only writer here cited to have eschewed secular models of helping altogether. William B. Oglesby focused on reconciliation through relationship in his discussion of biblical themes as a resource for pastoral care. Wayne E. Oates, while focusing more on christological elements in pastoral relationships, presupposed the reconciliation-sanctification sequence as an important aspect of his work. Although not a central feature of his work, this sequence also formed an important part of the background against which Seward Hiltner worked out his reconstruction of pastoral theology as a discipline.

Conservative evangelicals have entered the discussion, with John D. Carter's linking of self-actualization motifs, particularly as found in the work of C. G. Jung, to his understanding of biblical teaching about sanctification.

Edward P. Wimberly has developed a distinctive understanding of pastoral care in the black churches set against a modified understanding of the Pauline-Augustinian position, which emphasizes more the corporate nature of persons and the salvatory process. In his focus on the concept of "soul" Wimberly retained a primary focus on the individual's relationship to God, however.

Since Vatican II, Roman Catholics have increasingly entered the discussion. Earlier contributors included Charles A. Curran, Raymond Hostie, and W. C. Bier. Eugene C. Kennedy has developed an understanding of the total work of the priest, including both sacramental and extrasacramental aspects, as redemptive in intent. While his work is not specifically focused upon pastoral care as usually understood in the pastoral care movement, this element is clearly included.

b. The Eastern Orthodox tradition. Based more on Johannine and Irenean thinking than is the case in the Western tradition, the Orthodox approach to salvation emphasizes participation in the divine-human community and *theosis*, or growth in godlikeness. Little has been published that relates pastoral care, informed by modern understandings of personality and modes of helping, to this understanding of salvation. The state of the discussion in Eastern Orthodoxy suggests that such work will soon be forthcoming.

c. Liberation theology. Based on the work of Latin American theologians such as Juan Luis Segundo and Gustavo Gutierrez, liberation theology emphasizes salvation as corporate freedom from oppressive social and political structures. Following the analysis of the human situation first announced by Karl Marx, either rather closely or at some distance from its more radical implications for political and social revolution, these theologians see these structures as dividing the world into the powerful rich and the powerless poor, and as the source of almost all human ills.

Implications for pastoral care of liberation theology in its original Latin American form have been stated by Rubem Alvez, a Brazilian Protestant theologian. Alvez holds that pastoral care, like all other functions of the church as presently constituted, reflects the basic political situation of oppression and serves primarily the ends of the oppressors, even though it might have a mitigating effect in some instances in its effort to mediate grace, provide interpretation, and give moral guidance. Therefore it should be offered only by and to those who are "wholly committed to the creation of a new world" (Alvez, p. 136).

Liberation theology has become an important source for some persons in the black, mainline Protestant, and Roman Catholic churches who are committed to social and political change. Little attention has been paid to pastoral care, as such, by liberation theologians who differ greatly from the analysis presented by Alvez. But foundations for a more positive view of pastoral care than Alvez's offers are found in the work of Archie Smith on the relational self. Smith views the problems of individuals as due primarily to oppressive social structures, as the self is a product in large measure of society. But he stresses the role of "mediating structures" that can be modified while also offering help to individuals and families. The church is seen as an important mediating structure.

d. Process theology. Building on a foundation of the reflections of A. N. Whitehead on post-Newtonian physics, their interpretation by Charles Hartshorne, the radical empiricism of William James, and the evolutionary theology of Teilhard de Chardin, process theologians in mainline Protestant and Roman Catholic churches have offered a view of human beings and of God that is basically relational and developmental in character. Salvation is conceived as a complex of individual actualization and participation, cultural change toward the development of structures that enhance such actualization and participation, and the enabling and preservation by God of these in the divine life.

Since in process theology relational networks are a primary constituent of reality itself — some would say *the* constituent — pastoral theologians who espouse this form of theology stress its relational character in a way that is more radical than the view of relationships found generally in other discussions of pastoral care. No one is without relationships; it is *quality* that is crucial in human and divine-human relationships.

From the perspective of constructive theology both Daniel Day Williams and John B. Cobb have made significant contributions to this approach in pastoral care. Among pastoral theologians Don Browning, working in part with process theology, has enhanced the discussion of pastoral care in relation to ethics; and James N. Lapsley has provided a treatment of the foundations of pastoral care in relation to salvation and human health. The most definitive work is Gordon E. Jackson's *Pastoral Care and Process Theology.*

2. **Salvation in Pastoral Perspective.** If the doctrine of salvation is viewed from the perspective of the concrete interpersonal processes of pastoral care and counseling, two aspects emerge: an ever-present salvific character,

and intermittent explicit doctrinal speech having salvific import, or "God talk."

a. The salvific character of pastoral care and counseling. The intent of the caregiver is always to be salvific, and if the caring is done well (or at least not poorly), it always has this potential effect. This is true whether the pastoral encounter is of the briefest sort or is long-term pastoral counseling with the transformation of personality in view. It also is true whether the recipient of the pastoral care is young or old, an individual or a family, relatively healthy, ill, or dying, consciously religious or secular in outlook.

There are costs as well as gains for both the caregiver and the recipient. Care may be received or felt to be a threat. Working through the sometimes painful visions of the self and its guises is also threatening. But where participation in the enhancement of human and divine life is effected or the quality of it is increased, and the effects of sin and crippling visions of finitude are diminished, salvation is the proper theological name for the process.

Not all pastoral theologians would agree with this way of putting the matter. Some would emphasize the transformational elements in the process as salvific, or at least more so than sustaining elements while others would stress spiritual elements, in the sense of enabling contemplation or enhancing a conscious relationship with Jesus Christ. Nevertheless, all would agree that pastoral care has a salvific intent, and that, as such, it is a vital aspect of the mission of the church, and not a peripheral concern.

b. "God talk." This rather colloquial sounding phrase has come to denote explicit reference to theology in the "texts" or dialogue of pastoral care. The idea that authentic pastoral care can be distinguished from inauthentic "secular" counseling done under the guise of ministry by the presence of explicit theological language is a false, though fairly widespread, notion. For a helpful discussion of "God talk" see Hulme (1981).

However, the use of theological language and concepts is often initiated by the recipients of pastoral care as a part or focus of their concerns, and caregivers need to be prepared to respond constructively to it when this occurs. Such response may be to the content, the attitude expressed, or perhaps to what the caregiver perceives to be another idea or concern lying behind the theological language, depending upon the circumstances involved in the care being offered. A general rule is that early in a pastoral care relationship the emotional and attitudinal components should be the focus of response, while later in a counseling relationship, after some clarification of personal concerns has been attained, a more content-centered response may be in order — correcting, challenging, affirming, or offering answers to theological questions when such answers are known.

At times, theological language also illumines phenomena or behavior that psychological or secular language ignores. For example, it may be appropriate for caregivers to initiate theological discussion in order to point out forms of idolatry that have not been so perceived, or to show that recipients of care have a tendency to try to atone for sin themselves. These are essentially attempts to correct self-perception in the earlier stages of pastoral care, but they also call attention to some fundamentals of the Christian faith. Discussion of the meaning of salvation often is appropriate in the latter stages of pastoral counseling. Prayer, as a specialized form of speech addressed to God, may be especially appropriate as a part of pastoral care in crisis situations. But like other forms of "God talk," its presence or absence is not in itself a criterion of authentic pastoral care.

Bibliography. R. Alvez, "Personal Wholeness and Political Creativity," *Pastoral Psychology,* 26 (1977), 124–36. D. Browning, *The Moral Context of Pastoral Care* (1976). A. V. Campbell, *Rediscovering Pastoral Care* (1981). J. B. Cobb, *Theology and Pastoral Care* (1977). J. R. Fleck and J. D. Carter, eds., *Psychology and Christianity* (1981). S. Hiltner, *Preface to Pastoral Theology* (1958); *Theological Dynamics* (1972). W. E. Hulme, *Pastoral Care and Counseling* (1981). G. E. Jackson, *Pastoral Care and Process Theology* (1981). E. C. Kennedy, *Comfort My People* (1968). J. N. Lapsley, *Salvation and Health* (1972). W. E. Oates, *Protestant Pastoral Counseling* (1962). T. C. Oden, *Kerygma and Counseling* (1966). W. B. Oglesby, *Biblical Themes for Pastoral Care* (1980). P. W. Pruyser, *The Minister as Diagnostician* (1976). A. Smith, *The Relational Self* (1982). E. E. Thornton, *Theology and Pastoral Counseling* (1964). E. Thurneysen, *A Theology of Pastoral Care* (1962). E. P. Wimberley, *Pastoral Care in the Black Church* (1979); *Pastoral Counseling and Spiritual Values* (1982).

J. N. LAPSLEY

CHRISTOLOGY; ESCHATOLOGY. *See also* FREEDOM AND BONDAGE; MINISTRY AND PASTORAL CARE (Orthodox Tradition); GRACE AND PASTORAL CARE; HUMAN CONDITION / PREDICAMENT (Clinical Pastoral Perspective); LIBERATION THEOLOGY AND PASTORAL CARE. *See also* REVELATION; SACRAMENTAL THEOLOGY AND PASTORAL CARE, ROMAN CATHOLIC.

SALVATION ARMY. *See* SECTARIAN PASTORAL CARE.

SANCTIFICATION/HOLINESS. Sanctification (Latin root) and holiness (Anglo-Saxon root) describe both present Christian life and the process and goal toward which faith is directed. Sanctification is "the holiness without which no one will see the Lord" (Heb. 12:14), and is at the same time "the goal for the prize of the upward call of God in Christ Jesus." Paul confesses, "Not that I have already obtained this or am already perfect; but I press on to make it my own, because Christ Jesus has made me his own" (Phil. 3:12).

1. Old Testament Meanings. *To sanctify* is in its root meaning to set apart for sacred purposes. Thus, the covenant people of Yahweh is set apart to serve him and manifest his rule in the world. The holiness which characterizes their communal existence is derived from the holiness of the One to whom they are covenanted. For the Hebrews, Yahweh's holiness is both awe-inspiring in its transcendence and moral in its character, as defined by the law of the covenant: "You shall be holy; for I the Lord your God am holy." Holiness is thus fundamentally a relational term and refers not only to right relations to God but to fellow human beings, "reaching right down to . . . the animals and to [the] natural environment" (von Rad, 1962, p. 370). It is closely associated, therefore, with justice.

2. New Testament Meanings. Jesus redefined holiness in terms of the power of the Kingdom to break through the vicious circles of human sin and estrangement and open up new possibilities for positive relations. "You must be perfect, as your heavenly Father is perfect" follows a series of examples of the ways by which forgiveness, empowered by the anticipation of the Kingdom, can cut through the normal human round of reprisals with a radical alternative (Mt. 5:21–48). This "counsel of perfection" is translated by Luke as "Be merciful, even as your Father is merciful" (Lk. 6:36).

Paul also understands that human outgoingness is predicated upon receiving power from beyond the self to transcend self. Divine grace, communicated through Christ's love for us, affirms us in spite of who we are and opens up the possibility of reconciliation and trust which we could not initiate out of our insecure selves. This grace is given not just to the individual but to the community, and mediated to the individual by the Spirit through the community. Baptism and the Supper of the Lord incorporate us into the power sphere of the Spirit. We are "saints" (*hagioi,* holy ones, Paul's standard term for Christians) (Procksch in Kittel, 1964, p. 105). Having been granted redeemed creaturehood, Christians are admonished to live in a manner consistent with their new being in Christ (Rom. 6; I Cor. 11:17–33; II Cor. 5:14–21; Gal. 5). "The immeasurable riches of his grace in kindness toward us in Christ Jesus" is, to be sure, "not because of works, lest anyone should boast." Yet, the purpose is not only to restore us to divine favor (justification)—"by grace you have been saved"—but to empower us to give to others what we have received. "For we are his workmanship, created in Christ Jesus for good works, which God prepared beforehand that we should walk in them" (Eph. 2:4–10). Thus, justification and sanctification are intimately joined in one salvific history inaugurated by the new Adam, who opens up for humanity the possibility of reclaiming the image lost in the fall (Rom. 5:12–21).

3. Ancient and Medieval Christianity. Irenaeus continued Paul's theme of Christ as the restorer of human nature. As the new Adam, Christ recapitulates the history of humankind, this time in obedience, and thereby sanctifies human existence. According to Gregory of Nyssa and the Greek fathers, the goal of the drama of salvation is *theosis,* participation in the divine life through the Spirit. Genuine humanity is sanctified humanity.

Augustine paved the way for medieval developments by conceiving of grace as infused into the recipient through the sacraments. This made the process of sanctification effectively dependent upon the mediator, the church, although Augustine clearly believed that the purpose of the church's mediation was the increase of the love of God in the human heart. Thomas Aquinas developed further the Augustinian notion of sacramental grace that sanctifies and provides the ontological foundation in the soul on which the theological virtues (faith, hope, and love) can be built up (*De veritate* 7:27). Grace thus effects a reorientation of the soul toward God, in intellect as well as in will, perfecting the creature and enabling us to stand before God as righteous and just, deserving of eternal life, which is God's alone to give. Thus, St. Thomas is able to claim that all is grace and yet hold the Christian responsible for the degree of perfection attained in this life.

4. The Protestant Reformation. Luther despaired of the Christian ever achieving sufficient sanctification to merit God's declaring him or her just. The discovery that our justification is not dependent upon our own righteousness but solely upon Christ, who in his mercy pleads for us with the Father and covers our sins with his righteousness, came as a radically freeing realization to Luther. He likens it to a wedding in which Christ takes the sinner as his bride (Luther, 1943, p. 260). Our sanctification is thus in principle complete in Christ, insofar as we continue to trust him and him alone to guarantee our status before God. Sin is a persistent factor in the life of the Christian, who lives in the awareness of being at one and the same time justified and sinner (*simul justus et peccator*). This keeps us humble and conscious of the necessity to live constantly out of grace. The fact that "Christ is our righteousness" is not the occasion for license, however, for Christ is victorious over sin and enables us to treat it as that which "should cease to be, and is cast out" (Rupp, 1953, p. 246).

Calvin's doctrine of sanctification is rooted in the holiness of the sovereign God whose honor allows no traffic with unrighteousness and uncleanness (*Institutes* 3, 6, 2). God the Son has interceded for sinners, however, and cleansed us with his blood. "By his Spirit we are regenerated into a new spiritual nature, . . . delivered from the servitude of sin, . . . and made capable and able to do good works and not otherwise" (From the *Catechism of Geneva* 1536; Toon, 1983, p. 76). Thus, we belong not to ourselves but to Christ, and are called upon to deny ourselves and live for others, as he did (*Institutes* 3, 7, 4).

5. **Pietism.** John Wesley represents a combination of Lutheran piety, mediated to him by the Moravians, who testified to the radical grace of the God who justifies sinners; Calvinist piety, mediated through Wesley's own nonconformist forbears; eighteenth-century Anglicanism; and the ancient church fathers, who convinced him that the purpose of salvation is the restoration of the image of God in the fallen creature. Hence, we hear him defining salvation as "not barely, according to the vulgar notion, deliverance from hell, or going to heaven; but a present deliverance from sin, a restoration of the soul to its primitive health, its original purity; a recovery of the divine nature; the renewal of our souls after the image of God, in righteousness and true holiness, in justice, mercy and truth" (Wesley, 1975, p. 106). The tendency was strong in pietism to divide salvation into stages, the *ordo salutis*, and the Christian life into a series of identifiable experiences. Although this tendency is present in Wesley, he was clear that the foundation of Christian existence is divine grace; justification remains the constant source of our acceptance before God.

However, God intends that sin shall be not only forgiven but overcome, and enlists us in the struggle against every evil that degrades humankind. Opposed to quietism, he insisted that Christianity "is essentially a social religion" which accomplishes its purposes only as it gives expression in outgoing love to the grace which it has received (Wesley, 1984, p. 533). This love he identified as the *sine qua non* of sanctification. Faith has its roots in the divine quickening of the soul (regeneration), the " 'new creation,' the renewal of the soul 'in the image of God wherein it was created' " (Wesley, 1987, p. 147). Regeneration inaugurates a discipleship whose goal is perfection, interpreted by Wesley as perfect love toward

God and all creatures. This is not a perfection that avoids the limitations of finitude or the effects of the fall, but is that communion with God in the Spirit and service of neighbor that constitutes genuine humanity.

6. **Twentieth Century Developments.** Renewed interest in the doctrine of sanctification has emerged in contemporary theology. Karl Barth, who early noted the neglect of the doctrine (Barth, 1927, pp. 291ff.), saw sanctification as "the exaltation of man" in which God "turns man to Himself" "as faithful covenant partner who is well-pleasing to Him and blessed by Him. 'I will be your God' is the justification of man. 'Ye shall be my people' is his sanctification." Moreover, "are we not forced to say that teleologically sanctification [as the goal of God's intention] is superior to justification?" He concludes that justification and sanctification cannot be set over against each other because both are expressions of the "one grace of the one Jesus Christ" (Barth, 1958, pp. 499, 508). Yet Barth reopened here the issue of the teleology of God's saving activity, a theme more prominent, as we have seen, in the ancient fathers and Roman Catholicism than in popular Protestantism, where salvation has tended to be equated with justification.

Paul Tillich modified the traditional emphasis on justification by recognizing that the power which renews the human spirit, the power of the new being, begins to effect regeneration within the human heart before awareness of God's acceptance in justification is possible. This quickening activity of the Spirit, traditionally identified as prevenient grace, may be unconscious and not even connected with the conventional religious symbols and environment. Indeed, it may be present even in doubt and despair. But it is the hidden presence of the Ultimate, toward which human life is finally directed, which is at work. Sanctification is growth in the conscious awareness and naming of this power, which leads to increasing freedom, self-transcendence, and relatedness to others (Tillich, 1963, pp. 221–45).

Dietrich Bonhoeffer, with his polemic against "cheap grace" (Bonhoeffer, 1948), called the churches of the Reformation to recognize grace as a power which seeks to transform, rather than simply to forgive or bless the world (Bonhoeffer, 1955); he inquired how Christ can be the transformer of a secularized world as well as of the individual and the Christian community (Bonhoeffer, 1971, p. 280).

More recently Jürgen Moltmann sees genuine human life as eschatological, future-directed, empowered by hopes awakened by the vision and proleptic presence of the Kingdom. Because the good news of the Kingdom is always at odds with the present age, it comes as judgment, demanding change; because the good news of the Kingdom is "to seek and to save the lost" (Lk. 19:10), it comes as the power to change and to heal (Moltmann, 1974, pp. 291–316). If the gospel is only the message of forgiveness, "without criticism of what is, . . . the gospel becomes the uncritical compensation for existing evil"; if it is "the creative righteousness of God revealed in the resurrection of the crucified Jesus" (Moltmann, 1979, p. 171), it is the energy of the new age which transforms and sanctifies.

The Second Vatican Council, with its "Call to Holiness" in the *Dogmatic Constitution on the Church*, quotes St. Paul, "For this is the will of God, your sanctification" (I Thess. 4:3), and points out that holiness is the vocation of all members of the church, not just the clergy. All are "called to the fullness of Christian life and to the perfection of love, and by this holiness a more human manner of life is fostered also in earthly society." Everyday work is also a means to "rise to a higher sanctity . . . and promote the betterment of the whole of human society and the whole of creation," imitating Christ, "who plied his hands with carpenter's tools and is always working with the Father for the salvation of all" (*Vatican Council II*, 1975, pp. 396–402).

Liberation theology, in its feminist, black, and Third World forms, seeks the transformation of this world and its social, political, and economic structures. Sanctification is not the sanctifying of what is, but bringing the present order into conformity with the justice of God and the mind of Christ by either reformist or revolutionary means. Especially in its Latin American version, this involves Christians in concrete commitments to less than perfect political and economic alternatives to the status quo. To use the perfection of the Kingdom of God as an excuse for being unwilling concretely to work for change is viewed by these theologians as a misuse of the doctrine of the Kingdom, which intends that "Thy Kingdom come, Thy will be done *on earth* as it is in heaven." Obedience to this petition means solidarity with those movements seeking to bring greater justice (Runyon, 1981).

Charismatic and pentecostal inheritors of the nineteenth-century holiness movement characteristically attend primarily to the needs of individuals and see sanctification as the activity of the Spirit bringing physical and emotional healing to persons through religious experiences of tongues and other "gifts of the Spirit." However, many within these movements, and also among more traditional evangelicals, understand "holiness of heart and life" to include the perfecting not just of individuals but of society (Runyon, 1975).

7. **Sanctification and Pastoral Care.** For pastoral care justification and sanctification cannot be separated. When Hiltner (1949) said that pastoral counseling proceeds by understanding, not moralizing, coercing, etc., he was giving instructions for pastors to assist the counselee with both justification and sanctification. The issue of justification is found in the human need for self-acceptance — for example, when pastoral care communicates verbally and nonverbally the acceptability of feelings of grief or of anger. Pastors have a responsibility to assist in self-acceptance, and basic counseling guidelines are means to this end. Moreover, pastoral care and counseling attend to issues of justification not once but continually, as persons discover themselves more deeply, with attendant anxiety and dismay, or as they identify hidden resources and wonder why they have not used them better.

At the same time those instructions were about sanctification. The word *sanctification* is not used there, but the concept is present in the *expectation of actual improvement*, not only in the acceptance of oneself. The significance of persons in and of themselves is not diminished by attempts to help them become more whole and useful.

Interest in sanctification is also to be found in the *study of processes* which actually improve behavior and internal orientation. In fact, sanctification does not require

improvement, but even values the avoidance or delay of deterioration. The focus is not on accepting the reality simply as a given, but on making improvements or withstanding decline.

Pastoral attention to sanctification is also found in its *appreciative consideration of that which is truly human*. It therefore borrows freely from psychology (Erikson's stages, Maslow's hierarchy of needs, good grief, capacity for intimacy, the balance between fusion and distance in families, establishing and maintaining proper subsystem boundaries in families, individuation, proper maleness and femaleness, maturity, etc). But pastoral care also addresses the limits of sanctification in its clarity that it cannot achieve every therapeutic goal; there is a refractoriness in human nature. Thus, justification-sanctification move continually between open-ended hope and the fixed engravings of character.

Modern pastoral theology has tended not to identify any particular form of behavior or inner attitude as holy or as an expression of sanctification. Nevertheless, work in pastoral care and counseling can be understood as strictly analogous to Calvin's concept of sanctification, which expects actual improvement in human beings; a restoration of the truly human; a slow and difficult, though rewarding process; and incomplete and imperfect results (*Institutes* 3, 3, 9). Most interesting is the expectation of restoration. Both pastoral care and Calvin assert that there is a residue of the true human nature, from which humans have been estranged, that can be recovered by the pastoral care or, in terms of this article, the process of sanctification.

Recent developments in pastoral care have also begun to consider the social dimensions of human wholeness, pointing to some convergence with important recent developments in the theology of sanctification (cf. Clinebell, 1984; Gerkin, 1979).

Bibliography. K. Barth, *Church Dogmatics*, IV/2 (1958); "Rechtfertigung und Heiligung," *Zwischen den Zeiten*, 5 (1927), 281–309. G. C. Berkouwer, *Faith and Sanctification* (1952). D. Bonhoeffer, *The Cost of Discipleship* (1948); *Ethics* (1955); *Letters and Papers from Prison* (1971). J. Calvin, *Institutes of the Christian Religion* (2 vols., 1960). H. J. Clinebell, *Basic Types of Pastoral Care and Counseling* rev. ed. (1984). R. N. Flew, *The Idea of Perfection in Christian Theology* (1934). J. Fowler, *Faith Development and Pastoral Care* (1986). C. V. Gerkin, *Crisis Experience in Modern Life: Theory and Theology for Pastoral Care* (1979). S. Hiltner, *Pastoral Counseling* (1949). M. Luther, "A Treatise on Christian Liberty," in *Three Treatises* (1943). J. Moltmann, *The Crucified God* (1974); *The Church in the Power of the Spirit* (1977); *The Future of Creation* (1979). T. O'Meara, O.P., *Holiness and Radicalism in Religious Life* (1970). H. Perkins, *The Doctrine of Christian or Evangelical Perfection* (1927). O. Procksch, "Hagios," in G. Kittel, *Theological Wordbook of the New Testament*, vol. 1 (1964). G. von Rad, *Old Testament Theology*, vol. 1 (1962). T. Runyon, *What the Spirit Is Saying to the Churches* (1975); *Sanctification and Liberation* (1981). G. Rupp, *The Righteousness of God* (1953). P. Tillich, *Systematic Theology*, vol. 3 (1963). P. Toon, *Justification and Sanctification* (1983). *Vatican Council II*, A. Flannery, ed. (1975). J. Wesley, *Works*, vol. 1 (1984), vol. 4 (1987), vol. 11 (1975).

T. RUNYON
J. R. BURCK

CHRISTIAN LIFE; FORGIVENESS; SALVATION AND PASTORAL CARE. *See also* CHARACTER ETHICS; CHRISTOLOGY; FAITH AND WORKS; PERFECTIONISM; SIN/SINS. *Compare* DEVELOPMENTAL THEORY AND PASTORAL CARE; PILGRIMAGE METAPHOR; PROCESS, CONCEPT OF; *also* EARLY CHURCH, PASTORAL CARE AND COUNSELING IN; EVANGELICAL, LUTHERAN, METHODIST, REFORMED, *or* ROMAN CATHOLIC PASTORAL CARE; MINISTRY AND PASTORAL CARE (Orthodox Tradition); PIETISM AND PASTORAL CARE.

SANITY/INSANITY.

Terms referring to the soundness of mind. When used in the context of law, the definition may vary from jurisdiction to jurisdiction. Soundness of mind may be an issue in determining whether persons have the capacity or competency to make contracts, to dispose of property by will, to retain care of possessions, to take care of themselves without commitment, to cooperate with a lawyer in the event of trial, to be held criminally responsible, and to be executed.

The difficulty which courts have had in defining these terms is illustrated in the variety of meanings adopted in cases involving an insanity defense to avoid criminal responsibility. The House of Lords in a debate sparked by an English case in 1843 formulated the M'Naghten rule: "It must be clearly proved that at the time of the committing of the act the party accused was laboring under such a defective reason from disease of the mind as to not know the nature and quality of the act he was doing; or, if he did know it, that he did not know he was doing what was wrong." Known as the "right and wrong" test, this rule was applied by many English and American courts and permitted psychiatric testimony to be introduced to establish the relationship between criminal intent and the mental state of the offender. However, the rule was criticized for its emphasis on the cognitive functioning of the defendant at the expense of the consideration of emotional control. As a result, the "irresistible impulse test" was developed in some jurisdictions to supplement the M'Naghten rule. The defense was expanded to cover the person who knew the act was wrong but could not control the impulse.

Still another expansion of the rule came in the Durham decision that allows the defense if the act of homicide can be shown to be a "product" of a "mental disease or defect." A reaction to the broad definition of Durham resulted in many courts now adopting the American Law Institute proposed law, which adopts the combined M'Naghten and irresistible impulse test with the substitution of "appreciate" for "know" in order to include the emotional factor. Also, this test excludes by definition "an abnormality manifested only by repeated criminal or otherwise anti-social conduct." Because successful use of the defense may involve the defendant in longer confinement in a mental institution than would have resulted from imprisonment for a guilty verdict, other legal options may be used in the defense of a mentally ill offender.

The need to apply different rules when the intent of an act is different is at least as old as the Covenant Code (Exod. 21:12–14). The problem of the insane offender is illustrated in Saul's attack on David (I Sam. 18:10–11).

Bibliography. American Law Institute, *Model penal Code,* sec. 4.01 (1) (1955) L. Tancredi, J. Lieb, and A. Slaby, *Legal Issues in Psychiatric Care* (1975). R. L. Schwitzgebel and R. K. Schwitzgebel, *Law and Psychological Practice* (1980).

L. M. FOSTER

LEGAL DIMENSIONS OF PASTORAL CARE AND COUNSELING; MENTAL HEALTH AND ILLNESS. *See also* DEVIANT BEHAVIOR, THEORY OF; PSYCHOSIS.

SATANIC-RITUALISTIC ABUSE.

See CRUELTY/SADISTIC BEHAVIOR.

SCANDAL (Moral Theology).

A deed or word that is evil or appears to be evil and provides an occasion of sin to others. According to traditional Roman Catholic moral teaching based on Scripture, a person is obliged in conscience to refrain from any deliberate action that would give scandal to another even if that action is not gravely sinful in itself but has the "appearance of evil" or could easily be interpreted as evil by another. Giving scandal can be grievously sinful when it is directly intended and leads to another's spiritual damage.

Bibliography. B. Häring, *The Law of Christ* (1961).

W. M. NOLAN

MORAL THEOLOGY AND PASTORAL CARE; SIN/SINS.

SCAPEGOATING.

See FAMILY THEORY AND THERAPY; SACRIFICIAL BEHAVIOR.

SCHARFENBERG, JOACHIM

(1927–   ). German practical theologian, practicing psychoanalyst, author of several important books and articles, and editor of the journal, *Wege zum Menschen.* Educated in Jena, Halle, Tübingen, Kiel, and Cambridge, Mass., Scharfenberg served from 1953–63 as parish pastor, hospital chaplain, and director of the Protestant Counseling Services in Berlin. Between 1956 and 1961, he underwent training as a psychoanalyst. In 1964 he moved to Stuttgart to lead the Protestant Center for Marriage Counseling. Upon completing his *Habilitationsschrift* in 1967, he became lecturer at the University of Tübingen. Since 1971 Scharfenberg has been professor for practical theology in Kiel. Most notable among his many publications in the field of pastoral psychology are *Sigmund Freud und seine Religions-kritik als Herausforderung für den Christlichen Glauben* (1968, ET 1988); *Seelsorge als Gespräch* (1971, ET 1987); *Religion zwischen Wahn und Wirklichkeit* (1972); *Mit Symbolen leben* (1980, with Horst Kämpfer); *Einführung in die Pastoralpsychologie* (1985).

Scharfenberg's life and work are best captured by the image of a bridge-builder, mediating as he has been for a long time between theology and psychology, and between theory and practice. In both respects, Scharfenberg has been something like a forerunner, part of a small avant-garde of thinkers in Germany who carefully opened the discipline of theology to the insights of psychology, particularly depth psychology, without selling out and with careful and critical evaluation, at a time when some saw all the answers in psychology and others rejected it entirely. Thus, Scharfenberg's work is marked by a great sensitivity and great care for preserving the authenticity and relevance of theology and religion. At the same time, Scharfenberg is mining the riches of psychological theory and practice for insights that can be made fruitful for the theory and practice of pastoral care. An underlying concern of his always appears to be the improvement of communication, be it between university disciplines—as visible in his earlier works—or between counselor and counselee—as evidenced, for instance, by his 1980 book on the use of symbols.

N. F. HAHN

PSYCHOANALYSIS AND PASTORAL CARE; WESTERN EUROPEAN PASTORAL CARE MOVEMENT.

SCHIZOPHRENIA. A term commonly used to describe a group of five behavioral health disorders that include a loss of contact with reality. This is evidenced, at some point in the illness, by the prominent presence of hallucinations, delusions, severely deranged behavior, or markedly disrupted thinking. This group of schizophrenic disorders is characterized by severe disorganization of the person's personality, often requiring acute management and treatment in a hospital during the more active phases of the illness. Hypotheses and theories concerning the possible causes of these disorders range from demon possession to inherited biochemical abnormalities and include various psychological factors of traumatic events. Schizophrenia exists and poses a major health problem within all cultures where behavioral health disorders have been systematically studied. The heterogeneous nature of the schizophrenic syndrome requires a multimodal treatment plan, incorporating somatic therapy, psychotherapy, socialization opportunities, and spiritual support. Pastoral care and counseling can assist the healing process of persons with acute schizophrenic symptoms and can provide ongoing support to persons with chronic impairments related to schizophrenia.

1. **History.** Persons with symptoms of schizophrenia have been present since the beginning of civilization. In 1400 B.C., a Hindu author wrote about "wild men that were greedy, foul, naked, uneasy." Devils were believed to cause this condition. In the first and second centuries, clinical descriptions and serious attempt at treatment were attempted. A Greek physician differentiated between "maniacs" and other ill persons who were "stuporous, absent, and musing." The Roman physician Soranus wrote about patients "who believed they were God and refused to urinate for fear of causing a deluge." During the Middle Ages, society saw mentally ill persons as possessed by evil and either destroyed the person or confined him or her to asylums, where no clinical observation or treatment was undertaken. The Bedlam Asylum in England gave rise to the term *bedlum,* applied to chaotic conditions. Many persons were burned at the stake or jailed, but some attempts were made to eliminate the "madness" believed to be caused by pressure on the brain, with blood-letting or purging.

The philosophy of humanism is thought to have prompted some efforts at treating patients in asylums. Therapies included use of camphor, ether, turning on a suspended stool until they became unconscious, and being dropped through a trap door into an icy lake. Cruel as these efforts sound, they were serious attempts to stimulate and motivate those who today would be regarded as regressed patients. Possibly, the greatest gain was to separate true sufferers from malingerers.

In the eighteenth and nineteenth centuries, a "moral" or instructional therapy provided individual treatment and support, with some success. In the late nineteenth and early twenty-ninth centuries, physicians began to study and classify symptoms of the "insane." Bénédict-Augustin Morel first applied the term *dementia praecox* to a fourteen-year-old boy who had become sober, taciturn, withdrawn, and silent. This concept was further developed by descriptions of hallucinations and hebephrenia, and catatonia. In 1896, Emil Kraepelin combined a variety of clinical/mental syndromes—commonly thought of as representative of separate diseases—under the single entity he termed *dementia praecox.* Kraepelin's paper, "The Diagnosis and Prognosis of Demential Praecox" (1898), elaborated on his central premise that all primary and secondary dementia were manifestations of a single disease entity. His clinical symptoms included lack of external cause, occurrence in young and previously healthy persons, hallucinations, delusions, stereotypes, and disordered affects. Major emphasis was placed on the observation of ultimate deterioration and hence, the prognostic factor or outcome became central to Kraeplin's nosology.

In his 1911 paper entitled "Dementia Praecox or the Group of Schizophrenias," Eugen Bleuler developed a new concept of dementia praecox and relabeled it "schizophrenia." Instead of incurability and deterioration, Bleuler placed central importance on the "splitting of the personality, a nonintegrated and disharmonious state of mind in which most contradictory tendencies, thoughts, and potentialities existed together" (Kolb and Brodie, 1982, p. 346). Bleuler was influenced by Freud's dynamic insights and applied them to his patients thoughts and actions. Hence he conceptualized schizophrenia as both a disease entity and a psychopathological reaction that consisted of primary symptoms and secondary symptoms, from which he expected some patients to deteriorate, some to recover with defect, and others to recover without defect.

Adolf Meyer did not accept Kraeplin's or Bleuler's classification systems or Freud's dynamic concepts. Rather, he saw schizophrenia as a habit pattern of nonadaptive responses, developed over time, in reaction to traumatic events of a physical, social, and/or emotional nature. He emphasized the idiosyncratic nature of each patient's disorder and insisted on detailed individual study of each patient.

The early concepts of Kraeplin, Bleuler, and Meyer are no longer adequate. However, even with the development of new concepts and hypotheses, the clinical description or picture of the patient continues to be the most important factor in the diagnosis of schizophrenia.

2. **Epidemiology.** It is commonly accepted that schizophrenia exists and poses a major health problem within all cultures where psychiatric disorders have been systematically studied. Estimates of the incidence and prevalence rates of schizophrenia for various cultures do exist; however, both intracultural and cross-cultural comparisons of these rates are exceptionally difficult to accomplish. European and Asian studies, employing a narrow criterion for schizophrenia, have produced rates ranging

from 0.2 percent to almost 1.0 percent of the population. While U.S. studies, using a broader criterion for schizophrenia and examining an urban population, have found rates greater than 1.0 percent (DSM III, 1980, p. 186; Babigian, 1980, p. 1117), in summarizing the U.S. prevalence data available, states that between 2.3 percent (i.e., 500,000 persons) and 4.7 percent (i.e., 1 million persons) of the total U.S. population will need treatment for schizophrenia in any one year. As estimated, two million Americans (males and females equally) currently suffer from schizophrenia. Schizophrenia has been found to occur within all races and socioeconomic classes; however, prevalence rates are generally higher among nonwhites and highest among the lower socioeconomic strata. Specific reasons for these findings do not exist, but it has been variously hypothesized that downward social drift, lack of upward social mobility, high stress, and diagnostic biasing are involved. Studies investigating the prevalence of schizophrenia among family members of a diagnosed schizophrenic have yielded higher rates within these families. Several results substantiate the existence of genetic factors; however, it should be kept in mind that a sufficient discordance rate (even among monozygotic twins) does exist and that this discordance rate may be interpreted as evidence for the existence of nongenetic factors (*DSM III*, 1980, p. 186).

3. Etiology. Numerous hypotheses an theories exist concerning the possible causes of the schizophrenic disorders. Likewise, empirical data exist supporting each of these hypotheses and theories. Unfortunately, there continues to be insufficient data to conclusively prove or disprove any one hypothesis or theory.

It is commonly accepted that schizophrenia is a heterogeneous illness in which multiple factors interact and by their interaction precipitate the various symptoms that have been identified as composing the schizophrenic syndrome. Scientific opinion accepts that genetic factors are involved in predisposing various persons to, at least, some forms of schizophrenia. Exactly how this takes place and what specific nature or form this innate predisposition takes is not yet known. What appears to be "inherited" or transmitted is a vulnerability for or tendency toward the development of particular symptoms of schizophrenia — if, and only if, specific conditions are present. These conditions may include such factors as parental bonding, family dynamics, multiple environmental stressors, traumatic emotional events, opportunities for basic socialization and healthy ego-development, physical health, and any number of additional social, biochemical, emotional, and environmental factors that are yet to be identified.

As with the majority of other illnesses, the schizophrenic syndrome is not only a heterogeneous entity in which both the predisposing and initiating factors are multiple but also one in which these factors are non uniform (Weiner, 1980, p. 1148). It is true that an individual with a family history of schizophrenia is at greater risk for developing a schizophrenic disorder; however, this is not to say that he or she will invariably become schizophrenic. What is necessary is the predisposition for the syndrome and the existence of the appropriate biochemical and external factors (in the appropriate intensity and combination) to elicit the symptoms of schizophrenia.

The specific mechanisms involved or their combinations have not yet been clearly identified.

4. Clinical Symptoms. The various symptoms of schizophrenia can be grouped into five basic categories: perceptual disorders, cognitive disorders, disorders of verbal behavior, behavioral disorders, and disorders of affect. Perceptual disorders include: hypersensitivity to light, sound, smell, or taste; changes in objects' dimensions; sensations of bodily changes; extension or contraction of time; and a variety of auditory and visual hallucinations.

Cognitive disorders include disturbances in content and form of thought. False ideas that cannot be corrected by reasoning and that are idiosyncratic for the patient (Lehman, 1980, p. 1156), are typically fragmented, bizarre, grotesque, multiple, and involve themes of persecution, control by others, sex, and bodily functioning (Kolb and Brodie, 1982, p. 366). Somatic, grandiose, religious, and nihilistic delusions occur but less frequently than delusions about thoughts that can be heard by other people, inserted into one's mind, withdrawn from one's mind, or the delusion that one can be controlled by another person or object.

Another common feature in schizophrenic disorders is the patient's perplexity and his or her identity and sense of self. Such loss of ego boundaries reinforces patient's delusions about being controlled by external sources. Disturbances in form of thought appear as unrelated ideas with no awareness of the illogical and, at times, incoherent messages communicated. Or the patient may use an adequate amount of speech but produce abstract, concrete, and vague material.

Verbal disturbances include symbolism, blocking of affect-laden words, incoherent speech, mutism, neologisms, echolalia, and repetition of words or phrases. Behavioral changes can occur in areas such as work, social relations, self-care, and manners. Other behavioral disorders include attention deficits, withdrawal, anergia, negativism, poor impulse control, pronounced ambivalence, and a wide variety of mannerisms of speech and movement. Disorders of affect include both quantitative and qualitative changes. Blunted affect and flat affect are common. Many patients experience anhedonia, a state in which they are emotionally barren without feeling depressed (Lehman, 1980, p. 1164). Inappropriate affect and unpredictable changes in mood are not uncommon. Extremely intense mood states of euphoria, omnipotence, religious ecstasy, horror, or terror may also be present.

5. Types. According to the third edition of the *Diagnostic and Statistical Manual of Mental Disorders* (*DSM III*, 1980), five types of schizophrenia are recognized (i.e., disorganized, catatonic, paranoid, undifferentiated, and residual).

Disorganized (Hebephrenic) Type. The onset of this type typically occurs in early adolescence and is extremely insidious. Essential clinical symptoms include significant incoherence, loose associations, and flat, inappropriate, or silly affect. No elaborate delusional system is present; instead, fragmentary bizarre delusions or hallucinations or a disorganized nature are frequent. Regressive features of wetting and soiling are common. Other associated features may include mannerisms, grimacing, extreme social introversion and withdrawal, unmannerly eating habits, and hypochondrial complaints. Extreme social impairment and a chronic course without significant remissions are typical.

Catatonic Type. This type most frequently appears between the ages of fifteen and twenty-five. Catatonia most frequently has an acute onset that has been preceded by some type of emotional trauma. The essential clinical symptom is significant psychomotor disturbance which may include stupor, negativism, rigidity, excitement, and posturing. A rapid alternation between the extremes of excitement and stupor may be present. Other associated features may include mannerisms, stereotypes, and waxy-flexibility; mutism is common. The prognosis for recovery after a single catatonic episode is more favorable than for recovery from the other types of schizophrenia. However, after several catatonic episodes, the prognosis for recovery decreases significantly.

Paranoid Type. This type of schizophrenia tends to occur later in life; it typically appears after adolescence and most frequently manifests itself at around age thirty. Essential clinical symptoms include persecutory or grandiose delusions, hallucinations (typically auditory) with either persecutory or grandiose content, and delusional jealousy. Associated features of homophobia, gender identity, confusion, unfocused anger or anxiety, and violent tendencies may be present. Functional impairment may be minimal if the delusional material is encapsulated and is not overly acted upon. Speech may be of a stilted /formal quality, and extreme intensity in interpersonal interactions may be present (*DSM III*, 1980, p. 191).

Undifferentiated Type. Prominent psychotic symptoms (i.e., delusions, hallucinations, incoherence, or severely disorganized behavior) are present. However, the patient's clinical picture either does not meet the criteria for any of the three differentiated forms of schizophrenia (i.e., disorganized, catatonic, or paranoid) or it does meet the criteria for more than one of the differentiated types.

Residual Type. This diagnosis is applied when a documented history of at least one schizophrenic episode (with prominent psychotic symptoms) exists, but the current evaluation of the patient no longer indicates the existence of any significant psychotic symptoms. However, symptoms of the illness continue to be evident. Typical symptoms include social withdrawal, apathy and emotional blunting, some behavioral eccentricities, and associated loosening. Delusions or hallucinations may also be present; however, they are not the prominent clinical features at the current time and are not accompanied by strong affect (*DSM III*, 1980, p. 192).

6. **Illness Course and Prognosis.** Three phases in the schizophrenic process have been noted. By definition, a patient must exhibit signs of illness for at least six months and must also exhibit psychotic symptoms during the active phase of the illness (*DSM III*, 1980). However, a prodromal phase (i.e., the phase preceding the active phase) and a residual phase (i.e., the phase succeeding the active phase) are also usually present.

During the prodromal phase, clear deterioration in a previous level of functioning (e.g., social, self-care, work) is evident. In addition, one or more of the following features may be observed: social withdrawal, odd behavior, blunted or inappropriate affect, changes in personality, communication problems, impaired role functioning, a decrease in personal hygiene and grooming, patient reports of unusual perceptual experiences, or evidence of bizarre ideation. Onset of this initial phase of the schizophrenic process is difficult to date. The length of this phase has been shown to be quite variable.

Onset of the active phase of the schizophrenic process is typically associated with some type of significant psychosocial stressor. It is during this phase that florid psychotic features become evident. Common psychotic symptoms include delusions, hallucinations, incoherence, evidence of a formal thought disorder (i.e., loosening of associations and illogical thought), severely disorganized behavior, catatonia, and poverty in content of speech. Following the active phase of the schizophrenic process one commonly observes, in the patient, a state quite similar to that of the prodromal phase. In this residual phase, however, blunting and flattening of affect and impaired role functioning are more frequent and more apparent than in the prodromal phase. Further, certain psychotic features (e.g., delusions, hallucinations, thought disorganization) may continue, but without the strong affect found in the active phase.

There is no definite means of predicting the outcome of a schizophrenic episode; disabilities have been found to range from none (with full reintegration into society) to severe (requiring institutionalization). Kolb and Brodie (1982, p. 388) state that with each year of continued hospitalization, expectancy of recovery decreases. In addition, they report that of those patients hospitalized in the first year of illness, one-third make a fairly complete recovery; one-third improve to the point that they are able to return to outside life, but do exhibit some permanent personality damage and may require additional hospitalization at some point; and one-third require indefinite psychiatric care. Further, of this final third, approximately ten percent will probably need protective institutionalization (Kolb and Brodie, 1982, p. 388).

Several factors have been shown to correlate with a positive prognosis (*DSM III*, 1980, p. 185; Kolb and Brodie, 1982, p. 386). These include: good premorbid adjustment (including no evidence of a premorbid personality disorder and adequate premorbid social functioning), precipitating factors (typically, psychosocial in nature), sudden onset, onset in mid-life, clinical features of confusion and prominent affectivity, and a family history that may include a history of affective disorders but excludes a history of schizophrenic disorders.

7. **Treatment Methods.** Due to the complexity and hypothesized multiple/interactive causes of schizophrenia, no one specific or universally accepted "cure" exists. Basically, three major methods of treatment, typically employed in combination, are currently available. Each has its strengths as well as its limitations.

a. Milieu therapy. Hospital care employing the milieu approach to healing can offer the schizophrenic not only medical treatment but a social system in which he or she may begin to reestablish social contact. Opportunities for gradual, supportive growth — emotionally, physically, socially, and spiritually — can be offered through the modalities of psychotherapy (both individual and group), recreational therapy, occupational therapy, physical therapy, and chaplaincy. In addition, the staff can offer the schizophrenic patient healthy role models with whom communication and identification can be accomplished.

b. Psychotherapy. Both individual and group psychotherapy are important adjuncts to somatic therapy, as is the growing field of family therapy. These various forms of psychotherapy play a significant role in the milieu approach to treatment. Psychotherapy with a schizophrenic patient must initially focus on the building of trust and the maintenance of an extremely fragile relationship with the patient. As therapy progresses, the therapist must assist the patient in clarifying his or her feelings concerning day-to-day events and in developing socially adaptive methods of dealing with thoughts and feelings. It is essential that clarity of content and genuine support of the patient be maintained. Group psychotherapy can be particularly effective. The social milieu of the group can allow for increased opportunities for learning adaptive social responses. Further, the group context may be particularly effective as a basis of support and confrontation for the patient. Family therapy is a third and increasingly popular form of psychotherapy. The influence of family dynamics on the family member who has become schizophrenic is generally accepted as a significant variable in the development of the patient's illness. Consequently, if clarity can be brought to a confusing illness, encouraging family dynamics, new insights and directions presented, and fundamental "pathological" interactions confronted and changed through the family therapeutic process, then the schizophrenic patient may gain an additional sense of support and clarity concerning his or her role in the family and be further supported in positive emotional and social growth.

c. Somatic therapy. The use of psychotropic medications has radically changed the treatment of schizophrenic persons. A number of neuroleptics, particularly the phenothiazines, are currently in use. Schizophrenic patients exhibiting tension, psychomotor overactivity, agitation, antagonism, and aggressiveness typically respond well to treatment with these neuroleptics. In addition, phenothiazine therapy with acutely ill patients experiencing hallucinations and delusions usually brings about the cessation of these symptoms within two weeks of administration (and regular use) of the medication. Parkinsonian-like side effects are common in patients being treated with neuroleptics; however, antiparkinsonian agents are available and are generally effective in reducing these unwanted side effects. Due to the discovery and use of psychotropic medications, many patients who would have previously needed long-term institutional care now are able to function in society with appropriate outpatient psychiatric treatment.

d. Pastoral care. The pastor can especially bring unconditional acceptance and caring to the severely disturbed life of a person with a schizophrenic disorder. Such patients are often rejected and avoided by those close to them. The intensity of the emotional, mental, and behavioral aberration is usually beyond the abilities or willingness of the family and friends to understand and accept. Consistent visits by a pastoral counselor who values the patient and expresses acceptance of the person without agreeing with the delusional material can be therapeutic and provide a model for families and friends.

False beliefs of a schizophrenic patient affect self, self-worth, and relationship with God. It is not uncommon for a patient to believe that he or she is damned, is being persecuted by God, has lost the love of God, or can never be worthy of God's love or forgiveness again. Unless a patient is totally out of contact with reality, the times of awareness of the illness process and its impact on self and others bring intense feelings of guilt, hostility, frustration, and futility. Even the person with grandiose beliefs of godlike powers is often reacting to internal feelings of insecurity, powerlessness, and insignificance. Into this pain and confusion, pastoral care can bring the agape love and forgiveness of God. Pastoral counseling can open channels of communication and support while assisting the psychotherapy process.

The pastor should maintain contact with the primary therapist and treatment team for the particular patient. There are times for "just being there" and times to be actively working with the patient. The particular modes of interaction with the patient are best coordinated by the behavior health professional trained and licensed to assess, manage, and treat persons with illnesses as severe as the schizophrenic disorders.

Bibliography. E. Bleuler, *Dementia Praecox or the Group of Schizophrenias* (ET, J. Zinkin, 1950). *Comprehensive Textbook of Psychiatry/III* 3d ed., vol. 2, ch. 15, "Schizophrenic Disorders" (1980), 1093–1287. *Diagnostic and Statistical Manual of Mental Disorders* 3d ed. (1980). I. Kaplan, A. M. Freedman, B. J. Sadock, H. M. Babigian, "Schizophrenia: Epidemiology," pp. 1113–21. Kolb and Brodie, *Modern Clinical Psychiatry* (1982), pp. 344–403; *Modern Clinical Psychiatry* 10th ed. (1982). E. Kraepelin, *Dementia Praecox*, (ET, R. M. Barclay, 1919). H. E. Lehman, "Schizophrenia: Clinical Features," pp. 1153–92, Report of the "International Pilot Survey of Schizophrenia," World Health Organization, Geneva vol. 1 (1973). H. Weiner, "Schizophrenia: Etiology," pp. 1121–52.

S. MAYHUGH
A. J. STROM

PSYCHOPATHOLOGY, THEORIES OF; PSYCHOSIS. *See also* EVALUATION AND DIAGNOSIS, PSYCHOLOGICAL; MENTAL HEALTH AND ILLNESS; PSYCHOPATHOLOGY AND RELIGION. *Compare* BORDERLINE PERSONALITY; DEMONIC; MULTIPLE AND DISSOCIATIVE PERSONALITY; PERSONALITY, BIOLOGICAL DIMENSIONS OF; SUSPICIOUSNESS AND PARANOIA.

SCHLEIERMACHER, FRIEDRICH (1768–1834). Often referred to as the "father of modern theology," Schleiermacher was born in Breslau in Silesia. Through his parents, he came early under the influence of the Moravian Pietists. He studied at Halle and became a Reformed pastor in Berlin. he later became a professor of theology at Halle, but returned to Berlin where he became dean of the university's theological faculty.

In 1799 he published the first edition of his *On Religion: Speeches to Its Cultured Despisers,* which stressed that the heart of religion is not dogma but "intuition and feeling." In this remarkable volume he attempted to persuade the cultured among the despisers of religion that despite the authoritarianism of the orthodox and the skepticism of the rationalists, being religious is rooted in the very experience of being a sensitive and responsive human being. This new emphasis upon experience reflected the influence of his earlier Pietism, which was similar to the romanticism of Coleridge, and it was to become important for many of the theologians of the nineteenth century.

In 1811 he published the first edition of his *Brief Outline of the Study of Theology*. In it he described each of the various theological disciplines, grouping them as philosophical, historical, or practical; and he suggested that they were like a tree, with roots and trunk and branches, flowering in "practical theology," understood as the preparation of scholarly pastors for the church.

His major work was his systematic theology, titled *The Christian Faith* (1821–22), in which he creatively rethought and reorganized the discussion of the various traditional doctrines, arranging them according to those religious experiences that he saw as their generative bases. Religious consciousness is, therefore, truly rooted in an authentic "sense of being utterly dependent." This sense, Schleiermacher argues, is truly universal and characteristically human, though it was, he affirms, uniquely and perfectly present in Jesus of Nazareth.

Schleiermacher was undoubtedly the most creative theologian in the nineteenth century, and despite the respectful protests of such twentieth century theologians as Karl Barth, his influence has continued in theology, as well as proving formative in the development of such disciplines as the philosophy and psychology of religion.

J. E. BURKHART

PRACTICAL THEOLOGY, PROTESTANT; THEOLOGY AND PSYCHOLOGY.

SCIENTOLOGY. *See* NEW RELIGIOUS MOVEMENTS; POPULAR THERAPEUTIC MOVEMENTS AND PSYCHOLOGIES; SECTARIAN PASTORAL CARE.

SCII (Strong-Campbell Interest Inventory). *See* EVALUATION AND DIAGNOSIS, PSYCHOLOGICAL.

SCOTUS, JOHN DUNS (ca. 1270–1308). Franciscan philosopher and theologian, one of the sharpest medieval minds.

Scotus's work is important for the theory of pastoral care and counseling as a domain of practical theology.

In connection with the question concerning the nature of theology, Scotus was the first medieval thinker to employ the concept of *praxis* philosophically or theologically and the first to raise the question about the nature of "practice."

In that context, he recovered and sharpened the Aristotelian notion of *praxis*, albeit deleting its political dimension and downplaying the difference between "doing" and "making." Thus, Scotus left to his theological successor a thoughtful, though controversial, argument for theology as *scientia practica* which, in scholastic thought, will be contrasted and juxtaposed, with Thomas's notion of theology as *scientia speculativa*. Scotus anticipated what will turn out to be the animating center of much of theology in the 1990s, namely, the primacy of *praxis* over theory, and the hermeneutical circle of action and reflection.

N. F. HAHN

PASTORAL THEOLOGY, ROMAN CATHOLIC; THEORY AND PRAXIS.

SCRIPT. A term in Eric Berne's transactional analysis used to depict an individual's unconscious life plan in totality. It consists of one's fantasies, attitudes, and "games" derived from early experiences that serve to shape the style of present interactions between self and environment.

M. DOLINSKY

TRANSACTIONAL ANALYSIS.

SCRIPTURE. *See* BIBLE; OLD TESTAMENT AND APOCRYPHA; NEW TESTAMENT.

SCRUPULOSITY. Habitual doubt and anxiety about moral decisions. It is usually centered around small details rather than large moral issues (hence the word "scruple" from the Latin word for a small sharp pebble such as travelers used to get in their shoes).

People who suffer from scruples are never at peace and are constantly worried over the slightest details of their behavior, convinced that they have sinned and will be punished by God. The sacrament of reconciliation (penance) becomes a means of ritual purification for them. They are compulsive in confessing minutiae, terrified of forgetting a sin and never convinced that they have made a "good confession." They are momentarily relieved by absolution but will inevitably be back to confession in a few days or a few hours. These same people are often totally unconcerned about such important issues as Christian charity and kindness. They frequently ignore serious responsibilities without any apparent concern.

In the Middle Ages scrupulosity was considered a trial allowed by God for the purification of a soul. But regardless of its origin it was treated by insisting that the scrupulous person exercise complete unquestioning obedience to the confessor. This often led to infantile dependence and resulted in more scruples about this obedience to the confessor. It was an ineffective treatment, dealing only with symptoms. The attempt to deal with this problem by theological reeducation about the mercy of God or other such logical approaches also proved futile. Scrupulous people may understand intellectually but will remain completely without insight about the source of their anxiety.

Today scrupulosity is considered an obsessive-compulsive disorder, displacement of anxiety, or the result of faulty learning, and so it belongs in the domain of clinical psychology, requiring therapeutic treatment. But many scrupulous people refuse to trust anyone except a clergyperson and will not submit to psychotherapy. In this case, the confessor (or other clergy) can work with the psychotherapist to help the scrupulous person become aware of the underlying conflicts that are taking the conscious form of obsession with sin and mistakes.

Scrupulosity seems to be related to an age variable, with puberty as the peak period, but it can occur at any time during life. The precise cause of this disorder is still a matter of theory, but some form of psychotherapy is always needed.

Bibliography. A. Snoeck, *Confession and Pastoral Psychology* (1961).

W. M. NOLAN

CONSCIENCE (Roman Catholicism); LEGALISM AND ANTINOMIANISM; OBSESSIVE- COMPULSIVE DISORDER; RIGHTEOUSNESS/BEING RIGHT. *Compare* CASUISTRY; PERFECTIONISM; SANCTIFICATION/HOLINESS.

SEAL OF CONFESSION. Everything revealed in the sacrament of reconciliation for the purpose of receiving absolution is "under the seal," kept inviolably secret by the priest. Nothing may be revealed (a) to third person(s); (b) to the penitent outside of the sacrament; (c) by action or omission on the part of the priest, to the disadvantage of the penitent. Betrayal of the seal is punishable by automatic excommunication removable only by the Holy See of the pope. The seal is mitigated only by the penitent's freely expressed permission. Anyone else who obtains knowledge of whatever is under the seal is also bound by the seal.

G. S. HARAK

BLESSING AND BENEDICTION; PENANCE, SACRAMENT OF. *Compare* CONFIDENTIALITY.

SEANCE. *See* SPIRITUALISM; SURVIVAL (Occult).

SECOND COMING OF CHRIST. *See* ESCHATOLOGY.

SECOND VATICAN COUNCIL. *See* VATICAN COUNCIL II AND PASTORAL CARE.

SECONDARY GAIN. In classical psychoanalysis, secondary gain (epinosis) referred to the positive effects of the "symptoms" (verbal expressions and motor behaviors) of a neurosis, particularly phobias, conversion reactions, and depression—for example, the sympathy one receives for being "sick." Secondary gain was contrasted to primary gain (paranosis), which is the reduction in anxiety and intrapsychic conflict that occurs when a neurosis is formed and maintained. Neurotic symptoms and the secondary gain from them are varied. For example, the depressive's symptoms (e.g., crying) may result in attention not usually received in a non-depressive state. Furthermore, neurotic behavior may be used as an "excuse" for avoiding stressful situations (e.g., sexual relationships), or to obtain control over people or situations.

In modern behavioral therapy, particularly in applications to the newer fields of health psychology and behavioral medicine, secondary gain is the reinforced state of a person wherein the probability of certain somatic and pain behaviors (e.g., moaning, limping) is increased, and the probability of aversive behaviors (e.g., going to a stressful job) is decreased. Many cases of chronic pain with minimal tissue damage are due, at least in part, from secondary gain.

R. H. FORMAN

HEALTH AND ILLNESS; PSYCHOPATHOLOGY, THEORIES OF. *See also* BEHAVIOR THERAPIES; NEUROSIS; PSYCHOANALYSIS; PSYCHOSOMATIC ILLNESS. *Compare* MALINGERING; SIN AND SICKNESS.

SECONDARY INFERTILITY. *See* INFERTILITY.

SECONDARY PROCESS. *See* PRIMARY AND SECONDARY PROCESS.

SECTARIAN PASTORAL CARE. Pastoral care in sectarian churches takes its character from the life of the religious community and concomitantly its carefully defined distance from "secular" society. Sectarianism refers to any group with relatively well defined boundaries, a common ideology and a sense of mission. The nature, clarity and sharpness of sectarian boundaries varies across groups and eras. Pastoral care and counseling is influenced by whether the sectarian separation is based on perceived intrinsic differences between the community and the rest of society, whether there is a difference in terms of confessions or loyalties, or whether the separation is a consequence of the unique customs of the religious community. In the first case, pastoral care focuses on maintaining separation while in the second it is concerned to develop behavior consistent with a religious confession. In the third case, pastoral care seeks to nurture individual growth through the exercise of communal rituals.

Sectarian groups tend to reject the institutionalized means of salvation and their life together constitutes an ethical protest. The community is held together by a common set of beliefs and a common history of experiences which legitimate pastoral authority (whether lay or clergy). Pastoral care encourages the development of a new personal identity, a commitment to the group, and a new view of the external world. Pastoral care involves the creation of alternative ethical communities. The following analysis of sectarian pastoral care will focus only on the sectarian groups in their most traditional stances. Various sectarian groups are clearly in different stages of transition from semi-seclusion to greater assimilation, though it is not assumed that this is an inevitable process.

1. **Types of Sects.** Wilson (1970) made a useful distinction between sects based on how they respond to the world, how they develop solutions to the problem of evil, and the kind of search for salvation they find acceptable. The following analysis makes some use of Wilson's typology and examines the corresponding mode of pastoral care.

a. Conversionist sects (Salvation Army, the Assemblies of God, some conservative Evangelical groups) assume there is a fundamental difference between believers and unbelievers by reason of an internal change of heart. This change is supernatural in source and primarily emotional in nature. It is a response to evil in society. The focus of pastoral care is nurturance of this inward state in members. Ministry means helping members develop a personal relationship with God. Evil in society is best dealt with in terms of conversion rather than social reform and hence pastoral care is concerned more about personal than social ethics. Secular modes of counseling are seen as questionable and pastors tend not to be formally educated.

b. Revolutionary sects (Jehovah's Witnesses, Christadelphians, Third World movements) respond to the evil of the world by awaiting a cataclysmic intervention of God or advocating the radical reordering of social, political, and economic structures. For Christadelphians, pastoral counseling is based on biblical prophecy. Pastoral care from a Third World perspective has a strongly prophetic character and is based on a critical evaluation of historical events. There is a distinct ideological interpretation of history and members are encouraged to live in the light of that perspective. The revolutionary sect assumes the inevitability of suffering but not destiny (Alves, 1977). Pastoral care is the comforting of the poor, the oppressed or the socially rejected community. Pastoral care is never seen as confirmation of the status quo but rather springs from a vision of a liberated or reformed society.

c. Isolationist sects (Exclusive Brethren, Doukhobor, Hutterian, Amish) also see the world as evil but do not expend much energy in proselytizing. The focus is the development of the colony. Pastoral care is devoted exclusively to developing the purity of the community relative to the external world (language, dress, beliefs, wealth, sexuality, pacifism, etc.), responding to community needs, and socializing the next generation into the ethos of the group. The life of the community is seen as salvation in and of itself and pastoral care is the maintenance of this community. Pastoral care may involve the excommunication of members. Generally, the function of pastoral care is distributed over the membership rather than localized in the religious leadership. The communities tend to be unaware of and do not consult counseling services external to the community.

d. Gnostic sects (Christian Science, Scientology) are set apart from society by an abstract, esoteric knowledge which tends to be an extension of traditional religious teachings or a combination of traditions. Corporate worship and community development are not central to "pastoral care" but are seen as means to the ends of education, health and happiness. The nature of pastoral care is not well-defined in these rather urban, secular sects. Christian Science practitioners function much like secular therapists to members of the community. Pastoral care is primarily didactic rather than affective or relational, initiating new recruits into the teachings of the group.

e. Reformist sects (Quakers) clearly seek to change the society in which they live on the basis of collective religious convictions. When agreement among the Quakers emerged over ethical issues (e.g., pacifism and slavery) members were censured if they violated the consensus. In the reformist sect there is a significant place for the authority of the group in individual decision making. Membership in the community is not dependent upon having had a particular religious experience (in contrast to conversionist sects) but on a willingness to search for inner wisdom, submit to the discernment of the community in contrast to all other communities (e.g., the state) and serve the larger common good. The reformist movements tend to reject the hierarchism of the traditional church and hence expect that pastoral care be exercised not by a single individual but by the community. It is assumed that perfection and freedom are possible in the present world. The positive view of human nature of Quakers implicit in reformist pastoral care is evident in the goal "to answer that of God in every one."

f. Communitarian / Utopian sects (Oneida Community, Bruderhof, Anabaptist-Mennonites) focus on the quality of the religious community as an alternative to the world. Anabaptists believe the church is to be a voluntary group of adult believers willing to follow Christ in word and deed. The organization of the Oneida or the Bruderhof communities has been founded on the model NT church. Strong internal discipline exists among Mennonites, including the use of the ban (separation). The goal of pastoral care can be summarized as follows: true teaching, proper use of Christian rituals (baptism, the Lord's Supper, foot-washing), separation from the world, mutual admonition, keeping all commandments, accepting suffering and persecution, and nurturing faith and community. The communitarian sects tend to engage in greater interaction with society than the isolationist sects but still view professional pastoral counseling with suspicion.

2. **Themes.** *a. Centrality of the believer community.* Cultural and geographic isolation and theological warrant tend to create a greater sense of importance for community life. The group may be seen as the elect of God (conversionist), the faithful remnant (revolutionist), the NT church (communitarian), or a society of friends (reformist). With the exception of the gnostic sects, group life is central. The congregation is the point of departure for religious life. The implication for pastoral care in sectarian groups is that the congregation itself becomes the self-sufficient resource of care-giving (e.g., Hutterite communities). Members are not encouraged to find emotional, financial, or spiritual support elsewhere. Crises are managed internally. The resources of the community are distributed according to the needs of the individual.

Furthermore, the laity are seen as primary caregivers. Lay shepherds assist with emotional distress, financial problems, doctrinal confusion and vocational guidance. The care-giving skills of laity are developed. As these groups lose their sectarianism, they tend to move to the traditional single pastor system.

b. Integration and separation. The goal of pastoral care in sectarian groups is the integration of the individual into the cognitive, emotional, and social dimensions of the community and separation from society. The whole is assumed to be greater than the parts and hence pastoral care is the renewal of and encouragement to communal life and sacrifice. This tends less to be the case in more gnostic sects which are more individualistic in contrast to the other sects where the believing community is perceived as the primary community for the creation of personal identity. Generally there is a rejection of unbridled autonomy and a call to service to and on behalf of the community. The relationship to external society receives careful attention and may be monitored.

Pastoral care in conversionist sects consists in the verification of the experience of being born again, acceptance of the Scriptures as authoritative, release from guilt for sins committed, and an expectation of changed behavior. When doctrine is more crystallized, as in the gnostic sects and less sectarian groups, the unique ideological perspective on the meaning of tragedy, emotional distress, healing, death, sickness, parenting, etc., is made the salient goal of pastoral counseling. In the more gnostic sects (Christian Science), pastoral care takes the form of initiating new recruits into the esoteric revelations of the community and assisting members as they move through various stages of enlightenment. When the sect is reformist in nature (Quaker), there is a shift away from doctrinal orthodoxy to a faithfulness in action to inner illumination.

c. Ethics. Sectarian groups tend to assume that the will of God can be known and that it is absolute. In the Anabaptist and Quaker traditions the religious community is seen as the context in which the will of God is discerned. Specifically, orthopraxy is developed regarding such issues as military service, flag salute, medical regulations, nutrition, dress, forms of amusement, acceptable occupations, sexuality, taxes, foods, endogamy, oath-swearing, voting, legal sanctions of marriage, labor unions and public education. As a result there is a greater emphasis on accountability and discipline. With the exception of the gnostic sects, it is assumed that there is a clear connection between ethics and pastoral care.

d. Distance from secular helping professions. In the early stages of development of sectarian groups there is a clear distrust of clerical learning. Manuals of pastoral care make little reference to sources of help external to the community. External helpers tend to be suspect. In some sects, secular knowledge is acceptable provided it does not contravene the particular knowledge of the community. Many of the sectarian groups described above have tended not be aware of or participate in the mainstream pastoral counseling movement in America. However, among those sects that have moved more into denominational status there is more frequent borrowing from the literature of the social sciences.

Bibliography. R. Alves, "Personal Wholeness and Political Creativity: The Theology of Liberation and Pastoral Care," *Pastoral Psychology,* 26 (1977), 124–136; H. Brinton, *Friends for 300 Years* (1952). D. Browning, *The Moral Context of Pastoral Care* (1976). D. John, *The Christian Science Way of Life* (1962). F. Littell, *The Origins of Sectarian Protestantism: A Study of the Anabaptist View of the Church* (1964). B. Wilson, *Religious Sects: A Sociological Study* (1970).

A. C. DUECK

PASTORAL CARE (History, Traditions, and Definitions). *See also* ECCLESIOLOGY AND PASTORAL CARE; HISTORY OF PROTESTANT PASTORAL CARE (United States). *Compare* CHARISMATIC, CHRISTIAN SCIENCE, FUNDAMENTALIST, MORMON, PIETIST, *or* QUAKER PASTORAL CARE.

SECTS. *See* CHURCH-SECT DIFFERENCES; NEW RELIGIOUS MOVEMENTS.

SECULAR PRIESTHOOD. *See* MINISTRY (Roman Catholic Tradition).

SECULARIZATION/SECULARISM. *Secularization* (from *saeculum,* world) can refer to: (1) the expropriation of ecclesiastical properties by civil authorities; (2) that post-Enlightenment development in which intellectual life increasingly freed itself from the tutelage of the church and supranatural revelation in order to base knowledge on intramundane authorities, classically described by Dietrich Bonhoeffer as that "one great development which leads to the idea of the autonomy of the world . . . [in which] there is no longer any need for God as a working hypothesis." (1972, p. 359); (3) the waning credibility of the religious worldview under the impact of the alternative worldview of modern science,

with religion regarded as a purveyor of superstitions (Marx) or as an early explanation of phenomena now better explained by the natural sciences (Comte); and (4) in contemporary sociology, the fact that religion no longer provides the common assumptions and values that bind a culture together. According to Max Weber, increased religious *pluralism* results in competing centers of value, no one of which can provide a binding world view. Pluralism requires tolerance as the one universally held value. But tolerance tends to undermine the cohesiveness of a culture. Some sociologists (e.g., R. Bellah, D. Martin, T. Luckmann) claim that religion in other guises still plays a significant part in the social ethos. The fact remains, however, that secularization always means decreased general acquaintance with religion, and that pastoral care can no longer assume in the *general* population familiarity with, and convictions rooted in, biblical religion and traditional religious values.

1. Theological Developments Since World War II.
a. Contributions of Gogarten. Religious institutions have quite naturally opposed and decried the historical development of *secularization,* with its accompanying decline in the authority and power of the church and religious ethos. After World War II, however, a more positive appreciation of secularization emerged, sparked by Bonhoeffer's reflections (1972) but most fully developed by Friedrich Gogarten (1970). Gogarten distinguishes between legitimate "secularization," whose roots he sees in the Christian gospel itself, and "secularism," the ideological distortion of secularization. Genuine secularization, claims Gogarten, begins in the Bible itself, with the Hebrew demystification of the nature gods of surrounding tribes and the NT's insistence that the principalities and powers have been overcome by the cross of Christ. This "disenchantment" (*Entzauberung,* M. Weber) of the creation makes it possible to view the world as an object for investigation and ordering rather than as the sacred province of the gods, and gives rise to the objective and analytical attitudes of modern science.

Secularization, however, becomes secularism, an *ideology,* says Gogarten, when this-worldly authorities are absolutized and the management of the world is removed from the Christian faith context of stewardship and answerability to the transcendent Source. The motivations for secularist ideology vary. It may arise in resistance to the authority of the church, especially when the church confuses itself with the Absolute to which it testifies, and seeks to extend arbitrary control over all aspects of life. It may arise, as in Marxism, out of a doctrinaire materialism or out of the practical necessity to disabuse the peasantry of religious superstitions in order to rationalize agricultural production. In capitalist countries, secularism may not take such an aggressively doctrinaire form, but the *laissez-faire* economy assumes god-like qualities —all-powerful, unpredictable, fateful, yet trusted as ultimately benevolent (Adam Smith's "Invisible Hand") —while the witness and function of religion are restricted to the realm of the personal and private.

The result of these modern developments, according to Gogarten, has not been the disappearance of religion but the emergence of pseudo-religions and idolatrous substitutes. The wholeness and unity to life, once supplied by religion, must now be introduced by either secular authorities, who rely on propaganda and the power of the state to enforce a total vision, or sectarian messiahs, who promise order out of pluralistic confusion for those who submit to their authority. Thus, totalitarianisms on the right and left become the ironic quasi-religious products of secularism. The relative is absolutized because no genuinely transcendent point of reference functions to keep the relative relative and self-critical.

b. Theological development in America. Harvey Cox takes as his point of departure (1965) a more optimistic evaluation of secularization and celebrates the "world come of age" (Bonhoeffer) as the world of human responsibility freely accepted. Viewing the development from a historian's perspective, Gabriel Vahanian talks instead of *The Death of God,* while Thomas Altizer (1966) rejoices in the Dionysian possibilities for human self-expression opened up by this reputed death. Conservative Christians respond with attempts to roll back "secular humanism" by political efforts to restore marks of a religious ethos — e.g., prayer in public schools — or by creating alternative subcultures and Christian schools.

2. **Implications for Pastoral Care.** From the standpoint of pastoral care, secularization has implications as complex and multifaceted as they are unavoidable.

First, the waning of "Christian culture" means that knowledge of Christian imagery and values no longer permeates the general population. Viewed more positively, this general ignorance of Christian tradition may open a window of opportunity for theological interpretations to enter with the force of new, fresh insights.

Second, personal distress can take new forms — the shift that Tillich, for example, sees from the "guilt and condemnation" of an earlier age that understood itself *vis à vis* God, to the "emptiness and meaninglessness" of today's "culture of narcissism" (C. Lasch), which lacks any *vis à vis.*

Third, identity problems arise because, in a pluralistic culture of many competing worldviews, there exists no one generally accepted norm for social relations and social identity. As each person is left to shape his or her own identity, confusion reigns. Individuals feel claimed by multiple identities without any transcendent standard to determine the validity of various claims. Commitments are hard to make and harder to keep (R. Hunter).

Fourth, parenting becomes more difficult because the society no longer serves as the religious co-educator of children (John Westerhoff, *Will Our Children Have Faith?*), and no "cognitive community" (P. Berger) exists to reinforce the plausibility of religious values. Moreover, children breathe deeply of the autonomy and individualism of secular culture, and therefore tend to discredit traditional values in favor of those arrived at independently from parents, usually under the influence of peers. This results in horizontal value structures, inherently unstable and subject to breakdown with changes in peer groups.

Fifth, pastoral care itself has not remained unaffected by these same relativizing and secularizing tendencies. Pastoral counseling has taken over not only the methods but also many of the values of the secular disciplines of psychology and sociology. In comparison with scientific analysis, the language of theology, the Bible, and religious tradition may appear archaic, imprecise and obfus-

cating. "How can pastoral counseling be at the same time both an authentically theological and a scientifically psychological discipline?" asks Charles Gerkin (1984, p. 11). The temptation is to abandon pastoral care's traditional task of guidance within a theological framework (D. Browning, 1976) in favor of value-neutral analysis. But this results in the loss of a distinctive identity and contribution by the pastoral counselor.

The alternative is a conscious reappropriation of the theological, communal, and therapeutic resources of the faith, employing the means of grace — the sacraments, the appropriate use of prayer, biblical stories that function hermeneutically, and a supportive covenantal community of mutual responsibility (T. Oden, A. Campbell, J. Fowler).

Thus, although unalterably opposed to secularism, Christianity does not reject secularization as such but itself "secularizes" by bringing all loyalties under the control of one overarching covenantal relation that opens up the possibilities for human freedom, identity, community, and responsibility in a properly relative world.

Bibliography. T. Altizer, *The Gospel of Christian Atheism* (1966). R. Bellah, *Beyond Belief* (1970). P. Berger, *The Sacred Canopy* (1969). D. Bonhoeffer, *Letters and Papers from Prison* (1972). D. Browning, *The Moral Context of Pastoral Care* (1976). A. V. Campbell, *Rediscovering Pastoral Care* (1981). H. Cox, *The Secular City* (1965). J. Fowler, *Faith Development and Pastoral Care* (1986). C. Gerkin, *The Living Human Document* (1984). F. Gogarten, *Despair and Hope for Our Time* (1970). R. Hunter, "Commitment as Psychological Process: Theory and Pastoral Implications," *Pastoral Psychology,* 24 (1976), 190–205. C. Lasch, *The Culture of Narcissism* (1980). T. Luckmann, *The Invisible Religion* (1970). D. Martin, *A General Theory of Secularization* (1978). T. C. Oden, "Recovering Lost Identity," *J. of Pastoral Care,* 34 (1980), 4–19. D. S. Pacini, *The Cunning of Modern Religious Thought* (1987). G. Vahanian, *The Death of God* (1966). M. Weber, *The Sociology of Religion* (1963); *From Max Weber* (1946). J. Westerhoff, *Will Our Children Have Faith?* (1976).

T. RUNYON

DOUBT AND UNBELIEF; RELIGION; WORLD VIEW. *See also* CULTURAL ANTHROPOLOGY OF RELIGION; INTERPRETATION AND HERMENEUTICS, PASTORAL; PHILOSOPHY AND PSYCHOLOGY, WESTERN; SOCIOLOGY OF RELIGIOUS AND PASTORAL CARE. *Compare* APOSTASY; MATERIALISM; VALUES RESEARCH.

SEELSORGE. The task of watching over and caring for souls, first shared by all members of the Christian community (Gal. 6:1–2), later expected of elders (Heb. 13:17), and ultimately conferred on the priest at ordination. Reformers such as Luther and Bucer reasserted *Seelsorge* as a mutual obligation of believers, and gave it prominence in their writings.

A. L. MEIBURG

PASTORAL CARE (History, Traditions, and Definitions); WESTERN EUROPEAN PASTORAL CARE MOVEMENT. *See also* CARE OF SOULS.

SEGREGATION, RACIAL, AND PASTORAL CARE. *See* RACISM. *See also* PROPHETIC/PASTORAL TEN-

SION IN MINISTRY; SOCIAL CHANGE AND DISLOCATION; SOCIAL JUSTICE ISSUES.

SEIZURES. *See* EPILEPSY.

SELF, PHILOSOPHY OF. What differentiates a person or makes one the being one is.

1. Concepts of Selfhood. On a materialist view the self is the body, or some part of it, e.g., the brain. Few hold this in an outright form, but there is wide support for the "identity thesis" which acknowledges that there are both mental and physical processes but refuses to drive a wedge between them (Strawson, 1959, ch. 3; Hirst, 1959). Some impressive versions of this theory tend to culminate in physicalism (O'Shaughnessy, 1980). Such views are sharply opposed to dualism which holds that mental processes are essentially distinct from material ones, whether the latter are thought to exist in their own right or, as in forms of idealism, in some ultimately mind-dependent way.

Some, like Hume, refuse to look for the self beyond the flow of some association or pattern of mental processes themselves. Others, such as Plato, Augustine, Descartes, and Kant think of the self as some "owner" of experiences beyond the events themselves, the entity that has or enjoys the experiences. They occasionally, as with Kant, place the self so much outside the events themselves that it is timeless. The self, as other than the experiences, is sometimes thought to be identical in all persons, a "pure self" which is also the Supreme Self, as in some mysticism (Stace, 1980, ch. 5). It is a view which has prominence in Oriental religions, notably Hinduism. This has also some affinity with the thought of Hegel and nineteenth-century idealism. The self here is a "center of unification" within the whole of experience (the Absolute). It is the complete self or person, inclusive of all others.

2. The Problem of the Reality of the Self. A renowned modern view is behaviorism which reduces the self to behavior as prescribed by tendencies or dispositions (Ryle, 1949). There is, thus, no self as entity. As with outright materialism this view is hard to accommodate to the worth we place on various experiences and on moral actions which seem to require an "inner" reality altogether distinct from mere bodily existence.

Views which confer on the self some reality beyond the actual course of mental occurrences are attractive; this is what the most distinctive forms of dualism offer. The self, on such views, is a "something," which has or owns the experiences and has genuine initiative in action. (Ward, 1977, ch. 15). But the issue here is peculiarly difficult to handle. For if the self is more than dispositional tendencies or character or the actual course of mental existence, there is no way in which it can be described or identified as other things are. What is an entity of which nothing can be said? How can it be known? The answer seems to be in terms of each one's immediate awareness in one's own case. In the stock example, I am aware of a pain in having it—and also that it is *my* pain. To ask how I know, in such case, is absurd. In the case of persons other than oneself there must be evidence—screams, groans, wounds or, sometimes, mere dependable affirmation, etc. I may note such things in my own case too, but that is not how I know that I am in pain—that it is *me*. I feel the pain, and I can only feel it as my own. It is meaningful to add to there being the pain that it is mine, and so for all experience. One recognizes in one's own case a distinctness which one cannot describe, an elusive "deep further fact," as Derek Parfit puts it (Lewis, 1982).

Intimations of this are found in the way the unified character of experience, the way we make sense of things, presupposes, as Kant especially taught, an abiding subject distinct from all the particular items apprehended in this way. However it is doubtful whether we can carry this through (and avoid the pitfalls of a 'timeless self' which can hardly be alive and active in the real world where we are) without the initial immediate and peculiar awareness of self which each one has and ascribes to others in ascribing experience to them.

3. Selfhood and Temporal Continuity. The main guarantee of the continuity of the self which one is through various experiences is the memory we have of past experiences as having the same awareness of oneself. Around this is built all that we independently know of the course of our lives to establish our continued existence as the same persons. This seems to have far-reaching implications, although some thinkers (including many today) are content with describing identity in terms of patterns and connectedness of experience, or they regard these as all that matters for what is of worth or interest to us (cf. Parfit, 1971).

This is well seen in questions of survival or further existence. Is it enough that there should be some connectedness of our experience now and hereafter? Will it suffice if a replica reproduces and continues all I would expect to be and do? Or is it important in some further deeper way that it should be me? This is the main divide in major worldviews and religions. The Semitic tradition and subsequent Christian and Muslim attitudes start with the notion of beings maintained by God as distinct from God and from one another. The normal Oriental view, to which nineteenth-century idealism was close, was the notion of one all-inclusive system of being of which all are limitations or appearances. The "no-soul" doctrine of Buddhism tends to the same elimination of any final distinctness of persons, but it also recognizes the elusiveness of persons, and proposes *nirvana* which is *emptiness and fullness too.*

The elimination of the distinctness of self as the hallmark of a person, in various forms of monism, mysticism, and reductionism common today, seems out of accord with much that we deem to be of greatest concern. Survival, if thought to be important at all (and most persons seem to think it is), is survival of the particular being that each of us seems to be. It is to the real friends "we have lost awhile" that we look to be united.

4. Selfhood and Responsibility. Likewise in morals, as usually in law, we do not shed responsibility with change and the passage of time. I may have repented of vicious deeds and been forgiven, but I remain now the person who was guilty at the time in doing them. We should not try to shed that fact in coping with guilt and its implications. Our past does not wholly drop out of the picture, and it remains our own. It has its involvement in the redeemed state itself. It is also the self as more than its character at one time that can be the agent in freedom of choice between genuinely open alternatives — the supreme condition of properly moral good and evil (Campbell, 1967). All healing involves these matters. Forgiveness is not, as some suppose, a mere matter of exculpation but of bringing genuine guilt within the ambit of love. We are not transitory features of a passing scene but creatures who have to live out our lives as a rounded whole.

For the same reason we should not cast our responsibilities on others or on society, much though we are involved with one another and dependent on society. We must answer "one by one"; and our other achievements are those of the beings we severally are.

5. Self and Others. It is also essential in all personal relations to be deeply sensitive to the genuine inner existence of one another. Perversions, like cruelty or sadism and tragic estrangements come about through trying to force ourselves beyond the barrier of each one's personal existence, and thus to possess and dominate rather than be in communication with a genuine other. When love is most deep and intimate it must also distance itself in respect and reverence. Those we love are not actors in a private drama of our own; they exist as other selves in their own right. We need this realism, not the world of fantasy. We otherwise lapse into passionate excitation without tenderness. That in turn easily drives us to frustration and the horror of ultimate loneliness, the "somber solitude" to which Bertrand Russell (1968, pp. 157, 160) gives moving testimony.

6. Self and God. God loves us with reverence for what we are; God does not overwhelm or annihilate. God comes in the gentle ways of disclosure within our own deepest awareness. God draws us with bonds of reverent love, not violence, and this is why God's proper transcendence must be seen to involve our own distinctness as created beings. It is the same terms we bring to the marvel and the finality of incarnation.

This is not an extension of some divinity we all have in measure. We are not divine but finite beings, notwithstanding being made in the image of God. But this calls us also to take God's transcendence seriously, and in that way we may take the irreducible mystery of God's being to allow for something we cannot in any way understand in itself, but to which we are irresistibly impelled in our sensitive assimilation of the long course of divine disclosure and of the appropriate evidence of Scriptures.

Bibliography. A. J. Ayer, *The Concept of a Person* (1963). C. A. Campbell, *On Selfhood and Godhood* (1957); *In Defense of Free Will* (1967). R. G. Hirst, *Problems of Perception* (1959). J. N. Lapsley, "The Self: Its Vicissitudes and Possibilities: An Essay in Theological Anthropology," *Pastoral Psychology*, 35:1 (1986), 23–45. H. D. Lewis, *The Elusive Mind* (1969); *The Elusive Self* (1982); *Self and Immortality* (1973). G. Madell, *The Identity of the Self* (1981) B. O'Shaughnessy, *The Will* (1980). B. L. Mijuskovic, *Loneliness in Philosophy, Psychology, and Literature* (1979). D. Parfit, *Personal Identity* (1977); "Personal Identity," *Philosophical Review*, 80 (1971), 3–27. T. Penelhum, *Survival and Disembodied Existence* (1970). A. O. Rorty, ed., *The Identities of Persons* (1976). B. Russell, *Autobiography*, vol. 2 (1968). G. Ryle, *The Concept of Mind* (1949). S. Shoemaker, *Self-Knowledge and Self-Identity* (1963). W. T. Stace, *Mysticism and Philosophy* (1980). I. Stevenson, *Twenty Cases Suggestive of Reincarnation* (1966). P. G. Strawson, *Individuals* (1959). G. N. A. Vesey, *Body and Mind* (1964); *The Embodied Mind* (1965). J. Ward, *Psychological Principles* (1977).

H. D. LEWIS

PERSON (Philosophical Issues); PHILOSOPHY AND PSYCHOLOGY. *See also* EGO, PSYCHOLOGICAL MEANINGS AND THEORY OF; I AND THOU; PERSONAL, CONCEPT OF, IN PASTORAL CARE; PERSONALITY THEORY (Varieties, Traditions, and Issues); RESPONSIBILITY/IRRESPONSIBILITY, PSYCHOLOGY OF; SELF PSYCHOLOGIES; TIME/TIME SENSE. *Compare* MIND; PSYCHE; SOUL.

SELF, PSYCHOLOGICAL THEORIES OF. *See* PERSONALITY THEORY; SELF PSYCHOLOGIES. *See also* ANALYTICAL PSYCHOLOGY; EXISTENTIAL PSYCHOLOGY; HUMANISTIC PSYCHOLOGY; NEOFREUDIAN PERSONALITY THEORIES; OBJECT RELATIONS THEORY; PHENOMENOLOGICAL PSYCHOLOGY; PSYCHOANALYSIS.

SELF-ACTUALIZATION/SELF-REALIZATION. Refers to a drive or tendency evident within all organic and human life to grow, develop, mature, and thereby actualize or realize the potentialities of the organism and the self. Carl Rogers and Abraham Maslow developed the notion of self-actualization/self-realization in the 1960s, through their separate but similar growth-oriented personality theories.

For Carl Rogers, a human relationship of complete acceptance and understanding—"unconditional positive regard"—is prerequisite to actualizing the self's inherent potentialities. If a person receives conditional regard—socially imposed "conditions of worth"—then self-actualization is compromised. The individual will defend himself or herself against societal disapproval by denying or distorting the natural unfolding of his or her true potential. Rogers recognizes the need for some social constraints and states that a relationship of respect and acceptance can counter the need for defense.

Within an accepting relationship, a self-actualized, "fully functioning person" will develop. Such persons are characterized by emotional depth, spontaneity, flexibility, confidence, creativity, and openness to new experience. Because a self-actualized person is fundamentally self-accepting, she or he will value and accept others as well.

Abraham Maslow's main difference with Rogers is that he sees the satisfaction of a hierarchy of needs as prerequisite for self-actualization. At the bottom of the hierarchy are basic physiological needs essential to survival. Building upon these basic needs are affiliative needs for belonging, love, and social acceptance. When these foundational needs are met, the push toward actualization of the person's unique capabilities occurs.

Critics of self-actualization argue that this theory underestimates the extent to which larger social systems or forces interfere with or block an individual's growth. The assumption that growth will occur spontaneously given a loving human relationship, is also naive and fails to recognize the powerful resistance to growth that is operative at an unconscious level. Finally, self-actualization does not address the human need for explicit cultural and religious values and norms for moral living or personal growth.

The Christian tradition's view of the human propensity toward sin and evil offers a corrective to the naive optimism of self-actualization. However, the Christian tradition also reflects a dialectical tension. On the one hand, one Genesis story presents humanity as "fallen" and henceforth inclined toward evil (Genesis 3). On the other hand, another creation account emphasizes that humanity (male and female) is created in the image of God (Genesis 1).

A third position offered in the NT helps bridge these seemingly contradictory views of human nature. This position also offers another vantage point from which to view self-actualization. Even though we have the *imago dei* within us, we need divine help in realizing this potential. According to the NT tradition, humanity needs liberation—made possible through the death and resurrection of Jesus Christ—from those individual and systemic forces of sin that block our growth toward becoming all that God created us to be. The Christian tradition also asserts that we need the community of faith which is empowered by the Holy Spirit and that it is within the body of Christ that potentialities for human wholeness can be realized by the calling forth of each member's gifts.

Bibliography. H. J. Clinebell, *Contemporary Growth Therapies* (1981). S. Maddi, *Personality Theories* 4th ed. (1980). C. Rogers, *On Becoming a Person* (1961).

D. L. SILVER

PERSONALITY DEVELOPMENT; HUMANISTIC PSYCHOLOGY; SELF. *See also* BEING/BECOMING RELATIONSHIP; CAUSALITY IN PSYCHOLOGY, FORMS OF; DEVELOPMENTAL THEORY AND PASTORAL CARE; PHILOSOPHY AND PSYCHOLOGY. *Compare* HAPPINESS; HUMANNESS/HUMANISM; INDIVIDUATION; PROCESS, CONCEPT OF; SELF-TRANSCENDENCE.

SELF-ANALYSIS. An aspiration accompanied by an attempt, on the part of an individual, to be patient and analyst simultaneously. It can also be described as a person's systematic striving for self-knowledge in order to be able to deal more effectively with life and to develop one's potential.

Karen Horney outlined the ways in which the discoveries of psychoanalysis could both significantly enhance the process of self-analysis as well as reveal the formidable difficulties and limitations of such an endeavor. According to her, the three main tasks confronting a person in self-analysis are: (1) expression of feelings as honestly and completely as possible; (2) awareness of unconscious driving forces and their impact on life; and (3) development of a capacity to change disturbing relations with others and oneself.

The process of open, unreserved, true expression of feelings is the basis of self-analysis. Horney suggests the following to enhance free association: (1) express actual feelings, not only acceptable feelings; (2) give as free and wide a range to feelings as possible; and (3) be as spontaneous as possible, abstaining from logical reasoning. Inevitably, if one is honest in this process, one discovers patterns of dealing with one's "resistances," as various hurts and painful memories arise, expressing themselves in the form of: (1) open fights against provoking problem; (2) defensive emotional reactions; and (3) evasive

maneuvers. Concerning the first two expressions listed, a person typically finds it much easier to appeal to a "right" to be angry than to examine what vulnerable spot has been touched. There is no doubt that it is in one's best interests to proceed in this examination even if another person actually has been unfair or cruel. Regarding the third form, the defensive inhibitions and evasions operate in a devious manner. They may cause one to intellectualize about one's feelings rather than allow one to associate freely. Or, they may produce a nonchalant attitude toward the process.

The belief that people are largely helpless regarding their resistances and, therefore, cannot overcome them without professional help, is the strongest argument against self-analysis. This is further corroborated by reports of both patients and therapists who have experienced the subtle and complex nature of such phenomena. This brings to light the fact that psychoanalysis is a process which is affected by more than the sum of the patient's work and the therapist's work, but it is affected also by their relationship. Horney therefore cautions that it is preferable for one to have had a therapeutic relationship with an expert psychoanalyst before proceeding into self-analysis. She also says that self-analysis can legitimately replace psychoanalysis, in the traditional sense, as one specific means of personal growth (K. Horney, *Self-Analysis*, 1942).

KIRK A. KENNEDY

SELF-EXAMINATION; SELF-HELP PSYCHOLOGIES; SELF-UNDERSTANDING.

SELF-CENTEREDNESS. *See* EGOTISM; NARCISSISM; PRIDE AND HUMILITY.

SELF-CONCEPT. A complex configuration of beliefs and attitudes about the self, constituting a basic structure of personality, with important interactional, motivational, and cognitive attributes. The term generally refers to the self as object of the individual's knowledge and evaluation. Self-concept and related self referents (e.g., perceived self, ego-identity, self-image) have been assigned a central role in most modern theories of personality development and functioning by such theorists as Allport, Angyal, Cattell, Erikson, Fromm, Horney, Jung, Maslow, Rogers, and Sullivan. It is the supra-moderator of perception and functioning, which must include a relative degree of internal consistency, self-acceptance, and objectivity for healthy adjustment. While technical definitions vary, the term is most commonly associated with Rogerian personality theory, where it has been most thoroughly operationalized and developed.

In Carl Rogers's view, the self-concept is a structure of conscious and unconscious beliefs about the self, including (1) self characteristics, (2) self in relation to others, (3) personal values, and (4) personal ideas and goals. It begins to evolve as soon as the infant becomes aware of his or her distinct physical and social self and starts to experience differentiated interaction with others. Cognitions and awareness are integrated psychologically on the basis of the child's inherent "organismic" valuing system, or on a scale introduced by significant others. Because in early development the individual is vitally dependent on others, he or she tends to accept information and labels from others, even when it disagrees with his or her internal discriminations. Thus, all perceptions of the self at this stage are strongly influenced by information originating outside the organism, and the fundamentals of the self-concept are introjected from significant others.

Whatever the nature of the basic self-concept, it will tend to resist challenge and change, since it is primarily associated with conditions of self-worth. Thus, later perceptions that do not agree with it will be unconsciously distorted and denied, while perceptions more consistent with it will be more accurately experienced and accepted. In this way, the self-concept may become increasingly inaccurate, unrealistic, and rigid. Moreover, to the degree that the self-concept is incongruent with the "objective" or real self, maladjustment will occur, since awareness must be inhibited to avert discrepant information.

A major explicit goal of Rogerian therapy, and implicit within most other psychotherapies, is to make the self-concept more inclusive, more flexible, and more discriminating. This will increase adaptability and reduce defensiveness, and thus facilitate mental health and self-actualization.

Bibliography. C. Rogers, *On Becoming a Person* (1961). C. S. Evans, "The Concept of the Self as the Key to Integration," *J. of Psychology and Christianity*, 3:2, 4–11.

W. BECKER

IDENTITY; SELF. *See also* PERSONALITY THEORY. *Compare* SELF-ESTEEM.

SELF-CONFIDENCE. *See* SELF-ESTEEM.

SELF-CONTROL. *See* SELF-EXPRESSION/SELF-CONTROL.

SELF-DECEPTION. *See* DENIAL; SELF-UNDERSTANDING. *See also* COGNITIVE DISSONANCE; REPRESSION.

SELF-DENIAL. Normally, the sacrifice of egoistic desires in order to affirm a higher personal loyalty or ideal.

1. Self-Denial and Self-Fulfillment. Both psychologically and theologically, self-denial can be viewed as a form of behavior oriented ultimately toward self-fulfillment. By refusing to follow the voices within and without which offer direct or immediate gratification, we seek to affirm ourselves in another, presumably more worthy or significant way, thereby aiming implicitly or indirectly at self-fulfillment. Self-denial can, however, also be motivated by hostile, punitive attitudes toward oneself. Thus, self-fulfillment seems impossible without self-denial, but without some form of self-affirmation and self-fulfillment as its underlying impetus, self-denial becomes pathological and life-denying.

Everyday human endeavors exemplify the complex motivational possibilities in self-denial, from its self-destructive forms to those aimed at realizing self-fulfillment: losing weight, overcoming alcoholism, excelling in athletics, developing necessary work discipline, restraining and directing sexual desire. All these can involve, at times, an element of ascetic or even heroic self-denial in the interest of

self-fulfillment, as well as negative meanings related to guilt, shame, and self-deprecation.

Positive self-denial (as distinguished from self-hatred) implies a transformation of self. The self, gratified solely by the sating of solipsistic biological and emotional needs, seeks to be transformed into a self that loves not for itself alone, but rather for itself in union with others and in continuity with enduring human values. Perhaps nowhere is this more easily and universally seen than in love relationships. True self-fulfillment in love is found only by a self that bears the qualities of love, that orders its desires in relation to the welfare and needs of the one who is loved. To become a loving person in this sense requires a daily transformation of one's "old self"; one struggles to leave behind or "die" to narcissistic attitudes and behaviors that prevent this transformation from taking place.

2. Pathological Self-Denial. Seen from this perspective, neurosis and personality disorders are distortions or, in some instances, even inversions of this transformative process. According to some theorists (for example humanistic and neo-Freudian psychologists), the etiology of neurosis and personality disorders consists, at least in part, in becoming alienated from one's true self, from the potential to transcend oneself in authentic love relationships and commitment to enduring human values by consciously and/or unconsciously clinging to a false self. A syndrome of such maneuvers is often learned in childhood to win the love and approval of others (Horney, 1950).

Because this false self is inauthentic and detrimental to personal growth it causes various forms of psychic distress and (sometimes) bodily pain. But, blinded, as it were, to the truth about authentic self-fulfillment, these self-denying tendencies are perceived as representing reality and being necessary for survival. Thus, one believes that the need to be submissive or in control, or worthy of love in ways destructive to self and others, is necessary to psychological survival and therefore cannot be relinquished, however painful it may be to maintain them. Such pathological convictions can leave one feeling trapped and helpless, though psychotherapy can provide the means of freeing oneself from this confining and confusing impasse.

3. Theological Perspective. Biblically and theologically, the mystery of personal identity, of what it means to be a self, is rooted in our origin as creatures of God and in that special relation to God which is God's unique gift to us. Theologically the true self is in a relationship of likeness to God (*imago dei*) sharing perfectly in the life of the Word, in the unity of the Holy Spirit, and through this relationship in fellowship with one another. Apart from this union we are nothing (John 1; Col. 1:15–20; Eph. 1:3–6).

Human suffering and death are revealed in Scripture as having their origin in humanity's free decision to refuse to be the true self that exists in relationship to God (Genesis 3). In opposition to and alienation from God, a distorted, false form of selfhood is born that experiences itself not in the truth of ontological relationship to God, sustaining one's being, but in the illusion of being an absolute, autonomous ego capable of defining itself out of its own choices. From this alienation spring violence, injustice and all that is symptomatic of humanity's ignorance of and alienation from the true meaning of persons created in God's image and likeness.

Religious faith is rooted in a personal awakening and response in relationship to God. In specifically Christian terms this awakening is understood in terms of the indwelling Spirit opening one's eyes to the Lordship of Jesus as the one in and through whom one's new life comes. That is, Jesus of Nazareth is recognized spiritually as the Eternal Word through whom we were created and through whom we as sinners are forgiven and created anew through our participation in his cross and resurrection.

The response to this awakening is understood in terms of a discipleship that entails a daily dying to the illusory self apart from God in order to enter more deeply into a living, existential awareness of one's true self "hid with Christ in God" (Col. 3:3) and into loving, peaceful, just and redemptive relations with fellow humanity. Self denial—taking up one's cross and following him (Lk. 14:27) — is therefore intrinsic to Christian life, not as an expression of contempt for our created nature, much less as a masochistic, pathological attitude toward self, but as a grateful affirmation of authentic selfhood in rightly ordered divine and human relationship which God in Christ has made possible for us.

4. Counseling Approaches. The Christian committed to this faith conviction finds within every personal struggle a paradox. On one hand, suffering in union with Christ is purifying and redemptive; only if we die with Christ can we rise with him (II Cor. 4:7–12). The Christian knows that in an earthly condition in which one's only certitude about the future is death, true happiness and fulfillment cannot be found in living on one's own terms. On the other hand, even while "knowing" these things, one can still become enmeshed in anger, resentment, fear, or other negative feelings and desires that exert a dominating influence incompatible with what one professes to believe.

This living paradox dictates the central task of the Christian counselor: namely, to help the counselee to deny that self which denies the truth of God's Word at a level where it impinges upon the deepest forces of human existence. The task of the Christian counselor is to lead the counselee to die to a separate and ultimately unreal self that is blind to the unconditional love, the ever faithful presence that sustains in every trial, supports with mercy in every failing, and gives birth to hope, even in death itself.

This approach to pastoral counseling assumes three things: (1) that the counselee encounters Christ's presence not simply in Bible quotations and sermonettes, but in the compassion of the counselor who is willing to suffer with the client and struggle with him or her in the search for wholeness; (2) that the Christian counselor knows the symptoms indicative of disorders requiring competent clinical intervention, and employs these measures where appropriate or refers the person to someone capable of doing so; (3) that the counselee is given assistance in recognizing the means available to grow in personal faith and in awareness of life in union with God. The possibilities for growth in daily prayer, love relationships, and service to others, for example, should be carefully explored.

Bibliography. D. Allen, *Love: Christian Romance, Marriage, Friendship* (1987). P. J. Caplan, *The Myth of Women's Masochism* (1985). T. Hora, *Existential Metapsychiatry* (1977). K. Horney, *Neurosis and Human Growth* (1950). S. Kierkegaard, *Purity of Heart* (1948). J. B. McCandless, "Christian Commitment and a 'Docetic' View of Human Emotions," *J. of Religion and Health,* 23 (1984), 125–137. R. May, *Freedom and Destiny* (1981). M. S. Peck, *The Road Less Traveled* (1978). P. Tillich, *The Courage To Be* (1952).

J. FINLEY
F. GONZALEZ

ASCETICAL PRACTICES; CHRISTIAN LIFE; SELF-ESTEEM; SELF-EXPRESSION/SELF- CONTROL. *See also* LIFESTYLE ISSUES IN PASTORAL CARE; PHYSICAL FITNESS DISCIPLINES; SELF-ACTUALIZATION/SELF-REALIZATION; SELF-ANALYSIS; SELF-EXAMINATION; SELF-TRANSCENDENCE. *Compare* GIVING AND RECEIVING.

SELF-DESTRUCTIVE BEHAVIOR. Actions or tendencies that harm or destroy oneself. The most familiar forms include those behavioral manifestations that result in death or injury and that are usually consciously inflicted upon the self. Such behavior is classified as direct self-destructive behavior because it is visible and its effect is immediate. Indirect self-destructive behavior differs from direct in relation to two important criteria: time and awareness. The effect is not immediate but long-range, and the behavior may cover many years. The person involved in indirect self-destructive behavior may be unaware, only partially aware, or not concerned about the effects of the behavior. Also, the person usually does not view such behavior as self-destructive. Thus, as Norman Farberow (1980) has summarized, self-destruction occurs in many ways, some obvious, some disguised or unconscious, but always hastening, in one way or another, a person's own death. Emile Durkheim, in his classic work on suicide, pointed out that suicides were not unrelated to certain other forms of destructive conduct, the difference being one of degree and a lesser chance of death. This theme reappeared in Freud's concept of the death instinct and was the focus of Karl A. Menninger's *Man Against Himself.*

1. Interpretation. Freud sought to explain self-destructive behavior as the result of close and constant interaction between two basic instinctual drives — *Eros* (life) and *Thanatos* (death). Freud believed that everyone is vulnerable to self-destructive activity because of certain general features of the human condition. The journey from birth toward death is an inescapable progression described by Freud as a catabolic process that often operates unconsciously and exerts a variable influence in bringing about eventual termination. He noted the tendency toward "constancy" in that the human organism, as a result of its instinctually motivated activity, moves toward a state of lesser tension. Death, then, when it eventually comes, is the ultimate relief from tension. Further, the death instinct focuses on aggressive activities, and Freud contended that much aggression is originally directed against the self and is only directed in an outward way when the aggressive energy is deflected. Karl A. Menninger expanded the concept of the death instinct and postulated a state of balance between life and death forces. He suggested that this state of balance constantly changes under the influence of guilt, aggression, and eroticism, resulting in the production of a number of self-injurious or self-limiting behaviors.

2. **Self-Destructive Activities.** Self-destructive behaviors include a large group of activities that extend from failure to follow a prescribed medical treatment regimen to participation in high-risk sports. Alcoholics and drug abusers have generally been viewed as following a self-destructive course because of the negative impact of the abused substances on health and life in all its relationships. Hyperobesity, excessive cigarette smoking, self-mutilation, accident-proneness, resistance to recovery from certain diseases, compulsive gambling, and criminal behavior are other forms of self-destructive activity that are prominent today. Individuals involved in these activities, or with these tendencies, do not see these actions and tendencies as meant to injure them.

Persons from all age groups are involved in self-destructive behavior. Children and adolescents are increasingly resorting to self-destructive acts that previously had been considered typical only of adults. If indirect self-destructive behaviors are taken into consideration in viewing depressed children, the extent of the problem increases greatly. Further, as Wells and Stuart state, many professionals recognize behaviors such as eating disturbances, substance abuse, running away, promiscuity and prostitution, and repeated unwanted pregnancies as possible manifestations of self-destructive wishes in children and adolescents. Because self-destructive behavior has both intrapsychic and interpersonal symbolic determinants, family members may be involved in this activity and may also interfere with treatment because of their own needs, fears, and guilt.

3. **Motivation and Behaviors.** Many motivational factors are identified in one's effort to understand psychodynamically indirect self-destructive behavior. This behavior may be a defense used to ward off the pervasive pain of depression. Feelings of helplessness, hopelessness, and worthlessness are common factors in or leading to depression. Self-destructive behavior may have a positive value in defending against depression when the behavior that is substituted enhances self-esteem.

Masochism, asceticism, drug and alcohol abuse, and certain psychosomatic illnesses are easily seen as self-injurious and self-defeating. They may represent a defensive mechanism to handle the impact of chronic depression on the psyche, as well as cope with anxiety, self-directed anger, dependency, or the fear of dependency.

Physical illness may be used against the self. When it occurs it may force a radical change in the way one lives. The person is forced to examine choices and may be left with a new self-image that now means limited activity, increased dependency, change in lifestyle, and a loss of or a change in vocation, hobbies, and sexual interaction. The response to these choices and changes may range from bland acquiescence to bitterness, anger, and depression. Such emotions serve as a means of establishing feelings of control over one's life. The diabetic patient, for example, may adapt easily to the rituals related to controlling and living with the illness or rebel and sabotage all treatment methods and thereby increase disability and hasten death.

Alcohol and harmful drug use, overeating, and cigarette smoking represent pleasure-oriented, tension-reducing activities. These activities require individual control over the degree to which they are practiced. The step from moderation to self-destructive involvement may be short and quick. The personality profile of these individuals often includes a low level of frustration tolerance and a need for immediate gratification. Moreover, addictive behaviors are self-generating of self-destructive activity in that the abuse frequently serves to manufacture excessive guilt or depression, which in turn is escaped by further abuse.

An important dimension of substance abuse relates to family dynamics. The abuser, especially if young, can become the scapegoat on whom the family blames its problems and displaces its anger and disappointments. Because the family is more important than the individual member, the abuser is sacrificed or chooses to be sacrificed in order to hold the family together.

Self-mutilation, accident-proneness, and compulsive gambling have a potential for physical injury as well as for damaging occupational, social, and mental functioning. Self-mutilation may serve the purpose of helping the person come out of a depersonalized state and make contact with reality. It may also expiate some overwhelming guilt or serve the purpose of offering a part of oneself in a self-injurious act rather than offering all of the self. A sense of guilt, usually unconscious, and a need to atone for such guilt feelings may provide the motivation for many unintended accidents. Conflicts involving aggressive drives and a defensive sense of guilt seeking expiation form the matrix in which accidents can occur. Thus, the link is between unexpressed aggression and a sense of guilt. Further, the accident may help a person avoid new responsibilities by providing a convenient and acceptable rationale for not entering into a new situation where self-esteem or the esteem of others could be lost. A simple example often cited is that of the person who has a wreck on the way to a job interview, thereby avoiding the possible humiliating experience of being turned down for the job.

Stress-seeking behavior can play an important role in indirect self-destructive behavior. Its negative potentialities become manifest when the search for excitement and the degree of risk-taking begin to exceed the boundaries of safety, survival, and self-preservation. Thus, society tries to set some constraints on activities such as high-risk sports, because the dangers are obvious when such activities are uncontrolled. In defining the limits of high-risk sports, society is saying that beyond a particular point such behavior becomes unacceptable and attains a level that is self-destructive.

Actually, indirect self-destructive behavior is a part of everyone's repertoire and is, in fact, widespread. It becomes dangerous or life-threatening when it is repetitive and habitual. Such a behavioral pattern often begins as an effort to defend against or cope with psychic pain. A conscious intention of self-injury or death is not present. Thus, efforts to survive (cope) today may incapacitate tomorrow or forever. As is frequently said, to know about self-injury is to understand some of the ways in which individuals strive and fail without intending or wanting to fail.

4. **Intervention.** Intervention is difficult in indirect self-destructive behavior because society does not pre-

sume that thinking and judgment have been impaired as it does in direct suicidal behavior. Thus, persons involved in indirect self-destructive behaviors are usually permitted to follow, with little or no interference, a path leading to damaged health, talents, and life. These behaviors fall into what is usually referred to as one's rights — rights that society respects despite the high toll exacted in honoring such rights. At the same time, professionals in ministry and medicine, through counseling, teaching, and confrontation, have done much to make known the hidden determinants of such behavior. Through these efforts individuals often learn to substitute adjustment mechanisms that are more adaptive and less likely to produce self-injury or personal defeat.

Bibliography. E. Durkheim, *Suicide* (1897). N. L. Farberow, ed., *The Many Faces of Suicide: Indirect Self-Destructive Behavior* (1980). S. Freud, "Beyond the Pleasure Principle," *SE* vol. 18 ([1955] 1920) pp. 7 – 64. K. A. Menninger, *Man Against Himself* (1938). C. F. Wells and I. R. Stuart, *Self-Destructive Behavior in Children and Adolescents* (1981).

J. A. KNIGHT

SUICIDE. *See also* HOPE AND DESPAIR; PSYCHOANALYSIS (Personality Theory and Research); SADNESS AND DEPRESSION; UNCONSCIOUS; VIOLENCE. *Compare* SACRIFICIAL BEHAVIOR; SELF-ESTEEM; WILL TO LIVE.

SELF-DISCIPLINE. *See* ASCETICAL PRACTICES; SELF-EXPRESSION/SELF-CONTROL. *See also* PHYSICAL FITNESS DISCIPLINES.

SELF-DISCLOSURE. *See* SELF-EXPRESSION/SELF-CONTROL; SHAME.

SELF-ESTEEM. A self-evaluation or judgment, constituting the combined private and subjective appraisals of the self. It expresses approval or disapproval. The term has been referred to as the single most significant key to behavior (Branden, 1969) and the mainspring that launches every child for success or failure in living (Briggs, 1970).

Two major convictions — significance (worthiness) and personal efficacy (competence) — constitute self-esteem. Significance is an attitude of intrinsic value, acceptance, and affection toward the self. Personal efficacy is the level of success and mastery in meeting demands for achievement. Two secondary convictions — virtue and power — are also relevant. Virtue concerns adherence to moral and ethical standards. Power involves the ability to influence and control others.

1. **Characteristics.** Self-esteem is expressed in the following characteristics: (1) A relationship with anxiety. When the self-esteem is threatened, the individual feels anxious as it is threat that releases the self's anxiety. (2) An integration with overt behavior. Behavior seldom represents independent, surface activity. Linking behavior patterns to the underlying self-esteem helps to render meaning and importance to patterns which otherwise might appear strange or unexplainable. (3) Consciousness or unconsciousness. An individual need not be aware of his or her self-attitudes, though these will nonetheless find overt expression such as through voice, posture, gesture, and performance. Therefore, inferences about

self-esteem may be made by observing overt behavior. (4) Unidirectionality rather than causality of behavior. Self-esteem is both an antecedent and consequence of a wide range of personal and interpersonal characteristics. (5) Durability. Self-esteem is highly resistant to change, although limited situational shifts in self-evaluation may occur. This resistance is because people are generally unwilling to accept new evidence of themselves, resolving any dissonance between the evidence and their judgment of self in favor of their customary judgment (Aronson and Mills, 1959). In addition, individuals have a need for psychological consistency (Lecky, 1945). (6) A judgmental process based upon personal, moral, ethical, and value standards. Positive and negative affective connotations directed toward the self as object often represent biased subjective convictions rather than valid objective information. (7) A readiness to respond to external stimuli along predetermined lines. A personal conviction of inferiority, for example, may lead to a conclusion of helplessness in a given situation. (8) A capacity for healthiness. Learned rather than innate, the self-esteem has the potential to flourish depending upon the psychological environment where the individual resides. (9) Independence of social prestige. Personal affection and value rather than personal wealth, level of education, ethnic group affiliation, religion, or occupation is more intimately associated with self-esteem.

2. **Theoretical Foundations.** The theoretical origins of the concept can be traced to psychologist William James and sociologists Charles Cooley and G. H. Mead. Several theorists have included self-esteem as an important construct in their systems of personality. Only two, however, Adler and Maslow, have assigned it a central role in their theories.

Other theorists have contributed less directly. These include the neo-Freudians — Sullivan, Horney, and Fromm — who treat the concept as peripheral rather than central to their respective theories. The ego psychologists — e.g., Hartman, Erikson and Jacobson—have posited ideas related to self-esteem, though their conceptions carry a complex structure of unrelated assumptions. The self psychologists such as Rogers have been more preoccupied with the general nature of the subjective experience rather than external validation. Two researchers, Coopersmith and Rosenberg, have made major empirical contributions.

3. **Expressions of Unhealthy Self-Esteem.** Two antithetical expressions characterize unhealthy self-esteem. One is the special-person misconception (Raimy, 1975). The chief psychological mechanism, an exaggerated self-importance, takes on a variety of referents — superiority complex, arrogance, vanity, conceit, egotism, to name a few. The principal manifestation of the special person is found in compulsive attempts to wrest confirmation of one's superiority from others. If exaggerated self-esteem is threatened, vigorous efforts are made to defend it; if it is shattered, serious psychological difficulties occur. While reduction in anyone's self-esteem is hazardous, reducing the exaggerated self-esteem of the special person is often a mental health disaster.

An antithetical expression, low self-esteem, is equally unhealthy. The major psychological core, an exaggerated self-devaluation, takes on a variety of referents — inferiority

COMPARISON OF TRUE HUMILITY, PRIDE, AND FALSE HUMILITY

True Humility	*Pride*	*False Humility*
1. Based in self-worth.	1. Based in self-doubt.	1. Based in self-depreciation.
2. Accepts both strengths and weaknesses.	2. Denies weaknesses.	2. Rejects strengths.
3. Is open to both positive and negative feedback.	3. Is closed to corrective and negative feedback.	3. Is closed to affirmation and positive feedback.
4. Results in accurate appraisal.	4. Results in unrealistic appraisal (attitude of superiority).	4. Results in unrealistic appraisal (attitude of inferiority).

From C. W. Ellison (Ed.), *Your Better Self: Christianity, Psychology and Self-Esteem.* New York: Harper & Row, 1983. Reprinted by permission of Harper & Row, Publishers, Inc.

complex, inadequacy, self-doubt, unworthiness, to name a few. The principal manifestation is found in compulsive attempts to wrest confirmation of one's inferiority from others. If the inadequacies are confirmed by others, reinforcement occurs in a self-fulfilling prophecy. If the inadequacies are contradicted, further entrenchment in those beliefs and efforts to disprove the contradiction may occur (Driscoll, 1982).

Four major factors contribute to the development of self-esteem. The most commonly recognized cause is indulgence given during childhood. Pampered children develop an unrealistic, inflated value of their worth. Disregarded children develop an equally unrealistic, deflated value of their worth. A second determinant of self-esteem is early identification, usually with parents of significant others, or even fantasized heroes or heroines. Illustrative models in movies, stories, or television often provide fertile ground for identifying with worthy or unworthy characters. Third, formal or informal indoctrination may contribute to the development of self-esteem. Individuals who experience unusual adulation often develop a faulty sense of self-importance, while those who experience unusual derogation often develop a faulty sense of unworthiness. Finally, self-esteem evolves from the type of demands placed on the self. Demands which are unrealistic and impossible to achieve eventuate in low self-esteem. Children, for instance, seldom question parental expectations; instead, they question themselves (Briggs, 1970). Similarly in adulthood, low self-esteem is associated with the judgment of self against irrational standards of perfection.

4. Theological Foundations. Confusion reigns over the biblical view of self-esteem and its relationship to pride, true humility, and false humility. Several NT verses are especially useful, however, in delineating the biblical principles involved (Mk. 12:31; Rom. 12:3; Eph. 5:1–2). True humility, not pride, is the biblical counterpart of positive self-esteem (Ellison, 1983). Humility is based upon self-love, not self-negation, and owes its affirmation to God's unconditional regard for humankind. Pride is connected with achievement and attempts to arrogate glory due to God for one's self. False

humility, the counterpart of negative self-esteem, is a reverse form of pride in one's badness.

Thinking more highly of ourselves than we ought to think is pride. Thinking less highly of ourselves than we ought to think is false humility. Thinking about ourselves soberly ("with sober judgment") is true humility (Hoekema, 1983). Clarification of these concepts is illustrated in the chart above.

Bibliography. E. Aronson and J. Mills, "The Effects of Severity of Initiation on Liking for a Group," *J. of Abnormal and Social Psychology,* 59 (1959), 177–81. N. Branden, *The Psychology of Self-Esteem* (1969). D. C. Briggs, *Your Child's Self-Esteem: The Key to His Life* (1970). R. Driscoll, "Their Own Worst Enemies," *Psychology Today,* 6 (1981), 45–49. C. W. Ellison, "Self-Esteem: An Overview," in C. W. Ellison, ed., *Your Better Self: Christianity, Psychology and Self-Esteem* (1983). A. Godin, "Mental Health in Christian Life," in D. Belgum, ed., *Religion in Medicine* (1967). A. A. Hoekema, "The Christian Self-Image: A Reformed Perspective," in C. W. Ellison, ed., *Your Better Self: Christianity, Psychology and Self-Esteem* (1973). E. Jacobson, "The Self and the Object World," *Psychoanalytic Studies of the Child,* 9 (1954), 75–128. P. Lecky, *Self-Consistency: A Theory of Personality* (1945). V. Raimy, *Misunderstandings of the Self: Cognitive Psychotherapy and the Misconception Hypothesis* (1975). D. S. Ryan, "Self-Esteem: An Operational Definition and Ethical Analysis," *J. of Psychology and Theology,* 11 (1983), 295–302.

C. R. RIDLEY

LOVE. *Compare* EGO STRENGTH; EGOTISM; HAPPINESS; MIND-CURE MOVEMENT; NARCISSISM/NARCISSISTIC PERSONALITY; SELF-DENIAL.

SELF-EXAMINATION. The moral evaluation of one's acts, particularly the process of reviewing one's acts (thoughts, words, deeds, and omissions) during a definite period of time, e.g., one day, or the span of time since the previous celebration of the sacrament of reconciliation (confession). Though he did not originate it, Ignatius of Loyola in the sixteenth century systematized and popularized the *examen of conscience,* a practice of devoting between ten and fifteen minutes, once or twice a day, to a form of prayer in which, in God's presence and with the guidance of the Holy Spirit, one reflects on one's response to divine grace, with the purpose of becoming increasingly faithful to its promptings. Ordinarily, *examen* refers to the daily examination as a separate prayerful exercise, while the *examination of conscience* refers to the self-examination which precedes the celebration of the sacrament of reconciliation. Ignatius of Loyola also popularized the *particular examen*, in which one daily concentrates prayerfully on a particular aspect in which one especially needs to grow in responsiveness to God's grace, on faithfulness to a particular duty of one's state in life, or on an individual fault.

1. **History and Development.** The notion of self-examination, that is, of conscience or self-consciousness in its role of making moral judgments, antedates Christianity. Self-examination depends on the conviction that persons have a knowledge of the moral quality of their actions and of their responsibility for choices between good and evil acts. Often the emphasis may be on the detection of evil actions, although Cicero wrote of self-examination more positively, describing as the greatest joy in life "the consciousness of a life well spent and the remembrance of numerous needs well done" (*De Senectute*, 3:9). For Socrates, the sense of self-examination was inclusive: "A man who is good for anything ought not to calculate the chance of living or dying; he ought only to consider whether in doing anything he is doing right or wrong — acting the part of a good man or a bad" (*Phaedo*, 85). Seneca introduced the connection between self-examination and the divine: "God is near you, he is with you, he is within. . . . a sacred and august spirit resides within us and takes stock of our good and evil actions and is a guardian or avenger of our deeds. Just as he is trusted by us so does he trust us" (*Letters*, 41:1).

The people of Israel understood that their special relationship with God who had chosen them demanded of them a personal and communal commitment to the observance of the Law, i.e., an interior disposition expressed in external behavior. Frequently there was a tension between the dispositions of the heart and the mere external observance of ritual, and the psalmists (Ps. 40:4–8) and the prophets (Isa. 1:10–20; Joel 2:12–14) called the people back to a right relationship between the two dimensions. The psalmists acknowledged the need for God's help in searching the heart (Ps. 26:2), in order to stand worthily before their Lord (Ps. 24:3–4). Perhaps Psalm 139 most eloquently developed the prayer for self-examination in the OT: "O Lord, you have probed me and you know me; with all my ways you are familiar. Probe me, O God, and know my heart; try me and know my thoughts; see if my way is crooked and lead me in the way of old" (vss. 1, 3, 23–24, *NAB*).

In the NT, the teaching of Jesus Christ clearly states the need for conscience and its examination (Mt. 7:3–5), but the emphasis is on interior dispositions, which influence subsequent external behavior (Mt. 15:7–20; Lk. 11:39–42). An omniscient God seeks and values most highly purity of intention within the hearts of human sons and daughters (Mt. 6:1, 4, 6, 18, 33).

In the theology of Paul, conscience is for pagans what the law is for Jews (Rom. 2:14–16, 14:12). Indeed, for all persons conscience regulates moral activity, and the one who acts against conscience sins (Rom. 14:23). C. A. Pierce (1955) points out that Paul adopted the Greek idea of conscience for Christianity, but at the same time perceived its liability to error through defects in the knowledge of the moral quality of actions or through the influence of environment and habit, as well as its major defect as an ethical norm, its negativity. For the Christian, then, conscience needs the practical guidance of Christian wisdom, which instructs it in the revealed will of God, perceived in the light of faith (Rom. 13:1–10). This faith leads the Christian to a vision of the world and of human life within it, a vision which always governs and conditions one's reaction to moral situations, and which establishes love of God and love of neighbor as the supreme principles which regulate conduct and condition the exercise of freedom for the Christian. Conscientious self-examination is not an absolute norm, but is to be tested in the light of faith, with God as ultimate judge (I Cor. 14:3; II Cor. 13:5). Paul values highly a self-examination instructed and guided by faith, and he explicitly suggests that it precede participation in the Eucharist (I Cor. 11:27–28).

Among the fathers of the church, John Chrysostom recommended daily examination of conscience for all Christians, as did Augustine: "It is necessary every day to call our life to judgment and examine what we have done, night and day" (*De Spiritu et anima*, 51 PL 40, 817b). Both Basil and Benedict provided for examination of conscience in the rules for their monks. Thomas Aquinas saw conscience as the application of faith to living every day in Christ, and described it as the voice of God within (*Summa Theologica*, Ia 79, 12, 13). In the fourteenth century, the Brothers of the Common Life developed formulas for the practice of the examination of conscience among the laity.

After the Reformation, the principles of personal freedom and private judgment were emphasized as guides for personal living. In England, Jeremy Taylor stated that "daily examination of our actions is the whole course of our health preparatory to our death bed" (*The Rule and Exercise of Holy Dying*, 1651). Among Roman Catholics, Ignatius of Loyola was developing the schemata for the general and particular *examens*.

From the seventeenth century onward, there developed a departure from the ancient tradition of Christian self-examination. Traditionally the church had insisted that the individual Christian's conscience was subject to, and to be instructed by, objective truth and the demands of the divine order of things. The revelation of divine will, proclaimed and interpreted by the teaching of the church, guided the individual in the formation and examination of conscience, aided by the virtue of prudence. In the seventeenth century, manuals appeared which claimed to supersede prudence as a guide to conscience; these authors guided conscience by means of a casuistic legalism and regarded such a conscience as an inviolable subjective norm for moral choice. The earlier tradition was thus challenged by a complete subjectivity coupled with a complete mechanization of conscience formation and examination.

Since the Second Vatican Council, moral and spiritual theologians have sought to return the art of conscience formation and the practice of self-examination to their traditional NT and patristic roots, i.e., faith, charity, and the Christian virtue of prudence, or graced practical wisdom. The most promising and popular practical development in this direction is the *consciousness examen*.

2. A Renewed Model—*Consciousness Examen*. G. Aschenbrenner, S.J., claims that the *consciousness examen* is true to the spirit of the Ignatian *examen* of conscience, while avoiding the narrow and dangerous focus on introspection and negativity which at times had characterized its practice in recent centuries. The practice of the *consciousness examen* involves taking about fifteen minutes each day to bring to awareness prayerfully what the Lord is accomplishing in one's life, how the Holy Spirit is present and working and drawing one, and how other interior and exterior promptings are present and active as well.

Aschenbrenner retains the classic five steps of the *examen* of Ignatius: (1) *prayer for enlightenment*—the individual prays for the knowledge and understanding of God's ways and his or her own manner of responding to them, praying that the Holy Spirit may help to see oneself more and more as God does; (2) *reflective thanksgiving*—awareness and acknowledgment of inherent spiritual poverty and God's daily generosity, with emphasis upon the Lord's presence, invitations of grace, and gifts of this day; (3) *practical survey of actions*—not a merely negative listing of moral failings, but a survey of the day, asking how has the Lord been working in the individual's life; (4) *contrition and sorrow*—one expresses sorrow because of a lack of courage and honesty in responding to God's call of grace (especially regarding the specific matter of the *particular examen*), and also expresses faith that nonetheless nothing separates one from the love of Christ; (5) *hopeful resolution for the future*—based on what one is able to do with the constant powerful love of God enlightening one's way.

Bibliography. G. Aschenbrenner, S. J., "Consciousness Examen," *Review for Religious*, 31 (1972), 14–21. H. Jaeger, J. Guillet, *et al.*, "Examen de Conscience," *Dictionnaire de Spiritualité*, IV (2), (1978) pp. 1790–1838. I. Loyola, *The Spiritual Exercises of St. Ignatius*, C. Lattey, ed., (1928). C. A. Pierce, *Conscience in the New Testament* (1955). J. B. Wall, "Conscience, Examination of," *New Catholic Encyclopedia*, 4 (1970). C. Williams, "Conscience," *New Catholic Encyclopedia*, 4 (1970).

G. NIEDERAUER

CHRISTIAN LIFE; CONSCIENCE. *See also* IGNATIAN SPIRITUALITY. *Compare* JOURNAL KEEPING; MEDITATION; SELF-ANALYSIS; SELF-UNDERSTANDING.

SELF-EXPRESSION/SELF-CONTROL. The classic tension within pastoral care, counseling, theology, and supervision between the person's need to maintain flexibility and communication by freely expressing thoughts and feelings, and the need to maintain order, responsibility, and boundaries through limiting what is expressed.

The pastoral care movement, largely under the influence of the psychoanalytic and humanistic psychologies, has adopted the belief that to be "in touch" with one's feelings is indispensable to health, growth, and at least the visible signs of salvation. There is much empirical and experiential evidence for this. Freud and Rogers have taught us that a reliable indicator of a person's emotional health is the speed with which they become aware of an emotion they are experiencing. Knowing and naming the emotion greatly enhances the ability to respond usefully to whatever is stimulating it.

Self-expression is important because it enhances knowing one's own emotions, hence it deepens self-knowledge. Psychoanalysis has shown that freely saying what comes to mind reveals more and more of one's emotional and symbolic reality. Gestalt and bio-energetics therapies have demonstrated that allowing the body to move in response to its subtle aches and tensions unveils much emotional and historical data that otherwise remains hidden.

Were we to think only of individuals, the importance of self-expression might be limited to relatively brief periods of distress and their appropriate therapies, and to those few persons with a major interest in artistic creation. But relationships, especially close ones, require a high level of emotional disclosure if their members are to know enough about one another for the relationship to be mutually enjoyable and productive. The work of marriage and family therapists such as Virginia Satir and David and Vera Mace has demonstrated definitively that one's spouse has a far greater chance of meeting one's needs if he or she knows what they are. Communication of both the content and intensity of feelings keeps both partners current on the other's inner state, hence more able to behave in a way that complements it. George Bach and Barbara Wyden argued convincingly that the expression of a spouse's anger both exerts a powerful claim on a committed partner and provides indispensable and otherwise unavailable information about the importance of an issue to the one reacting.

All of this has powerful implications for pastoral care. For instance, recovery from a personal loss happens more quickly and at greater depth if the bereaved give vent to their pain overtly and demonstratively. Pastors can intervene better in most marital conflict situations if they encourage spouses to let one another know and feel the full scope of their thoughts and emotions about their conflict issues.

Nevertheless, self-expression is not the whole of health. Psychoanalysis, humanistic psychologies, and pastoral care agree that there are appropriate and necessary limits to both emotionality and the sharing of ideas. There are many other influences that join in that caution: behaviorist and cognitive psychologies, most of American psychiatry, and much of our cultural tradition.

Much of the maturation out of human infancy proceeds by limiting immediate expression. We learn that crying does not by itself produce the milk we hunger for, and that having a tantrum will not persuade mommy to let us stay up another hour. The ability to delay meeting our individual emotional needs and act instead to strengthen the family or community, which in the long run can meet them better, is a developmental achievement of the first importance.

Uncoordinated individual self-expression is either infancy or psychosis, and uncoordinated self-expression by a group is chaos. Pastorally there are many situations where it is necessary to help people restructure their defenses, limit their expression, and regain their control. Acute wailing grief is destructive and dangerous in an intensive care unit, as is acting out sexual impulses in an inappropriate context.

An important part of the pastor's expertise is knowing when the situation calls for self-expression and when for self-control. Self-control is necessary when important activities of other people would be interrupted or made more difficult by one person's self-expression, unless the cost of foregoing that expression is monumental. But most such expressions can be delayed. The pastor does well to get the grieving family out of the hospital to the safety of their home before they let their tears flow, but once there they will profit from encouragement to do so.

The other central indicator for self-control is when self-expression would reveal things about the person that would later be a source of embarrassment or disruption of relationships. Again, it is a matter of the pastor's expertise in knowing the most useful time and place. It may be very valuable for the pastor to hear about a prospective committee chairperson's lust for the associate minister, as part of working through either those feelings or the decision about their working together; but the same feelings shared with that person's spouse or the whole committee may cause needless pain and disruption.

In a healthy, mature person, a balance exists between self-expression and self-control. There is the capacity for powerful self-expression when it is needed to further personal or communal goals. Such persons trust their ability to express themselves well enough that fear of self-expression never limits their self-knowledge; hence their actions are usually well informed by a correct assessment of their own emotional states. Their self-expression serves goals beyond exhibitionism. It builds relationships, establishes claims on others, offers solutions, produces art, and pursues the objectives of the individual. It does so under the control of central objectives and of the ego. There are times in which such persons are aware of strong feelings or interesting ideas in themselves, but choose not to act on them in a visible way. They are able to decide not to punish with their anger, or woo with their sexual attraction, or be reduced to tears by their sadness. And they are able to decide, later, when the time and place are right, to do all of those things.

These variables are especially important in the pastor's self, since he or she is a model for those who are served. The pastor who lacks either self-expression or self-control will be limited in effectiveness, and will distort the attitudes of those who receive his or her care. The pastor who is insufficiently controlled will frighten people who expect their boundaries to be in jeopardy when they are together. Unnecessary opposition may be generated if people feel they must defend themselves actively or be swept away. Others are in danger of having their own poorly established defenses undermined, with resulting fear of inappropriate behavior.

The pastor who has too little self-expression will set a climate that subtly limits the self-expression of the receivers of care. In the pastor's lack of emotional range, for instance, they will see a subtle demand for adherence to an unemotional style. They may find certain emotionally intense subjects too dangerous to talk about with such a minister.

Ideally, the pastor will communicate complete, matter of fact confidence that he or she can express emotions and ideas powerfully and without reservation, and will know exactly when to do so; and can completely subsume

the need for that to a faithful decision to neither indulge themselves nor exploit those they serve.

Bibliography. G. Bach and B. Wyden, *The Intimate Enemy* (1968). D. Mace and V. Mace, *How to Have a Happy Marriage* (1977). V. Satir, *Conjoint Family Therapy* 3d ed. (1983).

B. W. GRANT

CATHARSIS; RESPONSIBILITY/IRRESPONSIBILITY, PSYCHOLOGY OF. *See also* ASCETICAL PRACTICES; GIVING AND RECEIVING; PHYSICAL FITNESS DISCIPLINES; PROFANE LANGUAGE; SUPPRESSION. *Compare* INTIMACY AND DISTANCE; SELF-ACTUALIZATION/SELF-REALIZATION; SELF-DENIAL; SELF-TRANSCENDENCE.

SELF-HELP GROUPS. *See* SELF-HELP PSYCHOLOGIES; SUPPORT GROUPS. *See also* ALCOHOLICS ANONYMOUS.

SELF-HELP PSYCHOLOGIES. Self-help psychologies are those practical strategies and activities by which individuals and small groups, usually without the aid or involvement of professionals, attempt to solve problems, meet needs, and change behavior or attitudes. The words "self help" may include the personal and practical assistance available through meditation, reading of books or articles, listening to tapes or sermons, watching films and television, or similar activities that can be done alone. More often, "self-help group" refers to the mutual aid that comes through peers who meet together, usually in small groups, to work at solving common problems.

It is impossible to estimate the prevalence and influence of self-help psychologies and groups based upon them. Self-help books and seminars are common, and it has been suggested that close to a million mutual-aid groups currently exist in North America alone. Many of these — including Bible study, prayer and sharing groups, Alcoholics Anonymous, and even some weight control programs — have a strong religious emphasis.

Self-help psychologies are not unique creations of the twentieth century. Family members and friends have helped each other for centuries, and for many years sermons and books have helped those who attempted to apply the preachers' or writers' principles to life. The NT writers repeatedly urged believers to help and care for one another, and the early church appeared to consist of supportive groups of caring people. More structured self-help groups can be traced to early Methodism, Quaker communities, and the Oxford Group Movement in England. Each of these united the teachings and practices of Christianity with the giving and receiving of help. Many modern self-help approaches descended from Christian beginnings and maintain strong religious emphases.

1. **Characteristics.** Self-help books, seminars, and sermons tend to be practical, easily understood, and relevant to the needs of the people who read or listen. Often there are formulas for solving problems or changing behavior, and invariably there is a strong element of hope, an expectation that situations will improve, and a belief that help can come apart from the involvement of professional counselors. Similar attitudes permeate the mutual-aid groups where, in addition, there is compassion, acceptance of one another, informality, a sharing of common needs and experiences, self-reliance, a desire to help one another, and sometimes resistance to what par-

ticipants may regard as the cold, ineffective, unnecessary, and expensive influence of professionals. Self-help psychologies embody a basic and ancient principle for meeting life's stresses: in times of need, we can help ourselves and we can help one another.

This self-help principle has been applied to a wide variety of human problems and numerous mutual-aid groups. According to Gartner and Riessman, the groups can be divided into four general categories. (1) The *"anonymous" groups* involve people who have persisting problems and need help in their attempts to change. Alcoholics Anonymous is well known; related groups include Gamblers Anonymous, Parents Anonymous (for parents who abuse their children), Overeaters Anonymous (and a variety of other weight loss programs), Neurotics Anonymous, and Narcotics Anonymous. (2) The *"expatient" groups* include people who have been hospitalized, often for psychiatric reasons, and who now give support, care, and post-hospitalization help to one another. (3) *"Life-transition" groups* include widows, parents without partners, pregnant women's groups, the recently divorced, retired people, those who have been released from prison, and a variety of youth groups. (4) In *"living with" groups,* the members help one another to live with difficult situations or family members. Examples include Al-Anon and Alateen for the families of alcoholics, as well as groups for heart patients, handicapped persons, families of prisoners, persons with high IQs, stutterers, and people living with family members who have arthritis, mental retardation, cancer, multiple sclerosis, and a variety of other diseases.

To this list one might add "spiritual growth" and other religious groups that exist for prayer, study, and mutual support, and "natural" groups such as families, gangs, neighborhood coffee klatches, and informal groups of fellow workers. These rarely organize formally, but they give considerable help, information, and encouragement in times of need.

2. **Strengths.** The fact that self-help psychologies exist in such abundance is evidence that they must serve some useful functions. There is, for example, *reassurance*. A group, book, or seminar leader can give hope, the assurance that "all is not lost," and the recognition that one's problems are not unique. Self-help psychologies also give *guidelines for action*. Admitting a problem and talking about it is a good step toward recovery, but the self-help approaches often give practical instruction also. Leaders or established group members model success in dealing with a problem. This instills new confidence in people who may feel helpless, hopeless, and confused.

A third strength, *involvement* with others, gets people to work on their problems, provides encouragement, and sometimes pulls people away from brooding, self-pity, and other self-destructive attitudes and actions. Almost all of the self-help psychologies also emphasize *responsibility* and promote this as a step toward change and growth. As they take responsibility for what can be changed, people develop more effective strategies for coping with existing problems and preventing future relapses or the development of new problems. Recently, there has been emphasis on what has been termed the *helper-therapy* principle. This is the view that the best way to help yourself is to reach out to help others. Self-help psychol-

ogies that encourage caring bring benefits both to the giver and to the receiver of help.

It is difficult to design research on the effectiveness of self-help psychologies, but the few studies that have been done are encouraging. There is clear evidence from surveys that both professionals and lay persons believe that self-help psychologies are effective and significant in promoting mental health. Professional counselors often refer counselees to self-help resources, and the prevalence of self-help psychologies suggests that many people are in fact being helped.

3. **Limitations and Risks.** Perhaps the chief risk of self-help psychologies is the tendency for people with serious or developing problems (including physical problems) to assume that there is no need for professional help or that professionals (including pastoral counselors) are incompetent. Self-help approaches also may encourage overdependence on small group support or on simplistic solutions. Often there is an unwillingness or failure to seek for and deal with underlying causes of problems. Writers of self-help materials, leaders of seminars, and group participants sometimes fail to see that many people are not capable, emotionally or intellectually, of listening to self-help suggestions, adapting them and applying them to life. When there is failure to improve, or when self-help psychologies blame people for their problems, the result may be increased guilt, frustration, and lowered self-esteem. Others have criticized their egocentric emphases, unrealistic idealism, tendencies to criticize society without working to bring social changes, and the implied idea that people can usually handle their own problems effectively without also relying upon faith in God.

4. **Self-Help and the Church.** Impressed by the prevalence and influence of self-help psychology, and concerned about the psychological harm that sometimes comes from non-professional attempts to give help, counselors and church leaders can be tempted to direct, dominate, and control self-help groups and their leaders. Such efforts, however, stifle the spontaneity, vitality, and flexibility of self-help psychology and can stimulate increased resistance to "outside influences."

Instead, there are benefits when counselors work cooperatively with people involved in the self-help movement. This may involve initiating, encouraging, or consulting with self-help groups, providing places in the church where groups could meet, promoting self-help seminars, referring counselees to useful self-help materials and mutual aid groups, developing self-help books or other materials, and helping people critique self-help approaches. While there are risks involved, self-help psychology does provide the first line of aid for many people and is likely to be at the forefront of future mental health and spiritual growth movements. If there is understanding and cooperation, the church and self-help psychology can work together to improve pastoral care in the decades ahead.

Bibliography. A. H. Katz and E. I. Bender, *The Strength In Us* (1976). G. Caplan and M. Killilea, eds., *Support Systems and Mutual Help* (1976). G. R. Collins, "Popular Christian Psychologies," *J. of Psychology and Theology,* (1975), 127–32. J. W. Drakeford, *People to People Therapy* (1978). A. Gartner and F. Riessman, *Self-Help in the Human Services* (1977). E. R. Rodolfa and L. Hungerford, "Self-Help Groups," *Professional*

Psychology 13 (1982), 345–53. G. H. Weber and L. M. Cohen, eds., *Beliefs and Self-Help* (1982).

G. R. COLLINS

POPULAR THERAPEUTIC MOVEMENTS AND PSYCHOLOGIES. *Compare* GROWTH GROUPS; SELF-ANALYSIS; SELF-UNDERSTANDING; SUPPORT GROUPS; THEORY AND PRAXIS.

SELF-IMAGE. *See* SELF CONCEPT.

SELF-INVOLVEMENT. *See* COMMITMENT; EGO INVOLVEMENT; EXISTENTIALISM.

SELF-KNOWLEDGE. *See* SELF-UNDERSTANDING.

SELF-LOVE. *See* LOVE; NARCISSISM; SELF-ESTEEM.

SELF PSYCHOLOGIES. Psychologies that place the self at the center of personality and make the growth or actualization of the self the primary goal both of life in general and of psychotherapy and counseling in particular. Self psychologies share all or most of the following characteristics:

(1) an emphasis on the conscious self as an integrated (or potentially integrated) system; (2) an emphasis on the true self as having almost unlimited capacity for change through freely made decisions. This process of choosing brings about self-actualization, the ideal way of being; self-actualization is an ongoing process of change, not a finished state; (3) an emphasis on the self as innately good, with no natural tendency to aggress against or exploit others or to make self-indulgent or narcissistic choices to its own detriment or to that of others. Such undesirable phenomena are attributed to a false self created by external factors, such as the family, traditional religion, society, or the economic system; (4) an emphasis on personality prior to self-actualization as primarily the result of social learning. That is, personality, particularly the false self, is the product of roles derived from family and cultural experiences — roles of an essentially arbitrary kind; (5) an emphasis on breaking with the past, especially with commitments to others, with tradition, and with all fixed moral codes. Morality is interpreted as personal, subjective, and relative; (6) an emphasis on getting in touch with and expressing feelings. This promotes a presumed greater awareness of the true self and greater self-acceptance and trust in one's deep instincts. The particular emotions — anger, sexual desire — do not matter a great deal. What counts is emotional expression as evidence of a break with presumably destructive inhibitions caused by a repressive past; (7) an emphasis on short-term counseling of relatively normal adult clients in contrast to therapy focused on children or on such problems as schizophrenia, manic-depressive symptoms, or alcoholism.

Examples of self psychology are those proposed by Carl Rogers (1961), Abraham Maslow (1954), and Erich Fromm (1947). Rollo May's writings and the Gestalt psychology of Fritz Perls are also closely related. Much of the immensely popular psychology in the U. S. during the 1960s and 1970s (e.g., Transactional Analysis) was a form of self psychology. Movements such as Erhard Seminar Training (EST) combine many features of self psychology with other elements, usually from Eastern religions.

Because of their rejection of pessimistic and deterministic psychologies, such as psychoanalysis and behaviorism, the self psychologies have often been called "humanistic psychology." A more neutral, descriptive term is probably "self psychology." Moreover, in view of its serious deficiencies and failings (noted below), especially the absence of emphasis on committed long-term relationships with others, it may be fairly charged that these theories generally fall far short of an adequate humanism.

1. Relation to Other Psychologies. Traditional psychoanalysis is in important respects the opposite of self psychology. Freud's theory emphasized the unconscious. His focus was on the client's past, especially childhood; his approach was analytic rather than integrative. In general Freud was pessimistic about the possibilities for much change in personality. Freud also gave theoretical importance to biology and to a philosophy of science based on determinism rather than on free will. Certain later developments in psychoanalysis (e.g., ego-psychology) have been more in line with self psychology. The ego theorists emphasize an autonomous ego (much like the self) with its own sphere of operation free of unconscious conflicts. These and related theorists (e.g., Erikson), however, are to be distinguished from self theorists because their concept of the ego remains embedded in a basically psychoanalytic framework.

The analytical psychology of Carl Jung has strong affinities with self psychology: individuation culminating in self-realization is proposed as the highest goal. However, certain important Jungian concepts and concerns such as the collective unconscious, dream analysis, the interpretation of symbols, and a fundamental interest in religion, are not characteristic of the self psychologies.

Alfred Adler is the major theorist who laid the foundation for self psychology with his "individual psychology," his concept of the "creative self," and the understanding of personality as expressed in a "style of life." Adler gave early emphasis to the role of the social environment in determining personality. Within Christianity, various liberal Protestant writers also articulated a kind of self psychology (Fosdick, 1943; Peale, 1937).

2. Origins and Ethos. The philosophical origins of self psychology lie in the Enlightenment's idea, expressed in Rousseau's image of the noble savage, that humans are born good only to be corrupted by civilization's inhibitions. The nineteenth century contributed many additional sources, for example, a belief in progress and the philosophies of Feuerbach, Nietzsche, and Emerson. In the twentieth century, John Dewey's philosophy of education shaped much psychological thinking and directly influenced Rogers. Existential philosophy's idea of the authentic person as one who creates the self and its values by making choices free of outside influences also had an important impact on the self psychologies.

The popularity of this psychology in the U. S. in recent decades owes much to social, economic, and cultural factors. The familiar American traditions of declaring one's independence, striving to be a "self-made man" or rugged individualist, American optimism about human nature, and the frontier mentality that avoids long-term commitments — always moving on — all support aspects of self psychology

(Kilpatrick, 1983). Thus, in spite of its hostility to tradition, self psychology is, in fact, part of a familiar one. In addition, the long history of American economic prosperity has made a psychology of self-growth appear reasonable to many Americans.

3. Critique. Self psychology has made a number of positive contributions to the understanding of personality and the counseling process: (1) its emphasis on the conscious, reflective self capable of making important life-changing decisions (hence on free will, choice, and personal responsibility) has served as a bulwark against an overemphasis on determinism in psychology; (2) its view of the self as an integrated or wholistic system has provided an alternative to analytic and reductive psychologies that interpret personality in terms of separate elements (e.g., drives and response tendencies) exerting their influence below consciousness; (3) its stress on the present has been a corrective to theories that have tended to interpret the person as a prisoner of the past and to neglect or undervalue the possibility of making changes in the present; (4) its emphasis on an empathic, nonjudgmental identification with clients in counseling reveals much research evidence showing that effective change begins with a sensitive, sympathetic understanding of the client's problem, while a cold, objective, distancing or judgmental attitude usually hinders therapeutic change; (5) optimistic, encouraging attitudes toward the self are beneficial for those relatively normal clients who, however, suffer from neurotic guilt or from extreme inhibitions.

Because of the great popularity of self psychology in pastoral care and counseling, however, it is important to give attention also to the weaknesses of this approach to psychology and psychotherapy. The following criticisms have been advanced: (1) the assumption that human nature is good and without an intrinsic capacity for evil is unconvincing; there is simply too much evidence of a human capacity to hurt, to aggress against, and to exploit others to warrant self psychology's optimism (Becker, 1973; Lorenz, 1966; Wilson, 1976). Furthermore, research has shown that in making decisions the self suffers from intrinsic illusions of overconfidence (Myers, 1981); (2) self theory has contributed greatly to the social pathology of narcissism and self-indulgence, facilitating, for example, the breakdown of the family by encouraging divorce and contributing to the withholding of interpersonal and social commitment (Lasch, 1979). In addition, self psychology ignores the fact that the cathartic expression of emotion, especially anger, can have many negative consequences for both self and society (Tavris, 1983); (3) the self psychologies fail to understand the importance of traditional moral codes and inhibitions for personality development and individual well-being. These structures have probably evolved because of their social and biological utility (Campbell, 1974) and should not be casually overthrown. (In general, the self psychologies seriously neglect the effects of biological factors in psychological problems); (4) self psychology can show little empirical support for key concepts like self-actualization, and should not represent such ideas, which are really moral ideals, as scientific in character. Moreover, the poorly formulated concept of self-actualization begs the question of what the self is;

(5) self-actualization theory views other persons and their environment in subjective terms; the downplaying of objective ethical standards and the role of external reality results in a seriously inadequate explanation of motivation (Frankl, 1967); (6) though well-meaning, self theory provides only a vague approach to theory and therapy, which has eroded the legitimate scientific and professional standards of clinical psychology (Strupp, 1976); (7) it is an especially American expression of the economic and political needs of a late stage of capitalism, the consumer economy; thus, self psychology is a social ideology serving the interests of large-scale economic and political powers (Lasch, 1979; Vitz, 1977).

Religious critics (Vitz, 1977; Bobgan and Bobgan, 1979; Bergin, 1980; Kilpatrick, 1983) have noted further that self psychology: (1) rejects God by assuming that the self is the center and origin of personality — thus directly encouraging self-worship, a kind of psychological or narcissistic idolatry, instead of the worship of God. At times the self is explicitly proposed as a substitute for God (Sartre, 1956; Frederick, 1974). Self-knowledge and self-actualization are often considered as a kind of salvation; (2) self psychology assumes that morality is subjective and relative since each self chooses its own morality, in fundamental opposition to traditional religious morality; (3) self psychology cannot cope with suffering and death; it can only interpret them as mistakes or misfortunes to be assimilated and ultimately let go, or to be forgotten and avoided in the future; (4) self psychology has no strong, theoretical concern for commitment to others, although some self-theorists, (e.g., Maslow and Fromm) do place a modest emphasis on loving others. This emphasis is based on the assumption that the self will freely *choose* to love others; there is a complete neglect of interpersonal or social *duties*. Hence, self theory in many ways is intrinsically at odds with family and social structure — and with the commandment to love one's neighbor as oneself.

Bibliography. A. Adler, *The Practice and Theory of Individual Psychology* (1927). E. Becker, *The Denial of Death* (1973). A. E. Bergin, "Psychotherapy and Religious Values," *J. of Consulting and Clinical Psychology*, 48 (1980) 95–105. M. Bobgan and D. Bobgan, *The Psychological Way/The Spiritual Way* (1979). D. T. Campbell, "On Conflicts Between Biological and Social Evolution and Between Psychology and Moral Tradition," *American Psychologist*, 30 (1975) 1103–26. H. E. Fosdick, *On Being a Real Person* (1943). V. E. Frankl, *Psychotherapy and Existentialism* (1967). C. Frederick, *EST: Playing the Game the New Way* (1974). E. Fromm, *Man for Himself* (1947). H. Hartmann, *Ego Psychology and the Problem of Adaptation* (1958). W. K. Kilpatrick, *Psychological Seduction* (1983). C. Lasch, *The Culture of Narcissism* (1979). K. Lorenz, *On Aggression* (1966). A. Maslow, *Motivation and Personality* 2d ed. (1970 [1954]). R. May, *Man's Search for Himself* (1953). D. Myers, *The Inflated Self* (1981). N. V. Peale, *The Art of Living* (1937). C. R. Rogers, *On Becoming a Person* (1961). J.-P. Sartre, *Existentialism* (1947). H. H. Strupp, "Clinical Psychology, Irrationalism, and the Erosion of Excellence," *American Psychologist*, 31 (1976) 561–71. C. Tavris, *Anger: The Misunderstood Emotion* (1982). P. C. Vitz, *Psychology as Religion: The Cult of Self-Worship* (1977). E. O. Wilson, *Sociobiology: The New Synthesis* (1977).

P. C. VITZ

HUMANISTIC PSYCHOLOGY; PERSON; PERSONALITY THE-ORY; SELF, PHILOSOPHY OF. *See also* GESTALT PSYCHOLOGY AND PSYCHOTHERAPY; INDIVIDUAL PSYCHOLOGY; INTER-PERSONAL THEORY; NEOFREUDIAN PERSONALITY THE-ORY; OBJECT RELATIONS THEORY; PHENOMENOLOGICAL PSYCHOLOGY AND PSYCHOTHERAPY. *Compare* ANALYTICAL (JUNGIAN) PSYCHOLOGY; EGO PSYCHOLOGY AND PSYCHO-THERAPY; PSYCHOANALYSIS; PSYCHOLOGY IN AMERICAN RELIGION. *Biography:* FROMM; HORNEY; JUNG; MASLOW; MAY; PERLS; ROGERS, CARL R.; SULLIVAN.

SELF PSYCHOLOGY, PSYCHOANALYTIC. *See* OBJECT RELATIONS THEORY.

SELF-REALIZATION. *See* SELF-ACTUALIZATION/SELF-REALIZATION.

SELF-SACRIFICE. *See* SACRIFICIAL BEHAVIOR.

SELF-TRANSCENDENCE. To surpass the self. The term may refer to experiences of realities that are beyond the self or to experiences in which the self goes beyond itself. It usually connotes presence to the self that goes beyond the self, and it consequently has the overtone of both radical transition and of being manifest.

Accounts of self-transcendence are characterized by a normative understanding of the self. If the self is taken to be human personality, its transcendence is found in any present state that is not circumscribed by human personality, for example, anonymous desires, dreams in which the person plays a non-originating part, a sense of unity that is not defined by personality, or participation in community spirit or consensus that originates in non-human revelation. If self is conceived as the whole of human awareness, its transcendence is found in events in which that awareness is ruptured or taken beyond itself, for example, in the revealed presence of God, the disclo-sure of radical absence, participation in something other than self. One might also speak of self-transcendence as being with a divine self that is greater than but like human selfhood, or one might speak of being self-aware and outside of the self in a non-determinate way, as in experiences of awe or Buber's account of I-Thou.

Certain symbols or images may be experienced as self-transcending. The symbol or image is within human awareness, but it carries power or meaning that tran-scends the self. As one communicates with the symbol/image or relates closely with it, the person might expe-rience transcendence of human selfhood, for example, dreams that reveal power or powers beyond the self or meanings that express reality beyond the self.

The self might be thought of as transcending itself as it develops into a state of being that is foreign to its familiar life. If the self is essentially changed through conversion or trauma, for example, one might speak of such radical transformations as experiences of self-transcendence: the self goes beyond itself by radical, inter-nal changes. Or one might speak of the self-transcending quality of the self and mean that the self goes beyond itself by means of possibilities, aspirations, memories, creative drive, etc.

Realities that might be characterized in terms of self-transcendence are present to the self, but are outside of it. God is conceived relative to self-transcendence, for

example, if God is found to be revealed (to be present with human awareness) in terms of otherness. The soul has been considered self-transcending in its immortal presence with the mortal self. Nature in which the self finds itself, or universal reason, or the universe might be spoken of as self-transcending. They are present to or in the self, but they surpass it. The unconscious in both Freudian and Jungian traditions can be considered self-transcending unless the self is defined so as to include the unconscious.

One might consider self-transcendence to be norma-tive for the self in the sense that the self occurs always as limited in the presence of what it is not. How a person relates to the limits of the self in the presence of the non-self in this conception would be an essential aspect of all forms of health and pathology.

Bibliography. M. Buber, *I and Thou* (1970). J. W. Conn and W. E. Conn, "Self-Sacrifice, Self-Fulfillment or Self-Transcen-dence in Christian Life?" *Human Development*, 3:3 (1982), 25–28. W. E. Conn, *Conscience: Development and Self-Transcendence* (1981). W. James, *Varieties of Religious Experience* (1902). J. E. Loder, *The Transforming Moment: Understanding Convictional Experiences* (1981). R. Otto, *The Idea of the Holy* (1958). J.-P. Sartre, *Being and Nothingness* (1956). C. E. Scott, *Boundaries in the Mind* (1982). M. Watkins, *Waking Dreams* (1976).

C. E. SCOTT

PERSON (Philosophical Issues); PHILOSOPHY AND PSYCHOLOGY, WESTERN; SELF; SPIRIT, HUMAN; THEOLOGICAL ANTHRO-POLOGY. *See also* BEING/BECOMING RELATIONSHIP; CON-SCIOUSNESS; FREEDOM AND DETERMINISM; IMAGINATION; LOVE; MEMORY; NATURE AND GRACE. *Compare* SELF-ACT-UALIZATION/SELF-REALIZATION; SELF-DENIAL; TRANSCEN-DENCE, DIVINE; TRINITY AND PERSONHOOD.

SELF-UNDERSTANDING. Operationally, the capac-ity to observe and interpret one's past, present and future motivations and behavior. In most contemporary secular psychotherapies and approaches to pastoral counseling, self-understanding is a major therapeutic aim. While the sufficiency of self-understanding for personal change has been questioned on many grounds, it remains a central goal with the majority of pastoral counselors. Self-under-standing, from a pastoral point of view, must include an integrated relation to transcendent values and meanings from one's religious tradition.

1. **History.** Self-understanding has been intimately connected with living the "good life" since classical Greek times (Alexander and Selesnick, 1966). Overcom-ing religious superstition and developing the rational powers of the mind have been cardinal points in the development of Western culture.

The biblical tradition, however, emphasizing revealed truth and covenantal, communal relationships, gave lit-tle specific attention to individual self-understanding in the modern sense. The understanding of self was through membership in the community and its traditions, and ultimate self-understanding was believed to be given through divine revelation and the power of the Spirit rather than through rational self-examination.

Subsequent history merged Greek and biblical approaches, developing disciplines of self-understanding involving subtle psychologies and methods of care, as in the ascetic and mystical traditions and in later Protestantism. Calvin, in a celebrated statement, asserted the inseparability of knowledge of God and knowledge of self (*Institutes* I: 1), and later Calvinism stressed conscientious self-examination, as did much Catholic piety.

2. Self-Understanding in Modern Psychology. *a. Sigmund Freud and the analytic tradition.* Twentieth-century psychology lost confidence in the therapeutic power of conscience, but self-understanding in a more rational and analytical form, reminiscent of the early Greek tradition, has been a pivotal concept. In this development Freud was the formative figure.

Freud's early formulation of the purpose of psychotherapy was to make the unconscious conscious, i.e., to work through the various impediments to knowing the truth about one's motivation and behavior. Freud taught that most psychological symptoms result from a kind of ignorance which the conscious mind imposes on itself as a compromise between the punitive conscience (superego) and the impulsive instinctual demands of the id. Such ignorance and resulting compromise formations (symptoms and works of culture) protect the personality against disintegration and provide for a degree of gratification of forbidden impulses.

An early, somewhat naive, confidence in the power of rational understanding soon gave way in Freud's writings to the realization that true self-understanding could not be gained from rational knowledge about one's inner life but only through the gradual, anxiety-provoking work of uncovering the feelings and experiences associated with repressed or denied memories, thoughts, and feelings (Freud, 1914). Self-understanding was thus contrasted with intellectualization and rationalization, two major defensive postures against the awareness of internal conflict and personal growth. In analytic thought and practice, this process of uncovering and working through of emergent material is mediated by the working alliance between therapist and client. The process of interpreting the various defensive maneuvers which the psyche employs to remain in ignorance, plus — most importantly — the effort to develop, interpret, and "work through" the "transference relationship" with the therapist, comprise the central tasks of these therapies aimed at developing self-understanding. Only caricatures and superficial understandings of these processes can support the notion that the therapeutic process is merely an intellectual adventure. With few exceptions psychoanalytically oriented writers maintain the centrality of self-understanding as the key factor in therapeutic change (Chessick, 1974; DeWald, 1964; Fromm-Reichmann, 1950).

b. Carl Rogers and the humanistic tradition. The other major tradition of contemporary psychology stressing the therapeutic power of self-understanding is humanistic psychology, especially the psychology of Carl Rogers. Like Freud, Rogers explained symptoms as the result of self-ignorance and viewed therapy as the search for self-understanding. But for Rogers true self-knowledge is not essentially rational as in analytic therapy; it is more wholistic, emotional, spontaneous, and "experiential." Rather than resolving transference, Rogerian therapy involves a nonjudgmental trusting relationship with a therapist whose "unconditional positive regard" enables the client to value his or her own experience more fully. The person is thus able to recover aspects of the self

disowned in childhood in deference to the "conditions of worth" imposed by powerful but loved and needed authority figures. As one recovers the capacity to experience oneself more fully (or "congruently") one recovers vitality and wholeness. Therefore a better term than self-understanding, which connotes explanatory or analytic insight, might be "self-experiencing" or "self-awareness" in Rogerian psychology.

3. Self-Understanding in Contemporary Pastoral Care and Counseling. Before the modern pastoral care and counseling movements, self-understanding was primarily moral self-examination. The modern clinical movement, however, influenced by psychotherapeutic developments, produced models for pastoral care and counseling which emphasized the development of analytic and experiential self-understanding, self-acceptance, and personal growth (e.g., Wise, 1950; Hiltner, 1951). In all cases both the self-understanding of the pastoral counselor and that of the client or parishioner were emphasized. This basic theory was consonant both with client centered and psychodynamic approaches to therapy — that one's conflicts, problems, and feelings *are* understandable and that through growing self-understanding persons *can* become more fully themselves. To the great credit of these and later writers in the field, self-understanding was never viewed in a magical, simplistic, or mechanical way (Wise, 1950, p. 119).

A growing number of persons come for pastoral counseling and psychotherapy who suffer not so much from classical problems of repression and oedipal difficulties as from moderate to severe developmental defects (e.g., "narcissistic" and "borderline" personalities). Traditional approaches seeking to develop insight with these persons are fraught with major difficulties and demand new ways of therapeutic thinking (Chessick 1977; Kohut 1971, 1977).

Many writers have also challenged the adequacy of self-understanding as a primary goal in the therapy of more traditionally disordered persons. Such criticisms have come from Gestalt therapy, behavior therapists of many orientations, hypnotic therapies (both direct and indirect), paradoxical therapies, and systems-oriented family therapies. Questions have arisen from theology as well. Reinhold Niebuhr (1955), for example, giving contemporary expression to the Augustinian tradition in which the "will" is held to be in bondage, questioned how the self can be saved through a deepened understanding of corrupt inner motives. Such "bondage of the will" often seems to ring true in clinical pastoral experience.

At the same time growth in psychological self-understanding, if it includes emotional and not merely cognitive understanding, is often emotionally liberating or unexpectedly helpful in practical ways, at least for many people. And most pastors continue to feel that a quest for truthfulness in relation to oneself is an important part of the quest for right relationship with God and other persons. Thus, despite certain theological critiques, the influence of the newer psychotherapies, and concerns about the changing psychology of contemporary selfhood, pastoral practice continues to employ the notion of self-understanding widely and in different forms, though the term is perhaps less explicit in pastoral theory than it was earlier in this century.

Self-understanding is thus a frontier question for the pastoral field today. Is self-understanding necessary for personal transformation, and what is the relationship between them? Should pastoral counseling and psychotherapy aim at self-understanding, or at empowering the self, and is the one a means to the other? If self-understanding is necessary for personal transformation, how does it come about psychologically, and how is it to be understood theologically?

Bibliography. F. Alexander and S. Selesnick, *The History of Psychiatry* (1966). R. Chessick, *Intensive Psychotherapy of the Borderline Patient* (1977); *The Technique and Practice of Intensive Psychotherapy* (1974). P. DeWald, *Psychotherapy* (1964). F. Fromm-Reichmann, *Principles of Intensive Psychotherapy* (1950). S. Freud, "Recollecting, Repeating, and Working Through" *SE*, vol. 12, pp. 146 ff. S. Hiltner, *Self-Understanding* (1951). H. Kohut, *The Analysis of the Self* (1971); *The Restoration of the Self* (1977). R. Niebuhr, *The Self and the Dramas of History* (1955). C. Rogers, *Client Centered Therapy* (1951). C. Wise, *Pastoral Counseling Theory and Practice* (1950).

R. G. BRUEHL

PSYCHOTHERAPY. *See also* HUMANISTIC PSYCHOLOGY; PHILOSOPHY AND PSYCHOLOGY; PSYCHOANALYSIS; REVELATION AND PASTORAL CARE. *Compare* INSIGHT; INTUITION; SELF-ANALYSIS; SELF-EXAMINATION.

SELF-WORTH. *See* SELF-ESTEEM.

SELFISHNESS. *See* AVARICE AND GENEROSITY; EGOTISM; NARCISSISM.

SEMINARY/SEMINARY STUDENT. *See* THEOLOGICAL EDUCATION; THEOLOGICAL STUDENTS.

SENILITY. *See* OLDER PERSONS, MENTAL DISORDERS OF.

SENSITIVITY/SENSITIVITY TRAINING. *See* COMPASSION; HUMAN RELATIONS TRAINING; PERCEPTIVENESS AND SENSITIVITY, PASTORAL.

SENSORY DEPRIVATION RESEARCH. Throughout history people have sought out isolation and self-imposed sensory deprivation to increase inspiration and meditation. Moses sought isolation at Mount Sinai prior to receiving the Ten Commandments (Exodus 19) and Jesus often sought solitude for prayer and meditation (e.g., Lk. 4:1–13; 6:12). Such extended deprivation has been viewed as beneficial in clearing one's mind for meditation and guidance. More recently, the negative impacts of sensory deprivation have become increasingly recognized. Following World War II, many prisoners of war experienced deleterious side-effects of prolonged sensory deprivation brought on by prison isolation. Labeled by some as brainwashing, these prison experiences often involved prolonged periods of isolation and minimal sensory input, making the prisoner more susceptible to making confessions.

Hebb and his co-workers in Montreal began early experimentation into controlled deprivation of sensory input. These researchers utilized a variety of methods of restricting sensory input including total immersion in lukewarm water and isolation in a darkened and soundproof room. Early results were scattered, but there appeared a growing consensus that extended periods of sensory deprivation could lead to increased suggestibility as well as increased anxiety, tension, and inability to concentrate. Extended deprivation often led to heightened imagery, frequently including visual hallucinations and sensory input with delusional quality. There was a general consensus that such extended periods of sensory deprivation had generally negative effects.

The negative effects of sensory deprivation have also been observed in daily life. Long-haul truckers, who view similar terrain along monotonous highways, are subject to increased fatigue and danger as a result of reduced sensory input. Assembly line workers are victims of diminished sensory input and are subject to increased accidents and errors in judgment. Additionally, many patients with extended hospital stays often experience the negative effects of their reduced sensory input. So called "cardiac psychosis" and "postoperative psychosis" are thought to be largely related to the starkness of intensive care rooms without windows and limited visitation. Finally, in the years when certain forms of polio were treated with extended treatment in a respirator or iron lung, it was observed that many of the patients who were in treatment for extended periods of time developed hallucinations as a direct result of their reduced sensory input.

In the last several years there has been a reawakening of the awareness of positive effects of sensory deprivation, particularly in controlled settings for the treatment of mental disorders. Peter Suedfeld (1980) has developed what he has termed *REST* — an acronym for "Restricted Environmental Stimulation Therapy or Technique." He utilized darkened isolation chambers and flotation tanks to provide patients with an opportunity for reflection and retreat from the stresses and cares of daily life. Used as an adjunct with other treatment approaches, *REST* seems to be effective in modifying undesirable behaviors such as excessive drinking, smoking, and overeating. Additionally, *REST* has been used as an adjunct to traditional psychotherapy for persons experiencing anxiety and certain stress-related physical disorders such as essential hypertension and asthma.

Bibliography. W. Heron, W. H. Bexton, and D. O. Hebb, "Cognitive Effects of a Decreased Variation in the Sensory Environment," *American Psychologist*, 8 (1953), 366. P. Suedfeld, *Restricted Environmental Stimulation: Research and Clinical Applications* (1980).

D. K. SMITH

PERSONALITY THEORY (Empirical Studies, Methods, and Problems). *Compare* BRAIN RESEARCH; ECOLOGICAL PSYCHOLOGY; PSYCHEDELIC DRUGS AND EXPERIENCE.

SEPARATION, MARITAL. *See* DIVORCE (Care and Counseling); MARRIAGE COUNSELING AND MARITAL THERAPY.

SEPARATION, MARITAL (Roman Catholicism). While recognizing the obligations and privilege spouses have to maintain conjugal living, the Catholic Church understands such is not always feasible. Serious danger of spirit or body to the other spouse or the children is legitimate cause for separation. Ideally, forgiveness should be given an adulterous spouse; however, the other has the right to separate. Provision for support and education of children must be arranged. With the diocesan bishop's permission, a permanent separation may be legally obtained. Canon law specifies procedures for separations: temporary or permanent. Notwithstanding a separation, the couple is still married.

J. MILLER

CODE OF CANON LAW (Roman Catholicism); DIVORCE AND REMARRIAGE (Roman Catholicism).

SEPARATION ANXIETY. The sense of care, foreboding, restlessness, or uneasiness observed in infants when removed from persons to whom there is a significant attachment, especially the mother. Thus, early separation creates a situation in which fears are easily aroused and the prospect of separation yields varying degrees of anxiety. The concept is associated with such persons as Freud, Rank, Klein, Fairbairn, Kris, Spitz, and especially John Bowlby. Some theorists understand separation anxiety and its subsequent manifestations in mourning and defense as the key to anxiety and neurosis. Others suggest that there is no single cause of neurosis but insist that separation anxiety is a key and a common ingredient in psychological distress.

Bibliography. J. Bowlby, *Separation: Anxiety and Anger* (1973), ch. 2, Appendix 1.

L. O. MILLS

ANXIETY; ANXIETY DISORDERS; NEUROSIS; SOCIAL ISOLATION.

SERVANT, PASTOR AS. *See* PASTOR (Normative and Traditional Images).

SERVICE OF ANOINTING (Orthodox). *See* MINISTRY AND PASTORAL CARE (Orthodox Tradition).

SERVICES AND AGENCIES, COMMUNITY. *See* SOCIAL SERVICES.

SETON, ELIZABETH, ST. *See* HISTORY OF ROMAN CATHOLIC PASTORAL CARE (United States); WOMEN IN PASTORAL MINISTRIES, HISTORY OF.

SEVEN DEADLY SINS. Those vices which tradition singled out as likely to produce further, usually serious sins. The list most often given includes pride, avarice, envy, anger, sloth, lust, and gluttony.
1. **Sin Lists.** The concept of human sinfulness or sin, while essential to Christianity, is too indeterminate to warn against the variety of human failings. On the other hand, a list of all human sins is impossible. Intermediate between sin and concrete sins are the vices or disordered affections which motivate specific sins. The most significant of these vices are called "capital sins." They are the sources of others sins. The popular term "deadly sins" is misleading since these disordered affections or the sins

they motivate are not always damning evils. Still, the vices can lead to major disturbances in relation to God, others, world, and self.

Scripture contains many sins lists. Subsequently church writers devised other lists. The number and kind of vices included have varied greatly, and no particular list of vices seems inevitable or exhaustive. The stress given to a particular sin varies among authors and from age to age. Though pride is often thought to be the source of all the others, it seems that any one vice might give rise to the others, and several may be involved as "motives" for a given act. Authors also note omissions in the list, for example, apathy, disloyalty, ingratitude, or hatred.
2. **Disordered Loves.** The seven vices are best understood as forms of aberrant loves. Human affections either may be directed to the wrong object or have an inappropriate depth or intensity. Thus pride is a love for a falsely exalted self; gluttony is an excessive love of food or drink. It should be noted that some items, like anger or pride, are not always disordered and can even be virtuous.

While the topic of the "seven deadly sins" has often served as a sermon topic, today the theme is only infrequently encountered. The ethical importance of character, however, ensures that some list of major vices will always be useful for a serious examination of the heart.

Bibliography. M. Bloomfield, *Seven Deadly Sins* (1952). D. Capps, *Deadly Sins and Saving Virtues* (1987). H. Fairlie, *Seven Deadly Sins Today* (1978). S. Lyman, *Seven Deadly Sins* (1978). W. F. May, *Catalogue of Sins* (1967). K. Olsson, *Seven Sins and Seven Virtues* (1962). B. Whitlow, *Hurdles to Heaven* (1963).

E. C. VACEK

ANGER AND MEEKNESS; AVARICE AND GENEROSITY; ENVY AND GRACIOUSNESS; GLUTTONY AND TEMPERANCE; LUST AND CHASTITY; PRIDE AND HUMILITY; SLOTH AND ZEAL. *See also* CHRISTIAN LIFE; LIFESTYLE ISSUES IN PASTORAL CARE; MORAL THEOLOGY AND PASTORAL CARE; REASON AND PASSION; SIN/SINS.

SEVENTH DAY ADVENTISTS. *See* SECTARIAN PASTORAL CARE; WHITE, ELLEN.

SEX. *See* SEXUAL ISSUES IN PASTORAL CARE; SEXUALITY.

SEX COUNSELING. *See* SEXUAL DYSFUNCTION AND SEX THERAPY.

SEX EDUCATION. Sex education is designed to deal with and minimize the confusion and anxiety many people in our culture experience in regard to sexuality. It is an attempt to provide direction and control for the powerful personal and social forces of sexuality. As discussed here, sex education does not include counseling in relation to sexuality nor parental efforts to direct and shape the sexuality of their children. Sex education refers to designed activities for a group under the direction of leaders. There are, of course, many other activities and experiences which educate in relation to sexuality.

The age of reason and our commitment to educate made it inevitable that education and sex would be linked and the problems of sex would be addressed by education. It is not clear, however, that education's more and better facts will result in a more mature, happier life. Indeed the excessive rationality of education tends to treat sex separately from personhood and results in sex being viewed as incidental to the person. Sex and sexuality are not discrete portions of the self; sexuality is pervasive and central to the self. An issue for sex education is how to avoid excessive rationality and preserve the mystery and centrality of sexuality to personhood.

The excessive rationality of education tends to focus attention on the conscious processes of the self. The goal of some sex education programs seems to be the development of conscious responsible decision making. This tends to overlook or ignore unconscious processes. The unconscious repression of ideas and facts which are perceived as alien to the self sometimes serves the self well. However, repression may be a barrier to sex education. Repression by the adolescent is at least one significant factor in the report by adolescents that their parents fail to talk with them about sex and sexuality. How is sex education to deal with unconscious aspects of the self in regard to sexuality?

Perhaps sex education inevitably directs the attention of participants to reproduction and reproductive issues. However, the more human and personal issue of human sexuality has to do with affection for self and others. The adolescent must relax the exclusive affectional bonds with parents in order to feel and express affection for others. The adolescent must learn to feel affection, must learn to differentiate degrees or levels of affection, must learn to combine commitment and continuity with affection and must learn personally and socially appropriate expressions of affection. This is an exceedingly difficult and complex series of tasks. It involves far more than rationality and conscious processes. How does sex education assist persons, especially adolescents, to differentiate levels of affection and appropriate expressions of affection? Are there ways to expand the affectional and expressional repertoire of persons?

A prevalent moral value in our culture is "permissiveness" with affection. This value holds that consenting adults who feel affection for each other may express that affection sexually. This value can be seen as a liberating response to the excessive repression of sexuality of the nineteenth century. However, as this value has spread throughout the culture, inadequacies have become apparent. First, affection is not a very restrictive guide and sexual permissiveness has become general. Second, this cultural norm has encouraged widespread sexual intercourse among adolescents.

Permissiveness with affection as a cultural norm is linked with the way in which our culture has "genitalized" the expression of affection. This "genitalization" of affectional expression can be clearly seen on prime-time TV. The general rule for TV seems to be that any positive relationship, no matter how superficial, or how temporary, will be expressed genitally (either implicitly or explicitly). Permissiveness and genitalization combine to make it exceedingly difficult for persons to differentiate levels or degrees of affection and to learn appropriate differentiated affectional responses. Given the cultural permissiveness and genitalization of affection, how can sex education effectively help persons to make more responsible sexual decisions? And, how will sex education define responsibility in light of cultural sexual norms?

In a cultural context of repression and denial of sexuality and of clear moral judgments and social sanctions, sexual education for rational decision making was appropriate. However, our culture, today, is a culture of considerably greater sexual freedom, a lack of clear, compelling moral standards, and the loss of socially accepted sanctions. The moral values related to self-restraint are generally lacking. Given these social and personal factors, there is no social / moral context within which responsible decisions can be made. There are no effective restraining factors for the decision process. What are the values and restraints to sexual activity which sex education promotes?

Finally, there are the issues posed by AIDS; some of these are known. But this disease, in addition to threatening epidemic disaster, will threaten a variety of assumptions, perspectives, and behaviors. AIDS makes clear the inadequacy of permissiveness with affection. AIDS propels into public discussion the description of a variety of explicit sexual behaviors. One response to AIDS proposes "safe sex" as an explicitly moral guide. And AIDS presents us with untold human suffering. What will be the consequences of the AIDS epidemic on sex education, and how quickly and thoroughly can sex education respond to those consequences?

L. RIPPY

CONTRACEPTION; PARENTS/PARENTHOOD. *See also* FAMILY PLANNING. *Compare* PARENT EDUCATION; PREMARITAL COUNSELING.

SEX ETHICS. *See* SEXUALITY, CHRISTIAN *or* JEWISH ETHICS AND THEOLOGY OF.

SEX RESEARCH. *See* SEXUALITY, BIOLOGICAL AND PSYCHOSOCIAL THEORY OF.

SEX THERAPY. *See* SEXUAL DYSFUNCTION AND SEX THERAPY.

SEXISM. Discrimination against, and domination and exploitation of women by men.

Sexism may be condemned or condoned according to one's beliefs about the relative worth and function of women and men. Although generally used pejoratively, the term "sexism" is the expression of attitudes about the relationship between the sexes which many people deem legitimate or right; for example, women are naturally more emotional than men; women should stay out of the labor force because they take jobs away from men; woman's place is in the home. Those who hold such views would generally regard them not as "sexist," but as valid statements of fact or truth. General usage, however, both in common parlance and in dictionary definitions, asserts that all beliefs and practices which confine women to particular spheres or denigrate their status in relation to men are discriminatory, arbitrary, prejudicial, restrictive, exploitative, and therefore sexist.

1. Origins of Sexism. Scholarship in feminist anthropology, archeology, and theology affords convincing evidence that sexism and its underlying misogyny (hatred of women) and gynephobia (fear of women) are of relatively recent advent in human history. Data, both tangible and mythological, from Paleolithic and Neolithic times, document the existence of cultures which were both egalitarian and biophilic. In the high civilization of the Keph (Minoan) people of ancient Crete, and at Çatal Hüyük in Anatolia, for example, no evidence of weapons or violence can be found. The earliest deity all over the world was female, the great Earth Mother, at first undifferentiated, later the One Goddess of Many Names. No evidence exists of domination of one sex by the other. There is clear evidence of respect for women, often awe of their life-giving powers. Excavations and artifacts from late Paleolithic and early Neolithic sites in many parts of the world suggest many-faceted cultural characteristics shared in an endless variety of ways between women and men. It is increasingly clear that women played an active role in the evolution of human civilization, not only in domestic arenas but in public ones. The invention of agriculture by women is well documented. Also, because the first deity was female, the earliest priests were female.

It is still unclear, however, whether the concept of male superiority grew as a result of a growing human awareness that men had a part in reproduction, or whether spreading populations began competing for resources and war was invented; nevertheless, with these developments came the devaluing and denigration of women. Mythologically, the creation story underwent several transformations from a world created solely by a goddess, to the world created by the goddess and her consort, to the world created from the body of a goddess by a male god, to the world created by a male god without benefit of female. Nearly every culture carries a story of the takeover of power by men, who wrest the secrets of life from women by violence or trickery. Most of such stories, which accompany the rise of male deity, are comparatively recent in evolutionary time — within the last five thousand years.

Thus in Semitic tradition, Yahweh replaces Iahu as creator and life-giver. Yahweh at first co-creates Lilith and Adam. Lilith (in Babylonian tradition the earth aspect of the great goddess Ishtar) refuses to be dominated by Adam; when God supports Adam's appeal, Lilith flies away, unwilling to submit. In Jewish tradition she becomes an evil spirit. In Christian tradition she is scarcely heard of and a new myth arises: Adam is created first and Eve second, taken from man's side and named by him. Man is responsible to God and woman to man. Woman is the first to sin; therefore, man will rule over her.

This second myth is incorporated into the OT and the myth of feminine evil is codified. In spite of the obvious biological fact of birth as woman's process, and even today in spite of current knowledge that the embryo is female for the first six weeks after conception, a male God as Father Creator prevails. Man has become the normative human, woman is "other." As the myth is sanctioned socially and politically and transformed into divine revelation by a father god, dominance of the male is assured; woman becomes property.

With the rise and spread of Christianity, woman is increasingly defined by her sexuality. Her worth is determined by her role as birth medium; she is dutiful daughter, faithful wife, devoted mother, or she is seductress and whore. Virginity and its loss are determined by the male. Woman is inferior to man. She becomes the embodiment of those qualities which man himself wishes to deny: carnality, vulnerability, emotionality, mortality. What becomes encoded as woman's "innate natural physiological and intellectual inferiority" and mythical responsibility for evil are used to justify misogyny and gynephobia not only in Jewish and Christian tradition, but in cultural and religious traditions all over the world. These are manifested in a variety of atrocities against women throughout patriarchal times: torture and burning of witches, genital mutilation, footbinding, suttee (widow burning), rape, battering, incest, and sexual slavery.

Debate over what, if any, gender distinctions are innate and what are learned is far from resolution. Although some things are understood about biological difference, little is understood about the effects of biological difference on other human characteristics. There is no conclusive research data to suggest that there are innate differences in intelligence or emotional and psychological characteristics. No behavioral traits or role assignments have been found to be common to all known cultures. There is more evidence which points to a wider spectrum of difference *within* sexes than *between* them.

2. Effects of Sexism. Beyond the simple and arbitrary divisions of sex roles, a pervasive sexual identity affects every aspect of women's and men's lives. Women are objectified and victimized psychically, physically, and socially. Men are cut off from those qualities they have assigned to women—nurturance, vulnerability, emotionality, attachment. As Ruether (1984) points out, although women are more victimized by patriarchal culture, men are more dehumanized.

Since power continues to reside with men, women are overtly victimized in many ways: (1) discrimination on the basis of sex is not explicitly prohibited by the U.S. Constitution; (2) in spite of their advancing educational level, women hold few elite and powerful positions in governing bodies, in business and industry or in educational, health, and social service institutions; (3) the pauperization of women continues to accelerate. Seventy-five percent of the country's poor are women and children. Two thirds of the adult poor are women. Eighty-four percent of fathers fail to pay court-ordered child support; (4) women earn sixty-eight cents to every dollar earned by men overall; the figure is even lower among the less affluent. A female college graduate can expect to earn less in her lifetime than a male high school dropout; (5) violence against women continues to be overtly and covertly sanctioned. In all but six states, a husband cannot be charged for raping his wife. One in three women will experience attempted or completed violent sexual assault at least once in her lifetime (this figure takes into account the fact that between twenty and fifty percent of such crimes go unreported). Six of ten women in marriage or cohabitation will be battered while in the relationship. One in three girls will be victims of incest before they are eighteen (and minority women are disproportionately represented). (See U.S. Department of Justice entries in bibliography; also Bagelow, 1984); (6) women still must fight to control their own bodies. Choice to bear or not bear children is not controlled by the woman herself. Unnecessary surgery, drug experimentation, victimization by prescribed drugs, and major responsibility for birth control all affect women predominantly; (7) woman as sexual object, as victim, and as servant continues to dominate media images; (8) language continues to exclude and subsume woman. She bears her father's and her husband's names. The man remains the norm for both the universal human and the individual male. Father and Son continue to be the prevailing images of deity.

3. Sexism and Racism. These are inextricably linked in complicated ways. Both are founded on the institutionalized belief in the superior humanity of the white male. In white Western culture all who can be defined as "other"—women, all people of color, and often those of non-European ethnic origin or non-Christian heritage—are exploited or oppressed. White woman's racism stems from her identification with and loyalty to white males. The woman of color lives in double jeopardy. Racism and sexism combine to make her social and political struggle unique. Women of color and women of no color are set against each other by conflicting loyalties and patriarchal policies which keep women emotionally identified with "their men" rather than with each other. Davis (1983) points out that "racism nourishes sexism," causing white women to be indirectly victimized by the special oppression of their sisters of color. Sexual oppression and violence also link sexism and racism. Rape of the women belonging to "the other," for example, in slavery and its continuing aftermath in this country and with regard to the relationship between Vietnamese women and American soldiers, are legitimized both by sexism, which makes woman "other," and by racism, which makes all who are different "the other."

Sexism and racism are also economically related. While the overwhelming percentage of the poor are women, the overwhelming percentage of poor women are women of color.

4. Sexism and Homophobia. These are closely allied and reinforce each other. Homophobia (*homo:* same, *phobia:* fear) is also a recently coined word reflecting the emergence of homosexual and lesbian identity as vital human options. The heterosexual bias of the culture is closely linked to sexism. Rich (1980) raises the issue of heterosexuality as a political institution. Male dominance requires the heterosexual control of women, either benevolently or violently. The lesbian who chooses to relate emotionally and/or sexually to women (and to a lesser extent the male homosexual) is a profound threat to male power and dominance. Rape, battering, incest, pornography, economic dependence of women, all are partly manifestations of compulsory heterosexuality. The violence, both psychic and physical, with which male dominance and heterosexuality is often enforced suggests an attempt to control something fearful and potentially powerful.

5. Reverse Sexism. This is the cry often heard in response to affirmative action programs directed toward improving opportunities for women in education and employment, and as women begin to assert their rights across the political and social scene. Cone sees black or reverse racism as a myth created by whites to ease their guilt feelings; the facts do not support the charge. Likewise reverse *sexism* is a deception. Indeed, when women and men compete on equal terms, some men will have to wait longer to achieve their goals as women move into equal participation in the culture. However, this cannot be equated with the sexist assertion that women are inferior and therefore men have the right to dominate. The insistence of women on equal participation in society does not suggest that women wish to dominate men or to discriminate against them.

Ruether (1984) asserts that sexism is primarily a male problem that men have imposed on women. The attempt of women to right that wrong is not reverse sexism, but the inevitable struggle of an oppressed group to gain equal access to all that society has to offer. Assertions of male superiority and institutionalized dominance are attempts to prevent women from having equal participation in decision making and to deny full humanity to women. Women's assertion of their rights is an affirmation of the full humanity of women rather than an attempt to assert female superiority or to deny the humanity of males.

6. Relevance for Pastoral Care. All that has been said about sexism in the culture as a whole is reflected in the church, both as institution and as theological environment. In churches, as in other institutions, the largest percentage of authorities are men, and the largest percentage of participants are women. Ministers and pastoral counselors, therefore, must be aware both of their own sexist biases and of the ways in which the church or pastoral counseling setting perpetuates the dominance of men and the denial of woman's humanity.

Bibliography. M. D. Bagelow, *Family Violence* (1984). R. Bleier, *Science and Gender: A Critique of Biology and Its Theories on Women* (1984). J. Cone, *Black Theology and Black Power* (1969). M. Daly, *Beyond God the Father* (1973); *Gyn/Ecology* (1978). A. Davis, *Women, Race and Class* (1983). V. Gornick and B. Moran, eds., *Women in Sexist Society* (1971). G. Lerner, *The Creation of Patriarchy* (1986). R. Ruether, *Sexism and God Talk: Toward a Feminist Theology* (1984). A. Rich, "Compulsory Heterosexuality and Lesbian Experience," *Signs,* 5 (1980): 631–60. P. Sanday, *Female Power and Male Dominance: On the Origins of Sexual Inequality* (1981). For government crime statistics see: Federal Bureau of Investigation, *Uniform Crime Reports* (1986); Bureau of Justice Statistics, U.S. Department of Justice, *Sourcebook of Criminal Justice Statistics* (1986).

C. ELLEN

EXPLOITATION/OPPRESSION; FEMINIST ISSUES IN PSYCHOLOGY; FEMINIST THEOLOGY AND PASTORAL CARE; PREJUDICE; SOCIAL JUSTICE ISSUES IN PASTORAL CARE; WOMEN, PASTORAL CARE OF. See also CONSCIOUSNESS RAISING; ETHICS AND PASTORAL CARE; MEN, PASTORAL CARE OF; PORNOGRAPHY; SOCIAL CONSCIOUSNESS AND RESPONSIBILITY; SOCIAL PERCEPTION, JUDGMENT, AND BELIEF; WOMEN IN PASTORAL MINISTRIES, HISTORY OF; VICTIMIZATION. Compare AUTHORITARIANISM; CULTURAL AND ETHNIC FACTORS IN PASTORAL CARE; RACISM.

SEXTRO, HEINRICH PHILIPP (1746–1838). Creator of experience-based education for ministry. Observing that even thoroughly educated candidates were insufficiently prepared for ministry, Sextro advocated the "art of use or application" (Piper), calling it "pastoral theology." He saw pastoral theology as a science in its own right, requiring its own educational theory and method, and not as something that can be studied in the abstract. According to Sextro, pastoral theology deals with experiences which can usually only be communicated verbally, with communal consideration of these experiences, with one's own practical efforts, and with their immediate assessment. Additional analogies to modern clinical supervision include (1) the relationship to persons as the primary concern; (2) precise oversight leading from experience to insight (Piper); (3) the employment of a notebook for recording clinical encounters; and (4) the reactions of students. To avoid distortion, Sextro felt that the student needed to experience the immediate effect of his activity as preacher and pastor and to make appropriate corrections.

Sextro established an institution for practical preparation in Göttingen in 1781, and later extended his educational innovations to vocational and adult education. His plan of 1797 for the *Predigerseminar* in Hannover omits clinical education, but retains his practical emphasis by linking education for catechetics there with a school for schoolteachers (Piper).

Bibliography. P. Zimmerman, "Sextro: Heinrich Philipp S. (Sextroh)," *Allgemeine deutsche Biographie*, vol. 34, (1892), pp. 77–9. H. C. Piper, *Kommunizieren lernen in Seelsorge und Predigt* (1981), pp. 14–27. H. P. Sextro, *Über praktische Vorbereitungsanstalten zum Predigtamt. Nebst einer Nachricht vom Königlichen Pastoralinstitut in Göttingen*, (1783) (cited in Piper).

J. R. BURCK

CLINICAL PASTORAL EDUCATION; PASTORAL THEOLOGY, PROTESTANT.

SEXUAL DEVIANCE. *See* SEXUAL VARIETY, DEVIANCE, AND DISORDER.

SEXUAL DYSFUNCTION AND SEX THERAPY.
Sexual dysfunction as defined by the *Diagnostic and Statistical Manual of Mental Disorders* (3d ed., 1980) is a disorder "characterized by inhibitions in sexual desire or the psychophysiological changes that characterize the sexual response cycle." Sex therapy is a systematic approach which retrains a couple (or individual) to communicate and behave with one another in a way that reduces demand, enhances pleasure, and facilitates natural physiological sexual response. Its goals are limited to the relief of patients' sexual symptoms. It differs from traditional techniques of treating sexual dysfunction by employing a combination of prescribed sexual experiences and psychotherapy (Kaplan, p. 187).

1. **The Sexual Response Cycle.** Sexual experience exhibits a cyclical pattern consisting of four phases. The appetitive phase (I) has to do with the thoughts, feelings and fantasies which urge one toward sexual activity. The excitement-plateau phase (II) includes both the feelings and the physical changes of growing sexual response which occur prior to, or as a result of, sexual-physical pleasuring. The plateau is an intensification of the sexual arousal as the tension of excitement increases. In the orgasmic phase (III) sexual tension and pleasure peak and trigger a rhythmic reflex reaction resulting in ejaculation for a man and pelvic release for a woman. This orgasmic phase is brief, intense, intrapsychic, and is the climax of sexual fulfillment. Women have the capacity for, and may need, more than one orgasmic release. In the resolu-

tion phase (IV) a sense of relaxation and general wellbeing occurs as bodies return to their prestimulated state.
2. **Sexual Dysfunction.** Diagnosis and evaluation of sexual dysfunction must be precise and detailed. The following must be identified: each partner's experience of the problem; the onset and history of the problem; when in the sexual response cycle the problem occurs; what happens in each phase of the sexual response cycle; what settings or occurrences seem to provoke it; whether it is complete or partial impairment; how family and developmental history may contribute to it; and what the desired results of sex therapy may be. Specific disorders are best understood by how they disrupt the normal response cycle. The earlier in the cycle the disruption occurs, the more difficult it is to reverse it.

Inhibited sexual desire (related to phase I of the response cycle) is reported by about forty percent of sex therapy clients (Kaplan; Penner and Penner). This is equally true for men and women. Among women sexual conflict, usually due to erotic ambivalence, is the primary source of inhibited desire. A woman may be very responsive once she gets into the sexual pleasuring, but she may resist that development intensely. This resistance seems to be connected with a lack of trust, a history of alcoholism or unstable parenting, a previous sexual trauma (rape or molestation), or the experience of pleasure as sinful.

For both men and women a lack of sexual desire may be secondary to unsatisfactory sexual experience in phases II and III. Unresponsiveness, ritualistic or mechanical sexual encounters, or lack of emotional connection with one's partner may lead to lack of desire. Or, a person who lacks desire may be diverting sexual energy toward the accomplishment of other goals, e.g., work. Of course, any external interference such as depression, anxiety, stress, illness, drugs, or alcohol will inhibit desire in both men and women.

The sexually naive male may lack desire because of feelings of inadequacy and an underdeveloped capacity for emotional expression. He has probably been raised in an overprotected home with little emotional intensity and has likely missed the usual childhood and adolescent experimentation. Deeper emotional-sexual blocks are seen when this situation is combined with a lack of closeness with father and a male-deprecating mother. The homosexually oriented male who has chosen to function in a heterosexual relationship may lack desire for his wife because of his general lack of sexual attraction to women.

Inhibited sexual excitement for a woman (phase II), once negatively labeled frigidity, is usually emotional rather than physical. She lacks the feelings of excitement even though the physical responses of arousal are present. For a man, difficulty with the excitement-plateau tends to manifest itself physically. Impotence, the inability to achieve or maintain an erection, is experienced by all men at some time, however, chronic anxiety about this involuntary response will make it an ongoing problem.

With the orgasmic phase (III), men and women tend to experience opposite difficulties. Men often respond too quickly — premature ejaculation — whereas many women have difficulty allowing a full response — orgasmic inhibition. A small percentage of men also have difficulty with inhibition of orgasm (retarded ejaculation). Some men have never ejaculated except in their sleep; others cannot ejaculate with a woman in any way; and for still others the inhibition of ejaculation is limited to intercourse.

Premature ejaculation for men and orgasmic inhibition for women are two of the most commonly experienced dysfunctions. Many men do not have control of ejaculation and thus ejaculate before they intend to, interrupting their own and often their partner's enjoyment. Some women have never experienced release from any form of stimulation; others have not experienced orgasm with their partner; and still others have been unable to be orgasmic during intercourse. Because of self-consciousness, fear, or discomfort with the building of sexual intensity these women consciously or unconsciously inhibit natural bodily responses. This leaves women feeling emotionally and physically frustrated. The buildup of congestion in the genitals and breasts causes physical tension and a feeling of heaviness.

Phase IV difficulties, i.e., with resolution, result from inhibition in phase III. When there has not been orgasmic release, return of the body to its prestimulated state will take longer and be accompanied by frustration rather than relaxation.

Painful intercourse (dyspareunia), which can be a part of all four phases of the response cycle, is often not taken seriously as a deterrent to satisfactory sexual enjoyment. Emotional tension, physical trauma, or infection can be the source of the pain.

The first experience of intercourse for a woman may be painful. In addition to the breaking of the hymen (the band around the opening of the vagina), there may be tightness due to eagerness which interferes with relaxation of the muscles of the vagina. When there has been past sexual trauma for a woman there may be an involuntary tightening of the outer third of the vagina (vaginismus) which prevents insertion of the penis.

Sexual dysfunctions cause extreme stress in marriages and self-doubt in individuals. Fortunately, sexual problems are amenable to change through education, self-help programs or books, and sex therapy. Others may require longer term psychotherapy for resolution. While most sexual problems are based on anxiety and inhibition, they differ in the degree to which physical and psychodynamic factors contribute.

3. Therapy. Sex therapy may be a short-term intensive process in which the couple is seen every day for ten to fourteen days away from their normal responsibilities, or it may be ongoing therapy in which the couple is seen once or twice a week, continuing with their regular life. The assessment period takes into account each partner's experience and history with the sexual dysfunction, including medical tests when needed.

Regardless of differences in style of treatment, the goals of sex therapy are to distract from anxiety, remove demand, eliminate negative or failure experiences and feelings, and build new patterns of sexual relating, both verbally and physically.

These goals are best met: (1) by becoming knowledgeable about one's own and each other's bodies and how they function; (2) by developing an awareness of and taking responsibility for one's own needs and feelings; (3) by learning to focus on sensations of pleasure without a demand to respond or please; (4) by opening effective communication within and about the sexual experience; and (5) by recognizing that sex is *not* limited to intercourse and orgasm but includes all enjoyment of each other's bodies, minds and spirits.

During the retraining-therapy process the therapist is actively in control. Intercourse or attempts at intercourse are usually ruled out. Teaching and touching experiences are assigned and selected. Two-and-a-half to three hours are allowed for each experience, though the couple is instructed to turn all clocks away and disregard time in order to listen to their internal desire for contact. The spouses are assigned responsibility for choosing and creating the setting for the experience, initiating the event, and being the first one to experience pleasure. The experiences themselves are vital to producing the necessary changes. They are described and given in written form during the therapy session, then experienced by the couple while they are alone together. Examples of the experiences that are assigned include sensate focus exercises of foot, hand, face and total body caresses that have the purpose of learning the enjoyment of the other person's body and the enjoyment of soaking in pleasure when being "pleasured." Thus both touching and being touched will be pleasurable. Other exercises include learning about each other's bodies and the type of touch that is most enjoyed. It is these behaviorally oriented prescriptions that characterize sex therapy and differentiate it from the usual psychotherapy and marital therapy. In sex therapy, emotional issues that surface are dealt with psychotherapeutically, and behavioral assignments are adjusted to work around the barriers. At all times the couple is encouraged to share their feelings with each other, as well as with their therapist or therapists to avoid any further sexual miscommunication.

Each sexual dysfunction has its own special treatment. When premature ejaculation is the problem, either the "squeeze technique" or the "stop-start" method will be employed. With impotence, re-focus and distraction are necessary. With female orgasmic dysfunction, the couple works to extend the length and intensity of the arousal. Vaginal dilators and P.C. muscle exercises are used to treat vaginismus.

Much change can take place in a relatively short period of time. How well that change is integrated into the couple's ongoing life depends upon their commitment to scheduling quality sexual experience times for themselves each week. Reviewing the principles that brought about the change and planning creative non-demand sexual times are vital. Follow-up sexual therapy sessions are necessary.

Many have gained sexual fulfillment after years of frustration. Kaplan has found that approximately eighty percent of sexually dysfunctional patients can be relieved of their symptoms through sex therapy.

Bibliography. H. S. Kaplan, *Disorders of Sexual Desire* (1979); *The New Sex Therapy* (1974). E. Kennedy, *Sexual Counseling* (1977). W. Masters and V. Johnson, *Human Sexual Inadequacy* (1970).

C. PENNER
J. PENNER

MARRIAGE COUNSELING AND MARITAL THERAPY; SEXUALITY, BIOLOGICAL AND PSYCHOSOCIAL THEORY OF. *See also* MEN; WOMEN. *Compare* BEHAVIOR THERAPIES.

SEXUAL IDENTITY/ORIENTATION/PERVERSION. *See* HOMOSEXUALITY; IDENTITY; SEXUALITY, BIOLOGICAL AND PSYCHOSOCIAL THEORY OF.

SEXUAL ISSUES IN PASTORAL CARE. Pastoral responsibility for dealing with sexual issues involves an awareness of the pastor's own sexuality and how it may affect relationships, the ability to listen with understanding to the explicit and implicit sexual concerns of parishioners and counselees, and the perceptiveness to discern the relationship between a counselee's sexual concerns and other issues in his or her life. It is expressed through the pastor's knowing enough to understand the parishioner's or counselee's concern and being able to suggest resources for dealing with those concerns that involve more knowledge and ability than the pastor has.
1. Focus and Limits of Pastoral Responsibility. Because sexuality is a central fact of life and relationship there are many sexual issues in pastoral care. The pastor may be involved in assisting parishioners to explore the implications of their decisions about sexual behavior and in dealing with their sexual feelings in a variety of situations. Pastors need not, however, feel obligated to function as sex therapists or to give specific advice on the conduct of sexual relationships. It is important that a pastor not be so anxious about or overly interested in the sexual issue presented that she or he is unable to care for the *person* as well as the problem. For example, a young man may come to the pastor with concerns about his sexual orientation. He may have had a recent homosexual experience or become aware of sexual feelings in the locker room of the gymnasium. Pastoral responsibility involves knowing something about homosexuality, but not a great deal. The pastor must know enough to understand what the counselee is anxious about and how he or she perceives it as a problem, but the pastor is required only to respond sensitively and professionally to the human predicament that is common to us all, not to be an expert at whatever issue is presented, sexual or otherwise.

The importance of this placing of sexual issues in pastoral perspective may be more clearly seen by focusing upon the pastor's primary area of professional expertise: defining, understanding, and responding to the human condition from a faith perspective — not abstractly, but as it is expressed in a particular person or group for whom she or he has responsibility. For instance, a pastor may be consulted by a troubled person who happens also to be sexually attractive. The pastor needs to be fully aware of that attraction, but, at the same time, able to avoid being physically expressive of the sexual fantasies he or she may have about the counselee and thus failing to respond to the human problem the person is expressing. As one professionally responsible for articulating the human condition in the light of religious tradition, understanding it, and responding appropriately to it, the pastor is not functioning competently when she or he responds only to the sexual issues present in a relationship. Pastoral competence involves having the ability to relate to the person as well as to his or her sexuality.

A related issue — one that is not fundamentally a sexual one but which often presents itself in a sexual form — is the human tendency to relate to persons in the present as if they were persons from the past. Psychologically, in the minds of others, a pastor is not only an individual human being but also a representative of other significant authority figures — parents, teachers, and so forth. This means that parishioners and counselees often relate to him or her on the basis of their experience with other authority figures who were important to them. A parishioner may be "in love" with her or his pastor or feel rejected by her or him because of prior rejecting experiences. Although pastors who have become skilled in psychotherapy have been supervised in using this "transference" from the past in their work, the relatively untrained pastor deals with this phenomenon by concentrating upon the practical dimensions of the problems presented rather than the relationship with the counselee and by limiting the time spent with the counselee.
2. Responding to Sexual Concerns. If the pastor can be clear about the central focus and limits of his or her professional responsibility, he or she can respond appropriately to a variety of sexual concerns. This may be done either in the interview with the concerned person or through an informed referral to another professional person or relevant literature. In the process of pastoral care he or she may be faced with confusion and misinformation about sexual facts, for example, the effectiveness of present-day contraceptive methods, from pills to periodic abstinence. The pastor cannot be expected to have correct, up-to-date information on all sexual subjects, but does need to be able to recognize possible misinformation and correct it, usually by a referral. Pastors can also be helpful in clearing up confusion between sexual feeling and sexual behavior. People still need to know that Mt. 5:28 does not mean that sexual feeling and behavior are the same thing. Some knowledge of the religious tradition's historic and contemporary views on sexuality is also important to have and to be able to interpret. Interpreting the religious tradition's attitude toward masturbation, for example, is important in the light of sex research and therapy since the early 1960s.

In a day when, for instance, young women may feel embarrassed about being virgins, pastors need to have formulated their point of view on issues like sexual expression in singleness. He or she may be consulted by a divorced woman of forty who is trying to decide whether sexual intercourse is appropriate for her outside of a marital relationship. Again, the pastor's expertise lies not in being able to give an authoritative "yes" or "no" but in hearing and responding to the larger human problem implicit in the question and to the feelings that are a part of that problem. This principle applies as well in difficult ethical dilemmas like abortion. Although abortion is certainly more than an emotional problem, it is clearly a sexual issue that must be dealt with in terms of the personal meanings, values, and feelings involved. This is important also in relation to concerns about sexually transmitted disease and the mechanics and manipulation of infertility treatment and its effects on a couple's sexual relationship. The most important principle in dealing with sexual issues in pastoral care, however, is the pastor's ability to maintain a pastoral perspective whether the issue is sexual or not.

Bibliography. L. S. Cahill, *Between the Sexes: Foundations for a Christian Ethics of Sexuality* (1985) is a useful discussion of Christian sexual ethics. M. Carrera, *Sex: the Facts, the Acts and Your Feelings* (1981) is the type of omnibus book that pastors need to have available to provide a wide variety of sexual information. J. Patton, *Pastoral Counseling: A Ministry of the Church* (1983) offers a brief discussion of transference phenomena in the parish.

J. PATTON

FAITH AND INTEGRITY, PASTOR'S; MORAL DILEMMAS IN PASTORAL PERSPECTIVE; PERSONHOOD OF THE PASTOR, SIGNIFICANCE OF. *See also* COUNTERTRANSFERENCE; GUIDANCE, PASTORAL; PERSONAL, CONCEPT OF, IN PASTORAL CARE; SEXUALITY; TRANSFERENCE.

SEXUAL PROMISCUITY. *See* SEXUALITY, CHRISTIAN *or* JEWISH THEOLOGY AND ETHICS OF; SEXUAL ISSUES IN PASTORAL CARE; SEXUAL VARIETY, DEVIANCE, AND DISORDER.

SEXUAL VARIETY, DEVIANCE, AND DISORDER. The term "sex" comes from medieval Roman Catholic Latin referring to the commandment against adultery. It has many meanings: sexual, sexual intercourse, coitus, sex organs of male and female, sexual intimacy of marital partners, masculinity and femininity, gender description, conception and reproduction of the species, immoral and unethical sexual relations (i.e., adultery, fornication, rape, etc.), and psychiatrically defined deviant behavior.

1. *Sexual Variety.* With human beings, the range of pleasure-returning behavior is limited only by imagination, time, and energy. However, the forms of sexual behavior are learned, not instinctive. "One only has to reflect that normal heterosexual behavior," writes Sandor Lorand, "has itself to be accounted for as a product of learning in social interaction during the early years, and then sees that all of sexual behavior can be explained in terms of very obvious 'symbolic' patterns." (p. 192). Karlen summarizes, "so far, the most reasonable explanation of this is the incredible human capacity for learning. Human beings are born with a minimum of programmed behavior; they must learn a great deal, coordinate what is programmed and what is learned, and do it in interaction with other humans" (Karlen, Arno, 1971, p. 395).

Sex is, however, more than genetics and biology and learning. As Hyder insists, "sex is a gift from God . . . It is the most complete way of total giving of oneself to the other. It is the most personal, intimate, and sacramental outward expression of the inner physical and spiritual love which God has given. Sexual intercourse within Christian marriage is the highest symbolic act which our mortal bodies are capable of performing, and as such represents worship and thanksgiving to the God of love who created us" (1975, p. 162).

Although any comprehensive theory of deviant behavior must be based on some comprehensive theory of sexuality, we do not have to know everything about its "ultimate nature" any more than we must know the nature of light in order to know the laws of optics. Deviation, in statistics, means the distance of any measure from the mean or average. Behavior which is "far out" thus is deviant. Again, behavior which is not tolerated by the culture is deviant, cruelty for sexual purposes for instance. Finally, sexual behavior which fails to measure up to the ideal such as unhealthy actions may be deviant, thus health, purity of action, and happiness would be "normal" while sickness, impurity, or unhappiness deviant.

A psychiatric dictionary describes *deviant* as "the ways in which sex gratification is obtained, mainly or exclusively, without penile-vaginal intercourse. Perversions may occur by the individuals selecting an abnormal sexual object or by engaging in abnormal relations with a usual sex object" (Hinsie, *et. al.*, p. 802).

Actions that are damaging or destructive against persons or property are described as *crimes*, i.e., rape. Behavior that ignores or breaks religious commandments are listed as *sins*, i.e., adultery. In psychiatry, deviance refers to what are known as *paraphilias*, being characterized by "arousal in response to sexual objects or situations that are not part of normative arousal activity patterns and that in varying degrees interfere with the capacity for reciprocal, affectional sexual activity." *Sexual dysfunctions,* on the other hand, are defined as "inhibitions in sexual desire or the psychophysiologic changes that characterize the sexual response cycle" (*DSM III-R*, 1987, p. 279).

From a biological standpoint, the primary aim of sex is pleasure and reproduction and includes, at some stage, coitus between a man and woman. As Clifford Allen (in Ellis and Abarbanel, vol. 2, 1961, p. 802) writes: "When these aims are entirely sidetracked and, out of fear or fixation, the usual modes of heterosexual intercourse are completely omitted, then the individual's behavior is considered deviant." While many deviant personalities report that they suffer extreme shame, guilt, and depression from their behavior, others are only distressed because of the society's reaction. The paraphilias are almost never diagnosed in females except in sexual masochism, where the ratio is estimated to be twenty males for each female.

2. *Sexual Deviant Behavior Diagnosed in the DSM III-R* (1987). (1) *Exhibitionism:* intense, recurrent, sexual urges and sexually arousing fantasies of at least six months duration, resulting in the exposure of genitals to strangers.

(2) *Fetishism:* recurrent, intense, sexual urges and sexual arousing fantasies, of at least six months duration, in which sexual arousal results from the use of nonliving fetishes or objects. Almost any object may serve as a fetish, the deviant person usually masturbates while smelling, holding, or rubbing the fetish object.

(3) *Frotteurism:* recurrent, intense, sexual urges involving rubbing and touching a nonconsenting person. Thus usually occurs in crowded places such as public transportation or on busy sidewalks.

(4) *Pedophilia:* intense, recurrent sexual urges involving sexual activity with a prepubescent child, usually thirteen years old or younger. The instigator often rationalizes that the child was "sexually provocative," "derived sexual pleasure from the actions," or that the activities have "educational value" for the child.

(5) *Sexual masochism:* recurrent, intense, sexual urges involving the real act of being humiliated, bound, beaten, or otherwise made to suffer. The person is usually markedly distressed by these actions. Sexual masochism includes fantasies of being raped and may include physical bondage, sensory bondage, paddling, spanking, flagellation, electrical shocks, cutting, and humiliation. The term "infantilism" describes being treated as a helpless infant.

(6) *Sexual sadism:* intense, recurrent sexual urges and fantasies which include psychological and physical suffering, including humiliation of the victim. Sexual sadism is usually chronic in its extreme form. The intensity of the cruelty inflicted usually increases with time.

(7) *Transvestic fetishism:* recurrent, intense sexual urges and sexually arousing fantasies involving cross-dressing, with anticipated arousal of other males. This has been described chiefly in heterosexual but also in homosexual males and varies from only a single garment of the opposite sex to passing as a woman.

(8) *Voyeurism:* recurrent, intense, sexual urges and sexually arousing fantasies which involve the act of observing unsuspecting people either naked, in the process of disrobing, or engaging in sexual activity. "Peeping Tom" behavior is limited to the purpose of achieving sexual excitement with no sexual contact sought or desired.

(9) *Paraphilia:* telephone scatologia; necrophilia (with corpses); partialism (exclusive focus on parts of the body); zoophilia (sex with animals) though uncommon, occurs particularly among males who are isolated from society and live in farming and herding occupations. Since animals interact sexually in response to the chemical stage in their estrus cycle in the female, there can be little resemblance with human activity, except in romantic fables, since only humans are involved in sexual activity without the possibility of conception. "Sex for fun" is strictly human, as is sexual variety and sexual deviance.

Other forms of paraphilia are coprophilia (with feces); klismaphilia (using enemas); urophilia (with urine). Armand M. Nicholi, Jr., psychiatrist at Harvard Medical School would add: *erotomania,* the pathological preoccupation with erotic fantasies or activities and *nymphomania,* the abnormal and excessive need for sexual intercourse, used to describe female behavior.

Allen would add *abnormal orificial sexuality,* using the fissure beneath the breast, the armpit and the folds between the thighs as *main* and *exclusive* sources of gratification (1961, p. 804). *Sexual analism* is the use of the anus and lower bowel as a substitute vagina, legally known as buggery or sodomy, common in homosexual behavior and a primary transmission channel for AIDS. Usually there must be considerable conditioning before there is any pleasure for the passive recipient but it is a common sexual method for homosexual rape in all-male institutions such as prisons and penitentiaries.

(10) *Homosexuality:* the disposition to seek sensory pleasure through genital bodily contact with persons of one's own sex in preference to sexual relations with the opposite sex. This behavior is generated not by sensory endings or body chemistry but by choice and conditioning, by what persons have learned as desirable. (Editor's note: However, it should be noted that these views, outside of *DSM III-R,* no longer reflect recent research and understanding. Homosexuality is now widely held to result from particular body chemistry, and is increasingly not considered as a "deviant" expression of sexuality.)

In the development phase of *gender identity,* we must distinguish between *homosocial* and *homosexual.* Freud called the period of pre-adolescence, *latency,* when boys relate to boys and girls to girls, which is a *homosocial* period, and not *homosexual* unless genital exploration is used. Friendships continue of same-sex relationships, companionable, supportive, David-and-Jonathan types of *homosocial* kinds. *Homosexual* relations are deviant here, and include sexually oriented and libidinal contacts with orgasm as the goal. It confuses the issue and is inaccurate to refer to this *pre-heterosexual* period as a *homosexual* period.

Deviancy is a part of civilized and religious standards. While Masters and Johnson (1979), might try to argue that any goal of pleasure is "normal and natural" when it brings pleasurable sensation and orgasm, civilization and culture necessitate the curbing of dangerous deviances, first by education of its young, then by legal means, then by religious commandments.

From this, we define deviance, as Talcott Parsons does, as "a departure from the normative standards which have come to be set up as the common culture" (Thio, 1978, p. 3).

The American Psychiatric Association (APA) removed homosexuality from its list of mental disorders after 1968 and limited the psychiatric diagnosis for homosexual persons, under 302.90, "sexual disorder not otherwise specified," to "persistent and marked distress about one's sexual orientation" (*DSM III-R,* 1987, p. 296). Ruth Tiffany Barnhouse, M.D., describes the process of change in the APA as partly the result of a vote influenced by a letter written and paid for by the National Gay Task Force and thought to be from the APA Board. "Many of the voting doctors, earnestly deploring the punitive laws and harsh social treatment of homosexuals, were persuaded to vote as they did by the argument that the elimination of homosexuality as an official illness might do something to improve these regrettable conditions" (1977, p. 45).

For the pastoral counselor, Richard F. Lovelace writes in *Homosexuality and the Church,* "What should we conclude concerning homosexuality from new scientific data interpreted in the context of biblical teaching? Homosexual behavior is uniformly condemned and nowhere commended wherever it is mentioned in Scripture. All other forms of sexual expression outside heterosexual marriage are condemned and nowhere commended throughout Scripture. We conclude that heterosexual activity outside marriage and homosexual activity under any circumstances are viewed in Scripture as destructive to the family and the rest of the social order. The Bible opposes private involvement in these forms of sexual behavior and warns that their public affirmation within the church is even more dangerous (see II Pet. 2:1–22; Jude vss. 4–13, 22–24)," (p. 146).

Continued study is necessary to overcome this serious situation of homophobia (an irrational fear and hatred of homosexual persons) and heterophobia (irrational fear and hatred of heterosexual persons and individuals of the opposite sex).

Certainly the Bible is not against sex, but the overall thrust is in favor of *legitimate* sexuality and pleasure. Like eating and drinking and comfort, sexuality is presented positively in the Scriptures where the activity is moral and permissible. God saw the creation as good. Scripturally, Lovinger writes, homosexuality is clearly and explicitly prohibited, particularly, "male homosexuality (Rom. 1:26–27, I Cor. 6:9–10) is strongly and clearly condemned" (p. 243).

Pastors may involve acceptance and empathy in counseling but not at the expense of standards of right and wrong, of helping people measure themselves by God's standards, as Christians, pastors can never be satisfied with "value-free sex education or behavior."

3. Conclusion. Pastors face many counseling relationships in which sexuality plays a major part. While psychotherapists, especially sex counselors, see persons with dysfunctions, pastors counsel persons with sexual problems of sin and guilt, or marital disharmony, and of sexual misdeed in both pre- and marital relationships.

Hatterer, a New York psychiatrist, points out that at least a third of homosexuals practicing during teen years and into their twenties, move into heterosexual behavior by their late twenties through religious experience, the love of a heterosexual person, ordinary maturing, or psychotherapy.

The pastor is in a most favorable position in counseling with persons with sexual problems, in that he or she can bring understanding and insight, like the psychologist, and also forgiveness of self and from God, and the pastor can offer a support group, the congregation, to stabilize the newfound healing experience. In today's world, more people of both sexes find freedom in speaking to a pastor about the intimate experiences of their lives. This is particularly helpful with a pastor who is at home with her or his own sexuality.

The pastor is a key person in cultivating healthy and moral sexual attitudes both in and out of his or her congregation and in the community. Religious faith does not create sexual deviance, it only defines it and educates persons in developing (learning) healthy and satisfying and moral forms of sexual expression.

It is the common experience of professional psychotherapists including pastoral counselors that sexually deviant behavior is just as responsive to religious conversion and psychotherapy as any other neurotic behavior or attitude. It is only when the individual is convinced that his or her perversion is inborn and refuses to cooperate in counseling or to admit that his or her behavior is immoral or a perversion, that it remains fixed in the personality, just as any neurotic attitude.

Bibliography. American Psychiatric Association, *Diagnostic and Statistical Manual of Mental Disorders* 3d ed., rev. (1987). R. T. Barnhouse, *Homosexuality: A Symbolic Confusion* (1977). A. P. Bell and M. S. Weinberg: *Homosexualities: A Study of Diversity Among Men and Women* (1978). A. P. Bell, M. S. Weinberg, and S. K. Hammersmith, *Sexual Preference, Its Development in Men and Women* (1981). J. R. Cavanagh, *Counseling the Homosexual, Our Sunday Visitor* (1977). N. S. Cryer, Jr., and J. M. Vayhinger, eds., *Casebook in Pastoral Counseling* (1962). A. Ellis and A. Abarbanel, *The Encyclopedia of Sexual Behavior*, 2 vols. (1961). J. R. Fleck and J. D. Darter, eds., *Psychology and Christianity: Integrative Readings* (1981). Group for the Advancement of Psychiatry, *Assessment of Sexual Function: A Guide to Interviewing* (1974). E. Goode and R. Troiden, eds., *Sexual Deviance and Sexual Deviants* (1974). G. W. Henry, *Sex Variants: A Study of Homosexual Patterns* (1948). L. E. Hinsie and R. J. Campbell, *Psychiatric Dictionary* (1976). J. S. Hyde, *Understanding Human Sexuality* (1979). O. Q. Hyder, *The People You Live With* (1975). S. Lorand, ed., *Perversions, Psychodynamics and Therapy* (1956). R. F. Lovelace, *Homosexuality and the Church* (1978). R. Lumiere and S. Cook, *Healthy Sex and Keeping It That Way: A Complete Guide to Sexual Infections* (1983). J. Marmor, ed., *Sexual Inversion: The Multiple Roots of Homosexuality* (1965). J. L. McCary, *Sexual Myths and Fallacies* (1971). W. H. Masters and V. E. Johnson, *Homosexuality in Perspective* (1979). R. E. L. Masters, *Forbidden Sexual Behavior and Morality* (1966). J. Money, ed., *Sex Research: New Developments* (1965). M. Oraison, *The Homosexual Question* (1977). M. Ostow, ed., *Sexual Deviation: Psychoanalytic Insight* (1974). C. Penner and J. Penner, *The Gift of Sex, A Christian Guide to Sexual Fulfillment* (1981). W. D. Rodgers, *The Gay Invasion, A Christian Look at the Spreading of Homosexual Myth* (1977). S. Sapp, *Sexuality, the Bible and Science* (1977). I. Singer, *The Goals of Human Sexuality* (1973). E. T. Rueda, *The Homosexual Network: Private Lives and Public Policy* (1982). L. B. Smedes, *Sex for Christians* (1976). E. Wheat and G. Wheat, *Intended for Pleasure* (1977). M. Weinberg, ed., *Sex Research, Studies from the Kinsey Institute* (1976). R. J. Wicks, R. D. Parson, and D. E. Capps, eds., *Clinical Handbook of Pastoral Counseling* (1985). A. Thio, *Deviant Behavior* (1978).

J. M. VAYHINGER

SEXUALITY. *See also* BISEXUALITY; INCEST; HOMOSEXUALITY; MASTURBATION. *Compare* SEXUAL DYSFUNCTION AND THERAPY.

SEXUAL VIOLENCE. *See* FAMILY VIOLENCE; INCEST; RAPE AND RAPE COUNSELING.

SEXUALITY, BIOLOGICAL AND PSYCHOSOCIAL THEORY OF. Biological and psychosexual development of humans is a continuously changing process. From conception to shortly after birth, biological and physical determinants play a major role in the process of growth. Very soon the impact of socialization, family and culture exert an ever-increasing influence on psychosexual development. With all these converging determinants, a relatively fixed pattern of psychosexuality is developed in the adult.

Even at this stage of development we are in a changing process because of our sexual values, orientations, religious beliefs, life experiences, new education and a change in our life expectations. This process will continue to evolve throughout our life cycle.

1. Biological. Biology of sex is the study of the functioning of the human body in relationship to the physical development of the male and female body and brain. Regardless of the genetic coding, during the first weeks of development male and female embryos are anatomically identical. At fertilization, when the male sperm and female egg unite to form a zygote, the initial programming for sexual differentiation is set in place. The sperm carries an X or a Y sex chromosome, while the egg always has an X chromosome. When the twenty-three chromosomes of the egg combine with the twenty-three chromosomes of the sperm, the zygote has a total of forty-six chromosomes. Generally a forty-six, XX chromosome pattern is the genetic code for a female and a forty-six, XY pattern creates a pattern for the male.

As the development of the embryo progresses two primitive gonads form during the fifth and sixth weeks of pregnancy, first as ridges of tissue and then as more distinct structures of male or female genitals. There are also two paired primitive duct systems that form in both male and female embryos during this time. These are the Müllerian ducts and the Wolffian ducts (Masters, Johnson and Kolodny, 1988).

For the testes to develop, there must be one further step in genetic control. A chemical substance called H-Y antigen, controlled by the Y chromosome, starts the transformation of the primitive gonads into testes (Wachtel, 1979). If H-Y antigen is not present, the primitive gonads will always develop into ovaries (Wachtel).

At this point of development of the embryo, sexual differentiation occurs at three different levels. These are the internal sex structures, the external genitals, and the brain. This differentiation is controlled mostly by hormones. Even if the embryo is genetically an XY male, if there is not enough testosterone the anatomic development will be female.

The female sexual differentiation does not depend on hormones. Ovaries generally develop at about the twelfth week after conception, but even if they do not, the Müllerian duct system will proceed to develop into the uterus, Fallopian tubes, and inner third of the vagina (Money and Ehrhardt).

2. The Development of the Brain.

Within the first weeks of gestation the androgen, if present, will begin to masculinize the brain. The action of the androgen is to organize the immature central nervous system into the patterns of maleness. When androgen, which is also testosterone, is absent the ongoing process toward femaleness continues in its natural course.

It is thought that because of the delicate process of change for the male fetus from female into male there is a greater prevalence of divergent sexual behavior among males. This divergent sexual behavior can be in the form of sadism, bestiality, masochism, pedophilia, and necrophilia, among others.

The masculinizing effect of testosterone in the developing embryo or fetus appears to be exerted upon the hypothalamus of the brain. Certain areas of the hypothalamus show distinct anatomical differences between the sexes. These differences can be altered by manipulation of testosterone (Gersh and Gersh 1981).

According to Byer, Shainberg and Jones, "The consequences of sexual differentiation in the fetal brain become evident during and after puberty. Physiologically, the brain differentiation influences cyclic sex hormone production, menstrual cycles, and cyclic fertility in the female, while it has a role in preserving the relatively constant level of sex hormone production and fertility in the male."

3. Differences in Adolescent Sexuality.

There are noticeable physical differences at puberty. True puberty is seen by changes in the ovaries and testes and the production of hormones from each. Soon after the first ejaculation most males produce viable spermatozoa. The ability to become pregnant does not always occur with the beginning of the female puberty. Menstruation does not always include ovulation.

There is a physical reason why pubescent males are aware of their sexual needs. The male receives sexual stimulation, this increases the production of sperm and the flow of secretions from the sex glands causing pressure on the ejaculatory reflex. His sexual tensions can be relieved only by ejaculation. The male has a local reaction. His increased adolescent sexuality is genitally oriented.

For the pubescent female there is a diffused reaction to sexual stimulation. When the female eggs begin to mature completely they mature one at a time, in most cases. The female sexual reaction is dominated by her cerebral cortex. Her sexuality is often socially oriented toward love and marriage. Females mature earlier than males. Often the young girl will find boys her age awkward and socially inept. She will seek older boys to meet her social needs.

4. Adult Attitudes Toward Sexuality.

Most males can achieve sexual gratification independent of love and commitment. In the past, for many women, sex and love have been inseparable. Robert O. Blood in his book, *Marriage,* states, "Married men rate sexual intercourse with the woman for whom they feel affection as the most important feature of their marriage. Most married women tend to rank sexual intercourse lower than security. For them a home and children are the most important elements of marriage. The wise husband will seduce his wife romantically rather than erotically" (Blood, p. 360). Such statements now appear outrageously biased to many.

"Acquiring a sex life these days is hardly difficult, either for women or for men. Having a love life, or a love life that endures, is less easy to come by" (Shaevitz, 1987). Sexuality does not seem as simple as it was in our grandparents' day. There were expected roles, behavior, and oftentimes an unquestioned commitment. We were never told that intimate sex is so complicated. It encompasses our bodies, our minds, our attitudes and our childhood beliefs. Developing intimacy with a partner is a lifelong process. This process is at times smooth, depressing, confusing, fulfilling, and it is never ended even when the commitment ends.

Men and women always seem to have had a different attitude toward sexuality. Tony Grant speaks of the myths in male-female relationships when she says sexual sameness in attitudes about sexuality is one of the liberation movements. "This lie of liberation, largely perpetrated by the sexual revolution, is particularly devastating in that it suggests that men and women are capable of enjoying sex in the same way. In reality, most women simply cannot separate sex from love as easily as men can. Casual sex leaves most women feeling sad and unfulfilled" (Grant, 1988). Sexual intercourse is an act of deep significance to a woman. She may begin a new life. She experiences this act physically as well as psychically. "The lie of sexual equality has led to widespread promiscuity among women, detachment from their bodies, and indeed, from their souls" (Grant, 1988).

5. Differences in the Degree of Sexual Response.

Among women, the variations in the degree of sexual responses are greater than among men. Some women, perhaps ten percent, never reach an orgasm until they are thirty or forty. Among men, this is very rare. At the other end of the scale, women far exceed men in number of orgasms they can achieve in a given time period (Kinsey).

Males and females reach their peaks of sexual activity and need at different ages. The average male in *this* culture reaches his peak before he is twenty. The average female begins sexual activity later and increases her responses to a peak around thirty to thirty-five. There are individual variations because human sexual response is most complicated (Masters, Johnson and Kolodny, 1988).

6. Psychological Differences in Sexual Arousal. Men and women are not equally aroused by the same stimuli. Men are more stimulated by nudity, erotic movies, and sexual literature. Women seem to be more easily aroused by romantic movies and literature. Sexual fantasies are more common among men than women. Men fantasize more than women during masturbation and intercourse (McMahon and McMahon).

The difference in men and women in their sexual needs can be partly attributed to the female physiology. Many women report increased sexual desire before the beginning of menstruation. These women may be stimulated by the pelvic congestion caused by the increased amount of blood in the genital area. Because a woman is generally in a monthly cycle she is influenced by her brain and body. The male reproductive function shows no such cycles. Androgen organizes the hypothalamus of the brain of the male embryo to behave differently.

7. Differences in the Desire for Intercourse. How often do married couples have sexual intercourse? There is no rule but there are some factors that influence sexual expression in the marriage. Some of these factors are, how old the couple were when they married, what their individual needs are, what their religious background is, how their health is, what their educational level is, and what their expectations of marriage and sex are.

Kinsey reported that the average married man has intercourse 2.8 times a week and the woman 2.6 times a week by the time they are twenty years old. By the age of thirty they have intercourse 2.2 times a week and by forty it has decreased to about 1.5 times a week. At age sixty the rate was 0.6 times a week (Kinsey). The majority of women report that they prefer intercourse less often than their husbands. There are some women, however, who wish for more sexual intercourse. The frequency of intercourse is not as important as the frequency of rejection and how the rejection is handled.

8. Differences in Sexual Performance. There is a significant difference between male and female sexual performance. The male's psychosexual structure seems to be comparatively fragile. "Aside from ejaculation, there are two major areas of physiological differences between male and female orgasmic expression. First, the female is capable of rapid return to orgasm immediately following an orgasmic experience if restimulated before tensions have dropped below plateau-phase response levels. Second, the female is capable of maintaining an orgasmic experience for a relatively long period of time" (Masters and Johnson).

Women can be multiorgasmic and they experience longer orgasms than men. Women do not have to undergo profound nervous system organization to prepare themselves physically for intercourse. For the man,

an erection is a prerequisite for intercourse. The man cannot submit as a woman can, he always has to perform. As women age they are capable of enjoying sex sometimes even more than when they were younger. They no longer have young children to tire them and are not so concerned about becoming pregnant. Young men are able to have several orgasms and ejaculations closely following the first intercourse. This capacity begins to decrease after the age of thirty.

9. The Psychosocial Theory of Sexuality. The definition of psychosocial relates to the process in which our peers, parents, environment, and society in general mold us psychologically and socially. This molding then relates to how we behave sexually.

Many students of human sexuality look to the environmental explanation for psychosexual development. Most agree that sexual attitudes and behavior are basically determined by familial, social, and cultural experiences. The learning theorist interprets psychosexual development in the context of the overall socialization process. This is the process by which the child is given approval for having the proper attitudes, roles, and for fulfilling expectations that are in harmony with his or her gender. The child learns to be shaped in an acceptable direction. This process is continuous.

The process is sometimes subtle and sometimes forced. Children acquire appropriate sex role characteristics by observing and imitating the behavior of others. They are rewarded for good behavior and punished for inappropriate behavior (McMahon and McMahon). At about the age of eighteen months children begin to form a strong concept of their gender identity. This feeling usually crystallizes by the age of two-and-a-half.

10. Sex Differences. Beyond the basic biological differences of male and female, there seem to be innate differences in the relationship to the child's behavior or personality characteristics. It has been observed that little boys show more aggression and little girls respond to smiling and talking from people around them. However, absolute differences in cognitive functioning and in social behavior in the first two years of life have not been conclusively demonstrated.

Several differences in cognitive abilities emerge in middle to late childhood. An example of this is that girls often show greater verbal abilities while boys often reveal better spatial abilities and sometimes mathematical abilities (Corey, 1978). One gender difference that appears in most cultures is that boys display aggressive behavior more than girls do. Aggression can be a biological component because of the androgen produced in the male more than in the female. Females do produce small amounts of androgen (McMahon and McMahon).

11. The Sociobiological Debate. An important variable in the consideration of sex differences is that males are rewarded for aggressive behavior and thus it is a learned behavior. Females learn early in their lives to use more oblique and covert forms of aggression, such as verbal injury, rejection, or manipulation (Grant). Females develop language skill to get what they want rather than using physical aggression.

Males begin school at a disadvantage to females. Males have more testosterone, therefore they are more aggressive and disruptive in school. They find it difficult to sit still, and often they do not have the verbal abilities of females of the same age. However, in the peer group, males mostly reward males for aggressive "masculine" behavior and females are rewarded for polite "feminine" behavior.

Males are socialized into being masculine in many other ways. A male who exhibits feminine behavior is often criticized by his peers and parents. When we talk of young children we often speak of the boy's future career possibilities and about a girl's physical attributes. Girls are pretty, delicate and petite and boys are tough, strong and active.

On the other side of the question girls soon learn to play their roles. Girls develop after female role models whom they observe pleasing others, nurturing, and being generally agreeable. If a girl does not wish to play the female role she is often made to feel she will not be accepted by a male later in life. A recent report showed that seventy-three percent of the books for use by young children are written about boys (McMahon and McMahon).

Another survey noted that adult females rarely appear in children's text books, though adult males are quite visible. The stories about girls are shorter, less interesting and more stereotyped than stories about boys. If a young girl wishes to be a neurosurgeon or a police officer it is difficult for her to find acceptance or a role model for patterning her life.

Girls may wonder about the value of being a female. One of the worst things that can be said about a person is "don't act like a sissy girl," or in later life, "they drive like a woman."

Some of the most impressive evidence in support of the social learning viewpoint in male and female behavior comes from a study researched by John Money and his colleagues. The study concerned children whose external genitals represent such a mixture of male and female characteristics that biological sex identification is difficult. The Money study found that in most of the cases they evaluated, children whose assigned sex did not match their chromosomal sex, developed a gender identity consistent with the manner in which they were reared (Money).

12. Androgyny and Sexuality. In the sociobiological debate we see an interesting development. In our present-day acceptance of people in general choosing the lifestyle they prefer we have the phenomenon of androgyny. Humans have varying degrees of masculine and feminine characteristics. The androgynous person has the balance of both traits. We all can be assertive or nurturers. The androgynous personality represents the most healthy and well-balanced personality in male or female. Androgynous people show more self-esteem and are more self-actualized than sex-role-stereotyped people. The androgynous female has a more positive attitude toward sexuality than the feminine female. The androgynous female would be less sexually inhibited and would tend to be assertive and see herself as a sexual person (Corey).

The androgynous person tends to be more flexible and can give and receive without worry about roles they are expected to play. The androgynous male can feel he does not have to prove himself in bed or by asserting masculine power over others. He could pass up a potential sex partner unless he felt genuine desire or love. The androg-

ynous woman will be freer to initiate sexual encounters instead of waiting for her partners to approach her. Masters, Johnson, and Kolodny argue that more women entering into heterosexual situations as equal, responsible, and responsive participants might help to diminish male performance anxiety and fears of failure. They state that sexual emancipation depends on personal and social emancipation.

Bibliography. O. Blood, *Marriage* (1969). O. Byer, L. W. Shainberg, and K. L. Jones, *Dimensions of Human Sexuality* (1985). G. Corey, *I Never Knew I Had A Choice* (1978). E. S. Gersh and I. Gersh, *Biology of Women* (1981). T. Grant, *Being a Woman* (1987). A. Kinsey, *Sexual Behavior in the Human Female* (1953). W. H. Masters and V. E. Johnson, *Human Sexual Response* (1966). W. H. Masters, V. E. Johnson, and R. C. Kolodny, *Human Sexuality* (1988). F. McMahon and J. W. McMahon, *Psychology, The Hybrid Science* (1986). J. Money and A. A. Ehrhardt, *Man and Woman, Boy and Girl* (1972). S. S. Wachtel, *Genetic Mechanisms of Sexual Development* (1979).

F. Y. FEHLMAN

BISEXUALITY; HOMOSEXUALITY; MEN, PSYCHOLOGY OF; PERSONAL, CONCEPT OF; SEXUAL VARIETY, DEVIANCE, AND DISORDER; WOMEN, PSYCHOLOGY OF. *See also* PERSONALITY, BIOLOGICAL DIMENSIONS OF; BODY; IDENTITY; PERSON. *Compare* SEXISM; SEXUAL DYSFUNCTION AND THERAPY.

SEXUALITY, CHRISTIAN THEOLOGY AND ETHICS OF. Sexuality includes but is not limited to genital expressions and procreative capacities. More broadly, it is the human way of being in the world as female or male persons, including varied experiences and understandings of sex roles, sexual-affectional orientations, perceptions of one's own embodiedness and that of others, and capacities for sensuousness, emotional depth, and interpersonal intimacy. Christian ethics and theology of sexuality attempt to interpret the meanings and expressions of sexuality in light of the Bible, Christian tradition, and contemporary thought. At the same time, it is also important to understand the ways in which the sexual experience and perceptions of Christians give shape to their understandings of Scripture, tradition, and the present life of faith.

1. Sexuality in Roman Catholicism. Throughout the centuries Roman Catholic theology has been ambivalent about sexuality. Though sexuality was seen as good because God was its source, it was also typically viewed as both inferior to the life of the spirit and as a primary arena for human sin. Throughout Christian history two alienating sexual dualisms have been present—in Protestant life and thought as well as in Roman Catholic. The first is spiritualistic or Hellenistic dualism, so-called because it reflects the body-spirit split that pervaded Greek thought at the beginning of the Christian Era. The other is sexist or patriarchal dualism, which marked Jewish culture and of which Christians are inheritors. The two dualisms intertwined as men assumed that the superior aspects (spirit and male) were intended to discipline and govern the inferior (body and female).

Traditionally, Catholic teaching viewed the natural purpose or end of sexual expression to be procreation and saw sexual ethics governed by natural law knowable through reason. While the "unitive" or relational purpose of sexuality was recognized, it was considered secondary to procreation (the latter including not only the producing of offspring but also their nurture). On this natural law basis it was possible to derive clear moral judgments about various sexual acts. If procreation was the natural purpose of sexual expression, then masturbation, homosexual intercourse, bestiality, and artificial birth control — all non-procreative — violated the natural order. While heterosexual incest, rape, fornication, and adultery did not violate the procreative possibility, nevertheless they were judged sinful because they denied the nurture of offspring.

In recent years this traditional view has been criticized by some Roman Catholic moral theologians on a variety of counts: its static, nonhistorical view of human nature; its judgments of sexual morality based upon the physical contours of acts rather than upon their relational meanings to persons; its legalistic and sex-negative tendencies; and its disproportionate focus upon genital sexuality.

A change from the traditional view received some ecclesiastical endorsement with the Second Vatican Council and its document *The Church in the Modern World* (1965), in which the unitive, relational meanings of sexuality were given equal standing with the procreative. Although a number of American Catholic theologians have pressed the analysis of sexuality even further into the centrality of the relational wholeness of the person, the Vatican's recent pronouncements have tended to retreat from the council's statement back toward an emphasis upon procreative primacy.

Nevertheless, changes in Catholic thought are continuing. They can be seen particularly in attitudes toward homosexuality and the status of women. Many Catholic theologians now refuse to label homosexual acts as intrinsically evil. While such acts are seen as "essentially imperfect" compared to the heterosexual ideal, they are to be evaluated on the basis of the meanings and moral responsibility of the particular relationship. The official Roman Catholic view, however, maintains that homosexual acts are essentially disordered, against the natural law, contrary to scripture, and can in no case be approved.

While the Catholic tradition long assumed the ontological inferiority of women, it has now evolved to a position that maintains the essential equality and complementarity of the sexes while insisting upon the different duties of the spouses in marriage. Women's rights must be defended in the social sphere, but their admission to full priesthood is forbidden. Reformist and radical Catholic feminists, however, have systematically criticized the church for being dualistic and hierarchical. These critics relate its masculinist theological language, its exclusion of women from church leadership, and its teachings on marriage and family to a pervasive worldview falsified by masculinist ideology.

Regarding artificial contraception, liberal Catholic theologians insist that the ethical difference between the rhythm method and artificial means is insignificant. The morality of married sexual expression, they insist, must be based upon the couple's relationship and their responsible parenting. Though a significant majority of Catholic couples in this society consider it a matter of personal conscience, official teaching still maintains that artificial contraception is an offense against nature.

2. Sexuality in Protestantism. If in Roman Catholicism there are divergent views and emphases, in Protestantism this is multiplied manyfold. In addition to great denominational diversities and the absence of a central ecclesiastical teaching authority, Protestants differ widely in their methods of biblical interpretation as well as in their views upon the weight to be given to tradition and to contemporary sexuality research. Nevertheless at least six commonalities might characterize the majority of Protestants, particularly in the "mainline" denominations.

(1) Sexuality is a good gift of the Creator. Even though it has been distorted by human sin, it is to be seen as God's invitation to communion. (2) However, the two alienating dualisms — spiritualism (spirit over body) and sexism (man over woman) — characterize Protestant history as well as Catholic. (3) A third Protestant feature, different from the Roman Catholic tradition, is the absence of the exaltation of virginity and celibacy over married life. The sixteenth-century Reformation undercut salvation by good works (including the works of virginity and celibacy) and, simultaneously, elevated the theological significance of Christian marriage. (4) Beginning in the seventeenth century, Protestantism began to abandon the idea that procreation was the primary purpose of marriage and sexual intercourse. Instead, the fundamental aim was to be seen as the expression of faithful love. (5) Protestants (with the exception of ultraconservative groups) have demonstrated considerable openness to recent empirical knowledge about sexuality, the culturally relative nature of sexual norms, feminist consciousness, and, to some extent, gay and lesbian consciousness. (6) Within mainstream Protestantism there has been a strong tendency to move from a negative approach to sexuality to a positive one, from a physically oriented focus upon the categories of sexual acts to a more interpersonal focus upon the meanings of sexual expression.

Protestant "evangelicals" call for a particular comment. Characteristically, evangelicals emphasize personal religious conversion, evangelism, and the centrality of the Bible in morals and doctrine. Yet, there are important differences on sexuality among them. In recent years many fundamentalist evangelicals have moved into ultraconservative political activism, giving major attention to sexuality issues, especially the condemnation of homosexuality, abortion, pornography, and feminism, and maintaining that the male-dominated nuclear family is normative. "Left-wing evangelicals," however, while insisting upon personal religious experience and the centrality of Scripture, have been open to feminist and gay-lesbian concerns as well as other sexuality issues having social justice implications.

3. Toward a New Paradigm for Sexual Theology. There are indications that a significant shift in Christian thinking about sexuality may now be taking place in elements of both Catholic and Protestant thought. If these tendencies continue, a new paradigm will emerge. Five marks of that new pattern might be discerned.

a. Toward sexual theologies. While the vast majority of theological reflections on sexuality in the past have assumed a one-way question (what does the Christian faith say *about* human sexuality?), there is an increasing recognition of the importance of also asking the question in the other direction as well; what does our experience as sexual beings tell us about the ways in which we experience God, interpret our religious tradition, and attempt to live faithfully? The prompting to press this second direction as well as the first has come from Christian feminists, lesbians, and gays, and (more indirectly) from other liberation theologies.

b. Toward sexuality as intrinsic to divine-human relationship. Under the impact of spiritualistic or Hellenistic dualism, there has been a strong tendency to view "the life of the spirit" as separate from or even antithetical to sexuality. However, the recovery of a more incarnational emphasis in Christian theology has insisted upon the centrality of embodied and relational experience in the experience of God. Thus, Christology can maintain the paradigmatic centrality of God's incarnation in Jesus of Nazareth while, at the same time, affirming the significance of the continuing incarnational reality in our bodily lives. And this has vast implications for the Christian understanding of sexuality.

c. Toward sexual sin as alienation from human sexuality. The crucial theological insight that sin is fundamentally alienation or estrangement and only secondarily specific acts has only recently been applied to sexuality. Increasingly, however, it is recognized that the twin sexual dualisms provide the basic dynamics of sexual sin. Spiritualism makes the sexual body either foreign and suspect or an unintegrated pleasure machine. Sexist dualism alienates men and women from each other and each gender from half of its humanity, for example, males from their affective and nurturing capacities and females from their intellectual and assertive strengths. Sexual alienation, however, just as surely disrupts the communion of self with all other beings, with the earth, and with God. Such alienation often will give rise to harmful sexual acts, but it is the alienation that is the root dynamic.

d. Toward salvation as recovery of sexual wholeness. Throughout the greater part of Christian history, most Christian thought suggested that salvation meant release from the realm of the body into the "higher" life of the spirit. Now, however, we are beginning to understand that salvation includes the process of recovering sexual wholeness, a "resurrection of the body." This includes growth in positive and bodily self-acceptance, in the capacity for sensuousness, in the diffusion of the erotic sense throughout bodily life (instead of the genitalization of most sexual feeling), in the breaking away from rigid sex-role stereotypes and sexual oppressions, and in the awakening of the self to its destiny as an embodiment of divine love.

e. Toward church as sexual community. The growing recognition of the sexual dimensions of corporate Christian existence includes an awakening awareness to the ways in which sexual understandings (both for good and for ill) pervade all theology and ethics, all understandings of spirituality, all orientations to worship and sacramental life, all perceptions of pastoral care, and all interpretations of social as well as interpersonal moral issues.

4. **Foundations for Christian Sexual Ethics.** *a. Insights from non-theological sources.* Traditional sexual norms have been challenged by varied sources. Historians have revealed the historical contingency of both sexual norms and their foundations (e.g., the strong role of Stoic philosophy in the rise of the procreative ethic). Modern biological knowledge has undercut some long-held sexual assumptions (e.g., that the male sperm was the sole life-carrying agent in reproduction). Studies of animal sexual behavior have challenged certain assumptions of what is "natural" and "unnatural" (e.g., masturbation and homosexual activity occur in many higher forms of animal life). Cross-cultural anthropological studies have revealed wide variations in sexual norms (e.g., homosexual expression is affirmed in numerous societies). Behavioral studies together with expanding medical knowledge have caused many to question certain long-held sexual assumptions (e.g., the supposed physical harmfulness of masturbation or of intercourse during the menstrual period). Modern psychological insights have revealed the centrality of human sexuality to individual emotional development, well-being, and creativity. Finally, the significant rise of feminist consciousness and gay/lesbian self-affirmation has challenged the double standards common in a Christian sexual tradition dominated by heterosexual males. The net result of all these and other influences has been a contemporary relativization of numerous sexual norms and a challenge to rethink Christian sexual ethics. (See Farley, 1978, pp. 1583–85.)

b. The centrality of love. In spite of the relativizing forces discussed above, the legalistic assumption—that objective standards can be applied in the same way to whole classes of sexual acts without regard to specific meanings and contexts—still has appeal to numerous Christians. The alternative is an ethic finding its center and direction in love. Such sexual ethics will take the bible seriously and at the same time will understand that in Scripture not only are authentic revelations of God's intention for human sexuality reflected, but also ancient sexual mores inappropriate to Christian life today. A love-centered sexual ethic understands that human nature is grounded in the will to communion and that our sexuality itself is a crucial means of that destiny. Even in its distortions and misuse, sexuality displays its power —in such instances its power to oppress and to destroy.

Love's source is God, and a Christian sexual ethic of love takes its content from faith's perceptions of God's ways with humankind—in divine creativity, in reconciliation, and in sustaining, fulfilling, liberating, and justice-making activity. Sexual love ought to be multidimensional: *epithymia* or libido (sexual desire); *eros* (aspiration for fulfillment through the beloved); *philia* (mutuality and friendship); and *agape* (freely offered self-giving). Each of these dimensions of love needs the other. Thus, at best, sexual desire (*epithymia*) is mated with desire for communion with and fulfillment in the other (*eros*), and with a strong element of mutuality and friendship (*philia*), and with the transformative power of self-giving (*agape*).

Further, other-love and self-love are indivisible. Self-love has been a particular problem in Christian ethics, often mistakenly confused with egocentrism and selfishness, thus condemned. Hence, many Christians have had considerable difficulty dealing with sexual pleasure. Without positive self-love, however, genuine intimacy is impossible, for intimacy depends upon each person's sense of self-worth.

A sexual ethic centered in love can express itself in various values, criteria by which specific sexual acts might be measured. Thus, sexual love ought to be self-liberating (expressing one's own self-affirmation and desire for growth). Sexual love should be other-enriching (displaying a genuine concern for the well-being and growth of the partner). Sexual love should be honest (expressing as truthfully as possible the meaning of the relationship between the partners). Such love should be faithful (committing itself to an ongoing relationship with this partner, yet without crippling possessiveness). Authentic sexual love is socially responsible (concerned that any specific sexual act express values that enhance the larger community). Sexual love will be life-serving (the power of renewed life being shared by the partners). And appropriate sexual love is joyous (exuberant in appreciation of love's mystery, life's gift, and the playfulness of good sex). (See Kosnick, *et al.*, 1977, pp. 9295.) Love-centered sexual ethics are inseparable from justice. Recognizing the ways in which so much sexuality has been distorted by abusive power relations, such ethics are radically committed to the liberation of sexual expression as mutual empowerment rather than as dominance and submission.

Such sexual ethics centered in love can give principled structure without legalistic absolutes. They will press toward the principle of single standards (not double ones) for sexual morality: the same basic considerations apply equally to the male and female, to the aged and the young, the married and unmarried, the able-bodied and differently-abled, the homosexual and the heterosexual. A further principle is that sexual expression with another person ought to be appropriate to the level of shared commitment. In addition to general principles, such sexual ethics can have specific sexual rules. Yet, most of these rules will be understood neither as exceptionless absolutes nor simply as "rules of thumb." They will express the wisdom of the Christian community and will serve as checks upon our finitude and sin. Christians can presume in their favor without making the rules absolute.

A sexual ethic of this type will be neither legalistic nor normless. It will place considerable responsibility upon the individual and it will not guarantee protection from mistakes in the sexual life. It will be sensitive to concrete situations, motivations, and relationships. It will be centered upon persons more than abstract concepts. If past Christian sexual ethics were often rooted in a deep suspicion of the body and its desires and hence placed primary emphasis upon the discipline and channeling of sexual expression, the present task is to shape an ethic which, without ignoring its destructive capacity, seeks fundamentally to enhance sexuality's power to contribute to human fulfillment in communion.

c. Illustrations of specific sexual issues. Christian ethics of marriage and family have been marred by several things: for example, interpreting "the image of God" as heterosexual co-humanity; ascribing absolute status to culturally relative (and frequently dehumanizing) sex roles; and proclaiming the ethically normative status of the nuclear family (which is a rather recent historical development). Positively, Christian sexual ethics affirms marriage as a covenant of love, always in process. It is centered in fidelity: the bonding of trust, honesty, mutual care, and primary commitment. Generally,

Christians uphold monogamous marriage as the appropriate place for total sexual intimacy, but there is some recognition that pre-marital genital expressions ought not be categorically condemned but rather evaluated in terms of the depth of the covenanting process. Regarding extra-marital sex with consent of the spouse, a minority argues that marital fidelity may or may not include genital exclusivity.

Masturbation can have a variety of meanings and often can be positively affirmed. Even if it lack the fullness of interpersonal sharing, it can be a significant means of self-exploration and affirmation. All forms of consensual, mutually pleasing sexual expressions that enrich both the relationship and the self between covenanted partners can be affirmed and have the capacity to express gratitude to the Creator of our sexuality.

The range of theological-ethical opinion on homosexuality is considerable. The biblical evidence is inconclusive at best. Perhaps the majority of denominational statements and theological opinions are divided between a "rejecting-but-non-punitive" position and one of "qualified acceptance." The former believes that homosexuality is unnatural and contrary to God's design but that lesbians and gay men should be treated with pastoral sensitivity. They should be directed toward sexual reorientation if possible and celibacy if not. The "qualified acceptance" position, while holding that homosexual orientation falls short of God's intent, recognizes that it is usually irreversible. Thus, gay men and lesbians should be supported in their attempts to live their sexual lives responsibly — celibacy is preferable, but same-sex monogamy is acceptable for those who cannot remain celibate. A growing (still minority) opinion, however, affirms that the full acceptance of homosexuality is viable within Christian faith. While homosexual expression is not biologically procreative it is, in the judgment of these Christians, fully capable of realizing the central purpose of human sexuality: responsible intimacy and love.

Christian feminism is having significant effects upon the church, including the movement toward sexually inclusive language and metaphors, an expanded use of the varied senses in worship, the full acceptance of women at all levels of church leadership, and the reform of hierarchical male institutional patterns in church and society. A movement among men for the reassessment of their own male sexuality and masculine spirituality is a further result. Such directions may be more potentially far-reaching than any church reform in several centuries.

Numerous persons have felt themselves "sexually disenfranchised," having been told in one way or another that they are not really sexual beings. They include those who have chosen celibacy, other single adults (never married or formerly married), children, the aging, the seriously ill, the differently-abled, the mentally retarded, and certain others whose sexual self-perceptions do not conform to traditional norms (e.g., transvestites and transsexuals). All of these need pastoral care in their sexuality, together with the church's understanding and affirmation. All human beings are sexual—from before birth until death. The worsening AIDS crisis is a particular challenge to Christian sexual theology and ethics today. It calls for sexual justice and compassion. And, in the face of its capacity to evoke an antisex hysteria by linking the fears of sex and death, it challenges the church to reaffirm sexuality as a fundamental arena of God's invitation out of isolation into communication and communion.

Bibliography. W. Abbot, ed., *The Documents of Vatican II* (1966). G. W. Albee, S. Gordon, and H. Leitenberg, eds., *Promoting Sexual Responsibility and Preventing Sexual Problems* (1983). D. S. Bailey, *Common Sense About Sexual Ethics: A Christian View* (1962). J. E. Boswell, *Christianity, Social Tolerance, and Homosexuality* (1980). L. S. Cahill, *Between the Sexes* (1985). W. G. Cole, *Sex in Christianity and Psychoanalysis* (1955). W. G. Countryman III, *Dirt, Greed, and Sex* (1988). C. E. Curran, *Moral Theology: A Continuing Journey* (1982). M. A. Farley, "Sexual Ethics," in W. T. Reich, ed., *Encyclopedia of Bioethics* (1978). B. W. Harrison, *Making the Connections* (1985). C. Heyward, *Touching Our Strength: The Erotic as Power and the Love of God* (1989). J. M. Holland, *Religion and Sexuality: Judaic-Christian Viewpoints in the U.S.A.* (1981). P. S. Keane, *Sexual Morality: A Catholic Perspective* (1977). M. M. Kellner, ed., *Contemporary Jewish Ethics* (1978). A. Kosnick, W. Carroll, A. Cunningham, A. Modras, and J. Schulte, *Human Sexuality: New Directions in American Catholic Thought* (1977). J. J. McNeill, *The Church and the Homosexual*, 3d ed. (1988). J. B. Nelson, *The Intimate Connection: Male Sexuality, Masculine Spirituality* (1988); *Embodiment: An Approach to Sexuality and Christian Theology* (1978). J. Plaskow and C. Christ, *Weaving the Visions: New Patterns in Feminist Spirituality* (1988). R. Scroggs, *The New Testament and Homosexuality* (1983). H. Thielicke, *The Ethics of Sex*, J. V. Doberstein, trans. (1964). P. Trible, *God and the Rhetoric of Sexuality* (1978).

J. B. NELSON

PERSON. *See also* CELIBACY; INCEST; ETHICS AND PASTORAL CARE; HOMOSEXUALITY; PERSONAL, CONCEPT OF, IN PASTORAL CARE; SEXISM; SEXUAL VARIETY, DEVIANCE, AND DISORDER. *Compare* FAMILY; MARRIAGE.

SEXUALITY, JEWISH THEOLOGY AND ETHICS OF.

The Jewish attitude toward sexuality is a reflection of the spiritual purity and religious discipline promulgated by the written Mosaic code at Mount Sinai and perpetuated by the rabbinic Oral Law or *Halakha.* In this tradition all humans have a timeless need for intimacy, love, and meaningful human relationships, and sexuality is one aspect of this need. Jewish tradition also believes that a strict code of sexual morality exists in definite terms in the Bible. Since early biblical times the Jewish people have firmly believed in the institution of marriage, sanctioned sexual intercourse only within the legal framework of marriage, and prohibited it otherwise. Marriage is not simply a civil ceremony but an act of divine sanctity under Jewish law. Sexual expression finds full meaning only in marriage; to practice it outside the marital bond of love desecrates the *"Kiddushin"* (holiness) of marriage. The survival of the Jewish family for millennia is regarded as evidence of the beauty and truth of this philosophy.

Today's Jewish laws and customs represent an unbroken continuation of Jewish religious tradition as practiced in the ancient Middle East, and many of these ancient laws and customs have been formative in the general development of Western morality and ethics.

Theologically, Jewish law encourages people to enjoy life and nature and to derive pleasure from all that is God-given, even pleasures of the body. In this way,

Jewish discipline attempts to lead human beings along the path to holiness and sanctification. In the Bible, for Israel to be a holy nation it must imitate God, who is immanent and transcendent — within the world and yet beyond it. Holiness, according to the Torah, implies a capacity to be part of nature, and yet capable of transcending it. Hence the Jewish tradition of sex morality in every age not only remained a sound guide for refined and pure sexual conduct, organically affirming psychobiological needs through marital love and mutuality, but also maintained a spiritual ideal for understanding the religious depth and significance of sex.

1. Pre-exilic Period. Biblical pre-exilic admonitions on sex were directed mainly against the sexual practices that were a part of heathen fertility rites and phallic worship. These denunciations were directed more against idolatrous paganism than against sexual immorality, however. During the First Commonwealth, sexual matters were viewed realistically as a natural human need, and the Pentateuchal laws regulating sexual morality were often not enforced except in cases of flagrant public violations such as incest, rape, and adultery. Moreover, the fact that the biblical terminology used for sexual morality was employed also for other sins suggests that the pretalmudic Jew was not preoccupied with sexual matters but viewed them as a normal, integral aspect of human life.

Men and women were seen as interdependent, and it was believed that a man discovers himself only through union with a woman and vice versa. In becoming "one flesh," man and woman are led to the building of a family. The ideal in the sexual act was propagation of the species through the creation of family, the stabilizing factor of society.

2. Postexilic and Talmudic Periods. Jewish attitudes toward sexual morality were radically altered in the postexilic period. Jewish society changed from being predominantly agricultural to being a commercial urban community in which the cities tended to be centers of immorality. In an effort to minimize these influences, the men of the Great Synagogue instituted additional ascetic laws. Persons were conceived as helpless and weak, whose *yetzer hara* — the Evil Inclination—incites them to immorality.

In opposition to this asceticism, the teachers of the talmudic period treated sexuality more moderately. The rabbis viewed the sexual drive as a healthy source of energy for properly sublimated acitivities. Men and women were to enjoy life, while orgiastic forces were to be subjected to wise rule and mastery. Without endorsing unbridled sexual freedom, they embraced a pansexual outlook: "Were it not for the Evil Inclination no man would build a house or marry a woman or engage in any occupation" (Midrash Rabbah, Genesis 9:9). The rabbis denied that flesh is evil, except through its corruption. The body, claims Hillel, is created by the Lord and is to be seen as a divine representation; it is part of the Creation, just like the *Yetzer hara,* and to be interpreted as "very good." Strongly opposed to celibacy, the Talmud views marriage as the only legitimate institution sustaining the family and fulfilling the biblical command of procreation; indeed, this is an imperative for humanity.

Talmudic Judaism therefore considered sex with one's marriage partner as natural. It was not to be glorified or exaggerated—nor was it to be degenerated or over-indulged. Prudery was unknown in the Talmud. To the contrary, the rabbis were outspoken in all matters of sexual education and in techniques enhancing the knowledge and mastery of the subject in the spirit of tradition. For only through marriage comes the actualization of the first commandment in the Bible, "Be fruitful and multiply" (Gen. 1:28). Indeed, in its opposition to asceticism, Talmudic teaching declares that "In the World-to-Come every person will be called to account for all the legitimate pleasures one has not partaken" (Jer. Talmud end of Kiddushin).

3. Post-Talmudic Period. A new pietistic and moralistic sexual regimen was developed in the Post-Talmudic period, in which disciplined standards of conduct were embellished by strict guidelines aimed at moral perfection. The Jewish Code of Law prescribed, along with sexual modesty and reticence, specific regulations as to the frequency and timing of sexual activity for the married couple, with positive provisions for adequate sexual fulfillment of the wife's needs. Rabbinic law also instituted a detailed hygienic regimen of "family purity," still practiced today and considered a cornerstone for perpetuating Jewish tradition and authentic Jewish existence and survival.

This trend toward ascetic rigidity, intended to achieve the elevation of the soul, was inherent in the spiritual *zeitgeist* of the Middle Ages. Medieval Jewish philosophers such as Saadyah Gaon, Yehuda Halevi, and Bahyah Ibn Paquda contended that sexual union could not be inherently reprehensible or shameful; otherwise the Lord Himself would have restrained the prophets from engaging in it. The sexual appetite, therefore, should be satisfied, not abused, and sexual intercourse was even considered to have therapeutic value as an antidote against melancholy.

In his medical treatise *On Sexual Intercourse,* Moses Maimonides, the great medieval philosopher and codifier, introduced the idea that sexual intercourse is not only a physiological process but basically a psychological activity, "a process of the soul," which is deeply related to the emotional state of the persons involved. Activities, including sex, have, as their keynote, the preservation of a healthy body in order to serve God better. Maimonides, however, counsels sexual moderation, encouraging sexual enjoyment so long as the man does not deny his wife's conjugal rights.

In the mystical tradition Nachmanides, a Kabbalistic exegete, declared that "the act of sexual union is holy and pure. . . for whatever the Lord created cannot possibly be shameful or ugly. . . When a man is in union with his wife in a spirit of holiness and purity, the Divine Presence is with them" (The Holy Epistle 2). Thus, man and woman were considered sublime symbols of mystic partnership with God in the act of Creation.

4. Contemporary Applications. In a society where marriage is increasingly regarded as merely a vehicle for personal growth, Judaism teaches a broader and more challenging conception. It emphasizes neither the exaggeration of nor aversion to sex, and considers sex to be neither evil nor base. Neither is sex in itself the magical key to all meaning and fulfillment, though it is profound in its spiritual significance. Rather, sex is considered essential for cementing a healthy relationship between husband and wife. It requires education, tact, and modesty and is to be approached in a natural and wholesome way, yet controlled by self-discipline.

From a Jewish perspective, sex counseling as a practical application of these principles requires empathy and a supportive approach in directing a balance between the ecstasy and agony of the troubled individual or the family system. Its goals are to help the sexually inadequate person build a more positive self-image and become aware of his or her partnership with the Almighty, in whose image we are all created.

Bibliography. The Babylonian Talmud (1956–61). Palestinian Talmud (1922). Midrash Rabbah (1921). The Zohar (1960). J. Karo, *The Shulhan Arukh* (1911). L. M. Epstein, *Sex Laws and Customs in Judaism* (1948). M. M. Brayer, *The Jewish Woman in Rabbinic Literature, A Psychosocial and Psychohistorical Perspective,* 2 vols. (1986); "The Role of Jewish Law Pertaining to the Jewish Family, Jewish Marriage and Divorce," in *Jews and Divorce* (1968).

M. M. BRAYER

JEWISH LIFE; JEWISH CARE AND COUNSELING; MARRIAGE AND MARITAL CARE (Jewish Perspective); PERSON (Jewish Perspective). *Biography:* MAIMONIDES (MOSES BEN MAIMON).

SEXUALLY TRANSMITTED DISEASE. *See* GONORRHEA; HERPES; SYPHILIS.

SHADOW. In analytical psychology, that aspect of the Self restricted to the personal unconscious and referring to those qualities of the same sex as the physical individual, which are totally unacceptable to the person; frequently the basis for the strong like or dislike of another of the same sex. It is to be distinguished from the *anima* or the *animus* which represents an aspect of the collective unconscious.

I. R. STERNLICHT

ANALYTICAL (JUNGIAN) PSYCHOLOGY (Personality Theory and Research).

SHALOM. *See* MEDIATION/CONCILIATION.

SHAMAN. A specialist in the well-being of the human soul who restores and maintains its health by means of archaic techniques of ecstasy. Through ecstatic experiences the shaman can "see" the soul's wanderings, and by means of magical techniques is able to recover it when it has been stolen or lost.

In the strict sense, shamanism is a religious phenomenon of Siberia and Central Asia, where ecstatic experiences and soul restoration are considered to be central religious rituals. By cultural diffusion, it came to be one of, if not the dominant religious expressions, among the Eskimo of Asia and North America, among many of the North and South American Indians, and among certain peoples in Tibet and China. Similar phenomena are found in Southeast Asia and Oceania.

Shamanism is commonly associated with a religious worldview in which there are several cosmic regions. The shaman knows the mysteries that enable him or her to break through from one such plane to another in pursuit of the soul—from the earth to the sky or to the underworld. This the shaman does by passing through an opening found in central sacred places associated with such symbols as a cosmic mountain, world tree, or central pole.

Both men and women may be shamans. The chief methods of their recruitment are heredity and/or special calling. The validation of their new status as a person "chosen by the spirits" comes through an ecstatic experience that involves their suffering, "death," and "resurrection." Commonly this takes the form of an illness that brings the novice close to death, followed by an encounter with a spirit and a miraculous healing. In other cases, the initial ecstatic experience may be sought by means of a quest involving a period of seclusion in the wilderness, a symbolic burial and descent into the underworld, ordeals, or drug-induced hypnotic sleep. Through this encounter the shaman acquires a tutelary spirit, and knows that he or she has been "called" for the new office.

Through the initiation the shaman acquires the ability to have immediate concrete experiences with spirits and gods. Since the shaman's soul can safely abandon its body during an ecstatic rite, the shaman can enter their world and talk with them face to face. Because the soul is seen as a precarious psychic unit that is inclined to leave the body, it is an easy prey for demons and sorcerers. The resulting soul loss leads to illness and even death. In his or her ecstatic state, the shaman diagnoses the case, goes in search of the patient's soul, captures it, and returns it to animate the body it has left. If the shaman finds it near the village, its retrieval is easy, but if it is at the bottom of the sea, or in the realm of the dead, the shaman must make a dangerous and exhausting journey with the aid of the tutelary spirit to retrieve it. When death occurs, it is the shaman who conducts the soul safely to the underworld.

Bibliography. M. Eliade, *Shamanism: Archaic Techniques of Ecstasy* (1964). I. M. Lewis, *Ecstatic Religion: A Study of Shamanism and Spirit Possession* (1989). J. McCown, "Shamanism: the Art of Ecstasy," *Encounter,* 39 (1978), 435–46.

P. HIEBERT

CULTURAL ANTHROPOLOGY OF RELIGION; SOCIOLOGY OF RELIGIOUS AND PASTORAL CARE; SPIRITUAL MASTERS AND GUIDES. *See also* AFRICAN, NATIVE AMERICAN *or* WEST INDIAN TRADITIONAL RELIGION; ECSTASY; TRANCE. *Compare* FAITH HEALING; PASTOR; PSYCHOTHERAPY.

SHAME. A painful feeling of being exposed, uncovered, unprotected, vulnerable. Etymologically, the Indo-European roots from which *shame* derives mean "to cover."

Three forms of shame may be distinguished (L. Wurmser, 1981, p. 50ff.): (1) *Shame anxiety,* a painful affective state regarding something which is anticipated. Shame anxiety is evoked by sudden exposure and signals the threat of contemptuous rejection. (2) *Being ashamed,* a complex affective and cognitive pattern in reaction to something that has already happened, variously called "disgrace-shame" (Schneider) or "shame about." (3) The *sense of shame,* a motive of behavior (H. Lewis, 1971) or a character attitude. Wurmser calls this "shame protecting," or more technically, shame as a reaction formation. The

"sense of shame" refers to the adaptive use of shame affect as a restraint on one's behavior. It is akin to a sense of modesty, reticence, or tact.

There is no consensus at present regarding the dynamics, meaning, valuation, or even terminology for shame. Thus it is necessary to consider several perspectives on the subject.

1. The Phenomenal and Structural Nature of Shame. *a. Shame and guilt.* Shame is frequently confused with, and even more frequently associated with, guilt. Shame and guilt are linked like ham and eggs. As Erik Erikson has noted: "Shame is an emotion insufficiently studied, because in our civilization it is so early and easily absorbed by guilt (Erik Erikson, 1963, p. 252). The connection, however, is culture-bound. Historically and cross-culturally, shame is just as intrinsically connected to other affects such as awe. For the Greeks, for example, "the feeling of shame. . . originates as the reaction which the holy excites in a man" (Snell, 1953, pp. 167–8).

Given the widespread confusion about shame and guilt, it is nevertheless useful to identify the commonly accepted distinctions between them: (1) First we recognize two quite distinct phenomenological "worlds" of shame and guilt. The family of shame-related experiences includes embarrassment, humiliation, disgrace, mortification, shyness, modesty, pride, vanity, ridicule, dishonor and honor, weakness and strength, and narcissism. The world of guilt involves a quite different arena of experience: debt, transgression, injury, responsibility, duty, obligation, offense, culpability, wrong, good or bad, and the obsessive/compulsive.

(2) There are further, *physiological* differences between shame and guilt. We blush and redden in shame. Shame involves greater body awareness than guilt (H. Lewis, 1971, p. 34). The shame response is universal: one wishes to cover one's face, to sink into the ground, to flee.

(3) Beyond this, Gerhard Piers (1953) set forth what has become the standard *psychoanalytic* distinction between shame and guilt. Both are defined structurally as the products of tension between ego and superego. Shame is response to failure and the shortcomings of the self in relation to the ego ideal; guilt is response to transgression. In the words of Franz Alexander (1939), guilt represents the psychology of conscience and thus the threat of punishment, while shame exhibits the psychology of narcissism and thus the threat of loss of love.

(4) This formulation, shame as failure, was extended by Helen Merrell Lynd (1958), who suggested that shame occurs along a *strong-weak* continuum, while guilt falls along a good-bad continuum. In shame, the self is perceived as small, inadequate, or lacking. This sense of felt inadequacy is often more salient for people than any feeling of wrong-doing; the sense of not being good-enough, i.e., acceptable, is often more deep-rooted and longstanding than any awareness of not being good in terms of morality.

(5) Shame is more inseparably connected to feeling than guilt. A person can *be* guilty, without *feeling* guilty. Alternately, she may *feel* guilty without *being* guilty. But if a person *feels* ashamed, he or she *is* ashamed (G. Thrane, 1979, p. 141).

(6) Another major distinction involves the *object-structure* of shame. Guilt need not have an object. One may simply feel guilty. But one is always ashamed *of* something. And, as Sartre notes, that something is *me* (Sartre, 1956, pp. 221–2). Shame involves the whole self. Guilt appears to be more discrete and specific, while shame has a global character. Guilt is about something I did or did not *do,* while shame is the revelation of something which I *am.* The experience of guilt, in turn, is more ideational than shame, which tends to be more difficult to put into words (Lewis, 1971, pp. 251–2).

(7) Guilt may also involve the whole person, but it involves a different aspect of the self-other relation. "Shame guards the boundary of privacy and intimacy; guilt limits the expansion of power . . . Shame protects the vulnerability of and integral image of the self; guilt protects and limits the integrity of an object . . . Shame is the basic protection mechanism in the field of expressive-communicative and perceptual-attentional interchange. Guilt has the parallel function in the motor-active and motor-aggressive field. . . ." (Wurmser, 1981, p. 67).

(8) Finally, shame seems peculiarly social, inseparable from one's sense of "face" and "losing face." To say that to be ashamed is to be ashamed of oneself is to point to the connection of shame and one's *identity.* What one is, of course, is broader than simply what one has consciously chosen. It involves all that one *identifies* with, or wishes to be identified with.

b. Beyond psychology. As valuable as psychology and psychoanalytic literature are in giving us increased understanding of the dynamics, development, and pathology of shame in individuals, they remain a limited perspective in need of the correction and context of the historical, philosophical, and sociological disciplines. Many of the best minds of the nineteenth century — Darwin, Scheler, Nietzsche, Havelock Ellis — wrestled with the significance of shame for what it means to be human.

Perhaps the most fundamental contribution to our understanding of shame in this century is Norbert Elias's monumental work, *The Civilizing Process* (1978), a study of the decisive role played in the civilizing process of Western societies from the medieval-feudal period to today by a shift in the feelings of shame. Elias's goal is specifically to correct the clinicians' bias of a "closed personality" independent of society. Instead, Elias documents how long-term changes in human personality involving a consolidation and differentiation of affect control are related to basic changes in the social structure (increased interdependence; consolidation of state controls).

3. Biblical and Theological Perspectives. Although the Western Christian tradition in the postbiblical period has neglected the phenomenon of shame and has failed to give it sustained reflection, the Scriptures are filled with references to shame. In the RSV, shame and its derivatives appear 195 times in the OT and forty-six times in the NT (Noble, 1975, p. 26; cf. Lynd, 1958, p. 25; Schneider, 1977, p. 113ff.).

a. Old Testament. Particularly in the OT, shame is at the heart of Israel's response as it again and again is confronted both by its own betrayal of the covenant relationship with Yahweh and by its idolatrous neighbors' defilement of the holy law of Yahweh (Jer. 3:24–25).

There are recurrent entreaties by the Israelites that they not be put to shame or disgrace by their enemies. Much of the OT also shares the world of taboo and shame-defilement. The preponderance of OT references to shame occur in the Psalms and the prophetical books, especially Jeremiah, Isaiah, and Ezekiel. There is a rich cluster of shame-related terms used in Scripture: to dishonor, disgrace, ridicule, humiliate, scorn, reproach, confound, taunt, scoff, naked, and face (e.g., Ps. 44:13–15; Noble, 1975, p. 27). Though shame is associated with many sins, from theft to prostitution, it is most centrally the result of *idolatry:* "All of them are put to shame and confounded, the makers of idols go in confusion together" (Isa. 45:16). The relation of shame and sin is complex. Sin is regarded as shameful, and the word shame became in Scripture a synonym for the name of the gods (i.e., Bosheth [shame] for Baal, Jer. 3:24–25). Shame is in turn regarded as a form of punishment for sin: "Let the wicked be put to shame" (Ps. 31:17; 35:4; 35:26).

The connection between shame and sin is more than merely verbal. As we have seen, guilt relates more to acts while shame involves one's sense of identity. Recognizing that sin in its full biblical sense is probably more often associated with the experience of shame enables us to transcend a moralistic view of sin as only wrong acts.

In Scripture shame also represents the possibility of repentance and redemption. The presence of shame is a sign of hope, its absence a mark of depravity (Jer. 6:15; 8:12; 3:3). One of the complaints brought against Judah is that it is shameless. We find shame present in its positive dimension in the OT. Many figures manifest that quality of awe and reverence which characterizes the sense of shame.

b. New Testament. Shame occupies a much less prominent place in the NT. Almost all NT references speak of shame as disgrace (e.g., "who . . . endured the cross, despising the shame" Heb. 12:2). The absence of the sense of shame is most strikingly evident in the original Greek. *Aidos,* the Greek word for the positive sense of shame, which links it with awe and the sacred, appears but once. This omission of *aidos* is accompanied by an unabashed shamelessness in the attitudes and actions of the NT. There are no holy places that one may no longer enter into; there is no temple in the Revelation of John. There are no holy things that one may no longer touch: Peter, with his OT scruples about unclean animals, is told that there are no unclean things now.

When Jesus dies, the veil of the temple is rent in two. Jesus does away with special holy places and permits free access to God (Heb. 10:19). He transcends the sacredness of time as well as place in his actions on the Sabbath. He teaches the disciples to address God with the undue familiarity of "Abba" ("Daddy"). It is this apparently shameless quality in Jesus that his enemies found blasphemous.

The "shamelessness" of the NT, however, does not negate the importance of a sense of shame in the face of the sacred, but it adds an important dynamic to the picture. The religious encounter is not only one of reticence before that which one venerates; it also involves the revelation of what is hidden. Religion may be understood as the dialectic of covering and uncovering of the sacred in time and space. The shamelessness of the NT must be understood in the context of the strong reticence of the OT. The freedom and intimacy of the NT presuppose the restraint and respect of the OT. The invitation to address God as "Abba" is issued to those who dared not to utter his name.

4. **Normative Anthropological Perspective on Shame.** Most cultures distinguish two kinds of shame: *being ashamed* (disgraced) and the *sense of shame* (modesty or discretion). Much contemporary work on shame is marred by its failure, on the one hand, to acknowledge the positive dimension of shame even in "being ashamed" and, on the other hand, to attend to the *sense* of shame. These defects have directly affected the contemporary estimate of shame, which tends to view it as the product of socialization (school, family, society) which should be overcome on one's journey toward maturity.

a. Being ashamed. Unquestionably there is much shame that is pathological and unconscious, involving rigid and brittle defensiveness. But much as psychoanalysis focused on pathology in its early years, only much later developing a general and normative psychology, so too have studies of shame traced the pathologies of shame without simultaneously recognizing the constructive role played by shame in normal development.

Disgrace-shame, or "shame about" some discrediting fact or quality, is disruptive, disorienting, and elicits a painful self-consciousness. Yet even this shame ought not to be understood as merely a negative phenomenon. Shame-as-disgrace is the immediate awareness that who we are is not who we want to be. It is the emotional price we pay for our encounter with the discrepancy between our ideals and our reality.

b. The sense of shame. The core of shame as a positive sense of covering or protection is even more apparent in the second kind of shame, "the sense of shame," or "shame protecting" which is more akin to a sense of modesty or discretion. This is the sense in which we implore someone, "Have you no shame?"

Two root cultures of Western civilization—Hebrew and Greek—are especially sensitive to the concept of shame as discretion. In a beautiful passage of the Talmud we read: "A sense of shame is a lovely sign in a man. Whoever has a sense of shame will not sin so quickly; but whoever shows no sense of shame in his visage, his father surely never stood on Mount Sinai" (Nedarim, fol. 20a). Plato, in the *Laws*, also speaks positively of shame, referring to "that divine fear which we have called reference and shame."

Does a healthy human being need covering? Some think not. But there are times in development and places in all phases of human life where covering is needed not because something is amiss, or wrong, but because it *is* appropriate—i.e., "fitting," "proper" (T. L. Gibson, 1988). Human beings are, in Bachelard's phrase, "half-open beings," always partly exposed, partly covered. Human experience, always vulnerable to violation, needs protection. Thus an element of reticence is always present and appropriate to human relationships, including one's relation to oneself.

To comprehend the role of such protective shame it is essential to recognize that this integrity is not a static "thing" to be preserved; rather, the achievement of a sense of self is an ongoing process, a dynamic balance of the many parts of ourselves and the identifications we have made.

The maintenance of a sense of self is much like learning to juggle. One needs to practice, to have a space to oneself within which to develop before one can maintain one's balance in front of others. The self needs some time off-stage, a private space, before it is ready to go public. Rehearsal is a process which becomes more sophisticated and differentiated as people mature, but throughout life it is a human need.

The sense of shame protects this process. This protection is in relation to others, for what is sheltered is not something already finished, but a becoming, a creative process. Shame functions like a protective covering during the period of gestation until the embryo—whether seed or soul—has come to full term and is ready to emerge. Such experiences deserve protection from intrusion and from premature exposure.

Shame thus plays its most prominent role during childhood and adolescence, times of formative growth and vulnerability (E. Erikson, 1963). The emerging values and half-formed commitments of these periods need time to mature. To intrude on that process, to yank up the roots to see how they are growing, can destroy the plant. Shame protects the *ongoing process of integrating* the self.

Respect for a private realm of experience and for a person's right to have control over that realm is an indispensable component in the process of achieving an integrated self and in the dynamics of maintaining healthy relationships (O. Strunk, 1982). At heart, human meeting and relations are always simultaneously disclosing and concealing. In meeting, participants both make contact yet remain separate. The sense of shame involves respect for the reality of our separateness and the space that is there between us. Language both discloses and covers in all encounters. The sense of shame implies respect for this depth and resonance of human meeting.

5. **Clinical Pastoral Perspective.** Perhaps the most relevant example of a mature sense of shame is its role in the counselor's and counselee's sense of shame in clinical practice. So much is vulnerability to exposure and violation heightened in therapy that an awareness of shame becomes indispensable. Indeed, many clients in psychotherapy remain shamed for years even over the fact that they are coming to counseling.

a. The vulnerability of clients. There are at least three structural components to the vulnerability of clients. First of all, clients are enjoined to speak whatever comes to mind at the same time that the counselor maintains a studied neutrality. Normal relationships involve a process of mutual, measured self-disclosure: this break in the pattern of normal relationships is at best unsettling for most clients.

Second, therapy involves an asymmetrical power relationship. Third, the client is vulnerable through the disclosure of a diminished sense of self. Being in therapy is like being seen during an illness: people are forced to encounter others when they feel less than themselves. As such, they are especially vulnerable to intrusion, violation, and degradation. The client is at the mercy of the therapist's sensitivity and sense of shame. The therapist must be able to respect the client at a time when the client may be unable to experience, maintain, or claim such self-respect.

b. The value of the counselor's sense of shame. The counselor's capacity to extend a protective covering is critical if the client is not to be shamed. Leon Wurmser (1981), following Freud, has spoken of this mature sense of shame in the clinician as a sense of "analytic *tact*," which he defines as the capacity "to protect the patient's narcissism from undue hurt and thus to enhance his curiosity" (p. 285). Such tact, far from being a simple trait, involves the capacity to balance several dynamic elements.

First, therapeutic tact involves the ability to balance the tension between surface and depth. It is not enough simply to uncover the truth and present it to clients. Freud himself labeled this tactic "wild" analysis and required that the therapist deal with clients in a spirit of tact and consideration. The capacity to monitor and match interpretations to what clients themselves are ready to hear and "discover" is an integral part of this requirement. Freud thought that "a fairly long period of contact" was needed to achieve a working alliance with a client.

Second, a mature sense of shame, of analytic tact, involves the capacity to handle sensitively the interplay between the public and the private in clinical work. The paradox of the therapeutic profession is that it invites and, in analysis, requires that people talk of what is most private with someone who is a professional—a public figure. Focused attention—both negative *and* positive—can be overwhelming and shameful. In therapy that discomfort is intensified as another human being devotes herself or himself solely to attending to oneself.

How then does one handle a setting so potentially charged with shame? The fundamental rules of technique in analytic therapy can be understood (though they seldom are) as rules for how to conduct therapy in the face of the ever-present potential for shame. The cardinal shift in technique from an emphasis on the uncovering of repressed material to a focus on "interpreting defense before content" is a recognition of the shaming potential of uncovering therapy.

To state this less technically, correct interpretations are not necessarily good interpretations. A correct interpretation can be experienced by a client as an attack and a humiliation. The core of the psychoanalytic contribution to the understanding of the clinical task is that information, data, and correct theory are not enough. In an age that has largely lost any sense of this, psychoanalysis insists that truth is inseparably *personal*.

Freud helped us see the depth in our speaking. Personal speech is not flat and linear, except when used as a defense. Human speech always refers beyond itself. Personal speech has an inherent doubleness: at the time that our speaking gives explicit expression to our experience, it also reminds us how much of reality's fullness remains unvoiced and implicit. In articulating some themes, it remains mute to others.

This *hidden-shown* character of both consciousness and language places a special burden on clinicians. They practice a strange discipline, simultaneously affirming the disclosive, revelatory power of human speech while knowing also and always the capacity of language to obscure and cover. This dialectic cannot be eliminated, for it is the essence of our humanity.

They are called on to maintain a mature sense of shame, because they practice in a field marked by the dynamic interplay between covering and uncovering, between the tacit and the explicit. The proper therapeutic stance is finally one of awe and deep respect, for the therapist stands on holy ground—engaging in an encounter that involves doubleness—the experience of both mystery and revelation, of reticence before the indescribable and of the revelation of that which is concealed.

Bibliography. F. Alexander, "Remarks About the Relation of Inferiority Feelings to Guilt Feelings," *International J. of Psychoanalysis*, 19 (1938), 41–9. S. Bok, *Secrets* (1986). C. Capps, *Life Cycle Theory and Pastoral Care* (1983). N. Elias, *The Civilizing Process* (1978). E. Erikson, *Childhood and Society* (1963). T. L. Gibson, "Secrets and Soul: A Jungian Fable About Pastoral Care," *J. of Pastoral Care*, 42 (1988), 3–12. G. Kaufman, *Shame* (1980). H. Lewis, *Shame and Guilt in Neurosis* (1971). H. M. Lynd, *On Shame and the Search for Identity* (1958). A. Noble, *Naked and Not Ashamed* (1975). J. Patton, *Is Human Forgiveness Possible?* (1985). G. Peterson, "Conscience and Caring," *Pastoral Psychology*, 33 (1982), 143. G. Piers and M. Singer, *Shame and Guilt* (1971). P. Pruyser, "Anxiety, Guilt and Shame in the Atonement," *Theology Today*, 21 (1964), 15–33. J.-P. Sartre, *Being and Nothingness* (1956). C. D. Schneider, *Shame, Exposure and Privacy* (1977). B. Snell, *The Discovery of the Mind* (1953). O. Strunk, Jr., *Privacy: Experience, Understanding, Expression* (1982). G. Thrame, "Shame," *J. Theory of Social Behavior*, 9 (1979), 139–66. "Shame and the Construction of the Self," *Annual of Psychoanalysis*, 7 (1979), 321–41. L. Wurmser, *The Mask of Shame* (1981).

C. D. SCHNEIDER

SELF-ESTEEM; SHYNESS. *See also* ACCEPTANCE; RESPONSIBILITY/IRRESPONSIBILITY, PSYCHOLOGY OF. *Compare* GUILT; HUMAN CONDITION/PREDICAMENT (Clinical Pastoral Perspective); SIN/SINS.

SHAPING. A behavior modification process by which new behavior is added to a person's repertoire by the reinforcement of successive repetitions of the desired behavior until it is established. This involves differentially reinforcing a series of behaviors that are successively similar to the target behavior.

J. W. FANTUZZO

BEHAVIOR THERAPIES (Methods and Research); CONDITIONING.

SHARING GROUPS. *See* GROWTH GROUPS; SUPPORT GROUPS.

SHAVUOT. *See* JEWISH HOLY DAYS AND FESTIVALS.

SHELTERS. *See* FAMILY VIOLENCE.

SHEDD, WILLIAM G. T. (1820–94). American Presbyterian pastor and theologian. Shedd taught at Auburn, Andover, and Union (New York) seminaries, and served as a pastor in both Presbyterian and Congregational churches.

His *Homiletics and Pastoral Theology* (1869) represented a conservative Calvinist emphasis on preaching and visitation as the primary pastoral tasks. A critic of the liberal biblical critic C. A. Briggs, Shedd argued that pastoral activity should serve both the needs of the parishioner and the canons of traditional Christian truth.

E. B. HOLIFIELD

PASTORAL THEOLOGY, PROTESTANT.

SHEPHERD/SHEPHERDING. A pastoral care metaphor which attempts to integrate the notions of healing, sustaining, and guiding, as well as other characteristics of the ancient shepherd of Old and New Testament times. The roots of the term "shepherding" go back to the agrarian lifestyle of the OT. "The Lord is my shepherd," marks the opening sentence of the twenty-third Psalm; "All we like sheep have gone astray," notes the prophet Isaiah (53:6). Likewise, in the NT the imagery of the shepherd is utilized in many places. One of the so-called "I am" statements of Jesus is "I am the good shepherd" (Jn. 10:14). The writer of Hebrews in a concluding ascription refers to Jesus as "the great shepherd of the sheep" (13:20).

Even though in contemporary urban life the familiarity of the shepherd is obscured, the concept is nonetheless of primary importance in the work of pastoral care and counseling. Seward Hiltner, among others, has stressed the "shepherding perspective" on ministry. The very use of the terms "pastor" and "pastoral" reflects the shepherding dimension of ministry.

The marks of the shepherd which draw on the biblical material as well as the development of pastoral care through the years are instructive for contemporary ministry. The shepherd knows the flock and is known by the flock. This statement, simplistic enough on its face, touches on the profound significance of personal relationships. In order truly to be a pastor there is the necessity for significant involvement in the life of the people of God. By the same token, the pastor demonstrates an openness which ultimately bears witness to strengths and weaknesses and the power and grace of God to transform and renew.

Again, the shepherd is one who genuinely loves the flock and is willing to sacrifice for their welfare. In the graphic portrayal of the "good shepherd" in John 10, Jesus calls attention to the fact that the good shepherd lays down his or her life for the sheep. This is in contrast with the behavior of the "hireling" who flees in the face of danger and does not truly care for the sheep.

From still another perspective, the shepherd is one who takes initiative in seeking and rescuing the sheep who are in danger. The imagery of the shepherd leaving the "ninety-nine" to go in search of one sheep that is lost (Mt. 18:12–14, Lk. 15:3–7) attests to the particular care and concern which mark effective pastoral ministry. The rejoicing which follows the finding of the lost sheep is identified as representing the genuine love which the shepherd manifests in relationship to the sheep. In sum, the concept of shepherding represents the "Incarnational model" of ministry in contrast with the model which has the caregiver waiting until the potential care-receiver takes the initiative to come seeking help. Rather, out of

concern and love for the care-receiver, the pastoral caregiver takes the initiative in such areas as home visitation, calling on those confined to institutions, and identifying with human hurt and suffering.

There is, to be sure, the possibility of a negative implication in the concept of shepherding. From this perspective, the shepherd is perceived to possess all wisdom, knowledge, and skill while the flock or sheep are seen as naive at best and stupid at worst. Thus it is that some pastoral care interpreters have called for a new image, feeling that the biblical notion of the shepherd feeds dependency needs on the part of the parishioner and triggers countertransference tendencies in the pastoral caregiver (Wise, 1951, 1980: pp. 223–4). Such a notion, however, is not inherent in the imagery to convey the whole of meaning when transferred from one setting to another (Oden, 1983, ch. 5). Thus, the caring, compassionate love and concern of the pastor for the people of God affirms the value, the dignity, and the integrity of the people of God. It is in this sense that the imagery of shepherding breaks down in the conviction that caring love is the gift of God to the people of God and not simply to the clergy or professional religious workers. All are burden bearers as the Galatian letter makes clear (6:2), and the process of bearing one another's burdens enables each person to bear his or her own load (Gal. 6:5). Pastoral shepherding care occurs wherever and whenever the people of God are supported and support in their pilgrimage toward wholeness.

Bibliography. S. Hiltner, *Preface to Pastoral Theology,* (1958); *The Christian Shepherd* (1959). T. Oden, *Pastoral Theology: Essentials of Ministry* (1983), ch. 5. C. A. Wise, *Pastoral Counseling* (1951); *Pastoral Psychotherapy: Theory and Practice* (1980).

W. B. OGLESBY, JR.

PASTOR (Normative and Traditional Images); POIMENICS.

SHERRILL, LEWIS J. (1892–1957). Presbyterian pastor and educator. Sherrill contributed to the development of pastoral care and counseling primarily by his attention to developmental psychology. After receiving his doctorate from Yale, Sherrill served as a pastor in Tennessee before becoming the professor of religious education in 1925 at Louisville Presbyterian Seminary, of which he was dean for two decades. In 1950 he became the Skinner and McAlpin Professor of Practical Theology at Union Theological Seminary in New York, and in the following year he published his influential *Struggle of the Soul,* a book in which he defined personal growth as a series of transitions through specifiable stages as one moves toward fulfillment.

He viewed maturation as the accomplishment of a series of developmental tasks: the child's struggle for individuation, the adolescent's effort to achieve independence, the young adult's task of identifying the self in relation to other persons and values, the middle-aged adult's striving to formulate a clear vision of life and the universe, and the older adult's struggle to discern appropriate ways of simplifying both vision and aspiration. He was especially interested in the capacity of the church to recognize such developmental stages and to respond fittingly in its education programs.

Sherrill also wished to integrate psychological and theological reflection, and his *Guilt and Redemption* (1945) established a conceptual setting within which he explored the theme of development. Deeply interested in theological education, he helped establish the American Association of Theological Schools.

Sherrill represented the preoccupation with developmental theory that marked the religious education movement during the 1930s and which began during the 1950s to inform the literature of pastoral care and counseling.

E. B. HOLIFIELD

THEOLOGICAL EDUCATION AND THE PASTORAL CARE MOVEMENT, PROTESTANT. *See also* DEVELOPMENTAL THEORY AND PASTORAL CARE.

SHIVAH. *See* GRIEF AND MOURNING, JEWISH CARE IN; JEWISH CARE AND COUNSELING.

SHLOSHIM. *See* JEWISH CARE AND COUNSELING.

SHOCK TREATMENT. *See* ELECTROCONVULSIVE THERAPY.

SHORT TERM COUNSELING. *See* BRIEF THERAPY AND COUNSELING.

SHRINES. Places of special religious devotion found in all parts of the world. They are maintained and frequented by nearly all the religions of humankind. Shrines constitute a distinct, virtually universal institution of religious care, offering spiritual renewal, the strengthening of faith and hope, experiences of ecstasy or worship, and sometimes specific blessings, especially healing.

Christian shrines fall into different categories, depending upon the reason for their veneration by the Christian people.

The so-called Holy Places in Palestine are those places associated with events in the life of Jesus. Among them, the highest place belongs to the holy sepulcher in Jerusalem from which Christ's resurrection is said to have taken place. It is enclosed in a basilica, which also houses the supposed site of Calvary, the place of Jesus' crucifixion. The alleged sites of the cenacle (the upper room in which the Last Supper was eaten and the Pentecost event occurred), Jesus' agony in the garden of Gethsemane, his painful journey from condemnation to execution, and his ascension into heaven — all in or near Jerusalem—have attracted pilgrims for centuries.

In early Christian history when the Roman persecutions were producing martyrs, their tombs (especially those of the apostles) became shrines to which the faithful flocked. The city of Rome is particularly associated with this kind of shrine, evidenced by the great basilicas and churches erected over the tombs of Saints Peter and Paul, Bartholomew, Agnes, Lawrence, and some others.

With the excavations done in Jerusalem by authority of Constantine I and his mother, Helen, a great devotion arose throughout Christendom to the relics of the passion of Christ: the cross, nails, crown of thorns, shroud, and

so forth. These objects were thought to have been found and authenticated; many of them were then fragmented into relics that are now to be found throughout the Christian world. Recent scientific investigations of the alleged shroud of Jesus, preserved in the cathedral of Turin, Italy, have received wide attention. A popular shrine in Rome houses the Santa Scala (holy staircase), thought to have been in the fortress Antonia in Jerusalem during the first century and to have been used by Jesus during his trial.

During the Middle Ages, pilgrimages were a popular form of religious devotion; two of their principal goals were the tomb-shrines of St. James the apostle at Compostela in Spain and that of St. Thomas à Becket at Canterbury in England.

In modern times some of the most frequently visited shrines are those associated with alleged apparitions of the Virgin Mary. Just outside Mexico City she is said to have appeared in 1531 to a catechumen upon whose cloak her image was imprinted. The place of the apparitions, now called Guadalupe, and the cloak continue to attract great numbers from Mexico and abroad.

Perhaps the most popular of all Christian shrines in the past century has been that of Lourdes in the Pyrenees mountains of southwestern France. In 1858 the mother of Jesus is alleged to have appeared there about fifteen times to a peasant girl, Bernadette Soubirous. The apparition identified herself as "the Immaculate Conception" (that dogma had been defined by Pius IX in 1854), and directed the seeress to "drink of the spring and wash there." The fourteen-year-old girl, seeing no spring where "the Lady" had indicated, dug into the earth, and water began to well up. That spring continues to flow to the present time; its waters — chemically identical with the drinking water of Lourdes — have become famous as an instrument of miraculous healings. A medical commission has been set up to examine the water. Some two million pilgrims visit Lourdes each year.

In several instances of shrines housing sacred icons, images, statues, and so forth, crowns have been donated by popes, reigning houses, or other dignitaries. Hence the "crowned shrines" that are to be found in various countries.

Bibliography. H. M. Gillet. "Shrines," *New Catholic Encyclopedia* (vol. 13, 1967), p. 181.

V. B. BROWN

PASTORAL CARE (History, Traditions, and Definitions). *See also* FAITH HEALING; LITURGICAL AND DEVOTIONAL LIFE, ROMAN CATHOLIC TRADITION OF; MARY, VENERATION OF; MEDIEVAL CHURCH, PASTORAL CARE IN; SAINTS, VENERATION OF. *Compare* PILGRIMAGE METAPHOR.

SHUT-INS. *See* CALLING AND VISITATION; CHRONIC ILLNESS; SICK, PASTORAL CARE OF.

SHYNESS. Although the term shyness has various meanings, at its core are the following characteristic reactions: excessive self-preoccupation, fear of certain social situations, feeling awkward and uncomfortable around particular types of people, inability to express one's thoughts and feelings to others, lack of social skills, low self-esteem, inhibition of actions which are normally desirable and familiar, and uncontrollable physical arousal, such as marked increases in heart rate and respiration. These behavioral, cognitive and physical reactions arise as a consequence of anxiety over being evaluated by others, presumably negatively, and thus judged to be unacceptable, unlovable, and be rejected. In the extreme, shyness becomes a phobia of associating with others—despite a desire to be sociable.

About forty percent of the more than ten thousand American adults surveyed (Zimbardo, 1977) report that they consider themselves to be currently shy, that is, for them shyness is a personal trait or disposition. An equal percentage report having been shy in the past, but no longer. An additional 15 percent think of themselves as "situationally shy"—they respond to certain social situations, such as blind dates or having to give a speech, with feelings of shyness, but shyness is not seen to be a personal characteristic. Only a small minority of people, about five percent, report no past or current shyness under any conditions.

Some research suggests that shyness may be inherited, but only for a rather small proportion of children (ten to fifteen precent). It is more typically a learned pattern of reactions stemming from a variety of causes, often social experiences involving being labelled negatively, being ridiculed, having poor social models, being rejected, and having a lack of basic social skills.

The obvious negative consequences of being shy include not having friends, difficulty in communicating with others, not presenting oneself as effectively as possible, and avoiding intimate contact with others. When shyness persists over a long time and comes to exert a dominant impact on behavior, the negativity of its consequences escalates. It may contribute to social isolation, loneliness, depression and agoraphobia (a fear of public places that confines the shy to the "prison" of their homes). Low self-esteem is a correlate of shyness, but it may act as a causal agent or be a consequence of the negative feedback associated with shy behaviors.

One maladaptive way of coping with the stress of shyness-eliciting situations attempts to reduce social anxiety by means of alcohol or drugs — which then may become a problem of addiction. Sexual impotence and frigidity may also arise due to the performance anxieties associated with the uncertainty and intimacy of sexual encounters. There is a large body of growing evidence that the best strategy for coping with the inevitable stresses of modern life is to be part of a social support network of family, friends, and co-workers. An effective social support system acts both as a prophylaxis against the debilitating effects of stress and as an adjunct in treating many forms of mental and physical illness. Because many shy people are outside of such supportive social environments they do not derive the benefits that they can provide. Thus shyness may be indirectly linked to a variety of psychological and physical health problems.

Despite the often serious and pervasive impact that shyness can have, it can be treated to minimize or overcome its inhibiting effects. The treatment of choice is one involving cognitive-behavioral modification strategies. Negative self-statements are directly altered, positive ones practiced, effective social skills are taught, and means of reducing shyness-related anxiety and physio-logical arousal are utilized. In extreme cases, professional care should be sought from a therapist who understands and treats shyness. Many shy people can be helped by actively following the exercises in some of the more reputable shyness self-help books available.

Although shyness is experienced as a personal problem, it is also a universal problem, since its isolating and inhibiting effects on social relations weaken the bonds of the human connection. By preventing, weakening, or overcoming shyness, we help reaffirm the social network so essential for living a full life as responsive social beings.

Bibliography. B. G. Gilmartin, *Shyness and Love: Causes, Consequences, and Treatment* (1987). W. H. Jones, J. M. Cheek, and S. R. Briggs, *Shyness: Perspectives on Research and Treatment* (1986). P. G. Zimbardo, *Shyness, What It Is, What To Do About It* (1977). P. G. Zimbardo, S. Radl, *The Shy Child* (1981).

P. G. ZIMBARDO

ANXIETY; SHAME; SOCIAL ISOLATION. *Compare* ALIENATION/ESTRANGEMENT; INHIBITION; FEAR.

SIBLINGS/SIBLING RIVALRY. *See* CHILDREN; COMPETITIVENESS.

SICK, PASTORAL CARE OF. (1) In a broad sense, the attitudes and actions of a Christian community in response to suffering caused by sickness. (2) More narrowly, an office or function of ordained ministry concerned with the spiritual and emotional support, and (at times) the healing, of persons and families experiencing disease or illness.

The transition from health to illness is experienced by most persons as undesirable, stressful, and often traumatic. The course of any debilitating illness is likely to involve pain, suffering, worry, fear, anxiety, bitterness, unfamiliar surroundings, bedrest and consequent physical weakening, family and financial strains, lack of privacy, relative social isolation, and a sense of human vulnerability and frailty. Further, the patient and his or her family may be faced with experiences involving guilt and forgiveness, diminished self-image, limited future prospects, and questions concerning the meaning of life, death, and theodicy. None of these experiences is unique to the sick; all can be known in the best of health. But in illness they are intensified. For this reason, pastoral care of the sick presents a significant challenge to the larger enterprise of pastoral care and counseling.

Historically, pastoral care of the sick evolved from many sources, both pre-Christian and Christian, and has exhibited a rich variety of traditions and emphases. Some of these practical traditions have presumed a unity of body and spirit while others have presupposed their separateness. Likewise, the ministry of the Word has been stressed in some traditions, the sacramental ministry in others. Current theory and practice still include approaches developed around both Word and Sacrament, but have added at least two others. One is the use of psychologically informed clinical methods derived from the secular healing arts. The other is a renewed appreciation of the community's sharing of suffering.

In the best contemporary understanding sickness is viewed as having objective ("disease") and subjective ("illness") aspects, interpenetrated by physical, social, and religious dimensions. Such a view of sickness makes possible an equally broad pastoral perspective embracing these four current approaches to the pastoral care of the sick. This perspective, derived from the complex and systemic nature of sickness and the dynamics of Christian community, regards the pastoral care of the sick as an organically interactive process of healing within Christ's Body, the church.

1. **Historical Overview.** Every major religious tradition has evolved and practiced methods of caring for the sick. Christian pastoral care of the sick, although given distinctive importance in the ministry of Jesus and the early church, had roots reaching deep into ancient traditions, especially those of Jewish and Greek culture. The Jewish valuing of life and health and the Jewish tradition of community care of the sick as well as the wholistic healing practices of the Greek Asclepian temples and the Hippocratic tradition of healing all provided resources for the early Christian pastoral tradition of care for the sick.

Into this rich heritage Jesus brought his ministry, seeing particularly in the "pastoral" role of shepherd the paradigm for his own ministry of caring (Jn. 10:1–30). A significant portion of the gospel accounts of Jesus' ministry is devoted to his caring for the sick. He is pictured as a compassionate and charismatic healer, attending to body, mind, and spirit, often without distinction between the three (Mt. 8:16, 28–34; 10:5–8; Mk. 1:34; 6:7–13; Lk. 4:16–21; 7:2–10; 9:1–2; 10:8–9). Yet he is moved to such pastoral care not simply from personal compassion, understood as human empathy or altruism; his care is also a sign of the coming of God's Kingdom and a call to repentance for the entire community. In Jesus' ministry, healing points beyond itself to God's comprehensive work of salvation, illumining the sickness of the spirit as well as of the body, and the sickness of the community as well as of its individual members. Jesus' ministry is depicted as a revelatory event showing forth God's redemptive promise for the whole world.

In Acts and the pastoral Epistles, the focus of pastoral care of the sick is on the activity of Jesus' Spirit ministering within the newly formed Christian communities. There was at first a communal, interactive, and reciprocal cast to this care in which the caring act passed back and forth among community members as the sick regained health and the carers became sick.

Yet there is evidence, even at this time, of the growing specialization and role definition in these ministries anticipating the formal institutional roles that became common in later periods. In some churches, certain persons were appointed to minister specifically to the sick as the needs of body and spirit increasingly began to be differentiated under Greek influence. The early rite of the sacrament of the sick reflects this growing tension (see Palmer). While it had not yet acquired the heavy emphasis on forgiveness of sins (*viaticum*) which later transformed this ministry into the "last rites" (extreme unction) of the Roman Catholic Church, the sacrament of the sick did envision a two-step action of pastoral care. Healing oils of presumed medical efficacy, blessed in the name of Christ, were administered liberally to a parishioner's ailing organs. The intent was to cure the illness and, by curing the illness, to enable the parishio-

ner to leave the sick bed and rejoin the community for the celebration of the Eucharist.

The assumption that bodily cure and spiritual care comprise a single pastoral function is evident in Christian writings from the earliest periods, a tradition that continued through the Middle Ages. As churchmen became the sole inheritors of medical knowledge and the primary practitioners of medical skills, pastoral care could embrace both cure and care wholistically and without significant division. But even in this period there were voices which commended the differentiation of spiritual care from less esteemed ministries to physical illness. Two ancient ideas emerged to support this dualistic outlook and to challenge the unitary or wholistic tradition. The first was the belief that illness is caused by sin, which oddly enough had the effect not of reinforcing a sense of continuity between body and spirit, but of emphasizing the moral and spiritual aspects through the priestly rites of confession, forgiveness, and absolution as a function of sacramental ministry (see 2.b. below). The second was the view that illness, however caused, provides an occasion for spiritual testing and strengthening. The effect of this view was to emphasize the evangelical and pastoral functions of admonition, exhortation, and advising for the purpose of moral reform or spiritual conversion (see 2.a. below).

Interwoven through the myriad of pastoral treatises, rites, councilar pronouncements, and homilies on the pastoral care of the sick dating from the early church fathers through the post-Reformation period, one finds various mixtures and weightings of these wholistic and dualistic themes. The trend, however, was to give increasing emphasis to dualistic views, thus accenting formal, ritual methods of care aimed explicitly—and often exclusively—at moral and "spiritual" rather than physical needs. Faithful pastors continued to visit their sick and undoubtedly exercised their human caring, counseling skills, and healing arts. Yet historical sources suggest that these pastors were increasingly pressed to concentrate on the moral and spiritual aspects of illness and to legitimate their ministries through use of the formal, institutionalized rites of the church.

Thus ritual became the principal pastoral method in the care of the sick. This persisted, together with the soul-body dualism which grounded it, through the Reformation and early modern periods. Only in the nineteenth and early twentieth centuries did more conversational methods and more wholistic conceptions of illness develop, largely through the discovery of hypnosis and advances in psychiatry and psychosomatic medicine (Lapsley, 1972, chap. 2). Modern clinical pastoral care, with its wholistic emphasis and psychological sophistication, emerged from this development, known in the early years as the religion and health movement.

2. **Contemporary Approaches.** In the contemporary church it is possible to identify at least four general approaches to the pastoral care of the sick:

a. The neo-classical and evangelical-pietistic approach. It is likely that in conservative churches earlier styles of pastoral care of the sick have continued, relatively unaffected by the clinical pastoral movement that has substantially impacted the more liberal churches. But there has also been something of a revival of traditional approaches in the so-called moderate or mainline church in recent years, embracing an increasing number of pastoral theologians and pastors. Its care of the sick resembles a bedside evangelical Protestant worship service. The pastor leads the parishioner-patient in prayer and in the reading of the Bible and exhorts the parishioner-patient to believe, to repent, and to accept God's gracious forgiveness. Eduard Thurneysen (ET 1962), an influential proponent of this approach, sees pastoral care as essentially a "communication of the Word." He further states that "not a single pastoral conversation can do without admonishing, even rebuking and chastising in some way." More recently, Thomas C. Oden (1986), after a long journey through various psychologically-oriented views of pastoral care, returns for guidance to traditionalist sources that range from Cyprian in the third century to the nineteenth century writings of J. H. Newman and F. P. Maurice. Among the correlative pastoral practices that Oden suggests are intercessory prayer, self-discipline, moral self-examination, evangelical witness, fasting, and spiritual direction.

This approach constitutes a return to a modified separatist tradition of classical Christian pastoral theory and practice; it also emulates and affirms the approach to pastoral care of the sick followed today by many evangelical, pietistic, and fundamentalist Christian churches. The distinctive Protestant contribution to this approach is rooted in the doctrine of total depravity, by which sin and sickness are seen as separate maladies yet in "correlation" (Thurneysen), belonging to human nature itself and overcome only in forgiveness.

b. The priestly-sacramental approach. In some ways the most traditional of all modern pastoral ministries to the sick is the priestly ministry, epitomized by the figure of the lone priest making the rounds of hospital beds, bringing a brief word of greeting, perhaps a pamphlet or a prayer, and the offer of sacramental ministry later in the day. The logistics of his practice require that he see between five and ten patients an hour in order to visit all the patients of his denomination or parish. There is little time for in-depth conversation. While this routine proves frustrating and tiring for many priests, the traditional priestly understanding of pastoral care of the sick supports this approach to ministry by weighting strongly the role of sacramental administration; this includes principally the hearing of confession and celebrating the Eucharist, but also giving last rites and administering the sacrament of the sick.

The English physician-theologian R. A. Lambourne once speculated that the rationale for both sacramental ministry and acute medical care of the sick derives from the same Augustinian notion of grace; i.e., a substance imparted and infused by those so ordained for the rescue of those in peril. Whether or not St. Augustine is the common parent of modern medicine and sacramental ministry, this view evokes compellingly similar images of priest and physician hurrying from room to room, offering brief ritualized contacts with each patient and their ministrations of life-giving substances. Performed by either a parish-based priest or a hospital duty chaplain, this traditional form of sacramental ministry constitutes a preeminently "doctoring" approach to the pastoral care of the sick.

Its highly ritualized form provides a certain emotional security and distance for the pastor, and offers the patient the security and rich meaning of religious symbolism in a time of uncertainty, anxiety, and change. If performed hurriedly and mechanistically, however, it also loses the personal values that come from more individualized care through a personally cultivated pastoral relationship.

c. The psychotherapeutic counseling approach. A distinctive style of pastoring the sick has developed through the modern clinical pastoral education movement with its roots in the late nineteenth and early twentieth century psychiatry, psychotherapy and religion and health movements. Unlike traditionalist approaches which principally adapted parish theology and practices to the sickroom, the clinical pastoral care movement was born in the sickroom and has now made deep inroads into general parish pastoral care and theology. In both practice and theory, the movement owes much to secular psychiatry and psychotherapy (Freud, Jung, Sullivan, Horney, and Rogers especially), to modern studies in psychosomatic medicine (e.g., Helen Flanders Dunbar), and to the creative work of the clinical pastoral education (CPE) pioneers like Anton Boisen, Richard Cabot, and Russell Dicks, who sought to apply these insights to the care of sick and troubled persons.

In the clinical tradition of pastoral care of the sick, the fully developed pastoral visit is essentially an in-depth counseling relationship developed between a "counselor" and a "counselee." Of course, not all care of the sick actually becomes fully developed in this sense. The counseling model, however modified in certain respects, remains the general aim or ideal. Among its distinctive features are: (1) careful in-depth listening for the unique meanings of the illness to the patient; (2) an attempt to draw out "eductively" and support the patient's emotional strengths; (3) an appreciation of the healing power of attending appropriately to negative or conflicted aspects of the experience (such as anxiety, guilt, and shame) rather than avoiding or reacting defensively against them; (4) attending to the interpersonal and family-related dimensions of the illness instead of viewing it individualistically; (5) the involvement and "use" of the pastor's own "personhood," and the pastor's personal relationship with the patient, as a means of facilitating a therapeutic process; and (6) selective, psychologically realistic use of prayer, sacrament, and scripture when appropriate as "religious resources" (though actual use of them varies widely among clinically trained pastors).

The clinical pastoral approach became institutionally embodied in clinical pastoral education programs which have trained large numbers of divinity students, parish ministers, and hospital chaplains since its beginnings in the twenties. CPE emphasizes learning from the patient in a supervised encounter with "living human documents" (Boisen) and follows the "medical model" in large measure, though obviously with great differences from the traditional "doctoring" approach of the sacramentalist pastor. The clinical pastoral approach to care of the sick has acquired great sophistication and has produced a major new form of specialized ministry, the hospital chaplain, as well as an administrative superstructure of nationally accredited training centers, rigorous certification processes, and specialty journals, which at times seems to obscure its affinities with traditional Christian thought and practice.

d. The lay community-kenosis approach. Most difficult of all to describe is another neo-traditionalist approach to the pastoral care of the sick, which has been taking shape during the past few decades. It shares elements and adherents of the other three approaches described yet is radically different. A lay movement emphasizing community and wholistic spirituality, it is non-individualistic, non-professional, non-authoritarian, non-ritualized, and unscientific. The central paradigm around which its philosophy and practice are organized is the archetypal "wounded healer" of Greek, Babylonian, and Hindu mythology, most recently applied to pastoral practice by Henri J. M. Nouwen from an old Talmudic legend (Nouwen, 1979). The wounded healer has no special knowledge, power, skill, authority, sanctity, or wholeness. In fact, it is precisely the lack (*kenosis*) of these esteemed qualities that enables the healer to experience the condition of the sick and to know and heal their suffering through his or her own. Often, the "wounded healer" is a healing *community* where "sharing of pain" takes place and mutual bearing of sufferings "become openings and occasions for a new vision." Lay visitation, corporate prayer, sitting vigils, the laying on of hands, words of sympathy and even humor — all practices central to the Jewish congregational tradition of ministering to the sick — are ways that "deepen the pain to a level where it can be shared." Its variety, informality, and unpretentiousness suggest the ministering ways of Jesus and the earliest Christian communities. Lacking identifiable outward form, this approach requires the discipline of a deeply contemplative view of life embracing active social and political as well as solitary dimensions. In this same vein, Leroy T. Howe (1981) envisions a community-centered pastoral care of the sick in which the sickest are enabled to minister to the less sick by being those best able to confront their own suffering and hopelessness "as the primary. . . setting in which the Kingdom of God and its promises are to be apprehended."

There may be other approaches to pastoral care of the sick deserving description but these four reflect a rich diversity of theological understanding and pastoral practice. Good pastoral theology appreciates such diversity and seeks to incorporate it into styles of practice, taking from each what is most important for the pastoral task at hand. Therefore it may be possible, on the basis of this descriptive typology, to suggest a richer and more comprehensive perspective which does justice to, but goes beyond, the enumerated types. Discerning the outlines of such a synthesis requires further reflection on the nature of sickness itself, however.

3. The Nature and Meaning of Sickness: Preliminary Considerations. a. Illness and disease. Sickness is a human condition involving physical or mental impairment sufficient to cause suffering. Every sickness presupposes a norm of health in respect to which it falls short. This norm of health has both objective and subjective determinants — as does sickness. Objectively, health can be defined by certain established parameters of physical, mental, and emotional functioning. Subjectively, health is usually described as a general sense of well-being, or simply as "feeling good." When sickness

is defined objectively it is usually called "disease," given a diagnostic name, and rated according to severity. "Illness" is the way we often refer to sickness experienced subjectively.

As may be imagined, there can be a close correlation between disease and illness (especially in acute treatment situations) as well as very little correlation (typical of some chronic illnesses). In parts of the world where whole populations bear parasitic diseases from birth to death, there is little awareness of *being* ill, while some medically healthy hypochondriacs in the Western world may spend most of their lives *feeling* ill. Further, being sick in Western society is a social role, sometimes assumed by persons wanting to be regarded as "sick" (for financial or personal reasons, consciously or unconsciously), and sometimes assigned by families or institutions wishing to stigmatize individuals or limit their access to employment or to social independence.

b. Christian interpretations of sickness. Ideas about and attitudes toward sickness have varied widely in Christianity. On the one hand sickness has been regarded as an unnatural and undesirable state, and thus the object of special care and compassion. The gospels record how Jesus gave high priority to curing and comforting the sick. His parable of the Good Samaritan (Lk. 10:29–37) expresses this succinctly. But Jesus' ministry to the sick did not always take precedence over his other concerns; sometimes bodily fatigue, the need to pray, or the call to preach drew him away from the pressing crowds of sick persons around him (Mt. 8:18; 14:23; Mk. 1:32–38; Lk. 5:15–16). From the earliest days of the church, Christians have visited the sick, cared for them in their homes and in later centuries have established hospices and hospitals to alleviate their suffering.

Nevertheless, sickness has also been regarded by Christians as natural, normal, and at times desirable. St. Paul accepted his "thorn. . . in the flesh" (II Cor. 12:7), thought by some scholars to be epilepsy; St. Francis befriended his numerous illnesses; and many other Christians through the centuries have welcomed illness as a God-sent test and purifier of the soul. Others have simply regarded sickness as a concomitant of original sin, if not causally related to it. Thurneyson claims that "sickness actually belongs to the nature of man." Willingness to bear sickness personally for reasons of chastisement, purification, or strengthening has usually not gone hand in hand with a willingness to impose sickness on or be thankful for sickness in others. But it is just as true that theologians and pastors have never been comfortable with a view that sickness in others is entirely bad (or good). A redemptive dimension can loom behind even the most tragic illness, confounding the urge to denounce it as unmitigated evil.

4. Toward a More Comprehensive Approach. Pastoral tradition has proceeded on the assumption that pastoral care of the sick is something that one person does to or for another. But the assumption is in fact questionable. To look to Jesus as the Good Shepherd, or as the prime exemplar of the "shepherding perspective" (Hiltner) implies a one-way process in which a single "shepherd" cares unilaterally for the "sheep." However, both the nature of sickness and the nature of the church suggest the need for a more complex, comprehensive, interactive model of pastoral care. Sickness occurs in families and communities; its disease aspect affects different members at different times but its illness aspect to some degree touches all members at all times. Healing is also an interactive process. When one member of a body, a family, or community suffers from disease, all suffer; but because all suffer, all are in some sense concerned with and affected by the need to address the malady of the diseased member.

The functioning of the human body provides a striking example of this complex interdependency. When an organ (or even a cell) is damaged by disease, an alarm is sounded throughout the body by means of chemical, hormonal, and nervous signals. In response, the rest of the body gives up precisely the substances needed to repair, heal, and nourish the diseased part. Healthy cells break down their own structural proteins in order to pass these through their outer membranes where they are then reassembled and rushed to the site where needed. When in turn the donor organs and cells become diseased, the process is reversed, with the now-recovered parts drawn to help and give of their substance. This is the nature of organic functioning.

In Christian pastoral care of the sick, we have to do with the organic functioning of the Body of Christ. Acts 2:44–47 and 4:32–5:16 gives an idealized but theologically significant picture of how the early Christian communities practiced an interactive pastoral caring among themselves (and the Epistles perhaps a more realistic view). In the Gospel of John the act by which Jesus' Spirit passed from his resurrected body into the many bodies which constituted his Church (Jn. 20:19–23) transferred to that new Body the same organic, reciprocal, interactive principle of love that was the unique characteristic of His life among us (Jn. 16:7–15; 17:20–23). Such is the infrastructure, the ontology, of Love Incarnate — both before and after his resurrection. There is perhaps something distinctive in the nature of pastoring, particularly to the sick, that enables it to illumine with special clarity this important feature of Christian life; it suggests a way that otherwise meaningless suffering can become redemptive. The implications of such a perspective for pastoral practice are many, but they certainly entail an enabling of members within the Christian community to exercise a preeminently active ministry to one another without regard to ordination or special training and in a way that corresponds with the functional nature of both the human body and the Body of Christ.

5. Conclusion. Pastoral care of the sick has flowered in this century in a variety of approaches. Each has its roots in some aspect of traditional thought and practice; and each has its contribution to make. Yet the nature of both sickness and the church prompts us to seek a more comprehensive view of these approaches, a perspective on them that does justice to the dynamics of sickness within the Christian community. In the writer's view, such a perspective would closely approximate the pastoral principles and practices seen in the life of Jesus and in the early Christian communities.

Bibliography. A. H. Becker, The Compassionate Visitor (1985). A. Boisen, Out of the Depths (1960). R. C. Cabot and R. L. Dicks, The Art of Ministering to the Sick (1936). R. Dayringer, Pastor and Patient: A Handbook for Clergy Who Visit the Sick (1982). H. Faber, Pastoral Care in the Modern Hospital (1971). J. Fichter, Religion and Pain: The Spiritual Dimensions of Health Care (1981). G. M. Furniss, "Healing Prayer and Pastoral Care," J. of Pastoral Care, 38 (1984), 107–19. S. Hiltner, Preface to Pastoral Theology (1958); Theological Dynamics (1972), ch. 4. E. B. Holifield, A History of Pastoral Care in America: From Salvation to Self-Realization (1983). L. F. Holst, ed., Hospital Ministry: The Role of the Chaplain Today (1985). L. Howe, "Where Are We Going in Pastoral Care?" Christian Century, 98 (1981), 1160–63. J. A. Knight, "The Minister as Healer, the Healer as Minister." J. of Religion and Health, 21 (1982), 100–114. J. N. Lapsley, Salvation and Health (1972). J. T. McNeill, A History of the Cure of Souls (1951). H. Nouwen, Creative Ministry (1978); The Wounded Healer (1979). T. Oden, Pastoral Theology (1983); "Recovering Lost Identity," J. of Pastoral Care, 34 (1980), 423; Crisis Ministries (1986). P. F. Palmer, "The Purpose of Anointing the Sick: A Reappraisal," Theological Studies, 19 (1958), 309–44; Pastoral Care of the Sick, Publ. No. 878, U.S. Catholic Conference (1983). R. C. Powell, CPE: Fifty Years of Learning Through Supervised Encounter With Living Human Documents, A.C.P.E., Inc. (1975). L. D. Reimer and J. T. Wagner, The Hospital Handbook: A Practical Guide to Hospital Visitation (1984). D. E. Saylor, ". . . And You Visited Me" (1979). A. Siirala, The Voice of Illness (1964). B. Spilka, J. D. Spangler, and C. B. Nelson, "Spiritual Support in Life Threatening Illness," J. of Religion and Health, 22 (1983), 98–104. E. E. Thornton, Professional Education for Ministry: A History of Clinical Pastoral Education (1970). E. Thurneysen, A Theology of Pastoral Care (1962); K. L. Vaux, This Mortal Coil: The Meaning of Health and Disease (1978). C. A. Wise, Pastoral Counseling: Its Theory and Practice (1951).

D. C. DUNCOMBE

HEALING; HEALTH AND ILLNESS; HOSPITALIZATION, EXPERIENCE OF; PATIENCE/PATIENTHOOD; SALVATION, HEALING, AND HEALTH; SIN AND SICKNESS. See also ANOINTING OF THE SICK, SACRAMENT OF; BLESSING AND BENEDICTION; FAITH HEALING; PAIN; PRAYER IN PASTORAL CARE; SUFFERING. Also CANCER PATIENT; HEART PATIENT; SURGICAL PATIENT. Compare CHRONIC ILLNESSES.

SICK, SACRAMENT OF THE ANOINTING OF.
See ANOINTING OF THE SICK, SACRAMENT OF.

SICK AND DYING, JEWISH CARE OF.
Judaism is guided by the fundamental concept of the supreme sanctity of human life. Persons created in the image of God assume an inherent dignity. That life is sacred is the locus of all other values. This concept is embodied and actualized through the halakha (Jewish law), the ritual and the way of life of the Jew. Mitzvot, divinely given commandments, obligate individuals to preserve their life and health, the physician to cure them, and the community to care for them in illness. Since each human life has infinite value, any fraction of it is equally of infinite worth and must be preserved as long as possible. Hence the person who is sick must seek treatment. Ritual law, even the Sabbath, is suspended not only for the sake of such treatment in the face of definite threats to life, but also in the presence of "possible" or "questionable" danger.

The tradition obligates physicians to deliver medical care not only in life-threatening situations, but even when such care is required simply for the alleviation of pain or preservation of physical well-being. They are mandated not only to effect a physical cure, but to bring hope and caring, and to alleviate the patient's emotional distress as well. The physician who refrains from healing is held guilty of shedding blood.

Jewish law endows *Bikkur Holim*, visiting the sick, with the fulfillment of a divine commandment. This rests upon every individual. The sick must be given support, comfort, and hope. The *halakha* presents guidelines as to whom, and when, and for how long the visit should be made. The primary purpose of visiting the sick is to make them comfortable, cheer them up, and pray for their recovery.

The Jewish community does not leave matters entirely to the benevolence and piety of the individual. Every community has a *Bikkur Holim* Society. These societies often function through the synagogue, not limiting their work to mere visiting. They may be available to relieve the exhausted family members of attending to the needs of the sick and often help financially, too.

Even more important than visiting the sick is the supreme obligation to preserve life as long as it is possible. This includes forbearing from hastening death, no matter how serious the illness. Hence euthanasia is forbidden. This raises questions: Is the preservation of life absolute and unconditional? Are there times when one is not obligated to preserve and prolong life, but is even advised to help terminate it? Since human life is sacred it may not be terminated or shortened for even a moment, except in situations of self-defense or martyrdom.

Considerations of the patient's convenience, usefulness, or even suffering where cure is plausible are not decisive. Active hastening of the dying process is absolutely forbidden. Only in a case of irreversible terminal illness and intractable pain would most Rabbinic authorities advocate passive euthanasia. Thus the physician may refrain from using artificial means to keep the patient alive, merely letting nature take its course. Drugs may be administered to control and alleviate pain even if this means shortening life, provided the intention is pain relief.

At the approach of death the patient is encouraged to say the *Viddui* (confession). Care is taken not to distress the patient. It is explained to patients that this does not necessarily mean that death is imminent. They pray for healing, confess their sins, and pray for the welfare of their family. Dying persons are not left alone so that they will not feel abandoned. Even after death, respect and reverence are due to the body, the abode of God's spirit. A *shomer* (guard) sits near the body and recites prayers and psalms until the funeral service.

Bibliography. I. Jakobovits, *Jewish Medical Ethics* (1975). F. Rosner and J. D. Bleich, *Jewish Bioethics* (1979). N. Schecter, "Pain and the Jewish Patient," *J. of Psychology and Judaism*, 1 (1976), 35–43. R. Schindler, "Truth Telling and Terminal Illness: A Jewish View," *J. of Religion and Health*, 21 (1982), 42–48. M. H. Spero, "Death and the 'Life Review' in Halakhah," *J. of Religion and Health*, 19 (1980), 313–19.

P. KRAUSS

JEWISH PRAYERS (Significance for Personal Care); JEWISH CARE AND COUNSELING (History, Tradition, and Contemporary Issues). *See also* DYING, PASTORAL CARE OF; RITUAL AND PASTORAL CARE.

SICK CALL (Roman Catholicism). A pastoral visit by a priest to a sick person either at home or in an institutional setting. The sick call may consist entirely of nonsacramental pastoral care and counseling. It may also be an occasion for the sick person to go to confession, to receive holy communion, and to receive the anointing of the sick. The sick call is often an occasion for the priest to help the sick person prepare for death. The 1983 "Rite of Anointing", (a revision of the 1974 post-Vatican II Rite), envisions the priest making more than one pastoral visit to an individual. The anointing of the sick is preferably celebrated at the beginning of a serious illness. Holy communion (*viaticum*) is the primary sacrament for the dying.

G. McCARRON

ANOINTING OF THE SICK, SACRAMENT OF; ROMAN CATHOLIC PASTORAL CARE. *See also* CALLING AND VISITATION.

SICKNESS. *See* HEALTH AND ILLNESS; SICK, PASTORAL CARE OF; SIN AND SICKNESS.

SIDDUR. The Jewish prayerbook. It contains the fixed liturgy for the three daily services (evening, morning, and afternoon), the four Sabbath services (evening, morning, additional, and afternoon), and usually a selection of individual prayers and meditations. A second prayerbook, called "Mahzor" contains the liturgies for the major festivals (Tabernacles, Passover, and Pentecost). The daily and Sabbath prayers are obligatory for Traditional Jews and are recited privately if no congregational worship is available.

P. J. HAAS

JEWISH PRAYERS (Significance for Personal Care).

SIGN OF THE CROSS. The marking of persons or objects with the primary symbol of the Christian faith has a long history within the church. In the *Apostolic Tradition* (ca. 215 A.D.), Hippolytus speaks of making the sign of the cross on one's forehead and eyes during times of temptation, "presenting it like a breastplate" to the Devil.

In most Christian denominations the sign of the cross is used to signify that a person claims identity as a follower of Jesus Christ. The first signation of an individual Christian is usually given at baptism, where one is "marked as Christ's own forever" (*Book of Common Prayer*, 1979, p. 308). Other pastoral occasions in which the sign of the cross is an integral part are Confirmation, the imposition of ashes on Ash Wednesday, healing and funeral services, and the consecration of buildings or vessels.

The sign of the cross has as its theological motivation the sacramental principle that material realities (including gestures) can disclose and make present spiritual realities.

S. J. WHITE

BLESSING AND BENEDICTION; RELIGIOUS LANGUAGE AND SYMBOLISM, PSYCHOLOGY OF; SYMBOLISM/SYMBOLIZING.

SILENCE. Capable of conveying many meanings, silence in and of itself has no particular meaning. The meaning of a particular episode or period of silence comes from its *context*: within what kind of relationship is silence maintained? which person in the relationship is maintaining silence? does the silence have a conscious or unconscious purpose? It is often the task of the pastor or pastoral counselor to understand silence — one's own or that of another person—but the task may also be simply to "live in" the silence, to experience it alone or with another person.

In addition, silence, whatever its intent or motivation, may be experienced anywhere on a "comfort scale" from deep comfort to extreme discomfort; it is often valuable to know how another person is experiencing a time of silence, as well as to be aware of one's own experience of it.

1. **Silence in Pastoral Counseling.** In pastoral counseling, silence is surrounded by a variety of other phenomena which may convey meanings in regard to the silence itself. The most important of these include the latent and/or manifest content of the last remark made; the "body language" of the persons present in the silence; and associations to similar silences in similar contexts. By recalling or examining these elements, the pastor may move closer to an accurate interpretation of the silence.

a. Silence on the part of help-seekers. When a person seeking help maintains a noticeable silence, the source of the silence may often be found in one of four (not mutually exclusive) areas.

i. Embarrassment. The help-seeker may be deeply embarrassed by material that needs to be revealed, or would be revealed if the client or parishioner were to speak. The fear of exposing oneself as a fool or as "the chief of sinners" can easily create a charged silence. The embarrassment would be present no matter who was hearing the parishioner; it does not specifically have to do with the pastor.

ii. Resistance. Here the specific relationship to the counselor or the pastor plays a somewhat larger part. The help-seeker knows (perhaps unconsciously) that if the silence is broken, he or she will be brought face to face with a key issue, and may have to face the possibility of changing. It is sometimes said that counseling consists essentially of the process of working through resistance.

iii. Transference. If the help-seeker believes (consciously or unconsciously) that to break the silence would be to threaten or to alter the significant relationship with the pastor or counselor, it may be terrifying to consider breaking the silence. The relationship is based on the transference neurosis.

iv. Work. During a silence, the parishioner or client may be making connections, reflecting on what has just been said, allowing himself or herself to experience feelings previously denied to conscious awareness, or doing other kinds of work appropriate to the counseling setting.

The pastor's correct understanding of the source of a silence can enhance the counseling process; misunderstanding can inhibit it. Silence caused by embarrassment can often eventually be overcome by the development of a trustworthy and trusting relationship; but silence coming out of resistance or transference will seldom be changed by simple relationship-building. Indeed, the existence of a trusting relationship may be a factor in causing "transference silences."

When the issue is resistance or transference, interpreting the resistance or transference as the cause is the most useful tactic, so long as the pastor or counselor does not expect that the help-seeker will immediately or gracefully accept the interpretation. On the other hand, if the silence represents work on the help-seeker's part, it is urgent that the silence be respected and maintained by the pastor.

b. The counselor's silence. In a formal counseling process, the counselor may maintain silence for one of two main reasons: as an outgrowth of countertransference, or as a consciously chosen means of help.

Countertransference includes such phenomena as anger at the help-seeker, boredom (which is a form of anger), sexual feelings, unwillingness to disturb the even tenor of the relationship, anxiety, and other feelings about the client or the situation. The pastor or counselor finds it difficult to break the silence lest one or more of these feelings be forced out into the open where it will be difficult or painful to deal with. Such a phenomenon is of course a mirror image of the phenomenon of transference in the help-seeker.

But the pastor or counselor may also *choose to remain silent* as a means of therapeutic intervention. We have already observed, for example, that maintaining a silence may be a means of respecting the counselee's work. In another situation, silence in response to a question may meet with a rueful but amused comment from the counselee: "You're not going to answer that question, are you?" In maintaining a well chosen silence, the pastoral counselor may heighten the transference of the counselee or parishioner or may throw the help-seeker back upon her or his own resources. Maintaining such tactical silences is an early lesson in the training of most counselors. The important thing, as with clients, is to know *why* one is remaining silent, and to understand what one expects to happen as a result of doing so.

2. **Silences in Pastoral Care.** Thus far we have been treating silence as something taking place within the boundaries of a formal counseling situation. But silence takes place in other situations — calling on the sick in hospitals and in grief ministry, among others — and in such situations silence may have other meanings not yet touched upon.

In grief ministries, for example, it is often quite appropriate for pastor and parishioner to spend long periods of time in silence. (The Jewish custom of "sitting shiva" after a death includes such silences.) The silence may have none of the meanings discussed above; it happens because in the face of deep loss words are inadequate or inappropriate. In such situations, silence may even be appropriate as a response to specific "why" questions, because "Why?" is more an expression of grief than a true theological question, and silence is a better answer than any effort to discuss the doctrine of providence.

The same is often true in ministry to the sick. Sharing short or long silences with a sick or dying parishioner is often a means of deepening a relationship or of expressing the depths already present.

Such silences have theological and psychological meanings closely related to the use of silence as a religious discipline. Among Quakers, silence is a means of "centering down" in the expectation that God's Spirit (Inner Light) is present and may be made known in the silence. In the disciplines of Ignatius of Loyola, silence is used with similar intent. Liturgical or meditational silence is much less well-known in most Protestant groups.

A deliberately cultivated silence and an unconsciously motivated silence are both experienced as having great power. Silence, particularly when shared with one or more other human beings, permits thoughts and feelings ordinarily kept out of conscious awareness to come to our attention. The pastor's challenging task is to learn to discriminate, and to help others discriminate, between the various voices which may be "heard" in the silence. Jewish and Christian traditions alike have confessed that what comes to consciousness can be the "still, small voice" of God; but those same traditions suggest (cf. I Jn. 4:1) that what arises could also be the voice of illness.

K. R. MITCHELL

LISTENING; MEDITATION; PRESENCE, MINISTRY OF. *See also* COUNTERTRANSFERENCE; RESISTANCE; SYMBOLIC DIMENSIONS OF PASTORAL CARE RELATIONSHIPS; TECHNIQUE AND SKILL IN PASTORAL CARE; TIMING; TRANSFERENCE; WORKING THROUGH.

SIMONS, MENNO (1496–1561). Religious reformer. After ordination to the Catholic priesthood, Simons was converted to the Reformation in 1536. Ordained as an Anabaptist elder, he labored in northern Holland and Germany. He was a reconciling spirit for Dutch and German Anabaptists as he distanced himself and his followers from the more radical and contentious wings of the Reformation like the Münster insurgents. His greatest accomplishment, wrought through his writings and his missionary activity, was to gather together the peaceful Anabaptists of Germany and northern Holland. His theology put a strong emphasis on the interior rebirth of Christ in the soul and a blameless life of external sobriety and godliness. Only such reborn souls were admitted to membership in the church, hence the exclusion of mixed marriages and the use of excommunication of the unworthy.

By the seventeenth century the word "Mennonite" became the common term for all Anabaptists in Europe except for the Hutterites. The frequent persecution of these groups led to their widespread diffusion in Europe, and, in the nineteenth century to North and South America. Like the Society of Friends, they have had a long and noble commitment to social service and pacifism.

Bibliography. W. Keeney, *The Development of Dutch Anabaptist Thought and Practice from 1539–1564* (1968).

L. S. CUNNINGHAM

PASTORAL CARE (History, Traditions, and Definitions).

SIN/SINS. The most comprehensive and distinctive term in ancient Israelite religion and its modern heirs (Judaism, Christianity, Islam) which describes the human predicament as a state of corporate and individual moral corruption originating in the human being's inclination to ignore, disobey, or replace God, plus the acts and dispositions prompted by that state.

Human beings throughout history have pondered the mysteries of creation and destiny, the mysteries that concern themselves and why they are what they are. All religious faiths respond to these mysteries by offering interpretations of human misery and human evil. Ancient Israelite religion experienced the human predicament in relation to the one, true God, the creator, whose requirements and relations to Israel had primarily a moral character. Obligations to this God were at the same time obligations to promote the welfare, acknowledge the rights, and meet the needs of other human beings. The fundamental insight at work here is the interconnection between the experience of the sacred and moral obligation, an insight which appears in Zoroastrianism, Islam, Judaism, and Christianity. Accordingly, sin has a double connotation of disobedience toward God and corruption of human beings. Sin occurs both as the distortedness or wrongness of human history as such in which all individuals participate and as specific acts originating in human self-determination. Sin thus is both fated or tragic and voluntary. Hence, that which relieves or reduces sin likewise has the double character of a corporate redemption aimed to break the historical power of sin, and a moral, cultic discipline able to transform the inclinations, acts, and pieties of the individual.

1. The Symbol and the Doctrine. The theme of sin is either explicitly treated or presupposed by the literature of ancient Israel and early Christianity, the Christian Scriptures. The collected writings of Israel begin with an account of the creation of the world and human beings immediately followed by a narrative of a primordial act of disobedience which transplants human beings from the condition of innocence into a radically corrupted human history. The prophets of Israel explicitly connect impending catastrophic political events with the moral corruption of the Israelite nation, and they connect that corruption with Israel's inclination to treat the nation and other mundane securities as if they themselves were the creator. In the NT, Jesus' prophetic ministry pressed the reality of sin back behind its embodiment in law and tradition to the secret intentions of the heart, and Paul used the ancient narrative of Adam to describe the character and course of history itself and the slavery or unfreedom this corrupted history works on all human beings.

This view of the human predicament as centrally and primarily a condition of sin contains at least these four features. First, the problem of the human being is determined in relation to God, the transcendent, righteous Creator. When human beings do not live from and centered in the Creator, they invariably develop idolatrous or absolutizing relations to the world. Second, these idolatrous relations in turn have disastrously distortive effects on the human being. They invade and corrupt reason, the emotions, community, language, and embodiment. These effects have to do with moral experience because they disrupt the conditions and ways of being normatively and communally human, and because they are promoted in acts of voluntary human self-interest. Third, the effects of idolatrous transformation accumulate not merely in the individual self, but find expression in the social relations and institutions in which human life endures over time. Finally, because sin reaches and corrupts the deepest realities of human history and society, the human self as we know it is formed in that corruption. Hence, sin is a bondage which influences the will as well as an act promoted by the will.

These four features of sin are present in various ways in the symbolism, narratives, and proclamations of the Bible. However, during the early centuries of the Christian church, these features called for interpretation in a predominantly hellenistic environment in which they were anything but self-evident. Conflict occurred between the Christian and the prevailing hellenistic ways of viewing the human predicament. Two issues were especially prominent and both obtained expressions weighted more on the hellenistic than the Christian side. According to the first, human sin is radical slavery, universally and unavoidably present in all human history, it owes its origin to the ignorance, weakness, and miseries which constitute human finitude. In this Manichaean formulation, sin is only a mask for the deeper problem of finitude itself. According to the second, sin is a matter of human freedom and responsibility, and there is nothing inevitable about it. In this Pelagian interpretation, sin is always a willful act, hence it is misleading to think of it as a bondage or slavery. Much of the work of the church fathers in these early centuries was an attempt to retain the distinctive Hebraic insights into the nature of sin in the face of these two "natural heresies" (Schleiermacher).

The attempt to solve these problems pushed the church into levels of language which were not mere repetitions of the Adamic story of Pauline passages but which discovered new paradigms and doctrinalizations able to relate these insights to the hellenistic ethos. More than any other early figure, it was Augustine who reformulated the Hebraic notion of sin into doctrine and paradigm. The result was the classical Catholic doctrine of sin, which persisted in Protestant Christianity with only minor changes. This doctrine included at least the following: Sin does not originate from a natural inclination in human nature, but in freedom. Nothing in creation, human or otherwise, explains or causes sin. At the same time, sin is inevitable because all of humankind participate in the disastrous effects of the sin of the first parents in which human nature itself lost its orientation or relation to God. The effects of this loss of divine presence was twofold. The natural harmony of various powers of the human self (soul) as well as the harmony of the human community in history were corrupted. Since it is corrupted human nature which is propagated in human birth, this corruption reaches every generation of human beings thus making sin universal to the human race. Human misery and mortality are secondary effects of the first.

Attending this essentially Augustinian doctrinalization were several paradigms which served as the framework of the doctrine. The most important was the historical story of Adam and Eve, the factuality of which was not only taken for granted, but was used to show that sin does not originate with the creation of human being but enters as a later interruption. A second paradigm is a legal one. It portrays sin as a violation of a divinely ordained order, the violation of which inevitably incurs guilt and punishment. The third paradigm is biological and serves as the framework for understanding how sin is transmitted to all generations and therefore is the basis for affirming sin's universality. The classical concept, therefore, results from a translation of the Hebraic notion of sin into a conceptuality free from Manichaean and Pelagian distortions.

2. Secular Critiques and Theological Revisions. It seems evident that the ancient Hebrew-Christian symbols of sin and the Augustinian doctrinalization are not characteristic of twentieth-century Western ways of understanding the human being. With the exception of enclaves of Protestant and Catholic orthodoxy, contemporary Christian theology has not retained the classical doctrinalization. Within theology itself, the doctrine has been eroding since the Enlightenment. Two of the three paradigms were targets of Enlightenment and post-Enlightenment criticisms; the biological way of understanding the transmission of sin and the literal-historical retention of the primordial fall as an actual event in time. Recently, severe criticism has been directed (by Paul Ricoeur) at the legal paradigm, the "myth of punishment." Discredited, then, are the traditional devices by which the Christian church prevented the image of sin from being transformed into Manichaism or Pelagianism. In the wake of this discreditation came the kind of liberalism which allied itself with modern progressivist and optimistic views of human nature and its capabilities. According to those views, human beings may have a predicament but it is clearly not a severe one.

Optimistic and trivialized depictions of the human predicament are only one strand of the modern West. The nineteenth and twentieth centuries have seen a renaissance of the ancient tragic view (in fiction, poetry, and philosophy), pessimistic apocalypses (Spengler, Heilbroner, Schell), and social and economic radicalism (Marx, Habermas). Furthermore, contemporary forms of the older paradigms have emerged. Psychological and social interpretations of guilt replace the objective, cosmic order of divine law. The Adamic story gives way to social and biological versions of the deterministic weight of history. Lorenz and other "instinctivists" offer a modern form of biological model.

These secularized versions of Fall, evil, and human culpability are not without their influence on theology itself. Modern European and American theologies use Freud, Marx and existential philosophy to criticize liberal theology and to restate the doctrine of sin. Liberation theology has been receptive to an approach to human evil assisted by Marxist-type hermeneutics of praxis and oppression. Freudian psychologies have contributed to the theological criticism of the primacy of the intellect affirmed by classical theology.

Acknowledging this pluralism of secular approaches to the human problem should not obscure what may be an underlying and pervasive way of understanding the human predicament ever more prominent in contemporary technocratic society. This therapeutic understanding, named so by Phillip Reiff, grasps the human problem in largely non-moral, non-religious categories. Instead of seeing a distinctive human predicament, this view grasps only the myriad of ways in which human beings are buffeted about by the whips and pangs of outrageous fortune. Various destructive causalities wreak damage on the human being, and if that damage is severe enough or enduring enough, the appropriate act is to seek the (physical, psychiatric, familiar, geriatric, etc.) therapist.

With this development, we are beyond Enlightenment criticisms of the ancient paradigms as the framework for understanding sin. What is removed in therapeutic understanding is the notion of sin itself, the very content which constitutes the original Hebraic insight. Accordingly, any contemporary person who would retrieve this ancient notion inherits a multiplicity of criticisms, substitutes, and attempted recoveries. Before us for assessment are the Enlightenment challenges of the old paradigms, the secular correction of liberal views, the pervasive presence of therapeutic understanding as a new paradigm, and the persisting claims of the original Hebraic and Christian symbol. In such a situation, can sin continue to be a way of understanding the human predicament? The question calls for two major explorations: a reformulation of sin in the face of these criticisms and alternatives, and a specific attempt to disentangle sin from its therapeutic rivals and resemblances.

3. A Contemporary Restatement. A contemporary theology of sin faces the formidable task of reformulating this way of viewing the human predicament without depending on the discredited paradigms, and yet avoiding the "natural heresies" which either reduce sin to tragic finitude, or trivialize it as immoral behavior. According to the older symbolism, the human predicament is a historical condition which invades every level of human life and whose character is an idolatrous or absolutizing relation to the worldly environment resulting in the corruption of moral experience.

A contemporary retrieval and restatement of these insights might include the following. (a) As personal, linguistic, and self-transcending beings, humans not only live in a perpetually threatening world, but are reflectively aware of their imperiled situation. Accordingly, they constantly ward off what threatens them and discern and resist their perilous situation. Hence, constituting the very center and structure of the self is a built-in anxiety and a striving for relief, peace, security, understanding, and love; in short, a striving for satisfaction and well-being.

(b) Human beings as we know them do not live in a clear and indisputable relation with the transcendent Creator, but rather in a situation of ambiguity. Accordingly, they respond to their imperilled finitude not on the basis of a divinely wrought security but in a situation of non-security. Unable to tolerate this situation of imperilled finitude and the inescapable anxiety which attends it, human beings "solve" their problem by discovering in their worldly environment the security, peace, and satisfaction which they seek. In other words, fear, anxiety, and yearning blind human beings to the limitations and vulnerabilities of the worldly entity (cause, event, person, style, object, nation, etc.) and, by attributing to it the power to remove the threats to life and being, bestow on it the features of deity.

(c) Insofar as something historical, relative, and vulnerable is grasped as deity, the subject becomes the one for whom the deity is deity, and this centered subject with its idol takes on a false centrality. All the human being's relations to the world are filtered through this anxiety-driven relation of self and idol. The self-idol becomes the reference point for dividing the world into those who promote and those who challenge the idol. This transforms humanizing, sympathetic, and obligatory inclinations (moral experience) into dispositions and acts of control, malice, and destruction.

(d) The human being has inherited from its genetic past biological equipment enabling it to be aggressive in its own self-defense and in its pursuit of the conditions of life and survival. When fear and anxiety lure the human being to absolutizing or to idolatrous relations, this constitutive or "benign" aggressiveness is transformed into inclinations of malice, avarice, distrust, and cupidity which in turn predispose the person toward acts which violate others.

Human being as we know it in history exists in a condition marked by the interrelation between fundamental (ontological) anxiety, the yearning for security and satisfaction, the genetic equipment, and absolutizing ways of being. Instead of originating in a particular time in history, this web of interrelations describes what happens when a self-transcending and imperilled being exists in unsecured ambiguity. The pattern of idolatry (sin) is itself neither an ontological feature like human temporality or embodiment, nor a product of genetically based aggressiveness, but a feature of self-transcending being unable to avoid absolutizing attachments in a situation where the presence of God is ambiguous.

These five brief formulations exemplify one way to recover the content of the symbol, sin, which does not depend on the outmoded literal-historical and biological paradigms. It avoids the Manichaean identification of sin and finitude because it makes sin a response on the part of a self-aware human being to its own situation of anxiety and imperilment. Anxiety and imperilment are the environment and background but not the "cause" of sin. It avoids the Pelagian moralization of the human predicament because it traces immoral inclinations and behaviors back to a pervasive condition of human being in history.

4. Sin in a Therapeutic Age. Can a reformulated theology of sin help clarify sin's relation to and distinction from other dimensions of the human problem? This is a pressing problem for pastoral care, diagnosis, counseling, and psychology because these undertakings all occur in a time and culture which is prone to regard therapeutic as the exhaustive paradigm for understanding the human predicament. There were impelling historical reasons for pastoral care's early alliance with psychology. Psychological knowledge helped care and counseling to correct the tendency to moralize. It facilitated the recognition of pathological elements at work in the situation of care and helped alert the minister to the changing dynamics of age groups, subcultures, and social stratifications. It introduced a new sophistication into the minister's relation to individuals and groups.

But the new psychologies did not lend themselves to limited use. Freudian, Rogerian and other similar approaches are not mere instruments but comprehensive ways of understanding the human problem. At the same time, the cultures as a whole, prompted especially by the social sciences, moved toward a therapeutic ethos and a managed society in which the human predicament is reduced to problems (marital conflict, child abuse, worry and stress, etc.). These problems in turn are grasped as symptoms of distorted social systems. The solution is the management of the social systems and the therapeutic treatment of the symptoms.

In addition, pastoral care was closely associated with the relatively independent academic field of pastoral theology and pastoral psychology in clergy education. The result of these converging events was the displacement of sin and redemption as guiding, interpretive symbols or concepts. This displacement had many forms; e.g., naive identification of redemption with human potential development and the replacement of the content of sin with categories from modern psychological anthropologies. Such a situation especially fosters the need to clearly identify basic paradigms of the human problematic (Freudian, Marxist-political, existentialist, Christian) as well as different strata or dimensions of the human problem.

At least three dimensions appear to be distinguishable: the ontological, the psychopathological, and the theological. The *ontological* dimension describes the problem of the human being at the level of what it means to be an organic, historical, self-transcending being. From hellenic times to the present, literary and philosophical works have depicted this ontological level in *tragic* terms. Thus, the powers, satisfactions, and accomplishments of the human being are tragically interwoven with vulnerability and suffering. The classical theological tradition saw this tragic (suffering) dimension as the consequence of sin. Modern restatements of the dynamics of sin (e.g., by Kierkegaard) see it as the presupposition and matrix of sin. The fear of death, ontological anxiety, the perennial experience of loss and grief, and the constant imperilment of human life are all themes of the ontological problem.

The *psychopathological* dimension describes what happens when the human being responds unsuccessfully to various biological, social, and even ontological victimizations. The role of human responsiveness is stressed or minimized in the current debate over the adequacy of a medical or illness model to interpret this level of problem. Whatever position one takes on that issue, psychopathology names some sort of enduring damage, loss, or dysfunction in human behavior or relations which has at least part of its origin in a "causality," having the character of a victimization; thus, the effects of a traumatic event, a controlling family structure, a body-chemical imbalance, an oppressive institution.

The *theological* dimension of the human predicament is what is under discussion here. The Hebrew-Christian paradigm of sin offers an account of what happens when human beings attempt to escape the ontological problem (anxiety, death) by means of absolutizing attachment.

If pastoral theology as *theology* is to transcend the modern psychologizing of sin and redemption by discerning how the paradigm of sin functions in the activities of care and diagnoses, it needs at least the following: (a) an anthropology which will enable it to sort out and discern various dimensions of the human predicament; (b) an anthropology able to interpret human sociality so as to understand how sin and redemption dispose and structure communities and thus how care can be socially mobilized; (c) an anthropology in which the human

being is both subject to and transcendent of the causalities of its environment; (d) a contemporary formulation of a theology of sin and redemption; (e) a general theory of both the ontological and psychopathological dimensions of the human problem as they relate to sin; (f) an anthropology which clarifies the dimensions of sin itself: thus sin as a pervasive, collective historical condition, as residing in fundamental inclinations, and as occurring in acts and decisions; (g) a theology which clarifies the relations between sin, guilt, and psychological guilt.

Bibliography. St. Anselm, Various essays in *Theology Treatises*, J. Hopkins and H. Richardson, eds. St. Augustine, *The Anti-Pelagian Writings*, NPNF. V. C. Becker, *The Structure of Evil* (1968). J. Calvin, *The Institutes of the Christian Religion* (1762) 2, ch. 1–3. J. Edwards, "Original Sin" in *Works* (1970) 3. P. Hallie, *The Paradox of Cruelty* (1969). P. Homans, *Theology after Freud* (1970). S. Kierkegaard, *Sickness unto Death* (ET 1975 [1944]); *The Concept of Anxiety* (ET 1980). L. Levalle, *Evil and Suffering* (1963). S. MacIsaac, *Freud and Original Sin* (1974). J. Müller, *The Christian Doctrine of Sin*, 2 vols., (1852). P. Ricoeur, "Original Sin: a Study in Meaning", in *The Conflict of Interpretations* (1974); *The Symbolism of Evil* (1967); *Fallible Man* (1965). H. Rondet, *Original Sin: the Patristic and Theological Background* (1972). H. S. Smith, *Changing Conceptions of Original Sin* (1955). F. R. Tennant, *The Origin and Propagation of Sin*, Lectures I and II (1902); *The Sources of the Doctrines of the Fall and Original Sin* (1903). M. F. Thelen, *Man as Sinner in Contemporary American Realistic Theology* (1946). N. P. Williams, *The Idea of the Fall and Original Sin* (1927).

E. FARLEY

FREEDOM AND BONDAGE; GUILT; LEGALISM AND ANTINO-MIANISM; SEVEN DEADLY SINS; TEMPTATION; UNPARDON-ABLE SIN. *See also* CASUISTRY; FORGIVENESS; GRACE, *or* MORAL THEOLOGY, *or* SALVATION, AND PASTORAL CARE; PENANCE, SACRAMENT OF; REPENTANCE AND CONFESSION. *Compare* ALIENATION/ESTRANGEMENT; ANOMIE/NORMLESSNESS; DOUBT AND UNBELIEF; HUMAN CONDITION/PREDICAMENT; RESISTANCE.

SIN, CONVICTION OF. *See* GUILT; REPENTANCE AND CONFESSION; SIN/SINS.

SIN, UNPARDONABLE. *See* UNPARDONABLE SIN.

SIN AND SICKNESS. The nature of pastoral care in the Hebrew and Christian communities since before the writing of Job has been shaped by the way the relationship between these realities has been understood. Every pastoral theology has had to choose a stance concerning that relationship, which has occasioned major controversies and has been pivotal in determining the nature of ministerial function.

1. Introduction and Historical Overview. All of Hebrew-Christian history has been concerned about this question. The ancient story that provides the framework for the book of Job asks whether suffering is always caused by sin. It appeared in response to a cultural setting that saw God's justice represented by a direct connection between consciously chosen evil and concrete physical suffering. The prophets broadened and politicized this view. The theme continues with the disciples' question in John 9:2: "Who sinned, this man or his father?" Jesus' response, "It was not this man who sinned, nor his parents," suggests that a different view was developing, though Paul's conviction that the wages of sin is death reveals a direct connection between sin and physical deterioration in the mind of the early church. The linkage persisted into modern times in the stigma associated with psychiatric illness into the nineteenth century, and with cancer in the first half of the twentieth century.

Since pastoral practice in every century has centered on freeing persons from the consequences of sin, identifying sin and its signs has always been a major task. Common themes of that discussion include: (1) Sin always carries negative consequences, and some of those are felt immediately after the sin, in this life; (2) those consequences typically include physical suffering, mental conflict and distress, and spiritual emptiness and estrangement; and (3) though much suffering is caused by sin, some suffering is independent of it.

There is now emerging a wholistic and naturalistic understanding of the link between sin and sickness, providing new clarity as to the means by which the sins of the families are visited upon the offspring to the seventh generation. A particular type of habitual living pattern, a mixture of sin and health, makes heart attack more likely; another increases the risk of cancer; another potentiates ulcers, and so on. Psychologically, a given variety of family sin predisposes children to schizophrenia; another to character disorder; another to chronic depression; another to hysteria, etc.

2. Sickness and Judgment. Throughout the theological spectrum, wherever any connection is seen between sin and sickness, the sickness is related to or part of God's judgment upon the sin. There are at least three prototypical ways to conceive that relationship, and three modes of pastoral activity follow from them.

a. Classical theism. At the right-hand end of the theological spectrum, where God is seen as unambiguously personal and omnipotent, sickness and other suffering can only be understood as God's choice. Much of that God-chosen sickness is judgment for sin. The only other possibility, given a good God, is the revelation of some good greater than the evil of the sickness. This position requires a belief that God exercises minute control of most natural process, but holds persons tightly responsible for disobedience in areas allotted to personal sovereignty.

Pastoral activity, when directed by this theology, has held that the illness is a sign that repentance is urgently needed; and has sought to identify the sin and seek repentance. It has seen healing as a natural consequence of restored right relation to God, and God as the personal agent of the healing. Or, conversely, it has sought to discern God's purpose in allowing the pain, if no judgment is seen, since "it must be God's will."

b. Dualism. In this worldview, there is one realm of existence where physical law always rules, and another in which God's judgment and spiritual strength operate. Atheism is a special case of this position, in that the second realm is canceled out and the former stands alone. In the atheistic perspective, most physical suffering is unrelated to sin or God, and is considered completely the result of natural forces. In the theistic worldview, psychological illness is often seen as a direct sign of moral failure or insufficient faith.

Pastoral practice under this theology is largely sustaining in the face of inevitable suffering. It is inspirational, suppressive, and other-worldly. It also provides guidance in avoiding the escapable material ills; and identifies those points, largely marked by the breaking though of the unconscious, where God's judgment was to be seen. Faithfulness is identified with holding uplifting conscious attitudes.

c. The wholistic position. Here it is understood that the psychological, spiritual, and physical aspects of life interpenetrate one another, so there is no point at which all are not operating together. Spiritual emptiness and psychological disequilibrium always increase physical vulnerability and/or pain; physical injury or illness always increase the obstacles to spiritual and psychological health. Sin directly weakens and damages sinners, cutting them off from the source of strength; no personal intervention of God is required. Sickness is rarely present without estrangement from God and self having first weakened the sufferer.

Pastoral activity is concerned primarily with helping the sufferer locate the causal links and change damaging behavior, so the healing connection with the divine and the neighbor can be reestablished. It focuses on reconciling and healing, with special attention to resolving grief and guilt, which are two spiritual-psychological pains with strong influence on physical health.

3. Salvation and Healing. Sin and sickness are deviant conditions, revealing the individual's failure or inability to be governed by those forces which make for wholeness. The reverse processes are repentance of and redemption from specific sins, or salvation from the state of sin; and healing from sickness. Both denote the reestablishment of a right relationship with that which makes for health, be it God and/or physical self-repair. The terms used differ with the theological options.

In classical theism, salvation and healing are closely and sequentially connected. Salvation is the primary concern. When it is achieved, healing is expected to follow, if the illness was God's judgment. If not judgment, then opportunity for revelation is seen in the distress. The revelation locates a message in the sickness, either for the sufferer or another; and becomes an aid to salvation for one or both.

In the dualistic position, salvation and healing are separated. As sickness does not come from sin, release from sin is seen as having no influence on physical healing. Man as machine and medicine as mechanics are independent of the spirit, and the mind and soul can be purified without reference to social or physical conditions. This view has encouraged Christians to seek release from physical and social ills in faith and hope for the hereafter, and has difficulty accounting for points where faith seems affected by social or psychological factors; or where healing results from interventions as much spiritual as mechanical.

From the wholistic stance, healing and salvation are seen as similar and/or closely intertwined processes. Any action that enhances one area of life enhances all. Salvation and healing describe different aspects of the same process. For the wholistically oriented pastor, salvation typically means a state and process of reciprocal and freely flowing interchange and cooperation with the physical world, other persons, and God; with the eschatological component left as mystery and the communal ecological aspects predominant.

4. Pastoral Care of the Sick and Sinful. This has typically been the top priority for most pastors, though the emphasis varies from era to era.

a. In physical illness. Parishioner expectations and the pastor's calling to be comforter or liberator in the face of danger, pain, and potential death make this the first call on most pastors' time. This is true across the theological spectrum, as serious illness represents a crucial chance for repentance and reassessment of lifestyle for the pastor, and for others. The crisis may be seen by all as a point of possible liberation.

The CPE movement developed in part from pastors' commitment to be more effective in this ministry. It spawned an educational arm in the Association for Clinical Pastoral Education, and contributed to the development of a group specializing in clinical services in medical settings: the College of Chaplains of the American Hospital Association.

b. In psychological illness. Conditions marked by intensely unpleasant feelings and thoughts have also been a major pastoral priority. Though there are influences from heredity and chemistry, most "mental illness" is as close to the traditional concept of sin as to that of sickness. It flows from the choice and/or development of a way of life that generates the symptoms.

The first signs of these difficulties are often brought to the pastor: depression, anxiety, and anger. They are often visible to the pastor in administrative or pastoral care settings. Both conditions make clergy an important resource for identification and treatment, which typically consists of identifying long-forgotten decisions that unknowingly eliminated major avenues to satisfaction; and reinstituting the possibility of a new choice. The clergy's commitment to a treatment so close to its traditional function has produced the pastoral counseling movement, and its primary accrediting body, The American Association of Pastoral Counselors.

c. In overt and explicit sin. Prior to the last century, the countering of obvious sin has been the clergy's dominant concern. This emphasis bore visible and misguided fruit in the excesses of the Inquisition and the Protestant theocracies, but was a fundamental part of Christian practice through the Catholic confessional and Protestant moralism for ages. The revulsion against the former and the trivialization of the latter have led to a reduced emphasis on sin in the liberal churches, though the evangelical wing continues its attention to individual morality. As Menninger pointed out, liberals now identify what used to be called sin as either illness or crime. This led to a dangerous situation in which individual sin is rarely discussed in the liberal church, and corporate sin goes largely unnoticed on the conservative side. There is a clear need for liberals to reclaim the idea of sin, to give it content that expresses current theology, and to restore it to use as a diagnostic term that can enable, not condemnation, but conviction, repentance, and newness of life. This is a large and fertile field for today's pastoral theology.

d. An emerging resynthesis. The wholistic health movement, the humanistic psychologies, and a new pastoral attentiveness to sin appear to be working together to produce a shared understanding of human pathology. All center around the choice and development of character. Aarne Siirala stated in *The Voice of Illness*, "a way of life is also a way of death." Starting with childhood, an individual faces a given environment with finite resources, information, and dangers. Each one chooses, on the basis of constitutional factors plus the available information and resources, a way to cope with the dangers and to reach for safety and satisfaction. Each choice influences later choices, and ultimately produces a characteristic way of addressing life; and each way includes practices that endanger the body, damage communion with God and neighbor, and carry the potential for psychological distress. It increasingly appears that the same choices damage in all three ways.

The pastoral response is to lovingly locate the points of deviation from a godly and joyous line of development; to help the individual identify the sources of hopelessness that led to the deviation; to reclaim the hope that would make a new risk possible; and to support the resulting growth toward abundant life in communion with God and the creation.

Bibliography. D. Browning, *Moral Context of Pastoral Care* (1976). A. Boisen, *Out of the Depths* (1960). B. W. Grant, *From Sin to Wholeness* (1982). S. Hiltner, *Preface to Pastoral Theology* (1958); *Theological Dynamics* (1972). J. McNeill, *History of the Care of Souls* (1951). C. Menninger, *Whatever Became of Sin?* (1979). A. Siirala, *The Voice of Illness* (1964).

B. W. GRANT

HEALTH AND ILLNESS; RELIGION AND HEALTH; SALVATION, HEALING, AND HEALTH; SUFFERING. *See also* CREATION, DOCTRINE OF, AND PASTORAL CARE; EVIL; FAITH HEALING. *Compare* PSYCHOSOMATIC ILLNESS; SECONDARY GAIN.

SINGING. *See* MUSIC AS MODE OF CARE; WORSHIP AND CELEBRATION.

SINGLE PARENTS. A single parent, narrowly defined, is someone who has unshared responsibility for the care and direction of his or her child or children. More broadly, a single parent is someone who lives in a separate household with his or her child or children and who has no partner living with them to share directly in the parenting responsibilities.

In some ways the phrase "single parent" is both misleading and culturally biased. Except in situations of death or abandonment, family systems continue to affect and be affected by the parent who does not live within the household. There continues to be an interdependence and relationship around parenting that makes the phrase misleading. In many ways, parents are forever, even if the structure of the family changes. The use of the phrase may also contribute to the prejudice against the "other parent." There seems to be clear and emerging evidence that access to and involvement with both parents is beneficial to children and to both parents (Pepper, 1982). The sanctioning of the "single parent" makes the other parent more invisible and increases the burden on the parent with whom the children primarily live.

It seems wiser to view the single parent as someone who has a separate household and who has no partner living there to share daily in the direct and immediate responsibilities of parenting. The more narrow definition of the single parent as someone who has unshared responsibilities for the care and direction of his or her children would apply accurately to only a small percentage, primarily to those widowed, never married, or abandoned. The majority of single-parent households are created by marital separations and divorce, and thus represent a reorganized family system in which relationships between parents and children are transformed and redefined. Both parents must face parenting singly while the children live with them (Goldsmith, 1982).

Single-parent households have sharply increased since 1970, with an increase of over fifty percent. Currently twenty percent of the children in the U.S. live primarily with only one parent. The increase may best be attributed to the dramatic increase in marital separations and divorces and to the increasing number of unmarried mothers who are choosing to have and keep their babies. The number of single-parent households created by the death of the spouse has not changed appreciably. Between eighty and ninety percent of single-parent households are headed by mothers. For blacks, the single-parent household is three times more common—forty-five percent compared to fifteen percent for whites (Weiss, 1979; Peterson, 1982).

1. **Emotional and Social Adjustments.** The emotional and social adjustments that single parents must make is colored by the route by which the family became a single parent household. The experience of grief, bereavement, and mourning over the loss of a partner, husband, lover, and family member is different, depending on the kind of relationship that existed prior to the loss. In widowhood, death may be felt as a deep wound and sad loss yet need not carry with it the ambivalence or sense of living with one's own choices that can be present in divorce or parenthood without marriage. Widowhood is viewed as an occasion to rally community support, to share sadness over loss, to feel compassion and empathy for those left. If there are bitter or angry feelings, these are seen as appropriate and expectable and are tolerated. Financially, insurance may help the family through an initial adjustment period.

The experience of loss in separation and divorce and parenthood without marriage is viewed differently. It is clear that grief is a part of the experience, whether the decision was made by or for the parent. Yet the element of choice seems to make community response less sympathetic, less supportive, less understanding. There is an attitude of moral indignation, "So you've made your bed, now lie in it." This makes grieving all the more difficult. The element of choice makes it harder to complain. Financially, too, there are fewer resources, and everyone ends up living at a lower economic standard. The guilt, anger, feelings of rejection, and ambivalence that go into separations, divorces, and decisions to raise children alone are intense and profound. Widows and widowers thus have a difficult time understanding the experience of these single parents.

One experience that all single parents have in common is their beginning a new life amidst disruption. Death, the breakup of a marriage, pregnancy, and the pressures to decide what to do all create a situation of confusion and disorganization. It is in the midst of all this that signifi-

cant reorganization and restructuring needs to occur in order for the family to cope. The work of running a home, providing child care, and providing an income to live on call for a reorganization and redistribution of responsibilities. Other adults may need to be brought into the family (relatives, housekeepers, friends) and adjustments made to these new adults. Questions of authority and boundaries are rampant.

Routines must be changed and adjusted to the new situation with its available personnel. Older children may be called on to help out. Times when children are without supervision (e.g., latchkey children) are frequent. The requirement to return to work or continue work with a different sense of necessity puts the single parent under new pressures. Out of the crisis created by the necessities to adapt and change, a restructuring of the family usually occurs. Things cannot and do not go on as before.

The most significant structural change has to do with the ending of the parental echelon (Weiss, 1979). It is difficult, if not impossible, to keep the same distance and authority without a parental partner; and it is probably not desirable or functional. It is clear that sharing responsibility for family management with children is the most common pattern. Parents become closer to their children. The family is run more democratically. Children's self-reliance and capacity to function in adult ways are fostered. There are clear benefits and disadvantages to this family reorganization and restructuring.

2. **Benefits.** Common prejudice labels single-parent homes as broken, deviant, or high risk. While indeed a healthier situation exists when there are both a mother and father who care for and are supportive of one another and who form a team in caring for their children, there can also be some benefits to raising children in a single-parent household under certain circumstances. In situations of separation and divorce, the reduction of tensions and conflicts between partners creates better home situations for children. They are able to relate to each parent with less divided loyalty and more spontaneity. If adequate access to both parents is maintained, children can grow and prosper. In situations of parents who have never married, the decision not to marry may be made with the judgment that a fruitful, viable marriage would not be possible. Thus, the possibilities of future tensions and conflicts are avoided. Many people who divorce, separate, or decide not to marry do so for sound reasons. The decision can be an opportunity to improve self-esteem, to take more conscious control and responsibility over one's life, and to grow and develop. Both fathers and mothers are called to reappraise their relationships with their children. With limited time, the possibility of greater intentionality in developing a special relationship is there. This development of a special, closer, more egalitarian relationship with children seems to be the benefit that crosses most single-parent households, irrespective of the route taken in becoming such. The possibility for personal development and growth seems to be the second benefit.

3. **Problems.** Along with these benefits, however, there are also some clear problems. Most single parents experience being overwhelmed at times. There is too much work to be done. There isn't enough time or energy. There isn't enough help and no one to turn to when

limits are reached, both physically and emotionally. Children tend to have intense reactions to loss. They experience confusion, feelings of guilt and rejection.

Judith Wallerstein's Divorce Project (Wallerstein, 1989) found that the pain and sense of loss experienced by children of divorce was severe. Most of the children felt isolated, had strong feelings of powerlessness and confusion, and had a multitude of symptoms from school problems to more severe psychiatric symptoms that reflected anxieties about their own survival. Parents in the midst of coping for themselves are called upon also to handle their children's pain and problems. The guilt many single parents feel makes these challenges that much more difficult.

Finally, the disappearance of the other parent, the loss of contact in families where death has not occurred, brings with it additional problems. Wallerstein found that all of the 131 children she studied intensely longed for the absent parent's return. Too often, the single parent with primary care or custody is left with full responsibility for the children, emotionally, physically, and financially. The other parent becomes more and more peripheral. The other parent, who is usually the father, must also deal with a painful sense of loss, of having few and circumscribed times to be with his children. His sense of roots is disturbed, his home is lost, his routine with his family is changed (Roman, 1979). Both parents and children can end up hurt by the breakup. The process of healing may take from two to four years or longer.

4. Coping Strategies and Ministry. If guidelines for coping with parenting alone can be offered, they would probably focus on four areas: developing a support base; lowering and changing expectations; balancing personal and family needs; and seeing the new situation as an opportunity for growth and grace. The need for support to the parent has always been there. In the single-parent household, new sources of support need to be found. Extended families, friends, support groups, and the other parent can all help. The use of relatives seems obvious, yet the ethic of self-sufficiency may make it hard for many to feel comfortable asking for help. Friends can be invaluable. Support groups, such as Parents Without Partners, Young Single Parents, or Phoenix groups provide adult company and support. The single most important resource can be the other parent. This requires distinguishing spousal from parental relationships and a commitment to the children's best interest (Ricci, 1980; Galper, 1978). Co-parenting has real potential for reducing the burdens both parents and children experience. Co-parenting need not mean fifty-fifty physical sharing. Rather, it means psychological parenting by both and a commitment to provide stability and consistency in the parent-child relationships.

The second challenge for the single parent involves understanding the changes in structure, organization, and functioning of the family. Accepting these changes and lowering the expectations for how things *should* be requires some growth and maturity. Roles, distribution, exercise of authority, times together, material wants and needs, and personal freedoms are just some of the areas where expectations face revision.

A third challenge is basically a moral one, namely, how to balance the needs of the family and the personal needs of the parent. Recognizing the needs of the parent for adult companionship and time away from the family is often difficult when guilt is present for being responsible for the children's loss of the other parent. Still, it is critical for the parents to care for themselves so that they will have something to give to their children.

The fourth challenge is a spiritual one, namely, being able to see opportunity amidst loss and grace amidst disruption. To see hope rather than despair calls for a personal search within.

The church and its ministry can help the single parent on many fronts. It can provide needed backup and support in terms of child care, support groups, and acceptance of single parent households in the life of the congregation. It can soften the judgments against single parents and promote understanding. It can help single parents to put their guilt into perspective and learn from their new situations that grace is possible. It can offer love, acceptance, and hope, both to the children and to the parent or parents. The largest challenge for ministry, however, lies in overcoming the prejudices that prevent effective co-parenting to be fostered and encouraged.

Bibliography. P. Ashdown-Sharp, *A Guide to Pregnancy and Parenthood for Women on Their Own* (1977). E. Atkin and E. Rubin, *Part Time Father* (1976). B. Barnes and J. Coplon, *The Single-Parent Experience: Workshop Models for Family Life Education* (1980). D. Davenport, *One Parent Families: A Practical Guide to Coping* (1979). M. Galper, *Co-Parenting* (1978). R. Gardner, *The Parents Book About Divorce* (1977). J. Goldsmith, "The Postdivorce Family System," in F. Walsh, ed., *Normal Family Processes* (1982). C. Klein, *The Single Parent Experience* (1973). A. Pepper, *Single Again: This Time with Children* (1982). See especially summary of 1979 Kentucky Fried Chicken Institute Single Parent Study, pp. 202–10. L. Peterson, "Single Parents and Working Mothers," in *Family Therapy News* 13:6 (1982). I. Ricci, *Mom's House/Dad's House* (1980). M. Roman and W. Haddad, *The Disposable Parent* (1979). M. Shepard and G. Goldman, *Divorced Dads* (1980). J. S. Wallerstein, *Surviving the Breakup* (1980). J. S. Wallerstein and S. Blakeslee, *Second Chances: Men, Women and Children a Decade After Divorce* (1989). R. Weiss, *Going It Alone* (1979).

J. H. SHACKELFORD

FAMILY, JEWISH *or* PASTORAL CARE AND COUNSELING OF. *See also* DIVORCE (Care and Counseling); DIVORCED PERSONS; GRIEF AND LOSS; PARENTS/PARENTHOOD; SINGLE PERSONS.

SINGLE PERSONS, JEWISH CARE AND COUNSELING OF. In a tradition that valued family as a cornerstone of community, a decision to remain single was, in effect, not only a denial of a sacred obligation "to be fruitful and multiply" but was tantamount to turning one's back on the Jewish community. From a traditional vantage point, to remain single was not an option but a disgrace. For this reason, the existence of single persons as an identifiable group within the Jewish community is a comparatively recent phenomenon.

Traditionally, the Jewish community recognized children and adults. At puberty children became adults with the adult responsibility of establishing their own families. Marriages tended to take place relatively early in life, frequently with financial support from the bride's parents, or as soon as it was possible for a young man to establish himself. The matchmaker (*shadhan*), who can be looked upon as a semi-official functionary of the Jewish community, performed an essential service for the unmarried by seeking out an appropriate mate. Maiden aunts or bachelor uncles who had defied the efforts of the matchmaker were regarded as parts of the families they lived with, not as entities in their own right.

One of the first clearly identifiable groups of Jewish singles was that which emerged on the modern college campus. To meet the needs of Jewish college youth, the first B'nai Brith Hillel Foundation was established on the campus of the University of Illinois in 1923. Today, Hillel offers a wide variety of religious, educational, cultural, and social programs at over 415 colleges where about 400,000 students are enrolled. Jewish students are encouraged to seek out the Hillel director, who is usually a rabbi, to discuss personal issues and problems.

With the 1960s another group of Jewish singles began to emerge, as Jews who attended college away from home never returned home to live and postponed marriage to the mid- or late twenties. While at first this phenomenon applied only to Jewish males, in the late 1960s it came to be increasingly true for Jewish females. In response, Jewish community centers and synagogues initiated social, educational, and cultural programs and Jewish family service offered individual and group counseling sessions for these Jewish singles.

While the Havurah movement (a *havurah* is any group or association but usually one that joins together for a specific purpose) was not primarily created either by singles or marrieds, it tended to serve both of these groups who were often isolated from their home communities and whose sense of alienation was high. It was an attempt on the part of young people to identify with Jewishness.

It is only within the past decade that the synagogue has both incorporated the Havurah movement and addressed itself to the large number of Jews who remain single into their late twenties and early thirties. This population has grown significantly in recent years because of later first marriages, later childbearing years, an increasing divorce rate among Jewish couples, and the large investment of energy now required to explore career opportunities. As a result, the number of Jewish adults who are not married is now so large that no Jewish institution can ignore them. Jewish community centers and synagogues now almost invariably have a wide variety of educational, cultural, religious, and social programs for singles. Quite often, particularly in the larger synagogues and centers, specialized programs for groups of singles have been offered in specific age categories. In addition, these institutions are becoming more and more sensitive to the need for sponsoring programs where singles can come together and talk about their loneliness, insecurities, and frustrations.

Programs to help singles cope more effectively respond to a vital personal need and also serve to reinforce Jewish identity. The rabbi is often instrumental in initiating many of these programs but is usually not directly involved in their implementation. While the rabbi customarily makes hospital visits and provides office time for singles seeking counsel, regular home visitations are not the norm except in response to specific requests.

As the Jewish community has come to embrace the concept of zero population growth philosophically and practically, with most Jews limiting their families to one or two children, childbearing years can legitimately begin at thirty. The sacred obligation to have children is still important but increasing attention is being given to enhancing the quality of one's own life and improving the quality of life for the next generation. Thus, as the number of Jewish singles has increased, as society has given recognition to the legitimacy of being single, and as Judaism has come to reaffirm individual growth as a basic value, Jewish singles have emerged as a separate identifiable entity within the Jewish community.

I. H. FISHBEIN

JEWISH CARE AND COUNSELING (History, Traditions, and Contemporary Issues); PERSON (Jewish Perspective). *See also* FAMILY, JEWISH THEOLOGY AND ETHICS OF; HAVURAH. *Compare* COMMUNITY, FELLOWSHIP, AND CARE; RELATIONSHIP NETWORK.

SINGLE PERSONS, PASTORAL CARE AND COUNSELING OF. Those who have never married, are separated, divorced, or widowed. Beyond this simple definition, however, no common profile of the single person is possible, and generalizations are often misleading. Singles may live alone, within families or intentional communities, or with their children. They may have no children, have joint custody, or be prevented from seeing their children. They may live with a housemate or be cohabitating or have a "committed relationship." They also vary regarding economic situation and the period of life in which they are single. Their singleness may be temporary or permanent, voluntary or involuntary. In all cases, however, "single" is a term denoting social status that acquires meaning largely by negation of the legal term "married". It is a residual category suggesting that alternative lifestyles are contrary to the assumed or prescribed social norm.

1. Social and Cultural Background. *a. Statistics.* For every married couple in the U.S. there is a single adult. Since 1950, singles have increased from one-fourth to one-third of the U.S. population over nineteen. While these figures do not take homosexual couples into account, they do reflect that single-person households have increased from 10.9 percent in 1950 to 22.6 percent in 1980. This trend is explained in part by the increase of elderly persons, especially widows who maintain their own homes; later first marriages; and the higher incidence of divorce. Of the population over nineteen, singles comprise 28 percent of the men and 35 percent of the women. Of *singles* over nineteen, 42 percent are men and 58 percent are women.

b. Stereotypes. Singles are stereotypically pictured as young, attractive, and having fun, and in our culture are often looked upon with envy. But while this image of the single person is approximately true for some, it leaves more out than it puts in. It is important to remember that this image is a stereotype laden with fantasy, not an accurate depiction of single persons or the single life in all or even most instances. Many single persons are in their middle or later years, and many that are young have social, economic, and personal situations far removed from the stereotype. In any case singles, even those who approximate the popular image, share in the general human condition. They celebrate triumphs, suffer failures, enjoy pleasures, and bear disappointments, anxieties, and losses. Like most human beings today, including married persons, singles must struggle to find a sense of meaning and purpose, to satisfy and reconcile their divergent needs for intimacy and autonomy, and to find ways to give something back to life.

2. **Pastoral Issues and Concerns.** *a. Social relationships and isolation.* Unfortunately, there is little research literature on the psychosocial issues of single living. It seems likely, however, that forming and maintaining social relationships in the absence of immediate family ties constitutes a major ongoing task for many single adults. Most human beings have a deep need for primary social interaction—the human touch. When there is no nuclear or extended family to meet this need, singles must find alternative networks of care and nurture. The workplace is a frequent source, as are recreational and avocational clubs and church-sponsored groups. Such contexts, however, have other dynamics and limitations that often do not satisfy deeper longings for community. In addition, older singles who lack such opportunities or the means to take advantage of them may consequently suffer serious social isolation. (Some research suggests that the isolated elderly person is also a stereotype.) Some young urban singles frequent "singles bars," though many are not happy with the unimaginative settings and disappointing results. For singles of all ages there is in fact a dearth of acceptable settings where single persons can meet their needs in creative, nonabusive ways.

b. Emotional and sexual issues. Singles may nor may not feel lonely, depending on personality strengths and social conditions; but there is little doubt that single persons must come to terms with their aloneness. For younger persons the role may seem normal and familiar, especially since the age at which first marriages occur is gradually increasing in our society. However, many who are single again, through death or divorce, feel like strangers in a strange land. Social patterns, opportunities, and expectations are at once exciting, frightening, and confusing. While their friends may be dealing with an empty nest, they may have no nest at all. And for those who have never married, singlehood may entail anxieties about finding a marriage partner or feelings of being inferior and unlovable. On the other hand, some singles clearly enjoy the greater freedom and mobility of the single life when finances permit, often gaining their principal pleasure through work and career or avocational pursuits.

Sexuality and sexual expression are uniquely problematic issues for single person. Sexual relationships can be meaningful and congruent with the level of commitment. As with those who are married, however, sex may also be compensatory, used as an antidepressant to soften pain, as a substitute for intimacy, as an expression of anger or hostility, or for reassurance. Undoubtedly, the failure of the church to provide a constructive sexual ethic for single persons contributes to the problems and uncertainties in the sex life of many singles.

Unfortunately, discussions of sex ethics in the church usually focus on adolescent premarital sex, extramarital sex, and to a lesser degree on homosexuality. Churches typically avoid discussing sex in relation to adult single life. Thus some singles may struggle with guilt under traditional restrictive ethics. Others may turn to the popular values portrayed in mass media or practices of various subcultures, and suffer the consequences of superficial and distorted value systems. What is needed is a biblically grounded understanding of sexuality not only as a need inherent in human nature, but as a way of being in the world as male and female. Such an understanding would also involve a way of being in friendship and community, participating in God's passion for right relationship, and experiencing God's gracious compassion toward all members of the human family. Working out such a sexual ethic as a part of the task of defining singlehood is necessary not only for the future of the church as a diverse, accepting community of faith, but also for the care and counseling of individuals whose struggles, as single persons, are in part derived from uncertain and unclear normative understandings of their life situations.

c. Developmental issues and family context. A capacity for intimate, caring human relationships is a complex developmental achievement perhaps never attained completely by anyone, single or married. But it is important for the pastor to understand that just as being married does not assure that one has the capacity for intimacy, so never having married does not in itself indicate that one has failed at this developmental task. Genuine, mature intimacy, the realistic capacity to love and care, can take many social and cultural forms besides marriage and family. By the same token, some persons apparently do remain single in part because of unresolved developmental issues, just as some persons marry for similar reasons. A lingering unconscious family dependency or anger, unresolved guilt or grief, a fear of genuine intimacy, excessive need for emotional distance and control, or questions of sexual identity are among the factors that may be involved.

In evaluating such possibilities for counseling purposes it is helpful also to consider the family context or "system" as well as the individual developmental history. Some nuclear families are structured around "invisible loyalties," such that one or more children find it difficult to form committed relationships beyond the family. Thus family therapy may prove more helpful than individual counseling in situations where a person experiences singleness itself to be a problem and seeks help.

d. Social and cultural factors. It is important to remember that social and economic circumstances, demographic distributions, cultural patterns, and other sociological factors all play a part in determining whether individuals marry, remarry, or remain single. The disproportionately large number of single women in relation to single men in midlife and later life, for instance, is a powerful factor influencing remarriage possibilities for bereaved and divorced women. Thus it is possible to overemphasize psychological factors in forming evaluative impressions of particular individuals for whom singleness presents itself as a source of pain or difficulty. Furthermore, being single in itself is not, or should not be, a problem or a curse, as such judgments may imply. The problem may lie as much or more with the culture that defines authentic personhood in terms of marriage as with anything in particular to the individual, though individual factors may also be present.

e. Moral and religious issues. It would be misleading to suggest that single persons experience moral and religious questions utterly unique to their social status, but it may well be true that single living does tend to accent certain themes and questions of a religious or moral character, despite the wide variety of circumstances in which a person can be single—young, old, bereaved, divorced, and so forth. Probably the most common of these concerns is the uncertain moral status attributed to singlehood as such. Because marriage is so pervasively experienced as the norm, those who are single, even perhaps aged widows and widowers, may experience a subtle rejection, suspicion, or stigmatization from married people (or even other singles), which reflects the fact that singlehood has not received a positive moral interpretation in our society. This in turn inevitably raises questions of self-worth and concomitant questions about the meaning and importance of marriage, family, and community. The underlying issue is how one can experience the love of God in a culture in which one's social status and identity are felt to be somehow under question or suspicion. This may overstate the experience for many singles, but there may be an element of truth here that applies more widely and deeply to the single experience than is commonly acknowledged.

Other moral and religious concerns commonly related to singlehood include questions concerning sexuality as well as the nature and importance of friendship, intimacy, and community. There are also questions concerning what Erik Erikson calls "generativity," the capacity to work and care for persons, projects, and values beyond oneself. When parenting is not involved, single living can offer many opportunities for commitment and service to wider human values, or it can become an invitation to self-absorption or self-centered pursuits under the guise of self-fulfillment. On the other hand, singles who have parenting responsibilities easily become exhausted by the task and often need, for their children's sake as well as their own, to claim more time and space for themselves within their moral commitment to parenthood. Other single parents resent their children and long for the real or imagined freedoms of childless living. Probably most single parents experience some of both feelings. In either case, however, the dilemma is more than a purely emotional or psychological problem; it involves understandings of what it means to be a responsible, mature human being, the value of generativity (in the form of parenthood), the purpose of life, and the nature of human fulfillment.

3. Pastoral Responses. *a. Leadership and care.* Pastoral response to the needs of singles, within the context of the whole church, needs to relate flexibly and empathetically to the inner meaning as well as outer circumstances of the single's world. This may mean leadership and challenge along with support and care, and education along with nurture. It may mean helping singles achieve the capacity to deal creatively with their particular uncertainties, disappointments, and failures: to be hurt without becoming hard, to develop a faith that embraces life openly (but not naively), to experience a sense of acceptance and Providence in their lives.

It may also mean helping singles find a meaningful place in the work and worship of the religious community, which is typically centered on marriage and two-parent family relationships, to the neglect or exclusion of single persons and single parents. Obviously this task requires pastoral vision and leadership to help the whole community find forms of common life, worship, and witness that are as much accepting of single persons as of those who are married. This, as much or more than individual care and counseling, defines the pastoral task relating to singles today. But while support groups can address the special needs of singles, care must be taken to avoid unnecessarily segregating and thereby stigmatizing single persons. Meanwhile, the church that continues to focus its ministry exclusively on married people and families perpetuates traditional prejudices against singles and contributes to the social pressure to marry.

b. Toward an ethic of single life. The degree to which being single will become more accepted and institutionalized in church and society is currently not clear. But there is clearly a need for the church to give leadership in defining the meaning and value of singlehood (and single parenthood) in a way that affirms its dignity and worth without undermining the value of marriage and two-parent family life. One creative way of doing this might be to develop an understanding of singlehood as a calling or "vocation" related to specific times and circumstances and to the unique gifts and limitations of individuals. Such a vocation would represent, like other callings, a particular way of entering into a hearty and ameliorative participation in and service to God's world. It would differ from the traditional Catholic concept of religious life in its departure from the ideal of celibacy and the taking of irrevocable, lifelong vows. It would be similar in distinguishing a form of Christian life in which love, care, commitment, and service are not defined in terms of marriage and family as the explicit or implicit norm. As a task of practical theology, the work could be conceived as that of developing the biblical notion that covenant or a mutually faithful relationship is of the essence of God, God's relation to humankind, and the relation of human beings to one another, and by envisioning ways in which this truth might be fulfilled apart from (as well as through) marriage. Recognizing that most adults in contemporary Western society will be single at some time during their adult lives, that some young people are postponing marriage, and that many widowed and divorced persons for various reasons will not remarry, it becomes clear that a major practical theological challenge of our time is to integrate these new realities into the cherished values of the tradition. This will require exploring anew the meaning of personhood, of community, of singleness, and of marriage.

Bibliography. R. K. Brown, *Reach Out to Singles* (1979). N. B. Christoff, *Saturday Night, Sunday Morning* (1978). J. R. Landgraf, *Creative Singlehood and Pastoral Care* (1982). W. Lyon, *A Pew for One, Please* (1977). P. J. Stein, ed., *Single Life: Unmarried Adults in Social Context* (1981). H. Vande Kemp and G. P. Schreck, "The Church's Ministry to Singles: A Family Mode," *J. of Religion and Health,* 20 (1981), 141–55.

R. O. EVANS
R. J. HUNTER
A. R. OSTROM

DIVORCED PERSONS; SINGLE PARENTS. *See also* COHABITATION; COMMUNITY, FELLOWSHIP, AND CARE; FAMILY THEORY AND THERAPY; LONELINESS; RELATIONSHIP NETWORK; SEXUAL ISSUES IN PASTORAL CARE; SEXUALITY, CHRISTIAN *or* JEWISH THEOLOGY AND ETHICS OF; SOCIAL ISOLATION. *Compare* MARRIAGE (Christian *or* Jewish Theology and Care).

SISTER, PASTOR AS. *See* PASTOR (Normative and Traditional Images); WOMEN IN PASTORAL MINISTRIES, HISTORY OF.

SISTERS/SISTERHOOD. *See* WOMEN, PSYCHOLOGY OF.

SITUATION ANALYSIS. *See* EVALUATION AND DIAGNOSIS, PSYCHOLOGICAL; INTERPRETATION AND HERMENEUTICS, PASTORAL; THEORY IN PASTORAL CARE AND COUNSELING, FUNCTION OF.

SITUATION ETHICS. *See* ETHICS AND PASTORAL CARE; MORAL DILEMMAS IN PASTORAL PERSPECTIVE.

SIXTEEN PERSONALITY FACTORS TEST. *See* EVALUATION AND DIAGNOSIS, PSYCHOLOGICAL.

SKILL/SKILLS. *See* TECHNIQUE AND SKILL. *See also* EDUCATION IN PASTORAL CARE AND COUNSELING; VIRTUE, CONCEPT OF; WISDOM AND PRACTICAL KNOWLEDGE.

SKINNER, B.F. *See* BEHAVIORISM.

SLEEP AND SLEEP DISORDERS. Sleep is one of the basic physiological states of the human being usually associated with periodic and temporary diminution of sensation, awareness, and sensorimotor activity. Normally, sleep is thought to provide rest and restoration for the body and the psyche. *Sleep disorders* include any disruption of the onset or termination of sleep, or any of a number of behaviors that occur during sleep, which disrupt the normal sleep cycles.

Proper sleep is necessary for normal intellectual and emotional functioning. Falling asleep, regulating the amount of sleep, and certain behaviors that occur during sleep can all become problematic enough to cause the individual to seek professional help. Many disturbing activities that occur during sleep may be normal phenomena, or may be common symptoms of psychological disturbance. In other cases, sleep disturbances may reflect serious neurologic diseases, requiring medical evaluation and intervention. Among persons with psychiatric disturbance, it is estimated that approximately forty-five percent experience some sleep disorder. In the general population, nearly twenty-five percent of adults experience some form of sleep disturbance in their lifetime. In recent years, great strides have been made in the understanding of the physiological processes involved in sleep, but the understanding of the psychological aspects of sleep has not kept pace.

There are large individual differences in the amount of sleep required for proper health. Babies sleep a great deal more than adults. An infant may sleep as much as sixteen

hours per day, whereas the average middle-aged adult sleeps approximately 7.5 hours per day. The need for sleep apparently continues to decline with advancing age so that the average 70-year-old individual may sleep only six to seven hours per night. Some individuals appear to function adequately on as little as three to four hours per night. Others require nine to ten hours per night for adequate functioning. These differences may not be indicative of pathology.

1. **Stages of Sleep.** Years ago the method of measuring sleep was primarily the amount of stimulation required to arouse the sleeper. More recently the development of the electroencephalogram (EEG) has allowed much more sophisticated measuring of central nervous system activity during sleep. Sleep can be classified into two major categories: rapid eye movement sleep (REM) and non-rapid eye movement sleep (NREM). REM sleep is characterized by frequent bursts of rapid, jerky eye movements associated with slow, low-voltage brain waves. These eye movements occur very infrequently in NREM sleep, which is associated with slow brain waves of higher voltage and frequency than those associated with REM sleep. NREM stages appear to be important in recovery from muscular fatigue while REM sleep appears to be more important in learning and psychological adjustment. Dreaming usually occurs during REM sleep. REM sleep is usually preceded by at least an hour of NREM sleep.

Most researchers further divide NREM sleep into four stages based on subtle differences in brain-wave patterns. In the light sleep of stage 1 NREM, there is a slowing of the overall EEG pattern. Normal persons may have brief, shock-like movements, may experience an associated sense of falling, and may be aroused to a more awake state by the convulsive movements. No epileptic activity appears on the electroencephalogram with these movements. In stage 2 NREM sleep sinusoidal wave patterns called sleep spindles appear on the EEG. In stage 3 NREM, sleep spindles and very slow wave activity account for nearly twenty percent of the brain wave activity. This increases to fifty percent in stage 4 NREM.

Normal sleep has four or five ninety-minute cycles of NREM sleep alternating with REM sleep in periods lasting an average of fifteen minutes. REM periods get longer later at night, so most of the total REM time is in the last third of sleep, while most stage 4 NREM sleep occurs during the first third of sleep.

2. **Sleep Disorders.** *Insomnia*, including decreased sleep duration, delays in onset of sleep, and repeated waking during sleep occurs in about two percent of individuals over eighteen years of age. The incidence of sleep problems among individuals seeking medical or psychological attention is substantially higher, perhaps as high as twenty percent. Before concluding that anxiety or depression account for a sleep disorder, however, a variety of organic causes must be ruled out. For this reason, the nonmedical practitioner is advised to seek medical consultation if sleep disturbance is a prominent feature of the person's complaint.

Insomnia is present in eighty to ninety percent of depressed patients, including alterations in the total amount of sleep, difficulty in falling asleep, or early morning wakening. Anxiety-related insomnia is more often characterized by difficulty in falling asleep and frequent nocturnal awakenings. A number of sleep-related phenomena may trigger complaints of insomnia even though the real problem is a worrisome symptom appearing during efforts to sleep.

Family patterns may also foster complaints of insomnia. If both parents in a family complain of insomnia, forty-eight percent of the offspring will also have difficulty falling asleep. This falls to twenty-nine percent if insomnia is a problem for one parent, and to eighteen percent if it is a problem for neither parent. This probably does not reflect a genetic basis for the disorder, but rather a learning of behavioral patterns. Nicotine, caffeine, and alcohol commonly produce sleep disturbances, and patients who have used sleep medications for prolonged periods of time may experience extremes of sleeplessness when the drug is withdrawn. Hypersomnia (excessive sleeping) may be associated with dissociative reactions and neurotic fatigue, but may also be due to metabolic problems or neurological disorders. Hypersomnia in the elderly may be associated with potentially lethal conditions and warrants prompt medical attention.

Sleep apnea (cessation of breathing) arouses the patient from sleep when arterial blood gases become abnormal. Apneic periods usually last from twenty to 150 seconds, occurring in clusters over a twenty to thirty minute time span. This disorder can be fatal.

Narcolepsy, a form of epilepsy, is an easily recognized disorder characterized by recurrent sleep attacks appearing abruptly and inappropriately even during the day. Referral to a competent neurologist is strongly recommended.

A number of *aberrant behaviors* during sleep may be troublesome. Sleepwalking and sleeptalking occur primarily in stage 4 of NREM sleep. This phenomenon is much more common in children than in adults. In children it is usually not associated with physiologic disturbance, but in adults may reflect significant central nervous system disorder. Sleepwalking in adults may be associated with psychomotor seizures. Enuresis (bed wetting), also occurs in stage 4 NREM sleep. Most cases are entirely benign, especially if there is a high family incidence of enuresis. Spinal cord damage or other central nervous system abnormalities must be considered when enuresis appears with no associated family history.

Restless leg syndrome is a disagreeable sensation of "cramping" or "aching" deep in the leg associated with an irresistible urge to move the legs. The person feels compelled to get up and walk about. One-third of patients with this syndrome have relatives with the same problem and the disorder is thought to have a hereditary basis. In the majority of individuals the disorder is benign and disturbs nothing more than their sleep.

Nocturnal leg cramps are distinctly different from the restless leg syndrome. These interfere with sleep by making the patient so uncomfortable that he or she cannot relax. In most cases there is no apparent physiological basis and the problem is often decreased by simple stretching of the calf muscle just before sleeping.

Sleep disorders may produce psychological disturbances as well as being symptoms of such disturbance. Mild sleep deprivation impairs intellectual functioning and more severe deprivation can lead to ego disorganization, hallucinations, and delusions.

3. Therapy. Sleep medications are among the most widely prescribed medications in the U.S. About ten percent of the population uses some form of medication at some time in their lives to help them fall asleep. Of patients using sleep medication, thirty-nine percent are over the age of sixty. Sleep medications are easily abused and may create more difficulty than they alleviate. If insomnia is a symptom of depressive illness, sedatives will often aggravate the depression and provide little relief from the sleep disorder.

Problems with sleep are common and are often caused by stress. A careful physical and neurological examination is appropriate for all persons with sleep problems, even if there is obvious stress in the individual's life. Once physiological problems have been ruled out, careful psychological counseling is preferable to simply masking the symptoms with medication. Behavioral approaches are helpful in cases where disturbed sleep is a function of poor sleep habits or maladaptive cognitions.

Bibliography. E. Hartman, "Sleep Disorders," in A. Freedman, H. Kaplan, B. Sadock, eds., *Comprehensive Textbook of Psychiatry*, II, 3d ed. (1980), pp. 2014–29. A. Kales and R. Berger, "Psychopathology of Sleep," in C. Costello, ed., *Symptoms of Psychopathology* (1970), pp. 418–47. R. Lechtenberg, *The Psychiatrist's Guide to Diseases of the Nervous System* (1982), pp. 326–51.

J. H. JENNISON

PERSONALITY, BIOLOGICAL DIMENSIONS OF; BRAIN RESEARCH; CONSCIOUSNESS; DREAM THEORY AND RESEARCH. *Compare* HYPNOSIS; UNCONSCIOUS.

SLOTH AND ZEAL (Moral Theology). *Sloth (acedia* in Latin) is one of the seven deadly or capital sins, consisting of apathy, boredom, the turning away from God and creation out of what St. Thomas called "sorrow in the divine Good."

Zeal, the virtue opposite to sloth, is the attitude of eagerness for activity that carries one toward God and Creation.

Christian tradition has understood sloth to be something more profound and pervasive than the popular meaning of laziness. Traditionally, sloth has carried with it the absence of hope in the possibility of useful action, so the slothful person is not only inactive, but lacks hope that there is any point to activity. John of Damascus used the phrase "an oppressive grief" for sloth.

This sin bears much in common with depression as a life stance, where sadness is woven around the failure to identify meaningful objectives. Though May disputes this position by citing St. Thomas (above), the depressive's turn inward is precisely a rejection of both God and Creation as sources of joy.

Yet it is more tragic than sins that elicit condemnation for the sinner, in that its narrowing of view and restriction of activity diminish the chance of the slothful person's seeing the way out of the malaise. Indeed, when hope is thus lost, activity seems foolish. The sin brings out its own punishment in the restriction of the capacity for joy and a deathward slide into torpor.

Renaissance and Victorian moralists were particularly alert to the dangers of sloth, as is that segment of the American church which sees virtue largely in activity and production. In societies where economic, artistic, and moral expansiveness have been identified with God's work and will, the failure to contribute actively has been stigmatized as an obstacle to the creative work of God.

Critics of this tendency have suggested that it misunderstands sloth as primarily a sin of bodily inactivity, rather than seeing its center rightly in the soul's despair about investment in life. They have further suggested that sloth can exist in a person who is physically energetic but who has yielded initiative and direction to others; it is self-direction and choice that reflect hope and purpose.

One of the typical signs and costs of sloth is a lack of awareness of one's own wishes and needs. Slothful persons, having lost hope that they will be gratified, become so habituated to looking first to the wishes of others that they abdicate their own will and spend little time doing what they want to do, which further feeds their sadness and diminishes their activity.

Zeal, the opposite life position, expects life, God, and the Creation to reward effort. As such, it differs from compulsive activity, which is typically motivated by the avoidance of pain, not the expectation of a good outcome. The zealous person invests energy in the world and in God, not in a tense and driven way but with joyous expectation that action will be a pleasure in itself as well as the bearer of rewards beyond itself.

This more natural and balanced condition is not marked by constant or frenetic activity, but by the self-regulating alternation of rest and effort. Unlike the rest of the slothful person, which more often serves as escape from efforts expected to be futile, the zealous person's rest is both pleasure and preparation. A sign of zeal is that its bearer feels rested after resting and chooses to return to activity in the expectation that it will be productive and enjoyable. Neither workaholic nor malingering, either of which the slothful may be, the zealot will be productive but free of the temptation to make an idol out of work.

Bibliography. H. Fairlie, *Seven Deadly Sins* (1978). B. W. Grant, *From Sin to Wholeness* (1982).

B. W. GRANT

CHRISTIAN LIFE; LIFESTYLE ISSUES IN PASTORAL CARE; SEVEN DEADLY SINS. *See also* CHARACTER ETHICS; LIFE/ALIVENESS; MORAL THEOLOGY AND PASTORAL CARE; REST AND RENEWAL; SIN/SINS; TEMPTATION.

SMALL GROUPS. *See* GROUP COUNSELING AND PSYCHOTHERAPY; GROUP DYNAMICS, PROCESS, AND RESEARCH; GROWTH GROUPS; SUPPORT GROUPS.

SMITH, PAUL I. *See* INSTITUTE OF PASTORAL CARE.

SOCIAL ADJUSTMENT. *See* ADJUSTMENT, CONCEPT OF; PSYCHOSOCIAL DEVELOPMENT.

SOCIAL AGENCIES. *See* SOCIAL SERVICES.

SOCIAL CASEWORK. A helping process begun in the early 1900s, traditionally used by professional social workers, enabling persons to find solutions to specific problems presented by a client or identified by the helper. Generally practiced in social service and health institutions, methods range from referrals for concrete

services (e.g., financial, health, or vocational services) to therapeutic intervention in emotional and behavioral issues.

A. C. HUNTER

SOCIAL SERVICES AND PASTORAL CARE; SOCIAL WORKER. *See also* INTERPROFESSIONAL TEAMS AND RELATIONSHIPS; MIGRANT WORKERS AND FAMILIES; POOR PERSONS. *Compare* VOCATIONAL REHABILITATION.

SOCIAL CHANGE AND DISLOCATION. Refers to conscious or unintended modification of patterns of human behavior through time. Social change includes more than change in the personalities of individuals but less than change in cultures. It refers to movements or modifications in social relationships, the nature and/or location of collectives, and/or institutions of a particular society through time. In general the nature of the unit said to change must display enough continuity to be recognizable as having some common properties with the initial unit.

Theories of social change deal with the causes, mechanisms, and consequences of modifications within a particular society. Sources within a society include planned change, conflicts between interest groups, and unanticipated strains or inconsistencies among parts of a model of society as a system. New ideas and/or practices may originate outside the society and produce change through diffusion. Industrialization, social differentiation, bureaucratization, and cultural imperialism have been among the major mechanisms of change. Consequences of social change include the elimination or modification of existing patterns of social behavior. At the lowest level in groups of two or more, patterns of interaction and the rights and duties associated with particular positions change. Within a society group boundaries and the relations between groups change. In the world system a comprehensively different type of society emerges or the pattern of relations between societies changes. Social theorists such as Marx, Spencer, Durkheim, Toennies, and Bell have suggested that societies progress or evolve from pre-industrial patterns emphasizing familial and communal relationships to industrial patterns emphasizing a division of labor based on relationships to the means of production to (perhaps) a "post-industrial" society where knowledge becomes an important resource in structuring human relationships.

Individuals often are affected by change as the patterns of behavior which they were trained to believe appropriate become inappropriate due to changes in the social order. For example, the "liberation of women" provides a basis for criticizing all aspects of male-female relationships before, during and after marriage. Yet the institutionalized patterns of dating, household division of labor, worker compensation, and divorce court judgments take decades to reflect this modification. Thus a large-scale trend or pattern which is the subject of much public debate may give rise to very personal problems for a given individual. The resolution of an individual problem will not change the glacial movement of the social order. In a similar fashion revolutions or social unrest and protest are thought to occur not when absolute deprivation is at its worst but when changing social conditions produce expectations which cannot be fulfilled.

Bibliography. R. A. Nisbet, *Social Change and History* (1969). W. E. Moore, *Social Change* (1963). H. Strasser and S. C. Randall, *An Introduction to Theories of Social Change* (1981).

T. C. HOOD

GRIEF AND LOSS; SOCIAL SERVICES AND PASTORAL CARE; SOCIAL STATUS AND CLASS FACTORS IN PASTORAL CARE. *See also* MIGRANT WORKERS. *Compare* DISASTER, PUBLIC; SOCIAL ISOLATION; SOCIOLOGY OF RELIGIOUS AND PASTORAL CARE; WARTIME PASTORAL CARE.

SOCIAL CLASS. *See* SOCIAL STATUS AND CLASS FACTORS.

SOCIAL CONSCIOUSNESS AND RESPONSIBILITY. Awareness of living in and being influenced by a community (social consciousness) and a sense of being accountable to and for that community (social responsibility). In some contexts social consciousness implies social responsibility.

A person's location within a community or network of interpersonal relationships has a profound influence on his or her attitudes and behavior. Many persons, however, are not aware of such influences and consequently lack insight into their own attitudes and behavior and that of others. This lack of social consciousness inhibits social responsibility. Pastors can use consciousness-raising techniques to help individuals better understand themselves and to enhance their self-conceptions, and as leadership strategies causing the congregation to become more socially responsible.

1. The Influence of Interpersonal Networks. An individual's understanding of himself or herself and of the surrounding world is influenced by that individual's interpersonal networks. Many social psychologists, especially those influenced by George Herbert Mead, see the individual's conscious self as originating in interaction with the social environment and continually being influenced by that environment. Individuals take upon themselves the attitudes of others around them. Education and other socialization processes shape the individual's consciousness in accord with the expectations and values of the group. Because these processes are interactive, however, individuals sometimes influence the expectations and values of the group and change the community itself.

In each of these networks of social action persons learn values and are subject to varying degrees of social influence or control. To the extent that all the social influences on an individual are similar that individual becomes more rigid in attitude and behavior. Communities in which persons in one social group do not associate with those in other social groups have a higher potential for conflict because of these rigidities.

2. Individuals' Lack of Social Awareness. Despite the demonstrated importance of social influences, most people appear to have little awareness of them. The literature on attribution of causes of behavior describes a tendency to overestimate the importance of personal or individualistic factors relative to situational or environmental influences. One clear evidence that people generally are not aware of influences from social networks comes from the study of Americans' understanding of the sources of poverty. A national survey has shown that causes of poverty seen as most important are those (such as lack of thrift, lack of effort) that place blame on the individual for his or her poverty. Similar responses have been obtained from a large sample of members of mainline churches. Ministers, however, appear much more socially conscious than lay members. The causes of poverty which ministers rated most important were all structural causes (prejudice and discrimination, low wages in some businesses and industries, and the failure of society to provide good schools).

3. Consciousness-Raising as a Counseling Strategy. The term "consciousness-raising" gained currency because of its use by social movements during the 1960s. Consciousness-raising is a process of altering persons' understandings of themselves and of society. The women's liberation movement stressed small groups in which women could share their thoughts and experiences in a supportive environment. Such groups enabled women to become more fully aware of the societal constraints directed specifically at women and to make a freer choice about the roles they would occupy and how they would perform these roles. Ideally the groups facilitated not only social consciousness but also social responsibility, as women began to feel accountable for other women.

The concepts and practices of consciousness-raising are relevant to the pastor's roles as counselor and as leader. It can be deeply rewarding to understand the role of interpersonal relations in forming one's self-concept and to manage those relations so that they reinforce ideals that have intrinsic meaning. According to Milton Rokeach, the fact that certain values do and others do not enhance one's self-conceptions provides leverage for value change. He contends that value change is most likely to occur in the direction that enhances one's self-conceptions as a moral and competent person. It may well be, then, that church experiences, from childhood memories of the parables and teachings of Jesus to contemporary participation in worship, are, or through consciousness-raising can become, keys to personality change.

4. Consciousness-Raising as a Leadership Strategy. Carl Rogers asserts a tendency for individuals when stripped of social influence to develop in a socially responsible direction. This assertion is compatible with Rokeach's theory. Gunnar Myrdal represents a more sociological approach to social responsibility, pointing out that institutions often channel people toward their more universalistic values rather than toward their more particularistic ones. When ordinary people act through their orderly collective bodies they act more as Americans, as Christians, and as humanitarians than if they were acting independently. Referring specifically to racial prejudice, Myrdal argues that people act differently in institutions than when following their personal prejudices because they have placed their highest ideals in their institutions. Since the church is one of those institutions in which people have placed their highest values, Myrdal's view suggests an important dimension of ministerial leadership aimed at social responsibility.

Studies of church members have shown that their attitudes toward their church's social action are often influenced more by expectations learned outside the church than by those learned from the church. But though church members sometimes seek their own self-interests through the church, the fact that they participate in the church likely means that at some level they share the deepest values of the church and that they are potentially subject to influence by those values. Ministers can take opportunities such as prayers, sermons, discussions in committee meetings and conversations with individual members to bring to consciousness members' beliefs in Christian values, encouraging them to apply those values to specific issues.

Ministers and socially conscious lay people can help the church shape social action policies that reflect biblical concepts such as those depicting the church as the servant of a just and compassionate God. The church moves in a more socially responsible direction as social policies gain legitimacy from such values and as members become more aware of how their resistance to policies based on such universalistic values is anchored in the vested interests of their various social groups. Of course, the pursuit of Christian values and the ability to put the interests of one's social groups in proper perspective do not guarantee the success or even the appropriateness of specific social actions. The socially responsible church learns from failures as well as successes.

Social responsibility adds a spirit that permeates the church's ministry and is facilitated by leaders who, affirming that they do not have all the answers, search for answers with their people, always leading them to examine critically the ready answers provided by their various social groups. In the church perhaps more than in any other major social institution processes that raise individuals' social consciousness and channel their energies in socially responsible ways can operate in a supportive community that ministers to a wide variety of each individual's needs. Rogers's insights imply that when the stress is on God's love and acceptance in the context of a loving, accepting community individuals can become free of the grip of social constraints and become socially responsible. Myrdal, however, implies that social constraints are necessary to pull individuals in a universalistic and responsible way. Though research is needed to clarify this issue, with proper leadership churches can provide a supportive context that gives individuals the security to break from the grip of such socially reinforced behaviors as racism at the same time that it provides the proper cues and stimuli for moving in the direction of universalistic, socially responsible values.

Bibliography. R. N. Bellah, et al., Habits of the Heart: Individualism and Commitment in American Life (1985). D. Courtier, "The Capacity to Promote Justice," Human Development, 6:3 (1985), 34–40. J. E. Dittes, When the People Say No (1979). J. Freeman, ed., Women: A Feminist Perspective (1975). I. H. Frieze, D. Bar-Tal, and J. S. Carroll, eds., New Approaches to Social Problems (1979). G. Myrdal, An American Dilemma (1964). P. Pfuetze, Self, Society, Existence (1961). C. R. Rogers, Freedom to Learn (1969). M. Rokeach, The Nature of Human Values (1973). J. R. Wood, Leadership in Voluntary Organizations: The Controversy Over Social Action in Protestant Churches (1981).

J. R. WOOD

CONSCIOUSNESS RAISING; RESPONSIBILITY/IRRESPONSIBILITY, PSYCHOLOGY OF; SOCIAL JUSTICE ISSUES IN PASTORAL CARE. See also LIFESTYLE ISSUES IN PASTORAL CARE; PEACEMAKING AND PASTORAL CARE; PROPHETIC/PASTORAL TENSION IN MINISTRY; SOCIAL PERCEPTION, JUDGMENT, AND BELIEF.

SOCIAL DEVELOPMENT. See PSYCHOSOCIAL DEVELOPMENT.

SOCIAL ETHICS. See ETHICS AND PASTORAL CARE; SOCIAL JUSTICE ISSUES.

SOCIAL GOSPEL. See RAUSCHENBUSH, Walter; see also HISTORY OF PROTESTANT PASTORAL CARE (United States); SOCIAL JUSTICE ISSUES IN PASTORAL CARE.

SOCIAL ISOLATION. The subjective perception of being emotionally disconnected from someone with whom an intimate relationship is desired. People may be generally lonely, with few or no close relationships, or may be lonely in relation to a particular person. Loneliness may be chronic, a relatively enduring experience usually related to personality and social skill deficits, or acute and event-related with a shorter duration. In contrast to social isolation, intimacy is a sense of closeness and togetherness between people in which there is mutual sharing and acceptance.

Social isolation in its more chronic and intense expression appears to be related to depression and other psychological dysfunctions, terminal illness, antisocial behavior, substance abuse, pessimism, and lower spiritual well-being.

Loneliness may be seen as spiritually, sociologically, and interpersonally generated. The biblical account of human creation in the image of God indicates that human beings are fundamentally social in nature (Gen. 1:26; Gen. 2:18) but that the intrusion of sin introduced alienation and isolation between human beings, as well as in the God-human relationship. Sin introduced a variety of ego defense mechanisms which destroy human intimacy. These include blaming, denial, and scapegoating. Sin also introduced the dynamic of egocentric individualism and attempts at self-preservation which move counter to the vulnerability and self-giving of intimacy. Other spiritually related causes of loneliness are a function of prophetic servanthood, human finitude, and doubt.

Although many tend to evaluate loneliness in terms of personal inadequacies, the widespread experience of loneliness in Western civilization suggests that broader sociological factors are promoting the phenomena. Certainly one of the most significant is the societally endorsed value of individualism. In contrast to the Eastern emphasis on the fundamental unity of each individual with the whole and upon harmony, Western society stresses separateness and independence as of the highest value. A persuasive emphasis on personal rights gives certain benefits but also has resulted in the deterioration of *Gemeinschaft*, or community, built on primary, intimate social relationships. Other sociological underpinnings of contemporary loneliness include the revised social structure occasioned by the industrial revolution, specialization, television programming, and the elevation of values such as achievement and acquisition as signs of worth when such values only promote competitiveness and manipulation. Urbanization and design factors associated with it have also distanced people from one another.

Interpersonal causes of loneliness include active and passive rejection by parents, peers, or significant authority figures, role isolation, in which people are unable to enter into authentic and unguarded, emotionally open relationships with others because their role does not permit it, and the lack of understanding between people. A lack of understanding may occur in any relationship and is one of the key factors behind the occurrence of loneliness within marriage. It is primarily due to faulty, distancing communication patterns.

Perhaps the most commonly recognized cause of loneliness is interpersonal loss. The loss of or prevention of close relationships due to moves is a generally unrecognized, but tremendously important cause of loneliness in our nomadic society. Death and divorce are also tremendously traumatic triggers of loneliness in the lives of millions.

Pastoral counseling approaches for social isolation need to be shaped on the basis of the intensity and duration of the experience, and its major contributing causes.

Bibliography. C. W. Ellison, *Saying Goodbye to Loneliness and Finding Intimacy* (1983). J. Hartog, J. R. Andy, and Y. A. Cohen, *The Anatomy of Loneliness* (1980). J. J. Lynch, *The Broken Heart: The Medical Consequence of Loneliness* (1977). C. E. Moustakas, *Loneliness* (1961); *Loneliness and Love* (1972). L. A. Peplau and D. Perlman, *Loneliness: A Sourcebook of Current Theory, Research, and Therapy* (1982). R. Tournier, *Escape from Loneliness* (1962).

C. ELLISON

ALIENATION/ESTRANGEMENT; LONELINESS AND ISOLATION; SHYNESS. *Compare* COMMUNITY, FELLOWSHIP, AND CARE.

SOCIAL JUSTICE ISSUES IN PASTORAL CARE.
The concept of justice is the fundamental normative principle for evaluating and harmonizing conflicting claims of rights, duties, and responsibilities. Social justice issues come to focus most clearly with respect to *distributive* justice, the impartial taxing and distribution of values, so as to achieve the common good. (Social justice may also be concerned with equal treatment in three other forms of justice: commutative justice, which adjudicates conflicts between parties within the state; retributive justice, which is imposed by the state; and remedial justice, which requires the present redress of past injustice.)

Social justice advocacy and pastoral care may be perceived as in four possible relationships with each other: (1) autonomous, (2) competing, (3) compensatory, i.e., common parts of a whole ministry, or (4) supplementary, i.e., mutually corrective and enabling.

1. **Autonomous.** Social justice claims autonomous authority when it claims one of these three bases: (a) civil law, (b) natural law, and (c) utilitarianism.

a. Justice as conformity to the law. Civil law is a conception of great moral and social importance, for the rule of law is a major achievement in human history, creating justice by mitigating the arbitrary and exploitive exercise of power by those with political and economic advantage. Yet the law's claim to autonomous authority must be challenged by the recognition that the codification of law and its interpretation remain subject to political and other power. Theologically speaking, even as law limits human sinfulness, it also reflects human sinfulness. Law tries to adjust for this by systems of checks and balances and by respect for due process. But it still must rely for justice on factors outside of law, including the commitment to justice of individuals who create and implement law.

b. Justice as the harmonization of values. One basis for appeal beyond civil law is to the natural law concept of the harmonization of values; the primary categories of this concept are *merit* (to be contrasted below with *need*) as the just basis for what is due, and the impartiality of rational judgments in terms of fairness and proportionality. However, limits on this natural law remain; since there are competing claims even among the values of a good creation, and since there are competing interpretations of the principles of harmonization, social justice issues remain even after the appeal to this natural law basis.

c. Justice as the maximization of values. This utilitarian definition of justice circumvents the distributional issue by adopting the market metaphor of capitalism. Since freedom ensures the right to determine one's own values, and to pursue them without restraint, values are privatized and public issues are reducible to supposedly value free, technical determinations of the productivity of means. This technical, quantitative definition of justice has been widely espoused in Western capitalistic countries where economic productivity has been great and the advantages of maximizing values through this process are clearly evident. This conception of justice, based on an ever-expanding pie of resources and values, has not, however, always created justice; great inequities have developed. It is a conception which requires correction, as from other views of justice, and from the regard of more human, less technical perspectives.

(A fourth basis for justice, grounded in the righteousness of God, will be discussed below.)

These legal and technical bases, then, leave issues of social justice still subject to essentially political struggles. Different groups appeal to the same concepts of law and justice to legitimate their own demands. Groups and individuals must be relied on for commitment to justice and to the meeting of essential human needs, along with their more restricted self-interest. In this sense, social justice advocacy is not independent of the concerns of pastoral care (see below).

At the same time, it is equally limited to suppose that pastoral care's promotion of personal empowerment and wholeness can be effective in the absence of socially just distribution of resources.

2. **Competing.** Social justice advocacy and pastoral care are commonly perceived as competing, in at least these aspects: (1) In practice, each is supremely demanding of time, energy, and commitment; it is difficult for a person or group to expend the requisite resources on more than one such demanding enterprise. (This itself becomes an issue of distribution of resources, a social justice issue,

and an issue of role conflict and identity diffusion, a pastoral care issue.)

(2) Social justice advocacy is traditionally addressed to social structures and institutions, pastoral care to individuals and primary relationships. The inherent and classically recognized conflict to interest between individual and collective welfare, then, generates some inevitable conflict between the practice of social justice advocacy and of pastoral care.

(3) Social justice advocacy typically focuses on human sinfulness and is more often perceived as an activity of law and judgment; pastoral care focuses on resources and is more often perceived as an activity of grace.

(4) Social justice advocacy is more often directed toward the disruption or transformation of established patterns, pastoral care more toward the reestablishment of what is ruptured, or the conservation of what is precarious. Pastoral care may be a silent supporter of an unjust status quo; social justice advocacy may be the active disrupter of social systems on which individuals have come to rely as supports of identity.

3. **Complementary.** Social justice advocacy and pastoral care can be described in language which makes them analogous or closely complementary parts of the same ministry. Both individual health and the social health of justice can be understood as grounded in the righteousness of God—an alternative basis for justice to those cited above. The Judeo-Christian heritage points ultimately to a righteous God whose justice is redemptive, liberating, and remedial. God's righteousness empowers the powerless and justifies those who are without merit, on the basis of *need*. Pastoral care and social justice advocacy are similarly engaged in this enterprise of empowerment and of liberation from the oppression of need. Both aspire to empower the powerless and to loosen the grip of existing powers. Both aspire to a wholeness (whether of individual or of society) which emphasizes interdependence and mutuality. Both attack the limited idolatries and addictions to which people cling and by which they define their lives, and both encourage more "faith"-ful adventurous, vulnerable, even sacrificial postures.

4. **Supplementary.** Even given statements more limited than the general common goals just expressed about the aims of social justice advocacy (to promote equitable distribution of resources and values) and of pastoral care (to promote the wholeness of individuals and their relationships with others), it is possible to identify ways in which the work and the perspective of social justice and the work and perspective of pastoral care become indispensable to each other. Both are value-laden, value-driven enterprises which need the corrective of the other's values.

(1) The wholeness of individuals, to which pastoral care aspires, depends greatly on the satisfaction of elemental human needs by the fair availability of economic and other resources, i.e., on social justice. In particular, the interpretation of particular pastoral care situations may benefit from the kind of assessment of social realities that consideration of social justice requires; e.g., the effects of social location or social role, the oppressiveness of some social conditions, the destructiveness of the withholding of some social resources.

(2) Wholeness of individuals is incomplete without a consciousness raised and tuned to issues of justice and injustice, without a capacity to relate even to remote others with compassionate identification.

(3) The processes of social justice—such as the just implementation of law, the awareness of the need to transcend and transform law, the capacity to make impartial judgments in adjudicating and harmonizing value conflicts, the readiness to recognize the special claims of need and the needy—require the participation of moral actors who are as whole as possible, relatively free of prejudices, defensiveness, fears (especially fears triggered by social differences) and other such characteristics which are impediments both to close personal relationships and to participation in social justice.

(4) The tactics and structures for the delivery of pastoral care, themselves part of social structures, may participate in and support unjust characteristics of their parent institution as, e.g., in the selective attention to individuals, or in providing merely palliative support to victims of injustice. The enterprise of pastoral care itself needs a corrective from the perspective of social justice.

(5) The tactics and structures of social justice advocacy may be carelessly destructive of individual wholeness, as, e.g., in reckless use of guilt-inducing tactics, or in paternalistic manipulation, and themselves need a corrective from the perspective of pastoral care.

Bibliography. T. Aquinas, *Summa Theologica*, vols. I–II, q. 90, 91, and 93–5, (1952). J. Bennett, *The Radical Imperative* (1975), ch. 5. P. DeVos, "Justice" in C. Henry, ed., *Baker's Dictionary of Christian Ethics* (1973). J. Macquarrie, "Justice," *Dictionary of Christian Ethics* (1967). R. Niebuhr, *The Nature and Destiny of Man*, vol II (1941), ch. 9. Plato, *The Republic*, F. Cornford, trans., (1945). P Ramsey, *Basic Christian Ethics* (1950), pp. 1–24. J. Rawls, *A Theory of Justice* (1971), par. 1–4, 11–17, 20–30. P. Tillich, *Love, Power, and Justice* (1954).

D. RHOADES

ADVOCACY; BLACK THEOLOGY AND PASTORAL CARE; CONSCIOUSNESS RAISING; EXPLOITATION/OPPRESSION; FEMINIST *or* LIBERATION THEOLOGY, AND PASTORAL CARE; PROPHETIC/PASTORAL TENSION IN MINISTRY; SOCIAL CONSCIOUSNESS AND RESPONSIBILITY. *See also* HEALTH CARE DELIVERY; PAROLEES AND EX-CONVICTS; POOR PERSONS; RICH PERSONS; SOCIAL CHANGE AND DISLOCATION; SOCIOLOGY OF RELIGIOUS AND PASTORAL CARE. *Compare* ETHICS AND PASTORAL CARE; JEWISH CARE AND COUNSELING; LIFESTYLE ISSUES; MORAL DILEMMAS IN PASTORAL PERSPECTIVE.

SOCIAL LEARNING THEORY. *See* PERSONALITY THEORY (Varieties, Traditions, and Issues).

SOCIAL PERCEPTION, JUDGMENT, AND BELIEF. The process of coming to know and understand other people, which is a major task of social interaction. Images of persons or groups are profoundly important in shaping how one relates to others. Perceptions shape beliefs but beliefs also influence perceptions. Observations of other people's skin color, sex, height, and style of dress will form individual impressions of them. Observations of their behavior and interpretations of its causes result in attributing personality traits to them. While such perceptions are often accurate, research also indicates that systematic error distorts social judgments and beliefs.

1. Impression Formation. *a. Primacy effect.* Not all information received is equally important in one's judgments of others. Research indicates, however, that greater weight is typically given to information that is obtained first. This may be due to being more attentive when initially meeting someone. In addition, first impressions may influence subsequent perceptions by establishing a central theme around which subsequent information is organized and interpreted. Such preconceived notions, called *schemata*, may bias the way one views, interprets, and remembers information received about another.

b. Schemata. An important schema that influences social perception is one's implicit "personality theory." Through experience we develop intuitive notions about how personality traits are related to one another. Thus learning that a person is intelligent may lead to a conclusion that he or she is also industrious. In general, knowing something favorable about another typically leads one to infer other desirable qualities. For example, many studies have shown that physically attractive persons are perceived as being more sensitive, kind, strong, poised, and sociable than those less attractive (Schneider, Hastorf, and Ellsworth, 1979).

c. Stereotypes. Implicit personality theories are closely related to stereotypes, which are generalizations about groups of people that distinguish those people from others. These generalizations may be an inevitable consequence of normal perceptual and thought processes. The tendency to form categories and make inferences on the basis of category membership reflects the need to simplify and find meaning in a complex world. Unless generalizations are made, one has difficulty in anticipating the future and coping adequately with the environment. At the same time, stereotypes often give an overly simplistic view of reality and lead to overestimation of differences between groups and underestimation of variations within them. In addition, they are often ethnocentric judgments and thus provide a major mechanism by which prejudice is sustained. Once formed, stereotypes perpetuate themselves by influencing attention, interpretations, and memories. We are more likely to notice instances that confirm rather than disconfirm our expectations. Memory is also selective; we remember those facts best that support our beliefs.

d. Self-fulfilling prophecies. Impressions of others may constitute self-fulfilling prophecies. Once formed, social beliefs may guide behavior and influence the responses of others in ways that are consistent with prior expectations. For example, if we judge another to be unfriendly we may maintain our distance, which in turn increases the likelihood that the person will respond in ways that confirm our original evaluation. Similarly, studies of teacher expectations indicate that the erroneous belief that certain students are unusually capable can lead teachers to give special treatment to those students (Rosenthal and Jacobsen, 1968). This may elicit superior performance and confirm a belief that was initially false.

e. Clinical judgments. David Myers (1980) has explored how these principles of social perception may influence and at times distort the clinician's judgment.

For example, studies have indicated that professional clinicians may perceive expected associations (e.g., between responses to Rorschach inkblots and homosexuality) even when the expected associations are demonstrably absent or contrary to what was expected. Once a client is diagnosed, clinicians may also be subject to hindsight bias, in which they search for and find incidents in the client's life history and present behavior that "confirm" and "explain" the diagnoses. Such selective attention and interpretation may contribute to overconfidence in one's judgments. When interacting with clients, erroneous diagnoses may be self-confirming since interviewers tend to seek and recall information that illustrates and verifies their initial assessments. Clients' actions readily come to fit their therapists' theories.

2. Attribution Theory. *a. Perceiving causality.* Another's actions are typically attributed to either an internal or an external cause, that is, to a person's disposition or to some situational factor. Some theorists have indicated that we interpret the causes of behavior in fairly rational ways. Harold Kelley (1973) has suggested that in explaining someone's behavior, (for example, why John is arguing with his employer) we use information about "consistency" (Does John often argue with his employer?), "distinctiveness" (Does John argue with others?), and "consensus" (Do others argue with John's employer?). If we learn that John and John alone frequently argues with his employer, and with many others in his life, we will likely attribute the behavior to John's disposition, that is, to his personality or attitudes.

b. Attributional biases. i. The fundamental attribution error. While people often provide reasonable explanations for behavior, they also are prone to certain systematic errors in the attribution process. One of the most common errors is the tendency for observers to underestimate the impact of situational influences, and to overestimate the influence of dispositional influences upon another's behavior. For example, research indicates that even when a person has been assigned or otherwise coerced into behaving in a particular way, observers will still interpret that behavior as indicative of the actor's underlying traits or attitudes (Fiske and Taylor, 1984). Perhaps the most unfortunate implication of this fundamental attribution error is that victims of situational forces may be held accountable for their fate. For example, poverty may be viewed only as a reflection of insufficient motivation and not as due to economic conditions beyond the victim's control.

ii. Actor-observer bias. While we may see other people's behavior as caused by relatively enduring dispositional factors, we tend to attribute our own behavior to external factors and to perceive it as more variable from situation to situation. This difference in the perceived causes of behavior may be an important cause of conflict. Parents who admonish their children for being late may hear how heavy the traffic was. Both the fundamental attribution error and actor-observer bias have been explained in terms of our tendency to attribute causality to wherever our attention is focused. When we watch another person act, that person occupies the center of our attention and is thus viewed as the cause of the action. However, when *we* act, our attention is usually on the situation and thus we are more aware of external influences upon ourselves. Interestingly, empathy-set instructions, in which one is told to pretend to observe oneself as another person might, or is told to assume the role of another person, reverse the actor-observer effect. (This is one result of the double-chair technique used in Gestalt therapy.)

iii. Self-serving bias. Different lines of research indicate a strong tendency to perceive oneself favorably. For example, studies have found that persons readily accept credit when they perform well, typically attributing success either to ability or effort; however, responsibility for failure will be denied by attributing it to "bad luck" or other situational factors (Myers, 1980). Moreover, in studies where people are asked to compare themselves to others, most see themselves as better than average on nearly every dimension that is both subjective and socially desirable (Myers, 1980). For example, most community residents see themselves as more tolerant than their neighbors, most business people view themselves as more ethical than the average business person, and most college students believe they will outlive their actuarially predicted age of death by about ten years. While the self-serving bias may reflect the need to protect and enhance self-image, it may also be the result of how we process information about ourselves. We intend to succeed and are likely to see ourselves as more responsible for intended than unintended results. Our efforts often produce positive results; thus it is not unreasonable to attribute an occasional failure to unusual circumstances. The pervasiveness of the self-serving bias suggests that pride, rather than low self-esteem, may be the more common human problem.

Bibliography. C. Antaki and C. Brewin, *Attributions and Psychological Change* (1982). S. Asch, "Forming Impressions of Personality," *J. of Abnormal and Social Psychology*, 41 (1946), 258 –90. S. Fiske and S. Taylor, *Social Cognition* (1984). I. Frieze, D. Bar-Tal, and J. Carroll, *New Approaches to Social Problems: Applications of Attribution Theory* (1979). D. Hamilton, *Cognitive Processes in Stereotyping and Intergroup Behavior* (1981). J. Harvey, W. Ickes, and R. Kidd, eds., *New Directions in Attribution Research*, vol. 3 (1981). E. Jones, D. Kanouse, H. Kelley, R. Nisbett, S. Valins, and B. Weiner, *Attribution: Perceiving the Causes of Behavior* (1972). E. Jones and R. Nisbett, *The Actor and the Observer: Divergent Perceptions of the Causes of Behavior* (1971). H. Kelley, "The Process of Causal Attribution," *American Psychologist*, 28 (1973), 107–28. D. Myers, *The Inflated Self* (1980). R. Nisbett and L. Ross, *Human Inference: Strategies and Shortcomings of Social Judgment* (1980). R. Rosenthal and L. Jacobson, *Pygmalion in the Classroom* (1968). D. Schneider, A. Hastorf, and P. Ellsworth, *Person Perception* (1979).

M. BOLT

LOCUS OF CONTROL RESEARCH; PREJUDICE; SOCIAL CONSCIOUSNESS AND RESPONSIBILITY; SOCIAL PSYCHOLOGY, DISCIPLINE OF. *See also* AUTHORITARIANISM; RACISM; SEXISM. *Compare* CONSCIOUSNESS RAISING; CULTURAL AND ETHNIC FACTORS *or* SOCIAL STATUS AND CLASS FACTORS, IN PASTORAL CARE; EVALUATION AND DIAGNOSIS; DISCERNMENT OF SPIRITS.

SOCIAL PSYCHOLOGY, DISCIPLINE OF.
Study of the influence, real or perceived, which social interactions, relationships, or institutions have upon the thoughts, feelings, and actions of persons.

1. Origin of Social Psychology. In the nineteenth century the special sciences of psychology, sociology, political science, and economics came to be recognized as independent disciplines. These sciences had no sooner come to be distinguished from each other than hybrid disciplines began to form. Social psychology is one such hybrid discipline. It draws in the special themes of the various social sciences for the purpose of studying persons in social contexts.

The beginning of widespread interest in social psychology in America coincides with the era between World War I and World War II during which social change and its attendant uncertainties created demand for a science which could be applied to the solving of social problems.

2. Major Approaches. Included within social psychology is a broad range of theoretical perspectives, of which four in particular account for the great bulk of what constitutes social psychological theory.

a. The behavioralist approach. Many social psychologists define their discipline by its method. The method to which they subscribe is a logical-empiricist view for the verification of theory. As a result the behavioralist approach studies publicly observable behaviors which occur in social situations or in response to social stimuli.

b. The constructivist approach. Concern with the cognitive features of social actions has characterized the growth of social psychology during the 1970s; this includes the ways in which persons form perceptions of others and the ways in which persons construe social events.

c. The psychoanalytic approach. Many psychologists recognize that there is tension between the needs of the individual (the id) and the demands which society places on the individual (the superego). Of interest are social forms which are developed as a compromise between these forces and the strategies which are devised to cover up failures in harmonizing the conflicting forces within the person.

d. The Marxist approach. This approach to social psychology critically examines both social actions and theories of social action in terms of how they function in the dynamics of power. For example, many Marxist theorists analyze the way in which social habits or perceptions function to validate oppression. Others are interested in the way in which the social institutions which are historical products of human action eventually may come to enslave the persons who believe that they need to maintain them.

3. Social Psychology and Religious Practice. Attempts have been made to integrate the specific insights of social psychology with a religious vision. This venture has had both a critical and a constructive side. It has been critical inasmuch as it has been shown that parts of modern psychology are not compatible with the teachings of traditional religion, for example, the psychological view that religion is a form of neurosis and belief in any god a function of projection. Constructive effort may be found in the increasing number of writings which attempt to make explicit what the relation between religious belief and science ought to be.

Along with other social scientists, social psychologists have studied religious institutions and practices as they are perceived by persons and as they influence the actions, attitudes, and perceptions of persons. The findings of social psychology have been put to technical use in the church. Theories of attitude formation and persuasion have been applied in attempts to improve teaching and preaching in the church. In addition, insights gained from social psychology are widely used in pastoral care and counseling.

As the church has taken on the responsibility to act as a social agent for its members, social psychological theory (especially Marxist theory) has come to be used in the criticisms which the church makes of society.

Bibliography. G. W. Allport, "The Historical Background of Modern Social Psychology," in Lindzey and Aronson, eds., *The Handbook of Social Psychology,* (1968). T. R. Sarbin, "Contextualism: A World View for Modern Psychology," in *Nebraska Symposium on Motivation* (1976). B. Ollman and E. Vernoff, eds., *The Left Academy: Marxist Scholarship on American Campuses* (1982).

M. VANDER GOOT

PSYCHOLOGY, WESTERN; SOCIAL PERCEPTION, JUDGMENT, AND BELIEF. *Compare* SOCIAL SCIENCE; SOCIOBIOLOGY; SOCIOLOGY OF RELIGIOUS AND PASTORAL CARE; SOCIOLOGY OF RELIGION.

SOCIAL PSYCHOLOGY OF RELIGION. *See* PSYCHOLOGY OF RELIGION.

SOCIAL SCIENCES.

Focus upon the social behavior of individuals within a group or interaction between people. The seventeen-volume *International Encyclopedia of the Social Sciences* has articles in the disciplines of anthropology, economics, geography, history, law, political science, psychiatry, psychology, sociology, and statistics.

There is disagreement among social scientists as to what qualifies a discipline as a social science. Some argue that a discipline is not a science unless it has an accumulated integrated body of knowledge which contains identifiable laws in the same sense as the physical sciences. The more usual view is to consider use of the scientific method in the study of social behavior as the qualifying feature of a social science.

There are many social scientists who believe that it is impossible to apply the scientific method, as it was developed in the natural sciences, to the study of social behavior. They prefer to think of their work as humanistic "social sciences," being content to view their craft more as an art than a science.

Since the 1950s, it has become increasingly popular to use the term "behavioral science" in place of, or interchangeably with, the older term "social science." This is especially true of psychology, where behaviorism as a school of thought has made the greatest inroads.

Research in the social sciences is commonly divided into the "pure" and the "applied," where the goal of the former is to obtain knowledge for the sake of knowledge, and the goal of the latter is to learn something about social behavior which can be useful and beneficial to human society. Those social scientists who hold a purist position often argue that social science is to social work as physics is to engineering. In recent years, however, social scientists have been challenged to demonstrate the usefulness of their research activity, resulting in an increased emphasis on policy or evalua-

tive research and a decreased distinction between the "pure" and the "applied."

The social sciences represent a rich primary source for the development and continued formation of pastoral care and counseling. This is especially true as increasing amounts of social science research have come to focus upon the social conditions which detrimentally affect personal adjustment and well-being.

Bibliography. J. Gould and W. Kolb, eds., *A Dictionary of the Social Sciences* (1964). D. Sills, ed., *International Encyclopedia of the Social Sciences* (1968).

J. BALSWICK

BEHAVIORAL SCIENCE; CULTURAL ANTHROPOLOGY; PSYCHOLOGY; SOCIOLOGY. *Compare* HUMAN NATURE, PROBLEM OF; THEOLOGICAL ANTHROPOLOGY; PHILOSOPHICAL ANTHROPOLOGY.

SOCIAL SCIENCES, JOURNALS IN. *See* JOURNALS IN RELIGION, THEOLOGY, AND THE SOCIAL SCIENCES, INTERDISCIPLINARY.

SOCIAL SERVICES AND PASTORAL CARE.

Social services may generally be described as help offered through agencies to individuals and families experiencing immediate or long-term problems affecting their physical and/or emotional well-being. Such problems include, but are not limited to, financial distress caused by unemployment, divorce, death, alcohol and drug abuse, mental illness, mental retardation, child abuse and neglect, learning disabilities, and such medically related concerns as infant and child health, family planning, infertility, genetic counseling, and geriatrics.

This article concerns the nature and availability of such social services as a resource in pastoral care. In order to understand their relationship one needs to acknowledge the interdependent relationship between a person's emotional and spiritual well-being and that person's physical, social, and environmental situation. Recognizing an intertwining of needs, the pastor is able to help persons solve problems within the pastoral relationship and through appropriate referrals to social agencies.

Historically, especially in urban and black congregations, pastoral care has involved considerable direct social service work by pastors assisting persons with concrete needs. As social service agencies have proliferated, the pastoral role has increasingly focused on referral, often combined with a sort of advocacy function of helping parishioners relate effectively to governmental and other social service agencies. Such pastors, for instance, may accompany their parishioners to the welfare office or county health department and help "walk them through" the often complicated bureaucratic maze and interpret their needs and problems to agency officials. But whatever form the interface with social services may take, ministry in all socioeconomic strata of society is intimately involved with social needs and inevitably must relate to the many social service agencies of modern society.

1. Identifying Problems Responsive to Social Services Intervention. At first glance some of the problems noted above may not appear specifically social service-oriented. However, the complexity of social problems illustrates the importance of interprofessional problem-solving. For example, a family with a critically ill child decidedly has medical and pastoral care needs. Financial difficulties and child care needs for siblings also may be problems. This family's pastor can help them solve some obvious problems by appropriate referrals to social service agencies, which then frees pastor and family to deal with the emotional, moral, and religious dimensions of their situation.

A minister's involvement with social services generally occurs under two circumstances: an individual or family may request the pastor's help with a specific problem (e.g., need for food or rent money), or the minister may discover during a pastoral relationship that a person's emotional distress, ill health, or moral and religious concerns are related to specific social problems. A pastoral issue like feelings of isolation, for instance, may be part of a problem of spouse abuse, including the need for financial resources, legal aid, and health care. In both circumstances the pastor has an opportunity to help clarify and assess the problem, to provide and interpret referral information about possible sources of help, and to support the persons in their decision making.

2. **Locating Referral Information.** An excellent general source book is *The Church and Community Resources*. But because the task of locating appropriate social services varies by community, pastors must locate specific referral sources for their own situations. Each community has its own informational resources. State agencies administering federal Department of Health and Human Services programs have information numbers. Local health and welfare departments have staff assigned to provide referral information. Metropolitan areas often have community resource books published by organizations like United Way. Yellow Pages listings usually include social service organizations. Public libraries may have references on local agencies.

More importantly, as the pastor gains experience in making social service referrals, he or she has the opportunity to cultivate working relationships with other community services professionals. Besides offering specific referral information, such persons can become the pastor's colleagues and consultants.

Bibliography. M. Bryant and C. Kemp, *The Church and Community Resources* (1977).

A. C. HUNTER

SOCIAL CASEWORK; SOCIAL WORKER. *See also* ADVOCACY; INTERPROFESSIONAL TEAMS AND RELATIONSHIPS; POOR PERSONS; REFERRAL; SOCIOLOGY OF RELIGIOUS AND PASTORAL CARE. *Compare* SOCIAL JUSTICE ISSUES IN PASTORAL CARE.

SOCIAL STATUS AND CLASS FACTORS IN PASTORAL CARE.

Status and class refer to social stratification. The terms are used to account for differences in power, prestige, and privilege among persons in a social system. Status relates to prestige factors and refers to social position. Class involves groups of persons with similar social profiles and shared perceptions and interests. Status and class, then, reflect the ways a population ranks its members in hierarchical groups, some higher and some lower. Since one's location in the social system has a decided, some would say a determinative, influence

on one's life, awareness of this system and its implications are essential considerations for pastoral care.

1. **Criteria, Class, and Profile.** American sociologists have given considerable attention to the criteria which form the basis for social stratification in a given society. Traditionally social differences among persons were explained as inherent, as the fruit of talent and virtue. But social scientists have sought more tangible clues to explain uneven and hierarchical social structures and have, since Marx, agreed that the economic clue is the most reliable. To be sure, some argue that the income factor must be supplemented with other criteria to achieve an adequate picture of status and class. Hollingshead, for example, uses occupation and years of schooling as primary criteria with sex and marital status as secondary ones. And Warner supplements income with occupation, education, dwelling area, family name, and group memberships. Still others add ethnicity to occupation, education, and income. But in each instance the central criterion is finally economic, however amplified.

These criteria serve as guides to a person's, group's, or institution's status and place in society. Generally the classes are delineated as lower, middle, and upper, though some would subdivide each group for greater precision. Colloquially the groupings are referred to as "haves" and "have nots" or as the "elite" versus the "average" versus those "having a hard time." But what the system means is that a person's income, occupation, education, etc. are similar enough to others to make him or her identifiable as part of a more or less distinct group. It also means that such persons share understandings, values, and perceptions. And finally it means that some are more highly prized than others and that in the U.S. persons should aspire to "better themselves," i.e., ascend the scale so as to claim the rewards of power, prestige, and privilege which the system promises.

In addition to the delineation of status and class, the criteria may also serve to predict the quality of life of a given individual or group and thereby provide a class profile. Peter Berger suggests that any good sociologist, given a person's income and occupation, can with reasonable assurance characterize that person's life. For example, class determines life's opportunities in terms of the amount of education one's children are likely to receive, the standards of medical care one may anticipate, and one's life expectancy. The social scientist can make intelligent guesses about where a person will live, the size and style of their home, how it is decorated, and what books or magazines will be found there. He or she can speculate on the individual's vocabulary, political affiliation, number of children and where or whether the individual attends church or temple and how often.

2. **Reflections on Status/Class.** What these observations about status and class make clear is that each person dwells in a particular social world. Persons are formed in that world and its rituals, values, and symbols are the spectacles through which they tend to view life. Thus, beliefs about ourselves and others, about what we may aspire to or hope for, and about the proper, i.e., "right" way of striving are related to class. How we regard ourselves as male and female, as husband and wife, and as parents differs according to our place in society. The rituals we observe in rearing our children, marrying our

young, buying our clothes, whether we drink at a bar or a club, and the ways we bury our dead reveal our social world. Where we go for help, to a clinic or a private physician, to a private hospital or a state facility, and how we are diagnosed and what treatment we receive relates to our social position.

The above are the symbolic accoutrements of status and class. They reflect power in terms of opportunities for decision and action, prestige in terms of how one is regarded, and privilege in terms of prerogatives and access. Obviously these symbols designate relative importance and value; they become an index to one's worth and identity. Those who aspire to "climb the ladder," to assume a different place in society, need both a vehicle and courage. Education has always been one acceptable path to higher status. The courage required involves sacrificing accustomed relationships and patterns to adopt new and different symbols and rituals, e.g., joining another church, going to concerts. The courage also mandates a certain defiance of the sanctions whereby the system maintains itself, i.e., police, courts, economic sanctions, persuasion, gossip, and ridicule. The lower-class woman who wants an education is not so far removed as some imagine from the corporate wife who wants to do social work. Each must deal with the social pressure which seeks to define her.

Lest these comments seem too neat, some allowance must be made for variations. Social structures differ in different communities. For example, some suggest that in large urban areas power hierarchies, both political and economic, and interest groups are more accurate indicators of community influence than classical social theory. Again, recent attention to alternative lifestyles seems to point to dissatisfaction with the value systems and role models society's structure reflects. The advent of the two-career marriage certainly mirrors this dissatisfaction. Also, some social stratification is more rigid and functions in many instances as a caste system. Race is fixed at birth. And though Native Americans and blacks may fulfill all the requisites for social acceptance, they remain Native Americans and blacks and so are constrained in many instances to live outside the mainstream. At the same time, these communities reflect social stratifications of their own which also are hierarchical and coercive. Finally, status is not always commensurate with income. The president of the Teamsters Union enjoys both power and privilege but not social prestige. Archbishop Desmond Tutu receives social prestige and a certain measure of privilege, but he possesses little real power.

3. Status/Class and Pastoral Care. Issues of social class have been largely unattended in pastoral care. Accusations that the pastoral care movement reflects a middle-class orientation ring true when one surveys its identification with the psychological sciences, the sixty-minute hour, structured relationships, and the minister as a professional. The social turmoil of the 1960s, the emergence of systems theory, and the discovery of the poor focused some attention on issues of justice and the wider range of behaviors and relationships. But by and large ministers have not demonstrated any deep sense of the ways the social system affects individuals, groups, and their dilemmas.

Perhaps the basic axiom for pastors is that an awareness of status and class must precede ministry in any given setting. Ministers are just as much a part of the system as anyone else. They reflect patterns, beliefs, values, and ways of understanding that make them uncomfortable with difference. Studies show that ministers and other helping persons relate best and provide the most assistance to those who are like them, and this is understandable. But such identification with a given class or orientation fosters the temptation to perceive *our* solution as *the* solution, as the better and perhaps even the more moral way, without appreciating the intuitions, values, and understandings others bring. It also fosters a sense of intimidation of those perceived to be "above" us and arrogance for those perceived to be "beneath" us. Congregational expectations of pastors and their understandings of religious symbolism do indeed reflect class and status. But such perceptions also reflect their understanding of the meaning of their lives and deserve to be taken seriously.

Awareness of status and class is also important as the pastor seeks to understand the dimensions of a given problem. As often as not marital problems are rooted in differing perceptions of what is proper and desirable, and these in turn are rooted in what we have learned to be acceptable behavior. Thus loneliness is frequently related to "making it"; conflicts over social life and the use of leisure time, whether to go bowling or to the symphony, may be symbolic of coming to terms with "who we are"; problems in communication, table manners, and how the couple views its "lot in life" are often related to class.

Finally, attention to status and class in any society raises immediately questions of social justice. Although pastoral care as such must always attend the individual and his or her distress, it must also acknowledge that much human distress stems from the inequalities of the social system. At this point pastoral care specialists may be in an unusually good position to be aware of the destructive power of social structures. Inequalities in health care delivery, in the judicial system, in the marketplace, in higher education, and in the religious community take their toll and eventuate in much human misery and frustration.

What the religious community at its best seeks is to cause persons to locate their security and sense of worth in some other reality than the class system. This begins to transpire when the pastor has learned not to identify with a given class and to foster a community of persons whose locus of value transcends any given social system.

Bibliography. R. Bendix and S. Lipset, *Class, Status and Power* (1953). P. Berger, *Invitation to Sociology: A Humanistic Perspective* (1963). K. Bloomquist, "Toward a Theological Engagement with Working-Class Experience," *Word and World*, 2:3 (1982). E. Goldberg, T. Macey, and L. Sata, "Socio-Economic Factors Which Influence Labeling of Mental Illness," *Psychological Reports*, 44 (1979), 1021–22. A. Hollingshead and F. C. Redlich, *Social Class and Mental Illness* (1958). E. Johnson, "Social Pastoral Care in the Urban Setting," *J. of Pastoral Care*, 32:4 (1978), 251–55. J. Myers and L. Bean, *A Decade Later: A Follow-Up of Social Class and Mental Illness* (1968). W. L. Warner, *Social Class in America: A Manual of Procedure for the Measurement of Social Status* (1949). B. Zablocki and R. Kanter,

"The Differentiation of Life-Styles," *American Review of Sociology*, 2 (1976).

L. O. MILLS

SOCIOLOGY OF RELIGIOUS AND PASTORAL CARE. *See also* BLACK, FEMINIST, *or* LIBERATION THEOLOGY AND PASTORAL CARE; MONEY; POOR PERSONS; POWER; RICH PERSONS; SOCIAL JUSTICE ISSUES; SOCIAL PERCEPTION, JUDGMENT, AND BELIEF. *Compare* CHURCH-SECT DIFFERENCES; CULTURAL AND ETHNIC FACTORS; LIFESTYLE ISSUES; RACISM; SEXISM.

SOCIAL WORKER. One who assists individuals and families in solving a variety of social, economic, educational, and health-related problems, usually through social agencies and institutions. The term is often applied broadly to persons such as welfare-eligibility caseworkers who provide concrete services (usually implementation of programs) but who frequently have no advanced professional training. In its more proper professional meaning "social worker" denotes a professionally educated person capable of assessing complex social needs and problems, evaluating assets and liabilities, identifying and utilizing problem-solving resources, coordinating other professionals, institutions, and agencies, and, most importantly, helping individuals and families psychologically.

Social work in the latter sense has evolved into a distinct profession with specific educational criteria, standards of practice, professional organizations, and a tradition of research. The profession's major organization in the U.S., the National Association of Social Workers, publishes a journal (*Social Work*) and recognizes advanced qualifications through its Academy of Certified Social Workers (ACSW). The ACSW certification requires two years of supervised postgraduate (M.S.W.) experience and the passing of a written examination.

Social workers' roles and responsibilities vary closely with education. *Bachelor-level (B.S.W.) social workers* generally offer concrete services and referrals for basic needs such as financial assistance, food, job training, employment, housing, health care, and child protection.

Masters-level (M.S.W.) social workers, by far the largest segment of the profession, typically engage in more complex problem solving in addition to involvement with concrete services. Frequently this entails facilitating psychosocial changes in matters such as marital or family conflict, substance abuse, juvenile delinquency, and resistance to medical, legal, or other professional help. In recent years social work has given increasing emphasis to psychological and psychiatric dimensions; today a number of social workers are essentially psychotherapists or marriage and family counselors, with many of these in private practice. Masters-level social workers also fill many administrative, supervisory, and consultative positions in health and educational institutions and in social agencies.

Another smaller branch of the profession, generally at the masters level, engages in community development, planning, and organizing, often working in impoverished communities to develop community resources. The social work profession itself originated in such community-based work in the late nineteenth and early twentieth-century through the pioneering efforts of social workers like Jane Addams of Chicago's Hull House.

Doctoral-level social workers generally function as senior administrators, educators, and researchers; the D.S.W.

is essentially a research and teaching degree. The field's major journals in the U.S., *Social Work* and *Social Casework,* publish much of this research and offer many psychologically and therapeutically oriented articles of value to pastoral counselors and researchers.

A. C. HUNTER

INTERPROFESSIONAL TEAMS AND RELATIONSHIPS; SOCIAL SERVICES AND PASTORAL CARE. *Compare* CLINICAL PSYCHOLOGIST; MARRIAGE AND FAMILY THERAPIST; PSYCHIATRIST/PSYCHIATRY; PSYCHOLOGIST; PSYCHOTHERAPIST.

SOCIALIZATION. *See* PSYCHOSOCIAL DEVELOPMENT; SOCIOLOGY OF RELIGIOUS AND PASTORAL CARE.

SOCIETY AND PERSONALITY. *See* PERSONALITY, SOCIETY, AND CULTURE.

SOCIETY OF FRIENDS. *See* QUAKER TRADITION OF CARE.

SOCIOBIOLOGY. A discipline of study in which principles derived from evolutionary biology are applied to the study of social behavior. Biologists have traditionally employed evolution to explain the structure and function of living things; only recently, however, have they begun to employ similar principles to the understanding of behavior—most strikingly, complex patterns of social behavior. It should be noted that sociobiology is not a theory; rather, it is a discipline that involves the unification of ecology, ethology (the biological study of animal behavior), and evolution.

Sociobiologic research has cast new light on previously unexplained patterns in animal behavior and, given the underlying biologic commonality between human beings and other living things, similar light may well be shed on humans. For example, animal altruism has long been an evolutionary conundrum; according to the precepts of Darwinian natural selection, living things should never behave in a manner that reduces their own success in projecting genes into the future (i.e., that reduces their "fitness"). And yet, apparent altruism is commonly observed in nature, as when individuals give an alarm call upon approach of a predator, thereby making themselves more susceptible to death, but at the same time increasing the chances that another individual, hearing the alarm call, might be saved. Sociobiologists now postulate that such cases of apparent altruism can be explained as representing underlying genetic selfishness, since the apparent altruist can be alerting genetic relatives, who have a certain probability of carrying the gene that is responsible for the alarm-calling itself. Thus, behavior that appears to be superficially altruistic is often revealed as genetic selfishness. This generalizes to the principle of "inclusive fitness," which recognizes that the important evolutionary unit is not the individual *or* the species, but rather, the individual's genes, which are represented in varying proportion in the individual's relatives. As a general rule, living things seem to behave in a manner that maximizes their inclusive fitness, regardless of the effect on their personal lives.

This principle may have significant ramifications for human beings, providing an explanation for the universal human tendency toward nepotism, and a wide array of family-centered biases in human behavior, including the diversity of kinship systems so widely studied by anthropologists. In addition, it suggest a new perspective on human moral and ethical systems, since these systems may well have the function of leavening the otherwise socially destructive human tendencies toward genetic selfishness.

The biology of male-female differences provides another striking example. Because males are defined as that sex which produces a large number of very small sex cells (sperm) whereas females produce a relatively small number of large sex cells (eggs), sociobiologists have interpreted significant trends in male-female behavior as due to the differing pressures of natural selection, operating via fitness maximization, on each sex. Males are typically more aggressive, competing among themselves for access to the females, which become a scarce and sought-after reproductive resource. Human beings frequently show similar tendencies, beginning in early childhood and continuing with patterns in adulthood.

A similar sociobiologic perspective provides new insights into family structure, parental inclinations, parent-offspring conflict, patterns of mate choice, etc. In each case, behavior is viewed as a "strategy" (not consciously plotted) directed toward maximizing genetic representation in the future. Human beings are clearly cultural as well as biological creatures, and in some cases, our inclinations may be in conflict. In other cases they may be surprisingly congruent, since culture itself seems to be one of our most important adaptations. The interface between biology and culture may prove to be one of the most mysterious yet important phenomena in human behavior; in the meantime, sociobiology offers a fresh perspective especially on the former, and aims at a unified scientific understanding of "human nature."

Bibliography. D. P. Barash, *The Whisperings Within* (1981); *Sociobiology and Behavior*, 2d. ed. (1982). G. S. Stent, ed., *Morality as a Biological Phenomenon*, rev. ed. (1980). E. O. Wilson, *On Human Nature* (1978).

D. BARASH

PERSONALITY, BIOLOGICAL DIMENSIONS OF; SOCIAL SCIENCES. *See also* AGGRESSION AND ASSERTION; HUMAN NATURE, PROBLEM OF; PERSONALITY, SOCIETY, AND CULTURE; SEXUALITY, BIOLOGICAL AND PSYCHOSOCIAL THEORY OF.

SOCIOLOGY OF RELIGION. The sociology of religion is often defined as a subdiscipline of sociology focusing particularly on religious institutions and collectivities. This is a useful, but limited, way of delineating coverage of the sociology of religion. A broader definition more in keeping with classical approaches to the sociology of religion treats the field as more integral to the discipline of sociology itself. This perspective is exemplified by writings of Peter Berger and Thomas Luckmann (1963), who present a view of sociology which treats religion as crucial to the operation of society, especially in the legitimation of knowledge and institutional structures in society. This perspective has since been developed in other writings by Berger (1967) and Luckmann (1967) that have become modern classics in the field.

1. Classical Theories. Classical theorists of the sociology of religion such as Emile Durkheim and Max Weber treated religion as a key variable in understanding how society works. These and other classical theorists would have had difficulty conceptualizing a society in which religion did not play a major role, and they sought to understand that role. Popular conceptions of the time also attributed an important place in the culture of societies to religion, and this contributed to the attention paid to religion by early theorists.

Durkheim believed that religion was a major factor leading to social solidarity, integration, and cohesion. His *Elementary Forms of Religious Life* (1965) focused on these issues, using the Australian aborigines as the vehicle of study. In this work he offered what has become the most-cited definition of religion in the field of sociology:

> A religion is a unified system of beliefs and practices related to sacred things, that is to say, things set apart and forbidden—beliefs and practices which unite into a single moral community called a Church, all those who adhere to them (1965, p. 62).

This definition contains Durkheim's important sacred-profane distinction, and also includes the essential social element. According to Durkheim, religion is not religion unless it is represented in a collective way. And, in an ironic and controversial twist, Durkheim seemed to assert that "religious belief was a representation of the morphological properties of the society in which it was located and that religious practice was a 'celebration' of the social sphere, binding the participants together" (Robertson, 1970, p. 15). This notion of society worshiping itself through religious beliefs and rituals was illustrated by Durkheim using the Australian aboriginal practice of totemism.

Max Weber believed that studying religion would lead to an understanding of the basic differences between Western and Eastern societies. His empirically based efforts to demonstrate that belief led to the most cited of his works, *The Protestant Ethic and the Spirit of Capitalism* (1904). In this work he focused on Calvinism as a wellspring for Western thought practices that eventually led to the development of capitalism as an economic form. His view stressed the contribution of Western religious thought to the growing *rationalization* of the West. This movement toward rationalization was in sharp contrast to the impact of the other religious traditions of the East, such as Hinduism and Confucianism.

Weber's theoretical bent was partially a response to Marxism, which treated religious beliefs in general as derivative of material concerns. Marxist thought seemed to dismiss religion as ideological and designed only to promote the position of the dominant classes in any society. Weber was convinced that this treatment of religion concealed the fact that religious ideas could and did have a strong influence on the development of societies. Thus, he is often said to have turned Marx on his head and treated religion as a powerful influence on human affairs, rather than as almost an afterthought cynically developed to rationalize and justify certain power arrangements. The debate over this issue continues to this day in the sociology of religion (see Robertson, 1970, for a review).

Weber also contributed other ideas of import to the sociology of religion. He made use of an "ideal type" methodology which allowed a focus on key facets of any social phenomenon, and he stressed the importance of the researcher truly understanding that which was being researched. Weber wrote of the differences between *exemplary* and *ethical* prophecy, with the latter used for major cultural breakthroughs, while the former was indicative of more traditional, status quo leadership. His work has also contributed to the development of a line of research on differences between types of religious organizations.

After the auspicious beginning of the sociology of religion through the works of Durkheim, Weber, and others, interest in the field (and in the view of religion as important to the understanding of society) waned markedly. Until recently, religion was relegated to a minor issue, particularly in American sociology. Thus, for fifty years or so, sociology, especially of the American variety, virtually ignored religion as an important variable. Only since the 1960s has religion been treated as important, with social theorists integrating religion into sociological theorizing.

2. **Definitional Issues.** A crucial issue to be faced by sociology of religion concerns the basic definition of religion. Weber, who wrote five books dealing with religion, refused to define it, saying that this should be done at the conclusion of his studies. Durkheim offered the definition above, which, although containing a substantive element (sacredness), has given rise to the *functional* approach to defining the phenomena of study. This approach is inclusive of virtually any system of thought that divides cultural elements into sacred and profane, and which is promoted within a collectivity.

While potentially useful, this broad approach has been criticized by many as not allowing adequate differentiation among systems of thought. Many of the critics of broad functional views espouse a *substantive* definition of the phenomena of study. In other words, a religion must contain specific beliefs in order to qualify as a religion. A substantive requirement favored by many concerns positing an omniscient and/or supernatural being. But even this limited substantive approach has been criticized as being too Western in application. Excellent discussions of definitional problems in the sociology of religion are found in Robertson (1970, pp. 34–51) and Berger (1967, pp. 175–85); both eventually adopt an approach that combines substantive and functional aspects.

Instead of floundering on the definitional issue, most contemporary scholars adopt an analytical approach to religion that focuses on specific aspects of religion, while seeking to avoid statements about ultimate truth or falsity of any particular religious belief. For instance, one popular text book (McGuire, 1987) uses a four-part approach, which discusses separately religious beliefs, religious rituals, religious experience, and religious communities. This uses the traditional analytical breakdown of cognitive, behavioral, and emotional levels, and adds the collective level as a special area of study for the sociologist.

Another popular approach within the discipline has been that of Charles Glock and Rodney Stark (1965),

who developed an analytical scheme referred to as the "dimensions of religiosity." This scheme includes: the *experiential* dimension (subjective religious experience and emotion); the *ritualistic* dimension (behaviors expected of religious people); the *ideological* dimension (beliefs held by the religious); the *intellectual* dimension (knowledge of the basic tenets of the religion); and the *consequential* dimension (effects of religion in everyday life). This broad analytical approach has led to a tremendous amount of research in the sociology of religion, and has generally proved quite useful.

3. **Modern Sociology of Religion.** In the past few decades there has been renewed interest in the sociology of religion, especially in America. That new interest has been given great impetus by the rise of many new religious movements and the growing involvement in the nation's political life of religious groups, especially those of a more conservative bent.

Major interest sparked by the rise of new religions, commonly referred to as "cults," has focused on ethnographic-like studies of a number of the newer religions. Also, there has been a major research concern with the conversion of individuals to the new religions. Popular concern with the movement of many youth into new religions has led to scholarly interest by sociologists of religion in questions about who joins, and why. Studies of the conversion/recruitment process have been done, often complemented by studies of organizational development and change in the new groups.

The growing political sophistication and involvement of religious people and groups who had not normally participated in politics to the degree of other groups has led to many studies of this process. Also, the growth of media evangelism and its involvement in politics has attracted the attention of sociologists. Thus the relationship between politics and religion has become fertile ground for studies by sociologists of religion.

Bibliography. P. Berger, *The Sacred Canopy* (1967). P. Berger and T. Luckmann, "Sociology of Religion and Sociology of Knowledge," *Sociology and Social Research*, 47 (1963), 417–27. E. Durkheim, *The Elementary Forms of Religious Life* (1961 [1915]). C. Glock and R. Stark, *Religion and Society in Tension* (1965). T. Luckmann, *Invisible Religion* (1967). M. McGuire, *Religion: The Social Context* (1987). R. Robertson, *The Sociological Interpretation of Religion* (1970). M. Weber, *The Protestant Ethic and the Spirit of Capitalism* (1958 [1904]).

J. T. RICHARDSON

AFRICAN, NATIVE AMERICAN, *or* WEST INDIAN TRADITIONAL RELIGION, PERSONAL CARE IN; CHURCH-SECT DIFFERENCES IN PASTORAL CARE; MORAL BEHAVIOR AND RELIGION; NEW RELIGIOUS MOVEMENTS; RELIGION; RELIGIOUS BEHAVIOR; RITUAL AND PASTORAL CARE; SOCIAL SCIENCES. *See also* COMMUNITY, FELLOWSHIP, AND CARE; JOURNALS IN RELIGION, THEOLOGY, AND THE SOCIAL SCIENCES, INTERDISCIPLINARY; PERSONALITY, SOCIETY, AND CULTURE. *Compare* CULTURAL ANTHROPOLOGY; PASTORAL SOCIOLOGY; PSYCHOLOGY OF RELIGION; SECULARIZATION/SECULARISM.

SOCIOLOGY OF RELIGIOUS AND PASTORAL CARE. Pastoral care and counseling take part in the developing relationship between religious institutions and the rest of society. The sociology of pastoral care, as distinguished from its cultural anthropology, therefore

stresses the *evolution* of its historical forms within larger social and historical processes. These involve a movement from relatively simple configurations of religious and social life to the complex forms of the modern world, marked by progressive differentiation or specialization of social institutions, and by the increasing rationalization and pluralism of culture. An anthropological approach, on the other hand, seeks to understand the contemporary functions of religious care and counseling in terms of the interdependence of religion and society, seen with special clarity in "primitive" societies. In this perspective, religion participates pervasively in forming social identity and transmitting a unified, continuous cultural perspective to new generations.

This article discusses both points of view, focusing first on religious care in primitive and traditional societies where its fundamentally unifying functions are prominent, then describing the changes that have occurred in modes of pastoral care and counseling as society has become more individualistic, differentiated, and complex.

1. **Ritual Care in Primitive Societies.** In the simplest human societies, moral and religious care are virtually synonymous with participation in the community's collective rites and rituals. Emile Durkheim's classic vision in *The Elementary Forms of the Religious Life* shows how such collective rites — the ceremonies, rituals, and sacred events of a community — stimulate and order the most intensely shared emotions and moral sentiments of a people. By stimulating powerful group emotion or "collective effervescence" and giving it symbolic representation and order, ritual cements the moral integrity of every society by nurturing the inner conscience of its members and forging the objective authority of its institutions. Similarly, Bronislaw Malinowski showed how religious rites of passage and supplication shape persons' emotions and relationships from birth through puberty and marriage to death, thus transmitting social traditions across biological boundary lines. Malinowski argued that human beings in every society, faced with natural limits and fateful contingencies beyond control by technical means, rely on the ritual enactment of religious belief to ground in experience the shared self-awareness and bonds of mutual aid and affection vital to society.

More recently, Claude Lévi-Strauss has analyzed the symbolic power of shamanistic healing to reinterpret personal experience in collective myth and transform it in ritual. This takes place, he observes, through processes of abreaction and transference parallel to those found in psychoanalysis. The shaman narrates a timelessly fixed group myth which the patient absorbs as the truth of his or her present condition, just as the analyst listens as the patient constructs an individual myth of pieces drawn from his or her own past. Both cures induce an experience and recreate a myth that the patient must live out, or relive, as a means of gaining wholeness.

2. **Pastoral Care in Traditional and Early Modern Societies.** Within the matrix of traditional Western societies, from classical antiquity to the beginnings of modern statehood and industry, religious caring grew more elaborately developed and differentiated, but it continued to find primary expression in corporate ritual

and moral regulation. As religious institutions became differentiated from kinship, politics, technology, and the economy in more complex societies, pastoral care took on a more distinctive life of its own in the religious realm.

With the rise of prophetic religions such as Judaism and Christianity, Max Weber saw pastoral care, "the religious cultivation on the individual," moving away from magical aid and the sacramental provision of consoling grace toward more rationalized forms of religious instruction based on ethical casuistry. Unlike preaching, which comes to prominence in periods of moral crisis and change, pastoral care exerts a primary influence on the routine conduct of everyday life in the workaday world. The chief instance of such influence for Weber was pastoral care's crucial role in promoting capitalism. In *The Protestant Ethic and the Spirit of Capitalism* Weber's argument for the religious foundations of modern capitalism turns on the pastoral psychology of ascetic Protestantism, which offered a practical response to the suffering caused by the dogma of predestination. Pastors encouraged the faithful to attain certainty of their divine election through intense worldly activity. Thus the Calvinist's inner loneliness and spiritual isolation before an awesome and distant God gave rise to "a restless and systematic struggle with life" through methodical, disciplined activity aimed at fulfilling a divine calling in the workaday world.

In Marxist analysis, by contrast, religious care *derives* from economic interests: pastoral care enacts religious ideas that seek to justify class-specific interests and social structures. For the oppressed at the bottom of the social order, religion, "the opium of the people," simultaneously expresses, protests, and masks real suffering caused by alienating and exploitative institutions. Religion offers otherworldly consolation and compensation in place of social criticism and transformation. For the middle class in capitalist societies, religion inspires individual industry and justifies its economic rewards as the fruits of moral virtue. For wealthy, powerful elites, religion depicts good fortune as moral desert instead of social injustice, while interpreting subjective feelings as universal truths in mystical or therapeutic terms.

In recent decades Marxist critiques of religion, and hence religious care, have combined with predominantly Freudian psychology in the work of Theodor Adorno, Erich Fromm, Herbert Marcuse, Jürgen Habermas, and others of the "Frankfurt School" of critical sociology. These theorists and their successors stress the role of "conformist psychology" in fostering "social amnesia," as Russell Jacoby puts it. In contrast to Freud, who sought to *expose* the fundamental antagonism between self and society, the therapeutic and pastoral psychologies of recent years are said to hide it. They cloak the economic and social-structural sources of human suffering and alienation in the guise of popular ideals of individual autonomy, interpersonal adjustment, and the integrity of bourgeois cultural values. This deception promises private self-fulfillment and intimacy in return for the repression of true individuality and justice. Corporate capitalism demands that the individual be reduced to a "one-dimensional" instrument of production and consumption, the "psychic commodity of the commodity society." Through such "repressive desublimation," argues Marcuse, capitalism prevails by transforming the original Puritan spirit of capitalism. Therapeutic translation divests religion of moral truth, turning it into a pragmatic tool to strengthen individual self-esteem and social synchronization. In this analysis, then, pastoral care and counseling's recent emphasis on individuality, self-expression, intimate relationships, psychic growth, and the like are all self-deceived attempts to subordinate individuals to the inner demands of corporate capitalism, evading the true sources of human suffering in the political and economic organization of society.

3. Pastoral Care in Modern Societies. In the modern state of "religious evolution," which Robert Bellah finds in advanced Western societies, a symbolically self-conscious and "multiplex" structure of religious meaning that *accepts* the world replaces the world-rejecting metaphysical dualism of historic orthodoxy. Flexible patterns of denominational membership predominate, functioning within large-scale democratic societies. Such societies are politically committed to the freedom and equality of individuals and to universal rights rather than traditional hierarchies of social strata fixed by birth and by rigidly prescribed reciprocal duties. In this situation religious life is marked by high degrees of pluralism, fluidity, and sometimes vividly contrasting patterns of progressive and reactionary modes of thought and action. Here the more liberal forms of theology of the mainline churches attempt to "ground religion in the structure of the human situation itself." And here pastoral psychology takes on special importance and novel forms aimed at therapeutically enhancing the self's capacity to comprehend and integrate its experience of a complex world. Pastoral psychologies tend therefore to join in sociocultural trends, encouraging individuals to reinterpret doctrine and take responsibility for moral choice in the search for personal maturity and social relevance. Insofar as such themes have typified the contemporary pastoral care and counseling movements, they have functioned as important sources of modernizing and morally relativizing forces in recent social history.

4. Emerging Issues and Criticism. According to cultural critics like Ernest Troeltsch, Philip Rieff, and Peter Berger, the assimilation of social-scientific psychology into pastoral care in American religion over the past century reflects a synthetic openness to the larger culture consonant with the modern need for self-integration in a complex, specialized, intricately coordinated society. But this "triumph of the therapeutic" also threatens to identify Christianity with an entirely individualized and inwardly spiritual religion indifferent to social and ethical concerns. Pastoral care in mainline churches, others add, is socially biased toward verbal, insight-oriented methods and individualistic values specific to the educated white middle class in first-world nations, and to its male members in particular. Although theologically conservative and evangelical Christians criticize secularizing developments in pastoral care, they, too, share in them.

Countering such criticisms are, on one hand, a welter of humanistic, transpersonal, and other religious psychologies, aimed at overcoming the reductionist and secularizing force of establishment psychology. On the other hand, pastoral psychologies of moral development

and virtue, operating through disciplined social practices in community, seek to counter the dominant individualistic piety of the culture. The latter points of view stress the congregation itself as a community of caring and character formation that can help to mediate and ethically interpret the reciprocal relationship between ostensibly "private" persons and the public world. In this perspective the work of the pastor focuses less on individual and family counseling than on leadership in the formation of congregations as "caring communities" defined by their common moral and religious purpose.

Undoubtedly, personal counseling will continue to be a necessary and important expression of the pastoral role, and specialized pastoral therapies will continue to have their place in the larger life of the churches in modern society. But there may well be a growing emphasis in future pastoral care on liturgy and congregational life in the mainline denominations, especially if these corporate forms of care can be combined with and supported by nonreductionist forms of pastoral psychology. Such a combination, in response to the unique freedoms, tensions, and structural divisions of modern society, could foster distinctively modern, yet unified, experiences of those deeply shared human emotions and reflections that inspire moral and religious life.

Bibliography. T. Adorno, M. Horkheimer, and H. Marcuse, *Kritische Theorie der Gesellschaft* (1969). R. Bellah, *Beyond Belief* (1970). P. Berger, *The Sacred Canopy* (1967). D. Browning, *The Moral Context of Pastoral Care* (1976). E. Durkheim, *The Elementary Forms of the Religious Life* (1965 [1912]). E. Fromm, *Escape From Freedom* (1941). J. R. Haule, "The Care of Souls: Psychology and Religion in Anthropological Perspective," *J. of Pastoral Theology*, 11, 108–16. D. Held, *Introduction to Critical Theory: Horkheimer to Habermas* (1980). J. Hunter, *American Evangelicalism* (1983). R. Jacoby, *Social Amnesia* (1975). C. Lévi-Strauss, "The Effectiveness of Symbols," in *Structural Anthropology*, C. Jacobson and B. G. Schoepf, trans., (1963). B. Malinowski, *Magic, Science, and Religion* (1948). H. Marcuse, *One-Dimensional Man* (1964). K. Marx, "Contribution to the Critique of Hegel's Philosophy of Right: Introduction" [1844], in K. Marx, *The Early Texts*, D. McLellan, ed. (1971). P. Rieff, *The Triumph of the Therapeutic* (1966). E. Troeltsch, *The Social Teaching of the Christian Churches* (1931 [1911]). V. Turner, *The Ritual Process* (1969). M. Weber, *The Protestant Ethic and the Spirit of Capitalism* (1958 [1904–5]). M. Weber, *The Sociology of Religion* (1963 [1922]).

S. M. TIPTON

CHURCH-SECT DIFFERENCES; CULTURAL AND ETHNIC FACTORS; CULTURAL ANTHROPOLOGY OF RELIGION, DISCIPLINE OF; PASTORAL SOCIOLOGY; PERSONALITY, SOCIETY, AND CULTURE; SOCIAL PSYCHOLOGY, DISCIPLINE OF; SOCIAL STATUS AND CLASS FACTORS. *See also* PERSONAL, CONCEPT OF, IN PASTORAL CARE; RITUAL; SECULARIZATION/SECULARISM; SHAMAN; SPIRITUAL MASTERS AND GUIDES; SUGGESTION, PERSUASION, AND INFLUENCE; WORLD VIEW. *Compare* POPULAR THERAPEUTIC MOVEMENTS AND PSYCHOLOGIES; PSYCHOLOGY IN AMERICAN RELIGION; SOCIAL JUSTICE ISSUES; *also* AFRICAN, NATIVE AMERICAN, *or* WEST INDIAN TRADITIONAL RELIGION, PERSONAL CARE IN.

SOCIOPATHIC PERSONALITY. *See* ANTISOCIAL PERSONS.

SOCRATES (ca. 469–399 B.C.). Greek philosopher who developed the "Socratic method"—a style of discussion which has found entry into thought and method in teaching and counseling. This philosophical method consists of creating an aura of doubt, perplexity, and self-distrust concerning accepted truths by means of raising questions in the fashion of dialectic cross-examination. Dubbed "midwifing" of ideas, it exposes unexamined presuppositions, inadequate knowledge, the questions of motives, means, and ends in order to lead to more enlightened decisions and conduct. Socrates's fervent practice of this method is grounded in two assumptions: A moral one views the soul as the lord over the body, reason as guiding conduct. Thus, knowledge affects virtuousness. A religious assumption calls for the immortal soul's preparation for eternity through knowledge and wisdom (salvation by education).

It has been said that Socrates's overarching concern with and care for the soul left its mark on the Greek way of life and influenced the emergence of the idea of care of souls in Christianity. There are echoes of his thought in the ethical and hermeneutical themes of pastoral care in the 1980s.

N. F. HAHN

PSYCHOTHERAPY; PHILOSOPHY AND PSYCHOLOGY, WESTERN.

SODOMY. *See* SEXUAL VARIETY, DEVIANCE, AND DISORDER.

SOLITUDE. *See* PRIVACY AND SOLITUDE. *See also* MEDITATION.

SOMATIZING/SOMATOFORM DISORDERS. *See* PSYCHOSOMATIC ILLNESS.

SOMATOTYPE. A term used to designate a general body type or physique. Somatotype is used most often in connection with the work of Sheldon (1942), who attempted to relate physique to personality and psychopathology. Sheldon postulated three general body types: *endomorphs* are the larger and more obese persons, and are believed to love comfort, be relaxed and sociable, and love eating; *mesomorphs* are muscular and strong, of medium weight, and are believed to love adventure, exercise, and activities that demand boldness and courage; *ectomorphs* are frail and slender, and are described as withdrawn and concerned with intellectual matters.

Sheldon's work has received limited validation (e.g., Cortes and Gatti, 1965), but the bulk of the research has failed to support his predictions. Although physique may partially account for the development of personality and psychopathology, the relationship appears to be indirect.

Bibliography. J. B. Cortes and F. M. Gatti, "Physique and Self-Description of Temperament," *J. of Consulting Psychology*, 29 (1965), 432–39.

R. E. BUTMAN

PERSONALITY THEORY; TEMPERAMENT. *Compare* BODY; BODY IMAGE.

SOMNAMBULISM. *See* SLEEP AND SLEEP DISORDERS.

SORROW. *See* GRIEF AND LOSS; SADNESS AND DEPRESSION.

SOUL. Term referring to the spiritual side of human existence. It indicates both the life principle which animates the body and the individuality of the person as expressed in thought, will and emotion. Soul is, thus, the seat of human activity and the source of moral judgment.

1. Biblical Usage. The scriptural view of human nature points away from a radical body-soul dualism toward a "psychosomatic unity." Nevertheless, the human being is a creature of polarities: the imagery of the OT can describe clay animated by "breath" (*ruah*) and can term the nonphysical pole of humanity "spirit" (*nephesh*). The *nephesh* can be described as going down to Sheol or Hades upon the death of the person: those in Sheol are "shades" (*rephaim*). *Nephesh* can also, by extension, refer to the whole person. The OT presents a fairly clear picture of the human being as an animated being, an embodied life. That the OT contains a wholistic anthropology but equally a sense of physical-spiritual polarity is seen from passages like Ezekiel 37 where bones and flesh come together but live only when the animating *ruah* comes upon them. *Ruah* tends to indicate the animating principle, *nephesh* the animated being.

In the intertestamental literature a sense of duality is reinforced. The Wisdom of Solomon in particular argues the distinction of soul and body as well as the preexistence and immortality of souls (2:23; 3:1ff; 7:17, 20; 8:20). This is usually viewed as the result of Greek influence upon Hebrew thought, but it is also the result of a meditation on the problem of *rephaim* in Sheol and the presence, even there, of God (cf. Pss. 86:13; 139:8; Prov. 15:11).

The NT turns still more clearly toward the Greek usage of "body and soul" (*soma* and *psyche*) but also uses the more Hebraic phrases "flesh and spirit" (*sarx* and *pneuma*) or "body and spirit" (*soma* and *pneuma*). The dualistic direction of the intertestamental literature has, however, been arrested and the NT points toward the human being as a unity: redemption does not refer to soul as abstracted from body but to the whole person. In many instances *psyche* indicates "life" or the human person rather than "soul" (cf. Mt. 6:25; Mk. 3:4; 8:35–37) while the more Greek meaning, "soul," appears in Rev. 6:9. There is no indication in the NT that the soul or "life" escapes by nature the corruptibility of the body. Immortality of soul rests, like resurrection of the body, on God. There is no implication, moreover, of a trichotomous humanity composed of body, soul, and spirit in the NT: the human being is a unified, though bipolar being, an embodied life.

2. Soul in Greek Philosophy. The more detailed speculation concerning soul which influenced the development of Christian thought came from the Greeks. We note two basic positions: the Platonic, which was most influential during the patristic period, and the Aristotelian, which shaped later medieval theology. Plato, drawing both on Socrates and on Orphic theology with its doctrine of the immortality of the soul, taught that human beings were composed of body and soul, the latter being the immaterial guide or ruler of the body. Soul or *psyche* consisted in the rational function, the moral courage and the appetites or affections with only the rational function being immortal. This essentially dualistic sense of body and soul carries over from Plato into Neoplatonism, the church fathers, and (in modern philosophy) the Cartesians. The tendency in all these thinkers was to identify soul with mind and its functions.

Aristotle offers a radically different perspective: he viewed the human being as a composite and identified *psyche* as the animating principle, the consciousness and life of the body. The soul, thus, is immaterial or spiritual. In contrast to Plato, however, no dualism of body and soul is implied: the body is the matter of which the soul is the form. Soul is the real "substance," the formal principle, the source of physical motion, and the final cause or inward goal-regulator (*entelechy*) of the body. In the case of humans, the soul is also the intellectual or rational function of the individual.

Neither the biblical writers nor the Greek philosophers will permit the view of soul as mere epiphenomenon of the body. Soul is a spiritual, immaterial reality which is essentially simple and indivisible, identifiable with the life of the human being and the intellectual functions. It need not be located at any point in the body since it is the life or, for Aristotle, the form of the body.

3. Soul in the History of Christian Thought. The fathers of the first five centuries of the Common Era recognized three theories of the origin of the soul: preexistence, creationism, and traducianism. The first is essentially Platonic. The soul, as a spiritual substance neither created nor destroyed, pre-exists the created body and must be embodied—perhaps because of a premundane fall of souls from divine perfection. This view, as denying the doctrine of creation *ex nihilo*, was rejected by all but the most platonizing of the fathers (e.g., Origen). The majority were creationists, arguing that souls are created by God for bodies and are joined with the body at conception. A smaller number, including Tertullian, held that the soul, like the body, is inherited from the parents: this view is termed traducianism. In both of these latter views, the Platonic dualism of body and soul is modified in favor of a view approaching that of Scripture.

If the fathers believed in the separation of body and soul at death, they viewed this as unnatural, as the result of sin, and they held to the doctrine of the Resurrection as descriptive of the destiny intended by God for humanity: both body and soul were destined for immortality since the person functions as a living whole. This latter point is particularly clear in the thought of Justin Martyr, Athenagoras, Tertullian, and Augustine. In addition to their modification of Platonism, the fathers must also be credited with the addition of a strong emphasis on the faculty of will to the doctrine of soul.

In the Middle Ages, after the rediscovery of Aristotle and the incorporation of Aristotelian thought into Christian philosophy by Thomas Aquinas, the Aristotelian notion of soul as *entelechy* prevailed over the Platonic position and the view of the human being as a living unity received a powerful philosophical impetus. The creationist view of the origin of soul became normative in Roman Catholicism and among the Reformed at the time of the Reformation, while the traducian position was favored by Lutheranism. Return to an essentially dualistic view occurs in the thought of Descartes who identified soul with thought and body with "extension." The great philosophical problem faced by Cartesianism, and one of the reasons that Descartes's philosophy was not readily accepted by theologians, was the difficulty it encountered in explaining the interaction of body and soul.

A renewed interest in "soul" is manifest in nineteenth-century German philosophy and theology, together with a preference for trichotomy on the part of authors like Lotze and Delitzsch. A distinction is here made between soul (*psyche, Seele*) and spirit (*pneuma, Geist*), according to which spirit is a higher principle than soul: soul is merely the life principle, spirit is the "unity of our being" or our "ego." This form of trichotomy does not, therefore, deny but rather presses the unity of the person under the three forms of body, soul, and spirit. The importance of this philosophical development for theology, philosophy, and the new discipline of psychology is that, for the first time in the history of thought, it identifies fully the issue of an ego, of the individual as conscious self, and maintains the polarity of the human being as a psychosomatic unity which cannot simply be reduced to protoplasm and its functions. Soul and spirit now become the seat of personality as well as the locus of intellect, will and affections.

The concepts of ego and self deriving from this philosophic history have been widely employed in certain branches of modern psychology (especially psychoanalysis and humanistic psychology), but "soul" has been almost universally rejected with the primary exception of Carl Jung and his school. Jung disavowed the religious and the philosophical meanings that "soul" has had in the West, which he regarded as projections, but found the term psychologically valuable and often employed it. His intent was to assert the nonreductive reality and mystery of psychic life, especially the unconscious, against the materialistic and rationalist spirit of modern psychology. He also made a technical distinction in some writings between soul, as a "soul-complex" in the unconscious (related to the anima), and psyche, the latter referring to the whole of psychic life (Jung, 1953, p. 201).

In modern clinical pastoral care and counseling and pastoral theology, "soul" has also been generally replaced by the more psychological "ego" and "self," though the growing influence of Jung's psychology may lead to a recovery of its use and importance. From a more psychoanalytic and theological perspective, Charles V. Gerkin (1984, ch. 5) has proposed a revised concept of soul, similar to the modern concept of spirit, related to hermeneutical process.

Bibliography. G. C. Berkouwer, *Man: The Image of God* (1962). G. S. Brett, *The History of Psychology*, 3 vols. (1912–21); abr. ed., 1 vol. (1965). C. Brown, "Soul/Spirit," in *New International Dictionary of New Testament Theology*, III, pp. 676–709. F. Copleston, *A History of Philosophy*, 9 vols. (1946–74). F. Delitzsch, *Biblical Psychology* (1875). C. V. Gerkin, *The Living Human Document* (1984). C. G. Jung, *Two Essays in Analytical Psychology* (1953). H. W. Robinson, *The Christian Doctrine of Man*, 3d ed. (1926). E. Rohde, *Psyche: The Cult of Souls and Belief in Immortality Among the Greeks* (1925).

R. Seeberg, *Text-Book of the History of Doctrines*, ET, C. Hay (1956).

R. A. MULLER

PERSON; PHILOSOPHY AND PSYCHOLOGY, WESTERN; PSY-CHE; SELF. *See also* ESCHATOLOGY AND PASTORAL CARE; I AND THOU; LIFE/ALIVENESS; PERSONAL, CONCEPT OF, IN PASTO-RAL CARE; SURVIVAL (Occult); THEOLOGICAL ANTHROPOL-OGY, DISCIPLINE OF. *Compare* EGO, PSYCHOLOGICAL MEAN-INGS AND THEORY OF; IMAGO DEI; SELF-TRANSCENDENCE.

SOUL (Black Church). Refers to the emotional, rhythmic, expressive character of black culture as well as to an ethos of solidarity, endurance, and honest appreciation of the ambiguities of black life. Soul is the essential sense of being that pulsates in the life of the black community.

The term does not have a specifically religious meaning. While soul is sometimes used to refer to the essence and uniqueness of what it means to be black, it is not simply a synonym for black. Rather, the term is used as an inclusive way to apply to food, music, and persons, and often connotes a bitter-sweet quality. Soul's musical, theatrical, or linguistic expression is an affirmation of black life as it is.

Alfred Pasteur and Ivory Toldson (1982) defined soul as the ability to express feelings in deeply creative ways. For many, the greatest expression of soul occurs through black secular and sacred music. Not just an aspect of soul, the mystic is the integrative force that unifies other aspects; it contains spontaneity, emotion, and rhythm.

Soul has adaptive qualities; some have seen it as having a sustaining impact enabling blacks to survive racial and economic hardships. Thus there is a strong theme of endurance and perseverance in the sermons and songs of black culture.

Bibliography. U. Hannerz, *Soul Side: Inquiries Into Ghetto Culture and Community* (1969). B. Pasteur and I. L. Toldson, *Roots of Soul* (1982).

W. E. GOODEN

BLACK AMERICAN PASTORAL CARE. *Compare* AFRICAN *or* WEST INDIAN TRADITIONAL RELIGION; PERSONAL, CONCEPT OF, IN PASTORAL CARE; SELF.

SOUL-MAKING. *See* ARCHETYPAL PSYCHOLOGY.

SOUTH AFRICAN PASTORAL CARE MOVE-MENT. It has taken a long time for the pastoral care movement to take root in South Africa. There are probably three main reasons for this. First, South Africa long regarded psychology with a certain reserve. This in turn was due to Freud's condemnation of religion — and also to the ideas of Jung, who at first appeared to view religion in a much more positive light but eventually seemed to regard it as a purely individual and intrapsychic event. A second cause would certainly be the methodology and prejudiced point of departure, amounting to an "exclusion de la transcendance," (Flournoy), employed by the original psychology of religion. Third, it was long feared that the pastoral care movement, while securely based psychologically, did not rest on a very solid theological foundation. Fortunately all this is long past, and most South African theological faculties and

colleges have for a considerable time been making grateful use of the knowledge, results, and methods of the pastoral care movement.

In general, pastoral care in South Africa has been influenced by two models. The first is that of Eduard Thurneysen (following Karl Barth), who basically saw pastoral care as an extension of preaching — in other words, as proclamation. This model made use of the word of God in an effort to do justice to the theological side of pastoral care; but it did so at the risk of underemphasizing human needs. The second model is that of pastoral counseling, which brought the vital supplementary insight that a failure to bring the word of God home to an individual in his or her own unique situation would also mean a failure to do justice to the theological aspect.

These two models between them, however, appear to have created a balance view, so that the two poles — God and humanity, poised in their bipolar tension—both receive their due. In the first (and most important respect, then, pastoral care is seen and practiced as a theological discipline; but this is given concrete form by a vigorous use of the knowledge placed at its disposal by the other human sciences.

During the past two decades, certain South African ministers have worked hard to make the findings of the pastoral care movement even more accessible and appropriate. A number of them have received training in psychology and are officially registered as psychologists, but practice as pastoral psychologists. While all pastors in South Africa may counsel, professional counseling may be performed only by persons registered with the Medical Council. These pastors work for the church, for other organizations, and also as members of psychiatric teams in clinics. However, this work on psychiatric teams still has its unsatisfactory side in that these ministers are accepted and welcomed for their psychological expertise rather than from any recognition that theology or the church—the pastor in fact—may have something uniquely valuable to contribute.

A project was accordingly launched by the Dutch Reformed hospital chaplains in Cape Town (in collaboration with the Theological Seminary at Stellenbosch) to equip pastors to counsel the sick (as well as for general counseling) by providing clinical training in both general and psychiatric hospital situations. The sole object of this course is to turn out better equipped *pastors*. The major training input for this program comes from the pastoral care movement. It is expected that other, similar programs will be developed elsewhere, such as at the University of South Africa (Unisa), possibly expanding such training to all fields of pastoral work.

Another important development is the founding of the Association for Clinical Pastoral Education of Southern Africa in 1970. The Rev. S. Abrahamse and the Rev. V. Msomi were the first two internationally qualified supervisors. CPE has since been in its groundbreaking stage, facing the challenge of the "indigenization" of CPE to the South African setting. While ACPESA has offered a number of multicultural as well as interdenominational courses across the country, it is felt to be a shortcoming of the local CPE Association that their academic entrance requirements are too low, and that these courses pay too much attention to the enrichment of personality and not enough to the increase of knowledge.

M. JANSON

INTERNATIONAL PASTORAL CARE MOVEMENT; PASTORAL CARE MOVEMENT; PASTORAL THEOLOGY, PROTESTANT. *Compare* AFRICAN PASTORAL CARE MOVEMENT.

SOUTH ASIAN PASTORAL CARE MOVEMENT.

South Asia includes the geographical regions of Southeast Asia (Philippines, Indonesia, Singapore, Malaysia, Thailand, Burma, Laos, Cambodia, and Vietnam), and the Indian subcontinent (India, Pakistan, Bangladesh, and Sri Lanka). These countries have a long and rich cultural heritage but suffer from socioeconomic problems, intercultural conflicts, and religious superstitions. Christians constitute a very small minority except in the Philippines. Modern pastoral care movements in these countries had their beginning only since the 1960s and were influenced by Western models of pastoral care and counseling. However, new attempts to develop contextual approaches have led to the adoption of indigenous models of care, such as *Yoga*, and to incorporate them in the development of the theory and practice of pastoral care and counseling.

1. **Southeast Asia.** The first country in Southeast Asia to develop a modern pastoral care movement was the *Philippines*. The Philippines Association for Pastoral Care was formed in 1965 by the Rev. J. Albert Dalton of the U.S. The first fully accredited CPE training program was conducted in 1966 at the St. Luke's Hospital, Manila. There are now nine CPE centers. Students work in hospitals, parishes, and with trade unions. Pastoral care and counseling has become a part of theological curriculum in all major theological colleges. The headquarters of the Philippines Association for CPE is at St. Luke's Hospital, Manila.

Indonesia has not yet developed a full-fledged modern pastoral care movement. Students at the Universitas Kristen Satya Wacana can major in pastoral counseling as part of the B.D. degree. A proposal is being put before the University to start CPE as one of its programs.

In theological colleges in *Singapore*, courses in pastoral care and counseling have been included for a long time; however, CPE was started only in 1974 by the Rev. J. Albert Dalton. The CPE training program is parish-centered. In 1983, it was moved from the church's Counseling Center to Mt. Alvernia Hospital. The Counseling and Care Center continues to provide services and training in human relations and counseling. The Association for Theological Education in Southeast Asia started the Institute for Advanced Pastoral Studies which prepares candidates for the degree of Doctor of Pastoral Studies.

There is no accredited CPE program in *Malaysia*; however, theological seminaries offer courses in pastoral care and counseling.

It was not until very recently that CPE training programs were started in *Thailand* at McCormic Hospital, Chiangmai, Bangkok Sanitarium, and Bangkok Christian hospital.

In *Burma, Laos, Cambodia,* and *Vietnam* there is no sign of the modern pastoral care movement.

2. **The Indian Subcontinent.** There is no CPE program in India, but there are programs similar to the CPE program in the West, which are growing very fast. The Christian Counselling Centre, Vellore, started in 1969 by the Church of South India, is the pioneer institution in this field. Frank Lake, an English physician and former missionary to India, was instrumental in starting it. The center uses both Western and Eastern approaches in training counselors at various levels. Its services are open to Protestants, Roman Catholics, and even to non-Christians. An M.Th. program in pastoral counseling was started in 1976 at the United Theological College, Bangalore. One of its major concerns is to develop theory and practice in pastoral counseling within the framework of the Indian church and culture.

The Rev. Salim Sharif started a counseling center at the Free Church in New Delhi in 1978. His concerns are to involve the church in the world as well as to develop preventive methods of counseling for use in a context of poverty and social injustice. Another program, known as *Vyakti Vikas Karayakaram* (Program for Personal Growth), was begun by the Rev. Carlos Welch and his wife Saroj Welch in 1980. It is a program of pastoral care of pastors which involves visiting the clergy and helping them with their personal and pastoral problems.

There is no CPE program in *Sri Lanka*. However, there is a very significant program known as *Deva Suva Sevawa* (Divine Healing Ministry), begun in 1971 by the Rev. Theodore Perera, who was inspired by Dr. Lake. This ministry uses medical, psychiatric, and spiritual resources in healing people not only from physical ailments but also from emotional and spiritual sickness.

D. D. PITAMBER

INTERNATIONAL PASTORAL CARE MOVEMENT; PASTORAL CARE MOVEMENT. *Compare* EAST ASIAN PASTORAL CARE MOVEMENT; PSYCHOLOGY AND PSYCHOTHERAPY (East-West Comparison).

SOUTHERN BAPTIST ASSOCIATION FOR CLINICAL PASTORAL EDUCATION. An organization which existed from 1957 through 1967, composed predominantly of Southern Baptists who had an interest in or taught clinical pastoral education.

In the 1930s, the idea for clinical pastoral training at the Southern Baptist Theological Seminary was conceived by Professor Gaines Dobbins who had the support of President W. O. Carver. The most significant event leading toward the formation of a separate association was the denial of supervisory status to Wayne Oates in 1946 by the Council for Clinical Training. Shortly thereafter, Oates went on to establish a clinical pastoral training program for the Southern Baptist Theological Seminary and became the central figure for CPE in the South.

Subsequently, three major training centers were established which provided the impetus for the formation of an association. Each held a common commitment to missionary objectives and to a professional model for theological education. At the same time, each represented a different tradition: pastoral theological tradition under Oates at the Southern Baptist Theological Seminary; pastoral healer tradition under Richard Young at North Carolina Baptist Hospital; and religious educator tradition under John Price at New Orleans Baptist Theological Seminary.

By 1956, Southern Baptist leaders recognized that the clinical pastoral education movement was moving toward unification without them. Their concern to become a visible and influential force led them to unite as an association. In 1957, as part of the fourth annual Southern Baptist Counseling and Guidance Conference in Nashville, Tennessee, eighteen persons actively involved in clinical pastoral education met, discussed, and formed the Southern Baptist Association for Clinical Pastoral Education (the Association).

By 1967, the Association, which had changed its name to the Association of Clinical Pastoral Educators in 1965, had experienced tremendous growth. It now claimed nearly one third of the nation's clinical pastoral educators. Moreover, non-Baptists composed twenty-five percent of its supervisors. Having participated in the move toward unification, the members of the Association voted at the annual meeting in 1967 to dissolve the Association in order to fully participate in the nationally unified Association for Clinical Pastoral Education effective January 1, 1968.

Bibliography. Minutes of the Annual Meeting, Southern Baptist Association for Clinical Pastoral Education, 1960–1967, located at the Southern Baptist Convention Historical Commission, Nashville, TN. E. Thornton, *Professional Education for Ministry: A History of Clinical Pastoral Education* (1970).

S. D. KING

CLINICAL PASTORAL EDUCATION; PASTORAL CARE MOVEMENT. *See also* ASSOCIATION FOR CLINICAL PASTORAL EDUCATION.

SPE (SUPERVISED PASTORAL EDUCATION). *See* HISTORY OF PROTESTANT PASTORAL CARE (Canada).

SPECIALIZATION IN PASTORAL CARE. This is both a new and an old notion in the history of the Judeo-Christian tradition. It is new in the sense that contemporary secularization and its resulting technologies in the helping professions have forced the church to develop specialized forms suited to the new conditions of society — to extend dramatically its ministry to *all* the world. It is old in that there has never been a time in the history of the church when pastoral care has been limited to a parish or a parochial setting. The topic itself often has been approached in terms of "specialized ministries," or, more recently, "ministry in specialized settings."

The subject may be viewed from at least three perspectives: (1) specialization within pastoral care that gets its forms from the specific techniques and operations characterizing the project (e.g., counseling/psychotherapy); (2) specialization that gets its *raison d'être* by virtue of the *setting* in which it takes place (e.g., a mental hospital); and (3) specialization in pastoral care that depends on both operations and setting (e.g., genetic counseling in an inner city social agency).

1. Background of Specialization. Pastoral care in its inclusive as well as its classical sense has been one of the "offices" of the ministry. Called *poimenics*, it stood in contrast, for example, to *homiletics* (preaching) or to *catechetics* (religious instruction). In more recent times the general term "pastoral care" has usually referred to the broad activities of a pastor in his or her relationships with parishioners, particularly those relationships in which crises or life transitions are manifest. Max Weber, the sociologist, once defined pastoral care as "the religious cultivation of the individual," but such an individualistic notion no longer characterizes the *full* meaning of pastoral care in a time when systemic notions pervade the field.

Pastoral care, however, does embrace a broad notion of expressing specific caring acts toward those persons with special needs and in crises. A major assumption of pastoral care amid crises is that of *presence*. In the care of souls, *being there* to provide an empathic presence is the presupposition of all other pastoral acts (Oden, 1986).

In his study of crisis ministry, theologian Thomas Oden lists six key questions that may guide an understanding and appreciation of pastoral care. Although Oden raises these questions as crucial issues for the general pastoral care giver, they represent as well the very conditions that often have given rise to specializations in pastoral care:

"(1) How shall the pastor best function in interpersonal conflict mediation, and in such critical moments as *vocational* decision, *addictive* and compulsive behaviors, and thoughts of *suicide*? (2) How shall the pastor most effectively visit and care for the *physically* ill? (3) If God is proclaimed and unsurpassably powerful and good, how shall the pastor deal with the *suffering* of parishioners, and what sort of care and reasoning shall be provided for inquiries concerning the justice of God amid suffering, temptation, and inequality? (4) How shall the pastor minister to crises in *marriage and family* living; premarital counsel, marital counsel, divorce counsel, celibacy counsel, parental counsel, youth counsel, abortion counsel, and adultery counsel? (5) How shall the pastor effectively care for the *poor* and needy, the stranger, those deprived of familial and economic resources, orphans, widows, the destitute, the imprisoned, and the enslaved? (6) Finally, how shall the pastor care for souls amid the crisis of terminal illness, *death*, and burial, and the grieving process?" (Oden, 1986, p. 1).

Even this extensive list of concerns is only part of the story in that the world is no longer organized around religious institutions, nor are such caring concerns in any sense limited to the expressions of religious meaning systems. Science, and particularly technology, have exercised an enormous influence on the methods and institutions providing services to those in need. The development of the behavioral and social sciences, for instance, has brought with it such fields as psychology, psychiatry, social work, counseling and psychotherapy. Based primarily on humanistic and naturalistic assumptions — not religious ones — these new ways of caring have developed a wide range of caring modes that have demonstrated a high degree of effectiveness.

At the same time, in its desire to offer *all* persons the *full* ministry of the gospel of Jesus Christ, the church's pastoral care has moved beyond the local congregation or parish into the wider world. Its ministers, priests, and specially trained laypersons have adopted many of the technologies developed by science in an attempt to strengthen the traditional modes of helping in the religious traditions. It has been this interface that partly explains the growth of specializations in pastoral care.

2. Contemporary Examples of Specialized Ministries. Simply cataloguing the varieties of specializations in pastoral care is itself a mammoth task and certain to be incomplete. Those commonly noted are ministers, priests, and nuns who serve in hospitals, jails, prisons, mental institutions, military service, schools, homes for disturbed children, pastoral counseling centers, and business and industrial complexes.

But such a list touches only the edge of the contemporary expression of ministry in specialized settings. For example, it is little known that there are chaplains on police forces or at racetracks; clergy also offer pastoral care at motels, to football teams, and to the U.S. Senate.

Added to this variety is the situation in the Roman Catholic church, where entire religious orders may be dedicated to a particular area of service beyond a local parish; for example, teaching, nursing, or spiritual direction. And in very recent times the rise and proliferation of many ministries make even more complex and extensive the reality of specialization in pastoral care.

If one takes seriously the rationale offered by those in such specializations — that is, that the church must reach out into every nook and cranny of the world—then there are indeed no boundaries, and the varieties of specializations are bound to expand and continue to challenge parochial notions of ministry and pastoral care. In fact, the realities of such specializations have confronted traditional understandings of ministry in ways never before confronted by parish-oriented church structures. "Chaplains in special ministries," one study observes, "are helping focus on the critical aspects of a theological foundation for ministry. The primary question they put to the conventional understanding of Christian ministry is whether what is going on in the churches is related to what God is doing in the whole creation and among all people" (Boozer, 1984, p. 223).

In the past this sort of rhetoric has ignited deep conflicts between those involved in specializations and those in parish-based ministry, but such strains have also resulted in a greater awareness that specializations in pastoral care are in fact a significant reality in the church's overall mission, one that needs to be confronted and addressed by all religious denominations.

3. Special Issues Relative to Pastoral Counseling as a Specialized Ministry. Specialization in pastoral care is a natural evolution of several conditions. First, the mission of the church in the second half of the twentieth century has moved beyond explicit conversion-oriented activities on foreign soil to a service-oriented project in secular society. Although the denominational factor looms large in determining the degree and awareness of this shift in mission, its reality is inevitable for all religious groups that do not elect to withdraw in the face of increased secularization of society.

Second, the decision to engage in serving the needs of all people in the world, not only those in the identified parish, leads to the realization that such an expression of mission carries with it certain consequences having roots in professional and state agencies relative to education and training of those offering such services; that is, specialization carries

with it an educational form that goes beyond the traditional theological training of clergy.

Perhaps the most notable and clear sign of this sort of realization may be seen in the development of the Clinical Pastoral Education movement (CPE; see Thornton, 1970). Although the original rationale for the movement was not primarily one that stressed specialization, the training centers were mostly in general and mental hospitals, not parishes. The idea was that persons under stress would provide young ministers with opportunities to perceive and understand dynamics made clear through the condition of crisis. These understandings could then be transferred to parish settings, thus increasing the effectiveness of the religious professional, providing him or her with new tools to deal with the "human document."

In this process, of course, seminarians came into contact with other helping professionals — psychiatrists, psychologists, social workers, mental health counselors, and so forth, many of whom demonstrated special skills gained through a different kind of education than that of traditional theological education and training. Through such associations clergy became more aware not only of the value of such training for parish work but for the needs of ministry within the settings where the training was taking place. Most CPE students still returned to their seminary classes and later to parishes, but a growing number made decisions to receive additional clinical training to become chaplains in these institutional settings, which required a level of specialization beyond the traditional education and training at the first professional degree.

This dynamic or movement does not account fully for the rise of specializations in pastoral care, of course; but certainly the general strain on the relationship between religion and health, captured well in the CPE development, must be counted as a significant factor in the specialization propensity.

Nowhere is this more true, or better illustrated, than in the evolution of pastoral counseling as a specialized form of ministry and as a specialization in pastoral care. The following is a brief and simplified sketch of its development.

(1) Counseling by parish pastors and priests always has been one function of their general ministry.

(2) The rise in counseling in the secular world following World War II achieved acceptance in the higher education project and in the mental health revolution, leading to its professionalization.

(3) Religious professionals began interfacing with these new professional counselors, particularly in the CPE centers.

(4) Identification with the technologies, art forms, and worldviews of these new professionals at times endangered the *theological* identity of the minister.

(5) The new expressions of ministry (e.g., counseling) began requiring special education and training beyond the traditional first professional degree; and certification, licensing, and so forth, became important, often moving the religious professional further away from his or her religious base.

(6) The new specialized training led to the forming of guilds and accreditation bodies, partly to develop standards and partly to assist in clarifying the identity confusion.

(7) The denominations began to see the specialization (pastoral counseling) as a legitimate mission and outreach, and a new dialogue developed between the new form of ministry and the base system from which it originally sprung.

This sort of scenario is not unique in the development of pastoral counseling as a specialization in pastoral care, but it does offer a broad sweep of circumstances of particular interest in the expression of the church's mission and provides one with a framework for making sense out of what at times appears to be a confused and strained situation within and between religious institutions and their many evolving forms of ministry.

4. The Current Organizational Dialogue on Ministry in Specialized Settings. As noted above, specialization in pastoral care usually leads to the formation of professional associations that define and enforce standards and identity. The following list, though not complete, clearly represents the tendency for those involved in specialized ministries to form guilds that provide practitioners with professional and political power:

American Association for Mental Deficiency
American Association of Pastoral Counselors
American Correctional Chaplains Association
American Protestant Correctional Chaplains Association
Association of Clinical Pastoral Education
Association of Mental Health Clergy
The Catholic Health Association/Pastoral Care
The College of Chaplains of the American Protestant Health Association
International Conference of Police Chaplains
National Association of Catholic Chaplains
National Conference on Ministry in the Armed Forces
National Institute of Business and Industrial Chaplains
Race Track Chaplains Association

Although such organizations were formed to provide those in specialized pastoral care a forum to discuss their common concerns and to establish identity criteria and support, they equally have served to set standards of professional practice in the particular setting and to provide a structure that can connect with the faith groups out of which the specialists have come.

Perhaps one of the most active developments in recent years has been the recognition among such groups that although they are often differentiated by methods and settings, they have a common identity in *pastoral care*. This realization has taken form in a dynamic dialogue among the various organizations. The forums for these discussions have been the Inter-Organizational Consultation in the 1970s and in the formation of the Joint Issues in Pastoral Care Organization (JIPCO) and the Council on Ministry in Specialized Settings (COMISS) in the early 1980s.

Symbolic of these active cooperative conversations was Dialogue '88, a massive conference for persons involved in specialized ministries, which met in Minneapolis, Minnesota, to share common concerns, to celebrate their form of ministry in specialized settings, and to provide a forum for dialogue and collaboration among the members of clinical pastoral care, counseling, and education associations; representatives of various interreligious groups; and agencies that use pastoral services. Clearly, Dialogue '88 was a conspicuous and focused expression of what has been happening in specializations in pastoral care and what these developments might mean for the wider vision of ministry.

5. Theological, Ecclesiastical, and Political Issues. The theological foundations of Christian ministry have also received wide attention in the church during the second half of the twentieth century. These various formulations have been influenced by biblical scholarship and by massive movements in the economic, social, and political spheres. There is, of course, no single theology of pastoral care that has given focused meaning to these developments. It is probably safe to observe, however, that every type of theology has within it a perspective which gives impetus and legitimation to special forms of ministry.

Theologies that have been formed in liberal traditions seem on the whole to have provided a more solid base for pastoral care specializations than have those which fall closer to the conservative end of the theological spectrum. Pastoral care itself has not generated a great deal of theological literature.

This absence of an articulate theological exposition supporting pastoral care generally was one of the primary criticisms of Seward Hiltner (1958). Fortunately, his challenge is presently being met by theological clinicians who have been able to integrate certain theological and clinical materials in creative ways; for example, John Patton in *Pastoral Counseling: A Ministry of the Church* (1983), and Merle R. Jordan in *Taking on the Gods: The Task of the Pastoral Counselor* (1986). The latter is an example of how a theological notion—idolatry—can serve as a guiding fiction for the practice of a particular specialization, that is, pastoral counseling.

Regardless of the particular setting in which a person *does* pastoral care, his or her roots are in some sort of ecclesiastical structure. Usually the parish minister or the parish priest has a relatively clear route of accountability to such structures, and often a relatively unambiguous relationship to figures within the ecclesiastical structure, for example, bishops, district superintendents, provincials, or superiors. But pastoral care specialists frequently are well removed from such structures and authorities and have between them and their faith group other—often secular—structures that impact their ministries and their loyalties far more directly. Thus it is that much of the discussion and the literature dealing with pastoral care specializations are focused on issues of accountability, responsibility, and loyalty.

Perhaps in this regard the most conspicuous example is that of the military chaplain. The conflict and the tension of the topic was captured well by Harvey Cox in the early 1970s: "How does a chaplain proclaim the prophetic gospel when he is wearing the uniform of the military, is paid by the state, and furthermore is dependent on his superior officers for advancement? . . . The question of how one speaks the truth to power is not a question that chaplains alone must grapple with. In a sense their difficult situation has the merit of being at least *clearly* difficult one. . . " (Cox, 1971, p. xi).

Cox saw the dilemma in broad terms affecting all ministers, but properly noted that in the case of the military chaplain (and, indeed, many other specialized ministries) the dilemma and tensions are open and clear.

At the administrative level of the ecclesiastical establishment the issue is often one of accountability and power. How does the pastoral care specialist relate to his or her ecclesiastical superior? What ways are there for chaplains or the pastoral counselors to retain and enhance their involvement in the faith groups from which one's religious authority derives?

At the grass-roots level of the ecclesiastical establishment, the strain often is blatant and lucid. The local parish pastor may ask, "How is it possible for the pastoral counseling specialist to have a salary three times greater than mine and at the same time stand clear of the direct authority of my superiors?" "What justice is there in the fact that a fellow seminary graduate is now a commander in the Navy with a great pension plan and I am still serving a three-point charge on minimum salary?"

Although these sorts of questions may sound like simplifications and exaggerations, the pastoral care specialist and the parish pastor have had, and still have, such issues between them. Often this schism has been denied and minimized; but in recent years, particularly since the dialogue among the specialized pastoral care organizations has begun, realistic programs and conversations have been initiated.

Certainly one of the perspectives that has emerged from these encounters is the opinion that it may be in the nature of pastoral care specialization to be on the edge of the ecclesiastical establishment. Indeed, that its form and peculiar power may partly be traced to its borderline status, not really in *or* out of the religious community. The argument is that this borderline status, if truly articulated, valued, and accepted, represents a new and exciting expression of mission — one which can connect most effectively with the growing nonchurched in the society while at the same time holding firmly to its primary identity as a *religious* project.

How such complex and interacting meanings and activities can take form is surely part of the current interorganizational dialogue on ministry in specialized settings and why the religious endorsing bodies need to play an important role in the future of specialized ministry.

6. A Note of the Future of Specialization. No one can predict with precision the destiny of pastoral care specializations. Much depends on the future propensities of the religious establishment. Some futurists see institutional religion withdrawing from the world, providing only a sort of sanctuary in which like-minded believers may huddle together while the rest of the world goes rushing by. If that should indeed happen, specializations in pastoral care surely would dwindle, perhaps disappear.

If, on the other hand, faith groups move outward into the world offering the full good news to all, then certainly the offering of pastoral care will take a variety of forms to meet the needs of the particular settings in which persons work, play, and love.

Perhaps just as significant will be the nature and extent of the relationships among the great meaning systems — religious, political, scientific — particularly as they get expressed in the helping and healing projects of humankind.

Bibliography. J. S. Boozer, *Edge of Ministry . . . The Chaplain Story* (1984). H. Clinebell, *Basic Types of Pastoral Care and Counseling* (1984). H. Cox, ed., *Military Chaplains: From a Religious Military to a Military Religion* (1971). S. Hiltner, *Preface to Pastoral Theology* (1958). E. B. Holifield, *A History of Pastoral Care in America* (1983). M. R. Jordan, *Taking on the Gods: The Task of the Pastoral Counselor* (1986). T. C. Oden, *Crisis Ministries* (1986). J. H. Patton, *Pastoral Counseling: A Ministry of the Church* (1983). A. Stokes, *Ministry After Freud* (1985). E. E. Thornton, *Professional Education for Ministry: A History of Clinical Pastoral Education* (1970).

O. STRUNK, JR.

CLINICAL PASTORAL EDUCATION; EDUCATION IN PASTORAL CARE AND COUNSELING; PASTORAL COUNSELING; SOCIOLOGY OF RELIGIOUS AND PASTORAL CARE; SUPERVISION, PASTORAL. *See also* GRADUATE EDUCATION IN PASTORAL THEOLOGY; THEOLOGICAL EDUCATION.

SPECIALNESS, SENSE OF. The feeling that one's burdens and/or gifts are unique; that one has been or should be singled out for special treatment; also the feeling of being the one who is loved.

Tensions exist between the damaging effects of believing one's situation is unlike anyone else's, and therefore one is entitled to a special dispensation; the frustration of believing one ought to have a visibly unique place, and the recognition that one does not; the pastoral and psychotherapeutic attempt to grant exclusive attention to the individual for the duration of the contracted time; and the Christian affirmation that each of us is uniquely known and loved by God.

In most sin and most psychopathology, the individual believes that he or she either does or should have a special place, and that said exaltation or its absence relieves the sufferer of the responsibilities that others must carry. Because of the specialness, such persons may believe they should not have to work, or should be taken care of without anything being asked in return, or should not be required to consider other people's feelings. When unpleasant things happen to them, they often experience themselves as being singled out by God or the fates for singular abuse. That, in turn, justifies resentment and retaliation.

Healing for such persons consists in part in coming to see themselves as a person like other persons, no more or less singled out for blessing or curse than they. That enables them to receive good fortune humbly, as a gift rather than a right; and to take misfortune as their share in the common lot of humanity. It further allows them to see some unpleasant outcomes as coming from their own error or misdeed, which in turn allows them to learn from them, rather than to see them as the product of an unpredictable and arbitrary malevolence.

Though to believe oneself singularly privileged or cursed almost always damages the believer and others, the belief is close to a central value of Christianity, pastoral care, and psychotherapy. The Judeo-Christian tradition has long held that God singles out each one of us for individualized love and care, numbers every hair of our heads, knows when we lie down and rise up. An important pastoral act is the reminder to recipients of care that they have this special status. The difference between this specialness and that which damages is the tradition's clear statement that every person receives it, not as a right but as a gift. It is neither earned by one's own act nor bestowed because of family or nation, but given. As such it can neither be a source of pride, since it comes unearned; nor of comparison, since it comes to all. This claim of our faith is healing, in that the same gift that invites us to love and esteem ourselves also binds us in community with our neighbor, who is offered the same benefit.

In the psychotherapeutic and pastoral care traditions, a contracted, temporary specialness plays a similar healing role. Part of the ethos of both relationships is the pastor's honoring the recipient's special claim for exclusive attention and investment during the contracted period. Confidentiality is a part of that specialness, honoring the individual's claim over the community's. Some therapists' commitment to never see any member of the client's family is another way this claim is honored. The therapist attempts to create a relationship that represents and, to an extent, compensates for the lack of a special enough relationship between the client and his or her parent. The attempt is to build into the client the experience of a relationship in which he or she is truly special, even if the specialness is paid for. That experience produces new structures within the person, artifacts of the attention of the therapist as representative of the caring of God, which in turn remove the need for the false specialness that places persons at odds with themselves and their neighbors.

B. W. GRANT

NARCISSISM/NARCISSISTIC PERSONALITY; PASTORAL COUNSELING; SELF-ESTEEM. *Compare* EGOTISM; IDENTITY; IMAGO DEI; MAGICAL THINKING; PERSONAL, CONCEPT OF; PRIDE AND HUMILITY (Moral Theology); RIGHTEOUSNESS/BEING RIGHT.

SPEECH DISORDERS AND THERAPY.

The term *speech disorder* is generally used to cover all disorders of communication. Such disorders are variously classified in terms of causation, symptomatology, and nature. Most communication deficiencies are in the areas of perception (both visual and auditory), motor functions (particularly of the speech muscles), symbolic formulation and expression, and sound production. Common designations are voice disorders, stuttering, language disabilities, cleft palate speech, impaired hearing, laryngectomy speech, retarded speech development, cerebral palsy speech, and malformation and omissions of speech sounds.

The speech pathologist or speech therapist as he or she may be called, serves in the public schools, hospitals, colleges and universities, various clinics, and in private practice. This specialist is grounded in human anatomy and neurophysiology, psychology, phonetics, acoustics, and psychotherapy, and usually has either an M.A., Ph.D., D.D.S., or some combination of these degrees. As a rule, he or she belongs to the American Speech-Language-Hearing Association. This relatively new discipline, founded in 1925, supports the publication of three journals devoted to theory, research and practice.

Since its inception, speech pathology has emphasized scientific research into all the aspects of communication disorders. Yet is has not neglected the practical aspects of the field, spending much energy in the development of ever more effective language and speech therapeutic techniques. Diagnostic studies of the speech defective must be thorough and complete before a remedial procedure can be considered. The causes and the nature of the trouble must be as completely understood and evaluated as possible. Many communication disorders are largely psychosomatic and it is essential that the therapist knows how much they may be due to organic factors and to what degree they may be psychosocial. For instance, stuttering is probably basically neurological but elicited and maintained by psychosocial forces. This kind of thinking is appropriate with voice disorders and most other communication troubles including reading disabilities.

Speech therapy is a blend of psychotherapy, educational procedures, surgery, relaxation and meditation, and guided mental imagery. Most people suffering from handicaps in communicating with others can be helped. Most public schools have at least one speech therapist on their staff. Children who are handicapped in speech make up the largest group of exceptional children in the public schools of America. There are more than twice as many children with speech defects as there are any other type of handicapped children. Most universities and colleges have training programs to prepare qualified speech pathologists to serve in all of the various specialties in the large field of speech-language-hearing troubles.

L. E. TRAVIS

DEVELOPMENTAL DISABILITIES; LANGUAGE DEVELOPMENT. *Compare* ADJUNCTIVE THERAPIES; COMMUNICATION.

SPENCER, ICHABOD

(1798–1854). Pastor of the Second Presbyterian Church in Brooklyn and lecturer at Union Theological Seminary (New York). In 1850 and 1853 Spencer published two celebrated volumes of *A Pastor's Sketches*, which provided verbatim accounts of selected pastoral conversations that tried to combine the virtues of gentility, refinement, and scrupulous honesty. Widely read in his own time, Spencer was rescued from obscurity in the twentieth century when Seward Hiltner published a *Preface to Pastoral Theology* (1958) in which he analyzed several of Spencer's accounts.

E. B. HOLIFIELD

HISTORY OF PROTESTANT PASTORAL CARE (United States).

SPENER, PHILIP JACOB

(1635–1705). German Lutheran Pietist leader, theologian, teacher, and pastor.

In reaction to laxity and routineness in contemporary *cura animarum*, and against the austere doctrinalism and scholasticism of Lutheran Orthodoxy, Spener advocated and implemented a religious *habitus* that stressed spiritual rebirth, a personal faith decision, the ongoing nurturing of faith in group Bible study, and practical fruits of the spirit. These ideas were clustered around his recovery of the notion of "the priesthood of all believers." The implications for the theory and practice of pastoral care concern two areas: private confessions and disciplinary measures. In regards to the improvement of the mechanistic, impersonal, and shallow practice of private confessions, Spener suggested replacing or augmenting it with a personal, conversational tone between confessor and penitent, free choice of one's confessor, appointments in the house of the pastor, and housecalls by the pastor in order to facilitate caring conversation. Further, Spener mapped out plans for support and Eucharist preparation groups.

Discipline, also, becomes a communal matter for all the pastors. It must always be helpful and not a punishment.

N. F. HAHN

PIETISM AND PASTORAL CARE. *See also* LUTHERAN PASTORAL CARE.

SPIRIT, DIVINE. *See* HOLY SPIRIT.

SPIRIT, HUMAN. *See* PERSON (Christian Perspective).

SPIRIT POSSESSION. *See* The DEMONIC; EXORCISM; CHARISMATIC EXPERIENCE.

SPIRITUAL COUNSEL. *See* SPIRITUAL DIRECTION; PASTORAL COUNSELING. *See also* EVALUATION AND DIAGNOSIS, RELIGIOUS; SPIRITUAL MASTERS AND GUIDES.

SPIRITUAL DIRECTION, HISTORY AND TRADITIONS OF. Spiritual direction implies a relationship and process whereby a person's particular spiritual gifts and graces are discovered, nurtured and developed, in association with another who is deemed to be expert in this aspect of pastoral ministry. Such skilled guidance has been described as both art and science: art insofar as it necessitates certain intuitive insights into spiritual and psychological processes, and science in that Christian prayer has to be grounded in biblical and systematic theology.

A large part of direction is thus concerned with the maintenance of spiritual health, providing the necessary conditions for growth: "I planted the seed, and Apollos watered it; but God made it grow. Thus it is not the gardeners with their planting and watering who count, but God, who makes it grow" (I Cor. 3:6–7 NEB). The Pauline analogy is pertinent, for gardening implies art, an intuitive sense or feeling for natural fertility, while it also involves much science. But neither Paul nor Apollos, nor anyone else save God, can produce growth; we can only provide those conditions favorable to growth.

Spiritual direction, therefore, is largely concerned with the application of the central Christian doctrines to an individual life of prayer; the maintenance, for example, of a trinitarian balance which avoids deism on the one hand and pantheism on the other. Or with the application to meditative prayer of a Christology which expresses a proper balance between Christ's divinity and his sacred humanity. It would also involve an ecclesiology that induces a balance or synthesis between the corporate and liturgical aspects of spirituality and the unique individualism of personal devotion.

1. **Pastoral Context.** *a. Moral theology.* This has a positive and a negative side, since it deals with virtue and spiritual gifts and also with sin and its divisions and remedies. Traditional theology sees a progression from the cardinal, or natural, virtues — justice, temperance, fortitude, prudence — to the theological virtues — faith, hope, love — to the gifts of the Spirit—holy fear, godliness, wisdom, understanding, knowledge, counsel,

ghostly strength. It is noticeable that these groups of virtues gradually increase in subtlety and religious content, from what most intelligent people would accept as basic human goodness to specifically Christian ideals. These latter groupings impinge on prayer and consequently play a major part in spiritual direction.

Sin is also an essentially theological, rather than a moral term, for its immediate impact is to frustrate prayer, understood as a living and continuous relationship between a person and God. The traditional classifications and categories of sins, such as mortal and venial sin, malice, and frailty, together with treatment of conscience and casuistry, seem artificial and over-sophisticated to many. But such criticism is diffused as soon as it is realized that we are dealing with spiritual direction rather than with basic human morality. In spiritual direction, sin is seen primarily as that which strains or diminishes a personal relationship with God.

b. Confession. It follows that the eradication of sin by confession and absolution has played a large part in traditional spiritual direction. But in certain times and traditions distortion has crept in through exaggeration of sacramental confession. This largely disciplinary and ecclesiastical injunction has led to a narrowing of values whereby confession and spiritual direction have been seen as one and the same thing, and the confessional has been regarded as the one proper environment for the exercise of direction.

For those Christian traditions which provide for and accept sacramental confession, it can play an important if minor part in the far wider process of direction. On the other hand, those Christian bodies that object to sacramental confession, or reject the theology behind it, need not for that reason forego creative direction. It is important clearly to recognize both the interrelation and the distinction between the two.

c. Counseling. Even worse confusion arises through the comparatively recent popularity of counseling as a pastoral technique, and its confusion with spiritual direction. Christian counseling is largely concerned with the solution or alleviation of day-to-day human problems, emotional difficulties, or stresses. With a serious Christian content, based on the Gospel, it is nevertheless largely dependent on psychological and psychiatric techniques. Serving the sick in heart and mind is a true expression of love for one's neighbor, yet while counseling is concerned with the solution of an immediate problem, or restoration of the *status quo*, direction offers more positive guidance aimed at the development of creative gifts of the spirit. Direction is concerned primarily with developing love for God, secondly with love for neighbor — it is aimed at the strong and healthy rather than the weak and sick — and ultimately it is concerned with the creation, not simply of good healthy Christians but of saints of redemptive power. It has been said, with some irony, that the strong and faithful form the most neglected group within any Christian community.

Nevertheless, despite these plain differences in approach, an interplay between counseling and direction is both possible and desirable: the most gifted of the faithful could still benefit from counsel, and, if only as by-product to its primary object, prayer can be therapeutic. Or perhaps direction could be regarded as the consummation and conclusion of counseling; Christian living, based on the gospel and assisted by subsidiary sciences, is a composite whole, with prayer as the synthesizing catalyst. In competent pastoral care, it is important to understand the parts which make up the whole.

2. The Spiritual Direction Relationship. The relationship between the spiritual director and those who are directed is complex, and it has varied from age to age and place to place. *a. Historical development.* From NT times to the early Middle Ages, direction was a loose and natural part of pastoral care; people talked about prayer, freely and uninhibitedly, as part of daily life. In the Scholastic period, spirituality became more formally studied and analyzed—direction became more of a science than an art. The Protestant Reformation produced different emphases, concluding with seventeenth-century pietism, which on the whole has been unhappy with spiritual direction as a legitimate aspect of pastoral care. In violent reaction the counter-reformation stressed the spiritual director as pedagogic, autocratic, and paternal, to whom total obedience was due. The *Spiritual Exercises* of St. Ignatius Loyola typify this viewpoint, in which those directed in prayer undergo strictly composed spiritual meditations, constantly supervised by their director, and possibly leaving everyone in a holy state of penitential exhaustion: sacramental confession was compulsory.

The seventeenth-century English church (the so-called Caroline Divines) did much to restore the sane balance, expressed in the current motto—"true piety with sound learning." The directorial emphasis was softened by the domestic ethos of the times; spiritual direction was a relation between father and son, mother and daughter, rather than that between master and servant or pedagogue and pupil. The period produced great spiritual directors, including many lay men and especially women, and considerable writings relevant to this pastoral skill. But it suffered a little by an overemphasis on morality rather than spiritual development.

b. Contemporary understanding. These historical emphases are still discernible in modern times; Roman Catholicism and Eastern Orthodoxy, though greatly varying from country to country, still incline toward the authoritarian, paternalistic side. Protestantism seems still largely neglectful of spiritual direction as an essential aspect of pastoral care, while the Anglican-Episcopalian pastoral tradition continues to uphold the English Caroline approach. And without prejudice this would appear to be the approach most consistent with modern aspiration: the relation between director and directed is one of mutual rapport, of equal respect for persons as persons, and of brothers and sisters in Christ. It is domestic rather than military, with a stress on freedom, not servitude, and love, not duty.

In the classic tradition the relation is expressed in various analogies. One is medical—the director is "physician of the soul," emphasizing the moral and the confessional. Others are the nuptial analogy, father and son or daughter; and the military analogy, soldiers of Christ under their commander. But the most significant could be the original, and most contemporary, in I Cor. 9:24–27, where St. Paul likens the spiritual director to the coach in charge of the spiritual athlete. The athletic coach is not quite a teacher, not quite a trainer, certainly

not a master or a superior, but one whose job is to develop the natural gifts and aptitude of the athlete he is coaching, and who in all likelihood is better at the game than he, the coach, is himself.

Perhaps a further distinguishing analogy is that the counselor is the trainer, salving the bruises and mending the muscles, while the coach, the spiritual director, gets on with teaching the techniques of the game itself.

3. The Schools of Prayer. It has been noted that spiritual direction is based on an application of the Gospel, crystallized into theology, to the particular needs of individual people. There are fundamental principles of Christian prayer that apply to all, and yet one such fundamental principle is that each and every person is a unique creation of God. So, while heeding doctrinal orthodoxy, spiritual direction is concerned with the most creative guidance of the individual.

This points to another essential synthesis: human individuality can only express itself in community—"no man is an island"—and so there can be no dichotomy between corporate worship and liturgical involvement and personal devotion: spiritual direction has to include both because the Christian life is one life, and prayer embraces both aspects. The technical word for this composite whole is *regula*, better translated "system" or "pattern" rather than the more literal "rule." An important initial aspect of spiritual direction is to construct a personal *regula* with due discipline but without undue regimentation; with bondage to Christ but with freedom to love.

This basic Christian doctrine of corporate-individual synthesis is classically expressed by St. Paul in I Corinthians 12, and Rom. 12:4–20. The church is the organic body of Christ, made up of individual members, cells, all of whom are unique in character yet wholly dependent one upon another. From this doctrine arise the multifarious schools of prayer throughout Christian history, and it is the study of these schools which plays the prominent part in spiritual direction as it concerns itself with the development of individuality.

The schools, initially monastic such as the Benedictines, Cistercians, Cluniacs, Franciscans, Dominicans, Carmelites, etc., and latterly secular like the Salesian, *devotio moderna*, English, Caroline, Protestant and so on, issue from accepting the whole faith, the whole creed, while centering their spirituality on one particular aspect of it: the Trinity or the persons comprising it, Christology, creation, atonement, or any other credal clause. This leads into an individual ethos, character, or stamp, into which individual Christians tend to fit. Direction as to which school or approach best supports individuality becomes an important part of the directorial process.

In order to explain this personal approach, Baron Friedrich von Hügel is attributed with having invented the term *attrait*: literally, attraction; but more technically, a leaning toward, or predisposition for, certain types of prayer or spiritual emphases. As a fundamental example, there is the *apophatic* and the *kataphatic* approaches to spirituality. The former is that which rejects symbolism or created images, either real or imaginary, in favor of detachment from all material things; sometimes called *via negativa* or the negative way. The latter is centered on the doctrine of creation, regarding the material universe as conducive to the divine disclosure, and employing human artifacts, like the crucifix, icons, or pictures as devotional symbols, i.e., a wide sacramentalism. Another such distinction is between the speculative, or intellectual approach to prayer, and the affective, or emotional outlook; the one might opt for discursive meditation, leading to doctrinal understanding; the other to simple, loving contemplation of the person of Jesus.

Such major distinctions, and multifarious minor ones, finally point to a person's *attrait*, his or her natural spiritual stance or approach to prayer.

4. **Progression.** Spiritual direction is primarily concerned with the maintenance of spiritual health, leading to maturity, while growth may confidently be expected through the grace of God. Progression is the technical term explaining how such growth is to be assessed and measured. This concept has given rise to a substantial body of writings, the titles of which invariably employ such words as scale, ladder, degree, and journey, all pointing to the notion of movement.

The biblical basis for this movement or development is, first, the covenant relation between God and the chosen people in the OT: moral obedience to divine law; second, the NT encounter with the incarnate Lord, and third, the Pauline conception of baptismal incorporation into the sacred humanity of Jesus: being "in Christ." This has been classically interpreted as the "Three Ways," that is, purgation, or the moral struggle against sin; illumination, or a prophetic understanding of our relation with God; and finally, unity with God, or the state of perfection. St. Thomas Aquinas rendered this scheme into more pastoral and personal terms: beginners, proficients, and perfect, signifying the stages of experiment, maturity, and the mystical union.

In the hands of competent spiritual directors, such progressions are of considerable value, while they are in danger of serious misapplication. They should therefore be regarded more as phenomenological, rather than strictly theological categories, purporting to describe the church's corporate experience as to how spirituality might be expected to develop, rather than as routes to follow or ladders purposefully to try to climb.

Two further provisos need to be pointed out. The first is that spiritual progress may develop in terms of either scale or value; scale implies changes in spiritual status, for example, a movement from simple vocal prayer to meditation or affective contemplation, while value means that prayer of any type may simply improve in depth and devotion. Many Christians move towards a contemplative *attrait*, allowing vocal and meditative prayer to diminish as time goes by, while many another's prayer ever remains in an elementary, vocal state, nevertheless improving in depth and value. Both mystical contemplation of the blessed Trinity and a perfect rendering of the Lord's Prayer, may imply technical perfection.

The second proviso is that ultimately the only sure test for spiritual progress is moral theology; affective stirrings, heightened religious experience, and penitential emotion all have their rightful and valuable place in the spiritual pilgrimage, but, quite simply and bluntly, progress is made when fewer sins are committed.

5. **Cultural Factors.** Since the spiritual life is carried out within a particular environment in this world, cultural factors have to be taken into account. Despite common principles, spiritual direction has to offer a different approach, involving different moral, pastoral and theological concepts, as between, for example, a Christian peasant family in Sicily and a financial executive on Wall Street. Under God, there is no reason why both should not achieve sanctity — in technical terms, perfection — but they will reach it by different routes, and by varying directorial techniques. The corporate devotion of the Orthodox monks on Mt. Athos will not be the same as that of the family commune in California: both need spiritual direction. which will be founded on a common systematic theology, but its interpretation must vary to suit the cultural divergence.

This cultural factor continues to pose a problem. Spiritual direction has always involved a balance or synthesis between theology and psychology; even before the researches of Freud or Jung, St. Augustine was a psychologist to be reckoned with. In the Christian world of the modern West, America has tended to place the emphasis on the psychological side, while Europe has been inclined to give priority to the ancient wisdom of the classical tradition—Patristic and Scholastic theology — with modern psychological studies as supportive adjuncts. The contemporary problem for modern spiritual direction is to restore or reconstitute the balance.

Recent American writing on the subject would appear to play down, and undervalue, the traditional wisdom of the saints, doctors, and acknowledged masters of the directorial art. On the other hand, the European outlook could be seen to be reactionary and irrelevant, giving undue prominence to medieval modes of thought. Further and continued interplay is desirable; whatever their outmoded idiom, outlook and philosophical framework, the wisdom of two thousand years of sanctity cannot be lightly dismissed. On the other hand, the teaching of the church's saints and fathers needs radical re-interpretation and updating to serve the needs of the spiritual direction of modern Western people. St. Benedict has much to say about the prayer and spiritual development of computer technicians and airline pilots, but it is not immediately obvious from a superficial reading of the *Regula*.

Yet Augustine, Anselm, and Aquinas would have been thrilled and excited by contemporary psychological insights, which they would unquestionably have utilized in their spiritual-theological studies. The cultural factor remains of much importance, and further studies are required. The present religious climate indicates a return to spiritual direction as central to pastoral care. This present article has been written, without undue apology, from the European theological angle. It should be supported and completed by studies from the other — psychological — side.

Bibliography. E. W. Trueman Dicken, *The Crucible of Love* (1963). St. Gregory the Great, *Liber Regulae Pastoralis* (ET, various). U. T. Holmes, *Spirituality for Ministry* (1982). St. Ignatius of Loyola, *Spiritual Exercises* (ET, 1919), pp. 271–348. St. John of the Cross, *Complete Works* I (ET, 1947), pp. 144–8, 182–4, 353–5; III pp. 75–91, 176–94. M. T. Kelsey, *Companions on the Inner Way* (1983). K. Leech, *Soul Friend* (1977). G. B. Scaramelli, *Directorium Asceticum* (1924). J. Taylor, *Works* I

(ET 1837), pp. 229–32; III pp. 283–6, 642–8. St. Teresa of Avila, *Complete Works* (ET 1949), 1: pp. 79–83, 2: pp. 19–22, 313–5, 3: pp. 250–1; also on training, 1: pp. 80–83, 2: pp. 22–26. M. Thornton, *Spiritual Direction* (1984); *Pastoral Theology: A Reorientation* (1956), pp. 131–46.

M. THORNTON

CARE OF SOULS; PASTORAL CARE; SPIRITUAL THEOLOGY AND PASTORAL CARE. *See also* PASTORAL THEOLOGY; RETREATS (Roman Catholic); SPIRITUAL DISCIPLINE AND GROWTH; SPIRITUALITY; THEOLOGICAL METHODOLOGY. *Compare* COUNSELING, ROMAN CATHOLIC; FORMATIVE SPIRITUALITY; HASIDIC CARE AND COUNSELING; JEWISH CARE AND COUNSELING; PASTORAL COUNSELING; PASTORAL PSYCHOTHERAPY; PSYCHOLOGY AND PSYCHOTHERAPY (East-West Comparison); THEOLOGY AND PSYCHOTHERAPY.

SPIRITUAL DIRECTION AND PASTORAL CARE.

Spiritual direction is the art, usually identified with the Catholic, Orthodox, and Anglican traditions, of the guidance of souls through the vicissitudes of the inner life. The shape of this life is delineated in various classical texts (notably in *The Ascent to Mount Carmel* by St. John of the Cross and *The Interior Castle* by St. Teresa of Avila).

Spiritual direction is to be understood as taking place within the household of faith. It is quasi-liturgical in that it openly acknowledges the presence of God as the third in the midst of an encounter between two people. It specifically invokes the Holy Spirit as director and guide and is, in a sense, an act of worship. This is in contrast to pastoral counseling, which need not necessarily make *conscious* acknowledgement of the presence of God. Still less does pastoral counseling need specifically to invoke the guidance of the Holy Spirit. Indeed, in some circumstances it would be unwise and even damaging to do so (for example, in the case of someone seeking care after a brutalizing experience with aggressively "religious" people).

Spiritual direction is usually, although not always, conducted on a one-to-one basis and has, until recently, been seen as one element of pastoral care. There are signs, however, of spiritual direction taking a more prominent role in the overall concern for pastoral care. It is true that Protestantism, with its historical emphasis on the doctrine of justification, has not as developed a tradition of spiritual direction as Catholicism. The companion doctrine of sanctification is now being given more attention and the whole realm of spirituality is being seen in a more sympathetic light by Protestants as the churches move closer together.

1. Relationship to Pastoral Counseling. *a. Definitions.* It has become a common practice to use the terms "pastoral care" and "pastoral counseling" interchangeably. With the growing interest in spiritual direction, it might be well to begin to use the term "pastoral care" as an overall term to include not only spiritual direction and pastoral counseling but also the whole process of Christian formation in its communal as well as its individual aspects. This will involve concern for social, political, and ecological issues as well as private and personal ones, since pastoral care has also to do with the formation of persons in community.

Pastoral counseling and spiritual direction would then be understood as two branches of pastoral care; the former's emphasis being on the psyche, the latter's on the spirit. *Psyche* may be said to act as the "container" of *spirit*, in that sound psychological development is the best preparation for spiritual formation. There are those who are psychologically well-adjusted who, nevertheless, have a sickness and sadness of spirit. Their psyche is like a well-scoured bowl in which there is very little life. On the other hand, there are those who have a rich spiritual life but whose psyche can barely hold life together with any kind of integrity. Their psyche is like a colander: a poor container from which things tend to drain away. It is evident that *psyche* and *spirit* need each other. In the same way, pastoral counseling and spiritual direction are complementary.

Another model might be to place pastoral care, spiritual direction and pastoral counseling in some kind of hierarchy with pastoral care at the top and pastoral counseling as an adjunct to spiritual direction. The argument for this arrangement is that the goal of spiritual direction (the formation of persons to be healing and holy presences in a broken world) is a "higher" one than that of pastoral counseling. Or we might prefer to think of their mutual relations in terms of a large circle: pastoral care being the whole circle, pastoral counseling being the inner circle and spiritual direction being the core. But these distinctions are only helpful up to a point since there is no consensus regarding the specific goals of either discipline. There is every indication that the two will be working in closer and closer cooperation in the future.

The Protestant tradition has always shown a marked interest in pastoral care and has done a great deal to foster the development of pastoral counseling in the U.S. As we have seen, pastoral counseling may be defined as an important ingredient within the total art of spiritual direction and the former's growing interest in the latter now makes rapprochement possible. Pastoral counseling has tended to emphasize the clinical, therapeutic, and psychological aspects of inner growth. Indeed, both spiritual direction and pastoral counseling are susceptible to the accusation that they are overly individualistic and somewhat Pelagian in their approach. Little is said about community formation and there is a tendency to make the pursuit of self-knowledge and self-development into a *work*, an end in itself.

b. Contemporary developments. Up until about 1970 the two traditions knew little of each other. Those concerned with mysticism and the life of prayer tended to be both ignorant and suspicious of the psychological emphasis of pastoral counseling and of the way in which the whole of pastoral care had been absorbed by this narrow counseling model. This approach was so dominated by twentieth-century theories of psychological development and the contribution of the behavioral sciences in general that it had no time for older traditions of pastoral care. Spiritual direction and pastoral care were cut off not only from each other but also from basic discussions in systematic theology, partly because the latter had developed into an overintellectualized activity which had little to say about the problems and opportunities (let alone the possibilities of tragedy and glory) of everyday life for the person of faith.

We are now enjoying a period of convergence of the various disciplines. On the one hand, modern spiritual direction embraces not only an interest in, but also a firm commitment to, the insights of depth psychology. Spiritual directors are prepared to take seriously the social and psychological pressures which give shape to the inner life. On the other hand, those who work in the area of psychology are, more and more, willing to acknowledge and work within the deeper dimension of life animated by the Holy Spirit.

Pastoral counselors, consequently, are moving away from their total dependence on therapeutic and clinical models. There is less fear of spiritual escapism and of psychological determinism (the twin enemies of a truly free inner life). Both dangers are still present but there is a greater awareness of the pitfalls. Both spiritual direction and pastoral counseling need the critical and guiding eye of systematic theology if they are to remain informed by the great themes of salvation. The latter needs the experiential grounding of pastoral concerns because of the necessity of its bringing its theological formulations to practical use. The ancient goal was to bring people to the *cognitio experimentalis Dei* (the experimental or experiential knowledge of God). This goal should surely be claimed by both traditions.

c. Differences. In addition to the basic distinction of *psyche* vs. *spirit*, the field of pastoral counseling is highly organized while that of spiritual direction is less so. The former has to do with skills for ministry, the latter with the discernment of a charisma for a particular vocation within the body of Christ. Programs in spiritual direction in seminaries are comparatively rare and then usually found only in Roman Catholic and Anglican institutions. Part of the reason for the developed organization of the one and the comparative lack of organization in the other is precisely that pastoral counseling requires the acquisition of skills, techniques, and expertise. These are verifiable and measurable. A spiritual director's role, on the other hand, is more intuitive. It relies on the gift of discernment, which is the heart of spiritual direction. This gift cannot be taught. All that can be done is to prepare the ground for further self-knowledge on the part of the person who appears to display this particular charisma.

Nevertheless, current approaches to spiritual direction recognize that certain things can be learned which can help those so gifted to function with greater clarity and presence. Spiritual direction is as much concerned with acquiring a sound knowledge of the psychological and behavioral sciences as is pastoral counseling. A deep immersion in the classic spiritual traditions is taken for granted as is a thorough grounding in the foundations of theology.

Another distinction lies in the tendency of pastoral counseling to emphasize self-expression and self-fulfillment. It is concerned with the functioning of the ego so that it can cope and flourish in the world. Spiritual direction, on the other hand, while acknowledging the importance of the above, puts its energy in the direction of self-surrender and self-abandonment in its concern for the discipline and glory of the life promised by the death and resurrection of Christ. Sometimes the two traditions seem in conflict, but there is no point in encouraging persons on a path of self-transcendence until they have developed a *self* to transcend. It is, therefore, useful to think of pastoral counseling as a necessary preparation for

spiritual direction and to see both under the general heading of pastoral care. Both are under pressure from the culture to endorse people's sense of disappointment and outrage at not getting what they want. In short, both disciplines have to deal with people's naive and infantile expectations with regard to personal happiness and religious life.

d. The goal of pastoral care. All this raises the question of whether the goal of pastoral care is merely to help people cope, to feel better about themselves, and to blunt the pain of their hurts and disappointments, or whether it is also as much concerned with ego-surrendering as it is with ego-coping and ego-development. Because spiritual direction focuses on the aspect of surrender and has traditionally not only helped people face "dark nights" but has often encouraged them to wait in the darkness rather than prematurely attempt to rescue them, its goal might be said to center on grace, on simple and attentive waiting on God. The essence of pastoral counseling is in giving direct assistance while spiritual direction concentrates on offering companionship.

2. The Task of Integration. All the distinctions outlined above are highly debatable. Much of the problem is a semantic one, and the task of the next decades will be to integrate the two vocabularies and see that the two disciplines serve but one end. Both will have to give up the tendency to make religion a private affair. Such privatization and individualism are enemies to both psychological development and spiritual growth from the Christian point of view. North American culture takes for granted the separation of church and state and sees religion as essentially a private matter. This is both theologically unsound and spiritually contradictory. There is no strictly "private" reality; and spiritual direction and pastoral counseling, when undergirded (for example) with a sound trinitarian theology, are as much concerned with the formation and development of communities as they are with individuals. Both would naturally be concerned with social justice and world peace.

In the light of the above the trend is toward the integration of the two traditions and a greater willingness to reflect theologically on the goals which are envisioned for the abundant life promised in the Gospel. Everyone needs some form of spiritual guidance and pastoral counseling since we do not live entirely unto ourselves. We need help in maintaining good interpersonal relations and finding ways through the conflicts of the inner life.

Possible models. Both spiritual direction and pastoral counseling take seriously the dramatic shape of a person's or a community's life. Each has a story to tell and every individual story is tested by and finds its meaning in the Gospel story. In spiritual direction there is a four-fold model which involves: (i) the telling of the story; (ii) the sharing of one's vision for the future; (iii) the placing of the life and the vision in the context of the Gospel story; and, finally, (iv) discerning the next step along the way.

Self-knowledge is very important if these questions are to be answered honestly, and our capacity for self-deception is almost boundless. In this four-fold model one can see that psychological skills are as essential as the gift of spiritual discernment. In fact, this model has much in common with one well suited for pastoral counseling which begins with the identification and clarification of a problem, moves on to the development of new perspectives and the setting of goals, and ends with some design for the implementation of these goals. The shift in language, however, from the "spiritual" to the "clinical" makes a great deal of difference to the way in which we understand what is going on.

3. **Summary.** There are signs that the art of spiritual direction is being recovered by the various denominations. It should be seen as an important aspect of pastoral care and a clear distinction should be made between pastoral care and pastoral counseling. Spiritual direction and pastoral counseling are, therefore, to be understood as two complementary disciplines under the general heading of pastoral care. Two things should be kept in mind: (i) useful distinctions between the two arts (the difference between the psyche and the spirit) are to be maintained; and (ii) a commitment to understanding their complementarity and mutual dependence is to be encouraged.

Bibliography. H. Clinebell, *Growth Counseling* (1979). T. Edwards, *Spiritual Friend* (1980). E. G. Hinson, "Recovering the Pastor's Role as Spiritual Guide," in G. Borchert and A. Lester, *Spiritual Dimensions of Pastoral Care* (1985). E. B. Holifield, *A History of Pastoral Care in America* (1983). U. T. Holmes, III, *Spirituality for Ministry* (1982). A. Jones, *Exploring Spiritual Direction: An Essay in Christian Friendship* (1982). M. Kelsey, *Companions on the Inner Way* (1983). D. Kenny, "Clinical Pastoral Education — Exploring Covenants with God," *J. of Pastoral Care* 34:2 (1980), 109 – 113. K. Leech, *Soul Friend* (1977). G. May, *Care of Mind, Care of Spirit* (1982); *Will and Spirit* (1982). J. Neufelder and M. Coelho, eds., *Writings on Spiritual Direction* (1982). H. Nouwen, *The Living Reminder* (1977). W. Pannenberg, *Christian Spirituality* (1983). K. Rahner, *The Practice of Faith* (1983). M. Robbins, "The Desert-Mountain Experience: The Two Faces of Encounter with God," *J. of Pastoral Care,* 35:1 (1981), 18 – 35. H. W. Stone, *The Word of God and Pastoral Care* (1988), ch. 5. N. S. T. Thayer, *Spirituality and Pastoral Care* (1985).

A. JONES

PASTORAL CARE (History, Traditions, and Definitions); SPIRITUAL THEOLOGY AND PASTORAL CARE. *See also* FORMATIVE SPIRITUALITY; PASTORAL THEOLOGY; ROMAN CATHOLIC PASTORAL CARE; SPIRITUAL DISCIPLINE AND GROWTH; SPIRITUALITY. *Compare* AUTHORITY, PASTORAL; GUIDANCE, PASTORAL; HASIDIC CARE AND COUNSELING; PASTORAL COUNSELING; PASTORAL PSYCHOTHERAPY.

SPIRITUAL DIRECTOR. A person of innate gifts, aptitude, learning, and experience who becomes involved in the guidance of others regarding prayer and the things of the spirit.

In the NT it would appear that St. Paul acted in such a manner to a group of disciples including Timothy, Titus, and Onesimus (I, II Timothy; Titus; Philemon). Priscilla and Aquila acted as directors to the zealous but inadequately instructed Apollos (Acts 18:24 – 26; 19:1 – 7.) As the *Parousia* expectation diminished, spiritual experimentation and theory developed, and the spiritual director took on a narrower and more professional character.

The Egyptian desert fathers provided the first truly spiritual theology, producing well-defined directors such as Cassian and Palladius. As monasticism developed, the abbot — spiritual father — was primarily seen as spiritual director to his community.

An important impetus came with the early medieval, largely Anglo-Germanic development of the solitary vocation; the anchorite and anchoress. Without the corporate support of a spiritual community, more personal and specialized guidance was required. The *Ancrene Riwle* (ca. 1200) and Walter Hilton's *Scala Perfectionis* (ca. 1300) are examples of such manuals for the director.

During the Reformation and Counter-Reformation period, Christian spirituality became more of a lay movement, and serious attention was given to the problems of prayer in a secular and domestic environment. As with the earlier solitary, the devout laity need more, not less, direction than the professed religious. St. Francis de Sales (1567–1622) is generally cited as the instigator of such lay direction.

The notion of a spiritual director varies throughout the religious world, developing its most esoteric mystique in such as the *guru* in Hinduism. Within Christianity the Orthodox East resembles this tradition in the *starets* and *poustinik.* Post-Tridentine Roman Catholicism stresses the director's authority, exemplified in the *Spiritual Exercises* of St. Ignatius of Loyola, while Anglicanism softens the concept into a more domestic emphasis on mutual cooperation, of which the coach of the spiritual athlete (see I Cor. 9:24ff) offers the best analogy. In the modern West, the spiritual director is primarily a theologian, founding the life of prayer upon sound doctrine, rather than a psychological technician.

Pronounced in the Anglican tradition is the fact that spiritual direction is no clerical preserve, and lay directors have been prominent from Julian of Norwich in the fourteenth century to Evelyn Underhill in the twentieth. Contemporary trends suggest that this emphasis will expand in pastoral care.

Bibliography. K. Leech, *Soul Friend* (1977). M. Thornton, *Christian Proficiency,* 2d ed. (1961), pp. 25 – 44; *Pastoral Theology,* 2d ed. (1958) pp. 132 – 46.

M. THORNTON

PASTOR; SPIRITUAL DIRECTION; SPIRITUAL MASTERS AND GUIDES. *See also* AUTHORITY, PASTORAL; ROMAN CATHOLIC PASTORAL CARE. *Compare* CHRISTIAN PSYCHOTHERAPIST; CONFESSOR; PASTORAL COUNSELOR; STARETS.

SPIRITUAL DISCERNMENT. *See* DISCERNMENT OF SPIRITS.

SPIRITUAL DISCIPLINE AND GROWTH. Focus on the deliberate efforts that believers make to advance in the life of faith. These terms have roots in the Bible, have changed with the shifts of the imperial, medieval, and modern ages, and today come in for reconsideration, partly due to Protestantism's renewed contact with Catholic and Orthodox spiritual traditions. The normative index in all Christian discipline and growth is love, the life of divine *agape.* Unless personal or church regimes serve this love and help it flourish, they are but "noisy gongs and clanging cymbals" (I Cor. 13:1) For pastoral guidance this norm suggests practices that balance challenge with encouragement, acceptance of self with service of neighbor, trust in God with solid hard work.

1. **Nature and History of Discipline.** There is no flourishing religious life without discipline. Unless the personality is under control, the passions serve reason and genuine love and an individual or group is able to pursue worthy goals, spirituality degenerates into enthusiasm, emotionalism, and narcissism. Discipline is not an end in itself, but it is a main requisite of all spiritual ventures (intellectual, artistic, or religious). With this requisite discipline, inspiration (the leading of the Spirit) can work wonders. Without it, growth will be spotty and virtue unreliable. People beginning a spiritual venture usually have high hopes and high energy. Without dashing these, pastors do well to help such people work out practical times, places, and methods for prayer, penance, and social service. When such regimes are apt and flexible, they become very helpful channels or instruments of growth.

Biblically, discipline runs together with chastisement. In most OT contexts, the head of the family had a responsibility to keep the household and children on the straight path. For Pauline theology the law was a discipline that brought an awareness of sin. In the grace of Christ the new discipline is following the Holy Spirit. Both testaments teach that God uses adversity to refine and discipline people's faith. The Pastoral Epistles give church leaders the responsibility of disciplining their flocks in solid doctrine and morality.

In early Christianity the sacraments focused on a common discipline and growth. Baptism was an initiation into Christ's death and resurrection. Confirmation strengthened this initiation. Penance provided for the forgiveness of sins and amendment of life. In later periods of church history confessors or spiritual directors helped pious laypeople, monks, and nuns to regularize their spiritual efforts. Fasting, stripes, long prayers, and self-denying services to the poor or sick were popular disciplines. In the monastic context a rule laid out much of the communal discipline and praying the liturgical hours was a central concern. In addition, many monks accepted hard physical work in a penitential and disciplinary spirit. The vows of poverty, chastity, and obedience were geared to helping religious become selfless servants and instruments of God. The liturgical seasons of Advent and Lent mediated discipline or mortification to the church at large.

Medieval Christianity focused much of its religious energy on the cross of Christ, making that the central symbol of Christian self-denial. There God's love stood most fully revealed. A disciple without a cross was no disciple. Such classics of devotional literature and spiritual formation as *The Imitation of Christ* by Thomas à Kempis and the *Spiritual Exercises* by Ignatius of Loyola communicated this conviction to late medieval and early modern Christians. À Kempis counseled the pious to shun the seductions of the world and keep their eyes on Christ crucified. Loyola urged acting against one's selfish desires and accepting the invitation of Christ the King to fight under the standard of the cross.

Reformed spirituality hearkened back to biblical themes, rejecting monastic developments and making Bible-reading itself a main discipline. Eastern Orthodoxy retained a demanding, at times almost harsh monastic life, and continued to depreciate worldly pleasures. Modernity forced Christians to wrestle with rationalism and romanticism, puritanism and free-thinking. It also brought questions of social justice to the fore. Today many groups across the ecumenical board are seeking a blend of prayer and social service that will at once be in the world and an affront to worldliness. Women, Blacks, Asians, and others apart from the White European mainstream are asking for models of Christian discipline and growth that better reflect their special experiences. The result is considerable pluralism and confusion.

2. **Pastoral Implications.** Were Christians now to go back to basics, a demanding love would stand spotlighted at center stage. Against all idolatry, spiritual discipline and growth would focus on loving the one holy God utterly, often through a deep contemplative prayer that went to the foundations of creation and brought forth a thorough self-abnegation. In dark nights and "clouds of unknowing," serious spiritual strivers would understand and suffer the wastelands of current Western culture, the threats of anomie, war, and the earth's pollution, as symptoms of humanity's deep refusal to accept the demanding love of its Creator. Against all false self-love and isolationism, spiritual discipline and growth would similarly develop thorough-going politics identifying with the wretched of the earth. Recalling the judgment scene in Matthew 25 and such traditional Christian convictions as "No one has the right to luxuries as long as anyone lacks necessities," they would make economic and social justice new forms of Christ's second command.

These would not, of course, be counsels to or ways of grimness. A discipline and growth coming from the Spirit bear unmistakable signs of joy and peace. But in a materialistic, indulged culture, such joy and peace are bound to be astringent. In cultures shadowed by death squads, they seal the miracle of martyrdom. Then losing one's life in order to gain it becomes quite literal. Then passion and resurrection are a daily passover. With the world becoming smaller, and its interconnectedness becoming more manifest, such facts of life on other continents cannot but shape believers in North America. Christians untroubled by brutalities in Latin America, Eastern Europe, and Africa, like Christians untroubled by threats of nuclear war and ecological pollution, are, under spiritual disciplines, highly suspect. As sexism and racism cry out for personal and communal correction, so do the buildups of arms, the spread of acid rain, the gap between the affluent and the starving.

Communities, no less than individuals, may test themselves by the criteria of radical contemplation and radical social service. Without violence or discouragement, they too may hope to progress in witness, political influence, and prayerful wisdom. Such growth will show in a greater realism about the vast reforms needed, and increased willingness to suffer patiently for supporting the poor and marginal. Regular prayer and regular charitable works will be the best insurance of an ebb and flow of healthy faith. The wisdom of the saints will be the best discipline for a creativity and freedom that are lively without being unbridled.

When discipline is fitting, people feel good but not complacent or self-satisfied. Like John the Baptist, they are happy to be decreasing that their Lord may increase. Thus Christian spiritual growth is no enlargement of the ego. What enlarges is the believer's horizon, which opens out toward the unlimited mystery of God, whom it wants to be all in all. This horizon of the mysterious God explains the Christian call to perfection, which it softens with widespread compassion. We are all simply people and our lives are short. None of us has ever seen God; so we all depend on God's mercy, and must all mainly give thanks. Good spiritual discipline and growth therefore readily turn eucharistic: thankful to God for the beautiful world, the divine love, the chance to help the suffering.

Bibliography. T. à Kempis, *The Imitation of Christ*, L. Sherley-Price, ed. (1952). S. Bolshakoff and M. B. Pennington, *In Search of True Wisdom* (1979). R. M. Brown, *Creative Dislocation — The Movement of Grace* (1980). J. T. Carmody, *Reexamining Conscience* (1982). D. L. Fleming, ed., *The Spiritual Exercises of St. Ignatius* (1978). K. Rahner, *The Practice of Faith* (1983).

J. CARMODY

SACRAMENTAL *or* SPIRITUAL THEOLOGY AND PASTORAL CARE; SANCTIFICATION; SPIRITUAL DIRECTION; SPIRITUALITY. *See also* BAPTISM AND CONFIRMATION; FORMATIVE SPIRITUALITY; GRACE AND PASTORAL CARE; LITERATURE, DEVOTIONAL; JOURNAL KEEPING; LITURGICAL AND DEVOTIONAL LIFE, ROMAN CATHOLIC TRADITION OF; MEDITATION; NATURE AND GRACE; PILGRIMAGE METAPHOR; PRAYER; RELIGIOUS LIFE; RENEWAL MOVEMENTS AND PROGRAMS; REST AND RENEWAL, RELIGIOUS TRADITIONS OF. *Compare* ASCETICAL PRACTICES; PHYSICAL FITNESS DISCIPLINES; SPIRITUAL FORMATION.

SPIRITUAL EXERCISES. *See* IGNATIAN SPIRITUALITY; SPIRITUAL DISCIPLINE AND GROWTH.

SPIRITUAL FORMATION. The process by which a person becomes mature in matters of personal religion, faith, or sense of purpose. In organizations (for example, religious orders) that have a particular spiritual tradition, formation usually is directive; members are guided along relatively definite paths by spiritual directors and prescribed devotions. For others, the process tends to coincide with a general human and religious maturation in realism, self-control, and appreciation of the mysteriousness of life and of God. Christian spiritual formation implies imitation of Christ and an effort to obey Christ's twofold command: love of God and love of neighbor as self.

J. CARMODY

FORMATIVE SPIRITUALITY; GRACE AND PASTORAL CARE; SPIRITUAL DISCIPLINE AND GROWTH; SPIRITUAL THEOLOGY AND PASTORAL CARE. *Compare* CHRISTOTHERAPY.

SPIRITUAL GIFTS (CHARISMATA). *See* CHARISMATIC EXPERIENCE; HOLY SPIRIT.

SPIRITUAL GROWTH. *See* SPIRITUAL DISCIPLINE AND GROWTH.

SPIRITUAL GUIDE. *See* GURU; PASTORAL COUNSELOR; SAGE; SPIRITUAL DIRECTOR; SPIRITUAL MASTERS AND GUIDES; ZADDIK. *See also* GUIDANCE, PASTORAL.

SPIRITUAL HEALING. *See* FAITH HEALING.

SPIRITUAL LIFE. *See* CHRISTIAN LIFE; JEWISH HOLY DAYS AND FESTIVALS; JEWISH PRAYERS; LITURGICAL AND DEVOTIONAL LIFE, ROMAN CATHOLIC TRADITION OF; SPIRITUAL DISCIPLINE AND GROWTH; SPIRITUALITY. *See also* FAITH AND INTEGRITY, *or* PRAYER AND WORSHIP LIFE, PASTOR'S.

SPIRITUAL MASTERS AND GUIDES. The spiritual master mediates a distant and ambivalently experienced God within the particularity of human understanding and need. In the person of the master the mystery and otherness of the divine is gathered in comprehensible and approachable form. Male or female, the master occupies an intermediary position, participating in the full reality of two levels of existence and through his or her person representing their integration. Metaphors employed such as midwife, usher, ferryman, and shepherd communicate a sense of the master who serves as a facilitating agency attending the precarious passage of the disciple into higher levels of spiritual understanding (Brown, 1971).

Notwithstanding variations of culture, language, and theological expression, the person of the spiritual master can be recognized as serving a common sociological role within different religious systems. Across history and context there is a striking similarity in the teaching methods used in their function as spiritual guides. The Western world is most familiar with the title of spiritual master through Eastern use of the designation "guru." Literally translated as "weighty" or "heavy one," a guru is the personal spiritual mentor whose guidance assists the disciple along the path to enlightenment. The instrument of direction is an intense interpersonal relationship characterized by acceptance, affection, and discipline. The spiritual master himself or herself serves as the text of instruction.

Spiritual masters have played important sociological roles in the organization and maintenance of their societies. Embodying the essence of their respective religion's traditions yet peripheral to ruling political loyalties, they were awarded community authority to arbitrate bitter divisions on both local and regional levels. Stories are told of governors, monarchs, and caliphs who kneeled before the word of the spiritual master, acknowledging a wisdom and power anchored in a reality that superseded their own.

The importance of a guide for individual spiritual growth is repeatedly emphasized by all traditions. Bernard of Clairvaux (1090–1154) commented, "He who takes himself for master, becomes the disciple of a fool." The necessity of a spiritual guide is a central tenet of Sufism. Buddhist masters stress the importance of an authoritative transmission of teachings from generation to generation through the living testimonies of the masters. The Upanishadic text of Hinduism underscores the need for a personal teacher in gaining spiritual knowledge. What is considered crucial is not the hearing of learned instruction but rather the experience of the master's soul in relationship.

The high authority given to a personal transmission of teachings is metaphorically conceived as wisdom made visible, truth revealed through the life of a spiritual master who incarnates the tradition. Such tacit knowledge is practical wisdom reaching beyond words to encompass a range of acts and expressions that render the divine accessible in the everyday experience of men and women.

The master-disciple relationship so emphasized in Eastern religious thought became decentralized in much of the Christian tradition. The hierarchical model of the master-disciple relationship was reconceived within a familial metaphor expressive of the theologically perceived status of equality of all pilgrims on a common journey of faith, and thus "Abba" was the term of choice by the Desert Fathers and Mothers of early Christianity to designate a personal spiritual guide. The only true master in the Christian tradition is Christ, who serves as the model for all spiritual guides.

The written experience of the masters has expressed itself in largely androgynous form, yet the question remains why so few women have been acknowledged among the spiritual elite. The answer may be a sociological and cultural reflection of the times, but it may also hint at a gendered form of female spiritual experience that cannot be fully captured by the master-disciple paradigm.

Juxtaposition of the spiritual master tradition with contemporary pastoral care and counseling raises interesting questions. How is the overt therapeutic agenda of pastoral counseling different from or similar to the spiritual/ethical agenda of the master-disciple relationship? Functionally, are the ritualized and structured "holding environments" of pastoral counseling, and the counselor-counselee relationship analogous to the relational personal bond and interchange between master and disciple? A consideration of the classic figure of the spiritual master or guide requires thoughtful reflection on the nature and frame of our work as self-conscious interpreters of God's truth through relationship.

Bibliography. P. Brown, "The Rise and Function of the Holy Man in Late Antiquity," *J. of Roman Studies*, 61 (1971), 80–101. *J. of Dharma*, Special Issue: "Spiritual Journeys," 11:1 (1986). J. R. Sommerfeldt, ed., *Abba: Guides to Wholeness and Holiness East and West*, Cistercian Studies Series, 38 (1982). *Studia Missionalia*, Special Issue: "Spiritual Masters," 36 (1987).

P. J. JOHNSON, III

PASTORAL COUNSELOR; SHAMAN; SPIRITUAL DIRECTOR; STARETS; ZADDIK. *See also* AUTHORITY, PASTORAL; GUIDANCE, PASTORAL; SOCIOLOGY OF RELIGIOUS AND PASTORAL CARE. *Compare* CHRISTIAN PSYCHOTHERAPIST; CHRISTIAN SCIENCE PRACTITIONER; PASTOR; PSYCHOTHERAPIST.

SPIRITUAL PSYCHOLOGIES. Systems which view the techniques, phenomena, and goals of spiritual/religious practice from a psychological perspective. The tendency is to perceive spiritual/religious practice as forms of mind training and spiritual realization as a state of consciousness. Examples include Buddhist, Hindu, Christian, and transpersonal psychologies. Such an approach is sometimes called "the perennial psychology" because of many commonalities in approach across cultures and centuries.

Bibliography. G. G. May, *Will and Spirit: A Contemplative Psychology* (1983).

R. N. WALSH

PSYCHOLOGY AND PSYCHOTHERAPY (East-West Comparison); PSYCHOLOGY, EASTERN. *Compare* PARAPSYCHOLOGY; POPULAR THERAPEUTIC MOVEMENTS AND PSYCHOLOGIES; TRANSPERSONAL PSYCHOLOGIES.

SPIRITUAL THEOLOGY AND PASTORAL CARE. "Spiritual theology" is a comparatively modern term embracing the older categories of ascetical, moral, and mystical theology. As such it has the advantage of being a comprehensive phrase indicating that the Christian spiritual life is a totality, an all-embracing commitment to Jesus Christ.

Spiritual theology is therefore a pastoral application of the whole theological corpus to the life of prayer, which may be defined as that continuous and unbreakable relationship between God and humanity which God initiates and maintains, or, in Christian terms, the relationship which issues from our baptismal incorporation into the sacred humanity of Christ. The spiritual life of prayer, as thus defined, is perhaps best illustrated by the nuptial analogy which is central to the Western tradition of spirituality. Our relationship with God is analogous to the human relation between husband and wife, infinitely variable in personal response and intensity, embracing every aspect of the relationship, mental, intellectual, emotional, physical, and contemplative, yet permanent and inviolable, even unbroken by absence.

The important principles concerned are that spiritual theology should be seen as application, in pastoral care, of the whole of divine learning and not as another departmental and isolable subject: it is the translation of biblical and systematic theology into practical and pastoral terms through the mediation of prayer. It follows that, although it is legitimate and convenient to subdivide prayer into its various manifestations—namely, vocal, meditative and contemplative, personal and liturgical, recollective and penitential, and so on—prayer is an essentially singular, not a plural concept. Prayer is a God-given state which we are in and to which we respond, rather than a series of isolated exercises which we perform from time to time. Spiritual theology points to a spiritual life, not to a series of pious acts inserted into another, secular life.

These emphases, associated with the modern term spiritual theology, are of value in eliminating a certain departmental artificiality associated with the older terminology, which can be confusing and pastorally unreal. Nevertheless it risks the disadvantage of being so comprehensive as to become vague and ambiguous. When spiritual theology is contracted to "spirituality," as it frequently is in contemporary writing and preaching, we risk being left with vagary which is pastorally unproductive. Therefore the older terminology should not be entirely abandoned, for despite its shortcomings it is able to illuminate and clarify the newer one. The three-fold division of spiritual theology, given above, is thus worthy of further consideration.

1. **Ascetical Theology.** That body of doctrine which subserves to the development of prayer, together with those mental, physical, and psychological disciplines

that tend to support it. It is unfortunate that in common converse, "ascetic" has come to be almost synonymous with extreme and irrational austerity like pain and discomfort as values in their own right. But here we are concerned with a technical term of theology derived from St. Paul's analogy of the training of the spiritual athlete (I Cor. 9:24–27). Classical expositions of ascetical theology will therefore contain much about the traditional Christian disciplines: fasting, self-denial, mortification, penitential renunciation, and so on, but always subservient to the development of prayer, as response to our given relationship with God.

Nevertheless, ascetical theology is concerned, above all, with personal development and spiritual growth, with the discovery and nurture of the gifts and graces with which every human being has been endowed. It will therefore deal with such aspects as prayer and its divisions —vocal, liturgical, meditative, contemplative—with spiritual progression, or the study of the manner in which the life of prayer develops; with the discernment of spirits or the tests for, and interpretation of, spiritual experience; and with the development of virtue in response to grace.

Ascetical theology has developed over the ages, meeting the needs of changing cultures, diverse human temperament, and particular spiritual aspiration. So it must continue to be studied with a view to pastoral development and reinterpretation into this century and the next. The historical result of all this accumulated wisdom issues in the multifarious "schools of prayer" which make up the rich diversity of Christian spiritual expression: Benedictine, Cistercian, Franciscan, Salesian, Ignatian, Carmelite, and so on. The study becomes immensely complex, yet it is based upon the glorious and incontrovertible fact that all people are uniquely different. For that reason alone it must remain central to pastoral care.

It is only to be expected that at certain periods, and according to prevailing theological fashion, the subject has suffered from a certain overcomplexity of artificial theological hairsplitting. It must be strongly reiterated that it should not be considered as a departmental subject, but as application of the biblical revelation to the life of prayer.

For example, the fundamental pattern of catholic prayer, initiated by St. Basil and St. Benedict—set forms of praise supporting the Eucharist and issuing in personal devotion—has been judged as monastic, artificial, and dull. Yet it is not only biblical (Mt. 6:6; 6:9–13), but a living and practical expression of trinitarian doctrine. In the scholastic tradition, discussion on the theological virtues leading into the gifts of the spirit may likewise appear to be complex and unreal, yet properly interpreted it is pastoral and biblical (I Cor. 13; Isa. 11:2–3; Gal. 5:22–4).

Underlying the classical tradition is the study of spiritual development as progress through the three ways or ages of Christian life; the initial purification from serious sin, illumination by grace, and a final union with God. This basic pattern is also open to misinterpretation either through oversophistication or oversimplification. But it is again biblically based since it follows the unfolding relation between God and humanity which is the central theme of the Scriptures: the covenant relation of the OT

implying moral obedience, illuminating encounter with God in Christ as expressed in the Gospel, and finally incorporation into the sacred humanity of Jesus as expounded by St. Paul. Correctly interpreted and applied, especially when the scheme is reduced to the personal version of St. Thomas Aquinas—beginners or "babes in Christ" (I Cor. 3:1), then proficients in prayer, and finally the perfected or sanctified—all such studies remain of much constructive value in pastoral care.

While such a vast corpus of learning may look a little daunting to the contemporary pastor or student, its basis is still biblical and systematic theology approached in a special way. Whatever branch of theology is studied, the ascetical theologian's perennial question is: How does this impinge on prayer?

2. Moral Theology. Something like the obverse of ascetical theology, they are as two sides of one coin, with obvious interrelations and interaction; growth in the spiritual life, progress in prayer, and the practice of the theological virtues inevitably involve moral improvement as well. Conversely, the Christian struggle against sinful tendencies and emotional distortion must involve a response to God's redemptive grace. But within the overall context of spiritual theology the distinction, albeit an artificial one, makes for clarity.

A further distinction is also called for, especially as applicable to pastoral care. This is between moral theology and the more modern and popular term Christian ethics. The latter is of much contemporary significance in that it is firmly grounded upon a wider moral philosophy, thus attempting to justify Christian moral standards by what to many are more acceptable criteria than ecclesiastical or biblical authority. In the modern Western world it thus has considerable apologetic value, hoping to demonstrate that Christian thought can produce reasoned and objective judgments on the stupendous moral issues of the day. But by and large such judgments are issued in terms of general philosophically grounded guidelines, which can have impact upon public opinion and secular authority. It is a moral theology which is still required in the pastoral guidance of individuals within a particular situation.

At first sight the older discipline of moral theology— which inevitably needs continual updating—suffers from the same failing as traditional ascetical theology: a hairsplitting sophistry which looks removed from and irrelevant to everyday living. Sin—a strictly theological rather than moral term—is divided and subdivided into innumerable categories of type, gravity, motive, and circumstance. Grace, which in pastoral practice may adequately be defined as God's help toward human sanctification, is divided by some scholastic theologians into seventeen different kinds, all operating in different ways. Conscience, which every reasonable person experiences every day, is equally analyzed in much detail.

But if other ages and theological fashions appear remote from modern pastoral needs, the core of all this traditional speculation and wisdom should not be summarily dismissed. As against Christian ethics, important as that is, moral theology still offers authoritative assistance to the contemporary exercise of pastoral care. Depending on context, expositor, or provenance, Christian ethics may be completed without any reference to sin, grace, conscience, penitence, redemption, confession, prayer, or, pervading it all, Christian anthropology.

The irony is that it is the contemporary study of Christian ethics that produces these general principles, basic standards, the much maligned blanket judgments, that causes modern society to castigate Christian morality as harsh, unbending, and lacking in compassion. It is scholastic moral theology that tries to understand human frailty, that assists individuals to make responsible moral decisions in the face of existing circumstances. In pastoral care the question is seldom what is right or wrong, but which is the best choice between evils or which is the best choice amongst comparable goods.

Latterly, Christian moralists have struggled with this question in the context of situational or existential ethics; circumstances alter cases, moral decision has to take cognizance of the actual and particular situation; there can be no Kantian imperative. Such reinterpretation is to be welcomed, but it is reinterpretation rather than a new invention, since traditional moral theology has always included a casuistry to assist individual people to make responsible moral decisions within their unique situations. Questions common in modern pastoral care, such as emotional disturbance and immaturity, psychiatric illness, depression, and diminished responsibility through stress are by no means unknown to the traditional casuist. The older moral theology still has much to offer to the contemporary pastor.

3. **Mystical Theology.** It differs from moral and ascetical theology in one important respect. Christian ascetical and moral endeavor assumes active human free will, comprising a purposeful response to God's grace. Christian prayer is normally mediated through intellect, imagination, and symbol, whether words, created things, or religious mandala like pictures, icons, or the crucifix. Mysticism claims a direct and unmediated activity of God upon chosen recipients who respond with complete renunciation. The word is much misused in general conversation, often signifying quite ordinary contemplative prayer and normal religious experience. But the true mystic is sufficiently rare to be on the outer fringe of ordinary pastoral care. In day-to-day work, the Christian pastor should be competent to guide others in progressive vocal, liturgical, meditative, and contemplative prayer, together with the moral theology which supports it. He or she should gain sufficient understanding of mysticism to recognize it if and when it occurs. Continued guidance is then a very specialized art.

Bibliography. J. Aumann, *Spiritual Theology* (1980). L. Bouyer, ed., *A History of Christian Spirituality* (1982). J. de Guibert, *The Theology of the Spiritual Life* (ET, 1954). B. Haring, *The Law of Christ* (ET, 1963); *Free and Faithful in Christ* (1978–81). F. P. Harton, *The Elements of the Spiritual Life* (1960). F. Heiler, *Prayer* (1938). F. von Hugel, *The Mystical Element of Religion* (1908). K. E. Kirk, *The Vision of God* (1977); *Conscience and Its Problems* (1927); *Some Principles of Moral Theology* (1921). R. C. Mortimer, *The Elements of Moral Theology,* 2d ed. (1953). A. Poulain, *The Graces of Interior Prayer* 5th ed. (1950). P. Pourrat, *Christian Spirituality* (ET, 1922). J. B. Scaramelli, *Directorium Asceticum* (1924). E. Underhill, *Mysticism* (1911).

M. THORNTON

SPIRITUAL DIRECTION AND PASTORAL CARE; SPIRITUALITY, ROMAN CATHOLIC. *See also* ASCETICAL PRACTICES; CHRISTOTHERAPY; FORMATIVE SPIRITUALITY; GRACE AND PASTORAL CARE; MYSTICISM; RELIGIOUS LIFE. *Compare* MORAL THEOLOGY AND PASTORAL CARE; PASTORAL THEOLOGY, ROMAN CATHOLIC; SACRAMENTAL THEOLOGY AND PASTORAL CARE, ROMAN CATHOLIC.

SPIRITUAL TRADITION OF CARE. *See* DISCERNMENT OF SPIRITS; SPIRITUAL DIRECTION.

SPIRITUALISM. A belief in and practice of communicating with spirits or non-corporeal intelligence. With roots in mid-nineteenth-century America, modern spiritualism is significantly concerned with essentially "pastoral" issues of health and wholeness. Indeed, one essential purpose of spirit contact is to aid in healing close friends and relatives residing on the "earth plane." Mediums, shaman-like individuals purportedly having the ability to communicate with the spirit world, act as liaisons, making contact with spiritual entities that assume forms which are recognizable to kin and friends.

1. **Spiritual Beliefs.** The spirit world is conceived as an indeterminate number of spiritual planes arranged in a hierarchy (V. Skultans, 1974). Contact with the spirit world is believed to occur between the earth plane and lower spiritual planes. Spiritualism is unlike most belief systems in that during the weekly church service, which otherwise resembles Protestant worship in a number of respects, believers are accorded the privilege of experiencing, firsthand, sacred aspects of their belief system (R. Fishman, 1979). Believers develop personal relationships with spiritual entities during the "message service," that section of the service in which spirit contact is made (see Macklin, 1974).

Mediums prepare themselves through various techniques, some involving elaborate and dramatic rituals. Each medium brings a "test" to the individual receiving the message, believed to be a scientific proof that the medium is actually in contact with the spirit world. The medium discloses the gender, the deceased's name, the way the individual died, or something equally personal to the believer. Mediums may take on symptoms of the illness the deceased suffered before dying. These proofs are usually sufficient to assure the believer that contact has been made, and provide a reason for following any advice passed on to the living.

Messages usually offer practical advice on matters relating to the well-being of church members, often advising on how to release negative thoughts and begin the healing process or warning believers of potential medical problems (Fishman, 1979). This experience of an alternate reality, the spirit world, validates two basic spiritualist beliefs: (1) that life is continuous so that, under proper conditions, one may communicate with deceased loved ones; and (2) that one may heal and teach through divine power.

2. **Modern Medical Beliefs.** Western medicine is embedded in a worldview of scientific materialism, which regards spiritual experiences to be epiphenomenal. However, recent evidence from non-Western cultures indicates that the materialist biomedical model alone is, at times, inadequate in dealing with the diversity of physical and emotional illnesses. Generally the

patient's epistemological beliefs are ignored; medical professionals treat physical problems and ignore other significant elements of the illness episode, including spiritual experiences.

Spiritual beliefs place illness into a different context by wholistically integrating the maintenance of physical health with social, spiritual, and emotional well-being. Thus the cause of illness is often viewed within the context of personal experiences and the mind-body dichotomy is sequentially reversed; unlike the biomedical model, body is made secondary to mind.

Bibliography. R. Fishman, "Spiritualism in Western New York: A Study in Ritual Healing," *Medical Anthropology* (1979), 1–22; "Transmigration, Liminality and Spiritualist Healing," *J. of Religion and Health*, 19 (1980), 217–25. J. Macklin, "Belief, Ritual and Healing: New England Spiritualism and Mexican American Spiritism Compared," in *Religious Movements in Contemporary America*, I. Zaretsky and M. Leone, eds. (1974). For a discussion of the origins of Spiritualism in the U.S. see G. Nelson, *Spiritualism and Society* (1969). L. Schwartz, "The Hierarchy of Resort in Curative Practice: The Admiralty Islands, Melanesia, *JHSB* 10 (1969), 201–9. V. Skultans, *Intimacy and Ritual* (1974). See also J. J. Heaney, *The Sacred and The Psychic* (1984).

R. G. FISHMAN

PARAPSYCHOLOGY; SURVIVAL (Occult). *See also* ESCHATOLOGY AND PASTORAL CARE; FAITH HEALING; SHAMAN; SOUL; SPIRIT, HUMAN. *Compare* TRANCE; WITCHCRAFT.

SPIRITUALITY (Jewish Tradition). *See* JEWISH HOLY DAYS AND FESTIVALS; JEWISH PRAYERS; THEOLOGY, JEWISH.

SPIRITUALITY (Orthodox Tradition). The term *spirituality* is unknown in classical Eastern Orthodox tradition. A modern concept, it has come to refer to a person's life and activity in relationship to God, and to oneself, other people, and all things in reference to God. It specifically refers to the life which God gives through Jesus Christ and the Holy Spirit in the Christian church.

1. Life in Relationship to God. Human beings are created in God's image for unending life. The content of life is the knowledge of God through a union of love.

According to Eastern Orthodoxy, the God who creates has an uncreated image, also called his Son and Word. He also has a personal Holy Spirit. Human beings, male and female, receive God's Spirit in order to be conformed to his image and so to participate in his divine life. Through willful disobedience by the abuse of their godlike freedom, human beings have distorted their nature made in God's image and have lost communion with God. This fact, symbolized in the biblical story of Adam and Eve, was foreseen by God as inevitable. Thus the coming of God's uncreated image as the human being, Jesus of Nazareth, the Messiah of Israel and Savior of the world, is understood as being at the center of God's plan for creation from the beginning.

In Jesus Christ human beings are restored to their God-given dignity by the indwelling of God's Spirit. They are given life, which is communion with God the Father through the Son in the Holy Spirit, which is a literal *theosis*, deification. The names for the persons of the divine Trinity are not debatable, according to Orthodoxy, since to change the names, images, and symbols given in the Judeo-Christian tradition is to change the content of the spiritual reality and mystical experience to which they testify.

2. The Life of the Church. The life of communion with God is, for Eastern Orthodoxy, the life of the church in her sacramental nature as the body and bride of Christ, the "fullness of him who fills all in all". (Eph. 1:23) In this sense the church is understood to be the Kingdom of God on earth, the kingdom which Jesus proclaimed and established by his crucifixion and glorification. It is life enabled by the Holy Spirit sent from God. Thus understood, God's kingdom is identified with the indwelling of the Holy Spirit, and with the Spirit himself, the acquisition of whom is the goal and content of life. Spiritual life is thus grounded in the life of the church where the Holy Spirit guarantees communion with God through Christ.

Baptism is the sacramental death and resurrection of a person in Christ, the dying and rising with Jesus to newness and fullness of life. In baptism one is mystically "born again" into the divine life of the Kingdom of God. Human nature is renewed. It is a person's Easter.

Chrismation (confirmation) is the sacramental sealing of new life in Christ by the Holy Spirit. It follows immediately after baptism as the person's Pentecost, the gift of the power to live the life into which one is baptismally born.

The *Eucharist* is the sacrament of the Kingdom of God where the Holy Spirit comes upon the community and its offering of bread and wine to transform the entire assembly into the body of Christ: It is the foretaste of the age to come, the new creation. It is the eating and drinking at the table of the kingdom, the marriage supper of the Lamb described in the Apocalypse. In the Orthodox church infants in the care of believing adults are baptized, sealed and brought to communion at the eucharistic supper. Spiritual life thus begins in its fullness from infancy.

Marriage is the sacramental participation of the love of a man and woman in God's love for the world which is consummated in the union of Jesus, the divine bridegroom with the church, his deified bride. Sexual love is perfected only in marriage, according to the tradition, and the spiritual life of the faithful couple signifies the divine life of God's kingdom, as does consecrated celibacy which the tradition affirms and glorifies.

The Anointing of the sick is the sacramental consecration of human suffering and death to the glory of God. There is no life in the fallen world without suffering, no life which does not end in physical death. The victory of Christ on the cross is the destruction of death by death. The spiritual life of a person is fulfilled in the transformation of suffering and death into an act of victory and life.

3. The Life of Prayer and Spiritual Warfare. Spiritual life is the everyday actualization of what is sacramentally given in the church. It is, therefore, a continual dying and rising in Christ, a continual reception of the Holy Spirit, a continual act of communion with God, a continual struggle to overcome suffering and death with the help of the power of God. As such, the spiritual life is a life of unceasing prayer which is traditionally defined as the conscious act of union of the whole person—mind and heart, body and soul—with God. It is also, because of human fallenness, a constant warfare against falsehood and sin, the devil, and death.

Techniques of prayer and spiritual warfare are developed in Eastern Orthodox tradition by a multitude of spiritual masters, both men and women, whose teachings are recorded in such writings as the *Lives of the Saints*, the *Sayings of the Fathers*, and the *Philokalia*. The testimony is that it is already possible to live the resurrected life of God's kingdom through constant prayer rooted in the church's liturgical worship, psalmody, and meditation on the Word of God. There is no specific method of prayer and spiritual warfare which is applicable in the same way to everyone. In this sense there are as many spiritualities as there are human beings made to be temples of God. But there are certain principles which are applicable to all.

The essential element in the spiritual life is the pure desire to see things clearly and to live rightly. In the church this means to know God as God really is and to glorify God by accomplishing God's will. In secular terms this means to search honestly for whatever is true, honorable, just, pure, lovely, gracious, excellent, and worthy of praise (cf. Phil. 4:8). With a pure desire, everything is possible by God's grace and guidance. Without it, there is no life.

The great enemy to life is self-deceit and delusion which are born of pride and self-will. Even such apparently good things as pure prayer, mystical union, holiness and spiritual perfection must be set aside as possible temptations of self-seeking to be conquered by God's grace.

Authentic life is proved by the acquisition of God's Spirit and his fruits, scripturally listed as "love, joy, peace, patience, kindness, goodness, faithfulness, gentleness, self-control" (Gal. 5:22). The gifts (*charismata*) of the Spirit in themselves prove nothing since they may be received unto judgment through prideful misuse.

The perfection of spiritual life is love, the fulfilling of the law and the direct sharing in the divine nature. Love alone is the proof of genuine mystical experience; love for God and neighbor, especially the enemy. To love with the love with which God loves the world is spiritual perfection.

The path to perfection requires guidance. The only master is in Christ who acts through God's Spirit. The living tradition of the Christian church, expressed in dogmas and doctrines, scriptures and saints, sacraments and symbols, councils and canons, icons and hymns bears the authority of the master. Obedience to this tradition guarantees the avoidance of delusion and the attainment of *discernment* (*diakrisis*), which is lucid insight into reality; *dispassion* (*apatheia*), which is perfect spiritual freedom; and *deification* (*theosis*), which is becoming divine by God's grace.

Bibliography. N. Arseniev, *Revelation of Life Eternal* (1982 [1963]); *Mysticism and the Eastern Church* (1979 [1926]). A. Schmemann, *For the Life of the World* (1973 [1963]). K. Ware, *The Orthodox Way* (1979).

T. HOPKO

CHRISTIAN LIFE; SANCTIFICATION/HOLINESS; SPIRITUAL DISCIPLINE AND GROWTH. *See also* ASCETICAL PRACTICES; MYSTICISM; RELIGIOUS EXPERIENCE; SACRAMENTAL THEOLOGY AND PASTORAL CARE. *Compare* MINISTRY AND PASTORAL CARE (Orthodox Tradition).

SPIRITUALITY, PASTOR'S. *See* FAITH AND INTEGRITY, PASTOR'S; PRAYER AND WORSHIP LIFE, PASTOR'S.

SPIRITUALITY (Protestant Tradition). Usually referred to as devotion or piety. The Protestant reformers rejected key elements of medieval Catholic spirituality: the Mass, oral confession, devotional reading, devotion to the saints and Mary, ascetic practices, and a variety of prayer forms. They closed monasteries, which had served as guides in spirituality and retreat centers for centuries. In place of these aids, they emphasized forgiveness of sins on account of grace (God's unmerited favor) received by faith, study of the Bible, and simple forms of prayer. Anglicans, standing somewhere between Catholic and Protestant traditions, held on to a number of elements of medieval piety as reflected particularly in *The Book of Common Prayer*. Major reformers such as Luther and Calvin also retained some, but radical reformers (Ana-baptists, spiritualists, rationalists) sought to restore primitive Christian piety with a minimum of later accretions.

1. History. *a. Puritanism.* The impoverishment of Protestant spirituality which accompanied these changes in the sixteenth century led to significant reassessments in the seventeenth century. In England Puritans, convinced the Church of England was only "halfly reformed," sought "further reformation" by way of a revival of medieval devotional practices. Zealous for "heart religion" manifested in transformed lifestyle and reform of society, the Puritans produced a profusion of manuals urging watching, fasting, praying, reading the Scriptures, keeping the Sabbaths, hearing sermons, receiving communion, relieving the poor, exercising works of piety and self-conscious attention to outward behavior. As they watched their dreams of a holy commonwealth fade in England, they turned with enthusiasm to the New World where they hoped to establish in the "wilderness of this world" a "Protestant Zion," a testing ground for living in the heavenly City itself. In numerous ways their spirituality paralleled that of medieval monks in both asceticism and contemplation. Whereas monks tried to make saints of those in monasteries, however, the Puritans sought to make saints of every person living within their society.

b. Pietism. In Europe Pietism arose during the late seventeenth century. Rooted partly in German and Dutch mysticism by way of Jakob Boehme (1575–1624), and partly in Puritanism, it represented a reaction against Protestant scholasticism and indifference following the Thirty Years' War (1618–48). Although restricted as a self-conscious movement to the careers of two persons—Philipp Jacob Spener (1635–1705) and August Hermann Francke (1633–1727), Pietism exerted continuing influence through the evangelical revivals of the eighteenth century. Spener's plan for the renewal of the Lutheran churches in his day, outlined in *Pia Desideria* in 1675, consisted of five major points: (1) earnest Bible study both privately and in small cell groups; (2) the establishment and diligent exercise of a "spiritual priesthood"; (3) the practice of piety, especially love, toward one another; (4) avoidance of arrogance and censoriousness in religious controversies and exercise of love toward unbelievers and heretics; and (5) training of ministers not only in academic subjects but in spirituality. The fifth proposal resulted in the founding of the first Protestant seminary in 1688; previously ministers were educated in the universities.

c. Revivalism and the social gospel. In North America Protestant spirituality has exhibited a marked effect of both Puritanism and Pietism as well as features characteristic of various traditions. In the "Great Awakening" (1720–50) and in the frontier revivals (1790–1820; 1857), however, the Puritan-Pietist models suffered some erosion as revivalism dominated the scene. As the U.S. progressed from a largely rural to a predominantly urban society, Protestant spirituality acquired a keener social sensitivity, concerned about prison reform, temperance, the plight of laborers, and numerous other issues. This development reached a peak in the "social gospel" movement of the late nineteenth and early twentieth centuries.

2. Contemporary Expressions. Years of societal confusion and turmoil in the twentieth century caused many Protestants to question the adequacy of their heritage in spirituality. Simultaneously a radical change in the ecumenical situation with the entrance of Roman Catholics into the ecumenical stream opened new options. At least four responses can be detected.

a. Radical or secular spirituality. This emerged from reflections on Dietrich Bonhoeffer's *Letters and Papers from Prison.* Rejecting otherworldly piety typical in many periods of Christian history, secular spirituality sounded a call for engagement with the world and "going through the world to God." It de-emphasized some traditional modes of cultivating piety and redefined others. Prayer, for instance, would be not so much "for" another as "to be with" another. The key, however, was to be "in" the world where the Kingdom of God is "the Beyond in the midst" of life.

b. Charismatic spirituality. This represented a reaction against formalistic and rationalistic religion. Although it had antecedents in the Pentecostal churches, the charismatic movement sprang up with renewed vigor in mainline Protestantism during the 1950s. Charismatics emphasized experiential religion, speaking in tongues or glossolalia being only one, though an important, expression.

c. Neo-Oriental or quasi-Oriental Christian spirituality. This moved in the same direction as charismatic spirituality. Especially attractive to college students, it drew heavily from major religions such as Buddhism or Hinduism to supplement Christian methods of prayer or meditation. New cults such as the Unification Church ("Moonies") combined both Christian and Oriental features.

d. Ecumenical influences. As Roman Catholics and Orthodox joined the ecumenical movement in the 1960s, they brought with them a wealth of traditional resources which proved attractive to Protestants. These included emphasis on the liturgy, retreat centers, spiritual direction and formation, prayer forms, methods of meditation, devotional writings, and thousands of persons equipped for spiritual guidance.

3. Challenges. Two basic presuppositions of Protestantism have created serious problems in spirituality. First, Protestants have defined grace as God's unmerited favor in forgiveness of sinners and, until recently, have rejected the traditional understanding of grace which underlies the whole tradition of spirituality; that is, grace as the Spirit working within the life of believers to transform them and to effect growth. The consequence has been an erosion of a sense of obligation to grow in grace since the final outcome, salvation, is assured. It was lack of assurance for which the reformers faulted Roman Catholicism, but in virtually guaranteeing salvation (of course, for the "Elect") from the start, they undercut the motive for human effort (even cooperation with God).

Second, Protestants have placed responsibility for growth almost entirely on the shoulders of individuals and have de-emphasized corporate means and duties. The more radical Protestants, for instance, have forbidden instruction in such practices as prayer, assuming that the Spirit alone will teach individuals without any help from the community of faith. The net effect has been a plethora of approaches and frantic search to find useful methods without the guidance which Christian history itself offers.

Changes in the ecumenical climate have opened a way out of these difficulties. Modern biblical studies have enabled both Protestants and Catholics to recognize the validity of the others' understanding of grace. At the same time they have moved closer to one another in their appreciation for both individual and corporate responsibility for the life of the Spirit. Protestants, for instance, not only speak about but seek spiritual direction from Roman Catholics. Since the Second Vatican Council (1962–65), meantime, Catholics now reject authoritarian approaches to direction and emphasize adaptation of guidance to individual personalities and circumstances.

Bibliography. D. Bonhoeffer, *Letters and Papers from Prison* (1972). L. Bouyer, *Orthodox Spirituality and Protestant and Anglican Spirituality,* vol. 3 of *A History of Christian Spirituality* (1982). E. G. Hinson, "American Spirituality," in *The Westminster Dictionary of Christian Spirituality,* G. S. Wakefield, ed., (1983); *Seekers After Mature Faith* (1968). U. T. Holmes, *A History of Christian Spirituality* (1981). W. Pannenberg, *Christian Spirituality* (1983). D. V. Steere, "Common Frontiers in Catholic and Non-Catholic Spirituality," in *Together in Solitude* (1983), D. Steere, ed.

E. G. HINSON

CHRISTIAN LIFE; SANCTIFICATION/HOLINESS; SPIRITUAL DISCIPLINE AND GROWTH. *See also* ASCETICAL PRACTICES; BORN-AGAIN EXPERIENCE; MYSTICISM; PILGRIMAGE METAPHOR; RELIGIOUS EXPERIENCE; RETREATS (Protestantism). *Compare* MINISTRY (Protestant Tradition). *Biography:* BONHOEFFER; SPENER.

SPIRITUALITY (Roman Catholic Tradition). Roman Catholicism tends to think of spirituality as one's distinctive way of following Christ, communing with God, and growing in the life of faith. Historically, Roman Catholic spirituality has been much shaped by the various religious orders, almost all of which owe a large debt to early monasticism. Doctrinally, the Catholic effort to balance reason and faith, nature and grace, has wrought different combinations of work and prayer, contemplation and action. Recently, Roman Catholic spiritual writers have been paying more attention to politics, solidarity with the poor, and Eastern religious disciplines.

1. **Basic Description.** In saying that Roman Catholicism tends to think of spirituality as one's distinctive way of following Christ, the intention is to foreclose discussion of any negative overtones that spirituality might bear. Spirituality in the Roman Catholic context is a wholly positive way or style of making faith existential (personally engaging), prayerful, and virtuous. Whatever deficiencies a given school or historical epoch may show, the intent or ambition is to fill the adherent with the love of Christ.

In general, the Roman Catholic accent has been individualist or personal, although members of the same group (e.g., Benedictines, Franciscans) tend to speak of their distinctive common tradition. Psychologically, then, one who joined such a group had the sense of submitting to a given outlook and discipline for religious growth. Theologically, all Roman Catholic spirituality accepts the priority of God's grace, the dominance of the Holy Spirit, but most schools also insist on regular prayer, penance, and reformation of character. Many contemporary commentators feel that the traditional emphases slighted ethical and social dimensions, so contemporary Catholic spiritualities tend to concentrate on practice and social implications (as well as prayer). Such notions as the fruits of the Spirit, the gifts of the Spirit, and *charismata* come to the fore when Roman Catholics speak of more mature spiritual stages.

2. **The Three Ways.** The most popular Catholic staging of the spiritual life speaks of three "ways": the purgative, the illuminative, and the unitive. The purgative way takes beginners from vice to virtue. It is a time of penance, training in prayer, and self-abnegation. Since it has often coincided with studenthood, apprenticeship, or time spent in a religious novitiate, it has dealt more with the self than the group to be ministered unto, been a matter more of personal development than social service. Usually meditative prayer dominates the purgative period.

The illuminative way usually means a shift to contemplative prayer — something simpler, less mind-oriented, more affective. Where Christian meditation means trying to get clear the values of Christ and discipleship, illuminative prayer means letting the love of Christ enlighten one's mind and heart, draw one's *joie de vivre*. In the illuminative way rules become less rigid and important, nuance and prudence flesh things out. Grace becomes more important than works. Listening to the Spirit sensitizes one's conscience and deepens one's awareness of every creature's smallness.

The unitive way connotes a nearly habitual sense of God's presence, a personal covenant or marital bond. In the mystics it is the fruit of deep purification. It may emphasize God's otherness or the rich humanity of Christ. It is the crown of all Catholic spiritualities, fulfilling the Pauline faith that Christ is the believer's inmost life (Gal. 2:20).

3. **Historical Sketch.** A Catholic spirituality ideally is the fruit of Orthodox doctrine (with special emphasis on the theology of grace) and generous practice. It articulates how one may best live out one's faith. As such it is

practical, the expression of an ongoing discernment of spirits. When a spirituality does not fit a given person or age, it stands ready for reform and regeneration. Roman Catholicism has tended to build its spiritualities organically, letting each age adapt the ascetical and mystical traditions of the past. Thus on the basis of NT counsels to poverty and chastity, and their own need for solitude, the early desert monks fashioned a life in pursuit of union with God. Their experience suggested the wisdom of communal ventures, under the guidance of practiced elders and a directive rule. Western monasticism, most powerfully shaped by Benedict of Nursia, has relied on the vows of poverty, chastity, and obedience to take Christians out of the sinful, seductive world and point them toward union with God. The monastic spiritualities try to penetrate the mystery of salvation so deeply that prayer becomes honestly social, one's passions become the sufferings of the world. In recent times Thomas Merton translated this traditional monastic spirituality effectively for many Catholics.

The more active religious orders gave Roman Catholicism spiritualities geared to apostolic service in the world. Thus the Franciscan, stressing poverty, and the Dominican, stressing study, both evolved followings of Jesus that were more mobile than the Benedictine, with its vow of stability. Jesuit spirituality is in the same mode, aiming at developing the ability to find God in all things. The mystical writings of the sixteenth century Spanish Carmelites Teresa of Avila and John of the Cross have made all Roman Catholic spiritualities aware of the *via negativa* or impact of the divine otherness. This was a theme of the influential fourteenth-century English classic, *The Cloud of Unknowing,* but the Spaniards made it more concrete and precise. In their wake Catholic spirituality has stressed that the way to unitive love of God is stark detachment. Another form of Catholic spirituality is that reflected in the book *The Imitation of Christ.*

4. **Contemporary Issues.** Today, liberation theology is the loudest voice in a Roman Catholic chorus that would have spirituality become less elitist, more political, and engaged with the sufferings of the world's downtrodden masses. For while the various Catholic religious orders developed profound spiritual traditions, the Catholic church did relatively little for the vast majority of its members who led lay lives in the world. After counseling them to receive the sacraments regularly and pray such devotions as the Rosary, it resorted to trying to refit (if not water down) an originally monastic spirituality for a life of parenthood and worldly work. By way of reaction Catholic spirituality is now coming to mean but an intensification of the whole life of faith: politics and economics, sex and work, prayer and solidarity with the suffering poor. Women are asking for spiritualities that take into account their special histories, psychologies, and needs. Blacks, Asians, Latin Americans and others are seeking alternatives to the White European styles that have dominated the Catholic mainstream. This is causing some confusion at the Roman Catholic center, where church officials are delighted that their people want vital religious growth but alarmed that these people often criticize traditional spiritualities as privatistic. Thus behind the debates over liberation theology lurk sizeable spiritual implications.

Currently, Roman Catholic spirituality is also opening to the wisdoms of other religious traditions, especially those of India and East Asia. As its demographics make the Catholic Church look away from a European basin to a future in the Third World, the spiritualities of the Third World are becoming more attractive. Thus the yogic techniques of Hinduism, the meditations of Buddhism, the vitality of African spirituality, and the like are making an increasing impact. The psychologies of the West have also made a mark, causing current Roman Catholic spirituality to be sensitive to the masochism or repression that sometimes marred its past forms. Above all, though, the current desideratum is a spirituality that helps the believers find God in the world of suffering humanity. This spirituality would make a great deal of poverty and prayer, less of celibacy and obedience to a religious superior than past Catholic spiritualities did. Its touchstone, however, would remain quite traditional: love of God with whole mind, heart, soul, and strength; love of neighbor as self. This could mean a radical contemplation of the divine mystery joined to a radical service of the world's dispossessed.

Bibliography. Anon., *The Cloud of Unknowing* (ET, 1912). P. Brooks, ed., *Christian Spirituality* (1975). L. Bouyer, *A History of Christian Spirituality,* 3 vols. (1982). D. L. Carmody, *Seizing the Apple* (1984). J. Carmody, *Holistic Spirituality* (1983). O. Chadwick, *Western Asceticism* (1958). G. Gutierrez, *We Drink from Our Own Wells* (1984). T. à Kempis, *The Imitation of Christ* (1418; ET, 1952). W. Johnston, *Christian Mysticism Today* (1984).

J. CARMODY

CHRISTIAN LIFE; LITURGICAL AND DEVOTIONAL LIFE, ROMAN CATHOLIC TRADITION OF; SANCTIFICATION; SPIRITUAL DISCIPLINE AND GROWTH. *See also* ASCETICAL PRACTICES; CHRISTOTHERAPY; FORMATIVE SPIRITUALITY; GRACE AND PASTORAL CARE; IGNATIAN SPIRITUALITY; LIBERATION THEOLOGY; MYSTICISM; RELIGIOUS EXPERIENCE; RELIGIOUS LIFE; RETREATS (Roman Catholicism); SPIRITUAL DIRECTION; VOCATION (Roman Catholicism). *Compare* ROMAN CATHOLIC PASTORAL CARE. *Biography:* JOHN OF THE CROSS; THERESA OF AVILA.

SPLIT PERSONALITY. *See* MULTIPLE AND DISSOCIATIVE PERSONALITY.

SPONTANEITY. *See* SELF-EXPRESSION/SELF-CONTROL.

SPOUSE ABUSE. *See* FAMILY LAW; FAMILY VIOLENCE.

STAFF MINISTRY. *See* MULTIPLE STAFF MINISTRIES AND RELATIONSHIPS.

STAGES/STAGE THEORY. *See* DEVELOPMENTAL THEORY; FAITH DEVELOPMENT RESEARCH; LIFE CYCLE THEORY; STRUCTURALISM.

STANDARDS FOR PASTORAL COUNSELING. Standards for a particular type of service are understood to be criteria set by a recognized authority for the purpose of maintaining the quality of service rendered and thus protecting the interests of those who make use of it. The authority for setting standards for pastoral counseling in the U.S. rests with the American Association of Pastoral Counselors (AAPC), a professional association of pastoral counselors which has developed criteria: (1) for assessing the competency of counselors; (2) for the operation and administration of pastoral counseling centers; and (3) for clinical training programs in pastoral counseling. Committees or commissions established by the AAPC oversee the adherence to these standards.

The standards for assessing counselor competence include academic and clinical training and experience plus the demonstration of one's competence before a committee of pastoral counselors who have already been certified by the professional association. The practice of pastoral counseling is defined in the statement of purposes in the *Handbook* of the AAPC as the "exploration, clarification and guidance of human life, both individual and corporate, at the experiential and behavioral levels through a theological perspective." Pastoral counseling requires, according to AAPC, "knowledge of theological and behavioral sciences and their integration at both theoretical and operational levels." This specialized knowledge includes: "Familiarity with a wide variety of approaches to the conceptualization of personality and interpersonal relationships; mastery of a coherent theory of personality and the counseling relationship which is useful in interpreting the intra- and interpersonal dynamics of counselees and the counseling process; ability to use the language and methodology of differential diagnosis and to relate diagnosis to counseling practice; understanding of the dynamics of religious experiences, and the implications for pastoral counseling; ability to think theologically about the counseling task and the relation of counseling to the total task of the religious community; ability to relate the contributions of various disciplines to the counseling task in coherent and useful ways, and to make appropriate use of interpersonal collaboration to meet the needs of counselees."

Professionalism in pastoral counseling means also acquiring a specialized skill: the "ability to assess a client's therapeutic need, to establish a therapeutic relationship, and to conduct, complete, and evaluate that therapy." This skill is acquired and demonstrated in the actual experience of counseling under supervision. An applicant for Fellow level in AAPC must have completed a minimum of 1,375 hours of actual counseling while having received at least 250 hours of interdisciplinary supervision of that counseling. In addition, applicants for the Fellow level are also required to "give evidence of having undergone sufficient theological and psychotherapeutic investigation of one's own intrapsychic and interpersonal processes so that one is able to protect the counselee from the pastoral counselor's problems and to deploy oneself to the maximum benefit of the counselee." This may be accomplished by a personal analysis or psychotherapy.

AAPC established standards for the demonstration of continued professional competence. Members of AAPC are "expected to maintain an active pastoral counseling practice, participate in a responsible program of continuing education and maintain a consultative relationship with peers."

For the operation and administration of pastoral counseling centers the standards include requirements for the structure of the governing board of the center, for the qualifications of the staff, for financial and personnel policies and procedures, etc. The standards for training programs in pastoral counseling include expectations about the nature of the curriculum, the type of supervision provided, and the interdisciplinary nature of the teaching staff, etc. These standards are continually monitored and changed by the professional association to meet the changing needs of pastoral counselors and those whom they serve.

Pastoral counseling as well as secular psychotherapy clinical training programs are usually conducted in freestanding training and service centers, clinics, or institutes. Clergy, psychiatrists, psychologists, and social workers usually have obtained their graduate degrees before completing clinical psychotherapy training. During the past sixty years seminaries and universities have rarely included Fellow level pastoral counseling or secular psychotherapy clinical training programs within their educational programs, given academic credit for clinical training, or accepted case studies as dissertations. Thus, D.Min., M.D., Ph.D., M.S.W. and other degrees do not necessarily indicate completion of clinical training to the Fellow level in AAPC.

Bibliography. C. S. Aist, "Standards: A View from the Past and Prospects for the Future," *J. of Pastoral Care*, 37 (1983), 60 – 7. American Association of Pastoral Counselors, *Handbook*.

J. PATTON

ACCREDITATION; CERTIFICATION. *Compare* AMERICAN ASSOCIATION OF PASTORAL COUNSELORS; LICENSURE.

STARBUCK, EDWIN DILLER (1866 – 1947). American psychologist of religion. A devout Quaker who studied psychology under Hugo Munsterberg and William James at Harvard, Starbuck taught philosophy and served as director of the Institute of Character Research at the University of Iowa and the University of Southern California.

Starbuck argued that students of religion should attend not to doctrines or institutions but to affective experiences. His *Psychology of Religion* (1899) was the first volume of a nascent movement, and his interest in conversion experiences and use of questionnaires typified much of the early work in the new discipline.

He believed that conversion was a natural experience, normally accompanying the physical changes of adolescence, through which men and women entered into a larger social environment. He advertised the value for pastors of such an understanding of religion, arguing that the knowledgeable minister would avoid narrow dogmatism, refuse to press for premature religious decision, and refrain from encouraging morbid introspection. Religious feelings, he thought, would ripen in their own time, and would, if properly guided, take the form of an "unselfing" within "a larger spiritual environment" (*The American J. of Psychology*, 8 [1896–97], 270 – 307).

E. B. HOLIFIELD

PASTORAL COUNSELING MOVEMENT; PSYCHOLOGY OF RELIGION (Theories, Traditions, and Issues).

STARETS. Spiritual guides within the Russian Orthodox Tradition. Usually devoted and spiritually experienced men, many of them laymen, whose lives reflected saintliness and charity and who served as guides to distressed souls. Theirs was essentially a non-sacramental ministry which appeared in the Middle Ages and flourished during the rise of asceticism in the nineteenth century following the secularizing emphasis of Peter the Great. Over the centuries these staretsy served as "the natural born guides of the Russian people" at all levels of society. Their gospel was one of unlimited charity especially to the poor.

Bibliography. J. T. McNeill, *A History of the Cure of Souls*, (1951), pp. 311–14.

L. O. MILLS

MINISTRY AND PASTORAL CARE (Orthodox Tradition); SPIRITUAL DIRECTOR; SPIRITUAL MASTERS AND GUIDES. *Compare* ZADDIK.

STATIONS OF THE CROSS. *See* LITURGICAL AND DEVOTIONAL LIFE, ROMAN CATHOLIC TRADITION OF. *See also* SPIRITUALITY (Roman Catholic Tradition).

STATUS, MENTAL. *See* MENTAL STATUS.

STATUS, SOCIAL. *See* SOCIAL STATUS AND CLASS FACTORS.

STEALING. *See* DEVIANT BEHAVIOR; DISORDERS OF CHILDHOOD; RESPONSIBILITY/IRRESPONSIBILITY, PSYCHOLOGY OF.

STEPFAMILIES. Families in which at least one of the spouses is a stepparent. The relationship of stepparent to stepchild is based on marriage, not blood. A stepfamily is created by a marriage when at least one of the partners brings children into the relationship, usually from a previous marriage.

Although exact figures are not available, it is estimated that one out of seven children is a stepchild and the number is growing rapidly (Visher and Visher). In some areas of the United States, nearly half of the population do not live in what is sometimes assumed to be a "normal" family (i.e., a mother, father, and children living together in a first-marriage family).

Stepfamilies face complex and difficult issues in addition to the normal problems faced by any family. (It is often very reassuring to let stepparents know that not all their problems are caused by living in a stepfamily.) These include:

1. **Loss.** Most members of a stepfamily face the complete or partial loss of a primary relationship. In this situation the children are no longer living full-time with both of their natural parents; spouses are no longer living with their previous partners. Even if the previous primary relationship is perceived negatively, loss is still experienced. For example, a couple who have been together for a period of time have, to some degree, become bonded

together. The breaking of this bond (even when considered a positive step) occasions the experience of loss. For children experiencing divorce there is generally a deeply felt hope that somehow their parents will reunite. It is often the remarriage of one of the parents (to a new partner) that shatters this hope and brings on the experience of loss.

In regard to the pastoral care and counseling of a stepfamily, it is crucial to focus on this (often denied) experience of loss. Sometimes this can be facilitated best by working with individuals outside the stepfamily setting. However, eventually, it is important for the stepfamily to learn to hear and accept the grieving of its members for their former families. Only as this loss is experienced and accepted can the stepfamily be open to strengthen their own relationships with one another.

2. The Role of Stepparent. The stereotypical image of the stepparent is a decidedly negative one (i.e., the common portrayal in folktales of the wicked stepmother and the cruel stepfather). The role is particularly difficult since there is no common agreement on what a stepparent is (or should be). For example, a stepmother cannot become a stepchild's natural mother; that role is already taken. Yet, in carrying out family responsibilities certain mothering activities are taken over by the stepmother. From the child's perspective, the stepparent is often seen as attempting to usurp the position of the natural parent.

In pastoral work with stepparents, it is important to help them understand that they cannot replace the natural parent. However, a stepparent should clearly assure the stepchild that he or she is very interested in becoming a loving, nurturing adult in the child's life. The relationship between stepparent and stepchild requires time, patience, and a willingness to offer love with no guarantee of reciprocity.

3. The Primacy of the Couple's Bond. Often lost sight of within the complexity of the stepfamily is the reason for the family's existence: the relationship between the stepparents themselves. The nurturing of this bond requires time, attention, and privacy; it is the foundation for the success of the stepfamily. It can also serve as a powerful demonstration to the stepchildren that marriage, in fact, can work. Effective pastoral care and counseling often need only to focus on strengthening this bond in order to make a major contribution to the well-being of the stepfamily.

Bibliography. R. Gardner, *The Boys' and Girls' Book about Divorce* (1971). R. Roosevelt and J. Lofas, *Living in Step* (1976). E. Visher and J. Visher, *Stepfamilies: A Guide to Working with Stepparents and Stepchildren* (1979); *How to Win as a Stepfamily* (1982).

D. R. BARSTOW

FAMILY; PARENTS/PARENTHOOD; REMARRIAGE (Issues in Pastoral Care). *Compare* DIVORCE, CHILDREN AND ADOLESCENTS IN; FOSTER CHILDREN AND FOSTER PARENTS.

STEREOTYPES/STEREOTYPING. *See* PASTOR (Popular Stereotypes and Caricatures); PREJUDICE; SOCIAL PERCEPTION, JUDGMENT, AND BELIEF.

STEWARDSHIP. *See* COMMITMENT; LEADERSHIP AND ADMINISTRATION; MONEY; RESPONSIBILITY/IRRESPONSIBILITY, PSYCHOLOGY OF.

STIGMATA. *See* LITURGICAL AND DEVOTIONAL LIFE, ROMAN CATHOLIC TRADITION OF; SPIRITUALITY (Roman Catholic Tradition).

STILLBIRTH. *See* MISCARRIAGE.

STIMULUS-RESPONSE THEORY. *See* BEHAVIORISM.

STOICISM. *See* PHILOSOPHY AND PSYCHOLOGY.

STOLLBERG, DIETRICH. *See* PASTORAL THEOLOGY, PROTESTANT.

STOLZ, KARL RUF (1884–1943). Congregationalist professor of religious education and dean of the School of Religious Education at Hartford Seminary Foundation from 1927 to 1943. Stolz influenced the pastoral care movement especially through an emphasis on psychological and religious adjustment derived from James, Dewey, Jung, and Adler. His *Pastoral Psychology* (1932) argued that it was the pastor's task to help persons reorganize themselves through appropriate adjustments to other persons and God.

E. B. HOLIFIELD

ADJUSTMENT, CONCEPT OF; HISTORY OF PROTESTANT PASTORAL CARE (United States).

STORY. *See* PERSONAL STORY, SYMBOL, AND MYTH IN PASTORAL CARE. *See also* MYTHOLOGY AND PSYCHOLOGY.

STREET PEOPLE. *See* HOMELESS PERSONS; POOR PERSONS.

STRESS AND STRESS MANAGEMENT. The debilitating and maladaptive physiological, emotional, and behavioral responses resulting from the appraisal of a situation and the ensuing belief that one does not possess adequate mechanisms and resources for coping. The eliciting stimulus, along with the mediating cognitive activity and responses taken together make up what is described as the stress process. The eliciting stimulus is labeled as a "stressor" while the person's specific responses to the cognitively mediated belief are labeled as "stress".

1. The Concept of Stress. The stress concept was first used by Hans Selye to identify a specific syndrome of physical symptoms that resulted from the prolonged activation of the body's defensive "fight or flight" mechanism. These symptoms are the enlargement and hyperactivity of the adrenal cortex, shrinkage (atrophy) of the thymus gland and lymph nodes, and appearance of gastrointestinal ulcers.

In addition to this constellation of physiological symptoms a large number of other physical dysfunctions have been identified as potential stress reactions. The concept has been broadened to encompass emotional and behavioral manifestations as well.

Psychological research has been instrumental in demonstrating that situations themselves are not the direct causes of stress responses. This is apparent from the recognition that the same situation or stimulus does not result in a stress response in all individuals exposed to that situation. Mediating between a situation and a person's stress response must be an evaluation of that situation as exceeding his or her ability to cope. For example, a new and demanding job assignment can lead to depression, excessive alcohol use, and ulcers in one person who perceives the task as beyond his or her capability, while another individual of comparable training and skill who perceives it as a challenge and opportunity can be prompted to enthusiasm and increased effectiveness.

The problem of stress has become increasingly important as other threats to health, such as bacterial infections, have been reduced. Also, the increased complexity of society has led to rapid change which sometimes surpasses acquired skills to meet new demands and tests people's confidence in themselves. The majority of current health problems threatening life and well-being in developed nations are a result of excessive stress.

2. **Symptomatology.** Stress responses can be grouped into physical, emotional, and behavioral symptoms. Physiological stress reactions often receive the greatest attention because they generally pose the most immediate threat to survival. However, the emotional and behavioral reactions can have an even greater impact on the quality of life and precipitate physical reactions.

Physical stress symptoms are most accurately diagnosed as psychophysiological disorders, thereby emphasizing their development from the stress process. They include tension and migraine headaches, gastrointestinal disorders, essential hypertension, increased heart rate (tachycardia), cold extremities, and muscle spasms and pain. In many other physical conditions stress has been proven to be a major contributing factor—for example, bronchial asthma, respiratory allergies, heart arrhythmias, and dermatological disorders. Increasing scientific evidence suggests a relationship between psychological stress processes and a general suppression of the body's immunological system. This may result in an increased susceptibility to infection and degenerative diseases and suggests a link to cancer.

The emotional manifestations of stress can be varied and are often overlooked or minimized. They can include anxiety, depression, irritability, and rapid mood swings. A rather specific cluster of emotional stress associated with persons in the helping professions has been labeled as "burnout" and is characterized by emotional exhaustion, over-depersonalization, and a reduced sense of personal accomplishment.

The behavioral symptoms of stress include hyperalertness, hyperactivity, insomnia, hyperventilation, nail biting, teeth grinding (bruxism), throat clearing, stuttering, excessive use of drugs and alcohol, and social withdrawal. These behavioral signs are primarily a consequence of hyperarousal of the autonomic nervous system.

All of the above signs of stress can be treated symptomatically, resulting in temporary relief or remission. However, symptomatic treatment alone is inadequate in that it does not address the factors that elicit stress. When the sources of stress are identified, more effective management becomes possible.

3. **Sources of Stress.** Sources of stress refer to the eliciting stimuli which lead to the cognitively mediated appraisal that effective coping is hopeless or unlikely. Almost any stimulus or situation is a potential stressor. Stressors can be categorized as physical/environmental stressors, organizational stressors, interpersonal stressors, and intrapersonal stressors.

Physical/environmental stressors include such physical/environmental factors as crowding, noise, and freeway driving. It is not the direct effect of these stimuli which elicit stress, as occurs when loss of hearing is caused by exposure to a sound that is above a specific decibel level. Rather, it is the interpretation that a specific sound is noxious and intolerable which elicits the stress syndrome, even though it may be below the decibel level which causes direct physical damage. Anyone who has a teenage son or daughter knows that what is one person's music is another person's noise.

Organizational stressors are the demands and expectations imposed on an individual from those groups of which they are a part. These include deadlines, role definitions, quotas, expectations for participation, etc. They are generally found in association with job settings, families, and social groups such as churches and clubs.

Interpersonal stressors most frequently involve negative situations such as dealing with angry, demanding, aggressive, or pessimistic persons. However, important intimate relationships which can elicit fears of disapproval and rejection can be particularly stress producing.

Lastly, intrapersonal stressors include the thoughts, beliefs, expectations, and demands one places on oneself. They represent the single largest group of stressors for most persons, and are the least well recognized. Sometimes referred to as "self-talk" or "internal tapes," these personal conversations often impose unrealistic expectations, irrational guilt, and distorted evaluations of self and situation. Among religious persons intrapersonal stressors are frequently imbedded in theological beliefs and values which leave little room for forgiveness, grace, and repentance.

Recognizing and understanding the nature of stressors in one's life is an important first step in stress management. The last section discusses other resources and methods for reducing stress.

4. **Stress Management.** Human beings need not be helpless victims of the ill effects of stress. Stress symptoms can be signals to mobilize physiological, behavioral, and cognitive resources which can effectively reduce adverse symptoms and improve the quality of life.

a. Physiological resources. The human body is equipped with impressive physiological normalizing, restorative, and healing mechanisms which can be activated to combat stress. These God-created health resources are elicited when humans act to establish certain conditions.

The *autonomic relaxation* response is the body's means of reversing the "fight or flight" response and leads to a reduction in blood pressure, heart rate, muscle tension, and other stress reactions. It can be thought of as the body's own biological tranquilizer. Without periods of relaxation the body adapts to higher levels of physiological arousal which eventually leads to illness. Although the body has been created with the capacity to relax, this restorative response can be maximized through activities such as meditative prayer and specific relaxation exercises.

Depression and pain symptoms often associated with stress can be significantly reduced through biochemical alterations in the brain resulting from increased *physical exercise.* A consistent program of aerobic conditioning at least three times per week can greatly increase stress resistance.

All of the body's metabolic processes to sustain health and combat stress require adequate *nutrition* in the form of a balanced diet from the four basic food groups. Research suggests that additional B-complex vitamin is needed during periods of heightened stress and that refined sugar should be reduced and foods, beverages, and drugs that are stimulants avoided.

b. Behavioral resources. Often the experiences associated with stress emerge from situations where an individual lacks appropriate behavioral responses to certain demanding situations. The acquisition of specific behavioral skills such as *assertiveness, time management,* and *effective communication* can enhance stress management. An appraisal of one's current life stressors will often lead to the identification of behavioral deficits which if acquired or polished will increase one's effectiveness. These may include aspects of parenting, employment functioning, socializing, or response to intimacy. Programs for developing behavioral skills can be implemented through self-direction or professional coaching.

c. Cognitive resources. Individuals who are able to mentally frame their life situations in such a way that they perceive a personal sense of control, are challenged by demands as providing an opportunity, and cling to an enduring belief of hope consistently demonstrate less adverse stress irrespective of their environment. As indicated earlier, an essential element of eliciting stress is a negative imbalance in the cognitively perceived demands of a situation and one's coping resources.

Often this imbalance results from unrealistic or irrational beliefs concerning the situation, for example, "this is a terrible, hopeless dilemma"; other people's thoughts, that is, "people are dissatisfied with me"; or self-evaluation, for example, "I should always be able to make people happy." Learning to restructure one's self-talk in a realistic and yet positive framework is a crucial element in managing stress.

The utilization of faith dimensions such as confession, forgiveness, grace, empowerment, presence, and the value of each individual person can be powerful beliefs in establishing more healthy cognitive structures. Enhancing and integrating a healthy faith system into one's daily life provides the Christian with a distinctive and encouraging perspective in confronting life's demands.

Bibliography. G. S. Every, *The Nature and Treatment of the Stress Response* (1981). W. E. Hulme, *Managing Stress in Ministry* (1985). R. S. Lazarus, *Psychological Stress and the Coping Process* (1980). L. J. Mason, *Guide to Stress Reduction* (1980). C. L. Rassieaur, *Stress Management for Ministers* (1982).

P. J. PETERSON

PLAY; POST-TRAUMATIC STRESS DISORDER; RELAXATION, PSYCHOLOGY AND TECHNIQUES OF. *See also* HUMOR; WIT AND HUMOR IN PASTORAL CARE; WORK AND CAREER. *Compare* ANXIETY; REST AND RENEWAL, RELIGIOUS TRADITIONS OF.

STRESS, DELAYED. *See* POST-TRAUMATIC STRESS DISORDER.

STROKE. *See* NEUROLOGIC ILLNESSES.

STRONG- CAMPBELL INTEREST INVENTORY. *See* EVALUATION AND DIAGNOSIS, PSYCHOLOGICAL.

STRUCTURAL INTEGRATION. *See* POPULAR THERAPEUTIC MOVEMENTS AND PSYCHOLOGIES.

STRUCTURALISM. A composite term which variously characterizes a set of methods of analysis, a cluster of social scientific and linguistic theories, and, at times, a philosophical worldview (Gardner). In all these uses structuralism refers to the search for general patterns in the operations of the human mind through the analysis either of its functioning or its products. Kant's philosophy anticipated structuralism in its identification of the *a priori* categories by which pure theoretical reasoning does its work. Gestalt psychology contributed to the emergence of structuralism with its attention to the mind's imposition of patterns on the random objects of sense-perception. In linguistics the structuralist perspective arose in the identification of basic elements of all languages, which makes possible the comparison of different language systems in terms of the basic structural units common to all. And in anthropology structuralism enables analysts of particular tribes or groups to discern systematic linkages between elements of their worldviews and patterns in many aspects of their everyday life such as art, architecture, costumes, patterns of food preparation and display, and the like.

In each of these instances *structuralism* is based upon several key assumptions: (1) The human mind is an active organ which performs "operations" on the data of sense perception to compose or construe meanings. (2) Examined in terms of the operations underlying or constituting thought, there are likely to be patterns common to the structuring activities of *all* human beings. (3) It is possible to characterize the patterns of these fundamental operations of composition in *formal* terms, that is, in terms that are descriptive of the mind's working regardless of differences in the *contents* of knowing or thought.

In one branch of twentieth century psychology the structuralist point of view has been wedded to a *developmental* perspective. Influenced by Hegel's philosophy of the dialectical development of *Geist* (Spirit, intelligence) in history, and of evolutionary theory in biology, this movement can be called *structural-developmental* psychology. James Mark Baldwin and John Dewey in the U.S., and Jean Piaget in Europe, are generally taken to be the founders of structural-developmental psychology. Piaget's *genetic structuralism* achieved great conceptual precision through the formal representation of cognitive operations by his use of mathematical and logical models.

While relinquishing some of Piaget's precision, others have been inspired by his work to extend the structural-developmental paradigm into such areas as the developing structural bases of moral reasoning (Lawrence Kohlberg), of social perspective-taking (Robert Selman), of ego development (Jane Loevinger, Robert Kegan), and of faith (James Fowler).

These theories, based on considerable empirical research, offer pastoral counselors perspectives which focus on the patterns underlying persons' constructions of self-other relations (including God), and on their constructions of life-meanings. A "stage" in these perspectives is the integrated set of operations characterizing a person's constructions of meaning at a given point in his or her development. These theories identify an invariant, sequential, and hierarchical series of such structural-developmental stages. In this regard they hold the promise of new diagnostic resources for pastoral counseling (Ivy). Their illumination of the dynamics and directions of transition offer fresh approaches and methods for counseling and pacing in helping relationships.

Bibliography. J. W. Fowler, *Stages of Faith* (1981); *Faith Development and Pastoral Care* (1986). H. Gardner. *The Quest for the Mind* 2d ed. (1981). S. Ivy, "The Structural-Developmental Theories of James Fowler and Robert Kegan as Resources for Pastoral Assessment," doctoral dissertation, Southern Baptist Theological Seminary (1985). L. Kohlberg, *Essays on Moral Development*, 3 vols. (1982–86).

J. W. FOWLER

DEVELOPMENTAL THEORY AND PASTORAL CARE. *See also* COGNITIVE DEVELOPMENT; FAITH DEVELOPMENT RESEARCH; MORAL DEVELOPMENT; PSYCHOLINGUISTIC THEORY IN PSYCHOLOGY AND COUNSELING.

STRUCTURING. As applied to pastoral care and counseling, the developing of proper conditions for pastoral work. It is similar in meaning to Seward Hiltner's concept of pre-counseling (1949), referring to the pastor's clarification of what the person is seeking and why the person wishes to address this concern at the present time. It may also involve determining whether the spouse and other family members should be present, and securing an adequate time and place for dealing with the issues presented.

J. PATTON

PASTORAL COUNSELING. *See also* ASSERTIVENESS IN MINISTRY; COVENANT AND CONTRACT; LEADERSHIP AND ADMINISTRATION; LIMIT-SETTING IN PASTORAL CARE AND COUNSELING. *Compare* CONFRONTATION (Pastoral and Therapeutic).

STRUGGLE/STRUGGLE OF THE SOUL. *See* EXISTENTIALISM; MYSTICISM; PATIENCE/PATIENTHOOD; PILGRIMAGE METAPHOR.

STUDENTS. *See* COLLEGE STUDENTS AND COLLEGE CHAPLAINCY; THEOLOGICAL STUDENTS.

STUTTERING. *See* BEHAVIORAL DISORDERS OF CHILDHOOD; SPEECH DISORDERS AND THERAPY.

The SUBSCONSCIOUS. Sometimes called the preconscious, co-conscious, paraconscious, and by some practitioners, unconscious. In the majority understanding it is that part of the mind which contains all the psychic material not immediately available in the conscious realm. However, this material can be called into awareness by virtue of its position on the periphery of consciousness. Thus it is best synonymous with the preconscious.

M. A. WOLTERSDORF

UNCONSCIOUS.

SUBLIMINATION. In psychoanalytic theory, the unconscious process by which socially unacceptable impulses or desires are gratified through cultural activity. The instinctual drive is qualitatively altered, permitting gratification without anxiety or guilt. Examples include: aggressive impulses sublimated through becoming a soldier or a football player; exhibitionistic impulses sublimated through becoming a choreographer. Sublimation is considered a healthy and often creative means of instinctual control, though Freud believed it could master only a portion of the personality's instinctual desires.

C. KOVEROLA

DEFENSE MECHANISMS. *See also* DEFENSE AND COPING THEORY; IMAGINATION; SEXUALITY, BIOLOGICAL AND PSYCHOSOCIAL THEORY OF.

SUBMISSIVENESS. *See* DEPENDENCE/INDEPENDENCE; PASSIVE-AGGRESSIVE PERSONALITY.

SUBSTANCE ABUSE. *See* ALCOHOL ABUSE *or* DRUG ABUSE, ADDICTION, AND THERAPY; EATING AND DRINKING; GLUTTONY AND TEMPERANCE.

SUFFERING. The experience of any kind of pain or distress. Suffering is pervasive, intrinsic to the human condition, and raises perennial religious and psychological questions. This essay begins by summarizing some contemporary theological themes relevant to suffering, then discusses human suffering under four aspects: loss, injustice and oppression, self-hatred and guilt, and physical pain. No attempt to do justice to historical treatment of these topics is possible, nor can the issue of suffering in non-monotheistic contexts (i.e., Buddhism) be included here.

1. **God's Suffering.** Traditional prophetic monotheism asked the question, "Why do the righteous suffer?" and expected a response from a God held to be both "mighty to save" and Lord of the world's moral order. Systematic and philosophical theologies refined this issue, providing answers such as "Suffering is punishment for sin," or "Suffering is due to evil, a privation of good, not a force in itself." These traditional formulations assumed that God exists beyond suffering—transcendent to it—a motif known as "divine impassibility." Suffering was thus defined as a *human* problem (although occasionally the issue of animals' pain was also raised). However, in contemporary religious thought, impassibility is widely challenged and repudiated. In this view it is asserted that the deepest strand of Jewish and Christian experience of

God knows the divine as deeply affected by pain, suffering with God's people.

This contemporary insight came, it seems, out of the experience of mass suffering during World War II. Totalitarian leaders mimicked traditional images of God as One who inflicts suffering for some cause or ideal beyond human comprehension. In revulsion against such views, various thinkers drew on their own experiences of intense suffering to revise the traditional belief. "Where is God?" asks a witness to an execution at a Nazi concentration camp. "Here he is — he is hanging here on this gallows!" comes the answer. This scene from Elie Wiesel's *Night* is pivotal for twentieth-century affirmations of divine solidarity with humans' suffering.

In addition to Wiesel, religious thinkers such as Simone Weil, Kazoh Kitamori, Dorothy Soelle, and Jürgen Moltmann have developed theologies of divine suffering. They stress the centrality of the cross, the death of Jesus, the *Logos* as full identification with human pain and death, as the fundamental response of God to human anguish. These ideas, although by no means shared by all religious thinkers, powerfully challenge traditional formulations of the theodicy problem and affect the permissible range of practical guidance offered to sufferers. No longer is suffering to be simply accepted as ordained by a God who remains personally remote from it.

This discussion of God's suffering, however, is related to the insight that it is never the sheer quantity of suffering, but *meaningless* suffering, that poses the deepest threat to humanity. Through his experiences as a concentration camp inmate, Viktor Frankl came to realize "He who has a *why* to live for can bear with almost any *how*." Thus in any discussion of suffering the dichotomy between pain and comfort, unhappiness and happiness, is less crucial than that of despair and meaning. The involvement of God with human anguish is one way to affirm the meaningfulness of suffering and to sustain hope in the midst of affliction.

2. Suffering as Human Grief and Loss. Contemporary psychological and practical religious reflection focuses upon various strands of suffering — death, bereavement, unemployment, and divorce, for example — as experiences of loss. "How can I endure loss?" and "What can I learn from loss?" are questions that dominate the contemporary literature.

One powerful paradigm is provided by Elisabeth Kübler-Ross's "five stages of dying" (denial, anger, bargaining, depression, and acceptance), which are often taken to be applicable to all experiences of loss. These are "stages" in a normative, not sequential, sense: "acceptance" is the goal and is "better" than denial, etc. In this model, loss is an intrapsychic process that an individual "moves through," and it is assumed that all loss must be "accepted" in order to maintain contact with reality. Although some criticize the "ethical naturalism" behind this model, the paradigm's persuasiveness has given it widespread appeal. In answering the "how" of endurance, it implicitly answers "What can I learn from loss?" by emphasizing yieldedness, acceptance of one's limits, and compassion. Humans are finite beings; loss is intrinsic to finitude. Loss is real, as is the suffering it creates, but Kübler-Ross's paradigm and

similar process models hold out hope for deepened appreciation of life through grief experience. The vast majority of secular and pastoral literature dealing with death and bereavement follows this approach.

3. Suffering as Injustice and Oppression. A different strand of suffering evokes an entirely different response in many contemporary persons. Because of the World War II phenomenon of mass death—that is, the Holocaust and Hiroshima — it is almost impossible to maintain that suffering is "punishment for sin," especially suffering that appears to be brought on by political and economic oppression and exploitation. The revolution against colonial empires in Africa, Asia, and Latin America has intensified an understanding of suffering as injustice and created various theologies of liberation to speak to this experience. God is not and could not be the upholder of oppressive regimes, racism, or class or caste systems. The God of the Bible always sides with the poor and oppressed.

Significantly, this form of suffering is not assimilated into a process paradigm moving from "denial to acceptance," for the ideal human response to this suffering is to struggle against it. "Acceptance" would mean capitulation to the forces of evil—the "rulers of this age." Pastoral psychological writings often ignore or downplay this aspect of suffering, implicitly adopting the public-private, political-individual dualism that pervades postindustrial societies. However, models of human brokenness and healing that take seriously the social context of individual life also make reference to factors of injustice and oppression operating to perpetuate suffering at the individual level. This point is obviously relevant to pastoral counseling in a minority group setting, where objective factors such as discrimination intertwine with the subjective despair they engender. But such issues ought also to be taken into account when dealing with problems among the "oppressors" (e.g., white middle-class North Americans). In the case of white middle-class North American *women*, however, theologies of liberation can see them as either "oppressors" (beneficiaries of a prosperity built on the backs of Third World peoples) or (as in feminist theology) themselves the victims of sexism, a powerful oppressive force.

As these remarks reveal, the dualistic division between oppressor and oppressed risks becoming Manichaean, projecting all evil onto the oppressor, and seeing oneself as the innocent victim. However, deeper reflections on this form of suffering seek the redemption of the oppressor, while at the same time repudiating the "sacrificial" model of suffering as inappropriate for victims of injustice. Although the suffering of the poor and exploited may be redemptive, this possibility should never be an excuse to perpetuate it.

4. Suffering as Self-Hatred and Guilt. This strand of suffering has preoccupied psychotherapists and counselors, and has been described in a wide range of psychological theories. Depth psychologies, existential psychology, and humanistic theories of personal growth all interpret the facts of self-hatred and guilt slightly differently but would agree on the pervasiveness of these facts in contemporary personality. Self-hatred may arise from internalization of injustice and oppression, even in such relatively apolitical forms as rigid parental expectations.

Or, the pervasive anomie of modern society may be internalized as a sense of inner emptiness and worthlessness, often conjoined with barely suppressed narcissistic rage. The individual may be born with an urge toward growth, but this is blocked or suppressed at an early age, resulting in a state of inner tension, disharmony, and sense of failure. For many therapists and psychological theorists, the religious tradition's focus upon guilt, sinfulness, and self-denial has been a source for such feelings, rather than a solution for them. For others, such as Erich Fromm, the injunction to "Love thy neighbor as thyself" implies that "self-love" is the proper foundation for healthy ethical action and personhood.

Debates about the meaning of "guilt" and its relation to "health" emerge when the latter position is taken as normative. Is all guilt neurotic? Is it the therapist's task to alleviate all guilt feelings, to make the client "feel better about himself?" Or are there "objective" forms of guilt, masked or denied by much psychotherapy? Recent contributors to this debate are now far more critical of the norms of the psychotherapies and of the importation of these norms into the church. Don S. Browning's *The Moral Context of Pastoral Care*, for example, emphasizes the important constructive normative role of the religious tradition and community in providing practical guidance and a necessary framework for therapeutic growth. From this one might draw the conclusion that not *all* self-hatred is unwarranted and that the call to repentance is Christianity's central response to the issue of guilt. However, the background for this call is the biblical affirmation that God declared the whole creation "very good" (Gen. 1:31). Against all self-hatred one must affirm, in the touching words of a ghetto child, that "God don't make no junk." Without this foundation, neither therapy nor the hope for redemption makes much sense. Thus, within contemporary thought, the suffering of self-hatred and guilt is what God redeems us *from*; it is not in itself "redemptive."

5. Suffering as Physical Pain. In traditional discussions, evil was divided into "natural" and "moral"—that is, the Lisbon earthquake and the torture of children. Today, much less is said about the first of these, and in our context, very little is available that deals with suffering as sheer physical hurt. Perhaps because of modern medical advances, dying is viewed primarily as a psychic loss rather than as a situation of intense or unrelieved physical pain. Since it is not the quantity of suffering but its meaninglessness that poses the deepest threat, physical pain, in itself, need not destroy the soul as can loss, oppression, or self-hatred. Nevertheless, no one writing for Americans today holds that physical pain in itself is beneficial. Ironically, since most dying hospital patients are kept semi-comatose by painkillers, advocates for the terminally ill must often plead for a reduction of medication so that the patient may, in full conscious alertness, say good-bye to relatives or complete some final tasks.

6. Conclusion. It may be that any specific experience of suffering contains all three major strands discussed here. A death in a car accident, for example, is, for the survivors a loss, a possible instance of injustice, and also a potential source of self-accusation and guilt. Child abuse clearly involves all dimensions, too. In North America today, the injustice-oppression model often results in demands for legal protection of victims and punishment of those responsible for helping create conditions where suffering is possible (for example, lawsuits against manufacturers of faulty or dangerous equipment). The enormous increase in medical malpractice suits shows how the experience of suffering as loss can be transformed into the experience of suffering as injustice. Behind this trend may lurk the deceptive hope for a world without suffering, for human life freed from vulnerability to loss, exploitation, guilt, and pain. Here, religious traditions can speak empathetically but critically to this hope. Without advocating masochism, they can convey a sense of God's redemptive presence in the midst of suffering.

Bibliography. D. Browning, *Atonement and Psychotherapy* (1966); *The Moral Context of Pastoral Care* (1976). V. Frankl, *Man's Search for Meaning* (1963). E. Fromm, *Escape From Freedom* (1969 [1941]). E. Kübler-Ross, *On Death and Dying* (1969). H. S. Kushner, *When Bad Things Happen to Good People* (1981). C. Lasch, *The Culture of Narcissism* (1978). A. C. McGill, *Suffering: A Test of Theological Method* (1982 [1968]). W. McWilliams, "Divine Suffering in Contemporary Theology," *Scottish J. of Theology*, 33 (1980), 35–53. J. Moltmann, *The Crucified God* (ET, 1974). O. H. Mowrer, *The Crisis in Psychiatry and Religion* (1961). D. Soelle, *Suffering* (1975). S. Weil, *Waiting for God* (1973 [1951]). E. Wiesel, *Night* (1960).

L. BREGMAN

EVIL; PAIN; PROVIDENCE, DOCTRINE OF, AND PASTORAL CARE. *See also* COMPASSION; DEATH, MEANING OF; DYING, PASTORAL CARE OF; EXPLOITATION/OPPRESSION; GRIEF AND LOSS; GUILT; HOLOCAUST; LIBERATION THEOLOGY AND PASTORAL CARE. *Compare* HOPE AND DESPAIR; PATIENCE/PATIENTHOOD; SIN AND SICKNESS.

SUFI CARE AND COUNSELING. *See* ISLAMIC CARE AND COUNSELING.

SUGGESTION, PERSUASION, AND INFLUENCE. *Suggestion* refers, in this context, to ways in which pastoral counselors and therapists may attempt to change or influence their counselees by indirect, largely unconscious and unacknowledged methods such as by charm or nonverbal communications—methods that play upon the parishioner's or counselee's suggestibility. *Persuasion*, by contrast, refers to attempts at influence and change by relatively more direct, conscious, and intentional (sometimes explicitly rational) means. *Influence* is used here as a generic term denoting all forms of pastoral or therapist impact for change whether or not intended or recognized by the counselor. Taken together, the three terms point to a basic and important question in contemporary pastoral care and counseling: how much and what kind of direct and indirect influence ought pastoral counselors to exercise (or do they in fact exercise) upon their counselees?

The question is basic and important for several reasons: (1) Pastoral counseling, following widespread psychotherapeutic theory and practice, generally seeks to minimize or restrict the direct, controlling influence of the counselor on the counselee; instead, it aims generally at facilitating a process that will stimulate the *counselee's* initiative, responsibility, and creativity in contrast to passive reception of influences or compliance with directives. This is consistent with the widespread belief that therapeutic change of major significance, i.e., characterological change as distinguished from behavioral change or symptom relief, cannot be achieved by suggestion or persuasion, but requires the emotionally difficult task of self-discovery and a struggle to achieve new patterns of behavior and relationship for oneself.

(2) Research studies have shown, however, that counseling and psychotherapy actually entail subtle but powerful suggestive and persuasive influences by the counselor on the counselee; nonverbal gestures and even silence all have their effect, for example, even when concerted efforts are made to be "nondirective" or "value neutral" (Shapiro and Morris, 1978). Moreover, the research of Jerome Frank (1974) and others has raised the possibility that all psychological healing may entail a process of influence in which factors like the social status of the therapist, levels of client expectation, and the presence of shared meanings and values operate silently but pervasively as the dominant determinants of therapeutic outcome (see also Orlinsky and Howard, 1986).

(3) Theologically, the question is further complicated by the consideration that pastoral care and counseling, as forms of Christian ministry, represent Christian faith and values and therefore are not and cannot appropriately be "value neutral." Religious conviction must not only undergird and direct pastoral care and counseling in some fundamental sense; it must also seek certain general outcomes and therefore aim at exerting certain kinds of influence. At the same time Christian faith itself may support the importance of restricting certain kinks of direct influence in the interest of facilitating individual responsibility, healing and growth.

These issues and their interrelationships have been recognized but not carefully examined in pastoral care and counseling, and it would be premature to offer solutions. It may be of practical value to pastoral counselors, however, to be aware of several general points. First, all care, counseling and psychotherapy is value-laden and entails a process of social influence whether acknowledged or not; thus it is important for the sake of professional responsibility to attempt to be aware and take critical responsibility for the way one may be influencing the lives of others. Second, the pastoral role contains powerful possibilities for subliminal, magical, and other forms of placebo-like influence which can significantly divert care and counseling by seeking to instill changes or good feelings in parishioners and counselees without the work of authentic self-examination and constructive personal change.

But finally, suggestion, persuasion and influence may also have positive value for religious care including pastoral psychotherapy and may even be essential to the healing of the soul. If so, this may be because it draws upon the relational nature of selfhood—the possibility that we are all somehow interrelated and interpenetrating in even our deepest personal subjectivity. We are thus dependent upon one another even in those times when we must also attempt to claim deep levels of responsibility for ourselves as individuals. The practical issue of managing influence in the counseling situation (or in parishioner relationships) may therefore be best formulated as how to combine a respect for the individuality of those in one's pastoral or professional care with

a responsible, if inevitable, exercise of personal and cultural influence upon them.

Bibliography. J. D. Frank, *Persuasion and Healing: A Comparative Study of Psychotherapy*, rev. ed. (1974). S. Hiltner, *The Counselor in Counseling* (1951). D.E. Orlinsky and K. I. Howard, "Process and Outcome in Psychotherapy," in S. L. Garfield and A. E. Bergin, eds., *Handbook of Psychotherapy and Behavior Change*, 3d ed. (1986), pp. 311–81. A. K. Shapiro and L. A. Morris, "The Placebo Effect in Medical and Psychological Therapies," in S. L. Garfield and A. E. Bergin, eds., *Handbook of Psychotherapy and Behavior Change*, 2d ed. (1978), pp. 369–410.

R. J. HUNTER

AUTHORITY, PASTORAL; POWER; REASONING AND RATIONALITY IN PASTORAL CARE; TECHNIQUE AND SKILL IN PASTORAL CARE. *See also* PSYCHOTHERAPY; SOCIOLOGY OF RELIGIOUS AND PASTORAL CARE. *Compare* GUIDANCE, PASTORAL; MAGICAL THINKING; MANIPULATION.

SUICIDE (Ethical Issues). The considerations relative to the right of a person to terminate his or her own life and to one's duty to the plans of another person to terminate his or her own life. The question of suicide as an ethical issue is at least as old as the Greek philosophers by whom it was discussed at great length. The topic was of surprisingly little concern, however, to the biblical writers who did not think of suicide as a moral or ethical issue. There are few incidents of suicide in either the OT or NT and those which are reported are without moral judgment. It was during the time of the early church when some were seeking martyrdom too easily that the issue became relevant. St. Augustine was among the first to take the position that suicide is an affront to God, and so the faithful should not seek their own death. In the following centuries the church took an increasingly strong position against suicide.

1. **One's Own Suicide.** *a. State of mind.* Most questions involving ethics assume a rational state of mind. Thus we recognize in children and in the insane a limited ability and therefore limited responsibility in making rational and ethical decisions. If suicidal behavior is defined as evidence *per se* of mental derangement (as the church has come to hold) then the suicided person is to be forgiven on the ground that he or she could not have decided otherwise. If it is possible to be suicidal rationally (as many others hold) the ethical question is relevant. This issue is further complicated by the concept of emotional crisis. Some hold that sane persons can have moments of severe emotional stress during which they may manifest behaviors for which they should not be held responsible. This is because, during the time of the crisis, they are unable to make rational decisions or control impulses. Others maintain that individuals are always accountable for their actions.

Assuming accountability, some hold that suicide is always a cowardly act which seeks the easy way out of difficulty and pain and is therefore in violation of a high ethical standard of human dignity (Pythagoras, *et al.*). Others hold that suicide is a basic right (Stoics, Epicureans, *et al.*) and even in some circumstances a duty (e.g., Asian and Eskimo culture).

b. Ownership of life. The right of disposition depends upon ownership. If persons consider their lives as their own they may feel justified in disposing of them as they wish. If persons accept God as the author of life and as the One who retains ownership, the ethical decisions of life and death are God's alone. In many circumstances the state is acknowledged as holding ownership of life (having the power of imprisonment, conscription, execution) as did Aristotle, and thus persons have no right to deprive the state of its property. Still others consider that our lives are subordinated to family, clan, or other social unit and these units alone have the right to terminate life.

c. Effect on survivors. The burden that death by suicide normally places on the survivors (both on those immediately touched and on society as a whole) is often cited as an ethical issue. In most cases of a suicidal death, the resulting grief is greatly complicated for those who mourn by strong feelings of guilt, rage, and bewilderment far beyond those experienced after a death from natural causes. In addition, it has been established that one suicide can often set the pattern for suicidal behavior of others, especially children. Others maintain that suicide can often be an ethical act of love if it serves as an alternative to a long, painful illness that produces suffering to the dying person and is emotionally and financially expensive to family members.

2. **Another's Suicide.** In considering the ethical principles relating to the possible suicide of another person, one balances that person's right of privacy, integrity, and right of self-determination against the duty to come to another's aid when they are in distress and in danger.

a. Answering the cry for help. Some hold that suicidal behavior is always a sign of emotional and mental distress and that suicidal communication by word or act is always a cry for help. To turn one's back or to fail to do all one can, including the canceling of the civil rights of the other by involuntary hospitalization if necessary, is a failure of compassion. There are times when we know better than others what is good for them, and it is ethical to enforce our will upon them during these times.

b. Self-responsibility. The other view holds that although we should express love for others who are considering suicide by showing our concern and by attempting to persuade them to reconsider the suicidal act, there must be limits to our action. We should at all times respect the individuals' right of choice, and if we fail in this respect we rob them of what is essential to their humanity. Even if they choose to die, we do them better honor by respecting this decision than we would by forcing the indignity of hospitalization and unasked-for drug or shock therapy.

Bibliography. N. L. Farberow and E. Shneidman, *The Cry For Help* (1961). L. D. Hankoff and B. E. Einsidler, *Suicide: Theory and Clinical Aspects* (1979). C. L. Hatton and S. M. Valente, *Suicide: Assessments and Interventions* (1984). J. Hillman, *Suicide and the Soul* (1964). P. W. Pretzel, *Understanding and Counseling The Suicidal Person* (1972).

P. W. PRETZEL

ETHICS AND PASTORAL CARE; MORAL THEOLOGY AND PASTORAL CARE. *See also* DEATH AND DYING, MORAL DILEMMAS IN; DEATH RESEARCH AND EDUCATION; MORAL DILEMMAS IN PASTORAL PERSPECTIVE; SELF-DESTRUCTIVE BEHAVIOR; WILL TO LIVE. *Compare* SACRIFICIAL BEHAVIOR; SELF-TRANSCENDENCE.

SUICIDE (Pastoral Care). Suicide is the deliberate human act of self-inflicted, self-intentioned death. It is to be distinguished from the instinctive activity of some animals which leads to their death, and from the self-destructive activities of humans who are not consciously intending to die. Therefore this discussion does not consider concepts of unconscious motivation, death instinct, self-destructive carelessness, and accident proneness. The term refers only to a fully conscious human act carried out with the intention of terminating one's own life in the immediate future.

The question of why some people are suicidal is as complex as is the etiology of any human behavior, and any explanation depends on the viewpoint of the person offering the explanation. Suicide has been described as a weakness, a noble act, a sin, a crime, a disease, and a natural choice. It has been discussed by philosophers, theologians, anthropologists, sociologists, psychologists, novelists, and poets. The 25,000 annual suicides in the U.S. leave in their wake confusion, fascination, aggravated grief reactions, and often additional suicides. Usually an intensive, lonely activity, it is sometimes performed in consort with a beloved in a love pact, and sometimes in mass numbers. It is often the result of mental disease such as psychotic depression or schizophrenia.

1. **Historical Attitudes.** *a. Greek.* The early Greeks (Homer and others before 700 B.C.) regarded the act of suicide as being good and admirable, whereas the later Greeks began to think of it as a political offense because it deprived the state of a citizen. Pythagoras (582–507 B.C.) thought all men were soldiers of God and had no right to take their own lives. Socrates, Plato, and Aristotle (569–322 B.C.) wrote against suicide except in cases of extreme poverty, sorrow, or disgrace, or unless it was ordered by the state. Still later in Greek tradition thinking was again changed and the Stoics and Epicureans encouraged suicide as a quite natural solution to many problems.

b. Religious. The OT records six suicides (Judg. 9:54; Judg. 16:28–31; I Sam. 31:1–6; II Sam. 17:23; I Kings 16:18, 19) and the NT one (Mt. 27:3–5), neither making any value judgment. Suicide was a fairly common occurrence in the early church which tended to approve of self-sacrifice and martyrdom, and it was not until St. Augustine (354–430 A.D.) wrote strongly against it that the church began taking a different view. Several church councils from 533 A.D. then condemned suicide, and St. Thomas Aquinas (1225–74) reaffirmed the Augustinian view that suicide is a sin.

c. Contemporary. Another shift in attitude began with Sir Thomas More (1468–1535) and continued through the writings of Donne, Hume, and Kant, all of whom opposed the church's condemnation of suicide as a sin and began to think of it as an aberration of mind which should be treated tolerantly. From this tolerance grew the modern view that suicide represents disease and should be treated as such. There is today, however, a strong minority view that holds that suicide represents neither a sin nor a disease, but is rather a rational choice.

2. **Pastoral Understanding.** *a. Depression and isolation.* Most suicidal persons are lonely, depressed individuals experiencing strong feelings of hopelessness and

helplessness, usually with strong underlying anger. Characteristically they have been experiencing suicidal thoughts for months or years as they have tried a variety of solutions for their emotional pain. Work, prayer, medication, and alcohol have failed as solutions, and they experience their lives withering away along with a diminishing capacity to cope with their pain and stress. Usually the depression is in response to some loss or series of losses which are emotionally significant to them, such as loss of a relationship, job, health, or reputation.

b. Ambivalence. Even at advanced stages of the development of suicidal ideation, most suicidal persons are highly ambivalent about dying. That is, simultaneous desires for life and death are in conflict. This ambivalence is seen in conflicting behavior (making suicide attempts in places where rescue is likely); in suicide notes ("if you love me, wake me up"); and in interviews with those who have survived serious attempts ("I finally decided to take the pills and leave it up to fate"). Most suicidal persons are not so much wanting to die as they are willing to die as a necessary price to escape the seemingly endless pain.

c. Crisis. Most suicidal persons will make a serious attempt only during a relatively brief period of time when the emotional pain peaks and when coping skills are low. The duration of this emotional crisis may be only a few hours, or at the most a few weeks. Clinical experience has consistently shown that if the crisis is survived because of someone's intervention or because of some other factor, the suicidal person does not soon return to the high risk stage.

d. Communication. As desperate and depressive feelings develop, suicidal persons make many covert and overt attempts at communicating their pain and their suicidal thoughts. This attempt at communication has been called "the cry for help." Verbal expressions of depression and uselessness, visits to physicians with complaints of vague symptoms, making a new will, giving away valued possessions, being careless in the use of medications and other drugs, and non-lethal suicide attempts and gestures can all be attempts on the suicidal persons' part to communicate their distress and their developing resolution to take their own life. They are all examples of the cry for help aimed toward loved ones, the general community, or to God. Contrary to the popular myth that the person who talks about suicide seldom commits it, the fact is that most persons who commit suicide have expressed their intention to do so.

3. **Pastoral Intervention.** *a. Listening.* Because most suicidal talk and behavior is at heart an attempt to communicate distress, most suicidal people respond well when that communication is received by a sensitive, concerned listener. If the listener can put aside all other concerns and gently inquire into the suicidal thoughts of the distressed person, the first important step in the intervention process will be achieved.

b. Evaluating suicidal risk. Because not every person who is depressed or who thinks about suicide represents a high suicidal risk, it is important to determine who among that population is about to take action so that appropriate response can be made. The key element in this determination is the suicidal plan the person has developed. Most persons who are seriously suicidal have thought carefully about the way they plan to die, and

have carefully prepared the means and the time, perhaps even having rehearsed the act. Because they are ambivalent about dying, most suicidal persons will be honest about the extent of their planning when a listener with genuine concern inquires. The more specific, deadly, and available the means are, the higher the risk will be. The use of pills is the most common means of suicide in the U. S., with guns the second most common. Both represent high risk means. Other factors to be considered in evaluating suicidal risk include high stress factors, low personal resources, a history of previous suicide attempts, and the use of alcohol.

c. Intervention plan. Because most people in a suicidal crisis represent a high risk for a relatively short period of time, the intervention plan should focus on immediate issues and be implemented quickly. The plan should take into consideration areas of perceived stress, present crisis factors, and should seek to develop immediate, if temporary, solutions. A list of all existing resources should be developed, including personal relationships, professional relationships, and community resources. The suicidal person should participate fully in every phase of plan development and implementation. Good follow-through is essential so there is no opportunity for feelings of abandonment.

d. Referral. In all high risk situations, and in all situations in which there is doubt about the severity of risk, professional consultation should be sought. In many communities suicide prevention centers have been established and these are normally excellent resources for consultation or referral. Some are twenty-four-hour telephone services and others provide walk-in capacity. Community mental health centers and private psychiatric and psychological services are also available in most communities.

Bibliography. L. D. Hankoff and B. E. Einsidler, *Suicide: Theory and Clinical Aspects* (1979). C. L. Hatton, S. M. Valente, and A. Rink, *Suicide: Assessment and Intervention* (1977). J. Hewett, *After Suicide* (1980). E. S. Shneidman and N. L. Farberow, *Clues to Suicide* (1957); *The Cry for Help* (1961). E. S. Shneidman, N. L. Farberow, and R. L. Litman, *The Psychology of Suicide* (1976).

P. W. PRETZEL

CRISIS MINISTRY; GUIDANCE, PASTORAL; HOT-LINE CRISIS MINISTRIES; MORAL DILEMMAS IN PASTORAL PERSPECTIVE. *See also* GRIEF AND LOSS; HOPE AND DESPAIR; SADNESS AND DEPRESSION; SELF-DESTRUCTIVE BEHAVIOR; WILL TO LIVE. *Compare* EMERGENCY, PSYCHOLOGY OF PASTOR IN.

SUICIDE PREVENTION. Preventive actions related to suicide are defined by the sequential phases in which they occur. *Prevention* refers to those primary preventive acts in which helping professionals, through education and counseling, seek to dissuade persons from killing themselves. *Intervention* involves secondary acts of prevention specifically intended to stop suicidal acts already in progress. *Postvention,* or after-care for surviving family and friends, is a tertiary preventive measure, since survivor-victims are at greater risk for suicide themselves than the general population. Edwin Shneidman has drawn a rough but helpful analogy between these phases of prevention and the traditional health concepts of immunization, treatment, and rehabilitation (1973).

This discussion offers a pastoral strategy for primary and secondary suicide prevention structured around the following seven comprehensive guidelines for ministry.

1. **Know the Diagnostic Signs.** Suicidal persons exhibit a variety of prodromal clues to significant others. Some are *verbal*, ranging from oblique hints ("I can't go on like this") to direct statements ("I'm going to kill myself"). Verbal clues should be taken seriously; most suicidal persons *do* talk about suicide before acting. Other clues are *behavioral*. Indirect behavioral signals — giving away possessions, rewriting a will, preplanning a funeral — should be closely noted. Direct clues, like suicidal actions, are the most serious indicators of the suicidal state. Eighty percent of persons who complete suicide attempt it at least once previously.

Situational clues are more difficult to recognize. These are visible in situations of extreme distress. The patient told of his terminal illness, the husband served with divorce papers, the executive fired from her job — these persons are staggering from heavy emotional blows. Pastors must be able to discern when situations such as these become contexts for suicidal thoughts and move to help diminish accumulated stress.

Syndromatic clues are signals given by physical and emotional symptoms. Three syndromes should be carefully watched: depression, disorientation, and defiance. Depression is the single most important signal, occurring in at least one-third of all suicides. Disorientation raises the possibility of drug abuse, psychosis, or brain disease and should be seriously regarded. Defiant persons who are vengeful toward significant others or who act to retain control over events in the midst of deteriorating conditions may be signaling the presence of suicidal thoughts. Pastors have the opportunity to teach these clues clearly to caring laypeople who can then join the ministry team within the church.

2. **Establish a Relationship.** Pastors and other counselors must take initiative in expressing concern for suicidal individuals. Sensitive pastors will (a) encourage suicidal persons to express their feelings without fear of judgmental responses; (b) raise the question of suicide themselves if they sense others are contemplating it; (c) affirm the choice for continued living; (d) contract with suicidal persons to continue the pastoral relationship, even in the midst of crisis; and (e) pray with and for them as a sincere expression of pastoral concern. If suicidal persons come for help, their decision should be affirmed through active availability. Pastors must always respect the desire and need for confidentiality while at the same time avoiding agreements which bind them to silently countenance suicide and prevent the engagement of other possible helpers.

3. **Identify the Cause(s).** Suicidal persons need help in recognizing and clarifying the central problems and secondary issues which have precipitated the suicidal crisis. Active listening and focused reflection are the most effective pastoral tools in untangling the rush of thought and emotion which evidence suicidal thoughts and feelings.

4. **Assess the Risk.** The central factors of *perturbation, lethality,* and *inimicality* must be assessed by the pastoral diagnostician. Perturbation refers to how emotionally upset the person is. Lethality is a gauge of the probability of direct suicidal action. Inimicality involves the presence of self-destructive tendencies in the person's lifestyle.

The chief factor to be considered in risk assessment is lethality. Suicide lethality grows in proportion to the persistence of ambivalence. Criteria for evaluating lethality include age and sex; existence of a suicide plan, including the lethality of the proposed method, its availability, and the details for using it; stress; symptoms; support systems; lifestyle; communication with significant others; reactions of significant others; and medical status. No single criterion is considered to elevate lethality with the exception of the suicide plan. The pastoral diagnostician evaluates suicide potential on the basis of a general profile of all the criteria.

The pastor must work to reduce lethality first, for elevated lethality (not heightened perturbation) leads to suicide. An informed pastoral discrimination can usually sense the differences between an impulsive suicide threat or gesture and a calculated suicidal act.

5. **Marshal Inner Strengths.** Counselors are to avoid the assumption that only external helps exist for suicidal persons. Family, friends, and caring institutions are important aids in the journey back to emotional health and stability, but points of contact for pastoral ministry also exist *within* the suicidal person. Sensitive pastors can help suicidal persons clarify feelings, look closer at real alternatives, and affirm the personal resources and spiritual gifts previously neglected. As order is brought forth out of confusion, suicidal persons may experience positive emotions which have been buried by anxiety. These will serve as a most effective deterrent to suicidal actions and should be given appropriate weight in the balance of personal strengths.

6. **Develop a Therapeutic Plan.** Progress toward stability can best be accomplished in the pastoral relationship through specific, teachable steps in altering behavior and responses to problems. Such a therapeutic plan secures the person's own involvement in reconstructing a life pattern free from the urge to self-destruct. The pastor helps the person identify the problems and seek solutions or coping strategies. This plan can provide a structure for personal re-creation if depression is not so deep that it deprives the process of momentum.

As a professional amid the caring community, the pastor is able to mobilize resources within it as well as within the social structures of the suicidal person's life. Referral is always indicated for serious emotional and physical distress. Each pastor should have reciprocal relationships with trusted physicians, psychiatrists, psychologists, and social workers. These persons enlarge the pastor's own capability to deal with the problem of suicide. Initiative should also be taken to convene significant others who will play important roles in the therapeutic plan. Every available support group should be brought into the new base of care and concern being provided for the suicidal person. The pastor can be the architect of this process.

7. **When Suicidal Crisis Occurs, Intervene.** In spite of the best efforts at intentional ministry, suicidal persons still attempt and complete suicide. Pastors should decide well in advance how they will act when this happens. The option of doing nothing is ruled out by the

pastor who has already demonstrated ongoing concern throughout the counseling process. The pastor's own ethical questions about suicide prevention need to be resolved *before* the moment of crisis and communicated clearly to persons in his or her care when necessary.

Bibliography. B. Blackburn, *What You Should Know About Suicide* (1982), pp. 35–124. H. Clinebell, "First Aid in Counseling: The Suicidal Emergency," *Expository Times* (1966), 328–32. E. Grollman, "Pastoral Counseling of the Potentially Suicidal Person," *Pastoral Psychology*, 16 (1966), 46–52; *Suicide: Prevention, Intervention, Postvention* (1971). C. Hatton, S. Valente, and A. Rink, eds., *Suicide: Assessment and Intervention* (1977). P. Pretzel, "Role of the Clergyman in Suicide Prevention," *Pastoral Psychology*, 21 (1970), 47–52; *Understanding and Counseling the Suicidal Person* (1972). E. S. Shneidman, "Preventing Suicide," *American J. of Nursing*, 65 (1965), 111–16; *Deaths of Man* (1973), pp. 33–41; "Suicide," *Modern Synopsis of Comprehensive Textbook of Psychiatry/II*, 2d ed. (1976), pp. 870–74. E. Stein, "Clergyman's Role with the Suicidal Person," *J. of Pastoral Care*, 19 (1965), 74–83. W. Stevens, *Suicidal Crisis in Your Rural Parish* (1977), pp. 68–95.

J. H. HEWETT

DEATH RESEARCH AND EDUCATION; HOT-LINE CRISIS MINISTRIES; HOPE AND DESPAIR; SADNESS AND DEPRESSION.

SUICIDE RESEARCH. Suicide is one of the top ten causes of death in the industrialized world and yet the number of suicides may be under-estimated since many accidental deaths may actually be suicides. For every person that completes a suicide there are eight to ten others that attempt and fail. As many as 200,000 people attempt suicide in the U.S. each year and about one in ten succeed. While more women than men attempt suicide and fail (3 to 1), men complete suicide more often than women (3 to 1). The higher rate of completed suicides among men is due in part to the fact that men use more lethal means for suicide. Men use guns more often than women do while women prefer to use pills.

While suicide occurs in most periods of the life cycle from childhood to old age, the dynamics and frequency differ from stage to stage. Among college students, for example, suicide is the third leading cause of death; it is twice the rate of persons not in college. In later adulthood men outnumber women in committing suicide ten to one, and divorced and widowed persons have a much higher suicide rate than married persons.

There are also differences in suicide rates among various ethnic groups. Chinese Americans and Native Americans have the highest rates of suicide. Black men between the ages of 25 and 35 kill themselves at two times the rate of white males in the same age group. This proportion changes in later years as suicide increases sharply with age among white men, and remains fairly stable among black men.

1. Motivation for Suicide. The suicidal crisis is typically triggered by a recent experience of loss or failure that leaves the person feeling hopeless and helpless. The role of the loss of a relationship with a person on whom one depended is very prominent in cases of suicide (Bowlby, 1980). Feelings of helplessness and the belief that in the future things will be no better than they are at present typifies the suicidal mind-set (Beck, Kovacs,

and Clessman, 1975). Suicidal persons faced with loss or failure also tend to be inflexible in their approach to their problems. The self-destructive solution is often the only one they see (Neuringer, 1964; Levinson, 1972). They seem incapable of thinking of alternative solutions to problems and may settle on suicide as the only way out (Patsiokas, Clum, and Luscomb, 1979).

2. Depression and Suicide. Studies have shown repeatedly that of all the categories of mental illness, depression is most frequently associated with suicide. Depressed persons express more suicidal thoughts and wishes and complete suicide at a greater rate than non-depressed persons. Some studies estimate that up to 80 percent of those who kill themselves are depressed (Baraclough, 1974). In one important study of 100 cases of suicide, 70 percent of the sample were depressed and 15 percent alcoholic. Alcoholism and depression, then, accounted for 85 percent of the suicides. An important aspect of depression is a sense of hopelessness and helplessness. Paradoxically, persons who are severely depressed are at greater risk for suicide when the depression lifts. This is so because while in the depth of depression they are unable to act on the wish to kill themselves. As the depression lifts they may gain enough energy to carry out the wish.

3. Theories of Suicide. Early psychoanalytic explanations of suicide saw it primarily as the result of rage turned inward upon the self. The person was seen as unable to direct anger at the appropriate external target and turned it on an internalized object instead. The internalized other was experienced as sadistic yet the person clung to him or her ambivalently. The act of suicide was intended to get rid of guilt and tension by murdering the original object.

Later psychoanalytic theorists saw suicide as motivated by more than inner-directed rage. Menninger (1983) suggests three broad motivational categories for understanding suicide. Some suicides exhibit hate, aggression, blame, and a wish for revenge. This set of motives Menninger labels "the wish to kill." Other suicides are characterized by guilt, submission, self-blame, and self-accusation. This set of motives Menninger labels as "the wish to be killed." The person wishes to destroy self in order to assuage powerful feelings of guilt. Finally, some suicides exhibit a sense of hopelessness, discouragement, and despair. The person, experiencing severe illness or great pain decides that life is not worth living. This set of motives Menninger labels "the wish to die."

Leonard (1967), in an elaboration of the intrapsychic misunderstanding of suicide, proposes three types of suicidal personalities tied to early developmental difficulties. He suggests that inadequate resolution of separation / individuation issues between the second and third years of life may lead to lack of a separate sense of identity, inadequate impulse control, and dependence on external control and rigid adaptation patterns that lack flexibility under stress.

The person with an inadequate sense of self as a separate person under stress may engage others in constant struggles of dependency and control. He or she cannot live with or without people. He or she may strike at self, thinking that this will hurt the external other. This person Leonard labeled as "Dependent Dissatisfied."

The person who early in life depended on others to provide controls for his or her impulses developed a pattern of conformity and dependency at the expense of individuality. When this person's fused sense of identity is disrupted or approval and control lessens because of loss, hostility, or rejection by a loved one, a suicidal crisis may be precipitated. In the absence of external support and control the person feels overwhelmed by rage and despair which is vented on the self. This type Leonard labeled "Satisfied Symbiotic."

The person who in early childhood is prematurely pushed toward independence often represses feelings of inadequacy and fear. She or he becomes independent in order to gain parental approval. This person develops a rigid style of approval seeking which is based on what one can do rather than on who one is. Because the person represses feelings he or she typically has little self-understanding and poor control of inner impulses. This person is particularly vulnerable to loss of status, and failure. Such occurrences may precipitate a suicidal crisis for this type which Leonard labeled "The Unaccepting Type." This typology is particularly valuable because it provides a model that takes into account the stressors which in conjunction with such vulnerability may trigger the suicidal crisis.

The best-known alternatives to the intrapsychic theory of suicide are sociological ones proposed first by Durkheim. Durkheim's typology took account of sociological factors that contributed to suicide. Shneidman has integrated the intrapsychic and sociological theories and suggested three categories. The first category, "Egoistic Suicide," involves an intrapsychic debate which is concerned with the person's existential struggles rather than with environmental issues. The suicide results when the person decides to end the inner torment by killing his or her personality.

The second category, "Dyadic Suicide," involves deep unfulfilled interpersonal needs and wishes. The person may feel hateful, angry, resentful, guilty, etc., and the suicide may reflect a range of feeling in the victim, from a wish for revenge to self-punishment. Most suicides fall into the dyadic category, and it is in this category we would place Leonard's three types and at least the first of Menninger's three types.

The third category, "Ageneretic Suicide," occurs when a person no longer feels he belongs or has a place in the sequence of generations. The person loses a sense of membership and feels psychologically old. Suicide results from feelings of alienation, emptiness, and disengagement.

4. Prevention. The pastor, counselor, friend or relative can play a critical role in preventing suicide. It is important, first of all, to determine the degree of risk present when one comes in contact with a potential suicide victim. Several factors are important in evaluating risk. The probability of suicide increases with age. Post-midlife men who are widowed or divorced are at greatest risk. Most suicides have a history of suicidal attempt. Prior attempts increase the risk. Persons with clear, well-thought-out suicidal plans are in more danger than those whose plans are vague. Persons who have direct access to lethal weapons are in greater danger. Persons who are in stressful situations, who have lost loved ones, experience disharmony at home, have chronic illness and poor ego strength are at higher risk. After determining the degree

of risk the helper must intervene. If the contact is by telephone the helper should maintain contact and work to establish a relationship by showing interest, concern, and self-assurance. This contact helps the person explore alternative solutions to the problems. The helper must get necessary information such as name, address, telephone, and demographic information. The helper gets information to determine the seriousness of the caller and helps to clarify the nature of the stressor or focal problem. The helper attempts to assess the strengths and resources of the potential victim and helps the person get in touch with her or his strengths and resources.

Finally the helper recommends and initiates a plan of action. The helper may have to take steps to ensure the physical safety of the potential victim. This may include hospitalization, removal of the means of suicide, or ensuring that the potential victim is never left alone.

Bibliography. B. Baraclough, B. Bunch, B. Nelson, and D. Sainsbury, "A Hundred Cases of Suicide: Clinical Aspects," British J. of Psychiatry, 125 (1974), 355–73. A. T. Beck, et al., "Hopelessness and Suicidal Behavior," J. of the American Medical Association, 234 (1975), 1146–49. J. Bowlby, Loss, Sadness, and Depression (1980). K. Menninger, Man Against Himself (1983). C. Neuringer, "Rigid Thinking in Suicidal Behavior," J. of Consulting Psychology, 28 (1964), 54–8. A. T. Patsiokas, G. A. Clum, and R. Luscomb, "Cognitive Characteristics of Suicide Attempters," J. of Consulting and Clinical Psychology, 47:3 (1979), 478–84. E. S. Shneidman, ed., On the Nature of Suicide (1969).

W. E. GOODEN

SUICIDE (Pastoral Care); SUICIDE PREVENTION. See also SADNESS AND DEPRESSION; PSYCHOPATHOLOGY, THEORIES OF; SELF-DESTRUCTIVE BEHAVIOR. Compare DEATH RESEARCH AND EDUCATION; DYING, MORAL DILEMMAS IN; MENTAL HEALTH AND ILLNESS.

SUKKOT. See JEWISH HOLY DAYS AND FESTIVALS.

SULLIVAN, HARRY STACK (1892–1947). Originator of the interpersonal theory of psychiatry and human development. Sullivan's interpersonal theory has had significant influence on many types of therapy, perhaps most notably family therapy, with its emphasis on the relationships between people rather than intrapsychic life. His view of the significance of preadolescence in human development was a direct challenge to the widely accepted psychoanalytic theory that nothing of major developmental significance occurred between the phallic stage, around age five or six, and adolescence. Sullivan argued that it was during preadolescence that people learned to develop genuine interpersonal relationships and to care for others as they cared for themselves.

Other contributions of Sullivan have come more indirectly. Perhaps most important is his "one genus hypothesis" of mental illness. He developed this view after working in the early part of his career with schizophrenic patients whom most others felt were untreatable. He found these patients to be "more like himself than otherwise" and affirmed a broad view of humankind that broke down some of the barriers between the helping person and patient. Although there are important differences, his work has significant parallels to that of Anton Boisen in its attending to "the voice of illness."

Expressed in general terms, Sullivan conceived of the human predicament as a struggle to cope with anxiety on the one hand and loneliness on the other. Interpersonal relationships inevitably involve anxiety, which people try to avoid, but without such relationships people must cope with the more painful experience of loneliness. Anxiety, as Sullivan viewed it, created complex interpersonal relationships loaded with multiple meanings, whereas his norm for human functioning was "simple" relationships with others. His therapeutic theory was designed to simplify complicated interpersonal relationships.

Considerable indirect influence from his work has come through pastoral supervisors and teachers who have encouraged their students to modify their "Rogerian" passivity and become more active and real in their pastoral interventions. Sullivan's norm for the interpersonal helper was that such a person be sensitive to the anxiety of all parties in the relationship, including his or her own anxiety; he or she must be able to convey security through the interpersonal relationship; and the helping person must not just be playing a role but must be genuine and real.

Bibliography. A. H. Chapman, *The Treatment Techniques of Harry Stack Sullivan* (1978). G. Chrzanowski, *Interpersonal Approaches to Psychoanalysis* (1977). L. Havens, *Participant Observation* (1976). P. Mullahy, *Psychoanalysis and Interpersonal Psychiatry: The Contributions of Harry Stack Sullivan* (1970). H. S. Sullivan, *The Collected Works of Harry Stack Sullivan.*

J. PATTON

INTERPERSONAL THEORY; NEOFREUDIAN PERSONALITY THEORIES AND PASTORAL CARE.

SUPEREGO. The last of the three mental agencies to develop according to Sigmund Freud's structural theory of personality. Its energies derive from the archaic id; it is shaped by the child's internalization of parental methods of controlling their own sexual and aggressive urges. It speaks through the voice of conscience; it controls the ego by inflicting guilt, shame and other psychic sufferings.

V. P. GAY

CONSCIENCE; PSYCHOANALYSIS (Personality Theory and Research).

SUPERIORITY, SENSE OF. *See* ANTISOCIAL PERSONS; HUMOR.

SUPERSTITION. The word superstition derives from *superstitio,* meaning to stand over; hence superstition refers to awe, amazement, fear, or dread. Eventually the term came to mean both excessive devotion or ritual in religion, and the survival of old religious habits in the midst of a new order of things. In contemporary Western religion the term is used to denigrate beliefs and practices which are out of touch with the scientific age (though what is sheer superstition to a Westerner may still be truth to someone in an animistic society).

Contemporary superstition may express magical beliefs, rituals and practices of primitive cultures which have survived into the modern period, usually in dimin-

ished or distorted form. The links with the distant past are usually not a conscious part of contemporary superstitious expressions. For example, to "knock on wood" is connected to a primitive belief in a great ancestor tree, now forgotten. This conservative tendency to revert to primitive, archetypal modes of thought typically appears when the outcome of an important situation is in the balance and events are beyond human control.

The cognitive psychologist, Jean Piaget, observed that superstitious thought resembles the thinking of young children, and that nearly every adult engages in some degree of superstitious thinking, especially in response to stress which often triggers reversions to childhood behavior. Freud believed that the superstitious rituals of obsessive-compulsive neurotics are a defense against the anxiety aroused by repressed desires, which differ from everyday magical and superstitious behaviors only in degree.

Bibliography. E. Maple, "Superstition," in R. Cavendish, ed., *Man, Myth and Magic* (1985).

D. GILLILAND

FEAR; MAGICAL THINKING. *Compare* WITCHCRAFT.

SUPERVISED PASTORAL EDUCATION. *See* HISTORY OF PROTESTANT PASTORAL CARE (Canada).

SUPERVISION, PASTORAL. Pastoral supervision is a dimension of the overall ministry of the religious community carried out by a pastor who offers both administrative oversight and a pastoral relationship to one or more persons engaged in developing ministerial competency and identity through actual ministerial practice. It expresses the two essential meanings of the term *pastor*: responsible administrator and caring person. One of the central contributions of Clinical Pastoral Education (CPE) to the ministry of the religious community and to education for that ministry is the reaffirmation that pastoral supervision is a significant dimension of ministry with theory and practical knowledge which the pastor may develop. The uniqueness of pastoral supervision, in contrast to other types of supervision, lies in its being understood as ministry, not as a practical technique designed to accomplish a more important task, such as preaching, teaching, or parish visitation.

1. **Relationship to Supervision in Other Disciplines. *a. Social work and education.*** Pastoral supervision has been related to supervision in other disciplines primarily in two ways: through the literature of those disciplines that dealt with supervision; and through the encounter and comparison with other disciplines in a training institution. With respect to the literature, social work, through its emphasis upon supervision as a significant part of professional work, was the first of the professions to influence the development of pastoral supervision (Towle, 1954). More recently the CPE movement's concern to be understood by the public as a particular type of educational procedure, in contrast to on-the-job training, has caused it to make more explicit use of learning theory in its supervisory methods. Thus, the teaching profession has become influential, particularly in supervisory CPE (Bigge, 1976).

b. Psychotherapy. Most significant for the understanding of pastoral supervision, however, has been the influence of psychotherapy supervision and the theoretical discussions of the relationship between supervision and psychotherapy. The relevance of the supervisory literature of psychotherapy for understanding pastoral supervision rests only secondarily in the historical fact of Clinical Pastoral Education's having developed in psychiatric institutions that were concerned, along with other treatments, with psychotherapy. Rather, it is based upon what is essentially a theological judgment—that ministry necessarily involves the whole person of the minister, not just what he or she knows or does. Therefore, clinical education for ministry requires theoretical resources that deal with the most profound psychosocial as well as theological understanding of the person. Most influential from this literature has been the psychoanalytically based work by Rudolf Ekstein and Robert S. Wallerstein, *The Teaching and Learning of Psychotherapy*, with its concepts of "parallel process," "clinical rhombus," "emergency," etc.

2. Relationship to Pastoral Consultation. Because both functions share a common methodology, pastoral supervision is sometimes confused with pastoral consultation. The essential distinction is administrative. In supervision, the supervisor has ultimate responsibility for the ministry being performed and, as part of his or her professional function, is required to oversee the work of the supervisee. The successful performance of the supervisee reflects upon the supervisor. In pastoral consultation, the consultant may be overseeing the same type of ministry, that is, chaplaincy, pastoral counseling, etc., but he or she has no responsibility for it. Moreover, the person seeking consultation has freely chosen to be in consultation and may accept or reject the consultative response that has been offered (Patton and Warkentin, 1971). In supervision, once the supervisor and supervisee are in the supervisory structure together, supervision is not voluntary. Whereas the need for supervision is associated with the early stages of ministry or other professions, the need for consultation is lifelong, both professionally and personally. One of the valuable contributions of pastoral supervision is assisting persons in becoming aware of their longer-term need of other persons in a consultative relationship.

3. The Development of Pastoral Supervision in CPE. *a. The Council and the Institute.* The development of pastoral supervision as a distinct discipline and function of ministry emerged out of Clinical Pastoral Education in the second twenty-five years of its history, most prominently in the 1950s and 1960s. Only after the value of clinical experience in an institutional setting became more generally recognized among clergy and theological educators were the specific factors necessary for satisfactory Clinical Pastoral Education examined. The two major clinical training organizations, the Council for Clinical Training and the Institute for Pastoral Care, developed standards for what constituted a satisfactory training setting and what qualifications a supervisor of clinical training needed to have. It was in the development of these standards, in the process of designating persons as qualified to be supervisors, and in the previously unpublished writing, printed in conference proceedings, through which chaplains attempted to share with each other what was involved in supervising students, that the discipline of pastoral supervision emerged.

Historian Brooks Holifield (1983) has identified two theoretical streams of development in Clinical Pastoral Education. One was associated with Richard Cabot and his sharp distinction between illness and health, the Institute of Pastoral Care, and Boston personalism's relatively optimistic view of human nature. The other was identified with Anton Boisen and his concern with psychopathology as a means of understanding persons, the Council for Clinical Training, and a more pessimistic view of human nature informed by psychoanalysis.

b. Therapeutic issues and pastoral skills. Although there was considerable overlapping of methodology and, to some degree, of theory, each clinical training group developed its own way of working with students, and with it, an emerging understanding of what constituted pastoral supervision. Although Boisen became concerned about the increasing concern of supervisors with the "therapeutic issues" of their students, the developing supervisory focus of the Council was more upon the person of the student and upon change precipitated by the clinical experience than upon learning pastoral methodology. The Institute, on the other hand, emphasized the development of "specifically pastoral skills by testing them with real people and submitting the results for evaluation."

Although far too broad to be fully accurate, the emphases of the two groups can with some accuracy be expressed by the generalization that the emphasis of the Council was upon the student's *being* whereas the Institute's was upon her or his *doing*. The Council and Institute no longer exist, having been merged in 1967 along with Southern Baptist and Lutheran organizations into the Association for Clinical Pastoral Education (ACPE), but the programmatic emphases on *being* or upon *doing* continue. Although virtually every pastoral supervisor would affirm the importance of both, his or her emphasis is usually upon one or the other.

4. Essential Features of Pastoral Supervision. *a. Supervision as educational and professional.* Although there have been a number of attempts to identify the essential features of pastoral supervision, the most useful and influential is the essay of Thomas Klink (1966) which identifies six essential features of supervision. The importance of these generalizations involves their context as well as content. In contrast to most of the writing about pastoral supervision prior to this time, Klink was addressing theological educators who were not interested in CPE as such but in the educational principles that could be derived from it. Moreover, his own ministry took place in an interprofessional setting committed both to education and service; therefore he was concerned to present generalizations about supervisory learning that would apply to professions other than his own.

i. An educational procedure. In the first of his identifying features, Klink insists that supervision is an educational procedure in its own right, not simply a dimension of something else, for example, the supervision of pastoral care or of psychotherapy, where it may be understood as a part of what is being supervised.

ii. Supervisors who are qualified. Klink insists upon supervision being done by persons who are involved in the practice of the profession or function of what is being supervised and who have become qualified to supervise that practice. The supervisor is not only an educator but a practitioner and, in effect, a model.

iii. Commitment to a profession. The persons supervised are not simply being looked at in terms of the work they are doing now, but that work is a part of a longer-term commitment—becoming qualified in a profession or in a practice recognized as important by them and by a larger community.

iv. A "contract" for supervision. Supervision involves a setting in which there are both clearly defined roles and yet some flexibility in the understanding of how those roles are to be carried out. Thus, within a clearly defined structure, there is in supervision a "contract" or mutual understanding between supervisor and supervisee about moving toward the supervisee's broader professional concerns.

v. Appropriate role function. The roles of both supervisor and supervisee must be appropriate to their particular profession, that is, in the supervisory process they are functioning within the profession, not apart from it.

vi. The presence of other professionals. The supervisory environment should include persons in other professions or with other concerns beyond their immediate tasks which challenge the supervisee to clarify his or her particular identity and professional concern.

These principles have been widely discussed and used both within CPE and in a variety of contexts where professional (in contrast to academic) education has been a major concern. An important example was the move toward the professionalization of theological education in the late 1960s and early 1970s, which involved the reconceptualization of traditional field work placements into programs of "supervised ministry" and the initiation of professional doctorates in ministry. Evidence of the concern with pastoral supervision beyond the CPE context is found in materials published by the Association for Theological Field Education (Beisswenger and McCarty, 1983).

Whether all of Klink's features are necessary for pastoral supervision remains a matter of debate among persons in the pastoral care field, theological educators, and those responsible for the supervision of ministry in parish and other contexts. To what degree and in what way, for example, does a supervisor need to be qualified to supervise? Or, particularly for those concerned with the supervision of laity (Southard, 1982), what is comparable for the layperson to the clergy's becoming a competent member of the profession of ministry? Can that larger goal be specific enough for a "contract" with laity to be adequately formed?

b. Supervision as pastoral and relational. i. Relevant for all ministry. Patton (1969) has attempted to broaden the concept of pastoral supervision beyond the context of professional education, viewing pastoral supervision as part of the task of all ministers whatever their context for ministry or whatever the category of ministry for which they have responsibility. In his generalizations Patton acknowledged that pastoral supervision is an educational procedure, but argued that it may take place in relationship with persons, laity or clergy, whose conscious focus is more upon the task of ministry than upon the process

of becoming minister. In this latter case, the "contract for learning" is more implicit than explicit but does exist and should gradually emerge and become more evident during the process of supervision. If the larger issue of "becoming minister" does not emerge and if the persons supervised—for example, laypersons in a parish—avoid looking at their identity as "minister," then the task of ministry itself suffers.

ii. Immersion in the human situation. Following Klink, but emphasizing the relational more than the professional and educational dimensions, Patton (1969) describes the optimum situation for pastoral supervision as one in which supervisees are so "immersed in the human situation that they cannot fail to experience it as a predicament rather than a problem." The supervisee's own humanity is such that he or she tends to view life as something that can be broken down into problems that can be solved if only one can learn the right procedure. The pastoral supervisor has a similar temptation— showing the supervisee how to solve the problem rather than allowing him or her to experience it in a relationship and move on, strengthened by that relationship, to minister in a situation where there is no clearly correct procedure. Pastoral supervision is pastoral, in its relational sense, because the supervisee needs not only what the supervisor knows, but he or she also needs the significant relationship that the supervisor may offer.

iii. Administrative oversight and pastoral relationship. The importance of relationship is perhaps the major way in which pastoral supervision differs from other types of supervision. While all supervision involves administrative oversight of the work being done and the task being learned, pastoral supervision provides a relationship in which the supervisees can look at themselves in the light of the task performed. In fact, many of the discussions within the CPE movement, as the role and identity of the pastoral supervisor was emerging, emphasized the self-understanding of the student and sought to clarify the relationship between supervision and psychotherapy. Actually, that issue was but one expression of the more central issue for pastoral supervision—the tension between administration and relationship. Other expressions of the same issue included determining what specific things supervisees need to know or do in relation to how they develop their own styles of ministry, and knowing how to relate the apparent needs of the parish or institution to the learning that supervisees need to do —and can only do—from what their failures reveal about themselves. In actual supervision the tension between administration and relationship is sometimes resolved in one direction, sometimes in the other. It is never fully resolved, however, and that fact is essential to the pastoral identity of supervision.

5. **Models of Supervision.** One of the ways of describing supervision both within and outside of the pastoral field has been in terms of models or modes of supervision. Donald F. Beisswenger (1974), writing from the point of view of theological field education, has provided a useful example of this. Beisswenger describes seven modes of supervision which offer both an image of the supervisor and a description of how the supervisor functions. (1) In the *work evaluation* mode the supervisor focuses upon the tasks that the student has been

assigned. (2) The *instructor* mode places responsibility upon the supervisor to establish an educational context and climate in which the student can grow in ways felt by the supervisor to be important. (3) The *apprentice* mode is one in which the student is not necessarily given a particular work but shares in the same duties as the pastor/supervisor. Learning is largely done through observing, mirroring, and modeling, taking place more by osmosis than structured contact. (4) Supervision in the *training* mode requires that the supervisor establish an educational context in which the student can be trained as a professional and may be seen in the previous discussion of Klink's point of view. (5) The *resource* mode may be seen in the supervisor who sees his or her role as providing resources of various kinds for the student at the student's initiative. Usually this mode is related to a particular interest which the student has, such as ministry to the elderly or to uninvolved church members. (6) The *consultative* mode is one in which student and supervisor contract to work on the concerns of the student and for which the supervisor, as consultant, bears no responsibility (as noted above). (7) The mode of *spiritual guide* is one in which the supervisor assists the student in attending to the task of discerning the presence of God within the pattern of daily life and work.

6. **Theological Images of the Pastoral Supervisor.** If pastoral supervision is understood as ministry, and if the religious community to which it is related is Christian, then according to Christian tradition pastoral supervision must be interpreted theologically as an extension of the ministry of Christ. Historical criticism prevents simple identification of what occurs in contemporary pastoral supervision with events recorded in the Gospels. Nevertheless, Christian tradition has broadly insisted that all ministry expresses essential continuity with the ministry of Christ. In the case of pastoral supervision this continuity can be interpreted in relation to several NT images.

a. The unity of person and work in Christ. Thematic continuity with the person and work of Christ may be seen in the pastoral supervisor's focus upon supervisees' quests for unity between what they are and what they do. Every human being is asked to "take the form of Christ," but this does not mean mocking specific traits from the biblical picture. Jesus as the Christ must be viewed wholistically. He "is the bearer of the New Being in the totality of his being, not in any special expressions of it" (Tillich, 1957). He is the Christ in resisting the temptation to claim ultimacy for any aspect of his finite nature, that is, any one thing that he was or did. He is the Christ in correctly perceiving the world as it is — undistorted by personal need — and acting appropriately in relation to it.

This understanding of Christ as one in whom there is an essential unity between what he was and what he did contrasts radically with the lack of unity in other human beings. The words of the hymn, "though what I dream and what I do in my weak days are always two," express the human condition that persons other than Christ do not exemplify unity, only a quest for it. This quest for unity is, perhaps, the image of the Christian life and ministry most relevant for pastoral supervision. In supervising, the pastor oversees and becomes related to the supervisee's quest for unity between action and being,

between what he or she is and does in ministry. In making this quest the supervisee comes as close as is possible to expressing continuity between his or her ministry and the ministry of Christ. Whatever specific acts of ministry may be examined in supervision, the pastoral supervisor's primary task is to interpret them in terms of this quest for the wholeness exemplified in Christ.

b. Parabolic teacher. Another theological theme that may be related to pastoral supervision is the image of Jesus as being a parable and a teller of parables. A parable is a story/event that breaks into and breaks down the most cherished assumptions of its hearers (Crossan, 1975). Jesus' life did that to those with whom he came in contact. It was an event that changed the meaning of Messiah from triumphant world ruler to suffering servant. His life was parabolic like the stories he told. He took the religious and cultural tradition of his hearers and contradicted it with Samaritans who were "good guys," not bad, or vineyard workers who "unfairly" received more wages than they deserved. The pastoral supervisor expresses this image of the parable teller in challenging the assumptive world of the supervisee in the context of a relationship in which he or she shares that world. Pastoral supervision involves pointing to the unexpected in the ordinary events of life and ministry.

c. Equipper of saints. A theological theme in the Pauline Epistles that is demonstrated in pastoral supervision is the juxtaposition of theological understanding with the practical, sometimes petty, concerns of the persons and churches whom he addressed. Paul's practical solutions to the problems of marriage and divorce, competitiveness and interpersonal conflict, decisions about the effect of certain actions upon the life and welfare of others are probably no more useful than solutions to practical problems today. His commitment to viewing those concerns in the light of the person and the work of Christ, however, provides a valuable image for pastoral supervision. Whatever the issue in human experience to be examined, a practical or technical solution is in itself inadequate. All that persons do and are is to be understood in the light of the God revealed in Jesus Christ. Just as the last half of Paul's letters must be read in the light of the first half, a particular pastoral action, in supervision, must be examined in relation to who the supervisee is in relation to his or her faith.

d. Deacon, shepherd, and overseer. A final theological theme that seems in continuity with modern pastoral supervision may be found in those NT letters subsequent to Paul, which focused on the structure of church and ministry and, therefore, on the role of the shepherd or overseer. The first letter of Peter, for example, describes Christ as shepherd and overseer of the Christian community. Other NT writings describe a similar function being carried out by members of and ministers to that community. The fact that the words for "shepherd" and "overseer" are consistently associated with each other in the NT adds support to the thesis that within Christian ministry the administrative and pastoral functions are not to be separated. Another interesting suggestion from the NT is that the need for pastoral supervision became evident only after the apostles — the charismatic leaders or ones who had direct knowledge of the Christ—had died out or moved on to another place. At that point an overseer was needed to be sure that the work begun by the apostles was continued and developed. One can surmise that the earliest pastoral supervisors were less likely to have been dynamic preachers of the gospel than faithful deacons left behind to keep things going.

This rather humble role of the first Christian pastoral supervisors resonates strongly with one of the most important understandings of the term "clinical" in modern pastoral care. It refers to common, not ostensibly religious, experience. The pastoral supervisor is one who is able to look at the ordinary events of life and ministry and interpret them within the relationship to those whose work he or she oversees. The early CPE students were involved in "humble" work not unlike that of the early church deacons. They functioned as orderlies, recreational assistants, etc., performing routine tasks in the institutional setting. Their "clinical" training occurred as they found meaning in their ordinary interaction with patients and in the stories of those persons whom the mental health system had labeled as "insane," but whom Anton Boisen could see as "living human documents."

Bibliography. D. F. Beisswenger, "Differentiating Modes of Supervision in Theological Field Education," *Theological Education*, 11 (1974), 50–58. D. F. Beisswenger and D. C. McCarty, *Pastoral Theology and Ministry* (1983). R. L. Bigge, *Learning Theory for Teachers* (1976). J. D. Crossan, *The Dark Interval* (1975). R. Ekstein and R. S. Wallerstein, *The Teaching and Learning of Psychotherapy* (1963). R. D. Fallot, "Metaphor and Change in the Supervision of Psychotherapy and Pastoral Counseling," *J. of Supervision and Training in Ministry*, 6 (1983), 23–32. G. A. Fitchett, "The Paradoxical Nature of CPE," *J. of Supervision and Training in Ministry*, 3 (1980), 57–72. B. M. Hartung, "The Capacity to Enter Latency in Learning Pastoral Psychotherapy," *J. of Supervision and Training in Ministry*, 2 (1979), 46–59. A. K. Hess, ed., *Psychotherapy Supervision* (1980). E. B. Holifield, *A History of Pastoral Care in America* (1983). T. W. Klink, "Supervision," in *Education for Ministry*, C. R. Fielding, ed. (1966). W. J. Mueller and B. B. Kell, *Coping With Conflict: Supervising Counselors and Psychotherapists* (1972). J. H. Patton, "A Theological Interpretation of Pastoral Supervision," in *The New Shape of Pastoral Theology*, W. B. Oglesby, ed. (1969). J. H. Patton and J. Warkentin, "A Dialogue on Supervision and Consultation," *J. of Pastoral Care*, 25 (1971), 165–74. K. H. Pohly, *Pastoral Supervision* (1977). H. F. Searles, "The Informational Value of the Supervisor's Emotional Experiences," *Collected Papers on Schizophrenia and Related Subjects* (1965). D. B. Schuster, J. J. Sandt, and O. F. Thaler, *Clinical Supervision of the Psychiatric Resident* (1972). S. Southard, *Training Church Members for Pastoral Care* (1982). P. Tillich, *Systematic Theology*, vol. II (1957). C. Towle, *The Learner in Education for the Professions: As Seen in Education for Social Work* (1954).

J. PATTON

CLINICAL PASTORAL EDUCATION; EDUCATION, NURTURE, AND CARE; MINISTRY. *See also* ACTION/BEING RELATIONSHIP; CERTIFICATION; CERTIFIED SUPERVISOR. *Compare* CONSULTATION; PASTORAL THEOLOGY, GRADUATE EDUCATION IN; LEADERSHIP AND ADMINISTRATION; PASTORAL CARE (History, Traditions, and Definitions); SPECIALIZATION IN PASTORAL CARE; THEOLOGICAL EDUCATION AND THE PASTORAL CARE MOVEMENT.

SUPERVISOR. *See* CERTIFIED SUPERVISOR.

SUPPORT. *See* COMFORT/SUSTAINING; COMMUNITY, FELLOWSHIP, AND CARE; SUPPORT GROUPS; TOUCHING/PHYSICAL SUPPORT.

SUPPORT GROUPS. Intentional gatherings of people, committed to meet regularly, for the direct purpose of caring, listening, and sharing. Within such a group, help and encouragement, information and emotional nurture may be provided for whatever life task or situation the group members are facing in common, for example, the positive resolution of grief, relating one's faith to one's job, coping with a terminal illness, or enhancing personal and spiritual growth. As part of the interpersonal, small-group, and self-help movements, support groups can be an effective resource for pastoral care by expressing and implementing the values of one's religious heritage.

1. **Small Groups.** While support groups are neither encounter nor therapy groups, they may be challenging and therapeutic. They have working within them the usual group dynamics involving trust level, hidden agendas, question of leadership, group emotional climate, and patterns and levels of participation and communication. Though large groups may emphasize the communication of intellectual information and/or emotional encouragement under the leadership of an expert, small groups focus on the sharing of experience and feeling by all participants under shared leadership. The two emphases are sometimes combined by having the large group meet as a whole, then breaking up into small peer groups for more personal, intimate communication. More intimate sharing among participants occurs in a small group where there is a high level of trust and affirmation, involving open communication among those meeting together regularly over a period of time.

2. **Religious Values and Importance for Ministry.** The use of support groups in pastoral care and in the ministry of the faith community can express many of the values of Christian faith heritage: the mandate to love one another and to carry one another's burdens, the need for fellowship and nurturing life and in growth and health, the importance of speaking the truth in love, and the worth and effectiveness of laity in giving care.

Support groups can augment pastoral care by meeting a wider range of human needs than individual care. They also offer laity the opportunity to use their gifts and experience and to enhance their growth and self-esteem by being responsible for one another.

As an arm of pastoral care, support groups can be used for referrals by the faith community and for inclusion within its own program. Groups outside the faith community can provide support for people facing cancer, alcoholism, stress, overeating, asthma, grief, divorce, or those wanting to take part in social action, for example, on issues of world hunger and peace.

Pastors and lay leaders may initiate different support groups in their congregations by inviting people to form a group around their particular concern. In the formation of such groups, care is taken in stating clearly the purpose of the group, its size, its frequency of meeting, and the guidelines and disciplines of participation. As these groups function within the faith congregation, concern is given not only to the content of their meetings but also to their dynamics, such as group climate, patterns and quality of participation, trust level, and leadership and power conflict.

By having a support group for themselves, pastoral care-givers can deal more readily with "burnout," enhance their professional effectiveness, and increase their sense of personal fulfillment in ministry. Whether composed of professional colleagues or of members of the faith community, such a group can be a special place where pastors find trust, care and affirmation, receive positive and negative feedback, and ask for the support they need.

Bibliography. J. L. Casteel, ed., *The Creative Role of Interpersonal Groups in the Church Today* (1968). H. Clinebell, *Growth Groups* (1977); *The People Dynamic* (1977). D. Klass, "Self-help Groups for the Bereaved: Theory, Theology, and Practice," *J. of Religion and Health*, 21 (1982), 307–24. C. Reid, *Groups Alive — Church Alive* (1969).

K. HANSEN

COMMUNITY, FELLOWSHIP, AND CARE; CONGREGATION, PASTORAL CARE OF; LAY PASTORAL CARE AND COUNSELING. *See also* GROUP DYNAMICS, PROCESS, AND RESEARCH; SELF-HELP PSYCHOLOGIES. *Compare* ALCOHOLICS ANONYMOUS; COMFORT-SUSTAINING; GROUP COUNSELING AND PSYCHOTHERAPY; GROWTH GROUPS; HAVURAH; PIETISM AND PASTORAL CARE; RAPE AND RAPE COUNSELING; RELATIONSHIP NETWORK; THERAPEUTIC COMMUNITY.

SUPPORTIVE THERAPY.

A type of counseling in which the primary purpose is to support the individual—socially, emotionally and spiritually. This type of counseling stands in contrast to uncovering, insight-oriented therapy, whose primary purpose is to facilitate personality change. This distinction is somewhat arbitrary, because all good counseling involves some elements of both.

Most of the care and counseling done by the parish pastor is supportive therapy. Bereavement, handicaps, illness, and other crises are typical situations in which the primary pastoral function is support. Supportive therapy is also an important tool for helping the dry alcoholic maintain his or her commitment to abstinence.

The methods of supportive therapy begin with good listening skills, especially those that listen for feelings and those that elicit the verbalization of feelings. The use of prayer, Scripture, and meditation are empowering methods that enable people to find strength, motivation, stability and direction in difficult times. Small groups are also an effective and efficient way to provide a ministry of support.

R. S. SULLENDER

COMFORT/SUSTAINING; PSYCHOTHERAPY. *See also* SUPPORT GROUPS; THERAPEUTIC COMMUNITY. *Compare* COMMUNITY, FELLOWSHIP, AND CARE; CONSOLATION.

SUPPRESSION.

A psychoanalytic term referring to the conscious avoidance of thoughts and feelings which are threatening to the individual's self-concept and likely to result in an experience of anxiety. Suppression contrasts with another defense mechanism, repression, which is the unconscious avoidance of threatening, anxiety-producing ideas and impulses; when repressed, unconscious material is not allowed into conscious awareness.

KEVIN R. KENNEDY

DEFENSE AND COPING THEORY; DEFENSE MECHANISMS. *Compare* REPRESSION; SELF-EXPRESSION/SELF-CONTROL.

SURGICAL PATIENT.

Pastoral care of the surgical patient brings into sharp focus the importance of longitudinal relationships among the patient, family, minister, and religious community. If the crisis of surgery can be experienced as an event in which there is continuity of care both "pre-op" and "post-op" then the shock of the hour(s) of actual surgery will be minimized. A "pre-op" visit the night before surgery becomes most helpful to patient and family if it is part of ongoing contacts between minister and patient with discussion and prayers on the larger questions of the reason for and feelings about the surgery. Regular follow-up visits likewise should be made, not just one visit to ascertain if the surgery was a "success."

On the day of the surgery, the family's needs are probably greater than the patient's. Family tensions usually will be great and the family system may prove itself as adequate or inadequate. The pastor and others from the faith community know the family and will be of great assistance.

After many surgical procedures there are myriad tubes, monitors, pumps, etc., and the family should be prepared for this via explanation by hospital staff. Many hospitals have extensive preparations for the patient by nursing, anesthesia, medical, and other staff; encourage this for the family as well.

There is usually a difference in patient and family anxiety depending upon whether the surgery is elective or emergency. In some cases, the crisis may be *both* the crisis of surgery and the crisis of uncertainty around why surgery is so suddenly required. In all cases, communication with the surgeon is crucial. Ideally this should be between the surgeon and patient; the minister's primary function should be encouraging the patient and family to ask the surgeon questions. If at all possible, the pastor should not get involved in relaying messages, but turn everyone toward direct dyadic communication with the appropriate person: husband/wife; patient/surgeon; surgeon/patient's wife, husband, daughter, etc. On the other hand, direct minister/surgeon talk is encouraged for the purpose of sorting out distortion, assumption, and denial.

Surgery, more than prolonged medical illness, serves to raise questions about the patient's body and body image. Viewing one's body as "friend," "strong ally," or "temple of God" will help with the healing process. A view of one's body as "fragile," "fat," "something-I-have-mistreated," or "always giving me trouble," signals a less favorable recovery. These predispositions cannot be changed at this last hour, but they are important matters for pastoral conversation, and may represent an opportunity for healthy change in lifestyle after the surgery, thus bringing the patient (and family) into the ongoing long-term issues of care of self and body.

D. C. DeARMENT

CRISIS MINISTRY; SICK, PASTORAL CARE OF. *See also* HEALING; HOSPITALIZATION, EXPERIENCE OF; PAIN; PATIENCE/PATIENTHOOD; SUFFERING. *Compare* CANCER PATIENT; HEART PATIENT.

SURRENDER TO CHRIST. *See* BORN-AGAIN EXPERI-ENCE; CONVERSION; EVANGELICAL PASTORAL CARE.

SURVIVAL (Occult). The belief that the individual personality remains after death and can communicate with the living. Survival is the basic tenet of spiritualism. In the practice of spiritualism a medium, sensitive to the spirit world (and generally in a state of trance), serves as an intermediary who passes on messages or assists the spirit in actively communicating with the living.

The birth of the modern spiritualist movement is said to date from March 31, 1848, when in Hydesville, New York, two sisters, Margaret and Katharine Fox, reported having had the first of a series of spirit conversations with a poltergeist they believed to inhabit their home. This event became the founding stone of the spiritualist organizations which sprang up in the U. S. and Great Britain for the purpose of communicating with spirits of the dead. Christian churches have continued their long tradition, rooted in the Bible, of opposing the practice, and the early spiritualistic movement was frequently denounced by the clergy in the press, public prayer meetings, and through lecture tours organized for that purpose. Today, belief in occult survival forms the basis for the world wide existence of spiritualist societies, newspapers and religious groups.

Scientific study of survival was inaugurated with the founding of the British Society for Psychical Research in 1882. Harvard and Duke Universities have been prominent in psychic research and course offerings. Researchers have included William James, William McDougall, and Gardner Murphy.

Present day research attempts to document celestial music, deathbed visions, "remembrances" of past lives and specific tests of otherworldly presences. Karlis Osis, director of research for the American Society for Psychical Research, gathered data from ten thousand doctors and nurses who stated that their patients reported seeing the spirits of dead persons at their bedsides. Research on voices captured on tape when no human present is speaking was published in 1971 by Konstantin Raudive in his book *Breakthrough*. The September 1977 volume of the distinguished psychiatric publication *Journal of Nervous and Mental Disease* included Ian Stevenson's research in children's recall of past lives. However, these and other research studies have produced no conclusive proof of occult survival.

Bibliography. I. Grattan-Guinness, *Psychical Research* (1982). J. J. Heaney, *The Sacred and the Psychic* (1984). D. Lorimer, *Survival? Body, Mind, and Death in the Light of Psychic Experience* (1984). G. McHargue, *Facts, Frauds and Phantasms* (1972). R. Miller and N. Malony, "The Agasha Temple: Modern Spiritualism Revisited," *J. of Altered States of Consciousness*, 4 (1978–79), 277–90. G. Nelson, *Spiritualism and Society* (1969).

J. Z. CLARK

SPIRITUALISM. *Compare* DEATH RESEARCH AND EDUCATION; ESCHATOLOGY AND PASTORAL CARE; PARAPSYCHOLOGY; SOUL.

SURVIVOR PSYCHOLOGY. The study of behavior patterns in individuals following their experience of man

made or natural disaster. Disasters are unexpected; life-threatening events produce devastation and social disruption. Examples of such disasters include war, nuclear reactor accidents, physical assault, rape, and transportation accidents (man made); and earthquakes, floods, hurricanes, tornadoes, and fires (natural). Following traumatic exposure involving death, physical injury and environmental destruction, individual responses often follow predictable patterns. Contrary to popular belief, difficulty in psychological readjustment following disaster is primarily related to the severity of the traumatic experience, *not* the pre-existing personality structure or psychological adjustment of the survivor (see Foy, *et al.*, 1984).

Several factors related to the degree of emotional impact have been identified, and some of the psychological needs of survivors are predictable. Individuals in lay or professional helping roles can facilitate the process of trauma mastery for others through: (1) understanding that the reaction is normal (even desirable) and predictable; and (2) providing encouragement and support during what may be, for some, an extended period of psychological vulnerability.

1. Patterns of Reactions to Trauma. The course of psychological reactions to trauma is often divided into three phases—impact, recoil, and reorganization. The impact phase includes reactions during the first few hours; the recoil phase occurs over a period of the next few months; and longer-term reactions, labeled the reorganization phase, over after eight months (Frieze, *et al.*, 1987).

Shortly after the occurrence of the disaster (impact phase) most survivors show some signs of what has been termed "disaster syndrome" (Wallace, 1956): absence of emotion, inhibition of activity, lack of responsiveness and automatic behavior, and indecisiveness. Disorientation, denial, disbelief, and helplessness, along with physical reactions of diarrhea, headaches, and aggravation of previous medical problems are often seen during this stage as well (Frieze, *et al.*, 1987). Initial shock and disbelief may be followed by detachment from others and regressive behaviors.

In the weeks following the disaster (recoil phase) other psychological signs become common, including: acute grief, anger, anxiety, hostility, depression, and loss of ambition (adults); phobias, nightmares, school avoidance, and lack of responsibility (children). Fears of being abandoned or alone, of helplessness, of recurrence of the event, and of death are commonly experienced during this phase. Blaming oneself, someone else, or blaming fate for the victimization and feelings of rage at the perceived source are also frequently reported (Frieze, *et al.*, 1987). These reactions represent *normal* responses to an abnormal or overwhelming event. They do not immediately indicate the presence of psychopathology requiring psychiatric diagnosis and extensive treatment.

The task for victims in the reorganization phase is to modify their perception of their life circumstances so that everyday life can go on without continued feelings of victimization. Becoming a "survivor" is accomplished by establishing more effective defensive behavior, changing expectancies toward more realistic appraisal of environmental danger, and mastery of related feared situations.

Continuing occasional symptoms, especially during times of increased stress, are common. Depression, intrusive thoughts about the traumatic incident, sleep disturbance, poor self-esteem, anxiety and relationship difficulties are frequent long-term psychological consequences. In addition, substance abuse and angry outbursts when under stress indicate the use of maladaptive coping responses which increase symptoms and inhibit constructive efforts at trauma mastery.

2. Trauma Intensity Factors. Current research on trauma shows that the various characteristics of a disaster contribute to different levels of psychological distress. Some of the factors related to traumatic emotional impact of an event include: witnessing death and exposure to dead and injured; duration of the event; intensity; unexpectedness; degree of threat posed; proportion of the community involved; depth of the individual's involvement; likelihood of recurrence; and separation from family members (Baum, *et al.*, 1983). In general, greater degrees of exposure on each of these factors can be expected to contribute to higher levels of distress.

3. Trauma as Shattered Life Assumptions. Recent research on cognitive processes in victimization indicates that major changes in the individual's basic life assumptions may occur. These assumptions involve the security and meaningfulness of the world and one's sense of self-worth in relation to perception of the environment (Janoff-Bulman, 1979). Specifically, these assumptions are: (1) that one's environment is physically and psychologically safe; (2) that events are predictable, meaningful and fair; (3) that one's own sense of self-worth is positive in relation to experiences with other people and events.

4. Victim Coping Strategies. Reducing psychological stress to tolerable limits, improving self-image and achieving a realistic outlook on the traumatic experience are objectives many victims need to attain in becoming survivors. Overcoming the negative feelings associated with being victimized is accomplished through the use of identifiable coping strategies.

Cognitive reappraisal is coping through positively changing the perception of threat, harm, and meaning of the traumatic experience. Redefining the degree of harm experienced by comparing one's own experience with those who are less fortunate is an example. Similarly, comparing actual outcome with a "worst possible" outcome is often used. Searching to find personal spiritual meaning from the experience may be especially beneficial to positive coping. However, the challenge of growth can be misconstrued as God's punishment for individual sins committed by otherwise well-meaning members of the social support network. Such blame of the victim can serve to intensify already existing feelings of self-blame.

Characterologic self-blame occurs when the individual attributes victimization to personality (e.g., "I was a careless person"), focused on a past, unchangeable, timeframe. A more positive form of coping occurs through the use of *behavioral self-blame* which focuses upon specific precautionary behaviors to be taken in the future (Janoff-Bulman, 1979).

If the overall task of the victim is to reorganize or rebuild shattered life assumptions, then the role of family, friends, and lay or professional helpers is to provide positive social support during the process. The most important assistance is to be available to *listen* as the victim talks about the traumatic event. The need for emotional expression of depression, sadness, and anger may continue for several months. Support can also be provided by giving assistance in problem solving—for example, filing insurance claims and applying for federal disaster relief funds—and victims can be supported as they deal with their fears of being victimized again. This could mean accompanying the individual during return visits to the trauma site or realistic discussion of additional precautionary measures to be taken in the future.

Bibliography. A. Baum, R. Fleming, and J. E. Singer, "Coping with Victimization by Technological Disaster," *J. of Social Issues*, 39 (1983), 117–38. D. W. Foy, R. C. Sipprelle, D. B. Rueger, and E. M. Carroll, "Etiology of Posttraumatic Stress Disorder in Vietnam Veterans: Analysis of Premilitary, Military and Combat Exposure Influences," *J. of Counseling and Clinical Psychology*, 52 (1984), 79–87. I. H. Frieze, S. Hymers, and M. S. Greenberg, "Describing the Crime Victim: Psychological Reactions to Victimization," *Professional Psychology: Research and Practice*, 18 (1987), 299–315. R. Janoff-Bulman, "Characterological Versus Behavioral Self-blame: Inquiries into Depression and Rape," *J. of Personality and Social Psychology*, 37 (1979), 1798–1809. R. J. Lifton, *Death in Life* (1976); *The Broken Connection* (1979), esp. ch. 21. A. F. C. Wallace, "Tornado in Worcester: An explanatory study of individual and community behavior in an extreme situation," National Academy of Sciences Publication, 392 (1956).

D. W. FOY

HOLOCAUST. *See also* DISASTER, PUBLIC; RAPE AND RAPE COUNSELING; VICTIMIZATION. *Compare* POST-TRAUMATIC STRESS DISORDER.

SUSPICIOUSNESS AND PARANOIA.

Suspiciousness is the characteristic of suspecting guilt in or harmfulness from others with little or no supporting evidence. Paranoia is most appropriately understood as a mental disorder characterized by extreme suspiciousness and delusions of persecution, but in popular usage the adjectival form, "paranoid," is often used as a hyperbolic way of describing one's distrust of a person or situation, as in the phrase, "I'm paranoid about _____."

1. Suspiciousness and Paranoia as Symptom and Category of Mental Illness. In the current manual for psychiatric diagnosis (DSM III-R, 1987), suspiciousness is one of the features commonly associated with the paranoid conditions: paranoid personality disorder, paranoid disorder, and schizophrenia, paranoid type. A paranoid personality disorder is judged to be present when a person inflexibly and maladaptively exhibits pervasive and unwarranted suspiciousness and mistrust, hypersensitivity and restricted affect, but with no delusions or hallucinations. A paranoid disorder is characterized by an unshakable delusional system, but with no disorder of thought. In schizophrenia, paranoid type, there are delusions and hallucinations as in the paranoid disorder, but they are accompanied by significant deterioration from a previous level of function along with disorganization of thought and inappropriateness of affect.

2. Suspiciousness and Paranoia as Characteristics of the Human Condition. Although suspiciousness and paranoia are important indicators of mental illness, they also provide a more general insight into the nature of the human condition. Harold Searles (1965) describes suspicious persons as unable to let themselves experience their feelings spontaneously, managing instead only to search for the "why" of anything that happens. Things must be slowed down, controlled and explained rather than experienced and trusted. Persons who defend themselves against the uncertainty of life in this way severely constrict the type of life that they are able to live.

A more recent theorist, W. W. Meissner (1978), notes that whether in its pathological forms or in its more acceptable and adaptive forms, the paranoid construction of a person's world provides a context in which an individual can find some sense of purpose and belonging. Paranoid projections serve as a means of removing from the person's sense of self elements which are intolerable, repulsive or excessively painful. These elements are driven out of consciousness and divorced from their sense of self, externalized and attributed to others. All of this serves to sustain the individual's sense of himself or herself as a persecuted victim.

The psychological theorist whose work presents the paranoid condition not only as pathology but as a central feature in life and development is Melanie Klein. Klein viewed what she called the "paranoid-schizoid" position as the infant's first attempt to organize experience. The paranoid-schizoid world of the infant is a nonreflective state of being in which thoughts and feelings are not personal creations, but, simply, events that happen. One's symbols are identical with what they stand for. The infant in this position does not interpret experience, but reacts to it, splitting off that which he or she is unwilling or unable to experience in the self. This is not pathology but a necessary process which establishes discontinuity between loved and feared aspects of self and others and without which the infant could not feed safely and would die.

Klein's other major "position" or state of being is the depressive position. As Thomas H. Ogden interprets the relation between the two, one does not "leave the paranoid-schizoid position behind at the 'threshold' of the depressive position; rather, one establishes more or less successfully a dialectical relationship between the two, a relationship in which each state creates, preserves, and negates the other, just as the conscious and unconscious mind do in Freud's topographic model" (1986, p. 67).

In the paranoid-schizoid position sadness is simply not a part of one's emotional vocabulary. The omnipotence of that position allows for everything to be "taken back" when a new emotional state is entered. The "depression" of the depressive position is a feeling of sadness that, in fact, one's omnipotence is not real. History cannot be rewritten. Feelings of loss, guilt, sadness, remorse, compassion, empathy, and loneliness are all burdens that are unavoidable. One does not overcome the depressive position; it is a realistic orientation to life as it is.

3. Suspiciousness and Paranoia as a Message to be Understood and Addressed by the Pastor. It is appropriate to think of a pastoral response to suspiciousness and paranoia as twofold. First, the pastor needs to be able to recognize them as possibly indicative of serious mental illness. The lack of ability to put oneself in another's place, unusually rigid definition of all problem situations as external, blamable on someone else, and the

inability of the parishioner to share himself or herself with the pastor in any emotional way except, perhaps, with suppressed rage, all point in the direction of mental illness. If these signs are accompanied by delusions and obvious disorder of thought and flatness of affect, they suggest that the most important pastoral responsibility is to work with the parishioner's family or other responsible persons to seek psychiatric treatment and, possibly, hospitalization.

Second, a pastor can also view suspiciousness and paranoia as useful indicators of the human pain of life, a temporary regression from the depressive position and its painful realism. When the pastor finds himself or herself talking frequently about what "they" are doing to ruin the church or how the church hierarchy has consistently been unfair, this may be the sign that he or she is lacking in significant relationships and should seek one or more of them to help overcome the separation he or she feels. In response to a parishioner or counselee, rigidity, literal-mindedness, separation into a clear-cut good guys and bad guys view of life, all may indicate a temporary regression to a paranoid position. The pastor's response to this is to offer a significant relationship which can help the parishioner or counselee risk moving to a more relational position in life.

Bibliography. American Psychiatric Association, *Diagnostic and Statistical Manual of Mental Disorders, III-R* (1987). F. Flach, ed., *Diagnostics and Psychopathology* (1987). W. W. Meissner, *The Paranoid Process* (1978). T. H. Ogden, *The Matrix of the Mind* (1986). H. F. Searles, *Collected Papers on Schizophrenia and Related Subjects* (1965). Segal, *Klein: Theories and Techniques of the Pioneer of Child Analysis* (1979).

J. PATTON

ANXIETY; FEAR; NEUROSIS; PSYCHOSIS. *See also* EVALUATION AND DIAGNOSIS, PSYCHOLOGICAL; PSYCHOPATHOLOGY, THEORIES OF.

SUSTAINING. *See* COMFORT/SUSTAINING.

SWEARING. *See* PROFANITY; VOWS/VOWING.

SYMBOL, PERSONAL. *See* PERSONAL STORY, SYMBOL, AND MYTH.

SYMBOLIC BEHAVIORISM. *See* BEHAVIORISM.

SYMBOLIC COMMUNICATION. *See* COMMUNICATION; SYMBOLIC DIMENSIONS OF PASTORAL CARE RELATIONSHIPS; SYMBOLISM/SYMBOLIZING.

SYMBOLIC DIMENSIONS OF PASTORAL CARE RELATIONSHIPS. Clergy role responsibility mixes explicit, conscious representations of God and the community of believers with implicit, nonconscious presentations of the meaning and means of life (Frank, 1973) or the dimension of depth (Tillich, 1959).
1. Psychological Dimensions. In the face of finitude, the clergyperson serves as an ambiguous attachment figure (Reed, 1978) onto whom people project their deepest longings and anxieties and from whom they derive images of order and form to transform confusion and

chaos (Holmes, 1978). These anxieties and longings, and the expectations of order and form, often reflect immature assumptions about an all-knowing, ever-loving, infallible, protective authority or an all-powerful, always-vigilant, invincible moral authority. However, they may also express more mature expectations of the pastor as symbol-bearer. These more mature expectations are distinguished by the way in which they simultaneously express the contradictions, paradoxes, and ambiguities of life while drawing these divergent themes together into a vital unity that renews the meaningfulness of the whole. Thus the pastoral role at deep levels of intuition and perception may symbolize nature's ageless rhythms (e.g., Eccl. 3:1–8) side by side with the salvific inbreaking of the Transcendent into nature and history (Exodus, Kingdom of God, Easter, Pentecost).

2. Pastoral Dimensions. Every pastor can recount incidents in which he or she was the object — or target — of such deeply felt, contradictory, nonrational expectations, mature or immature, conscious or unconscious. Such expectations powerfully shape pastoral relationships and may function as an obstacle and hindrance or as a rich opportunity for personal ministry (or both), depending largely on the pastor's own maturity, discernment, and skill in allowing his or her own "person" to serve as a bearer of symbolic meaning.

This task is especially complex when the nonconscious, symbolic forces are conflicted or under stress. They may then distort or undermine conscious, rational thought and action, triggering fight-or-flight panic (essentially a turning to oneself for control) or hostile demandingness, anger, and guilt toward perceived authority (turning to others for control; see Colman and Bexton, 1975). Insofar as such conflicts can be resolved, or insofar as the unconscious symbolic forces are unconflicted to begin with (Ullanovs, 1975), pastoral care relationships, precisely because of their symbolic character, are able to call forth deep expressions of the courage to be as oneself, that is, authentic individuality, and the courage to be as a part, that is, dependency on life-giving (and threatening) forces that one can neither control nor contain (Tillich, 1959). Such movements of the human spirit can also have profound healing effects (Frank).

3. Religious Meanings. As symbolic bearers of God, clergy have a unique opportunity to help their parishioners and counselees transform immediate contexts of limitation—the ordinariness and struggle of everyday life — into larger contexts of potentiality, that is, a widened sense of what is real and what is possible and a deepened sense of the universal in the particular. This requires artful, discerning attempts to bring rational, conscious reflection (e.g., on moral issues; see Browning, 1976) into the arena of the church's symbolic life, clarifying and critiquing symbolic meanings, while at the same time allowing the numinous depth of the symbols themselves — the Bible, the cross, the special language of liturgy and faith, even the church building and the clerical collar — to open up, deepen, nourish, and transfigure everyday meanings and liberate deeper healing and saving forces.

Because historical expressions overlie transhistorical content, the symbolic dimensions present a "threshold" presence between divinity and humanity that eludes explanation (Eliade, 1964; Turner, 1969). In the pastoral figure people can experience those images of meaning that illumine darkness, restore hope, clarify distortions, and remind them of righteousness, that is, the whole-making dimension of depth within every person.

Bibliography. D. Browning, *The Moral Context of Pastoral Care* (1976). A. D. Colman and W. H. Bexton, eds., *Group Relations Reader* (1975). M. Eliade, *Shamanism* (1964). J. D. Frank, *Persuasion and Healing*, rev. ed. (1973). S. Hiltner and L. Colston, *The Context of Pastoral Counseling* (1961). U. T. Holmes, *The Priest in Community* (1978). B. Reed, *The Dynamics of Religion* (1978). P. Tillich, *Theology of Culture* (1959), pp. 3–9; *The Courage to Be* (1952). V. W. Turner, *The Ritual Process* (1969). A. Ullanov and B. Ullanov, *Religion and the Unconscious* (1975).

J. B. ASHBROOK

INCARNATIONAL PASTORAL CARE; PASTOR (Normative and Traditional Images *or* Stereotypes and Caricatures); PRESENCE, MINISTRY OF; SYMBOLISM/SYMBOLIZING. *See also* The HOLY; INTERPRETATION AND HERMENEUTICS, PASTORAL; PERSONAL STORY, SYMBOL, AND MYTH IN PASTORAL CARE; PERSONHOOD OF THE PASTOR, SIGNIFICANCE OF; RELIGION; The UNCONSCIOUS. *Compare* RELIGIOUS LANGUAGE IN PASTORAL CARE; SECULARIZATION/SECULARISM; SILENCE; TECHNIQUE AND SKILL IN PASTORAL CARE.

SYMBOLISM/SYMBOLIZING. Symbol may be defined as a double-meaning expression, linguistic or visual, requiring an interpretation. Symbols are a special kind of sign that include a second level of meaning in addition to the primary, literal meaning. This definition is based on that of Paul Ricoeur and it is the fruit of a long debate over the meaning of "symbol" and the role of symbolizing in human thought. Langer's *Philosophy in a New Key* holds that "symbol" is indeed the key to twentieth-century reflection. This essay discusses the philosophical concept of symbol, two psychological approaches to symbols, and the concept's religious significance.

1. The Nature of Symbols. The issue of symbolism arose early in the twentieth century among theorists of culture. In a positivist worldview, all language was either an accurate duplication of nonlinguistic reality, or superstitious, fanciful, and erroneous. But in an epistemological shift, this fanciful and emotionally loaded language was perceived to have its own kind of reality, objectivity, and proper scope. The concept of "symbol" became a tool to clarify this reality.

Ordinary language depends on a relation between the signifier and the thing signified. There is the concept "water," the substance itself, and the words for "water" in various languages. These are all involved in the primary, literal meaning of "water." But the concept "water" also evokes a number of additional meanings, concerned with birth and purification. These are not erroneous confusions, but symbolic elaborations expressive of a second level of significance. Myth, ritual, and art centered around water depend on such second-level meanings. These are not, therefore, to be dismissed as childish, meaningless, or unscientific. They depend on a use of language different from that of science but equally valid. Although intense debate has raged over the exact relations among concept, word, and thing signified, and over the separability of primary and second-level meanings, the topic is clearly of central importance to religion.

A second element in the definition is "interpretation." A naive realist asks whether a concept held corresponds to some entity in the real world. This is inappropriate if one wishes to understand symbolism. "How do we interpret this symbol?" means "To what second-level meanings does it refer?" The unicorn never existed as a zoological specimen, but as a symbol it was rich in meanings for medieval Europeans. Symbols belong to culture and are vulnerable to cultural changes: they are often said to "decay" or "die" as they lose their meanings over time.

2. **Psychologies of Symbols.** *a. The psychology of unmasking.* Because the question of interpretation is so crucial, we follow Ricoeur in classifying psychologies according to their interpretive style. Freud believed that interpretation should be an unmasking. In his view of dreams, the remembered, manifest dream-images serve as disguises for the real, latent, repressed dream-thoughts. The primary meaning is a false screen which hides the second-level meaning. The latter is so unacceptable to the conscious mind that symbolization must occur in order to defend oneself against it. The interpreter must be suspicious of manifest meanings and undo the defensive distortions of the symbolizing process.

This view of symbolism as calling for a "hermeneutic of suspicion" (Ricoeur), also influences the Freudian view of the therapeutic situation, where the goal is to gain insight into repressed psychic contents. The role of the therapist, through the concept of "transference," is in part to serve as a symbol for the patient's hidden attitudes toward parental figures. Yet unmasking interpretations always raise questions about the degree to which the interpreter imposes his or her meanings onto the symbol. The experiencer's perspective is often devalued, insofar as the defensive function of symbolism is stressed.

b. Restorative psychologies. The alternative to an unmasking interpretation is one which seeks to restore the fullness of the symbol's multiplicity of meanings. These are not assumed to be disguised or distorted through the appearance of the symbol. In psychology, the best example of such an approach is that of C. G. Jung. In Jungian theory, the latent dream-content is not at war with the manifest content. Interpretation proceeds through "amplification" of the experiencer's images, by means of mythological and other collective associations. The patient is encouraged to view his or her own symbolizing in the context of myth-making. A numinous, powerful dream-image of a tree is not a disguise for some personally unacceptable repressed psychic content, but expressive of the same mystery and wholeness conveyed by the cosmic trees of mythology and religion (i.e., Yggdrasil, the Cross). The goal of interpretation is to restore those levels of meaning lost to a rationalistic and literal-minded culture.

In this view, the symbolizing process is a natural and spontaneous function of the psyche. Without it, we would be unable to apprehend or respond to the depth, complexity, and beauty of the universe. Although symbols can be used defensively, this is not their primary function. Many non-Jungians and non-psychologists share this view of symbols. Neo-Freudian Robert J. Lifton and anthropologist Mary Douglas are examples of many non-Jungian theorists who give priority to the constructive and positive aspects of symbolization. Yet restorative interpretations are vulnerable to the same criticism leveled at the suspicious mode. The interpreter may impose a particular scheme of "amplifications" upon the experiencer's own symbols.

Some exponents of restorative interpretations assert that they are uncovering primordial, universal patterns of symbolism, rather than imposing meanings. This idea of a storehouse of symbolic meanings to which the interpretation gives access has been held by Jung and, in phenomenology of religion, by Mircea Eliade. These universal patterns, or "archetypes," are among the more debatable points in the entire study of symbolism.

3. **Religious Significance of the Concept of "Symbol."** The philosophical reformulation described in (1) above greatly changed traditional views about the function of religious language and its truth. An emphasis on symbolic meanings gives priority to worship and storytelling over abstract theological formulation—a shift that has prompted renewed interest in liturgy among both Protestants and Roman Catholics.

Calling religious language essentially "symbolic," however, raises many questions. Unmasking interpretations would claim that all symbolism is a disguise for unacceptable truth, a claim defenders of religion vigorously reject. But to assert, as restorative interpreters sometimes do, that all symbols are automatically "valid," is just as dubious. The most destructive twentieth-century ideologies have also relied on symbols for their impact, often in a blatantly manipulative fashion. The question of how one can distinguish between "authentic" and "idolatrous" uses of symbols is pursued by theologians Paul Tillich, Owen Barfield, and others.

Moreover, intrinsic to the construct of "symbol" is a sense of symbolism's cultural relativity. Symbols, as cultural creations, are vulnerable to historical change. Liberation theologians, feminists, and others have addressed this issue, hoping to free faith from its dead symbols. Yet most advocates of this approach to religious language grant that because symbols draw on those deeper levels of the psyche least amenable to rational control, it is difficult deliberately to replace one set of symbols with another. Another expression of this basic issue arises in rethinking relations among the world's faiths. Those who utilize "symbol" as a key construct find pervasive similarities among the major religious traditions, and stress these, often at the risk of overlooking basic theological differences.

Counselors working within their particular traditions, and aware of the cultural relativity of their symbols must attend to the intersection between the counselee's own private set of self-generated symbols and those normative within their religious tradition. The problems of granting validity and of distinguishing "authentic" symbols remain a central concern; and the task appears to require a synthesis of unmasking and restorative interpretations.

Bibliography. O. Barfield, *Saving the Appearances: A Study in Idolatry* (1965). M. Daly, *Beyond God the Father* (1973).

M. Douglas, *Purity and Danger* (1966); *Natural Symbols* (1970). M. Eliade, *Patterns of Comparative Religion* (1963). S. Freud, *The Interpretation of Dreams*, SE 4, (1958 [1900]); *Totem and Taboo*, SE 13, ([1912]). C. G. Jung, *Symbols of Transformation, Collected Works* 5, 2d ed. (1970); *Man and His Symbols* (1964); *Psychology and Religion: West and East, Collected Works* 11, 2d ed. (1969). S. Langer, *Philosophy in a New Key* (1960 [1942]). R. J. Lifton, *The Broken Connection* (1979). P. Ricoeur, *Freud and Philosophy* (1970); *The Symbolism of Evil* (1967); *The Conflict of Interpretations* (1974). D. Sperber, *Rethinking Symbolism* (1975). P. Tillich, *Dynamics of Faith* (1957).

L. BREGMAN

PERSONAL STORY, SYMBOL, AND MYTH IN PASTORAL CARE; RELIGIOUS LANGUAGE AND SYMBOLISM, PSYCHOLOGY OF. *See also* ANALYTICAL (JUNGIAN) PSYCHOLOGY AND RELIGION; COMMUNICATION; DREAM THEORY AND RESEARCH; INTERPRETATION AND HERMENEUTICS, PASTORAL; PSYCHEDELIC DRUGS AND EXPERIENCE; PSYCHOANALYSIS AND RELIGION. *Compare* PSYCHOLINGUISTIC THEORY IN PSYCHOLOGY AND COUNSELING; RITUAL AND PASTORAL CARE; SACRAMENTAL THEOLOGY AND PASTORAL CARE.

SYMPATHY. *See* COMFORT/SUSTAINING; COMPASSION; EMPATHY.

SYMPTOM/SYMPTOMS. *See* EVALUATION AND DIAGNOSIS, PSYCHOLOGICAL; HEALTH AND ILLNESS; PSYCHOPATHOLOGY, THEORIES OF.

SYNAGOGUE. *See* JEWISH CARE AND COUNSELING. *See also* COMMUNITY, FELLOWSHIP, AND CARE; CONGREGATION, PASTORAL CARE OF.

SYPHILIS. A chronic or acute disease spread primarily by sexual contact and caused by *Treponema palidum*. The early localized lesions are called chancres. The advanced stages of syphilis involve destructive changes in the central nervous system and cardiovascular system. Syphilis can be effectively treated with antibiotics.

D. THOMAS

SEX EDUCATION. *Compare* NEUROLOGIC ILLNESSES.

SYRIAN ORTHODOXY. *See* MINISTRY AND PASTORAL CARE (Orthodox Tradition).

SYSTEMATIC DESENSITIZATION. A behavior therapy for the treatment of phobias usually involving a graded list of situations providing closer and closer contact with the feared object (the anxiety hierarchy) combined with training in muscle relaxation. The patient imagines an item from the anxiety hierarchy and then relaxes. This decreases the fear and allows the patient to move to progressively more threatening items.

D. G. BENNER

BEHAVIOR THERAPIES (Methods and Research); CONDITIONING.

SYSTEMS THEORY. "A set of elements standing in interaction" (von Bertalanffy, 1969), the combination of parts to form a whole, which work together for the good of the whole.

(1) An example for mechanical systems is a pump, made up of cylinder, piston, and valves which are connected to a pipe and some lever or engine to provide power. The various parts work together to draw water from a well.

(2) An example for a physiological system is the animal circulatory system, made up of a pump (muscle of heart, nerves, and pipes — arteries and veins) which work together to circulate blood throughout the body. The circulatory is one of several systems within the animal's body which interact for the smooth functioning of the whole.

(3) The psychological system consists of the parts of the human psyche which function together for the good of the whole person. Murray Bowen (1978) explains that the human being's psyche is made up of an emotional system which is shared with other animals, the intellectual system which sets him or her apart because of a highly developed cerebral cortex, and the feeling system, the bridge between the two. To become mature and differentiated is to become more in control of one's life and less dependent upon the authorities of childhood and adolescence. M. Rokeach (1960), a social psychologist, has demonstrated how the psyche as a system may be open or closed and the consequences for interpersonal as well as institutional relationships.

(4) The social system is a particular form of societal organization in which members band together, giving up certain individual privileges so as to benefit from the power of the group to satisfy social needs. Examples are the family system, the work system, the school system, the church, city, state, and nation.

(5) A philosophical and theological system is an organized set of presuppositions, methods, principles, doctrines and/or beliefs, meant to explain the functioning of a universe. Examples are the doctrine of God, the doctrine of salvation through the cross of Christ, the theory of good and evil.

Family systems theory and therapy have brought ministers an awareness of systems thinking. Early systems theorists — Gregory Bateson (1978), Don Jackson (1978), Virginia Satir (1967) — placed the emphasis on communication between family members. Verbal and nonverbal feedback, homeostasis (the tendency of the family system to seek balance), and the identified patient (the family's projection of guilt on a family scapegoat) were early emphases. Later systems theorists — Murray Bowen (1978), Salvadore Minuchin (1976), and the Milan School — emphasized the structure of the family, multi-generational transmission of emotional process, and strategic or paradoxical intervention into family process.

E. M. Pattison (1972; 1977) has detailed the implications of general systems theory for pastoral care and for parish-based pastoral functioning. In practical terms, general systems notions stress the importance of the pastor in visiting the individual parishioner in family, school, and work contexts. In appraising problems, the pastor should interview the troubled person with other significant persons in his or her life, i.e., spouse, children, parents, or working colleagues.

Rather than attempting linear analysis of cause and effect, the pastor observes interactions, communication channels, authority patterns. The pastor involves himself or herself directly in the social system and intervenes actively to introduce change. The pastor reflects upon situations theologically to guide the parishioner to see his or her life as a whole, and as within God's purpose.

Bibliography. G. Bateson, D. Jackson, J. Haley, and J. Weakland, "Toward a Theory of Schizophrenia," in M. M. Berger, ed., *Beyond the Double Bind* (1978). L. von Bertalanffy, *General Systems Theory: Essays on Its Foundation and Development* (1969). M. Bowen, *Family Therapy in Clinical Practice* (1978). L. Hoffman, *Foundations of Family Therapy* (1981). S. Minuchin, *et al.,* *Problem Solving Therapy* (1976). E. M. Pattison, *Pastor and Parish—A Systems Approach* (1977); "Systems Pastoral Care," *J. of Pastoral Care,* 26 (1972), 2–14. M. Rokeach, *The Open and Closed Mind* (1960). V. Satir, *Conjoint Family Therapy: A Guide to Theory and Technique* (1967); *Peoplemaking* (1972).

C. W. STEWART

CONGREGATION, PASTORAL CARE OF; FAMILY THEORY AND THERAPY. *Compare* CYBERNETIC THEORY IN PSYCHOLOGY (Principles, Applications, and Issues); HOMEOSTASIS; THEORY AND PRAXIS.

T

TABERNACLES. *See* JEWISH HOLY DAYS AND FESTIVALS.

TALMUD. *See* JEWISH CARE AND COUNSELING; JEWISH LITERATURE IN CARE AND COUNSELING.

TAOIST SOUL CARE. *See* PSYCHOLOGY, EASTERN; PSYCHOLOGY AND PSYCHOTHERAPY (East-West Comparison).

TAT (Thematic Apperception Test). *See* EVALUATION AND DIAGNOSIS, PSYCHOLOGICAL; MURRAY, Henry.

TAYLOR, CHARLES. *See* CANADIAN PASTORAL CARE MOVEMENT.

TAYLOR, JEREMY (1613–67). English bishop, royal chaplain, and theologian. Taylor influenced seventeenth- and eighteenth-century conceptions of pastoral topics especially through the publication of his *Holy Living* (1650) and *Holy Dying* (1651). His books encouraged an intense devotional life marked by the "practice" of the presence of God and helped to inaugurate a tradition of piety designated by the phrase "holy living." As a theologian, Taylor was critical of High Calvinism, which he deemed incompatible with the pastoral task of engendering and sustaining piety. He objected to the view that God's justifying grace produced no alteration of the internal temper and dispositions of the Christian.

After serving as a chaplain to Archbishop William Laud and to King Charles I, he suffered imprisonment in Wales, during which time he wrote his pastoral works. At the Restoration in 1660, Charles II named him a bishop in Ireland. His pastoral writings continued to influence Anglican piety throughout the eighteenth century.

E. B. HOLIFIELD

ANGLICAN PASTORAL CARE.

TEACHER, PASTOR AS. *See* EDUCATION, NURTURE, AND CARE; PASTOR (Normative and Traditional Images); TEACHING.

TEACHING. Under the impact of Clinical Pastoral Education (CPE), teaching in the parish from a pastoral perspective takes into account persons as well as content. Like the best in Christian education (Groome; Nelson; cf. Oden), pastoral teaching involves "making sense" of what is happening to people in specific situations. It gives cognitive focus to personal experience by drawing upon the resources of faith and belief. In short, proclamations about "truth" emerge from and are shaped by manifestations of "meaning."

How something is learned, when it is learned, with whom it is learned, and for what purpose it is learned are as basic as what is learned. Knowledge for its own sake is secondary. The process by which teaching occurs and the situations that call forth the necessity of understanding are primary.

1. **How?** Methods of pastoral teaching are related integrally to content embedded within specific contexts. Clinical Pastoral Education was born in and nurtured by immediate involvement in concrete situations. Reflection, analysis, and action follow from the precipitating experiences.

a. Concrete situations. "Living human documents" was Boisen's focus, even as the medical setting was Cabot's and the social agency was Keller's (Thornton). Detailed case reports and verbatims provided the basic data from which meaning was drawn and to which understanding was directed (*J. of Pastoral Care*, 1975). In line with experiential education (à la John Dewey), pastoral teaching encourages people to struggle with who they are and what life means. Through face-to-face encounters they explore immediate experience. Such teaching is shaped by leading questions, for example, "What is going on here?" "What is triggered off or awakened in you by this situation?" "What are you experiencing?"

b. Reflective exploration. Both enlarges and deepens what is presented. Pastoral teaching amplifies the experience by discovering parallel or similar associations. Contrasts and comparisons quicken a perspective without deserting the primary concern. The use of metaphorical language opens many levels of meaning and holds paradoxical ideas together (Watzlawick). As people elaborate their experience, they discover more reality than they initially discerned. In this mode the teaching develops through reflective questioning, e.g., "What feelings, thoughts, and fantasies do you have about this situation?" "What biblical images, stories, or sayings come to mind" (cf. Wingeier)? "Are there theological themes awakened by this event" (cf. Capps)? "What similar situations have you struggled with?"

c. Analytic refinement. Carries conceptual formulations to another level of significance. Beyond the sharing of personal reflections lies a wealth of accumulated knowledge. Pastoral teaching identifies cognitive structures. These organize the rich data of understood experience. Theological and theoretical ideas are now linked with basic human conditions. Truths and situations are juxtaposed in dynamic equilibrium (Hiltner, 1972; Tillich; Tracy). The explanations or "naming" (Gen. 2:19–20a) bring order out of chaos. However, analytic questions abound, for example, "Are there pieces missing in what we have considered?" "How do the seeming contradictions hold together?" "What are the relationships among the parts?" "How does knowledge of human development, personality dynamics, patterns of belief, and theology add to your grasp of this situation?" "What ideas or clues are suggested here that might apply in other situations?"

d. Applied action. The final step is "doing the truth." Pastoral teaching moves from disclosing what is, to amplifying what it means, to crystallizing how it matters, to declaring "what is to be done" (Mt. 7:21–22). Cognitive structure provides a rationale for new behavior and new experience (Frank). And here questions shift from abstract generalizations to specific actions. "Based on what you know, what options do you have?" "What can you do now?" "How will you go about it?"

2. When. Normal developmental stages and disruptive crises provide opportunities for pastoral teaching. Intensified experience calls for making sense of the meaning of life existentially (Kierkegaard). These are the ripe moments, those rich *kairoi*, pregnant with possibility. Pastoral teaching connects what confronts people with what life has meant through the ages and can mean in the present, that is, the two classical shapes of religious expression, namely, manifestations of God's presence and proclamations of God's purposes (Tracy).

a. Life cycle transitions represent the normal changes and primary events of birth and death, commitments and convictions, maturing and mastering, and belonging and becoming, which are the core of our human journey (Erikson; Fowler; Gilligan; Gould; Lowenthal; Wright).

Giving birth and parenting offer special expectancy about the manifestation of mystery. A pastor can meet with a couple or with groups to sort through the hopes and fears of nurturing the bearers of the future. What does a child mean in terms of lifestyles, priorities, relationships? To ask parents why they "bother" to bring their child for baptism (or parent dedication) is to open up the many meanings of belonging to the "household of faith."

To explore confirmation (or adult baptism) with adolescents, who are seeking identity through larger devotion, requires dealing with paradox. How do they deal with their family of origin (Mt. 10:34–39)? Where do they give themselves unconditionally?

To explore with a couple about to be married the necessity of leaving parents to cleave to one another (Gen. 2:24) focuses on their task of differentiating themselves. How do they take their parents seriously (Exod. 21:12), and extend their own identification with the whole family of God (Mk. 3:31–33)?

The ritualizations of the life cycle present the ripest occasions for pastoral teaching. They are sacramental in transmitting what is essentially human (Worgul), reinforcing and celebrating meaningfulness.

b. Life-crisis disruptions. Normal patterns invariably are transformed by unexpected disruption. These events call into question the meanings with which people have managed to live (Gerkin). Loss, however it appears, attacks one's sense of self and undermines one's capacity to cope. Life's painful passages cry out for understanding.

In the midst of tragedy pastoral teaching activates the reassuring rhythms of ritual (cf. Ps. 23; d'Aquili and Laughlin). This holds people until the subsequent work of guiding, to use a perspective of Hiltner's (1958), permits the pastor to participate in the suffering of others in ways that allow the meaning of their soul's agony to show itself. In such disruptions pastoral teaching permits nothing to be wasted. Everything can contribute to people's becoming *if* they can trust in ways that draw upon the providential, saving purposiveness of God (Rom. 8:28). Personal experience eventually flows into universal experience. The parish itself constitutes a place of agony and ecstasy within which people learn to transform pain into promise (Ashbrook, 1971).

3. With Whom. While "everyone is much more simply human than otherwise" (Sullivan), people differ in ways that affect the teaching and learning process. These differences are as important for education as they are for therapy.

a. Personality patterns. Take account of what a person brings, that is, motivations, personality types, and value orientations.

i. Motivational dynamics (d'Ydewalle and Lens) include instinctual drives and interactional defenses, purposive striving and power relationships. To the degree the non-rational forces are conflicted, to that degree pastoral therapy is more appropriate than pastoral teaching (Murphy).

ii. Personality types, as conceptualized by Jung (cf. Keirsey and Bates), contrast ways by which people become aware of the world and come to conclusions about the world. Some understand through what they receive through their five senses, while others bring their own intuition. Some arrive at conclusions based upon logical thought, while others decide whether something is personally meaningful. Some keep life expanding with possibilities, while others mobilize resources to get specific tasks accomplished.

iii. Value orientations, reflective of social class constraints, sharpen the perceived world in which people live. What they say (ideas) and do (interactions) have been represented on a series of continua: (a) activity (flux and change) and passivity (stability and security); (b) rationalism (order and logic) and traditionalism (pragmatic and traditional); (c) universalism (equality) and particularism (personalized); (d) individualism ("I" and primary group ("us"); and (e) the future (planning and change) and the present (immediate and tangible). Lundberg (1974) demonstrated that there is a systematic and positive relationship between personality development and social class position, with lower-class people developing more slowly and less completely than middle-class people. Some educators counter the social class argument with testimony to the richness of soul which comes from (for example) black expressiveness (Pasteur and Toldson) or the empowerment of victims which comes from "the pedagogy of the oppressed" (Freire).

b. Educational patterns. These are as much a consideration in pastoral teaching as in Christian education. The concern is cognitive clarity, a recognition of the importance of conceptual frameworks for understanding, naming, and interpreting experience (Ashbrook, 1975).

i. Learning styles. People learn differently (Kolb, Rubin, and McIntyre; Knowles). Perhaps a minority are oriented to a formal-conceptual style. They exhibit concern about accuracy, adequacy, and underlying rationale in primarily systematic ways. For them the issue is "truth." Probably more people, however, are oriented to an informal-concrete style. They are concerned about immediacy, excitement, and reality in impressionistic ways. They want to know the "meaning of things."

Each of these styles reflects varied learning processes. The formal pattern prefers analytic and common-sense learning; the informal pattern concentrates on concrete and reflective learning. Although pastoral teaching invariably begins with concrete situations, the fullest learning sequence includes all four processes: concrete, reflective, analytic, and common sense.

ii. Cerebral processing. Knowing something about the way the brain works helps the educator (Wittrock), pastoral or otherwise, to organize personality types, value orientations, and learning styles into two basic patterns: (1) an all-at-once participation in symbolic expressiveness, and (2) a one-step-at-a-time analysis of conceptual explanation. Two biblical experiences suggest images for these patterns: Moses's bush, which was not consumed (Exod. 3:1–3), evokes the experience of rich amplifications of primary data by the right brain. And Jacob's ladder with angels (ideas?) moving up and down (Gen. 28:12) implies organizing ideas in an orderly way by the left brain.

Furthermore, people use different re-presentational systems in experiencing and expressing reality (Grinder and Bandler). The major systems are seeing, hearing, and sensing. These preferences can be discerned in the ways people talk, for example, "What do you see?" "What do you hear?" "How do you feel?" Usually, one system is preferred, another is auxiliary, and a third remains neglected. But they can all be activated by various combinations of questions, for instance, "As you look at what you feel, what thoughts come to mind?"

The Bible emphasizes that people are cut off from God and one another when they "look without seeing and listen without hearing" and so sense without feeling (Mt. 13:13). Thus, pastoral teaching seeks to recover full functioning in which holistic and rational processing are activated for all three systems, as in the event of Pentecost when people saw something, heard something, and felt something (Acts 2:1–12).

Neither a wholistic approach nor a rational approach is sufficient in pastoral teaching. Both are needed. Being able to love God, neighbor, and self with all that one is (Mk. 12:29–31) requires using "both sides of the brain" (Buzan).

4. **For What Purpose?** Pastoral teaching is not the accumulation of information nor the articulation of doctrine. The cognitive task contributes to restoring a meaningfully moral context of personal and communal responsibility.

a. Personal growth. Individuals are able to transform painful or perplexing experience by renewing their minds (Rom. 12:1–2). Stones of stumbling become stepping stones or, in especially powerful events, chief cornerstones in building an edifice of the genuinely human (I Pet. 2:8). Nothing interferes with the realization of meaningfulness — not death, nor the principalities of racism, sexism, classism, and ageism — and neither life itself nor things to come (Rom. 8:31–39). Just as nothing can separate people, so everything can unite them to the love of God in Christ Jesus. All experience is salvageable in the personal growth that pastoral teaching fosters.

b. Communal enhancement. Small groups provide a unique vehicle for pastoral teaching (Clinebell; Leslie). Geared for persons in specific stages of the life cycle or for significant others affected by those stages, such groups can be structured for growth. Intimacy enriches illumination; meaning is enhanced by meeting. The special needs of parents, single adults, couples, and consciousness-raising seekers can be addressed. People learn to know life's meaning as they give and receive from one another.

c. Social witness. While pastoral teaching's primary emphasis is understanding, its intended impact is witness to the transforming power of God in individual and corporate life. Right living and right relationships require moral inquiry within a framework of commitment (Browning). In order to break through the dividing walls of hostility, a confused culture needs a vision of new humanity (Eph. 2:14–16).

5. **Manifestations of Meaningfulness.** More than the methodology and rationale of pastoral teaching, its distinctive feature seems to be the settings in which it occurs. These are moments of manifestation in which the meaning of life is on the line. Whether in the pastor's study, parishioners' homes, or institutions of accountability, the teaching task engages people immediately. Explanation clarifies experience. What has been proclaimed through the ages is made manifest in particular places, for particular people, at particular times; in short, "something which has existed since the beginning, that we have heard, and . . . seen . . . and . . . touched . . . the Word, who is life" (I John 1:1 JB).

Bibliography. Educational resources: T. Buzan, *Using Both Sides of Your Brain* (1980). T. Groome, *Christian Religious Education* (1980). S. Hauerwas, "The Gesture of a Truthful Story," *Theology Today*, 42 (1985), 181–89. M. Knowles, *The Adult Learner* (1978). D. Kolb, I. Rubin, and J. McIntyre, *Organizational Psychology* (1974). C. Nelson, *Where Faith Begins* (1967). M. Wittrock, ed., *The Human Brain* (1977).

Interpretive resources: J. Ashbrook, *Responding to Human Pain* (1975), pp. 57–61. A. Boisen, *The Exploration of the Inner World* (1962). D. S. Browning, ed., *Practical Theology* (1983). D. Capps, *Pastoral Care: A Thematic Approach* (1979). J. Frank, *Persuasion* and Healing, rev. ed. (1973). C. Gerkin, *Crisis Experience in Modern Life* (1979). S. Hiltner, *Theological Dynamics* (1972). P. Tillich, *The Dymanics of Faith* (1957); *Systematic Theology* (1951–63). D. Tracy, *The Analogical Imagination* (1981). P. Watzlawick, *The Language of Change* (1978). D. Wingeier, *Working Out Your Own Beliefs* (1980).

Developmental and personality resources: E. Erikson, *Toys and Reasons: Stages in the Ritualization of Experience* (1977). J. Fowler, *Stages of Faith* (1981). C. Gilligan, *In A Different Voice* (1982). R. Gould, *Transformations: Growth and Change in Adult Life* (1978). J. Grinder and R. Bandler, *The Structure of Magic II: A Book About Communication and Change* (1976). D. Keirsey and M. Bates, *Please Understand Me: Character and Temperament Types* (1978). S. Kierkegaard, *Fear and Trembling* and *Sickness Unto Death* (1954). M. Lowenthal, *et al.*, *Four Stages of Life: A Comparison Study of Men and Women Facing Transitions* (1975). M. Lundberg, *The Incomplete Adult: Social Class Constraints on Personality Development* (1974). J. Murphy, "Ministry to the Total Person," *J. of Pastoral Care*, 34 (1980), 235–43. J. Wright, *Erikson: Identity and Religion* (1982). G. d'Ydewalle and W. Lens, eds., *Cognition in Human Motivation and Learning* (1981).

Contextual and parish resources: E. d'Aquili and C. Laughlin, eds., *The Spectrum of Ritual* (1979). J. Ashbrook, *In Human Presence — Hope* (1971), pp. 65–83. H. Clinebell, *The People Dynamic* (1972). P. Freire, *The Pedagogy of the Oppressed* (1970). S. Hiltner, *A Preface to Pastoral Theology* (1958). R. Leslie, *Sharing Groups in the Church* (1971); "Living Issues in CPE: Dialogue," *J. of Pastoral Care*, 29 (1975), 148–56. T. Oden, *Pastoral Theology* (1983), ch. 10. A Pasteur and I. Toldson, *Roots of Soul* (1982). D. A. Phillipy, "Hearing and Doing the Word: An Integrated Approach to Bible Study in a Maximum Security Prison," *J. of Pastoral Care*, 37 (1973), 13–21. E. Thornton, *Professional Education for Ministry* (1970). G. Worgul, *From Magic to Metaphor: A Validation of the Christian Sacraments* (1980).

J. B. ASHBROOK

EDUCATION, NURTURE, AND CARE; LEARNING THEORIES; MORAL DEVELOPMENT; RELIGIOUS DEVELOPMENT. *See also* BIBLE, PASTORAL USE AND INTERPRETATION OF; BRAIN RESEARCH; CLINICAL PASTORAL PERSPECTIVE; EXPERIENTIAL THEOLOGY; FAITH DEVELOPMENT RESEARCH; IMAGINATION; INTERPRETATION AND HERMENEUTICS, PASTORAL; LIFE CYCLE THEORY AND PASTORAL CARE; ROLE PLAY; THEORY AND PRAXIS; TIMING; VALUES RESEARCH. *Compare* COGNITIVE PSYCHOLOGY AND PSYCHOTHERAPY; EVANGELIZING; PREACHING; REASON AND RATIONALITY IN PASTORAL CARE; RITUAL AND PASTORAL CARE; SUPERVISION; VALUES CLARIFICATION.

TEAM MINISTRIES. *See* INTERPROFESSIONAL TEAMS AND RELATIONSHIPS; MULTIPLE STAFF MINISTRIES AND RELATIONSHIPS; ROMAN CATHOLIC PASTORAL CARE.

TECHNIQUE AND SKILL IN PASTORAL CARE.

The methods or procedures employed in carrying out the work of the minister and /or the ministering community, as distinguished from the theory that guides and informs it. The ability to utilize specific techniques is skill, which can be developed through training, practice, and experience.

1. The Problem. In contemporary pastoral care and counseling technique and skill present an important, largely unresolved issue. For while there are specific techniques that can be learned, the church has historically sensed that care and counseling require qualities of faith, integrity, and wisdom in the pastor that exceed any mere application of technique. The pastoral care movement has added to this tradition the view that pastoral care and counseling also require psychological qualities of selfhood and capacities for interpersonal relationship which cannot be reduced entirely to the exercise of technique. The issue is therefore how the learnable methods of pastoral care and counseling are related to these crucial intangibles of faith, integrity, wisdom, selfhood, and interpersonal relationship.

Historically, pastoral technique varies widely and appears, in any given age, to be a direct expression of the dominant philosophical, theological and psychological systems of the culture (cf. Clebsch and Jaekle; Holifield; McNeill). This connection points to the integral relation between technique and theory (whether recognized by practitioners in given situations or not), and makes it difficult to argue that there ought to be a single universal set of techniques for all pastors.

2. Two Orientations. Jay Haley offers a description of the problem of technique and skill in psychotherapy that may be helpful in understanding the related problem in pastoral care and counseling. Haley contrasts two fundamentally different understandings of technique in contemporary counseling training which he labels orientations "A" and "Z" respectively. Within orientation "A" the responsibility of change resides with the client, the goal of therapy is the development of the person, the specific development involved is self-awareness, and a fundamental issue is the personal growth of the therapist, which makes him or her a better therapist. Within orientation "Z", it is the therapist who must make plans to determine what is to happen in the interview, the goal of the therapy is to solve problems, the specific means of problem solving is the planning of new behavior, and a fundamental issue is the therapist's practice of making specific and concrete interventions that stimulate behavior change. Orientation "A" almost universally assumes the personal therapy of the counselor; orientation "Z" assumes that the therapist will become a better therapist by practice and improvement of his or her behavioral skills. Translating this into the pastoral care arena, does the pastor learn pastoral care by learning technique, or by becoming a more "whole" person?

While the issue is not neatly resolvable into one side or another, it is clear that the dominant modes of clinical education of clergy in the Association of Clinical Pastoral Education and the American Association of Pastoral Counselors have focused around the personal growth and awareness orientation characteristic of Haley's orientation "A". The value of the development of the person who is the pastor has been widely recognized as almost the condition without which effective pastoral care would not take place. The learning of specific techniques, whatever they may be as mandated by the pastor's worldview, has taken a back seat to the personal growth of the pastor, consistent with the dictum that if a person appropriately understands himself or herself, technique will naturally flow from that person.

The tensions involved in consciously linking one's technique in pastoral care with one's worldview, and between growth as a person and the learning of behavioral techniques, are tensions that will likely continue to flourish and perhaps are best left as opposing positions which stimulate creative dialogue and mutual correctiveness.

Bibliography. W. Clebsch and C. Jaekle, *Pastoral Care in Historical Perspective* (1964). J. Haley, *Problem-Solving Therapy: New Strategies for Effective Family Therapy* (1976). E. B. Holifield, *A History of Pastoral Care in America* (1983). J. McNeill, *A History of the Cure of Souls* (1951). E. Thurneysen, *A Theology of Pastoral Care* (1963). C. Wise, *The Meaning of Pastoral Care* (1966).

B. M. HARTUNG

CLINICAL PASTORAL PERSPECTIVE; PASTORAL CARE (Contemporary Methods, Perspectives, and Issues); PROBLEM SOLVING; WISDOM AND PRACTICAL KNOWLEDGE. *See also* CONSULTATION; CONVERSATION, PASTORAL; FEELING, THOUGHT, AND ACTION IN PASTORAL COUNSELING; INITIATIVE AND INTERVENTION; LIMIT-SETTING; LISTENING; PERSONAL STORY; PHENOMENOLOGICAL METHOD IN PASTORAL CARE; REASONING AND RATIONALITY IN PASTORAL CARE; REFERRAL; SILENCE; SUGGESTION, PERSUASION, AND INFLUENCE; TELEPHONE, PASTORAL USE OF; WIT AND HUMOR.

TEENAGE PREGNANCY. *See* PREGNANCY. *See also* MORAL DILEMMAS IN PASTORAL PERSPECTIVE.

TEENAGERS. *See* ADOLESCENTS.

TEKAKWITHA, KATERI. *See* WOMEN IN PASTORAL MINISTRIES, HISTORY OF.

TELEOLOGY. *See* CAUSALITY IN PSYCHOLOGY, FORMS OF.

TELEPATHY. *See* PARAPSYCHOLOGY.

TELEPHONE, PASTORAL USE OF. The telephone is becoming an increasingly sophisticated tool of pastoral communication. Presently available is the innovation of conference calling whereby more than two callers may be connected from different places, thereby expanding the conditions under which families may use pastoral counseling. For example, grandparents or children away at college may represent important dynamics in the extended family and thus be necessary members in a pastoral encounter with a couple in a stalemated marriage. On the other hand, accepting the telephone's limits may also be a pastoral gain. Often a person is so ambivalent about seeking pastoral help that the telephone allows him or her to make contact while maintaining the necessary distance from the pastor.

A well-known example of the structured use of the telephone to provide pastoral support to persons needing such distance is the telephone crisis counseling service pioneered by Alan Walker under the name *Life Line*. It arose out of this Australian urban pastor's frustrated efforts to reach the isolated individuals who lacked the spiritual resources for survival in a secular, mobile society where traditional church supports were absent or no longer functional. This model was duplicated and adjusted to the needs of metropolitan areas worldwide, and supplemented the church's pastoral ministry to the unchurched.

Using the telephone to counsel people in crisis will ideally be preparatory for a face-to-face encounter, but such an encounter may never take place or else be postponed. A depressed or suicidal person will be especially reticent to call the pastor, since such a person fears imposing upon others. If, however, the person has received indica-

tion from the pastor that such a request is welcomed, he or she may ask. Even then the pastor needs to initiate in the conversation and not be anxious about pauses. By directing the person into a safer place (the presence of others) the pastor appeals to the part of the person that wants help. It must be assumed that any attempt to call indicates ambivalence, and even if they call to say they have swallowed a bottle of sleeping pills, they can be reminded that the call is evidence of ambivalence. In order to dispatch help the pastor also needs to ask simple, direct questions of information about the location and identity of the caller.

Sometimes the telephone continues to be the ideal primary means of pastoral contact owing to the particular needs or circumstances of the caller. If, for example, a person is out of town but in need of ongoing pastoral support, the pastor may do this on the telephone. If the person is agoraphobic and not able to venture out of the house, regular contact by telephone may help. Bereaved persons, new parents, and people in other rites of passage all appreciate pastoral telephone calls. Such calls, as in the case of hospital patients, may supplement actual visits by the pastor, enabling the pastor to be available to more people in a more consistent way.

Bibliography. A. Walker, *As Close as the Telephone* (1967). R. MacKinnon and R. Michels, "The Role of the Telephone in the Psychiatric Interview," *The Psychiatric Interview in Clinical Practice* (1971), 431–50.

D. DURSTON

HOT-LINE CRISIS MINISTRIES; TECHNIQUE AND SKILL IN PASTORAL CARE. *See also* INITIATIVE AND INTERVENTION, PASTORAL.

TEMPER / TEMPER TANTRUMS. *See* SELF-EXPRESSION/SELF-CONTROL. *See also* ANGER; RAGE AND HOSTILITY.

TEMPERAMENT. A constitutional tendency toward certain types of emotional reactions and levels of sensitivity. Some people are more active than others, some more high-strung, and some more placid. These differences are most likely rooted in the individual's biology since they are often apparent at birth. Research has shown consistent differences in such factors as response to loud noises, sensitivity to light, and pain threshold at birth, and this finding has been interpreted to support the notion of innate temperament.

Historically, Hippocrates (ca. 460 – 377 B.C.) was the first to classify and systematically study these individual differences. He theorized that four basic body "humours" (blood, phlegm, black bile, and yellow bile) were the basis of four corresponding basic temperaments (sanguine, phlegmatic, melancholic, and choleric). Hippocrates also felt that imbalances among these humors lay at the basis of many of the mental illnesses; thus his treatments consisted of attempts to alter the balance of the humours through herbs, purgatives, and blood letting.

More recent work on temperament grows out of Gordon Allport's understanding of the concept. Allport defined temperament as "the characteristic phenomena of an individual's nature, including his susceptibility to emotional stimulation, his customary strength and speed of response, the quality of his prevailing mood, and all the peculiarities of fluctuation and intensity of mood (1961, p. 34)." This definition suggests four temperaments: emotionality, activity, sociability, and impulsivity. These have been the basic temperaments in the major current model of temperament, that of Robert Plomin and his colleagues (Buss and Plomin, 1975).

Plomin's research has suggested that activity level is largely inherited from parents and is fairly stable over an individual's life span. Sociability also seems to be largely inherited and stable, these being the criteria of temperament as determined by Plomin. However, emotionality and impulsivity have thus far not been shown to be as stable or as strongly genetically determined.

A major research group led by Alexander Thomas has conducted in-depth longitudinal observations of a relatively small group of children and has identified nine temperaments: activity level, rhythmicity, approach-withdrawal, adaptability, intensity of reactions, threshold of responsiveness, quality of mood, distractibility, and attention span and persistence. These can be further classified in three basic patterns: the easy child, the difficult child, and the slow-to-warm-up child. The easy child usually is positive in outlook, has low intensity responses, and exhibits an approach orientation towards novel stimuli. In contrast, the difficult child's pattern involves negative mood, high intensity responses, and a withdrawal orientation toward novel stimuli. Finally, the slow-to-warm-up child is characterized by a somewhat negative mood and a withdrawal orientation, but a low activity level and low intensity reaction (Thomas *et al.*, 1963; Thomas and Chess, 1977).

Another widely used approach for describing temperament was developed from extensive research by Isabel Briggs Myers, using the basic categories of personality type advanced by C. G. Jung. Her Myers-Briggs Type Indicator employs sixteen possible combinations of introversion and extroversion, sensing and intuition, thinking and feeling, and judging or perceiving to explain personality preferences and their effects on vocational choice, activities, and relationships (see Kiersey and Bates, 1978).

The religious writings of Tim F. LaHaye (1966) on the subject of temperament have been popular in conservative Protestant circles. LaHaye accepts Hippocrates's four basic temperaments (although not his body humor theory of etiology) and attempts to document strengths, weaknesses, and possibilities for change within each. He also discusses the ways in which a Christian should expect "spirit-controlled" temperaments to differ from those of nature. However, lacking a research base and not being reflective of nor consistent with the current models based on research, the limitations of this approach are substantial.

Bibliography. G. Allport, *Pattern and Growth in Personality* (1961). T. F. LaHaye, *Spirit-Controlled Temperament* (1966). A. Buss and R. Plomin, *A Temperament Theory of Personality Development* (1975). A. Thomas, S. Chess, H. Birch, M. Hertzig, and S. Korn, *Behavioral Individuality in Early Childhood* (1963). A. Thomas and S. Chess, *Temperament and Development* (1977). D. Kiersey and M. Bates, *Please Understand Me: Character and Temperament Types* (1978).

D. G. BENNER

PERSONALITY, BIOLOGICAL DIMENSIONS OF. *Compare* PERSONALITY TYPES AND PASTORAL CARE.

TEMPTATION. A term for "testing" that carries very specific biblical and theological content, as well as having psychodynamic implications. In both the Old and New Testaments, the term appears in the context of God's testing of a person or persons in order to clarify the strength of their loyalty or faith. Thus, a good end is intended. Awareness seems to be the object of temptation—to expose the inner core of the person. The exposure leads to an understanding of one's own nature and then opens a pathway to deeper faith. One's limits, or finitude, become known. The way is open to forming more accurate understanding of and participation in a right relationship with God. Great care is exercised theologically in stating that God's temptation of human beings is for good, while temptation aimed toward evil comes from other sources.

Temptation reveals the solidity and stability of one's process of identity formation. As identity becomes more focused, commitments are made to certain values. Situations arise in one's external environment or in one's inner personal experience that "test" those values. The test may involve commitments to family, marriage, friends, institutions, or one's own perception of self. In any case, the temptation, or testing, does lead to greater awareness about oneself. The possibility then exists to open pathways to growth or to succumb to a lesser view of self and to avoid further awareness and growth.

Popular understanding of temptation often focuses on the presence of a tempter. "Seducing" a person into denial or desertion of values and commitments implies an external source for temptation. It is important to remember, however, that temptation can arise from within. Confused identity, lack of differentiation, family history, competing claims for loyalty, and multiple commitments can "test" a person in ways that seldom show a readily identifiable external source. The conflicts within that are part of our nature as human beings make us vulnerable to temptation aimed toward bad ends just as temptation aimed toward good ends can be an opportunity for growth and clearer sense of direction.

A pastoral perspective on temptation should include an awareness of identity formation, the influence of family systems, and an adequate theological understanding of human nature. Pastoral opportunities are numerous for working with people who, faced with new opportunity or crisis, must decide who they will be. The temptations they face in making these decisions are indeed a "test" of their self-understanding and commitment. Often it is important for the pastor to take the initiative toward people who are probably wrestling with such decisions, because there may be a sense of shame about some of the options that have occurred to them. At the same time, there is often gratitude for a "willing ally" to accompany them in their process of growing self-awareness and clarification of values and commitments.

Bibliography. C. S. Lewis, *The Screwtape Letters* (1943).

W. V. ARNOLD

CONSCIENCE; IDENTITY; RESPONSIBILITY/IRRESPONSIBILITY, PSYCHOLOGY OF. *See also* SELF EXAMINATION; SIN /SINS. *Compare* MORAL DEVELOPMENT; MORAL THEOLOGY AND PASTORAL CARE; SCANDAL (Moral Theology); VALUES.

TEN COMMANDMENTS. The Ten Commandments contain a distinctive summary of those kinds of human conduct demanded by the God of Israel (observance of the Sabbath and honoring of parents) and of the kinds of action prohibited by Israel's God (the remaining eight). There is widespread agreement on many points of interpretation today: that the commandments to some extent do go back to Moses; that they probably were ten in number originally and were remembered by reference to the ten fingers; that they were addressed to individual members of the community but also applied to the community as a whole; that they were intended to be a pithy summary of the minimal requirements of Israel's obligation to God, not a law code but a summary of the ethos within which the community was to live out its existence under God.

In the life of church and synagogue this remarkable summary of God's demands and prohibitions has had a checkered history. Treated as a divine law code to regulate individual conduct, they have often fostered the development of a legalistic spirit, or they have been rejected by those who would have nothing to do with legalism. When treated as a central element of the religious ethos of Judaism and Christianity they have sometimes functioned in what seems to be their proper way: as a liberating set of demands and prohibitions, listing actions that in principle were ruled out, framing thereby the moral and religious structure of the people's lives, allowing personal decisions to concentrate on the concrete implications and inferences from the common starting point.

Divisions of the commandments have varied greatly. One helpful distinction is to group those commandments stating God's exclusive claims upon the people as together providing the ground of the entire list: it was God who delivered the slaves from Egyptian bondage; Israel is to have no other God as rival to the Lord; is to make no plastic representation of the Lord; and is not to use God's divine name to work violence or mischief upon others. The remaining commandments deal with personal and social ethics, apart from two that seem to have a special status. They are the commandments now appearing in positive form: observation of the Sabbath and the honoring of parents.

The command to cease from all normal labor on one day in seven is unique to Israel and has not yet been explained in a satisfactory way with regard to its antecedents and origin. The explanations given in the two different places where the Ten Commandments are listed (Exod. 20:1–17 and Deut. 5:6–21) ground Sabbath observance in God's own rest after completing the acts of creation in six days (Exodus) and in the human and animal need for rest from labor (Deuteronomy). Basically, Sabbath observance demands that one cease from normal activities one day in seven; the command is not to do certain kinds of acts on the Sabbath but to cease to do what one does six days in the week. It is highly probable that Israel's devotion to God, the community's care and concern for the family and for the neighbor, and indeed the very development of such a set of guidelines as the Ten Commandments owe their existence to the institution of the Sabbath.

The other positive commandment has in view not the obedience of small children to their parents but the care of aged parents by their adult children. While old age was honored in Israel, this commandment makes evident the strain placed upon family life by conflicts between the generations. The adult generation was often kept under too close control by an aged generation that would not yield the appropriate power and heritage to their children. The commandment underscores as well the fact that life consists in more than productivity; when aged persons no longer contribute positively to the community's life, they have not forfeited their right to live. The sanctity of life is clearly in view in both of these commandments — Sabbath observance and honoring parents.

The other commandments do not settle questions of what is murder, what is adultery, what constitutes theft or false testimony or coveting. The community must make such definitions, and it has the freedom to do so. But the prohibitions uphold God's claim upon the life of individual and community, God's demand that life be enhanced and not damaged. Religious history reveals well enough the danger that such guidelines will be used to stifle the freedom and creativity of individuals and groups. But rightly applied, such guidelines are an immensely positive force within a society. They can give direction to personal and social life, uphold life's sanctity, and offer a common point of departure for those within the religious communities that have preserved the commandments and those outside such communities.

Since the Ten Commandments are among the building blocks of contemporary culture in many, if not in most, parts of the world, their significance for pastoral care is obvious. For not only do they form the backdrop for the moral code of parishioners, they also reflect those values which the Judeo-Christian tradition has insisted to be constitutive of human life. They remind us that one dimension of pastoral care and counseling is moral and that coming to terms with values is an essential aspect of care.

Bibliography. D. Browning, *The Moral Context of Pastoral Care* (1983). W. Harrelson, *The Ten Commandments and Human Rights* (1980). E. Nielsen, *The Ten Commandments in New Perspective* (1968).

W. HARRELSON

BIBLE, PASTORAL USE AND INTERPRETATION OF. *See also* OLD TESTAMENT AND APOCRYPHA, TRADITIONS AND THEOLOGY OF CARE IN; INTERPRETATION AND HERMENEUTICS, PASTORAL; RELIGIOUS LANGUAGE IN PASTORAL CARE. *Compare* BIBLICAL LITERALISM; ETHICS AND PASTORAL CARE; FAITH AND WORKS; LEGALISM AND ANTINOMIANISM.

TENSION. *See* ANXIETY; BIOFEEDBACK; STRESS.

TERESA, MOTHER. *See* MOTHER TERESA OF CALCUTTA.

TERESA OF AVILA, ST. *See* THERESA OF AVILA, ST.

TERMINAL ILLNESS. *See* DYING, PASTORAL CARE OF; DYING CHILD AND FAMILY; SICK AND DYING, JEWISH CARE OF. *See also* DEATH AND DYING, MORAL DILEMMAS IN *or* PSYCHOSOCIAL THEORIES OF; SICK, PASTORAL CARE OF.

TERMINOLOGY. *See* COUNSELEE/CLIENT/PARISHIONER; PASTORAL CARE AND COUNSELING; PRAXIS/PRACTICE; SACRAMENTS, ORDINANCES, AND RITES.

TERTULLIAN OF CARTHAGE (ca. 160–ca. 220). Earliest known Christian theologian, African moralist, and apologist. A valuable mirror of early Christianity in North Africa, he reflects the struggle of the church in the first and second centuries to come to terms with exomologesis, that is, the public confession of sin and public performance of penance.

Because he granted only one postbaptismal repentance and completely excluded idolaters, murderers, and adulterers from it, Tertullian is considered a rigorist who laid the foundations for practices in years to come. Historically relevant and a reflection of his detachment from pagan society is Tertullian's strict opposition to the lax readmission of believers who lapsed under persecution into idolatry.

While his writings on penitence do reveal a form of pastoral care that is earnestly concerned with the issue of reconciliation through exomologesis and its profound psychological and spiritual value, Tertullian's repeated slips into extremism, rigidity, and sarcasm detract from his greatness.

N. F. HAHN

EARLY CHURCH, PASTORAL CARE AND COUNSELING IN; EXEMOLOGESIS.

TESTING, PSYCHOLOGICAL. *See* EVALUATION AND DIAGNOSIS, PSYCHOLOGICAL.

TESTING, SPIRITUAL. *See* SPIRITUAL DISCIPLINE AND GROWTH; SUFFERING.

THANATOLOGY. *See* DEATH RESEARCH AND EDUCATION. *See also* DEATH AND DYING, PSYCHOSOCIAL THEORIES OF.

THANKFULNESS/THANKSGIVING. *See* GRATITUDE; WORSHIP AND CELEBRATION.

THEFT. *See* DEVIANT BEHAVIOR; RESPONSIBILITY/IRRESPONSIBILITY, PSYCHOLOGY OF.

THEMATIC APPERCEPTION TEST. *See* EVALUATION AND DIAGNOSIS, PSYCHOLOGICAL.

THEODICY. *See* EVIL; PROVIDENCE; SUFFERING.

THEODORET OF CYHRRUS. *See* EARLY CHURCH, PASTORAL CARE AND COUNSELING IN.

THEOLOGICAL ANTHROPOLOGY, DISCIPLINE OF. The section of systematic theology that deals with human beings or any theological account of human nature and destiny. The content of theological anthropology ordinarily includes the human as created, the human as sinner, and the human as redeemed.

As a theological discipline theological anthropology presupposes and involves the understanding of the human (*anthropos*) in relation to the divine reality (*theos*). This means that theological anthropology is generally the locus of theology's interchange with the behavioral sciences. Depending upon its methodological presuppositions, the theological understanding of human beings may draw upon the insights of psychology, sociology, cultural anthropology, and other studies of human life and culture. Theological anthropology may also contribute insights to other modes of understanding the human phenomenon as well as propose limits or cautions to those sciences.

Bibliography. W. Pannenberg, *Anthropology in Theological Perspective* (1985).

C. B. KLINE

PERSON; THEOLOGY. *See also* HUMAN CONDITION /PREDICAMENT; HUMAN NATURE, PROBLEM OF; IMAGO DEI; SOUL. *Compare* BIBLICAL ANTHROPOLOGY, DISCIPLINE OF; PHILOSOPHY AND PSYCHOLOGY.

THEOLOGICAL EDUCATION AND THE PASTORAL CARE MOVEMENT, JEWISH. Jewish seminaries have only recently included pastoral care ("counseling" and "human relations") in core curricula. Strong interest in this role has developed rapidly since the 1960s, with students taking clinical pastoral training, classroom seminars including intensive case analysis of actual experiences in counseling members of student congregations, and elective courses dealing with psychology and religion. Graduates of Jewish seminaries often continue their training by attending workshops and institutes in counseling, psychotherapy, and family therapy. A small but growing number of rabbis make pastoral counseling a significant part of their master role as religious leaders, but notably few leave the rabbinate to become full-time specialists in counseling and therapy.

Jews have long been prominent in the field of psychotherapy and psychoanalysis. Although the Jewish community accepted therapy as a popular aspect of health care, rabbis were slow to integrate psychology and religion. Rabbi Joshua Loth Liebman of Boston, author of *Peace of Mind* (1976), was the first to attempt to integrate Judaism and psychoanalysis. Traditional as well as liberal seminaries now supplement the historic emphasis on Bible, commentaries, and rabbinic literature (Midrash, Talmud, and Codes), with so-called "practical" courses because of the example of the Protestant pastor, the recognition that individual salvation calls for more than instruction in the Torah, the growing expectation of laypersons that rabbis concern themselves with interpersonal and family relations, and because the age of psychology made "talking cures" attractive. Historically, the commandments of visiting the sick and caring for the bereaved, as well as many other aspects of caring for individual needs, were incumbent on all Jews, lay and rabbinic. With growing specialization in our culture and greater assimilation of Jewish life and institutions into larger social patterns, Jewish clergy are now perceived as givers of rabbinic ("pastoral") care, and the earlier concept of "commandment" or *mitzvah* tends to be replaced by an expectation of rabbinic responsibility.

Jewish life is expressed in communal as well as in specifically religious institutions like the synagogue; the Jewish community has long sponsored forms of counseling such as family service bureaus and agencies specializing in the needs of particular groups, such as the sick or the aged. Staffing of such programs and agencies has typically included professionally trained laypersons like social workers, psychologists, physicians, and psychiatrists.

In the earlier phase of theological training for pastoral care, seminaries tended to rely on models of psychiatrists, particularly on psychoanalysts, clinical psychologists, and social workers. The earliest clinically trained supervisor was an Orthodox rabbi, I. Fred Hollander, associated with the Yeshiva University. At the Hebrew Union College the Department of Human Relations was established in 1948, and courses in counseling were formally developed beginning in 1950 by Rabbi Robert L. Katz, who continued the pioneer work of Rabbi Abraham Cronbach (Jewish social studies) and Dr. Abraham Franzblau (pastoral psychology).

As Christian pastors have been influenced by Carl R. Rogers, rabbis have assimilated the insights of Sigmund Freud. Only since the 1960s has there emerged greater independence from the authority and prestige of psychoanalysis and a more critical examination of the unique role of the clergyperson, as well as a greater concern for theological and ethical issues in the counseling relationship. Jewish seminaries, as much and perhaps more than Christian seminaries, continue to experience a tension between classical studies and empirical training in counseling.

Bibliography. J. L. Liebman, *Peace of Mind* (1976).

R. L. KATZ

JEWISH CARE AND COUNSELING (History, Tradition, and Contemporary Issues); JUDAISM AND PSYCHOLOGY; PASTORAL CARE MOVEMENT. *See also* ECUMENICAL RELATIONSHIPS IN THE PASTORAL CARE AND COUNSELING MOVEMENTS; EDUCATION IN PASTORAL CARE AND COUNSELING.

THEOLOGICAL EDUCATION AND THE PASTORAL CARE MOVEMENT, PROTESTANT.

The term "pastoral care movement" refers in this article, as it often does in contemporary discussion, to the concentrated interest in pastoral care and counseling, the relationship of religion and health, and the clinical pastoral training of clergy which had its roots in the early decades of the twentieth century and its full flowering as a major movement in North American Protestantism following the Second World War. This article traces the relationship between this movement, whose educational expressions have been largely derived from and centered in clinical contexts, and the academic theological education of the seminaries, with which it has had a varied and at times tense relationship.

1. **The Pastoral Care Movement.** There were certain antecedents to the beginning concentration of the late 1940s and the early 1950s which gave rise to the pastoral care movement. Perhaps the primary impetus came from the emergence of the behavioral sciences and particularly the advances in psychology, psychotherapy, sociology, and the related so-called human sciences. Psychology in the modern era began in the laboratory with the work of Wilhelm Wundt but gradually found a place in clinical settings both in and out of institutions. The work of Sigmund Freud and others produced what was termed the "new psychology," whereby concentrated scrutiny was given to procedure in alleviating human suffering. The so-called insane asylums began to take on marks of therapeutic institutions rather than simply being custodial in nature. In the early 1920s doctoral dissertations began to appear in theological schools with such titles as "Jesus and the New Psychology."

In the mid-1920s there emerged what has been called the Clinical Education Movement for Clergy (CPE). Variously attributed to the work of Anton Boisen and others, the procedure involved bringing seminary students into mental hospitals to study, in Boisen's phrase, the "living human documents." In this context students worked directly with patients and received supervision from chaplains and persons in the healing disciplines. The pattern that developed included direct involvement with patients, a peer learning group, and a supervisor who assisted students in assessing their growing competence to deal with persons in difficulty.

A more concentrated emphasis on pastoral care and counseling in American theological education emerged following World War II when returning military chaplains and others began to search for opportunities to learn more effective means for care delivery. Few, if any, of the theological schools had extensive offerings in pastoral care and counseling although interest in the subject matter was gaining attention. In the late 1940s and early 1950s it is possible to discern growing evidence of the emergence of a pastoral care movement as such seen in the establishing of professorships, the organization of associations and guilds, the publication of books and journals and the increasing curriculum offerings available to seminary students and continuing education participants in the matter of enhancing effectiveness in the bearing of burdens.

2. **Early Relationship.** The pastoral care movement grew up, by and large, outside the theological schools and to some extent outside the church as such. Many of the early leaders found themselves out of step with the more traditional forms of ministry as well as the didactic procedures of theological education and discovered in the institutional settings a challenge and opportunity for ministry and for learning care delivery which they had not found in the seminary or parish. This bifurcation often led to tension between the CPE people and the people in the theological schools. The fact that the hospital rather than the church became the nurturing setting for the learning of pastoral theology in theory and practice raised questions among those whose experience had not included such procedures. In many theological schools the students who had participated in CPE (or "clinical training" as it was often called) were looked upon askance when they returned to the campus following a summer sojourn in a hospital. This type of reception often tended to produce a reaction that set the CPE students apart and at times eventuated in their developing a kind of elitism which did little to endear them to faculty, students, and judicatories.

Alongside the growing interest in clinical training was the introduction of case material as a part of the educational procedure. Russell Dicks and Seward Hiltner early on stressed the importance of case notes as the means for developing theory and skill in pastoral care. Just as the sermon had long been identified as the unit of preaching which could be evaluated, analysed, and improved, so the case study became the unit of pastoral care that made for effective reflection on what had actually transpired in the pastoral conversation. In the early days most if not all of the case material took the form of notes or narrative descriptions of the pastoral care situation. Gradually there developed a verbatim simulation in which the actual words used between pastor and parishioner were set forth in the form of a brief excerpt or drama. This was followed by the employment of tape recorders which could reproduce the exact words and voice tones. Still later, video recordings made possible the evaluation and analysis of body language including facial expression, posture, and the like alongside the verbal communication.

As has already been noted, the initial reaction of many theological schools to the emerging interest in pastoral care and counseling studies was often marked by suspicion and resistance. Many persons were skeptical about introducing the data of the behavioral sciences into theological study. A considerable Barthian influence became evident, which took the position that to focus on what the minister does in the pastoral care conversation was in error in that by definition the emphasis had been diverted from what God does in the restoration of persons. In addition, the development of clinical training in the hospital setting at times led to what was called, rightly or wrongly, the "medical model," which influenced some students to abandon pastoral calling and to post office hours whereby the parishioners would come to seek help on a determined schedule. In the view of many these and related practices moved away from the historical pastoral role of the minister.

In the mid-1950s a concerted study of theological education in the U.S. and Canada was conducted, resulting in several publications, including *The Advancement of Theological Education* (1957), by H. Richard Niebuhr, Daniel Day Williams, and James M. Gustafson. Drawing on surveys, interviews, and consultations, the authors presented the state of theological education and made suggestions and recommendations for improvement in theological studies. The developing place of pastoral studies both in and out of the theological schools was noted and attention was called to the opportunities and values as well as the obstacles and problems. One issue explored in the study was the relationship between the traditional theological disciplines and the so-called practical studies. The writers concluded that both needed the other and deplored the implication that such areas as Bible and theology were somehow "impractical" and that pastoral care, education, and preaching had no "body of knowledge." One year following the release of the report on theological education, Seward Hiltner published his monumental *Preface To Pastoral Theology* (1958), which explored the relationship between the "Logic-centered" fields and the "Operation-centered" fields. These two publications, among others, attested to the establishment of pastoral care and counseling as a part of theological education even though continued growth would occur and varieties of emphases would be explored in the years to follow.

3. Recent Relationship. By the mid-1980s such phrases were being used as "pastoral care come of age." Implied in this type of statement was the recognition of the fact the vast majority of seminaries in the U.S. and Canada listed extensive curricular offerings and continuing education events in the minister's function of care delivery. Much of the early suspicion had dissipated, a factor caused in part by the fact that more and more theological professors had by then had courses in care and counseling and many had participated in CPE. Books and articles appeared which dealt with the biblical and theological dimensions of pastoral care and counseling as well as exploration of the relationship between pastoral care and related functions of ministry such as worship, preaching, education, and administration. The involvement of the traditional means of grace such as prayer, devotion, and sacrament in the pastoral relationship became an increasing aspect in the overall care delivery procedure.

This shift of climate within the theological schools was accompanied by a growing relationship between the campus and the clinic. Many saw that it was profitable for the student to experience education for ministry both in the academic classroom and in the institutional setting where multidisciplined teams worked to alleviate human suffering. In addition, the accrediting guilds were incorporating into their structure not only professors from theological seminaries but also parish ministers. On these occasions for conversation, consultation, and mutually shared service, the value of the wider spectrum came more clearly into focus. Still another aspect of the closer ties between pastoral care and theological education could be seen in the growing instances of those with roots in the pastoral care movement assuming administrative responsibilities in the theological schools. Persons certified by one or more of the guilds became deans, presidents, and principles of seminaries, which marked a shift from their earlier function as mere members of the faculty. Many seminaries became corporate members of one or more of the guilds not only contributing financial resources to the work of CPE but also seeing members of their faculty serving the guilds as officers at local, regional, and national levels.

Such emerging relationships between theological education and the pastoral care movement do not signify that all tension has now been resolved, but it has taken on a much more constructive nature. As was set forth in the study of theological education in the 1950s and in Hiltner's thesis regarding "Logic-centered" and "Operation-centered" fields, the tension has become more and more a means whereby the several aspects of theological education can contribute to and receive from all other aspects. The diminution of a defensive stance and the increase of collegial conversation and discussion have opened the way for a more creative understanding of the pastoral responsibilities of ministry and the sense in which these functions could be informed both by the researchers in the behavioral sciences and by the heritage of faith emerging from biblical and theological studies.

Bibliography. C. W. Brister, *Pastoral Care in the Church* (1964). S. Hiltner, *Preface to Pastoral Theology* (1958). E. B. Holifield, *A History of Pastoral Care in America* (1983). J. T. McNeill, *A His- tory of the Cure of Souls* (1951). H. R. Niebuhr, D. D. Williams, and J. M. Gustafson, *The Advancement of Theological Education* (1957). E. Thornton, *Clinical Pastoral Education* (1970).

W. B. OGLESBY, JR.

CLINICAL PASTORAL EDUCATION; HISTORY OF PROTESTANT *or* ROMAN CATHOLIC PASTORAL CARE (Canada *or* United States); INTERNATIONAL PASTORAL CARE MOVEMENT; PASTORAL CARE MOVEMENT. *See also* EDUCATION IN PASTORAL CARE AND COUNSELING; JOURNALS IN PASTORAL CARE AND COUNSELING; PASTORAL THEOLOGY, GRADUATE

EDUCATION IN. *Compare* PSYCHOLOGY IN AMERICAN RELIGION. *Biography:* BOISEN; CABOT; DICKS; DUNBAR; HILTNER; KELLER; VAN OOSTERZEE.

THEOLOGICAL EDUCATION AND THE PASTORAL CARE MOVEMENT, ROMAN CATHOLIC.

The relationship of the pastoral care movement to theological education in the Roman Catholic church in the U.S. was shaped by shifting understandings of the task of theological education and of the nature of pastoral care in Roman Catholicism.

1. Prior to the Second Vatican Council. From the Council of Trent until the Second Vatican Council the understanding of pastoral care and of the task of theological education was significantly shaped by the strength of the sacramental tradition combined with the understanding of grace as an ontological reality having nothing to do with experience. During this period in the Roman Catholic church pastoral care centered on the administration of the sacraments, with the sacrament of confession having particular importance. Courses on pastoral care and pastoral theology were not included as a regular part of the seminary curriculum, nor were there field education programs. While courses designated as pastoral theology began to appear in the late 1940s, these courses dealt with the administrative details of running a parish and the external details of sacramental preparation. The pastoral care dimensions of priestly ministry were addressed in courses on moral theology, canon law, sacramental theology, and homiletics. The humanistic disciplines, including psychology, were considered unimportant in the seminary curriculum, and any relationship between the pastoral care movement and theological education was largely coincidental.

2. The Second Vatican Council. The Second Vatican Council contained two shifts in perspective of particular significance for the relationship between the pastoral care movement and theological education in Roman Catholicism. The first of these was the growing appreciation of the concrete, historical nature of the church's embodiment in the world. The second was the growing appreciation of grace as not only an ontological but also an experiential reality. These two shifts in perspective led to major changes in the understanding of the nature of pastoral care and of the task of theological education. "The Decree on Priestly Formation" issued by the council insists on the importance of pastoral concern permeating all segments of the theological curriculum, highlights the importance of subjects such as psychology and sociology, and underscores the importance of the integration of theory and practice. *The Program of Priestly Formation* (PPF), the official document prescribing the implementation of "The Decree on Priestly Formation" for the U.S., fully incorporates this concern that the historical and pastoral dimensions of theology permeate the entire curriculum. Concretely these shifts took the form of the introduction of courses in pastoral theology, pastoral care, and pastoral counseling, the inclusion of a pastoral focus in all subjects in the curriculum, and the requirement that every seminary include a field education program to serve as a primary locus for theological reflection and integration.

3. The Pastoral Care Movement. Catholic seminaries in the U.S. turned to the pastoral care movement for assistance in implementing the shifts in perspective, which the council had introduced. Here they found well-established, effective programs for integrating the practical, pastoral dimensions of theological education and reflection into the overall curriculum and the life experience of the ministerial student. The pastoral care programs most commonly used in this process have been the Clinical Pastoral Education (CPE) programs, which are "highly recommended" in the PPF and frequently required in seminary curricula. These programs have helped effect an increased awareness of the sociocultural factors impacting theology and ministry, an increased sensitivity to human needs and concerns, and an increased appreciation of the role of the humanistic sciences in theological education. The task yet to be accomplished is to reach a deeper integration of the richness and strength of the sacramental tradition with a well-grounded pastoral care, an integration which would yield a vital, effective pastoral care fundamentally shaped by the sacramental tradition so central to the Roman Catholic church.

Bibliography. A historical overview of shifting perspectives on the nature of pastoral care can be found in W. Clebsch and C. Jaekle, *Pastoral Care in Historical Perspective* (1975). The key resources for understanding the impact of the Second Vatican Council on the shape of theological education in Roman Catholicism today are "The Pastoral Constitution on the Church in the Modern World" and "The Decree on Priestly Formation" in *The Documents of Vatican II*, W. Abbot, ed. (1966) and *The Program of Priestly Formation* of the National Conference of Catholic Bishops (1971; 2d ed., 1976; 3d ed., 1981).

M. McCARTHY

COUNSELING, ROMAN CATHOLIC; HISTORY OF ROMAN CATHOLIC PASTORAL CARE (Canada *or* United States); PASTORAL CARE MOVEMENT; VATICAN COUNCIL II AND PASTORAL CARE; EDUCATION IN PASTORAL CARE AND COUNSELING; PASTORAL THEOLOGY, GRADUATE EDUCATION IN. *Compare* CLINICAL PASTORAL EDUCATION; PSYCHOLOGY IN AMERICAN RELIGION.

THEOLOGICAL METHODOLOGY. *See* PASTORAL THEOLOGICAL METHODOLOGY.

THEOLOGICAL REFLECTION. *See* PASTORAL THEOLOGICAL METHODOLOGY; PASTORAL THEOLOGY; THEORY IN PASTORAL CARE AND COUNSELING, FUNCTIONS OF.

THEOLOGICAL SCHOOL INVENTORY (TSI). *See* EVALUATION AND DIAGNOSIS, PSYCHOLOGICAL; THEOLOGICAL STUDENTS, EVALUATION AND EMPIRICAL STUDIES OF.

THEOLOGICAL STUDENTS, EVALUATION AND EMPIRICAL STUDIES OF.

Empirical evaluations of theological students—those persons in post-baccalaureate programs of study preparing for ministry-related vocations—can be classified into two broad groups. The first deals with their general psychological characteristics. The second evaluates the effects theological education has on them.

This article draws from a selected sample of the many empirical studies of theological students conducted during the past twenty years. Few studies used a systematic random sampling of theological students. Most employed convenient samples of persons attending a particular institution or belonging to a denomination to which the researcher had access. Many studies employed reliable measuring devices, others used instruments constructed for a specific study without estimates of their validity or reliability.

1. Psychological Characteristics of Seminary Students. Empirical studies attempting to identify psychological characteristics of seminary students have most frequently used the Minnesota Multiphasic Personality Inventory (MMPI) or the Myers-Briggs Type Indicator (MBTI).

a. MMPI studies. Summaries of MMPI studies suggest some relatively consistent patterns. Theological students, over a fifteen-year period, from a variety of denominations and schools tended to score higher on several scales than the general population. These included the K, Hy, Pd, Mf, and Ma Scales. The interpretations placed on these scores, however, have varied more than the scores. The complexity and clinical insight the MMPI represents make it difficult to interpret, especially when attempting to identify basic characteristics of groups rather than individuals. Nonetheless, the following interpretations have been suggested.

The K scale was originally intended to detect defensiveness. It tends to be slightly elevated in college populations, and some interpreters take the slight elevation of K scores for postcollege theological students as a sign of generally good adjustment. K was shown to be positively related to self-acceptance and to positive self-concept in at least one study of seminarians. The Pd scores, which are also higher in studies of theological students than the general population, may suggest aggressiveness, anxiety, or greater degrees of prior family conflict. The higher than average Ma scores can be interpreted as indicating a tendency to be more verbal and enthusiastic than the general population. Theological students also tend to have higher than typical Hy scores and lower than average Si scores. In college populations, where a similar pattern has been observed, these scores have been interpreted as indicating good general adjustment with reference to social relations, verbal skills, and ability to reason. The higher than typical Mf scores have been interpreted variously. While this scale was originally intended as a measure of homosexual tendencies, it was the "least well validated of any of the original MMPI scales" (Drake and Oetting). Men in educational settings typically score higher on this scale. Some have suggested that this score, particularly when combined with higher Hy and lower Si scores, indicates a good general environmental adjustment. Higher Mf scores may suggest a degree of control over aggressive adjustment patterns.

Nauss has concluded that the MMPI studies, as a group, lead to a relatively positive assessment of theological students' personality characteristics. It can be inferred from these data that seminarians have "ego strength, and good emotional adjustment, are friendly, enthusiastic, self-confident, showing initiative, showing ease of oral expression and leadership qualities, extroverted and socially at ease with others." While such a characterization may seem overly positive, it reflects realistic interpretation of MMPI studies across schools, denominations, and decades. However, less positive interpretations can be derived from the same data. The more positive interpretation would seem most appropriate in light of the technical work during the 1950s and 1960s, which sought to reevaluate MMPI scales from their more narrow origins as indications of psychopathology to broader use as indicators of both good and bad psychological adjustment.

b. MBTI studies. The influence of Jungian thinking in American seminaries has precipitated a number of studies of theological students using the Myers-Briggs Type Indicator. Unlike the MMPI, it did not originate in attempts to diagnose psychopathology. It assumes that personality can be expressed typologically. The MBTI attempts to assess the individual's location on four continua with the following sets of poles: (1) *extrovert* (E) —a preference for the exterior world of people and events, as opposed to *introvert* (I)—a preference for the interior world of concepts and ideas; (2) *sensing* (S)— perceiving the external world more readily in factual, practical ways, as opposed to *intuition* (N)—perceiving it in thematic or theoretical ways; (3) *thinking* (T)— making decisions using a logical, rationalistic approach, as opposed to *feeling* (F)—decision making based heavily on values and perceived consequences on people; and (4) *judging* (J)—a preference to live in a more planned, orderly fashion, as opposed to *perceiving* (P)—a more spontaneous, accept-what-comes approach.

Studies using the MBTI indicate that theological students show a marked preference for F over T in their decision-making process. A majority also express a preference for E over I, and for J over P. Less dramatic preferences exist for the S or N dimensions. These results suggest that theological students are more likely oriented to the external world of tasks and people than the internal world of ideas; more inclined to live in a planned and ordered way than a spontaneous, adapting way; and more likely to be influenced in their decisions by the values they hold and the impact of decisions on people than by a more rationalistic, pro/con assessment.

c. Relationships among personality and other variables. Other studies have sought to relate psychological characteristics to other variables as a way to classify theological students. Characteristics such as open-mindedness, flexibility, and self-described liberalism have been positively correlated with higher scores on scales measuring complexity, autonomy, and personal integration.

When ministry students have been compared to social work and counseling students, they were interpreted as being less likely to live in the present, less inner-directed, less flexible in the application of their values, less sensitive to their own needs and feelings, possessing less self-regard, less able to accept self with its weaknesses, and less willing to accept aggression. Seminarians have been shown to have a more highly uniform set of personality variables than samples of other, nonseminary students. They appear to have more benevolent values than students in other programs of study. They were similar to counselor trainees in their level of authoritarianism and concept of human nature. Theological students have been interpreted as perceiving death in friendlier terms than other students, and as more inclined to think that anger is wrong. They also have been shown to be more likely to inhibit aggressive responses.

d. Conclusions. Theological students do appear to have some common characteristics. They tend to be reasonably adjusted, expressive, and verbal people; less comfortable with anger and aggression than other groups in the society; more value-oriented and people-oriented; less self-accepting; and, to some extent, less inner-directed. These traits are not uncommon to people in other helping professions.

Characteristics that may be seen as strengths can also be the basis for problems. For example, orientation toward other people and a sensitivity to their needs may cause individuals to be less than maximally inner-directed. Or, a rightful concern about the proper expression of anger and aggression can degenerate into an avoidance of conflict or inappropriate expressions of anger.

The literature includes enough contradictory evidence to suggest that theological students are best perceived as a heterogeneous group. They differ from each other on almost every dimension that has been explored. The "ministerial personality" has been elusive. Where one has been identified, it reflects the reasonable tendencies and approaches one would easily associate with the practice of ministry or priesthood. Psychological evaluations demonstrate a range of health represented among theological students, with the majority being as well adjusted as other people in our society.

2. Seminar Education and Theological Students.

a. Motivations. The most consistent empirical inquiry of persons' motivations for entering theological study has been in studies of the *Theological School Inventory* (TSI). This instrument has been used, with revisions, since the early 1960s. The TSI identifies seven areas of motivation for entering ministry or priesthood. They include: (1) service to persons, (2) evangelistic witness, (3) social reform, (4) intellectual interest, (5) leadership success, (6) acceptance of others, and (7) self-fulfillment. Over the years, the rank order of strength of these areas of motivations has varied. Variance can also be noted among schools and denominations. The Service to Persons scale, however, has consistently been among the highest rated for students entering seminary over the past twenty years.

The TSI also has attempted to identify empirically how ministerial students perceive their vocational calling to Christian ministry. In the original norm group, as well as in reference groups since, students were about equally divided in how they perceived their call. For many it was experienced through natural gifts, abilities, and desires. For many others, call was interpreted as a special intervention or summons in their lives. TSI studies in individual seminaries have shown some variation in motivation or perception of call over the years. These variations are best interpreted, however, against a background of stable and consistent motivations across two decades.

b. Persisters and nonpersisters. Studies comparing students who persist through theological education into career ministry or priesthood with those who drop out of seminary have generally produced idiosyncratic information. Variations in conclusions seem to be related to the variables investigated and students' denomination. Demographic variables distinguish very little between the two

groups. One of the earlier, although more sophisticated, studies of this issue concluded that both groups are heterogeneous. People stay in seminary for a variety of reasons, and people leave seminary for a variety of reasons as well.

The most extensive research in this area has been conducted on Roman Catholic seminarians. These studies suggest, among other things, that persisters (1) are more submissive, have higher musical and social interests; (2) have either as great, or a slightly greater, degree of overall personality adjustment; (3) have a balanced and realistic view of celibacy; and (4) have a somewhat more authoritarian orientation.

c. Effects of theological education. Studies have identified discernable shifts in assessed personality characteristics such as self-concept and expressed self-actualization during the years pursuing a theological degree. Some studies focusing on short-term interventions, such as a group dynamics course or a Clinical Pastoral Education (CPE) experience, have shown less obvious shifts in personality factors. However, CPE has been demonstrated to have a major influence on how individuals perceive their ministry task and go about it. There is evidence that the goals and values an institution holds as most important will be reflected in the attitudes of students graduating from these institutions.

Apparently, theological education produces measureable shifts in the students who experience it. The longer the exposure, the greater the likelihood of shifts. The most readily measureable shifts occur in the areas of skill, knowledge, attitudes, values, and tendencies. Psychological characteristics such as self-concept and self-awareness can also be positively influenced.

d. Effects of role. A great deal has been speculated and bemoaned about the role into which theological students are thrust as they perceive themselves and are perceived as ministers or priests. Some research indicates that individuals who feel a great deal of conflict in their ministerial role may be more inclined to drop out of theological training. Conversely, the more individuals assume a "ministerial" role during training, the more they are likely to continue training. Some research also suggests that the congruence between positive self-concept and acceptance of clergy role is present in ministerial candidates who also see themselves as very similar to lay people. Theological students may be reflecting a healthy adjustment when they accept the ascription of a role others place on them.

e. Women and theological education. Perhaps the most dramatic shift in Protestant theological education over the past decade has been the emergence of women students. While women remained a relatively small percentage of ordained clergy in most Protestant denominations (range of 1.3 percent to 7.8 percent in nine selected denominations in 1981), the percentage of total students who are women in those same denominations ranged from 21 percent to 45 percent. Women are a dramatic and influential part of contemporary theological education. In a comparison of motivations, women were more inclined to enter seminary with their primary motivation being "discovering in which ways to best serve Christ in the church and world" or "personal spiritual growth and faith development," rather than "preparing to be a parish minister." Men, on the other hand, overwhelmingly rated this third motivator as highest of the three. Women students are more likely to reflect a stronger feminist orientation than men students or women laity.

Women report problems, at times, because of an ineffective socialization to ministerial role. They have been excluded from the events, mentor relationships, and support many male theological students receive, and are therefore less skilled in their response to ministerial expectations and role. More frequently than is true for men, women students use seminary education as a means to mid-adulthood career change. Seminaries seem to have adjusted to the increased presence of women students, and women graduating in the early eighties report more satisfactory experiences than women graduating in the early seventies (Carroll, Hargrove, and Lummis).

Bibliography. Empirical research on clergy and theological students prior to 1965 is abstracted and summarized in R. Menges and J. Dittes, *Psychological Studies of Clergymen* (1965). A good review of studies of personality is available in A. Nauss, "The Ministerial Personality: Myth or Reality," *J. of Religion and Health,* 12 (January 1973). Interpretation of the MMPI is based on L. Drake and E. Oetting, *An MMPI Codebook for Counselors* (1959 [1929]). A thorough study of women theological students is included in J. W. Carroll, B. J. Hargrove, and A. Lummis, *Women of the Cloth* (1983). See also S. W. Cardwell, "The Theological School Inventory: After Ten Years," *J. of Pastoral Care,* 28 (1974), 267–79; B. N. Ekhardt and W. M. Goldsmith, "Personality Factors of Men and Women Pastoral Candidates, Part I: Motivational Profiles," *J. of Psychology and Theology,* 12 (1984), 109–18; "Part II: Sex Role Preferences," *J. of Psychology and Theology,* 12 (1984), 211–21.

D. ALESHIRE

CALL TO MINISTRY; READINESS FOR MINISTRY STUDIES; THEOLOGICAL EDUCATION AND THE PASTORAL CARE MOVEMENT. *Compare* CLERGY, RABBIS, *or* RELIGIOUS, EMPIRICAL STUDIES OF; EVALUATION AND DIAGNOSIS, PSYCHOLOGICAL; MENTAL HEALTH, PASTOR'S; PERSONHOOD OF THE PASTOR, SIGNIFICANCE OF; ROLE, MINISTERIAL.

THEOLOGICAL STUDENTS, PASTORAL CARE OF.
Students in divinity schools and theological seminaries require pastoral care as do members of any Christian community, but their needs are specialized due to their particular function and task within that community. Unfortunately, the tendency in many theological schools is to treat students as if their status as learners of theological and pastoral skills implies that they have few or no needs for pastoral care.

1. **Significant Factors.** Theological students often experience fairly strong conflict between the school as a community of faith and as an academic institution. Theological inquiry and critical scholarship can challenge the overly simple faith assumptions which students bring to theological education. Such conflicts in their external world parallel and sometimes foster internal conflicts between faith and doubt; often, students feel constrained to deny the existence of such conflicts.

Many theological students hope to find seminary a comfortable community with few value conflicts. But some students may have attended large universities where a wide variety of values competed for attention and

loyalty. Others, from enmeshed families or enmeshed religious communities whose values are almost entirely unquestioned, will have attended colleges that largely adopted those same values. Value conflicts in theological schools can be quite sharp indeed.

Until relatively recently, students in theological education were almost without exception unmarried males in their early twenties. Now they include people of all ages, married and single, male and female. Theological institutions, despite excellent intentions, tend to treat students as though they were still the same population that existed in the late 1940s. Students are often credited with less maturity and less responsibility than in undergraduate schools. This pattern is reflected in everything from academic assignments to school housing policies.

Yet theological institutions tend to treat students, and the students tend to treat themselves, as though they have almost no pastoral needs. Chaplaincy programs, often provided by faith groups to college students, are rare in theological seminaries. Faculties and trustees regularly vote down proposals to provide a pastor or a chaplain to students.

Two factors play significant parts in such a pattern. First, there exists the completely unwarranted assumption that since most seminary faculty members are themselves clergy, they can provide whatever pastoral care is needed. This is particularly true for those who teach pastoral care. Faculty members' teaching function is compromised when they act as pastors to students. Second, there is the equally unwarranted assumption that, as developing providers of pastoral care, students are less likely to need pastoral care for themselves.

The general pattern in theological education, with a few exceptions, is that pastoral care to students is provided on a catch-as-catch-can basis, almost never as a part of a program supported by the institution. Students may consult a trusted faculty member, a pastor in their field education setting, or the pastor of their own home church.

2. **Pastoral Care Issues for Theological Students.**
a. Confidentiality. Always an issue in pastoral care, confidentiality is particularly important in ministry to theological students. The understanding that pastoral conversations are utterly confidential is of special importance in a close-knit community. In other settings, a faith crisis or a love affair can be discussed with many people, including pastors; in seminary, sharing such problems may result in others questioning the student's staying in school or continuing to prepare for ministry.

b. Intimacy issues. In terms of emotional development, many students are wrestling with their capacity to experience and express intimacy. Psychological research has repeatedly suggested that clergy, as a group, have particular difficulties with appropriate intimacy. The relationship to the church often takes the place of relationships to spouse and family. That pattern often begins in theological school.

c. Individuation. Most human beings struggle to become differentiated individuals, owners of their own thoughts and feelings, independent from the families and communities in which they had their origins. Sometimes the reason that individuating is such a struggle is that the family of origin does not want the person to become a differentiated self or to leave home in the emotional and spiritual sense.

For the theological student, the issue may be still more complicated. The church may have become the agent of leaving home, that is, the individual may have discovered that service in the church is one way of leaving home that will be accepted without question by the family. But the church, to whom new loyalties are attached, may also demand that the student not become a differentiated self. Faith issues may actually hide a continuing struggle to become one's own person.

d. Spirituality. Perhaps because matters of faith must be approached technically in a theological school, maintaining a lively spiritual life often becomes problematic for students. At the same time, adhering to spiritual patterns learned at an earlier stage of development can serve as a defense against spiritual or intellectual learning. Pastoral care for theological students often faces the task of helping a student come to a new spirituality and a new approach to relationships, both to God and to other people. To be identified as a sensitive and effective pastor is to invite the sharing of profound religious experience, some of which is still new, raw, and undigested. It is appropriate for the pastoral care of theological students to take the form of spiritual direction, and those extending pastoral care to theological students should be familiar with both the classic and contemporary forms of that art.

Bibliography. H. J. M. Nouwen, *Reaching Out* (1975). D. S. Browning, *Generative Man* (1975).

K. R. MITCHELL

CALL TO MINISTRY; THEOLOGICAL STUDENTS, EVALUATION AND EMPIRICAL STUDIES OF. *See also* VOCATION (Protestantism). *Compare* CAREER DEVELOPMENT AND GUIDANCE (For Pastors); PASTOR, PASTORAL CARE OF; READINESS FOR MINISTRY STUDIES; RELIGIOUS, PASTORAL CARE OF.

THEOLOGICAL VIRTUES. See VIRTUE, CONCEPT OF. *See also* MORAL THEOLOGY; SPIRITUAL THEOLOGY.

THEOLOGY, BIBLICAL. See OLD TESTAMENT AND APOCRYPHA; NEW TESTAMENT.

THEOLOGY, CHRISTIAN. (1) Theology in general is disciplined reflection about God as the ultimate origin, meaning, and goal of the world and human life. This reflection is usually done in the context of a religious community united by the conviction that God is known, experienced, trusted, and served in light of some normative revelation of divine activity and purposes given in particular events, experiences, and persons in the past history of the community. (2) Christian theology is a form of theology that seeks to understand the world and human life in light of faith in the creative, reconciling, and renewing purposes of God revealed in the history of ancient Israel and in Jesus, as that history is interpreted in the Bible and further interpreted in the past and present thought of the Christian church. Theological reflection always involves a mutually informative dialogue between its normative sources and human experience in a particular political, economic, cultural, and historical environment.

S. C. GUTHRIE

PASTORAL THEOLOGICAL METHODOLOGY. *See also* CONTEXTUAL, EMPIRICAL, EXPERIENTIAL, LIBERATION, MORAL, NEOORTHODOX, PASTORAL, PROCESS, *or* SPIRITUAL THEOLOGY.

THEOLOGY, JEWISH. There is a good deal of debate about whether or not Judaism even has a theology. It does not, of course, present a creed that is salvific or a dogmatic structure that determines membership in a believing church. But from the core of Deuteronomy through the rabbinic *aggadah* (nonlegal passages), and from Maimonides's Thirteen Articles of Belief to the modern day epigones of Germany's Franz Rosenzweig and Martin Buber, there is abundant evidence of theological reflection.

The three principles of Jewish theologizing are God, Torah, and the people of Israel. About God's inner nature not much is asserted (except for theosophical mysticism in the Kabbalah and Hasidism). Judaism is much more concerned with what God wants than with who God is. Monotheism means, in practice, a single-minded love and fear of One who can never be known fully. The false gods of paganism or of contemporary chauvinisms are the real enemies of the Jewish Creator who loves all humankind, and offers himself to them.

Torah means, in widening circles of reference, the Five Books of Moses, which are the central documents of both Jewish law and Jewish theology, the whole of Scripture, its oral interpretation, which is asserted to be as primary as written doctrine, and finally all of Jewish tradition even to the last question of the last student. Torah is both revelation and law, both doctrine and way. It is God's anthropology more than human theologizing. It constitutes the parameters of Jewish obedience, as well as the central issue of debate between Orthodox and non-Orthodox thinkers in modern times.

The people of Israel and the land of Israel are at the center of Jewish thinking. Deuteronomy already knows of the scandal of Jewish particularity and Judah Halevi puts it at the forefront of his medieval existentialist version of theology, the Kuzari. God is everyone's God but still this God chooses the Jewish community as symbol and servant, commanded to perform prodigies of obedience and to live both separate from and in service to the whole world. Jewish theology wrestles with reconciling a universal vision with an insistence on the prerogatives and hopes of the beleaguered people itself. Persecution and, finally, holocaust are the sharpest edge of this problem. The state of Israel is the other crucial present-day problem for Jewish theologians of all stripes. But more intimate concerns, like family and diet and the dilemmas of living in several civilizations simultaneously, have their place in modern Jewish speculation as well. Since the Emancipation, at the beginning of the nineteenth century, the old consensus, which never reached unanimity in any case, has been broken. If there is any unity at all now, it is the unity of the Jewish spiritual landscape and the consistency of millennial concerns.

A. J. WOLF

JUDAISM AND PSYCHOLOGY. *See also* FAMILY, JEWISH THEOLOGY AND ETHICS OF; MARRIAGE (Jewish Theology and Care); PERSON (Jewish Perspective).

THEOLOGY, JOURNALS IN. *See* JOURNALS IN RELIGION, THEOLOGY, AND THE SOCIAL SCIENCES, INTERDISCIPLINARY.

THEOLOGY AND PERSONALITY, DISCIPLINE OF. *See* PASTORAL THEOLOGY, PROTESTANT.

THEOLOGY AND PSYCHOANALYSIS. *See* PSYCHOANALYSIS AND THEOLOGY.

THEOLOGY AND PSYCHOLOGY. This essay describes different types of relationship which may pertain between the two disciplines of theology and psychology in the effort to lay a systematic interdisciplinary foundation for ministry.

The discipline of theology here refers to constructive thematized reflection by the Christian community upon its own nature and life. The movement of theological reflection, then, is from conviction to systematic expression in relation to culture and back again to deepening conviction. Thus, the emphasis will be upon systematic theology as distinct from doctrinal, historical, or biblical theology.

The discipline of psychology, understood as the study of the human personality, includes academic psychology, social psychology, and clinical psychology, chiefly variations on the psychoanalytic tradition. Excluded here is popular psychology or any form of psychological reflection that does not have behind it a body of empirical research.

The interdisciplinary methodologies set forth are ways in which these two disciplines have been related so as to allow both to be treated with integrity. Methodologies that violate the integrity of one discipline for the sake of the other are excluded. Moreover, certain subdisciplines such as psychology of religion and theological anthropology are not dealt with as such.

Historically, the modern concern to relate theology to psychology for ministry began with Schleiermacher in his classic encyclopedia of theological studies, *Brief Outline of the Study of Theology*. The essence of his position was that theology, philosophical and historical, be the overarching rationale for all that is done in practical theology as aided by the human sciences.

Schleiermacher viewed human sciences, and psychology in particular, not only as a practical tool for the application of philosophical and historical theology to the pragmatic issues of ministry, but also as an aid to keep the circle of ministerial practice and theological reflection itself constructive and alive to new developments. However, Schleiermacher did not precisely engage the questions addressed here: how is psychology to interact with theology for the sake of ministerial practice, and how is this interaction to be guided, maintained, and enhanced without distortion on either side?

1. Unsatisfactory Methods. *a. Semantic connections.* Systematically, the common tendency to cross-fertilize the disciplines by finding semantic connections — the same word in both disciplines is thought to bridge the two — must be rejected as trivializing and distorting. Here are some examples of obvious difficulties: (1) Anxiety, clinically understood, is a signal that something is wrong; but in existentialist theology, anxiety, as a recognition of one's finitude and the emergence of the human spirit, is a sign that something is right; (2) *object relations* in clinical language refers to interpersonal relationships, which are both positive and negative; but *object* applied to persons in theology implies distancing and depersonalization of relationships. Terms and concepts must be kept within their own larger disciplinary contexts if they are to be the focus of an interdisciplinary study.

b. Reductionism. Also to be rejected are radical reductionistic methods in which one discipline states, in effect, that the substance of the other discipline is "nothing but" a subcategory of its own structure, and, consequently, the fundamental claims of the other discipline are explained away. On the surface, Freud's reductionistic treatment of religion makes theology "nothing but" a symptom of regression and neurotic behavior. On the other side, the early work of Karl Barth reduced all secular disciplines to total ignorance where the truth of God and humanity were concerned; they are "nothing but" unredemptive expressions of human fallenness.

Less obvious but more pervasive is the popular use of Carl Jung's analytical psychology as a way of interpreting biblical and theological concerns to the human condition. These interpretations tend to focus on the biographies of key figures who range from the patriarchs, to St. Paul, and St. Theresa. Where theological themes are permitted a genuine interaction with Jungian understanding of the psyche, these particular forms of interdisciplinary dialogue can be fruitful, but where Jung's thought claims the final word on the significance of theological matters, a radical reductionism takes over. Specifically, Jung's attempt to make Christ a symbol of the self is a reduction of the ontological reality of his nature to a psychic phenomenon. By this basic claim, Jungian Christology drifts toward gnosticism, and a reduction of Christian salvation to the individuation process.

2. Types of Relationship. Because theology and psychology as disciplines are developed from fundamentally different premises and reflect on distinctly different levels of generality, a wide variety of methodological approaches to relating them and their findings prevails. All approaches tend to stress one side or the other, so the following section will indicate where theological perspectives are dominant and where psychological perspectives predominate. The major emphasis is given to the theologically dominant perspective because theologians seem to have given considerably more attention to the possibilities and problems in interdisciplinary methodology than most psychologists. None of these positions is definitive since the overall endeavor to do this sort of interdisciplinary work is still very young.

a. Tillich's correlational method. A fundamental generic type of interdisciplinary methodology is the correlational method developed by Paul Tillich as the foundation for his systematic theology. Here existential questions raised by the inherent ambiguities of the human situation were to be answered by the gospel, whose center for human existence is the new being in Jesus as the Christ. Tillich made considerable use of depth psychology to articulate the nature of the questions raised by human existence, but it should be noted that he saw the issues as fundamentally existential, not functional and adaptational. Thus, the contribution of depth psychology in the correlational method is to point to the deeper ontological issues of human existence, which only the gospel of Christ can address.

b. Hiltner's perspectual method. In fundamental agreement with Tillich's concern for correlation, but finding the actual dynamics of the method unclear and potentially too static, Seward Hiltner developed a perspectual approach which treats theology and psychology as separate perspectives on a given experiential phenomenon. The phenomenon (e.g., psychopathology) is first viewed theologically (e.g., under the aspect of "sin") then the phenomenon is interpreted from a psychodynamic viewpoint (e.g., the pathological potential in chronic blame and guilt) with the aim that the theological understanding will become more sensitive and relevant to the concrete human situation. "What is religiously important about sin is not that somebody, we or our forefathers, did bad things. Of course they did and we have done so too. It is that the decisions of human life even when they turn out badly, are not above repair if they are seen within the context of the God who unambiguously wills the fulfillment of human kind so long as he does not have to remove man's freedom in the providential process of assistance" (Hiltner, p. 107).

This move from theology to psychology and back to theology keeps the interdisciplinary circle intact with respect to a given phenomenon, but ontological and existential concerns are turned toward pragmatic and empirical criteria. Hiltner's view is not inconsistent with the Chicago school of empirical theology, but is better understood metaphysically from the standpoint of process theology.

c. Transcendental neo-Thomism. In Roman Catholic theology, the traditionally positive relationship between nature and grace has made the correlation of psychology and theology less problematic. The clearest and most influential approach which stresses interdisciplinary methodology is that of Bernard Lonergan. Lonergan's transcendental neo-Thomism is based on an epistemology which claims to be operative in all disciplines because it pertains to how we know *anything*. There are four phases of the knowing process which are necessary and sufficient in any field, but these phases have to be restated depending on the field in question. Generally, these phases are *experience, understanding, reflection*, and *judgment*. Lonergan's approach uses the necessary structure of cognition (the transcendental argument) as the basis for interdisciplinary study on the metaphysical ground that only such an approach yields true knowledge of Being.

Three conversions (intellectual, moral, and religious) are required to comprehend the inner coherence of Lonergan's theological position. The third (which may occur first) involves primarily submission to the otherworldly love of God. This conversion, which shapes and undergirds the others, puts all knowledge, moral and intellectual, in its ultimate context of meaning and being. Thus, Lonergan views psychology as a neo-Thomist for whom theology is distinct from, but completes without contradiction, the understanding of nature which the human sciences provide.

Lonergan's discussion of the psychology of human development in this context is illuminating since he moves well beyond those who want to establish direct one-to-one connections between stages of human development and theological doctrines or virtues.

Empirical studies make the experiential aspects of human development understandable, but Lonergan's reflective powers find the qualities of development at all levels, from inorganic to biological and psychological, to be isomorphically related to each other and proportionate to Being itself. Each higher level of integration emerges from lower levels and is successively transformed in the course of development toward an actualization of Being. Development is not a mere succession of stages, psychologically or theologically delineated; rather, the larger context of intelligible Being is the basis for psychological claims about the development of the human personality, as it is also the basis for the formulations of systematic theology. Thus, the intelligibility of Being is the foundation for transcending disciplinary boundaries and correlating theological and psychological claims about human nature. By the exercise of *judgment*, a transcendentally determinant decision emanating from experience, understanding, and reflection, Lonergan conceives of human development as following certain elementary laws (integrity, limitation, transcendence etc.,) in basic conformity to the development inherent in Being itself, finally completed only by the love of God. The definite "Yes" or "No" of judgment is, however, always open to further investigation in light of new experience, understanding, and reflection.

d. Phenomenology. Although no one figures as its main proponent, the phenomenological method technically interpreted through the work of Brentano, Husserl, Heidegger, Sartre, and Merleau-Ponty provides a distinctively different philosophical foundation for relating theology and psychology. Since the main thrust of phenomenology as a method is to bracket the worlds constructed by disciplinary structures, the method proposes to gain, via an intuition of Being (e.g., Heidegger), what the sciences of both psychology and theology obscure *a priori* by their disciplinary systems. Here it may be important to note that Heidegger makes a sharp distinction between "calculative thinking" which is intrinsic to all disciplinary systems and is preeminent in a scientific and technologically oriented society, and "meditative thinking" in which one recovers a profound sense of the Being in which the languages of psychology and theology are grounded and by which they are transcended.

Some persons use phenomenology as a method for exposing the nature of the human situation, but then turn to theology and revelation as a way of developing a response to the phenomenological situation. See Thomas Oden's *Structure of Awareness* as an example of this. Others want to make a full scale attempt to interpret theology and its relation to social and cultural realities phenomenologically. Edward Farley's project, carried out in *Ecclesial Man, Ecclesial Reflection*, and *Theologia*, is the foremost example.

In *Ecclesial Reflection* Farley works a Foucaultian purge of theological consciousness, deconstructing the "house of theological authority" in order to disclose the nature of theological judgment or "criteriology." It is from such a standpoint that faith recognizes and employs "ecclesial universals" and can thereby assess the significance of the sciences for ministerial practice. Farley's project establishes that some such ministerial judgment emerging from theology as *habitus* is necessary, but precisely what that implies for the interpretation of situations is not yet evident.

Others use phenomenology as a way of interpreting the spiritual life for which both psychology and theology provide modes of reflection and sources of insight. The writings of the Roman Catholic psychologist Adrian Van Kaam are an example of this use of phenomenology.

e. New hermeneutic. Emerging from the phenomenology of Being is the concern for language and the hermeneutical approach to interdisciplinary issues. Here the focus is upon the later Heidegger, Gadamer, and the new hermeneutic.

The ultimate inseparability of speech, meaning, and Being implied in this new hermeneutical discussion may be assimilated by theology to its doctrine of the Word; however, in psychology language is more narrowly conceived. Its analytical approaches tend to reduce language to its basic components and to their dependence on other aspects of the personality such as neurological, developmental, and cultural influences. But the new hermeneutic argues that the disciplines of psychology and theology are themselves "languages." Thus, in language broadly conceived we have the most fundamental way of interpreting interdisciplinary relationships.

Both empirical and classical disciplines are basically linguistic ways of expressing the fundamental intentionality of human consciousness toward knowledge. Moreover, this intentionality is not merely the property of the individual but is expressive of the entire history of human existence as it has responded with sensitivity and self-understanding to its place in Being. Since it is language that brings knowledge into existence in any discipline, the ultimate hermeneutical position is that the truth of Being continually emerges as both disciplines create new linguistic worlds of meaning. However, this continues only so long as those worlds do not lose their rootedness in history and Being. No discipline *qua* discipline has any reality in and of itself; thus, dialogue between disciplines should be the sort of conversation or interplay in which the linguistic foundations for their participation become increasingly generative and creative of what is fundamentally true about humanity (cf. Gadamer, *Truth and Method*, p. 345.). Such truth, however, can only be generated by such an interplay, not structured *a priori* by any system.

This hermeneutical approach is sometimes given its bearings in terms of "root metaphors" by which disciplinary boundaries are transcended, and the governing approach is said to be controlled and directed by a deep underlying metaphor such as the notions of "machine" or "organism" might suggest. Perhaps one of the most provocative root metaphors is that of "the artist" suggested by Gadamer and carried further by Gibson Winter. The root metaphor of the artist includes but transforms technical mastery suggested by the machine as well as concerns for wholeness suggested by the organism, and it suggests, supports and guides a fundamental mode of interaction by which new expressions of reality may be created through dialogical exchange among disciplines.

f. Structuralism. The prominence of structuralism stems in part from the quest for mind, which has been the perennial preoccupation of the French intellectual tradition. However, structuralism is a diverse phenomenon and has strong advocates in other parts of Europe and the U.S. Chief figures in France are anthropologist Claude Lévi-Strauss and psychoanalyst Jacques Lacan; in Switzerland, genetic epistomologist, Jean Piaget. Followers in the U.S. are Lawrence Kohlberg, Carol Gilligan, Robert Kegan, and James Fowler. Structuralism has made its major contributions to the human sciences, and it has not been especially concerned with theological matters. Of course, in the effort to understand the universal structures of mind, structuralism is implicitly coming to an understanding of the structures of the theologian's mind and its product, theology, as well.

The essence of the position is that all thought including the discipline of psychology and theology is governed by innate structural potentials. In psychology, the developmental emergence of the formal properties of intelligence, language, moral judgment, and other dominant registers of behavior is constructed out of the interaction of the personality with its environment. Moreover, they emerge according to an invariant sequence which moves the individual's adaptational competence to ever higher levels of complexity management. Piaget's genetic epistemology has had its predominant influence in psychology and his work has gained theological significance only indirectly through Kohlberg, Fowler, and, to some extent, Kegan. Lévi-Strauss's analyses of myth and narrative structure have found some currency in biblical theology, especially in the analysis of OT stories and NT parables, but not yet in systematic theology.

The simplest illustration of structuralism applied to theological considerations is James Fowler's attempt to describe "faith" as having formal structural properties apart from but immanent in whatever the content of faith might be. The maturation of these formal properties toward increased internal complexity and universality of scope indicates how mature one's "faith" actually is. The interpretative value of this position lies in its capacity to classify persons according to their cognitive competence in structuring meaning. Consequently the position is heavily criticized as to both its theological and its psychological adequacy. Nevertheless, structuralism is receiving increased attention, and with advances in research on neurological structures, more sophisticated attempts to interpret psychopathology as well as attempts to understand theological notions in structuralist categories are emerging.

g. Developing approaches. Several points of view should be mentioned which are derivative from or revisions of these five positions. Most notable is David Tracy's constructive use of "analogical imagination" to make the move between theology and a contemporary pluralistic culture of which the discipline of psychology is an aspect. He employs a "revised correlational method," which he envisions as less one-sided than Tillich's and more reciprocal. His position critically correlates both questions and answers that come from various secular or non-Christian interpretations of existence, with interpretations of the questions and answers conveyed in Christian revelation. This makes the exchange in the correlational method more diversified and active than Tillich's use of the method, without compromising depth. Notable is Tracy's recognition of Jesus Christ as the master analogy for relating the divine and the human. Thus his more vital correlational exchange is to be governed and perpetuated by both the critical and constructive power of this analogy. This is consistent with those positions which take as a premise the "unity of truth" as revealed in Christ (e.g., Narramore and Carter, *Integrating Psychology and Theology*), but it raises the issue of methodology to a more explicit and sophisticated level of operation.

Also utilizing analogy and a "revised correlational method" is Don Browning. His early, ground-breaking work in *Atonement and Psychotherapy* developed the analogical relationship between a Rogerian approach to healing and the atonement. More recently in the context of practical theology, he has worked out five levels of practical moral thinking: (1) a deep metaphorical level; (2) an obligational level; (3) a tendency-need level; (4) a contextual level; and (5) a rule-role level. These levels govern interdisciplinary reflection and action as he has demonstrated in part in his book *Religious Thought and the Modern Psychologies*.

Following the emergence of process thought as the metaphysical basis for relating theology and psychotherapy is the work of James Lapsley. Moving beyond Hiltner in his explicit dependence upon process theology, Lapsley, in *Salvation and Health*, envisions six stages of adult participation being actualized with increased complexity. In addition to process theology, ego psychology and relational motifs in soteriology influenced this position.

Related to the transformational pattern implied in Lonergan, in the hermeneutical approach, and in the stage transition process as embedded in structuralist thinking, James Loder (1981) has argued that transformation *per se* has its own grammar or logic, and this serves as an interdisciplinary methodology that not only connects theology and psychology at points central to both disciplines but also extracts a theme common to most other interdisciplinary methodologies.

3. Conclusions. It is evident from this brief survey that the two disciplines of theology and psychology are not easily combined, and that for responsible connections to be made between them some methodological formulations need to be made explicit. If not, reductionism or a vague methodological syncretism is the result.

Methodology in most cases makes definite philosophical assumptions which are developed either in the direction of epistemology or metaphysics or both. Whether such philosophical intervention in the interdisciplinary discussion results in a new sort of *tertium quid* reductionism is still an open question.

What seems evident is that no single methodology will do the job satisfactorily. It is perhaps best to view the task of methodology in relating psychology and theology as an effort to make connections between the disciplines explicit, cognitively reversible, and subject to public scrutiny. The aim of the task of relating theology and psychology should be mutual correction for the sake of a mutually enlightening contribution to the disclosure of what is most fully and truly human about our common humanity.

Bibliography. D. Browning, *Atonement and Psychotherapy* (1966); *Religious Thought and the Modern Psychologies* (1987); D. Browning ed., *Practical Theology* (1983). E. Farley, *Ecclesial Man* (1975); *Ecclesial Reflection* (1982); *Theologia* (1983). H. G. Gadamer, *Truth and Method* 2d ed., (1979). S. Hiltner, *Preface*

to *Pastoral Theology* (1958); *Theological Dynamics* (1980). J. Lapsley, *Salvation and Health* (1972). J. Loder, *The Transforming Moment* (1981). B. J. F. Lonergan, *Method in Theology* (1972). B. Narramore and J. Carter, *The Integration of Psychology and Theology* (1979). T. Oden, *The Structure of Awareness* (1969). F. Schleiermacher, *Brief Outline of the Study of Theology* (1850).

J. LODER

PASTORAL THEOLOGICAL METHODOLOGY; PHILOSOPHY AND PSYCHOLOGY; THEOLOGY; THEOLOGY AND PSYCHOTHERAPY. *See also* ANALYTICAL (JUNGIAN) PSYCHOLOGY AND THEOLOGY; HUMANISTIC PSYCHOLOGY AND THEOLOGY; PSYCHOANALYSIS AND THEOLOGY; *also* FAITH DEVELOPMENT RESEARCH; INTEGRATION OF PSYCHOLOGY AND THEOLOGY; INTERPRETATION AND HERMENEUTICS, PASTORAL; PHENOMENOLOGICAL PSYCHOLOGY; PSYCHOTHEOLOGY; STRUCTURALISM. *Compare* JUDAISM AND PSYCHOLOGY; PASTORAL THEOLOGY; PRACTICAL THEOLOGY. *Biography:* HILTNER; LONERGAN; TILLICH.

THEOLOGY AND PSYCHOTHERAPY. 1. Historical Development. If psychotherapy can be defined as the treatment of emotional or spiritual difficulties by verbal and symbolic means (as opposed to chemical, surgical, and physical therapies), then theology was the theoretical base for psychotherapy from ancient times until the Enlightenment. The richest flourishing of that theory-practice relationship can be seen in the fifteenth-century *Malleus Maleficarum*, a treatise on the healing of spiritual ills by driving out the demons presumed to be the cause of the trouble.

In the eighteenth century, such a theological assumption about the nature of illness and therapy disappeared for the most part in the Western world. Demon possession as a cause of illness, and exorcism or similar symbolic treatments as a cure, now have a small following among certain Christians popularly called "charismatic" and some Westerners deeply influenced by Eastern, non-Christian faiths.

In the eighteenth and most of the nineteenth centuries, emotional illness was thought of as lacking in any particular cause or meaning, and psychotherapy as defined above was not a prevalent aspect of treatment. (Asylum, rather than treatment, was what was provided to the sick.) When psychodynamic assumptions about emotional ills began to be accepted, and psychotherapy became an important form of treatment, theological questions could be asked about psychotherapy. This time, however, psychotherapy had its theoretical roots in a thoroughly secular understanding of human beings, and emotional ills were traced to conflicts between forces within the personality. Thus theology, rather than being a "queen of the sciences" that could offer a fundamental explanation for illness, became an interested commentator: sometimes admonishing, sometimes admiring, but never at the center of the struggle to deal verbally and symbolically with emotional troubles.

2. Contemporary Thought. A high point in the dialogue between theology and psychotherapy was reached in the late 1950s and early 1960s when Karl Barth and Paul Tillich dominated the theological landscape, and the particular therapeutic modality of Carl R. Rogers's client-centered therapy engaged the interest of clergy almost exclusively. The views of Barth and Tillich concerning the relation of theology to human culture and experience were radically different. Tillich took a keen interest in psychotherapy, and particularly in the analytic psychotherapies, believing that they had a contribution to make to theological dialogue. Barth may have respected psychotherapy as a human process, but accorded it no place in theology.

Don S. Browning and Thomas C. Oden, who were both well versed both in Barth's theology and in Rogers's therapeutic theory, saw a possibility of pulling the two sets of ideas into dialogue with each other. At first glance, it seems to be an odd juxtaposition: the therapy of Rogers was founded upon a thoughtful but insistent optimism about human nature, while Barth held a classical, almost Augustinian, concept of sin. To Rogers, telling someone something for that person's own good was anathema, while Barth's understanding of ministry put proclamation (kerygma) in first place.

Yet Browning and Oden saw subtle parallels between the thinking of Barth and that of Rogers. The empathy of a good Rogerian therapist, which should lead to self-understanding, was seen as parallel to the doctrine of the humanity of Christ, which theologically supports the faith that one is known fully by God. Similarly, the therapist's acceptance of the client, designed to open the door to self-acceptance, has its parallel in God's forgiveness which, when appropriated, leads to a sense of being forgiven.

Both Browning and Oden can be said to have been theologizing about the strategy and tactics of the psychotherapeutic process. Since the 1960s, however, no major efforts of a similar kind have been mounted, although important issues about psychotherapy have arisen which call for theological comment and interpretation.

Paul Tillich's work foreshadowed, in a way, these more contemporary questions. Tillich saw profound questions raised in a thoroughgoing psychotherapeutic process concerning the nature of human existence and suggested that beyond the neurotic anxiety dealt with by therapists there existed an existential anxiety which required theological understanding. As a theologian, Tillich viewed psychotherapy as a process which could clarify profound questions, but which could not be expected to provide answers to fundamental questions about human existence.

3. Continuing Challenges. In the meantime, new methods of psychotherapy were being proposed, many of which developed in popularity and influence. In addition to client-centered therapy and psychodynamically based therapies, one now sees reality therapy, family therapy, transactional analysis, primal scream, behavior modification, and a number of other treatments. Some alternative therapies are fads; certainly, many are more clever than profound. Such a variety implies increasing difficulty in examining therapy from a theological viewpoint, since each system has its own assumptions about human nature and helping behavior. A theological examination of the strategy and tactics of psychotherapy is no longer practicable.

A different kind of question seriously addressed by a few psychotherapists and fermenting among a few theologians seems to be a new challenge. This new dialogue concerns the goals and purposes, the *telos* of psychotherapy. Discussions in this area include a number of specific themes, including economic questions as well as questions clustering around the nature of health.

The economic questions focusing around psychotherapy have become a moral and theological problem. It is difficult for therapists, pastoral or secular, to offer psychotherapy at a cost many people can afford. (In the 1980s many church-related agencies reported that it cost upwards of $35-40 to deliver one hour of therapy.) This fact limits psychotherapy to persons in relatively high socioeconomic brackets. Although this issue is not, on its surface, directly related to the nature of psychotherapy, it has a subtle but profound impact upon the practice of psychotherapy.

The nature of health and wholeness is another issue undergoing theological examination. Under the impact of such theologians as Jürgen Moltmann, deeper recognition of the brokenness of our world is growing; this in turn raises the question of what it means to be a whole person in such a broken world.

This question arises at a time when Sigmund Freud's familiar formula about the goals of therapy, *lieben und arbeiten* (to love and to work), has received increasingly selfish interpretation in American culture. Freud's original formulation involved not only sexuality and productivity but a whole outlook on human interrelatedness now set aside by many psychotherapists as outmoded. Persons seeking therapy, as well as therapists, often bring to therapy expectations that the process should produce complete fulfillment; some theologians have dubbed this the "Bronze Dream." The relationship between theology and psychotherapy demands continuing theological commentary on this understanding of health and wholeness.

Bibliography. D. G. Benner, "The Incarnation as a Metaphor for Psychotherapy," *J. of Psychology and Theology*, 11(1983), 287–94. D. S. Browning, *Atonement and Psychotherapy* (1966). J. Moltmann, *The Crucified God* (1974). T. C. Oden, *Contemporary Theology and Psychotherapy* (1967); *Kerygma and Counseling: Toward a Covenant Ontology for Secular Psychotherapy* (1966). D. Roberts, *Psychotherapy and a Christian View of Man* (1950). W. S. Sabom, "Heresy and Pastoral Counseling," *J. of Pastoral Care*, 36 (1982), 76–86. A. Siirala, *The Voice of Illness* (1964). P. Tillich, *The Courage to Be* (1952); *Theology of Culture* (1959). R. D. Vanderploeg, "Imago Dei as Foundational to Psychotherapy: Integration versus Segregation," *J. of Psychology and Theology*, 9 (1981), 299–304. D. D. Williams, *The Minister and the Care of Souls* (1961).

K. R. MITCHELL

PASTORAL COUNSELING; PASTORAL PSYCHOTHERAPY; THEOLOGICAL METHODOLOGY; THEOLOGY AND PSYCHOLOGY. *See also* COUNSELING, ROMAN CATHOLIC; EXPERIENTIAL THEOLOGY; JUDAISM AND PSYCHOLOGY; PASTORAL THEOLOGY. *Compare* CURE OF SOULS TRADITION; PHILOSOPHY AND PSYCHOLOGY, WESTERN; RELIGION AND PSYCHOTHERAPY; SPIRITUAL DIRECTION, HISTORY AND TRADITIONS OF; VALUES IN COUNSELING AND PSYCHOTHERAPY. *Biography:* BARTH; ROBERTS; TILLICH; WILLIAMS.

THEOLOGY OF PASTORAL CARE AND COUNSELING. *See* PASTORAL THEOLOGICAL METHODOLOGY; PASTORAL THEOLOGY.

THEORY AND PRAXIS. Near the beginning of the nineteenth century, the philosopher Immanuel Kant wrote an essay entitled, "On the Old Saw: It May Work in Theory, but It Won't Work in Practice." The essay summarized the Enlightenment's attitude toward a philosophical issue that it had inherited from classical Greek philosophy and set the stage for what would prove to be a far-reaching recasting of the issue in nineteenth-century thought. In brief: What is the relation between those forms of knowledge and activity that are concerned with knowing for its own sake, and those that pertain to ethical and political life?

1. **Aristotle.** The origins of the distinction between theory and practice derive from Aristotle, who distinguished between *theoria* and *praxis*. Strictly speaking, *praxis* is "doing proper," whose end is not the production of an artifact but the performing of a particular activity in a certain way. Aristotle thereby sought to underscore the disciplines and activities in human ethical and political conduct, whose proper end is living well in the *polis*. To be sure, *theoria* for Aristotle is a form of life that requires strenuous disciplined activity, but since its end is knowing or wisdom for its own sake, it represents a distinct dimension of the free human life.

A good measure of confusion finds its way into the distinction Aristotle struck when it is recast as a *contrast* between theory and practice. Practice and the practical tend to strike us as referring to "nuts and bolts," the basic "how-tos" that are required for the maintenance of life. When practice and the practical are so understood, they stand not so much as a dimension of the free human life that differs from the theoretical as they do opposed to it: one who is concerned with the "practical" in this sense has little regard for the "theoretical."

2. **Kant and the "Left-Wing Hegelians."** This way of construing the issue was precisely what Kant opposed in certain strands of Enlightenment thinking. He argued instead that all human beings become aware of the possibility of acting freely, i.e., in accord with a self-legislated universal moral law. And he held further that this awareness consists in nothing other than pure reason (theoretical reason) becoming practical, i.e., reason directing human conduct to its highest (moral) end.

The force of Kant's arguments have had far-reaching appeal and have provided an interpretive basis for what was occurring politically in the American and French revolutions for freedom. For these and other reasons, Kant's concept of praxis had almost hypnotizing appeal among the radical young followers of Hegel who came to be known as the Left-Wing Hegelians. Desiring to "go beyond" Hegel, whom they regarded as being too ethereal, the Left-Wing Hegelians sought to develop a conception of philosophy that exercised a direct influence on the practices of social life. Following the lead of Feuerbach, Marx attempted to "materialize" the concept of praxis, outlining its actual role in the "economy" of social life. Accordingly, Marx thought that praxis was the process of production of objects, which when having mastery over humans alienates them from themselves; but, when becoming the means for free social and human expression, praxis becomes the source for overcoming this alienation. Indeed, in its most heightened form, praxis becomes revolutionary practice or the radical transformation of the alienating conditions of labor into the possibility of a humanized world.

However much the concept of praxis has come to be associated with the tradition of Marxist philosophies, its prominence has not been limited to Marxism. Other philosophical traditions—some more closely allied with Marxist thought (e.g., Sartrian existentialism) and some of quite disparate conception (e.g., contemporary Anglo-American analytic philosophy)—have accorded the notion of praxis a pivotal role. Moreover, the distinctly American tradition of pragmatism, as articulated by Dewey and Pierce, has been preoccupied with the nature of human action and practice and is itself a development in the line of thinking about the nature of praxis, deriving from critical revisions of proposals first set out by Hegel and Kant.

3. **Modern Theological Traditions of Praxis.** In a parallel fashion, traditions of theological thinking have evolved in the wake of Kant that also have accorded a pivotal role to the concept of praxis. Schleiermacher's *Brief Outline* and *Christian Faith* recognized the central role of the principles of church governance in the formation of Christian consciousness. In his view, ethics, or the systematic articulation of the principles that govern the shaping of consciousness, is the field from which the first propositions are to be derived in the interpretation of the nature of the church. Following this line of thinking, Ritschl claimed that there is a distinctive form of value judgment not bound to the historically mediating forces of culture—what he called an independent value judgment—that enables human beings to discern the distinctive course of conduct directing them to their highest (moral) ends. Ritschl identified such independent value judgments with the moral teachings of Jesus and claimed that these had a direct transformative effect upon human consciousness and conduct. Similarly, Hermann taught that one's encounter with the force of Jesus' personality as depicted in Scripture had a transformative effect.

More recent liberation and political theologies have radicalized these proposals, either by extending them, as in the case of Moltmann, or by breaking with them and adapting certain Marxist insights to the concrete social experiences of suffering and oppression, as in the cases of Gutierrez, Metz, and Bonino. Among contemporary liberation theologians, the pragmatist approach to decentering the concept of the self and its action and developing new approaches to the conception of praxis has found a new advocacy in the work of Rebecca Chopp.

The interpretation of these concerns in the field of pastoral theology has achieved prominence particularly in the last decade, especially through the efforts of Donald Capps (1984), Charles Gerkin (1984), and Charles Winquist (1979). A common thread in these endeavors is the growing preoccupation with narrative theology, or story, as a way of transforming the fragmentation of contemporary consciousness. Although Gerkin draws largely from the work of the hermeneutical tradition (especially the interpretation of that tradition by Gadamer), as does Capps (although inclining more to the views of Ricoeur), and Winquist has moved increasingly in the direction of deconstructive criticism, all three of them are allied in their fundamental insight that certain configurations of language already dispose humans to distinct conceptions of the world and of human conduct in that world, which the pastoral counselor must both engage and, by suggestive intervention, help to transform. In such thinking, accordingly, the locus of praxis is in the formation and transformation of "language games" that predispose the self, and in the enabling of the self to participate in the transformation of such language games.

Bibliography. R. J. Bernstein, *Praxis and Action* (1971). D. Capps, *Pastoral Care and Hermeneutics* (1984). C. V. Gerkin, *The Living Human Document* (1984). F. Schleiermacher, *Brief Outline of the Study of Theology* (1850); *The Christian Faith* 2d ed (1830; ET, 1928). C. Winquist, *Practical Hermeneutics* (1979).

D. S. PACINI

WISDOM AND PRACTICAL KNOWLEDGE. *See also* PRACTICAL THEOLOGY; PRAXIS / PRACTICE (Terminology). *Compare* PHILOSOPHY AND PSYCHOLOGY; PRAGMATISM AND PASTORAL CARE.

THEORY IN PASTORAL CARE AND COUNSELING, FUNCTIONS OF.

The practice of pastoral care and counseling presupposes an undergirding theory or theories in regard to the nature of the human being in relationship to God, the meaning of human distress or dysfunction, and the factors involved in enabling persons to move toward health and wholeness. The theory, whether examined or unexamined, is always operating and involves the functions of analysis, perspective, praxis, and comprehensive understanding, or interpretation, all of which interact simultaneously.

The function of *analysis* helps the pastor separate and explore three foci which constitute the helping process. One focus is examining who the person (couple/family) is in terms of his or her human nature as a person in relationship to God, significant others, and self. Emphasis is placed on the unique qualities, characteristics, and circumstances that are involved as these persons describe their lives. A second focus is assessing the "tragic flaw" that causes these persons discomfort or pain — what is amiss in their lives, family network, or social system. The third focus is determining the intervention which best enables healing to take place through the caring process. These three foci constitute a sequential process, clear awareness of which can assist a pastor to become more conscious of how he or she actually goes about caring for and counseling other persons more perceptively and responsibly.

Perspective is that function which relates explicitly to how a person sees himself or herself as a care deliverer in the process of analyzing a given situation. Every caring person brings to the process specific ideas, values, and motivations, conscious and unconscious, which directly affect style, strategy, and sensitivity to health and wholeness. Thus, a pastor utilizes knowledge of the divine-human relationship involved in an understanding of God, humankind, sin, and salvation. This perspective, along with the incorporation of learnings from the behavioral sciences, gives meaning to the way a pastor constructively engages another's faith and value structure in the caring process. Because effective pastoral care and counseling continually brings theory under scrutiny and evaluation in order that the practice may be more productive, further education, the use of clinical material, and collegial and supervisory critiques of one's ongoing work are essential aids in assessing the pastoral perspective in healing.

Praxis is that function which builds upon analysis and perspective to inform the actual application of knowledge and learning. The practice of pastoral care and counseling is effective not simply by reason of good intention, but by being informed regarding theological, psychological, and systemic understanding of human need and deliverance. What a pastor believes about the responsibility of a person seeking help determines the ways he or she attempts to help. If a pastor thinks that volition is the key to wholeness, then he or she will exhort. By contrast, if the pastor believes that understanding leads to constructive solutions, then he or she will instruct or seek to draw out insight. Again, if the pastor is convinced that reconciliation is essential for renewal, then he or she will seek to facilitate forgiveness. Thus, the pastor's concept of the nature and function of the "tragic flaw" (for instance) influences the practical approach to the caring, though praxis most find specific and concrete ways of implementing it.

Comprehensive understanding is that function which pulls together analysis, perspective and praxis into a single, meaningful whole, and thus constitutes one's most inclusive, overarching principle of practice. Presumably such understanding for the pastor is or ought to be theology. (This does not mean that actual counseling must move immediately or always to the use of theological or religious language, though at some point that may well be in order.) It does mean that the pastoral counselor should be critically aware of his or her most basic operating theory because that conception of the meaning of care (and perhaps of life itself) shapes and colors the other functions at deep psychic and operational levels. At the same time it is possible that comprehensive understanding may in turn also be shaped and colored by the other functions. In this case the attempt to grasp what is going on through analysis, the recognition and forming of one's own perspectival slant, and even the search for specific means of implementing care (praxis) may all impact one's comprehensive or fundamental principle of understanding, creating a multifaceted dialectical relationship between theory and practice.

Bibliography. L. T. Howe, "Theology in the Practice of Ministry," *J. of Pastoral Counseling*, 19 (1984 [misprinted 1985]), 128–35. R. L. Kinast, "A Process Model of Theological Reflection," *J. of Pastoral Care*, 37 (1983), 144–55; "How Pastoral Theology Functions," *Theology Today*, 37:4 (1981), 425–38. D. A. Schön, *The Reflective Practitioner: How Professionals Think in Action* (1983). J. D. Whitehead and E. E. Whitehead, *Method in Ministry* (1980).

S. R. BROWN

WISDOM AND PRACTICAL KNOWLEDGE. *See also* PASTORAL THEOLOGY; PRAXIS/PRACTICE (Terminology); RELIGIOUS LANGUAGE IN PASTORAL CARE; PASTORAL THEOLOGICAL METHODOLOGY; THEORY AND PRAXIS. *Compare* PHENOMENOLOGICAL METHOD IN PASTORAL CARE; PRACTICAL THEOLOGY; REASONING AND RATIONALITY IN PASTORAL CARE.

THERAPEUTIC COMMUNITY.

A systems approach to treatment that uses natural social relationships as major agents of therapeutic change. The current meaning of the term *therapeutic community* designates many things. The original intent was to develop treatment modalities that were similar to the natural world by recognizing that group processes not only caused maladaptive behavior but also could reverse such trends. Helping clients to adapt to society was believed possible if a therapeutic environment could approximate the real world.

Originally the term was applied by Maxwell Jones during the post–World War II era to the rapid resocialization of prisoners of war in a small face-to-face residential community. Historically, the four primary goals included use of a democratic process, reality confrontation, permissive tolerance of disturbed behavior, and egalitarianism.

Today the term is applied to life in the hospital ward or within a community-based setting. The community is viewed not merely as a gathering of isolated patients for individual treatment, but as a cohesive group in which all interpersonal relationships are used for therapeutic purposes. Everyone is made to feel a part of the community since change is believed more likely to occur when everyone shares perceptions that certain changes are desirable. Therapeutic communities aim for group discussion and negotiation rather than strict reliance upon authoritative decision making.

Development of the therapeutic community has led to use of a social systems approach and expansion of treatment to the neighborhood (e.g., group therapy, community outreach education, day treatment, drop-in centers, and halfway houses).

The concept of therapeutic community enhances an understanding of how God's divine nature is seen in the created world. First, there is equality among group members with no divisions based upon education or background, just as all stand equal before God under grace and all are equally important in the church. Second, there is unity in diversity; individual members separately exercise unique gifts, and balanced leadership leads to the common good. Third, the dignity and unconditional worth of each individual is preserved, congruent with creation in God's image. Fourth, individuals are responsible not only for their own actions but also for the process of ministering to others (Gal. 6:1–5). Fifth, relationships are central in the life of the community. This reflects the priority that God places on relationships: divine-human relationships primarily and human-human relationships secondarily (Mt. 22:37–40). The expression of this truth for therapeutic communities is in the application of trust and cooperation between persons in need of care and healing.

Bibliography. M. Jones, *Beyond the Therapeutic Community: Social Learning and Social Psychiatry* (1968).

J. J. FOG
J. V. GILMORE

COMMUNITY, FELLOWSHIP, AND CARE; GROUP COUNSELING AND PSYCHOTHERAPY; PSYCHOTHERAPY (Varieties, Traditions, and Issues). *See also* CHRISTIAN THERAPY UNIT; GROUP DYNAMICS, PROCESS, AND RESEARCH; HAVURAH. *Compare* GROWTH GROUPS; HALFWAY HOUSE; MILIEU THERAPY; RELIGIOUS AND UTOPIAN COMMUNITIES; SELF-HELP PSYCHOLOGIES; SUPPORT GROUPS.

THERAPEUTIC CONDITIONS. The psychologically relevant circumstances, provided by the psychotherapist or counselor to the client in the context of their immediate relationship, which facilitate constructive personality change in the client.

1. The Therapeutic Triad. Research in the field of psychotherapy (see Truax and Carkhuff) has indicated that client outcome or benefit relates significantly to the levels of certain conditions provided by the therapist. Probably the most widely researched of these conditions if the "therapeutic triad" of self-congruence, respect, and accurate empathy.

a. Self-congruence refers to the relationship between the therapist's inner experience and outward behavior. A congruent therapist genuinely is what he or she *is* — without facade, defensiveness, or playing a role. The congruent therapist is aware of his or her own feelings, accepts and lives them, and communicates them to the client if appropriate.

b. Respect refers to the therapist's ability to prize or care for the other simply because he or she is a human being, and not on the basis of performance or other criteria. However, while suspending critical judgment or evaluation, the therapist nevertheless appreciates the person's human potentials and is committed to enabling the other to actualize those potentials. In this process the therapist sees the other as self-determining and refuses to take responsibility for the client. Whereas congruence relates to the *therapist's* freedom to be himself or herself, respect involves the therapist's ability to create a safe, accepting environment in which the *client* is free to be. Called "unconditional positive regard" by Carl Rogers, this dimension may involve nonpossessive warmth as one aspect of the therapist's caring.

c. Accurate empathy may be defined as the therapist's ability accurately and sensitively to understand the client's experiences and feelings and their meaning to the client in the moment-to-moment encounter. As therapist, one does not isolate oneself from the other but rather actively enters into the client's feelings in order to experience life from that person's perspective. The empathic therapist attends not only to the verbal expressions of the client but also to the subtler cues available in the client's voice qualities and body language, as well as within the therapist's own intuition. Empathy thus includes awareness not only of the client's overtly expressed feelings but also of the veiled feelings and experiences of which the client may not even be conscious. Furthermore, merely understanding the client's inner world is not sufficient. The therapist must also be able to communicate this understanding to the other in such a way that the client can grasp and use it to further his or her own self-awareness.

This triad of factors, which grew out of studies by Rogers and others (1967), forms the backbone of client-centered approaches to therapy. Indeed, Rogers hypothesizes (1957) that these three conditions are both necessary and sufficient (if provided over a period of time) to bring about constructive personality and behavioral change in the client.

2. Other Therapeutic Conditions. Some writers see Rogers's triad as too simplified an analysis of the helping process. Accordingly, other conditions have been advanced (see Carkhuff) as important aspects of effective therapy. Among these are: concreteness or specificity of expression (the therapist's ability to steer away from vague and anonymous generalities and to focus on specific, personally meaningful material); self-disclosure (appropriate sharing of the therapist's own values, attitudes, and experiences); confrontation (pointing out discrepancies in the client's behavior); and immediacy of relationship (the therapist's ability explicitly to relate to the expressions of the client which reflect the client's feelings toward the therapist in the present moment).

In addition, as therapist one must be able to time one's responses to the needs of the client and to the client's ability to grasp one's interpretations experientially. Thus Egan and others propose that effective therapy moves through stages—for instance, from simpler to more advanced (or "deeper") levels of empathy, confrontation, and so forth.

While there are many ways of conceptualizing the important conditions for effective therapy, the implications of the research are clear: how the therapist relates to the client affects the client and the results of therapy.

Bibliography. R. R. Carkhuff, *Helping and Human Relations,* vol. 1 (1969). G. Egan, *The Skilled Helper* (1975). C. R. Rogers, E. Gendlin, D. Kiesler, and C. B. Truax, eds., *The Therapeutic Relationship and Its Impact* (1967); "The Necessary and Sufficient Conditions of Therapeutic Personality Change," *J. of Consulting Psychology,* 21 (1957), 95–103. C. B. Truax and R. R. Carkhuff, *Toward Effective Counseling and Psychotherapy* (1967).

B. VAN DRAGT

PSYCHOTHERAPY; PSYCHOTHERAPY AND COUNSELING (Research Studies and Methods). *Compare* RITUAL AND PASTORAL CARE.

THERAPEUTIC MOVEMENTS. *See* POPULAR THERAPEUTIC MOVEMENTS AND PSYCHOLOGIES.

THERAPIST. *See* PSYCHOTHERAPIST. *See also* CHRISTIAN PSYCHOTHERAPIST *or* PSYCHOLOGIST; MARRIAGE AND FAMILY THERAPIST; PSYCHIATRIST/PSYCHIATRY.

THERAPY/THERAPIES. *See* PSYCHOTHERAPY. *See also* PASTORAL COUNSELING; PASTORAL PSYCHOTHERAPY; POPULAR THERAPEUTIC MOVEMENTS AND PSYCHOLOGIES.

THERESA OF AVILA, ST. (1515–82). Religious foundress, mystic, and writer. Born into an aristocratic family in Avila (Spain), Theresa entered a convent in her hometown at the age of twenty. Two decades later (in 1555) she underwent a "true conversion," which led her to found convents across Spain dedicated to a life of austerity and contemplative prayer. She was aided in this effort by St. John of the Cross. These convents were known as discalced (i.e., "shoeless") Carmelite convents because of the characteristic sandals worn with rough brown habits.

Encouraged by her spiritual directors, Theresa wrote, in a vigorous vernacular, a number of books: her autobiography; *The Way of Perfection* (a manual of piety for her nuns); and her most mature work, *The Interior Castle,* which was a treatise on contemplative prayer. Noted for her intelligence, deep faith, and quick wit, Theresa was the first woman (along with St. Catherine of Siena) to be named, in 1970, as a

Doctor of the Church, this honor coming three-and-a-half centuries after her canonization.

Bibliography. H. Hatzfeld, *Santa Teresa de Avila* (1969).

L. S. CUNNINGHAM

MYSTICISM; SPIRITUAL MASTERS AND GUIDES; SPIRITUALITY (Roman Catholic Tradition).

THERESA, MOTHER. *See* MOTHER TERESA OF CALCUTTA.

THINKING. *See* COGNITIVE PSYCHOLOGY AND PSYCHOTHERAPY; FEELING, THOUGHT, AND ACTION IN PASTORAL COUNSELING; REASONING AND RATIONALITY IN PASTORAL CARE.

THIRD FORCE PSYCHOLOGY. *See* HUMANISTIC *or* EXISTENTIAL PSYCHOLOGY AND PSYCHOTHERAPY.

THOMAS À KEMPIS (ca. 1380–1471). Monk and spiritual writer. Educated by the Brethren of the Common Life, Thomas entered the monastery of the Canons Regular of Mount St. Agnes in Holland in 1399. He lived there for the remainder of his long life, serving for periods in various monastic offices. He was an assiduous copyist of manuscripts and a prolific writer of treatises on spiritual matters and hagiographical works.

Thomas is credited as the author of *The Imitation of Christ,* a work which has gone through three thousand editions, with translations into nearly a hundred languages. The work reflects the then popular *devotio moderna,* that is, an interiorized piety focused on the humanity of Christ and a dedication to the interior cultivation of Christ's virtues. The work recommends a strongly interior piety with a concomitant depreciation of external works of piety such as pilgrimage and the cults of the saint's relics. It recommends the imitation of the humility and self-giving of Christ, especially as those virtues are reflected in the passion of Christ.

The long-term influence of this work cannot be overestimated. It was a decisive text for Ignatius of Loyola, thus bringing its emphasis on meditation on the humanity of Christ into Catholic Reformation spirituality via the Jesuits. The work was often reprinted in Protestant countries, sometimes with excisions of its more Roman Catholic elements such as the doctrine of transubstantiation.

Bibliography. R. R. Post, *The Modern Devotion* (1968).

L. S. CUNNINGHAM

SPIRITUALITY (Roman Catholic Tradition).

THOMAS AQUINAS, ST. (1224–74). Italian Dominican theologian and philosopher, teacher at Paris.

From the rich life and the erudite writings—notably, the famous *Summa theologiae*—of this medieval thinker, two items merit particular attention for their relevance for pastoral care. One, in response to his theological predecessors' unresolved problem of penance, Aquinas, like some of his contemporaries, supplied definitions of the four parts of penance as well as elaborations of its sacramental character. Second, although his scholarship is credited with founding theology as a science, his elevation of the *vita contemplativa* over the *vita activa* has led, at least in continental Catholic theology, to negative consequences: to a false superiority of theory over praxis and even a hostility to praxis. Although somewhat modified in the scholastic debate with Duns Scotus's *theologia practica*, currents of Thomas's concepts have shaped pastoral and practical theology until challenged by liberation theology in the twentieth century.

N. F. HAHN

PASTORAL THEOLOGY, ROMAN CATHOLIC; PHILOSOPHY AND PSYCHOLOGY, WESTERN.

THILO, HANS-JOACHIM. *See* PASTORAL THEOLOGY, PROTESTANT.

THOMISM. *See* PHILOSOPHY *or* THEOLOGY AND PSYCHOLOGY; PASTORAL THEOLOGY, ROMAN CATHOLIC.

THOMPSON, MURRAY. *See* CANADIAN PASTORAL CARE MOVEMENT.

THORNTON, EDWARD. *See* PASTORAL THEOLOGY, PROTESTANT.

THORNTON, MARTIN. *See* PASTORAL THEOLOGY, PROTESTANT.

THOUGHT DISORDERS. *See* COGNITIVE DEVELOPMENT; COGNITIVE PSYCHOLOGY AND PSYCHOTHERAPY; ORGANIC MENTAL DISORDER AND ORGANIC BRAIN SYNDROME.

THOUGHT PROCESSES. *See* COGNITIVE PSYCHOLOGY AND PSYCHOTHERAPY; FEELING, THOUGHT, AND ACTION IN PASTORAL COUNSELING; REASONING AND RATIONALITY IN PASTORAL CARE.

THURMAN, HOWARD (1900–81). Professor and dean of the chapels at Howard University (1932–44) and Boston University (1953–65), and pastor of the first U.S. church that was racially integrated in its membership and leadership (1944–53). In addition to his popularity as a speaker, Thurman's twenty-three books prove him to be the most prolific black American interpreter on the centrality of personality to matters of spiritual formation.

Central themes of his thought are "the underlying unity of life" and "the conscious intent of life" toward wholeness (*Disciplines of the Spirit*, 1963, p. 104). Building upon these themes, Thurman asserted that the nurture of personality is inextricable from concerns of the social order. He often elucidated this conviction by focusing on the importance of racial reconciliation to the individual's proper sense of self. His ideas on nonviolence, reconciliation, and inclusive community significantly influenced the thinking of civil rights leaders of the 1950s and 1960s.

L. E. SMITH

BLACK AMERICAN PASTORAL CARE.

THURNEYSEN, EDUARD (1888–1974). Swiss Protestant pastor and theologian. He occupied pastorates in Switzerland, including the Münster at Basel, and was professor of practical theology at the University of Basel, 1927–59. From 1913 he was closely associated with Karl Barth, whose dialectical theology he elaborated in terms of its pastoral implications. His book, *A Theology of Pastoral Care* (ET, 1962), is a significant volume in the literature of pastoral care.

Thurneysen was thoroughly versed in the Freudian tradition, but seems not to have considered developmental and humanistic approaches of American psychology. Throughout his career he worked with "an unnecessary cynicism toward all secular healing" (Oden, p. 73), advocating pastoral care and counseling as best conducted within the church. These features condition all details in Thurneysen's theology of pastoral care.

In *Theology* Thurneysen clearly separates pastoral care from psychotherapy. The study of the "profane" sciences — psychology, sociology, law — may assist in developing proper pastoral attitudes, but it will not make the clergyman a pastoral counselor. Psychotherapeutic approaches endanger ministerial performance. For Thurneysen pastoral care and counseling is "a special discourse" distinguished from "profane and natural speech" (Oden, p. 105). Pastoral care is self-sufficient, not dependent upon secular wisdom. In fact, psychotherapy is potentially a dangerous poison which threatens religious health.

Thurneysen moves upon this assumed dichotomy between psychotherapy and pastoral care and interprets the latter in terms of the traditional methods of ministry. Thus, pastoral care is fundamentally proclamation and instruction. He believed pastoral conversation is distinctive in so far as it clarifies the Bible and exhorts counselees to hear its instruction. The counselor is "to be a listener — a patient, concentrated, attentive, alert, and understanding listener and nothing else" (Oden, p. 127). Yet the end of listening is exhortation. What is heard must be challenged by "the divine judgment which rules over everything human" (Oden, p. 132).

Thurneysen makes little, if any, room for the Word of God to be mediated through interpersonal relationships without being made verbally explicit or to come through a "secular" psychotherapist. He understands pastoral care to be basically homiletical, that is, identical to public preaching, aimed toward gaining a response. Although he makes room for listening, ultimately the Bible must be opened, its message interpreted with authority, and gratitude given to God for guidance. Bible, not feeling, is the focus of pastoral care and counseling and the ministerial office is to preserve that priority. "Thurneysen's whole line of argument is sorely tempted, despite itself, to take the Word of God captive, limit it only to that occasion in which it is captured in man's speech, as if the Word were not effectually present amid the structures of the world and even amid the notorious failures of human works and words" (Oden, p. 78). Nonetheless Thurneysen sought to relate modern pastoral care and theology to the major psychological developments of the early twentieth century, at least by clarifying their distinctive natures and roles from a Barthian theological perspective.

Thurneysen's work has exerted great influence on the continent for many years.

Bibliography. T. C. Oden, *Contemporary Theology and Psychotherapy* (1967), pp. 73–80.

R. W. CRAPPS

NEOORTHODOX THEOLOGY AND PASTORAL CARE; PASTORAL THEOLOGY, PROTESTANT.

TIBBS, A. E. *See* BAPTIST PASTORAL CARE.

TILLICH, PAUL (1886–1965). Protestant systematic theologian. After leaving Germany in 1933, Tillich taught at Union Theological Seminary (New York), Harvard University, and the University of Chicago. In his sermons, his writings on the theology of culture, and his systematic theology, he often sought to find correlations between theological and psychological themes.

One of Tillich's most important contributions to the pastoral care tradition was his method of correlation, according to which the philosophical or psychological analysis of existence and the questions it raised shaped the form of the Christian answer presented by the theologian. Since 1929, when the neurologist Kurt Goldstein and the psychologist Adhemar Gelb at the University of Frankfurt encouraged Tillich to study psychiatric theory, he had incorporated a psychological vocabulary into his thought. His method of correlation permitted him to seek the inner continuities between the psychological language and traditional theological concepts. Hence the Protestant notion of justification by grace could be reinterpreted, in the light of clinical psychiatric experience, as the insight that the unacceptable were accepted. The psychoanalytic method, Tillich said, had taught him what it meant to speak of accepting the unacceptable. And that knowledge, in turn, provided a new insight into the notion of justification. Yet at the same time, the method of correlation also redefined acceptance by locating it within a wider theological vocabulary that deepened its significance. It enabled Tillich to say that the acceptance offered by counselors represented and embodied a "power of acceptance" that transcended any finite relationship.

Tillich also enhanced the understanding of pastoral care by his careful exploration of such notions as anxiety, freedom, guilt, and courage. His work influenced the existential and phenomenological psychologists who sought to understand such themes without simply retracing them to childhood origins or viewing them as merely surface manifestations of deeper psychic processes. Tillich's single most important contribution to the theory of pastoral care might well have been his *Courage to Be* (1952), in which he explored, among other topics, the relationships between ontological and pathological anxiety.

After moving to New York, Tillich took an active part in the New York Psychology Group, which contained theologians, psychologists, sociologists, and psychoanalysts. The group, which sometimes met in Tillich's apartment, served as an important resource for some of the leaders of the modern pastoral care movement, including Seward Hiltner, David Roberts, Rollo May, and Harrison and Grace Elliott. He also became an influential theological consultant for the journal *Pastoral Psychology* and often wrote for it. Tillich carried on a continuing dialogue with psychologists and psychoanalysts, always urging them to recognize the ontological — and ultimately theological—implications of their psychological categories.

Indeed, during the two decades following the Second World War, no theologian exercised more influence than Tillich on the theological and theoretical interpretation of pastoral care, especially in North America.

E. B. HOLIFIELD

HISTORY OF PROTESTANT PASTORAL CARE (United States); PSYCHOLOGY IN AMERICAN RELIGION; PASTORAL THEOLOGY, PROTESTANT; PASTORAL THEOLOGICAL METHODOLOGY; THEOLOGY AND PSYCHOLOGY. *See also* EXISTENTIALISM; NEOORTHODOX THEOLOGY; PSYCHOANALYSIS AND THEOLOGY.

TIME / TIME SENSE. Time is the sequential dimension of reality in terms of which change, movement, and alterations in relationships of specifiable phenomena occur.

1. **Theories.** Of several, these may be noted: time as linear progression, only the present is real (common sense); time as unreal or appearance (Saṁkara, Parmenides, McTaggart); time as an objective ontic reality (Newton, Alexander); time as a necessary mode of human understanding, but of uncertain ontological status (Kant); time as duration (Bergson), and generated by phenomena in their succession (Leibnitz, Whitehead).

In this century, with notable exceptions, time is generally regarded as a "dimension" of space-time (Minkowski), hence the "space-time continuum." Cognitively we can separate them, but in reality there is no space without time or vice versa. Nor can there be space-time without phenomena.

Inevitably we utilize common sense notions of time as a stream or string, but this raises insuperable contradictions for science and philosophy and, indeed, for self-understanding. Most temporal metaphors are spacial and, while useful for making one point, misleading as strict analogies.

2. **Time Sense.** This is the awareness and interpretation of one's experience of sequentiality, contemporaneity, and anticipation. It selects, contorts, and emphasizes objective sequentiality. So Heidegger restricts time to human experience: without humans there is no time.

Time may seem to race or crawl, as Shakespeare emphasized. Also we measure time with reference to our own being. As a doorknob is high to a child and low to a giant, so a year is relative. To a sixty-year-old, one year is a sixtieth of a lifetime; to a six-year-old it is a sixth or less. Hence, experientially one year passes by the oldster ten times as fast, however much individual days have dragged. In counseling, the sense of time relative to a person's experience must be recognized and appreciated.

3. **The Past.** Past events are recalled with an accompanying sense of "pastness." When this feeling of pastness accompanies a present experience, it causes a strange sense of *déjà vu*. That is commonplace, but chronic temporal disorientation may pose serious problems.

Few things are more important in pastoral care than the perception people have of the past. Here the space-time concept is helpful. The past is not unreal. It has fixed actuality although real in a different way than the present (Hartshorne). In this regard time is more like a snowball than a string, for much of the past is carried along in the present. It distorts reality to view the past as having evaporated and the future as imaginary.

Although the past is fixed, the mode of relating to it permits great variation. Some attempt escape, others are prisoners of the past. Thus the crucial insight is realization that our use, interpretation, and response to the past can be creative, liberating, and redemptive. Life is lived betwixt the preciousness of time and deliverance from its relentless pressures.

4. The Future. The future does not exist except as present durations impinge upon the succeeding future. Future events, whatever they may be, are not facts in the same sense that past events are. This dissolves some of the puzzles that plagued theologians, who imagined that if God knows everything, God must know the future. But to the degree that there is freedom, the hypothetical future is not factual or a datum for knowledge. Medieval theologians were clear about this and did not include things that were false or nonexistent among the knowable. It is not a meaningful limitation upon God to have boundaries that exclude absurdity.

Psychologically, however, the future has a different status. Although not factually real, it is psychologically efficacious and has a quasi-reality in the mind. Human beings are intentional, which means that we are powerfully affected by this extension of purpose and vision into the future. The projection may be one of fear, hope, helplessness, courage, or some admixture of these and other qualities. Thus an important contribution of faith to life quality is the type of envisagement that can enliven the reality of past experience. This way we have of living partially in the future is not mere fantasy but is among the effective determinants of character. One of the important contributions of pastoral counseling is the attempt to engender a creative and affirming outlook toward the future, including, when necessary, a hopeful adjustment in the face of inexorable, delimiting circumstances, where someone is "afflicted in every way" but need not be "crushed" (II Cor. 4:8).

Among the many theories about the nature of this expectancy are: ideals as refined future projections of present realities (Dewey); the future as a lure attracting us toward more significant fulfillment (Whitehead); existing (living) in the anticipation of possibilities (Heidegger); the future as having reality in that our hunger becomes hope grounded in the not-yet (Ernst Bloch). In all such views there is the necessary claim of some degree of human freedom, that is, of self-determination. This contrasts with all strictly deterministic models. The task of engendering hope in relation to awareness of the future is often not one of theory, but a psychological mind-set that clings to the security of hopelessness or helplessness.

Bibliography. Augustine, *Confessions*, bk. IX, 13; XI, 13–41. F. Brentano, "Psychology," in R. M. Chisholm, ed., *Realism and the Background of Phenomenology* (1960). M. Heidegger, *Being and Time* (1962); *On Time and Being* (1972). T. C. Oden, *The Structure of Awareness* (1969). J.-P. Sartre, *Being and Nothingness* (1953), part 4, 2. J. J. C. Smart, ed., *Problems of Space and Time* (1964). A. N. Whitehead, *Aims of Education* (1929), ch. 7 *Adventures of Ideas* (1933), chs. 19, 20.

C. S. MILLIGAN

HOPE AND DESPAIR; MEMORY. *See also* ESCHATOLOGY AND PASTORAL CARE; PHILOSOPHY AND PSYCHOLOGY. *Compare* BEING/BECOMING RELATIONSHIP; FREEDOM AND DETERMINISM; REMINISCENCE THERAPY.

TIMING. In the pastoral sense, the intuitive knowing of the right moment to offer oneself to another person in a particular way. Called "prudence" or "wisdom" in Aristotelian and medieval theory, a sense of the timely, fitting response has been recognized as critical in the art of the cure of souls over the centuries.

Whether the response is an action or a verbal communication, if well timed it will be precisely tuned to the processes of the person being helped. Proper timing shapes when and how something is done, what is said, and how something is said. Factors involved include the nature of the contractual agreement, role definition, level of trust, receptivity or resistance, ego strength of the person involved, and his or her stage of development. How the person hears what is said or experiences what is done acts as a perceptual grid, influencing the timeliness of a pastoral act. Staying in contact with these realities and being attuned to the person's unique rhythms, the pastor looks for the right moment.

In the more structured counseling relationship, timing is principally related to the question of when to make an interpretation or give feedback. Many believe the moment to be when the ground has been prepared and the counselee almost sees the linkage spontaneously; the counselor merely helps in taking the last step. The optimal moment occurs, however, when there is both a cognitive and an affective resonance. When these factors are not present and the timing is off, either resistance or a lack of impact results.

Knowing the right time to act is largely an intuitive matter, depending significantly on the pastor's own internal responses. Effective pastors listen to the "guiding voice" within themselves, silently asking such questions as, What do I know personally about what this person is going through? What have I myself learned about this along the way? What vibrations are set off in me? What associations? What feelings? Such reflections mix together in a subtle, intuitive blend. Then, out of this attunement between what they hear in themselves and what they hear in the other, a sense of the right moment often emerges spontaneously.

When the timing is right, a caring act can support, challenge or invite in a way exactly suited to the individual's needs. The right words at the right time can broaden awareness, bring what was hidden or obscure to clarity, and make possible qualitatively new kinds of decisions that are more personally authentic, creative, and profound.

It was this deeper significance of timing that Tillich pointed to in his exposition of the NT concept of *kairos*, the "fulfillment of time," "the demand of the historical moment" (*Systematic Theology*, 3, pp. 369–72). In Tillich's understanding *kairos* is "the right time in which something can be done," "the fertile moment." Kairotic moments derive from, and are judged by, the "great *kairos*" of the appearance of the Christ in human history. "Awareness of a *kairos* is a matter of vision," says Tillich, "not analysis and calculation." "*Kairoi* are rare and the great *kairos* is unique," but through the relative *kairoi* of human experience the great *kairos*, the Kingdom of God, becomes manifest, though such moments are always subject to misperception and demonic distortion.

Bibliography. E. Berne, *Transactional Analysis in Psychotherapy* (1961). E. Gendlin, *Focusing* (1978). K. Menninger, *Theory of Psychoanalytic Technique* (1958). E. Polster and M. Polster, *Gestalt Therapy Integrated* (1974). T. Reik, *Listening With the Third Ear* (1948). P. Tillich, *Systematic Theology*, vol. 3 (1963). L. Wolberg, *The Technique of Psychotherapy* (1954).

G. E. CRISWELL

TECHNIQUE AND SKILL IN PASTORAL CARE; WISDOM AND PRACTICAL KNOWLEDGE. *See also* INITIATIVE AND INTERVENTION; INTUITION; PRUDENCE; WIT AND HUMOR IN PASTORAL CARE.

TODDLERS. *See* CHILDREN; PARENTS/PARENTHOOD.

TOKEN ECONOMY. A behavior modification program that involves three elements: (1) tokens; (2) backup reinforcers; and (3) specific reinforcement contingencies. Tokens are conditioned reinforcers (points, stars, or other tangible items), that acquire their reinforcing properties as a result of their relationship to backup reinforcers (i.e., natural, unlearned reinforcers, such as food). Tokens are given when desired behavior occurs. Tokens are then exchanged for backup reinforcers.

J. W. FANTUZZO

BEHAVIOR THERAPIES (Methods and Research); CONDITIONING.

TOLSTOY, LEO. *See* CLASSIC LITERATURE IN CARE AND COUNSELING (Orthodoxy).

TOOMBS, GORDON. *See* CANADIAN PASTORAL CARE MOVEMENT.

TORAH/TORAH STUDY. *See* THEOLOGY, JEWISH.

TOUCHING/PHYSICAL SUPPORT. *Touching* is physical contact between persons, usually for the purpose of communicating positive attitudes, values, and intentions toward the person touched.

Physical support may be alternately defined as: (1) an expanded form of touching expressed in carrying, embracing, assisting, or holding; or (2) the provision of material resources such as money, food, shelter, and clothing to persons in need.

Developmental studies of infancy and childhood clearly demonstrate the importance of reliable touching and physical support on the part of the caretaker as a basis for trust in the goodness of life, and for the capacity to love and to hope for a meaningful future. In some cases, physical survival itself depends upon the satisfactory experience of touching and physical support. There is evidence that even for adults the lack of human companionship and its expression in touching may contribute significantly to the onset of life-threatening illness, while the presence of touch and physical support may contribute positively to human health and to the recovery of the sick.

The therapeutic use of touch is disputed. Some dismiss it because it fosters inappropriate dependencies, sexual expectations, and magical thinking such as that connected with certain forms of faith healing. Others see it as central to the therapy process, regarding it as an important means to establish rapport, communicate acceptance, overcome repressions, and promote self-disclosure and openness to therapeutic exploration.

Pastoral care draws heavily upon touching and physical support in ministering to persons suffering from major material and interpersonal losses, acute anxiety and depression, and serious illness. By these and other means, pastoral care transcends an exclusive reliance upon the written and spoken Word in making present and furthering a sense of hope and of God's providence, by which a capacity to love and certain forms of healing and religious fellowship may emerge.

Guidelines for the pastoral use of touching include awareness of the purpose for which the touching is intended, naturalness of expression, responsiveness to the community standards in which touching occurs, freedom to refuse touching and to allow touching to be refused or discontinued, exploration of the meaning of touching (or not touching) to the parishioner, chastity and emotional fidelity to primary relational commitments, and public accountability.

Bibliography. J. J. Lynch, *The Broken Heart: The Medical Consequences of Loneliness* (1977). E. E. Mintz, "On The Rationale of Touch in Psychotherapy," *Psychotherapy: Theory, Research and Practice*, 6 (1969), 232–34. J. Pattison, "Effects of Touch on Self-Exploration and The Therapeutic Relationship," *J. of Consulting and Clinical Psychology*, 40 (1973) 2: 170–75.

L. K. GRAHAM

COMFORT/SUSTAINING; INTIMACY AND DISTANCE; TECHNIQUE AND SKILL IN PASTORAL CARE. *See also* BODY; PERSONAL, CONCEPT OF.

TOURNIER, PAUL (1888–1974). Physician and clinical psychologist in Geneva, Switzerland. Tournier brought to pastoral care and counseling the perspective of a physician with an intense appreciation for the Bible. His experience as a doctor led him to understand the psychodynamic meaning of illness, while he found in the Bible illustrations for his interpretation of personhood.

In *A Doctor's Casebook in the Light of the Bible* (1960) Tournier maintains that physicians have two diagnostic tasks: determining the patient's physiological disease and then discovering the meaning which the experience of illness has for the person. As a Christian he believes that in either case healing in the final analysis follows a biblical pattern.

Tournier's analysis of personhood in *The Meaning of Persons* (1957) is dualistic. He distinguishes between *person*, that "invisible reality in the image of God" (p. 102) and *personage*, the exteriority of the person. The two categories are reflected in the French title of the work, *Le Personnage et la Personne*. The doctor's task in healing, and presumably the minister's, is to search for the authentic person and enable the patient to construct an adequate personage.

Crucial to healing is the relationship between the physician and the patient on the one hand and between God and the person on the other. In the final analysis

God is healer, providing a more adequate personage as Adam's fig leaf was replaced with skin clothing (p. 76).

For healing to occur persons must have a place where they are loved and accepted unconditionally (*A Place For You*). Ideally this happens in the family. If a place is found in the family or its substitute, persons will be able to extend this place to include the whole human race under a loving heavenly Father.

R. W. CRAPPS

PERSON; SALVATION, HEALING, AND HEALTH, THEOLOGY OF. *Compare* RELIGION AND HEALTH MOVEMENT.

TRADITION, SPIRITUAL. *See* SPIRITUAL DIRECTION; SPIRITUAL DISCERNMENT.

TRADITIONAL RELIGIONS. *See* AFRICAN, NATIVE AMERICAN, *or* WEST INDIAN TRADITIONAL RELIGION, PERSONAL CARE IN. *See also* CULTURAL ANTHROPOLOGY OF RELIGION, DISCIPLINE OF; SOCIOLOGY OF RELIGIOUS AND PASTORAL CARE.

TRADITION AS A MODE OF CARE. We live in a time when our views on pastoral care are more strongly influenced by psychotherapeutic theories than by theological systems and concepts. One effect of this shift in emphasis from theology to psychotherapy has been the failure to give adequate attention to some traditional pastoral acts and practices which, for many parishioners, are their primary experience of pastoral care.

Only a minority of parishioners seek pastoral counseling (i.e., regularly scheduled counseling sessions) from their pastors. Thus, for many, their main, even sole experience of pastoral care is by other kinds of pastoral acts and initiatives, ones which bear slight resemblance, in form and process, to the psychotherapeutic hour, such as the performing of marriages, conducting of funerals, hospital visitation, and home visitation. If pastoral counseling, with its openness to contemporary psychotherapeutic methods, is the area of pastoral care that most interfaces with modernity, then such ritual and ritualized activities as these comprise the area of pastoral care which faces toward tradition. For many parishioners, pastoral care is actually defined by these ritualized activities.

1. **Care Through Rites and Sacraments.** These traditional rites or observances of the church—baptism, Holy Communion, the marriage ceremony, the burial service —afford opportunities for significant pastoral care to occur. But over the centuries, those that have become recognized as having greatest pastoral care potential or overtones are ones that assist persons in coping (1) with broken, severed, or attenuated relationships, whether between human selves or between selves and God, and (2) with the threatened disintegration or extinction of the self through natural aging, illness, and death.

a. Pastoral care through confession and assurance. The act of confession, followed by assurance of forgiveness, most often occurs in a regularly appointed worship service, but it may also occur in private. If private, it may follow a set form or procedure, or it may be improvised. In public confession a set form is usually followed, with some variation in language usually allowed.

In confession, individuals are given opportunity to examine themselves and to attempt, honestly and without resistance, to discern ways in which they have contributed to the weakening or undermining of human relationships, and frustrated the purposes and intentions of God. Following the act of confession, the pastor proclaims, to those who are genuinely sorry, that God has forgiven them. From the penitent's side, the key elements are self-examination, a spirit of remorse, and the desire to change. From the pastor's side, the key elements are the assurance that God has accepted the penitent's confession and is nurturing the penitent's intention to change. While the self-examination of the penitent is usually concerned with matters that evoke a sense of guilt (from wrongs committed against other purposes), it may also include feelings of shame (failure to live up to one's standards and ideals for oneself).

b. Pastoral care of the sick. The sick and infirm of the congregation are typically remembered in the regularly scheduled worship service through the pastoral prayer, often mentioned by name, and visited by the pastor and members of the congregation. Thomas C. Oden (1983), a strong advocate of traditional forms of pastoral care, notes that "The pastoral tradition is well furnished with prayers, litanies, and services that have been used and revised for centuries in ministry to the sick. Many are commendable even to low church or free church ministries that normally do not use much ceremony" as they "often capture the essence of pastoral conversation in spare and beautiful language" (p. 257–58). Oden specifically commends the Anglican "Order for Visitation of the Sick," which includes the option of offering Communion to the sick, the Catholic practice of anointing the sick, especially those who are at the point of death, and Martin Luther's instructions on spiritual healing and pastoral anointing. These rituals are understood to be an extension of the congregational worship with the pastor acting both as personal comforter and as the congregation's representative.

c. Pastoral care of the dying and bereaved. An important tradition in the pastoral care of the dying is the reading of selected biblical texts, typically one of the Psalms (e.g., Psalm 23, 42, 131), portions of Romans 8 and of I Corinthians 15. In addition, most Protestant books of worship include special prayers for the dying. The Methodist "Canticle of Conquest Over Death," for instance, is a prayer for trust addressed to the "everlasting rock" who keeps one in perfect peace and "swallows death up forever," which assures the grieving that God is the One who "wipes away tears from all faces." The Lutheran prayer emphasizes the peaceful departure of the "ransomed soul," as does the Eastern Orthodox prayer, which asks God to loose "this servant from every bond and receive his [or her] soul in peace." The Anglican "Ministration at the Time of Death" includes a prayer for mercy, the Lord's Prayer, and a simple commendation of the soul of the sufferer to God, concluding with the words, "May your rest be this day in peace, and your dwelling-place in the Paradise of God."

The Catholic service includes penance, anointing (with oil), and the Viaticum. *Viaticum* means "with you on the way" and is thus a litany of the journey which a person, unlikely to experience bodily restoration, embarks upon "on the way" to life with God. During this service, Holy Communion is received by the persons present in the room (Oden, p. 306).

The burial service has always served to offer consolation to the bereaved and to provide a community context of support and loss. But its focus should not be primarily upon "human companionship," vulnerable as it is to death and separation, but on our companionship with God, which does not end in death (Oden, p. 308–9). Moreover, the burial service is intended not only for the grieving family but also for the others present, to prepare for their own future grief situations and to deal with their own unfinished grief from previous bereavements (Willimon, p. 114).

d. The pastoral blessing. A common element in all traditional forms of pastoral care is the pastoral blessing. In each of these rites the pastor communicates God's blessing, assuring the penitent, sick, dying, and bereaved that they and their loved ones even now, in their deepest despair, are the objects of God's living attention and participants in God's everlasting peace. Paul W. Pruyser (1969, pp. 352–65) stresses the importance of the pastoral blessing to many troubled persons, noting how this blessing frequently gives parishioners a palpable sense of God's supportive presence. He notes, however, that many pastors tend to neglect this ancient practice, especially in ministry to the sick.

2. **New Traditions.** For decades, pastoral theologians have argued that pastoral care is too enmeshed in traditional forms, and that it fails to minister to troubled persons in fresh and innovative ways. They point out that we have well-formulated practices and procedures for ministry to the sick, the dying, and the bereaved, but have no comparable rites and practices for such devastating experiences as divorce, retirement, infertility, miscarriage, accidents, bankruptcy, nest emptying, and various forms of victimization (e.g., rape, child abuse, unemployment). While it is doubtful that laity would desire public rituals for all these situations, and some of these experiences may be deemed inappropriate for mention in public pastoral prayers, pastoral theologians have encouraged continuing assessment of traditional forms and the development of rites intended to address experiences which have not received the attention traditionally accorded the personal sense of sin, sickness, and death. They have also encouraged us to ask whether these experiences are best addressed through private informal acts of pastoral care or through new public ritual practices.

Pastoral care needs to adapt to a changing society and to changing perceptions of what kinds of experiences deserve more intentional pastoral care initiatives. By giving certain of these experiences more public attention through well-conceived ritual enactments, they will be less ignored or minimized, and thus less neglected even in the more private sphere of pastoral care. On the other hand, laity have come to expect that pastors will be especially responsive to their need for comfort and reassurance in situations involving sin, sickness, and death. Pastors who neglect these areas of ministry are running the risk of being perceived as lacking in basic pastoral care skills and sensitivities. And, contrariwise, pastors who are effective in responding to such expectations typically find that effective-ness in these traditional expressions of pastoral care enables them also to be more effective in the newer and less traditional areas of care and counseling.

Tradition is often viewed as the enemy of progress and change. But while it is true that advocates of traditional practices in pastoral care are often adversaries of change, tradition, as such, is not the enemy of progress and is not inherently opposed to change. In fact, its purpose is to initiate and foster change in the individual penitent. If effectively embodied, traditional forms of pastoral care can be the most consistently reliable impetus for change in the pastor's whole repertory of ministerial practices.

Bibliography. T. C. Oden, *Pastoral Theology: Essentials of Ministry* (1983). P. W. Pruyser, "The Master Hand: Psychological Notes on Pastoral Blessing," in W. B. Oglesby, Jr., ed., *The New Shape of Pastoral Theology: Essays in Honor of Seward Hiltner* (1969).

D. CAPPS

ECCLESIOLOGY AND PASTORAL CARE; REST AND RENEWAL, RELIGIOUS TRADITIONS OF; RITUAL AND PASTORAL CARE; SOCIOLOGY OF RELIGIOUS AND PASTORAL CARE. *Compare* DRAMA AS MODE OF CARE; JEWISH CARE AND COUNSELING; LITURGICAL CHANGE AND REFORM (Pastoral Issues); MUSIC AS MODE OF CARE.

TRAGEDY. *See* CRISIS; DISASTER, PUBLIC; GRIEF AND LOSS; SUFFERING.

TRAIT THEORY. *See* PERSONALITY THEORY (Varieties, Traditions, and Issues).

TRANCE. A state of mind, characterized by profound absorption or concentration, and increased susceptibility to agreeable suggestions.

When a person is experiencing a trance he or she also may be experiencing hypnosis. One of the thinking-process characteristics of the trance is increased susceptibility to suggestion, and some believe that hypnosis is only a form of increased suggestibility. Thus, the so-called trance may not be a distinct phenomenon but merely a reflection of the condition of hypersuggestibility. Trance is difficult to observe or measure scientifically, though there is evidence that trance states exist and that they are different from normal consciousness, as well as sleep, coma, and other unconscious states. Some discernible characteristics are: (1) acceptance of statements in a relatively literal way; (2) "trance-logic," i.e., the bypassing of the censoring or critical judgment of logical thinking; (3) self-reports by subjects that they were indeed experiencing a unique state of mind, other than consciousness or sleep; (4) the effectiveness of posthypnotic suggestions.

While there are physiological conditions associated with trance—such as the whites of the eyes turning slightly red, increased lacrimation, dilation of the pupils, reduced respiration, reduced pulse, and sometimes gurgling of the digestive system—it cannot be claimed that such characteristics are proof of trance, because they also exist when a person is physically relaxed.

Trance is not a discrete state as much as it is a position on a continuum of grades of awareness. Thus, a person can be in a light trance, (being preoccupied) at one end of the continuum, or in a very deep state resembling somnambulism at the other. Further, the relative depth of the trance depends upon many factors, such as one's mental and physical condition and—if the trance is induced by another person, for convenience's sake called the hypnotist—the persuasive skills and confidence of the hypnotist. The trance is enhanced by consent, rapport, communications, and freedom from fear of trance.

When experiencing a trance a person is not only susceptible to acceptable suggestions, he or she is also able to focus intently on a subject. Visual and auditory distractions can be shut out, and the mind's ability to understand phenomena, resolve conflicts, and be susceptible to mature solutions is enhanced.

The deeper or more profound the trance, the more phenomena can be experienced, such as control of pain, phobia, habits, and other apparent instances of mind-over-matter. It appears that mind-over-matter phenomena, including remarkable feats of strength or rapid healing of physical ills, entail a removing of false restrictions more than an enactment of extraordinary abilities. That is, the trance state can help persons reach their potential by tapping the power of the subconscious mind.

R. R. KING, JR.

RELIGIOUS BEHAVIOR; RELIGIOUS EXPERIENCE. *Compare* ASCETICAL PRACTICES; CHARISMATIC EXPERIENCE; ECSTASY; HYPNOSIS; MYSTICISM; PEAK EXPERIENCE; VISIONS AND VOICES.

TRANQUILIZERS. *See* DRUGS; MEDICATION; SLEEP AND SLEEP DISORDERS.

TRANSACTIONAL ANALYSIS. A theory of personality and systematic psychotherapy for personal growth and social change developed by psychiatrist Eric Berne (1910–70). TA consists in a set of concepts and techniques designed to enable individuals to consciously identify, understand, and change or control certain patterns of interpersonal interaction which the theory holds to be the source of psychological difficulties and unhappiness.

TA contends that people often experience problems in living because of decisions made in early childhood, called *scripting*, which result in their assuming an "I'm Not OK" life position. This negative self-concept impacts their interpersonal relationships through the various roles they take in dealing with others. Seeing themselves as basically "losers," they may assume a defensive attitude in both internal and social interactions, leading toward lonely isolation and avoidance of intimacy with others and with God. An overall goal of TA therapy is for each person to take control of his or her own life (rather than to be restricted by a negative script) through a redecision to claim an "I'm OK" life position.

The basic conceptual tools of TA—the Parent, Adult, and Child ego states — may seem to resemble the psychoanalytic concepts of superego, ego, and id, while actually they are quite different. In TA theory the Parent, Adult, and Child are each manifestations of the Freudian ego (hence the name *ego states*), and thus they are conscious, visible behaviors, in contrast to the unconscious activity of the superego and id in psychoanalytic theory.

Since its development by Berne and his associates in the 1950s, TA has been practiced extensively in clinical,

industrial, and church contexts and has been used successfully with couples and families as well as with individuals. Its rapid growth in popularity is probably due to the fact that TA is relatively easy to learn, oriented to conscious understanding and control, adaptable to a wide variety of settings, and free of psychiatric jargon (one of Berne's special emphases). The TA movement was incorporated in 1965 as the International Transactional Analysis Association (ITAA), and has since grown to include over six thousand members worldwide. The Association publishes the *Transactional Analysis Journal* and has its own training and certification procedures for TA therapists. Many pastoral counselors hold certified membership in ITAA.

1. **Structural Analysis.** In TA theory, personality is composed of three basic structural units, or ego states, each of which is conscious, though the three states are distinct from one another and have different contents and functions. The goal of structural analysis is to define and distinguish these ego states clearly so that their respective functions do not overlap or "contaminate" one another.

The Parent (P) ego state is the incorporation of the specific parental figures—and other authority figures, including God—which each person experiences when young. Hence, in the present this ego state expresses itself outwardly toward others in value judgments which may be nurturing and/or critical (or prejudicial). Such behavior may be identical or very similar to that of the original parenting figures.

The Adult (A) ego state is concerned with the autonomous collecting and processing of data and the logical estimation of probabilities as a basis for action, problem solving, and social cooperation. It organizes information based upon input and computes dispassionately. It is not related to a person's chronological age.

The Child (C) ego state contains all the natural needs, feelings, impulses, and potentialities of an infant, as experienced in the present. It consists of creative, manipulative, and intuitive capacities as well as the adaptational feelings and behavior learned in childhood, such as compliance and rebellion. In each person the Parent ego state generally conducts an internal dialogue with the Child ego state, continually telling it what to do or to avoid doing.

2. **Transactional Analysis Proper.** Transactional analysis proper involves determining which ego state in one person is transacting—or interacting—with which ego state in another person. Its goal is social control, that is, the enabling of each individual to exercise autonomy by using whatever ego state is appropriate for healthy communication. Thus, problems in communication must be noted and clarified. To achieve this, TA conceives of communication in terms of exchanges or *transactions*. There are three basic forms of transaction:

Complementary transactions occur in healthy relationships, that is, when people transact openly and directly from any ego state and receive responses that are expected and appropriate. Figure 1 represents a complementary Adult-Adult transaction. In this diagram the vectors of sending and receiving are parallel and communication is depicted as open with respect to stimulus and response expectations:

Figure 1

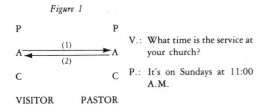

V.: What time is the service at your church?

P.: It's on Sundays at 11:00 A.M.

VISITOR   PASTOR

Crossed transactions occur between any ego states when a message sent from one person receives an inconsistent, unexpected response, as in Figure 2; hence the vectors cross. Communication may then be impaired, and the individual may feel misunderstood, hurt, or angry. Gestures, facial expressions, body posture, voice tone, and vocabulary may all contribute to the meaning conveyed.

Figure 2

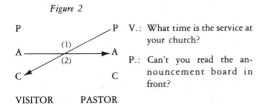

V.: What time is the service at your church?

P.: Can't you read the announcement board in front?

VISITOR   PASTOR

Ulterior transactions have a hidden agenda. Along with the spoken words (the social level) a nonverbal message is sent (the psychological level). Very often the verbal stimulus and the nonverbal stimulus are quite different. In Figure 3 broken lines convey the ulterior message.

V. (seductively): What time is the service at your church? (You're really handsome— I'd like to see more of you.)

Figure 3

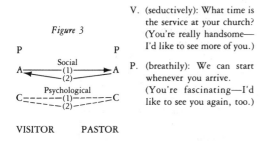

P. (breathily): We can start whenever you arrive. (You're fascinating—I'd like to see you again, too.)

VISITOR   PASTOR

Ulterior transactions are not always double-leveled or *duplex* (as in the diagram). They may also be *angular*, as when a particular ego state in one person makes contact with two ego states in another. Ulterior transactions may or may not produce ongoing communication, depending upon whether both persons receive all the messages sent and whether the messages receive a favorable response.

3. Game Analysis. A *game* in TA terminology refers to a series of ongoing transactions that appear to be complementary, but which include ulterior transactions designed to set the stage for a well-defined *payoff*, or climax. Payoffs are usually uncomfortable feelings such as fear, anger, sadness, or embarrassment experienced by the person in a one-down position, while the one-up person enjoys the advantage. The goal of game analysis is for persons to gain awareness of the games they play, how they initiate these games, and how they get hooked into them by others. The goal also includes awareness of how games can be broken up by moving into the Adult ego state in order to achieve appropriate autonomy while making relationships more satisfying.

Games are played at various levels of intensity and by any number of people, though usually by just two persons. It is helpful to analyze the process enacted in games in terms of the Drama Triangle, which involves the roles of Victim, Rescuer, and Persecutor; as professional helpers, pastors are especially vulnerable to becoming caught in the Triangle. The action in the Drama Triangle sequence calls for an eventual switch in roles (with subsequent bad feeling payoff) as indicated by arrows in Figure 4.

Figure 4

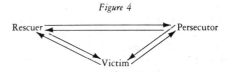

The following exchange shows how it works in a game that might be called "Gee, You're Wonderful, Pastor":

> **Parishioner** (played from adoring Victim role): "Gee, Pastor, I don't know how you ever find the time in your busy schedule to look after all the people in our church. How do you do it?"
> **Pastor** (played from benevolent Rescuer role): "Well, I really care about people as we are all God's children, so I just make time to see everyone in need."
> **Parishioner** (angrily switching to Persecutor role): "Well, then, how come you never visited me when I was in the hospital?"

Usually the Victim is played from the Child ego state, with the Rescuer and Persecutor played from the Parent.

Game roles are commonly played outside of Adult awareness. The uncomfortable feelings involved in games are exploited by players to justify their behavior. But while most games are detrimental, Berne also lists some good ones; these involve a positive exchange of *strokes*, or units of recognition.

4. Script Analysis. A script is one's life plan, written by a person's own early decisions, growing out of transactions with parents. The repeated games people play, living out the roles of Victim, Persecutor, and Rescuer, serve to advance the script drama. Scripts may be constructive (winners), destructive (losers), or "going nowhere" (banal). The goal of script analysis is to change nonproductive scripts into winners' scripts through deeplevel redecisions for personal autonomy. In pastoral work such redecisions have been compared to the process of repentance and conversion.

5. Theological Critique. The clinical effectiveness of TA, especially when allied with Gestalt therapy, has been recognized throughout the U.S. and around the world, and its literature is now translated into many foreign languages. It also has found many followers in the pastoral counseling movement, where its appeal has been both practical and theological. Many pastoral counselors have seen a significant similarity, for instance, between TA's theory of Parent, Adult, and Child interaction and the Pauline concept of internal personality conflict. Thus Paul's anguished lament that "I do not do the good I want, but the evil I do not want is what I do" (Rom. 7:19) appears to express a tension which, from the perspective of TA, could be considered a Parent-Child conflict—a psychological description of sin. Similarly,

Paul's experience of freedom and new life in Christ (Romans 8) may be viewed as a movement into Adult awareness, the emergence of realistic strength. Such parallels between TA and biblical or theological themes need not result in the reduction of theological categories to psychology, but may be viewed as evidence of a significant compatibility or congruence between TA theories and Christian theology, and thus provide warrants for their use in pastoral care and counseling.

On the other hand, TA has been criticized by some theologians for its "humanistic" presuppositions, its particular value assumptions, and its own form of "ingroup" language, which arguably substitutes for and impoverishes the language of the religious tradition (Oden, 1974; Reuter, 1974). Basically, religious critics point out the need to see "OKness" as the work of God's transcending grace, mercy, and forgiveness, rather than as the result of human script redecision alone — in theological terms, the problem of Pelagianism. As a secular therapy TA does not, of course, utilize such theological categories as sin, grace, repentance, and confession. The question is therefore whether TA's methods and theories are implicitly consistent with religious convictions or contrary to them.

In evaluating TA theologically, however, it is important to avoid misreading the theory as some Christian writers have done, for example by (1) identifying "OKness" and "NOT-OKness" with feelings alone, rather than understanding them as comprehensive, assumed life positions independent of feelings, or (2) holding that script messages are unilaterally imposed on individuals by significant authority figures rather than being individually decided upon by each person, even though this occurs during childhood when the child's view of the world is incomplete and premature.

Though continued theological discussion of TA is needed, it is clear that many pastors, pastoral counselors, and Christian psychologists have found TA's categories of Parent, Adult, and Child compatible with their religious understanding of human nature, and have also found it pastorally useful in many situations of human hurt, conflict, and difficulty.

Bibliography. E. Berne, *Transactional Analysis in Psychotherapy* (1961); *Games People Play* (1964); *Principles of Group Treatment* (1966); *What Do You Say After You Say Hello?* (1972). T. Harris, *I'm OK — You're OK* (1967). M. James and D. Jongeward, *Born to Win: Transactional Analysis with Gestalt Experiments* (1971). M. James, *Born to Love: Transactional Analysis in the Church* (1973). C. Steiner, *Scripts People Live* (1974). M. and R. Goulding, *Changing Lives Through Redecision Therapy* (1979). *For critique see* T. Oden, *Game Free* (1974). A. Reuter, *Who Says I'm OK?* (1974).

J. C. LANDRUD

PSYCHOTHERAPY. *See also* COMMUNICATION; COMPETITIVENESS; EGO; SELF. *Compare* GESTALT PSYCHOLOGY AND PSYCHOTHERAPY; INTERPERSONAL THEORY; MODELS IN PSYCHOLOGICAL AND PASTORAL THEORY; PSYCHOANALYSIS; OBJECT RELATIONS THEORY.

TRANSCENDENCE, DIVINE. The independence of the Divine in the Divine-world relation. Used concretely it names one dimension of ongoing interaction between the Divine and the world, for example, sustaining, for-giving. Divine transcendence is always understood in relation to its contrast term, *divine immanence*, which names another dimension of the same relationship.

Divine transcendence has been understood in various ways. Each is generated by a root metaphor. The following five metaphors have been especially influential. *First*, the divine transcends us *as a sculptor transcends the sculpture*. This metaphor lays stress on the sculptor's personal efficacy. The sculptor imposes a form on the material intentionally. This has been the root metaphor for classical Christian understanding of the Divine's continuing action in the world. The Divine as cause transcends its effects in the same way as the sculptor. Transcendence points to an asymmetry in the Divine-world relation. The world depends on the Divine to be what it is, while the Divine does not depend on the world to be what it is. Here, transcendence does not contradict divine immanence. The Divine is ongoingly "in" its effects, literally in-forming them.

Second, the Divine transcends us *as the watchmaker transcends the watch*. Here, stress lies on the watchmaker's technical skill manipulating mechanical causality to make the watch. Transcendence points not to asymmetry in a relationship, but to radical separateness of coercive power. Here, transcendence does contradict immanence. As its mechanical cause, the watchmaker is not in the watch, but stands separate from it as it continues to operate mechanically according to its own principles; they are wholly separate beings.

Third, the Divine transcends us *as the body transcends its organs*. The metaphor stresses the complex relationship between whole and parts in living organisms. Here, transcendence points to a relation that is both asymmetrical and reciprocal. It implies immanence. On the one hand, the body is comprised of, and can be changed by, many distinct organic systems that are in varying degrees semiautonomous. On the other hand, the body is a whole greater than they and greater than the mere sum of them. As a whole it can affect them. The same is true for the Divine-world relation. As a whole embracing a multitude of semiautonomous realities, the Divine influences these realities to grow toward its goals for them and is itself so influenced by their responses that it grows (reciprocity), but in such a way that its basic character does not change and its capacities to achieve its goals are not diminished (asymmetry).

Fourth, the Divine transcends us *as Thou transcends I*. Stress lies on the freedom of genuine loving. In an interpersonal encounter, the more deeply I know the other in love, the more deeply I know that the other's freedom makes him or her inexhaustible. Here, transcendence implies immanence, for it is precisely to the degree that we enter each other's lives that I know how utterly the other transcends my ability to comprehend him or her. So too with the Divine's transcending of us. The more deeply we experience divine love, the more we know its transcendent freedom.

Fifth, the Divine transcends us *as a horizon transcends the scene*. Stress falls on the way all seeing is delimited by a horizon that is not itself part of what is seen but frames it and makes it visually graspable. It is at once integral to the scene, and yet transcends it. That is a metaphor for the Divine's relation, not to perception, but to all experiencing.

The Divine is the limit of our experience, constantly apprehended along with every particular thing, experienced as the ground of its meaning and worth, but always transcending experience in never itself being directly experienced.

D. H. KELSEY

GOD, DOCTRINE OF, AND PASTORAL CARE; GOD, IDEAS AND IMAGES OF; The HOLY. *See also* REVELATION AND PASTORAL CARE. *Compare* SELF-TRANSCENDENCE.

TRANSCENDENCE, HUMAN. *See* PERSON; SELF-TRANSCENDENCE. *See also* IMAGO DEI; SACRIFICIAL BEHAVIOR.

TRANSCENDENCE THERAPY. *See* FORMATIVE SPIRITUALITY.

TRANSCENDENTAL MEDITATION. *See* MEDITATION; POPULAR THERAPEUTIC MOVEMENTS AND PSYCHOLOGIES.

TRANSFERENCE. A psychoanalytic term which defines the phenomenon of the transfer of feelings and thoughts from one person to another and one circumstance to another. It includes all unconscious material in the psychotherapeutic setting which the client places onto the therapist, the origin of which is in the internal psychic structure of the client. Given a natural tendency to repeat old experiences of relationships, the client reacts to the new experience of therapy and the new person of the therapist as if the therapy were a previous experience and the therapist were a previously encountered historical person.

B. Moore and B. Fine (1967) define transference as follows: "The *displacement* of patterns of feelings and behavior, originally experienced with significant figures of one's childhood, to individuals in one's current relationships. This *unconscious* process thus brings about a repetition, not consciously perceived, of attitudes, *fantasies* and emotions of love, hate, anger, etc. under many different circumstances." Thus transference exists both inside and outside of the psychotherapeutic relationship, and has relevance for the practice of psychotherapy and the understanding of all other human relationships as well. Transference theory is also helpful in understanding the pastor-parishioner relationship (Ordway, 1970).

1. **Transference as a Psychotherapy Phenomenon.** If there is a basic human tendency to repeat old experiences in the present, there is, as H. Nunberg points out, always a readiness for transference. However, the psychoanalytic situation is "particularly suited" for the development of transference, for in the consistency of meeting and the relative neutrality of the therapist, material from the inner life of the client emerges more readily than in other, less intense, relationships. The analytic situation facilitates the development of the transference with the goal of understanding the phenomenon, not acting upon it.

Undergirding the work of psychotherapy is the development of a positive transference, in which the client develops a grounded basic hopefulness, trust, and confidence in the therapist rooted in a positive mother-child bonding experienced by the patient. Where there is no basic positive transference, psychotherapy is seen to be extremely difficult if not impossible, as the client will be responding to the therapist initially as unhelpful and therapy will likely be disrupted. The development of a negative transference during the course of the psychotherapy, once a positive transference has been established, is considered to be a natural course of development, but the therapeutic relationship will be able to remain intact because of the earlier positive bonding.

In the analysis of the transference, the therapist and the client work together to discover the kind of infantile wish upon which the transference is based. Such wishes, in classical psychoanalytic theory, are either of an aggressive or sexual nature. The understanding of these transferred responses of the client to the therapist produces insight in the client related to the vicissitudes of object attachment of libidinal drives. The client comes to recognize the existence of these libidinal drives within himself or herself, the historical persons toward whom these drives were directed, and the resultant place of these drives in the working of current interpersonal relationships. The emergence of these transferred responses in the contemporary relationship with the therapist allows movement from the present back to the past and forward again to the present as the ongoing dialog between present and past illuminates the current functioning of the client. It is the present reality of the transference experience which makes psychoanalytic therapy existentially vital rather than historically intellectual and cognitive. An insight about historical functioning outside of the context of the transference experience with the therapist always runs the risk of being only an intellectual formulation. In this sense psychoanalytic therapy, contrary to the popular view of it, is a "here and now" method which uses the present experience with the therapist to search for historical truth to expand present meaning.

2. **Interpretable Transference in Ego Psychology.** Questions have been raised in contemporary ego psychology concerning the actual definition of transference and its capacity to be interpreted and therefore to be used constructively in the ongoing psychotherapy. Thus the Blancks argue that if the primary psychological problem lies in a pre-Oedipal stage of development, then a level of development in which whole objects are present within the psyche of the individual has not been achieved. "Where the therapist is perceived as a potential gratifier of symbiotic need, for example, or as narcissistically perceived parts of a self-object unit, then long-held formulations of transference do not apply in the traditional way" (Blanck, 1979, p. 99).

G. and R. Blanck formulate the basic question in the following manner: "When is the analyst real, when is he truly a transference figure, when is he experienced as part of a self-object unit fantasied to be a potential gratifier of unfulfilled need?" (Blanck, 1979, p. 101). When the fundamental psychological problem is one of ego organization, the transfer of attitudes and feelings to the therapist is not based on a historical person to present person transfer, but is based rather on the transfer of unfulfilled needs of the ego organization into the therapeutic relationship. The Blancks suggest that the term *transference* be reserved for the well-organized and functioning ego, while the terms *need replication* (gratification of the need) and *object replication* (an object as part of the self) be used for the earlier phenomenon.

3. Interactive Understanding of Transference. R. Langs has suggested that the notion of transference can be used both as a way to understand a client's use of the therapeutic relationship and also as a way for the therapist to defend against the truth of the client's perception of the therapist. He argues for the therapist first looking to himself or herself, then to the interaction of the relationship, and only after that to the pathology of the client to understand the nature of meaning of the client's response to the therapist. This may also be a helpful procedure for pastors.

Defensively, transference can become a tool to insure the therapist's position of power and authority in the therapeutic relationship. Using a classic understanding of transference, any therapist can, if enough of the history of the client is known, link contemporary behavior to a past relationship or even to a past need or self-object unit, leaping over reflection about the appropriateness of the client's response to the actual behavior of the therapist. In Langs's system, the more the therapist generates problems in the therapeutic relationship born of the therapist's psychopathology, the more likely it is for the client to respond to the therapist in nontransference ways. In a defensive relationship, it is also more likely for the therapist to interpret the client's nontransference response as transference, thus making the problem the client's rather than the therapist's. The net effect of this kind of distortion by the therapist is for the client to distrust his or her own perceptions, thereby experiencing him- or herself as even more psychologically ill than was first believed. On the other hand, if a therapist can receive the client's nontransference communications and correct the problem in the therapy, then the client will more likely develop transference communications with the therapist, since that is the arena in which the psychotherapy proper takes place.

In like manner, a popular understanding of the notion of transference can be used to establish a position of power in any interpersonal relationship. The defensive use of the notion of transference relationships can be seen when a husband behaves toward his wife in a certain way, says she, because he sees in her his mother; or if a parishioner, in the pastor's view, constantly objects to a pastor's leadership style because the parishioner dislikes authority figures in general due to a bad relationship with a parent. Again, the therapist is to consider the possibility of the difficulty lying in the other person only after a serious consideration of the difficulty being his or her own or in the nature of the relationship.

4. Transference in Pastoral Care. The potential relevance of the concept of transference for all human relationships and its special importance in psychotherapy have led to discussions of transference in pastoral care and counseling (see C. Wise, L. Rulla, D. Williams). Most of these discussions deal with the classical understanding of transference and suggest that the minister or educator understand the nature of the phenomenon and work to either use it positively and growthfully for the parishioner where possible, or avoid it as much as possible by being as "real" as one can be in relationships with people.

The works of G. and R. Blanck and R. Langs caution against a too simplistic use of the concept of transference

as either an explanation for behavior rooted in a previous relationship or as a defense against unpleasant realities about the pastor which the parishioner may be communicating. Central to both discussions is the pastor's willingness to understand in fuller measure the meaning of the parishioner's response to him or her. Given the inflated notion of transference as its importance has become more evident in all interpersonal relationships, not simply the psychotherapeutic, it would be well to take more seriously the idea of distortion or "transference-like" behavior, retaining the term transference in its now technical sense where its unconscious properties become paramount (see R. R. Lee, 1980).

Bibliography. G. Blanck and R. Blanck, *Ego Psychology: Theory and Practice* (1974); *Ego Psychology II: Psychoanalytic Developmental Psychology* (1979). J. Edward, N. Riskin, and P. Turrini, *Separation-Individuation: Theory and Application* (1981). R. R. Lee, *Clergy and Clients: The Practice of Pastoral Psychotherapy* (1980). B. Moore and B. Fine, *A Glossary of Psychoanalytic Terms and Concept* (1967; 2d ed., 1968). H. Nunberg, *Principles of Psychoanalysis* (1955). J. A. Ordway, "Transference Reactions in Parishioners," *J. of Pastoral Care,* 24 (1970), 56–59. L. Rulla, *Depth Psychology and Vocation* (1971). D. Williams, *The Minister and the Care of Souls* (1961). C. Wise, *Religion in Illness and Health* (1942).

B. M. HARTUNG

PSYCHOANALYSIS (Therapeutic Method and Research). *See also* ANALYTICAL (JUNGIAN) PSYCHOLOGY AND PASTORAL CARE; CONFRONTATION (Pastoral and Therapeutic); INTERPRETATION AND HERMENEUTICS, PASTORAL; PSYCHOANALYSIS AND PASTORAL CARE; RESISTANCE; SUGGESTION, PERSUASION, AND INFLUENCE. *Compare* COUNTERTRANSFERENCE.

TRANSFORMATION, PERSONAL. *See* CONVERSION; DEVELOPMENTAL THEORY; SANCTIFICATION/ HOLINESS; SELF-TRANSCENDENCE.

TRANSITIONS. *See* CRISIS MINISTRY; CRISIS, DEVELOPMENTAL; DEVELOPMENTAL THEORY; LIFE CYCLE THEORY; PSYCHOTHERAPY; RITUAL AND PASTORAL CARE.

TRANSPERSONAL PSYCHOLOGIES. Approaches to psychological and spiritual well-being and potential in which experiences and behavior that extend beyond (*trans*) the personal (persona, personality, or ego) are considered. Higher mental processes and altered states of consciousness are emphasized. A broad nonsectarian integration of schools, perspectives, and techniques, both Eastern and Western is attempted.

R. N. WALSH

PERSONALITY THEORY (Varieties, Traditions, and Issues); PSYCHOLOGY OF RELIGION (Theories, Traditions, and Issues). *Compare* HUMANISTIC PSYCHOLOGY AND THEOLOGY; PARAPSYCHOLOGY; PSYCHOLOGY, EASTERN; PSYCHOLOGY AND PSYCHOTHERAPY (East-West Comparison); SPIRITUAL PSYCHOLOGIES.

TRANSPLANT SURGERY. *See* MORAL DILEMMAS IN PASTORAL PERSPECTIVE.

TRANSVESTISM/TRANSSEXUALISM. *See* HOMO-
SEXUALITY; SEXUAL VARIETY, DEVIANCE, AND DISOR-
DER.

TRAUMA. *Physical Trauma* is an injury or wound produced violently, and the resulting physical and psychological condition. *Psychic Trauma* is an emotionally
shocking experience which has a lasting psychic effect,
usually categorized as posttraumatic stress disorder (see
Kaplan).

Physical trauma is a widespread and destructive phenomenon; it is the third leading cause of death in the
U.S. and the leading cause among persons aged one to
forty-four. Trauma is responsible for 150,000 deaths
annually and leaves ten to seventeen million persons
disabled, with almost half a million of these disabled
permanently.

1. Effects of Physical Trauma. While the particular
areas of the body affected need immediate attention in
major physical trauma, the most important medical issue
is maintaining or resuscitating the victim's cardiopulmonary functions. A common problem is shock, a generalized state in which the bodily systems are disturbed by
severe inadequacy of blood circulation. Immediate stabilization is necessary, followed by initial treatment of
specific injuries.

Emotional responses to major physical trauma may
include psychotic, neurotic, and behavioral reactions. The
traumatized person must deal with overwhelming helplessness, humiliation, impaired body image, and possible mental symptoms. The rapidity and completeness of emotional
recovery depends on a host of variables, including the meaning of the event to the victim, pretrauma personality
strengths and weaknesses, the strengths of the support
system, and the quality and timeliness of crisis intervention
in physical and psychic processes.

2. Pastoral Care. The process of pastoral crisis intervention is making contact, focusing the crisis, and assisting with coping. In addition, pastoral presence, active
listening, and ritual are important. *Presence* means that
the pastor, as a representative of God and church, may be
a stabilizing and sustaining figure simply by being present in the midst of pain, fear, and "psychic numbing."
The minister may be a symbol of hope, help, and comfort. *Active listening* enables affected persons to break out
of the overwhelming isolation of intense emotions, to
socialize their experience and thus share the burden, to
ventilate, and to begin to gain perspective. Familiar
rituals often reach the overwhelmed victim at deep levels.
Prayer, brief Scripture phrases or passages, and sacraments may be appropriate.

Guilt is ubiquitous in times of trauma. The pastor
may help involved parties sort out realistic from unrealistic guilt and seek forgiveness for any valid guilt feelings. The pastor may also be a consultant and guide
during the long period of grief and adjustment after the
incident, as the victim and/or family seek to interpret the
event and put it in perspective in their faith pilgrimage.

Bibliography. W. F. Ballinger, R. B. Rutherford, G. D.
Zuidena, eds., *The Management of Trauma* (2d ed., 1973; 4th
ed., 1985). R. A Crowley and C. M. Dunham, eds., *Shock
Trauma/Critical Care Manual* (1982). H. I. Kaplan *et al.*, eds.,
Comprehensive Textbook of Psychiatry IV (1985), chs. 25, 27. R. J.
Lifton, *The Broken Connection* (1979). N. Schnaper and R. A.
Crowley, "Overview: Psychiatric Sequelae to Multiple
Trauma," *American J. of Psychiatry*, 133:8 (1976), 883–90.
D. K. Switzer, *The Minister as Crisis Counselor* (1974).

W. R. MONFALCONE

CRISIS INTERVENTION THEORY; CRISIS MINISTRY; EMER-
GENCY, PSYCHOLOGY OF PASTOR IN; POST-TRAUMATIC
STRESS DISORDER; VICTIMIZATION. *See also* BIRTH TRAUMA;
DISASTER, PUBLIC; RAPE AND RAPE COUNSELING.

TRINITY AND PERSONHOOD. The doctrine of the
Trinity points to the central Christian mystery of the
community of the Creator, the Redeemer, and the Holy
Spirit in the unity of the Godhead. Throughout Christian thought, reflection on this subject has intertwined
with developments in the understanding of personhood.

In the West the classical formula, received from Tertullian through Augustine, has been one "substance" in
three *persons*. However, the doctrine's bearing upon personhood has less to do with the technical term *person* than
with the doctrine as a whole, in its evocation of the rich
internal complexity of God.

Derived from a Greek term originally meaning an
actor's mask, the Latin term *persona* came to designate the
human individual. Understandably, the abstract language of "substance" and "person" has led many modern
theologians to regard the doctrine as an historically late
development overly influenced by Greek metaphysics,
and thus as a dispensable appendage to the faith.

This common impression may be corrected by considering the roots of the doctrine in the church's worship.
The community knew God as the one whom Jesus dared
address as *Abba*, i.e., "Father" or "Parent." It also knew
God as the one who raised Jesus from the dead, making
Jesus present to the community "in the Spirit." All this
and more was brought together in the church's practice
of praying to the Father, with the Son, in the Spirit. Such
prayer was of a piece with the message of salvation — so
much so that it became a way of naming God, of saying
who God is (see Jenson, 1982). The community testified
that the very Godhead is, in its own right, a community of
self-giving love, and that the worshipping church is simply
a reflection and result of that primary community.

Traces of this dynamic, personalistic vision may be
found in Augustine, e.g., when he sets forth an analogy
between the Trinity and the coexistence in a single
human individual of "being," "intellect," and "will."
Augustine's penetrating meditations on the internal
complexity of the self, at times approaching a notion of
the unconscious, and his affirmation of the will in particular, marked a turning point in the Western understanding of personhood.

To a large extent, however, Augustine and the Western theology which followed him obscured the richness
of the Trinity by an excessive stress on divine unity. This
orientation was often in the service of an authoritarian
view of society: one God, one pope, one ruler. Contemporary feminists have raised awareness of the need to find
alternative ways of speaking about God which do not
invite such patriarchal distortion.

Drawing upon the Eastern Orthodox tradition, Jürgen
Moltmann has argued that the doctrine is profoundly
opposed to the notion of a solitary, unfeeling deity. Rather,

it proclaims "the passionate God" who participates intimately in Jesus' abandonment on the cross and who identifies thereby with all of human suffering.

Bibliography. L. Hodgson, *Doctrine of the Trinity* (1943). R. Jenson, *Triune Identity* (1982). J. Moltmann, *Trinity and the Kingdom* (1981). K. Rahner, *Trinity* (1969). C. Welch, *Trinity in Contemporary Theology* (1953). See also T. Hopko, "The Trinity in the Cappadocians," in B. McGinn and J. Meyendorff, eds., *Christian Spirituality: Origins to the Twelfth Century* (1985); and in a more popular vein, A. McGill, *Suffering: A Test of Theological Method* (1968, 1982).

W. J. LOWE

GOD, DOCTRINE OF, AND PASTORAL CARE; TRANSCENDENCE, DIVINE. *Compare* PERSON.

TROELTSCH, ERNST (1865–1923). Born in Augsburg, Troeltsch studied at various German universities and was influenced by the work of Albrecht Ritschl. He became professor of systematic theology at Heidelberg in 1894 and professor of philosophy of religion at Berlin in 1915.

He was a leader in "the history of religions" school and a friend and intellectual colleague of Max Weber. His insights influenced the work of H. Richard Niebuhr and others. Among Troeltsch's many important publications was a remarkable study of *The Social Teaching of the Christian Churches,* in which he formulated and developed descriptions of, and the significant contrasts between, *church,* *sect,* and *mysticism.* Troeltsch struggled philosophically with the theological consequences of understanding *history* (and its relativities) as a decisive category. He also explored the question whether and in what ways it is appropriate to speak of the uniqueness and finality of any historical religion.

J. E. BURKHART

CHURCH-SECT DIFFERENCES IN PASTORAL CARE. *Biography:* NIEBUHR, H. RICHARD.

TRUST IN PASTORAL RELATIONSHIPS. Reliance upon the integrity, compassion, ability, or strength of another person and confidence in the caring process. In pastoral care the sharing of anxious longings, contradictory emotions, and secrets can only be risked in an atmosphere of trust. While often in tension with doubt, trust enables persons to share their stories, gain insight into situations of conflict, and receive guidance and strength for creative living. Akin to hope, trust relies on future possibilities as well as current realities and is a necessary foundation for all caring ministries.

Trust is not only a personal quality but a corporate possibility. The Christian congregation ideally offers a community in which the individuals' needs and hopes are understood and sustained by faith in God. At its best, the church lives by the trust it teaches and fidelity it proclaims.

1. **Theological Perspective.** In Christian perspective it is through Jesus Christ that God has provided a new possibility for trusting relationships. The Apostle Paul expressed this new potential for life together thus: "Christ Jesus . . . has broken down the dividing wall of hostility . . . that he might create in himself one new man in place of two, so making peace" (Eph. 2:13–15).

The removal of this barrier enables an end to enmity, distrust, and animosity, and opens the possibility of trust as a gift available through faith. This trust affirms God's immanence, concern, and willingness to help.

Trust is multifaceted: it involves some risk-taking in human relationships as well as in the human-divine relationship. Trust allays suspicion, self-consciousness, and fear of betrayal. It creates community, a bond of privacy in friendship, and privileged communication in pastoral conversations. Trust expresses confidence in a helper's character and competence, trust anticipates help in discovering resources, overcoming difficulties, and learning how to live responsibly in the future. Yet this motive is often mixed.

2. **Trust and Conflict.** Conflict is the vantage point from which trust's value and function may be viewed in life. One learns to believe the hard way—through broken promises, violated values, and betrayals of confidence. Life lets one down; cosmic order appears to fail; confusion gnaws at the human spirit. It is because care is usually sought in such circumstances of conflict that trustworthiness is so crucial in pastoral procedures. In these situations the sensitive pastor helps the parishioner or counselee maintain certain limits of confidentiality and disclosure and does not betray confidences. Rather, the pastor pursues the truth as a freeing force in life and hears confessions in assured confidentiality.

3. **Trust as Commitment.** A relational concept, trust gives order, meaning and a sense of permanence to one's life. Without trust, life becomes lonely, chaotic, and lacking in direction. Yet committed reliance upon another's care cannot be bargained for but must be received as a gift. Thus, Jesus spoke of a person laying down his life for his friends as an expression of ultimate care (Jn. 15:13). This may mean sacrificing one's own preferences, energies, and time for the sake of another, but in any case involves a significant giving of self as the basis of trust. Pastors develop trustworthiness as they become accessible to congregants' lives, vulnerable to their needs, faithful in initiating concern and in "standing by," and professionally skillful in responding to their hurts and needs when appropriate.

Bibliography. C. W. Brister, *The Promise of Counseling* (1978). C. Gratton, *Trusting: Theory and Practice* (1982). W. E. Oates, *The Christian Pastor* 3d ed. (1982). D. D. Williams, *The Minister and the Care of Souls* (1961).

C. W. BRISTER

FAITH/BELIEF; MORAL DEVELOPMENT; PERSONALITY DEVELOPMENT; THERAPEUTIC CONDITIONS. *See also* FAITH DEVELOPMENT RESEARCH; MORAL BEHAVIOR AND RELIGION. *Compare* ACCEPTANCE.

TRUTH-TELLING. Refers to the moral duty of professional persons to be honest and forthright with any person over whom they have potential or actual control. The principle applies to a wide variety of professional relationships (including those that involve human experimentation), but the present article considers only the physician-patient relationship and the counselor-counselee relationship.

1. **Physician-Patient Relationship.** Truth-telling rests on the principle that patients have a right to self-

determination and should have control over what happens to their bodies in the course of treatment. To exercise this right, patients must have adequate and usable knowledge about the diagnosis, treatment, and prognosis of their illness. Increased concern for the right to self-determination and increased desire of patients to know the truth have put pressure on physicians to share relevant information.

From the physician's point of view, truth-telling is a relative rather than an absolute duty. Four factors influence what, when, and how information should be shared with the patient. First, physicians are often aware of the uncertainty of their knowledge. To share that uncertainty with the patient may undermine the patient's trust in the doctor; to emphasize what is known and pretend that it is the whole truth is deceptive and may prove to be false as more data are obtained. Second, many patients have difficulty understanding their medical condition, however much the physician tries to explain. Third, the physician's time is limited, and time spent with one patient to explain a medical condition may take time away from another patient. Fourth, telling patients the truth may actually do harm by making them less able to cope with their illness or less willing to undergo treatment.

Given these factors, physicians often appeal to the principle of "therapeutic privilege," that is, the right to withhold information when truth-telling could be detrimental to the patient's welfare. In the past, law courts have tended to protect the physician's privilege by using as a criterion of truth-telling the "prevailing standard practice," namely, what the reasonable medical practitioner would disclose under the same or similar circumstances? Increasingly, law courts have shifted to the "reasonable person standard," namely, what the reasonable person must know to make an informed decision about his or her illness or treatment. This shift in criteria attends to the patient's right to self-determination, but pays less heed to the patient who has difficulty assimilating information.

2. Counselor-Counselee Relationship. Truth-telling as an issue in therapeutic relationships also involves a person's right to self-determination. Unlike the physician, though, the counselor is concerned with self-determination in a twofold sense, with both (a) what the counselee needs to know to make an informed decision, and (b) how to increase the counselee's degree of self-determination.

Most counselors would say that they should clarify the terms and expectations of the counseling relationship for the counselee. A more difficult issue concerns sharing factual or even privileged information relevant to the counselee's current struggle. Most therapists would do so

as long as it is vital to the therapeutic process and does not violate rules of confidentiality.

The basic intent of counseling—to help persons become more self-determinative—raises the question whether counselors should share insights into the counselee with him or her directly. Most counselors would be concerned not only about the timing of such sharing but also about the value of it, given the assumption that it is more helpful to counselees if they gain insight into themselves rather than being told by a therapist.

A related issue is whether counselors should share personal reactions to a counselee with the counselee. Some schools (like psychoanalysis) see countertransference in such reactions and recommend that counselors consult professional colleagues to overcome the countertransference. Others (like Rogerian counseling) see incongruity in such reactions and maintain that counselors must take whatever steps necessary to become genuine in counseling relationships, even discussing reactions with the counselee.

Truth-telling in therapeutic relationships, then, has many dimension and no absolute guidelines beyond doing what will help the client know himself or herself.

Bibliography. T. Beauchamp and J. Childress, *Principles of Biomedical Ethics* (1979). S. Bok, "Truth-Telling: Ethical Aspects," *Encyclopedia of Bioethics*, 4 (1978), pp. 1682–88. F. Harron, J. Burnside, and T. Beauchamp, *Health and Human Values* (1983). R. Veatch, *Death, Dying, and the Biological Revolution* (1976).

L. O. MILLS

ETHICS, PROFESSIONAL; FAITH AND INTEGRITY, PASTOR'S; MORAL DILEMMAS IN PASTORAL PERSPECTIVE. *See also* CONFRONTATION (Pastoral and Therapeutic); CONSCIENCE; DYING, MORAL DILEMMAS IN; RESPONSIBILITY/IRRESPONSIBILITY, PSYCHOLOGY OF. *Compare* LYING; THERAPEUTIC CONDITIONS; VALUES IN COUNSELING AND PSYCHOTHERAPY.

TSI (Theological School Inventory). *See* EVALUATION AND DIAGNOSIS, PSYCHOLOGICAL; THEOLOGICAL STUDENTS, EVALUATION AND EMPIRICAL STUDIES OF.

TWINS/TWINSHIP. *See* PERSONALITY, BIOLOGICAL DIMENSIONS OF.

TYPE A/B BEHAVIOR PATTERNS. *See* STRESS.

TYPES/TYPOLOGIES. *See* PERSONALITY TYPES AND PASTORAL CARE. *See also* CHURCH-SECT DIFFERENCES; SOMATOTYPE.

TYRRELL, BERNARD J. *See* CHRISTOTHERAPY.

U

UHSADEL, WALTER. *See* PASTORAL THEOLOGY, PROTESTANT.

UNBELIEF. *See* DOUBT AND UNBELIEF.

UNCERTAINTY. *See* DECISION/INDECISION, PSYCHOLOGY OF; DOUBT AND UNBELIEF.

UNCHURCHED PERSONS. *See* EVANGELISM; SECULARIZATION/SECULARISM.

UNCONDITIONAL POSITIVE REGARD. *See* CLIENT-CENTERED THERAPY; THERAPEUTIC CONDITIONS.

UNCONSCIOUS, THE. That part of the mind or psyche containing information that has never been conscious, or that was once conscious but is no longer. The unconscious has received both philosophic and psychological analysis. Psychological evidence indicates that both affective and cognitive processes occur unconsciously and may be either adaptive or disruptive. Freud, James, Jung, and Piaget have explored different aspects of the unconscious. Eastern psychology has a parallel but quite different viewpoint. The unconscious, as locus of both spiritual and demonic forces, has been recognized by theologians like Paul Tillich and Jacques Ellul.

1. **The Existence of the Unconscious.** Philosophically, the qualities of consciousness and unconsciousness cannot be understood except in relation to one another. A concept of consciousness indirectly implies the existence of unconscious processes. The unconscious is something we infer and reconstruct from signs derived from consciousness. The unconscious may thus be described philosophically as a state of unperceived existence which is in contrast to states of perceived existence occurring within consciousness.

Psychological studies also offer evidence for the existence of the unconscious. Studies of ordinary sense perception reveal that a significant amount of our cognitive and affective activity goes on in the absence of conscious awareness. This unconscious system of sensory input

processing is grounded in neural structures. One is often aware of the end result of this sequence of information processing but rarely of the process itself.

2. **Western Psychological Perspectives.** One of Freud's most important claims was that such unconscious processing occupies the larger part of our psyche and has a strong influence upon our perception and action. Freud often focused upon affective unconscious processes, but in *The Interpretation of Dreams*, he explains how complex thought processes may also occur in the absence of conscious awareness. Freud described the rationale and the psychological processes (defense mechanisms such as repression) for excluding certain material from consciousness. He emphasized, however, that although various thoughts and experiences are excluded from consciousness, this material nevertheless exerts important influences upon conscious life and behavior. Freud and his disciples employed techniques such as hypnosis, free association, dream analysis, and projective testing to uncover unconscious psychological processes, and based psychoanalytic therapy upon the skilled interpretation of these materials. By gaining awareness of disruptive processes within the unconscious, patients could be helped to achieve emotional resolutions of their problems.

Other psychologists such as Piaget have explored the cognitive aspects of the unconscious. Persons are often aware of the initial stimulus as well as the result of a sequence of problem solving operations and yet remain unaware of the processing activity which gave rise to the solution or decision. Sometimes perceptual information is kept out of awareness so as not to interfere with ongoing, complicated cognitive processes. Such occurrences may be helpful, for if these repressed materials became conscious, the result would be disruptive. For example, in the affective domain, uncontrolled biological impulses would make it impossible for one to adjust to reality. In cognitive activities such as reading or writing, awareness of first-order sensory perceptions or early levels of sensory processing might well be distracting and wasteful of our limited processing capability—such awareness might well interfere with our reading or writing ability. A sizable amount of cognitive and affective activity is thus seen to take place in the absence of cognitive awareness; at times, this lack of awareness is clearly helpful

3. Eastern Psychology, Spirituality, and the Unconscious. In traditional Eastern yoga psychology the unconscious has been understood in terms of *samsakāras* or repressed memory traces. In the Eastern view, the unconscious is nothing other than the sum total of memory traces left behind by actions and thoughts in this and previous lives. Yoga and the various esoteric meditative disciplines are simply psychological techniques for raising such memory traces from the unconscious to consciousness where they can be critically examined and either purged or retained. Rigorous practice of yoga can, according to Eastern psychology, gradually root out the unconscious traces (including even the instincts) until all have been made conscious. Then the unconscious would cease to exist, and the resultant personality would be thoroughly spiritual. Western psychologists, preeminently the depth psychologists, do not agree with this optimistic Eastern assessment concerning the degree to which the unconscious can be made conscious, but have attempted to give their own account of such spiritual intuitions. Freud, for instance, restricted the unconscious to the id, with its basic biological instincts, along with repressed materials from the ego. In *Civilization and Its Discontents* (1962) Freud examined the Eastern belief in an identity between individuals and the Divine, and concluded that the seemingly universal human feeling of identity with a higher order was not inherent in the unconscious or any other aspect of the personality. Rather, it is a shrunken residue of early prenatal and infancy experiences of an all-embracing intimate bond between ourselves and the world about us. The religious impulse — our sense of spirituality — says Freud, is the persistence of such immature "oceanic" feelings of world-absorption from infancy.

In his *Varieties of Religious Experience* (1978) William James, on the other hand, identified the unconscious as that part of the personality through which the divine impinges on human experience, while Rudolf Otto, in *The Idea of the Holy* (1958), postulated a mental "divination faculty" responsive to divine stimulation, just as the eye is responsive to light. Though Otto did not clearly locate the divination faculty, it would seem to share in the unconscious to the degree that the other sense organs do.

It is Carl Jung, however, who has given the most careful attention to the question of spirituality and the unconscious. Jung assumes Freud's theory of the unconscious but, under Eastern influence, enlarges it to include the "God archetype" as the cornerstone of personality. For Jung the psyche in its relation to the conscious and unconscious dimensions may be thought of as a series of expanding concentric circles with the ego at the center. Surrounding the ego is consciousness, which in turn is surrounded by the personal unconscious containing specific personal acquisitions and forgotten, repressed or subliminally perceived contents. All of this is then enclosed within the collective unconscious which expands outward in every direction toward infinity. Jung's collective unconscious is based upon the idea of an inherited potential for psychic functioning, out of which

contents arise which are common to all humans. It is the collective or shared foundation out of which consciousness ever arises afresh. Consequently, the fundamental human psychic activity is the activity of the unconscious. Within it reside the potential dynamics which, when structured by individual growth, represent humankind's universal reactions to typical human situations (e.g., fear, danger, relationships between the sexes, between children and parents, between persons and the divine). These are the archetypes, and it is the God archetype — the Spirit within — which is the integrating principle for all psychological growth through the levels of the collective unconscious, the personal unconscious, and the conscious. For Jung, then, it is via the unconscious that one experiences the Divine.

4. Theological and Pastoral Appropriation. Though deeply influenced by Freud, Christian theologian Paul Tillich has paid particular attention to Jung's analysis of the unconscious. In the third volume of his *Systematic Theology* Tillich helpfully examines the sacramental function of the Spirit in relation to the unconscious. Apprehension of the Spirit through consciousness alone is not sufficient. For the sacramental power of the Spirit to be effective, the unconscious must be engaged as well. In another vein, theologian Jacques Ellul has applied Jung's insights regarding the unconscious to an assessment of the impact of modern technology upon the personality.

The modern "discovery of the unconscious" — more accurately, the systematic exploration of and theorizing about the unconscious — has enlarged the role of pastors to include helping people discover the presence and power of the Spirit within the unconscious. For modern persons, conditioned by a scientific worldview to see nature and themselves mechanistically and rationalistically, it may be (as Jung believed) that the unconscious is the remaining dimension through which the Spirit can be most powerfully experienced. This, however, requires developing new modes of perception and experience attuned to the ways of the unconscious — especially its expression through symbol, myth, ritual, and dreams — and to the many deeply felt but easily overlooked ways in which the Spirit, as Paul puts it, "intercedes for us with sighs too deep for words" (Rom. 8:26).

Bibliography. N. Caputi, *Unconscious: A Guide to the Sources* (1985). H. G. Coward, "Jung's Encounter with Yoga," *J. of Analytical Psychology,* 23 (1978), 339–57. J. M. Davidson and R. J. Davidson, eds., *The Psychobiology of Consciousness* (1980). R. C. Fuller, *Americans and the Unconscious* (1986). J. Ellul, *The Technological Society* (1964). S. Freud, *New Introductory Lectures on Psychoanalysis* (1964 [1930]). R. C. Fuller, *Americans and the Unconscious* (1986). N. S. Goldman, "The Unconscious in Pastoral Psychology: A Rabbinic Perspective," *Pastoral Psychology,* 34:3 (1986), 193–209. C. S. Hall, *A Primer of Freudian Psychology* (1957). J. Jacobi, *The Psychology of C. G. Jung* (1962). W. James, *The Varieties of Religious Experience* (1978 [1902]). C. G. Jung, *Man and His Symbols* (1968). E. Kohak, "Forest Lights: Notes on the Conceptualization of the Unconscious," *J. of Religion and Health,* 22 (1983), 49–57. W. Lowe, *Evil and the Unconscious* (1983). R. L. Munroe, *Schools of Psychoanalytic Thought* (1955). R. Otto, *The Idea of the Holy* (1958 [1923]). P. Ricoeur, *Freud and Philosophy* (1970). P. Tillich, *Systematic Theology* vol. 3 (1963). A. Ulanov and B. Ulanov, *Religion and the Unconscious* (1975). V. White, *God and the Unconscious* (1953).

H. COWARD

ANALYTICAL PSYCHOLOGY; PSYCHOANALYSIS; PSYCHOLOGY, EASTERN; REPRESSION. *See also* PHILOSOPHY AND PSYCHOLOGY; SPIRIT. *Compare* CONSCIOUSNESS; MIND; RESISTANCE.

UNCTION. *See* ANOINTING OF THE SICK, SACRAMENT OF.

UNDERHILL, EVELYN (1875–1941). Writer and spiritual director. Born into an upper-class English family of nominal religious observance, Underhill underwent a profound religious conversion in 1914 while on retreat at a Catholic convent. Because of her disapproval of the antimodernist stance of the Roman Church, and in consideration of her husband's wishes, she remained in the Church of England. She formally affiliated with that body in 1921, the same year that Baron Friedrich von Hügel became her spiritual director.

Underhill's *Mysticism* (1911) and *Worship* (1936) are her most notable books, with the former still much consulted. She also wrote a number of monographs and edited many spiritual classics. Underhill was an expert spiritual director in her own right, counseling many of her clients both personally and through correspondence. From 1924 on she also gave retreats and days of recollection to many audiences. Throughout her active life she was keenly interested in political and social affairs. Her manifesto *The Church and War* (1941), published just a few months before her death, was a declaration of her total pacifism, a stance she found as a natural consequence of her mystical life. She was the first woman to be invited to give a series of theological lectures at Oxford (1921). Named a Fellow of King's College (Cambridge) in 1928, she also received the Doctor of Divinity degree from Aberdeen University in 1938.

Bibliography. M. Cropper, *Evelyn Underhill* (1958). C. Williams, ed., *The Letters of Evelyn Underhill* (1943).

L. S. CUNNINGHAM

MYSTICISM; SPIRITUAL DIRECTION.

UNDERSTANDING, PASTORAL. *See* EMPATHY; INSIGHT; INTERPRETATION AND HERMENEUTICS; PERCEPTIVENESS AND SENSITIVITY; THEORY IN PASTORAL CARE AND COUNSELING, FUNCTIONS OF.

UNDERSTANDING, SELF. *See* SELF-UNDERSTANDING. *See also* INSIGHT; SELF-ANALYSIS; SELF EXAMINATION.

UNDERTAKER. *See* FUNERAL DIRECTOR.

UNDOING. In psychoanalytic theory, an unconscious defense mechanism in which repressed painful feelings of guilt and remorse are controlled by the use of a magical gesture (ritual) which attempts to annul or atone for a forbidden act (while unconsciously also gratifying it). The person tries to undo offenses by symbolic means, such as compulsive hand washing, or monotonous repetition of a prayer. A more extreme example is the catatonic schizophrenic person seeking to undo the sins of the world by holding his or her arms in a gesture of blessing for days on end.

M. DOLINSKY

DEFENSE AND COPING THEORY; DEFENSE MECHANISM; OBSESSIVE-COMPULSIVE DISORDER. *See also* FORGIVENESS; GUILT; PSYCHOANALYSIS (Personality Theory and Research); REPRESSION. *Compare* FAITH AND WORKS; PENANCE, SACRAMENT OF; REPETITION COMPULSION

UNEMPLOYED PERSONS. In a culture which makes occupation a major mark of personal identity and high income a principal measure of personal worth, unemployment can be an emotionally devastating experience. The unemployed experience a traumatic disruption in the daily routines that largely define life, a sense of powerlessness, social rejection, and loss of self-esteem. One readily assumes being the object of social disdain or pity—which may or may not be true—and assumes that the unemployment is a symptom of some fundamental personal defectiveness, which may or may not be true. These feelings often compel the unemployed person to seek isolation and otherwise to lessen the very motivation and social skills that would help find employment and cope with the unemployment.

Thus, pastoral care for the unemployed person begins with the recognition of the emotional trauma associated with the experience. This trauma often manifests itself in emotional depression, which contributes to a strong sense of alienation from one's family, church, and community. Because of this alienation the unemployed person often seeks a lifestyle of social isolation. The movement toward isolation becomes the greatest obstacle to coping with and overcoming unemployment. Providing personal support is the basis for all ministry to unemployed persons.

At the level of individual pastoral care the professional can, first, provide an "open ear", listening to the spoken and unspoken needs of each person. In this sense pastoral care for the unemployed involves a receptive and compassionate listening to the pain surrounding the experience of the unemployed, a pain that usually includes the arousal of past traumata.

But helping the unemployed to move from the pain of the past to the experience of the present is crucial. An important function of pastoral care is helping the jobless person develop a strategy for assuming control of his or her life in the present. Developing a regular structure and setting attainable goals is very helpful. For example, one might set up a daily routine and set goals of obtaining a given number of interviews per week. This regular structure and goal setting will enable one to assume some personal power in a situation that creates the feeling of powerlessness.

Finally, pastoral care involves encouragement and hope for the future. This can best be realized when unemployed people are gathered together in a support group. The sharing of mutual concerns and job networking provides one with a community of support and resources. A support/resource group can open a future that often feels closed and limited.

In the church, responsive and sensitive parishioners can reinforce the work of the professional. They can do so by communicating to the jobless person that her or his worth is not bound up in work, but rather who he or she is. The church can say to the unemployed person: "We love you apart from your work. You are not alone. We will stand with you."

R. V. THOMPSON

SOCIAL CHANGE AND DISLOCATION; WORK AND CAREER. *See also* ADVOCACY; SOCIAL SERVICES; SOCIAL STATUS AND CLASS FACTORS. *Compare* SOCIAL JUSTICE ISSUES; STRESS AND STRESS MANAGEMENT; POOR PERSONS; VOCATION.

UNFORGIVABLE SIN. *See* UNPARDONABLE SIN.

UNHAPPINESS. *See* SADNESS AND DEPRESSION.

UNIFICATION CHURCH. *See* NEW RELIGIOUS MOVEMENTS.

UNITARIAN-UNIVERSALIST PASTORAL CARE. Unitarian-Universalists were part of the liberal movement in American religion which took place in the first three decades of this century and laid the groundwork for the modern understanding of pastoral care. Although not large in number, they contributed greatly to breaking the shackles of biblical literalism and theological naïveté which blocked the integration of the developing behavioral sciences into pastoral care. Along with this important contribution, they also were pioneers in the development of a new emphasis on social ethics.

A Unitarian physician and surgeon, Richard C. Cabot, issued the first call for a clinical experience for theological students in 1925, and went on to begin the actual organization and promotion of Clinical Pastoral Education at Massachusetts General Hospital. In the 1930s he coauthored with a minister, Russell L. Dicks, *The Art of Ministering to the Sick,* a book that is a classic statement of the beginning of the new approach to pastoral care. Cabot was the first president of the Council for Clinical Training. His work is indicative of the Unitarian-Universalist contribution to the liberalism which made possible the modern approach to pastoral care, and which continues to push forward its development.

One distinction with regard to pastoral care among Unitarian-Universalists is that it tends to be linked with social action. There is a strong emphasis on the fact that we are not persons in isolation, and that while a Unitarian-Universalist may quite freely utilize understandings about personality and counseling from any relevant resource, there still appears to be an incompleteness about pastoral care if it does not take into account the contemporary social and ethical concerns that are part of the society in which one lives. Another rather general characteristic of pastoral care in Unitarian-Universalism is that it champions human rights and the use of reason, and tends toward almost complete nonjudgmentalism in regard to such pastoral concerns as abortion, birth control, and issues concerning the termination of life.

Unitarian-Universalists do not seek to develop definitive criteria in regard to pastoral care but remain open to continuing development. This attitude was aptly reflected by the Universalist historian Ernest Cassara who, in responding to the question of where Unitarians stand, stated that the only response to that question is that Unitarians do not stand, but move.

Bibliography. J. Adams and S. Hiltner, *Pastoral Care in the Liberal Churches* (1970). R. Cabot and R. Dicks, *The Art of Ministering to The Sick* (1936). E. Cassara, *Universalism in America* (1971). D. Parke, *The Epic of Unitarianism* (1957).

W. A. KNIGHTS

PASTORAL CARE (History, Traditions, and Definitions).

UNITED STATES, HISTORY OF PASTORAL CARE AND COUNSELING IN. *See* HISTORY OF PROTESTANT *or* ROMAN CATHOLIC PASTORAL CARE (United States); JEWISH CARE AND COUNSELING (History, Traditions, and Contemporary Issues).

UNIVERSITY STUDENTS. *See* COLLEGE STUDENTS AND COLLEGE CHAPLAINCY.

The UNKNOWN. *See* ANXIETY; FEAR; MATERIALISM; The UNCONSCIOUS.

UNMARRIED COUPLES. *See* COHABITATION.

UNPARDONABLE SIN. A term often used by persons whose whole life is hobbled by scrupulosity, who seek to be perfect in minute and trivial ways. Their preoccupation, in psychiatric terms, is obsessive-compulsive addiction to the fixed idea that they have committed or are about to commit the unpardonable sin. These persons may also be clinically depressed. They are often undergoing radical changes in their life due to common crises such as the birth of a child (particularly a first child), the death of a spouse or the first experience of a sexual relationship.

These persons want repeated reassurance in a given interview or telephone call with a pastor. Many times such a person may be talking with several pastors sequentially without telling any one pastor that he or she is doing so. They read much self-help literature. They read certain passages in the Bible repeatedly and quote them.

Examples of such passages are as follows: II Thess. 1:9 assures Christians who are being persecuted that their persecutors "shall suffer the punishment of eternal destruction and exclusion from the presence of the Lord." Also, in Mk. 3:29, Jesus says, "But whoever blasphemes against the Holy Spirit never has forgiveness, but is guilty of an eternal sin." Furthermore, in Heb. 6:4–6, the Christian who is only superficially mature in the gospel and deliberately remains so is told: "It is impossible to restore again to repentance those who . . . have tasted the goodness of the word of God and the powers of the age to come, if they then commit apostasy, since they crucify the Son of God on their own account and hold him up to contempt."

When seen from a pastoral hermeneutical point of view, the contexts of these scriptures specifically are aimed at three conditions. First, they are meant to comfort Christians who are being persecuted by people without any cause other than that they profess faith in Jesus as Lord. Second, they point to the hazard of shallow, nominal, and deliberately ignorant external assent to a few elementary doctrines of the gospel with a conscious and deliberate intention to remain this way. Third, they pronounce a stern judgment on the deliberate refusal of an enemy of the gospel to change his or her hardness of heart to the tutelage of the Holy Spirit.

However, persons who come for help with the obsession that they have committed the unpardonable sin are usually not in one of these categories. They are scrupulous to a fault and have often been Christians since childhood. The pastor can give historical and biblical interpretations *ad nauseam* with no avail. More nonrational and less intellectualized understanding is needed in these cases.

First, these ideas reflect the profound terror of the person at the thought of or fear of change and separation from people upon whom they feel totally dependent, especially a parent or spouse. Second, some temptations are "mashed" by this idea, such as the temptation to commit suicide, to kill someone else, or to divorce their spouse. To the pious, scrupulosity-ridden person, even anger itself may be unpardonable.

Pastoral patience is needed to listen to such persons carefully and to explore their underlying temptations. If he or she is actually suicidal or has a history of such in the past, then psychiatric help can be sought. The idea of the unpardonable sin in pastoral practice is symbolic of the person's temptations more than it represents the God and Father of our Lord Jesus Christ.

W. E. OATES

FORGIVENESS; GUILT; SCRUPULOSITY; SIN/SINS. *Compare* GRACE AND PASTORAL CARE; MORTAL SIN.

UNPLANNED PREGNANCY. *See* PREGNANCY.

UNWED MOTHERS. *See* SINGLE PARENTS.

UTOPIAN COMMUNITIES. *See* RELIGIOUS AND UTOPIAN COMMUNITIES.

VALUE, CONCEPT OF. Value is the attribute of worth assigned to some entity, factor, quality, or experience (from the Latin *valere,* be strong, well). There are two distinct aspects: the personal judgment of worth on the part of the evaluator and the objective quality of worthfulness in the thing prized. Philosophers have debated about the nature of value; since values are not verifiable in the same way that facts are, the debate is not likely to be settled. Yet there tends to be substantial agreement about those qualities of character and appropriation which are of value.

1. Theories. Theories of the concept of value include *realism* (objective immaterial realities — Plato), *eudaemonism* (realized purpose — Aristotle), *hedonism* (forms of pleasure — Epicurus), *formalism* (determination by rational will—Kant), *utilitarianism* (contributes to happiness or well being—Mill), *voluntarism* (fulfills interests — Perry), *emotivism* (projections of emotional preferences).

The conventional distinction between intrinsic and instrumental values (means and ends) is not particularly helpful, since intrinsic values nevertheless are means toward human enrichment and are held to be of worth on that account. Process philosophy regards all values as both intrinsic and instrumental, since every actuality has value for itself and at the same time participates in the universal relativity. Thus Whitehead states: "The purpose of God is the attainment of value in the temporal world."

The process view affirms the subjective pole of appreciative appropriation and the objective pole of qualitative enrichment, both being necessary for actualization of value.

2. Religious Values. Most theologians regard God as source or ground of value and sanction for authentic valuations, although they differ in explication of this. Evil is the destruction of value (disvalue) or obstruction of potential value. One need not accept Augustine's view, "To Thee [God] there is no such thing as evil," in order to see the validity of his argument that the term *evil* can have no meaning except in relation to some notion of value or the good.

Many recent theologians have stressed the continuity of religious values with all life values, perceiving the faith contribution as illuminating and vivifying the value dimension of all experience, and providing an interpretive context of integrity and depth.

3. Pastoral Care. Value is a collective, abstract term that easily becomes vacuous. The pastor is in a special position to give the concept particular content, disclosing to people the neglected preciousness within their lives. There are many forms of value (Perry lists eight), and many people would be helped if contrasting types were brought into better balance, if worth were seen as collecting experiences more than things, and if quality of relationships replaced confused multiplicity. Especially important is enabling people to discover practical ways of reordering their valuations, to see that "true" values enhance other values, remain precious in retrospect, often require delayed gratification, yet at times are quite serendipitous.

Bibliography. Augustine, *Enchiridion* (1961). B. Blanshard, *Reason and Goodness* (1961). R. Frondizi, *What Is Value?* (1963). R. B. Perry, *Realms of Value* (1968). C. L. Stevenson, *Ethics and Language* (1944). A. N. Whitehead, *Religion in the Making* (1927).

C. S. MILLIGAN

ETHICS AND PASTORAL CARE. *See also* MORAL BEHAVIOR AND RELIGION; MORAL DEVELOPMENT. *Compare* MONEY.

VALUE NEUTRALITY. *See* ETHICS AND PASTORAL CARE; VALUES IN COUNSELING AND PSYCHOTHERAPY.

VALUES CLARIFICATION. Methods of determining the actual evaluations that function in an individual's decisions and attitudes, as contrasted with presumed valuations which are in fact inoperative. Analysis is not limited to isolated value judgments, but seeks also to discover the pattern of one's valuational system, the relative importance of particular values, and the procedure by which one's value judgments are made.

1. **Values Clarification Movements.** In recent years values clarification has denoted a program for carrying out these tasks, especially by Sidney B. Simon and associates since 1966. The basic assumption is that people have values but often are confused about them. The aim is to begin where people are in their valuations and to clarify their situation for better self-understanding, elimination of needless internal conflict, and intentionality toward continued growth. This is done not by indoctrination, but by eliciting responses to cases, simulation, and role playing. It is designed for use in schools where there is the dilemma of avoiding imposition of the teacher's value system, yet a need to illumine the realization that educational subject matter contains valuations as well as facts and concepts.

The literature is admittedly simplistic. The supposition that the program is not a morality is dubious, for normative principles are involved. However, it has been useful to teachers in situations where sophistication is less important than effectiveness, and it is a corrective for moral teaching that has been either memorization or dodging valuational issues.

Lawrence Kohlberg is noteworthy for developing a theory and methodology for determining the formal or structural level at which persons operate in value judgments. Critics have claimed hidden biases and unexamined presuppositions in Kolberg's theory, although others have found his analysis helpful. His underlying assumption that formal levels of maturity are discernible across cultures is empirically defensible, at least in part, despite legitimate questions raised about strategies and conclusions derived from the theory.

2. **Definitions.** The term *value* is ambiguous because in ordinary discourse it refers to two distinctly different things: *evaluations* that we make and *qualities* that we experience. Judgment about the nutritional benefit of certain foods is quite different from being nourished by those foods. The foregoing discussion refers to values in the evaluating sense: one's scale of values. But an adequate philosophy of values must also deal with the nature of value as experienced or possessed, and with criteria for valuational claims. Thus values clarification may also refer to investigation of authentic values and the basis for such claims.

Values as possessed goods are factors that sustain and enhance the significance of life. This is tautological, since enhancement and significance are quasi-synonyms for value. If values are not reducible to any other class of entities (values are not equivalent to facts or psychological states), then the tautological feature is unavoidable. Of course, if value terms are pseudoexpressions for phenomena that can be described more accurately by other modes of discourse, there is little point in valuational analysis. Value discourse requires valuational presuppositions, about which there is great diversity of opinion.

Although definitions must be abstract, actual values occur as concrete qualities in individual lives. They do so with a high degree of relativity, conditioned by particular circumstances and realistic possibilities, cultural patterns, and idiosyncrasies of taste and aversion. Hence a central question is whether value claims have any universal validity. That there are cultural and individual diversities does not settle the question whether there are any universals that underlie such variation. The clarification of values in this sense has the unending task of shedding light on a crucial area.

3. **Pastoral Care.** It is beneficial for people to discover their operative evaluations as distinct from merely verbal ones. A Steinbeck character held that most people do not know what they want, how to get it, or that they have it when they do. Many pastors would agree. Frequently in what appear to be value conflicts, the real disagreement is over the procedures that will achieve the goal. In that case, the issue is not about values but effectiveness.

Particularly important is clarification of those values which are owned but without appreciative awareness. For example, insightful rediscovery of blessedness is often what is lacking in people who find life meaningless. This is usually achieved best by processes of disclosure, whether in preaching or counseling.

Bibliography. L. Kohlberg, *The Philosophy of Moral Development* (1981). K. N. Lewis and D. A. Lewis, "A Biblical Analysis of Values Clarification," *J. of Psychology and Theology*, 10 (1982), 40–46. T. Lickona, ed., *Moral Development and Behavior* (1976). S. B. Simon and J. Clark, *More Values Clarification* (1975). P. W. Taylor, *Normative Discourse* (1961).

C. S. MILLIGAN

MORAL DILEMMAS IN PASTORAL PERSPECTIVE. *See also* AXIOTHERAPY; ETHICS AND PASTORAL CARE; GUIDANCE, PASTORAL; LIFESTYLE ISSUES IN PASTORAL CARE; MORAL DEVELOPMENT; MORAL THEOLOGY AND PASTORAL CARE. *Compare* ADVOCACY; CONSCIOUSNESS RAISING.

VALUES IN COUNSELING AND PSYCHOTHERAPY.

It is generally accepted today that values — beliefs that determine specific conduct or goals of existence — are inherent in the practice of psychotherapy. Until recently there has been an emphasis on the value neutrality of the therapist. It is now realized that such a neutrality is not possible since therapy involves education, social influence, and persuasion (Beutler). Some even maintain that psychotherapy is a contemporary religious system in that it defines existence and meaning in life (Pattison). Therapeutic change at any level — physical, emotional, behavioral, rational, interpersonal, or spiritual—involves the changing of values in some sense.

All the major therapeutic systems are based upon scientifically unprovable value assumptions. This does not negate the use of empirical research, but it does demand a recognition of the presuppositions foundational to every investigation. Philosophical orientations that underpin mental health approaches are usually humanistic, naturalistic, social, or existential (Lowe). Examples of humanistic approaches are client-centered and rational-emotive therapies; naturalistic approaches are behavioral and social learning therapies; social approaches are some group therapies and family therapies; existential approaches are existential analysis and logotherapy.

Criteria that describe value presuppositions are based on what a therapist believes about the nature of reality, the nature of human beings, the nature of mental health, and the way it is achieved (Van Leeuwen). The following summary statements are given as examples of value assumptions concerning the nature of reality and humanness: identity and truth are rooted in the values of the body (Alexander Lowen—bioenergetic therapy); intrinsic to human beings is the organismic valuing process, which is trustworthy (Carl Rogers—client-centered therapy); human beings are predisposed to both irrationality and rationality, the latter being the measure of reality (Albert Ellis—rational-emotive therapy); human beings both influence and are shaped by their social context, and reality is largely determined by the family (Salvador Minuchin—structural family therapy); identity belongs to both the natural and supernatural orders with truth residing in God (Paul Tournier—Christian therapy). These assumptions are beyond the scope of empirical investigation, and yet in the therapeutic process they determine which questions are significant, what information is relevant, what assessment is made, what alternatives are considered, what objectives and goals are set, and what attitudes and actions therapists take toward their clients.

There has been some research on the transmission of values in individual therapy. Change that occurs without a shift in values tends to be transient; successful therapy, therefore, inevitably involves some change in the client's value system (Beutler). Moreover, some degree of compatibility between the values of client and therapist seems necessary to bring about change. During the therapeutic process clients tend to acquire their therapist's interest patterns, attitudes, and view of life. Clients also assume their therapist's goals and evaluate the success of their therapy on this basis.

Recent research increasingly emphasizes the importance of values in therapy. G. H. Zuk regards family problems as essentially conflicts between disparate value positions. He provides a framework that focuses on the dominant value positions involved in family conflicts by exploring and utilizing such variables as the family's expectations and engagement in therapy, and the power differential in the family. H. H. Strupp argues that some values are *essential* to the therapeutic process; these are deeply experienced by the client. Other values he designates as *optional* and *idiosyncratic*. If therapists distinguish between these kinds of values in their own practice then they will be less likely to impose optional or idiosyncratic values on clients. G. M. Abroms presents a hierarchy of value development that enables the therapist to assist clients in moving from less satisfactory, or lower value functioning, to more productive and creative higher value functioning. Among others, A. E. Bergin calls for a recognition of the legitimacy of religious values in the profession. He points out that a large number of clients have theistic systems of belief that differ in important ways from much of the profession, and that these need to be respected. He presents a number of hypotheses to investigate the impact of theistic values on therapeutic outcome. These articles and many others attest to the fact that values are inescapably central to the therapeutic process.

Bibliography. G. M. Abroms, "The Place of Values in Psychotherapy," *J. of Marriage and Family Counseling,* 4 (1978), 3–17. A. E. Bergin, "Psychotherapy and Religious Values," *J. of Consulting and Clinical Psychology,* 48 (1980), 95–105. L. E. Beutler, "Values, Beliefs, Religion and the Persuasive Influence of Psychotherapy," *Psychotherapy: Theory, Research and Practice,*

16 (1979), 432–40. P. Brickman, *Commitment, Conflict, and Caring* (1987). L. D. Goodstein, "The Place of Values in the World of Counseling," *The Counseling Psychologist,* 4 (1973), 63–66. B. S. Hagner, "Values in Psychotherapy: A Study of the Presence and Impact of Value Assumptions in the Counseling Process," (Doctoral dissertation, Northern Illinois University, 1980), *Dissertation Abstracts International.* R. J. Lovinger, *Working with Religious Issues in Therapy* (1984). C. M. Lowe, *Value Orientations in Counseling and Psychotherapy: The Meanings of Mental Health* 2d ed. (1976). E. M. Pattison, "Forward: Making Paths Through the Forest of Life," in R. H. Cox, ed., *Religious Systems and Psychotherapy* (1973). M. Stern, ed., *Psychotherapy and the Religiously Committed Patient* (1985). H. H. Strupp, "Humanism and Psychotherapy: A Personal Statement of the Therapist's Essential Values," *Psychotherapy: Theory, Research and Practice,* 17 (1980), 396–400. M. S. Van Leeuwen, "The View from the Lion's Den: Integrating Psychology and Christianity in the Secular University Classroom," *Christian Scholar's Review,* 5 (1976), 364–73. B. E. Wolfe, "Moral Transformations in Psychotherapy," *Counseling and Values,* 23 (1978), 43–48. G. H. Zuk, "Values in Family Therapy," *Psychotherapy: Theory, Research and Practice,* 15 (1978), 48–55.

B. S. HAGNER

ETHICS AND PASTORAL CARE; EVALUATION AND DIAGNOSIS; MORAL DEVELOPMENT; PSYCHOTHERAPY AND COUNSELING (Research Studies and Methods); RELIGION AND PSYCHOTHERAPY. *See also* AXIOTHERAPY; BLACK *or* FEMINIST ISSUES IN PSYCHOLOGY; CHRISTIAN PSYCHOTHERAPIST; FEMINIST THERAPY; FORMATIVE SPIRITUALITY; PASTORAL COUNSELING; PASTORAL PSYCHOTHERAPY. *Compare* ADVOCACY; CONSCIOUSNESS RAISING; ETHICS, PROFESSIONAL; JOURNALS IN RELIGION, THEOLOGY, AND THE SOCIAL SCIENCES, INTERDISCIPLINARY; LIFESTYLE ISSUES IN PASTORAL CARE; MORAL DILEMMAS IN PASTORAL PERSPECTIVE; MORALIZING; MORAL THEOLOGY AND PASTORAL CARE.

VALUES RESEARCH. The definition of values most commonly held is "an enduring belief that a specific mode of conduct or end-state of existence is personally and socially preferable to alternative modes of conduct or end-states of existence" (Rokeach, 1969, p. 160). Five dimensions of values have been identified: they can (1) have emotional significance; (2) express desire for future preferences; (3) be implicit or explicit; (4) mold the course of behavior; and (5) highlight importance of means and goals of action (Ehrlich and Weiner, 1961). Moreover, values are influencing agents and can be differentiated from other concepts such as goals, desires, normative statements, traits, and attitudes. While general in scope, values can be isolated and categorized (Allport, Vernon, and Lindzey, 1951; Kilmann, 1981). Values serve as backdrop, an overarching "should", for the above concepts and determine what desires, traits, or attitudes are meaningful.

Rokeach (1969) has defined two types of individual values, instrumental and terminal. *Instrumental* values are beliefs about preferred behavior which direct an individual *to reach* a desired state such as behaving in a "loving" manner. *Terminal* values are beliefs that direct an individual *to strive for* a desired state such as becoming "perfect" as a Christian. While all persons seem to possess terminal and instrumental values, the difference in values among persons is derived from how these values are patterned (Williams, 1979). Values can be patterned according to hierarchy, degree of devotion, degree of universality, and consistency.

Recent research has found that the concept of values is equally applicable to the larger social structure (Rokeach, 1979). Value specialization is the concentration on a particular set of values by an institution in order to limit its functions. As an institution determines its functions or goals, it will adopt values that support its goals, while simultaneously relinquishing values which run counter to its functions. Value-sharing is the identification of common values which exist among institutions of differing functions.

Psychology is concerned with how individual values influence behavior. Many people come for pastoral and psychological counseling because they struggle with questions related to meaning. Since values do influence attitudes, philosophy of life, preferences, and goals, it behooves clinical and pastoral practitioners to understand a client's value system and the varied meanings attached to behavior.

Contemporary psychology is also beginning to ask how the existing values of a therapist inform his or her clinical expertise and how this expertise in turn influences the values, and subsequently, the behavior of the client (Bergin, 1980).

Bibliography. A. E. Bergin, "Psychotherapy and Religious Values," *J. of Consulting and Clinical Psychology,* 48 (1980), 95–105. D. Ehrlich and D. N. Wiener, "The Measurement of Values in Psychotherapeutic Settings," *J. of General Psychology,* 64 (1961), 359–72. G. Allport, P. E. Vernon, and G. Lindzey, *A Study of Values* (1960). M. Rokeach, "From Individual to Institutional Values," in *Understanding Human Values* (1979), 47–70; *Beliefs, Attitudes, and Values* (1969). R. H. Kilmann, "Toward a Unique/ Useful Concept of Values For Interpersonal Behavior: A Critical Review of the Literature on Value," *Psychological Reports,* 48 (1981), 939–59. R. M. Williams, "Change and Stability in Values and Value Systems: A Sociological Perspective," in M. Rokeach, ed., *Understanding Human Values* (1979), 15–46.

H. C. STEVENSON

ETHICS AND PASTORAL CARE; MORAL BEHAVIOR AND RELIGION; MORAL DEVELOPMENT. *See also* MATERIALISM; SECULARIZATION/SECULARISM; WORLD VIEW. *Compare* CONSCIENCE.

VAN OOSTERZEE, JOHN JACOB (1817–82). Dutch Reformed applied (practical) theologian, author of a comprehensive, discerning, and insightful, two-volume *Practical Theology* (1878), which is marked by wisdom, a respect for psychiatry, ample attention to the private care of souls through pastoral visitation, and a wide acquaintance with the pastoral care literature of its time. It is concerned primarily with the gathering and ordering of rules and guidelines for the application of theological truths to the pastoral practice, in the fashion of practical theology understood as applied theology.

N. F. HAHN

PASTORAL THEOLOGY, PROTESTANT.

VAN KAAM, ADRIAN. *See* FORMATIVE SPIRITUALITY.

VATICAN COUNCIL II AND PASTORAL CARE. The Second Vatican Council contained significant shifts in the understanding of anthropology and of revelation and grace which had a profound influence on the practice of pastoral care in the Roman Catholic tradition, bringing about a broadened understanding of care, an expanded sense of mission, and a renewed sacramental practice.

1. Pastoral Care Prior to Vatican II. Prior to the Second Vatican Council, pastoral care in the Roman Catholic tradition focused almost exclusively on the priestly sacramental ministry, with the sacrament of penance and its concern for the moral life of individual Christians holding particular prominence. This era of pastoral care in the church was marked by an extrinsic approach to revelation and grace. A technical concept of sacrament, which equated the sacrament with the rite, prevailed. Strongly influenced by Cartesian dualism, the theology of the church issued in a pastoral care which was informed by sharp dichotomies between body and soul, nature and grace, church and world. Natural and supernatural revelation were seen as completely divorced from each other. Revelation was understood as a body of truths handed down in Scripture and tradition, and the category of experience was deliberately excluded from theological reflection.

2. Key Documents Affecting Pastoral Practice in the Church. While all the documents of the Second Vatican Council are addressed at some level to pastoral practice, two have had particular importance in effecting a change in the overall understanding and practice of pastoral care in the church. These are the pastoral constitution "On the Church in the Modern World" (*Gadium et Spes*) and the constitution "On Divine Revelation" (*Dei Verbum*). *Gadium et Spes,* the only major conciliar document to have originated from the council floor, is identified by the council as a "pastoral" constitution, a designation unprecedented in the history of the church. In addressing the relationship between church and world, the document manifests a striking openness to the intellectual climate of the twentieth century and to the new understandings of the human person made available through advances in the historical, social, and psychological sciences. In the opening paragraph of the document the council advances a vision of the integral relationship between church and world, a relationship which is rooted in continuity rather than dichotomy.

The constitution "On Divine Revelation" parallels in striking ways the movements present in the pastoral constitution "On the Church in the Modern World." Like *Gadium et Spes, Dei Verbum* moves away from the Cartesian dualism which informed so much of pre-Vatican II theology. It avoids the language of natural and supernatural, reclaiming instead the category of experience in revelation. In moving to a dynamic, experiential, and personalist language, the document speaks of revelation as personal disclosure rather than as truths disclosed. It presents divine revelation as a dynamic, historical process in which the church is constantly moving toward the fullness of divine truth.

These two documents articulated new understandings of theological anthropology and the theology of grace and revelation which have had a significant impact on the theory and the practice of pastoral care in the Roman Catholic tradition.

3. A Renewed Anthropology. The Second Vatican Council presented a renewed understanding of Christian anthropology, focusing on the historical, dynamic, relational, and unified character of the human person. The council moved away from the pessimistic view of human nature characteristic of preconciliar theology, emphasizing the theme of the human person as being in the image of God and linking this theme explicitly with the category of relation. Thus, the human person was understood as one who is called to establish and maintain right relations with self, nature, others, and God.

a. A historical view of the person. The anthropology underlying *Gadium et Spes* was rooted in a reclamation of the historical character of human existence which had been eclipsed by the dualism, ritualism, and jurisprudence of previous centuries. In reincorporating the historical dimension of human life into its understanding of the human person, the council affirmed the essential and intimate link between humankind and its history and emphasized the continuity between social and cultural transformation and the religious dimension of all life.

b. A dynamic view of the person. This reclamation of the historical dimension of the human person was accompanied by an emphasis on the subject character of human existence. A dynamic vision of the human person as relational and free was foundational to the vision of the human person which emerged from the council. The council documents moved away from the essentialist and static view of the human person which typified much of Western anthropology to a dynamic, evolutionary view of reality in general and of the human person in particular. The anthropology of Vatican II presents the human person as possessed of an inner dynamism and an active self-transcendence which includes the longing for and openness to Being as such, and to the possibility of revelation.

c. A unified view of the person. A final feature which undergirds the anthropology presented in the conciliar documents was a return to a biblical view of the human person as a unified whole. The Platonic and Cartesian dualism of body and soul, matter and spirit are set aside. Instead, a unified vision of the human person "whole and entire, body and soul, heart and conscience, mind and will" is presented (*Gadium et Spes, 3*).

4. A Renewed Theology of Revelation and Grace. The understanding of revelation and grace which was advanced by the Second Vatican Council represented a significant shift from the pre–Vatican II approach to these issues, a shift which was foundational to the entire theological framework of the council and which has had far-reaching consequences for pastoral practice in the church.

a. Understanding of nature and grace. The council, in writing *Gadium et Spes,* deliberately avoided the use of the terms *nature* and *supernature* and, thereby, shifted the whole framework of the discussion of revelation, abandoning the extrinsic approach to grace which had informed neoscholastic theology. The council affirmed a theology of revelation and grace rooted in a vision of the intrinsic relation between nature and grace, and posited a fundamental continuity between self-understanding, human experience, and grace, viewing grace as an experiential as well as an ontological reality.

b. A reclamation of experience. One of the most significant shifts which occurred in the theology of revelation articulated by the council was the recovery of experience as a central theological category. The reaction against modernism, which had involved a deliberate isolating of Catholic theology from historical, social, and cultural developments, was remedied in the constitution "On Divine Revelation" which restored experience to a proper place in the process of revelation. The council affirmed the sacramental principle that the spiritual is embodied and communicated through the material, pointing to the Incarnation as the archetypal instance of this principle and acknowledging this principle as the only basis for contact or encounter between God and the human community.

Thus, the council affirmed the principle that the place of revelation is in the concrete, lived experience of the historical and conditioned human subject, and that revelation can occur only in and through the ordinary categories of human experience. The understanding of revelation and grace presented by the council is one which affirms one's fulfillment in grace as also and necessarily one's fulfillment as a human person and which locates the place of revelation and grace within human history and struggle. Our development and growth as human persons in human communities is the place of the experience of grace and revelation in our lives.

5. A Renewed Pastoral Practice. The Christian anthropology and the theology of revelation and grace which were advanced by the Second Vatican Council have had important consequences for the practice of pastoral care within the church. Once the historical, dynamic, and unified character of the human person is acknowledged and the category of experience is reclaimed in theology, the church must expand its understanding of care, of sacrament, and of the interpretation of moral precepts. In moving from a view of revelation as a body of truths to revelation as an interpersonal communication which is dynamic, historical, and experiential, the council pointed to the necessity of attending to the concrete, sociohistorical factors of people's lives in community. The shifts which the Council effected have impacted pastoral care in two distinct but interrelated realms, the sacramental dimension of our ordinary lives, and the dynamic, human, care dimensions of our sacramental lives.

a. A broadened understanding of care. The understanding of anthropology and revelation advanced by the council call for a broadening of the understanding of care within the ministry of the church. If revelation occurs in and through the ordinary categories of human experience, and if one's fulfillment in grace is also and necessarily one's fulfillment as a person, then the care of the church must attend to the daily circumstances of our lives —the joys and sorrows, successes and failures, the deep and unquenchable yearnings, the moments of fulfillment and the dark and terrifying regions of human experience —in and through which God's presence among us is made known.

Concretely, this has meant that theology as a whole, and pastoral practice in particular, has had to engage in a serious dialogue with the social sciences which shed light on the historical, dynamic, and relational character of human existence. In taking seriously the affirmation that grace builds on nature, pastoral practice within the church has recognized the necessity of attending to that nature and the myriad ways in which it can be disabled. This has led to the retrieval of the psychological traditions with their insights into individual, interpersonal, and social dynamics and to the increasing involvement of both clergy and laity in the CPE movement, in ministry within the hospital setting, and in the ministry of pastoral counseling. The shift which the Second Vatican Council effected in the practice of pastoral care is readily evident in these last two instances. Hospital chaplaincy is no longer conceived of primarily as the administration of the sacraments but is rather understood as ministration to the whole person, which may or may not include sacramental ministry. Likewise, pastoral counseling is now understood as an important and dynamic ministry in its own right rather than as the giving of concrete advice—often in conjunction with the sacrament of penance—on how to fulfill objective moral precepts.

b. An expanded sense of mission. The council also brought about a deeper and more inclusive sense of mission for the whole Christian community. Both the dogmatic constitution on the church (*Lumen Gentium*) and the pastoral constitution on the church in the modern world (*Gadium et Spes*) speak of the church as "the People of God" and emphasize the "priesthood of all believers." In so doing they issue a call to all members of the church to an energetic involvement in the mission and ministry of the church. The effects of this call can be seen in the ever-increasing involvement of the laity in a broad range of pastoral care activities and in the increasing commitment of individuals, of groups, and of the church as a whole to the causes of social justice and of personal and social transformation. To be a Christian, in the vision of the council, is to be actively involved in the mission of the church, the building up of the world in truth, in justice, and in love.

c. The renewal of the sacramental tradition. The broadened understanding of pastoral care which emerged from the Second Vatican Council was paralleled by a renewal of the sacramental tradition of the church. The move to a dynamic understanding of revelation and the reclamation of the category of experience as central to revelation called for a sacramental theology and praxis which was attentive to the concrete social and historical circumstances of peoples' lives. Sacramental activity came to be understood as a dynamic activity which embraces not only the moment of the rite but the entire dynamic, developmental process leading up to and flowing from the rite. By incorporating insights from the human sciences concerning symbolic action, ritual behavior, and human dynamics, the revision of text and rite aimed at touching the community and the individuals who constitute it at the deepest levels of meaning and experience.

d. The task ahead. Since the Second Vatican Council significant progress has been made in renewing the pastoral care of the church. Care is now understood in a broad context which involves attending to the dynamic, historical, and social circumstances of peoples' everyday lives. The sacramental rites have been revised so as to touch us more readily at the deepest levels of meaning in our lives. The task which remains is to effectively integrate the various dimensions of care and sacrament, so that the church might practice a pastoral care which is fully and integrally shaped by the sacramental tradition.

Bibliography. W. Abbot and J. Gallagher, ed., *The Documents of Vatican II* (1966). D. Lane, *The Experience of God* (1981). R. McBrien, *Catholicism* (1981). G. McCool, ed., *A Rahner Reader* (1975). R. Vaillancourt, *Toward a Renewal of Sacramental Theology* (1979).

M. MCCARTHY

HISTORY OF ROMAN CATHOLIC PASTORAL CARE (Canada *or* United States); LITURGICAL CHANGE AND REFORM (Pastoral Issues); MINISTRY (Roman Catholic Tradition); PASTORAL THEOLOGY, ROMAN CATHOLIC; ROMAN CATHOLIC PASTORAL CARE. *See also* ANOINTING OF THE SICK, SACRAMENT OF; DIVORCE AND REMARRIAGE (Roman Catholicism); INCARNATIONAL THEOLOGY AND PASTORAL CARE (Roman Catholicism); PENANCE, SACRAMENT OF; SACRAMENTAL THEOLOGY AND PASTORAL CARE, ROMAN CATHOLIC. *Compare* ECCLESIOLOGY AND PASTORAL CARE; PERSON; REVELATION; THEOLOGY AND PSYCHOLOGY.

VATICAN COUNCIL II AND PASTORAL THEOLOGY. *See* PASTORAL THEOLOGY, ROMAN CATHOLIC.

VENERATION OF MARY AND SAINTS. *See* MARY, *or* SAINTS, VENERATION OF.

VENEREAL DISEASE. *See* GONNORHEA; HERPES; SYPHILIS.

VENIAL SIN. That sin whereby one's positive relationship with God in virtue of saving grace is impaired without being destroyed. In Roman Catholic tradition it is considered different in kind from mortal sin. One guilty of venial sin is not obliged to confession, although recourse to the sacrament is encouraged. In conceding that sinfulness coexists with justification, it is to venial sin that Catholics refer, regarding its prevalence as evidence of a moral weakness deriving from the Fall. The distinction between venial and mortal sin is easier in theory than in practice, and the casuistry devoted to it has lately been viewed with increasing skepticism.

J. GAFFNEY

MORAL THEOLOGY AND PASTORAL CARE; SIN/SINS. *Compare* MORTAL SIN.

VENTILATION OF FEELINGS. *See* CATHARSIS; FEELING, THOUGHT, AND ACTION IN PASTORAL COUNSELING; SELF-EXPRESSION/SELF-CONTROL.

VERBATIM. A document, written from memory, recording a conversation in approximately the dialogical form in which it occurred. Typically a verbatim also includes: (1) description of the setting, the persons involved, and the expectations for the conversation; (2) the dialogue; (3) reflection on the relationship. Current usage identifies a product, "the verbatim," but early usage recognized a process synonomous with Cabot and Dicks's "note-writing": "verbatim recording of visits" or "recording of direct discourse as it took place during the call" (Guiles).

Akin to the data employed in clinical-pathological conferences in medicine, verbatims are the characteristic learning instruments of clinical pastoral education and of much contemporary pastoral theology (theological reflection on pastoral acts — Hiltner, 1958) and pastoral psychology. Throughout the world, nascent pastoral care movements have employed collections of verbatims to display and interpret the new pastoral care.

Russell Dicks initiated modern verbatim-writing, making notes on his pastoral calls and recording his prayers. According to A. P. Guiles, Dicks introduced it into pastoral education, its current *Sitz im Leben*, to solve a problem: "The student's description of his calls failed to preserve the overtones and undertones, the veiled emotion or intentions of the patient, a sort of double-talk, which was fully as significant as the patient's outright pronouncements." (Guiles, p. 47) By 1945 "note-writing" had become part of the standards of clinical pastoral training (p. 57).

Audio and video recording provide closer access to the nuances of live caregiving and to the complexities of systems, yet verbatims remain ideal for brief or public encounters or for situations that discourage technological recording. Although verbatims bring the frustrations of incompleteness and inaccuracy, they teach students that they can learn from what they imperfectly remember. In fact, one pillar of contemporary pastoral care is the study of incomplete and partially distorted memories of pastoral caregiving.

Verbatims disclose not only the pastoral partner, but also the pastor. In verbatims, students reveal their problems in caregiving. Verbatims produce anxiety, particularly about self-exposure; hence the eye of a censor, not altogether unconscious, guides discourse-recording. Nevertheless, verbatims are like expressionistic paintings, which reveal how painters have experienced themselves and their world (Zijlstra, 1971, p. 40). In verbatim-writing Cabot and Dicks identify some of the moral rigor and low-keyed spirituality of modern pastoral care, calling verbatim-writing self-criticism, self-revelation, preparation for self-improvement, meditation made effective, and sometimes prayer — noting that writing entails "new acts of forgiveness, of one-hundred-percent veracity with ourselves."

Bibliography. R. Burck, "Pastoral Expressionism: Verbatims in the Pastoral Paradigm," *J. of Supervision and Training in Ministry*, 3 (1980), 39–56. R. C. Cabot and R. L. Dicks, *The Art of Ministering to the Sick* (1936) pp. 24–61. A. P. Guiles, in S. Hiltner, ed., *Clinical Pastoral Training* (1945) pp. 47–57. S. Hiltner, *Preface to Pastoral Theology* (1958). W. Zijlstra, *Seelsorge-Training — Clinical Pastoral Training* (1971).

J. R. BURCK

CASE STUDY METHOD; CLINICAL PASTORAL EDUCATION. *Compare* RECORD KEEPING.

VERDERY, E. A. *See* BAPTIST PASTORAL CARE.

VETERANS. *See* MILITARY SERVICE AND MILITARY CHAPLAINCY; POST-TRAUMATIC STRESS DISORDER.

VIANNEY, ST. JEAN MARIE BAPTISTE (1786–1859). French Roman Catholic parish priest and spiritual director. Considered the great charismatic of pastoral care in nineteenth century Catholicism, Vianney lived a highly ascetic, unconventional lifestyle, intense at prayer and penance. His pastoral ministry reflected the contemporary understanding of spiritual direction, i.e., confession, correction, and guidance, on both a communal and individual level.

Vianney functioned as a sort of public spiritual director to the village of Ars, whose lax religious life he transformed through heavy family visitation and strong preaching about morality. In private spiritual direction, what appeared to be an ability to "read hearts" gained him greatest fame as a confessor. He executed both functions with such great success that in 1929 he was declared the patron saint of all pastors and priests.

N. F. HAHN

SPIRITUAL DIRECTION, HISTORY AND TRADITIONS OF.

VICE/VICES. *See* CHARACTER ETHICS; MORAL THEOLOGY; SEVEN DEADLY SINS.

VICTIMIZATION. The process whereby an individual or group of individuals (especially one identified by a distinctive characteristic, such as race, sex, socioeconomic background) is unjustly harmed or has their rights violated. Historically, a victim was a person or animal used as a sacrifice in a religious ritual. Currently, however, the term often connotes criminal or immoral behavior. A victim is one who is put to death or tortured; subject to oppression, deprivation or suffering; tricked or duped; or otherwise subjected to hardship or manipulation.

1. **Victimology.** The term *victimology* was coined in 1947 by B. Mendelsohn, and the first major study was carried out by Hans von Hentig. Victimology has steadily grown as a distinct field of study within criminology. In 1973 the First International Symposium on Victimology was held in Jerusalem and resulted in the issuing of five volumes of papers under the title *Victimology: A New Focus*. Since 1976 the international journal *Victimology* has been published. The field is still in its infancy with many scholars recognizing the importance of the victim-criminal relationship, but considerable debate exists regarding the precise boundaries of the field. The British penal reformer, Margery Fry, is responsible for initiating much of the popular interest in the plight of victims and their demand for just compensation.

2. **Victimization.** *a. Cultural factors.* Who is considered a victim is historically and culturally relative. Entire classes of people may emerge as victims with a change in social outlook. In one setting, wife or child beating may be acceptable. Blacks may be denegrated slaves in one era and pitied victims in another. Victimization is a social process and the definition of who is a victim changes as societal values change.

b. Types of victims. There are many types of victims, not all of whom are objects of criminal intention. First, there are victims of disease and natural disasters (e.g., cancer, floods, hurricanes, fires). Second, there are accident victims (e.g., auto, hiking, industrial). Third, some victimization is self-inflicted (e.g., substance abuse, suicide). Fourth, there are victims of institutional and cultural patterns (e.g., women, racial minorities). Fifth, there are victims of group and intergroup conflict (e.g., wars, gang violence). Sixth, there are victims of personal assault (rape, murder, child abuse).

c. Characteristics of victims. Powerlessness is one characteristic of almost all victims. One is a victim when one is unable to control one's circumstances. The route to overcoming victimization is empowerment, whether this be physical, psychological, or spiritual. The process of victimization involves the stripping of power from persons. Victimization may involve stereotyping or narrowly or inappropriately defining roles. Although victimization is socially defined, there is always a social interaction between subject and object or victim and environment. Passivity enhances and prolongs victimhood. Changes in victim status occur when power is seized and applied against the oppressive force.

3. **Victim Compensation.** *a. Historical context.* Much of the literature dealing with victimization is directed toward the issue of victim compensation. In more ancient and primitive civilizations, if one was wrong it was the responsibility of the victim (or his or her family) to seek recompense. The response might be revenge or it might be direct restitution. The ancient law of "an eye for an eye" was a way of recognizing the direct relationship between a victim and the offender. With the process of modernization, the state has increasingly interceded between victim and offenders so that now the victim may have very little actual contact with the offender. On one hand, this is a very positive occurrence in that it may prevent family feuds and personal vendettas. But it also means that the victim has almost been lost sight of in the attention given to prosecuting the offender. Also, whereas financial recompense formerly might pass directly to the victim, now the fine, if there is one, usually goes directly to the state, and the state becomes the beneficiary rather than the victim who experienced the loss.

b. Legislation. The first legislation for compensation of victims occurred in New Zealand with the establishment of a compensation tribunal in 1963. Similar legislation followed in England in 1964 and then in the U.S. in California in 1965, in New York in 1966, Hawaii in 1967, and so on. Although states and countries differ, often there is compensation to a victim (above a specific minimum, such as $100) for medical expenses (not covered by insurance) incurred as a result of an assault, earnings lost while an individual is recuperating from a criminally inflicted injury, and funeral and burial expenses. Compensation has been directed specifically to victims of criminal assault and not to other types of victims.

c. Opposition. Victim compensation is a highly debated issue and very likely legislation has passed more as a way of allaying potential victim anxiety than in response to the philosophical merits of victim compensation. The common objections to victim compensation are that it is simply another means of redistributing public tax money. Critics ask why victims of crimes should be compensated while victims of fires or floods are not.

Other critics argue that money for victim compensation would be better spent on prevention of crime.

d. Proponents. Proponents of victim compensation often state that the issue is one of fairness and equity: is it fair for the state to spend money to rehabilitate the criminal while doing nothing to assist the victim? Proponents argue that victim compensation programs help rehabilitate the victim so that he or she may once again become an active and functional member of society. Perhaps a more basic argument supporting victim compensation, however, is that it is the task of the state to protect its citizens. When it fails to do so, the state owes its citizens recompense. A variation of this argument is that compensation assists in making victims feel less alienated from society, and therefore victim compensation programs contribute to a more harmonious and integrated society. Victim compensation programs become particularly important when the public feels that crime is reaching epidemic proportions.

e. Financing. There are a variety of ways in which victim compensation programs may be financed. It is possible to allocate a portion of the offender's fine to the victim. The earnings resulting from paid labor while in prison could go to the victim. The offender could be required to pay a portion of his or her noninstitutionalized earnings to the victim. Alternatively, the state could compensate the victim. Finally, the suggestion has been made that there could be a form of either public or private insurance that would compensate victims of criminal offenses.

f. Reparation. Victim compensation programs certainly extend beyond payment made in connection with individual offenses. The notion of reparations paid by governments to victim populations, especially as a result of genocide or unjust relocations, has been demonstrated in the case of the German government's payment of reparations to Jews; the issue is a matter of current legal debate in connection with the U.S. government's relocation of the Japanese during World War II. Reparations are also being sought by Armenians deported from Turkey during the First World War.

4. **Conclusion.** Victimization is a very complex process and much research is still needed in the emerging field of victimology. For example, much attention by victimologists is being directed toward understanding the victim's role in being victimized. Victims are often blamed for being the source of their own injustice (especially in the case of rape). It has also been noted that victimizers have themselves often been victims (e.g., in the case of child abusers).

Sensitive pastoral care and counseling of victims usually requires a suspension of the pastor's assumptions about the victim's possible role in the victimization. Victims may experience a wide range of emotions, including grief, guilt, and anxiety, and need to fully explore and express these emotions in a trusted relationship. Further, victims may need guidance toward resources to relieve immediate needs, such as shelter or financial assistance. The longer term goal of care is to facilitate the necessary social, political, spiritual, or psychological empowerment needed to help prevent future victimization.

Bibliography. I. Drapkin and E. Viano, eds., *Victimology: A New Focus*, 5 vols. (1974). S. Katz and M. A. Mazur, *Understanding the Rape Victim* (1979). W. Parsonage, ed., *Perspectives on Victimology* (1979). R. Reiff, *The Invisible Victim* (1979). S. Salasin, *Evaluating Victim Services* (1981). J. Scherer and G. Shepherd, *Victimization of the Weak* (1982). E. Viano, ed., *Victims and Society* (1976). H. Von Hentig, *The Criminal and His Victims* (1948).

D. E. MILLER

ADVOCACY; CRISIS MINISTRY; DISASTER, PUBLIC; HOLOCAUST; POST-TRAUMATIC STRESS DISORDER; SURVIVOR PSYCHOLOGY; TRAUMA; VIOLENCE. *Compare* ANTISOCIAL PERSONS; DEPROGRAMMING; EXPLOITATION/OPPRESSION; INDOCTRINATION.

VICTIMS ANONYMOUS. *See* INCEST; SUPPORT GROUPS; VICTIMIZATION.

VIETNAM VETERANS. *See* POST-TRAUMATIC STRESS DISORDER. *See also* HOLIDAY DEPRESSION; MILITARY SERVICE AND MILITARY CHAPLAINCY.

VIGIL LIGHT. *See* LITURGICAL AND DEVOTIONAL LIFE, ROMAN CATHOLIC.

VINCENT DE PAUL, ST. (ca. 1581–1660). Religious founder and worker of charity. Vincent was ordained a Catholic priest at the early age of nineteen. After service as a court chaplain and parish priest, he founded the Congregation of the Mission (1625), a society of priests who forswore church preferment to work in priest-poor villages and parishes. Known more commonly today as the Vincentians, they soon became involved both in foreign missionary work and in education, especially education of the clergy. In 1633 the congregation received the church of Saint Lazare in Paris (hence their other name, the Lazarists), which was to headquarter their work.

In his priestly life Vincent's works of charity were so legendary that "Monsigneur Vincent" became a national hero in France. Vincent organized an auxiliary of wealthy Parisian women to aid his work in the hospitals, galleys of convicts, prisons, slums, and hostels of France. He sent chaplains with armies who were at war and organized relief services during wars and other disasters.

With Louise de Marillac, he founded the Sisters of Charity, the first order of women religious who were not bound to the cloister. Their charitable work was to become an important part of French Catholic life and later was to extend throughout the world. In 1830, inspired by Vincent's life, Frederick Ozanam, a Parisian university professor, and some friends founded the St. Vincent de Paul Society—a lay group organized to work with the poor—which still flourishes in the Catholic church. Vincent de Paul was canonized a saint in 1737 by Pope Clement XII.

Bibliography. P. Coste, *The Life and Works of St. Vincent de Paul* 3 vols. (1952). J. Leonard, ed., *Letters of St. Vincent de Paul* (1937).

L. S. CUNNINGHAM

SPIRITUALITY (Roman Catholic Tradition); PASTOR (Normative and Traditional Images).

VINDICTIVENESS. *See* ANTISOCIAL PERSONS.

VINET, ALEXANDER (1797–1847). From 1839 on, professor of practical theology at Lausanne and Basel after teaching French literature and serving as a minister in Basel. Vinet was a Swiss liberal Protestant apologist, a man of high talent, great sensitivity, deep spirituality, and genuine interest in promoting the cure of souls. His pastoral significance rests on two pillars: (1) his personal openness and availability to ordinary people and their hurts as well as to troubled peers, and (2) his sketchy formulation of a theology of experience.

Widely used in its time and read even into the 20th century, Vinet's manual for the personal cure of souls, *Pastoral Theology* (1853), treats the *cura animarum* in the theoretical context of pastoral theology, but in a most sagacious manner. He strives for a balance between the rights of individuals and the task of clerics and the demands of the gospel and a balance between, for example, passivity and aggressiveness, overbearing and withholding —always depending on the circumstances.

N. F. HAHN

PASTORAL THEOLOGY, PROTESTANT.

VIOLENCE. Involves the use of force against persons or objects. While often being physical in nature, the term may also refer to verbal abuse. Physical violence ranges on a continuum from superficial injury to death, while verbal violence involves violation of character or dignity. Analyses of violence generally are of two types: *personal violence*, as in the case of rape, homicide, child abuse, and wife battering, and *collective violence*, as in the case of strikes, riots, rebellions, revolutions, terrorist activities, and wars. The focus in the following sections will be primarily on sociological interpretations of violence.

1. **Social Context of Violence.** Violence is most pronounced in social contexts where cultural norms are in question and the political structure is undergoing rapid change. Violence, in such contexts, is an expression of protest, often by groups within a society whose members feel inadequately represented in the political process and who feel discriminated against economically. Violence predictably increases in periods of social stress or transition and declines in periods of social stability. For example, Hovland and Sears have shown that lynchings increased during economic depressions and declined in periods of prosperity. Viewed individualistically or psychologically, violence may appear to occur for personal gain, but viewed sociologically, violence (particularly an increase in the level of violence) coincides with the breakdown of societal norms and changes in subgroup expectations. Alienation and anomie are consistent correlates of increases in collective violence.

2. **Theories of the Cause of Violence. a. *Relative Deprivation.*** The relative deprivation theory is perhaps the most widely held view regarding the source of violence (see Gurr). According to this theory, collective violence is the result of the perceived discrepancy between one's value expectations and the social and polit-

ical restraints within which one lives (value capabilities). Violence is a product of discontent or frustration with what one feels are unjust and inequitable circumstances. Such deprivation is relative insofar as it is one's perception of the situation that determines how discontent one is. Deprivation is often experienced when one social group makes economic gains while another group appears to stagnate. Advertising often plays a considerable role in indiscriminately raising the expectations of all social groups while, in fact, only selected populations may have the economic ability to purchase given goods and services. According to the relative deprivation hypothesis, violence is an expression of frustration as a result of holding unachievable expectations. If people did not feel deprived, they would not be discontent.

b. Biological. A second interpretation explains violence in terms of instinctual reactions. Just as animals are known to defend territorial space aggressively — sometimes sacrificing their lives for their young — likewise it has been postulated that threats to personal territory (including home or nation) arouse in individuals an aggressively defensive violent reaction. Furthermore, numerous studies have been done with animals demonstrating that conditions of overcrowding generate violence, the parallel being extended to slum dwellings and impacted urban environments.

c. Self-interest. A third view, rooted more in theological and philosophical premises (see Hobbes and Niebuhr), as opposed to biological theories, states that humankind is inherently evil and self-interested. Except for the existence of coercive institutions such as the state, men and women would plunder, rob, and violate each other indiscriminately. Hence, a stable social order emerges out of protective self-interest, not humankind's good nature. In Christian theology, violence is a product of the Fall of humankind, but the human proclivity toward evil is a widely held perception. Freud, for example, believed that the masses would destroy each other except for their fear of divine retribution or civil restraint.

d. Learned response. A fourth view on the roots of violence is based on social learning theory (see Bandura and Walters). Individuals observe that strategically enacted violence enables them to achieve specific goals. Thus, violence is "rationally" enacted as one pursues particular ends. Violence is not an irrational or instinctual response in that the individual may be very calculating about rewards and punishments before performing a violent act. In short, violence is viewed as a means to a specific end.

e. Frustration reduction. Realizing that none of the above theories is mutually exclusive, but indeed may be complementary, it has been suggested that aggressive behavior may reduce one's level of frustration or anger (see Berkowitz). If one attacks what one perceives to be the source of one's problems — or some symbolic representative of it—then one may experience a reduction in the level of one's hostility even if one's attack does not make a substantial change in the circumstances causing the frustration. On occasion, the object of attack may actually serve as a scapegoat for frustrations that stem from an entirely unrelated source.

3. Cultural Conditioning. Violence always occurs within a given cultural context of values and norms.

Beliefs of a religious or secular nature play an enormous role in determining whether violence is justified, in what circumstances, and for what ends. Violence may be absolutely proscribed in all circumstances, as many sectarians for example, have held, or its use may be carefully stipulated as belonging to the police or military. These are culturally conditioned values and vary from culture to culture and subculture to subculture.

Values are tied to socially constructed belief systems (see Berger and Luckmann), often rooted in elaborate cosmological and historical myths. Violence is legitimated and inspired according to mythically based views of superiority and subordination, traditionally having impacted women and racial minorities in particular. Culturally based norms may also encourage violence against one's own person, as in the case of altruistic suicide. Also, it is certainly in the service of culturally defined values that wars are waged and ideals are defended. Violence is respected and even rewarded if it either is performed by a legitimate authority or if it is justifiable according to publically approved goals.

4. Violence and Social Change. Historically, violence has often accompanied social change. Revolutions mark the history of every nation, as do revolts, strikes, riots, etc. As expectations are raised through increased literacy, introduction of modernizing ideologies (missionaries being a not infrequent source), programs of reform (especially those which are announced but not enacted), and the inclusion of new elements within the political process, violence is often the instrument which forces those protecting tradition and personal self-interest to change.

Riots, terrorism, and other collective acts of violence are communicative expressions whose intent need not be interpreted as wanton destruction, but instead as statements of subgroup plight of redress of grievances. Violence is seldom the first attempt to articulate a concern; rather, it is more often born of desperation, a feeling that all other avenues of communication have failed.

5. Apologists for Nonviolence. Those championing nonviolence argue that humanity is not inherently evil: a better world can only be realized through nonviolent means regardless of how expedient violence might appear in realizing short-term goals. Proponents of nonviolence may also rest their case on moral rules or principals which proscribe violence regardless of any consideration of the ends to be realized. Nonviolence may be advocated as an effective political strategy in particular circumstances without the proponent eschewing violence in all situations.

Reinhold Niebuhr (1932) argued that coercion is used in both violent and nonviolent political practices. Niebuhr states, "The chief difference between violence and nonviolence is not in the degree of destruction which they cause, though the difference is usually considerable, but in the aggressive character of the one and the negative character of the other" (p. 240). For example, a boycott is a nonviolent tactic, but it may cause unemployment and even loss of life.

6. Selected Commentators. *a. Karl Marx.* Marx should not be viewed as an advocate of violence. He was aware of the historical linkage between violence and revolution, but violence plays an effective role in societal change only if the political contradictions within the society have established the appropriate preconditions for change. In short, violence does not cause revolutionary change, but it may be one of the birth pangs of societal transformation.

b. Max Weber. In his famous address, "Politics as a Vocation," Weber says that "the state is a relation of men dominating men, a relation supported by means of legitimate (i.e. considered to be legitimate) violence" (p. 78). Elsewhere in the address, Weber states that violence is the decisive means for politics, and the politician cannot responsibly shy away from the use of force. Domination, he says, has historically stemmed from three justifications: tradition, personal charisma, and law. Weber does not indiscriminately approve of violence, he rather believes the person with a "calling for politics" must realize the nature of the state.

c. Georges Sorel. In *Reflections on Violence* Sorel reveals himself to be an apocalyptic utopian in which strategically employed violence by the proletarian class will result in a radical socialism. On the last page Sorel states "It is to violence that Socialism owes those high ethical values by means of which it brings salvation to the modern world" (p. 249). Sorel has been an often quoted proponent by revolutionaries for the use of violence. Sorel was himself, however, more a theoretician and supported violence, chiefly in the form of the strike, only as it might contribute to the attainment of a utopian socialism.

d. José Ortega y Gasset. In *The Revolt of the Masses,* Ortega y Gasset states that violence is "the Magna Carta of barbarism" (p. 74). Violence used to be the means of final resort after one had exhausted all other means in the defense of justice. However, now that "the masses" are engaging in direct political action, states Ortega y Gasset, violence appears to be more readily practiced than reason and rational debate.

e. Hannah Arendt. Arendt is one of the most provocative recent commentators in that her slim volume *On Violence* surveys a number of theorists discussing violence and also critiques the emergence during the 1960s of violent protest as a dominant political form. She agrees with Sorel and Pareto that the bureaucratization of public life leads to an increase in violence. In her words, "In a fully developed bureaucracy there is nobody left with whom one can argue, to whom one can present grievances, on whom the pressures of power can be exerted" (p. 8). But while it is understandable why violence has increased, and even that violence may in the short term be a means for individuals to dramatize injustice, she rejects the use of violence. Violence begets violence; it should not be used as a means to end violence. Arendt rejects many of the modern apologies for violence, especially those based on biological models and those views linking violence and creativity.

7. **Violence and Liberation Theology.** Liberation theologians have broadened the definition of violence so as to include the violence implicit in institutional and political forms such as colonialism and sexually defined role expectations. From this perspective, violence is an act or set of rules which denies one's humanity and freedom to express oneself creatively. Violence need not assume an overt active expression, as in physical violence.

It may be implicit in various forms of oppression supported by stable governments and established customs.

Ruben Alves relates violence specifically to one's view of the future and attitude toward change. He states that there are two completely different understandings of violence. First, for the person who is afraid of the future and new definitions of reality, "violence is everything that disturbs or threatens the world . . . fear has built. Everything that tends to usher in the new, that moves toward change, everything that opposes the structures that claim to be destined for eternity is violence" (p. 111). But for the person who is free to meet the future, violence has a totally different meaning. "It is whatever denies him a future, whatever aborts his project to create a new tomorrow; it is the power that keeps him prisoner of the futureless structures of a futureless world" (p. 111–12). Violence, for Alves, is that which denies people the possibility of exercising their freedom.

8. **Conclusion.** To summarize, violence has a number of different connotations, but it would surely be wrong to conclude that violence is universely condemned. Quite the contrary, violence is seen as a by-product of a society in transition, where value definitions are changing and expectations are in flux. Descriptively, violence has often times accompanied constructive changes in government or culture. While few commentators would deny either the linkage between violence and social change, or that violence should never be an end in itself, the question seems much more open to debate as to whether violence is a justifiable means to an end. It is at this point that religious tradition and argumentation play an important role.

Bibliography. R. Alves, *A Theology of Human Hope* (1969). H. Arendt, *On Violence* (1970). A. Bandura and R. Walters, *Social Learning and Personality Development* (1963). P. Berger and T. Luckmann, *The Social Construction of Reality* (1966). L. Berkowitz. "The Concept of Aggressive Drive," in L. Berkowitz, ed., *Advances in Experimental Social Psychology,* vol. 2 (1964). T. Gurr, *Why Men Rebel* (1970). M. F. Hirsch, *Women and Violence* (1981). T. Hobbes, *Leviathan* (1947). C. Hovland and R. Sears, "Minor Studies in Aggression," *J. of Psychology,* 9, 301–10. P. Marsh and A. Campbell, eds., *Aggression and Violence* (1982). R. Niebuhr, *Moral Man and Immoral Society* (1960 [1932]); *The Nature and Destiny of Man* (1964 [1941]). J. Ortega y Gasset, *The Revolt of the Masses* (1932). J. Short, Jr., and M. Wolfgang, eds., *Collective Violence* (1972). G. Sorel, *Reflections on Violence* (1950). M. Weber, "Politics as a Vocation," in H. Gerth and C. Mills, eds., *From Max Weber* (1946), 77–128.

D. EARL MILLER

AGGRESSION AND ASSERTION; ANGER; ANTISOCIAL PERSONS; DEVIANT BEHAVIOR; FAMILY VIOLENCE. *See also* HOLOCAUST; JUVENILE CRIME AND DELINQUENCY. *Compare* CONFLICT AND CONFLICT MANAGEMENT; PEACE-MAKING AND PASTORAL CARE; VICTIMIZATION.

VIP, PASTORAL CARE OF. VIPs (very important persons) are persons who because of achievement, status, or position are prominent in the community. Pastoral care of the VIP personality may be looked at developmentally from the perspective of the individual needing the care, or from the concern of the provider. This article, however, is based on the needs of the VIP common to all people, needs created by the nature of the VIP circumstance, and the underlying dynamic of the care required by a VIP.

The VIP shares needs common to all persons. For the VIP, however, the stance of prominence will magnify the need. Anxiety reaction, for example, may be more observed in the VIP because there are more and strange places from which unrecognized threats may emerge. Other needs that come to all people, but are heightened by the VIP position in society, include stress, the experience of "passages," and depersonalization by society.

Studies in stress indicate the intensity of types of stress caused by such experiences as job changes, death in a family, and moving. Whereas the non-VIP may have these stress producing categories stretched out over a period of time, the VIP finds the major ones often repeated. The types of problems with which the VIP must deal are constantly changing. The VIP may have to travel considerably. The expectations "dumped" on the VIP constantly increase. As stress increases in society generally — as in a war or economic crisis — the expectations of the VIP to solve those problems increase.

The VIP not only moves through life stages, but also moves through them publically. He or she also has developmental experiences that are generic to that public stance. The "Big Man" or "Big Woman" on campus carries with it expectations or promise of future status. Nomination to high office does the same. Retirement, defeat in an election, loss of a competition carry a unique experience of grief. In every arena of VIP experience, there can thus be identified certain stages that are superimposed on the traditional stages of growth that carry trauma.

Therefore, VIPs both share the usual need for pastoral care with those in the rest of society and have their own special needs for integration and separation. For those "on the way up," these needs usually center on integration of new experience or what David Riesman calls the problem of consumption. Yet the problem of separation from past circumstances is still there. For those "on the way down," those needs usually center on problems of separation, but the necessity for reintegration is not lost. The very nature of the stress and anxiety increases the need for that care of soul which allows one to deal with the experiences that press in daily, to maintain a sense of confidence and worth, and to let go when the VIP status is changed.

Specialized needs of the VIP which may be identified include the problem of identity ("Who am I?"—the public image or expectation of someone else), the target of rejections (including projections by the pastor), the "loneliness at the top" experience, and the need for freedom to handle both success and failure.

Basic elements of pastoral care of VIPs include helping the individual to be in touch with some sense of the cosmic and of the deeply personal. Awareness that one is part of something bigger frees the person to be a person and cope with the pressures. Prayer and spiritual discipline help as therapeutic tools. A sense of call, a sense that one's work is a ministry, and a sense that one is part of a purpose that began before and will continue after oneself, all fit into this cosmic dimension.

Opportunity to experience the deeply personal—what might be called "the cosmic within"—is also critical. Those aspects of pastoral care that allow one to be aware of self, of the nearness of God ("the kingdom of heaven within"), and the love of Christ are important. It is often a temptation to make requests of a VIP rather than to meet him or her as a person. Instead, pastoral care of VIPs means offering a supporting, healing, sustaining presence.

Bibliography. H. Selye, *The Stress of Life*, 2d ed. (1978).

J. G. EMERSON

LIFESTYLE ISSUES; SOCIAL STATUS AND CLASS FACTORS IN PASTORAL CARE; RICH PERSONS. *See also* ANTISOCIAL PERSONS; POWER; SOCIAL CONSCIOUSNESS AND RESPONSIBILITY.

VIRGIN MARY. *See* MARY, VENERATION OF.

VIRTUE, CONCEPT OF. (1) Expressing or pertaining to the excellence of a thing, idea, or social practice; (2) a set of historically defined skills and dispositions whose embodiment helps shape a particular character in individuals and societies.

The classical treatment of the concept of virtue saw virtues as skills of the good life, which vices represented failures in the good life or the pursuit of lesser or inappropriate goods. Virtue relates degrees of excellence within a particular thing, and that excellence itself is judged in relation to a wider constellation of goods often understood to be in a hierarchical relationship. It was a matter of much debate whether there were primary virtues such as justice or love which expressed true human nature and whose excellence ordered all others. In modern times attention has focused on virtues as goods in themselves or on virtue as a thing to be possessed. In either case the larger moral context seemed lost in the generally uncritical acceptance of abstractly (or conventionally) defined virtues. Partly in reaction to this distortion, mid-twentieth-century moral theory contrasted virtue with obligation, seldom favorably, and often with the understanding that true morality lay in obligations defined apart from human nature or history, while the concept of virtue was at best useful for motivating a proper response to duty.

Contemporary thought continues the suspicion of virtue as the central feature of moral theory, but has been increasingly concerned to recover its historical and relational qualities and to focus on its role in forming character in ways obligation language fails to do. This discussion is less willing than its predecessors to stake claims about "the" virtue of human nature, and is more critically aware of the social location and history of virtues. Virtues represent practical skills of the good life, as well as dispositions that help to shape the character of those who practice them. They are thus always relational terms dependent on the normative vision of the good they seek to embody. This in turn makes the acquisition of virtues something disciplined by the historical narratives in which they are depicted and by contact with the lives of others in which they are embodied. Attention to the often conflicting virtues offered by different stories and communities can help establish the moral context and possibilities of transformation in both theological ethics and pastoral care.

Bibliography. S. Hauerwas, *A Community of Character* (1981), esp. pp. 111–52, relation of virtue to virtues, connection with character of individual and community. A. MacIntyre, *After Virtue* (1981), historical treatment of shift in use of language of virtue. T. Oden, *Care of Souls in the Classic Tradition* (1984), is a good example of using virtue language in reclaiming traditions of pastoral care. E. Erikson, "A Schedule of Virtues," in *Insight and Responsibility* (1964), is an insightful and influential interpretation of virtue from an ego-psychoanalytic perspective.

RICHARD BONDI

CHARACTER ETHICS AND PASTORAL CARE; ETHICS AND PASTORAL CARE. *See also* WISDOM AND PRACTICAL KNOWLEDGE.

VIRTUES AND VICES. *See* CHARACTER ETHICS; MORAL THEOLOGY.

VISIONS AND VOICES. The Bible portrays visions and voices as legitimate means of divine revelation to the people of God. Visions were revelations of sight which made known the mysteries of God. Often they intersected with reality in such a way as to fill it with religious significance. Amos's vision of the plumb line, for instance, indicated that Israel had been judged (Amos 7:7). Usually it was the OT seer (*hōzêh*) or prophet who received visions, hence the most common Hebrew term for vision was the derivative *hāzôn*. Examples are found throughout Israel's prophets (e.g., I Sam. 3:1; Isa. 1:1; Hab. 2:2–3) and wisdom literature (Ps. 89:19; Prov. 29:18; Job 33:15–18).

Voices figured prominently in Jeremiah "to whom the word of the Lord came" (Jer. 1:2, 11, 13; 2:1; etc.). The rabbinic term *bath qôl* signified the divine voice unaccompanied by visible manifestations. It was applied to such occurrences as the voice from heaven relieving Nebuchadnezzar of his kingdom (Dan. 4:31).

Visions and voices were linked when the vision disclosed the word of Yahweh. Thus, Isaiah *saw* a vision and proclaimed what Yahweh had *spoken* (Isa. 1:1–2). So, too, Obadiah's vision was announced under the prophetic messenger formula, "Thus says the Lord" (Obad. 1:1; cf. Nah. 1:1; Hab. 1:1).

The record concerning visions and voices in the NT runs parallel to that in the OT. The most frequently used Greek terms for *vision* are *horama* (Acts 9:10–12; 10:3; etc.) and *horasis* (Acts 2:17; Rev. 9:17), derivatives of the verb *horaō*, "to see, behold". Occasionally, the noun *optasia* describes the visionary experience (Lk. 1:22, 24:23, II Cor. 12:1).

Visions in the NT appear most frequently in Luke's writings. They brought good news to Zechariah (Lk. 1:19–22) and the women at Jesus' tomb (Lk. 24:23), as well as comfort to Paul (Acts 18:9). They also provided instruction and guidance to such persons as Ananias (Acts 9:10), Cornelius (Acts 10:3), Peter (Acts 10:9–20), and Paul (Acts 16:9).

The *bath qôl* appears as a voice (*phōnē*) from the heavens at critical times in Jesus' ministry. It comes first at his baptism (Mt. 3:17; Mk. 1:11; Lk. 3:22), again at the transfiguration (Mt. 17:5; Mk. 9:7; Lk. 9:35), and

finally in response to Jesus' prayer prior to the Last Supper (Jn. 12:28). Similarly, Paul met the voice of the risen Jesus on the Damascus Road (Acts 9:4–6).

Voice and vision appear together in the Apocalypse. While in the Spirit on the Lord's day, John the Revelator heard "a loud voice like a trumpet" instructing him to write to the seven churches (Rev. 1:10–11). John "turned *to see the voice* that was speaking." What he saw was the vision of the seven golden lampstands in the midst of which stood "one like a son of man" (Rev. 1:12–16).

Visions and voices are frequently cited in places where the Holy Spirit is thought to be active and worship is enthusiastic. Among the Montanists (Tertullian, *Treatise on the Soul* 9; *Veiling of Virgins* 17), in the acts of martyrs (cf. *Passion of Perpetua* 4, 7–8, 10, 11) and even among certain Gnostics (Irenaeus, *Against Heresies* 3.2.1; Hippolytus, *Refutation of All Heresies* 6:37; 7:26; 10:16) such phenomena were common. Cyprian, bishop of Carthage (A.D. 248–58) appointed others to leadership (*Epistles* 33, 34), comforted the confessors (*Epistles* 76, 78), exhorted his congregation to unity in his absence (*Epistle* 7), and received personal guidance (*Epistle* 9:4; *Life and Passion* 7) through them. Similar phenomena have occurred among mystics, enthusiasts, and pietists throughout the history of the church, most recently among Pentecostals and those touched by charismatic renewal.

Visions and voices are thought to proceed from the Spirit of God, and are understood as coming in fulfillment of Joel's promise (Joel 2:28–29; cf. Acts 2:15–18). Hence, they are sometimes associated with dreams and the gift of prophecy and the gift of discerning of spirits can reveal the source of the experience. Testing is important in that appeal is made to these experiences not only to bring about "upbuilding and encouragement and consolation" (I Cor. 14:3), but also to manipulate and deceive (Jer. 14:14; 23:16; II Cor. 11:14; I Thess. 5:19–22; I John 4:1–3).

Modern psychology and psychiatry tend to treat visions and voices within a pathological arena, usually as visual or auditory hallucinations. Psychological understandings of such phenomena—particularly when they take on a religious bent—often center around the idea of a hierarchy of realities which receive their continuous power from some sort of social reinforcement (Pruyser, 1968). A contemporary historian of psychology, however, has hypothesized a rather different and startling explanation of auditory "hallucinations" in biblical times by suggesting that ancient peoples from Mesopotamia to Peru could not "think" as do modern humans and were therefore not conscious. Unable to introspect, they experienced auditory hallucinations—voices of gods which were actually heard and then faithfully reported in such documents as found in the Old Testament. Coming from the brain's right hemisphere, these voices told an individual what to do in circumstances of stress and novelty. This type of mentality, called the bicameral mind, was left behind as humankind learned consciousness, although a residue may still be witnessed in modern cases, which are now called deviant or pathological (Jaynes, 1976).

Whatever the origin of these voices or visions, persons who claim to experience such phenomena need to be taken seriously. The pastor or psychologist faced with such persons must be prepared to help them test their experiences, distinguishing between the psychological and revelatory factors. The person's relationship to God is as important as his or her understanding of reality. Reality is not distorted in the thinking of those who experience God. They can separate themselves from their experience and engage in the testing process (I Cor. 14:37–40). Hence in divinely given visions and voices, they retain their identity over against God, they are not overpowered in the experience, and they function in an orderly manner (I Cor. 14:30–33, 40).

Bibliography. E. Ash, *Faith and Suggestion* (1912). J. Ennemoser, *The History of Magic,* 2 vols. (1854). J. Jaynes, *The Origin of Consciousness in the Breakdown of the Bicameral Mind* (1976). P. W. Pruyser, *A Dynamic Psychology of Religion* (1968).

C. M. ROBECK, JR.

EVALUATION AND DIAGNOSIS; GUIDANCE, DIVINE; PSYCHOPATHOLOGY AND RELIGION; RELIGIOUS EXPERIENCE. *See also* ILLUMINATION; PSYCHEDELIC DRUGS AND EXPERIENCE; PSYCHOSIS; RELIGIOUS LANGUAGE AND SYMBOLISM, PSYCHOLOGY OF; SCHIZOPHRENIA. *Compare* CHARISMATIC EXPERIENCE; ECSTASY; HALLUCINATION.

VISITATION. *See* CALLING AND VISITATION; CONGREGATION, PASTORAL CARE OF.

VOCATION (Protestantism). Though widely used today as a synonym for occupation, vocation (*vocatio,* a calling; *vocare,* to call) is fundamentally a theological term referring to (1) the call to salvation, (2) the call to service within the church, and (3) the call to serve God in whatever station of life one has. Before the Protestant Reformation *vocation* was used to describe the monastic life exclusively. Luther and Calvin, interpreting the NT references to vocation, objected to this narrowing of the term and applied it broadly to the Christian's calling in society, a development that led to the modern secularization of the term.

1. New Testament. *Kaleo, klatos,* and *klasis* are the three Greek words which, with their derivatives, are translated "vocation." *Kaleo* refers to God's call of persons into salvation, into fellowship with Christ, out of "darkness into light." "After you have suffered a little while, the God of all grace, who has called you to his eternal glory in Christ . . ." (I Pet. 5:10). "God is faithful, by whom you were called into the fellowship of his Son, Jesus Christ our Lord" (I Cor. 1:9). "And those whom he predestined he also called; and those whom he called he also justified." (Rom. 8:30). (See also I Tim. 6:12, I Pet. 2:9; II Thess. 2:14.)

Klatos denotes a special and specific invitation. "Paul . . . called to be an apostle" (Rom. 1:1). "To all . . . who are called to be saints" (Rom. 1:7). "To the church of God which is at Corinth, to those sanctified in Jesus Christ, called to be saints . . ." (I Cor. 1:2) (See also Mt. 22:14).

Klasis refers usually to the invitation to enter the Kingdom of God, but in one passage (I Cor. 7:20) it refers to position or station in life, a usage found in

classical Greek literature. "For the gifts and the call of God are irrevocable" (Rom. 11:29). ". . . that you may know what is the hope to which he has called you" (Eph. 1:18). ". . . just as you were called to the one hope." (Eph. 4:4). "I press on toward the goal for the prize of the upward call of God in Christ Jesus" (Phil. 3:14). "Everyone should remain in the state in which he was called" (I Cor. 7:20). "Therefore, holy brethren, who share in a heavenly call . . ." (Heb. 3:1).

2. Reformation. Luther and Calvin, confronted by a concept of vocation that reserved the term to those who were committed to a monastic life, refused to accept a compartmentalization of life into sacred and secular. The Christian, according to Luther, lives his or her vocation in the various stations of life. I Cor. 7:14–17 was critically important to Luther. He focused upon the servant aspect of all of life and saw the various roles of father, mother, son, and daughter, as well as specific jobs, to be related to one's vocation, that is, as ways to express response to vocation, the call to servanthood before God and neighbor. A vocation is a position or station which by its nature is helpful to others. The presence of service and love determined whether the station qualified as a vocation. These could be part of any serviceable work, and there was no secular order from which God was excluded. The emphasis shifted from the "what" to the "why" and "how" of the station or work. The cobbler, blacksmith, farmer, in faith, serves *in vocation* as surely as the priest. A parent, or homemaker, serves in a vocation as surely as the judge, lawyer, or doctor.

Calvin emphasized stewardship of all of life as the vocation of the Christian. More than simply as an opportunity for service, he saw work as a required mode of service assigned, not by random accident, but according to the purposes of God. Such lawful modes are part of the sovereign action of God. Vocation, for Calvin, meant neither spiritual nor worldly distinctions but the total claim of the Lord upon daily life. His is an ethic of vocation: living the whole of one's life in response to one's calling.

Because work consumed so much of life, the Reformers' emphasis upon servanthood and stewardship led their followers to emphasize work as the major expression of vocation. This led eventually to the secularization of the term to mean simply one's occupation or profession. This was not the intent of the Reformers. Their intent was rather that vocation be perceived as the call to discipleship, with work as a major, but not the only, response to that call. Nevertheless, work gradually came to be regarded as *the* expression of vocation, and vocation became a synonym for profession or occupation.

3. Contemporary Meanings. Roman Catholics continue to use the term "to have a vocation" to refer to specifically religious callings, though general usage thus emphasizes employment as vocation and suggests that other activities be referred to as avocations. However, there is still a recognition in secular dictionaries and encyclopedias of the concept of calling as one meaning of the word. Some theorists in the field of vocational psychology, therefore, distinguish between vocation and other work on the basis of the sense of commitment, which vocation implies, and the individual's desire (usually in the classical professions—law, ministry, medicine, teaching) to obtain more than economic meaning from work activity. Ego satisfaction, "fulfillment of one's potential," and service to the broader community are among the benefits derived from vocation. Such usage, which is not universal, does not fully recognize the theological nature of the concept, but does convey some of the original intent.

4. Vocational Counseling. Pastoral counselors, other clergy, and professional personnel in the church have an opportunity to engage in ministry as *vocational* counselors. The church has paid less attention to this aspect of ministry than it has to other forms of counseling. Very little has been written about the relationship between pastoral and vocational counseling (though the two specialties developed with parallel chronology), and pastoral counselors in general have shown only slight professional interest in vocational counseling. This may be due to the unique knowledge requirements involved in occupational sociology and vocational psychology. Vocational counseling, in theological conception if not in secular practice, is comprehensive in its concern for the whole life of the individual—that is, for the stewardship of life in various arenas: work, family, community, friendship, leisure, and religious practice. Most vocational counselors, however, are simply career counselors and are appropriately named such since they do not touch upon vocation in the theological sense.

Pastors who wish to use vocational counseling as a way to express pastoral concern for the whole life of the individual need to study occupational sociology, vocational psychology, and the processes of counseling as applied to occupational decision making, as well as to develop an integrative approach that will put work issues in context with the other, more traditional concerns of pastoral care. Awareness of age-related factors, work satisfaction measurements, discovery of interest procedures, impact of personality, values clarification, needs assessment, and ability analysis are all important. The same variables function in marriage, child-raising, community and church participation, and even in leisure-time pursuits. Their impact upon, or opportunity for satisfaction in, the various arenas of life is the way in which vocation gets acted out. For example, an ability to work with people in nurturing ways can be seen as part of one's call, as one of the resources of which one has to be steward. This may lead to a choice of occupation, in early life or later, which is nurturing by its nature, such as teaching. Alternatively, one's work may be machinery-oriented, and the use of nurturing abilities would be carried out in church, community, or family activities.

A principle of complementarity functions in this regard. It is the task of vocational counseling in the theological sense to assist persons in discovering that complementarity. This cannot be engaged in responsibly, however, unless there is special knowledge about occupations and careers; the tendency in the absence of such knowledge is to ignore the possibility that a change in work is indicated. Some pastors, recognizing this but not wishing to become expert in occupational variables, consult with and refer persons to vocational counselors who are sensitive to the concerns of the pastor, much in the same way that referrals are made to mental health counselors. The pastor and vocational counselor can then work as a team to provide a more wholistic approach to the person's decision making.

Bibliography. W. A. Beardslee, *Human Achievement and Divine Vocation in the Message of Paul* (1961). E. Brunner, *The Christian Doctrine of Creation and Redemption* (ET, O. Wyon, 1952). J. Calvin, *Commentary on First Corinthians* (ET, J. Pringle, 1948); *Institutes I and II*, (ET, H. Beveridge, 1957); see especially bk. 3, secs. 7 and 10; bk. 4, sec. 13. J. E. Dittes, *Vocational Guidance of Theological Students* (1964); *When Work Goes Sour* (1987). J. H. Fichter, *Religion as an Occupation: A Study in the Sociology of Professions* (1961). G. Harkness, *John Calvin: The Man and His Ethics* (1958 [1931]). C. F. Kemp, *the Pastor and Vocational Counseling* (1961). M. Luther, *Works* I (Muhlenberg, 1943) and II and III (ET, Holman, 1916, 1931); see especially "Treatise on Christian Liberty" and "To the Christian Nobility" (II). P. S. Minear, *To Die and to Live: Christ's Resurrection and Christian Vocation* (1977). J. C. McLelland, *The Other Six Days* (1961). J. O. Nelson, ed., *Work and Vocation* (1954); *Vocation and Protestant Religious Occupations* (1963). G. H. Ranson, "The Christian Doctrine of Vocation," *Review and Expositor*, 54 (1957). A. Richardson, *The Biblical Doctrine of Work* (1952). C. A. Schleck, *The Theology of Vocation* (1963). G. Wingren, *Luther on Vocation* (1957).

T. E. BROWN

CHRISTIAN LIFE; WORK AND CAREER. *See also* CALL TO MINISTRY; CAREER DEVELOPMENT AND GUIDANCE (For Pastors); MINISTRY. *Compare* GOD'S WILL, ACCEPTANCE OF; PLAY.

VOCATION (Roman Catholicism). The Roman Catholic understanding of vocation is linked with the notion of vocation or call in the OT and NT. In the OT, people were called into existence, they were invited to cooperate with the ongoing process of creation, and they entered a covenanted relationship. In the NT vocation was closely related to the Greek word *kalein*, which most often carried the meaning of being called but also meant "to name" or "to invite." According to the new covenant, Jesus Christ came as God's call to humankind, and from that point onward the individual's response to the call of God was linked with a response to Jesus Christ who was the *kalon*, or caller. Fittingly in the NT, those who accepted the call of Christ were designated as *kalloumenoi*; namely, those who were called.

1. Personal Vocation. A vocation or call from God presupposes a personal God who actively invites men and women to commit themselves to the gospel of Jesus Christ in unique ways. A sense of personal vocation as a call to growth and holiness in the Christian life was reinforced in the documents of the Second Vatican Council and subsequent statements by recent popes which stress the co-responsibility of everyone and the interdependence of each person to become a mature and committed disciple of Jesus Christ.

The Catholic Christian responds to God's call in Christ in baptism, and the baptismal commitment empowers the Christian to continue the revelation of God's call to all of creation. The emphasis on the centrality of the call to holiness and service as derived through baptism is most congenial with the "inclusive" ecclesiology of the Second Vatican Council, which defined church as the people of God, avoiding a narrow understanding of vocation based on hierarchical status and/or ecclesiastical office. In this broader understanding of ministry, everyone has a vocation to serve the Kingdom of God.

2. The Clergy/Laity Distinction and Vatican II. It is true, however, that this notion of a personal vocation or call to growth in the Christian life has been obscured in the past when the separateness of clerical and lay vocations was stressed, occasionally suggesting that clergy and vowed religious were called to perfection and laity to mediocrity. Such unfortunate emphases tended to denigrate the laity, fostering an unwarranted and inaccurate consciousness of second class citizenry, and limiting the development of personal vocation to the ordained priesthood or the canonical religious life. An unintentional (one supposes) example of this type of gap is the choice of entries under *vocation* in the 1967 edition of the *New Catholic Encyclopedia*, volume 14, where an essay on "Vocation, Religious and Clerical" has no lay counterpart. While it is true that a subsequent entry called "Vocation to the Supernatural Life" is included, the theme of that essay also bypasses the laity for specific consideration.

In this connection, O'Connell (1979) and Deck (1987) offer evidence to substantiate the claim that in both popular and sophisticated literature the terms *vocation/ vocations* almost always have as their referent the ordained priesthood and religious life.

Without any ambiguity, however, the documents of the Second Vatican Council call attention to the universality of the term *vocation*. The church is a community of disciples who share a universal call to holiness, whatever their condition or state of life may be. The universal call to holiness is addressed to laity, religious, and clergy without distinction, but it is to be lived out in and through different vocations. Different members of the church pursue their vocations in different ways, of course, because each member receives particular gifts to exercise on behalf of the furtherance of the kingdom of God. "From the acceptance of these charisms, there arise for each believer the right and duty to use them in the Church and in the world for the good of all persons and the building up of the Church" ("Apostolicam Actuositatem," #3).

In his first encyclical, Pope John Paul II wrote of the church as the community of the people of God "which is so vast and so extremely differentiated" that "we must see first and foremost Christ saying in a way to each member of the community: 'Follow me'" ("Redemptor Hominis," #21). The key insight into the transforming power of the church rests with the individual Christian's discernment, acceptance, and faithful fulfillment of his or her vocation. "The Pope too and every Bishop must apply this principle to himself. Priests and religious must be faithful to this principle. It is the basis on which their lives must be built by married people, parents and women and men of different conditions and professions, from those who occupy the highest posts in society to those who perform the simplest tasks ("Redemptor Hominis," #21).

In this light, no choice of a state of life as such is superior to any other. Each call has its own dignity and is a gift of grace to be appraised in dialogue with one's unique life situation in the light of the teachings and traditions of the church.

Of the many documents spawned from the Second Vatican Council, a most helpful one in framing a theology of vocation is the final document of the Latin American bishops' conference at Puebla in 1979. In this document (nos. 852–58), the bishops suggest that vocation should be understood in three ways: first, as the call to be fully man or woman, the vocation to be human; second, as the baptismal call to follow Christ; third, as the specific call within that larger baptismal call. Succinctly, the Latin American bishops offer a precise and suitable framework that fairly represents the Roman Catholic theology of vocation.

3. The Common Priesthood of the Faithful. While all Christians share the universal and common call to holiness, each person discerns the specificity of that vocation. By baptism, all Christians touch base with the source of the common priesthood of all the faithful in the action of Christ who is the model of sanctity for every human being. Ninety-nine percent of the faithful follow this lay vocation which, according to the Vatican II document, "Lumen Gentium," has as its purpose to offer spiritual sacrifices and proclaim the power of Christ, to participate in the sacraments, to offer prayer and thanksgiving, to give witness to the world by a holy life and to engage in self-denial and active charity. The universal priesthood, or priesthood of all believers, is called upon primarily to contribute to the sanctification of the world, seeking primarily to enhance the holiness of the universe. Most Catholics exercise this common priesthood in their families and occupations, doing their part to transform the social order in family, in work, in the marketplace, in public life, and occasionally by sharing with vowed religious and clergy the pastoral, educational, and administrative ministries in service of the community.

The Catholic church teaches that the common priesthood of the faithful, which all share, and the ordained or ministerial priesthood, while interrelated, "differ from one another in essence and not only in degree" ("Lumen Gentium," #10). The ministerial priest, acting in the person of Christ, "brings about the Eucharistic sacrifice, and offers it to God in the name of all the people. For their part, the faithful join in the offering of the Eucharist by virtue of their royal priesthood" (ibid.).

Others within the Catholic Christian community are called to live in obedience to the word of God, in poverty and dependence upon divine mercy, and in chaste love in a manner that becomes a sign of the whole Christian community. Through their formal consecration and vows, canonical religious men and women are a public sign or witness to the universal call to holiness.

4. Discerning One's Vocation. One determines or discerns the specificity of one's vocation with prayerful attention to the call of God and community, conscious that one's vocation is not a static entity but that it will unfold. Like conversion in the Christian life, vocation is ongoing. In the practical order of things, a contemporary theology of vocation points to a general call from God to which an individual gives an active, self-determined response, depending upon his or her own personal history and the capacity one has cultivated for hearing the promptings and murmurings of God in one heart and life.

Bibliography. Documents: "Apostolicam Actuositatem," and "Lumen Gentium," in A. Flannery, O.P., ed., *Vatican Council II: The Conciliar and Post Conciliar Documents* (1980). *Redemptor Hominis* (1978). *Puebla and Beyond: Documentation and Commentary* (1979).

Studies: A. F. Deck, "Ministry and Vocations: Going Back to the Drawing Board," in *America* (March 14, 1987), 212–18. A. Godin, *The Psychology of Religious Vocations* (1983). G. Grisez, "Personal Vocation: A Key to Authentic Renewal of the Church," in *Homiletic and Pastoral Review*, 4 (1985), 10–20. L. J. O'Connell, "God's Call to Humankind: Towards a Theology of Vocation," in *Chicago Studies*, 18 (1979), 147–60. D. E. Pilarczyk, "The Changing Image of Priest," in *Origins*, 16 (1986), 137–46. S. Schneiders, I.H.M., "Evangelical Equality," parts 1 and 2, *Spirituality Today*, 38 (1986), 293–302, and 39 (1987), 56–67.

D. DONNELLY

MINISTRY (Roman Catholic Tradition); RELIGIOUS LIFE (VOWED LIFE). *See also* CALL TO MINISTRY; CHRISTIAN LIFE. *Compare* GOD'S WILL, ACCEPTANCE OF; LAICIZATION; WORK AND CAREER.

VOCATIONAL COUNSELING. *See* VOCATION (Protestantism).

VOCATIONAL REHABILITATION. A federally funded program to help handicapped persons return to competitive employment. Since it is usually a public program, broad guidelines for vocational rehabilitation are set by the federal government, but the program is administered by the states and funding is on a federal and state matching funds basis.

The rationale for these programs is economic: if handicapped people return to work, tax revenues increase and public assistance correspondingly decreases.

Eligibility for federal vocational rehabilitation is determined by two requirements: (1) the documented presence of a disability (mental or physical) that is a handicap to employment, and (2) a reasonable expectation that through vocational rehabilitation services individuals may become more employable.

Vocational Rehabilitation Counseling. At the point of referral, the vocational rehabilitation counselor makes a diagnostic study to determine if the applicant is eligible for services and, if so, the extent of his or her disability. This diagnostic work-up may include one, but not all, of the following: a general practitioner's physical examination, lab tests, vocational evaluation, hearing evaluation, psychological examination, other evaluations by specialists, and diagnostic hospitalization. During this phase, the counselor will also offer counseling, vocational testing, and referral as appropriate. These diagnostic services are offered regardless of the applicant's income level.

If the client is eligible for services, the client and the counselor together outline a program of services, which may include services paid for by the government as well as services provided directly by the counselor. Services may include medical treatment, convalescent care, prostheses, transportation, personal needs, maintenance, clothing, and formal training of all types.

Services provided directly by the counselor include personal counseling, training in job-seeking skills, voca-

tional education information, setting up on-the-job training programs, job placement assistance and coordination of services from other agencies. After the client returns to work, the counselor provides follow-up for a minimum of sixty days to help the client maintain employment, but services can be provided after this time if necessary.

Bibliography. H. Rusalem and D. Malikin, eds., *Contemporary Vocational Rehabilitation* (1976).

R. E. HONOUR

SOCIAL SERVICES AND PASTORAL CARE. *See also* HANDICAP AND DISABILITY; LOSS OF FUNCTION; WORK AND CAREER. *Compare* UNEMPLOYED.

VOICES. *See* VISIONS AND VOICES.

VOLUNTEERS, PASTORAL CARE OF. The term *volunteer* denotes nonprofessionals whose service activities supplement the functioning of full-time staff workers. It is used here to distinguish such services from those of professionals: clergy, institutional chaplains, and pastoral counselors.

In contrast to professional clergy who are obligated as paid employees under contract to parishes or centers, volunteers may withdraw the offer to serve, just as it was voluntarily made. Further, whereas professionals undertake their service functions as their vocational choices, with the tangible rewards of payment for services, the functions of volunteers are usually secondary to vocational choices and other personal activities. The question as to whether the term *volunteers* may be applied validly to the functioning of laypeople within the congregation's pastoral care ministry hinges on a theological question: Is that service activity a voluntary commitment that may be withdrawn at will, or is it a ministry that is entailed by virtue of being a member of the community of faith?

1. Lay Ministries in the Congregation. Despite the theological argument that the term volunteer has no place in the vocabulary of the Christian community, it still receives wide acceptance. Lay people are called to assume their respective ministries. Care should be exercised in the selection and training of lay people for specific roles in the congregation.

The keystone of effective lay ministry is the intensity and consistency of supervision, which is exercised by the full-time staff or by other laypeople who are competent to provide supervision of lay ministries. Support of lay ministers by the clergy staff provides for the pastoral needs of those providing ministry, whether as caregivers, youth counselors, committee members, etc., as well as serving as a model for the various ministries.

One of the foci of NT theology is the notion that each baptized member is gifted for ministry. This devolves upon the congregation as one of its responsibilities, namely, assisting each member of the congregation to recognize his or her gift and calling each member to the exercise of that gift.

Supervision of the respective lay ministries is usually provided in the context of committee meetings or leadership training events. Members should be encouraged to acknowledge their accountability to the congregation for their respective activities, which should be reported for supervision by clergy staff and peers. Clergy supervisors may also request individual supervisory sessions in order to address the needs or actions of particular members.

It is appropriate to conclude a training event with the presentation of the participants to the congregation in the context of a commissioning service, in which the congregants commit themselves to support the ministry which will be offered in their behalf.

2. Lay Ministries in Institutional Settings. Hospital pastoral care departments may recruit volunteers whose functions are delineated in contrast to the duties of paid staff members. Their levels of functioning are likely to be part-time, less intensive, less informed, and subject to fewer expectations than those of the clergy. Growing numbers of laypeople are participating in CPE with a view to serving in a voluntary capacity. Whether their ministries are perceived as equivalent to those of clergy, or secondary and supplementary, will vary in accordance with the policies of the respective institutions and the role perceptions of the senior staff chaplains under whose supervision they serve.

With respect to involvement of volunteers in pastoral counseling services, a strong caveat must be entered. There exist some schools of theological thought, usually the more conservative, that argue for peer counseling by less than professionally trained volunteers, who may be supervised by clergy with little professional training themselves and no training in supervision. The question of the role and efficacy of volunteer counselors will then depend upon the theological stance of the proponent, rather than on the level of professional training and supervision deemed necessary for the well-being of both counselor and client.

Pastoral counselors from mainstream denominations are likely to require stringent restrictions on the functioning of volunteers in counseling centers, and be disposed to challenge the validity of such a role under any circumstances, since it does not meet their professional criteria. On the other hand, clergy who propose a significant role for volunteers in pastoral counseling will do so on the basis that this concept meets relevant theological criteria.

Bibliography. D. Johnson, *The Care and Feeding of Volunteers in the Church* (1978).

R. H. SUNDERLAND

CONGREGATION, PASTORAL CARE OF. *Compare* LAY PASTORAL CARE AND COUNSELING; VOCATION; WORK AND CAREER.

VOWED LIFE. *See* RELIGIOUS LIFE.

VOWS/VOWING. A vow is a solemn promise that binds one to a particular intention. Although the word *vow* can be used simply to strengthen one's assertion or emphasize the depth of one's intention, the customary usage conveys a degree of solemnity not found in the simple notion of promising, due to the fact that a vow is made ordinarily either to God or before God. A vow to God can be a promise to perform a particular action (for example, to make a pilgrimage or to give a portion of one's money to the poor) or a promise to devote oneself to a particular way of living. A vow to God must be a vow to do something or to be something that is both possible and better than what is already morally required or otherwise obligatory. Vowing oneself to God can be said to be synonymous with consecrating oneself to God and to God's service. By consecrating oneself a person sets his or her life apart out of a sense of call or mission or obedience to God's desires for the person.

1. Origins. Vowing is not peculiar to Christians. It is also practiced among Jews and Muslims, and was known before Judaism. It continues to be part of such religious traditions as Hinduism, Buddhism, and Jainism. Vows to the gods, furthermore, were not unknown in the pagan religions. It is difficult to extricate vowing from making promises of votive offerings in the ancient religions. Ancients, by votive offerings, promised to offer a sacrifice to one of the gods if a certain circumstance turned benign for them.

The Hebrew Scriptures show that the custom of making vows and votive offerings antedates Israel, since these Scriptures are concerned not to exhort the hearer into taking vows but stress rather the need for purification about the whole process of vowing. If one is prone to make a vow to God, it is essential that one fulfill that vow (Deut. 23:21–23). At times vows were accompanied by oaths that invoked a curse upon one's self or others if the vow were not fulfilled (I Sam. 14:24). The prophets frequently called the people to task for the lightness with which they made vows before God and the distance between what their lips said, what their hearts intended, and what their hands did. Vows and consecration are closely linked in these scriptures. A person could be consecrated by another person. For example, Samuel was consecrated while he was still in his mother's womb (Judg. 13:4–14). The notion of one's person being consecrated to God for a specific length of time is also not unknown in Israel (Num. 6:1–21). Such persons were known as Nazirites.

The concept of vowing as such does not win any attention in the Gospels. The closest Jesus' words come to the subject communicates his disdain for the abuse of setting some part of one's possessions aside (hypocritically) consecrating them to God so that they cannot be used to serve the needs of one's mother and father. What is dedicated to God is called *korban* (Mk. 7:9–13). In general, Jesus is more concerned with what he sees in the hearts of his hearers than he is with what they avow by their speech before God. Vows were not unknown to Paul of Tarsus. At one point in his ministry Paul shaved his head because of a vow he had taken (Acts 18:18).

Early in Christian tradition, around the year 100, we have evidence of Christians pledging themselves to being Christian in very specific ways, for example, by continence. By the fourth century the monastic vocation had become sufficiently stable that one finds monks permanently obligating themselves to a life in a monastery. This is accompanied by a vow of virginity and a vow to keep the rule of life. By the time of St. Benedict monks were making promises of stability, obedience, and a conversion of morals as the content of their consecration to God. It is not until the twelfth century with the hermits of St. Augustine that we find a profession of three vows — poverty, chastity, and obedience. By the time of the Middle Ages vowing, not in the solemn public sense but in the sense of personal vowing to God, was common.

2. Theology of Vowing. The rationale for taking vows in religious congregations and monasteries of the Catholic tradition derives from a particular way of seeing and imitating the life of Jesus. It also understands Jesus' invitation to a select few to follow him in a distinct way to be one which has continued since his resurrection. Hence poverty, chastity, and obedience are taken to be "evangelical counsels" before they constitute matter for vows. They are counsels because they entail a degree of commitment to Christ over and above what is essential to being Christian. They are called evangelical because their inspiration is the Gospels and the submission of Jesus to his Father's will.

The Reformers, especially Calvin, Luther, and Wycliffe, took issue with this development within the Christian tradition. Luther, for example, found vows a form of works-rightousness which deludes people into thinking that they can earn salvation by their faithfulness to their vows. Luther's concern was to preserve the gratuity of the justification of sinners by God in Christ. His own experience in early life placed great stock in keeping his vows so that his fidelity would assure his salvation. His disillusionment led him to excoriate the notion of monastic vows altogether, along with the two other institutions of Catholic Christianity, the Mass as it was understood in his day, and the papacy. He considered vows useless since one cannot guarantee one's ability to fulfill the vows taken. Furthermore, he complained that entrance into religious life was being proclaimed a new form of baptism, which he found a derogation of the uniqueness of baptism. Finally, he insisted that to demand a pledge of chastity from those who would be ministers of the church was a diabolical tyranny.

A more frequent objection to the notion of taking vows is a concern about the possible reduction of freedom in one's subsequent actions and choices. This objection is valid to the extent that the vowing person can lose heart in doing that which was vowed. Subsequent action, if done at all, can be performed out of a grudging sense of duty to fulfill the vow taken. Notwithstanding the force of the objection, however, there must also be an appreciation of the fact that vowing makes a formal statement about one's sense of self and gives a degree of stability to that which is seen to be a good. A vow can also be a social statement about how one feels led by God to relate to God and neighbor. By vowing, one is willing to place oneself beyond the swaying power of mood or adverse circumstance in order to continue to pursue both what one sees as ideal and one's ideal self. A vow has the value of indicating a deeper submission to God precisely because of its long-term duration. Vowing is based on the premise that human freedom is given to us to be used; not to use one's freedom to particularize life makes it likely that one will lose the freedom one has. By using our freedom to make irrevocable choices something eternal is made.

There are a number of ways in which vows can cease to be binding: if the fulfillment of a vow is connected with a particular time frame and the time expires; if one's means of fulfilling the vow undergoes a substantial change (for example, if a person vowed to tithe becomes penniless); or if the condition on which the fulfillment of a vow depends is not fulfilled. The Catholic church, furthermore, has historically exercised the power to commute, dispense, or annul vows when there appears to be a legitimate impediment to their being fulfilled.

Bibliography. L. Gerke, *Christian Marriage: A Permanent Sacrament* (1965). J. C. Haughey, *Should Anyone Say Forever* (1975). See also various articles on "Vow" in the *New Catholic Encyclopedia* (1967). S. Hendrix, *Luther and the Papacy* (1981). K. Rahner, *Grace in Freedom* (1969).

J. C. HAUGHEY, S.J.

CELIBACY; COMMITMENT; PROMISING; RELIGIOUS LIFE. *See also* BAPTISM AND CONFIRMATION; HOLY ORDERS; MATRIMONY, SACRAMENT OF; OBEDIENCE; SPIRITUAL DISCIPLINE AND GROWTH. *Compare* APOSTASY; BORN-AGAIN EXPERIENCE; INFIDELITY, MARITAL; PROFANE LANGUAGE; SELF-EXPRESSION/SELF-CONTROL.

VOYEURISM. *See* SEXUAL VARIETY, DEVIANCE, AND DISORDER.

VULNERABILITY. *See* DEPENDENCE/INDEPENDENCE; INTIMACY AND DISTANCE; SHAME.

WAITING. *See* PATIENCE/PATIENTHOOD.

WARD, MARY. *See* WOMEN IN PASTORAL MINISTRIES, HISTORY OF.

WARMTH, PERSONAL. *See* THERAPEUTIC CONDITIONS.

WARTIME PASTORAL CARE. Ministry to those who are both the perpetrators and the victims of war. Armed military conflict is the ever present reality of modern life; at this writing, conflict continues in the Near East, the Far East, Central America, South America, and elsewhere.

1. Psychological Effects of War. There is a vestigial remnant of the heroic warrior; we see him in armor or on his horse. His byword is valor, and his creed is chivalry. With the advent of modern technology, however, the fable of the heroic warrior has faded. The facts of war, the mutilation of millions, the socialization of sadism, and the threat of universal extinction, has helped to destroy it. Paradoxically, as war has come closer via television, it has seemed ever more distant. We see it portrayed almost every night in some corner of the globe. We see the men in uniform, the guns, planes, and explosions, and yet the whole affair has the quality of a fantasy, as though there is no distinction between television news and television drama. The ego defends itself against the reality of death with a fantasy. Freud called it identification with the aggressor. These defenses distance us from the fact that we support aggression, and that the fantasy has become a reality.

For the majority, war is something to know about as an observer, as with professional football, which we watch while others play the game. For a minority, war is something to experience as a perpetrator who becomes a victim of his or her own violence, or as a victim who then responds in violence only to exchange roles with the perpetrators. Always present are the spectators who support the play. In a transformation, the watchers become perpetrators, the perpetrators become victims, and the victims become spectators. War touches everyone in an exchange of roles; no one is innocent and no one is untouched.

2. Biblical and Theological Understanding. To the extent that the pastor understands the human condition from the biblical perspective, he or she will see it as potential perfection marred by the tragedy of separation from God and the failure to realize health and optimal human development.

From the theological perspective, the human condition is marked by the reality of both sin and grace and of necessity and freedom. In this perspective Christian faith hopes for transformation of the dichotomies of existence while preserving the reality of both poles of the dichotomy. The dichotomy of necessity and freedom bears correspondence in human existence in other human dichotomies: passivity and activity, law and gospel, individuality and community, service to God and service to state, and even consciousness and unconsciousness. The tragedy is that humanity attempts to reconcile these dichotomies in self-destructive ways. The tension they produce becomes unbearable. One pole becomes identified within the self while the other is projected outward. My group and I become "good, right, and righteous — the elect," while the others become "bad, the damned, the sinners." They must be destroyed while I must be confirmed. Aggression against the other is the basis for war. This decision is based on a judgment which projects the dark side of the dichotomy and internalizes the light side. This decision is the theological and psychological basis for socialized aggression against the other, "the enemy." Humanity is thus torn between the poles, separated and broken. This separation is sin in theological terms, and war is its socialized manifestation. The pastor's vantage point within this context will help to determine the response. To the extent that the pastor is conscious of his or her own conflicts and tendencies toward projection there is the possibility that these may be transcended. To the extent that the pastor is unconscious of his or her own conflicts and projections, there may appear a tendency to be trapped in the conflict and drawn in as a pawn, blessing the forces of light in their struggle against the forces of darkness.

3. **Pastoral Psychological Understanding.** There is the ministry of word and of sacrament within the community of the church. But all of these can be contaminated by the conflict and dichotomy already depicted. The ministry of the word brings to the dichotomy of necessity and freedom the healing love of God. This is a "tough love" in that it faces squarely the realities of both sin and separation with the all powerful and ever present realities of forgiveness and reparation. The love of God, as of self and neighbor, transcends the dichotomy of necessity and freedom and heals through its transcendence. This is manifested physically and materially in sacrifice — in crucifixion and resurrection. It is symbolized sacramentally in the transcendence of the dichotomy through baptism where the dichotomy of life and death is celebrated. In the eucharistic feast, wine becomes blood and bread becomes flesh. The material is transformed into the spiritual. The transformation is accomplished by the historical and material sacrifice of Jesus called Christ. This sacrifice is the material transformation of the dichotomy of existence. To the extent that the pastor presents through word and sacrament this transcendence, he or she represents the actions of Jesus Christ. This representation forms the basis for both the community of the church and the ministry of pastoral care. In the issue of war, one clearly finds the dichotomous nature of human existence.

This ministry is informed and amplified by the knowledge of modern psychology and psychiatry. Geen (1972) reviewed twenty years of research on aggression and concluded that: (1) Frustration can lead to aggression on the part of humans. While this is mitigated by social situations, it appears that frustration leads to an internal readiness to perform aggression. (2) Observation of aggression by others in reality or drama facilitates the expression of aggression by the observer. (3) One effect of the observation of aggression may be the direct imitation of the aggression witnessed. (4) Aggression may be reduced by teaching a rationally measured aggressive response, decreasing positive reinforcement for aggression, and reducing the use of harsh punishments.

The Vietnam War offered an opportunity to study the effect of armed military conflict on those veterans involved (Getsinger, 1975; Williams, 1980). Participation in this war has been shown to be related to the development of posttraumatic stress disorder. The symptoms of this condition are depression, isolation, rage, alienation, avoidance of emotion, guilt over survival, anxiety reactions, sleep disturbance with nightmares, and the intrusion of traumatic memories.

4. **Pastoral Response.** The pastor can have an active role in the reduction of aggression and violence in our society. This must grow out of his or her psychotheological framework for ministry and might include: (1) developing an action plan for parish education on the sources of violence including reduction of the frustrations of poverty and ignorance and reducing the use of harsh and sadistic punishments; (2) teaching the constructive use of measured aggression and force as well as the technique of nonviolence; (3) activation of the church community for the healing of victims and perpetrators of violence

including individual and group counseling. Because the traumas of combat were experienced in a group, group counseling has proven to be an effective means of healing. Referral is important when serious psychiatric disturbances are seen (Getsinger, 1975).

Getsinger notes that survivors of combat experience major changes in their self-concept and in their attitude toward life. As with the grief reaction, the war veteran faces problems of readjustment to civilian life as a person with a new identity. A major component of this adjustment is dealing with the guilt of being a survivor after watching one's friends die. The redemptive community of the church can help to proclaim the good news of forgiveness to the veteran who has violated his or her moral standards in the face of war.

Bibliography. P. Bourne, *Men, Stress, and Vietnam* (1970). R. G. Geen, *Aggression* (1972). S. H. Getsinger, "Pastoral Counseling and the Combat Veteran," *J. of Religion and Health* 14, (1975), 214 – 19. T. Williams, *Post-Traumatic Stress Disorders of the Vietnam Veteran* (1980).

S. H. GETSINGER

CRISIS MINISTRY; DISASTER, PUBLIC; POST-TRAUMATIC STRESS DISORDER; SURVIVOR PSYCHOLOGY; VICTIMIZATION.

WATSON, JOHN (1850 – 1907). Very successful Scottish Presbyterian minister and prolific fiction author.

His most famous and most influential theological work was published in several books around the turn of the century. Best known are his Yale lectures, *The Cure of Souls (1896).* Though characterized by an almost cavalier disinterest in systematic theory and little originality, it is still a skillful work of true insight and common sense, steeped in rich experience, emphasizing pastoral visitation and private consolation, and featuring helpful suggestions for pastoral work. Particularly beneficial is the chapter on "the work of the pastor," which provides good rules for personal interviews.

N. F. HAHN

PASTORAL THEOLOGY, PROTESTANT; REFORMED PASTORAL CARE.

The WAY INTERNATIONAL. *See* NEW RELIGIOUS MOVEMENTS.

WEALTH. *See* LIFESTYLE ISSUES; POWER; RICH PERSONS; SOCIAL STATUS AND CLASS FACTORS; VIPs.

WEATHERHEAD, LESLIE (1893–1976). English Methodist pastor and writer. As pastor of the City Temple in London, Weatherhead established a Church Psychological Clinic in collaboration with psychiatrists, psychologists, and physicians, and he worked to acquaint the English clergy with the theories and techniques of modern psychotherapy. His service as a staff officer in World War I prompted him to study the relation between the New Psychology and the work of the ministry, and when he went to Leeds in 1925, he sought the cooperation of physicians. He became deeply interested in the church's ministry of healing, whether through psychotherapy, intercessory prayer, or the curative power of religious faith. When he went to the City Temple in 1936, he created not only the medical psychiatric clinic but also a regular program of intercessory prayer and spiritual healing.

While serving as the pastor of City Temple, Weatherhead completed work on a doctoral degree at the University of London, and in 1951 he published his thesis under the title *Psychology, Religion and Healing*, a comprehensive survey of nonphysical methods of healing throughout the history of the church. The book was one of many that he published on psychological themes. His writings in the 1930s on human sexuality, though quite conservative by later standards, evoked considerable debate.

Weatherhead was particularly effective in promoting renewed attention to pastoral care in English Methodism. He was the founding co-president in 1946 of the Methodist Society for Medical and Pastoral Practice, which emerged from the earlier Methodist Spiritual Healing Committee, appointed at his instigation in 1937 to examine the topic of "spiritual healing." He also successfully proposed to the Methodist conference that all students for the Methodist ministry should have sufficient psychological training to help them diagnose psychological illness, and that ministers and physicians should cooperate whenever possible in experimental clinics.

E. B. HOLIFIELD

SALVATION, HEALING, AND HEALTH, THEOLOGY OF. *See also* HEALING; PASTORAL COUNSELING MOVEMENT.

WEDDING CEREMONY, CHRISTIAN. In Christian tradition, the wedding ceremony is seen as a rite of passage and an act of worship which celebrates the love of God as witnessed by the covenant being made between a man and a woman. It differs from a purely civil service in that the officiant is usually an ordained minister and it is conducted within the context of the community of faith, which reinforces the couple's commitment to God and to each other in love.

Planning for the wedding ceremony involves an important pastoral opportunity. While the forms for the ceremony vary widely, there are specific elements found in almost all of them. These reflect the crucial elements of marriage itself: that it is a combination of cultural and religious definition; that the commitment carries importance far beyond the pledges of husband and wife; that the man and woman are declaring a very specific kind of faithfulness to each other; and that the relationship is indeed blessed by God and the community of faith. In addition to providing a focus for preparation for the ceremony itself, these elements also serve as a guide for the pastor in educating couples about marriage, both prior to and following the ceremony.

The first element is a statement by the officiant about the nature and intent of marriage broadly understood. Discussion of the couple's understanding of their planned relationship serves as a vehicle for planning the ceremony, but more importantly, there is opportunity to explore the perceptions that the man and woman have of their roles with each other. The personal goals/ hopes/ dreams that each partner holds are crucial and should be compared with those of the intended spouse. Further, the cultural understanding of marriage is included because the commitment holds meaning for a wider community of parents, friends, and extended family. The stability of a culture is often tied, perceptually, to the strength of commitments between marital partners and family members. Such a statement of the nature and intention of marriage also involves a theological perception about marriage, including emphasis on such characteristics as permanence, nurture, sexual exclusivity, shared responsibility, and faithfulness in adversity.

A second element in the wedding ceremony is the statement of intent made by the bride and the groom to the officiant. It is at this point in the service that each partner declares to the officiant, and thus to the community, their intention to incorporate a particular understanding of marriage into their own relationship. Here, too, the symbolic affirmation is made that the couple is accountable to a larger community. Often, at this point in the ceremony, the bride is "given away" by the father or some other family member. While that act may reflect older conceptions of wives being "property," there is also the possibility of having the act more broadly understood and acted out to reflect the community's participation in this ceremony.

A prayer of thanksgiving and petition often follows these statements of intent. The content of the prayer is often an acknowledgment of the histories that have brought these persons together, an expression of gratitude for the love they share, and a petition for God's grace to sustain them in the pledges they are making in this ceremony.

The element of vows made to each other follows the vows made to the officiant. Having acknowledged the broader understanding of marriage and affirmed their willingness to continue in that tradition, the bride and groom face each other and "particularize" the pledge directly to each other in some form. A typical form begins, "I _____ take you _____ to be my wedded wife/husband." The content of these vows is intended to be personal. While there are standard forms, many couples prefer to write their own vows to reflect the intimacy and unique character of the relationship. A symbol of the commitment, ordinarily a ring, is exchanged to signify the concrete nature of this ritual.

With the vows exchanged, the final element is the pronunciation by the officiant that the marriage is "done." A charge to the couple often follows, encouraging them to maintain their pledge and assuring them of support by God's grace and the acknowledged interest of the wider community.

Bibliography. P. H. Biddle, Jr., *Abingdon Marriage Manual* (1974). J. L. Christensen, *The Minister's Marriage Handbook* (1974). C. Lamont, *A Humanist Wedding Service* (1972). R. L. Morgan, "A Ritual of Remarriage," *J. of Pastoral Care*, 37:4 (1983), 292–301. W. E. Oates and W. Rowatt, *Before You Marry Them* (1975).

W. V. ARNOLD

MARRIAGE; MATRIMONY, SACRAMENT OF; RITUAL AND PASTORAL CARE; WORSHIP AND CELEBRATION.

WEDDING CEREMONY, JEWISH. The Hebrew word for marriage is *qidushin*, derived from *qadosh* (holy). This accurately describes the Jewish understanding of marriage as enunciated in Hebrew Scriptures: "Hence a man leaves his father and mother and clings to his wife, so that they become one flesh" (Gen. 2:24, JPS), and by the rabbis: "He who is without a wife dwells without blessings" (Midrash, Tihilim [Psalms] 59).

The ceremony customarily is held in the temple or synagogue, or in the home of the bride or groom, and is performed by a rabbi, often assisted by a cantor. The wedding party gathers under a *hupah* (a canopy suspended on four poles), which symbolizes the home that the couple will establish together. The service begins with recitation of traditional prayers. The rabbi then may give a brief charge to the couple, following which he reads the *k'tubah* (marriage contract). In ancient times, this contract delineated the financial responsibilities to be assumed by the groom, as well as other marital obligations of the couple. While the *k'tubah* is still a legal agreement for Orthodox Jews, most Conservative and Reform Jews have revised the wording, so that it is a statement of the spiritual bond of mutuality between a man and a woman.

The service continues as the bride and groom share a cup of wine (*qidush*), symbolic of their sharing and thereby enriching the joys of life together. Traditionally this is followed by the cantor chanting seven blessings, sanctifying the covenant into which the bride and groom are entering.

The next ritual act is the exchange of rings, accompanied by vows of love and loyalty. In the more traditional ceremony, only the groom presents a ring, symbolic of his acceptance of the dowry which the bride brings with her.

The Jewish wedding ceremony concludes as the rabbi pronounces the couple husband and wife and blesses them with the priestly benediction (Num. 6:24–26). The groom usually crushes the wine glass by stepping on it, symbolic in old days of mourning the destruction of the first and second Temples, even while we rejoice on such happy occasions. Presently the custom continues with a variety of new interpretations by rabbis. The assembled relatives and friends then shout, "Mazel Tov!" (good luck), and the service is concluded.

Prior to the wedding, the rabbi has usually held several counseling sessions with the couple, individually and together. The focus in premarital counseling by most rabbis is on marriage as a covenant to which both the man and woman make commitment. Many rabbis encourage the couple to return for a postnuptial counseling session six months to a year after the wedding.

Traditionally, the couple also is called to the pulpit and blessed at a Sabbath service preceding their wedding. Since home, family, and community are considered the foundations of Jewish life, the wedding is a sacred occasion, in which the spiritual dimensions of the relationship between husband and wife, and their relationship to God, are emphasized and are shared with the congregation.

Bibliography. M. Bial, *Liberal Judaism at Home* rev. ed. (1971). S. Maslin, *Gates of Mitzvah* (1979).

R. M. FALK

JEWISH HOLY DAYS AND FESTIVALS; MARRIAGE AND MARITAL CARE (Jewish Perspective); RITUAL AND PASTORAL CARE; WORSHIP AND CELEBRATION.

WESLEY, JOHN (1703–91). Anglican priest and founder of Methodism. Wesley's chief contribution to the tradition of pastoral care was his innovative use of small groups for purposes of spiritual formation. After establishing his first United Society in London in 1739, Wesley divided each society into classes of about twelve persons, led by a layperson who was to assist them in fulfilling their expressed intention to do good, refrain from harm, and evidence their desire for salvation. He also created smaller "bands," in which members were encouraged to assist and confide in one another. Wesley assigned the leadership of both the classes and the bands to ordinary members of the societies, but carefully regulated their activities through regular supervision and detailed rules.

The classes became the instruments of further Christian care when Wesley began to designate a set number of "visitors" from each class, who were to assume responsibility for visiting the sick two or three days each week, to care for their spiritual and temporal needs. Wesley's further innovation was his preoccupation with health and healing within his movement, which led him to establish medical dispensaries in English cities and to train himself as an amateur physician to meet the medical needs of the poor.

His classes, reflecting both pietistic and earlier Anglican traditions, remained the central setting for pastoral care in Methodism until the mid-nineteenth century.

E. B. HOLIFIELD

METHODIST PASTORAL CARE. *See also* PASTORAL CARE (History, Traditions, and Definitions); EVANGELICAL PASTORAL CARE; PIETISM AND PASTORAL CARE.

WEST INDIAN TRADITIONAL RELIGION, PASTORAL CARE IN. The West Indian *soul* personality is complex because it is drawn from many cultures and is still in the process of formation. The dilemma might best be illustrated by a simple grammatical question. Do we write the West Indies *is* or the West Indies *are*? And it is this dilemma which creates a difficulty for pastoral care.

The diversity of cultures is basically drawn from the residual Amerindian bases, the overlay of Western Europeanism (Christianity) in its several forms (Spanish, French, English, Danish, and Dutch), later the overlay of African traditional religions, and in more recent times the newer Christian sects from the U.S.

This religious potpourri also includes Hinduism and Islam in the larger English-speaking Caribbean area. At times of crisis there are many human and religio-cultural responses within the larger traditionally orthodox Christian environment.

Traditional (folk) religion is based upon West African sources. Voodoo (Haiti), obeah (Jamaica), shango (Trinidad), and santeria (Cuba) each display the dual role of remedy for societal dysfunction, as well as personal healing and comfort in times of distress. All derive their strength from a belief in a total unity of all things (not to be confused with pantheism) in which all the world is invested with a spiritual life-force. This invisible power (life-force) might be used for good or for evil since by its very nature it is neutral. This bifocal nature may be seen in the practice of obeah and Myal in the Jamaican context, in which it might be interpreted in traditional Western European terminology as black and white magic. In fact, each is a tapping of the life-force for specific purposes. So that obeah is used in healing, to seek certain benefits, and also to produce death, while Myal tends wholly toward healing and counteracts the nonbeneficial elements in obeah. The rituals resemble each other so that it is only the trained eye which can discern the differences (Morrish, 1982).

It has recently been suggested that myalism formed an alliance with orthodox Christianity, particularly the Baptists, during the 1840s, and elements of African traditional religion are very much a part of pastoral care even within the mass-orientated Caribbean church membership (Schuler, *Alas, Alas, Kongo,* 1980). Examples of this might be seen in the development of revivalism, Pocomania, and even Rastafarianism at the extreme end of the spectrum (Barrett, 1976). Revivalism (Zion Revival, 1861) took its rise from the Moravian revival in 1860 and has a distinct Christian orientation, while Pocomania (whose origins are more deeply Africa-rooted) uses Christian rituals such as hymns and certain prayers. Obeah and myal rely upon an expert knowledge of the use of herbal medicine, and are not so deeply rooted in Christian faith.

Shango (Trinidad) has definite affinities with Yoruba religious practices. In *Religious Cults in the Caribbean* G. E. Simpson has documented and commented on its belief system and its influence. For the devotees it serves the same need as xango (Brazil) in its syncretistic tendencies blending elements of Yoruba traditional religion with Roman Catholicism and the Baptist faith, as it was derived from the Great Awakening in the U.S. and brought to Trinidad by the freed slaves. Like obeah and myal it serves both a psychological and social function but is more elaborate in its organization. Its emphasis upon spirit possession and healing resembles the characteristics of revivalism.

The *Spiritual Baptists* are perhaps closest to other Afro-Christian groups. They bear similarities to the black churches of the U.S. They maintain (1) the inerrancy of the Bible, (2) the Virgin Birth, (3) the supernatural atonement, (4) the physical resurrection, and (5) the reality of the miracles of Jesus. At the same time symbolic writing, as may be seen in voodoo, is present. The baptismal ceremony is a departure from the power of Satan and the defeat of the powers of evil by the dance and other baptismal preparations.

West Indian traditional religion deals with the elemental events of life, the rites of passage. Birth is celebrated by blessings, baptisms, namings, and horoscopes depending on the island culture. Marriage, puberty, and menopause each finds its place in religious celebration. Sometimes the influences are those of Western Christianity in its several forms. At other times they are African or Indian oriented and in some instances bear an Islamic stamp as, for example, the Jordanites of Guyana. Death is celebrated also in all these forms, as the markings on the shrines or tombs of the departed in each territory illustrate. The ceremonies surrounding death, the mourning, the anointing, the wake, the "nine night", the forty-day, the memorial service, the direction of the funeral procession, and the libations each have a part to play.

Soul care then is not an individualistic exercise in the first place but the healing, reorganization, and arranging of a new society. It is wholistic in its approach and method. At the same time, chosen individuals play important roles, and in them both the corporate and individual are integrated. Thus the priest, the politician (recently), and the doctor complement each other in the healing of the society. And in this regard the sex, social status, and background of the individual are not of greatest significance. Rather it is if they can tap the life-force, the energy that controls life and death. And this is true both for West Indian (folk) traditional religion and for the more Orthodox Christian Churches.

Bibliography. L. E. Barrett, *The Sun and Drum: African Roots in Jamaican Folk Tradition* (1976). I. Morrish, *Obeah, Christ, and Rastaman: Jamaica and Its Religion* (1982). G. E. Simpson, *Religious Cults in the Carribean* (1970). M. Schuler, *"Alas, Alas Kongo"* (1980). "Religion and Spiritism," *Caribbean Quarterly,* 24 (1978), 3–4.

H. O. RUSSELL

CULTURAL ANTHROPOLOGY; SHAMAN; SOCIOLOGY OF RELIGIOUS AND PASTORAL CARE; SOCIOLOGY OF RELIGION. *Compare* AFRICAN *or* NATIVE AMERICAN TRADITIONAL RELIGION; BLACK AMERICAN PASTORAL CARE; RELIGION; SOUL (Black Church).

WESTBERG, GRANGER (1893–1976). A Lutheran clergyman noted for his contributions to religion and health and to theological education. Westberg was ordained on a call to Bloomington, Illinois, in 1939, and after five years became the first full-time chaplain at Augustana Lutheran Hospital in Chicago. Eight years later he went to Billings Hospital, University of Chicago, as chaplain. In 1956 he was appointed Associate Professor of Religion and Health with a joint position in the Divinity School and the Medical School of the University of Chicago. In 1964 he became dean of the Institute of Religion at the Texas Medical Center in Houston, and three years later was appointed professor of practical theology at Hamma School of Theology of Wittenberg University, Springfield, Ohio. As professor of medicine and religion in the Department of Preventive Medicine and Community of the University of Illinois College of Medicine at Chicago, he became founder and director of Wholistic Health Centers in 1972, where he remained until his retirement in 1981.

The main activity of Wholistic Health Centers has been coordinating the establishment of centers where a family physician, nurse, and pastoral counselor work together on a full-time basis as a health team. The emphasis is on prevention and first-order intervention in the context of honoring the patient as an active member of the health team. Through this model of health ministry, Westberg challenged the tendency in modern medical specialization to neglect the relation of the dynamics of the whole person to the onset and progress of the disease process. His major contribution to pastoral care lies clearly in his creative experimentation with interdisciplinary cooperation between religious and health professions. Dr. Westberg is the author of many articles and several books, the most popular being *Good Grief,* which provides guidance through the grief process.

Bibliography. G. E. Westberg, *Community Psychiatry and the Clergyman* (1966); *Good Grief* (1962); *Minister and Doctor Meet* (1961); *Premarital Counseling: A Manual for Ministers* (1958). G. E. Westberg, ed., *Theological Roots of Wholistic Health Care* (1979). N. L. Tubesing, *Whole Person Health Care: Philosophical Assumptions* (1977); *Wholistic Health Care: The Process of Engagement* (1976).

R. L. UNDERWOOD

PASTORAL CARE MOVEMENT; WHOLISTIC HEALTH CARE.

WESTERN EUROPEAN PASTORAL CARE MOVEMENT. The pastoral care and counseling movement in Western Europe has developed through several discernible stages.

1. Background and Early Years. At the beginning of the 1950s, as theological students and pastors from Western Europe traveled to the U.S. in order to participate in courses which were part of a program for clinical pastoral training, the situation of pastoral care in their home countries was as follows:

In the *Lutheran churches,* pastoral care was understood as the proclamation of God's Word transmitted "in the form of a dialogue from man to man through direct confrontation" (H. Asmussen, 1937). In the *Reformed tradition,* Karl Barth's identification of law and gospel was introduced into pastoral care, and therefore the only legitimate theological basis for pastoral care was thought to be ecclesiastical discipline. Pastoral care was understood as a kind of *"Rückfrage"* (reverberated questioning) in which the human individual is questioned. Thus there should be no pastoral care without admonishing, even scolding, and punishing (Thurneysen, 1962). For pastoral care in a *pietistic* manner, religious awakening and conversion were the decisive catchwords, for in pastoral care a struggle for salvation of the individual takes place, shaking him or her up and bringing the person at all costs and with great seriousness to the point of decision.

In the middle of the nineteenth century, the German pastor Johann Christoph Blumhardt requested that pastoral care should also have a healing effect. Based in a "medical-priestly attitude," the command "Heal the sick" should be taken seriously again, as it was partially realized in the St. Luke's Order, especially in England and Scandinavia. From then on Blumhardt's plea was never completely ignored. Dietrich Bonhoeffer also took this course when he supplemented the concept of pastoral care as proclamation by emphasizing the service of listening (*Dienst des Zuhörens*).

This summary partly explains why for such a long time a pastoral counseling movement did not develop in Europe as it did in the U.S. During the 1920s in Berlin, however, a lively group called "Doctor and Pastoral Counselor" had been formed, and the first steps towards a pastoral psychology were developed and discussed with the old Psychoanalytical Institute. The Nazi regime put an end to this, however, and efforts toward developing a pastoral psychology became solely the matter of individual scholars.

2. The Postwar Years. Beginning in 1944 Gute Bergsten, in collaboration with psychiatrists and psychologists, directed the "Institute for Spiritual Counsel and Psychological Treatment" of the St. Luke's Foundation in Stockholm. He wrote about his development as being the way from *"Medica Clerica"* to pastoral psychology. In 1953, Willibald Demal in Vienna published a practical pastoral psychology as a science of the soul for minister and educators. These were, however, singular efforts which had little influence on the theological discussion of pastoral care or the pastoral practice of clergy.

This was altered when approximately ten years after the end of the war, a sufficient number of theologians, having been trained in the U.S., set out to apply to the European situation what they had learned in the CPE movement. The first training centers were opened in the Netherlands, and this led to a pilgrimage of German and Scandinavian pastors to Holland for clinical training in addition to those who had been trained in the U.S.

In West Germany, at the end of the 1950s, the pervasive attitude was still such that pastoral psychologists could seldom make use of the clinical training which they had acquired either in congregations or hospitals. The sixties, therefore, were a kind of incubation period for the pastoral counseling movement. Not a few of those who had enjoyed an initial training period in the U.S. used the time of "latency" to expand their competence through degrees in psychology or to complete psychoanalytical training.

A significant setback for the European pastoral counseling movement was the decision of the German Society for Depth Psychology and Psychotherapy not to admit any more theologians for psychoanalytical training. This led to the foundation of the German Society for Pastoral Psychology in 1972, which was constituted from the beginning as a society combining three sections: depth psychology, CPE, and group dynamics—social psychology. The society's task was to develop comparative standards of knowledge and capacities which were organized according to the following principles: (1) self-experience (analysis or group experience), (2) theoretical learning, and (3) practical work under supervision. A fourth section called "Behavioral and Communication Psychology" was added later.

3. The Seventies and Eighties. The decisive breakthrough toward a real clinical pastoral movement occurred in the 1970s. More and more qualified pastoral psychologists returned from the U.S. and strived for further qualification as supervisors. Training centers in West Germany, Scandinavia, and Switzerland were opened. Gradually church leadership made available funds and personnel for qualified initial and continued training.

In 1971 at Bad Segeberg a pastoral psychological seminar was started and has continued through subsequent years. At the beginning there were participants from West Germany, Scandinavia, and Finland. Soon the seminar also included participants from the Netherlands, the United Kingdom, East Germany, and Poland.

A first meeting of West Germans and Americans in Arnoldshain in 1971 still reflected the gratitude of the Europeans for the stimulation and inspiration that they had received from the U.S. Four years later at Ruschlikon in Switzerland it was possible to speak of a genuinely international exchange of experiences. The Americans, however, were still unsure as to whether the training standards of the Europeans were comparable to those in the U.S. In 1977 at Eisenach (East Germany) there was for the first time a reciprocal learning experience between pastoral counseling movements in the Western and Eastern worlds. The first large international conference in 1979 at Edinburgh made evident the opportunities of an equal partnership and widened the scope to include Africa, Asia, and Latin America. The special atmosphere of the 1981 conference at Lublin in Poland finally gave many participants the impression that the international pastoral psychological movement could gradually overcome the barriers of limitation due to its individualistic disposition by branching out into the political area and worldwide activities.

For the European clinical pastoral movement the 1970s will remain the "golden" age. The rapidity of its spreading has, slowed down noticeably in the 1980s. An unfavorable economic situation and budget cuts have resulted in stagnation in many areas. A theological counter-drift causes a resisting wind. In many cases this is understood as a possibility for deepening and developing an independent identity, even where expansion at the same rate is no longer possible.

Bibliography. H. Asmussen, *Die Seelsorge* (1937). G. Bergsten, *Pastoral Psychology* (1951). D. Bonhoeffer, *Life Together* (1965). R. Burck, "Begleitende Seelsorge in East and West Germany," *J. of Pastoral Care*, 37 (1983), 136–43. W. Demal, *Practische Pastoral-psychologie* (1953). O. Haendler, *Die Predigt* (1942). B. Martin, *Die Heilung der Kranken als Dienst der Kirche* (1955). O. Pfister, *Christianity and Fear* (1948). H. C. Piper, *Kommunizieren lernen in Seelsorge und Predigt* (1981). J. Scharfenberg, "The Babylonic Captivity of Pastoral Theology," *J. of Pastoral Care*, 8 (1954), 125–34. E. Thurneysen, *A Theology of Pastoral Care* (1962).

J. SCHARFENBERG

INTERNATIONAL PASTORAL CARE MOVEMENT; PASTORAL CARE MOVEMENT. *See also* PASTORAL THEOLOGY, PROTESTANT. *Compare* BRITISH *or* EASTERN EUROPEAN PASTORAL CARE MOVEMENT.

WHINING. *See* BEHAVIORAL DISORDERS OF CHILDHOOD.

WHITE, ELLEN H. (1827–1915). Seventh-Day Adventist prophetess and co-founder. Born in Maine, Ellen Harmon suffered a traumatic injury at about age nine that ended her formal schooling and left her a semi-invalid. Raised a Methodist, in 1840 she joined the Millerites, who expected the Second Coming of Christ in 1844. Following the "Great Disappointment" when Christ did not return, she experienced the first of many trance-like "visions," during which she claimed to receive divine illumination. In 1846 she married James White, with whom, in the 1860s, she organized the Seventh-Day Adventist Church. Although she never assumed formal leadership of the organization, she wielded enormous theological and administrative influence, especially after the death of her husband in 1881. Her voluminous publications include thirty-seven volumes of *Testimonies for the Church* (1855–1909), in which she relayed doctrinal and behavioral counsel, often of a personal nature, which she had received in visions. The work *Steps to Christ* had a circulation of five million copies and was translated into eighty-five languages.

Bibliography. For a nonapologetical interpretation that focuses on her health-related activities, see R. L. Numbers, *Prophetess of Health: A Study of Ellen H. White* (1976).

R. L. NUMBERS

SECTARIAN PASTORAL CARE; WOMEN IN PASTORAL MINISTRIES, HISTORY OF.

WHOLENESS. *See* HEALTH AND ILLNESS; HEALING; WHOLISTIC HEALTH CARE.

WHOLISTIC HEALTH CARE. An interdisciplinary approach to health care in which patients play an active part in their own health planning. The emphasis is as much on health as on treating illness and involves treating the whole person physically, emotionally, and spiritually.

There are four primary models of wholistic health care. All provide for some adjunct to regular medical practice. One typically involves a physician, nurse, and pastoral counselor operating as a team out of a local church. Another model has its origin in CPE programs and departments of pastoral care. These are clinic-oriented practices reflecting a more traditional health care delivery system, and may involve such professionals as psychologists, social workers, biofeedback technicians, psychiatrists, nurse-practitioners as well as family practice physicians, internists, and pastoral counselors. Usually, after an initial screening by one or more of the professional groups, one professional will work with the patient.

A third model operates in free-standing clinics where a variety of professionals work cooperatively with a referral and consultation system. Where patients are treated in common, there often is a multidisciplinary team that consults on treatment plan and interventions. Frequently, but not always, the patient participates in the staffing or case conference. A fourth model involves a pastoral counseling practice operating in a church setting with a physician as a consultant, rather than as a joint practitioner.

Innovative techniques involved in wholistic health care include pain control through meditation, sensory awareness, autogenics, exercise, relaxation and biofeedback, fighting cancer and other chronic ailments through visualization, goal setting, and building emotional support systems. Self-healing through dream interpretation, keeping journals, and spiritual discipline are also practiced. Nutrition, physical fitness, handling stress, and personal transformation also play an important part in wholistic health care.

Wholistic health care treatments are often related to Jungian therapy techniques. Through dream analysis and journal keeping patients are encouraged to see how their illnesses function consciously and unconsciously, and how they can serve secondary functions like getting attention or atoning for guilt. Consequently, patients may be able to make personal or lifestyle changes that can effect the course of their illness.

Lifestyle, or pace, is another concern of wholistic care. People are taught how to control what they do—from choosing how fast they go to the setting of personal goals. They are also taught how to control their environment through the way they relate to other people, for example, by learning to say no or by asserting their feelings. They also learn to change attitudes by relabeling events more positively, enjoying themselves by using humor, and letting go of the unnecessary.

Wholistic health care is based on a very positive attitude, which asserts that people can make a difference in their health or illness. The movement is criticized, however, for a tendency to equate illness with sin and health with salvation, for making people feel guilty for causing their illness, and for putting too much emphasis on individualism and "feeling good." Most institutions that provide wholistic health care are sensitive to these criticisms and try to provide a balanced approach within the standards for good medical and religious practice.

J. L. FLORELL

HEALTH AND ILLNESS; MENTAL HEALTH AND ILLNESS; RELIGION AND HEALTH; SALVATION, HEALING AND HEALTH. *See also* ANALYTICAL (JUNGIAN) PSYCHOLOGY (Therapeutic Method and Research); LUTHERAN PASTORAL CARE.

WICKES, FRANCES. *See* NEW YORK PSYCHOLOGY GROUP.

WIDE RANGE ACHIEVEMENT TEST. *See* EVALUATION AND DIAGNOSIS, PSYCHOLOGICAL.

WIDOWS/WIDOWERS. Persons who have lost a marital partner through death and have not remarried. The nature of the marital relationship and the circumstances of the death influence the kind of care the remaining partner may need, but there are common tasks which must be faced. These tasks are similar to those which confront persons who have lost a partner through separation or divorce. They include: grieving the loss, coping with life without the partner, rebuilding a self-image and sources of self-esteem, and learning to love again in spite of the pain of loss and the difficulties of living alone. Sociocultural trends in the U.S. make the caring resources of pastor and congregation increasingly important. A brief description of these trends and the problems which confront the remaining partner will suggest some of the resources which are needed for pastoral care.

1. The Sociocultural Context of Widowhood. Patterns of marriage and family life which are increasingly common in this country both increase the difficulty of the problems produced by the loss of a mate and reduce the available resources for assistance. In our society, couples are usually expected to center their social life and to find their primary emotional satisfactions in their relationship with each other. That relationship is also expected to be their chief resource for coping with the pressure of life. The loss of a partner, then, means disorganization of social life, loss of major source of emotional satisfaction, and loss of a primary resource for coping with life. If the couple has children, their relationship is expected to be the emotional foundation of the family, and their children are dependent on them for protection and support. The loss of one of the marital partners means a serious disruption of the emotional life of each family member and of the coping patterns which have become part of the family system. Friends, neighbors, and members of the extended family may be of help but often cannot be consistently available for the long-term

individual and family tasks of grieving and coping with the loss. The remaining partner must grieve and cope more or less alone, unless new resources can be found in congregation and community.

From another perspective, our society places a high value on freedom and independence, and being single again may be experienced as an opportunity for more independent living. For some, who have found marriage to be a burden or "trap," release from the marriage bond may be welcomed even though real grief is felt. The price of independence, however, is the development of new levels of competence, and for some, especially older persons, the necessary competence may be difficult to achieve.

2. Problems Following the Loss of a Partner. *a. Physical.* A traumatic loss may produce a variety of physical symptoms evidenced in difficulties in breathing, eating, sleeping, relaxing, concentrating, etc. Normally these symptoms disappear in time, but the continued stress of having to cope with problems which once could be shared may contribute to ongoing physical problems. As the years go by, symptoms associated with living alone in social isolation may develop, such as malnutrition or obesity, insomnia, hypertension, loss of muscle tone, and general physical deterioration.

b. Psychological. Unresolved grief and the stress of living alone may lead to a variety of psychological as well as physical problems. Moreover, the loss of the couple identity confronts the remaining partner with the task of reworking his or her identity, both as an individual and as a social being. This is a particular problem for the woman who has never had a real identity of her own and has defined her place in life in terms of her relationship with her mate. A man may discover how dependent he has been on his wife to care for his food and clothing and his social needs. The task of developing new patterns of coping may be difficult for both men and women, particularly for persons who have strong dependency needs.

c. Social. The reorganization of social relationships around the identity of widow or widower may be a difficult task. The remaining partner may find that the couples with whom he or she was friendly in the past are no longer comfortable with the relationship. Withdrawal from social contacts can be a normal reaction to loss but becomes pathological if continued over time. The social isolation of many men and women living alone in our society is an increasing problem. The parent without a partner may also have social problems, finding little time or energy for social contacts because of the demands of work and family. More men than women remarry, and the incidence of remarriage for women decreases as they grow older. Men die younger, and across the country widows outnumber widowers about five to one. Deaths among widowers age 45 to 64 outnumber those of widows in the same age range almost three to one.

d. Familial. Both the presence and absence of family can lead to problems for the widowed. The responsibilities of supporting a family and being a single parent can be overwhelming. The absence of family may mean a pattern of lonely, isolated living, which can lead to physical, emotional, and spiritual deterioration. For older persons the isolation may be complicated by illness or physical handicaps and/or by low income, poor housing, unsafe environments, inadequate medical care, lack of transportation, etc.

e. Religious. The struggle to develop a new sense of self and to find new meaning and purpose for life has important spiritual dimensions. The losses and burdens of widowhood may lead to resentment and bitterness toward God and withdrawal from life. The religious task is to be able to accept and transcend the pain and burdens of loss and loneliness and to trust in values and relationships which cannot be lost. The task of loving, losing, and learning, through successful grieving, to love again is one of the basic lessons of religious life. Grief can be the pain that heals, and the meaning of love can become the infinite ground of continuing life and relationships in spite of the pain of particular losses.

3. **Resources for Pastoral Care.** *a. The pastoral relationship.* The pastor has the resources of his/her religious heritage to offer to the widowed, and with the decreasing presence of family, friends, and neighbors as a resource for sharing and coping with widowhood, the pastor is often the only person who can keep in touch with individuals and family through the various stages of the process of coming to terms with the loss. If the grieving and coping process does not go well, the pastor needs to know when and how to intervene. Rather than being the only "rescuer," the pastor needs to know how to help people make use of available resources; and if adequate resources do not exist, to take responsibility for helping to develop appropriate resources.

b. Caring networks. When the extended family is not available for assistance, the natural resources for caring and support are found in friends who are emotionally close to the family and its members. Pastors need to be able to identify such caring networks, support their efforts to assist the widow or widower and the children, to assess their effectiveness, and to supplement their efforts if necessary.

c. The extended family. The family has been the most important resource for mutual assistance, historically, and continues to be in many instances. The history of a particular family may interfere with the effectiveness of the assistance available, however, and the geographical dispersion of many families limits the help they can offer.

d. The congregation. The regular worship services, prayer groups, church school, and youth programs, men's and women's groups, and other congregational activities can be important resources. Members of the congregation and church groups can offer various kinds of support during the critical period following a death. For the long-term tasks a group of carefully selected, trained, and supervised lay ministers of pastoral care may need to be developed, particularly to assist those who cannot participate regularly in church activities.

e. Support groups. The sociocultural situation has led to the development of a variety of support groups for the widowed. The availability of such groups varies in different parts of the country, and they often do not exist in rural areas, but the pastor needs to know about such groups and the possibility of developing similar resources in his or her area. Parents Without Partners, NAIM groups for Roman Catholics, Widow-to-Widow programs, groups for single parents and "women in transition," and grief therapy groups are illustrations of the kinds of groups which have been developed. Also important are educational and supportive resources for persons who need to enter or reenter the work force or need some kind of vocational training.

Bibliography. L. Cain, *Widow* (1974). C. S. Lewis, *A Grief Observed* (1984). H. Lopata, *Women as Widows* (1979); "The Widowed Family Member," in N. Datan and N. Lohman, eds., *Transitions of Aging* (1980). J. Phipps, *Death's Single Privacy* (1974). L. Pincus, *Death and the Family* (1981). P. Silverman, *Helping Women Cope with Grief* (1981). P. Silverman *et al.*, *Helping Each Other in Widowhood* (1974). R. Weiss, *Marital Separation* (1975).

H. L. JERNIGAN

COMFORT/SUSTAINING; GRIEF AND LOSS; LONELINESS AND ISOLATION; SINGLE PERSONS.

WIEMAN, HENRY NELSON (1884–1975). American philosopher and psychologist of religion. Wieman helped to define and popularize a theological conception of "adjustment" that had considerable influence among pastoral theologians in America during the 1930s. As a professor at the Divinity School of the University of Chicago, he not only coauthored (with Regina Westcott-Wieman) a *Normative Psychology of Religion* (1935), but also insisted that the task of the theologian was to discover the features in the universe that would promote the maximal fulfillment for persons who adjusted themselves properly to those features. For Wieman, God was the power and process within the world, which, by promoting value, unity, and mutuality, produced the greatest good and thus deserved the highest devotion. He viewed the psychology of religion as an instrument in the quest for appropriate adjustment to God.

E. B. HOLIFIELD

EMPIRICAL THEOLOGY AND PASTORAL CARE.

WIFE. *See* MARRIAGE; WOMEN, PASTORAL CARE OF.

WIFE, PASTOR'S. The female person married to a male clergyman who serves a parish as its pastor.

A variety of models may be identified for a pastor's wife. Sweet (1983) lists models which he found in his study of pastor's wives from the sixteenth to the nineteenth century: the companion, the sacrificer, the assistant, and the partner. Buckingham (1981) lists four identities for pastors' wives in her table of contents: woman, wife, mother, minister.

As the role of pastor's wife has evolved, new styles of response to the role have produced additional models. The "partner" model of pastor's wife gives her a position of honor and prestige equal with the pastor as they share the symbols of leadership. The "social chair" model is quite close to the "partner," except that her identity is separate in the social duties she directs as pastor's wife. The "servant-of-ministry" model has most of the elements of the traditional role in it. The pastor's wife pours out her life in the duties of the church and the needs of her husband with no claims for the rights of her own personhood.

The "parallel" model is adopted by women who have their own careers apart from the marriage and the church but join in the activities of the church much as other employed women of the church. The "isolated" model is a style practiced by pastors' wives who see themselves as separate and distinct from their husband's vocation. They pursue careers or interests of their own and may not involve themselves at all in the life of the church, or their involvement may be casual with complete detachment from the work of the minister.

For some pastors' wives, the boundary between their persons and their roles as wives of pastors is so blurred the two become identical. The "partner" and the "servant-of-ministry" models exhibit such an absence of boundary between the person and the role. The "social chair" model may or may not be one of enmeshed boundary. The "parallel" and the "isolated" models manifest a separate boundary for the wife. The "isolated" model exhibits almost a closed boundary from the role of the pastor.

Practitioners of these various models will manage quite differently the relevant issues for pastors' wives. Two major clusters of issues confront the pastor's wife. One cluster focuses on the wife as a person and on the management of her needs as well as those of the family. The pastor's wife must make choices about whether to have personal friends within the membership of the congregation or to have friends outside the congregation, if at all. Closely related is the issue of the need for confidants in whom the pastor's wife can develop an emotional support network. The pastor's wife has a need to be loved and respected for herself alone, but many report this missing. Response to criticism of herself or her husband forces mostly unsatisfactory options for wives of pastors. The pastor's wife can often ill afford to fight for herself or defend her husband. The encroachment of church responsibilities into the pastor's time and energy so as to deprive the family is a difficult issue. Financial and other limitations also invade the domestic well-being of the pastor's wife and family.

The other cluster of issues centers about the pastor's wife's relationship to the church and her husband's ministry. Because pastors occupy leadership roles, their wives must make decisions about their public image — whether they will concern themselves with it and how or if they will manage it. Related to this issue is their response to requests (or demands) from the church or the community for service or leadership. Thus, the issue of acceptable social participation is always before them. The fishbowl syndrome for the pastor's wife is well established. Likewise, the pastor's wife must decide how much and what kind of entertaining is required or desired. For those pastors' wives who embrace a "parallel" or an "isolated" model, the issue of acceptable vocational or social activist participation must be evaluated. Mention must also be made of the issue of how the pastor's wife handles information about persons and the church that naturally flows through the pastor's home and conversations. Each of these issues and others related to the pastor's role could be enlarged.

Although the list of issues is formidable, many pastors' wives report the relish of their role. They find immense satisfaction in what they deem to be their calling as clearly as do their husbands. Few other roles of society require as much personal maturity and internal security as does the role of pastor's wife.

Few studies have been done on the role. Denton's Columbia University study is probably the most comprehensive recent study. Denton found five categories of literature available on the minister's wife: (1) self-help works, (2) autobiography, (3) biography, (4) fiction, and (5) general works. Sweet has produced a historical study of the evolution of the role. The women's liberation movement has had its impact on the pastor's wife, but no definitive study of that phenomena has been done to date.

Bibliography. M. Buckingham, ed., *Help, I'm A Pastor's Wife* (1981). B. J. Coble, *The Private Life of the Minister's Wife* (1981). W. Denton, *The Role of the Minister's Wife* (1962). M. L. Haines, *This Ministry We Share* (1986). D. Longberg, *Counsel for Pastor's Wives* (1988). J. H. Morgan and L. B. Morgan, *Wives of Priests* (1980). B. J. Niswander, "Clergy Wives of the New Generation," *Pastoral Psychology*, 30:3 (1982), 160–69. F. Nordland, *The Unprivate Life of a Pastor's Wife* (1972). K. Norheim, *Mrs. Preacher* (1985). T. A. Peck, ed., *The Minister's Mate* (1986). D. H. Pentecost, *The Pastor's Wife and the Church* (1964). C. Ross, *Who Is The Minister's Wife?* (1980). D. Sinclair, *The Pastor's Wife Today* (1980). L. Sweet, *The Minister's Wife* (1983). R. White, *What Every Pastor's Wife Should Know* (1986).

E. WHITE

MARRIAGE AND FAMILY LIFE, PASTOR'S. *Compare* CLERGY COUPLES; HUSBAND, PASTOR'S.

WILL/WILLING. Will is commonly defined as that power or capacity of the person which makes choices and executes purposeful actions. A more comprehensive, fundamental, and clinically helpful definition, however, would understand will as the energy of human being and the enactment of this energy.

Will is distinguished from personal desire, emotion, and motivation. It names a power basic for personal affections, but not identical with those affections. In Platonic thought, for example, will may be thought of as the desire of the soul, which is distinguished from the desires of individuals in their day-to-day lives. By virtue of understanding will as human energy we may distinguish between issues that have to do with the will to be and those concerning personal interests.

1. **The Nature of Human Will.** Does human will have a nature? How one answers this question will be significant for how one defines the goals of pastoral counseling and psychotherapy. If will is pure passion without any goal other than the expression of itself, the therapist will seek to allow the maximal expression of life-force within the existing circumstances. Which values a person lives out will be of secondary importance to the intensity of willing. If will is teleological, seeking, let us say, union with God or obedience to God, then knowledge of the telos and the conditions necessary for achieving the desired goal will have primary importance for psychotherapy. Therapy would then involve a profound, experiential education of human will. If the will has a nature, but that nature is hidden to human beings except in special revelation, then therapy's relation to the special revelation will be crucial. In the first instance — will as pure passion seeking its own expression — a therapeutic

situation would be one that frees the will from constraints on its expression. In the second instance, therapy would occur as the conditions develop in which the will discovers its forgotten or ignored direction.

2. Commitment. Does human will discover itself by means of its own energy? If it does, the therapist might attempt to encourage an intensification of will by encouraging commitment of any kind. Commitment limits and focuses will. It tends to intensify energy, to narrow human direction, and thereby to increase the power of will. As it comes to expression with greater energy, the self-developing will would find greater or less satisfaction in the objects of its commitment. The dissatisfied will would look for its satisfaction in relation to something more appropriate for its emerging discrimination. If, for example, the human will is created for divine filiation, it would be profoundly unhappy or, as Augustine says, restless until it is free from commitments to finite things and finds its suitable relation with God. Or if the will is without divine moorings, it would come to reject those commitments that restrict its energy, and it would seek out those relations in which it finds its life increased or maximally expressed.

3. Resentment. Resentment is one term that can name oppressed willing. Oppressed human will can turn against itself and express its energy as a negative force that intends either weakness or destruction. It might, for example, be hostile to lively energy in others, or it might be hostile to its own oppressed life. In the first instance a person would oppose people who had freer and more energetic lives. Such opposition could take the form of oppressive rules or subtle and destructive undercutting of life-giving attitudes and relationships. In the second, it would cause its own sickness and death. Forms of resentment are expressions of suppressed will in which its life-affirming power has been distorted.

4. Willpower. People experience different degrees of willpower. In everyday language we speak of willpower as an individual's ability to set and hold autonomous directions. A person who does not and cannot live out the values that he or she affirms is "weak." One might, for example, want to stop drinking or to show his or her spouse loving-kindness and be unable to carry out those projects. Or one might want to live with dedication and interest, but experience boredom and apathy. Willpower in the sense of firm determination in these kinds of situations is often not possible, and we cannot understand the issue adequately if we interpret it as a person's lack of willpower in the everyday sense of the word.

When one thinks, on the other hand, of willpower as human energy and not solely as personal decisiveness, one can approach the issue in terms of basic conflicts that are not within an individual's control. Human being appears to seek life and self-fulfillment unless the very energy of life is stifled or oppressed. What is the meaning of a person's involvement in a destructive addiction or a person's inability to express love and kindness? Perhaps the person has not experienced deep appreciation for his or her life, the freedom of nonjudgmental love, or life-affirming discipline in a context of nurturance. In such cases, the power of will has grown in a context of rejection or fear. One has come to be, yet with a nonvoluntary suspicion of the value or importance of one's own being.

The power of life-affirmation is consequently experienced as suspect. This suggests that the therapist's task is to create conditions in which the will as the power of human life may will itself to be. Strength of will as life-affirmation would be a necessary condition for a person's discovering personally, in his or her life, the will's teleology or the will's drive to self-expression. Or if one is persuaded that self-sacrifice is the culmination of human health, the act of giving up personal intention in favor of a higher intentionality would be a life-affirming action which, to be truly self-giving, would need to be free of resentment against life itself. Otherwise self-sacrifice would be in the service of hostility to the very condition of self-sacrifice: a life-affirmation strong enough to yield positively before divine intention for human life.

These observations suggest that will, when taken as the life-energy of human being, finds both its positive development and its fulfillment in experiences of life-affirmation. These experiences constitute the conditions in which individuals are able to pursue their own interests with a will to be and a contingent sense for the value of being in all of its instances.

Bibliography. Aristotle, *On the Soul.* Augustine, *Confessions.* V. Frankl, *The Doctor and the Soul* (1955). S. Kierkegaard, *Either/Or* (1971). J. N. Lapsley, ed., *The Concept of Willing* (1967). F. Nietzsche, *Genealogy of Morals* (1956). R. May, *Love and Will* (1969). Plato, *Protagoras.* P. Tillich, *The Courage to Be* (1952).

C. E. SCOTT

CAUSALITY IN PSYCHOLOGY, FORMS OF; DECISION /INDECISION, PSYCHOLOGY OF; FAITH/BELIEF; FREEDOM; GRACE; PHILOSOPHY AND PSYCHOLOGY, WESTERN. *See also* ACTION / BEING RELATIONSHIP; COMMITMENT; HUMAN CONDITION / PREDICAMENT; PERSON (Philosophical Issues); RESISTANCE; SACRIFICIAL BEHAVIOR. *Compare* MOTIVATION; SELF-ACTUALIZATION /SELF-REALIZATION; SELF-TRANSCENDENCE.

WILL, DIVINE. *See* GOD'S WILL, ACCEPTANCE OF; GUIDANCE, DIVINE.

WILL POWER. *See* WILL / WILLING.

WILL THERAPY. A therapy usually associated with Otto Rank (1884–1939), which stresses the capacity to direct one's own actions.

Rank was a member of Freud's inner circle but severed his ties with Freud and psychoanalysis by stressing the role of consciousness and self-directedness in personality development. For Rank, the loss of blissful union with the mother in the birth experience, rather than Oedipal conflicts, is the primal source of anxiety and psychopathology. Thus the goal of therapy is to assist the client in accepting him or herself as a unique, separate individual capable of choosing to express his or her own emotionality and creativity.

Will, according to Rank, is a "positive guiding organization and integration of the self, which utilizes creativity as well as inhibits and controls the instinctual drives." As with Adlerian psychotherapy, the task of the therapist is to help clients assume responsibility for their own lives, creatively transcending heredity and environment. This is anxiety-producing, however, since it forces the individual to face up to the separation anxiety entailed in every creative act.

Bibliography. F. Karpf, *The Psychology and Psychotherapy of Otto Rank* (1953). O. Rank, *Will Therapy and Truth and Reality* (1972).

R. E. BUTMAN

PSYCHOTHERAPY. *See also* SEPARATION ANXIETY; WILL/ WILLING. *Compare* ASSERTIVENESS TRAINING AND THERAPY; EXISTENTIAL PSYCHOLOGY AND PSYCHOTHERAPY; INDIVIDUAL PSYCHOLOGY; PARADOXICAL INTENTION; RATIONAL-EMOTIVE PSYCHOTHERAPY; *Biography:* RANK.

WILL TO LIVE. The survival motive. In humans, it denotes the persistent desire, intent, and purpose to retain indefinitely the vitality and integrity of the person, including those unique characteristics which define the individual personality. Expressed negatively, the will to live is the motivation to avoid death or disintegration. The opposite of the will to live — a "death wish" is sometimes also posited as part of human nature — may be expressed in life-destructive behavior such as mental or physical illness, substance abuse, or suicide.

A will to live may be posited as a single fundamental instinct for survival — either of the individual or of the species — embedded in the structure of each living creature. In a liberal theological perspective, such an instinct may be relied on in pastoral care as a resource generating and directing adaptive and healthy behavior; and pastoral care may try to address the acquired impediments, such as anxiety or poverty, that impair its free exercise. Theologically, such pastoral care attempts to minimize the effects of fallenness or sin (of the individual and of the species) so as to liberate the life-enhancing forces inherent in Creation. From a more conservative theological standpoint, however, reliance on a natural, creaturely "will to live" may be viewed as an act of unfaith, an idolatrous turning to the creation instead of the Creator, and a failure to find one's true life not in oneself or one's inherent powers but in Christ alone through the power of the Holy Spirit (Gal. 2:20; Col. 3:3 – 4; cf. Mt. 16:25; Phil. 1:21).

Alternatively, the will to live may be regarded as the effect of one or more of various motives and attitudes, such as hope, a sense of meaning or purpose, a sense of personal identity, a sense of group identity and membership, a sense of support and commitment in a human relationship or with God. Such attitudes are presumably acquired and enhanced during a person's development and socialization, and it can be a purpose of pastoral care to strengthen a will to live by the nurture of hope, meaning, identity, relationship, etc. This might include tactics as diverse as expressing supportive personal acceptance to a depressed counselee, advising an aimless teenager or a middle-aged early retiree on locating vocational (re)training, encouraging a battered woman to esteem and protect herself in recourse to a shelter and legal aid, advising an oppressed group to a greater sense of their own identity and rights, preaching vigorously of God's covenant and faithfulness.

A will to live may become distorted by becoming exaggerated, as in pride or narcissism; by becoming dependent on too fallible and unreliable sources — idols, theologically speaking — such as vocational success or

idealized family relationships; or by becoming a pathological fear of death.

Bibliography. V. Frankl, *Man's Search for Meaning* (1963 [1959]). C. Solomon, *Counseling with the Mind of Christ* (1977). P. Tournier, *The Meaning of Persons* (1957). D. Tweedie, Jr., *Logotherapy and the Christian Faith* (1965 [1961]).

B. E. ATKINSON

HOPE AND DESPAIR; LIFE/ALIVENESS; MOTIVATION; WILL/ WILLING. *See also* DEATH AND DYING, PSYCHOSOCIAL THEORIES OF; DYING, PASTORAL CARE OF; EXISTENTIALISM; FREEDOM; HEALTH AND ILLNESS; LOGOTHERAPY; SICK, PASTORAL CARE OF; SURVIVOR PSYCHOLOGY. *Compare* GOD'S WILL, ACCEPTANCE OF; SADNESS AND DEPRESSION; SELF-ACTUALIZATION/SELF-REALIZATION; SELF-DESTRUCTIVE BEHAVIOR; SUICIDE.

WILLIAMS, DANIEL DAY (1910 – 73). A Congregational Church minister, author, lecturer, and a theology professor at Chicago Theological Seminary and the University of Chicago 1939 – 54, and Union Seminary (New York), 1954 – 73. Influenced by the process philosophy of Whitehead and Hartshorne, his early writing (*God's Grace and Man's Hope,* 1949) struck an intermediate position between the liberal and neoorthodox traditions. Later he produced what has been called the first systematic process theology (*The Spirit and the Forms of Love,* 1968). His continuing concern to interpret the Christian faith in relation to human thought and experience led to a particular emphasis on theology and psychotherapy (*The Minister and the Care of Souls,* 1961). A sensitive pastor and counselor, Williams's most significant contribution to pastoral counseling has been in the area of theological methodology. Specifically, he calls for a pastoral method that goes beyond a simple linguistic linking of theological and psychological categories to a deeper exploration of the metaphysical realities which inform them both.

C. M. MENDENHALL, III

PROCESS THEOLOGY AND PASTORAL CARE; THEOLOGY AND PSYCHOTHERAPY.

WISDOM AND PRACTICAL KNOWLEDGE IN PASTORAL CARE. *Wisdom* refers to a deep or insightful understanding of life achieved through experience; *practical knowledge* is knowledge about how to do things or how to proceed in certain situations, also achieved through experience. The two are closely related and fundamental to all care and counseling.

Wisdom is primarily existential, a quality of undeceived understanding and experience won through struggle and effort over time. It is therefore largely tacitonly partly reducible to speech and writing — and is marked by qualities of self-knowledge, maturity, perspective, judgment, a sense of the whole, and a capacity to find a certain dialectical wholeness in the contradictory aspects of experience (e.g., good and evil). In written form, wisdom from ancient times to the present is typically the literature of aphorism, proverb, parable, and story, in contrast to philosophy's rational and systematic synthesizing.

One must love and seek wisdom to become wise and must ground one's seeking in a fundamental reverence and faith: "The fear of the Lord is the beginning of wisdom" (Ps. 111:10; Prov. 9:10). To be wise is to understand life's ultimate or universal features through the particular symbols of a moral and religious culture. Theologically, however, wisdom is also a gift of God (Prov. 2:6), who is truly wise and who created the world through wisdom (Proverbs 8), though its deepest expression, paradoxically, is the cross, the very "wisdom of God" (I Cor. 1:18–31).

Practical knowledge, by contrast, knows how to do things, as distinguished from wisdom's understanding of the way things are. As used here, the term applies to the "knowing how" involved both in specific skills and in very complex activities with moral ends (Aristotle's *phronesis*), e.g., the "practical wisdom" involved in doing psychotherapy and in the most comprehensive human actions (living, suffering, or dying well). Though some practical knowledge can be reduced to writing (as in how- to books), in its complex moral forms like pastoral care it is mainly existential, gained through experience, experiment, and practice. Because practical knowledge entails a distinctive slant on the world, it both complements and merges with wisdom in its more complex forms; knowing how to live well, for example, or how to die, both reflects and embodies a certain wisdom about life.

Wisdom and practical knowledge are fundamental to pastoral care and counseling. Caring in any form (parental, pastoral, etc.) requires both how-to knowledge and insightful understanding. These come through practice and experience, and from living out, through varied experiences, the meanings and values of one's religious and psychological worldview. Moreover, while modern pastoral care and counseling have tended to define their primary goals therapeutically, as a kind of healing endeavor, their goals may also be regarded as sapiential, the seeking of wisdom and the development of morally and spiritually profound forms of practical knowing (e.g., how to love, how to suffer). Finally, pastoral theology, including its related psychological theories, can perhaps be best understood as a form of wisdom and practical knowledge rather than as formal theology, philosophy, or science.

Bibliography. D. Capps, *Life Cycle Theory and Pastoral Care* (1983), chap. 5. W. J. Harrelson, "Wisdom and Pastoral Theology," *Andover Newton Quarterly*, 7 (1966), 6–14.

R. J. HUNTER

PRACTICAL THEOLOGY; PRAGMATISM AND PASTORAL CARE; PRUDENCE (Moral Theology); TECHNIQUE AND SKILL IN PASTORAL CARE; THEORY AND PRAXIS; WISDOM TRADITION, BIBLICAL. *See also* EXPERIENCE; PHILOSOPHY AND PSYCHOLOGY, WESTERN.

WISDOM TRADITION, BIBLICAL. In biblical literature (especially in Proverbs, Job, Ecclesiastes, Sirach, and Wisdom of Solomon) wisdom is understood as the mode of God's creative activity by which the orderliness and dependability of the world is achieved. For human beings to possess wisdom is to have insight into this world order (both physical and moral) and so to be able to live successfully and harmoniously. Wisdom affirms the goodness of creation and believes that the good life, in a modest material sense, is not in essential conflict with the good life in the moral sense. Although much of

wisdom's advice initially appears strongly individualistic and success-oriented, wisdom always understands the individual to be a person in relationship, an individual in community. The essence of wisdom is to appreciate the relationship between one's acts and their consequences — for oneself and for others. An action which is truly good for oneself will also produce good for one's community. An action which is destructive for the community will also prove destructive for the individual who performs it, although the consequences may not be immediately apparent. Wisdom is thus essentially concerned with the creation of a good and moral society in the family, in the local community, and in the larger social structure.

Theologically, this moral concern is grounded in God's activity as Creator. Wisdom affirms that the created world is not morally neutral, but that it tends to reward good and punish evil. (This view is critically examined within the wisdom tradition in the books of Job and Ecclesiastes.) Human beings as moral agents do not instinctively know, however, how to act in harmony with God's created order. While wisdom does not have a doctrine of original sin, wisdom does view people as being innately selfish beings — greedy, hot-tempered, rash, violent, stubborn, arrogant, deceitful, lazy. The *fool*, a technical term in wisdom, is the person in whom these natural tendencies have hardened into established character traits. To become wise, to transcend one's obstinately self-regarding nature, is understood by wisdom to be a process of education. Such education is not behavioral training but the acquisition of new insight into the divinely ordained structure of the world, into its deep interrelatedness, into the relation between acts and their consequences, and into the fact that human beings are ultimately communal and not individual. The person whose character and behavior are shaped by this new insight is known in the wisdom literature as one who "fears the Lord."

Bibliography. W. Brueggemann, *In Man We Trust* (1972). D. Capps, *Biblical Approaches to Pastoral Counseling* (1981); *Life Cycle Theory and Pastoral Care* (1983), ch. 5. J. Crenshaw, *Old Testament Wisdom: An Introduction* (1981). G. von Rad, *Wisdom in Israel* (1972).

C. A. NEWSOM

OLD TESTAMENT AND APOCRYPHA, TRADITIONS AND THEOLOGY OF CARE IN. *Compare* CHARACTER ETHICS; EXPERIENCE; PRACTICAL THEOLOGY; PRUDENCE; RELIGION AND MORAL BEHAVIOR.

WISE, CARROLL A. (1903–85). Methodist chaplain, pastor, clinical educator, and pastoral theologian. As one of the theological leaders of the American pastoral care movement, Wise explored the function of religious symbols for the integration of personality and developed an interpretation of pastoral care as the art of communicating the inner meaning of the gospel to persons at the point of their need through relationships in which deep feelings could find expression and acceptance.

Such a conception of pastoral care led Wise to adopt the methods of client-centered counseling proposed by the therapist Carl Rogers. He thought that communication in counseling occurred more through the pastor's acceptance and understanding of the parishioner than through any efforts at verbal reassurance. In his *Pastoral Counseling: Its Theory and Practice* (1951) and *The Meaning of Pastoral Care* (1966) he argued that the condition for success in pastoral counseling was the quality of the relationship between the pastor and the person in need, and he therefore urged that pastors consider their "general pastoral relationships" as the setting within which effective counseling could take place. Wise developed his views partly through his work as a counselor for the YMCA, through a four-year appointment as the counseling minister of the Hennepin Avenue Methodist Church in Minneapolis and through his teaching as professor of pastoral psychology and counseling at Garrett Biblical Institute.

Having received clinical pastoral training under Anton Boisen at Worcester State Hospital, Wise became Boisen's successor in 1931 as chaplain and clinical training supervisor at that institution. He worked within the Council for Clinical Training and defended its use of mental hospitals for purposes of clinical training. He also supported the psychodynamic orientation that characterized the work of the council. He later became the president of the council and a supporter of plans for its merger with the Institute for Pastoral Care. Thus he contributed to the formation of the Association of Clinical Pastoral Education in 1967. He also supported the creation of an American Association of Pastoral Counselors in 1963.

The publication of his *Religion in Illness and Health* (1942) stimulated interest in the therapeutic functions of religion. Impressed by the work of Helen Flanders Dunbar and Walter B. Cannon in psychosomatic medicine, Wise explored the function of religious symbolism in the understanding of illness and the promotion of health. He believed that an appropriate religious worldview would lead toward the integration and growth, and hence the health, of the personality. He had an interest, as well, in the unhealthy use of religious symbols as means of self-deception and concealment. The book represented the growing acceptance of psychodynamic theories among Protestant pastoral writers.

Wise had studied theology at Boston University, and his work represented an expansion and modification of theological personalism. Arguing that the gospel was revealed through a person and could be communicated only through personal relationship, Wise was critical of any moralism or intellectualism that imposed static categories on dynamic relationships. He urged pastoral counselors to value the person rather than attempt to change the person's values.

Wise was among the most influential of the American pastoral theologians after the Second World War. His emphasis on interaction and relationship found wide acceptance in seminaries and clinical centers.

E. B. HOLIFIELD

HISTORY OF PROTESTANT PASTORAL CARE (United States); PASTORAL CARE MOVEMENT; PASTORAL COUNSELING MOVEMENT; PASTORAL THEOLOGY, PROTESTANT; PSYCHOLOGY IN AMERICAN RELIGION; THEOLOGICAL EDUCATION AND THE PASTORAL CARE MOVEMENT, PROTESTANT. *See also* PASTORAL PSYCHOTHERAPY.

WISE FOOL. *See* PASTOR (Normative and Traditional Images).

WISH/ WISHING. *See* HOPE AND DESPAIR; WILL / WILLING.

WIT AND HUMOR IN PASTORAL CARE. The creatively playful dimension of caring that can be a part of pastoral interaction. At the heart of humor is the surprise marriage of incompatibles that lifts a situation into a fresh frame of reference and often allows the discharge of laughter. Paradoxically, what is ultimately serious can at the same time be hilariously funny; as Irvin S. Cobb puts it, "Humor is tragedy standing on its head with its pants torn!" (Koestler, 1964). Even in the midst of pain, joy can erupt as the fruit of discovery, the recognition of the absurdity in an illusion, the glimpsing of a solution to an insoluble dilemma, the jumping over to a new perspective that permits greater self-acceptance, or as the rippling affect of expanded awareness. Humor can be the bubbling to the surface of a theology of hope in what resignation had concluded was a personal swamp. Laughing together can be the overflow of the shared intimacy of the pastoral relationship.

In the pastoral relationship, humor may wear different costumes and play a variety of roles. Sigmund Freud saw humor as an instinctive coping mechanism used by persons under stress. In this view, when repression is being lifted, humor may erupt with a free play of ideas, double meanings, condensations, plays on words, the released inner child weaving a new vision of connections. The sense of moving in tune with one's processes can carry an innate pleasure, as contrasted with the dispirited quality of feeling stuck. In the initial phases of counseling, humor can sometimes help to melt resistances and establish rapport. Well-timed humor can ease the tensions of a moment. It can defeat habit with originality, break through the crust of the familiar, stir up depressed energy, shift the ground of the interaction in a more fruitful direction, and invite persons up into the bleachers for a better look at what is happening.

The best humor is tuned to the processes of the moment and has the spark of immediacy. Sometimes the humor is saying out loud what usually is only thought. The counselor may use humor as a means of engaging the counselee by overstatement, understatement, contextual switches, playing on multiple meanings, exaggerating an element of incongruity, or leaping into a melodramatic role. What appears to make sense can be unclothed as nonsense. A joke or humorous story may give added emphasis to a point being made. Sometimes a metaphor or incident from the material of the counselee becomes a humorous meta-language that can be a quick reminder of their persistent dynamics. The disarming surprises of humor provide a means for facilitating the reflections of the parishioner or counselee and for keeping the energy of the interactions moving. Humor contains the possibility of transcendence, through which the essential paradoxes of life are grasped and transformed.

The sensitive use of humor takes into account the vulnerability of the person being engaged. The pastor will exercise care so that the counselee does not feel laughed at. Humor can have a hostile intent, or be a seductive ploy or a means of avoidance, by either the client or the counselor. The pastor will be alert to these negative uses and meanings of humor.

Pastors can, at times, assume the role of court jester, poking fun at themselves and others. At the heart of such humor is a love of persons, an attitude of acceptance of what is, and a transcending affirmation, in the midst of suffering or struggle, of the creative possibilities for human life.

Bibliography. A. Ellis, *Humanistic Psychotherapy: The Rational-Emotive Approach* (1973). S. Freud, *Wit and Its Relation to the Unconscious*, in A. Brill, *Basic Writings of Sigmund Freud* (1938), and *SE*, vol. 3. M. Goulding and R. Goulding, *Changing Lives Through Redecision Therapy* (1979); "Humor and Illumination," *Voices*, (winter, 1981). H. Greenwald, *Direct Decision Therapy* (1973). A. Koestler, *The Act of Creation* (1964). B. Parrott, *God's Sense of Humor* (1983). F. Perls, *In and Out of the Garbage Pail* (1969). J. Zinker, *Creative Process in Gestalt Therapy* (1977).

G. E. CRISWELL

HUMOR; TECHNIQUE AND SKILL IN PASTORAL CARE. *Compare* CONVERSATION, PASTORAL; INTERPRETATION AND HERMENEUTICS, PASTORAL; PERSONAL STORY, SYMBOL, AND MYTH IN PASTORAL CARE.

WITCHCRAFT. The term possesses multiple meanings designating a cross-cultural phenomenon with deep historical roots and widespread distribution. In its most familiar usage witchcraft refers to the late medieval belief in the practice of malevolent magic through supernatural powers gained from the establishment of a voluntary pact with Satan. In a broader anthropological sense the word is used without the diabolical pact to denote the exercise of a wide spectrum of magical arts in predominantly harmful pursuits. In this regard witchcraft is closely akin to sorcery, involving incantations and ritual manipulation of symbolic objects. Yet it is distinct, as witchcraft contains an inherited, internal quality. One is born a witch, whereas one learns to become a sorcerer. In contemporary parlance witchcraft may additionally denominate the particular belief structure of neopagan religious groups distinguished by polytheistic nature-centered sacraments. The word is rich in archetypal associations, conjuring forth potent images which serve as focal lenses for projections of the unconscious.

1. **European History.** Over a period of five centuries, from the early witch trials of the thirteenth century to the last legal execution in Poland in 1793, Europe was obsessed with a witchcraft ideology that brought about the episodic persecution and death of an unknown number of women and men. As the execution fires were burning out in England and the Continent, a witch panic flared in the colonies in seventeenth-century New England. Suggested estimates of those indicted under the charge of witchraft range from a hundred thousand to more than a million. Analysis of available court records reveal that of those accused approximately ninety-two percent in England and eighty percent in the rest of Europe were women.

For more than half a millennium an enormous amount of pastoral energy was explicitly directed toward the identification and persecution of witches. A number of major theologians both Catholic (e.g., Aquinas) and Protestant (e.g., Luther, Calvin, Wesley) lent support to these activities. Their theological testimonies can be viewed as reflections of the irrefutable logic of a cultural climate wherein witchcraft was viewed as a normal and reasonable belief and contrary convictions were irrational and heretical.

There is no consensus concerning reasons for the witch mania. The development of printing and literacy, the judicial revolution, the change in the status of women and the Christianization of the peasantry have been, among others, offered as proximate causes. Significant among suggested preconditions allowing for the persecution was the gradual shift in religious and legal perspective which turned to consider witchcraft as a heresy and capital crime endangering both church and state. Prior to the late medieval and early modern periods witches were generally regarded by the church as benign figures who made magical use of morally neutral supernatural energies and whose self-confessed supernatural escapades were considered delusional. Accusations of being a follower of Satan changed the witch into a diabolical enemy of God participating in a secret and extensive conspiracy bent on the destruction of the Church.

Central to the persecution and prosecution of witches was the *Malleus Maleficarum* (*The Hammer of Witches*). Authored by Dominican clerics James Sprenger and Heinrich Kramer, the *Malleus* was a handbook for witchhunters meticulously detailing procedures for the identification, prosecution, and sentencing of suspected witches, including proper application of torture for the extraction of confession and the naming of confederates. First printed in 1486, it was republished twenty-nine times between its first edition and 1669. During this period the *Malleus* could be found in every courtroom and in every pastor's study. The work was prefaced with a copy of the papal bull of 1484 by Innocent VII granting unbridled authority for the pursuit of witches wherever their practice might be suspected.

Biblical passages cited as scriptural evidence of the existence of witches offer dubious support at best. The so-called witch of Endor (I Sam. 28:7ff) does not meet minimum medieval criteria for definition as a witch. The Hebrew word is appropriately translated as 'medium.' The Old Testament does not recognize the idea of a diabolical pact with Satan. The New Testament holds scattered indirect references to activities that bear slight resemblances to witchcraft and which are contextually related to the accepted magical practices of the time.

2. **Current Practice.** Witchcraft is a common phenomenon in modern Africa where tribal cosmologies continue to provide a supportive context for a belief in the operation of magic. It should be noted that the traditional witchdoctor functions as an opponent of witchcraft, which is viewed as morally evil. Witchcraft in Africa is the pursuit of harmful ends by supernatural means, usually directed toward family members and neighbors. Belief in witchcraft and its persecution is closely related to the social and psychological strains experienced by members of a culture. One theory of witchcraft views its social function as a scapegoating mechanism allowing expression of societal tensions. An increase in witch hunting can be expected when a society is threatened by natural or cultural pressures requiring the reconfiguration of foundational ideologies.

Contemporary witchcraft in the U.S. and Great Britain, commonly referred to as the religion of Wicca, bears no similarity to the historic understanding and is properly viewed as a neopagan nature religion emerging out of the pluralism of New Age beliefs. In a desire for legitimacy its practitioners have alluded to their craft as a continuation of an ancient religion dating back to pre-Christian Europe. The writers upon whom these assertions depend, primarily Margaret Murray and Gerald Gardner, have been discredited as manufacturing fraudulent historical evidence. Modern neopagan witchcraft is distinctive for its antiauthoritarian structure, feminist emphasis, creativity, and depth psychological orientation. Its linkage to ancient religious practices is now conceived metaphorically rather than literally.

3. **Broader Pastoral Issues.** Christina Larner spoke in the 1982 Gifford Lectures of the operation of temporal ethnocentrism in historical studies of past cultures, illustrating her concern with a focus on the European era of witchcraft. Larner lamented our inability to view past systems of thought as complex, integrated wholes. She noted an inevitable selective perception operating in the examination of historical cultures reflective of a hermeneutical bias. The metaphysical cosmology of late medieval and early modern Europe provided a rationally coherent structure for a belief in witches. From a position several hundred years removed we judge such an ideology as tragically flawed. As pastors we must be resistant of tendencies to absolutize contemporary understandings and be mindful of an ongoing creation beyond our limited, temporal window of vision.

There may well be over a hundred thousand Wicca practitioners meeting regularly in small group settings known as covens. Such a membership suggests the increasing likelihood of pastors coming into contact with aspects of the Wicca belief system. Neopagan witchcraft believers have been characterized as ecologically oriented promoters of pluralistic, antiauthoritarian ideologies. Their antipatriarchal beliefs offer a conception of the feminine principle that has often been disregarded in the masculine symbolism of historic Christianity. As a result neopagan witchcraft has become a nurturing, spiritual sanctuary for women and men who have felt estranged and victimized by traditional theologies.

As a belief system, Wicca continues a trend of greater member visibility and of professionalism in the training of its leaders. Seminary students with admitted witchcraft beliefs are beginning to be found in attendance at liberal divinity schools. Margot Adler notes the struggle of Wicca for recognition as a legitimate religious group and projects licensing possibilities of Wicca priestesses as pastoral counselors. We cannot dismiss neopagan witchcraft as a psychological aberration embodied by its practitioners but must recognize it as an integrated metaphysical system perhaps necessitating dialogue.

Bibliography. M. Adler, *Drawing Down the Moon* (1986). N. Cohn, *Europe's Inner Demons* (1975). C. Larner, *Witchcraft and Religion* (1984). M. Marwick, ed., *Witchcraft and Sorcery* (1982). G. Parrinder, *Witchcraft: European and African* (1963). R. H. Robbins, *Encyclopedia of Witchcraft and Demonology* (1959). G. Scarre, *Witchcraft and Magic in 16th and 17th Century Europe* (1987). M. Summers, trans., *Malleus Maleficarum* (1951).

P. J. JOHNSON, III

NEW RELIGIOUS MOVEMENTS; PASTORAL CARE (History, Traditions, and Definitions). *See also* CULTURAL ANTHROPOLOGY OF RELIGION, DISCIPLINE OF; SEXISM.

WITHDRAWNNESS. *See* AUTISM; SHYNESS; SOCIAL ISOLATION.

WITNESSING, EVANGELICAL. *See* EVANGELICAL PASTORAL CARE; EVANGELIZING.

WOMEN, ORDINATION OF. *See* MINISTRY; RABBI/RABBINATE; WOMEN IN PASTORAL MINISTRIES.

WOMEN, PASTORAL CARE OF. Since both the theory and practice of pastoral care come predominantly from a male perspective, it is crucial that pastoral care be reexamined in order to take full account of the particular issues of the pastoral care of women. The pastor's theology of humanity is fundamental to this. Instead of making assumptions about who women are and what they need, attention must be focused on finding out and understanding what women's experience actually is.

1. **Reexamination.** Education of pastors and congregations for effective pastoral care of women will include a prophetic conviction that God desires the full development of *all* persons. The congregational affirmation of women is only complete when women are fully included in all aspects of congregational life. Such pastoral care of women requires a new level of self-awareness from pastors and an increased awareness of the vast range of women's experiences of growing up, education, work, and sexuality. Pastors may mistakenly assume one woman's experience to be women's experience. The female pastor, for instance, may take her experience or the male pastor his wife's experience, as normative. Self-awareness also includes recognition and reexamination of one's attitudes regarding the nature of female and male roles and relationships. When pastors hold rigid role expectations for women and men, the effectiveness of pastoral care is limited. The options which pastors affirm influence the choices parishioners make. When pastors see women only in support roles, they reinforce the denial of other possibilities for women.

2. **Theology of Humanity.** Theology has a significant influence in defining women and men and in shaping the roles that each play. Traditional theologies have functioned to reinforce socially defined female and male roles rather than using Christian values to define roles. Pastor's attitudes toward women are derived from their understanding of Scripture's concept of the nature of humanity. However, neither of the Genesis creation stories makes any statement about roles. At the heart of the stories are messages concerning identity—who God is as Creator and who we are as God's creation. Also of concern is our relationship with the rest of creation. One understanding of sexual differentiation is that men and women are meant to be interdependent. We are dependent on one another for our existence and the rest of creation for sustenance.

That we are created as relational and interdependent beings does not necessitate hierarchy. Differences have been perceived as determining order and value. The creation stories emphasize that female and male are created from the same substance (Gen. 2:23). Created as "other" does not make men and women "opposite" (Trible, 1978, pp. 98–101).

Goldstein has suggested that humanity has been beset with two major temptations to sin that are shared unequally by the sexes. Men have had a greater temptation toward pride and women toward sloth. Both inclinations tempt us to refuse to be who we are. Pride tempts us to be more, and sloth tempts us to be less than we are. In either case, the result is a denial of God's gift of humanity. Extremes of independence and dependence parallel these temptations. Pastors who encourage women to renounce pride will reinforce women's tendency toward sloth.

Paul emphasizes that each of us is held accountable for our lives before God (Rom. 14:10 – 12). God calls women to live faithfully, according to the gifts we receive. These gifts might be demonstrated in a career or in homemaking. Pastoral care helps parishioners to live faithfully by helping women examine the gifts they are using and claim all of the gifts God has given them.

3. Reexamining Assumptions. False assumptions can seriously undermine effective pastoral care of women. For example, when a woman reports her husband's abuse, the pastor may assume that the woman is at fault by having done something to cause the abuse. Instead, the woman may be seeking support, understanding, and possible referral to community resources that will assist her.

Further, the assumption that women are responsible for the primary care of children in a home with one working parent no longer fits the reality of contemporary society. In fact, this "traditional" type of family is in the minority in light of the increased number of families with single parents, both parents working, and parents exchanging roles. Family tasks are not, and need not be, accomplished only within stereotypical roles.

Linguistic and communication studies have challenged false assumptions about language and its effects. While men often assume that women talk too much and thus their words can be ignored, Kramarae (1981) found that men and women use words differently. Language is never value free. Miller and Swift (1976) showed that when the generic terms *he* or *man* are used, people think *male*. The exclusion of women from language also promotes their exclusion from other aspects of society.

Reexamining false assumptions can have several practical implications for pastoral care. When women are taken seriously, it will be realized that jokes about women in sermons and other communications can be hurtful rather than humorous and can damage the pastor's credibility and trustworthiness.

Fair treatment of women will result in appropriate referrals with pastoral follow-up when a pastor realizes that he or she cannot give all the help that is needed.

Respect for women will result in women being given the authority their positions deserve. Both men and women find it difficult to give women authority and will often criticize a woman more than a man in the same position. Effective pastoral care can raise sensitivity to the distinction between person and position.

Primarily, women want choice, which involves seeing each woman as an individual worthy of God's love and care. Choice takes pain seriously, regardless of the reality of the situation. Feelings are real, even when they seem inconsistent with reality. It is only as women can affirm the reality of their feelings, needs, and situation that they will realize their full potential.

4. Women's Experience. Traditionally female experience has been defined in terms of male experience. Women do this as well as men. With male experience defined as normative, women mistrust the reality and deny the value of their own experiences.

Incest and other forms of violence against females of all ages occur across all socioeconomic, ethnic, racial, educational, and religious lines. Families that appear to be ideal often harbor the damage and pain of abuse. Pastoral response that recognizes the reality of these women's experiences can enable women to respond appropriately to their situation.

Women of color experience discrimination on two fronts: color and sex. Assumptions about women's experience that ignore women of color are incomplete. While white women struggle to gain a place in the work force, black women are expected to be employed, thus forced to work outside the home. The pastor is challenged to examine commonalities and differences of women's experience (Coles and Coles; Joseph and Lewis). The close connection between sexism and racism requires that both be addressed simultaneously.

Gender-related differences need to be carefully distinguished from cultural expectations of female and male. For example, Gilligan (1982) discovered that women make ethical decisions as systematically as men, but with a different set of concerns. Women decide the ethics of a situation within a web of concern that considers the complexity of relationships and seeks to maintain relationships rather than (as for men) to conform to abstract norms. Women making ethical decisions need pastors who can recognize this style of moral reflection characteristic of a woman's decision-making process.

While the expression of emotions is considered more acceptable for women than men, there are important distinctions. Women are permitted public expression of such emotions as sadness, joy, and love, but not anger. (The reverse tends to be true for men.) Both women and men deny women's anger, though women's anger seems particularly difficult for men to tolerate.

Some women experience and express sexual attraction to other women. Lesbian women represent another dimension of the variety among women within the church. While convictions about homosexuality vary widely and are the occasion for intense controversy, it is generally true that lesbians share a double discrimination, that of sex and of sexual preference. Pastors working with lesbians can easily deny lesbian experience by ignoring the intensity of both forms of discrimination.

Women going through processes of growing feminist awareness may experience and express anger. Recognition of one's status as a victim in oppressive situations causes anger and rejection of the system's values. As these women proceed by stages toward a fuller form of liberation, pastoral responses must be appropriate to each stage. Appropriate responses include challenging women who are not fully using their gifts, letting go of women who are angry and rejecting, and supporting women in their often difficult struggle toward liberation.

5. Sexuality. Sexuality is present in pastoral care situations regardless of the sex of the pastor. A pastoral care setting is an intimate setting, and this intimacy lends itself to being sexually charged. Men tend to trade intimacy for sex, and women tend to trade sex for intimacy. Recognition of sexual barter can defuse potentially dangerous circumstances.

Pastors can make clear ethical decisions in the midst of sexually charged situations. They need to consider sexual issues and have strategies in place for handling situations that arise. Through careful forethought, clear, consistent sexual boundaries are maintained. The fact is, however, that some pastors do engage in sexual intimacy with parishioners (Rassieur). Once this has happened, the pastor abdicates the pastoral role with that parishioner. The person with greater role authority—the pastor—has the greater responsibility to maintain appropriate boundaries.

Pastors' beliefs about women's sexuality will determine how sexual situations are handled. If pastors believe that women are the source of sexual temptation, then they are likely to blame women for innocent situations. For example, the pastor who does not call before visiting and is met at the door by a woman in her robe may blame the woman for being seductive. Culture has assigned women the responsibility for sexual relations. The double standard that holds women accountable for sexual involvement and encourages men in sexual activity is damaging to all.

Incest, sexual abuse, and rape are realities of women's lives. Rape is a crime of violence, and, as in other sexual crimes, the victim is often blamed. While sexual abuse is only infrequently discussed in the church, victims of sexual abuse do exist in each congregation. Many women conceal painful secrets. The pastor can help break the conspiracy of silence by naming sexual abuse as a reality. The woman who is victim and the family that rejects her both need pastoral care.

As long as sex is used to sell products from toothpaste to vacations, women will be seen as sex objects and undervalued. Pastoral care strategies demand social action against practices that deny women's worth. In summary, each person should be taken seriously as a gifted individual. This is as important for men as for women. That which separates women and men from God must be the focus of pastoral care. Rigid perceptions of what women experience and expectations regarding what women want form barriers that prevent effective pastoral care. Pastoral response needs to be freed from these perceptions and thus enable women's movement toward liberation.

Bibliography. N. Chodorow, *The Reproduction of Mothering* (1978). R. Coles and J. H. Coles, *Women of Crisis: Lives of Struggle and Hope* (1978). M. M. Fortune, *Sexual Violence* (1983). C. Gilligan, *In A Different Voice* (1982). V. S. Goldstein, "The Human Situation: A Feminine View," *J. of Religion* (1960). B. W. Harrison, *Our Right to Choose* (1983). J. Johnston, *Lesbian Nation* (1973). G. Joseph and J. Lewis, *Common Differences: Conflicts in Black and White Feminist Perspectives* (1981). E. Justes, *The Pastoral Care of Women* (in press). C. Kramarae, *Women and Their Speaking* (1981). H. Lips and N. L. Colwill, *The Psychology of Sex Differences* (1978). C. Miller and K. Swift, *Words and Women* (1976). J. B. Miller, *Toward a New Psychology of Woman* (1976). C. Moraga and G. Anzaldua, eds., *This Bridge Called My Back* (1981). C. Rassieur, *The Problem Clergymen Don't Talk About* (1976). C. A. Rayburn, "Psychotherapy and Counseling with Religious Women: Some Ethical Concerns," *J. of Pastoral Counseling*, 20 (1985), 18 – 30. R. R. Ruether, *Sexism and God-Talk* (1983). A. W. Schaef, *Women's Reality* (1981). P. Trible, *God and the Rhetoric of Sexuality* (1978). A. Walker, *The Color Purple* (1982).

P. L. T. GARRISON
E. J. JUSTES

CULTURAL AND ETHNIC FACTORS IN PASTORAL CARE; LIFE CYCLE THEORY AND PASTORAL CARE; PASTORAL CARE (Contemporary Methods, Perspectives, and Issues). *See also* CHILD-BIRTH; CONSCIOUSNESS RAISING; IDENTITY; MENOPAUSE; PREGNANCY; RAPE; SEXISM; SEXUAL ISSUES IN PASTORAL CARE; SEXUALITY. *Compare* MEN, PASTORAL CARE OF.

WOMEN, PSYCHOLOGY OF. The psychology of women developed out of perceived deficits in the theory and research of psychology as a whole. Since from the beginning most psychologists have been male, and when society has been patriarchal, the science of mind and behavior has concentrated on the male experience, many of the theories that were formed about human behavior were actually describing male behavior (Freud, Erikson). The assumption was that either the female experience was identical, or females were an inferior and different species that did not warrant the attention of researchers and theorists. The advent of societal changes in the perception of women's nature, behavior, and experience, and the infiltration of women into the field of psychology naturally gave birth to the subspeciality of the psychology of women. Its purpose is to identify and address the errors, misconceptions, and deficits of a male-dominated field of psychology. It also seeks to develop and advance the field by focusing on particular research topics pertinent to the science of women's minds and behavior.

1. History. *a. Innate versus learned behavior.* The field of psychology of women began to emerge in the early 1900s. Prior to this time, women had been regarded almost as a separate species from men. Characteristics such as rationality and originality that were highly valued as "exclusively human" were evident in men, but seemed to be relatively lacking in women. During this era, evolutionary theory was popular, and psychology was attempting to integrate evolutionary "truths" into its data, theories, and concepts.

This school of thought, called functionalism, applied evolutionary theory to explain the differences between women's and men's natures. Women were assumed to be lower on the evolutionary scale and thus incapable of the intellectual pursuits of men. Thus, women were assumed to possess innate qualities that explained their absence from academic and business life. Woman's nurturing behavior was explained as maternal instinct, similar to that of animals. This emphasis on innate biological traits became an integral part of early psychological theories.

In the mid-1920s, psychology began a paradigm shift to a new school of thought known as behaviorism. Behavior was viewed as learned rather than innate. Most human behavior, both male and female, could be explained as a product of social conditioning. Behavior was thus relative to one's social context. However, despite the widespread effects of learning theory on the field, a tendency still remains in psychology to assume that socially conditioned behavior in women is innate.

b. Psychoanalysis. The emphasis on innateness of behavior received heavy backing in Freudian personality theory. Sigmund Freud held that due to their lack of a penis, women were biologically inferior to men, and he essentially saw the female as an inadequate male. Freud largely ignored the social context of people and their behavior. He considered the male experience as normative, developed his theory of personality with this value, and then labeled women deviant for not conforming to "normal" development. Freud's work came to be widely accepted in psychiatry, clinical psychology, and pastoral counseling, and thus the myth of women's innate inferiority was perpetuated.

As women entered the field of psychology, theories following Freud began to focus on and make sense of the female experience. It was not until the early 1950s, though, that psychologists, influenced by the work of anthropologist Margaret Mead and psychoanalyst Karen Horney, began to emphasize the importance of social and cultural values as the context for understanding women's behavior. Mead's cross-cultural work denied the myth that certain behavioral patterns of women were innate, by revealing that women in other cultures did not behave in similar ways. Horney reformulated the psychoanalytic theory of "penis envy" in terms of social status and power issues and effectively refuted ideas about female masochism by pointing out the cultural factors encouraging women to behave in ways considered masochistic.

Despite these corrective influences, psychoanalytic theory remains both sex-biased and popular. Erik Erikson's psychosocial developmental stages, for instance, were developed through a study of male children, and yet are accepted as valid among both sexes by many psychologists and pastoral care specialists.

2. Content. The field of psychology of women has evolved through several stages.

a. Sex differences. In its inception, the major focus of the psychology of women was on the differences between men and women. At first, this interest centered mainly around sexual development differences and concerns over whether conclusions made about behavior and ability based on research could be generalized to women. Unfortunately, research indicating the existence of sex differences usually resulted in future study of males only (e.g., Kohlberg, 1969).

More research has been conducted in this area of psychology of women than any other. The classic work summarizing the major findings is Maccoby and Jacklin's *Psychology of Sex Differences* (1974). Highlights of the results include the following, which have been shown to be unfounded beliefs about sex differences: (1) girls are more "social" than boys; (2) girls are more "suggestible" than boys; (3) girls have lower self-esteem; (4) girls are better at role learning and simple tasks and boys better at higher cognitive processing; (5) boys are more "analytic"; (6) girls are more affected by heredity and boys by environment; (7) girls lack achievement motivation; and (8) girls are auditory and boys are visual.

Four sex differences, however, have been fairly well established: (1) girls have greater verbal ability than boys; (2) boys excel in visual-spatial ability; (3) boys excel in mathematical ability; and (4) males are more aggressive. Areas such as competitiveness, dominance, compliance, and nurturance have ambiguous findings.

b. Oppression and psychotherapy. This second stage developed in the late 1960s as a natural outgrowth of the woman's movement. Of central concern was explaining female "inferiority" and women's subordinate position in society. Consciousness was raised as to how psychology contributed to the oppression of women, especially through its research biases. In addition, attention was turned to the psychotherapeutic process.

Phyllis Chesler's (1972) work purported that men drive women "mad" in order to maintain their privileged position. Gove and Tudor's study (1973) indicated women's role in our society possesses characteristics that promote mental illness. Broverman *et al.* (1970) found that among mental health professionals, the profile for a "mentally healthy adult" and a "mentally healthy man" were identical, while the comparison of the "adult" profile with that of a "mentally healthy woman" showed large discrepancies. Essentially, the message to women from the mental health professionals was "to be a healthy woman is not to be a healthy person."

c. Sex roles. During the third stage, a closer examination was made of male and female sex roles. The concern revolved around such issues as biological and sexual aspects of sex roles, social and cultural influences in role devaluation, traditional versus alternative models, and consequences of implementing these models. Specific studies were conducted to examine the effects of maternal employment (Hoffman, 1974), role conflict, and dual career families (Rapaport and Rapaport, 1971). Also, work was begun on definitions and measures of masculine, feminine, and androgynous traits (Bem, 1974).

d. Societal expectations. The focus of this fourth stage was threefold: (1) the different expectations for individuals based on their sex; (2) the process by which these different expectations affect the behavior of males and females; and (3) the consequences of these expectations for both sexes. Research on these areas indicates that widely held differences in expectations exist in both sexes. For instance, investigators (e.g., Deaux and Taylor, 1973) have regularly found that identical performance in males and females is evaluated differently and that different attributions as to what causes success or failure are made depending on the sex of the subject. Research further indicated that people respond differently to a person based on whether they label the individual as male or female, and these differential responses are more harmful to women than men.

e. Environment and mainstreaming. Current work in the psychology of women points toward a future emphasis on the interaction of sex and the situation. Research is focusing on the effects of "mainstreaming," that is, males and females entering each other's traditional worlds and equally sharing responsibility in both the private and public sectors.

3. Research Bias and Methodology. Of concern to those in the field of psychology of women is not only what is studied, but also how it is examined. One of the most obvious biases is the dearth of research dealing with females; most studies are still performed using male subjects. When research does include both men and women, often the investigator fails to test for sex differences and thus misses a possible confounding variable influencing the results. Even when differences are found, often the data from females is ignored in the building of a theory.

Many researchers, of both sexes, lack knowledge about sex roles and how they influence behavior and thus do not design experiments sensitive to these factors. Exclusive use of male investigators is a problem, as is ignoring experimental and situational influences such as the cause of male biased tasks. Many researchers make the mistake of viewing behavior as dichotomous, especially when they conceptualize masculinity and femininity as mutually exclusive categories.

Although it is recognized that no research is value-free, investigators of human behavior must be wary of unconsciously incorporating the present prevalent value system of this culture into their research design and interpretation of results. Those who read psychological research literature need to be aware of these biases as well, in order to make decisions regarding the validity, appropriateness, and applicability of the conclusions.

4. **Implications for Pastoral Care.** *a. Sociological factors.* The psychology of women offers a rich field of theory, data, and concepts for integration into the discipline of pastoral care and counseling. One of its most crucial contributions is its challenge to pastors to become informed of and sensitized to the effects of the various sociological/cultural factors that influence the behavior and status of women and men. Women constitute over half of the average church congregation, and it seems imperative that pastors begin to appreciate and empathize with their experiences.

Recognizing sociological factors is critical in the counseling situation. Counselors often look for internal pathology as the source of an individual's distress, when much of the difficulty may stem from situational, social, and cultural limitations. Several issues particularly significant to women that need to be considered from the vantage point of societal influences include: eating disorders; sexual/physical violence; incest; alcoholism; premenstrual syndrome; pregnancy and childbirth; body image; issues of power, entitlement, self-esteem; and decisions regarding career, lifestyle, and family. Pastors become more effective counselors by educating themselves concerning such societal influences and their effect on their counselee's behavior. In addition, the psychology of women offers a challenge to pastors to evaluate the church for its limiting social/subcultural influences on the lives of women.

b. Values and attitudes. Psychological studies have well documented the fact that a counselor's values and attitudes are more influential in therapeutic outcome than other counselor characteristics or particular techniques and orientations. This conclusion offers yet another invitation to self-examination. The counseling pastor should ask himself or herself the following questions: Do I value stereotypical sex-role expectations over and above individual choice? Do I have goals and methods of counseling that constrict women's and men's growth and breadth of self-knowledge? Do I encourage dependency in women in their relationships with others, including their relationships with me? Do the women I

counsel leave with a passive, adjustive stance or an active, self-determining one? What behaviors and values do I directly and indirectly reinforce in my female counselees in our time together? Admittedly, no human interchange is value-free, nor is total objectivity necessarily a goal. Self-awareness is crucial, however, for responsible counseling.

c. Restriction of women and men. The psychology of women recognizes that traditional theories and values are restrictive to both men and women. The challenge for pastors is to be leaders in developing the church's prophetic voice to the culture by modeling healthy, egalitarian relationships based on mutual respect and care. Within the context of counseling, pastors can challenge their male counselees to explore and struggle with the issues raised by psychology of women and be a model of encouragement by sharing the conflicts they have experienced themselves.

d. Power. The issue of power and its use in relationships is a topic of concern in the psychology of women. Power is a given in all human interchanges, and its mere existence has no moral implications. However, individuals are held accountable for their uses and abuses of power, and this is where the danger of oppression seeps in. Pastors are challenged to recognize their power to influence both women's and men's capacities to grow and to validate the direction their growth takes. Pastoral counselors need to be wary of an "adjustment" model of health that uses the white male as its norm and standard. With Christ as their model, pastors, once they recognize and are comfortable with their power, can share it by empowering others.

e. Image of God. Finally, psychology of women encourages pastors to recognize that the church desperately needs the leadership, participation, and integration of women's experiences of God into its life. Together, women and men express the fullness of humanity, which is a reflection of the image of God. In continuing to deny and devalue women's active participation and leadership, the church is only partially experiencing the fullness of God.

Bibliography. S. L. Bem, "Measurement of Psychological Androgyny," *J. of Consulting and Clinical Psychology*, 42 (1974), 155–62. I. K. Broverman *et al.*, "Sex-role Stereotypes and Clinical Judgments of Mental Health," *J. of Consulting Clinical Psychology*, 34 (1970), 1–7. P. Chesler, *Women and Madness* (1972). K. Deaux and J. Taylor, "Evaluation of Male and Female Ability," *Psychological Reports*, 32 (1973), 261–62. E. Erikson, *Childhood and Society* (1963); *Identity: Youth and Crisis* (1968). W. R. Gove and J. F. Tudor, "Adult Sex Roles and Mental Illness," in J. Huber, ed., *Changing Women in a Changing Society* (1973). L. W. Hoffman, "Effects of Maternal Employment on the Child," *Developmental Psychology*, 10 (1974), 204–28. K. Horney, *Feminine Psychology* (1967). L. Kohlberg, "Stages and Sequence: The Cognitive-Developmental Approach to Socialization," in D. A. Goslin, ed., *Handbook of Socialization Theory and Research* (1969). E. E. Maccoby and C. N. Jacklin, *The Psychology of Sex Differences* (1974). M. Mead, *Sex and Temperament in Three Primitive Societies* (1935). R. Rapaport and R. Rapaport, *Dual Career Families* (1971). Compare S. W. Cardwell, "Why Women Fail/Succeed in Ministry: Psychological Factors," *Pastoral Psychology*, 30:3 (1982), 153–62.

A. B. Ulanov, *Receiving Woman: Studies in the Psychology and Theology of the Feminine* (1981).

C. E. SCHULER

PERSONALITY, BIOLOGICAL DIMENSIONS OF; IDENTITY; SEXISM; SEXUALITY. *See also* PERSONALITY THEORY; PSYCHOANALYSIS; PSYCHOTHERAPY; VALUES IN COUNSELING AND PSYCHOTHERAPY.

WOMEN IN PASTORAL MINISTRIES, HISTORY OF. Throughout the church's history, women have been involved in its caring ministries, even when they were excluded from the pastoral office. The history of women in pastoral ministries thus cannot be simply confined to the history of their ordination.

1. Primitive and Early Church. Specific pastoral offices in the early church developed in the transition from the charismatic Jesus movement to the institutional church. The charismatic ministries of prophet and apostle (I Cor. 12:4–11) were highly regarded, the charism of the spirit being received by women as well as men (Acts 2:17). The four daughters of Philip (Acts 21:9) were prophetesses, as were women in the Corinthian congregation, although attempts were made to regulate their prophesying (I Cor. 11:2–16). The most influential of all the early women apostles were those associated with Paul, especially Prisca (I Cor. 16:19; Rom. 16:3; Acts 18:2, 18, 26; II Tim. 4:19) and Phoebe (Rom. 16:1–2), who served the congregation at Cenchreae, not only as deacon, but as presiding elder (*prostatis*).

Despite the participation of women on all levels of pastoral ministry in the early church, regulations restricting their participation seem to have been promulgated fairly early. Besides the Pauline injunction for women to be veiled when praying or prophesying (I Cor. 11:2–16), there are later restrictions upon their speaking in assemblies (I Cor. 14:33b–36) and against their having any form of authority over men, especially in teaching (I Tim. 2:9–15; 5:1–17; Tit. 2:3–5).

In the second through the fourth centuries, there were two main opportunities for the exercise of women's ministries: through the ascetic life or through service in the orders of deaconess, canoness, widow, or virgin, as they were newly defined in the third and fourth centuries by the *Didascalia Apostolorum* and *Apostolic Constitutions*. Prominent Roman women used their family wealth to endow churches, support male clergy, and to found new monastic communities of men and women. Marcella (325–410), an ascetic widow, scholar, and friend and advisor of Jerome, was the leader of a community of like-minded women. Three of these, the elder Paula, the elder Melania, and her daughter Albina, founded and supervised communities of celibate women. The deaconess Macrina, sister of Basil and Gregory of Nyssa, according to the biography written by Gregory, was also their spiritual counselor.

In the fourth century, specific women's orders were created. The diaconate, an ordained clerical office for women (*Didascalia* XVI:3:12) lasted until the eleventh century. The order of widows, mentioned first in Acts 6:1ff and I Tim. 5:9–15, was confirmed by the Councils of Nicea (325) and Chalcedon (451) as a group of women over sixty whose principal function was to support the church by prayer and charitable works. Consecrated virgins were confirmed as a separate ministry (*Apostolic Constitutions* III:2:15).

2. Medieval Period (500–1500). Female presbyters were forbidden in the fourth century (Council of Laodicea, Canon 11). Teaching (*Didascalia* III:6:2) and Eucharistic ministries (*Apostolic Church Order* XXIV:1–28) were also forbidden for women. Nevertheless, female heads of religious communities had considerable pastoral authority in spiritual and temporal matters. Bridget of Ulster (453–523), foundress of a dual monastic community in Kildare, is said by her biographer Cogitosus, to have been ordained a bishop, while Hilda (614–80), foundress of a double abbey at Whitby, presided over the Synod of Whitby in 664.

The mystical piety of medieval holy women, lay and religious, enabled them to function as counselors to both sexes and all ranks of religious and lay persons. Such women included ascetics and mystics like Angela of Foligno (1248–1309); Clare of Assisi (1194–1253), foundress of the Poor Clares; Bridget of Sweden (1303–73), foundress of the Brigittines; and the Dominican Catherine of Siena (1347–80). The latter two were instrumental in persuading the Avignonese pope, Gregory XI, to return to Rome. Despite the spiritual and physical care afforded by these women, however, their activities were frequently limited by the church hierarchy. In the thirteenth century, Pope Boniface VIII attempted to cloister all religious women, a decision effectively limiting the active service of members of tertiary orders, like Angela of Foligno. An association of religious laywomen, the Beguines, which began in the Netherlands in the twelfth century, was noted for its philanthropic work, but was condemned as heretical by the Council of Vienna (1311).

3. Reformation and Counter-Reformation. In the sixteenth century, save for emergency baptism by midwives and the hearing of confessions and the granting of absolution by abbesses with quasi-episcopal jurisdiction, women continued to be excluded from the pastoral office, except in some sects of the radical Reformation. However, women like Argula von Grumbach (1492–1563), who continued her reforming activities until her imprisonment, defied limitation by traditional female roles. Jadwige Gnoinskiej of Poland founded a Unitarian community of Polish Brethren at Rakow, unique in its dedication to egalitarianism and equality of the sexes.

The institution of a married clergy in the Protestant Reformation had a significant impact, the pastor's wife being conceived of as his co-worker in ministry. Perhaps the most influential pastor's wife was Katherine Zell (1497–1562), wife of the Strasbourg cleric Matthew Zell. After his death, Katherine continued his ministry, as well as her own, visiting the sick and imprisoned, and writing Protestant tracts.

In the Catholic Counter-Reformation, opportunities for women's ministries slightly increased, with the founding or reformation of active as well as contemplative orders. Teresa of Avila (1515–82) was influential, not only for her mystical experiences, but also for her founding of the Reformed (Discalced) Carmelite order. Angela of Brescia (1474–1540) founded the oldest Catholic women's teaching order, the Ursulines, in the same period.

4. **Modern Period.** In the seventeenth and eighteenth centuries, Catholic religious orders continued to provide a place for the exercise of women's pastoral ministries. Jeanne Françoise de Chantal (1572–1640) and English Catholic Mary Ward (1585–1645) founded active orders of women devoted to the care of the sick and the poor. In the French New World, Marie-Marguerite d'Youville (1707–71) founded a similar order, the Grey Nuns of Charity. Mohawk convert Kateri Tekakwitha (1656–80) was the first Native American to adopt a life of chastity, prayer, and ministry. In Spanish America, women of tertiary orders were responsible for the assistance of the poor, the sick, and the hungry, and for women's education.

The Quaker and Methodist movements in England and the First Great Awakening in English America afforded Protestant women an active ministry validated by spiritual experience. Women's Meetings of the Society of Friends were instituted by Quaker leader Margaret Fell (1614–1702) for assisting the poor and imprisoned, and for overseeing education. Many Quaker women suffered persecution and imprisonment simply for speaking in public. Mary Dyer, a supporter of the "Antinomian" Anne Hutchinson (1591–1643), was hanged for Quakerism in America in 1660. Ann Lee (1736–84), a visionary member of the "Shaking Quakers," fled persecution in England to found the first community of the United Society of Believers in Christ's Second Coming (Shakers) in Watervliet, New York.

During the Methodist revival in England, John Wesley appointed women class leaders, itinerants, and local preachers. One of the most influential Methodist women was Selina Hastings, Countess of Huntingdon (1707–91), who founded her own body of Calvinistic Methodists, the Countess of Huntingdon's Connexion. In New York City, Barbara Heck (1734–1804) was responsible for organizing the first Methodist Society of the U.S. and Canada.

In the nineteenth century, despite the confinement of women to the home and their restriction in the church, American Protestant laywomen founded and participated in numerous female charitable societies and missions, supported and conducted religious education, and played an active role in reform movements. Many of the women who were involved in the antislavery movement, like abolitionists Sarah Grimké (1792–1873) and Frances Wright (1795–1850), and in the temperance movement, like Frances E. Willard (1839–98), were also involved in the women's rights movement. Missions were also a major area of involvement for American Protestant women. In 1800, the Boston Female Society for Missionary Purposes (Baptist and Congregational) was founded, and by the end of the century, two-thirds of missionaries were women. "Women's Work for Women" included evangelism, education, and medical assistance and training.

Sectarian and revivalist movements like the revival begun in upstate New York in the 1820s by Charles Grandison Finney convinced women of their anointing to ministry by the spirit. Among these women were the black evangelists Julia Foote (1823–1900?), self-taught A.M.E. Zion preacher, missionary, and the first female deacon and elder of the A.M.E. Zion Church; and

Amanda Berry Smith (1837–1915), evangelist to the U.S., Great Britain, India, and Africa. Phoebe Palmer (1806–74), prominent Methodist lay evangelist and editor of *The Guide to Holiness,* was author of *The Promise of the Father* (1859), arguing that women's ministry was validated by the Holy Spirit. Among new sects, three were founded by women: the Pentecostal Pillar of Fire Church, founded by Alma Bridewell White (1862–1946), who served as its first bishop, and the Seventh-Day Adventists, founded through the revelations of Ellen Gould White (1827–1915), who became its prophet and leader. Mary Baker Eddy (1821–1910) founded Christian Science and became its first pastor.

The deaconess order was revived in the Lutheran, Episcopal, Methodist, and Presbyterian churches after 1849, inspired by the model Kaiserswerth of German pastor Theodor Fliedner, where Protestant women trained as missionaries, nurses, and social workers. New Catholic women's religious orders for teaching and healing ministries were begun by Elizabeth Seton (1774–1821), foundress of the Sisters of Charity and of the first free parochial school in the U.S. (1800), and by Frances Xavier Cabrini (1850–1917), foundress of the Missionary Society of the Sacred Heart.

In the twentieth century, lay women's involvement and leadership in charities, missions, and religious education led to agitation for their admission to pastoral offices. Already in the nineteenth century, women has been ordained, beginning with Antoinette Brown (Congregationalist) in 1853. After World War II, most other Protestant denominations began ordaining women. The first meeting of the World Council of Churches in 1948 set up a Commission on the Life and Work of Women in the Church, for which Kathleen Bliss wrote the landmark document, *The Service and Status of Women in the Churches.* In 1956, Maude Keister Jensen was the first woman elder given full conference rights by the Methodist Church. The Presbyterian Church in the U.S. ordained women as ministers of word and sacrament in 1955. While the American Baptist Convention began ordaining women in the 1890's, the Southern Baptist Convention, basing its decision on I Tim. 2:12, condemned the ordination of women to the pastoral ministry in 1980 and 1984, but permitted women to serve in the ministries of evangelism and religious education. The Lutheran Church in America ordained its first woman pastor, Elizabeth Platz, in 1970. The Lutheran Church, Missouri Synod, continues to hold the view that Scripture forbids women to serve in the pastoral office, while allowing them full lay participation. In the Protestant Episcopal Church, the "irregular" coordination of women to the priesthood in 1974 led to the vote to ordain women by the General Convention of 1976. Most recently, in 1989 Barbara Harris became the first female Episcopal bishop in North America.

Although new active religious orders for Catholic women were opened in 1914 (Maryknoll Sisters) and in 1915 (Sisters of the Blessed Sacrament), restrictions were imposed by the 1917 Code of Canon Law, preventing American Catholic women religious from taking a major role in social activism until the Second Vatican Council. Catholic laywomen, however, like Dorothy Day (1897–1980), who founded the Catholic Worker Movement in

America, became increasingly involved in social action. On ordination of women to the priesthood, however, Pope John Paul II reaffirmed his opposition in the "Declaration on the Question of Admission of Women to the Ministerial Priesthood," February 29, 1977.

Twentieth-century Jewish women continued the pioneering work of philanthropist Rebecca Gratz (1781–1869), who founded the first Hebrew Sunday school in America. Despite serious resistance to the participation of women in rabbinical study, Sally Priesand became the first ordained woman rabbi (Reform) in 1972.

Bibliography. R. Bainton, *Women of the Reformation*, 3 vols. (1970–77). K. Bliss, *The Service and Status of Women in the Churches* (1952). C. Perkins Gilman, *His Religion and Hers* (1923). R. Gryson, *The Ministry of Women in the Early Church* (1976). N. Hardesty, *Great Women of Faith* (1982). J. Irwin, *Womanhood in Radical Protestantism, 1525–1675* (1979). P. Jewett, *The Ordination of Women* (1980). H. B. Montgomery, *Western Women in Eastern Lands* (1910). J. Morris, *Against Nature and God* (1973). R. R. Ruether and R. S. Keller, eds., *Women and Religion in America*, 3 vols. (1981–86). R. R. Ruether and E. McLaughlin, eds., *Women of Spirit: Female Leadership in the Jewish and Christian Traditions* (1979). E. Schüssler Fiorenza, *In Memory of Her* (1983).

G. P. CORRINGTON

ECCLESIOLOGY AND PASTORAL CARE; MINISTRY; PASTOR (Definition and Functions); PASTORAL CARE (History, Traditions, and Definitions); RABBI/RABBINATE. *See also* EARLY CHURCH, PASTORAL CARE AND COUNSELING IN; MEDIEVAL CHURCH, PASTORAL CARE IN; HISTORY OF PROTESTANT *or* ROMAN CATHOLIC PASTORAL CARE; JEWISH CARE AND COUNSELING. *Compare* FEMINIST THEOLOGY AND PASTORAL CARE; PASTOR (Normative and Traditional Images *or* Popular Stereotypes and Caricatures); SEXISM. *Biography:* DAY; DIX; DUNBAR; EDDY; MARILLAC; MOTHER TERESA OF CALCUTTA; THERESA OF AVILA; UNDERHILL; WHITE.

WOOLMAN, JOHN (1720–72). American Quaker minister and social reformer. Woolman's *Journal* reflects a person of simplicity, strong religious feeling, and devotion to action growing out of personal conviction. Woolman supported himself by working as a tailor, enabling him to serve without remuneration. He did not condemn wealth, but wanted nothing to interfere with the cultivating of his own spirituality and counseling others who agreed or disagreed with his perspective.

Woolman preferred individual appeal over public proclamation as a method of change. On thirty occasions he traveled the eastern seaboard of the U.S., conferring, advising, and persuading individuals to act responsibly, particularly in resolving social problems. Slavery was especially offensive to Woolman, and he spent much of his time in personally persuading slaveholders. His essay *Some Considerations on the Keeping of Negroes* is one of the first antislavery documents, and four years after his death, Quakers became the first denomination to prohibit its members to own slaves.

Woolman's *Journal* is rich with dreams and other material which provide a fascinating glimpse into the inner life of an extraordinary religious personality.

R. W. CRAPPS

QUAKER PASTORAL CARE.

WORCESTER, ELWOOD (1862–1940). Rector of the Emmanuel Episcopal Church in Boston and founder of the Emmanuel Movement. Worcester inaugurated in 1905 the first serious effort to transform pastoral care in the light of the New Psychology and liberal theology. Trained in theology at General Theological Seminary in New York and in experimental psychology under Wilhelm Wundt in Leipzig, Worcester formed alliances with physicians and created small therapeutic groups to provide spiritual and psychological healing. Through the journal *Psychotherapy,* the movement introduced liberal American Protestants to such European therapists as Pierre Janet and Sigmund Freud.

Deeply influenced by William James, Worcester believed that the pastor could develop suggestive techniques to influence the subconscious and thereby engender health through the relaxation of hidden tensions. He viewed his program as an alternative to Christian Science.

E. B. HOLIFIELD

EMMANUEL MOVEMENT; HISTORY OF PROTESTANT PASTORAL CARE (United States); PASTORAL CARE MOVEMENT; PSYCHOLOGY IN AMERICAN RELIGION; RELIGION AND HEALTH MOVEMENT.

WORK AND CAREER. *Work* is a task-oriented, purposeful activity in pursuit of personal or economic objectives, synonymous with *job, employment,* and *occupation. Career* is the sequence of positions one holds in reference to work, from student preparation days to and through retirement. One's career is usually singular and lifelong, involving the continuum of decisions about type of work, job, and profession. One does not literally "change careers," then, but rather makes changes in the path of life called career. *Career counseling* is consultation about one's decision in reference to work success and satisfaction along the career path.

1. **Biblical Perspective.** The Bible presents work as essential to the fulfillment of human purpose; in the OT it is something that is shared with God: the creative making of the world. "Man goes forth to his work and to his labor until the evening" (Ps. 104:25). In the NT reference to work is found mostly in the "house tables" of Paul's epistles, in which attitudes of diligence, honesty, and faithfulness in the stewardship of gifts is admonished (Col. 3:22–4:1; Eph. 6:3–9, I Tim. 6:1ff.; Tit. 2:9ff.; I Pet. 2:18–25). Work as a response to the new covenant in Christ removes any sense of burdensomeness from it (Mt. 11:28–30); it is one part of vocation.

Career, however, is not a biblical term, though its original meaning in English, from the French *carrière,* meaning the ground on which a race is run, is approximated in the Hebrew *merots* (Eccl. 9:11: "The race is not to the swift") and *orach* (Ps. 19:5: ". . . like a strong man runs its course with joy") and in the Greek *agōn* (Heb. 12:1: "Let us run with perseverance the race that is set before us"). As a race or race course, a path, a way, or custom, *career* was used only figuratively to refer to a person's life.

2. **Sociological and Psychological Perspectives.** Work is a dominant force in the lives of individuals. Durkheim predicted that the social and political organization of culture would ultimately be determined by the

division of labor. Sociological studies reveal that in developed nations work does indeed influence the organization of life in pervasive ways, functioning in the shaping of values, choice of friends, type and location of housing (thus of community), children's education, political affiliation, religious participation, family life patterns, and leisure time activities.

Psychologists point to the impact of work upon the self-concept, indicating that in the choice of an occupation one is seeking a way to express a self-concept and then, as the work is pursued, that the self-concept changes in response to the work. Some studies reveal that this change begins to occur in anticipation of entrance into high commitment occupations such as ministry, law, medicine, teaching. Ability to work is generally viewed in psychology as one criterion of mental health, while overwork can become an addicting defense used to avoid other equally important aspects of life, such as personal relationships (Oates, 1972).

Adaptation to work is now recognized as a lifelong process which is experienced differently at certain discernible stages. In general terms, with many individual exceptions, these stages are: growth (0 – 14), exploration (15 – 24), establishment (25 – 44), maintenance (45 – 65), decline (65 +). In the growth stage the self-concept is being formed through various life experiences while awareness of work and its meaning in life develops. During exploration tentative choices are explored and a decision is reached; preparation is pursued and entry into an occupation is gained. The period of establishment is a time for training, development of competence, stabilization, and advancement. Maintenance is marked by continuity sustained by commitment, inservice training, and organizational wisdom. Decline is a time of letting go due to physical and mental changes.

Many persons repeat the stages of exploration and establishment in mid-life. For some, due either to their own preference or economic forces, the maintenance stage is never reached as far as a single occupation is concerned. These persons explore and establish themselves several times, following a sequential occupations career much the way some engage in sequential marriages. Maintenance tasks have to do with the sustaining of a lifestyle rather than maintenance in a single occupation. Career decision-making thus becomes an ongoing activity through middle and even later life, as recent trends in mid-life career changes suggest.

3. **Work Satisfaction.** Decision-making relative to work satisfaction involves a series of compromises, affected by both internal and external factors. Internal factors describe the individual in terms of abilities and skills, interests, values, commitments, the "rules of life" one follows, personality characteristics, and knowledge. No occupation or job is likely to satisfy all of the requirements; this requires compromise for most persons. Inadequately discerned compromise leads to great unrest and perhaps a search for a new occupation.

In external factors the necessary compromises become more complex and difficult. Such factors include socioeconomic conditions, including the current or future job market; costs and length of training to meet skill and credential demands; family needs; age restrictions; and political climate. The individual functions not only in relation to one context or environment but to a series of overlapping, contradicting, competing, and complementary contexts. The objective is to make integrative compromises that contribute to wholeness in work and in the rest of one's life and which, in mid-life, will reflect an emerging ego-integrity (Erikson). Unfortunately, many persons reach mid-life without a developing ego-integrity, largely (if not entirely) due to ill-decided compromises related to work. The eventual result, according to Erikson, is despair. Persons may engage in deliberate and often desperate efforts to change this process, often by seeking a change in job, occupation, or profession, though others seek such changes for positive developmental reasons, in order to fulfill another aspect of themselves.

Sometimes despair is precipitated by unemployment. Whether the result of inadequacies in the individual or changing technology and economy, the response to unemployment is the same as to any other major loss in life: denial, despair, anger, acceptance, resolution. Some are able to manage the process in positive adaptive ways and utilize their skills to regroup, find another position, and continue on with life, using unemployment as an opportunity for self-evaluation and career planning. Others are maladaptive — unable to mobilize their resources in their own behalf, and thus unable effectively to seek new employment or plan for the future. They often become seriously depressed. A third group does not despair but nevertheless fails to develop an effective approach to the problem of unemployment; they passively accept the situation and assume a reactive response pattern, waiting to be rescued. In any case unemployment and retirement are critical opportunities for reflecting upon the meaning and significance of work in the totality of one's life. In addition to pastoral conversation, this topic needs to be explored in pastoral preaching and teaching, since one aspect of the anguish felt in work and career crises is often the idolatrous significance given to work and career in contemporary middle and upper-class society (cf. Dittes, 1987; Oates, 1972; Raines and Day-Lower, 1986).

4. **Pastoral Response.** Pastors and pastoral counselors can be significantly helpful to persons in all stages of career decision-making and in times of unemployment by utilizing the counseling skills that are applied to any life crisis. Beyond this, special needs are present that require of the counselor specific knowledge and awareness. Knowing personally the competent referral resources in the community and being able to work in complementarity to them is very important. In cases of unemployment, it is appropriate to organize support groups, seek financial aid from the church to assist with professional consultation, engage in creative problem solving to overcome negative resistances, and warn that "self-help" methods may lead to unperceived errors in the job search and actual delay in obtaining a position.

Theologically, the pastor's task is to enable persons to see work in a wholistic perspective which, like any other aspect of life, is subject to the grace of God. This perspective will help to prevent the idolatry of work or a person's dependence upon work as the sole criterion for self-worth or identity.

Bibliography. T. E. Brown, "Career Counseling as a Form of Pastoral Care," *Pastoral Psychology*, (1971), 15–20, 22, 212;

"Career Planning," in J. Biersdorf, ed., *Creating An Intentional Ministry* (1976). T. Caplow, *The Sociology of Work* (1954). J. O. Crites, *Vocational Psychology* (1969). J. E. Dittes, *When Work Goes Sour* (1987). E. Durkheim, *The Division of Labor in Society*, ET, G. Simpson (1933). E. H. Erikson, *Childhood and Society* (1950). E. Ginzberg, "Toward a Theory of Occupational Choice: A Restatement," *Vocational Guidance Quarterly*, (1972), 169–76. C. C. Healy, *Career Development: Counseling Through the Life Stages* (1982). J. L. Holland, *Making Vocational Choices: A Theory of Careers* (1973). A. M. Kroll, L. B. Pinklage, J. Lee, E. B. Morely, and E. H. Wilson, *Career Development: Growth and Crisis* (1970). B. C. Lane, "Stalking the Snow Leopard: A Reflection on Work," *Christian Century*, 101 (1984), 13–16. D. J. Levinson, *The Seasons of a Man's Life* (1978). W. H. Norman and T. J. Scaramella, eds., *Mid-Life: Developmental and Clinical Issues* (1980). W. E. Oates, *Confessions of a Workaholic* (1972). J. C. Raines and D. C. Day-Lower, *Modern Work and Human Meaning* (1986). D. E. Super, *Career Education and the Meaning of Work* (1976). D. V. Tiedman and R. P. O'Hara, *Career Development: Choice and Adjustment* (1963).

T. E. BROWN

CHRISTIAN LIFE; DUAL CAREER MARRIAGE; LIFESTYLE ISSUES IN PASTORAL CARE; VOCATION. *See also* CAREER DEVELOPMENT AND GUIDANCE (For Pastors); MIGRANT WORKERS AND FAMILIES; UNEMPLOYED; VOCATIONAL REHABILITATION.

WORKAHOLISM. *See* WORK AND CAREER.

WORKING THROUGH. A term which indicates the client's repetitive attempts to utilize an insight discovered in the psychotherapy process in relationship to a fuller understanding of both present and historical relationships. It is the client's trying out a new way of looking at himself or herself in a variety of relationships and experiences.

Basic to an understanding of working through is the clinical reality that a single insight does not, in and of itself, produce lasting change. While something of a break-through might be seen to occur when an insight is achieved, it is the working through process that deepens the understanding as the meaningfulness of the insight is practiced and tested in relationships both inside and outside of the psychotherapy. Thus, the working through process is the most time-consuming work of the psychotherapy as it is the client's attempt to utilize and apply the understanding that was gained through the insight.

Knowledge of the necessity of working through is of significance to both the professional counselor and the pastor. Often there is an implicit expectation that if a person comes to a specific understanding of a previously unintegrated fact (e.g., that the client developed symptomatology which was then focused upon by his or her parents and had the effect of uniting the parents who were otherwise highly conflicted), then the person will be able to apply that knowledge immediately (e.g., be more able to handle being in the middle of conflicted relationships more rationally and not develop symptomatology) and experience relief from the development of distressing symptoms. This implicit expectation is not supported by clinical evidence. Rather, the person must come back to this issue again and again, working and reworking the insight, testing and applying it in situation after situation. As the insight gets practiced, dis-

cussed, and practiced again, it becomes a more significant and grounded part of the client's reality.

By forming realistic expectations of the client, the pastor can then develop a patient attitude toward the client's progress in counseling. The pastor will expect a client to move in and out of "progress" around a given problem, even after an insight concerning that problem has been achieved. The practice in applying the meaning of an insight will sometimes involve successes and other times failures. Movement will be both forward and backward, toward resolution and away from it again. However, it is only with this repetitive attempt to apply an insight that the insight can lead to what Greenson calls "a stable change in behavior or attitude."

Bibliography. S. Freud, "Remembering, Repeating, and Working-Through," *SE*, 12, pp. 145–56. R. Greenson, *The Technique and Practice of Psychoanalysis* (1967). L. Wolberg, *The Technique of Psychotherapy*, 2d ed. (1967).

B. M. HARTUNG

CONFRONTATION (Pastoral and Therapeutic). *See also* PSYCHOANALYSIS (Therapeutic Method and Research); PSYCHOANALYTICALLY-ORIENTED PSYCHOTHERAPY. *Compare* ACTING OUT; RESPONSIBILITY/IRRESPONSIBILITY, PSYCHOLOGY OF.

WORKS OF MERCY. *See* COMPASSION; MORAL THEOLOGY AND PASTORAL CARE.

WORKS RIGHTEOUSNESS. *See* FAITH AND WORKS; LEGALISM AND ANTINOMIANISM; RIGHTEOUSNESS/BEING RIGHT.

WORLDVIEW. The most basic and comprehensive concepts, values, and unstated assumptions about the nature of reality shared by people in a culture. It is the way they characteristically interpret the universe of human experience.

1. Kinds of Worldview Assumptions. Worldview assumptions fall roughly into three categories. (1) There are existential assumptions that provide the cognitive foundations for ordering the world meaningfully. These have to do with such things as the nature of time, space, causation, personhood, society, invisible beings and forces, birth and death, and other aspects of reality. They also provide the root metaphors (e.g., organic and mechanistic) that people use to interpret their experiences. Existential assumptions provide people with a sense of order and meaning in a world that often appears to be chaotic and senseless. They serve as the basis upon which explicit explanation systems such as religion, science, politics, economics, and medicine are built. Precisely because worldview assumptions are so foundational, they are largely unquestioned and implicit. To challenge them is to threaten the people's faith in meaning itself. There are few fears so great as when people lose confidence that there is order and meaning in the universe.

(2) Worldviews also include affective assumptions. These relate to the tone, character, and quality of life, to desirable and undesirable states of affairs in the culture, and to aesthetic styles and moods that characterize a society. Worldviews provide people with a feeling of security in the face of the profound insecurity found at the root of the human experience, and a sense of awe and

mystery in the face of the transcendent nature of the universe. Affective assumptions tend to be manifested most clearly in the expressive forms of culture — in the arts, music, dance, and drama.

(3) Finally, there are normative assumptions that provide a sense of moral order: of good and evil, righteousness and sin. From these arise the value systems of a culture.

2. Worldview Functions. A worldview serves several important functions within a culture. It integrates the whole range of concepts, feelings, values, and behavior patterns into a more or less unified way of seeing and accounting for the world. It reinforces faith in the culture by reinforcing its deepest assumptions with strong emotional attachments that make them resistant to change. A worldview also provides a psychological reinforcement to individuals during periods when fear and anxiety rise sharply within the community. At such times people tend to fall back upon their most deeply held beliefs to find security, support, and a clearer perspective of reality.

Worldviews are able to reduce internal structural contradictions that occur in the processes of cultural change by modifying their assumptions. For this reason they are remarkably resilient and endure over time. Nevertheless, in times of special crisis, rapid change and high cultural stress, they may no longer provide people with an adequate understanding of their world. In such cases cultures may collapse, or the people may convert to a new and more satisfactory worldview in what may be referred to as a major paradigm shift.

3. Cross-Cultural Differences. The deepest differences between cultures are found at the level of worldview. People in different cultures do not see the same world and use different languages to speak about it. Western cultures see time as linear and are concerned with beginnings and endings. Other societies see time as cyclical, pendular, or episodic in nature. Modern societies see land as secular property owned privately or by governments; tribal societies, like Israel in the OT and the American Indians, often see land as sacred and inalienably owned by the tribe or community.

One of the greatest differences in worldviews is that between modern and traditional ones. The latter tend to see the world in terms of organic analogies: trees, rocks, and even the world itself are alive. Modernity, however, as Peter Berger (1974) and others have pointed out, is based on a mechanical view of the world. The epitomy of modernity is the factories that manipulate nature as if it were lifeless matter controlled by predetermined laws, and the bureaucracies that treat humans as parts of a machine. A second difference is the emergence of secularism and materialism in modern societies. These arise from the widespread denial of transempirical realities that cannot be seen or observed directly.

4. Pastoral Implications. Worldview enters deeply, though often imperceptibly, into the way problems and crises are experienced and dealt with, and the way care is given. Because they are a part of the way humans construct their sense of the world itself, worldview assumptions seem natural, true, and beyond question, though they can be hidden but powerful sources of difficulty in human life. Persons, for example, who simply assume the modern secular, materialistic outlook on life may be inclined to expect medical or mechanistic-behavioral

solutions to personal difficulties which, in some situations, may be more effectively and appropriately understood in psychological, social, or religious terms; or again, sex role assumptions which may be entirely unrecognized by family members may play a significant role in marriage and family difficulties. Thus pastoral care and counseling must be alert to the role worldview plays in defining the possibilities, limits, and meanings of human experience. Needless to say, this is especially urgent in cross-cultural ministries where worldview assumptions between pastor and people may radically differ. In either case, however, it is important that worldviews be critically identified and their role understood in care and counseling situations.

Bibliography. P. L. Berger, *et al.*, *The Homeless Mind: Modernization and Consciousness* (1974). S. Diamond, ed., *Primitive Views of the World* (1964). T. W. Jones, "World Views: Their Nature and Their Function," *Current Anthropology*, 13 (1972), 79–91. W. J. Ong, "World as View and World as Event," *American Anthropologist*, 71 (1969), 634–47. *For pastoral care implications see* D. W. Augsburger, *Pastoral Counseling Across Cultures* (1986). C. V. Gerkin, *Crisis Experience in Modern Life* (1979).

P. HIEBERT

CULTURAL AND ETHNIC FACTORS IN PASTORAL CARE; INTERPRETATION AND HERMENEUTICS, PASTORAL; SOCIAL PERCEPTION, JUDGMENT, AND BELIEF. *See also* CROSS-CULTURAL PASTORAL CARE; MATERIALISM; SECULARIZATION / SECULARISM; LIFESTYLE ISSUES IN PASTORAL CARE; PSYCHOLOGY AND PSYCHOTHERAPY (East-West Comparison).

WORRY. *See* ANXIETY.

WORSHIP AND CELEBRATION. Worship, broadly defined, is the human response of praise, adoration, thanksgiving, and supplication to the mystery of God's being and self-communication. The activity of worship characteristically takes place within a gathered community of faith, involving time, space, symbols, ritual actions, speaking, music, and silence. In Jewish and Christian traditions, corporate patterns of prayer and ritual action are mutually related to intimate personal prayer and to levels of interior worship as well. This article focuses upon theological and anthropological dimensions of meaning in the forms and historical patterns of public worship found in the Christian tradition, concluding with key pastoral implications for the celebration of worship in an age of liturgical reform and renewal.

1. The Nature of Worship. Authentic worship both forms and expresses human beings in relation to the Divine. True worship seeks that which is truly holy. In the prophet Isaiah's vision in the temple (Isaiah 6), heavenly beings cry out, "Holy, holy, holy" in ceaseless praise of God. At the same time the prophetic seer senses personal limit and unworthiness. The quality of the divine presence forms and illuminates human life. Acknowledging God as holy involves the self-perception of unholiness and creatureliness. True worship of God involves the formation of particular dispositions, attitudes, and conceptions of God, the world, self, and community. In the language of Martin Buber, worship occurs when God becomes a "Thou" and is no longer an object of speculation or cognitive inquiry alone. Worshiping God is a matter of passional commitment and relatedness. Yet worship also involves learning concepts and teachings, and participates in a common history, recalled and retold in acts of remembrance and proclamation. Thus, in exploring the pastoral dimensions of how worship both forms and expresses human beings in a living faith, we must attend to the intimate mutual relations between experience and doctrine, symbol and historical claim, emotion and thought, feeling and ritual pattern.

In acknowledging such divine attributes as holiness, righteousness, and mercy the community of worship manifests basic human attitudes and emotions such as awe, gratitude, humility, reverence, and joy. These are learned and expressed precisely in and through the specific images, teachings, and interpreted memories which form the identity and history of the faith community. In some communities there may be little or no critical reflection or appropriation of the memories, while in others the formation and expression of such object-directed emotions as gratitude, humility, or holy love may be highly self-reflective. These differences depend, of course, upon inherited patterns of piety and the various ways in which theological learning has been assimilated into preaching, Scripture study faith-formation, and moral reflection in that particular denomination or local church's own history. Pastoral sensitivity to the style and substance of particular worshiping communities requires a mature understanding of these dimensions which are often hidden beneath the surface of how the worshipers regard themselves. Every tradition and every local community of worship inherits a culturally patterned way of worshiping. The style and character of faith-experience in particular denominations are results of this complex process of liturgical formation and expression, whether "free" or canonically liturgical.

The public worship of God touches upon matters which are essential to our humanity: memory and identity, praise and thanksgiving, truth-telling before God and neighbor, forgiving and receiving forgiveness, feeding and being fed, being healed, and offering ourselves to God for the sake of others. Time, place, words, and rituals are set apart from ordinary use in worship and point to the central mystery inherent in authentic liturgical action: the ordinary elements of life — water, bread, wine, light, breath, touching, posture — become the bearer of the extraordinary. Everyday acts of speaking and listening, embracing, feeding and being fed, working and resting are brought to focus in the intentional activity of becoming aware of the reality and presence of God. This is especially true of the meaning of Christian sacramental worship where ordinary things such as bread, wine, water, and oil become the "means of grace," acts of God's own self-giving, according to most Christian traditions.

2. Historical Patterns and Styles of Celebration.

Historical forms and patterns of public worship show an immense variety across traditions, from ecstatic dances to elaborate, often highly stylized liturgical ritual, to simple communal silence, as with the Quakers. Whether highly structured or free, the essence of worship is wholehearted acknowledgment and response to the One who has created and redeemed the world. Particular denominational traditions shape and express the faith of the community in differing ways, though all Christian patterns involve time, place, the Scriptures, symbols, a gathered assembly, and the acts of proclaiming, witnessing, and receiving. Different liturgical patterns and worship forms are closely related to particular types of spirituality as well as to denominational identity.

In recent ecumenical discussions of Christian worship three fundamental types of public worship are usually mentioned: "altar-centered" or sacramental, "pulpit-centered" or proclamatory, and "waiting upon the Spirit." The first is associated with the Roman Catholic, Orthodox, and Anglican traditions; the second with main-line and evangelical Protestantism; and the third with Pentecostals, certain charismatic renewal movements, and the Quakers. While such types are by no means mutually exclusive, each worship pattern and style has a different center of gravity. The sacramental traditions involve the reading of Scripture and preaching the word of God, but their central focus of worship is upon God's incarnational self-giving in Jesus Christ. Emphasis is upon the saving mystery of Christ's death and resurrection, which is most intensely recognized in the holy meal. Christ is understood to be both the one sacrificed for the salvation of the world and the one who is truly present in the words and sign-actions of the gathered church. Great stress is placed upon the continuity of the church's practice and of those authorized to celebrate the sacraments. In the more sacramentally oriented traditions, the church itself is thought of as being a sacrament to the world, extending the incarnation of Christ in the form of a community of faith, love, and service. There has been a tendency in these traditions to relegate preaching and congregational participation, except for receiving sacramental grace, to a secondary role.

In proclamation or word-oriented traditions, the sermon is regarded as central to worship, hence the leaders of worship are characteristically referred to as "preachers" or, less often, "pastors," rather than as priests. The teaching and preaching authority of the clergy is seen as that which can rightly open the Scriptures, proclaim the word, and also celebrate the sacraments. The church is in this view often regarded principally as a herald of Good News, and the community is primarily directed toward serving the world. Often in such traditions the emphasis is placed upon the "priesthood of all believers" and the function of the church is a witnessing community of the word. Here forms of worship have sometimes come, ironically, to be dominated by the preachers, while nevertheless emphasizing the people's role in hymns, responses, and the fellowship of believers.

The third type of worship, "waiting on the Spirit," covers a wide range, from concentration on speaking in tongues and other congregational manifestations of being acted upon by the Holy Spirit, to the Quaker meeting in which persons are moved to speak only after the "discipline" of silence and contemplative prayer. In all these, emphasis is clearly on human experience of the divine presence and on expressing what one is experiencing or discerning. The tendency in some forms of this type is toward strong discontinuity of behavior from ordinary life. Worship and "being religious" often refer to special experiences which may not relate very clearly to ordinary daily life. Black and Hispanic traditions often combine enthusiastic worship in the Spirit with vital preaching and, in some cases, with considerable formal liturgy.

The most interesting developments in the twentieth century are occurring where these three types are beginning to appreciate one another and where the laity discover aspects of their own traditions which lack what has been more central in one of the others. Thus, Roman Catholicism since the Second Vatican Council (1963–65) has recovered biblical preaching and, in some instances, has witnessed charismatic renewal flourishing alongside other forms of a renewed participation of the laity in liturgical life. Protestant traditions have been gradually rediscovering the importance of sacramental celebration. Within the past fifteen years significant renewal within mainline Protestant churches has been related to the restoration of the classical balance between word and sacramental celebration.

In American culture within the last century, we can identify four major periods of change in the pattern and style of Protestant worship, most of which reflect changes in the surrounding shifts in American society. From the Civil War era until the turn of the century most Protestant worship was dominated by revivalism. In this period worship served the end of converting people to the faith. Sunday worship patterns focused upon preaching for a decision and inculcating a profile of expected evangelical experience. Methodists, Baptists, Presbyterians, and others invariably concluded Sunday services of worship with a hymn of preparation, the sermon, a call to conversion or to commitment during the singing of a hymn, and a concluding prayer of blessing. The characteristic style was warm, informal, and folksy. Shortly after the turn of the century, a marked change occurred, especially in urban settings, which James White has called the beginning of the "era of respectability." Attention was being given to more refined, aesthetic taste, and the emotional experience of revivalism was replaced by more dignified and learned preaching. Choirs began to sing Mendelssohn, Bach, and other classical composers, and "good taste" came to influence the environment of church sanctuaries. The era of respectability in Protestant worship developed, in the 1940s and early 1950s, into a period of concern for historical roots of Protestant liturgy. Many denominations rediscovered their Reformation roots and began to use patterns of prayer and sacramental services which were based on the models of the sixteenth and seventeenth centuries. Then, in the mid-1960s churches experienced a sudden and widespread period of experimentation with nearly every aspect of worship, from new musical forms drawn from popular culture to the introduction of multimedia, drama, dance, and colloquial language. This was a period of cultural pluralism, and the sudden realization of the splintering and diversity of cultures within society is still a factor influencing the style and its counter-reaction in several traditions. The hallmark words were *relevancy* and *expressive celebration*. This was a time of Harvey Cox's *Feast of Fools* and articles such as "Liturgies when Cities Burn."

In light of these cultural and social shifts, Christian worship now faces a range of unprecedented issues for teachers, celebrants, and congregations. Significant growth in worship life in the churches in our culture today requires sustained teaching and reflection on the impact and significance of this very recent history in American culture on the way we worship and our expectations. Even today many local Protestant churches exhibit all four strata of these shifts of style and emphasis: revivalism, "good taste," historical identity and order, and relevance/experimentation.

3. **Reform and Renewal of Worship Today.** Such considerations of theology, human religious needs, and historical developments set the context for the task of reform and renewal in Christian worship as we move toward the twenty-first century. Reform and renewal are different, though related tasks. Reform of the patterns and texts and music with which we worship may or may not lead to genuine renewal of worship as faithful liturgy. New music and new language do not necessarily immediately transform individual and communal lives. At the same time many of our inherited patterns and styles of worship were biblically impoverished and did not reflect an adequate understanding of the larger Christian tradition. Churches which emphasized preaching services but celebrated the Lord's Supper quarterly were not, in fact, fulfilling the Reformers' wishes — neither Luther, Calvin, nor Wesley. Similarly, sacramental celebrations which were not grounded in the people's study of Scripture and in lively, biblical preaching were not adequate to the mystery of the "Word made visible" and proclaimed in eucharist, or to the "audible sacrament" of authentic preaching.

Concern for reforming our liturgical patterns which has emerged in the past twenty years, stimulated initially by the liturgical reforms of the Second Vatican Council, must now be related to the more difficult task of renewing the depth and quality of worship. This is the task of education and pastoral liturgy in the heart of every denomination and every local church. Questions have been raised about the adequacy and depth of our patterns and styles of worship both from a deeper knowledge of the Jewish and Christian traditions, and by the social and cultural crises of modern life — from the threat of nuclear holocaust to the disillusion of many with inherited images of church in relation to the essential questions of human existence, personal and communal. When worship becomes disconnected from the realities of life and death in our world, the question of renewal is paramount.

Perhaps the most hopeful sign in our present explorations of the meaning and point of worship concerns the recovery of the roots of Christian worship in the Scripture and the formative period of the early church. We cannot simply appeal to what the early church did as the best way for judging contemporary efforts of reform and renewal. Still, the early period serves as a reminder that without the essentials of grounding in Scripture and the richness of the whole tradition, and the mutuality of common prayer and service to the world, Christian worship cannot be adequate to its own gospel or to "all sorts and conditions" of humanity today.

Recent discussions by theologians and historians of Christian worship have spoken of the need to understand and recover the whole "canon" of Christian worship. That is, just as there is a canon of Scripture in which the church decided which books were of primary importance for the life and faith of the church, so there is a similar canon of essential elements in Christian worship. These four basic structures form a body of defining elements which the Christian tradition has used over the centuries. While not always understood and practiced with equal weight in each tradition, these four structures or elements are indispensable to a full and organically whole approach to worship. The four are: the rites of Christian initiation (baptism, confirmation, and the whole process leading thereto), the Lord's Supper or Eucharist, the cycles of time (feasts and seasons which are unfolding the story of God in Christ), and the patterns of daily prayer. In addition, we may speak of a fifth element of the canon which flows from teaching and practicing these essentials, namely, "pastoral" services of worship such as marriage and funeral rites, services of penitence and reconciliation, and various forms of prayer with the sick and the dying.

In our age of reform and renewal of Christian worship and life, the study of the whole meaning and range of Christian worship is absolutely central to growth and deeper unity among the churches. Each of the major denominational bodies and, indeed, many ethnic and third-world churches are in the process of reappropriating the whole canon of Christian worship. At that same time, traditions are learning from each other. Each tradition has something to contribute to the others.

4. Implications for Pastoral Liturgy. If it is true that Christian worship both forms and expresses human beings in the mystery of God in Christ, then the linkage between worship and pastoral care becomes crucial. Becoming a faithful person and a more mature community of faith is not a matter of gaining new information. It is a matter of *formation* in a whole range of capacities. Christian nurture is a gradual process of change in the heart of our personal being. Worship itself is a "school of prayer." Yet there are various levels of maturity and levels of capacity to participate in the whole range of worship.

A distinctive phrase from the *Constitution on the Sacred Liturgy* of Vatican II has been influential in much Protestant reflection on the future direction of worship: the church must teach and nurture Christians for "full, conscious, and active participation" in the liturgy. The early church took the matter of formation and training for worship very seriously. The catechumenate, or preparation process for Christian initiation, was an intensive period of being formed in Scripture, in prayer, fasting, self-reflection, and in the patterns of Christian life and devotion. This was often a three-year period, as described by Hippolytus in the third century. The laity had various roles in instructing and encouraging those who were preparing for baptism. The Lenten period became a time of preparation for the whole community to participate in the great Easter celebration, thereby witnessing with the newly baptized and reaffirming their own baptismal covenant.

The current practices of easy infant baptism and the lack of intentional training period for church membership must be reevaluated, and a pattern of preparation for "full, conscious and active participation" be undertaken by the whole congregation. At the same time, worship is a profoundly intergenerational experience, and the practice of infant baptism by many traditions requires that training and formation in the meaning and ways of participation in worship take seriously the various levels of human development, moral and emotional. Children are often able to respond to levels of nonverbal symbol in surprisingly strong ways. Focusing upon the wider range of visual, acoustical, and bodily forms of participation in early experiences of worship is of crucial importance to the formation of faith. Many churches have developed programs involving the whole family in common experiential learning with respect to worship and to sacramental participation. Musical training is, of course, one of the most important ways of forming younger persons in the prayer, praise, memory, and hope which constitute the heart of Christian worship.

Because Christian worship involves the whole community, and the recent reforms of our patterns and styles of worship demand more thoughtful preparation of both the participants and the worship service itself, several concluding implications are in order. First, the future directions of worship will require lay participation in planning and in the various ministries within the gathered community. Education in reading and the study of Scriptures, in theology and the practice of leading prayer, of serving communion, of sponsorship of candidates for initiation (baptism and confirmation) is part of worship renewal. Second, new catechetical structures and processes are emerging which take seriously the moral development of persons at different age levels and in different life passages. In this way, worship can be linked with the continual deepening faith-life of the whole congregation without imposing a single regimented style of education. Third, the new emphasis on restoring the balance between word and sacrament, and the increasingly fruitful ecumenical awareness among various churches create a need for better adult education in the history of worship. Finally, the future direction of Christian worship is radically dependent upon recovering the inner connection between worship and service, between love of God and love of neighbor, between prayer and work. By recovering these four aspects of the pastoral dimension of worship we may restore the ancient and venerable root meaning of liturgy as the "work of the people of God." At the same time, we may learn again what St. Augustine said of faithfully participating in the Eucharist: "It is your own mystery you receive."

Bibliography. J. E. Burkhart, *Worship* (1892). P. W. Hoon, *The Integrity of Worship* (1971). R. Hovda, *Strong, Loving and Wise: Presiding in Liturgy* (1977). D. E. Saliers, *Worship and Spirituality* (1984). J. F. White, *Introduction to Christan Worship*, rev. ed., (1990).

D. E. SALIERS

CONGREGATION, PASTORAL CARE OF; JEWISH HOLY DAYS AND FESTIVALS, PASTORAL DIMENSIONS OF; JEWISH PRAYERS (Significance for Personal Care); LITURGICAL CALENDAR; LITURGICAL CHANGE AND REFORM (Pastoral Issues); MINISTRY; PRAYER; PREACHING; RITUAL AND PASTORAL CARE; SACRAMENTAL THEOLOGY. *See also* BAPTISM AND CONFIRMATION; CHRISTIAN LIFE; COMMUNION (EUCHARIST); DRAMA; FUNERAL; JEWISH LIFE; MUSIC; SYMBOLISM/SYMBOLIZING; TRADITION. *Compare* MEDITATION; REST AND RENEWAL (Religious Traditions).

WORSHIP LIFE, PASTOR'S. *See* PRAYER AND WORSHIP LIFE, PASTOR'S.

WOUNDED HEALER. *See* PASTOR (Normative and Traditional Images).

YAHRZEIT. The anniversary of the death of one's immediate relative (generally a parent, sibling, or child). According to tradition, the Yahrzeit is commemorated by the mourner's lighting a small candle to be left burning throughout the day and by attending synagogue worship on the Sabbath immediately following the anniversary to recite the mourner's prayer, the Kaddish. There are various other customs associated with the commemoration of the Yahrzeit, including giving extra charity on that day, fasting the night before, and leading the daily synagogue service.

P. J. HAAS

GRIEF AND MOURNING, JEWISH CARE IN; JEWISH HOLY DAYS AND FESTIVALS, PASTORAL DIMENSIONS OF; MOURNING CUSTOMS AND RITUALS. *Compare* ANNIVERSARY DEPRESSION.

YELCHANINOV, ALEXANDER (1891–1934). A Russian, Yelchaninov (or Elchaninov) studied history and philosophy at the University of St. Petersburg where he taught after his graduation. In 1921 he had to leave Russia with his wife and daughter and settled in southern France. Continuing the attempts that began in Russia before his exile, Yelchaninov taught Russian language and history to the many emigrés that fled the Communists and participated in various organized religious and philosophical discussion groups with other Russian professors and writers. In 1926 he accepted ordination and was entered into the Orthodox priesthood.

The most famous source (the only one in English) on the life and thought of Father Alexander Yelchaninov is his *Diary of the Russian Priest*. The *Diary* presents to us, in a pastoral perspective, the most intimate thoughts about how the Christian life is to be applied to the concrete circumstances in which people live. This perspective in Yelchaninov's *Diary* is distinctly Orthodox in spirituality and Russian in culture. It was compiled by his wife Helen from his various notes, letters, and sermon outlines shortly after his death in 1934, and it has since served as a guide to the many Orthodox priests who seek to grow in their pastoral life.

Father Alexander stands at the cutting edge of the venerable spiritual tradition of Orthodoxy and the contemporary life of its people. He became especially known in two areas: as a spiritual director and as an exceptional preacher. As a spiritual director, he demonstrated the gift of "attention" and charity, of self-forgetfulness and sensitive human understanding. His words of guidance cut through all the phenomena that people brought to him, so that he influenced people toward the "shortest way to God."

J. L. ALLEN

PASTOR (Normative and Traditional Images); SPIRITUALITY (Orthodox Tradition).

YIZKOR. Literally, "May [God] remember". Jewish communal memorial service. This brief liturgy is recited four times a year: on the Day of Atonement, at the conclusion of Tabernacles, at the conclusion of Passover, and on Weeks. It is centered around the recitation of the names of the deceased members of the congregation or community, now often including reference to the victims of the Holocaust. The service reaffirms the link between the present, surviving community and its past members who founded the community and gave it its character.

P. J. HAAS

GRIEF AND MOURNING, JEWISH CARE IN; JEWISH HOLY DAYS AND FESTIVALS, PASTORAL DIMENSIONS OF; JEWISH PRAYERS; MOURNING CUSTOMS AND RITUALS.

YOGA. *See* MEDITATION; PSYCHOLOGY, EASTERN.

YOM KIPPUR. *See* JEWISH HOLY DAYS AND FESTIVALS.

YOUNG, R.K. *See* BAPTIST PASTORAL CARE.

YOUNG ADULTS. Postadolescent persons still becoming fully mature; human beings in the early period of adulthood. The period of young adulthood is still emerging as a recognized psychosocial era having a distinctive character in the life span. Legal demarcation by age for entry into young adulthood ranges from sixteen to twenty-one, as the threshold of this era is variously determined by factors such as driver's license, the right to vote, military registration, unmediated access to medical care, economic independence, the establishment of a residence separate from family of origin, a career, marriage, and parenthood. Psychologically one becomes a young adult when the tasks of adolescence — individuation from family and the capacity for critical reflection on self and world—have been achieved. Young adulthood is determined by its capacity to enter into adult roles such as those of parent and critical thinker, while yet being a novice and apprentice in relation to the high educational and emotional demands of a postindustrial society. The young adult has achieved a measure of differentiation from family but is not yet fully incorporated into adult society.

1. Developmental Issues. One typically becomes a young adult in the context of events that challenge one's most basic life assumptions. The collapse of inherited and/or assumed structures of meaning, intellectual or emotional, compels the young adult to seek a reformulation of faith that will meet the test of his or her ongoing lived experience. The young adult is one who begins to take responsibility for his or her understanding of truth. The young adult does not accept outside authority uncritically, even in relation to faith.

This era is also typically marked by ambivalence. The searching, wary, and divided nature of the young adult is the manifestation of his or her relative freedom, still fragile autonomy, passion for the ideal, and tendency toward dichotomous thought. The yearnings to stand alone and also to belong are each strong and often experienced as a dichotomous tension that cannot be resolved. This conflict may take the form of marriage vs. career, collaborations vs. competition, personal life vs. vocational demands, social acceptability vs. social protest, the life of contemplation vs. social action, and freedom vs. commitment. Faith communities that incarnate a vision of inclusiveness, in which the particularity of the individual is also prized, may offer an anchoring and educational context, safeguarding the premature or too final collapse of the young adult's dichotomies in one direction or the other. The end of young adulthood is marked by a tested and less ambivalent relation to self and society, which may emerge in the late twenties or early thirties.

The young adult recomposes meaning using elements from personal and cultural history in conjunction with the best images of the "ideal" and of the futures that are available in his or her environment. In traditional religious terms, this era is the time of "formation" and is an optimum period for envisioning the Kingdom (or Commonwealth) of God and one's relation to it. But as the young adult imagination is dependent upon the images available to it, the effort to "make sense" and find that which is "consistent" or "pure" in a critically reflected upon and relativized world can result in the adopting of

an amoral hedonism, a cynical moral nihilism, or any ideological fanaticism as well as in a transcendent religious faith and an ethic of responsibility.

While no longer embedded in an adolescent dependence on conventional peer groups or heroes, the young adult is yet dependent upon a self-chosen authority or a mentor and requires an ideologically confirming network of affiliation. Therefore, the young adult may be at once critically distanced from conventional or inherited religious tradition while simultaneously vulnerable to charismatic religious leadership and to the religious appropriation of political, professional, or other ideology. Persons or communities that function as guide, guru, or mentor may provide images of a viable and worthy vision of hope and a community of support that call into being the young adult's passion and competence and may form the ground for the most profound and responsible of adult commitments. The potential for abuse is also clear as influential persons and movements can take advantage of the young adult's search for commitment. Historically, religious orders and other religious and social movements have typically found their genesis in these dynamics. Therefore, it is crucial to recognize that the energies of the young adult have a particular capacity to serve the renewal of human life in every generation.

2. Response of Faith Community. Young adults seek a religious faith community for two primary reasons: spiritual transcendence and social belonging. This double yearning is manifest in the search for vocation—finding one's strength and fittingness (identity) in relation to the whole of being. The community of faith formation, therefore, should seek to be sensitive to the following needs.

(1) Opportunities for the experience of transcendence: liturgy, music, meditation, critical reflection and insight, the ambience of architecture, participation in meaningful and inspiring action.

(2) Opportunities for belonging or social affiliation that recognize but are not controlled by issues of sexual intimacy (thus not dividing young adults into single and married groupings): action projects; artistic expression and appreciation; study opportunities in which exploration and differing opinions do not threaten inclusion; occasions of ritual and worship; athletic, artistic, and dining events, with meeting times and arrangements that are sensitive to both work schedules and child care.

(3) Opportunities to test one's vocation: short-term commitments with structures of accountability; challenging and meaningful responsibilities that recognize emerging talents and test one's competency, while still providing guidance and honoring exploration; the space in which to discover and speak one's own word; confirmation, both informal and ritualized; financial subsidy for those exploring vocations not otherwise supported by the culture, that is, work among the poor, artistic development and travel as a means of education.

3. Pastoral Care of the Young Adult. In a religiously pluralistic culture, the young adult may intensely explore alternatives to established tradition in order to reflect critically on his or her inherited faith while simultaneously maintaining a means of religious expression. One consequence is the interfaith marriage and/or the formation of vocation in a tradition other than that of the young adult's inheritance; pastoral care needs to be particularly attentive to issues of continuity with the past at the time of an enlargement of perception, recognizing the potential of this era for either a deepening of one's faith in dialogue with others or a distancing from religion because its forms do not accommodate the search for truth in the young adult's experience.

During this transition between late adolescence and mature adulthood, the young adult may need to withdraw temporarily from all of the inherited traditions and values of his or her family of origin, engaging in what Erikson (1968) describes as a "psychosocial moratorium." While this causes frustration for parents and caregivers, it is often necessary in order for the young adult to adopt a set of values and beliefs that are felt to be his or her own. While the end result is often similar to the "inherited tradition," the moratorium allows for the testing of the meaning of tradition in the context of one's own world.

The beginning of parenthood, which is often a part of the young adult era, may open one of the most powerful moments of readiness for new faith formation, deepening one's consciousness of vocation in continuity with the generations. Young adults are also particularly mobile, and travel or other social dislocation may serve to prompt the restructuring of the meaning of faith. But whether in relation to these critical factors or others, religion for the young adult must make strong and fitting connections with immediate experience, both personal and social. The character of the faith community itself, as well as the particularity of its forms — ritual, political orientation, modes of education, style of sociability — must make sense in young adult experience and cannot find its justification in tradition alone. At the same time, it is meaningful connection with tradition — a meaning that embraces a history and a future beyond the boundaries of the self alone — that the young adult seeks.

Pastoral care must therefore focus simultaneously on both the emerging strength of the young adult and the vulnerability to loneliness and despair during an era in the life cycle when the soul is seeking so much. Pastoral care must not simply assume that the young adult will inevitably return to church, synagogue, or temple which, in fact, may come to be perceived as "outgrown." Rather, prizing the potential of young adult faith, pastoral care must focus both on the particular needs and contributions of the young adult within the community of faith. Recognizing that young adult faith experience is shaped by critique and distance as well as by search for communion, ministry to and with young adults must extend beyond the parish into the primary arenas in the culture in which young adult faith is both tested and formed: higher education, marriage, low-paying jobs and apprenticeships, military service, and even prisons.

The critical explorations of young adulthood are essential for the development of a clearer sense of identity; this, in turn, allows for the achievement and maintenance of intimate relationships. Until identity is reasonably secure, the young adult will be reluctant, or unable, to make firm commitments in relationships or in vocational choice. Thus, effective pastoral care provides an authentic, accepting, but positive atmosphere in which the young adult can form and adopt the "basic identifications" (Sherrill) upon which life as a mature adult can be established.

Bibliography. E. Erikson, *Identity: Youth and Crisis* (1968; *Insight and Responsibility* (1964). J. W. Fowler, *Stages in Faith* (1981). C. Gilligan, "Moral Development in the College Years," *The Modern American College,* A. Chickering, ed. (1981). R. Gribbon, *The Problem of Faith Development in Young Adults* (1977; *When People Seek the Church* (1983). D. Heath, *Growing Up in College: Liberal Education and Maturity* (1968). R. Kegan, *The Evolving Self* (1982). K. Keniston, "Prologue: Youth as a Stage of Life," *Youth and Dissent* (1971 [1960]). S. Parks, *The Critical Years: The Young Adult Searches for a Faith to Live By* (1986). W. G. Perry, *Forms of Intellectual and Ethical Development in the College Years: A Scheme* (1970 [1968]). L. Sherrill, *The Struggle of the Soul* (1963 [1951]).

S. D. PARKS

LIFE CYCLE THEORY AND PASTORAL CARE. *See also* COMMITMENT; FAMILY; IDENTITY; PARENTS/PARENTHOOD; PERSONALITY DEVELOPMENT; VOCATION. *Compare* ADOLESCENTS; MIDLIFE PERSONS.

YOUTH. *See* ADOLESCENTS.

Z

ZADDIK. Literally, "righteous one." The word is used in a general sense in the biblical literature to refer to a just or righteous person. In rabbinic Judaism the term has become more technical, being used to refer to unusually pious and righteous individuals. According to rabbinic legend there are only thirty-six true zaddikim alive at any one time and it is for their sake that the world survives. In the Hassidic communities of the eighteenth and nineteenth centuries, the term was sometimes used to refer to the Hassidic group's leader, or *rebbe*. Because of this leader's piety and scholarship, he was deemed to have special abilities to intercede in heaven for this followers.

P. J. HAAS

JEWISH CARE AND COUNSELING (History, Tradition, and Contemporary Issues); HASIDIC CARE AND COUNSELING; SPIRITUAL MASTERS AND GUIDES. *Compare* RABBI/RABBINATE; SPIRITUAL DIRECTOR; STARETS.

ZEAL. *See* SLOTH AND ZEAL.

ZEDEKAH. *See* JEWISH CARE AND COUNSELING.

ZELL, KATHERINE. *See* WOMEN IN PASTORAL MINISTRIES, HISTORY OF.

ZEN BUDDHIST SOUL CARE. *See* PSYCHOLOGY, EASTERN; PSYCHOLOGY AND PSYCHOTHERAPY (East-West Comparison).

ZINZENDORF, COUNT NICOLAUS LUDWIG VON (1700–60). German theologian and reformer, organizer of the Moravian church. In 1722 Zinzendorf organized a religious assembly in his home, a group including descendents of the Bohemian Brethren. Five years later he resigned his government post and gave himself entirely to the pastoral care of this assembly. The group ultimately became the Moravian church in 1749.

Under the influence of Jacob Spener, Zinzendorf promoted fraternal care by laypersons. The religious community was divided into subgroups under the supervision of elders. Within these groups each person became confessor to other members in the spirit of *Unitas Fratrum*, the unity of brethren.

Zinzendorf's emphasis on the role of feeling in religion sometimes produced excesses in the hands of undisciplined laypersons with limited intellectual restraints. Nonetheless it breathed new enthusiasm into German orthodoxy and, through F. D. E. Schleiermacher, profoundly influenced Protestant theology.

R. W. CRAPPS

PIETISM AND PASTORAL CARE.

ZWINGLI, ULRICH (1484–1531). Swiss Protestant theologian and reformer. As a Roman Catholic priest, Zwingli was an admirer and student of Erasmus, with whom he shared strong humanistic leanings. He served as chaplain to Swiss soldiers in papal service and in 1516 moved to Einsiedeln, where abuses of the shrine there stirred desires for reform.

In 1518 Zwingli became People's Preacher at Zurich's Old Minster where he remained for the rest of his life and where his commitment to reform ideals emerged. The Reformation movement in German Switzerland became full blown in 1522 with the publication of Zwingli's tracts *Von Erkiesen und Fryheit der Spysen* and *Architeles*, the latter calling for freedom of clergy from control by pope and bishops.

Another important Reformation document, and the earliest Protestant guide for pastors, was Zwingli's *Der Hirt (The Pastor)*. The work utilizes the shepherd metaphor for the pastor. In the first of two parts the good shepherd is admonished to preach for salvation, but also to instruct and serve the flock. He must love people passionately and guard them against falling away. The shepherd's reward is the upbuilding of the church. The second part warns against false prophets, who must be identified and either corrected or expelled. False shepherds must either return to their tasks of caring for the sheep or suffer punishment like the prophets of Baal.

Zwingli's *Pastor* does not attempt a full description of the pastoral office, but it is a significant document in developing Protestant conceptions of ministry.

R. W. CRAPPS

CLASSIC LITERATURE IN CARE AND COUNSELING (Protestantism); MINISTRY (Protestant Tradition); REFORMED PASTORAL CARE.